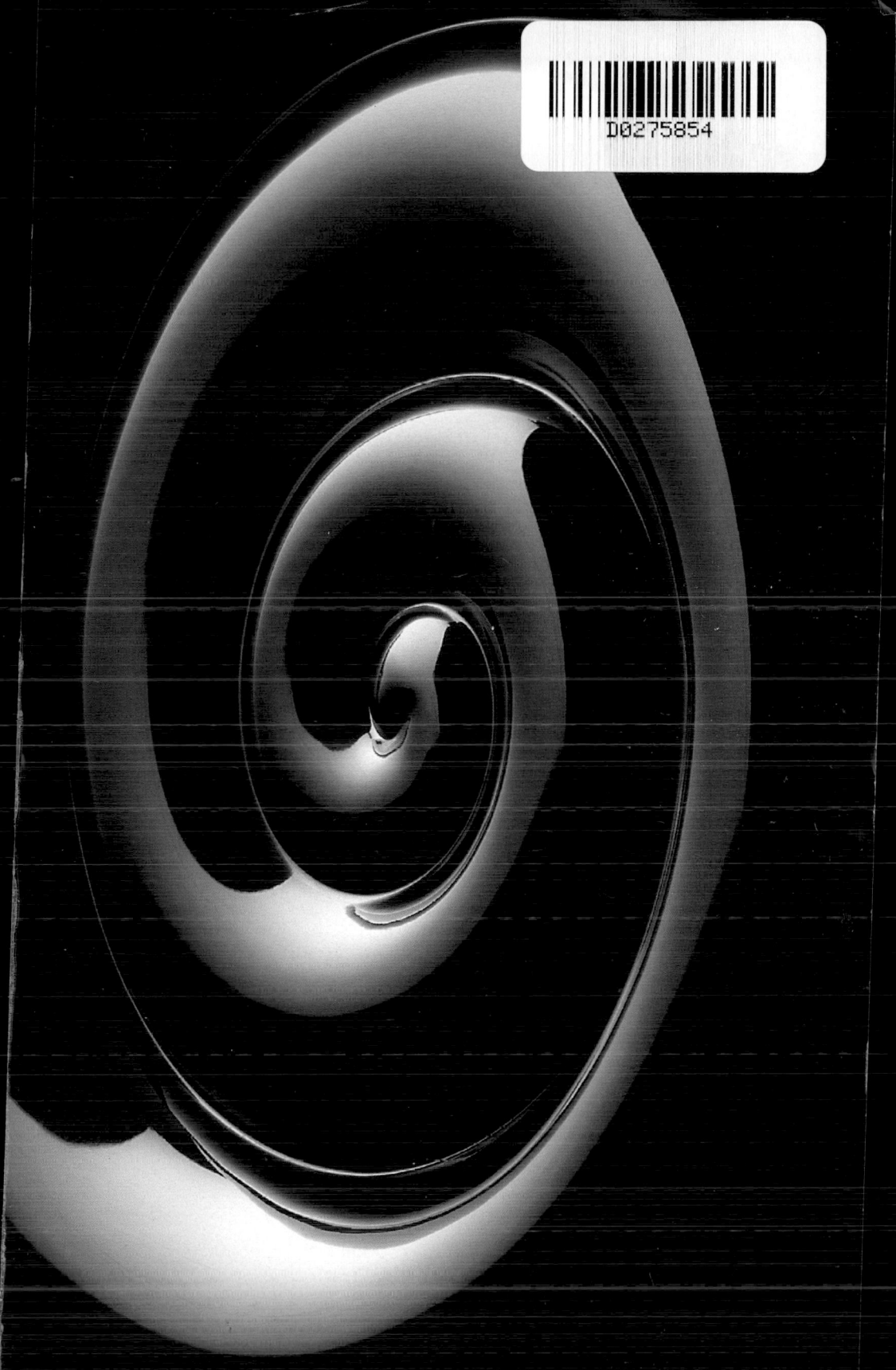

The B&W Nautilus is absolutely the most ideal speaker I have ever heard. It can be limited or coloured by the sources, amplifiers and cables, without any coloration of its own. This is the best loudspeaker that money can buy – Hi-Fi Review Japan

Special award for component of the year – Stereo Sound Japan

Special award for Grand Prix component of the year– Radio Gijutsu Japan

At B&W, music is our very reason for being. In our search for the perfect music reproduction, the B&W Nautilus, has pioneered technologies such as the hollow pole magnet drivers and the transmission pipe principle, which will shape the direction of the audio industry well into the next millennium.

It symbolises all the innovation, dedication and love of music which have inspired B&W engineers ever since the company was established 30 years ago.

In the search for transparency of sound, the Nautilus represents a true audio miracle. It can only be limited or coloured by the source, amplifiers and cables, without any colouration of its own.

Hailed as 'the best loudspeaker that money can buy', the Nautilus enables the listener to hear nuances and subtle dynamics hitherto unattainable, offering a level of sonic accuracy unmatched by any other speaker.

The Nautilus offers a unique chance to hear music exactly as recorded – detailed, vibrantly alive, full of power and unhindered by driver distortion or cabinet diffraction.

Listen and you'll see!

DM601

*The 601s sound like
the voice coils of God.*

CDM1

*For a domestic loud-
speaker that knows how
to groove, our European
Award is an honestly-
bestowed plaudit.*

P4

*These classy British
boxes leave you in
no doubt either physi-
cally or sonically about
how your money's
being spent.*

*B&W's patented method
of using Kevlar for loud-
speaker cones, has been
a major factor in reduc-
ing unwanted standing
waves. Kevlar's unique
woven fibres along with
further 'doping' by B&W
provide a remarkably
near perfect solution
to this problem.*

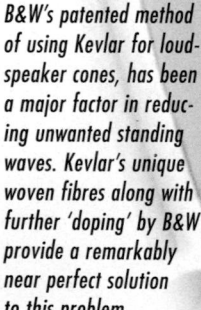

The result for the problem of resonances inside budget speaker cabinets is B&W's Prism construction. The solution involves a series of tapered wedges on the rear panel. Sound waves reflect off these wedges in a random fashion, reducing the build up of resonances and so contributes to clearer, uncoloured sound.

prism system®

B&W

DM302

European loudspeaker
of the year 1996/97

WHAT HI·FI?

This is a hard-nut
speaker, but it's edu-
cated and decisive too.
Dynamic and controlled
– there's not a lot to
touch it at the price.

Listen and you'll see

For more information please contact:-
B&W Loudspeakers (UK) Ltd +44 (0)1903 750 750
B&W Loudspeakers of America (508) 664 2870
http://www.bwspeakers.com.

Gramophone

Classical

GOOD CD GUIDE

1997

Sales and distribution

Book trade North America **Music Sales Corporation**
257 Park Avenue South,
New York, NY 10010, USA.
Telephone (212) 254 2100
Fax (212) 254 2013

UK and Rest of World **Mitchell Beazley**
81 Fulham Road,
London SW3 6RB, Great Britain.
Telephone +44 (0)171 581 9393
Fax +44 (0)171 225 9424

Record trade and private North America **Music Sales Corporation**
257 Park Avenue South,
New York, NY 10010, USA.
Telephone (212) 254 2100
Fax (212) 254 2013

UK and Rest of world **Gramophone Publications Limited**
135 Greenford Road, Sudbury Hill, Harrow,
Middlesex HA1 3YD, Great Britain.
Telephone +44 (0)181 422 4562
Fax +44 (0)181 869 8400

Gramophone
Classical
GOOD CD GUIDE
1997

Gramophone magazine, founded by the novelist and writer Compton Mackenzie and the broadcaster Christopher Stone, has been published monthly since 1923. As one of the first magazines devoted to the discussion of recorded music, *Gramophone* has maintained its position as the most informed and influential publication of its kind. Calling on the wealth of talent of a panel of the world's leading writers on music, *Gramophone* is the record collector's bible and it is from these writers and in the tradition of *Gramophone* that this book is published. Each month the magazine carries over 200 reviews of music across a wide spectrum and talks to the leading performers of the day. This year we are delighted to be publishing the *Good CD Guide* in association with a fellow British company, B&W Loudspeakers, whose dedication to producing fine loudspeakers closely matches the ideals of *Gramophone* itself: expertise drawing on experience, consistency and an awareness of the requirements of the consumer.

Published by

**Gramophone Publications Limited,
135 Greenford Road,
Sudbury Hill, Harrow,
Middlesex HA1 3YD,
Great Britain.**

Editorial Director	**Christopher Pollard**
Editor	**Máire Taylor**
Reviews Editor	**Jonathan Swain**
Editorial Consultants	**Harriet Smith** **Michael Stewart**
Editorial Assistant	**Ann Marks**
Production	**Dermot Jones** **Ivor Humphreys** **Janis Nicholls**
Design	**Dinah Lone**

Contributors

Andrew Achenbach · Nicholas Anderson · Mary Berry · Alan Blyth · Joan Chissell · Robert Cowan · Peter Dickinson · John Duarte · Adrian Edwards · Richard Fairman · David Fallows · David Fanning · Iain Fenlon · Hilary Finch · Fabrice Fitch · Jonathan Freeman-Attwood · Edward Greenfield · David Gutman · Douglas Hammond · Christopher Headington · Michael Jameson · Stephen Johnson · James Jolly · Lindsay Kemp · Robert Kenchington · Tess Knighton · Andrew Lamb · Robert Layton · Ivan March · Peter Marchbank · James Methuen-Campbell · Ivan Moody · Bryce Morrison · Patrick O'Connor · Michael Oliver · Richard Osborne · David Patmore · Stephen Plaistow · Nicholas Rast · Guy Rickards · Marc Rochester · Julie-Anne Sadie · Stanley Sadie · Lionel Salter · Alan Sanders · Edward Seckerson · Robert Seeley · Harriet Smith · John Steane · Michael Stewart · Jonathan Swain · John Warrack · Arnold Whittall · Mark Wiggins · Richard Wigmore

Cover illustration Oliver Betts,
BA Student, Bath College of Higher Education
Printed in England by William Clowes Limited,
Beccles, Suffolk, NR34 9QE

Contents

Introduction

by David Mellor, MP QC

Collectors of classical recordings are living through a veritable golden age of choice. The eye, the mind, not to say the wallet boggle as you enter a record store to see the staggering range of material available.

When CDs started, some cynics said the new technology would cherry pick. There would be endless versions of the *New World*, but the more arcane repertory would be left on black disc, or might even disappear all together. What nonsense. Not only are there myriad versions of the *New World* in the catalogue, but masses of obscure music as well, a lot of which never appeared in the LP era at all.

What's more, the choice fully reflects a century of recording. You are not merely confined, as you are in the concert-hall, to the tyros of today. If you want to hear Grieg playing the piano, it's available, or Caruso in his very first recordings is there too. If you want to rediscover, in excellent sound, the magic of Toscanini, Beecham, Stokowski, Schnabel, Edwin Fischer, Callas, Ponselle or Heifetz, they are there in abundance, with hundreds of their colleagues, whether celebrated or half forgotten, alongside them.

The best of today rub shoulders on the shelves with the greats of yesterday, and versions good, bad and indifferent all lie waiting for you. But the question is, where do you begin, or having begun, where do you then go on to? CDs are not cheap and, for most people, need to be chosen with care. I do not myself complain about the price – especially now that 'twofers' are available, often containing marvellous performances of a mass of material that was previously spread over three or four CDs – for not much more than a tenner if you shop around. And the format, unlike the old click-ridden black discs, or rustly 78s, offers a lifetime of unblemished musical enjoyment.

No, you don't need to complain about the price if you wish to be fair. But what you do need is a reliable guide to ensure that you can negotiate these endless shoals of choice, and end up with CDs that release as much as possible of the musical substance of the pieces recorded and hopefully in good quality sound as well.

That, of course, is where this Guide comes in. *Gramophone* is the most authoritative of all classical music magazines. Its team of reviewers are unrivalled and are at your service here in a volume portable enough to carry along to the shop with you.

There is rarely any such thing, thank goodness, as the only good version. There are usually several, and often many. But there are some bad ones, and some of those are at premium price as well. So buyers beware. No book should ever become a substitute for your own taste. But sensible people allow their taste to be shaped by experts. That's what I have done. I have 50 years of back copies of *Gramophone* at home and I frequently browse through them. I never feel it's other than time well spent.

So enjoy this volume. It will help you to a lifetime of musical pleasure, and could save you many hours of expensive disappointments. Used sensibly, it will very quickly justify its modest outlay.

Suggested basic library

Albéniz
Iberia
Allegri
Miserere
Bach
Brandenburg Concertos
Cantatas Nos. 78, 82, 140, 147
Goldberg Variations
Mass in B minor
St Matthew Passion
Toccata and Fugue in D minor (organ)
Violin Concertos
Barber
Adagio for Strings
Bartók
Concerto for Orchestra
Piano Concertos Nos. 1-3
Violin Concertos Nos. 1 and 2
Beethoven
Fidelio
Missa solemnis
Piano Concertos Nos. 1-5
Piano Sonatas Nos. 8, "Pathétique", 14,
    "Moonlight", 21, "Waldstein" and 23,
    "Appassionata"
Piano Trio No. 7, "Archduke"
Symphonies Nos. 1-9
33 Variations on a Waltz by Diabelli
Violin Concerto
Violin Sonatas Nos. 5, "Spring" and 9,
    "Kreutzer"
Berg
Three Orchestral Pieces
Violin Concerto
Berlioz
Grand messe des morts
Symphonie fantastique
Bernstein
West Side Story
Bizet
L'Arlésienne – Concert Suites Nos. 1 and 2
Carmen
Symphony in C major
Borodin
Prince Igor – Polovtsian Dances
Brahms
Clarinet Quintet
Ein deutsches Requiem
Hungarian Dances
Piano Concertos Nos. 1 and 2
Piano Quintet
Symphonies Nos. 1-4
Variations on a Theme by Haydn, "St Antoni
    Chorale"
28 Variations on a Theme by Paganini
Violin Concerto
Britten
Les illuminations
Peter Grimes – Four Sea Interludes
Serenade for Tenor, Horn and Strings
War Requiem
The Young Person's Guide to the Orchestra
Bruch
Violin Concerto No. 1
Bruckner
Symphonies Nos. 3, 4, 5, 8 and 9

Byrd
Mass for four voices
Mass for five voices
Canteloube
Chants d'Auvergne
Chabrier
España
Chopin
Piano Concertos Nos. 1 and 2
Piano Sonatas Nos. 2 and 3
Various Solo Piano Works
Copland
Appalachian Spring
Rodeo – Four Dance Episodes
Debussy
Images
La mer
Nocturnes
Piano Préludes
Prélude à l'après-midi d'un faune
String Quartet
Delibes
Coppélia
Delius
Brigg Fair
In a summer garden
On hearing the first cuckoo in Spring
Sea Drift
A Village Romeo and Juliet   Walk to the
    Paradise Garden
Dohnányi
Variations on a Nursery Theme
Donizetti
L'elisir d'amore
Lucia di Lammermoor
Dowland
Various Solo Lute Works
Dukas
Sorcerer's Apprentice
Dvořák
Cello Concerto
Piano Quintet
Piano Trio No. 4, "Dumky"
Serenade for Strings
Slavonic Dances
String Quartet No. 12, "American"
Symphonies Nos. 7, 8 and 9, "From the New
    World"
Elgar
Cello Concerto
The Dream of Gerontius
Introduction and Allegro for Strings
Pomp and Circumstance Marches
Symphonies Nos. 1 and 2
Variations on an Original Theme, "Enigma"
Violin Concerto
Falla
Noches en los jardines de España
El sombrero de tres picos
Fauré
Requiem
Franck
Symphonic Variations
Symphony in D minor
Gershwin
An American in Paris

The reviews

Using the guide

The presentation and design of this guide is similar to that of its parent publication, *Gramophone*. The rating system – one, two or (the top accolade) three **G**s, is applied to releases which the reviewers consider to be recordings of particular distinction, having attained or deserving to attain classic status. It may sometimes appear to be anomalous when recordings under "Additional recommendations", for example, are deemed to be deserving of a higher rating than the full review of the same work. This is simply because it is the guide's policy to review as many new releases as possible each year and constraints of space often mean that we can have only one review of a particular work. As with previous editions, works which merit attention but not, perhaps, a full review, are provided under "Suggested listening" and "Further listening". The original *Gramophone* review date is provided for readers who might wish to investigate further. Generally, where more than three composers are represented on a single disc, if it receives a full review this appears in the Collections section which starts on page 1076 and the reader is referred to the Index to Reviews starting on page 1213. The Index to Artists, starting on page 1311, applies mainly to those represented by full reviews.

The title for each review contains the following information:

Composer(s), work(s), artist(s), record company or label, price range and disc number. The text within the brackets indicate the number of discs (if there is more than one), timing, mode of recording and the original review date in *Gramophone*. Period-instrument performances are highlighted by the use of a symbol. If the issue under review is a reissue, details are given of its provenance. Recording dates are also provided, when available.

Key to symbols

Ⓕ   Full price £10 and over   Ⓜ   Medium price £7 – £9·99
Ⓑ   Bargain price £5 – £6·99   Ⓢ   Super bargain price £4·99 and below

---

AAD/ADD/DDD denote analogue or digital stages in the recording/editing or mixing/mastering or transcription processes in CD manufacture.

✔   Recordings where period instruments are used.

*   Where this appears after a disc number, it is an indication that the recording quality may not be up to the highest standards. This generally applies to pre-1960 recordings.

oas   discs (reviewed as a set) which are only available singly

---

Some titles also highlight the following information:

Gramophone Classical 100 – a selection of the 100 greatest classical recordings of all time which have become corner-stones of the catalogue. This features some of the leading names in classical music this century, including Furtwängler, Karajan, Solti, Beecham, Heifetz and Callas (the selection is based on a book of the same name which is currently out of print).

Gramophone Award winner – the list of Award winners from 1977 to 1995 starts on page 1194.

Gramophone Editor's choice – in every issue of *Gramophone* ten outstanding discs are selected from the month's reviews, one of which also becomes *Record of the month*.

Selected by Sounds in retrospect – *Gramophone*'s listening panel appraises recordings from the technical standpoint and singles out those which are notable for their particularly excellent sound quality (from January 1996 this panel selection became known as *Soundings*).

Abbreviations

alto	countertenor/male alto	**mndl**	mandolin
anon.	anonymous	**narr.**	narrator
arr	arranged	**ob**	oboe
attrib.	attributed	**Op.**	opus
b	born	**orig.**	original
bar	baritone	**org**	organ
bass-bar	bass-baritone	**perc**	percussion
bn	bassoon	**pf**	piano
c	circa (about)	**picc**	piccolo
cl	clarinet	**pub.**	publisher/published
clav	clavichord	**rec**	recorder
cont	continuo	**rev.**	revised
contr	contralto	**sax**	saxophone
cor ang	cor anglais	**sngr**	singer
cpsr	composer	**sop**	soprano
cpte(d)	complete(d)	**spkr**	speaker
d	died	**stg**	string
db	double bass	**synth**	synthesizer
dig pf	digital piano	**tbn**	trombone
dir	director	**ten**	tenor
ed.	edited (by)/edition	**timp**	timpani
exc	excerpt	**tpt**	trumpet
fl	flute	**trad.**	traditional
fl	flourished	**trans.**	transcribed
fp	fortepiano	**treb**	treble
gtr	guitar	**va**	viola
harm	harmonium	**va da gamba**	viola da gamba
hn	horn	**vars.**	variations
hp	harp	**vc**	cello
hpd	harpsichord	**vib**	vibraphone
keybd	keyboard	**vn**	violin
lte	lute	**voc**	vocal/vocalist
mez	mezzo-soprano	**wds.**	words

Carl Friedrich Abel
German/British 1723-1787

Suggested listening ...

...Symphonies, Op. 7 – No. 1 in G major; No. 2 in B flat major; No. 3 in D major; No. 4 in
F major; No. 5 in C major; No. 6 in E flat major. **Cantilena / Adrian Shepherd.** Chandos
CHAN8648 (6/89).

...Symphonies, Op. 10 – No. 1 in E major; No. 2 in B flat major; No. 3 in E flat major; No. 4 in
C major; No. 5 in D major; No. 6 in A major. **La Stagione / Michael Schneider.** CPO CPO999
207-2 (7/95).

...Symphonies, Op. 17 – No. 1 in E flat major; No. 2 in B flat major; No. 3 in D major; No. 4 in
C major; No. 5 in B flat major; No. 6 in E flat major. **Hanover Band / Anthony Halstead.** CPO
CPO999 214-2 (7/95). ✐

...String Quartet in A major, Op. 8 No. 5. *Coupled with works by* **Shield, Marsh, Webbe** and
S. Wesley Salomon Quartet. Hyperion CDA66780 (3/96). *See review in the Collections section;
refer to the Index to Reviews.*

...Flute Sonatas, Op. 6 – No. 5 in F major; No. 6 in G major. Seven pieces for Viola da gamba.
Trios for Two Flutes and Continuo – F major; G major. Cello Sonata in A major, WKO148.
La Stagione. CPO CPO999 209-2 (7/95).

Peter Abélard
French 1079-1142

Abélard Hymns and Sequences for Heloïse – O quanta qualia; Dolorum solatium; Suscipe; Mater
salvatoris; Ne derelinquas me; Sponsus (with Winchester Cathedral Choristers). Epithalamica;
Magnum salutis gaudium; Quam pium; Felicite me floribus; Dum esset rex; De profundis;
Samson dux fortissime. **Schola Gregoriana / Mary Berry.** Herald Ⓔ HAVPCD168 (79 minutes:
DDD: 3/95). Texts and translations included. Recorded 1993. Ⓖ

This is a beautiful and fascinating collection. Peter Abélard is famous as lover, heretic and poet. His
treatise on ethics, his *Story of a calamity* (the calamity of his love for his pupil Heloïse, their marriage
and enforced separation and his castration by her infuriated relatives) are classics of medieval Latin
literature. So are his hymns, over 100 of them, many written for the community of nuns of which
Heloïse became Abbess. He wrote music as well as words for a great number of them, but until a short
time ago it was thought that only two of these melodies had survived. Recent scholarship has now
added several more. In this collection six hymns and sequences by him (plus a seventh, setting his
words to a plainchant melody) are placed in the context of music that he and Heloïse very probably
knew. Reading too much of Abélard's life-story into this music is an agreeable pitfall into which
Dr Berry herself lures us by inviting us to hear in *Dolorum solatium* David's lament for Saul and
Jonathan, something of the "utter despair in which he found himself after his parting from Heloïse".
The exquisite and moving close, a single voice crying "My hands are wounded by playing the harp,
my voice is harsh from lamenting, my breath fails" does indeed sound like a message. *Sponsus* and
Samson dux fortissime are dramas of a more public kind, each of the characters in the former having
their own melodies, and brief spoken lines that seem to call for staged action. And in *Samson dux
fortissime* the robust choral declamation, the long and powerful narrative for Samson (warrior
prototype of Christ) and the sudden use of a high tenor for Delilah have a pungent theatricality. After
hearing the whole collection you have to remind yourself that throughout you have heard nothing but
monody, a single line discreetly shared between solo voice and a 'chorus' of at most three. Subtlety of
word-setting, flexible variation of melody, supple rhythm – all these need responsive but not assertive
singing. Once or twice one or other singer sounds a touch stressed by the chosen pitch; otherwise the
performances are pretty well ideal, and the acoustic of Winchester Cathedral frames them beautifully.

Hans Abrahamsen
Danish 1952-

Suggested listening ...

...Symphony[a]. *Coupled with* **Gade** Echoes from Ossian, Op. 1[a]. **Horneman** Gurre Suite[b].
Nørgård Twilight[b], Aarhus Royal Academy of Music Orchestra / [a]Ole Schmidt, [b]Søren
K. Hansen. Kontrapunkt 32194 (7/95).

Antón García Abril
Spanish 1933-

New review

Abril Three Sonatas for Orchestra. Hemeroscopium. Piano Concerto[a]. [a]Guillermo González (pf);
Madrid Symphony Orchestra / Enrique García Asensio. Marco Polo Ⓔ 8 223849 (65 minutes:
DDD: 6/96). Recorded live in 1994.

Who, those outside Spain may be asking, is Abril? A prolific composer in many fields – a partial list
is given in the insert-booklet – he has taught at the Madrid Conservatoire since the age of 24, was a
co-founder in 1958 of the influential New Music group, and has received numerous prizes and

honours. This disc documents a highly successful concert in his honour when, at the age of 61, he was awarded the Guerrero Foundation Prize (previous recipients of which had been Rodrigo and Montsalvatge). *Hemeroscopium* ("watchtower of the day"), a concerto for large orchestra, was completed in 1972 (when Asensio conducted the première, as here) and only slightly revised subsequently. It is a grandiloquent work in three connected sections, only occasionally recognizably Spanish and revealing some influences from Bartók and Petrassi (with whom Abril studied). Basically melancholy, its course is punctuated by shatteringly loud and violent outbursts. The *Three Sonatas* are transcriptions of harpsichord movements by Soler. Minor changes from the original in matters of accidentals are of no great consequence, but the scoring for full orchestra (at first for a ballet in 1984) leads to a rather vulgar, inflated image of Soler. The Piano Concerto is an earlier work but was scrapped in favour of a radical revision in 1994. Showily extrovert, it is easy on the ear, with a lively light-hearted first movement akin to Françaix, a more lyrical "Coral" which harmonically is somehow reminiscent of John Ireland, and a diffuse, rather noisy finale. Guillermo González clearly revels in the work's bravura, and the recording throughout (particularly in *Hemeroscopium*'s immense climaxes) is spectacular.

Adolphe Adam
French 1803-1856

Adam Giselle. Slovak Radio Symphony Orchestra / Andrew Mogrelia. Naxos Ⓢ 8 550755/6 (two discs: 114 minutes: DDD: 4/95). Recorded 1994.

Naxos offer this complete version of Adam's classic ballet score to challenge comparison with Bonynge's recording for Decca. Give or take some seeming slight variances in the Act finales, both offer essentially the same text, complete with traditional interpolations attributed to Burgmüller and Minkus. In the ultimate comparison there can be little doubt that Bonynge gives more point to the contrasts in the score, and that the playing of the Covent Garden orchestra and Decca's recorded sound give just the edge over the Naxos disc. Yet it is on any count a highly enjoyable alternative, with some especially rewarding passages such as the Act I "Pas seul". Many, of course, may well prefer a single-CD abridged version. For them either of the admirable alternatives might suit, though they will not come cheaper than this super-budget set. Light of step and light on the pocket, it is also commendably economical on shelf-space in its sensible single-CD-width case. The others listed below are also highly recommendable.

Additional recommendations ...

…**Vienna Philharmonic Orchestra / Herbert von Karajan.** Decca Ovation Ⓜ 417 738-2DM (60 minutes: ADD).

…**Royal Opera House Orchestra, Covent Garden / Richard Bonynge.** Decca Ovation Ⓜ 433 007-2DM2 (two discs: 124 minutes: DDD: 12/91).

…**Royal Opera House Orchestra, Covent Garden / Mark Ermler.** Royal Opera House Records Ⓕ ROH007 (74 minutes: DDD: 4/94).   Ⓖ

Further listening ...

…**Le corsaire. English Chamber Orchestra / Richard Bonynge.** Decca 430 286-2DH2 (10/92).

John Adams
American 1947-

New review

Adams Violin Concerto[a]. Shaker Loops[b]. [a]**Gidon Kremer** (vn); [a]**London Symphony Orchestra / Kent Nagano;** [b]**Orchestra of St Luke's / John Adams.** Nonesuch Ⓕ 7559-79360-2 (59 minutes: DDD: 6/96). Recorded 1994-5.   Ⓖ

A superb CD that displays two very different aspects of John Adams's evolving art, *Shaker Loops* dancing to a minimalist pulse, lean, fidgety and cleverly designed (the accelerating 'take-offs' in "A final shaking" are extremely effective), and the altogether deeper, more intimate Violin Concerto. In the concerto Adams keeps up the momentum for the entire duration of his long first movement, shifting colours constantly until 11'44" when a brief solo passage marks a slowing down in preparation for the ensuing Chaconne. Here, a quiet chiming suggests parallels with Arvo Pärt, while Adams floats his mysterious textures above a quietly undulating accompaniment. The Sibelius of *Tapiola* seems to hover somewhere around 5'49" into the first movement (just as parts of *Shaker Loops* suggest an up-tempo *Lemminkaïnen*) and the concerto ends with a fast dancing Toccata. As to the solo line, Adams himself admits that it is "almost never ending", but in the hands of Gidon Kremer – whose sinewy, lightly-bowed tone suits the piece perfectly – it is a compelling monologue. Adams's Violin Concerto takes its spiritual theme from poet Robert Hass's *Body through which the dream flows*. *Shaker Loops* is an earlier, easier and rather less durable piece. It started life as a string quartet (*Wavemaker*), then – beyond drastic recomposition – filled out to a septet which, suitably augmented, is how we hear it here. The term "Shaker" refers to the frenzied dancing of a religious sect and

Adams's four-part structure sets up a varied roster of tempos and textures. There have been other recordings of the work, but this is surely the best – agile, precise and extremely well balanced. The sound is excellent.

New review

J. Adams Short ride in a fast machine (arr. L.T. Odorn)[a]. Grand Pianola Music[b].
D. Lang Are you experienced?[c] Under Orpheus[d]. [c]**David Lang** (narr); [b]**Lindsay Wagstaff**, [b]**Kym Amps**, [b]**Ruth Holton** (sops); [bd]**Ellen Corver**, [bd]**Sepp Grotenhuis** (pfs); **Netherlands Wind Ensemble / Stephen Mosko.** Chandos New Direction Ⓕ CHAN9363 (76 minutes: DDD: 10/95). Text included. Recorded 1994-5.

The rocky suspension of John Adams's 'Fast machine' (as refurbished for wind band by Lawrence T. Odorn) makes for a rougher 'Short ride' than, say, the composer himself provided; yet either serves as a thrilling concert opener. The sound on this new Chandos recording is pleasingly open and 'up-front', with prominent brass, bright percussion and a realistic dynamism. Likewise in the spaciously rolling *Grand Pianola Music*, where a tangy blend of two pianos, three sopranos and an ensemble of woodwind, brass and percussion works through sundry "elements of the composer's heritage" (quoting from Keith Potter's useful notes) until we reach the vistaed home straight "On the Dominant Divide". Here, the two antiphonally placed pianos throw a maddeningly memorable tune between them, excitably supported by the band – and especially by the bass drum. The augmented Netherlands Wind Ensemble play extremely well for Stephen Mosko but create a heavier body of sound than Adams himself commands via the London Sinfonietta, while Elektra's recording achieves the finer balance of textures. As to choices, Adams adds his madcap *Chamber Symphony*, whereas Mosko presents two works by another young American composer, David Lang (b.1957). The first takes its lead from the Jimi Hendrix album "Are you experienced?" and starts with a spoken confession from the composer himself, who calmly informs us that while he was "busy setting up, someone crept up silently behind you [that's *you*, the listener] and dealt a quick blow to the side of your head". The musical upshot of this unfortunate piece of enforced biography is a Nymanesque dance, a violent encounter with the 'Voice of God', and a consolatory "Siren's Song" – most of it crafted along vaguely minimalist lines, with texts spoken rather than sung. Lang's narrative is surreal yet unpretentious, an entertaining sequence that draws you into its zany world with considerable ease. The music, too, is appealing, whereas *Under Orpheus* – a fleshed-out re-working of a 1989 piece for two pianos – backs insistent two-piano tremolos with shifting support from wind and brass. It's fascinating stuff, but less immediate than the companion work. All in all, a disc that should be heartily welcomed by those for whom modern music means – among other things one hopes – pulse, harmony and a guaranteed level of accessibility.

Additional recommendation ...

...Grand Pianola Music. Chamber Symphony. **London Sinfonietta / John Adams.** Elektra Nonesuch Ⓕ 7559-79219-2 (53 minutes: DDD: 3/95). Recorded 1993. Ⓖ

J. Adams Harmonielehre. The Chairman Dances. Two Fanfares – Tromba lontana; Short Ride in a Fast Machine. **City of Birmingham Symphony Orchestra / Sir Simon Rattle.** EMI Ⓕ CDC5 55051-2 (62 minutes: DDD: 6/94). Recorded 1993.

Harmonielehre was inspired by a dream vision of a massive tanker that suddenly took flight, displaying a "beautiful brownish-orange oxide on the bottom part of its hull"; the 'setting' was just off San Francisco Bay Bridge. "Those pounding E minor chords are like a grinding of gears," says John Adams of its violent, gunshot opening. Scored for a huge orchestra and structured in three contrasted sections, *Harmonielehre* is probably the nearest thing on offer to a minimalist symphony, and for that reason alone it could well appeal beyond the élite coterie of minimalist-fanciers. Rattle's recording has great heft and dynamic range, an informative balance and a vivid sense of aural perspective. The brass components of those opening chords (horns, trumpets, trombones and tubas) have enormous weight and presence, and the ringing marimbas thereafter, a bright complexion. Adams's frequent requests for subtle tempo transitions ("Tempo gradually picks up", "Slightly faster ... but still very flexible and fluid" and so on) are subtly honoured by the conductor. Rattle gives us three fill-ups: the Copland-inspired *Short Ride in a Fast Machine* and *Two Fanfares*, and *The Chairman Dances*, a 'foxtrot for orchestra' that utilizes material from Adams's opera, *Nixon in China*. Searching for a metaphor, one might suggest that Rattle's Mao does his foxtrot in tweeds and a pair of brogues. Rattle's view of Adams is recommended particularly to mainstream collectors who aren't yet sold on minimalism.

Additional recommendation ...

...The Chairman Dances. **Bernstein** West Side Story – Mambo. **Kernis** New Era Dance. **Schiff** Stomp **Larsen** Collage: Boogie. **Harbison** Remembering Gatsby. **Torke** Black and White – Charcoal. **Moran** Points of Departure. **Agento** The Dream of Valentino – Tango. **Daugherty** Desi. **Rouse** Bonham. **Baltimore Symphony Orchestra / David Zinman.** Argo Ⓕ 444 454-2ZH (71 minutes: DDD: 7/95).

Further listening ...

...Hoodoo Zephyr. Coast. Disappointment Lake. Tourist Song. Tundra. Bump. Cerulean. **John Adams** (bar/synth). Elektra Nonesuch 7559-79311-2 (4/94).
...The Death of Klinghoffer. **Soloists; London Opera Chorus; Lyon Opera Orchestra / Kent Nagano.** Elektra Nonesuch 7559-79281-2 (3/93).

Richard Addinsell
British 1904-1977

Addinsell Goodbye Mr Chips – Theme. Ring around the moon – Invitation Waltz. Smokey
Mountains Concerto[a]. The Isle of Apples. The Prince and the Showgirl – potpourri. Tune in
G major[b]. Tom Brown's Schooldays – Overture. Festival[a]. Journey to Romance. Fire over
England – Suite. A Tale of Two Cities – Theme[b]. [a]**Philip Martin,** [b]**Roderick Elms** (pfs);
BBC Concert Orchestra / Kenneth Alwyn. Marco Polo Ⓕ 8 223732 (68 minutes: DDD: 4/95).
Recorded 1994.

Universally known for the *Warsaw Concerto* from the wartime film *Dangerous Moonlight*, Richard
Addinsell composed a good deal else for British films and radio. The film scores represented here range
chronologically from *Fire over England* (1937), through *Goodbye Mr Chips* (1939), *Tom Brown's
Schooldays* (1951) and *The Prince and the Showgirl* (1957) to *A Tale of Two Cities* (1958), and all
present music of the same undemanding, sensitive, relaxing and highly melodic nature. The high-
spirited selection from *The Prince and the Showgirl* is especially cheering. Besides four individual
numbers not connected with films, there is also the *Smokey Mountains Concerto*, with three curiously
contrasted movements that are each effective in their very different ways. Addinsell himself composed
only for piano, being celebrated also as accompanist and arranger for Joyce Grenfell. The original
orchestrations of his music were done by the likes of Leonard Isaacs and Douglas Gamley, and much
of the orchestral material for this recording has been prepared by Philip Lane, who also provides the
informative notes. The music here is meat and drink to this British orchestra, conductor and piano
soloists and they combine to provide a very attractive release.

Further listening ...
...Warsaw Concerto. *Coupled with works by* **Gottschalk, Litolff** and **Rachmaninov** Cristina
Ortiz (pf); **Royal Philharmonic Orchestra / Moshe Atzmon.** Decca 414 348-2DH (9/86). *See review
in the Collections section; refer to the Index to Reviews.*   Ⓖ
...Blithe Spirit – Prelude and Waltz. Passionate Friends – Suite. *Coupled with works by*
**C. Williams, Brodszky, C. Parker, J. Addison II, Arnold, Allan Gray, Frankel,
Greenwood, Alwyn, Spoliansky, P. Green** and **Vaughan Williams** Various orchestras and
conductors. EMI mono CDGO2059* (9/94). *See review in the Collections section; refer to the
Index to Reviews.*

Dionysio Aguado
Spanish 1784-1849

Suggested listening ...
...Menuett. Andante. Guitar Method Lessons – Nos. 15, 19, 24, 26 and 29. Guitar Method Studies
– No. 17. *Coupled with* **Sor** Minuet, Op. 11 No. 6. Studies, Op. 6 – No. 6 in A major; No. 9 in
D minor; No. 11 in E major; No. 12 in A major. Study in A major, Op. 31 No. 19. Studies, Op. 35
– No. 13 in C major; No. 17 in D major; No. 22 in E minor. Minuetto, Op. 22. **Tárrega** Rosita.
Four Mazurkas. Estudio brillante de Alard. Gran vals. Preludios – No. 1 in E major; No. 8 in
E major (Lágrima); No. 9 in D minor (Endecha); No. 11 in D major. Alborada. Recuerdos de la
Alhambra. Maria. **Norbert Kraft** (gtr). Naxos 8 553007 (1/95).

Kalevi Aho
Finnish 1949-

Aho Symphony No. 9[a]. Cello Concerto[b]. [a]**Christian Lindberg** (tbn); [b]**Gary Hoffman** (vc); **Lahti
Symphony Orchestra / Osmo Vänskä.** BIS Ⓕ CD706 (62 minutes: DDD: 2/96).

The psychology of ninth symphonies is a problem area for composers. Reaching the common tally of
Beethoven, Schubert and Dvořák often heralds the footfalls of mortality, as with Mahler, who
declined to number *Das Lied von der Erde* – though the 'No. 9' curse still got him anyway – or
Miaskovsky, who penned his Ninth and Tenth concurrently. Qualitatively, Beethoven's cycle either
forces a challenge on an epic scale or its evasion. Few seem able to take the hurdle in their stride, as
Havergal Brian and Robert Simpson have managed to do. Typically, the Ninth (1993-4) by Kalevi
Aho – still only in his forties – is wholly individual. Coming with scarcely a pause for him to catch his
breath after the monumentality of No. 8 (1993), No. 9 is a polystylistic symphony-cum-trombone
concerto whose expressive world reaches back to the baroque (necessitating the excellent Christian
Lindberg to double up on the sackbut). Aho's best work has an incalculable quality that Haydn would
have appreciated, found for instance in the second movement's majestic fusion of the seemingly
incongruous elements set in opposition in the first. The concluding celebration of the third span does
not, however, quite scale the same heights. Aho's Cello Concerto (1983-4) is a dark affair and,
although more unified in manner than the symphony, a much tougher nut to crack. But as with the
rather brighter Violin Concerto, repeated acquaintance pays dividends. The performances are
exemplary and the recording, capturing everything from the quietest whisper to quite the loudest
climax you are likely to hear in a cello concerto, of demonstration quality. It is also excellent news that
BIS plan to record all of Aho's output.

Further listening ...
...Symphony No. 8[a]. Pergamon[b]. [b]Lilli Paasikivi, [b]Eeva-Liisa Saarinen, [b]Tom Nyman, [b]Matti Lehtinen (narrs); [a]Hans-Ola Ericsson, [b]Pauli Pietiläinen (orgs); **Lahti Symphony Orchestra / Osmo Vänskä**. BIS CD646 (3/95).

Jehan Alain

French 1911-1940

Suggested listening ...
...Intermezzo. Litanies, Op. 79. *Coupled with* **Dupré** Preludes and Fugues, Op. 7. **Franck** Prélude, fugue et variation in B minor, Op. 18. Fantaisie in A major. **Tournemire** Petite rapsodie improvisée. Cantilène improvisée. Improvisation sur le Te Deum. **Jane Watts** (org). Priory PRCD286 (9/90).

...Trois Danses. *Coupled with* **Langlais** Trois Paraphrases Grégoriennes, Op. 5. **Messiaen** Messe de la Pentecôte. **Catharine Crozier** (org). Delos DE3147 (2/95).

...Litanies, Op. 79. *Coupled with works by* **Sibelius, Sløgedal, Mulet, Lindberg, Mozart, Lefébure-Wély, Nielsen** and **Elgar** Christopher Herrick (org). Hyperion CDA66676 (8/94). *See review in the Collections section; refer to the Index to Reviews.*

...Deuxième fantaisie. Le jardin suspendu. *Coupled with works by* **Franck, Mendelssohn, Schumann, Andriessen, Saint-Saëns** and **Messiaen** Piet Kee (org). Chandos CHAN9188 (10/93). *See review in the Collections section; refer to the Index to Reviews.*

Isaac Albéniz

Spanish 1860-1909

Albéniz (orch. Halffter). Rapsodia española, Op. 70.
Falla Noches en los jardines de España.
Turina Rapsodia sinfónica, Op. 66. **Alicia de Larrocha** (pf); **London Philharmonic Orchestra / Rafael Frühbeck de Burgos**. Decca Ⓕ 410 289-2DH (52 minutes: DDD: 10/84). From 410 289-1DH (6/84).   Ⓖ

The three magically beautiful nocturnes which make up Falla's *Nights in the gardens of Spain* express the feelings and emotions evoked by contrasted surroundings, whilst Albéniz's enjoyably colourful *Rapsodia española* is a loosely assembled sequence of Spanish dances such as the *jota* and the *malagueña*. Like Falla's *Nights* the work was conceived as a piano solo, but this disc contains a version with orchestra arranged by Cristobal Halffter. The disc is completed by Turina's short, two-part work for piano and strings. All three pieces are excellently performed, but it is the Falla work which brings out the quality of Larrocha's artistry; her ability to evoke the colour of the Spanish atmosphere is remarkable. Frühbeck de Burgos supports her magnificently and persuades the LPO to produce some very Latin-sounding playing. The recording is suitably atmospheric.

Albéniz Iberia[a] (arr. Gray) – El Albaicín; Triana; Rondeña.
Granados Valses poéticos (trans. Williams).
Rodrigo Invocación y Danza. En los trigales.
Anonymous (arr. Llobet). Ten Catalan Folk-songs. **John Williams** (gtr); [a]**London Symphony Orchestra / Paul Daniels**. Sony Classical Ⓕ SK48480 (71 minutes: DDD: 7/92). Recorded 1989-91.   Ⓖ

The amalgam of technical guitaristic perfection in the face of daunting demands, fluid musicality and exemplary tone-production, caught in this exceptionally lifelike recording, represents a landmark in the instrument's march towards true parity with other instruments. Granados's *Valses* are unabridged, Rodrigo's moody *Invocación y Danza* comes in its original and more effective form, and two of the charming settings of Catalan folk-songs arranged by Llobet have no other recording. Nothing in Albéniz's virtuosic *Iberia* is accessible to the solo guitar, but with the aid of the London Symphony Orchestra and Gray's enchantingly evocative arrangements, Williams shows three of its movements in a new and colourful light. To anyone with the slightest interest in the guitar or Spanish romantic music this disc is a required purchase.

Additional recommendations ...
...Iberia. Navarra (compl. de Séverac). Suite española, Op. 47. **Alicia de Larrocha** (pf). Decca Ⓕ 417 887-2DH2 (two discs: 126 minutes: DDD: 6/88).   ⒼⒼ

...Iberia (orch. Arbós). **Falla** El sombrero de tres picos – ballet[a]. [a]**Jill Gomez** (sop); **Philharmonia Orchestra / Yan Pascal Tortelier**. Chandos Ⓕ CHAN8904 (72 minutes: DDD: 4/91).

...Iberia. Cantos de España, Op. 232. **Rafael Orozco** (pf). Auvidis Valois Ⓕ V4663 (two discs: 112 minutes: DDD: 11/92).

New review
Albéniz Iberia[a]. Navarra[a].
Granados Goyescas[b]. **Alicia de Larrocha** (pf). Double Decca Ⓜ 448 191-2DF2 (two discs: 141 minutes: ADD: 4/96). Items marked [a] from SXL6586/7 (10/73), [b]SXL6587 (12/77). Recorded 1972-6.   Ⓖ

Alicia de Larrocha has been playing these works, the greatest in the repertoire of Spanish piano music, all her life; and immersed as she was from her earliest childhood in the authentic tradition (her mother, her aunt and she herself were all trained at Granados's own school, of which she later became director), she has several times been asked to re-record them. She once said, rather wistfully, that she didn't consider herself a specialist but that Spanish music was what the public constantly demanded of her. One can sympathize with her if she feels inescapably cast in this mould – but then she shouldn't be so wonderfully persuasive in it! Complete technical assurance in these extremely demanding works (Albéniz himself, a brilliant pianist, was on the verge of withdrawing some of the *Iberia* pieces, such as "Lavapies", on the grounds that they were unplayable) has now become taken for granted, and Larrocha is not unique in mastering their terrors; but though there have been other distinguished interpreters, her readings have consistently remained a touchstone. She employs plenty of subtle rubato (for example in Albéniz's "Almería" and Granados's "Los requiebros") but possesses the ability to make it sound as natural as breathing; yet she can also preserve a stimulating tautness of rhythm, as in "El puerto". In the true sense of that much-misused word, this is *classical* playing, free from any superimposed striving for effect but responding fully to the music's sense of colour; and even in the densest of textures (as in "Eritaña") she is able to control conflicting tonal levels. *Goyescas*, which can tempt the unwary into exaggerated 'expressiveness', brings forth a wealth of poetic nuance, without losing shape – as for instance in the splendid "El amor y la muerte". The recorded quality throughout always was good and here emerges as fresh as ever. Anyone who does not already possess these recordings in one of their previous issues should not hesitate to acquire them now – all the more so since the two discs together cost the same as one full-price one.

Albéniz Mallorca, Op. 202. Suite española, Op. 47. Cantos de España, Op. 232 – Córdoba.
Granados Cuentos de la juventud – Dedicatoria. 15 Tonadillas – El majo Olvidado. 12 Danzas españolas, Op. 37 – Villanesca; Andaluza (Playera). 7 Valses poéticos.
Rodrigo Tres Piezas españolas. **Julian Bream** (gtr). RCA Navigator Ⓢ 74321 17903-2 (77 minutes: DDD: 3/95). Recorded 1982-3.   Ⓖ

In 1982 Julian Bream recorded a solo recital of music by Albéniz and Granados in his favourite recording venue, Wardour Chapel in Wiltshire. It offers playing of extraordinary magnetism and an almost total illusion of the great guitarist seated in the room making music just beyond one's loudspeakers; this effect is particularly striking in Albéniz's *Cordoba* and the *pianissimo* reprise of the central section of the Granados *Danza española* No. 5, which is quite magical. The other works included are all played with comparable spontaneity. RCA here reissue this disc at super-bargain price on their enterprising Navigator label; moreover, they have added another 15 minutes of music in the form of Rodrigo's *Tres Piezas españolas*, recorded a year later. The second of these, a seven-minute "Passacaglia", is quite masterly, while the final "Zapateado" brings characteristically chimerical virtuosity from the soloist. It is difficult to identify another recital of Spanish guitar music that surpasses this, and it is now one of the great bargains in the Navigator catalogue.

Additional recommendations ...

...Suite española – No. 1, Granada; No. 3, Sevilla; No. 4, Cádiz; No. 5, Asturias. Piezas caracteristicas, Op. 92 – No. 7, Zambra Granadina; No. 12, Torre bermeja. Cantos de España, Op. 232 – No. 4, Córdoba. Tango, Op. 163 No. 2, Mallorca, Op. 202. **John Williams** (gtr). Sony Classical Ⓕ SK36679 (44 minutes: DDD: 4/84).

...Suite española. **Granados** Goyescas – excerpts. **Falla** El amor brujo. **New Philharmonia Orchestra / Rafael Frühbeck de Burgos.** Decca Ⓜ 417 786-2DM (69 minutes: ADD: 10/89).

...Suite española – No. 1; No. 2, Cataluña. Cantos de España, Op. 232. **Granados** 12 Danzas españolas, Op. 37. Allegro de concierto. **Alicia de Larrocha** (pf). Decca Ⓜ 433 923-2DM2 (two discs: 119 minutes: DDD: 9/92).

...(arr. Byzantine). Suite española. Recuerdos de viaje, Op. 71. **Julian Byzantine** (gtr). Classics for Pleasure Ⓑ CD-CFP4631 (78 minutes: DDD: 4/94).

...Suite española – Sevilla; Cádiz; Aragón; Castilla. Pavana capricho, Op. 12. Iberia – Triana. Navarra. *Coupled with works by* **Falla, Lecuona** and **Infante** Katia and **Marielle Labèque** (pfs). Philips Ⓕ 438 938-2PH (59 minutes: DDD: 9/94). *See review in the Collections Section; refer to the Index to Reviews.*

Further listening ...

...Piano Sonatas – No. 3, Op. 68; No. 4, Op. 72; No. 5, Op. 82. L'automne, Op. 170. **Albert Guiovart** (pf). Harmonia Mundi Iberica HMI98 7007 (12/94).

...Navarra. *Coupled with works by* **Debussy, Szymanowsksi, Prokofiev, Villa-Lobos** and **Schumann** Artur Rubinstein (pf). RCA Victor Gold Seal 09026 61445-2 (10/93). *See review in the Collections section; refer to the Index to Reviews.*   ⒼⒼⒼ

Pere Alberch Vila   Spanish 1517-1582

Suggested listening ...

...Reyna soberana. Con voz llorosa. O Virgen sancta. El bon jorn. *Coupled with works by* **Flecha** and **Brudieu** La Colombina Ensemble. Accent ACC94103D (11/95). *See review under Brudieu; refer to the Index to Reviews.*

Sebastiàn de Albero
Spanish 1722-1756

Suggested listening ...
...14 Keyboard Sonatas. Three Keyboard Sonatas (misattributed to D. Scarlatti) – F sharp minor, Kk142; C major, Kk143; G major, Kk144. **Joseph Payne** (hpd). BIS CD629 (4/94). ✎   ⓔ

Stephen Albert
American 1941-1992

S. Albert Cello Concerto[a].
Bartók Viola Concerto, Sz120[b].
Bloch Schelomo[a]. **Yo-Yo Ma** ([a]vc/[b]alto vn); **Baltimore Symphony Orchestra / David Zinman.** Sony Classical ⓔ SK57961 (78 minutes: DDD: 3/95). Recorded 1993.   ⓖ
The Albert Concerto is a gritty, Barber-style tussle, with its various participants scored on more or less equal terms; whereas Bartók's transparent dialogue (as played here on an alto violin) has soloist and orchestra co-exist rather than interrelate, and Bloch's sumptuous evocation of King Solomon alternates candid incantation with huge, tonally complex orchestral tuttis. Albert composed a number of orchestral works, including two symphonies – the second of which lay unfinished at the time of his death. As it happens, this four-movement Cello Concerto (1990) is also conceived on a symphonic scale. Fairly cosmopolitan in overall style, it opens with an intense, rhapsodizing solo, before a blast of brass and a flurry of strings make way for a good deal of agitated argument. Ideas throughout are darkly colourful but conventional; there's a scurrying scherzo, a pensive *Larghetto* and a ten-minute finale that occasionally suggests Bartók or the Stravinsky of the *Symphony in Three Movements*. Although initial encounters hardly suggest a revelatory masterpiece, the combination of Albert's inventive music, Ma's intense delivery and Zinman's alert conducting makes for a pretty riveting experience. As to the Bartók Concerto, Ma's decision to use a vertical viola, or alto violin stems from his apparent dissatisfaction with "the registral displacement" of the authorized cello version. Using the alto violin also meant honouring the work's original pitch, although Wolfram Christ's superb DG recording (reviewed under Bartók) is both richer in tone and more urgently communicated. Zinman appears to have been working from a revision that incorporates certain re-interpretations of Bartók's original sketches. It's a good performance, strongly accompanied and it 'fits' well – in programming terms, that is – between Albert and Bloch. *Schelomo* himself wails or prays to theatrical effect. Zinman's superbly recorded Baltimore players rise to survey Bloch's towering climaxes with a combination of bravura and finesse.

Tomaso Albinoni
Italian 1671-1751

Albinoni Concerti a cinque, Op. 7 – No. 3 in B flat major; No. 6 in D major; No. 9 in F major; No. 12 in C major. Concerti a cinque, Op. 9 – No. 2 in D minor; No. 5 in C major; No. 8 in G minor; No. 11 in B flat major. **Anthony Robson** (ob); **Collegium Musicum 90 / Simon Standage** (vn). Chandos Chaconne ⓔ CHAN0579 (72 minutes: DDD: 5/95). ✎ Recorded 1993.   ⓖⓖ
Exaggerated attention to one of a composer's works can breed neglect of the others, as seems to have been the case with Albinoni and the famous (and spurious) *Adagio*. Recordings of this piece occupy over seven column inches in *The Gramophone Classical Catalogue*, at the expense of other more worthy compositions. All the concertos of Op. 7 and Nos. 2, 5, 8 and 11 of Op. 9 are for solo oboe and strings or, better, for strings *with* oboe: the soloist complements rather than 'opposes' the ripieno, interacting with it and eschewing 'spotlit' virtuosity. Albinoni treats the oboe like a voice (another wind instrument), whereas Vivaldi (whose oboe works were written at about the same time) has the agile violin more in mind. There isn't one 'filler' in either set, which means that there isn't one in the programme either, and the slow movements have tunes that stay in the mind. Anthony Robson is velvet-toned but with the hint of an edge (matching that of the strings), phrasing flawlessly and alert to lyricism and poetry where they appear over the parapet. Collegium Musicum 90 are one of the very best baroque bands to emerge in recent years and here they are in their element. The recorded balance is just right, keeping soloist and strings in equal perspective. In every positive sense these are listener-friendly works, and this recording bids strongly for a place on every shelf. It is good news indeed that Chandos intend to complete both of these sets.
Additional recommendations ...
...Op. 7 Nos. 3, 6, 9 and 12. Op. 9 Nos. 2, 5, 8 and 11. **London Harpsichord Ensemble / Sarah Francis** (ob). Unicorn-Kanchana ⓔ DKPCD9088 (74 minutes: DDD: 3/90).
...Op. 9 – No. 2; No. 6 in G major; No. 9 in C major. Concerto in C major. **Vivaldi** Concertos – C major, RV560; F major, RV457; C major, RV559. **Paul Goodwin** (ob); **King's Consort / Robert King.** Hyperion ⓔ CDA66383 (70 minutes: DDD: 6/91). ✎
...Op. 7 – No. 1 in D major; No. 2; No. 3; No. 4 in G major; No. 5; No. 6; No. 7 in A major; No. 8; No. 9; No. 10 in B flat major; No. 11; No. 12r. Sinfonie e concerti a cinque, Op. 2 – No. 5 in D major; No. 6 in G minor. **Heinz Holliger, Maurice Bourgue** (obs); **I Musici.** Philips ⓔ 432 115-2PII2 (two discs: 94 minutes: DDD: 1/93).

...Op. 9 – No. 2; No. 3 in F major[a]; No. 5; No. 8; No. 9[a]; No. 11. **Anthony Camden,** [a]**Julia Girdwood** (obs); **London Virtuosi / John Georgiadis.** Naxos Ⓢ 8 550739 (64 minutes: DDD: 3/94).
...Op. 7 No. 3 (transcribed for trumpet). *Coupled with works by* **Corelli, Vivaldi, Torelli, A. Marcello, Viviani, Franceschini** and **Baldassare** Håkan Hardenberger (tpt); **I Musici.** Philips Ⓕ 442 131-2PH (54 minutes: DDD: 5/95). *See review in the Collections section; refer to the Index to Reviews.* Ⓖ

New review

Albinoni Concerti a cinque, Op. 10 – No. 1 in B flat major; No. 2 in G minor; No. 3 in C major; No. 4 in G major; No. 5 in A major, No. 6 in D major, No. 7 in F major; No. 8 in G minor; No. 9 in C major; No. 10 in F major; No. 11 in C major; No. 12 in B flat major. **Piero Toso, Giorgio Carmigola** (vns); **I Solisti Veneti / Claudio Scimone.** Erato Ⓜ 0630-11222-2 (two discs: 108 minutes: ADD: 2/96). Recorded 1981.

Albinoni's 12 Concertos (*Opera decima*), Op. 10 represent a comparatively recent discovery. Although their existence has long been known (as listed by the Amsterdam publisher, Le Céne), they only reappeared in the 1960s when the music was found in a Swedish library at the Castle of Leufsta. Four of the set are violin concertos (Nos. 6, 8, 10 and 12), three *concerti grossi* with a small *concertino* group (Nos. 2, 3 and 4), while the remainder have no soloists. The works date from the mid 1730s, 13 years after the splendid Op. 9 and are of additional interest in demonstrating the development of the string *sinfonia* (all are in the three-part format of the Italian overture – quick-slow-quick). But it is for their melodic warmth that these concertos are to be cherished – readily demonstrated by the lovely slow movement of the D major Violin Concerto (No. 6), the serene *Adagio* of the C major *Concerto grosso* (No. 3) and the gracious, Boccherini-like Minuet finale of the same work. They also have an outgoing vitality that is entirely engaging. The playing (directed by Claudio Scimone – Piero Toso and Giorgio Carmigola are the soloists) – on modern instruments – is warm, polished and musical and the recording has an ample acoustic. Some may prefer more sharply etched detail of the kind associated with period performance (particularly in the *concerti grossi*). However, the resonant string timbres are agreeably natural and immaculately transferred to CD.

Albinoni Six Sonate da chiesa, Op. 4. 12 Trattenimenti armonici per camera, Op. 6. **Locatelli Trio** (Elizabeth Wallfisch, vn; Richard Tunnicliffe, vc; Paul Nicholson, hpd/org). Hyperion Ⓕ CDA66831/2 (two discs: 159 minutes: DDD: 4/95). 🎵 Recorded 1991-2. Ⓖ

All the pieces on these discs are violin sonatas rather than trio sonatas but, sensibly, the keyboard continuo player Paul Nicholson uses harpsichord for Op. 6 and organ for Op. 4, thereby providing the listener with variety in colour. This variety is maximized by a sensible decision to intermingle the two sets. Each sonata is cast in the four movement slow-fast-slow-fast *da chiesa* pattern though, as with Corelli but to an even greater extent, Albinoni far from keeps to the *da chiesa* spirit, introducing a wealth of dance measures. Almost invariably the music is graceful in character, melodically appealing – above all, as so often with Albinoni – in the slow movements such as the *Adagio* of Op. 4 No. 6, and expressively restrained. These qualities are not lost on the violinist, Elizabeth Wallfisch who affectingly captures the limpid, reflective content of slow movements, on the one hand, and the brilliance of the faster ones on the other. Her continuo cellist, Richard Tunnicliffe, gives her discreet and sensitive support throughout. Perhaps a dimension of playful virtuosity has not perhaps been fully realized. In all essentials, though, this is an enjoyable and very worthwhile release, illuminating less familiar aspects of Albinoni's music.

Further listening ...

...Concerti a cinque, Op. 5. **I Musici.** Philips 422 251-2PSL (11/88).
...Il nascimento dell'Aurora. **Soloists; I Solisti Veneti / Claudio Scimone.** Erato 4509-96374-2 (7/95). Ⓖ

Hugo Alfvén
Swedish 1872-1960

Alfvén Swedish Rhapsodies – No. 1, Op. 19, "Midsummer Vigil"; No. 2, Op. 24, "Upsala-rapsodi"; No. 3, "Dalarapsodi". A Legend of the Skerries, Op. 20. Gustav Adolf II, Op. 49 – Elegy. **Iceland Symphony Orchestra / Petri Sakari.** Chandos Ⓕ CHAN9313 (70 minutes: DDD: 3/95). Recorded 1993.

Petri Sakari gives us the most natural, unaffected and satisfying *Midsummer Vigil* to be heard on disc. He is light in touch, responsive to each passing mood and every dynamic nuance, self-effacing and completely at the service of the composer. Moreover in the *Upsala-rapsodi* and its later companion, he is fresher and more persuasive than any of his rivals on record. Even the Wagnerian-Straussian echoes from the skerries sound convincing. The only reservation concerns the *Elegy* from the incidental music to Ludwig Nordström's play about Gustav Adolf II, which might have benefited from greater reticence. Unusually for Sakari, he does not tell the tale simply or let the music speak for itself. The recorded sound is refreshingly free from analytical point-making; everything is there in the right perspective, though listeners whose first response is to find the recording recessed will find that a higher level of playback than usual will produce impressively natural results on high-grade equipment.

Additional recommendation ...
...A Legend of the Skerries. Symphony No. 4, Op. 39, "From the Outermost Skerries"[a]. [a]**Soloists; Stockholm Philharmonic Orchestra / Neeme Järvi.** BIS Ⓕ CD505 (64 minutes: DDD: 8/92).

Alfvén Symphony No. 5 in A minor, Op. 54. The Mountain King – Suite. Gustav II Adolf, Op. 49 – Elegy. **Royal Stockholm Philharmonic Orchestra / Neeme Järvi.** BIS Ⓕ CD585 (68 minutes: DDD: 1/94). Recorded 1992.
The first movement of the Fifth Symphony (1942-52) is a long one lasting over 17 minutes, with echoes of Wagner and Sibelius – and in the second group a reminder of Bax. Given the fervent advocacy it receives here from Neeme Järvi and the Royal Stockholm Philharmonic, it makes a strong impression. So, too, do the dreamy musings of the slow movement. Järvi is also at his most persuasive and gets marvellously responsive and committed playing from the Stockholm orchestra especially in the first two movements and *The Mountain King* – and the touching "Elegy" from *Gustav II Adolf*, perhaps Alfvén's most affecting and deeply felt piece. The BIS team have come up with a state-of-the-art recording, natural and lifelike. The perspective could hardly be improved upon and each orchestral strand has presence and is effortlessly truthful in timbre.

Further listening ...
...Symphony No. 2 in D major, R28. Midsummer Vigil – Swedish Rhapsody No. 1, R45. **Stockholm Philharmonic Orchestra / Neeme Järvi.** BIS CD385 (7/88).
...Songs, Op. 28 – No. 3, I kiss your hand; No. 6, The forest sleeps. *Coupled with works by* **Rangström, Stenhammar, Peterson-Berger, Sigurd von Koch** and **Sjögren** Anne Sofie **von Otter** (mez); **Bengt Forsberg** (pf). DG 449 189-2GH (5/96). *See review in the Collections section; refer to the Index to Reviews.* ⒼⒼ

Charles-Valentin Alkan

French 1813-1888

Alkan 25 Préludes dans les tons majeurs et mineur, Op. 31.
Shostakovich 24 Preludes, Op. 34. **Olli Mustonen** (pf). Decca Ⓕ 433 055-2DH (76 minutes: DDD: 10/91). Recorded 1990. *Gramophone Award Winner 1992.* ⒼⒼ
It was brave of Decca to launch the career of their then newly-signed pianist with a disc of miniatures few people actually know since the *oeuvre* of Charles-Valentin Alkan is usually confined to specialist labels and second rate executants. The 25 Préludes are a reasonably benign introduction to Alkan's idiosyncratic world – elusive and quirky to be sure but less ruthlessly barnstorming than much of his output. They are by no means easy pieces to bring off, but you wouldn't know it from Mustonen's exceptionally assured, brilliantly poised readings. Where rival versions are content to offer the 25 Préludes without coupling, Mustonen adds deft and sparkling performances of Shostakovich's not exactly insubstantial Op. 34 Preludes. Exceptional pianism, excellent, bright recording and helpful notes.

Alkan Transcription de Concert (Beethoven's Piano Concerto No. 3 in C minor, Op. 37 – first movement). Three Etudes, Op. 76.
Busoni Sonatina No. 6 super Carmen (Kammerfantasie).
Chopin/Alkan Piano Concerto No. 1 in E minor, Op. 11 – Romanza.
Medtner Danza festiva, Op. 38 No. 3. **Marc-André Hamelin** (pf). Hyperion Ⓕ CDA66765 (72 minutes: DDD: 3/95). Recorded live in 1994. ⒼⒼ
The solo transcriptions on the first half of this disc are not intended as substitutes for the real thing, at least not in the context of this disc, but are presented here as supreme examples of the art of piano transcription in the late nineteenth century. In addition, they are superb display pieces, revealing not only the subtleties of the transcriber's art and, in this case, the pianist's ability to render them audible, but also Hamelin's extraordinary ability to make the pieces sound like originals rather than transcriptions. Indeed, in the Alkan transcription of the first movement of Beethoven's Third Piano Concerto, the absence of the orchestra never becomes a concern. The principal glory of the disc, however, is Hamelin's account of Alkan's *Etudes*, Op. 76, for the hands separately and reunited – an exceptionally formidable opus (one that Ronald Smith claims "alone establish[es] Alkan as the rival, if not indeed the peer, of Liszt as the joint architect of transcendental piano technique") which here receives an equally formidable and awe-inspiring performance. We also have the added frisson of knowing that what we hear is a single take before a live audience; listen to the hair-raising final study, a blistering, unbroken five-minute salvo of *prestissimo* semiquavers. The remaining items on the disc, a scintillating account of Busoni's *Sonatina* No. 6 and Medtner's ebullient *Danza festiva* from Op. 38, provide further evidence that Hamelin is a considerable presence in the pianistic world. The recorded sound varies a little from piece to piece (they were recorded over three evenings in the Wigmore Hall in London) but all are excellent in quality and have a natural, intimate ambience.

New review
Alkan 12 Etudes dans les tons mineurs, Op. 39. Nocturne, Op. 22. Etude in F major, Op. 35 No. 5. Assez vivement, Op. 38 No. 1. Préludes, Op. 31 – No. 8, La chanson de la folle au bord de la mer; No. 12, Le temps qui n'est plus; No. 13, J'étais endormie, mais mon coeur veillait. Esquisses,

Op. 63 – No. 2, La staccatissimo; No. 4, Les cloches; No. 11, Les soupirs; No. 61, En songe. Gros temps, Op. 74, First Suite No. 2. Barcarolle, Op. 65 No. 6. **Jack Gibbons** (pf). ASV Ⓔ CDDCS227 (two discs: 155 minutes: DDD: 11/95). Recorded 1995.   ⒺⒺ

ASV and Jack Gibbons enter the Alkan arena with this extremely generous two-CD set. "Comme le vent" ("Like the wind"), the opening *Etude* from Op. 39, is a real baptism of fire for the pianist. Marked *prestissimamente* it is an unrelenting deluge of notes which, if played at Alkan's specified metronome marking, travels at the rate of 160 bars per minute, or to put it another way, traverses 20 densely packed pages in just 4'30". Gibbons throws caution to the wind, and completes the whirlwind in a staggering 4'38". Despite the odd occasion when he comes perilously close to tumbling into the abyss this ranks among the most exhilarating feats of pianism on disc. Listening to these commanding and exceedingly sure-footed performances one is left with the feeling that Gibbons has grown with and nurtured these pieces for some time. The following four *Etudes* make up the Symphony for Solo Piano, and if anything Gibbons is even more impressive in his reading of this striking work. Comparision with Ringeissen reveals a closer adherence to Alkan's tempo and metronome markings and thus gives the Symphony a much greater sense of impetus and rhythmic drive compared with Ringeissen's more spacious, airy account. Moving on to the Concerto for Solo Piano (*Etudes* Nos. 8-10) Gibbons faces daunting competition from Marc-André Hamelin. Technically their readings are pretty well matched; however, Hamelin is crisper and more classical in approach compared with Gibbons's more wildly romantic reading. More extraordinary feats of virtuosity await the listener in the twelfth *Etude* ("Le festin d'Esope") and the *Allegro barbaro* from the Op. 35 *Etudes*, but the delightful selection of miscellaneous pieces with which Gibbons fills the remainder of the set shows not only the more introverted side of Alkan's creativity but also allows Gibbons to display a less ostentatious and more directly poetic aspect of his playing. The simple *Nocturne* in B major, with its Chopinesque heartbeat, is beautifully rendered as are "Les soupirs" and "En songe" from the *Esquisses*, Op. 63 and the *Barcarolle* Op. 65 No. 6. However, the highlight of these miniatures comes with Gibbons's sensitive and effective delivery of the potently atmospheric "La chanson de la folle au bord de la mer" ("Song of the mad woman on the seashore"), surely one of the most curious piano pieces to emerge from the nineteenth century. All in all, an exceptionally impressive issue that can be highly recommended to both Alkan devotees and newcomers alike. The recorded sound is excellent.

Additional recommendations ...

...Etudes dans les tons mineurs, Op. 39 Nos. 8-10. Concerto pour piano seul. **Marc-André Hamelin** (pf). Music and Arts Ⓕ MACD724 (50 minutes: DDD: 8/93).

...Etudes dans les tons mineurs, Op. 39 Nos. 3 and 12. 12 Etudes dans les tons majeurs, Op. 35. **Bernard Ringeissen** (pf). Marco Polo Ⓕ 8 223351 (78 minutes: DDD: 11/93).

New review

Alkan Grande sonate, Op. 33, "Les quatre âges". Sonatine, Op. 61. Barcarolle, Op. 65 No. 6. Etudes dans les tons mineurs, Op. 39 – No. 12, "Le festin d'Esope". **Marc-André Hamelin** (pf). Hyperion Ⓕ CDA66794 (70 minutes: DDD: 12/95). Recorded 1994.   Ⓔ

Alkan's *Grande sonate*, subtitled "The four ages", is an extraordinary piece in many respects, not least in its rather unconventional layout of four movements, each employing progressively slower tempos. Perhaps for this reason it has never attained a place in the repertoire – the *Extrêmement lent* finale is hardly the sort of movement to ignite an overwhelming response from an audience, despite the feats of hair-raising bravura required in the first two movements. Hamelin's performance is everything one could wish for. The crispness and precision of his finger-work in the dazzling first movement (Alkan's portrait of the man in his twenties) is quite breathtaking and the sometimes superhuman feats of pianism demanded in the Faust-inspired second movement are executed with astounding ease. His reading of the third movement (Alkan's imagined picture of domestic bliss) is beautifully poised and charmingly rendered whilst the tragic, Promethean finale is most effectively and powerfully projected, though it should be noted that here Hamelin is no less than 2'46" faster than Ronald Smith, whose reading is perhaps closer to Alkan's written tempo indication of *Extrêmement lent*. The *Sonatine*, Op. 61 is an entirely different matter, "concise and concentrated in the extreme" is how François Luguenot describes it in his informative booklet-note. Hamelin's direct, finely articulated no-nonsense reading brings out the clarity and economy of the writing, and he is quick, too, to underscore the work's more classical stance. A beautifully serene and hypnotic account of the seductive "Barcarolle" follows, and the disc closes with a stunning display of pianistic gymnastics in the shape of "Le festin d'Esope" from the Op. 39 *Etudes*. Recorded sound is excellent. Another Hyperion/Hamelin must.

Additional recommendation ...

...Grande sonate, "Les quatre âges". **Ronald Smith** (pf). EMI CDM7 64280-2 (5/92).

Further listening ...

...Concerti da Camera, Op. 10 – No. 1 in A minor; No. 2 in C sharp minor. *Coupled with works by* **Henselt** **Marc-André Hamelin** (pf); **BBC Scottish Symphony Orchestra / Martyn Brabbins.** Hyperion CDA66717 (8/94). *See review under Henselt; refer to the Index to Reviews. Gramophone Editor's choice.*   ⒺⒺ

...Grand duo concertante in F sharp minor, Op. 21. Sonate de concert in E major, Op. 47. Trio in G minor, Op. 30. **Trio Alkan.** Marco Polo 8 223383 (8/93).   Ⓔ

...Quatre impromptus, Op. 32 (1). Deuxième recueil d'impromptus, Op. 32 (2). Salut, cendre du pauvre!, Op. 45. Alleluia, Op. 25. Rondeau chromatique, Op. 12. Variations on a theme from

Steibelt's Orage Concerto, Op. 1. Super flumina Babylonis, Op. 52. **Laurent Martin** (pf). Marco Polo 8 223657 (4/95).
...Esquisses, Op. 63. **Laurent Martin** (pf). Marco Polo 8 223352 (4/95).
...Sonatine, Op. 61. Zorcico (Spanish Dance). 12 Etudes dans les tons mineurs, Op. 39 – No. 3, Scherzo diabolico. Two Nocturnes, Op. 57. Gigue et air ballet dans le style ancien, Op. 24. Marches, quasi da cavalleria, Op. 37 – No. 1. Quatrième recueil de chants, Op. 67 – No. 6. Saltarelle, Op. 23. **Bernard Ringeissen** (pf). Harmonia Mundi Musique d'abord HMA190 927 (11/88).
...13 Prières, Op. 64. Petits préludes sur les gammes du plainchant. Impromptu dur le choral de Luther, Op. 69. **Kevin Bowyer** (org). Nimbus NI5089 (5/89).

Gregorio Allegri Italian c1582-1652

New review
Allegri Miserere mei (two versions). Missa Vidi turbam magnam. De ore prudentis[a]. Repleti sunt omnes[a]. Cantate domino[a]. **A Sei Voci / Bernard Fabre-Garrus** with [a]**Dominique Ferran** (org). Auvidis Astrée Ⓕ E8524 (62 minutes: DDD: 9/95). Texts and translations included. Recorded 1994.

Gregori Allegri's fame rests upon a single piece, a simple enough setting of the psalm *Miserere mei* into which extravagantly ornamented passages for a second choir of soloists are interpolated. In practice it was these passages, which for centuries remained a jealously guarded secret of the papal choir who alone had access to the music and performed it once a year (during Holy Week), that ensured Allegri's reputation. This record presents two versions of the piece. The first is sung with ornamentation added by the French musicologist Jean Lionnet following seventeenth-century models, while the second presents the Burney-Alfieri version familiar from the classic 1963 recording made by King's College Choir directed by David Willcocks. The curiously named group A Sei Voci (in fact there are ten of them) produce a rather varied sound, at times somewhat flat and white but at its best with an appropriate Italianate edge. For the most part the embellishments are negotiated with style and verve; just occasionally (in the first *Miserere*) they are fuzzy or insecure. *Miserere mei* apart, hardly any of Allegri's music is heard either liturgically or in the concert-hall. By training a pupil of Nanino, a distinguished follower of Palestrina, his best music is confidently written in the High Renaissance contrapuntal manner. The six-voice *Missa Vidi turbam magnam*, composed on one of his own motets, is a fine work, and shows that the *stile antico*, far from being a mere academic exercise, could still be vividly sonorous and dramatic, qualities which are successfully brought out in this reading. The record is nicely rounded out with a selection of short continuo motets in the popular new manner, well-established in Northern Italy, which was then becoming fashionable in Rome.

Additional recommendations ...
...Miserere mei. **Palestrina** Stabat mater a 8. Hodie beata virgo. Senex puerum portabat. Magnificat a 8. Litaniae de Beata Vergine Mariae I a 8. **Roy Goodman** (treb); **King's College Choir, Cambridge / Sir David Willcocks**. Decca Ovation Ⓜ 421 147-2DM (56 minutes: ADD: 5/89).   Ⓖ
...Miserere mei. **Lotti** Crucifixus. **Palestrina** Missa Papae Marcelli. Stabat mater a 8. **The Sixteen / Harry Christophers**. Collins Classics Ⓕ 5009-2 (56 minutes: DDD: 10/90).   Ⓖ
...Miserere mei. *Coupled with works by* **B. Rose, Brahms, Britten, Harvey, Mendelssohn, Stanford, Tavener** and **Wise** Jeremy Budd (treb); St Paul's Cathedral Choir / John Scott with **Andrew Lucas** (org). Hyperion Ⓕ CDA66439 (76 minutes: DDD: 10/91). *See review in the Collections section; refer to the Index to Reviews.*
...Miserere mei. *Coupled with works by* **Palestrina, Byrd, Parsons, Viadana, Tallis, Philips, G. Gabrieli, Lotti, Tye, Victoria** and **Monteverdi** Soloists; Westminster Cathedral Choir / James O'Donnell. Hyperion Ⓕ CDA66850 (72 minutes: DDD: 5/96). *See review in the Collections section; refer to the Index to Reviews.*

Francisco António de Almeida Portuguese c1702-1755

Almeida La Giuditta. **Lena Lootens, Francesca Congiu** (sops); **Axel Köhler** (alto); **Martyn Hill** (ten); **Cologne Concerto / René Jacobs**. Harmonia Mundi Ⓕ HMC90 1411/2 (two discs: 121 minutes: DDD: 11/92). 🖊 Text and translation included. Recorded 1992.   ⒼⒼ

Francisco António de Almeida is a name that will be unfamiliar to all but the most ardent *aficionados* of baroque music. Born in Portugal, he spent some time in Rome which led to the composition of several comic operas and a large amount of sacred music, most of which has been lost. *La Giuditta*, based on the biblical story of Judith's victory over Holofernes, is his only surviving oratorio. Stylistically he is closest to Handel, with those characteristic Handelian harmonies in "Quella fiamma" on track 3, though *Giuditta* was written before any of Handel's oratorios except *La Resurrezione*. But Almeida establishes a style very much his own from the very first chord, here brilliantly brought to life by René Jacobs and his Cologne Concerto. Martyn Hill as Holofernes is appropriately war-like, though he is occasionally choppy, notably in "Invitti miei guerrieri". Axel

Köhler as Ozia, beseiged by Holofernes's armies, is, however, superb, with a fine dramatic range: the gentleness of his "Tortorella, se rimira" is particularly moving. Lena Lootens in the title-role is wonderfully stylish, pure of voice throughout "Sento che dice al cor", with great strength and clean *fioriture* in her plea to God to defeat her enemies, "Dalla destra onnipotente". It is perhaps a pity that the part of Achiorre should have been written for a soprano: Francesca Congiu has a hard time convincing listeners that she is indeed Commander of the Ammonites, though this illusion would probably be easier to sustain on stage. René Jacobs guides the work with an unerring sense of pace and drama. From the attention-grabbing Overture through to the final notes, this is a totally committed, totally compelling performance of a newly discovered masterpiece.

William Alwyn
British 1905-1985

Alwyn (arr. Palmer) Odd Man Out – Suite. The History of Mr Polly – Suite. The Fallen Idol – Suite. The Rake's Progress – Calypso Music. **London Symphony Orchestra / Richard Hickox.** Chandos Ⓕ CHAN9243 (72 minutes: DDD: 3/94). Recorded 1993.   Ⓖ

William Alwyn, like Malcolm Arnold, made his name as a composer of film music in the great days of British cinema. In the immediate post-war years he wrote the scores on the present disc. British films in those days had 'symphonic' scores and were awash with orchestral sound. *Odd Man Out* inspired the most powerful and lyrically poignant music here, while *The History of Mr Polly* (a much-liked movie, with John Mills memorable in the title-role) is charmingly lightweight, especially in the "Punting scene", and is really rather touching in the "Utopian sunset" of the finale. *The Fallen Idol* (an outstanding movie, written by Graham Greene) is about a small boy who witnesses a death and is in danger of implicating his friend, the Butler (Ralph Richardson). The music subtly underlines the action and feelings of the characters. The original scores were unwittingly destroyed at Pinewood Studios but Christopher Palmer has lovingly restored each one for this disc. Hickox conducts all this music with total commitment and it is beautifully played and recorded.

Additional recommendation ...

...The Rake's Progress – Calypso Music. *Coupled with works by* **Arnold, Vaughan Williams, Addinsell, C. Williams, Brodszky, C. Parker, J. Addison II, Allan Gray, Frankel, Greenwood, Spoliansky** and **P. Green** Various orchestras and conductors. EMI mono Ⓔ CDGO2059* (65 minutes: ADD: 9/94). *See review in the Collections section; refer to the Index to Reviews.*

Alwyn Miss Julie. **Jill Gomez** (sop) Miss Julie; **Benjamin Luxon** (bar) Jean; **Della Jones** (mez) Kristin; **John Mitchinson** (ten) Ulrik; **Philharmonia Orchestra / Vilem Tausky.** Lyrita Ⓕ SRCD2218 (two discs: 118 minutes: ADD: 3/93). Notes and text included. From SRCS121/2 (12/83). Recorded 1979. *Gramophone Editor's choice.*   Ⓖ

A magnificent recorded presentation of Alwyn's strong and characterful adaptation of August Strindberg's drama which was three years in the making and first performed in 1977 for a BBC Radio 3 broadcast. The composer himself wrote the fluent (if somewhat over-sanitized) libretto, creating in the process an extra character in the personage of Ulrik, the gamekeeper; in the opera, Ulrik (off-stage) shoots the lap-dog Miss Julie wants to take with her when she elopes with her manservant Jean, whereas in Strindberg's original it is Jean who (on on-stage) horrifically kills Miss Julie's pet finch – both dramatically and symbolically a far more pungent gesture. As ever, Alwyn's idiom is approachable (there are strong echoes of Puccini and Walton) and impeccably crafted; certainly the Philharmonia seem to revel in the confident orchestral writing, and Vilem Tausky directs proceedings with real passion and conviction. The cast, too, is uniformly excellent: Benjamin Luxon is on commanding form as Jean, whilst Jill Gomez in the title-role produces the most ravishing sounds throughout (try sampling her gorgeous delivery of the Midsummer Night aria at the end of Act 1 Scene 1). The Kingsway Hall sessions took place over a four-day period in January 1979. The expertly-annotated booklet may say "ADD", but this is, technically speaking, as realistic a recording as you will ever hear, with soloists set in perfect relief against an impeccably balanced orchestral backdrop. From every conceivable point of view, then, this welcome CD reissue represents an unqualified success.

Further listening ...

...Concerto for Flute and Eight Wind Instruments[a]. Suite for Oboe and Harp[b]. Music for Three Players[d]. Trio for Flute, Cello and Piano[e]. [ace]**Kate Hill** (fl); [d]**Joy Farrall** (cl); [d]**Leland Chen** (vn); [e]**Caroline Dearnley** (vc); [c]**Ieuan Jones** (hp); [bde]**Julius Drake** (pf); [a]**London Haffner Wind Ensemble / Nicholas Daniel** ([b]ob). Chandos CHAN9152 (10/93).

...Violin Concerto[a]. Symphony No. 3. [a]**Lydia Mordkovitch** (vn). **London Symphony Orchestra / Richard Hickox.** Chandos CHAN9187 (1/94).

...Concerto for Oboe, Harp and Strings[a]. Concerti grossi – No. 1 in B flat major; No. 2 in G major; No. 3. [a]**Nicholas Daniel** (ob); **City of London Sinfonia / Richard Hickox.** Chandos CHAN8866 (9/92).

...Clarinet Sonata[a]. Flute Sonata[b]. Oboe Sonata[c]. Divertimento[d]. Crépuscule[e]. Sonata impromptu[f]. [bd]**Kate Hill** (fl); [c]**Nicholas Daniel** (ob); [a]**Joy Farrall** (cl); [e]**Ieuan Jones** (hp); [f]**Leland Chen** (vn); [f]**Clare McFarlane** (va); [abc]**Julius Drake** (pf). Chandos CHAN9197 (11/94).

...String Quartets – No. 1 in D minor; No. 2, "Spring Waters". **London Quartet.** Chandos CHAN9219 (5/94).
...Symphonies – No. 1 in D major; No. 4. **London Philharmonic Orchestra / William Alwyn.** Lyrita SRCD227 (7/92). Ⓖ
...Symphony No. 1 in D major. Piano Concerto No. 1[a]. [a]**Howard Shelley** (pf); **London Symphony Orchestra / Richard Hickox.** Chandos CHAN9155 (5/93).
...Symphonies – No. 2; No. 3; No. 5, "Hydriotaphia". **London Philharmonic Orchestra / William Alwyn.** Lyrita SRCD228 (10/92). Ⓖ
...Lyra Angelica[a]. Autumn Legend[b]. Pastoral fantasia[c]. Tragic Interlude. [a]**Rachel Masters** (hp); [b]**Nicholas Daniel** (cor ang); [c]**Stephen Tees** (va); **City of London Sinfonia / Richard Hickox.** Chandos CHAN9065 (10/92). Ⓖ
...Invocations[a]. A Leave-taking[b]. [a]**Jill Gomez** (sop); [b]**Anthony Rolfe Johnson** (ten); [a]**John Constable**, [b]**Graham Johnson** (pfs). Chandos CHAN9220 (6/94).

Joan Albert Amargós
Spanish 1950-

New review
Amargós Clarinet Concerto[a]. Trio for Flute, Clarinet and Cor Anglais[b]. Sonata for Two Flutes[c]. Flute Sonata in E major[d]. [bcd]**Jaume Cortadellas**, [c]**Patrizia Mazo** (fls); [a]**Walter Boeykens**, [b]**Xavier Figuerola** (cls); [b]**Philippe Vallet** (cor ang); [d]**Lluís Vidal** (pf); [a]**Chamber Orchestra of the Teatre Lliure, Barcelona / Josep Pons.** Harmonia Mundi Ⓕ HMC90 5232 (75 minutes: DDD: 6/96). Recorded 1994-5.
Determined efforts are being made in Spain to bring its contemporary composers to the notice of the outside world, which hears relatively little of their works; the present disc is helpful in throwing light on the activities of one of them. Joan Albert Amargós (who is also a clarinettist) belongs to a generation that represents a less severe vein and less radical, far more accessible idiom than some of the older composers. As exemplified in his skilfully written, rhythmically vital Clarinet Concerto (composed last year and brilliantly played by the Belgian virtuoso Walter Boeykens), that idiom is individual and decidedly eclectic, with influences of all kinds, including stylized jazz elements. The three inventive chamber works again show real understanding of the nature of the instruments employed, and are couched in an elaborately contrapuntal style – the Sonata for flute and piano being the most dissonant whose description in the booklet as "neo-classical" is altogether too restrictive. What should make Amargós appealing to music-lovers in general is that he seems to possess a sense of humour.

Alearco Ambrosi
Italian 1931-

Suggested listening ...
...Messa.*Coupled with* **Bettinelli** Toccata Fantasia. **Galliera** Venerdi Santo dal "Trittico". **Bossi** Stunde der Wehie, Op. 132 No. 4. Stunde der Freude, Op. 132 No. 5. **Petrali** Messe solennelle – Gloria. **Luigi Benedetti** (org). Priory PRCD427 (4/95).

Firket Amirov
USSR 1922-1984

Suggested listening ...
...Six Pieces. *Coupled with works by* **Gubaidulina, Feld, Taktakishvili** and **Martinů** Leslie Newman (fl); Amanda Hurton (pf). Cala CACD88026 (6/96). *See review in the Collections section; refer to the Index to Reviews.*

Martin Amlin
American 1953-

Suggested listening ...
...Time's Caravan. *Coupled with* **Carter** Emblems. The harmony of morning. Heart not so heavy as mine. Musicians wrestle everywhere. **McKinley** Four Text Settings. **Sheng** Two folksongs from Chinhai. **John Oliver Chorale / John Oliver.** Koch International Classics 37178-2 (5/95).

John Amner
British 1579-1641

Suggested listening ...
..."Cesar's" Service – Te Deum[ac]. Second Verse Service[ac] – Magnificat; Nunc dimittis. I will sing unto the Lord as long as I live[ac]. Blessed be the Lord God[ac]. O ye little flock[ab]. Sing, O heav'ns[ac]. Variations for keyboard on "O Lord in Thee is all my trust"[c]. Consider, all ye passers by[abc]. Hear, O Lord and have mercy[ac]. My Lord is hence removed[abc]. I will sing unto the Lord, for He hath

triumphed gloriously[ac]. Glory be to God on high[ac]. O sing unto the Lord[ac]. [a]**Ely Cathedral Choir;** [b]**The Parley of Instruments / Paul Trepte** with [c]**David Price** (org). Hyperion CDA66768 (7/95).

Charles Ancliffe
British 1880-1952

Suggested listening ...

...*Nights of Gladness. Coupled with works by* **Binge, Williams, Coates, Toye, Collins, Farnon, Baynes, Curzon, Lutz, Gibbs, White, Ketèlbey, Joyce** and **Ellis** New London Orchestra / **Ronald Corp.** Hyperion CDA66868 (7/96). *Gramophone Editor's record of the month. See review in the Collections section; refer to the Index to Reviews.* ⑥

Leroy Anderson
American 1908-1975

New review

Leroy Anderson The belle of the ball. Phantom Regiment. The First Day of Spring. Sleigh Ride. Plink, Plank, Plunk! Blue Tango. Forgotten dreams. Bugler's holiday. The Penny-whistle Song. Clarinet Candy. Horse and Buggy. The trumpeter's lullaby. Fiddle-faddle. Jazz Pizzicato. Jazz Legato. The Syncopated Clock. The Sandpaper Ballet. The Typewriter. The Waltzing Cat. Promenade. Saraband. Serenata. Balladette. Arietta. Home Stretch. **St Louis Symphony Orchestra / Leonard Slatkin.** RCA Victor Red Seal ⑥ 09026 68048-2 (72 minutes: DDD: 1/96). ⑥

Light music connoisseurs will doubtless already have invested in Frederick Fennell's sparkling Mercury collection which contains many of the items heard here. Enter Leonard Slatkin and his superbly polished St Louis Symphony to lavish equally affectionate, witty treatment on Anderson's treasurable miniatures. What is more, Slatkin's generous selection includes a handful of particularly indelible offerings (*Bugler's holiday, The Sandpaper Ballet* and *The trumpeter's lullaby* amongst them) omitted from Fennell's anthology. Slatkin and his excellent band clearly relish every opportunity afforded by Anderson's colourful, stunningly crafted orchestrations, with marvellous solo contributions throughout and consistently pliant work from those sumptuous St Louis strings. Indeed, everything about this release is beyond reproach: the glowing Powell Symphony Hall acoustic; Richard Dyer's informed and enthusiastic notes; and, last but not least, the striking jewel-case artwork (tilt the CD case slightly and the typewriter springs into life before your very eyes). Great fun!

Jurriaan Andriessen
Dutch 1925-

Suggested listening ...

...*Concerto for Bassoon and Wind Ensemble*[c]. *Coupled with* **Downey** Edge of Space[a]. **Jacob** Concerto for Bassoon, Strings and Percussion[b]. **Robert Thompson** (bn); [a]**London Symphony Orchestra;** [b]**English Chamber Orchestra;** [c]**English Chamber Orchestra Wind Ensemble / Geoffrey Simon.** Chandos CHAN9278 (10/94).

Louis Andriessen
Dutch 1939-

L. Andriessen De Stijl[a]. M is for Man, Music, Mozart[b]. [a]**Gertrude Thoma,** [b]**Astrid Seriese** (sops); [a]**Schoenberg Ensemble;** [a]**Asko Ensemble / Reinbert de Leeuw;** [b]**Volharding Orchestra / Jurjen Hempel.** Elektra Nonesuch ⑥ 7559-79342-2 (55 minutes: DDD: 2/95). Text included. Recorded 1993-4. ⑥⑥

The Dutch composer Louis Andriessen may have embraced minimalism as the fundamental feature of his mature musical language but his personal brand of it is not for the faint-hearted. There is little trace of the laid-back, hypnotic gentleness of the likes of Adams, Glass or Reich, and some may find Andriessen's no-holds-barred, grab-you-by-the-throat directness off-putting. Others will find it exhilarating. Andriessen's stylistic antecedents here are 1920s Hindemith and Weill, Stravinsky, Bachian polyphony, rock and jazz. This heady mix is particularly apposite in *De Stijl* ("Style"), composed in 1984-85. Here and in *M is for Man, Music, Mozart* the hard-hitting thrust and momentum of Andriessen's music never slackens and the composer exhibits considerable skill in avoiding restlessness. The latter work was written in 1991 in collaboration with the film director Peter Greenaway for BBC2 television. There is greater variety of mood and texture than in *De Stijl* and its seven sections alternate song with instrumental music. Divorced from Greenaway's exuberantly provocative images, *M is for Man, Music, Mozart* creates a rather meditative impression and proves a viable concert work, unlike many film-originated scores. Performance and recording are stunning.

Further listening ...

...*Hout. Hoketus. Coupled with works by* **Wolfe, D. Lang** and **Gordon** Bang on a Can All-Stars. Sony Classical SK66483 (2/96). *See review in the Collections section; refer to the Index to Reviews. Selected by Soundings.*

Jean-Henri d'Anglebert   French 1635-1691

New review
D'Anglebert Pièces de clavecin – Suites: G major; G minor; D minor. **Brigitte Tramier** (hpd).
  Pierre Verany Ⓕ PV795012 (61 minutes: DDD: 9/95). 🗡 Recorded 1994.
It is astonishing that until now we have had no recordings of the main three of d'Anglebert's four
suites (from his 1689 volume, his only publication) since Kenneth Gilbert's now 20-year-old version.
For this musician at the French court since 1622, who was a pupil of Chambonnières, was the greatest
of Couperin's predecessors – in fact, he has been hailed by one musicologist as "representing the
highest development of French harpsichord music, even more than François Couperin". The fullness
of his textures, his harmonic boldness, his elaborate ornamentation (for which he provided a table of
indications on how to interpret his signs) mark him as a major figure; and his improvisational
unmeasured preludes are exceptionally interesting, that in D minor being truly splendid. Brigitte
Tramier's Hemsch instrument allows great delicacy and finesse and she brings a natural grace and
dance spirit. She makes the rhythmic subtleties of the G minor Gigue convincing, and is poetic in the
strangely un-gay Gaillardes of the G minor and G major Suites. This is a highly recommendable issue,
marred only by an extraordinary and unfortunate muddle over the listing of tracks 15-20.

Anonymous

Anonymous The Play of Daniel. **Estampie / Michael Popp.** Christophorus Ⓕ CHR77144
  (51 minutes: DDD: 2/95). Texts and translations included. Recorded 1993.   Ⓖ
Michael Popp has dressed up *The Play of Daniel* in 1970s pop garb and turned it into something that
is effectively his own composition, but it actually works. His anodyne-looking list of ten performers
– four singers and six players, all playing instruments with well-behaved historical names – produces
a range of sounds and rhythms that truly startles the ear. One can't be sure how much double-tracking
and electronic enhancement is involved here; apparently quite a lot. But there is without question a
large quantity of spellbindingly virtuosic playing and some thoroughly satisfying singing. What is
good is that Popp has kept fairly strictly to the surviving notes as his basis. Everything is scored with
imagination and verve. Some dazzling colours and rhythms are added to articulate the sections of the
drama: there is a magical sound to represent the appearance of the hand; the various characters are
strikingly characterized by the orchestration; there are certain moments where the textures are
reduced to become something that might even have happened in the original performance. But
nobody is using that much misused word 'authenticity' here; and the whole musical impact benefits
enormously from the plainly well-informed freedom that results. It's honest and it's good; the
individual performers are excellent, and the play comes across with special power. It's also refreshingly
different.

George Antheil   American 1900-1959

New review
Antheil Airplane Sonata. Sonata sauvage. La femme 100 têtes – I-XIII; XXIV-XXVI; XL; XLIII-
  XLV. Little Shimmy. Transatlantic – Tango. Piano Sonata No. 4. 11 Valentine Waltzes.
  Marthanne Verbit (pf). Albany Ⓕ TROY146-2 (68 minutes: DDD: 11/95). Recorded 1994.
The subtitle of this CD is "Bad Boy of Music", which is the title of Antheil's 1945 autobiography. He
loved this role, scandalizing Paris and New York in the 1920s; going on tour as a brutal pianist with
an armoury of tone-clusters, splashy *glissandos* and mechanical rhythms; and persuading his patron
to support him for 19 years. Antheil's *Ballet mécanique* (listed below) was a landmark and before that
his solo recitals had convinced the intelligensia of Paris that this brash American was something big.
In 1926 Copland felt that Antheil possessed "the greatest gifts of any young American now writing".
This promise wasn't quite fulfilled, at least in terms of the values which maintained in the years up to
and after Antheil's early death in 1959. His bubble seemed to have burst by the later 1920s, but he went
on to write operas that were staged in Europe, then he worked for Hollywood and brought a new
romanticism into his concert music. Russian influences are strong in Antheil – he approached
Stravinsky like a mad kleptomaniac and he overdid his borrowings to the point of crazy extravagance.
In the 1990s, with the calculated exaggerations of Schnittke and others, Antheil seems to have been
ahead of his time. So this anthology of piano music is well timed, bringing together percussive classics
like *Airplane Sonata* and *Sonata sauvage*, which make interesting comparisons with those of Cowell.
Marthanne Verbit is immersed in the whole Antheil scene and has painstakingly wrestled with his
casual manuscripts, full of missing accidentals and inconsistencies. She is overwhelmingly convincing,
relishing Antheil's quixotic style-modulations and treating the later *Valentine Waltzes* with rare
pianistic charm. Antheil's jazz phase is represented by a shimmy and a tango with more than a nod

to Weill. Verbit has chosen 20 out of 45 concentrated but eloquent miniatures comprising the set called *La femme 100 têtes*. Altogether a most enjoyable portrait of yet another American eccentric.
Further listening ...
...Ballet mécanique[a]. A Jazz Symphony[b]. Sonata No. 2 for Violin, Piano and Drum[c]. String Quartet No. 1[d]. [c]**Charles Castleman** (vn); [b]**Ivan Davis**, [c]**Randall Hodgkinson** (pfs); [a]**Rex Lawson** (pianola); [d]**Mendelssohn Quartet; New Palais Royale** [a]**Percussion Ensemble and** [ab]**Orchestra / Maurice Peress.** MusicMasters 67094-2 (4/94).

Antonius de Civitate Austrie   Italian fl. 1420-1425

Suggested listening ...
...Clarus ortu/Gloriosa mater. *Coupled with works by* **Tapissier, Velut, Anonymous, Ciconia, Philipoctus de Caserta, Johanne Egidius, Matheus de Sancto Johanne, Bartolomeus da Bologna, Zacharias, Brassart** and **Dufay** Orlando Consort. Metronome METCD1008 (11/95). *See review in the Collections section; refer to the Index to Reviews.* Ⓖ

Jean-Baptiste Arban   French 1825-1889

Suggested listening ...
...Variations on a theme from Bellini's "Norma". Variations on a Tyrolean Theme. *Coupled with works by* **Sarasate, Waxman, Falla, Saint-Saëns, Paganini, Tchaikovsky, Fauré** and **W. Brandt** Sergei Nakariakov (tpt); Alexander Markovich (pf). Teldec 4509-94554-2 (6/95). *See review in the Collections section; refer to the Index to Reviews.* ⒼⒼ

Anton Arensky   USSR 1861-1906

New review
Arensky Piano Concerto in F minor, Op. 2. Fantasia on Russian Folksongs, Op. 48.
Bortkiewicz Piano Concerto No. 1 in B flat major, Op. 16. **Stephen Coombs** (pf); **BBC Scottish Symphony Orchestra / Jerzy Maksymiuk.** Hyperion Ⓕ CDA66624 (71 minutes: DDD: 3/93). Recorded 1992. Ⓖ
It is suggested in the insert-note which accompanies this recording that "there must always be a place for those like Arensky and Bortkiewicz who reflect so elegantly and expertly on what has gone before, rather than shake us by the ears and grab us (sometimes screaming) into the future". This observation is most pertinent to the works here. All three are reminders of the pleasures of easy-listening music from an age before the whole concept was hijacked by commercialism. If this is the sort of thing you like, you'll surely like this sort of thing, as they say. Both concertos fall pleasantly on the ear. Arensky's early Op. 2 (1881) is an engaging cocktail with overtones of Liszt, Chopin and Grieg. Bortkiewicz's First Concerto is a true product of Russia's Silver Age, the scent of the Nicholas and Alexandra era evoked by a blend of Rachmaninov and Wagner. Stephen Coombs and the BBC Scottish SO present the music with wholehearted advocacy. Hyperion's engineering has the piano rather backward, not allowing it to sparkle quite as it should; otherwise this is a model issue from this ever-enterprising source.

Arensky Piano Trios – No. 1 in D minor, Op. 32; No. 2 in F minor, Op. 73. **Beaux Arts Trio** (Ida Kavafian, vn; Peter Wiley, vc; Menahem Pressler, pf). Philips Ⓕ 442 127-2PH (63 minutes: DDD: 6/95). Recorded 1994. Ⓖ
The presence of Tchaikovsky hovers benignly over Arensky in many pieces, not least in the First Trio: though Arensky does not have Tchaikovsky's felicity of invention, he can actually solve the problems of writing for piano and strings more steadily, and the work would surely have a more secure place in the repertory were it attached to a more famous name. While it has become something of a popular item, his Second languishes, with only two recorded versions available. Both are fine works, and the Beaux Arts Trio on Philips give beautiful, perceptive performances. Again, comparisons with Tchaikovsky's Piano Trio are inevitable, and by no means odious. Arensky may not have Tchaikovsky's distinctive musical personality, but he can write at least as effectively for the difficult medium, sometimes more originally, and he never lapses into the mighty chordal piano textures with which Tchaikovsky can make problems for his players. Moreover, he has a melodic charm that is much in the manner of Tchaikovsky, who, with some reservations, was appreciative. The *Elegy* of the First Trio and the *Romanza* of the Second are beautiful inventions, and both *Scherzos* speed along delicately and wittily. Another influence for the good was Mendelssohn. It is important not to overplay the resemblances in performance, and indeed not to overplay at all: less makes more in this

music, and does so in these admirable interpretations. Balance is very well managed throughout by both players and the producer.

Additional recommendation ...
...No. 1. **Tchaikovsky** Piano Trio in A minor, Op. 50. **Cho-Liang Lin** (vn); **Gary Hoffman** (vc); **Yefim Bronfman** (pf). Sony Classical Ⓔ SK53269 (76 minutes: DDD: 9/94). *See review under Tchaikovsky; refer to the Index to Reviews.* **Gramophone** *Editor's choice.*

Further listening ...
...String Quartet No. 2 in A minor, Op. 35. *Coupled with* **Tchaikovsky** Souvenir de Florence, Op. 70. **Raphael Ensemble.** Hyperion CDA66648 (2/94).
...Silhouettes (Suite No. 2), Op. 23. *Coupled with* **Scriabin** No. 3 in C minor, Op. 43, "Le divin poème". **Danish National Radio Symphony Orchestra / Neeme Järvi.** Chandos CHAN8898 (10/91).
...Suites for Two Pianos – No. 1 in F major, Op. 15; No. 2, Op. 23, "Silhouettes"; No. 3, Op. 33, "Variations"; No. 4, Op. 62. **Stephen Coombs, Ian Munro** (pfs). Hyperion CDA66755.
...Intermezzo in F minor, Op. 36 No. 12. Le ruisseau dans la forêt. Romance, Op. 53 No. 5. *Coupled with works by* **Glazunov, Liadov, Rachmaninov, Taneyev** and **Tchaikovsky** **Margaret Fingerhut** (pf). Chandos CHAN9218 (4/94).

Dominik Argento
American 1927-

Suggested listening ...
...The Dream of Valentino – Tango. *Coupled with* **Moran** Points of Departure. **Torke** Black and White – Charcoal. **Harbison** Remembering Gatsby. **Larsen** Collage: Boogie. **Schiff** Stomp. **Kernis** New Era Dance. **J. Adams** The Chairman Dances. **Bernstein** West Side Story – Mambo. **Daugherty** Desi. **Rouse** Bonham. **Baltimore Symphony Orchestra / David Zinman.** Argo 444 454-2ZH (7/95).

Attilio Ariosti
Italian 1666-c1729

Suggested listening ...
...La rosa. *Coupled with works by* **Corelli, Torelli, Bononcini** and **Steffani** Ann Monoyios (sop); **Berlin Barock Compagney.** Capriccio 10 459 (10/95). ✍ *See review in the Collections section; refer to the Index to Reviews.* Ⓖ

Thomas Arne
British 1710-1778

Arne Favourite Concertos – No. 1 in C major (solo hpd version)[a]. Keyboard Sonatas – No. 1 in F major[a]. Trio Sonatas – No. 2 in G major; No. 5; No. 6 in B minor; No. 7 in E minor. **Le Nouveau Quatuor** (Utako Ikeda, fl; Catherine Weiss, vn; Mark Caudle, vc; [a]Paul Nicholson, hpd). Amon Ra Ⓔ CD-SAR42 (58 minutes: DDD: 5/90). ✍ Recorded 1989.

If the music history books offer little more than a passing reference to the slim repertoire of enchanting chamber music by Thomas Arne, the ordinary man in the street, who can at least whistle *Rule Britannia*, is unlikely even to have heard that any exists. This disc comes therefore as something of a revelation. The members of the Nouveau Quatuor perform on instruments dating from the composer's lifetime, tuned down a semitone. The trio sonatas, originally published for two violins and continuo, are played here by a mixed quartet: flute, violin, cello and harpsichord, which is believed to have been what the composer really intended. The introduction of the flute adds colour, brightness and definition to these charming pieces and gives the listener a chance to savour the admirable tone and phrasing of the flautist, Utako Ikeda. Paul Nicholson's harpsichord solos are distinguished as much by their elegance as by their extraordinary power and brilliance. A word, finally, in praise of Peter Holman's excellent insert-notes: they are both scholarly and extremely readable.

Arne Comus – By the rushy-fringed bank; Brightest Lady; Thrice upon thy Finger's Tip[a]. Rosamond – Rise, Glory, rise[a]. The Tempest – Ariel's song[a].
Handel Ariodante – Neghittosi or voi che fate?[a]. Alcina – Credete al mio dolore; Tornami a vagheggiar[a]. Alexander's Feast – War, he sung, is toil and trouble[a]. L'Allegro, il penseroso ed il moderato – Sweet bird[a]. Saul – Capricious man[a]. Overture, Alessandro Severo, HWVAnh13. Hornpipe in D major, HWV356. March in D major, HWV345.
Lampe Britannia – Welcome Mars[a]. Dione – Pretty warblers[a]. [a]**Emma Kirkby** (sop); **Academy of Ancient Music / Christopher Hogwood.** L'Oiseau-Lyre Ⓔ 436 132-2OH (72 minutes: DDD: 7/93). ✍ Texts and translations included. Recorded 1991. Ⓖ

Emma Kirkby's voice has no longer the *ingénue* air, the charmingly demure quality through which a hint of passion enticingly peeps, with which she delighted so many of us in her earlier recordings. It is now fuller, and used with less inhibition (or pretence of it); and that means that a wider repertory, not to say a wider interpretative range, is open to her. The virtues of taste and technique and impeccable tuning however remain, still supported by a prodigious musical intelligence and a natural feeling for early eighteenth-century style (among others). This disc casts her in music composed, for the most part, for one of the most celebrated English singers of that era, Cecilia Young, one of several talented singing sisters and for a time the wife of Thomas Arne – famed in her day for the "sweetness and simplicity" (Dibdin's words) of her singing and her character. The impersonation seems a convincing one, to judge by the result here, which is uniformly delightful. Christopher Hogwood conducts in direct and unaffected fashion. A true desert island disc.

New review

Arne Artaxerxes. **Christopher Robson** (alto) Artaxerxes; **Ian Partridge** (ten) Artabanes; **Patricia Spence** (mez) Arbaces; **Richard Edgar-Wilson** (ten) Rimenes; **Catherine Bott** (sop) Mandane; **Philippa Hyde** (sop) Semira; **The Parley of Instruments / Roy Goodman.** Hyperion Ⓕ CDA67051/2 (two discs: 140 minutes: DDD: 6/96). ☞ Notes and text included. Recorded 1995.

A warm welcome to the first recording of this opera, a work of great historical importance and musically fascinating. Thomas Arne, the leading English composer of his time for the theatre, wanted to write serious as well as comic English operas, and decided that Italian *opera seria* should serve, on the literary side, as his model; he chose the most famous of all the Metastasio librettos, *Artaserse*, as the basis for his first (and last) attempt at the genre. English vocal music of this period has quite a distinctive manner, tuneful, rather short-breathed, often with a faintly 'folky' flavour. It does not naturally reflect the exalted emotional manner of an *opera seria* text. Nevertheless, the music is enormously enjoyable, full of good melodies, richly orchestrated, and never (unlike Italian operas of the time) long-winded. The story of *Artaxerxes* is a typical Metastasian one, with 'treasonous designs' and misunderstandings, and plenty of opportunity for the expression of strong and varied emotion. Much of the best and most deeply felt music goes to Arbaces, originally a castrato role written for the famous Tenducci, at mezzo-soprano pitch: here it is very finely and expressively sung by Patricia Spence. She uses more vibrato than anyone else in the cast but her warmth of tone and expressive power are ample justification. Mandane, Arbaces's beloved, composed for Arne's mistress Charlotte Brent, is another rewarding part and is finely sung here by Catherine Bott, bright in tone, true in pitch and scrupulous in her verbal articulation, who can encompass both the charming English ditties and the more Italianate virtuoso pieces. The original score does not survive complete, a victim (like so many) of the frequent theatre fires of the time; Peter Holman has done a predictably unobtrusive and stylish job of reconstructing some of the lost recitatives for this recording which is recommended to anyone curious about this byway of eighteenth-century opera, and to anyone who is drawn to Arne's very individual and appealing melodic style.

Richard Arnell

British 1917-

Arnell Punch and the Child – ballet[a].
Berners The Triumph of Neptune – ballet suite[b].
Delius Paris: The Song of a Great City[c]. [b]**Robert Grooters** (bar); [ac]**Royal Philharmonic Orchestra;** [b]**Philadelphia Orchestra / Sir Thomas Beecham.** Sony Classical British Pageant mono
Ⓜ SMK46683* (68 minutes: ADD: 11/94). Item marked [a] from Columbia LX1391/3 (5/51. Recorded 1950), [b]CBS 61431 (7/74. 1952), [c]Philips ABL3089 (2/56. 1955). Ⓖ

Delians everywhere will rejoice at the reappearance of Beecham's 1955 recording of *Paris*. Comparison with this conductor's marvellous 1934 version (listed below) shows his earlier offering to be the better co-ordinated of the two (both orchestrally and structurally), yet there are moments to treasure in this RPO performance and Beecham's poetic instincts do not desert him – witness his surpassingly lovely treatment of Delius's secondary lyrical material when it reappears at 15'21". Richard Arnell's ballet, *Punch and the Child*, dates from 1948, a commission for the American company, Ballet Caravan (later known as the New York City Ballet). Beecham conducted the English concert-hall première in 1949 and recorded it the following year with the RPO in Kingsway Hall. It's an attractively rumbustious creation, reminiscent at times of Bliss in ballet mode, and delivered here with much gusto. Beecham twice recorded music from Lord Berners's 1926 ballet, *The Triumph of Neptune*. The present 1952 account of the Suite with the Philadelphia restores those two substantial numbers ("Cloudland" and "The Frozen Forest") not found on Beecham's earlier 1937 LPO set. Again, good transfers, though in *Paris* the sound has not the extraordinary richness and depth that distinguishes Anthony Griffith's superb restoration of that earlier Columbia production.

Additional recommendation ...

...Paris. Eventyr. Fennimore and Gerda – Intermezzo. Over the Hills and Far Away. Irmelin Prelude. **London Philharmonic Orchestra / Sir Thomas Beecham.** Sir Thomas Beecham Trust mono Ⓜ BEECHAM2* (61 minutes: ADD: 6/89).

Sir Malcolm Arnold

Arnold Clarinet Concertos – No. 1, Op. 20; No. 2, Op. 115. You know what sailors are – Scherzetto (arr. Palmer).
Britten (orch. Matthews). Movement for Clarinet and Orchestra.
Maconchy Concertinos Nos. 1 and 2. **Thea King** (cl); **English Chamber Orchestra / Barry Wordsworth.** Hyperion Ⓕ CDA66634 (65 minutes: DDD: 12/93). Recorded 1992.   Ⓖ
Designed in part as a tribute to Frederick Thurston, who died 40 years ago, this collection of short *concertante* works for clarinet makes an exceptionally attractive disc, beautifully recorded and superbly performed, with Thurston's widow and star-pupil, Thea King, as soloist. With her ever-seductive tone, at once sensuously beautiful yet clear, never letting you forget that this is a reed instrument, King perpetuates the qualities he sought to instil, not least in the works on the disc written for him. These include the first of Arnold's concertos and the first of Maconchy's concertinos, while the *Scherzetto,* a delightfully jaunty piece adapted by Christopher Palmer from Arnold's music for the film, *You know what sailors are*, also seems to have been inspired directly by Thurston's playing. The other direct influence here is Benny Goodman. He turned in 1942 to the young Benjamin Britten, then in the United States, to write a concerto for him. It is a highly attractive short piece, alternately energetic and poetic, with material adroitly interchanged, and with percussion used most imaginatively. The second of the Arnold concertos was written for Goodman too and it shows Arnold at his most endearing, with sharp ideas leading to broad, memorable melodies that echo popular music, without ever cheapening the result. Both King and the ECO under Barry Wordsworth bring out the warmth as well as the rhythmic drive of all this music.

Additional recommendations ...
...Clarinet Concerto No. 1[b]. Double Violin Concerto, Op. 77[d]. Flute Concerto No. 1, Op. 45[a]. Horn Concerto No. 2, Op. 58[c]. [a]**Karen Jones** (fl); [b]**Michael Collins** (cl); [c]**Richard Watkins** (hn); [d]**Kenneth Sillito**, [d]**Lyn Fletcher** (vns); **London Musici / Mark Stephenson.** Conifer Ⓕ CDCF172 (56 minutes: DDD: 8/89).
...Clarinet Concertos Nos. 1 and 2[a]. Three Shanties, Op. 4[b]. Sonatina, Op. 29[c]. Fantasia, Op. 87. Divertimento, Op. 37[d]. **Emma Johnson** (cl); [bd]**Jaime Martin** (fl); [bd]**Jonathan Kelly** (ob); [b]**Claire Briggs** (hn); [b]**Susanna Cohen** (bn); [c]**Malcolm Martineau** (pf); [a]**English Chamber Orchestra / Ivor Bolton.** ASV Ⓕ CDDCA922 (61 minutes: DDD: 7/95).

Arnold Flute Concerto No. 2, Op. 111[a]. Clarinet Concerto No. 2, Op. 115[b]. Horn Concerto No. 1, Op. 11[c]. Piano Duet and Strings, Op. 32[d]. [a]**Karen Jones** (fl); [b]**Michael Collins** (cl); [c]**Richard Watkins** (hn); [d]**David Nettle**, [d]**Richard Markham** (pfs); **London Musici / Mark Stephenson.** Conifer Ⓕ CDCF228 (72 minutes: DDD: 12/93). Recorded 1993.
Of the brief concertos which Arnold wrote for a whole range of instruments, the Horn Concerto No. 1 is the earliest work here. Written in 1946 for Charles Gregory, then Arnold's colleague in the London Philharmonic, it is also the longest of the works here, with an extended central *Andante* with dark overtones and a hunting-rhythm finale. Richard Watkins, Principal Horn of the Philharmonia, plays it with great panache and glorious tone. Karen Jones, Principal Flute of the Bournemouth orchestra and Shell/LSO prize-winner in 1985, is equally sympathetic in the Flute Concerto No. 2, the most original work on the disc, with a central scherzo flanked by an equivocal *Allegro moderato* and a final lyrical *Allegretto*. The Concerto for Piano Duet is full of characteristic Arnold touches. After an emphatic first movement a central Passacaglia brings craggy contrasts, leading to a jazzy finale with relaxed episodes. Nettle and Markham play as one at their single keyboard, and under Mark Stephenson the young musicians of London Musici perform throughout with understanding and precision.

Arnold Four Scottish Dances, Op. 59 (arr. Farr). Four English Dances, Op. 27 (arr. Farr). Four English Dances, Op. 33 (arr. Farr). Four Cornish Dances, Op. 91. Little Suites – No. 1, Op. 80; No. 2, Op. 93. Fantasy, Op. 114. The Padstow Lifeboat, Op. 94[a]. **Grimethorpe Colliery Band / Elgar Howarth;** [a]**Sir Malcolm Arnold.** Conifer Ⓕ CDCF222 (66 minutes: DDD: 12/93). Recorded 1993.   Ⓖ
The composer was present throughout these recordings and he conducted the final item, the *Padstow Lifeboat* march with its insistent off-key foghorn. The sheer ebullience of the playing is immediately breathtaking in the first of the *Scottish Dances*, and in the second the 'drunken' solo bass trombone is in the best tradition of the British brass experience. The eight *English Dances* are played with equal sophistication and brilliance. The *Mesto* (Op. 27 No. 3) is quite haunting and the players get round the colour problem in the first dance in Op. 33 by whistling the air themselves! The more melancholy atmosphere of the *Cornish Dances* is touchingly caught. The two *Little Suites* demonstrate how well the composer – once a trumpeter himself in the LPO – understands the medium. The finest of the original band works is the *Fantasy,* a highly imaginative series of joined vignettes. The recording is natural, and beautifully balanced, making the most of the hall's ambience without any loss of detail.

Additional recommendations ...
...Cornish Dances. English Dances – Op. 27; Op. 33. Irish Dances, Op. 126. Scottish Dances. Solitaire – Sarabande; Polka. **London Philharmonic Orchestra / Malcolm Arnold.** Lyrita Ⓕ SRCD201 (61 minutes: ADD/DDD: 12/90).   ⒼⒼ

...*As Lyrita.* **Philharmonia Orchestra / Bryden Thomson.** Chandos Ⓕ CHAN8867 (48 minutes: DDD: 10/90).

...Four Scottish Dances[c]. **Vaughan Williams** Job[a]. The Wasps – Overture[b]. **London Philharmonic Orchestra /** [ab]**Sir Adrian Boult,** [c]**Sir Malcolm Arnold.** Everest Ⓕ EVC9006 (57 minutes: ADD: 5/95).

Arnold A Sussex Overture, Op. 31. Beckus the Dandipratt, Op. 5. The Smoke, Op. 21. The Fair Field, Op. 110. Commonwealth Christmas Overture, Op. 64. **London Philharmonic Orchestra / Sir Malcolm Arnold.** Reference Recordings Ⓕ RRCD48 (63 minutes: DDD: 6/92). Recorded 1991.

Four of the overtures here are early pieces composed before 1960, while *The Fair Field* (written for the Fairfield Halls in Croydon, Surrey) dates from 1972. The earliest piece is *Beckus the Dandipratt* (a dandipratt was an Elizabethan coin, but the word was also used for a cheeky small boy) and was inspired by a youngster that the composer and his wife befriended on a wartime Cornish holiday. *The Smoke* (a Cockney term for London) has raucous jazz elements, while the *Commonwealth Christmas Overture* places cosy English chimes alongside the more urgent Christmas music of a Caribbean pop group. Though much of this music is cheerfully extrovert, by no means all of it is, and for all its tunefulness it is not easy-listening music in the usual sense. Under the composer, the London Philharmonic play it brilliantly and lovingly, and the recording is rich and detailed. The booklet note by the producer, the late Christopher Palmer, is a model of information, enthusiasm and style and complements a splendid issue.

Arnold Symphonies – No. 1, Op. 22; No. 2, Op. 40. **London Symphony Orchestra / Richard Hickox.** Chandos Ⓕ CHAN9335 (61 minutes: DDD: 3/95). Recorded 1994.

Here is an entirely appropriate coupling of the first two symphonies, superbly played by the LSO and given demonstration sound in what is surely an ideal acoustic for this music, with striking depth and amplitude and a wholly natural brilliance. The dynamic range is wide but the moments of spectacle, and there are quite a few, bring no discomfort. Richard Hickox shows himself thoroughly at home in both symphonies and the readings have a natural flow and urgency, with the two slow movements bringing haunting, atmospheric feeling. The First Symphony opens with thrusting confidence on strings and horns and at its climax, where the strings soar against angry brass ostinatos, the playing generates great intensity; then at the start of the slow movement the purity of the flute solo brings a calm serenity which returns at the close. There are only three movements and the plangent lyrical melancholia of the expansive march theme of the finale is filled out by some superb horn playing which is enormously compelling. The first movement of Symphony No. 2 brings a most winning clarinet solo (Arnold's fund of melodic ideas seems inexhaustible), there is an energetic, bustling scherzo to follow, but again it is the slow movement which one remembers for its elegiac opening, its arresting climax and lovely epilogue-like close. Above all these are real performances without any of the inhibitions of 'studio' recording.

Additional recommendations ...

...No. 2[a]. No. 5, Op. 74[b]. Peterloo – overture, Op. 97[b]. [a]**Bournemouth Symphony Orchestra / Sir Charles Grooves;** [b]**City of Birmingham Symphony Orchestra / Sir Malcolm Arnold.** EMI Studio Ⓜ CDM7 63368-2 (71 minutes: ADD: 6/90).

...No. 1, Op. 22[b]. Concerto for Two Pianos[ac]. Solitaire[b] – Sarabande; Polka. Tam O'Shanter – Overture, Op. 51[d]. English Dances[d] – No. 3, Op. 27 No. 3; No. 5, Op. 33 No. 1. [a]**Phyllis Sellick,** [a]**Cyril Smith** (pfs); [b]**Bournemouth Symphony Orchestra,** [c]**City of Birmingham Symphony Orchestra;** [d]**Philharmonia Orchestra / Malcolm Arnold.** EMI British Composers [abc]stereo/[d]mono Ⓜ CDM7 64044-2* (76 minutes: ADD: 10/91).   Ⓖ

...Nos. 1 and 2. **National Symphony Orchestra of Ireland / Andrew Penny.** Naxos Ⓢ 8 553406 (56 minutes: DDD: 5/96).

Arnold Symphonies – No. 3, Op. 63; No. 4, Op. 71. **London Symphony Orchestra / Richard Hickox.** Chandos Ⓕ CHAN9290 (74 minutes: DDD: 9/94). Recorded 1993.

These two Arnold symphonies share comparatively little of the amiable optimism which distinguishes so many of his shorter works. Instead they reflect his experience of life over a broader span, with disillusion and even tragedy as part of their symphonic ethos. As it happens the Third Symphony does have an exuberant, upbeat finale, but even here there is a last-minute change of mood in the coda, with a sudden Holst-like, plangent rhythmic warning; nevertheless the final few bars are distinctly positive. The work, commissioned by the Royal Liverpool Philharmonic Society and first performed in 1957, produces a long, striking and expressively bleak string melody in the opening movement, while the despairing isolation of its *Lento* slow movement is similarly harrowing. The first movement of the Fourth Symphony is dominated by one of those entirely winning Arnoldian lyrical tunes even though there is jagged dissonance in the central episode, and it has been suggested that this ambivalence was prompted by the contemporary Notting Hill race-riots, which also may have brought the Caribbean percussion instruments into the orchestra. Richard Hickox has the full measure of both symphonies and the Chandos recording is superb, full of colour and atmosphere.

Additional recommendations ...

...No. 4. **London Philharmonic Orchestra / Sir Malcolm Arnold.** Lyrita Ⓕ SRCD 200 (54 minutes: DDD: 11/90).

…No. 3[a]. **Vaughan Williams** Symphony No. 9 in E minor[b]. **London Philharmonic Orchestra / [a]Sir Malcolm Arnold, [b]Sir Adrian Boult.** Everest Ⓕ EVC9001 (70 minutes: ADD: 4/95).

New review

Arnold Symphonies – No. 5, Op. 74; No. 6, Op. 95. **London Symphony Orchestra / Richard Hickox.** Chandos Ⓕ CHAN9385 (58 minutes: DDD: 12/95). Recorded 1995.   Ⓖ

Arnold's Fifth Symphony is one of his most accessible and rewarding works and the composer's own EMI recording (listed earlier), made in 1972, a decade after the music was composed, is special. The acoustics of the De Montfort Hall, Leicester seem quite admirable in terms of Arnold's own presentation of a work which, with its *Tempestuoso* first movement and essentially lyrical, pain-filled *Andante* (which the composer described as an emotional cliché), brings a balance between deep personal feeling and an expression of irony at life's unrelenting dance. A characteristically brash and exuberant *Con fuoco* scherzo precedes the high-spirited 'pipe and tabor' finale which brings back the main theme of the slow movement and ends obliquely: it sounds as if it is being composed in the presence of the listener. The inspiration for the symphony was the early deaths of several of the composer's friends and colleagues: Dennis Brain, Frederick Thurston, David Paltenghi and Gerard Hoffnung. They are all remembered in the first movement and Hoffnung's spirit clearly pops up in the third and fourth. The Chandos recording is more richly resonant than the EMI version, and that reinforces the impression that in Hickox's hands the *Andante* has an added degree of acceptance in its elegaic close, while the last two movements are the more colourfully expansive. The reading overall is clearly modelled on the composer's own and if it conveys a slightly less potent underlying anguish, the playing is certainly no less deeply felt. The Sixth Symphony (1967) is nothing like as comfortable as the Fifth, with a bleak unease in the unrelenting energy of the first movement, which becomes even more discomfiting in the desolate start to the *Lento*. This leads to a forlorn suggestion of a funeral march, which then ironically quickens in pace but is suddenly cut down; the drum strokes become menacingly powerful and the despairing mood of the movement's opening returns. Hickox handles this quite superbly and grips the listener in the music's pessimism, which then lifts completely with the energetic syncopated trumpet theme of the rondo finale. Although later there are moments of ambiguity, and dissonant reminders of the earlier music, these are eclipsed by the thrilling life-asserting coda. In both symphonies the splendidly expansive Chandos recording increases the weight and power of utterance and though Handley's earlier version of the Sixth is riveting, Hickox is even more compelling.

Additional recommendation …

…No. 6, Op. 95. Fantasy on a theme of John Field, Op. 116[a]. Sweeney Todd, Op. 68a. Tam O'Shanter, Op. 51. [a]**John Lill** (pf); **Royal Philharmonic Orchestra / Vernon Handley.** Conifer Ⓕ CDCF224 (78 minutes: DDD: 2/94). *Gramophone Editor's choice. Selected by Sounds in Retrospect.*

New review

Arnold Symphony No. 9, Op. 128. **National Symphony Orchestra of Ireland / Andrew Penny.** Naxos Ⓢ 8 553540 (57 minutes: DDD: 5/96). Includes an interview between the composer and the conductor. Recorded 1995. *Gramophone Editor's choice.*   Ⓖ

Arnold's Ninth Symphony has become something of a mystery work, and it is good to have this superb first recording to confirm that here is a culmination to his symphonic series both characteristic and distinctive. As Arnold explains in his interview with the conductor, included as a supplement to the 47-minute symphony, Sir Charles Groves took it up just before he died, giving a trial performance, and then one with the BBC Philharmonic. Since then conductors have fought shy. Registering the baldness of the arguments, with two-part writing the general rule and with structure built on repetition and juxtaposition rather than thematic development, one can perhaps understand the reservations of traditionalists. What that fails above all to take into account is Arnold's continuing mastery of the orchestra, the actual sounds. As the late Hugo Cole put it in his survey of Arnold's music (Faber: 1989), "Arnold composes with his ear. His music speaks to us first of all through its sounds." If at the start and elsewhere one is reminded of Shostakovich, the instrumentation is quite distinctive. The ear is regularly tweaked by the terracing of sounds, at extremes of register as well as of dynamic, culminating in the long slow finale, almost as long as the other three movements combined. With two poignant themes, the mood of tragedy and disillusion is clear. The parallel with the final *Adagio* of Mahler's Ninth Symphony comes obviously to mind. Yet unlike Mahler the music conveys no hint of neurosis or self-pity. The other three movements are just as direct, bald in their arguments but ever pointful, not facile, built on instantly memorable material. Andrew Penny draws not just a concentrated, consistently committed performance from the Irish players, but a warmly resonant one, with the strings sounding glorious and the woodwind and brass consistently brilliant. The recording is rich and full.

Further listening …

…Guitar Concerto, Op. 67.*Coupled with* **Rodrigo** Concierto de Aranjuez. **Takemitsu** To the Edge of Dream. **Julian Bream** (gtr); **City of Birmingham Symphony Orchestra / Sir Simon Rattle.** EMI CDC7 54661-2 (7/93).   Ⓖ

…A Grand Grand Overture, Op. 57. Concerto for Two Pianos (three hands), Op. 104[a]. Carnival of Animals, Op. 72. Symphony No. 2, Op. 40. [a]**David Nettle,** [a]**Richard Markham** (pfs); **Royal**

Philharmonic Orchestra / Vernon Handley. Conifer CDCF240 (12/94). *Gramophone Editor's choice.*

...Sinfoniettas – No. 1, Op. 48; No. 2, Op. 65; No. 3, Op. 81. Flute Concerto No. 1, Op. 45[a]. Oboe Concerto, Op. 39[b]. [a]**Edward Beckett** (fl); [b]**Malcolm Messiter** (ob); **London Festival Orchestra / Ross Pople.** Hyperion CDA66332 (3/90).

...Symphonies – No. 7, Op. 113; No. 8, Op. 124. **Royal Philharmonic Orchestra / Vernon Handley.** Conifer CDCF177 (3/91).   ⒼⒼ

...Film Suites (arr. Palmer) – The Bridge on the River Kwai; The Inn of the Sixth Happiness; Hobson's Choice; Whistle down the Wind. The Sound Barrier, Op. 38. **London Symphony Orchestra / Richard Hickox.** Chandos CHAN9100 (2/93).

...The Sound Barrier, Op. 38. *Coupled with works by* **Vaughan Williams, Addinsell, C. Williams, Brodszky, C. Parker, J. Addison II, Allan Gray, Frankel, Greenwood, Alwyn, Spoliansky** and **P. Green Various orchestras and conductors.** EMI mono CDGO2059* (9/94). *See review in the Collections section; refer to the Index to Reviews.*

...String Quartets – No. 1, Op. 23; No. 2, Op. 118. **McCapra Quartet.** Chandos CHAN9112 (10/92).

...Allegro in E minor. Three Piano Pieces. Serenade in G major. Day dreams. Two Piano Pieces. Piano Sonata. Three Piano Pieces. Prelude. Variations on a Ukrainian folk-song, Op. 9. Children's Suite, Op. 16. Two Bagatelles, Op. 18. Eight Children's Pieces, Op. 36. Three Fantasies, Op. 129. **Benjamin Frith** (pf). Koch International Classics 37162-2 (2/95).

Juan Crisóstomo Arriaga   Spanish 1806-1826

New review

Arriaga Symphony in D major. Los esclavos felices – Overture.
Voříšek Symphony in D major, Op. 24. **Scottish Chamber Orchestra / Sir Charles Mackerras.** Hyperion Ⓕ CDA66800 (58 minutes: DDD: 11/95). Recorded 1995. *Gramophone Editor's choice.*   ⒼⒼ

A curious set of parallels links the two composers here. Both were child prodigies who died, within two months of each other, at an early age, of tuberculosis, in a foreign country (Arriaga, a Spaniard, in France at the age of 19, Voříšek, a Bohemian, in Austria at 34). And each wrote his only symphony around 1823 – in the key of D. Both composers show themselves fond of Schubertian modulations and key shifts, but whereas Arriaga's chief influences seem to be Mozart (in the symphony's elegant *Andante*) and Rossini (in the sparkling *Allegro* of his Overture and the orchestral crescendo towards its end), Voříšek, who was brought up on Mozart and was in fact taught philosophy by Mozart's first biographer, plainly was already entering Beethoven territory, with striding bass figures in the first movement and, particularly, with the fiery scherzo (whose Trio features a solo horn). Arriaga calls his third movement a Minuet, but this too is in fact a scherzo, unusually constructed in one span rather than in binary form: the Trio here is devoted to a flute solo. The outer movements of this work are agitated, in the *Sturm und Drang* tradition, and Mackerras makes the most of the initial *Allegro vivace*'s abrupt dynamic contrasts – more vividly dramatic than Savall. He secures considerable finesse in the SCO's performances – the lovingly phrased introduction to Arriaga's Overture and the ingratiating start of the Voříšek are seductive – but it is the excitable energy of the latter that brings forth the most spectacular playing: the tremendous vigour of its finale makes this a demonstration track. Wholeheartedly recommended.

New review

Arriaga String Quartets – No. 1 in D minor; No. 2 in A major; No. 3 in E flat major. **Sine Nomine Quartet** (Patrick Genet, François Gottraux, vns; Nicolas Pache, va; Marc Jaermann, vc). Claves Ⓕ CD50-9501 (75 minutes: DDD: 9/95). Recorded 1994. *Gramophone Editor's choice.*   Ⓖ

In any roster of gifted composers tragically cut off in their youth – for example Pergolesi and Norbert Burgmüller (considered "another Schubert") at 26, Lili Boulanger and Reubke at 24, Lekeu the day after his twenty-fourth birthday – there is no more striking figure than Juan Crisóstomo Arriaga. He had written an octet (among other things) by 11, had had an opera performed when he was 13, and three months after entering the Paris Conservatoire (aged 15) was declared to have "completely mastered harmony": two years later the highly critical Cherubini called an eight-part choral piece of his a masterpiece. By that time, however, Arriaga had already composed much, including, in a genre then greatly in vogue in Paris, the present three quartets. (An extraordinary slip in the translation states that Arriaga had hoped to have them performed at the court of King Edward VII – who had yet to be born! The king in question was in fact Fernando VII of Spain.) These quartets are written with a sureness and maturity of technique and a felicitous flow of invention that almost justify Arriaga having been called "the Spanish Mozart" (apart from his having been born 50 years to the day after his great predecessor): indeed, there is a Mozartian shadow over the dramatic opening movement of the D minor work. Other influences have been adduced but particularly in the E flat Quartet, notably in the remarkable second and third movements, a distinctive personality is unmistakable. Even more than those other teenage phenomena, Rossini's string sonatas and Mendelssohn's string symphonies, these quartets have a right to be judged by the highest criteria. The young Swiss ensemble Sine Nomine offer unquestionably the best performances of these now available: at times pushing speeds but their playing shows real commitment as well as considerable polish and nuance.

Alexander Arutiunian

Armenian 1920-

Suggested listening ...
...Trumpet Concerto. *Coupled with* **L. Mozart** Trumpet Concerto in D major. **Hummel** Trumpet
Concerto in E flat major. **A. Sandoval** (orch. Zelanti) Trumpet Concerto. **Arturo Sandoval** (tpt);
London Symphony Orchestra / Luis Haza. GRP Classical GRK75002 (1/95).

Hugh Aston

British c1485-1558

Suggested listening ...
...A Hornepype. *Coupled with works by* **Anonymous, Tomkins, Gibbons, Byrd** and **J. Bull**
Sophie Yates (virg). Chandos Chaconne CHAN0574 (12/95). ✐ *See review under Byrd; refer to
the Index to Reviews.*

Kurt Atterberg

Swedish 1887-1974

Suggested listening ...
...Piano Quintet, Op. 31ᵃ. Suite No. 1, "Orientale"ᵇ. Horn Sonata in B minor, Op. 27ᶜ. ᶜ**Imre
Magyari** (hn); ᵇ**György Kertész** (vc); ᵃᵇ**Ilona Prunyi** (pf); ᵃ**New Budapest Quartet.** Marco Polo
8 223405 (9/93).

Daniel-François-Esprit Auber

French 1782-1871

New review
Auber Le domino noir. **Sumi Jo** (sop) Angèle d'Olivarès; **Isabelle Vernet** (sop) Brigitte de San
Lucar; **Bruce Ford** (ten) Horace de Massarena; **Patrick Power** (ten) Count Juliano; **Martine
Olmeda** (mez) Jacinthe; **Jules Bastin** (bass) Gil Perez; **Doris Lamprecht** (mez) Ursule; **Jocelyne
Taillon** (mez) La tourière; **Gilles Cachemaille** (bar) Lord Elfort; **London Voices.**
Auber Gustav III, ou Le bal masqué – Overture; Ballet Music. **English Chamber Orchestra /
Richard Bonynge.** Decca Ⓕ 440 646-2DHO2 (two discs; 144 minutes: DDD; 1/96). Notes, text
and translation included. Recorded 1993-5. *Gramophone Editor's choice.*   Ⓖ Ⓖ
Auber's operas were tremendously successful in the nineteenth century, but have hardly been performed
in the twentieth at all. *Le domino noir* clocked up 1,200 performances in Paris alone, after its 1837
première, and was soon seen in London and in New Orleans. This spiffing new recording – the only
previous one was a much-abridged affair from French radio – is the surest blow yet to be struck for a
revival of Auber's popularity in our time. The music is tuneful, danceable, constantly surprising in its
form, and full of interesting orchestration. The story is a variation on the usual masked-ball romantic
comedy. The heroine, Angèle, is sung by Sumi Jo who sounds even more confident than she did in the
recital of French arias ("Carnival!", reviewed in the Collections section; refer to the Index to Reviews)
which she and Bonynge recorded at the same time as this. As the young man in pursuit of the
beautiful masked stranger, Bruce Ford sings with a good deal of elegance, he takes the high notes in
full voice, rather than the head tone which was probably customary in the 1830s. Both he and Sumi
Jo deal pretty well with the French language – most of the rest of the cast consists of distinguished
French singers: Isabelle Vernet as Angèle's confidante, Martine Olmeda splendid as the housekeeper,
Jacinthe, and the veteran Jules Bastin as Gil Perez, porter at the convent.
    One of Auber's most successful tragic operas was another masked ball – *Gustave III*, the libretto of
which, also by Scribe, later served for Verdi's *Un ballo in maschera*. As a fill-up on the second disc we
get the ball scene from that opera, which is a ballet in itself. Richard Bonynge conducts with his usual
flair, keeping everything going at a sparkling pace and encouraging some really imaginative singing.
Gilles Cachemaille has a cameo as one of those satirical English milords who were so much a part of
nineteenth-century Parisian comedy. Hopefully this will be the beginning of an Auber series – he and
Scribe produced 50 operas together. No wonder the streets on either side of the Paris Opéra are
named after them.
Additional recommendation ...
...Gustav III. **Soloists; Intermezzo Vocal Ensemble; French Lyrique Orchestra / Michel Swierczewski.**
    Arion Ⓕ ARN368220 (three discs: 184 minutes: DDD: 9/93).
Further listening ...
...Overtures – Le Cheval de bronze. Fra Diavolo. La Muette de Portici. *Coupled with* **Suppé**
    Overtures – Die schöne Galathee. Pique Dame. Leichte Kavallerie. Dichter und Bauer. Ein

Morgen, ein Mittag, ein Abend in Wien. Boccaccio. **Detroit Symphony Orchestra / Paul Paray.**
Mercury 434 309-2MM.

...Fra Diavolo. **Soloists; Jean Laforge Chorale Ensemble; Monte Carlo Philharmonic Orchestra /**
Marc Soustrot. EMI CDS7 54810-2 (1/94).

Louis Aubert   French 1887-1968

New review
J. Aubert Suites de concerts de symphonies en trio, Op. 8 – No. 2 in D major; No. 5 in F major.
Concertos for Four Violins, Op. 17 – No. 1 in D major; No. 6 in G minor. Concerto in G minor,
Op. 26 No. 4, "Le carillon". **Collegium Musicum 90 / Simon Standage.** Chandos Chaconne
Ⓕ CHAN0577 (74 minutes: DDD: 2/96). ✔ Recorded 1994.
Rameau's contemporary, Jacques Aubert's unwieldily-titled Suites of 1730 are regarded as
antecedents of the French symphony (the preface sanctions performance by a larger body than a trio,
justifying the approach here), but both the present works from the set commence with a French
Overture, continue with half a dozen dance forms, and end in a chaconne whose refrain is interspersed
with episodes. Texturally and harmonically simple, with alternating major and minor sections to
provide contrast, the suites are unfailingly cheerful and lively – even the one Sarabande here – and,
probing no depths, are content to be elegant and charming. The advance publicity for Aubert's book
of six concertos for four violins, four years later, claimed them as "the first works of this genre to
come from the pen of a Frenchman", though in fact Corrette had anticipated him by six years.
Musically more varied and interesting than the suites, they adopt the Vivaldian three-movement form
and begin with a Vivaldian unison passage; though described as being "for four violins", only the first
violin has a solo part – ornate and relatively virtuosic, with multiple-stops in the Gavotte of No. 1. *Le*
carillon, from a later set, reverts to the *sonata da chiesa* pattern (slow-fast-slow-fast), distributes
interest among the instruments less unevenly, and ends in a French character piece. The crisply neat,
rhythmically vital playing throughout of Simon Standage and his colleagues is altogether admirable,
and the disc is accompanied by exemplary notes by Nicholas Anderson, its producer.

Georges Auric   French 1899-1983

Suggested listening ...
...Ouverture. *Coupled with* **Milhaud** Le boeuf sur le toit. **Satie** Parade. **Françaix** Piano
– Concertino[a]. **Fetler** Contrasts for Orchestra. [a]**Claude Françaix** (pf); **London Symphony Orchestra**
/ Antál Dorati. Mercury 434 335-2MM.   Ⓖ

Charles Avison   British 1709-1770

Avison 12 Concerti grossi after D. Scarlatti. **The Brandenburg Consort / Roy Goodman.** Hyperion
Ⓕ CDA66891/2 (two discs: 151 minutes: DDD: 4/95). ✔ Recorded 1994.   Ⓖ
Charles Avison was the most active English composer of concertos during the first half of the eighteenth
century, and his 12 *Concerti grossi* of 1744 among the most interesting of them. Five years earlier,
Thomas Roseingrave had published in London 42 harpsichord sonatas by Domenico Scarlatti and it was
these which provided Avison with the bulk of his material for these *Concerti grossi*. These are appealing
concertos, in no sense mere arrangements of Scarlatti's music but revealing a skilful and inventive
composer at work. Nevertheless, Scarlatti shines through most of the time, a constant delight to the
listener who, at least from time to time, will find a happy point of contact with the original source. The
booklet, incidentally, helpfully indicates, where possible, the Scarlatti sonata on which each movement is
based. Goodman's band is usually spirited and stylish, if not always endowed with aural finesse. Choice
between Goodman and the reissued Marriner (listed below) probably depends more upon the exchequer
and preferences for period instruments versus modern ones than on the respective merits of each
recording, for both sets are thoroughly enjoyable. Goodman's acoustic is spacious and reverberant. The
effect is closer to a performance in a large church than to one in an eighteenth-century music room.
Additional recommendation ...
...**Iona Brown, Malcolm Latchem** (vns); **Denis Vigay** (vc); **Nicholas Kraemer** (hpd); **Academy of St**
Martin in the Fields / Sir Neville Marriner. Philips Duo Ⓜ 438 806-2PM2 (two discs: 143 minutes:
ADD: 8/94).   Ⓖ

Milton Babbitt   American 1916-

Suggested listening ...
...Fanfare for all. *Coupled with works by* **Van Vliet, Wheeler, Zappa, Stravinsky, J. Nelson,**
Shemaria, H. Hancock and **London.** **Meridian Arts Ensemble.** Channel Classics Channel
Crossings CCS8195 (4/96). *See review in the Collections section; refer to the Index to Reviews.* Ⓖ

Grázyna Bacewicz

Suggested listening ...
...Violin Sonata No. 4[a]. Piano Sonata No. 2[b]. Concerto for String Orchestra[c]. Violin Concerto
No. 7[d]. [a]**Edward Statkiewicz,** [d]**Piotr Janowski** (vns); [a]**Aleksandra Utrecht,** [b]**Krystian Zimerman**
(pfs); [c]**Polish Chamber Orchestra / Jerzy Maksymiuk;** [d]**Warsaw Philharmonic Orchestra / Andrzej
Markowski.** Olympia OCD392 (12/93).
...String Quartets[a] – No. 3; No. 5. Piano Quintet No. 2[b]. [a]**Wilanow Quartet;** [b]**Warsaw Piano
Quintet.** Olympia OCD387 (8/93).
...String Quartet No. 4. *Coupled with* **Szymanowski** String Quartets – No. 1 in C major, Op. 37;
No. 2, Op. 56. **Maggini Quartet.** ASV Ⓔ CDDCA908 (59 minutes: DDD: 2/95).

Carl Philipp Emanuel Bach

C.P.E. Bach Cello Concertos – A minor, Wq170; B flat major, Wq171; A major, Wq172. **Anner
Bylsma** (vc); **Orchestra of the Age of Enlightenment / Gustav Leonhardt.** Virgin Classics Veritas
Ⓔ VC7 59541-2 (70 minutes: DDD: 2/90). ✏ Recorded 1988.
During his many years at the court of Frederick the Great, C.P.E. Bach composed these three cello
concertos. The fact that they also exist in his transcriptions for harpsichord and flute hardly suggests
very idiomatic writing for the cello and in a way the implied comment is true; nevertheless, they go
very well on the tenor instrument and Anner Bylsma brings out their quirky charm (a quality never
in short supply with this composer) while coping adequately with some tricky figuration in the quicker
movements; he's also eloquent in the highly expressive slower ones that are especially characteristic of
this Bach. This is perhaps not a CD for a basic collection, even of cello music, but it should give the
pleasure which is itself audible in the music-making by players completely at home in the idiom. The
recording was made in the well-tried location of All Saints' Church in Petersham in the UK; it places
the cello rather far back, but convincingly, and has an agreeably warm sound. The period pitch is
about a quarter of a tone lower than a modern one and the booklet gives the date and maker's name
of the orchestra's 23 instruments, though, oddly, not those of the soloist's baroque cello.
Additional recommendation ...
...**Miklós Perényi** (vc); **Liszt Chamber Orchestra / János Rolla.** Harmonia Mundi Musique d'abord
Ⓑ HMA190 3026 (70 minutes: DDD: 8/94).

C.P.E. Bach Flute Concertos – D minor, H484 No. 1; A major, H438; G major, H445. **Jennifer
Stinton** (fl); **Orchestra of St John's Smith Square / John Lubbock.** Collins Classics Ⓕ 1373-2
(67 minutes: DDD: 10/93). Recorded 1992.
The three concertos on this disc all exist in versions for solo instruments other than the flute. Which
versions reflect Bach's original intentions is not clear but, bearing in mind his employer, Frederick the
Great's passion for the flute, and the composer's equally fervent commitment to the keyboard, we may
perhaps adjudge an element of expediency in the flute concerto versions. The flautist Jennifer Stinton
finds plenty of interest in the music and interprets it with spirit and virtuosity. Her phrases are well
thought out and her articulation clear and effective. It is in the outer movements that these
performances are at their best with crisp, responsive orchestral playing, well-chosen tempos and clean,
incisive ensemble, and the brooding intensity of the middle movements is at times startling. These are
modern-instrument performances, but none the worse for that. The recording balance is pleasing, too,
achieving an even dialogue between soloist and ripieno, without artificially highlighting the flute and
the sound is clear and effective.
Additional recommendations ...
...A minor, H431; H438. Harpsichord Concerto in D minor, H425. **Eckart Haupt** (fl); **CPE Bach
Orchestra / Hans Haenchen.** Capriccio Ⓔ 10 104 (69 minutes: ADD: 10/88).
...G major, H445; H438; H484 No. 1. **James Galway** (fl); **Württemburg Chamber Orchestra / Jorg
Faerber.** RCA Victor Ⓔ RD60244 (69 minutes: DDD: 2/91).

New review
C.P.E. Bach Sinfonias, H663-6 – No. 1 in D major; No. 2 in E flat major; No. 3 in F; No. 4 in
G major.
W.F. Bach Sinfonia in F major. **Salzburg Chamber Philharmonic Orchestra / Yoon K. Lee.** Naxos
Ⓢ 8 553289 (52 minutes: DDD: 4/96). Recorded 1994. *Gramophone Editor's choice.*   Ⓖ
The exhilarating C.P.E. Bach symphonies presented here are not the more frequently recorded,
surprise-filled string symphonies of 1773 (H657-62), but the set of four for strings, flutes, oboes,
bassoons and horns which Bach wrote a couple of years later. They are no less astonishing.
Bewildering changes of direction, disorientating rhythmic games and unexpected solos all turn up in
this nervous, excitable music, which for originality and sheer life-force could surely only have been
matched in its day by that of Haydn. The Salzburg Chamber Philharmonic, under their founder Yoon
K. Lee, turn in crisp, spirited and (the odd moment of slack tuning apart) disciplined performances
which do the music full justice. They are not timid about making the most of Bach's strong contrasts,
although they produce them more by the release of some thunderous *forte* passages than by the

pursuit of too many unearthly *pianissimos*. The overall effect is wholly convincing, and only in the symphony by Emanuel's older brother Wilhelm Friedemann – more old-fashioned and less successful as a piece, though in its way just as determinedly unorthodox – does the use of modern instruments begin to get in the way of the spirit of music. This is an undeniably good buy.

New review

C.P.E. Bach Trio Sonatas for Two Violins and Continuo – A minor, H582; F major, H576; E minor, H577; B flat major, H584; D minor, H590. **London Baroque** (Ingrid Seifert, Richard Gwilt, vns; Charles Medlam, vc; Richard Egarr, hpd). Harmonia Mundi Ⓕ HMC90 1511 (62 minutes: DDD: 9/95). ✏ Recorded 1994.   Ⓖ

It seems rather difficult to associate C.P.E. Bach, Johann Sebastian's most talented and in some ways most adventurous of composing sons, with a form as deeply rooted in his father's time as the trio sonata – yet he wrote some 25 of them during his time at home in Leipzig and then in Berlin in the late 1740s and early 1750s. Some of them look backwards to the more democratic instrumental dialogues of baroque chamber music, while others look forward to the simpler textures of the classical period, but needless to say all are constructed with the craftsmanship we are entitled to expect from a Bach. London Baroque have made quite a speciality of playing the music of Bach's offspring over the last few years. Ingrid Seifert and Richard Gwilt bring to the music a rich and colourful sound quite distinct from that of rival trio sonata groups. But it is what the whole ensemble does which really matters, of course, and they could hardly make a more impressive start to the disc than with the opening of the A minor Sonata, in which an explosive violin line is driven along by throbbing repeated bass notes, a texture that could have come straight out of one of the composer's sparkier symphonies. There is similar energy in the last movement of the E minor Sonata too, dealt with in equally virtuosic fashion. Elsewhere there is more lyrical music to be enjoyed. The first movement of the F major Sonata has elegance and a constantly evolving texture, while the middle movement of the B flat major work features an eloquent melody for muted violins (here spiced with a saucy portamento or two), mixed with some exquisitely charming pizzicato passages. And, of course, there are surprises, those moments of startling unorthodoxy that are such a C.P.E. Bach trademark, including a crashing cadence that almost brings things to a complete halt in the F major's slow movement. "C.P.E.Bach Trio Sonatas" probably doesn't look all that promising an album title, but in London Baroque's hands it spells delight.

C.P.E. Bach Viola da gamba Sonatas – C major, Wq136; D major, Wq137; G minor, Wq88[ab]. Keyboard Sonatas – E major, H26[b]; A minor, H30[b]. **London Baroque** ([a]Charles Medlam, William Hunt, vas da gamba; [b]Richard Egarr, hpd). Harmonia Mundi Ⓕ HMC90 1410 (68 minutes: DDD: 1/93). ✏ Recorded 1991.

C.P.E. Bach's three sonatas for viola da gamba must be among the very last solo pieces outside France for an instrument which had gradually been supplanted by the cello. Two of the sontatas (Wq136/137) are of the continuo accompaniment type and date from the mid-1740s. The third (Wq88) written in 1759 is, by contrast more up-to-date in style with a fully written out harpsichord part on an equal footing with the gamba. From the gambist's viewpoint all three works are virtuoso pieces which explore pretty widely the expressive and technical range of the instrument. The partnership of Charles Medlam and Richard Egarr, with William Hunt in the two continuo sonatas, is an effective one. Medlam's tone is well-focused, he articulates clearly and has a lively rapport with the north German *Empfindsamer Stil*, present to a greater or lesser extent in almost all C.P.E. Bach's music after 1740 or so. Medlam responds to the music with a happy blend of head and heart, realizing at the same time one of Bach's own tenets for a good performance, "the ability through singing or playing to make the ear conscious of the true content and affect of a composition". Two keyboard sonatas complete this entertaining programme, one from the *Prussian* set, the other from the *Württemberg*. Richard Egarr plays them stylishly with a lively response to ornaments. Some listeners may find the interpretations understate Bach's characteristically temperamental gestures but the virtuosity of the playing is admirable.

Additional recommendation ...

...Sonatas – Wq88; Wq136; Wq137. Fantasia in C major, Wq59 No. 6. **Siegfried Pank** (va da gamba); **Christiane Jaccottet** (clav/fp). Capriccio Ⓕ 10 102 (56 minutes: DDD: 10/88). ✏

C.P.E. Bach Flute Sonatas – C major, H504; D major, H505; E major, H506; G major, H508; G major, H509; C major, H515; G minor, H542 No. 5 (BWV1020); B flat major, H543; E flat major, H545 (BWV1031); B flat major, H578. **Barthold Kuijken** (fl); **Bob van Asperen** (hpd). Sony Classical Vivarte Ⓕ S2K53964 (two discs: 140 minutes: DDD: 5/94). ✏ Recorded 1993.   Ⓖ

This album contains C.P.E. Bach's five sonatas for flute with obbligato harpsichord. The playing is lively in spirit. Kuijken's tone is warmly coloured, softly spoken and pleasingly rounded and he clearly has much affection for Bach's expressive idiom. The balance between flute and harpsichord is effective, too, with Bob van Asperen proving himself an ideal partner both on account of his playing, which is particular in and attentive to detail, and his sympathy with the music. A first-rate recital, stylishly played with outstanding virtuosity and sympathetically recorded.

C.P.E. Bach Keyboard Sonatas – "Prussian", H24-29[a]; "Württemberg", H30-35[b]. Harpsichord Concerto in C major, H190[c]. **Bob van Asperen** (hpd). Teldec Das Alte Werk Ⓜ 9031-77623-2 (three discs: 175 minutes: ADD: 7/93). *✐* Items marked [ac] recorded 1977-9, new to UK, [b]EK6 35378 (6/79). **G**

C.P.E. Bach Keyboard Sonatas – B minor, H35; E major, H39; F minor, H40; C major, H41; B flat major, H51.**Colin Booth** (hpd). Olympia Ⓕ OCD433 (78 minutes: DDD). *✐* From Soundboard Records SBCD921 (8/93). Recorded 1992.

C.P.E. Bach's sets of *Prussian* and *Württemberg* Sonatas played by Bob van Asperen typify why back catalogues are as important as ever; not only have these veracious performances of the earlier *Prussian* Sonatas never reached these shores before, but neither of these sets are currently available complete. In the *Württemburg* Sonatas van Asperen's playing is of the utmost brilliance and he rarely misses a trick in communicating Bach's variegated style with exuberance and refinement. Such qualities abound too in the dazzling *Concerto per il Cembalo solo*. The recorded sound is suitably clear and fresh throughout. One interesting feature of these keyboard sonatas is the stylistic variety that is contained within individual movements. Recitative-like passages jostle with orchestrally conceived ideas, lyricism with more robust, challenging gestures, counterpoint with homophonic texture and baroque disciplines with *galant* phraseology. Rhythmic and harmonic uncertainties abound and all this is placed at the service of expression. Colin Booth plays with technical fluency and a ready awareness of all the little quirks and pitfalls in Bach's style which can be the undoing of players with a more prosaic outlook. He plays his own copy of a two-manual Mietke harpsichord – he was the maker who supplied an instrument to the Cöthen court during J.S. Bach's time there. This is a worthy single disc alternative and a recital well worth becoming acquainted with, above all for the music but also for the sympathetic playing and the distinctive sound of the harpsichord.

Further listening ...

...Organ Concertos[a] G major, H444; E flat major, H446. Prelude in D major, H107. Fantasia and Fugue a 4 in C minor, H103. **Roland Munch** (org); [a]**CPE Bach Orchestra / Hartmut Haenchen.** Capriccio 10 135 (10/88).

...Concerto for Harpsichord, Two Flutes and Strings in F major, H454. Concerto for Harpsichord and Strings in B minor, H440. Concerto for Harpsichord, Two Horns and Strings in C minor, H448. **Les Amis de Philippe / Ludger Rémy** (hpd). CPO CPO999 350-2 (2/96). *✐*

...Sinfonias – E flat major, H654; F major, H656; C major, H649; F major, H650; E minor, H653. **CPE Bach Orchestra / Hartmut Haenchen.** Capriccio 10 103 (9/87).

...Symphonies, Wq183 – No. 1 in D major; No. 2 in E flat major; No. 3 in F major; No. 4 in G major. **CPE Bach Orchestra / Hartmut Haenchen.** Capriccio 10 175 (10/88).

...Pièces Caractéristiques[b] – La Borchward, H79; La Pott, H80; La Gleim, H89; La Bergius, H90; La Stahl, H94; La Boehmer, H81; La Louise, H114. *Coupled with* **Schulz** Diverses pièces, Op. 1[b] – No. 5, Allegretto; No. 6, Larghetto con Variazioni. **Fasch** Andantino con Variazioni[a]. **Benda** Keyboard Sonatinas[a] – Rondeau; Allegro; Allegretto; Allegretto; Allegretto moderato. **Graun** Keyboard Sonata in D minor[a]. **Hasse** Keyboard Sonata in E flat major[a]. **Christine Schornsheim** ([a]hpd/[b]fp). Capriccio 10 424 (4/95). *✐*

...Fantasia and Fugue a 4 in C minor, H103. Organ Prelude in D major, H107. Organ Sonatas – F major, H84; A minor, H85; D major, H86; G minor, H87. **Jacques van Oortmerssen** (org). BIS CD569 (5/93).

...Magnificat in D minor, H772 – Quia respexit. *Coupled with works by* **J.S. Bach, Telemann, Handel, Brahms, Schumann** and **Schubert** Elly Ameling (sop); Various soloists. Deutsche Harmonia Mundi 74321 26617-2 (12/95). *See review in the Collections section; refer to the Index to Reviews.*

...Die Auferstehung und Himmelfahrt Jesu, H777. **Hillevi Martinpelto** (sop); **Christoph Prégardien** (ten); **Peter Harvey** (bass); **Ghent Collegium Vocale Choir; Orchestra of the Age of Enlightenment / Philippe Herreweghe.** Virgin Classics Veritas VC7 59069-2 (9/92). *✐*

Johann Christian Bach

German 1735-1782

New review
J.C. Bach Six Harpsichord Concertos, Op. 1 – No. 1 in B flat major; No. 2 in A major; No. 3 in F major; No. 4 in G major; No. 5 in C major; No. 6 in D major. **Graham Cracknell, Adrian Butterfield** (vns); **Angela East** (vc); **Anthony Halstead** (hpd). CPO Ⓕ CPO999 299-2 (66 minutes: DDD: 7/96).

The Op. 1 Keyboard Concertos were published in 1763: they are chamber works, played here, as they should be, with just two solo violins and a cello. They are slight pieces, neatly and gracefully formed but for the most part slender in musical content and often harmonically rather static. Nos. 1, 2, 3 and 5 are in the *galant* two-movement form, the second usually an extended minuet showing J.C. Bach's characteristic warmth of invention. The first movements, which vary in tempo from *Andante* to *Allegro*, are embryonic versions of the concerto form familiar to us from Mozart. Nos. 4 and 6, which Bach called "Concerto o Sinfonia", are quite different: each is in three movements, fast-slow-fast, the first of them not in concerto form at all but with the material shared equally between strings and keyboard, and fully integrated, more like a true keyboard quartet. The opening *Allegro* of No. 4 is a particularly good piece, with a vitality and momentum to the music that is otherwise in short supply. And the slow movements of both these two have an expressive keyboard cantilena that is very appealing. The finale of No. 6 is a charming set of variations on *God save the King*. Anthony Halstead gives plain and direct performances, with many delicate touches of timing and articulation. There is some quite brilliant playing in the first movement of No. 4. Here and there one might wish for a shade more flexibility in rhythm; it's always worth thinking, in music of this kind, in terms of a vocal line. However, the music is finely represented, and this augurs well for future discs in this projected complete recording of J.C. Bach's keyboard concertos.

New review

J.C. Bach Six Symphonies, Op. 6 – No. 1 in G major; No. 2 in D major; No. 3 in E flat major; No. 4 in B flat major; No. 5 in E flat major; No. 6 in G minor. **Hanover Band / Anthony Halstead.** CPO Ⓟ CPO999 298-2 (56 minutes: DDD: 3/96). ✍ Recorded 1994.

In the Op. 6 Symphonies, the frothy Italianate music of the composer's Italian and early London years was behind him; these pieces, dating from the late 1760s, though still of course Italian-influenced in their formal clarity and their melodic style, are sturdier music, more carefully composed, more symphonic in feeling. Both the E flat works in this set have something of the solidity and warmth associated with that key, and each has a C minor *Andante*; the G major's first movement has the confident ring and thematic contrasts of his mature music, and the D major contains Mannheim crescendos and some delightful textures, with flutes and divided violas, in its charming and slightly playful middle movement. The set ends with Bach's single minor-key symphony in G minor, very similar in spirit to Mozart's No. 25; this piece, often recorded before, shows an unfamiliar side to his musical personality. Anthony Halstead and his players convey the strength and the spirit of the music convincingly. The lively finales all go with a swing, and the opening movements have plenty of energy. The slow movements are not always quite so persuasive: the third C minor slow movement of the G minor Symphony is a little over-deliberate and becomes detached and modest in expressive impact. But generally these are strong and appealing performances of some attractive and unfamiliar music, clearly, slightly drily recorded, and admirers of the London Bach and his music need not hesitate.

J.C. Bach Adriano in Siria – Overture. Six Grand Overtures, Op. 18 – No. 1 in E flat major; No. 4 in D major. Symphony in G minor, Op. 6 No. 6. Sinfonia concertante in C major, T289 No. 4 (ed. Maunder). **Academy of Ancient Music / Simon Standage** (vn). Chandos Chaconne Ⓟ CHAN0540 (65 minutes: DDD: 12/93). ✍ Recorded 1993.

The G minor Symphony is a magnificently fiery piece, similar in manner to Haydn's No. 39 and Mozart's No. 25; it is done here with plenty of *Sturm und Drang*, notably in the very forceful finale, and the fine, noble ideas of the slow movement are well caught too. The opening item is a three-movement D major Symphony, in effect, with a well-worked first movement and an *Andante* with rich wind writing. No other composer, besides of course Mozart, seems to have had as keen a feeling as J.C. Bach for the sensuous beauty of wind textures. The *Sinfonia concertante* isn't quite as successful a piece, being rather repetitive, but it is never less than charming and enjoyable music, again with some beautiful windy textures in the *Larghetto* and a delightful "Two lovely black eyes" theme in the rondo. The solo playing is admirable. Recommended to anyone sympathetic to J.C. Bach's music.

Further listening ...

...Keyboard Concertos – Op. 1; Op. 7. **Ingrid Haebler** (fp); **Vienna Capella Academica / Eduard Melkus.** Philips 438 712-2PM2 (2/94).

...Keyboard Concerto in B flat major, Op. 13 No. 4[d]. *Coupled with* **Mozart** Serenade No. 10 in G major, K525, "Eine kleine Nachtmusik"[e]. **Bach** Orchestral Suite No. 2 in B minor, BWV1067[a]. Harpsichord Concerto in F minor, BWV1056[b]. **Vivaldi** Violin Concerto, Op. 8 No. 3, "Autumn"[c]. [b]**Agi Jambor,** [d]**Marinus Flipse** (pfs); **Concertgebouw Orchestra / Willem Mengelberg.** Archive Documents Mengelberg Edition mono ADCD112* (5/95).

...Keyboard Sonatas – Op. 5 Nos. 5 and 6; Op. 17 Nos. 2, 3 and 5. **Virginia Black** (hpd). CRD CRD3453 (2/90). ✍

...Amadis des Gaules (sung in German). **Soloists; Stuttgart Gächinger Kantorei; Stuttgart Bach Collegium / Helmuth Rilling.** Hänssler Classic 98 963 (9/93).

Johann Sebastian Bach   German 1685-1750

Bach Harpsichord Concertos – D minor, BWV1052[a]; D major, BWV1054[a]. Concerto for Flute, Violin, Harpsichord and Strings in A minor, BWV1044[a]. Das Wohltemperierte Klavier, BWV846-93 – Preludes and Fugues: F major, BWV880; B major, BWV892. [a]**Le Concert Français / Pierre Hantaï** (hpd). Auvidis Astrée Ⓟ E8523 (70 minutes: DDD: 1/95). ✍ Recorded 1993.   ⓖⓖ

Gramophone Editor's record of the month.

The concertos come over well. Ensemble is tautly controlled and the string playing effectively articulated, though on occasion the first violin is a little too favoured in the recorded balance. However, the string playing is so unanimous in sound and purpose that there is little to worry about in this department. Hantaï himself is impressive for his wonderfully rhythmic playing, the clarity with which he interprets both his own keyboard textures and those which support and punctuate it, and not least for his supple, muscular concept of the music. These are extraordinarily invigorating performances, which draw the listener deep into the harmonic and contrapuntal complexities and conceits of Bach's art. Take for instance the elusive *Adagio* of BWV1052, where careful punctuation and sensitive interaction between solo and tutti make for a rewarding coherence. In the A minor Triple Concerto, Hantaï is joined by his flautist brother, Marc and François Fernandez (violin), the leader of the ensemble. The work is a Leipzig arrangement of movements from earlier pieces not in concerto form, whose extent sources were almost certainly copied after Bach's death. The opening *Allegro* is a little too heavy, but the essentially three-part texture of the middle movement is realized with affection. This is a stimulating disc which makes one eagerly look forward to further instalments from these gifted musicians.

Additional recommendations ...

...BWV1052; E major, BWV1053; BWV1054; F minor, BWV1056; F major, BWV1057; G minor, BWV1058; D minor, BWV1059. **Amsterdam Baroque Orchestra / Ton Koopman** (hpd). Erato Bonsai Ⓑ 4509-91930-2 (two discs: 107 minutes: DDD). ✍

...BWV1052; BWV1053; BWV1054; **Hae-won Chang** (pf); **Camerata Cassovia / Robert Stankovsky.** Naxos Ⓢ 8 550422 (62 minutes: DDD).

...BWV1052, E major, BWV1053; BWV1054; **The English Concert / Trevor Pinnock** (hpd). Archiv Produktion Ⓕ 415 991-2AH (58 minutes: DDD: 9/87). ✍

...BWV1052[a]. Concerto for Two Harpsichords in C major, BWV1061[b]. Concerto for Three Harpsichords in C major, BWV1064[c]. Concerto for Four Harpsichords in A minor, BWV1065[d]. [b]**Eduard Müller,** [cd]**Gerhard Aeschbacher,** [d]**Heinrich Gurtner** (hpds); **Ansbach Bach Week Soloists / Karl Richter** (hpd). Teldec Ⓑ 4509-99873-2 (73 minutes: ADD: 5/96). *See review in the Collections section; refer to the Index to Reviews.*

New review

Bach Violin Concertos – No. 1 in A minor, BWV1041; No. 2 in E major, BWV1042. Double Violin Concerto in D minor, BWV1043[a]. Triple Violin Concerto in D major, BWV1064[ab]. [a]**Linda Melsted,** [b]**David Greenberg** (vns); **Tafelmusik / Jeanne Lamon** (vn). Sony Classical Vivarte Ⓕ SK66265 (62 minutes: DDD: 2/96). ✍ Recorded 1995.

Although only three of Bach's violin concertos (BWV1041-3) have been preserved in their original form there were undoubtedly a great many more. Several have survived in later versions as harpsichord concertos while individual movements from lost concertos almost certainly survive within the body of Bach's cantatas. As well as the three familiar violin concertos by Bach, Tafelmusik and their soloist/director Jeanne Lamon have included a concerto better known in its version in C major for three harpsichords and strings (BWV1064). The reconstruction by Wilfried Fischer, following the assumption that the work in its original form was for three violins, transposes the music up a tone to D major – Bach's normal practice was to transpose his original down a tone to accommodate the harpsichord range. Yet there are still features of this concerto, above all in its conjectural version for three violins, which do not quite ring true. Nevertheless Lamon and her two solo partners, Linda Melsted and David Greenberg, make out a strong case for accepting the piece as genuine Bach. The two solo violin concertos and the concerto for two violins have been thoroughly and painstakingly rehearsed and the results are rewarding. Some readers may find Lamon's tone a little astringent at times but she is also capable of producing a warm sound, especially in the lower part of her tessitura. What you may like most about these performances, however, is the way in which she shapes and punctuates her phrases without ever losing sight of the poetry of the music. The finale of the A minor Concerto, for instance, is not the breathless conversation it so often sounds in performance but an articulate exposition of its subtle counterpoint. Indeed, clarity of musical argument is a strong feature of the playing in each of these concertos.

Additional recommendations ...

...Nos. 1[a] and 2[a]. Double Violin Concerto in D minor, BWV1043[b]. Concerto for Three Violins, BWV1064[c]. [b]**Alison Bury,** [c]**Pavlo Beznosiuk,** [c]**Catherine Mackintosh** (vns); **Orchestra of the Age of Enlightenment / Elizabeth Wallfisch** ([abc]vn). Virgin Classics Veritas Ⓕ VC7 59319-2 (63 minutes: DDD). ✍

...Nos. 1 and 2. Double Violin Concerto. Violin and Oboe Concerto in C minor, BWV1060. **Jaap Schröder, Christopher Hirons** (vns); **Academy of Ancient Music / Christopher Hogwood.** L'Oiseau-Lyre Ⓕ 400 080-2OH (45 minutes: DDD: 3/83). ✍

...Nos. 1 and 2. Double Violin Concerto. Violin and Oboe Concerto. **Anne-Sophie Mutter** (vn); **English Chamber Orchestra / Salvatore Accardo** (vn). EMI Ⓕ CDC7 47005-2 (53 minutes: DDD: 2/84).

...Nos. 1 and 2. Double Violin Concerto. **Simon Standage, Elizabeth Wilcock** (vns); **The English Concert / Trevor Pinnock** (hpd). Archiv Produktion Ⓕ 410 646-2AH (46 minutes: DDD: 8/84). ✍

...Nos. 1 and 2. Double Violin Concerto. Violin and Oboe Concerto. **Arthur Grumiaux, Herman Krebbers** (vns); **Heinz Holliger** (ob); **Les Soloists Romands / Arpad Gerecz.** Philips Ⓜ 420 700-2PSL (61 minutes: DDD: 5/88). Ⓖ

...Nos. 1 and 2[a]. Double Violin Concerto[b]. **Beethoven** Romances[c] No. 1 in G major, Op. 40; No. 2 in F major, Op. 50. **Brahms** Violin Concerto in D major, Op. 77[d]. **Tchaikovsky** Violin Concerto in D major, Op. 35[d]. **David Oistrakh,** [b]**Igor Oistrakh** (vns); [a]**Vienna Symphony Orchestra;** [bc]**Royal Philharmonic Orchestra / Sir Eugene Goossens;** [d]**Staatskapelle Dresden / Franz Konwitschny.** DG The Originals [abc]stereo/[d]mono Ⓜ 447 427-2GOR2* (two discs: 142 minutes: ADD: 6/95).

...No. 1. Harpsichord Concertos – E major, BWV1053; A major, BWV1055; G minor, BWV1058. **Christophe Rousset** (hpd); **Jaap Schröder** (vn); **Academy of Ancient Music / Christopher Hogwood.** L'Oiseau-Lyre Ⓕ 443 326-2OH (57 minutes: DDD: 10/95). ✐

Bach Double Concertos – D minor for Two Violins, BWV1043[a]; C minor for Violin and Oboe, BWV1060[b]; C minor for Two Harpsichords, BWV1060[c]; C minor for Two Harpsichords, BWV1062[c]. [a]**Jaap Schröder**, [a]**Christopher Hirons**, [b]**Catherine Mackintosh** (vns); [b]**Stephen Hammer** (ob); [c]**Christophe Rousset** (hpd); **Academy of Ancient Music / Christopher Hogwood** ([c]hpd). L'Oiseau-Lyre Florilegium Ⓕ 421 500-2OH (58 minutes: DDD: 9/89). ✐ Item marked [a] from DSDL702 (8/82), [b] and [c] new to UK.

The concept of a concerto with two or more soloists grew naturally out of the *concerto grosso*, and Bach was among those baroque composers who explored its possibilities. The Concerto in D minor, BWV1043 for two violins is perhaps the best known of his works in the *genre*, which Bach himself reworked as a Concerto for Two Harpsichords, BWV1062, in the key of C minor. No alternative version has survived in the case of the two-harpsichord Concerto BWV1060, also in C minor, but musicological evidence suggests that it was originally intended for two single-line instruments – two violins or one violin and an oboe. The work has thus been notionally reconstructed in the latter form. Baroque music never sounds better than when it is played on period instruments, in proper style, and by performers of the quality of those in this recording, not least the well matched soloists. The famous slow movement of BWV1043 is taken a little faster than usual, convincingly stripped of the specious sentimentality with which it is often invested. The recording is of suitably high quality.

Additional recommendations ...

...Harpsichord Concerto in A major, BWV1055. Concerto for Four Harpsichords and Strings in A minor, BWV1065[a]. Triple Harpsichord Concerto, BWV1060-62[b]. Double Harpsichord Concertos, BWV1063-64[c]. [abc]**Tini Mathot**, [ac]**Patrizia Marisaldi**, [a]**Elina Mustonen** (hpds); **Amsterdam Baroque Orchestra / Ton Koopman** (hpd). Erato Bonsai Ⓑ 4509-91929-2 (two discs: 118 minutes: DDD). ✐

...BWV1043. *Coupled with works by* **Mozart, Schubert, Berlioz** and **Borodin**. **Louis Zimmerman** (vn); **Concertgebouw Orchestra / Willem Mengelberg**. Pearl mono Ⓜ GEMMCD9154* (76 minutes: ADD: 3/96).

Bach Oboe Concertos – F major, BWV1053; A major, BWV1055; D minor, BWV1059. **Chamber Orchestra of Europe / Douglas Boyd** (ob, ob d'amore). DG Ⓕ 429 225-2GH (46 minutes: DDD: 4/90). Recorded 1989.

Although Bach is not known to have written any concertos for the oboe he did entrust it with some beautiful *obbligato* parts, so he clearly did not underrate its expressive capacities. He did however rearrange many of his works for different instrumental media and there is musicological evidence that original oboe concertos were the (lost) sources from which other works were derived. The Harpsichord Concerto in A major, BWV1055, is believed originally to have been written for the oboe d'amore, whilst the other two Oboe Concertos have been reassembled from movements found in various cantatas. Whatever the validity of the academic reasoning, the results sound very convincing. Douglas Boyd is a superb oboist, with a clear sound that is free from stridency, and a fluency that belies the instrument's technical difficulty. He plays the faster, outer movements with winsome lightness of tongue and spirit, and with alertness to dynamic nuance; the slow ones, the hearts of these works, are given with sensitivity but without sentimentality – which can easily invade that of BWV1059, taken from Cantata No. 156, *Ich steh mit einem Fuss im Grabe*. The Chamber Orchestra of Europe partners him to perfection in this crisp recording.

Bach Brandenburg Concertos, BWV1046-51 – No. 1 in F major; No. 2 in F major; No. 3 in G major; No. 4 in G major; No. 5 in D major; No. 6 in B flat major. **Tafelmusik / Jeanne Lamon** (vn). Sony Classical Vivarte Ⓕ S2K66289 (two discs: 93 minutes: DDD: 4/95). ✐ Recorded 1993-4. ⓐ

New review

Bach Brandenburg Concertos, BWV1046-51. **Boston Baroque / Martin Pearlman** (hpd). Telarc Ⓕ CD80354/68 (two discs, oas: 52 and 41 minutes: DDD: 2/96). ✐ ⓐ *CD80368* – No. 1 in F major; No. 2 in F major; No. 3 in G major. *CD80354* – No. 4 in G major; No. 5 in D major; No. 6 in B flat major.

Tafelmusik's *Brandenburgs* come straight from the heart and as such they are performances which invite repeated listening and are furthermore both easy and enjoyable to live with. There are no startling novelties here and nothing which attempts to impede the natural course of musical flow. Tempos are sensibly chosen and, once chosen, consistently adhered to. That is not to say that there is an absence of affective gesture or a lack of rhetorical awareness. Everything in fact is punctuated in a way that allows the listener to follow the subtly shaded nuances of Bach's dialogue. Some readers may feel that these interpretations lack the stamp of a strong personality at the helm but any such fears of interpretative neutrality are largely dispelled by the sensibility of the players and their hitherto proven skill at reaching the heart of the music without the assistance either of pretension or muddled intellectual clutter. Reservations chiefly concern minutiae of tuning and to a much lesser extent, ensemble. Neither these weaknesses, nor the occasional blip or thwack, hindering the production of clean notes from oboe, horns or trumpet, spoil enjoyment of Tafelmusik's Nos. 1 and 2. It is a pity that the first movement of No. 3 is marred by indifferent tuning in the lower strands of the texture and, more disturbingly, by a marked acceleration in speed beginning at bar 84 (3'26"); but the second *Allegro* of the work is so well done that you are inclined to forgive them. Tafelmusik's account of this brilliant binary movement – a unique example of the form among Bach's concertos as Malcolm Boyd remarks in an excellent accompanying essay – is not to be missed.

Boston Baroque are a close-knit group of highly accomplished and stylish instrumentalists. On their discs their enthusiasm is clear in the bustling outer movements; it's a wise leader who knows his team, in this case Martin Pearlman, who no doubt set the tempos. In the slow movements there is the breathing-space which is often found lacking. The soloists are first-class (though Friedemann Immer's trumpet trills in Concerto No. 2 sound a mite uncomfortable) and the multi-talented Daniel Stepner (violone piccolo in No. 2, violin soloist in Nos. 4 and 5, and viola soloist in No. 6) and Pearlman himself (harpsichord) are especially impressive. It is, however, the ensemble, supported by a finely balanced recording, that makes these accounts so outstanding, and those who are allergic to thin or nasal string sounds will find nothing to cringe from in the warmth of tone that characterizes these performances. The annotation states (but without explanation) that Concerto No. 6 "must remain a chamber piece with one player to a part": whether it must or not, the recording shows it to be wholly effective played in that way. We are also told that "it includes the transparent sounds of gambas" and so it does, but we are left to guess who their players might be. No matter how many horses enter a race the winner is usually clear, but it is not so with oft-recorded works such as the *Brandenburgs* (as is evidenced by the list which follows). There can be no clear 'best', but the Telarc set, at once thoughtful, sensitive, stylish and joyous, is likely to remain amongst those which will prove to be enduring.

Additional recommendations ...

...Nos. 1-3. **Academy of St Martin in the Fields / Sir Neville Marriner.** Philips Ⓔ 400 076-2PH (45 minutes: ADD: 3/83)

...Nos. 1-6[a]. Orchestral Suites, BWV1066-9[b]. **The English Concert / Trevor Pinnock.** Archiv Produktion Ⓜ 423 492-2AX3 (three discs: 173 minutes: DDD/ADD: 10/88). ✍   Ⓖ

...Nos. 1-6. **Orchestra of the Age of Enlightenment.** Virgin Classics Veritas Ⓔ VCD7 59260-2 (two discs: 93 minutes: DDD: 7/89). ✍

...Nos. 1-6. Orchestral Suites. **Adolf Busch Chamber Players / A. Busch.** EMI Références mono Ⓜ CHS7 64047-2* (three discs: 195 minutes: ADD: 12/91).

...Nos. 1, 2 and 4. Orchestral Suite No. 2. **Vienna Concentus Musicus / Nikolaus Harnoncourt.** Teldec Digital Experience Ⓜ 9031-75858-2 (73 minutes: DDD: 9/92). ✍   Ⓖ

...Nos. 3, 5 and 6. Orchestral Suite No. 3. **Vienna Concentus Musicus / Nikolaus Harnoncourt.** Teldec Digital Experience Ⓜ 9031-75859-2 (75 minutes: DDD: 9/92). ✍

...Nos. 1-6. **Vienna Concentus Musicus / Harnoncourt.** Teldec Das Alte Werk Ⓜ 9031-77611-2 (two discs: 105 minutes: ADD: 7/93). ✍

...No. 3[c]. **Haydn** Symphony No. 45 in F sharp minor, "Farewell"[b]. **Schubert** Symphony No. 8 in B minor, "Unfinished", D759[b]. **Litolff** Concerto symphonique No. 4 in D minor, Op. 102 – Scherzo[ab]. **Rachmaninov** (arr. Wood) Prelude in C sharp minor, Op. 3 No. 2[e]. **Bruckner** Overture in G minor[d]. **Beethoven** Symphony No. 5 in C minor, Op. 67[d]. **Brahms** Variations on a Theme by Haydn, "St Antoni", Op. 56a[d]. **Dvořák** Symphonic Variations, B70[d]. [a]**Irene Scharrer** (pf); [b]**London Symphony Orchestra**; [c]**British Symphony Orchestra**; [d]**Queen's Hall Orchestra**; [e]**symphony orchestra / Sir Henry Wood.** Dutton Laboratories mono Ⓜ 2CDAX2002* (two discs: 138 minutes: ADD: 9/94).

...Nos. 1-6. **New London Consort / Philip Pickett.** L'Oiseau-Lyre Ⓔ 440 675-2OH2 (two discs: 95 minutes: DDD: 1/95). ✍

...Nos. 1-6. Orchestral Suites – No. 2 in B minor, BWV1066; No. 3 in D major, BWV1067. **Vienna Concentus Musicus / Nikolaus Harnoncourt.** Teldec Ⓜ 4509-95980-2 (two discs: 148 minutes: DDD: 5/95). ✍

...Nos. 1-6. **La Petite Bande / Sigiswald Kuijken.** Deutsche Harmonia Mundi Ⓔ 05472 77308-2 (two discs: 97 minutes: DDD: 6/95).

Bach Orchestral Suites, BWV1066-69 – No. 1 in C major; No. 2 in B minor[a]; No. 3 in D major; No. 4 in D major. [a]**Wilbert Hazelzet** (fl); **Amsterdam Baroque Orchestra / Ton Koopman.** Deutsche Harmonia Mundi Ⓔ RD77864 (two discs: 79 minutes: DDD: 1/90). ✍ Recorded 1988.
Gramophone Award Winner 1990.   ⒼⒼⒼ

Bach's Orchestral Suites are deservedly well represented in the catalogue, with versions in plenty by orchestras of period and modern instruments alike. Koopman captures the contrasting colours and textures of these works with a sure feeling for orchestral sonority, but over and above that he is most persuasive in his gestures, graceful at times, ceremoniously pompous at others. Thus the Sarabande of the B minor Suite is one of the high-water marks of the entire set, exquisitely poised and lovingly articulated by the flautist, Wilbert Hazelzet, an artist of rare sensibility. Other dances in this suite fare equally well, with a Menuet redolent of courtly gesture and a Polonaise with an easy, carefree gait. As a general rule, Koopman favours rather slower tempos than many of his rival colleagues and he is to be applauded for doing so. The Rondeau of the B minor Suite is, comparatively speaking, slow yet avoiding monotony; the Forlane of the C major Suite is delightfully airy, as are the two Bourrées and the pleasingly leisurely Passepieds. Loveliest of all, perhaps, in this performance of the C major Suite, are the relaxed and affectingly articulated Courantes and the refined Menuets, whose kinetic energy is subtly realized under Koopman's direction. Koopman draws the strongest contrast between lighter textured dances and galanteries such as these, and the grandiose music contained in the two D major Suites. The Overtures in both instances are magnificent with commendably vibrant timpani and snarling trumpets which sets the blood coursing through the veins. This is robust Bach playing but without a hint of vulgarity and in no sense lacking in appropriate restraint. This is a considerable achievement and if some listeners are mildly irked by Koopman's own brilliant but perhaps over-busy keyboard continuo realizations, they are unlikely to be able to resist the subtle inflexions and ravishing inner-part understanding of Suite No. 2; and, it should be added, the sheer exuberant spirit of occasion which shines through the performances of the other three suites. The recorded sound is splendid.

Additional recommendations ...

...Nos. 1-4. **Cologne Musica Antiqua / Reinhard Goebel.** Archiv Produktion Ⓕ 415 671-2AH2 (two discs: DDD: 10/86). ✐   ⒼⒼ

...Nos. 1-4. **Academy of St Martin in the Fields / Sir Neville Marriner.** Decca Serenata Ⓜ 430 378-2DM (78 minutes: ADD: 7/91).

...No. 2 in B minor, BWV1067. Harpsichord Concerto in F minor, BWV1056. **Vivaldi** Violin Concerto, "Autumn", Op. 8 No. 3. **J.C. Bach** Keyboard Concerto in B flat major, Op. 13 No. 4. **Mozart** Serenade No. 13 in G major, K525, "Eine kleine Nachtmusik". **Agi Jambor, Marinus Flipse** (pfs); **Concertgebouw Orchestra / Willem Mengelberg.** Archive Documents Mengelberg Edition mono Ⓕ ADCD112* (69 minutes: AAD: 5/95).

...Nos. 1-4. Cantata No. 110, Unser Mund sei voll Lachens – Unser Mund sei voll Lachens[a]. Cantata No. 174, Ich liebe den Höchsten von ganzem Gemüte – Sinfonia Concerto. Easter Oratorio, BWV249 – Sinfonia. Cantata No. 42, Am Abend aber desselbigen Sabbats – Sinfonia. Cantata No. 52, Falsche Welt, dir trau ich nicht – Sinfonia. [a]**The English Concert Choir; The English Concert / Trevor Pinnock.** ✐ Archiv Produktion Ⓕ 439 780-2AH2 (two discs: 121 minutes: DDD: 12/95).

Bach Orchestral Suite No. 4 in D major, BWV1069. Concerto for Three Violins and Strings in D major, BWV1064. Cantata No. 42, Am Abend aber desselbigen Sabbats – Sinfonia. **Vivaldi** Concertos – Strings in A major, RV158; Four Violins and Strings in B minor, Op. 3 No. 10. L'Olimpiade – Overture. **Freiburg Baroque Orchestra / Thomas Hengelbrock.** Deutsche Harmonia Mundi Ⓕ 05472 77289-2 (64 minutes: DDD: 4/94). ✐ Recorded 1991-2.   Ⓖ

The Freiburg Baroque Orchestra score ten out of ten for vitality in their pleasingly varied programme. Bach's Orchestral Suite No. 4 is heard in what is probably a pre-Leipzig version, which excludes trumpets and drums. That may not sound too promising for readers who like their 'fix' of brass and timpani, yet the immensely rewarding sonorities created by strings, three oboes and bassoon together with invigorating rhythmic patterns, provides wonderful mental and aural refreshment. However, the two Menuets in the Leipzig version are also missing. Of the two Vivaldi concertos, the A major piece for ripieno strings foreshadows the style of the early Mannheim symphonists, with its tremolos, breaks and short runs punctuated by trills in the outer movements and the B minor, the tenth of the 12 which Vivaldi published under the title *L'estro armonico*, is among the most inventive of the set. This enjoyable release is well recorded and helpfully documented.

Bach The Art of Fugue, BWV1080[a]. A Musical Offering, BWV1079[b]. Canons, BWV1072-8; 1086-7[a]. **Cologne Musica Antiqua / Reinhard Goebel.** Archiv Produktion Ⓕ 413 642-2AH3 (three discs: 140 minutes: ADD: 4/85). ✐ Items marked [a] from 413 728-1AH2 (4/85); [b]2533 422 (11/79).   ⒼⒼ

The great compilation of fugues, canons and a trio sonata which Bach dedicated to King Frederick the Great is one of the monuments of baroque instrumental music. Every contrapuntal device of canon at various intervals, augmentation, inversion, retrograde motion and so on is displayed here, and the performances are splendidly alive and authentic-sounding. It goes without saying that period instruments or modern replicas are used. The intellectually staggering *Art of Fugue* is a kind of testament to Bach's art and for this recording the instrumentation, unspecified by the composer, has been well chosen. The 14 miniature Canons which close this issue are for the most part a recent discovery and were written on a page of Bach's own copy of the *Goldberg Variations*; of curiosity value certainly but not much more than that. Excellent recording for these performances which have great authority.

Additional recommendations ...

...The Art of Fugue. **Hespèrion XX / Jordi Savall.** Auvidis Astrée Ⓕ E2001 (two discs: 92 minutes: ADD: 11/88). ✐

...The Art of Fugue. **Amsterdam Bach Soloists.** Ottavo Ⓕ OTRC48503 (72 minutes: DDD: 8/89). ✐

See further on in this section for The Art of Fugue (harpsichord and organ versions).

| New review |

Bach Musikalisches Opfer, BWV1079. **Ensemble Sonnerie** (Wilbert Hazelzet, fl; Paul Goodwin, ob/ob d'amore/ob da caccia; Frances Eustace, bn; Monica Huggett, vn; Pavlo Beznosiuk, vn/va;

Sarah Cunningham, va da gamba; Gary Cooper, hpd). Virgin Classics Veritas Ⓟ VC5 45139-2
(72 minutes: DDD: 7/96). 🎵   Ⓖ
Ensemble Sonnerie have looked beyond the instrumentations employed for most performances of this
work (for instance, Cologne Musica Antiqua, reviewed above) and have welcomed in a variety of
colourful combinations, right up to a rich consort realization of the six-part Ricercar (though we do
get the keyboard version of this piece as well). This is not quite as cavalier as it might appear; many
of the sounds will be familiar enough to Bach enthusiasts, from the fruity presence of the oboe da
caccia to the delicious doubling of flute and violin. Some must have caused the engineers problems of
balance, but the greater clarity achieved certainly helps the listener to follow closely Bach's remarkable
contrapuntal ingenuity. The overlapping of different instrumental combinations in the canons also
allows Ensemble Sonnerie to lengthen the work, as does their willingness to follow Bach's invitation
to investigate a few extra contrapuntal possibilities. The result is about 20 more minutes of music than
usual. The playing itself is of as high a standard as one would expect from the names above, with
everyone taking part as if this were music to be enjoyed rather than just admired. This must be the
most purely enjoyable *Musical Offering* for a long time.

Bach Flute Sonatas – No. 1 in B minor, BWV1030; No. 2 in E flat major, BWV1031; No. 4 in
C major, BWV1033; No. 5 in E minor, BWV1034; No. 6 in E major, BWV1035. Violin Sonata in
G minor, BWV1020 (arr. fl). **James Galway** (fl); **Sarah Cunningham** (va da gamba); **Philip Moll**
(hpd). RCA Victor Red Seal Ⓟ 09026 62555-2 (75 minutes: DDD: 6/95). Recorded 1993.
Gramophone Editor's choice.   Ⓖ
The basic six flute sonatas, BWV1030-35, can be accommodated on a single disc, but Galway plays
safe by keeping to what Bach (or someone else) actually wrote, omitting the unfinished A major
Sonata, BWV1032, which other players have chosen to present in variously completed forms. There
is, from the purist's point of view, still a 'risk' since it remains unproven that Bach was the composer
of BWV1031, 1033 and 1020 – with the last of which Galway replaces BWV1032; however, their
quality justifies their inclusion – if Bach didn't write them one doubts that he would have disowned
them. The booklet-notes mention the doubts concerning the authenticity of BWV1020, but not those
of BWV1031 and 1033. Galway is at his warm, velvet-toned best, phrasing immaculately, caressing
the slow movements and fleet of tongue in the quicker ones. His tempos are well chosen and he never
allows virtuosity to get the better of his judgement. The 'supporting cast' are no less beyond reproach,
but whilst the flute and viola da gamba are well balanced the harpsichord might profitably have been
allowed a rather more equal say in BWV1030 and BWV1031, in which it has an obbligato role. This
will serve well as an introduction to this repertory, but you may prefer to have a complete account of
this *oeuvre*, such as that by Janet See (baroque flute) and Davitt Moroney (listed below), albeit at the
expense of a second disc.

Additional recommendations ...
...BWV1030-35. Partita in A minor, BWV1013. **Stephen Preston** (fl); **Trevor Pinnock** (hpd); **Jordi
Savall** (va da gamba). CRD Ⓟ CRD3314/5 (two discs: 98 minutes: ADD: 1/90). 🎵
...BWV1030-35. G minor, BWV1020. **Janet See** (fl); **Davitt Moroney** (hpd); **Mary Springfels** (va da
gamba). Harmonia Mundi Ⓟ HMU90 7024/5 (two discs: 114 minutes: DDD: 11/91). 🎵
...BWV1030-35. **William Bennett** (fl); **George Malcolm** (hpd); **Michael Evans** (vc). ASV Quicksilva
Ⓢ CDQS6108 (77 minutes: ADD: 3/94).   Ⓖ

New review
Bach (arr. Palladian Ens.) Trio Sonatas, BWV525-30 – No. 1 in E flat major; No. 3 in D minor;
No. 5 in G major; No. 6 in G major. Four Duets, BWV802-05. 14 Verschiedene Canones,
BWV1087. **Palladian Ensemble** (Pamela Thorby, recs; Rachel Podger, vn; Susanna Heinrich,
va da gamba; William Carter, gtr/archlte/theorbo). Linn Records Ⓟ CKD036 (75 minutes:
DDD: 8/95). 🎵 Recorded 1994.
The Palladian Ensemble consists of young early-music players whose fluent techniques have been
directly developed on period instruments and who are well informed and imaginative – "We've read
all the books on performance practice and style, but we're not overawed by them. This is how we *feel*
the music, and we're very well equipped to do it *our* way." The Trio Sonatas are 'properly' transposed
to keys more suited to the chosen instruments, and the Four Duets are given to the violin and viola
da gamba: the annotator describes them as "too rarely performed" – he should look in *The
Gramophone Classical Catalogue*! How do you bring a perpetual canon to an end? One way is by
means of a fade-out, as happens with the fourteenth of the *Goldberg* canons, the colourful
presentation of which as a whole drives a horse and cart through any notion that canons are just dry,
academic exercises. Hairpin dynamics sometimes comes close to sounding mannered and Rachel
Podger does not always wash the tonal acid from her etched lines, but these are very tiny flies in the
ointment of performances that are refreshingly committed and which stray from old paths in
stimulating and revealing ways. Enjoy them, and feel compassion for anyone who is unable to do so.

New review
Bach Violin Sonatas, BWV1014-19 – No. 1 in B minor; No. 2 in A major; No. 3 in E major; No. 4
in C minor; No. 5 in F major; No. 6 in G major. **Fabio Biondi** (vn); **Rinaldo Alessandrini** (hpd).
Opus 111 Ⓟ OPS30-127/8 (two discs: 90 minutes: DDD: 7/96). 🎵 Recorded 1995.

Biondi and Alessandrini are probably the two most fêted members of Italy's growing early music community, but interest in them so far has depended a lot on the fact that they have been performing Italian music, in which, it is felt, caprice and a little bit of red-blooded passion have an important part to play. Such qualities are not so easy to apply to Bach, even if you wanted to; better here to play intelligently, in tune and with good articulation, and let Bach's robust notationally more complete music speak for itself. This is just what Biondi and Alessandrini do, though at the same time bringing a moving lyricism to slow movements, and above all a bold and biting energy to faster ones such as the last movement of BWV1014, the second movement of BWV1015 with its upward arpeggios, or the finale of the same sonata. Alessandrini, better known internationally as the Director of Concerto Italiano, is a crisp harpsichordist and shows considerable dexterity in the last movement of BWV1016, among others. The recording is fairly close for both instruments, which it needs to be for the harpsichord if it is to contribute much to the music's dialogue; but perhaps the violin could have been given a little more space, so that we do not have to hear Biondi breathing or the friction of his bow on the string. This really is a small complaint, however, and does not detract from a warm recommendation.

Additional recommendations ...

...BWV1014-19. **Arthur Grumiaux** (vn); **Christiane Jaccottet** (hpd). Philips 426 452-2PBQ2 (two discs: 129 minutes: DDD).

...BWV1014-19. **Susanne Lautenbacher** (vn); **Leonore Klinckerfuss** (hpd). Bayer Ⓕ BR100086/7 (two discs: 98 minutes: DDD: 10/90). ✐

...BWV1014-19. **Sigiswald Kuijken** (vn); **Gustav Leonhardt** (hpd). Deutsche Harmonia Mundi Editio Classica Ⓜ GD77170 (two discs: 94 minutes: ADD: 10/90). ✐

...BWV1014-19. Sonata in G major, BWV1019a. Sonatas for Violin and Continuo – G major, BWV1021[a]; E minor, BWV1023[b]. **Elizabeth Blumenstock** (vn); **John Butt** (hpd) with [a]**Elisabeth Le Guin** (vc); [b]**Steven Lehning** (va da gamba). Harmonia Mundi Ⓕ HMU90 7084/5 (two discs: 120 minutes: DDD: 10/93). ✐

Bach Six Keyboard Partitas, BWV825-30. Italian Concerto in F major, BWV971. Overture in the French style in B minor, BWV831. **Andreas Staier** (hpd). Deutsche Harmonia Mundi Ⓕ 05472 77306-2 (three discs: 184 minutes: DDD: 2/95). ✐ Recorded 1993.   ⒼⒼ

On which level these wonderfully rich pieces speak to us is, of course, largely in the hands of the performer: now we have persuasive accounts from, amongst others, Christophe Rousset, Ketil Haugsand and Andreas Staier. The latter is a performer with a keen understanding of decorum though it is the darkly imbued suites where he is especially penetrating. He takes a stark and disturbing view of the C minor Partita. The opening is remarkably powerful and rhetorical but the way he juxtaposes this with an almost ironically free-flowing *andante* before setting into an exacting and exhilarating fugato is musicianship of real conviction and flair. Staier's impeccable digital facility and steadiness is often at the root of the colourful devices which he imparts to the A minor Partita with an energetic, almost Scarlattian Burlesca and before that a rounded and genial Sarabande, and finally a dreamy Gigue – a rare thing indeed! What more could one want from this music? Often, not much. But acquaintance with the more radical and 'off piste' playing of Ketil Haugsand keeps Staier's and Rousset's distinguished achievements in check. Impetuosity and disencumbered emotional boundaries can bring serious detractors, and there are moments where Staier's more finely honed and regulated approach will win many friends whilst Haugsand's will perhaps be considered too idiosyncratic (though the harpsichord sonority welcomes all ye who are unsure of its most beautiful properties). Rousset is exceptional in the First Partita, and of course in others too, though he does not deliver the emotional range which these pieces afford in the hands of either Haugsand or Staier. Let's make no mistake: Staier's performances are still in the very top bracket, always thought-provoking and clearly argued, with moments of matchlessly vital and exquisite playing (the Gigue of the G major Partita, for instance). Each of these versions has its moments of unique magic and there is no question that these three are the leaders in the present field. Staier's set also includes Part Two of the *Clavier-Übung*, an extra disc with the *Italian Concerto* and the B minor *Overture in the French style*, both beautifully played. Here, as elsewhere, his Keith Hill harpsichord after German examples gives a clearly defined attack and a focus which will have you on the edge of your seat.

Additional recommendations ...

...Four Duets, BWV802-05. Italian Concerto. French Overture. **Kenneth Gilbert** (hpd). Harmonia Mundi Musique d'abord Ⓑ HMA190 1278 (56 minutes: DDD: 2/90). ✐

...Four Duets. Italian Concerto. French Overture. Chromatic Fantasia and Fugue. **Christophe Rousset.** L'Oiseau-Lyre Ⓕ 433 054-2OH (68 minutes: DDD: 5/92). ✐ *Selected by Sounds in Retrospect.*

...Four Duets. French Overture. Italian Concerto. Prelude, Fugue and Allegro in E flat major, BWV998. **Davitt Moroney** (hpd). Virgin Classics Veritas Ⓕ VC7 59272-2 (71 minutes: DDD: 9/92). ✐

...Keyboard Partitas. **Christophe Rousset** (hpd). L'Oiseau-Lyre Ⓕ 440 217-2OH2 (two discs: 154 minutes: DDD: 9/93). 🖅

...Keyboard Partitas. Preludes, BWV924-29, BWV930. Six Little Preludes, BWV933-38. Preludes and Fughettas – D minor, BWV899; E minor, BWV900; G major, BWV902. Preludes and Fugues – A minor, BWV895; G major, BWV902*a*. Two Fugues in C major, BWV952 and BWV953. Fughetta in C minor, BWV961. **Glenn Gould** (pf). Sony Classical Glenn Gould Edition Ⓜ SM2K52597* (two discs: 148 minutes: ADD: 11/94).

...Partita in B flat major, BWV825. *Coupled with works by* **Mozart, Schubert** and **Chopin** Waltzes – No. 1 and Nos. 3-14. **Dinu Lipatti** (pf). EMI Références mono Ⓜ CDH5 65166-2* (73 minutes: ADD: 12/94). *See review in the Collections section; refer to the Index to Reviews.* ❻❻❻

...Partita, BWV825 – Menuets I and II; Gigue. **Beethoven** Piano Concerto No. 4 in G major, Op. 58[a]. Piano Concerto No. 5 in E flat major, Op. 73, "Emperor"[b]. **Walter Gieseking** (pf); [a]**Saxon State Orchestra / Karl Böhm;** [b]**Vienna Philharmonic Orchestra / Bruno Walter.** APR mono Ⓜ APR5512* (68 minutes: ADD: 3/96).

...Italian Concerto. Chromatic Fantasia and Fugue in D minor, BWV903. Toccata in D minor, BWV912. French Suites No. 5 in G major, BWV816. *Coupled with works by* **Paradis, Daquin, Rimsky-Korsakov, Rameau, F. Couperin, Temploton** and **Malcolm.** George Malcolm (hpd). Decca Ⓜ 444 390-2DWO (75 minutes: ADD: 11/95). 🖅

Bach The Art of Fugue, BWV1080. **Davitt Moroney** (hpd). Harmonia Mundi Ⓕ HMC90 1169/70 (two discs: 99 minutes: DDD: 5/86). 🖅 *Gramophone Award Winner 1986.* ❻❻

Bach died before the process of engraving his last great work had been completed, thus leaving a number of issues concerning performance in some doubt. However, Davitt Moroney is a performer-scholar who has a mature understanding of the complexity of Bach's work; in a lucid essay in the booklet, he discusses the problems of presenting *The Art of Fugue* whilst at the same time explaining his approach to performing it. Certain aspects of this version will be of particular importance to prospective buyers: Moroney, himself, has completed Contrapunctus 14 but he also plays the same Contrapunctus in its unfinished state as a fugue on three subjects. He omits Bach's own reworkings for two harpsichords of Contrapunctus 13 on the grounds that they do not play a part in the composer's logically-constructed fugue cycle; and he omits the Chorale Prelude in G major (BWV668*a*) which certainly had nothing to do with Bach's scheme but was added in the edition of 1751 so that the work should not end in an incomplete state. Moroney's performing technique is of a high order, placing emphasis on the beauty of the music which he reveals with passionate conviction. Exemplary presentation and an appropriate recorded sound enhance this fine achievement.

Additional recommendations ...

...The Art of Fugue. **Gustav Leonhardt** (hpd). Vanguard Classics Bach Guild mono Ⓜ 08.2012.72* (two discs: 97 minutes: ADD).

...The Art of Fugue (earlier version). **Kenneth Gilbert** (hpd). Archiv Produktion Ⓕ 427 673-2AH (59 minutes: DDD: 4/90). 🖅

...The Art of Fugue. Overture in the French style in B minor, BWV831. Italian Concerto in F major, BWV971. Prelude, Fugue and Allegro in E flat major, BWV998. **Gustav Leonhardt, Bob van Asperen** (Art of Fugue) (hpds). Deutsche Harmonia Mundi Editio Classica Ⓜ GD77013 (two discs: 132 minutes: ADD: 12/90). 🖅

...The Art of Fugue, Contrapunctus 1-12, 14, 15. **Wolfgang Rübsam** (org). Naxos Ⓢ 8 550703 (72 minutes: DDD: 1/94).

...The Art of Fugue, Contrapunctus 13 and 17-19. Passacaglia and Fugue in C minor, BWV582. Sei gegrüsset, Jesu gütig, BWV768.**Wolfgang Rübsam** (org). Naxos Ⓢ 8 550704 (78 minutes: DDD: 1/94).

Bach Sonatas and Partitas for Solo Violin, BWV1001-06. Sonatas – No. 1 in G minor; No. 2 in A minor; No. 3 in C major. Partitas – No. 1 in B minor; No. 2 in D minor; No. 3 in E major. **Arthur Grumiaux** (vn). Philips Duo Ⓜ 438 736-2PM2 (two discs: 113 minutes: ADD: 2/94). From A02205/7L (3/62). Recorded 1960-61. *Gramophone Editor's choice.* ❻❻❻

The totally innocent ear, deprived of any comparison, could be forgiven for judging Grumiaux's to be definitive performances of Bach's Partitas and Sonatas. There is little of the sweetness of a Heifetz, the passing whimsy of a Shumsky here. And yet they define, indeed, as few other performances do, the structural frame and rhythmic working-out of each movement with extraordinary determination and authority. The purity of intonation is absolute; the energy locked into the sheer sound of the instrument startling. *And* two discs, as they say, for the price of one! Those who know and love the performances of the Belgian violinist Arthur Grumiaux will be thrilled to rediscover these Berlin recordings of the early 1960s, sharply remastered and sounding out in a roomy acoustic. The platinum gleam glancing off every moment of double-stopping, and the flinty brightness struck where contrapuntal voices meet ring out as never before. The arpeggios of the *Presto* of the G minor Sonata flash like light from the many facets of a prism; and the same mesmeric steadiness of *moto perpetuo* makes for a heady finish to the C major Sonata. What dominates, though, is the rhythmic rigour of Grumiaux's playing. His perfectionism, fused with a real sense of struggle, brings sheer might to the fugues of the Sonatas: it is rather like watching a climber scaling a vast rock face, securing himself with a pick and leaping across the next crevasse.

Additional recommendations ...

...**Sigiswald Kuijken** (vn). Deutsche Harmonia Mundi Editio Classica Ⓜ GD77043 – (two discs:
128 minutes: ADD). ✐   ⒺⒺⒺ
...**Yehudi Menuhin**. EMI Rouge et Noire mono CZS7 67810-2* (two discs: 140 minutes: ADD).
...**Oscar Shumsky** (vn). ASV Ⓕ CDDCD454 (two discs: 147 minutes: ADD: 9/87).   ⒺⒺ
...**Nathan Milstein** (vn). EMI mono Ⓜ ZDMB7 64793-2* (two discs: 114 minutes: ADD: 5/94).
                                                                            ⒺⒺⒺ
...Partitas Nos. 1-3. **Viktoria Mullova** (vn). Philips Ⓕ 434 075-2PH (77 minutes: DDD: 6/94). ⒺⒺ
...(trans. North) Sonatas and Partitas, BWV1001-06. **Nigel North** (lte). Linn Records Ⓕ CKD013,
CKD029 (two discs, oas: 70 and 68 minutes: DDD: 4/95). *Gramophone Editor's choice.*

Bach (arr. Bream) Prelude, Fugue and Allegro in E flat major, BWV998. Suite in E minor,
BWV996. Partita No. 2 in D minor, BWV1004 – Chaconne. Partita No. 3 in E major, BWV1006.
Julian Bream (gtr). EMI Ⓕ CDC5 55123-2 (70 minutes: DDD: 1/95). Recorded 1992.
One so readily associates the names of Bream and Bach that it comes as a surprise to find that he has
not previously recorded either the Partita, BWV1006a, the *Prelude, Fugue and Allegro*, BWV998, or the
Chaconne from BWV1004. The Suite in E minor, BWV996 is to be found on RCA in the version he
recorded in the 1960s, but the years have wrought changes in his view of the work. He relishes the music
at slightly easier tempos, often closer to those adopted by many lutenists: in BWV1006a the
correspondence is close, but in BWV996 he takes a more spacious view of the ('French') Courante,
whilst the Sarabande proceeds with slow dignity and, like several other movements on this record, is
treated to more embellishment than Bream has hitherto been wont to introduce. Various guitarists have
treated the *Chaconne* in ways ranging from the 'religious' awe of Segovia to the 'Grand Prix' approach
of sundry others; Bream, adding enhancing appoggiaturas at 1'45" and 2'47", treats it with the greatest
respect, and if his 15'47" seems slow on paper it does not *sound* so. Violinist Oscar Shumsky (listed
above), praised for his performance, takes it at about the same generous pace. The clarity of Bream's
thought emerges from his fingers in an equally unhurried BWV998. If his recorded archive with EMI
does not ultimately reach the proportions of that with RCA it will still be one to treasure.

Bach Solo Cello Suites, BWV1007-12 – No. 1 in G major; No. 2 in D minor; No. 3 in C major;
No. 4 in E flat major; No. 5 in C minor; No. 6 in D major. **Anner Bylsma** (vc). Sony Classical
Vivarte Ⓕ S2K48047 (two discs: 115 minutes: DDD: 1/93). ✐ Recorded 1992.
This is the second complete version of Bach's six Cello Suites recorded by the Dutch virtuoso Anner
Bylsma (the first is listed below). In a period of some 13 years between the first and second recordings,
Bylsma's concept of these works has not undergone any fundamental changes. The difference between
them is rather one of degree for, as Byslma himself says in a lively note accompanying the discs, "one
keeps finding new relationships between the notes and every motif can be played in so many different
ways – and always with meaning, too". In the new version Bylsma intensifies the musical gestures
which characterized the earlier one. He is, if anything, more spontaneous in his playing here and he
takes greater risks. What we have, in fact, are 'performances' as opposed to studio-correct readings;
and so listeners concerned with niceties of intonation, for instance, may sometimes be mildly
disconcerted by what they hear. But from a purely interpretative standpoint the new set is bolder,
more relaxed and more broadly expressive. Indeed, were it not for his impeccable 'early music'
credentials Bylsma might be targeted by critics for excessive romanticism. Pierre Fournier was thus
condemned for his Bach playing, yet his performances of the *Preludes* of these Suites, made three
decades ago, were in many respects far stricter than those of Bylsma. All this and much else make it
clear that convenient generalizations and tidy compartments are less acceptable than ever. Bylsma is
an artist who is not afraid to express himself individually, intensely and even, at times audaciously.
Open-minded readers will find much to admire and much that is satisfying in these passionate, warmly
expressive performances. But neither the noble Fournier nor Bylsma's earlier recording is lightly to be
cast aside, not to mention all the other recommendable recordings in the catalogue.

Additional recommendations ...

...**Heinrich Schiff** (vc). EMI Ⓕ CDS7 47471-8 (two discs: ADD).
...**Yo-Yo Ma** (vc). Sony Classical Ⓜ S2K37867 (two discs: 125 minutes: DDD).
...**Anner Bylsma** (vc). RCA Ⓕ RD70950 (two discs: 126 minutes: DDD). ✐
...**Pierre Fournier** (vc). DG The Originals Ⓜ 449 711-2GOR2 (two discs: 139 minutes: ADD: 3/89).
ⒺⒺ
...**Pablo Casals** (vc). EMI Références mono Ⓜ CHS7 61027-2* (two discs: 130 minutes: ADD:
3/89). *Gramophone classical 100.*   ⒺⒺⒺ
...**Paul Tortelier** (vc). EMI Ⓑ CZS5 68148-2* (two discs: 125 minutes: ADD: 3/92).
...**Mischa Maisky** (vc). DG Ⓕ 445 373-2GH2 (two discs: 157 minutes: DDD: 10/94).
...**Lluís Claret** (vc). Auvidis Valois Ⓕ V4695 (two discs: 130 minutes: DDD: 3/95).
...**Ralph Kirshbaum** (vc). Virgin Classics Ⓕ VCD5 45086-2 (two discs: 140 minutes: DDD: 4/95).
...**Mstislav Rostropovich** (vc). EMI Ⓕ CDS5 55363-2 (two discs: 147 minutes: DDD: 6/95).
...*Coupled with works by* **Kodály, Dohnányi, Boccherini, Haydn, Schumann, Saint-Saëns,
Dvořák, Fauré, Milhaud** and **Prokofiev**. **János Starker** (vc); **Gerald Moore** (pf); **Philharmonia
Orchestra / Carlo Maria Giulini, Walter Susskind**. EMI mono/stereo Ⓜ CZS5 68485-2* (six discs:
398 minutes: ADD: 12/95). *See review in the Collections section; refer to the Index to Reviews.*

Bach Harpsichord works. **Wanda Landowska** (hpd). RCA Victor Gold Seal mono Ⓜ GD60919* (two discs: 150 minutes: ADD: 3/93). Recorded 1945-57.
Goldberg Variations, BWV988 (from HMV ALP1139, 5/54). Concerto in D major, BWV972 (HMV DB6819, 12/48). Fantasias – C minor, BWV906 (RB16068, 9/58); C minor, BWV919. Prelude, Fugue and Allegro in E flat major, BWV998 (both from ALP1246, 6/55). Two-Part Inventions, BWV772-86. Three-Part Inventions, BWV787-801 – No. 1 in C major; No. 2 in C minor; No. 5 in E flat major; No. 11 in G minor; No. 13 in A minor; No. 14 in B flat major; No. 15 in B minor (all from RB16193, 7/60). Capriccio sopra la lontananza del suo fratello dilettissimo in B flat major, BWV992. Partita No. 2 in C minor, BWV826 (RB16068).			ⒼⒼⒼ
The woman who played for Tolstoy, who rediscovered the harpsichord for a modern listening audience and who enchanted generations of music-lovers with her engaging personality, was also one of the century's great Bach interpreters. But her grand, flamboyant and highly demonstrative style is largely out of step with modern theories on Bach performance, so these two discs – which are beautifully transferred from late 78s and early tape originals – are likely to annoy as well as inspire. However, the *Goldberg Variations* (the second of Landowska's two recordings of the work) are deeply poetic and chock-full of imagination, while few keyboard players since have injected quite so much pathos and personality into Bach's autobiographical *Capriccio sopra la lontananza del suo fratello dilettissimo* ("Capriccio on the Departure of His Beloved Brother") – his "departure" being *a* journey, as opposed to *the* journey! – or the Concerto in D major "After Vivaldi". Landowska's 'harpsichord Pleyel' makes a big, exciting sound, very unlike the softer, less dynamic sonority of a genuine period instrument. Few apologies need be made for the later recordings on the album, which come across with considerable presence, albeit in mono. One woman's Bach, perhaps ... but very much worth listening to.
Additional recommendations ...
...Prelude and Fugue in A minor, BWV894. Toccatas – F sharp minor, BWV910; C minor, BWV911; G minor, BWV915. Aria variata in A minor, BWV989. Capriccio sopra ... .
Kenneth Gilbert (hpd). Archiv Produktion Ⓕ 437 555-2AH (70 minutes: DDD: 6/93). ✍
...Two Part-Inventions. Three-Part Inventions. **Glenn Gould** (pf). Sony Classical Glenn Gould Edition Ⓜ SMK52596 (50 minutes: ADD: 6/93).

Bach Das Wohltemperierte Klavier, "The Well-tempered Clavier", Books 1 and 2 – 48 Preludes and Fugues, BWV846-893. **Kenneth Gilbert** (hpd). Archiv Produktion Ⓕ 413 439-2AH4 (four discs: 256 minutes: DDD: 2/87). ✍ From 413 439-1AH5 (9/84). Recorded 1983.			ⒼⒼ
In Book 1 there are virtually no markings and so the performer carries heavy responsibility for phrasing and articulation. Gilbert's blend of scholarship and technique with artistic sensibility makes for notably convincing, often poetic playing. The D minor Prelude is one of many instances where his interpretation haunts the memory. Gilbert's vital rhythmic sense and love of refinement are qualities in his artistry which can be strongly felt throughout this vast project. Some readers may feel that he is comparatively unadventurous in his registration – others, for example, make a greater point of differentiation through instrumental colour – but it is one of the features of Gilbert's performance that is particularly praiseworthy, since he clearly and effectively achieves his contrasts through interpretation, renouncing the facility to emphasize them by more artificial means. In textural clarity he yields nothing to his competitors in this repertoire and, in short, arrives at a solution which is refined, lyrical and sometimes dazzlingly virtuosic, as in the Prelude in B flat, BWV866. The acoustic of the Musée de Chartres, where the *48* were recorded, is pleasantly resonant. Gilbert plays a seventeenth-century Flemish harpsichord enlarged first by Blanchet and then by Taskin in the following century. A satisfying achievement and an important issue.
Additional recommendations ...
...Books 1 and 2. **Edwin Fischer** (pf). EMI Références mono Ⓜ CHS7 63188-2* (three discs: 237 minutes: ADD: 3/90).			Ⓖ
...Books 1 and 2. **Colin Tilney** (clav/hpd). Hyperion Ⓕ CDA66351/4 (four discs: 304 minutes: DDD: 10/90). ✍ *Selected by Sounds in Retrospect.*
...Books 1 and 2. **Tatyana Nikolaieva** (pf). Mezhdunarodnaya Kniga Ⓕ MK418042/3 (two sets of two discs, oas: 130 and 154 minutes: DDD: 5/92).
...Book 1. **Ton Koopman** (hpd). Erato Duo Bonsai Ⓜ 4509-95304-2 (110 minutes: DDD: 2/95). ✍
...Book 2. **Ton Koopman** (hpd). Erato Duo Bonsai Ⓜ 4509-95305-2 (141 minutes: DDD: 2/95). ✍
...Das Wohltemperierte Klavier – Preludes and Fugues: C major, BWV846; C sharp minor, BWV849; D major, BWV850; D minor, BWV851; E flat minor/D sharp minor, BWV853. *Coupled with works by* **Haydn, Schubert, Chopin, Schumann, Debussy, Scriabin, Rachmaninov** and **Prokofiev** Sviatoslav Richter (pf). DG Double Ⓜ 447 355-2GDB2 (two discs: 150 minutes: ADD: 12/95).

New review
Bach Six English Suites, BWV806-811. **Glenn Gould** (pf). Sony Classical Glenn Gould Edition Ⓜ SM2K52606 (two discs: 112 minutes: ADD: 4/96). From CBS 79208 (3/78).
No more original genius of the keyboard has existed than Glenn Gould, but this can lead to drawbacks as well as thrilling advantages. You may, for instance, sense how Gould can sacrifice depth

of feeling for a relentless and quixotic sense of adventure. Yet love it or deride it, every bar of these lovingly remastered discs (dating from 1971 and 1973; the hiatus is explained in some riveting accompanying notes) tingles with *joie de vivre* and an unequalled force and vitality. Try the opening of the First Suite. Is such freedom glorious or maddening, or is the way the odd note is nonchalantly flicked in the following sustained argument a naughty alternative to Bach's intention? The pizzicato bass in the second Double from the same Suite is perhaps another instance of an idiosyncracy bordering on whimsy, an enlivenment or rejuvenation that at least remains open to question. But listen to him in virtually any of the sarabandes from the Suites and you will find a tranquillity and equilibrium that can silence such criticism and even at his most piquant and outrageous his playing remains, mysteriously, all of a piece. The Gigue from the Second Suite is taken at a spanking *Presto* and the Prelude from the Third Suite is a gloriously true *vivace*, never rigid or merely metronomic. The fiercely chromatic, labyrinthine argument concluding the Fifth Suite is thrown off with a unique brio, one of those moments when you realize how Gould can lift Bach out of all possible time-warps and make him one of music's truest modernists. Sony's presentation is superb.

Additional recommendations ...

...English Suites Nos. 1-6. **Andras Schiff** (pf). Decca Ⓔ 421 640-2DH2 (two discs: 129 minutes: DDD: 12/88).

...English Suites Nos. 3, 4 and 6. French Suites Nos. 2, 4 and 6. Toccatas – D minor, BWV913; G major, BWV916. Fantasia in C minor, BWV906. Clavier-Ubung – Italian Concerto in F major, BWV971; Overture in the French style in B minor, BWV831. Four Duets, BWV802-5. **Sviatoslav Richter** (pf). Philips Ⓔ 438 613-2PH3 (three discs: 214 minutes: DDD: 8/94).   Ⓖ

New review

Bach Six French Suites, BWV812-17. Sonata in D minor, BWV964. Five Preludes, BWV924-28. Prelude in G minor, BWV930. Six Preludes, BWV933-8. Five Preludes, BWV939-43. Prelude in C minor, BWV999. Prelude and Fugue in A minor, BWV894. **Angela Hewitt** (pf). Hyperion Ⓕ CDA67121/2 (two discs: 151 minutes: DDD: 2/96). Recorded 1995. *Gramophone Editor's choice*. Ⓖ

Even the most out-and-out purists who blench at the thought of Bach on so alien an instrument as the piano (as if Bach himself ever showed any reluctance at transferring his work from one instrument to another!) will find it hard not to be won over by Angela Hewitt's artistry. This Canadian pianist, eschewing all hieratic pretentiousness on the one hand and self-regarding eccentricities on the other, gives us Bach performances that are not only admirable in style but marked by poise and what used to be called a 'quiet hand': 'chaste' might not be too fanciful a term, so long as that does not suggest any lack of vitality. There is intelligence in her carefully thought-out phrasing and subtle variety of articulation: gradations of sound are always alive without their becoming precious. The bulk of this recording is devoted to the *French Suites* (in which Hewitt includes a second Minuet in No. 2 and, more controversially, a Prelude and a vivacious second Gavotte in No. 4). Particlarly enjoyable is the lightness of her treatment of the Airs of Nos. 2 and 4, the vigour of No. 5's Bourrée and the freshness of No. 6's Allemande; the extra decorations she adds in repeats everywhere sound properly spontaneous and are in the best of taste; ornaments are always cleanly played (though her mordents sometimes fall before, rather than on, the beat) and matched up in imitative voices.

Bach Six French Suites, BWV812-17. Suite in A minor, BWV818*a*. Suite in E flat major, BWV819*a*. **Davitt Moroney** (hpd). Virgin Classics Veritas Ⓔ VCD7 59011-2 (two discs: 144 minutes: DDD: 4/91). ✍ Recorded 1990.

Bach Six French Suites, BWV812-17. **Andrei Gavrilov** (pf). DG Ⓔ 445 840-2GH2 (two discs: 93 minutes: DDD: 7/95). Recorded 1993.

Bach compiled his *French Suites*, so-called – the composer himself did not give them this title – towards the end of his Cöthen period and at the beginning of his final appointment at Leipzig. As well as performing the customary six suites, five of which have survived in Bach's own hand, Davitt Moroney includes two further suites prepared by Bach's pupil, Heinrich Nikolaus Gerber, in 1725. These and extra movements to the well-known six suites belong to various surviving sources and though we can be sure that Bach himself had good reason to discard them from his final thoughts, so-to-speak, their presence in this album is nonetheless welcome. Moroney has given careful thought and preparation to the project and the results are often illuminating. His interpretations are relaxed, articulate and show a lively awareness of the music's poetic content. There is a clarity in these performances which stems from lucid punctuation highlighting the significance of every phrase. Shorter dance movements have poise and are allowed to breathe while longer ones, notably *allemandes,* have a taut rhythmic elasticity which enable the listener to savour their eloquent often pensive inflexions. Perhaps *sarabandes* are sometimes a little too weighty, but this is to some extent a matter of taste and few will be disappointed by Moroney's stylistically informed and technically fluent playing. The recording is excellent.

Like others before him (including András Schiff) Andrei Gavrilov acknowledges his debt to Glenn Gould, sensing a fellow spirit throwing down the gauntlet and challenging convention at every turn with his fearless mix of directness and idiosyncrasy. Yet as his performances so eloquently convey, there are depths and subtleties in these ever-fascinating cosmopolitan Suites which are often erased by Gould's manic determination to redefine the parameters of Bach interpretation. Gavrilov has a way, for instance, of casting light on even the simplest, least polyphonic of the composer's arguments.

He may retain some of his former headstrong pugnacity yet in the Sarabandes, which like pools of reflection form the nodal and expressive centre of each Suite, he finds an often glorious ease, repose and gently luminous sense of texture. Even those for whom such open-hearted espousal of the modern piano's resources ("the piano wins hands down" exclaims Gavrilov of arguments concerning harpsichord versus piano) is anachronistic will surely be touched and convinced. Predictably there are moments when Gould has the razor's edge over Gavrilov and, indeed, every other pianist, when it comes to clarity and dexterity. Yet even in the volleys of notes in, say, the Courante from the Sixth Suite, his dayglo, acidic brilliance is more arresting than poetically engaging. Touchingly and endearingly and by his own admission, Gavrilov sees Bach as "the key to comprehending the universe". The DG sound quality is exemplary.

Additional recommendations ...

...French Suites. **Gustav Leonhardt** (hpd). RCA Victor Seon Ⓜ GD71963 (two discs: 78 minutes: ADD: 5/90). ✎

...French Suites. Overture (Partita) in the French style in B minor, BWV831. **Glenn Gould** (pf). Sony Classical Glenn Gould Edition Ⓜ SM2K52609 (two discs: 85 minutes: ADD: 7/95).

Bach Goldberg Variations, BWV988. **Pierre Hantaï** (hpd). Opus 111 Ⓕ OPS30-84 (77 minutes: DDD: 4/94). ✎ *Gramophone Award Winner 1994*. **Gramophone** *Editor's choice*. Recorded 1992. ⒼⒼ

New review

Bach Goldberg Variations, BWV988. **Christophe Rousset** (hpd). L'Oiseau-Lyre Ⓕ 444 866-2OH (77 minutes: DDD: 11/95). ✎ Recorded 1994. Ⓖ

Pierre Hantaï's approach to the *Goldberg Variations* is tremendously spirited and energetic but also disciplined. What is most appealing about this playing, though, is that Hantaï clearly finds the music great fun to perform; some players have been too inclined to make heavy weather over this music. He makes each and every one of the canons a piece of entertainment while in no sense glossing over Bach's consummate formal mastery. Other movements, such as Var. 7 (gigue) and Var. 11, effervesce with energy and good humour and he is careful to avoid anything in the nature of superficiality. Not for a moment is the listener given the impression that his view of the music is merely skin deep. Indeed, there is a marked concentration of thought in canons such as that at the fourth interval (Var. 12). Elsewhere his feeling for the fantasy and poetry of Bach's music is effective and well placed (such as in Var. 13). The character of Bruce Kennedy's copy of an early eighteenth-century instrument by the Berlin craftsman, Michael Mietke is admirably captured by the effectively resonant recorded sound.

Some artists, notably Hantaï and those listed below, have helped to change public perception of the Variations, and Rousset joins their number in presenting the work as something that would have entertained the insomniac Count Keyserling than than sending him to sleep again. As the proverb has it, it's the first step that counts; and nowhere is this more true than here. Even Pinnock, whose account of the Variations is stimulatingly lively, states the theme at a funereal pace quite out of keeping with what follows. Rousset treats it as the sarabande it is, with the stateliness of that dance yet with a subtle freedom. From then on, the music exudes cheerfulness – the first variation has an engaging light-hearted energy – and speeds are fast throughout (which incidentally allows all repeats to be included on the disc). Variation 7 is a real gigue (as it has now been established to be), and the fughetta of Var. 10 is positively chirpy: the *alla breve* Var. 22, crisply articulated, has an invigorating spring. There is no undue slowing-down for the minor-key variations, and no sentimentalizing of the famous 'black pearl' Var. 25; but Rousset brings a true *affettuoso* feeling to Var. 13. All the complex passagework of the Variations is nimbly and cleanly played: a slight overhang of resonance noticeable in the theme and at the start of the minor Var. 21 is undetectable elsewhere. There is a robust sound from the Hemsch instrument employed, and Rousset is sparing in changes of registration. Some people may accuse him of a lack of *gravitas* overall, but this issue is still extremely recommendable.

Additional recommendations ...

...Goldberg Variations. **Trevor Pinnock** (hpd). Archiv Produktion Ⓕ 415 130-2AH (61 minutes: ADD: 8/85). ✎ Ⓖ

...Goldberg Variations. **András Schiff** (pf). Decca Ⓕ 417 116-2DH (73 minutes: DDD: 12/86).

...Goldberg Variations. **Kenneth Gilbert** (hpd). Harmonia Mundi Ⓕ HMC90 1240 (77 minutes: DDD: 6/87). ✎ ⒼⒼ

...Goldberg Variations. **Maggie Cole** (hpd). Virgin Classics Veritas Ⓜ VER5 61153-2 (79 minutes: DDD: 2/92). ✎ ⒼⒼ

...Goldberg Variations. **Glenn Gould** (pf). Sony Classical Glenn Gould Edition mono Ⓜ SM2K52594* (46 minutes: ADD: 4/93). ⒼⒼⒼ

...Goldberg Variations. **Glenn Gould** (pf). Sony Classical Glenn Gould Edition Ⓜ SMK52619* (51 minutes: DDD: 8/93). *Gramophone classical 100.* ⒼⒼ

...Goldberg Variations. 14 Three-Part Inventions, BWV788-801. **Glenn Gould** (pf). Sony Classical Glenn Gould Edition Ⓜ SMK52685* (61 minutes: ADD: 11/94).

...(arr. Sitkovetsky) Goldberg Variations. **New European Strings Chamber Orchestra / Dmitry Sitkovetsky** (vn). Nonesuch Ⓕ 7559-79341-2 (60 minutes: DDD: 9/95).

...Goldberg Variations. Das Wohltemperierte Klavier – Preludes and Fugues: E flat major, BWV876; E major, BWV878; F sharp minor, BWV883; B flat minor, BWV891. **Glenn Gould** (pf). CBC Records Perspective Series mono Ⓕ PSCD200/* (66 minutes: ADD: 1/96).

Bach Goldberg Variations, BWV988. **Konstantin Lifschitz** (pf). Denon Ⓕ CO-78961 (79 minutes:
   DDD: 9/95). *Gramophone Editor's choice*. Recorded 1994.
Bach Goldberg Variations, BWV988.
Mozart Keyboard Sonata in C major, K330/K300*h*.
Schoenberg Suite, Op. 25.
Sweelinck Fantasia. **Glenn Gould** (pf). Sony Classical mono Ⓜ SMK53474* (76 minutes: ADD:
   9/95). Recorded live in 1959.

A mere 18 years old when his disc was recorded the Lifschitz *Goldberg Variations* are already among
the most assured and exultant on record. Variations such as Nos. 6, 9 and 21 are formidably articulate
and blaze with the most characterful virtuosity. Occasionally a certain severity – a fear of moving
outside self-imposed limits – colours the playing (Var. 14, for example). Yet already Lifschitz evinces
a conviction and maturity, a high seriousness that pianists twice his age may well envy. Denon's
recording is of great vividness and immediacy.

   Glenn Gould's recordings of Bach's *Goldberg Variations* are scattered like gold-dust throughout the
catalogue, and there are still more to come. Any other pianist would risk a sense of duplication, but
such is Gould's nature and pianism that each and every reading casts its own spell; creates its own
ambience and fascination. Here, his performance forms the major part of his legendary 1959 Salzburg
recital, given when he was 27 and already near the end of his brief but dazzling public career. Elfin
and teasing Gould has rarely worn his astonishing expertise more lightly or engagingly, or illuminated
every facet of Bach's timeless masterpiece with a more nonchalant sense of its glory. His 'black pearl'
(Var. 25) is lightened with a silvery clarity that he would later darken with greater speculation and time
and again Bach's polyphony is playfully but never irresponsibly pointed and coloured. His virtuosity
in Vars. 5 and 6 is ethereal rather than pressured and, throughout, the constant play of light and shade
suggests only the most transcendental pianism and musicianship. As a bonus you can hear Sweelinck's
solemnities offered with rare significance, Schoenberg's Op. 25 spun off with hallucinatory magic, and
Mozart's K330 Sonata played with a truly extraordinary cunning, elegance and artifice. Here, indeed,
is a "sensually charged but intellectually controlled artistic temperament", an assuaging alternative to
later utterances which sometimes crystallized into pendantry and affectation. This is a disc beyond
price; a crowning touch to Gould's endlessly fascinating discography.

Bach Fantasia in C minor, BWV906. 15 Two-Part Inventions, BWV772-86. 15 Three-Part
   Inventions, BWV787-801. Chromatic Fantasia and Fugue in D minor, BWV903. **Angela Hewitt**
   (pf). Hyperion Ⓕ CDA66746 (63 minutes: DDD: 11/94). Recorded 1994. *Gramophone Editor's
   choice*.

Angela Hewitt's approach may be gleaned from her refreshingly lucid annotation, or simply by
listening to what she does. "A skilful player can [bring out the different voices] with different colours"
and "To be capable of producing a true legato without using the pedal will serve a pianist well in any
repertoire": Hewitt puts her fingers where her thoughts are, to signal effect. She never upsets the
balance of the lines that it is in the nature of the harpsichord (Bach's chosen instrument) to yield, and
her economy with the sustaining pedal helps to preserve their clarity. The two- and three-part
Inventions are treated as music in their own right, not simply as the invaluable exercises they are; each
is given its distinctive character, with a wonderful variety of sensitive touch and shapely rubato that
never once threatens to become anachronistic. Her readings of the C minor *Fantasia* and the *Chromatic
Fantasia and Fugue* are as eloquent and stimulating as any yet recorded by a harpsichordist.
Additional recommendation ...
...BWV772-86. BWV787-801. Anna Magdalena Notenbüch – Minuets: G major, BWVAnh114,
   F major, BWVAnh115, G major, BWVAnh116, F major, BWVAnh132; Polonaises: G minor,
   BWVAnh119, G minor, BWVAnh125; March in D major, BWVAnh122; Musette in D major,
   BWVAnh126. **János Sebestyén** (pf). Naxos Ⓢ 8 550679 (58 minutes: DDD: 6/94).
See the end of the J.S. Bach section for details of availability of Complete Organ Works.

Bach Fantasias and Fugues – C minor, BWV537; G minor, BWV542; C minor, BWV562;
   G major, BWV572. Preludes and Fugues – D major, BWV532; F minor, BWV534; A major,
   BWV536; G major, BWV541; A minor, BWV543; B minor, BWV544; C major, BWV545;
   C minor, BWV546; C major, BWV547; E minor, BWV548, "Wedge"; E flat major, BWV552,
   "St Anne". **Christopher Herrick** (org). Hyperion Ⓕ CDA66791/2. (two discs: 150 minutes:
   DDD: 4/94). Played on the organ of the Jesuitenkirche, Lucerne, Switzerland. Recorded 1993.
                                                                              ⒼⒼ

These 15 works constitute some of the finest and most important music ever written for the organ.
They are such mainstays of the repertory that no serious lover of organ music could consider a world
without them. Herrick's performances are authoritative, scholarly and perceptive, but if that were all
it would merely be putting Bach on a pedestal, making him accessible only to those who already
possess the key to the door. Herrick's genius is in bringing the music vividly to life, injecting it with a
sense of fun and a directness of appeal without for a moment compromising artistic integrity. Few
could fail to be captivated by the wonderfully vibrant and smiling countenance of the great E flat

Prelude while those of us who have laboured long and hard just to get our feet round that most ankle-twisting of all fugue subjects must surely surrender in the face of Herrick's effortless fluency in BWV542. The glorious Swiss instrument has been brilliantly recorded, portraying not just the instrument itself but its sumptuous aural setting.

Additional recommendations ...

...Fantasia and Fugue, BWV542. Fugue in G minor, BWV578. Canzona in D minor, BWV588. Preludes and Fugues – C major, BWV531; A minor, BWV543; BWV544. Fantasias and Fugues – BWV562; G major, BWV570; BWV572. Passacaglia and Fugue in C minor, BWV582. **Ton Koopman** (org). Teldec Das Alte Werk Ⓕ 4509-94458-2 (74 minutes: DDD). ✍

...Prelude and Fugue, BWV532. Clavier-Ubung III, BWV669-89 – Christe, aller Welt Trost, BWV670. *Coupled with works by* **Bonnal, Langlais, B. Ferguson** and **Dupré Roger Sayer** (org). Priory Ⓕ PRCD495 (76 minutes: DDD: 4/96). *See review in the Collections section; refer to the Index to Reviews.*

Bach Orgelbüchlein, BWV599-644. **Simon Preston** (org). DG Ⓕ 431 816-2GH (76 minutes: DDD: 3/92). Played on the Lorentz organ of Sorø Abbey, Denmark. Recorded 1989.

New review

Bach Orgelbüchlein, BWV599-644. **Christopher Herrick** (org). Hyperion Ⓕ CDA66756 (72 minutes: DDD: 9/95). Played on the Metzler organ in the Stadtkirche, Rheinfelden, Switzerland. Ⓖ

Bach's *Orgelbüchlein* ("Little Organ Book") contains 46 short preludes based on the chorale melodies used in the Lutheran church. It is arranged to follow the course of the church's year, beginning in Advent, passing through Christmas, Lent, Easter, Ascension, Pentecost and Trinity and ending with those miscellaneous areas classified in most hymn-books as "General". But Bach was not merely providing the church organist with something useful (although its enduring usefulness is still evident today – walk into almost any church and at some point you are likely to find the organist delving into a copy of Bach's *Orgelbüchlein*), he also intended these as teaching pieces. The title page describes them as offering "instruction in the various ways of working out a chorale, and also practice in the use of the pedals". What wonderful teaching pieces these are for any organ student – training exercises of this calibre would surely be enough to tempt anyone into learning how to play the organ! On the DG disc with that accomplished organist, Simon Preston, playing a ravishing Danish instrument sumptuously recorded, the full genius of Bach is revealed.

The fifth volume in Hyperion's ongoing Bach series finds another wonderful Swiss organ. With just two manuals and 32 speaking stops it's relatively small but still offers sufficient scope for Herrick to find a different registration for each of these 45 Preludes. The softer sounds used for *Herr Jesu Christ, dich zu uns wend* are preferable to the rather coarse *pleno* (*In dir ist Freude*) but it makes an undeniably ravishing sound. The *Orgelbüchlein*'s 46 Chorale Preludes (here the almost identical pair on *Liebster Jesu* are merged, accounting for the disc's 45 tracks) are so brief that listening to them all in one sitting is the musical equivalent of eating salted peanuts one at a time in quick succession. In an attempt to make it all more palatable Herrick tries two tricks. First, he plays remarkably fast – which some people may not find particularly rewarding – *Der Tag der ist so freudenreich* has as much of a relaxed air as an athletics track. Secondly, he revises the playing order, interspersing those Preludes based on 'general' themes between those for particular times in the church's year, and even mixing up the ones within each group. However, the booklet thoughtfully provides the tracking order to programme into your player if you wish to hear the pieces in the original sequence. On the subject of the booklet, suffice it to say it deserves paeans of praise. Robin Langley's notes are the perfect match for Herrick's playing: scholarly, erudite, infinitely rewarding and so easily communicative one is barely aware one is absorbing some of the most complex and intellectually demanding ideas. If the *Gramophone* Awards were to include a category for CD booklets this would be a strong contender.

Bach Organ works, Volume 1 – Fantasia and Fugue in G minor, BWV542. Trio Sonata No. 1 in E flat major, BWV525. Toccata and Fugue in D minor, BWV565. Pastorale in F major, BWV590. Organ Concerto No. 1 in G major, BWV592. Chorale Prelude – Erbarm' dich mein, O Herre Gott, BWV721. Organ Chorale – Aus tiefer Not schrei ich zu dir, BWV1099. **Kevin Bowyer** (org). Nimbus Ⓕ NI5280 (67 minutes: DDD: 10/92). Played on the Marcussen organ of St Hans Kirke, Odense, Denmark. Recorded 1991.

Organist Kevin Bowyer and record company Nimbus have set out to record every note Bach wrote for the organ, is believed to have written or is now known not to but in the past was thought to have written. It is a mammoth project planned to take several years. The first disc, perhaps inevitably, includes the best-known of all Bach's organ pieces – although some would dispute that it is an organ piece or even that Bach wrote it; Bowyer's account of the *Toccata and Fugue* in D minor is invigorating, exciting and very fast. It sets the scene for a CD of virtuoso performances and sound musicianship. The whole is a well-chosen, self-contained programme which also includes an indisputably 'great' organ work, a Trio Sonata, a transcription Bach made of an effervescent concerto by Ernst, a youthful chorale prelude as well as one from a collection only discovered in 1985 and one real oddity. Much thought has gone into the choice of organ and this instrument serves its purpose admirably; roaring magnificently in the *Fantasia* and emulating the tranquil sounds so characteristic of the *Pastorale*. If the remaining discs are going to be this good then it's a series well worth collecting.

Additional recommendations ...

...Toccata and Fugue, BWV565. Fantasia and Fugue, BWV542. Preludes and Fugues – A major,
  BWV536; E minor, BWV548. Passacaglia and Fugue in C minor, BWV582. Fantasia in G major,
  BWV572. **Anton Heiller** (org). Vanguard Classics Ⓕ 08.2005.71 (65 minutes: ADD).
...Toccatas and Fugues – BWV565; F major, BWV540; D minor, BWV538, "Dorian". Toccata,
  Adagio and Fugue in C major, BWV564. Passacaglia and Fugue in C minor, BWV582.
  Christopher Herrick (org). Hyperion Ⓕ CDA66434 (64 minutes: DDD: 4/91).
...Organ works, Volume 3. Preludes and Fugues – F minor, BWV534; A minor, BWV543. Trio
  Sonata No. 2 in C minor, BWV526. Organ Concerto No. 5 in D minor, BWV596. Sei gegrüsset,
  Jesu gütig, BWV768. **Kevin Bowyer** (org). Nimbus Ⓕ NI5290 (64 minutes: DDD: 6/93).

Bach Organ works, Volume 4: Toccatas – G minor, BWV915; G major, BWV916. Fugues on
  themes of Albinoni – A major, BWV950; B minor, BWV951. Fugue in C minor, BWV575.
  Preludes and Fugues – C major, BWV553; D minor, BWV554; E minor, BWV555; F major,
  BWV556; G major, BWV557; G minor, BWV558; A minor, BWV559; B flat major, BWV560.
  Fantasia con imitazione in B minor, BWV563. **Kevin Bowyer** (org). Nimbus Ⓕ NI5377
  (74 minutes: DDD: 2/94). Played on the Marcussen organ of Sct. Hans Kirke, Odense,
  Denmark. Recorded 1992.

While critical opinion and academic argument may deter others, Bowyer is content to let the music
speak for itself, whether it is "by J.S. Bach, J.L. Krebs or A.N. Other". On this disc the music speaks
with absolute conviction. One thinks of the gloriously dramatic rhetoric Bowyer brings to the two
Toccatas (BWV915 and 916). Harpsichordists may claim these as their own but who could deny this
lovely Odense organ the opportunity to glitter with such flamboyant music? The eight 'short' Preludes
and Fugues have a muscular, clean-shaven feel to them underlined by plain and simple registrations.
While other recordings of such indefinable pieces seem like scraps from the cutting-room floor,
Bowyer sets them firmly in the mainstream of high baroque organ music.

Additional recommendation ...

...Toccatas – F sharp minor, BWV910; C minor, BWV911; D major, BWV912; D minor, BWV913;
  E minor, BWV914; G minor, BWV915; G major, BWV916. **Glenn Gould** (pf). Sony Classical
  Glenn Gould Edition Ⓜ SM2K52612 (two discs: 81 minutes: ADD: 9/94).

Bach Organ works, Volume 1 – Toccata and Fugue in D minor, BWV565. Herzlich tut mich
  verlangen, BWV727. Fugue in G major, BWV577. Erbarm' dich mein, O Herre Gott, BWV721.
  Fugue on a theme by Corelli in B minor, BWV579. Prelude and Fugue in G major, BWV541.
  Pastorale in F major, BWV590. Clavier-Ubung III, BWV669-89 – Wir glauben all'an einen Gott,
  BWV680. Orgel-Büchlein, BWV599-644 – O Mensch, bewein' dein Sünde gross, BWV622.
  Passacaglia and Fugue in C minor, BWV582. **Peter Hurford** (org). EMI Eminence
  Ⓜ CD-EMX2218 (63 minutes: DDD: 3/94). Played on the organ of Martinikerk, Groningen,
  Holland. Recorded 1993.   Ⓔ

"Peter Hurford playing organs of Bach's Time". For his earlier recordings on Argo, Hurford played
mainly modern, neo-baroque instruments and while Bach on 'authentic' instruments is no novelty, we
certainly don't hear enough of the wondrous Ahrend organ which begins this new series in such style.
Ahrend? Builders of Bach's time? Well we're obviously going to have to take the title with a hefty
pinch of salt. Although it dates back over 500 years, in its present form the organ dates back only as
far as 1984. Bach never played it, and even if he had he certainly wouldn't recognize it now, but it
sounds wonderful; Henry Mitton and Mark Nations have recorded it magnificently, closely focusing
the sound within an aura of spaciousness. Splendid playing by Hurford too, of course. He begins (as
everyone does) with the ubiquitous Toccata and Fugue in D minor. But what a performance!
Everything else is given warmly communicative, unpretentious and immensely appealing
performances. Hurford knows and loves his Bach, something which shines out of every note he plays.

Bach Organ works, Volume 2 – Concerto in D minor after Vivaldi's Op. 3 No. 11, BWV596. Vater
  unser im Himmelreich, BWV737. Aria in F major, BWV587. Der Tag, der ist so freudenreich,
  BWV719. Trio Sonata No. 5, BWV529. Nun danket alle Gott, BWV657. Liebster Jesu, wir sind
  hier, BWV731. Fantasia super Valet will ich dir geben, BWV735. Nun freut euch, lieben Christen
  gmein, BWV734. Toccata, Adagio and Fugue in C major, BWV564. **Peter Hurford** (org). EMI
  Eminence Ⓜ CD-EMX2226 (66 minutes: DDD: 12/94). 🎵 Played on the Schnitger organ in the
  Ludgerikirche, Norden, Germany. Recorded 1993.   ⒺⒺ

Hurford continues his tour of Bach's organ works on an organ that dates from Bach's own time. There
may be stylistic quibbles: for instance, given the virtues of the marvellous Schnitger organ at Norden
(a clear, 'oakey' brilliance, imposing but not austere) it is perhaps a mite surprising that Hurford still
occasionally shows a liking for frothy, high-pitched registrations which may be too neo-baroque for
some tastes. But set against that, and far more important, is his increased ability to convey energy
without haste. Indeed, his relaxed control (without any diminution of authority or personality) in
quick movements, especially the outer movements of Sonata No. 5 and the Toccata, Adagio and
Fugue, results in performances that are, without exception, more mellow, humane and witty than his
earlier ones. And in terms of textual clarity they are exemplary. The close marriage of music and
instrument is most fruitful in the chorale settings (BWV737, 719, 657 and 735), all of them displaying

rather formulaic imitative techniques. But, of course, Hurford knows exactly what he is about: with registrations carved from the meat of the instrument – solid choruses and reeds – these works are revealed as quintessential meditations for the Lutheran liturgy, dogma in music, patient, strong and assured. *Nun danket alle Gott*, in particular, is given an outstandingly trenchant performance. The engineering is first-rate, the slightly recessed pedal balance reflecting (but not distractingly so) the unusual layout of the instrument, which is fully explained in the insert-notes.

Additional recommendation ...

...BWV565. BWV709/726. BWV727. Preludes and Fugues – E minor, BWV533; D minor, BWV539; C major, BWV531; C minor, BWV549; G major, BWV550. Wo soll ich fliehen hin, BWV694. Nun komm, der Heiden Heiland, BWV699. Gottes Sohn ist kommen, BWV703. Herr Christ, der einig Gottes Sohn, BWV698. Lob sei dem allmächtigen Gott, BWV704. Gelobet seist du Jesu Christ, BWV697; Vom Himmel hoch, da komm ich her, BWV701. Christum wir sollen loben schon, BWV696. In dulci jubilo, BWV751. **Lorenzo Ghielmi** (org). Deutsche Harmonia Mundi Ⓟ 05472 77278-2 (58 minutes: DDD: 7/93).

Bach Trio Sonatas, BWV525-30 – No. 1 in E flat major. No. 2 in C minor. No. 3 in D minor. No. 4 in E minor. No. 5 in C major. No. 6 in G major. **Christopher Herrick** (org). Hyperion Ⓟ CDA66390 (72 minutes: DDD: 11/90). Played on the Metzler organ of the Parish Church of St Nikolaus, Bremgarten, Switzerland. Recorded 1989.   ⒼⒼⒼ

The common assumption is that Bach wrote his six Trio Sonatas as training studies for his son Wilhelm Friedmann, and certainly to this day young organists regard the ability to play these pieces as a prerequisite in establishing proper organ technique. But if ever the notion that this is music "first to practise and secondly to admire" was shown to be false, this stunning disc presents an unanswerable argument. Christopher Herrick's performances are immense fun, brimming over with real affection for the music. He allows himself occasional displays of enthusiasm (adding a few exuberant glissandos in the last movement of the E flat major Sonata, for example) and he chooses his stops both to enhance the vitality of the quick movements and to underline the sheer beauty of the slower ones. Never has this music sounded less like a training study! The Hyperion recording of the sumptuous Swiss instrument makes this disc a worthwhile buy if only for its glorious sound; the organ speaks into a rich, opulent acoustic which treats each note as a priceless jewel, to be enhanced by its setting but not in any way to be obscured. A disc of rare beauty and a real gem in any collection.

New review

Bach Schübler Chorales, BWV645-50[a]. Chorales, BWV651-68[b]. Chorales[a] from Cantatas Nos. 36, 59, 62 and 180. Wenn wir in höchsten Nöten sein, BWV431[b]. Du heiliger Brunst, süsser Trost, BWV226 No. 2[b]. An Wasserflüssen Babylon, BWV267[b]. Herr Jesus Christ, dich zu uns wend', BWV332[b]. O Lamm Gottes, unschuldig, BWV401[b]. Nun danket alle Gott, BWV386[b]. Von Gott will ich nicht lassen, BWV418[b]. Allein Gott in der Höh' sei Ehr', BWV260[b]. Jesus Christus, unser Heiland, BWV363[b]. Komm, Gott Schöpfer, heiliger Geist, BWV370[b]. [a]**Amsterdam Baroque Choir / Ton Koopman** ([b]org). Teldec Das Alte Werk Ⓟ 4509-94459-2 (two discs: 142 minutes: DDD: 6/96). Organ works played on the organ of the Grote Kerk, Leeuwarden. Texts and translations included. Recorded 1994.

Koopman's performances have a glorious sense of spontaneity born of the understanding that, with a cantata and a fistful of chorale preludes to compose and perform every week, Bach was hardly involved here in deep, painstaking creativity. Koopman seems totally attuned to the essential practicality of this music. As a result he can indulge in outrageously ebullient ornamentation, which from any other organist might seem merely bad taste, and maintain his light, dispassionate approach even through those Preludes usually afforded particular emotional significance, yet make it all sound stylistically convincing. A link between organ and cantata cycles is forged here by pairing each prelude with its chorale, sung by the choir with whom Koopman is currently working his way through the complete cantatas for Erato. The complete unity of approach between organist and singers is ingeniously underpinned by the use of organ accompaniment where unaccompanied singing might create a sense of dissociation. There is occasional variation but throughout, the singing of the Amsterdam Baroque Choir is an unalloyed joy. Koopman isn't going to be everybody's cup of tea every time, but with this beautifully recorded pair of discs any reservations are completely outweighed by the sheer musical integrity of what are truly wonderful performances.

New review

Bach Cantatas – No. 4, Christ lag in Todesbanden[c]; No. 131, Aus der Tiefen rufe ich, Herr, zu dir[b]; No. 182, Himmelskönig, sei willkommen[a]. [b]**Julianne Baird**, [a]**Christine Brandes**, [c]**Judith Nelson** (sops); [a]**Judith Malafronte** (mez); [b]**Drew Minter**, [c]**Daniel Taylor** (altos); [c]**Benjamin Butterfield** (ten); [c]**Kurt-Owen Richards**, [ab]**James Weaver** (basses); **American Bach Soloists / Jeffrey Thomas** ([a]ten). Koch International Ⓟ 37235-2 (67 minutes: DDD: 3/96). ✍ Texts and translations included. Recorded 1994.

This programme contains three early works from Mühlhausen and Weimar. These are the cantatas that benefit most from scaled-down forces since they are, in most cases, more closely related to the Lutheran sacred concerto and motet of the late seventeenth century. Thomas, following in Joshua Rifkin's steps, adheres strictly to the one-to-a-part principle. Judith Malafronte's beautifully coloured voice has a timbre, clarity and understanding of Bach's melodic demands that make you long to hear her in many more of Bach's cantatas. Sadly, she sings in only one work on the disc, Bach's Annunciation/Palm Sunday Cantata, *Himmelskönig, sei willkommen*. The equivalent vocal range in the remaining two cantatas is served by countertenor Drew Minter who also makes a fine contribution though a less satisfying one than Malafronte. There is in fact much good singing throughout, James Weaver and Julianne Baird being but two whose expressive warmth enhances the music. Thomas and his team apply a wealth of effective stylistic ideas. There is, for instance, a wonderfully lyrical approach by the recorder player in the alto aria of No. 182; the shaping of phrases is carefully thought out, he leans slightly on all the notes that call for it and punctuates the music with all the skill of a seasoned rhetorician. Thomas himself, in the extended declamatory tenor aria from the same work, has similarly persuasive ideas though occasionally lacks the assured vocal technique to see him through. In summary, there is plenty of food for thought here and much that is both stylistically apposite and emotionally satisfying. Some readers will want a stronger vocal presence in the choral movements but, this apart, the performances and the recorded sound can be warmly recommended.

Additional recommendations ...

...(Nos. 1-199, excluding Nos. 15, 53, 118, 141, 142, 189, 190, 191 and 193.) **Soloists; Tölz Boys' Choir; Vienna Boys' Choir; Hanover Boys' Choir; Choir of King's College, Cambridge; Ghent Collegium Vocale; Chorus Viennensis; Leonhardt Consort / Gustav Leonhardt; Vienna Concentus Musicus / Nikolaus Harnoncourt.** Teldec Das Alte Werk Ⓑ 4509-91765-2 (60 discs: ADD/DDD: 2/95). ✍ Texts and translations included. Also available as ten six-disc mid-price sets, as follows: *4509-91755-2* (387 minutes): Nos. 1-14 and 16-19. *4509-91756-2* (385 minutes): Nos. 20-36. *4509-91757-2* (416 minutes): Nos. 37-52 and 54-60. *4509-91758-2* (389 minutes): Nos. 61-78. *4509-91759-2* (385 minutes): Nos. 79-99. *4509-91760-2* (369 minutes): Nos. 100-117. *4509-91761-2* (371 minutes): Nos. 119-137. *4509-91762-2* (403 minutes): Nos. 138-140, 143-159, 161 and 162. *4509-91763-2* (366 minutes): Nos. 163-182. *4509-91764-2* (299 minutes): Nos. 183-188, 192 and 194-199.

...(Nos. 1-200, excluding Nos. 15, 53, 118, 141, 142 and 189.) Christmas Oratorio, BWV248. Easter Oratorio, BWV249. **Soloists; Frankfurt Kantorei; Indiana University Chamber Singers; Stuttgart Gächinger Kantorei; Stuttgart Gedächtniskirche Choir; Stuttgart Bach Collegium, Württemberg Chamber Orchestra / Helmuth Rilling.** Hänssler Classic Ⓜ 98 841 (69 discs: AAD/DDD: 2/95).

...Volume 5 – No. 5, Wo soll ich fliehen hin; No. 26, Ach wie flüchtig, ach wie nichtig; No. 38, Aus tiefer Not schrei ich zu dir; No. 55, Ich armer Mensch, ich Sündenknecht; No. 56, Ich will den Kreuzstab gerne tragen; No. 60, O Ewigkeit, du Donnerwort; No. 70, Wachet! betet! seid bereit allezeit; No. 80, Ein feste Burg ist unser Gott; No. 96, Herr Christ, der einge Gottessohn; No. 106, Gottes Zeit ist die allerbeste Zeit; No. 115, Mache dich, mein Geist bereit; No. 116, Du Friedefürst, Herr Jesu Christ; No. 130, Herr Gott, dich loben alle wir; No. 139, Wohl dem, der sich auf seinen Gott; No. 140, Wachet auf, ruft uns die Stimme; No. 180, Schmücke dich, o liebe Seele. **Soloists; Munich Bach Choir and Orchestra / Karl Richter.** Archiv Produktion Ⓕ 439 394-2AX5 (five discs: 342 minutes: ADD: 1/95).

...No. 7, Christ unser Herr zum Jordan kam[a]; No. 11[b]; No. 30, Freue dich, erlöste Schar[c]; No. 68, Also hat Gott die Welt geliebt[d]; No. 104, Du Hirte Israel, höre[b]. [b]**Hedy Graf**, [c]**Emiko Iiyama**, [d]**Agnes Giebel** (sops); [abc]**Barbara Scherler**; [d]**Claudia Hellmann** (mezzos); [a]**Georg Jelden**, [bd]**Kurt Huber**; [c]**Theo Altmeyer** (tens); [abd]**Jakob Stämpfli**; [c]**Bruce Abel**, [d]**Erik Wenk** (basses); **Heinrich Schütz Choir, Heilbronn; Pforzheim Chamber Orchestra / Fritz Werner.** Erato Ⓜ 0630-12978-2 (two discs: 140 minutes: ADD). Ⓖ

...Volume 4 – No. 8, Liebster Gott, wann werd' ich sterben; No. 9, Es ist das Heil uns kommen her; No. 17, Wer Dank opfert, der preiset mich; No. 27, Wer weiss, wie nahe mir mein Ende!; No. 33, Allein zu dir, Herr Jesu Christ; No. 45, Es ist dir gesagt, Mensch, was gut ist; No. 51, Jauchzet Gott in allen Landen!; No. 78, Jesu, der du meine Seele; No. 100, Was Gott tut, das ist wohlgetan; No. 102, Herr, deine Augen sehen nach dem Glauben; No. 105, Herr, gehe nicht ins Gericht mit deinem Knecht; No. 137, Lobe den Herren, den mächtigen König der Ehren; No. 148, Bringet dem Herrn Ehre seines Namens; No. 178, Wo Gott der Herr nicht bei uns hält; No. 179, Siehe zu, dass deine Gottesfurcht; No. 187, Es wartet alles auf dich; No. 199, Mein Herze schwimmt im Blut. **Soloists; Munich Bach Choir and Orchestra; Ansbach Bach Week Soloists Ensemble / Karl Richter.** Archiv Produktion Ⓕ 439 387-2AX6 (six discs: 358 minutes: ADD: 1/95).

...No. 12, Weinen, Klagen, Sorgen, Zagen; No. 18, Gleich wie der Regen und Schnee; No. 61; No. 132; No. 152, Tritt auf die Glaubensbahn; No. 172, Erschallet, ihr Lieder; No. 182, Himmelskönig, sei willkommen; No. 199, Mein Herze schwimmt im Blut; No. 203, Amore traditore. Quodlibet, BWV524. **Soloists; Amsterdam Baroque Choir and Orchestra / Ton Koopman.** Erato Ⓕ 0630-12598-2 (three discs: 183 minutes: DDD: 5/96). ✍ *Selected by Soundings.*

...Volume 1 – No. 13, Meine Seufzer, meine Tränen[adfhj]; No. 28, Gottlob! nun geht das Jahr zu Ende[aefhj]; No. 58, Ach Gott, wie manches Herzelied[bh]; No. 61, Nun komm, der Heiden Heiland[afhj]; No. 63, Christen, ätzet diesen Tag[adfhj]; No. 64, Sehet, welch eine Liebe[adhj]; No. 65, Sie werden aus Saba alle kommen[gij]; No. 81, Jesus schläft, was soll ich hoffen?[dhj]; No. 82, Ich habe genug[h]; No. 111, Was mein Gott will, das g'scheh allzeit[adfij]; No. 121, Christum wir sollen loben schon[adfhj]; No. 124, Meinen Jesum lass ich nicht[cegij]; No. 132, Bereitet die Wege, bereitet die Bahn[adfij]; No. 171, Gott, wie dein Name, so ist auch dein Ruhm[aefhj]. [a]**Edith Mathis,** [b]**Sheila Armstrong,** [c]**Lotte Schädle** (sops); [d]**Anna Reynolds,** [e]**Hertha Töpper** (mezzos); [f]**Peter Schreier,** [g]**Ernst Haefliger** (tens); [h]**Dietrich Fischer-Dieskau** (bar); [i]**Theo Adam** (bass-bar); **Munich Bach** [j]**Choir and Orchestra / Karl Richter.** Archiv Produktion Ⓑ 439 369-2AX4 (four discs: 278 minutes: ADD: 3/94). Texts and translations included. All from 2722 005 (11/72) except No. 82, 198477 (4/70).   Ⓖ

...No. 36, Schwingt freudig euch empor[a]; No. 61, Nun komm, der Heiden Heiland; No. 62, Nun komm, der Heiden Heiland[a]. **Nancy Argenta** (sop); [a]**Petra Lang** (mez); **Anthony Rolfe Johnson** (ten); **Olaf Bär** (bar); **Monteverdi Choir; English Baroque Soloists / John Eliot Gardiner.** Archiv Produktion Ⓕ 437 327-2AH (61 minutes: DDD: 2/93). 🗲 Texts and translations included.

...No. 54, Widerstehe doch der Sünde[a]; No. 170, Vergnügte Ruh', beliebte Seelenlust[a]. Mass in B minor, BWV232 – Agnus Dei[a]. **Handel** Orlando – Ah Stigie larve![b]. Jephtha, HWV70 – 'Tis Heaven's all-ruling pow'r[b]. Theodora, HWV68 – Kind Heav'n, if Virtue be thy care; Sweet Rose, and Lilly, flow'ry Form[b]. **Alfred Deller** (alto); [a]**Leonhardt Baroque Ensemble / Gustav Leonhardt** (org); [b]**Handel Festival Orchestra / Sir Anthony Lewis.** Vanguard Classics Alfred Deller Edition Ⓜ 08.5069.71* (59 minutes: ADD: 1/95). 🗲   ⒼⒼ

...No. 56, Ich will den Kreuzstab gerne tragen; No. 82, Ich habe genug. **Max van Egmond** (bar); **St Bavo's Cathedral Boys' Choir; Baroque Instrumental Ensemble / Frans Brüggen.** RCA Seon Ⓜ GD71956 (40 minutes: ADD: 10/89). 🗲

...Nos. 56, 82 and 158. **Peter Kooy** (bass); **La Chapelle Royale Choir and Orchestra / Philippe Herreweghe.** Harmonia Mundi Ⓕ HMC90 1365 (52 minutes: DDD: 10/92). 🗲

...Nos. 56, 82 and 158. **Olaf Bär** (bar); **Scottish Chamber Orchestra / Peter Schreier.** EMI Ⓕ CDC7 54453-2 (48 minutes: DDD: 6/93).

...No. 82[a]. **Brahms** Lieder[b]. **Hans Hotter** (bass-bar); [b]**Gerald Moore** (pf); [a]**Philharmonia Orchestra / Anthony Bernard.** EMI Références mono Ⓜ CDH7 63198-2* (69 minutes: ADD: 1/90).   Ⓖ

...No. 82[a]. **Brahms** Lieder – Vier ernste Gesänge, Op. 121. Feldeinsamkeit, Op. 86 No. 2. Minnelied III, Op. 71 No. 5. Sapphische Ode, No. 94 No. 4. Botschaft, Op. 47 No. 1. Sommerabend, Op. 85 No. 1. Mondenschein, Op. 85 No. 2. Ständchen, Op. 106 No. 1. O wüsst ich doch den Weg zurück, Op. 63 No. 8. Auf dem Kirchhofe, Op. 105 No. 4. In Waldeseinsamkeit, Op. 85 No. 6. **Hans Hotter** (bass); [b]**Gerald Moore** (pf); [a]**Philharmonia Orchestra / Anthony Bernard.** EMI Références mono Ⓜ CDH7 63198-2* (69 minutes: ADD: 4/90).

...No. 198, Lass, Fürstin, lass noch einen Strahl (Trauer Ode)[a]; No. 158, Der Friede sei mit dir[b]; No. 27, Wer weiss, wie nahe mir mein Ende![c]. [ac]**Rotraud Hansmann** (sop); [ac]**Helen Watts** (contr); [a]**Kurt Equiluz** (ten); **Max van Egmond** (bass); **Monteverdi Choir; Concerto Amsterdam / Jürgen Jurgens.** Teldec Das Alte Werk Ⓜ 4509-93687-2 (67 minutes: ADD: 10/94). 🗲   ⒼⒼ

New review

Bach Cantatas – No. 6, Bleib' bei uns, denn es will Abend werden; No. 41, Jesu, nun sei gepreiset; No. 68, Also hat Gott die Welt geliebt. **Barbara Schlick** (sop); **Andreas Scholl** (alto); **Christoph Prégardien** (ten); **Gotthold Schwarz** (bass); **Accentus Chamber Choir; Limoges Baroque Ensemble / Christophe Coin** (vc). Auvidis Astrée Ⓕ E8555 (63 minutes: DDD: 5/96). 🗲 Texts and translations included. Recorded 1995.

These three cantatas are Leipzig compositions dating from 1725. No. 41 is a New Year piece, No. 6 an Easter one, while No. 68 was written for Whitsun. Though belonging to the same year, these cantatas are varied in structure, only No. 41 adhering to that unifying thematic pattern which was such a distinctive feature of the chorale-based works of the 1724-5 annual cycle. The many illuminating features of Coin's lively direction elsewhere ensure a high level of enjoyment; and his own violoncello piccolo solos convey the poetry of the music with wonderfully intuitive expression and grateful gesture. Happily, the four vocal soloists are outstanding and the small choir sound well, on the whole, though they do not always make their presence sufficiently felt. The opening chorus of No. 6, Schweitzer's "masterpiece of poetry in music", is handled with extraordinary sensibility by Coin, who brings out details in Bach's scoring, such as the throbbing quavers of the upper and middle string parts, with loving tenderness. This gentleness of approach, together with a close identity and warm rapport with Bach's kaleidoscopic tonal palette, are virtues common to all three discs and sterling qualities that will survive the fickleness of changing fashion. And what is so refreshing about these recordings is the absence of intrusive mannerism. There are no empty gestures here, just total absorption in the music, and a disarming humility. A release of great distinction.

Bach Cantatas – No. 8, Liebster Gott, wann werd' ich sterben[a]; No. 26, Ach wie flüchtig, ach wie nichtig[b]; No. 43, Gott fähret auf mit Jauchzen[c]; No. 61, Nun komm, der Heiden Heiland[d]; No. 85, Ich bin ein guter Hirt[e]; No. 130, Herr Gott, dich loben alle wir[b]; No. 182, Himmelskönig, sei willkommen[f]. [abcdf]**Frederike Sailer,** [e]**Ingeborg Reichelt** (sops); [abcdf]**Claudia Hellmann,** [e]**Hertha Töpper** (mezzos); **Helmut Krebs** (ten); [abf]**Erik Wenk,** [cd]**Jakob Stämpfli,** [e]**Franz Kelch** (basses); **Heinrich Schütz Choir, Heilbronn;** [a]**South-West German Chamber Orchestra,** [bcdef]**Pforzheim**

Chamber Orchestra / Fritz Werner. Erato Ⓜ 4509-97407-2* (two discs: 147 minutes: ADD: 5/95). Item marked [a] from STU70086 (recorded 1961), [bd]STU70085 (1961), [cf]STU70087 (1961), [e]STU70042 (1959). Ⓖ

Bach Cantatas – No. 6, Bleib' bei uns, denn es will Abend werden[a]; No. 31, Der Himmel lacht! die Erde jubiliert[c]; No. 67, Halt im Gedächtnis Jesum Christ[b]; No. 76, Die Himmel erzählen die Ehre Gottes[a]; No. 80, Ein feste Burg ist unser Gott[a]; No. 87, Bisher habt ihr nichts gebeten in meinem Namen[a]. [ab]**Ingeborg Reichelt**, [c]**Agnes Giebel** (sops); [a]**Hertha Töpper**, [b]**Marga Hoffgen**, [c]**Claudia Hellmann** (mezzos); **Helmut Krebs** (ten); [ab]**Franz Kelch**, [c]**Erich Wenk** (basses); **Heinrich Schütz Choir, Heilbronn; Pforzheim Chamber Orchestra / Fritz Werner.** Erato Ⓑ 4509-98525-2* (two discs: 149 minutes: ADD: 6/95). Recorded 1960-64. Texts and translations included.

Fritz Werner, conductor and composer, died in 1980 and were it not for enterprising releases such as these, we would have little cause to remember a man who championed Bach's cantatas in the 1960s and early 1970s with rare integrity and unaffected eloquence. The first disc comprising reissues of seven cantatas, chosen from over 50 he recorded from 1958-74, is skilfully conceived to cover all the important seasons of the church calendar. The Advent cantata is the magnificent *Nun komm, der Heiden Heiland*, which is touchingly natural in its expression. The soloists here feature the sensitive singing of tenor, Helmut Krebs, who may not have an effortless vocal technique but his open-throated and committed performances are full of personality and his recitatives nobly delivered. Jakob Stämpfli, too, is a fine and highly consistent Bachian. The Heinrich Schütz Choir are also well suited to Werner's spontaneous and smooth transitions and classical pacing. How thrilling are the trumpets and drums in the bass aria of No. 130, no holds barred, crackling articulation and an inimitable moment when in the excitement of it all they get slightly out. And the free-flowing flute obbligato in the same cantata (again, with Krebs on top form) has a recognizable personality gently coaxed by a sympathetic, untyrannical director. Other than Nos. 61 and 130, No. 8, *Liebster Gott*, is another outstanding all-round performance. The opening chorus is instilled with compassion and radiant phrasing. The substantial *Himmelskönig, sei willkommen* for Palm Sunday (No. 182) is less consistent overall. To sum up: this is a sobering release of near 'historical' (in its true sense) Bach cantatas, conceived by musicians whose innate perception of what they were doing relied principally on good artistry. Recorded sound transfers are good on the whole. Documentation is not up to scratch for such an important release.

The second volume of Werner's cantatas is to be welcomed as more than simply an interesting antiquarian exercise. Werner was at his most incisive, lean and prescient (in the best way) in the earlier stages of his recording career. The six cantatas in this generously filled selection were recorded between 1960-64, something of a golden period in Bach performance. Werner's strengths are exhibited to the full here in works which enshrine the Sundays around Easter and Easter Day itself which is celebrated with No. 31. He gives this piece a racy and dynamic lift at the outset of the sort we can recall in No. 130 from the first volume, with instrumental playing which boasts in the brass department no less distinguished exponents than Maurice André and Hermann Baumann. The choral singing of the Heinrich Schütz Choir is less well projected than is ideal in the more robust movements, though in the slow middle section of the opening chorus and the gloriously judged solo-oriented Cantata, No. 87, Werner's strategy is clear for all to see as he gently coaxes his musicians, never drilling them to hard-driven exclamation. The singers are a constant joy. Helmut Krebs, as noted above, is not a musician whose technical facility impresses on its own terms, but his soft-grained sound is remarkably sympathetic. Sadly, Agnes Giebel appears only once, though her shimmeringly old-fashioned strains in the soprano aria of No. 31 are alone worth the price of the discs (even if in any other hands it would be considered intolerably slow) and if Ingeborg Reichelt does not float quite so ethereally, she is secure at the very least and accompanied by an agile August Wenzinger on the violoncello piccolo in the memorable chorale, "Bleib' bei uns" (from No. 6), as Bach conveys the comfort of Christ's presence in the preparation for death. Hertha Töpper is a fine contralto. If a touch ripe for some people's taste, her nobility of expression in "Hoch gelobter Gottes Sohn" from No. 6 is admirable. Werner delivers a fine account of this cantata though it is perhaps prone to drag its feet a little. No. 76 is a little short on drama though it is finely wrought whilst No. 67 imparts committed direction as do the splendid duets in *Ein feste Burg* (No. 80). A release of great significance then, on several fronts. Documentation is greatly improved with this second volume. The recorded transfers are outstanding.

Additional recommendations ...

...No. 4, Christ lag in Todesbanden (with appendix); No. 21, Ich hatte viel Bekümmernis (with appendix); No. 31; No. 71, Gott ist mein König; No. 106, Gottes Zeit ist die allerbeste Zeit, "Actus tragicus"; No. 131, Aus der Tiefe rufe ich, Herr, zu dir; No. 151, Nach dir, Herr, verlanget mich; No. 185, Barmherziges Herze der ewigen Liebe; No. 196, Der Herr denket an uns. **Barbara Schlick** (sop); **Kai Wessel** (alto); **Guy de Mey** (ten); **Klaus Mertens** (bass); **Amsterdam Baroque Choir and Orchestra / Ton Koopman.** Erato Ⓕ 4509-98536-2 (three discs: 198 minutes: DDD: 9/95).

...No. 5, Wo soll ich fliehen hin; No. 6; No. 7, Christ unser Herr zum Jordan kam; No. 8. **Paul Esswood** (alto); **Kurt Equiluz** (ten); **Max van Egmond** (bass); **Vienna Boys' Choir; Chorus Viennensis; Vienna Concentus Musicus / Nikolaus Harnoncourt; Regensburger Domspatzen; King's College Choir, Cambridge; Leonhardt Consort / Gustav Leonhardt.** Teldec Ⓜ 2292-42498-2 (two discs: 87 minutes: ADD: 9/85). ✍   Ⓖ

...No. 8[a]; No. 156, Ich steh mit einem Fuss im Grabe[b]; No. 198, Lass, Fürstin, lass noch einen Strahl, "Trauer-Ode". [a]Julianne Baird, [c]Judith Nelson (sops); [c]Judith Malafronte (mez); [ab]Steven Rickards (alto); [c]William Sharp (bar); [ab]James Weaver (bass); American Bach Soloists / Jeffrey Thomas (ten). Koch International Classics Ⓕ 37163-2 (68 minutes: DDD: 4/93).

New review

Bach Cantatas – No. 7, Christ unser Herr zum Jordan kam[a]; No. 11, Lobet Gott in seinen Reichen[b]; No. 30, Freue dich, erlöste Schar[c]; No. 68, Also hat Gott die Welt geliebt[d]; No. 104, Du Hirte Israel, höre[b]. [b]Hedy Graf, [c]Emiko Iiyama, [d]Agnes Giebel (sops); [abc]Barbara Scherler, [d]Claudia Hellmann (mezzos); [a]Georg Jelden, [bd]Kurt Huber, [c]Theo Altmeyer (tens); [abd]Jakob Stämpfli, [c]Bruce Abel, [d]Erik Wenk (basses); Heinrich Schütz Choir, Heilbronn; Pforzheim Chamber Orchestra / Fritz Werner. Erato Ⓜ 0630-12978-2 (two discs: 140 minutes: ADD: 6/96). Texts and translations included. Item marked [a] from STU70342 (recorded 1970), [b]STU70341 (1970), [c]STU70665 (1971), [d]STU70181 (1963). Ⓖ

Followers of this splendid series of reissues will already have gathered why Erato feel compelled to continue their quick-fire release strategy (see reviews above). Each disc serves as evidence that Bach performance in the 1950s, 1960s and, to a certain extent, 1970s can boast qualities which have eluded many modern-day practitioners. Yet, above all, what these performances implore from the listener is that we distinguish between fashion and taste – what is a sign of its time and what transcends it, in the process begging a few questions regarding what constitutes 'the real thing' if we take the concept of authenticity to its logical conclusion. Most persuasive of all in Werner's Bach is the ingenuous reading of the musical line as dictated by the sentiments of the text. We can witness this in the arias of No. 30, magnificently sung by Bruce Abel and Barbara Scherler (how deft is the pacing and articulation here as slothful and decadent sinners are brought into line – but done with such grace), as well as the long-breathed direction in the gentle, pastoral lilt of the opening chorus of No. 104. Whether one looks upon these traits as an embodiment of the uncomplicated self-expression found in the German provinces (Heilbronn and Pforzheim are hardly metropolitan), or just a director blessed with an intuitive sense of Bach's emotional world, it is hard to know. Easier to recognize is the extent of the fine singing on display: Kurt Huber is typical of the musicianly singer Werner seems to have attracted: sensitive and instinctively able to colour the music with memorable nuances (only Emiko Iiyama is disappointing). Better known is the quietly distinguished Jakob Stämpfli who comes up trumps every time, as indeed throughout the series has the inimitable and gleaming voice of Agnes Giebel; No. 68, a fine cantata for Pentecost, reveals a singer who transports the familiar sense of frolicking joy of "Mein glaubiges Herze" ("My heart ever faithful") on to a new shining plateau, reinforced by the delightfully performed instrumental interlude which follows. There is much else to admire here including a notable Ascension Oratorio (No. 11) boasting a brilliant opening chorus, if a less compelling final one (a monstrously hard movement) where Werner rather runs out of steam. His performance of No. 7 is still valid for its robust energy, even if there are details in continuo realization which are harder to reconcile in modern times. The accompanying booklet is satisfyingly complete but it is a pity that more care wasn't taken to transfer details correctly from the original format. Again, the sound transfers are outstanding – the best so far – and no less than these wonderful performances deserve.

Bach Cantatas – No. 11, Lobet Gott in seinen Reichen; No. 43, Gott fähret auf mit Jauchzen; No. 44, Sie werden euch in den Bann tun. Barbara Schlick (sop); Catherine Patriasz (contr); Christoph Prégardien (ten); Peter Kooy (bass); Collegium Vocale / Philippe Herreweghe. Harmonia Mundi Ⓕ HMC90 1479 (67 minutes: DDD: 3/94). ✍ Texts and translations included. Recorded 1993.

Gott fähret auf mit Jauchzen is resonant in its joyful celebration of Christ's Ascension to Heaven and the right hand of God the Father. The orchestra includes three trumpets, drums and two oboes, as well as the basic string band, and these all play a part in the majestic opening chorus. By comparison, Sie werden euch in den Bann tun is a modestly conceived piece. The Ascension 'Oratorio' (No. 11), though listed among Bach's cantatas, is an oratorio in more than just name, making use of a narrator who relates the events surrounding Christ's Ascension. Like Bach's two other oratorios, this one makes extensive use of music which had previously been written for other contexts. It also contains the music which eventually was to become the Agnus Dei of the B minor Mass. Herreweghe paces all three works with assurance and fluency and is supported by the excellence of his singers and instrumentalists. Fine recorded sound and an informative booklet set the seal on an accomplished issue.

Bach Cantatas – No. 39, Brich dem Hungrigen dein Brot; No. 93, Wer nur den lieben Gott lässt walten; No. 107, Was willst du dich betrüben. Agnès Mellon (sop); Charles Brett (alto); Howard Crook (ten); Peter Kooy (bass); Collegium Vocale Chorus and Orchestra / Philippe Herreweghe. Virgin Classics Veritas Ⓕ VC7 59320-2 (61 minutes: DDD: 3/94). ✍ Texts and translations included. Recorded 1991. Ⓖ

The three pieces included here are mature examples of Bach's cantata writing; two of them, Nos. 93 and 107, were written in 1724 for the Fifth and Seventh Sundays after Trinity respectively, and thus belong to Bach's great second cycle in which he concentrated on a chorale-based scheme. The remaining cantata, No. 39, is a masterly work, above all in the concerto-like construction of the opening chorus, scored for voices with treble recorders, oboes and strings. Agnès Mellon is beguiling both in her three arias – one per cantata – and in her duo with Charles Brett. Both Crook and Kooy are on characteristically fine form. Enjoyable, too, are the contributions from the chorus and orchestra, and, as usual, the oboe playing of Marcel Ponseele is a constant pleasure, above all for his poetic phrasing and communicative articulation. An excellent recorded sound sets the seal on a fine issue.

Bach Cantatas – No. 49, Ich gehe und suche mit Verlangen; No. 115, Mache dich, mein Geist
   bereit; No. 180, Schmücke dich, o liebe Seele. **Barbara Schlick** (sop); **Andreas Scholl** (alto);
   Christoph Prégardien (ten); **Gotthold Schwarz** (bass); **Concerto Vocale; Limoges Baroque Ensemble
   / Christophe Coin** (vc). Auvidis Astrée Ⓕ E8530 (71 minutes: DDD: 2/95). 🖉 Texts and
   translations included. Recorded 1993.   ⓖⓖ

Three of Bach's Leipzig church cantatas form a characteristically well thought-out programme from the French gamba player, cellist and director, Christophe Coin. *Schmücke dich, o liebe Seele* (No. 180) and *Mache dich, mein Geist, bereit* (No. 115) are among the most overlooked of the cantatas, outside 'complete editions'; but they are towering masterpieces which deserve to be as popular as, for instance, *Wachet auf!* (No. 140) or any of the others which find their way, albeit infrequently, into concert programming. There is a more particular reason, however, beyond that of sheer musical excellence, why Coin has chosen to perform these works: it is that in each of them Bach has included a movement calling for the obbligato presence of a small, five-stringed cello, the violoncello piccolo. Nine of Bach's cantatas contain a part for this distinctive-sounding instrument, in each of which the composer employs it with telling effect. No. 180 is a delicately scored piece for two recorders, oboe, oboe da caccia and strings, with an affecting undercurrent of elegy. Coin's direction, his overall grasp of the musical idiom and his evident care over textual detail lead to the heart of the piece. Not everything is refined – there are, for example, some rough moments in the instrumental tuttis – but the spirit of the performance carries everything along with it. This much is true for the remaining cantatas, too. No. 115 contains music of quite extraordinary inventive richness and nowhere more so than in its two *da capo* arias for alto and soprano, respectively: the second, in B minor, seems to lead us into almost uncharted emotional territory in its contemplative profundity. This heart-rending trio for soprano, flute, violoncello piccolo and continuo is one of the most astounding achievements in the entire canon; and it is beautifully sung by Barbara Schlick. The Leipzig Concerto Vocale (a mixed choir of men's and women's voices), and the Limoges Baroque Ensemble have gathered under Coin's direction in performances which probe far beyond musical superficialities.

Additional recommendation ...

...No. 49. No. 58, Ach Gott, wie manches Herzelied. No. 82, Ich habe genug. **Nancy Argenta** (sop);
   Klaus Mertens (bass); **La Petite Bande / Sigiswald Kuijken** (vn). Accent Ⓕ ACC9395D (63 minutes:
   DDD: 3/94). 🖉   ⓖ

Bach Cantatas – No. 51, Jauchzet Gott in allen Landen![a]; No. 202, Weichet nur, betrübte Schatten,
   "Wedding Cantata"[b]; No. 209, Non sa che sia dolore[c]. [ac]**Teresa Stich-Randall**, [b]**Anny Felbermayer**
   (sops); [b]**Hilde Rössl-Majdan** (mez); [b]**Waldemar Kmentt** (ten); [a]**Helmut Wobisch** (tpt); [ac]**Vienna
   State Opera Orchestra / Anton Heiller;** [b]**Vienna Bach Guild Choir and Orchestra / Felix Prohaska.**
   Vanguard Classics Bach Guild Ⓜ 08.2028.71* (65 minutes: ADD: 10/94). Items marked [a] and [c]
   from PVL7078 (11/58), [b]PVL7004 (12/55). Recorded 1953-4.   ⓖ

This Vanguard reissue retains all of its interest today for lovers of Bach's music and for anyone mindful of the evolution of performing practice. The present disc does not quite measure up to the one reviewed further on but nevertheless has features which should appeal to collectors. Chief among them is the voice of Teresa Stich-Randall who sings two of the three cantatas for solo soprano assembled here (Nos. 51 and 209). Her clear-sounding, lightly textured voice and almost unfailingly secure technique were particularly suited to this repertoire, only her poor diction detracting from performances of considerable merit. Anton Heiller, who directs a section of the Vienna State Opera Orchestra in these two cantatas, chooses tempos somewhat more leisurely than those favoured by most performers of today. The soprano, Anny Felbermayer was, like Stich-Randall a regular singer with the Vienna State Opera, and her voice, more intimate than the other, is admirably suited to the beautiful Wedding Cantata (No. 202). She, at least, seldom lets us down but the accompaniment, especially continuo, is often too heavy, the harpsichord too prominent, and the recorded sound (1953) does, of course, show its age. But though Felix Prohaska's direction is a little stolid there is much to savour from the obbligato oboe playing and from Felbermayer's sunny side up view of the piece. The transfer to CD has been well mastered.

Additional recommendation ...

...No. 51. No. 82, Ich habe genug. No. 199, Mein Herze schwimmt in Blut. **Nancy Argenta** (sop);
   Ensemble Sonnerie / Monica Huggett (vn). Virgin Classics Veritas Ⓕ VC5 45038-2 (62 minutes:
   DDD: 12/94). 🖉

Bach Cantatas – No. 67, Halt im Gedächtnis Jesum Christ[a]; No. 108, Es ist euch gut, dass ich hingehe[a]; No. 127, Herr Jesu Christ, wahr' Mensch und Gott[b]. [b]**Antonia Fahberg** (sop); [a]**Lilian Benningsen** (contr); **Sir Peter Pears** (ten); **Kieth Engen** (bass); **Munich Bach Choir; Munich State Opera Orchestra / Karl Richter.** Teldec Das Alte Werk Ⓜ 9031-77614-2* (61 minutes: ADD: 5/93). Texts and translations included. Recorded 1958. New to UK.   ⊖⊖⊖
Collectors of Bach's choral music have strong views on Richter's performances, especially the church cantatas which represented the majority of his recorded output for Archiv. Most would agree that Richter's special affinity with Bach's music found its mark most persuasively in the 1960s before his mysterious adoption of the cloudy neo-romantic sound which did little to project his profound understanding of Bach's inner strength. Here we have a rarity from the late 1950s (a 'one-off' from Teldec not available in this country before) which forces us to revise our opinions about Richter's rigidity. These three cantatas were caught before the Munich Bach Orchestra had been formed though you would not know that they were not Bachians to the core; this is a state opera orchestra inspired by invigorating musical expression, blessed with an ignorance of self-conscious fashion. Certainly there are a few distracting mannerisms and a voice, notably Lilian Benningsen, which in hindsight seem somewhat out of place but they never detract from the prevailing conviction of the performances. In Cantata No. 67 the spirit of the text is directly and lucidly communicated by a spruce and well-balanced choral group, supported by the inimitable Peter Pears (a treasure or two here for his fans). The bass Keith Engen is also a Bach singer out of the top drawer; the opening aria of Cantata No. 108 is lovingly sung and the legendary Edgar Shann delivers an obbligato oboe line which is worth the cost of the disc alone, even without the other priceless revelations here.

Bach Cantatas – No. 73, Herr wie du willt, so schicks mit mir; No. 105, Herr, gehe nicht ins Gericht mit deinem Knecht; No. 131, Aus der Tiefen rufe ich, Herr, zu dir. **Barbara Schlick** (sop); **Gérard Lesne** (alto); **Howard Crook** (ten); **Peter Kooy** (bass); **Ghent Collegium Vocale Chorus and Orchestra / Philippe Herreweghe.** Virgin Classics Veritas Ⓔ VC7 59237-2 (58 minutes: DDD: 5/93). ✒ Texts and translations included. Recorded 1990.
Philippe Herreweghe's choir consists of some 16 voices to which he has added four excellent soloists, all of whom are experienced artists in this repertory. *Aus der Tiefen rufe ich* is one of Bach's earliest cantatas dating back to 1707 or 1708. The text is a setting of Psalm 130, *De profundis* with additional verses from a Lenten hymn. Herreweghe conveys the sombre intensity of the piece and is especially well served by his soloists, choir and solo oboist, with a particularly lyrical contribution from Howard Crook. Harmonically, No. 73 is a work of considerable strength. The Gospel-based text underlines the contrasting states of human frailty on the one hand and God's omnipotence on the other. Counterpart and subtle instrumentation play a part in the work's dark climax, a bass recitative and aria in which Bach's extraordinary gifts at evoking musical-textual imagery are on display. Peter Kooy is resonant, declamatory and affecting and is well supported on the whole by the strings, though the violins are thin at times. The beautiful *Herr, gehe nicht ins Gericht* is masterly from start to finish. The text focuses on two themes, the parable of the unjust steward and St Paul's warning to the Corinthians against idolatry and pride. Barbara Schlick is on top form, making this perhaps the interpretative high point of the entire recording; Bach's musical concept, furthermore, is breathtakingly original. She is affectingly partnered by Marc Ponseele whose delicately shaded oboe playing is all that one could wish for. Kooy declaims with firm control and a feeling for the poetry, and Crook is effective in his aria dispelling the emotional intensity of the earlier sections. Herreweghe manages all with tenderness and emotional restraint, achieving a sustained often deeply affecting performance. Three wonderful works, affectionately realized with solo contributions of distinction.

Bach Cantatas – No. 78, Jesu, der du meine Seele; No. 106, Gottes Zeit ist die allerbeste Zeit. **Teresa Stich-Randall** (sop); **Dagmar Hermann** (mez); **Anton Dermota** (ten); **Hans Braun** (bar); **Vienna Bach Guild Choir and Orchestra / Felix Prohaska.** Vanguard Classics Bach Guild mono/stereo Ⓜ 08.2009.71* (49 minutes: ADD: 9/93). Texts and translation included. From Top Rank 35/008 (1/60). Recorded 1954. *Gramophone* classical 100.   ⊖⊖⊖
This reissue effortlessly earns itself a place of distinction in the recorded heritage of Bach's sacred cantatas. One could even go further and say that Prohaska's performance of *Jesu, der du meine Seele* (No. 78) remains unrivalled to this day for its cohesive overall concept and for the great distinction of its soloists. This is a very fine performance indeed and one which no lover of Bach's music should be without. In the intervening years since this record was made, we have changed our ideas about many aspects of performance style; unlike No. 78 the other piece here, the *Actus Tragicus* (No. 106) falters a little from Prohaska's view that, since it is funeral music it must therefore be slow. The choral passages suffer accordingly, though the intimately scored and profoundly touching *Sonatina* is tenderly executed with an evident concern for historical veracity. Indeed, this recording may well have been among the very first to have used recorders and gambas as Bach required. Recordings of this calibre require no apologia in the wake of 'authenticity' and are a firm reminder that there was life in Bach performance before Karl Richter or Nikolaus Harnoncourt. Patchy, they may be but the finest things here shine out with a radiancy and a sensibility that deserves our approbation. Among the many wonderful elements to be found in No. 78 mention must be made, above all, of Anton Dermota's affecting account of the supplicatory tenor recitative with its confident aria "Dein Blut, so

meine Schuld durchstreit", limpidly accompanied by Hans Reznicek (flute), the lyrical and almost perfectly balanced partnership of Stich-Randall and Hermann in the duet "Wir eilen mit schwachen", supported by a lively continuo realization by Anton Heiller (organ), and the accompagnato "Die Wunden, Nägel, Kron und Grab" finely sustained by Braun. And the noble, elegiac sweep with which Prohaska imbues the opening chorus is on a par with all that follows. In short, a great release.

Bach Cantatas – No. 84, Ich bin vergnügt mit meinem Glücke; No. 202, Weichet nur, betrübte Schatten; No. 209, Non sa che sia dolore. **Nancy Argenta** (sop); **Ensemble Sonnerie / Monica Huggett.** Virgin Classics Veritas Ⓕ VC5 45059-2 (54 minutes: DDD: 6/95). ✒ Texts and translations included. Recorded 1993.   Ⓖ

Of the three works on this disc, No. 84 is the only sacred cantata. Unlike the better-known *Ich habe genug* (No. 82), its two alternating recitatives and arias are followed by a four-part chorale set to a melody which occupies an important place in Bach's work, *Wer nur den lieben Gott lässt walten*. Nos. 202 and 209 are, respectively, a wedding cantata – though not one which is linked in any way to the marriage service – and a piece commemorating the departure on a journey of an unidentified friend, presumably of the composer, whoever he may have been, since Bach's authorship is also sometimes questioned. Bach or not, it is a very engaging work with an extended concerto movement for flute and strings in B minor in which Bach unquestionably must have had at least a hand. The performances are very good indeed. Both Nos. 84 and 202 are dominated by oboe writing rich in fantasy and this aspect is well understood by oboist Paul Goodwin, above all in the wonderfully expressive opening arias of each work. Argenta's youthful voice is well suited to all this music yet it is, perhaps, especially alluring in the Italian cantata, No. 209, in whose more galant idiom she sounds completely at home. This is a captivating performance in which Argenta is sensitively partnered by the limpid flute playing of Lisa Beznosiuk.

Bach Cantatas. [a]**Allan Bergius,** [b]**Christoph Wegmann,** [a]**Helmut Wittek,** [d]**Stefan Gienger** (trebs); [e]**Kurt Equiluz** (ten); **Thomas Hampson** (bar); **Vienna Concentus Musicus / Nikolaus Harnoncourt.** Teldec Ⓕ 9031-74798-2 (55 minutes: DDD: 4/92). ✒ Recorded 1983-87.

No. 140, Wachet auf! ruft uns die Stimme – Wann kommst du, mein Heil?[a]; Mein Freund ist mein![a]. No. 146, Wir müssen durch viel Trübsal in das Reich Gottes eingehen – Wie will ich mich freuen[e] (all from 6 35653, 1/85). No. 147, Herz und Mund und Tat und Leben – Ich will von Jesu Wundern singen (6 35654, 7/85). No. 152, Tritt auf die Glaubensahn – Tritt auf die Glaubensbahn; Wie soll ich dich, Liebster der Seelen[b]. No. 153, Schau, lieber Gott, wie meine Feind – Fürchte dich nicht, ich bin bei dir. No. 154, Mein liebster Jesus ist verloren – Wisset ihr nicht (6 35656, 4/86). No. 185, Barmherziges Herze der ewigen Liebes – Das ist der Christen Kunst (2292-44179-2, 9/89). No. 192, Nun danket alle Gott – Der ewig reiche Gott[c]. No. 194, Höchsterwünschtes Freudenfest – Was des Höchsten Glanz erfüllt; O wie wohl ist uns geschehn[d] (2292-44193-2, 5/90). No. 196, Der Herr denket an uns – Der Herr segne euch[e] (2292-44194-2, 5/90).

This disc is both an alluring shop window for Teldec's complete series of Bach cantatas – though in no sense a substitute – and an attractive programme in its own right. Bach's sacred cantatas are richly endowed with vocal duets and the present issue offers only a selection from them. The common factor is the baritone, Thomas Hampson, who is partnered by some of the talented boy trebles who made such a distinctive contribution to the complete edition, and by the tenor, Kurt Equiluz. Hampson joined the team when the series was already two-thirds of the way through, so the earliest cantata to feature here is No. 140, *Wachet auf! ruft uns die Stimme*. That work, however, provides an auspicious starting-point since it contains two especially fine duets which are also among the most popular with audiences. Much else, though, will be comparatively unfamiliar to all but well-seasoned Bach cantata enthusiasts. In short, a very attractive compilation which, if it draws unsuspecting listeners into Bach's sacred dramatic wonderland will have more than fulfilled its purpose. Texts are not included, alas, but an accompanying note provides useful signposts to travellers in a strange land.

Additional recommendations ...

...No. 19, Es erhub sich ein Streit; No. 40, Dazu ist erschienen der Sohn Gottes; No. 70, Wachet, betet, seid bereit allezeit; No. 140; No. 149, Man singet mit Freuden vom Sieg; No. 180, Schmücke dich, o liebe Seele. **Soloists; Heinrich Schütz Choir, Heilbronn; Pforzheim Chamber Orchestra / Fritz Werner.** Erato Ⓜ 0630-11223-2 (two discs: 146 minutes: ADD: 2/96).   Ⓖ

...No. 4, Christ lag in Todesbanden; No. 150, Nach dir, Herr, verlanget mich; No. 196. **Soloists; Bach Collegium Japan / Masaaki Suzuki.** ✒ BIS Ⓕ CD751 (45 minutes: DDD: 6/96).

Bach Cantatas – No. 211, Schweigt stille, plaudert nicht, "Coffee"; No. 212, Mer hahn en neue Oberkeet, "Peasant". **Emma Kirkby** (sop); **Rogers Covey-Crump** (ten); **David Thomas** (bass); **Academy of Ancient Music / Christopher Hogwood.** L'Oiseau-Lyre Ⓕ 417 621-2OH (52 minutes: DDD: 10/89). ✒ Texts and translations included.   Ⓖ

These two most delightful of Bach's secular cantatas here receive sparkling performances fully alive to the humour and invention of the music. The *Coffee* Cantata illustrates a family altercation over a current enthusiasm, the drinking of coffee. A narrator tells the story whilst the soprano and bass soloists confront each other in a series of delightful arias. Thomas brings out the crabby dyspeptic side of Schlendrian's character imaginatively and Kirkby makes a charming minx-like Lieschen.

Covey-Crump's sweet light tenor acts as a good foil. The *Peasant* Cantata also takes the form of a dialogue, here between a somewhat dull and simple young man and his sweetheart Mieke, a girl who intends to better herself. Through the 24 short movements Bach conjures up a wonderfully rustic picture with some vivid dance numbers and rumbustious ritornellos. The soloists' nicely rounded characterizations emerge with great humour and Hogwood directs with vitality and sprightly rhythmic control. The recording is excellent.

Additional recommendations ...

...No. 202, Weichet nur, betrübte Schatten, "Wedding Cantata"[a]. No. 209, Non sa che sia dolore[a]. Nos. 211 and 212[abc]. [a]**Elly Ameling** (sop); [b]**Gerald English** (ten); [c]**Siegmund Nimsgern** (bass); **Collegium Aureum.** Deutsche Harmonia Mundi Editio Classica Ⓜ GD77151 (two discs: 106 minutes: ADD: 10/90). ✍

...No. 211. No. 213, Hercules auf dem Scheidewege. **Barbara Bonney** (sop); **Ralf Popken** (alto); **Christoph Prégardien** (ten); **David Wilson-Johnson** (bar); **Orchestra and Choir of the Age of Enlightenment / Gustav Leonhardt.** Philips Ⓕ 442 779-2PH (74 minutes: DDD: 7/95). ✍

...No. 82, Ich habe genung – Ich habe genug!; Schlummert ein; No. 202, Weichet nur, betrübte Schatten; No. 209, Non sa che sia dolore; Nos. 211 and 212 – excerpts. Anna Magdalena Notenbuch – Bist du bei mir. *Coupled with works by* **C.P.E. Bach, Telemann, Handel, Brahms, Schumann** and **Schubert Elly Ameling** (sop); **Various soloists;** Deutsche Harmonia Mundi Ⓕ 74321 26617-2 (four discs: 239 minutes: ADD: 12/95). *See review in the Collections section; refer to the Index to Reviews.*

Bach Motets – Singet dem Herren, BWV225; Der Geist hilft unsrer Schwachheit auf, BWV226; Jesu meine Freude, BWV227; Fürchte dich nicht, BWV228; Komm, Jesu, komm, BWV229; Lobet den Herren, BWV230. **Greta de Reyghere, Katelijne van Laetham** (sops); **Martin van der Zeijst, Sytse Buwalda** (altos); **Hans Hermann Jansen** (ten); **Johannes-Christoph Happel** (bar); **La Petite Bande Choir; La Petite Bande / Sigiswald Kuijken.** Accent Ⓔ ACC9287D (65 minutes: DDD: 5/93). ✍ Texts and translations included. Recorded 1992.

Bach Motets – Singet dem Herren, BWV225; Der Geist hilft unsrer Schwachheit auf, BWV226; Jesu meine Freude, BWV227; Fürchte dich nicht, BWV228; Komm, Jesu, komm, BWV229; Lobet den Herren, BWV230. **Netherlands Chamber Choir / Ton Koopman.** Philips Ⓕ 434 165-2PH (63 minutes: DDD: 5/93). ✍ Texts and translations included. Recorded 1986-7.

These two approaches to Bach's Motets differ strongly from one another. Sigiswald Kuijken directs performances with *colla parte* instrumental support, that is to say with instruments doubling each of the vocal strands. Ton Koopman, on the other hand, prefers the vocal strands *a cappella* with instruments providing only the basso continuo. The choir in each version is made up of women sopranos and countertenors with the men's voices. Choosing between the versions is difficult and, to a large extent must be a matter of which approach you prefer. Kuijken's performances are more relaxed than those of Koopman. He avoids anything in the nature of over-direction and, while neither singing nor playing is always quite as tidy as it might be, there is a lively spontaneity, especially rewarding in the radiant performance of *Singet dem Herren*. Koopman draws more sharply articulated singing than Kuijken from the Netherlands Chamber Choir though sometimes at the expense of natural declamation and spontaneity. But there is greater linear clarity here than in the other and it pays off handsomely in *Komm, Jesu, komm*. It is a pity that Koopman does not avail himself of the surviving instrumental parts for *Der Geist hilft* but, in other respects, the strengths and weaknesses of the two performances are fairly evenly distributed and both are highly recommended.

Additional recommendations ...

...*As above.* O Jesu Christ, meins Lebens Licht, BWV118. **Agnès Mellon, Greta de Reyghere** (sops); **Vincent Darras** (alto); **Howard Crook** (ten); **Peter Kooy** (bass); **Collegium Vocale; La Chapelle Royale Chorus and Orchestra / Philippe Herreweghe.** Harmonia Mundi Ⓕ HMC90 1231 (67 minutes: DDD: 12/86). ✍

...*As above.* **Trinity College Choir, Cambridge / Richard Marlow** with **Graham Jackson and Richard Pearce** (orgs). Conifer Ⓕ CDCF158 (66 minutes: DDD: 12/88).

Bach Magnificat in D major, BWV243[a].
Vivaldi Ostro picta, RV642[b]. Gloria in D major, RV589[c]. [abc]**Emma Kirkby**, [ac]**Tessa Bonner** (sops); [ac]**Michael Chance** (alto); [a]**John Mark Ainsley** (ten); [a]**Stephen Varcoe** (bar); **Collegium Musicum 90 Chorus and Orchestra / Richard Hickox.** Chandos Chaconne Ⓕ CHAN0518 (64 minutes: DDD: 7/91). ✍ Texts and translations included. Recorded 1990.   Ⓖ

This issue was the first CD release featuring the then newly founded Collegium Musicum 90 under its directors Richard Hickox and Simon Standage. The Collegium embraces both choir and orchestra who are joined in this programme of Bach and Vivaldi by a comparably fine team of soloists. Hickox sets effective tempos in Bach's *Magnificat* and points up the many striking contrasts in colour and texture with which the piece abounds. From among the many successful features of the recording Stephen Varcoe's "Quia fecit mihi magna" and the "Et misericordia" sung by Michael Chance and John Mark Ainsley stand out. Vivaldi's *Gloria*, RV589 is the better known of two settings by the composer in D major. In this programme it is prefaced by an introductory motet *Ostro picta*, which may well in fact belong to the *Gloria* and here sung with warmth and radiance by Emma Kirkby. Hickox's performance of this evergreen vocal masterpiece comes over with conviction. It is gracefully phrased, sensitively sung and affectingly paced with an admirable rapport between vocalists and instrumentalists. The recorded sound is first-rate.

Additional recommendations ...

...Magnificat. Cantata No. 51, Jauchzet Gott in allen Landen!. **Soloists; English Baroque Soloists / John Eliot Gardiner.** Philips Ⓕ 411 458-2PH (41 minutes: DDD: 9/85). 🖋

...Magnificat. Cantata No. 21, Ich hatte viel Bekümmernis. **Soloists; Netherlands Chamber Choir; La Petite Bande / Sigiswald Kuijken.** Virgin Classics Veritas Ⓕ VC7 59528-2 (73 minutes: DDD: 2/90). 🖋

...Magnificat. **Vivaldi** Gloria. **Soloists; Academy of St Martin in the Fields Chorus and Orchestra / Sir Neville Marriner.** EMI Ⓕ CDC7 54283-2 (56 minutes: DDD: 3/92).

...Magnificat. Cantata No. 10, Meine Seele erhebt den Herrn. **Soloists; Stuttgart Gächinger Kantorei; Stuttgart Bach Collegium / Helmuth Rilling.** Hänssler Classic Ⓕ 98 921 (50 minutes: DDD: 2/96).

Bach Mass in B minor, BWV232. **Nancy Argenta** (sop); **Catherine Denley** (mez); **Mark Tucker** (ten); **Stephen Varcoe** (bar); **Collegium Musicum 90 Chorus and Orchestra / Richard Hickox.** Chandos Chaconne Ⓕ CHAN0533/4 (two discs: 108 minutes: DDD: 1/93). 🖋 Texts and translations included. Recorded 1992. ⒼⒼ

The reputation of Chandos's early music label Chaconne is now firmly established. Richard Hickox, his soloists and the Collegium Musicum 90 Chorus and Orchestra deliver a performance of this Mass which is satisfying on many levels. Hickox has a proven track-record with choirs and here he comes across as an effective disciplinarian in his firm control both of voicse and instruments. Yet he avoids imposing that autocratic will on his forces which sometimes lessens the spontaneity of rival performances. Perhaps his strength lies more in the handling of the extrovert and most joyful sections of the Mass than in the deeply contemplative ones. Thus the *Et in terra pax*, for instance, comes over especially well with articulate and transparently textured choral singing supported by robust but none the less sympathetic orchestral playing. The solo vocalists make a strong, even team and the use of a mezzo-soprano offers a welcome alternative in the *Agnus Dei* which, in most period instrument performances has unjustly become the sole preserve of countertenors. It may be that some other versions intermittently achieve greater heights of intensity but, taken as a whole, this lively, spontaneous and consistently accomplished version is a fine achievement.

Additional recommendations ...

...**Soloists; Taverner Consort; Taverner Players / Andrew Parrott.** EMI Reflexe Ⓕ CDS7 47293-8 (two discs: 103 minutes: DDD: 8/86). 🖋 Ⓖ

...**Monteverdi Choir; English Baroque Soloists / John Eliot Gardiner.** Archiv Produktion Ⓕ 415 514-2AH2 (two discs: 105 minutes: DDD: 2/86). 🖋 Ⓖ

...**Soloists; Ghent Collegium Vocale Chorus and Orchestra / Philippe Herrweghe.** Virgin Classics Veritas Ⓕ VCD7 59517-2 (two discs: 107 minutes: DDD: 8/89). 🖋

...**Soloists; Netherlands Bach Society Collegium Musicum; La Petite Bande / Gustav Leonhardt.** Deutsche Harmonia Mundi Editio Classica Ⓜ GD77040 (two discs: 111 minutes: ADD: 6/90). 🖋 Ⓖ

...**Soloists; The Sixteen Choir and Orchestra / Harry Christophers.** Collins Classics Ⓕ 7032-2 (two discs: 106 minutes: DDD: 11/94). 🖋

...**Soloists; Vienna Boys' Choir; Viennensis Chorus; Vienna Concentus Musicus / Nikolaus Harnoncourt.** Teldec Das Alte Werk Ⓜ 4509-95517-2 (two discs: 107 minutes: ADD: 4/95). 🖋

...**Soloists; Bavarian Radio Chorus; Baverian Radio Symphony Orchestra / Eugen Jochum.** EMI Forte Ⓜ CZS5 68640-2 (two discs: 122 minutes: ADD: 5/96).

Bach Masses – A major, BWV234; G minor, BWV235. Sanctus in D major, BWV238. **Agnès Mellon** (sop); **Gérard Lesne** (alto); **Christoph Prégardien** (ten); **Peter Kooy** (bass); **Ghent Collegium Vocale Chorus and Orchestra / Philippe Herreweghe.** Virgin Classics Veritas Ⓕ VC7 59587-2 (64 minutes: DDD: 1/91). 🖋 Texts and translations included. Recorded 1989.

That Bach's four short Masses have excited so little interest is doubtless a result of the bad press they have attracted over the years: "more barbaric parodies cannot be imagined" was Albert Schweitzer's opinion, and his evaluation – if rather blunt – is typical of the disdain felt for these works by Bach scholars who could not forgive the composer for re-cycling a few of his cantatas and thereby treading on their romantic notions of the original creative artist. But unless the B minor Mass itself – just as much a patchwork of secondhand material – is also to be classed as 'barbaric', few listeners today will be able to find much to object to in these charming pieces, in which Bach's personality shines through just as strongly as in any of his more reputable creations. And how many people *know* Cantata No. 187? Philippe Herreweghe's recordings of the Masses in G minor and A major – along with the sprightly (and original) D major Sanctus, BWV238 – should not, then, be of interest only to Bach enthusiasts. Both Masses share the same formal outline, the main contrast between them arising instead from their instrumental colouring, as Bach supplements the strings with oboes in BWV235, and flutes in BWV234. Herreweghe maximizes this gentle distinction by fixing his efforts on achieving a smooth blend and a rich, reverberant sound, in which he is undoubtedly helped by the echoing church acoustic of the Abbaye aux Dames in Saintes. If the sheer nobility and tenderness of Bach's church music appeals to you then you will have no problems with this disc.

Additional recommendations...

...BWV235[a]; G major, BWV236[b]. **Soloists; Stuttgart Gächinger Kantorei; [a]Stuttgart Bach Collegium; [b]Stuttgart Chamber Orchestra / Helmuth Rilling.** Hänssler Classic Ⓕ 98 962 (52 minutes: DDD: 10/93).

...F major, BWV233; BWV234; BWV235; G major, BWV236. Sanctus in C major, BWV237. Sanctus, BWV238. Sanctus in D minor, BWV239. Sanctus in G major, BWV240. Sanctus in D major, BWV241. Christe eleison in G minor, BWV242. **Lausanne Vocal Ensemble and Chamber Orchestra / Michel Corboz.** Erato Ⓕ 4509-97236-2.

...BWV233[a]; BWV234[b]. **Soloists; Stuttgart Gächinger Kantorei; [a]Franz Liszt Chamber Orchestra; [b]Stuttgart Bach Collegium / Helmuth Rilling.** Hänssler Classic Ⓕ 98 924 (55 minutes: DDD: 2/96).

New review

Bach St John Passion, BWV245 (sung in English). **Sir Peter Pears** (ten) Evangelist; **Gwynne Howell** (bass) Jesus; **Heather Harper, Jenny Hill** (sops); **Alfreda Hodgson** (contr); **Robert Tear, Russell Burgess, John Tobin, Adrian Thompson** (tens); **John Shirley-Quirk** (bar); **Wandsworth School Boys' Choir; English Chamber Orchestra / Benjamin Britten.** Double Decca Ⓜ 443 859-2DF2 (two discs: 130 minutes: ADD: 7/95). Recorded 1971.

Britten's recording of the *St John Passion* is very special indeed. He apparently preferred to perform this Bach choral work because of its natural potential for drama. With Sir Peter Pears a superb Evangelist (and you can hear every word!) this account takes over the listener completely. The soloists are all splendid, though one must single out the glorious contribution of Heather Harper, and the choral response is inspirational in its moments of sheer fervour. Britten's direction is both urgent and volatile, the Wandsworth School Boys' Choir sing out full-throatedly and the English Chamber Orchestra underpin the whole performance with gloriously rich string textures. (Listening to this unique recording one is tempted to conclude that the 'authentic' string sound, for all its clarity and bite, is less desirable than modern instruments in an expansive work of this kind.) Then there is the analogue recording itself which, even after a quarter of a century, offers a demonstration of ambient fullness, vividness of detail and natural balance. In fact, one gets the impression that a live performance at The Maltings, Snape has been transported to the area just beyond one's speakers – an amazing achievement! As a bonus it is available at mid price.

Additional recommendations ...

...**Soloists; Monteverdi Choir; English Baroque Soloists / John Eliot Gardiner.** Archiv Produktion Ⓕ 419 324-2AH2 (two discs: 107 minutes: DDD: 2/87). 🎵   Ⓖ

...**Soloists; Ghent Collegium Vocale; La Chapelle Royale Orchestra / Philippe Herreweghe.** Harmonia Mundi Ⓕ HMC90 1264/5 (two discs: 115 minutes: DDD: 5/88). 🎵

...**Soloists; La Petite Bande Choir and Orchestra / Sigiswald Kuijken.** Deutsche Harmonia Mundi Editio Classica Ⓜ GD77041 (two discs: 122 minutes: ADD: 6/90). 🎵

Bach St Matthew Passion, BWV244. **Anthony Rolfe Johnson** (ten) Evangelist; **Andreas Schmidt** (bar) Jesus; **Barbara Bonney, Ann Monoyios** (sops); **Anne Sofie von Otter** (mez); **Michael Chance** (alto); **Howard Crook** (ten); **Olaf Bär** (bar); **Cornelius Hauptmann** (bass); **London Oratory Junior Choir; Monteverdi Choir; English Baroque Soloists / John Eliot Gardiner.** Archiv Produktion Ⓕ 427 648-2AH3 (three discs: 167 minutes: DDD: 10/89). 🎵 Text and translation included. *Gramophone Award Winner 1990.*   ⒼⒼⒼ

New review

Bach St Matthew Passion, BWV244. **Christoph Prégardien** (ten) Evangelist; **Klaus Mertens** (bass) Jesus; **Monika Frimmer, Veronika Winter** (sops); **Susanne Norin** (mez); **Wilfried Jochens** (ten); **Hans-Georg Wimmer** (bass); **Rheinische Kantorei; Das Kleine Konzert / Hermann Max.** Capriccio Ⓕ 60 046-2 (two discs: 153 minutes: DDD: 7/96). 🎵 Text and translation included.

What makes John Eliot Gardiner's *St Matthew Passion* stand out in the face of stiff competition is perhaps more than anything his vivid sense of theatre. Bach's score is, after all, a sacred drama and Gardiner interprets this aspect of the work with lively and colourful conviction. That in itself, of course, is not sufficient to ensure a fine performance but here we have a first-rate group of solo voices, immediately responsive choral groups in the Monteverdi Choir and the London Oratory Junior Choir – a distinctive element this – and refined obbligato and orchestral playing from the English Baroque Soloists. Anthony Rolfe Johnson declaims the Evangelist's role with clarity, authority and the subtle inflexion of an accomplished story-teller. Ann Monoyios, Howard Crook and Olaf Bär also make strong contributions but it is Michael Chance's "Erbarme dich", tenderly accompanied by the violin obbligato, which sets the seal of distinction on the performance. Singing and playing of this calibre deserve to win many friends and Gardiner's deeply-felt account of Bach's great Passion does the music considerable justice. Clear recorded sound.

There is much to be said in favour of Capriccio's recording of Bach's 'Great Passion'. The solo vocal group are mainly excellent, the voices of the Rheinische Kantorei often outstandingly affecting, and the instrumental playing on period instruments, warm in sound and technically fluent. And, from a practical and budgetary viewpoint, it is also appealing, for the entire Passion is contained on two discs rather than the customary three. The role of the Evangelist is entrusted to that most ubiquitous of tenors, Christoph Prégardien. His is a voice that has steadily developed since his earlier recording with Gustav Leonhardt. Klaus Mertens, too, is affecting through his sensitive colouring of the words. Each has notably clear diction and a lively ear for subtle nuances of tone. By and large, the remainder of the soloists are also appealing. The lioness's share of the solo soprano work is taken by Monika Frimmer. Her youthful-sounding, unaffected voice is attractive although can can detect occasional insecurity of technique and unsteadiness in her declamation of recitatives. Susanne Norin manages her several arias with a vocal and emotional restraint which complements the overall approach in this performance. Wilfried Jochens is effective, bringing a sense of theatre to his interpretations; Hans-Georg Wimmer is more of a baritone than a bass and it is the middle range of his voice which impresses most. In some of the arias you might feel that Hermann Max pushes the tempo along just a shade too fast but the drama is well paced and stylishly executed. In summary, this is a reading which satisfies one's sensibilities on several different levels. Traditionalists may not like it much but others should consider it, for it is certainly the most impressive of any recent newcomers.

Additional recommendations ...

...Soloists; **Ghent Collegium Vocale; La Chapelle Royale Chorus and Orchestra / Philippe Herreweghe.** Harmonia Mundi Ⓕ HMC90 1155/7 (three discs: 171 minutes: DDD: 11/85). ✒ Ⓖ

...Soloists; **Tölz Boys' Choir; La Petite Bande Men's Chorus and Orchestra / Gustav Leonhardt.** Deutsche Harmonia Mundi Ⓕ RD77848 (three discs: 172 minutes: DDD: 5/90). ✒

...Soloists; **Breda Sacraments Choir; Netherlands Bach Society Choir; Amsterdam Baroque Orchestra / Ton Koopman.** Erato Ⓕ 2292-45814-2 (three discs: 174 minutes: DDD: 5/93). ✒ Ⓖ

...Soloists; **Munich Boys' Choir; Munich Bach Choir; Munich Bach Orchestra / Karl Richter.** Archiv Produktion Ⓜ 439 338-2AX3 (three discs: 197 minutes: ADD: 6/94).

...Soloists; **Hungarian Festival Chorus; Hungarian Radio Children's Choir; Hungarian State Philharmonic Orchestra / Géza Oberfrank.** Naxos Ⓢ 8 550832/4 (three discs: 163 minutes: DDD: 8/94).

Bach Christmas Oratorio, BWV248. **Theo Altmeyer** (ten) Evangelist and arias; **Hans Buchhierl** (treb); **Andreas Stein** (boy alto); **Barry McDaniel** (bar); **Tölz Boys' Choir; Collegium Aureum / Gerhard Schmidt-Gaden.** Deutsche Harmonia Mundi Editio Classica Ⓜ GD77046 (three discs: 163 minutes: ADD: 4/88). Notes, text and translation included. From EMI CDS7 49119-8 (4/88). Recorded 1973. Ⓖ

This performance of Bach's *Christmas Oratorio* possesses a radiance and a spontaneity perhaps unrivalled by more modern and carefully contrived versions. It is not without its weaknesses, which lie mainly in passages of insecure instrumental playing; but these are outweighed by its merits chief among which, perhaps, are the contributions, both solo and choral, of the Tölz Boys' Choir. All the soprano and alto solos are sung by boys and in the choruses it is boys rather than countertenors who sing the alto line. Gerhard Schmidt-Gaden, the chorusmaster and conductor, effectively relaxed tempos which may at first sound too leisurely to ears accustomed to the frenetic pace chosen by some rival versions. Occasionally, he is a little too slow as, for instance, in the opening chorus of Part Four but for the most part he directs a performance free from intrusive mannerisms which bedevil too many performances of baroque music today. The treble, Hans Buchhierl and the alto, Andreas Stein, are outstanding, and the tenor Theo Altmeyer and the baritone, Barry McDaniel, are hardly less impressive. With its ingenuousness, its spirit of innocent joy and in its simple but sensitive response to the music this performance comes closer than most to the contemplative heart of Bach's Christmas masterpiece.

Additional recommendations ...

...Soloists; **Vienna Boys' Choir; Chorus Viennensis; Vienna Concentus Musicus / Nikolaus Harnoncourt.** Teldec Ⓕ 9031-77610-2 (two discs: 155 minutes: DDD: 12/86). ✒

...Soloists; **Monteverdi Choir; English Baroque Soloists / John Eliot Gardiner.** Archiv Produktion Ⓕ 423 232-2AH2 (two discs: 140 minutes: DDD: 12/87). ✒

...Soloists; **Munich Bach Choir and Orchestra / Karl Richter.** Archiv Produktion Ⓜ 427 236-2AX3 (three discs: 168 minutes: ADD: 3/89).

...Soloists; **Ghent Collegium Vocale Chorus and Orchestra / Philippe Herreweghe.** Virgin Classics Veritas Ⓕ VCD7 59530-2 (two discs: 150 minutes: DDD: 12/89). ✒ Ⓖ

...Soloists; **Frankfurt Vocal Ensemble; Cologne Concerto / Ralf Otto.** Capriccio Ⓕ 60 025-2 (two discs: 141 minutes: DDD: 4/92). ✒

...Soloists; **Munich Bach Choir and Orchestra / Karl Richter.** Teldec Ⓑ 4509-97902-2 (three discs: 169 minutes: ADD: 5/96). *See review in the Collections section; refer to the Index to Reviews.*

Bach Easter Oratorio, BWV249. Cantata No. 11, Lobet Gott in seinen Reichen (Ascension Oratorio). **Monika Frimmer** (sop); **Ralf Popken** (alto); **Christoph Prégardien** (ten); **David Wilson-Johnson** (bar); **Choir and Orchestra of the Age of Enlightenment / Gustav Leonhardt.** Philips Ⓕ 442 119-2PH (73 minutes: DDD: 10/94). ✒ Texts and translations included. Recorded 1993. Ⓖ

Bach Easter Oratorio, BWV249. Cantata No. 66, Erfreut euch, ihr Herzen. **Barbara Schlick** (sop); **Kai Wessel** (alto); **James Taylor** (ten); **Peter Kooy** (bass); **Collegium Vocale / Philippe Herreweghe.** Harmonia Mundi Ⓕ HMC90 1513 (73 minutes: DDD: 5/95). ✒ Texts and translations included. Recorded 1994. Ⓖ

The Easter Oratorio does not quite fulfil traditional expectations of what constitutes an oratorio: no grand proportions like Christmas (though one might also argue the extent to which that series of tableaux conforms to the medium), no biblical text like the compact Ascension Oratorio or indeed named 'personae' as in the Passions. One might assume, moreover, that the greatest feast in the Christian calendar should have goaded Bach to a more extended effort than an average-sized cantata. That aside, we are left with a work of customary Bachian brilliance in the quality of individual movements, even if the whole is not entirely satisfying. It does, however, carry a unique flavour and one with which Leonhardt clearly feels a close affinity. This is evident in the way he handles the exuberant Sinfonia with knowing and stately bravura, gently nudging the dance-inspired meter with subtle accentuation, also providing copious insights into the phrasing of the wonderful wind dialogues – all played with fastidious clarity and *élan* by the OAE. The chorus is fairly streamlined and although the quality of singing goes without saying, Herreweghe's Collegium Vocale bring greater breadth to Bach's choruses in the second work, despite a less convincing recorded sound. If Herreweghe appears to push the tempos in these movements, Leonhardt is inclined to rest on his laurels with a distinctly laid-back approach. The soloists are variable. Only Ralf Popken in "Saget, saget mir" gives cause for celebration. Christoph Prégardien is not at his best in "Sanfte soll mein Todeskummer" from the Easter Oratorio, where his voice sounds remarkably colourless and flat. Monika Frimmer, too, struggles to find a 'gracious countenance' to accompany her Ascension aria, "Jesu, deine Gnadenblicke". Despite some minor misgivings, Leonhardt's Easter Oratorio is appealing. As for the Ascension Oratorio, Herreweghe's has some exceptional solo singing but Leonhardt is still a front-runner and this recording certainly has its revelatory moments.

In the Easter Oratorio Herreweghe has the edge over his competitors in the quality of his solo contributions. Unlike his peers, he takes the version Bach made for 1725 (he revised the work again in 1735) where specific characters express the text: Mary Magdalen, say, rather than merely "Soprano" as Bach preferred it ten years later – though, ironically, having dropped the characters he then called the work 'oratorio' for the first time! The difference is minimal but one cannot help identifying more easily with the Easter story when Barbara Schlick represents "Mary Mother of James", especially when the music is sung as involvingly as it is here. The centrepiece of the work is the exquisite pastoral *sommeil*, "Sanfte soll", which James Taylor, if tonally a touch reticent in places, performs with considerable charm. The three fine arias in this work are capped by the uplifting "Saget" aria, where Mary Magdalen searches gleefully for the risen Christ. Herreweghe catches the spirit of this like no one else and Kai Wessel is an invigorating advocate for this magnificent creation. Herreweghe includes the sparkling and distinctive Easter work, *Erfreut euch*, also derived from a secular source, where he revels both in the textural contrasts and the inimitable vocalized homogeneity of his group, Collegium Vocale.

Further listening ...

...Harpsichord Concertos – A major, BWV1055; F minor, BWV1056; F major, BWV1057. **Hae-won Chang** (pf); **Camerata Cassovia / Robert Stankovsky.** Naxos 8 550423.

...Trio Sonatas   D minor, BWV1036; C major, BWV1037; G major, BWV1038; G major, BWV1039. **London Baroque.** Harmonia Mundi HMC90 1173 (6/86). 🖎

...Three Sonatas for Viola da gamba and Harpsichord, BWV1027-29. **Kim Kashkashian** (va); **Keith Jarrett** (hpd). ECM New Series 445 230-2 (1/95).

...An Wasserflüssen Babylon, BWV653. Von Gott will ich nicht lassen, BWV658. Wer nur den lieben Gott lässt walten, BWV690 and BWV691. Vom Himmel hoch, da komm ich her, BWV700 and BWV701. Jesus, meine Zuversicht, BWV728. Liebster Jesu, wir sind hier, BWV730 and BWV731. Meine Seele erhebt den Herren, BWV733. Fantasia and Fugue in C minor, BWV537. Preludes and Fugues – B minor, BWV544; C major, BWV547. Fugue in G minor, BWV578. Trio in D minor, BWV583. **Nicholas Danby** (org). Sony Classical Digital Club SMK64239 (5/95).

Complete Organ Works:

...**Kevin Boyer** (org) – *Volume 1* (reviewed above). *Volume 2*, Nimbus NI5289.

...**Michel Chapuis** (org) – Auvidis Valois V4425-2 (1-4). *Also available separately.*

...**Hans Fagius** (org) – *Volume 1*, BIS CD235/6 (11/86). *Volume 2*, BIS CD308/9. *Volume 3*, BIS CD329/30. *Volume 4*, BIS CD343/4 (10/91). *Volume 5*, BIS CD379/80. *Volume 6*, BIS CD397/8. *Volume 7*, BIS CD439/40 (10/91). *Volume 8*, BIS CD443/4. *Volume 9*, BIS CD445 (10/91).

...**André Isoir** (org) – Calliope CAL9703/17 (*Volumes 1-5*). *Volume 6*, CAL9708. *Volume 7*, CAL9709. *Volume 8*, CAL9710 (8/89). *Volume 9*, CAL9711 (4/88). *Volume 10*, CAL9712. *Volume 12*, CAL9714. *Volume 13*, CAL9715. *Volume 14*, CAL9716. *Volume 15*, CAL9717.

Wilhelm Friedemann Bach   German 1710-1784

New review

W.F. Bach Harpsichord Concertos – D major, F41; F minor, F44; A minor, F45. **London Baroque** (Richard Egarr, hpd; Ingrid Seifert, Richard Gwilt, vns; Irmgard Schaller, va; Charles Medlam, vc). Harmonia Mundi Ⓟ HMC90 1558 (54 minutes: DDD: 5/96). 🖎 Recorded 1995.

W.F. Bach wrote four concertos for harpsichord and strings. Two of the works, F41 and F44, belong to Bach's Dresden period (1733-46), a third, F45, may pre-date these, though the matter has long been controversial, while a fourth, F43, is probably the latest. Harpsichordist Richard Egarr, with London Baroque, has chosen three of them and is partnered by single strings. The approach has its merits but the chief strengths of this release lie in a perceptive understanding of those highly individual gestures, inner tensions and swift changes of mood which embody the ethos of the *Empfindsamer Stil*. Not that this highly gifted member of the Bach clan embraced *Empfindsamkeit* wholeheartedly, for one of the many fascinating aspects of his style – and one of its most distinctive – is its constant oscillation between past and present. His feeling for melody is more apparent than that of Carl Philipp Emanuel and more effortless, too – the sustained beauty of the *Adagio molto* of the F major Concerto is an example – but there is also a darker, brooding side to this music. Wilhelm Friedemann's style seems to reflect much of what we know about his unsettled disposition. The performances are fluent, vital and idiomatically perceptive. To begin with you may find the violins a little astringent in tone but you will soon adjust to that and find yourself enjoying the clarity of texture afforded by the one-to-a-part approach. The players all have an awareness of just how much every little gesture counts in this music and this both enlivens and enriches their performances.

W.F. Bach Keyboard Sonatas – G major, F7; No. 2 in A major, F8; No. 7 in C major, F2.
Eight Fugues, F31. March, F30. Prelude, F29. Suite in G minor, F24. **Christophe Rousset** (hpd).
Harmonia Mundi Musique d'abord Ⓑ HMA190 1305 (65 minutes: DDD: 8/94). ✔ Recorded
1989.   Ⓖ
This disc confirms the independence and originality of one of the least known of J.S. Bach's sons – Wilhelm Friedemann. His remarkable Fantasia in C major, F2 brings a darkly dramatic opening, then immediately evokes memories of Johann Sebastian's Chromatic Fantasia, BWV903 in its florid brilliance, yet has a voice very much its own. Two sonatas are hardly less striking: the G major, F7 has a thoughtful "Lament" at its centre and an engaging finale, which Rousset despatches with fine dash, while the A major, F8 brings a closing Presto – a flowing moto perpetuo – that could almost become a lollipop if given more exposure. Rousset was only 19 when he recorded this recital. Yet he plays with remarkable maturity and discernment throughout. He certainly reveals the diversity of the eight succinct miniature Fugues which readily demonstrate Wilhelm's contrapuntal mastery.

W.F. Bach Cantatas, Volume 1 – Lasset uns ablegen die Werke der Finsternis, F80; Es ist eine
Stimme eines Predigers in der Wüste, F89. **Barbara Schlick** (sop); **Claudia Schubert** (contr);
Wilfried Jochens (ten); **Stephan Schreckenberger** (bass); **Rheinische Kantorei; Das Kleine Konzert /
Hermann Max.** Capriccio Ⓕ 10 425 (54 minutes: DDD: 11/94). ✔ Texts and translations
included. Recorded 1991.   ⒼⒼ
W.F. Bach Cantatas, Volume 2 – Sinfonia in D major, F64; Dies ist der Tag, F85[a]; Erzittert und
fallet, F83[a]. [a]**Barbara Schlick** (sop); [a]**Claudia Schubert** (contr); [a]**Wilfried Jochens** (ten); [a]**Stephan
Schreckenberger** (bass); [a]**Rheinische Kantorei; Das Kleine Konzert / Hermann Max.** Capriccio
Ⓕ 10 426 (60 minutes: DDD: 11/94). ✔ Texts and translations included. Recorded 1991.   ⒼⒼ
These two discs of sacred cantatas by Bach's eldest son, Wilhelm Friedemann, make a valuable contribution towards a fuller understanding of this highly gifted but complex and somewhat enigmatic member of the Bach clan. The stylistic vocabulary is both rich and varied, often harking back to a strong paternal influence – what better one has there ever been? – but with equal fluency reflecting the current *galant* style, fragrantly seasoned from time to time with the spirit of the more northerly German *Empfindsamer Stil*. The cantatas are rich in points of interest. The athletic trumpet and vocal writing of the opening chorus of the St John's Day cantata, *Es ist eine Stimme eines Predigers in der Wüste* ("The voice of him that crieth in the wilderness") are immediately arresting; so, too, is the wonderfully rhapsodic organ obbligato which accompanies the *galant*, virtuoso soprano aria of the same work. By contrast, the cello part of the following continuo aria for bass, though virtuosic, has its foot firmly in baroque phraseology. The cantatas, *Dies ist der Tag* ("This is the day") and *Erzittert und fallet* ("Tremble and fall") probably date from the late 1750s and are less Janus-like in their musical stance. The Whitsun cantata, *Dies ist der Tag* is a particularly festive piece which is prefaced by a three-movement Sinfonia scored for horns, flutes, oboes, bassoon and strings. This in fact replaces the more usual elaborate choral movement, choral writing being confined to a simple concluding hymn verse. The two arias, one with limpid writing for two flutes, the other with horns, are beguiling and thoroughly *au courant* with the developing style of early classicism. *Erzittert und fallet* was composed for Easter Day and begins with a vocally demanding chorus foreshadowing Telemann's "Es rauscht" at the beginning of the second part of his oratorio, *Der Tag des Gerichts* (1762). The three arias are in strong contrast with one another. One, for tenor, is lightly accompanied by two flutes, the second, a ravishing pastoral duet for soprano and baritone with oboe d'amore, the third, for soprano, a turbulent evocation of "floods and thunderous lightnings". Imaginative programming, sympathetic performances and, all in all, something of a musical revelation. Full texts and informative notes set the seal on recordings of distinction.

Further listening ...
...Sinfonia in F major. *Coupled with* **C.P.E. Bach** Sinfonias, H663-6 – No. 1 in D major; No. 2 in
E flat major; No. 3 in F major; No. 4 in G major. **Salzburg Chamber Philharmonic Orchestra /
Yoon K. Lee.** Naxos Ⓢ 8 553289 (52 minutes: DDD: 4/96). *Gramophone Editor's choice. See
review under C.P.E. Bach; refer to the Index to Reviews.*   Ⓖ

Heinrich Baermann
German 1784-1847

Suggested listening ...
...Quintet in E flat major, Op. 23 – Adagio. *Coupled with* **Brahms** Clarinet Quintet in B minor, Op. 115. **Mozart** Clarinet Quintet in A major, K581. **Alfred Boskovsky** (cl); **Vienna Octet.** Decca Ovation 417 643-2DM (9/88).

Tadeusz Baird
Polish 1928-1981

Suggested listening ...
...Colas Breugnon – suite[b]. *Coupled with* **Szymanowski** Violin Concertos[a] – No. 1, Op. 35; No. 2, Op. 61. **Górecki** Three Pieces in the Old Style[b]. [a]**Konstanty Kulka** (vn); [a]**Polish National Radio Symphony Orchestra,** [b]**Polish Chamber Orchestra / Jerzy Maksymiuk.** EMI Matrix CDM5 65418-2 (3/96).
...Voices from Afar[a]. Goethe-Briefe[b]. Scene[c]. Canzona[d]. [a]**Jerzy Artysz,** [b]**Andrzej Hioski** (bars); [c]**Klaus Storck** (vc); [c]**Helga Storck** (hp); [a]**Warsaw National Philharmonic Symphony Orchestra / Witold Rowicki;** [c]**Katowice Radio Symphony Orchestra / Wojciech Michniewski;** [d]**Cracow Radio and Television Chorus and Orchestra;** [d]**Polish National Symphony Orchestra / Jan Krenz.** Olympia OCD388 (9/93).

Sir Edward Bairstow
British 1874-1946

Suggested listening ...
...Blessed City, heavenly Salem. The Lamentation. Jesu, the very thought of Thee. Lord, Thou has been our refuge. Let all mortal flesh keep silence. Lord, I call upon Thee. When Israel came out of Egypt. Jesu, grant me this I pray. Save us, O Lord. If the Lord had not helped me. A Blessed Virgin's Cradle Song. Evening Service in D major. **York Minster Choir / Philip Moore** with **John Scott Whiteley** (org). Priory PRCD365 (6/93).
...Prelude in C major. Evening Song. Scherzo in A flat major. Nocturne. Prelude on "Vexilla Regis". Elegy. Toccata and Prelude on "Pange Lingua". Meditation. Three Short Preludes. Legend. Organ Sonata in E flat major. **Francis Jackson** (org). Mirabilis MRCD902 (4/91).
...Organ Sonata in E flat major. *Coupled with works by* **Elgar** and **Harris John Scott** (org). Priory PRCD401 (8/94).

David Baker
American 1931-

Suggested listening ...
...Roots II. *Coupled with* **Rochberg** Summer, 1990. **Rorem** Spring Music. **Beaux Arts Trio.** Philips 438 866-2PH (8/94).

Osvaldas Balakauskas
Lithuanian/USSR 1937-

New review
Balakauskas Like the touch of a sea wave[a].
Barkauskas Partita.
Pärt Fratres[a]. Spiegel im Spiegel[a].
Schnittke Violin Sonata No. 1[a]. **Rusné Mataityté** (vn); [a]**Margrit-Julia Zimmermann** (pf). Proud Sound ℗ PROUCD139 (57 minutes: DDD: 7/96). Recorded 1995.
The big news here is Balakauskas's *Like the touch of a sea wave* (1976), a delicate example of musical Post-Impressionism, reminiscent of Debussy and Hindemith. It's a finely chiselled offering that suggests light on glistening crystals and the performances here are splendid, with the Lithuanian-born violinist Rusné Mataityté and Russian-German pianist Margrit-Julia Zimmermann underlining the score's many stylistic subtleties. Balakauskas himself was born in Lithuania, whereas Vytautas Barkauskas (with whom Balakauskas is bound to be confused, at least in the West) was born six years earlier, in Kaunas. His playful unaccompanied violin *Partita* (1967) was popularized by Gidon Kremer, whose violinistic wit must have made real mischief of its many jokes and surprises. Not that Mataityté can be found wanting. Her tonal palette is both wide and accommodating and she makes great play with the syncopated "Toccata" fourth movement. Schnittke's First Violin Sonata (1963) is made of fairly angry stuff. The first movement projects solo declamations over powerful piano chords; the second makes aggressive fun rather in the manner of Prokofiev; the lyrical third mirrors the *Largo* from Shostakovich's Second Piano Trio, and the finale reintroduces an element of playfulness. Maximum contrast is afforded by Arvo Pärt, whose now-ubiquitous *Fratres* variations (1977-80) and simple but serene *Spiegel im Spiegel* (1978) end the programme. Again, the performances are extremely convincing, while the music itself casts a quieting spell. The recordings are perfectly adequate.

Further listening ...
...Ostrobothnian Symphony. *Coupled with* **Vasks** Symphony for Strings, "Stimmen". **Narbutaite**
Opus lugubre. **Ostrobothnian Chamber Orchestra / Juha Kangas.** Finlandia 4509-97892-2 (11/95).

Mily Balakirev   USSR 1837-1910

Balakirev Piano Concertos – No. 1 in F sharp major, Op. 1; No. 2 in E flat major, Op. posth.
Rimsky-Korsakov Piano Concerto in C sharp minor, Op. 30. **Malcolm Binns** (pf); **English
Northern Philharmonia / David Lloyd-Jones.** Hyperion Ⓕ CDA66640 (61 minutes: DDD: 7/93).
Recorded 1992.   Ⓖ
'Op. 1' and 'Op. posth.' say a lot about Balakirev's two piano concertos. The First is a single
movement only, composed at the age of 18 and massively indebted to the Chopin concertos. The
Second was begun not long after, in 1861, but abandoned after the first movement; he was only
persuaded to write the other movements down near the end of his life. At his death in 1910 the finale
had to be completed by Lyapunov, which may be partly why it sounds so splendidly rambunctious, so
close in places, to Gershwin. The concerto was certainly worth the efforts of all concerned; the first
movement's fugal episodes and the slow movement's tinges of Russian Orthodox gloom stay in the
mind, compensating for Balakirev's occasional recourse to inflating and over-decorating short sub-
phrases. The First Concerto, too, has little flashes of individuality which keep you listening despite
the obvious naïvety and derivative quality of the material. The Rimsky-Korsakov has come and goes
from the catalogue over the years. It is in effect more of a folk-song fantasia than a concerto, but there
is much post-Liszt-and-Griegian charm, as well as a striking foretaste of Rachmaninov's *Paganini*
Rhapsody (Paganini's famous opening motif coincidentally also begins the second strain of Rimsky's
chosen theme). These three works make an excellent programme, then. And Malcolm Binns, though
not the most sparkling of soloists, plays with commendable solidity. The quality of the orchestra's
contribution is high, and all in all this is an admirably conceived and executed disc.

Additional recommendation ...
...No. 1[a]. **Rimsky-Korsakov** Piano Concerto[b]. **Medtner** Piano Concerto No. 1 in C minor,
Op. 33[a]. **Igor Zhukov** (pf); **USSR TV and Radio Large Orchestra /** [a]**Alexander Dmitriev,** [b]**Gennadi
Rozhdestvensky.** Mezhdunarodnaya Kniga Ⓕ MK417087 (62 minutes: ADD: 2/94).

New review
Balakirev Fantasy on themes from Glinka's "A Life for the Tsar"[b].
Paderewski Piano Concerto in A minor, Op. 17[a].   ·
F.X. Scharwenka Piano Concerto No. 1 in B flat minor, Op. 32[c]. **Earl Wild** (pf); [c]**Boston
Symphony Orchestra / Erich Leinsdorf;** [a]**London Symphony Orchestra / Arthur Fiedler.** Elan
Ⓕ CD82266 (73 minutes: ADD: 7/96). Item marked [a] from RCA SB6843 (5/71), [bc]SB6815 (2/70).
Recorded 1969-71.   Ⓖ
Earl Wild is among the most brilliant pianists of our time. However, the major record companies, in
particular, have been slow off the mark and so all credit to Elan for reissuing these vintage
performances first recorded by RCA. Capturing Wild on peak form is not easy and there have been
times when that extraordinary motor (once compared to a perfectly tuned Ferrari) has been left
unaccompanied by the keenest musical engagement. But here everything operates at maximum
voltage and with a spine-tingling wit and precision. In Scharwenka's second movement scherzo Wild
cuts some of the most scintillating capers you are ever likely to encounter. Balakirev's very Lisztian
Fantasy takes over the intermission, so to speak, and, again, the performance is of an awe-inspiring
verve and perfection. The notes stream and cascade from his fingers like diamonds; you may well be
listening to one of the most infallible of all keyboard mechanisms. The Paderewski is a more domestic
creation but the themes are attractively homespun, their treatment as engaging as you would expect
from a pianist of such stature. Wild fills out some of the more opulent gestures for added effect and
his champagne brilliance makes every page sharp, and buzzing with a vitality all his own. All recorded
rivals are chased into the shadows and the transfers are excellently managed.

Further listening ...
...Symphony No. 1 in C major. Tamara – symphonic poem. **Royal Philharmonic Orchestra / Sir
Thomas Beecham.** EMI Beecham Edition CDM7 63375-2* (7/90).
...Symphony No. 1 in C major. Russia – symphonic poem. **Philharmonia Orchestra / Evgeni
Svetlanov.** Hyperion CDA66493 (12/91).
...Symphony No. 2 in D minor. Tamara – symphonic poem. Overture on the themes of three
Russian songs. **Philharmonia Orchestra / Evgeni Svetlanov.** Hyperion CDA66586 (9/92).
...Symphony No. 2 in D minor. Russia – symphonic poem. **Russian State Symphony Orchestra /
Igor Golovschin.** Naxos 8 550793 (9/94).
...Islamey. *Coupled with works by* **Mussorgsky, Rachmaninov, Liadov** and **Medtner** Boris
Berezovsky (pf). Teldec 4509-96516-2 (7/96). *See reviews in the Collections section; refer to the
Index to Reviews.*
...20 Songs – The bright moon; My heart is torn; Song of Selim; When I hear thy voice. Three
Forgotten Songs – Thou art so captivating; Spanish song. 10 Songs – Over the lake; I loved him.
Coupled with **Mussorgsky** What are words of love to you?. Night. **Borodin** The false note. The

sea princess. **Rimsky-Korsakov** The octave, Op. 45 No. 3. The clouds begin to scatter, Op. 42 No. 3. Of what I dream in the quiet sky, Op. 40 No. 3. Enslaved by the rose, the nightingale, Op. 2 No. 2. In spring, Op. 43 – No. 1, The lark sings louder; No. 2, Not the wind, blowing from the heights. **Cui** I remember the evening. 25 Songs, Op. 57 – No. 11, "You" and "Thou"; No. 17, The statue of Tsarskoie Selo; No. 25, Desire. Ici-bas. I touched the bloom lightly, Op. 49 No. 1. It's over. **Olga Borodina** (mez); **Larissa Gergieva** (pf). Philips 442 780-2PH (8/95).

Claude-Béninge Balbastre French 1727-1799

Suggested listening ...
...Quatre Sonates en quatuor, Op. 3. **Concerto Rococo.** Pierre Verany PV794043 (3/95). ✒

Pietro Baldassare Italian c1690-c1768

Suggested listening ...
...Sonata for Cornett, Strings and Continuo in F major (transcribed for trumpet). *Coupled with works by* **Franceschini, Viviani, A. Marcello, Torelli, Albinoni, Corelli** and **Vivaldi Håkan Hardenberger** (tpt); **I Musici.** Philips 442 131-2PH (5/95). *See review in the Collections section; refer to the Index to Reviews.*

Michael William Balfe Irish 1808-1870

Suggested listening ...
...The Bohemian Girl. **Soloists; Radio Telefis Eireann Philharmonic Choir; National Symphony Orchestra of Ireland / Richard Bonynge.** Argo 433 324-2ZH2 (8/92).

Adriano Banchieri Italian 1568-1634

New review
Banchieri Festino nella sera del Giovedi grasso avanti Cena, Op. 18.
Striggio Il cicalamento delle donne al bucato. La caccia. **Concerto Italiano / Rinaldo Alessandrini.**
Opus 111 ⓔ OPS30-137 (60 minutes: DDD: 3/96). Texts and translations included. Recorded 1995.
The centrepiece of this record is Adriano Banchieri's depiction of an entertainment on the evening of a major holiday (*Giovedi grasso* – literally "fat Thursday") during the sixteenth century. In common with his other 'madrigal-comedies', this is an ingeniously constructed sequence of short, pithy and for the most part lighthearted madrigals (some of them strophic) arranged around the lightest of narrative frameworks. In practice this music could have been sung in a domestic context simply as music in its own right; equally it could have been performed in a staged version, the added action being improvised along the lines of the short characterizations which precede each madrigal (and which on this record are usefully declaimed). For all its lightheartedness (the result is a sort of *commedia dell'arte* with music), Banchieri's writing is varied, effective and often achieves its results by quite subtle means. Descending from the Olympian heights of their much acclaimed records of Monteverdi, Rinaldo Alessandrini and Concerto Italiano do not lose a single opportunity to squeeze every ounce of wit from the text, from the out-of-tune singing and cracked voices of the old men from Chioggia to the imitations of the sound of the Jew's harp and the hilarious medley of animal sounds in the "Contrappunto bestiale alla mente". The result is exhilarating and supremely entertaining – it is difficult to imagine a more effective reading. The outer layers of the sandwich are provided by two of Alessandro Striggio's sequences of descriptive madrigals whose less imaginative, more conventional writing is expertly and sensitively rendered. All in all this makes for the perfect piece of light listening for any renaissance enthusiast

Sir Granville Bantock British 1868-1946

Bantock Pagan Symphony. Fifine at the Fair. Two Heroic Ballads. **Royal Philharmonic Orchestra / Vernon Handley.** Hyperion ⓕ CDA66630 (80 minutes: DDD: 3/93). Recorded 1992. ⓖ
Granville Bantock was a man born at the wrong time. He wrote colourful, hedonistic late-romantic music well into the second quarter of the twentieth century, and has been neglected for many years as an anachronism. At times he recalls Strauss, at others Bax, but if he lacks that personal utterance that would stamp every page with his name and no other, there's plenty of compensation in his sheer craftsmanship. With some composers that word means a worthy but rather dull demonstration of technical facility, but Bantock has the gift of communicating his own pleasure in his craft. He will take a scale, twist it, bend it slightly, and we are not only delighted by the fine melody that he has made

(and there are many of them) but also by the cleverness of the process. This could lead to mere garrulousness, an endless succession of pretty tricks, but Bantock's resource also ensures that the impulse of the two big pieces here (and they are both very big, single movement structures lasting half-an-hour) never flags. His scoring is particularly beautiful, sumptuous yet clean throughout, with many ingeniously original sonorities that work perfectly in such fine performances as these. The recordings are clear and spacious.

Additional recommendation ...

...Fifine at the Fair. **Bax** The Garden of Fand. **Berners** The Triumph of Neptune – Ballet Suite[a]. [a]**Robert Alva** (bass); **Royal Philharmonic Orchestra / Sir Thomas Beecham.** EMI Beecham Edition mono CDM7 63405-2* (64 minutes: ADD: 6/92)

Further listening ...

...Celtic Symphony. The Witch of Atlas. The Sea Reivers. Hebridean Symphony. **Royal Philharmonic Orchestra / Vernon Handley.** Hyperion CDA66450 (5/91).

Samuel Barber

New review

Barber Cello Concerto, Op. 22[a]. Violin Concerto, Op. 14[b]. Capricorn Concerto, Op. 21[c]. [a]**Steven Isserlis** (vc); [b]**Kyoko Takezawa** (vn); [c]**Jacob Berg** (fl); [c]**Peter Bowman** (ob); [c]**Susan Slaughter** (tpt); **St Louis Symphony Orchestra / Leonard Slatkin.** RCA Victor Red Seal Ⓕ 09026 68283-2 (65 minutes: DDD: 5/96). Recorded 1994-5.

The Cello Concerto is a restless work touched through and through by the shock, uncertainty and fragile optimism of a world just coming out of war. Steven Isserlis is in many respects just the player for the piece. His agility is a boon in ensuring that it never becomes overly strenuous, that its capriciousness, its touches of irony (all those quizzical pizzicato *glissandos* and harmonics) are not lost in the shadows. The slow movement's *cantilena* really does warm to his personal touch, his long, canonic duet with oboe for once not a mismatch. Isserlis's cello is the lightest of Lieder baritones with the flexibility and imagination to fine-spin phrases as very few can and do. Listen to his withdrawal into the heart of the slow movement. Isserlis reflecting, Isserlis lost in thought, is always special. Kyoko Takezawa is not a player to keep much to herself. The casual opening page of the Violin Concerto, starting as it does mid sentence through a shared confidence, is soon impatient to go public. Her sound – intense and focused – seems to reach way beyond the length of each phrase. She is mindful, too, of the fiercer contrasts, seeking always to maximize them. It's a very 'operatic' performance, the lyric and dramatic elements grippingly interacted. The big 'aria' – in which the first oboe gets to be the envy of all the surrounding players – comes, of course, with that ravishing principal subject of the slow movement, and when Takezawa does finally come to embrace it, the feeling of release, of fulfilment in her tone (sung right from the heart, from the chest-voice of her G string) is worth the wait. Slatkin responds with a gloriously full-throated tutti in the strings. All of which is wickedly offset by that mad, mordant, highland fling of a finale, twirling woodwinds and fractured trumpet fanfares as belligerent as you could wish. Between the two main courses comes the sorbet. Barber's *Capricorn Concerto* (for flute, oboe, trumpet and strings) is a playful *concerto grosso* for the New World, a sharp take on baroque procedures, a streetwise *Brandenburg* No. 2.

Additional recommendation ...

...Cello Concerto. **Shostakovich** Cello Concerto No. 1 in E flat major, Op. 107. **Raphael Wallfisch** (vc); **English Chamber Orchestra / Geoffrey Simon.** Chandos Ⓕ CHAN8322 (DDD: 2/85).

Barber Violin Concerto, Op. 14[a].
Korngold Violin Concerto, Op. 35[a]. Much ado about nothing, Op. 11[b] – The maiden in the bridal chamber; Dogberry and Verges; Intermezzo; Hornpipe. **Gil Shaham** (vn); [a]**London Symphony Orchestra / André Previn** ([b]pf). DG Ⓕ 439 886-2GH (71 minutes: DDD: 9/94). Recorded 1993. *Gramophone Editor's choice.*
Barber Violin Concerto, Op. 14.
Bernstein Serenade.
Foss Three American Pieces. **Itzhak Perlman** (vn); **Boston Symphony Orchestra / Seiji Ozawa.** EMI Ⓕ CDC5 55360-2 (67 minutes: DDD: 6/95). Recorded 1992.

Though the conjunction of Barber and Korngold might not seem pointful, it works splendidly here. The performance of the Barber, warm and rich, with the sound close and immediate, brings out above all the work's bolder side, allowing moments that are not too distant from the world of Hollywood music (no disparagement there) and aptly the Korngold emerges as a central work in that genre. There have been subtler readings of Barber's lovely concerto, with the soloist not always helped by the close balance, but it is good to have a sharp distinction drawn between the purposeful lyricism of the first movement, marked *Allegro*, and the tender lyricism of the heavenly *Andante*. In the *moto perpetuo* finale Shaham brings out the fun behind the movement's manic energy, with Previn pointing the Waltonian wit. In the Korngold, Gil Shaham may not have quite the flair and panache of its dedicatee, Jascha Heifetz, in *his* incomparable reading (see review under Korngold; refer to the Index to Reviews), but what emerges in comparison is how electric the playing of the LSO is under Previn here, rich and full as well as committed, echoing vintage Previn/LSO recordings of the 1970s. The recording is clear and immediate, the balance of the soloist not as close as with Heifetz. It is striking how Previn gives a rhythmic lift to the dashing *moto perpetuo* of the finale, where Wallenstein for Heifetz tends to make it a mad dash in pursuit of the soloist. The suite from Korngold's incidental music to *Much ado about nothing*, dating from his early period in Vienna, provides a delightful and apt makeweight, with Previn, as pianist, just as understanding and imaginative an accompanist.

Perlman plays not just with unrivalled power but with rare passion in what are arguably the two finest *concertante* works for violin written by American composers, adding an attractive makeweight in the colourful Foss pieces. Not that the claims of the rival versions of the Barber and Bernstein are completely outshone. Next to them Perlman may initially seem almost too confident, missing an element of fantasy in his total sureness. Yet increasingly through the five contrasted movements the purposefulness as well as the masterful power of Perlman's playing adds to the work's impact, eliminating any thought that the piece might be too episodic. He demonstrates the more tellingly the way in which each movement leads thematically out of the preceding one, until the final movement, much the longest, completes the circle in its references back to the opening. He makes it seem a warmer piece too, thanks to his range of incomparably rich tone-colours. Perlman produces an equally warm tone in the Barber Concerto. If in the first movement Shaham sounds more carefree, bringing out the fantasy of the opening theme, the extra weight of Perlman's sound brings dividends too in this sumptuously romantic concerto. Previn and the LSO for Shaham may give a sharper, cleaner edge to their accompaniment, but, as in the Bernstein, Ozawa and the Boston orchestra play with a passion to match that of their soloist. For Perlman the central slow movement is the kernel of the work. When the soloist enters after the extended orchestral introduction, he plays with a warmth and intensity that even he has rarely matched, making the return of the main theme on the G string a wonderful resolution, with vibrato so perfectly controlled that there is no hint of soupiness. Weight, power and virtuoso brilliance then come together in Perlman's dazzling account of the finale. The Lukas Foss pieces, as the title suggests, have a strong element of Copland-like folksiness, married to sweet, easy lyricism with some Stravinskian echoes. Though, in the recording, textures could be more open, the rich tapestry of Boston sound is beautifully moulded to the fullness of Perlman's violin.

Barber Essays for Orchestra – No. 1, Op. 12; No. 2, Op. 17; No. 3, Op. 47.
Ives Symphony No. 1. **Detroit Symphony Orchestra / Neeme Järvi.** Chandos Ⓟ CHAN9053
(70 minutes: DDD: 3/92). Recorded 1991.

This issue comes with a booklet celebrating Neeme Järvi's 100th disc for Chandos and a remarkable joint achievement by this conductor and company. Järvi's wide ranging sympathies are proved yet again in the music of these two American composers, but there is a paradox here in that it is the innovator Ives who is the more conventional and the conservative Barber who challenges the ear. The explanation is that Ives's First Symphony is a graduation work from his years at Yale University, representing a compromise between his natural boldness and the discipline that he grudgingly accepted from his teacher Horatio Parker. The result is romantically expansive, often fascinating and occasionally beautiful, with influences including Brahms and Dvořák (there are echoes of the *New World* Symphony in the slow movement) but also a bold homespun element in places suggesting the Ivesian innovations that were yet to come. Samuel Barber seemed unhappy with the symphony as a form, writing a one-movement First Symphony in 1936 and eventually destroying all but one movement of his wartime Second (1944). Instead he wrote three impressive *Essays for Orchestra* that have been called "surrogate symphonies" and of which No. 3 was his final work before his death. Each has a sequence of moods and tempos, the *First Essay* being partly elegiac (recalling his *Adagio for Strings*), the Second having some vigorously busy music and the Third being the most enigmatic. While none of these works sound especially American, the performances are convincing and the recording offers rich sound.

Barber Symphony No. 1, Op. 9. The School for Scandal Overture, Op. 5.
Beach Symphony in E minor, Op. 32, "Gaelic". **Detroit Symphony Orchestra / Neeme Järvi.**
Chandos Ⓟ CHAN8958 (72 minutes: DDD: 10/91). Recorded 1991.   Ⓖ

Amy Beach (or Mrs H.H.A. Beach, as she was known professionally in her lifetime) was born in Henniker, New Hampshire in 1867. By all accounts she was a prodigiously talented youngster – she could sing 40 tunes by the age of two, and at four she was composing small pieces for the piano. She made her 'official' début as a pianist at the age of 16 playing Chopin's Rondo in E flat and Moscheles's G minor Piano Concerto, but after her marriage to a noted Boston surgeon in 1885 she abandoned her concert career and devoted her time exclusively to composition. The *Gaelic* Symphony (her only work in the genre) dates from 1896. Like Dvořák's *New World* Symphony, which had received its American première just a few years earlier, it draws its inspiration from folk material; though Beach's sources are drawn not from native America but rather from her Gaelic forebears. The writing reveals a remarkable degree of craftsmanship and maturity, and although the music contains perhaps more imitation than originality (Brahms, Tchaikovsky and Parry spring to mind) there is nevertheless plenty of enjoyment to be had from this fresh and engaging work. Barber's First Symphony made a welcome return after a protracted absence from the catalogue. Slatkin's account (listed below) might in some ways be more satisfactory as his orchestra seems more comfortable, and the American conductor clearly has an innate grasp of the music's style. This one-movement, highly compact work deserves to be much better known as it contains some of Barber's most invigorating and memorable material. Stylistically it finds allegiance with the post-romanticism of symphonies such as Walton's First and Howard Hanson's Second (*Romantic*). The disc also includes Barber's equally engaging Overture to *The School for Scandal*. Committed performances.

Additional recommendations ...

...School for Scandal Overture. Symphony No. 2, Op. 19. Music for a Scene from Shelley, Op. 7. Essay No. 1. Adagio for Strings. **New Zealand Symphony Orchestra / Andrew Schenck**. Stradivari Ⓕ SCD8012 (66 minutes: DDD: 8/89).

...No. 1[a]. Piano Concerto, Op. 38[b]. Souvenirs, Op. 28[c]. [bc]**John Browning** (pf); [ab]**St Louis Symphony Orchestra / Leonard Slatkin** ([c]pf). RCA Victor Red Seal Ⓕ RD60732 (70 minutes: DDD: 11/91). Ⓖ

...No. 1. Adagio for Strings. Essays for Orchestra, Nos. 1 and 2. Music for a Scene from Shelley, Op. 7. School for Scandal Overture. **Baltimore Symphony Orchestra / David Zinman**. Argo Ⓕ 436 288-2ZH (64 minutes: DDD: 1/93).

Barber String Quartet, Op. 11.
Britten String Quartet No. 2 in C major, Op. 36.
Takemitsu A Way A Lone. **Tokyo Quartet** (Peter Oundjian, Kikuei Ikeda, vns; Kazuhide Isomura, va; Sadao Harada, vc). RCA Victor Red Seal Ⓕ 09026 61387-2 (61 minutes: DDD: 2/94). Recorded 1992.   ⒼⒼ

Three very different minds grappling with the intricacies of four-way musical dialogue. Takemitsu, a habitual aesthete wandering in the thick of sensual Bergian textures; Barber, a compelling New World Romantic revelling among memories of Dvořák and, perhaps, Nielsen; and then Britten, a bold, incandescent voice in prime condition, proclaiming during the year (1945) that also witnessed *Peter Grimes* and *The Holy Sonnets of John Donne*. All are summoned among the sonorous ranks of the Tokyo Quartet for performances that combine rigour, warmth and textual acuity. It's a compelling mix, the standard of playing is uniformly high, the recording pleasingly full-bodied and the programme itself well chosen. This and the CD listed below are the result of very different programming concepts: the Tokyos offering "the responses of three composers to the challenge of tradition", the Emersons, a conspectus on American quartet writing in the first half of the century. Which makes a choice relatively easy and the chances of disappointment correspondingly remote.

Additional recommendations ...

...String Quartet. *Coupled with works by* **Wirén, A. Tchaikowsky** and **Hugh Wood** Lindsay Quartet. ASV Ⓕ CDDCA825 (77 minutes: ADD: 1/93). *See review in the Collections section; refer to the Index to Reviews.*

...String Quartet – Adagio. *Coupled with works by* **Piazzolla, Maraire, B. Johnston, Reich, Górecki, Riley, Crumb, Glass, Tahmizyan, Pärt, R. Scott, S. Johnson, Daugherty** and **Hendrix. Dumisani Maraire** (ngoma/hosho); **Astor Piazzolla** (bandoneon); **Patty Manning**, [c]**John Taylor, Larry Caballero** (vocs); **Djivan Gasparian** (duduk); **Kronos Quartet**. Nonesuch Ⓕ 7559-79394-2 (two discs: 101 minutes: DDD: 2/96). *See review in the Collections section; refer to the Index to Reviews.*

Barber Ballade, Op. 46. Excursions, Op. 20. Nocturne, Op. 33. Piano Sonata, Op. 26. Souvenirs, Op. 28. **Eric Parkin** (pf). Chandos Ⓕ CHAN9177 (63 minutes: DDD: 10/93). Recorded 1992.

This is not quite the Complete Works for Solo Piano, as claimed in the title, nor is it "the entire output for solo piano, save for a single childhood essay" as stated in the booklet. This is the complete published piano music, apart from *Three Sketches*, and there are quite a lot of unpublished pieces. None of this matters when the playing is as polished and sympathetic as Parkin's. He responds wonderfully to the nostalgic melancholia of Barber. The ballet score, *Souvenirs*, is available in the orchestral and piano-duet versions, but this solo piano treatment is just as engaging. Parkin knows exactly how to present this side of Barber and his treatment of the *Four Excursions* based on different popular idioms is equally convincing. A performer as well versed as Parkin in British post-romantics such as Ireland and Bax finds home ground again in Barber's *Nocturne* and the late *Ballade*. In Barber's classic, the Sonata, Parkin is in competition with several other recordings including Horowitz's (listed below), Peter Lawson's and Joanna MacGregor's (both reviewed elsewhere in this *Guide*; refer to the Index to Reviews.) Parkin treats the work lyrically and never forces us to regard the finale, especially, as a hard-hitting block-buster in the way that so many young pianists do. He is transparent in the scherzo; sings in the *Adagio*; and the final fugue subject has exactly the catchy, swinging quality that many players miss. At times there is a lack of brilliance, which the rather dull recording emphasizes, but this is a winning anthology of this major American romantic.

Additional recommendations ...

...Piano Sonata. **Prokofiev** Piano Sonata No. 7. **Kabalevsky** Piano Sonata No. 3 in F major, Op. 46. *Also includes works by* **Fauré, Prokofiev** and **Poulenc** Vladimir Horowitz (pf). RCA Victor Gold Seal mono/stereo Ⓜ GD60377* (65 minutes: ADD: 7/94).   ⒼⒼⒼ

...Ballade. **Beach** Five Improvisations, Op. 148. **Bernstein** Five Anniversaries. **Cage** Bacchanale for Prepared Piano. **Copland** Four Piano Blues. **Gershwin** Three Preludes.

Gottschalk Manchega, RO143. Le Banjo, RO22. **M. Gould** Boogie Woogie Etude.
Joplin The Entertainer. Maple Leaf Rag. **MacDowell** New England Idylls, Op. 62.
Nancarrow Prelude. **Michel Legrand** (pf). Erato Ⓕ 4509-96386-2 (77 minutes:
DDD: 7/95).

Barber Vocal and Chamber Works – Dover Beach, Op. 3[ac]; Serenade, Op. 1[c]; Three Songs, Op. 2[ab];
Three Songs, Op. 10[ab]; Four Songs, Op. 13[ab]: Sure on this shining night; Nocturne. Despite and
Still, Op. 41: Solitary Hotel[ab]; Three Songs, Op. 45[ab]; String Quartet, Op. 11[c]. [a]**Thomas Allen**
(bar); [b]**Roger Vignoles** (pf); [c]**Endellion Quartet** (Andrew Watkinson, Ralph de Souza, vns;
Garfield Jackson, va; David Waterman, vc). Virgin Classics Ⓕ VC5 45033-2 (64 minutes: DDD:
10/94). Texts included. Recorded 1990-93.   Ⓖ

The *Serenade*, Op. 1 was written when Barber was only 19 and the first two of its three brief
movements belie the implication in the title of a lightweight work. The slow introduction to the pithy
first movement echoes late Beethoven, and leads to a compressed *Allegro* similarly dark in its minor
key colourings. Even the central *Andante* is as melancholy as it is brief, with the rhythmic finale alone
lightening the mood, music one might easily attribute to an English composer of the time. The
Endellion play that music with the hushed gravity and clear intensity that it deserves, no mere student
work, and their reading of the Op. 11 Quartet – best known as the original source of Barber's
celebrated *Adagio* for strings – is a big-scale, thrustful account and altogether admirable. Thomas
Allen's account of *Dover Beach* not only conveys more mystery and a keener feeling for atmosphere
than the one with Thomas Hampson and the Emerson Quartet, it points the contrasts of mood more
clearly, and builds to a thrilling climax on the poet's expression of love. In the solo songs, Allen and
Vignoles opt for consistently faster speeds than their rivals, so that the slow tango of the Joyce setting,
"Solitary Hotel", is more clearly established. If Vignoles cannot quite match the velvety
persuasiveness of Browning's spontaneous-sounding accompaniments, Allen compensates with
singing even more consistently purposeful and varied in expression than Hampson's, and no less
beautiful in tone. In their different ways both are revelatory. Only three of the songs – "With Rue my
Heart is Laden", Op. 2 and the two songs from Op. 13 – are ones which Studer sings (reviewed below),
with the male voice more purposeful, the woman's often more sensuous. With splendid sound and an
excellent balance, both open and clear, this is an outstanding disc to recommend to anyone wanting
to investigate beyond the celebrated *Adagio*.

Barber A Slumber Song of the Madonna[ac]. There's Nae Lark[bc]. Love at the door[bc]. Serenades[bc].
Love's Caution[ac]. Night Wanderers[bc]. Oh that so sweet imprisonment[ac]. Strings in the Earth and
Air[bc]. The Beggar's song[bc]. In the dark pinewood[bc]. Three Songs, Op. 2[bc]. Three Songs, Op. 10[abc].
Four Songs, Op. 13[ac]. Dover Beach, Op. 3[bd]. Two Songs, Op. 18[ac]. Nuvoletta, Op. 25[ac]. Mélodies
passagères, Op. 27[bc]. Hermit Songs, Op. 29[ac]. Despite and Still, Op. 41[bc]. Three Songs, Op. 45[bc].
[a]**Cheryl Studer** (sop); [b]**Thomas Hampson** (bar); [c]**John Browning** (pf); [d]**Emerson Quartet** (Eugene
Drucker; Philip Setzer, vns; Lawrence Dutton, va; David Finckel, vc). DG Ⓕ 435 867-2GH2 (two
discs: 110 minutes: DDD: 5/94). Notes and texts included. Recorded 1991-2. *Gramophone Award
Winner 1994. Gramophone Editor's choice.*   ⒼⒼ

Sung in chronological order these songs are almost an autobiography and the set provides a
compelling argument for regarding Barber's songs as his art at its most complete. There's hardly a
weak song in the collection. Hampson brings to this music a remarkable range of expression and
colour, a subtle use of words and a conviction that not a few of these songs are masterpieces. Studer
has a slightly cooler approach, but often provides the vocal glamour, the ability to sketch long curves
and floated high notes, that Barber (singer himself and connoisseur of singing) so often demanded.
And John Browning, to whose virtuosity Barber tailored his Piano Concerto, sounds not only like a
man who has yearned to accompany these singers in these songs for a long while, but like a
considerable accompanist indeed, matching Hampson's dynamic range and expressive flexibility and
Studer's seamless line with resourceful sympathy. The recorded sound is flawless.

Additional recommendations ...

...Knoxville: Summer of 1915. Dover Beach. Hermit Songs. Andromache's Farewell, Op. 39.
**Soloists; Juilliard Quartet; Dumbarton Oaks Orchestra / William Strickland; New York
Philharmonic Orchestra / Thomas Schippers.** CBS Masterworks Portrait Ⓜ MPK46727*
(51 minutes; AAD: 10/91).   Ⓖ
...Nocturne, Op. 13 No. 4. Hermit Songs[d]. Sleep now, Op. 10 No. 2[a]. The dainies, Op. 2 No. 1[a].
Nuvoletta[a]. Knoxville[b]. Antony and Cleopatra[b] – Give me some music; Give me my robe.
Leontyne Price (sop); [a]**Samuel Barber** (pf); [b]**New Philharmonia Orchestra / Thomas Schippers.**
RCA Victor Gold Seal Ⓜ 09026 61983-2* (63 minutes. ADD: 8/94).   Ⓖ

Further listening ...

...Piano Concerto[a]. Medea – Media's Meditation and Dance of Vengeance. Adagio for Strings.
[a]**Tedd Joselson** (pf); **London Symphony Orchestra / Andrew Schenck.** ASV CDDCA534 (6/86).
...Knoxville: Summer of 1915, Op. 24. *Coupled with works by* **Gershwin** *and* **Previn Kathleen
Battle** (sop); **Orchestra of St Luke's / André Previn.** DG Ⓕ 437 787-2GH (46 minutes: DDD:
1/96). *See review under Previn; refer to the Index to Reviews.*   Ⓖ
...Vanessa – Intermezzo; Under the Willow Tree. Music for a scene from Shelley, Op. 7. Medea's
Meditation and Dance of Vengeance, Op. 23a. *Coupled with* **Chadwick** Symphony No. 3 in

F major. **Detroit Symphony Orchestra / Neeme Järvi.** Chandos CHAN9253 (10/94). *See review under Chadwick; refer to the Index to Reviews.*

...Adagio for Strings, Op. 11. Medea's Meditation and Dance of Vengeance, Op. 23. *Coupled with* **Elgar** Introduction and Allegro for String Quartet and String Orchestra, Op. 47. **Tchaikovsky** Serenade in C major, Op. 48. **Boston Symphony Orchestra / Charles Munch.** RCA Victor Gold Seal 09026 61424-2 (9/93).

...Adagio for Strings, Op. 11. Symphony No. 2, Op. 19. *Coupled with* **Bristow** Symphony No. 2 in F sharp minor, Op. 26. **Detroit Symphony Orchestra / Neeme Järvi.** Chandos CHAN9169 (10/93).

...Prayers of Kierkegaard, Op. 30. The lovers, Op. 43. **Sarah Reese** (sop); **Dale Duesing** (bar); **Chicago Symphony Chorus and Orchestra / Andrew Schenck.** Koch International Classics 37125-2 (3/92).

...Agnus Dei, Op. 11. *Coupled with* **Bernstein** Chichester Psalms[a]. **Copland** In the Beginning[b]. Four Motets. [a]**Dominic Martelli** (treb); [b]**Catherine Denley** (mez); [a]**Rachel Masters** (hp); [a]**Gary Kettel** (perc); [a]**Thomas Trotter** (org); **Corydon Singers / Matthew Best.** Hyperion CDA66219 (9/87).

...With rue my heart is laden. *Coupled with works by* **L. Berkeley, Butterworth, Horde, Ireland, Moeran** and **C.W. Orr** Anthony Rolfe Johnson (ten); Graham Johnson (pf). Hyperion CDA66471/2 (8/95). Includes various poems from Housman's "A Shrophire Lad" read by Alan Bates. *See review in the Collections section; refer to the Index to Reviews.*

...A Hand of Bridge[ae]. Essay for Orchestra No. 2, Op. 17[e]. Music for a Scene from Shelley, Op. 7[e]. A Stopwatch and an Ordnance map, Op. 15[be]. Serenade for String Orchestra, Op. 1[e.] Adagio for Strings, Op. 11[d]. Let Down the Bars, O Death, Op. 82 No. 2[c]. [a]**Patricia Neway** (sop) Geraldine; [a]**Eunice Alberts** (contr) Sally; [a]**William Lewis** (ten) Bill; [a]**Philip Maero** (bar) David; [b]**Robert De Cormier Chorale;** [c]**Washington DC Cathedral Choir;** [d]**Zagreb Soloists / Antonio Janigro;** [e]**Symphony of the Air, New York / Vladimir Golschmann.** Vanguard Classics 08.4016.71 (8/92).

...Vanessa. **Soloists; New York Metropolitan Opera Chorus and Orchestra / Dimitri Mitropoulos.** RCA Victor Gold Seal GD87899 (7/90).

Francisco Barbieri

Spanish 1823-1894

New review

Barbieri El Barberillo de Lavapiés. **Lola Casariego** (mez) Paloma; **Maria Bayo** (sop) Marquesita del Bierzo; **Manuel Lanza** (bar) Lamparilla; **José Sempere** (ten) Don Luis de Haro; **Juan Pons** (bass-bar) Don Juan de Peralta; **Stefano Palatchi** (bass) Don Pedro de Monforte; **La Laguna University Polyphonic Chorus; Reyes Bartlet Choir, Puerto de la Cruz; Tenerife Rondalla and Symphony Orchestra / Victor Pablo Pérez.** Auvidis Valois Ⓟ V4731 (67 minutes: DDD: 2/96). Notes, text and translation included. Recorded 1994. ⊚⊚

Much of the sparkle in this performance of one of the pillars of the *zarzuela grande* repertoire – which first saw the light three months before both *Carmen* and *Trial by Jury* – is due to the young conductor, Victor Pablo Pérez who secures orchestral playing of a finesse all too rare in this sphere. Shorn of the raucous and crude sonorities with which many *zarzuela* performances have been fobbed off, this classic work – heard here in Barbieri's original orchestration – is given a chance to reveal its quality, which, however different in style, bears comparison with the best Viennese operettas (it is exactly contemporaneous with *Die Fledermaus*). Pablo Pérez has the advantage of a well-trained, fresh-voiced chorus and a cast of good singers, all with commendably clear enunciation – which lends point, for example, to the scene where the two women imitate the low-life speech of Madrid *majas* (more or less the equivalent of Cockney sparrows). Chief vocal honours go to Manuel Lanza in the title-role of the "little barber" who, like his Rossinian forebear, gets caught up in intrigue, though here of a political rather than an amorous nature: the parallel with Figaro is heightened on this occasion by the role being sung by a baritone instead of the usual tenor; and he is well partnered by Lola Casariego as his seamstress sweetheart. Their music, imbued with popular dance flavours, is contrasted with the more Italianate style allotted to the two aristocratic principals, Don Luis and the Marquesita. The recording is of the music only, without any of the extensive dialogue, but the big gaps in the plot are summarized in synopses, which are also translated. A firm recommendation.

Woldemar Bargiel

German 1828-1897

Suggested listening ...

...Octet in C minor, Op. 15*a. Coupled with* **Mendelssohn** Octet in E flat major, Op. 20. Divertimento. Hyperion CDA66356 (4/90).

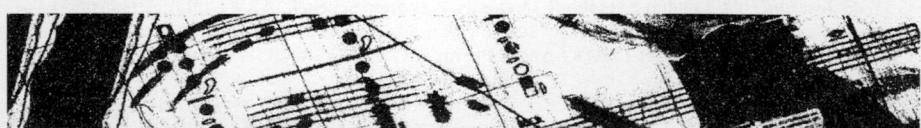

Augustin Barié
French 1884-1915

Suggested listening ...
...Trois pièces, Op. 7. Symphonie in B flat minor, Op. 5. *Coupled with* **Dupré** Le tombeau de Titelouze, Op. 38. **Peter Wright** (org). Priory PRCD406 (10/94).
...Trois Pièces. *Coupled with works by* **R. Vierne, d'Indy, Roussel, Honegger, Dupré, Langlais** and **L. Vierne** Marie-Bernadette Dufourcet (org). Priory PRCD422 (6/95). *See review in the Collections section; refer to the Index to Reviews.*

Vytautas Barkauskas
USSR 1931-

Suggested listening ...
...Partita. *Coupled with works by* **Balakauskas, Pärt** and **Schnittke** Rusné Mataityté (vn); [a]**Margrit-Julia Zimmermann** (pf). Proud Sound PROUCD139 (7/96). *See review under Bulakauskas; refer to the Index to Reviews.*

Wayne Barlow
American 1912-

Suggested listening ...
...The Winter's Past. *Coupled with works by* **Bloom, Corigliano** and **Wilder** Humbert Lucarelli (ob); **Brooklyn Philharmonic Orchestra / Michael Barrett.** Koch International Classics 37187-2 (7/94). *See review under Wilder; refer to the Index to Reviews.*

Agustín Barrios
Paraguayian 1885-1944

New review
Barrios Las abejas. Aconquija Maxima. Aire de Zamba. Le catedral. Choro da saudade. Cueca. Julia florida. Una limosna por el amor de Dios. Maxixa. Mazurka appassionata. Medallon antiquo. Un sueno en la floresta. Villancico de navidad. Preludes – C minor; G minor. Waltzes, Op. 8 – No. 3; No. 4. **John Williams** (gtr). Sony Classical [c] SK64396 (67 minutes: DDD; 9/95). Recorded 1994.

New review
Barrios Un sueno en la Floresta. Gavota Madrigal. Danza Paraguaya. Jha che valle! London carapé. Julia florida. Waltzes, Op. 8 No. 3; No. 4. Vals de Primavera. Vals Tropical. Las Abejas. Fabiniana. Mazurka appassionata. País de Abanico. Cueca. Le catedral. A Mi Madre. Caazapá. Una limosna por el amor de Dios. **David Russell** (gtr). Telarc [c] CD80373 (70 minutes: DDD; 1/96). Recorded 1994.

John Williams was by no means the first guitarist to play Barrios's music in the post-war years but he was the first to draw sustained attention to it and, from his position of authority, to ensure its place in the limelight and a popularity that would probably have amazed and gratified Barrios himself (who died in 1944). Two decades have passed since Williams's first all-Barrios disc was issued and, since interest has been sustained by the musicological delvings of Richard Stover, by the reissue of recordings made by Barrios and by the quality of the music itself, it is appropriate that he should repeat the exercise, taking advantage of the longer playing time of CD. Most of the items from the LP are included on the present recording and there are several 'extras'. Though there is very little that is not already available on some other recording there is very good reason for bringing them all together on a disc of the highest musical and technical quality, which this one certainly is. Recordings suggest that Barrios's own playing was less polished than that of Segovia but his other qualities amply compensated for this. This is a touchstone recording, essential to all gramophilic guitarists and lovers of the instrument. Nine items appear in both Russell's and Williams's programmes. Of the remainder, nine of those on Russell's disc and six on Williams's have no other recording (at the time of going to press). It is the 'unique' items that invalidate any question of choice between the two, since in both cases the performers, interpretations and recording quality are of the highest quality. One may feel Williams's tone to be the more solid, Russell's to embrace greater warmth in its spectrum, but this is a purely subjective matter. The complementary status of the two recordings extends to their annotation, Russell's being written by Richard Stover and Williams providing an interesting and more generalized essay.

Gerald Barry
Irish 1952-

Suggested listening ...
...Au Milieu[b]. Sur les Pointes[b]. Triorchic Blues[b]. Swinging Tripes and Trillibubkins[b]. Triorchic Blues[a]. Piano Quartet[ac]. Bob[ac]. "_____"[ac]. Sextet[ac]. [a]**Michael d'Arcy** (vn); [b]**Noriko Kawai** (pf); [c]**Nua Nós / Dáirine Ní Mheadhra.** NMC NMCD022 (4/95).

John Barry
British 1933-

Suggested listening ...
...The Classic John Barry – Film Scores: Zulu; Out of Africa; Midnight Cowboy; The Last Valley;
Eleanor and Franklin; Hanover Street; Born Free; Chaplin; Dances with Wolves; Raise the
Titanic; Indecent Proposal; The Persuaders; Robin and Marian; Body Heat; Somewhere in Time;
The Lion in Winter. **City of Prague Philharmonic Orchestra / Nic Raine.** Silva Screen
FILMCD141 (8/94).
...The Lion in Winter – original film soundtrack. Columbia Legacy CK66133.

Lionel Bart
British 1930-

New review
Bart (orch. W.D. Brohn) Oliver! **1994 London Palladium Cast** including **Gary Bradley, Adam Searles,
Sally Miles, Jonathan Pryce, Sally Dexter and Miles Anderson / Martin Koch.** First Night Records
Ⓕ CASTCD47 (71 minutes: DDD: 8/95). Notes and text included.
This recording of *Oliver!* based on the stage production at the London Palladium is full of good
things, not least in the successful casting of Gary Bradley in the title-role, the trickiest part to bring
off. Bradley's Oliver is no wimp – as his clear, well-focused rendition of the potentially embarrassing
"Where is love?" makes plain; and for once the scales are tipped evenly between him and the Artful
Dodger, a more or less infallible part to which Adam Searles brings his own infectious charm. The
two principal roles, of course, are haunted by memories of the past. It says much for their successors
that their performances ring true too. Sally Miles brings a sincerity and warmth to her big ballad "As
long as he needs me", whilst revelling in her music-hall ditty "Oom-pah-pah", where Bart's rhyme
about pretty little Sally displaying "her garters but not for free and gratis", always brings a smile.
Jonathan Pryce initially seems too young for this role, but save a momentary step into stock Jewish
humour in "You've got to pick a pocket" (miscued in the accompanying booklet), he comes through
with a refreshing portrayal of a rather one-dimensional character. The workhouse boys make up in
gusto for what they sometimes lack in tuning, whilst their elders and lessers make a lusty bunch in the
parlour and workhouse scenes. William Brohn's orchestrations are played with relish by the band, and
Martin Koch conducts with a real sympathy for the needs of his big cast. The recording lacks some
atmosphere considering the diverse locations that arise in the story, but it does capture every word of
Bart's enduringly popular piece.
Additional recommendation ...
...**Soloists; National Symphony Orchestra / John Owen Edwards.** TER Classics Ⓕ CDTER1184
(63 minutes: DDD: 10/92).

Béla Bartók
Hungarian 1881-1945

Bartók Piano Concertos – No. 1, Sz83; No. 2, Sz95; No. 3, Sz119. **Peter Donohoe** (pf); **City of
Birmingham Symphony Orchestra / Sir Simon Rattle.** EMI Ⓕ CDC7 54871-2 (77 minutes: DDD:
11/93). Recorded 1990-92. *Gramophone Editor's choice.*   ⒼⒼⒼ
Making Bartók's First Piano Concerto sound fun must have taken some doing, but Donohoe and
Rattle have certainly managed it. The recording blends the instrument in among the orchestra, so that
Rattle's sensitivity to nuance, Donohoe's lightness of touch and the accommodating acoustic of
Birmingham's Symphony Hall transform what we frequently hear as an angular confrontation into
something genuinely palatable. The Second Concerto, in this impressively urgent account, could hold
its own in any company, even though there are one or two passages where articulation momentarily
falters. The rest is either pungent or evocative: the second movement's 'night music' *Adagio* sections
are beautifully sustained and the finale has terrific *élan.* Taken overall, this is a marvellous trio of
performances and serves as a fresh reminder of just how great these works are.
Additional recommendations ...
...Nos. 1 and 2. **Maurizio Pollini** (pf); **Chicago Symphony Orchestra / Claudio Abbado.** DG
Ⓕ 415 371-2GH (52 minutes: ADD: 9/86).   ⒼⒼ
...Nos. 1-3. **Zoltán Kocsis** (pf); **Budapest Festival Orchestra / Iván Fischer.** Philips Ⓕ 446 366-2PH(74
minutes: DDD: 12/95).   ⒼⒼⒼ
...Nos. 1-3[a]. **Stephen Kovacevich** (pf); [a]**London Symphony Orchestra; BBC Symphony Orchestra / Sir
Colin Davis.** Philips Silver Line Ⓜ 426 660-2PSL (77 minutes: ADD: 5/91).   Ⓖ
...Nos. 1-3. **Géza Anda** (pf); **Berlin RIAS Symphony Orchestra / Ferenc Fricsay.** DG The Originals
Ⓜ 447 399-2GOR* (78 minutes: ADD: 5/95).   ⒼⒼ
...Nos. 1-3. **Zoltán Kocsis** (pf); **Budapest Festival Orchestra / Iván Fischer.** Philips Ⓕ 446 366-2PH
(74 minutes: DDD: 12/95).

New review
Bartók Piano Concerto No. 3, Sz119[a].
Schumann Symphony No. 4 in D minor, Op. 120. [a]**Géza Anda** (pf); **Staatskapelle Dresden /**

Herbert von Karajan. DG Ⓜ 447 666-2GX (55 minutes: ADD: 10/95). Recorded live in 1972.
Gramophone Editor's choice.
Trying to imagine the broader profile of Herbert von Karajan's approach to this sunniest of Bartók concertos isn't at all difficult and, sure enough, its constituent virtues include the expected executive refinement, lustrous string tone, cosseting legato and heavily weighted tutti. So far as tempo is concerned, things are more or less comparable with Anda's legendary recording under Fricsay, and although the live performance is marginally slower, there's plenty of arresting detail. For example, start at 4'48" into the *Adagio religioso* and witness how Anda softens his tone and how Karajan builds towards a seething *tremolando* on the strings. Then there is the sheer beauty of it all, be it Anda's supremely cultured pianism or Karajan's stylishly shaped accompaniment. The finale, in particular, is far darker than usual, more beefy, while the sheer force of Anda's playing reminds us of Bartók's Lisztian pedigree. In the Schumann there is much sensitive phrase shaping, most especially from the strings, while the transition from *Scherzo* to finale has a Furtwänglerian aura, replete with vivid premonitions of Bruckner and beyond. The finale itself (without repeat) is remarkably pliant: a broadly paced, ruminative affair, infinitely flexible, yet tensing its limbs for an exultant coda. As in the Bartók, there are a few executive mishaps, but all are significantly outweighed by the players' commitment. The recording is decent save for underprojected horns. This CD is a refreshing, even heartening experience, and light years removed from so many chromium-framed Karajan studio sessions that hail from the same period.

Bartók Viola Concerto, Sz120[a]. Music for Strings, Percussion and Celesta, Sz106[b]. [a]**Wolfram
Christ** (va); **Berlin Philharmonic Orchestra / Seiji Ozawa.** DG Ⓕ 437 993-2GH. (52 minutes:
DDD: 4/94). Item marked [a] recorded in 1989, [b]recorded live in 1992. ⓖⓖ
The performing edition of this affecting but uncompleted Viola Concerto takes obvious heed of Bartók's other 'late' works: yet Tibor Serly's 'completion' relates a strongly individual brand of musical poetry, not least via the lonely *più dolce* passage for viola and bassoons (4'02") and the sinister *Lento parlando* (12'25") that precedes the slow movement. The *Adagio religioso* visits an unruffled calm parallel to that in the Third Piano Concerto's similarly named centre-piece, while the finale achieves a lilting, 'folksy' sense of release. Wolfram Christ and Seiji Ozawa take a fairly gentle view though they offer us manifold interpretative insights and Christ's instrument has the textural warmth of seasoned mahogany. Neither the performance nor the (clean but close) recording can be found wanting: both do justice to the music's subtle but pensive sense of tonal fantasy. This recording of the *Music for Strings, Percussion and Celesta* has pin-point definition, a rich bass and a startlingly realistic piano sound. It is a compelling performance and a worthy coupling for the most wholly recommendable version of the Viola Concerto currently available.

Additional recommendations ...
...Viola Concerto. **Hindemith** Der Schwanendreher (Concerto after folk-songs). **Tabea
Zimmermann** (va); **Bavarian Radio Symphony Orchestra / David Shallon.** EMI Ⓕ CDC7 54101-2
(48 minutes: DDD: 3/93).
...Viola Concerto. *Coupled with works by* **S. Albert** and **Bloch.** Yo-Yo Ma (alto vn); **Baltimore
Symphony Orchestra / David Zinman.** Sony Classical Ⓕ SK57961 (78 minutes: DDD: 3/95). *See
review under Albert; refer to the Index to Reviews.* ⓖ
...Music for Strings, Percussion and Celesta. **Janáček** Capriccio[a]. **Martinů** Concerto for String
Quartet and Orchestra. [a]**Joela Jones** (pf); **Cleveland Orchestra / Christoph von Dohnányi.** Decca
Ⓕ 443 173-2DH (70 minutes: DDD: 4/95).
...Music for Strings, Percussion and Celesta[b]. Dance Suite, Sz77[a]. The wooden prince, Sz60[a].
Scriabin Le poème de l'extase, Op. 54[a]. [a]**New York Philharmonic Orchestra,** [b]**BBC Symphony
Orchestra / Pierre Boulez.** Sony Classical Boulez Edition Ⓜ SM2K64100 (two discs: 123 minutes:
ADD: 9/95).

Bartók Violin Concertos – No. 1, Sz36[a]; No. 2, Sz112[b]. **Kyung-Wha Chung** (vn); [a]**Chicago
Symphony Orchestra;** [b]**London Philharmonic Orchestra / Sir Georg Solti.** Decca Ovation
Ⓜ 425 015-2DM (59 minutes: ADD/DDD: 2/91). Item marked [a] from 411 804-1DH (10/84),
[b]SXL6212 (4/78). Item marked [a] recorded 1984, [b]1977. ⓖ
Bartók Violin Concerto No. 2, Sz112. Rhapsodies – No. 1, Sz87; No. 2, Sz90. **Kyoko Takezawa**
(vn); **London Symphony Orchestra / Michael Tilson Thomas.** RCA Victor Red Seal
Ⓕ 09026 61675-2 (63 minutes: DDD: 12/93). Recorded 1992-3. ⓖ
Bartók Violin Concerto No. 2, Sz112. Rhapsodies – No. 1, Sz87; No. 2, Sz90. **Kyung-Wha Chung**
(vn); **City of Birmingham Symphony Orchestra / Sir Simon Rattle.** EMI Ⓕ CDC7 54211-2
(59 minutes: DDD: 6/94). *Gramophone Award Winner 1994.* ⓖ
Long gone are the times when Bartók was thought of as an arch-modernist incapable of writing a melody and the young Yehudi Menuhin was considered daring in championing his Violin Concerto. Today this work is listed as his second in this form, but four decades ago it stood alone because the composer had suppressed an earlier one dating from 1908, or more precisely reshaped it into another work called *Two Portraits*. When this earlier piece was finally published in its original form some 30 years ago, it became his First Concerto and the more familiar one of 1938 his Second. The First was inspired by a beloved woman friend, but it does not by any means wear its heart on its sleeve, being a complex and edgy work to which Kyung-Wha Chung brings a passionate lyricism. Her conductor Sir

Georg Solti is the composer's compatriot and was actually his piano pupil as well, so that he too knows how to make this music breathe and sing. Chung and Solti are equally at home in the more obviously colourful and dramatic Second Concerto, giving it all the range, expressive force and occasional violence, driving momentum and sheer Hungarian charm that one could desire. The London Philharmonic Orchestra play as if inspired and the recordings (in two locations, seven years apart) are subtle yet lit with the right brilliance. Kyoko Takezawa's reading of the Second has a tonal bloom and sense of purpose that place it securely among the best available versions, while Michael Tilson Thomas and the London Symphony follow her every move, etching orchestral detail – and this score is particularly rich in incident – with obvious care and considerable imagination. The *Rhapsodies*, too, are crisply turned, and the recording well balanced.

It is rare indeed to encounter a concerto recording where the critical honours can be evenly distributed, but the EMI recording really does suggest a strong team spirit. Heard purely for its own sake, Chung's playing is sinewy, agile and occasionally a mite brittle: phrasing is always judicious, but tone production is generally less physically engaging than Takezawa's. Yet one soon realizes that every passage has been carefully thought through – the opening sequence, for example, which Chung traces as a continuous line of monologue. However, it is when soloist and conductor grapple in dialogue that the sparks really start to fly. Rattle and his players make the very most of Bartók's orchestral commentary: instrumental interplay is always alert, rhythms are keenly focused and his way of cushioning Chung, palpably convincing. The well-matched *Rhapsody* recordings are, again, revealing. The solo line is nicely attenuated, and the overall approach one of fine-tuned improvisation. Detail is legion (note the way solo violin and woodwinds intertwine at the beginning of the Second *Rhapsody*'s second movement) and Rattle compounds the rhapsodic idea by shaping his phrases with imaginatively applied rubato. So, it's a strong recommendation, with the sole proviso that Takezawa has a rather more ingratiating tonal profile than Chung. However, Chung is certainly a more probing Bartókian than she was at the time of her recording under Solti; and her poignantly expressed intelligence will doubtless prove a durable virtue.

Additional recommendations ...

...No. 2. **Moret** En rêve. **Anne-Sophie Mutter** (vn); **Boston Symphony Orchestra / Seiji Ozawa.**
DG Ⓕ 431 626-2GH (58 minutes: DDD: 11/91).   Ⓖ

...Nos. 1 and 2. **Gerhard Hertzel** (vn); **Hungarian State Symphony Orchestra / Iván Fischer.** Nimbus
Ⓕ NI5333 (63 minutes: DDD: 7/93).   ⒼⒼ

...No. 2[a]. Sonata for Solo Violin, Sz117. **Bruch** Violin Concerto No. 1 in G minor, Op. 26[a].
Mendelssohn Violin Concerto in E minor, Op. 64[b]. **Tchaikovsky** Violin Concerto in D major,
Op. 35[b]. **Ivry Gitlis** (vn); **Vienna Pro Musica Orchestra /** [a]**Jascha Horenstein,** [b]**Hans Swarowsky.**
Vox Legends mono Ⓑ CDX2 5505* (two discs: 159 minutes: ADD: 11/93).   ⒼⒼⒼ

...No. 2[c]. Piano Concertos Nos. 1-3[ab]. Concerto for Orchestra[d]. [c]**Henryk Szeryng** (vn); [ab]**Stephen
Kovacevich** (pf). [a]**London Symphony Orchestra;** [b]**BBC Symphony Orchestra / Sir Colin Davis;**
[cd]**Concertgebouw Orchestra / Bernard Haitink.** Philips Duo Ⓜ 438 812-2PM2 (two discs:
151 minutes: ADD: 2/94).   ⒼⒼⒼ

...Rhapsody No. 1. Contrasts, Sz111. *Coupled with works by* **Bloch, Debussy, Ives** and
Schubert Joseph Szigeti (vn); Béla Bartók (pfs). Biddulph mono Ⓜ LAB070/71* (two discs:
129 minutes: ADD: 7/94). *See review in the Collections section; refer to the Index to Reviews.* ⒼⒼ

New review

Bartók The Miraculous Mandarin[a]. Two Portraits, Sz37[b].
Janáček Sinfonietta[c]. [b]**Shlomo Mintz** (vn); [a]**Ambrosian Singers;** [ab]**London Symphony Orchestra,**
[c]**Berlin Philharmonic Orchestra / Claudio Abbado.** DG Masters Ⓜ 445 501-2GMA (66 minutes:
DDD: 12/94). Items marked [ab] from 410 589-1GH (8/83). Recorded 1982-7.   Ⓖ

It is scarcely surprising that Bartók's ballet *The Miraculous Mandarin* failed to reach the stage for some years after it was composed in 1918-19, for the plot concerns three ruffians who force a girl into luring men from the street up to a shabby garret. The first two men, an old rake and a shy youth, have no money and are thrown out; the third is a mysterious mandarin who strikes fear into the girl. She tries to elude his embraces and the ruffians attempt to rob and kill him, but he seems indestructible until the girl finally yields to his advances, at which point he dies. Those who normally find this score too pungently aggressive may enjoy Abbado's splendid account of the complete ballet (including the wordless chorus in the finale). He conveys the music's full power and extraordinary vividness with enormous energy and knife-edge playing from the orchestra; unlike some performances, the ear is never overtaxed, partly because the orchestra are slightly recessed. No greater contrast could be provided than the first of the *Two Portraits*, where in the most tender and ethereal fashion Bartók expresses his love for the young violinist Steffi Geyer. Here Shlomo Mintz plays most beautifully. The second *Portrait* is a brief, boisterous transcription of a piano *Bagatelle*. For this reissue DG have added to the original coupling a comparably vibrant version of Janáček's *Sinfonietta*. Here the brass sonorities are superbly resonant and the Berlin Philharmonic's playing is full of colouristic detail. The recordings are all first-class.

...The Miraculous Mandarin[a]. **L. Weiner** Suite on Hungarian Folk-tunes, Op. 18. [a]**London Voices; Philharmonia Orchestra / Neeme Järvi.** Chandos Ⓕ CHAN9029 (62 minutes: DDD: 3/92). Ⓖ

Bartók Concerto for Orchestra, Sz116[a]. The Miraculous Mandarin, Sz73[b]. **City of Birmingham Symphony** [b]**Chorus and Orchestra / Sir Simon Rattle.** EMI Ⓕ CDC5 55094-2 (70 minutes: DDD: 1/95). Item marked [a] recorded live in 1993, [b]1992. *Selected by Sounds in Retrospect.* ⒼⒼ
Bartók Concerto for Orchestra, Sz116. Kossuth (1903). **San Francisco Symphony Orchestra / Herbert Blomstedt.** Decca Ⓕ 443 773-2DH (59 minutes: DDD: 7/95). Recorded 1993.

Rattle's tone and texture in *The Miraculous Mandarin* are securely on target. There is an appropriate suggestiveness to the "Seduction Games", the strings and winds project with impressive confidence throughout, the trumpets prior to "The Chase" are more rhythmically secure than most, and the various dramatic incidents that succeed the closing pages of the Suite (and which include some of Bartók's most powerful music for the stage) are given with a genuine sense of pathos. The chorus is well balanced, the percussion, too – while Rattle himself drives all with a combination of animal vigour and teeming imagination. However, the disc's main claim to distinction is a live recording of the *Concerto for Orchestra* that, for sheer character and communicative power, virtually sweeps the board – certainly as far as the digital field is concerned. Right from the opening *Andante non troppo*, it is clear that everyone is wholly engaged in the task in hand. The "Elegia" is especially intense, with a positively outraged return of the first movement's initial *forte* idea – the dotted trumpet lending a genuinely Magýar tang to the proceedings. Again, a rhapsodizing, folk-like spontaneity spices the viola passages and, most especially, its mirror image on the winds a little later. The closing minute or so of the "Intermezzo" is more tender than any other encountered in recent years, while the finale is full of witty incident: the trilling violas at 2'01", the expressive *divisi* strings at 2'26", the ensuing *accelerando* and fugue – every little variation played for all it's worth and the whole brimming over with life and energy. The closing moments are thrilling, with a lacerating final chord tailed by a grateful volley of applause.

Blomstedt's cogently argued *Concerto for Orchestra* which, although less overtly characterful than Rattle's and less virtuosic than Reiner's, boasts a clarity, intelligence and calm sense of purpose that lend the work an almost symphonic logic. The engineering, too, is usefully revealing. Don't expect a high-octane, tough-fisted *tour de force* (although the closing pages have plenty of impact), but readers in search of a lively, keen-eyed and, particularly, a superbly recorded overview are unlikely to be disappointed. *Kossuth* was Bartók's first completed orchestral work To be quite honest, it's a pretty weak piece, full of obvious derivations (Strauss, Wagner, Liszt and so on) although you do occasionally hear intimations of Bartók's own First Suite, and even *Bluebeard's Castle*. Lajos Kossuth was, to quote Decca's notes, "the soul and motor for the campaign for Hungarian independence one and a half centuries ago". The campaign failed but Kossuth remained a hero, especially for the youthful nationalist Bartók, who commemorated him in a programmatic mini-epic, the synopsis for which reads like a sequence of silent film subtitles. *Tristan und Isolde* looms large in Section 6, while the approaching Austrian troops mutter among the bassoons and enter into a very clumsily wrought musical battle. 'Good fun' might seem a rather half-hearted, even patronizing form of commendation, but the performance serves as a sobering reminder of a great composer's unpromising immaturity. A valuable, artistically accomplished coupling.

...Concerto for Orchestra. Music for Strings, Percussion and Celesta. **Oslo Philharmonic Orchestra / Mariss Jansons.** EMI Ⓕ CDC7 54070-2 (68 minutes: DDD: 1/91).
...Concerto for Orchestra[a]. Dance Suite, Sz77. Two Portraits, Sz37. Mikrokosmos – From the diary of a fly. [a]**London Symphony Orchestra; Philharmonia Hungarica / Antál Dorati.** Mercury Ⓜ 432 017-2MM* (72 minutes: ADD: 11/91). ⒼⒼⒼ
...Concerto for Orchestra. **Enescu** Romanian Rhapsodies, Op. 11 – No. 1 in A major; No. 2 in D major. **Royal Scottish Orchestra / Neeme Järvi.** Chandos Ⓕ CHAN8947 (66 minutes: DDD: 2/92).
...Concerto for Orchestra[a]. The miraculous mandarin, Sz73 – Suite[b]. [a]**Boston Symphony Orchestra / Rafael Kubelík;** [b]**Boston Symphony Orchestra / Seiji Ozawa.** DG Ⓜ 437 247-2GGA (58 minutes: ADD: 1/93).
...Concerto for Orchestra. Four Pieces, Sz51. **Chicago Symphony Orchestra / Pierre Boulez.** DG Ⓕ 437 826-2GH (60 minutes: DDD: 3/94). Ⓖ
...Concerto for Orchestra[a]. Music for Strings, Percussion and Celesta, Sz106[b]. Hungarian Sketches, Sz97[b]. **Chicago Symphony Orchestra / Fritz Reiner.** RCA Victor Living Stereo Ⓜ 09026 61504-2 (76 minutes: ADD: 3/94). *Gramophone classical 100.* ⒼⒼⒼ
...Concerto for Orchestra. The Miraculous Mandarin. Two Pictures, Sz46. **Philharmonia Orchestra / Hugh Wolff.** Teldec Ⓕ 9031-76350-2 (76 minutes: DDD: 9/94).
...Concerto for Orchestra. The Miraculous Mandarin, Op. 19[a]. [a]**Tanglewood Festival Chorus; Boston Symphony Orchestra / Seiji Ozawa.** Philips Ⓕ 442 783-2PH (70 minutes: DDD: 8/95).
...Concerto for Orchestra. *Coupled with works by* **Beethoven** and **Rossini** Soloists; London Voices; World Orchestra for Peace / Sir Georg Solti. Decca Ⓕ 448 901-2DH (62 minutes: DDD: 3/96). *Gramophone Editor's record of the month. See review in the Collections section; refer to the Index to Reviews.*

...Concerto for Orchestra[a]. Music for Strings, Percussion and Celesta[b]. [a]**Berlin Radio Symphony Orchestra**, [b]**Berlin RIAS Orchestra / Ferenc Fricsay.** DG mono The Originals Ⓜ 447 443-2GOR* (65 minutes: ADD: 5/96).

Bartók The wooden prince, Sz60. Cantata profana, Sz94[a]. [a]**John Aler** (ten); [a]**John Tomlinson** (bass); **Chicago Symphony** [a]**Chorus and Orchestra / Pierre Boulez.** DG Ⓕ 435 863-2GH (73 minutes: DDD: 3/93). Recorded 1991.   ⒼⒼⒼ

Bartók's parable of fathers, sons and fleeing the nest, his 1930 *Cantata profana* is a mesmerizing, symmetrically designed masterpiece, where words and music are forged into an action-packed 18 minutes. Boulez provides what is by far the best studio recording the work has ever had (also the first to be digitally recorded), and truly state-of-the-art in terms of sound. Boulez is able to command a shimmering, hushed *pp* yet the battle-hardy *Allegro molto* with its hectoring syncopations and warlike percussion is full of grit and muscle. John Aler is wonderfully adroit with Bartók's high-flying solo tenor line, John Tomlinson sounds like an authentic Magyar, and the Chicago Symphony Chorus egg the proceedings on with tireless zeal. Turn then to *The wooden prince* and you confront the final flowering of Bartók's post-romantic phase; it's an effulgent, exotic piece, full of wistful, melancholy wind solos (clarinet and saxophone figure prominently) and billowing, heavily-scored climaxes. How astonishing to reflect that it was written *after* the composer's trail-blazing opera, *Bluebeard's Castle*. Again, the soft music is wonderfully atmospheric: the *ppp* muted violins in the Prelude have a ghostly pallor that is so typical of this orchestra's quiet string playing, yet when all are engaged at full throttle, the effect is shattering. Detail is legion throughout: the basses, brass and drums have immense presence. Järvi and the Philharmonia Orchestra are also very good, if rather more reverberantly recorded.

Additional recommendation ...

...The wooden prince. Hungarian Sketches, Sz97. **Philharmonia Orchestra / Neeme Järvi.** Chandos Ⓕ CHAN8895 (66 minutes: DDD: 10/91).

Bartók String Quartets – No. 1, Sz40[a]; No. 2, Sz67[b]; No. 3, Sz85[a]; No. 4, Sz91[a]; No. 5, Sz102[a]; No. 6, Sz114[b]. **Tokyo Quartet** (Koichiro Harada, Kikuei Ikeda, vns; Kazuhide Isomura, va; Sadao Harada, vc). DG 20th Century Classics Ⓜ 445 241-2GC3 (three discs: 159 minutes: ADD: 10/94). Items marked [a] from 2740 235 (4/81), [b]2530 658 (2/78). *Gramophone Award Winner 1981*. Recorded 1975-80.   ⒼⒼ

Bartók String Quartets – No. 1, Sz40[a]; No. 2, Sz67[a]; No. 3, Sz85[b]; No. 4, Sz91[b]; No. 5, Sz102[c]; No. 6, Sz114[c]. **Novák Quartet** (Antonín Novák, Dušan Pandula, vns; Josef Podjukl, va; Jaroslav Chovanec, vc). Philips Duo Ⓜ 442 284-2PM2 (two discs: 158 minutes: ADD: 10/94). Items marked [a] from SAL3686 (1/70), [b]SAL3693 (1/70), [c]SAL3694 (1/70). Recorded 1965.

Both these reissued sets totally outclass almost all their digital rivals, and yet initial comparisons between the two reveal a number of telling differences: the Novák Quartet's mellow reserve, for example, is in marked contrast to the Tokyo's febrile, acutely responsive attack; while Philips's warm-textured sound is quite unlike the harder profile and sharper focusing favoured by DG. Sometimes the Novák rather dull the cutting edge of Bartók's more acerbic writing (in the Third and Fourth Quartets, particularly), but then the last two quartets are wonderfully communicative: the Fifth with its shimmering *Adagio* and *Andante*, the Sixth with its sorrowful predominance of *Mesto* ("sad"). Not that the Tokyo lack heart. In fact, of the two quartet leaders, Koichiro Harada has the more vibrant tone, and his contribution to the Sixth Quartet in particular wrings every ounce of emotion from the score. And when it comes to the work's closing pizzicato chords, his players are the more lovingly attentive, arpeggiating the phrase so as to highlight its relationship to crucial episodes earlier on in the movement. The first two quartets find the Novák strong on mystery, the Tokyo on dynamic inflexion (theirs is by far the more vivid account of the Second's *Allegro molto capriccioso*, the closing *prestissimo* most especially). Still, when the cards are down and a final reckoning to hand, the Tokyo have the edge: their searing intensity, acute sense of colour and total commitment to each score combine for maximum impact which, if you don't already know the music, can't fail to win you over. If you do, then the Novák's manifold insights and affecting *Innigkeit* should make for an enlightening extension of your experience (and, of course, the format and price impose minimum financial and spatial sacrifices). The DG recordings were taped at various locations but have been fairly well matched, whereas Philips's (excellent) engineering is more wholly consistent. Both sets represent, in their very different ways, superb value for money, although it is a pity that DG didn't follow Philips's lead and issue the six works on two CDs.

Additional recommendations ...

...Nos. 1-6. **Végh Quartet.** Auvidis Astrée Ⓕ. Nos. 1 and 2: E7717 (57 minutes: DDD: 3/87). Nos. 3 and 4: E7718 (38 minutes: DDD: 3/87). Nos. 5 and 6: E7719 (60 minutes: DDD: 3/87).   ⒼⒼ

...Nos. 1-6. **Emerson Quartet.** DG Ⓕ 423 657-2GH2 (two discs: 149 minutes: DDD: 12/88). *Gramophone Award Winner 1989*.   ⒼⒼ

...Nos. 1-6. **Lindsay Quartet.** ASV Ⓕ CDDCS301 (three discs: 163 minutes: DDD: 3/89).   ⒼⒼ

...Nos. 3-5. **Chilingirian Quartet.** Chandos Ⓕ CHAN8634 (78 minutes: DDD: 6/89).   Ⓖ

...Nos. 1–6. **Chilingirian Quartet.** Chandos Ⓜ CHAN7013/14 (two discs: 151 minutes: DDD: 9/95).

...Nos. 1-6. **Janáček** String Quartets – No. 1, "Kreutzer Sonata"; No. 2, "Intimate Letters". **Tokyo Quartet.** RCA Victor Red Seal Ⓕ 09026 68286-2 (three discs: 199 minutes: DDD).

New review
Bartók String Quartets – No. 1, Sz40; No. 2, Sz67; No. 3, Sz85; No. 4, Sz91; No. 5, Sz102; No. 6, Sz114. **Keller Quartet** (András Keller, János Pilz, vns; Zoltán Gál, va; Ottó Kertesz, vc). Erato Ⓕ 4509-98538-2 (two discs: 149 minutes: DDD: 2/96). Recorded 1993-4

"I was delighted to hear the Keller Quartet's recordings ... and discover the extent to which [the musicians] have entered into the very soul of these works and, by living every moment of them, conveyed that soul to their listeners." So writes Sándor Végh in Erato's well-prepared booklet-note. András Keller (the Quartet's leader) is in fact a Végh pupil and it is indeed fitting that these 1993-4 sessions should have been recorded at the Salle de musique de la Chaux-de-Fonds – the very location where the Végh Quartet recorded their second (stereo) cycle. Both sets parade a lifelike body of tone, although digital technology assures the Kellers an extra degree of dynamism. As to the newer performances, what impresses most is the Kellers' naturalness, commitment and an apparent ability to survey even the most complex passages with absolute assurance. Take, for example, the Fifth Quartet's opening *Allegro*, a veritable minefield of violent rhythmic contrasts and a high point of the Végh's Astrée set; here too the attack is powerful without sounding in the least uptight while the Kellers' intonation is truer than that of their distinguished forebears. Note, also, the subtlest hint of *glissando* at the *pizzicato* start of the "Alla bulgarese" *Scherzo* (and the subtlest hint of jazz, too). The Third Quartet starts very well, though some of the *pizzicato* writing later on is occasionally a little unfocused (for example in the "Seconda parte") and the closing *Allegro molto* isn't quite as cathartic as it is with the Véghs. The first two quartets, however, are given excellent performances, the First especially, with its unmistakable premonitions of the Sixth (try 1'51" into the *Allegretto*). The Second Quartet's opening *Moderato* is sensitively shaped and displays a genuine sense of forward motion, while the *Allegro molto capriccioso*'s sudden (muted) *prestissimo* flies off at a terrific speed. In the Sixth Quartet, the Kellers balance pathos and humour with due respect for Bartók's cyclic structure (each appearance of the salient 'thematic cell' seems more meaningful than the last). Bartók's prescribed dynamics are largely respected, although his suggested timings are more less precisely realized. What matters is that the spirit is right and that this most magnificent of post-Beethoven quartet cycles emerges for all its worth as the pre-eminent achievement of twentieth century chamber music.

Bartók Violin Sonatas – No. 1, Sz75; No. 2, Sz76. Contrasts, Sz111[a]. **György Pauk** (vn); [a]**Kálmán Berkes** (cl); **Jenö Jandó** (pf). Naxos Ⓢ 8 550749 (75 minutes: DDD: 9/94). Recorded 1993.
Gramophone Editor's choice.   Ⓖ

Readers who habitually fight shy of Bartók's provocatively astringent piano writing – especially as exemplified in the Piano Sonata, *Out of doors* and *Three Studies* – might initially find these endlessly fascinating works rather unpalatable, the First Sonata especially. But careful scrutiny reveals manifold beauties which, once absorbed, tend to haunt one's memory and prompt repeated listening. Jandó's piano playing is forthright yet without the naked agression of, say, Sviatoslav Richter. Furthermore, it provides an effective foil for Pauk's warm tone and fluid solo line, especially in the First Sonata, where the interpretation is at once thoughtful and well shaped, and fully appreciative of the mysterious 'night music' that sits at the heart of the *Adagio*. The Second Sonata is both gentler and more improvisatory, its language and structure – although still pretty formidable – somewhat in the manner of a rhapsody. Pauk and Jandó again hit the target, and the full-bodied recording makes for an homogeneous sound picture. To have a spirited performance of the multi-faceted *Contrasts* as a bonus certainly helps promote this well-annotated CD to the front line of competition, especially as no other rival presents the two sonatas in tandem with such a generous coupling. A confident mainstream recommendation, then, and superb value for money.

Additional recommendations ...

...No. 1. **Janáček** Violin Sonata. **Messiaen** Theme and Variations. **Gidon Kremer** (vn); **Martha Argerich** (pf). DG Ⓕ 427 351-2GH (57 minutes: DDD: 1/91).   Ⓖ

...No. 1[a]; No. 2, Sz76b. For Children, Sz42 (trans. Szigeti)[c] – No. 28, Parlando; No. 18, Andante non molto; No. 42, Allegro vivace; No. 33, Andante sostenuto; No. 38. [ac]**David Oistrakh**, [b]**Gidon Kremer** (vns); [ac]**Frida Bauer**, [b]**Oleg Maisenberg** (pfs). Praga Ⓕ PR250038 (60 minutes: ADD: 10/93).

...No. 1. Rhapsody No. 2, Sz89. 15 Hungarian Peasant Songs, Sz71 (trans. cpsr and Országh). Piano Sonatine, Sz55 (trans. Gertler). Hungarian Folktunes, Sz66 (trans. Szigeti). **Susanne Stanzeleit** (vn); **Gusztáv Fenyö** (pf). ASV Ⓕ CDDCA883 (69 minutes: DDD: 6/94).   Ⓖ Ⓖ

...No. 2[bg]. Solo Violin Sonata, Sz117[d]. Contrasts, Sz111[acg]. [a]**Elmar Schmid** (cl); [b]**Lorand Fenyves**, [c]**Arvid Engegard**, [d]**Hans Heinz Schneeberger**, [e]**Yuuko Shiokawa** (vns); [f]**Zoltán Rácz**, [f]**Zoltan Váczi** (perc); [g]**András Schiff**, [h]**Bruno Canino** (pfs). Decca Ⓕ 443 893-2DH (64 minutes: DDD: 11/94).

Bartók Sonata for Two Pianos and Percussion, Sz110.
Ravel (arr. Sadlo) Ma mère l'oye – Pavane de la Belle au bois dormant; Les entretiens de la belle et la bête; Petit Poucet; Laideronette, Imperatrice des Pagodes; Le jardin féerique. Rapsodie espagnole. **Martha Argerich, Nelson Freire** (pfs); **Peter Sadlo, Edgar Guggeis** (perc). DG Ⓕ 439 867-2GH (56 minutes: DDD: 10/94). Recorded 1993. *Gramophone Editor's choice.*   Ⓖ Ⓖ Ⓖ

The Bartók is an extremely impetuous affair, with excitable tempos, alarmingly wide dynamics and the odd smudged detail. However, it is also one of the most compelling performances ever recorded, with the emphasis placed firmly on continuous argument and a level of intensity that extends as much to the quieter moments as, for example, to the fraught climax of the first movement's fugue. What is particularly wonderful here is the degree of subtle rubato that Argerich and Freire allow themselves, treating the music as music, and not as some modernist manifesto. As to the Ravel, the arrangements are remarkably respectful of Ravel's originals, *Ma mère l'oye* resembling Gaston Choisnel's two-piano version of 1911, the *Rapsodie* also reducing well to this particular instrumental formula (the "Habanera" was in any case originally composed for the two-piano medium). Sadlo's pitched-percussion garnishings are based largely on those that Ravel himself concocted for his orchestrations, but even those that aren't work wonderfully well. Aside from the expected tam-tam and xylophone in "Empress of the pagodas", there is the most exquisite high percussion in "The fairy garden", so beautifully handled that the absence of strings is hardly noticed. This CD should be considered an inspired 'one-off', where four top-ranking players teamed-up purely for the fun of making wonderful music together. Considered as such, it's a disc in a million.

Additional recommendation ...

...Sonata for Two Pianos and Percussion[a]. Suite for Two Pianos, Sz115a. **Jean-François Heisser, Georges Pludermacher** (pfs); [a]**Guy-Joel Cipriani,** [a]**Gérard Perotin** (perc). Erato Ⓕ 2292-45861-2 (58 minutes: DDD: 4/93).   ⒼⒼ

New review

Bartók Solo Violin Sonata, Sz117. 44 Duos, Sz98[a]. **György Pauk,** [a]**Kazuki Sawa** (vns). Naxos Ⓢ 8 550868 (73 minutes: DDD: 5/96). Recorded 1994.

György Pauk's masterful account of the Solo Sonata reminds one of thematic parallels both between the opening motif of the "Melodia" and the initial bars of the *Concerto for Orchestra* and between the *Presto* finale and parts of the Second Violin Concerto's last movement (there are side-glances at the *Concerto for Orchestra* in that movement, too). These references suggest unusually clear focusing on the part of the interpreter. Pauk – a confident and consistently perceptive Bartókian – is particularly impressive in the fugue, where his voicing is extremely secure and his tone nicely rounded. Elsewhere, treacherous double-stoppings and sighing harmonics pose him no obvious problems, while his handling of the central call to arms in the "Melodia" (so typical of Bartók's 'night music') sounds especially convincing. He doesn't hurry, he doesn't over-project, and one is grateful to join him for what sounds like an act of profound inward communion. Thereafter Pauk is joined by the Japanese violinist Kazuki Sawa for an ethnically aware account of the 44 *Duos*. Here the accent is securely on folk inflexions – the closing "Transylvanian Dance", for example, where both players effect a forwardly wailing tone. Their keen rhythmic sense is well illustrated in the snappy "Runthenian Kolomejka" and their expressive potential in "Sorrow". Naxos's recordings are entirely satisfactory.

Additional recommendations ...

...Duos. **Sándor Végh, Albert Lysy** (vns). Auvidis Astrée E7720 (50 minutes: ADD: 3/88).   ⒼⒼ
...Duos. **Fuchs** 20 Duos, Op. 55. **Eugene Drucker, Philip Setzer** (vns). Biddulph Ⓜ LAW007 (74 minutes: DDD: 3/95).   ⒼⒼ

Bartók Contrasts, Sz111[ab]. Rhapsodies – No. 1, Sz86; No. 2, Sz89[b]. Six Romanian Folk Dances, Sz56 (arr. Székely)[b]. Solo Violin Sonata, Sz117. [a]**Michael Collins** (cl); **Krysia Osostowicz** (vn); [b]**Susan Tomes** (pf). Hyperion Ⓕ CDA66415 (72 minutes: DDD: 4/91). Recorded 1990.   Ⓖ

Unusually for a composer who wrote so much fine chamber music Bartók was not himself a string player. But he did enjoy close artistic understanding with a succession of prominent violin virtuosos, including the Hungarians Jelly d'Arányi, Joseph Szigeti and Zoltán Székely, and, towards the end of his life, Yehudi Menuhin. It was Menuhin who commissioned the Sonata for solo violin, but Bartók died before he could hear him play it – Menuhin was unhappy with the occasional passages in quarter-tones and the composer had reserved judgement on his proposal to omit them. It was Menuhin's edition which was later printed and which has been most often played and recorded; but Krysia Osostowicz returns to the original and, more importantly, plays the whole work with intelligence, imaginative flair and consummate skill. The Sonata is the most substantial work on this disc, but the rest of the programme is no less thoughtfully prepared or idiomatically delivered. There is the additional attraction of an extremely well balanced and natural-sounding recording. As a complement to the string quartets, which are at the very heart of Bartók's output, this is a most recommendable disc.

Additional recommendations ...

...Solo Violin Sonata. Rhapsody No. 1. Violin Sonata No. 2, Sz76. Romanian Folk Dances, Sz56. **Susanne Stanzeleit** (vn); **Gustáv Fenyö** (pf). ASV Ⓕ CDDCA852 (64 minutes: DDD: 6/93).
...Rhapsodies Nos. 1 and 2[a]. Solo Violin Sonata. Six Romanian Folkdances (arr. Székely)[a]. For Children, Sz42 – Seven Hungarian Folktunes (arr. Szigeti)[a]. **Mark Kaplan** (vn); [a]**Bruno Canino** (pf). Arabesque Ⓕ Z6649 (62 minutes: DDD: 12/94).
...Solo Violin Sonata (arr. viola). **Shostakovich** Viola Sonata, Op. 147[a]. **Stravinsky** Elegy. **Raphael Hillyer** (va); [a]**Reinbert de Leeuw** (pf). Koch Schwann Ⓕ 311612 (74 minutes: DDD: 5/95).

Bartók Solo Piano Works. **György Sándor** (pf). Sony Classical Ⓜ SX4K68275 (four discs: 287 minutes: DDD: 11/95). Recorded 1993-5.
For Children, Sz42. The first term at the piano, Sz53. 15 Hungarian Peasant Songs, Sz71. Three Hungarian folksongs from the Csík district, Sz35a. Hungarian Folktunes, Sz66. Eight Improvisations on Hungarian Peasant Songs, Sz74. Three Rondos on (Slovak) Folktunes, Sz84. Romanian Christmas Carols, Sz57. Six Romanian Folkdances, Sz56. Two Romanian Dances, Sz43. Suite, Sz62, with original Andante. Piano Sonata, Sz80. Sonatina, Sz55. 14 Bagatelles, Sz38. Four Dirges, Sz45. Petite Suite, Sz105. Violin Duos, Sz98 (arr. Sándor) – No. 1, Teasing Song; No. 17, Marching song; No. 35, Ruthenian kolomejka; No. 42, Arabian song; No. 44, Transylvanian dance. 10 Easy Pieces, Sz39. Allegro barbaro, Sz49. Out of doors, Sz81. Seven Sketches, Sz44. Two Elegies, Sz41. Three Burlesques, Sz47. Nine Little Pieces, Sz82. Three Studies, Sz72.

There can't be many pianists on the current circuit whose fund of experience extends to working with a major twentieth-century master; but of those still recording, György Sándor must surely take pride of place. Sándor prepared Bartók's first two piano concertos under the composer's guidance and gave the world premières of the Third Concerto and the piano version of the *Dance Suite*. The present collection is Sándor's second survey of Bartók's piano music and he programmes all the major works apart from *Mikrokosmos*. Many of the new performances are exceptionally fine, even though the passage of time has witnessed something of a reduction in Sándor's pianistic powers, mostly where maximum stamina and high velocity fingerwork are required (as in the first *Burlesque*). However, you may be astonished at the heft, energy and puckish humour of Sándor's 1994 recording of the Piano Sonata, a more characterful rendition than its predecessor, with a particularly brilliant account of the folkish *Allegro molto* finale. The *Allegro barbaro* is similarly 'on the beam', while Sándor brings a cordial warmth to the various collections of ethnic pieces, the *Romanian Christmas Carols* especially. His phrasing, rubato, expressive nuancing, attention to counterpoint and command of tone (sample the *15 Hungarian Peasant Songs*) suggest the touch of a master, while his imagination relishes the exploratory nature of the *Improvisations*, *Bagatelles* and *Miraculous Mandarin*-style *Studies*.

Viewed overall, Kocsis (reviewed below) offers the more painstakingly precise reportage of Bartók's notation and a rather more sharply focused presentation of the music's multi-faceted rhythmic personality. He is also the more adroit technician, whereas his acute musical intuition guarantees a high level of interpretative individuality. Like Sándor, he approaches the texts (either written or recorded) as guide-lines, and it is fair to say that in this respect at least, the differences between the two pianists are more a matter of degree than principle. Both give their all wherever Hungarian folk music predominates: sample Kocsis in the first of the *Csík* Folksongs, Sz35a or Sándor in "Evening with the Széklers" from *Ten Easy Pieces* and you'd be hard pressed to choose between them. Which leaves scant space to promote the music's abundant qualities, be they harmonic or rhythmic innovation, powerful emotion telescoped into a minute time-span (*For Children* and the various sequences of short pieces), humour (*Burlesques*), introspection (*Dirges*), autobiography (the various manifestations of Steffi Geyer's theme), ethnic variety (Hungarian, Romanian, Ruthenian, Arabic, etc.) or the sheer scope and complexity of Bartók's piano writing in general. Sándor connects with it all, much as he did 30 years ago, while he now enjoys the added advantage of full-bodied digital sound. His principal rivals are, for the moment at least, severely compromised by being 'incomplete'. In sum, intuitive interpreters, especially those who knew and understand the composers they perform, are becoming an increasingly rare breed. In that respect alone, György Sándor's Bartók deserves an honoured place in every serious CD collection of twentieth-century piano music.

Bartók For Children, Sz42. **Zoltán Kocsis** (pf). Philips Ⓕ 442 146-2PH (75 minutes: DDD: 6/95). Recorded 1994. ⒼⒼ
Bartók's piano cycle *For Children* may be beautiful, varied and harmonically challenging, but it's certainly not 'easy' – at least not in comparison with, say, *First Term at the Piano* or the first two books of the later *Mikrokosmos*. Musically, though, there is much to hold the interest, whether in the sheer tunefulness of the material, or the 'user-friendly' presentation of its occasionally complex rhythms, the richness of Bartók's modulations, or even the narrative skill that transforms certain pieces into miniature tone-poems. And yet only a major recreative talent could successfully string this particular collection of pearls as a single sweeping sequence. Zoltán Kocsis triumphs on all fronts. His mature technique allows for superior timing, a warmer touch (chords in particular are expressively weighted) and a potent blend of scholarship and musical spontaneity.

Additional recommendation ...
...For Children. Mikrokosmos, Sz107 – progressive pieces for piano in six volumes (complete, Books 1-6). **Dezsö Ránki** (pf). Teldec Ⓜ 9031-76139-2 (three discs: 200 minutes: ADD: 10/92). Ⓔ
...For Children. **Géza Anda** (pf). Testament mono Ⓕ SBT1065* (79 minutes: ADD: 10/95). *See review in the Collections section; refer to the Index to Reviews.*

Bartók Piano works, Volume 1 – 14 Bagatelles, Sz38. Two Elegies, Sz41. Sonatine, Sz55. Six Romanian Folk Dances, Sz56. Three Hungarian Folk Tunes, Sz66. **Zoltán Kocsis** (pf). Philips Ⓕ 434 104-2PH (54 minutes: DDD: 1/94). Recorded 1991. ⒼⒼⒼ

Bartók himself admitted that his *Bagatelles* (1908) were largely experimental, and indeed at least half-a-dozen of them could easily have fallen from a jazz-pianist's copybook (Nos. 7, 11 and 12, particularly), their sensual harmonies and capricious rhythimic computations prophetic of so much that was to happen in that world. Debussy, too, is much in evidence (No. 3), as is Bartók's love of folk-song (Nos. 4 and 5). The *Elegies* would sit nicely among the shorter works of Busoni. These virtuosic effusions recall the moon-flecked world of late Liszt, albeit flushed with a Hungarian rather than a gipsy complexion. Folk-song proper informs Kocsis's last three selections: the familiar *Six Romanian Folk Dances*, the cheerful and ingenious *Sonatine* and the relatively dense *Hungarian Folk Tunes*, Sz66 – the last bringing us to the far edge of the Great War. It's a cliffhanger of a finale, and has us eager for more. Kocsis's readings are absolutely on target. A peach of a disc.

Bartók Piano Works, Volume 2 – Two Romanian Dances, Sz43. Three Hungarian folksongs from the Csík district, Sz35*a*. Allegro barbaro, Sz49. Four Dirges, Sz45. Suite, Sz62. Romanian Christmas Carols, Sz57. Three Studies, Sz72. Three Rondos on Folktunes, Sz84. The first term at the piano, Sz53. **Zoltán Kocsis** (pf). Philips Ⓕ 442 016-2PH (71 minutes: DDD: 11/94). Recorded 1993. *Gramophone Editor's choice.*   Ⓖ
The spontaneous nature of Bartók's own recorded performances is a quality that Kocsis achieves in his own playing. He also displays an ecstatic involvement in Bartók's harmonic writing, most particularly in the delicious, eloquently voiced *Three Hungarian folksongs from the Csík district* and the exploratory *Three Studies*, the first as violent as the Miraculous Mandarin's murder, the third, a shifting sequence of computations that anticipates the player-piano studies of Conlon Nancarrow. Kocsis's performances are never mere replications of Bartók's own; rather, they take the composer's lead in generating energy without aggression, poetry without indulgence and accuracy without pedantry. The rest of the programme of Vol. 2 is as varied as the incidents within each individual opus. The *Two Romanian Dances*, both of them rich in novel variation, are thrust forwards in heady excitement, the first breaking half-way for a darkly rhapsodic central section, the second, a sort of mad-cap burlesque. The *Allegro barbaro* discards its customary metallic sheen (mistakenly applied by pianists who have no understanding of Bartók's idiom) and, instead, assumes more authentically Hungarian characteristics. Then there are the deeply expressive *Four Dirges*, the varied and instantly memorable *Romanian Christmas Carols* and the masterly Suite, Sz62 (the best place to start if you're at all sheepish about tackling the musical complexion of Bartók's major piano works). The disc contents are imaginatively varied, the interpretations beyond criticism, the recordings superb (warm, close and lifelike, as per Philips's 'house' style) and the documentation highly informative.

New review
Bartók Piano works. **Béla Bartók** (pf). Pearl mono Ⓜ GEMMCD9166* (69 minutes: ADD: 6/96). From HMV, Patria, Columbia and Continental originals; recorded 1929-42.
László Somfai observed how Bartók's manner of playing was "fortified with his rich experiences of Classical interpretation and adopted very carefully the truly personal 'accentuations' of his own music". In most instances, Bartók didn't so much transcend his own rules as allow himself maximum freedom within them: time and again one notices minute adjustments in matters of rhythm, dynamics or inflexion, none of which disrupts the flow or distorts the character of the music. This compilation, the most comprehensive available on a single disc, offers full-bodied transfers of some fascinating commercial recordings, not least of Liszt's "Sursum corda" (*Années de pèlerinage – Troisième année*) which, in contrast with, say, Alfred Brendel's beautifully delineated account on Philips (2/96), sounds like a spontaneous transcription of an orchestral piece – such is its rugged grandeur. The next track (17) finds Bartók unsteady at the start of *Mikrokosmos*'s "Staccato", but how thrilling are the hungry, almost Schnabelian 'snatched' phrases of the succeeding "Ostinato" and the wicked caprices of that underrated masterpiece, *Improvisations on Hungarian Peasant Songs* (which Bartók recorded only in excerpt). There are 38 tracks in all on this disc, with the Suite, Op. 14 and the First *Romanian Dance* taking pride of place as Bartók's finest solo recordings. The *Allegro barbaro* is also good, though nowhere near as barbaric as some – a significant fact given a plethora of fierce-fisted Bartókians, all of whom should make an effort to hear this invaluable CD.

Bartók Duke Bluebeard's castle. **Siegmund Nimsgern** (bass-bar) Bluebeard; **Tatiana Troyanos** (mez) Judith; **BBC Symphony Orchestra / Pierre Boulez.** Sony Classical Boulez Edition Ⓜ SMK64110 (61 minutes: ADD: 3/95). Notes, text and translation included. From CBS 76518 (9/76). Recorded 1976.   ⒼⒼⒼ
Bartók Duke Bluebeard's castle. **Walter Berry** (bass-bar) Bluebeard; **Christa Ludwig** (mez) Judith; **London Symphony Orchestra / István Kertész.** Decca The Classic Sound Ⓜ 443 571-2DCS (59 minutes: ADD: 4/95). Notes, text and translation included. From SET311 (5/66). Recorded 1965.   ⒼⒼ
The crux of the drama, its emotional thrust and potent symbolic allusions, all are unequivocally realized by Siegmund Nimsgern, Tatiana Troyanos and Pierre Boulez. Troyanos's Judith has more credibility than most. For example, that wonderful passage 3'21" into the "First Door", when Bluebeard asks Judith why she must open all the doors, and she responds with a confession of love – is seethingly intense, although the frenzied string writing that tails her candid "because I love you" rather loses focus in all the steam. Yet Boulez captures to perfection the ambiguous nature of Bartók's

heated response, whether Judith really is in love – or just plain curious. Again, at the "Third Door" ("Now behold my spacious kingdom"), the impact is colossal, even though digital technology would have stretched the dynamic curve even further. Judith's triumphant, heroically sustained C sounds more genuinely wonder-struck than any other on record, while Boulez's pacing is ideally judged – in fact, throughout this memorable performance, he balances the constituent parts of Bartók's rich tonal palette with a meticulous ear, patiently scaling the score's many texturally complex climaxes. Nimsgern is a tortured, yet commanding Bluebeard, vocally excellent and interpretatively compelling, although the recording does sometimes lend his voice an untypically cavernous quality.

Readers in search of sharp-edged instrumental accents or the texture and tang of native Hungarian singers would be better advised to search out Dorati's 1962 version for Mercury. Kertész, on the other hand, favours a far richer sound-stage, with softer contours (his armoury suggests more weight than glinting steel, his torture chamber, anxiety rather than cruelty) and a passionate swell to the string writing. When it comes to the husband-and-wife team of Walter Berry and Christa Ludwig, one senses more a woman discovering sinister aspects of the man she loves than an inquisitive shrew intent on plundering Bluebeard's every secret. Here, Judith seems perpetually poised to take Bluebeard's arm and linger lovingly about him, while Berry's assumption of the title-role – which is beautifully, if not terribly idiomatically, sung – suggests neither *Angst* nor impatience. Ludwig, too, was in wonderful voice at the time of this recording, and instances of her eloquence are far too numerous to list individually. Placing this classic recording in the context of its finest rivals is fairly easy, in that Kertész represents the opera's compassionate core, whereas Boulez opts for maximum drama, Dorati, mobility and native inflexion. If you don't already know the piece and are happiest when listening to mainstream romantic opera, then try either this splendid-sounding reissue or the (sonically inferior) Boulez. The current transfer is superb, with a thunderous organ beyond the fifth door and merely the odd rogue edit or spot of tape hiss to betray the passing years.

Additional recommendations ...
...**Soloists; Bavarian State Orchestra / Wolfgang Sawallisch.** DG 20th Century Classics Ⓜ 423 236-2GC (58 minutes: ADD: 9/88). ⒼⒼ
...**Duke Bluebeard's castle**[a]. [a]**Olga Szönyi** (sop) Judith; [a]**Mihály Székely** (bass) Bluebeard. **Berg** Wozzeck – excerpts[b]. [b]**Helga Pilarczyk** (sop); **London Symphony Orchestra / Antál Dorati.** Mercury Living Presence Ⓜ 434 325-2MM (73 minutes: ADD: 7/93). ⒼⒼ
...**Soloists; Frankfurt Radio Symphony Orchestra / Eliahu Inbal.** Denon Ⓕ CO-78932 (60 minutes: DDD: 10/95).
...**Soloists; Stravinsky** Oedipus rex[a]. [a]**North German Radio Chorus;** [a]**Berlin RIAS Chamber Choir; Berlin Radio Symphony Orchestra / Ferenc Fricsay.** DG Double mono Ⓜ 445 445-2GX2* (two discs: 112 minutes: ADD: 11/95).

Further listening ...
...**Divertimento for Strings, Sz113.** *Coupled with* **Schoenberg** Verklärte Nacht. **Hindemith** Trauermusik for Viola and Strings[a]. [a]**Cecil Aronowitz** (va); **English Chamber Orchestra / Daniel Barenboim.** EMI Matrix CDM5 65079-2 (12/94). Ⓖ
...**Five Songs, Sz61**[a]. **Five Songs, Sz63**[a]. Hungarian Folksongs, Sz64 – Black is the earth; My God, my God; Wives, let me be one of your company; So much sorrow; If I climb the rocky mountains. Five Songs, Sz61 (orch. Kodály)[b]. Five Hungarian Folksongs, Sz101[b]. **Júlia Hamari** (contr); [a]**Ilona Prunyi** (pf); [b]**Hungarian State Orchestra / János Kovacs.** Hungaroton HCD31535 (7/93). ⒼⒼⒼ
...**Sonatina, Sz55.** *Coupled with works by* **Liszt** and **Delibes/Dohnányi** Géza Anda (pf); **Philharmonia Orchestra / Alceo Galliera.** Testament mono SBT1067* (10/95). *See review in the Collections section; refer to the Index to Reviews.*
...**Rhapsody, Sz27. Scherzo, Sz28.** *Coupled with* **Dohnányi** Variations on a Nursery Theme, Op. 25. **Zoltán Kocsis** (pf); **Budapest Festival Orchestra / Iván Fischer.** Philips 446 472-2PH (4/96).
...**Dance Suite, Sz77. Ravel** La valse. **Satie** Parade. **Busoni** Tanzwalzer, Op. 53. **Liadov** Kikimora, Op. 63. **Chabrier** Le roi malgré lui – Fête polonaise. **Liszt** Mephisto Waltz No. 2, S111. **Philharmonia Orchestra / Igor Markevitch.** Testament mono Ⓕ SBT1060* (77 minutes: ADD: 2/96).
...**Dance Suite, Sz77. Two Pictures, Sz46. Hungarian Sketches, Sz97. Divertimento, Sz113. Chicago Symphony Orchestra / Pierre Boulez.** DG Ⓕ 445 825-2GH (72 minutes: DDD: 9/95).
...**Two Pictures, Sz46.** *Coupled with* **Stravinsky** Le baiser de la fée. **La Scala Philharmonic Orchestra, Milan / Riccardo Muti.** Sony Classical SK58949 (61 minutes: DDD: 9/95).

Antoine-Edouard Batiste

French 1820-1876

Suggested listening ...
...**Offertoire in D minor.** *Coupled with works by* **Bossi, Dubois, Dupré, Jolivet, Lefébure-Wély, Lemare** and **Saint-Saëns** Christopher Herrick (org). Hyperion CDA66457 (9/91). *See review in the Collections section; refer to the Index to Reviews.* ⒼⒼⒼ

Alison Bauld
Australian 1944-

Suggested listening ...
...*Farewell Already. Coupled with works by* **Connolly, P.P. Nash, Weir, Elias, Payne** and
A. Gilbert Jane Manning (sop); **Jane's Minstrels / Roger Montgomery.** NMC Artists' Series
NMCD025 (10/95). *See review in the Collections section; refer to the Index to Reviews.*

Sir Arnold Bax
British 1883-1953

Bax Symphonies – No. 1 in E flat major[a]; No. 7[b]. **London Philharmonic Orchestra /** [a]**Myer**
Fredman, [b]**Raymond Leppard.** Lyrita Ⓕ SRCD232 (78 minutes: ADD: 12/92). Item marked [a] from
SRCS53 (8/71), [b]SRCS83 (11/75).   Ⓖ
Few English composers have expressed such intense and fiercely passionate emotions as Bax has in
the first two movements of his First Symphony. Such rage and grief as can be found there seem to
suggest a psycho-drama being played out, and when we learn that at the time of its composition
(1921) Bax may still have been coming to terms with the aftermath of the Great War, the loss of
friends in the Easter Rising in Ireland and the irretrievable breakdown of his marriage, it is tempting
to imagine that the symphony is indeed exercising some kind of personal exorcism on these events.
Bax himself, however, was always reluctant to admit the existence of such a 'programme' behind the
symphony, and in many ways he was probably right to do so. Whatever personal experiences Bax had
poured into it, the end result is unquestionably a powerful, cogent symphony of universal appeal. The
Seventh and last of Bax's symphonies makes an intelligent and well contrasted coupling. The first
movement, though not without tension and some storm-tossed passages (very much a Baxian
seascape this) has a prevailing mood of hope and expectation – as though embarking on some
adventurous seaward journey to new lands, whilst the second movement finds Bax in wistful
'legendary' mood so evocative of the early tone-poems. The last movement begins by echoing the
optimism of the first movement, but finally gives way, in the long and beautiful epilogue, to a mood
of autumnal nostalgia and sad farewell. These are classic Lyrita recordings, with exceptionally fine
performances from Fredman and Leppard and superb digital transfers.
Additional recommendation ...
...Nos. 1-7. **London Philharmonic Orchestra; Ulster Orchestra / Bryden Thomson.** Chandos
   Ⓕ CHAN8906/10 (five discs: 300 minutes: DDD).

Bax Symphony No. 3 in C major. Four Orchestral Sketches – Dance of Wild Irravel. Paean.
London Philharmonic Orchestra / Bryden Thomson. Chandos Ⓕ CHAN8454 (59 minutes:
DDD: 12/86). Recorded 1986.   Ⓖ
Bax's Third Symphony has a long and gravely beautiful epilogue, one of the most magical things he
ever wrote: a noble processional with a disturbing, motionless glitter at its centre and, just before the
very end, a sudden bitter chill. It is pure Bax, and will haunt you for days. We may associate some of
the Symphony with the lonely sands and the shining sea of Morar in Invernessshire (where the work
was written), the impassioned string music that rises from that sea in the centre of the slow movement
with deep emotion, the war-like dance of the finale with conflict or war and the frequent violent
intercuttings of lyricism and darkness with what we know about Bax's temperament. But it is harder
to explain in programmatic terms why lyric can become dark or vigour become brooding within
startlingly few bars, why that epilogue seems so inevitable, why the Symphony for all its wild
juxtapositions does not sound like a random sequence of vivid memories and passionate
exclamations. That it is a real symphony after all, powered by purely musical imperatives, is suggested
by this finely paced and tautly controlled performance, one of the finest in Thomson's Bax cycle. The
enjoyable racket of *Paean* and the glittering colour of *Irravel* respond no less gratefully to the
sumptuousness of the recording.

New review
Bax Nonet[a]. Oboe Quintet[b]. Elegiac Trio[c]. Clarinet Sonata[d]. Harp Quintet[e]. **Nash Ensemble**
([ac]Philippa Davies, fl; [ab]Gareth Hulse, ob; [ad]Michael Collins, cl; [abe]Marcia Crayford, [be]Iris Juda,
[a]Elizabeth Wexler, vns; [abce]Roger Chase, va; [abe]Christopher van Kampen, vc; [a]Duncan McTier,
db; [ce]Skaila Kanga, hp; [ad]Ian Brown, pf). Hyperion Ⓕ CDA66807 (73 minutes: DDD: 5/96).
Recorded 1995. *Gramophone Editor's choice.*   ⒼⒼ
A truly first-rate modern recording of Bax's Nonet. What a bewitching creation it is, overflowing with
beguiling invention and breathtakingly imaginative in its instrumental resource (the sounds created
are often almost orchestral). Bax worked on the Nonet at the same time (1929-30) as he was
composing his Third Symphony and there are striking similarities between the two works. The Nash
Ensemble (under the direction of Ian Brown) give a masterly, infinitely subtle reading – a worthy
successor to the classic 1937 recording with the Griller Quartet and distinguished colleagues (now
beautifully refurbished by Dutton Laboratories). The remainder of the disc brings comparable
pleasure. The delightful Oboe Quintet (written for Leon Goossens in 1922) receives immensely
characterful treatment, especially the jaunty, Irish-jig finale (such sparkling, richly communicative
playing). The same is true of the lovely Harp Quintet, which is essayed here with a rapt intensity and

delicious poise. In the hands of these stylish artists, the *Elegiac Trio* possesses a delicacy and gentle poignancy that are really quite captivating. That just leaves the engaging Clarinet Sonata, a work that has fared well in the recording studio over the last few years. Suffice to report, Michael Collins and Ian Brown are compelling advocates, and theirs is a performance to set beside (if not supersede) those of Emma Johnson and Malcolm Martineau and Janet Hilton and Keith Swallow. Beautiful sound and expert balance throughout.

Additional recommendations ...

...Clarinet Sonata. **Bliss** Clarinet Quintet **Vaughan Williams** Six Studies in English folk song. **Janet Hilton** (cl); **Lindsay Quartet.** Chandos Ⓕ CHAN8683 (52 minutes: DDD: 2/89).

...Oboe Quintet. **Bliss** Oboe Quintet. **Britten** Phantasy for Oboe Quartet, Op. 2. **Pamela Woods** (ob); **Audubon Quartet.** Telarc Ⓕ CD80205 (55 minutes: DDD: 10/89).

...Clarinet Sonata. **Ireland** Fantasy-Sonata in E flat major[a]. **Vaughan Williams** Six Studies in English folk song[a] . Three Vocalises for Soprano Voice and Clarinet[b]. **Bliss** Pastoral (posth)[a]. Two Nursery Rhymes[b]. **Stanford** Clarinet Sonata, Op. 129*Af*. [b]**Judith Howarth** (sop); **Emma Johnson** (cl); [a]**Malcolm Martineau** (pf). ASV Ⓕ CDDCA891 (74 minutes: DDD: 7/94).

...Nonet[a]. **Delius** Violin Sonata No. 3[b]. **Ferguson** Octet, Op. 4[c]. **Moeran** String Trio in G major[d]. [a]**Joseph Slater** (fl), [a]**Leon Goossens** (ob); [a]**Frederick Thurston**, [c]**Pauline Juler** (cls); [c]**Dennis Brain** (hn); [c]**Cecil James** (bn); [b]**Albert Sammons**, [d]**Jean Pougnet** (vns); [d]**Frederick Riddle** (va); [d]**Anthony Pini** (vc); [c]**James Edward Merrett**, [a]**Victor Watson** (dbs); [a]**Maria Korchinska** (hp); [b]**Kathleen Long** (pf); [ac]**Griller Quartet.** Dutton Laboratories mono Ⓜ CDAX8014* (72 minutes: ADD: 12/95).

New review

Bax Piano Trio in B flat major.
Holst Short Piano Trio in E major.
Stanford Piano Trio No. 2 in G minor, Op. 73. **Pirasti Trio** (Nicholas Miller, vn; Alison Wells, vc; Jeffrey Sharkey, pf). ASV Ⓕ CDDCA925 (72 minutes: DDD: 9/95). Recorded 1994.

A valuable, uncommonly rewarding collection. Especially impressive here is the Stanford Second Piano Trio of 1899 (there are two others, dating from 1889 and 1918). This is immensely civilized music, solidly constructed, inventive, eloquent (especially in the *Andante* slow movement) and always distinguished by impeccable craft. Holst completed his Trio in E in 1894, a year into his studies at the Royal College of Music. Stanford was his composition tutor from 1893 to 1898, and the present work (one of his "early horrors", as he later labelled his student efforts) is melodious, neat and unpretentious – only at the rapt close of the central *Adagio* do we catch just the merest whiff of the composer's mature style. Bax's Trio, on the other hand, dates from towards the end of his career (the score was finished in January 1946). It is a most attractive, engagingly tuneful creation, its comparatively relaxed demeanour characteristic of Bax's later manner. These are fervent, beautifully accomplished performances and the sound is admirably natural.

Bax Cello Sonata in E flat major. Folk Tale. Cello Sonatina in D major. Legend-Sonata in F sharp minor. **Bernard Gregor-Smith** (vc); **Yolande Wrigley** (pf). ASV Ⓕ CDDCA896 (76 minutes: DDD: 8/94). Recorded 1993.

There are three beautiful slow movements here, and all three of them are wistful backward glances; quotes from *Spring Fire*, *The Garden of Fand*, and, in the *Sonatina*, Delius's *Brigg Fair*. Poignant regret for the vanished past is one of the things one expects from Bax; another is that unstable alternation of mood out of which he paradoxically wove some of his most powerful symphonic structures. That is here too, most overtly in the first movement of the E flat Sonata. Old Bax hands will know his way of reducing a melody to its basic rhythm and then allowing that to sprout new melodic ideas. That happens here; so does that other Bax ploy of touching an apparently new vein, but only in order to spark a coda. The outer movements of the *Sonatina* are problem- and shadow-free Bax; the *Folk Tale* is no such thing, but another haunted recollection, grave, poignant and angry by turns. The Irish dream? Lost love? Vanished youth? The essence of Bax would perhaps vanish if we were able to put a precise label on his nostalgias, sorrows and regrets. All four pieces are given strong and eloquent performances, and are cleanly recorded; Gregor-Smith's tone is sinewy rather than plummily rich, which serves the composer well.

New review

Bax Epithalamium[a]. I sing of a maiden. Lord, thou hast told us. [a]Magnificat. Mater ora filium. This worldës joie.
Villette Attende Domine. Hymne à la Vierge. O magnum mysterium. O sacrum convivium. Salve regina. **Rodolfus Choir / Ralph Allwood** with [a]**Christopher Hughes** (org). Herald Ⓕ HAVPCD176 (60 minutes: DDD: 9/95). Recorded 1993.

This is rather special. The Rodolfus Choir's members, aged between 16 and 25, are graduates of Ralph Allwood's popular Eton Choral Courses for young singers. Allwood has the gift of exploiting the vocal colour of young voices to thrilling effect (only the tenors are very occasionally betrayed by their youth), but he also manages to harness the sense of zeal that characterizes the best endeavours of young people together with a remarkable corporate musical intelligence and sensitivity. The sound is lovely within a wide dynamic and tonal spectrum but there is real understanding also, not just of text and mood, but of musical processes as well. That is just as well since this programme is a sumptuous pudding of rich choral textures and harmonic elaboration. Pierre Villette (b.1926) was Director of the Besançon and Aix-en-Provence Conservatoires, and his Latin motets written between 1944 and 1983 mine a harmonic vein somewhat akin to Poulenc at his most consistently gorgeous. In other hands it might all seem just too self-indulgent, but here the added-note harmonies are balanced with painstaking delicacy and the phrasing is controlled eloquently and without exaggeration. The meat of the programme is in the Bax works. The unaccompanied works are masterpieces, in particular *This worldës joie* and above all *Mater ora filium*, which makes technical demands almost equal to those of the big Richard Strauss motets while possessing greater emotional truth and urgency. Fine though the performances by Paul Spicer's Finzi Singers are, Allwood's direction has even more poetry and the Rodolfus Choir rise above the technical challenges to convey a sense of radiance and elation. There is a perceptive accompanying note by David Goode and, despite the varied size of the choir in different pieces, the recording (made in Eton College Chapel) of the *a cappella* works is perfectly judged in perspective, acoustic and clarity. A marvellous disc.

Additional recommendation ...

...I sing of a maiden. This worldës joie. Mater ora filium. Five Greek Folk-Songs. **Howells** Two
   Madrigals. Long, long ago. The summer is coming. Take him, earth, for cherishing. **Finzi Singers
   / Paul Spicer.** Chandos Ⓕ CHAN9139 (63 minutes: DDD: 6/93).

Further listening ...

...Cello Concerto[a]. Northern Ballad No. 3 – Prelude for a Solemn Occasion. Cortège.
   Mediterranean. Overture to a Picaresque Comedy. [a]**Raphael Wallfisch** (vc); **London Philharmonic
   Orchestra / Bryden Thomson.** Chandos CHAN8494 (11/87).
...Violin Concerto. Legend. Romantic Overture. Golden Eagle – incidental music. [a]**Lydia
   Mordkovitch** (vn); **London Philharmonic Orchestra / Bryden Thomson.** Chandos CHAN9003
   (4/92).   Ⓖ
...Symphonic Variations in E major. Morning Song, "Maytime in Sussex". **Margaret Fingerhut** (pf);
   London Philharmonic Orchestra / Bryden Thomson. Chandos CHAN8516 (2/88).
...The Garden of Fand. *Coupled with* **Bantock** Fifine at the Fair. **Berners** The Triumph of
   Neptune[a]. [a]**Robert Alva** (bass); **Royal Philharmonic Orchestra / Sir Thomas Beecham.** EMI
   CDM7 63405-2* (6/92).
...On the sea-shore (ed./orch. Parlett). *Coupled with* **Bridge** The Sea. **Britten** Peter Grimes – Four
   Sea Interludes; Passacaglia. **Ulster Orchestra / Vernon Handley.** Chandos CHAN8473 (3/87).
...Northern Ballad No. 1. Mediterranean. The Garden of Fand. Tintagel[a]. November Woods.
   London Philharmonic Orchestra / Sir Adrian Boult. Lyrita SRCD231 (9/92).   Ⓖ
...Spring Fire. Symphonic Scherzo. Northern Ballad No. 2. **Royal Philharmonic Orchestra / Vernon
   Handley.** Chandos CHAN8464 (9/86).   ⒼⒼ
...Winter Legends. Saga Fragment. **Margaret Fingerhut** (pf); **London Philharmonic Orchestra /
   Bryden Thomson.** Chandos CHAN8484 (2/87).   Ⓖ
...Festival Overture[a]. Christmas Eve on the Mountains[b]. Dance of Wild Irravel[c]. Paean[c].
   Nympholept[d]. Tintagel[e]. [abcd]**London Philharmonic Orchestra,** [e]**Ulster Orchestra / Bryden
   Thomson.** Chandos CHAN9168 (2/94). *Selected by Sounds in Retrospect.*   Ⓖ
...Tintagel[a]. *Coupled with* **Vaughan Williams** Symphony No. 5 in D major[b]. [a]**London Symphony
   Orchestra;** [b]**Philharmonia Orchestra / Sir John Barbirolli.** EMI British Composers CDM5 65110-2
   (3/95).
...The Boar's Head. *Coupled with works by* **Elgar, Vaughan Williams, Howells, Delius, Warlock,
   Britten** and **Holst. London Madrigal Singers / Christopher Bishop; Baccholian Singers of London;
   Philip Jones Brass Ensemble; English Chamber Orchestra / Ian Humphris.** EMI British Composers
   CMS5 65123-2 (2/96). *See review in the Collections section; refer to the Index to Reviews.*
...Piano Quintet[a]. String Quartet No. 2 in E minor. [a]**David Owen Norris** (pf); **Mistry String Quartet.**
   Chandos CHAN8795 (4/91).
...Violin Sonatas – No. 1 in E major; No. 2 in D major. **Erich Gruenberg** (vn); **John McCabe** (pf).
   Chandos CHAN8845 (9/90).
...Legend for Viola and Piano. *Coupled with works by* **Britten, Vaughan Williams, R. Clarke,
   Grainger** and **Bridge** **Paul Coletti** (va); **Leslie Howard** (pf). Hyperion CDA66687 (10/94). *See
   review in the Collections section; refer to the Index to Reviews.*   Ⓖ
...Piano Sonatas – No. 1 in F sharp minor; No. 2 in G major. Lullaby. Country Tune. Winter
   Waters. **Eric Parkin** (pf). Chandos CHAN8496 (12/87).
...Two Russian Tone Pictures – Nocturne, "May Night in the Ukraine"; Gopak, "National Dance".
   The Maiden with the Daffodil – Idyll. The Princess's Rose Garden – Nocturne. Apple Blossom Time.
   On a May Evening. O Dame get up and bake your pies – Variations on a North Country Christmas
   carol. Nereid. Sleepy Head. A romance. Burlesque. **Eric Parkin** (pf). Chandos CHAN8732 (7/90).
...Enchanted Summer[a]. Walsinghame[b]. Fatherland[c]. [a]**Anne Williams-King,** [ab]**Lynore McWhirter**
   (sops); [bc]**Martyn Hill** (ten); **Brighton Festival Chorus; Royal Philharmonic Orchestra / Vernon
   Handley.** Chandos CHAN8625 (10/89).   Ⓖ

Sydney Baynes
British 1879-1938

Suggested listening ...
...Destiny. *Coupled with works by* **Binge, Williams, Coates, Toye, Collins, Farnon, Curzon, Lutz, Gibbs, White, Ketèlbey, Joyce, Ellis** and **Ancliffe** New London Orchestra / Ronald Corp. Hyperion CDA66868 (7/96). *See review in the Collections section; refer to the Index to Reviews.* **Gramophone** *Editor's record of the month.*

Antonio Bazzini
Italian 1818-1897

Suggested listening ...
...La Ronde des lutins, Op. 25. *Coupled with works by* **Wieniawski, Paganini, Kreisler, Bloch, Tchaikovsky, Messiaen** and **Sarasate** Maxim Vengerov (vn); Itamar Golan (pf). Teldec 9031-77351-2 (4/94). *See review in the Collections section; refer to the Index to Reviews.*

Amy Beach
American 1867-1944

Suggested listening ...
...Piano Concerto in C sharp minor, Op. 45[a]. *Coupled with* **MacDowell** Piano Concerto No. 2 in D minor, Op. 23[b]. [a]**Mary Louise Boehm**, [b]**Eugene List** (pfs); **Westphalian Symphony Orchestra / Siegfried Landau.** Vox 115718-2 (5/93).
...Symphony in E minor, Op. 32, "Gaelic". *Coupled with works by* **Barber** Detroit Symphony Orchestra / Neeme Järvi. Chandos CHAN8958 (10/91). *See review under Barber; refer to the Index to Reviews.* Ⓖ
...Piano Trio in A minor, Op. 150. *Coupled with works by* **C. Schumann, Tailleferre, Boulanger, Mendelssohn-Hensel, Carreño** and **Chaminade** Macalester Trio. Vox Box 115845-2 (10/94). *See review in the Collections section; refer to the Index to Reviews.*
...Violin Sonata, Op. 34[a]. *Coupled with* **R. Clarke** Cello Sonata[a]. Epilogue[b]. Three Compositions, Op. 40[b]. **Pamela Frame** (vc); [a]**Barry Snyder**, [b]**Robert Weirich** (pfs). Koch International Classics 37281-2 (3/95).
...Piano Quintet in F sharp major, Op. 67. *Coupled with* **R. Clarke** Piano Trio. Viola Sonata. **Martin Roscoe** (pf); **Endellion Quartet.** ASV CDDCA932 (10/95). *See review under Clarke; refer to the Index to Reviews.* **Gramophone** *Editor's choice.*
...Five Improvisations, Op. 148. *Coupled with* **Barber** Ballade, Op. 46. **Bernstein** Five Anniversaries. **Cage** Bacchanale for Prepared Piano. **Copland** Four Piano Blues. **Gershwin** Three Preludes. **Gottschalk** Manchega, RO143. Le Banjo, RO22. **M. Gould** Boogie Woogie Etude. **Joplin** The Entertainer. Maple Leaf Rag. **MacDowell** New England Idylls, Op. 62. **Nancarrow** Prelude. Michel Legrand (pf). Erato 4509-96386-2 (7/95).
...Cabildo[a]. The Hermit Thrush at Eve, Op. 92 No. 1. Give me not love, Op. 61. In the Twilight, Op. 85. Shakespeare Songs, Op. 37 – O mistress mine. Dark is the Night, Op. 11 No. 1. Jeune fille et jeune fleur, Op. 1 No. 3. **Soloists;** [a]**New York Concert Singers;** [a]**Mark Peskanov** (vn); [a]**Carter Brey** (vc); **Christopher O'Riley** (pf). Delos DE3170 (12/95).

Robert Beaser
American 1954-

Beaser Chorale Variations. Seven Deadly Sins[a]. Piano Concerto[b]. [a]**Jan Opalach** (bass-bar); [b]**Pamela Mia Paul** (pf); **American Composers Orchestra / Dennis Russell Davies.** Argo Ⓕ 440 337-2ZH (77 minutes: DDD: 8/94). Texts included. Recorded 1992. Ⓠ
That Beaser is an eclectic can be taken as read. The *Chorale Variations*, which opens this CD, is a terrific piece: dazzlingly colourful, fearless of gesture and visited by countless identifiable influences. The guest-list is surprisingly varied: Copland, Berg, Mahler, Tchaikovsky, Janáček and with Stravinsky, Vaughan Williams, Steve Reich and John Adams, arriving together – notable elements in a beautifully fashioned and ingeniously constructed composition. The *Seven Deadly Sins* are as many masterly settings of Anthony Hecht's abstruse but haunting poetry. Some vices occasionally appear to reflect each other – "Wrath" and "Avarice" seem like half-brothers – while Beaser extends Hecht's "Dies Irae" idea, wrapping it in deep purple. For "Lust", he has his imaginary protagonist edge off the scene as if fazed either by shame or by calm acceptance. Bernstein is a probable influence, Adams too; but it's an excellent piece and would make a fine programme companion for, say, Bernstein's *Songfest*. In the 34-minute Piano Concerto, which annotator Steven Ledbetter sees as "a genuine recreation of the grand virtuoso Romantic concerto for our time", there are original touches, and Pamela Mia Paul is a highly accomplished soloist, but the virtuoso element (Tchaikovsky, Litolff, Bartók, *et al*) rings rather shallow and a 15-20 minute condensation would work wonders. It's the *Chorale Variations* and *Seven Deadly Sins* that most effectively trumpet Robert Beaser's arrival on our music scene. The performances and recordings are superb, and the documentation is mostly perceptive and informative.

Conrad Beck

Suggested listening ...
...Drei Epigramme für Paul Sacher. *Coupled with works by* **Henze, Fortner, Ginastera, Boulez, Dutilleux, Lutosławski, Berio, C. Halffter, Britten, K. Huber** and **Holliger** Patrick **Demenga** (vc). ECM New Series 445 234-2 (8/95).

Walter Beckett

Suggested listening ...
...String Quartet No. 1. *Coupled with works by* **Kinsella, I. Wilson** and **Boydell** Vanbrugh **Quartet.** Chandos CHAN9295 (10/94).

David Bedford

Suggested listening ...
...Song of the White Horse[a]. Star Clusters, Nebulae and Places in Devon[b]. [a]**Soloists;** [a]**Queen's College Choir, Cambridge;** [a]**Nash Ensemble / Stuart Bedford;** [b]**London Philharmonic Chorus;** [b]**London Philharmonic Orchestra Brass / John Alldis.** Voiceprint VP110CD.
...Fridiof Kennings. *Coupled with works by* **Nyman, Corea, W. Gregory** and **R. Powell** Apollo **Saxophone Quartet; Mike Hamnett** (perc). Argo 443 903-2ZH (8/95). *See review in the Collections section; refer to the Index to Reviews.*

Ludwig van Beethoven

Beethoven Piano Concertos – No. 1 in C major, Op. 15; No. 2 in B flat major, Op. 19; No. 3 in C minor, Op. 37; No. 4 in G major, Op. 58; No. 5 in E flat major, "Emperor", Op. 73. **Maurizio Pollini** (pf); **Berlin Philharmonic Orchestra / Claudio Abbado.** DG Ⓕ 439 770-2GH3 (three discs: 174 minutes: DDD: 6/94). Recorded live in 1992-93.   ⓖⓖⓖ
Whilst Gilels was alive, Pollini was one of the heirs apparent; now that Gilels is gone he is king – in Beethoven, at least. There may be more individual and idiosyncratic interpreters of the music but there is none whose command, at best, is sovereign. The Fourth Concerto has a keenly felt sense of the evolving drama, and a slow movement where the dialogue between piano and orchestra is spellbinding in its intensity. Maybe Pollini is not yet entirely reconciled to Beethoven's prankish first concerto, the Concerto No. 2 in B flat. In the outer movements, he can seem brusque: ill-at-ease with Beethoven in his rumbustious, amorous, Hooray Henry mood. By contrast, the performance of the Third is a joy from start to finish. Abbado and Pollini are hand-in-glove, which gives this cycle a cohesiveness which Pollini's previous set (1/89) with Böhm and Jochum rather obviously lacked, though the Berliners don't play the first movement of the *Emperor* Concerto as commandingly as Böhm and the Vienna Philharmonic on the earlier recording. But the slow movement goes well, and the finale is more jovial than before. Musically, though, there are evident gains – in these live recordings – moments where the tension is palpable in a way that it rarely is in the recording studio. The sound is full-bodied and immediate, with applauses, a few squeaks, bumps and ill-timed coughs.
Additional recommendations ...
...Nos. 1-5[a]. Triple Concerto in C major, Op. 56[b]. [a]**Leon Fleisher,** [b]**Eugene Istomin** (pfs); [b]**Isaac Stern** (vn); [b]**Leonard Rose** (vc); **Philadelphia Orchestra / Eugene Ormandy.** Sony Classical Ⓑ SB3K48397 (three discs: 205 minutes: ADD).
...Nos. 1-5. **Claudio Arrau** (pf); **Dresden Staatskapelle / Sir Colin Davis.** Philips Ⓕ 422 149-2PH3 (three discs: 189 minutes: DDD: 1/89).   ⓖⓖ
...Nos. 1-5. Choral Fantasia[a]. **Daniel Barenboim** (pf); [a]**John Alldis Choir; New Philharmonia Orchestra / Otto Klemperer.** EMI Ⓜ CMS7 63360-2 (three discs: 211 minutes: ADD: 3/90).   ⓖ
...Nos. 1-5. 25 Bagatelles. Presto in C minor, Wo052. Allegretto in C major, Wo056. **John Lill** (pf); **City of Birmingham Symphony Orchestra / Walter Weller.** Chandos Ⓕ CHAN9084/6 (three discs: 235 minutes: DDD: 1/93).
...Nos. 1-5. Rondos, Op. 51. **Wilhelm Kempff** (pf); **Berlin Philharmonic Orchestra / Paul van Kempen.** DG Dokumente mono Ⓜ 435 744-2GDO3* (189 minutes: ADD: 4/93). *Gramophone classical 100.*   ⓖⓖⓖ
...Nos. 1-4. Romances. **Stephen Kovacevich** (pf); **Arthur Grumiaux** (vn); **BBC Symphony Orchestra / Sir Colin Davis; Concertgebouw Orchestra / Bernard Haitink.** Philips Duo Ⓜ 442 577-2PM2 (two discs: 152 minutes: ADD: 8/95).
...Nos. 1-5[a]. Two Rondos, Op. 51. Piano Sonatas – No. 8 in C minor, Op. 13, "Pathetique". No. 14 in C sharp minor, Op. 27 No. 2, "Moonlight". **Radu Lupu** (pf); [a]**Israel Philharmonic Orchestra / Zubin Mehta.** Decca Ⓜ 448 000-2DM3 (three discs: 225 minutes: ADD/DDD: 3/96).
...Nos. 2[a], 3[b], 4[c] and 5[d]. Piano Sonata No. 14 in C sharp minor, Op. 27 No. 2, "Moonlight". **Solomon** (pf); **Philharmonia Orchestra /** [ac]**André Cluytens;** [d]**Herbert Menges;** [b]**BBC Symphony**

Orchestra / Sir Adrian Boult. EMI Références mono Ⓜ CHS5 65503-2* (two discs: 150 minutes: ADD: 11/95).

Beethoven Piano Concertos – No. 1 in C major, Op. 15[a]; No. 2 in B flat major, Op. 19[b]. **Wilhelm Kempff** (pf); **Berlin Philharmonic Orchestra / Ferdinand Leitner.** DG Galleria Ⓜ 419 856-2GGA (65 minutes: ADD: 9/88). Item marked [a] from SLPM138774 (6/62), [b]SLPM138775 (9/62). ⒼⒼ
The Second Piano Concerto was in fact written before the First, and recent research suggests that an initial version of the so-called Second Concerto dates back to Beethoven's teenage years. If the Second Concerto inevitably reflects eighteenth-century classical style, it has Beethoven's familiar drive and energy and a radical use of form and technique. The First Concerto pre-dates the revolutionary *Eroica* Symphony by some eight years and still shows classical influences, but it is on a larger scale than the Second Concerto, and has greater powers of invention. Kempff's recording of these two works dates from the early 1960s, but the sound quality is pleasingly open and full-bodied, so that the soloist's pearly, immaculate tone quality is heard to good effect. Kempff and Leitner enjoy what is obviously a close rapport and their aristocratic, Olympian but poetic music-making suits both works admirably.
Additional recommendations ...
...No. 1[a]. **Mozart** Piano Concerto No. 9 in E flat major, K271[a]. Keyboard Sonata in B flat major, K570. **Walter Gieseking** (pf); [a]**Berlin State Opera Orchestra / Hans Rosbaud.** APR mono Ⓜ APR5511* (75 minutes: ADD).
...Nos. 1 and 2. **Murray Perahia** (pf); **Concertgebouw Orchestra / Bernard Haitink.** CBS Ⓕ SK42177 (70 minutes: DDD: 4/87).
...Nos. 2 and 3. **Till Fellner** (pf); **Academy of St Martin in the Fields / Sir Neville Marriner.** Erato Ⓕ 4509-98539-2 (66 minutes: DDD: 9/95).

New review
Beethoven Piano Concertos – No. 3 in C minor, Op. 37; No. 4 in G major, Op. 58[a]. **Mitsuko Uchida** (pf); **Royal Concertgebouw Orchestra / Kurt Sanderling.** Philips Ⓕ 446 082-2PH (72 minutes: DDD: 5/96). Recorded 1994, item marked [a] recorded live. Ⓖ
This pairing of Beethoven's Third and Fourth Piano Concertos is formidable, the playing at once brilliant and sensitive, rigorous and free-spirited. Of the two performances, that of the Fourth Concerto is perhaps the more memorable. Uchida re-creates the solo part with flair and imagination, and dazzling technique. And what a wonderful voyage of discovery the slow movement is here. If the performance seems a touch mellower and more confiding than that of the C minor Concerto, it is perhaps because it was being played live to an audience in the Concertgebouw, a hall whose famous acoustic can be a shade severe when empty. What we have here in the Fourth Concerto is a first-rate concert-hall perspective (with the applause edited out). Some might argue that the C minor Concerto is a severe piece. Certainly, this appears to be Sanderling's and Uchida's view of the first movement (until the cadenza, where Uchida becomes much more confiding in the *dolce* and *espressivo* passages). The performance is wonderfully alive, which is more than can be said for 75 per cent of extant recordings of this music, but there are pianists – Kovacevich and Kempff for example – who have made the music of the first movement move a shade more gracefully and songfully than Uchida does here. The slow movement, by contrast, emerges as a wonderfully rapt soliloquy for the solo pianist, the orchestra doing little more than make simple acts of obeisance before the soloist. (Rather stiff acts of obeisance: throughout the C minor Concerto Sanderling is inclined to make the orchestra sit rather heavily on down-beats and *sforzandos*.) The recording of the C minor Concerto is best heard at a safe distance. Played too loud or heard too close it can seem unduly fierce and odd blemishes show up. Where this coupling is concerned, Stephen Kovacevich is a strong rival, more so than Brendel. Kempff's is also very fine, though he uses his own cadenzas and the recordings are now over 30 years old.
Additional recommendations ...
...Nos. 3 and 4. **Wilhelm Kempff** (pf); **Berlin Philharmonic Orchestra / Ferdinand Leitner.** DG Galleria Ⓜ 419 467-2GGA (67 minutes: ADD: 9/87).
...Nos. 3 and 4. **Alfred Brendel** (pf); **London Philharmonic Orchestra / Bernard Haitink.** Philips Silver Line Classics Ⓜ 420 861-2PSL (69 minutes: ADD: 5/88).
...Nos. 3 and 4. **Vladimir Ashkenazy** (pf); **Chicago Symphony Orchestra / Sir Georg Solti.** Decca Ovation Ⓜ 417 740-2DM* (71 minutes: ADD: 5/88).
...Nos. 3 and 4. **Stephen Kovacevich** (pf); **BBC Symphony Orchestra / Sir Colin Davis.** Philips Concert Classics Ⓑ 426 062-2PCC (69 minutes: ADD: 12/89).
...No. 3. Andante favori in F major. 25 Bagatelles. **Vladimir Ashkenazy** (pf); **Vienna Philharmonic Orchestra / Zubin Mehta.** Decca Ⓜ 436 471-2DM (68 minutes: DDD: 7/93).
...No. 3[a]. Piano Trio in B flat major, Op. 97, "Archduke"[b]. [b]**Henry Holst** (vn); [b]**Anthony Pini** (vc); **Solomon** (pf); [a]**BBC Symphony Orchestra / Sir Adrian Boult.** Dutton Laboratories mono Ⓜ CDLX7015* (71 minutes: ADD: 11/95).

Beethoven Piano Concertos – No. 4 in G major, Op. 58[a]; No. 5 in E flat major, Op. 73, "Emperor"[b]. **Wilhelm Kempff** (pf); **Berlin Philharmonic Orchestra / Ferdinand Leitner.** DG The Originals Ⓜ 447 402-2GOR* (71 minutes: ADD: 5/95). Item marked [a] from SLPM138775 (9/62), [b]SLPM138777 (5/62). Recorded 1961. ⒼⒼ

Kempff was never a heavyweight among Beethoven pianists. What he had was intellect and imagination in perfect balance, a fabulous touch, great rhythmic *élan*, and a kind of improvisatory zeal that – translated into other terms – can best be described as a true and abiding sense of wonder. In the Fourth Piano Concerto you may be less than happy with his decision to use his own cadenzas, for all that they are an earnest of Kempff's own improvisatory instinct. But the performance as a whole is such a joy, so light-filled, that even that qualification tends to fade into insignificance. And how beautifully Leitner and the Berlin Philharmonic accompany Kempff. This was the new young Berlin Philharmonic of the early 1960s, poet-musicians to a man, trained to listen and respond and then, in performance, take wing into precisely those areas of mind and imagination that were Kempff's own natural habitat. The 1961 Fourth sounds especially radiant in the new transfers. Despite a touch of gruffness in some of the orchestral tuttis in the *Emperor* it, too, generally comes up with glistening clarity, the balances between solo and orchestral voicings flawlessly judged by the balance engineer and the musicians themselves. A record like this is a joy to return to and it is to be hoped that it remains in the catalogue indefinitely.

Additional recommendations ...

...No. 5[a]. **Schumann** Piano Concerto in A minor, Op. 54[b]. **Walter Gieseking** (pf); [a]**Berlin Radio Orchestra / Artur Rother;** [b]**Berlin Philharmonic Orchestra / Wilhelm Furtwängler.** Music and Arts [a]stereo/[b]mono Ⓕ CD-815* (67 minutes: ADD).

...No. 5. Piano Sonata in E major, Op. 109. **Stephen Kovacevich** (pf); **BBC Symphony Orchestra / Sir Colin Davies.** Philips Concert Classics Ⓑ 422 482-2PCC (59 minutes: ADD: 12/89).

...No. 5. **Arturo Benedetti Michelangeli** (pf); **Vienna Symphony Orchestra / Carlo Maria Giulini.** DG Ⓕ 419 249-2GH (42 minutes: ADD: 2/88).   ⒼⒼ

...No. 5. Choral Fantasia in C minor, Op. 80[a]. **Melvyn Tan** (fp); [a]**Schütz Choir of London; London Classical Players / Roger Norrington.** EMI Reflexe Ⓕ CDC7 49965-2 (52 minutes: DDD: 4/90). ✏

...No. 5. Triple Concerto in C major, Op. 56[a]. **Leon Fleisher** (pf); **Cleveland Orchestra / George Szell; Eugene Istomin** (pf); [a]**Isaac Stern** (vn); [a]**Leonard Rose** (vc); [a]**Philadelphia Orchestra / Eugene Ormandy.** Sony Classical Essential Classics Ⓜ SBK46549 (74 minutes: ADD: 8/91).   ⒼⒼⒼ

...No. 5. Grosse Fuge in B flat major, Op. 133 (arr. string orch.). **Australian Chamber Orchestra / Stephen Kovacevich** (pf). EMI Eminence Ⓜ CD-EMX2184 (53 minutes: DDD: 3/92).   ⒼⒼ

...No. 5. Choral Fantasia[a]. **Alfred Brendel** (pf); **London Philharmonic** [a]**Choir and Orchestra / Bernard Haitink.** Philips Insignia Ⓜ 434 148-2PM (61 minutes: ADD: 7/92).

...Nos. 4[a] and 5[b]. **Bach** Keyboard Partita in B flat major, BWV825 – Menuets I and II; Gigue. **Walter Gieseking** (pf); [a]**Saxon State Orchestra / Karl Böhm;** [b]**Vienna Philharmonic Orchestra / Bruno Walter.** APR mono Ⓜ APR5512* (68 minutes: ADD: 3/96).

Beethoven Violin Concerto in D major, Op. 61. Two Romances – No. 1 in G major, Op. 40; No. 2 in F major, Op. 50. **Gidon Kremer** (vn); **Chamber Orchestra of Europe / Nikolaus Harnoncourt.** Teldec Ⓕ 9031-74881-2 (57 minutes: DDD: 12/93). Recorded live in 1992.   ⒼⒼⒼ

Gidon Kremer offers one of his most commanding performances, both polished and full of flair, magnetically spontaneous from first to last. Rarely do you hear such consistently pure tone in this work and the orchestral writing too is superbly realized, with magical sounds in the slow movement in particular. It has become customary to treat the long first movement as expansively as possible – Chung and Perlman provide outstanding examples – but Kremer takes a much more urgent view and after his thoughtful and dedicated, slightly understated reading of the slow movement, he and Harnoncourt round the performance off magically with a finale that skips along the more infectiously thanks to light, clean articulation and textures. Traditional performances seem heavyweight by comparison. The controversial point for some will be the cadenza in the first movement where he uses a transcription of the big cadenza which Beethoven wrote for his piano arrangement of the work. However, this is altogether one of the most refreshing versions of the concerto ever committed to record, backed up by crisp, unsentimental readings of the two *Romances*.

Additional recommendations ...

...Violin Concerto[a]. **Mozart** Violin Concerto in A major, K219, "Turkish". **Berlin Philharmonic Orchestra / Wolfgang Schneiderhan** (vn); [a]**Eugen Jochum.** DG The Originals Ⓜ 447 403-2GOR* (75 minutes: ADD).

...Violin Concerto. **Itzhak Perlman** (vn); **Philharmonia Orchestra / Carlo Maria Giulini.** EMI Ⓕ CDC7 47002-2 (44 minutes: DDD: 2/84).

...Violin Concerto[a]. **Mendelssohn** Violin Concerto in E minor, Op. 64[b]. **Yehudi Menuhin** (vn); [a]**Philharmonia Orchestra;** [b]**Berlin Philharmonic Orchestra / Wilhelm Furtwängler.** EMI Références Ⓜ CDH7 69799-2* (71 minutes: ADD: 10/89).   ⒼⒼ

...Violin Concerto. Two Romances. **Itzhak Perlman** (vn); **Berlin Philharmonic Orchestra / Daniel Barenboim.** EMI Ⓕ CDC7 49567-2 (61 minutes: DDD: 11/89).

...Piano Concerto in D major, Op. 61 (transcribed by the composer from the Violin Concerto)[a]. Two Romances[b]. [a]**Daniel Barenboim** (pf); [b]**Pinchas Zukerman** (vn); [a]**English Chamber Orchestra,** [b]**London Philharmonic Orchestra / Daniel Barenboim.** DG Galleria Ⓜ 429 179-2GGA (61 minutes: ADD: 4/90).

...Violin Concerto. **Bruch** Violin Concerto No. 1 in G minor, Op. 26[a]. **Kyung Wha Chung** (vn); **Royal Concertgebouw Orchestra;** [a]**London Philharmonic Orchestra / Klaus Tennstedt.** EMI Ⓕ CDC7 54072-2 (70 minutes: DDD: 6/92).

...Violin Concerto. Piano Sonata No. 10 in G major, Op. 96[a]. [a]**Marc Neikrug** (pf); **Pinchas Zukerman** (vn); **Los Angeles Philharmonic Orchestra / Zubin Mehta.** RCA Victor Ⓕ 09026-61219-2 (73 minutes: DDD: 11/92).

...Violin Concerto. *Coupled with works by* **Bach, Mendelssohn, Brahms, Scott, Schumann, Debussy, Falla, Corelli, Bizet** and **Kreisler. Fritz Kreisler** (vn); **Berlin State Opera Orchestra / Leo Blech.** Biddulph mono Ⓜ LAB049/50* (two discs: 155 minutes: ADD: 9/92).

...Violin Concerto. Romance No. 2. **Oscar Shumsky** (vn); **Philharmonia Orchestra / Andrew Davis.** ASV Quicksilva Ⓑ CDQS6080 (54 minutes: ADD: 12/92). ⓆⒼ

...Violin Concerto. **Mendelssohn** Violin Concerto in E minor, Op. 64. **Kyung-Wha Chung** (vn); **Vienna Philharmonic Orchestra / Kyrill Kondrashin.** Decca Ⓜ 430 752-2DM (71 minutes: DDD: 2/93).

...Violin Concerto[a]. **Bruch** Violin Concerto No. 1 in G minor[b]. **Georg Kulenkampff** (vn); **Berlin Philharmonic Orchestra /** [a]**Hans Schmidt-Isserstedt,** [b]**Joseph Keilberth.** Teldec Historic Series mono Ⓜ 9031-76443-2* (69 minutes: ADD: 11/93).

...Violin Concerto. Two Romances. **Stephanie Chase** (vn); **Hanover Band / Roy Goodman.** Cala Ⓕ CACD1013 (55 minutes: DDD: 12/93). 🎵

...Violin Concerto. Two Romances. **Dmitri Sitkovetsky** (vn); **Academy of St Martin in the Fields / Sir Neville Marriner.** Virgin Classics Ⓕ VC5 45001-2 (62 minutes: DDD: 3/94). Ⓠ

...Violin Concerto. **Sibelius** Violin Concerto in D minor, Op. 47. **David Oistrakh** (vn); **Stockholm Festival Orchestra / Sixten Ehrling.** Testament mono Ⓕ SBT1032* (75 minutes: ADD: 7/94).

...Violin Concerto. Two Romances. **Salvatore Accardo** (vn); **La Scala Philharmonic Orchestra, Milan / Carlo Maria Giulini.** Sony Classical Ⓕ SK53287 (63 minutes: DDD: 1/95).

...Two Romances[b]. **Bach** Violin Concertos[a] – A minor, BWV1041; E major, BWV1042. Double Violin Concerto in D minor, BWV1043[b] (with Igor Oistrakh, vn). **Brahms** Violin Concerto in D major, Op. 77[c]. **Tchaikovsky** Violin Concerto in D major, Op. 35[d]. **David Oistrakh** (vn); [a]**Vienna Symphony Orchestra;** [b]**Royal Philharmonic Orchestra / Sir Eugene Goossens;** [c]**Dresden Staatskapelle / Franz Konwitschny.** DG The Originals [ab]stereo/[c]mono Ⓜ 447 427-2GOR2* (two discs: 142 minutes: ADD: 6/95).

New review

Beethoven Violin Concerto in D major, Op. 61 (with first movement cadenzas by Auer, Beethoven, Busoni, David, two by Joachim, Kreisler, Laub, Milstein, Saint-Saëns, Schnittke, Vieuxtemps, Wieniawski and Ysaÿe). **Ruggiero Ricci** (vn); **Chianti Orchestra / Piero Bellugi.** Biddulph Ⓜ LAW017 (78 minutes: DDD: 6/96). Recorded 1994.

In some respects, this is the ultimate CD bargain: a single concerto recording that can be reprogrammed to incorporate any one of 14 separate cadenzas. It's a brilliant idea, though whether this particular performance will bear such frequent repetition is open to doubt. Ruggiero Ricci's playing is bright, fairly agile and occasionally sharp; his vibrato is less insistent than it once was, and although signs of frailty surface here and there, his cultivated musicianship remains intact. The main problem, however, is with the half-hearted orchestral accompaniment – not the sort of thing to inflict on this of all concertos. As to the cadenzas themselves, Ricci gives each piece his best shot – which is no mean feat for a 76-year-old, especially given the copious technical demands involved. Musically, there is much to savour. The sound is adequate. An invaluable compilation, but if the concerto alone is your main priority, you would be better advised to look elsewhere.

Beethoven Triple Concerto in C major, Op. 56[a]. Choral Fantasia in C minor, Op. 80[b]. **Beaux Arts Trio** ([a]**Ida Kavafian,** vn; [a]**Peter Wiley,** vc; **Menahem Pressler,** pf); [b]**Mid-German Radio Chorus; Leipzig Gewandhaus Orchestra / Kurt Masur.** Philips Ⓕ 438 005-2PH (52 minutes: DDD: 6/94). Recorded 1992-3. ⒼⒼⒼ

New review

Beethoven Triple Concerto in C major, Op. 56[a]. Choral Fantasia in C minor, Op. 80[b]. [a]**Itzhak Perlman** (vn); [a]**Yo-Yo Ma** (vc); [b]**Chorus of the Deutsche Oper, Berlin; Berlin Philharmonic Orchestra / Daniel Barenboim** (pf). EMI Ⓕ CDC5 55516-2 (55 minutes: DDD: 12/95). Text and translation included. Recorded live in 1995. Ⓠ

Kurt Masur has rarely conducted more electrifying Beethoven performances on disc. The opening tutti of the concerto establishes a speed markedly faster than usual, and if the three soloists modify it slightly, the characteristic which marks this performance is its urgency. But there is no feeling of breathlessness, simply exhilaration. The evenness and clarity of Pressler's articulation in scales and passagework is a delight. As for the brief central meditation, led – like most main themes in this work – by the cello, it flows very warmly and naturally, with Peter Wiley just as rich and positive an artist as Pressler. This now stands as one of the very finest versions of a work which at last looks like being appreciated, not as a rarity, but as an important pillar of the Beethoven canon. The *Choral Fantasia* is hardly likely to establish itself in a comparable niche, but this performance is most persuasive. The variations on the corny main theme are regularly pointed with engaging wit, not just by Pressler but by the wind soloists, and the brass sound is glorious. It is rather like having the choral finale of the Ninth anticipated with tongue-in-cheek. Balances are always difficult, not just in this work but notoriously in the Triple Concerto. The soloists are well-focused and the orchestral sound is warm and full.

Though EMI's Berlin sound for Barenboim is warm with plenty of presence, and the soloists are justly balanced not too far in front, the textures grow opaque in tuttis. There is also an edge on the solo violin and cello tone, particularly the former, which is occasionally distracting. Even so, anyone responding to the zestful, infectiously sprung Berlin performance is unlikely to be overcritical of the sound, and the brass is very well caught. In this concerto the cellist is the leader, and Yo-Yo Ma's cello tone here is not as ample as, for example, Rostropovich's in an earlier EMI recording from Berlin, along with David Oistrakh and Sviatoslav Richter and with Karajan conducting. Yet Ma's sound brings positive advantage in the tender, hushed intensity of his big opening solo in the slow movement. Choice between this and the Philips disc is hard to assess, and might well be left to a preference between crisp co-ordination and the inspiration of the moment. Unlike many so-called 'live performances' put on disc, these Berlin readings keep a few seconds of applause at the end of each work. If that for the *Fantasia* is markedly more enthusiastic than for the Concerto, the larger forces with chorus may partly account for that, as well as Barenboim's Furtwängler-like whipping up of speed in the final coda, an endearing touch.

Additional recommendations ...

...Triple Concerto[a]. Choral Fantasia[b]. [a]**Christian Funke** (vn); [a]**Jürnjakob Timm** (vc); [a]**Peter Rösel**, [b]**Jörg-Peter Weigle** (pfs); [b]**Leipzig Radio Chorus; Dresden Philharmonic Orchestra / Herbert Kegel.** Capriccio Ⓕ 10 150 (54 minutes: DDD: 9/87).   ⒼⒼ

...Triple Concerto[a]. **Brahms** Double Concerto in A minor, Op. 102[b]. [a]**Rudolf Serkin** (pf); [a]**Jaime Laredo**, [b]**Isaac Stern** (vns); [a]**Leslie Parnas**, [b]**Leonard Rose** (vcs); [a]**Marlboro Festival Orchestra / Alexander Schneider;** [b]**Philadelphia Orchestra / Eugene Ormandy.** CBS Masterworks Portrait Ⓜ CD44842 (71 minutes: ADD: 11/89).   ⒼⒼⒼ

...Triple Concerto[a]. **Brahms** Double Concerto in A minor, Op. 102[b]. [ab]**David Oistrakh** (vn), [ab]**Mstislav Rostropovich** (vc); [b]**Sviatoslav Richter** (pf); [a]**Berlin Philharmonic Orchestra / Herbert von Karajan;** [b]**Cleveland Orchestra / George Szell.** EMI Studio Plus Ⓜ CDM7 64744-2 (70 minutes: ADD: 7/93).   ⒼⒼ

Beethoven Symphonies – No. 1 in C major, Op. 21. No. 2 in D major, Op. 36. No. 3 in E flat major, Op. 55, "Eroica". No. 4 in B flat major, Op. 60. No. 5 in C minor, Op. 67. No. 6 in F major, Op. 68, "Pastoral". No. 7 in A major, Op. 92. No. 8 in F major, Op. 93. No. 9 in D minor, Op. 125, "Choral"[a]. [a]**Charlotte Margiono** (sop); [a]**Birgit Remmert** (mez); [a]**Rudolf Schasching** (ten); [a]**Robert Holl** (bass); [a]**Arnold Schoenberg Choir; Chamber Orchestra of Europe / Nikolaus Harnoncourt.** Teldec Ⓕ 2292-46452-2 (five discs: 358 minutes: DDD: 11/91). Recorded live in 1990-91. *Gramophone Award Winner 1992.*   ⒼⒼⒼ

Beethoven Symphonies. [a]**Lucia Popp** (sop); [a]**Carolyn Watkinson** (contr); [a]**Peter Schreier** (ten); [a]**Robert Holl** (bass); [a]**Netherlands Radio Chorus; Concertgebouw Orchestra / Bernard Haitink.** Philips Bernard Haitink Symphony Edition Ⓑ 442 073-2PB5 (five discs: 725 minutes: DDD: 9/94). Recorded 1987.

No. 1 in C major, Op. 21. No. 2 in D major, Op. 36. No. 3 in E flat major, Op. 55, "Eroica". No. 4 in B flat major, Op. 60 (all from 416 822-2PH6, 6/88). No. 5 in C minor, Op. 67 (420 540-1PH, 10/87). No. 6 in F major, Op. 68, "Pastoral" (416 822-2PH6). No. 7 in A major, Op. 92 (420 540-1PH). No. 8 in F major, Op. 93. No. 9 in D minor, Op. 125, "Choral"[a]. Egmont, Op. 84 – Overture (all from 416 822-2PH6).   ⒼⒼ

Brimful of intrepid character and interpretative incident, Nikolaus Harnoncourt and the splendid Chamber Orchestra of Europe give us what is surely one of the most stimulating Beethoven symphony cycle of recent times. As Harnoncourt himself states in a lively interview for the accompanying booklet to this set: "It has always been my conviction that music is not there to soothe people's nerves ... but rather to open their eyes, to give them a good shaking, even to frighten them". So it transpires that there's a re-creative daring about his conducting – in essence an embracement of recent scholarly developments and Harnoncourt's own pungent sense of characterization – which is consistently illuminating, thus leaving the listener with the uncanny sensation that he or she is in fact encountering this great music for the very first time. In all of this Harnoncourt is backed to the hilt by some superbly responsive, miraculously assured playing from the COE: their personable, unforced assimilation of Harnoncourt's specific demands (complete with period-style lean-textured strings and bracingly cutting brass and timpani), allied to this conductor's intimate knowledge of the inner workings of these scores, make for wonderfully fresh, punchy results. In this respect Symphonies Nos. 6-8 in particular prove immensely rewarding, but the *Eroica* and (especially) the Fourth, too, are little short of superb. In sum, it's a cycle which excitingly reaffirms the life-enhancing mastery of Beethoven's vision for the 1990s and into the next century beyond.

Haitink's second Beethoven cycle was greeted warmly when it first appeared; his virtues of textural rhythmic clarity well in evidence. He is often at his most impressive in the allegedly 'lighter' symphonies; Nos. 1, 8 and especially No. 4 are very enjoyable – vital, flexible, elegantly shaped and balanced, and thoroughly civilized. Perhaps the problem with the *Eroica*, Fifth, Seventh and *Choral* Symphonies is that they are a degree *too* civilized. This is no vision of a Beethoven – as one critic put it – "storming heaven with his boots on". Still, there is more than one way of approaching any great work, and for most of the set the phrase "intensely agreeable" seems a good, bite-sized summary. Tempos almost always seem well-chosen – except perhaps the slowish *Scherzos* of Nos. 2 and 4 – and it's good to find Haitink taking a less extreme view of scherzo-trio contrasts in No. 7 (and observing all the repeats in the *Scherzo*). The recordings have lost none of their virtues – breadth, depth, clarity, warmth of tone – in the transfers.

Additional recommendations ...

...Nos. 1-9. **Cleveland Orchestra / George Szell.** Sony Essential Classics SB5K48396.

...Nos. 1-9. Overtures – Die Geschöpfe des Prometheus, Op. 43. Coriolan. Egmont. **London Classical Players / Roger Norrington.** EMI Ⓜ CMS5 65184-2 (six discs: 353 minutes: DDD: 11/89). ⚟   ⒼⒼ

...Nos. 1-9. **Berlin Philharmonic Orchestra / Herbert von Karajan.** DG Ⓜ 429 036-2GX5 (five discs: 332 minutes: ADD: 1/90).

...Nos. 1-9. Overture – Leonore No. 3, Op. 62*a*. **NBC Symphony Orchesta / Arturo Toscanini.** RCA Gold Seal mono Ⓜ GD60324* (337 minutes: ADD: 5/90).   ⒼⒼⒼ

...Nos. 1-9. **Leipzig Radio Chorus; Leipzig Gewandhaus Orchestra / Kurt Masur.** Philips Ⓕ 426 290-2PH5 (five discs: 355 minutes: DDD: 6/93).   ⒼⒼ

...Overtures[a] – Coriolan; Egmont; König Stefan; Die Geschöpfe des Prometheus; Fidelio; Leonora No. 1, Op. 138; Leonora No. 2, Op. 72*a*; Leonora No. 3. The Consecration of the House, Op. 124. Namensfreier, Op. 115. Die Ruinen von Athen, Op. 113. 12 Menuets, WoO7[b]. 12 German Dances, WoO8[b]. 12 Contredanses, WoO14[b]. [a]**Leipzig Gewandhaus Orchestra / Kurt Masur;** [b]**Academy of St Martin in the Fields / Sir Neville Marriner.** Philips Duo Ⓜ 438 706-2PM2 (two discs: 155 minutes: ADD: 5/94).

...Nos. 1-9. **Orchestre Révolutionnaire et Romantique / John Eliot Gardiner.** Archiv Produktion Ⓕ 439 900-2AH5 (five discs: 328 minutes: DDD: 11/94). ⚟ *Gramophone Editor's choice.*   Ⓖ

...Nos. 1-9. Coriolan, Op. 62 – Overture. **Soloists; Kaunas State Choir; Sinfonia Varsovia / Sir Yehudi Menuhin.** IMG Records Ⓢ 30368 00025 (five discs: 359 minutes: DDD: 4/96).

New review

Beethoven Symphonies – No. 1 in C major, Op. 21; No. 2 in D major, Op. 36; No. 3 in E flat major, Op. 55, "Eroica"[a]; No. 4 in B flat major, Op. 60; No. 5 in C minor, Op. 67; No. 6 in F major, Op. 68, "Pastoral"; No. 7 in A major, Op. 92; No. 8 in F major, Op. 93; No. 9 in D minor, Op. 125, "Choral"[b]. Overtures – Egmont, Op. 84[a]; Leonore No. 3, Op. 72*a*. [b]**Sharon Sweet** (sop); [b]**Jadwiga Rappé** (contr); [b]**Paul Frey** (ten); [b]**Franz Grundheber** (bar); [b]**Dresden State Opera Chorus; Staatskapelle Dresden / Sir Colin Davis.** Philips Ⓜ 446 067-2PH6 (six discs: 403 minutes: DDD: 12/95). Text and translation included. Items marked [a] from 434 120-2PH (3/93). Recorded 1991-3. *Gramophone Editor's choice.*   ⒼⒼ

There has not been a Beethoven cycle like this since Klemperer's heyday, or Bruno Walter's, a sequence of performances that form a certain sense of fundamental wholeness, the conductor and his fellow musicians sufficiently at ease with themselves and the music they are playing to render the task of performing it nothing less than a physical pleasure and a private joy. It is easy to forget nowadays how physically gratifying Beethoven's music can and should be. We have a tendency in this country to find sensual gratification, the sound source itself, suspect; which perhaps explains why we have of late become more addicted than most to the slimline, high speed, prosily talkative Beethoven of the so-called authenticists.

The trick, of course, is to marry sound with substance which is where this new Dresden cycle of the nine symphonies is a *locus classicus* of good practice. It is difficult to imagine any orchestra – not even the Berliners, the Vienna Philharmonic or Masur's Leipzig Gewandhaus Orchestra – who play Beethoven with a richer, fuller, darker, warmer sound than the Staatskapelle Dresden. The Berliners playing for Karajan in his 1976 set produced a rich, visceral sound, but one that related to a rather different performing tradition, the Toscanini influence still glistening through. Davis is clearly more a Klemperer man (Klemperer in his prime, that is). Like the latter, Davis has mastered the difficult trick of sustaining broad tempos and infusing them with a rhythmic impetus – now dancing, now marching, now simply bowling along – which is unforced, unflagging and utterly at ease with itself. One of the great joys of the new set – perhaps *the* great joy and one that will commend it to a wide constituency of more mature collectors – is the feeling of inevitability about so much of the music-making.

By giving himself and the players, and the music, time to sound and to breathe, Davis is also able to reproduce beautifully the written phrasing of the music. How mannerly this all is, like a great actor bothering to ensure that we hear every word as the verse rhythms rise and fall. And what a rich cargo of melodic beauty it brings with it, too. It is here that the analogy with Bruno Walter comes in, for he was one of the last conductors who really made the Beethoven symphonies sing in a way that befits this great master of articulate song. Walter was also a man of temperament, not afraid to shape a paragraph rhetorically to his own ends. Davis does this too at times. And again it usually seems 'right'. Not right for all time, but right in its own way now, true to itself. Günter Wand in his fine RCA set rarely takes this kind of risk. Harnoncourt does so rather more frequently but in a way that often sounds arbitrary and which becomes irksome on repeated hearings. The sound is glorious, full and forward and beautifully clear, with just enough reverberation to allow the music its necessary aura. Davis's old knack of allowing winds and strings to speak on equal terms is very much in evidence throughout. Oboe, flute and bassoon all ravish sense.

The *Pastoral* Symphony is a joy from first to last, a performance to set beside those of Klemperer, Böhm and more recently Giulini. All it lacks is the proper old-fashioned division of the violins left and right. (The Seventh lacks this, too, but the recording is so good that it is at least possible to hear the two groups as separate entities.) There are places where a potentially controversial steadiness brings fresh insights: the oboe-led *Poco andante* towards the end of the finale of the *Eroica* ushering in what is almost a Mahlerian backward glance to the great Funeral March, or the second movement of the Eighth Symphony not so much replicating the new-fangled metronome as anticipating Mahler's jangling rustic excursion at the start of his Fourth Symphony. As for the Fifth Symphony, Davis circumvents its aggressively heroic elements by playing the first movement, with its germinal four-note idea, as though it were the work of Haydn in seven-league boots. The scherzo is played with a Furtwängler-like slowness (is our leading Berliozian thinking here of Berlioz's phrase about the scherzo having the "gaze of a mesmeriser"?) but the finale, denying all kinship with what has gone before, has plenty of its own life-enhancing *Schwung*.

Is anything, then, amiss in the cycle? As it progresses, there are a few lapses, the odd orchestral raspberry, that may or may not be there as an earnest of the musicians' humanity, their essential fallibility. In the finale of the Ninth, the choir and to some extent the soprano and alto solos are too backwardly placed. Davis allows time for the words to be articulated, yet we have to strain to hear them. The tenor is excellent, but one has heard the baritone solos better sung (to put it mildly). And the Ninth's first movement is not quite the apotheosis of Davis's intense, steady, visionary, singing way with Beethoven one had hoped for.

The performances of the overtures *Egmont* and *Leonore* No. 3 reveal in microcosm the set's qualities. Both are miniature music-dramas charged with extra-musical meaning, but they are often carelessly played by conductors and orchestras. Too few conductors get the balance right between the dramatic and the symphonic elements in the music. Davis is able to adjudicate between the two elements in masterly fashion, not least – one comes back finally to this – because of the strength and purity of the orchestral response: a steady pulse buoyantly articulated, fabulous, soft *pianissimos*, *sforzandos* that are properly stressed and sounded, *fortissimos* that are burnished and full-bodied. Here, as in Klemperer's performances or Walter's, codas and victory symphonies are triumphant homecomings rather than sudden acts of military conquest.

Beethoven Symphonies – No. 1 in C major, Op. 21; No. 3 in E flat major, Op. 55, "Eroica". **Royal Concertgebouw Orchestra / Wolfgang Sawallisch.** EMI Ⓕ CDC7 54501-2 (77 minutes: DDD: 6/95). Recorded 1993.
Collectors who swear by their fine old 1950s mono LPs of the Beethoven symphonies made in the Concertgebouw under conductors like Erich Kleiber, Eugen Jochum, Eduard van Beinum or Pierre Monteux will find Sawallisch's Concertgebouw recording of the First Symphony to be a great delight. True, the slow movement is rather comatose – *Andante cantabile* but barely *con moto* – but all three quicker movements are played with a clarity and zest that you will not find, for instance, in Harnoncourt's performance, where the first movement is played in a way that is oddly tired-sounding: mannered and circumspect. The EMI recording for Sawallisch is of a piece with the playing, electrically alive. In the *Eroica*, Sawallisch does one or two old-fashioned things. There is no exposition repeat and there are some expressive slowings in the course of the exposition. What follows is, though, of a piece with this: a reading that has an irresistible and continuing sense of forward motion but not one that is bought at all cost, as Sawallisch's direction of the long and musically profound lead-back to the recapitulation makes abundantly clear.

Additional recommendations ...
...Nos. 1 and 4. Egmont Overture. **Berlin Philharmonic Orchestra / Herbert von Karajan.** DG Galleria Ⓜ 419 048-2GGA (64 minutes: ADD: 4/88).   ⒼⒼ
...Nos. 1 and 6. **London Classical Players / Roger Norrington.** EMI Reflexe Ⓕ CDC7 49746-2 (66 minutes: DDD: 9/88). ✐   ⒼⒼ
...Nos. 1 and 2. **Cleveland Orchestra / Christoph von Dohnányi.** Telarc Ⓕ CD80187 (59 minutes: DDD: 6/89).   Ⓖ
...Nos. 1 and 7. **Royal Philharmonic Orchestra / Barry Wordsworth.** Tring International Royal Philharmonic Collection Ⓢ TRP033 (64 minutes: DDD: 8/95).

Beethoven Symphonies – No. 2 in D major, Op. 36; No. 4 in B flat major, Op. 60. **North German Radio Symphony Orchestra / Günter Wand.** RCA Victor Red Seal Ⓕ RD60058 (68 minutes: DDD: 9/89). Recorded 1988.   ⒼⒼ
Seldom has Beethoven's Second Symphony sounded as fresh, dynamic or persuasive as this. The work occupies a transitional place in the symphonic line as begun by Mozart and Haydn; on the one hand it forms the climax of that line, on the other it looks forward to new beginnings. Günter Wand's stance clearly leans towards those new beginnings, with a reading that is more 'Beethovian' in approach than most, highlighting the fingerprints of his future symphonic style. The Fourth Symphony has always tended to be eclipsed by the towering edifices of the Third and Fifth Symphonies, but the Fourth takes stock, and with the maturity gained in the writing of the Third, looks back once more in an act of homage to the triumphs of the past. Wand's performances are inspired; he is a conductor who never imposes his own ego and never does anything for the sake of effect, resulting in performances that are honest, direct and unpretentious. His tempos are superbly judged; brisk, but not hurried, allowing the pristine articulation of the strings to come shining through (this needs to be heard to be believed; orchestral playing such as this is rare indeed). The orchestral balance is ideal, with

woodwind textures nicely integrated into the orchestral sound, and this is supported by the excellent recorded sound which approaches demonstration quality. A very fine issue indeed.

Additional recommendations ...

...Nos. 2 and 4. **Philharmonia Orchestra / Otto Klemperer.** EMI Studio Ⓜ CDM7 63355-2* (73 minutes: ADD: 8/90). ⒼⒼ

...Nos. 2 and 8. **Royal Philharmonic Orchestra / James Lockhart.** Tring International Royal Philharmonic Collection Ⓢ TRP039 (62 minutes: DDD: 11/95).

Beethoven Symphony No. 3 in E flat major, Op. 55, "Eroica"[a]. Overture – Leonore No. 3, Op. 72a[b]. **North German Radio Symphony Orchestra / Günter Wand.** RCA Victor Ⓕ RD60755 (65 minutes: DDD: 10/91). Recorded live in [a] 1989, [b]1990. ⒼⒼ

Günter Wand's live performance of the *Eroica* represents a worthy alternative to Klemperer's 1955 landmark recording. In many ways Wand stands as a legitimate successor to Klemperer as one of the holders of the great Teutonic tradition of interpreting Beethoven in terms of struggle and triumph. Certainly he launches into the symphony with tremendous vigour and power and he sustains these characteristics throughout. Following an opening movement in which the tension never relaxes at all, Wand leads a reading of the Funeral March which is deeply felt but without self-indulgence. The scherzo and trio provide well-pointed relief prior to an epic reading of the triumphant final movement, which carries all before it. The fill-up, an equally powerful reading of the *Leonore* Overture No. 3, precedes the performance of the *Eroica* and acts as an excellent curtain-raiser and introduction to Wand's interpretative style: genuine and powerful and wholly without self-indulgence. The North German Radio recording is excellent, capturing the involved atmosphere of a live performance without any of the distractions normally encountered. Highly recommended.

Additional recommendations ...

...No. 3. Leonore Overture No. 1. **Berlin Philharmonic Orchestral / Rafael Kubelík.** Belart Ⓕ 450 037-2 (66 minutes: ADD).

...No. 3. Grosse Fuge in B flat major. **Philharmonia Orchestra / Otto Klemperer.** EMI mono Ⓜ CDM7 63356-2* (70 minutes: ADD: 8/90). ⒼⒼⒼ

...No. 3. Leonore Overtures Nos. 2 and 3. **Philharmonia Orchestra / Otto Klemperer.** EMI mono Ⓜ CDM7 63855-2* (76 minutes: ADD: 4/92). *Gramophone classical 100.* ⒼⒼⒼ

...No. 3. **Mozart** Symphony No. 40 in G minor, K550. **NBC Symphony Orchestra / Arturo Toscanini.** RCA Victor Gold Seal Ⓜ GD60271* (69 minutes: ADD: 10/92).

...Nos. 3, 5 and 6. **Schubert** Symphony No. 9 in C major, D944, "Great". **Berlin Philharmonic Orchestra / Wilhelm Furtwängler.** Tahra mono Ⓜ FURT1008/11* (four discs: 243 minutes: ADD: 3/95). Also includes previously unpublished recordings of works by Brahms, Dvořák, Mendelssohn, Schubert, Schumann and R. Strauss; recorded 1930-54.

...Nos. 3, 7 and 8. The Consecration of the House, Op. 124. **Berlin Philharmonic Orchestra / Paul van Kempen.** Philips Ⓜ 438 533-2PM2* (two discs: 124 minutes: ADD: 3/94). ⒼⒼ

...No. 3. **Mussorgsky** A Night on the Bare Mountain. **London Philharmonic Orchestra / Klaus Tennstedt.** EMI Ⓕ CDC5 55186-2 (63 minutes: DDD: 11/94).

...No. 3. *Coupled with works by* **Schubert, Brahms, Tchaikovsky, Ravel** and **Debussy** Concertgebouw Orchestra / Pierre Monteux. Philips The Early Years Ⓜ 442 544-2PM5 (five discs: 311 minutes: ADD: 12/94). *See review in the Collections section; refer to the Index to Reviews.* ⒼⒼⒼ

...No. 3; No. 9[a]. Overtures – Egmont; Coriolan; Der Geschöpfe des Prometheus. [a]**Dame Gwyneth Jones** (sop); [a]**Tatiana Troyanos** (mez); [a]**Jess Thomas** (ten); [a]**Karl Ridderbusch** (bass); [a]**Vienna State Opera Chorus; Vienna Philharmonic Orchestra / Karl Böhm.** DG Double Ⓜ 437 368-2GX2 (two discs: 146 minutes: ADD: 4/95).

New review

Beethoven Symphonies – No. 4 in B flat major, Op. 60; No. 5 in C minor, Op. 67. **La Scala Philharmonic Orchestra / Carlo Maria Giulini.** Sony Classical Ⓕ SK58921 (73 minutes: DDD: 11/95). Recorded 1993.

Giulini's Fifth, which ends with a piccolo singing high in the stratosphere as C major sounds majestically beneath, is not a performance in the histrionic (or historic) sense of the word. Rather, it is a meditation on the work's informing vision, what Goethe called "the Fall upwards", the transition from dark to light, the seeds of spiritual regeneration planted in the very ground of despair. And that is not an elaborately periphrastic way of saying that the performance is a bit dull, that the old boy is not quite what he was. Giulini's desire is to give the music time to breathe and be heard. And he is absolutely the master of how best to bring that about. You hear this in the time he allots to the opening fermatas (and in the fineness of their sound, rich and unforced); you hear it in the slight 'lift' he imparts to the rhythm, the time they are given to dance; and you hear it in the steady, unflustered pulse of the whole. The final two movements are treated as a seamless robe. Logically – since there is no repeat of the *Scherzo*'s first half – Giulini omits the finale's exposition repeat. The music is thus allowed to move forward with a simple momentum of its own. Climaxes are finely judged, and rarely has the *Scherzo*'s unexpected return within the finale seemed so fine an invention as it does here. The symphony's slow movement, incidentally, is played as though it is first cousin to Schubert's *Unfinished* Symphony. Giulini has never previously recorded the Fourth Symphony and coming to it late has its risks. The slow introduction, the slow movement and the still points of the *Allegro vivace*'s turning world are wonderfully well reimagined and realized. The word *vivace*, though, implies a slightly more spirited gait than Giulini allows. But if parts of the first movement seem a touch lumpy, the finale is a miracle of unforced motion, the La Scala playing relaxed, the mood gamesome as it invariably is when the conductor takes note of Beethoven's written instruction: *Allegro ma non troppo*. (Klemperer was always very persuasive in this movement, Gardiner on his recent Archiv recording is ruinously quick.) Sony's Milan recordings place the orchestra a shade distantly, giving a slightly veiled quality to the string tone, but since this is consonant with the sound Giulini draws from the orchestra it is hardly a matter of great concern.

Additional recommendation ...
...Nos. 4 and 6. **NBC Symphony Orchestra / Arturo Toscanini.** RCA Gold Seal Ⓜ GD60254*
(69 minutes: ADD).   ⒼⒼⒼ

Beethoven Symphonies – No. 5 in C minor, Op. 67[a]; No. 7 in A major, Op. 92[b]. **Vienna Philharmonic Orchestra / Carlos Kleiber.** DG The Originals Ⓜ 447 400-2GOR (72 minutes: ADD: 5/95). Item marked [a] from 2530 516 (6/75), [b]2530 706 (9/76). *Gramophone classical 100.*   ⒼⒼⒼ
The recording of the Fifth, always very fine, comes up superbly in this new transfer. What, though, of the Seventh Symphony, an equally distinguished performance though always perceptibly greyer-sounding on LP, and on CD? Well, it too is superb. What the Original-Image Bit-Processing has done to it, heaven only knows, but the result is a performance of genius that now speaks to us freely and openly for the first time. In some ways this is a more important document than the famous Fifth. Great recordings of the Seventh, greatly played and greatly conducted, but with first and second violins divided left and right, are as rare as gold-dust. Freshly refurbished, this Kleiber Seventh would go right to the top of any short list of recommendable Sevenths. It is wonderful to have these two legendary performances so expertly restored and placed together on one disc for the first time.

Additional recommendations ...
...Nos. 5 and 7. **Vienna Philharmonic Orchestra / Rafael Kubelík.** Belart Ⓕ 450 038-2 (75 minutes: ADD).
...Nos. 5 and 7. *Coupled with works by* **Brahms, Dukas, Gluck, Haydn, Mendelssohn, Mozart, Rossin, Verdi** *and* **Wagner** Philharmonic Symphony Orchestra of New York / **Arturo Toscanini.** Pearl mono GEMMCDS9373* (three discs: 230 minutes: ADD: 3/90). *Gramophone classical 100.*   ⒼⒼⒼ
...No. 7. Overtures – Der Geschöpfe des Prometheus, Op. 43; Coriolan, Op. 62; Egmont, Op. 84. **Vienna Philharmonic Orchestra / Karl Böhm.** DG Ⓑ 429 509-2GR (62 minutes: ADD: 10/90).
...Nos. 5 and 7. **Philharmonia Orchestra / Vladimir Ashkenazy.** Decca Ovation Ⓜ 430 701-2DM (77 minutes: DDD: 8/91).   Ⓖ
...No. 7. **Haydn** Symphony No. 101 in D major, "Clock". **Mendelssohn** A Midsummer Night's Dream – incidental music, Op. 61: Scherzo. **New York Philharmonic Orchestra / Arturo Toscanini.** RCA Gold Seal mono Ⓜ GD60316* (66 minutes: ADD: 11/92).
...Nos. 5 and 7. **Royal Liverpool Philharmonic Orchestra / Sir Charles Mackerras.** EMI Eminence Ⓜ CD-EMX2212 (68 minutes: DDD: 12/93).
...Nos. 5 and 6. **Berlin Philharmonic Orchestra / Herbert von Karajan.** DG Ⓑ 439 403-2GCL (67 minutes: ADD: 1/94).
...No. 5[d]. **Litolff** Concerto symphonique No. 4 in D minor, Op. 102 – Scherzo[ab]. **Bruckner** Overture in G minor[d]. **Haydn** Symphony No. 45 in F sharp minor, "Farewell"[b]. **Bach** Brandenburg Concerto No. 3 in G major, BWV1048[c]. **Schubert** Symphony No. 8 in B minor, "Unfinished", D759[b]. **Rachmaninov** (arr. Wood) Prelude in C sharp minor, Op. 3 No. 2[e]. **Brahms** Variations on a Theme by Haydn, "St Antoni", Op. 56a[d]. **Dvořák** Symphonic Variations, B70[d]. [a]Irene Scharrer (pf); [b]London Symphony Orchestra; [c]British Symphony Orchestra; [d]Queen's Hall Orchestra; [e]symphony orchestra / Sir Henry Wood. Dutton Laboratories mono Ⓜ 2CDAX2002* (two discs: 138 minutes: ADD: 9/94).

Beethoven Symphonies – No. 5 iḥ C minor, Op. 67; No. 6 in F major, Op. 68, "Pastoral". **North German Radio Symphony Orchestra / Günter Wand.** RCA Victor Red Seal Ⓕ 09026 61930-2 (79 minutes: DDD: 5/94). Recorded live in 1992.   ⒼⒼ
Beethoven Symphony No. 6 in F major, Op. 68, "Pastoral". Overtures – Coriolan, Op. 62; Egmont, Op. 84. **La Scala Philharmonic Orchestra, Milan / Carlo Maria Giulini.** Sony Classical Ⓕ SK53974 (65 minutes: DDD: 5/94). Recorded 1993. *Gramophone Editor's choice.*   ⒼⒼ
To judge from this live performance of the Fifth Symphony, Wand has the trick of keeping something back for the performance itself; a remarkable skill in repertory as familiar as this after so much detailed preparation. In matters of rhythm and phrasing and the balancing of lines, Wand is difficult to fault. Indeed, you will hear things in these performances – from the basses and bassoons, and, in the Fifth Symphony, from the trombones – which are all too often glossed over. Apart from a curiously measured *Scherzo*, the Fifth Symphony goes exceptionally well. The first movement is not over-driven, yet the finale has real *élan*, the reading, for want of a better word, suddenly and surprisingly rather Furtwänglerish. In the *Pastoral* Symphony it is Wand's exemplary account of the Scene by the Brook that most obviously stands out. Here he has the knack of marrying the music's necessary forward movement with the murmurous beauty of its inner detailing. Wand's *Pastoral* gives

profound pleasure, as, in its very different way, does Giulini's, his third recording of the Symphony and, by some distance, his finest. Superbly sustained and expressively moulded, this is a performance in which every sentence is gloriously phrased and where individual string lines are always richly distinct; not a note is extraneous to Beethoven's purpose. The whole performance is wonderfully at odds with the hell-for-leather spirit of an agnostic age. It is, in the end, a deeply *spiritual* performance of a work which was conceived by Beethoven, first and last, as an essentially spiritual experience. The disc begins with a profoundly satisfying *Coriolan* Overture and the dramatic opening of the *Egmont* Overture is played with a near-ideal blend of trenchancy and *espressivo* intensity. As for the coda, the so-called 'Victory Symphony', few have brought out as vividly as Giulini its musical and moral sure-footedness.

Additional recommendations ...

...No. 6. Overtures – Der Geschöpfe des Prometheus, Op. 43; Coriolan, Op. 62. **Northern Sinfonia / Richard Hickox.** ASV Quicksilva Ⓢ CDQS6053 (59 minutes: DDD).

...Nos. 6 and 8. **Vienna Philharmonic Orchestra / Hans Schmidt-Isserstedt.** Decca Ⓜ 433 622-2DSP (55 minutes: ADD: 3/90).   Ⓖ

...No. 5[d]. **Litolff** Concerto symphonique No. 4 in D minor, Op. 102 – Scherzo[ab]. **Bruckner** Overture in G minor[d]. **Haydn** Symphony No. 45 in F sharp minor, "Farewell"[b]. **Bach** Brandenburg Concerto No. 3 in G major, BWV1048[c]. **Schubert** Symphony No. 8 in B minor, "Unfinished", D759[b]. **Rachmaninov** (arr. Wood) Prelude in C sharp minor, Op. 3 No. 2[e]. **Brahms** Variations on a Theme by Haydn, "St Antoni", Op. 56a[d]. **Dvořák** Symphonic Variations, B70[d]. [a]**Irene Scharrer** (pf); [b]**London Symphony Orchestra**; [c]**British Symphony Orchestra**; [d]**Queen's Hall Orchestra**; [e]**symphony orchestra / Sir Henry Wood.** Dutton Laboratories mono Ⓜ 2CDAX2002* (two discs: 138 minutes: ADD: 9/94).

New review

Beethoven Symphony No. 6 in F major, Op. 68, "Pastoral"[a].
Schubert Symphony No. 5 in B flat major, D485[b]. **Vienna Philharmonic Orchestra / Karl Böhm.** DG The Originals Ⓜ 447 433-2GOR (74 minutes: ADD: 1/96). Item marked [a] from 2530 142 (2/72, recorded 1971), [b]2531 279 (11/80, recorded 1979). *Gramophone classical 100.*   ⒼⒼⒼ

Karl Böhm's Beethoven is a compound of earth and fire. His VPO recording of Beethoven's Sixth of 1971 dominated the LP catalogue for over a decade, and has done pretty well on CD on its various appearances. His reading is generally glorious and it remains one of the finest accounts of the work ever recorded. It still sounds well (perhaps the bass is a bit lighter than on LP) and the performance (with the first movement exposition repeat included) has an unfolding naturalness and a balance between form and lyrical impulse that is totally satisfying. The brook flows untroubled and the finale is quite lovely, with a wonderfully expansive climax. This latest coupling (the Schubert Fifth) is as unexpected as it is successful and dates from the end of Böhm's recording career. It is a superb version of this lovely symphony, another work that suited Böhm especially well. The reading is weighty but graceful, with a most beautifully phrased *Andante* (worthy of a Furtwängler), a bold Minuet and a thrilling finale. The recording is splendid. If you admire Böhm this is a worthy way to remember his special gifts.

Additional recommendation ...

...Nos. 6-8[a]; Overtures[b] – Fidelio; Leonore No. 3. [a]**Vienna Philharmonic Orchestra;** [b]**Dresden Staatskapelle / Karl Böhm.** DG Double Ⓜ 437 928-2GX2 (two discs: 130 minutes: ADD: 4/95). *No. 6 is the same recording as the one reviewed above.*   ⒼⒼⒼ

Beethoven Symphony No. 6 in F major, Op. 68, "Pastoral"[a]. Egmont, Op. 84 – Overture[b]; Die Trommel gerühret[b]; Freudvoll und leidvoll[c]; Klärchens Tod bezeichnend[b]. Der Geschöpfe des Prometheus, Op. 43 – Overture[d]. [c]**Birgit Nilsson** (sop); [abc]**Philharmonia Orchestra;** [d]**New Philharmonia Orchestra / Otto Klemperer.** EMI Studio Ⓜ CDM7 63358-2* (69 minutes: ADD: 8/90). Items marked [a] from SAX2260 (10/58), [bc]33CX1575 (11/58), [d]HMV SXLW3032 (6/77). Recorded 1957.   ⒼⒼⒼ

Klemperer's most revered Beethoven recordings date from the middle and late 1950s. In its day, his account of the *Pastoral* was notorious for the slow *Scherzo* – "it's a Ländler" – he is said to have retorted grumpily – but once again the performance as a whole offers a wonderful example of Klemperer's ability to sustain dramatic interest within generously conceived spaces. The result is an overwhelming sense of vital but unhurrying reflection. The *Egmont* numbers on this disc are also very fine. Birgit Nilsson is wonderfully fresh in the two arias, and the rarely recorded "Klärchens Tod bezeichnend" is very affecting. As for the famous overture, Klemperer's account is steadily paced, and as cogent and gauntly explicit a reading of this symphonic music-drama as any on disc. It is a reading of great power and nobility in which nothing is overdone; in this respect the coda is a particular success.

Additional recommendation ...

...No. 6. Menuet in G major, WoO10 No. 2[ad] (arr. db/pf). **Koussevitzky** Valse miniature, Op. 1 No. 2[ad]. Concerto for Double-bass and Orchestra in F major, Op. 3 – Andante[ad] (arr. db/pf). Chanson triste, Op. 2[ad] (1929). **Eccles** (arr. Koussevitzky) Violin Sonata in G minor – Largo (arr. db/pf Two versions, [bd]1928 and [ad]1929). **J. Strauss II** Wiener Blut, Op. 354[c], Frühlingsstimmen, Op. 410[c]. **Laska** Wiegenlied[ad] (arr. db/pf.) [a]**Pierre Luboshutz,** [b]**Bernard Zighera** (pfs);

[c]**Boston Symphony Orchestra / Serge Koussevitzky** ([d]db). Biddulph mono Ⓜ WHL019*
(75 minutes: ADD: 9/94).

Beethoven Symphony No. 9 in D minor, Op. 125, "Choral". **Anna Tomowa-Sintow** (sop); **Agnes Baltsa** (mez); **Peter Schreier** (ten); **José van Dam** (bass-bar); **Vienna Singverein; Berlin Philharmonic Orchestra / Herbert von Karajan.** DG Galleria Ⓜ 415 832-2GGA (67 minutes: ADD: 4/87). Text and translation included. From 2740 172 (10/77). Recorded 1976.

Beethoven Symphony No. 9 in D minor, Op. 125, "Choral". **Alessandra Marc** (sop); **Iris Vermillion** (mez); **Siegfried Jerusalem** (ten); **Falk Struckmann** (bar); **Berlin State Opera Chorus; Berlin Staatskapelle / Daniel Barenboim.** Erato Ⓕ 4509-94353-2 (74 minutes: DDD: 7/94). Text and translation included.

All collections need Beethoven's *Choral* Symphony as one of the works at the very core of the nineteenth-century romantic movement. Within its remarkable span, Beethoven celebrates both the breadth and power of man's conception of his position in relation to the Universe; his sense of spirituality – especially in the great slow movement – and in the finale the essential life-enhancing optimism emerges, which makes human existence philosophically possible against all odds. Karajan lived alongside the Beethoven symphonies throughout his long and very distinguished recording career, and he recorded the Ninth three times in stereo. Sadly the most recent digital version, in spite of glorious playing in the *Adagio*, is flawed, but both analogue versions are very impressive indeed. His 1976 version is the best of the three. The slow movement has great intensity, and the finale brings a surge of incandescent energy and exuberance which is hard to resist. All four soloists are excellent individually and they also make a good team. The reading as a whole has the inevitability of greatness and the recording is vivid, full and clear. At mid-price this is very recommendable indeed.

Barenboim's is an important recording in that it re-establishes – in its own way and with a telling eloquence that is specially its own – that the Ninth is a work of the new romanticism, a prophetic work that cannot be adequately dealt with by so-called 'authenticists' desirous of tethering it either to the letter of the written text or to performance practice in Beethoven's own lifetime. The literalists and authenticists have had some powerful advocates on record – Toscanini, not easily gainsaid, and, for the authenticists, Norrington. Barenboim's Ninth starts deep in the *Urwald*, far away, wreathed in the mists of time. Yet it is a measure of his mastery that the reading never appears to meander or hold fire. On the contrary, the development and recapitulation blaze quietly, from within. 'Quietly' because the Erato recording, made in Berlin's Jesus-Christus Kirche, is rather soft-grained. Important solo voicings, human or instrumental, are neither obscured nor specifically 'lit'. In the finale, words sound clearly enough whilst at the same time being part of the performance's general euphony. The extreme inwardness of Barenboim's reading at key points – the symphony's opening bars, most of the slow movement, the very slow *molto pianissimo* start of the first instrumental statement of the "Joy" theme – is complemented by considerable ebullience in the *Scherzo* and in the later stages of the finale. The soloists are generally reliable, the choir first-rate, the orchestra more than adequate to the considerable task in hand.

Additional recommendations ...

...No. 9. **Soloists; Bayreuth Festival Chorus and Orchestra / Wilhelm Furtwängler.** EMI mono CDH7 69801-2* (75 minutes: ADD). *Gramophone classical 100.* ⒼⒼⒼ

...No. 9. **Soloists; London Symphony Chorus; Academy of Ancient Music / Christopher Hogwood.** L'Oiseau-Lyre Ⓕ 425 517-2OH (63 minutes: DDD: 11/89). ☞ *Selected by Sounds in Retrospect.*

...No. 9. **Soloists; Philharmonia Chorus and Orchestra / Otto Klemperer.** EMI Studio Ⓜ CDM7 63359-2* (72 minutes: ADD: 8/90). Ⓖ

...No. 9. **Soloists; Vienna Singakademie; Vienna Symphony Orchestra / Eliahu Inbal.** Denon Ⓕ CO-76646 (68 minutes: DDD: 3/91).

...No. 9. **Soloists; Royal Liverpool Philharmonic Choir and Orchestra / Sir Charles Mackerras.** EMI Eminence Ⓜ CD-EMX2186 (61 minutes: DDD: 12/91). *Selected by Sounds in Retrospect.* Ⓖ

...No. 9. **Soloists; Bruno Kittel Choir; Berlin Philharmonic Orchestra / Wilhelm Furtwängler.** Music and Arts mono CD653* (74 minutes: ADD: 5/94).

...No. 9. **Soloists; Lucerne Festival Chorus; Philharmonia Orchestra / Wilhelm Furtwängler.** Tahra mono Ⓕ FURT1003* (78 minutes: ADD: 3/95). *Gramophone Award Winner 1995.* Ⓖ

...No. 9. **Soloists; Amsterdam Toonkunst Choir; Concertgebouw Orchestra / Willem Mengelberg.** Archive Documents Mengelberg Edition mono Ⓕ ADCD113* (72 minutes: AAD: 5/95).

New review

Beethoven Quintet for Piano and Wind in E flat major, Op. 16[a].

Spohr Septet in A minor, Op. 147[b]. [b]**Chantal Juillet** (vn); [b]**Christopher van Kampen** (vc); **Pascal Rogé** (pf); **London Winds** ([b]Philippa Davies, fl; [a]Gareth Hulse, ob; Michael Collins, cl; Robin O'Neill, bn; Richard Watkins, hn). Decca Ⓕ 443 892-2DH (64 minutes: DDD: 4/96). Recorded 1994. Ⓖ

Beethoven modelled his Quintet on Mozart's Quintet, K452; however, the Decca coupling with Spohr's A minor Septet suggests comparisons with romantic models rather than classical ones. Perahia and the ECO on Sony (listed below) eloquently express the music's genial mood, presenting its civilized discourse with abounding charm and classical elegance. All the instruments are excellently balanced, and the ensemble is beautifully recorded in Sony's superb, naturally lit production, highlighting the piano's brilliance on the Decca disc. In the present instance, Pascal Rogé and London Winds produce a fuller, more robust sound, with the piano tone given a softer edge that emphasizes the music's romantic tendencies. Effusive phrasing and bold projection throughout imbue the first movement with greater dramatic potency, give the second movement increased warmth and expressive intensity and bring the work to a more exuberant close in the finale. Spohr's Septet was his last chamber work with piano, and its unusual instrumental forces inspired the composer to write music of astonishing freshness and vitality, which is conveyed in this performance with infectious enthusiasm and charm. The opening *Allegro* has a persuasive romantic sweep; the lush autumnal atmosphere of the "Pastorale" is vividly evoked; the *Scherzo*'s 'orchestral' richness is effectively captured, with the finale culminating in concerto-like brilliance.

Additional recommendations ...

...Quintet. **Mozart** Quintet for Piano and Wind in E flat major, K452. **Murray Perahia** (pf); members of the **English Chamber Orchestra**. Sony Classical Ⓕ SK42099 (53 minutes: DDD: 12/86).

...Quintet[a]. **Mozart** Quintet[a]. Adagio and Rondo in C minor, K617[b]. [b]**Imre Kovács** (fl); **József Kiss** (ob); [a]**Béla Kovács** (cl), [a]**Jenö Kevoházi** (hn); [a]**Jozsef Vajda** (bn); [b]**György Konrád** (va); [b]**Tamás Koó** (vc); **Jenö Jandó** ([a]pf/[b]celesta). Naxos Ⓢ 8 550511 (59 minutes. DDD: 4/93)

...Quintet. **Mozart** Quintet. **Hansjörg Schellenberger** (ob); **Larry Combs** (cl); **Dale Clevenger** (hn); **Daniele Damiano** (bn); **Daniel Barenboim** (pf). Erato Ⓕ 4509-96359-2 (49 minutes: DDD: 12/94).

Beethoven Septet in E flat major, Op. 20. Sextet in E flat major, Op. 81*b*. **Vienna Chamber Ensemble.** Denon Ⓕ CO-75373 (57 minutes: DDD: 11/93). Recorded 1992.   ⒼⒼ

New review

Beethoven Septet in E flat major, Op. 20[a]. Piano Trio in B flat major, Op. 11[b]. **Walter Boeykens Ensemble** (Walter Boeykens, cl; [a]Brian Pollard, bn; [a]Jacob Slagter, hn; [a]Marjeta Korosec, vn; [a]Therese-Marie Gilissen, va; Roel Dieltiens, vc; [a]Etienne Siebens, db; [b]Robert Groslot, pf). Harmonia Mundi Ⓕ HMC90 1518 (65 minutes: DDD: 12/95). Recorded 1995.

Beethoven's Septet is a charming work whose importance lies not only in its consolidation of its composer's style before its composition in 1799/1800 but also in its anticipation of his further development as a composer. Moreover, its scoring for clarinet, bassoon, horn and strings and its divertimento structure offer music which is exquisite both in form and textural diversity. Its eternal popularity makes it one of the most frequently recorded chamber works: its fluency of invention and freshness of instrumentation provide the ever-tempting opportunity for groups to offer new insights. The performance by the Vienna Chamber Ensemble is distinguished by interpretative and acoustical refinement which is sensational. The ensemble is ideally matched and the phrasing is elegantly shaped. Clarinettist Norbert Täubl achieves a wonderful smoothness of line, and his playing in the second movement, in particular, sounds heavenly. The Sextet's classical balance and charm, designed to delight the aristocratic audiences of the time, are winningly caught by this Viennese group.

The Walter Boeykens Ensemble reveal the work's exquisitely proportioned balance between its six movements. Though not as dynamic nor as fluid as the Vienna Chamber Ensemble, the Boeykens do play with stronger determination and brilliance than the Gaudier. In the first movement, for example, the Boeykens' focused ensemble sounds lively and spontaneous, enhanced by a pronounced contrast of tempo between the *adagio* slow introduction and the following *allegro*. The Gaudier's relaxed, civilized approach is clear and well balanced, but it lacks the panache of either the Vienna Chamber Ensemble or the Boeykens versions. If, however, the Vienna Chamber Ensemble's mellifluous, smoothly recorded sound is not to your taste, try the Boeykens – most notably in the fourth movement variations and virtuoso finale – whose incisive edge highlights the textural diversity of the music's different instrumental combinations with natural clarity. Beethoven wrote his Op. 11 Trio in 1798, and its scoring is identical with that of the composer's own 1805 arrangement of the Septet. For the Trio clarinettist Walter Boeykens is joined by Roel Dieltiens on cello and Robert Groslot on piano in a performance of engaging verve and energy.

Additional recommendations ...

...Septet. **Mendelssohn** Octet in E flat major, Op. 20. Members of the **Vienna Octet**. Decca Ⓜ 421 093-2DM* (74 minutes: ADD: 5/88).   Ⓖ

...Septet. Sextet. **Gaudier Ensemble**. Hyperion Ⓕ CDA66513 (57 minutes: DDD: 7/92).

...Septet. String Quintet in C major, Op. 29. **Hausmusik**. EMI Reflexe Ⓕ CDC6 54656-2 (72 minutes: DDD: 6/93).

Beethoven Sextet in E flat major, Op. 71. March in B flat major, WoO29. Octet in E flat major, Op. 103. Rondino in E flat major, WoO25. Duets, WoO27 – No. 1 in C major. **Charles Neidich** (cl); **Mozzafiato** (Gerard Reuter, Marc Schachman, obs; Charles Neidich, Ayako Oshima, cls; Dennis Godburn, Michael O'Donovan, bns; William Purvis, Stewart Rose, hns). Sony Classical Vivarte Ⓕ SK53367 (65 minutes: DDD: 8/94). ✈ Recorded 1992-3.

Beethoven composed the Octet, Op. 103 and *Rondino*, WoO25 some time around 1792 and, although it was published separately, there is evidence to suggest that the *Rondino* was originally intended as the fourth movement of a five-movement work. Mozzafiato play the *Rondino* after the Octet, suggesting that the *Presto* finale was written to replace the *Rondino*. Their full-bodied tone-quality creates a warm, broadly conceived result: the oboe and bassoon solos which open the *Andante* second movement sound heavenly; the Minuet and Trio is cheerfully witty; a more flexible approach to the *Presto* finale produces a heightened dramatic effect and, in the *Rondino*, they deliciously reveal the music's textural diversity. In the Sextet, Op. 71 Neidich's clarinet playing is stupendous and his mellifluous virtuosity, especially in the faster outer movements, is well matched by the other performers to demonstrate this group's fine soloistic skills as well as their strong corporate identity. Enchanting performances of the March, WoO29 and the Duo for clarinet and bassoon, WoO27 No. 1 complete a delightful and immensely enjoyable concert.

Beethoven Piano Quartet in E flat major, Op. 16.
Schumann Piano Quartet in E flat major, Op. 47. **Isaac Stern** (vn); **Jaime Laredo** (va); **Yo-Yo Ma** (vc); **Emanuel Ax** (pf). Sony Classical Ⓕ SK53339 (65 minutes: DDD: 10/94). Recorded 1992.
ⒼⒼ

Sixteen recordings of Beethoven's Op. 16 in its original Mozart-inspired quintet version for piano and wind against only two for the piano quartet arrangement in which it rapidly re-emerged – that's the current *Gramophone Classical Catalogue* listing. But this 1992 performance of the quartet from Isaac Stern and his eminent younger colleagues makes it hard to believe that it was conceived for any other combination than theirs – and what higher praise than that? The *Andante cantabile*, with its delicately embellished melodic strands, surely gains in expressive eloquence from the more personal inflexions of caressing strings. And with their bold dynamic contrasts and piquant accentuation, what drama all four players draw from the opening movement. As a brilliant young pianist himself, Beethoven entrusted the pianist with a load of responsibility, at once arrestingly and effortlessly discharged here by Emanuel Ax. As for Schumann's Piano Quartet, no longer is it dwarfed in popularity by its immediate predecessor in the same key, the Piano Quintet. This recording will surely win it a host of new friends – and not only for the mercurial lightness and grace of the Mendelssohnian sprites in the *Scherzo* and the glowing but essentially unsentimentalized intimacy of the *Andante cantabile* (as dedicated a love-song as Schumann ever wrote). The performers' impulse in the two flanking movements is unflagging and the overall impression is of spontaneous enjoyment – a group of friends making music together for their own delight rather than as just another professional engagement. The recording is as vibrant as the playing.

Beethoven Piano Quartets – E flat major, WoO36 No. 1; D major, WoO36 No. 2; C major, WoO36 No. 3; E flat major, Op. 16. **Raphael Oleg** (vn); **Miguel da Silva** (va); **Marc Coppey** (vc); **Philippe Cassard** (pf). Auvidis Valois Ⓕ V4715 (two discs: 88 minutes: DDD: 5/95). Recorded 1994.

This issue of the three piano quartets Beethoven completed at the age of 15 but subsequently suppressed, in double harness with the 26-year-old composer's piano quartet arrangement of his Op. 16 Quintet for piano and wind, is more than welcome – despite its shortish playing time. Indebted to the still youthful Mozart the teenage Beethoven may well (and should) have been, as also tempted to entrust too much to the piano. But the unpredictability of even immature genius is striking. Never can you for a second foretell what surprise, whether of key, harmony, rhythm or scoring, lies just around the corner. His fluent, confident craftsmanship makes you marvel no less. Even when borrowing the three-movement sequence of Mozart's G major Violin Sonata (K397) for his own E flat major work, Beethoven gives his chromatically intensified opening *Adagio assai*, his stormy minor-key *Allegro* and even the beguiling variations, an unmistakable stamp of his own. The playing itself of course contributes to the pleasure, with first praise to Philippe Cassard for never allowing the keyboard to dominate. But all four Paris Conservatoire-trained colleagues are artists of taste and finesse. Their characterization is most sensitively attuned to the music's own true scale. Never does point-making sound self-consciously inflated. In the more familiar Op. 16 work they are just as persuasive as Isaac Stern and his colleagues who opt for sharper accentuation and more urgency in the faster flanking movements. The Auvidis Valois recording itself has a pleasingly soft-grained intimacy.

Beethoven String Quartets – No. 3 in D major, Op. 18 No. 3; No. 7 in F major, Op. 59 No. 1, "Rasumovsky". **Orpheus Quartet** (Charles-André Linale, Emilian Piediacuta, vns; Emile Cantor, va; Laurentiu Sbarcea, vc). Channel Classics Ⓕ CCS6094 (68 minutes: DDD: 12/94). Recorded 1993.
Ⓖ

The Orpheus do not use this music as a vehicle for their virtuosity or prowess; and they do not draw attention to their spot-on ensemble, immaculate intonation and tonal finesse, though they possess all these qualities in no small measure. Take the *Presto* finale of the D major: we are not presented with the headlong rush favoured by many ensembles. The sense of pace is in harmony with the horse-drawn rather than the jet-driven; every note speaks, every phrase tells and the overall effect is all the more exhilarating. Generally speaking, the Orpheus find the *tempo giusto* throughout. They remain attuned to the sensibility of the period and relate their pace to a dance movement in a manner that their rivals have lost. There is something very natural about the players' music-making. They are inside these scores and convey their involvement; no auto pilot, no *ersatz* feeling, no exaggerated or mechanized *sforzatos*. What a relief! All the same, they are not preferable in the slow movement of the F major *Rasumovsky* to the Végh or the Talich (on a seven-disc set), or in the first movement to the Tokyo, who have a symphonic breadth which conveys just how revolutionary this movement is. The recording is bright and clean, and enhances the claims of this impressive issue.

Additional recommendations ...

...Complete Quartets: Op. 18 Nos. 1-6. No. 7 in F major, Op. 59 No. 1, "Rasumovsky", No. 8 in E minor, Op. 59 No. 2, "Rasumovsky". No. 9 in C major, Op. 59 No. 3, "Rasumovsky". No. 10 in E flat major, Op. 74, "Harp". No. 11 in F minor, Op. 95, "Serioso". No. 12 in E flat major, Op. 127. No. 13 in B flat major, Op. 130. No. 14 in C sharp minor, Op. 131. No. 15 in A minor, Op. 132. No. 16 in F major, Op. 135. **Talich Quartet.** Calliope Ⓕ CAL9633/9 (seven discs: 502 minutes: AAD: 1/89). ⒼⒼ

...Complete Quartets. Grosse Fuge in B flat major, Op. 133. **Hungarian Quartet.** EMI Ⓜ CZS7 67236-2* (seven discs: 476 minutes: ADD).

...Nos. 1-6. **Quartetto Italiano.** Philips Ⓜ 426 046-2PM3 (three discs: 163 minutes: ADD: 2/90).

...Nos. 3, 4 and 6. **New Budapest Quartet.** Hyperion Ⓕ CDA66402 (75 minutes: DDD: 10/90).

...Nos. 1, 3, 4, 10, 12, 13 and 14. **Alban Berg Quartet.** EMI Ⓕ CDS7 54587-2 (four discs: 242 minutes: DDD: 10/92).

...Nos. 2, 5, 6, 8, 9, 11, 15 and 16. Grosse Fuge. **Alban Berg Quartet.** EMI Ⓕ CDS7 54592-2 (four discs: 259 minutes: DDD: 10/92).

...Nos. 1-6. String Quartet in F major, H34 (transcribed from Piano Sonata in F major, Op. 14, No. 1). String Quintet in C major, Op. 29. **Tokyo Quartet** with **Pinchas Zukerman** (va). RCA Victor Red Seal Ⓕ 09026 61284-2 (three discs: 204 minutes: DDD: 9/93). Ⓖ

...Nos. 4-6. **Brandis Quartet.** Nimbus Ⓕ NI5353 (75 minutes: DDD: 9/94).

...Nos. 1, 9 and 11-16. Violin Sonata in E flat major, Op. 12 No. 3[a]. **Schubert** String Quartet in B flat major, D112. **Mendelssohn** Capriccio in E minor, Op. 81 No. 3. [a]**Rudolf Serkin** (pf); **Busch Quartet.** EMI mono Ⓜ CHS5 65308-2* (four discs: 270 minutes: ADD: 1/95).

...Nos. 1 and 14. **Petersen Quartet.** Capriccio Ⓕ 10 510 (66 minutes: DDD: 3/95). *Gramophone Editor's choice.*

...Nos. 3 and 13; Grosse Fuge in B flat major, Op. 133. **Emerson Quartet.** DG Ⓕ 449 505-2GY (70 minutes: DDD: 4/96).

...No. 13. Grosse Fuge, Op. 133. **Brandis Quartet.** Nimbus Ⓕ NI5465 (61 minutes: DDD: 4/96).

New review

Beethoven String Quartets – No. 4 in C minor, Op. 18 No. 4; No. 15 in A minor, Op. 132. **Petersen Quartet** (Conrad Muck, Gernot Süssmuth, vns; Friedemann Weigle, va; Hans-Jakob Eschenburg, vc). Capriccio Ⓕ 10 722 (63 minutes: DDD: 4/96). Recorded 1995. ⒼⒼ

The Petersen Quartet possess impeccable technical address, immaculate ensemble, flawless intonation and tonal finesse. Tempos are judged with real musicianship, and dynamic markings are observed without being exaggerated. The C minor Quartet, Op. 18 No. 4 has dramatic tension without loss of lyrical fervour and the *Scherzo* has wit. When we move to the first movement of the A minor Quartet the sound-world changes as if youth has given way to wisdom and experience. They hardly put a foot wrong here and their *Heiliger Dankgesang* is rapt and inward-looking. They press ahead fractionally in one or two places – on the reprise of the main section in the second movement and when the main theme returns in the finale. But one or two minor reservations apart, theirs is quite simply the most satisfying late Beethoven to have appeared in recent years. Above all the Petersen do not invite you to admire their prowess. They appear to be untouched by the three 'g's (Gloss, Glamour and Glitz) and their concern is with truth rather than beauty.

Beethoven String Quartets, Op. 18 – No. 5 in A major; No. 6 in B flat major. **Quatuor Mosaïques** (Erich Höbarth, Andrea Bischof, vns; Anita Mitterer, va; Christophe Coin, vc). Auvidis Astrée Ⓕ E8541 (58 minutes: DDD: 7/95). 🎙 Recorded 1994. *Gramophone Editor's choice.*

Of the Op. 18 works the A major probably has most to gain from a responsive performance on period instruments. Its light, sometimes spare textures and air of amiable, slightly abstracted elegance are particularly resistant to the high-voltage brilliance of certain modern-instrument ensembles; and the Mosaïques, most imaginative and penetrating of 'original' quartets, give an almost ideal reading. As you might expect, the imitative interplay of the finale gains particularly from the textural clarity easier to achieve on period instruments played with sparing vibrato. The tempo, characteristically, is on the broad side here. But few ensembles have brought such wit and grace, such a subtle variety of colour and bowing, to the quicksilver instrumental dialogues. Yet the Mosaïques' delicacy and intimacy do not preclude an authentic Beethovenian trenchancy in the development, bows biting deeply into gut strings in those vehement *fortissimo* exchanges. The *Andante* variations, on one of Beethoven's bare scale themes, can often outstay their welcome; but these players bring an unusual grave eloquence to the theme itself. In the B flat Quartet they are hardly less persuasive. The epigrammatic opening *Allegro* is as lithe, spring-heeled and quick-witted as you could wish (the dialogue at the start of the development deliciously handled), yet avoids the clipped, relentlessly sportive approach heard in many performances. In the *Adagio ma non troppo* Erich Höbarth brings a rare sense of fantasy to the conventional-looking violin fioriture; and the protracted ending is, for once, witty rather than tedious. For musical insight the Mosaïques' beautifully recorded readings of these quartets hold their own with any of the modern-instrument versions in the catalogue.

Beethoven String Quartets – No. 7 in F major, Op. 59 No. 1, "Rasumovsky"; No. 8 in E minor, Op. 59 No. 2, "Rasumovsky"; No. 9 in C major, Op. 59 No. 3, "Rasumovsky". **Lindsay Quartet**

(Peter Cropper, Ronald Birks, vns; Roger Bigley, va; Bernard Gregor-Smith, vc). ASV
Ⓜ CDDCS207 (two discs: 115 minutes: DDD: 4/95). From CDDCA554 (1/89).　Ⓖ
In the few years that separate the Op. 18 from the Op. 59 quartets, Beethoven's world was shattered
by the oncoming approach of deafness and the threat of growing isolation. The Op. 59 consequently
inhabit a totally different plane, one in which the boundaries of sensibility had been extended in much
the same way as the map of Europe was being redrawn. Each of the three quartets alludes to a
Russian theme by way of compliment to Count Rasumovsky, who had commissioned the set. The
immediate impression the F major Quartet conveys is of great space, breadth and vision; this is to the
quartet what the *Eroica* is to the symphony. The neglect of Beethoven's C major Quintet is
unaccountable for it is a rewarding and remarkable score, written only a year before the First
Symphony. At one time the presto finale earned it the nickname "Der Sturm", doubtless on account
of the similarity, or rather anticipation of the storm in the *Pastoral* Symphony. Although the Lindsays
may be rivalled (and even surpassed) in some of their insights by the Végh and the Talich, taken by
and large, they are second to none and superior to most. In each movement of the E minor they find
the *tempo giusto* and all that they do as a result has the ring of complete conviction. The development
and reprise of the first movement are repeated as well as the exposition and how imaginatively they
play it too! The *pp* markings are scrupulously observed but are not obtrusively pasted on as they are
in some sets. The C major is not quite in the same class though the opening has real mystery and awe
and some listeners might legitimately feel that the whole movement could do with a little more
momentum. On the other hand, they move the second movement on rather too smartly. Yet how
splendidly they convey the pent-up torrent of energy unleashed in this fugal onrush. Even if it does
not command quite the same elevation of feeling or quality of inspiration that distinguishes their F
major and E minor quartets, it is still pretty impressive.

Additional recommendations ...
...Nos. 8 and 9. **Végh Quartet.** Auvidis Valois Ⓕ V4404 (71 minutes: ADD: 4/88).　ⒼⒼⒼ
...Nos. 7 and 8. **Budapest Quartet.** Sony Classical Essential Classics Ⓑ SBK46545* (70 minutes:
ADD: 8/91).
...Nos. 7-11. **Quartetto Italiano.** Philips Ⓜ 420 797-2PM3 (three discs: 165 minutes: ADD: 2/90).
　ⒼⒼ
...Nos. 12-16. Grosse Fuge in B flat major, Op. 133. **Quartetto Italiano.** Philips Ⓜ 426 050-2PM4
(four discs: 216 minutes: ADD: 2/90). *Gramophone classical 100.*　ⒼⒼⒼ
...Nos. 7-9 and 11. **Tokyo Quartet.** RCA Victor Red Seal Ⓕ RD60462 (three discs: 170 minutes:
DDD: 3/92).
...Nos. 7-9. **Brandis Quartet.** Nimbus Ⓕ NI5382 (72 minutes: DDD: 6/94).

Beethoven String Quartets – No. 11 in F minor, Op. 95, "Serioso"[a]; No. 15 in A minor, Op. 132[b].
Végh Quartet (Sándor Végh, Sándor Zöldy, vns; Georges Janzer, va; Paul Szabó, vc). Auvidis
Valois Ⓕ V4406 (68 minutes: ADD: 4/88). Item marked [a] from Telefunken EX6 35041 (8/76);
[b]EX6 35040 (10/74).　ⒼⒼⒼ
Beethoven String Quartets – No. 15 in A minor, Op. 132[a]; No. 16 in F major, Op. 135[b]. **Talich
Quartet** (Petr Messiereur, Jan Kvapil, vns; Jan Talich, va; Evzen Rattai, vc). Calliope
Ⓕ CAL9639 (68 minutes: ADD: 12/86). Item marked [a] from CAL1639, (6/80), [b]CAL1640
(6/80).　ⒼⒼ
After the expansive canvas of the Op. 59 Quartets and the *Eroica*, Beethoven's F minor Quartet,
Op. 95, displays musical thinking of the utmost compression. The first movement is a highly
concentrated sonata design, which encompasses in its four minutes almost as much drama as a full-
scale opera. With it comes one of the greatest masterpieces of his last years, the A minor, Op. 132.
The isolation wrought first by his deafness and secondly, by the change in fashion of which he
complained in the early 1820s, forced Beethoven in on himself. Opus 132 with its other-worldly
Heiliger Dankgesang, written on his recovery from an illness, is music neither of the 1820s nor of
Vienna, it belongs to that art which transcends time and place. Though other performances may be
technically more perfect, these are interpretations that come closer to the spirit of this great music
than any other on CD. Collectors need have no doubts as to the depth and intelligence of the Talich
Quartet's readings for they bring a total dedication to this music: their performances are innocent of
artifice and completely selfless. There is no attempt to impress the listener with their own virtuosity
or to draw attention to themselves in any way. The recordings are eminently faithful and natural, not
'hi-fi' or overbright but the overall effect is thoroughly pleasing.

Additional recommendations ...
...Nos. 11 and 15. **Végh Quartet.** Auvidis Valois Ⓕ V4406 (68 minutes: DDD: 4/88).
...No. 11 (arr. Mahler). **Mahler** Symphony No. 2 in C minor, "Resurrection"[a]. [a]Tina Kilberg (sop);
[a]Kirsten Dolberg (mez); [a]Danish National Radio Choir; **Danish National Symphony Orchestra /
Leif Segerstam.** Chandos Ⓕ CHAN9266/7 (two discs: 116 minutes: 10/95).

Beethoven String Quartets. **Végh Quartet** (Sándor Végh, Sándor Zöldy, vns; Georges Janzer, va;
Paul Szabó, vc). Auvidis Valois Ⓕ V4405, V4408 (two discs, oas: 71 and 66 minutes: ADD: 6/87).
Items marked [a] from Telefunken EX6 35041 (8/76), [b]Telefunken SKA25113T/1-4 (10/74).
V4405 – No. 10 in E flat major, Op. 74, "Harp"[a]; No. 12 in E flat major, Op. 127[b]. *V4408* –
No. 14 in C sharp minor, Op. 131[b]; No. 16 in F major, Op. 135[b].　ⒼⒼⒼ

Beethoven stepped both outside and beyond his period nowhere more so than in the late quartets and the last five piano sonatas. The Op. 127 has been called Beethoven's "crowning monument to lyricism", whilst the Op. 131 is more inward-looking. Every ensemble brings a different set of insights to this great music so that it is not possible to hail any single quartet as offering the whole truth – yet these are as near to the whole truth as we are ever likely to come. The Végh give us music-making that has a profundity and spirituality that completely outweigh any tiny blemishes of intonation or ensemble. One does not get the feeling of four professional quartet players performing publicly for an audience but four thoughtful musicians sharing their thoughts about this music in the privacy of their own home. They bring us closer to this music than do any of their high-powered rivals.

Additional recommendations ...

...(orch. Mitropoulos/Bernstein) Nos. 14 and 16. **Vienna Philharmonic Orchestra / Leonard Bernstein.** DG Ⓕ 435 779-2GH (77 minutes: ADD/DDD: 11/92). ⒼⒼ

...No. 12. **Mozart** String Quartet No. 19 in C major, K465, "Dissonance". **Amadeus Quartet**. Orfeo mono Ⓔ C358941B* (63 minutes: ADD: 10/95).

...Nos. 14 and 15. **Capet Quartet**. Biddulph mono Ⓜ LAB099* (78 minutes: ADD: 12/95).

Beethoven String Quartets – No. 13 in B flat major, Op. 130[a]; No. 8 in E minor, Op. 59 No. 2, "Rasumovsky"[b]. **Talich Quartet** (Petr Messiereur, Jan Kvapil, vns; Jan Talich, va; Evzen Rattai, vc). Calliope Ⓕ CAL9637 (73 minutes: ADD: 3/87). Item marked [a] from CAL1637/40, [b]CAL1634/6. ⒼⒼ

The Beethoven quartets are one of the greatest musical expressions of the human spirit and they must be represented in any collection. The advantage of this Talich recording is that it couples a masterpiece from Beethoven's middle period, the great E minor Quartet, with one of the greatest of his last years. The B flat was the third of the late quartets to be composed and at its first performance in 1826 its last movement, the *Grosse Fuge*, baffled his contemporaries. Later that same year, he substituted the present finale, publishing the *Grosse Fuge* separately. The Talich Quartet have a no less impressive technical command than other ensembles but theirs are essentially private performances, which one is privileged to overhear rather than the over-projected 'public' accounts we so often hear on record nowadays. At 73 minutes this is marvellous value too.

Beethoven Piano Trios – E flat major, Op. 1 No. 1; G major, Op. 1 No. 2; C minor, Op. 1 No. 3; B flat major, Op. 11; D major, Op. 70 No. 1, "Ghost"; E flat major, Op. 70 No. 2; B flat major, Op. 97, "Archduke"; B flat major, WoO39; E flat major, WoO38; E flat major, Op. 44; G major, Op. 121a. **Beaux Arts Trio** (Daniel Guilet, vn; Bernard Greenhouse, vc; Menahem Pressler, pf). Philips The Early Years Ⓜ 438 948-2PM3 (three discs: 235 minutes: ADD: 11/94). From SAL3527/30 (1/66). Recorded 1965. ⒼⒼ

Beethoven Piano Trios – C minor, Op. 1 No. 3; B flat major, Op. 11[a]. Allegretto in B flat major, WoO39. [a]**Wolfgang Meyer** (cl); **Erich Höbarth** (vn); **Christophe Coin** (vc); **Patrick Cohen** (pf). Harmonia Mundi Ⓕ HMC90 1475 (60 minutes: DDD: 1/95). ✏ Recorded 1993.

Beethoven Piano Trios – B flat major, Op. 11; B flat major, Op. 97, "Archduke". **Chung Trio** (Kyung-Wha Chung, vn; Myung-Wha Chung, vc; Myung-Whun Chung, pf). EMI Ⓕ CDC5 55187-2 (61 minutes: DDD: 1/95). Recorded 1992.

It's the immediacy and freshness, the wholehearted commitment of the playing by the Beaux Arts Trio that holds you spellbound in almost every context. To begin with, in the *joie de vivre* of the E flat and G major Op. 1 Trios, it's so good to be reminded that a colossus like Beethoven was once so young at heart – in the persuasive lyricism of slower tempos no less than the teasing, devil-may-care sparkle and wit of their finales (taken at a breathless pace without for a moment sounding gabbled). The crowning performance is nevertheless the *Archduke*. The players' expansive yet so warmly human nobility in the opening *Allegro moderato*, their urgent, mercurial response to the undertones of the *Scherzo*, their raptness in the visionary serenity of the slow movement and their pungency in the finale convince you that no greater piano trio has ever been written. Here, too, you're given the fullest chance to enjoy the silken beauty of Guilet's violin and the velvet richness of Greenhouse's now legendary 1707 Stradivari cello; also the wonderful blend of tone achieved by all three in contexts like the pizzicato/staccato of the first movement's development, or the eerie chromatic start to the trio of the *Scherzo*. Hailed in the booklet as "the soul of the entire ensemble", Pressler himself (incidentally the only one of the original three still at his post today) achieves many miracles of delicacy and fleetness.

Harmonia Mundi give us a welcome recording of Beethoven's original version of the Trio, Op. 11. Although Beethoven later adapted the work for the more frequently chosen violin, nothing can capture the opening movement's hiding and seeking quite like the clarinet. Meyer marks, teases and imitates with glee just as he phrases and articulates with high mischief in the first variation of Beethoven's nine on Joseph Weigl's aria, *Pria ch'io l'impegna*. Cohen's fortepiano here is, as the note cryptically puts it, "Clarke d'après Walter, 1986". This was the Viennese Anton Walter, whose early pianos, with their hammer-heads resting directly on the keys, Mozart grew to favour. In the Op. 1 No. 3 Trio, its sweet, short metallic resonance brings a sting to the accents and raging scale passages in an uncompromising opening movement of a work Haydn much admired, but warned Beethoven not to publish. Its dangers and disturbances, as well as the delicate patterning of its slow movement, shine out anew in this entirely engaging performance. Six-and-a-half minutes' worth of the single *Allegretto* movement of Beethoven's B flat Trio make up an hour's listening on this irresistible disc.

The playing of Kyung-Wha Chung on the EMI disc – sweet, sentient and sharply defined – almost persuades you again of the violin's adapted and adopted role in the Op. 11 Trio. And what the modern piano loses in the immediacy of its own voice and its empathy with the others is generously compensated by Myung-Whun's nimble, light-filled playing. This piano's warmer resonance comes into its own in the long distances of the rolling crescendos and decrescendos which form the heart of the *Adagio*, and lift it into the major. The real wonder of this disc, though, is the Chungs' performance of the Op. 97 Trio in B flat. Beethoven dedicated it "in deep reverence" to Austria's Archduke – and Myung-Whun never forgets it, whether in his awed, reverential opening, or in the simplicity of the wonderfully hushed frame of his slow movement theme. Violin and cello merely brush, rather than gush, against it, and lead it into a dream sequence of variations. The Chungs' gentle unfolding and nourishing of this opening movement – everything is done within a veiled undertone – leaves plenty of fuel unburned for the scherzo, which starts on tiptoe, and whose dark chromatic shadows in the trio are never over-briskly dissipated by what can often be an over-assertive waltz. This is chamber-music-making at its most perceptive and rewarding.

Additional recommendations ...

...Complete Piano Trios. Variations in G major on "Ich bin der Schneider Kakadu", Op. 121*a*. Variations, Op. 44. Allegretto in E flat major. **Vladimir Ashkenazy** (pf); **Itzhak Perlman** (vn); **Lynn Harrell** (vc). EMI Ⓕ EX290834-3 (four discs: 257 minutes: DDD: 3/87).

...Complete Piano Trios. Variations Op. 121*a*. Variations, Op. 44. Allegretto in E flat major. **Borodin Trio.** Chandos Ⓕ CHAN8352/5 (four discs: 271 minutes: DDD: 7/87).

..."Archduke". Variations, Op. 121*a*. **Robinson Trio.** IMP Classics Ⓜ PCD874 (63 minutes: DDD: 1/88).

...Op. 1 Nos. 1 and 2. **London Fortepiano Trio.** Hyperion Ⓕ CDA66197 (58 minutes: DDD: 11/87) ✍

...Op. 1 Nos. 1-3. "Ghost". "Archduke". Variations, Op. 121*a*. 14 Variations, Op. 44. Allegretto in E flat major. **Pinchas Zukerman** (vn); **Jacqueline du Pré** (vc); **Daniel Barenboim** (pf). EMI Studio Ⓜ CMS7 63124-2 (three discs: 230 minutes: ADD: 8/89).

..."Archduke". "Ghost". **Henryk Szeryng** (vn); **Pierre Fournier** (vc); **Wilhelm Kempff** (pf). DG Ⓜ 429 712-2GGA (71 minutes: ADD: 9/90).

...Op. 1 Nos. 1-3. B flat major, Op. 11. D major after Symphony No. 2, Op. 36. E flat major, Op. 44. E flat major, Op. 38 (after Septet, Op. 20). "Ghost". E flat major, Op. 70 No. 2. "Archduke". G major, Op. 121*a*. E flat major, WoO38. B flat major, WoO39. Trio movement in E flat major, Hess 48. **Beaux Arts Trio.** Philips Ⓜ 432 381-2PM5 (five discs: 359 minutes: ADD/DDD: 3/92).

..."Ghost"; E flat major, Op. 70 No. 2. **Solomon Trio.** IMP Classics Ⓕ MCD44 (65 minutes: DDD: 11/92).

..."Archduke"[b]. Op. 1 No. 3[a]. "Ghost"[c]. Cello Sonatas – F major, Op. 5 No. 1[d]; G minor, Op. 5 No. 2[e]; F major, Op. 17[g]; C major, Op. 102 No. 1[f]. [abc]**Sándor Vegh.** (vn); **Pablo Casals** (vc); [c]**Karl Engel,** [abefg]**Mieczyslaw Horszowski,** [d]**Wilhelm Kempf** (pfs). Philips Ⓜ 438 520-2PM3 (three discs: 200 minutes: ADD: 3/94).

..."Archduke". Allegretto in E flat major, Hess 48. Variations, Op. 121*a*. **Solomon Trio** (Rodney Friend, vn; Timothy Hugh, vc; Yonty Solomon, pf). IMP Masters Ⓕ MCD69 (66 minutes: DDD: 3/94). Ⓖ

..."Archduke". B flat major, Op. 11. **Alexander Schneider** (vn); **Pablo Casals** (vc); **Eugene Istomin** (pf). Sony Classical Casals Edition mono Ⓜ SMK58990* (65 minutes: ADD: 5/94).

...E flat major, Op. 1 No. 1. G major, Op. 1 No. 2. **Stuttgart Piano Trio.** Naxos Ⓢ 8 550946 (63 minutes: DDD: 7/94).

...C minor, Op. 1 No. 3. E flat major, WoO38. E flat major, Op. 44. Trio movement in E flat major, Hess No. 48. **Stuttgart Piano Trio.** Naxos Ⓢ 8 550947 (60 minutes: DDD: 7/94).

..."Ghost". Op. 70 No. 2. **Stuttgart Piano Trio.** Naxos Ⓢ 8 550948 (57 minutes: DDD: 12/94).

..."Archduke". **Brahms** Piano Trio No. 1 in B major, Op. 8. **Viktoria Mullova** (vn); **Heinrich Schiff** (vc); **André Previn** (pf). Philips Ⓕ 442 123-2PH (75 minutes: DDD: 8/95).

...B flat major, Op. 11. **Brahms** Piano Trio in A minor, Op. 114. **Mozart** Trio for Clarinet, Viola and Piano in E flat, K498, "Kegelstatt". **Richard Stoltzman** (cl); **Yo-Yo Ma** (vc); **Emanuel Ax** (pf). Sony Classical Ⓕ SK57499 (70 minutes: DDD: 1/96).

...Op. 1 Nos. 1 and 2. **Erich Hobarth** (vn) **Christophe Coin** (vc); **Patrick Cohen** (fp). Harmonia Mundi HMC190 1361 (70 minutes: DDD: 2/96). ✍

Beethoven String Trios – E flat major, Op. 3; Op. 9 – No. 1 in G major; No. 2 in D major; No. 3 in C minor. Serenade in D major, Op. 8. **Itzhak Perlman** (vn); **Pinchas Zukerman** (va); **Lynn Harrell** (vc). EMI Ⓕ CDS7 54198-2 (two discs: 143 minutes: DDD: 2/93). Recorded live 1989-90. Ⓖ

Beethoven String Trios, Op. 9 – No. 1 in G major; No. 2 in D major; No. 3 in C minor. **L'Archibudelli** (Vera Beths, vn; Jürgen Kussmaul, va; Anner Bylsma, vc). Sony Classical Vivarte Ⓕ SK48190 (68 minutes: DDD: 9/92). ✍ Recorded 1991. Ⓖ

Whereas the last of Beethoven's six Piano Trios, the *Archduke*, was not written until he was 41, all five of his String Trios date from his twenties, with the six-movement E flat Trio, Op. 3, appearing in 1792, to be followed by the *Serenade* in D, Op. 8, some five years later. But after banishing all such eighteenth-century entertainment connotations in his three next classically designed, four-movement String Trios (Op. 9) of 1798, he thereafter preferred to write not for three but rather, four strings in what grew into a legendary, life-long cycle of string quartets. The double-stopping in the noble slow movement of the high-powered C minor String Trio already portends pursuit of richer textures. So it is essentially the artist as a young man that we meet on the EMI set, and what a revelation of youthful genius they offer in imaginative range. Recorded live in New York, the playing is eloquent testimony to that little extra piquancy and boldness of characterization that an audience can draw from artists even as studio-friendly as Perlman, Zukerman and Harrell – perhaps all the more fresh in their approach because not in daily harness as an ensemble. Tone is splendidly vibrant. And incidentally they score over their also excellent, but less succulently reproduced DG rivals, by including the arresting extra trio Beethoven subsequently provided for the *Scherzo* of the G major Trio.

A group with "a special love for historical stringed instruments" is how L'Archibudelli is described, as might be gleaned from their name (an Italian compilation of bows and strings) plus the fact that Anner Bylsma plays a 1835 Gianfrancesco Pressenda cello, Vera Bath a 1727 Stradivari violin and Jürgen Kussmaul a 1785 William Forster viola. But though striving for a special period quality of sound they are anything but antiquarian in their approach to these works, all of them striking enough to have placed Beethoven among the immortals even if he had written nothing else. With their brisk tempo, strong dynamic contrast and piquant accentuation, they leave no doubt of the urgency inherent in the key of C minor for this composer. The other two Trios in major keys are equally imaginatively characterized and contrasted. Some listeners might even feel they are over-volatile in their response to every detailed innuendo, at the expense of firmly drawn, classical line. But their relish of the music wins the day. Once or twice busy figuration in the lower strings emerge a bit bottom-heavy. The recording is true to life.

Additional recommendations ...

...*As EMI.* **Anne-Sophie Mutter** (vn); **Bruno Giuranna** (va); **Mstislav Rostropovich** (vc). DG Ⓔ 427 687-2GH2 (two discs: 139 minutes: DDD: 7/89).

...E flat major. Serenade, Op. 8. **L'Archibudelli.** Sony Classical Vivarte Ⓔ SK53961 (71 minutes: DDD: 5/94). 🎵

New review

Beethoven Cello Sonatas – No. 1 in F major, Op. 5 No. 1; E flat major, Op. 64. Variations on Handel's "See the conqu'ring hero comes", WoO45. **Anssi Karttunen** (vc); **Tuija Hakkila** (fp). Finlandia Ⓔ 4509-95584-2 (71 minutes: DDD: 11/95). 🎵 Recorded 1992.

This is the first volume of Beethoven's complete works for cello and fortepiano, works which were, in turn, the first of their kind – sonatas in which the cello found its own, proud voice, liberated at last from trotting dutifully along the continuo bass-line. And it is the 'firstness' which these performances so excitingly celebrate. With their 1770 Benjamin Banks cello and reproduction 1795 Walter fortepiano, Anssi Karttunen and Tuija Hakkila play as if they really are exploring ideas of startling novelty, daring each other on, and pushing their instruments to the limits of their capabilities. In the F major Sonata they re-create the energy of those two itinerant virtuosos, Beethoven and Duport, in whose hands the work first came to life. Rhythms snap one against the other, as the sudden mischiefs and secret moments of brief song, so prophetic of the compact dramas of the Op. 10 Piano Sonatas, spring to new life. The Op. 64 Sonata – an arrangement of the String Trio, Op. 3 – is a totally different creature, with its six sharply contrasted movements. Karttunen and Hakkila revel in their differences. Every note bites into place in their ferocious outer movements, always tempered with the good humour of tiny subtleties and graces of phrasing. The range of detail and dynamic nuance in a single piano scale or repeated note is remarkable: so are the disorientating silences and offbeats of the first Menuetto. Both performers remember that, for Beethoven, Handel was the greatest composer who ever lived; and they do both proud in their buoyantly inflected, mischievously competitive *Variations on "See the conqu'ring hero comes"*.

Additional recommendations ...

...Nos. 1 and 2. 12 Variations in F major on "Ein Mädchen oder Weibchen" from "Die Zauberflöte", Op. 66. Seven Variations in E flat major on Mozart's "Bei Männern, welche Liebe fühlen" from "Die Zauberflöte", WoO46. **Mischa Maisky** (vc); **Martha Argerich** (pf). DG Ⓔ 431 801-2GH (66 minutes: DDD: 2/92). ⊙⊙

...Nos. 1-5. Variations, WoO46. Variations, Op. 66 **Pablo Casals** (vc); **Rudolf Serkin** (pf). Sony Classical Casals Edition mono Ⓜ SM2K58985* (two discs: 158 minutes: ADD: 5/94).

...Nos. 1-3. **Timothy Hugh** (vc); **Yonty Solomon** (pf). IMP Masters Ⓔ MCD80 (76 minutes: DDD: 9/94).

...Nos. 1-5. Variations, Op. 66. Variations, WoO46. Variations, WoO45. **Mischa Maisky** (vc); **Martha Argerich** (pf). DG Ⓔ 439 934-2GH2 (two discs: 139 minutes: DDD: 2/95).

Beethoven Cello Sonatas – No. 1 in F major, Op. 5 No. 1[a]; No. 2 in G minor, Op. 5 No. 2[b]; No. 3 in A major, Op. 69[c]; No. 4 in C major, Op. 102 No. 1[d]; No. 5 in D major, Op. 105 No. 2[e]. Menuet in G major, WoO10 No. 2 (arr. vc/pf)[f].

Brahms Cello Sonata No. 2 in F major, Op. 99[g]. **Pablo Casals** (vc); [abdeg]**Mieczyslaw Horszowski,** [cf]**Otto Schulhof** (pfs). EMI Références mono Ⓜ CHS5 65185-2* (two discs: 136 minutes: ADD: 10/94). Item marked [a] from HMV DB3908/10, [b]DB3911/13 (both recorded 1939), [c]DB1417/19 (10/31), [d]DB3065/6 (7/37), [e]DB3914/16 (4/41), [f]DB1419, [g]DB3059/62 (8/40). ⊙⊙⊙

Sensitive phrasing was the very hub of Pablo Casals's art, and these CDs are more revealing than many of how this most communicative of cellists could mould and energize a musical line, reducing his tone to a soulful tenor then thrusting a powerful *sforzando* for maximum dynamic contrast. The Beethoven sonatas are endlessly rewarding in this respect, but even they must bow to the marginal supremacy of Casals's 1936 account of the Brahms F major Sonata, one of the truly great cello recordings. No one since has projected the work's heroic opening with as much confidence (the repeat is observed, by the way), nor brought greater suppleness or tonal variety to the *Adagio affetuoso*. Note, too, how both Casals and Horszowski explore the winding musical thickets of the *Allegro passionato* (Brahms at his most mischievous) and make play with the closing *Allegro molto*. The Beethoven sonatas are equally indelible, the Op. 5 works sounding very much their innovatory selves, and those of Op. 102 more probing and explosive than most. Both players invest Op. 102 No. 2's searching *Adagio con molto sentimento d'affetto* with an intriguing sense of the numinous, then dig deep into the succeeding *Allegro fugato* – a gritty debate on the preceding mystery, and parallel in effect to the last movement of the *Hammerklavier*. Casals recorded the Op. 69 Sonata some nine years before Opp. 5 and 102, not with Horszowski, but with the stylish and facilitating Otto Schulhof. It differs from its companions in being more songful than soulful and with a *bel canto* solo line that extends to the charming Menuet makeweight. Recordings of this unique quality deserve painstaking restoration, and Andrew Walters's transfers are excellent. Surface levels are low, the solo cello sounds clean and immediate, and the piano is more recognizably itself than on some 78s from the 1930s.

Beethoven Violin Sonatas – No. 1 in D major, Op. 12 No. 1 (from SXL6790, 7/77); No. 2 in A major, Op. 12 No. 2 (SXL6632, 2/75); No. 3 in E flat major, Op. 12 No. 3 (SXL6789, 12/76); No. 4 in A minor, Op. 23; No. 5 in F major, Op. 24, "Spring" (both from SXL6736, 7/76); No. 6 in A major, Op. 30 No. 1; No. 7 in C minor, Op. 30 No. 2 (both from SXL6791, 12/77); No. 8 in G major, Op. 30 No. 3 (SXL6789); No. 9 in A major, Op. 47, "Kreutzer" (SXL6632); No. 10 in G major, Op. 96 (SXL6790). **Itzhak Perlman** (vn); **Vladimir Ashkenazy** (pf). Decca Ovation Ⓜ 421 453-2DM4 (four discs: 239 minutes: ADD: 1/89). Recorded 1973-5.   Ⓖ

New review

Beethoven Violin Sonatas – No. 1 in D major, Op. 12 No. 1; No. 2 in A major, Op. 12 No. 2; No. 3 in E flat major, Op. 12 No. 3; No. 4 in A minor, Op. 23; No. 5 in F major, Op. 24, "Spring"; No. 6 in A major, Op. 30 No. 1; No. 7 in C minor, Op. 30 No. 2; No. 8 in G major, Op. 30 No. 3; No. 9 in A major, Op. 47, "Kreutzer"; No. 10 in G major, Op. 96. **Petr Messiereur** (vn); **Stanislav Bogunia** (pf). Calliope Ⓕ CAL9251/3 (three discs: 217 minutes: DDD: 3/96). Recordėd 1994-5.

Although Beethoven designated these works as "for piano and violin", following Mozart's example, it is unlikely that he thought of the piano as leading the proceedings, or the violin either, for that matter: both instruments are equal partners and in that sense this is true chamber music. Perlman and Ashkenazy are artists of the first rank and there is much pleasure to be derived from their set. Such an imaginative musician as Ashkenazy brings great subtlety to these works composed by a supreme pianist-composer. And the better the pianist is in this musc, the better does the violinist play. Discernment is matched by spontaneity and the whole series is remarkably fine, while their celebrated performance of the *Kreutzer* Sonata (also available separately, listed below) has quite superb eloquence and vitality. The recording boasts unusually truthful violin sound capturing all the colour of Perlman's playing – and that is saying something. Ashkenazy's vivid attack is always faithful to the Beethoven idiom.

Messiereur and Bogunia rightly do not dress up the fresh-faced youthful sonatas – and all but Op. 96 are youthful, with the *Kreutzer* dating from Beethoven's thirty-third year – and one becomes increasingly won over by the directness and clear focus of the playing, where briskness comes without roughness and energy without loss of poise. How admirably vivid and alert is a movement such as the *Allegro piacevole* finale of the A major Sonata, how keen and crisp the ensemble in the *Presto* opening movement of the A minor work, how innocent and insouciant the corresponding movement of the *Spring* Sonata, where Kremer and Argerich on DG are self-consciously winsome. The *Adagio molto espressivo* of this sonata also flowers as it should, proving that these artists can indeed relax their tight rein where they feel it necessary. There's a sunny humour in the *Scherzo* of the C minor Sonata and throughout its successor in G major. Apart from the quality of the performances, the Calliope recording is both natural and pleasing: try the start of Op. 30 No. 1 to hear sound with both impact and delicacy. The duo give the later sonatas more warmth and flexibility than they accord to the early ones, and clearly their whole approach has been carefully thought out. However, the safest recommendation perhaps remains the warmly thoughtful Perlman and Ashkenazy set.

Additional recommendations ...

...Nos. 5 and 9. **Itzhak Perlman** (vn); **Vladimir Ashkenazy** (pf). Decca Ⓕ 410 554-2DH (62 minutes: ADD: 11/83).

...Nos. 1-10. **Sir Yehudi Menuhin** (vn); **Wilhelm Kempff** (pf). DG Ⓜ 415 874-2GCM4 (four discs: 272 minutes: ADD: 6/87).

...Nos. 8-10. **Jascha Heifetz** (vn); **Emmanuel Bay** (pf). RCA Victor Gold Seal mono Ⓜ GD87706* (72 minutes: ADD: 11/88).   ⒼⒼ

...Nos. 5 and 9. **Takako Nishizaki** (vn); **Jenö Jandó** (pf). Naxos Ⓢ 8 550283 (56 minutes: DDD: 3/91).

...Nos. 5, 9 and 10. **Zino Francescatti** (vn); **Robert Casadesus** (pf). Sony Classical Essential Classics Ⓑ SBK46342* (76 minutes: ADD: 3/91).

…Nos. 5 and 9. **Thomas Zehetmair** (vn); **Malcolm Frager** (fp). Teldec Digital Experience Ⓜ 9031-75856-2 (59 minutes: DDD: 6/92). ✒

…Nos. 5, 8 and 9. **Pinchas Zukerman** (vn); **Daniel Barenboim** (pf). EMI Studio Plus Ⓜ CDM7 64631-2 (78 minutes: ADD: 3/93).

…Nos. 1–10. **Gidon Kremer** (vn); **Martha Argerich** (pf). DG Ⓕ 447 058-2GH3 (three discs: 226 minutes: DDD: 1/96).　　　　　　　　　　　　　　　　　　　　　　　　　Ⓖ

…Nos. 3, 5 and 7. **Adolf Busch** (vn); **Rudolf Serkin** (pf). APR mono Ⓜ APR5541* (60 minutes: ADD: 5/96).

…Nos. 7, 8 and 9. **Olivier Charlier** (vn); **Brigitte Engerer** (pf). Harmonia Mundi Ⓕ HMC90 1580 (79 minutes: DDD: 6/96).

Beethoven Violin Sonatas – No. 6 in A major, Op. 30 No. 1; No. 7 in C minor, Op. 30 No. 2; No. 8 in G major, Op. 30 No. 3. **Gidon Kremer** (vn); **Martha Argerich** (pf). DG Ⓕ 445 652-2GH (64 minutes: DDD: 1/95). Recorded 1993. *Gramophone Editor's choice*.　　　ⒼⒼ

Beethoven's Op. 30 violin sonatas are three irresistibly lively and individual spirits in the hands and imaginations of Martha Argerich and Gidon Kremer. The first, in A major, has that particular quality of blithe and elusive joy reminiscent of the *Spring* Sonata, and created here by the lightest and truest touch on string and key, fused with bright rhythmic clarity. The slow movement is a tremulous song of long-forgotten, far-off things, in which violin and piano find an intimate balance of tone. The second sonata of the group is here less an heroically clenched C minor fist, more the unfolding of a gripping and tense *Märchen*: a dark children's fairy-tale told through the rapid tapering of a phrase-ending on the violin, the gutsy ebb and flow of a piano crescendo, the sudden *pianissimo* picking up after the loud chords of a second theme. At the start of the development, Argerich even seems to be asking if her listeners are sitting comfortably – and rather hoping they are not. The G major Sonata's centrepiece is its Minuet and Trio, which Argerich and Kremer cunningly tease and charm into revealing its archaic qualities: a dance glimpsed through a lace veil. It is framed by two fast movements that would identify their performers anywhere, with their high-voltage velocity and wittily imaginative anticipation of each other's every move.

Beethoven Variations on Handel's "See the conqu'ring hero comes", WoO45. 12 Variations on Mozart's "Ein Mädchen oder Weibchen", Op. 66. Seven Variations on Mozart's "Bei Männern, welche Liebe fühlen", WoO46. Horn Sonata, Op. 17 (arr. vc). **Pieter Wispelwey** (vc); **Lois Shapiro** (fp). Channel Classics Ⓕ CCS6494 (45 minutes: DDD: 4/95). ✒ Recorded 1994.

There may be only 45 minutes of it, but this recital of Beethoven variations teems with fresh insights in the irresistible serendipity of its playing. Lois Shapiro partners Pieter Wispelwey's 1701 cello on a 1780 Viennese fortepiano whose wiry energies she unleashes without more ado in an attention-grabbing opening theme for Handel's *See the conqu'ring hero comes*. Her bright-eyed first variation glints as phrases dart from dynamic shadow to light and back again. Then the cello's lean, slightly astringent voice makes itself felt in no uncertain terms before the keyboard gets its own back in mercurial scale passages. The players' delight in teasing, sparring and debating with each other comes into its own in the variations on *Ein Mädchen oder Weibchen*. The theme itself struts forward cheekily, only to peck its way through the first variation, before the cello makes the most of the wry harmonic subtext of the second. In the seventh, one half of a shared phrase caresses and preens the other; the tenth casts the shadow of Papageno's noose. Each player's imagination and technique is tested to the full in an absorbing account of the more abstracted *Bei Männern* variations. The world of *Singspiel* is not far away, either, in this performance of the Sonata in F major, Op. 17: Wispelwey and Shapiro summon up the nascent world of Marzelline and Jacquino in their quick, ardent responses to the music and to each other's playing.

Beethoven Six Variations in F major on an Original Theme, Op. 34[a]. Six Variations in D major, Op. 76. 15 Variations and a Fugue on an Original Theme in E flat major, Op. 35, "Eroica"[a].
Chopin Four Scherzos[b] – No. 1 in B minor, Op. 20; No. 2 in B flat minor, Op. 31; No. 3 in C sharp minor, Op. 39; No. 4 in E major, Op. 54.
Schumann Etudes symphoniques, Opp. 13 and posth[a]. Bunte Blätter, Op. 99[b]. **Sviatoslav Richter** (pf). Olympia Ⓕ OCD339[a] and OCD338[b] (two discs, oas: 77 and 75 minutes: ADD: 4/94). Recorded by Eurodisc 1970-77.　　　ⒼⒼ

Remarkably well-recorded considering the source, one performance after another here is so memorable as to rank among the best versions around of the piece in question. There is such richness in the Beethoven Variations that it seems pointless and unfair to highlight any one in particular. Nevertheless, the *Eroica* Variations end with Richter playing most pianists under the table. He is not usually thought of as a very credible Chopin player, and yet he strides through the four *Scherzos* with an abundance of technique and deftly coloured textures that make this version a definite front-runner. His Schumann, on the other hand, has always been dazzling, because he has a temperament that convincingly responds to the extreme swings in mood. The reading of the *Etudes symphoniques* is an

overwhelming experience. The fourth of the supplementary variations emerges as an exotic lament of ravishing beauty and the pianist's very large hands enable him to attack the chords of the finale with ferocious confidence. Well-chosen and excellent in sound, these performances should not be missed.

Additional recommendations ...

...Variations, Op. 34. 15 Variations, Op. 35, "Eroica". Rondos, Op. 51 – No. 1 in C major; No. 2 in G major. Bagatelle in A minor, WoO59, "Fur Elise". **Louis Lortie** (pf). Chandos Ⓕ CHAN8616 (58 minutes: DDD: 10/90).

...Variations, Op. 34. Six Variations, WoO70. 15 Variations and a Fugue. 32 Variations on an Original Theme in C minor, WoO80. **Jenö Jandó** (pf). Naxos Ⓢ 8 550676 (54 minutes: DDD: 9/93).

Beethoven 33 Variations in C major on a Waltz by Diabelli, Op. 120. Piano Sonata No. 28 in A major, Op. 101. **Peter Donohoe** (pf). EMI Ⓕ CDC7 54792-2 (64 minutes: DDD: 8/94). Recorded 1992.

"Weird and wonderful" is about the right description of Beethoven's last great set of variations – though with the emphasis on "wonderful". It's the perfect counter to the old canard that Beethoven had no sense of humour, or that if he did, it was applied with the subtlety of a sledgehammer. The humour ranges from deliciously childlike *forte-piano* alternations (Var. 13), to sly, self-mocking quotation (the invocation of Mozart's Leporello in Var. 22 – "Night and day I labour"), to a joke on a cosmic scale – the break-up of the fugue (Var. 32) into eerie stillness and harmonic ambiguity, followed by the sudden, mock-innocent reappearance of the theme in Mozartian peruke and lace (Var. 33). A good performance can leave you wondering, for just a moment, where on earth – or anywhere – you are. At the same time there are moments of inner intensity that match anything in the late piano sonatas; and behind it all is the same sense of powerful structural unfolding. A recommendable performance has to hold all these elements in balance. Time and time again Donohoe's brilliance, his scintillating staccato and unfailing sense of textural clarity are a delight. Donohoe, too, registers the deepest sense of shock at the fugue's astonishing conclusion than many of his rivals. However, he convinces least where Barenboim is often most successful – the slow variations. If sound quality is not your main concern then Schnabel remains the front-runner, currently available on Pearl – not always perfectly accurate, sometimes quirky, but always absorbing.

Additional recommendations ...

...Diabelli Variations. **Artur Schnabel** (pf). Pearl Ⓕ GEMMCD9378* (ADD).   ⒼⒼ

...Diabelli Variations. **Alfred Brendel** (pf). Philips Ⓕ 426 232-2PH (53 minutes: DDD: 8/90).   ⒼⒼ

...Diabelli Variations. **Stephen Kovacevich** (pf). Philips Concert Classics Ⓑ 422 969-2PCC (54 minutes: ADD: 8/90).

...Diabelli Variations. Piano Sonata No. 31 in A flat major, Op. 110. *Coupled with works by* **C.P.E. Bach, Bach, Chopin, Mozart** and **Schubert Mieczyslaw Horszowski** (pf). Pearl Ⓕ GEMMCDS9979 (two discs: 155 minutes: ADD: 12/93).

...Diabelli Variations. **Daniel Barenboim** (pf). Erato Ⓕ 4509-94810-2 (58 minutes: DDD: 8/94).

...Diabelli Variations. 15 Variations and Fugue on an original theme in E flat major, Op. 35, "Eroica". **Tatyana Nikolaieva** (pf). Olympia Ⓜ OCD570 (65 minutes: ADD: 6/95).

...Diabelli Variations. **William Kinderman** (pf). Hyperion Ⓕ CDA66763 (55 minutes: DDD: 8/95).

New review

Beethoven 33 Variations in C major on a Waltz by Diabelli, Op. 120. 32 variations on an Original Theme in C minor, WoO80. **Benjamin Frith** (pf). ASV Quicksilva Ⓢ CDQS6155 (62 minutes: DDD: 2/96). Recorded 1990.   Ⓖ

This bargain on ASV's super-budget Quicksilva label offers a currently almost unbeatable coupling of the *Diabelli* Variations and the *32 Variations on an Original Theme*. Benjamin Frith is one of those artists whose musical perceptions are not to be doubted, and whose playing is almost never troubled by technical blemishes, and certainly not here. In short, both performances are masterly, the interpretations clearly thought through, concentrated in tension and feeling. With excellent recording this disc is unsurpassed, even by Brendel or Kovacevich who, of course, both have their own insights to offer in the *Diabelli*. But then so has Frith, and very impressive they are too.

Beethoven Complete Piano Sonatas. **Richard Goode** (pf). Elektra Nonesuch Ⓕ 7559-79328-2 (ten discs: 608 minutes: DDD: 3/94). Items marked [a] from 7559-79213-2 (4/92), [b]979 212-2 (9/90), [c]979 211-2 (9/89). Remainder new to UK.

No. 1 in F minor, Op. 2 No. 1; No. 2 in A major, Op. 2 No. 2; No. 3 in C major, Op. 2 No. 3; No. 4 in E flat major, Op. 7; No. 5 in C minor, Op. 10 No. 1[a]; No. 6 in F major, Op. 10 No. 2[a]; No. 7 in D major, Op. 10 No. 3[a]; No. 8 in C minor, Op. 13, "Pathétique"; No. 9 in F major, Op. 14 No. 1; No. 10 in G major, Op. 14 No. 2; No. 11 in B flat major, Op. 22; No. 12 in A flat major, Op. 26; No. 13 in E flat major, Op. 27 No. 1, "quasi una fantasia"; No. 14 in C sharp minor, Op. 27 No. 2, "Moonlight"; No. 15 in D major, Op. 28, "Pastoral"; No. 16 in G major, Op. 31 No. 1[b]; No. 17 in D minor, Op. 31 No. 2, "Tempest"[b]; No. 18 in E flat major, Op. 31 No. 3[b]; No. 19 in G minor, Op. 49 No. 1; No. 20 in G major, Op. 49 No. 2; No. 21 in C minor, Op. 53, "Waldstein"; No. 22 in F major, Op. 54; No. 23 in F minor, Op. 57, "Appassionata"; No. 24 in F sharp major, Op. 78; No. 25 in G major, Op. 79; No. 26 in E flat major, Op. 81a, "Les adieux"; No. 27 in E minor, Op. 90; No. 28 in A major, Op. 101[c]; No. 29 in B flat major, Op. 106, "Hammerklavier"[c]; No. 30 in E major, Op. 109[c]; No. 31 in A flat major, Op. 110[c]; No. 32 in C minor, Op. 111[c]. ⓖⓖⓖ

Until the last few years Richard Goode was active principally as an ensemble player, in chamber music, a field in which he excels. He is American and his reputation in the USA is considerable, but less so in the UK. Whoever commissioned the long essay for the Nonesuch booklet from Michael Steinberg did the set a fine service. The production and engineering are credited to Max Wilcox and his expertise and care leaves one with little to quibble with. The sound and microphone balances rates from good to very good and they're pretty consistent over the ten CDs. The lower end of the dynamic range is very well defined, perhaps better than the other. In the first movement of the *Hammerklavier* Sonata and the *Scherzo* of the A flat Sonata, Op. 110, Wilcox hasn't been completely successful in dissuading Goode from stamping on the pedal, but this Serkinesque habit is not obtrusive elsewhere. There is some unevenness of achievement in Goode's playing but the level, in general, is wonderfully high, with no lapses from grace. Everything demands assessment in the company of the best there is. The interpretation of the A major Sonata, Op. 101 is one of the finest ever put on record. Reservations? You may have a doubt as to whether the playing in this sonata or that represents everything Goode is capable of: sometimes he disappoints, slightly, by appearing to hold back from the listener – through temperamental reserve? – the boldness and fullness of communciation the greatest players achieve. One might say that, for all their insight and illumination, some of the performances lack the final leap and a degree of transcendence. In the first movement of the A flat, Op. 110 Goode sounds as if he's trying too hard. Yet he is marvellous later in the sonata, at the close of the reprise of the *Arioso*, taking the listener through the 'heartbeat' chords into the inversion of the Fugue and by way of the difficult transition (which gave Beethoven much trouble) to the serentiy and triumph of the final pages with a sureness and quality of imagination that are exceptional. If this isn't Beethoven interpretation of the highest class it is impossible to say what is. One might prefer an even stiller slow movement of the *Hammerklavier* Sonata, but that and a few other small regrets are probably attributable to the business of record making.

Consideration of that enormous span of slow music in the *Hammerklavier* brings to mind the great 'set-piece' slow movements of the early sonatas as well: in Op. 2 Nos 2 and 3, Op. 7, Op. 10 Nos. 1 and 3. Those processional, inward, even monumental and ineluctable qualities which they share demand intense concentration on both sides of the microphone and Goode makes them eloquent, even though they could smile a little more. In Op. 14 No. 2 in G he is delicious – perfect. There is abundant wit, as he plays it, in the first movement of Op. 10 No. 2 in F too. A quality often to be observed in Goode is allure. Maybe that is why his playing is so very likeable: the finish of his playing, technical and musical, is immaculate but on top of that he is exciting. His sound always makes you listen. His feeling for it and for fine gradations of sound from one end of his wide dynamic range to the other are those of a virtuoso and inform everything he does. And when he's more obviously on virtuoso territory, as in the *Waldstein* and *Appassionata*, he responds to their demands for brilliance and thrilling projection as to the manner born. He is constantly inside the music, not on the outside looking in, and what a lively, cultivated, lucid and stimulating guide he is. There is nothing diffident or half-hearted about the way he makes this cycle of Beethoven resound wonderfully, the earlier sonatas appearing as no less masterly or characteristic of their composer than the later.

Additional recommendations ...

...Nos. 1-32. **Alfred Brendel** (pf). Philips Ⓕ 412 575-2PH11 (11 discs: 659 minutes: ADD: 1/85). ⓖⓖ

...Complete Piano Sonatas. **Daniel Barenboim** (pf). EMI Ⓑ CZS7 62863-2 (ten discs: 687 minutes: ADD: 10/90). ⓖⓖ

...Nos. 1-32. **Wilhelm Kempff** (pf). DG Ⓡ 429 306-2GX9 (nine discs: 594 minutes: ADD: 3/91). ⓖⓖ

...Nos. 1-32. **Artur Schnabel** (pf). EMI Références mono Ⓜ CHS7 63765-2* (eight discs: 605 minutes: ADD: 7/91). *Gramophone classical 100.* ⓖⓖⓖ

...Nos. 1-32. Piano Variations. **Claudio Arrau** (pf). Philips Ⓜ 432 301-2PM11 (11 discs: 739 minutes: ADD: 1/92). ⓖ

...Nos. 1-10. **Jean-Bernard Pommier** (pf). Erato Ⓕ 2292-45598-2 (three discs: 215 minutes: DDD: 9/93).

...No. 5. *Coupled with works by* **Mozart** Till Fellner (pf); [a]Lausanne Chamber Orchestra / Uri Segal. Claves Ⓕ CD50-9328 (62 minutes: DDD: 9/94). *See review under Mozart; refer to the Index to Reviews.*

...Nos. 5-7. **Louis Lortie** (pf). Chandos Ⓕ CHAN9101 (56 minutes. DDD: 3/93).

...Nos. 7, 9, 30 and 31. **Awadagin Pratt** (pf). EMI Ⓕ CDC5 55290-2 (74 minutes: DDD: 5/96).

...Nos. 7-10. **Tatyana Nikolaieva** (pf). Olympia Ⓕ OCD563 (74 minutes: ADD: 1/95).

...Nos. 11-14. **Tatyana Nikolaieva** (pf). Olympia Ⓕ OCD564 (76 minutes: ADD: 1/95).

...Nos. 11-20. **Jean-Bernard Pommier** (pf). Erato Ⓕ 2292-45812-2 (three discs: 191 minutes: DDD: 9/93).

...Nos. 1, 5, 6, 9, 10, 13, 14, 15 and 25. **Alfred Brendel** (pf). Vox Box Ⓑ 115772-2 (two discs: 145 minutes: ADD: 9/93).

...Nos. 8, 14, 15 and 24. **Wilhelm Kempff** (pf). DG Galleria Ⓜ 415 834-2GGA (60 minutes: ADD: 8/87).

...Nos. 8, 14, 23 and 26. **Arthur Rubinstein** (pf). RCA Victor Gold Seal Ⓜ 09026 61443-2 (76 minutes: ADD: 10/93).

...Nos. 14, 21 and 23. **Vladimir Ashkenazy** (pf). Decca Ovation Ⓜ 417 732-2DM (66 minutes: ADD: 12/87).

...Nos. 28-32. **Maurizio Pollini** (pf). DG Ⓕ 419 199-2GH2 (two discs: 126 minutes: DDD: 12/86). ⒼⒼ

...Nos. 15-17. **Tatyana Nikolaieva** (pf). Olympia Ⓜ OCD565 (69 minutes: ADD: 6/95).

...Nos. 18-22. **Tatyana Nikolaieva** (pf). Olympia Ⓜ OCD566 (78 minutes: ADD: 6/95).

...Nos. 23-27. **Tatyana Nikolaieva** (pf). Olympia Ⓜ OCD567 (76 minutes: ADD: 6/95).

...Nos. 28 and 29. **Tatyana Nikolaieva** (pf). Olympia Ⓜ OCD568 (67 minutes: ADD: 6/95).

...Nos. 30-32. 32 Variations on an original theme in C minor, WoO80. **Tatyana Nikolaieva** (pf). Olympia Ⓜ OCD569 (76 minutes: ADD: 6/95).

Jenö Jandó's reliable complete super-bargain set of the sonatas is available on Naxos on two sets comprising five CDs each (8 505002 and 8 505003). They are also available on ten separate CDs, the details of which follow (the volume numbers do not indicate the numerical order of the sonatas).

...(Vol. 3) Nos. 1-3. Naxos Ⓢ 8 550150 (67 minutes: DDD: 12/90).

...(Vol. 5) Nos. 5, 6, 7 and 25. Naxos Ⓢ 8 550161 (63 minutes: DDD: 12/90).

...(Vol. 8) Nos. 4, 13, 19, 20 and 22. Naxos Ⓢ 8 550167 (68 minutes: DDD: 12/90).

...(Vol. 6) Nos. 9, 10, 24, 27 and 28. Naxos Ⓢ 8 550162 (72 minutes: DDD: 12/90).

...(Vol. 1) Nos. 8, 14 and 23. Naxos Ⓢ 8 550045 (56 minutes: DDD: 2/91).

...(Vol. 10) Nos. 15 and 33-38. Naxos Ⓢ 8 550255 (69 minutes: DDD: 2/91).

...(Vol. 2) Nos. 17, 21 and 26. Naxos Ⓢ 8 550054 (63 minutes: DDD: 2/91).

...(Vol. 7) Nos. 12, 16 and 18. Naxos Ⓢ 8 550166 (64 minutes: DDD: 6/91).

...(Vol. 9) Nos. 11 and 29. Naxos Ⓢ 8 550234 (64 minutes: DDD: 6/91).

...(Vol. 4) Nos. 30, 31 and 32. Naxos Ⓢ 8 550151 (64 minutes: DDD: 6/91).

New review

Beethoven Complete Piano Sonatas. **Wilhelm Kempff** (pf). DG Dokumente mono Ⓜ 447 966-2GDO8* (eight discs: 511 minutes: ADD: 4/96). From DG originals reviewed between 4/56 and 12/59, and previously unpublished (Sonata No.11; recorded 1956). Includes bonus disc, "Wilhelm Kempff – An All-Round Musician". Recorded 1951-6. ⒼⒼ

Wilhelm Kempff was the most inspirational of Beethoven pianists. Those who have cherished his earlier stereo cycle for its magical spontaneity, will find Kempff's qualities even more intensely conveyed in this mono set, recorded between 1951 and 1956. Amazingly the sound has more body and warmth than the stereo, with Kempff's unmatched transparency and clarity of articulation even more vividly caught, both in sparkling *Allegros* and in deeply dedicated slow movements. If in places he is even more personal, some might say wilful, regularly surprising you with a new revelation, the magnetism is even more intense, as in the great *Adagio* of the *Hammerklavier* or the final variations of Op. 111, at once more rapt and more impulsive, flowing more freely. The bonus disc, entitled "An All-Round Musician", celebrates Kempff's achievement in words and music, on the organ in Bach, on the piano in Brahms and Chopin as well as in a Bachian improvisation, all sounding exceptionally transparent and lyrical. Fascinatingly, his pre-war recordings of the Beethoven sonatas on 78s are represented too. Here we have his 1936 recording of the *Pathétique*, with the central *Adagio* markedly broader and more heavily pointed than in the mono LP version of 20 years later.

Beethoven Piano Sonatas, Op. 2 – No. 1 in F minor; No. 2 in A major; No. 3 in C major. **Alfred Brendel** (pf). Philips Ⓕ 442 124-2PH (70 minutes: DDD: 7/95).

Brendel reminds us here that, in their different ways, these works of Beethoven's first maturity are as finished and as characteristic as the later ones, and it's a measure of his artistry that he makes us aware of the Op. 2 trilogy as three "highly profiled individuals" – the description in the notes – and not just as generalized 'early' Beethoven. You need to play this disc at a reasonably high level to savour the full range of Brendel's dynamics and colouring. Perhaps not everything is communicated here as vividly as Brendel habitually achieves in the concert-hall. The playing conveys a total vision and is musically alive as few can rival, but one is inclined to regret that no place had been found for a passing breeze of impetuosity. The spellbinding inner worlds of the great slow movements in the A major and C major Sonatas of Op. 2 are as demanding for the player as any. The piano has to be transcended. Brendel treats the *Largo appassionato* of the A major as a processional, and keeps it nicely on the move; even finer is his control of nuance and movement in the E major *Adagio* of Op. 2 No. 3 – the end is marvellous. His simpler, sculpted eloquence in the slow movement of the F minor Sonata is also touching, and in general, he allows himself plenty of time for reflectiveness and quasi-improvisatory exploration. The first movement of the A major Sonata is a particularly interesting journey: *Allegro vivace* certainly, two in a bar, but never a rush, so one can be all the more aware of the teeming incident on the way. The radiant finale of this Sonata is another high spot, clearly hugely enjoyed by him in this affectionate account of it. This is fresh, youthful Beethoven in which there is room for caprice and laughter and good humour as well as profundity and the shocks of the new. It is all the more attractive for that – early Beethoven should surely be allowed to smile a little.

Additional recommendations ...

...Nos. 1-3. **John O'Conor** (pf). Telarc Ⓕ CD80214 (67 minutes: DDD: 9/90).

...Nos. 1-3. **Tatyana Nikolaieva** (pf). Olympia Ⓕ OCD561 (71 minutes: ADD: 1/95).

...Nos. 3, 11, 18, 23, 24, 29 and 30. Bagatelle in A minor, WoO59, "Für Elise". Six Ecossaises, WoO83. Variations – F major, Op. 34; D major on "Rule Britannia", WoO79; G major, WoO70

on "Nel cor più non mi sento"; 33 in C major on a Waltz by Anton Diabelli, Op. 120; 15
Variations, Op. 35, "Eroica ". Andante favori, WoO57. Bagatelles, Op. 126. Piano Concertos –
No. 4 in G major, Op. 58; No. 5 in E flat major, Op. 73, "Emperor". **Alfred Brendel** (pf); **Chicago
Symphony Orchestra / James Levine**. Philips Ⓜ 446 922-2PM5 (five discs: 373 minutes:
ADD/DDD: 2/96).

New review

Beethoven Piano Sonatas – No. 4 in E flat major, Op. 7; No. 15 in D major, Op. 28, "Pastoral";
No. 20 in G major, Op. 49 No. 2. **Alfred Brendel** (pf). Philips Ⓕ 446 624-2PH (65 minutes: DDD:
2/96). Recorded 1994. Recorded 1994. *Gramophone Editor's record of the month.*   Ⓖ
Brendel's interpretation of the *Pastoral* has changed – and its status has stratospherically soared – in
two interrelated respects. In the first place, the two outer movements are both slower than on either
the 1960s Turnabout recording or the 1970s Philips version. What we have here is not some amiable
musical ramble; rather, it is a multi-layered music-drama in which the pianist's relish in debating the
issues the music is already asking itself makes for the most exhilarating kind of listening. And what a
debate it is, substantial and charged with feeling. The lead back to the recapitulation – the lurch into
B major, the sudden silence, the restatement in B minor, a further silence, the unresolved question on
the home dominant – is realized with quite heart-stopping intensity. But, then, intensity is very much
the order of the day in this latest cycle of recordings, a throwing open of the gates, with a far greater
use of declamatory effects and rhetorical tropes than was the case in either of his two earlier cycles.
Not that Brendel has thrown overboard any of his wryness, wit or natural sense of balance. He plays
the two inner movements of the *Pastoral* Sonata every bit as elegantly as before. And yet here again
one notices sudden deepenings and new-found beauties. The performance of the E flat Sonata, Op. 7
is similarly grand, open and free-spirited. And here a word needs to be said about the recordings,
which are thrillingly loyal to the music-making. The sound, like the playing, can be both grand and
awesomely quiet. Above all, it offers a persistently clear view of the rich ensemble of inner voices that
is so vital to Brendel's purpose. The engagingly brief G major Sonata makes a delightful postlude. and
again Brendel has changed tack, playing the second of the two movements, the *Tempo di Menuetto*
much more swiftly than previously. Played like this is sounds wonderfully fresh and gamesome, the
perfect envoi to an enthralling disc.
Additional recommendations ...
...Nos. 4, 11 and 13. **John O'Conor** (pf). Telarc Ⓕ CD80363 (70 minutes: DDD: 8/94).
...Nos. 4-6. **Tatyana Nikolaieva** (pf). Olympia Ⓕ OCD562 (63 minutes: ADD: 1/95).
...No. 4; No. 8 – Adagio cantabile; No. 32 . Andante favori in F major, WoO57. Six Variations on
"Nel cor più non mi sento", WoO70. Heiligenstadt Testament[a]. **Elly Ney** (pf/[a]spkr). Biddulph
mono Ⓜ LHW033* (80 minutes: ADD: 3/96).

Beethoven Piano Sonatas – No. 8 in C minor, Op. 13, "Pathétique"[a]; No. 23 in F minor, Op. 57,
"Appassionata"[b]; No. 31 in A flat major, Op. 110[c].
Handel Keyboard Suite in D minor, HWV428[d] – Prelude; Air and Variations; Presto. Chaconne
and Variations in G major, HWV435[e]. **Edwin Fischer** (pf). APR Signature mono Ⓜ APR5502*
(72 minutes: AAD: 12/94). Item marked [a] from HMV DB3666/7 (12/38), [b]DB2517/19 (10/35),
[c]DB3707/08 (recorded 1938), [d]DB2378 (9/35), [e]HMV DA4401 (12/32).   Ⓖ
On this invaluable APR disc, expertly grouped and presented, are some of Fischer's finest and most
legendary performances. His very first published recording (1931) of the Handel Chaconne, for
example, was made at a time when his matchless *leggiero* and radiant tone were unimpeded by
obvious blemishes or erratic pianism. Both this performance and that of the pieces from the Suite
No. 3 have an improvisatory magic, a strength and grace and supreme assurance. Fischer commences
the *Pathétique* with a scrupulous adherence to Beethoven's *fp* marking, a sudden shift of sound that
is fascinatingly modernist or prophetic. The *Allegro di molto e con brio* is exactly that, dancing with
an irrepressible lightness and urgency; and if one listens to the slow octave descent just before the final
outburst one will hear a rapt 'all-passion-spent' quality, something Fischer could achieve with
supreme naturalness, without even a hint of artifice or calculated effect. All past vicissitudes are
finally resolved in Op. 110 in a blaze of heroic glory, and time and again he makes you pause to
consider key points and details that somehow elude others. There is here a richness and humanity, a
sheer quality that was uniquely Fischer's.

Beethoven Piano Sonatas – No. 8 in C minor, Op. 13, "Pathétique". No. 14 in C sharp minor,
Op. 27 No. 2, "Moonlight". No. 15 in D major, Op. 28, "Pastoral". No. 17 in D minor, Op. 31
No. 2, "Tempest". No. 21 in C major, Op. 53, "Waldstein". No. 23 in F minor, Op. 57,
"Appassionata". No. 26 in E flat major, Op. 81a, "Les Adieux". **Alfred Brendel** (pf). Philips Duo
Ⓜ 438 730-2PM2 (152 minutes: ADD: 4/94). Recorded 1970-77.   ⒼⒼ

New review

Beethoven Piano Sonatas – No. 8 in C minor, Op. 13, "Pathétique"[a]; No. 23 in F minor, Op. 57,
"Appassionata"[b]. Fantasia in C minor, Op. 80[c]. Bagatelles[a] – Op. 33 Nos. 3 and 5; Op. 119
Nos. 2, 7 and 9; Op. 126 Nos. 1, 4 and 6. **Sviatoslav Richter** (pf); [c]**Russian State Academic Choir;**
[c]**Moscow Radio Symphony Orchestra / Kurt Sanderling**. Melodiya mono Ⓜ 74321 29462-2*
(80 minutes: ADD: 6/96). Items marked [a] recorded 1959, [b]1960, [c]1952.

The Philips reissue, containing seven of Beethoven's most popular named sonatas admirably played by Alfred Brendel, is in every way an outstanding bargain, well worth obtaining, even if duplication is involved. All the performances are authoritative and offer consistently distinguished playing, while the recording is very realistic indeed. The *Tempest* resonates in the memory and the central movements of the *Pastoral* are most beautifully shaped. The *Pathétique, Moonlight* and *Appassionata* all bring deeply satisfying readings that are compellingly conceived and freshly executed. This set can be recommended without any reservations whatsoever. The booklet-notes with the Melodiya reissue claim that Richter's live 1960 Moscow *Appassionata* is his favourite among his recorded performances of the work, and from the elemental power it unleashes one can well believe it. The *Pathétique* is magnificently implacable, while the *Choral Fantasia* is a remarkable curiosity – cavernous acoustic, fierce recording, the text in Russian, sung with intimidating gusto. The mono sound is acceptable.

Additional recommendations ...

...Nos. 8, 14, 21 and 23. **Wilhelm Kempff** (pf). DG The Originals Ⓜ 447 404-2GOR (79 minutes: ADD: 9/95).

...Nos. 8, 14 and 17. **Cristina Ortiz** (pf). Tring International Ⓢ TRP027 (57 minutes: DDD: 10/95).

...Nos. 12, 21, 24 and 26. **Dénes Várjon** (pf). Capriccio Ⓕ 10 714 (71 minutes: DDD: 3/96).

...Nos. 21, 23 and 26. **Emil Gilels** (pf). DG Ⓕ 419 162-2GH (ADD: 8/86).   ⒼⒼ

...Nos. 21 and 31. **Stephen Kovacevich** (pf). EMI Ⓕ CDC7 54896-2 (53 minutes: DDD: 2/94).
Gramophone Editor's choice.

...Nos. 21, 23 and 27. **Barry Douglas** (pf). RCA Victor Red Seal Ⓕ 09026 61280-2 (66 minutes: DDD: 6/94).

...Nos. 30, 31 and 32. **Vladimir Feltsman** (pf). MusicMasters Ⓕ 67098-2 (66 minutes: DDD: 6/94).

...Nos. 14, 21 and 23. **Vladimir Horowitz** (pf). RCA Victor Gold Seal Ⓜ GD60375 (65 minutes: ADD: 7/94).

...Nos. 23, 24, 25 and 27. **Alfred Brendel** (pf). Philips Ⓕ 442 787-2PH (59 minutes: DDD: 11/95).

Beethoven Piano Sonatas – No. 9 in E major, Op. 14 No. 1[a]; No. 11 in B flat major, Op. 22[b]; No. 12 in A flat major, Op. 26[c]; No. 27 in E minor, Op. 90[c].
Haydn Keyboard Sonatas[c] – No. 39 in D major, HobXVI/24; No. 62 in E flat major, HobXVI/52.
Weber Piano Sonata No. 3 in D minor, J206[c]. **Sviatoslav Richter** (pf). Philips Ⓕ 438 617-2PH2 (two discs: 131 minutes: ADD/DDD: 8/94). Item marked [a] from SAL3457 (9/64), [b]SAL3456 (9/64), remainder new to UK. Items marked [ab] recorded 1963, [c]1994.   ⒼⒼ

Richter's greatness is due partly to his limitless artistic and technical ability and partly to his extraordinarily wide range of repertoire. His unique capacity to surprise derives from a profound understanding of musical processes, and his concerts are events in a continuous sequence of musical discovery. In Haydn's E flat Piano Sonata, Richter's extreme sensitivity to detail produces a captivating performance of great delicacy and charm. Haydn's D major Sonata provides further evidence of Richter's wholly unselfconscious approach: the opening movement is expressed with transparent clarity; the *cantabile Adagio* is beautifully judged, and the finale has an engaging ethnic gait. He recorded the Beethoven sonatas in 1963 and, though there is a noticeably drier quality to the sound, the performances have retained a remarkable freshness of resonance. The dramatic intensity of the E major work, for example, is heightened by Richter's tendency to controversial extremes of tempo in both directions. Specifically, Richter rejects the *Allegretto* marking for the second movement in favour of a speed that is closer to *Adagio* to which the finale provides a scintillating conclusion. His wide dynamic and expressive range in both of these sonatas creates effects that are quite simply miraculous. The versions of the Sonatas, Op. 26 and Op. 90 are digital recordings, but there are no signs that Richter has lost any of his interpretative power or originality. His command of broad structural relationships is as assured as ever, as is his scrupulous attention to the music's harmonic and motivic detail. His comprehensive exploitation of the music's intrinsic possibilities generates great energy and pace as a means of intensifying its natural warmth and expressiveness. The set concludes with a startling performance of Weber's Third Piano Sonata. The first movement, marked *Allegro feroce*, contrasts a powerfully driven opening with music of simple melodic charm which, after a richly diverse variation slow movement, culminates in a bravura finale of breathtaking virtuosity. As is so often the case with Richter's performances, then, these are landmarks in piano playing which no lover of piano music should be without.

Additional recommendations ...

...No. 9. **Liszt** Hungarian Rhapsody in C sharp minor, S244 No. 12. **Brahms** Piano Concerto No. 2 in B flat major, Op. 83[a]. Variations on a Theme by Paganini, Op. 35 – Book 2. **Gina Bachauer** (pf); [a]**London Symphony Orchestra / Stanislaw Skrowaczewski.** Mercury Living Presence Ⓜ 434 340-2MM (77 minutes: ADD: 9/95).

...Nos. 27, 28 and 32. **Stephen Kovacevich** (pf). EMI Ⓕ CDC7 54599-2 (60 minutes: DDD: 10/92).

Beethoven Piano Sonatas. **Artur Schnabel** (pf). Pearl mono Ⓜ GEMMCDS9123* (two discs: 141 minutes: AAD: 11/94). Recorded 1932-8.
No. 14 in C sharp minor, Op. 27 No. 2, "Moonlight" (from HMV DB2089/90. Recorded 1933); No. 15 in D major, Op. 28, "Pastoral" (DB1953/5, 8/33); No. 16 in G major, Op. 31 No. 1 (DB3154/7, 9/37); No. 17 in D minor, Op. 31 No. 2, "Tempest" (DB2649/51, 4/36); No. 18 in E flat major, Op. 31 No. 3 (DB2358/60. 1932). Variations on an Original Theme in F major, Op. 34 (DB3623/4, 2/39). Seven Bagatelles, Op. 33 (DB3783/6, 8/39).   ⒼⒼⒼ

Heavy background hiss is a small price to pay for a greater sense of Schnabel's immediacy and quality, and both of these discs, the original material transferred with a courageous candour and honesty, do much to reconvince one that Beethoven and Schnabel are, indeed, synonymous. How characteristic is that gruff but musicianly refusal in Op. 27 No. 2 of all undue solemnity, all notion of romantic, moonlit effusion. Such robust eloquence will hardly appeal to those who long for a prolonged gaze into the infinite (the first movement is over almost before you realize it), but the balance of sense and sensibility provides a superbly authoritative alternative. Of course, there are moments when Schnabel's impetuosity can cause momentary confusion: in the whirling finale of Op. 31 No. 3 altogether too many corners are taken on two wheels. Yet the odd snatched phrase or telescoped rhythm pales into oblivion when you consider Schnabel's overall achievement, his salty brio and the profound eloquence of his slow movements. Time and again he wears his immense learning lightly and in, say, the dazzling wit and repartee of Op. 31 No. 1 the dust of ages seems to fall away before one's very eyes and ears. The Op. 33 *Bagatelles* – diamond-chippings from the master's workshop – also prove that Schnabel was as much at home in concentrated aphorism as in lengthy working-out.

New review

Beethoven Piano Sonatas – No. 16 in G major, Op. 31 No. 1; No. 17 in D minor, Op. 31 No. 2, "Tempest"; No. 18 in E flat major, Op. 31 No. 3. **Stephen Kovacevich** (pf). EMI Ⓕ CDC5 55226-2 (64 minutes: DDD: 11/95). Recorded 1994. *Gramophone Editor's choice.* ⓖⓖ

The Op. 31 Sonatas offer a wonderful way into the Beethoven sonatas, not least because they have done unusually well on record. And what to buy? Well, this offering from Stephen Kovacevich from his emergent Beethoven sonata cycle is very brilliant, an exceptional record in every way. There is stiff competition from Brendel and Richard Goode, to name just two. With Goode, the D minor Sonata, the *Tempest*, is wonderfully well done, finely painted on the keyboard. There is much in the festive E flat Sonata that is gloriously right – the *Scherzo* is played to perfection – but after that *tour de force* Goode gives an inexplicably laboured account of the *Menuetto*. Brendel is measured here, too. Kovacevich finds a middle way in this *Menuetto* that seems effortlessly right. His tempo is more or less exactly what one imagines a *moderato e grazioso* should be, and it serves Minuet and Trio equally well. The preceding *Scherzo* is a touch fiercer than Goode's or Brendel's, the finale a show-stopping *Presto, con fuoco* which Goode attempts and which Brendel rather capriciously avoids. Brendel's performances of the G major and E flat Sonatas offer a fine mixture of caprice and intellectual rigour. There are more fluctuations of pulse than with Kovacevich and a much greater use of diversionary tactics. There are more zig-zags of emotion, too, in the *Tempest*, which Brendel plays in a fit of high passion that borders on outright anger. Kovacevich's playing can be just as angry but it is always terrifically focused. EMI have been obliged to take on board some pretty ferocious playing. The recording occasionally threatens to fray at the edges but never quite does. War-weary and battle-hardened it bears these marvellous performances triumphantly home.

Additional recommendations ...

...Nos. 17, 18 and 26. **Murray Perahia** (pf). CBS Masterworks Ⓜ MK42319 (61 minutes: DDD: 2/88).

...Nos. 16-18. **Richard Goode** (pf). Elektra Nonesuch Ⓕ 7559-79212-2 (68 minutes: DDD: 9/90).

...Nos. 16-18. **Alfred Brendel** (pf). Philips Ⓕ 438 134-2PH (72 minutes: DDD: 7/93).

...Nos. 17, 25 and 28. **Bruno-Leonardo Gelber** (pf). Denon Ⓕ CO-75245 (54 minutes: DDD: 1/94).

Beethoven Piano Sonatas – No. 16 in G major, Op. 31 No. 1; No. 32 in C minor, Op. 111. Six Bagatelles, Op. 126. **Mia Chung** (pf). Channel Classics Ⓕ CCS7195 (72 minutes: DDD: 6/95). Recorded 1994.

For Mia Chung, Beethoven's music offers special challenges that compel her to explore her own expressive potential to its limits. Indeed, Chung's carefully observed, exquisitely crafted playing in the *Six Bagatelles* reveals a wealth of detail, but some may find her playing too civilized. Try the Fourth or Sixth *Bagatelle*, for example, where Stephen Kovacevich gives a more potently effective version of the music's dramatic contrasts. However, there are no such quibbles with the G major Sonata. Here, Chung's fluent response to gesture comprehensively captures Beethoven's vivacity and wit in the first movement. The second movement's overtly theatrical character inspires John Lill to take a challengingly slow tempo: presumably to discharge his powerful aggression in the opening *Allegro*. By contrast, Chung unfolds the music's operatic lyricism with balletic grace to create a deliciously ornate centre-piece to the sonata; while sparkling, transparent textures and lithe phrasing winningly convey the finale's charming simplicity. Jenő Jandó's clear formal grasp of the C minor Sonata (listed above) is very impressive, but Chung's performance is inspired. She compellingly portrays the work's opposition of earthly and heavenly elements identified in the insert-notes. Subtly controlled dynamics and beguiling spontaneity give the first movement startling freshness and originality and, by playing the *Arietta* slower than Jandó, Chung creates the opportunity for some surprising detail. Sensitive characterization of the variations which reaches a striking, jazz-like climax in the third, and Chung's ethereal tone in the final pages, make this outstanding performance a totally absorbing musical experience.

Beethoven Piano Sonatas – No. 19 in G minor, Op. 49 No. 1; No. 20 in G major, Op. 49 No. 2; No. 22 in F major, Op. 54; No. 23 in F minor, Op. 57, "Appassionata"; No. 30 in E major,

Op. 109; No. 31 in A flat major, Op. 110; No. 32 in C minor, Op. 111. **Sviatoslav Richter** (pf).
Philips Ⓕ 438 486-2PH2 (two discs: 122 minutes: DDD: 8/94). Recorded 1992.   Ⓖ
Beethoven Piano Sonatas – No. 18 in E flat major, Op. 31 No. 3; No. 28 in A major, Op. 101. Two
Rondos, Op. 51. Piano Trio in B flat major, Op. 97, "Archduke"[a]. Quintet for Piano and Wind in
E flat major, Op. 16[b]. **Sviatoslav Richter** (pf); [a]members of the **Borodin Quartet**; [b]members of the
Moraguès Quintet. Philips Ⓕ 438 624-2PH2 (two discs: 131 minutes: DDD: 8/94). Recorded
1986-92.   Ⓖ

There are times in a reviewer's working life when he or she folds away the notebook, discards the score,
and just listens – the performance demands it. This was one such event. Those whose chief pleasure
as critics is to pounce on minute blemishes (preferably blemishes no one else has noticed) would no
doubt have a joyous time here – Richter is no chromium-plated perfectionist. But to go glitch-hunting
in the face of playing of this quality would surely require a heroic degree of insensitivity. Granted,
Richter would hardly be Richter if there wasn't something bizarre to pick out, and there is one detail
that does call for comment. In the Quintet for piano and wind, Op. 16, Richter and the four members
of the Moraguès Quintet repeat not only the first movement exposition, but the exposition plus the
slow introduction. For those who listen for structural signposts it is disorientating; and yet it is all so
wonderfully played – the colour, the vitality, the sense of creative give-and-take between the players
are all you could wish for in this sunny, in every sense young piece. Throughout these two sets the
sheer aliveness of the playing can be breathtaking – no exaggeration. It doesn't matter whether the
territory is the most searching late Beethoven or an early, 'easy' sonata (Beethoven's own description)
such as the G minor, Op. 49 No. 1. One could make endless lists of favourite details – little touches
that show how thorough Richter's understanding is, but what finally distinguishes Richter's
Beethoven is a quality ... the word is 'improvisatory': it is as though you were hearing the music not
merely played, but composed. This is what holds the attention even when Richter's conscious
decisions go against what you expect of the music – the slow tempos in the scherzo and fugue of Op.
110, for instance. These four discs form another valuable counterweight to the modern nostalgists'
claim that great playing – and especially great Beethoven playing – is a thing of the remote past. The
transfers serve Richter excellently: intrusive audience noise is minimal, in fact in Op. 111 you might
only realize that there is an audience at all when the clapping and cheering thunders in at the end. The
engineering is good.

Beethoven Piano Sonatas – No. 21 in C major, Op. 53, "Waldstein"; No. 24 in F sharp major,
Op. 78; No. 31 in A flat major, Op. 110. **Stephen Kovacevich** (pf). EMI Ⓕ CDC7 54896-2
(53 minutes: DDD: 2/94). Recorded 1992.   Ⓖ
Few pianists today – not Brendel, not Ashkenazy, not Serkin – can free themselves of self-awareness
enough to find the tender simplicity of the opening *Moderato cantabile* of Beethoven's Op. 110.
Kovacevich can, and he goes on to fill each moment of figuration and trilling with light. His finale
has a mesmeric inwardness generated by the seemingly infinite nuances he can find in a single repeated
note. A steadiness of purpose in the *Arioso* leads naturally into the quiet self-assurance of the
effortless building of the Fuga. The coupling – with the little Op. 78 and the *Waldstein* – makes for a
sensitively built recital in its own right. Again, Kovacevich's skill at drawing the listener in marks the
Op. 78 Sonata, with its effervescent figurework and spontaneous major-minor changes. The same
nimble fingerwork, over a thrumming bass, makes the *Waldstein* positively tingle with life:
Kovacevich's joy in the physical excitement and momentum of the writing is equalled by his strength
in delineating the song at its heart.
Additional recommendation ...
...Nos. 21, 23 and 26. **Melvyn Tan** (fp). Virgin Classics Ⓜ VER5 61160-2 (63 minutes: DDD:
5/88). ✒

New review
Beethoven Piano Sonatas – No. 27 in E minor, Op. 90[a]; No. 28 in A major, Op. 101[b]; No. 29 in
B flat major, Op. 106, "Hammerklavier"[c]. **Sviatoslav Richter** (pf). Praga Ⓑ CMX354003
(75 minutes: ADD: 6/96). Item marked [a] recorded 1965, [b]1986, [c]1975.
These entirely unedited performances feel not only live but somehow extraordinarily real. Not that
Richter ever gives the impression of playing for the microphone, and his vision of musical structures
remains constant whether he is in the studio or the concert-hall. Nevertheless the atmosphere within
which that vision is realized differs from venue to venue, and in Prague it seems to have been
extraordinarily conducive. This is outstanding Beethoven playing, though frustratingly the 1965
Hammerklavier has a little memory black-out at 8'20" in the first movement, without which it might
have grown into something even more extraordinary.

Beethoven Piano Sonata No. 29 in B flat major, Op. 106, "Hammerklavier". **Emil Gilels** (pf). DG
Ⓕ 410 527-2GH (49 minutes: DDD: 2/84). From 410 527-1GH (12/83). *Gramophone Award
Winner 1984.*   ⒼⒼ
The great Soviet pianist Emil Gilels died in 1986, not many months before his seventieth birthday, and
left behind him a major legacy of recorded performances. This account of the *Hammerklavier* is a fine
memorial. The work is very long and exceedingly taxing technically and the pianist must plumb its
often turbulent emotional depth, not least in the enormous 20-minute slow movement which requires

deep concentration from player and listener alike. After the recording was made in 1983, the pianist told his producer: "I feel that the weight has been lifted, but I feel very empty". Gilels manages to give it more tonal beauty and warmth than most pianists, without any loss of strength or momentum. His is measured and beautiful playing, and finely recorded too.

Additional recommendations ...
...Nos. 27-29. **John O'Conor** (pf). Telarc Ⓕ CD80335 (73 minutes: DDD: 8/93).
...Nos. 28 and 29. **Vladimir Ashkenazy** (pf). Decca Ⓕ 436 735-2DH (66 minutes: DDD: 4/94).

Beethoven Piano Sonatas. **Maurizio Pollini** (pf). DG Ⓜ 429 569/70-2GH (two discs, oas: 63 and 62 minutes: AAD: 7/90). From 419 199-2GH2 (12/86). Recorded 1975-77.
  429 569-2GH – No. 28 in A major, Op. 101; No. 29 in B flat major, Op. 106, "Hammerklavier".
  429 570-2GH – No. 30 in E major, Op. 109; No. 31 in A flat major, Op. 110; No. 32 in C minor,
  Op. 111.   ⒼⒼ
If Beethoven's 32 piano sonatas may be likened to a range of foothills and mountains, then these five sonatas are the last lofty pinnacles, difficult of access but offering great rewards to both pianist and listener. No library is complete without them. Pollini's playing must be praised for its interpretative mastery as well as its exemplary keyboard skill. These are prizewinning issues which have been widely admired, not least for the magnificent last sonata, Op. 111, and the recordings hardly show their age.

Additional recommendations ...
...Nos. 30-32. **John O'Conor** (pf). Telarc Ⓕ CD80261 (65 minutes: DDD: 11/92).
...Nos. 27-32. **Solomon** (pf). EMI Références mono/stereo Ⓜ CHS7 64708-2* (two discs:
  141 minutes: ADD: 7/93). *Gramophone classical 100. Gramophone Editor's choice.*   ⒼⒼⒼ
...Nos. 27-32. **Alfred Brendel** (pf). Philips Duo Ⓜ 438 374-2PM2 (two discs: 148 minutes: ADD:
  8/93).
...Nos. 27-32. **Charles Rosen** (pf). Sony Classical Essential Classics Ⓑ SB2K53531 (two discs:
  150 minutes: ADD: 11/94).
...Nos. 30-32. **Inger Södergren** (pf). Calliope Approche Ⓑ CAL6648 (68 minutes: ADD: 11/95).

New review
Beethoven Songs from the British Isles. **Elaine Woods** (sop); **Carolyn Watkinson** (contr); **Josef Protschka** (ten); **Richard Salter** (bar); **Christian Altenburger** (vn); **Julius Berger** (vc); **Helmut Deutsch** (pf). Sony Classical Ⓕ SK64301 (70 minutes: DDD: 12/95). Texts included. Recorded 1987.
  Scottish Songs, Op. 108   No. 1, Music, Love and Wine; No. 2, Sunset; No. 3, Oh! sweet were the hours; No. 5, The sweetest lad was Jamie; No. 7, Bonnie laddie, highland laddie; No. 9, Behold my love how green the groves; No. 13, Come fill, fill, my good fellow; No. 18, Enchantress, farewell; No. 19, O swiftly glides the bonny boat; No. 20, Faithfu' Johnie; No. 25, Sally in our Alley. Scottish Songs, WoO156 – No. 2, Duncan Gray; No. 5, Cease your funning. Irish Songs, WoO152 – No. 7, His boat comes on the sunny tide; No. 8, Come draw we round a cheerful ring; No. 20, Farewell bliss and farewell Nancy. Irish Songs, WoO153 – No. 6, Sad and luckless was the season; No. 12, I'll praise the Saints; No. 13, 'Tis sunshine at last. Irish Songs, WoO154 – No. 4, The pulse of an Irishman; No. 8, Save me from the grave and wise; No. 12, He promised me at parting. Welsh Songs, WoO155 – No. 2, The Monks of Bangor's March; No. 4, Love without Hope; No. 8, Farewell, thou noisy town; No. 9, To the Aeolian Harp; No. 20, To the Blackbird. Songs of various nationality, WoO157 – No. 3, O Charlie is my darling; No. 7, Robin Adair, "Since all thy vows false maid".
One does not usually fancy that it would be seemly or even thinkable to nod to Beethoven in the street, supposing that time and place permitted. But hearing these arrangements is like looking over his shoulder as he works. At his least forbidding here, he smiles, sings to himself and from time to time gets up to dance. The work is incidental, its scope, aspirations and rewards all strictly limited. It comes mostly from Scotland, from Herr Thomson, who tends to ask for a song without words: that is, he sends the tune he wants arranged for voice (or voices) and piano trio but regrets that the lyrics are not yet available. A pity, but the melodies are such charmers, have such unassuming strength and grace, that their arrival is like that of good company: wholesome stimulants of a composer's wit and skill, his heart too. Beethoven wrote 140 such arrangements, and here are 29 of them, each one a delight. The absence of words (if indeed George Thomson did fail to provide them on these occasions as on others) seems not to have constituted much of a drawback: sometimes the accompaniment takes an odd form, as with the clip-clop of *Sally in our Alley* or the rollicking energy of *Enchantress, farewell*, but there are happy chances too, such as the sympathetically sighing phrases of the instruments in *I'll praise the Saints* which, though nominally a song of rejoicing, tells also of anxious prayers. Usually it is some rhythmic figure in the melody that gets him going (*O Charlie is my darling* for instance) and then he adds syncopations of his own and alternating *piano* and *forte* figures till his studio is peopled with dancers and drinkers, "light in the eye and a song in the air". The performances are excellent: good singing and playing by all concerned, and though we may not have expected to find Josef MacProtschka among them he is welcome none the less. Texts are provided, and German translations to which ("er schiesst sich tot" being easier than "lowpin o'er a lim") one sometimes turns for enlightenment. The record is the most genial of musical companions, and none but the grumpy heart will want to miss it.

Beethoven An die ferne Geliebte. Op 98ª. Adelaide, Op. 46ª. Zärtliche Liebe, WoO123ª. L'amante
impaziente, Op. 82 Nos. 3 and 4ª. In questa tomba oscura, WoO133ª. Maigesang, Op. 52 No. 4ª.
Es war einmal ein König, Op. 75 No. 3ª.
Brahms Vier ernste Gesänge, Op. 121ᵇ. O wüsst' ich doch den Weg zurück, Op. 63 No. 8ᶜ. Auf
dem Kirchhofe, Op. 105 No. 4ᶜ. Alte Liebe, Op. 72 No. 1ᶜ. Verzagen, Op. 72 No. 4ᶜ. Nachklang,
Op. 59 No. 4ᶜ. Feldeinsamkeit, Op. 86 No. 2ᶜ **Dietrich Fischer-Dieskau** (bar); **Jörg Demus** (pf).
DG Ⓔ 415 189-2GH* (71 minutes: ADD: 9/85). Text and translations included. Items marked ª
from SLPM139216/18 (2/67), ᵇSLPM138644 (10/61), ᶜSLPM138011 (5/59).   ⒼⒼⒼ
Beethoven's small oeuvre of songs is rich and varied. The six songs of *An die ferne Geliebte* follow the
unrequited lover's reflections on his beloved, with the piano weaving its way between the individual
songs setting the mood and gently assisting the narrative; indeed, it even has the last word. Fischer-
Dieskau's intelligent and intense delivery are assisted by his warm tone and easy legato. He adds
Beethoven's great song *Adelaide* and, among others, three Italian settings, lightening the tone and
raising the spirits for the second half of the programme. Brahms's *Vier ernste Gesänge*, drawn from
the image-laden texts of the Old Testament, reflect on man's fate in the great order of life and more
particularly on death. The songs have a solemn character and settle in the lower register of the
baritone's vocal range, a range that finds a particularly appropriate tone-colour in Fischer-Dieskau's
expressive voice. The remainder of the recital draws on similarly severe songs, making for a well-
devised programme with a consistent theme. Jörg Demus accompanies sensitively and the elderly
recordings sound well.

Additional recommendations ...
...Lieder, Op. 52 – Das Liedchen von der Ruhe; Maigesang (Mailied); Die Liebe; Marmotte. Lieder,
Op. 75 – Neue Liebe, neues Leben; Aus Goethes Faust; Der Zufriedene. Drei Lieder, Op. 83.
Sechs Lieder, Op. 48. Adelaide, Op. 46. Andenken, WoO136. Lied aus der Ferne, WoO137.
Sehnsucht, WoO146. Der Wachtelschlag, WoO129. An die Hoffnung, Op. 94. Der Kuss, Op. 128.
Abendlied unterm gestirnten Himmel, WoO150. Resignation, WoO149. Zärtliche Liebe (Ich liebe
dich), WoO123. In questa tomba oscura, WoO133. **Dietrich Fischer-Dieskau** (bar); **Hertha Klust**
(pf). Testament mono Ⓔ SBT1057* (77 minutes: ADD: 10/95).
...Lieder, Op. 75 – No. 2, Neue Liebe, neues Leben; No. 3, Es war einmal ein König. Mailied,
Op. 52 No. 4. *Coupled with works by* **Amalia, Reichardt, Zelter, Schumann, Schubert,
Brahms, R. Strauss, Schoeck, Reger, Busoni** and **Wolf. Dietrich Fischer-Dieskau** (bar);
Karl Engel (pf). Orfeo D'Or mono Ⓔ C389951B* (72 minutes: ADD: 2/96).

New review
Beethoven Cantata on the death of the Emperor Joseph II, WoO87. Cantata on the accession of
the Emperor Leopold II, WoO88. **Bodil Arnesen** (sop); **Markus Schäfer** (ten); **Alan Titus** (bass);
Berlin Radio Symphony Chorus and Orchestra / Karl Anton Rickenbacher. Koch Schwann
Ⓕ 314352 (67 minutes: DDD: 10/95). Texts and translations included. Recorded 1993.
Beethoven's twin cantatas on the death of Joseph II and the accession of Leopold II (the Emperor is
dead; long live the Emperor) are never going to be repertory pieces, nor even get more than very
occasional concert outings; but they certainly earn a hearing, and Rickenbacher has a strong feeling
for music that fascinatingly adumbrates much that lay ahead. Beethoven was only 20 when he wrote
them, to a commission to mark the events in Bonn, and it was partly the demands posed by the music
that prevented their performance. Probably still more responsible was a text that celebrated Joseph's
liberal policies by attacking, in true Enlightenment vein, his defeat of "a monster named Fanaticism".
This was a scarcely veiled dig at clerical excesses, and needless to say the Church took affront. But the
appeal to the young Beethoven's humanist idealism drew from him music in a vein that he was to mine
deeper when he came to write *Fidelio* not many years later, and even the Ninth Symphony near the
end of his life. The darkness of the opening chorus on Joseph's death and the exaltation of the finale
to the Leopold cantata, both finely sung and played here, take us straight to the Dungeon Scene
and to the embrace of the world's millions at the end of Ninth. Not all the music is of this
quality, and, like so many young composers, Beethoven had not yet learnt the virtues of economy. The
two long arias, "Hier schlummert" and "Fliesse, Wonnezähre" are somewhat out of proportion, and
make heavy demands upon the soprano: Bodil Arnesen sounds in rather insecure command of them,
and has a little trouble at the top of the range, as does Alan Titus at the bottom of the range in his
bass contributions. But for anyone thinking about a Beethoven 'What next?', here is an interesting
answer.

Beethoven Mass in D major, Op. 123, "Missa solemnis". **Charlotte Margiono** (sop); **Catherine
Robbin** (mez); **William Kendall** (ten); **Alastair Miles** (bass); **Monteverdi Choir; English Baroque
Soloists / John Eliot Gardiner.** Archiv Produktion Ⓕ 429 779-2AH (72 minutes: DDD: 3/91). 🎵
Text and translation included. Recorded 1989. *Gramophone Award Winner 1991.*   ⒼⒼ
Beethoven Mass in D major, Op. 123, "Missa solemnis". **Cheryl Studer, Jessye Norman** (sops);
Plácido Domingo (ten) **Kurt Moll** (bass); **Leipzig Radio Chorus; Swedish Radio Chorus; Eric
Ericson Chamber Choir; Vienna Philharmonic Orchestra / James Levine.** DG Ⓕ 435 770-2GH2
(two discs: 83 minutes: DDD: 11/92). Text and translation included. Recorded 1991. *Selected by
Sounds in Retrospect.*   Ⓖ

Beethoven Mass in D major, Op. 123, "Missa solemnis". **Julia Varady** (sop); **Iris Vermillion** (mez); **Vinson Cole** (ten); **René Pape** (bass); **Berlin Radio Chorus; Berlin Philharmonic Orchestra / Sir Georg Solti.** Decca Ⓕ 444 337-2DH (77 minutes: DDD: 6/95). Text and translation included. Recorded live in 1994. Ⓖ

New review

Beethoven Mass in D major, Op. 123, "Missa solemnis". **Rosa Mannion** (sop); **Birgit Remmert** (contr); **James Taylor** (ten); ᵇ**Cornelius Hauptmann** (bass); **Chapelle Royale Chorus; Collegium Vocale; Orchestra of the Champs-Elysées Théâtre, Paris / Philippe Herreweghe.** Harmonia Mundi Ⓕ HMC90 1557 (77 minutes: DDD: 12/95). 🗫 Text and translation included. Recorded live in 1995. Ⓖ

The *Missa solemnis* is generally agreed to be one of the supreme masterpieces of the nineteenth century, but attempts to record a genuinely great performance have over many years run into difficulties. Usually the greatness itself is flawed, perhaps in the quality of the solo singers or in some particular passages where the conductor's approach is too idiosyncratic or momentarily not up to the challenge of Beethoven's inspiration (an example is Klemperer's heavy-handedness in the fugues). The strain upon the choir, especially its sopranos, is notorious; similarly the technical problems of balance by producer and engineers. In the last several years many recordings have appeared, all of which rank with the best as performances. The version under John Eliot Gardiner remains a very probable first choice. It combines discipline and spontaneous creativity, the rhythms are magically alive and the intricate texture of sound is made wonderfully clear. The great fugues of the *Gloria* and *Credo* achieve at the right points their proper Dionysiac sense of exalted liberation.

These are qualities which the Levine recording shares, but the means are sharply contrasted. Gardiner uses a choir of 36 and an orchestra of 60 playing on period instruments, aiming at a "leaner and fitter" sound. Levine has the traditional large forces of singers and players. Gardiner's soloists are admirable but they are not major stars, whereas Levine has a quartet that constitutes what the record's promoters claimed as "the most luxurious of our time". That may create more suspicion than confidence, for singers who are at home in *Aida* do not necessarily fit the bill in the *Missa solemnis*. These four, however, sing magnificently and their opulence of tone proves a genuine enrichment. In some respects, Harnoncourt's performance is finer still. Though he, like Levine, is working in the Grosses Festspielhaus at Salzburg and is recorded live, his performance has the greater clarity, partly because of the forces used: his period timpani, for instance, do not boom like Levine's later ones. Then, in comparison with Gardiner, Harnoncourt's way sometimes has more humanity about it: the march of his *Credo*, for instance, is less military than Gardiner's.

In 1977 Solti recorded a taut, well-braced performance in Chicago; here, by just a half-turn of the screw, nothing excessive, he intensifies the concentration of spirit. In doing so he takes a calculated risk, for there are perilous moments in the *Missa solemnis*, yet the control is absolute and the gain in excitement palpable. With this go an additional clarity of recorded sound, so that the separate strands are more readily followed, and a better balance is obtained. With Gardiner, the exceptional clarity of his smaller body of singers and players, their meticulous responsiveness to direction and concentrated attention to detail is as impressive as ever; yet one is very aware of it *as* a performance. Sometimes, as in the first sounding of drums and trumpets signifying war, Gardiner's extra intensity brings a real gain, but often Solti produces the effect without so insistently making the point. Of both of these, one wonders, do they, with all their energy, answer Beethoven's request: *Bitte um innern und äussern Frieden* ("Please, with inward and outward peace")? Harnoncourt, with his slower speeds and weightier style, achieves that more successfully (as Klemperer did). Excellent playing and choral work distinguish Solti's performance. The soloists are good individually and (more remarkably) give evidence of listening to one another and recognizing the growths and diminutions of their own importance in the general weave. An essay by H. Robbins Landon enriches the booklet, and the record has an advantage over most of its rivals (though not Gardiner or Herreweghe) in its confinement to a single disc.

Herreweghe's live recording of the *Missa solemnis* vies with Gardiner's studio performance, also with period forces. Herreweghe's speeds in the *Kyrie* and *Agnus Dei* are closer to latter-day convention, and more than Harnoncourt he conveys the work's deeply spiritual intensity: here one registers a great sense of live, tense communication. From the start there is no mistaking the inner quality conveyed, the *Innigkeit*, the sense of embarking on a visionary journey. Only in those outer movements, the *Kyrie* and *Agnus Dei*, is there a substantial difference between Herreweghe and Gardiner over speeds, so that Harmonia Mundi have been able to fit the whole work on to a single CD – as indicated above – a substantial advantage. The four young soloists for Herreweghe make an excellent team, most satisfyingly topped by the sweet, firm tone of the Canadian soprano, Rosa Mannion. The American tenor, James Taylor, clear and fresh, makes his mark strongly too as another relative newcomer to disc, incisive rather than weighty in the great statement of "Et homo factus est". Curiously it is the most experienced of the four as a recording artist, the bass Cornelius Hauptmann, who slightly disappoints in his rough tone in the key solo which opens the *Agnus*. After that Herreweghe finds a spring-like release in the compound time of the *Dona nobis pacem*, even if the military interruptions are not quite as dramatic as one wants. In sum, a good alternative to the Gardiner for a period-instrument performance.

Additional recommendations ...

...Missa solemnis. **Mozart** Mass in C minor, K427/K417*a*. **Soloists; Atlanta Symphony Chorus and Orchestra / Robert Shaw.** Telarc Ⓕ CD80150 (two discs: 139 minutes: DDD: 11/88).

...Missa solemnis[a]. Choral Fantasia in C minor, Op. 80[b]. **Soloists; [a]New Philharmonia Chorus; [b]John Alldis Choir; New Philharmonia Orchestra / Otto Klemperer.** EMI Ⓜ CMS7 69538-2 (two discs: 100 minutes: ADD: 12/88). ⒼⒼ

...Missa solemnis. **Soloists; Arnold Schöenberg Choir; Chamber Orchestra of Europe / Nikolaus Harnoncourt.** Teldec Ⓕ 9031-74884-2 (two discs: 81 minutes: DDD: 4/93). 🎖 ⒼⒼ

...Missa solemnis. Mass in C major, Op. 86. **Soloists; London Symphony Chorus and Orchestra / Sir Colin Davis.** Philips Duo Ⓜ 438 362-2PM2 (two discs: 136 minutes: ADD: 8/93).

...Missa solemnis. **Soloists; Chicago Symphony Chorus and Orchestra / Daniel Barenboim.** Erato Ⓜ 4509-91731-2 (two discs: 84 minutes: DDD: 6/94).

Beethoven Fidelio. **Christa Ludwig** (mez) Leonore; **Jon Vickers** (ten) Florestan; **Walter Berry** (bass) Don Pizarro; **Gottlob Frick** (bass) Rocco; **Ingeborg Hallstein** (sop) Marzelline; **Gerhard Unger** (ten) Jacquino; **Franz Crass** (bass) Don Fernando; **Kurt Wehofschitz** (ten) First Prisoner; **Raymond Wolansky** (bar) Second Prisoner; **Philharmonia Chorus and Orchestra / Otto Klemperer.** EMI Ⓕ CDS5 55170-2 (two discs: 128 minutes: ADD: 1/90). Notes, text and translation included. From Columbia SAX2451/3 (6/62). Recorded 1962. *Gramophone* classical 100. ⒼⒼⒼ

Fidelio teems with emotional overtones and from the arresting nature of the Overture, through the eloquence of the quartet, through the mounting tension of the prison scene to the moment of release when the wrongly imprisoned Florestan is freed, Beethoven unerringly finds the right music for his subject. Klemperer's set has been a classic since it first appeared way back in 1962. The performance draws its strength from his conducting: he shapes the whole work with a granite-like strength and a sense of forward movement that is unerring, while paying very deliberate attention to instrumental detail, particularly as regards the contribution of the woodwind. With the authoritative help of producer Walter Legge, the balance between voices and orchestra is faultlessly managed. The cumulative effect of the whole reading is something to wonder at and shows great dedication on all sides. Most remarkable among the singers is the humanity and intensity of Christa Ludwig's Leonore. In her dialogue as much as in her singing she conveys the single-minded conviction in her mission of rescuing her beleaguered and much-loved husband. Phrase after phrase is given a *frisson* that has the ring of truth about it. As her Florestan, Jon Vickers convincingly conveys the anguish of his predicament. One or two moments of exaggeration apart this is another memorable assumption. Walter Berry, as Pizarro, suggests a small man given too much power. Gottlob Frick is a warm, touching Rocco, Ingeborg Hallstein a fresh, eager Marzelline, Gerhard Unger a youthful Jacquino and Franz Crass a noble Don Fernando. This is a set that should be in any worthwhile opera collection. (Incidentally, this latest reissue has now inexplicably reverted from mid to full price.)

Additional recommendations ...

...Fidelio. **Soloists; Vienna State Opera Chorus; Vienna Philharmonic Orchestra / Leonard Bernstein.** DG Ⓕ 419 436-2GH2 (two discs: 135 minutes: ADD: 6/87).

...Fidelio. **Soloists; Chorus of the Deutsche Oper, Berlin; Berlin Philharmonic Orchestra / Herbert von Karajan.** EMI Ⓜ CMS7 69290-2 (two discs: 119 minutes: ADD: 4/88).

...Fidelio. **Soloists; Dresden State Opera Chorus; Dresden Staatskapelle / Bernard Haitink.** Philips Ⓕ 426 308-2PH2 (two discs: 133 minutes: DDD: 1/91). *Selected by Sounds in Retrospect.*

...Fidelio. **Soloists; Chorus; NBC Symphony Orchestra / Arturo Toscanini.** RCA Victor Gold Seal mono Ⓜ GD60273* (two discs: 112 minutes: ADD: 10/92).

...Fidelio. Leonore Overture No. 3, Op. 72[a]. **Soloists; Bavarian State Opera Chorus; Bavarian State Orchestra; [a]Berlin Philharmonic Orchestra / Ferenc Fricsay.** DG Dokumente Ⓜ 437 345-2GDO2* (two discs: 128 minutes: ADD: 5/93).

...Fidelio. **Soloists; Vienna State Opera Chorus; Vienna Philharmonic Orchestra / Wilhelm Furtwängler.** EMI Références mono Ⓜ CHS7 64496-2* (two discs: 133 minutes: ADD: 5/93).

...Fidelio[a]. **Weber** Oberon – Ozean du Ungheuer![b]. **Soloists; [b]Hilde Konetzni** (sop); [a]**Vienna State Opera Chorus and Orchestra / Karl Böhm;** [b]**Vienna Symphony Orchestra / Leopold Ludwig.** Preiser mono Ⓕ 90195* (two discs: 146 minutes: AAD: 8/94).

...Fidelio – Final Scene[a]. **Bartók** Concerto for Orchestra, Sz116. **Rossini** Guillaume Tell – Overture. [a]**Soloists; [a]London Voices; World Orchestra for Peace / Sir Georg Solti.** Decca Ⓕ 448 901-2DH (62 minutes: DDD: 3/96). *See review in the Collections section; refer to the Index to Reviews.*

New review

Beethoven Fidelio. **Charlotte Margiono** (sop) Leonore; **Peter Seiffert** (ten) Florestan; **Sergei Leiferkus** (bar) Pizarro; **László Polgár** (bass) Rocco; **Barbara Bonney** (sop) Marzelline; **Deon van der Walt** (ten) Jacquino; **Boje Skovhus** (bar) Don Fernando; **Reinaldo Macias** (ten) First Prisoner; **Robert Florianschütz** (bass) Second Prisoner; **Arnold Schoenberg Choir; Chamber Orchestra of Europe / Nikolaus Harnoncourt.** Teldec Ⓕ 4509-94560-2 (two discs: 119 minutes: DDD: 10/95). Notes, text and translation included. Recorded 1994. ⒼⒼ

The fact has to be faced that *Fidelio* hasn't received a really satisfying recording for at least 20 or so years and the old favourites are beginning to show their age. Next to this superb Teldec recording, even Klemperer sounds less than immediate and occasionally a shade heavy-handed; however, as suggested above, his reading still presents an alternative, grander, more romantic view of the work than this new set, although it in turn yields in theatrical excitement to the Furtwängler and Böhm historic versions. That said, one also has to say that everything that Harnoncourt touches leaves one with a sense of a country rediscovered: we listen to the piece in hand with new ears. So it is again here. With one exception, Beethoven's sole but intractable opera has seldom emerged from the recording studio, or indeed the theatre, with such clarity of texture, such promptness of rhythm, such unity of purpose on all sides. Even more than with Klemperer, this is a reading that gives full play to winds and horns, making one aware, whether it's in the Overture, Pizarro's aria, Leonore's big scena or the Prelude to Act 2, just how important they are both to the structure and character of each movement. Accents, as ever with this conductor, tend to be strong, as for instance the very pronounced marking of the rhythm in the 6/8 section in Rocco's aria (giving it a rustic feeling) or the *sforzandos* in "Ha, welch ein Augenblick".

Where tempos are concerned, Harnoncourt is almost bound to be controversial somewhere. If many speeds are to the work's advantage just on the measured side of the customary, as in the Dungeon quartet, allowing us for once to hear every strand of the argument, that for "O namenlose Freude" is uncommonly moderate: if it isn't twice as slow as that chosen by such an experienced Beethovenian as Böhm, it feels as though it is. At this pace, Leonore and Florestan seem to be conducting a gentle exchange of deeply felt emotions on an interior level rather than allowing their pent-up emotions to burst forth in an explosion of joy, as is more usual. This may have something to do with Harnoncourt's view of the piece as a personal rather than a universal drama. Two vocal interpretations stand out for excellent singing and pungent characterization. Once Leiferkus's Pizarro takes centre-stage the action lifts on to a new, more tense plane. This vicious, little dictator with his incisive diction, spoken and sung, and his biting, vital voice is a commanding presence. But Evil is up against an equally arresting advocate of Good in Margiono's gloriously sung and read Leonore. Everything she does, that dialogue apart, bespeaks at once Leonore's desperation and determination. Everything is there in her diction and in her warm, appealing tone. Hers isn't the quasi-dramatic soprano usually associated with the part, but she never sounds either strained or overparted in the context of a more lyrical, smaller-scale performance.

Seiffert has reached Florestan at a critical point in his career as he moves towards heroic roles. He fills it with more refulgent tone than any other tenor on recent recordings – the high tessitura of his aria's close causes him no distress at all – but one has to admit that there is little of the *Schmerz* in the tone found, quite differently, in the recordings of Vickers (Klemperer) or Patzak (Furtwängler). In that sense, though, he fits into Harnoncourt's well-ordered scheme of things. Polgár turns in a well-rounded but not very individual Rocco. Bonney is her customary stylish self as Marzelline but a trifle cool in expression. Van der Walt is a more than adequate Jaquino. There has, however, been a major piece of miscasting where Don Fernando is concerned. A role that needs a solid bass with strong low notes has been cast with a high baritone who sounds anything but authoritative. Harnoncourt has opted for a professional chamber choir to second the superb Chamber Orchestra of Europe. Its members certainly give us the most well-groomed, securely sung Prisoners' Chorus and finale on any version. But by the same token they don't quite sound the note of anguish in the former which those schooled in theatre performances of the piece can achieve. By far the nearest in concept to Harnoncourt is Fricsay, the exception referred to earlier, in terms of size and character of performance and indeed of casting. If you listen to the Act 1 trio in both versions side by side, and to the following March, the similarities are plain to hear, with Fricsay just having the edge in terms of a more characterful Marzelline in Seefried and Rocco in Frick. Pacing, care for orchestral balance and a fresh look at the score as a whole were also Fricsay's attributes. And, wonder of wonders, the 1957 DG recording yields very little in presence to the new one. So this mid-price set, so recently refurbished, is a strong rival to the new one.

Further listening ...

...Der Geschöpfe des Prometheus. **Scottish Chamber Orchestra / Sir Charles Mackerras.** Hyperion CDA66748 (11/94). 🄖

...Egmont – incidental music, Op. 84. Symphony No. 5 in C minor, Op. 67. **Sylvia McNair** (sop); **Will Quadflieg** (narr); **New York Philharmonic Orchestra / Kurt Masur.** Teldec 9031-77313-2 (1/94). 🄔

...Grosse Fuge in B flat major, Op. 133. *Coupled with* **Schubert** String Quintet in C major, D956[a]. **Hagen Quartet;** [a]**Heinrich Schiff** (vc). DG 439 774-2GH (11/94). *Gramophone Editor's choice.*

...Duets, WoO27 – No. 1 in C major[a]. Trio in G major, WoO37[b]. Serenade in D major, Op. 25[c]. **Susan Milan** (fl); [ab]**Sergio Azzolini** (bn); [c]**Levon Chilingirian** (vn); [c]**Louise Williams** (va); [b]**Ian Brown** (pf). Chandos CHAN9108 (4/93).

...Seven Bagatelles, Op. 33. 11 Bagatelles, Op. 119. Fantasia in G minor, Op. 77. Seven Variations in C major on "God save the King", WoO78. Five Variations in D major on "Rule Britannia", WoO79. **Melvyn Tan** (fp). EMI Ⓟ CDC7 54526-2 (71 minutes: DDD: 12/92). 🖉 🄖

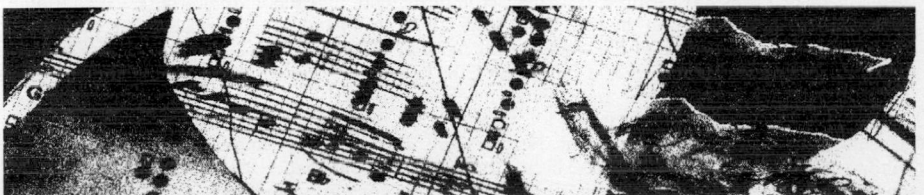

Vincenzo Bellini

Bellini I Capuleti ed i Montecchi. **Edita Gruberová** (sop) Giulietta; **Agnes Baltsa** (mez) Romeo;
Dano Raffanti (ten) Tebaldo; **Gwynne Howell** (bass) Capellio; **John Tomlinson** (bass) Lorenzo;
Royal Opera House Chorus and Orchestra, Covent Garden / Riccardo Muti. EMI Ⓜ CMS7 64846-
2 (two discs: 130 minutes: DDD: 2/95). Text and translation included. Recorded live in 1984.
From EX270192-3 (12/85).

When Covent Garden revived this work in April 1984, for the first time since 1848, praise for the
opera, Muti's conducting and the singing was almost universal. That same enthusiasm can now be
extended to this reissue. Muti and his two principals, caught at white heat on the stage of Covent
Garden, offer a rendition of Bellini's supple, eloquent score that gave the work a new definition and
standing in the Bellini canon. Away from the limbo of studio recording, the music lives at a
heightened level of emotion and the sound reflects a true opera-house balance. Muti persuades his
singers and the Royal Opera House players to noble utterance. Baltsa's Romeo has a Callas-like
conviction of phrase and diction: here is a Romeo who will go to his death for the love of his Juliet.
Who wouldn't do that when that role is sung so delicately and affectingly as by Gruberová, then at
the absolute height of her powers, as indeed was Baltsa? Raffanti's open-throated Italian tenor is just
right for Tebaldo's bold incursions. Gwynne Howell and John Tomlinson both contribute effectively
to what is a wholly engrossing performance.

Additional recommendations ...

...I Capuleti ed I Montecchi – Eccomi in lieta vesta ... Oh! quante volte. La sonnambula[a] – Oh! se
una volta sola ... Ah! non credea mirarti ... Ah! non giunge. **Donizetti** Don Pasquale – Quel
guardo il cavaliere ... So anch'io la virtu magica. Linda di Chamounix – Ah! tardai troppo ... o
luce di quest' anima. **Rossini** Tancredi[b] – Gran Dio! Deh! tu proteggi ... Giusto Dio. Il viaggio a
Reims[b] – Partir, oh ciel! desio. **Kathleen Battle** (sop); [a]**Randi Stene** (contr); [a]**Richard Croft** (ten);
[a]**Mark S. Doss** (bass); [b]**Ambrosian Opera Chorus; London Philharmonic Orchestra / Bruno
Campanella.** DG Ⓕ 435 866-2GH (56 minutes: DDD: 12/93).

Bellini Norma. **Maria Callas** (sop) Norma; **Ebe Stignani** (mez) Adalgisa; **Mario Filippeschi** (ten)
Pollione; **Nicola Rossi-Lemeni** (bass) Orovesco; **Paolo Caroli** (ten) Flavio; **Rina Cavallari** (sop)
Clotilde; **Chorus and Orchestra of La Scala, Milan / Tullio Serafin.** EMI mono Ⓕ CDS7 47304-8*
(three discs: 160 minutes: ADD: 3/86). Notes, text and translation included. From Columbia
mono 33CX1179/80 (11/54). Recorded 1954.

Norma may be considered the most potent of Bellini's operas, both in terms of its subject – the secret
love of a Druid priestess for a Roman general – and its musical content. It has some of the most
eloquent music ever written for the soprano voice and two duets that show Bellini's gift for liquid
melody. The title-role has always been coveted by dramatic sopranos, but there have been few in the
history of the opera who have completely fulfilled its considerable vocal and histrionic demands: in
recent times the leading exponent has been Maria Callas. The mono recording comes up sounding
remarkably forward and immediate on CD, and it captures Callas's commanding and moving
assumption of the title part, the vocal line etched with deep feeling, the treatment of the recitative
enlivening the text. Stignani is a worthy partner whilst Filippeschi is rough but quite effective. Serafin
knew better than anyone since how to mould a Bellinian line to best effect.

Additional recommendations ...

...**Soloists; London Symphony Chorus and Orchestra / Richard Bonynge.** Decca Ⓜ 425 488-2DM3
(three discs: 171 minutes: ADD).

...**Soloists; Chorus and Orchestra of La Scala, Milan / Tullio Serafin.** EMI Ⓜ CMS7 63000-2*
(three discs: 161 minutes: ADD: 7/89). Highlights from the above recording are also available
separately. Details are as follows: Casta diva; Va, crudele; O rimembranza; O non tremare;
Introduction, Act 2; Mira, o Norma; Guerra, guerra; In mia man' alfin tu sei; Taci, ne ascolta
appena. EMI Ⓜ CDM7 63091-2* (64 minutes: ADD: 7/89).

Bellini La sonnambula. **Maria Callas** (sop) Amina; **Nicola Monti** (ten) Elvino; **Nicola Zaccaria**
(bass) Count Rodolfo; **Fiorenza Cossotto** (Mez) Teresa; **Eugenia Ratti** (sop) Lisa; **Giuseppe
Morresi** (bass) Alessio; **Franco Ricciardi** (ten) Notary. **Chorus and Orchestra of La Scala, Milan /
Antonino Votto.** EMI mono Ⓕ CDS7 47378-8* (two discs: 121 minutes: ADD: 9/86). Notes text
and translation included. From Columbia 33CX51469, 33CX1470/1 (10/57). Recorded 1957.

Dramatically this opera is a tepid little mix which might be subtitled *The mistakes of a night* if that
did not suggest something more amusing than what actually takes place. Musically, the promise of a
brilliant finale keeps most people in their seats until the end, and there are half-a-dozen charming,
sometimes exquisite items on the way. But it is all a little insubstantial, and much depends upon the
performance, especially that of the soprano. The name of Maria Callas is sufficient to guarantee that
there will be a particular interest in the work of the heroine. As usual, her individuality is apparent
from the moment of her arrival. Immediately a character is established, not an insipid little miss but
a woman in whom lurks a potential for tragedy. This is the pattern throughout and much has
exceptional beauty of voice and spirit. Nicola Monti has all the sweetness of the traditional lyric
tenor; the pity is that what might have been a most elegant performance is marred by the intrusion of
unwanted aspirates. Nicola Zaccaria sings the bass aria gracefully, and carrying off her small role

with distinction is Fiorenza Cossotto, at the start of her career. The orchestral playing is neat, the conducting sensible and the recording clear.

Additional recommendation ...

...Soloists; London Opera Chorus; National Philharmonic Orchestra / Richard Bonynge. Decca
Ⓟ 417 424-2DH2 (two discs: 141 minutes: DDD: 4/87).

Further listening ...

...Oboe Concerto in E flat major. *Coupled with works by* **Rossini, Cherubini** and **Donizetti**
Roger Lord (ob); Academy of St Martin in the Fields / Sir Neville Marriner. Double Decca 443
838-2DF2 (7/95). *See review under Rossini; refer to the Index to Reviews.*

...I Puritani. Soloists; Chorus and Orchestra of La Scala, Milan / Tullio Serafin. EMI mono CDS7
47308-8* (4/89).

...I Puritani. Soloists; Chorus of the Royal Opera House, Covent Garden; London Symphony
Orchestra / Richard Bonynge. Decca 417 588-2DH3 (4/95).

...I Puritani. Soloists; Chorus and Orchestra of the Teatro Massimo, Catania / Richard Bonynge.
Nuova Era 6842/44 (10/91).

Benatz de Ventadorn   French ?c1130/40-c1190/1200

Suggested listening ...

...Le Fou sur le Pont. Troubadour Songs: Can vei le lauzta mover; Non es meravilla s'eu chan; Pos
me pregatz seignor; Tant ai mo cor ple de joya; Lanquan vei la foilla; Bel m'es can eu vei la
brolha; En Cossirer et en esmai; Era'm cosselhatz, senhor; Amics Benatz de Ventadorn; Per
melhs cobrir lo mal pes; Can l'erba fresch'el folha par; Lo gens temps de pascor; Cantarai
d'aqueszt trobadors. **Camerata Mediterranea / Joel Cohen.** Erato 4509-94825-2 (11/94).
Gramophone Editor's choice.   Ⓖ

Georg Benda   Bohemian 1722-1795

Suggested listening...

...Flute Concerto in E minor. *Coupled with works by* **C.P.E. Bach, Frederick the Great** and
Quantz Patrick Gallois (fl); CPE Bach Chamber Orchestra / Peter Schreier. DG 439 895-2GH
(2/95). *See review in the Collections section; refer to the Index to Reviews.*

...Keyboard Sonatinas[a] – Rondeau; Allegro; Allegretto; Allegretto; Allegretto moderato. *Coupled*
with **Graun** Keyboard Sonata in D minor[a]. **Hasse** Keyboard Sonata in E flat major[a]. **Fasch**
Andantino con Variazioni[a]. **Schulz** Diverses pièces, Op. 1[b] – No. 5, Allegretto; No. 6, Larghetto
con Variazioni. **C.P.E. Bach** Pièces Caractéristiques[b] – La Borchward, H79; La Pott, H80; La
Gleim, H89; La Bergius, H90; La Stahl, H94; La Boehmer, H81; La Louise, H114. **Christine**
Schornsheim ([a]hpd/[b]fp). Capriccio 10 424 (4/95). ✐

...Du, kleine Blondine, bezauberst ja schon![b]. Du fehlest mir[a]. Venus, wenn du willst mich rühren[a].
Cephalus und Aurore[a]. Philint ist still, und flieht die Schönen[b]. Philint stand jüngst vor Babets
Thur[b]. Ich liebte nur Ismenen[b]. Mein Thyrsis! dürft ich dir doch sagen[a]. Belise starb, und sprach
im Scheiden[a]. Lieber Amor, leihe mir[b]. Mein Geliebter hat versprochen[a]. Faulheit, itze will ich
dir[b]. Ein trunkner Dichter leerte[b]. Mir Armen, den des Fiebers Kraft[b]. Von nun an, O Liebe,
verlass' ich dein Reich[b]. Das Andenken[a]. Piano Sonatinas – No. 3 in A minor; No. 9 in
A minor; No. 16 in G minor; No. 21 in F major; No. 29 in E flat major; No. 32 in A major.
[a]**Emma Kirkby** (sop); [b]**Rufus Müller** (ten); **Timothy Roberts** (fp). Hyperion CDA66649 (1/94). ✐

Cesare Bendinelli   Italian c1686-1757

Suggested listening ...

...Sonata CCC-XXXIII. Sarasinetta. *Coupled with works by* **G. Gabrieli, A. Gabrieli** and
M. Thomsen Gabrieli Players / Paul McCreesh. Virgin Classics Veritas VC7 59006-2 (5/90). ✐
Gramophone Award Winner 1990. See review in the Collections section; refer to the Index to
Reviews.   Ⓖ Ⓖ

Xavuer Benguerel   Spanish 1931-

Suggested listening ...

...Tempo. *Coupled with* **Cruz de Castro** Guitar Concerto. **Marco** Concierto Guadiana. **Wolfgang**
Weigel (gtr); European Masters Orchestra / Peter Schmelzer. Koch Schwann 312362 (5/95).

Paul Ben-Haim

Suggested listening ...
...Violin Concerto. *Coupled with* **Castelnuovo-Tedesco** Violin Concerto No. 2, Op. 66,
   "I profeti". **Itzhak Perlman** (vn); **Israel Philharmonic Orchestra / Zubin Mehta.** EMI CDC7
   54296-2 (5/93).
...The Sweet Psalmist of Israel[b] *Coupled with* **Bloch** Sacred Service[a]. **Foss** Song of Songs[c].
   [a]**Robert Merrill** (bar); [b]**Sylvia Marlowe** (hpd); [c]**Jennie Tourel** (mez); **New York Metropolitan
   Synagogue Choir;** [a]**New York Philharmonic Orchestra / Leonard Bernstein.** Sony Classical
   Bernstein Royal Edition SM2K47533 (11/92).

George Benjamin

G. Benjamin Sudden Time. **London Philharmonic Orchestra / George Benjamin.** Nimbus (special
   price) NI1432 (16 minutes: DDD: 11/94). Recorded 1994. *Gramophone Editor's choice.*   Ⓖ
Sudden Time is a subtle, refined piece, as one would expect from the composer of *At First Light* and
Antara. It is also much more than a highly-polished miniature; yet no one should find its imaginative,
constantly shifting textures in the least forbidding. The earlier stages may promise rather more in the way
of boldly dramatic characterization than the piece as a whole actually delivers – the opening has a hushed
sense of ominous anticipation reminiscent of Schoenberg's *Five Orchestral Pieces* and also his
Accompaniment to a Film Scene. Yet the more aggressive moments of *Sudden Time* achieve their
particular impact through being reined in rather than allowed to run riot, and to this extent the
composition keeps its distance from simple reflections of any *Martial Cadenza,* the title of the Wallace
Stevens poem in which the phrase "sudden time" is to be found. Performance and recording are excellent.
Further listening ...
...At first light[a]. Ringed by the flat horizon[b]. A Mind of Winter[c]. [c]**Penelope Walmsley-Clark** (sop);
   [a]**Gareth Hulse** (ob); [b]**Ross Pople** (vc); [c]**P. Archibald** (cl); [ac]**London Sinfonietta / George Benjamin;**
   [b]**BBC Symphony Orchestra / Mark Elder.** Nimbus NI5075.
...Antara. *Coupled with* **Boulez** Dérive. Memoriale[a]. **J. Harvey** Song Offerings[b]. [b]**Penelope
   Walmsley-Clark** (sop); [a]**Sebastian Bell** (fl); **London Sinfonietta / George Benjamin.** Nimbus
   NI5167 (10/89). *Gramophone Award Winner 1990.*   Ⓖ
...Piano Sonata. **George Benjamin** (pf). Nimbus NI1415 (CD single).

Richard Rodney Bennett

Bennett Guitar Concerto[a].
Arnold Guitar Concerto, Op. 67[b].
Rodrigo Concierto de Aranjuez[c]. **Julian Bream** (gtr); **Melos Ensemble /** [c]**Sir Colin Davis.**
   RCA Julian Bream Edition Ⓕ 09026 61598-2 (62 minutes: ADD: 6/94). Item marked [a] recorded
   in 1972, [b]1959, [c]1963.
Sir Malcolm Arnold's Concerto was written for Julian Bream in 1957. Bream made his record in
partnership with the composer – directing the Melos Ensemble – two years later and the results are in
every way definitive. The recording was made for RCA by Decca engineers and is beautifully balanced
and strikingly warm and atmospheric. The couplings include Bream's first stereo recording of the
Rodrigo *Concierto de Aranjuez* with Sir Colin Davis in charge of the accompaniment and Richard
Rodney Bennett's Guitar Concerto, written in 1970 and also dedicated to Bream. Its imaginative
variety of texture, lustrous and transparent, consistently titillates the ear. The performance, like that
of the Arnold, is definitive and the 1972 recording is excellent. Bream has since recorded both the
Arnold and the Rodrigo for EMI with Simon Rattle (CDC7 54661-2, 7./93), although the earlier disc
is by no means superseded.
Further listening ...
...Concerto for Stan Getz[b]. *Coupled with* **Myers** Concerto for Soprano Saxophone and Orchestra[a].
   Torke Concerto for Soprano Saxophone and Orchestra[c]. **John Harle** (sax); [a]**Argo Symphony
   Orchestra / James Judd;** [b]**BBC Concert Orchestra / Barry Wordsworth;** [c]**Albany Symphony
   Orchestra / David Alan Miller.** Argo 443 529-2ZH (7/95).
...Saxophone Concerto. *Coupled with works by* **Debussy, Glazunov, Heath, Ibert** and **Villa-
   Lobos** John Harle (sax); **Academy of St Martin in the Fields / Sir Neville Marriner.** EMI CDC7
   54301-2 (1/92). *See review in the Collections section; refer to the Index to Reviews.*

Alban Berg

Berg Violin Concerto.
Rihm Gesungene Zeit. **Anne-Sophie Mutter** (vn); **Chicago Symphony Orchestra / James Levine.**
   DG Ⓕ 437 093-2GH (52 minutes: DDD: 1/93). Recorded 1992. *Selected by Sounds in
   Retrospect.*   ⒼⒼ

Berg Violin Concerto[a].
Janáček Violin Concerto, "Pilgrimage of the soul"[a].
Hartmann Concerto funebre[b]. **Thomas Zehetmair** (vn/[b]dir); [a]**Philharmonia Orchestra / Heinz Holliger;** [b]**Deutsche Kammerphilharmonie.** Teldec Ⓜ 4509-97449-2 (60 minutes: DDD: 6/95). Recorded 1990-91.

New review
Berg Violin Concerto[a].
Ravel Tzigane[b].
Stravinsky Violin Concerto in D major[a]. **Itzhak Perlman** (vn); [a]**Boston Symphony Orchestra / Seiji Ozawa;** [b]**New York Philharmonic Orchestra / Zubin Mehta.** DG The Originals Ⓜ 447 445-2GOR (57 minutes: [a]ADD/[b]DDD: 7/96). Items marked [a] from 2531 110 (3/80), [b]423 063-2GH (12/87).   ⊕⊕

One of the very few 12-note pieces to have retained a place in the repertory, Berg's Violin Concerto is in fact a work on many levels. Behind the complex intellectual facade of the construction is a poignant sense of loss, ostensibly for Alma Mahler's daughter, Manon Gropius, but also for Berg's own youth; and behind that is a thoroughly disconcerting mixture of styles which resists interpretation as straightforward Romantic consolation. Not that performers need to go out of their way to project these layers; given a soloist as comprehensively equipped as Anne-Sophie Mutter and orchestral support as vivid as the Chicago Symphony's they simply cannot fail to register. Their recording, then, makes a fine demonstration-quality recording alternative to the even more idiomatically insightful historic version of Krasner and Webern.

In their less flamboyant but equally persuasive way, Zehetmair and Holliger are very much in the same class; the Teldec recording is not quite so brightly lit as DG's, but if anything it is more realistically balanced. In other words, choice can safely be left to the couplings; in which respect honours are again fairly even. In recent years Mutter has made a point of seeking out effective new *concertante* pieces as couplings to established repertoire concertos. The latest of these, by the 40-year-old German composer Wolfgang Rihm, is more or less in a historical line from Berg and his fellow-expressionists. *Gesungene Zeit* means "Time Chanted", and the music reflects the mystical implications of the title. It steers clear of the extremes of avant-garde hermeticism and post-modernist opportunism and should prove rewarding to anyone who can take Berg in their stride and is curious to discover what lies beyond. Zehetmair's choice is adventurous in a different way. Janáček's 12-minute Concerto, recently reconstructed from the fragmentary state in which he abandoned it in 1926, is related to his opera *From the House of the Dead*. Not a major addition to the repertory, it nevertheless has enough authentic late-Janáčekian passion to merit occasional performances. No less worthy of preservation is the 1959 Concerto by the Webern-pupil Karl Amadeus Hartmann. This is an energetic and assertive work, rather like radically intellectualized Prokofiev; performances and recording are again fine.

Perlman's account of the Berg Violin Concerto with the Boston orchestra under Ozawa has long occupied a respected place in the catalogue. The original reviewer in *Gramophone* in March 1980 was completely convinced by Perlman's "commanding purposefulness". As to the recording, he wrote that "though Perlman's violin – beautifully caught – is closer than some will like, there is no question of crude spotlighting". Sixteen years later on and in a different competitive climate, his verdict ("These are both performances to put with the very finest") still holds good. Perlman is also a little too close in the *Tzigane*, the recording of which sets him very firmly front-stage again. All the same, this is playing of stature and still among the best available versions. There are, however, probably more desirable recordings now available of the Stravinsky Concerto.

Additional recommendation ...
...Violin Concerto[a]. Lyric Suite[b]. [a]**Louis Krasner** (vn); [b]**Galimir Quartet;** [a]**BBC Symphony Orchestra / Anton Webern.** Testament Ⓔ SBT1004* (57 minutes: ADD: 6/91). *Gramophone Award Winner 1991.*   ⊕⊕

Berg String Quartet, Op. 3. Lyric Suite. **Alban Berg Quartet** (Günther Pichler, Gerhard Schulz, vns; Thomas Kakuska, va; Valentin Erben, vc). EMI Ⓔ CDC5 55190-2 (46 minutes: DDD: 11/94). Recorded 1991-2.

The appearance of this disc brings into focus the interpretative rivalry of the Alban Berg and Schönberg Quartets in Berg's two masterpieces for the medium. There's an obvious difference in sound quality. The Koch Schwann performances (listed below), recorded in 1985, are warm yet intimate, the ensemble homogenous to a fault: so well-blended, in fact, that clarity of detail occasionally suffers in the interests of a well-rounded whole. By comparison EMI offer a much broader perspective, the four players more forward and more distinct. Here details may at times seem too intrusive for the good of an integrated interpretation, and the concern to make every emotional nuance tell risks spilling the music over into melodrama. In general the Berg Quartet probe the extremes of the music more determinedly, and their unfailingly bright sound can seem larger than life when set against the Schoenberg's relative reticence. There's no doubting the emotional power of this

EMI recording. Only if you feel it goes over the top are you likely to have an outright preference for the Schönberg's less forceful brand of musical poetry.

Additional recommendations ...

...String Quartet. Lyric Suite. **Schönberg Quartet.** Koch Schwann 310005 (47 minutes: DDD: 12/89).

...String Quartet. **Liszt** Am Grabe Richard Wagners, S135[a]. **Webern** Five Movements, Op. 5. **Kronos Quartet;** [a]**Marcella deCray** (hp); [a]**Aki Takahashi** (pf). Elektra Nonesuch (special price) 7559-79318-2 (33 minutes: DDD: 1/94).

...String Quartet. **Schoenberg** String Quartet No. 2 in F sharp minor, Op. 10[a]. **Webern** Five Movements, Op. 5. Langsamer Satz. [a]**Christiane Oelze** (sop); **Brindisi Quartet.** Metronome Ⓕ METCD1007 (70 minutes: DDD: 6/95).

Berg Piano Sonata, Op. 1.
Liszt Piano Sonata in B minor, S178. Nuages gris, S199. R.W. – Venezia, S201. Schlaflos, Frage und Antwort, S203. Elegie No. 2, S197.
Webern Variations, Op. 27. **Barry Douglas** (pf). RCA Victor Red Seal Ⓕ 09026 61221-2 (61 minutes: DDD: 12/92). Recorded 1991.

Liszt's Piano Sonata leads something of a double life in the musical world. First of all it is a calling card for virtually every young virtuoso seeking to make a big impression; secondly it is recognized as one of the great path-breaking achievements in terms of compositional innovation, since its four-movements-in-one structure is a source of inspiration for the early works of Schoenberg. Even more strikingly, the near-atonal intensity of the late piano works prepares for the harmonic explorations of Schoenberg, Berg and Webern. So Barry Douglas has been extremely astute in planning this recital. Berg's single-movement Sonata shares its home tonality with the Liszt Sonata and its main motif with that of *Nuages gris*, while the Webern *Variations* show the distant consequences of essentially the same line of thought. The outstanding performance is of the Berg, where Douglas is more responsive to the expressive ebb and flow than any current rival. His Liszt Sonata does not approach the heights of a Zimerman or a Brendel, but it is still an impressive achievement and the other works give much satisfaction too. The warm acoustic of Watford Town Hall lends a welcome glow to the recorded sound.

Additional recommendations ...

...Piano Sonata. *Coupled with works by* **Krenek** and **Webern** Marcelo Bratke (pf). Olympia Ⓕ OCD431 (57 minutes: DDD: 4/94).

...Piano Sonata. **Schoenberg** Piano Concerto, Op. 42[a]. Drei Klavierstücke, Op. 11. Suite, Op. 25. **Webern** Piano Variations, Op. 27. **Glenn Gould** (pf). [a]**CBC Symphony Orchestra / Jean-Marie Beaudet.** CBC Records Perspective Series mono Ⓕ PSCD2008* (65 minutes: ADD: 1/96).

...Piano Sonata. *Coupled with works by* **Ravel, Stravinsky, Scriabin, Messiaen, Britten** and **Copland** Shura Cherkassky (pf). Decca Ⓕ 433 657-2DH (79 minutes: ADD: 2/96). *See review in the Collections section; refer to the Index to Reviews.*   Ⓖ

New review

Berg Seven Early Songs[a]. Der Wein[a]. Three Orchestral Pieces, Op. 6. [a]**Anne Sofie von Otter** (mez); **Vienna Philharmonic Orchestra / Claudio Abbado.** DG Ⓕ 445 846-2GH (49 minutes: DDD: 7/96). Texts and translations included.   ⒼⒼ

It is only two years since Anne Sofie von Otter included the *Seven Early Songs* on a recital disc (reviewed below), a programme glowing in the sunset of German romanticism. Making comparisons between that and this new recording of the orchestral version has been a test of self-discipline. There is so much to delight in the earlier performance that it is difficult to tear oneself away, whatever the different pleasures to be encountered here. Singing with orchestra, von Otter naturally works on a larger scale. The words are more firmly bound into the vocal line; there is not the detailed give-and-take that was possible with a pianist. But the outline of her interpretation remains that of a true Lieder singer, always lighting upon unexpected subtleties of colour and emphasis to inflect the poetry. In all this Abbado is an equal partner. Von Otter needs careful accompaniment in the concert-hall if she is to dominate an orchestra and Abbado, in co-operation with DG's technical team, has produced a balance that never drowns her, but still sounds fairly natural. The other leading collaboration on record is Pierre Boulez and Jessye Norman. In *Der Wein*, Berg's late concert aria, von Otter and Abbado catch the lilt of the jazz rhythms. In the *Seven Early Songs* are von Otter and Abbado a touch too cool? Perhaps, but in the final song, "Sommertage", they throw caution to the winds and end the cycle on a passionate high. Abbado has recorded the *Three Orchestral Pieces* before and his main rival is his younger self. His 1970s recording has long been one of the standard versions of this work and the opportunity to see how his thoughts have developed since then brings more surprises than one might have expected. In short, his outlook is progressing from the Italianate to the Germanic. No doubt the influence of the Vienna Philharmonic Orchestra has much to do with that and their marvellously eloquent playing is one of the prime attractions of the disc. In their company Abbado finds more depth and complexity in the music than before, although that does mean that the March loses the Bartókian attack and driving rhythms that made his first version so exciting. The earlier performance, now available at mid-price, is coupled with Margaret Price in ravishing readings of the *Altenberg Lieder* and *Lulu* Suite. On this disc von Otter makes an equally enticing vocal attraction, though prospective purchasers should note that the playing time is under 50 minutes.

Additional recommendations ...

...Three Orchestral Pieces. Lulu Suite[a]. Altenberg Lieder, Op. 4[a]. [a]**Dame Margaret Price** (sop);
London Symphony Orchestra / Claudio Abbado. DG 20th Century Classics Ⓜ 423 238-2GC
(67 minutes: ADD: 8/88). Ⓖ

...Seven Early Songs[a]. Funf Orchesterlieder nach Ansichtkartentexten von Peter Altenberg,
Op. 4[a]. Wo der Goldregen steht[b]. Lied des Schiffermädels[b]. Sehnsucht II[b]. Geliebte Schöne[b].
Vielgeliebte, schöne Frau[b]. Ferne Lieder[b]. Schattenleben[b]. Vorüber![b]. Liebe[b]. Mignon[b].
Grabschrift[b]. Schliesse mir die augen beide Nos. 1 and 2[b]. Er klagt, dass der Frühling so kortz
blüht[b]. **Jessye Norman** (sop); [b]**Ann Schein** (pf); [a]**London Symphony Orchestra / Pierre Boulez.**
Sony Classical Ⓕ SK66826 (48 minutes: DDD: 3/95).

Berg Seven Early Songs.
Korngold Liebesbriefchen, Op. 9 No. 4; Sterbelied, Op. 14 No. 1; Gefasster Abschied, Op. 14
No. 4; Drei Lieder, Op. 18; Glückwunsch, Op. 38 No. 1; Alt-spanisch, Op. 38 No. 3; Sonett für
Wien, Op. 41.
R. Strauss Wie sollten wir geheim sie halten, Op. 19 No. 4; Ich trage meine Minne, Op. 32 No. 1;
Der Rosenband, Op. 36 No. 1; Hat gesagt – bleibt's nicht dabei, Op. 36 No. 3; Meinem Kinde,
Op. 37 No. 3; Befreit, Op. 39 No. 4; Die sieben Siegel, Op. 46 No. 3. **Anne Sofie von Otter** (mez);
Bengt Forsberg (pf). DG Ⓕ 437 515-2GH (64 minutes: DDD: 6/94). Texts and translations
included. Recorded 1991-3. *Gramophone Editor's choice.*
The chosen Strauss songs here are characteristically gentle and affectionate, a mood in which von
Otter is often at her best. Not that, having captured a mood, she is content to let it lie dully over as
much as a verse or a line. In *Der Rosenband* she is always sensitive to the modulations; in *Ich trage
meine Minne* the voice darkens with the change of tonality in verse two; in *Wie sollten wir geheim sie
halten* she captures the subdued excitement of the opening as she does the frank exultation of the
close. For lightness of touch, the Op. 38 songs endear themselves among the Korngold group:
Glückwunsch has an unaffected, comfortable way with it (a little adaptation could turn it neatly into
Roger Quilter or even Jerome Kern), and *Alt-spanisch* (with its reminiscence of "On yonder hill there
stands a maiden") is a charmer. At the centre of the recital are the *Seven Early Songs* of Alban Berg.
The first, "Nacht", which is also the longest and most readily memorable, is taken rather more slowly
than usual, but gaining in its subtler evocations of the mists and then the silvered mountain paths.
Von Otter's draining the voice of all vibrato also helps create the sense of watchful stillness, just as in
the sixth song, "Liebesode", it makes for an almost other-worldly dreaminess, deepening to a full-
bodied passion as the rose scent is borne to the love-bed. Always the mezzo-soprano voice is
resourcefully used, able to colour deeply at such points, to float a pure head-tone in "Traumgekrönt"
or launch a radiant high A in "Die Nachtigall".

Berg Wozzeck. **Franz Grundheber** (bar) Wozzeck; **Hildegard Behrens** (sop) Marie; **Heinz Zednik**
(ten) Captain; **Aage Haugland** (bass) Doctor; **Philip Langridge** (ten) Andres; **Walter Raffeiner**
(ten) Drum-Major; **Anna Gonda** (mez) Margret; **Alfred Sramek** (bass) First Apprentice;
Alexander Maly (bar) Second Apprentice; **Peter Jelosits** (ten) Idiot; **Vienna Boys' Choir; Vienna
State Opera Chorus; Vienna Philharmonic Orchestra / Claudio Abbado.** DG Ⓕ 423 587-2GH2
(two discs: 89 minutes: DDD: 2/89). Notes, text and translation included. Recorded live in 1987.
ⒼⒼⒼ
A live recording, in every sense of the word. The cast is uniformly excellent, with Grundheber, good
both at the wretched pathos of Wozzeck's predicament and his helpless bitterness, and Behrens as an
outstandingly intelligent and involving Marie, even the occasional touch of strain in her voice
heightening her characterization. The Vienna Philharmonic respond superbly to Abbado's ferociously
close-to-the-edge direction. It is a live recording with a bit of a difference, mark you: the perspectives
are those of a theatre, not a recording studio. The orchestra is laid out as it would be in an opera
house pit and the movement of singers on stage means that voices are occasionally overwhelmed. The
result is effective: the crowded inn-scenes, the arrival and departure of the military band, the sense of
characters actually reacting to each other, not to a microphone, makes for a grippingly theatrical
experience. Audiences no longer think of *Wozzeck* as a 'difficult' work, but recordings have sometimes
treated it as one, with a clinical precision either to the performance or the recorded perspective. This
version has a raw urgency, a sense of bitter protest and angry pity that are quite compelling and
uncomfortably eloquent.

Additional recommendations ...

...Wozzeck. Lulu (two-act version). **Soloists; Chorus and Orchestra of the Deutsche Oper, Berlin /
Karl Böhm.** DG Ⓜ 435 705-2GX3 (three discs: 217 minutes: ADD: 1/93). ⒼⒼ

...Wozzeck. **Soloists; Vienna State Opera Chorus. Schoenberg** Erwartung, Op. 17. **Anja Silja**
(sop); **Vienna Philharmonic Orchestra / Christoph von Dohnányi.** Decca Ⓕ 417 348-2DH2
(two discs: 123 minutes: DDD: 2/89). ⒼⒼⒼ

Berg Lulu (orchestration of Act 3 completed by Friedrich Cerha). **Teresa Stratas** (sop) Lulu; **Franz
Mazura** (bar) Dr Schön, Jack; **Kenneth Riegel** (ten) Alwa; **Yvonne Minton** (mez) Countess
Geschwitz; **Robert Tear** (ten) The Painter, A Negro; **Toni Blankenheim** (bar) Schigolch, Professor
of Medicine, The Police Officer; **Gerd Nienstedt** (bass) An Animal-tamer, Rodrigo; **Helmut**

Pampuch (ten) The Prince, The Manservant, The Marquis; **Jules Bastin** (bass) The Theatre Manager, The Banker; **Hanna Schwarz** (mez) A Dresser in the theatre, High School Boy, A Groom; **Jane Manning** (sop) A 15-year-old girl; **Ursula Boese** (mez) Her Mother; **Anna Ringart** (mez) A Lady Artist; **Claude Meloni** (bar) A Journalist; **Pierre-Yves Le Maigat** (bass) A Manservant; **Paris Opéra Orchestra / Pierre Boulez.** DG Ⓟ 415 489-2GH3 (three discs: 172 minutes: ADD: 11/86). Notes, text and translation included. From 2740 213 (10/79).
Gramophone Award Winner 1986. Recorded 1979. ⓠⓠ

Now here's a masterpiece that fulfils all the requirements needed for a commercial smash hit – it's sexy, violent, cunning, sophisticated, hopelessly complicated and leaves you emotionally drained. *Lulu* was Berg's second opera and easily matches his first – *Wozzeck* – for pathos and dramatic impact. The meaningful but gloriously over-the-top story-line, after two tragedies by Frank Wedekind, deserves acknowledgement. Lulu, mistress of Dr Schön, is married to a medical professor. An artist also has the hots for her, but just as his passion gets interestingly out of hand, her husband walks in, catches them approaching the act and dies of shock. She marries the artist, who learns about Dr Schön and kills himself; then she marries the jealous Dr Schön, and eventually kills *him*. Smuggled out of prison by an adoring lesbian, she sets up home in Paris with Schön's son, gets blackmailed and ends up in London as one of Jack the Ripper's victims! And that's not the half of it – but we'll spare you the rest. What matters is that Berg's music is magnificent, romantic enough to engage the passions of listeners normally repelled by 12-tone music, and cerebral enough to keep eggheads fully employed. It's opulent yet subtle (saxophone and piano lend the score a hint of jazz-tinted decadence), with countless telling thematic inter-relations and much vivid tonal character-painting. Berg left it incomplete (only 390 of the Third Act's 1,326 bars were orchestrated by him), but Friedrich Cerha's painstaking reconstruction is a major achievement, especially considering the complicated web of Berg's musical tapestry. This particular recording first opened our ears to the 'real' Lulu in 1979, and has transferred extremely well to CD. The booklet contains a superb essay by Boulez which in itself is enough to stimulate the interest of a potential listener. Performance-wise, it is highly distinguished. Teresa Stratas is an insinuating yet vulnerable Lulu, Yvonne Minton a sensuous Gräfin Geschwitz and Robert Tear an ardent artist. Dr Schön is tellingly portrayed by Franz Mazura (who also turns up as Jack the Ripper), Kenneth Riegel is highly creditable as Schön's son and that Boulez himself is both watchful of detail and responsive to the drama, hardly needs saying. It's not an easy listen, but it'll certainly keep you on your toes for a stimulating, even exasperating evening.

Further listening ...

...(trans. Schnittke) Four-part Canon. *Coupled with* **Schnittke** String Trio. Concerto for Three. Minuet. **Gidon Kremer** (vn); **Yuri Bashmet** (va); **Mstislav Rostropovich** (vc); **Moscow Soloists.** EMI CDC5 55627-2 (5/96). *See review under Schnittke; refer to the Index to Reviews.*

...Chamber Concerto for Piano, Violin and 13 Wind Instruments[a]. Four Pieces for Clarinet and Piano, Op. 5[b]. Piano Sonata, Op. 1. **Daniel Barenboim** (pf); [a]**Pinchas Zukerman** (vn); [b]**Anthony Pay** (cl); [a]**Ensemble InterContemporain / Pierre Boulez.** DG The Originals 447 405-2GOR (7/95).

...Lulu. **Soloists; French National Orchestra / Jeffrey Tate.** EMI Ⓟ CDS7 54622-2 (three discs: 172 minutes: DDD: 1/93).

...Lulu – Symphonie. *Coupled with* **Weill** Die sieben Todsünden[a]. **Angelina Réaux** (sop); [a]**Hudson Shad; New York Philharmonic Orchestra / Kurt Masur.** Teldec Ⓟ 4509-95029-2 (12/94). *See review under Weill; refer to the Index to Reviews.*

...Four Pieces, Op. 5[ae]. Chamber Concerto – Adagio (arr. cpsr)[abe]. *Coupled with* **Schoenberg** Piece in D minor[be]. String Trio, Op. 45[bcd]. Phantasy, Op. 47[be]. **Mahler** Quartet in A minor[bcde]. **Webern** Two Pieces for Cello and Piano[de]. Four Pieces, Op. 7[bc]. Three Little Pieces, Op. 11[de]. Cello Sonata[de]. [a]**Sabine Meyer** (cl); [b]**Gidon Kremer** (vn); [c]**Veronika Hagen** (va); [d]**Clemens Hagen** (vc); [e]**Oleg Maisenberg** (pf). DG 447 112-2GH (4/96). *See review in the Collections section; refer to the Index to Reviews.*

Erik Bergman

Finnish 1911-

Suggested listening ...

...The Singing Tree. **Soloists; Dominante Choir; Tapiola Chamber Choir; Finnish National Opera Orchestra / Ulf Söderblom.** Ondine ODE794-2D (5/93).

Luciano Berio

Italian 1925-

New review

Berio Continuo[b].
Carter Partita[a].
Takemitsu Visions[b]. **Chicago Symphony Orchestra / Daniel Barenboim.** Teldec Ⓟ 4509-99596-2 (52 minutes: DDD: 8/95). Recorded live in 1993-4.

This disc might create expectations of neo-baroque tendencies, in compositions entitled *Partita* and *Continuo*. On the contrary, however, these works demonstrate that what makes Berio and Carter such giants on the contemporary stage is their ability to compose coherently and attractively without creating echoes of the distant past (or even of the earlier twentieth century). The two works are well contrasted: *Continuo* an eloquent, searching slow movement, *Partita* bold, even balletic in its concentrated yet playful instrumental dialogues. Carter's note, whimsically contrasting the speed of present-day travel by air with the horses and marching armies of earlier times, nevertheless adds an 'old' dimension by quoting the seventeenth-century Richard Crashaw's poetic celebration of bubbles. Taking 'Partita' in the Italian sense of game or match, Carter's bubbling fantasy is the more powerful for projecting a flamboyant surface against a much darker background, and the main point of the piece could be the tension which results when playfulness knows itself to be under constant threat: every bubble is about to burst. Berio's work, though sounding quite different, is comparable in the sense that the sustained continuity which is its most immediately obvious feature exists to be challenged in confrontations whose varied densities ensure an intricate kaleidoscope of rich colours as the music steadily unfolds. Takemitsu's two-part *Visions* is not on the same level as *Partita* or *Continuo*. Here echoes and associations – expressionist, impressionist – are all too apparent, and the prevailing slowness seems self-indulgent when substance is relatively slight. The disc nevertheless makes a major contribution to the contemporary repertory on record, and is technically immaculate in every way.

New review

Berio Notturno[a].

Haydn String Quartets, Op. 77, "Lobkowitz" – No. 1 in G major; No. 2 in F major. **Alban Berg Quartet** (Günther Pichler, Gerhard Schulz, vns; Thomas Kakuska, va; Valentin Erben, vc). EMI Ⓟ CDC5 55191-2 (72 minutes: DDD: 10/95). Item marked [a] recorded live. Recorded 1993-4.

The subtle, civilized discourse of Haydn's last two complete quartets is here improbably juxtaposed with Luciano Berio's brooding, fragmentary third quartet, written in 1993 for the Alban Berg Quartet. *Notturno* seeks to defy notions of perceptible form: in complete antithesis to Haydn's methods, it meditates on the possibility of non-dialectic musical narrative. With its reluctance to resolve or to reach conclusions, there is a precarious, evanescent quality to this music; even its most violent, obsessive ideas tend to fade away with apparent inconsequentiality. At times we seem to hear a fragment of singable melody; but every aspiration to lyrical expansion is jeopardized by silence or by desultory activity, frantic, ominous or anguished. The Alban Berg give a stunning account of this enthralling, disquieting, enigmatic work. They rise to the challenge of Berio's daunting, ceaselessly inventive string writing with astonishing unanimity, sureness of intonation and command of a huge range of colours and dynamics. And they are acutely responsive to the mystery and desolation which lie at the heart of *Notturno*, taking their cue from the work's epigraph, a line from Paul Celan's *Argumentum e silencio* ("A Testimony from Silence") alluding obliquely to the victims of the Holocaust. Moving with a jolt to more familiar and reassuring territory, the Alban Berg's accounts of Haydn's Op. 77 Quartets are certainly impressive in their assurance, control and finish. Both *Scherzos* and finales are notably successful, rhythmically taut and alive, with a keen feeling for the element of Slavonic astringency and abandon. Both first movements are shaped with a strong sense of their architecture, though that of No. 1 can seem a shade relentless, short on wit and whimsy, while the opening *Allegro moderato* of No. 2 suffers from moments of impatience and over-forceful attack familiar in other Alban Berg performances of the classical repertoire. In the sublime slow movements the Alban Berg, for all their beauty of sonority, strike one as wanting in warmth and flexibility. The Mosaïques Quatuor, with their greater expressive variety and improvisatory freedom, draw you far more deeply into this music (see review under Haydn; refer to the Index to Reviews). The recording is pleasingly natural, though with a slight bias in favour of the first violin.

Berio Recital I for Cathy[a]. 11 Folk Songs[b].

Weill (arr. Berio. Sung in English) Der Dreigroschenoper – Ballade von der sexuellen Hörigkeit[c]. Marie Galante – Le grand Lustucru[c]. Happy End – Surabaya-Johnny[c]. **Cathy Berberian** (mez); [a]**London Sinfonietta**; [b]**Juilliard Ensemble / Luciano Berio**. RCA Victor Gold Seal Ⓜ 09026 62540-2 (65 minutes: ADD: 7/95). Texts included. Items marked [a] from SER5665 (4/73), [b]SB6850 (3/72), [c]new to UK. Recorded 1972. ⊕⊕

These are classic recordings that no contemporary music enthusiast or Berberian/Berio admirer will want to be without. This disc could be regarded as a fitting tribute to Cathy Berberian and her inimitable vocal genius. As an artist she was unique. As a champion of contemporary music (particularly music by her one-time husband Luciano Berio) she was second to none – not only for her interpretative prowess but also the inspirational quality of her highly individual style; many composers (including Stravinsky) wrote music specifically with her voice in mind. The recordings gathered together here were all composed, or arranged for her, by Luciano Berio. The two principal items are perhaps among the most famous of the Berberian/Berio collaborations. *Recital I for Cathy* makes use of Berberian's dramatic training in a composition (or decomposition?) in which the vocalist, frustrated by the non-appearance of her pianist, struggles through the programme whilst simultaneously sharing a Beckett-like stream-of-consciousness monologue with her audience. Berberian's performance here is a monumental *tour de force*. Another example of the extraordinary qualities of Berberian's voice can be found in the celebrated *Folk Songs* of 1964. The three songs by Kurt Weill reveal Berberian as a natural Weill interpreter (perhaps the best since Lotte Lenya). They are something of a find, this being their first ever release on disc. All in all, this is a wonderful tribute to a phenomenal talent

Additional recommendation ...

...11 Folk Songs[a]. Formazioni. Sinfonia[b]. [a]**Jard van Nes** (mez); [b]**Electric Phoenix; Royal Concertgebouw Orchestra / Riccardo Chailly.** Decca Ⓕ 425 832-2DH (70 minutes: DDD: 8/90). Ⓖ

Further listening ...

...Sinfonia[a]. Eindrücke. [a]**Regis Pasquier** (vn); [a]**New Swingle Singers; French National Orchestra / Pierre Boulez.** Erato 2292-45228-2 (7/88). Ⓖ

...Les mots sont allés. *Coupled with works by* **Lutosławski, Dutilleux, Beck, Henze, Fortner, Ginastera, Boulez, C. Halffter, Britten, K. Huber** and **Holliger** Thomas Demenga (vc). ECM New Series 445 234-2 (8/95).

...Les mots sont allés. *Coupled with works by* **Britten, Kodály** and **Henze** Matt Haimovitz (vc). DG 445 834-2GH (12/95).

...Lied per clarinetto solo. Sequenza IX. *Coupled with* **Stravinsky** Three Pieces for Solo Clarinet. **Stockhausen** In Freundschaft. **Jolivet** Ascèses. **Messiaen** Quatuor pour la fin du temps – Abîme des oiseaux. **Boulez** Domaines. **Paul Meyer** (cl). Denon CO-78917 (7/95).

...Coro for Voices and Instruments. **Cologne Radio Chorus and Symphony Orchestra / Luciano Berio.** DG 20th Century Classics 423 902-2GC (10/88). Ⓖ

...Laborintus II. **Soloists; Chorale Expérimentale; Ensemble Musique Vivante / Luciano Berio.** Harmonia Mundi Musique d'abord HMA190 764 (12/87).

Sir Lennox Berkeley
British 1903-1989

Berkeley Piano Sonata, Op. 20. Six Preludes, Op. 23. Five Short Pieces, Op. 4. Palm Court Waltz, Op. 81 No. 2[a]. Sonatina for Piano Duet, Op. 39[a]. Theme and Variations, Op. 73[a]. **Raphael Terroni,** [a]**Norman Beedie** (pfs). British Music Society Ⓕ BMS416CD (58 minutes: DDD: 3/94). Recorded 1993.

This is some of the finest British piano music of the century. If you find Bax turgid, Ireland too sweet, Tippett gawky or repetitive, Britten and Walton virtually non-existent in the solo repertoire, then Sir Lennox Berkeley's consistently melodic piano writing should be a real discovery. Both Terroni and Headington (listed below) really understand the Berkeley style: the latter pianist was Berkeley's first pupil at the Academy. The outer movements of the Sonata demand a special feeling for flow to give quite diverse material continuity. Both Terroni and Headington achieve this. Terroni's finale is excellent, and the overwhelming impression confirms Malcolm Williamson's description: "a flawless masterpiece". There are real delights, too, in the rest of Terroni's offering. His *Six Preludes* are just right, musically dedicated and unidiosyncratic. The *Five Short Pieces* are a microcosm of Berkeley's style in the 1930s, as are the *Preludes* for the 1940s. Terroni gauges them beautifully – the balance of melody and accompaniment in No. 4 is sheer perfection. And his duo with Norman Beedie is everything one could ask for in the *Sonatina* and *Theme and Variations*, exquisite piano duets in the great tradition of Schubert, Fauré or Satie.

Additional recommendation ...

...Piano Sonata. Six Preludes. Five Short Pieces. Three Pieces, Op. 2. Polka, Op. 5a. Three Mazurkas, Op. 32 No. 1. Paysage (1944). Improvisation on a Theme of Falla, Op. 55 No. 2. Mazurka, Op. 101 No. 2. **Christopher Headington** (pf). Kingdom Ⓕ KCLCD2012 (61 minutes: DDD: 6/89).

Further listening ...

...Symphony No. 3, Op. 74[b]. Serenade, Op. 12[a]. Divertimento in B flat major, Op. 18[a]. Partita, Op. 66[a]. Sinfonia concertante, Op. 84 – Canzonetta[a] (with Roger Winfield, ob). **Berkeley/Britten** Mont Juic, Op. 9[c]. **London Philharmonic Orchestra / Sir Lennox Berkeley.** Lyrita SRCD226 (3/93).

...Because I liked you better. He would not stay for me. *Coupled with works by* **Barber, Butterworth, Horder, Ireland, Moeran** and **C.W. Orr** Anthony Rolfe Johnson (ten); Graham Johnson (pf). Hyperion CDA66471/2 (8/95). Includes various poems from Housman's "A Shrophire Lad" read by Alan Bates. *See review in the Collections section; refer to the Index to Reviews.*

Michael Berkeley
British 1948-

Suggested listening ...

...Clarinet Concerto[a]. Pere du doux repos[b]. Flighting[c]. [ac]**Emma Johnson** (cl); [b]**Henry Herford** (bar); [a]**Northern Sinfonia / Sîan Edwards.** ASV (special price) CDDCB1101 (2/94).

...Baa Baa Black Sheep. **Soloists; Chorus of Opera North; English Northern Philharmonia / Paul Daniel.** Collins Classics 7036-2 (4/95).

Irving Berlin

Suggested listening ...

...**Annie get your gun. Soloists; Ambrosian Chorus; London Sinfonietta / John McGlinn.** EMI CDC7 54206-2 (11/91).

Hector Berlioz

Berlioz Harold in Italy, Op. 14[a]. Tristia, Op. 18[b]. Les troyens à Carthage – Act 2, Prelude[c]. [a]**Nobuko Imai** (va); [b]**John Alldis Choir; London Symphony Orchestra / Sir Colin Davis.** Philips Ⓕ 416 431-2PH (70 minutes: ADD: 12/86). Texts and translations included. Item marked [a] from 9500 026 (3/76), [b]9500 944 (6/83), [c]SAL3788 (3/70).   ⒼⒼ

Berlioz was much influenced by the British romantic poet, Byron, and his travels in Italy – where he went in 1831 as the winner of the Prix de Rome – led him to conceive a big orchestral work based on one of Byron's most popular works, *Childe Harold's Pilgrimage*. Like Berlioz's earlier *Symphonie fantastique*, *Harold in Italy* was not only a programme work but brilliantly unconventional and imaginative in its structure and argument. A commission from the great virtuoso, Paganini, led him to conceive a big viola concerto, but the idea of a Byronic symphony got in the way of that. Though there is an important viola solo in the symphony as we know it – richly and warmly played on this recording by Nobuko Imai – it is far from being the vehicle for solo display that Paganini was wanting. Sir Colin Davis's 1975 performance, beautifully transferred to CD, emphasizes the symphonic strength of the writing without losing the bite of the story-telling. The shorter works are also all valuable in illustrating Berlioz's extraordinary imagination. Excellent sound on all the different vintage recordings.

Additional recommendations ...

...Harold in Italy. **Yuri Bashmet** (va); **Frankfurt Radio Symphony Orchestra / Eliahu Inbal.** Denon Ⓕ CO-73207 (40 minutes: DDD: 12/89).

...Harold in Italy. Rêverie et caprice, Op. 8. **Yehudi Menuhin** (vn/va); **Philharmonia Orchestra / Sir Colin Davis.** EMI Studio Ⓕ CDM7 63530-2 (53 minutes: ADD: 11/90).   Ⓖ

...Harold in Italy (arr. Liszt)[a]. **Liszt** Romance oubliée, S132[a]. Hymne à Sainte Cécile (Gounod), S491. Le Moine (Meyerbeer), S416. Festmarsch zu Schillers Jähriger Geburtsfeier (Meyerbeer), S549. **Leslie Howard** (pf); [a]**Paul Coletti** (va). Hyperion Ⓕ CDA66683 (73 minutes: DDD: 11/93).

...Harold in Italy[a]. La Damnation de Faust, Op. 24[b] – Hungarian March; Ballet des Sylphes; Menuet des Follets. Les Troyens – Trojan March[c]; Royal Hunt and Storm[d]. [a]**Joseph de Pasquale** (va); **Philadelphia Orchestra /** [ac]**Eugene Ormandy,** [b]**Charles Munch;** [d]**Orchestre de Paris / Daniel Barenboim.** Sony Classical Essential Classics Ⓑ SBK53255 (74 minutes: ADD: 8/94).

Berlioz Le carnaval romain, Op. 9[a]. Béatrice et Bénédict – Overture[a]. Le corsaire, Op. 21[a]. Les troyens – Royal Hunt and Storm[a]. Benvenuto Cellini – Overture[a]. Roméo et Juliette, Op. 17 – Queen Mab scherzo[b].

Saint-Saëns Le rouet d'Omphale in A major, Op. 31[c]. **Boston Symphony Orchestra / Charles Munch.** RCA Victor Gold Seal Ⓜ 09026-61400-2* (61 minutes: ADD: 11/93). Items marked [a] from SB2125 (10/61), [b]LDS6098 (10/62), [c]SB2041 (9/59). Recorded 1957-61.

This particular Berlioz concert has long enjoyed classic status. Munch secures an electrifying response from his great Boston orchestra, whose playing is virtuosic and tender by turns. Highlights include truly exhilarating renderings of *Le corsaire* and *Benvenuto Cellini* as well as a quite riveting Royal Hunt and Storm, which attains a breathtaking poetry in the horn-led moments of repose. The bonus item, Saint-Saëns's colourful tone-poem, *Le rouet d'Omphale*, is also superbly managed here: its central climax has surely never sounded more gripping. Recordings are a bit thin in the treble, but not enough to take the shine off what is an irresistible mid-price anthology.

Additional recommendations ...

...Overture – Le carnaval romain. *Coupled with works by* **Weber, Brahms, Mozart, Wagner** and **Rossini London Philharmonic Orchestra / Sir Thomas Beecham.** Dutton Laboratories mono Ⓜ CDLX7009* (75 minutes: ADD: 10/94). *See review in the Collections section; refer to the Index to Reviews.*

...Le carnaval romain. Le corsaire, Op. 21. **Bizet** Jeux d'enfants. **Saint-Saëns** Danse macabre, Op. 40. Le rouet d'Omphale, Op. 31. **Ibert** Divertissement. **Paris Conservatoire Orchestra / Jean Martinon.** Decca Classic Sound Ⓜ 448 571-2DCS (64 minutes: ADD: 2/96).

New review

Berlioz Symphonie fantastique, Op. 14.

Dutilleux Métaboles. **Orchestra of the Opéra-Bastille, Paris / Myung-Whun Chung.** DG Ⓕ 445 878-2GH (67 minutes: DDD: 4/96). Recorded 1993.   Ⓖ

Not many versions of the *Symphonie fantastique* rival Myung-Whun Chung's in conveying the nervously impulsive inspiration of a young composer, the hints of hysteria, the overtones of nightmare in Berlioz's programme. He makes one register it afresh as genuinely fantastic. The volatile element in this perennially modern piece is something which Chung brings out to a degree you will rarely have heard before, and that establishes his as a very individual, sharply characterized version with unusually strong claims. The rapport between the conductor and the Bastille orchestra is so complete that all the subtleties of expression, the highly complex rubato, sound natural and spontaneous, regularly making one register this – despite the nationality of the conductor – as a very French performance. It is characteristic of Chung that where the slow introduction is unusually spacious, with tension carried over long pauses, the main *Allegro* is impulsively fast, with a degree of wildness that sounds totally idiomatic. The second movement waltz, another performance of extremes, has a delectable lilt, and works to an exciting conclusion. The long meditation of the "Scène aux champs" flows easily, and the opening dialogue between cor anglais and distant oboe has rarely sounded more atmospheric. Only at the start of the finale does tension momentarily slacken, and Chung's fast tempo for the clarinet's grotesque version of the motto theme pushes the players to the limit, but the conclusion brings all the expected thrills in its impulsiveness, with the bass drum vividly caught. The coupling is the set of five brief and brilliant pieces which Dutilleux wrote for Szell and the Cleveland Orchestra in 1964. Chung's view is both poetic and atmospheric, bringing out the subtly contrasting timbres in each piece, with the different sections of the orchestra brought together in the final *Presto*, where Chung relishes the marking "Flamboyant", underlining jazzy syncopations in fractional anticipation to make this even more exciting than Rostropovich's weightier but equally volatile reading. This is a makeweight to welcome, for it is sure to surprise and delight many who buy the disc primarily for Chung's inspired reading of the Berlioz.

Additional recommendation ...

...**Dutilleux** Métaboles[b]. Mystère de l'instant[a]. Timbres, espace, mouvement[b]. [a]**Collegium Musicum / Paul Sacher;** [b]**French National Orchestra / Mstislav Rostropovich.** Erato MusiFrance Ⓕ 2292-45626-2 (46 minutes: ADD/DDD: 8/92).

Berlioz Symphonie fantastique, Op. 14[a]. Le carnaval romain, Op. 9[b]. Le corsaire, Op. 21[b]. Harold in Italy, Op. 16[c]. Symphonie funèbre et triomphale, Op. 15[d]. [c]**Nobuko Imai** (va); [d]**John Alldis Choir; London Symphony Orchestra / Sir Colin Davis.** Philips Duo Ⓜ 442 290-2PM2 (two discs: 150 minutes: ADD: 10/94). Item marked [a] from SAL3441 (5/64), [b]SAL3573 (10/66), [c]9500 026 (3/76), [d]SAL3788 (3/70). Recorded 1963-75.   Ⓖ

Davis's performances of Berlioz remain among the finest of our time, and in the days when there was still a cause to be won they played a crucial part in establishing a central place in the repertory for that wayward romantic genius. The recordings offered to us here have long been favourites with collectors and it is splendid, and splendid value, to have them here assembled in Philips's convenient two-disc Duo format. The oldest, the *Symphonie fantastique*, has been more sumptuously recorded since, but not conducted more perceptively or more excitingly, not least since Davis never goes for mere excitement: his charge of energy comes from a deeper involvement with the music, so that the liveliness of "Un bal" can emerge from a tinge of the sinister in the opening figures and the "Marche au supplice" thuds with menace beneath the crack of the rhythms. Nobuko Imai's performance of *Harold* is confident, warm and smooth and it is a fine performance, as is that of the *Symphonie funèbre et triomphale*. The two overtures make up a full pair of discs in a highly recommendable package.

Additional recommendations ...

...Symphonie fantastique. **London Classical Players / Roger Norrington.** EMI Reflexe Ⓕ CDC7 49541-2 (53 minutes: DDD: 4/89). ✎   Ⓖ

...Symphonie fantastique. Le corsaire. **Royal Philharmonic Orchestra / André Previn.** RPO Ⓕ CDRPO7016 (62 minutes: DDD: 5/92).

...Symphonie fantastique. **Vienna Philharmonic Orchestra / Sir Colin Davis.** Philips Ⓕ 432 151-2PH (56 minutes: DDD: 5/92).   ⒼⒼ

...Symphonie fantastique. **Orchestre Révolutionnaire et Romantique / John Eliot Gardiner.** Philips Ⓕ 434 402-2PH (53 minutes: DDD: 6/93). ✎

...Symphonie fantastique. Overtures – Le carnaval romain; Le corsaire, Op. 21. La Damnation de Faust – Hungarian March. Les Troyens – Trojan March. **Detroit Symphony Orchestra / Paul Paray.** Mercury Ⓜ 434 328-2MM (73 minutes: ADD: 9/93).

...Symphonie fantastique[a]. Lélio, Op. 14*b*[b]. Béatrice et Bénédict[c] – Overture; Entr'acte. Les Troyens – Royal Hunt and Storm[c]. Benvenuto Cellini – Overture[c]. Le carnaval romain[c]. Les nuits d'été, Op. 7[d]. La mort de Cléopatre[e]. [e]**Jean-Louis Barrault** (narr); [de]**Yvonne Minton** (mez); [d]**Stuart Burrows**, [b]**John Mitchinson** (tens); [b]**John Shirley-Quirk** (bar); **London Symphony** [b]**Chorus and** [ab]**Orchestra;** [c]**New York Philharmonic Orchestra;** [de]**BBC Symphony Orchestra / Pierre Boulez.** Sony Classical Boulez Edition Ⓜ SM3K64103 (three discs: 199 minutes: ADD: 3/95).

...Symphonie fantastique[a]. Roméo et Juliette[b] – Love scene; Queen Mab scherzo. [a]**Concertgebouw Orchestra,** [b]**London Symphony Orchestra / Sir Colin Davis.** Philips Solo Ⓜ 446 202-2PM (80 minutes: ADD: 6/96).

...Symphonie fantastique[a]. Le carnaval romain, Op. 9[b]. **Saint–Saëns** Symphony No. 3 in C minor, Op. 78, "Organ"[c]. Carnaval des animaux[d]. [d]**John Ogden, Brenda Lucas** (pfs); [c]**C. Robinson** (org); [a]**Berlin Philharmonic Orchestra,** [b]**Vienna Philharmonic Orchestra /** [ab]**Rudolf Kempe;** [cd]**City of Birmingham Symphony Orchestra / Louis Fremaux.** EMI Seraphim Ⓜ CES5 68525-2 (two discs: 120 minutes: ADD: 11/95).

New review
Berlioz Herminie[a]. Les nuits d'été, Op. 7[b]. [a]**Mireille Delunsch** (sop); [b]**Brigitte Balleys** (mez); **Orchestre des Champs-Elysées, Paris / Philippe Herreweghe.** Harmonia Mundi Ⓕ HMC90 1522 (54 minutes: DDD: 10/95). Texts and translations included. Recorded 1994. Ⓖ

It is possible to hear pre-echoes in *Herminie* of Cassandra's fateful, searing music (quite apart from the dry-run for the *Symphonie fantastique*'s main motif). This extraordinary work of 1828, almost as arresting as its near-contemporary *Cléopâtre*, received a grand, dramatic rendering from Plowright, one somewhat vitiated by the backward recording of the voice. Mireille Delunsch sings it in a more compact, direct manner. Her tone is narrower and better focused than Plowright's, her French diction clearer. Herreweghe and his orchestra adopt a leaner, less vibrato-ridden sound, surely nearer to that of Berlioz's time, than that of their British counterparts. Delunsch also enters into the inner agony of the distraught, frustrated Herminie with a will. All in all the interpretation is absorbing from start to finish. The recording imparts a beautiful bloom to her tone as it does to that of Balleys in the much more familiar *Nuits d'été*, and this adds great atmosphere to an idiomatic, unfussy reading of this oft-recorded work. Her voice does not luxuriate in the more sensual moments of the cycle as does Crespin's in her famous version, but it has a clarity of profile, a definition of phrase that brings it close to de los Angeles's ever-attractive reading and, where strength of feeling is called for, Balleys provides it, as in "Au cimitière" and "Absence". All the other versions of the work are coupled differently. This one makes a sensible pairing with the cantata. What may also influence your choice is, again, Herreweghe's lean, well-pointed support which often emphasizes, rightly, the striking originality of Berlioz's scoring.

Additional recommendations ...

...Les nuits d'été. *Coupled with works by* **Ravel, Debussy** and **Poulenc** Régine Crespin (sop); **Suisse Romande Orchestra / Ernest Ansermet.** Decca Ⓕ 417 813-2DH (68 minutes: ADD: 11/88). *See review in the Collections section; refer to the Index to Reviews.*

...Roméo et Juliette[a]. Les nuits d'été[b]. [b]**Victoria de los Angeles** (sop); [a]**Soloists;** [a]**Harvard Glee Club;** [a]**Radcliffe Choral Society; Boston Symphony Orchestra / Charles Munch.** RCA Victor Gold Seal mono Ⓜ GD60681* (two discs: 122 minutes: ADD: 4/93).

...Herminie[a]. Béatrice et Bénédict – Overture. La mort de Cléopâtre[a]. King Lear, Op. 4. [a]**Rosalinde Plowright** (sop); **Philharmonia Orchestra / Jean-Philippe Rouchon.** ASV Ⓕ CDDCA895 (68 minutes: DDD: 8/94).

New review
Berlioz L'Enfance du Christ, Op. 25. **Jean Rigby** (mez); **John Aler, Peter Evans** (tens); **Gerald Finley, Robert Poulton** (bars); **Alastair Miles, Gwynne Howell** (basses); **St Paul's Cathedral Choir; Corydon Singers and Orchestra / Matthew Best.** Hyperion Ⓕ CDA66991/2 (two discs: 101 minutes: DDD: 12/95). Text and translation included. Recorded 1994. *Selected by Soundings.*

Gardiner, while acknowledging the drama of *The infant Christ*, classified it as "theatre of the mind";Best, however, is anxious to get away from "the rather pious oratorio approach in favour of something more human and dramatic". He therefore treats the work as overtly operatic, not so much by cast movements or varied microphone placings as by his pacing of the action and by encouraging his artists to throw themselves wholeheartedly into the emotions of the story. He gets off to a tremendous start with a superb reading by a black-voiced Alastair Miles as a Herod haunted by his dream and startled into belligerent wakefulness by the arrival of Polydorus. Later, there is desperate urgency in the appeals for shelter by Joseph (an otherwise gently lyrical Gerald Finley), harshly rebuffed by the chorus. And, throughout, there are spatial perspectives – the soldiers' patrol advancing (from practically inaudible pizzicatos) to centre stage and going off again; a beautifully hushed and atmospheric faraway "Amen" at the end. The angels' warning to the Holy Family in Part 1, however, is miscalculated by the voices being too distantly placed for their words to be audible. Balance in general is excellent, a notable passage being the duet in the tender scene at the manger. The clear enunciation (in very good French) of nearly everyone is a plus point: only Jean Rigby, sweet toned and radiating innocence as Mary, might have given her words greater precision. The chorus's response to the mood and meaning of words is always alert and sensitive, matched by the nuanced orchestral playing. The scurrying of the Ishmaelite family to help, played really *pianissimo*, is vividly graphic; and their home entertainment on two flutes and a harp, which sometimes marks a drop in the interest, here has great charm. But overall it is Best's pacing, already mentioned, which makes this recording distinctive. This recording of Berlioz's appealing work well stands comparison with its much-praised predecessors listed below.

Additional recommendations ...

...L'enfance du Christ. **Soloists; Monteverdi Choir; Lyon Opéra Orchestra / John Eliot Gardiner.** Erato Ⓕ 2292-45275 2 (two discs: 96 minutes: DDD: 1/88). ✒

...L'enfance du Christ[a]. Tristia, Op. 18 – Méditation religieuse; La mort d'Ophélie[b]. Sara la baigneuse, Op. 11[c]. La mort de Cléopâtre[d]. **Soloists;** [abc]**St Anthony Singers;** [a]**Goldsbrough Orchestra;** [bcd]**English Chamber Orchestra / Sir Colin Davis.** Double Decca Ⓜ 443 461-2DF2 (two discs: 142 minutes: ADD: 12/94).

Berlioz Messe Solennelle (also includes revised version of Resurrexit). **Donna Brown** (sop); **Jean-Luc Viala** (ten); **Gilles Cachemaille** (bar); **Monteverdi Choir; Orchestre Révolutionnaire et**

Romantique / John Eliot Gardiner. Philips Ⓕ 442 137-2PH (61 minutes: DDD: 4/94). ✒ Text and translation included. Recorded live in 1993. *Gramophone Editor's choice.*   ⒼⒼ
The reappearance of Berlioz's lost Mass of 1824 is the most exciting musical discovery of modern times. Why did Berlioz abandon the work? Only the *Resurrexit* was retained, though it was rewritten: both versions are included here. Some of it, but not much, is dull, some is awkward, but the best of the work is superb: among this one may count the *Incarnatus*, the *O Salutaris* and the lovely *Agnus Dei*. The latter was too good to lose, and survives in another form in the *Te Deum*. So do other ideas: it is at first disconcerting to hear the chorus singing "Laudamus te, benedicamus te", to the Carnival music from *Benvenuto Cellini*, more so than to hear the slow movement of the *Symphonie fantastique* in the beautiful *Gratias*. Once these and other associations are overcome, the work coheres remarkably well. Yet perhaps it did not do so well enough for Berlioz, and perhaps he was dissatisfied with the conjunction of some rather academic music with ideas that were too original, indeed too beautiful, to make a satisfying whole. All the same, no wonder the precocious 20-year-old was embraced after the first performance by his teacher, old Le Sueur, with the promise that he would be a great composer. Who knows whether he might have been made to think twice about abandoning the work had he heard a performance such as this, almost certainly more perceptive and assured than he would have got from the Opéra orchestra in 1825? His far-seeing imagination, especially with extraordinary textures and conjunctions of novel ideas, is now understood better than it could have been then. This applies to the wonderful Monteverdi Choir (their sopranos never sounding better), to an orchestra including serpent, ophicleide and the nobly dragon-headed buccin, and above all to Gardiner himself. This is a record of a great musical event, not to be missed.

Berlioz Grande messe des morts[a]. Symphonie funèbre et triomphale[b]. [a]**Ronald Dowd** (ten); [b]**Dennis Wick** (tb); [a]**Wandsworth School Boys' Choir;** [b]**John Alldis Choir; London Symphony Chorus**[a] **and Orchestra / Sir Colin Davis.** Philips Ⓕ 416 283-2PH2 (two discs: 127 minutes: ADD: 4/86). Notes, texts and translations included. Item marked [a] from 6700 019 (9/70), [b]SAL3788 (3/70).   Ⓖ
Berlioz's Requiem is not a liturgical work, any more than the *Symphonie funèbre* is really for the concert hall; but both are pieces of high originality, composed as ceremonials for the fallen, and standing as two of the noblest musical monuments to the French ideal of a *gloire*. The Requiem is most famous for its apocalyptic moment when, after screwing the key up stage by stage, Berlioz's four brass bands blaze forth "at the round earth's imagin'd corners"; this has challenged the engineers of various companies, but the Philips recording for Sir Colin Davis remains as fine as any, not least since Davis directs the bands with such a strong sense of character. He also gives the troubled rhythms of the *Lacrymosa* a stronger, more disturbing emphasis than any other conductor, and time and again finds out the expressive counterpoint, the emphatic rhythm, the telling few notes within the texture, that reveal so much about Berlioz's intentions. The notorious flute and trombone chords of the *Hostias* work admirably. Ronald Dowd is a little strained in the *Sanctus*, but the whole performance continues to stand the test of time and of other competing versions. The same is true of the *Symphonie funèbre et triomphale*, which moves at a magisterial tread and is given a recording that does well by its difficult textures. A fine coupling of two remarkable works.

Additional recommendations ...
...Grande messe[a]. Te Deum, Op. 22[b]. [a]**Stuart Burrows,** [b]**Jean Dupouy** (tens); [b]**Jean Guillou** (org); [a]**French Radio Chorus;** [b]**Paris Orchestra Chorus;** [b]**Paris Enfante Choir;** [b]**Maîtrise de la Résurrection;** [a]**French National Orchestra;** [a]**French Radio Philharmonic Orchestra / Leonard Bernstein;** [b]**Paris Orchestra / Daniel Barenboim.** CBS Maestro Ⓜ M2YK46461 (two discs: 127 minutes: ADD: 9/91).
...Grande messe[a]. Symphonie fantastique[b]. [a]**Léopold Simoneau** (ten); [a]**New England Conservatory Chorus; Boston Symphony Orchestra / Charles Munch.** RCA Victor Red Seal Ⓕ RD86210 (two discs: 130 minutes: [a]stereo/[b]mono: ADD: 2/88)

New review

Berlioz La damnation de Faust, Op. 24. **Susan Graham** (sop); **Thomas Moser** (ten); **José van Dam** (bass-bar); **Frédéric Caton** (bass); **Chorus and Orchestra of Opéra de Lyon / Kent Nagano.** Erato Ⓕ 0630-10692-2 (two discs: 122 minutes: DDD: 11/95). Text and translation included. Recorded 1994.   Ⓖ
New versions of *Faust* have been appearing more or less annually in recent years, but it is rare to encounter one as good as Kent Nagano's. At its centre is a perception of Berlioz's extraordinary vision, in all its colour and variety and humour and pessimism, and the ability to realize this in a broad downward sweep while setting every detail sharply in place. *La damnation* is a work about the steady failure of consolations in a romantic world rejecting God, until all Faust's sensations are numbed and Mephistopheles has him trapped in the hell of no feeling. Every stage of the progress is mercilessly depicted here. The chorus are brilliant in all their roles, offering in turn the lively charms of peasant life, raptures of faith in the Easter Hymn, beery roistering in Auerbach's Cellar that grows as foul as a drunken party, cheerful student Latin bawls (those were the days); later they sing with delicacy as Mephistopheles's spirits of temptation and finally become a vicious pack of demons. Nagano takes the Hungarian March at a pace that grows hectic as the dream of military glory turns hollow. These are sharp perceptions, brilliantly realized. There is the same care for orchestral detail. Nagano seems to be conducting from the New Berlioz Edition score, and he uses his imagination with

it. He has an unerring sense of tempo, balancing weight of tone against speed, and he can light upon the telling contrapuntal line, or point a detail of instrumental colour (like the viola tremolo that 'betrays' the will-o'-the-wisps as the devil's creatures) or even a single note (like the snarl in the Ride to the Abyss), elements that give Berlioz's marvellous orchestration its expressive quality. José van Dam is an outstanding Mephistopheles, curling his voice round phrases with hideous elegance, relishing the mock-jollity of the Serenade and the Song of the Flea, taunting Faust with lulling sweetness on the banks of the Elbe, yet also disclosing the sadness of the fallen spirit. Thomas Moser sings gravely and reflectively as he is first discovered on the plains of Hungary, and rises nobly to the challenge of the Invocation to Nature (*très large et très sombre*, as Berlioz wanted), but is almost at his finest in the many recitative passages as he twists and turns in Mephistopheles's tightening grasp. Susan Graham does not match these two superb performances, but she sings her two arias simply and well. This is, all round, the best version since that of Sir Colin Davis made in 1973, and sets Nagano among the outstanding Berlioz conductors of the day.

Additional recommendations ...

...Soloists; **Wandsworth School Boys' Choir; Ambrosian Singers; London Symphony Chorus and Orchestra / Sir Colin Davis.** Philips Ⓟ 416 395-2PH2 (two discs: 131 minutes: ADD: 1/87).

...Soloists; **Edinburgh Festival Chorus; Lyon Opera Orchestra / John Eliot Gardiner.** Philips Ⓟ 426 199-2PH2 (two discs: 124 minutes: DDD: 3/90).

...Soloists; **Cologne Radio Chorus; Stuttgart Radio Chorus; North German Radio Chorus, Hamburg; Frankfurt Radio Symphony Orchestra / Eliahu Inbal.** Denon Ⓟ CO-77200/01 (two discs: 127 minutes: DDD: 7/91).

Berlioz Béatrice et Bénédict. **Susan Graham** (sop) Béatrice; **Jean-Luc Viala** (ten) Bénédict; **Sylvia McNair** (sop) Héro; **Catherine Robbin** (mez) Ursule; **Gilles Cachemaille** (bar) Claudio; **Gabriel Bacquier** (bar) Somarone; **Vincent Le Texier** (bass) Don Pedro; **Philippe Magnant** (spkr) Léonato; **Lyon Opera Chorus and Orchestra / John Nelson.** Erato MusiFrance Ⓟ 2292-45773-2 (two discs: 111 minutes: DDD: 6/92). Notes, text and translation included. Recorded 1991.

We have to note that the title is not a French version of *Much Ado about Nothing*, but that it takes the two principal characters of Shakespeare's play and constructs an opera around them. The comedy centres on the trick which is played upon the protagonists by their friends, producing love out of apparent antipathy. Much of the charm lies in the more incidental matters of choruses, dances, the magical "Nocturne" duet for Béatrice and Héro, and the curious addition of the character Somarone, a music-master who rehearses the choir in one of his own compositions. There is also a good deal of spoken dialogue, the present recording having more of it than did its closest rival, a version made in 1977 with Sir Colin Davis conducting and Dame Janet Baker and Robert Tear in the title-roles (see below). Perhaps surprisingly, the extra dialogue is a point in favour of the new set, for it is done very effectively by good French actors and it makes for a more cohesive, Shakespearian entertainment. John Nelson secures a well-pointed performance of the score, comparing well with Davis's, and with excellent playing by the Lyon Orchestra. Susan Graham and Jean-Luc Viala are attractively vivid and nimble in style, and Sylvia McNair makes a lovely impression in Héro's big solo. The veteran Gabriel Bacquier plays the music-master with genuine panache and without overmuch clownage. There is good work by the supporting cast and the chorus and the recording is finely produced and well recorded.

Additional recommendation ...

...Soloists; **John Alldis Choir; London Symphony Orchestra / Sir Colin Davis.** Philips Ⓟ 416 952-2PH2 (two discs: 98 minutes: DDD: 9/87).

Berlioz Les Troyens. **Françoise Pollet** (sop) Dido; **Gary Lakes** (ten) Aeneas; **Deborah Voigt** (sop) Cassandra; **Gino Quilico** (bar) Choroebus; **Hélène Perraguin** (mez) Anna; **Jean-Philippe Courtis** (bass) Narbal; **Michel Philippe** (bass) Pantheus; **Catherine Dubosc** (sop) Ascanius; **Jean-Luc Maurette** (ten) Iopas; **René Schirrer** (bar) Priam, Soldier I; **Claudine Carlson** (mez) Hecuba; **John Mark Ainsley** (ten) Hylas; **Marc Belleau** (bass) Hector's Ghost, Soldier II, Greek Captain; **Gregory Cross** (ten) Sinon; **Michel Beuachemin** (bass) Mercury; **Montreal Symphony Chorus and Orchestra / Charles Dutoit.** Decca Ⓟ 443 693-2DH4 (four discs: 238 minutes: DDD: 12/94). Notes, text and translation included. Recorded 1993. *Gramophone Editor's record of the month. Selected by Sounds in Retrospect.* Ⓖ

It is a tribute to the quality of Sir Colin Davis's pioneering set of Berlioz's epic opera that it remained unchallenged by any rival on record for a quarter-century, the 1969 sound superbly focused, giving a vivid sense of presence. Then came Dutoit and the Montreal Symphony Orchestra, who have established themselves as second to none in the French repertory, not only because of their idiomatic responsiveness to the music, but because of the consistent warmth and richness of their sound. Add to that a largely French-speaking cast, on balance even more sensitive and tonally more beautiful than Davis's, plus two minor but valuable textual additions, and the advantage of the new over the old is clear. Interpretatively, the contrasts between Dutoit and Davis are quickly established at the very start of "La prise de Troie". Dutoit launches in at high voltage, more volatile than Davis, conveying exuberance, consistently preferring faster speeds. Davis may be marginally less exciting, but he often compensates in the extra crispness and clarity of the playing of the Covent Garden orchestra. The advantage of Dutoit's faster speeds – reflecting the metronome markings – comes not just in thrilling

*Allegro*s, but in flowing *Andante*s. So Cassandra's first solo is more persuasively moulded at a flowing speed, with Deborah Voigt far warmer than Berit Lindholm for Davis, both in her beauty of tone and in her *espressivo* phrasing.

As Aeneas Gary Lakes may not have so richly heroic a voice as Jon Vickers for Davis, being rather more easily stressed at the top, but among today's tenors he is the most experienced of all in this role, having sung it close on two-dozen times on both sides of the Atlantic. His big advantage over Vickers, most of all in the great love scene with Dido in Act 3, is that he shades his voice far more subtly. Though the role of Dido very often goes to a mezzo – Josephine Veasey on the Davis set, Dame Janet Baker on EMI's set of excerpts with Sir Alexander Gibson conducting (listed below) – here Decca firmly opt for a soprano, Françoise Pollet. One of the most exciting French singers to have appeared in years, she is in many ways an ideal choice. Very much attuned to the idiom, she sings consistently with full, even tone, so that, matching Dutoit's expressiveness and the richness of the Montreal sound, she brings out the feminine sensuousness of the role more than a mezzo normally would. Such a passage as the central section of the Dido/Anna duet in Act 3 inspired her to legato of velvet beauty when, persuaded by Anna, she lets herself think of new love. That is one of the few passages in either half of the opera where Dutoit is significantly slower than Davis, and the tender beauty of the number is all the more intense, one of the loveliest passages of all.

Throughout the opera Dutoit's degree of rhythmic freedom, notably in heavily syncopated passages, intensifies the controlled frenzy behind much of the most dramatic writing, and here Dido's hysteria, like Cassandra's earlier on, is most tellingly conveyed. She may not have the dark colourings of a Baker or a Veasey, but her dramatic power is just as intense. There is barely a weak link in the rest of the huge cast. Though on balance the Covent Garden Chorus for Davis sing with even crisper ensemble, the passionate commitment of the Montreal chorus matches the fire of Dutoit's whole reading. This is a thrilling set to have one marvelling afresh at the electric vitality of Berlioz's inspiration, and marvelling too that the formidable problems of recording so massive a work have been accomplished so confidently. It is a tribute to the performance and the beauty of the recording, as well as to Berlioz, that this massive four hours of music seems so short, with no *longueurs* whatsoever.

Additional recommendations ...

...Soloists; Wandsworth School Boys' Choir; Royal Opera House, Covent Garden Chorus and Orchestra / Sir Colin Davis. Philips Ⓕ 416 432-2PH4 (four discs: 241 minutes: ADD: 12/86). *Gramophone classical 100.*   ⊛⊛⊛

...Act 5, scenes 2 and 3ᶜ. Les nuits d'été, Op. 7ᵃ. La mort de Cléopâtreᵇ. **Dame Janet Baker** (mez); ᶜ**Bernadette Greevy** (contr); ᶜ**Keith Erwen** (ten); ᶜ**Gwynne Howell** (bass); ᶜ**Ambrosian Opera Chorus;** ᵃ**New Philharmonia Orchestra / Sir John Barbirolli;** ᵇᶜ**London Symphony Orchestra / Sir Alexander Gibson.** EMI Studio Ⓜ CDM7 69544-2 (78 minutes: ADD: 11/88).

Further listening ...

...Rêverie et caprice, Op. 8ᵃ. *Coupled with* **Lalo** Symphonie espagnole, Op. 21ᵃ. **Saint-Saëns** Violin Concerto No. 3 in B minor, Op. 61ᵇ. **Itzhak Perlman** (vn); **Orchestre de Paris / Daniel Barenboim.** DG Digital Masters 445 549-2GMA (7/95).

...Benvenuto Cellini. **Soloists; Royal Opera House Chorus, Covent Garden; BBC Symphony Orchestra / Sir Colin Davis.** Philips 416 955-2PH3 (1/89).

...Te Deum, Op. 22. **Soloists; London Symphony Chorus; London Philharmonic Choir; Wooburn Singers; St Alban's School Choir; Desborough School Choir; Haberdashers' Aske's School Choir; Southend Boys' Choir; Forest School Choir, Winnersh; High Wycombe Parish Church Choir; European Community Youth Orchestra / Claudio Abbado.** DG 410 696-2GH (2/84).

Baronet Lord Berners   British 1883-1950

New review

Berners A Wedding Bouquetᵃ. Luna Park. March. ᵃ**RTE Chamber Choir; RTE Sinfonietta / Kenneth Alwyn.** Marco Polo Ⓕ 8 223716 (52 minutes: DDD: 7/96). Recorded 1994.

These ballet scores – two choreographed by Balanchine and three by Ashton – can now stand beside the best of Bliss and Lambert. This is particularly true of *A Wedding Bouquet* (not *Wedding Bouquet* as on the CD). Written for chorus and orchestra – the version for speaker and orchestra was purely an economy measure and should not be perpetuated – *A Wedding Bouquet* was premièred at Sadler's Wells in 1937 (not 1936 as stated in the vocal score). It was an extraordinary combination of elements: a shockingly nonsensical text taken from Gertrude Stein's *They must be wedded to their wife*, set to music by Berners – who also designed the costumes and décor – and choreographed by Frederick Ashton. It works brilliantly in the theatre, where at times it feels rather like Stravinsky's *Les noces* translated to the home counties, although the official location is in France. *A Wedding Bouquet* has never gone out of the ballet repertoire, but only two excerpts have been recorded. The whole work comes out wonderfully in this effervescent performance, with all the sparkle of the champagne being liberally drunk on stage. Both soloists and chorus are well balanced, although a real *pianissimo* is lacking. The tunes are extremely catchy, especially the tango and the crazy waltz, and there is every justification now for regarding *A Wedding Bouquet* as Berners's masterpiece – a real discovery in British music of the inter-war period, and destined to become a classic. Alongside it, *Luna Park*, although a great bonus on record for the first time, seems more conventional. Like *The Triumph of*

Neptune, it is impeccably crafted and radiates balletic enjoyment. The filler is an isolated *March*, which Philip Lane has scored, but the *Fanfare* he refers to in his informative notes is not included.

Further listening ...

...The Triumph of Neptune – Suite. Fugue. Nicholas Nickleby. Three Morceaux. Fantaisie espagnole. **Royal Liverpool Philharmonic Orchestra / Barry Wordsworth.** EMI British Composers CDM5 65098-2 (8/94).

...The Triumph of Neptune – Schottische; Hornpipe; Polka; Harlequinade; Dance of the Fairy Princess; Intermezzo; Apotheosis of Neptune. *Coupled with works by* **Bantock** and **Bax Robert Alva** (bar); **London Philharmonic Orchestra / Sir Thomas Beecham.** EMI Beecham Edition mono CDM7 63405-2* (6/92).

...The Triumph of Neptune. *Coupled with works by* **Arnell** and **Delius** Royal Philharmonic Orchestra / Sir Thomas Beecham. Sony Classical British Pageant mono SMK46683* (11/94). *See review under Arnell; refer to the Index to Reviews.* Ⓔ

...Les sirènes[a]. Caprice péruvien. Cupid and Psyche. [a]**Miriam Blennerhassett** (contr); **RTE Sinfonietta / David Lloyd-Jones.** Marco Polo 8 223780 (4/96).

Elmer Bernstein

American 1922-

Suggested listening ...

...The Great Escape – film score. **orchestra / Elmer Bernstein.** Intrada MAF7025D (5/93).

...Kings Go Forth. Some Came Running – Original film soundtracks. **orchestra / Elmer Bernstein.** Cloud Nine CNS5004 (5/93).

...The Magnificent Seven – film score. The Hallelujah Trail – Overture. **The Phoenix Symphony / James Sedares.** Koch International 37222-2 (11/94).

Leonard Bernstein

American 1918-1990

Bernstein Songfest[a]. Chichester Psalms[b]. [a]**Clamma Dale** (sop); [a]**Rosalind Elias**, [a]**Nancy Williams** (mezzos); [a]**Neil Rosenshein** (ten); [a]**John Reardon** (bar); [a]**Donald Gramm** (bass); [b]soloist from the **Vienna Boys' Choir**; [b]**Vienna Jeunesse Choir**; [a]**National Symphony Orchestra of Washington**, [b]**Israel Philharmonic Orchestra / Leonard Bernstein.** DG Ⓔ 415 965-2GH (62 minutes: ADD: 5/86). Texts and, where appropriate, translations included. Item marked [a] from 2531 044 (11/78), [b]2709 077 (9/78). Recorded 1977.

"I, too, am America", is the message of Leonard Bernstein's orchestral song-cycle *Songfest*. The subject of the work is the American artist's emotional, spiritual and intellectual response to life in an essentially Puritan society, and, more specifically, to the eclecticism of American society and its many problems of social integration (blacks, women, homosexuals and expatriates). As expected from a composer/conductor equally at home on Broadway or in Vienna's Musikverein, the styles range widely. The scoring is colourful, occasionally pungent, always tuneful. Bernstein's soloists are well chosen and sing with feeling. This vivid live recording of the *Chichester Psalms* offers the full orchestral version and the performers all give their utmost.

Additional recommendation ...

...Chichester Psalms[a]. **Barber** Agnus Dei. **Copland** In the Beginning[b]. Four Motets. [a]**Dominic Martelli** (treb); [b]**Catherine Denley** (mez); [a]**Rachel Masters** (hp); [a]**Gary Kettel** (perc); **Corydon Singers / Matthew Best.** Hyperion Ⓔ CDA66219 (54 minutes: DDD: 9/87).

Bernstein On the Town. **Frederica von Stade** (mez) Claire; **Tyne Daly** (sngr) Hildy; **Marie McLaughlin** (sop) Ivy; **Thomas Hampson** (bass) Gabey; **Kurt Ollmann** (bar) Chip; **David Garrison** (sngr) Ozzie; **Samuel Ramey** (bass) Pitkin; **Evelyn Lear** (sop) Madame Dilly; **Cleo Laine** (sngr) Nightclub singer; **London Voices; London Symphony Orchestra / Michael Tilson Thomas.** DG Ⓔ 437 516-2GH (75 minutes: DDD: 10/93). Notes and text included. Recorded 1992. ⒼⒼ *Gramophone Award Winner 1994.*

On the Town is a peach of a show, a show which positively hums along on the heat of its inspiration, a show rejoicing in the race of time, but regretful of its passing, a show which lovingly encapsulates those transitory moments seized and then lost amidst the impatient, pulsating heart and soul of the lonely city – the Big Apple. On two amazing nights Michael Tilson Thomas and this starry cast brought New York City to the Barbican in London. Recording this semi-staged performance live must have been a living nightmare for DG's engineers, but one wonders if they might not have pulled off a more up-front balance for the voices. Only Cleo Laine gets to be really intimate with her bluesy nightclub song "Ain't got no tears left". You'll hang on every breath Laine takes. Many of the notes are threadbare, but who needs the notes when you've got instincts like hers. As to the major roles there are happily no grave misjudgements in casting such as marred the composer's by now infamous *West Side Story* on this label. Mind you, you know you're in big-league production when you get Samuel Ramey delivering (gloriously) the Brooklyn Navy Yard Workers' ode to morning "I feel like I'm not out of bed yet". And Ramey was an inspired choice for Clare's monumentally boring boyfriend, Pitkin. His "Song", a masterpiece of arch formality, is very funny indeed. In performance, Tyne

Daly's cab-driving Hildy knocked 'em in the aisles with her huggable personality, and the three sailors, Gabey, Chip, Ozzie – Thomas Hampson, Kurt Ollmann, David Garrison – are just perfect. Not only are they well-matched vocally, but you could put them on any stage and never look back. Hampson's two big numbers – "Lonely Town" and "Lucky to be Me" – are handsomely sung with careful avoidance of that peculiarly 'operatic' articulation. The real heroes of this dizzy enterprise are Tilson Thomas and the London Symphony Orchestra, every last player a character, an individual. John Harle's soaring, throaty sax and rhythms are so hot, tight and idiomatic that you'd never credit this wasn't an American band. The playing here is stunning, there's no other word.

Bernstein West Side Story. **Tinuke Olafimihan** Maria; **Paul Manuel** Tony; **Caroline O'Connor** Anita; **Sally Burgess** Off-stage voice; **Nicholas Warnford** Riff; **Julie Paton** Rosalia; **Elinor Stephenson** Consuela; **Nicole Carty** Francisca; **Kieran Daniels** Action; **Mark Michaels** Diesel; **Adrian Sarple** Baby John; **Adrian Edmeads** A-rab; **Garry Stevens** Snowboy; **Nick Ferranti** Bernardo; **chorus and National Symphony Orchestra / John Owen Edwards.** TER Ⓕ CDTER2 1197 (two discs: 101 minutes: DDD: 2/94). Recorded 1993.   Ⓔ

To cap the composer's own recording of *West Side Story,* even given his controversial casting of opera stars, is something of an achievement. The set starts with the major advantage of being inspired by a production at the Haymarket, Leicester, so that many of the cast are really inside their roles. They have youth on their side, too. Paul Manuel from that company may not have a large voice, but his sympathetic portrayal of Tony, both in his solos and duets with Maria, makes one feel that he identifies totally with the part. Moreover, the way in which he can float a high note, as at the end of the alternative film version of "Something's coming" puts him on a par with Carreras (for Bernstein). His Maria, Tinuke Olafimihan, is a gem. Her ability to interact with him and to express the laughter and the tragedy of the heroine is very real. At the heart of the "Somewhere" ballet, Sally Burgess voices the lovers' plea for peace with a magnificent rendition of its famous soaring tune. Nicholas Warnford as leader of the Jets gives no less than his rival in the tricky "Cool" sequence and Jet song. John Owen Edwards directs Bernstein's score as if he believes in every note of it. Moreover, he has imparted to his players the very pulse that sets this music ticking.

Additional recommendation ...

...**Dame Kiri Te Kanawa** (sop); **José Carreras** (ten); **Tatiana Troyanos** (mez); **Kurt Ollmann** (bar); composite chorus and orchestra from 'on and off' Broadway / **Leonard Bernstein** with **Marilyn Horne** (mez). DG Ⓕ 415 253-2GH2 (two discs: 98 minutes: DDD: 4/85).

Bernstein Candide (1988 final version). **Jerry Hadley** (ten) Candide; **June Anderson** (sop) Cunegonde; **Adolph Green** (ten) Dr Pangloss, Martin; **Christa Ludwig** (mez) Old lady; **Nicolai Gedda** (ten) Governor, Vanderdendur, Ragotski; **Della Jones** (mez) Paquette; **Kurt Ollmann** (bar) Maximilian, Captain, Jesuit father; **Neil Jenkins** (ten) Merchant, Inquisitor, Prince Charles Edward; **Richard Suart** (bass) Junkman, Inquisitor, King Hermann Augustus; **John Treleaven** (ten) Alchemist, Inquisitor, Sultan Achmet, Crook; **Lindsay Benson** (bar) Doctor, Inquisitor, King Stanislaus; **Clive Bayley** (bar) Bear-Keeper, Inquisitor, Tsar Ivan; **London Symphony Chorus and Orchestra / Leonard Bernstein.** DG Ⓕ 429 734-2GH2 (two discs: 112 minutes: DDD: 8/91). Notes and text included. Recorded 1989. *Gramophone* Award Winner 1992.   Ⓔ

Here it is – all of it – musical comedy, grand opera, operetta, satire, melodrama, all rolled into one. We can thank John Mauceri for much of the restoration work: his 1988 Scottish Opera production was the spur for this recording and prompted exhaustive reappraisal. Numbers like "We Are Women", "Martin's Laughing Song" and "Nothing More Than This" have rarely been heard, if at all. The last mentioned, Candide's 'aria of disillusionment', is one of the enduring glories of the score, reinstated where Bernstein always wanted it (but where no producer would have it), near the very end of the show. Bernstein called it his "Puccini aria", and that it is – bittersweet, long-breathed, supported, enriched and ennobled by its inspiring string counterpoint. And this is but one of many forgotten gems. It was an inspiration on someone's part (probably Bernstein's) to persuade the great and versatile Christa Ludwig and Nicolai Gedda (in his sixties and still hurling out the top Bs) to fill the principal character roles. To say they do so ripely is to do them scant justice. Bernstein's old sparring partner Adolph Green braves the tongue-twisting and many-hatted Dr Pangloss with his own highly individual form of *sprechstimme*, Jerry Hadley sings the title role most beautifully, *con amore*, and June Anderson has all the notes, and more, for the faithless, air-headed Cunegonde. It is just a pity that someone didn't tell her that discretion is the better part of comedy. "Glitter and Be Gay" is much funnier for being played straighter, odd as it may sound. Otherwise, the supporting roles are all well taken and the London Symphony Chorus have a field-day in each of their collective guises. Having waited so long to commit every last note (or thereabouts) of his cherished score to disc, there are moments here where Bernstein seems almost reluctant to move on. His tempos are measured, to say the least, the score fleshier now in every respect: even that raciest of Overtures has now acquired a more deliberate gait, a more opulent tone. But Bernstein would be Bernstein, and there are moments where one is more than grateful for his indulgence: the grandiose chorales, the panoramic orchestrascapes (sumptuously recorded), and of course, that thrilling finale – the best of all possible Bernstein anthems at the slowest of all possible speeds – and why not (prepare to hold your breath at the choral *a cappella*). It's true, perhaps, that somewhere in the midst of this glossy package there is a more modest show trying to get out, but let's not look gift horses in the mouth.

Additional recommendations ...

...Candide – Overture. On the Town. Trouble in Tahiti. On the Town – Three Dance Episodes. Fancy Free. West Side Story – Symphonic Dances. On the Waterfront – Symphonic Suite. Facsimile choreographic essay. **Soloists; Columbia Wind Ensemble; New York Philharmonic Orchestra / Leonard Bernstein.** Sony Classical Portrait Ⓜ SM3K47154 (three discs: 203 minutes: ADD: 5/92). 🄖🄖

...Candide – Overture. West Side Story – Symphonic Dances. **Gershwin** An American in Paris. Rhapsody in Blue[a]. **New York Philharmonic Orchestra / Leonard Bernstein** ([a]pf). Sony Classical Ⓜ SMK47529 (60 minutes: ADD: 11/92).

Further listening ...

...Serenade. *Coupled with works by* **Barber** *and* **Foss** Itzhak Perlman (vn); **Boston Symphony Orchestra / Seiji Ozawa.** EMI Ⓕ CDC5 55360-2 (6/95). *See review under Barber; refer to the Index to Reviews. Gramophone Editor's choice.* 🄖

...Halil. *Coupled with works by* **Martin, Nielsen** *and* **Ibert** Michael Faust (fl); **Cologne Radio Symphony Orchestra / Alun Francis.** Capriccio 10 495 (12/94). *See review in the Collections section; refer to the Index to Reviews.*

...Clarinet Sonata. *Coupled with works by* **Gershwin, Ives** and **Kirchner** Yo-Yo Ma (vc); Jeffrey Kahane (pf). Sony Classical SK53126 (4/94). *See review in the Collections section; refer to the Index to Reviews* 🄖

...Symphonies – No. 1, "Jeremiah"[af]; No. 2, "The Age of Anxiety"[bf], No. 3, "Kaddish"[acf]. Chichester Psalms[cdf]. Serenade after Plato's Symposium[ef]. Prelude, Fugue and Riffs[g]. [a]Jennie Tourel (mez); [d]John Bogart (alto); [e]Felicia Montealegre (spkr); [e]Zino Francescatti (vn); [g]Benny Goodman (cl); [b]Philippe Entremont (pf); [c]Camerata Singers; [c]Columbus Boy Choir; [f]New York Philharmonic Orchestra; [f]New York Philharmonic Orchestra; [g]Columbia Jazz Combo / Leonard Bernstein. Sony Classical SM3K47162 (3/92).

...Symphony No. 1, "Jeremiah"[a]. Songfest[b]. Anniversaries – In Memoriam: Nathalie Koussevitzky[c]. [b]Linda Hohenfeld (sop); [a]Nan Merriman, [b]Wendy White, [b]Patrice Spence (mezzos); [b]Walter Planté (ten); [b]Vernon Hartman (bar); [b]John Cheek (bass); [ab]St Louis Symphony Orchestra / [a]Leonard Bernstein, [b]Leonard Slatkin ([c]pf). RCA Victor Red Seal [a]mono/[b]stereo 09026 61581-2* (6/94)

...Five Anniversaries. *Coupled with* **Barber** Ballade, Op. 46. **Beach** Five Improvisations, Op. 148. **Cage** Bacchanale for Prepared Piano. **Copland** Four Piano Blues. **Gershwin** Three Preludes. **Gottschalk** Manchega, RO143. Le Banjo, RO22. **M. Gould** Boogie Woogie Etude. **Joplin** The Entertainer. Maple Leaf Rag. **MacDowell** New England Idylls, Op. 62. **Nancarrow** Prelude. Michel Legrand (pf). Erato Ⓕ 4509-96386-2 (77 minutes: DDD: 7/95).

...West Side Story. Original film soundtrack. Sony SK48211.

...West Side Story – I feel pretty. Candide – Glitter and be gay. The Madwoman of Central Park West – My new friends. *Coupled with works by* **Weill, Sondheim** *and* **Blitzstein** Dawn Upshaw (sop); **orchestra / Eric Stern.** Elektra Nonesuch 7559-79345-2 (12/94). *See review in the Collections section; refer to the Index to Reviews.* 🄖🄖

...West Side Story – Mambo. *Coupled with* **J. Adams** The Chairman Dances. **Kernis** New Era Dance. **Schiff** Stomp. **Larsen** Collage: Boogie. **Harbison** Remembering Gatsby. **Torke** Black and White – Charcoal. **Moran** Points of Departure. **Agento** The Dream of Valentino – Tango. **Daugherty** Desi. **Rouse** Bonham. **Baltimore Symphony Orchestra / David Zinman.** Argo 444 454-2ZH (7/95).

...Wonderful Town. **Original TV cast.** Sony Broadway SK48021.

Franz Adolf Berwald
Swedish 1796-1868

New review

Berwald Symphonies – No. 1 in G minor, "Sinfonie sérieuse"; No. 2 in D major, "Sinfonie capricieuse"; No. 3 in C major, "Sinfonie singulière"; No. 4 in E flat major. Estrella de Soria – Overture. The Queen of Golconda – Overture. Symphony in A (cptd. Druce). **Swedish Radio Symphony Orchestra / Roy Goodman.** Hyperion Ⓕ CDA67081/2 (two discs: 145 minutes: DDD: 6/96). Recorded 1995. 🄖

New review

Berwald Orchestral works. [a]Niklas Sivelöv (pf); Helsingborg Symphony Orchestra / Okko Kamu. Naxos Ⓢ 8 553051/2 (two discs, oas: 71 and 78 minutes: DDD). Recorded 1995.
8 5530511 – Symphonies: No. 1 in G minor, "Sinfonie sérieuse"; No. 2 in D major, "Sinfonie capricieuse". Estrella de Soria – Overture. *8 553052* – Symphonies: No. 3 in C major, "Sinfonie singulière"; No. 4 in E flat major. Piano Concerto in D major[a].

New review

Berwald Symphonies – No. 1 in G minor, "Sinfonie sérieuse"; No. 2 in D major, "Sinfonie capricieuse"; No. 3 in C major, "Sinfonie singulière"; No. 4 in E flat major. **Gothenburg Symphony Orchestra / Neeme Järvi.** DG Masters Ⓜ 445 581-2GMA2 (two discs: 112 minutes: DDD). From 415 502-2GH2 (12/85). Recorded 1995.

Goodman's set is of exceptional interest in that it offers a realization by Duncan Druce of the surviving fragment of the early A major Symphony. This will be new to readers, and is complemented by the overtures to *Estrella de Soria* and *The Queen of Golconda*. The Helsingborg set on Naxos gives us the D major Piano Concerto of 1855 as well as the four symphonies under the consistently underrated but artistically consistent Okko Kamu. Goodman's performances of the symphonies are as alive and intelligent as one would expect from him and radiate an enthusiasm for Berwald's music that is inspiriting. The wind of the fine Swedish Radio Symphony certainly shine. However, one longs, particularly in the slow movement of the E flat Symphony, for the strings to sing more ardently, and to speak with greater weight and eloquence. They sound a little inhibited, as if playing against their natural inclination and their lightness also rather emphasizes the top-heaviness of Berwald's scoring. All the same, the felicities in the Hyperion set far outweigh any reservations one might have, and Berwaldians will certainly want to have it on their shelves.

Järvi's set with the Gothenburg Symphony Orchestra now appears at half its original price – two CDs for the price of one, and packaged economically as one disc. The sound has plenty of warmth and presence, and is full-bodied. Järvi's advocacy of these works is totally committed and his orchestra play splendidly, with some fine wind articulation. The *Sinfonie capricieuse* is particularly satisfying and arguably still the best on disc. Although it is inexpensive, the Naxos set is not short on quality, either in terms of performance or recording. Okko Kamu gets very acceptable results from the Helsingborg Symphony Orchestra and although they do not sweep the board, they are sound, thoughtful performances, free from eccentricity and with no lack of character. The Helsingborg strings do not produce quite the polished, finely integrated sonority as the Gothenburg orchestra but they play well.

Further listening ...

...Symphonies – No. 1 in G minor, "Sinfonie sérieuse"; No. 4 in E flat major. **San Francisco Symphony Orchestra / Herbert Blomstedt.** Decca Ⓟ 436 597-2DH (63 minutes: DDD: 1/94).

...The Queen of Golconda – Overture. Piano Concerto in D major[b]. The Festival of the Bayadères. Violin Concerto in C sharp minor, Op. 2[a]. Serious and joyful fancies. [a]**Arve Tellefsen** (vn); [b]**Marian Migdal** (pf); **Royal Philharmonic Orchestra / Ulf Björlin.** EMI Matrix CDM5 65073-2 (6/94).

...Septet in B flat major. *Coupled with* **Hummel** Septet in D minor, Op. 74. **Nash Ensemble.** CRD CRD3344 (6/89).   Ⓖ

...Piano Quintet No. 1 in C minor. Piano Trios – No. 1 in E flat major; No. 3 in D minor. **Stefan Lindgren** (pf); **Berwald Quartet.** Musica Sveciae MSCD521 (10/93).

...String Quartet No. 1 in G minor. *Coupled with* **Wikmanson** String Quartet No. 2 in E minor, Op. 1 No. 2. **Chilingirian Quartet.** CRD CRD3361 (3/95).

...String Quartets – [ab]No. 2 in A minor; [c]No. 3 in E flat major. [a]**Skåne Quartet;** [b]**Ericson Quartet;** [c]**Kyndel Quartet.** Caprice CAP21506.

Bruno Bettinelli

Italian 1913-

Suggested listening ...

...Toccata Fantasia. *Coupled with* **Galliera** Venerdi Santo dal "Trittico". **Bossi** Stunde der Wehie, Op. 132 No. 4. Stunde der Freude, Op. 132 No. 5. **Petrali** Messe solennelle – Gloria. **Ambrosi** Messa. **Luigi Benedetti** (org). Priory PRCD427 (4/95).

Heinrich Biber

Bohemian 1644-1704

New review

Biber Sonatae tam aris quam aulis servientes. **Purcell Quartet** (Catherine Mackintosh, Catherine Weiss, vns; Richard Boothby, violone; Robert Woolley, hpd/org); **Katherine McGillivray, Jane Rogers, Tim Cronin** (vas); **Mark Bennett, Michael Laird** (tpts). Chandos Chaconne Ⓟ CHAN0591 (67 minutes: DDD: 6/96). Recorded 1995. ✍ *Gramophone* Editor's choice.   Ⓖ

The Purcell Quartet are experienced interpreters of Biber, having recorded the composer's complete *Harmonia artificiosa* sonatas (listed below) to deserved plaudits. *Sonatae tam aris* is perhaps a less arcane collection overall: the violins are tuned normally and the emphasis is on a more pithy ensemble sonata, rather than a projection of subtle and sophisticated solo effects. Five of the works employ either one or two trumpets, working typical motifs into an imaginative web of violins and violas, each with lines of true polyphonic integrity. The Purcell Quartet give these wonderfully striking and noble textures a sense of space and composure. If the all-string works, like Sonata No. 6, are less deliberately calculated and theatrical than with the Freiburg consort (listed below), then the Purcells certainly communicate a soft warmth which says much about the simple freshness of these delightful works; the group also provide the dance-like sections with enough of an uplift to allude to the odd rustic root without, as the Freiburgers do – very convincingly, revelling in rustic and gipsyish antics. The Purcells take more 'as read' than the free-spirited Germans. Whilst the virtuosity of the Freiburg group has the listener on the edge of the seat in the Fourth Soanta, one is drawn to the sheer beauty and intimacy of the ensemble playing here, enhanced by the impeccable trumpet playing of Mark Bennett and Michael Laird. If not as cultivated or polished as the Germans, the English group have special things to say about this music and they display a pure, unadulterated pleasure in Biber's delicious creations.

Biber Sonatae tam aris, quam aulis servientes – No. 1 in C major; No. 4 in C major; No. 6 in
F major; No. 7 in C major; No. 8 in G major; No. 10 in G minor; No. 12 in C major.
Schmelzer Sonata a 3 in B minor, "Lamento. Duodena selectarum sonatarum – No. 2 in A minor;
No. 8 in B flat major. Sonata sopra la morte Ferdinand III. Lamento a 3 in B flat major.
Harmonia a 5 in B flat major. **Freiburg Baroque Orchestra Consort.** Deutsche Harmonia Mundi
Ⓟ 05472 77348-2 (74 minutes: DDD: 7/96). ✍

The glowing incandescence of Austrian mid-baroque instrumental music could hardly be more
effectively demonstrated than in the choice of repertoire and the performances on this disc. The
harmonically sumptuous and tonally exotic programme is shared between the Vienna court musician,
Schmelzer, and his younger Bohemian contemporary, Biber. Few if any of the pieces here are new to
the catalogue but there are few others that match the feeling for tonal colour and expressive nuance
shown here by the Freiburg Baroque Orchestra Consort. The Schmelzer items have been selected from
a variety of sources, among them the *Duodena selectarum sonatarum* (1659), while the sonatas by
Biber belong to his first published work, the *Sonatae tam aris, quam aulis servientes* (1676). The menu
has been thoughtfully chosen, capitalizing upon the vivid contrasts that exist at the two extremes,
between the scintillating trumpet-dominated pieces by Biber, on the one hand, and Schmelzer's
affecting *Sonata sopra la morte Ferdinand III* on the other. Emperor Ferdinand was Schmelzer's
musically gifted employer, and his death in 1657 prompted not only this outstandingly beautiful piece
by his Hofkapellmeister but also a comparable impressive keyboard *Lamentation* by his court
organist, Froberger. This sonata is the most touching of Schmelzer's three elegiac pieces assembled
here, all of which however are harmonically distinctive and of sustained interest. Biber's *Sonatae tam
aris* are in the church sonata tradition and call to mind Schmelzer's *Sacro-profanus concentus musicus*
(1652). The first and last sonatas of the set, both included here, contain parts for two trumpets, as
does the Seventh Sonata, largely built upon a ground-bass. The Fourth and Tenth Sonatas, on the
other hand, call for a single trumpet, while the remaining two on the disc, the Sixth and Eighth, are
purely string textured. Violas play a significant role in all but one of them (No. 7), providing a vital
element in Biber's skilfully deployed and colourfully contrasted instrumental groupings. The Freiburg
musicians seem to revel in the wonderfully varied sonorities inherent in Biber's consort textures,
responding sympathetically to the composer's colourfully imaginative tonal palette. The sonatas with
trumpet are likely to have instant appeal but it is the more sorrowful utterances of Schmelzer which
make a deeper impression on the senses.

Biber Sonatae tam aris quam aulis servientes – No. 2 in D major; No. 3 in G minor; No. 5 in
E minor; No. 9 in B flat major.
Georg Muffat Armonico tributo – No. 2 in G minor; No. 5 in G major. **Freiburg Baroque
Orchestra Consort.** Deutsche Harmonia Mundi Ⓟ 05472 77303-2 (59 minutes: DDD: 10/94). ✍
Recorded 1993. 🔊🔊

This is a well-chosen programme of sonatas by Biber and Muffat. Biber is represented by four pieces from
his 1676 collection *Sonatae tam aris quam aulis servientes* ("Sonatas intended for use both at the altar
and at court"), Muffat by two sonatas, suites to all intents and purposes, from a set of five published
in 1682 under the title *Armonico tributo*. For sheer *élan*, the Freiburg Baroque Orchestra Consort have
no rivals. Their playing has an effective bite to it, the rhythms are taut and the sonorities rewarding. In
the Biber, above all, the instrumentalists seem fired by the music's fantasy and by the composer's
irresistible feeling for dance measures. They engage a harpsichord throughout and limit the remaining
continuo instruments to a cello and double-bass. Biber and Muffat heavies will require the complete
sets but readers who spread their affections more evenly are likely to be captivated by this anthology.

Biber Eight Sonatas for Violin and Continuo (1681) Sonata violino solo representativa in
A major. Sonata, "La Pastorella". Passacaglia for Solo Lute[n]. Mystery Sonatas – Passacaglia in
G minor[b]. **Romanesca** ([b]Andrew Manze, vn; [a]Nigel North, lte/theorbo; John Toll, hpd/org).
Harmonia Mundi Ⓟ HMU90 7134/5 (two discs: 127 minutes: DDD: 2/95). ✍ Recorded
1993-4. *Gramophone Award Winner 1995. Gramophone Editor's choice Selected by Sounds in
Retrospect.* 🔊🔊

Whilst the more famous *Mystery Sonatas* have quickly found friends with their touching cameo-
representations of the 15 Mysteries, the 1681 set is still largely unknown amongst players and listeners
alike. Yet what is immediately noticeable from this première recording of the sonatas is that Biber is
not only a legendary virtuoso, probably never bettered in the seventeenth or eighteenth centuries, but
one of the most inventive composers of his age: bold and exciting, certainly but also elusive, mercurial
and mysterious. The majority of the works comprise preludes, arias and variations of an unregulated
nature: improvisatory preludes over naked pedals and lucid arias juxtaposing effortlessly with
eccentric rhetorical conceits are mixed up in an unpredictable phantasm of contrast, and yet at its best
it all adds up to a unified structure of considerable potency. Whatever the philosophical key to Biber's
intangible and unstable world may be, Andrew Manze is the protagonist *par excellence* for music
which requires a notable degree of considered response to complement the adventurous spirit of the
virtuoso. In short, this is masterful playing in which Manze has enough confidence in his subject not
to over-characterize Biber's volatile temperament. Hence the preludes are often sweet and restrained

and yet often there is also a held-back, almost smouldering quality, which is skilfully pitched against the free-wheeling energy of the fast music. The range of super-sensitive nuance from Romanesca, as a whole, and Manze's distinctive virtuosity put this amongst the finest baroque chamber music discs to have appeared in recent years.

Additional recommendation ...

...Sonata violino solo representativa[a]. Mensa sonara. **Cologne Musica Antiqua / Reinhard Goebel** ([a]vn). Archiv Produktion Ⓕ 423 701-2AH (62 minutes: DDD: 11/89).

Biber Mystery Sonatas. **John Holloway** (vn); **Davitt Moroney** (org/hpd); **Tragicomedia** (Stephen Stubbs, lte/chitarrone; Erin Headley, va da gamba/lirone; Andrew Lawrence-King, hp/regal). Virgin Classics Veritas Ⓕ VCD7 59551-2 (two discs: 131 minutes: DDD: 5/91). ✐ Recorded 1989. *Gramophone* Award Winner 1991.   ⓖⓖ

Biber was among the most talented musicians of the late seventeenth century. He was a renowned violinist and his compositions, above all for the violin, are technically advanced and strikingly individual. The 15 *Mystery Sonatas* with their additional *Passacaglia* for unaccompanied violin were written in about 1678 and dedicated to Biber's employer, the Archbishop of Salzburg. Each Sonata is inspired by a section of the Rosary devotion of the Catholic Church which offered a system of meditation on 15 Mysteries from the lives of Jesus and His mother. The music is not, strictly speaking, programmatic though often vividly illustrative of events which took place in the life of Christ. All but two of the 16 pieces require *scordatura* or retuning of the violin strings; in this way Biber not only facilitated some of the fingerings but also achieved sounds otherwise unavailable to him. The Sonatas are disposed into three groups of five: Joyful, Sorrowful and Glorious Mysteries whose contrasting states are affectingly evoked in music ranging from a spirit reflecting South German baroque exuberance to one of profound contemplation. John Holloway plays with imaginative sensibility and he is supported by a first-rate continuo group whose instruments include baroque lute, chitarrone, viola da gamba, a 15-string lirone, double harp and regal.

Additional recommendation ...

...**Cologne Musica Antiqua / Reinhard Goebel** (vn). Archiv Produktion Ⓕ 431 656-2AH2 (two discs: 114 minutes: DDD: 10/91). ✐

Further listening ...

...Harmonia artificiosa – ariosa: diversi modi accordata. **Purcell Quartet / Elizabeth Wallfisch.** Chandos Chaconne CHAN0575/6 (11/94). ✐

...Harmonia artificiosa – ariosa. **Tafelmusik / Jeanne Lamon.** Sony Classical Vivarte SK 58920 (5/95). ✐

...Missa alleluja[ab]. *Coupled with* **Schmelzer** Vesperae sollennes[ab]. Sonata per Chiesa et Camera. Sacro-Profanus Concentus Musicus – Sonata XII. **Palestrina** Coelestis urbs Jerusalem. **Froberger** Fantasia II in A minor. **Anonymous** Gregorian Chant for the Dedication of a Church – Mass Propers[a]. Gregorian Chant for Vespers[a].[a]**Vienna Hofburgkapella Schola;** [b]**Concerto Palatino; Gradus ad Parnassum / Konrad Junghänel.** Deutsche Harmonia Mundi 05472 77326-2 (7/95). ✐

...Requiem in F minor. *Coupled with* **Valls** Missa Scala Aretina. **Sandrine Piau, Mieke van der Sluis** (sops); **Bouke Lettinga, David Cordier** (altos); **John Elwes** (ten); **Harry van der Kamp** (bass); **Netherlands Bach Society Choir and Baroque Orchestra / Gustav Leonhardt.** Deutsche Harmonia Mundi 05472 77277-2 (8/93). ✐

...Requiem a 15 in A major. Vesperae a 32[a]. Els Bongers, Anne Grimm (sops); Kai Wessel, [a]Peter de Groot (altos), [a]Marcel Reyans, Simon Davies (tens); René Steur (bass); Kees-Jan de Koning (bass); **Amsterdam Baroque Choir and Orchestra / Ton Koopman.** Erato 4509-91725-2 (9/94). ✐   ⓖ

...Arminio. Soloists; Salzburg Hofmusik / Wolfgang Brunner. CPO CPO999 258-2 (6/95). ✐   ⓖ

William Billings   American 1746-1800

Suggested listening ...

...The New-England Psalm-Singer. The Singing Master's Assistant. The Psalm-Singer's Amusement. The Suffolk Harmony. The Continental Harmony. The Lord is ris'n indeed. **His Majesties Clerkes / Paul Hillier.** Harmonia Mundi HMU90 7048 (10/92).

Gilles Binchois   French c1400-1460

Suggested listening ...

...Rondos and Ballades. *Coupled with* **Dufay** Rondeaux, Ballades and Lamentations. **Ensemble Gilles Binchois / Dominique Vellard.** Virgin Classics Veritas VC7 59043-2.   ⓖ

...Qui veut mesdire si mesdie. Amoureux suy et me vient toute joye. Adieu mon amoureuse joye. Ay douloureux disant helas. Magnificat secundi toni. Se la belle n'a le voloir. *Coupled with works by* **Anonymous, Bittering, Cardot, Dunstable, Fontaine, Johannes de Lymburga, Legrant, Machaut, Power** and **Velut. Gothic Voices / Christopher Page.** Hyperion CDA66783 (1/96). *See review in the Collections section; refer to the Index to Reviews.*

Ronald Binge

Suggested listening ...
...Saxophone Concerto[a]. Elizabethan Serenade. Scottish Rhapsody. Miss Melanie. Las Castañuelas. Madrugado. The Red Sombrero. Trade Winds. Faire Frou-Frou. String Song. The Watermill. Scherzo. The dance of the snowflakes. High Stepper. The Whispering Valley (with Silvia Cápová, pf). Venetian Carnival. Sailing by. [a]**Kenneth Edge** (sax); **Slovak Radio Symphony Orchestra, Bratislava / Ernest Tomlinson.** Marco Polo British Light Music 8 223515 (11/94).
...Elizabethan Serenade. The Watermill. *Coupled with works by* **Williams, Coates, Toye, Collins, Farnon, Baynes, Curzon, Lutz, Gibbs, White, Ketèlbey, Joyce, Ellis** and **Ancliffe New London Orchestra / Ronald Corp.** Hyperion CDA66868 (7/96). *See review in the Collections section; refer to the Index to Reviews.* **Gramophone** *Editor's record of the month.* Ⓖ

Sir Harrison Birtwistle

Birtwistle The Triumph of Time. Gawain's Journey. **Philharmonia Orchestra / Elgar Howarth.** Collins Classics Ⓕ 1387-2 (55 minutes: DDD: 7/93). Recorded 1993. ⒼⒼ
Gawain's Journey offers a substantial set of extracts from Birtwistle's opera *Gawain* (vocal lines allotted to instruments) which forms a convincing whole and reinforces the impression that this is one of the weightiest dramatic scores of this or any other age. It has the immediate, unmediated forcefulness so typical of Birtwistle. It may verge on the unremitting, but there's no mistaking the visceral theatrical power. In no sense is *The Triumph of Time* operatic, but its structure and material (which Birtwistle linked to the Bruegel engraving) is vividly dramatic, the sure-footed skill and economy of its gradual accumulation of tension and density still unsurpassed in Birtwistle's output – this triumphant return to the catalogue of a 1970s masterwork is cause for jubilation.

New review
Birtwistle Secret Theatre. Nenia: the Death of Orpheus[a]. Ritual Fragment. [a]**Rosemary Hardy** (sop); **Musikfabrik NRW / Johannes Kalitzke.** CPO Ⓕ CPO999 360-2 (52 minutes: DDD: 5/96). Text included. Recoded 1994-5.
Kalitzke and Musikfabrik NRW offer performances of great virtuosity and character. The two works they have chosen to go with *Secret Theatre* are an ideal introduction both to it and to Birtwistle's style. *Secret Theatre* is a powerful drama, with each instrument acting a part in it. The same is true of *Ritual Fragment*, but here the instrumental characters appear successively, each with its own tribute or reflection. *Nenia* is a grave monologue, one of a group of works that can be seen as 'studies' for Birtwistle's second opera, *The Mask of Orpheus*. *Nenia* and *Ritual Fragment* provide clues to the rite enacted in *Secret Theatre*, where the instruments not only step forward for monologues but also group themselves into parties or alliances, one concerned primarily with melodic material, the other with harmony. There are tensions, therefore, between solo and corporate statement, and mysterious but powerful forces drawing individual instruments from one group to another. All of which may sound dry, but the seamless argument is grippingly dramatic throughout. It is Birtwistle at his most compelling, and the players on this recording are obviously convinced of that. The two shorter pieces, both beautiful laments, are finely done. Rosemary Hardy is as virtuoso in her rapid alternation of words and non-verbal exclamations as she is moving in her cries of "Euridice!" and the gravity of her final narration. It is a pity that CPO have omitted four lines of the text from their booklet. The recording, however, is excellent.

New review
Birtwistle Tragoedia. Five Distances. Three Settings of Celan[a]. Secret Theatre. [a]**Christine Whittlesey** (sop); **Ensemble InterContemporain / Pierre Boulez.** DG Ⓕ 439 910-2GH (76 minutes: DDD: 9/95). Texts included. Recorded 1993.
We in the West are used to approaching music harmonically, but no one in their right mind would call Birtwistle a great harmonist – one doesn't rush to the piano to try and work out his chords (as one might with, say, Lutosławski, Knussen or Reich). Rhythm is much more important: repeated patterns that hold obsessively, change or decay, are superimposed so that they support or clash with one another, creating tensions and resolutions of their own – a parallel with Western harmonic thinking, but in effect quite different. Sonority is important too. In the earlier works, like *Tragoedia*, the up-down movements of the instrumental lines often feel more like changes in colour than significant intervals. In *Tragoedia* the results on occasions can be dry – the bare bones, with little flesh or sinew. But in this acutely focused performance a lot of it makes immediate sense. The actors in Birtwistle's tragedy may not be warmly, palpably human, but they are definitely enacting *something* – a drama for shadowy, skeletal forms, perhaps. Scenes like this might still take place on dark, deserted nights among the ruins of classical theatres. The two shorter works, *Five Distances* and *Three Settings of Celan*, show how much Birtwistle has changed since then. The polyphony can be denser, more active, but the lines themselves have also become more expressive. Of course it helps to have a singer like Christine Whittlesey, who not only gets the notes but understands the shape of the lines and their relation to the words. But it's the final work, *Secret Theatre*, that leaves the strongest and most

detailed impression. That sense of journeying, however strange or dream-like the territory, is very striking. The soloists of the Ensemble InterContemporain clearly relish the twists and turns of Birtwistle's lines, whether foreground or background. The recording offers clarity but not dryness, with colours and textures distinct but also nicely blended.

New review

Birtwistle Gawain. **Marie Angel** (sop) Morgan Le Fay; **Anne Howells** (mez) Lady de Hautdesert; **Richard Greager** (ten) Arthur; **Penelope Walmsley-Clark** (sop) Guinevere; **Omar Ebrahim** (bar) Fool; **Alan Ewing** (bass) Agravain; **John Marsden** (ten) Ywain; **François Le Roux** (bar) Gawain; **Kevin Smith** (alto) Baldwin; **John Tomlinson** (bass) Green Knight, Bertilak; **Chorus and Orchestra of the Royal Opera House, Covent Garden / Elgar Howarth.** Collins Classics Ⓕ 7041-2 (two discs: 136 minutes: DDD: 5/96). Notes and text included. Recorded live in 1994. *Gramophone Editor's choice. Selected by Soundings.*   Ⓖ

Gawain marks a climactic point in Birtwistle's output, combining dramatic strategies from his four earlier stage works with a clearer narrative than any of them and drawing together aspects of his musical language that he had been exploring in concert works for 15 years or more. It is an opera of compelling power and grandeur. Opera it most certainly is, and its magnificent opening gesture immediately promises that it will be an epic one. The First Act ends with the characteristic Birtwistle device of a fivefold cycle of the seasons, symbolically portraying Gawain's preparation for his confrontation with the Green Knight, while Act 2 turns on a threefold cycle of lullabies, hunting scenes and seductions in which he learns how few of the knightly virtues for which he is famed he in fact possesses. Another long-term constituent of Birtwistle's style is those long, sinuous, ranging lines that underlie so much of his music. The very opening gesture, a craggy descent, is one mode that it adopts here; another is the intense, often ornate, wide-spanning lyricism heard soon afterwards as Morgan Le Fay and Lady de Hautdesert begin their plot to subvert King Arthur's court with Gawain as their unwitting instrument. Morgan's lullabies in Act 2, each of them sinking Gawain deeper into enthralment, have a sinister beauty to them that is the very image of witchcraft. Indeed, although none of the characters in this fable is a rounded personality – *Gawain* is no *verismo* opera – each of them is boldly and tellingly portrayed.

It is an opera whose drama often takes place in the wonderfully rich and strange sounds of Birtwistle's orchestra: massive, striding bass-lines, whooping brass, the prominent cimbalom at times almost as central as it once was in Stravinsky's imagination. The solo singers must achieve extremes of intensity to stand out in relief. Among them John Tomlinson is in outstandingly noble voice as the Green Knight and François Le Roux, when not obliged to force, is moving in the title-role. Marie Angel is fearless though often bitingly shrill as Morgan, Anne Howells a voluptuous Lady de Hautdesert. The recording brings the voices forward, which helps comprehension of the text, but does not diminish Elgar Howarth's masterly control of the score's burnished splendours. The whole enterprise is a huge achievement, a worthy and commendably prompt recording of one of the most powerful operas of the late twentieth century.

Further listening ...

...Antiphonies[a]. Nomos[b]. An Imaginary Landscape[b]. [a]**Joanna MacGregor** (pf); [a]**Netherlands Radio Philharmonic Orchestra / Michael Gielen;** [b]**BBC Symphony Orchestra / Paul Daniel.** Collins Classics 1414-2 (12/94).

...Melencolia I[a]. Ritual Fragment. Meridian[b]. [b]**Mary King** (mez); [a]**Antony Pay** (cl); [b]**Michael Thompson** (hn); [b]**Christopher van Kampen** (vc); [a]**Helen Tunstall** (hp); [b]**London Sinfonietta Voices; London Sinfonietta / Oliver Knussen.** NMC NMCD009 (8/93).

...Endless Parade[a]. *Coupled with* **Blake Watkins** Trumpet Concerto. **Maxwell Davies** Trumpet Concerto. **Håkan Hardenberger** (tpt); [a]**Paul Patrick** (vib); **BBC Philharmonic Orchestra / Elgar Howarth.** Philips 432 075-2PH (6/91).   ⒼⒼ

...Earth Dances. **BBC Symphony Orchestra / Peter Eötvös.** Collins Classics 2001-2 (3/92). *See review in the Collections section; refer to the Index to Reviews.*   ⒼⒼ

Cesare Andrea Bixio   Italian 1898-1978

Suggested listening ...

...Mamma. Vivere. Parlami d'amore, Mariù. La mia canzone al vento, with a selection of Italian songs. **Luciano Pavarotti** (ten); **Andrea Griminelli** (fl); **Chorus and Orchestra / Henry Mancini.** Decca 411 959-2DH (8/84).

Georges Bizet   French 1838-1875

Bizet Symphony in C major. L'Arlésienne – Suites Nos. 1 and 2. **Academy of St Martin in the Fields / Sir Neville Marriner.** EMI Ⓕ CDC5 55118-2 (66 minutes: DDD: 8/94). Recorded 1992.
This effervescent youthful symphony is in excellent hands here. Vivacity and elegance are present in full measure, and one can only admire a violin section that can play the finale up to speed without hazard or apparent strain. Indeed, tempos are finely judged throughout. The first movement dances

agreeably and comes complete with its exposition repeat, the *Adagio*'s lovely oboe solo (which occurs twice) is coaxingly played by Celia Nicklin, who rightly earns a credit on the jewel-case, the scherzo bounds along in pastoral mood and the finale affirms *joie de vivre* in a manner hard to resist. The two suites from *L'Arlésienne* also come off well, conveying the vigour, colour and occasional peasant toughness of Bizet's incidental music to Daudet's play. The recording, made in EMI's Abbey Road Studio No. 1, is detailed and well balanced, complementing the stylish playing.

Additional recommendations ...

...Symphony. Jeux d'enfants – petite suite. **Debussy** Danse sacrée et danse profane. **Vera Badings** (hp); **Concertgebouw Orchestra / Bernard Haitink.** Philips Ⓕ 416 437-2PH (50 minutes: ADD: 10/86).

...Symphony[a]. L'Arlésienne – Suite No. 1[b]; Suite No. 2 (arr. Guiraud)[b]. [a]**French Radio National Symphony Orchestra,** [b]**Royal Philharmonic Orchestra / Sir Thomas Beecham.** EMI Ⓕ CDC7 47794-2* (65 minutes: ADD: 11/87). Ⓖ

...L'Arlésienne – Suites. Carmen – Suites Nos. 1 and 2. **Montreal Symphony Orchestra / Charles Dutoit.** Decca Ⓕ 417 839-2DH (73 minutes: DDD: 6/88).

...Symphony. **Britten** Simple Symphony, Op. 4. **Prokofiev** Symphony No. 1 in D major, Op. 25, "Classical". **Orpheus Chamber Orchestra.** DG Ⓕ 423 624-2GH (64 minutes: DDD: 1/89).

...Symphony. **Ravel** Ma mère l'oye. **Scottish Chamber Orchestra / Jukka-Pekka Saraste.** Virgin Classics Virgo Ⓑ VJ7 59657-2 (64 minutes: DDD: 12/91).

...Symphony. L'Arlésienne – Suites. **Lyon National Orchestra / Emmanuel Krivine.** Denon Ⓕ CO-75471 (70 minutes: DDD: 2/94).

...Symphony in C major. Roma. Patrie, Op. 19. **Toulouse Capitole Orchestra / Michel Plasson.** EMI Ⓕ CDC5 55057-2 (73 minutes: DDD: 5/95).

...L'Arlésienne – Suite No. 1. Carmen – Suite. **Saint-Saëns** Danse macabre, Op. 40. Samson et Dalila – Bacchanale. Le carnaval des animaux (with Olga Barabini, Mary Binney Montgomery, pfs). **Philadelphia Orchestra / Leopold Stokowski.** Biddulph mono Ⓜ WHL012* (72 minutes: ADD: 8/95).

Bizet Carmen. **Julia Migenes** (mez) Carmen; **Plácido Domingo** (ten) Don José; **Faith Esham** (sop) Micaëla; **Ruggero Raimondi** (bass) Escamillo; **Lilian Watson** (sop) Frasquita; **Susan Daniel** (mez) Mercédès; **Jean-Philippe Lafont** (bar) Dancairo; **Gérard Garino** (ten) Remendado; **François Le Roux** (bar) Moralès; **John Paul Bogart** (bass) Zuniga; **French Radio Chorus; French Radio Children's Chorus; French National Orchestra / Lorin Maazel.** Erato Ⓕ 2292-45207-2 (three discs: 151 minutes: DDD: 9/85). Notes, text and translation included. From NUM75113 (3/84). ⒼⒼⒼ

New review

Bizet Carmen. **Béatrice Uria-Monzon** (mez) Carmen; **Christian Papis** (ten) Don José; **Leontina Vaduva** (sop) Micaëla; **Vincent le Texier** (bass-bar) Escamillo; **Maryse Castets** (sop) Frasquita; **Martine Olmeda** (mez) Mercédès; **Franck Leguérinel** (bar) Dancaïre; **Thierry Trégan** (ten) Remendado; **Olivier Lallouette** (bass) Moralès; **Lionel Sarrazin** (bass) Zuniga; **Paul Renard** (spkr) Lillas Pastia; **Bordeaux CNR Children's Choir; Bordeaux Theatre Chorus; Bordeaux Aquitaine Orchestra / Alain Lombard.** Auvidis Valois Ⓕ V4734 (two discs: 142 minutes: DDD: 10/95). Notes, text and translation included. Recorded 1994.

With some justification, *Carmen* is reckoned to be the world's most popular opera. Its score is irresistible, its dramatic realism riveting, its sense of *milieu* unerring, though it has to be remembered that the work was not an immediate triumph. Too many recordings have blown up the work to proportions beyond its author's intentions but here Maazel adopts a brisk, lightweight approach that seems to come close to what Bizet wanted. Similarly Julia Migenes approaches the title part in an immediate, vivid way, exuding the gipsy's allure in a performance that suggests Carmen's fierce temper and smouldering eroticism, and she develops the character intelligently into the fatalistic person of the card scene and finale. Her singing isn't conventionally smooth but it is compelling from start to finish. Plácido Domingo has made the part of Don José very much his own, and here he sings with unstinting involvement and a good deal of finesse. Ruggero Raimondi is a macho Toreador though Faith Esham is a somewhat pallid Micaëla.

Any performance has to be considered on its own merits, but since competition on disc is so intense with a work like *Carmen*, there has to be something special to make it appear high on a list of recommendations. Having a French singer in the title-role is one of the advantages of the Auvidis set. Béatrice Uria-Monzon is a young singer who has been making her name in recent seasons. A full-bodied Mediterranean mezzo, her Carmen is bold and earthy, with thrilling contralto-like tone for such important moments as the "Tra-la-la" replies to her interrogators in Act 1. She handles the dialogue with Don José very well, before the Séguidille, in which she pretends that, like him, she is

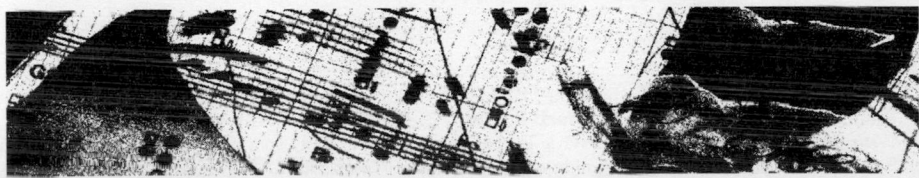

from Navarre (this is usually cut). This weight of voice rather tells against her where charm is concerned, with the "Chanson bohème" sounding haughty rather than festive. The version of *Carmen* used here reverts to spoken dialogue rather than the spurious recitatives. The singers all deal with this efficiently. Leontina Vaduva is a good Micaëla but Christian Papis's Don José isn't really a match for either of his leading ladies. In "Parle-moi de ma mère" he exhibits an unfortunate beat in the voice that makes it all sound too tragic – after all he should really just seem nostalgic and quite happy to be talking to his young visitor, although he can produce effective, soft notes, as at the end of "Là bas, là bas". One has nothing but sympathy for Carmen's preference for Vincent le Texier's Escamillo whose performance is the best among the other principals. For a quick summing-up, this is a well-recorded, authentically French *Carmen*, conducted with flair by Alain Lombard.

Additional recommendations ...

...**Soloists; Schoenberg Boys' Choir; Paris Opera Chorus; Berlin Philharmonic Orchestra / Herbert von Karajan.** DG Ⓕ 410 088-2GH3 (three discs: 170 minutes: ADD: 12/83).

...**Soloists; Les Petits Chanteurs de Versailles; French National Radio Chorus and Orchestra / Sir Thomas Beecham.** EMI Ⓕ CDS7 49240-2* (three discs: 161 minutes: ADD: 6/88).

...**Soloists; Ambrosian Singers; London Symphony Orchestra / Claudio Abbado.** DG Ⓕ 419 636-2GH3 (three discs: 157 minutes: 2/88).   Ⓖ

...**Soloists; Radio France Maîtrise and Chorus; French National Orchestra / Seiji Ozawa.** Philips Ⓕ 422 366-2PH3 (three discs: 159 minutes: DDD: 8/89).

...**Soloists; Manhattan Opera Chorus; Metropolitan Opera Children's Chorus and Orchestra / Leonard Bernstein.** DG Ⓕ 427 440-2GX3 (three discs: 160 minutes: ADD: 9/91).

...**Soloists; René Duclos Choir; Jean Pesneaud Children's Choir; Paris Opera Orchestra / Georges Prêtre.** EMI Ⓕ CDS7 54368-2 (two discs: 146 minutes: ADD: 5/92).   Ⓖ

Bizet Les pêcheurs de perles. **Barbara Hendricks** (sop) Leïla; **John Aler** (ten) Nadir; **Gino Quilico** (bar) Zurga; **Jean-Philippe Courtis** (bass) Nourabad; **Toulouse Capitole Chorus and Orchestra / Michel Plasson.** EMI Ⓕ CDS7 49837-2 (two discs: 127 minutes: DDD: 1/90). Notes, text and translation included. Recorded 1989.

Let a tenor and a baritone signify that they are willing to oblige with a duet, and the cry will go up for *The Pearl Fishers*. It's highly unlikely that many of the company present will know what the duet is about – it recalls the past, proclaims eternal friendship and nearly ends up in a quarrel – but the melody and the sound of two fine voices blending in its harmonies will be quite sufficient. In fact there is much more to the opera than the duet, or even than the three or four solos which are sometimes sung in isolation; and the EMI recording goes further than previous versions in giving a complete account of a score remarkable for its unity as well as for the attractiveness of individual numbers. It is a lyrical opera, and the voices need to be young and graceful. Barbara Hendricks and John Aler certainly fulfil those requirements, she with a light, silvery timbre, he with a high tenor admirably suited to the tessitura of his solos. The third main character, the baritone whose role is central to the drama, assumes his rightful place here: Gino Quilico brings genuine distinction to the part, and his aria in Act 3 is one of the highlights. Though Plasson's direction at first is rather square, the performance grows in responsiveness act by act. It is a pity that the accompanying notes are not stronger in textual detail, for the full score given here stimulates interest in its history. One of the changes made in the original score of 1863 concerns the celebrated duet itself, the first version of which is given in an appendix. It ends in a style that one would swear owed much to the 'friendship' duet in Verdi's *Don Carlos* – except that Bizet came first.

Additional recommendations ...

...**Soloists; Paris Opéra Chorus and Orchestra / Georges Prêtre.** Classics for Pleasure Ⓑ CD-CFPD4721 (two discs: 104 minutes: ADD: 10/91).

...**Soloists; Chorus and Orchestra of the Opéra-Comique, Paris / André Cluytens.** EMI mono Ⓜ CMS5 65266-2* (two discs: 107 minutes: ADD: 9/95).

Further listening ...

...Jeux d'enfants. *Coupled with* **Prokofiev** Peter and the wolf, Op. 67[a]. **Saint-Saëns** Le carnaval des animaux. [a]**Sir John Gielgud** (narr); **Royal Philharmonic Orchestra / Andrea Licata.** Tring International Royal Philharmonic Collection TRP046 (11/95).

...Jeux d'enfants. *Coupled with* **Saint-Saëns** Danse macabre, Op. 40. Le rouet d'Omphale, Op. 31. **Ibert** Divertissement. **Berlioz** Le carnaval romain, Op. 9. Le corsaire, Op. 21. **Paris Conservatoire Orchestra / Jean Martinon.** Decca The Classic Sound Ⓜ 448 571-2DCS (2/96).

...Djamileh. **Soloists; Bavarian Radio Chorus; Munich Radio Orchestra / Lamberto Gardelli.** Orfeo C174881A (4/89).

Boris Blacher   German 1903-1975

Suggested listening ...

...Alla marcia[a]. Dance Scenes[b]. Chiarina[a]. Partita, Op. 24[c]. Piano Sonatina, Op. 14 No. 2[d]. Drei Psalmen[e]. *Coupled with works by* **Shortall, Weill, B. Goldschmidt, Milhaud** and **Vaughan Williams** [e]**Michael Kraus** (ten); [d]**Sylvie Lechevalier**, [e]**Walter Moore** (pfs); [a]**Berlin Radio Symphony Orchestra**, [b]**London Philharmonic Orchestra / Noam Sheriff**; [c]**Poznan Philharmonic**

Orchestra / **Andrzej Borejko.** Largo 5130 (7/95). *See review in the Collections section; refer to the Index to Reviews.*

Christopher Blake
New Zealand 1949-

Suggested listening ...
...Till human voices wake us. *Coupled with works by* **A. Ritchie, A. Watson, Lilburn, Whitehead, Jenny McLeod, Farquhar, Pruden** and **Carr** Christopher Doig (ten); New Zealand Symphony Orchestra / **Kenneth Young.** Continuum (special price) CCD1073 (5/96). *See review in the Collections section; refer to the Index to Reviews.*

Howard Blake
British 1938-

Suggested listening ...
...Violin Concerto, "The Leeds"[a]. A Month in the Country – suite. Sinfonietta. [a]**Christiane Edinger** (vn); **English Northern Philharmonia / Paul Daniel.** ASV CDDCA905 (12/94).

Michel Blavet
French 1700-1768

Suggested listening ...
...Flute Concerto in A minor. *Coupled with* **Buffardin** Flute Concerto in E minor. **Boismortier** Five Sonatas for Cello, Viol, Bassoon and Continuo, Op. 26 – No. 6 in D major. **Corrette** Concerto comique 25. **Quentin** Flute Sonata in D major. Violin Concerto in A major. **Cologne Musica Antiqua / Reinhard Goebel.** Archiv Produktion 447 286-2AMA.
...Flute Sonatas: Op. 2 – No. 2 in D minor; No. 4 in G minor, "La lumague"; No. 5 in D major, "Lachauvet". Op. 3 – No. 2 in B minor; No. 6 in D major. **Masahiro Arita** (fl); **Wieland Kuijken** (bass viol); **Chiyoko Arita** (hpd). Denon Aliare CO-79550 (9/92).

Sir Arthur Bliss
British 1891-1975

Bliss Music for Strings. Pastoral: Lie Strewn the White Flocks[a]. [a]**Della Jones** (mez); [a]**Sinfonia Chorus; Northern Sinfonia / Richard Hickox.** Chandos Ⓕ CHAN8886 (61 minutes: DDD: 7/91). Text included. Recorded 1990.
Surely *the* disc with which to start a Bliss collection. Here is a pairing of two of the composer's very strongest works in sensitive, ideally disciplined accounts from the ever-responsive Northern Sinfonia under Richard Hickox. Brimful of fine invention as well as the most swaggeringly idiomatic (and technically demanding) writing, Bliss's athletic *Music for Strings* is a mightily impressive achievement: its enviable fluency and consummately argued progress mark it out as another in the long line of superb string works British composers have produced this century. It was first performed in 1935 at the Salzburg Festival by the strings of the Vienna Philharmonic (no less) under Sir Adrian Boult; suffice to report, Hickox draws playing of splendidly full-blooded tone and unanimous skill from his Tyneside group that would not disgrace even the string section of that same great orchestra. The classically-inspired idyll *Pastoral: Lie Strewn the White Flocks* dates from seven years earlier and constitutes perhaps the first fully characteristic example of Bliss's mature style. It's a most beguiling song cycle, limpidly scored for small choir, mezzo-soprano, flute, strings and timpani, and some of the individual numbers are hauntingly lovely, not least that ravishing setting of Robert Nichols's "The Pigeon Song" (with Della Jones a touchingly tender soloist). A valuable coupling, then, complemented by ideally warm-toned, transparent Chandos sonics throughout.

Further listening ...
...Piano Concerto, Op. 58[a]. March, Op. 99, "Homage to a Great Man". [a]**Philip Fowke** (pf); **Royal Liverpool Philharmonic Orchestra / David Atherton.** Unicorn-Kanchana Souvenir UKCD2029 (8/90).
...Cello Concerto[a]. The Enchantress[b]. Hymn to Apollo. [b]**Linda Finnie** (mez); [a]**Raphael Wallfisch** (vc); **Ulster Orchestra / Vernon Handley.** Chandos CHAN8818 (7/91).
...String Quartets – No. 1 in B flat major; No. 2. **Delmé Quartet.** Hyperion CDA66178 (11/89).
...Checkmate – Suite. *Coupled with* **Lambert** Horoscope – suite. **Walton** Façade – Suites Nos. 1 and 2. **English Northern Philharmonia / David Lloyd-Jones.** Hyperion CDA66436 (3/91). *Selected by Sounds in Retrospect.*
...A Colour Symphony. Checkmate – Suite. **Ulster Orchestra / Vernon Handley.** Chandos CHAN8503 (4/87).
...Checkmate – excerpts[b]. *Coupled with* **Rubbra** Symphony No. 5 in B flat major, Op. 63[a]. **Tippett** Little Music for Strings[c]. [a]**Melbourne Symphony Orchestra;** [b]**West Australian Symphony Orchestra;** [c]**Soloists of Australia /** [c]**Ronald Thomas;** [ab]**Hans-Hubert Schönzeler.** Chandos Collect CHAN6576 (6/92).

...Morning Heroes[a]. Investiture Antiphonal Fanfares[b]. Prayer of St Francis of Assisi[c]. [a]**Brian Blessed** (narr); [ac]**East London Chorus;** [a]**Harlow Chorus;** [a]**East Hertfordshire Chorus;** [ab]**London Philharmonic Orchestra / Michael Kibblewhite.** Cala CACD1010 (2/93).

Marc Blitzstein   American 1905-1964

New review
Blitzstein The Airborne Symphony[a]. Native Land – Dusty sun[b]. [a]**Charles Holland** (ten); **Walter Scheff** (bar); [a]**Robert Shaw** (narr); [a]**Victor Chorale;** [a]**New York City Symphony Orchestra / Leonard Bernstein** ([b]pf). RCA Victor Gold Seal mono Ⓜ 09026 62568-2* (59 minutes: ADD: 7/95). Texts and translations included. Recorded 1946.   Ⓖ

Blitzstein's style – at least as represented here – might be described as 'American-eclectic', looking sideways to Copland and Harris, and forward to Bernstein (a personal friend) and, very occasionally, John Adams. A serving member of the US Air Force during the Second World War (and stationed in the UK), Blitzstein was temporarily relieved of his usual duties so that he could finish his "big symphony, on flight" which, although initially performed only "for an assortment of majors and colonels", was eventually given its full première on April 1st, 1946 by the New York City Symphony under Bernstein's baton. *The Airborne* isn't so much a symphony as a notably macho symphonic oratorio, with a narrator (in this case, a particularly fervent Robert Shaw), two male singers, and a large chorus and orchestra. Each of the three movements is sub-divided into either four or five sections: the first movement traces the history of flight and documents the Wright brothers' early triumphs; the second deals more specifically with images of war (Hitler's strutting armies, bombed cities, the personal reverie of a British pilot), while the third recalls aircrews preparing for aborted sorties, a bombardier writing to his loved one (the song "Emily"), a bombing raid and – last but by no means least – Blitzstein's own stern warning to future generations. Musically, there is more action than substance and a suggestion or two of Walton's *Belshazzar's Feast* and Vaughan Williams's *A Sea Symphony*. The caricatures of the Nazis (with "Ay-dolf" [*sic*] Hitler prominent among them) are pertinent and biting, the character portraits knowingly written and the scoring appropriately cinematic. There are tender moments too, most specifically in "The Open Sky", and the work is consistently catchy and tuneful. Youngsters keen on war stories or the idea of air combat will probably love it. Although various sections of the printed libretto are missing from the original recording, it remains a gripping period piece, one that is interpreted here with real conviction and fairly well recorded for the time. *Native Land* is a kind of spiritual used in a scene involving two sharecroppers, one white, the other black, who were murdered after requesting an extra ten cents for their cotton. Walter Scheff and Bernstein deliver a touching performance. Some of the 78 sides sound better than others, and there is occasional 'popping' from the closely recorded singers; but taken overall, this is a most valuable addition to Leonard Bernstein's discography.

Further listening ...
...Juno – I wish it so. No for an Answer – In the clear. Reuben, Reuben – Never get lost. *Coupled with works by* **Sondheim, Weill** and **Bernstein** **Dawn Upshaw** (sop); **orchestra / Eric Stern.** Elektra Nonesuch 7559-79345-2 (12/94). *See review in the Collections section; refer to the Index to Reviews.*   ⒼⒼ

Ernest Bloch   Swiss/American 1880-1959

Bloch America[a]. Concerto grosso No. 1[b]. **Patricia Michaelian** (pf); [a]**Seattle Symphony Chorale and Orchestra / Gerard Schwarz.** Delos Ⓕ DE3135 (61 minutes: DDD: 8/94). Text included. Recorded 1993.   Ⓖ

Ernest Bloch's "Epic Rhapsody for Orchestra", *America,* is a warming musical flight across the history of the United States, and uses the anthem of the same name as a leitmotif that helps bind English, American Indian and Jewish-style themes into a homogeneous and hugely accessible whole. There are three variegated movements, each a dramatic tone-poem reflecting such universal ideas as "Struggle and Hardships" or "Hours of Joy – Hours of Sorrow" (the second movement's subtitle), with the third visiting the world of jazz and culminating in a full-throated choral celebration of the anthem itself. However, Bloch's 'programme' is fairly specific. *America* might be best described as a great film score that never was, a highly emotive thanksgiving from a man who had himself only recently arrived in his new home, with tender references to such perennial favourites as *John Brown's Body* and *Dixie*. There are also veiled references to other of Bloch's works, including *Schelomo* and the delightful *Concerto grosso* that Gerard Schwarz programmes as *America*'s coupling. Demonstration standard sound.

Additional recommendations ...
...America. **American Concert Choir; Symphony of the Air / Leopold Stokowski.** Vanguard Classics Ⓕ 08.8014.71* (53 minutes: ADD).
...Concerto grosso[a]. **Barber** Adagio for Strings, Op. 11. **Grieg** Holberg Suite, Op. 40. **Puccini** Crisantemi (arr. string orchestra). [a]**Irit Rob** (pf); **Israel Chamber Orchestra / Yoav Talmi.** Chandos Ⓕ CHAN8593 (62 minutes: DDD: 8/88).

...Concerti grossi Nos. 1 and 2. **Q. Porter** Ukrainian Suite. **San Diego Chamber Orchestra / Donald Barra.** Koch International Classics Ⓕ 37196-2 (52 minutes: DDD: 12/94).

Bloch Symphony in C sharp minor. Schelomo[a]. [a]**Torleif Thedéen** (vc); **Malmö Symphony Orchestra / Lev Markiz.** BIS Ⓕ CD576 (78 minutes: DDD: 5/93). Recorded 1990-92. *Gramophone Editor's choice.*

Ernest Bloch's early symphony is an endearing and at times impressive showcase for a young composer (he was 23) endowed by nature and nurture with all the gifts save individuality (though there are hints in the later movements that that too is on the way). He can write impressively strong, expansive melodies, develop them with real ingenuity and build them into monumental climaxes. Climax-building, indeed, is what young Bloch seems most interested in at this stage of his career, that and a love for all the rich contrasts of colour and texture that a big orchestra, imaginatively used, can provide. He is so very good at his craft, so adept at pulling out still more stops when you thought there could hardly be any left, so sheerly and likeably clever that one is scarcely ever made impatient by the occasional feeling that this or that movement could have ended two or three minutes earlier. It's a pleasure, too, to listen for fulfilled echoes of that youthful exuberance in the mature 'biblical rhapsody' *Schelomo*. Just as Lev Markiz adroitly avoids any impression of over-padded grossness in the symphony, so he and his fine soloist find more than richly embroidered oriental voluptuousness in this portrait of King Solomon; there is gravity and even poignancy to the music as well, and Thedéen's subtle variety of tone colour gives the work shadow and delicacy as well as richness. Typically BIS reproduce a truthful aural equivalent of the modern concert hall experience.

Additional recommendations ...

...Schelomo. **Georges Miquelle** (vc); **Eastman Rochester Orchestra / Howard Hanson.** Mercury Ⓜ 432 718-2MM (63 minutes: ADD: 11/91).

...Schelomo[a]. **R. Strauss** Don Quixote, Op. 35[b]. **Emanuel Feuermann** (vc); **Philadelphia Orchestra /** [a]**Leonard Stokowski,** [b]**Eugene Ormandy.** Biddulph mono Ⓜ LAB042* (58 minutes: ADD: 12/91).

...Schelomo. *Coupled with works by* **S. Albert** and **Bartók** Yo-Yo Ma (vc/); **Baltimore Symphony Orchestra / David Zinman.** Sony Classical Ⓕ SK57961 (78 minutes: DDD: 3/95). *See review under S. Albert; refer to the Index to Reviews.*   Ⓖ

Further listening ...

...Violin Concerto. Baal Shem. *Coupled with* **Serebrier** Momento psicológico. Poema elegíaca. **Michael Guttman** (vn); **Royal Philharmonic Orchestra / José Serebrier.** ASV CDDCA785 (5/92).

...Three Jewish Poems. Two Last Poems ... (Maybe ...)[a]. Evocations, [a]**Alexa Still** (fl); **New Zealand Symphony Orchestra / James Sedares.** Koch International Classics 37232-2 (9/94).

...Piano Quintets Nos. 1 and 2. **American Chamber Players.** Koch International 37041-2.

...Baal Shem. *Coupled with works by* **Bartók, Debussy, Ives, Schubert,Bach, Brahms, Corelli, Debussy, Dvořák, Falla, Hubay, Kodály, Lalo, Milhaud, Mussorgsky** and **Schubert** Joseph Szigeti (vn); Andor Foldes (pf). Biddulph mono LAB070/71* (7/94). *See review in the Collections section; refer to the Index to Reviews.*   ⒼⒼ

...Sacred Service[a]. *Coupled with* **Ben Haim** The Sweet Psalmist of Israel[b] **Foss** Song of Songs[c]. [a]**Robert Merrill** (bar); [b]**Sylvia Marlowe** (hpd); [c]**Jennie Tourel** (mez); **New York Metropolitan Synagogue Choir;** [a]**New York Philharmonic Orchestra / Leonard Bernstein.** Sony Classical Bernstein Royal Edition SM2K47533 (11/92).

Karl-Birger Blomdahl   Swedish 1916-1968

Suggested listening ...

...Symphonies – No. 1; No. 2; No. 3, "Facetter". **Swedish Radio Symphony Orchestra / Leif Segerstam.** BIS CD611 (8/94).

Robert Bloom   American 1908-

Suggested listening ...

...Requiem. Narrative. *Coupled with works by* **Barlow, Corigliano** and **Wilder** Humbert Lucarelli (ob); **Brooklyn Philharmonic Orchestra / Michael Barrett.** Koch International Classics 37187-2 (7/94). *See Review under Wilder; refer to the Index to Reviews.*

John Blow   British 1649-1708

New review

Blow God spake sometime in visions. How doth the city sit solitary. The Lord is my shepherd. God is our hope and strength. I beheld and lo! a great multitude. Turn thee unto me, O Lord. Blessed is the man. Lift up your heads. O Lord I have sinned. O give thanks unto the Lord. O Lord, thou hast searched me out. Cry aloud and spare not. Lord, who shall dwell in thy tabernacle. I said in the cutting off of my days **Robin Blaze** (alto); **Joseph Cornwell, William Kendall** (tens); **Stephen**

Varcoe, Stephen Alder (bars); **Winchester Cathedral Choir / David Hill; The Parley of Instruments / Peter Holman.** Hyperion Ⓔ CDA67031/2 (two discs: 116 minutes: DDD: 3/96). ✒ Texts included. Recorded 1995.

In choosing a range of Blow's best and most representative anthems, Peter Holman and David Hill have had quite a task on their hands: Blow was even more prolific than Purcell in this domain. They have sensibly cast their critical eyes over those works written in the 'golden' age of Charles II, several of whose reputations go before them. The dignity and sobriety of the fine coronation anthem *God spake sometime in visions* is a joy to behold and it is given a grand and spacious reading here. David Hill, ever the choral director to sustain and shape a line, is peerless in the opening paragraph. Here, as in other distinguished works like *I beheld and lo!*, the success of these performances is determined by deft recognition of the structural strengths and solecisms of Blow's music. As with a number of Purcell's symphony anthems, Blow cannot always find the exit and needs a helping hand to get back on track. Hill has a breezy approach in such circumstances which serves him well, as in the overlong, if imaginative *O give thanks unto the Lord*. He is helped too by a pleasing integration between soloists, choir and instruments – caused as much by the sensitivity of soloists as adept recording – which ensures that occasional formal disparity does not find an ally in the textural isolation of 'groups' from one another. Blow's particular attraction is the disarming tunefulness of *The Lord is my shepherd* in the tradition of airiness which Pelham Humfrey had introduced to the chapel following his French sojourn, and touchingly performed by excellent soloists (even if the work does rather tail off towards the end). So, too, the idiomatic simplicity of expression of *Turn thee unto me*, where the fine treble soloist is complemented by a cathedral choir whose feel for the work's gentle and intimate contours has a resigned elegance. In a similar vein is the tormented *O Lord I have sinned*, a work which has a distinctive Purcellian flavour with its chromatic inflexions and unpredictable contrapuntal movement. Yet it fails to plumb the depths as in the similar type of piece which became something of a Purcell speciality. Indeed, for all Blow's quality there are several works here that just miss the mark despite their distinctive place in English Restoration musical life. Whether or not such a state of affairs warrants two discs is arguable, but there is no doubt that this is an important addition to Hyperion's English Orpheus series.

Blow Venus and Adonis. **Catherine Bott** (sop) Venus; **Michael George** (bass) Adonis; **Libby Crabtree** (sop) Cupid; **Julia Gooding** (sop) Shepherdess, Grace 1; **Andrew King** (ten) Shepherd 1; **Simon Grant** (bass) Shepherd 2, Huntsman 3, Grace 3; **Christopher Robson** (alto) Shepherd 3, Huntsman 1, Grace 2; **Paul Agnew** (ten) Huntsman 2; **Westminster Abbey School Choristers; New London Consort / Philip Pickett.** L'Oiseau-Lyre Ⓔ 440 220-2OH (57 minutes: DDD: 7/94). ✒ Notes and text included. Recorded 1992. *Gramophone Editor's choice.*   Ⓖ

This recording reveals Blow's opera (and lamentably one of only two real 'all-sung' dramas to emerge from England in the Restoration period), to be a work of rare quality and pathos with Philip Pickett at his most luminous. Whilst Charles Medlam and London Baroque (listed below) take a robust and homespun view of the overture, Pickett has his listener mentally prepared from the outset for the opera's solemn denouement. The noble and eloquent opening (with some minor ensemble infelicities) sets the scene in more ways than one since Pickett is not content to see the Prologue's traditional machinations undermine the cultivated expression he believes this work merits. Consequently, the introduction of *Venus and Adonis* emerges sumptuously from Blow's skilful preparations, notably in the beautifully sung chorus refrain "In these sweet groves" and an ethereal Act Tune of three recorders which delivers the doomed lovers to their first intimate exchanges. Catherine Bott is the most telling and sensual Venus imaginable, her singing always captivating in its tonal variety and emotional nuance. Her relationship with Adonis is never mannered but tense and simmering, and in its chilling realism allows the listener to experience the brutal psychology of an anonymous adaptation. (Story line: Venus insists that Adonis goes hunting and the former suffers incessant grief when he meets his match with an Aedalian boar.) Michael George, as Adonis, plays his part thoughtfully in the striking immediacy of the tragedy, elegantly shaping his lines with a prescient tinge of melancholy before he is led in wounded at the start of Act 3.

Additional recommendation ...

...**Soloists; Chorus; London Baroque / Charles Medlam.** Harmonia Mundi Musique d'abord Ⓑ HMA190 1276 (50 minutes: DDD: 9/88). ✒

Further listening ...

...Awake, my lyre. Salvator mundi. Stay, gentle Echo. Poor Celadon, he sighs in vain. St Cecilia's Day Ode, "Begin the song" – Music's the cordial of a troubled heart. Go, perjur'd man. Help, Father Abraham. Chloe found Amintas. Whilst on Septimnius's panting breast. Gloria patri, qui creavit nos. Paratum cor meum. Sing ye Muses. Sonata in A[a]. Ground in G minor[a]. **Red Byrd;** [a]**The Parley of Instruments.** Hyperion CDA66658 (1/94). ✒

...No more the dear, lovely nymph's no more. The Self-banished. Lovely Selina, innocent and free. O turn not those fine eyes away. Fairest work of happy nature. Flavia grown old. O that mine eyes would melt into a flood. O mighty God, who sit'st on high. Sabina has a thousand charms. O all the torments, all the cares. The Queen's Epicedium, "No, Lesbia, no, you ask in vain". A Choice Collection of Lessons[a]: Suite No. 1 in D minor; Suite No. 3 in A minor. Prelude in G major[a]. Morlake Ground[a]. Grounds: G minor[a]; C major[b]. Voluntary in G minor[c]. **John Mark Ainsley** (ten); **Paula Chateauneuf** (theorbo/gtr); **Timothy Roberts** ([a]spinet/[b]hpd/[c]org). Hyperion CDA66646 (10/93). ✒ *Gramophone Editor's choice.*

Felix Blumenfeld

New review
Blumenfeld Etude in A major, Op. 2 No. 1. Three Etudes, Op. 3. Valse-Etude in F major, Op. 4.
Etude, Op. 14, "Sur mer". Etude de concert in F sharp minor, Op. 24. Two Etudes-Fantaisies,
Op. 25. Two Etudes, Op. 29. Etude for the left hand in A flat major, Op. 36. Four Etudes, Op. 44.
Etude-Fantaisie in F minor, Op. 48. Etude in F sharp major, Op. 54. **Daniel Blumenthal** (pf).
Marco Polo Ⓔ 8 223656 (73 minutes: DDD: 12/95). Recorded 1993.

Blumenfeld's *Etude for the left hand* is the only one of his 18 studies to remain in the repertoire,
occasionally surfacing from pianists with a masochistic taste for the super-virtuoso repertoire. So how
good it is to hear the complete set, each and every one packed with luscious Slavonic melody entwined
in ferocious and frequently double-note figurations. Blumenfeld (born in Russia in 1863) was a
formidable pianist and teacher (his pupils included Horowitz) and he set out with a vengeance to
challenge and ensnare even the most athletically equipped players. Daniel Blumenthal, working his way
through some thorny and not always grateful stretches of the repertoire, plays with an imposing breadth,
even if he lacks the sort of magical technical and poetic resource to lift such music, untrammelled, from
its sometimes mundane origins. In the D flat *Etude* (Op. 3 No. 1) he relishes the graceful melody set in
its glittery arpeggio surround, and he storms the impassioned declamation of Op. 3 No. 3 with a full-
blooded sense of rhetoric. He is at his best in the dramatic duet of Op. 44 No. 2 as well as in the greater
richness and harmonic adventure of all the later studies. Cautious listeners should first try tracks 12-18,
where the music acquires its greatest individuality and transcends the influence of Chopin and a wide
variety of Russian romantic composers (notably Glazunov and Lyapunov). The recordings are warmer
than usual from this source and all lovers of high-born virtuosity will want to have this disc.

Luigi Boccherini

Boccherini Cello Concertos – No. 1 in E flat major, G474; No. 2 in A major, G475; No. 3 in
D major, G476; No. 4 in C major, G477; No. 5 in D major, G478; No. 6 in D major, G479;
No. 7 in G major, G480; No. 8 in C major, G481; No. 9 in B flat major, G482; No. 10 in
D major, G483; No. 11 in G major, G573; No. 12 in E flat major. **David Geringas** (vc); **Orchestra
da Camera di Padova e del Veneto / Bruno Giuranna.** Claves Ⓔ CD50-8814/16 (three discs:
204 minutes: DDD: 7/89). Recorded 1988.
Boccherini Cello Concertos[a] – No. 3 in D major, G476; No. 7 in G major, G480; No. 9 in B flat
major, G482. Concert aria – Se d'un amor tiranno, G557[b]. [b]**Marta Almajano** (sop); **Limoges
Baroque Ensemble / Christophe Coin** (vc). Auvidis Astrée Ⓔ E8517 (62 minutes: DDD: 4/94). ✍
Recorded 1993.

"Boccherini: 12 Concerti per il Violoncello" proclaims the cover, a little ambitiously, perhaps – for
Boccherini probably didn't compose that many. David Geringas has had to exercise a little ingenuity
to reach this figure (two of the concertos are almost certainly spurious), but it was probably worth the
effort, and his set is a thoroughly enjoyable one in its undemanding way. His intonation is virtually
perfect, even high up on the A string, his passage-work is clean, his rhythms are crisp, and he produces
(not using a period instrument) a light but pleasingly resonant tone. Listen in particular to the slow
movements (such as those of G477 or G483) for eloquence and neatly timed detail. Geringas provides
his own cadenzas, including one that quotes Mozart. A very pleasing release. The recording quality
and balance are exemplary. Christophe Coin throws off in the deftest fashion the typical Boccherinian
filigree figuration, the little ornamental flourishes perfectly placed and timed, the numerous
stratospheric excursions above the treble stave sweet-toned and delicate. And with it he shows a
command of Boccherini's style, affectionately graceful, sometimes with a faintly quizzical air. The
tone of Coin's instrument is light and translucent, and with this small orchestra the sound in the solos,
which are anyway lightly accompanied, is particularly sweet: in the first movement of G482 (the
concerto known from the Grützmacher version) the unassuming handling of the virtuoso writing has
a special kind of charm and the rather grander manner called for in the D major work G476 is also
very happily caught, not without a hint of the romantic at times, for Coin is no austere stylist. The
aria that completes his disc is a large-scale duet for cello, in its full concerto manner, and soprano; the
lines are full of eloquent appoggiaturas and there is some beguiling duetting for the voice and the
instrument. Marta Almajano has a big, clear top register and plenty of drama to her singing.

Additional recommendations ...
...Nos. 4 and 6-8. **Anner Bylsma** (vc); **Concerto Amsterdam / Jaap Schröder.** Teldec Das Alte Werk
Ⓜ 9031-77624-2 (61 minutes: ADD: 7/93).
...No. 9. *Coupled with works by* **Bach, Kodály, Dohnányi, Haydn, Schumann, Saint-Saëns,
Dvořák, Fauré, Milhaud** and **Prokofiev** János Starker (vc); Philharmonia Orchestra / Carlo
Maria Giulini, Walter Susskind. EMI mono/stereo Ⓜ CZS5 68485-2* (six discs: 398 minutes:
ADD: 12/95). *See review in the Collections section; refer to the Index to Reviews.*

Boccherini Symphonies – No. 4 in D minor, G506, "La casa del diavolo" (Op. 12); No. 4 in
F major, G512 (Op. 12); C minor, G519 (Op. 41). **Academy of Ancient Music / Christopher
Hogwood.** L'Oiseau-Lyre Ⓕ 436 993-2OH (58 minutes: DDD: 2/95). ✔ Recorded 1992.
In this issue of three Boccherini symphonies by the Academy of Ancient Music, the more incisive
edge of the orchestra's period instruments offers a vivid expression of the music's dramatic content.
In *La casa del diavolo* (G506), for example, the AAM match the radiance of the German Academy
(listed below) in the opening *Allegro* and gentle pathos in the second movement, but crisper, clearer
textures in the finale create a more chilling representation of the music's diabolical character. The
AAM's stylish response to Boccherini's imaginative rhythms and inventively varied textures is
delightfully apparent in the F major Symphony, where the finale's sudden diversion into a minuet is
deftly handled. The four-movement C minor Symphony is the most expansive and truly 'symphonic'
of the three works recorded here. The AAM's taut control of the opening movement's dialogue
between various instrumental groupings, the engagingly pastoral tone in the *Lentarello*, the suitably
rustic minuet and trio and astonishing brilliance in the tarantella-like finale, produce a genuinely
compelling result. These fresh, vigorous accounts are attractively presented in resonant recorded
sound.

Additional recommendation ...

...Symphonies, Volumes 3-6. **German Chamber Academy, Neuss / Johannes Goritzki.** CPO
Ⓕ CPO999 173/6-2 (four discs, oas: 55, 61, 49 and 52 minutes: DDD: 1/94). *CPO999 173-2 –*
Op. 12: No. 4 in D minor, G506; No. 5 in B flat major, G507; No. 6 in A major, G508. *CPO999
174-2 –* Op. 21: No. 1 in B flat major, G493; No. 2 in E flat major, G494; No. 3 in C major, G495;
No. 4 in D major, G496; No. 5 in B flat major, G497. *CPO999 175-2 –* Op. 21: No. 6 in A major,
G498. Op. 35: No. 1 in D major, G509; No. 2 in E flat major, G510; No. 3 in A major, G511.
CPO999 176-2 – Op. 35: No. 4 in F major, G512; No. 5 in E flat major, G513; No. 6 in B flat
major, G514. Op. 37: No. 1 in C major, G515.

New review
Boccherini Six String Quartets, G201-6 (Op. 32) – No. 1 in E flat major, G201; No. 2 in E minor,
G202; No. 3 in D major, G203; No. 4 in G minor, G204; No. 5 in D minor, G205; No. 6 in
A major, G206. **Esterházy Quartet** (Jaap Schröder, Alda Stuurop, vns; Wiel Peeters, va; Wouter
Moeller, vc). Teldec Das Alte Werk Ⓜ 4509-95988-2 (two discs: 93 minutes: ADD: 10/95). From
EK6 35337 (12/77). Recorded 1976. *Gramophone Editor's choice.*
Among Boccherini's 100 or so string quartets, this particular set, written in 1780, is probably the most
polished and most original – quite stunningly original, really, when you consider that these pieces pre-
date Haydn's Op. 33 set and all of Mozart's mature quartets. The range of expression they embody is
astonishing: most of it sombre and pathetic, conveyed with characteristic refinement and nuance, but
there are spirited and witty movements too, and a couple of quite rumbustious ones. You have only
to listen to the first of the quartets to be charmed – an E flat work, its opening movement very gentle
and touching in its curiously epigrammatic way (and played with great delicacy of timing), a minuet
whose trio's subtle wit is a particular delight, a C minor *Grave* of some power and an ebullient finale
with typically ingenious handling of quartet textures. There is a remarkable, deeply pathetic slow
movement to open the E minor Quartet (No. 2); a vivacious *Allegro vivo*, full of sparkling rhythms
and dialogues and with much high cello writing, to open the next; an elegantly worked-out first
movement to the G minor work, No. 5; while No. 6 is a joy throughout with its dancing first
movement, its highly chromatic second, its bagpipe-textured minuet and its brilliant finale. These
Dutch players, who made this recording 20 years ago, have a true feeling for the temper of
Boccherini's music, especially its delicate half-lights and its hints of ambiguous emotion, as their
sensitive timing and shading repeatedly shows. This pair of CDs is quite outstanding and you should
certainly buy them.

Boccherini String Quintets, Op. 11 – No. 4 in F minor, G274; No. 5 in E major, G275; No. 6 in
D major, G276. **Smithsonian Chamber Players** (Marilyn MacDonald, Jorie Garrigue, vns;
Anthony Martin, va; Anner Bylsma, Kenneth Slowik, vcs). Deutsche Harmonia Mundi
Ⓕ RD77159 (67 minutes: DDD: 4/92). Recorded 1988.✔   Ⓖ
Boccherini was a virtuoso cellist and often played together with a family string quartet in Madrid and
the experience was obviously a very pleasant one, for he wrote 100 quintets for two violins, viola and
two cellos. He was never at a loss for ideas: the quintets are richly varied in form and texture, the latter
enhanced by Boccherini's intimate knowledge of the techniques and sound-qualities of the bowed-
string instruments. Many of us know the famous Minuet – but how many are familiar with the work
from which it comes? The Quintet in E, the fifth of the six Quintets of his Op. 11 (1775), of which it
is the third movement, is one of those in this recording. The bucolic Quintet in D, *dello l'uccelería*,
("The aviary") is a cyclic work with bird-song, shepherd's pipes and hunting sounds. If Boccherini
was, as Giuseppe Pupo described him, "the wife of Haydn", his music has the charm, grace and poise
of the best wives, and there is nothing wrong with that"! The Smithsonian Players play like good
Italians, which none of them is, and are superbly recorded in this irresistibly attractive album. They
all use Stradivarius instruments, producing clear sounds and textures such as may have been heard in
Boccherini's time.

Boccherini Cello Sonatas – No. 2 in C minor, G2b[b]; No. 4 in A major, G4[a]; No. 10 in E flat major, G10[a]; No. 17 in C major, G17[a]; No. 23 in B flat major, G565[b]. **Richard Lester** (vc); [a]**David Watkin** (vc continuo); [b]**Chi-Chi Nwanoku** (db). Hyperion Ⓟ CDA66719 (67 minutes: DDD: 1/96).

Richard Lester's slightly impetuous playing of these sonatas seems to capture very happily their character: their somewhat wayward invention, their sense of being formalized versions of a cellist's improvisations. The momentary hesitancies hint at the player-composer who is deciding as he goes which of the ideas in his mind to try out next. Yet beneath it is a strong rhythm and a very sure compositional technique. The music is very high lying: the cellist has prolonged spells in high thumb positions with quite rapid passagework, and these Lester executes with great brilliance and crispness – there is just one passage, in the finale of the C major work, where accuracy of intonation momentarily eludes him, but otherwise one cannot imagine playing of greater exactitude. The opening movement of that sonata is a particularly fine piece, with its pensive moments and its sudden flights of fancy; there is an eloquent central *Largo* and a dashing, witty finale. The E flat work has jaunty syncopations, the A major a first movement of particular brilliance and again there is an intensely expressive slow movement. The final sonata here is the B flat work that was evidently the model for the outer movements of the famous Boccherini-Grützmacher Concerto – it sounds vastly better without the late-romantic harmonizations of the concerto version and with the curious array of tempo changes in the finale that Grützmacher ironed out. Lester's bowing is vigorous, his tone warm and sharply defined with very little vibrato. Usually these sonatas are accompanied by a keyboard but here the practice, undoubtedly very common in Boccherini's day, of using another string instrument is preferred. In two sonatas a double-bass is used: the effect is a bit gruff, with something of a chasm between top and bottom when the cello is in its upper reaches. The two cellos are much more persuasive, especially when the second is as supportively played as it is here.

Additional recommendation ...
...No. 2[a]; No. 8 in B flat major, G8[b]; No. 9 in F major, G9[c]; No. 9 in G major, G15[e]; No. 10[d]. Six Fugues, G73 – No. 2 in F major; No. 3 in B flat major; No. 5 in A major[f]. **Anner Bylsma**, [abdef]**Kenneth Slowik** (vcs); [bce]**Bob van Asperen** (fp). Sony Classical Vivarte Ⓟ SK53362 (77 minutes: DDD: 3/94). ☞

Further listening ...
...Symphonies – D major, G490; C major, G491; C major, G523. **German Chamber Academy, Neuss / Johannes Goritzki.** CPO CPO999 084-2 (12/94).

...Boccherini Edition, Volumes 1-5. **Soloists; Petersen Quartet; New Berlin Chamber Orchestra / Michael Erxleben** (vn). Capriccio (5/93) available as follows: *Volume 1 – 10 450:* String Sextets, Op. 23 – No. 1 in E flat major, G454; No. 3 in E major, G456; No. 4 in F minor, G457; No. 6 in F major, G459. *Volume 2 – 10 456:* Sextets (Divertimentos), Op. 16 – No. 1 in D major, G461; No. 4 in E flat major, G464; No. 5 in A major, G465; No. 6 in C major, G466. *Volume 3 – 10 457:* Symphonies, Op. 37 – No. 1 in C major, G515; No. 3 in D minor, G517; No. 4 in A major, G518. *Volume 4 – 10 458:* Symphonies – C minor, Op. 41, G519; D major, Op. 42, G520; D major, Op. 43, G521; D minor, Op. 45, G522. *Volume 5 – 10 451:* String Quartets – D major, Op. 15 No. 1, G177; G minor, Op. 24 No. 6, G194; A major, Op. 39, G213; F major, Op. 64 No. 1, G248.

...String Sextets, Op. 23 – No. 1 in E flat major, G454; No. 2 in B flat major, G455; No. 5 in D major, G458. **Ensemble 415.** Harmonia Mundi HMC90 1478 (6/94). ☞

...Guitar Quintets – No. 1 in D minor, G445; No. 2 in E major, G446; No. 3 in B flat major, G447; No. 4 in D major, G448; No. 5 in D major, G449; No. 6 in D major, G450; No. 7 in E minor, G451; No. 9 in C major, "La ritrata di Madrid", G453. **Pepe Romero** (gtr); **Academy of St Martin in the Fields Ensemble.** Philips 438 769-2PM2 (4/94).

...Guitar Quintets – No. 5 in D major, G449[a]; No. 7 in E minor, G451[b]. String Quintet in A major, G308 (Op. 20 No. 2)[c]. [ab]**David Starobin** (gtr); **Pina Carmirelli**, [a]**Joseph Genualdi**, [b]**Philip Setzer**, [c]**Michaela Paetsch** (vns); [ab]**Philipp Naegele**, [c]**Toby Hoffman** (vas); [a]**Marcy Rosen**, [b]**Peter Wiley**, [c]**Ramon Bolipata**, [c]**Gary Hoffman** (vcs). Sony Classical SMK47298 (9/92).

...Piano Quintets, Op. 56 – No. 1 in E minor, G407; No. 2 in F major, G408; No. 5 in D major, G411. **Patrick Cohen** (fp); **Quatuor Mosaïques.** Auvidis Astrée E8518 (4/94). ☞   Ⓖ

...Piano Quintets, Op. 57 – No. 2 in B flat major, G414; No. 3 in E minor, G415; No. 6 in C major, G418. **Patrick Cohen** (fp); **Quatuor Mosaïques.** Auvidis Astrée E8721 (12/92). ☞

...String Quintets – Op. 13 No. 4 in D minor, G280. Op. 31 No. 2 in G major, G326. Op. 60 No. 3 in A major, G393. Op. 62 No. 5 in D major, G401. **Petersen Quartet; Ulrich Knorzer** (va); **Guido Schiefen** (vc). Capriccio 10 452 (4/94).

...String Quintets[a] – Op. 30 No. 6 in C major, "La musica notturna delle strade di Madrid", G324. Op. 36 No. 6 in F major, "Quintetto dello Scacciapensiero", G336. String Quartet in G major, Op. 44 No. 4, "La Tiranna", G223[b]. Duet for Two Violins in E flat major, "La bona notte", G62. **Mayumi Seiler, Silvia Walch** (vns); [ab]**Diemut Poppen** (va); [ab]**Richard Lester**, [a]**Howard Penny** (vcs). Capriccio 10 453 (4/94).

...Oboe Quintets – No. 1 in G major. No. 2 in F major. No. 3 in D major. No. 4 in A major. No. 5 in E flat major. No. 6 in D minor. **Lajos Lencsés** (ob); **Parisii Quarte.** Capriccio 10 454 (4/94).

...Stabat mater, G532 (1781 version)[a]. String Quintet in C minor, G328 (Op. 31 No. 4). [a]**Agnès Mellon** (sop); **Ensemble 415.** Harmonia Mundi HMC90 1378 (9/92). ☞

Jerry Bock

Suggested listening ...
...She Loves Me. **Original 1994 London revival cast.** First Night CASTCD44.

Léon Boëllmann

Suggested listening ...
...Piano Quartet in F minor, Op. 10[a]. Piano Trio in G major, Op. 19. **Béla Bánfalvi** (vn); [a]**János Fejérvári** (va); **Károly Botvay** (vc); **Ilona Prunyi** (pf). Marco Polo 8 223524 (11/93).
...Deuxième Suite, Op. 27. 12 Pièces, Op. 16. Suite gothique, Op. 25. **Patrice Caire** (org). REM Editions REM311053 (7/89).
...Suite gothique, Op. 25. *Coupled with works by* **Guilmant, Vierne, M-A. Charpentier, Langlais, Bonnet, de Maleingreau** and **Widor** Simon Lindley (org). Naxos 8 550581 (3/93).
See review in the Collections section; refer to the Index to Reviews.

Georg Böhm

Böhm Suites – No. 1 in C minor[a]; No. 2 in D major; No. 6 in E flat major; No. 8 in F minor[a]. Prelude, Fugue and Postlude in G minor. Capriccio in D major. Wer nur den lieben Gott lässt walten. Ach wie nichtig, ach wie flüchtig. **Gustav Leonhardt** (hpd/[a]clavichord). Sony Classical Vivarte Ⓕ SK53114 (63 minutes: DDD: 9/93). 🖉 Recorded 1992.   Ⓖ
Georg Böhm was one of the leading German organists of his day and his craft is brilliantly reflected in this disc of his keyboard music. At the heart of the recital are two chorale *partite* on the famous Lutheran hymns, *Wer nur den lieben Gott lässt walten* and *Ach wie nichtig, ach wie flüchtig.* These consist of sets of seven and eight variations, respectively, and are intended for harpsichord rather than organ. Leonhardt's beautifully spoken account of the variations, clear-textured, eloquently phrased and animated in delivery, is one of the greatest delights in the recital; but throughout the programme you cannot fail to admire the sheer nobility of statement and the refinement of his taste. These are qualities, admittedly, which you find to a greater or lesser extent in all Leonhardt's work but when they are placed at the service of music with which he seems to have a close personal affinity then the performances enter the realms of magic. The disc is admirably recorded and well documented.
Additional recommendation ...
...No. 1; No. 3 in E flat major; No. 4 in F major; No. 5 in F minor; No. 11 in E flat major. Partitas Nos. 1-10. Prelude, Fugue and Postlude in G minor. Capriccio in D major. **Rinaldo Alessandrini** (hpd). Auvidis Astrée Ⓕ E8526 (68 minutes: DDD: 8/95). 🖉

François Boieldieu

New review
Boieldieu Harp Concerto in C major.
Parish Alvars Harp Concerto in G minor, Op. 81.
Viotti (arr. Nordmann) Adagio non troppo in C minor. **Marielle Nordmann** (hp); **Franz Liszt Chamber Orchestra / Jean-Pierre Rampal.** Sony Classical Ⓕ SK58919 (61 minutes: DDD: 10/95). Recorded 1993.
Boieldieu's instrument was the piano. However, in late-eighteenth-century France, the harp was much in favour and he took a marked interest in it, one product of which was his Harp Concerto (*c*1895). It takes the form of the classical concerto of the time and the writing for the harp is 'pianistic'; the harp was then regarded as a viable substitute for the piano, particularly as an accompanying instrument, with the approval of no less than Marie-Antoinette herself. Viotti's concertos were all written for the violin but several were reworked (not all by the same arranger) as piano concertos; the *Adagio non troppo* in this recording is based on Daniel Steibelt's arrangement of Concerto No. 19 as a piano concerto, the solo part being adapted for the harp by Marielle Nordmann. Once again the writing is pianistic and the musical language poses no serious problems in making the transition. Both of these works have great charm. After Erard's invention of the double-action harp in 1811 the instrument became more versatile (but also more difficult for a non-playing composer to write freely for!) and a succession of harp-virtuoso-composers appeared, ready and able to take advantage of the new possibilities. Parish Alvars, an Englishman taught by Frenchmen, was the father of modern harp technique, complete with its battery of special effects. His is a full-blown romantic concerto, in which the (again) pianistic writing recalls Berlioz's description of Parish Alvars as "the Liszt of the harp". Nordmann's eloquent performances, Rampal's refined control of the orchestra, and the crystal-clear and well-balanced recording, leave nothing to be desired – except the possession of this most attractive disc.
Further listening ...
...Le Calife de Bagdad. **Soloists; Camerata de Provence Chorus and Orchestra / Antonio de Almeida.** Sonpact SPT93007 (9/94).

Joseph Bodin de Boismortier   French 1689-1755

Suggested listening ...
...Five Sonatas for Cello, Viol, Bassoon and Continuo, Op. 26 – No. 6 in D major. *Coupled with*
   Blavet Flute Concerto in A minor. **Buffardin** Flute Concerto in E minor. **Corrette** Concerto
   comique 25. **Quentin** Flute Sonata in D major. Violin Concerto in A major. **Cologne Musica**
   Antiqua / Reinhard Goebel. Archiv Produktion 447 286-2AMA. ☞
...Sonata in G minor, Op. 34 No. 1. *Coupled with works by* **Leclair** and **Corrette** Florilegium
   Ensemble; Scott Pauley (theorbo). Channel Classics CCS7595 (12/95). ☞ *See review under*
   Leclair; refer to the Index to Reviews.

Arrigo Boito   Italian 1842-1918

Boito Mefistofele. **Cesare Siepi** (bass) Mefistofele; **Mario del Monaco** (ten) Faust; **Renata Tebaldi**
   (sop) Margherita; **Floriana Cavalli** (sop) Elena; **Lucia Danieli** (mez) Marta, Pantalis; **Piero De**
   Palma (ten) Wagner, Nereo; **Chorus and Orchestra of the Santa Cecilia Academy / Tullio Serafin.**
   Decca Grand Opera Ⓜ 440 054-2DMO2* (two discs: 141 minutes: ADD: 4/94). Notes, text and
   translation included. From SXL2094/6 (6/59). Recorded 1958.
This recording has in Siepi a real Italian bass with a fine sense of line and a genuine enjoyment of
Boito's words. Phrases that are often merely snarled are here truly sung, and Siepi's is the only devil
to suggest in the quartet that he is trying to seduce Martha, and that he will very probably succeed.
There is incisiveness and grain there, too, to add menace to his suavity. Tebaldi gives one of the best
accounts of "L'altra notte" on record, strongly sung and very touching in its suggestion of grieving
guilt. Del Monaco sings "Dai campi, dai prati" without the slightest acknowledgement of its poetry,
but the splendour of the sound and his instinctive feeling for legato have their own allure, and they
give nobility to his finely phrased "Giunto sul passo estremo". The recording doesn't allow Serafin to
make a sonic spectacular of the outer scenes, but his care for Boito's often rather old-fashioned
cantabile, his quirky rhythms and orchestral colours is scrupulous throughout.
Further listening ...
...*See also the* **Great Singers at the Maryinsky Theatre** *review in the Collections section; refer*
   to the Index to Reviews. Nimbus NI7865 (3/95).

William Bolcom   American 1938-

Suggested listening ...
...Violin Sonata No. 2. *Coupled with works by* **MacMillan, Copland, Schnittke** and **Dresher**
   Maria Bachmann (vn); **Jon Klibonoff** (pf). Catalyst 09026 62668-2 (5/95). *See review in the*
   Collections section; refer to the Index to Reviews.   Ⓖ

Joseph Bonnal   French 1880-1944

Suggested listening ...
...Paysages Euskariens. *Coupled with works by* **Bach, Langlais, B. Ferguson** and **Dupré** Roger
   Sayer (org). Priory PRCD495 (4/96). *See review in the Collections section; refer to the Index to*
   Reviews.

Guillaume Boni   French died c1594

Suggested listening ...
...Rossignol mon mignon. Las! sans espoir. Quand je dors. Ha, bel accueil. Comment au départir.
   Coupled with works by **Regnard, J. de Castro, Monte** and **Rippe** Fantasie II. **Clément**
   Janequin Ensemble / Dominique Visse (alto). Harmonia Mundi HMC90 1491 (2/95). *See review in*
   the Collections section; refer to the Index to Reviews.

Joseph Bonnet   French 1884-1944

Suggested listening ...
...Pièces nouvelles, Op. 7 – No. 1, Clair de lune; No. 2, Etude de concert; No. 3, Pastorale; No. 4,
   Caprice héroïque. *Coupled with* **Dupré** Three Preludes and Fugues, Op. 36. **Peeters** Aria,

Op. 51. Concert Piece, Op. 52*a*. Elégie, Op. 38. Preludium, Canzona e Ciacona, Op. 83. **Jane Watts** (org). Priory PRCD377 (8/94).

…Romance sans paroles. *Coupled with works by* **Guilmant, Vierne, M-A. Charpentier, Langlais, de Maleingreau, Boëllmann** and **Widor Simon Lindley** (org). Naxos 8 550581 (3/93). *See review in the Collections section; refer to the Index to Reviews.*

Giovanni Bononcini
Italian 1670-1747

Suggested listening …

…Cantata e duetti[a] – Gia la stagion d'amore; Lasciami un sol momento; Misero pastorello; Siedi Amarilli mia. Sonata for Cello and Continuo in A minor. Sonata for Two Violins and Continuo in D minor. **Il Seminario Musicale / Gérard Lesne** ([a]alto). Virgin Classics Veritas VC5 45000-2 (12/94). ✍   **Ⓖ**

…Polifemo – Respira, alma, respira … Dove sei, dove t'ascondi; Non soffrirà, mai Circe … Pensiero di vendetta[a]. Cefalo e Procride – Cintia, il tuo nome invoco … Sacro dardo, in te confido; Numi del ciel pietosi … Bella auretta[a]. *Coupled with works by* **Torell, Ariosti, Corelli** and **Steffani** [a]**Ann Monoyios** (sop); **Berlin Barock Compagney.** Capriccio 10 459 (10/95). ✍ *See review in the Collections section; refer to the Index to Reviews.*   **Ⓖ**

Alexander Borodin
USSR 1833-1887

Borodin Symphonies – No. 1 in E flat major; No. 2 in B minor; No. 3 in A minor. Prince Igor – Overture; Dance of the Polovtsian Maidens; Polovtsian Dances[ab]. String Quartet No. 2 in D major – Notturno (orch. N. Tcherepnin). In the Steppes of Central Asia[b]. Petite Suite (orch. Glazunov). [a]**Torgny Sporsén** (bass); **Gothenburg Symphony** [a]**Chorus and Orchestra / Neeme Järvi.** DG Ⓕ 435 757-2GH2 (two discs: 148 minutes: DDD: 9/92). Items marked [b] from 429 984-2GH (3/91), others new to UK. Recorded 1989-91.   **Ⓖ**

While it is possible to imagine performances of even greater power and finesse in this strangely unfashionable repertoire, Järvi's Borodin set is arguably the best to have appeared in recent years. The extravagant layout means we get not just the symphonies but a rich supplement of orchestral works, including even the *Petite Suite* as arranged by Glazunov. Another rarity, Nikolay Tcherepnin's orchestration of the famous *Notturno* will astonish those familiar with the chaste original: Tcherepnin transforms it into an exotic Scriabin-like tableau, almost as remote from Borodin as its kitschy *Kismet* mutation. The more recognizable *Steppes* are negotiated with ample eloquence and the *Prince Igor* excerpts score by including a brief contribution from the great Khan himself, reminding us of the music's original operatic context. The main works are equally persuasive. The First Symphony emerges here as far more than a dry-run for the Second. Järvi plays the music for all its worth, with DG's big, resonant sound serving to boost the symphonic credentials of the piece. The unfinished Third is also tougher and more dramatic than usual, no mere pastoral reverie in Järvi's interventionist view. The Second Symphony is rather different, suitably epic and yet unusually long-drawn and thoughtful. Thus, the *Scherzo* is bubbling but sensibly articulate, while the *Andante* is daringly broad with a superbly sensitive horn solo.

Additional recommendations …

…No. 2. In the Steppes of Central Asia. Prince Igor – Overture; March; Dance of the Polovtsian Maidens; Polovtsian Dances. **John Alldis Choir; National Philharmonic Orchestra / Loris Tjeknavorian.** RCA Victor Silver Seal Ⓑ VD60535(64 minutes: ADD: 8/77).

…Nos. 1-3. **CSR Symphony Orchestra, Bratislava / Stephen Gunzenhauser.** Naxos Ⓢ 8 550238 (76 minutes: DDD: 8/91).

…No. 1. No. 3 (cptd Glazunov). Prince Igor – Overture (orch. Glazunov); Polovtsian March (orch. Rimsky-Korsakov). **Russian State Symphony Orchestra / Evgeni Svetlanov.** RCA Victor Red Seal Ⓕ 09026 61674-2 (72 minutes: DDD: 1/94).

…Nos. 1 and 2. In the Steppes of Central Asia. **Royal Philharmonic Orchestra / Vladimir Ashkenazy.** Decca Ⓕ 436 651-2DH (71 minutes: DDD: 8/94).

…Prince Igor – Overture[a]. No. 2[b]. *Coupled with works by* **Liadov, Shostakovich** and **Tchaikovsky Hallé Orchestra /** [a]**Leslie Heward,** [b]**Constant Lambert.** Dutton Laboratories mono Ⓜ CDAX8010* (67 minutes: ADD: 2/95).

…No. 2[a]. **Tchaikovsky** Manfred Symphony, Op. 58[b]. **Philharmonia Orchestra / Paul Kletzki.** Testament mono Ⓕ SBT1048* (78 minutes: ADD: 3/95).

…In the Steppes of Central Asia. *Coupled with works by* **Bach, Mozart, Schubert** and **Berlioz Louis Zimmerman, Ferdinand Hellmann** (vns); **Concertgebouw Orchestra / Willem Mengelberg.** Pearl mono Ⓜ GEMMCD9154* (76 minutes: ADD: 3/96).

Borodin String Quartets – No. 1 in A major; No. 2 in D major. **Borodin Quartet** (Mikhail Kopelman, Andrei Abramenkov, vns; Dmitri Shebalin, va; Valentin Berlinsky, vc). EMI Ⓕ CDC7 47795-2 (66 minutes: DDD: 5/88). From EMI Melodiya ASD4100 (3/82). *Gramophone Award Winner 1983.*   **ⒼⒼ**

These quartets are delightful music, and they are played here by the aptly-named Borodin Quartet with a conviction and authority that in no way inhibits panache, spontaneity and sheer charm. Doubtless the most popular music of Borodin and the other members of the Russian 'Five' will always be their colourful orchestral and stage music, but no CD collector should ignore these chamber works. Their style derives from a mid-nineteenth-century Russian tradition of spending happy hours in music-making at home and also from the refreshing musical springs of folk-song. This performance offers not only first-rate playing from artists who 'have the music in their blood' but also a warm and convincing recorded sound.

Additional recommendations ...

...No. 2ª. **Shostakovich** String Quartet No. 8 in C minor, Op. 110ª. **Tchaikovsky** String Quartet No. 1 in D major, Op. 11ᵇ. ªBorodin Quartet; ᵇGabrieli Quartet. Decca Ⓜ 425 541-2DM (76 minutes: ADD: 5/90).

...No. 2. **Glazunov** Five Novelettes, Op. 15. **Tchaikovsky** String Quartet No. 1 in D major, Op. 11. **Hollywood Quartet.** Testament mono Ⓕ SBT1061* (80 minutes: ADD: 8/95).

Borodin Prince Igor. **Mikhail Kit** (bar) Igor; **Galina Gorchakova** (sop) Yaroslavna; **Gegam Grigorian** (ten) Vladimir; **Vladimir Ognovenko** (bass) Prince Galitzky; **Bulat Minjelkiev** (bass) Khan Kontchak; **Olga Borodina** (mez) Kontchakovna; **Nikolai Gassiev** (ten) Ovlour; **Georgy Selezniev** (bass) Skula; **Konstantin Pluzhnikov** (ten) Eroshka; **Evgenia Perlasova** (mez) Nurse; **Tatyana Novikova** (sop) Polovtsian Maiden; **Kirov Opera Chorus and Orchestra / Valery Gergiev.** Philips Ⓕ 442 537-2PH3 (three discs: 209 minutes: DDD: 4/95). Notes, text and translation included. Recorded 1993. *Selected by Sounds in Retrospect.* Ⓖ

Borodin's limited time to devote to composition meant that many of his works often took years to complete. *Prince Igor* was no exception; even after 18 years of work it remained unfinished at his death in 1887, and it was finally completed by Rimsky-Korsakov and Glazunov. Borodin's main problem with *Prince Igor* was the daunting task of turning what was principally an undramatic subject into a convincing stage work. In many ways he never really succeeded in this and the end result comes over more as a series of epic scenes rather than a musical drama. Despite this, however, one is nevertheless left with an impression of a rounded whole, and it contains some of Borodin's most poignant and moving music, rich in oriental imagery and full of vitality. Curious things happen long before the official surprises of this vitally fresh *Prince Igor*, not least in the Overture, where Gergiev takes the horn's beautiful melody at a very slow pace. No doubt it would be different in a concert performance, but Gergiev is anxious to prepare us for the weighty events which follow and his particular point with the theme is to relate it to its place in the opera as the heart of Igor's great aria. There, in league with the bass-baritonal timbre of Gergiev's prince, Mikhail Kit, it solemnly underlines the fact that this is an aria of potency frustrated, sung by a hero who spends most of the opera in captivity; and that is further emphasized by a second aria which no listener will ever have heard before. It is the most significant of the passages discovered among Borodin's papers, rejected by Rimsky-Korsakov in his otherwise sensitive tribute to Borodin's memory but specially orchestrated for this recording by Yuri Faliek.

The other problem with the *Prince Igor* we already know is the way that Act 3 rather weakly follows its much more imposing Polovtsian predecessor. Gergiev obviates both that, and the problem of too much time initially spent in Igor's home town of Putivl, by referring to a structural outline of Borodin's dating from 1883 which proposes alternating the Russian and Polovtsian acts. In the theatre, we might still want the famous Polovtsian *divertissement* as a centrepiece; but on the recording the new order works splendidly, not least because Gergiev is at his fluent best in the scenes of Galitzky's dissipation and Yaroslavna's despair, now making up the opera's Second Act and no weak sequel to the exotica of Kontchak's entertainment. While Borodina executes Kontchakovna's seductive chromaticisms with astonishing breath control and focus of tone, Bulat Minjelkiev's Kontchak is a little too free and easy, at least in comparison with Ognovenko's perfectly gauged Galitzky, a rogue who needs the extra rebellion music of this new version to show more threatening colours. There's just the right degree of relaxation, too, about his drunken supporters Skula and Eroshka. It takes two Russian character-singers to make sense of this pair – "with our wine and our cunning we will never die in Russia", they tell us truthfully – and their comical capitulation on Igor's return wins respect for Borodin's daring happy-end transition here. It's beautifully paced by Pluzhnikov (rather strained by the awkward vocal writing, not inappropriately), Selezniev and their conductor, and crowned by a choral cry of joy which brings a marvellous rush of tearful adrenalin. That leaves us with Gorchakova, so touching in Yaroslavna's first aria – and her way is paved with a wonderful sense of atmosphere from the Kirov strings – but not always projecting the text very vividly and clearly not at her best in the big scena of the last act. Still, in terms of long-term vision, orchestral detail and strength of ensemble, Gergiev is far ahead of Tchakarov on Sony Classical, the only serious contender.

Additional recommendations ...

...**Soloists; Sofia National Opera Chorus; Sofia Festival Orchestra / Emil Tchakarov.** Sony Classical Ⓕ S3K44878 (three discs: 210 minutes: DDD: 6/90). Ⓖ

...Prince Igor (Act 3 omitted). Songs – Those people; Song of the dark forest; From my tears; The queen of the sea; The beauty no loves me; The magic garden; Arabian melody; The Fisher-maiden; Listen to my song, little friend; The sleeping princess; Arrogance; The sea; Why art thou so early, dawn? There is poison in my songs; The false note; For the shores of thy far native land. **Boris Christoff** (bass); **Soloists; Chorus and Orchestra of the National Opera Theatre, Sofia / Jerzy**

Semkov; [b]Lamoureux Concerts Orchestra / Georges Tzipine. EMI Studio Ⓜ CMS7 63386-2 (three discs: 203 minutes: ADD: 6/90).

Further listening ...

...The false note. The sea princess. *Coupled with* **Rimsky-Korsakov** The octave, Op. 45 No. 3. The clouds begin to scatter, Op. 42 No. 3. Of what I dream in the quiet sky, Op. 40 No. 3. Enslaved by the rose, the nightingale, Op. 2 No. 2. In spring, Op. 43 – No. 1, The lark sings louder; No. 2, Not the wind, blowing from the heights. **Mussorgsky** What are words of love to you?. Night. **Balakirev** 20 Songs – The bright moon; My heart is torn; Song of Selim; When I hear thy voice. Three Forgotten Songs – Thou art so captivating; Spanish song. 10 Songs – Over the lake; I loved him. **Cui** I remember the evening. 25 Songs, Op. 57 – No. 11, "You" and "Thou"; No. 17, The statue of Tsarskoie Selo; No. 25, Desire. Ici-bas. I touched the bloom lightly, Op. 49 No. 1. It's over. **Olga Borodina** (mez); **Larissa Gergieva** (pf). Philips 442 780-2PH (8/95).

Pietro Borrono da Milano   Italian fl. 1530-1540

Suggested listening ...

...Pavana chimata la Desparata. Tocha tocha la Canella. Pavana la Gombertina. Saltarello chiamato el Mazolo. Two saltarellos. Fantasia. *Coupled with works by* **Francesco Milano, Ripa** and **Dall'Aquila** Paul O'Dette (lte). Harmonia Mundi HMU90 7043 (10/95). 🖙 *See review in the Collections section; refer to the Index to Reviews.*   Ⓖ

Sergei Bortkiewicz   Austrian/USSR 1877-1952

Suggested listening ...

...Piano Concerto No. 1 in B flat major, Op. 16. *Coupled with* **Arensky** Piano Concerto in F minor, Op. 2. Fantasia on Russian Folksongs, Op. 48. **Stephen Coombs** (pf); **BBC Scottish Symphony Orchestra / Jerzy Maksymiuk.** Hyperion CDA66624 (3/93). *See review under Arensky; refer to the Index to Reviews.*

Dmitry Bortnyansky   Ukrainian 1751-1825

New review

Bortnyansky Choral Concertos – No. 4, Make a joyful noise unto the Lord; No. 6, Glory be to God in the highest; No. 15, Come o ye people; No. 27, I cried unto God with my voice; No. 32, Lord, make me know mine end; No. 34, Let God arise. Te Deum. The Hymn of the Cherubim No. 7. **St Petersburg Glinka State Choir / Vladislav Chernushenko.** Teldec Das Alte Werk Ⓜ 4509-93856-2 (70 minutes: DDD: 4/95). Texts and translations included.

Bortnyansky was one of the Russians sent off to Italy by Catherine the Great to learn their trade as opera composers. Of his operas, *The Falcon*, at any rate, has a certain charm; but it is for his church music that he is best known. These pieces, many of them so-called 'Sacred Concertos', once formed the staple diet of Russian churches, to the considerable despair of later composers. These included Tchaikovsky, who was very bored at being made by his publisher to work on them for a complete edition. "Commonplace trifles", he sniffed, declaring that a selection would be preferable. Here is a selection, very well sung, and conducted with a sympathetic hand, and showing why Tchaikovsky was irritated. If Tchaikovsky was suspicious, Berlioz loved these pieces. The pieces are strongly Italian-influenced in their polyphonic writing, and Russian almost only in their use of strong choral sonorities. Tchaikovsky was interested in something closer to the authentic Orthodox tradition. Yet he and others, including Rachmaninov, were influenced willy-nilly by Bortnyansky, and with the present growth of interest in Russian church music there is a case for hearing these works, which are not exactly commonplace nor trifling. They include a *Cherubic Hymn* (one which Tchaikovsky, whatever he may have said, is known to have rehearsed with his choir); otherwise the seven pieces are concertos. That is to say, they are cast in several movements in response to the dictates of the text. So the first here recorded, *Make a joyful noise*, has a fast movement followed by an *Adagio*, an *Allegro moderato*, an *Andante* and then an *Allegretto* finale. The last is a big setting of the *Te Deum* for double chorus. It is attractive music, lying somewhere between the Orthodox and Catholic worlds.

Additional recommendation ...

...Te Deum. **Plainchant** Seventeenth-century Russian Liturgy. **Moscow Patriarchal Choir / Anatoly Grindenko.** Opus 111 Ⓕ OPS30-79 (63 minutes: DDD: 4/94).

Further listening ...

...Many years. *Coupled with* **Sariyev** The Lord, our God. **Chesnokov** Come, let us entreat Joseph, Op. 9 No. 9. Bless the Lord, o my soul, Op. 27 No. 1. Joyous light, Op. 9 No. 21. Let us, mystically representing the Cherubim. Praise ye the name of the Lord in heaven. **Kastal'sky** Liturgy of St John Chrysostom. **Anonymous** Russian Orthodox Chant: Easter Stikhiras. From my youth. Stikhira to the Russian Holymen. **Bolshoi Theatre Children's Choir / Andrey Zaboronok.** Collins Classics 1443-2 (7/95).

Marco Enrico Bossi
Italian 1861-1925

Suggested listening ...
...Stunde der Wehie, Op. 132 No. 4. Stunde der Freude, Op. 132 No. 5. *Coupled with* **Petrali** Messe solennelle – Gloria. **Galliera** Venerdi Santo dal "Trittico". **Bettinelli** Toccata Fantasia. **Ambrosi** Messa. **Luigi Benedetti** (org). Priory PRCD427 (4/95).
...Pièce héroïque in D minor, Op. 128. Scherzo in D minor, Op. 49 No. 2. *Coupled with works by* **Batiste, Dubois, Dupré, Jolivet, Lefébure-Wély, Lemare** and **Saint-Saëns** Christopher Herrick (org). Hyperion CDA66457 (9/91). *See review in the Collections section; refer to the Index to Reviews.* ❻❻❻

Giovanni Bottesini
Italian 1821-1889

Suggested listening ...
...Ero e Leandro – Prelude. Concertino in C minor[a]. Il diavolo della notte – Sinfonia. Passione amorose[ac]. Elegie in D[a]. Ali Babà – Overture. Duo concertant on themes from Bellini's "I puritani" – Overture[ab]. [b]**Moray Welsh** (vc); [a]**Thomas Martin** (db); **London Symphony Orchestra / Franco Petracchi** ([c]db), [c]**Matthew Gibson**. ASV CDDCA907 (3/95).

Rutland Boughton
British 1878-1960

Suggested listening ...
...Symphony No. 3 in B minor. Oboe Concerto No. 1. **Sarah Francis** (ob); **Royal Philharmonic Orchestra / Vernon Handley.** Hyperion CDA66343 (1/90). ❻
...The Immoral Hour. **Soloists; George Mitchell Choir; English Chamber Orchestra / Alan G. Melville.** Hyperion CDA66101/2 (8/87). ❻❻

Lili Boulanger
French 1893-1918

Suggested listening ...
...Les sirènes. Renouveau. Hymne au soleil. Soir sur la plaine. Dans l'immense tristesse. Attente. Reflets. Le retour. *Coupled with* **Mendelssohn-Hensel** Gartenlieder, Op. 3. Nachtreigen; **C. Schumann** Three Geibel Part-songs. **Christine Friedek** (sop); **Mitsuko Shirai, Regine Böhm** (mezzos); **Bernhard Gärtner** (ten); **Hartmut Höll, Sabine Eberspächer** (pfs); **Heidelberg Madrigal Choir / Gerald Kegelmann.** Bayer BR100041 (4/90).

Pierre Boulez
French 1925-

Boulez Rituel (1974-75). Messagesquisse (1976). Notations I-IV (1945-78). **Orchestre de Paris / Daniel Barenboim.** Erato Ⓕ 2292-45493-2 (41 minutes: DDD: 10/90). Recorded 1988-9.
It goes without saying that this disc wins no prizes for length. It is nevertheless important in several significant respects. Only rarely do we have the chance to hear Boulez's music, not only under a conductor other than the composer, but a conductor whose whole artistic background is so different from Boulez's own. Barenboim clearly has his own point of view, and the technical skill to realize it convincingly with a first-class French orchestra. Boulez himself now tends to underline the public ceremonial of *Rituel* (a tribute to the Italian composer and conductor Bruno Maderna), whereas Barenboim, restraining the cumulative clangour of the music's dialogues between the implacable reiterations of gongs and tamtams and the seven other instrumental groups, preserves more of the intimacy of personal regret and loss. *Rituel* is unusual for Boulez in the clear-cut logic of its gradually evolving form, and Barenboim does well to convey that logic without making the whole design seem too predictable for its own good. He is equally attentive to the need to balance striking details with a feeling for overall shape in the shorter but no less personal structures of *Notations* and *Messagesquisse*. The recording is outstanding in its spaciousness and tonal range.

Additional recommendations ...
...Messagesquisse. *Coupled with works by* **Ginastera, Fortner, Henze, Beck, Dutilleux, Lutosławski, Berio, C. Halffter, Britten, K. Huber** and **Holliger** Thomas Demenga (vc); **Cello Ensemble / Jürg Wyttenbach.** ECM New Series Ⓕ 445 234-2 (two discs: 84 minutes: DDD: 8/95).

New review
Boulez 12 Notations[a]. Structures pour deux pianos, Livre 2[b]. ... explosante-fixe ...[c]. [c]**Sophie Cherrier**, [c]**Emmanuelle Ophèle**, [c]**Pierre-André Valade** (fls); [ab]**Pierre-Laurent Aimard**, [b]**Florent Boffard** (pfs); **Ensemble InterContemporain, Paris / Pierre Boulez.** DG Ⓕ 445 833-2GH (70 minutes: DDD: 12/95). Recorded 1993-4.

Though he may well disapprove of the designation, in ... *explosante-fixe* ... Pierre Boulez has written one of the great flute concertos of this or any other century. At nearly 37 minutes, it is also probably the longest, and the expansiveness of the score, dating from 1991-3, gives the lie to all those persistent tales about Boulez's reluctance to compose. He has never lacked for ideas: he's just been unusually fastidious in his concern to do those ideas full justice. This is music of prodigious melodic inventiveness – and if you believe Boulez incapable of lyricism, try ... *explosante-fixe* ... from as early as 1'50". It shares a relish for regular rhythmic patterns with other later works (*Messagesquisse*, *Répons*), but its primary concern is with the possibility of enhancing natural sound by electronic means. There are no sound effects, no 'funny noises', but a subtle enrichment of pitch and tone colour as the principal flute and its two satellites interact with ensemble and electronics in music that moves absorbingly between turbulence and poetic reflection in Boulez's uniquely personal way. This is a brilliantly engineered recording, though it is a pity that it wasn't possible to present it as a sequence of tracks cued to a fuller commentary in the notes. No less engaging are the performances of *Notations* and *Structures, Livre 2*, the former revealing the very early Boulez's debts to Debussy, Stravinsky and Bartók, the latter displaying the full, formidable power of his still-youthful originality. This is a superb disc. The energy and sensitivity of the works it contains puts a great deal of other contemporary music in the shade, and performances and recordings are equal to the music's stature.

New review

Boulez Piano Sonatas Nos. 1-3. **Idil Biret** (pf). Naxos ⑤ 8 553353 (64 minutes: DDD: 11/95).
  Recorded 1995.
It sometimes seems as if Pierre Boulez has spent a lifetime paying the penalty for having found composition so easy as a young man. The first two piano sonatas, works of his early twenties, are formidably assured in technique and tremendously rich in ideas. Those sections of the Third Sonata released for performance sound cold and tentative by comparison. Or is it that the Third Sonata's much more extreme rejection of tradition is itself a triumph, an authentic modernity that stands out the more prominently when so much else in contemporary music favours compromise and conformity? Such thoughts are inspired by Idil Biret's absorbing new disc. In the first movement of the First Sonata the broader picture proves to be well fleshed-out, the argument kept on the move, the young composer's impatience and arrogance palpable in Biret's steely touch and the rather dry but never merely harsh recorded sound. The Second Sonata is no less confidently played. While not superseding Pollini's magisterial account, this is a strong alternative, not least in those passages in the second and fourth movements where a strange kind of atonal Debussian reflectiveness can be heard. Is it in the Second Sonata's remarkably diverse finale that premonitions of the Third Sonata's rejections of continuity begin to appear? Quite possibly – and yet the immense power of the Second Sonata as a whole suggests why such experiments as No. 3 represents could never be a last word for Boulez. This disc is not the first to let us hear the three sonatas together, and Claude Helffer's recording has many virtues. But Biret's musical persuasiveness, and the up-to-date sound, earn this Naxos issue a strong recommendation.

Additional recommendations ...
...Nos. 1-3. **Claude Helffer** (pf). Auvidis Astrée ⑤ E7716 (55 minutes: ADD: 8/88).
...No. 2. *Coupled with works by* **Webern, Stravinsky** and **Prokofiev** Maurizio Pollini (pf).
  DG The Originals Ⓜ 447 431-2GOR (68 minutes: ADD: 6/95). *See review in the Collections section; refer to the Index to Reviews.*   ⊖⊖

New review

Boulez Le marteau sans maître[a]. Piano Sonata No. 1[b]. [a]**Linda Hirst** (sop); [b]**Marc Ponthus** (pf);
  [a]**Lontano / Odaline de la Martinez.** Lorelt ⑤ LNT108 (47 minutes: DDD: 3/96). Recorded 1992.
The dearth of alternative recordings of *Le marteau sans maître* in current catalogues could be taken as evidence that, even in the pluralistic 1990s, Boulez's uncompromising masterwork has had its day. It is therefore a particular virtue of this performance that no attempt is made to smooth over the texture's brittle surface, and Linda Hirst's account of the intermittent but crucial vocal part offers an ample variety of tone colour that reinforces *Le marteau*'s affinity with that earlier, equally uncompromising modern masterwork, *Pierrot lunaire*. Some listeners may be disconcerted by a lack of Gallic suavity, a sense of effort not inconsistent with a group of performers counting like mad as they weave their collective way through Boulez's intricate metrical maze. The whole nevertheless holds together well as an intensely dramatic experience – perhaps too dramatic, in the sense that the recording doesn't always allow the lighter tone colours (viola and guitar) to come through, and the xylorimba player seems to have some difficulty in shading down dynamics when required. As for the tam-tams and gong that preside ceremonially over the work's final stages – they can rarely have sounded more arresting, imposing than they do here. A dry, at times harsh, sound is apparent in this recording of the First Piano Sonata. Marc Ponthus attacks the extensive toccata-like sections with such bravura that the quieter episodes are in danger of sounding more disengaged than poetically restrained. It's a powerful performance, however: even if you already have another account of this

remarkably mature early work, this one provides a worthwhile alternative, and it fits well with Odaline de la Martinez's compellingly forceful *Marteau*.

Boulez Pli selon pli. **Phyllis Bryn-Julson** (sop); **BBC Symphony Orchestra / Pierre Boulez.** Erato
Ⓕ 2292-45376-2 (68 minutes: DDD: 3/89). From NUM75050 (5/83). Recorded 1981.
Gramophone Award Winner 1983.   ⒼⒼ

New review
Boulez Pli selon pli[a]. Livre pour cordes[b]. [a]**Halina Lukomska** (sop); [a]**BBC Symphony Orchestra,**
[b]**New Philharmonia Orchestra / Pierre Boulez.** Sony Classical Boulez Edition Ⓜ SMK68335
(71 minutes: ADD: 7/96). Text and translation included. Items marked [a] from 72770 (1/70),
[b]73213 (2/74). Recorded 1968-9.

Pli selon pli, composed between 1957-62, is one of the great pillars of post-war musical modernism. If that proclamation merely makes it sound forbidding, then it could scarcely be less appropriate. 'Pillar' it may be, but as exciting in its moment-to-moment shifts of colour and contour, and as compelling in its command of large-scale dramatic design as anything composed since the great years of Schoenberg and Stravinsky. Easy, no: enthralling and rewarding – yes. This is no grand, single-minded work in the great Germanic symphonic tradition, but a sequence of distinct yet balanced responses to aspects of the great symbolist poet Mallarmé. On the first disc here, his second recording of the piece, Boulez is prepared to let the music expand and resonate, the two large orchestral tapestries enclosing three "Improvisations", smaller-scale vocal movements in which the authority and expressiveness of Phyllis Bryn-Julson is heard to great advantage. The sound is brilliantly wide-ranging and well-balanced, and while the contrast between delicacy and almost delirious density embodied in *Pli selon pli* does take some getting used to, to miss it is to miss one of modern music's most original masterworks.

The first version of *Pli selon pli*, here reissued by Sony on CD for the first time, has a special historical status as embodying the composer's view of the work near the time of its actual completion, when forcefulness, and even ferocity, seemed to count for more as foils to the music's moments of relative restraint than the sustained densities so strongly emphasized in the Erato recording. Even if you have the latter disc, this reissue is of great significance; comparisons are always a fascinating exercise, and never more so than where Boulez's own music is concerned. Its value is enhanced by the addition of the potently expressive *Livre pour cordes*. This is only a part of what Boulez intends as a complete recasting of his youthful work for string quartet, and, as it happens, the first of the two movements we hear in this recording was superseded in 1989 by another reworking, as yet unrecorded. Such are the delights and frustrations of Boulez: fortunately he has not forbidden reissue of this initial and far from negligible version of *Livre*.

Further listening ...
...Structures pour deux pianos. **Alfons Kontarsky, Aloys Kontarsky** (pfs). Wergo WER6011-2 (6/93).
...Rituel in memoriam Bruno Maderna[a]. Eclat/Multiples[b]. [a]**BBC Symphony Orchestra** and
[b]**Ensemble InterContemporain / Pierre Boulez.** Sony Classical SMK45839 (8/90).
...Le visage nuptial[a]. Le soleil des eaux[b]. Figures, Doubles, Prismes. [ab]**Phyllis Bryn-Julson** (sop);
[a]**Elizabeth Laurence** (mcz); [ab]**BBC Singers; BBC Symphony Orchestra / Pierre Boulez.** Erato
2292-45494-2 (12/90).
...Domaines. *Coupled with* **Stravinsky** Three Pieces for Solo Clarinet. **Berio** Lied per clarinetto
solo. Sequenza IX. **Stockhausen** In Freundschaft. **Jolivet** Ascèses. **Messiaen** Quatuor pour
la fin du temps – Abîme des oiseaux. **Paul Meyer** (cl). Denon CO-78917 (7/95).

Derek Bourgeois   British 1941-

New review
D. Bourgeois Trombone Concerto, Op. 114*b*
Howarth Trombone Concerto.
Jacob Trombone Concerto. **Christian Lindberg** (tbn); **BBC National Orchestra of Wales / Grant
Llewellyn.** BIS Ⓕ CD658 (62 minutes: DDD: 10/95). Recorded 1993.

Gordon Jacob's Trombone Concerto is full of happy ideas, so well tailored for the instrument. The work opens with a drum roll and a bold solo cadenza that, just after the orchestral entry, aptly quotes the famous Holst arpeggio theme from *The Perfect Fool*. The *Adagio* brings a finely spun, atmospheric web from the strings, over which the soloist sings his mournful *cantilena*. This reaches a climax of considerable ardour, which subsides after a sinuous bassoon solo, and slowly winds down to effectively sustain its arch-like structure. Elgar Howarth wrote his concerto as a 23-year-old trumpet player at the Royal Opera, Covent Garden and then put it in a drawer and forgot all about it until Christian Lindberg heard of its existence and came looking. It would be agreeable to report that it is a hidden masterpiece but it is a rather patchy work. The finest part of the piece is the *Lento* where the trombone soars freely over an unassertive ostinato. The finale is a Stravinsky pastiche. Derek Bourgeois's extrovert, cultivated work matches Gordon Jacob in resource and melodic flair. The *Adagio* brings first a *nobilmente* idea and its sequential extension shows that its composer knows just what he is doing. The finale goes at a tremendous pace (here Rimsky's bumble-bee springs to mind). Lindberg's staccato articulation is something to marvel at; he is also a player of consummate musicianship, and is most sympathetically accompanied. If you want a collection of trombone concertos this one will be hard to beat, for the recording is well balanced and full, if a trifle over-resonant: the orchestral detail could be more sharply defined.

Guillaume Bouzignac   French c1592-c1641

Bouzignac Ecce festivitas amoris. Ecce homo. Unus ex vobis. In pace in idipsum. Ha, plange, filia Jerusalem. Vulnerasti cor meum. Alleluya, Venite amici. Flos in floris tempore. O mors, ero mors tua. Clamant clavi. Ecce aurora. Dum silentium. Jubilate Deo. Salve Jesus piissime. Ave Maria. Tota pulchra es. Te Deum. **Les Pages de la Chapelle; Orlando Gibbons Viol Ensemble; Les Arts Florissants Chorus and Instrumental Ensemble / William Christie.** Harmonia Mundi Ⓟ HMC90 1471 (63 minutes: DDD: 6/94). ✒ Recorded 1993.

If, by any chance, you should think that with another disc of French seventeenth-century church music from Les Arts Florissants you know what to expect, think again. Bouzignac is quite definitely, quite splendidly, different. Try *Unus ex vobis* on your friends and see if they can tell what century it comes from, let alone what country (its lugubrious dialogue between Christ and his disciples actually sounds more like something from the Russian Orthodox Church). This is music that abandons itself to its text in as absolute and direct a way as you are ever likely to encounter in the baroque period, and the results are sometimes gripping, sometimes haunting, and sometimes both. But that is not all. Bouzignac knew his counterpoint; he could write in joyous, celebratory vein, rather like a lightfooted Gabrieli (*Jubilate Deo*); and there is also music of aching beauty – *In pace in idipsum* should be enough to melt anyone into their chair. Christie marries an acute sense of drama to a sensitivity to words and to the music's lyrical qualities. He uses boy sopranos, and though their singing is hardly in the polished Arts Florissants mould, it does square nicely with this music's straightforward mode of communication.

Further listening ...

...Unus ex vobis. Ha, plange, filia Jerusalem. *Coupled with works by* **Carpentras, Gilles, Ceppede, Vitré** and **Godolin** Soloists; Boston Schola Cantorum; Boston Camerata / Joel Cohen. Erato 4509-98480-2 (11/95). ✒

York Bowen   British 1884-1961

New review

Bowen Piano Sonata No. 5 in F minor, Op. 72. Preludes, Op. 102 – No. 1 in C major; No. 2 in C minor; No. 6 in D minor; No. 7 in E flat major; No. 8 in E flat minor; No. 10 in E minor; No. 15 in G major; No. 16 in G minor; No. 18 in G sharp minor; No. 19 in A major; No. 20 in A minor; No. 21 in B flat major; No. 22 in B flat minor. Ballade No. 2, Op. 87. Berceuse in D major, Op. 83. Suite Mignonne, Op. 39 – Moto perpetuo. Toccata in A minor, Op. 155. Romances – No. 1 in G flat major, Op. 35 No. 1; No. 2 in F major, Op. 45. **Stephen Hough** (pf). Hyperion Ⓟ CDA66838 (77 minutes: DDD: 6/96). *Gramophone Editor's choice.*   🅖🅖

This disc comes as quite a revelation. York Bowen was, along with Arnold Bax, perhaps the most brilliantly gifted product of the Royal Academy of Music from the first decade of this century. Not only was Bowen a dazzlingly accomplished pianist, he quickly completed a healthy clutch of large-scale offerings that had Saint-Saëns hailing him as "the most remarkable of the young British composers"; indeed, by 1912, Bowen had written three piano concertos and two symphonies. After the First World War, however, Bowen's music went out of fashion and he drifted into a life of quiet academic security. This eloquent collection from Stephen Hough suggests that a radical reappraisal of Bowen's compositional achievement is long overdue. Certainly, a piece like the Fifth Sonata from 1923 (there are six in all) reveals a pianistic craft of the highest order. This red-blooded, lyrical creation is full of strong ideas, resourcefully worked out. Bowen's chosen idiom invites comparisons with Rachmaninov and (closer to home) Bax and Ireland, whereas the bewitching, harmonically searching *Berceuse* (1926) and achingly tender *Romances* (published in 1913 and 1917) inhabit an altogether more intimate world (both bear a dedication to the composer's wife). Hough also gives us 13 of the 24 Preludes which make up Bowen's Op. 102 (1950), and an extremely compelling sequence they form too: try the gently rocking No. 21 in B flat major (track 7), the winsomely delicate No. 10 in E minor (track 3) or the stormy, fearsomely tricky No. 18 in G sharp minor (track 13). Hough responds with his usual effortless technical mastery, rapt affection and intrepid panache. As is customary from this company, both production values and documentation are exemplary.

New review

Bowen 24 Preludes in all keys, Op. 102. Nocturne in A flat major, Op. 78. Rêverie in B major, Op. 86. Berceuse in D major Op. 93. Partita in D minor, Op. 156. **Marie-Catherine Girod** (pf). 3D Classics Ⓟ 3D8012 (74 minutes: DDD: 12/95).

Bowen stuck to his post-romantic guns in the tradition of Chopin, Scriabin and Medtner right up to his death in 1961 and Girod takes Bowen's pianism in the grand manner, which is the only thing to do since it needs a big technique and has a wide emotional range. Most of the CD is occupied with the

24 Preludes, Op. 102, dating from 1940 – one in each major and minor key, going upwards from C to B, although the CD booklet lists some keys incorrectly. The faster movements generally sound rather East European, but there is an attractive melodic approach in the lyrical pieces such as No. 2 in C minor and No. 6 in D minor. The inflexions feel English, especially in the way a phrase is repeated with decorations. By comparison the shorter pieces and the late *Partita* have less individuality but they are invariably idiomatic. Everything is played with zealous conviction. The booklet is so enthusiastic that "un romantique anglais" is translated as "a romantic Englishman"! This well-recorded disc is recommended to romantics of all nationalities.

Paul Bowles
American 1910-

Suggested listening ...
...Concerto for Two Pianos, Winds and Percussion[a]. Flute Sonata[b]. Music for a Farce[c]. Sonata for Oboe and Clarinet[d]. Hippolytos and Salome[e]. Scènes d'Anabase[f]. Night Waltz[g]. [f]**Martyn Hill** (ten); [be]**Dietmar Wiesner** (fl); [adef]**Catherine Milliken** (ob/cor ang); [ace]**Ib Hausmann,** [d]**Carol Robinson** (cls); [ace]**Bruce Nockles** (tpt); [abcefg]**Hermann Kretzschmar,** [ag]**Olga Balakleets** (pfs); [ace]**Rainer Römer,** [ace]**Peppie Wiersma** (perc). Largo 5131 (6/96).

William Boyce
British 1711-1779

Boyce Eight Symphonies, Op. 2. **Academy of Ancient Music / Christopher Hogwood.** L'Oiseau-Lyre Ⓔ 436 761-2OH (61 minutes: DDD: 4/94). ✒ Recorded 1992.
The Boyce *Eight Symphonys* (as he himself spelt the title) are one of the treasures of English eighteenth-century music, cheerful, unassuming and confident, full of good tunes, and typically English in style – their quirky lines, their refusal to follow the regular procedures, their mixture of baroque and classical features, with their fugues declining to remain fugal, their very un-French French overtures: all this is part of their particular charm. Hogwood catches the eccentric character of the music well and gives a great deal of attention to the textural depth of the music and its inner detail. All the fugal movements go well, done with vitality and a feeling for their logic.
Additional recommendations ...
...**The English Concert / Trevor Pinnock** (hpd). Archiv Produktion Ⓔ 419 631-2AH (60 minutes: DDD: 9/87). ✒
...**Bournemouth Sinfonietta / Ronald Thomas.** CRD Ⓔ CRD3356 (60 minutes: ADD: 4/85).
Further listening ...
...Overtures Nos. 1-9. **Cantilena / Adrian Shepherd.** Chandos CHAN6531 (10/91).
...Overtures Nos. 10-12. Concerti grossi – B minor; B flat major; E flat major. **Cantilena / Adrian Shepherd.** Chandos CHAN6541 (6/92).
...Anthems – O where shall widom be found?; Wherewithal shall a young man; I have surely built thee an house; O praise the Lord; Turn thee unto me; O give thanks; By the waters of Babylon; The Lord is King be the people never so impatient. Voluntaries[a] – Nos. 1, 4 and 7. **New College Choir, Oxford / Edward Higginbottom** with [a]**Gary Cooper** (org). CRD CRD3483 (10/92). ✒
...**Solomon** – serenata. **Bronwen Mills** (sop) She; **Howard Crook** (ten) He; **The Parley of Instruments / Roy Goodman.** Hyperion CDA66378 (11/90). ✒

Eugene Bozza
French 1905-1991

Suggested listening ...
...Pulcinella. *Coupled with* **Milhaud** Duo concertante, Op. 351. Caprice, Op. 335a. **Françaix** Tema con variazioni. **Honegger** Clarinet Sonatina, H42. **Hindemith** Clarinet Sonata in B flat major. **Vaughan Williams** Six Studies in English folk song. **Kupferman** Moonflowers, Baby!. **Jonathan Cohler** (cl); **Judith Gordon** (pf). Crystal CD733 (5/95).

Johannes Brahms
German 1833-1897

Brahms Violin Concerto in D major, Op. 77.
Sibelius Violin Concerto in D minor, Op. 47. **Tasmin Little** (vn); **Royal Liverpool Philharmonic Orchestra / Vernon Handley.** EMI Eminence Ⓜ CD-EMX2203 (72 minutes: DDD: 2/93). Recorded 1991. Ⓖ
New review
Brahms Violin Concerto in D major, Op. 77.
Schumann Violin Concerto in D minor, Op. posth. **Joshua Bell** (vn); **Cleveland Orchestra / Christoph von Dohnányi.** Decca Ⓔ 444 811-2DH (68 minutes: DDD: 5/96). Recorded 1994.
Tasmin Little admits that she prefers not to commit her interpretations to disc until she has "something to say and the means with which to say it". That is certainly the case with the Brahms

Concerto, a clear, considered reading (much aided in the slow movement by Jonathan Small's excellent oboe solo), quite without mannerism and beautifully accompanied by Vernon Handley and the Royal Liverpool Philharmonic. The Sibelius has even more character, and here Little adds to an impressive roster of the work's many great female interpreters (Neveu, Wicks, Bustabo, Ignatius, etc). Handley is an impressive Sibelian whose feel for the idiom is apparent in every bar, and both recordings are excellent. As a coupling the two performances are irresistible.

Bell's first entry in the Brahms instantly demonstrates the soloist's love of bravura display, his gift for turning a phrase individually in a way that catches the ear, always sounding spontaneous, never self-conscious. Regularly one registers moments of new magic, not least when, in the most delicate half-tones, *pianissimos* seem to convey an inner communion, after which the impact of bravura *fortissimos* is all the more dramatic. He rounds off the movement with his own big cadenza and a magically hushed link into the coda, rapt and intense. The slow movement, sweet and songful, gains too from Bell's love of playing really softly, not least in stratospheric registers. In the finale the vein of fantasy is less apparent. Next to others this seems a little plain, strong and clean but at a relatively modest pace, lacking some of the individuality of earlier versions, finely detailed and sharply focused though the playing is. Dohnányi and the Cleveland Orchestra provide weighty and sympathetic support throughout and the generous coupling of the Schumann Violin Concerto in another commanding performance adds to the attractions of the disc. There too Dohnányi and the Cleveland Orchestra add to the weight and dramatic impact of a performance that defies the old idea of this as an impossibly flawed piece, with Bell bringing out charm as well as power. The central slow movement has a rapt intensity rarely matched, and the dance-rhythms of the finale have fantasy as well as jauntiness and jollity, with Bell again revelling in the bravura writing. The recording is full-bodied and well-balanced.

Additional recommendations ...

...Violin Concerto[a]. **Sibelius** Violin Concerto in D minor, Op. 47[b]. **Ginette Neveu** (vn); **Philharmonia Orchestra / [a]Issay Dobroven, [b]Walter Susskind.** EMI mono Ⓜ CDH7 61011-2* (70 minutes: ADD: 3/88).

...Violin Concerto. **Mendelssohn** Violin Concerto in E minor, Op. 64. **Xue-Wei** (vn); **London Philharmonic Orchestra / Ivor Bolton.** ASV Ⓕ CDDCA748 (67 minutes: DDD: 4/91).

...Violin Concerto. **Itzhak Perlman** (vn); **Berlin Philharmonic Orchestra / Daniel Barenboim.** EMI Ⓕ CDC7 54580-2 (40 minutes: DDD: 2/93).

...Violin Concerto. **Tchaikovsky** Violin Concerto in D major, Op. 35. **Jascha Heifetz** (vn); **Chicago Symphony Orchestra / Fritz Reiner.** RCA Victor Living Stereo Ⓜ 09026 61495-2* (64 minutes: ADD: 4/93). ⓆⒼⒼ

...Violin Concerto[b]. Violin Sonata No. 1 in G major, Op. 78[a]. [a]**Isaac Stern, Pincas Zukerman** (vns); [b]**Orchestra de Paris / Daniel Barenboim** ([a]pf). DG Classikon Ⓑ 439 405-2GCL (70 minutes: ADD: 1/94).

...Violin Concerto. **Schumann** Violin Concerto in D minor, Op. posth. **Takayoshi Wanami** (vn); **London Philharmonic Orchestra / Adrian Leaper.** IMP Classics Ⓜ PCD1062 (71 minutes: DDD: 4/94).

...Violin Concerto. **Mendelssohn** Violin Concerto in E minor, Op. 64. **Johanna Martzy** (vn); **Philharmonia Orchestra / Paul Kletzki.** Testament mono Ⓕ SBT1037* (68 minutes: ADD: 9/94).

...Violin Concerto[a]. **Tchaikovsky** Violin Concerto in D major, Op. 35[b]. **Ida Haendel** (vn); [a]**London Symphony Orchestra / Sergiu Celibidache;** [b]**Royal Philharmonic Orchestra / Sir Eugene Goossens.** Testament mono Ⓕ SBT1038* (76 minutes: ADD: 10/94).

...Violin Concerto. **Viktoria Mullova** (vn); **Berlin Philharmonic Orchestra / Claudio Abbado.** Philips Ⓕ 438 998-2PH (40 minutes: DDD: 11/94).

...Violin Concerto[c]. **Beethoven** Romances[b] – No. 1 in G major, Op. 40; No. 2 in F major, Op. 50. **Bach** Violin Concertos[a] – A minor, BWV1041; E major, BWV1042. Concerto for Two Violins and Strings in D minor, BWV1043[b] (with Igor Oistrakh, vn). **Tchaikovsky** Violin Concerto in D major, Op. 35[c]. **David Oistrakh** (vn); [a]**Vienna Symphony Orchestra;** [b]**Royal Philharmonic Orchestra / Sir Eugene Goossens;** [c]**Dresden Staatskapelle / Franz Konwitschny.** DG The Originals [ab]stereo/[c]mono Ⓜ 447 427-2GOR2 (two discs: 142 minutes: ADD: 6/95).

...Violin Concerto. **Mozart** Violin Concerto No. 3 in G major, K216. **Frank Peter Zimmermann** (vn); **Berlin Philharmonic Orchestra / Wolfgang Sawallisch.** EMI Ⓕ CDC5 55426-2 (60 minutes: DDD: 5/96). *See review under Mozart; refer to the Index to Reviews.*

New review

Brahms Piano Concertos[a] – No. 1 in D minor, Op. 15; No. 2 in B flat major, Op. 83. Seven Piano Pieces, Op. 116[b]. **Emil Gilels** (pf); [a]**Berlin Philharmonic Orchestra / Eugen Jochum.** DG The Originals Ⓜ 447 446-2GOR2 (two discs: 125 minutes: ADD: 6/96). Items marked [a] from 2707 064 (12/72), [b]2530 655 (7/76). Recorded 1972-5. *Gramophone classical 100.* ⓆⒼⒼ

The booklet-notes make reference to Jerrold Northrop Moore's original *Gramophone* review, in which Gilels and Jochum were praised for "a rapt songfulness that in no way detracts from Brahms's heroism, and so comes closer to that unique and complex combination of attitudes that for me is Brahms more than any other performances of these concertos I have ever heard, on records or otherwise". One might add that Jochum and the Berlin Philharmonic make plain sailing where others struggle with choppy cross-currents (admittedly sometimes to Brahms's advantage) and that the recordings don't sound their age. And what of the situation since 1972? Abbado and Brendel have perhaps probed a little deeper here and there, Kovacevich and Sawallisch won a *Gramophone* Award for their recording of No. 1 and sundry reissues have reminded us of such contrasted partnerships as Rubinstein with Reiner in the First Concerto and, in the Second, Adrian Aeschbacher raging wild with Furtwängler and, also in the Second, Serkin with Szell. Neither concerto rests content with a single interpretation, the Second especially – and there one can additionally turn to Gilels's fiery first recording under Fritz Reiner, so much swifter than this Berlin remake. Some will prefer it, although RCA's 1958 recording is nowhere near as refined as on this DG set. As for the Seven Piano Pieces, Gilels viewed the opus as a single piece, a musical novella in several chapters.

Additional recommendations ...

...Nos. 1 and 2. Scherzo in E flat minor, Op. 4. Four Ballades, Op. 10. Eight Pieces, Op. 76. **Stephen Kovacevich** (pf); **London Symphony Orchestra / Sir Colin Davis.** Philips Ⓜ 442 109-2PM2 (two discs: 141 minutes: ADD/DDD).   Ⓖ

...No. 2ª. Variations on a Theme by Paganini, Op. 35 – Book 2. **Beethoven** Piano Sonata No. 9 in E major, Op. 14 No. 1. **Liszt** Hungarian Rhapsody in C sharp minor, S244 No. 12ᵈ. **Gina Bachauer** (pf); ªLondon Symphony Orchestra / Stanislaw Skrowaczewski. Mercury Living Presence Ⓜ 434 340-2MM (77 minutes: ADD: 9/95).

...No. 2. Variations on a Theme by Haydn, Op. 56a. **Emil Gilels** (pf); **Chicago Symphony Orchestra / Fritz Reiner.** RCA Silver Seal Ⓑ VD60536 (62 minutes: ADD).

...Nos. 1 and 2. Two Rhapsodies, Op. 79. Piano Pieces. **Wilhelm Backhaus** (pf); **Vienna Philharmonic Orchestra / Karl Böhm.** Decca Ⓜ 433 895-2DM2 (ADD).

...No. 1. **Alfred Brendel** (pf); **Berlin Philharmonic Orchestra / Claudio Abbado.** Philips Ⓕ 420 071-2PH (49 minutes: DDD: 11/87).

...No. 1ª. Variations on a Theme by Haydnᵇ. **Daniel Barenboim** (pf); ªPhilharmonia Orchestra, ᵇVienna Philharmonic Orchestra / Sir John Barbirolli. EMI Studio Ⓜ CDM7 63536-2 (70 minutes: ADD: 11/90).

...No. 1ª. Zwei Gesänge, Op. 91ᵇ. **Stephen Kovacevich** (pf); ᵇAnn Murray (mez); ᵇNobuko Imai (va); ªLondon Philharmonic Orchestra / Wolfgang Sawallisch. EMI Ⓕ CDC7 54578-2 (59 minutes: DDD: 10/92). *Gramophone Award Winner 1993. Selected by Sounds in Retrospect*   Ⓖ

...No. 2ª. Academic Festival Overture, Op. 80ᵇ. Tragic Overture, Op. 81ᵇ. **Daniel Barenboim** (pf); ªPhilharmonia Orchestra, ᵇVienna Philharmonic Orchestra / Sir John Barbirolli. EMI Studio Ⓜ CDM7 63537-2 (76 minutes: ADD: 11/90).

...No. 2. **Alfred Brendel** (pf); **Berlin Philharmonic Orchestra / Claudio Abbado.** Philips Ⓕ 432 975-2PH (49 minutes: DDD: 6/92).

...No. 2. Fantasias. **Emil Gilels** (pf); **Berlin Philharmonic Orchestra / Eugen Jochum.** DG Galleria Ⓜ 435 588-2GGA (*coupled with No. 1 and reviewed above*) (74 minutes: ADD: 9/92).   ⒷⒼⒼ

...No. 1ª. Rhapsody in B minor, Op. 79 No. 1ª. Capriccio in B minor, Op. 76 No. 2ᵇ. Intermezzo in E flat minor, Op. 118 No. 6ᵇ. **Artur Rubinstein** (pf); ªChicago Symphony Orchestra / Fritz Reiner. RCA Victor Gold Seal Ⓜ 09026 61263-2 (65 minutes: ADD: 2/93).

...No. 2. **Tchaikovsky** Piano Concerto No. 1 in B flat minor, Op. 23. **Vladimir Horowitz** (pf); **NBC Symphony Orchestra / Arturo Toscanini.** RCA Victor Gold Seal Ⓜ GD60319* (74 minutes: ADD: 9/93).

...No. 2. **Strauss** Burleske. **Rudolf Serkin** (pf); **Cleveland Orchestra / George Szell.** Sony Classical Ⓜ SBK53262 (67 minutes: ADD: 3/94).

...No. 1ª. Scherzo in E flat minor, Op. 4. Four Ballades, Op. 10 – No. 1 in D minor; No. 2 in D major. Waltzes, Op. 39 – No. 1 in B major; No. 2 in E major; No. 15 in A flat major. Hungarian Dances – No. 6 in D flat major; No. 7 in A major. **Wilhelm Backhaus** (pf); ªBBC Symphony Orchestra / Sir Adrian Boult. Biddulph mono Ⓜ LHW017* (67 minutes: ADD: 9/94).

...No. 2ª. Variations on an original theme in D major, Op. 21 No. 1. Variations on a Theme by Paganini, Op. 35. ªSaxon State Orchestra / Karl Böhm. Biddulph mono Ⓜ LHW018* (71 minutes: ADD: 9/94).

...No. 1. Variations and Fugue on a Theme by Handel, Op. 24ᵇ. **Solomon** (pf); ªPhilharmonia Orchestra / Rafael Kubelík. Testament mono Ⓕ SBT1041* (73 minutes: ADD: 10/94).   Ⓖ

...No. 2ª. Lieder, Op. 105ᵇ. **Stephen Kovacevich** (pf); ᵇAnn Murray (mez); ªLondon Philharmonic Orchestra / Wolfgang Sawallisch. EMI Ⓕ CDC5 55218-2 (62 minutes: DDD: 10/94). *Selected by Sounds in Retrospect.*

...No. 2ª. Intermezzos – B flat minor, Op. 117 No. 2ᵇ; C major, Op. 119 No. 3ᶜ. Rhapsody in G minor, Op. 79 No. 2ᵇ. **Solomon** (pf); ªPhilharmonia Orchestra / Issay Dobrowen. Testament mono Ⓕ SBT1042* (58 minutes: ADD: 10/94).   Ⓖ

...No. 1. **Dohnányi** Variations on a Nursery Theme, Op. 25. **Mark Anderson** (pf); **Hungarian State Symphony Orchestra / Ádám Fischer.** Nimbus Ⓕ NI5349 (75 minutes: DDD: 3/95). *See review under Dohnányi; refer to the Index to Reviews.*

...No. 2. Symphony No. 1 in C minor, Op. 68 – Adagio ... Allegro non troppo ma con brio. *Coupled with works by* **Beethoven, Bruckner and Wagner** Adrian Aeschenbacher (pf); Soloists; Berlin Philharmonic Orchestra / Wilhelm Furtwängler. Tahra mono Ⓜ FURT1004/07* (four discs: 263 minutes: ADD: 3/95).

...No. 2ª. Variations on a Theme by Paganini, Op. 35 – Book 2. **Beethoven** Piano Sonata No. 9 in E major, Op. 14 No. 1. **Liszt** Hungarian Rhapsody in C sharp minor, S244 No. 12. **Gina**

Bachauer (pf); [a]**London Symphony Orchestra / Stanislaw Skrowaczewski.** Mercury Living Presence
Ⓜ 434 340-2MM (77 minutes: ADD: 9/95).
…Nos. 1 and 2. Theme and Variations (from String Sextet No. 1, Op. 18). Four Ballades, Op. 10.
Schumann Kreisleriana, Op. 16. Kinderszenen, Op. 15. Fantasiestücke, Op. 12. Fantasie in
C major, Op. 17. Etudes symphoniques, Op. 13. Drei Romanzen, Op. 94[c]. Abendlied, Op. 85
No. 12[c]. Adagio and Allegro in A flat major, Op. 70[c]. Fantasiestücke, Op. 73[c]. Funf Stücke in
Volkston, Op. 102[c]. Piano Concerto in A minor, Op. 54[b]. **Alfred Brendel** (pf); [c]**Heinz Holliger**
(ob); [a]**Berlin Philharmonic Orchestra,** [b]**London Symphony Orchestra / Claudio Abbado.** Philips
Ⓜ 446 925-2PM5 (five discs: 334 minutes: ADD/DDD: 2/96).

New review

Brahms Piano Concerto No. 1 in D minor, Op. 15[a].
Franck Symphonic Variations[b].
Litolff Concerto symphonique No. 4 in D minor, Op. 102 – Scherzo[b]. **Sir Clifford Curzon** (pf);
[a]**London Symphony Orchestra / George Szell;** [b]**London Philharmonic Orchestra / Sir Adrian Boult.**
Decca The Classic Sound Ⓜ 425 082-2DCS (74 minutes: ADD: 4/95). Item marked [a] from
SXL6023 (12/62), [b]SXL2173 (2/60). *Gramophone classical 100.*   ⒼⒼⒼ
It is debatable as to whether there is any other recording of the D minor Concerto that so instantly
takes fire and which burns thereafter with so pure and steady a flame. To all outward appearances,
Curzon and Szell were an oddly contrasted couple; yet they worked wonderfully well together, in
Mozart and here in Brahms. The 1962 recording still comes up phenomenally well, despite some
occasional muzzling of the orchestra's bass texturing. A merciful muzzling, you might think, given the
frequency with which Szell detects and detonates the small arsenal of explosive devices Brahms has
hidden in the undergrowth. We obviously don't lack great recordings of this concerto but this 1962
Decca version remains as collectable as any. The fill-ups to this repackaged CD are also welcome. The
Franck is beginning to sound its age technically but the performance is charming. As for the Litolff,
it is irresistible, a gem of a performance, well recorded.

Brahms Double Concerto in A minor, Op. 102[a]. Piano Quartet No. 3 in C minor, Op. 60[b]. **Isaac
Stern** (vn); [b]**Jaime Laredo** (va); **Yo-Yo Ma** (vc); [b]**Emanuel Ax** (pf); [a]**Chicago Symphony Orchestra
/ Claudio Abbado.** CBS Masterworks Ⓔ MK42387 (68 minutes: DDD: 6/88).

New review

Brahms Double Concerto in A minor, Op. 102[a].
Schumann Cello Concerto in A minor, Op. 129. [a]**Ilya Kaler** (vn); **Maria Kliegel** (vc); **National
Symphony Orchestra of Ireland / Andrew Constantine.** Naxos Ⓢ 8 550938 (59 minutes:
DDD: 10/95). *Gramophone Editor's choice.*
The grave, declamatory utterances at the beginning of the Double Concerto tell us much about the
nature of what will follow. They can also reveal a great deal about the two soloists who enter in turn
with solo cadenzas separated by thematic orchestral material. On the CBS disc, perhaps surprisingly,
it is the much younger man, Yo-Yo Ma, who brings out most strongly the noble gravity of the
composer's inspiration, while the relatively veteran Isaac Stern is more melodious and spontaneous-
sounding. The music's steady but unhurried paragraphs are very well handled by Claudio Abbado
and the excellent Chicago Symphony Orchestra is responsive and pretty faithfully balanced with the
soloists. This is a performance to satisfy rather than to thrill, perhaps, but satisfy it does. The
recording is rich and rather reverberant, notably in orchestral tuttis. The powerful C minor Piano
Quartet is also well played and provides a substantial partner to the concerto. Apparently Brahms
once said that it had the mood of a man thinking of suicide, but one hastens to say that it is nothing
like as gloomy as that would suggest.
    The Brahms and Schumann concertos make an excellent and apt coupling, here on Naxos given
warmly spontaneous-sounding performances, very well recorded. The violinist, Ilya Kaler, is as clean
in attack and intonation as Maria Kliegel. Kliegel in her opening cadenza allows herself full freedom,
but any feeling that this is to be an easygoing, small-scale reading is dispelled in the main *Allegro*,
which is clean and fresh, sharp in attack, helped by full-bodied sound. Kaler and Kliegel make the
second subject tenderly expressive without having to use exaggerated rubato. Similarly there is no self-
indulgence in the soaring main melody of the central *Andante*, but no lack of warmth or tenderness
either. The finale is then unhurried but has dance-rhythms so beautifully sprung and such delicate
pointing of phrases that any lack of animal excitement is amply replaced by wit and a sense of fun.
A delightful performance. In the Schumann Kliegel takes a spacious, lyrical view of the first
movement, using a soft-grained tone at the start with wide vibrato. She then builds up the power of
the performance, and with Constantine and the Irish orchestra providing sympathetic
accompaniment, the spontaneous expression is most compelling. So, too, is the simple, dedicated
playing in the central *Langsam*, and, as in the Brahms, Kliegel brings witty pointing to the finale, not
least in the second subject. The balance of the soloist is good.
Additional recommendations …
…Double Concerto[b]. **Beethoven** Triple Concerto in C major, Op. 56[a]. [a]**Rudolf Serkin** (pf); [a]**Jaime
Laredo,** [b]**Isaac Stern** (vns); [a]**Leslie Parnas,** [b]**Leonard Rose** (vcs); [a]**Marlboro Festival Orchestra /
Alexander Schneider;** [b]**Philadelphia Orchestra / Eugene Ormandy.** CBS Masterworks Portrait
Ⓜ CD44842* (71 minutes: ADD: 11/89).   ⒼⒼⒼ

...Double Concerto[a]. **Strauss** Don Quixote, Op. 35[b]. [a]**Nathan Milstein** (vn); [b]**Joseph de Pasquale** (va); **Gregor Piatigorsky** (vc); [a]**Philadelphia Robin Hood Dell Orchestra / Fritz Reiner;** [b]**Boston Symphony Orchestra / Charles Munch.** RCA Ⓜ 09026 61485-2* (71 minutes: ADD: 10/93).

Brahms Serenades – No. 1 in D major, Op. 11; No. 2 in A major, Op. 16. **West German Sinfonia / Dirk Joeres.** IMP Classics Ⓜ PCD1024 (79 minutes: DDD: 5/93). Recorded 1992.
If the term serenade suggests something which is open-hearted and uncomplicated then Brahms's two compositions in this form follow classical conventions up to a point. Each work has an appealing geniality and mellow warmth, but Brahms had a perpetually serious side to his nature, and there's always a nearby cloud threatening to move over the sun. Such mixed characteristics are particularly evident in the Second Serenade, which is scored without violins, and lacks the brightness which upper strings bring to orchestral textures. It is no easy task for a conductor to balance the opposing elements in either work, but Dirk Joeres manages this very successfully. He has at his disposal a very fine body of players, who are given clear, high-quality recordings. In the faster, more outgoing sections of each score he points the rhythms very skilfully, and he shapes the slower, more inward movements in a highly sympathetic, attentive fashion. Even the First Serenade's long *Adagio no troppo* movement, which so easily loses direction, is kept on course through Joeres's subtle use of phrase and pulse.
Additional recommendation ...
...No. 1. **Elgar** In the South, Op. 50. **La Scala Philharmonic Orchestra, Milan / Riccardo Muti.** Sony Classical Ⓕ SK57973 (71 minutes: DDD: 1/95).

Brahms Orchestral Works. **Concertgebouw Orchestra / Bernard Haitink.** Philips Bernard Haitink Symphony Edition Ⓑ 442 068-2PB4 (four discs: 291 minutes: ADD: 9/94). Recorded 1970-80. Symphonies – No. 1 in C minor, Op. 68 (from 6500 519, 11/73); No. 2 in D major, Op. 73 (6500 375, 7/75); No. 3 in F major, Op. 90 (6500 155, 3/71); No. 4 in E minor, Op. 98 (6500 389, 10/73). Variations on a Theme by Haydn, Op. 56*a*, "St Antoni" (6500 375). Tragic Overture, Op. 81 (6500 155). Academic Festival Overture, Op. 80 (412 002-1PS, 8/84). Hungarian Dances – No. 1 in G minor; No. 3 in F major; No. 10 in F major (all new to UK. Recorded 1980). Serenades – No. 1 in D major, Op. 11 (9500 322, 2/78); No. 2 in A major, Op. 16 (412 002-1PS).   Ⓠ
Concertgebouw standards at the time of Haitink's survey (1970-80) left little to be desired; in other words, here is a level of individual artistry and collaborative accomplishment not to be taken for granted. Perhaps the clarinets don't always overcome reservations about their tone and intonation with the sensitivity of their phrasing, but the horns invariably do, and more often than not Brahms's favourite instrument is a source of joy in these recordings, blazing gloriously at appropriate moments (especially in the Fourth Symphony), or opening up and sustaining huge vistas in the 'dawn' of the First's finale. As to the strings, Haitink's insistence on firmly defined (though never over-emphatic) rhythms from the bass-lines up is altogether exceptional; there are countless examples, but most memorable of all is the cellos' and basses' ostinato that sees the Second Symphony's finale in the home strait. What an articulate, integrated Brahms sound this is, too; a case of conductor and engineers easily achieving their aims working in a familiar acoustic. Nor is that acoustic to be taken for granted; how unappealing is the equally informative but stark sound of Klemperer's Philharmonia and Toscanini's NBC tapings in comparison (see elsewhere). There is a degree of tape hiss, most noticeable in the Third Symphony where there is also a trace of hardness, and a chill to the string tone in parts of the Second Symphony, but none of this is serious. The only movement you may initially find overly sober is the first of the Third Symphony, taken very broadly, though it is determined and imposing, and the launching of the coda is stupendously powerful. All in all, there is no better way of getting to know the Brahms orchestral works on a budget.
Additional recommendations ...
...Nos. 1-4. Variations on a Theme by Haydn. Academic Festival Overture. Hungarian Dances Nos. 17-21. Tragic Overture. **Cleveland Orchestra / George Szell.** Sony Classical Ⓑ SB3K48398 (three discs: 214 minutes: ADD).
...Nos. 1[a]; No. 2[b]; No. 3[c]; No. 4[d]. Tragic Overture[e]. Variations on a Theme by Haydn[e]. **Berlin Philharmonic Orchestra / Rudolf Kempe.** Testament [bde]mono/[ac]stereo Ⓕ SBT3054* (three discs: 190 minutes: ADD: 4/95).
...Nos. 1-4. **North German Radio Symphony Orchestra / Günter Wand.** RCA Victor Ⓑ 74321 20283-2 (two discs: 158 minutes: DDD: 5/95).
...Hungarian Dances Nos. 1-21. **Budapest Symphony Orchestra / István Bogár.** Naxos Ⓢ 8 550110 (49 minutes: DDD).
...Tragic Overture. *Coupled with works by* **Mozart, Weber, Wagner, Berlioz** and **Rossini** **London Philharmonic Orchestra / Sir Thomas Beecham.** Dutton Laboratories mono Ⓜ CDLX7009* (75 minutes: ADD: 10/94). *See review in the Collections section; refer to the Index to Reviews.*
...Nos. 1-4. Variations on a theme by Haydn. Tragic Overture. Academic Festival Overture. **Chicago Symphony Orchestra / Daniel Barenboim.** Erato Ⓕ 4509-94817-2 (four discs: 212 minutes: DDD: 11/94).
...Variations and Fugue on a Theme by Haydn. *Coupled with works by* **Wagner, Shostakovich, R. Strauss** and **Smetana** The Solti Orchestral Project, Carnegie Hall / **Sir Georg Solti.** Decca Ⓕ 444 458-2DH (77 minutes: DDD: 12/95). *See review in the Collections section; refer to the Index to Reviews.*   Ⓖ

...Nos. 1-4. Variations on a Theme by Haydn[a]. Hungarian Dances[a] – No. 1 in G minor; No. 3 in F major; No. 10 in F major. **Beethoven** Overtures – Coriolan, Op. 62[a]; Leonore No. 2, Op. 72[b]. [a]**Vienna Philharmonic Orchestra;** [b]**Berlin Philharmonic Orchestra / Wilhelm Furtwängler.** EMI Références mono Ⓜ CHS5 65513-2* (three discs: ADD: 2/96).

Brahms Orchestral and Vocal Works. **NBC Symphony Orchestra / Arturo Toscanini.** RCA Victor Gold Seal mono Ⓜ GD60325* (four discs: 267 minutes: ADD: 5/90). Texts and translations included.
Symphonies – No. 1 in C minor, Op. 68 (from HMV ALP1012, 11/52); No. 2 in D major, Op. 73 (ALP1013, 11/52); No. 3 in F major, Op. 90 (ALP1166, 10/54); No. 4 in E minor, Op. 98 (ALP1029, 6/53). Double Concerto in A minor, Op. 102 (with Mischa Mischakoff, vn; Frank Miller, vc. RB16066, 7/58). Variations on a Theme by Haydn, Op. 56*a* (ALP1204, 12/54). Tragic Overture, Op. 81 (VCM3, 4/67). Academic Festival Overture, Op. 80 (VCM3, 4/67). Hungarian Dances – No. 1 in G minor; No. 17 in F sharp minor; No. 20 in E minor; No. 21 in E minor (ALP1235, 5/55). Gesang der Parzen, Op. 89 (Robert Shaw Chorale. AT125, 4/74). Liebeslieder-Walzer, Op. 52 (Chorus; Artur Balsam, Joseph Kahn, pfs. Recorded 1948. New to UK).   ⒼⒼⒼ
Despite many reissues, technical tinkerings, and critical re-evaluations, the recordings of the great Italian maestro Arturo Toscanini still stand head and shoulders above those which have the unenviable task of rivalling his genius as conductor and interpreter. This generous Brahms set is an excellent example of why Toscanini's recordings are still essential. The readings of the four symphonies must stand as benchmarks against which others are compared, and generally are found wanting. Toscanini's command of this music is total: his sense of architecture is unfailing, his control of tempos and rubato is masterly, and his ability to persuade the NBC Symphony Orchestra to play with extraordinary dynamic variety and tonal beauty is proof of his genius. In addition to the symphonies the set contains a fiery performance of the Double Concerto with the orchestra's principals as eloquent, if occasionally overshadowed, soloists and excellent readings of the essential shorter works of Brahms: the *Haydn Variations, Academic* and *Tragic* Overtures and *Hungarian Dances.* And to round off the set there are good, if not perfect, performances of two choral works, the rarely performed *Song of the Fates* and the *Liebeslieder Waltzes,* Op. 52. The transfer to CD of the original tapes has been handled particularly well: the worst tonal excesses have been successfully tamed, and there is a fine sense of balance throughout (the recordings range from 1948 to 1953). With such a giant as Toscanini recommendation really becomes superfluous. Suffice it to say that these recordings are testimony to the genius of one of the greatest conductors this century has ever known.
Additional recommendation ...
...Hungarian Dances. **Dvořák** Symphonic Variations, B70. Czech Suite, B93. **North German Radio Symphony Orchestra / John Eliot Gardiner.** DG Ⓕ 437 506-2GH (62 minutes: DDD: 6/93).

Brahms Symphony No. 1 in C minor, Op. 68. Gesang der Parzen, Op. 89[a]. [a]**Berlin Radio Chorus; Berlin Philharmonic Orchestra / Claudio Abbado.** DG Ⓕ 431 790-2GH (58 minutes: DDD: 10/91). Recorded 1990.   Ⓖ
Brahms Symphony No. 1 in C minor, Op. 68[a].
Wagner Siegfried Idyll[bc]. Siegfried – Siegfried's horn-call[c]. [c]**Dennis Brain** (hn); [ab]**Philharmonia Orchestra / Guido Cantelli.** Testament mono Ⓕ SBT1012* (62 minutes: ADD: 2/93). Item marked [a] from HMV ALP1152 (7/54), [b]HMV DB9746/7 (4/52), [c]HMV C3622 (11/47). Recorded 1947-53.   Ⓖ
Claudio Abbado's 1990 recording of Brahms's First Symphony achieves the sort of musical and sonic impact that Karajan's first DG version did in the mid-1960s. That too was with the Berlin Philharmonic, a rich, grandly imposing performance that sung and stamped, culminating in a massively jubilant finale. Abbado's tempos are generally broad: his first movement (without its repeat) is as boldly emphatic as Klemperer's but he never stints on affection, and few would find fault with his warm, lyrical handling of the beautiful *Andante,* 'sostenuto', indeed! Abbado ventures between the score's little nooks and crannies (in that respect at least, he's Karajan's superior), highlighting small details without impeding the music's flow or weakening the performance's overall structure. When the finale breaks from *Più Andante* to *Allegro non troppo, ma con brio* (not *too* fast, but with plenty of spirit), Abbado really goes for the burn, very much as Furtwängler did before him. It's a truly inspired reading, grand but never grandiose; appreciative of Brahms's thick-set orchestration, but never stodgy. The fill-up is of enormous import, and opens with one of the composer's most inspired musical gestures: a bold, burgeoning *Maestoso,* anticipating the words "The gods should be feared/by the human race ...". *Gesang der Parzen,* or "Song of the Fates" is a setting of a particularly unsettling poem by Goethe, one that warns how the uplifted have particular reason to fear the gods, those who "turn their beneficent eyes away from whole races." Abbado surely sensed the terrible truth of that prophesy, and his reading of Op. 89 breathes a deeply disquieting air.
    Cantelli conducts an interpretation of the Symphony which is free of any idiosyncrasy. Yet there is an extraordinary electricity in his conducting, a sense of concentration and conviction which lifts the

performance into one of the greatest ever set down on record. The fiery young Italian makes the vintage Philharmonia play in an inspired fashion, and the 1953 mono recording is very acceptable. A slightly edgy string sound betrays the 1951 origin of the *Siegfried Idyll* recording, but the performance has a tenderness, warmth and eloquence which has never been surpassed. Dennis Brain's exuberant horn-call completes a very desirable Testament disc.

Additional recommendations ...

...Nos. 1-4. Variations on a Theme by Haydn. Academic Festival Overture. Hungarian Dances Nos. 17-21. Tragic Overture. **Cleveland Orchestra / George Szell.** Sony Classical Ⓑ SBK48398 (three discs: 214 minutes: ADD).   Ⓖ

...No. 1. Tragic Overture. Academic Festival Overture. **Philharmonia Orchestra / Otto Klemperer.** EMI Studio Ⓜ CDM7 69651-2 (67 minutes: ADD: 1/90).

...No. 1. **Schumann** Overture, Scherzo and Finale, Op. 52. **Berlin Philharmonic Orchestra / Herbert von Karajan.** DG Privilege Ⓑ 431 161-2GR (63 minutes: ADD: 8/91).   ⒼⒼⒼ

...No. 1. Variations on a Theme by Haydn. **London Classical Players / Roger Norrington.** EMI Ⓕ CDC7 54286-2 (61 minutes: DDD: 10/91). 🎵

...No. 1. Serenade No. 2 in A major, Op. 16. **NBC Symphony Orchestra / Arturo Toscanini.** RCA Victor Gold Seal Ⓜ GD60277 (71 minutes: ADD: 11/92).   ⒼⒼ

...No. 1. **Royal Liverpool Philharmonic Orchestra / Marek Janowski.** ASV Quicksilva Ⓢ CDQS6101 (46 minutes: DDD: 9/93).

...No. 1. Variations on a Theme by Haydn. **North German Radio Symphony Orchestra / Wilhelm Furtwängler.** Tahra mono Ⓕ FURT1001* (69 minutes: ADD: 3/95).

...Nos. 1-4. **North German Radio Symphony Orchestra / Günter Wand.** RCA Ⓑ 74321 20283-2 (two discs: 158 minutes: DDD: 5/95).   Ⓖ

...No. 1. **Schumann** Symphony No. 1 in B flat major, Op. 38, "Spring". **Berlin Philharmonic Orchestra / Herbert von Karajan.** DG The Originals Ⓜ 447 408-2GOR (76 minutes: ADD: 7/95).

Brahms Symphony No. 2 in D major, Op. 73. Tragic Overture, Op. 81. **Boston Symphony Orchestra / Bernard Haitink.** Philips Ⓕ 432 094-2PH (62 minutes: DDD: 10/92). Recorded 1990.

Brahms Symphony No. 2 in D major, Op. 73. Academic Festival Overture, Op. 80. **New York Philharmonic Orchestra / Kurt Masur.** Teldec Ⓕ 9031-77291-2 (50 minutes: DDD: 5/93). Recorded 1992.   Ⓖ

Brahms's Second Symphony is the warmest, most lyrical of the four, and on the Philips disc it receives a performance which brings out those qualities to the full. Haitink's reading is very straightforward and unselfconscious: he allows the first movement to blossom attractively, but he ensures that this process is achieved within a strong framework – one is always aware that detail has its secure place within the musical argument. The second movement's basic pulse is on the slow side, but Haitink's affectionate, watchful conducting ensures that the music flows naturally. The third movement is brought to life quite gently too, but accents are light and rhythms are sharp enough to ensure that the mood is still outgoing. In the finale Haitink sets a fast initial tempo, but he allows the music to breathe through the use of subtle inflexions and changes of pulse. There's plenty of excitement, but nothing is too hectic. In the Overture Haitink's basic tempo is quite measured, but again accents are sharp, and the score's dramatic element is well brought out. Throughout both works the playing of the Boston Symphony Orchestra is superlative, and the recording is excellent, with just a slight reservation that there is an occasional moment of slightly acid string tone.

Masur also brings warmth and affection to the symphony. In the first movement he maintains a strong sense of line, and paces the music more objectively than Haitink. The structure is clearer, but there's also a natural, unforced lyricism. The *Adagio* has a natural ebb and flow, and once again Masur makes the listener aware of the music's shape and argument very clearly. After a neatly pointed *Allegretto* the finale is given a beautifully balanced, strongly argued reading which eschews superficial excitement, but satisfies through the feeling of a symphonic argument brought to a logical conclusion. To sum up, Haitink caresses the music with more subjective warmth than Masur, whose reading by no means lacks affection, but is more architectural and objective. The New York Philharmonic respond to their musical director with highly sensitive, very accomplished playing, and Teldec's attractively warm but clearly recorded disc is completed by a genial, uplifting *Academic Festival Overture*.

Additional recommendations ...

...No. 2. Alto Rhapsody, Op. 53[a]. [a]**Christa Ludwig** (mez); [a]**Philharmonia Chorus; Philharmonia Orchestra / Otto Klemperer.** EMI Studio Ⓜ CDM7 69650-2 (51 minutes: ADD: 1/90).   ⒼⒼ

...No. 2. Alto Rhapsody[a]. [a]**Marjana Lipovšek** (contr); [a]**Ernst Senff Choir; Berlin Philharmonic Orchestra / Claudio Abbado.** DG Ⓕ 427 643-2GH (60 minutes: DDD: 2/90).   Ⓖ

...No. 2. **Schumann** Symphony No. 2 in C major, Op. 61. **Berlin Philharmonic Orchestra / Herbert von Karajan.** DG Ⓜ 435 067-2GGA (75 minutes: ADD: 11/91).

...No. 2. **Royal Liverpool Philharmonic Orchestra / Marek Janowski.** ASV Quicksilva Ⓢ CDQS6102 (58 minutes: DDD: 11/93).

...No. 2. Tragic Overture. **London Classical Players / Roger Norrington.** EMI Reflexe Ⓕ CDC7 54875-2 (55 minutes: DDD: 12/93). 🎵

...No. 2. Academic Festival Overture. Tragic Overture. *Coupled with works by* **Beethoven, Debussy, Ravel, Schubert** and **Tchaikovsky** London Symphony Orchestra / Pierre Monteux.

Philips The Early Years Ⓜ 442 544-2PM5* (five discs: 311 minutes: ADD: 12/94). *See review in the Collections section; refer to the Index to Reviews.*   ⒼⒼⒼ

Brahms Symphony No. 3 in F major, Op. 90. Tragic Overture, Op. 81. Schicksalslied, Op. 54[a].
   [a]**Ernst-Senff Choir; Berlin Philharmonic Orchestra / Claudio Abbado.** DG Ⓕ 429 765-2GH
   (68 minutes: DDD: 1/91).   Ⓖ
Brahms Symphony No. 3 in F major, Op. 90.
Schoenberg Chamber Symphony No. 1, Op. 9. **Royal Concertgebouw Orchestra / Riccardo**
   Chailly. Decca Ⓕ 436 466-2DH (58 minutes: DDD: 9/93). Recorded 1991-2.

Abbado's disc is gloriously programmed for straight-through listening. He gets off to a cracking start with an urgently impassioned *Tragic Overture* in which the credentials of the Berlin Philharmonic to make a richly idiomatic, Brahmsian sound – already well accepted – are substantially reaffirmed. A wide-eyed, breathtaking account of the *Schicksalslied* ("Song of Destiny") follows to provide sound contrast before the wonders of the Third Symphony are freshly explored. This is a reading of the Symphony to be savoured; it is underpinned throughout by a rhythmic vitality which binds the four movements together with a forward thrust, making the end inevitable right from the opening bars. Even in the moments of repose and, especially, the warmly-felt *Andante*, Abbado never lets the music forget its ultimate goal. Despite this, there are many moments of wonderful solo and orchestral playing along the way in which there is time to delight, and Abbado seems to bring out that affable, Bohemian-woods, Dvořák-like element in Brahms's music to a peculiar degree in this performance. The Symphony is recorded with a particular richness and some may find the heady waltz of the third movement done too lushly, emphasized by Abbado's lingering tempo. Nevertheless, this is splendid stuff, and not to be missed.

Chailly's No. 3 is a very likeable, impressive reading which just seems to lose confidence in itself from time to time. The recording is outstanding, as is the playing of the full orchestra. Chailly's account of the first movement is well-conceived, although lacking a certain natural flow. The basic tempo is ideal, there is plenty of spirit and expression, but the music seems slightly ill at ease with itself. Matters improve greatly in the second movement, which moves forward calmly and easily, with plenty of natural warmth. Only an occasional awkwardness in the phrasing disturbs an otherwise almost ideal account of the third movement, and the finale is very impressively managed throughout. Although Abbado and Walter on CBS/Sony at mid-price remain the top recommended versions, this disc is very desirable, perhaps mainly for the coupling. Schoenberg's *Chamber Symphony* dates from an early stage in his development, and shows tonality under severe pressure and in fact cracking apart under the composer's assault. This feeling of pressure, of music somehow fighting to get out, is something which needs to be brought out strongly in performance, and Chailly succeeds brilliantly in conveyingthe score's wild intensity. He drives the music very hard, chooses fast, almost hectic tempos, and gets superbly committed playing from his 15 orchestral soloists. The influence of the older composer is apparent not only in the work's few quieter passages, which are shaped very beautifully by Chailly, but in certain rhythmic characteristics, which sound rather like Brahms caught up in a nightmare. The ensemble must be a brute to balance successfully, but the engineers have succeeded brilliantly.

Additional recommendations ...
...No. 3. Variations on a Theme by Haydn. **Columbia Symphony Orchestra / Bruno Walter.**
   CBS Masterworks Ⓜ CD42531* (52 minutes: ADD: 9/86).   ⒼⒼ
...No. 3. Variations on a Theme by Haydn. **Hallé Orchestra / Stanislaw Skrowaczewski.** IMP
   Classics Ⓜ PCD906 (60 minutes: ADD: 4/89).
...Nos. 3 and 4. **Philharmonia Orchestra / Otto Klemperer.** EMI mono Ⓜ CDM7 69649-2*
   (76 minutes: ADD: 1/90).
...No. 3. Variations on a Theme by Haydn. **Vienna Philharmonic Orchestra / Carlo Maria Giulini.**
   DG Ⓕ 431 681-2GH (61 minutes: DDD: 8/91).
...No. 3. Serenade No. 1 in D major, Op. 11. **Belgian Radio and Television Philharmonic Orchestra,**
   Brussels / Alexander Rahbari. Naxos Ⓢ 8 550280 (77 minutes: DDD: 1/92).

New review
Brahms Symphony No. 3 in F major, Op. 90[a].
Schubert Symphony No. 5 in B flat major, D485[b].
Mendelssohn The Hebrides, Op. 26[c]. **Chicago Symphony Orchestra / Fritz Reiner.** RCA Victor
   Gold Seal Ⓜ 09026 61793-2 (69 minutes: ADD: 9/95). Items marked [a] from SB2007 (12/58),
   [b]SB2134 (1/62), [c]SB2059 (2/60).   Ⓖ

Perhaps the very opening of the Brahms is unexceptional; it's not very passionate; maybe there is a little too much of what Reiner called his "self-controlled control". However, slowly but surely, the benefits of that control make themselves felt. The first movement is tautly drawn; no undue roaming in the pre-recapitulation gloaming. Speaking of control and pivotal points, as we turn into this movement's coda, the reins are loosened and the ride is fabulously exciting. The slow movement's mellow (here, very autumnal) pastoral takes its time, and is wonderfully phrased and shaded. The concentration is so intense you can almost sense the falcon eye surveying the scene. And this is how to record Brahms: forget the over-ripe textures and fudged balances of many a modern Brahms symphony recording; here one-and-all is for all to hear (with, admittedly, a moderate amount of tape hiss). No small thanks to Reiner, this is a lean, athletic, supremely articulate, eloquent and well-tempered Brahms sound. With slimmed-down strings, the Schubert is as light on its feet, as perfectly balanced, as poised and as stylishly pointed as any period-instrument or chamber orchestra performance, and very few of them are as immaculately precise. As in the Brahms, there are no repeats, except in the Minuet and Trio, where the repeats are subtly varied and the *ritardandos* consummately handled. The whole is suave and sleek, but shaped, savoured and illumined by the hand of an epicure. As to *The Hebrides*, the way Reiner holds on to the long notes in those wind calls about a third of the way in is very striking indeed, as is the timpani playing, superbly forthright (and very clear) but always musical. Drawbacks? Well, it's as Reiner commented on receipt of the news that he and his orchestra had become box office: "One must take the good with the good".

Brahms Symphony No. 4 in E minor, Op. 98. **Vienna Philharmonic Orchestra / Carlos Kleiber.**
DG Ⓕ 400 037-2GH (39 minutes: DDD: 9/85). From 2532 003 (4/81). Recorded 1980.
Gramophone classical 100.   ⓖⓖⓖ
Brahms Symphony No. 4 in E minor, Op. 98. Variations and Fugue on a Theme by Handel,
Op. 24 (orch. Rubbra). **Cleveland Orchestra / Vladimir Ashkenazy.** Decca Ⓕ 436 853-2DH
(70 minutes: DDD: 11/94). Recorded 1994.
Brahms Symphony No. 4 in E minor, Op. 98. Variations on a Theme by Haydn, Op. 56a, "St
Antoni". **Boston Symphony Orchestra / Bernard Haitink.** Philips Ⓕ 434 991-2PH (62 minutes:
DDD: 9/94). Recorded 1992.

Carlos Kleiber's reading of Brahms's Fourth Symphony is highly individual and thought-provoking but those listeners who know Kleiber from his thrilling recordings of Beethoven's Fifth and Seventh Symphonies and are expecting similarly uncompromising, high-tension performances with enormous muscular energy are in for a surprise!. His reading certainly has plenty of muscle, but he shows considerable patience and generosity in his handling of Brahms's long, constantly developing melodic lines. Sound is generally good, though the bass may need assistance on some equipment. Ashkenazy manages a skilful blend of classical strength and lyrical warmth in the first movement, whose basic tempo, perfectly chosen, is underpinned by a strong pulse. The rocking accompaniments in the bass (1'47" and onwards) register clearly and cleanly, and provide a vital rhythmic commentary on the melodic line. In the *Andante*, the ebb and flow of the musical argument, the rise and fall of tension, are conveyed with the greatest fidelity, and considerable beauty of utterance. It is in the third movement alone that Ashkenazy falls below par. Everything is just as it should be in a way, but there's a slight lack of boisterous Brahmsian energy and weight. In the finale Ashkenazy draws the passacaglia 'variations' together very adroitly, bringing out the differing personality of each episode, but maintaining overall shape and momentum towards a well-judged climax. Ultimately it doesn't possess greatness of the kind provided by Kleiber and Toscanini, whose performances really do burn in the imagination and memory. Decca's issue has, however, an enterprising coupling in the shape of a bright, characterful account of Rubbra's curiously un-Brahmsian orchestration of the *Handel* Variations.

There is a little more separation of timbre in the sound of Haitink's Boston Brahms Fourth and *Haydn* Variations than in his previous 1972-73 Amsterdam recordings; perhaps marginally less ambient warmth in tuttis, though certainly more than in Kleiber's famously lean and exciting 1981 Vienna recording of the symphony. However, the 20 years that separate Haitink's accounts have brought some much more marked musical changes, not only in his overall view – he adds a minute to each of the symphony's first two movements – but in a more acute moment-by-moment control (comparable, at times to Carlos Kleiber's), pliant pacing and communicative phrasing. The first movement is now not so much an older man's Brahms as an older Brahms, more poignantly reflective, more given to mysterious depths, less heroic and purposeful in overall cast though still able to bestir himself mightily, and when the coda arrives, to declaim with the terrifying rage of age. The second movement (smoother clarinet tone in Boston), now serene and very slow indeed has a timeless Brucknerian tread. The *Scherzo* is quite as fearsomely jocular as before, though with more interesting shadings. This is Brahms playing, conducting and recording of real stature, not as intensely dramatic in the symphony as the exacting Kleiber (who has no coupling), but worthy to stand alongside him.

Additional recommendations ...
...No. 4. Variations on a Theme by Haydn. **Hallé Orchestra / James Loughran.** Classics for Pleasure
Ⓑ CD-CFP4614 (59 minutes: ADD: 3/93).
... No. 4. Variations on a Theme by Haydn. **Boston Symphony Orchestra / Bernard Haitink.** Philips
Ⓕ 434 991-2PH (62 minutes: DDD: 9/94).
...No. 4. Academic Festival Overture. **Chicago Symphony Orchestra / Daniel Barenboim.** Erato
Ⓜ 4509-95194-2 (51 minutes: DDD: 11/94).
...No. 4. *Coupled with works by* **Klemperer, Ravel** and **Vaughan Williams** New Philharmonia
Orchestra **/ Leopold Stokowski.** BBC Radio Classics Ⓑ BBCRD9107 (74 minutes: ADD: 3/95).
See review in the Collections section; refer to the Index to Reviews.   ⓖ

Brahms String Sextets – No. 1 in B flat major, Op. 18; No. 2 in G major, Op. 36. **Raphael Ensemble**
(James Clark, Elizabeth Wexler, vns; Sally Beamish, Roger Tapping, vas; Andrea Hess, Rhydian
Shaxson, vcs). Hyperion Ⓕ CDA66276 (74 minutes: DDD: 1/89). Recorded 1988.   ⓖ

Completed after the First Piano Concerto, but still comparatively early works, the Sextets are typified by lush textures, ardent emotion, and wonderfully memorable melodic lines. The first is the warmer, more heart-on-the-sleeve piece, balancing with complete naturalness a splendidly lyrical first movement, an urgent, dark set of intricate variations, a lively rustic dance of a *Scherzo*, and a placidly flowing finale. The Second Sextet inhabits at first a more mysterious world of half-shadows, occasionally rent by glorious moments of sunlight. The finale, however, casts off doubt and ends with affirmation. Both works are very susceptible to differing modes of interpretation, and the Raphael Ensemble has established very distinctive views of each, allowing the richness of the texture its head without obscuring the lines, and selecting characteristically distinct tone qualities to typify the two works. The recording is clear and analytic without robbing the sound of its warmth and depth. Altogether an impressive recording début for this ensemble.

Additional recommendations ...

...Nos. 1 and 2. **Academy of St Martin in the Fields Chamber Ensemble.** Chandos Ⓕ CHAN9151 (78 minutes: DDD: 8/93).

...No. 1[a]. Piano Trio No. 1 in B major, Op. 8[b]. **Isaac Stern**, [a]**Alexander Schneider** (vns); [a]**Milton Katims**, [a]**Milton Thomas** (vas); **Pablo Casals**, [a]**Madeline Foley** (vcs); [b]**Dame Myra Hess** (pf). Sony Classical Casals Edition mono Ⓜ SMK58994* (77 minutes: ADD: 5/94).   ⒼⒼ

Brahms Clarinet Quintet in B minor, Op. 155.
Mozart Clarinet Quintet in A major, K581. **Harold Wright** (cl); **Boston Symphony Chamber Players** (Malcolm Lowe, Laura Park, vns; Burton Fine, va; Jules Eskin, vc). Philips Ⓕ 442 149-2PH (72 minutes: DDD: 9/94). Recorded 1993.

Harold Wright was a long-serving and much respected principal with the Boston Symphony Orchestra and with the Boston Chamber Players. The closeness of sympathy between him and the string players is doubtless the product of many years of musical companionship, but that 'orchestral' quality of being aware of everything that is happening with every other player and the 'chamber' quality of mutually exploring music as if anew combine here to create beautiful performances. The two works have in common something that Brahms had clearly observed in Mozart, namely the way the clarinet is not simply the soloist with accompaniment but how its tonal qualities can enhance the textures and enrich the middle registers and sing in duet with different string instruments. Wright and the first violin, Malcolm Lowe, share phrasing and a warmth and sweetness of tone, in Brahms's Quintet especially, in a manner that one can hardly imagine being more sensitively done. This is a gentle, elegiac performance, but also one of intelligence. Mozart's Quintet is also played in reflective vein, with liveliness in the minuet and finale restrained to bright textures and springing rhythms rather than anything more superficially exciting; and the *Larghetto* is sung with a romantic warmth that keeps within classical bounds. The recording is properly responsive to the details of texture, close enough for a few intakes of breath to be heard.

Additional recommendations ...

...Clarinet Quintet. Clarinet Trio in A minor, Op. 114. **Thea King** (cl); **Gabrieli Quartet; Karina Georgian** (vc); **Clifford Benson** (pf). Hyperion Ⓕ CDA66107 (65 minutes: DDD: 2/87).

...Clarinet Quintet[a]. **Mozart** Clarinet Quintet in A major, K581[b]. **Gervase de Peyer** (cl); Members of the **Melos Ensemble.** EMI Ⓜ CDM7 63116-2 (65 minutes: ADD: 11/89)   Ⓖ

...Clarinet Quintet[a]. Clarinet Trio[ab]. **József Balogh** (cl); [a]**Csaba Onczay** (vc); [b]**Danubius Quartet;** [a]**Jenö Jandó** (pf). Naxos Ⓢ 8 550391 (59 minutes: DDD: 9/93).

Brahms Piano Quintet in F minor, Op. 34[a]. String Quartet No. 2 in A minor, Op. 51 No. 2. **Borodin Quartet** (Mikhail Kopelman, Andrei Abramenkov, vns; Dimitri Shebalin, va; Valentin Berlinsky, vc); [a]**Elizo Virzaladze** (pf). Teldec Ⓕ 4509-97461-2 (77 minutes: DDD: 5/95). Recorded 1990.   ⒼⒼ

These were recorded at The Maltings, Snape which provides warm, reverberant reproduction very much in keeping with these players' vision of the well-nourished composer in middle age, a Brahms aglow yet at the same time more traditionally Germanic than the acutely susceptible, highly charged Viennese Brahms from the translucently textured Alban Berg Quartet (listed further on). Always the Borodins prefer the longer line (as in the opening of the slow movement), the broader view, to the Bergs' spontaneous response to detail. Choice is very much a matter of taste since it goes without saying that in all matters of intonation, balance and interplay, both world-renowned teams are exemplary. With the incisive Elizo Virzaladze at the keyboard, the Piano Quintet emerges with magisterial strength and breadth. Not even an earthquake could disrupt the rhythmic stability underpinning each movement (and not least the *Scherzo*), or shake the absolute certainty of each player's conviction. If the Brahms as guardian of classical tradition looms larger than the romanticist, there are still memorable reminders of the vulnerable heart behind it all – as notably in the stabbing intensity they bring to the finale's *poco sostenuto* introduction and temperamental coda.

Additional recommendations ...

...Piano Quintet. **Maurizio Pollini** (pf); **Quartetto Italiano.** DG Ⓕ 419 673-2GH (43 minutes: AAD: 6/87). *Gramophone Award Winner 1980.*   ⒼⒼⒼ

...Piano Quintet. **Schumann** Piano Quintet in E flat major, Op. 44. **Jenö Jandó** (pf); **Kodály Quartet.** Naxos Ⓢ 8 550406 (67 minutes: DDD: 2/91).

...Piano Quintet[a]. String Quartet No. 3 in B flat major, Op. 67. [a]**Piers Lane** (pf); **New Budapest Quartet.** Hyperion Ⓕ CDA66652 (78 minutes: DDD: 4/93).

Brahms Piano Quartets – No. 1 in G minor, Op. 25; No. 2 in A major, Op. 26; No. 3 in C minor, Op. 60. **Isaac Stern** (vn); **Jaime Laredo** (va); **Yo-Yo Ma** (vc); **Emanuel Ax** (pf). Sony Classical Ⓕ S2K45846 (two discs: 128 minutes: DDD: 3/91). Recorded 1986-9. *Gramophone Award Winner 1991. Selected by Sounds in Retrospect.* Ⓖ

These three piano quartets belong to the middle of Brahms's life. They have all the power and lyricism that we associate with his music, as well as the fine craftsmanship that he acquired when young and, with the high standards he set himself, demonstrated in every work thereafter. The mood of the music is again Brahmsian in that alongside a wealth of melodic and harmonic invention there are some shadows: all we know of Brahms's life suggests that he was never a happy man. But if this is reflected in the music, and especially the C minor Quartet, we can recognize the strength of intellect and will that keeps all in proportion so that there is no overt soul-bearing. These quartets are big pieces which often employ a grand manner, though less so in No. 2 than the others. For this reason, the present performances with their exuberant sweep are particularly telling, and although no detail is missed the players offer an overall strength. Top soloists in their own right, they combine their individual gifts with the ability to play as a well integrated team. The recording is close but not overwhelmingly so. Only the booklet, with notes in four languages, mars at least some copies of this issue, for it has some blank pages and details of the movements are missing, as are parts of the English and Italian notes.

Additional recommendations ...

...Nos. 1 and 3. **Domus.** Virgin Classics Ⓕ VC7 59248-2 (76 minutes: DDD: 6/88).

...No. 2. **Mahler** Movement for Piano Quartet. **Domus.** Virgin Classics Ⓕ VC7 59144-2 (61 minutes: DDD: 1/89).

...No. 1. Variations and Fugue on a Theme by Handel, Op. 24 (orch. Rubbra). **London Symphony Orchestra / Neeme Järvi**. Chandos Ⓕ CHAN8825 (71 minutes: DDD: 2/91).

...Nos. 1-3. String Quartet No. 2 in A minor, Op. 51 No. 2. Piano Quintet in F minor, Op. 34. **Schumann** Piano Quintet in E flat major, Op. 44. **Victor Aller** (pf); **Hollywood Quartet.** Testament mono Ⓕ SBT3063* (three discs: 220 minutes: ADD: 1/95).

New review

Brahms Piano Quartet No. 1 in G minor, Op. 25ᵃ. Four Ballades, Op. 10ᵇ. **Emil Gilels** (pf); members of the **Amadeus Quartet** (Norbert Brainin, vn; Peter Schidlof, va; Martin Lovett, vc). DG The Originals Ⓜ 447 407-2GOR (65 minutes: ADD: 6/95). Item marked ᵃ from 2530 133 (11/71), ᵇ2530 655 (7/76).

We have to thank members of the Amadeus Quartet for two outstanding performances of Brahms's G minor Piano Quartet – a comparatively recent one with Murray Perahia (below), unforgettable for its spontaneity and uninhibited romantic warmth and verve, and this much earlier (1971) version with Gilels, here reissued at medium price in DG's Originals series. The booklet reminds us that the recording made history at that date since "a contract between an artist from the Soviet Union and a Western label was a sensational event in cultural diplomacy". Reproduced with respect for the sound quality of its time, the playing has a glowing strength and intensity throughout, while never allowing the composer's heart to rule his head. Only in the first movement's opulent textures does the keyboard occasionally dominate. From Gilels we're also given a maturely unhurried, essentially 'inward' recording (made some five years later) of Brahms's four youthful *Ballades*, with their strange, almost supernatural undertones. A bargain.

Additional recommendation ...

...No. 1. **Murray Perahia** (pf); members of the **Amadeus Quartet.** CBS Ⓕ CD42361 (40 minutes: DDD: 12/87).

Brahms String Quartets – No. 1 in C minor, Op. 51 No. 1; No. 3 in B flat major, Op. 67. **Borodin Quartet** (Mikhail Kopelman, Andrei Abramenkov, vns; Dimitri Shebalin, va; Valentin Berlinsky, vc). Teldec Ⓕ 4509-90889-2 (69 minutes: DDD: 11/94). Recorded 1993. ⒶⒶ

Brahms String Quartets, Op. 51 – No. 1 in C minor; No. 2 in A minor. **Cleveland Quartet** (William Preucil, Peter Salaff, vns; James Dunham, va; Paul Katz, vc). Telarc Ⓕ CD80346 (68 minutes: DDD: 2/95). Recorded 1993.

It's essentially the mature, middle-aged composer that the Borodin Quartet evoke in their full-bodied, spacious and firmly-contoured performance of the C minor Quartet. Comparing it with the Alban Berg Quartet (listed below), the first and most obvious difference is the Borodin's more deliberate tempo for the powerful flanking movements in the home key. They prefer breadth to their rivals' urgency. In the *Romanze*, richly romantic from both teams, the Borodin favour a riper sound-world, warmly fortified by their viola and cello, as against the Berg's more translucent sonority, with its ethereal *pianissimo* often evoking the rapt magic of moonlight. Differences in the B flat Quartet are less marked: both readings are vividly characterful. But again – and perhaps most of all in the finale – the overriding impression is of more traditionally Germanic romanticism from the Russians, whereas from the Viennese team we meet a more minutely impressionable as well as a more highly-strung composer. The Teldec recording, made in this company's Berlin studio, is as full, warm and open as the playing. Whichever group you choose, you will not be disappointed.

Though the Cleveland Quartet have changed both their leader and viola player in recent years, all their old tonal opulence (rooted in the exceptionally full-bodied Guarneri cello of Paul Katz) is still very much there. So is all the old fire, and equally, their determination to wring the last drop of expression from even the most intimate confession. In short, you could go many a long day without encountering a more overtly romantic composer than the Brahms you meet here. In the C minor Quartet's *Romanze* some listeners might in fact prefer the very mellow but more emotionally reticent Borodin Quartet, or the Alban Berg with their ethereally withdrawn *pianissimo*. In the bolder flanking movements they are as compulsive as the highly-strung, impressionable Alban Berg while often finding a broader, suaver, melodic sweep. The venue was their favoured Mechanics Hall at Worcester, Massachusetts, a warmly reverberant building – as the sheer fullness of the sound immediately makes plain.

Additional recommendations ...

...Nos. 1 and 2. **Gabrieli Quartet.** Chandos Ⓕ CHAN8562 (61 minutes: DDD: 4/88).
...Nos. 1-3. **Takács Quartet.** Decca Ⓕ 425 526-2DH (66 minutes: DDD: 9/90).
...Nos. 2 and 3. **Orlando Quartet.** Ottavo Ⓕ OTRC68819 (75 minutes: DDD: 6/90).
...Nos. 1 and 2. **New Budapest Quartet.** Hyperion Ⓕ CDA66651 (67 minutes: DDD: 4/93).
...No. 3. Piano Quintet in F minor, Op. 34ᵃ. ᵃ**Piers Lane** (pf); **New Budapest Quartet.** Hyperion Ⓕ CDA66652 (78 minutes: DDD: 4/93).
...Nos. 1-3. **Alban Berg Quartet.** EMI Ⓕ CDS7 54829-2 (two discs: 102 minutes: DDD: 2/94).   Ⓖ
...Nos. 1 and 2. **Carmina Quartet.** Denon Ⓕ CO-75756 (66 minutes: DDD: 6/94).
...Nos. 1-3. **Sine Nomine Quartet.** Claves Ⓕ CD50-9404/5 (two discs: 99 minutes: DDD: 10/94).
...Nos. 1-3. **Dvořák** String Quartet No. 13 in G major, B192ᵇ. **Alban Berg Quartet.** Teldec Ⓜ 4509-95503-2 (two discs: 134 minutes: ADD: 2/95).
...No. 2. **Schumann** String Quartet No. 3 in A major, Op. 41 No. 3. **Vogler Quartet.** RCA Victor Red Seal Ⓕ 09026 61866-2 (66 minutes: DDD: 7/95).

Brahms Piano Trio No. 1 in B major, Op. 8.
Mendelssohn Piano Trio No. 1 in D minor, Op. 49. **Chung Trio** (Kyung-Wha Chung, vn; Myung-Wha Chung, vc; Myung-Whun Chung, pf). Decca Ⓕ 421 425-2DH (65 minutes: DDD: 4/95). Recorded 1987.   Ⓖ

New review

Brahms Piano Trios – No. 1 in B major, Op. 8; No. 2 in C major, Op. 87. **Augustin Dumay** (vn); **Jian Wang** (vc); **Maria-João Pires** (pf). DG Ⓕ 447 055-2GH (67 minutes: DDD: 5/96). Recorded 1994-5.   Ⓖ

The Chung Trio give us real connoisseur performances. It is the streamlining, the new clarity and economy of idea and structure in Brahms's revision of the Op. 8 which the Chungs uniquely reveal. As timbres blend gently at each confluence, it is the journey rather than the destination which really matters to them in the first movement. The care with which the piano feels its way into the second subject prepares for the subtlest nuances of detail and variation in the development, so that the first idea resurfaces in its final form under bright, new light. The scherzo is one of the sharpest on disc; the clarity of the *Adagio*'s quiet playing is as much a credit to Christopher Raeburn's direction as to the performers' sensitivity. The Mendelssohn *Molto allegro agitato* restrains its tendency to romp ahead too early: the Chungs' antennae focus on the underlying melancholy within the music's dark wash, built up by the cello's introduction of both first and second subjects. They give space and time enough for the maximum clarity of articulation of shorter note values, and create a substantial head of steam for their first joint statement. The restrained tempo means that Myung-Whun's piano can glory in its strength of direction, and in the quiet beauty of its linking passages, while Kyung-Wha's violin can sing its heart out. The slow movement follows as a continuing though becalmed song. And the scherzo, Ariel-like, drinks the air before it and, in turn, influences the finale whose dactylic dance barely touches the ground.

In the Chinese cellist Jian Wang, the duo of Augustin Dumay and Maria-João Pires have found themselves a true soul mate as this, their first record of piano trios together, engagingly shows. The B major Trio doesn't quite topple the Chungs' recording but it comes pretty close to it. And in comparison with the recently reissued Grieg Trio performance, this has a greater tendency to linger, more rubato and more vibrato, with a bright, exultant glow as the violin joins the ground-swell of the great opening melody. The *Scherzo*'s trio, likewise, pulls back to form a slow, soupy centrepiece. Here the rubato is a little mannered, with neither the instinctive lilt of, say, the Beaux Arts, nor the directness of the more plain-speaking Griegs. Everything, though, can be traded in for the sheer wonder of this *Adagio*. As slow as any on disc, it reveals the real empathy between Dumay and Wang in moments of great beauty where the Milstein legacy in Dumay's playing is wonderfully apparent. For the C major Trio, Dumay, Pires and Wang offer a generally broad and spacious performance, with a suppleness of repartee in the slow movement's variations which matches their fluency of invention. The *Scherzo*'s niggling is as compact and securely balanced as any, before the players glide, then stride, into the bright sunlight of the Trio.

Additional recommendations ...

...No. 1; No. 2 in C major, Op. 8; No. 3 in C minor, Op. 101; A major, Op. posth. (attrib. Brahms). **Beaux Arts Trio.** Philips Duo Ⓜ 438 365-2PM2 (two discs: 119 minutes: DDD: 1/88).
...Nos. 1-3; A major, Op. posth; Horn Trio E flat major, Op. 40ᶜ; Clarinet Trio in A minor, Op. 114ᶜ. **Odeon Trio;** ᶜ**Rainer Moog** (va). Capriccio Ⓕ 10 633 (three discs: 175 minutes: DDD: 7/93).

...Nos. 1-3[a]; A major, Op. posth. Horn Trio in E flat major, Op. 40[b]. Clarinet Trio in A minor,
Op. 114[c]. [ad]**Beaux Arts Trio;** [c]**George Pieterson** (cl); [b]**Francis Orval** (hn); [b]**Arthur Grumiaux** (vn);
[b]**Gyorgy Sebok** (pf). Philips Duo Ⓜ 438 365-2PM2 (two discs: 130 minutes: ADD: 8/93).

...No. 1[a]. String Sextet No. 1 in B major, Op. 18[b]. **Isaac Stern,** [b]**Alexander Schneider** (vns); [b]**Milton
Katims,** [b]**Milton Thomas** (vas); **Pablo Casals,** [b]**Madeline Foley** (vcs); [a]**Dame Myra Hess** (pf). Sony
Classical Casals Edition mono Ⓜ SMK58994* (77 minutes: ADD: 5/94).

...No. 1. **Beethoven** Piano Trio No. 7 in B flat major, Op. 97, "Archduke". **Viktoria Mullova** (vn);
Heinrich Schiff (vc); **André Previn** (pf). Philips Ⓕ 442 123-2PH (75 minutes: DDD: 8/95).

...Nos. 1 and 2. **Grieg Trio.** Virgin Classics Ⓕ VC5 45184-2 (64 minutes: DDD: 4/96).

Brahms Horn Trio in E flat major, Op. 40. Piano Quintet in F minor, Op. 34. **Nash Ensemble**
(Marcia Crayford, Elizabeth Layton, vns; Roger Chase, va; Christopher van Kampen, vc; Frank
Lloyd, hn; Ian Brown, pf). CRD Ⓕ CRD3489 (73 minutes: DDD: 9/94). Recorded 1991.

It would be hard to imagine more amiable performances of these two strongly characterized Brahms
works. The Nash Ensemble's comfortable approach is intense as well as warm, plainly derived from
long experience performing this music in concert. The speeds in both works are markedly slower than
on other versions, and the ensemble is a degree less polished, but in their expressive warmth they are
just as magnetic, with a sense of continuity that the higher-powered readings do not always convey.
The romanticism of the Nash approach comes out particularly strongly in the opening *Andante* of the
Horn Trio, with the horn soloist, Frank Lloyd, producing an exceptionally rich, braying tone,
reminiscent of Dennis Brain. After relaxed accounts of the first three movements the galloping finale
is then given with great panache, conveying more fun than the more virtuoso reading from Ashkenazy,
Perlman and Tuckwell. Thanks partly to the CRD recording, the Nash performances are made to
sound satisfyingly beefy, almost orchestral, though some may find the full-bodied sound a degree too
reverberant, with the piano rather in front of the strings. The disc can be strongly recommended,
particularly as this is the only available coupling of these two works.

Additional recommendations ...

...Horn Trio[a]. **Beethoven** Horn Sonata in F major, Op. 17. **Krufft** Horn Sonata in F major.
Lowell Greer (hn); [a]**Stephanie Chase** (vn); **Steven Lubin** (fp). Harmonia Mundi Ⓕ HMU90 7037
(65 minutes: DDD: 9/92). ✍

...Horn Trio. **Franck** Violin Sonata. **Schumann** Adagio and Allegro in A flat major, Op. 70.
Saint-Saëns Romance in E flat major, Op. 67. **Itzhak Perlman** (vn); **Barry Tuckwell** (hn);
Vladimir Ashkenazy (pf). Decca Ⓜ 433 695-2DM (73 minutes: ADD: 9/92). Ⓖ

...Horn Trio[a]. **Schumann** Andante and Variations[b]. Adagio and Allegro, Op. 70. **Radovan
Vlatkovic** (hn); [a]**Hans Maile** (vn); [b]**George Donderer,** [b]**Mathias Donderer** (vcs); **Vladimir
Ashkenazy,** [b]**Vovka Ashkenazy** (pfs). Decca Ⓕ 433 850-2DH (56 minutes: DDD: 10/93).

Brahms Cello Sonatas – No. 1 in E minor, Op. 38; No. 2 in F major, Op. 99. Violin Sonata No. 1
in G major, Op. 78 (arr. Klengel). **Karina Georgian** (vc); **Pavel Gililov** (pf). Biddulph Ⓜ LAW014
(two discs: 88 minutes: DDD: 9/94). Recorded 1989-90.

The two true cello sonatas are keenly contrasted. Unhurried tempos for the flanking movements of
the earlier E minor work help to emphasize its gravity: these artists also find the droll charm of the
Allegretto quasi Menuetto and the nostalgia of its trio without a trace of self-conscious coquetry.
Balance, finely judged in the E minor work, sometimes goes against the mellifluously lyrical but not
outsize-toned cello in the passionate F major Sonata, with its turbulently rich-textured keyboard part.
Yet the two artists are so closely attuned in spirit that this does not seriously disturb: so often Gililov
brings an Ashkenazy-like translucency to the piano's upper register by way of amends. The laden
Adagio is played with a totally committed intensity by them both and the songful finale has an
endearing spring-like freshness. The bonus included is Paul Klengel's cello transcription of the
G major Violin Sonata, Op. 78. All three recordings were made at The Maltings, Snape with an over-
reverberant sounding bass in this last work, but with a clear and natural sound quality in the two
Cello Sonatas proper. The playing itself is refined and affectionate.

Additional recommendations ...

...Nos. 1[a] and 2[a]. Intermezzos – C sharp minor; Op. 117 No. 3; A major, Op. 118 No. 2; E flat
minor, Op. 118 No. 6; E minor, Op. 119 No. 2; C major, Op. 119 No. 3. [a]**Gregor Piatgorsky** (vc);
Artur Rubinstein (pf). RCA Victor Gold Seal Ⓜ 09026 62592-2* (74 minutes: ADD/mono)

...Nos. 1 and 2. **Mstislav Rostropovich** (vc); **Rudolf Serkin** (pf). DG Ⓕ 410 510-2GH (58 minutes:
DDD: 9/83). Ⓖ

...Nos. 1 and 2. **Steven Isserlis** (vc); **Peter Evans** (pf). Hyperion Ⓕ CDA66159 (50 minutes: DDD:
4/86).

...Nos. 1 and 2. Violin Sonata No. 3 in D minor, Op. 108 (trans. cello). **Yo-Yo Ma** (vc); **Emanuel Ax**
(pf). Sony Classical Ⓕ SK48191 (75 minutes: DDD: 11/92).

...Nos. 1 and 2. **Pieter Wispelwey** (vc); **Paul Komen** (pf). Channel Classics Ⓕ CCS5493 (53 minutes: DDD: 1/94). 🖉   Ⓖ

...No. 2. *Coupled with works by* **Beethoven** Pablo Casals (vc); **Mieczyslaw Horszowski** (pf). EMI Références mono Ⓜ CHS5 65185-2* (two discs: 136 minutes: ADD: 10/94). *See review under Beethoven; refer to the Index to Reviews.*   ⒼⒼⒼ

...Nos. 1 and 2. **Mendelssohn** Song without words, Op. 109. **Schumann** Fantasiestücke, Op. 73. **Nathaniel Rosen** (vc); **Doris Stevenson** (pf). John Marks Records Ⓕ JMR5 (70 minutes: DDD: 3/95).

...Nos. 1 and 2. **János Starker** (vc); **György Sebök** (pf). Erato Ⓜ 4509-96950-2 (54 minutes: ADD: 7/95).

New review

Brahms Clarinet Sonatas, Op. 120 – No. 1 in F minor; No. 2 in E flat major. Clarinet Trio in A minor, Op. 114[a]. **Michel Portal** (cl); [a]**Boris Pergamenschikow** (vc); **Mikhail Rudy** (pf). EMI Ⓕ CDC7 54466-2 (70 minutes: DDD: 5/93).

To be given the Clarinet Trio as well as the two sonatas is generous measure in itself. So how good to be able to say that this disc is an even greater bargain in terms of quality. The insert-notes remind us of the inspirational source of all three works, specifying the "polish and almost feminine sensitivity" as the qualities in the playing of Richard Mühlfeld (principal clarinettist of the Meiningen Court Orchestra) that Brahms so much admired. One feels that he would feel just the same about Michel Portal. His tone is as liquid as his playing is super-sensitive. Mikhail Rudy and Boris Pergamenschikow are ideally attuned partners for him: all three respond with a loving intimacy to the music's glowing and nostalgic lyricism. Yet there is no lack of strength when required. These very finely balanced performances banish all misconceptions of the composer as a brusque and burly academic. Instead, we're reminded of his acutely vulnerable heart – such as in the magically ethereal coda of the Trio's first movement. The recording is excellent.

Additional recommendations ...

...Clarinet Sonatas. **Thea King** (cl); **Clifford Benson** (pf). Hyperion Ⓕ CDA66202 (43 minutes: DDD: 10/87).

...Clarinet Sonatas. **Gervase de Peyer** (cl); **Gwenneth Pryor** (pf). Chandos Ⓕ CHAN8563 (43 minutes: DDD: 3/88).

Brahms Viola Sonatas, Op. 120 – No. 1 in F minor; No. 2 in E flat major.
Joachim Variations on an Original Theme in E major, Op. 10. **Rivka Golani** (va); **Konstantin Bogino** (pf). Conifer Ⓕ CDCF199 (71 minutes: DDD: 9/92). Recorded 1991.

The Brahms Viola Sonatas belong to the last years of his life and were originally written for clarinet. But the composer always saw them as alternatively for viola and this version goes further than just transposing notes as necessary: for example, some figuration is different, there is double-stopping, and sometimes the viola even plays where the clarinet does not. Rivka Golani brings plenty of tonal flexibility to the music and demonstrates her understanding of Brahms's autumnal style, with its smouldering passions and hints of regret. So does her pianist Konstantin Bogino. The recording successfully balances the two players and instruments, and if the piano bass has a heavyish sound, that suits the music quite well. Golani comes across here as an essentially serious artist, which is perhaps right, although she might have brought more pace to the opening *Allegro appassionato* of the F minor Sonata and more of a smile to its *grazioso* third movement. She is also a little deliberate in the two *allegro* movements in the E flat major Sonata although its finale has fine vigour. But in compensation she offers much tonal beauty. Joachim was a friend of Brahms and the first interpreter of his Violin Concerto, and his Variations are here recorded for the first time. Their style suggests something between Schumann and Elgar and no very strong individuality emerges, but he wrote beautifully for the instrument and Golani's playing is as refined and expressive as one could wish for.

Additional recommendations ...

...Viola Sonatas[a]. Lieder, Op. 91[b]. **Pinchas Zukerman** (va); [b]**Marilyn Horne** (mez); [b]**Martin Katz**, [a]**Marc Neikrug** (pfs). RCA Victor Red Seal Ⓕ 09026 61276-2 (57 minutes: DDD: 9/94).

...Viola Sonata No. 2[a]. **Casadesus** Viola Concerto in B minor[b]. **Mozart** Sinfonia concertante in E flat major, K364/K320d[c]. [c]**Albert Spalding** (vn); **William Primrose** (va); [a]**Gerald Moore** (pf); [b]**chamber orchestra / Walter Goehr**; [c]**New Friends of Music Orchestra / Fritz Stiedry.** Pearl mono Ⓜ GEMMCD9045* (64 minutes: AAD: 9/94).

New review

Brahms Violin Sonatas – No. 1 in G major, Op. 78; No. 2 in A major, Op. 100; No. 3 in D minor, Op. 108. **Nicolas Chumachenco** (vn); **Daniel Levy** (pf). Edelweiss Ⓕ ED1036 (72 minutes: DDD: 4/96).

Polish-born violinist Nicolas Chumachenco was raised in Argentina and attended masterclasses with Heifetz before graduating in 1967 and settling in Switzerland, where he now teaches. On the evidence of this disc, he is a fine musician as well as a skilful player, while his partner Daniel Levy is also an artist of quality. They take the G major Sonata spaciously, but do not forfeit momentum in the process and the delicate warmth of the music comes across convincingly, helped by a warm, well-balanced recording. Their essentially lyrical approach is not unlike that of Augustin Dumay and

Maria-João Pires, who perhaps have the edge on them in that they paint a still richer picture expressively: arguably, Chumachenco is too sweet-toned to bring out the full depth of passion here, and perhaps especially in the final D minor Sonata. However, no one who buys this Edelweiss issue will be disappointed. It glows with affection, and, beyond that, does so in a Viennese way. It would be wrong to suggest that the necessary intensity is lacking or that flames only smoulder – try the development of the *Allegro amabile* in the A major Sonata to prove otherwise. The best test is probably the D minor Sonata, which receives a fine performance even if these players' strengths are best revealed in gentler music. Indeed, Chumachenco and Levy are impressive artists whose natural eloquence well suits this repertory.

Additional recommendations ...

...Nos. 1-3. **Arthur Grumiaux** (vn); **György Sebök** (pf). Philips Solo Ⓜ 446 570-2PM (66 minutes: ADD).

...Nos. 1-3. **Itzhak Perlman** (vn); **Vladimir Ashkenazy** (pf). EMI Ⓕ CDC7 47403-2 (70 minutes: DDD: 2/87). Ⓖ

...Nos. 1-3. **Krysia Osostowicz** (vn); **Susan Tomes** (pf). Hyperion Ⓕ CDA66465 (68 minutes: DDD: 11/91).

...Nos. 1-3. **Augustin Dumay** (vn); **Maria-João Pires** (pf). DG Ⓕ 435 800-2GH (72 minutes: DDD: 3/93).

...Nos. 1 and 2[a]; No. 3[b]. **Gioconda De Vito** (vn); [a]**Edwin Fischer**, [b]**Tito Aprea** (pfs). Testament mono Ⓕ SBT1024* (71 minutes: ADD: 12/93).

Brahms (arr. Piatti) 21 Hungarian Dances.
Schmidt Drei Phantasiestücke nach ungarischen Nationalmelodien. **Nancy Green** (vc); **Frederick Moyer** (pf). Biddulph Ⓕ LAW010 (66 minutes: DDD: 5/95). Recorded 1993.

Brahms's *Hungarian Dances*, originally scored for piano duet, comprise two separate groups of pieces: the first ten were completed in 1868, the remainder finished in 1880. These arrangements by cello virtuoso, Alfredo Piatti, offer colourful versions that highlight the composer's startlingly varied approach to his source material. These compelling performances convey in a beguiling way the extent of the composer's nourishment of the gipsy folk idiom. Green and Moyer demonstrate a genuine sympathy for these pieces that sounds wholly appropriate to Piatti's own sensitive arrangements. Virtuoso techniques, such as multiple stopping, harmonics and octave doubling, and dramatically conceived registral contrast (most notably in No. 10), vividly display this excellently matched duo's intuitive response to the music's mood swings. The balance tends to favour the cello in dances Nos. 1 to 10, but Green and Moyer sound ideally matched in the second group, where the piano plays a more equal role and Brahms's creative influence is more evident. The performers luxuriate in the remarkable array of textural and subtly coloured effects created by Piatti's arrangements. Try the delightful exchange between cello and piano in No. 15, the spacious, long-lined melody of No. 17, or the atmospheric cello harmonics in No. 18. Schmidt's *Three Fantasy Pieces*, in which Green's intelligent and perceptive phrasing of the cello's ornate melodic lines is deftly accompanied by Moyer, complete this unusual and rewarding programme.

Additional recommendation ...

...21 Hungarian Dances (arr. Joachim). **Joachim** Andantino in A minor. Romance in B flat major. **Marat Bisengaliev** (vn); **John Lenehan** (pf). Naxos Ⓢ 8 553026 (67 minutes: DDD: 2/96).

New review

Brahms Variations on a Theme by Paganini, Op. 35.
Schumann Arabeske in C major, Op. 18. Etudes symphoniques, Opp. 13 and posth. **Jean-Yves Thibaudet** (pf). Decca Ⓕ 444 338-2DH (65 minutes: DDD: 10/95).

This is a refreshingly individual, though never quirky, display of imaginative vitality in the two most virtuosic works for solo piano that Schumann and Brahms ever wrote. Predictably the technical challenges of Brahms's *Paganini* Variations hold few fears for Thibaudet. Even Horowitz once admitted that in Liszt's *Faust* Waltz he'd heard Thibaudet's fingers do things that his own couldn't in dexterity, clarity of articulation and general command. But virtuosity is never an end in itself. What surprises and pleases most is Thibaudet's readiness to relax and revel in the romance, the mystery, the lyrical charm and the sheer tonal seductiveness of the less demonstrative, the more personally expressive, variations. Some listeners may of course find his whole approach too fancifully Gallic, insufficiently Germanic. But more than one road leads to Rome, and arguably even Brahms himself would succumb to the spring-like allure of this one. Schumann's *Arabeske*, delectably liquid (despite its over-hasty second A minor episode) brings brief respite before the *Etudes symphoniques*, which, like nearly everyone today, Thibaudet plays in the posthumously published 1861 edition (reinstating the two numbers excluded by Schumann in his own 1852 revision though retaining its tautened finale). His leisurely unfolding of the theme, followed by an uncommonly brisk first variation (marked only *un poco più vivo*) typifies his immediacy of response to every changing mood, which once more, as in the Brahms, results in a reading perhaps more memorable for variety than continuity. But again his fingers sing as finely as they sparkle. He wisely plays the five posthumously published, rejected early variations as a separate group at the end of the work, rightly reserving his most intimately poetic revelations for the last two, both beautifully done. Sound reproduction throughout is at once natural and never too forward for comfort in your own room.

Brahms Piano works. **Gerhard Oppitz** (pf). Eurodisc Ⓕ RD69245 (five discs, also available separately: 74, 73, 73, 76 and 76 minutes: DDD: 10/90).
RD69246 – Piano Sonata No. 1 in C major, Op. 1. Four Piano Pieces, Op. 119. Variations and Fugue on a Theme by Handel, Op. 24. *RD69247* – Four Ballades, Op. 10. Variations on an Original Theme, Op. 21 No. 1. Variations on a Hungarian Song, Op. 21 No. 2. Six Piano Pieces, Op. 118. *RD69248* – Three Intermezzos, Op. 117. Piano Sonata No. 2 in F sharp minor, Op. 2. Eight Piano Pieces, Op. 76. *RD69249* – Two Rhapsodies, Op. 79. Scherzo in E flat minor, Op. 4. Seven Fantasias, Op. 116. Variations on a Theme by Paganini, Op. 35. *RD69250* – Variations in F sharp minor on a Theme by R. Schumann, Op. 9. 16 Waltzes, Op. 39. Piano Sonata No. 3 in F minor, Op. 5.

Aaron Copland once called Fauré "the French Brahms", and we can find the same reticent warmth, harmonic subtlety and pianistic refinement, together with the ability to say much in little, in a Brahms intermezzo as we do in one of his nocturnes. But the comparison falls away as soon as we turn to Brahms's earlier piano music, and it's worth remembering that most of his solo pieces are either early or late – there's nothing save for the Eight Pieces, Op. 76 and the Two Rhapsodies, Op. 79, in the three decades and 80 opus numbers between the *Paganini* Variations in 1863 and the Fantasias, Op. 116, in 1892. There's also a marked contrast between the fire of the young Brahms writing big virtuoso pieces and the mellower emotions that a man nearing the end of his life expressed in fewer (but no less telling) notes. In the three sonatas, all written before the composer reached 21, Gerald Oppitz convinces us at once in the big gestures over the whole keyboard that characterize the opening of each, yet he is a gentle giant, too, in the tender moments that invariably follow by the next page. We are in safe interpretative hands, for Oppitz is at one with the ebb-and-flow of tempo and tone, while pedalling (not always easy in this music) is convincing too. He also manages the sometimes naïve figuration well, as in the trio in the *Scherzo* of the First Sonata. His technical command is excellent. The other two sonatas have the same strength and high seriousness. He takes a predictably stern view of the E flat minor Scherzo and the Ballades, Op. 10, although perhaps the *Handel* Variations and the other variation sets could have done with a little more fantasy and playfulness. However, the taxing *Paganini* Variations have sureness and strength. Oppitz is also pretty well at home in the late music. The sorrowful B minor and E flat minor Intermezzos are compelling, though the former is taken slower than usual, as are the First and Third Intermezzos of Op. 117. This serious artist sometimes fails to lighten his heart enough, e.g. in the B minor Capriccio, Op. 76 and the C major Intermezzo, Op. 119, with its markings of *grazioso, giocoso* and *leggiero*. Nevertheless, the pianist is so good at conveying the Brahmsian dour or questioning seriousness that with that one reservation, no collector getting these CDs will be disappointed. Not quite everything is here – there are studies and other smaller items that have not yet entered the concert repertory.

Additional recommendations ...

...Piano works. **Julius Katchen** (pf). Decca Ⓜ 430 053-2DM6 (six discs: 388 minutes: ADD: 2/91).

...Four Ballades. **Schubert** Piano Sonata in A minor, D537. **Arturo Benedetti Michelangeli** (pf). DG Ⓕ 400 043-2GH (48 minutes: ADD: 3/83).

...Four Ballades. Four Scherzos. **Vladimir Ashkenazy** (pf). Decca Ⓕ 417 474-2DH (74 minutes: ADD: 2/87).

...Four Ballades. **Weber** Piano Sonata No. 2 in A flat major, J199. **Alfred Brendel** (pf). Philips Ⓕ 426 439-2PH (53 minutes: DDD: 6/91).

...Variations and Fugue on a Theme by Handel. Rhapsodies. Six Piano Pieces, Op. 118. **Emanuel Ax** (pf). Sony Classical Ⓕ SK48046 (68 minutes: DDD: 10/92).

...Variations on an Original Theme. Variations on a Hungarian Song. Five Piano Studies. **Idil Biret** (pf). Naxos Ⓢ 8 550509 (56 minutes: DDD: 8/94).

...Piano Sonatas – No. 1; No. 2 in F sharp minor, Op. 2. Variations on a Theme by Paganini. Capriccio in C major, Op. 76 No. 8. Intermezzo in E minor, Op. 116 No. 5. Ballade in G minor, Op. 118 No. 3. Rhapsody in E flat major, Op. 119 No. 4. *Coupled with works by* **Schumann** **Sviatoslav Richter** (pf). Philips Ⓕ 438 477-2PH3 (three discs: 184 minutes: DDD: 8/94). *See review under Schumann; refer to the Index to Reviews.*

...Variations and Fugue on a Theme by Handel. Two Rhapsodies, Op. 79. Variations on a Theme by Paganini. **Gerhard Oppitz** (pf). RCA Victor Red Seal Ⓕ 09026 61811-2 (69 minutes: DDD: 9/94).

...Two Rhapsodies, Op. 79. *Coupled with works by* **Chopin, Prokofiev, Ravel** and **Liszt** **Martha Argerich** (pf). DG The Originals Ⓜ 447 430-2GOR (71 minutes: ADD: 6/95). *See review in the Collections section; refer to the Index to Reviews.*   ⒼⒼ

...Variations on a Theme by R. Schumann. Variations and Fugue on a Theme by Handel,. Variations on a Hungarian song. Theme and Variations in D minor. **Mikhail Rudy** (pf). EMI Ⓕ CDC5 55167-2 (64 minutes: DDD: 7/95).

...Variations on a Theme by Paganini – Book 2. *Coupled with works by* **Mendelssohn, Bach, Tchaikovsky** and **Rachmaninov**. **Shura Cherkassky** (pf). Decca Ⓕ 433 655-2DH (68 minutes: ADD: 2/96). *See review in the Collections section; refer to the Index to Reviews.*

...Piano Pieces, Op. 76 – No. 2, Capriccio in B minor; No. 3, Intermezzo in A flat major. Capriccio in D minor, Op. 116 No. 7. Intermezzo in E flat major, Op. 117 No. 1. Intermezzo in C major, Op. 119 No. 3. *Coupled with works by* **D. Scarlatti, Schumann, Matthay, Bach** and

Ferguson Dame Myra Hess (pf). Biddulph mono Ⓜ LHW025* (76 minutes: ADD: 3/96). *See review in the Collections section; refer to the Index to Reviews.* Ⓖ
…Variations on a Theme by R. Schumann. Variations and Fugue on a Theme by Handel. Four Ballades, Op. 10. **Jorge Federico Osorio** (pf). ASV Quicksilva Ⓢ CDQS6161 (68 minutes: DDD: 5/96).

New review

Brahms Piano Sonata No. 3 in F minor, Op. 5[a]. Intermezzos[b] – E flat major, Op. 117 No. 1; C major, Op. 119 No. 3.
Schubert Piano Sonata No. 21 in B flat major, D960[b]. **Sir Clifford Curzon** (pf). Decca The Classic Sound Ⓜ 448 578-2DCS (77 minutes: ADD: 7/96). Item marked [a] from SXL6041 (5/63), [b]SXL6580 (12/73).

It took wild horses to drag Curzon into the studio, at least in his last years, and he was a record company's nightmare when it came to agreeing what might be issued. One could say that Curzon was not a natural pianist, yet he developed a technique which admirably served the force of his will: and when the two were in harness and in good shape the transcendental aspects of his playing could produce an indelible musical experience. These recordings have lost none of their freshness. The little holes and imperfections are quite unimportant because at every moment Curzon is conveying an exactitude of character and sense. His sound 'speaks' and persuades you to listen to something precise. Nothing is generalized. Yet the overview is there as well as the detail, particularly in the Schubert. As with every great pianist, the quality of his sound is distinctive: tightly focused, crystalline, refulgent. With his sovereign control of line and timing, the pianism seems at all times to be perfectly weighted and to have everything within its sights. You could say that about other great interpreters, no doubt, but there is a special attractiveness about Curzon's ability to delight the senses while penetrating to the heart of the matter. When he was on form he could talk of the most serious things while singing at you like a nightingale. How crude most performances of the Brahms F minor Sonata seem when compared with his. All the climaxes well up from within (and how they glow), yet its scale and range are thrillingly made manifest. This is terrific value at mid price. The sound is fair to good in both the big pieces – and only slightly inferior in the earlier recording. The two Brahms *Intermezzos* are in a very dry acoustic as if Curzon had recorded them at home (perhaps he did?); but so they were on the original LP.

Additional recommendations …
…Piano Sonata No. 3. Four Ballades, Op. 10. **Idil Biret** (pf). Naxos Ⓢ 8 550352 (63 minutes: DDD: 12/92).
…Piano Sonata No. 3. Intermezzo. Romance in F major, Op. 118. No. 5. Four Ballades, Op. 10. **Artur Rubinstein** (pf). RCA Victor Gold Seal mono/stereo Ⓜ 09026 61862-2* (63 minutes: ADD: 9/94).
…Piano Sonata No. 3. Four Ballades, Op. 10. **Grigory Sokolov** (pf). Opus 111 Ⓕ OPS30-103 (67 minutes: DDD: 3/95).

Brahms Piano Sonata No. 3 in F minor, Op. 5.
Liszt Années de pèlerinage, deuxième année, Italie, S161 – Après une lecture du Dante (fantasia quasi sonata).
Schumann Toccata in C major, Op. 7. **Mark Anderson** (pf). Nimbus Ⓕ NI5422 (67 minutes: DDD: 7/95). Recorded 1993. *Gramophone* Editor's choice.

Following hard on the heels of his much-praised concerto début for Nimbus (see review under Dohnányi; refer to the Index to Reviews), Mark Anderson continues with a no less impressive recital disc. Brahms is once again his favoured composer and it is easy to see why, for here is playing aglow with warmth and sincerity, a far cry from the glib, impersonal expertise of many other winners of glittering prizes. The opening is magnificently forthright and imperious and, whether in ardent rhetoric or cloudy introspection, Anderson is stylish and assured. Some momentary failures of concentration (at 8'39", for example) and an occasional lack of impetus (the perennial problem, particularly in the vast spans of this work, of reconciling 'line' and detail) are marginal concerns given such strength of purpose, such essential *gravitas*. Liszt's Dante Sonata is, if anything, an even greater success. The absence of all obvious display and the concentration on purely musical values are deeply impressive. From Anderson, Liszt's fulminating response to Dante emerges in all its first glory and the performance is quite without the fustian and bombast that so often seem inseparable from this piece. The Schumann *Toccata* is, again, notable for sensitive as well as athletic virtues, its bustling and headlong flight poetically and brilliantly realized. Even in a market place crowded with celebrities, Anderson's Brahms has a special validity and authority, while his Liszt and Schumann are among the finest available. The recordings, made in Nimbus's splendid new concert-hall, are a far cry from some of their earlier efforts.

Brahms 16 Waltzes, Op. 39. Ten Hungarian Dances. **Idil Biret** (pf). Naxos Ⓢ 8 550355 (52 minutes: DDD: 10/94). Recorded 1992.

Both the *Waltzes* and the *Hungarian Dances* are extremely demanding in their two-hand form, and in the latter collection one could often believe that the 20 fingers of two duettists must be involved, so many notes are being played in all registers (for an example, try No. 8 in A minor). However, the technical problems evidently hold no terrors for this pianist and her performances are both convincing and attractive. What more need be said about this playing of music in which Brahms portrayed, in turn, sophisticated Vienna and untamed Hungary? Well, not a great deal. The quicker *Waltzes* have plenty of vivacity, and the slower ones are lyrical in an aptly Viennese manner. Tempos, textures, phrasing, rubato and pedalling are well managed and the playing has a very convincing blend of subtlety and simplicity. She treats these 16 pieces as a sequence, as Brahms's key structure allows, and leaves relatively little gap between them. The *Hungarian Dances* have a darkly surging Magyar energy and sound that are very pleasing: indeed, Biret seems totally at home in this music. The recording is a bit larger than life, but perfectly acceptable.

Additional recommendations ...

...16 Waltzes. 21 Hungarian Dances. **Yaara Tal, Andreas Groethuysen** (pf duet). Sony Classical Ⓕ SK53285 (68 minutes: DDD: 4/94).

...16 Waltzes. Pieces, Op. 76 – No. 2, Capriccio in B minor; No. 7, Intermezzo in A minor; No. 8, Capriccio in C major. Two Rhapsodies, Op. 79. Pieces, Op. 116 – No. 1, Capriccio in D minor; No. 2, Intermezzo in A minor; No. 4, Intermezzo in E major. Pieces, Op. 117 – No. 1, Intermezzo in E flat major; No. 2, Intermezzo in B flat minor. Six Pieces, Op. 118. Pieces, Op. 119 – No. 1, Intermezzo in B minor; No. 2, Intermezzo in E minor; No. 3, Intermezzo in C major. **Wilhelm Backhaus** (pf). Biddulph mono Ⓜ LHW019* (77 minutes: ADD: 9/94).

...16 Waltzes. Variations on a Theme by Haydn, Op. 56*b*, "St Antoni Chorale". Sonata in F minor, Op. 34*b*. **Martha Argerich, Alexandre Rabinovitch** (pfs). Teldec Ⓕ 4509-92257-2 (64 minutes: DDD: 1/95).

Brahms Two Rhapsodies, Op. 79 – No. 1 in B minor; No. 2 in G minor. 16 Waltzes, Op. 39. Six Piano Pieces, Op. 118. **Stephen Kovacevich** (pf). Philips Ⓕ 420 750-2PH (53 minutes: DDD: 4/88). From 6514 229 (4/83). Ⓖ

Brahms 16 Waltzes, Op. 39. Eight Piano Pieces, Op. 76. Two Rhapsodies, Op. 79 – No. 1 in B minor; No. 2 in G minor. **Mikhail Rudy** (pf). EMI Ⓕ CDC7 54233-2 (59 minutes: DDD: 5/93). Recorded 1991-2.

The Op. 79 *Rhapsodies* have been described as the "most temperamental" of all Brahms's later keyboard works. It would certainly be hard to imagine more vehement performances than those given by Kovacevich, thanks to his robust tone, trenchant attack and urgent tempos – perhaps even a shade too fast for the *Molto passionato, ma non troppo allegro* of the Second. But the pleading second subject of No. 1 in B minor brings all the requisite lyrical contrast. The Waltzes, too, have their tenderer moments of *Ländler*-like sentiment and charm. However, they emerge faster and more excitable than usual, as if Kovacevich were trying to remind us of Brahms's old love of Hungary no less than his new love of Vienna. "It is wonderful how he combines passion and tenderness in the smallest of spaces" was Clara Schumann's comment on the miniatures and the phrase fits Kovacevich's warmly responsive account of the Op. 118 set just as well. The piano is faithfully and fearlessly reproduced in what sounds like a ripely reverberant venue.

Mikhail Rudy's account of the Two *Rhapsodies* and the 16 Waltzes makes a pleasing alternative to Stephen Kovacevich's disc. For a start, the younger pianist has been exceptionally well recorded in the Salle Wagram in Paris, and he also plays a fine instrument that is in perfect condition. Of course that is not all: Rudy brings great character to the Eight Pieces, Op 76, with each one fully (but not exaggeratedly) characterized, not least in matters of texture, dynamics and pedalling. Similarly, this pianist effortlessly encompasses the blend of passion and gentler poetry that we find in the *Rhapsodies*. As for the Waltzes, this golden chain of Viennese melody and lilting charm comes across with affection and panache, as well as idiomatic rubato, not least in the famous A flat major Waltz which is the penultimate number. Repeats, too, are never mechanical, but often reveal something subtly new about the music which we could not have with a single playing. Finally, the frequent difficulty of Brahms's idiosyncratic piano writing, both here and in the other pieces, presents no more than a pleasing challenge to this intelligent and sensitive artist and all proceeds fluently, though never in a routine way.

Additional recommendation ...

...Two Rhapsodies. Three Intermezzos, Op. 117. Six Piano Pieces. Four Piano Pieces, Op. 119. **Radu Lupu** (pf). Decca Ⓕ 417 599-2DH (71 minutes: ADD: 8/87). ⒼⒼ

New review

Brahms Two Motets, Op. 74. Fest- und Gedenk-sprüche, Op. 109. Three Motets, Op. 110. Missa Canonica. Two Motets, Op. 29. **RIAS Chamber Choir, Berlin / Marcus Creed.** Harmonia Mundi Ⓕ HMC90 1591 (61 minutes: DDD: 5/96). Texts and translations included. Recorded 1994-5.

These are wonderful pieces, which, hearing, you would suppose to be all heart, looking at, you think must be all brain, and in fact are compounded of both, the one feeding upon and stimulating the other. In no other department of his work is Brahms quite so conscious of his heritage. Writing in the midday of romanticism, he finds the great formal, contrapuntal tradition not a weight upon him but a refreshment. He draws upon Schütz as upon Bach, and from the Italian polyphonists and masters of the double choir as well as from his own German background. The innocent ear would never suspect the mathematical intricacies, the sheer musical logic, and yet it tells, even without conscious recognition: one senses the workmanship, and the emotion which would in any case go out to greet such strong, vivid word-setting is immeasurably enhanced. A striking example is provided by the three movements, all that survive, from the *Missa Canonica*, undertaken in 1856. The *Sanctus* is set in deeply reverential mood and, like the flowing triple-time *Benedictus*, betrays nothing of its origin as an academic exercise. The *Agnus Dei* is overtly polyphonic yet that too gives way to a gently lyrical mode, in the "Dona nobis pacem". They were published in 1984 and this is their first recording. The motets, of course, have been recorded many times and very well too, yet, on balance, no more satisfyingly than they are here. The RIAS Chamber Choir produce a fine quality of homogeneous tone and, under Marcus Creed, show themselves fully responsive to both words and music. In the exciting "Wenn ein starker Gewappneter" movement of Op. 109 the Trinity College forces are preferable, in terms of clarity and immediacy, but the RIAS disc remains a strong recommendation, especially for its inclusion of the surviving *Missa Canonica* fragments.

Additional recommendation ...
...Two Motets, Op. 74. Two Motets, Op. 29. Three Motets, Op. 110. Three Motets, Op. 37. Psalm 13, Op. 27. Ave Maria, Op. 12. Fest- und Gedenkspruche. Geistliches Lied, Op. 30. **Trinity College Choir, Cambridge / Richard Marlow.** Conifer Ⓕ CDCF178 (65 minutes: DDD: 2/90).

Brahms Gesang der Parzen, Op. 89. Nänie, Op. 82. Schicksalslied, Op. 54. Begräbnisgesang, Op. 13. Alto Rhapsody, Op. 53ᵃ. ᵃ**Jard van Nes** (mez); **San Francisco Symphony Chorus and Orchestra / Herbert Blomstedt.** Decca Ⓕ 430 281-2DH (63 minutes: DDD: 8/90). Texts and translations included. Recorded 1989.

Brahms is such a familiar figure that it is salutary to be reminded that one area of his work, choral music, remains mostly unknown to collectors save for the *German Requiem* and *Alto Rhapsody*. This is a pity, for this composer who was also a distinguished choral conductor drew some of his finest inspiration from this medium. This issue includes the *Rhapsody*, warmly and movingly sung by Jard van Nes, but its importance lies in the fact that it also does much to give us a better knowledge of other big pieces too. Don't be put off by the sombre subject matter – including *Begräbnisgesang*, "A Song of the Fates" (a tremendous piece), another work about fate itself and not one but two funeral hymns! – but listen instead to thrilling choral singing and orchestral playing under the direction of a conductor who believes passionately in the music. "Plenty of strength, light and drama" is what *Gramophone*'s critic found in this programme when it first came out, and to that one would add that the San Francisco Symphony Chorus sing the German texts with complete conviction. If this music makes us regret that Brahms wrote no opera, we may at least feel that here is something not far short of it even though it was not intended for the stage; to see this, listen only to the *Schicksalslied* which is the first work performed. A good recording complements the quality of performance, though ideally the choral textures could be clearer.

Additional recommendations ...
...Triumphlied, Op. 55. Schicksalslied. Nänie. Alto Rhapsodyᵃ. ᵃ**Brigitte Fassbaender** (mez); **Prague Philharmonic Choir; Czech Philharmonic Orchestra / Giuseppe Sinopoli.** DG Galleria Ⓜ 435 066-2GGA (70 minutes: DDD: 11/91).
...Marienlieder, Op. 22. Schicksalslied. Alto Rhapsodyᵃ. Nänie. Gesang der Parzen. ᵃ**Nathalie Stutzmann** (contr); **Bavarian Radio Chorus and Symphony Orchestra / Sir Colin Davis.** RCA Victor Red Seal Ⓕ 09026 61201-2 (67 minutes: DDD: 5/93).
...Schicksalsliedᵃ. **Reger** An die Hoffnung, Op. 124ᵇ. **Rihm** Hölderlin-Fragmenteᶜ. **R. Strauss** Drei Hymnen, Op. 71ᵇ. ᵇ**Karita Mattila** (sop); ᶜ**Johannes M. Kösters** (bar); ᵃ**Leipzig Radio Chorus; Berlin Philharmonic Orchestra / Claudio Abbado.** Sony Classical Ⓕ SK53975 (58 minutes: DDD: 3/95).

Brahms 15 Romanzen aus "Die schöne Magelone", Op. 33. **Brigitte Fassbaender** (mez/narr); **Elisabeth Leonskaja** (pf). Teldec Ⓕ 4509-90854-2 (78 minutes: DDD: 10/94). Texts and translations included. Recorded 1993. *Gramophone Editor's choice.*   Ⓖ

Fassbaender has conceived the rewarding idea of marrying Brahms's cycle with the tale, by Ludwig Tieck, that inspired it. Thus, she prefaces every song with the appropriate section of the story, so that we are involved in the adventures of Peter and his beautiful love Magelone. We see before us the lovely girl, the handsome knight who entrances her and Magelone's go-between nurse; then follow their courtship, so rudely interrupted by natural forces (an interfering raven, always a symbol of evil in this imaginary world), Peter's adventures in a Moorish country, his escape and eventual and improbable reunion with his beloved for the happy end. Each of Brahms's songs captures the mood – happy, histrionic and sad – of the moment it illustrates in the text. It makes for a fascinating essay in narrative and music, and nobody is better equipped than Fassbaender to play the dual role of speaker and singer. She reads the high romantic text with as much emotional and intellectual control as she sings Brahms's pieces, which are greatly improved by being heard in context. She is partnered by the like-minded Leonskaja, something of a Brahms specialist, who plays the piano parts with welcome authority. She is nicely balanced with the singer in an exemplary recording. The whole project is a success and certainly the best way to encounter this music. Accept no substitutes.

Brahms Liebeslieder, Op. 52. Neue Liebeslieder, Op. 65. Three Quartets, Op. 64. **Edith Mathis** (sop); **Brigitte Fassbaender** (mez); **Peter Schreier** (ten); **Dietrich Fischer-Dieskau** (bar); **Karl Engel, Wolfgang Sawallisch** (pf duet). DG Ⓕ 423 133-2GH (55 minutes: DDD: 12/88). Texts and translations included. From 2740 280 (6/83).   ⒼⒼ

These delightful works will be eagerly snapped up by lovers of these seemingly simple but, in fact, quite complex settings for one, two or four voices. The performances are thoroughly idiomatic, both as regards the singers and pianists, with full value given to the words and their meaning. It is not merely a question of fine singing, which with this quartet one may more or less take for granted: the subtlety and charm of the interpretations makes what can all too often be a dreary sequence of three-four numbers into a poetic response to the nature of the waltz. There is an intelligent give-and-take between the soloists, so that voices move in and out of the limelight, as the skilful recording allows, and an extra dimension of the music is disclosed here that is too often obscured. The immediate sound is here a great advantage. This is a very worthwhile and welcome reissue of a most attractive individual record.

Additional recommendation ...

...Liebeslieder. Neue Liebeslieder. **Schumann** Spanische Liebeslieder, Op. 138. **Barbara Bonney** (sop); **Anne Sofie von Otter** (mez); **Kurt Streit** (ten); **Olaf Bär** (bar); **Bengt Forsberg, Helmut Deutsch** (pf duet). EMI Ⓕ CDC5 55430-2 (64 minutes: DDD: 10/95).

Brahms Lieder. **Dame Margaret Price** (sop); **Graham Johnson** (pf). RCA Victor Red Seal Ⓕ 09026 60901-2 (61 minutes: DDD: 5/94). Notes, texts and translations included. Recorded 1992.
Op. 96 – No. 1, Der Tod, das ist die kühle Nacht; No. 3, Es schauen die Blumen; No. 4, Meerfahrt. Op. 85 – No. 1, Sommerabend; No. 2, Mondenschein. Es liebt sich so lieblich im Lenze!, Op. 71 No. 1. Op. 14 – No. 1, Vor dem Fenster; No. 2, Vom verwundeten Knaben; No. 7, Ständchen; No. 8, Sehnsucht. Mädchenfluch, Op. 69 No. 9. Klage, Op. 105 No. 3. Op. 148 – No. 4, Gold überwiegt die Liebe; No. 6, Vergangen ist mir Glück und Heil. Op. 84 – No. 4, Vergebliches Ständchen; No. 5, Spannung. Deutsche Volkslieder, WoO33 – No. 4, Da unten in Tale; No. 15, Schwesterlein, Schwesterlein; No. 37, Du mein einzig Licht. Op. 97 – Dort in den Weiden, No. 4. Zigeunerlieder, Op. 103 – No. 1, He, Zigeuner, greife; No. 2, Hochgetürmte Rimaflut; No. 3, Wisst ihr, wann mein Kindchen; No. 4, Leiber Gott, du weisst; No. 5, Brauner Bursche führt zum Tanze; No. 6, Röslein dreie in der Reihe; No. 7, Kommt dir manchmal; No. 11, Rote Abendwoken ziehn.

With Graham Johnson to devise intelligent, logical programmes, Dame Margaret Price and himself to interpret them, a remarkable unanimity of thought and confidence of manner is being achieved, the delights there for the taking. Here we begin with six contrasted settings of Heine, all reasonably familiar songs, each given with a nice balance between breadth of phrasing and warmth of feeling. The account of *Mondenschein* fully realizes its autumnal melancholy in phrases that seem to linger endlessly in the air. The judicious choice of *Volkslieder* settings once more indicates Brahms's deep understanding of the originals and just how to clothe them in appropriate harmonies, as in the antique Dorian mode of *Sehnsucht* and *Vergangen ist mir Glück und Heil*, both sung and played here with an exquisite sense of longing. Finally, the partnership lavish a winningly uninhibited *élan* on the *Zigeunerlieder*. If we are occasionally aware of a momentary strain on Price's present resources, we are consoled by the passionate spontaneity of the results. The recording is ideally balanced, intimate yet open.

Additional recommendations ...

...Spanische Lied, Op. 6 No. 1. Lieder, Op. 7 – Anklänge; Volkslied; Die Trauernde. Sehnsucht, Op. 14 No. 8. Von ewiger Liebe, Op. 43 No. 1. An die Nachtigall, Op. 46 No. 4. Gold überwiegt die Liebe, Op. 48 No. 4. Wiegenlied, Op. 49 No. 4. Lieder, Op. 59 – Regenlied; Dein blaues Auge. Junge Lieder I – Meine Klage ist grun, Op. 63 No. 5. Klage I – Ach, mir fehlt, Op. 69 No. 1. Lieder, Op. 86 – Therese; Nachtwandler. Lieder, Op. 95 – Das Mädchen; Bei dir sind meine Gendanken; Schön war, das ich dir weihte. Five Lieder, Op. 105 – Wie Melodien zieht es mir; Klage. Mädchenlied, Op. 107 No. 5. **Schumann** Liederkreis, Op. 39. **Edith Mathis** (sop); **Gerard Wyss** (pf). Denon Ⓕ CO-78947 (60 minutes: DDD: 11/95).

...Lieder, Op. 57 – No. 2, Wenn du nur zuweilen lächelst; No. 3, Es träumte mir; No. 4, Ach, wende diesen Blick; No. 8, Unbewegte laue Luft. Deutsche Volkslieder, WoO33 – No. 12, Feinsliebchen, du sollst mir nicht barfuss geh'n; No. 15, Schwesterlein, Schwesterlein; No. 33, Och Moder, ich well en Ding han!; No. 41, Es steht ein' Lind'; No. 42, In stiller Nacht, zur ersten Wacht. Lieder, Op. 107 – No. 3, Das Mädchen spricht; No. 5, Mädchenlied. Vergebliches Ständchen, Op. 84 No. 4. Ständchen, Op. 106 No. 1. Am Sonntag Morgen, Op. 49 No. 1. Trennung, Op. 97 No. 6. Während des Regens, Op. 58 No. 2. O kühler Wald, Op. 72 No. 3. Von ewiger Liebe, Op. 43 No. 1. *Coupled with works by* **Telemann, C.P.E. Bach, Bach, Handel, Schumann** and **Schubert** Elly Ameling (sop); **Various soloists;** Deutsche Harmonia Mundi Ⓕ 74321 26617-2 (four discs: 239 minutes: ADD: 12/95). *See review in the Collections section; refer to the Index to Reviews.*

...Deutsche Volkslieder, WoO33 – No. 6; No. 12, Feinsliebchen; No. 42, In stiller Nacht. Die Trauernde, Op. 7 No. 5. *Coupled with works by* **Schumann** Irmgard Seefried (sop); **Erik Werba** (pf). Orfeo D'Or Salzburg Festspieldokumente mono Ⓕ C398951B* (77 minutes: ADD: 3/96). *See review under Schumann; refer to the Index to Reviews.*

Brahms Lieder – Vier ernste Gesänge, Op. 121. Vergebliches Ständchen, Op. 84 No. 4. Vorschneller Schwur, Op. 95 No. 5. Das Mädchen spricht, Op. 107 No. 3. Alte Liebe, Op. 72 No. 1. Meine Liebe ist grün, Op. 63 No. 5. Dein blaues Auge, Op. 59 No. 8. Sapphische Ode, Op. 94 No. 4. Nachtigall, Op. 97 No. 1. Komm bald, Op. 97 No. 7. Herbstgefühl, Op. 48 No. 7.
Schumann Liederkreis, Op. 39. **Brigitte Fassbaender** (mez); **Elisabeth Leonskaja** (pf). Teldec
Ⓟ 9031-74872-2 (69 minutes: DDD: 10/94). Texts and translations included. Recorded 1992. **Ⓖ**

Because Fassbaender is such an idiosyncratic singer, no one who loves her art will want to be without this fresh manifestation of her impulsive, spontaneous skills. Likewise those unlucky ones who abhor her voice and style will remain unconvinced. The very first song of the Schumann cycle shows many of Fassbaender's singular ways – her use of portamento and vibrato, her underlining of specific words are there for all to hear. In the second song, "Intermezzo", the emphasis she gives to "Mein Herz" at the start of the second verse and the repetition of the opening "Dein Bildnis" go to the heart of the matter. Leonskaja proves an ideal partner for this singer. Her big, strong playing in "Waldesgespräch" matches Fassbaender's operatic approach to this romantic outpouring but she can be just as effective in more delicate matters, as "Schöne Fremde" reveals. So, all in all this is, as one would expect, an absorbing, thought-provoking interpretation, yet one that is always held within the bounds of sensible speeds and forward-moving rhythms. The scale of the pair's reading of Brahms's *Vier ernste Gesänge* is announced in the first song, again operatic in its breadth and strength of expression (the extreme pessimism of the second song is achieved partly through harsh tone and forceful vibrato). Urgency in *Vergebliches Ständchen*, with a subtle rubato at the close; a wonderful joy in voice and piano in *Das Mädchen spricht*; a rich melancholy about love gone by forever in *Alte Liebe*; a dark richness in *Sapphische Ode* are typical of the insights on display, typical too of the full, ideally balanced recording of voice and instrument.

Brahms Lieder. **Anne Sofie von Otter** (mez); **Bengt Forsberg** (pf). DG Ⓟ 429 727-2GH (61 minutes: DDD: 4/91). Texts and translations included. Recorded 1989.
Zigeunerlieder, Op. 103 – No. 1-7 and 11. Dort in den Weiden, Op. 97 No. 4. Vergebliches Ständchen, Op. 84 No. 4. Die Mainacht, Op. 43 No. 2. Ach, wende diesen Blick, Op. 57 No. 4. O kühler Wald, Op. 72 No. 3. Von ewiger Liebe, Op. 43 No. 1. Junge Lieder I, Op. 63 No. 5. Wie rafft' ich mich auf in der Nacht, Op. 32 No. 1. Unbewegte laue Luft, Op. 57 No. 8. Heimweh II, Op. 63 No. 8. Mädchenlied, Op. 107 No. 5. Ständchen, Op. 106 No. 1. Sonntag, Op. 47 No. 3. Wiegenlied, Op. 49 No. 4. Zwei Gesänge, Op. 91 (with Nils-Erik Sparf, va).

Many of the Lieder here are but meagerly represented in current catalogues, so that this recital is all the more welcome, particularly in view of the perceptive musicality of both singer and pianist. They show a fine free (but unanimous!) flexibility in the *Zigeunerlieder*, with a dashing "Brauner Bursche" and "Röslein dreie" and a passionate "Rote Abendwolken"; but there is also lightness, happy in "Wisst ihr, wann mein Kindchen", troubled in "Lieber Gott, du weisst"; and Otter's coolly tender tone in "Kommt dir manchmal in den Sinn" touches the heart. Also deeply moving are the profound yearning and the loving but anxious lullaby in the two songs with viola obbligato (most sensitively played). Elsewhere, connoisseurs of vocal technique will admire Otter's command of colour and legato line in the gravity of *O kühler Wald*, the stillness of *Die Mainacht* and the intensity of *Von ewiger Liebe*, and her lovely *mezza voce* in the *Wiegenlied* and the partly repressed fervour of *Unbewegte laue Luft*; but to any listener her remarkable control, her responsiveness to words and, not least, the sheer beauty of her voice make this a most rewarding disc, aided as she is by Forsberg's characterful playing.

New review
Brahms Ein deutsches Requiem, Op. 45. **Sylvia McNair** (sop); **Håkan Hagegård** (bar); **Westminster Symphonic Choir; New York Philharmonic Orchestra / Kurt Masur.** Teldec Ⓟ 4509-98413-2 (60 minutes. DDD: 2/96). Text and translation included. Recorded 1995.

The first word of the *Deutsches Requiem* is "selig"; the last movement reiterates it, and throughout there recur images of this happiness ("reap in joy", "joy and gladness", "rejoice in the living God", "your heart shall rejoice", "Death is swallowed up in Victory"). This recording is the first to seize on this, not as an element in the *Requiem* but as its prevailing spirit. Even the subdued opening carries an intimation of it in the treatment of the dotted note, and the choir wear a happy face – they sound as though they *mean* their "selig" and their "kommen mit Freuden". In the second movement, "Denn alles Fleisch", the universal funeral processes briskly, the dotted notes giving now almost a jaunty movement. And why not? For this is not a funeral *march* but a *Trauermusik* in 3/4, the time-signature of waltz, and (this recording seems to say) we acknowledge death, accept it with fortitude and know that a modulation to triumphant B flat major lies immediately ahead. Nor is this an exercise in stoical stupidity: "Death is a fearful thing" all right, and the shudder of recognition comes, with much more truth in it, after the baritone, the voice of the individual, has sung of mortality in the third movement and the orchestra enter suddenly on a bleak *fortissimo*. On the other hand, the musings which follow ("Ach, wie gar nichts") are not dwelt upon and the "Der Gerechten" fugue is given strong rhythmic impulse, almost primitive in its excitement over the long-held pedal note.

In short, this is not 'just any old Brahms *Requiem*' but a rather special one. Among the many recordings, few take Brahms's original metronome markings seriously; this one does, and so ranges itself for comparison with the versions under Norrington and Gardiner. As usual, there are pros and cons. Gardiner has the best recorded sound and the best choral singing; his way with the score is also compelling and powerful. Norrington too is strong in ideas. Masur's Teldec recording could do with more bloom and body. Sylvia McNair brings lovely tone but a less compassionate feeling to the soprano solo than did Lynne Dawson with Norrington: a young sister-comforter rather than a mother. Håkan Hagegård is a little dry of voice, and his 'character' is that of the average man rather than Fischer-Dieskau's more spiritual philosopher type for Klemperer. The choir respond well to Masur's call for energy and alertness. If the more familiar and perhaps more comforting approach, with slower speeds, is wanted, then the recommendation would be for Hickox; for quicker speeds and more bracing rhythms, Gardiner; for the *Seligkeit*, perhaps unrecognized before in performances of the *Deutsches Requiem*, Masur.

Additional recommendations ...

...Ein deutsches Requiem. **Dame Elisabeth Schwarzkopf** (sop); **Dietrich Fischer-Dieskau** (bar); **Philharmonia Chorus and Orchestra / Otto Klemperer.** EMI Ⓕ CDC7 47238-2 (69 minutes: ADD: 6/87). *Gramophone classical 100.*   ⒼⒼⒼ

...Ein deutsches Requiem. **Charlotte Margiono** (sop); **Rodney Gilfry** (bar); **Monteverdi Choir; Orchestre Révolutionnaire et Romantique / John Eliot Gardiner.** Philips Ⓕ 432 140-2PH (66 minutes: DDD: 4/91). 🎜   Ⓖ

...Ein deutsches Requiem. **Felicity Lott** (sop); **David Wilson-Johnson** (bar); **London Symphony Chorus and Orchestra / Richard Hickox.** Chandos Ⓕ CHAN8942 (74 minutes: DDD: 1/92).

...Ein deutsches Requiem[a]. Begräbnisgesang, Op. 13. [a]**Lynne Dawson** (sop); [a]**Olaf Bär** (bar); **Schütz Choir of London; London Classical Players / Roger Norrington.** EMI Reflexe Ⓕ CDC7 54658-2 (68 minutes: DDD: 4/93). 🎜

...Ein deutsches Requiem. **Elizabeth Norberg-Schulz** (sop); **Wolfgang Holzmair** (bar); **San Francisco Symphony Chorus and Orchestra / Herbert Blomstedt.** Decca Ⓖ 443 771-2DH (71 minutes: DDD: 7/95).

Further listening ...

...Piano Trio in A minor, Op. 114. *Coupled with* **Beethoven** Piano Trio in B flat major, Op. 11. **Mozart** Trio for Clarinet, Viola and Piano in E flat major, K498, "Kegelstatt". **Richard Stoltzman** (cl); **Yo-Yo Ma** (vc); **Emanuel Ax** (pf). Sony Classical SK57499 (1/96).

...Piano Transcriptions – Theme and Variations in D minor. Two Sarabandes. Two Gigues. Two Gavottes. Kleine Klavierstück. Canon in F minor. Rákóczy March. Ländler by Franz Schubert. Study on Impromptu in E flat major, D935 No. 2 (Schubert). *Coupled with* **Gluck** Iphigenie en Aulide – Gavotte. **Schumann** Piano Quintet in E flat major, Op. 44 – Scherzo. **Idil Biret** (pf). Naxos 8 550958 (5/95).

...11 Chorale Preludes, Op. 122. O Traurigkeit, O Herzeleid. Preludes and Fugues – A minor; G minor. Fugue in A flat minor. **Robert Parkins** (org). Naxos 8 550824 (12/94).

...Duets – Op. 20: Weg der Liebe I; Weg der Liebe II; Die Meere; Op. 66: Am Strande; Jägerlied. Four Duets, Op. 61. Guter Rat, Op. 75 No. 2. *Coupled with* **Dvořák** 13 Moravian Duets, B107. **Reger** Three Duets, Op. 111*a*. **Juliane Banse** (sop); **Brigitte Fassbaender** (mez); **Cord Garben** (pf). Koch Schwann 312592 (8/95).

...Zwei Lieder, Op. 91. *Coupled with works by* **R. Strauss, A. Busch, Loeffler, Dargomïzhsky, Marx, Reutter** and **Gounod** Mitsuko Shirai (mez); Tabea Zimmermann (va); Hartmut Höll (pf). Capriccio 10 462 (9/95). *See review in the Collections section; refer to the Index to Reviews.* Ⓖ

Johannes Brassart   French fl. 1420-1445

Suggested listening ...

...Te dignitas presularis. *Coupled with works by* **Zacharias, Antonius de Civitate Austrie, Tapissier, Velut, Anonymous, Ciconia, Philipoctus de Caserta, Johanne Egidius, Matheus de Sancto Johanne, Bartolomeus da Bologna** and **Dufay** Orlando Consort. Metronome METCD1008 (11/95). *See review in the Collections section; refer to the Index to Reviews.* Ⓖ

Walter Braunfels   German 1882-1954

Suggested listening ...

...Verkündigung. **Soloists; Cologne Symphony Chorus and Orchestra / Dennis Russell Davies.** EMI CDS5 55104-2 (7/94).

Nicolae Bretan   Romanian 1887-1968

Suggested listening ...

...Golem. Arald. **Soloists; chorus; Moldova Philharmonic Orchestra / Cristian Mandeal.** Nimbus NI5424 (10/95).

Tomás Bréton

New review

Bretón La verbena de la Paloma. **Maria Bayo** (sop) Susana; **Plácido Domingo** (ten) Julián; **Raquel Pierotti** (mez) Seña Rita; **Silvia Tro** (sop) Casta; **Rafael Castejón** (sngr) Don Hilarión; **Jesús Castejón** (bass-bar) Don Sebastian; **Ana Maria Amengual** (sngr) Tia Antonia; **Milagros Martin** (folk sngr) Cantaora; **Enrique Baquerizo** (bass) Watchman; **Madrid Comunidad Chorus; Madrid Symphony Orchestra / Antoni Ros Marbà.** Auvidis Valois Ⓔ V4725 (46 minutes: DDD: 9/95). Notes, text and translation included. Recorded 1994. Ⓖ

Entering the orchestra pit to conduct the first performance of his light-hearted one-acter *La verbena de la Paloma* in 1894, Tomás Bretón, a highly cultured musician with his heart set on writing serious operas (his *Los amantes de Teruel* the previous year had had a very mixed reception), leant over to his first violin and murmured, "I think I've made a terrible mistake this time". He could not have been more wrong. The piece was not only immediately acclaimed with the utmost enthusiasm, but has become a classic at the core of the *género chico* zarzuela repertoire: its habanera *¿Dónde vas con mantón de Manila?* is familiar from birth to every single Spaniard. The plot, slight as it is but skilfully developed, concerns the young typesetter Julián's jealousy when he sees his beloved, Susana, and her sister taken to the fair by the randy old chemist Don Hilarión on the eve of the festival of Our Lady of the Dove (August 14th). Like the earlier recording under Moreno Torroba, this version omits the dialogue connecting the musical numbers (but includes the watchman's scene, mostly spoken over strings), and there is an attempt to create a theatrical atmosphere by crowd noises, etc. The orchestral playing and the choral singing (particularly in the famous *seguidillas*) show a polish and sensitivity that are unfortunately far from usual in zarzuela performances; and to capture the authentic scenic setting the producer has reverted to the original score and presented the *soleá* with piano and the *mazurka* on piano and violin, as would have been the practice in the cafés. Domingo is in excellent voice in his only solo; Maria Bayo has little to do except in the quintet (an unusual feature in such pieces); the biggest part, that of Don Hilarión, is as usual taken by a character actor who sings after a fashion. It is all very engaging and cheery. (By the way, when Auvidis's hapless translator more than once writes, in her own peculiar brand of English, of a "cut for voice and piano", she actually means a vocal score.)

Further listening ...

...Piano Trio in E major[a]. String Quartet in D major[b]. [a]**György Oravecz** (pf); **New Budapest Quartet.** Marco Polo 8 223745 (6/95).

Havergal Brian

New review

Brian Fantastic Variations on an Old Rhyme. Symphonies – No. 20 in C sharp minor; No. 25 in A minor. **National Symphony Orchestra of Ukraine / Andrew Penny.** Marco Polo Ⓔ 8 223731 (63 minutes: DDD: 6/96). Recorded 1994.

The *Fantastic Variations* (the 'Old Rhyme' on which they are based is *Three Blind Mice*) are early Brian, exuberant music written when he had only just turned 30, but although Symphony No. 20 dates from over 55 years later it is not so much a late work as one of his 'middle period', when he was still experimenting and developing. Only Symphony No. 25, completed just before his ninetieth birthday in 1966, really counts as 'late' Brian. The *Variations* are hugely resourceful, already fantastic before the theme has even been properly stated. Of course Brian is showing off his orchestral mastery, and the range of grotesque, bizarre and troubling ideas that he can draw from such an unpromising theme, but only once or twice do you get the feeling that the contrast between material and treatment is getting a little extreme. The two symphonies are descendants of the *Variations* in their ingenuity of thematic development. Both are intensely dramatic, but their drama is never mere gesture; both are impressive in their long-term strategy, the way that themes are recalled by subtle allusion instead of mere recurrence. Symphony No. 25 is a fine example of this, sowing a new and beautiful melody in the midst of the first movement's development, but only revealing that melody in its full form at the end, where it becomes an obvious, satisfying and moving conclusion. Once or twice the Ukrainian players sound a bit baffled by the idiom, but they clearly believe in the Symphony No. 25, the finest work here, and give it an absorbing, vivid reading. There is a touch of rawness to the sound at times, but Andrew Penny is alert to the often striking, often surprising colours of Brian's orchestra.

Further listening ...

...The Jolly Miller. Violin Concerto in C major[a]. Symphony No. 18. [a]**Marat Bisengaliev** (vn); **BBC Scottish Symphony Orchestra / Lionel Friend.** Marco Polo 8 223479 (8/94).

...Symphony No. 1, "Gothic". **Soloists; Slovak Philharmonic Choir; Slovak National Theatre Opera Chorus; Slovak Folk Ensemble Chorus; Lucnica Chorus; Bratislava Chamber Choir; Bratislava Children's Choir; Youth Echo Choir; Czechoslovak Radio Symphony Orchestra, Bratislava; Slovak Philharmonic Orchestra / Ondrej Lenárd.** Marco Polo 8 223280/1 (7/90).

...*8 223447:* Symphonies – No. 4, "The Song of Victory"[a]; No. 12[b]. *8 223481[c]:* Symphonies – No. 17; No. 32 in A flat major. In Memoriam. Festal dance. [a]**Jana Valásková** (sop); [a]**Slovak Philharmonic Chorus; [a]Brno Philharmonic Chorus; [a]Cantus Choir; [a]Slovak Opera Chorus; [a]Youth**

Echo Choir; [ab]Bratislava Radio Symphony Orchestra; [c]Ireland National Symphony Orchestra /
Adrian Leaper. Marco Polo 8 223447/223481 (2/93).
...Symphonies Nos. 7 and 31. Comedy Overture – The Tinker's Wedding. **Royal Liverpool
Philharmonic Orchestra / Sir Charles Mackerras.** EMI British Composers CDM7 64717-2 (9/93).

Frank Bridge   British 1879-1941

Bridge Oration – Concerto elegiaco, H180.
Britten Cello Symphony, Op. 68. **Steven Isserlis** (vc); **City of London Sinfonia / Richard Hickox.**
   EMI Ⓜ CDM7 63909-2 (68 minutes: DDD: 2/92). From CDC7 49716-2 (5/88).   Ⓖ
Steven Isserlis's decision to couple these two English masterpieces on one disc was a particularly
intelligent one: not only because Frank Bridge was one of Britten's most influential teachers and
mentors, but also because both works reflect, in their different ways, the two composers' strong pacifist
beliefs and their deep concern at man's inhumanity to man. *Oration* (subtitled *Concerto elegiaco*) dates
from 1930 and is both an explicit outcry against the futility of war and a vast lament for the many
friends and colleagues that Bridge had lost as a result of the Great War. Indeed, throughout its 30-
minute span the work is constantly haunted by images of war – sometimes in mocking parody (as in
the central march section, or the martial fanfares that erupt violently into orchestral climaxes), and
sometimes in sombre, grief-stricken episodes of moving intensity. Isserlis gives us an exceptionally fine
performance that fully captures the intensity and vision of this richly rewarding and shamefully
neglected masterpiece. Britten's own masterpiece in the idiom – the Cello Symphony – was composed
some 30 years later, but the influence of *Oration* can be clearly discerned both in its emotional content
(if perhaps less overtly displayed than in the former) and in the similar way that it eschews the
conventions of a formal concerto. Again both soloist and conductor deserve the highest praise for a
performance that matches the profundity and vision of the music. Well recorded.

Bridge Three Idylls, H67.
Elgar String Quartet in E minor, Op. 83.
Walton String Quartet in A minor. **Coull Quartet** (Roger Coull, Philip Gallaway, vns; David Curtis,
   va; John Todd, vc). Hyperion Ⓕ CDA66718 (73 minutes: DDD: 10/94). Recorded 1993.
The Elgar and Walton Quartets make an apt and attractive coupling, as several rivals have
demonstrated, playing with biting precision and warm understanding. Here the Coull have a clear
advantage in adding a fine example of Frank Bridge's quartet writing. The *Three Idylls* date from
1906, soon after Bridge's first regular quartet. As this superb, purposeful performance shows, the
separate pieces make up a composition which in its sharp changes of mood is closely akin to the
fantasy works by Bridge and others which were encouraged by the Cobbett Prize. The three crisply
conceived movements hang together so well that at a later period the composer might well have
counted them as a quartet proper, despite the flouting of sonata form. Even making no allowance for
that significant bonus, the Coull performances of the two main works compare very favourably with
those of the Britten Quartet. Though in the Elgar their reading sounds almost too comfortable, less
successful at conveying Elgar's volatile mood-changes, its relaxed warmth is still very persuasive.The
Walton has never had a performance that so movingly captures the spirit of characteristic melancholy,
an element which finds one of its supreme expressions in the extended *Lento*. Here the Coull players
sustain exceptionally slow speeds with a hushed intensity that makes even the Britten Quartet's
performance seem relatively extrovert. Recommended warmly to everyone wanting masterly and
highly individual examples of quartet writing by three of the most positive British composers.

New review
Bridge Cello Sonata in D minor, H125. Four Short Pieces, H104 – Spring Song. Melodie, H99.
   Scherzo, H19*a*.
Britten Cello Sonata, Op. 65. **Steven Doane** (vc); **Barry Snyder** (pf). Bridge Ⓕ BCD9056
   (52 minutes: DDD: 4/96). Recorded 1994.
A good pairing, of course. Bridge's increasingly progressive European outlook after the First World
War seems to have held back his career. However, the two-movement Cello Sonata of 1917 is very
English in its rich eloquence, although there is an affinity with Fauré, a composer with whom Bridge
shared qualities of quietly glowing passion and unerring craftsmanship. The sonata's deeply
emotional second movement is masterly. Collectors already possessing the outstandingly played and
recorded 1968 performance by Rostropovich and Britten (see review under Britten) will already know
the worth of this music, but this performance by the American duo of Steven Doane and Barry
Snyder is warmly sympathetic and thoroughly enjoyable. The Bridge miniatures that accompany it are
equally effective. Britten's Sonata, written for Rostropovich, is equally unconventional in having five
movements of which Nos. 2, 4 and 5 each last less than three minutes but are none the less
characterful and telling. This duo also respond keenly to the younger man's crisper invention and here
is another strong yet sensitive performance. Again, of course, collectors may already have
Rostropovich and the composer, playing with an authority impossible to surpass. But if you want
these two sonatas together this attractive disc provides a safe recommendation and Steven Doane is
clearly a cellist to watch. The recording favours the cello, but is otherwise faithful and pleasing.

Additional recommendations ...
...Cello Sonata. Four Short Pieces – Meditation; Spring song. **Debussy** Cello Sonata. **Dohnányi**
Cello Sonata in B flat minor, Op. 8. **Bernard Gregor-Smith** (vc); **Yolande Wrigley** (pf). ASV
Ⓟ CDDCA796 (68 minutes: DDD: 9/92).
...Cello Sonata. **Schubert** Sonata for Arpeggione and Piano in A minor, D821. **Mstislav
Rostropovich** (vc); **Benjamin Britten** (pf). Decca The Classic Sound Ⓜ 443 575-2DCS
(52 minutes: ADD: 4/95).   ⒼⒼ

Further listening ...
...**Phantasm.** *Coupled with* **Ireland** Piano Concerto; **Walton** Sinfonia concertante (original
version). **Kathryn Stott** (pf); **Royal Philharmonic Orchestra / Vernon Handley.** Conifer CDCF175
(1/90).   Ⓖ
...Sir Roger de Coverley, H155. *Coupled with* **Purcell** Chacony in G minor for strings, Z730.
Delius Two Aquarelles. **Elgar** Introduction and Allegro, Op. 47. **Britten** Simple Symphony,
Op. 4. Prelude and Fugue, Op. 29. **English Chamber Orchestra / Benjamin Britten.** Decca The
Classic Sound 448 569-2DCS (2/96).
...The Sea. *Coupled with* **Bax** On the Sea-Shore (orch. Parlett). **Britten** Four Sea Interludes,
Op. 33*a*. Passacaglia, Op. 33*b*. **Ulster Orchestra / Vernon Handley.** Chandos CHAN8473 (3/87).
...Elegy, H47. Scherzetto, H19. *Coupled with* **Ireland** Cello Sonata in G minor; **Stanford** Cello
Sonata No. 2 in D minor, Op. 39. **Julian Lloyd-Webber** (vc); **John McCabe** (pf). ASV
CDDCA807 (2/93).
...Pensiero, H53*a*. Allegro appassionato, H82. *Coupled with works by* **Britten, Vaughan
Williams, R. Clarke, Grainger** and **Bax** Paul Coletti (va); **Leslie Howard** (pf). Hyperion
CDA66687 (10/94). *See review in the Collections section; refer to the Index to Reviews.*   Ⓖ
...A Sea Idyll, H54*a*. Capriccios – No. 1 in A minor, H52; No. 2 in F sharp minor, H54*b*. Three
poems – Ecstasy, H112*b*. The Hour Glass, H148. Piano Sonata, H160. Vignettes de Marseille,
H166. **Kathryn Stott** (pf). Conifer CDCF186 (9/91).
...Day after day. Speak to me my love. Dweller in my deathless dreams. Journey's End. *Coupled with
songs by* **Warlock, Ireland, Howells** *and* **Holst** Sarah Leonard (sop); **Malcolm Martineau** (pf).
Cala United Recordings 88016-2 (3/95).

George Bristow   American 1825-1898

Suggested listening ...
...Symphony No. 2 in F sharp minor, Op. 26. *Coupled with* **Barber** Symphony No. 2, Op. 19.
Adagio for Strings, Op. 11. **Detroit Symphony Orchestra / Neeme Järvi.** Chandos CHAN9169
(10/93).

Estâvão Brito   Portuguese c1575-1641

Suggested listening ...
...Lamentations of Jeremiah – Incipit lamentatio Jeremiae. *Coupled with* **F. Vásquez** In te,
Domine, speravi. (attrib.) **Morales** Vigilate et orate. **Victoria** Et egressus est. Ecce vidimus eum.
Amicus meus. Unus ex discipulis. Eram quasi agnus. Seniores populi. Benedictus Deus Dominus
Israel. Vere languores nostros. **Lienas** Coenantibus autem. **Cardoso** Magnificat Primi Toni. **La
Colombina.** Accent ACC9394D (8/94).

Benjamin Britten (Lord Britten of Aldeburgh)   British 1913-1976

Britten Piano Concerto in D major, Op. 13ᵃ. Violin Concerto, Op. 15ᵇ. ᵇ**Mark Lubotsky** (vn);
ᵃ**Sviatoslav Richter** (pf); **English Chamber Orchestra / Benjamin Britten.** Decca London Ⓜ 417
308-2LM (67 minutes: ADD: 10/89). From SXL6512 (8/71). Recorded 1970.   Ⓖ
Britten Piano Concerto in D major, Op. 13ᵃ. Soirées musicales, Op. 9. Matinées musicales, Op. 24.
ᵃ**Ralf Gothóni** (pf); **Helsingborg Symphony Orchestra / Okko Kamu.** Ondine Ⓟ ODE825-2
(71 minutes: DDD: 1/95). Recorded 1994. *Gramophone Editor's choice.*   Ⓖ
Just after Britten's performances were released on LP in 1971, the composer admitted with some pride
that Sviatoslav Richter had learned his Piano Concerto "entirely off his own bat", and had revealed
a Russianness that was in the score. Britten was attracted to Shostakovich during the late 1930s, when
it was written, and the bravado, brittleness and flashy virtuosity of the writing, in the march-like
finale most of all, at first caused many people (including Lennox Berkeley, to whom it is dedicated)
to be wary of it, even to think it somehow outside the composer's style. Now we know his music better,
it is easier to accept, particularly in this sparkling yet sensitive performance. The Violin Concerto
dates from the following year, 1939, when Britten was in Canada, and it, too, has its self-conscious
virtuosity, but it is its rich nostalgic lyricism which strikes to the heart and the quiet elegiac ending is
unforgettable. Compared to Richter in the other work, Mark Lubotsky is not always the master of its
hair-raising difficulties, notably in the scherzo, which has passages of double artificial harmonics that

even Heifetz wanted simplified before he would play it (Britten refused), but this is still a lovely account. Fine recordings, made in The Maltings at Snape.

From Ondine comes a perceptive, at times daring, always thought-provoking account of Britten's Piano Concerto. Indeed, pungent characterization is the order of the day, especially in the two middle movements. Here the "Waltz" is teased out with sly seduction by Okku Kamu and his excellent orchestra, yet at the same time the ominous undertones of this music have never been more unnervingly projected. Even more distinctive is Ralf Gothóni's provocatively expansive way with the opening of the "Impromptu", Britten's theme emerging like some ravishingly intimate meditation. As on the admirable performance by Joanna MacGregor for Collins Classics, we are also offered the concerto's original slow movement, a sharply inventive, highly capricious "Recitative and Aria". Ondine rather jarringly programme this movement between the "Waltz" and "Impromptu", whereas Collins allot it a separate track after the concerto proper – an altogether preferable arrangement. No complaints, though, about the fizz and bravura on show in the opening "Toccata", nor about the mock-banal finale, whose *largamente* climax struts forth in superbly grim fashion here. Welcome contrast is afforded by the two Rossini-inspired suites, and Kamu does them both proud. Ondine's sound is first-rate.

Additional recommendations ...

...Piano Concerto[a]. Violin Concerto[b]. [a]**Joanna MacGregor** (pf); [b]**Lorraine McAslan** (vn); **English Chamber Orchestra / Steuart Bedford.** Collins Classics Ⓕ 1301-2 (66 minutes: DDD: 9/92).

...Violin Concerto[a]. Canadian Carnival, Op. 19. **Britten/Berkeley** Mont Juic, Op. 12. [a]**Lorraine McAslan** (vn); **English Chamber Orchestra / Steuart Bedford.** Collins Classics Ⓕ 1123-2 (58 minutes: DDD: 12/90).

...Piano Concerto. **Copland** Piano Concerto. **Gillian Lin** (pf); **Melbourne Symphony Orchestra / John Hopkins.** Chandos Collect Ⓜ CHAN6580 (51 minutes: ADD: 3/93).

Britten Gloriana, Op. 53a. Four Sea Interludes, Op. 33a. The Prince of the Pagodas, Op. 57a – Pas de Six. **Royal Liverpool Philharmonic Orchestra / Takuo Yuasa.** EMI Eminence Ⓜ CD-EMX2231 (53 minutes: DDD: 3/95). Recorded 1993.

This is a first-rate Britten collection. Takuo Yuasa's *Grimes* Interludes are a match for the finest available: with the RLPO on powerfully responsive form, his sensitive reading steers a satisfying middle course between Slatkin's cool objectivity and Hickox's more warmly expressive manner. Certainly, "Sunday Morning" attains a marvellous, bustling climax, notable for some sparkling work from superbly assertive Liverpool trumpets, whilst both "Dawn" and "Moonlight" are at once pleasingly atmospheric yet immensely refined of texture. Yuasa's "Storm" undoubtedly generates great physical excitement. The six numbers which comprise the "Pas de Six" from Act 3 of *The Prince of the Pagodas* contain some of that ambitious ballet's most engaging invention. Yuasa and his colleagues positively relish all the music's drama, glitter and poise, and prove themselves no less dashingly committed exponents of the *Gloriana* concert suite. Here the opening fanfares and popular sequence of "Courtly Dances" are delivered with genuine panache, whilst RLPO principal oboist Jonathan Small creates a ravishing impression in the second movement "Lute Song" (which utilizes Essex's hauntingly wistful aria "Happy were he"). Indeed, the whole performance possesses memorable vibrancy, polish and swagger. The only complaint about this disc is its duration: just 53 minutes of music is a touch on the stingy side.

Additional recommendations ...

...Four Sea Interludes. Passacaglia, Op. 33b. **Bridge** The Sea. **Bax** On the Sea-Shore (orch. Parlett). **Ulster Orchestra / Vernon Handley.** Chandos Ⓕ CHAN8473 (52 minutes: DDD: 3/87).

...Four Sea Interludes. Johnson over Jordan. The Young Person's Guide to the Orchestra. Suite on English Folk Tunes (A time there was ...), Op. 90. **Bournemouth Symphony Orchestra / Richard Hickox.** Chandos Ⓕ CHAN9221 (67 minutes: DDD: 3/94).

<hr>

New review

Britten The Young Person's Guide to the Orchestra, Op. 34[a]. Simple Symphony, Op. 4[b]. A Spring Symphony, Op. 44 – Spring, the sweet spring[c]. Noyes Fludde[d] – Noye, Noye, take thou thy company ... Sir! heare are lions. Serenade for Tenor, Horn and Strings, Op. 31 – Nocturne[e]. Folk Songs[c] – The Plough Boy; Early One Morning. Billy Budd – Interlude and Sea Shanties[f]. A Ceremony of Carols, Op. 28 – Adam lay i-bounden[g]. A Hymn to the Virgin[g]. War Requiem – Lacrimosa[f]. Peter Grimes – Interlude (Dawn)[h]. [ce]**Sir Peter Pears** (ten); [e]**Barry Tuckwell** (hn); [cdfgh]**various soloists; choirs, choruses and orchestras,** [aef]**London Symphony Orchestra,** [bd]**English Chamber Orchestra / Benjamin Britten** (pf); [d]**Norman Del Mar.** Decca Ⓜ 436 990-2DWO (74 minutes: ADD: 6/93). Item marked [a] from SXL6110 (9/64), [b]SXL6405 (6/69).   ⒼⒼ

Although when dealing with the music of a single composer Decca's "World of ..." series tends to offer a series of single movements rather than complete works, this reissue, "The World of Britten", is very welcome as it includes the composer's own 1963 recording of *The Young Person's Guide to the Orchestra* with the LSO and his complete 1968 ECO version of the *Simple Symphony*. The latter is delightfully fresh and is unforgettable for the joyful bounce of the "Playful Pizzicato", helped by the resonant acoustic of The Maltings, Snape. *The Young Person's Guide*, adapted from a theme by Purcell, came about through a film which would demonstrate to children the instruments of the orchestra. Here, Britten wisely omits the now rather dated text. He adopts quick tempos that must have been demanding even for the LSO players, with more spacious ones for the more introspective sections. This is beautiful playing, possessing wit and brilliance, with all kinds of memorable touches. If this transfer is a little dry in sonority this disc is invaluable for these two performances alone. As a bonus we also get ten short excerpts from other major Britten works, including *Billy Budd*, the *War Requiem*, *Peter Grimes* and the haunting, echoing "Nocturne" from the *Serenade* (sung by Peter Pears with Barry Tuckwell playing the horn obbligato). We also get Pears's singing of Britten's arrangements of *Early One Morning* and *The Plough Boy* (with the boisterous whistling refrain heard in the upper register of the piano accompaniment). The only curious inclusion here is the exuberant excerpt from Norman Del Mar's now deleted recording of *Noyes Fludde*.

Additional recommendations ...

...The Young Person's Guide to the Orchestra. Cello Symphony[a]. Peter Grimes – Four Sea Interludes, Op. 33a. **Pärt** Cantus in memory of Benjamin Britten. [a]**Truls Mørk** (vc); **Bergen Philharmonic Orchestra / Neeme Järvi.** BIS Ⓕ CD420 (75 minutes: DDD: 6/89).

... The Young Person's Guide to the Orchestra[b]. **Saint-Saëns** Le carnaval des animaux[a]. **Grieg** Peer Gynt – Suites Nos. 1 and 2[c]. **Gounod** March funèbre d'une marionette. **Loesser** Hans Christian Anderson – musical film. [ab]**Hugh Downs** (narr); [a]**Leo Litwin**, [a]**Samuel Lipman** (pfs); [c]**Eileen Farrell** (sop); **Boston Pops Orchestra / Arthur Fiedler.** RCA Victor Living Stereo Ⓜ 09026 68131-2 (76 minutes: ADD: 12/95).

Britten Cello Symphony, Op. 68[a]. Sinfonia da Requiem, Op. 20[b]. Cantata misericordium, Op. 69[c]. [a]**Mstislav Rostropovich** (vc); [c]**Sir Peter Pears** (ten); [c]**Dietrich Fischer-Dieskau** (bar); [c]**London Symphony Chorus and Orchestra**, [a]**English Chamber Orchestra**, [b]**New Philharmonia Orchestra / Benjamin Britten.** Decca London Ⓜ 425 100-2LM (75 minutes: ADD: 9/89). Text and translation included. Item marked [a] from SXL6138 (12/64), [bc]SXL6175 (9/65). Recorded 1964.

Ⓖ Ⓖ Ⓖ

This mid-price disc offers two of Britten's finest works, the *Cello Symphony* and the *Sinfonia da Requiem*. The latter was written in 1940 and is one of the composer's most powerful orchestral works, harnessing opposing forces in a frighteningly intense way. From the opening drumbeat the *Sinfonia* employs sonata form in a dramatically powerful way, though the tone is never fierce or savage; it has an implacable tread and momentum. The central movement, "Dies irae", however, has a real sense of fury, satirical in its biting comment – the flutter-tongued wind writing rattling its defiance. The closing "Requiem aeternam" is a movement of restrained beauty. On this recording from 1964 the New Philharmonia play superbly. The Cello Symphony, written in 1963 as part of a series for the great Russian cellist Mstislav Rostropovich, was the first major sonata-form work written since the *Sinfonia*. The idea of a struggle between soloist and orchestra, implicit in the traditional concerto, has no part here; it is a conversation between the two. Rostropovich plays with a depth of feeling that has never quite been equalled in other recordings and the playing of the ECO has great bite. The recording too is extraordinarily fine for its years. The *Cantata misericordium*, one of Britten's lesser known works, was written in 1962 as a commission from the Red Cross. It takes the story of the Good Samaritan and is scored for tenor and baritone soloists, chorus, string quartet and orchestra. It is a universal plea for charity and here receives a powerful reading. This is a must for any collector of Britten's music.

Additional recommendations ...

...Sinfonia da Requiem. The Young Person's Guide to the Orchestra, Op. 34. Peter Grimes – Four Sea Interludes; Passacaglia. **Royal Liverpool Philharmonic Orchestra / Libor Pešek.** Virgin Classics Ⓜ CUV5 61195-2 (63 minutes: DDD: 4/90).

...Cello Symphony. **Bridge** Oration – Concerto elegiaco, H180. **Steven Isserlis** (vc); **City of London Sinfonia / Richard Hickox.** EMI Ⓜ CDM7 63909-2 (68 minutes: DDD: 2/92). *See review under Bridge; refer to the Index to Reviews.* Ⓖ

New review

Britten Prelude and Fugue, Op. 29[a]. Lachrymae – Reflections on a Song of Dowland, Op. 48a[b]. Elegy[c]. Simple Symphony, Op. 4[a]. Variations on a theme of Frank Bridge, Op. 10[d]. [bc]**Lars Anders Tomter** (va); [abd]**Norwegian Chamber Orchestra / Iona Brown.** Virgin Classics Ⓕ VC5 45121-2 (78 minutes: DDD: 10/95). Item marked [d] from Simax PSC1035 (1/89). *Gramophone Editor's choice.* Recorded 1988-91. Ⓖ

The *Frank Bridge* Variations are finely disciplined, strongly characterized and benefit from sumptuous engineering. The hushed intensity achieved in such variations as the "Adagio" and "Chant" recalls Britten's own remarkable interpretation – and there can be no higher praise than that! In the *Simple Symphony* the infectious "Playful Pizzicato" could perhaps have been given with a greater sense of fun; elsewhere, though, there can be no complaints about the outer movements (both wonderfully crisp and vital), whilst the lovely "Sentimental Sarabande" has surely seldom enjoyed such tenderly expressive advocacy. The *Prelude and Fugue* is brought off with exhilarating poise and panache, and it is difficult to imagine a more eloquent contribution than that of violist Lars Anders Tomter in the early solo *Elegy* and haunting, Dowland-inspired *Lachrymae*. Consistently superior sound, Michael Oliver's admirable booklet-notes and an uncommonly generous playing time add to the considerable attractions of this Virgin Classics release.

Additional recommendations ...

...Simple Symphony. **Bizet** Symphony in C major. **Prokofiev** Symphony No. 1 in D major,
Op. 25, "Classical". **Orpheus Chamber Orchestra.** DG Ⓕ 423 624-2GH (64 minutes: DDD: 1/89).
...Variations on a Theme of Frank Bridge. **Butterworth** Two English Idylls. A Shropshire Lad.
The banks of green willow. **Warlock** Capriol Suite. **Academy of St Martin in the Fields / Sir
Neville Marriner.** Decca London Ⓜ 421 391-2LM (62 minutes: ADD: 8/89).
...The Young Person's Guide to the Orchestra. Variations on a Theme of Frank Bridge. Peter
Grimes – Four Sea Interludes, Op. 33a; Passacaglia. **BBC Symphony Orchestra / Andrew Davis.**
Teldec British Line Ⓕ 9031-73126-2 (68 minutes: DDD: 8/91). *Selected by Sounds in Retrospect.*
...Simple Symphony. Variations on a theme of Frank Bridge. Prelude and Fugue for String
Orchestra, Op. 29. **Bournemouth Sinfonietta / Ronald Thomas.** Chandos Collect Ⓜ CHAN6592
(51 minutes: ADD: 11/93).
...Simple Symphony. Prelude and Fugue, Op. 29. **Bridge** Sir Roger de Coverley, H155. **Delius** Two
Aquarelles. **Elgar** Introduction and Allegro, Op. 47. **Purcell** Chacony in G minor for strings,
Z730. **English Chamber Orchestra / Benjamin Britten.** Decca The Classic Sound Ⓜ 448 569-2DCS
(58 minutes: ADD: 2/96).

<hr>

New review
Britten Temporal Variations[a]. Six Metamorphoses after Ovid, Op. 49. Two Insect Pieces[b].
Phantasy, Op. 2[c].
Poulenc Oboe Sonata[d]. Trio for Oboe, Bassoon and Piano[e]. **François Leleux** (ob); [e]**Jean-François
Duquesnoy** (bn); [c]**Guillaume Sutre** (vn); [c]**Miguel da Silva** (va); [c]**Marc Coppey** (vc); [abde]**Emmanuel
Strosser** (pf). Harmonia Mundi Les Nouveaux Interprètes Ⓑ HMN91 1556 (76 minutes: DDD:
2/96). Recorded 1995.   Ⓖ
The pairing of these composers is apt, for they were friends and their musical high spirits – frequent in
the Parisian, less so in the uneasy East Anglian – often have a darker side. The oboist here, French and
very young (he was born in 1971), possesses an excellent technique and is a deeply sensitive artist. Both
qualities quickly become evident in the flowing, quietly poignant opening melody of Poulenc's Sonata,
where Leleux's tone is not only beautiful but also admirably responsive to the subtle dynamic shading
and rhythmic flexibility. Yet this is far from the whole story, and the *grotesquerie* of the passage starting
at 2'16" shows that there is more to his playing than gentleness – as does the mercurial *Scherzo*, delivered
with delightful point and relish. The final *Déploration* of this sonata, as played here, is infinitely moving
and nothing less than superb. Fortunately Leleux and his pianist partner, who is equally attuned to
Poulenc's world, have been extremely well recorded. This performance and that of the bouncy Trio both
give keen pleasure. So do the Britten pieces, three of them early (the characterful *Six Metamorphoses*
being the exception) and edgy. Performed as vividly as this, they are undoubtedly worth having. The
booklet gives no information on the music beyond titles and timings. Otherwise there is only praise for
a fine, generously filled disc, recommended even if you already possess some of the music.
Additional recommendation ...
...Phantasy, Op. 2[ac]. Holiday Diary, Op. 5[b]. Six Metamorphoses after Ovid[a]. Temporal
Variations[ab]. Five Waltzes[b]. Two Insect Pieces[ab]. Night Piece (Notturno)[b]. [a]**Sarah Francis** (ob);
[b]**Michael Dussek** (pf); [c]members of the **Delmé Quartet.** Hyperion Ⓕ CDA66776 (75 minutes:
DDD: 2/96).

<hr>

Britten String Quartets – No. 1 in D major, Op. 25[a]; No. 2 in C major, Op. 36[c]; No. 3, Op. 94[c].
String Quartet in D major[d]. Rhapsody[d]. Quartettino[d]. Elegy[e]. Phantasy in F minor[bf]. Phantasy,
Op. 2[b]. Three Divertimentos[a]. Alla marcia[a]. [abcdf]**Endellion Quartet** (Andrew Watkinson, James
Clark, vns; [e]Garfield Jackson, va; David Waterman, vc); [f]**Nicholas Logie** (va); [b]**Douglas Boyd**
(ob). EMI British Composers Ⓜ CMS5 65115-2 (three discs: 169 minutes: DDD: 7/95). Items
marked [ab] from CDC7 47695-2, [c]CDC7 47696-2 (5/88), [def]CDC7 47694-2 (7/87). Recorded 1986.
EMI's mid-price reissue of these recordings adds up to an outstanding compilation. Britten's three
numbered quartets have been much recorded, but this is the only issue that puts these works in the
fullest possible context, and the performances as a whole remain unsurpassed in their skill and
sensitivity. In the various early compositions, most published posthumously, the Endellion's only
significant rival is the Gabrieli Quartet with oboist Derek Wickens (listed below). In the *Rhapsody*
(1929) and *Quartettino* (1930) the Endellion have the field to themselves, and it's tempting to say that
the *Quartettino* alone would justify the purchase of this set. At just over 15 minutes it is far from tiny,
and the style – elements from Bridge, Ravel and Bartók, even Berg or early Schoenberg, all given a
genuinely Brittenish colouring – makes it a fascinating piece, and remarkably well composed for a 16-
year-old. If we add the D major Quartet of 1931 to the three numbered works the main competition
the Endellion face is from the Britten Quartet on Collins Classics. The Britten Quartet's readings are
distinguished by their weight and seriousness, qualities that can turn to ponderousness, especially in
the 1931 Quartet, which needs a lighter touch if the music is not to seem laboured in places. The
Britten Quartet give a performance of Op. 25 which is magnificent of its kind, but the huge finale of
No. 2 seems very long and drawn-out, and No. 3 lacks some of the nuances of expression which
distinguish the Endellion's fine performance. For an overview of Britten's quartet music (and not
forgetting Douglas Boyd's characterful participation in Op. 2) the Endellion Quartet, and these EMI
recordings, will take some beating.

Additional recommendations ...

...Sinfonietta, Op. 1[a]. String Quartets Nos. 2 and 3[b]. [a]**Vienna Octet;** [b]**Amadeus Quartet.** Decca London Ⓜ 425 715-2LM (68 minutes: ADD: 9/90).

...No. 2 in C major, Op. 36. No. 3. **Alberni Quartet.** CRD Ⓕ CRD3395 (55 minutes: ADD: 3/89).

...Nos. 2 and 3. **Britten Quartet.** Collins Classics Ⓕ 1025-2 (64 minutes: DDD: 12/90).

...Temporal Variations[a]. Two Insect Pieces[a]. Phantasy in F minor[c]. Alla marcia[d]. Three Divertimentos[d]. Phantasy, Op. 2[e]. [ae]**Derek Wickens** (ob); [a]**John Constable** (pf); [cd]**Gabrieli Quartet.** Unicorn-Kanchana Souvenir Ⓜ UKCD2060 (58 minutes: DDD: 6/93).

New review

Britten Solo Cello Suites[a] – No. 1, Op. 72; No. 2, Op. 80. Cello Sonata, Op. 65[b]. **Mstislav Rostropovich** (vc); [b]**Benjamin Britten** (pf). Decca London Ⓜ 421 859-2LM (68 minutes: ADD: 10/89). Items marked [a] from SXL6393 (6/70), [b]SXL2298 (1/62).   ⒼⒼ

This is a classic recording of the Cello Sonata, with Rostropovich and the composer playing with an authority impossible to surpass, and is here coupled with the unaccompanied First and Second Cello Suites. The Sonata is unconventional in having five movements of which Nos. 2, 4 and 5 each last less than three minutes but are none the less characterful and telling. The suggestive, often biting humour, masks darker feelings. However, Britten manages, just, to keep his devil under control. Rostropovich's and Britten's characterization in the opening *Dialogo* is stunning and their subdued humour in the *Scherzo-pizzicato* also works well. In the *Elegia* and the final *Moto perpetuo*, again, no one quite approaches the passion and energy of Rostropovich. This work, like the two Suites, were written for him and he still remains the real heavyweight in all three pieces. Their transfer to CD is remarkably successful; it is difficult to believe that the recording of the Sonata is nearly 35 years old and that of the Suites 26 years.

Additional recommendations ...

...Suite, Op. 6[a]. Elegy[b]. Cello Sonata[c]. Six Metamorphoses after Ovid, Op. 49[d]. [d]**Roy Carter** (ob); [a]**Alexander Barantschik** (vn); [b]**Paul Silverthorne** (va); [c]**Moray Welsh** (vc); [a]**John Alley,** [c]**John Lenehan** (pfs). EMI Anglo-American Chamber Music Series Ⓕ CDC5 55398-2 (59 minutes: DDD: 7/95).

...Cello Sonata. *Coupled with works by* **Mayer** *and* **Rubbra** **Timothy Gill** (vc); **Fali Pavri** (pf). Guild Ⓕ GMCD7114 (79 minutes: DDD: 4/96). *See review under Mayer; refer to the Index to Reviews.*

...Cello Sonata. **Bridge** Cello Sonata in D minor, H125. Four Short Pieces, H104 – Spring Song. Melodie, H99. Scherzo, H19a. **Steven Doane** (vc); **Barry Snyder** (pf). Bridge Ⓕ BCD9056 (52 minutes: DDD: 4/96). *See review under Bridge; refer to the Index to Reviews.*

New review

Britten Solo Cello Suites – No. 1, Op. 72; No. 2, Op. 80; No. 3, Op. 87. **Robert Cohen** (vc). Decca London Ⓕ 444 181-2LH (69 minutes: DDD: 6/96). Recorded 1994.

As a whole the performance of the First Cello Suite is the least persuasive: some tempos are on the slow side, and there is an occasional lack of dynamic contrast, for example in the finale. Even so, one is soon won over by Cohen's ability to characterize the music vividly while avoiding the exaggerated emphases that creep into certain other recordings. Cohen's reading of No. 2 is especially fine, with an expressiveness and sense of drama which are the more compelling for being projected against an appropriately restrained background. The version of the Russian *Hymn for the Departed*, with which Britten's Third Cello Suite ends, is heartbreaking in its raw simplicity, and Robert Cohen plays it perfectly. He is aided by an excellent recording, the instrument not overbearingly close or excessively resonant.

Britten Four Cabaret Songs[a]. When you're feeling like expressing your affection[a]. On this Island – As it is, plenty[a]. Blues (arr. Runswick)[b] – The Spider and the Fly; Blues; The clock on the wall; Boogie-Woogie.

Porter Paris – Let's do it[a]. Gay Divorce – Night and Day[a]. Leave it to Me – My heart belongs to daddy[a]. Miss Otis Regrets[a]. Nymph Errant – The Physician[a]. [a]**Jill Gomez** (sop), [a]**Martin Jones** (pf); [b]**instrumental ensemble** (David Roach, cl/sax; Graham Ashton, tpt; Beverley Davison, vn; Chris Lawrence, db; John Constable, pf; Gregory Knowles, perc). Unicorn-Kanchana Ⓕ DKPCD9138 (52 minutes: DDD: 9/93). Texts included. Recorded 1992. *Gramophone Editor's choice.*   Ⓖ

Britten's cabaret songs were written for the singing actress Hedli Anderson; there were more than four, but these are the only ones to have seen publication so far. The texts by Auden are full of the spirit that William Coldstream described, writing about one of Anderson's performances, "teaching of carefree lucidity and the non-avoidance of banality". *When you're feeling like expressing your affection*

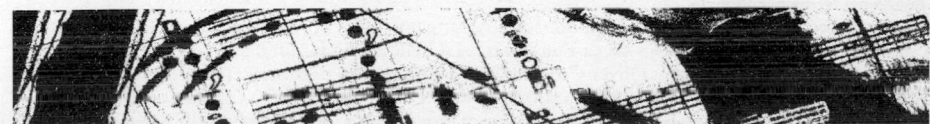

which is published and performed here for the first time is one of the results of Auden and Britten's work for the GPO in the 1930s. Apart from the references to "any telephone kiosk" and "Press button A" it would still serve well as an encouragement to make use of the telephone. "As it is, plenty", the last song from *On this Island*, being also in the ironic popular-music style, rounds off the group nicely. Jill Gomez's performances are perfect in every nuance, her beautiful tone, clear diction and just hinted-at irony, never overdoing it, give the songs the exact weight they need. The Cole Porter encores and Daryl Runswick's arrangements of four *Blues* by Britten complete a quite delicious record.

Britten A Spring Symphony, Op. 44[a]. Cantata Academica, Op. 62[b]. Hymn to St Cecilia, Op. 27[c].
[ab]**Jennifer Vyvyan** (sop); [a]**Norma Procter,** [b]**Helen Watts** (contrs); [ab]**Sir Peter Pears** (ten); [b]**Owen Brannigan** (bass); [a]**Emanuel School Boys' Choir;** [a]**Chorus and Orchestra of the Royal Opera House, Covent Garden / Benjamin Britten; London Symphony** [bc]**Chorus and** [b]**Orchestra / George Malcolm.** Decca London Ⓜ 436 396-2LM (74 minutes: ADD: 9/93). Texts and translation included.
Item marked [a] from SXL2264 (5/61), [bc] L'Oiseau-Lyre SOL60037 (10/61). Recorded 1960-61.ⒼⒼ
Britten's performance of the *Spring Symphony* fairly leaps out of one's loudspeakers, and the 1960 sound is as crisp and alive as the performance and the work itself. In the last two pieces George Malcolm's direction is as vivid as Britten's elsewhere. The *Cantata Academica* (1959) is one of Britten's happiest pieces, bubbling over with warmth, jollity and good fellowship. Indeed the Latin title is only one of mock-solemnity. Try "Tema seriale con fuga" to hear how this composer could make living music out of the most perniciously academic device of our troubled century. Further high points are Owen Brannigan's marvellously pompous bass aria and the boisterous "Canone ed ostinato". The performance of the *Hymn to St Cecilia* is skilful, idiomatic and touching.
Additional recommendation ...
...A Spring Symphony[a]. Four Sea Interludes, Op. 33[ab]. The Young Person's Guide to the Orchestra, Op. 34[b]. [a]**Jo Vincent** (sop); [a]**Kathleen Ferrier** (contr); [a]**Sir Peter Pears** (ten); [a]**St Willibrord's Boys' Choir**; [a]**Netherlands Radio Chorus**; **Concertgebouw Orchestra, Amsterdam / Eduard van Beinum.** Decca Historic Series mono Ⓜ 440 063-2DM* (75 minutes: ADD: 9/94).

New review
Britten Folk-song Arrangements[a]. Folk-song Arrangements – orchestral versions[b]. King Herod and the Cock[c]. The Twelve Apostles[d]. The Holly and the Ivy[e]. [a]**Felicity Lott** (sop); [abcd]**Philip Langridge** (ten); [ab]**Thomas Allen** (bar); [a]**Carlos Bonell** (gtr); [a]**Osian Ellis** (hp); [a]**Christopher Van Kampen** (vc); [a]**Graham Johnson,** [cd]**David Owen Norris** (pfs); [cd]**Wenhaston Boys' Choir / Christopher Barnett;** [e]**BBC Singers / Simon Joly;** [b]**Northern Sinfonia / Steuart Bedford.** Collins Classics Ⓕ 7039-2 (three discs: 199 minutes: DDD: 11/95). Texts included.
Those who bought the attractive Hyperion set of Britten's 'complete' folk-song arrangements probably thought that they had at least one area in their collection which was complete and need not be reconsidered. Now comes another set, on three CDs rather than two. So the questions run: "What is the extra material?", "How good is it?" and "How do the performances compare?" Eight unpublished settings for solo or duet, one for choir and tenor and one unidentified folk-song setting plus 14 of the published songs rearranged for voice and orchestra: that is the tally. Additions to the voice-and-piano repertoire include *Greensleeves* and *The Crocodile* (the song of a sailor who spins a yarn for landsmen gullible enough to swallow the 500-mile length of croc with attendant wonders). *I wonder as I wander*, a favourite encore in Sir Peter Pears's concerts, is here on record for the first time. These and two light-hearted duets all give pleasure, though perhaps not so acute as to make the purchase imperative. More unexpected, perhaps, is the setting which goes under the title of *The Stream in the Valley* and which turns out to be *Da unten im Tale*, best known today in the arrangement by Brahms. In this Britten introduces to very lovely effect a part for cello. Interest, then, begins to add up. The orchestrations may not add much more, though it is striking to find that the remoteness of tonality in *Fileuse* and to some extent *Eho* (Vol. 2) seems increased. The choral settings are fun (perhaps more than that), and the great discovery among them is the unfinished, comparatively large-scale arrangement of *The Bitter Withy*, a fascinating piece and apparently going so well that it is astonishing to find Britten putting it aside and never returning to it. Certainly for first-time buyers this is the set to have. As to the performances, much in a Britten collection of this kind depends on the tenor, and Philip Langridge quickly establishes himself as a worthy successor to Pears, a singer of intelligence and bold, distinctive character. In most of the volumes he shares with Felicity Lott, who is comparably sensitive to modulations and underlying feeling. Thomas Allen makes only a brief appearance, but it is good to hear his warm tone and fine legato in the version of *The Sally Gardens* with strings. Fine playing by Osian Ellis and the guitarist Carlos Bonell and a strong contribution from the Wenhaston Boys' Choir are further attractions. Graham Johnson's playing, as we now almost take for granted, is uniformly excellent. The set is well recorded, the Collins engineers skilfully aligning the acoustics of their five different locations.
Additional recommendations ...
...The Rape of Lucretia (abridged)[a]. Folk-song Arrangements[b] – Voici le printemps; Fileuse; Quand j'étais chez mon père; Le roi s'en va-t'en chasse; La belle est au jardin d'amour; The Salley Gardens; Little Sir William; Oliver Cromwell; The Bonny Earl o' Moray; The ash grove; Quand j'étais chez mon père; There's none to soothe; Sweet Polly Oliver; Le roi s'en va-t'en chasse; The plough boy; The foggy foggy dew; Come you not from Newcastle?; O waly waly. **Soloists;** [b]**BBC**

Theatre Chorus; [a]**English Opera Group Chamber Orchestra,** [b]**Orchestra of the Royal Opera House, Covent Garden / Sir Reginald Goodall.** EMI British Composers mono Ⓜ CMS7 64727-2* (two discs: 156 minutes: ADD: 2/94). *Gramophone Editor's choice.* Ⓖ

…Folk Song Arrangements. **Lorna Anderson, Regina Nathan** (sops); **Jamie MacDougall** (ten); **Bryn Lewis** (hp); **Craig Ogden** (gtr); **Malcolm Martineau** (pf). Hyperion Ⓕ CDA66941/2 (two discs: 125 minutes: DDD: 2/95).

…Folk Song Arrangements[b] – The Salley Gardens; Little Sir William; The ash grove; Oliver Cromwell. Seven Sonnets of Michelangelo, Op. 22[a]. Introduction and Rondo alla burlesca, Op. 23 No. 1[c]. Mazurka elegiaca, Op. 23 No. 2[c]. Serenade for Tenor, Horn and Strings[d]. **McPhee** Balinese Ceremonial Music[e]. [abd]**Sir Peter Pears** (ten); [d]**Dennis Brain** (hn); [e]**Colin McPhee,** [c]**Sir Clifford Curzon** (pfs); [d]**Boyd Neel String Orchestra / Benjamin Britten** ([abce]pf). Pearl mono Ⓜ GEMMCD9177* (78 minutes: ADD: 10/95).

New review

Britten Harmonia Sacra – Lord! I have sinned; Hymn to God the Father; A Hymn on Divine Musick. This way to the Tomb – Evening; Morning; Night. Night covers up the rigid land. Fish in the unruffled lakes. To lie flat on the back with the knees flexed. A poison tree. When you're feeling like expressing your affection. Not even summer yet. The red cockatoo. Wild with passion. If thou wilt ease thine heart. Cradle song for Eleanor. Birthday song for Erwin. Um Mitternacht. The Holy Sonnets of John Donne, Op. 35. **Ian Bostridge** (ten); **Graham Johnson** (pf). Hyperion Ⓕ CDA66823 (65 minutes: DDD: 1/96). Texts included. Recorded 1995. *Gramophone Editor's record of the month.* ⒼⒼ

Bostridge is in the royal line of Britten's tenor interpreters. Indeed his imaginative response to words and music may come closer than any to Pears himself. He is heard here in a veritable cornucopia of by and large unfamiliar and even unknown songs (the Donne cycle apart), mostly from the earliest period of Britten's song-writing career when his inspiration was perhaps at its most free and spontaneous. The three settings from Ronald Duncan's *This way to the Tomb* nicely match that poet's florid, vocabulary-rich style as Britten was to do again two years later in *Lucretia*, with "Night", based on a B minor ground bass, a particularly arresting piece. The Auden settings, roughly contemporaneous with *On this Island*, all reflect Britten's empathy with the poet at that time. The third, *To lie flat on the back*, evinces Britten's gift for writing in racy mode, as does *When you're feeling like expressing your affection*, very much in the style of *Cabaret Songs*. Much deeper emotions are stirred by the two superb Beddoes settings (*Wild with passion* and *If thou wilt ease thine heart*), written when the composer and Pears were on a ship returning home in 1942. *The red cockatoo* itself is an early setting of Waley to whom Britten returned in *Songs from the Chinese*. All these revelatory songs are performed with full understanding and innate beauty by Bostridge and Johnson, who obviously have a close artistic rapport. They form a lengthy and rewarding prelude to their shattering account of the Donne Sonnets. They are as demanding on singer and pianist as anything Britten wrote, hence their previously small representation in the catalogue. Both artists pierce to the core of these electrifying songs, written after, and affected by, Britten's visit to Belsen with Menuhin in 1945 shortly after the war's end. Fully documented notes, and the skills of the recording team in catching the immediacy of these riveting performances complete one's pleasure in this richly satisfying issue.

Britten Serenade for Tenor, Horn and Strings, Op. 31[a]. Les illuminations, Op. 18[b]. Nocturne, Op. 60[c]. [abc]**Sir Peter Pears** (ten); [c]**Alexander Murray** (fl); [c]**Roger Lord** (cor ang); [c]**Gervase de Peyer** (cl); [c]**William Waterhouse** (bn); [ac]**Barry Tuckwell** (hn); [c]**Dennis Blyth** (timp); [c]**Osian Ellis** (hp); [ac]strings of the **London Symphony Orchestra;** [b]**English Chamber Orchestra /** [abc]**Benjamin Britten.** Decca London Ⓜ 436 395-2LM* (73 minutes: ADD: 9/93). Texts included. Item marked [a] from SXL6110 (9/64), [b]SXL6316 (11/67), [c]SXL2186 (5/60). Recorded 1959-66. ⒼⒼ

No other instrument was more important to Britten than the human voice and, inspired by the musicianship and superb vocal craftsmanship of his closest friend, Peter Pears, he produced an unbroken stream of vocal works of a quality akin to those of Purcell. Three of his most haunting vocal pieces are featured on this wonderful CD. The performances date from between 1959 and 1966 with Pears in penetratingly musical form, even if the voice itself was by now a little thin and occasionally unsteady. The ECO and LSO are superb in every way and of course Britten was his own ideal interpreter. The recordings are vintage Decca and excellent for their time. This welcome mid-price reissue is strongly recommended.

Additional recommendations …

…Les illuminations[a]. Simple Symphony, Op. 4. Phaedra, Op. 93[a]. [a]**Christiane Eda-Pierre** (sop); **Jean-Walter Audoli Instrumental Ensemble / Jean-Walter Audoli.** Arion Ⓕ ARN68035 (56 minutes: DDD: 6/89).

…Les illuminations[a]. Phaedra, Op. 93[b]. Folk Song Arrangements – Fileuse; La belle est au jardin d'amour; Eho! Eho!; Quand j'étais chez mon père; Le roi s'en va-t'en chasse[b]. [a]**Jill Gomez** (sop); [b]**Felicity Palmer** (mez); **Endymion Ensemble / John Whitfield.** EMI British Composers Ⓜ CDM5 65114-2 (50 minutes: DDD: 7/95).

…Les illuminations[bf]. **Duparc** L'invitation au voyage[cd]. Soupir[cd]. Testament[cd]. Sérénade florentine[cd]. La vague et la cloche[cd]. Lamento[cd]. La Vie antérieure[cd]. Phidylé[cd]. Extase[cd]. Elégie[cd]. Le Manoir de Rosemonde[cd]. Chanson triste[cd]. **Fauré** Requiem, Op. 48[ace]. La bonne chanson, Op. 61[cd]. **Ravel** Don Quichotte à Dulcinée[ce]. Shéhérazade[be]. **Debussy** Trois ballades de François Villon[ce]. [a]**Pierrette Alarie,** [b]**Janine Micheau** (sops); [c]**Camille Maurane** (bar); [d]**Lily Bienvenu** (pf); [a]**Elisabeth Brasseur Choir; Lamoureux Orchestra /** [e]**Jean Fournet,** [f]**Paul Sacher.** Philips The Early Years mono Ⓜ 438 970-2PM2* (two discs: 157 minutes: ADD).

...Les illuminations[a]. Sinfonia da Requiem, Op. 20[b]. Seven Sonnets of Michelangelo, Op. 22[c]. [ac]**Sir Peter Pears** (ten); [a]**CBS Symphony Orchestra / Benjamin Britten** ([c]pf); [b]**New York Philharmonic Orchestra / Sir John Barbirolli.** NMC mono Ⓔ NMCD030* (61 minutes: ADD: 2/96).

New review
Britten Les illuminations, Op. 18. Serenade for Tenor, Horn and Strings, Op. 31[a]. Nocturne, Op. 60. **John Mark Ainsley** (ten); [a]**David Pyatt** (hn); **Britten Sinfonia / Nicholas Cleobury.** EMI Eminence Ⓜ CD-EMX2247 (73 minutes: DDD: 7/96). Texts and translations included.
Gramophone Editor's choice.   Ⓖ
Ainsley is representative of the third generation of Britten interpreters with fewer of the inhibitions that inevitably afflicted those tenors who lived in the immediate shadow of the composer. Which is not to say that, in these absorbing performances, he is in any way flouting tradition: these are mainstream interpretations, but ones with their own validity. Ainsley is most compelling in the *Nocturne*, arguably the most difficult of the three to emcompass. Here he has nothing to fear in comparison with Sir Peter Pears. In his liquid tone, response to the texts and technical accomplishment of the challenging line, he is well-nigh faultless. More important still in this cycle, he catches the individual mood of each setting through finding the right timbre for each – floating line for the Shelley, nocturnal mystery for the Tennyson, with a wonderful *subito piano* on the final A flat (throughout the disc, Ainsley is faithful to all markings), pure legato for the Coleridge, mesmeric, hushed tone for the Wordsworth, light lyricism for the Keats and so on. With Cleobury and the highly skilled soloists of the Britten Sinfonia lending ideal support, this is a reading to savour. Apart from too many aspirates in the runs of "Hymn", the *Serenade* is almost on a par with *Nocturne*, the many facets of this still-amazing cycle fully realized both in terms of vocal refinement and textual acuity. He is helped by the most thrilling account yet of the horn solo from young David Pyatt. His playing is nothing short of masterly and magical. In *Les illuminations* he achieves the essential delicacy and sensuous erotic touch but his pace is too hectic in places. His French, though not wholly idiomatic, is clearly articulated. High praise is due to Cleobury, who seems to have found even more nuances in the orchestral parts of all three works than his predecessors. If you want these works together on a single mid-price CD in modern sound, you need not hesitate. The recording ensures that we hear everything in perfect perspective and the balance with the voice is commendable.

Britten Quatre chansons françaises[af]. Our Hunting Fathers, Op. 8[bf]. Les illuminations, Op. 18[af]. Serenade for Tenor, Horn and Strings, Op. 31[def]. Nocturne, Op. 60[dg]. Phaedra, Op. 93[cf]. [a]**Felicity Lott,** [b]**Phyllis Bryn-Julson** (sops); [c]**Ann Murray** (mez); [d]**Philip Langridge** (ten); [e]**Frank Lloyd** (hn); [f]**English Chamber Orchestra;** [g]**Northern Sinfonia / Steuart Bedford.** Collins Classics Ⓕ 7037-2 (two discs: 127 minutes: DDD: 12/94). Texts and translations included. Item marked
[b] from 1192-2 (4/92). Recorded 1990-94.   ⒼⒼ
To hear all these orchestral song-cycles at one sitting demonstrates the development from the raw invention of the recently published *Quatre chansons françaises* and *Our Hunting Fathers*, through the central three works for high voice, to the bleak, etiolated sounds of *Phaedra*. Listening to them one after another also suggests new relationships and the debt Britten owed to earlier composers. "Dance of Death" in *Our Hunting Fathers* surely has Shostakovich as an inspiration, as does the "Dirge" in the *Serenade*. The final song of *Les illuminations* might have been written by Poulenc himself, while at many points the influence of Mahler is paramount and, as Philip Reed and Donald Mitchell point out in their informative notes, the "Prologue" to the *Serenade* must have been inspired by the opening of the last act of Verdi's *Falstaff*. And yet all these derivations are subsumed in Britten's own musical persona. Each cycle is also *sui generis*: as with any of Verdi's works, each has its own *tinta*, its own very special world of sound. All these facets of the pieces are made manifest in these superb performances, part of Collins Classics's ongoing Britten edition, masterminded by Steuart Bedford, the composer's most faithful disciple among performing artists. While throughout following Britten's intentions to the letter, he manages to imprint his own interpretation on to each cycle, basically a taut, fine-grained, spare style that, with the help of the mostly well balanced and spacious recordings, allow us to hear even more detail of the scores than do the excellent Decca versions (reviewed above) with the composer on the podium. Those are now around 30 years old.

In all but one case Bedford has the ECO as his pliant and willing ally in these exemplary performances. On *Our Hunting Fathers,* recorded in 1991, three years earlier than the rest, neither the playing nor the recording is quite on a par with the later sessions. Bryn-Julson sings that extremely taxing cycle in a bravura manner, occasionally with a harsh tone not inappropriate to the searing message of this extraordinary work, which may well have had the burghers of Norwich twitching at its première back in 1936. Even today it can amaze with its direct brilliance. Lott takes on the two French pieces and constantly makes us aware of the intriguing and sensuous sounds in *Quatre chansons*, not least in "Nuits de Juin", the very first song, with its strong Bergian leanings. She is also a formidable interpreter of *Les illuminations*, she and the players revelling in its ecstatic sound-world, ever obedient to the composer's copious markings, perfect in her French. Pears will always remain the bench-mark in the two tenor cycles, but Langridge, without slavishly following the master, sings them with as much if not more verbal acuity and with dazzling tone and technique. Anyone wanting these works in portmanteau form need not hesitate. Britten is done full justice by these involving, faithful interpretations, recorded in truthful, modern sound.

Britten A Ceremony of Carols, Op. 28[a]. Missa brevis in D major, Op. 63[b]. A Hymn to the Virgin. A Hymn of St Columba[b]. Jubilate Deo in E flat major[b]. Deus in adjutorum meum. [a]**Sioned Williams** (hp); **Westminster Cathedral Choir / David Hill** with [b]**James O'Donnell** (org). Hyperion Ⓕ CDA66220 (49 minutes: DDD: 2/88). From A66220 (12/86). Texts included.

A Ceremony of Carols sets nine medieval and sixteenth-century poems between the "Hodie" of the plainsong Vespers. The sole accompanying instrument is a harp, but given the right acoustic, sensitive attention to the words and fine rhythmic control the piece has a remarkable richness and depth. The Westminster Cathedral Choir perform this work beautifully; diction is immaculate and the acoustic halo surrounding the voices gives a festive glow to the performance. A fascinating *Jubilate* and *A Hymn to the Virgin*, whilst lacking the invention and subtlety of *A Ceremony*, intrigue with some particularly felicitous use of harmony and rhythm. *Deus in adjutorum meum* employs the choir without accompaniment and has an initial purity that gradually builds up in texture as the psalm (No 70) gathers momentum. The *Missa brevis* was written for this very choir and George Malcolm's nurturing of a tonal brightness in the choir allowed Britten to use the voices in a more flexibile and instrumental manner than usual. The effect is glorious. St Columba founded the monastery on the Scottish island of Iona and Britten's hymn sets his simple and forthright prayer with deceptive simplicity and directness. The choir sing this music beautifully and the recording is first rate.

Additional recommendations ...

...Missa Brevis[c]. Festival Te Deum in C major, Op. 32[c]. Jubilate Deo in C major. Hymn to St Peter, Op. 56[ac]. A Hymn to the Virgin. A Hymn of St Columba[c]. Sweet was the Song the Virgin sang. A New Year Carol[b]. A Shepherd's Carol. A Ceremony of Carols[b]. **The Sixteen / Harry Christophers** with [a]**Sioned Williams** (hp); [b]**Stephen Westrop** (pf); [c]**Margaret Phillips** (org). Collins Classics Ⓕ 1370-2 (61 minutes: DDD: 7/93).

...A Ceremony of Carols. A Boy is Born, Op. 3. Friday Afternoons, Op. 7. Psalm 150, Op. 67. **Various choirs and soloists / Benjamin Britten.** Decca London Ⓜ 436 394-2LM* (74 minutes: ADD: 9/93).

...A Hymn to the Virgin. A Boy is Born, Op. 3[a]. Christ's Nativity[b]. A Shepherd's Carol. Jubilate Deo[c]. Te Deum in C major[c]. [b]**Susan Gritton** (sop); [c]**Catherine Wyn-Rogers** (contr); **Holst Singers;** [a]**St Paul's Cathedral Choristers / Stephen Layton** with [c]**David Goode** (org). Hyperion Ⓕ CDA66825 (67 minutes: DDD: 3/96).

New review

Britten The Rescue of Penelope. Phaedra, Op. 93[a]. [a]**Lorraine Hunt** (mez); **Alison Hagley** (sop) Athene; **Catherine Wyn-Rogers** (mez) Artemis; **John Mark Ainsley** (ten) Hermes; **William Dazeley** (bass) Apollo; **Dame Janet Baker** (narr); **Hallé Orchestra / Kent Nagano.** Erato Ⓕ 0630 12713-2 (52 minutes: DDD: 7/96). Notes and text included.

Soon after his return from America, at the height of the war in 1943, Britten wrote the incidental music for a radio play by Edward Sackville-West on the Homeric subject of Odysseus's return to Penelope. Drawn from the complete score with barely any amendment of the original, and compressed into a 36-minute cantata, with Chris de Souza tailoring the text and Colin Matthews, Britten's last amanuensis, most tactfully editing the music, the result is extraordinarily powerful. The most important role is that of the narrator, here masterfully taken by Dame Janet Baker who brings the story vividly to life despite the stylized classical language (e.g. "Odysseus, Lord of sea-girt Ithaca" or "His fair wife, white armed Penelope"). Rather confusingly Athene also appears as a soprano with the radiant Alison Hagley sounding totally unlike Dame Janet. She is one of a godly quartet of singers who contribute Greek-style commentaries – vocal passages which regularly add to the atmospheric beauty of the piece. The surprise is that the idiom is not for the most part very Britten-like, except in the vitality of the writing. Here with a bigger orchestra than was usual for him, he allows himself far richer sounds, with the strings in particular often sounding like Walton. The result is hugely enjoyable, and for all the unexpected echoes – not just of Walton's film music but also of Elgar and Wagner – the more one listens, the more one identifies Britten. Who else but Britten would have thought of giving the theme of the heroine, Penelope, most poignantly, to an alto saxophone? This is music which is not just illustrative but strong and purposeful in heightening the drama, in bringing home emotions. It is welcomes addition to the Britten *oeuvre*. It is apt that another encapsulated classical drama should provide the coupling, particularly one inspired by the singing of Dame Janet Baker. *Phaedra* was Britten's last vocal work, and after the richness of the early work the spareness of the writing hits one the more sharply. Lorraine Hunt's performance may not quite match that of Dame Janet in conveying the heroine's agony, but there is comparable intensity, with vocal colouring of similarly grave beauty and variety; with Hunt this is above all the portrait of a deranged woman,

chillingly powerful. In both works Kent Nagano draws strongly committed playing from the Hallé, with some fine solo work, instrumental as well as vocal. Though, reasonably enough, Dame Janet's narration is rather close in the bigger work, the sound is full and well-balanced.

Additional recommendation ...
...The Rape of Lucretia[a]. Phaedra[b]. **Soloists; English Chamber Orchestra / [a]Benjamin Britten, [b]Steuart Bedford.** Decca London Ⓕ 425 666-2LH2 (two discs: 124 minutes: ADD: 5/90).

Britten War Requiem, Op. 66[a]. Sinfonia da Requiem, Op. 20. Ballad of Heroes, Op. 14[b]. [a]**Heather Harper** (sop); [a]**Philip Langridge, [b]Martyn Hill** (tens); [a]**John Shirley-Quirk** (bar); [a]**St Paul's Cathedral Choir; London Symphony [ab]Chorus and Orchestra / Richard Hickox.** Chandos Ⓕ CHAN8983/4 (two discs: 125 minutes: DDD: 11/91). Texts and translations included. *Gramophone Award Winner 1992*. *Gramophone classical 100. Selected by Sounds in Retrospect.*   ⒼⒼⒼ
Britten's *War Requiem* is the composer's most public statement of his pacifism. The work is cast in six movements and calls for massive forces: full chorus, soprano soloist and full orchestra evoke mourning, supplication and guilty apprehension; boys' voices with chamber organ, the passive calm of a liturgy which points beyond death; tenor and baritone soloists with chamber orchestra, the passionate outcry of the doomed victims of war. The most recent challenger to the composer's classic Decca version offers up-to-date recording, excellently managed to suggest the various perspectives of the vast work, and possibly the most convincing execution of the choral writing to date under the direction of a conductor, Richard Hickox, who is a past master at obtaining the best from a choir in terms of dynamic contrast and vocal emphasis. Add to that his empathy with all that the work has to say and you have a cogent reason for acquiring this version even before you come to the excellent work of the soloists. In her recording swan song, Harper at last commits to disc a part she created. It is right that her special accents and impeccable shaping of the soprano's contribution have been preserved for posterity. Shirley-Quirk, always closely associated with the piece, sings the three baritone solos and duets with rugged strength and dedicated intensity. He is matched by Langridge's compelling and insightful reading, with his notes and words more dramatic than Pears's approach. The inclusion of two additional pieces, neither of them short, gives this version an added advantage even if the *Ballad of Heroes* is one of Britten's slighter works.

Additional recommendations ...
...War Requiem. **Soloists; Christ Church Cathedral Choir, Oxford; City of Birmingham Symphony Chorus and Orchestra / Sir Simon Rattle.** EMI Ⓕ CDS7 47034-8 (two discs: DDD: 12/84). *Selected by Sounds in Retrospect.*   Ⓖ
...War Requiem. **Soloists; Bach Choir; Highgate School Choir; London Symphony Chorus; Melos Ensemble; London Symphony Orchestra / Benjamin Britten.** Decca Ⓕ 414 383-2DH2 (two discs: 81 minutes: ADD: 4/85).   ⒼⒼⒼ
...War Requiem. **Soloists; Atlanta Symphony Chorus and Orchestra / Robert Shaw.** Telarc Ⓕ CD80157 (two discs: 83 minutes: DDD: 12/89).
...War Requiem. **Soloists; Monteverdi Choir; Tölz Boys' Choir; North German Radio Chorus and Symphony Orchestra / John Eliot Gardiner.** DG Ⓕ 437 801-2GH2 (two discs: 83 minutes: DDD: 11/93).

Britten Peter Grimes. **Sir Peter Pears** (ten) Peter Grimes; **Claire Watson** (sop) Ellen Orford; **James Pease** (bass) Captain Balstrode; **Jean Watson** (contr) Auntie; **Raymond Nilsson** (ten) Bob Boles; **Owen Brannigan** (bass) Swallow; **Lauris Elms** (mez) Mrs Sedley; **Sir Geraint Evans** (bar) Ned Keene; **John Lanigan** (ten) Rector; **David Kelly** (bass) Hobson; **Marion Studholme** (sop) First Niece; **Iris Kells** (sop) Second Niece; **Chorus and Orchestra of the Royal Opera House, Covent Garden / Benjamin Britten.** Decca Ⓕ 414 577-2DH3* (two discs: 144 minutes: ADD: 4/86). Notes and text included. From SXL2150/52 (10/59). Recorded 1958. *Gramophone Award Winner 1986*. *Gramophone classical 100. Selected by Sounds in Retrospect.*   ⒼⒼⒼ
New review
Britten Peter Grimes. **Philip Langridge** (ten) Grimes; **Janice Watson** (sop) Ellen Orford; **Alan Opie** (bar) Balstrode; **Ameral Gunson** (mez) Auntie; **John Graham-Hall** (ten) Bob Boles; **John Connell** (bass) Swallow; **Anne Collins** (contr) Mrs Sedley; **Roderick Williams** (bar) Ned Keene; **John Fryatt** (ten) Rector; **Matthew Best** (bass) Hobson; **Yvonne Barclay** (sop) First Niece; **Pamela Helen Stephen** (mez) Second Niece; **London Symphony Chorus; City of London Sinfonia / Richard Hickox.** Chandos Ⓕ CHAN9447/8 (two discs: 147 minutes: DDD: 5/96). Notes and text included. Recorded 1995. *Gramophone Editor's choice. Selected by Soundings.*   Ⓖ
The Decca set has long been regarded as the definitive recording which, in 1958, introduced this opera to many listeners and one which has never been superseded in its refinement or insight. Britten's conducting, lithe, lucid and as inexorable as "the tide that waits for no man", reveals his work as the complex, ambiguous drama that it is. Sir Peter Pears, in the title-role which was written for him, brings unsurpassed detail of nuance to Grimes's words while never losing sight of the essential plainness of the man's speech. The rest of the cast form a vivid portrait gallery. The recording is as live and clear as if it had been made yesterday and takes the listener right on to the stage. The bustle of activity and sound effects realize nicely Britten's own masterly painting of dramatic foreground and background. For Hickox on Chandos there is Langridge's tense, sinewy, sensitive Grimes. Predictably he rises to the

challenge of the Mad scene; this is a man hugely to be pitied, yet there is a touch of resignation, of finding some sort of peace at last, after all the agony of the soul. Earlier he doesn't quite match either Pears (Britten) or Rolfe Johnson (Haitink) in poetic tone for "What harbour" and the Pleiades solo, and he can't carry his voice over the ensemble later in that Inn scene as Vickers (Davis) easily does, but the compensations are appreciable. The portrayal is more tense and immediate than that of Rolfe Johnson, more accurate than, and just as anguished as, that of Vickers and a match for that of Pears in personal identification – listen to the eager touch at "We strained in the wind".

The next composite heroes are the members of the chorus. Electrifying as their rivals are, the LSO singers, trained by Stephen Westrop, seem just that much more arresting, not least in the hue-and-cry of Act 3, quite terrifying in its immediacy as recorded by Chandos. Hickox's whole interpretation has little to fear from the distinguished competition. Many details are placed with special care, particularly in the Interludes and the parodistic dances in Act 3, and whole episodes, such as the Grimes/Balstrode dispute in Act 1, have seldom sounded so dramatic. Once or twice one would have liked a firmer forward movement, as in the fifth Interlude (Britten's own direction of this Passacaglia is that bit more urgent), but the sense of total music-theatre is present throughout and it's excitingly laid before us by the City of London Sinfonia and the recording. Of the other soloists, the one comparative disappointment is Janice Watson's Ellen Orford. She sings the part with tone as lovely as any of her rivals on disc and with carefully wrought phrasing and is very much part of a convincing team but doesn't have the experience to stand out from the village regulars and sound important, as Ellen should. Britten's set remains *hors concours* (the composer's own taut conducting is unsurpassed), but that recording stretches over three CDs. Hickox is the finest of the modern recordings: as sound it is quite spectacular, vast in range, with well-managed perspectives and just enough hints of stage action to be convincing.

Additional recommendations ...

...**Soloists; Chorus and Orchestra of the Royal Opera House, Covent Garden / Sir Colin Davis.** Philips Ⓕ 432 578-2PM2 (two discs: 146 minutes: ADD: 11/91).

...**Soloists; Chorus and Orchestra of the Royal Opera House, Covent Garden / Bernard Haitink.** EMI Ⓕ CDS7 54832-2 (two discs: 145 minutes: DDD: 7/93). *Gramophone Editor's choice.*

Britten Gloriana. **Josephine Barstow** (sop) Queen Elizabeth I; **Philip Langridge** (ten) Earl of Essex; **Della Jones** (mez) Lady Essex; **Jonathan Summers** (bar) Lord Mountjoy; **Alan Opie** (bar) Sir Robert Cecil; **Yvonne Kenny** (sop) Penelope; **Richard Van Allan** (bass) Sir Walter Raleigh; **Bryn Terfel** (bass-bar) Henry Cuffe; **Janice Watson** (sop) Lady-in-waiting; **Willard White** (bass) Blind ballad-singer; **John Shirley-Quirk** (bar) Recorder of Norwich; **John Mark Ainsley** (ten) Spirit of the Masque; **Peter Hoare** (ten) Master of Ceremonies; **Welsh National Opera Chorus and Orchestra / Sir Charles Mackerras.** Argo Ⓕ 440 213-2ZHO2 (two discs: 148 minutes: DDD: 7/93). Notes and text included. Recorded 1992. *Gramophone Award Winner 1994. Gramophone Editor's choice.*   Ⓖ

Four decades on from the ill-fated première of Britten's Coronation opera where, instead of the staid pageant expected by the bejewelled and stiff audience assembled for a royal gala, they were given an intimate study of the ageing Queen's torment as she copes with the conflict of private emotions in the midst of public pomp, *Gloriana* has now at last been given a complete recording on CD. Sir Charles Mackerras presents it here with the utmost conviction, drawing together the motivic strands of the score into a unified, coherent whole (not an altogether easy task), appreciating the contrast of the public and private scenes, exposing the raw sinews of the writing for the two principal characters, and drawing superb playing from his own WNO Orchestra. Josephine Barstow crowns her career with her performance as Queen Elizabeth, commanding the opera by her vocal presence, her imposing, vibrant tone, her vital treatment of the text, and her attention to detail. Philip Langridge projects all the vehement impetuosity of Essex but also, in the famous lute songs, the poetic ardour of the handsome if unruly Earl. There is much discerning interpretation elsewhere and the recording is worthy of the performance. Any small reservations are as nothing before the triumph of the achievement as a whole.

Britten The Turn of the Screw. **Philip Langridge** (ten) Prologue, Quint; **Felicity Lott** (sop) Governess; **Sam Pay** (treb) Miles; **Eileen Hulse** (sop) Flora; **Phyllis Cannan** (mez) Mrs Grose; **Nadine Secunde** (sop) Miss Jessel; **Aldeburgh Festival Ensemble / Steuart Bedford.** Collins Classics Ⓕ 7030-2 (two discs: 106 minutes: DDD: 6/94). Notes and text included. Recorded 1993. *Gramophone Editor's choice. Selected by Sounds in Retrospect.*   ⒼⒼ

Arguably the tautest, most compact of all his scores for the stage, this version comes with a fascinating essay by Donald Mitchell, and letters from the composer revealing that, as a youth in 1932, Britten heard a dramatized version of James's story on the wireless and described it as "eerie and scary", adjectives that apply even more strongly to his own setting of 22 years later. Mitchell explains that the music discloses the Governess and Quint as two sides of the same character: "The Governess/Quint symbiosis (and its musical realisation) has its roots precisely in the pursuit of power, power to possess Miles ". Consciously or not, that struggle, once you are aware of it, is very much present in the forceful, histrionic portrayal of the roles here by Felicity Lott and Philip Langridge, coming to a climax in the final confrontation where the tension is almost unbearable in such a lifelike, big-scale recording. Both bring all their long stage experience to bear on giving character and verbal enlightenment to their roles. Steuart Bedford (who paces the work to within a minute of Britten's own timing) and his players have the advantage over the composer and his hand-picked ensemble in the ability of modern recording to open up the score and also subject it to the minutest scrutiny so that one is amazed again not only at the intricate skill with which it is woven but also by its extraordinary aptness in fitting individual instruments to evoke a mood, a situation, a place. The supporting singers offer arresting interpretations. Those who have lived with and loved the original version over 40 years are not going to let affection for it dim, but the new set is happily in the true tradition of the piece, and deserves a high placing among all the other recent performances of Britten's operas. The work itself will surely capture the imagination of any newcomer who hasn't yet been made aware of its greatness.

Additional recommendation ...
...**Soloists; English Opera Group Orchestra / Benjamin Britten.** Decca London mono Ⓔ 425 672-2LH2* (two discs: 105 minutes: ADD: 5/90).

Further listening ...
...**Tema Sacher.** *Coupled with works by* **C. Halffter, Berio, Lutosławski, Dutilleux, Beck, Henze, Fortner, Ginastera, Boulez, K. Huber** and **Holliger** Patrick and Thomas Demenga (vcs); **Cello Ensemble / Jürg Wyttenbach.** ECM New Series 445 234-2 (8/95).
...**String Quartet No. 3, Op. 94.** *Coupled with* **Tippett** String Quartet No. 4. **Lindsay Quartet.** ASV CDDCA608 (5/88).
...**Lachrymae, Op. 48.** *Coupled with works by* **Debussy, Honegger, Denisov** and **Takemitsu** Nobuko Imai (va); Naoko Yoshino (hp). Philips 442 012-2PH (12/94). *See review in the Collections section; refer to the Index to Reviews.*
...**Solo Cello Suite No. 3, Op. 87.** *Coupled with works by* **Kodály, Berio** and **Henze** Matt Haimovitz (vc). DG 445 834-2GH (12/95).
...**Solo Cello Suite No. 3, Op. 87.** *Coupled with* **Tavener** The Protecting Veil[a]. Thrinos. **Steven Isserlis** (vc); [a]**London Symphony Orchestra / Gennadi Rozhdestvensky.** Virgin Classics VC7 59052-2 (3/92). *Gramophone Award Winner 1992.* ⒼⒼ
...**Nocturnal after John Dowland, Op. 70.** *Coupled with* **Schafer** Le cri de Merlin. **Tippett** The blue guitar. **Norbert Kraft** (gtr). Chandos CHAN8784 (1/90).
...**Holiday Diary, Op. 5.** *Coupled with works by* **Messiaen, Berg, Ravel, Stravinsky, Scriabin** and **Copland** Shura Cherkassky (pf). Decca 433 657-2DH (2/96). *See review in the Collections section; refer to the Index to Reviews.*
...**Hölderlin Fragments, Op. 61** – No. 5, Hälfte des Lebens. *Coupled with works by* **Cornelius, Eisler, Fortner, Fröhlich, Hauer, Jarnach, Komma, Pfitzner, Ullmann** and **Reutter.** Mitsuko Shirai (mez); Hartmut Höll (pf). Capriccio 10 534 (12/94). *See review in the Collections section; refer to the Index to Reviews.*
...**Purcell Realizations. Soloists; Graham Johnson** (pf). Hyperion CDA67061/2 (11/95).
...**Antiphon, Op. 56b**[b]. Te Deum in C major[b]. A Wedding Anthem, Op. 46[b]. Rejoice in the Lamb, Op. 30[b]. The Sycamore tree. The Ballad of Little Musgrave and Lady Barnard[a]. Advance Democracy. Sacred and Profane, Op. 91. **The Sixteen / Harry Christophers** with [a]**Stephen Westrop** (pf); [b]**Margaret Phillips** (org). Collins Classics 1343-2 (6/93). *Gramophone Editor's choice.*
...**The Ballad of Little Musgrave and Lady Barnard.** *Coupled with works by* **Bax, Elgar, Vaughan Williams, Howells, Delius, Warlock** and **Holst** London Madrigal Singers / Christopher Bishop; Baccholian Singers of London; Philip Jones Brass Ensemble; English Chamber Orchestra / Ian Humphris. EMI British Composers CMS5 65123-2 (2/96). *See review in the Collections section; refer to the Index to Reviews.*
......**Saint Nicolas, Op. 42**[a]. Rejoice in the Lamb, Op. 30[b]. **Soloists;** [a]**Girls' Choir of Sir John Leman School, Beccles;** [a]**Boys' Choir of Ipswich School Preparatory Department;** [b]**Purcell Singers;** [a]**Aldeburgh Festival Choir and Orchestra / Benjamin Britten** with [a]**Ralph Downes,** [b]**George Malcolm** (orgs). Decca London mono 425 714-2LM* (9/90).
...**Deus in adjutorium meum**[f]. Chorale on an old French carol[f]. Cantata misericordium, Op. 69[bdfg]. *Coupled with* **Finzi** Requiem da camera[acdfg]. **Holst** Psalms, H117 – No. 86[aefg]; No. 148[efg]. [a]**Alison Barlow** (sop); [b]**John Mark Ainsley** (ten); [c]**David Hoult,** [d]**Stephen Varcoe** (bars); [e]**John Alley** (org); [f]**Britten Singers;** [g]**City of London Sinfonia / Richard Hickox.** Chandos CHAN8997 (3/92).
...**Paul Bunyan. Soloists; Plymouth Music Series Chorus and Orchestra / Philip Brunelle.** Virgin Classics VCD7 59249-2 (8/88). *Gramophone Award Winner 1988. Selected by Sounds in Retrospect.*
...**Albert Herring. Soloists; English Chamber Orchestra / Benjamin Britten.** Decca London 421 849-2LH2 (6/89).
...**Billy Budd.** The Holy Sonnets of John Donne, Op. 35. Songs and Proverbs of William Blake, Op. 74. **Soloists; Ambrosian Opera Chorus; London Symphony Orchestra / Benjamin Britten.** Decca 417 428-2LH3 (6/89). ⒼⒼ
...**Noye's Fludde**[a]. The Golden Vanity, Op. 78[b]. [ab]**Soloists;** [b]**Benjamin Britten** (pf); [a]**English Opera Group Orchestra; An East Suffolk Children's Orchestra / Norman Del Mar;** [b]**Wandsworth School Boys' Choir / Russell Burgess.** Decca London 436 397-2LM (11/93). Ⓖ
...**A Midsummer Night's Dream. Soloists; Choirs of Downside and Emanuel Schools; London Symphony Orchestra / Benjamin Britten.** Decca London 425 663-2LH2 (5/90). Ⓖ
...**A Midsummer Night's Dream. Soloists; Trinity Boys' Choir; City of London Sinfonia / Richard Hickox.** Virgin Classics VCD7 59305 (8/93).

…Curlew River. **Soloists; English Opera Group / Benjamin Britten** and **Viola Tunnard.** Decca
   London 421 858-2LM (9/89).
…Curlew River. **Soloists; Guildhall Chamber Choir and Ensemble.** Koch Schwann 313972 (5/96).
…The Burning Fiery Furnace. **Soloists; English Opera Group / Benjamin Britten.** Decca 414 663-
   2LM(10/90).   ⓖ
…The Prodigal Son. **Soloists; English Opera Group / Benjamin Britten.** Decca 425 713-2LM (9/90).
…Owen Wingrave[a]. Six Hölderlin fragments, Op. 61[b]. The Poet's Echo, Op. 76[c]. [a]**Soloists;**
   [a]**Wandsworth School Boys' Choir; English Chamber Orchestra / Benjamin Britten.** [b]**Sir Peter Pears**
   (ten); [c]**Galina Vishnevskaya** (sop); [c]**Mstislav Rostropovich** ([b]pf). Decca London 433 200-2LHO2
   (11/93).   ⓖ
…Death in Venice. **Soloists; English Opera Group Chorus; English Chamber Orchestra / Steuart
   Bedford.** Decca London 425 669-2LH2 (5/90).   ⓐⓖ

František Brixi   Bohemian 1732-1771

Suggested listening …
.. Organ Concertos – No. 2 in D major; No. 4 in C major; No. 5 in C major. **Jan Hora** (org); **Prague
   Chamber Orchestra / František Vajnar.** Supraphon 10 3029-2 (9/92).

Nicholas Brodszky   German/American 1905-1958

Suggested listening …
…The Way to the Stars – Suite. Carnival –Intermezzo. *Coupled with works by* **Addinsell,
   C. Williams, C. Parker, J. Addison II, Arnold, Allan Gray, Frankel, Greenwood, Alwyn,
   Spoliansky, P. Green** and **Vaughan Williams** Various orchestras and conductors. EMI mono
   CDGO2059* (9/94). *See review in the Collections section; refer to the Index to Reviews.*

Leo Brouwer   Cuban 1939-

Suggested listening …
…Guitar Sonata. *Coupled with works by* **Martin, Britten, Takemitou** and **Lutosławski** Julian
   Bream (gtr). EMI CDC7 54901-2 (4/94). *See review in the Collections section; refer to the Index to
   Reviews.*

Max Bruch   German 1838-1920

Bruch Violin Concerto No. 1 in G minor, Op. 26.
Mendelssohn Violin Concerto in E minor, Op. 64. **Maxim Vengerov** (vn); **Leipzig Gewandhaus
   Orchestra / Kurt Masur.** Teldec ⓕ 4509-90875-2 (51 minutes: DDD: 4/94). Recorded 1993.
   Gramophone Editor's choice.   ⓖ
As one might expect with Mendelssohn's own orchestra, the Leipzig Gewandhaus, under Kurt Masur,
there is a freshness and clarity in the Mendelssohn which ideally matches the soloist's playing, at once
keenly felt and expressive but clean and direct, with articulation of diamond precision and fine tonal
shading. If anyone has ever thought this work at all sentimental, this shatters any such idea, and
characteristically Masur encourages a flowing speed in the central *Andante*, which brings out the
songfulness of the main theme. It is consistent with this approach that in his expressiveness Maxim
Vengerov is more inclined to press ahead than to hold back, so that with a dashingly fast speed for
the finale one is left breathless at the end. The slow movement of the Bruch gains from being taken
at a flowing speed and Vengerov finds a rare depth of expressiveness, which makes the movement a
meditation rather than simply a lyrical interlude. With outstanding recorded sound, warm yet clear
and detailed, there is now no more recommendable disc of this coupling.

Additional recommendations …
…Violin Concerto. **Mendelssohn** Violin Concerto. **Nathan Milstein** (vn); **Philharmonia Orchestra
   / Leon Barzin.** Classics for Pleasure ⓑ CD-CFP4374 (48 minutes: ADD).   ⓒⓖ
…Violin Concerto. **Mendelssohn** Violin Concerto. **Anne-Sophie Mutter** (vn); **Berlin Philharmonic
   Orchestra / Herbert von Karajan.** DG ⓕ 400 031-2GH (57 minutes: DDD: 3/83).
…Violin Concerto. Scottish Fantasy, Op. 46. **Cho-Liang Lin** (vn); **Chicago Symphony Orchestra /
   Leonard Slatkin.** CBS Masterworks Ⓜ SMK42315 (53 minutes: DDD: 7/87). *Selected by Sounds
   in Retrospect.*   ⓐⓖ
…Violin Concerto. Scottish Fantasy, Op. 46. **Vieuxtemps** Violin Concerto No. 5 in A minor,
   Op. 37. **Jascha Heifetz** (vn); **New Symphony Orchestra / Sir Malcolm Sargent.** RCA Victor
   Ⓜ 09026 61778-2* (65 minutes: ADD: 3/88).
…Violin Concerto. **Mendelssohn** Violin Concerto. **Joshua Bell** (vn); **Academy of St Martin in the
   Fields / Sir Neville Marriner.** Decca ⓕ 421 145-2DH (54 minutes: DDD: 5/88).

...Violin Concerto. **Mendelssohn** Violin Concerto. **Schubert** Rondo in A major, D438. **Nigel Kennedy** (vn); **English Chamber Orchestra / Jeffrey Tate.** EMI Ⓕ CDC7 49663-2 (71 minutes: DDD: 1/89).

...Violin Concerto. **Dvořák** Violin Concerto in A minor, Op. 53. **Tasmin Little** (vn); **Royal Liverpool Philharmonic Orchestra / Vernon Handley.** Classics for Pleasure Ⓑ CD-CFP4566 (60 minutes: DDD: 7/90).

...Violin Concerto[c]. **Mendelssohn** Violin Concerto[b]. **Sarasate** Introduction et Tarantelle, Op. 43[a]. **Kreisler** Liebesfreud[a]. **Cho-Liang Lin** (vn); [a]**Sandra Rivers** (pf); [b]**Philharmonia Orchestra / Michael Tilson Thomas;** [c]**Chicago Symphony Orchestra / Leonard Slatkin.** CBS Masterworks Ⓜ CD44902 (61 minutes: DDD: 3/91).

...Violin Concertos – No. 1; No. 2 in D minor, Op. 44; No. 3 in D minor, Op. 58. Adagio appassionato, Op. 57. Romance, Op. 42. Scottish Fantasy[a]. Konzertstück, Op. 84. Serenade, Op. 75. In Memoriam, Op. 65. **Salvatore Accardo** (vn); [a]**Elizabeth Unger** (hp); **Leipzig Gewandhaus Orchestra / Kurt Masur.** Philips Silver Line Ⓜ 432 282-2PSL3 (three discs: 214 minutes: ADD: 7/91).

...Violin Concerto. **Beethoven** Violin Concerto in D major, Op. 61. **Kyung-Wha Chung** (vn); **Royal Concertgebouw Orchestra / Klaus Tennstedt.** EMI Ⓕ CDC7 54072-2 (70 minutes: DDD: 6/92).

...Violin Concerto. Scottish Fantasy. **Lalo** Symphonie espagnole, Op. 21. **Anne Akiko Meyers** (vn); **Royal Philharmonic Orchestra / Jesús López-Cobos.** RCA Victor Red Seal Ⓕ RD60942 (60 minutes: DDD: 9/92).

| New review |

Bruch Violin Concerto No. 2 in D minor, Op. 44.
Goldmark Violin Concerto No. 1 in A minor, Op. 28. **Nai-Yuan Hu** (vn); **Seattle Symphony Orchestra / Gerard Schwarz.** Delos Ⓕ DE3156 (60 minutes: DDD: 12/95). Recorded 1993-4.

Hu is a virtuoso in the best sense of that word, with uncommon lyrical gifts, who can shape phrases with a sense of gentle rapture and coax his violin to produce the most lovely sounds. Both performances come into direct competition with those of Itzhak Perlman (differently coupled), and when compared Hu by no means comes out second best. Perlman may at times be more dazzling (and in the passagework he achieves a stronger profile), but his preference for a very forward spotlight is a distinct minus point in a pair of warm-hearted concertos where the intimacy of feeling shared between soloist and orchestra is better caught by a more natural balance. Even though the Bruch was specifically written for Sarasate, neither of these concertos impresses primarily by its brilliance. Here both gain from the understanding partnership attained by Hu with Schwarz and his excellent Seattle orchestra within a kindly acoustic. Having attended the première of Bruch's Second Concerto, Brahms wrote to Simrock: "Hopefully a law will not be necessary to prevent any more first movements being written as an *Adagio*. That is intolerable for normal people." Bruch's riposte was, "If I meet with Brahms in heaven, I shall have myself transferred to Hell". He could not understand why the popularity of the First Concerto precluded performance of the others, "which are just as good if not better". Certainly Hu's superb reading here bears out the composer's evaluation of the D minor Concerto. The ardently simple presentation of the glorious main theme of that maligned *Adagio* goes right to the heart.

Additional recommendations ...

...Violin Concerto. Scottish Fantasy, Op. 46. **Itzhak Perlman** (vn); **Israel Philharmonic Orchestra / Zubin Mehta.** EMI Ⓕ CDC7 49071-2 (54 minutes: DDD: 6/88).

Bruch Scottish Fantasy, Op. 46.
Sibelius Violin Concerto in D minor, Op. 47. **Midori** (vn); **Israel Philharmonic Orchestra / Zubin Mehta.** Sony Classical Ⓕ SK58967 (63 minutes: DDD: 2/95). Recorded live in 1993.

Midori gives commanding performances of both works, at once pure in tone and warmly expressive. It is a tribute to her mastery that in concert her playing has all the precision one would expect in the studio, exceptionally clean and precise, not least above the stave. There is, then, the gain in tension one would expect in live performances, with the main lyrical themes of the first two movements of the Sibelius given rapt intensity, and with the coda of the first movement as thrilling as any on disc. The finale is remarkable for the clean precision of her playing, with detail sharply defined even in the most dense bravura passages. This may not be as fiery as some readings, but the sureness is very satisfying. In the Bruch, Midori displays the same qualities, and for whatever reason there is rather more bloom on the sound. So the cleanness of the articulation, not least in heavy double-stopping, makes for a light, rather than romantic approach, lean in tone. There is no lack of expressive warmth or temperament, for the lightness goes with a sense of fantasy. The rapt intensity of Midori's very first *pianissimo* entry in the slow introduction to the first movement is evidence enough of that, and the double-stopped first statement of the main theme in that movement ("Through the wood, laddie") is tender in its precision (track 5, 1'00"). There is also a magical moment at the very end when, as the culmination of a wonderfully clear and incisive account of the finale with its main "Scots wha hae" theme, her final slow cadenza has an ethereal purity leading to a momentary reference back to the theme of the first movement: at a whispered *pianissimo* it is breathtaking, and more intense than it could ever be in the studio. If the sound in the Mann Auditorium in Tel Aviv has less bloom on it than one would like, and the tuttis are at times constricted and aggressive, this is one of the better recordings made in that difficult acoustic, with fair presence given to the soloist: the disc can be safely recommended to anyone who finds this rare coupling appealing.

Bruch Symphonies – No. 1 in E flat major, Op. 28; No. 2 in F minor, Op. 36; No. 3 in E major, Op. 51. **Cologne Gürzenich Orchestra / James Conlon.** EMI Ⓔ CDS5 55046-2 (two discs: 103 minutes: DDD: 4/94). Recorded 1992-3.

Bruch's three symphonies are works whose rather reticent melodic style, at times dense scoring and formal stiffness, need affectionate help if their genuine qualities are to emerge and outweigh their flaws. Carefully handled there is real romantic charm (and some agreeably brusque sturdiness) to the first movement of the Third Symphony; its *Adagio* has sonorous solemnity and an ardent climax, and its *Scherzo* some fire. The Second Symphony, its over-extended finale apart, is stronger still. Conlon and his Cologne players cannot always disguise passages of awkwardly coarse scoring, but their sound, though full, is lean and that is in itself an advantage. Conlon is also more likely than Masur (listed below) to relax into Bruch's genial melodies, to linger and shape them with affectionate rubato. For some tastes Masur's urgency will compensate for his at times lumbering massiveness of sound. Although *longueurs* are obvious in both conductors' hands, Conlon seems the more concerned to persuade us not to mind them. For anyone wanting all the symphonies of this neglected but likeable composer his set is a pretty safe recommendation.

Additional recommendation:

...Nos. 1-3. Swedish Dances, Op. 63. **Leipzig Gewandhaus Orchestra / Kurt Masur.** Philips Ⓕ 420 932-2PH2 (two discs: 105 minutes: DDD: 3/89).

Further listening ...

...Clarinet and Viola Concerto in E minor, Op. 88[a]. *Coupled with* **Crusell** Introduction, Theme and Variations on a Swedish air, Op. 12[b]; **Mendelssohn** Two Concert Pieces[c] – F major, Op. 113; D minor, Op. 114. [abc]**Thea King** (cl); [a]**Nobuko Imai** (va); [c]**Georgina Dobrée** (basset hn); **London Symphony Orchestra / Alun Francis.** Hyperion CDA66022 (1/88).

...Double Piano Concerto, Op. 88a. *Coupled with* **Mendelssohn** Double Piano Concerto in E major. **Katia and Marielle Labèque** (pfs); **Philharmonia Orchestra / Semyon Bychkov.** Philips 432 095-2PH (7/93). Ⓖ

...String Quartets – No. 1 in C minor, Op. 9; No. 2 in E major, Op. 10. **Academica Quartet.** Dynamic CDS29 (5/94).

Anton Bruckner

Austrian 1824-1896

Bruckner Symphonies – No. 1 in C minor (Linz version); No. 2 in C minor (ed. Nowak. Both from 2740 264, 6/82); No. 3 in D minor (1889 version, ed. Nowak. 2532 007, 7/81); No. 4 in E flat major, "Romantic" (2530 674, 10/76); No. 5 in B flat major (2702 101, 10/78); No. 6 in A major (2531 295, 11/80); No. 7 in E major (2707 102, 4/78); No. 8 in C minor (ed. Haas. 2707 085, 5/76); No. 9 in D minor (2530 828, 6/77). **Berlin Philharmonic Orchestra / Herbert von Karajan.** DG Karajan Symphony Edition Ⓜ 429 648-2GSE9 (nine discs: 520 minutes: ADD/DDD: 3/91). Recorded 1975-81. ⒼⒼ

Bruckner Symphonies – No. 0 in D minor, "Die Nullte" (from SAL3602, 4/67); No. 1 in C minor (6500 439, 6/73); No. 2 in C minor (SAL3785, 5/70); No. 3 in D minor (SAL3506, 7/65); No. 4 in E flat major, "Romantic" (SAL3617, 2/68); No. 5 in B flat major (6700 055, 6/72); No. 6 in A major (6500 164, 11/71); No. 7 in E major (SAL3624/5, 9/67); No. 8 in C minor (6700 020, 10/70); No. 9 in D minor (SAL3575, 10/66). **Concertgebouw Orchestra / Bernard Haitink.** Philips Bernard Haitink Symphony Edition Ⓑ 442 040-2PB9 (nine discs: 592 minutes: ADD: 8/94). Recorded 1963-72. Ⓖ

It is often said that the essence of good Bruckner conducting is a firm grasp of structure. In fact that is only a half-truth. Of course one must understand how Bruckner's massive statements and counterstatements are fused together, but a performance that was nothing but architecture would be a pretty depressing experience. Karajan's understanding of the slow but powerful currents that flow beneath the surfaces of symphonies like the Fifth or Nos. 7-9 has never been bettered, but at the same time he shows how much more there is to be reckoned with: strong emotions, a deep poetic sensitivity (a Bruckner symphony can evoke landscapes as vividly as Mahler or Vaughan Williams) and a gift for singing melody that at times rivals even Schubert. It hardly needs saying that there's no such thing as a perfect record cycle, and Karajan's collection of the numbered Bruckner symphonies (unfortunately he never recorded "No. 0") has its weaknesses. The early First and Second Symphonies can be a little heavy-footed and, as with so many Bruckner sets, there's a suspicion that more time might have been spent getting to know the fine but elusive Sixth – and there's an irritating throwback to the days of corrupt Bruckner editions in the first big crescendo of the Fourth Symphony (high swooping violins – nasty!) – but none of these performances is without its major insights, and in the best of them – particularly Nos. 3, 5, 7, 8 and 9 – those who haven't stopped their ears to Karajan will find that whatever else he may have been, there was a side to him that could only be described as 'visionary'. As for the recordings: climaxes can sound a touch overblown in some of the earlier symphonies, but on the whole the image is well-focused and atmospheric. A valuable set, and a landmark in the history of Bruckner recording.

Reviewing Bernard Haitink's 1965 account of Bruckner's Fourth Symphony, Deryck Cooke wrote: "The more I listen to Haitink's Bruckner performances, the more I wonder if he isn't, really, after all, the answer to a Brucknerian's prayers". On another occasion he wrote: "And then there are Haitink's own great virtues: his feeling for the chaste nobility of Bruckner's music; his objective expressive intensity, without any undue intrusion of his own personality; and his preservation of an unswerving line, with only those slight tempo modifications necessary to allow the music to make its full expressive effect". Whether or not conductors actually get better with age, the best invariably do wonderful work when they are young. Certainly, the Bruckner and Mahler recordings Haitink made in the late 1960s and early 1970s come into this category. Right from the start, you sense here is a man who briefed his team, read the map and is raring to go. The cycle began in 1963 with Symphony No. 3. The playing is alert, rousing even, though inclined to edginess. This is partly to do with the sound of the post-war Concertgebouw (marginally more Francophone in those days), partly a matter of an as yet not-quite-symbiotic bond between Haitink and the players. The Fourth Symphony followed in 1965. This suggests some deepening and refining of the bond between conductor and orchestra and, as Cooke suggested, is a very fine performance. The *Scherzo* is particularly exciting. The Ninth Symphony (also 1965) came surprisingly early in the cycle. The performance explains why. Both conductor and orchestra play the symphony as if in the grip of a deep compulsion. The orchestral response alone has a terrific explicitness and immediacy. As for Haitink, he plays the work very dramatically, as a symphonic psycho-drama, "a vastation" as thinkers and theologians of Bruckner's time often termed breakdown and purgation of the spirit. When it comes to the great central tetralogy, Symphonies Nos. 5-8, there are some problems. Most problematic is the Eighth Symphony. The Seventh has a quick first movement; but it survives. Not so the Eighth. The first movement just about hangs together, thanks to some finely concentrated playing at critical junctions. But the *Scherzo* is absurdly quick, as is the finale. Haitink's account of the Sixth Symphony is less of a problem than it is with some rivals. The recording is exceptionally fine – everything thrillingly immediate, finely 'terraced'. It is a quicker performance than Klemperer's classic version for EMI. The *Adagio* always sounded well and so it remains, the keening Dutch oboe and bright trumpets the perfect foil for the Rembrandt-colourings of the strings and lower brass. Symphonies Nos. 1, 2, 5 and 6 were the last to be recorded. (Haitink actually ended with this rousing account of No. 1.) They are all very fine. This is one of the best Fifths ever made; dramatic where Karajan is epic but fascinatingly alive and well integrated. The Second Symphony also receives an exceptional performance (the text, as elsewhere in the cycle, is Haas). Philips's CD remastering realizes, as some of their drabber mid-1960s LPs never could, just how vivid and astonishingly natural these Concertgebouw-played, Concertgebouw-made recordings are. However, these are proper recordings: the coming together of a fine hall, a superb orchestra properly balanced at source by the conductor, and a recording team that knew everything about good sound but nothing about 'hi-fi'. You will need a supplementary account of the Eighth; but is this too much to ask when the set as a whole is being offered, new-minted, at a knock-down price?

Additional recommendations ...

...Nos. 1-9. **Cologne Radio Symphony Orchestra / Günter Wand.** Deutsche Harmonia Mundi Editio Classica Ⓜ GD60075 (ten discs: 559 minutes: ADD/DDD: 2/90).

...Nos. 1, 4 and 7-9 – **Berlin Philharmonic Orchestra; Nos. 2, 3, 5 and 6 – Bavarian Radio Symphony Orchestra / Eugen Jochum.** DG Ⓜ 429 079-2GX9 (nine discs: 552 minutes: ADD: 2/90).   Ⓖ

...No. 2. **Royal Concertgebouw Orchestra / Riccardo Chailly.** Decca Ⓕ 436 154-2DH (67 minutes: DDD: 3/94).

New review

Bruckner Symphony No. 1 in C minor (Linz version). **Chicago Symphony Orchestra / Sir Georg Solti.** Decca Ⓕ 448 898-2DH (47 minutes: DDD: 4/96). Recorded 1995. *Gramophone Editor's choice.*   ⒼⒼ

In its original 1866 Linz version, Bruckner's First Symphony is something of a cheeky chappy among the nine, a delightful romp of a symphony but also tender and affecting and rich in intimations of things to come. There have been times in the past when Solti has seemed a restless Brucknerian, inclined to harry the music or drive it too hard. Here there is a thrilling sense of forward propulsion, apt to a young man's work, yet nothing is forced or gratuitously aggressive. This is even true of the *Scherzo* which Solti takes extremely briskly. It is also a very sensitive performance and a very observant one. The slow movement's lovely counter-subject is most beautifully played, the phrasing levitated with all the care and grace one looks for at the equivalent moment of the Seventh Symphony's slow movement. Bruckner is, by and large, sparing of egregious gestures in this symphony as elsewhere, but where there is an unexpected harmonic or dynamic nuance to be registered, Solti and his players are as swift and sensitive in execution as they are musically observant. The Chicago players are on superb form. It is difficult to imagine the symphony being better played than it is here. The Barenboim performance on DG is fine enough, but the new reading has a vibrancy and beauty about it, a quality of flawless yet unassuming virtuosity that is the mark of an élite orchestra at the very height of its powers. The many difficult, high-lying violin passages are played

not only with confidence, but with imagination. The playing of the violas and cellos is consummate in its eloquence. In the circumstances, it would be difficult for the engineers to go wrong. But the recording, too, is of a piece with the rest. As Bruckner recordings go, it is of demonstration quality, ripe yet clear, immediate yet rich in atmosphere.

Additional recommendation ...

...No. 1. (1866 version)[a]. Te Deum[b]. [a]**Jessye Norman** (sop); [b]**Yvonne Minton** (mez); [b]**David Rendall** (ten); [b]**Samuel Ramey** (bass); **Chicago Symphony** [b]**Chorus and Orchestra / Daniel Barenboim.** DG Galleria Ⓜ 435 068-2GGA (70 minutes: DDD: 12/91).

New review

Bruckner (ed. Nowak) Symphonies – No. 3 in D minor[a] (1889 version); No. 4 in E flat major, "Romantic"[b]. **Vienna Philharmonic Orchestra / Karl Böhm.** Double Decca Ⓜ 448 098-2DF2 (two discs: 125 minutes: ADD). Item marked [a] from SXL6505 (10/71), [b]6BB171/2 (10/74). ⒼⒼⒼ
The 1973 Böhm Bruckner Fourth is a classic, widely praised and much reissued, but the 1970 recording of the Third Symphony (the tidied-up 1889 edition) is every bit as fine. Some slightly dusty, quiet string tone apart, the recording verges on the spectacular, as does the playing, sophisticated and folksy by turns. The VPO respond splendidly throughout (Bruckner's rustic trio section is inimitably Viennese in its earthy gait). There is something mountainously grand in their response in full cry under Böhm. They also have it game, set and match over their competitors in the Austrian dance subjects of the *Scherzo* and finale. The exemplary focus and spectacular dynamic range of this Sofiensaal production really does take one's breath away. As for the Fourth Symphony, that has been more or less *hors concours* for a generation. This is its third or fourth appearance on CD. Buy now if you missed it earlier.

Additional recommendations ...

...(1877 version). **Vienna Philharmonic Orchestra / Bernard Haitink.** Philips Ⓕ 422 411-2PH (62 minutes: DDD: 3/91).

...No. 3. **North German Radio Symphony Orchestra / Günter Wand.** RCA Victor Red Seal Ⓕ 09026 61374-2 (54 minutes: DDD: 3/93).

...Nos. 3 and 8 (both ed. Nowak). **Cleveland Orchestra / George Szell.** Sony Classical Ⓑ SB2K53519 (two discs: 136 minutes: ADD: 1/95).

Bruckner Symphony No. 4 in E flat major, "Romantic". **Philadelphia Orchestra / Wolfgang Sawallisch.** EMI Ⓕ CDC5 55119-2 (67 minutes: DDD: 9/94). Recorded 1993.   Ⓖ
The Philadelphians have always had their special sound, nurtured and lovingly preserved down the years by Stokowski, Ormandy and Muti; and to judge by this fine Bruckner Fourth it is something that Sawallisch will not willingly forego. Indeed, the genius of this particular reading lies in its Protean quality, the very way the sound is so interestingly adapted and applied. The Fourth is an odd work. Popular, certainly, but popular for certain specific moments: the mistily romantic opening, the fine hunting *Scherzo* and the finale's magnificent peroration. As for the larger structure – well, it is a work that undergoes something of a sea-change after the *Scherzo*. The finale does not so much round off the work as propose the kind of grounds on which it might originally have been built. Which is where Sawallisch's reading, and the Philadelphians' realization of it, is so interesting. Apart from one passage midway through the slow movement, where the mood darkens and the music mysteriously broods, the first two movements can have an almost straightforwardly classical feel. This seems to be Sawallisch's view. The Philadelphia playing here is lucid and eloquent – the feel of "clean stonework", to borrow Robert Simpson's helpful phrase. How different is the finale! Here we are deep in the Wagnerian forest – the dramatic change of mood graphically registered. "First make your palette", Karajan used to say. To judge by this performance, the orchestra have several palettes ready-prepared which Sawallisch has used to brilliant effect in this reading. After the clean stonework of the first three movements, the finale is a Wagnerian revel, Stokowski-style. What sounded at first light like just another Bruckner Fourth has proved to be anything but. The recording is glorious.

Additional recommendations ...

...No. 4. **Philharmonia Orchestra / Otto Klemperer.** EMI Studio Ⓜ CDM7 69127-2 (61 minutes: ADD: 12/88).   ⒼⒼ

...No. 4. **Berlin Philharmonic Orchestra / Eugen Jochum.** DG Ⓑ 427 200-2GR (65 minutes: ADD: 9/89).

...**Vienna Philharmonic Orchestra / Claudio Abbado.** DG Ⓔ 431 719-2GH (69 minutes: DDD: 4/91).   Ⓖ

...(original version). **Frankfurt Radio Symphony Orchestra / Eliahu Inbal.** Teldec Digital Experience Ⓜ 9031-77597-2 (68 minutes: DDD: 12/92).

...No. 4. **Vienna Philharmonic Orchestra / Karl Böhm.** Decca Ovation Ⓜ 425 036-2DM (68 minutes: ADD: 3/93).   ⒼⒼⒼ

...No. 4. **Berlin Philharmonic Orchestra / Herbert von Karajan.** DG Galleria Ⓜ 439 522-2GGA (64 minutes: ADD: 1/94).

...No. 4. **Berlin Philharmonic Orchestra / Daniel Barenboim.** Teldec Ⓕ 9031-73272-2 (68 minutes: DDD: 3/94).   Ⓖ

...No. 4[a], Overture in G minor[b]. **Philharmonia Orchestra / Lovro von Matačić.** Testament [a]mono/[b]stereo Ⓓ SBT1050[a] (76 minutes: ADD: 2/95).

…No. 4. **Smetana** The bartered bride – Overture. **Weber** Oberon – Overture. **NBC Symphony Orchestra / Bruno Walter.** Pearl mono Ⓜ GEMMCD9131* (74 minutes: AAD: 2/95).

…No. 4. **San Francisco Symphony Orchestra / Herbert Blomstedt.** Decca Ⓕ 443 327-2DH (67 minutes: DDD: 7/95).

Bruckner (ed. Nowak) Symphony No. 5 in B flat major. **London Philharmonic Orchestra / Franz Welser-Möst.** EMI Ⓕ CDC5 55125-2 (70 minutes: DDD: 4/95). Recorded live in 1993.

Welser-Möst has looked, listened, and decided 'enough is enough'. Enough pussy-footing around the Fifth as though it were some sacred monolith, enough of circumspection. This is a performance, sensual and exciting, that could have been filmed by Ken Russell or apostrophized by Dylan Thomas. Not everyone will approve, of course. You can already hear the drone of lobbyists urging the Home Secretary to outlaw the making of love to a Bruckner symphony in public. Certainly, this is not a CD for those of a nervous disposition or those who genuinely seek the longer view such as Karajan provides. Welser-Möst's reading is more in the Jochum style where analysis doesn't drive out passion, where what is contemplated in the study doesn't entirely predetermine what is experienced in performance. Welser-Möst takes risks with the finale, where the fugue is driven fiercely on, and in the *Adagio* where his observation of the *alla breve* marking gives a generous pendulum-swing to the crotchet-triplet accompaniment. This can make for a reading that is unconsidered and over-quick, but not here. The play of two against three is beautifully realized as the basis for one of the most richly expressive of all recorded accounts of this movement. In general, Welser-Möst favours an almost Beethoven-like drive and directness. Yet there is plenty of space around the lyric subjects and chorales. In the first movement the gearing of the transitions whereby this is achieved is especially elaborate. He is most obviously himself, the boy from Linz, in the *Scherzo* and Trio. It begins fiercely, as Bruckner requires, but then opens out in a wonderfully broad lolloping Upper Austrian dance. The London Philharmonic play gloriously throughout and the engineers get superb results from the Vienna Konzerthaus auditorium.

Additional recommendations ...

…No. 5. **Berlin Philharmonic Orchestra / Daniel Barenboim.** Teldec Ⓕ 9031-73271-2 (72 minutes: DDD: 3/93).

…No. 5. **Cleveland Orchestra / Christoph von Dohnányi.** Decca Ⓕ 433 318-2DH (74 minutes: DDD: 8/93). *Gramophone Editor's choice.*   Ⓖ

…No. 5. **Royal Concertgebouw Orchestra / Riccardo Chailly.** Decca Ⓕ 433 819-2DII (75 minutes: DDD: 11/93).

…No. 5. **Vienna Philharmonic Orchestra / Wilhelm Furtwängler.** EMI Salzburg Festival Edition mono Ⓜ CDH5 65750-2* (70 minutes: ADD: 1/95).

Bruckner (ed. Haas). Symphony No. 6 in A major. **New Philharmonia Orchestra / Otto Klemperer.** EMI Studio Ⓜ CDM7 63351-2 (55 minutes: ADD: 3/90). From Columbia SAX2582 (9/65). Recorded 1964.   ⒼⒼ

Bruckner Symphony No. 6 in A major.
Bach (orch. Webern) Musikalisches Opfer, BWV1079 – Fuga ricercarta a 6. **Cleveland Orchestra / Christoph von Dohnányi.** Decca Ⓕ 436 153-2DH (63 minutes: DDD: 10/94). Recorded 1991-3.   Ⓖ

No Brucknerian will want to be without Klemperer's legendary performance, indeed it has long been regarded as perhaps the finest recorded interpretation of this symphony. Part of Klemperer's success lies in his unerring ability to project the symphony's architectural and organic content through Bruckner's ever changing terrain. His vigorous and resolute approach is apparent from the outset, where the opening ostinato string figure, crisp and rhythmically assured, tell us that this is no routine performance. His handling of Bruckner's frequent *fortissimo* 'blaze ups' is always dramatic, exhilarating and sonorous, whilst never destroying the beautifully clear and lucid textures he achieves throughout the symphony. The adagio is one of Bruckner's most sublime creations. Klemperer's choice of tempo may seem fast here, but is entirely justified by the resulting sense of momentum and forward drive: and you will be hard pressed to find a better rendering of the tender and expansive second theme as it burgeons out of the sombre introduction. The Scherzo, with its incessant bass and cello ostinato tread is given a subtle and evocative reading, building the tension superbly before resolving into the haunting and mysterious trio section with its Tristanesque horn calls. The recording, made in the Kingsway Hall in 1964, is excellent.

Dohnányi's is an extraordinarily bold and vivid account and the Severance Hall sound is as analytical as ever; yet on this occasion it also provides the kind of multifaceted perspectives that help give a Bruckner symphony its special character. Listening to this recording, one is left in little doubt that this is Bruckner's most strikingly scored symphony to date, its "tumultuous surface sparkling like the Homeric seas" as Sir Donald Tovey put it many years ago. Recording after recording of the Sixth has come apart at the seams as a result of the conductor's inability to gauge the pulse of the two outer movements. Bruckner's tempo indications and his bowing marks both imply a certain breadth of utterance that has to be reconciled none the less with pulsing rhythms and demystified textures. No one sorts this out better than Klemperer; he has hawk-like patience and a hawk-like keenness of vision. Dohnányi sets a very good basic tempo in the first movement, which he then proceeds to modify in ways that don't always accord with Bruckner's carefully documented wishes; and quite a good tempo in the finale. The flux is not always Bruckner's. However, as Eugen Jochum often proved, a living response to Bruckner can be mightily effective. Dohnányi's reading of the two inner movements deserves nothing but praise. He allows the *Adagio* the space it needs. (Klemperer is quicker, though, from the keening start onwards, always wonderfully articulate emotionally.) The quality of the Cleveland sound in the grieving C minor funeral lament at fig. D (5'01") is such as to make one want to rank this slow movement alongside those of the better-known Seventh and Eighth Symphonies. And how beautifully the slow movement's coda is handled and characterized. This is pure *Meistersinger*, Bruckner dressed in Sachs's garb. The slowish, minor-key *Scherzo* is also perfectly judged. Rarely can the trio's sweet academic debate between horns, woodwinds and strings have sounded more irresistible or affecting than it does here. After so fabulously played a Bruckner Sixth, the finale all complexity and clamour, the sudden dip into the cooler waters of Webern's hallucinatorily beautiful orchestration of the Ricercar from Bach's *Musical Offering* is as welcome as a solitary stroll at eventide.

Additional recommendations ...

...No. 6. **Bavarian State Orchestra / Wolfgang Sawallisch.** Orfeo Ⓕ CO24821A (55 minutes: ADD: 6/84).

...No. 6. **North German Radio Symphony Orchestra / Günter Wand.** RCA Victor Red Seal Ⓕ RD60061 (55 minutes: DDD: 2/91).

...No. 6. **Berlin Philharmonic Orchestra / Daniel Barenboim.** Teldec Ⓕ 4509-94556-2 (55 minutes: DDD: 9/95).

...No. 6. **Berlin Philharmonic Orchestra / Herbert von Karajan.** DG Galleria Ⓜ 447 525-2GGA (58 minutes: ADD: 3/96).

New review

Bruckner (ed. Haas) Symphony No. 7 in E major. **Vienna Philharmonic Orchestra / Herbert von Karajan.** DG Karajan Gold Ⓕ 439 037-2GHS (66 minutes: DDD: 3/96). From 429 226-2GH (5/90). Recorded 1989. ⒼⒼ

The Vienna Philharmonic feature on what was Karajan's last recording, an idiomatic account of the Seventh Symphony, lighter and more classical in feel than either of his two Berlin recordings yet loftier, too. As for the new Original-image bit-processing you need go no further than the first fluttered violin *tremolando* and the cellos' rapt entry in the third bar to realize how ravishingly 'present' the performance is in this new reprocessing. Or go to the end of the symphony and hear how the great E major peroration is even more transparent than before, the octave drop of bass trombone and bass tuba 13 bars from home the kind of delightfully euphoric detail that in 1989 only the more assiduous score-reader would have been conscious of hearing. This remastered Bruckner Seventh is definitely pure gold.

Additional recommendations ...

...No. 7. **Berlin Philharmonic Orchestra / Herbert von Karajan.** EMI Studio Ⓜ CDM7 69923-2 (68 minutes: ADD: 6/89). ⒼⒼ

...No. 7. **Dresden Staatskapelle / Giuseppe Sinopoli.** DG Ⓕ 435 786-2GH (65 minutes: DDD: 9/93).

...No. 7. **Vienna Philharmonic Orchestra / Claudio Abbado.** DG Ⓕ 437 518-2GH (64 minutes: DDD: 5/94).

...No. 7. **Vienna Philharmonic Orchestra / Hans Knappertsbusch.** Music & Arts mono Ⓕ CD209* (62 minutes: AAD: 12/95).

...No. 7. **Concertgebouw Orchestra / Bernard Haitink.** Philips Solo Ⓜ 446 580-2PM (65 minutes: ADD: 6/96).

Bruckner (ed. Haas) Symphony No. 8 in C minor. **Vienna Philharmonic Orchestra / Herbert von Karajan.** DG Ⓕ 427 611-2GH2 (two discs: 83 minutes: DDD: 10/89). Recorded 1988. *Selected by Sounds in Retrospect.* **Gramophone** *classical 100.* ⒼⒼⒼ

Bruckner (ed. Nowak) Symphony No. 8 in C minor. **Vienna Philharmonic Orchestra / Carlo Maria Giulini.** DG Masters Ⓜ 445 529-2GMA2 (two discs: 88 minutes: DDD: 2/95). From 415 124-2GH2 (7/85). Recorded 1984. ⒼⒼⒼ

As if by some strange act of providence, great conductors have often been remembered by the immediate posthumous release of some fine and representative recording. With Karajan it is the Eighth Symphony of Bruckner, perhaps the symphony he loved and revered above all others. It is the sense of the music being in the hearts and minds and collective unconscious of Karajan and every one of the one hundred and more players of the Vienna Philharmonic that gives this performances its particular charisma and appeal. It is a wonderful reading, every bit as authoritative as its many predecessors and every bit as well played but somehow more profound, more humane, more lovable if that is a permissible attribute of an interpretation of this Everest among symphonies. The end of the work, always astonishing and uplifting, is especially fine here and very moving. Fortunately, it has been recorded with plenty of weight and space and warmth and clarity, with the additional benefit of the added vibrancy of the Viennese playing. The sessions were obviously sufficiently happy for there to shine through moments of spontaneous power and eloquence that were commonplace in the concert hall in Karajan's later years, but which recordings can't always be relied upon to catch.

Ten years on from its making in Vienna in 1984, Giulini's performance can confidently be claimed as one of the great Bruckner recordings of the age. It is an immensely long-breathed performance yet it is of a piece with itself and the music it serves. It is a reading that is suffused from start to finish with its own immutable logic, cast and voiced, you might say, like a great tenor bell. The playing of the Vienna Philharmonic is similarly whole: luminous as though lit from within, immensely strong, yet flawless in every aspect of tone and touch. You might argue that Giulini's case is helped by his use of the tidied Nowak text; that Karajan, in his last and greatest recording, goes one stage further by conjuring from the fuller Haas edition a performance of even greater grandeur and sweep. But the two are not in contention. Both is a miracle sufficient unto itself; the Karajan a shade earthier, perhaps, a shade rougher-hewn than the Giulini which glows, in this magnificent new transfer, like Carrara marble lit by the evening sun.

Additional recommendations ...

...No. 8. **Wagner** Lohengrin – Preludes, Acts 1 and 3. Parsifal – Preludes, Acts 1 and 3. **Berlin Philharmonic Orchestra / Herbert von Karajan.** EMI Seraphim Ⓜ CES5 69092-2 (two discs: 122 minutes: ADD).

...No. 8. **Bavarian Radio Symphony Orchestra / Rafael Kubelík.** Orfeo Ⓕ C203891A* (71 minutes: ADD: 8/90).

...No. 8 – Scherzo[a]; Adagio[a]; finale[b]. **Prussian State Orchestra / Herbert von Karajan.** Koch Schwann [a]mono/[b]stereo Ⓕ 314482* (71 minutes: ADD: 12/94).

New review

Bruckner Symphonies – No. 8 in C minor[a]; No. 9 in D minor[b]. **Concertgebouw Orchestra / Eduard van Beinum.** Philips The Early Years mono Ⓜ 442 730/1-2PM* (two discs, oas: 72 and 59 minutes: ADD: 3/96). Item marked [a] from ABL3086/7 (3/56), [b]6530 058 (12/77), recorded 1956.
Eduard van Beinum's Eighth received a guarded welcome in the columns of *Gramophone* in March 1956. Notwithstanding what many would now regard as the general tautness and discipline of his reading, the reviewer clearly viewed the work – as people were wont to do in those days – much as they might have viewed (in Dickens's graphic image) "a Megalosaurus, forty feet long or so, waddling like an elephantine lizard up Holborn Hill". So the van Beinum Eighth, which was also said to be in rather boxy sound, was rather forgotten about. To judge by the CD remastering, the 'boxy sound' was more a matter of poor LP pressings than inadequate recording. True, one is aware to some extent of the confines of the hall. But what a hall, and what bitingly vivid playing! The rather Frenchified sound of the orchestra's woodwinds and brass in those days brings Bruckner closer to Berlioz than to Wagner or Brahms. Yet, for all that, there is also a weight and majesty about the playing that is unmistakably Brucknerian. How does van Beinum dispatch the Eighth Symphony as speedily as he does here? Well, there is an intensely dramatic first movement that is quick but not overquick; a fast *Scherzo*, too fast for comfort; and a beautifully paced *Adagio*. What many collectors will like about this 1955 Eighth is the sense it conveys of live music-making, this astonishing orchestra playing with that mixture of tonal solidity, instrumental articulacy and edge-of-the-seat excitement that is uniquely their own.
The same quality of live music-making is also to be found in the 1956 Ninth. It is, by any standards, a great account of the Ninth, one that, again, is more dramatic than epic, a performance that anatomizes this great wounded giant of a symphony with a care that mixes pity and awe in almost equal measure. Throughout the performance the strings and brass play magnificently. As for the woodwinds, the playing of the first oboe has a truth and penetrating beauty that would be worth hearing for itself alone were it not so ineluctably part of a greater whole. The recording has a splendour, a clarity and a sense of rightness about it that almost makes one wonder why anyone ever bothered to convert to stereo.

Bruckner Symphony No. 9 in D minor. **Berlin Philharmonic Orchestra / Herbert von Karajan.**
DG Ⓕ 429 904-2GGA (62 minutes: ADD: 9/86). From 2530 828 (6/77). Recorded 1966.   ⒼⒼ
Karajan's 1976 recording has long been something of a classic, capturing the conductor and the Berlin Philharmonic on top form. From the opening of the titanic first movement to the final grinding dissonance of the lofty *Adagio* Karajan's control of phrase lengths, tempo and rhythmic swing are gloriously apparent. Compared with many more recent accounts of this solemn work, Karajan's beautifully recorded performance seems refreshingly urgent, cohesive and properly threatening. Exceptionally vivid, it was sometimes difficult to tame on LP, but the CD version gives unalloyed pleasure.

Additional recommendations ...

...No. 9. **Vienna Philharmonic Orchestra / Carlo Maria Giulini.** DG Ⓕ 427 345-2GH (68 minutes: DDD: 8/89).   ⒼⒼⒼ

...No. 9. **Berlin Philharmonic Orchestra / Daniel Barenboim.** Teldec Ⓕ 9031-72140-2 (63 minutes: DDD: 10/91).   ⒼⒼⒼ

...Nos. 7 and 9. **Berlin Philharmonic Orchestra / Wilhelm Furtwängler.** DG Double mono Ⓜ 445 418-2GX2* (two discs: 121 minutes: ADD: 1/95).

Bruckner String Quintet in F major[a]. Intermezzo in D minor[a]. Rondo in C minor. String Quartet in C minor. **L'Archibudelli** (Vera Beths, Lis Rautenberg, vns; Jürgen Kussmaul, [a]Guus Jeukendrup, vas; Anner Bylsma, vc). Sony Classical Vivarte Ⓕ SK66251 (76 minutes: DDD: 3/95). 🖉 Recorded 1994.

"Bruckner is long, he takes time", remarked Anner Bylsma in a *Gramophone* interview in March 1995; not exactly controversial, but it is important in understanding his, and his ensemble's approach to the Quintet. The first movement in particular is more spacious than any other version. But there is more to it than tempo. What matters here is the subtlety of phrasing and fineness of the shading, giving vitality and inner intensity to patterns that can easily sound repetitive, especially at this speed. Much of the Quintet is marked *p*, *pp* or *ppp*; L'Archibudelli show how magically suggestive so many of the quiet passages can be and how important it is to respect those dynamic gradings. They also make the work as a whole sound as unified and sublimely purposeful as the best of the symphonies. As for coupling: the 22-minute student Quartet, with its hints of Mendelssohn and rather more obvious debt to Haydn, is beautifully played, and there is more than one pre-echo of greater things to come. The spaciousness of the Sony sound suits the Quintet especially well, the more obviously 'chamber' textures of the Quartet perhaps less so.

Additional recommendations ...

...String Quintet. Intermezzo. **Sonare Quartet** with **Vladimir Mendelssohn** (va). Claves Ⓕ CD50-9006 (49 minutes: DDD: 2/91).

...String Quintet. Intermezzo. **Alberni Quartet** with **Garfield Jackson** (va). CRD Ⓕ CRD3456 (47 minutes: DDD: 6/91).

New review

Bruckner Masses – No. 1 in D minor[a]; No. 2 in E minor[b]; No. 3 in F minor[c]. [a]**Edith Mathis**, [c]**Maria Stader** (sops); [a]**Marga Schiml**, [c]**Claudia Hellmann** (mezzos); [a]**Wiesław Ochman**, [c]**Ernst Haefliger** (tens); [a]**Karl Ridderbusch**, [c]**Kim Borg** (basses); **Bavarian Radio Chorus and Symphony Orchestra / Eugen Jochum.** DG The Originals Ⓜ 447 409-2GOR2 (two discs: 148 minutes: ADD: 5/95). Item marked [a] from 2530 314 (7/73), [b]2720 054 (3/73), [c]SLPM138829 (3/63). Text and translation included. *Gramophone Classical 100.* ⒼⒼⒼ

Like Bruckner, Eugen Jochum came from a devout Catholic family and began his musical life as a church organist. He would have known the Mass texts more or less inside out, which explains why his readings focus not on the sung parts – which, for the most part, present the text in a relatively foursquare fashion – but on the orchestral writing which, given the gloriously full-bodied playing of the Bavarian orchestra, so lusciously illuminates familiar words. He approaches the Masses with many of the same ideas he so eloquently propounds in his recordings of the symphonies and the music unfolds with a measured, almost relaxed pace which creates a sense of vast spaciousness. This can have its drawbacks: one is so entranced by the beautifully moulded orchestral introduction to the *Benedictus* from the D minor Mass that the entry of a rather full-throated Marga Schiml comes as a rude interruption. DG's digital transfers are extraordinarily good – they really do seem to have produced a sound which combines the warmth of the original LP with the clarity of detail we expect from CD.

Bruckner Mass No. 1 in D minor. Te Deum in C major. **Joan Rodgers** (sop); **Catherine Wyn-Rogers** (contr); **Keith Lewis** (ten); **Alastair Miles** (bass); **Corydon Singers and Orchestra / Matthew Best** with **James O'Donnell** (org). Hyperion Ⓕ CDA66650 (67 minutes: DDD: 11/93). Texts and translations included. Recorded 1993. *Gramophone Editor's choice.* ⒼⒼ

Earth-shaking is the only way to describe Bruckner's great *Te Deum* – literally as well as metaphorically with, on this disc, the thundering Westminster Cathedral organ (sensitively superimposed). The considerably enlarged Corydon Singers sing with consummate skill, rooting out all the subtleties and nuances of Bruckner's magnificent score yet always faithful to Matthew Best's thrusting, athletic direction. It is followed with a performance of the D minor Mass of extraordinary power and strength. From the dazzling orchestral colour and the electrically charged climaxes piling in one on top of the other, to the opulent writing for voices encompassing a vast array of human emotions, Bruckner's debt to Wagner is everywhere apparent. This is very much Bruckner the symphonist – the orchestra certainly dominate the work – and this orchestra produce playing of the very highest calibre.

Additional recommendation ...

...Te Deum[a]. **Mozart** Mass in D minor, K626[b], "Requiem". [a]**Agnes Giebel**, [b]**Elisabeth Grümmer** (sops), **Marga Höffgen** (contr); [a]**Josef Traxel**, [b]**Helmut Krebs** (tens); **Gottlob Frick** (bass); **St Hedwig's Cathedral Choir, Berlin; Berlin Philharmonic Orchestra /** [a]**Karl Forster**, [b]**Rudolf Kempe.** EMI Références mono Ⓜ CDH5 65202-2* (80 minutes: ADD: 10/94).

Bruckner Mass No. 2 in E minor[bcd]. Afferentur regi[bcd]. Ave Maria in F major (1861)[bd]. Ave Maria (1882, with Peter King, org)[a]. Ecce sacerdos magnus[bcd]. Locus iste[bd]. Aequali for Three Trombones, Nos. 1 and 2[c]. [a]**Anne-Marie Owens** (mez); [b]**City of Birmingham Symphony Chorus;** [c]**Birmingham Symphony Orchestra Wind Ensemble /** [d]**Simon Halsey.** Conifer Ⓕ CDCF192 (64 minutes: DDD: 1/91). Texts and translations included. Recorded 1990. Ⓖ

Bruckner's religious works require for their full realization an elusive combination of classical restraint and romantic fervour. In this excellent recording by the City of Birmingham Symphony Chorus and Wind Ensemble this style is captured perfectly. Under conductor Simon Halsey the chorus's finely tuned singing and rich tone are ideally suited both to the E minor Mass of 1866 and the four brief but intense motets which provide an excellent makeweight. The CBSO Wind Ensemble's accompaniment in the Mass, and solo playing in the two *Aequali* for three trombones, is well-balanced and sonorous, qualities which are also shared by Conifer's atmospheric recorded sound. These choral works display a more personal side to Bruckner's character than the mighty symphonies, and so help to round out in a unique way the musical portrait of this great composer. Thus this finely prepared CD, completed by the first-ever recording of the *Ave Maria,* is an essential complement to the more well-known, and more public, works.

Additional recommendations ...

...Mass No. 2. Libera me in F minor (Colin Sheen, Roger Brenner, Philip Brown, tbns). Aequali for three trombones, Nos. 1 and 2 (Sheen, Brenner, Brown). **Corydon Singers; English Chamber Orchestra Wind Ensemble / Matthew Best.** Hyperion Ⓕ CDA66177 (53 minutes: DDD: 9/86).

...Afferentur regi. Ave Maria (1861). Christus factus est. Ecce sacerdos magnus[b]. In St Angelum custodem, "Iam lucis orto sidere". Inveni David. Libera me[b]. Locus iste. Os justi. Pange lingua. Salvum fac populum. Tantum ergo[b]. Tota pulchra es[a]. Vexilla regis. Virga Jesse floruit. [a]**Daniel Norman** (ten); **St Bride's Church Choir, Fleet Street / Robert Jones** with [b]**Matthew Morley** (org). Naxos Ⓢ 8 550956 (62 minutes: DDD: 7/95).

Bruckner Mass No. 3 in F minor. Psalm 150 in C major. **Juliet Booth** (sop); **Jean Rigby** (mez); **John Mark Ainsley** (ten); **Gwynne Howell** (bass); **Corydon Singers and Orchestra / Matthew Best.** Hyperion Ⓕ CDA66599 (68 minutes: DDD: 3/93). Texts and translations included. Recorded 1992.   ⓆⓆ

Bruckner, the devout Catholic who poured his very soul into his devotional, liturgical choral pieces often seems a very different being from Bruckner, the composer of gargantuan, almost self-indulgent symphonies rich in luscious orchestral colour and sensuous harmony. Where the two combine the result can be something almost other-worldly. The F minor Mass is certainly his finest choral work, if not the finest music he ever created. The intensity of religious feeling is heightened rather than diminished by the sumptuous orchestral support, and the soaring melodies and opulent harmonies are somehow purified and enriched by the devotional character of these familiar texts. Here is a performance which by understating the music's abundant richness gives tremendous point to the inner conviction of Bruckner's faith. This orchestra, brought together for this recording but sounding as if they have been playing this music all their days, plays with commendable discretion, balancing admirably with a relatively small choral body. As with everything the Corydon Singers and Matthew Best turn their hands to, it is an impeccable performance, infused with real artistry and sensitive musicianship. Enhanced by the glorious solo voices from a high-powered team this is a CD of rare depth and conviction.

Further listening ...

...Overture in G minor[d]. **Haydn** Symphony No. 45 in F sharp minor, "Farewell"[b]. **Bach** Brandenburg Concerto No. 3 in G major, BWV1048[c]. **Schubert** Symphony No. 8 in B minor, "Unfinished", D759[b]. **Litolff** Concerto symphonique No. 4 in D minor, Op. 102 – Scherzo[ab]. **Rachmaninov** (arr. Wood) Prelude in C sharp minor, Op. 3 No. 2[e]. **Beethoven** Symphony No. 5 in C minor, Op. 67[d]. **Brahms** Variations on a Theme by Haydn, "St Antoni", Op. 56a[d]. **Dvořák** Symphonic Variations, B70[d]. [a]**Irene Scharrer** (pf); [b]**London Symphony Orchestra;** [c]**British Symphony Orchestra;** [d]**Queen's Hall Orchestra;** [e]**symphony orchestra / Sir Henry Wood.** Dutton Laboratories mono 2CDAX2002* (9/94).

...Helgoland. *Coupled with* **Wagner** Das Liebesmahl der Apostel. **Ambrosian Chorus; Symphonica of London / Wyn Morris.** IMP Classics PCD1042.

...Requiem in D minor. Psalms – 112 in B flat major; 114 in G major. **Soloists; Corydon Singers; English Chamber Orchestra / Matthew Best.** Hyperion CDA66245 (1/88).

Joan Brudieu   French/Catalonian *c*1520-1591

New review

La Justa Madrigals and Ensaladas from Sixteenth-Century Catalonia.
Brudieu Madrigals – No. 13, Fantasiant, amor a mi descobre; No. 15, Ma voluntat amb la rahó s'envelopa; No. 16, Si l'amor en un ser dura.
Flecha La negrina. La justa.
Alberch Vila Reyna soberana. Con voz llorosa. O Virgen sancta. El bon jorn. **La Colombina Ensemble** (Maria Cristina Kiehr, sop; Claudio Cavina, alto; Josep Benet, ten; Josep Cabré, bass). Accent Ⓕ ACC94103D (68 minutes: DDD: 11/95). Texts and translations included. Recorded 1994.

This CD presents some pieces which have already been recorded by groups as diverse as The King's Singers, Hespèrion XX and the Huelgas Ensemble for example – the *ensaladas* of Mateu Fletxa (Flecha) – alongside previously unrecorded madrigals of two further sixteenth-century Catalan composers, Joan Brudieu and Père Alberch Vila. The Catalan orientation of this recording is perhaps not surprising given the fact that two of the singers (Josep Benet and Josep Cabré) are Catalans, but La Colombina's approach to this repertory is as different as it could be from that of that other well-established Catalan-based group, Hespèrion XX. They perform both *ensaladas* and madrigals unaccompanied, as was surely intended, and with a degree of musical seriousness that, in the case of the *ensaladas*, is lacking from the jokey, close-harmony approach adopted by The King's Singers.

These strange, pot-pourri style pieces are intended to be wittily onomatopoeic and often funny, but for the most part they also contain a serious message (usually the redemption of mankind) and require a certain amount of sensitive handling. The real discovery on this recording, however, is of the Catalan madrigal school. East-coast Spain was traditionally more open to Italian influence, and composers such as Brudieu and Vila were clearly familiar with madrigalian trends from across the Mediterranean. Like their Italian counterparts, they chose to set some of the finest poetry in their own language such as that by Austiàs March. Some of the texts are open to spiritual interpretations, while others are clearly devotional and, as in Vila's *Reyna soberana*, owe much to the motet style of the *Siglo de oro*, combined with a more madrigalian approach to textural changes which are well brought out by these singers. Similarly, their hushed rendition of the chromatic lines of Vila's *Con voz llorosa*, on the 'false world' theme, is very effective. Clearly a lot of thought has gone into this very interesting recording which can be thoroughly recommended, both for its polished performances and its presentation of a little known but fascinating repertory.

Nicolaus Bruhns
German 1665-1697

Suggested listening ...
...Organ Works – Praeludia: E minor No. 1; E minor, No. 2; G major; G minor. Nun komm, der Heiden Heiland. *Coupled with* **Buxtehude** Auf meinen lieben Gott, BuxWV179; Gott der Vater wohn uns bei, BuxWV190; Nun komm, der Heiden Heiland, BuxWV211; Nimm von uns, herr du treuer Gott, BuxWV207; Puer natus in Bethlehem, BuxWV217; Von Gott will ich nicht lassen, BuxWV220/1 **Piet Kee** (org). Chandos Chaconne CHAN0539 (10/93).

Antoine Brumel
French c1460-c1515

Brumel Missa "Et ecce terrae motus". Lamentations. Magnificat Secundi toni. **The Tallis Scholars / Peter Phillips.** Gimell Ⓔ CDGIM026 (73 minutes: DDD: 9/92). Texts and translations included. Ⓖ
Antoine Brumel was one of the French members of the great Franco-Flemish school of composers which flourished during the fifteenth and sixteenth centuries. His 12-part *Earthquake Mass* is one of the most glorious, if little-known products of this school – a work of colossal power whose rhythmic complexities and virtuoso vocal writing are exceptionally demanding. It is a great tribute to the excellent Tallis Scholars and their fine conductor Peter Phillips that their performance of this masterpiece leaves nothing to be desired. The choir enters fully into the spirit of this visionary work – balancing vocal ecstasy with musical discipline in equal parts. The recording was made in the warm but clear acoustic of the parish church of Salle in Norfolk, an ideal setting for music of this period. The most sympathetic recorded sound captures perfectly the atmosphere of this location. Two more restrained works by Brumel, a set of *Lamentations* and a *Magnificat*, complete a disc of great interest. The comparison of the *Earthquake Mass* with another work of great complexity, Thomas Tallis's 40-part motet *Spem in alium*, is unavoidable. For those who enjoy the grandeur of such choral music performed in a completely authentic style this disc can be strongly recommended.

Additional recommendation ...
...Missa "Et ecce terrae motus". Dies irae. **Huelgas Ensemble / Paul van Nevel.** Sony Classical Vivarte Ⓔ SK46348 (67 minutes: DDD: 5/91). ✐

Further listening ...
...Missa "Berzerette savoyenne". Laudate Dominum de caelis. Sicut lilium inter spinas. Heth: Cogitavit Dominus. Lauda Sion Salvatorem. **Josquin Desprez** Bergerette savoyenne. **Chanticleer.** Chanticleer Records CR-8805 (7/94).

Gaetano Brunetti
Italian/Spanish 1744-1798

Suggested listening ...
...Symphonies – No. 22 in G minor; No. 26 in B flat major; No. 36 in A major. **Cologne Concerto.** Capriccio 10 489 (7/95). ✐

Gavin Bryars
British 1943-

New review
Bryars String Quartets[a] – No. 1, "Between the National and the Bristol"; No. 2. Die letzten Tage[b]. [a]**Balanescu Quartet** ([b]Alexander Balanescu, [b]Claire Connors, vns; Andre Parker, va; Sian Bell, vc). Argo Ⓔ 448 175-2ZH (73 minutes: DDD: 2/96). Recorded 1995.
Restrained, elegiac and with an almost therapeutic consistency of pulse, "The Last Days" (the album's title) suggests a combination of commemorative and reconciliatory elements. The commemorative angle concerns both the First Quartet (1985), which Bryars revised at the time of his

sister's death, and *Die letzten Tage* ("The Last Days", 1991, for two violins), which takes its title from Karl Kraus's apocalyptic satire *The Last Days of Mankind*. Its first movement starts in unison before exploring further, whereas the effective core of the piece lies in the heightened expression of two four-minute "Intermezzos". Bryars's mastery of the medium transcends expected limitations (you'd hardly guess this to be the work of just two players), while the two quartets incorporate equal measures of poetry and textural innovation. The 'reconciliatory' axis already referred to concerns the Second Quartet (1990), which attempts to synthesize the various nationalities of the Balanescu's individual players. It starts where the First ends, among high harmonics, and incorporates more genuinely fast writing than in Bryars's previous work. Gently pulsing accompaniments and subtle harmonic development are common to both pieces (with significant major-key episodes in the First Quartet), the First plumbing greater depths than its equally arresting though more outwardly demonstrative successor. Asked to offer a very generalized impression of the 'sound' of these pieces, one might suggest a subtle blend of Janáček, Pavel Haas and Philip Glass. Certainly, the mood throughout evokes a quiet communion shared between friends. The entire programme was recorded in the presence of the composer and so, in the absence of any real grounds for criticism (at least on the performance front), this excellently recorded CD is enthusiastically commended as a prime sample of Bryars's patient, ethereal and highly accessible style.

Further listening ...

...Prologue. String Quartet No. 1, "Between the National and the Bristol". First Viennese Dance. Epilogue. **Pascal Pongy** (hn); **Charles Fullbrook, Gavin Bryars** (perc); **Arditti Quartet.** ECM New Series 829 484-2 (3/87).

...Incipit Vita Nova[a]. Glorious Hill[b]. Four Elements[c]. Sub Rosa[d]. [a]**Hilliard Ensemble;** [a]**Annemarie Dreyer** (vn); [a]**Ulrike Lachner** (va); [a]**Rebecca Firth** (vc); [c]**chamber ensemble;** [d]**Gavin Bryars Ensemble.** ECM New Series 445 351-2 (5/94).

...Jesus' Blood never failed me yet. **Tom Waits** (sngr); **Hampton Quartet; chorus; orchestra / Michael Riesman.** Point Music 438 823-2PTH (10/93). *Gramophone Editor's choice.* Ⓖ

...The Sinking of the Titanic. **Westhaston Boys' Choir; Camilla Thornton** (va); **Ziella Bryars, Orlanda Bryars, Lucy Thornion** (vcs); **Gavin Bryars Ensemble.** Point Music 446 061-2PTH (2/95).

John Bull

British ?1562/3-1628

New review

Bull In Nomines – IV; V; IX; XII. Pavan in the second tone. Galliard. Lord Lumley's galliard. The King's Hunt. Duke of Brunswick's alman. Germain's alman. English toy. Irish toy. Why ask you. Fantasias – X; XV. Dutch Dance. Fantastic Pavan and Galliard. Chromatic Pavan and Galliard. Melancholy Galliard. Dr Bull's goodnight. Salvator mundi Deus. **Pierre Hantaï** (hpd). Auvidis Astrée Ⓕ E8543 (74 minutes: DDD: 9/95). ✍ Recorded 1994.

In view of the fact that Bull was perhaps the greatest of Elizabethan keyboard virtuosos and writers, it is surprising that not more harpsichordists have leapt at the chance of recording his exceptionally diverse output. For sheer exuberant brilliance, outstanding here, apart from the variations of *Doctor Bull's goodnight*, are the galliards, especially No. 78 in the *Musica Britannica* volume (listed in the heading as *Galliard*). There are also virtuosic strings of thirds in *Lord Lumley's galliard* and the remarkable *In Nomine* that is No. 9 in the *MB* numbering, which is actually in 11/4 time. Of the other examples of this peculiarly English form rooted in polyphony, No. 4 is very fine and No. 5 notable for its rhythmic surprises. Observable in Bull's music too, however, is a strong vein of melancholy, even in such straightforward little pieces as the *English toy* or the *Dutch Dance*; and his famous bold harmonies and 'false relations' can be heard in the *Fantastic Pavan* and, above all, in the magnificent *Chromatic Pavan and Galliard* (thought to have been written in memory of Queen Elizabeth). Hantaï's enjoyment in the more extrovert pieces is evident, but he also enters fully into Bull's more contemplative moods. On a well-recorded Italian instrument of 1677, he is perhaps over-emphatic in *Why ask you*, and certainly very free in rhythm and pace in the *Chromatic Pavan*, but otherwise he compels nothing but wholehearted admiration: his diversity of articulation (legato, semi-staccato and staccato) in *The King's Hunt* is worth every harpsichordist's study.

Additional recommendations ...

...In Nomine. *Coupled with works by* **Anonymous, Aston, Tomkins, Gibbons** and **Byrd** **Sophie Yates** (virg). Chandos Chaconne Ⓕ CHAN0574 (71 minutes: DDD: 12/95). ✍ *See review under Byrd; refer to the Index to Reviews.*

...Chromatic Pavan and Galliard, "Queen Elizabeth's". Fantastic Pavan and Galliard. Melancholy Pavan. Pavan and Galliards, "St Thomas Wake". Trumpet Pavan. Italian Galliard. The Prince's Galliard. The Quadran Pavan and Galliard – No. 2; No. 3. Spanish Pavan. **Joseph Payne** (hpd). BIS Ⓕ CD729 (63 minutes: DDD: 3/96). ✍

John Buller

Suggested listening ...
...Proença. The Theatre of Memory. **Soloists; BBC Symphony Orchestra / Mark Elder.** Unicorn-
Kanchana Souvenir UKCD2049 (11/92).

Gioan Pietro del Buono

Suggested listening ...
...Sonata quinta. *Coupled with works by* **Picchi, Trabaci, A. Mayone, Giovanni de Macque,
Facoli, A. Valente, Frescobaldi, Lambardo, Merula, M. Rossi, Salvatore,
B. Storace, G. Strozzi, Stradella** and **A. Scarlatti** Rinaldo Alessandrini (hpd). Opus 111
OPS30-118 (4/95). ✍ *See review in the Collections section, refer to the Index to Reviews.*

Norbert Burgmüller

Suggested listening ...
...Symphony No. 2 in D major. *Coupled with* **Schumann** Symphony No. 4 in D minor, Op. 120
Berlin Radio Symphony Orchestra / Georg Schmöhe. Koch Schwann Musica Mundi 311010
(11/89).

Geoffrey Burgon

Suggested listening ...
...Magnificat. Nunc dimittis. Two hymns to Mary. This world from But have been found again.
Short Mass. At the round earth's imagined corners. A prayer to the Trinity. Laudate Dominum.
Michael Laird (tpt); **Jeremy Suter** (org); **Chichester Cathedral Choir / Alan Thurlow.** Hyperion
CDA66123 (9/84).
...Television Scores – Brideshead Revisited; Testament of Youth; Bleak House; Tinker, Tailor,
Soldier, Spy[a]; The Chronicles of Narnia. [a]**Lesley Garrett** (sop); **Philharmonia Orchestra / Geoffrey
Burgon.** Silva Screen FILMCD117 (5/93).

Adolph Busch

Suggested listening ...
...Nun die Schatten dunkeln. Wonne der Wehmut. Aus den Himmelsaugen. *Coupled with works by*
Brahms, R. Strauss, Loeffler, Dargomïzhsky, Marx, Reutter and **Gounod** Mitsuko
Shirai (mez); **Tabea Zimmermann** (va); **Hartmut Höll** (pf). Capriccio 10 462 (9/95). *See review in
the Collections section; refer to the Index to Reviews.*   **G**

Alan Bush

Suggested listening ...
...Nocturne, Op. 46[a]. Relinquishment, Op. 11[b]. Lyric Interlude, Op. 26[c]. Voices of the Prophets,
Op. 41[d]. English Suite, Op. 28[e]. [d]**Philip Langridge** (ten); [c]**Clio Gould** (vn); [ab]**Piers Lane,** [c]**Sophia
Rahman,** [d]**Lionel Friend** (pfs); [e]**Northern Chamber Orchestra / Nicholas Ward.** Redcliffe
Recordings RR008 (4/94).

Geoffrey Bush

New review
Bush Overture, "Yorick"[a]. Music for Orchestra[b]. Symphonies – No. 1[c]; No. 2, "Guildford"[d]. [a]**New
Philharmonia Orchestra,** [b]**London Philharmonic Orchestra /** [ab]**Vernon Handley;** [c]**London Symphony
Orchestra / Nicholas Braithwaite;** [d]**Royal Philharmonic Orchestra / Barry Wordsworth.** Lyrita
Ⓕ SRCD252 (79 minutes: ADD/DDD: 3/96). Item marked [a] from SRCS95 (1/80), [b]SRCS57
(10/72), [c]SRCS115 (5/82), [d]new to UK. Recorded 1972-94.
Geoffrey Bush's style is 'traditional', yet not over-indebted to any predecessor; certainly not, at least
in the orchestral music, to his teacher John Ireland. There is an audible affinity, at times, with Walton
in his exuberant vein, once or twice with Constant Lambert (the slow movement of the First
Symphony, a lament for Bush's boyhood hero, gracefully quotes him). Bush's individuality lies in his
sound, which is colourful, rarely lush, sometimes agreeably brusque and brassy (he loves fanfares and
sonorous major-key climaxes). This astringency of colour adds zest to his always fluent, generous

flow of melody. His ingenious use of form is personal, too, and when he decides to cast the first movement of the First Symphony as a rondo it is not long before you realize that he has the resource and the dramatic flair to make such a repetitive form eventful. The Second Symphony manages to be a single, extended sonata-form movement and a more or less conventional four-movement symphony at the same time. There is also what one might call a 'light music side' to Geoffrey Bush, exemplified by the cheerful overture *Yorick* (though with an elegy at its centre) which he wrote in memory of the comedian Tommy Handley. He has the shrewdness not to suppress this aspect of his musical personality when writing symphonies, just as when writing for children in the *Music for Orchestra* he refuses to patronize them. All four orchestras here seem to enjoy themselves a good deal. The reissued recordings sound a little on the thin side, but they have ample colour and impact.

Antoine Busnois
French c1430-1492

Suggested listening ...
...Victimae Paschali laudes. *Coupled with works by* **Ockeghem, Obrecht** and **Isaac** The Clerks' Group / Edward Wickham. ASV Gaudeamus CDGAU139 (3/95). *See review under Ockeghem; refer to the Index to Reviews.*
...Gaude coelestis Domina. In hydraulis. *Coupled with* **Obrecht** (attrib.): Humilium decus. **Ockeghem** Missa prolationum. **Pullois** Flos de spina. **Josquin Desprez** Illibata Dei Virgo nutrix. **The Clerks' Group / Edward Wickham.** ASV Gaudeamus CDGAU143 (3/96).

Ferruccio Busoni
Italian/German 1866-1924

Busoni Piano Concerto, Op. 39. **Garrick Ohlsson** (pf); Men's voices of the **Cleveland Orchestra Chorus; Cleveland Orchestra / Christoph von Dohnányi.** Telarc Ⓕ CD80207 (72 minutes: DDD: 4/90). Recorded 1989. ⒼⒼ
Busoni's Concerto is a thundering vehicle for virtuosity and one doubts while listening to this whether the concerto has ever been played so outstandingly, from the conductor and his players as well as the soloist. The second scherzo is so infectiously exciting that one feels tempted to cheat and play it all over again before proceeding to the finale, and the enormous central movement has a formidable sense of scale and pacing, to which Ohlsson's sonorous pianism is a bonus as well as a contributing factor. The orchestral sound is outstandingly beautiful and transparent and the piano (Ohlsson uses a Bösendorfer) produces crags of grandiose tone without ever seeming to approach its limit or giving any impression that the engineers have helped it.

Busoni Turandot – Suite, Op. 41.
Casella Paganiniana, Op. 65.
Martucci Nocturne in G flat major, Op. 70 No. 1. Novelletta, Op. 82 No. 2. Giga, Op. 61 No. 3.
La Scala Philharmonic Orchestra, Milan / Riccardo Muti. Sony Classical Ⓕ SK53280 (59 minutes: DDD: 4/94). Recorded 1992. ⒼⒼⒼ
Riccardo Muti takes time out here to present some of the lesser known, rarely heard orchestral scores of his fellow countrymen, and a superbly played, enjoyable concert it is too. Proceedings commence with a fine and spirited performance of Alfredo Casella's divertimento *Paganiniana* – not a great piece by any means but a work possessing plenty of charm and humour nevertheless; the outer movements are a bit of a romp (very *opera buffa*) and must have been as much fun to write as they clearly are for the La Scala Philharmonic to play. The tone and temperature rise a few degrees in Martucci's gorgeously lyrical *Nocturne*, Op. 70 No. 1 – a sort of Mahler-meets-Puccini-meets-Respighi love song – and this is nicely contrasted with the affable if somewhat lightweight musings of his *Novelletta* and *Giga*. The high point of the disc, though, must surely be Muti's account of Busoni's *Turandot* Suite, Op. 41, the work that, after several tinkerings, finally ended up forming the basis of his 1917 opera. The recording is exceptionally clear and well focused, if at times a little dry.
Additional recommendation ...
...Turandot – Suite. Nocturne symphonique, Op. 43. Rondo arlecchinesco, Op. 46. Divertimento for Flute and Orchestra, Op. 52ᵃ. Two Studies from "Doktor Faust", Op. 51. Clarinet Concertino, Op. 48ᵇ. Tanzwalzer, Op. 53. ᵃ**Jean-Claude Gérard** (fl); ᵇ**Ulf Rodenhäuser** (cl); **Berlin Radio Symphony Orchestra / Gerd Albrecht.** Capriccio Ⓕ 10 479 (76 minutes: DDD: 6/94). Ⓖ

New review
Busoni String Quartets – No. 1 in C minor, Op. 19; No. 2 in D minor, Op. 26. **Pellegrini Quartet** (Antonio Pellegrini, Thomas Hofer, vns; Charlotte Geselbracht, va; Helmut Menzler, vc). CPO Ⓕ CPO999 264-2 (54 minutes: DDD: 1/96). Recorded 1994.
The First Quartet is by a young composer who knows and loves Schubert, loves him for his serenity as well as his effortless flow of melody. But it was a young man who knew much more than how to imitate effectively who wrote the consistently absorbing development section of the first movement, who hit upon the striking, rather Nordic-sounding trio to the charming minuet-scherzo, and who played such exhilarating games of 'hunt the bar-line' in the finale. It is a lovely work, fully worthy of a

place in the repertory, and the fact that this appears to be its first recording is astonishing. And, believe it or not, Op. 26 is even finer. It is a work full of continuous change and diverting surprise, so packed with resource that you once or twice think that Busoni is showing off, until you reflect that any 21-year-old with gifts like these may be permitted to show off a little. And very often his surprises are quiet ones, in any case, not flashy at all: the gentle shadows that fall across the rather Dvořákian slow movement; the hushed lyrical idea that several times fades to silence between the finale's athletic bursts of counterpoint. Like Op. 19 it is a quartet of real stature whose neglect until now is inexplicable. In a strictly chronological catalogue of Busoni's works these two quartets would be Op. 208 and Op. 221 respectively. The more the music of his amazingly prolific youth is discovered, the more likely it seems that he was perhaps this century's most breathtakingly gifted prodigy. In that context these quartets are not really 'early Busoni' at all, but the works of a fully mature master. How good that for their first recording they should have found such players as these: the Pellegrini Quartet are quite superb, beautifully responsive to Busoni's subtleties, his wit and his melodic refinement. The recordings are excellent.

Busoni Fantasia contrappuntistica[a]. Fantasia nach J.S. Bach[a]. Toccata[b]. **John Ogdon** (pf). Continuum Ⓕ CCD1006 (60 minutes: AAD: 7/89). Items marked [a] from Altarus AIR-2-9074 (10/88), [b] new to UK. 🅖🅖🅖

Busoni's *Fantasia contrappuntistica* is of legendary difficulty, density and length and pianists are understandably very reluctant to learn it. John Ogdon plays it with consummate virtuosity, clarity and sustained concentration, and alongside the technical assurance there is in evidence a firm intellectual grasp of Busoni's prodigious structure and a lofty eloquence in expressing his faith. It is a formidable feat of musicianship as well as pianism. The two other pieces are more personal and many readers may find them even more moving. The *Fantasia nach J.S. Bach* is freer in structure than the *Fantasia contrappuntistica* and with its dedication to his father's memory it is as though Busoni has chosen particularly beloved and appropriate pages for his tribute, adding his own meditations on them. The very late *Toccata* is a resurgence of the Faustian vein that runs throughout Busoni's work, but now dark and pessimistic. The three works add up to a sort of triple self-portrait and Ogdon characterizes them finely. Busoni's piano-writing demands a huge range of sonority as well as endurance and sheer dexterity; in these performances (and this superb recording) Busoni's piano is rendered full-size.

Busoni Arlecchino. **Robert Wörle** (ten) Arlecchino (Peter Matié), Leandro; **Marcia Bellamy** (mez) Colombina (Katharina Koschny); **René Pape** (bass) Ser Matteo del Sarto; **Siegfried Lorenz** (bar) Abbate Cospicuo; **Peter Lika** (bass) Dottor Bombasto, **Berlin Radio Symphony Orchestra / Gerd Albrecht**. Capriccio Ⓕ 60 038 (67 minutes: DDD: 11/94). Notes and synopsis included. Recorded 1992. 🅖🅖

Albrecht's *Arlecchino* is one of the finest readings of a Busoni opera yet committed to disc. Fine as Nagano's reading is, Albrecht projects a greater feeling of drama and dramatic pace (as well as the *commedia dell'arte* aspects of the opera) and seems to have absorbed the Busoni spirit far more successfully; the presence of Busoni's final masterpiece, *Doktor Faust*, is exceptionally strong. Marcia Bellamy is a shade more suited to the role of Colombina than Susanne Mentzer (Nagano), and there are some exceptionally good performances from René Pape, Siegfried Lorenz and Peter Lika in the roles of Matteo, Abbate Cospicuo and Dottor Bombasto. The master-stroke, however, is the casting of Robert Wörle in both the Arlecchino and Leandro roles, an inspired idea and one which is delivered with great aplomb and panache – his Leandro is more sharply characterized than Stephan Dahlberg's for Nagano. Albrecht draws superb orchestral playing from the Berlin Radio Symphony Orchestra (especially in the wind and brass departments) and the recording is well balanced and atmospheric.

Additional recommendation ...

...Arlecchino. Turandot. **Soloists; Chorus and Orchestra of the Opéra de Lyon / Kent Nagano.** Virgin Classics Ⓕ VCD7 59313-2 (two discs: 137 minutes: DDD: 11/93). *Selected by Sounds in Retrospect.*

Further listening ...

...Violin Concerto in D major, Op. 35a[a]. Violin Sonata No. 2 in E minor, Op. 36a[b]. [ab]**Joseph Szigeti** (vn); [b]**Mieczyslaw Horszowski** (pf); [a]**Little Orchestra Society / Thomas Scherman.** Sony Classical mono MPK52537* (5/93).

...Concertino for Clarinet and Small Orchestra. *Coupled with works by* **Copland** *and* **Mozart** Paul Meyer (cl); **English Chamber Orchestra / David Zinman.** Denon CO-75289 (11/93). *See review under Copland; refer to the Index to Reviews.*

...Berceuse élégiaque, Op. 42[a]. *Coupled with* **Schoenberg** Chamber Symphony No. 2, Op. 38[a]. **Weill** Symphonies[b] – No. 1; No. 2. [a]**New Philharmonia Orchestra / Frederik Prausnitz;** [b]**BBC Symphony Orchestra / Gary Bertini.** EMI Matrix CDM5 65869-2 (4/96).

...Tanzwalzer. *Coupled with* **Satie** Parade. **Ravel** La valse. **Bartók** Dance Suite, Sz77. **Liadov** Kikimora, Op. 63. **Chabrier** Le roi malgré lui – Fête polonaise. **Liszt** Mephisto Waltz No. 2, S111. **Philharmonia Orchestra / Igor Markevitch.** Testament mono SBT1060* (2/96).

...Violin Sonatas – No. 1 in E minor, Op. 29; No. 2 in E minor, Op. 36*a*. **Lydia Mordkovitch** (vn); **Victoria Postnikova** (pf). Chandos CHAN8868.

...Sonatina No. 6 super Carmen (Kammerfantasie). *Coupled with works by* **Alkan, Chopin/Alkan** and **Medtner Marc-André Hamelin** (pf). Hyperion CDA66765 (3/95). *See review under Alkan; refer to the Index to Reviews.* ⊖⊖

...An die Jugend – Giga, bolero e variazione (study after Mozart). *Coupled with works by* **Liszt, Debussy, Mendelssohn, Schumann, Chopin, Scriabin, Rachmaninov** and **Weber.** **Anatol Ugorski** (pf). DG 447 105-2GH (3/96). *See review in the Collections section; refer to the Index to Reviews.*

...Suite Campestre, Op. 3. Fantasia in modo antico, Op. 33*b* No. 4. Elegies – No. 1, Nach der Wendung; No. 7, Berceuse élégiaque. Macchietti medioevali. Sonatinas – No. 4 in die Nativitas Christi MCMXVIII; No. 6 on "Carmen" (Kammerfantasie). *Coupled with* **Bach** (trans. Busoni) Orgel-Büchlein, BWV599-644 – Num komm' der Heiden Heiland, BWV599; Ich ruf' zu dir, BWV639. **William Stephenson** (pf). Olympia OCD461 (11/94).

...Doktor Faust. **Soloists; Bavarian Radio Chorus and Symphony Orchestra / Ferdinand Leitner.** DG 20th Century Classics 427 413-2GC3 (8/89).

...Turandot. **Soloists; Berlin RIAS Chamber Choir; Berlin Radio Symphony Orchestra / Gerd Albrecht.** Capriccio 60 039 (11/93). ⊖

George Butterworth
British 1885-1916

Butterworth A Shropshire Lad. Two English Idylls. The banks of green willow.
Coleridge-Taylor Ballade in A minor, Op. 33. Symphonic Variations on an African Air, Op. 63.
MacCunn The land of the mountain and the flood, Op. 3. **Royal Liverpool Philharmonic Orchestra / Grant Llewellyn.** Argo Ⓕ 436 401-2ZH (68 minutes: DDD: 6/93). Recorded 1991.

Grant Llewellyn's Butterworth is a model of sensitivity and poise and how tellingly he manages to convey the vulnerable poignancy behind this engaging music. The misty introduction to *A Shropshire Lad* is beautifully evocative, with scrupulously observed dynamics whilst the central portion brings just the right amount of pulse-quickening passion. Samuel Coleridge-Taylor completed his *Ballade* in 1898, the same year as the first scene of his once popular cantata *The Song of Hiawatha*. It's an enjoyable essay, full of effective orchestral bluster, but in no way distinctive – only the touchingly sweet secondary melody lingers in the memory. The *Symphonic Variations on an African Air* of 1906, on the other hand, show far greater imaginative scope. The African air in question is the resonant black spiritual *I'm troubled in mind*, and Argo's booklet-annotator rightly cites Delius's *Appalachia* as a kindred creation. Under Llewellyn, Hamish MacCunn's delightful Victorian concert overture, *The land of the mountain and the flood*, also receives crisp yet affectionate treatment, its 'big' tune most stirringly attended to. Argo's production is vivid and well-lit. A lovely collection.

Additional recommendation ...

...Two English Idylls. A Shropshire Lad. The banks of green willow. **Britten** Variations on a Theme of Frank Bridge, Op. 10. **Warlock** Capriol Suite. **Academy of St Martin in the Fields / Sir Neville Marriner.** Decca London Ⓜ 421 391-2LM (62 minutes: ADD: 8/89).

Butterworth Bredon Hill and other songs. A Shropshire Lad.
Finzi Let us garlands bring, Op. 18.
Ireland Sea Fever. The Vagabond. The Bells of San Marie.
Vaughan Williams Songs of Travel. **Bryn Terfel** (bass-bar); **Malcolm Martineau** (pf). DG Ⓕ 445 946-2GH (77 minutes: DDD: 8/95). Texts included. Recorded 1995. *Gramophone Editor's record of the month.* ⊖⊖⊖

There *is* a touch of genius about this man. To listeners who know some of these songs and have heard them well performed before, it will come – not quite as a revelation, because one might sense they had a life outside the normal condition and character of other performances – but more as the fulfilment of a deeply felt wish, instinctive rather than consciously formed. As in all the best Lieder singing, everything is specific: "Fly away, breath" we recite, thinking nothing of it, but with this singer it is visual – we see it in flight, just as in *Sea Fever* we know in the very tiniest of gaps that in that second he has *heard* "the seagulls crying". As in all the best singing of songs, whatever the nationality, there is strong, vivid communication: he will sometimes sing so softly that if he had secured anything less than total involvement he would lose us. There is breadth of phrase, variety of tone, alertness of rhythm, all the musical virtues are there; and yet that seems to go only a little way towards accounting for what is special. In more detail then. *Bredon Hill*: "a happy noise to hear" is the robust observation of a fulfilled and carefree man, "and come to church in time" is exultant *hubris*, "I hear you" has anger in it, "I will come" resentful submission. Finzi's "O mistress mine": "in delay there lies no plenty" is the free, open-throated call of lovers to make time run (since we can't make it stand still), and "Youth's stuff will not endure" is a lightly intimated *memento mori*, half seriousness, half joke. "When I was one-and-twenty" (*A Shropshire Lad*): the "wise man" who pedalled his tuppeny-ha'penny thought-for-the-day is a pompous loud-mouth, "but oh tis true" has the groan of acknowledgement, and the repeated "tis true" comes from the private recesses of the soul, which *knows* it is! One after another, these songs are brought to a full life. There is a boldness about Terfel's art that could be perilous (and he stands on the brink throughout *A Shropshire Lad*'s "Is my team ploughing?"), but which, as exercised here, is marvellously well guided by musicianship, intelligence and the genuine flash of inspiration. Malcolm Martineau's playing is also a delight: his touch, in its way, is as sure and illuminating as the singer's. From the recording you might prefer less hall-reverberance around the voice. From the songs themselves you could not possibly wish anything more: hearing them performed like this you probably won't swap them for half the German song repertoire or the whole of the French.

Additional recommendation ...

...Bredon Hill. When the lad for longing sighs. On the idle hill of summer. A Shropshire lad. *Coupled with works by* **L. Berkeley, Barber, Horder, Ireland, Moeran** and **C.W. Orr** **Anthony Rolfe Johnson** (ten); **Graham Johnson** (pf). Hyperion Ⓕ CDA66471/2 (two discs: 124 minutes: DDD: 8/95). Includes various poems from Housman's "A Shrophire Lad" read by Alan Bates. *See review in the Collections section; refer to the Index to Reviews.*

Dietrich Buxtehude   German c1637-1707

Buxtehude Sonatas: Op. 1 – No. 1 in F major, BuxWV252; No. 2 in G major, BuxWV253; No. 6 in D minor, BuxWV257. Op. 2 – No. 3 in G minor, BuxWV261. C major, BuxWV266. D major, BuxWV267. Passacaglia in D minor, BuxWV161. Ciacona in E minor, BuxWV160. Fried- und Freudenreiche Hinfarth, BuxWV76 – Klaglied. **Capriccio Stravagante / Skip Sempé.** Deutsche Harmonia Mundi Ⓕ 05472-77300-2 (64 minutes: DDD: 2/95). 🖉 Recorded 1992.   ⊕⊕

The majority of chamber works here constitute the only important publications made of Buxtehude's music in his lifetime. At his best, they are right up Sempé's street, "provoking the sense of wonder, the unusual" and encouraging the performer to engage in a free, spontaneous and concentrated rhetorical expression. The sonatas Nos. 1 and 6 from Op. 1 are cases in point, where Buxtehude presents an affecting juxtaposition of recitative-like proclamations, dances and tautly constructed figures, secretly worked out behind closed doors. Often, as in Op. 2 No. 3, this is an elusive cocktail, rarefied and stylistically paradoxical at times (in the way Purcell can be) and in the process highly satisfying and original. Of the unusual gems, there is a superb double-harpsichord Passacaglia with a theme very similar to Bach's monolithic organ piece of the same name; two harpsichords create a liberating and noble concoction, as lovers of BWV1061 will attest. A lively and imaginative programme of some fine music.

Additional recommendations ...

...Op. 1 – No. 3 in A minor, BuxW; No. 4 in B flat major, BuxWV255. Op. 2 – No. 3; No. 6 in E major, BuxWV264. **Boston Museum Trio.** Harmonia Mundi Musique d'abord Ⓑ HMA190 1089 (41 minutes: ADD).   ⓖ

...Op. 1 – Nos. 2, 4 and 6. Op. 2 – No. 2 in D major, BuxWV260; No. 3. **Trio Sonnerie.** ASV Gaudeamus Ⓕ CDGAU110 (47 minutes: DDD). 🖉

...Op. 1 – Nos. 1-7. **John Holloway** (vn); **Jaap ter Linden** (va da gamba); **Lars Ulrik Mortensen** (hpd). Da Capo Ⓕ 8 224003 (57 minutes: DDD: 1/96). 🖉

...Op. 2 – Nos. 1-7. **John Holloway** (vn); **Jaap ter Linden** (va da gamba); **Lars Ulrik Mortensen** (hpd). Da Capo Ⓕ 8 224004 (63 minutes: DDD: 1/96) 🖉

Buxtehude Nimm von uns, Herr, BuxWV78. Jesu, meines Lebens Leben, BuxWV62. Mit Fried und Freud, ich fahr dahin, BuxWV76. Führwahr, er trug unsere Krankheit, BuxWV31. Herzlich lieb, hab ich dich o Herr, BuxWV41. Der Herr ist mit mir, BuxWV15. **Claron McFadden** (sop); **Franciska Dukel** (mez); **Jonathan Peter Kenny** (alto); **Marius van Altena** (ten); **Stephan MacLeod** (bass); **Collegium Vocale; The Royal Consort; Anima Eterna Orchestra / Jos van Immerseel.** Channel Classics Ⓕ CCS7895 (65 minutes: DDD: 7/95). Texts included. Recorded 1994.

Gramophone Editor's choice.   ⊕ⓖ

This disc includes six of Buxtehude's vocal works, only two of which appear to have been previously recorded. Jos van Immerseel, more familiar to readers as a fortepianist and harpsichordist, here directs Philippe Herreweghe's Collegium Vocale together with his own instrumental ensemble, Anima Eterna, and a gamba quartet, The Royal Consort. The solo vocalists come from further afield but have been carefully chosen and are, in the main, effective. The North German middle ground between chorale concertato and the early cantatas of Bach is an interesting one, especially in the hands of composers of Buxtehude's stature. In these cantatas the disparate textual elements of bible passage, hymn and devotional poetry, typical of the time, are complemented by the composer's skill in drawing together the comparably disparate musical ones of sonata, concertato principles, aria and chorale. That in itself might give these cantatas only an ephemeral charm, but Buxtehude was a musician who was gifted in the art of word-painting and, above all, in the expression of deep, often grief-stricken emotions. He could be brilliant, too, in his lyrical approach to texts, but it is an all-pervading melancholy which seems to characterize most strongly much that is most profound in his sacred vocal music. These six works demonstrate Buxtehude's formal versatility with two large-scale chorale cantatas; a beautiful ostinato-based strophic aria, with an almost startling dissonance; the famous, austere and highly contrapuntal *Canticum Simeonis* ("*Mit Fried und Freud*") which Buxtehude performed at his father's funeral in 1674; and two *concertante* pieces, one consisting of a sinfonia and multisectional aria, the other of a sinfonia, aria and alleluia. The performances respond to the highly charged emotional outpouring of these works but occasionally lack polish. However, the music is first-rate (the ostinato- and chaconne-based movements make particularly strong appeal) and Immerseel's direction is stylish and sensitive. The cantata texts are in German only but there is a translation of Immerseel's interesting introductory essay.

Further listening ...
...Trio Sonatas – C major, BuxWV266; G major, BuxWV271; B flat major, BuxWV273. *Coupled with* **Pachelbel** Suite in G major. Musicalische Ergotzung – Suite No. 4 in E minor. Aria con variazoni in A major. Canon and Gigue in D major. **Cologne Musica Antiqua / Reinhard Goebel.** Archiv Produktion Galleria 427 118-2AGA (6/89). ✔
...Organ Works – Ach Gott und Herr, BuxWV177. Ach Herr mich armen Sünder, BuxWV178. Canzona in C major, BuxWV166. Canzonetta in C major, BuxWV167. Canzonetta in D minor, BuxWV168. Canzonetta in E minor, BuxWV168. Ciacona in C minor, BuxWV159. Jesus Christus, unser Heiland, BuxWV198. Komm, heiliiger Geist, Herre Gott, BuxWV199. Komm heiliger Geist, Herre Gott, BuxWV200. Prelude and Fugue in F major, BuxWV144. Prelude and Fugue in F major, BuxWV145. Prelude and Fugue in F sharp minor, BuxWV146. Prelude and Fugue in G minor, BuxWV150. Te Deum laudamus, Phrygian, BuxWV218. **Michel Chapuis** (org). Auvidis Valois V4431 (12/89).

William Byrd   British 1543-1623

New review

Byrd All in a garden green[a]. La volta No. 1 in G major, "Lady Morley". O mistress mine I must[a]. Wolsey's Wild[a]. O Lord, how vain are all our delights[bc]. Psalmes, Sonets and Songs – Who likes to love; My mind to me a kingdom is[bc]; Farewell, false love[bc]. Triumph with pleasant melody[bc]. Truth at the First[bc]. Ad Dominum cum tribularer[b]. Cantiones sacrae – Attollite portas; Da mihi auxilium; Domine secundum actum meum; Miserere mihi, Domine[b]. [a]**Sophie Yates** (virg); [b]**I Fagiolini / Robert Hollingworth;** [c]**Fretwork.** Chandos Chaconne Ⓔ CHAN0578 (73 minutes: DDD: 8/95). ✔ Texts and translations included. Recorded 1994.

This disc adopts an imaginative approach to programming Byrd's music by presenting works in different genres grouped together to demonstrate a single stage in his development. And how amazingly many-sided was the young Byrd, who burst like a star on the then somewhat enfeebled state of English music, not only being appointed organist of Lincoln Cathedral at the age of 20 and of the Chapel Royal ten years later but, with his teacher Tallis, embarking on an important publishing venture. This disc includes Latin motets, keyboard dances and variations on popular songs of the day, and sacred and secular songs (and a dialogue) with viols. There is so much here that wins our admiration: the dazzling contrapuntal elaboration of *Attollite portas*, the close-knit texture of *Da mihi auxilium* and the massive *Ad Dominum cum tribularer*; the exuberant variations on *O mistress mine* (neatly played by Sophie Yates) and Byrd's melodic gift in the strophic *O Lord, how vain*. The singers' adoption of period pronunciation of English – so that, for example, "rejoice" emerges as "rejwace" – affects the tuning and the musical sound, it is claimed here, but without rather clearer enunciation the point remains not proven. Probably more upsetting to many will be the Anglicized pronunciation of Latin favoured by lawyers and a few schoolmasters. The viol consort gives quiet, stylish support and is well balanced, the Fagiolini sopranos occasionally 'catch the mike' on high notes (e.g. in the passionate pleas of *Miserere mihi, Domine*), and the recorded level of the virginals might have been a little higher without falsifying its tone. But these are very minor criticisms of a most rewarding disc.

New review

Byrd Harpsichord works.
Gibbons Harpsichord works. **Laurent Stewart** (hpd). Pierre Verany Ⓔ PV795051 (62 minutes: DDD: 3/96). ✔ Recorded 1994.
    Byrd My Lady Nevell's Ground, BK57. French Corantos, BK21 – No. 1; No. 3. Pavan and Galliard in G minor, BK3, "Sir William Petre". Rowland, BK7. Volte in G major, BK91. Alman in G major, BK11. Prelude in A minor, BK12. Fantasia in A minor, BK13. **Gibbons** Fantasias – D minor, MBXX/5; G major, MBXX/6; D minor, MBBXX/8; A minor, MBXX/11; A minor, MBXX/12; C major, MBXX/14. Preludes – A minor, MBXX/1; A minor, MBXX/4. Galliard, MBXX/20, "Lady Hatton". Ground in A minor, MBXX/26. French Coranto, MBXX/38. Pavan and Galliard in A minor, MBXX/18-19, "Lord Salisbury". The Italian ground, MBXX/27. The Queen's command, MBXX/28.
Byrd and Gibbons form an ideal partnership for a two-composer programme of English virginals music. Byrd fanciers may regret that he occupies only about one-third of the playing time, but no one could suggest that Gibbons's more rarely recorded music is less worthy of an outing. In his short life Gibbons wrote far less than Byrd but, except in its inclusion of six of his ten splendid fantasias, the programme does not deal in quantities (quality is to be found in abundance) but rather in the presentation of both composers in a variety of genres. Byrd's many magnificent pavan-galliard pairings are central to his output, but Gibbons strangely wrote only one such – and it is not set against Byrd's genuflexion to the same dignitary. However, it is not the programme that is the most

remarkable feature of this recording (in the field one could hardly go wrong!), rather it is the performance. Stewart might have celebrated the triumphant return of Lord Willoughby (who shares the tune of *Rowland*) a little less soberly, but in every other respect his playing is of the highest order. His tempos are convincing, phrasing is lucid, rubato subtly absorbed within a firm pulse, choice of registration apt and economically varied, and real gravity or joy of spirit illuminates every item. He plays a copy of a Ruckers harpsichord of 1612 (a date within the life span of both composers), tuned with unequal temperament and, surprisingly, to A = 440; the sound is sumptuous but clear, with every contrapuntal line sharply etched. The recording is excellent.

New review
English Virginals Music Sophie Yates (virg). Chandos Chaconne Ⓟ CHAN0574 (71 minutes: DDD: 12/95). Recorded 1994.
   Byrd Prelude in A minor, BK12. Fantasia in A minor, BK13. Pavan, BK54. Galliard, BK55. Barley Break, BK92. Pavan and Galliard in G minor, BK3, "Sir William Petre". The Woods so wild, BK85. Hugh Ashton's Ground, BK20. The Bells, BK98. **Gibbons** Fantasia. **Anonymous** My Lady Carey's Dompe. **Tomkins** Barafostus' Dream. **Aston** A Hornepype. **J. Bull** In Nomine.
Sophie Yates provides an overview of the period that ended in the 1620s after the death of Byrd, its central figure, Gibbons and Bull, though Tomkins delayed the stylistic rigor mortis for another 30 years. The anonymous *My Lady Carey's Dompe* and Aston's *Hornepype* provide quasi-improvisational precursors (though they are not so placed in the programme) of the ubiquitous divisions upon whatever, including Byrd's or Aston's *Ground* – he looked both backwards to Aston and sideways to Dowland and Harding in writing divisions on their works. We are in the world of Byrd, the genres in the development of which he played a major role, and the contemporary composers he influenced. Byrd's *Fantasia* in A minor (FWVB52) is one of his finest early works and, coupled with its Prelude (FWVB100), is an excellent choice, as is that by Gibbons. Dowland's *Lachrymae Pavan* and Harding's *Galliard* are not thematically linked but Yates, noting their common key and adjacency in the Fitzwilliam Virginal Book (121 and 122), juxtaposes them; whether or not Tregian intended this, it works well here. Only Byrd's setting of Harding's *Galliard* lacks any other current recording, but duplications are unimportant in a programme that is as well conceived and executed as this one. Yates plays on a warm-toned virginals, a copy, broadly based on an Italian instrument *c*1600, tuned to an unequal temperament that lends spice to chromatic chords such as that in Byrd's *Fantasia* – at 0'10". Her grasp of style is secure, her delivery always expressive – but never to excess, and her shaping of the fantasias is clear-sighted.

William Byrd and his Age [a]Alfred Deller (alto); **Schola Cantorum Basiliensis / August Wenzinger.** Vanguard Classics Alfred Deller Edition Ⓜ 08.5068.71* (44 minutes: ADD: 4/95). Texts included. From PVL7035 (5/58). ✐ Recorded 1956.
   Anon. (arr. Warlock) Come tread the paths[a]. Ah, silly poor Joas[a]. O death, rock me asleep[a]. **Byrd** Care for thy soul (arr. le Huray and Dart)[a]. Ye sacred muse (arr. Fellowes)[a]. My sweet little darling (arr. Fellowes)[a]. Come, pretty babe[a]. Fantasia a 4 in G minor, BE17/4. **Corkine** (arr. Warlock) What booteth love?[a]. **A. Ferrabosco II** Fantasias – a 4; a 6. **R. Nicholson** (arr. Warlock) In a merry May morn[a]. **Parsons** (arr. Warlock) Pour down, you powr'rs divine (Pandolpho)[a]. **Whythorne** (arr. Warlock) Buy new broom[a].   ⓖⓖ
This is probably one of the most successful recordings Deller made and his programme, thoughtfully chosen as always, includes some of the loveliest songs of the period, arranged mainly by Edmund Fellowes and Peter Warlock. Interspersed among these are three *Fantasias* for viol consort, two of them by the English-born Alfonso Ferrabosco, and the remaining one by Byrd. Viol playing has changed a lot since then but August Wenzinger's consort of viols, drawn from the Schola Cantorum Basiliensis, played a pioneering role in the early music revival, and the performances are sensitive. It is for the songs and above all for Deller's interpretation of them, however, that this disc should be treasured. His singing of Byrd's "My sweet little darling, my comfort and joy", which begins his programme establishes a lyrical, sometimes elegiac mood which colours the entire recording, reaching a sustained climax in Robert Parsons's *Pandolpho*. It is probably unwise to listen to everything here without a break, but taken in 15-minute sessions Deller's voice and his often extraordinary sensibility to music and text make a strong impact. The recorded sound still comes over well and the balance between voice and instruments is usually effective.

Byrd Masses – Five Voices; Four Voices; Three Voices. Motet – Ave verum corpus a 4. **The Tallis Scholars / Peter Phillips.** Gimell Ⓟ CDGIM345 (67 minutes: DDD: 3/86). ✐ From BYRD345 (5/84).   ⓖⓖ
Byrd was a fervently committed Roman Catholic and he helped enormously to enrich the music of the English Church. His Mass settings were made for the many recusant Catholic worshippers who held services in private. They were published between 1593 and 1595 and are creations of great feeling. The contrapuntal writing has a much closer texture and fibre than the Masses of Palestrina and there is an austerity and rigour that is allowed to blossom and expand with the text. The beautifully restrained and mellow recording, made in Merton College Chapel, Oxford, fully captures the measure of the music and restores the awe and mystery of music that familiarity has sometimes dimmed.

Additional recommendations ...

...Mass for Five Voices. Mass Propers for the Feast of All Saints. Motets. **Christ Church Cathedral Choir, Oxford / Stephen Darlington.** Nimbus Ⓕ NI5237 (52 minutes: DDD: 12/90).

...Masses. **King's College Choir, Cambridge / Sir David Willcocks.** Decca Ⓜ 433 675-2DM (75 minutes: ADD: 10/92).

...Masses. Anglican Music – The Great Service. O Lord, make thy servant. O God, the proud are risen against me. Sing joyfully unto God our strength. **The Tallis Scholars / Peter Phillips.** Gimell Ⓕ CDGIM343/4 (two discs: 132 minutes: DDD: 7/93).

...Masses – Five Voices; Four Voices. Infelix ego. **Oxford Camerata / Jeremy Summerly.** Naxos Ⓢ 8 550574 (65 minutes: DDD: 7/93).

...Ave verum corpus. Civitas sancti tui. Haec dies. *Coupled with works by* **Lotti, Allegri, Palestrina, Parsons, Viadana, Tallis, Philips, G. Gabrieli, Tye, Victoria** and **Monteverdi** Soloists; Westminster Cathedral Choir / James O'Donnell. Hyperion Ⓕ CDA66850 (72 minutes: DDD: 5/96). *See review in the Collections section; refer to the Index to Reviews.*

Byrd Gradualia – The Marian Masses. **William Byrd Choir / Gavin Turner.** Hyperion Ⓕ CDA66451 (80 minutes: DDD: 11/91). 🖉 Texts and translations included. Recorded 1990.
Mass Propers – Feasts of the Purification of the BVM, the Nativity of the BVM, the Annunciation of the BVM, the Assumption of the BVM; Votive Masses of the BVM: Advent, Christmas to the Purification, Purification to Easter, Easter to Pentecost and Pentecost to Advent.

This useful recording explores the cycle of motets Byrd composed for English Roman Catholics to sing in their clandestine services. He began the project soon after writing the three Masses (which date from the mid 1590s), and took ten years to bring it to completion. Like so much of Byrd's late music, the *Gradualia* motets are compact and economical in expression: miniature masterpieces that glow with the warmth of the composer's personal religious convictions, and miraculously balance exquisite musical design with the most intelligent word-setting. Their chamber-music scale is nicely captured in these performances by the William Byrd Choir, headed by a superb team of five solo voices. Everything on the disc belongs to feasts of the Blessed Virgin, many of which share texts with one another. Byrd economized by setting each text once only, and to play them in their correct liturgical order the various tracks of the CD have to be pre-selected. This is great fun to do; but the disc also makes perfectly satisfying listening when played straight through from start to finish.

Additional recommendation ...

...Laudibus in sanctis. Gradualia – Volume 1/i: Feast of All Saints – Offertory: Iustorum animae; Volume 2: Easter Day. **Tomkins** My beloved spake. My shepherd is the living Lord. O sing unto the Lord a new song. **Gibbons** Almighty God, who by Thy Son. O clap your hands. **Blitheman** In pace. **Taverner** Dum transisset Sabbatum I. **Tallis** O nata lux de lumine. O salutaris hostia. **Wilbye** Homo natus de muliere. **W. Mundy** O Lord, the maker of all thing. **R. White** (attrib.) O praise God in His holiness. **Worcester Cathedral Choir / Donald Hunt** with **Raymond Johnston** (org). Abbey Alpha Ⓕ CDCA957 (69 minutes: DDD: 2/95).

Further listening ...

...Keyboard Works: Fantasias – No. 2 in C major; No. 2 in G major. Pavans and Galliards – No. 2 in F major, "Ph. Tregian"; No. 2 in G major; No. 3 in G minor. The Carman's Whistle; The Woods so Wild; Walsingham; All in a garden green. The Queen's Alman. The Bells. Ut re mi fa sol la. La volta – No. 1 in G major. **Ursula Duetschler** (hpd). Claves CD50-9001 (10/90). 🖉

...Keyboard Works: My Lady Nevell's Ground. O mistress mine I must. John must come kiss me now. Passamezzo Pavan and Galliard. The Carman's Whistle. Walsingham. Hugh Ashton's Ground. Fortune my foe. Sellinger's Round. **Elaine Thornburgh** (hpd). Koch International Classics 37057-2 (4/92). 🖉

...Pavan and Galliard a 6 in C major, BE17/15[d]. Fantasia a 6 in G minor No. 2, BE17/13[d]. In Nomine a 4 No. 2, BE17/17[d]. Fantasia a 4 in G minor, BE17/4[d]. Fantasia a 6 No. 3[d]. In Nomine a 5, BE17/18-22[d]. John come kiss me now, BK81[c]. Pavan in A minor No. 1, BK14[c]. Qui passe (Chi passa) for my Lady Nevell, BK19[c]. Susanna fair[ad]. Fair Britain Isle[ad]. Rejoice unto the Lord[ad]. In angel's weed[ad]. Have mercy upon me, O God[bd]. Triumph with pleasant melody[bd]. Christ rising again[bd]. [a]**Tessa Bonner** (sop); [b]**Red Byrd**; [c]**Timothy Roberts** (hpd); [d]**Rose Consort of Viols.** Naxos 8 550604 (6/95). 🖉

...Teach me, O Lord. Cantate Domino. Ave verum corpus. Sing joyfully unto God our strength. *Coupled with works by* **Weelkes, Tomkins, Tallis** and **Gibbons** Worcester Cathedral Choir / Donald Hunt with Raymond Johnston (org). Abbey Alpha CDCA943 (5/93). *See review in the Collections section; refer to the Index to Reviews.*

...The Great Service: Morning Service – Venite; Te Deum; Benedictus; Creed. Evening Service – Magnificat; Nunc dimittis. Anthems – O God, the proud are risen against me; O Lord make thy servants. Sing joyfully unto God our strength. **The Tallis Scholars / Peter Phillips.** Gimell CDGIM011 (6/87).

...Motets: In resurrectione tua; Aspice Domine de sede; Vide Domine afflictionem; Domine tu iurasti; Vigilate; Domine secundum multitudinem; Tristitia et anxietas; Ne irascaris Domine; O quam gloriosum. **New College Choir, Oxford / Edward Higginbottom.** CRD CRD3420 (12/91).

David Byrne
British 1952-

Suggested listening ...
...High Life. *Coupled with works by* **Moran, Lurie** and **Torke** Balanescu Quarte. Argo 436 565-2ZH (3/93). *See review in the Collections section; refer to the Index to Reviews.*

Juan Bautista José Cabanilles
Spanish 1644-1712

Suggested listening ...
...Pasacalles primero tono. Tiento de Batalla del octavo tono. *Coupled with works by* **A. de Cabezón, Ximénez, Coelho, Carreira** and **H. de Cabezón** Sophie Yates (hpd). Chandos Chaconne CHAN0560 (11/94). *See review in the Collections section; refer to the Index to Reviews.*

Hernando de Cabezon
Spanish 1541-1602

Antonio de Cabezon
Spanish 1510-1566

Suggested listening ...
...Diferencias sobre "La dama le demanda". Diferencias sobre el Canto llano del Caballero. Diferencias sobre la Gallarda Milanesa. Pavana con su glosa. Tiento del primer tono. Farbordon del primer tono. Obra sobre Cantus firmus. *Coupled with works by* **H. de Cabezón, Ximénez, Coelho, Carreira** and **Cabanilles** Sophie Yates (hpd). Chandos Chaconne CHAN0560 (11/94). *See review in the Collections section; refer to the Index to Reviews.*

John Cage
American 1912-1992

A Chance Operation The John Cage Tribute. **Various Artists.** Koch International Classics Ⓟ 37238-2 (two discs: 141 minutes: DDD: 8/94). Works performed by their composers unless indicated.
Cage 30 Pieces for String Quartet – excerpts (Kronos Quartet). Dance No. 1 for Two Prepared Pianos (Patrick Moraz, Charles Turner). Concert for Piano and Orchestra – Three Solos for Trumpet (Earle Brown). Living Room Music (David Van Tieghem). 4'33" (Frank Zappa). Aria (Meredith Monk). New York City – street noises outside Cage's apartment (Steven Smith). **Jackson Mac Low/Anne Tardos** First Four-Language Word Event in Memoriam John Cage. **Christian Wolff** Six Melodies Variation for Solo Violin (Roger Zahab). **Ken Nordine** A Cage Went In Search of a Bird. **Laurie Anderson** Cunningham Stories – At the Age of Twelve ... ; Merce Cunningham Phoned His Mother ... ; Every Morning ... ; The Cunningham Company ... . **Ryuichi Sakamoto** Haiku FM. **Larry Austin/Robert Black** art is self-alteration is Cage is ... (Robert Black, db). **David Tudor** Webwork – excerpts. **Yoko Ono** Georgia Stone. **Oregon** (group composition): Chance/Choice. **Takehisa Kosugi** 75 Letters and Improvisation. **James Tenney** Ergodos I. **Robert Ashley** Factory Preset. **John Cale** In Memoriam John Cage – Call Waiting.   🅖🅖

"Music was the main way John Cage made himself into who he was" writes David Revill, one of the many contributors to "A Chance Operation". And the Cagean aesthetic is indeed one of constantly shifting contexts for everything that 'sounds', be it interrupted silence, teeming radio signals, standard instruments employed in tonal exploration (including Cage's own prepared pianos) or that ongoing, undifferentiated improvisation that we habitually call noise. Cage remains the pivotal force, and the fulcrum for all 22 composers gathered together on these two CDs: most selections are either by him (texts or music), inspired by him or dedicated to him. His spirit is felt everywhere, yet rather than stifling or inhibiting, it served to liberate a veritable flood of invention. Indeed, it is both touching and apposite that Cage's legendary 4'33" of inhabited silence be entrusted to the late Frank Zappa who, the odd shuffle notwithstanding, simply sits by and lets it all happen. Laurie Anderson's quietly hypnotic *Cunningham Stories* (to texts by Cage himself) arrive in four short instalments, while the first CD ends with Yoko Ono's lengthy but accessible *Georgia Stone*, a montage comprising culturally significant voices (John Lennon, Martin Luther King, unnamed victims of political oppression, etc.), rhetorical sound patterns and sundry musical impressions. Then there are Meredith Monk's outlandish vocalizations, Ryuichi Sakamoto's ear-stretching *Haiku FM*, David Tudor's punishing *Webwork*, the mournful double-bass drone of *art is self-alteration is Cage is ...* by Larry Austin and Robert Black, after one of Cage's own key concepts. Koch International's method harbours an extra ace, one that you too can play. Each work is split into a number of tracks, which means that the first disc has 11 pieces divided by 98; the second a further 11 divided by 85. The idea is that by using the 'random' button on your CD player, you can prompt a totally 'new' programme consisting of freshly juxtaposed extracts from any of the 22 works included – a sort of DIY Cage kit, and immense fun to play with. Self-recommending for creative bold spirits.

New review

Cage Music for Three[a]. Eight Whiskus[b]. Four[c]. **Joan La Barbara** (sngr); [c]**John Cage** (voc); [ac]**Leonard Stein** (pf/voc/perc); [ac]**William Winant** (perc). Music & Arts Ⓔ CD875 (50 minutes: DDD).

This is a memento of an extraordinary occasion – John Cage's last concert appearance on July 23rd, 1992, in the Summerstage outdoor series held in New York's Central Park. It nearly failed to take place as a result of torrential rain for most of the day. Some of the introductory announcements are included, along with the three works performed, and the applause demonstrates the warmth with which Cage himself was received. Joan La Barbara has already recorded *Eight Whiskus* (pronounced 'Whiskoos', by the way) on a varied CD of Cage's vocal works with the same percussionist. The version here lasts less than five minutes and, as Cage warned La Barbara when he wrote it for her in 1984, it contains four-letter words in the text. *Music for Three* is one of a series of pieces for various groups defined by the number of players involved, some already recorded: this version lasts just over ten minutes. The major part of the CD is the première of *Four*, specially composed for the occasion and lasting almost half an hour. The three players joined by Cage had to choose 12 different sounds, including their own voices, and perform these within the time-scale provided. This is vintage Cage, naturally beyond criticism at this Last Supper of the American avant-garde, and there is perceptible interaction between the performers. The pace is leisurely, the unexpected is expected, and – which is not always the case in Cage performances – the amount of activity justifies the time-scale. You would hardly know this was an outside event from this recording, which everyone interested in Cage will want to possess.

Additional recommendation ...

...A flower[ad]. Mirakus[a]. Eight Whiskus[a]. The Wonderful Widow of Eighteen Springs[ad]. Nowth Upon Nacht[ad]. Sonnekus[f]. Forever and Sunsmell[ace]. Solo for Voice 49[a]. Solo for Voice 52[b]. Solo for Voice 67[a]. Music for Two (by One)[a]. **Joan La Barbara** ([a]voc/[b]perc); [c]**Scott Evans** (perc); **William Winant** ([d]pf/[e]perc); [f]**Leonard Stein** (pf). New Albion Ⓔ NA035CD (56 minutes: DDD: 9/91).

Cage Roaratorio: An Irish Circus on Finnegans Wake[a]. Laughtears[b]. Writing for the Second Time through Finnegans Wake[a]. **John Cage,** [b]**Klaus Schöning** (spkrs); [a]**Joe Heaney** (sngr); [a]**Matt Malloy** (fl); [a]**Seamus Ennis** (uilleann pipes); [a]**Paddy Glackin** (vn); [a]**Peadher Mercier,** [a]**Mel Mercier** (bodhrans). Mode Records Ⓔ Mode 28/9 (two discs: 149 minutes: DDD: 10/94).   Ⓖ

Cage's *Roaratorio* was performed at the Proms for his seventy-fifth birthday in 1987. Those in the Royal Albert Hall were entranced by the multiplicity of acoustical activity on to which was superimposed the visual exhilaration of Merce Cunningham's dance group. Some merely listening to the radio at home wrote to the BBC to complain of a concert which sounded like crossed wavelengths with liberal helpings of static and feedback. It is a rich assembly of involvements all stemming from James Joyce's last so-called novel. Cage started by making a text – a special kind of abridgement of the original – called *Writing for the Second Time through Finnegans Wake*. (This is published in its own right and is recorded here on its own by Cage, who also speaks it as the continuous element in *Roaratorio*.) Then Klaus Schöning of West German Radio in Cologne asked him if he would like to put music to it to make a kind of radio play. So Cage decided to superimpose on to the text specially recorded sounds referred to in *Finnegans Wake*, as well as a live group of Irish folk musicians. These genuine folk artists were surprised to find that they were expected to perform, like Merce Cunningham's dancers, regardless of whatever else happened to be going on at the time, but they soon got the hang of it. The traditional pieces they played are listed in the magnificent CD booklet, which has full texts of Cage's Joyce rewrite (still indestructibly Joycean) plus the text of the recorded interview between him and Schöning. *Roaratorio* was a great success in Schöning's radio series and won the Carl Sozuka Prize, with international broadcasts and performances to follow. All this took place in 1979 and what Mode have now released is the original production from West German Radio, which was supported by a variety of other organizations and required a large cast of technicians. *Roaratorio* is one of Cage's most attractive larger assemblages, completely logical if one approaches it, as he did, through the philosophy and sound-world of Joyce. Anyone interested in Joyce is bound to find it illuminating. The piece is a landmark in the composer's later output, and a credit to all involved in its elaborate realization.

Further listening ...

...Atlas eclipticalis. Concert for Piano and Orchestra[a]. [a]**Joe Kubera** (pf); **SEM Ensemble Orchestra / Petr Kotik.** Wergo John Cage Edition WER6216-2 (12/93).

...Winter Music[a]. Atlas eclipticalis[b]. [b]**Eberhard Blum** (fls); [a]**Mats Persson,** [a]**Steffen Schleiermacher,** [a]**Kristine Scholz,** [a]**Nils Vigeland** (pfs). Hat-Hut Now Series ARTCD6141 (10/94).

...String Quartet in four parts. Music for four. **Arditti Quartet.** Mode Records mode27 (12/93).

...Ten. Ryoanji. Fourteen. **Ives Ensemble.** Hat-Hut Hat Now Series ARTCD6159 (2/96).

...13 Harmonies. *Coupled with* **Zahab** Verging Lightfall. **Roger Zahab** (vn); **Eric Moe** (pf/hpd/org). Koch International Classics 37130-2 (11/95).

...Atlas eclipticalis. **Eberhard Blum** (fls). Hat Hut Now Series ARTCD6111 (12/93).

...In a Landscape. Music for Marcel Duchamp. Souvenir. A Valentine out of season. Suite for Toy Piano. Bacchanale. Prelude for Meditation. Dream. **Stephen Drury** (keybds). Catalyst 09026-61980-2 (7/95).

...Bacchanale for Prepared Piano. In a Landscape. Daughters of the Lonesame Isle. The Seasons. Suite for Toy Piano. Ophelia. In the Name of the Holocaust. Music for Piano No. 2. **Margaret Leng Tan** (pfs). New Albion NA070CD (7/95).

...Music for Marcel Duchamp. Bacchanale. The Perilous Night. *Coupled with* **Ives** Three Page Sonata. **Sessions** Piano Sonata No. 3, "Kennedy Sonata". **William Grant Naboré** (pf). Doron Music DRC3002.

...Etudes Australes. **Grete Sultan** (pf). Wergo WER6152-2 (7/93).

...Bacchanale for Prepared Piano *Coupled with.* **Barber** Ballade, Op. 46. **Beach** Five Improvisations, Op. 148. **Bernstein** Five Anniversaries. **Copland** Four Piano Blues. **Gershwin** Three Preludes. **Gottschalk** Manchega, RO143. Le Banjo, RO22. **M. Gould** Boogie Woogie Etude. **Joplin** The Entertainer. Maple Leaf Rag. **MacDowell** New England Idylls, Op. 62. **Nancarrow** Prelude. **Michel Legrand** (pf). Erato 4509-96386-2 (7/95).

...Souvenir. *Coupled with* **Pärt** Annum per annum. Pari intervalli. Mein Weg hat Gipfel und Wellentäler. Trivium I-III. **Scelsi** In nomine lucis. **Christoph Maria Moosmann** (org). New Albion NA074CD (2/96).

...The Perilous Night (1944)[a]. Four walls (1944)[b]. [b]**Joan La Barbara** (sop); **Margaret Leng Tan** ([a]prepared pf; [b]pf). New Albion NA037CD (1/91).

...20 Sonatas and Interludes for Prepared Piano. Music for Marcel Duchamp. The Wonderful Widow of Eighteen Springs[a]. [a]**Gerald English** (ten); **Nigel Butterley** (prepared pf). Tall Poppies TP025 (10/94).

Raffaele Calace
Italian 1863-1934

Suggested listening ...

...Works for Mandolin – Danza Spagnola, Op. 105[a]. Mattino d'autunno, Op. 164[a]. Concerto a plettro, Op. 155[a]. Impressionismo, "Momento lirico", Op. 145[b]. Intermezzo, "Mesto pensiero", Op. 146[b]. Suite[b] – Pavana, Op. 54; Bolero, Op. 26; Mazurka, Op. 41; Tarantella, Op. 18. Impressioni Orientali, Op. 132[b]. [a]**Raffaele Calace Quintet;** [b]**Brescia Mandolin and Guitar Orchestra / Claudio Mandonico.** Fonè 91FO2 (12/93).

Antonio Caldara
Italian c1670-1736

Suggested listening ...

...Cantatas[a]: Medea in Corinto. Soffri, mio caro Alcino. D'improvviso. Vicino a un rivoletto. 12 Suonate da camera, Op. 2 – No. 3 in D major. 12 Suonate a 3, Op. 1 – No. 5 in E minor. **Il Seminario Musicale / Gérard Lesne** ([a]alto). Virgin Classics Veritas VC7 59058-2 (11/91). ✧

...Madrigals – Fra pioggie, nevi e gelo. Dell'uom la vita. Fugge di Lot a moglie. Vedi co'l crine sciolto. Là su morbide. De piacari. Cantatas – Lungi dall'idol mio; Il Dario; La forriera del giorno; Stella ria; Il Gelsomino. **Wren Baroque Soloists / Martin Elliott.** Unicorn-Kanchana DKPCD9130 (2/93). ✧ ⓖ

Charles Camilleri
Maltese 1931-

New review

Camilleri Morphogenesis. Wine of Peace. L'amour de Dieu. Invocation to the Creator. **Kevin Bowyer** (org). Unicorn-Kanchana ⓕ DKPCD9151 (58 minutes: DDD: 11/95). Played on the organ of Ely Cathedral. Recorded 1993.

It may seem odd that a composer who has deliberately set out to create a 'pan-Mediterranean' musical language, fusing East and West, should be best known for his organ music – an instrument almost wholly associated with west European, specifically Christian, culture. But following a revelatory experience hearing Messiaen played in London on the Royal Festival Hall organ, he clearly saw in the instrument a personal means of expression. Any specifically Messiaen traits are confined to the exploration of exotic rhythmic patterns, most obviously in the *Invocation to the Creator* which, without undermining Camilleri's tempo markings, Bowyer manages to condense from the score's suggested length of 16 minutes into less than 13. Otherwise the language is very much Camilleri's own. Cultural juxtaposition is vividly depicted in *L'amour de Dieu* where the right hand describes a quasi-plainchant melody, the left hand static, oriental folk rhythms, and the pedals provide an organized rhythmic cycle rotating a symbolically significant three times during the course of the piece – the professed intention of the work being to convey spiritual and earthly reconciliation – and all that in a little over three minutes. At well over half an hour *Morphogenesis* is a far more substantial piece, its five movements each attempting to portray "the vast solitudes in which spaceship-earth navigates and all its quarrelsome denizens become one kin". Make of that what you will. Kevin Bowyer powerfully reveals the true essence of Camilleri's work. This is a thought-provoking and immensely stimulating disc.

Further listening ...

...Piano Concertos –No. 1, "Mediterranean"; No. 2, "Maqam"; No. 3, "Leningrad". **André de Groote** (pf); **Bournemouth Symphony Orchestra / Michael Laus.** Unicorn-Kanchana DKPCD9150 (11/94).

...Choral Works – Unum Deum. Requiem. Missa brevis. Sonus Spiritus. Lumen nivis. Pacem in Maribus. Amen. Malta Yok! Celestial Voices. **Joyful Company of Singers / Peter Broadbent.** Unicorn-Kanchana DKPCD9157 (3/95).

Thomas Campion   British 1567-1620

Suggested listening ...

...Ayres – Beauty, since you so much desire. Love me or not. Your faire lookes. Never love unlesse you can. O never to be moved. The sypres curten of the night is spread. Awake thou spring of speaking grace. Come you pretty false-ey'd wanton. So tyr'd are all my thoughts. Fire, fire. Pin'd I am and like to dye. Author of light. See where she flies. Faire if you expect admiring. Shall I come sweet love to thee? It fell on a sommers daie. Kinde are her answers. Beauty is but a painted hell. Sweet exclude me not. Are you what your faire lookes expresse? I care not for these ladies. Never weather-beaten saile. **Drew Minter** (alto); **Paul O'Dette** (lte). Harmonia Mundi HMU90 7023 (6/91). ✍

...Author of light, revive my dying spright. Never weather-beaten saile more willing bent to shore. The sypres curten of the night is spread. *Coupled with works by* **Ford, Danyel, Rosseter, Dowland** and **A. Holborne** Michael Chance (alto); **Christopher Wilson** (lte). Chandos Chaconne CHAN0538 (10/94). ✍   Ⓖ

André Campra   French 1660-1744

Campra Idoménée. **Bernard Delétré** (bass) Idoménée; **Sandrine Piau** (sop) Electre; **Monique Zanetti** (sop) Ilione; **Jean-Paul Fouchécourt** (bass) Idamante; **Marie Boyer** (mez) Venus; **Jérôme Correas** (bass) Eole, Neptune, Jealousy, Nemesis; **Richard Dugay** (ten) Arcas; **Jean-Claude Sarragosse** (bass) Arbas, Protée; **Mary Saint-Palais** (sop) Cretan Girl; **Anne Pichard** (sop) First Shepherd; **Anne Mopin** (sop) Second Shepherd, Trojan Girl; **Les Arts Florissants Chorus and Orchestra / William Christie.** Harmonia Mundi Ⓕ HMC90 1396/8 (three discs: 166 minutes: DDD: 9/92). ✍ Notes, text and translation included. Recorded 1991.   Ⓖ

André Campra was one of the leading lights on the French musical scene between Lully's death in 1687 and Rameau's operatic début in 1733. He was a pioneer of *opéra-ballet* and wrote a significant corpus of sacred music and several successful *tragédies en musiques*. One of these was *Idoménée* which was first staged in 1712 and revived in 1731 in this reworked version. Campra's librettist was Antoine Danchet whose text was later to serve as a prime source for *Idomeneo*, Mozart's *opera seria*. Campra's score is an attractive one with few weak moments and the same may be said of Danchet's adaptation of Crébillon's contemporaneous play of the same name. Campra shows much skill in his writing for the human voice and a greater degree of sympathy than some of his fellow French composers. There are passages of finely sustained dialogue, notably between Idoménée and his son Idamante (Act 2, Scene 4), and Idoménée and Priam's daughter, Ilione. The instrumental writing, which plays a prominent part in the texture throughout the opera is also very effective; Act 3, for instance, contains a captivating sailors' dance for piccolos, drums and strings. This opera quickly proves itself deserving of the loving attention paid it by Christie and his forces. Supple choruses, colourful *divertissements* and a profusion of beguiling airs sung by a strong cast of soloists set the seal on a fine issue.

Further listening ...

...Messe de Requiem. **Elisabeth Baudry, Monique Zanetti** (sops); **Josep Benet** (alto); **John Elwes** (ten); **Stephen Varcoe** (bar); **La Chapelle Royale Chorus and Orchestra / Philippe Herreweghe.** Harmonia Mundi HMC90 1251 (9/87). ✍

Joseph Canteloube   French 1879-1957

New review

Canteloube Chants d'Auvergne – Serie 1: La pastoura als camps; Baïlèro; L'ïo de rotso; Ound' onorèn gorda; Obal, din lou Limouzi; Serie 2: Pastourelle; L'Antouèno; La pastrouletta è lo chibalie; La delïssádo; N'aï pas iéu de mio; Lo calhé; Serie 3: Lo fiolaïré; Passo pel prat; Lou boussu; Brezairola; Maluros qu'o uno fenno. Serie 4: Jou l'pount d'o Mirabel; Oï, ayaï; Pour l'enfant; Chut, chut; Pastorale; Lou coucut; Serie 5: Postouro sé tu m'aymo; Quand z-éyro petituono; Té, l'co tèl; Uno jionto postouro; Hél beyla-z-y-dau fél; Obal, din lo combuèlo; Là-haut, sur le rocher; Lou diziou bé.

Villa-Lobos Bachianas Brasileiras No. 5. **Dame Kiri Te Kanawa** (sop); **English Chamber Orchestra / Jeffrey Tate.** Double Decca Ⓜ 444 995-2DF2 (two discs: 111 minutes: DDD: 1/96). Notes, text and translation included. Recorded 1982-3. Ⓖ

Although Canteloube's collection of the *Chants d'Auvergne* is well represented in the current catalogue,. Dame Kiri Te Kanawa's richly sensuous approach to these delightful songs is undoubtedly very seductive, especially when the accompaniments by Jeffrey Tate and the ECO are so warmly supportive and Decca's Kingsway Hall, London sound so opulent. Her account of the most famous number, "Baïlèro", must be the most relaxed on record, yet she sustains its repetitions with a sensuous, gentle beauty of line, supported by lovely wind playing from the orchestra which seems to float in the air. There is a resonance given to the sound, which means that certain of the brighter, more obviously folksy numbers, lose a little of their rustic sharpness. None the less there is no question that the overall effect is very appealing, particularly when Dame Kiri's voice (recorded in the early 1980s) is so young and fresh and the sound so lustrously beautiful. As an encore we are offered another famous lollipop which she makes her own in the same languorous, Scheherazade-like manner – the Villa-Lobos *Bachianas Brasileiras* No. 5, an "Aria" for soprano and cellos. She sings this in Portuguese and the result is ravishing, almost decadent at its softly intoned reprise. The following "Dança" from the same piece is hardly less enticing.

Additional recommendations ...

...Chants d'Auvergne – excerpts. **Marvis Martin** (sop); **Auvergne Orchestra / Jean-Jacques Kantorow.** Denon Ⓕ CO-75862 (51 minutes: DDD: 11/94).

...Chants d'Auvergne – excerpts. **Dawn Upshaw** (sop); **Orchestra of the Opéra de Lyon / Kent Nagano.** Erato Ⓕ 4509-96559-2 (47 minutes: DDD: 2/95).

André Caplet
French 1878-1925

New review

Caplet Suite Persane – Nihavend. Légende pour Orchestre. Marche triomphale et pompière.
Debussy (orch. Caplet) Children's Corner. Pagodes. Suite bergamasque – Clair de lune. **Rheinland-Pfalz State Philharmonic Orchestra / Leif Segerstam.** Marco Polo Ⓕ 8 223751 (56 minutes: DDD: 9/95). Recorded 1987.

The valuable services that André Caplet rendered his friend Debussy – besides the pieces orchestrated here he also completed *Gigues* and *Boîte à joujoux*, scored the *Martyre de Saint-Sébastien* and conducted its first performance – have overshadowed his own gifts as a composer. Colour plays a large part in Caplet's early (1901) *Nihavend*, despite its having originally been scored only for double wind quintet: it is a kind of Rimskian passacaglia or set of variations on a simple, and apparently authentic, Persian melody. The *Légende* of four years later is also an orchestral expansion, from a nonet: a solo saxophone has a prominent role in both versions. Highly charged emotionally and clearly structured (though rather too long), it is disquieting in mood: like the previous piece, it has nothing Debussian about it. The Debussy items are well done, especially *Pagodes*, which culminates in a shimmering web of exotic sound with its combination of celesta, string trills and *glissandos* in contrary motion from two harps. This orchestra's violins are not always totally secure in the upper register, but in general the performances are very persuasive.

Further listening ...

...Conte fantastique[a]. Two Divertissements[b]. Les prières[c]. Two Sonnets[d]. Septet[c]. [ce]**Sharon Coste,** [de]**Sandrine Piau** (sops); [e]**Sylvie Deguy** (mez); [abcd]**Laurence Cabel** (hp); [ace]**Musique Oblique Ensemble.** Harmonia Mundi HMC90 1417 (2/93).

...Myrrha[ade]. Tout est lumière[b]. *Coupled with* **Debussy** Printemps[b]. **Ravel** L'aurore[d]. Matinée de Provence[b]. Tout est lumière[c]. Les bayadères[b]. La nuit[c]. [a]**Sharon Coste,** [b]**Brigitte Desnoues,** [c]**Gaële Le Roi** (sops); [d]**Marc Duguay** (ten); [e]**Jean-François Lapointe** (bar); **Chorus and Orchestra of the Sorbonne, Paris / Jacques Grimbert.** Marco Polo 8 223755 (10/95).

Manuel Cardoso
Portuguese 1566-1650

Suggested listening ...

...Missa Regina caeli. Sitivit anima mea. Tulerunt lapides. Non mortui. *Coupled with* **D. Lôbo** Missa pro defunctis a 8. Audivi vocem de caelo. Pater peccavi. **The Sixteen / Harry Christophers.** Collins Classics 1407-2 (8/94).

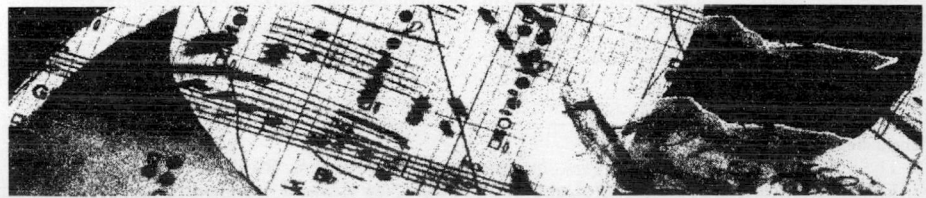

...Requiem. Non mortui. Sitivit anima mea. Mulier quae erat. Nos autem gloriari. Magnificat Secundi Toni a 5. **The Tallis Scholars / Peter Phillips.** Gimell CDGIM021 (10/90).

...Magnificat Primi Toni. *Coupled with* **Lienas** Coenantibus autem. **Victoria** Et egressus est. Ecce vidimus eum. Amicus meus. Unus ex discipulis. Eram quasi agnus. Seniores populi. Benedictus Deus Dominus Israel. Vere languores nostros. (attrib.) **Morales** Vigilate et orate. **Brito** Lamentations of Jeremiah – Incipit lamentatio Jeremiae. **F. Vásquez** In te, Domine, speravi. **La Colombina.** Accent ACC9394D (8/94).

...Lamentatio. Magnificat secundi toni. *Coupled with* **Lôbo** Audivi vocem da caelo. Pater peccavi. **Magalhães** Vidi acquam. Missa O soberana luz. Commissa mea pavesco. **Fonseca** Beata viscera. **Trosylho** Circumdederunt me. **Escobar** Clamabat autem mulier. **Ars Nova / Bo Holten.** Naxos 8 553310 (3/96).

Richard de Bellengues Cardot   French 1380-1470

Suggested listening ...

...Pour une fois et pour toute. *Coupled with works by* **Anonymous, Bittering, Binchois, Dunstable, Fontaine, Johannes de Lymburga, Legrant, Machaut, Power** and **Velut. Gothic Voices / Christopher Page.** Hyperion CDA66783 (1/96). *See review in the Collections section; refer to the Index to Reviews.*

Giacomo Carissimi   Italian 1605-1674

New review

Carissimi Jephte.
Marazzoli San Tomaso. Per il giorno della resurrezione. **Cantus Cölln** (Johanna Koslowsky, Maria Cristina Kiehr, Mona Spägele, sops; Gerd Türk, Wilfried Jochens, tens; Stephan Schreckenberger, bass; Carsten Lohff, hpd/org) / **Konrad Junghänel.** Deutsche Harmonia Mundi Ⓕ 05472 77322-2 (64 minutes: DDD: 10/95). Texts and translations included. 🎵 Recorded 1994.

Carissimi's name is inseparable from the origins and early history of the oratorio in Rome. Based for the most part on incidents from the Old Testament set to Latin texts, his best-known works in the genre attracted a wide public and were copied and transmitted throughout Italy and beyond. One of their distinctive features is the way that Carissimi divides up the text so that the narrative role is split between different characters and even, as in *Jephte*, is sometimes assigned to the chorus. Konrad Junghänel has responded sensitively to the possibilities of lively characterization that this structural feature encourages, and has selected his soloists with care. There is some fine singing here, notably from Johanna Koslowsky, who also adds improvised ornamentation with style and a good sense of period sound. The well-known final chorus, famous if only from Handel's re-use of it in *Samson*, was regarded in the seventeenth century as a masterpiece of vivid expression; it is rendered here with quiet conviction rather than theatrical intensity. Marazzoli's music is constantly being reassessed as new works come to light, but from the two oratorios on this disc it is clear that he was the equal of Carissimi in this genre. They are performed with authority and intelligence in a rather understated manner that from the rhetorical point of view is at times a little pedestrian for all that they are characterized by clear diction, technical proficiency and structural control. Once again these performers have uncovered hidden gems, and for that alone this CD is to be welcomed.

Additional recommendation ...

...Oratorios – Jepthe; Judicium Salomonis; Jonas. **Gabrieli Consort and Players / Paul McCreesh** (bass vn). Meridian Ⓕ CDE84304 (53 minutes: 7/87). 🎵

Further listening ...

...Vanitas vanitatum II. *Coupled with works by* **Marazzoli, Mazzocchi, Rossi, V. Mazzocchi, Landi** and **Anonymous. Tragicomedia / Stephen Stubbs.** Teldec Das Alte Werk 4509-98410-2 (3/96). 🎵 *See review in the Collections section; refer to the Index to Reviews.*

John Alden Carpenter   American 1876-1951

Suggested listening ...

...Piano Sonata No. 1 in G minor. Diversions. Nocturne. Polonaise américaine. Impromptu. Tango américain. Minuet. Litle Dancer. Little Indian. Twilight Reverie. Danza. **Denver Oldham** (pf). New World NW328/9-2 (7/88).

Edwin Carr   New Zealand 1926-

Suggested listening ...

...The Snow Maiden.*Coupled with works by* **Farquhar, C. Blake, A. Ritchie, A. Watson, Lilburn, Whitehead, Jenny McLeod** and **Pruden** New Zealand Symphony Orchestra /

Kenneth Young. Continuum (special price) CCD1073 (5/96). *See review in the Collections section; refer to the Index to Reviews.*

Antonio Carreira

Portuguese c1530-before 1597

Suggested listening ...
...Canção a Quatro glosada. *Coupled with works by* **A. de Cabezón, Ximénez, Coelho, H. de Cabezón** and **Cabanilles** Sophie Yates (hpd). Chandos Chaconne CHAN0560 (11/94). *See review in the Collections section; refer to the Index to Reviews.*

Teresa Carreño

Venezuelan 1853-1917

Suggested listening ...
...String Quartet in B minor. *Coupled with works by* **C. Schumann, Beach, Tailleferre, Boulanger, Mendelssohn-Hensel** and **Chaminade** Joseph Roche, Robert Zelnick (vns); **Tamas Strasser** (va); **Camilla Heller** (vc). Vox Box 115845-2 (10/94). *See review in the Collections section; refer to the Index to Reviews.*

Elliott Carter

American 1908-

Carter Gra[b]. Enchanted Preludes[ad]. Duo[cf]. Scrivo in Vento[a]. Changes[e]. Con Leggerezza Pensosa: Omaggio a Italo Calvino[bcd]. Riconoscenza per Goffredo Petrassi[c]. Cello Sonata[dg]. **The Group for Contemporary Music** ([a]Harvey Sollberger, fl; [b]Charles Neidich, cl; [c]Rolf Schulte, vn; [d]Fred Sherry, vc; [e]David Starobin, gtr; [f]Martin Goldray, [g]Charles Wuorinen, pfs). Bridge Ⓟ BCD9044 (79 minutes: DDD: 12/94). Recorded 1992-4.

The major work here is the *Duo* for violin and piano (1974), an epic exploration of co-existent incompatibilities which has the expressive scope and structural command of great drama. These may seem extravagant claims on behalf of a score some have found too unremitting, too gritty in its fractured syntax and forceful rhetoric. True, it takes time for the larger eloquence and coherence of the *Duo* to make their effect but, once perceived, they are irresistible. This performance starts with the violinist in danger of exaggerating the score's unusually detailed expressive markings, but it builds well and, as the piano comes increasingly into action, the co-ordination and interplay of the players arouses increasing admiration. The other major work, the Cello Sonata (1948) also makes a strong impression: a technical breakthrough for the composer, it is unambiguously direct and potent for the listener, despite an over-resonant recording. The recorded balance in the *Duo* (same venue, but different piano) is more successful. The remaining six works are all miniatures by comparison, and show Carter's extraordinarily spontaneous inventiveness reaching right up to *Gra* (1993), a witty, whimsical eightieth birthday present for Lutosławski.

Further listening ...
...Piano Concerto[a]. Variations for Orchestra. [a]**Ursula Oppens** (pf); **Cincinnati Symphony Orchestra / Michael Gielen.** New World NW347-2 (4/87).
...Partita. *Coupled with* **Berio** Continuo. **Takemitsu** Visions. **Chicago Symphony Orchestra / Daniel Barenboim.** Teldec 4509-99596-2 (8/95). *See review under Berio; refer to the Index to Reviews.*
...Emblems. The harmony of morning. Heart not so heavy as mine. Musicians wrestle everywhere. *Coupled with* **Amlin** Time's Caravan. **McKinley** Four Text Settings. **Sheng** Two folksongs from Chinhai. **John Oliver Chorale / John Oliver.** Koch International Classics 37178-2 (5/95).

Ferdinando Carulli

Italian 1770-1841

Suggested listening ...
...Andante affetuoso, Op. 320. *Coupled with works by* **Soler, Giuliani, Sor** and **Mertz** Marta Almajano (sop); **José Miguel Moreno** (gtr). Glossa GCD920202 (2/96). *See review in the Collections section; refer to the Index to Reviews.*

Robert Carver

British c1490-1550

Suggested listening ...
...Missa Dum sacrum mysterium. O bone Jesu. Gaude flore virginali. **Cappella Nova / Alan Tavener.** ASV Gaudeamus CDGAU124 (10/91).
...Missa L'Homme armé. Mass for Six Voices. **Cappella Nova / Alan Tavener.** ASV Gaudeamus CDGAU126 (10/91).
...Missa Fera pessima. Missa Pater creator omnium. **Cappella Nova / Alan Tavener.** ASV Gaudeamus CDGAU127 (5/92).

Alfredo Casella   Italian 1883-1947

Suggested listening ...
...Paganiniana, Op. 65. *Coupled with works by* **Busoni** and **Martucci** La Scala Philharmonic
  Orchestra, Milan / **Riccardo Muti.** Sony Classical SK53280 (4/94). *See review under Busoni; refer
  to the Index to Reviews.*   ⒼⒼⒼ
...Harp Sonata, Op. 68. *Coupled with works by* **Rosetti, Spohr, Debussy, Damase, Tournier,
  Prokofiev, Renié** and **Fauré.** Naoko Yoshino (hp). Philips 446 064-2PH (2/96). *See review in
  the Collections section; refer to the Index to Reviews.*

John Casken   British 1949-

Suggested listening ...
...Cello Concerto. **Northern Sinfonia / Heinrich Schiff** (vc). Collins 20th Century Plus 2006-2 (6/93).
...Darting the Skiff. Maharal Dreaming. Vaganza. **Northern Sinfonia / John Casken.** Collins
  Classics 1424-2 (5/95).   Ⓖ

Mario Castelnuovo-Tedesco   Italian/American 1895-1968

Castelnuovo-Tedesco Guitar Concerto No. 1 in D major, Op. 99.
Rodrigo Concierto de Aranjuez.
Villa-Lobos Guitar Concerto. **Norbert Kraft** (gtr); **Northern Chamber Orchestra / Nicholas Ward.**
  Naxos Ⓢ 8 550729 (60 minutes: DDD: 4/94). Recorded 1992.
The time has long passed when it was possible to point to any one recording of any of these concertos
(the Rodrigo in particular) as 'The Best'; as with players, one can only discern a 'top bracket' within
which choice depends finally on personal preference – or allegiance to one's favourite performer, or
indeed with the other works on the disc. Norbert Kraft's accounts of these concertos takes its place
therein. In this recording Kraft is placed forwardly enough for every detail to be heard, but not to
create an impression of artificiality. The Northern Chamber Orchestra plays with freshness and are
alert to every detail and the beautifully clear recording catches it faithfully.
Further listening ...
...Violin Concerto No. 2, "I profeti". *Coupled with* **Ferguson** Violin Sonata No. 1, Op. 2.
  Françaix String Trio in C major. **K. Khachaturian** Violin Sonata in G minor, Op. 1. **Jascha
  Heifetz** (vn); **Joseph de Pasquale** (va); **Gregor Piatigorsky** (vc); **Lilian Steuber** (pf); **Los Angeles
  Philharmonic Orchestra / Alfred Wallenstein.** RCA Victor Gold Seal GD87872 (9/90).   ⒼⒼⒼ

Ricardo Castillo   Guatemalian 1891-1966

Suggested listening ...
...Sinfonieta para Orquesta. Xibalbá. Guatemala I and II. *Coupled with* **Martínez-Sobral**
  Acuarelas Chapinas. **Moscow Symphony Orchestra / Antonio de Almeida.** Marco Polo 8 223710
  (5/95).

Alfredo Catalani   Italian 1854-1893

Suggested listening ...
...La Wally. **Soloists; Turin Lyric Chorus; Monte Carlo National Opera Orchestra / Fausto Cleva.**
  Decca 425 417-2DM2 (2/90).

Francesco Cavalli   Italian 1602-1676

New review
Cavalli Musiche sacre concernenti messa – Vespro della Beata Vergine. **Concerto Palatino / Bruce
  Dickey, Charles Toet.** Harmonia Mundi Ⓕ HMC90 5219/20 (two discs: 120 minutes: DDD: 5/96).
  ✒ Texts and translations included. Recorded 1994.   Ⓖ
Most of the music on this record is taken from Cavalli's *Musiche sacre* of 1656, a miscellaneous
collection of pieces which reflect his decades of involvement with St Mark's Basilica in Venice, an
association which began when he joined the choir as a chorister in 1616. In this sense the Vespers
music presented here is not to be thought of as a single unified work, but rather as a sequence of
movements, arranged in the correct liturgical order, which could have been heard at the Basilica at
Second Vespers on any feast of the Virgin. Comparisons with Monteverdi's *Vespers* of 1610 are
inevitable (he was, after all, Cavalli's teacher for a quarter of a century), and there can hardly be any
doubt that Cavalli knew the older work (a debt discreetly acknowledged by direct quotation in

"Laetatus sum"). The most important legacies are the traditional alternation style of psalm setting (here recast in a more modern idiom), common throughout north Italy but particularly associated with Venice, and the richness of the instrumental and vocal palette. As Bruce Dickey's informative notes explain, there are no indications in the *Musiche sacre* itself that cornetts are to be used; his decision to use them here to double the soprano lines in the tutti sections and occasionally to substitute for the violins on obbligato lines seems entirely justified both in terms of artistic results and also what is known of Venetian practice at this time. The effect, faultless and majestic as ever (Dickey surely remains without peer among cornettists), is well matched by some very elegant string-playing, shown off to particularly good advantage not only in the Vespers sequence itself but also in a number of canzonas and sonatas that have been inserted, following contemporary practice, as antiphon substitutes. Most of the vocal parts in these pieces were written for soloists, with the occasionally contrasting full sections clearly marked in the original edition. The team of experienced singers who have been assembled here is fully up to the task. The overall effect is both stunning and revelatory, an authoritative reminder of the quality of Cavalli's sacred music, so often overlooked in favour of his works for the stage. The recording is also excellent, sensitively realized in a warmly resonant acoustic that could almost be St Mark's Basilica itself.

Further listening ...
...Calisto. **Soloists; Concerto Vocale / René Jacobs.** Harmonia Mundi HMC90 1515/7. ✐ Ⓖ
...Calisto (realized Leppard). **Soloists; Glyndebourne Festival Chorus; London Philharmonic Orchestra / Raymond Leppard.** Decca 436 216-2DMO2.

Friedrich Cerha
Austrian 1926

Suggested listening ...
...Eine Art Chansons – 60 short songs. **Heinz Karl Gruber** (bar); **Robin McGee** (db); **Martin Jones** (pf); **James Holland** (perc). Largo 5126 (9/94).

Pierre Certon
French c1510-1572

Suggested listening ...
...La, la, la, je ne l'ose dire. *Coupled with works by* **Clemens non Papa, G. Coste, Compère, De Bussy, Fresneau, Gombert, Guiard, Hesdin, Josquin Desprez, La Rue, Ninot le Petit, Pipelare, Sermisy, Vermont le Jeune** and **Willaert** Clément Janequin Ensemble / **Dominique Visse.** Harmonia Mundi HMC90 1453 (5/95). *See review in the Collections section; refer to the Index to Reviews.*

Emmanuel Chabrier
French 1841-1894

Chabrier España. Suite pastorale. Joyeuse marche. Bourrée fantasque. Le Roi malgré lui – Fête polonaise; Danse slave. Gwendoline – Overture.
Roussel Suite in F major, Op. 33. **Detroit Symphony Orchestra / Paul Paray.** Mercury Ⓜ 434 303-2MM* (68 minutes: ADD). Recorded 1957-60. ⒼⒼⒼ

Paray's classic Chabrier collection radiates a truly life-enhancing spontaneity, an all-too-rare commodity in this day and age. His *España* has to be one of the most twinklingly good-humoured ever committed to disc – an account overflowing with rhythmic panache and unbuttoned exuberance – whilst the adorable *Suite pastorale* has rarely sounded so fresh-faced and sheerly disarming, even though Paray's very swift "Sous bois" does admittedly take some getting use to. The excerpts from *Le Roi malgré lui* are despatched with memorable theatrical charisma and huge gusto, qualities which extend to a blistering rendition of the remarkable, almost feverish overture to *Gwendoline*. But Paray reserves perhaps his finest achievement for the uproarious *Joyeuse marche* and *Bourrée fantasque* (an astonishingly quick-witted, vital conception). The orchestra respond with irrepressible spirit and characteristic Gallic poise, and the Mercury engineering astonishes in its intrepidly wide range of dynamic and full-blooded brilliance (just sample those wonderfully hefty bass-drum thwacks towards the end of *España*). All this and Roussel's bustling, neo-classical *Suite* too! An irresistible confection.

Additional recommendations ...
...Joyeuse marche. Suite pastorale. Bourrée fantasque. España. Gwendoline – Overture. Le roi malgré lui – Danse slave. **French National Orchestra / Armin Jordan.** Erato Ⓜ 4509-96370-2 (54 minutes: DDD).
...España. Suite pastorale. **Dukas** L'apprenti sorcier. La péri. **Ulster Orchestra / Yan Pascal Tortelier.** Chandos Ⓕ CHAN8852 (57 minutes: DDD: 2/91).

Chabrier Dix Pièces pittoresques. Pièces posthumes. Impromptu in C major. Trois valses romantiques (with Elizabeth Burley, pf). **Kathryn Stott** (pf). Unicorn-Kanchana Ⓕ DKPCD9158 (74 minutes: DDD: 5/95). Recorded 1994. ⒼⒼ

Listening to these delectable performances of piano pieces by Chabrier it is easy to see why alert musical minds like Ravel and Poulenc held him in such admiration. Cortot declared that his style of piano writing was unique; this may have been partly due to Chabrier's brilliance in keyboard improvisation, a talent which he was delighted to show off, and whose sometimes unstructured nature is illustrated in No. 8 of the *Pièces pittoresques* and, more particularly, in his early *Impromptu* in C major (described by Poulenc as "ravishing") and also in the "Caprice" of the *Pièces posthumes*. Throughout the disc Kathryn Stott is at her most sparkling and subtle best, with ebullient gaiety in the "Scherzo-valse", fragile delicacy in the gentle "Sous bois", rhythmic gusto in the "Danse villageoise", quiet lyricism in "Idylle" (all from the *Pièces pittoresques*), and wistful charm in "Feuillet d'album" and enchanting lightness in "Ballabile" (from the *Pièces posthumes*): there is freshness and imaginative nuance in evidence everywhere. She is joined by Elizabeth Burley in neat, scintillatingly spirited performances of the two-piano *Trois valses romantiques* – only the third of which really lives up to its title (with playful filigree decoration): the Second is coquettishly lyrical, the First just sheer fun. Aided by first-class recording, this is an immensely enjoyable disc.

Additional recommendations ...

...Dix Pièces pittoresques. Bourrée fantasque. Impromptu. **Richard McMahon** (pf). Pianissimo
Ⓜ PP10792 (52 minutes: DDD: 8/92).   ⒼⒼ

...Dix Pièces pittoresques[a]. Bourrée fantasque[a]. Cinq pièces posthumes[a]. Marche des Cipayes[a].
Impromptu[a]. Habanera[a]. Joyeuse Marche[ab]. Cortège burlesque[ab]. Trois valses romantiques[ab].
Air de Ballet[a]. Souvenirs de Munich[ab]. Suite de valses[a]. Souvenirs de Brunehaut[a]. Petite valse[a].
Capriccio in C sharp minor[a]. [a]**Pierre Barbizet,** [b]**Jean Hubeau** (pfs). Erato Ⓕ 4509-95309-2
(two discs: DDD).

New review

Chabrier Briséïs. **Joan Rodgers** (sop) Briséïs; **Mark Padmore** (ten) Hylas; **Simon Keenlyside** (bar)
Le Catéchiste; **Michael George** (bass) Stratocles; **Kathryn Harries** (mez) Thanastô; **Scottish Opera
Chorus; BBC Scottish Symphony Orchestra / Jean Yves Ossonce.** Hyperion Ⓕ CDA66803
(74 minutes: DDD: 8/95). Notes, text and translation included. Recorded live in 1994.

The name of Chabrier is so associated with vivacious, gaily extrovert music and with comic operas that we are apt to forget that he was a fervent admirer of Wagner, whose influence is patent in his opera *Gwendoline* and, to a rather lesser extent, in *Briséïs*, which was left with only its First Act complete. The story is based on Goethe's ballad *The Bride of Corinth*, but the original vampire heroine is replaced by a bride who returns from the dead to claim her promised husband. The rift between paganism and Christianity is bridged by her when she converts to the new faith to save her dying mother, but at the bitter price of taking a vow of chastity. What is Wagnerian in the opera is the overblown libretto (by the librettist of *Gwendoline*), Chabrier's ingeniously elaborate use of leitmotifs (though he rejected Wagnerian declamation as boring), some of the harmonies and modulations, and the very full orchestration at rapturous moments in the action. Nevertheless the basic language remains French, notably at the very start, with the young sailor Hylas on his galley, yearning for his beloved, and later when he sails away – a lovely passage sensitively handled here by the BBC's recording engineer (for this performance comes from a Radio 3 relay). The last scene of the act is very fine, with a lyrical orchestral prelude, a combination of the quasi-ecclesiastical pleas of the catechist with the grandiose gestures of the pagans, led by old Stratocles, Briseis's struggle between her vow to Hylas and her desire to save her mother, and a big triumphal conclusion. Joan Rodgers as the heroine copes brilliantly with her cruelly exacting, high-lying part. The initial scene between her and the fresh-voiced Mark Padmore is overlong by dramaturgical criteria, but both artists convincingly convey the two lovers' ecstasy. Except for Michael George, whose vibrato becomes disturbing, the whole cast's enunciation (in very good French) is admirably clear; and the orchestral playing is both eloquent and full of nuance. A decisive first British performance of this hitherto little-known work – which, however, Richard Strauss conducted in 1899 – and which modifies our overall view of Chabrier.

Further listening ...

...Piano Works, Volume 1 – Bourrée fantasque. Pièces posthumes – Ballabile; Caprice; Feuillet
d'album. Petite valse. Habanera. Dix Pièces pittoresques. **Georges Rabol** (pf). Naxos 8 553009
(2/95).

...Piano Works, Volume 2 – Marche des Cipayes. Julia, Op. 1. Impromptu in C major. Pièces
posthumes – Aubade; Ronde Champêtre. Capriccio in C sharp minor. Souvenirs de Brunehaut.
Georges Rabol (pf). Naxos 8 553010 (2/95).

...Piano Works, Volume 3 – España. Trois Valses romantiques. Prélude. Marche française. Cortège
burlesque[a]. Souvenirs de Munich: quadrille on themes from "Tristan und Isolde" (Wagner)[a]. Air
de ballet[a]. Suite de valses[a]. **Georges Rabol,** [a]**Sylvie Dugas** (pfs). Naxos 8 553080 (2/95).

...L'étoile – O petite étoile; Je suis Lazuli!. *Coupled with works by* **Sullivan, Lehár, Offenbach,
J. Strauss II, Romberg, Novello, Coward, Chabrier, Heuberger** and **Sullivan** Lesley
Garrett (sop); **Crouch End Festival Chorus; Royal Philharmonic Concert Orchestra / James
Holmes.** Silva Screen Classics SILKTVCD1 (2/96). *See review in the Collections section; refer to
the Index to Reviews.*

...Le Roi malgré lui. **Soloists; French Radio Chorus; French Radio New Philharmonic Orchestra /
Charles Dutoit.** Erato 2292-45792-2.

...Une education manquée. **Soloists; orchestra / Charles Bruck.** Le Roi malgré lui – Hélas, à l'esclavage. Chanson pour Jeanne. L'île heureuse. Gwendoline – Blonde aux yeux de pervenche. Ballade des gros dindons. Pastorale des cochons roses. **Christiane Castelli** (sop); **Hélène Boschi** (pf). Le Chant du Monde mono LDC278 1068* (8/92).

George Whitefield Chadwick
American 1854-1931

New review

Chadwick Symphonic Sketches. Melpomene – overture. Tam O'Shanter. **Czech State Philharmonic Orchestra / José Serebrier.** Reference Recordings Ⓕ RRCD-64 (63 minutes: DDD: 2/96). Recorded 1995.

In the sympathetic hands of Serebrier and the Czech (formerly Brno) State Philharmonic, Chadwick's *Symphonic Sketches* sound transformed, its warm-hearted, tuneful inspiration emerging as freshly as the day it was conceived. When the impressive *Melpomene* overture was first heard at a Boston Symphony concert in December 1887, the response was just as enthusiastic as it had been almost exactly a year earlier for the première of Chadwick's engaging Second Symphony. Taking its name from the Muse of tragedy, *Melpomene* is a fine, often eloquent achievement, whose slumbering, neo-Wagnerian character invites (and well withstands) comparison with, say, the tone-poems of Franck. However, the real discovery here is Chadwick's last important score, the 1915 symphonic poem, *Tam O'Shanter*. The adventures of Burns's "blithering, blustering, drunken" rogue are depicted in music of the utmost vividness and local colour. Chadwick's orchestral mastery is evident throughout, the wit and confidence of the writing at times reminiscent of Dukas's *L'apprenti sorcier*. A thoroughly enjoyable disc of late romantic music, with sumptuous, wide-ranging engineering.

Additional recommendation ...

...Symphonic Sketches. Symphony No. 2 in B flat major. **Detroit Symphony Orchestra / Neeme Järvi.** Chandos Ⓕ CHAN9334 (64 minutes: DDD: 4/95).

Chadwick Symphony No. 3 in F major.
Barber Vanessa – Intermezzo; Under the Willow Tree. Music for a scene from Shelley, Op. 7. Medea's Meditation and Dance of Vengeance, Op. 23a. **Detroit Symphony Orchestra / Neeme Järvi.** Chandos Ⓕ CHAN9253 (66 minutes: DDD: 10/94). Recorded 1993-4.

Well made and richly orchestrated, here is a thoroughly engaging, warm-hearted symphony, which only occasionally tends to a certain academic drabness. Though the influence of such European masters as Mendelssohn, Schumann and Brahms is obvious, Chadwick's language also possesses a native, 'folksy' feel in its rhythmic verve and imaginative harmonic resource. Readers who have enjoyed, say, Chandos's Stanford cycle should also find Chadwick very much to their liking. The remaining Barber items also show the Detroit orchestra to be in fine fettle, with rich, pliant strings, beautifully blended, characterful winds and full-throated brass. In the two orchestral excerpts from *Vanessa*, Järvi displays an appealing lightness of touch, but the climax of the "Intermezzo" lacks something in passion. The sumptuous *Music for a scene from Shelley* is finely done. Järvi undoubtedly impresses in the thrilling *Medea* portrait, but the sheer ferocity of the "Dance of Vengeance" never quite registers here. For this piece, Munch and the Bostonians remain about the best at the moment.

Further listening ...

...Symphony No. 2 in B flat major. **H. Parker** A Northern Ballad, Op. 49. **Albany Symphony Orchestra / Julius Heygi.** New World Ⓕ NW339-2 (51 minutes: DDD: 9/87).

Jacques Champion de Chambonnières
French 1601-1672

New review

Chambonnières Suites – D major; G major; D minor; F major.
Dumont Suite in D minor. Allemandes – C major; A minor; C major. Allemande grave in C major.
Member of the Hardel family Suite in D minor. **Jane Chapman** (hpd). Collins Classics Ⓕ 1422-2 (67 minutes: DDD: 8/95). 🎵 Recorded 1994.

Jane Chapman's commendable survey of the seventeenth-century Bauyn Manuscript reaches its conclusion with this third disc, consisting mainly of pieces by Chambonnières, the father figure of French harpsichord music, and Henry Dumont (who performed much the same role for the French motet). Dumont has been doing well on disc recently, but the chance to hear some of his harpsichord music is rare. The Pavanne, Courante and Allemandes offered here represent almost everything by him in the Bauyn Manuscript, and reveal a composer competent enough, though hardly memorable. More so is the great Chambonnières, represented in the collection by no less than 123 pieces, and on this disc by 19 gathered into four Suites which amply demonstrate his elegant melodic assurance. Chambonnières is still too little recorded for so fine a composer, but the same could also be said of the virtually unknown Monsieur Hardel, for whom the main obstacle to greater recognition seems to be that no one is sure what his first name was. Here he is represented by a single well-wrought Suite, including a Gavotte popular in his own day and furnished with varied repeats by Louis Couperin.

Anyone familiar with the first two discs in this series will already know that Jane Chapman has a neat and endearing way with the French repertoire, albeit one shown to better advantage in the jaunty sprung rhythms of the shorter and faster pieces (for instance, Chambonnièrre's *Gigue Bruscanbille* or the unusually titled *Brusque*) than in the longer and more reflective Pavannes and Allemandes, where she tends to be a little hasty. Her instrument – a delicate, much-rebuilt 1614 Ruckers – is less grand than we are perhaps used to in this kind of music, but historically at least, is entirely appropriate.

Additional recommendation ...
...C major[a]; G major[a]; A major[a]; D major[a]. **d'Anglebert** Tombeau de M. de Chambonnières.
Skip Sempé (hpd) with [a]**Brian Feehan** (theorbo). Deutsche Harmonia Mundi Ⓕ 05472 77210-2 (72 minutes: DDD: 4/93).

Cécile Chaminade
French 1857-1944

Suggested listening ...
...Piano Trio No. 1 in G minor, Op. 11. *Coupled with works by* **Carreño, C. Schumann, Beach, Tailleferre, L. Boulanger** and **Mendelssohn-Hensel Macalester Trio.** Vox Box 115845-2 (10/94). *See review in the Collections section; refer to the Index to Reviews.*
...Arlequine, Op. 53. Poème romantique, Op. 7 No. 1. Chanson Brétonne. Divertisse-ment, Op. 105. Six Pièces humoristiques, Op. 87 – Sous bois; Consolation. Passacaille in E major, Op. 130. Nocturne, Op. 165. Scherzo-Valse, Op. 148. Etude symphonique, Op. 28. Feuillets d'Album, Op. 98 – Elégie. Gigue in D major, Op. 43. Au pays dévasté, Op. 155. Pastorale, Op. 114. Libellules, Op. 24. Valse tendre, Op. 119. Tristesse in C sharp minor, Op. 104. Six Etudes do concert, Op. 35 – Impromptu; Tarantella. **Peter Jacobs** (pf). Hyperion CDA66706 (11/94).
...Air à danser, Op. 164. Air de ballet, Op. 30. Contes bleus No. 2, Op. 122. Danse créole, Op. 94. Six Etudes de concert, Op. 35 – No. 2, Automne. Feuillets d'album, Op. 98 – No. 4, Valse arabesque. Guitare, Op. 32. La lisonjera, Op. 50. Lolita, Op. 54. Minuetto, Op. 23. Pas des écharpes, Op. 37. Pas des sylphes: Intermezzo. Piéces humoristques, Op. 87 – No. 4, Autrefois. Pierette, Op. 41. Romances sans paroles, Op. 76 – No. 1, Souvenance; No. 3 Idyll; No. 6, Méditation. Sérénade, Op. 29. Sous le masque, Op. 116. Toccata, Op. 39. **Eric Parkin** (pf). Chandos CHAN8888 (8/91).

Gustave Charpentier
French 1860-1956

G. Charpentier Louise. **Berthe Monmart** (sop) Louise; **André Laroze** (ten) Julien; **Louis Musy** (bar) Father; **Solange Michel** (mez) Mother; **Paris Opéra-Comique Chorus and Orchestra / Jean Fournet.** Philips mono Ⓜ 442 082-2PM3* (three discs: 163 minutes: ADD: 9/94). Notes, text and translation included. Recorded 1956.   ⒼⒼ

The charms of *La vie parisienne, Manon* and *La bohème* notwithstanding, *Louise* is the essential opera set in, and about, Paris. This recording has the air of authority and authenticity throughout. All the principals were members of the company at the Opéra-Comique during the 1950s, when Jean Fournet was its Music Director. The appropriately-named Berthe Monmart who sings the title-role may not be the soprano of one's dreams, but her singing is full of charm, and she manages moments such as the leap to a soft high G at "des pétales de roses" in the opening love duet without apparent strain. Of course, every prima donna has recorded "Depuis le jour" (Melba, Callas, Price, Caballé, Sutherland, the list is endless) and it is useless to suggest that Monmart has such vocal allure, but she achieves complete conviction. All the singers have well-nigh perfect diction – essential in this supreme example of French *verismo*. What genius Charpentier mustered for this one work. When the Father makes his entrance in Act 1, to his 'tired' music and asks if the soup is ready, the psychological portrait is completed – mother/father/daughter, caught in this early picture of youth in rebellion. Musy's career had begun in the 1920s, and he had sung the entire baritone repertory at the Opéra-Comique before becoming its director of productions. André Laroze is the real thing – a French tenor. In the duet that follows "Depuis le jour" he and Monmart get up steam in fine ecstatic fashion. Fournet's pacing of the score achieves excitement at the climactic moments, the lovers' duets, Louise's almost hysterical apostrophe to Paris in the closing scene, while making the faintly mystical opening of Act 2 a miniature poem, with its street cries and little ripples of *chanson*. The mono sound is amazingly vivid – you are completely swept along by its fresh sense of theatricality and by the true *opéra-comique* style of all concerned.

Additional recommendations ...
...Soloists; Ambrosian Opera Chorus; New Philharmonia Orchestra / Georges Prêtre. Sony Classical Ⓕ S3K46429 (three discs: 172 minutes: ADD: 6/91).

Marc-Antoine Charpentier

New review

M-A. Charpentier Leçons de Ténèbres du Vendredi Saint. **Agnès Mellon** (sop); **Ian Honeyman** (ten); **Jacques Bona** (bar); **Il Seminario Musicale / Gérard Lesne** (alto). Virgin Classics Veritas Ⓕ VC7 59295-2 (71 minutes: DDD: 9/95). ✍ Texts and translations included. Recorded 1994.

Charpentier wrote many settings of the *Tenebrae*, or *Leçons de Ténèbres* as they were known in France, and they invariably inspired him to great heights of expressive intensity. Their texts come from the *Lamentations of Jeremiah the Prophet*, but are interspersed with affective, ornamental, melismatic phrases inspired by letters of the Hebrew alphabet. In addition to the *Leçons* the sequence includes Antiphons and Responses as well as plainchants with their faburdens for the Psalms, and occasional instrumental ritornellos. Not quite all of this music is by Charpentier. There are, for instance, pieces by Nivers, one of the greatest French organists of the time, included in the sequence; but though most of the assembled chants with their harmonizing faburdens were common property of the Catholic Church throughout Europe, one faburden at least is by Charpentier (H156). The French baroque *Leçons de Ténèbres* are deeply moving, with their distinctive blend of Italian monodic *lamentazioni* and French *air de cour*. The idiom allows for dramatically highly charged effects and, in the hands of composers like Charpentier and Couperin, such effects are often realized with thrilling suspensions, dissonances and impassioned declamation. Indeed, with Charpentier one often senses the composer's love of, and experience in writing for, the stage in the many theatrical gestures and in his vividly depictive handling of the texts. Certainly this highly emotive blend of sacred and secular ingredients resulted in music of extraordinary intensity, none of which is lost on Gérard Lesne and his ensemble, Il Seminario Musicale. Here are performances which discover the subtleties of Charpentier's muse effortlessly and gracefully. His style presents no problems for these artists; they are, in the main, sensible to the myriad expressive nuances suggested by the texts and realized in music of reflective intensity.

Additional recommendations ...

...Leçons de Ténèbres du Mercredi Saint. **Catherine Greuillet, Caroline Pelon** (sops); **Christopher Purves** (bass); **Il Seminario Musicale / Gérard Lesne** (alto). Virgin Classics Veritas Ⓕ VC5 45107-2 (64 minutes: DDD: 9/95). ✍

...Leçons de Ténèbres du Jeudi Saint. **Sandrine Piau** (sop); **Gérard Lesne** (alto); **Ian Honeyman** (ten); **Peter Harvey** (bass); **Il Seminario Musicale / Gérard Lesne** (alto). Virgin Classics Veritas Ⓕ VC5 45075-2 (66 minutes: DDD: 9/95). ✍

New review

Charpentier Vespres à la Vierge. **Le Concert Spirituel / Hervé Niquet.** Naxos Ⓢ 8 553174 (61 minutes: DDD: 3/96). Texts and translations included. Recorded 1995.   Ⓖ

Charpentier Beatus vir, H221. Laudate pueri, H149. Laetatus sum, H216. Nisi Dominus, H150. Lauda Jerusalem, H210. Ave maris stella, H60. Magnificat, H72. Salve regina, H24. **Nivers** Antiphonarium Monasticum, Antiennes I-VI.

This release offers a liturgical reconstruction of the Vespers office. The five Vesper psalms and *Magnificat* belong to different periods in Charpentier's life and the six antiphons are not by him at all but by Charpentier's organist-composer contemporary, Nivers. The reconstruction works well though the carelessly assembled documentation omits any catalogue identification either of the *Laetatus sum* (Psalm 122) or the *Nisi Dominus* (Psalm 127). The relevant numbers, without which the pieces are virtually impossible to identify, are given above. Le Concert Spirituel, under Hervé Niquet's direction, here demonstrate their rapport with Charpentier's music. The vocal sound is fresh and the wide range of musical *Affekt* shows off a greater diversity of tonal colour. Tenors and basses incline towards a roughness of timbre here and there – sections of the *Beatus vir* suffer from this – yet, overall, the bright and full-blooded choral sound is pleasing and vital. Some readers may feel that the recording balance of the psalms and canticle is a fraction too close, creating the atmosphere of a drawing-room Vespers rather than one in more spacious, ecclesiastical surroundings. The antiphons fare much better in this respect, being given a deeper aural perspective. In summary, this is a richly rewarding programme of music which, if not entirely vintage Charpentier, never disappoints. Some of the pieces are harmonically arresting and none, perhaps, more than the setting for three choral groups of the *Salve regina* with its passages of striking chromaticism. Warmly recommended.

New review

Charpentier La descente d'Orphée aux enfers. **Sophie Daneman** (sop) Euridice; **Paul Agnew** (ten) Orphée; **Jean-François Gardeil** (bar) Apollon, Titye; **Patricia Petibon** (sop) Daphné, Enone; **Monique Zanetti** (sop) Proserpine; **Katalin Károlyi** (mez) Aréthuze; **Steve Dugardin** (alto) Ixion; **François Piolino** (ten) Tantale; **Fernand Bernadi** (bass-bar) Pluton; **Les Arts Florissants / William Christie.** Erato Ⓕ 0630-11913-2 (56 minutes: DDD: 5/96). ✍ Notes, text and translation included. Recorded 1995. *Gramophone Editor's record of the month.*   Ⓖ

Charpentier's chamber opera *La descente d'Orphée aux enfers* may not be a work on the scale of *Médée* or *David et Jonathas*, but the familiar tale of Orpheus entering the Underworld to retrieve his lost love Euridice provides Charpentier (like so many others) with plenty on which to exercise his considerable dramatic skills. That is true, even without the customary denouement, for this two-act piece (composed in the mid 1680s for private performance at the residence of the Duchesse de Guise) ends with the triumph of Orpheus's music over the powers of the Underworld, and thus misses out the moment when he loses Euridice for a second time. The existing ending works quite well, however, and it is at least worth noting that in 1710 Clérambault's famous cantata, *Orphée*, ended at the same point in the story. As it is, Charpentier provides us with a chillingly sudden death for Euridice, an interesting scene in which three shades are charmed by some relatively minor examples of Orpheus's art, and a hero with all the desperation and impetuosity one would need to undertake as reckless a task as his. These last qualities are excellently conveyed by the unrestrained, dramatic singing of Paul Agnew, who is also equal to the task of characterizing Orpheus's musical entreaty to the Underworld, by turns artful and impassioned (and accompanied with great tenderness by two bass viols). Agnew's heart-on-sleeve approach is not always beautiful, but it never leaves good taste behind, and in this he is well matched by his colleagues. William Christie's direction shows its customary sure dramatic touch, and the result is a performance which seems unlikely to be bettered.

Charpentier Médée. **Lorraine Hunt** (sop) Médée; **Bernard Deletré** (bass) Créon; **Monique Zanetti** (sop) Créuse; **Mark Padmore** (ten) Jason; **Jean-Marc Salzmann** (bar) Oronte; **Noémi Rime** (sop) Nérine; **Les Arts Florissants / William Christie.** Erato Ⓕ 4509-96558-2 (three discs: 195 minutes: DDD: 6/95). ✐ Texts and translations included. Recorded 1994. ⒼⒼⒼ

William Christie himself answers the question that everyone is bound to ask: why has he chosen to make a new recording of this splendid (but still little-known) early opera – Charpentier's only *tragédie-lyrique* – only ten years after his previous version? For a start, the new issue is of the complete work and the experience of staging the opera has changed Christie's view of its pacing and sharpened the response of the orchestra (an unusually large one for its period) and continuo. Here we have an entirely new cast. Lorraine Hunt's Medea is something of a *tour de force*. She invests every word with meaning and produces the widest range of colour to express all the emotional nuances in Medea's complex character – jealousy, indignation, tenderness, sorrow, fury, malignity and outright barbarism: she is especially outstanding in Act 3, one of the most superb acts in all baroque opera, in which she has no fewer than four great monologues, the first with affecting chromatic harmonies, the second accompanied by feverish rushing strings, the third the sombre "Noires filles du Styx" with its eerie modulations, the fourth with dark orchestral colours. Charpentier's orchestration and texture, indeed, are wonderfully effective: string writing varies between extreme delicacy (beautifully played here) and savage agitation; the cool sound of the recorders is refreshing and the many dances featuring recorders and oboes – for of course the work had to create substantial opportunities for ballet, as well as spectacular stage effects – are enchanting. As Jason Mark Padmore, a real *haute-contre*, sings with admirable ease and intelligence and the tragic Creusa, poisoned by the vengeful Medea is the light-voiced Monique Zanetti, the very embodiment of youthful innocence and charm: her death scene, still protesting her love for Jason, is most moving. A notable detail in all the principals, incidentally, is their absorption of *agréments*, with Hunt showing special mastery in this regard. There is a large cast for the numerous minor roles, all well taken; and the chorus sing cleanly and with evident commitment. All told, a considerable achievement, and a triumph for Christie, whose decision to re-record the work is amply justified by the result.

Additional recommendation ...

...**Soloists; Les Arts Florissants Chorus and Orchestra / William Christie.** Harmonia Mundi Ⓕ HMC90 1139/41 (three discs: 182 minutes: AAD: 3/85). ✐ *Gramophone Award Winner 1985.* Ⓖ

Further listening ...

...Canticum in honorem Beatae Virginis Mariae inter homines et angelos, H400. Prélude a 3, H509. Pour la conception de la Vierge, H313. Nativité de la Vierge, H309. Prélude pour Salve regina a 3, H23*a*. Salve regina a 3, H23. Pour la fête de l'Epiphanie, H395. Prélude pour le Magnificat a 4, H533. Magnificat a 4, H80. Stabat mater pour des religieuses, H15. Litanies de la Vierge, H83. **Le Concert des Nations / Jordi Savall.** Auvidis Astrée E8713 (2/90). ✐ Ⓖ

...Litanies de la vierge, H83. Te Deum, H146. Missa Assumpta est Maria, H11. **Philidor, le Cadet** Marche de timbales[a]. **Les Arts Florissants Vocal and Instrumental Ensemble / William Christie** with [a]**Marie-Ange Petit** (perc). Harmonia Mundi HMC90 1298 (9/89) ✐

...Quatuor anni tempestatis, H335-8. Psalms – Quemadmodum desiderat cervus, H174. Nisi Dominus, H231. Notus in Judea, H179. **Françoise Semellaz, Noémi Rime** (sops); **Bernard Delétré** (bass); **Le Parlement de Musique / Martin Gester.** Opus 111 OPS30-9005 (9/91). ✐

...Office de ténèbres – Incipit oratio Jeremiae, H95. Leçons de ténèbres – Manum suam, H92; Ego vir videns, H93. Responsories – Eram quasi agnus, H116; O Juda, H119; O vos omnes, H134. Miserere, H157. **Le Parlement de Musique / Martin Gester** (org/hpd). Opus 111 OPS55-9119 (9/92). ✐

...Messe pour les trespassés. **Soloists; Lisbon Gulbenkian Foundation Choir and Orchestra / Michel Corboz.** Erato 4509-97238-2 (3/95).

...Messe des morts, H7. Litanies de la Vierge, H89. Psalms – Nisi Dominus, H160; Laudate pueri, H203; Confitebor tibi, H220. Elévation à 5 sans dessus de violon, "Transfige dulcissime Jesu", H251. **Le Concert Spirituel / Hervé Niquet.** Naxos 8 553173 (6/95). ✐

...Leçons de ténèbres du mercredi saint – Complete Services. Nine Tenebrae Responsories – Nos. 1-3. **Concerto Vocale.** Harmonia Mundi HMC90 1005.

...Le reniement de St Pierre. Méditations pour le Carême. **Les Arts Florissants Vocal and Instrumental Ensemble / William Christie.** Harmonia Mundi Musique d'abord HMA190 5151 (7/86). ✏   Ⓖ

...**Actéon. Soloists; Les Arts Florissants Vocal and Instrumental Ensemble / William Christie.** Harmonia Mundi Musique d'abord HMA190 1095 (5/83). ✏ *Gramophone Award Winner 1982-3.*   ⓆⓆ

...Le malade imaginaire. **Soloists; Les Arts Florissants Chorus and Orchestra / William Christie.** Harmonia Mundi HMC90 1336 (4/91). ✏ Included with this CD is a complementary CD (41 minutes) containing Charpentier's "'O' Anthems for Advent", H36-43; "In nativatem Domini nostri Jesus Christi canticum", H414; "Noëls dur les instruments", H534.

Ernest Chausson   French 1855-1899

Chausson Concert for Violin, Piano and String Quartet in D major, Op. 21.
Ravel Piano Trio. **Joshua Bell** (vn); **Steven Isserlis** (vc); **Jean-Yves Thibaudet** (pf); **Takács Quartet** (Gábor Takács-Nagy, Károly Schranz, vns; Gábor Omai, va; András Fejér, vc). Decca Ⓕ 425 860-2DH (62 minutes: DDD: 1/91). Recorded 1989.

New review

Chausson Concert for Violin, Piano and String Quartet in D major, Op. 21[a].
Franck Violin Sonata No. 1 in A major, Op. 13. **Pierre Amoyal** (vn); **Pascal Rogé** (pf); [a]**Ysaÿe Quartet** (Christophe Giovaninetti, Luc-Marie Aguera, vns; Miguel da Silva, va; Michel Poulet, vc). Decca Ⓕ 444 172-2DH (70 minutes: DDD: 2/96). Recorded 1994.   Ⓖ

Chausson's *Concert* for violin, piano and string quartet has an unusual force and scope for chamber music and the composer draws our attention to them from the start. Although a 'Concert' is not quite the same as a concerto, the full title rightly suggests that, along with the piano, one violin is more important than the other two; on the first Decca disc Joshua Bell's big, assertive D major tune in the first movement emphasizes this. The players give this music the right kind of forward surge. They are convincing, too, in the dreamily modulating slower music, which resists settling down to a definite theme and key yet remains positive, and is thus forward-looking for 1891. The players give this first movement plenty of space but there is no sense of unnecessary lingering. In the *Sicilienne* and the quiet, sombre *Grave* they are slightly muted and pastel-coloured, though their finale has plenty of fire. The recording is spacious and the sound of Thibaudet's piano (and fine playing) is well caught and balanced, but more textural detail from the members of the Takács Quartet would have been preferable; this is mainly because Bell's violin is placed a little too forward. The Ravel Trio is played by Bell and Thibaudet with Steven Isserlis in a sensitive and well-recorded performance with plenty of voltage. Here, too we find skill and a fine freshness.

This is repertory in which Decca artists have excelled over the years, but unlike the recording above, the second one is all French. Just as British artists respond intuitively to the needs of Elgarian rubato, in the Franck piece one recognizes the totally idiomatic response to this high romantic music in its own free use of rubato, natural and unaffected. It is remarkable how Amoyal and Rogé allow themselves great freedom over rhythm and tempo without ever seeming undisciplined. So the opening *Allegretto* emerges as a dreamy meditation, a happy preparation for more serious arguments later. This is a reading full of fantasy, giving the impression of music emerging spontaneously on the spur of the moment. The full and immediate recording helps, and so it does in the *Concert* for violin, piano and string quartet, which receives just as warmly spontaneous-sounding a performance. Although the recording producer here (Paul Myers) is common to both discs, the sound is strikingly different. On the first one it is slightly diffused and distant but on the more recent one the focus is far sharper, the sense of presence keener, and that adds to one's involvement, with contrasts of dynamic and texture, of light and shade, more clearly brought out. Here the string quartet is given its full weight, instead of being a mere addendum, and that owes much also to the playing of the Ysaÿe Quartet. As in the Franck, speeds tend to be broader in the newer performance, and the style more freely idiomatic, making it among the most persuasive of all recorded performances of this work, which is at last establishing its rightful place as a late romantic masterpiece.

New review

Chausson La légende de Sainte Cécile[a]. La tempête[b]. [a]**Isabelle Vernet**, [b]**Raphaëlle Farman** (sops); [b]**Marie-Ange Todorovitch** (mez); [b]**Laurence Dale** (ten); [b]**François Le Roux**, [b]**Jean-Philippe Lafont** (bars); [a]**women's voices of the French Radio Chorus; Paris Orchestral Ensemble / Jean-Jacques Kantorow.** EMI Ⓕ CDC5 55323-2 (79 minutes: DDD: 4/96). Notes, texts and translations included. Recorded 1994.

Admirers of Chausson's songs, particularly the *Poème de l'amour et de la mer*, will be familiar with the name of the poet Maurice Bouchor. For a three-act play he wrote (in somewhat inflated language) for a marionette theatre Chausson composed incidental music, consisting of 15 short numbers with some thematic interconnections. Predominantly slow, melancholy but also rapturous, they are expressively lyrical, with tinges both of archaism and of Wagnerism. Especially lovely is a *cantique* for unaccompanied cello followed by a soprano solo. Much of the music is cast for the angelic choir, represented in radiant tone (but not quite impeccable intonation) by female voices of the French Radio

Chorus. Except for one number condemning a blasphemer, in which Chausson introduces a tam-tam, the scoring is delicate, for only strings (beautifully played here) and celesta. Chausson's incidental music to a French version of Shakespeare's *Tempest* is a rather slighter score – nothing like as sparse in instrumentation, however, as stated by the note-writer, who couldn't have been listening – but it contains several delightful numbers, including charming interludes in Acts 3, 4 and 5 which could well be adopted generally as a little suite. All the singers are excellent. The ditties for Stephano and Caliban (the baritones) and Ariel's "Where the bee sucks" are unaccompanied, but "Come unto these yellow sands" (Dale) and the duet for Juno and Ceres (Todorovitch and Farman) are pearls that should rightly not have lain hidden until now.

Further listening ...

...Symphony in B flat major, Op. 20[a]. Poème, Op. 25[b]. *Coupled with* **Saint-Saëns** Introduction and Rondo capriccioso, Op. 28[b]. [b]**David Oistrakh** (vn); **Boston Symphony Orchestra / Charles Munch.** RCA Victor Gold Seal GD60683.   Ⓖ

...Symphony in B flat major, Op. 20. *Coupled with* **Fauré** Pélleas et Mélisande – concert suite, Op. 80. **Netherlands Radio Philharmonic Orchestra / Jean Fournet.** Denon CO-73675 (9/90).

...Piano Trio in G minor, Op. 3. *Coupled with* **Ravel** Piano Trio. **Beaux Arts Trio.** Philips 411 141-2PH (4/85).

...Quelques danses, Op. 26. Paysage, Op. 38. *Coupled with* **Franck** Prélude, Choral et Fugue. Les plaintes d'une poupée. Danse lente. Prélude, Aria et Final. **Dukas** Piano Sonata in E flat minor. Variations, interlude et final sur un thème de Rameau. La plainte, au loin, du faune ... . Prélude élégiaque. **Jean Hubeau** (pf). Teldec 4509-96221-2 (4/96).

...Poème de l'amour et de la mer, Op. 19[a]. Poème, Op. 25[b]. *Coupled with* **Fauré** Pelléas et Mélisande – Suite, Op. 80. Pavane, Op. 50[c]. [a]**Linda Finnie** (contr); [c]**Renaissance Singers; Ulster Orchestra / Yan Pascal Tortelier** ([b]vn). Chandos CHAN8952 (12/91).

...Le Roi Arthus. **Soloists; French Radio Chorus and New Philharmonic Orchestra / Armin Jordan.** Erato Libretto 2292-45407-2 (10/91).   Ⓖ

Carlos Chávez (Y Ramírez)   Mexican 1899-1978

New review

Chávez Toccata[a]. Paisajes mexicanos. La Hija de Cólquide[a]. Cantos de México. Baile. [a]**Claudia Coonce** (ob); **Mexico State Symphony Orchestra / Enrique Batiz.** ASV Ⓔ CDDCA927 (56 minutes: DDD: 5/96). Recorded 1994.

Those who may have been deterred by some of Chávez's often astringent and acerbic music now have the opportunity, with the present selection of his works, of hearing him in more approachable vein. Much the most attractive is the longest work here, the symphonic suite *The daughter of Colchis*, originally the score for the Martha Graham ballet *Dark meadow*. Its calm, pastoral atmosphere, spare texture and mostly diatonic and linear style make it sound very much like Copland, for whose work it could easily be mistaken. The *Toccata*, taken from some incidental music to a dramatized version of *Don Quixote*, also comes as a pleasant surprise: the first third of its six-and-three-quarter minutes is taken up by a pastoral oboe solo; gradually other woodwinds then enter, the pace quickening the while, until at about half-way through the piece the whole orchestra becomes involved in a vigorous scherzo. In contrast, the *Mexican landscapes* are full of thematically disjunct, noisily grandiose dramatic gestures masking nationalistic turns of phrase and dance rhythms. All the works so far mentioned were written in the 1940s: the earlier, brief *Songs of Mexico*, musically primitive, exploits an exotic orchestra of native instruments and ends in a dance of raw energy; the *Baile* ("Dance") of 1953 was the original finale of the Fourth Symphony, and progresses curiously in aggressive short jerks. The playing and recording throughout are both excellent.

New review

Chávez Sinfonia de Antigona[a]. Symphony No. 4, "Sinfonia romantica"[a].
Revueltas Caminos[b]. Musica para charlar[b]. Ventanas[b]. [a]**Royal Philharmonic Orchestra;** [b]**Mexico State Philharmonic Orchestra / Enrique Bátiz.** ASV Ⓔ CDDCA653 (71 minutes: DDD: 8/89).

All the music on this disc is refreshingly direct and unpretentious, with performances to match. In the three 1930s works by Revueltas, reflecting his skills as a theatre and film composer, there may be a tendency to go on for too long. But an almost Ivesian swagger counters any tendencies to Hollywood exoticism: and, as the end of *Musica para charlar* ("Music for chatter") shows, Revueltas's punchy sense of humour doesn't prevent him from generating powerful climaxes out of attractive melodic material. The earliest piece, *Ventanas*, is the most serious in tone, evoking a particularly bumpy train ride, and as the almost direct quote from *The Rite of Spring* towards the end shows, there is much more to Revueltas's style than folky post-impressionism. There is a far greater range of style in the two works by Chávez, written 20 years apart. *Sinfonia de Antigona* (1933) offers an unusual mixture of austere and lyrical music, and the sheer idiosyncrasy of the piece is striking, but is a bit let down by an attempt at faster music in modal style. The Symphony is much more conservative, with an easy-going but dull first movement; the other two are much more interesting: a *Molto lento* with a strong sense of line, and a genial, expansive finale with a raucously affirmative ending. The performances have panache but the sound is variable. Undoubtedly, though, this is a disc to sample.

Luigi Cherubini
Italian 1760-1842

Cherubini Requiem Mass No. 1 in C minor[a]. Marche funèbre. [a]**Corydon Singers; Corydon Orchestra / Matthew Best.** Hyperion Ⓕ CDA66805 (54 minutes: DDD: 4/96). Text and translation included. Recorded 1995. Ⓖ

This is a work that was profoundly admired by Beethoven and even by Berlioz, normally grudging and unfair where Cherubini was concerned. It would be an oversimplification to suggest that Matthew Best emphasizes the Beethoven rather than the Berlioz aspect of the work; but he does seem less interested in the fascinating use of colour as an element in the actual invention than in the rugged moral strength and the force of the statements. The recording reflects this emphasis, and is firm and clear without being especially subtle over orchestral detail. The choir deliver the *Dies irae* powerfully, and much dramatic vigour is recalled in the fugue traditionally reserved for "Quam olim Abrahae". Presumably this idea derives from the suggestion of generation upon generation of Abraham's children inheriting God's promise: whoever first thought of it, many composers have taken up the device. Berlioz, however, was satirical about Cherubini's fugues, and saved his admiration for the wonderful long *decrescendo* that ends the *Agnus Dei*. This is beautifully controlled here. Like Christoph Spering and the Cologne Chorus Musicus, who give a more colourful, 'Berliozian' performance, Best includes the tremendous *Marche funèbre*. There was inspiration here again for Berlioz (especially in his *Hamlet* funeral march). Best handles this superbly, opening with a merciless percussion crash and sustaining the pace and mood unrelentingly. In his hands, it sounds more original than ever, a funeral march that, rather than mourn or honour, rages against the dying of the light.

Additional recommendations ...

...Requiem Mass[a]. **Verdi** Messa da Requiem[b]. Soloists; [a]**Ambrosian Singers;** [b]**Ambrosian Chorus; Philharmonia Orchestra / Riccardo Muti.** EMI Forte Ⓜ CZS5 68613-2 (two discs: 135 minutes: [a]ADD/[b]DDD).

...Requiem Mass[a]. In Paradisium[a]. Marche funèbre. [a]**Cologne Chorus Musicus; Das Neue Orchester / Christoph Spering.** Opus 111 Ⓕ OPS30-116 (56 minutes: DDD: 2/95). ✍

Further listening ...

...Overtures – Eliza. Médée. L'hôtellerie portugaise. Les deux journées. Anacréon. Faniska. Les abencérages. Concert Overture. **Academy of St Martin in the Fields / Sir Neville Marriner.** EMI CDC7 54438-2 (9/92).

...Horn Sonata in F major. *Coupled with works by* **Rossini, Bellini** and **Donizetti** Barry Tuckwell (hn); **Academy of St Martin in the Fields / Sir Neville Marriner.** Double Decca 443 838-2DF2 (7/95). *See review under Rossini; refer to the Index to Reviews.*

...Mass in D minor[a], "Messe solennelle". *Coupled with* **Haydn** Mass in C major, "Missa in tempore belli", HobXXII/9[b]. [ab]**Soloists; Stuttgart Gächinger Kantorei;** [a]**Stuttgart Bach Collegium;** [b]**Stuttgart Chamber Orchestra / Helmuth Rilling.** Hänssler Classic 98 981 (two discs: DDD: 5/93).

...Requiem Mass No. 2 in D minor. **Ambrosian Singers; New Philharmonia Orchestra / Riccardo Muti.** EMI CMS7 63161-2.

Paul Chesnokov
USSR 1877-1944

Chesnokov Requiem No. 2, Op. 39. Come, let us worship. The Lord's Prayer. The good thief. Eternal remembrance. Let all flesh be silent, Op. 27. **Cantus Sacred Music Ensemble / Ludmilla Arshavskaya.** Olympia Ⓕ OCD482 (65 minutes: DDD: 1/96). Translations included. Recorded 1995.

Discovering anything about Pavel Grigoryevich Chesnokov is not easy: Soviet writers were under political restraint to avoid emphasis of the most important aspect of the career of this composer, his sacred music. On the evidence of this disc, Chesnokov seems to depart from the position inherited from Tchaikovsky by Rachmaninov and Grechaninov, in particular, by moving beyond their reconciliation of a personal idiom to liturgical and ecclesiastical demands, and using the materials of chant as a stimulus to his own invention. This is not to say that he rejects his heritage. Rather, he builds upon it with music that is inspired by Russian chant, but that is not afraid to use personal melodic developments and, in particular, some non-ecclesiastical chromatic romantic harmony. A beautiful example of the latter comes in the last piece on the record, *Let all flesh be silent*. That he can also write simply but convincingly within the idiom is shown by another beautiful setting, that of *The Lord's Prayer*. The Requiem is more strictly liturgical, and was composed in memory of Chesnokov's teacher, Stepan Smolensky. It is a powerful and touching piece. The strength and expertise of the performance show once again how much was quietly treasured during the years of religious repression.

Further listening ...

...Come, let us entreat Joseph, Op. 9 No. 9. Bless the Lord, o my soul, Op. 27 No. 1. Joyous light, Op. 9 No. 21. Let us, mystically representing the Cherubim. Praise ye the name of the Lord in heaven. *Coupled with* **Sariyev** The Lord, our God. **Bortnyansky** Many years. **Kastal'sky**

Liturgy of St John Chrysostom. **Anonymous** Russian Orthodox Chant: Easter Stikhiras. From my youth. Stikhira to the Russian Holymen. **Bolshoi Theatre Children's Choir / Andrey Zaboronok.** Collins Classics 1443-2 (7/95).

Thomas Chilcot   British c1700-1766

Suggested listening ...
...Harpsichord Concerto in A major, Op. 2 No. 2 (recons. R. Langley). *Coupled with works by* **Roseingrave, Handel, Nares, P. Hayes** and **Hook** The Parley of Instruments / **Paul Nicholson** (hpd). Hyperion CDA66700 (8/94). ✐ *See review in the Collections section; refer to the Index to Reviews.*

Fryderyk Chopin   Polish 1810-1849

New review
Chopin Piano Concertos[a] – No. 1 in E minor, Op. 11; No. 2 in F minor, Op. 21. Mazurkas – F minor, Op. 63 No. 2; F minor, Op. 68 No. 4. Waltz in E minor, Op. posth. **Evgeni Kissin** (pf); [a]**Moscow Philharmonic Orchestra / Dmitri Kitaienko.** RCA Victor Red Seal Ⓜ 09026 68378-2 (71 minutes: ADD: 2/96). From Olympia OCD149 (9/89). Recorded live in 1984.   Ⓖ
Here is a living rather than fabricated example of just what is possible from a 12-year-old genius. It is no exaggeration to say that these performances, taken from a 1984 Moscow concert, are among the most phenomenally assured and meteoric of any on record. Every page blazes with youthful confidence and a stylistic know-how that would be astonishing from a pianist twice Kissin's age. Even at that age he possessed the peculiar attributes of Russian pianism at its greatest, with flawless, even strength and the most full-bodied *cantabile*. At 10'18" in the first movement of the E minor Concerto you will hear playing of great expressive fullness; already he has all the time in the world to make his points (usually the hallmark of older, more experienced players). His punishing attack on Chopin's double-note elaboration at 5'27" in the finale will leave you breathless and so, too, will the way his playing so effortlessly takes wing at 2'07". True, there are moments (the opening of the F minor Concerto's central *Larghetto*) where he sounds too relentlessly upfront, too aggressively thrusting, and doubtless, when he comes to re-record these concertos in his maturity he will find an even wider spectrum of colour and nuance; a greater subtlety. However, it is doubtful whether he will ever surpass the infallible and propulsive brilliance of these performances. The concertos first appeared on Olympia in 1989, but RCA have trumped their ace, not only with three superbly played encores (the first emerging wraith-like from a storm of cheers) but in greatly improved, immaculate sound.
Additional recommendations ...
...Nos. 1 and 2. **Murray Perahia** (pf); **Israel Philharmonic Orchestra / Zubin Mehta.** Sony Classical Ⓕ SK44922 (76 minutes: DDD: 6/90).   ⓆⓆ
...No. 1[a]. No. 2[b]. **Tamás Vásáry** (pf). **Berlin Philharmonic Orchestra /** [a]**Jerszy Semkow,** [b]**János Kulka.** DG Privilege Ⓑ 429 515-2GR (75 minutes: ADD: 6/90).
...Nos. 1 and 2. **Emil Gilels** (pf); **Philadelphia Orchestra / Eugene Ormandy.** Sony Classical Essential Classics Ⓑ SBK46336 (72 minutes: ADD: 3/91).
...Nos. 1 and 2. Waltz in C sharp minor, Op. 64 No. 2. Nocturnes – Nos. 1-19. **Artur Rubinstein** (pf); **London Symphony Orchestra / Sir John Barbirolli.** EMI Références mono Ⓜ CHS7 64491-2* (two discs: 161 minutes: ADD: 7/93).   ⓆⓆ
...Nos. 1 and 2. **Nikolai Demidenko** (pf); **Philharmonia Orchestra / Heinrich Schiff.** Hyperion Ⓕ CDA66647 (73 minutes: DDD: 11/93).
...Nos. 1 and 2. **Martino Tirimo** (pf); **Philharmonia Orchestra / Fedor Glushchenko.** Conifer Ⓜ 75605 51247-2 (76 minutes: DDD: 6/95).
...No. 1[a]. 12 Etudes, Op. 25. Ballade No. 1 in G minor, Op. 23. **Géza Anda** (pf); [a]**Philharmonia Orchestra / Alceo Galliera.** Testament mono Ⓕ SBT1066* (80 minutes: ADD: 10/95). *See review in the Collections section; refer to the Index to Reviews.*   Ⓖ

Chopin Piano Concerto No. 1 in E minor, Op. 11[a]. Ballade in G minor, Op. 23[b]. Nocturnes, Op. 15 – No. 1 in F major[b]; No. 2 in F sharp minor[b]. Nocturnes, Op. 27 – No. 1 in C sharp minor; No. 2 in D flat major. Polonaise No. 6 in A flat major, Op. 53, "Heroic"[b]. **Maurizio Pollini** (pf); [a]**Philharmonia Orchestra / Paul Kletzki.** EMI Studio Plus Ⓜ CDM7 64354-2 (73 minutes: ADD: 11/92). Item marked [a]from ASD370 (11/60), recorded 1960, [b]ASD2577 (8/70), 1968.
Gramophone classical 100.   ⓆⓆⓆ
This disc is a classic. The concerto was recorded shortly after the 18-year-old pianist's victory at the Warsaw competition in 1959. Nowadays we might expect a wider dynamic range to allow greater power in the first movement's tuttis, but in all other respects the recording completely belies its age, with a near perfect balance between soloist and orchestra. This is, of course, very much Pollini's disc, just as the First Concerto is very much the soloist's show, but effacing as the accompaniment is, Pollini's keyboard miracles of poetry and refinement could not have been achieved without one of the most characterful and responsive accounts of that accompaniment ever committed to tape. The

expressive range of the Philharmonia on top form under Kletzki is at once, and continuously, exceptional, as is the accord between soloist and conductor in matters of phrasing and shading. The solo items are a further reminder of Pollini's effortless bravura and aristocratic poise. His tonal shading in the two accompanying Op. 27 *Nocturnes* is equally exquisite. Also on offer are the paired Op. 15 *Nocturnes*, the G minor *Ballade* and the recital ends stirringly with the A flat *Polonaise*.

Additional recommendations ...

...No. 1. **Liszt** Piano Concerto No. 1 in E flat major, G124. **Martha Argerich** (pf). **London Symphony Orchestra / Claudio Abbado**. DG The Originals Ⓜ 449 719-2GOR (55 minutes: ADD: 4/85). ⒼⒼ

...Nos. 1 and 2. **Krystian Zimerman** (pf). **Los Angeles Philharmonic Orchestra / Carlo Maria Giulini**. DG Ⓕ 415 970-2GH (72 minutes: ADD: 9/86). Ⓖ

...No. 1. Fantasia on Polish Airs, Op. 13. Andante spianato and Grande polonaise brillante in E flat major, Op. 22. **Idil Biret** (pf). **Czecho-Slovak State Philharmonic Orchestra, Košice / Robert Stankovsky**. Naxos Ⓢ 8 550368 (74 minutes: DDD: 4/92).

...No. 1[a]. Piano Sonata No. 2 in B flat minor, Op. 35. Also includes 23 other short works by Chopin. **Alexander Brailowsky** (pf); [a]**Berlin Philharmonic Orchestra / Julius Prüwer**. Danacord mono Ⓕ DACOCD336/7* (two discs: 135 minutes: ADD: 11/95).

Chopin Piano Concerto No. 2 in F minor, Op. 21[a]. Preludes, Op. 28. **Maria-João Pires** (pf); [a]**Royal Philharmonic Orchestra / André Previn**. DG Ⓕ 437 817-2GH (74 minutes: DDD: 10/94). Recorded 1992. Ⓖ

Here, beautifully and responsibly partnered by Previn and the Royal Philharmonic – the days of massacred tuttis and lax and indifferent orchestral partnerships seem mercifully remote – and recorded with the greatest warmth and clarity, Pires at last gets the treament she deserves. What gloriously imposing breadth as well as knife-edged clarity she brings to each phrase and note; absolutely nothing is taken for granted. To lift a phrase from Keats, she "loads every rift of her subject with ore" and the intricacy and stylishness of her rubato remind us that the inspiration behind the F minor Concerto was Constantia Gladkowska, a young singer and Chopin's first love. Listen to Pires's *fioritura* in the heavenly *Larghetto* or her way of edging into the finale's scintillating coda and you will gasp at such pianism and originality. Indeed, the opening of her finale may surprise you with its dreaminess (*Allegro vivace*?) but as with all great pianists, even her most extreme ideas are carried through with unshakeable conviction and authority. Pires's 24 Preludes, too, remind us that she is the possessor of one of the most crystalline of all techniques. More importantly, her way with the more interior numbers among Chopin's teeming and disparate moods is of exceptional drama and intensity. Understatement plays little part in her conception and those who prefer the more classically biased playing of artists such as Pollini are in for some surprises. In No. 4, for example, her reading is intensely 'laden', the *stretto* climax super-charged, the entire performance virtually choked by its own emotion. Yet how memorably she allows the central unease of No. 13 to dissolve into tranquillity, and, returning to fire and fury, what rhetorical force she unleashes in No. 18. In short, you will rarely hear Chopin playing of greater mastery or calibre. In her own scrupulously modern way Maria-João Pires surely embodies the spirit of the great pianists of the past; of Kempff, Edwin Fischer and, most of all, Alfred Cortot. Ashkenazy, Biret and Richter – amongst her modern rivals – are also highly recommendable.

Additional recommendations ...

...No. 2[a]. **Tchaikovsky** Piano Concerto No. 1 in B flat minor, Op. 23[b]. **Vladimir Ashkenazy** (pf); **London Symphony Orchestra / [a]David Zinman, [b]Lorin Maazel**. Decca Ovation Ⓜ 417 750-2DM (66 minutes: ADD: 1/89).

...No. 2. Variations on "Là ci darem le mano", Op. 2. Concerto Rondo in F major, Op. 14, "Krakowiak". **Idil Biret** (pf). **Czecho-Slovak State Philharmonic Orchestra, Košice / Robert Stankovsky**. Naxos Ⓢ 8 550369 (67 minutes: DDD: 4/92).

Chopin Piano Trio in G minor, Op. 8[a]. Cello Sonata in G minor, Op. 65[b]. Introduction and Polonaise brillant in C major, Op. 3 (versions for [d]pf, [c]vc and pf, arr. Feuermann). [a]**Pamela Frank** (vn); [abc]**Yo-Yo Ma** (vc); [abc]**Emanuel Ax**, [d]**Eva Osinska** (pfs). Sony Classical Ⓕ SK53112 (72 minutes: DDD: 6/95). Recorded 1989-92.

This most welcome reminder of the 'chamber music' Chopin of course starts with his G minor Piano Trio (1828-29) dedicated to his compatriot, the music-loving would-be composer-cum-cellist, Prince Radziwill. Rarely has it enjoyed what might be termed 'bigger-named' rescue on disc which is inexplicable. For even if Chopin's beloved piano gets the best of it, a performance as imaginatively characterized as this makes you salute the teenage work anew with those well-worn words (albeit in a different context) "Off with your hats, gentlemen – a genius". Despite the procrustean (for Chopin) demands of sonata-form, the minor-key challenges of the opening *Allegro con fuoco* are conveyed with appealing urgency before the amiable grace of the *Scherzo*, the smouldering romance of the *Adagio sostenuto* and the dance-like gaiety of the finale. Shortly after accepting the Trio's dedication, Prince Radziwill invited Chopin to stay at his country estate – hence the Op. 3 *Polonaise brillant* in C (the slow introduction came later) for the Prince to play with his bewitching 17-year-old pianist daughter. Here, Yo-Yo Ma chooses Emanuel Feuermann's reworking of the cello part – as Chopin himself might well have enhanced it with decorative *fioriture* had the Prince's fingers been as agile as his daughter's. More importantly, the disc offers what is thought to be the first recording of this work in a solo-piano version, recently discovered by the Polish pianist-musicologist, Jan Weber. It is played here with spirited affection by Weber's pupil, Eva Osinska. The mature Cello Sonata, written in 1845-46 for Chopin's good friend, August Franchomme, is no stranger to the catalogue. And it is good to say that this tactfully balanced, persuasively fluid performance from Yo-Yo Ma and Emanuel Ax ranks with the best of its rivals. The recording is vivid and true.

Additional recommendations ...

...Cello Sonata[i]. *Coupled with works by* **Haydn, Monn, Dvořák, Schumann, Saint-Saëns, Delius, Elgar, Franck, Fauré, Bruch, Bach, Handel** and **Beethoven** Jacqueline du Pré (vc); **Gerald Moore, Ernest Lush, Stephen Kovacevich** (pfs); **London Symphony Orchestra / Sir John Barbirolli; Royal Philharmonic Orchestra / Sir Malcolm Sargent; New Philharmonia Orchestra; Chicago Symphony Orchestra; English Chamber Orchestra / Daniel Barenboim** ([i]pf). EMI Ⓑ CZS5 68132-2 (six discs: 437 minutes: ADD: 8/94). *See review in the Collections section; refer to the Index to Reviews.*   ⒼⒼ

...Introduction and Polonaise brillant. *Coupled with works by* **Tchaikovsky, Rachmaninov, Offenbach, Moszkowski, Dvořák, Liszt, Grieg, Popper** and **Weber** Henri Demarquette (vc); **François-Frédéric Guy** (pf). Pierre Verany Ⓕ PV795101 (75 minutes: DDD: 4/96).

New review

Chopin Etude in F major, Op. 25 No. 3[c]. Waltz in A minor, Op. 34 No. 2[d].
Mussorgsky Pictures at an Exhibition (piano version[a]; orch. Ravel[b]). [acd]**Byron Janis** (pf); [b]**Minneapolis Symphony Orchestra / Antál Dorati.** Mercury Living Presence Ⓜ 434 346-2MM (66 minutes: ADD: 2/96). Item marked [a] new to UK, [b]AMS16051 (9/60), [cd]AMS16136 (5/63). Ⓖ
Byron Janis's admirers will snap up this release like gold-dust. Beginning with the encores, Chopin's *Etude*, Op. 25 No. 3 flashes and winks like summer lightning and in the A minor *Waltz* the playing is as patrician in style as it is crystalline in technique. The main items are the twin couplings of Mussorgsky's *Pictures* in the original piano version and Ravel's fascinating and resourceful orchestration. Yet it is a curious fact that while Mussorgsky's work is unpianistic – at least in conventional terms – positively crying out for added spice and colour, it remains impregnable. Of course, a great deal depends on the pianist and Janis is gloriously equal to the task. His actual performance (which omits the "Promenande") posseses a stupendous brio and his Horowitz-honed virtuosity in the final pages is overwhelming in its pace and dynamism. These performances are also a sad reminder of the loss we suffered when this great American pianist was stricken by ill-health early in his career.

Chopin Fantasie in F minor, Op. 49. Waltzes – No. 2 in A flat major, Op. 34 No. 1; No. 3 in A minor, Op. 34 No. 2; No. 5 in A flat major, Op. 42. Polonaise No. 5 in F sharp minor, Op. 44. Nocturnes – No. 1 in C sharp minor, Op. 27 No. 1; No. 2 in D flat major, Op. 27 No. 2; No. 10 in A flat major, Op. 32 No. 2. Scherzo No. 2 in B flat minor, Op. 31. **Evgeni Kissin** (pf); RCA Victor Red Seal Ⓕ 09026 60445-2 (67 minutes: DDD: 5/94). Recorded at performances in Carnegie Hall, New York in 1993. *Gramophone Editor's choice.*   ⒼⒼⒼ
Evgeni Kissin's playing at 21 (which he was when these performances were recorded) quite easily outmatches that of the young Ashkenazy and Pollini – and most particularly in terms of the maturity of his musicianship. The programme launches off with a reading of the great F minor *Fantasie*, which, though a bit measured, is integrated to perfection. The power and determination of the performance certainly make one sit up and listen, but at the same time it would be difficult not to be moved by the heartfelt lyricism of the melodic passages. Although Kissin may be a little unsmiling in the three waltzes, at least he has admirable sophistication in being able to work in detail from the accompaniments so as to add interest to the interpretations. His control in the tricky A flat, Op. 42 is quite amazing. Of all the items on the CD, however, the *Nocturne* in C sharp minor is the jewel. This reading is amongst the most darkly imaginative and pianistically refined on disc. The release is rounded off by a powerfully glittering performance of the Second *Scherzo*.

Additional recommendations ...

...Introduction and Variations in E major on a German air ("Der Schweizerbub"). Four Scherzos – No. 1 in B minor, Op. 20; No. 2; No. 3 in C sharp minor, Op. 39; No. 4 in E major, Op. 54. Variations in B flat major on "Là ci darem la mano", Op. 2. **Nikolai Demidenko** (pf). Hyperion Ⓕ CDA66514 (63 minutes: DDD: 1/92).

...Scherzos Nos. 1-4. **Howard Shelley** (pf). Chandos Ⓕ CHAN9018 (55 minutes: DDD: 7/92).

...Nocturnes Nos. 11-19. **Idil Biret** (pf). Naxos Ⓢ 8 550357 (55 minutes: DDD: 7/93).

...Fantasie. Marche funèbre in C minor, Op. 72 No. 2. Etudes, Op. posth. – No. 1 in F minor; No. 2 in A flat major; No. 3 in D flat major. Barcarolle in F sharp major, Op. 60. Berceuse in D flat major, Op. 57. Polonaise-fantaisie in A flat major, Op. 61. Contredanse in G flat major. Cantabile in B flat major. Feuille d'album. Fugue in A minor. Variations in A major, "Souvenir de Paganini". **Fou Ts'ong** (pf). Sony Classical Essential Classics Ⓑ SBK53515 (66 minutes: ADD/DDD: 12/94).

...Scherzos Nos. 1-4. *Coupled with works by* **Beethoven** and **Schumann** Sviatoslav Richter (pf). Olympia Ⓕ OCD338 (75 minutes: ADD: 4/94). *See review under Beethoven; refer to the Index to Reviews.*   ⒼⒼ

...Waltzes – No. 1 and Nos. 3-14. *Coupled with works by* **Bach, Mozart** and **Schubert** Dinu Lipatti (pf). EMI Références mono Ⓜ CDH5 65166-2* (73 minutes: ADD: 12/94). *See review in the Collections section; refer to the Index to Reviews.* ⒼⒼⒼ

Chopin Preludes Nos. 1-24, Op. 28. Scherzo No. 2 in B flat minor, Op. 31. Mazurkas – No. 13 in A minor, Op. 17 No. 4; No. 15 in C major, Op. 24 No. 2; No. 25 in B minor, Op. 33 No. 4. Polonaise No. 5 in F sharp minor, Op. 44. **Seta Tanyel** (pf). Collins Classics Ⓕ 1330-2 (69 minutes: DDD: 4/94). Recorded 1992-3.

Chopin Preludes Nos. 1-24, Op. 28. Preludes – No. 25 in C sharp minor, Op. 45; No. 26 in A flat major, Op. posth. (all from 2530 721, 2/78). Barcarolle in F sharp major, Op. 60 (SLPM138672, 1/68). Polonaise No. 6 in A flat major, Op. 53 (SLPM139317, 5/68). Scherzo No. 2 in B flat minor, Op. 31 (2530 530, 6/75). **Martha Argerich** (pf). DG Galleria Ⓜ 415 836-2GGA (62 minutes: ADD: 4/88). ⒼⒼ

Avoiding all overtly self-conscious point-making in pursuit of expression, Seta Tanyel gets to the heart of the matter with a stylish simplicity. And how beautifully she makes the piano sing within a sound-world that is wholly Chopinesque in its translucency. That said, there is certainly no lack of strength, either of motivation or sheer tonal weight, as the more demonstratively disturbed of the 24 Preludes make very clear. However stormy the outburst or complex the figuration she nevertheless always manages to reveal a hidden melodic thread. Slower numbers carry their weight of sentiment without being allowed to drag. Nothing in the first half of the recital is more pleasing than the three *Mazurkas*. Each tells its own personal tale while – with a spring-like tonal delicacy and freshness – never allowing you to forget its origin in the dance. In the flanking B minor *Scherzo* and F sharp minor *Polonaise*, darker undertones of disquiet and defiance are conveyed with an urgent nervous energy far more telling than bombast. And what beguiling *cantabile* she draws from her instrument in the gracious mazurka-like trio of the Polonaise. The Abbey Road reproduction is pleasing enough.

Professor Zurawlew, the founder of the Chopin Competition in Warsaw was once asked which one of the prizewinners he would pick as having been his favourite. Looking back over the period 1927-75, the answer came back immediately: "Martha Argerich". Her disc reviewed here could explain why. There are very few recordings of the 24 Preludes that have such a perfect combination of temperamental virtuosity and compelling artistic insight. Argerich has the technical equipment to do whatever she wishes with the music. Whether it is in the haunting, dark melancholy of No. 2 in A minor or the lightning turmoil of No. 16 in B flat minor, she is profoundly impressive. It is these sharp changes of mood that make her performance scintillatingly unpredictable. In the *Barcarolle* there is no relaxed base on which the melodies of the right hand are constructed, as is conventional, but more the piece emerges as a stormy odyssey through life, with moments of visionary awareness. Argerich, it must be said, is on firmer ground in the *Polonaise*, where her power and technical security reign triumphant. The CD ends with a rippling and yet slightly aggressive reading of the second Scherzo. This is very much the playing of a pianist who lives in the 'fast lane' of life. The sound quality is a bit reverberant, an effect heightened by the fact that Argerich has a tendency to over-pedal.

Additional recommendations ...

...Mazurkas Nos. 1-51. **Artur Rubinstein** (pf). RCA Victor Red Seal Ⓕ RD85171 (two discs: 140 minutes: ADD: 9/89).

...24 Preludes – No. 2 in A minor; No. 4 in E minor; No. 5 in D major; No. 6 in B minor; No. 7 in A major; No. 8 in F sharp minor; No. 9 in E major; No. 10 in C sharp minor; No. 11 in B major; No. 13 in F sharp major; No. 19 in E flat major; No. 21 in B flat major; No. 23 in F major. **Schumann** Novelletten, Op. 21 – No. 2 in D major; No. 4 in D major; No. 8 in F sharp minor. Fantasiestücke, Op. 12 – In der Nacht; Traumes-Wirren. **Sviatoslav Richter** (pf). Olympia Ⓕ OCD287 (63 minutes: DDD: 10/92).

...24 Preludes. Prelude in A flat. Piano Sonatas – No. 1 in C minor, Op. 4; No. 2 in B flat minor, Op. 35; No. 3 in B minor, Op. 58. Rondos – C minor, Op 1; F major, "à la mazur", Op. 5. Four Ballades. Introduction and Rondo in C minor/E flat major, Op. 16. Rondo in C major, Op. 73. **Garrick Ohlsson** (pf). Arabesque Ⓕ Z6628/30 (three discs, oas: 78, 66 and 64 minutes: DDD: 10/93).

...Preludes: Nos. 1-24; No. 25 in C sharp minor, Op. 45; No. 26 in A flat major. Op. posth. Spring, Op. 74 No. 2. Allegretto and Mazur. Two Bourées. Ecossaise, Op. 72 No. 3. Three Ecossaises, WN27. Boléro in C major, Op. 19. Contredanse in G flat major. Galop marquis in A flat major. Allegretto in F sharp minor. Feuille d'album in E major. Cantabile in B flat major. Fugue in A minor. **Cyprien Katsaris** (pf). Sony Classical Ⓕ SK53355(69 minutes: DDD: 10/93).

...24 Preludes – No. 6 in B minor; No. 7 in A major; No. 8 in F sharp minor; No. 9 in E major; No. 10 in C sharp minor; No. 11 in B major; No. 17 in A flat major; No. 19 in E flat major; No. 23 in F major; No. 24 in D minor. Barcarolle in F sharp major, Op. 60. Nocturne in F major, Op. 15 No. 1. Etudes – Op. 10: No. 1 in C major; No. 2 in A minor; No. 3 in E major; No. 4 in C sharp minor; No. 6 in E flat minor; No. 10 in A flat major; No. 11 in E flat major; No. 12 in C minor. Op. 25: No. 5 in E flat minor; No. 6 in G sharp minor; No. 7 in C sharp minor; No. 8 in D flat major; No. 11 in A minor; No. 12 in C minor. Polonaises – C sharp minor, Op. 26 No. 1; C minor, Op. 40 No. 2; A flat major, Op. 61. *Coupled with works by* **Liszt** Sviatoslav Richter (pf). Philips Ⓕ 438 620-2PH3 (three discs: 202 minutes: DDD: 8/94).

New review
Chopin Preludes Nos. 1-24, Op. 28. Etudes – Op. 10: No. 4 in C sharp minor; No. 5 in G flat major; No. 6 in E flat minor; Op. 25: No. 1 in A flat major; No. 2 in F minor; No. 6 in G sharp minor; No. 12 in C minor. **Dame Moura Lympany** (pf). Erato Ⓕ 0630-11726-2 (61 minutes: DDD: 2/96). Recorded 1995.

While it would be idle to pretend that Dame Moura Lympany still commands her former light-fingered grace and brilliance, her playing remains warmly affectionate and committed. Indeed, it could be argued that the passing years have brought an increased depth and widening poetic perspective. She commences Chopin's 24 Preludes in richly expansive style and inflects the insistent morbidity of No. 2 with an expressive freedom she might not have allowed herself some years ago. Yet everything is seen through a glass clearly rather than darkly. Nothing is rushed or effusive and if her journey through No. 5 is strenuous and her flight through the *presto* storms of No. 12 heavily laden, she can still cut a dash in, say, the brilliant fury of No. 16, and find the urgent romantic pulse beneath the Rachmaninovian swirl and glitter of No. 8. Particularly enjoyable is her spaciousness in No. 6 (a true *lento*), her touching inwardness in No. 13 and her unusual thoughtfulness in the normally carefree No. 21, with its central carillon of bells. In No. 24, on the other hand, she is truly *appassionato*, her performance as grandly conceived as it is restlessly surging. For her encores Dame Moura gives us no fewer than seven *Etudes*. No doubt in her heyday she could have tossed off both sets with all the ease and elegance for which she was celebrated. Yet, once again, her playing remains full of quality and interest, with no lack of pace or fluency in Op. 25 No. 2 and with a drama and propulsion in Op. 25 No. 12 that pianists half her age might envy. Fine alternative recordings notwithstanding, Dame Moura's disc is sufficiently personal and special to make comparisons more than usually odious. The recordings are warm and Philipps Simon's notes are lively and acute.

Chopin Nocturnes – Op. 9: No. 1 in B flat minor; No. 2 in E flat major; No. 3 in B major. Op. 15: No. 1 in F major; No. 2 in F sharp major; No. 3 in G minor. Op. 27: No. 1 in C sharp minor; No. 2 in D flat major. Op. 32: No. 1 in B major; No. 2 in A flat major; C minor. Op. 37: No. 1 in G minor; No. 2 in G major. Op. 48: No. 1 in C minor; No. 2 in F sharp minor. Op. 55: No. 1 in F minor; No. 2 in E flat major. Op. 62: No. 1 in B major; No. 2 in E major. No. 19 in E minor, Op. 72 No. 1; No. 20 in C sharp minor, Op. posth. Impromptus – No. 1 in A flat major, Op. 29; No. 2 in F sharp major, Op. 35; No. 3 in G flat major, Op. 51. Fantaisie-impromptu in C sharp minor, Op. 66. **Peter Katin** (pf). Olympia Ⓜ OCD254 (two discs: 140 minutes: DDD: 12/89).   Ⓖ

Katin is a quietly persuasive artist rather than a virtuoso and he brings an entirely appropriate sense of intimacy to this Chopin recital of nocturnes and impromptus. The approach is chronological and complete, so that in the nocturnes the E minor and the *Lento con gran espressione* in C sharp minor come first, although they were published posthumously, and we also hear the rarely played C minor (without opus number) which only came to light in 1937, a century after its composition. Rubato is used freely but tastefully and melodies really sing, so that a good balance is achieved between emotional richness and the fastidiousness that was also part of Chopin's musical nature. The impromptus are well done too, with the famous *Fantaisie-impromptu* played according to a manuscript source and so with rather fewer ornaments than usual. The recording was made in an Oslo church with a fine acoustic and an instrument that the pianist finds "exceptionally sympathetic", as the booklet tells us and his own programme notes are almost as poetic as the music itself, as when he writes of the E flat major Nocturne, Op. 55 No. 2, that "a coda of sheer magic seems to descend from a height and passes into infinity"

Additional recommendations ...

...Complete Nocturnes. **Livia Rév** (pf). Hyperion Ⓕ CDA66341/2 (112 minutes: DDD: 2/90). *Selected by Sounds in Retrospect.*

...Nocturnes Nos. 1-10, 20 and 21. **Idil Biret** (pf). Naxos Ⓢ 8 550356 (57 minutes: DDD: 7/93).

...Three Impromptus. Fantaisie-impromptu. Barcarolle in F sharp major, Op. 60. Piano Sonata No. 3 in B minor, Op. 58. **Howard Shelley** (pf). Chandos Ⓕ CHAN9175 (57 minutes: DDD: 11/93).

...Complete Nocturnes. Fantaisie-impromptu. Barcarolle in F sharp major, Op. 60. **Kathryn Stott** (pf). Unicorn-Kanchana Ⓕ DKPCD9147/8 (two discs: 124 minutes: DDD: 7/94).   Ⓖ

...Fantaisie-impromptu. *Coupled with works by* **Liszt, Busoni, Debussy, Mendelssohn, Schumann, Scriabin, Rachmaninov** and **Weber** Anatol Ugorski (pf). DG Ⓕ 447 105-2GH (62 minutes: DDD: 3/96). *See review in the Collections section; refer to the Index to Reviews.*

Chopin Waltz No. 2 in A flat major, Op. 34 No. 1 (from HMV DB1168, 2/30). Mazurkas Nos. 1-51 (DB3802/8, 9/39 and DB3839/45, 2/42). Four Scherzos (DB1915/8, 11/33). Barcarolle in F sharp major, Op. 60 (DB1161, 8/28). Berceuse in D flat major, Op. 57 (DB2149, 7/34). Polonaises – No. 1 in C sharp minor, Op. 26; No. 2 in E flat minor, Op. 26; No. 3 in A major, Op. 40, "Military"; No. 4 in C minor, Op. 40 No. 2; No. 5 in F sharp minor, Op. 44; No. 6 in A flat major, Op. 53, "Heroic"; No. 7 (DB2493/6, 7/36 and DB2497/9, 8/36). Andante spianato and Grand polonaise in E flat major, Op. 22 (DB2499/500, 8/36). **Artur Rubinstein** (pf). EMI Références mono Ⓜ CHS7 64697-2* (three discs: 233 minutes: ADD: 1/93). Recorded 1928-39.   ⒼⒼ

Artur Rubinstein is popularly remembered as Chopin's genial, sparkling elder statesman; but, up until now, only seasoned collectors have been aware of his many pre-war recordings – where "aristocratic poise" (Rubinstein's best-known interpretative attribute) went hand-in-hand with impulsiveness, spontaneity and dazzling virtuosity. To compare these 1932-35 versions of the *Scherzos* and Polonaises with Rubinstein's wise, elegant (and extremely musical) post-war recordings for RCA is to pit "emotion recollected in tranquillity" against the hot-headed impact of immediate experience. There's less of a contrast with the Mazurkas, although – again – these first recordings (Rubinstein made two subsequent sets) have that extra degree of 'lift' and tension. Readers will of course ask themselves whether transfers from old 78s really can deliver as much musical pleasure as modern recordings. But in this case, so-called 'surface noise' is never intrusive and the quality of the playing is so exceptional that the mono sound and relative lack of dynamic range soon cease to pose a problem.

Additional recommendations ...

...Polonaises Nos. 1-7. **Artur Rubinstein** (pf). RCA Victor Red Seal Ⓕ RD89814 (60 minutes: ADD: 12/86).

...Polonaises – No. 7 in A flat major, Op. 61, "Polonaise-fantaisie"; No. 12 in G flat major; No. 13 in G minor; No. 14 in A flat major; No. 15 in A flat major; No. 16 in G sharp minor. Bolero in A minor, Op. 19. Allegro de concert, Op. 46. Berceuse in D flat major, Op. 57. Tarantelle in A flat major, Op. 43. **Nikolai Demidenko** (pf). Hyperion Ⓕ CDA66597 (66 minutes: DDD: 11/92).

...Nocturnes, Op. 37 – No. 1 in G minor; No. 2 in G major. Polonaise No. 5. Berceuse in D flat major, Op. 57. Etude in G flat major, Op. 10 No. 5. *Coupled with works by* **Mozart** and **Ravel** **Konstantin Lifschitz** (pf). Denon Ⓕ CO-78908 (66 minutes: DDD: 12/94). ⒼⒼ

Chopin Four Ballades – No. 1 in G minor, Op. 23; No. 2 in F major, Op. 38; No. 3 in A flat major, Op. 47; No. 4 in F minor, Op. 52. Mazurkas – No. 7 in F minor, Op. 7 No. 3; No. 13 in A minor, Op. 17 No. 4; No. 23 in D major, Op. 33 No. 2. Waltzes – No. 1 in E flat major, Op. 18; No. 5 in A flat major, Op. 42; No. 7 in C sharp minor, Op. 64 No. 2. Etudes, Op. 10 – No. 3 in E major; No. 4 in C sharp minor. Nocturne in F major, Op. 15. **Murray Perahia** (pf). Sony Classical Ⓕ SK64399 (61 minutes: DDD: 12/94). Recorded 1994. *Gramophone Award Winner 1995.* *Gramophone Editor's choice. Selected by Sounds in Retrospect.* ⒼⒼⒼ

This is surely the greatest, certainly the richest, of Perahia's many exemplary recordings. Once again his performances are graced with rare and classic attributes and now, to supreme clarity, tonal elegance and musical perspective, he adds an even stronger poetic profile, a surer sense of the inflammatory rhetoric underpinning Chopin's surface equilibrium. In other words the vividness and immediacy are as remarkable as the finesse. And here, arguably, is the oblique but telling influence of Horowitz whom Perahia befriended during the last months of the old wizard's life. Listen to the First *Ballade*'s second subject and you will hear rubato like the most subtle pulsing or musical breathing. Try the opening of the Third and you will note an ideal poise and lucidity, something rarely achieved in these outwardly insouciant pages. From Perahia the waltzes are marvels of liquid brilliance and urbanity. Even Lipatti hardly achieved such an enchanting lilt or buoyancy , such a beguiling sense of light and shade. In the mazurkas, too, Perahia's tiptoe delicacy and tonal irridescence (particularly in Op. 7 No. 3 in F minor) make the music dance and spin as if caught in some magical hallucinatory haze. Finally, two contrasting *Etudes*, and whether in ardent lyricism (Op. 10 No. 3) or shot-from-guns virtuosity (Op. 10 No. 4) Perahia's playing is sheer perfection. The recording beautifully captures his instantly recognizable, glistening sound world as well as the immense grandeur of his conceptions.

Additional recommendations ...

...Ballades. Barcarolle in F sharp major, Op. 60. Fantasie in F minor, Op. 49. **Krystian Zimerman** (pf). DG Ⓕ 423 090-2GH (60 minutes: DDD: 10/88). ⒼⒼⒼ

...Ballades. Piano Sonata No. 2 in B flat minor, Op. 35. **Andrei Gavrilov** (pf). DG Ⓕ 435 622-2GH (57 minutes: DDD: 6/92).

...Ballades. Barcarolle. Berceuse. Fantasie. **Alexeï Lubimov** (fp). Erato Ⓕ 2292-45990-2 (63 minutes: DDD: 7/93). ✍

...Ballades. Piano Sonata No. 3. **Nikolai Demidenko** (pf). Hyperion Ⓕ CDA66577 (61 minutes: DDD: 11/93).

...Ballades. Mazurkas – A minor, Op. 7 No. 2; A minor, Op. 17 No. 4; C major, Op. 24 No. 2; C sharp minor, Op. 50 No. 3; C sharp minor, Op. 63 No. 3. **Ivan Moravec** (pf). VAI Audio Ⓕ VAIA1092 (55 minutes: ADD: 12/95).

...Ballades. Berceuse in D flat major, Op. 57. Impromptu No. 2 in F sharp major, Op. 36. Etude in A flat major, Op. 25 No. 1. 24 Preludes, Op. 28. **Alfred Cortot** (pf). Music & Arts mono Ⓕ CD871* (77 minutes: ADD: 6/96). Ⓖ

New review

Chopin Ballade No. 1 in G minor, Op. 23. Nocturne No. 1 in F major, Op. 15. 12 Etudes, Op. 10. Scherzo No. 2 in B flat minor, Op. 31. **Cécile Licad** (pf). MusicMasters Ⓕ 67124-2 (60 minutes: DDD: 10/95). Recorded 1993.

Chopin recitals may come in droves, but they are rarely of this richness, mastery and eloquence. Cécile Licad, Manila-born but US-based, compels one to think and feel again about every note, proving that in such hands great music can never become over-familiar. What imperiousness she finds in the first of the Op. 10 *Etudes* (Chopin's 'runaway chorale') and what a timeless malaise she achieves in the near Wagnerian chromaticism of No. 6. Her unusually dark colouring captures the underlying turbulence of No. 9 in a very special way, while her thunder in No. 4 relaxes into lightness and even a smile in the pentatonic scintillation of No. 5. Generally too intense (particularly in rubato) to take wing with, say, Cortot's irresistible wit and *élan* or Ashkenazy's early (1950s) legendary fleetness and elegance, Licad plays with a character and commitment entirely her own; a far cry from today's more fashionable austerity and circumspection. In the first *Ballade* she sounds a truly tragic and bardic note and her coda is launched with an awe-inspiring force and assurance (*appassionata* and *il più forte possible*, indeed), while in the Second *Scherzo* she seeks out a core of poetry all too frequently erased by other, lesser artists intent on little beyond surface brio and whimsy. Here, surely, are musicianship and virtuosity working in superb alliance. The recordings match the performances in their warmth and clarity.

Chopin Waltzes – No. 1 in E flat major, Op. 18. No. 2 in A flat major, Op. 34 No. 1. No. 3 in
   A minor, Op. 34 No. 2. No. 4 in F major, Op. 34 No. 3. No. 5 in A flat major, Op. 42. No. 6 in
   D flat major, Op. 64 No. 1. No. 7 in C sharp minor, Op. 64 No. 2. No. 8 in A flat major, Op. 64
   No. 3. No. 9 in A flat major, Op. 69 No. 1. No. 10 in E minor, Op. 69 No. 2. No. 11 in G flat
   major, Op. 70 No. 1. No. 12 in F minor, Op. 70 No. 2. No. 13 in D flat major, Op. 70 No. 3.
   No. 14 in E minor, Op. posth. No. 15 in E major, Op. posth. No. 16 in A flat major, Op. posth.
   No. 17 in E flat major, Op. posth. No. 18 in E flat major, Op. posth. No. 19 in A minor,
   Op. posth. **Jean-Bernard Pommier** (pf). Erato Ⓔ 4509-92887-2 (57 minutes: DDD: 3/94).
   Recorded 1993.

This pianist has given long and careful thought as to what aspect of the composer he feels these waltzes should reveal: while recognizing them as "fashionable" Chopin, he never allows his fingers just to trip their way along. The result is never less than pleasing for judicious choice of tempo, for several stimulating textual variants taken from original manuscripts, and a general surefootedness. Perhaps the disc doesn't haunt the memory in quite the same way as several CD reissues of legendary waltzers of yore. Lipatti (listed below) immediately springs to mind. Of these, the one with whom Pommier has least in common is the mercurial, light-fingered Lipatti, someone too loved by the gods to have time for second thoughts about some questionably breathless tempos or swiftness of internal vacillations of mood, but who so miraculously conveyed the "rapture and poignancy of first sensations". Maybe Pommier more often looked to Rubinstein's finely integrated last recording of these waltzes – though without wholly achieving the eloquent simplicity of phrasing and naturalness of rubato of that artist in later days – or indeed his life-long fingertip magic. But the trenchancy with which the French pianist makes his every point is undeniably impressive. Full, clear-toned recording.

Additional recommendations ...

...Nos. 1-14. **Artur Rubinstein** (pf). RCA Victor Red Seal Ⓔ RD89564* (ADD).   ⒼⒼ
...Nos. 1-14. Mazurka No. 32 in C sharp minor, Op. 50 No. 3. Barcarolle in F sharp major, Op. 60.
   Nocturne No. 8 in D flat major, Op. 27 No. 2. **Dinu Lipatti** (pf). EMI Références mono
   Ⓜ CDH7 69802-2* (65 minutes: ADD: 7/89).   Ⓖ ⒼⒼ
...17 Waltzes. Polonaises – G minor, Op. posth; B flat major, Op. posth. **Allan Schiller** (pf). ASV
   Quicksilva Ⓢ CDQS6149 (60 minutes: DDD: 4/95).

Chopin Etudes, Opp. 10 and 25. **Maurizio Pollini** (pf). DG Ⓕ 413 794-2GH (56 minutes: ADD:
   5/85). From 2530 291 (11/72).   ⒼⒼⒼ

New review

Chopin Etudes: Op. 10[a] – No. 4 in C sharp minor; No. 10 in A flat major; No. 11 in E flat major;
   Op. 25 – No. 5 in E minor; No. 8 in D flat major; No. 11 in A minor; No. 12 in C minor.
   Nocturnes[a] – E major, Op. 62 No. 2; E minor, Op. 72 No. 1. Polonaise in A flat major, Op. 61[a].
Scriabin Piano Sonatas[b] – No. 2 in G sharp minor, Op. 19; No. 5 in F sharp major, Op. 53.
   Sviatoslav Richter (pf). Praga Ⓑ CMX354007 (61 minutes: ADD: 6/96). Items marked [a] recorded
   live in 1988, [b]live in 1972.

The 24 *Etudes* of Chopin's Opp. 10 and 25, although dating from his twenties, remain among the most perfect specimens of the genre ever known, with all technical challenges – and they are formidable – dissolved into the purest poetry. With his own transcendental technique (and there are few living pianists who can rival it) Pollini makes you unaware that problems even exist – as for instance in Op. 10 No. 10 in A flat, where the listener is swept along in an effortless stream of melody. The first and last of the same set in C major and C minor have an imperious strength and drive, likewise the last three impassioned outpourings of Op. 25. Lifelong dislike of a heart worn on the sleeve makes him less than intimately confiding in more personal contexts such as No. 3 in E and No. 6 in E flat minor from Op. 10, or the nostalgic middle section of No. 5 in E minor and the searing No. 7 in C sharp minor from Op. 25. Like the playing, so the recording itself could profitably be a little warmer from time to time, but it is a princely disc all the same, which all keyboard *aficionados* will covet. Chopin Studies were never Richter's ideal repertoire. But in 1988, when the magisterial technique was starting to fray in some repertoire, he turned in some glorious sustained performances, and his wonderful hall-filling sound is finely captured here. Of the Scriabin sonatas, No. 5 is unbelievably daring and No. 2 has you hanging on every note.

...Etudes. **Liszt** Mephisto Waltz No. 1, "Der Tanz in der Dorfschenke", S514. **Vladimir Ashkenazy**
(pf). Melodiya mono Ⓜ 74321 33215-2* (72 minutes: ADD).

...Etudes. **Vladimir Ashkenazy** (pf). Decca Ⓕ 414 127-2DH (DDD: 1/85).   Ⓖ

...Etudes. **Louis Lortie** (pf). Chandos Ⓕ CHAN8482 (68 minutes: DDD: 1/87).

...Etudes. Trois nouvelles études, Op. posth. **Boris Berezovsky** (pf). Teldec Ⓕ 9031-73129-2
(68 minutes: DDD: 4/92).

...Etudes. **John Bingham** (pf). Meridian Ⓕ CDE84221 (67 minutes: DDD: 5/93).

Chopin Piano Sonata No. 2 in B flat minor, Op. 35. Nocturnes – F sharp major, Op. 15 No. 2;
C minor, Op. 48 No. 1; E major, Op. 62 No. 2; C sharp minor, Op. posth. Barcarolle in F sharp
major, Op. 60. Scherzo in B flat minor, Op. 31. **Mikhail Pletnev** (pf). Virgin Classics Ⓕ VC5
45076-2 (68 minutes: DDD: 3/95). From VC7 90738-2 (4/90). Recorded 1988. *Selected by Sounds
in Retrospect.*

These are superb and audacious performances. Love them or hate them you will never – not for a
minute, not for a second – remain indifferent. Is his *Barcarolle* daringly free or scrupulously true to
both the music's outer and inner manifestation? Dare one mention a glaring rhythmic distortion in
the closing octaves, a vulgarization of Chopin's nobility in the second bar of the C minor *Nocturne*,
or question the *forte* rather than *pianissimo* start to the *doppio movimento* in the same *Nocturne*? Such
questions are asked in a spirit of awe rather than impertinence and are, in any case, invariably silenced
by Pletnev's technical and musical imperiousness. The Second Sonata will have experts (and
particularly Polish experts) locked in furious debate when not mesmerized by the spine-tingling drama
Pletnev achieves at the start of the first-movement development, the sinister underlying waltz rhythm
he finds in the *Scherzo*, the chillingly exact 'timpani' rolls in the Funeral March and, most of all, the
terrifying miasma emanating from the finale, its linear texture clouded and engulfed in lavish yet
precise pedalling. Rarely, too, have the *Nocturnes*' passionate and erotic undertow surfaced so tellingly
through their civilized veneer. In short, not since Michelangeli's heyday has Chopin been played with
such compulsive brilliance, individuality and pianistic mastery. The recordings capture Pletnev's
sound-world to perfection and are of optimum range and clarity.

...Piano Sonatas Nos. 1-3. **Idil Biret** (pf). Naxos Ⓢ 8 550363 (75 minutes: DDD).

...Piano Sonatas – No. 2; No. 3 in B minor, Op. 58. Fantasie in F minor, Op. 49. **Shura Cherkassky**
(pf). Decca Ⓕ 433 650-2DH (63 minutes: DDD: 6/93).   ⒼⒼ

...Piano Sonata No. 2, 12 Etudes, Op. 25ᵇ, **Grigory Sokolov** (pf). Opus 111 Ⓕ OPS30-83
(59 minutes: DDD: 1/94).

...Barcarolle in F sharp major. Scherzo No. 3 in C sharp minor, Op. 39. *Coupled with works by*
Brahms, Prokofiev, Ravel *and* **Liszt** Martha Argerich (pf). DG The Originals Ⓜ 447
430-2GOR (71 minutes: ADD: 6/95). *See review in the Collections section; refer to the Index to
Reviews.*   ⒼⒼ

Chopin Piano Sonatas – No. 2 in B flat minor, Op. 35; No. 3 in B minor, Op. 58. **Maurizio Pollini**
(pf). DG Ⓕ 415 346-2GH (52 minutes: DDD: 8/86).   ⒼⒼ

These two magnificent romantic sonatas are Chopin's longest works for solo piano. The passion of
the B flat minor Sonata is evident throughout, as is its compression (despite the overall length) – for
example, the urgent first subject of its first movement is omitted in the recapitulation. As for its
mysterious finale, once likened to "a pursuit in utter darkness", it puzzled Chopin's contemporaries
but now seems totally right. The B minor Sonata is more glowing and spacious, with a wonderful
Largo third movement, but its finale is even more exhilarating than that of the B flat minor, and on a
bigger scale. Pollini plays this music with overwhelming power and depth of feeling; the expressive
intensity is rightly often disturbing. Magisterial technique is evident throughout and the recording is
sharp-edged but thrilling.

...Nos. 2 and 3. Fantaisie in F minor, Op. 49. **Artur Rubinstein** (pf). RCA Victor Red Seal
Ⓕ RD89812 (61 minutes: ADD: 2/87).   ⒼⒼ

...Nos. 2 and 3. **Murray Perahia** (pf). CBS Ⓕ MK76242 (50 minutes: ADD: 3/89).   ⒼⒼ

...Nos. 2 and 3. No. 1 in C minor, Op. 4. Etudes, Op. 10 – No. 6 in E flat minor. Etudes, Op. 25 –
No. 3 in F major; No. 4 in A minor; No. 10 in B minor; No. 11 in A minor. Mazurkas, Op. 17 –
No. 1 in B flat major; No. 2 in E minor; No. 3 in A flat major; No. 4 in A minor. **Leif Ove
Andsnes** (pf). Virgin Classics Duo Ⓜ VCK7 59072-2 (two discs: 111 minutes: DDD: 6/92).

Chopin Piano Sonata No. 3 in B minor, Op. 58. Mazurkas – A minor, Op. 17 No. 4; B flat minor,
Op. 24 No. 4; D flat major, Op. 30 No. 3; D major, Op. 33 No. 2; C sharp minor, Op. 50 No. 3;
C major, Op. 56 No. 2; F sharp minor, Op. 59 No. 3; B major, Op. 63 No. 1; F minor, Op. 63
No. 2; C sharp minor, Op. 63 No. 3; F minor, Op. 68 No. 4. **Evgeni Kissin** (pf). RCA Victor Red
Seal Ⓕ 09026 62542-2 (65 minutes: DDD: 11/94). Recorded live in 1993. *Gramophone Editor's
record of the month.*   ⒼⒼ

At 23 Kissin is unquestionably among the master-pianists of our time, and in their poise and maturity
all these performances seem light-years away from colleagues twice his age. What magnificence and

assertion he finds in the B minor Sonata's opening (for once truly *maestoso*), what menace in the following uprush of chromatic scales, his deliberate pedal haze capturing one of Chopin's most truly modernist moments. Kissin may relish left-hand counter-melody in the return of the second subject and elsewhere, yet such detail is always offered within the context of the whole, within the most bracing and invigorating sense of propulsion. A momentary failure of concentration at 1'04" in the *Scherzo*'s central section comes as reassuring evidence of human fallibility but elsewhere one can only marvel at a manner so trenchant, musicianly and resolutely unsentimental. The equestrian finale is among the most lucid on record (no Argerichian waving of fire-brands here) and concludes in a controlled triumph that has the audience cheering to the heavens. The 12 *Mazurkas* are no less remarkable for their strength and discretion. Nothing is rushed, everything is unfolded with complete naturalness and authority. Kissin's rubato is beautifully idiomatic yet so stylishly applied that you are only aware of a musical 'breathing', of the finest fluctuations of pulse and emotion. Few other pianists have gone to the heart of the matter with such assurance (always excepting Artur Rubinstein). The recording captures Kissin's clear, unnarcissistic sonority admirably and audience noise is kept to a minimum.

Further listening ...

...(trans. Franchomme) Grand Duo concertante in E major on Themes from Meyerbeer's "Robert le diable"[b]. *Coupled with* **Franchomme** Air auvergnat varié in A minor, Op. 26[d]. Caprices, Op. 7[a] – No. 2 in E minor; No. 4 in A minor; No. 7 in C major. Nocturne in G major (trans. Chopin)[b]. Grande valse, Op. 34[d]. Nocturne in A flat minor, Op. 15 No. 3[b]. Air russe varié No. 2 in D minor, Op. 32[d]. **Anner Bylsma** (vc); [b]**Lambert Orkis** (fp); [d]**L'Archibudelli** and **Smithsonian Chamber Players.** Sony Classical Vivarte SK53980 (4/95). ✍

...Rondo in C minor, Op. 1. Rondo "à la Mazur" in F major, Op. 5. Introduction and Rondo in C minor/E flat major, Op. 16. Rondo in C major, Op. 73. Mazurkas, Op. posth. – G major; B flat major; C major; A flat major; D major. Introduction and Variations in E major on "Der Schweizerbub". Introduction and Variations in B flat major on a theme from Hérold's "Ludovic", Op. 12. Souvenir de Paganini (Variations in A major). Variations No. 6 in E major on a March from Bellini's "I Puritani". Introduction, Theme and Variations (with Martin Sauer, pf). **Idil Biret** (pf). Naxos 8 550508 (5/93).

Johannes Ciconia   French/Italian c1335-1411

Suggested listening ...

...Amor por ti sempre. Caçando un giorno. O Padua, sidus praeclarum. Regina gloriosa. Aler m'en veus. Io crido amor. O rosa bella. Poy che morir. Ben che va dui donna. Le ray au soleyl (three versions). Pertrum Marcello Venetum/O petre antistes inclite. Chi nel servir antico. Per quella strada. Una panthera. Gli atti col dançar. Sus une fontayne. O Petre, Christe discipule. Doctorem principem/Melodia suavissima/Vir mitis. O virum omnimoda/O Lux et decus/O beate Nicholae. **Project Ars Nova Ensemble.** New Albion NA048CD (5/93).

...O Petre Christi discipule. Gloria "Suscipe trinitas". *Coupled with works by* **Philipoctus de Caserta, Anonymous, Johanne Egidius, Matheus de Sancto Johanne, Bartolomeus da Bologna, Velut, Tapissier, Antonius de Civitate Austrie, Zacharias, Brassart** and **Dufay Orlando Consort.** Metronome METCD1008 (11/95). *See review in the Collections section; refer to the Index to Reviews.*   ⓖ

Francesco Cilea   Italian 1866-1950

Cilea Adriana Lecouvreur. **Renata Scotto** (sop) Adriana Lecouvreur; **Plácido Domingo** (ten) Maurizio; **Sherrill Milnes** (bar) Michonnet; **Elena Obraztsova** (mez) Princesse de Bouillon; **Giancarlo Luccardi** (bass) Prince de Bouillon; **Florindo Andreolli** (ten) Abbe de Chazeuil; **Lillian Watson** (sop) Jouvenot; **Ann Murray** (mez) Dangeville; **Paul Crook** (ten) Poisson; Major-domo; **Paul Hudson** (bass) Quinault; **Ambrosian Opera Chorus; Philharmonia Orchestra / James Levine.** CBS ⒠ MZK79310 (two discs: 135 minutes: ADD: 3/90). Notes, text and translation included. From 79310 (6/78). Recorded 1977.

Adriana Lecouvreur is an archetypal prima donna vehicle. Look at the plot coldly, without reference to the music, and it is costumed hokum of an improbability that takes the breath away (of course there's jealousy, of course there's a death-scene, but what do you say to a bunch of poisoned violets as a murder weapon?). Even with the music, even allowing that Cilea was a much shrewder man of the theatre and a much more able musician than his detractors can bear to allow, it is still ... well, hokum with some damned good tunes. But Cilea wrote his opera in the full knowledge that an essential five per cent of its appeal would be added by the prima donna. Not with faultless vocalism, though that's a prerequisite too, but with the sort of allure of vocal personality that elsewhere would be called "star quality". With that extra five per cent, arguments about the artifice of the plot and the occasional thinness of the score fall away as the irrelevancies that they are. And you can tell very soon whether the soprano in question has that quality: after Cilea's brief but evocative scene-setting (telling us that we're back-stage at the Comédie Française in the eighteenth century, a world of glamour and intrigue), she enters, a prima donna portraying a prima donna, and tells us, to a sumptuous melody, that star though she is she's but the humble handmaid of her art. If you are not moved despite yourself, despite the obvious artifice (is it Adriana or the soprano herself speaking?) proceed no further; either this opera or this performance is not for you. Scotto has that magic quality, in abundance. That Domingo is an ardent hero, Milnes a touching elderly admirer, Obraztsova a baleful rival and Levine an enthusiastic exponent of the subtleties and ingenuities of a composer often despised for having written prima donna vehicles is all bonus, making this a performance that you can return to again and again. But the centre of its allure, its *raison d'être*, is Renata Scotto, glamour personified. Her entrance is electrifying, her death moving and everything between is more than life-size.

Additional recommendation ...

...Soloists; Welsh National Opera Chorus; Welsh National Opera Orchestra / Richard Bonynge.
Decca Ⓕ 425 815-2DH2 (two discs: 134 minutes: ADD: 9/90).

Domenico Cimarosa
Italian 1749-1801

Cimarosa Il matrimonio segreto. **Arleen Auger** (sop) Carolina; **Julia Varady** (sop) Elisetta; **Dietrich Fischer-Dieskau** (bar) Geronimo; **Júlia Hamari** (contr) Fidalma; **Ryland Davies** (ten) Paolino; **Alberto Rinaldi** (bar) Count Robinson; **English Chamber Orchestra / Daniel Barenboim**.
DG Ⓜ 437 696-2GX3 (three discs: 165 minutes: ADD: 8/93). Text and translation included. From 2709 069 (9/77). Recorded 1975. *Gramophone Editor's choice.* Ⓖ

The music may not have the more adventurous harmony or contrapuntal dexterity of Mozart (whose opening of the *Zauberflöte* Overture only four months earlier Cimarosa must almost certainly have cribbed), but it abounds in delightfully fresh melodic invention and rhythmic vitality – its bubbling patter-work too is worthy of Rossini at his best. Together with its construction, with as many ensembles as solo arias and with skilfully planned finales, and its scoring, primarily aimed at supporting the singers but giving the orchestra some independent interest, it marks not merely an expert craftsman but a composer of distinction whose wide popularity at the time is understandable. Barenboim makes the music dance along with the utmost sparkle, and he is fortunate in having a splendid cast, in whom it is almost invidious to praise Ryland Davies (with free tone-production, fine breath-control and native-sounding Italian) and the silver-voiced Arleen Auger as the young couple at the centre of the plot. But Alberto Rinaldi also brings a real sense of character to the blustering Count Robinson (was this personage intended as a dig at the British?), who sets his heart on the clandestinely married Caroline and ends up, most improbably, marrying her shrewish elder sister whom he had previously declared he would rather die than wed; and Julia Varady gives a stunning performance of that character's big florid aria in the last act. An issue not to be missed.

Mikolajus Ciurlionis
Lithuanian 1875-1911

Suggested listening ...

...Symphonic poems – The sea; In the forest. Five Preludes for String Orchestra. **Slovak Philharmonic Orchestra / Juozas Domarkas.** Marco Polo 8 223323 (6/91).
...Piano Works, Volumes 1 and 2. **Mûza Rubackyté** (pf). Marco Polo 8 223549/50 (2/95).
8 223549: 10 Preludes. Humoresque, VL162. Nocturnes – VL178; VL183. Impromptu, VL181. Chansonette, VL199. Mazurkas – VL222; VL234. Piano Sonata, VL155. *8 223550:* 16 Preludes. Pater Noster, VL260. Autumn, VL264. Three Pieces on a Theme. Fugue in B flat minor, VL345. String Quartet in C minor (trans. Rubackyté).

Jeremiah Clarke
British c1674-1707

Suggested listening ...

...I will love Thee. *Coupled with works by* **Goss, S.S. Wesley, Mendelssohn, Ouseley, Schubert** and **Parry** Chichester Cathedral Choir / Alan Thurlow with James Thomas (org).
Priory PRCD539 (5/96).

Rebecca Clarke
British 1886-1979

New review

R. Clarke Piano Trio[b]. Viola Sonata[c].
Beach Piano Quintet in F sharp major, Op. 67[a]. **Martin Roscoe** (pf); [a]**Endellion Quartet** ([b]Andrew Watkinson, Ralph de Souza, vns; [bc]Garfield Jackson, va; David Waterman, vc). ASV
Ⓟ CDDCA932 (74 minutes: DDD: 10/95). Recorded 1994.

Rebecca Clarke's beautiful Viola Sonata and her remarkable Piano Trio are deservedly becoming almost repertory pieces these days, but there has not been a previous recording of Amy Beach's Piano

Quintet. It is one of her best works, distinctly post-Brahmsian but with a softer lyrical vein and an individual talent for not doing the obvious. It satisfyingly balances an opening movement rendered similarly unstable by the return of its mysterious slow introduction. There is abundant melodic appeal, especially in the song-like middle movement, but although the Quintet is beautifully made and ingeniously planned it does not have quite enough identity to lodge in the memory. Ironically enough, this is especially noticeable when Beach is coupled, as here, with Clarke. Clarke's Trio is as much about the undercutting or assailing of lyricism as Beach's Quintet is, but here the language is so much more personal that the drama is immediately more gripping. The end of the Trio's first movement has a bleak quality of conflict unresolved that almost approaches Shostakovich, and when the apparently untroubled dance music of the finale (with a hint of folk melody to it) is first challenged by a mournful lyricism from earlier in the work, then by quite unexpected fanfares and march rhythms the sheer scale of the conflict is greater than anything Beach can encompass. It is a fine piece, and very beautifully played and it is difficult to imagine a better recorded performance of the Viola Sonata: Garfield Jackson is audibly grateful for a fellow-violist's idiomatic sympathy for the instrument's eloquence and its ability to sketch large gestures, and in the scherzo he is delighted to find Clarke in genial, exuberant mood (though even here there is a quiet corner of wistfulness). For anyone who doubts, or does not yet know, that Clarke was one of the most accomplished British composers of her generation there could be no better proof than this coupling, to which the Beach Quintet is an agreeable bonus. First-class recorded sound throughout.

Additional recommendation ...

...Viola Sonata. Lullaby. Morpheus. *Coupled with works by* **Britten, Vaughan Williams, Grainger, Bax** and **Bridge** Paul Coletti (va); Leslie Howard (pf). Hyperion Ⓕ CDA66687 (67 minutes: DDD: 10/94). *See review in the Collections section; refer to the Index to Reviews.*

Further listening ...

...Cello Sonata[a]. Epilogue[b]. Three Compositions, Op. 40[b]. *Coupled with* **Beach** Violin Sonata, Op. 34[a]. **Pamela Frame** (vc); [a]Barry Snyder, [b]Robert Weirich (pfs). Koch International Classics 37281-2 (3/95).

Clemens non Papa   French/Flemish c1510-c1556

Suggested listening ...

...Missa Pastores quidnam vidistis. Motets – Pastores quidnam vidistis; Tribulationes civitatum; Pater peccavi; Ego flos campi. **The Tallis Scholars / Peter Phillips.** Gimell CDGIM013 (12/87).

...Ego flos campi. Intemerata Dei mater. *Coupled with* **Anonymous** (attrib. Josquin) Nunc Dimittis. **Morales** Magnificat octavi toni. **Lhéritier** Surrexit pastor bonus. **Ockeghem** Intemerata Dei mater. **Rogier** Laboravi in gemitu meo. **Palestrina** Si ignoras te. **Lassus** Lauda mater ecclesia. **Victoria** Vadam, et circumibo civitatem. **Byrd** Laudibus in sanctis. **João IV** Crux fidelis. **Oxford Camerata / Jeremy Summerly.** Naxos 8 550843 (3/95).

...Une fillette bien gorriere; Du laid tetin; Imcessament suis triste et doloreux. *Coupled with works by* **Certon, G. Coste, Compère, De Bussy, Fresneau, Gombert, Guiard, Hesdin, Josquin Desprez, La Rue, Ninot le Petit, Pipelare, Sermisy, Vermont le Jeune** and **Willaert**. **Clément Janequin Ensemble / Dominique Visse.** Harmonia Mundi HMC90 1453 (5/95). *See review in the Collections section; refer to the Index to Reviews.*   Ⓖ

Muzio Clementi   Italian/British 1752-1832

New review

Clementi Piano Sonatas – B flat major, Op. 24 No. 2; F sharp minor, Op. 25 No. 5; B minor, Op. 40 No. 2; D major, Op. 40 No. 3. **Nikolai Demidenko** (pf). Hyperion Ⓕ CDA66808 (69 minutes: DDD: 10/95). Recorded 1994.

Several recent excellent releases – on period and modern instruments – have done much to counter Mozart's evaluation of Clementi as a "mere mechanicus". For those who remain unconvinced, Demidenko's issue of Clementi sonatas (on a modern piano) provides a comprehensive demonstration of the composer's skill and imagination that should ensure an enthusiastic following. The B flat Sonata, Op. 24 No. 2, which Clementi played at Joseph II's court in December 1781, is an exuberant exhibition piece. Demidenko's spontaneous keyboard virtuosity and delightful variety of touch underlines the music's surprising diversity. Indeed, the soft lighting of his performances in general heightens the emotional impact of his interpretations. Two of the Op. 40 Sonatas offer remarkable illustrations of Clementi's dramatic and expressive power. Demidenko's performance of the dazzling D major Sonata reveals its potent cocktail of Beethovenian boldness and Mozartian *dolce* in the first movement, and luxuriates in its poignant, improvisatory melody and rich harmony in the second. However, Demidenko's tonal range, technical polish and musical intelligence are even

more impressive in the B minor Sonata. Here, his apt characterization of the first movement's turbulent mix of icy reserve and fiery bravura, and deft handling of the second movement's fusion of *adagio* and finale, compellingly evoke the music's spirit of fantasy.

Additional recommendations ...

...F minor; F sharp minor; G minor, Op. 7 No. 3; B flat major, Op. 24 No. 2; D major, Op. 25 No. 6. **Peter Katin** (fp). Athene Ⓕ ATHCD4 (75 minutes: DDD: 12/93). ✓

...G minor, Op. 8 No. 1; F minor, Op. 13 No. 6; F sharp minor, Op. 25 No. 5; D major, Op. 40 No. 3. Batti, batti (after the aria from Mozart's *Don Giovanni*). **Maria Tipo** (pf). EMI Ⓕ CDC7 54766-2 (73 minutes: DDD: 2/94).

...B flat major, Op. 24 No. 2; Op. 25: No. 2 in G major, No. 5 in F sharp minor; D major, Op. 37 No. 2. Six Keyboard Sonatinas, Op. 36. **Balázs Szokolay** (pf). Naxos Ⓢ 8 550452 (71 minutes: DDD: 9/95).

Further listening ...

...Symphonies, Op. 18 – No. 1 in B flat major; No. 2 in D major. Minuetto pastorale in D major. Piano Concerto in C major. **Pietro Spada** (pf). **Philharmonia Orchestra / Francesco D'Avalos.** ASV CDDCA802 (2/93).

...Symphonies – No. 1 in C major; No. 3 in G major, "Great National Symphony". Overture in C major. **Philharmonia Orchestra / Francesco D'Avalos.** ASV CDDCA803 (2/93).

...Symphonies – No. 2 in D major; No. 4 in D major. Overture in D major. **Philharmonia Orchestra / Francesco D'Avalos.** ASV CDDCA804 (2/93). These three recordings are also available as part of a three-disc mid-price set (ASV CDDCS322).

Louis-Nicolas Clérambault
French 1676-1749

Suggested listening ...

...Cantatas – Orphée; Zéphire et Flore; Léandre et Héro. Sonata, "La Magnifique". **Julianne Baird** (sop); **Music's Recreation.** Meridian CDE84182 (1/91). ✓ *Selected by Sounds in Retrospect.*

Eric Coates
British 1886-1957

Coates Orchestral works. [a]**Royal Liverpool Philharmonic Orchestra / Sir Charles Groves;** [b]**London Symphony Orchestra / Sir Charles Mackerras;** [c]**City of Birmingham Symphony Orchestra / Reginald Kilbey.** Classics for Pleasure Ⓑ CD-CFPD4456* (two discs: 129 minutes: ADD: 9/89). From CFPD414456-3 (11/86). Recorded 1956-71.
Saxo-Rhapsody. Wood Nymphs. Music Everywhere (Rediffusion March). From Meadow to Mayfair. The Dam Busters – march ([a] all from Columbia TWO226, 12/68); London. Cinderella – phantasy. London Again ([a] TWO321, 12/70). The Merrymakers – Miniature Overture. Summer Days – At the dance. By the Sleepy Lagoon. The Three Men – Man from the sea. The Three Bears – Phantasy ([b] CFP40279, 3/78). Calling all Workers – March. The Three Elizabeths ([c] TWO361, 12/71). ⒼⒼ

Eric Coates reached a vast public through the use of his music as signature tunes for radio programmes such as "In Town Tonight" ("Knightsbridge" from the *London Suite*), "Music While You Work" (*Calling all Workers*) and "Desert Island Discs" (*By the Sleepy Lagoon*). The cinema furthered the cause with the huge success of *The Dam Busters* march. There is much more to his music, though, than mere hit themes. Suites such as *London, London Again, From Meadow to Mayfair* and *The Three Elizabeths* offer a wealth of delights and are all the better for the juxtaposition of their contrasted movements. The two tone-poems for children, *Cinderella* and *The Three Bears* are splendidly apt pieces of programme music – simple to follow, ever charming, never trite. The miniature overture *The Merrymakers* and the elegant waltz "At the dance" (from the suite *Summer Days* are other superb pieces of light music, whilst the *Saxo-Rhapsody* shows Coates in somewhat more serious mood. Throughout there is a rich vein of melody, and an elegance and grace of orchestration that makes this music to listen to over and over again with ever increasing admiration. The three conductors and orchestras featured adopt a no-nonsense approach that modestly suggests that his music should not be lingered over, never taken too seriously. Considering that the Mackerras items were first issued in 1956 (the rest being from 1968-71), the sound is of astonishingly good and remarkably uniform quality. This is a veritable feast of delightful music and, at its low price, a remarkable bargain.

Additional recommendations ...

...The Merrymakers. London. The Three Elizabeths. Calling all Workers. The Jester at the Wedding. The Dam Busters. The Green Hills o' Somerset[a]. Stonecracker John[a]. [a]**Ian Wallace** (bass); **BBC Concert Orchestra / Sir Adrian Boult.** BBC Radio Classics BBCRD9106 (76 minutes: ADD: 3/95). Ⓖ

...Calling All Workers. *Coupled with works by* **Binge, Williams, Toye, Collins, Farnon, Baynes, Curzon, Lutz, Gibbs, White, Ketèlbey, Joyce, Ellis** and **Ancliffe** New London Orchestra / Ronald Corp. Hyperion CDA Ⓕ CDA66868 (78 minutes: DDD: 7/96). *Gramophone Editor's record of the month. See review in the Collections section; refer to the Index to Reviews.* Ⓖ

New review

Coates Songs[a] – Rise up and reach the stars; At vesper bell; The young lover; The grenadier; Four old English songs; Because I miss you so; Sigh no more, ladies; Tell me where is fancy bred; The fairy tales of Ireland; Music of the night; Betty and Johnny; The mill o' dreams; When I am dead; The little green balcony; Ship of dream; The outlaw's song; Your name; Beautiful lady moon; Princess of the dawn. First meeting[b]. [a]**Richard Edgar-Wilson** (ten); [b]**Michael Ponder** (va); **Eugene Asti** (pf). Marco Polo Ⓔ 8 223806 (69 minutes: DDD: 4/96). Texts included. Recorded 1994.
This is very much a sequel to the existing ASV collection of Coates songs performed by Brian Rayner Cook and Raphael Terroni. The performers and label may be different, but the recording location and producer are the same. Most particularly, there is no overlap of programmatic content. Uncommonly for a sequel, this collection is every bit the equal of its predecessor both in content and performance. Richard Edgar-Wilson has a delightfully natural, free-ranging and expressive tenor voice, his words coming through with complete clarity, while Eugene Asti clearly revels in Coates's luxurious accompaniments. Such, moreover, is the consistency of Coates's inspiration and musicianship that, though his best-known songs are all in the ASV collection, the selection here is equally enjoyable. At the most obviously popular end of the spectrum *The grenadier* has one of those rousing Fred Weatherly lyrics after the fashion of *Stonecracker John*, while at the more ambitious end are some delightfully fresh Shakespeare settings, as well as the short song-cycle *The mill o' dreams*. By way of variety the collection also includes a piece for viola and piano that Coates composed for his teacher Lionel Tertis. This gives producer Michael Ponder a chance to step into the limelight, which he richly deserves for this utterly diverting collection.

Further listening ...
...The Seven Dwarfs. The Jester at the Wedding. Four Centuries. **East of England Orchestra / Malcolm Nabarro.** ASV White Line CDWHL2075 (8/93).
...Reuben Ranzo. I heard you singing. Brown eyes I love. I pitch my lonely caravan at night. The dreams of London. A song remembered. The green hills o' Somerset. Bird songs at eventide. A dinder courtship. Always as I close my eyes. Little lady of the moon. Through all the ages. Stonecracker John. At sunset. I'm lonely. Homeward to you. Today is ours. A song of summer. **Brian Rayner Cook** (bar); **Raphael Terroni** (pf). ASV White Line CDWHL2081 (3/87).

Jean Cocteau   French 1889-1963

Suggested listening ...
...Le bel indifférent[b]. *Coupled with* **Poulenc** La voix humaine[a]. [a]**Denise Duval** (sop) La Femme; [b]**Edith Piaf** (spkr); [a]**Paris Opéra-Comique Orchestra / Georges Prêtre;** [b]**instrumental ensemble.** EMI L'Esprit Français Ⓜ CDM5 65156-2* (10/94). *See review under Poulenc; refer to the Index to Reviews.*

Manuel Rodrigues Coehlo   Portuguese c1555-1635

Suggested listening ...
...Segunda Susana grosada a 4 sobre a de 5. Segunda Tento do primeiro tom. *Coupled with works by* **A. de Cabezón, Ximénez, Carreira, H. de Cabezón Cabanilles** and **Anonymous** **Sophie Yates** (hpd). Chandos Chaconne CHAN0560 (11/94). *See review in the Collections section; refer to the Index to Reviews.*

Samuel Coleridge Taylor   British 1875-1912

Suggested listening ...
...Scenes from "The Song of Hiawatha", Op. 30 – Onaway, awake, beloved[a]. *Coupled with* **Harty** A John Field Suite. **Ireland** A London Overture. **Gardiner** Shepherd Fennell's Dance. **Vaughan Williams** The Lark Ascending[b]. **Holst** The Hymn of Jesus, H140[c]. [a]**Webster Booth** (ten); [b]**David Wise** (vn); [c]**Huddersfield Choral Society; Liverpool Philharmonic Orchestra / Sir Malcolm Sargent.** Dutton Laboratories mono CDAX8012* (5/95).
...Hiawatha Overture, Op. 30. Petite Suite de Concert, Op. 77. Four Characteristic Waltzes, Op. 22. Gipsy Suite, Op. 20. Romance of the Prairie Lilies, Op. 39. Othello, Op. 79. **RTE Concert Orchestra / Adrian Leaper.** Marco Polo 8 223516 (1/96).
...Ballade in A minor, Op. 33. Symphonic Variations on an African Air, Op. 63. *Coupled with works by* **Butterworth** and **MacCunn** **Royal Liverpool Philharmonic Orchestra / Grant Llewellyn.** Argo 436 401-2ZH (6/93). *See review under Butterworth; refer to the Index to Reviews.*
...Petite suite de concert, Op. 77[d]. Ballade in D minor, Op. 4[bd]. 24 Negro Melodies, Op. 59[d] – Take Nabandji; Going Up; Deep River; Run, Mary, run; Sometimes I feel like a motherless child; The Bamboula. Clarinet Quintet in F sharp minor, Op. 10[ac]. [a]**Harold Wright** (cl); [b]**Michael Ludwig** (vn); [c]**Hawthorne Quartet** (Ronan Lefkowitz, Si-Jing Huang, vns; Mark Ludwig, va; Sato Knudson, vc); [d]**Virginia Eskin** (pf). Koch International Classics 37056-2 (10/92).

Cy Coleman

Suggested listening ...
...City of Angels. **Original London cast.** First Night CASTCD34.

Pascal Collasse

Suggested listening ...
...Cantiques spirituels tirez de l'Ecriture Sainte. **Agnès Mellon, Sandrine Piau** (sops); **Benoît Thivel**
(alto); **Les Talens Lyriques / Christophe Rousset** (hpd/org). Erato MusiFrance 4509-92860-2 (9/94).

Henri Collet

New review

Collet Cinco canciones populares castellanas, Op. 69^a. Siete canciones populares de Burgos,
Op. 80^a. Poema de un día, Op. 48^a. Los amantes de Galicia^a. La pena^a. Cantos de Castilla,
Op. 42. ^{a}**Rachel Yakar** (sop); **Claude Lavoix** (pf). Claves Ⓕ CD50-9506 (57 minutes: DDD: 10/95).
Texts and translations included.

If the name of Henri Collet rings any bells in musicians' minds, it is as the critic who was responsible
in 1920 for the tag *Les Six* (purely by accident, since his article was merely entitled "Les Cinq Russes,
Les Six Français et Erik Satie") and as the author of books and articles on Spanish music. A
precociously gifted Parisian, he became enamoured of Spain very early on, studied literature and
music in Madrid, and composed numerous works, nearly all of Spanish inspiration and with Spanish
titles: Falla praised him highly for capturing the authentic Spanish spirit. Of the numerous songs here
the most striking is "Mariana" (one of the Castilian set), with its harshly uncompromising guitar
thrumming: the most immediately appealing are the simple folksongs in Galician dialect. Rachel
Yakar's performances are full of intensity and rhythmic vigour, and her enunciation is extremely clear;
but, uncomfortably, she is slightly flat throughout the Castilian and Burgos songs (the translations of
which are, in places, so free as to be independent of the originals): for the others, presumably recorded
at a different session, there is no such flaw. Claude Lavoix is very persuasive in the ten highly pianistic
Cantos de Castilla keyboard solos, several of which deserve to be taken up more widely.

Anthony Collins

Suggested listening ...
...Vanity Fair. *Coupled with works by* **Binge, Williams, Coates, Toye, Farnon, Baynes,
Curzon, Lutz, Gibbs, White, Ketèlbey, Joyce, Ellis** and **Ancliffe** New London Orchestra
/ Ronald Corp. Hyperion CDA66868 (7/96). *See review in the Collections section; refer to the Index
to Reviews.* **Gramophone** *Editor's record of the month.*   Ⓖ

Loÿset Compère

Suggested listening ...
...Omnium bonorum plena. Se j'ay parlé. Seray je vostre mieulx amée. Ave Maria, gratia plena.
Alons fere nos barbes. Ne vous hastez pas. Asperges me, Domine. Che fa la ramacina. Scaramella
fa la galla. Missa in Nativitate, "Deus Noster Jesu Christie". **Orlando Consort.** Metronome
METCD1002 (6/94).

Edward Confrey

Suggested listening ...
...Kitten on the Keys. *Coupled with works by* **Grainger, Gershwin, Waller, Ellington,
J.P. Johnson, Gottschalk, Columbia, Rube Bloom, Cowell, Nancarrow, B. Powell,
Beiderbecke, Jelly Roll Morton, Joplin** and **Cervantes** Alan Feinberg (pf); **Daniel
Druckman** (marimba). Argo 444 457-2ZH (11/95). *See review in the Collections section; refer to
the Index to Reviews.*

Justin Connolly

Suggested listening ...
...Poems of Wallace Stevens II, Op. 14. *Coupled with works by* **P.P. Nash, Weir, Bauld, Elias,
Payne** and **A. Gilbert** Jane Manning (sop); **Jane's Minstrels / Roger Montgomery.** NMC

Artists' Series NMCD025 (10/95). *See review in the Collections section; refer to the Index to Reviews.* Ⓖ

...Sonatina in Five Studies, Op. 1. *Coupled with works by* **Tippett, Sackman** and **Saxton** Steven **Neugarten** (pf). Metier MSVCD92008 (1/96). *See review in the Collections section; refer to the Index to Reviews.*

Arnold Cooke
British 1906-

Suggested listening ...
...Clarinet Concerto. *Coupled with* **Jacob** Mini-Concerto. **Rawsthorne** Clarinet Concerto. **Thea King** (cl); **Seattle Northwest Chamber Orchestra / Alun Francis.** Hyperion CDA66031.

Aaron Copland
American 1900-1990

Copland Clarinet Concerto.
Busoni Clarinet Concertino, Op. 48.
Mozart Clarinet Concerto in A major, K622. **Paul Meyer** (cl); **English Chamber Orchestra / David Zinman.** Denon Ⓕ CO-75289 (56 minutes: DDD: 11/93). Recorded 1992.

One of Paul Meyer's most distinctive qualities as a clarinettist is the smoothness of his tone at all dynamic levels, together with his ability to initiate a soft note with a scarcely audible beginning and to let it die away until it loses itself almost inaudibly. This betokens, of course, immense technical control, and it is impressively displayed on this record; the variety of the tone is less remarkable. So the long, cool phrases at the start of Copland's Concerto are beautifully poised, and the rare atmosphere is sustained as by almost no other player, perhaps not even Benny Goodman. Goodman, for whom the work was written and who gave encouragement to Meyer, naturally had the swing manner as no one else did (once he had got round the technical difficulties, which seem to have rattled him). Meyer plays brightly, and this is a very fresh and pleasant performance. With Busoni's odd, eclectic *Concertino*, Meyer does his best to make sense of the welter of half-allusions and shifts in manner. It is not his fault if the piece remains somewhat unfocused. These two works will probably guide listeners in their choice rather than Mozart's Concerto, which has of course been recorded by pretty well every modern clarinettist of note. Meyer keeps it cool, fairly near the surface. He does not respond to the darker elements in the development of the first movement, nor to the tensions that clutch at the centre of the *Adagio*. He is at his best in the cheerful insouciance he brings to the finale.

Additional recommendations ...
...Clarinet Concerto. **Nielsen** Clarinet Concerto, FS129. **Lutosławski** Dances Preludes. **Janet Hilton** (cl); **Royal Scottish Orchestra / Mattias Bamert.** Chandos Ⓜ CHAN8618 (51 minutes: DDD: 10/88).

...Clarinet Concerto[a]. Connotations. El salón México. Music for the Theatre. [a]**Stanley Drucker** (cl); **New York Philharmonic Orchestra / Leonard Bernstein.** DG Ⓕ 431 672-2GH (74 minutes: DDD: 8/91). Ⓖ

New review
Copland Piano Concerto[a]. Appalachian Spring[b]. Symphonic Ode[c]. [a]**Lorin Hollander** (pf); **Seattle Symphony Orchestra / Gerard Schwarz.** Delos Ⓕ DE3154 (62 minutes: DDD: 4/96). Recorded 1993-4.

Schwarz locates an unadorned, deceptively powerful purity in *Appalachian Spring* which certainly accords with Copland's own assessment of Martha Graham's original choreography ("There's something prim and restrained, a strong quality about her, that one tends to think of as American; her style is seemingly, but only seemingly, simple and extremely direct"). At once invigorating and unsentimental, Schwarz's lucid reading carries less emotional pungency than, say, Bernstein's inspirationally intense Los Angeles account for DG, yet is no less moving in its cool understatement and quiet honesty. The concerto (Copland's final jazz-inspired composition) was roundly condemned by the conservative Boston critics following its January 1928 première ("A harrowing horror from beginning to end" was a fairly typical reaction). Nowadays, of course, the music's spiky lyricism and bracing rhythmic flair seem entirely endearing. Hollander and Schwarz form a fine partnership, less highly charged, perhaps, than the composer and Bernstein, but compelling for all that; many will prefer the newcomers' more playful, less abrasive manner in the outrageous bar-room antics of the jazzy finale. As for the imposing *Symphonic Ode*, Schwarz and his Seattle band do it proud. Exemplary, rich-toned work throughout from the Delos engineers (terrific bass-drum sounds in the *Symphonic Ode*) further enhances this high-class Copland collection.

Additional recommendations ...
...Piano Concerto. *Coupled with* **Britten** Piano Concerto. **Gillian Lin** (pf); **Melbourne Symphony Orchestra / John Hopkins.** Chandos Collect Ⓜ CHAN6580 (51 minutes: ADD: 3/93).

...Appalachian Spring. Billy the Kid – suite. Rodeo. Fanfare for the Common Man. **New York Philharmonic Orchestra / Leonard Bernstein.** Sony Classical Bernstein Royal Edition Ⓜ SMK47543 (63 minutes: ADD: 5/93). Ⓖ Ⓖ Ⓖ

Copland Concert Suites – The Red Pony; Our Town; Music for Movies. The Heiress – Prelude; Finale. Prairie Journal (Music for Radio). **St Louis Symphony Orchestra / Leonard Slatkin.** RCA Victor Red Seal Ⓕ 09026 61699-2 (67 minutes: DDD: 11/94). Recorded 1991-2.   Ⓖ

Though the front cover bears the title "Music for Films", the earliest offering here was written in 1936 following a commission from the CBS radio network. *Music for Radio* (also known as *Saga of the Prairies* or *Prairie Journal*) was one of Copland's first conscious efforts to attain a greater simplicity of utterance and stronger melodic appeal, and its clean-cut, out-of-doors demeanour is relished to the full by these performers. Copland wrote eight film scores in all, the first three of which – *The City* (1939), *Of Mice and Men* (1939) and *Our Town* (1940) – formed the basis for his 1943 concert suite, *Music for Movies*. Slatkin gauges the differing moods of each of the five tableaux with unerring perception. Perhaps Copland's most enduring achievement in this particular field remains his 1948 score for *The Red Pony*. Again, the performance is all one could wish and there's real swagger in the joyous "Happy Ending" number. In addition, Slatkin also gives us the heart-warmingly evocative concert suite Copland compiled from his score for *Our Town*, as well as a first commercial recording for Arnold Freed's idiomatic 1990 reconstruction of Copland's Academy Award-winning 1948 score for *The Heiress*, which happily restores the "Prelude" that director William Wyler rejected for the final print. With excitingly full-bodied sound, this is an unmissable Copland collection.

Copland El salón México[a]. Dance Symphony[a]. Fanfare for the Common Man[a]. Rodeo – Four Dance Episodes[a]. Appalachian Spring – suite[b]. **Detroit Symphony Orchestra / Antál Dorati.** Decca Ovation Ⓜ 430 705-2DM (74 minutes: DDD: 8/91). Items marked [a] from SXDL7547 (10/82), [b]414 457-2DH (6/86). Recorded 1981-84.   ⒼⒼ

This glorious disc shows how well Antál Dorati assimilated the music of Aaron Copland. The big-boned swagger of "Buckaroo Holiday" from *Rodeo* with its vision of open spaces and clear blue skies is established straightaway in Dorati's performance with keen rhythmic drive and fine orchestral articulation. The "Hoe Down" is properly exciting while the other two dance episodes are wonderfully expressive. In the 1945 suite of *Appalachian Spring* Dorati secures marvellous phrasing and dynamics but tends to understate the poetic elements of the score. Decca's sound quality is exemplary and is of demonstration standard in *Fanfare for the Common Man*, as it is in the enjoyable curtain-raiser, the sturdy, big-hearted *El salón México*. Dorati's vast experience as an interpreter of Stravinsky and Bartók pays fine dividends in Copland's gruesome *Dance Symphony*, music inspired by the vampire film fantasy, *Nosferatu*. This survey of Copland's most popular orchestral works is a welcome addition to the mid-price catalogue.

Additional recommendations ...

...El salón México[c]. Danzón cubano[e]. An Outdoor Overture[e]. Quiet City[e]. Our Town[e]. Las agachadas[c]. Fanfare for the Common Man[e]. Lincoln Portrait[be]. Appalachian Spring – suite[e]. Rodeo – Four Dance Episodes[e]. Billy the Kid – suite[e]. Music for Movies[d]. Letter from Home[e]. John Henry[e]. Symphony No. 3[d]. Clarinet Concerto[af]. [a]**Benny Goodman** (cl); [b]**Henry Fonda** (narr; [c]**New England Conservatory Chorus;** [d]**New Philharmonia Orchestra;** [e]**London Symphony Orchestra;** [f]**Columbia Symphony Orchestra / Aaron Copland.** Sony Classical Ⓜ SM3K46559 (three discs: 226 minutes: ADD: 7/91).   ⒼⒼ

...Fanfare for the Common Man. Lincoln Portrait[a]. Canticle of Freedom[b]. An Outdoor Overture. **R. Harris** American Creed. When Johnny comes marching home. [a]**James Earl Jones** (spkr); **Seattle** [b]**Chorale and Symphony Orchestra / Gerard Schwarz.** Delos Ⓕ DE3140 (61 minutes: DDD: 5/93).

...Fanfare for the Common Man. Billy the Kid – suite. El salón México. Rodeo – Hoe-Down. Appalachian Spring – suite. **Royal Philharmonic Orchestra / Philip Ellis.** Tring International Royal Philharmonic Collection Ⓢ TRP040 (65 minutes: DDD: 12/95).

...(arr. Bernstein) El salón México. *Coupled with works by* **Messiaen, Berg, Ravel, Stravinsky, Scriabin** and **Britten Shura Cherkassky** (pf). Decca Ⓕ 433 657-2DH (79 minutes: ADD: 2/96). *See review in the Collections section; refer to the Index to Reviews.*   Ⓖ

New review

Copland Organ Symphony[a]. Short Symphony. Dance Symphony. Orchestral Variations. [a]**Simon Preston** (org); **St Louis Symphony Orchestra / Leonard Slatkin.** RCA Victor Red Seal Ⓕ 09026 68292-2 (67 minutes: DDD: 6/96). Recorded 1993-5.

Copland's *Organ Symphony* is an oddly eclectic mix born of oddly eclectic elements. Russian immigrant parents, a French teacher, jazz – the new national identity: all have a hand in the composition. But still the voice which emerges most strongly is American. Something stirs in the great outdoors but, as yet, it's untamed and more than a little unpredictable. In the *Dance Symphony* young Copland taps once more into his French connections, to indulge himself, to bring on the cornets and two harps, to lend a Berlioz-like enchantment to the solo bassoon; the second movement's shadowy waltz is the one that never made it into the *Symphonie fantastique*. The fact is that the real Copland only fully emerges with the *Short Symphony* (No. 2) of 1932-3. The Stravinsky factor is strong, of course (wiry, angular, busy neo-classical tone and a folkloric homespun quality), but the true grit is entirely Copland's own. The rhythmic bounce and the sometimes belligerent syncopations are all his, too. Slatkin and his band are as spry as can be in that respect. The most exciting item on the disc, however, comes last in the chronology. Nearly three decades after Copland famously got tough with his *Piano Variations* (1930), he laid them out for orchestra. And they came up sounding like a brand-new piece. This is Copland outreaching himself, theoretical ingenuity allied to vision. And rather like this sharp, smart, punchy performance, the overriding impression is of evolution – onwards and upwards.

Copland Symphony No. 3. Music for a Great City. **St Louis Symphony Orchestra / Leonard Slatkin.** RCA Victor Red Seal Ⓕ RD60149 (67 minutes: DDD: 2/91). Recorded 1989.

Copland intended this symphony as a 'grand gesture' and there is no doubt at any point in Slatkin's performance that a big statement is being made. He is totally inside the music and he secures playing of great precision and refinement from an orchestra which has exactly the right timbre and style. In 1964 the London Symphony Orchestra asked Copland for a work to celebrate its sixtieth season. *Music for a Great City* refers to New York, however, not London, for instead of a new work Copland adapted music from the 1961 Carroll Baker film *Something Wild*, shot on location in New York, and he fashioned four episodes roughly in the shape of a symphony. Each 'movement' bears a descriptive title such as "Skyline" or "Subway Jam". Slatkin obviously revels in Copland's highly expressive writing, sometimes sentimental, sometimes tense or jaggedly aggressive, and he conducts a brilliantly effective account of the score, with virtuoso playing from his Saint Louis orchestra. The recording has impressive range and sonority, yet detail is beautifully clear.

Additional recommendation ...

...No. 3. Quiet City. **New York Philharmonic Orchestra / Leonard Bernstein.** DG Ⓕ 419 170-2GH (55 minutes: DDD: 11/86).

Copland The Tender Land. **Elisabeth Comeaux** (sop) Laurie; **Janis Hardy** (mez) Ma Moss; **Maria Jette** (sop) Beth; **LeRoy Lehr** (bass) Grandpa Moss; **Dan Dressen** (ten) Martin; **James Bohn** (bar) Top; **Vern Sutton** (ten) Mr Splinters; **Agnes Smuda** (sop) Mrs Splinters; **Merle Fristad** (bass) Mr Jenks; **Sue Herber** (mez) Mrs Jenks; **Chorus and Orchestra of The Plymouth Music Series, Minnesota / Philip Brunelle.** Virgin Classics Ⓕ VCD7 59253-2 (two discs: 107 minutes: DDD: 8/90). Notes and text included. Recorded 1989.

Aaron Copland was a father figure of American music, and Leonard Bernstein expressed a lifelong admiration when he called him "the best we have". Yet though a generation separates them, *The Tender Land* had its première in 1954 just three years before *West Side Story*. Both opened in New York, but while Bernstein's piece is set there and portrays a violent urban America, Copland's belongs to the wide Midwest and the quiet of a farming home. It was written for young singers and has a wonderful freshness, a clean 'plainness' which Copland compared to that of his ballet *Appalachian Spring*. The story tells how the young girl Laurie Moss falls in love with Martin, a travelling harvester who visits her mother's farm, and after being left by him still decides to leave home and make her own way in the world. It has been criticized as undramatic, and its partly spoken dialogue and small cast have also gone against it – Copland later wryly called opera "la forme fatale" and never wrote another – but whatever its viability on stage, on record it provides a satisfying experience and this Minnesota performance has just the right flavour, offering simplicity and sensitivity without affectation. The conductor is himself a Midwesterner who writes that his young cast "have their roots in this particular soil" which is the heartland of America. The recording is every bit as fresh as the music.

Further listening ...

...Ballets – Grohg[a]; Hear ye! Hear ye![b]. Prelude[b]. [a]**Cleveland Orchestra; [b]London Sinfonietta / Oliver Knussen.** Argo 443 203-2ZH (10/94). *Gramophone Editor's choice.*   Ⓖ

...Nocturne. *Coupled with works by* **Bolcom, MacMillan, Schnittke** and **Dresher** Maria **Bachmann** (vn); **Jon Klibonoff** (pf); **James Saporito** (perc). Catalyst 09026 62668-2 (5/95). *See review in the Collections section; refer to the Index to Reviews.*   Ⓖ

...Duo[a]. *Coupled with* **Glass** Einstein on the Beach – Suite. **Ornstein** Violin Sonata, Op. 31[b]. **Wernick** Cadenzas and Variations II. **Gregory Fulkerson** (vn); [a]**Robert Shannon**, [b]**Alan Feinberg** (pfs). New World 80313-2 (2/96).

...In the Beginning[b]. Four Motets. *Coupled with* **Barber** Agnus Dei. **Bernstein** Chichester Psalms[a]. [a]**Dominic Martelli** (treb); [b]**Catherine Denley** (mez); [a]**Rachel Masters** (hp); [a]**Gary Kettel** (perc); **Corydon Singers / Matthew Best.** Hyperion CDA66219 (9/87).

Chick Corea   American 1941-

Suggested listening ...

...Children's Songs Nos. 2-4, 6, 7, 11, 16 and 18[be]. *Coupled with works by* **Nyman, D. Bedford, W. Gregory** and **R. Powell** Apollo Saxophone Quartet; **John Harle** (keybds); **Mike Hamnett** (perc). Argo 443 903-2ZH (8/95). *See review in the Collections section; refer to the Index to Reviews.*

Arcangelo Corelli

Corelli 12 Concerti grossi, Op. 6 – No. 1 in D major; No. 2 in F major; No. 3 in C minor; No. 4 in D major; No. 5 in B flat major; No. 6 in F major; No. 7 in D major; No. 8 in G minor; No. 9 in F major; No. 10 in C major; No. 11 in B flat major; No. 12 in F major. **The English Concert / Trevor Pinnock.** Archiv Produktion Ⓕ 423 626-2AH2 (two discs: 130 minutes: DDD: 1/89). ✏ *Gramophone Award Winner 1989.* Ⓖ

In his working life of about 40 years Corelli must have produced a great deal of orchestral music, yet the 12 *Concerti grossi*, Op. 6 form the bulk of what is known to have survived. Their original forms are mostly lost but we know that those in which they were published in Amsterdam by Estienne Roger had been carefully polished and revised by the composer – and that they were assembled from movements that had been written at various times. The first eight are in *da chiesa* form, the last four in *da camera* form – without and with named dance movements respectively, and the number of their movements varies from four to seven. Each features the interplay of a group of soloists, the *concertino* (two violins and a cello) and the orchestra, the *ripieno*, the size of which Corelli stated to be flexible. These are masterpieces of their genre, one that was later developed by, notably, Bach and Handel, and they are rich in variety. The scores leave scope for embellishment, not least in cadential and lining passages, and the players of The English Concert take full advantage of them. Regarding the overall performances, suffice it to say that this recording won a *Gramophone* Award.

Additional recommendations ...

...**Ensemble 415 / Chiara Banchini** (vn); **Jesper Christensen** (hpd). Harmonia Mundi Ⓕ HMC90 1406/7 (two discs: 147 minutes: DDD: 6/92). ✏

...**Guildhall String Ensemble / Robert Salter** (vn). RCA Victor Red Seal Ⓕ RD60071 (two discs: 128 minutes: DDD: 9/91).

...Nos. 1, 3, 7, 8, 9 and 11. **Tafelmusik Baroque Orchestra / Jean Lamon** (vn). Deutsche Harmonia Mundi Ⓕ RD77908 (66 minutes: DDD: 12/89). ✏

...**Brandenburg Consort / Roy Goodman.** Hyperion Ⓕ CDA66741/2 (two discs: 138 minutes: DDD: 9/93). ✏

Corelli Trio Sonatas, Op. 3[a] – F major; D major[c]; B flat major; B minor; D minor[c]; G major. Trio Sonatas, Op. 4[b] – C major; G minor; A major; D major; A minor; E major. [c]**Jakob Lindberg** (theorbo); **Purcell Quartet** (Catherine Mackintosh, [a]Elizabeth Wallfisch, [b]Catherine Weiss, vns; Richard Boothby, vc); **Robert Woolley** ([a]hpd/[b]org). Chandos Chaconne Ⓕ CHAN0526 (76 minutes: DDD: 12/92). ✏ Recorded 1990 (Op. 3), 1992 (Op. 4).

Corelli's chamber music was reprinted 84 times during his lifetime and 31 more during the rest of the eighteenth century, a record that most composers would find enviable even today. The Sonatas of Op. 3 are *da chiesa*, those of Op. 4 are *da camera* (with dance-titled movements); the recording contains the first six of each set – the remaining ones are on another disc (Chandos CHAN0532), should you (as is probable) be tempted to add them to your collection. They are small gems: most have four movements and their durations range from five-and-a-half to seven-and-a-half minutes, within which they pack a wealth of invention, pure beauty and variety of pace and mood. Surviving evidence suggests that they were played at a much lower pitch than today's standard, the lower string tension adding warmth and opulence to the sound. Catherine Mackintosh takes full advantage of the works' opportunities for pliant phrasing and added embellishments; Elizabeth Wallfisch 'converses' with her in her own characteristic way, whilst Catherine Weiss (Wallfisch's replacement in Op. 4) follows her example more closely. The Purcell Quartet's oneness of thought and timing in these landmark works is a joy to hear and the recording is superb in all respects.

Additional recommendation ...

...Trio Sonatas – B flat major, Op. 3 No. 3; C major, Op. 4 No. 1. **A. Scarlatti** Humanità e Lucifero[u]. [a]**Rossana Bertini** (sop); [a]**Massimo Crispi** (ten); **Europa Galante / Fabio Biondi** (vn). Opus 111 Ⓕ OPS30-129 (61 minutes: DDD: 2/96). ✏ *See review under A. Scarlatti; refer to the Index to Reviews.*

Further listening ...

...Sonata in G minor, WoO2. Trio Sonata in G major, Op. 2 No. 12. *Coupled with works by* **Ariosti, Torelli, Bononcini** *and* **Steffani Ann Monoyios** (sop); **Berlin Barock Compagney.** Capriccio 10 459 (10/95). ✏ *See review in the Collections section; refer to the Index to Reviews.* Ⓖ

...Sonata for Trumpet and Strings in D major. *Coupled with works by* **Vivaldi, Albinoni, Torelli, A. Marcello, Viviani, Franceschini** *and* **Baldassare** Håkan Hardenberger (tpt); **I Musici.** Philips 442 131-2PH (5/95). *See review in the Collections section; refer to the Index to Reviews.* Ⓖ

John Corigliano

New review

Corigliano Troubadours.
Foss American Landscapes.
Schwantner From Afar ... . **Sharon Isbin** (gtr); **Saint Paul Chamber Orchestra / Hugh Wolff.** Virgin Classics Ⓕ CDC5 55083-2 (67 minutes: DDD: 8/96). Ⓖ

No concerto has done more for the prosperity of the guitar than Rodrigo's *Concierto de Aranjuez*, nor has any done more harm – by identifying the form with catchy tunes and Spanishness, and by freezing out newcomers. The USA is a famously diverse country and so too, potentially, is the territory of the guitar concerto, as this landmark recording demonstrates at a high level. Corigliano, a lover of strong programmatic images, looks back to the Europe of long ago, from which America itself sprang, evoking the time and world of the troubadours in a work that is deeply imaginative, marvellously scored and, for the soloist, highly demanding. It is quite simply the finest new guitar concerto in many decades. Though Schwantner is an erstwhile classical, jazz and rock guitarist, *From Afar* ... is his first composition to incorporate the instrument. He celebrates its unique qualities of seductive and diverse sound, and its sheer physicality (the player's immediate contact with the strings) in a work described as "sexy and savage" in which the soft-voiced guitar is skilfully integrated with the often violent sounds of the orchestra. It is not the language of rock music that marks *From Afar* ..., it is the extreme emotions it arouses. Foss's landscapes are 100 per cent American, drawing on folk tunes with serenity, tenderness, nostalgia, humour and abounding energy, showing that it is not only Spanish music that can bring out the best in the guitar. Given the space one could eulogize in detail about all three concertos, but suffice it to say that one can have only unreserved praise for Isbin's superb performances and, indeed, for everyone who played a part in the making of this disc which carries the highest recommendation.

Corigliano Violin Sonata. Works for Violin and Piano. **Maria Bachmann** (vn); **Jon Klibonoff** (pf).
  Catalyst Ⓕ 09026 61824-2 (69 minutes: DDD: 12/93). Recorded 1993.
  Pärt Fratres. **Moravec** Violin Sonata. **Glinsky** Toccata-Scherzo. **Messiaen** Quatuor pour la
  fin du temps – Louange à l'Eternité de Jésus.   Ⓖ
Here's a double-barrelled surprise: gripping new music for violin and piano and a performing style that revisits a sweet-scented immediacy more typical of previous generations. Maria Bachmann has a bright, winsome tone and a heart-warming interpretative manner. The works that particularly suit her are Corigliano's 1963 Violin Sonata and the two pieces that were written with her in mind, Albert Glinsky's Toccata-Scherzo and Paul Moravec's Sonata. Of the latter two, the Glinsky is the more memorable – a sort of Sarasate for the 1990s, its lyrical centre-piece flanked by brilliant outer sections. The Corigliano harbours the kind of juicy 'tunes' that modern players search for in vain but hardly ever find in contemporary music. The Lento is strikingly memorable, whereas elsewhere Corigliano demands all the tricks of the fiddler's trade – harmonics, pizzicatos, sul ponticello and so on, all couched in an appealing musical context that might best be described as Stravinsky-cum-Samuel Barber. Messiaen himself said of his "Praise to the Immortality of Jesus" that it "specifically addresses the second aspect of Jesus, namely His human aspect, the Word that has become flesh, resurrected immortal to give Him life." And it's as well to bear that in mind when listening to Bachmann's unusually sensuous performance. Bachmann receives sympathetic support from Jon Klibonoff and both are nicely recorded.

Additional recommendation ...
... Violin Sonata. **Beach** Violin Sonata, Op. 34.**Curtis Macomber** (vn); **Diane Walsh** (pf). Koch
  International Classics Ⓕ 37223-2 (64 minutes: DDD: 8/95).
Further listening ...
...Symphony No. 1. **Chicago Symphony Orchestra / Daniel Barenboim.** Erato 2292-45601-2
  (7/91).   ⒼⒼ
...Clarinet Concerto[a]. *Coupled with* **Barber** Third Essay for Orchestra, Op. 47. [a]**Stanley Drucker**
  (cl); **New York Philharmonic Orchestra / Zubin Mehta.** New World NW309-2 (5/88).   ⒼⒼ
...Aria. *Coupled with works by* **Barlow, Bloom** and **Wilder** Humbert Lucarelli (ob); [a]**Mark Wood**
  (perc); **Brooklyn Philharmonic Orchestra / Michael Barrett.** Koch International Classics 37187-2
  (7/94). *See Review under Wilder; refer to the Index to Reviews.*

Carl August Cornelius   German 1824-1874

Suggested listening ...
...Sonnenuntergang. *Coupled with music by* **Britten, Eisler, Fortner, Fröhlich, Hauer,**
  Jarnach, Komma, Pfitzner, Ullmann *and* **Reutter** Mitsuko Shirai (mez); Hartmut Höll (pf).
  Capriccio 10 534 (12/94). *See review in the Collections section; refer to the Index to Reviews.*

William Cornysh   British 1468-1523

Suggested listening ...
...Salve regina. Ave Maria, mater Dei. Gaude virgo mater Christi. Magnificat. Ah, Robin. Adieu,
  adieu, my heartes lust. Adieu courage. Woefully arrayed. Stabat mater. **The Tallis Scholars / Peter**
  Phillips. Gimell CDGIM014 (4/89).   Ⓖ
...Ave Maria, mater Dei. *Coupled with works by* **Davy, Lambe** and **Wilkinson** Credo in Deum/
  Jesus autem. Salve regina. **The Sixteen / Harry Christophers.** Collins Classics 1342-2 (7/93). *See*
  review in the Collections section; refer to the Index to Reviews.   Ⓖ

Michel Corrette

Suggested listening ...

...Concerto comique No. 25, "Les Sauvages et la Furstemberg". *Coupled with* **Boismortier** Five
Sonatas for Cello, Viol, Bassoon and Continuo, Op. 26 – No. 6 in D major. **Blavet** Flute
Concerto in A minor. **Buffardin** Flute Concerto in E minor. **Quentin** Flute Sonata in D major.
Violin Concerto in A major. **Cologne Musica Antiqua / Reinhard Goebel.** Archiv Produktion 447
286-2AMA. ✒

...Concerto comique No. 25, "Les Sauvages et la Furstemberg". *Coupled with works by*
Boismortier and **Leclair Florilegium Ensemble; Jane Rogers** (va); **Scott Pauley** (theorbo).
Channel Classics CCS7595 (12/95). ✒ *See review under Leclair; refer to the Index to Reviews.*

Napoléon Coste

Suggested listening ...

...Pièces originales, Op. 53 – No. 1, Reverie. Morceaux episodiques, Op. 23 – No. 7, Les soirées
d'Auteuil. Grande sérénade, Op. 30. *Coupled with* **Sor** Introduction and Variations on a theme
by Mozart, Op. 9. Fantasia élégiaque in C minor, Op. 59. Etudes – Op. 6 No. 11; Op. 31 No. 12;
Op. 35 No. 22. **Raphaëlla Smits** (gtr). Accent ACC29182D (8/93).

François Couperin

New review

Couperin L'art de toucher le clavecin – Prelude No. 6 in B minor. Troisième livre de clavecin[a] –
Treizième ordre; Quatorzième ordre; Quinzième ordre. **Robert Kohnen** (hpd); [a]**Barthold Kuijken**
(fl). Accent Ⓕ ACC9399D (64 minutes: DDD: 4/96). ✒ Recorded 1993.
Kohnen has chosen the first three *ordres* of Couperin's *Troisième livre de clavecin* which was published
in 1722; and he has prefaced his recital with the sixth of eight preludes from Couperin's didactic *L'art
de toucher le clavecin* which first appeared in 1716. His playing is rhythmically incisive, fastidious in
detail – Couperin was hot on that – and full of character. If, on first acquaintance, his realization of
Couperin's vignette "Les lis naissans" (*Ordre* No. 13) seems a shade spiky then his lyrical approach to
the flowing 6/8 melody of the rondeau "Les rozeaux", which follows, reassures us that Kohnen does
have the poetry of the music at heart, and intends that it should be so. Less appealing are Kohnen's
somewhat intrusive vocal introductions to "Les folies françoises". This information is provided in the
booklet so it hardly needs to be reiterated. In a concert recital such snatches of actuality can be
effective; on a disc, after repeated listening, they become an unwelcome interruption. Occasional
departures from the norm in the following two *ordres* are of an altogether more agreeable nature. In
"Le rossignol-en-amour" (*Ordre* No. 14) Kohnen takes Couperin up on his suggestion to use a
transverse flute, played here with a beautifully rounded tone by Barthold Kuijken. Likewise, in the
jaunty rondeau, "La Julliet", the trio texture is realized by flute and harpsichord rather than the more
usual two-harpsichord texture. This piece is beautifully done, as is the subtly bell-like "Carillon de
Cithère" which follows it. In short, a stylish and entertaining release – apart from the aforementioned
spoken prefaces – which is as likely as any to draw the cautious listener into Couperin's refined,
allusory and metaphor-laden idiom.

F. Couperin Quatrième livre de clavecin. **Christophe Rousset** (hpd). Harmonia Mundi Ⓕ HMC90
1445/6 (two discs: 152 minutes: DDD: 10/94). ✒ Recorded 1993.   ⒼⒼ
Couperin's Fourth Book of harpsichord pieces, his last, published in Paris in 1730 though completed
around three years earlier does not, perhaps, contain as many masterpieces as the First and Second
Books, but a high proportion of them possess a character nevertheless poignant and sometimes
enigmatic which both stimulates the imagination and haunts the memory. For example, pieces such as
"L'Amphibie", a noble passacaille, "L'Arlequine" bringing to mind Watteau's clown, "L'Epineuse",
a rondeau with an almost Schubertian melancholy (Couplet 3), and a rare excursion into the key of
F sharp major (Couplet 4) and "La Pantomime", whose deliciously angular gestures were probably
inspired by Scaramouche, the central figure in the Comédie Italienne popular in Paris in the early
eighteenth century. All this and, as they say, much more make this anthology a deeply rewarding one.
Rousset is fastidious in matters of ornament – for that he would have gained Couperin's wholehearted
approval – and has a lively response to the many and varied musical gestures, some of them of
enormous subtlety. He has, furthermore , the technique to implement Couperin's requirements with
absolute fluency, and the sense to eschew exaggerated or misplaced mannerisms.

Additional recommendations ...

...*HMA190 351/3* (152 minutes) – Premier livre de clavecin: Ordres 1-5. *HMA190 354/6* (191
minutes) – Deuxième livre de clavecin: Ordres 6-12. L'art de toucher le clavecin. *HMA190 357/8*
(150 minutes) – Troisième livre de clavecin: Ordres 13-19. *HMA190 359/60* (152 minutes) –
Quatrième livre de clavecin: Ordres 20-27. **Kenneth Gilbert.** Harmonia Mundi Musique d'abord
Ⓓ HMA190 351/60 (two triple- and two double-disc sets: ADD: 10/89). ✒

...Quatrième livre de clavecin. **Olivier Baumont** (hpd). Erato MusiFrance Ⓕ 2292-45824-2
(two discs: 142 minutes: DDD: 8/93). ✍

...L'art de toucher le clavecin: Préludes – C major; D minor; G minor; B flat major; F minor;
A major. Premier livre: Troisième ordre – Allemande La ténébreuse; Courantes I and II;
Sarabande La lugubre; L'espagnolète; Chaconne La favorite. Cinquième ordre – Sarabande La
dangereuse; Les ordes. Dixième livre: Sixième ordre – Les baricades mistérieuses. Huitième
ordre – La Raphaéle; Allemande L'Ausoniène; Courantes I and II. Sarabande L'unique; Gavotte;
Rondeau; Gigue; Passacaille. Troisième livre: Quinzième ordre – Le dodo ou L'amour au berçeau.
Quatrième livre: Vingt-troisième ordre – L'arlequine. Vingtquatrième ordre – Les vieux seigneurs.
Skip Sempé (hpd). Deutsche Harmonia Mundi Ⓕ RD77219 (72 minutes: DDD: 1/91). ✍

...Troisième livre de clavecin. **Olivier Baumont, Davitt Moroney** (hpds). Erato MusiFrance
Ⓕ 4509-92859-2 (two discs: 134 minutes: DDD: 2/94). ✍

...Deuxième livre de clavecin[a]. L'art de toucher le clavecin. **Olivier Baumont, [a]Davitt Moroney**
(hpds). Erato Ⓕ 4509-96364-2 (three discs: 178 minutes: DDD: 3/95). ✍ *Selected by Sounds in
Retrospect.*

...Deuxième livre de clavecin[a]. L'art de toucher le clavecin. **Christophe Rousset, [a]William Christie**
(hpds). Harmonia Mundi Ⓕ HMC90 1447/9 (three discs: 182 minutes: DDD: 3/95). ✍

...Deuxième livre de clavecin: Les Baricades Mistérieuses; Passacaille; Troisième livre: Les Folies
françoises, ou Les Dominos; Les Fauvétes Plaintives; Le Dodo, ou L'Amour en berceau; Le Tic-
Toc-Choc, ou Les Maillotins; La Muse-Plantine; Quatrième livre de clavecin: L'Arlequine; Les
Ombres Errantes. *Coupled with works by* **D. Scarlatti, Rameau** and **Rossini** Marcelle Meyer
(pf). EMI mono Ⓜ CZS5 68092-2* (four discs: 275 minutes: ADD: 6/95). *See review in the
Collections section; refer to the Index to Reviews.*　　　　　　　　　　　　　　Ⓖ Ⓖ Ⓖ

...Premier livre de clavecin: Ordres 1-5. **Christophe Rousset** (hpd). Harmonia Mundi Ⓕ HMC90
1450/2 (three discs: 182 minutes: DDD: 7/95).

...Troisième Livre de clavecin: Quatorzième ordre – Le Rossignol-en-amour; Le Carillon de Cithere.
Coupled with works by **Rameau, Rimsky-Korsakov, Daquin, Paradis, Bach, Templeton**
and **Malcolm** George Malcolm (hpd). Decca Ⓜ 444 390-2DWO (75 minutes: ADD: 11/95). ✍

Further listening ...

...Pièces de violes. Les goûts-réunis[a] – Douzième Concert in A major; Troisième Concert in
G major. **Wieland Kuijken, [a]Kaori Uemura** (vas da gamba); **Robert Kohnen** (hpd). Accent
ACC9288D (4/94). ✍　　　　　　　　　　　　　　　　　　　　　　　　　　　　Ⓖ

...Trois leçons de ténèbres. Motet – Victoria! Christo resurgenti. Magnificat. **Mieke van der Sluis**
(sop); **Guillemette Laurens** (mez); **Pascal Monteilhet** (lute); **Marianne Muller** (va da gamba);
Laurence Boulay (hpd, org). Erato MusiFrance 2292-45012-2 (8/90). ✍　　　　　　　　Ⓖ

...Les Nations. **Frans Vester** (fl); **Marie Leonhardt** (vn); **Amsterdam Quartet**. Teldec 4509-
93689-2. ✍

...Les Nations – La Française; Suite de Simphonie en Trio. Qu'on ne me dise[a]. Doux liens de mon
coeur[a]. *Coupled with* **Montéclair** Le Triomfe de la Constance[a]. Pan et Syrinx[a].
J-B. Forqueray Pièces de viole – La Forqueray; La Cottin; La Bellemont; La Portugaise; La
Couperin[c]. **Leclair** Sonata in D major, Op. 9 No 6[b]. **Marais** La Sonnerie de Sainte Geneviève du
Mont[bc]. Pièces de viole – Prélude; Allemande, La superbe; L'arabesque[c]. Le tableau de l'opération
de la taille[c]. [a]**Judith Nelson** (sop); [b]**Monica Huggett** (vn); [c]**Christophe Coin** (va da gamba);
Academy of Ancient Music / Christopher Hogwood. L'Oiseau-Lyre 436 185-2OH2 (10/94). ✍

Louis Couperin　　　　　　　　　　　　　　　　　　　　　　French c1626-1661

L. Couperin Harpsichord Works – Suites: D major; A minor; C major; F. Tombeau de M. de
Blancrocher. **Laurence Cummings** (hpd). Naxos Ⓢ 8 550922 (74 minutes: DDD: 3/95). Recorded
1993.

Cummings handles the ticklish problems of Couperin's free-rhythm Preludes with assurance,
producing very convincing readings; and his brisk lift to the rhythm of the "changement de
mouvement" in the F major and A minor Preludes (the latter "in imitation of M. Froberger") is
invigorating. He applies *inégalités* and stylish embellishments and variants with an easy spontaneity,
brings off the grandiose C major Passacaille with panache, and is neat at fitting in the intricate
rhythms of the C major Courante (for crossed hands). He is particularly happy in the high spirits of
"La Piémontaine" and the "Branle de Basque". But when his rhythm is so good, why does he disturb
the flow of the D major Sarabande by lingering overlong at the end of the second and fourth bar?
This apart, one can have little but praise for this disc; and at its low price it is a real bargain which
should be eagerly snapped up.

Additional recommendations ...

...A minor; D minor; Prélude in C major; Pavanne in F sharp minor. *Coupled with works by*
Froberger, Frescobaldi and **Anonymous** Jane Chapman (hpd). Collins Classics Ⓕ 1421-2
(71 minutes: DDD: 4/95). ✍ *See review in the Collections section; refer to the Index to Reviews.*

...Harpsichord Suites – complete. Pavanne in F sharp minor. Prelude and Chaconne in G minor; Two
Pieces in B flat major. Three Pieces in G minor. Four Pieces in G major. **Davitt Moroney** (hpd).
Harmonia Mundi Musique d'abord Ⓑ HMA190 1124/7 (four discs: 315 minutes: ADD: 4/90). ✍

Sir Noël Coward
British 1899-1973

...Bitter Sweet. **Soloists; New Sadler's Wells Opera Chorus and Orchestra / Michael Reed.** That's Entertainment Records CDTER2 1160 (11/89).

Henry Cowell
American 1897-1965

Cowell Hymn and Fuguing Tune No. 10. Air and Scherzo. Concerto grosso. Fiddler's Jig.
Persichetti The Hollow Men.
MacDowell Woodland Sketches, Op. 51 – To a wild rose. **Manhattan Chamber Orchestra / Richard Auldon Clark.** Koch International Classics Ⓔ 37282-2 (57 minutes: DDD: 7/95). Recorded 1994.
Unlike some of Cowell's other works, *Ongaku* and the *Persian Suite*, for example, the works here are more straightforward, even naïve, like some of Virgil Thomson. The *Hymn and Fuguing Tune* No. 10 (1955) sounds as if it might have been written by an eccentric baroque composer – some later Billings – and then arranged. Just as Cowell's ethnic pieces exist in a limbo between continents, so do his traditional pieces manage to hover between various musical traditions, sometimes lacking any compelling focus. The soloists in the Manhattan Chamber Orchestra are impressive, especially Gary Louie's alto saxophone in the *Air and Scherzo*, but Cowell was naughty to help himself to the opening glissando of Gershwin's *Rhapsody in Blue* at the start of the *Scherzo* (track4)! Cowell's family background was Irish and the *Fiddler's Jig* itself as well as the fourth movement of the *Concerto grosso* are unpretentious – an Irish-American Gordon Jacob? Persichetti's response to T.S. Eliot's poem follows Copland's *Quiet City* in drawing on the symbolism of the trumpet to represent man's experience of emptiness or loneliness in the twentieth century. The resemblance in mood is striking. There have been other recordings of *The Hollow Men*, one current in America. It works, especially played like this. It is less easy to see why an arrangement of MacDowell's evergreen *To a wild rose* needed to be used as a filler on this shortish CD. There is always plenty more Cowell, whose name is the only one on the front of the jewel-case.

Sir Frederic Cowen
British 1852-1935

...Symphony No. 3 in C minor, "Scandinavian". Indian Rhapsody. The Butterfly's Ball. **Košice State Philharmonic Orchestra / Adrian Leaper.** Marco Polo 8 223273 (2/91).

Laurence Crane
British 1961-

...Balanescu. *Coupled with works by* **N. Hayes, Hallgrimsson, Weir, Finnissy, G. Jackson, S. Harrison, A. Fisher** and **Skempton** Tapestry. British Music Label BML012 (12/95). *See review in the Collections section; refer to the Index to Reviews.*

Paul Creston
American 1906-1985

Creston Symphony No. 5, Op. 64[a]. Toccata, Op. 68[a]. Choreografic Suite, Op. 86*a*[b]. [a]**Seattle Symphony Orchestra;** [b]**New York Chamber Symphony Orchestra / Gerard Schwarz.** Delos Ⓔ DE3127 (69 minutes: DDD: 10/94). Recorded 1991-2. *Gramophone Editor's choice.*
The dashingly scored *Toccata* from 1957 makes a swaggering curtain-raiser here: its outer portions revel in passages of enormous rhythmic panache (a real Creston trademark) and writing of great soloistic flair, whilst the contrasting central *Andante* section luxuriates in a contemplative balm. First performed the previous year, the Fifth Symphony also boasts a largely extrovert demeanour. A feeling of restlessness pervades the *Con moto* opening movement which soon acquires a formidable propulsion, its surging string-lines, stamping rhythms and opulent, percussion-laden tuttis at times reminiscent of Ravel or Roussel (if lacking the innate good taste of both those French masters). The emotional quotient remains pretty high for the ensuing *Largo*, whose richly-woven, almost indecently lush climaxes are offset by some particularly ingratiating writing for solo wind. The most extended item is the 29-minute *Choreografic Suite* (1965). It has five movements, each of which contains much tuneful invention. The piece as a whole, however, does tend to outstay its welcome, for all the agreeable piquancy and lightness of Creston's transparent scoring. Schwarz obtains thoroughly decent results and the slightly dry, 'theatre-pit' ambience suits the music admirably.

Further listening ...
...Symphony No. 2, Op. 35. *Coupled with* **Ives** Symphony No. 2. **Detroit Symphony Orchestra /**
   Neeme Järvi. Chandos CHAN9390 (11/95).
...Symphony No. 3, Op. 48, "Three Mysteries". Invocation and Dance, Op. 58. Out of the Cradle.
   Partita for Flute, Violin and String Orchestra, Op. 12. **Iikka Talvi** (vn); **Scott Goff** (fl); **Seattle**
   Symphony Orchestra / Gerald Schwarz. Delos DE3114 (12/92).
...String Quartet, Op. 8c. *Coupled with works by* **Villa-Lobos, Turina, Debussy** and **Ravel**
   Arthur Gleghorn (fl); **Mitchell Lurie** (cl); **Ann Mason Stockton** (hp); **Hollywood Quartet; Concert**
   Arts Strings / Felix Slatkin. Testament mono SBT1053* (3/95). *See review in the Collections*
   section; refer to the Index to Reviews.   ⓖⓖ

William Croft   British 1678-1727

New review
Croft God is gone up with a merry noise. Hear my prayer, O Lord. I will sing unto the Lord.
   O Lord God of my Salvation. O Lord, I will praise Thee. O Lord, rebuke me not. We wait for
   Thy loving kindness. We will rejoice in Thy salvation. Voluntaries[a] – A minor; D major. **Choir of**
   New College, Oxford / Edward Higginbottom with **Timothy Morris** ([a]org). CRD ⓕ CRD3491
   (67 minutes: DDD: 8/95). Texts included. Recorded 1992.
The programme here very happily supplements the other recital of Croft's church music presently
available (listed below) which includes the fine and famous Burial Service. It is not unfitting that the
simple decorum of those funeral sentences should be so closely associated with his name, for in the
present collection we find him often at his best and most characteristic in the setting of penitential or
prayerful texts. His masterpiece is probably *O Lord, rebuke me not,* described by Dr Burney as "one
of the most masterly and grand compositions", working out its fugues with heart as well as brain, and
at the end, allowing his "Amen" the breadth, beauty and dignity of a great river flowing through
meadows. He was very conscious of "the solemnity and gravity which may properly be called the
Church style", and even in a joyful context he finds it natural to gravitate towards the minor tonality.
An instinct for reliable structure is also his; one never feels that material is either wasted or over-
extended. The longest work here is the verse-anthem *O Lord, I will praise Thee* (14'12"), its varied
sections finely balanced, its style neither light nor ponderous. The performances match the music:
unostentatious and highly capable. In music of this period the dry acoustic of the New College
Chapel is no disadvantage, and both the recording and its presentation are admirable.
Further listening ...
...Te Deum and Jubilate in D major. Musica sacra – Rejoice in the Lord, O ye righteous; The Burial
   Service. **St Paul's Cathedral Choir; Parley of Instruments / John Scott.** Hyperion CDA66606 (4/93).

William Crotch   British 1775-1847

Suggested listening ...
...Organ Concerto No. 2 in A major. Overture in G major. Sinfonias – E flat major; F major.
   Andrew Lumsden (org); **Milton Keynes Chamber Orchestra / Hilary Davan Wetton.**
   Unicorn-Kanchana DKPCD9126 (1/93).

George Crumb   American 1929-

Suggested listening ...
...Five Pieces. Gnomic Variations. Makrokosmos I. **Jeffrey Jacob** (pf). Centaur CRC2050 (4/91).
...Black Angels. *Coupled with works by* **Tallis, Marta, Ives** and **Shostakovich** Kronos Quartet.
   Elektra Nonesuch 7559-79242-2 (4/91). *See review in the Collections section; refer to the Index to*
   Reviews.
...Black Angels. *Coupled with* **Schubert** String Quartet in D minor, "Death and the Maiden",
   D810. **Brodsky Quartet.** Teldec 9031-76260-2 (9/93).
...Cello Sonata. *Coupled with* **Escher** Cello Sonata **Kodály** Cello Sonata, Op. 8. **Pieter Wispelwey**
   (vc). Globe GLO5089 (12/94).

Bernhard Crusell   Finnish 1775-1839

Crusell Clarinet Concerto No. 1 in E flat major, Op. 1.
L. Koželuch Clarinet Concerto in E flat major.
Krommer Clarinet Concerto in E flat major, Op. 36. **Emma Johnson** (cl); **Royal Philharmonic**
   Orchestra / Günther Herbig. ASV ⓕ CDDCA763 (67 minutes: DDD: 9/91).
The idiom of Stockholm-based composer Bernhard Crusell embraced elements of Mozart, Spohr,
Weber, Rossini and even Beethoven. But in the hands of the young woodwind virtuoso, Emma

Johnson, his music has a personality all its own. Here she turns her attention to his First Clarinet Concerto which is full of engaging ideas. The slow movement is beautifully done and in the finale the soloist is at her very best – full of impulsive charm and swagger. Although the Koželuch concerto, a recent discovery, seems less distinctive, the slow movement of the Krommer is undeniably affecting and its finale bounces along in fine style. Emma Johnson plays throughout with a winning spontaneity and the RPO, arguably just a shade tubby of timbre for such music, back her up with distinction. The generous acoustic is effectively caught.

Additional recommendation ...

...Clarinet Concertos – No. 1; No. 2 in F minor, Op. 5; No. 3 in B flat major, Op. 11. **Orchestra of the Age of Enlightenment / Anthony Pay** (cl). Virgin Classics Veritas Ⓔ VC7 59287-2 (72 minutes: DDD: 12/93). ✒

Further listening ...

...Clarinet Concerto No. 2 in F minor, Op. 5. *Coupled with* **Weber** Clarinet Concertino in E flat major, Op. 26. **Baermann** Quintet (Septet) in E flat major, Op. 23 – Adagio. **Rossini** Introduction, Theme and Variations in B flat major. **Emma Johnson** (cl); **English Chamber Orchestra / Sir Charles Groves**. ASV CDDCA559 (11/86). ⒼⒼ

Carlos Cruz de Castro
Spanish 1941-

Suggested listening ...

...Guitar Concerto. *Coupled with* **Benguerel** Tempo. **Marco** Concierto Guadiana. **Wolfgang Weigel** (gtr); **European Masters Orchestra / Peter Schmelzer**. Koch Schwann 312362 (5/95).

César Cui
USSR 1835-1918

Suggested listening ...

...25 Preludes, Op. 64. **Jeffrey Biegel** (pf). Marco Polo 8 223496 (11/94).

...Kaleidoscope, Op. 50. Violin Sonata in D major, Op. 86. **Peter Sheppard** (vn); **Aaron Shorr** (pf). Olympia OCD456 (12/95).

...I remember the evening. 25 Songs, Op. 57 – No. 11, "You" and "Thou"; No. 17, The statue of Tsarskoie Selo; No. 25, Desire. Ici-bas. I touched the bloom lightly, Op. 49 No. 1. It's over. *Coupled with* **Balakirev** 20 Songs – The bright moon; My heart is torn; Song of Selim; When I hear thy voice. Three Forgotten Songs – Thou art so captivating; Spanish song. 10 Songs – Over the lake; I loved him. **Mussorgsky** What are words of love to you?. Night. **Borodin** The false note. The sea princess. **Rimsky-Korsakov** The octave, Op. 45 No. 3. The clouds begin to scatter, Op. 42 No. 3. Of what I dream in the quiet sky, Op. 40 No. 3. Enslaved by the rose, the nightingale, Op. 2 No. 2. In spring, Op. 43 – No. 1, The lark sings louder; No. 2, Not the wind, blowing from the heights. **Olga Borodina** (mez); **Larissa Gergieva** (pf). Philips 442 780-2PH (8/95).

Frederic Curzon
British 1899-1973

Suggested listening ...

...The Boulevardier. Punchinello. In Málaga. Salterello[a]. Dance of an Ostracised Imp. Capricante. Galavant. Pasquinade. Simonetta. Cascade. Le Peinata. Robin Hood. Bravada. [a]**Silvia Capova** (pf); **Bratislava Radio Symphony Orchestra / Adrian Leaper**. Marco Polo British Light Music 8 223425 (6/93).

...The Boulevardier. *Coupled with works by* **Binge, Williams, Coates, Toye, Collins, Farnon, Baynes, Lutz, Gibbs, White, Ketèlbey, Joyce, Ellis** and **Ancliffe** New London Orchestra / Ronald Corp. Hyperion CDA66868 (7/96). *See review in the Collections section; refer to the Index to Reviews. Gramophone Editor's record of the month.* Ⓖ

Ingold Dahl
Swiss/American 1912-1970

New review

I. Dahl Concerto for Alto Saxophone and Wind Orchestra[ac]. Music for Brass Instruments[b]. Hymn orch. Morton)[c]. The Tower of Saint Barbara[c]. [a]**John Harle** (sax); [b]**New World Brass;** [c]**New World Symphony / Michael Tilson Thomas**. Argo Ⓔ 444 459-2ZH (72 minutes: DDD: 9/95). Recorded 1994. *Gramophone Editor's choice.*

Tilson Thomas's description of his teacher as "a musician's musician" seems entirely apt. Dahl's chosen idiom combines something of the elegance of Stravinsky, the craft of Hindemith, as well as the jagged, bracingly 'out-of-doors' manner of so much twentieth-century Americana. There's also more than a stylistic nod in the direction of jazz and big band music: annotator Anthony Linick informs us that the versatile Dahl worked as an arranger for Tommy Dorsey, an experience surely reflected in the wittily assured scoring in the vigorous finale of the Concerto for alto saxophone and wind orchestra (written for Sigurd Rascher in 1948-9, and revised in 1954). Again, in the impressive *Music for Brass Instruments* (1944) the sheer professionalism of the writing really stands out: its immaculately judged sonorities and ample opportunities for relaxed virtuosity must make it immensely satisfying to perform. Whilst on a year's sabbatical in 1952-3, Dahl lived in the village of Schruns in the Austrian Vorarlberg. Here he began work on his ballet score, *The Tower of Saint Barbara*, which was inspired by the local medieval legend of that early Christian martyr. Though eventually completed in 1954, the ballet was never staged. The present four-movement "Symphonic Legend" is an eloquent, often powerful creation which grows in stature on repeated hearings, and, once more, Dahl's superbly transparent, clean-limbed scoring gives very real pleasure. That just leaves *Hymn*: originally conceived for solo piano in 1957, this stately, impassioned essay is heard here in an effective new orchestration by Lawrence Morton, which was specially commissioned by Tilson Thomas a few years after Dahl's death. Performances throughout are as dashingly committed as they are dazzlingly accomplished. Stunning work, too, from the Argo recording team. Well worth exploring.

Luigi Dallapiccola   Italian 1904-1975

New review

Dallapiccola Canti di Prigionia[b]. Cinque frammenti di Saffo[ac]. Due Liriche di Anacreonte[ac]. Sex Carmina Alcaei[ac]. Tempus destruendi – Tempus aedificandi[b]. Due Cori di Michelangelo Buonarroti il Giovane[b]. [a]**Julie Moffat** (sop); [b]**New London Chamber Choir / James Wood;** [c]**Ensemble InterContemporain / Hans Zender.** Erato Ⓔ 4509-98509-2 (72 minutes: DDD: 5/96). Texts included. Recorded 1991-2.

This disc charts Dallapiccola's 40-year journey as a vocal composer, from the consonantly framed madrigalisms of the Michelangelo settings (1933) to the intense post-tonal strivings of *Tempus destruendi – Tempus aedificandi* (1970-71). It is a fascinating, thought-provoking odyssey, as the rather easygoing flow of the early style yields to more turbulent lines which seem to resist assimilation into conventionally balanced structures. The music that comes between these extremes confirms that Dallapiccola was at his best when his personal, Italianate lyricism was contained by small-scale forms and refined yet rigorous contrapuntal textures of the kind he so admired in Webern. On a larger scale, as in the *Canti di Prigionia* for chorus with pianos, harps and percussion (1938-41), whose ritualistic style has links with middle-period Stravinsky, his strongly expressive melodic lines do not always sustain a convincing sense of purpose, and the members of the New London Chamber Choir sound less at home here than in the *a cappella* works mentioned above. The contrast between the restrained, reflective idiom of the *Canti di Prigionia* and the intense yet eloquent cycles for solo voice and instruments from the 1940s which follow are striking. It is in the *Frammenti di Saffo*, the *Liriche di Anacreonte* and the *Carmina Alcaei* that Dallapiccola found his true musical identity, absorbing Webernian austerities into his own warmer and more rhythmically flexible idiom. These performances are generally excellent, though the recordings opt for atmosphere at the expense of the fullest clarity of texture.

Additional recommendation ...

...Il Prigioniero. Canti di Prigionia. **Soloists; Eric Ericson Chamber Choir; Swedish Radio Chorus and Symphony Orchestra / Esa-Pekka Salonen.** Sony Classical Ⓔ SK68323 (69 minutes: DDD: 3/96).

Marco Dall'Aquila   Italian c1480-after 1538

Suggested listening ...

...Ricercar. Il est bel est bon. Ricercar Lautre jour No. 101. Nous bergiers. La Traditora Nos. 2 and 3. Ricercars Nos. 16 and 33. La Battaglia. *Coupled with works by* **Ripa, Borrono da Milano** and **Francesco da Milano** Paul O'Dette (lte). Harmonia Mundi HMU90 7043 (10/95). ☞ *See review in the Collections section; refer to the Index to Reviews.*

Jean-Michel Damase   French 1928-

Suggested listening ...

...Variations on "Early one morning". Sonata for Flute and Harp. Quintet[a]. Trio[b]. **Anna Noakes** (fl); **Gillian Tingay** (hp); [a]**Richard Friedman** (vn); [a]**Jane Atkins** (va); [ab]**Ferenc Szucs** (vc). ASV CDDCA898 (10/94).

...Variations, Op. 22. *Coupled with works by* **Milhaud, Françaix, Ibert, Fauré, Debussy, Pi**erné and **Poulenc** Reykjavik Wind Quintet. Chandos CHAN9362 (10/95).

...Sicilienne variée. *Coupled with works by* **Tournier, Renié, Casella, Rosetti, Spohr, Debussy, Prokofiev** and **Fauré** Naoko Yoshino (hp). Philips 446 064-2PH (2/96). *See review in the Collections section; refer to the Index to Reviews.*

Jean-François Dandrieu

Dandrieu Premier livre d'orgue – Mass and Vespers for Easter Sunday[a].
Gregorian Chant Mass and Vespers for Easter Sunday[b]. [b]**Paris Gregorian Choir / Jaan-Eik Tulve**
with [a]**Jean-Patrice Brosse** (org). Pierre Verany Ⓟ PV794034 (59 minutes: DDD: 6/95). Texts and
translations included. Played on the organ of St Bertrand-de-Comminges, France. Recorded 1993.
A peculiarly French recording, this. Jean-Patrice Brosse plays Dandrieu's organ music for Easter Day
Mass on the splendid instrument at St-Bertrand-de-Comminges (the town where Herod Antipas is
supposed to have spent his last years), and the chant is supplied by the Paris Gregorian Choir.
Dandrieu's music is – while naturally more restrained than his harpsichord works – colourful and
inventive, though not as memorable as Couperin's Organ Masses, and is extremely well played by
Brosse. Certainly the most impressive piece is the "Offertoire sur les grands jeux on 'O filii et filiae'".
What makes the recording interesting is the liturgical context in which Dandrieu's music is placed.
Bells are rung, the choir sound suitably monkish, and there is a sense of connection between the chant
and the organ music which is of course essential (for example, in the *Kyrie* or the *Sanctus*), but in
practice extremely difficult to achieve on a recording. The sound quality itself is excellent.

Jan Yves Daniel-Lesur

Suggested listening ...
...Le cantique des cantiques[a]. Messe du Jubilé[ab]. In paradisum[b]. La vie intérieure[b]. *Coupled with*
Messiaen O sacrum convivium[ab]. [a]**BBC Symphony Chorus / Stephen Jackson** with [b]**Jeremy
Filsell** (org). ASV CDDCA900 (1/95).

Richard Danielpour

Suggested listening ...
...Metamorphosis[a]. *Coupled with* **Perle** Piano Concerto No. 2[a]. Six Etudes. **Michael Boriskin** (pf);
[a]**Utah Symphony Orchestra / Joseph Silverstein.** Harmonia Mundi HMU90 7124 (5/95).

John Danyel

Suggested listening ...
...The Complete Songs and Lute Music – Like as the lute delights[bg]; Time, cruel time[agh]; What
delight can they enjoy[abcd]; Mrs E. her funeral tears for the death of her husband[bgh]; Why canst
thou not?[agh]; Stay, cruel, stay![ag]; Coy Daphne fled[abgh]; Let not Chloris think[bg]; Eyes, look no
more[bgh]; Thou pretty bird[bg]; Dost thou withdraw thy grace?[ag]; He whose desires are still
abroad[bgh]; If I could shut the gate[bgh]; I die whenas I do not see[bg]; Can doleful notes?[bg]; Now the
earth, the skies, the air[abcegh]; Mistress Anne Grene her leaves be greene[g]; Passy-measures
Galliard[fg]; A Fancy[fg]; Pavan in C major[g]; Rosamund[g]; Monsieur's Almain[g]. [a]**Libby Crabtree**
(sop); [b]**Nigel Short** (alto); [c]**Charles Daniels,** [d]**Matthew Vine** (tens); [e]**Adrian Peacock** (bass); [f]**Jacob
Heringman,** [g]**David Miller** (ltes); [h]**Mark Caudle** (bass viol). Hyperion CDA66714 (1/96). ✍

Franz Danzi

Suggested listening ...
...Flute Concertos – No. 1 in G major, Op. 30; No. 2 in D minor, Op. 31; No. 3 in D minor, Op. 42;
No. 4 in D major, Op. 43. **András Adorján** (fl); **Munich Chamber Orchestra / Hans Stadlmair.**
Orfeo C003812H (8/88).
...Flute Concerto No. 2 in D minor, Op. 31[a]. Concertante for Flute, Clarinet and Orchestra in
B major, Op. 41[b]. Fantasia on "Là ci darem la mano" from Mozart's "Don Giovanni"[c]. [ab]**James
Galway** (fl); [bc]**Sabine Meyer** (cl); **Württemberg Chamber Orchestra / Jörg Faerber.** RCA Victor
Red Seal 09026 61976-2 (2/95).
...Three Wind Quintets, Op. 56 – B flat major; G minor; F major. Quintet for Piano and Wind in
D minor, Op. 41[a]. [a]**Love Derwinger** (pf); **Berlin Philharmonic Wind Quintet.** BIS CD552 (5/93).
...Three Wind Quintets, Op. 56 – B flat major; G minor; F major. Sextet in E flat major, Op. 10.
John Brudbury (cl); **Philip Tarlton** (bn); **Richard Berry** (hn); **Michael Thompson Wind Quintet.**
Naxos 8 553076 (11/95).
...Clarinet Sonata in B flat major. *Coupled with* **Mendelssohn** Clarinet Sonata in E flat major.
Weber Grand duo concertant, J204. **Charles Neidich** (cl); **Robert Levin** (fp). Sony Classical
SK64302 (9/95). ✍
...Horn Concerto in E major. *Coupled with works by Haydn and Rosetti.* **Hermann Baumann** (hn);
Concerto Amsterdam / Jaap Schröder. Teldec Das Alter Werk 0630-12324-2 (8/96). *See review
under Haydn; refer to the Index to Reviews.*

Louis-Claude Daquin
French 1694-1772

New review

Daquin Nouveau livre de noëls, Op. 2. **Christopher Herrick** (org). Hyperion Ⓟ CDA66816
(65 minutes: DDD: 12/95). Played on the organ of St Rémy, Dieppe. Recorded 1995.
Gramophone Editor's choice.   Ⓖ

Le coucou is probably the only thing many people know of Daquin, Louis XV's prized court organist, hailed by contemporaries such as Marchand as a supreme virtuoso and recognized even by Rameau (whom he defeated in a competition for an important organ post) as the finest improviser of his day. His only organ compositions to have survived are the present 12 *Noëls* – treatments of traditional Christmas carols – a genre dating from Lebègue's collection about 60 years earlier. Daquin's *Noëls*, written around 1740, employ a technique of variations of ever-increasing brilliance: they extend from the swaggering boldness of No. 1, the bucolic No. 3 over a long drone bass and the briskly breezy No. 4 to the charmingly naïve No. 9 (on flutes), the aggressively cheerful No. 10 and the stunningly exultant No. 12. This is something all organ lovers will want to have. The splendid instrument, almost exactly contemporary with the work presented (much rebuilt but in 1992 restored on historical lines), allows Christopher Herrick to display both his own virtuosity and the organ's rich range of colours (the specification is provided) with vividness – he has fun with multiple echo effects in Nos. 6 and 10 – and the recording (made under difficult circumstances) is wonderfully fresh in sound. Smashing!

Further listening ...

...Le coucou. *Coupled with works by* **Paradis, Bach, Rimsky-Korsakov, Rameau, F. Couperin, Templeton** and **Malcolm** George Malcolm (hpd). Decca 444 390-2DWO (11/95). ✏

Alexander Dargomïzhsky
USSR 1813-1869

Suggested listening ...

...Elegy, "She is coming". *Coupled with works by* **Loeffler, A. Busch, Brahms, R. Strauss, Marx, Reutter** and **Gounod** Mitsuko Shirai (mez); Tabea Zimmermann (va); Hartmut Höll (pf). Capriccio 10 462 (9/95). *See review in the Collections section; refer to the Index to Reviews.* Ⓖ

Michael Daugherty
American 1954-

Suggested listening ...

...Desi. *Coupled with* **Agento** The Dream of Valentino – Tango. **Moran** Points of Departure. **Torke** Black and White – Charcoal. **Harbison** Remembering Gatsby. **Larsen** Collage: Boogie. **Schiff** Stomp. **Kernis** New Era Dance. **J. Adams** The Chairman Dances. **Bernstein** West Side Story – Mambo. **Rouse** Bonham. **Baltimore Symphony Orchestra / David Zinman.** Argo 444 454-2ZH (7/95).

Antoine Dauvergne
French 1713-1797

Suggested listening ...

...Les Troqueurs[a]. Concert de simphonie in F major, Op. 3 No. 2. [a]**Mary Saint-Palais** (sop) Margot; [a]**Sophie Marin-Degor** (sop) Fanchon; [a]**Nicolas Rivenq** (bar) Lubin; [a]**Jean-Marc Salzmann** (bar) Lucas; **Cappella Coloniensis / William Christie.** Harmonia Mundi HMC90 1454 (8/94). ✏ Ⓖ

Carl Davis
American/British 1936-

Suggested listening ...

...(arr. Longstaff) A Christmas Carol – ballet suite. *Coupled with works by* **Muldowney** and **Feeney** Northern Ballet Theatre Orchestra / John Pryce-Jones. Naxos 8 553495 (3/96). *See review under Feeney; refer to the Index to Reviews.*

Richard Davy
British c1465-c1507

Davy The Passion according to St Matthew.
Lambe Nesciens mater.
Nesbet Magnificat. **Eton College Chapel Choir / Ralph Allwood.** Chatsworth Ⓟ FCM1004
(66 minutes: DDD: 5/95). Texts and translations included. Recorded 1991-4.

The Eton Choirbook, sung by the choir for which it was originally compiled, and recorded in Eton College Chapel: can you get any more authentic than that? While the historical connection does undoubtedly add an intellectual – even an emotional – *frisson* to the recording, and while it is good to have the opportunity of hearing the distinctive sound of boys' voices in this repertory, does it really take us any nearer to the late fifteenth-century experience? There is little doubt from the high standards of performance and sound engineering on this disc that it aspires to the same levels and probably similar goals of the recordings of mixed choirs such as The Sixteen. Indeed, it is impressive in these respects. The choice of repertory is interesting, too. This may not be the first recording of Richard Davy's *St Matthew Passion*, but it is nevertheless a piece that is rarely heard. Subsequent settings of the Passion, from Bach to Pärt, have undoubtedly influenced our expectations – we cannot escape this. Yet, with a little imagination and a performance of some intensity and beauty, as is this case here, we can recapture something of the work's original impact. The polyphonic settings of the *turba* (representing all those passages of dialogue not spoken by Christ) are inherently dramatic as they burst out of the restrained (by nature of the chant tone) telling of the events leading to the Crucifixion. The college choir respond well (or have been well trained to respond) to the words, its contributions being well paced and varied in degree of intensity and colour of tone. The larger-scale, more complex contrapuntal writing in Lambe's *Nesciens mater* and Nesbet's *Magnificat* more obviously tests the choir's limits, but overall the singers acquit themselves extremely well, especially the boys. This recording, however near it does or does not come to being truly authentic, makes the music live.

Further listening ...

...*Salve regina*. In honore summae matris. *Coupled with works by* **Lambe, Plummer** and **William, Monk of Stratford** The Sixteen / Harry Christophers. Collins Classics 1462-2 (3/96). *See review in the Collections section; refer to the Index to Reviews.*

William Levi Dawson   American 1899-

Suggested listening ...

...**Dawson** Negro Folk Symphony. *Coupled with works by* **Ellington** and **W.G. Still** Detroit Symphony Orchestra / **Neeme Järvi.** Chandos CHAN9226 (3/94). *See review under Still; refer to the Index to Reviews.*

Willem De Fesch   Dutch 1687-1761

New review

De Fesch Concertos – Op. 2a: No. 2 in C major[a]; No. 5 in F major[a]; No. 6 in D major. Op. 5: No. 2 in G minor; No. 5 in C minor[a]. Concertos, Op. 3a: No. 3 in E major; No. 4 in C major; No. 6 in A minor[a]. Concertos in seven parts, Op. 10 – No. 4 in D major; No. 5 in F major.
[a]**Gordan Nikolitch** (vn); **Auvergne Orchestra / Arie van Beek.** Olympia Explorer Ⓜ OCD450 (72 minutes: DDD: 7/96).

Willem De Fesch was a contemporary of Bach and Handel. His instrument was the violin, on which he established a considerable reputation as a virtuoso. In 1732 he settled in London, where he remained until his death in 1761, taking up the post of organist-choirmaster at the Venetian Embassy Chapel, and in 1746 he played first violin in Handel's orchestra. The Italian influence was in the air and De Fesch breathed it deeply. It's not difficult to hear echoes of Vivaldi and – for example, in the *Concerto grosso*, Op. 5 No. 2 – Handel. His violin concertos make great demands on the soloist, some crystallizing as full-blown cadenzas; that in the first movement of Op. 3 No. 6 may have been the first fully written-out cadenza ever published. De Fesch was, however, a transitional composer: he foreshadowed the development of sonata form, for example in the first *Allegro* of the *Concerto grosso*, Op. 10 No. 4. Notwithstanding outside influences, De Fesch was very much his own man, capable of producing strong thematic material and of treating it in clear-cut and attractive ways. Nikolitch and the Auvergne Orchestra present the music with impeccable style and a real sense of joy in discovering hitherto hidden treasure. Many of De Fesch's works remain to be rediscovered, holding out hope for much pleasure still to come. The recording quality is a model of clarity.

Claude Debussy   French 1862-1918

Debussy Images[a].
Ravel Boléro[b]. La valse[b]. Rapsodie espagnole[b]. **Boston Symphony Orchestra / Charles Munch.** RCA Victor Living Stereo Ⓜ 09026 61956-2 (74 minutes: ADD: 12/94). Item marked [a] from VICS1162 (3/66), [b]SB2019 (3/59). Recorded 1955-7.   Ⓖ

Munch, as one writer put it, "preferred 'taking-off' at concerts instead of nit-picking at rehearsals". Though he didn't generally live as dangerously in his studio recordings, you are unlikely to hear a more bracing "Rondes de Printemps". And his "Gigues" most certainly does 'take-off' as soon as the opportunity arises, after perhaps the most atmospheric opening on disc (whose secret is in the barely audible muted trumpet – what control! – and the flute vibrato). No matter what Munch does, he seems to be able to rely on an orchestra who move with him, with grace, at the speed of light, and with not a musical hair out of place. Brass playing in particular is truly 'legendary'; in other words, faultless, but expressive, not merely ostentatious. And was there ever a more hauntingly distant horn solo from 3'05" in the slow movement of "Ibéria", or a conductor and leader who drew more humour from the (here, delightfully tipsy) strolling fiddler in its last movement? There is marginally more fantasy, flair and fun in Munch's *Images* than any other. Boston's orchestra and its hall have rarely, if ever, had a more natural stereo showing on disc. Assuredly not from RCA themselves when, in the years following this recording, the microphone quota increased. Compared with other remakes, these older recordings have more detail, a more convincing balance, livelier timbres and more of the hall's acoustic. *Boléro* starts at Ravel's surprisingly fast marking, and gradually gets faster; and *La valse* finds Munch and the orchestra at their greatest (trumpets in a spin in the final bars – once heard never forgotten). There isn't today's dynamic range, of course (though the *Images* come very close).

Additional recommendations ...

...Images. Nocturnes[a]. [a]**Montreal Symphony Orchestra Chorus; Montreal Symphony Orchestra / Charles Dutoit.** Decca Ⓕ 425 502-2DH (60 minutes: DDD: 6/90).

...Images. Le martyre de St Sébastien – symphonic fragments. *Coupled with works by* **Beethoven, Brahms, Debussy, Schubert** *and* **Tchaikovsky. London Symphony Orchestra / Pierre Monteux.** Philips The Early Years Ⓜ 442 544-2PM5* (five discs: 311 minutes: ADD: 12/94).
See review in the Collections section; refer to the Index to Reviews.   ⒼⒼⒼ

...Images. **Elgar** Variations on an Original Theme, "Enigma", Op. 36. **Berlin Philharmonic Orchestra / James Levine.** Sony Classical Ⓕ SK53284 (67 minutes: DDD: 2/95).

Debussy Berceuse héroïque[a]. Images[b]. Danse sacrée et danse profane (with Vera Badings, hp)[b]. Jeux[c]. Nocturnes[c]. Marche écossaise sur un thème populaire[d]. Prélude à l'après-midi d'un faune[d]. La mer[d]. Première rapsodie (George Pieterson, cl)[d]. **Concertgebouw Orchestra / [a]Eduard van Beinum, Bernard Haitink.** Philips Duo Ⓜ 438 742-2PM2 (two discs: 141 minutes: ADD: 3/94). Items marked [a] from SABL130 (2/60), [b]9500 509 (5/79), [c]9500 674 (11/80), [d]9500 359 (4/78).
Gramophone classical 100.   ⒼⒼⒼ

Philips have repackaged Haitink's late-1970s recordings on two CDs for the price of one. Space has also been found for Debussy's last orchestral work, the short *Berceuse héroïque* conducted by Eduard van Beinum (in excellent 1957 stereo). In every respect this package is a genuine bargain. In *La Mer*, like the 1964 Karajan on DG Galleria, there is a concern for refinement and fluidity of gesture, for a subtle illumination of texture; and both display a colourist's knowledge and use of an individually apt variety of orchestral tone and timbre. It is the wind playing that you remember in Haitink's *Images*: the melancholy and disconsolate oboe d'amore in "Gigues"; and from "Ibéria", the gorgeous oboe solo in "Les parfums de la nuit", and the carousing clarinets and raucous trumpets in the succeeding holiday festivities. And here, as elsewhere in the set, the Concertgebouw acoustic plays a vital role. Haitink's *Jeux* is slower and freer than average, and possessed of a near miraculous precision, definition and delicacy. The jewel in this set, for many, will be the *Nocturnes*, principally for the purity of the strings in "Nuages"; the dazzling richness and majesty of the central procession in "Fêtes"; and the cool beauty and composure of "Sirènes". It is in this last movement where interpretation and balance differ most widely, with Haitink opting for an ethereal distance. With him, there may be passages where you are unsure if they are singing or not, but the effect is quite as magical as the entry of the offstage choir in "Neptune" from *The Planets*.

Additional recommendations ...

...La mer. **Rimsky-Korsakov** Scheherazade, Op. 35. **Chicago Symphony Orchestra / Fritz Reiner.** RCA Victor Gold Seal Ⓜ GD60875* (69 minutes: ADD).

...La mer. Prélude à l'après-midi d'un faune. Jeux. **London Philharmonic Orchestra / Serge Baudo.** EMI Eminence Ⓜ CD-EMX9502 (52 minutes: DDD: 10/87).   Ⓖ

...Printemps. Prélude à l'après-midi d'un faune. La mer. Nocturnes – Nuages; Fêtes. **Boston Symphony Orchestra / Charles Munch.** RCA Papillon Ⓜ GD86719 (62 minutes: ADD: 7/88).

...La mer. Prélude à l'après-midi d'un faune. **Ravel** Daphnis et Chloé – Suite No. 2. Boléro. **Berlin Philharmonic Orchestra / Herbert von Karajan.** DG Galleria Ⓜ 427 250-2GGA (64 minutes: ADD: 7/89). *Gramophone classical 100.*   ⒼⒼⒼ

...La mer. Prélude à l'après-midi d'un faune. Jeux. Le martyre de Saint Sébastien. **Montreal Symphony Orchestra / Charles Dutoit.** Decca Ⓕ 430 240-2DH (75 minutes: DDD: 2/91).

...Nocturnes – Nuages; Fêtes. Prélude à l'après-midi d'un faune. Le martyre de Saint Sébastien – symphonic fragments. La mer. **Philharmonia Orchestra / Guido Cantelli.** Testament mono Ⓕ SBT1011* (67 minutes: ADD: 10/92). *Gramophone classical 100.*   ⒼⒼⒼ

...La mer. Nocturnes. Prélude à l'après-midi d'un faune. Danse. **Philadelphia Orchestra / Eugene Ormandy.** Sony Classical Essential Classics Ⓑ SBK53256* (65 minutes: ADD: 3/94).

...La mer. Nocturnes[a]. Première rapsodie[b]. Jeux. [b]**Franklin Cohen** (cl); [a]**Cleveland Chorus and Orchestra / Pierre Boulez.** DG Ⓕ 439 896-2GH (71 minutes: DDD: 3/95). *Gramophone Editor's record of the month.*

...Danse sacrée et danse profane[b]. *Coupled with works by* **Ravel, Turina, Villa-Lobos** *and* **Creston Arthur Gleghorn** (fl); **Mitchell Lurie** (cl); **Ann Mason Stockton** (hp); **Hollywood Quartet;**

[b]**Concert Arts Strings / Felix Slatkin.** Testament mono Ⓕ SBT1053* (73 minutes: ADD: 3/95).
See review in the Collections section; refer to the Index to Reviews. ⒼⒼ
…Nocturnes. Prélude à l'après-midi d'un faune. Danse sacrée et danse profane. Préludes, Book 1 –
No. 10, La cathédrale engloutie. Estampes – Soirée dans Grenade (both orch. Stokowski). **Ravel**
Rapsodie espagnole. **Philadelphia Orchestra / Leopold Stokowski.** Biddulph mono Ⓜ WHL013*
(77 minutes: ADD: 8/95).
…La mer. **Respighi** The Pines of Rome. The Fountains of Rome. **Chicago Symphony Orchestra /
Fritz Reiner.** RCA Victor Living Stereo Ⓜ 09026 68079-2 (62 minutes: ADD: 9/95). Ⓖ
…La mer. Prélude à l'après-midi d'un faune. **Ravel** Pavane pour une infante défunte. Ma mère
l'oye. **Royal Concertgebouw Orchestra / Carlo Maria Giulini.** Sony Classical Ⓕ SK66832
(64 minutes: DDD: 11/95).
…La mer. **Mussorgsky** Pictures at an Exhibition. **Ravel** Boléro. **Berlin Philharmonic Orchestra /
Herbert von Karajan.** DG The Originals Ⓜ 447 426-2GOR (75 minutes: ADD: 12/95).

New review

Debussy Printemps. La boîte à joujoux. Children's Corner. La plus que lente. **Montreal Symphony
Orchestra / Charles Dutoit.** Decca Ⓕ 444 386-2DH (69 minutes: DDD. 8/95). Recorded 1992-4.
Children's Corner and the main work here – the ballet *La boîte à joujoux* – are variously linked. Both
were intended for Debussy's daughter ChouChou, whose toys were the inspiration for most of the
portraits of the former and also for the latter's "pantomime" (as Debussy originally called it) and both
were (very idiomatically) orchestrated by André Caplet. *La boîte à joujoux*, to quote David Cox, "has
not the sustained musical invention of *Children's Corner*, though with the interest focused on the stage
action it could undoubtedly be an attractive entertainment for children and adults alike". And indeed
it would be for the listener at home, if a full printed scenario and linked tracking (or indexing) points
were provided. Yet neither Decca's notes (otherwise excellent), nor those that accompany Tilson
Thomas's more artful and atmospheric account (reviewed below), give us much more than an outline
of the story. Still, even without moment-by-moment knowledge of the stage action, many will surely
respond to the gentle humour, whimsy, parody and the touching tenderness of the piece. Performance
and recording are generally up to Decca/Montreal standards – the very slow and dream-like "Jimbo's
lullaby" from *Children's Corner* is especially effective.

Debussy La boîte à joujoux. Prélude à l'après-midi d'un faune. Jeux. **London Symphony Orchestra /
Michael Tilson Thomas.** Sony Classical Ⓕ SK48231 (63 minutes: DDD: 11/92). Recorded 1991. ⒼⒼ
"Something to amuse the children, nothing more" wrote Debussy about *La boîte à joujoux* (mostly
written in 1913, but completed after his death by Caplet). The children would have been a lot more
amused by the goings-on of the occupants of Tilson Thomas's toy box had Sony provided a decent
synopsis, but his characterization, storytelling and evocation of atmosphere are so vivid that
foreknowledge of events is almost unnecessary. Strictly adult entertainment is provided by this
languorous *Prélude*, with particularly lovely, long-breathed playing from the LSO's principal flute;
and the suspect shenanigans of *Jeux*, where Tilson Thomas eschews some of Haitink's miraculous
acuity of rhythm and texture (reviewed above), in favour of greater urgency and spontaneity.
Recorded levels are higher for the *Prélude* than the rest of the programme, but this disc is superbly
engineered: the sound has both a fine bloom and a tactile presence.

Additional recommendation …
…La boîte à joujoux. **Prokofiev** Peter and the wolf, Op. 67[a]. [a]**Patrick Stewart** (narr); **Orchestra of
Opéra de Lyon / Kent Nagano.** Erato Ⓕ 4509-97418-2 (61 minutes: DDD: 8/95).

New review

Debussy Khamma.
Ravel Daphnis et Chloé[a]. [a]**Het Groot Omroepkoor; Royal Concertgebouw Orchestra / Riccardo
Chailly.** Decca Ⓕ 443 934-2DH (74 minutes: DDD: 10/95). Recorded 1994.
You would expect this *Daphnis* to sound superb, and, of course, it does. Rattle and EMI didn't have
the advantage of the Concertgebouw acoustic: the full flood of choral tone at the climax of Chailly's
"Daybreak" (the famous first scene of Part 3) has to be heard to be believed (Chailly's timing of this
sunburst is masterly), and it hardly needs saying that this new disc's ability to astonish with decibels
at climaxes is greater than Decca's previous Dutoit or Monteux recordings (all reviewed or listed
under Ravel). Possibly the wind machine is cranked with excessive enthusiasm, and the strange lights
scenes of *Daphnis* do not seem to be enjoyed or exploited for the strangeness that can result from even
the ordinary (i.e. musical) instruments being asked to play or phrase in unusual ways. Chailly is faster,
too, in the dance scenes where, if you are Sir Simon Rattle, lingering leads to marvels of
characterization (Daphnis's "Dance gracieuse", Chloé's "Dance of Supplication" and the
"Pantomime"), which is not to say that Chailly is bland. And blandness is emphatically the last word
to use in describing Chailly's way with Debussy's *Khamma* (Rattle's coupling is *Boléro*). This
immediately pre-*Jeux* (conceptually speaking) ballet is a sort of Egyptian *Salome-cum-Rite of Spring*,
in as much as Khamma dances herself to death for the Sun God Amun-Ra that he might be
persuaded to save the city from siege. The ominous opening pages here are immediately gripping: a
Nibelheim-like family of lower woodwind slithering around, marvellously focused drum, and trumpet
fanfares that genuinely do "give one the shivers" as Debussy once asserted. In general, Chailly, Decca

and these superb musicians realize more of the score's "discoveries of harmonic chemistry" and sheer theatre than one dared imagine possible. But why no linked tracking with the synopsis? When the piece is unfamiliar, and the musicians and recording team have gone to this much trouble, it won't do for post-production to relegate it to the status of a filler.

Debussy Images – Ibéria.
Ravel Rapsodie espagnole. Pavane pour une infante défunte. Valses nobles et sentimentales.
Alborada del gracioso. **Chicago Symphony Orchestra / Fritz Reiner.** RCA Victor Gold Seal
Ⓜ GD60179 (68 minutes: ADD: 1/90). Recorded 1956-57.   ⒼⒼ
These performances are seldom less than mesmeric. The extremes of tempo and dynamics are exploited to the full in the Spanish night/day pieces: has any other conductor managed the gradual transition from *Ibéria*'s "perfumes of the night" to the gathering brilliance of the succeeding morning's holiday festivities, with such a delicate, yet precisely focused tracery of sounds? This is the very stuff of a waking dream. And the disc opens with what has to be the slowest, most languid account of the "Prélude" from the *Rapsodie espagnole* ever recorded; the resulting total concentration of the players on their conductor for control of rhythm and dynamics can be felt in every bar; it's not just a musical stunt, it creates a unique tension and atmosphere. Just listen to the finesse of the playing throughout, particularly the percussion, and marvel at how Reiner balances the textures in even the most riotous outbursts of the *Rapsodie*'s explosive "Feria". And the sound? Normally this *Guide* carries caveats for discs recorded in the mid 1950s, and audio boffins might nod their heads at a minuscule degree of tape saturation and hiss, but it is difficult to think of any modern recording that renders the spectacle, colour and refinement of these scores with more clarity and atmosphere.

Additional recommendation ...
...Images – Ibéria. **Schubert** Symphony No. 4 in C minor, D417, "Tragic". **Tchaikovsky**
Francesca da Rimini, Op. 32. **New York Philharmonic Symphony Orchestra / Sir John Barbirolli.**
Dutton Laboratories Essential Archive mono Ⓑ CDEA5000* (69 minutes: ADD: 1/96).

Debussy String Quartet in G minor, Op. 10.
Ravel String Quartet in F major.
Webern String Quartet (1905). **Hagen Quartet** (Lukas Hagen, Rainer Schmidt, vns; Veronika
Hagen, va; Clemens Hagen, vc). DG Ⓕ 437 836-2GH (70 minutes: DDD: 6/94). Recorded
1992-3.   ⒼⒼ
The first movement of the Debussy is taken fastish, but its passionate urgency convinces and it is not forced tonally or tempo-wise. Indeed, the playing is beautifully polished, and this fine ensemble also fully understand the emotional world of the music, the slow movement (again more flowing than usual) offering an acid test which they pass easily. The finale is thrilling. In the Ravel, the playing is sensitive and skilful. Webern's one-movement Quartet was inspired by a painting entitled "Evolving, Being, Passing Away", and the music begins with a motif akin to Beethoven's "Muss es sein?" figure in his String Quartet, Op. 135. The scenario here is predictable: youthfully Germanic heart-searching and struggle, but with little that is memorable, and ultimately somewhat constipated. Still, this performance is persuasive, and the work deserves to be heard when played as well as this. The recording deserves praise: the sound is excellent, not least for viola and cello.

Additional recommendations ...
...String Quartet. **Ravel** String Quartet. **Quartetto Italiano.** Philips Silver Line Ⓜ 420 894-2PSL
(57 minutes: ADD: 10/88).   Ⓖ
...String Quartet. **Ravel** String Quartet. **Carmina Quartet.** Denon Ⓕ CO-75164 (53 minutes: DDD:
3/93).
...String Quartet. **Ravel** String Quartet. **Dutilleux** String Quartet, "Ainsi la Nuit". **Juilliard
Quartet.** Sony Classical Ⓕ SK52554 (74 minutes: DDD: 3/94).
...String Quartet. **Ravel** String Quartet. **Menu** Sonatine. **Parisii Quartet.** Auvidis Valois Ⓕ V4730
(68 minutes: DDD:10/95).
...String Quartet. **Ravel** String Quartet. **Stravinsky** Three Pieces for String Quartet. **Lindsay
Quartet.** ASV Ⓕ CDDCA930 (61 minutes: DDD: 12/95).

Debussy Violin Sonata[a]. Sonata for Flute, Viola and Harp[b].
Franck Violin Sonata in A major[a].
Ravel Introduction and Allegro[b]. [a]**Kyung-Wha Chung** (vn); [b]**Osian Ellis** (hp); [a]**Radu Lupu** (pf);
[b]**Melos Ensemble.** Decca Ⓜ 421 154-2DM (67 minutes: ADD: 1/89). Items marked [a] from
SXL6944 (9/80), [b]SOL60048 (9/62). Items marked [a] recorded in 1977, [b]1962.   Ⓖ
| New review |
Debussy Violin Sonata.
Franck Violin Sonata in A major.
Ravel Berceuse sur le nom de Gabriel Fauré. Pièce en forme de habanera. Tzigane. **Augustin Dumay**
(vn); **Maria-João Pires** (pf). DG Ⓕ 445 880-2GH (56 minutes: DDD: 10/95). Recorded 1993.   Ⓖ

New review
Debussy Violin Sonata.
Poulenc Violin Sonata.
Ravel Violin Sonata. Tzigane[a]. **Tasmin Little** (vn); **Piers Lane** (pf). EMI Eminence
Ⓜ CD-EMX2244 (61 minutes: DDD: 12/95). Item marked [a] from CD-EMX2196 (12/92).
Recorded 1991-5. *Gramophone Editor's choice.*   ⒼⒼ

The Decca disc must be one of the best CD bargains around, with three masterpieces from the French tradition in excellent performances that have won the status of recording classics. Kyung Wha Chung and Radu Lupu are a fine duo who capture and convey the delicacy and poetry of the Franck Sonata as well as its rapturous grandeur, and never can the strict canonic treatment of the great tune in the finale have sounded more spontaneous and joyful. They are no less successful in the different world of the elusive Sonata which was Debussy's last work, with its smiles through tears and, in the finale, its echoes of a Neapolitan tarantella. The 1977 recording is beautifully balanced, with a natural sound given to both the violin and piano. The Melos Ensemble recorded the Ravel *Introduction and Allegro* 15 years before, but here too the recording is a fine one for which no allowances have to be made even by ears accustomed to good digital sound; as for the work itself, this has an ethereal beauty that is nothing short of magical and Osian Ellis and his colleagues give it the most skilful and loving performance. To talk about this disc as one for every collection savours of cliché, but anyone who does not have it may safely be urged to make its acquisition.

On the DG disc there is a spacious, eloquent view of Franck's Sonata, in which Dumay's essentially sweet tone also has the requisite strength; as for Pires, she accompanies where necessary and yet can offer a partner's contribution too, as well as being equal to the composer's considerable pianistic demands, not least in terms of large stretches. Although the recorded balance favours the violinist, the brilliant second movement is very effective, and so is the flowing canonic finale, in which the players rightly think in long phrases. Debussy's emotionally fragile world fares even better: this playing has the right flexibility of time and tone, and the rapidly shifting moods of this essentially sad music, so different from Franck's with its emotional assurance, are unerringly captured; and the sound is excellent here. Dumay and Pires are also at home in Ravel's music with its characteristic delicate tenderness and – in *Tzigane* at least – glittering virtuosity.

Even by today's high standards EMI Eminence's disc is outstanding, perfectly recorded by Andrew Keener and Mike Hatch. It begins with Ravel's Sonata, of which the first movement is played with a crisp coolness that may be off-putting to ears expecting cajolery but rightly emphasizes the titillating acidity of the world-weary 1920s idiom. Indeed the playing has great subtlety and there can be nothing but praise for Tasmin Little's acutely judged sonority as well as the actual beauty of her tone. Piers Lane is no less admirable: listen, for example, how he shapes and textures the elegantly edgy phrases of the (finally) flagellatory central Blues. The duo bring the same insight, unselfishness and sheer affection to the very different worlds of Poulenc and Debussy. Time and again one notes details that come up freshly minted, and you might decide to upwardly reassess Poulenc's Sonata on hearing this performance, which goes beyond consistent skill to offer enormous energy and feeling. Debussy's wonderful but fragile Sonata again comes alive in a quite extraordinary way. Nothing is routine, and yet nothing is out of place. Little and Lane have all the virtues of sensitivity and virtuosity of Dumay and Pires plus an extra flair and intensity which puts them in a class of their own.

Additional recommendations ...
...Violin Sonata. Sonata for Flute, Viola and Harp. Syrinx. Cello Sonata. Première Rapsodie for Clarinet and Piano. Petite pièce for Clarinet and Piano. **Athena Ensemble.** Chandos
Ⓕ CHAN8385 (55 minutes: ADD: 5/87).
...Violin Sonata. **Lekeu** Violin Sonata in G major. **Schubert** Sonatinas – D major, D384; A minor, D385; G minor, D408. Violin Sonata in A major, D574. **Kreisler** Liebesleid. Liebesfreud. Schön Rosmarin. Caprice viennois. Tambourin chinois. **Tartini** (arr. Kreisler) Sonata in G minor, "Devil's Trill". **Corelli** (arr. Castagnone) Sonata in D minor, "La Follia", Op. 5 No. 12. **Vitali** (arr. Grumiaux) Ciacona in G minor. **Veracini** (arr. Castagnone) Sonata in A major, Op. 1 No. 7. **Paganini** Le Streghe, Op. 8. I palpiti, Op. 13. **Arthur Grumiaux** (vn); **Riccardo Castagnone** (pf). Philips The Early Years mono Ⓜ 438 516-2PM3* (three discs: 196 minutes: ADD: 11/93).   ⒼⒼ
...Violin Sonata. *Coupled with works by* **Ravel** *and* **Pierné** Gérard Poulet (vn); Noël Lee (pf). Arion Ⓔ ARN68228 (65 minutes: DDD: 9/94). *See review under Ravel; refer to the Index to Reviews. Gramophone Editor's choice.*   Ⓖ
...Sonata for Flute, Viola and Harp[ab]. *Coupled with works by* **Honegger, Denisov, Takemitsu** *and* **Britten** Aurèle Nicolet (fl); Nobuko Imai (va); Naoko Yoshino (hp). Philips Ⓕ 442 012-2PH (64 minutes: DDD: 12/94). *See review in the Collections section; refer to the Index to Reviews.*
...Rapsodie for Saxophone and Piano. Syrinx. Première rapsodie. Sonata for Flute, Viola and Harp. Le petit nègre. Petite pièce. Rapsodie. **Saint-Saëns** Odelette, Op. 162. Clarinet Sonata in E flat major, Op. 167. Feuillet d'album, Op. 81. Bassoon Sonata in G major, Op. 168. Caprice sur des airs danois et russes, Op. 79. Piano Sonata in D major, Op. 166. Romance in D flat major, Op. 37. Tarantelle in A minor, Op. 6. **Various artists.** Cala Ⓜ CACD1017 (two discs: 129 minutes: 2/95).
...Violin Sonata. **Fauré** Violin Sonata No. 1 in A major, Op. 13. **Franck** Violin Sonata in A major. **Pinchas Zukerman** (vn); **Marc Neikrug** (pf). RCA Victor Red Seal Ⓔ 09026 62697-2 (68 minutes: DDD: 5/95).

...Violin Sonata. **Fauré** Violin Sonata No. 1 in A major, Op. 13. **Poulenc** Violin Sonata. **Isabelle van Keulen** (vn); **Ronald Brautigam** (pf). Koch Schwann Ⓕ 315272 (56 minutes: DDD: 10/95).

Debussy Cello Sonata[a].
Schubert Sonata in A minor, D821, "Arpeggione"[b].
Schumann Fünf Stücke im Volkston, Op. 102[a]. **Mstislav Rostropovich** (vc); **Benjamin Britten** (pf).
Decca Ⓕ 417 833-2DH (59 minutes: ADD: 9/87). Items marked [a] from SXL6426 (10/70), recorded 1968, [b]SXL2298 (1/62), recorded1961.   ❻❻❻

As if being one of the greatest composers this country has produced was not enough, Benjamin Britten was also supremely gifted as a conductor and pianist and here we hear him interpreting the music of others. The bewildering concentration of mood and imagery in Debussy's avowedly classical temperamental 15-minute Sonata presents special challenges to the players and its subtleties reveal themselves only after many hearings. It is a piece which is never easy to bring off, with its *commedia dell'arte* transparency and specialized effects. Britten and Rostropovich bring to it and the other works a depth of understanding which it would be hard to imagine bettered. The Schubert Sonata is an engaging work, whilst the five Schumann pieces have a rustic simplicity and strength which these performers turn entirely to Schumann's advantage. Certainly a collector's item, this CD ought to be part of every chamber music collection. The analogue recordings have transferred extremely well.

Additional recommendations ...

...Cello Sonata. **Martin** Ballade. **Poulenc** Cello Sonata. **William Conway** (vc); **Peter Evans** (pf).
Linn Records Ⓕ CKD002 (51 minutes: DDD: 11/91).

...Cello Sonata. *Coupled with works by* **Bridge** and **E. Dohnányi** Bernard Gregor-Smith (vc);
Yolande Wrigley (pf). ASV Ⓕ CDDCA796 (68 minutes: DDD: 9/92).

...Cello Sonata[d]. **R. Strauss** Don Quixote, Op. 35[a]. **Tchaikovsky** Variations on a Rococo Theme in A major, Op. 33[b]. **Fauré** Elégie, Op. 24[c]. **Tortelier** Le pitre[d]. **Paul Tortelier** (vc); [a]**Leonard Rubens** (va); [d]**Gerald Moore** (pf); **Royal Philharmonic Orchestra /** [a]**Sir Thomas Beecham**, [bc]**Norman Del Mar**. EMI Références mono Ⓜ CDH5 65502-2* (78 minutes: ADD: 12/95).

New review

Debussy Complete Piano Works. **Walter Gieseking** (pf); [a]**Hessian Radio Orchestra, Frankfurt / Kurt Schröder**. EMI mono Ⓜ CHS5 65855-2* (four discs: 276 minutes: ADD: 6/96). Recorded 1951-55. Préludes, Books 1 and 2 (from Columbia 33CX1098, 1/54 and 33CX1304, 11/55). Pour le piano. Estampes. Images, Sets 1 and 2 (all from 33CX1137, 3/54). Children's Corner (Columbia 33C1014, 6/53). 12 Etudes. D'un cahier d'esquisses (both from 33CX1261, 2/57). Rêverie. Valse romantique (Columbia LX1598, 1/54). Masques. L'isle joyeuse. La plus que lente. Le petit nègre. Berceuse héroïque. Hommage à Haydn. Danse bohémienne. Mazurka. Deux Arabesques. Nocturne. Tarantelle styrienne. Ballade (33CX1149, 5/54). Suite bergamasque (HMV HQM1225, 11/70). Fantaisie[a] (previously unpublished. Recorded live in 1951).   ❻❻❻

Gieseking's insight and iridescence in Debussy are so compelling and hypnotic that they prompt either a book or a blank page – an unsatisfactory state where criticism or assessment is concerned! First and foremost, there is Gieseking's sonority, one of such delicacy and variety that it can complement Debussy's witty and ironic desire to write music "for an instrument without hammers", for a pantheistic art sufficiently suggestive to evoke and transcend the play of the elements themselves ("the wind, the sky, the sea ..."). Lack of meticulousness seems a small price to pay for such an elemental uproar in "Ce qu'a vu le vent d'Ouest", and Puck's elfin pulse and chatter (*pp aérian*) are caught with an uncanny deftness and precision. The final Debussian magic may not lie in a literal observance of the score, in the unfailing dotting and crossing of every objective and picturesque instruction, yet it is surely the start or foundation of a great performance. More domestically, no one (not even Cortot) has ever captured the sense in *Children's Corner* of a lost and enchanted land, of childhood re-experienced through adult tears and laughter. "Pour les tièrces", from the *Etudes*, may get off to a shaky start but, again, in Debussy's final masterpiece, where pragmatism is resolved into a fantasy undreamed of even by Chopin, Gieseking's artistry tugs at and haunts the imagination. Try "Pour les sonorités opposées", the nodal and expressive centre of the *Etudes*, and you may well wonder when you have heard playing more subtly gauged or articulated, or the sort of interaction with a composer's spirit that can make modern alternatives seem so parsimonious by comparison. So here is that peerless palette of colour and texture, of a light and shade used with a nonchalantly deployed but precise expertise to illuminate every facet of Debussy's teeming and insinuating imagination. An added bonus, a 1951 performance of the *Fantaisie* for piano and orchestra (an ecstatic and scintillating work, played here with a life-affirming chiaroscuro) completes an incomparable set of discs. The transfers are a triumph, with an immediacy much less obvious in the originals. These records should be in every musician's library, be they singer or conductor, violinist or pianist.

Debussy Préludes – Books 1 and 2. **Krystian Zimerman** (pf). DG Ⓜ 435 773-2GH2 (two discs: 84 minutes: DDD: 3/94). Recorded 1991. *Gramophone classical 100. Gramophone Award Winner 1994. Gramophone Editor's choice.*   ❻❻❻

Two discs, retailing at a high mid price and playing for a total of 84 minutes? The playing and the recording had better be in the luxury class. Fortunately they are. Zimerman is the very model of a modern virtuoso. His overrriding aim is vivid projection of character. His quasi-orchestral range of dynamic and attack, based on close attention to textual detail (there are countless felicities in his observation of phrase-markings) and maximum clarity of articulation, is the means to that end. As a result, he draws out the many connections in this music with the romantic tradition, especially in pianistic *tours de force* such as "Les collines d'Anacapri", "Ce qu'a vu le vent d'Ouest" and "Feux d'artifice", which are treated to a dazzling Lisztian *élan*. The instrument he has selected is itself something of a star and DG's recording combines opulence with razor-sharp clarity. At the other extreme Zimerman displays an exquisite refinement of touch that makes the quieter pieces both evocative and touching. Such sensitively conceived and wonderfully executed Debussy playing stands, at the very least, on a level with a classic recording such as Gieseking's, or a comparably idiomatic modern one such as Martino Tirimo's.

Additional recommendations ...

...Préludes. **Walter Gieseking** (pf). EMI Références mono Ⓜ CDH7 61004-2* (70 minutes: ADD: 4/88). ⒼⒼⒼ

...Préludes. **Martino Tirimo** (pf). IMP Masters Ⓕ MCD16 (78 minutes: DDD: 2/91).

...Préludes. Images – Sets 1 and 2. Estampes. **Claudio Arrau** (pf). Philips Ⓜ 432 304-2PM2 (two discs: 134 minutes: ADD: 2/92).

...Préludes. Deux Arabesques. Children's Corner. Estampes. Images – Sets 1 and 2. Mazurka, L'isle joyeuse. Pour le piano. **Werner Haas** (pf). Philips Duo Ⓜ 438-718-2PM2 (two discs: 157 minutes: ADD: 4/94).

| New review |

Debussy Préludes – Books 1[a] and 2[b]. Images[c]. Children's Corner[c]. **Arturo Benedetti Michelangeli** (pf). DG Ⓕ 449 438-2GH2 (two discs: 128 minutes: [ac]ADD/[b]DDD: 5/96). Item marked [a] from 2530 200 (11/78), [b]427 391-2GH (3/89), [c]2530 196 (12/71). Recorded 1971-88. Ⓖ

Of Debussy playing his own music Alfredo Casella said "he made the impression of playing directly on the strings of the instrument with no intermediate mechanism – the effect was a miracle of poetry". This is not Michelangeli's way. He can certainly be poetic and produce miracles but his manner is not ingratiating. Generalized 'atmosphere' doesn't interest him. His superfine control is put at the service of line and movement, above all, and the projection of perspectives. It is as if he were intent on defining the space the pieces occupy. He gives you a sense not just of foreground and background but of many planes in between. Try "Feux d'artifice", the last of the Second Book of *Préludes* (second disc, track 12), for instances of this: the murmuring ostinato at the beginning (*léger, égal et lointain*) is 'positioned' with absolute precision, and as you're drawn into the picture it's as if you can see exactly where everything is coming from. Michelangeli was capable of a transcendental virtuosity, not always noticed, that had nothing to do with playing fast and loud and everything to do with refinement, and it is very much in evidence here – in many other *Préludes* and especially in the first two *Images* of the Second Book; also, less expectedly, in "The snow is dancing" from *Children's Corner*. The clarity of texture and the laser-like delineation can sometimes be disconcerting if you're accustomed to a softer, more ethereal style, but they have a way of making Debussy's modernism apparent and thrilling. He sounds here as if he has had nothing to do with the nineteenth century. The *Images* and *Children's Corner* are among the finest versions ever recorded. But in some of the *Préludes*, particularly in Book 1, the sound is rather close and dry – maybe how Michelangeli wanted it. He uses as little pedal as he can get away with – Marguerite Long reported that Debussy, like Chopin, considered the art of the pedal as a "sort of breathing", but you don't get much sense of that here. In the Breton seascape "Ce qu'a vu le vent d'ouest" do you really *want* to hear every note? There are people who regard Gieseking as unparalleled in this music, but after a quarter of a century the best of Michelangeli, similarly, will run and run. Today's generation of Debussy pianists will be expected to work from a less corrupt text, quite rightly, but they will have far to go before they can rival the penetrating qualities of Michelangeli's Debussy at its best. He could take your breath away and he was illuminating in this repertoire in a rare way.

Additional recommendations ...

...Images – Hommage à Rameau; Poissons d'or. Préludes – La cathédrale engloutie; Ondine. *Coupled with works by* **Szymanowski, Prokofiev, Villa-Lobos, Schumann** and **Albéniz Artur Rubinstein** (pf). RCA Victor Gold Seal Ⓜ 09026 61445-2 (64 minutes: ADD: 10/93). *See review in the Collections section; refer to the Index to Reviews.*

...Children's Corner. *Coupled with works by* **Tchaikovsky** and **Schumann Idil Biret** (pf). Naxos Ⓢ 8 550885 (66 minutes: DDD: 10/94).

Debussy Suite bergamasque. Images oubliées. Pour le piano. Estampes. **Zoltán Kocsis** (pf). Philips Ⓕ 412 118-2PH (55 minutes: DDD: 4/85). *Selected by Sounds in Retrospect.* ⒼⒼ

Debussy Images – Sets 1 and 2. D'un cahier d'esquisses. L'isle joyeuse. Deux arabesques. Hommage à Haydn. Rêverie. Page d'album. Berceuse héroïque. **Zoltán Kocsis** (pf). Philips Ⓕ 422 404-2PH (62 minutes: DDD: 2/90). Recorded 1988. **Gramophone** *Award Winner 1990.* ⒼⒼ

Three decades ago you could have counted on the fingers of one hand the performers who really had the measure of Debussy's piano style. Today there are many, but even so the Hungarian pianist Zoltán Kocsis stands out as especially idiomatic. On the first disc here, he plays four relatively early sets of pieces of which all but the *Suite bergamasque* are in the composer's favourite triptych form that he also used in *La mer*. The most 'classical' of them are the oddly titled *Pour le piano*, in which the Prelude echoes Bach's keyboard writing, and the *Suite bergamasque* with its eighteenth-century dances, but even in the latter work we find the composer's popular "Clair de lune" memorably impressionistic in its evocation of moonlight. In the *Estampes*, the last pieces played, he displayed a still more fully developed impressionism in musical pictures of the Far East, Moorish Spain and lastly a mysteriously rainswept urban garden. The rarity here is the *Images oubliées*, pieces dating from 1894 that Debussy left unpublished, doubtless because he reworked material from them in the *Estampes* and very obviously in the Sarabande of *Pour le piano*, but they are fine in their own right and here we can compare the different treatments of the similar ideas. The second recital is also a revealing portrait of the composer, its items discerningly offsetting the familiar with the less-known. It also brings playing not only of exceptional finesse, but at times of exceptional brilliance and fire. The main work is of course *Images*, its two sets completed in 1905 and 1907 respectively, by which time the composer was already master of that impressionistic style of keyboard writing so different from anything known before. For superfine sensitivity to details of textural shading Kocsis is at his most spellbinding in the first two numbers of the second set, "Cloches à travers les feuilles" and "Et la lune descend sur le temple qui fût". He is equally successful in reminding us of Debussy's wish to "forget that the piano has hammers" in the atmospheric washes of sound that he conjures (through his pedalling no less than his fingers) in *D'un cahier d'esquisses*. The sharp, clear daylight world of *L'îsle joyeuse* reveals a Kocsis exulting in his own virtuosity and strength as he also does in the last piece of each set of *Images*, and even in the second of the two familiar, early *Arabesques*, neither of them mere vapid drawing-room charmers here. The recording is first rate. Both discs are highly recommendable. Zoltán Kocsis brings refinement and brilliance to all this music and the piano sound is exceptionally rich and faithful.

Additional recommendations ...

...Suite bergamasque – Prélude. Le petit nègre. Deux Arabesques. Images – Poissons d'or. Children's Corner. La plus que lente. Préludes – Des pas sur la neige; Les terrasses des audiences; Ondine; Feux d'artifice. Etudes – Pour les cinq doigts; Pour les arpèges composés. L'îsle joyeuse. **Dame Moura Lympany** (pf). Classics for Pleasure Ⓑ CD-CFP4653 (74 minutes: DDD: 10/94). Recorded 1993.

...Pour le piano. Estampes. **Ravel** Miroirs. Sonatine. Jeux d'eau. **Lilya Zilberstein** (pf). DG Ⓕ 439 927-2GH (74 minutes: DDD: 2/95).

...Images. Images oubliées. Estampes. **Georges Pludermacher** (pf). Harmonia Mundi Ⓕ HMC90 1503 (58 minutes: DDD: 3/95).

...Estampes. Préludes, Book 1 – Voiles; Le vent dans la plaine; Les collines d'Anacapri. *Coupled with works by* **Schumann, Schubert, Bach, Haydn, Chopin, Scriabin, Rachmaninov** and **Prokofiev** **Sviatoslav Richter** (pf). DG Double Ⓜ 447 355-2GDB2 (two discs: 150 minutes: ADD: 12/95).

...Suite bergamasque. Nocturne. Danse bohémienne. Rêverie. Mazurka. Deux arabesques. Valse romantique. Ballade. Tarantelle styrienne. Pour le piano. **François-Joël Thiollier** (pf). Naxos Ⓢ 8 553290 (71 minutes: DDD: 1/96).

Debussy Etudes – Books 1 and 2. **Mitsuko Uchida** (pf). Philips Ⓕ 422 412-2PH (47 minutes: DDD: 7/90). Recorded 1989.   ⒼⒼⒼ

Near the beginning of his career, Debussy's *Prélude à l'après-midi d'un faune* (1894) opened the door (so it is often said) for modern music. His late works, including three chamber sonatas and the set of 12 piano studies (1915), opened another door, through which perhaps only he could have stepped. But his death from cancer in 1918 at the age of 56 put paid to that prospect. The harmonic language and continuity of the *Studies* is elusive even by Debussy's standards, and it takes an artist of rare gifts to play them 'from within', at the same time as negotiating their finger-knotting intricacies. Mitsuko Uchida is such an artist. On first hearing perhaps rather hyperactive, her playing wins you over by its bravura and sheer relish, eventually disarming criticism altogether. This is not just the finest-ever recorded version of the *Studies*; it is also one of the finest examples of recorded piano playing in modern times, matched by sound quality of outstanding clarity and ambient warmth.

Additional recommendations ...

...Etudes – Books 1 and 2. Pour le piano. **Gordon Fergus-Thompson** (pf). ASV Ⓕ CDDCA703 (62 minutes: DDD: 7/90).

...Etudes – Books 1 and 2. Berceuse héroïque. Morceau de concours. D'un cahier d'esquisse. Suite bergamasque. **Lívia Rév** (pf). Saga Classics Ⓜ EC3383-2 (75 minutes: ADD: 4/92).

Debussy Le martyre de Saint-Sébastien. **Sylvia McNair** (sop); **Ann Murray** (mez); **Nathalie Stutzmann** (contr); **Leslie Caron** (narr); **London Symphony Chorus and Orchestra / Michael Tilson Thomas**. Sony Classical Ⓕ SK48240 (66 minutes: DDD: 3/93). Text and translation included. Recorded 1991. *Gramophone Award Winner 1993. Selected by Sounds in Retrospect.*   ⒼⒼ

"Archers aim closely, I am the target; whoever wounds me the most deeply, loves me the most. From the depths I call forth your terrible love ... again ... again! ...AGAIN!" cries the Saint in ecstasy. What Oscar Wilde did to the story of Salome, so the Italian writer D'Annunzio did to the story of Saint Sebastian (a young Roman officer ordered to be killed by his own archers because of his sympathy for persecuted Christians). This was the first modern recording, not of the complete play (which lasted five hours!), but of an intelligent and effective reduction of the written text using the Saint as narrator, and incorporating all of an hour's worth of Debussy's incidental music. And it must be deemed a triumph. Leslie Caron's Saint is quietly intense and a model of restraint; Sylvia McNair's *vox coelestis* is just that, a gift from God; and the chorus and orchestra respond with total conviction to what is evidently, from Tilson Thomas, direction with a mission. The sheer sorcery of Debussy's music, as strongly imbued as his *Pélleas* with Wagner's *Parsifal*, benefits enormously from the acoustic of, appropriately, All Saints' Church in Tooting, London.

Additional recommendation ...
...Le martyre de Saint-Sébastien. Images. Ibéria. **Boston Symphony Orchestra / Charles Munch.** RCA Victor Gold Seal Ⓜ GD60684* (73 minutes: ADD). ⒼⒼ

Debussy La damoiselle élue[a]. Prélude à l'après-midi d'un faune. Images, Ibéria. [a]**Maria Ewing** (sop) Damoiselle; [a]**Brigitte Balleys** (contr) Narrator; **London Symphony** [a]**Chorus and Orchestra / Claudio Abbado.** DG Ⓕ 423 103-2GH (49 minutes: DDD: 3/88). Text and translation included.
Selected by Sounds in Retrospect. Ⓖ
La damoiselle élue is scored for soprano, women's chorus and orchestra and sets verses from Dante Gabriel Rossetti's *The Blessed Damozel*. It is cast into four short movements and owes a clear debt to Wagner's *Parsifal*. The *Prélude à l'après-midi d'un faune* was Debussy's first real masterpiece and this evocation of Mallarmé's poem introduced a whole palette of new, supremely beautiful sounds, combining them into a musical structure both concise and subtly complex. Once heard it can never be forgotten. "Ibéria" is the central component of the orchestral set of *Images* and its three movements employ the rhythms and harmonies of Spanish music to conjure up a perfect picture of the Spanish/Mediterranean climate in its various moods. A fine Debussian, Abbado penetrates to the heart of all these works and is given fine orchestral support throughout. Maria Ewing is an impressive Damoiselle and the women of the LSO chorus are in excellent voice. The recording is most successful, with good atmosphere and clarity.

Additional recommendation ...
...La Damoiselle élue[a]. Nocturnes[b]. Le martyre de Saint Sébastien – La Cour de Lys; Danse extatique; La Passion; Le Bon Pasteur. [a]**Dawn Upshaw** (sop); [a]**Paula Rasmussen** (mez); [ab]**Los Angeles Master Chorale; Los Angeles Philharmonic Orchestra / Esa-Pekka Salonen.** Sony Classical Ⓕ SK58952 (68 minutes: DDD: 12/94).

New review
Debussy Rodrigue et Chimène (recons. Langham Smith and orch. Denisov). **Laurence Dale** (ten) Rodrigue; **Donna Brown** (sop) Chimène; **Hélène Jossoud** (mez); Iñez; **Gilles Ragon** (ten) Hernan; **Jean-Paul Fouchécourt** (ten) Bermudo; **José van Dam** (bass-bar) Don Diègue; **Jules Bastin** (bass) Don Gomez; **Vincent le Texier** (bass-bar) King; **Jean-Louis Meunier** (ten) Don Juan d'Arcos; **Jean Delescluse** (ten) Don Pèdre de Teruel; **Chorus and Orchestra of the Opéra de Lyon / Kent Nagano.** Erato Ⓕ 4509-98508-2 (two discs: 109 minutes: DDD: 10/95). Notes, text and translation included. Recorded 1993-4. *Gramophone Editor's choice.* ⒼⒼ
It may come as a surprise to many who treasure the unique magic of *Pelléas et Mélisande* that Debussy toyed with some 30 other plans for operas, and two years before *Pelléas* had all but completed his first operatic venture. Debussy very soon realized that the libretto's blustering tone was alien to his ideals of half-hinted action in short scenes, and became increasingly restive, finally abandoning it and claiming that it had been accidentally destroyed. In reality it survived complete in a sketch in short score, though some pages have since been lost. Richard Langham Smith reconstructed the work from the manuscripts in the Piermont Morgan Library in New York, it was completed and orchestrated, with a remarkable insight into Debussian style, by Edison Denisov, and in 1993 it was presented by the Opéra de Lyon to mark the opening of its new house. Inconsistencies of style reveal something of Debussy's uncertainties and doubts over a subject inappropriate for him. There is little in Act 3 that would lead anyone to identify him as the composer, and virtually the only sections of the work with a harmonic idiom that was later to become characteristic of him are Rodrigue's and Chimène's mutual declaration of love at the start of Act 1 (after a reflective modal prelude with a tinge of Russian influence), the orchestral prelude to Act 2 and the unexpected quiet interlude that precedes Rodrigue's mortal challenge to his beloved's father Don Gomez, who had shamed his own father. Debussy is less at home with the choral scene leading up to the angry conflict between the two initially friendly houses, the heroic and warlike atmosphere of much of Act 2, and the bombastic assembling of the royal court; but all these are tackled, if not with individuality, at least with vigour. Don Gomez's death scene is affecting, and the unaccompanied choral requiem for him makes an effective close to Act 2. Unlike *Pelléas*, there are a number of extended set pieces for the singers, including Rodrigue's dutiful dilemma, Don Diègue's hymn to the concept of honour, Chimène's lament for her father and her final anguish as she is torn between love and hate for Rodrigue. As a performance and recording, this is in the highest class. Nagano's orchestra play for him with finesse, and the work is cast from strength. Laurence Dale is a near-perfect Rodrigue youthful, ardent, sensitive to changes of mood, and with a free vocal production that is a constant pleasure to hear; Donna Brown makes a passionate Chimène, though occasionally just too close to the microphone for sudden outbursts and José van Dam is his always reliable self, with nobility in his

voice. Clarity of enunciation throughout (except, at times, from the chorus) is to be applauded. In sum, an intriguing addition to our knowledge of Debussy at an early stage of his career.

Debussy Pelléas et Mélisande. **Eric Tappy** (ten) Pelléas; **Rachel Yakar** (sop) Mélisande; **Philippe Huttenlocher** (bar) Golaud; **Jocelyne Taillon** (mez) Geneviève; **Colette Alliot-Lugaz** (sop) Yniold; **François Loup** (bass) Arkel; **Michel Brodard** (bass) Doctor, Shepherd; **Monte-Carlo National Opera Orchestra / Armin Jordan.** Erato Libretto Ⓜ 2292-45684-2 (three discs: 160 minutes: ADD: 12/91). Notes, text and translation included. From STU71296 (10/80). Recorded 1979.   Ⓖ
Maeterlinck's play was the inspiration for Debussy's sole masterpiece in the operatic genre. *Pelléas et Mélisande* tells of a medieval princess who falls in love with her husband Golaud's younger half-brother Pelléas, who is then killed by Golaud before Mélisande herself dies in childbirth. The story has a Wagnerian parallel in *Tristan und Isolde*, but the music is very different, being more restrained on the surface while suggesting no less powerful passions beneath. No modern performances have really succeeded in replacing the classic versions conducted by Roger Desormière and Ernest Ansermet (not currently available), both of which preserve a tradition of performing this elusive piece that has since been lost. Armin Jordan's performance at once conjures up and then sustains the strange half-lit world of Maeterlinck's tale. Despite the title, in some ways the chief role is that of Golaud, and Philippe Huttenlocher, who is a superb singer-actor, makes us believe in and feel for him. Rachel Yakar is mysterious, delicate and wholly feminine as Mélisande – indeed, sometimes maddeningly so, for in her passivity and reluctance to explain herself she positively invites Golaud's jealous suspicions. The role of Pelléas can be sung either by a high baritone or by a tenor: again it is the latter and Eric Tappy therefore sounds all the more youthful and innocent compared with the dark baritone quality of Golaud (he's supposed to be 20 years younger). The other principals have less to do but are also satisfying, not least the bass François Loup as the kindly old king, Arkel. The orchestra under Armin Jordan play as if inspired and the clear recording allows every word to be heard, which is what Debussy wanted but is hard to achieve in the theatre. One gladly agrees with the original *Gramophone* review which found this performance "profoundly moving" and it offers us a considerable and very agreeable mid-price bargain.

Additional recommendations ...
...Pelléas et Mélisande. Mélodies. **Soloists; Yvonne Gouverné Choir; symphony orchestra / Roger Desormière.** EMI Références mono Ⓜ CHS7 61038-2* (three discs: 196 minutes: ADD: 8/88). *Gramophone* classical 100.   Ⓖ Ⓖ Ⓖ
...**Soloists; Montreal Symphony Chorus and Orchestra / Charles Dutoit.** Decca Ⓕ 430 502-2DH2 (two discs: 151 minutes: DDD: 3/91). *Selected by Sounds in Retrospect.*
...**Soloists; Vienna State Opera Chorus; Vienna Philharmonic Orchestra / Claudio Abbado.** DG Ⓕ 435 344-2GH2 (two discs: 148 minutes: DDD: 3/92).   Ⓖ
...**Soloists; Raymond St Paul Chorus; French Radio National Orchestra / André Cluytens.** Testament mono Ⓕ SBT3051* (three discs: 161 minutes: ADD: 6/95).

New review

Debussy Pelléas et Mélisande. **Claude Dormoy** (ten) Pelléas; **Michèle Command** (sop) Mélisande; **Gabriel Bacquier** (bar) Golaud; **Roger Soyer** (bass) Arkel; **Jocelyne Taillon** (mez) Geneviève; **Monique Pouradier-Duteil** (sop) Yniold; **Xavier Tamalet** (bass) Doctor, Shepherd; **Burgundian Chorus; Orchestra of the Opéra de Lyon / Serge Baudo.** RCA Opera Ⓑ 74321 32225-2 (two discs: 147 minutes: ADD: 7/96). Synopsis and text included. From Eurodisc 452 266, recorded 1978.   Ⓖ Ⓖ
There have been many fine historic recordings of *Pelléas et Mélisande*: reissues have included Desormière's of 1941, Ansermet's of 1952, Cluytens's of 1956, and more recently Jordan's of 1979 – and now comes yet another, from Baudo, a conductor with a great reputation as an interpreter of French music and closely associated with this particular work. The excellence of this performance leaves one wondering why it has taken the best part of 20 years to emerge here. Baudo produces a warm sound from the Lyon orchestra, knows how to shape Debussy's subtle phrases, and is notably good at making use of silences. He is fortunate to have a cast without a single weak member. It is often the case that the central figure of Golaud, tortured by blind jealousy, steals the show, but Gabriel Bacquier is superb, capturing every nuance from tenderness to abrupt anger (at the news of the loss of the ring) or agonized frustration beside Mélisande's deathbed. Michèle Command, here at an early stage of her career, and entirely free from the undue weightiness that has sometimes characterized her work since, makes a shy, fey Mélisande who remains an enigmatic figure; she invests the famous solo about her long hair with a sense of melancholy. The big surprise of this set is the Pelléas, a sensitive singer who seems, inexplicably, to have appeared in only one other recording (*The merry wives of Windsor*), made in the year before this – in a bass role! Listed here as a tenor, he is more a high baritone (which is appropriate for the part), just occasionally sounding a trifle stretched on a high note. The part of Arkel is given nobility by Roger Soyer; and the Yniold sounds convincingly childlike. Care has been taken in the production, as can be heard in the hollower acoustic of the scene in the vaults; only the perspective of the sailors on the unseen ship – always a problem in recordings – is a little uncertain. Make no mistake: this is a very rewarding version of this masterpiece, and as a two-disc bargain-price issue is a real snip. Even at bargain price, however, there is no excuse for RCA's rank carelessness in listing a principal character as "Goulad".

Further listening ...

...(orch. Caplet) Children's Corner. Estampes – Pagodes. Suite bergamasque – Clair de lune. *Coupled with works by* **Caplet Rheinland-Pfalz State Philharmonic Orchestra / Leif Segerstam.** Marco Polo 8 223751 (9/95). *See review under Caplet; refer to the Index to Reviews.*

...Printemps[b]. *Coupled with* **Caplet** Myrrha[ade]. Tout est lumière[b]. **Ravel** L'aurore[d]. Matinée de Provence[b]. Tout est lumière[c]. Les bayadères[b]. La nuit[c]. [a]**Sharon Coste,** [b]**Brigitte Desnoues,** [c]**Gaële Le Roi** (sops); [d]**Marc Duguay** (ten); [e]**Jean-François Lapointe** (bar); **Chorus and Orchestra of the Sorbonne, Paris / Jacques Grimbert.** Marco Polo 8 223755 (10/95).

...Music for Two Pianos – En blanc et noir[a]; Petite Suite[a]; Six épigraphes antiques[a]; Lindaraja[a]; Marche écossaise[a]. Ballade slave. Berceuse héroïque. Danse. Danse Bohémienne. Etudes – Books 1 and 2. D'un cahier d'esquisses. Hommage à Haydn. Masques. Nocturne. Le petit nègre. La plus que lente. Rêverie. Suite bergamasque. Valse romantique. **Werner Haas,** [a]**Noël Lee** (pfs). Philips Duo 438 721-2PM2 (4/94).

...Premier Trio in G major. *Coupled with* **Ravel** Piano Trio. **Fauré** Piano Trio in D minor, Op. 120. **Solomon Trio.** IMP Classics MCD41 (7/92). Ⓖ

...Premier Trio in G major. *Coupled with* **Fauré** Piano Trio in D minor, Op. 120. **Saint-Saëns** Piano Trio No. 1 in F major, Op. 18. **Golub Kaplan Carr Trio.** Arabesque Z6643 (7/95).

...Premier Trio in G major. *Coupled with* **Ravel** Piano Trio. **Schmitt** Très lent. **Joachim Trio.** Naxos 8 550934 (8/95).

...Premier Trio in G major. **Ravel** Piano Trio. **Julie Rosenfeld** (vn); **Gary Hoffman** (vc); **André Previn** (pf). RCA Victor Red Seal 09026 68062-2 (11/95).

...(arr. Bozza) Le petit nègre. **Ibert** Trois pièces brèves. **Françaix** Wind Quintet No. 1. **Milhaud** La cheminée du roi René, Op. 205. **Damase** Variations, Op. 22. **Pierné** Pastorale, Op. 41 No. 1 (original version). **Poulenc** (arr. Emerson): Novelette No. 1 in C major. **Fauré** (arr. C. Williams) Dolly, Op. 56 – Berceuse. **Reykjavik Wind Quintet.** Chandos CHAN9362 (10/95).

...Mélodies – L'âme évaporée. Ariettes oubliées. Beau soir. Les cloches. Fêtes galantes, Sets 1 and 2. Mandoline. Musique. Noël des enfants qui n'ont plus de maison. Nuit d'étoiles. Proses lyriques. **Claudette LeBlanc** (sop); **Valerie Tryon** (pf). Unicorn-Kanchana DKPCD9133 (4/93).

...Ariettes oubliées. Cinq poèmes de Charles Baudelaire. Chansons de Bilitis. *Coupled with* **Ravel** Histoires naturelles. **Nathalie Stutzmann** (contr); **Cathérine Collard** (pf). RCA Victor Red Seal RD60899 (7/92).

Abel Decaux
French 1869-1943

New review

Decaux Clairs de lune.
Ravel Miroirs.
Schoenberg Drei Klavierstücke, Op. 11. **Frederic Chiu** (pf). Harmonia Mundi Ⓕ HMU90 7166 (67 minutes: DDD: 1/96). Recorded 1994.

Here is something special; a programme of 'reflections', of parallels rather than incongruities performed with rare elegance and finesse. For Frederic Chiu Debussy and Ravel, Schoenberg, Berg and Webern all "found their initial *élan* from the universal search for the post-Wagnerian aspirin". Abel Decaux, whose *Clairs de lune* predate Ravel's *Miroirs*, also falls within this category and his most intriguing modernity makes his presence in such company apt rather than arbitrary. Less academically, his "La ruelle" is an alley few would choose to visit after dark, and his "Le cimetière" is a sombre place indeed. Despite several technical relationships with *Miroirs* such bleakness is a far cry from that piece, where Ravel's expressionist writing reaches its height and finds its outlet in a dazzling interplay of night and day, or brightness and shadows. Chiu's "Noctuelles" are as light-winged as any on record. His "Une barque sur l'océan", too, has an authentically Ravelian sense of *luxe, calme et volupté*, a Mediterranean marinescape, dancing with pin-points of light – a magical evocation. Guitars twang and castanets snap with precision and aplomb (despite an uncharacteristic mis-hit at the end) in "Alborada", and in the central *plus lent* the clowning dissolves into a most subtly perceived sense of reverie. In the first of Schoenberg's *Drei Klavierstücke*, Chiu makes us specially aware of how the flickering half lights of Ravel's "Noctuelles" are reincarnated in a still-familiar form, and throughout all three pieces his playing is scrupulously sensitive and controlled. These recordings beautifully capture his delicate and precise sonority; anyone with an ear for the enterprising, intelligently planned and superbly played should investigate.

Juan Francés de Iribarren
Spanish 1698-1767

Suggested listening ...

...Quién nos dira de una flor. Viendo que Jil, hizo raya. *Coupled with works by* **F. Valls, J. de Torres, C. Galán, Literes** and **Anonymous Al Ayre Español / Eduardo López Banzo.** Deutsche Harmonia Mundi 05472 77325-2 (8/95). *See review in the Collections section; refer to the Index to Reviews.* Ⓖ

Michel Delalande

French 1657-1726

Suggested listening ...

...Sinfonies pour les soupers du Roi. **La Symphonie du Marais / Hugo Reyne.** Harmonia Mundi HMC90 1337/40 (four discs: 7/91). 🎵

...Cantate Domino, S72. De profundis, S23. Regina coeli, S53. **Ex Cathedra Chamber Choir and Baroque Orchestra / Jeffrey Skidmore.** ASV Gaudeamus CDGAU141 (7/95). 🎵 Ⓖ

...Trois Leçons de Ténèbres et le Miserere. **Michaëla Etcheverry** (mez); **Jean-Louis Charbonnier** (va da gamba); **Laurence Boulay** (hpd). Erato 4509-98528-2. 🎵

...Te Deum, S32. Super flumina. Confitebor tibi, Domine. **Véronique Gens, Sandrine Piau, Arlette Steyer** (sops); **Jean-Paul Fouchécourt, François Piolino** (tens); **Jérôme Corréas** (bass); **Les Arts Florissants / William Christie.** Harmonia Mundi HMC90 1351 (7/91). 🎵

...Petits Motets – Miserere a voix seule. Vanum est vobis ante lucem. Miserator et misericors. Cantique quatrième. *Coupled with* **Lemaire** Assumpta est Maria. **Morin** Regina coeli. **Soloists; Les Arts Florissants Chorus and Orchestra / William Christie.** Harmonia Mundi HMC90 1416 (4/93). 🎵 Ⓖ

...Dies irae, S31. Miserere mei Deus secundum, S27. **Linda Perillo, Patrizia Kwella** (sops); **Howard Crook** (alto); **Herve Lamy** (ten); **Peter Harvey** (bass); **Chorus and Orchestra of La Chapelle Royale / Philippe Herreweghe.** Harmonia Mundi HMC90 1352 (12/91). 🎵 Ⓖ

Leo Delibes

French 1836-1891

New review

Delibes Sylvia.
Saint-Saëns Henry VIII – Ballet-divertissement. **Razumovsky Sinfonia / Andrew Mogrelia.** Naxos Ⓢ 8 553338/9 (two discs: 114 minutes: DDD: 6/96). Recorded 1995. *Gramophone Editor's choice.*
Of Delibes's two full-length ballets, *Coppélia* is the more obviously popular, the one with the bigger tunes and the greater number of recordings. However, *Sylvia* is also a superbly crafted score, full of haunting melodies. Andrew Mogrelia's Naxos series is one to be collected and treasured: there is loving care applied to selection of tempos, shaping of phrases, orchestral balance and refinement of instrumental detail. Here you thrill to *Sylvia*'s Act 1 Fanfare, marvel at the control of tempo and refinement of instrumental detail in the "Valse lente" and "Entrée du sorcier", and revel in the sheer ebullience of Sylvia's return in Act 2. The inclusion of the ballet music from Saint-Saëns's *Henry VIII* was an admirably enterprising move, even though it doesn't amount to anything major apart from the "Danse de la gitane", being essentially a collection of mock 'Olde Britishe' dances. All the same, a quite remarkable bargain.

Additional recommendation ...

...Sylvia[a]. Coppélia[b]. [a]**London Symphony Orchestra / Anatole Fistoulari;** [b]**Minneapolis Symphony Orchestra / Antál Dorati.** Mercury Living Presence Ⓜ 434 313-2MM3 (three discs: 173 minutes: ADD: 3/93). Ⓖ

Delibes Coppélia. **Orchestra of the Opéra de Lyon / Kent Nagano.** Erato Ⓕ 4509-91730-2 (two discs: 99 minutes: DDD: 5/94). Recorded 1993. *Gramophone Editor's choice.* ⒼⒼ
Though the text played absolutely complete may be straightforward Delibes, the interpretation instantly announces itself as being anything but straightforward. Every phrase, every accent, every nuance seems to be newly considered, without losing the feel for the action that is taking place on the stage. The overriding impression here is of the rightness and naturalness of Nagano's whole reading. The rare quality of the performance is evident at once from the way the music lights up in the *cantando* section in the twelfth bar of the Prelude. Later, in Act 2, the Boléro has a rare dash and brio, while the opening March of Act 3 has a similarly compelling onward momentum. The sequence of speciality dances that makes up most of the final Act is delightfully turned, with a quite heavenly viola solo in "La Paix" and a thrilling final Galop. It is unfortunate that the recording is spread over two CDs, but anyone who loves this music should make a point of hearing Nagano's outstanding reading.

Additional recommendations ...

...**Orchestra of the Royal Opera House, Covent Garden / Mark Ermler.** Royal Opera House Ⓕ ROH006 (74 minutes: DDD: 7/93).

...Coppélia. La Source, ou Naïla – Suites Nos. 2 and 3; Intermezzo. **Slovak Radio Symphony Orchestra, Bratislava / Andrew Mogrelia.** Naxos Ⓢ 8 553356/7 (two discs: 130 minutes: DDD: 6/96).

Further listening ...

...Lakmé. **Soloists; Monte-Carlo Opera Chorus; Monte-Carlo National Opera Orchestra / Richard Bonynge.** Decca Grand Opera 425 485-2DM2 (12/89).

...*See also the* **Great Singers at the Maryinsky Theatre** *review in the Collections section; refer to the Index to Reviews.* Nimbus Prima voce mono NI7865*.

Frederick Delius

Delius Violin Concerto[a]. Two Aquarelles (arr. Fenby). On hearing the first cuckoo in Spring. Summer Night on the River. Fennimore and Gerda Intermezzo (arr. Fenby). Irmelin Prelude. Dance Rhapsodies Nos. 1 and 2. [a]**Tasmin Little** (vn); **Welsh National Opera Orchestra / Sir Charles Mackerras.** Argo Ⓕ 433 704-2ZH (75 minutes: DDD: 7/92). Recorded 1990-91. Ⓖ

This disc of the Violin Concerto should be played to friends who are not committed Delians; it is sure to persuade them that this concerto merits the same devotion as those by Elgar and Walton. Tasmin Little has the edge over Ralph Holmes (but only just) in coping with the work's technical difficulties; and under Mackerras's purposeful guidance, and with greater contrasts of pace between the various sections of its one movement form, the piece behaves more like a conventional concerto. If a certain amount of dream-like atmosphere is shed in the work's opening section in favour of classical rigour and vigour, at the heart of this account is the central accompanied cadenza: a minor miracle of flowing improvisation, with Mackerras and Little more freely rhapsodic than previous partnerships, and as twins in the seamless unfolding of the musical line. Argo's sound is very immediate, with a believable balance between soloist and orchestra, and excellent handling of the (albeit very few) orchestral climaxes. To the many shorter pieces that make up this disc's generous duration, only Beecham has brought a comparable feeling for texture and atmosphere. *Summer Night on the River*, in particular, is remarkable for its Debussian delicacy and the chamber-like intimacy of its sonorities.

Additional recommendations ...

...Violin Concerto. Suite. Légende. **Ralph Holmes** (vn); **Royal Philharmonic Orchestra / Vernon Handley.** Unicorn-Kanchana Ⓕ DKPCD9040 (53 minutes: DDD: 9/85).

...Appalachia[ce]. Koanga – Closing scene[de]. Hassan[e] Intermezzo; Serenade; Closing scene[b]. On hearing the first cuckoo in Spring[f]. Summer Night on the River[f]. Cradle Song[a]. Twilight Fancies[a]. The Nightingale[a].[a]**Dora Labbette** (sop); [b]**Jan van der Gucht** (ten); [c]**BBC Chorus;** [d]**London Select Choir;** [b]**Chorus of the Royal Opera House, Covent Garden;** [e]**London Philharmonic Orchestra,** [f]**Royal Philharmonic Society Orchestra / Sir Thomas Beecham** ([a]pf). Dutton Laboratories mono Ⓜ CDLX7011* (78 minutes: ADD: 10/94). ⒼⒼ

...Paris. In a Summer Garden. Summer Night on the River. Brigg Fair. On hearing the first cuckoo in spring. A Song of Summer. **London Symphony Orchestra / Anthony Collins.** Dutton Laboratories mono Ⓕ CDLXT2503* (76 minutes: ADD: 8/95).

...Dance Rhapsodies Nos. 1 and 2. North Country Sketches. In a Summer Garden. A Village Romeo and Juliet – Walk to the Paradise Garden. **Bournemouth Symphony Orchestra / Richard Hickox.** Chandos Ⓕ CHAN9355 (77 minutes: DDD: 9/95).

...Paris: The Song of a Great City[a]. Suite[b]. Fennimore and Gerda Intermezzo[c]. Arabesque[d]. [d]**Thomas Allen** (bar); [b]**Ralph Holmes** (vn); [d]**Ambrosian Singers; Royal Philharmonic Orchestra /** [a]**Norman Del Mar,** [b]**Vernon Handley,** [cd]**Eric Fenby.** Unicorn Kanchana Souvenir Ⓜ UKCD2076 (67 minutes: DDD: 4/96).

New review
Delius Fantastic Dance[a]. A Dance Rhapsody No. 1[b]. A Dance Rhapsody No. 2[c]. A Song of the High Hills[d]. Three Preludes[e]. Zum Carnival[e]. [d]**Maryetta Midgley** (sop); [d]**Vernon Midgley** (ten); [e]**Eric Parkin** (pf); [d]**Ambrosian Singers;** [abcd]**Royal Philharmonic Orchestra /** [acd]**Eric Fenby,** [b]**Norman Del Mar.** Unicorn-Kanchana Souvenir Ⓜ UKCD2071 (65 minutes: DDD: 8/95). Item marked [a] from DKP9008/09 (10/81), [b]DKPCD9108 (3/92), [cd]DKPCD9063 (1/88), [e]DKP9021 (7/83). Recorded 1981-90.

New review
Delius Irmelin Prelude[a]. A Song of Summer[a]. A Late Lark[b] . Piano Concerto in C minor[c]. Violin Concerto[d]. [b]**Anthony Rolfe Johnson** (ten); [d]**Ralph Holmes** (vn); [c]**Philip Fowke** (pf); **Royal Philharmonic Orchestra /** [ab]**Eric Fenby,** [d]**Vernon Handley,** [c]**Norman Del Mar.** Unicorn-Kanchana Souvenir Ⓜ UKCD2072 (71 minutes: DDD: 8/95). Items marked [ab] from DKP9008/09 (10/81), [c]DKPCD9108 (3/92), [d]DKP9040 (7/85). Recorded 1981-90.

New review
Delius Koanga – La Calinda (arr. Fenby)[a]. Idyll: Once I passed through a populous city[b]. Songs of Sunset[c]. A Village Romeo and Juliet – The Walk to the Paradise Garden[d]. [b]**Felicity Lott** (sop); [c]**Sarah Walker** (mez); [bc]**Thomas Allen** (bar); [c]**Ambrosian Singers; Royal Philharmonic Orchestra /** [abc]**Eric Fenby,** [d]**Norman Del Mar.** Unicorn-Kanchana Souvenir Ⓜ UKCD2073 (73 minutes: DDD: 8/95). Items marked [ab] from DKP9008/09 (10/81), [c]DKPCD9063 (1/88), [d]new to UK. Recorded 1981-90.

The unique insight that Eric Fenby would bring as an interpreter of Delius was the reason for many of these Unicorn recordings, but we owe the idea and its realization to their producer, the late Christopher Palmer. As well as providing Delians with some of the most illuminating and inspiring text on the music (in books and sleeve-notes), Palmer, in the studio, and especially in a work like *A Song of the High Hills*, was able to put his understanding (and Fenby's, of course) into practice. You don't need the score of *A Song of the High Hills* to tell you that the passage from 9'54" represents "The wide far distance, the great solitude". That to which you are listening – totally spellbound – could be nothing else (and by nobody else).

A few years ago, Ralph Holmes's recording of the Violin Concerto (with Vernon Handley) would have been a good reason for acquiring Vol. 2. It is a warm, leisurely reading (the peak distortion remains), though it lacks the planning and poise of the Little/Mackerras collaboration reviewed above (which achieves both greater purpose and repose). The Piano Concerto is another matter: as recorded here, it is a grand showstopper in the best romantic piano concerto tradition, yet Fowke and Del Mar alert you to all the Delian reverie in the making (the dynamic range of Fowke's piano is colossal). But the outlay for Vol. 2 is justified by Anthony Rolfe Johnson alone, in the all too brief six minute-long *A Late Lark* ("one of Delius's works that is surely entirely without flaw, a most moving farewell", as Trevor Harvey put it in his original review).

In Vol. 3, Fenby's control in *Songs of Sunset* does not always match his insight (choral work is often sloppy and too distantly recorded); the recent Hickox, or the 1957 Beecham is to be preferred. But without Fenby in the recording studio (or at Grez!), we would never have had *Idyll*: Whitman texts combined with a late reworking of music from an earlyish opera, *Margot la Rouge*, to provide a reflective then rapturous love duet that looks back to Delius's Paris as well as to his *Paris* – this makes Vol. 3 indispensable, especially as sung and played here. And a very considerable bonus in Vol. 3 is Del Mar's previously unissued *Walk to the Paradise Garden*. This is not the Beecham version for reduced orchestra, as stated in the otherwise excellent notes, though it incorporates many of Beecham's dynamics and tempo indications. It is, most assuredly, a *Walk* on the grandest (11'00" to Beecham's 8'38"), most passionate scale (not a bar-line in earshot, either), and turns out to be yet another of these three discs' memorials to inspired Delians who died in our, but before their, time.

Delius Over the hills and far away[a]. North Country Sketches[b]. Eventyr[c]. Koanga – Closing scene[d].
[d]**BBC Chorus; Royal Philharmonic Orchestra / Sir Thomas Beecham.** Sony Classical British Pageant mono Ⓜ SMK58934* (64 minutes: ADD: 11/94). Item marked [a] from Columbia 33C1017 (12/53), [b]Columbia LX1399/1401 (7/51), [c]LX8931/2 (9/52), [d]LX1502 (1/52). Recorded 1950-59.   ⊖⊖⊖

No one, it seems, could quite 'magick' the music of Frederick Delius the way that Sir Thomas Beecham did. Listen, if you will, to "Autumn, the wind soughs in the trees", the first of the wonderfully atmospheric, seldom-heard *North Country Sketches*: one doubts whether the desolate beauty of the Yorkshire uplands has ever been more hauntingly evoked, whilst in the closing bars time really does seem to stand still. Indeed, all this music-making undoubtedly distils a very real sense of enchantment: *Eventyr* has never been given with more poetry and *Over the hills and far away* (an early piece) is simply captivating, a performance which far outstrips Beecham's later stereo-remake in fantasy, joyful vigour and spontaneity. Lawrance Collingwood was the producer of all these Abbey Road sessions from 1949-51; transfers have been expertly managed, with one irritating exception – the very start of "The March of Spring" (the last of the *North Country Sketches*) has been fractionally clipped. In sum, a collection that should be in every self-respecting Delian's library, for none of this music has ever been surveyed with greater imagination and intuitive rapture than here.

Additional recommendations ...

...North Country Sketches. Florida – suite. **Ulster Orchestra / Vernon Handley.** Chandos
Ⓕ CHAN8413 (67 minutes: DDD: 12/86).

...Paris: The Song of a Great City. Eventyr. Fennimore and Gerda – Intermezzo. Over the hills and far away. Irmelin Prelude. **London Philharmonic Orchestra / Sir Thomas Beecham.** Sir Thomas Beecham Trust mono Ⓜ BEECHAM 2* (61 minutes: ADD: 6/89).

...Appalachia[a]. A Song of the High Hills[b]. Over the hills and far away. [b]**Rebecca Evans** (sop); [b]**Peter Hoare** (ten); [a]**Daniel Washington** (bar); **Welsh National Opera** [ab]**Chorus and Orchestra / Sir Charles Mackerras.** Decca London Ⓕ 443 171-2LH (78 minutes: DDD: 1/96). *Gramophone Editor's choice.*

Delius Paris: The Song of a Great City. Double Concerto[ab]. Cello Concerto[b]. [a]**Tasmin Little** (vn); [b]**Raphael Wallfisch** (vc); **Royal Liverpool Philharmonic Orchestra / Sir Charles Mackerras.** EMI Eminence Ⓜ CD-EMX2185 (64 minutes: DDD: 3/92). Recorded 1991.   ⊖

Paris is an extravagant nocturnal impression of the city where "Le grand anglais", as Delius was known to his friends (who included Gaugin and Eduard Munch) spent a decade of his life, during which he developed, as Eric Fenby put it, "a painter's sense of orchestral colour". Premièred in 1901, it shows Delius relishing the full palette of his Staussian-sized orchestra to conjure an intoxicating merry-go-round of the city's night-life. Mackerras's performance is very physical, propelling the dancing to wild, whirling climaxes, and his balance engineers place us firmly among the excitement. In the Cello Concerto, a personal favourite of Delius's, Raphael Wallfisch and Mackerras seek out the contrasts inherent in the score, and, for the first time on disc, its pervasive dreaminess is offset by faster decorative passages, and a genuine playfulness. In short, it dances as well as sings. They are joined by Tasmin Little for an account of the Double Concerto that has never before received teamwork of such confidence, security and unanimity of purpose. This Eminence disc is an essential acquisition for all Delians, especially at the modest asking price.

Additional recommendations ...

...Cello Concerto. **Holst** Invocation. **Vaughan Williams** Fantasia on Sussex Folk Tunes. **Philharmonia Orchestra / Vernon Handley.** RCA Victor Red Seal Ⓕ RD70800 (48 minutes: DDD: 7/87).

...Cello Concerto. *Coupled with works by* **Elgar, Saint-Saëns, Schumann, Dvořák, Haydn, Monn, Chopin, Franck, Fauré, Bruch, Bach, Handel** and **Beethoven** Jacqueline du Pré (vc) with various artists and orchestras. EMI ℗ CZS5 68132-2 (six discs: 437 minutes: ADD: 8/94). *See review in the Collections section; refer to the Index to Reviews.* 🅖🅖

…Paris[c]. *Coupled with works by* **Arnell** and **Berners** Robert Grooters (bar); **Royal Philharmonic Orchestra; Philadelphia Orchestra / Sir Thomas Beecham.** Sony Classical British Pageant mono Ⓜ SMK46683* (68 minutes: ADD: 11/94). *See review under Arnell; refer to the Index to Reviews.* 🅖

…Cello Concerto[e]. **Paradies** (arr. Dushkin) Sicilienne in E flat major[c]. **Schumann** Fantasiestücke, Op. 73[c]. **Mendelssohn** Song without words, Op. 109[c]. **Fauré** Elégie, Op. 24[c]. **Bach** Toccata, Adagio and Fugue in C major, BWV564 – Adagio[d]. **Saint-Saëns** Le carnaval des animaux – The swan[b]. **Falla** (arr. Maréchal) Suite populaire espagnole Jota[a]. **Bruch** Kol Nidrei, Op. 47[c]. **Jacqueline du Pré** (vc); [a]**John Williams** (gtr); [b]**Osian Ellis** (hp); [c]**Gerald Moore** (pf); [d]**Roy Jesson** (org); [e]**Royal Philharmonic Orchestra / Sir Malcolm Sargent.** EMI ℗ CDC5 55529-2 (73 minutes: ADD: 11/95).

Delius Brigg Fair. In a Summer Garden. Paris: The Song of a Great City. On hearing the first cuckoo in Spring. Summer Night on the River. A Village Romeo and Juliet – Walk to the Paradise Garden. **BBC Symphony Orchestra / Andrew Davis.** Teldec British Line ℗ 4509-90845-2 (77 minutes: DDD: 1/94). Recorded 1992. *Gramophone Editor's choice.Selected by Sounds in Retrospect.*

This *Brigg Fair* is unique. What a lovely surprise to hear real London sparrows sharing the air space of St Augustine's Church with Delius's translated Lincolnshire larks (flute and clarinet) in the opening minutes of the work, albeit much more distantly. Very effective too are those almost still pools of string sound (early morning mists?), given the extended boundaries of this acoustic, and the familiar warmth and depth of tone Davis draws from the orchestra's strings. In the final magnificently broad climax (pealing bells, for once, very clear), you cannot fail to be impressed by the depth, coherence and articulacy of the sound – hallmarks, indeed, of the entire disc. Davis's strings come into their own in the *Walk to the Paradise Garden*. For *In a Summer Garden*, Davis mutes his strings more often than Delius asks; but the reading's delicacy of texture and hazy, suffusing warmth are difficult to resist. And it will please those who don't respond to the more animated freshening up of the score by other conductors. As no other Delius disc has an identical programme, and very few such a generously extended one, this disc is the best of its kind currently available for those wanting state-of-the-art sound and wishing to start a Delius investigation; it will also bring many moments of joy and illumination to seasoned Delians.

Additional recommendation …

…Brigg Fair. In a Summer Garden. Eventyr. A Song of Summer. **Hallé Orchestra / Vernon Handley.** Classics for Pleasure Ⓑ CD-CFP4568 (56 minutes: DDD: 8/90).

New review
Delius Violin Sonatas Nos. 1-3[a]. Cello Sonata[b]. [a]**Ralph Holmes** (vn); [b]**Julian Lloyd Webber** (vc); **Eric Fenby** (pf). Unicorn-Kanchana Souvenir Ⓜ UKCD2074 (65 minutes: ADD/DDD: 8/95). Items marked [a] from RHS310 (5/73), [b]DKP9021 (7/83). Recorded 1972-81. 🅖

Here is selfless, utterly dedicated music-making, always spontaneous-sounding yet never losing the organic thread of Delius's remarkable, free-flowing inspiration. In the First Sonata there may never be a performance to match the extraordinarily fluid, re-creative rapture of May Harrison's 1929 recording (with composer Arnold Bax at the piano), but Holmes and Fenby come close. There is a slight fragility to Holmes's distinctive, silvery tone that is extremely moving, and Fenby, though no virtuoso practitioner, accompanies with intuitive sympathy. The recording of the piano (the instrument used is the three-quarter Ibach grand left to Fenby by Delius himself) remains a touch boxy and wanting in bloom, though the balance is otherwise natural and the overall effect nicely intimate. In the Cello Sonata Lloyd Webber and Fenby adopt a mellow, notably ruminative approach. Dedicatee Beatrice Harrison's 1926 recording (with Harold Craxton) should be sought out by all discerning Delians, for through the surface crackle emerge a rapt wonder, generous flexibility and instinctive sense of line that are something special. A small textual observation of note: Lloyd Webber (like Harrison before him) eschews the cello's final D major chord.

Additional recommendation …

…Violin Sonata No. 1[ag]. Cello Sonata[eh]. Hassan – Serenade[de]. **Brahms** Cello Sonata No. 1 in E minor, Op. 38[ef]. **Burleigh** Plantation (Southlands) Sketches, Op. 36[ci]. **Smetana** From the homeland, No. 2 in G minor[ci]. **Popper** Gavotte, Op. 23 No. 2[de]. Vito (Spanish dance), Op. 54 No. 5[be]. **Bach** Solo Cello Suite No. 3 in C major, BWV1009[c] – Prelude; Gigue. **May Harrison** ([a]vn/[b]pf); **Margaret Harrison** ([c]vn/[d]pf); [e]**Beatrice Harrison** (vc); [f]**Gerald Moore**, [g]**Sir Arnold Bax**, [h]**Harold Craxton**, [i]**Reginald Paul** (pfs). Symposium mono ℗ CD1140* (76 minutes: ADD: 3/93).

Delius Sea Drift[a]. Songs of Sunset[b]. Songs of Farewell. [b]**Sally Burgess** (mez); [ab]**Bryn Terfel** (bass-bar); **Waynflete Singers; Southern Voices; Bournemouth Symphony Chorus and Orchestra / Richard Hickox.** Chandos ℗ CHAN9214 (77 minutes: DDD: 11/93). Texts included. Recorded 1993. *Gramophone Award Winner 1994. Gramophone Editor's choice.* 🅖🅖

Sea Drift is a sublime conjunction of Whitman's poetry and Delius's music describing love, loss and unhappy resignation, with the sea (as Christopher Palmer put it) as "symbol and agent of parting".

Written in 1903-04 (the same years as Debussy's *La mer*), it is surely Delius's masterpiece; right from the swaying opening bars its spell is enduring and hypnotic. Hickox in his second recording of the work now gives us the finest recorded post-Beecham *Sea Drift*. The shaping of the opening falling woodwind figures at a slow tempo more than usually (and very beautifully) portends the sad turn of events; and the climax is broad and superbly co-ordinated. Terfel's bar-by-bar characterization (and glorious voice), conveys the full expressive range of the role from impassioned appeal to gentle call without artifice; and the choral singing from Hampshire's finest is superb. The whole is recorded with warmth, spaciousness, depth and clarity. If Hickox's Sally Burgess is taxed a little by the high notes in the *Songs of Sunset*, Hickox is greatly to be preferred to Fenby (see below) in the *Songs of Farewell*, where Fenby's chorus have difficulty with some of his broad tempos – there's a lot more life in Hickox's last three songs, particularly the "Old Sailor" of the final song. Strongly recommended.

Additional recommendations ...

...Sea Drift[a]. Florida – Suite. [a]**Thomas Hampson** (bar); **Welsh National Opera** [a]**Chorus and Orchestra / Sir Charles Mackerras.** Argo Ⓕ 430 206-2ZH (63 minutes: DDD: 12/91).

...Sea Drift[a]. A Village Romeo and Juliet. [a]**Gordon Clinton** (bar); **Soloists; chorus; Royal Philharmonic Orchestra / Sir Thomas Beecham.** EMI Beecham Edition mono Ⓜ CMS7 64386-2* (two discs: 124 minutes: ADD: 11/92).

...Songs of Sunset (with Maureen Forrester, contr; John Cameron, bar; Beecham Choral Society). Over the Hills and Far Away. Sleigh Ride. Irmelin Prelude. Dance Rhapsody No. 2. Summer Evening. Brigg Fair. On hearing the first cuckoo in Spring. Summer Night on the River. A Song before Sunrise. Marche Caprice. Florida – Suite. Fennimore and Gerda – Intermezzo. **Royal Philharmonic Orchestra / Sir Thomas Beecham.** EMI Ⓔ CDS7 47509-8* (ADD: 6/87). *Gramophone* classical 100. ⓖⓖⓖ

...Songs of Farewell[a]. Cynara[b]. Caprice and Elegy[c]. Two Aquarelles[d]. Lebenstanz[e]. Légende[f]. [b]**Thomas Allen** (bar); [f]**Ralph Holmes** (vn); [c]**Julian Lloyd Webber** (vc); [a]**Ambrosian Singers; Royal Philharmonic Orchestra /** [abcd]**Eric Fenby,** [e]**Norman Del Mar,** [f]**Vernon Handley.** Unicorn Kanchana Souvenir Ⓜ UKCD2077 (67 minutes: DDD: 4/96).

Further listening ...

...Piano Concerto in C minor. *Coupled with works by* **Finzi** and **Vaughan Williams** Piers Lane (pf); **Royal Liverpool Philharmonic Orchestra / Vernon Handley.** EMI Eminence CD-EMX2239 (11/95). *See review under Finzi; refer to the Index to Reviews.*

...Two Aquarelles. **Elgar** Introduction and Allegro, Op. 47. **Bridge** Sir Roger de Coverley, H155. **Britten** Simple Symphony, Op. 4. Prelude and Fugue, Op. 29. **Purcell** Chacony in G minor for strings, Z730. **English Chamber Orchestra / Benjamin Britten.** Decca The Classic Sound 448 569-2DCS (2/96).

...String Quartet. *Coupled with* **Elgar** String Quartet in E minor, Op. 83. **Brodsky Quartet.** ASV CDDCA526 (7/89).

...Twilight Fancies[bd]. Wine Roses[bd]. The Bird's Story[ad]. Let Springtime come[ad]. Il pleure dans mon coeur[cd]. Le ciel est par-dessus le toit[ad]. La lune blanche[cd]. To Daffodils[bd]. I-Brasil[cd]. Twilight Fancies[be]. The Violet[ae]. Let Springtime come[be]. In the Seraglio Garden[ae]. Silken shoes[e]. Young Venevil[ae]. Autumn[be]. Irmelin Rose[ae]. Il pleure dans mon coeur[e]. Le ciel est par-dessus le toit[e]. La lune blanche[ce]. Chanson d'automne[be]. Avant que tu ne t'en ailles[ae]. To Daffodils[be]. So white, so soft, is she[ce]. I-Brasil[ce]. [a]**Felicity Lott** (sop); [b]**Sarah Walker** (mez); [c]**Anthony Rolfe Johnson** (ten); [d]**Royal Philharmonic Orchestra / Eric Fenby** ([e]pf). Unicorn Kanchana Souvenir UKCD2075 (4/96).

...A Mass of Life[a]. Songs of Sunset[b]. Arabesque[c]. [abc]**Soloists;** [a]**London Philharmonic Choir;** [bc]**Liverpool Philharmonic Choir;** [a]**London Philharmonic Orchestra;** [bc]**Royal Liverpool Philharmonic Orchestra / Sir Charles Groves.** EMI CMS7 64218-2 (6/93).

Edison Denisov

USSR 1929-

Suggested listening ...

...Chamber Music for Viola, Harpsichord and Strings[a]. Concerto for Two Violas, Harpsichord and String Orchestra[b]. Epitaph. [a]**Nabuko Imai, Petra Vahle** (vas); **Annelie de Man** (hpd); **Amsterdam Neuw Sinfonietta / Lev Markiz.** BIS CD518 (9/92).

David Del Tredici

American 1937-

Suggested listening ...

...Steps[a] (1990). Haddock's Eyes[b] (1985). [b]**David Tel Tredici** (pf); [b]**Susan Naruki** (sop); [b]**Claire Bloom** (narr); [a]**New York Philharmonic Orchestra;** [b]**New York Philharmonic Ensemble / Zubin Mehta.** New World 80390-2.

Norman Dello Joio

Suggested listening...
...The Triumph of Saint Joan, "Symphony in Three Movements". Variations, Chaconne and Finale. *Coupled with* **Barber** Adagio for Strings, Op. 11. **New Zealand Symphony Orchestra / James Sedares.** Koch International Classics 37243-2 (9/94).
...Diversion of Angels (Serenade for Orchestra). Seraphic Dialogues (Triumph of St Joan Symphony). Lyric Dances (Exaltation of Larks). **Atlantic Sinfonietta / Edvard Tchivzhel.** Koch International Classics 37167-2 (1/95).

Henry Desmarets

Suggested listening ...
...Two Grand Motets Lorrains[a]. Mystères de Notre Seigneur Jesus Christ – oratorio[b]. **Soloists;** [a]**New College Choir, Oxford;** [a]**Fiori Musicali / Edward Higginbottom;** [b]**Lyon Vocal and Instrumental Ensemble / Guy Cornut.** Erato 4509 98529 2.

Paul Dessau

New review
Dessau Hagadah shel Pessach. **Sabine Ritterbusch, Renate Spingler** (sops); **Yvi Jänicke** (contr); **Peter Galliard, Gabriel Sade** (tens); **Jochen Schmeckenbecher, Bernd Weikl** (bars); **Johann Tilli, Alfred Muff, Matthias Hölle** (basses); **North German Radio Chorus; Carl Maria von Weber Men's Choir; Hamburg Philharmonic Orchestra / Gerd Albrecht.** Capriccio Ⓟ 10 590/91 (two discs: 91 minutes: DDD: 10/95). Text and translation included. Recorded live in 1994.

The choral forces are generous, the orchestra fairly large (percussion are enthusiastically employed), and the overall style suggests (*very* roughly speaking) a Hindemith-Bloch synthesis, fathered by Mendelssohn, toughened by Weill and with a smattering of Miklós Rózsa thrown in for good measure. Granted, Dessau's aural depiction of the Deity in dialogue with Moses ("The Mission") hardly matches Schoenberg's (in *Moses und Aron*), but as narrative epics go, *Hagadah shel Pessach* is something of a find – especially as presented here, in a keenly played, well-sung and powerfully recorded performance. Why, then, the neglect? History offers most of the answers. Paul Dessau was himself Jewish; he even composed for the synagogue. He left Germany for obvious reasons in 1933, and so *Hagadah shel Pessach*'s actual subject matter (freedom from slavery) was profoundly topical. The work itself, which was planned as early as 1934 and completed some two years later, recounts the Exodus story, initially in terms of the traditional Jewish Passover service (or Seder). Tragic to relate that what set out as a cry of optimism ("Next year we shall be in Jerusalem; and next year free!") was far from a prophecy. *Hagadah shel Pessach* deserves recognition not only for its purely musical qualities (which are fully on a par with, say, Walton's *Belshazzar's Feast*) but also for its topical relevance.

Further listening ...
...String Quartets Nos. 1-7. **New Leipzig Quartet.** CPO CPO999 002-2 (5/95).

François Devienne

Suggested listening ...
...Six Sonatas for Bassoon and Bass, Op. 24. **Danny Bond** (bn); **Richte van der Meer** (vc); **Robert Kohnen** (hpd). Accent ACC9290D (11/94). 🖊

Frédéric Devreese

Suggested listening ...
...Piano Concertos Nos. 2-4. **Daniel Blumenthal** (pf); **Belgian Radio and Television Orchestra / Frédéric Devreese.** Marco Polo 8 223505 (11/93).
...Benvenuta. Un soir, un train – Thème; Danse de l'auberge. L'oeuvre au noir suite. Belle – Prélude; Fagnes du Nord. **Belgian Radio and Television Philharmonic Orchestra / Frédéric Devreese.** Marco Polo 8 223681 (11/94).

Godfried Devreese

Suggested listening ...
...Tombelène. Violin Concerto No. 1[a]. Concertino for Cello and Orchestra[b]. [a]**Guido de Neve** (vn); [b]**Viviane Spanoghe** (vc); **Belgian Radio and Television Philharmonic Orchestra / Frédéric Devreese.** Marco Polo 8 223680 (11/94).

David Diamond
American 1915-

Suggested listening ...

...Symphony No. 1. The Enormous Room. Violin Concerto No. 2[a]. [a]**Ilkka Talvi** (vn); **Seattle Symphony Orchestra / Gerard Schwarz.** Delos DE3119 (1/94). *Selected by Sounds in Retrospect.*

...Symphonies Nos. 2 and 4[a]. Concerto for Small Orchestra[a]. [a]**Seattle Symphony Orchestra;** [b]**New York Chamber Symphony Orchestra / Gerald Schwarz.** Delos DE3093 (4/91).

...Symphony No. 3[c]. Romeo and Juliet[b]. Psalm[c]. Kaddish[ac]. [a]**János Starker** (vc); [b]**New York Chamber Symphony Orchestra;** [c]**Seattle Symphony Orchestra / Gerard Schwarz.** Delos DE3103 (4/93).

...TOM – suite. This Sacred Ground[a]. Symphony No. 8. [a]**Erich Parce** (bar); [a]**Seattle Girls' Choir;** [a]**Northwest Boychoir;** [a]**Seattle Symphony Chorale; Seattle Symphony Orchestra / Gerard Schwarz.** Delos DE3141 (4/95).

Peter Dickinson
British 1934-

Suggested listening ...

...Mass of the Apocalypse. Outcry. The Unicorns. **Soloists; London Consort Choir; City of London Sinfonia / Nicholas Cleobury; Solna Brass / Lars-Gunnar Björklund.** Conifer CDCF167 (5/89).

Alphons Diepenbrock
Dutch 1862-1921

Suggested listening ...

...The Birds – Overture. Suites – Marsyas; Electra. Hymne for violin and orchestra. **Emmy Verhey** (vn); **The Hague Residentie Orchestra / Hans Vonk.** Chandos CHAN8821 (8/90).

...Hymnen an die Nacht No. 2, Muss immer der Morgen wiederkommen. Die Nacht. Im grossen Schweigen. Wenige wissen das Geheimnis der Liebe. **Linda Finnie** (contr); **Christopher Homberger** (ten); **Robert Holl** (bass); **The Hague Residentie Orchestra / Hans Vonk.** Chandos CHAN8878 (4/91).

...Im grossen Schweigen[a]. *Coupled with* **Mahler** Symphony No. 7 in E minor. [a]**Håkan Hagegård** (bar); **Royal Concertgebouw Orchestra / Riccardo Chailly.** Decca 444 446-2DH2 (5/95). *See review under Mahler; refer to the Index to Reviews.* 🅖🅖

Charles Dieupart
French ?after 1667-c1740

Suggested listening ...

...Sopranino Recorder Concerto in A minor. *Coupled with works by* **Heinichen, Fasch, Pisendel, Quantz** and **Veracini** Cologne Musica Antiqua / Reinhard Goebel. Archiv Produktion 447 644-2AH (1/96). 🖎 🅖

James Dillon
British 1950-

New review

Dillon Ignis noster. Helle Nacht. **BBC Symphony Orchestra / Arturo Tamayo.** Auvidis Montaigne Ⓔ MO782038 (44 minutes: DDD: 8/95). Recorded 1994.

Dillon's titles could not be more elemental: *Helle Nacht* ("Bright Night") and *Ignis noster* ("Our Fire", or "Divine Fire") both encapsulate images of intense experience which are themselves paradoxical. *Helle Nacht* concerns a "moment of searing darkness which in its intensity becomes unbearably bright", while *Ignis noster* evokes the world of alchemy, an element of "consuming energy" which is also a force for transformation. It is not difficult to imagine how such ideas might prompt musical responses. But there is a sustained brilliance and inventiveness in Dillon's responses which engage the listener, and which offer immense rewards over repeated hearings, as the brightness becomes bearable without loss of intensity, and the consuming energy loses none of its initial mind-blowing impact. If successful avant-garde composition is that in which the possibility of total chaos and incoherence is triumphantly confronted and resisted, then Dillon is indeed successful. These performances, aided by expertly balanced and mixed recordings made at the BBC's Maida Vale studios, are impressively faithful to the spirit of the music, avoiding the impression of plodding stagnation that can afflict less committed renderings of such scores. The music may be elemental, but it has a richness of incident and an exuberant wealth of expression that give it a powerful humanity.

New review

Dillon Evening rain[a]. Sgothan[b]. A roaring flame[c]. Crossing over[d]. Come live with me[a]. ti.re-ti. ke-dha[f]. Spleen[g]. **Accroche Note** ([ace]Françoise Kubler, mez; [b]Cécile Daroux, [e]Claire Gentilhomme, fls; [e]René Bellier, ob; [d]Armand Angster, cl; [ce]Jean-Paul Celea, db; [eg]Bernhard Wambach, pf; [e]Guy

Frisch, efEmmanuel Séjourné, perc). Auvidis Montaigne Ⓟ MO782037 (69 minutes: DDD: 2/96). Texts and translations included. Recorded 1995.

The earliest work on this disc, *Crossing over* for clarinet (1978), already displays the essence of that highly personal blend of complexity and accessibility that is most fully explored in James Dillon's major orchestral works, and the remarkable *Nine rivers* cycle. *Crossing over* has its aggressive, fragmented moments, but it can also be playful, with references to traditional styles of vocal *coloratura* alongside avant-garde pitch-bendings and special effects. Almost all the pieces in this collection of relatively small-scale works, written between 1978 and 1984, reveal comparable qualities. Even in *ti.re-ti.ke-dha* for solo drummer (the title referring to "mnemonic patterns used in North Indian drumming") there's a firmly shaped musical design, and while *Sgothan* ("Clouds") for solo flute doesn't significantly transcend the limitations of the genre, the piano piece *Spleen* effects a remarkable transformation of Darmstadt-style percussiveness into something richer and more imaginative. Of the three vocal works, *Come live with me* is the most overtly lyrical, and although Dillon seems to have some difficulty in sustaining the melodic focus over its more-than-15-minute span, the final stages, with resonant bell-strokes recalling the magical ending of Stravinsky's *Les noces*, are hauntingly direct. *Evening rain* (recorded, as the notes acknowledge, during a heavy storm) is a neat working-out of relationships between older and newer kinds of vocal sounds, but for sheer inventiveness you will probably return most often to *A roaring flame*, a celebration of love whose weird combination of female voice and double-bass with Gaelic and Provençal texts sparks the most intensely memorable music on the entire disc. Performances and recordings are admirable.

Further listening ...
...East 11th St NY10003. La femme invisible. Windows and Canopies. **Music Projects London / Richard Bernas**. NMC NMCD004 (9/92).

Carl von Dittersdorf   Austrian 1739-1799

New review
Dittersdorf Six Symphonies after Ovid's Metamorphoses. **Failoni Orchestra / Hanspeter Gmür.** Naxos Ⓢ 8 553368/9 (two discs, oas: 64 and 73 minutes: DDD: 7/96). Recorded 1995.
 8 553368 – No. 1 in C major; No. 2 in D major; No. 3 in G major. *8 553369* – No. 4 in F major; No. 5 in A major; No. 6 in D major.

Among the most entertaining specimens of the descriptive programme symphony, popular in Austria and Bohemia during the late-eighteenth century, are those based on Ovid's *Metamorphoses* by Carl Dittersdorf (1786). Six of these survive intact, and while the programme element can be vague, with the music portraying generalized emotional states suggested by Ovid's verses, there is plenty of graphic, even dramatic, writing. The prime influence here is Gluck, with whom Dittersdorf took lessons and whom he accompanied on a trip to Italy in 1763. Gluck's Furies, especially the dance from *Don Juan* which he later reworked for the Paris *Orphée*, seem to lie behind several of the most theatrical movements in these symphonies. Under their Swiss conductor, the Budapest-based Failoni Orchestra give a very fair account of picturesque and inventive symphonies which deserve to be every bit as popular as, say, Haydn's early 'Times of Day' trilogy. Their tone and manner is sometimes a shade heavy for this music, and tempos can be on the sober side, but phrasing is shapely and gracious. If violins can sound a touch glassy above the stave, the recorded sound is perfectly acceptable, with well-defined wind and brass detail in the tuttis. No one who fancies venturing beyond Haydn and Mozart is likely to be disappointed here, especially at the alluring Naxos price.

Stephen Dodgson   British 1924-

Suggested listening ...
...Flute Concertoᵃ. Last of the Leavesᵇ. Duo Concertoᶜ. ᵇ**Michael George** (bass); ᵃ**Robert Stallman** (fl); ᵇ**John Bradbury** (cl); ᶜ**Anthea Gifford** (gtr); **Northern Sinfonia / Ronald Zollman**. Biddulph LAW013 (7/94).

Ernö Dohnányi   Hungarian 1877-1960

Dohnányi Piano Concertos – No. 1 in E minor, Op. 5; No. 2 in B minor, Op. 42. **Martin Roscoe** (pf); **BBC Scottish Symphony Orchestra / Fedor Glushchenko**. Hyperion Ⓟ CDA66684 (75 minutes: DDD: 5/94). Recorded 1993.   Ⓠ
This coupling provides a salutary reminder of two of Dohnányi's most substantial if sadly neglected works. Both concertos – separated by 50 years, but mildly rather than radically different in their musical language – burgeon with heartfelt melody and high-flying pianistics. And if Dohnányi hardly provides anything so important as a bridge between Liszt and Bartók, his alternation of dark and scintillating ideas is accomplished with an easy and professional aplomb. The Second Concerto's crisply accented finale in whirling and nationalistic duple time is notably attractive. Martin Roscoe's superbly authoritative performances are majestic and glittering as required, and his survival of his

recessed placing in relation to the orchestra is doubly to his credit. Fedor Glushchenko's partnership is excellent and, overall, the recordings are of high quality.

Dohnányi Variations on a Nursery Theme, Op. 25.
Brahms Piano Concerto No. 1 in D minor, Op. 15. **Mark Anderson** (pf); **Hungarian State Symphony Orchestra / Adám Fischer.** Nimbus Ⓕ NI5349 (75 minutes: DDD: 3/95). Recorded 1994.

Brahms had the good grace to say of Ernö Dohnányi's C minor Piano Quintet, "I could not have written it better". It was no use. Years later, when he came to write his wonderfully skittish *Variations on a Nursery Theme*, Dohnányi sent the old boy up something rotten. Like many of the best parodies, it is done with a completely straight face; so much so that Dohnányi's Variation No. 3 could probably go directly into the finale of Brahms's B flat Concerto without anyone noticing a thing. On this Nimbus disc, it is the D minor Concerto that plays Wise to Dohnányi's Eric Morecambe, so the joke is slightly obscured. Mark Anderson gives a glittering performance of the Dohnányi, and a spontaneous one; he is superbly accompanied by Adám Fischer and the Hungarian State SO. Nimbus's recording is admirable in everything but the backward placing of the woodwind in general and the bassoons in particular. One thing the Dohnányi *Variations* share with the D minor Brahms Concerto is a passionate minor key opening. Again Fischer and his Hungarian orchestra are superb, the playing incisive and gloweringly vivid. It is a measure, too, of the accord that exists between conductor and soloist that the pianist enters the fray with the perfectly groomed musical manners of a soloist in a baroque concerto. And it is the logic of Anderson's playing, his sweet reasonableness, that holds the attention, even though Brahmsians who, like farmers at market, look for a solid well-hung beast, may find Anderson a shade light-toned in bravura passages. The Brahms obviously faces tough competition, but the Dohnányi is a very fine performance in its own right.

Additional recommendations ...

...Variations on a Nursery Theme. **Bartók** Rhapsody, Sz27. Scherzo, Sz28. **Zoltán Kocsis** (pf); **Budapest Festival Orchestra / Iván Fischer.** Philips Ⓕ 446 472-2PH (77 minutes: DDD: 4/96).

...Variations on a Nursery Theme. **Rachmaninov** Piano Concerto No. 2 in C minor, Op. 18[a]. Rhapsody on a Theme of Paganini, Op. 43[b]. **Julius Katchen** (pf); [a]**New Symphony Orchestra / Anatole Fistoulari;** [b]**London Philharmonic Orchestra / Sir Adrian Boult.** Dutton Laboratories mono Ⓕ CDLXT2504* (79 minutes: ADD: 5/96).

New review
Dohnányi Sextet in C major, Op. 37[a].
Fibich Quintet in D major, Op. 42. **Endymion Ensemble** (Mark van de Wiel, cl; Stephen Stirling, hn; Krysia Osostowicz, vn; [a]Iris Juda, va; Jane Salmon, vc; Michael Dussek, pf). ASV Ⓕ CDDCA943 (66 minutes: DDD: 2/96). Recorded 1995.   Ⓖ

Both composers employ their chosen resources with great expertise, Dohnányi in a richly harmonized Sextet that opens among the clouds and ends in a mood of dance-like exuberance, Fibich with a more conventional structure and a genial stream of melody. Each work owes something to Brahms although in the case of Fibich's Quintet, Schumann seems as much in evidence, not only through the score's specific melodic complexion, but in a *Scherzo* that features two contrasting trios. Smetana is another possible point of reference, especially at the start of the finale, although – as Jan Smaczny usefully points out in his excellent booklet-note – the younger Fibich "often anticipated the achievements of the elder composer". Dohnányi's Sextet is a far darker piece, opening as it does among rolling string arpeggios and toughening for a fairly tense development. The "Intermezzo" second movement suggests (at least initially) Brahms as siphoned through the imagination of Schoenberg, whereas the eventful third movement suddenly breaks into a rhythmically upbeat finale that sounds as much Afro-Caribbean as Hungarian, albeit with a luscious 'big' tune to offset the fun. The Endymion Ensemble do both Fibich and Dohnányi proud and the recordings are excellent.

Further listening ...

...Konzertstück in D major, Op. 12. *Coupled with works by* **Bach, Kodály, Boccherini, Haydn, Schumann, Saint-Saëns, Dvořák, Fauré, Milhaud** and **Prokofiev** János Starker (vc); **Gerald Moore** (pf); **Philharmonia Orchestra / Carlo Maria Giulini, Walter Susskind.** EMI mono/stereo CZS5 68485-2* (12/95). *See review in the Collections section; refer to the Index to Reviews.*

...Konzertstück in D major, Op. 12. *Coupled with* **Dvořák** Cello Concerto in B minor, B191. **Raphael Wallfisch** (vc); **London Symphony Orchestra / Sir Charles Mackerras.** Chandos CHAN8662 (5/89).

...Piano Quintets[a] – No. 1 in C minor, Op. 1; No. 2 in E flat minor, Op. 26. Suite in the Old Style, Op. 24. [a]**Vanbrugh Quartet. Martin Roscoe** (pf). ASV CDDCA915 (5/95). Recorded 1994.   Ⓖ

...Piano Quintet No. 1 in C minor, Op. 1. String Quartet No. 2 in D flat major, Op. 15. **Wolfgang Manz** (pf); **Gabrieli Quartet.** Chandos CHAN8718 (5/89).

...Cello Sonata in B flat minor, Op. 8. *Coupled with* **Bridge** Cello Sonata in D minor, H125. Four Short Pieces, H104 – Meditation; Spring song. **Debussy** Cello Sonata. **Bernard Gregor-Smith** (vc); **Yolande Wrigley** (pf). ASV CDDCA796 (9/92).

...Four Pieces, Op. 2. Passacaglia in E flat minor, Op. 6. Variations and Fugue on a Theme by E.G., Op. 4. **Annette Servadei** (pf). Continuum CCD1064 (5/95).

Gaetano Donizetti

New review

Donizetti Sinfonia in G minor (recons. Päuler). Sonata in C minor (orch. Hoffmann). Oboe
Sonata in F major (orch. Hoffmann). Concerto for Violin, Cello and Orchestra in D minor
(recons. Wojciechowski). Cor Anglais Concerto in G major. Clarinet Concertino in B flat
(recons. Meylan). Sinfonia in D minor (recons. Andreae). **Budapest Camerata / László Kovács.**
Marco Polo Ⓕ 8 223701 (64 minutes: DDD: 10/95). Recorded 1994.

This is an intriguing issue of instrumental concertos, recorded for the first time. As in his string
quartets, Donizetti's dramatic flair and imaginative instrumentation provide the main points of
interest, while the G major Concerto for cor anglais – a theme and variations – provides an
opportunity to sample Donizetti's formal ingenuity and thematic invention. After a crisp performance
of the buoyant G minor *Sinfonia*, the Budapest Camerata offer a group of solo concertos featuring a
variety of instruments. The C minor flute *Concertino* and F major oboe *Concertino* – originally
intended as instrumental sonatas – are presented in Wolfgang Hoffmann's sensitive orchestrations.
Contrasts (textural, dramatic and dynamic) are well defined, with admirably clear recording. The
infectiously exuberant *allegros* are not especially profound, but Donizetti's slow movements are often
most effective. The D minor Concerto for violin, cello and orchestra is the longest and most
impressive work here. The Budapest Camerata balance solo and ensemble forces with subtle
refinement throughout this charming piece, whose brief *Andante* has genuine pathos, and smiling
finale has engaging wit.

Donizetti Anna Bolena. **Maria Callas** (sop) Anna Bolena; **Nicola Rossi-Lemeni** (bass) Enrico VIII;
Giulietta Simionato (mez) Giovanna Seymour; **Gianni Raimondi** (ten) Riccardo Percy; **Plinio
Clabassi** (bass) Rochefort; **Gabriella Carturan** (mez) Smeton; **Luigi Rumbo** (ten) Hervey;
Chorus and Orchestra of La Scala, Milan / Gianandrea Gavazzeni. EMI mono Ⓜ CMS7
64941-2* (two discs: 140 minutes: ADD: 1/94). Notes, text and translation included. Recorded
live in 1957. *Gramophone Editor's choice.*   Ⓖ

Here Callas gives one of her finest performances. The first impression is essentially a vocal one, in the
sense of the sheer beauty of sound, for recording reveals it to be so much better focused than
Simionato's. Then, in the first solo, "Come innocente giovane", addressing Jane Seymour, she is so
clean in the cut of the voice and the style of its usage, delicate in her *fioritura*, often exquisite in her
shading, that anyone, ignorant of the Callas legend, would know immediately that this is an artist of
patrician status. There are marvellous incidental moments, and magnificent crescendos, into, for
instance, "per pietà delmio spavento" and "segnata è la mia sorte", culminating in the Tower scene.
The singers at her side hardly measure up. Even so, the great ensembles still prove worthy of the event,
and the recording, which is clear without harshness or other distortion, conveys the special quality of
this memorable evening at the opera with remarkable vividness and fidelity.

Donizetti L'elisir d'amore. **Mariella Devia** (sop) Adina; **Roberto Alagna** (ten) Nemorino; **Pietro
Spagnoli** (bar) Belcore; **Bruno Praticò** (bar) Dulcamara; **Francesca Provvisionato** (mez) Giannetta;
Tallis Chamber Choir; English Chamber Orchestra / Marcello Viotti. Erato Ⓕ 4509-91701-2
(two discs: 129 minutes: DDD: 6/93). Notes, text and translation included. Recorded 1992.
Gramophone Editor's choice.   Ⓖ

A modern and completely recommendable set of this delightful piece, country cousin to *Don
Pasquale*, was badly needed – and here it is. It is a delight from start to finish, making one fall in love
all over again with this delightful comedy of pastoral life. The plot is a variant of the much used
theme of the fake love potion. Here the potion is supplied by the charlatan Doctor Dulcamara to the
shy young Nemorino to help him win the love of Adina. Roberto Alagna, disciple of Pavarotti, sings
Nemorino with all his mentor's charm and a rather lighter tone appropriate to the role. He also
evinces just the right sense of vulnerability and false bravado that lies at the heart of Nemorino's
predicament. Here is a tenor with a great future if only he stays with roles within his range. He is
partnered by Mariella Devia who has every characteristic needed for the role of Adina. With a fine
sense of buoyant rhythm, she sings fleetly and uses the coloratura to enhance her reading. She can
spin a long, elegiac line where that is needed, and her pure yet full tone blends well with that of her
colleagues. She also suggests all Adina's high spirits and flirtatious nature. The other principals,
though not as amusing in their interpretations as some of their more experienced predecessors, enter
into the ensemble feeling of the performance. All are helped by the lively but controlled conducting
of Viotti and by the ideal recording.

Additional recommendations ...

...Soloists; **Ambrosian Opera Chorus; English Chamber Orchestra / Richard Bonynge.** Decca
    Ⓕ 414 461-2DH2 (two discs: 141 minutes: ADD: 6/86).

...Soloists; **Turin Radio Symphony Chorus and Orchestra / Claudio Scimone.** Philips
    Ⓕ 412 714-2PH2 (two discs: 127 minutes: DDD: 6/86).   ⒼⒼ

...Soloists; **Chorus and Orchestra of the Metropolitan Opera, New York / James Levine.** DG
    Ⓕ 429 744-2GH2 (two discs: 119 minutes: DDD: 2/91).

...Soloists; **Chorus and Orchestra of La Scala, Milan / Tullio Serafin.** Classics for Pleasure
    Ⓑ CD-CFPD4733 (two discs: 111 minutes: ADD: 5/94).

...**Soloists; Chorus and Orchestra of the Maggio Musicale Fiorentino / Francesco Molinari-Pradelli.** Double Decca Ⓜ 443 542-2LF2* (two discs: 108 minutes: ADD: 7/95).

Donizetti Lucia di Lammermoor. **Cheryl Studer** (sop) Lucia; **Plácido Domingo** (ten) Edgardo; **Juan Pons** (bar) Enrico; **Samuel Ramey** (bass) Raimondo; **Jennifer Larmore** (mez) Alisa; **Fernando de la Mora** (ten) Arturo; **Anthony Laciura** (ten) Normanno; **Ambrosian Opera Chorus; London Symphony Orchestra / Ion Marin.** DG Ⓕ 435 309-2GH2 (two discs: 138 minutes: DDD: 4/93). Notes, text and translation included. Recorded 1990.

With 15 recordings currently available, *Lucia di Lammermoor*, once regarded as *passé*, appears to be in remarkably good health. Not so long ago it was dismissed as little more than a convenient vehicle for the latest coloratura soprano, who could enjoy a double success, first in the Fountain Scene where she would be applauded on entry and then able to warm up for the celebrated Mad Scene, which was the real culmination of the evening even to the extent (in Melba's day, for instance) of finishing the opera on Lucia's final high note and eliminating the tenor's big scene which is to follow. Nowadays, while the opera is still a *tour de force* for the soprano, the tenor shares the honours and the whole thing is much more of a company production. Its likely hero is Donizetti himself, whose music has strengths of many kinds, including expert and evocative orchestration. Recordings by Callas and Sutherland are generally respected as permanent classics of the gramophone, but recent versions deserve consideration, and this one, with Studer and Domingo in the leading roles, is certainly fit as a whole to stand alongside its eminent predecessors. The fine deep colours of the orchestra, the sturdy dramatic cohesion and well-wrought climaxes, are well brought out; passages traditionally omitted are in place (and deserve to be). The role of Lucia's confidante is sung with distinction by Jennifer Larmore, and though Juan Pons could do with more bite to his tone and Samuel Ramey with more expressiveness in his vocal acting these have their strengths too. Studer combines beautiful tone, technical accomplishment and touching pathos. Details include an extended cadenza in the Mad Scene, which ends on a not too exposed high E flat (D being the ceiling elsewhere). Domingo triumphantly overcomes the difficulties such a role must pose at this stage of his career: Edgardo di Ravenswood in this recording is as firmly at the centre of the opera as is its eponymous heroine.

Additional recommendations ...

...**Soloists; Royal Opera House Chorus and Orchestra, Covent Garden / Richard Bonynge.** Decca Ⓕ 410 193-2DH3 (three discs: 140 minutes: ADD: 11/85).

...**Soloists; Chorus of La Scala, Milan; Berlin RIAS Symphony Orchestra / Herbert von Karajan.** EMI mono Ⓜ CMS7 63631-2* (two discs: 119 minutes: ADD: 2/91).

...**Soloists; Ambrosian Singers; London Symphony Orchestra / Richard Bonynge.** Teldec Ⓕ 9031-72306-2 (two discs: 143 minutes: DDD: 11/92).

...**Soloists; Ambrosian Opera Chorus; New Philharmonia Orchestra / Jesús López-Cobos.** Philips Ⓜ 446 551-2PM2 (two discs: 143 minutes: ADD: 3/96).

Donizetti Don Pasquale. **Renato Bruson** (bar) Don Pasquale; **Eva Mei** (sop) Norina; **Frank Lopardo** (ten) Ernesto; **Thomas Allen** (bar) Malatesta; **Alfredo Giacomotti** (bass) Notary; **Bavarian Radio Chorus; Munich Radio Orchestra / Roberto Abbado.** RCA Victor Red Seal Ⓕ 09026 61924-2 (two discs: 120 minutes: DDD: 12/94). Notes, text and translation included. Recorded 1993. Ⓖ

Like the excellent Ferro (listed below), Roberto Abbado balances equably the witty and more serious sides of the score. If he and his orchestra don't quite achieve the brio of Ferro – for instance the lighter, faster Ferro touch in the famous "Cheti, cheti immatinente" duet is better at suggesting *sotto voce* plotting – Abbado finds a gratifying lightness in the "A quel vecchio" section of the Act 1 finale and creates a delightful sense of expectancy as Pasquale preens himself while awaiting his intended bride. Ferro, Abbado and the slightly po-faced Muti (listed below) play the score complete and respect Donizetti's intentions, banishing the traditional emendations added by his interpreters over the years. The new set has many strengths and few weaknesses: indeed it would be hard to cast the piece more successfully today. Pasquale is usually assigned to a veteran singer. In the case of Bruscantini (Muti) and Bacquier (Ferro), allowances definitely have to be made for the singer's age: both men cleverly compensate with the vocal equivalent of guying for failing voices. With Bruson you hear a voice hardly touched by time and a technique still in perfect repair. Apart from weak low notes, he sings and acts the part with real face, and his vital diction, particularly in recitatives, is a pleasure to hear. He works well with Thomas Allen's nimble, wily Malatesta, an unexpected piece of casting that proves to be inspired. Like Bruson, Allen sings every note truly and relishes his words, evincing a sense of comedy as he prepares, cruel to be kind, to gull his friend. Eva Mei's Norina is an ebullient creature with a smile in her tone, much more pointed and pert than the accurate but lacklustre Hendricks (Erato) or the admittedly warmer-voiced Freni (Muti). The edge to Mei's voice seems just right for Norina though others may find it tends towards the acerbic under pressure. Her skills in coloratura are as exemplary as you would expect from a reigning Queen of Night. Lopardo is that rare thing, a tenor who can sing in an exquisite half-voice, as in "Com' è gentil", yet has the metal in his tone to suggest something heroic in "E se fia", the cabaletta to "Cercherò lontana terra", which in turn is sung in a plangent, loving way, just right. As the recording here is exemplary as compared with the EMI (too reverberant) and the Erato (singers sometimes too backward), this version is now the outright recommendation.

Additional recommendations ...
...Soloists; **Ambrosian Opera Chorus; Philharmonia Orchestra / Riccardo Muti.** EMI Ⓔ CDS7
47068-2 (two discs: 123 minutes: DDD: 8/88).
...Soloists; **Lyon Opera Chorus and Orchestra / Gabriele Ferro.** Erato Ⓔ 2292-45487-2 (two discs:
120 minutes: DDD: 11/90).

Further listening ...
...String Quartets – No. 7 in F minor; No. 8 in B flat major; No. 9 in D minor. **Revolutionary
Drawing Room.** CPO CPO999 170-2 (10/95).
...String Quartet No. 13 in E minor. *Coupled with* **Puccini** Crisantemi. **Verdi** String Quartet in
E minor. **Alberni Quartet** CRD3366 (5/89).
...String Quartet in D major (1828). *Coupled with works by* **Rossini, Bellini** and **Cherubini**
Academy of St Martin in the Fields / Sir Neville Marriner. Double Decca Ⓜ 443 838-2DF2
(two discs: 112 minutes: ADD: 7/95). *See review under Rossini; refer to the Index to Reviews.*
...Italian Songs – Canto d'Ugolino; L'amor funesto; Il trovatore in caricatura; Spirito di Dio
benefico; Viva il matrimonio. French Songs – Le renégat; Noé, scène du Deluge; Le départ pour
la chasse; Un coeur pour abri; Le hart (chant diabolique). **Ian Caddy** (bass-bar); **Melvyn Tan** (fp).
Meridian CDE84183 (4/90). ✍
...Lucia di Lammermoor – Il dolce suono ... Ardon gli'incensi ... Alfin son tua ... Spargi d'amaro
pianto. *Coupled with works by* **Bellini, Gounod, G. Charpentier** and **Delibes** Mariella Devia
(sop); **Svizzera Italiana Orchestra / Marcello Rota.** Bongiovanni GB2513-2 (10/94).
...Gabriella di Vergy. **Soloists; Geoffrey Mitchell Choir; Royal Philharmonic Orchestra / Alun
Francis.** Opera Rara ORC3 (9/94).
...Ugo, Conte di Parigi. **Soloists; Geoffrey Mitchell Choir; New Philharmonia Orchestra / Alun
Francis.** Opera Rara ORC1 (12/90).
...Emilia di Liverpool. L'eremitaggio di Liverpool. **Soloists; Geoffrey Mitchell Choir; Philharmonia
Orchestra / David Parry.** Opera Rara ORC8 (5/92).
...Imelda de' Lambertazzi. **Soloists; Chorus and Orchestra of Swiss-Italian Radio and Television /
Marc Andreae.** Nuova Era 6778/9 (10/91).
...Lucrezia Borgia. **Soloists; London Opera Chorus; National Philharmonic Orchestra / Richard
Bonynge.** Decca 421 497-2DM2 (3/90).
...Lucrezia Borgia. **Soloists; RCA Italiana Opera Chorus and Orchestra / Jonel Perlea.** RCA Victor
Gold Seal GD86642 (9/90).
...Maria Stuarda. **Soloists; Bologna Teatro Communale Chorus and Orchestra / Richard Bonynge.**
Decca 425 410-2DM2 (9/90).
...L'Assedio di Calais. **Soloists; Geoffrey Mitchell Choir; Philharmonia Orchestra / David Parry.**
Opera Rara ORC9 (7/91).
...Gianni di Parigi. **Soloists; Chorus and Orchestra of RAI, Milan / Carlo Felice Cillario.** Nuova Era
6752/3 (10/91).
...La fille du régiment. **Chorus; Chorus and Orchestra of the Royal Opera House, Covent Garden /
Richard Bonynge.** Decca 414 520-2DH2 (11/86).
...La Favorita. **Soloists; Slovak Philharmonic Chorus; Italian International Opera Orchestra / Fabio
Luisi.** Nuova Era 6823/4 (10/91).
...Maria Padilla. **Soloists; Geoffrey Mitchell Choir; London Symphony Orchestra / Alun Francis.**
Opera Rara ORC6 (2/93).
...Roberto Devereux. **Soloists; Rhine Opera Chorus; Strasbourg Philharmonic Orchestra / Friedrich
Haider.** Nightingale Classics NC070563-2 (5/95).
...La favorite – Un ange, une femme inconnue; Je ne méritais pas ... Qui ta voix m'inspire; La
maîtresse du roi? ... Ange si pur. Messa da Requiem – Ingemisco. Gabriella di Vergy – Si compia
il sacrificio ... Io l'amai. *Coupled with works by* **Rossini** Justin Lavender (ten); **Bournemouth
Symphony Orchestra / Howard Williams.** IMP Classics 30367 0010-2 (3/96). *See review under
Rossini; refer to the Index to Reviews.*

Friedrich Dotzauer   German 1783-1860

Suggested listening ...
...String Quintet in D minor, Op. 134. Canon in G major. Six Pieces, Op. 104. Quartet for Cello
obbligato, Two Violins and Viola, Op. 64. Allegro in A minor, Op. 155 No. 2. Allegro non troppo
in B flat major, Op. 54 No. 2. Presto in D major, Op. 158 No. 2. **L'Archibudelli** and **Smithsonian
Chamber Players.** Sony Classical SK64307 (3/95).

John Dowland   British c1563-1626

Dowland Lachrimae, or Seaven Teares. **Christopher Wilson** (lte); **Fretwork** (Wendy Gillespie,
Richard Campbell, Julia Hodgson, William Hunt, Richard Boothby, viols). Virgin Classics
Veritas Ⓔ VC5 45005-2 (60 minutes: DDD: 7/94). ✍ From VC7 90795-2 (11/89), recorded 1987
and VC7 91117-2 (3/91), 1989.   Ⓖ

Did Dowland ever expect this collection to be played in its entirety, at one sitting? If so, in what order? Whatever your own 'answers' to these unanswerable questions may be, you can (if you feel strongly about it) easily impose them on any of the various integral versions on CD. Fretwork's reissue presents them as an entirety, with the dances in their original published order – the whole book 'as is'. The performances are laudable in their characterization (of the pavans in particular), discreet embellishment of the dances, clarity of detail (the product of pleasantly dry string sound and acoustic) and overall balance, in which the lute is neither backgrounded nor obtrusive. Christopher Wilson adds a firmly propulsive edge to the dances. This is the best available version of Dowland's monumental work, graced with Peter Holman's splendid notes and blessed with superbly engineered recording. The recording by The Parley of Instruments Renaissance Violin Consort is also recommended, being the only one to avail itself of Dowland's "or Violons" option; Holman directs the proceedings – you can't keep a good man down!

Additional recommendation ...

...Lachrimae[b]. Captain Digorie Piper his Pavan[b]. The King of Denmarke his Galliard, P40[a]. Moritz, Landgrave of Hessen-Kassel: Pavan[a]. [a]**Paul O'Dette** (lte); [b]**The Parley of Instruments Renaissance Violin Consort / Peter Holman.** Hyperion Ⓟ CDA66637 (69 minutes: DDD: 8/93). ✍

New review

Dowland The First Booke of Songes or Ayres – If my complaints could passions moue; Can she excuse my wrongs with vertues cloake; Deare if you change ile neuer chuse againe; Go Cristall teares; Sleepe wayward thoughts; All ye whom loue or fortune hath betraide; Come againe: sweet loue doth now enuite; Awake sweet loue thou art returnd. The Second Booke of Songes or Ayres – I saw my Lady weepe; Flow my teares fall from your springs; Sorrow sorrow stay, lend true repentant teares; Tymes eldest sonne, old age the heire of ease; Then sit thee down, and say thy "Nunc Dimitis"; When others sings "Venite exultemus"; If fluds of tears could clense my follies past; Fine knacks for Ladies, cheap, choise, braue and new; Come ye heavie states of night; Shall I sue, shall I seeke for grace. **Paul Agnew** (ten); **Christopher Wilson** (lte). Metronome Ⓟ METCD1010 (59 minutes: DDD: 5/96). Texts included. Recorded 1995.

New review

Lovesongs and Sonnets of John Donne and Sir Philip Sidney [a]**Paul Agnew** (ten); **Christopher Wilson** (lte). Metronome Ⓟ METCD1006 (62 minutes: DDD: 5/96). Texts included. Recorded 1994.

G. Tessier In a grove most rich of shade[a]. **Dowland** O sweet woods, the delight of solitarienesse[a]. Sweete stay a while, why will you?[a]. Preludium. **Morley** Who is it that this darke night[a]. **Coprario** Send home my long strayde eies to mee[a]. **A. Ferrabosco II** So breake off this last lamenting kisse[a]. **Corkine** The Fire to see my woes for anger burneth[a]. 'Tis true, 'tis day, what though it be?[a]. **Hilton II** A Hymne to God the Father[a]. **Anonymous** Come live with me[a]. So breake off this last lamenting kisse[a]. Goe my flocke, goe get you hence[a]. Goe and catch a fallinge star[a]. O deere life when shall it be[a]. Sir Philip Sidney's Lamentacion. Dearest love I doe not goe[a].

In the Dowland Paul Agnew is light of step in the quicker songs, and he languishes longer than most over the variously sorrowful ones; it says much for his artistry, that in "Flow my teares" and "I saw my Lady weepe" he protesteth neither too much nor too long. Many of his choices now enjoy 'pop' status, but his inclusion of the beautiful trilogy of which "Tymes eldest sonne" is the first part, commonly neglected in mixed programmes such as this, is particularly welcome. He receives the most sensitive of support from Wilson, clearly articulated, warm in tone, and perfectly complementary in completing the contrapuntal textures – neither intrusively nor coyly balanced with the voice. Dowland's lute songs have generated many fine recordings, as they richly deserve, and here is one more, beautifully presented, with a booklet containing first-class annotation and all the texts.

Love is a familiar peg on which to hang a song recital, and if there is a further focus it is usually on the composer of the music; Agnew and Wilson turn the tables, for once, by spotlighting the writers of the texts, namely Sir Philip Sidney and John Donne. Their poems are set by Tessier, Dowland, Morley, Coprario, Alfonso Ferrabosco II, Corkine, John Hilton and the ever-present Anonymous, the last being recovered from a variety of sources. Of the songs, only those by Tessier and Dowland, and one by Anon have any other current recording. Sidney's sonnets *Astrophel and Stella*, written between 1581 and 1583, may have been addressed to the daughter of the Earl of Essex but she was unwillingly married to Lord Rich in 1581, so Sidney may have had in mind the daughter of Sir Francis Walsingham, whom he married in 1583. The emotional range of Donne's *Songs and Sonets* may also mirror the fluctuating fortunes of his own, basically happy marriage. In both cases the operative word is 'may'. To the good features of the recording of the Dowland songs are to be added notably clearer diction and some graceful embellishments (trippingly lithe in *Dearest love I doe not goe*) from Agnew, and two well-chosen lute solos by way of interludes from Wilson.

Additional recommendations ...

...The First Booke of Songes. **Consort of Musicke / Anthony Rooley.** L'Oiseau-Lyre Ⓟ 421 653-2OH (76 minutes: DDD: 10/89). ✍   ⒼⒼ

...The First Booke of Songes. **Rufus Müller** (ten); **Christopher Wilson** (lte). ASV Gaudeamus Ⓟ CDGAU135 (74 minutes: DDD: 10/93). ✍

...The First Booke of Songes – Can she excuse my wrongs with vertues cloake. I saw my Lady weepe. Sorrow sorrow stay, lend true repentant teares. Shall I strive with words to move?. *Coupled with works by* **Campion, Ford, Danyel, Rosseter, A. Holborne** and **Anonymous Michael Chance** (alto); **Christopher Wilson** (lte). Chandos Chaconne Ⓕ CHAN0538 (65 minutes: DDD: 10/94). 🖊   Ⓖ

...The First Booke of Songes or Ayres. **John Elwes** (ten); **Matthias Spaeter** (lte). Pierre Verany Ⓕ PV794091 (79 minutes: DDD: 3/95). 🖊

Dowland The Second Booke of Songes. **The Consort of Musicke / Anthony Rooley** (lte). L'Oiseau-Lyre Ⓕ 425 889-2OH (70 minutes: ADD: 8/91). 🖊 Texts included. From DSLO528/9 (9/77). Recorded 1976.   ⓖⓖ

This recording originally appeared in 1977 as part of Florilegium's complete Dowland cycle. The "Second Booke of Songes" dates from 1600 and contains two of Dowland's most famous compositions *Flow my teares* and *I saw my Lady weepe*, though here these are presented unusually (and not entirely convincingly) as vocal duets. In fact there is a surprisingly wide variety of vocal and instrumental combinations throughout the disc, from consort song to four-part vocal to the more familiar sound of solo voice and lute, all of which were suggested as performance possibilities by Dowland himself. It is partly as a result of this that the recording retains its freshness in spite of its age, but it would be wrong to ignore the contribution made by the intelligent and sensitive singing of Emma Kirkby and Martyn Hill, both of whom sound completely in their element.

New review

Dowland Complete Solo Lute Works. **Jakob Lindberg** (lte/orpharion). BIS Ⓜ CD722/4 (four discs: 261 minutes: DDD: 11/95). 🖊 Recorded 1994.

New review

Dowland Complete Solo Lute Works, Volume 1. **Paul O'Dette** (lte/orpharion). Harmonia Mundi Ⓕ HMU90 7160 (64 minutes: DDD: 11/95). 🖊 Recorded 1994.

Pavan (Mylius 1622). Almains – The Lady Laitones Almone, P48; Almain, P49; Mistris Whittes thinge, P50; Almain, P51. Ballads and Other Popular Tunes – Orlando Sleepeth, P61; Go from my Window, P64; Lord Willoughby's welcome home, P66; What is a day, P79. Fantasies – Farwell, P3; Fantasie, P5. Galliards – Frog Galliard, P23 and P23*a*; Melancholy Galliard, P25; Galliard, P27; M. Gilles Hobies Galiard, P29; Galliard in G minor, P30; Galliard, P35; Mr Knights Galliard, P36; My Ladie Riches Galyerd, P43*a*; Galliard, P104. Jigs, Corantos, Toys – Mistris Winters Jumpe, P55; Mrs Whites Nothing, P56. Pavans – Dr Cases Pauen, P12; Pavan, P18; A Dream, P75.

What constitutes the 'complete' lute music of Dowland? Lindberg has chosen to put his cards on the table, whilst O'Dette is revealing his in instalments. Diana Poulton (*John Dowland*; London: 1972) lists 11 pieces as "anonymous, but probably by Dowland", four as "attributed to Dowland, probably incorrectly", and of the numerous alternative versions two, from foreign manuscript sources, are said to be "obviously poor". Therein lies the problem. Lindberg describes the choice of the best versions as "subjective" and even at this early stage it shows, for example, O'Dette playing both P23 and P23*a* whilst Lindberg offers only the latter, and they play only P66 and 66*a* respectively (and the list of differences continues). In the absence of solid evidence it is perhaps best to record every piece, leaving those to whom such things are important to come to their own conclusions. Lindberg groups the pieces according to the sources of his chosen versions, which is as good a way as any. If O'Dette's ordering is other than arbitrary he does not reveal its basis; it yields a nicely varied one hour plus of listening and avoids the placing of galliards back to back, which Lindberg does not always manage.

Both players are highly accomplished lutenists and tend to revel in more exuberant tempos in the galliards than dancers thereof would find comfortable, but it is O'Dette whose tempos inhabit the somewhat wider range. O'Dette's treatment of the pavans and *A Dream* (P75) is a little more spacious, as is his delivery of *Farwell* (P3), though neither artist extracts the same depth of pathos from this last or, in Lindberg's case, *Forlorne hope fancy* (P2) as does Julian Bream. Lindberg, who occasionally makes one aware of technical difficulties, does not quite match O'Dette's squeaky clean and effortless delivery, nor is his tone so consistently pure, but his set represents a considerable achievement that will be warmly welcomed by lovers of this music – so will O'Dette's as it unfolds, offering the advantages of the separate availability of the discs and the prospect of more comprehensive annotation. The *divers* lutes and wire-strung orpharion used by each player are excellently recorded.

Further listening ...

...Can she excuse my wrongs[abc]. Flow my teares[abe]. A fancy, P5[b]. Sorrow stay[abe]. Queene Elizabeth, her Galliard[b]. Goe nightly cares[abde]. Now, O now I needs must part[ab]. Preludium[b]. A Fantasie, P1[b]. Say love if ever thou didst finde[ab]. Frogg Galliard[b]. Awake sweet love, thou art returned[ab]. Tell me, true Love[abc]. *Coupled with works by* **Campion, Ford, Johnson, Ferrabosco, Danyel, Hunnis** and **Anonymous** [a]**James Bowman** (alto); [b]**David Miller** (lte); [c]**King's Consort of Viols**. Hyperion CDA66447 (10/91). 🖊

John Downey
American 1927-

Suggested listening ...

...Edge of Space[a]. *Coupled with* **J. Andriessen** Concerto for Bassoon and Wind Ensemble[c].
Jacob Concerto for Bassoon, Strings and Percussion[b]. **Robert Thompson** (bn); [a]**London
Symphony Orchestra;** [b]**English Chamber Orchestra;** [c]**English Chamber Orchestra Wind Ensemble /
Geoffrey Simon.** Chandos CHAN9278 (10/94).

Patrick Doyle
British 1953-

Suggested listening ...

...Henry V – original film soundtrack. **City of Birmingham Symphony Orchestra / Simon Rattle.**
EMI CDC7 49919-2 (2/90).
...Mary Shelley's Frankenstein – original film soundtrack. Epic MOODCD30.

Giovanni Draghi
Italian c1640-1708

Suggested listening ...

...Suites[b] – A major; G minor; C minor; G major. *Coupled with works by* **Gibbons** and **Purcell**
Davitt Moroney ([a]virg/[b]hpd). Virgin Classics Veritas VC5 45166-2 (5/95). ✏

Paul Dresher
American 1951-

Suggested listening ...

...Double Ikat – Part Two[a]. *Coupled with works by* **Schnittke, Copland, Bolcom** and
MacMillan Maria Bachmann (vn); **Jon Klibonoff** (pf); [a]**James Saporito** (perc). Catalyst 09026
62668-2 (5/95). *See review in the Collections section; refer to the Index to Reviews.*

Henri Du Mont
French 1610-1684

Suggested listening ...

...Sacred Choral Works – Memorare. Dialogus de anima. Magnificat. Super flumina Babylonis. **La
Chapelle Royale Chorus, Paris / Philippe Herreweghe.** Harmonia Mundi Musique d'abord
HMA190 1077 (3/91).

Théodore Dubois
French 1837-1924

Suggested listening ...

...Grand Choeur in B flat major. *Coupled with works by* **Batiste, Bossi, Dupré, Jolivet,
Lefébure-Wély, Lemare** and **Saint-Saën Christopher Herrick** (org). Hyperion CDA66457
(9/91). *See review in the Collections section; refer to the Index to Reviews.* ⓖⓖ

Guillaume Dufay
French c1400-1474

Suggested listening ...

...Triste plaisir et douleureuse joye – Rondeaux, Ballades and Lamentations. *Coupled with*
Binchois Rondeaux and Ballades. **Ensemble Gilles Binchois / Dominique Vellard.** Virgin Classics
Veritas VC7 59043-2. ✏   ⓖ
...Balsamus et munda cera/Isti sunt agni novelli. Supremum est mortalibus bonum. Ecclesie
militantis. *Coupled with works by* **Zacharias, Antonius de Civitate Austrie, Tapissier,
Velut, Anonymous, Ciconia, Philipoctus de Caserta, Johanne Egidius, Matheus
de Sancto Johanne, Bartolomeus da Bologna** and **Brassart Orlando Consort.**
Metronome METCD1008 (11/95). *See review in the Collections section; refer to the Index to
Reviews.*   ⓖ

Paul Dukas
French 1865-1935

New review
Dukas L'apprenti sorcier.
Saint-Saëns Symphony No. 3 in C minor, Op. 78, "Organ"[a]. [a]**Simon Preston** (org); **Berlin
Philharmonic Orchestra / James Levine.** DG Ⓟ 419 617-2GH (47 minutes: DDD: 8/87).   ⓖ

James Levine and the BPO, on cracking form, offer a performance of Saint-Saëns's Third Symphony which is still (nearly ten years on) among the best available. The balance between the orchestra and organ, here played powerfully by Simon Preston, is well judged and the overall acoustic very convincing. Levine directs a grippingly individual reading, full of drama and with a consistently imaginative response to the score's detail. The organ entry in the finale is quite magnificent, the excitement of Preston thundering out the main theme physical in its impact. The music expands and blossoms magnificently, helped by the spectacular dynamic range of the recording. Levine's choice of coupling is a happy one, especially as his account of Dukas's masterpiece is still the best in the catalogue. It was Stokowski who made *The sorcerer's apprentice* famous (with the help of Walt Disney) and his Philadelphia version remains the yardstick. Levine chooses a faster basic tempo than Stokowski, but justifies his speed by the lightness of his touch – this is a real orchestral scherzo – and, of course, the clean articulation and rhythmic bounce of the Berlin Philharmonic playing help more than a little. The big climax is thrilling, but Levine keeps something in reserve for the moment when the sorcerer returns to quell the flood. One feels that Levine must have Disney's imagery in his mind in the beautifully managed closing pages of the story, for the picture of the crestfallen Mickey handing back the broom to his master springs readily to mind. A marvellous finish to an altogether exhilarating listening experience.

Additional recommendation ...

...L'apprenti sorcier. **Franck** Symphony in D minor. Grande pièce symphonique in F sharp minor, Op. 17 – Andante. Panis angelicus. **Satie** Gymnopédies – Nos. 1 and 2. **A. Thomas** Mignon – Gavotte. **Berlioz** La damnation de Faust, Op. 24 – Hungarian March. **Philadelphia Orchestra / Leopold Stokowski.** Biddulph mono Ⓜ WHL011* (70 minutes: ADD: 8/95).

Dukas Symphony in C major. Polyeucte – overture. **BBC Philharmonic Orchestra / Yan Pascal Tortelier.** Chandos Ⓕ CHAN9225 (56 minutes: DDD: 6/94). Recorded 1993. *Selected by Sounds in Retrospect.*

Before *L'apprenti sorcier*, the tradition Dukas was following was that of Franck, and he was also heavily influenced by the Wagnerianism then holding French composers in thrall. Both models can be discerned in the overture *Polyeucte*: nevertheless, and despite extensive Wagnerian use of the brass, there is a clarity (even delicacy in the third of its five sections) and an imaginative sense of colour which are individual to him. The finely crafted Symphony composed four years later, in 1896 – daringly in C major at a time when tonality was undergoing such general buffeting – shows Dukas as essentially a classicist, although the middle section of the central movement reveals that Nature romanticism had not passed him by. The eloquent performance here gives the vigorous first movement a splendid *élan* (and a terrific ending) while also luxuriating in the Franckian secondary subjects, there is lovely warm, lyrical playing and sensitive nuance in the second movement, and the finale (even more Franckian in its harmonic thinking) bubbles over with nervous energy. Exemplary recording quality.

Additional recommendation ...

...Symphony. La Peri – ballet. L'apprenti sorcier. **Netherlands Radio Philharmonic Orchestra / Jean Fournet.** Denon Ⓕ CO-75284 (74 minutes: DDD: 6/93).

New review

Dukas L'apprenti sorcier (arr. Rabinovitch).
Ravel La valse (arr. cpsr).
R. Strauss Symphonia domestica, Op. 53 (arr. Singer). **Martha Argerich, Alexandre Rabinovitch** (pfs). Teldec Ⓕ 4509-96435-2 (62 minutes: DDD: 7/96). ⒼⒼ

Here is a disc to set the music world on fire, ablaze with the sort of pianistic panache and poetic empathy from which legends are made. However, those of a nervous disposition and with a bias towards serenity, should be warned that such fire is of an aptly sinister and engulfing nature. After all, Dukas's *L'apprenti sorcier* and Ravel's *La valse* both inhabit worlds of exuberant nightmare, and although one can marvel at the concentrated wit and verve of Argerich and Rabinovitch, it is their uncanny evocation of unsettled states where all equilibrium is lost and the "ceremony of innocence" is well and truly drowned that forms the most lasting impression. Such vividness brings parts of *La valse* to a near standstill before accelerating away and achieving an effect not unlike suddenly applied centrifugal force. The opening quivers with unease, the commencement of a vision where even the most opulent Viennese gaiety and extravagance is menacingly clouded and distorted. The Dukas, too, develops from sinister hints to a situation diabolically out of control yet one sustained by both players with an iron grip all the more remarkable when you consider the immense virtuoso resources involved. Otto Singer's skilful version of Strauss's autobiographical *Symphonia domestica* hardly transcends its orchestral origin yet it is illuminated at every point — whether in rhetorical uproar or flickering, Lisztian half-lights — by playing of an overwhelming brio and crystalline clarity. If anything Argerich's blow-torch incandescence has increased rather than diminished over the years. The recordings are close but unconfined, capturing with fine fidelity the dazzling impact of these performances.

Further listening ...

...Piano Sonata in E flat minor. Variations, interlude et final sur un thème de Rameau. La plainte, au loin, du faune ... . Prélude élégiaque. *Coupled with* **Chausson** Quelques danses, Op. 26.

Paysage, Op. 38. **Franck** Prélude, Choral et Fugue. Les plaintes d'une poupée. Danse lente. Prélude, Aria et Final. **Jean Hubeau** (pf). Teldec 4509-96221-2 (4/96).

…Variations, Interlude and Finale on a theme by Rameau. Prélude élégiaque. La plainte, au loin, du faune. Piano Sonata in E flat minor. **Margaret Fingerhut** (pf). Chandos CHAN8765 (1/90).

…Ariane et Barbe-Bleue. **Soloists; French Radio Chorus; French Radio New Philharmonic Orchestra / Armin Jordan.** Erato Libretto 2292-45663-2 (9/91).

Henry Dumont   French 1610-1684

Suggested listening …

…Suite in D minor. Allemandes – C major; A minor; C major. Allemande grave in C major. *Coupled with* **Chambonnières** Suites – D major; G major; D minor; F major. **Member of the Hardel family** Suite in D minor. **Jane Chapman** (hpd). Collins Classics 1422-2 (8/95). ✒ *See review under Chambonnières; refer to the Index to Reviews.*

John Dunstable   British c1390-1453

New review

Dunstable Descendi in ortum meum. Ave maris stella. Gloria in canon. Speciosa facta es. Sub tuam protectionem. Veni, Sancte spiritus/Veni creator spiritus. Albanus roseo rutilat/Quoque ferundus eras/Albanus Domini laudus. Specialis virgo. Preco preheminencie/Precursor premittitur/textless/Inter natos mulierum. O crux gloriosa. Salve regina mater mire. Missa Rex seculorum. **Orlando Consort.** Metronome Ⓕ METCD1009 (74 minutes: DDD: 2/96). Texts and translations included. Recorded 1995. *Gramophone Editor's choice.*　　　　　　　Ⓖ

Dunstable's career, as far as recordings are concerned, has been strange. A few of his pieces have appeared repeatedly, while many others have been almost entirely ignored. This new CD does contain three well-known motets – *Preco preheminencie, Veni, Sancte spiritus* and *Albanus* – but the rest are rarely performed. For some of the delicious antiphons, it is hard to see why. There are also some total novelties. The canonic *Gloria* was discovered very recently in Russia and has not yet been published: it is a hugely inventive work that adds a substantial new dimension to our knowledge of Dunstable. And *Descendi in ortum meum*, though discovered and published a quarter of a century ago, surely stands as the latest known work of its composer: a magnificent piece that builds an entirely new kind of edifice with the materials of his characteristic style. Most impressive of all, though, is the Mass, *Rex seculorum*, which ends the disc. This may or may not be by Dunstable – which is probably why it has never been recorded. Whoever the composer, though, it is a key work in the history of the polyphonic Mass cycle, one of the very few that prefigure the design and structure of the continental cycles later in the century. And it is a work brimming with invention. The Orlando Consort sound better every time they go into a recording studio. Here they have a wonderfully forward style that beautifully matches the music and helps the listener to understand why Dunstable achieved such an enormous reputation on the continental mainland. If they are occasionally a touch rough, these are classic performances that will be hard to challenge in the years to come.

Further listening …

…Beata Dei genitrix. *Coupled with works by* **Anonymous, Cardot, Bittering, Binchois, Fontaine, Johannes de Lymburga, Legrant, Machaut, Power** and **Velut. Gothic Voices / Christopher Page.** Hyperion CDA66783 (1/96). *See review in the Collections section; refer to the Index to Reviews.*

Marie Eugène Duparc   French 1848-1933

Duparc L'Invitation au voyage. Sérénade florentine. La Vague et la cloche. Extase. Phidylé. Le Manoir de Rosemonde. Lamento. Testament. Chanson triste. Elégie. Soupir. La Vie antérieure. Le Galop. Sérénade. Au pays où se fait la guerre[a]. Romance de Mignon[a]. La Fuite[a]. **José van Dam** (bass-bar); [a]**Florence Bonnafous** (sop); **Maciej Pikulski** (pf). Forlane Ⓕ UCD16692 (67 minutes: DDD: 1/94). Texts and translations included. Recorded 1993.

These songs may justly be held to represent the peak of development of the French *mélodie* in their sensitivity, intensity, scope of expression and unfaltering taste. Influences may be seen of his teacher César Franck in his emotionalism and chromatic texture, of Gounod in the rippling piano part of a song like *Chanson triste*, and particularly of Wagner in the harmonic colouring of *Soupir* and the almost Tristanesque *Extase*; but it has been well observed that the sinister drama of *Le Manoir de Rosemonde*, with its insistent rhythm, is worthy of Hugo Wolf, and that the bleak tints of *Lamento* show some foreshadowing of Ravel's *Le gibet*. Despite all this, however, Duparc is very much an individual genius; and the breadth of his stylistic range, from the passionate lyricism of *L'Invitation au voyage* or the haunting sensuousness of *Phidylé* to the simple heartbreak of *Au pays où se fait la guerre*, makes any *intégrale* of his songs of riveting interest. Particularly so when sung with such imaginative insight, commitment and verbal intensity as by José van Dam here. He is expertly partnered by a responsively musical young Polish accompanist, Maciej Pikulski.

Additional recommendations ...
...L'invitation au voyage[cd]. Soupir[cd]. Testament[cd]. Sérénade florentine[cd]. La vague et la cloche[cd]. Lamento[cd]. La Vie antérieure[cd]. Phidylé[cd]. Extase[cd]. Elégie[cd]. Le Manoir de Rosemonde[cd]. Chanson triste[cd]. **Fauré** Requiem, Op. 48[ace]. La bonne chanson, Op. 61[cd]. **Britten** Les illuminations, Op. 18[bf]. **Ravel** Don Quichotte à Dulcinée[ce]. Shéhérazade[be]. **Debussy** Trois ballades de François Villon[ce]. [a]**Pierrette Alarie**, [b]**Janine Micheau** (sops); [c]**Camille Maurane** (bar); [d]**Lily Bienvenu** (pf); [a]**Elisabeth Brasseur Choir; Lamoureux Orchestra /** [e]**Jean Fournet,** [f]**Paul Sacher.** Philips The Early Years mono Ⓜ 438 970-2PM2* (two discs: 157 minutes: ADD).

Jacques Duphly

French 1715-1789

Suggested listening ...
...Harpsichord Solos – La de Redemond. La du Buq. *Coupled with works by* **J-B. Forqueray, Leclair, Mondonville** and **Guillemain Simon Standage** (vn); **Lars Ulrik Mortensen** (hpd). Chandos CHAN0531 (6/93). ✍ *See review under Leclair; refer to the Index to Reviews.*
...Pièces de clavecin – Livre I: Allemande in D minor; Courante in D minor; La Damanzy; Allemande in C minor; La Boucon; La larare; Rondeau. Livre II: La Félix; La Lanza; La d'Héricourt. Livre III: La Forqueray; Médée; Les Grâces. Livre IV: La de Vaucanson; La Porthouin. **Mario Raskin** (hpd). Pierre Verany PV793021 (3/94). ✍

Marcel Dupré

French 1886-1971

Suggested listening ...
...Organ Symphony in G minor, Op. 25. *Coupled with* **Rheinberger** Organ Concerto No. 1 in F major, Op. 137. **Michael Murray** (org); **Royal Philharmonic Orchestra / Jahja Ling.** Telarc CD80136 (6/87).
...Three Preludes and Fugues, Op. 36. *Coupled with works by* **Bonnet** and **Peeters Jane Watts** (org). Priory PRCD377 (8/94).
...Preludes and Fugues, Op. 7. *Coupled with* **Alain** Intermezzo. Litanies, Op. 79. **Franck** Prélude, Fugue et Variation in B minor, Op. 18. Fantaisie in A major. **Tournemire** Petite rapsodie improvisée. Cantilène Improvisée. Improvisation sur le Te Deum. **Jane Watts** (org). Priory PRCD286 (9/90).
...Cortège et Litanie, Op. 19 No. 2. *Coupled with works by* **Dubois, Batiste, Bossi, Jolivet, Lefébure-Wély, Lemare** and **Saint-Saëns Christopher Herrick** (org). Hyperion CDA66457 (9/91). *See review in the Collections section; refer to the Index to Reviews.* ⒼⒼⒼ
...Le tombeau de Titelouze, Op. 38. *Coupled with works by* **Barié** Peter Wright (org) Priory PRCD406 (10/94).
...Scherzo, Op. 16. *Coupled with works by* **Roussel, d'Indy, R. Vierne, Barié, Honegger, Langlais** and **L. Vierne** Marie-Bernadette Dufourcet (org). Priory PRCD422 (6/95). *See review in the Collections section; refer to the Index to Reviews.*
...15 Versets sur les Vêpres de la Vierge, Op. 18[a]. *Coupled with* **Plainchant** Vespers Service[b]. [a]**Philippe Lefèbvre** (org); [b]**Schola Gregoriana / Mary Berry** with **David Hill** (org). Herald HAVPCD170 (4/95). *Gramophone Editor's choice.* ⒼⒼ
...15 Versets sur les Vêpres de la Vierge[a]. Seven Pieces, Op. 27. [a]**Choral Scholars of St Nicholas, Meerbusch-Osterath; Suzanne Chaisemartin** (org). Motette CD50251 (1/96).
...Evocation, Op. 37 – Allegro deciso. *Coupled with works by* **B. Ferguson, Langlais, Bonnal** and **Bach** Roger Sayer (org). Priory PRCD495 (4/96). *See review in the Collections section; refer to the Index to Reviews.*

Francesco Durante

Italian 1684-1755

New review
Durante Lamentationes Jeremiae Prophetae. **Monika Frimmer, Mechthild Bach** (sops); **Margarete Joswig** (contr); **Cologne Chamber Choir; Collegium Cartusianum / Peter Neumann.** CPO Ⓟ CPO999 325-2 (68 minutes: DDD: 4/96). ✍ Text and translation included. Recorded 1994. Ⓖ
The *Lamentations of the Prophet Jeremiah*, three in all, were probably composed in 1751, towards the end of Durante's life. They are a far cry from the earlier Italian *lamentazioni*, more closely resembling in their richly scored, vocally virtuosic arias sections of oratorio. These *concertante* pieces are striking above all for their stylistic variety. Harmonies are bold, sometimes daring and often wonderfully expressive, as in the opening section of the Third Lamentation or in the opening "De Lamentatione" of the First. Here the music is full of pathos, imaginatively scored and sympathetically inclined towards the voice. Each Lamentation has its own distinctive colouring, the First for soprano with pairs of flutes and horns with strings, the Second for soprano, alto and strings, and the Third for

soprano, alto, tenor and bass soloists with four-part choir, two horns and strings. This last Lamentation is particularly impressive for the way in which Durante intersperses and blends older contrapuntal disciplines with up-to-the-minute *galant* gestures resonantly proclaimed by the intermittent presence of the two *concertante* horns. When confronted with pieces such as this, it is not difficult to understand the praise lavished upon Durante by contemporaries such as Rousseau, who described him as "the greatest harmonist in Italy that is, in the whole world" (well he would, having been roundly snubbed by Rameau several years earlier). The performances are good, with an excellent period-instrument band, a responsive though not always incisive choir and mostly stylish soloists. Monika Frimmer does not always sound comfortable in the execution of ornaments but the vocal quality is pleasing and her intonation reliable. Director Peter Neumann infuses the music with fervour, attending to the many nuances that exist in Durante's setting of the texts. An unusual and stimulating release, well recorded and painstakingly documented.

Further listening ...

...Concerto for Two Violins, Viola and Continuo in G minor. *Coupled with* **Sarri** Concerto for Recorder, Two Violins, Viola and Continuo in A minor. **D. Scarlatti** Mandolin Sonata in D minor, Kk90. **A. Scarlatti** Sonata for Recorder, Two Violins and Continuo in A minor. **Mancini** Sonata for Recorder, two Violins and Continuo in D minor. **Il Giardino Armonico / Giovanni Antonini** (rec). Teldec Das Alte Werk 4509-93157-2 (11/94). ✍   Ⓖ

Sebastián Durón   Spanish 1660-1716

New review

¡Ay amor! Barroco Español, Volume 2. **Al Ayre Español / Eduardo López Banzo.** Deutsche Harmonia Mundi Ⓕ 05472 77336-2 (62 minutes: DDD: 1/96). ✍ Texts and translations included. Recorded 1994.   Ⓖ

Durón Veneno es de amor la envidia – Ondas riscos, pezes, mares. El impossible mayor en amor le venze Amor – Donde vas; Danae, cuya belleza; Oye, escucha, aguarda, espera. **Literes** Azis y Galatea – Seguidillas; Confiado gilguerillo; Monstruo, en quien ha sobrado; Pues del culto mi peidad; Coplas. Los elementos – Deydades que en el monte; Ay amor; Mas si fuese la planta fugitiva. El estrago en la fineza, o Jupiter y Semele – Pues soy abejuela; Yo he de enmudecer; Ven dulcissimo bien. **Martín y Coll** (arr. anon) Flores de musica – Ruede la Vola; Cancion Franzesa; Diferencias sobre la gayta.

This volume of Spanish baroque music concentrates on theatre music of the latter part of the seventeenth century and the first half of the eighteenth. The prevalent forms of entertainment at the Spanish court were the *zarzuela* and the *comedia*, both of which combined musical items with speech. The disc presents extracts from a number of such pieces by Sebastián Durón and Antonio de Literes, the leading Spanish court composers of the period, together with various instrumental pieces. The CD is very much a showcase for the soprano Marta Almajano (the excellent Catalan baritone Jordi Ricart is featured on only two items) who, as on the first disc, proves to be more than equal to the challenge, singing expressively and with bravura as the music demands. Given the nature of this music, the recording comprises a series of fairly short items, but each quickly establishes a distinctive character and Al Ayre Español once again are clearly well under the skin of the idiom. Castanets and drums are confined to the most overtly popular items – for instance, the *seguidillas* and *coplas* from Literes's renditon of the Acis and Galatea myth. His treatment of this theme is characteristic of the *zarzuela* with its mix of comic elements and allusions to mythology, making it quite different from Handel's more dramatic, *opera seria* approach. In other ways, Literes's musical idiom has many correspondences with Handel in Italianate vein. There are so many other gems on this disc that it is hard to single out individual items, but try Durón's "Ondas, riscos, pezes, mares" for plangent chromaticism – the Spanish composers were good at laments, one of the typical dramatic scenes that called for music. All in all, this is an enticing sample of the hitherto little explored Spanish baroque in highly convincing performances.

Maurice Duruflé   French 1902-1986

New review

Duruflé Sacred Choral and Organ Works, Volumes 1 and 2. [a]**Béatrice Uria-Monzon** (mez); [b]**Didier Henry** (bar); [c]**Eric LeBrun** (org); [d]**Michel Piquemal Vocal Ensemble**; [e]**Orchestre de la Cité / Michel Piquemal.** Naxos Ⓢ 8 553196/7 (two discs, oas: 67 and 62 minutes: DDD: 11/95). Texts and translations included. Recorded 1994.

8 553196 – Requiem, Op. 9[abcde]. Quatre Motets sur des thèmes grégoriens, Op. 10[d]. Scherzo, Op. 2[c]. Notre père, Op. 14[d]. Prélude et Fugue sur le nom d'Alain, Op. 7[c]. *8 553197* – Messe "Cum jubilo", Op. 11[bcde]. Prélude, Adagio et Choral varié sur le thème du "Veni Creator", Op. 4[c]. Suite, Op. 5[c].

There are certainly better recordings available of much of this music: John Scott's disc of the complete organ works still reigns supreme while for the *Quatre Motets* and the Requiem (the top recommendation is Matthew Best and the Corydon Singers at full price on Hyperion). But this pair of Naxos CDs is noteworthy for anyone who professes a deep love for Duruflé's music – on two counts. Firstly it includes a rare recording of the wonderful *Messe "Cum jubilo"* in its orchestral version. As with the Requiem, Duruflé was persuaded, probably against his better judgement, to make a version just with organ accompaniment – in which guise both works lose the greater part of their inherent beauty since Duruflé, with his innate sense of colour, was a masterly orchestrator. Secondly these performances probably come closer than any other to the essential spirit of Duruflé – this despite their manifest flaws. Regrettably the choir have a penchant for singing flat; Michel Piquemal doesn't always seem in complete control of events and has some very strange ideas about speeds and tempo changes; Eric LeBrun's enthusiasm for the faster solos, notably the *Alain* Fugue, rather outstrips his technical facility; and the Cavaillé-Coll organ of the church of Saint-Antoine des Quinze-Vingts in Paris is hardly in tiptop condition. The recordings, not without certain obvious rough edges, are nevertheless suitably rich and atmospheric. No one could accuse Piquemal of asserting his own interpretative individuality on these performances; instead he gives his musicians free rein to follow their natural inclinations in music which seems almost second nature to them. The singers trace the flowing plainsong-inspired lines with the kind of easy freedom that no amount of detailed practice could recreate, while the orchestral players possess that indefinable Frenchness which guides them through Duruflé's quasi-impressionistic mists with all the nonchalant self-assurance of a London bus driver in a January smog. Meanwhile Eric LeBrun plays with a mixture of extrovert passion and subtle sensitivity which is perfectly in tune with the distinctive style of Duruflé's organ music. Didier Henry's wonderfully expressive solos in the Requiem and, more particularly, the matchless *Benedictus* from the *Messe* (what depths of emotion Duruflé was able to pack into this tiny – two-minute – movement with its inescapable Messiaenic overtones) are unforgettable.

Additional recommendations ...

...Requiem[a]. Quatre Motets. [a]Ann Murray (mez); [a]Thomas Allen (bar); Corydon Singers; [a]English Chamber Orchestra / Matthew Best with [a]Thomas Trotter (org). Hyperion Ⓕ CDA66191 (51 minutes: DDD: 4/87).

...Quatre Motets[a]. Mass "Cum jubilo"[b]. **Fauré** Requiem, Op. 48[c]. Cantique de Jean Racine, Op. 11[d]. **Messiaen** O sacrum convivium. [c]Camilla Otaki (sop); [bc]Mark Griffiths (bar); Trinity College Choir, Cambridge; [bcd]Richard Pearce (org); [c]London Musici / Richard Marlow. Conifer Ⓕ CDCF176 (73 minutes: DDD: 10/90).

...Requiem[a]. Quatre Motets. Notre père. Mass "Cum jubilo"[b]. [a]Aaron Webber (treb); [ab]Simon Keenlyside (bar); [a]Natalie Clein (vc); Westminster Cathedral Choir / James O'Donnell with [ab]Iain Simcock (org). Hyperion Ⓕ CDA66757 (71 minutes: DDD: 6/95).

...Prélude sur l'introit de l'Epiphanie. Prélude et Fugue sur le nom d'Alain, Op. 7. Suite, Op. 5. Scherzo, Op. 2. Prélude, Adagio et Choral Varié sur le "Veni creator spiritus", Op. 4 (with the men's voices of St Paul's Cathedral Choir). Fugue sur le carillon des heures de la Cathédrale de Soissons, Op. 12. **John Scott** (org). Hyperion Ⓕ CDA66368 (70 minutes: DDD: 1/91).

Duruflé Prélude et Fugue sur le nom d'Alain, Op. 7[c]. Requiem, Op. 9[c]. Quatre Motets sur des thèmes grégoriens, Op. 10[b].
Fauré Requiem, Op. 9[a]. Cantique de Jean Racine, Op. 11[a]. Messe basse[b].
Poulenc Mass in G major[d]. Salve Regina[d]. Exultate Deo[d]. Litanies à la vierge noire[d]. **Jonathon Bond, Andrew Brunt, Robert King** (trebs); **Benjamin Luxon** (bar); **Christopher Keyte** (bass); St John's College Choir, Cambridge; Academy of St Martin in the Fields / George Guest with Stephen Cleobury (org). Double Decca Ⓜ 436 486-2DF2 (two discs: 149 minutes: ADD: 7/94). Items marked [a] from Argo ZRG841 (4/76), [b]ZRG662 (2/71), [c]ZRG787 (5/75), [d]ZRG883 (6/78). Recorded 1969-76.   **Ⓖ**

Here is almost two-and-a-half hours of bliss. These are recordings to set aside for the time when, as the prayer says, "the busy world is hushed". The two discs would make an excellent present and it would be necessary to buy a second copy (for yourself) while about it. Asked to characterize Fauré's and Duruflé's Requiems as compared with others, we might suggest words such as 'delicate', 'restrained', 'meditative', 'undramatic'; but that last would be a mistake. These performances certainly do not go out of their way to 'be' dramatic or anything else other than faithful to the music but one is struck by the power exercised by those rare moments that rise to a *forte* and above. In Fauré the orchestral crescendo introducing the baritone soloist has the effectiveness of a spotlight brought up gradually upon a motionless figure on stage; the entry of brass in the *Sanctus* has breadth and majesty incommensurate with its scoring and duration; the brief orchestral climax of the *Lux aeterna* looms imposingly like the front of a great cathedral. Duruflé too is dramatic, but in the way that (say) Westminster Cathedral is dramatic, with stillness and space, and the light of candles amid a brooding darkness. The choir is surely at its best, the trebles with their fine, clear-cut, distinctive tone, the tenors (so important in the Fauré) graceful and refined without being precious, the altos exceptionally good, and only the basses just occasionally and briefly plummy or obtrusive in some way. The Poulenc works further test a choir's virtuosity yet in the extremely difficult Mass, the choir seems secure, and in the *Salve Regina* they catch the necessary tenderness. Of the treble soloists, Andrew Brunt sings most beautifully in the *Messe basse*, while Jonathon Bond's high, well-floated tones have ethereal effect in the *Agnus Dei* of Poulenc's Mass in G. Christopher Keyte dramatizes almost too convincingly in Duruflé's "tremens factus", and Benjamin Luxon, his production less even, builds finely in Fauré's *Libera me*. Stephen Cleobury, the organist throughout, contributes an admirably played solo written by Duruflé as a tribute to the young organist Jehan Alain, killed early in the war. These recordings have a vividness, certainly in the choral sound, that modern recordings generally lack.

Jan Ladislav Dussek   Bohemian 1760-1812

New review

Dussek Piano Sonatas – A flat major, Op. 64, "Le Retour à Paris"; F sharp minor, Op. 61, "Elégie Harmonique". Fantasia and Fugue in F minor, Op. 55. **Andreas Staier** (fp). Deutsche Harmonia Mundi Ⓟ 05472 77334-2 (61 minutes: DDD: 7/96). ✗   ⒼⒼ

The second volume in Andreas Staier's Dussek series (Vol. 1 is listed below) includes two of the last and finest sonatas by this fascinating, wayward Bohemian. The F sharp minor, *Elégie Harmonique*, is a memorial to the composer's patron, friend and fellow-roisterer, Prince Louis Ferdinand of Prussia, who fell in the Battle of Saalfeld in 1806. Cast in two movements only, it opens with a brooding, quasi-improvisatory slow introduction and continues with a *Tempo agitato* of mingled pathos and protest, full of halting melodic lines, shadowy harmonies and disconcerting dynamic contrasts. The syncopations of the finale have an edgy obsessiveness, relieved only in a beautiful, consolatory G flat episode which distantly echoes the A flat episode in the finale of Beethoven's Third Piano Concerto. Dussek's characteristically rich pianistic effects are still more in evidence in the expansive four-movement A flat Sonata. The composer wrote this with a dual purpose in mind: to mark his final return to Paris in 1807 (hence the title), and to outdo the provocatively titled *Ne plus ultra* Sonata by one Joseph Woelfl, intended to be the last word in wrist-breaking pyrotechnics. Formidable the challenges of Dussek's first movement, in particular, may be, but there is never any question of vacuous virtuosity: from the opening theme the music cultivates a very individual vein of impassioned, rhapsodic romanticism. The *Molto adagio* justifies its marking *dolcissimo, con anima ed espressione*, the minuet-scherzo hints at a remote F sharp minor before confirming the tonic, A flat – a haunting effect, typical of Dussek's harmonic daring – and the brilliant, volatile finale opens with a theme which sounds as if it might be a folk-dance from the composer's native Bohemia. Staier uses a restored 1806 Broadwood grand, less refined but more vibrant and powerful than the contemporary Viennese piano. The purposely inefficient damping mechanism produces what the restorer, Christopher Clarke, describes in his note as an "elemental wash of sound", with a "permanent halo of harmonies". If here and there Staier's attack seems unduly aggressive, he, like the composer, palpably relishes the instrument's possibilities. In both the sonatas and the Fantasia and Fugue (which grows ever less fugal as it proceeds), his playing is brilliant, dramatic and richly imagined. The recording is vivid, though the close miking places the listener only a few feet from the instrument.

Further listening ...

...Piano Concertos[a] – B flat major, C97; G minor, C187. The Sufferings of the Queen of France, C98. [a]**Concerto Köln / Andreas Staier** (fp). Capriccio 10 444 (10/95). ✗

...Piano Sonatas – C major, Op. 9 No. 2; G minor, Op. 10 No. 2. Three Sonatas, Op. 35. **Geoffrey Govier** (pf). Olympia Explorer OCD430 (9/93).

...Piano Sonatas – Op. 35: No. 1 in B flat major; No. 2 in G major; No. 3 in C minor. D major, Op. 31 No. 3. **Andreas Staier** (fp). Deutsche Harmonia Mundi 05472 77286-2 (2/95). ✗   ⒼⒼ

Henri Dutilleux   French 1916-

Dutilleux Violin Concerto, "L'arbre des songes"[a]. Cello Concerto, "Tout un monde lointain"[b]. [a]**Pierre Amoyal** (vn); [b]**Lynn Harrell** (vc); **French National Orchestra / Charles Dutoit.** Decca Ⓕ 444 398-2DH (51 minutes: DDD: 3/95). Recorded 1993. *Selected by Sounds in Retrospect.* ⒼⒼ

It was high time that Dutilleux's two concertos were brought together on disc, and this fine new recording should help to win him new admirers. The Cello Concerto, first performed in 1970, was written for Rostropovich and Lynn Harrell boldly confronts this formidable precedent; there is certainly no sense of undue reticence or constraint in his playing. The many technical challenges present no problems: more significantly, Harrell the interpreter has the full measure of the music's tricky blend of boldness and delicacy. From the start of the "very free and flexible" first movement the undertones of mystery and menace which reflect the music's source in Baudelaire's poetry are fully in evidence, and Harrell has the advantage of first-class (1993) recorded sound. The cello is placed well forward, but the orchestra are never recessed to compensate. The Violin Concerto (1985) builds on the sultry, surreal Baudelairean spirit of the Cello Concerto – the 'tree' of the title seems tropical, the 'dreams' mainly unquiet – and Pierre Amoyal, with admirable support from Dutoit and the FNO, succeeds brilliantly in shaping the rhapsodic solo line with a mixture of intensity and fantasy, so that the piece works well as both structure and expression. Here, too, the production team have ensured that the concerto's rich textures can be heard without strain or artificiality. The whole enterprise can be warmly recommended.

Dutilleux Symphonies – No. 1; No. 2, "Le double". **BBC Philharmonic Orchestra / Yan Pascal Tortelier.** Chandos Ⓕ CHAN9194 (60 minutes: DDD: 11/93). *Gramophone Award Winner 1994. Selected by Sounds in Retrospect.*   Ⓖ

This pair of relatively early works by Henri Dutilleux, completed in 1951 and 1959 respectively, show him poised to inherit the Honegger/Martinů strand of the symphonic tradition. Yet, while an almost Simpsonian *élan* in the first movement of No. 2 promises a rich vein for further exploration, the Stravinskian strategies of the finale, ending with a virtual recomposition of the chorale that concludes the *Symphonies of Wind Instruments*, reveals a more modernist tendency, and leads away from the well-made, tonally-resolving symphony altogether. With their broad thematic vistas and persuasive adaptations of traditional forms, Dutilleux's symphonies offer considerable rewards to interpreters and listeners alike. Yan Pascal Tortelier and the BBC Philharmonic allow the music all the space it needs in strongly characterized, rhythmically well-sprung performances with uniformly excellent solo playing in No. 2, and the Chandos sound is rich and natural.

Additional recommendation ...

...No. 1. Timbres, espaces, mouvement. **Orchestre National de Lyon / Serge Baudo.** Harmonia Mundi Ⓕ HMC90 5159 (47 minutes: ADD: 3/87). *Selected by Sounds in Retrospect.*

Further listening ...

...Mystère de l'instant[a]. Métaboles[b]. Timbres, Espace, mouvement[b]. [a]**Zurich Collegium Musicum / Paul Sacher;** [b]**French National Orchestra / Mstislav Rostropovich.** Erato MusiFrance 2292-45626-2 (8/92).

...Métaboles. Timbres, espace, mouvement (rev. 1991). Symphony No. 2, "Le double". **Orchestre de Paris / Semyon Bychkov.** Philips 438 008-2PH (5/94).　　　　　　　　　　　　　　　Ⓖ

...Métaboles. *Coupled with* **Berlioz** Symphonie fantastique, Op. 14. **Paris Opéra-Bastille Orchestra / Myung-Whun Chung.** DG 445 878-2GH (4/96). *See review under Berlioz; refer to the Index to Reviews.*

...Sacher[e]. Ainsi la nuit ...[d]. Deux sonnets de Jean Cassou[e]. Les citations[f]. [e]**Gilles Cachemaille** (bar); [f]**Maurice Bourgue** (ob); [c]**David Geringas** (vc); [ah]**Geneviève Joy,** [be]**Henri Dutilleux** (pfs); [f]**Huguette Dreyfus** (hpd); [f]**Bernard Cazauran** (db); [f]**Bernard Balet** (perc); [d]**Sine Nomine Quartet.** Erato MusiFrance 4509-91721-2 (5/95).

...Trois strophes sur le nom de Sacher. *Coupled with works by* **Beck, Henze, Fortner, Ginastera, Boulez, Lutosławski, Berio, C. Halffter, Britten, K. Huber** and **Hollige** Patrick and **Thomas Demenga** (vcs); **Cello Ensemble / Jürg Wyttenbach.** ECM New Series 445 234-2 (8/95)

Antonin Dvořák　　　　　　　　　　　　　　　　　　　Czechoslovakian 1841-1904

Dvořák Cello Concerto in B minor, B191[a]. Silent woods, B173[b]. Rondo in G minor, B171[b]. Slavonic Dance in A flat major, B147 No. 8[b]. **Heinrich Schiff** (vc); [a]**Vienna Philharmonic Orchestra / André Previn** ([b]pf). Philips Ⓕ 434 914-2PH (54 minutes: DDD: 9/93). Recorded 1992.　　　　　　　　　　　　　　　　　　　　　　　　　　　　　Ⓖ

Schiff's cello is recorded in a more natural balance than is common in this concerto, so that the solo instrument's first entry does not give the impression of a super-cello, as most recordings do, but the concentration and tension bear witness to the scale and power of the interpretation. When it comes to the great second subject melody Schiff's hushed *pianissimo* is ravishingly gentle, and unlike almost every rival he avoids drawing the tempo out, observing Dvořák's *In tempo* marking at a very marginally broader speed. The result has a touching simplicity and tenderness. André Previn is a fresh and understanding partner, pointing rhythms even more crisply, and the Vienna Philharmonic brings out the Slavonic tang in the score. The bright detailed recording helps, with the Vienna horns – so important in this work from the opening tutti on – sounding glorious. Schiff's flowing speed in the slow movement again brings out the freshness of folk-based ideas. Only in the finale does the balance of the cello mean that the result is less biting. Few versions come near to matching this. The coupling is apt. These are not the usual orchestral arrangements but have Previn as a sparkling piano accompanist.

Additional recommendations ...

...Cello Concerto. **Schubert** Sonata in A major, D821, "Arpeggione". **Lynn Harrell** (vc); **London Symphony Orchestra / James Levine.** RCA Papillon Ⓜ GD86531 (67 minutes: ADD: 11/87).

...Cello Concerto[a]. **Bloch** Schelomo[b]. **Bruch** Kol Nidrei, Op. 47[c]. **Pierre Fournier** (vc); [ab]**Berlin Philharmonic Orchestra /** [a]**George Szell,** [b]**Alfred Wallenstein,** [c]**Jean Martinon.** DG Privilege Ⓓ 429 155-2GR (71 minutes: ADD: 5/90).

...Cello Concerto. **Elgar** Cello Concerto. **Maria Kliegel** (vc); **Royal Philharmonic Orchestra / Michael Halász.** Naxos Ⓢ 8 550503 (73 minutes: DDD: 9/92).

...Cello Concerto[a]. **Saint-Saëns** Cello Concerto No. 1 in A minor, Op. 33[b]. Le carnaval des animaux – Le cygne[c]. **Fauré** Elégie, Op. 24[d]. Berceuse, Op. 16[d]. **Debussy** Rêverie[d]. **Ravel** Pièce en forme de habanera[d]. **Pierre Fournier** (vc); [d]**Ernest Lush,** [c]**Gerald Moore** (pfs); **Philharmonia Orchestra /** [a]**Rafael Kubelík,** [b]**Walter Susskind.** Testament mono Ⓕ SBT1016* (77 minutes: ADD: 7/93).

...Cello Concerto[a]. Piano Concerto in G minor, B63[b]. [a]**Mstislav Rostropovich** (vc); [b]**František Maxián** (pf); **Czech Philharmonic Orchestra / Václav Talich.** Supraphon Historical mono Ⓜ 11 1901-2* (77 minutes: ADD: 3/94).

...Cello Concerto. Silent woods, B182. *Coupled with works by* **Delius, Elgar, Saint-Saëns, Schumann, Haydn, Monn, Chopin, Franck, Fauré, Bruch, Bach, Handel** and

Beethoven Jacqueline du Pré (vc) with various artists and orchestras. EMI Ⓑ CZS5 68132-2 (six discs: 437 minutes: ADD: 8/94). *See review in the Collections section; refer to the Index to Reviews.* ⒼⒼ

...Romance, B39[a]. Hussite, B132. Silent woods[b]. *Coupled with works by* **Fučík, Nedbal** and **Smetana** Malcolm Stewart (vn); Timothy Walden (vc); Alan Pendlebury (bn); Royal Liverpool Philharmonic Orchestra / Libor Pešek. Virgin Classics Ⓕ VC7 59285-2 (76 minutes: DDD: 11/94). *See review in the Collections section; refer to the Index to Reviews.*

...Cello Concerto. **Schumann** Cello Concerto in A minor, Op. 129. **Arto Noras** (vc); **Finnish Radio Symphony Orchestra / Sakari Oramo.** Finlandia Ⓕ 4509-98886-2 (64 minutes: DDD: 10/95).

...Cello Concerto in B minor, B191[a]. **Elgar** Cello Concerto in E minor, Op. 85[b]. Jacqueline du Pré (vc); [a]Chicago Symphony Orchestra / Daniel Barenboim; [b]London Symphony Orchestra / Sir John Barbirolli. EMI Ⓕ CDC5 55527-2 (72 minutes: ADD: 11/95). *The Elgar work is the same recording as the one reviewed under Elgar; refer to the Index to Reviews.* ⒼⒼⒼ

...Cello Concerto. *Coupled with works by* **Bach, Kodály, Dohnányi, Boccherini, Haydn, Schumann, Saint-Saëns, Fauré, Milhaud** and **Prokofiev.** János Starker (vc); Gerald Moore (pf); Philharmonia Orchestra / Carlo Maria Giulini, Walter Susskind. EMI mono/stereo Ⓜ CZS5 68485-2* (six discs: 398 minutes: ADD: 12/95). *See review in the Collections section; refer to the Index to Reviews.*

New review

Dvořák Cello Concerto in B minor, B191[a]. Symphony No. 9 in E minor, B178, "From the New World"[b]. [a]Pablo Casals (vc); Czech Philharmonic Orchestra / George Szell. Dutton Laboratories Essential Archive mono Ⓑ CDEA5002* (74 minutes: ADD: 1/96). Item marked [a] from HMV DB3288/92 (2/38), [b]HMV C2949/53 (12/37). Ⓖ

When there has been such an explosion in the field of historic recordings on CD, it is specially welcome that Dutton Laboratories, responsible for some of the most vivid transfers ever, have established an attendant bargain label, the Essential Archive. This issue, offering two recordings at a most attractive price, will, hopefully, tempt non-specialist collectors into investigating what magnetism the 78 era can hold for the music-lover. Casals's pioneering recording of the Cello Concerto is no stranger to CD and it has long been recognized as a classic of the recorded repertoire. Hailed in *Grove V* as "destined to mark a standard for generations" and described at the time as "seemingly played with a sword rather than a bow", it still exercises a powerful effect: the incandescent solo playing is mesmeric. Some of Casals's passionate quality may have been due to his decision to break out of his self-imposed restricted activities caused by the Spanish civil war: he had consented to appear with Szell in Prague and he was persuaded into making a recording the day after the concert. There is little to choose between the Dutton transfer and EMI's most recent one of the same performance, also using the Cedar process, with the Dutton marginally brighter and more forward. What makes this disc fascinating is having, instead of more Casals, the recording of the *New World* made in London by Szell and the Czech Philharmonic six months after the concerto. It is a bitingly powerful performance, crisp and intense, with pinpoint articulation, all the more valuable when Szell seems not to have returned to it in later commercial recordings. As Sir Compton Mackenzie (the first editor of *Gramophone*) said at the time, it is "trance-like" in the slow movement, having one forgetting the limited 78rpm dynamic range.

Additional recommendation ...

...Cello Concerto[a]. **Bruch** Kol Nidrei[b]. **Elgar** Cello Concerto in E minor, Op. 85[c]. **Pablo Casals** (vc); [a]Czech Philharmonic Orchestra / George Szell; [b]London Symphony Orchestra / Sir Landon Ronald; [c]BBC Symphony Orchestra / Sir Adrian Boult. EMI Références mono Ⓜ CDH7 63498-2* (75 minutes: ADD: 8/90). ⒼⒼ

Dvořák Cello Concerto in B minor, B191.

Tchaikovsky Variations on a Rococo Theme, Op. 33. **Mstislav Rostropovich** (vc); **Berlin Philharmonic Orchestra / Herbert von Karajan.** DG The Originals Ⓜ 447 413-2GOR (60 minutes: ADD: 5/95). From 139044 (10/69). Recorded 1968. *Gramophone classical 100.* ⒼⒼⒼ

This splendid disc offers a coupling that has justifiably held its place in the catalogue at full price (both on LP and CD) for nearly 30 years. The upper surface of the CD itself is made to look like a miniature reproduction of the original yellow label LP – complete with light reflecting off the simulated black vinyl surface. As can be seen from the above, there have been a number of outstanding recordings of the Dvořák Concerto since this DG record was made, but none to match it for the warmth of lyrical feeling, the sheer strength of personality of the cello playing and the distinction of the partnership between Karajan and Rostropovich. Any moments of romantic licence from the latter, who is obviously deeply in love with the music, are set against Karajan's overall grip on the proceedings. The orchestral playing is superb. You have only to listen to the beautiful introduction of the secondary theme of the first movement by the Principal Horn to realize that the Berlin Philharmonic are going to match their illustrious soloist in eloquence, while Rostropovich's many moments of poetic introspection never for a moment interfere with the sense of a spontaneous forward flow. The recording from 1969 is as near perfect as any made by DG in that vintage analogue era. The CD transfer has freshened the original and gives the cello a highly realistic presence, and if the passionate *fortissimo* violins lose just a fraction in fullness, and there seems to be, comparably, just a slight loss of resonance in the bass, the sound picture has an impressively clear and vivid focus. In the coupled Tchaikovsky *Rococo* Variations, Rostropovich uses the published score rather than the original version. However, he plays with such a masterly combination of Russian fervour and elegance that any criticism is disarmed. The music itself continually demonstrates Tchaikovsky's astonishing lyrical fecundity, as one tune leads to another, all growing organically from the charming 'rococo' theme. The recording here is marvellously refined and the illusion of the artists sitting out beyond one's speakers is very real indeed. The description 'legendary' is not a whit too strong for a mid-price reissue of this calibre.

Dvořák Violin Concerto in A minor, B108. Romance in F minor, B39. **Kyung-Wha Chung** (vn); **Philadelphia Orchestra / Riccardo Muti.** EMI Ⓕ CDC7 49858-2 (47 minutes: DDD: 11/89). Recorded 1988.

Considering the popularity of his Cello Concerto, Dvořák's Violin Concerto has never quite caught on with the general public. But a top class performance can convince us that the neglect is unfair. Kyung Wha Chung plays the concerto with the right blend of simplicity and brilliance, Slavonic warmth and folk-like quality, and the Philadelphia Orchestra under Riccardo Muti give her the right kind of support, unobtrusive enough to make us forget that the orchestral writing is not Dvořák at his most instrumentally imaginative, yet positive enough to provide more than just a discreet background. Ultimately, we probably enjoy the concerto most for its Bohemian lilt, a quality we feel in the violin's very first entry and that is present again in ample measure in the rondo finale – a movement of unfailingly dancing rhythm and considerable charm that here receives a sparkling performance. The delicately scored Romance in F minor that completes the programme is a slightly earlier work than the Violin Concerto and, it has been said, suggests a leisurely walk through the Bohemian countryside with someone who knows it well. The recorded sound is well defined and faithful, capturing Chung's fine tonal palette.

Additional recommendations ...

...Violin Concerto[a]. **Sibelius** Violin Concerto in D minor, Op. 47[b]. **Salvatore Accardo** (vn); [a]**Concertgebouw Orchestra;** [b]**London Symphony Orchestra / Sir Colin Davis.** Philips Silver Line Ⓜ 420 895-2PSL (68 minutes: ADD: 10/88).

...Violin Concerto. **Suk** Fantasy, Op. 24. **Josef Suk** (vn); **Czech Philharmonic Orchestra / Karel Ančerl.** Supraphon Crystal Collection Ⓑ 11 0601-2 (56 minutes: ADD: 9/89).

...Violin Concerto[a]. Romance, B39[a]. Carnival Overture. **Midori** (vn); **New York Philharmonic Orchestra / Zubin Mehta.** CBS Masterworks Ⓜ CD44923 (53 minutes: DDD: 11/89).

...Violin Concerto. **Bruch** Violin Concerto No. 1 in G minor, Op. 26. **Tasmin Little** (vn); **Royal Liverpool Philharmonic Orchestra / Vernon Handley.** Classics for Pleasure Ⓑ CD-CFP4566 (60 minutes: DDD: 7/90).

...Violin Concerto. Romance, B39. **Schumann** Violin Concerto in D minor, Op. posth. **Thomas Zehetmair** (vn); **Philharmonia Orchestra / Eliahu Inbal.** Teldec Ⓜ 4509-91444-2 (72 minutes: DDD: 7/93).

...Violin Concerto. **Glazunov** Violin Concerto in A minor, Op. 83. **Frank Peter Zimmermann** (vn); **London Philharmonic Orchestra / Franz Welser-Möst.** EMI Ⓕ CDC7 54872-2 (52 minutes: DDD: 3/94).

...Violin Concerto. **Lalo** Symphonie espagnole, Op. 21. **Christian Tetzlaff** (vn); **Czech Philharmonic Orchestra / Libor Pešek.** Virgin Classics Ⓕ VC5 45022 2 (63 minutes: DDD: 7/94).

...Romance, B39[a]. Ten Legends, B122. Nocturne in B major, B47. [a]**Stephanie Gonley** (vn); **English Chamber Orchestra / Sir Charles Mackerras.** EMI Eminence Ⓜ CD-EMX2232 (57 minutes: DDD: 3/95).

...Violin Concerto. Romance, B39. **Glazunov** Violin Concerto in A minor, Op. 82. **Ilya Kaler** (vn); **Polish National Radio Symphony Orchestra / Camilla Kolchinsky.** Naxos Ⓢ 8 550758 (63 minutes: DDD: 4/95).

...Violin Concerto[a]. Symphony No. 9 in E minor, B178, "From the New World". **Smetana** The bartered bride – Overture. [a]**Josef Suk** (vn); **Czech Philharmonic Orchestra / Karel Ančerl.** Orfeo Festspiel Dokumente mono Ⓕ C395951B* (78 minutes: ADD: 4/96).

New review

Dvořák Czech Suite, B93, Festival March, B88. The Hero's Song, B199, Hussite, B132. **Polish National Radio Symphony Orchestra / Antoni Wit.** Naxos Ⓢ 8 553005 (63 minutes: DDD: 8/95). Recorded 1993-4.

Wit's achievement, especially in the case of *The Hero's Song*, is considerable. This colourful, rather sprawling tone-poem was Dvořák's last orchestral work and is not an easy piece to bring off. Wit finds genuine nobility in it, while his gently, mellow way with the lovely *Czech Suite* also gives much pleasure. The opening "Praeludium" is just a touch sleepy, but there is no want of lyrical affection or rhythmic bounce elsewhere and the whole performance radiates an idiomatic, old-world charm that really is most appealing. As for the *Hussite* overture, Wit's clear-headed reading impressively combines dignity and excitement. Given such finely disciplined orchestral playing, the results are once again both eloquent and characterful. All of which just leaves the rousing *Festival March* of 1879, splendidly done here, with the excellent Katowice brass sounding quite resplendent in their introductory call-to-arms. Recordings throughout possess a most agreeable bloom and transparency.

Dvořák Overtures and Symphonic Poems – My home, B125a[a]. Hussite, B132[b]. In nature's realm, B168[b]. Carnival, B169[b]. Othello, B174[b]. The water goblin, B195[c]. The noon witch, B196[c]. The golden spinning-wheel, B197[d]. The wild dove, B198[d]. Symphonic Variations, B70[c]. **Bavarian Radio Symphony Orchestra / Rafael Kubelík.** DG Galleria Ⓜ 435 074-2GGA2 (two discs: 157 minutes: ADD: 11/91). Items marked [a] from 2530 593 (12/75), [b]2530 785 (2/78), [c]2530 712 (11/76), [d]2530 713 (11/76). Recorded 1973-6.   ⒼⒼⒼ

Writing about Richard Strauss's *Don Juan*, Tovey remarked that "programme music ... either coheres as music or it does not". Perhaps Dvořák's symphonic poems have never attained the popularity of those by Richard Strauss because there are a few too many seams in his musical narrative. Equally, the gruesome local folk ballads on which they are based (and which Dvořák gleefully brings to life) afforded him less range for depth of human characterization. But there are lots of good reasons to value them. There's his inimitable stream of heart-easing melody, and alongside the obvious debt to Liszt and Wagner, their harmonic boldness and magical instrumental effects look forward to Suk, Martinů and Janáček. Indeed, in the central section of *The golden spinning-wheel*, where the wheel and assorted paraphernalia are offered to the false queen in return for the various dismembered portions of the heroine's body, the repeated patterns on muted strings sound like pure Janáček. And the exquisite closing pages of *The wild dove* could be the best thing Martinů ever wrote. Also written when Dvořák was at the height of his power (in the 1890s), these two mid-priced discs offer the chance to hear his three concert overtures – *In nature's realm*, *Carnival* and *Othello* – as he originally conceived them: a thematically linked three movement 'symphonic' work on the theme of nature, life and love. The earlier and no less worthy *Symphonic Variations* and *My home* and *Hussite* overtures complete a set that would be fine value in terms of minutes for your money even if the performances were mediocre. As it is you won't find a finer account at any price. Knowing when to keep this music on the move is the secret of Kubelík's success, but the mobility is always marked by freshness of spirit rather than plain drive. The whole set is informed with his burning belief in the value of the music and his experience is drawing precisely what he wants from his own Bavarian players. DG's mid-1970s recordings project this with clarity and coherence and need fear nothing from more recent digital contenders.

Additional recommendations ...

...The golden spinning-wheel. The water goblin. Othello. Scherzo capriccioso, B131. **London Symphony Orchestra / István Kertész.** Decca Ovation Ⓜ 425 060-2DM (73 minutes: ADD).

...Symphonic Variations. The noon witch. Serenade in D minor, Op. 44. Hussite. **London Symphony Orchestra / István Kertész.** Decca Ovation Ⓜ 425 061-2DM (76 minutes: ADD).

...In Nature's Realm. Carnival. Othello. Scherzo capriccioso. **Ulster Orchestra / Vernon Handley.** Chandos Ⓕ CHAN8453 (53 minutes: DDD: 7/86).

...The water goblin. Piano Concerto in G minor, B63[a]. [a]**Jenö Jandó** (pf); **Polish National Radio Symphony Orchestra / Antoni Wit.** Naxos Ⓢ 8 550896 (62 minutes: DDD: 12/94).

Dvořák Slavonic Dances, B83 and B147. **Vienna Philharmonic Orchestra / André Previn.** Philips Ⓕ 442 125-2PH (71 minutes: DDD: 10/94). Recorded 1993.   Ⓖ

New review

Dvořák Slavonic Dances, B83 and B147. **Russian National Orchestra / Mikhail Pletnev.** DG Ⓕ 447 056-2GH (72 minutes: DDD: 11/95). *Selected by Soundings.*

Previn, with his rhythmic flair, brings out the playfulness of the *Slavonic Dances* as few others do. One is regularly reminded of the proximity of Dvořák's Bohemia to Vienna, when in the warm Musikverein acoustic, these dances become first cousins to the waltzes and polkas of the Strauss family. Previn also brings out more than his rivals the many warm cello descants which normally go unnoticed, but which here surge up in rich, yet transparent, textures. The energetic dances, too, regularly bring a rush of adrenalin at the climaxes, such as one gets from this orchestra every New Year's Day. In their different ways Szell and Dohnányi (listed below, both with the Cleveland Orchestra on peak form) are fiercer than Previn in such *Furiant* dances as Nos. 1 and 8, with their respective recordings adding weight of sound. Yet helped by the acoustic, Previn has more light and shade, and sounds just as easily idiomatic, if anything more so than Dohnányi, for whom the Cleveland Orchestra respond almost too precisely. Though Dohnányi's *allegros* and *prestos* are generally a shade brisker than Previn's, it is the reverse with the slower tempos, where Previn keeps the music flowing more, so that the *Lento grazioso* of the final dance, No. 8 in A flat of the second group, keeps its dance overtones.

Though Pletnev has Slavonic musicians, the results are not quite traditionally Czech, with refinement and crispness of ensemble the keynotes rather than earthier qualities. His is a distinctive and highly enjoyable version of Dvořák's colourful dances. These are, after all, works which for all their lack of pretension are open to all kinds of subtleties of interpretation, with different views totally valid. At times with such refined playing one might even dub Pletnev's approach as Mozartian, with elegance a regular element, and with even the wildest *furiants* kept under control. The crispness of ensemble and clarity of texture give a sharpness of focus that avoids any idea that these are performances lacking in bite, though after the Previn one might well feel they are on the cool side, with the extrovert joy of the music rather underplayed. So the Dumka lament of the second dance is lighter and cooler than with Previn, charming rather than warmly expressive. Dynamic contrasts are sharply defined through all the dances, and Pletnev and his Russian players consistently make one marvel at the beauty of the instrumentation. Like the Previn version, but in a totally different way, this is a disc to give a fresh view of well-loved music.

Additional recommendations ...

...Slavonic Dances, B78 and B145. **Artur Balsam, Gena Raps** (pf, four hands). Arabesque Ⓕ Z6559 (63 minutes: 3/87).

...Slavonic Dances, B83 and B147. **Rheineland-Pfalz State Philharmonic Orchestra / Leif Segerstam.** BIS Ⓕ CD425 (78 minutes: DDD: 7/89).

...Slavonic Dances, B83 and B147. **Cleveland Orchestra / Christoph von Dohnányi.** Decca Ⓕ 430 171-2DH (74 minutes: DDD: 12/90).

...Slavonic Dances, B83 and B147. Carnival – Overture, B169. **Czech Philharmonic Orchestra / Václav Talich.** Slavonic Dances. **Czech Philharmonic Orchestra / Václav Talich.** Music and Arts mono Ⓕ CD658* (75 minutes: AAD: 6/92).

...Slavonic Dance, B147 (arr. Clements). Serenade in D minor, B77. **Krommer** Partita in E flat major, Op. 45[a]. **Mysliveček** Octet in E flat major. [a]**Charles Kavalovski,** [a]**Scott Brubaker** (hns); **New York Harmonie Ensemble / Steven Richman.** Music and Arts Ⓕ CD691 (59 minutes: DDD: 8/92).

...Slavonic Dances, B83 and B147. **Cleveland Orchestra / George Szell.** Sony Classical Essential Classics Ⓑ SBK48161 (74 minutes: ADD: 11/92).

...Slavonic Dances, B83 and B147. **Berlin Radio Symphony Orchestra / Karel Ančerl.** Tahra mono Ⓕ TAH118* (70 minutes: DDD: 11/95).

Dvořák Complete Symphonies and Orchestral Works. **London Symphony Orchestra / István Kertész.** Decca Ⓑ 430 046-2DC6 (six discs: 431 minutes: ADD: 4/92). Recorded 1963-66. Symphonies – No. 1 in C minor, B9, "The Bells of Zlonice" (from SXL6288, 10/67); No. 2 in B flat major, B12 (SXL6289, 9/67); No. 3 in E flat major, B34 (SXL6290, 5/67); No. 4 in D minor, B41 (SXL6257, 4/67); No. 5 in F major, B54 (SXL6273, 3/67); No. 6 in D major, B112 (SXL6253, 11/66); No. 7 in D minor, B141; No. 8 in G major, B163 (SXL6044, 7/63); No. 9 in C minor, B178, "From the New World" (SXL6291, 11/67). Scherzo capriccioso, B131 (SXL6348, 7/63). Overtures – In nature's realm, B168 (SXL6290, 5/67); Carnival, B169 (SXL6253, 11/66); My home, B125*a* (SXL6273, 3/67).   ⒼⒼ

István Kertész recorded the Dvořák symphonies during the mid-1960s and his integral cycle was quick to achieve classic status, with his exhilarating and vital account of the Eighth Symphony (the first to be recorded in February 1963) rapidly becoming a special landmark in the catalogue. The original LPs, with their distinctive Breughel reproduction sleeves are now collectors' items in their own right, but these magnificent interpretations became available again in 1992, in glitteringly refined digitally remastered sound, and it is a tribute to the memory of this tragically short-lived conductor that this cycle continues to set the standard by which all others are judged. Kertész was the first conductor to attract serious collectors to the early Dvořák symphonies which, even today are not performed as often as they should be; and his jubilant advocacy of the unfamiliar First Symphony, composed in the composer's twenty-fourth year, has never been superseded. This work offers surprising insights into the development of Dvořák's mature style, as does the Second Symphony. Kertész shows that Symphonies Nos. 3 and 4 have much more earthy resilience than many commentators might have us believe, insisting that Dvořák's preoccupation with the music of Wagner and Liszt had reached its zenith during this period. The challenging rhetoric of the Fourth has never found a more glorious resolution than here, with Kertész drawing playing of gripping intensity from the London Symphony Orchestra. The Fifth Symphony, and to a still greater extent, its glorious successor, Symphony No. 6, both reveal Dvořák's clear affinity with the music of Brahms. Kertész's superb reading of the Sixth, however, shows just how individual and naturally expressive this underrated work actually is, whilst the playing in the great climax of the opening movement and the vigorous final peroration remains tremendously exciting, even almost 30 years after the recording first appeared. In the great final trilogy, Kertész triumphs nobly with the craggy resilience of the Seventh Symphony, and his buoyant ardour brings a dynamic thrust and momentum to the Eighth Symphony, whereas his New World is by turns indomitable and searchingly lyrical. The six-disc set also offers assertive and brilliant readings of the Overtures Carnival, In nature's realm and the rarely heard My home, together with a lucid and heroic account of the Scherzo capriccioso. These definitive performances have been skilfully reprocessed, the sound is astonishingly good, even by modern standards, and the playing of the London Symphony Orchestra is often daringly brilliant under the charismatic direction of one of this century's late-lamented masters of the podium.

Additional recommendations ...

...Nos. 1-9. **Royal Scottish Orchestra / Vernon Handley.** Chandos Ⓜ CHAN9008/13 (six discs: 378 minutes: DDD).

...Symphonies Nos. 1-9[a]. Scherzo capriccioso[b]. Carnival[b]. The wild dove[b]. [a]**Berlin Philharmonic Orchestra;** [b]**Bavarian Radio Symphony Orchestra / Rafael Kubelík.** DG Ⓜ 423 120-2GX6 (six discs: 425 minutes: ADD: 10/88).   ⒼⒼ

...No. 1. The Hero's Song, B199. **Scottish National Orchestra / Neeme Järvi.** Chandos Ⓕ CHAN8597 (74 minutes: DDD: 4/89).

...No. 2. Slavonic Rhapsody in A flat major, B86 No. 3. **Scottish National Orchestra / Neeme Järvi.** Chandos Ⓕ CHAN8589 (61 minutes: DDD: 7/88).

…No. 3. Carnival. Symphonic Variations. **Scottish National Orchestra / Neeme Järvi.** Chandos
Ⓕ CHAN8575 (63 minutes: DDD: 5/88).

…No. 4. Ten Biblical Songs, B185[a]. [a]**Brian Rayner Cook** (bar); **Scottish National Orchestra / Neeme
Järvi.** Chandos Ⓕ CHAN8608 (68 minutes: DDD: 12/88).

Dvořák Symphony No. 5 in F major, B54. Othello, B174. Scherzo capriccioso, B131. **Oslo
Philharmonic Orchestra / Mariss Jansons.** EMI Ⓕ CDC7 49995-2 (64 minutes: DDD: 7/90).
Recorded 1989.

Of all the romantic composers, it is probably Dvořák who best evokes a sunlit, unspoiled and
relatively untroubled picture of nineteenth-century country life. Light and warmth radiate from his
Fifth Symphony, composed in just six weeks of the year 1875 when he was in his early thirties. It has
been called his "Pastoral Symphony", and it is easy to see why, especially in a performance as fresh
and sunny as this one. Mariss Jansons brings out all the expressiveness and heart of the music without
exaggerating the good spirits and playful humour that are so characteristic of the composer, and one
would single out for praise the fine wind playing of the Oslo Philharmonic Orchestra (and not least
its golden-toned horns) were it not for the fact that the strings are no less satisfying. The lyrical
Andante con moto brings out the fine interplay of the instrumental writing, the bouncy *Scherzo* is
uninhibited without going over the top and the exciting finale has plenty of momentum. The other
two pieces are also nicely done, the *Scherzo capriccioso* having both lilt and vigour and the rarely
played *Othello* overture (a late work) being a suitably dramatic response to Shakespeare's tragedy. The
recording is warm and clear.

Additional recommendation …

…No. 5. The water goblin. **Scottish National Orchestra / Neeme Järvi.** Chandos Ⓕ CHAN8552
(61 minutes: DDD: 12/87). *Selected by Sounds in Retrospect.*

Dvořák Symphony No. 6 in D major, B112.
Janáček Taras Bulba. **Cleveland Orchestra / Christoph von Dohnányi.** Decca Ⓕ 430 204-2DH
(66 minutes: DDD: 7/91). Recorded 1989.   ⒼⒼ

With its obvious echoes of Brahms's Second Symphony, the Sixth Symphony is a work which, for all
its pastoral overtones, gains from refined playing, and quite apart from the imaculate ensemble, the
Cleveland violins play ethereally, as in the melody at the start of the slow movement. Dohnányi does
not miss the earthy qualities of the writing either, and the impact of the performance is greatly
enhanced by the fullness and weight of the recording. This is altogether a superb account. There is
also the bonus of an unusual makeweight, *Taras Bulba*. The account here is very Viennese in style and
warmly expressive against its opulent background. However, if Janáček is your first priority, then
Mackerras's version, coupled with the *Sinfonietta* (refer to the Index to Reviews) is the obvious choice,
for he characterfully persuades his truly Viennese musicians to sound more like Czechs, playing
brilliantly with a sharp attack very apt for the composer's music. But those who want a radiant
account of the Dvořák will find comparable joy in the characterful Janáček rhapsody.

Additional recommendations …

…No. 6. My Home. Hussite. Carnival. **Czech Philharmonic Orchestra / Karel Ančerl.** Supraphon
Ⓕ 11 1926-2 (75 minutes: ADD).   Ⓖ

…No. 6. **Suk** Serenade in E flat major, Op. 6. **Czech Philharmonic Orchestra / Václav Talich.** Koch
Legacy mono Ⓕ 37060-2* (72 minutes: AAD: 1/92).   Ⓖ

…No. 6. The wild dove. **Czech Philharmonic Orchestra / Jiří Bělohlávek.** Chandos Ⓕ CHAN9170
(63 minutes: DDD: 11/93).

Dvořák Symphonies – No. 7 in D minor, B141; No. 8 in G major, B163. **Oslo Philharmonic
Orchestra / Mariss Jansons.** EMI Ⓕ CDC7 54663-2 (74 minutes: DDD: 6/93). Recorded 1992.
Gramophone Editor's choice.   Ⓖ

Dvořák Symphonies – No. 7 in D minor, B141; No. 9 in E minor, B178, "From the New World".
London Philharmonic Orchestra / Sir Charles Mackerras. EMI Eminence Ⓜ CD-EMX2202
(79 minutes: DDD: 2/93). Recorded 1991.

Mariss Jansons's popular pairing makes most agreeable listening. With clean-cut playing from the fine
Oslo orchestra and natural, unexaggerated sonics, these are engagingly alive, refreshingly energetic
readings, if not quite as warm-hearted or openly affectionate as some Dvořákians might like.
Jansons's sophisticated sense of texture impresses throughout, however, and the outer movements of
No. 8 in particular emerge with genuinely vivid freshness. Jansons's clean-heeled direction brings with
it a certain endearing spontaneity and rhythmic resilience that will undoubtedly give pleasure. Sir
Charles Mackerras's long-standing authority in the Czech repertoire is of course well-known by now,
so his thoughts are not to be dismissed lightly, especially when, at nearly 80 minutes, Nos. 7 and 9
make a terrifically generous pairing. In the tragic Seventh, Mackerras concentrates largely on the
more endearingly lyrical side of Dvořák's invention; in this respect both inner movements are
particularly memorable in their open-hearted grace and charm. However, those who (rightly) crave a
greater degree of intensity and symphonic rigour in the two great flanking outer movements such as
one encounters with rival interpreters will perhaps come away not quite so satisfied. Similarly, this
New World is an affectingly unfussy traversal. The slow movement glows ravishingly at an
exceptionally broad tempo, and in the finale Mackerras draws Dvořák's structural threads together

with undemonstrative cogency. Overall, this is undoubtedly a fine account, if not quite as winningly spontaneous an experience as Kubelík's famous BPO recording for DG (reviewed below). With all that, Mackerras's are still warmly affectionate readings, superbly played and resplendently recorded. At mid-price the value is obvious.

Additional recommendations ...

...Nos. 7 and 8. **Czech Philharmonic Orchestra / Václav Talich.** Koch International Classics Legacy mono Ⓕ 37007-2* (ADD).

...Nos. 7 and 8. **Cleveland Orchestra / Christoph von Dohnányi.** Decca Ovation Ⓜ 430 728-2DM (73 minutes: DDD: 12/91).

...Nos. 7 and 8. **London Symphony Orchestra / Antál Dorati.** Mercury Living Presence Ⓜ 434 312-2MM (71 minutes: ADD). ⒼⒼ

...No. 8. Scherzo capriccioso. Legends, Op. 59 Nos. 4, 6 and 7. **Hallé Orchestra / Sir John Barbirolli.** EMI Phoenixa Ⓜ CDM7 64193-2* (61 minutes: ADD: 6/92). ⒼⒼ

...Nos. 7 and 9. **Royal Concertgebouw Orchestra / Carlo Maria Giulini.** Sony Classical Ⓜ SX2K58946 (two discs: 91 minutes: DDD: 11/94).

...No. 7[c], Piano Concerto in G minor, B63[a]. Cello Concerto in B minor, B191[b]. Slavonic Dances, B83 and B147[b] – No. 9 in B major; No. 16 in A flat major. [a]**František Maxián** (pf); [b]**Mstislav Rostropovich** (vc); [b]**Toronto Symphony Orchestra;** [ac]**Hessian Radio Orchestra, Frankfurt,** [d]**Czech Philharmonic Orchestra / Karel Ančerl.** Tahra Ⓕ TAH136/7 (two discs:153 minutes: ADD: 3/96).

Dvořák Symphony No. 8 in G major, B163. Symphonic Variations, B70. **London Philharmonic Orchestra / Sir Charles Mackerras.** EMI Eminence Ⓜ CD-EMX2216 (60 minutes: DDD: 4/94). Recorded 1992. Ⓖ

This is an unmissable account of the Eighth Symphony. Mackerras realizes all the score's indications of shading, pointing and phrasing, or to put it another way, all its elegance and bittersweet ambiguity. In this, amongst the listed comparisons above, he has no peers. He has a spirited and willing LPO in the palm of his guiding, illuminating hand. Articulation and emphasis are consistently light, and not only in the energetic tuttis In the flute solo some 40 seconds into the first movement the LPO principal, without disturbing the tranquillity of the scene, animates the solo to suggest birdsong (all the solo and ensemble flute work on the Mackerras disc is outstanding). It is this wide range of pictoral suggestion and emotion, and an orchestra audibly fired up by the occasion, that mark Mackerras's performance of the Symphony as an example of great Dvořák conducting. Has anybody, one wonders, made as much of the contrast between the joyous pealing of bells and fanfares that end the first appearance of the slow movement's second subject, and the abrupt hush for its chorale-like conclusion, as if the traveller has suddenly entered the dark interior of a church and encountered a solemn procession. And revelation follows revelation: you can't fail to notice the tension as the *ppp* strings prepare for the anguished transformation of the movement's opening theme. Mackerras relaxes in the *Symphonic Variations* but keeps the work flowing along and gives as fine a performance of this work as you are likely to hear. The Eminence sound for Mackerras (from London's Henry Wood Hall), is immediate and lively, with a wider dynamic range.

Additional recommendations ...

...No. 8. **Janáček** Sinfonietta, Op. 60. **New York Philharmonic Orchestra / Kurt Masur.** Teldec Ⓕ 4509-90847-2 (63 minutes: DDD: 12/94).

...No. 8. The noon witch. **Berlin Philharmonic Orchestra / Claudio Abbado.** Sony Classical Ⓕ SK64303 (51 minutes: DDD: 2/95).

...No. 8. **Franck** Symphony in D minor. **Haydn** Symphony No. 92 in G major, "Oxford". **Prokofiev** Symphony No. 1 in D major, Op. 25, "Classical". **Concertgebouw Orchestra / Karel Ančerl.** Tahra Ⓕ TAH124/5 (two discs: 116 minutes: ADD: 3/96).

New review

Dvořák Symphonies – No. 8 in G major, B163; No. 9 in E minor, B178, "From the New World". **Berlin Philharmonic Orchestra / Rafael Kubelík.** DG The Originals Ⓜ 447 412-2GOR (73 minutes: ADD). From 2720 066 (10/73). Recorded 1972. *Gramophone classical 100.* ⒼⒼⒼ

These accounts are quite magnificent and their claims on the allegiance of collectors remain strong. They have the kind of freshness and vigour that remind one of what it was like to hear these symphonies for the first time. The atmosphere is authentic in feeling and the sense of nature seems to be uncommonly acute. Kubelík has captured the enthusiasm of his players here and generates a sense of excitement and poetry. The playing of the Berlin Philharmonic is marvellously eloquent throughout and, as is so often the case, a joy in itself. The woodwinds phrase with great poetic feeling and imagination though, come to that, all the departments of this great orchestra respond with sensitivity and virtuosity. The recording has great dynamic range and encompasses the most featherweight string *pianissimos* to the fullest orchestral tutti without discomfort. The listener is placed well back in the hall so that the woodwind, though they blend beautifully, may seem a little too recessed for some tastes, though it should be said that there is no lack of vividness, power or impact. The balance and the timbre of each instrument is natural and truthful; nothing is made larger than life and Kubelík has a natural warmth and flexibility In so competitive a market as these, it would be wrong to speak of any single recording as a first choice but this will always remain high in any list of recommendations for it has a vernal freshness that is wholly reviving.

Additional recommendation ...

...Nos. 7-9[a]. The wild dove[b]. **Smetana** Má vlast – Vltava, B111[c]. [a]**Berlin Philharmonic Orchestra,** [b]**Bavarian Radio Symphony Orchestra;** [c]**Boston Symphony Orchestra / Rafael Kubelík.** DG Double Ⓜ 439 663-2GX2 (two discs: 146 minutes: ADD). *These are the same recordings as those reviewed above.*   ⒼⒼⒼ

Dvořák Symphony No. 9 in E minor, B178, "From the New World"[a]. American Suite[b]. [a]**Vienna Philharmonic Orchestra / Kyrill Kondrashin;** [b]**Royal Philharmonic Orchestra / Antál Dorati.** Decca Ⓜ 430 702-2DM (63 minutes: DDD: 8/91). Item marked [a] from SXDL7510 (7/80), [b]410 735-2DH2 (3/85). Recorded 1979-83.   ⒼⒼ
Kondrashin's *New World* caused something of a sensation when originally transferred to CD. Here was a supreme example of the clear advantages of the new medium over the old and the metaphor of a veil being drawn back between listener and performers could almost be extended to a curtain: the impact and definition of the sound is quite remarkable and the acoustic of the Sofiensaal in Vienna are presented as quite ideal for this score. The upper strings have brilliance without edginess, the brass – with characteristically bright VPO trumpets – has fine sonority as well as great presence, the bass is firm, full and rich and the ambience brings luminosity and bloom to the woodwind without clouding.

Additional recommendations ...

...No. 9. My home. In nature's realm. **Czech Philharmonic Orchestra / Karel Ančerl.** Supraphon Great Artists Series Ⓕ 11 1242-2 (64 minutes: ADD).

...No. 9. Symphonic Variations. **London Philharmonic Orchestra / Zdenek Macal.** Classics for Pleasure Ⓑ CD-CFP9006 (66 minutes: DDD: 9/87).

...No. 9. **Suk** Serenade in E major, Op. 6. **Czech Philharmonic Orchestra / Václav Talich.** Supraphon Historical mono Ⓜ 11 1899-2* (71 minutes: AAD: 2/94).

New review

Dvořák Piano Quintet in A major, B155[a]. String Quintet in G major, B49[b]. **Gaudier Ensemble** (Marieke Blankestijn, Lesley Hatfield, vns; Iris Juda, va; Christoph Marks, vc; [b]Stephen William, db; [a]Susan Tomes, pf). Hyperion Ⓕ CDA66796 (66 minutes: DDD: 4/96). Recorded 1995.   ⒼⒼ
The Dvořák Piano Quintet has received a high-powered performance from Menahem Pressler and the Emerson Quartet (reviewed below). The pianist on the Gaudier's disc is Susan Tomes, who matches even Pressler in imagination, encouraging a performance lighter than that for DG, full of mercurial contrasts that seem entirely apt. For example, in the second movement *Dumka* there is more light and shade, and the *Scherzo* sparkles even more, leading to a jaunty, exuberant finale. The G major String Quintet, the earliest of the two which Dvořák wrote, the one with extra double-bass, is similarly lighter than the Chilingirian and Coull Quartets (reviewed and listed below). If slower speeds and less crisp ensemble make the Coull version seem too heavy, the Chilingirian one is just as strongly characterized as the Gaudier, with a firmer, fuller tone. Marieke Blankestijn's violin is thinner than Levon Chilingirian's, but it can be just as beautiful, as in the lovely high-floating second subject of the slow movement. Altogether a fine disc, if this coupling appeals.

Dvořák Piano Quintet in A major, B155[a]. Piano Quartet No. 2 in E flat major, B162. **Menahem Pressler** (pf); **Emerson Quartet** (Eugene Drucker, [a]Philip Setzer, vns; Lawrence Dutton, va; David Finckel, vc). DG Ⓕ 439 868-2GH (75 minutes: DDD: 9/94). Recorded 1993.   ⒼⒼ
If the Piano Quintet, with its wealth of memorable melody, is by far the better-known, Pressler and the Emersons demonstrate how the Piano Quartet, sketched immediately after the other work and completed two years later in 1889, is just as rich in invention, in some ways even more distinctive in its thematic material. If there is one movement that above all proves a revelation, it is the *Lento* of the Quartet. Opening with a duet for cello and piano, it is here played with a rapt, hushed concentration to put it among the very finest of Dvořák inspirations. The following *grazioso* movement, almost like a Viennese waltz, is then given a delicious schmaltzy flavour, with one whole-tone motif particularly striking, not to mention another passage where the piano is made to sound like a musical-box. The performance of the Quintet, too, is comparably positive in its characterization. Many will prefer the easier, even warmer reading from Domus in the Piano Quartet (see below), which is neatly if not so generously coupled with the much earlier Piano Quartet in D, B53. In this music it is not always the high-powered reading that makes its mark most persuasively, and the Hyperion sound for Domus is far warmer than the DG New York recording for this disc, which gives an unpleasant edge to high violins, making the full ensemble abrasive. None the less, if the volume is curbed, one can readily enjoy these passionate and intense accounts of two of Dvořák's most striking chamber works.

Additional recommendations ...

...Piano Quintets – A major, B28; B155. **Rudolf Firkušný** (pf); **Ridge Quartet.** RCA Victor Red Seal Ⓕ RD60436 (67 minutes: DDD: 7/92).

...Piano Quartets – No. 1 in D major, B53; No. 2. **Domus.** Hyperion Ⓕ CDA66287 (70 minutes: DDD: 3/89).   Ⓖ

...Piano Quintet in A major, B155. **Martinů** Piano Quintet No. 2. **Peter Frankl** (pf); **Lindsay Quartet.** ASV Ⓕ CDDCA889 (70 minutes: DDD: 6/94). Ⓖ

Dvořák String Quintets – G major, B49[a]; E flat major, B180[b]. Intermezzo in B major, B49[c].
Chilingirian Quartet (Levon Chilingirian, Mark Butler, vns; Louise Williams, va; Philip De Groote, vc); [b]**Simon Rowland-Jones** (va); [ac]**Duncan McTier** (db). Chandos Ⓕ CHAN9046 (69 minutes: DDD: 11/92). Recorded 1990-91.

Dvořák's G major String Quintet is a thoroughly engaging affair, winning first prize in a competition for new chamber works organized by the Prague Artistic Circle. Originally in five movements, Dvořák subsequently removed the "Intermezzo" second movement, revising and publishing it separately eight years later as the haunting *Nocturne* for string orchestra. Enterprisingly, this Chandos disc includes that "Intermezzo" in its original string quintet garb. The E flat Quintet from 1893, on the other hand, is a wholly mature masterpiece. Completed in just over two months during Dvořák's American sojourn, it replaces the double-bass of the earlier Quintet with the infinitely more subtle option of a second viola. Brimful of the most delightfully fresh, tuneful invention, the score also shares many melodic and harmonic traits with the popular *American* Quartet – its immediate predecessor. The Chilingirian Quartet, ideally abetted by double-bassist Duncan McTier and violist Simon Rowland-Jones, are enthusiastic, big-hearted proponents of all this lovely material, and the excellent Chandos recording offers both a realistic perspective and beguiling warmth.

Additional recommendations ...

...String Quintet, B180. String Sextet in A major, B80. **Raphael Ensemble.** Hyperion Ⓕ CDA66308 (65 minutes: DDD: 8/89).

...String Quintet, B180. String Sextet, B80. **Josef Suk** (va); **Josef Chuchro** (vc); **Smetana Quartet.** Supraphon Ⓕ 11 1469-2 (68 minutes: DDD: 9/93).

...String Quintet, B180[a]. Terzetto. Bagatelles. [a]**Patrick Ireland** (va); **Lindsay Quartet.** ASV Ⓕ CDDCA806 (69 minutes: DDD: 9/93).

...String Quintet, B180[a]. Intermezzo[a]. String Sextet, B80[b]. **Panocha Quartet;** [b]**Josef Klusoň** (va); [b]**Michal Kaňka** (vc); [a]**Pavel Nejtek** (db). Supraphon Ⓕ 11 1461-2 (71 minutes: DDD: 5/94). Ⓖ

... String Quintet, B180. String Sextet, B80. **Vienna String Sextet.** EMI Ⓕ CDC7 54543-2 (67 minutes: DDD: 10/94).

...String Quintet, B180[a]. Intermezzo, B49[a]. String Quartet No. 10 in E flat major, B92. **Coull Quartet;** [a]**Peter Buckoke** (db). Hyperion Ⓕ CDA66679 (78 minutes: DDD: 10/94).

...String Quintet, B49. Serenade in D minor, B77. **Chamber Music Society of the Lincoln Center / David Shifrin.** Delos Ⓕ DE3152 (66 minutes: DDD: 8/95).

New review

Dvořák String Quartets – No. 12 in F major, B179, "American"; No. 13 in G major, B192. **Vlach Quartet, Prague** (Jana Vlachová, Ondřej Kukal, vns; Petr Verner, va; Mikael Ericsson, vc). Naxos Ⓢ 8 553371 (69 minutes: DDD: 4/96).

On the face of it, the credentials of the Vlach Quartet of Prague would seem to be impeccable – the group's leader, Jana Vlachová, is the daughter of the great Josef Vlach – and, indeed, the players make a most pleasing impression on this vividly recorded Naxos coupling. They certainly produce a beguilingly rich, beautifully blended sound and bring to this music a big-hearted, songful fervour as well as textural mastery. What is more, Dvořák's characteristic, chugging cross-rhythms are handled with particular felicity. Interpretatively, their approach contrasts strongly with other readings in that the Vlach team adopt a coaxing, lyrically expressive stance (with the gorgeous slow movement of the *American* a highlight). In the case of the masterly G major Quartet, these gifted newcomers show fresh insights (they are especially perceptive in those wistful reminiscences at the heart of the finale). All in all, this enjoyable Naxos offering represents a real bargain.

Additional recommendations ...

...No. 12. **Schubert** String Quartet No. 14 in D minor, D810, "Death and the Maiden". **Borodin** String Quartet No. 2 in D major – Notturno. **Quartetto Italiano.** Philips Silver Line Ⓜ 420 876-2PSL (75 minutes: ADD: 3/89).

...String Quartets – No. 1 in A major, B8. No. 2 in B flat major, B17. No. 3 in D major, B18. No. 4 in E minor, B19. No. 5 in F minor, B37. No. 6 in A minor, B40. No. 7 in A minor, B45. No. 8 in E major, B57. No. 9 in D minor, B75. No. 10 in E flat major, B92. No. 11 in C major, B121. No. 12. No. 13 in G major, B192. No. 14 in A flat major, B193. F major, B120 (Fragment). Cypresses, B152. Quartettsatz. Two Waltzes, B105. **Prague Quartet.** DG Ⓑ 429 193-2GCM9 (nine discs: 589 minutes: ADD: 8/90). ⒼⒼⒼ

...No. 12. **Barber** String Quartet, Op. 11. **Glass** String Quartet No. 1. **Duke Quartet.** Collins Classics Ⓕ 1386-2 (61 minutes: DDD: 1/94). Ⓠ

...No. 12. Piano Quintet in A major, B155[a]. **Janáček** String Quartet No. 1, "The Kreutzer Sonata". [a]**Pavel Štěpán** (pf); **Smetana Quartet.** Testament Ⓕ SBT1074 (79 minutes: ADD: 3/96). *See review in the Collections section; refer to the Index to Reviews.* ⒼⒼ

...No. 14. Terzetto in C major, B148. **Janáček** String Quartet No. 2, "Intimate Letters". **Smetana Quartet.** Testament Ⓕ SBT1075 (77 minutes: ADD: 3/96). *See review in the Collections section; refer to the Index to Reviews.* ⒼⒼ

...Nos. 12 and 13. **Vlach Quartet, Prague.** Naxos Ⓢ 8 553371 (69 minutes: DDD: 4/96).

Dvořák Piano Trios – No. 1 in B flat major, B51; No. 2 in G minor, B56. **Borodin Trio** (Rotislav Dubinsky, vn; Yuli Turovsky, vc; Luba Edlina, pf). Chandos Ⓕ CHAN9172 (75 minutes: DDD: 11/93). Recorded 1992.   Ⓖ

Of Dvořák's six piano trios, only four survive, and only two are at all familiar to most listeners. These here are the other two, written in 1875 and 1876 when he was in his mid-thirties. They are delightful works, even if they cannot match the quality of the F minor Trio and the *Dumky*; and are given splendid advocacy by the Borodin Trio, who sense their quality while not overstating claims. That is to say, the players do not try to milk the fine slow movements for more emotion than they actually contain, and by playing them with sensitivity and a light touch manage to draw the most from them. The two scherzos are similarly given a lively spring but not any kind of forced hilarity: they are in fact quite gentle movements. Luba Edlina opens the B flat Trio with a beautifully delicate exposition of the melody arpeggiated in a manner instantly recognizable as by Dvořák. These are attractive works, attractively played.

Dvořák Piano Trios – No. 3 in F minor, B130; No. 4 in E minor, B166, "Dumky". **Barcelona Trio** (Gerard Claret, vn; Lluís Claret, vc; Albert G. Attenelle, pf). Harmonia Mundi Ⓕ HMC90 1404 (70 minutes: DDD: 11/92). Recorded 1991.

There are considerably more recorded versions of the *Dumky* Trio than of its F minor forerunner which dates from nine years earlier. Obviously collectors prefer their Dvořák in national dress. The richly romantic F minor work comes primarily as a reminder of Dvořák's profound admiration for Brahms, who so gallantly championed his cause to the publisher, Simrock, when life was still an uphill struggle. The Barcelona Trio play it with loving care for textural detail while at the same time effortlessly sustaining tension throughout each movement's larger span. The *Dumky* was the last of his piano trios, written in 1891 at the age of 50. Before leaving for America the following year he and the violinist, Ferdinand Lachner, and the cellist, Hanuš Wihan, undertook a farewell concert tour of some 40 towns in his beloved Bohemia and Moravia with the *Dumky* always their central work. The sharp alternations of melancholy and dance-like gaiety giving this folk-genre its special character are met with splendid intensity and abandon by the Barcelona team.

Additional recommendation ...

...No. 4 in E minor, "Dumky", B166. **Smetana** Piano Trio in G minor, B104. **Rostislav Dubinsky** (vn); **Yuli Turovsky** (vc); **Luba Edlina** (pf). Chandos Ⓕ CHAN8445 (68 minutes: DDD: 5/86).

Dvořák Stabat mater[a]. Psalm 149. [a]**Lívia Aghová** (sop); [a]**Marga Schiml** (contr); [a]**Aldo Baldin** (ten); [a]**Luděk Vele** (bass); [a]**Prague Children's Choir; Prague Philharmonic Choir; Czech Philharmonic Orchestra / Jiří Bělohlávek.** Chandos Ⓕ CHAN8985/6 (two discs: 96 minutes: DDD: 2/92). Notes, texts and translations included. Recorded 1991.

The *Stabat mater* is a thirteenth-century Christian poem in Latin describing the Virgin Mary standing at the foot of the Cross. It has been set to music by many Catholic composers from Palestrina to Penderecki, and Dvořák's version, first heard in Prague in 1880, soon went on to other countries including Britain, where it had a number of cathedral performances and one in the Royal Albert Hall in London in 1884 that was conducted by the composer himself and used a choir of over 800 singers – "the impression of such a mighty body was indeed enchanting", he wrote. Its ten sections are well laid out for the different vocal and instrumental forces and so avoid the monotony which might seem inherent in a contemplative and deeply sombre text. This performance was recorded by Chandos with Czech forces in Prague Castle, and in it we feel the full dignity and drama of the work, an oratorio in all but name. The four solo singers convey genuine fervour and one feels that their sound, which is quite unlike that of British singers, must be akin to what the composer originally imagined. If they are a touch operatic, that doesn't sound misplaced and they perform well together, as in the second verse quartet "Quis est homo". The choral singing is no less impressive, and indeed the whole performance under Bělohlávek gets the balance right between reverent simplicity and intensity of feeling. Psalm 149 is a setting of "Sing unto the Lord a new song" for chorus and orchestra and its celebratory mood provides a fine complement to the other work.

Additional recommendations ...

...Stabat mater. Ten Legends, Op. 59[a]. **Soloists; Bavarian Radio Chorus and Symphony Orchestra;** [a]**English Chamber Orchestra / Rafael Kubelík.** DG 2CD Serie Ⓜ 453 025-2GTA2 (two discs: 128 minutes: ADD: 9/90).

...Stabat mater, B71. **Soloists; Oregon Bach Festival Choir and Orchestra / Helmuth Rilling.** Hänssler Classic Ⓕ 98 935 (two discs: 87 minutes: DDD: 8/96).

New review

Dvořák Rusalka. **Milada Subrtová** (sop) Rusalka; **Eduard Haken** (bass) Watergnome; **Marie Ovčačíková** (contr) Witch; **Ivo Zídek** (ten) Prince; **Alena Míková** (mez) Foreign Princess; **Jadwiga Wysoczanská** (sop) First Woodsprite; **Eva Hlobilová** (sop) Second Woodsprite; **Věra Krilová** (contr) Third Woodsprite; **Ivana Mixová** (sop) Turnspit; **Václav Bednář** (bar) Hunter; **Prague National Theatre Chorus and Orchestra / Zdeněk Chalabala.** Supraphon Ⓕ SU0013-2 (two discs: 149 minutes: ADD: 1/96). From SUAST50440/3 (9/64). Notes, text and translation included. Recorded 1961.   Ⓖ

This excellent set boasts Eduard Haken, one of the great interpreters of the Watergnome, in robust voice, infusing the somewhat enigmatic character with a rueful gentleness as well as a firmness of utterance. Ivo Zídek as the Prince was in his mid-thirties and in his prime at the time of this recording, singing ardently and tenderly and with a grace of phrasing that matches him well to Milada Subrtová's Rusalka. Hers is a beautiful performance, sensitive to the character's charm as well as to her fragility and pathos. The Slavonic tradition of the old watersprite legend places her in the line of the suffering heroine and it is a measure of Dvořák's success that her delicate appeal holds throughout quite a long opera, and her sinuous but never over-sensual lines and the piercing harmony associated with her give her a unique appeal. Subrtová sings the part with unfaltering sensitivity. Zdeněk Chalabala, who died only a couple of months after completing this recording, handles the score with great tenderness and an affection that shines through every bar. He was sometimes underrated as a conductor: this is a beautiful performance. The recording comes up remarkably well; and the booklet includes full text and translations into French, German, and – one or two unfortunate turns of phrase apart – quite reasonable English.

Additional recommendation ...

...Soloists; **Prague Philharmonic Chorus; Czech Philharmonic Orchestra / Václav Neumann.**
Supraphon Ⓕ 10 3641-2 (three discs: ADD: 7/86).

Dvořák The Jacobin. **Václav Zítek** (bar) Bohuš; **Vilém Přibyl** (ten) Jiří; **Daniela Sounová** (sop)
Terinka; **Karel Průša** (bass) Count Vilém; **René Tuček** (bar) Adolf; **Marcela Machotková** (sop)
Julie; **Karel Berman** (bass) Filip; **Beno Blachut** (ten) Benda; **Ivana Mixová** (mez) Lotinka;
Kantilena Children's Chorus; Kühn Chorus; Brno State Philharmonic Orchestra / Jiří Pinkas.
Supraphon Ⓕ 11 2190-2 (two discs: 155 minutes: ADD: 12/94). Notes, text and translation
included. From SUP2481/3 (2/80). Recorded 1977.

This was the first (and, so far, only) recording of Dvořák's charming village comedy – for the Jacobin of the title is not here a political activist but a young man, Bohuš, returning from exile in Paris to his stuffy old father, Count Vilém. The sub-plots include all manner of misunderstandings, and set in the middle of them is the touching figure of Benda, the fussy, rather pedantic but wholly moving music-master. Dvořák is known to have had in mind his own boyhood teacher, Antonín Liehmann, whose daughter gives her name, Terinka, to Benda's daughter. Beno Blachut celebrated his sixty-fourth birthday during the making of this set. His was a long career, as well as one of great distinction; he is still well able to get round the lines of this part, and gives an affecting picture of the old musician, never more so than in the rehearsing of the welcome ode. This is an idea that has cropped up in opera before, but it is charmingly handled here. Václav Zítek sings Bohuš pleasantly and Marcela Machotková trips away lightly as Julie. Vilém Přibyl sounds less than his most energetic, though his voice is in good fettle; and there is some lack of drive from Jiří Pinkas, who might have done more to bring out the often witty touches in Dvořák's scoring. Never mind: this revived version of a delightful piece can be safely recommended. There is a full libretto, with translations into French, German and rather stilted English.

Dvořák Kate and the Devil. **Anna Barová** (contr) Kate; **Richard Novák** (bass) Devil Marbuel; **Miloš Ježil** (ten) Shepherd Jirka; **Daniela Suryová** (contr) Kate's mother; **Jaroslav Horáček** (bass)
Lucifer; **Jan Hladík** (bass) Devil the Gate-keeper; **Aleš Stáva** (bass) Devil the Guard; **Brigita Sulcová** (sop) Princess; **Natália Romanová** (sop) Chambermaid; **Pavel Kamas** (bass) Marshall;
Oldřich Polášek (ten) Musician; **Brno Janáček Opera Chorus and Orchestra / Jiří Pinkas.**
Supraphon Ⓕ 11 1800-2 (two discs: 119 minutes: AAD: 9/94). Notes, text and translation
included. From 1116 3181/3 (3/82). Recorded 1979.

Kate and the Devil has never fared very well outside Czech lands. Record collectors have fared better, and it is high time to welcome back this version, originally recorded in 1979. Though this was never one of the best Supraphon recordings, it is perfectly serviceable. The plot is complicated, and broadly speaking concerns the bossy Kate who, finding herself a wallflower at the village hop, angrily declares that she would dance with the Devil himself. Up there duly pops a junior devil, Marbuel, who carries her off to hell, where her ceaseless chatter wearies Lucifer himself. The diabolical company is only too happy to allow the shepherd Jirka to remove her again. Jirka, attractively sung by Miloš Ježil, also manages to help the wicked but later repentant Princess to escape the Devil's clutches, and all ends well. The work has a proper coherence, and much good humour besides. Anna Barová's Kate is strong and full of character, but manages not to exclude the charm that should underlie her rantings at Marbuel, who is handsomely sung by Richard Novák. Brigita Sulcová similarly makes much of the not very sympathetic Princess. Jaroslav Horáček enjoys himself hugely as Lucifer and Jiří Pinkas accompanies them well.

Further listening ...

...Piano Concerto in G minor, B63. *Coupled with* **Schubert** Fantasy in C major, "Wanderer",
D760. **Sviatoslav Richter** (pf); **Bavarian State Orchestra / Carlos Kleiber.** EMI CDC7 47967-2
(11/87).

...Serenades – D minor, B77; E major, B52. **Academy of St Martin in the Fields / Sir Neville
Marriner.** Philips 400 020-2PH (4/83). Ⓖ

...Serenade in E major, B52. *Coupled with* **Janáček** Suite. **Martinů** Partita. **Prague Chamber
Orchestra / Břetislav Novotný.** Denon CO-78919 (7/95).

...Nocturne in B major, B47. Two Waltzes, B105. Humoresque in G flat major, B187. *Coupled with works by* **Sibelius, Tchaikovsky, Elgar** and **Grieg** Serenata of London / **Barry Wilde.** IMP Classics PCD1108 (2/95).

...String Sextet in A major, B80[a]. *Coupled with* **Martinů** Serenade No. 2. String Sextet[a]. **Academy of St Martin in the Fields Chamber Ensemble.** Chandos CHAN8771 (5/90).

...String Quartet No. 13 in G major, B192. *Coupled with* **Brahms** String Quartets – No. 1 in C minor, Op. 51 No. 1; No. 2 in A minor, Op. 51 No. 2; No. 3 in B flat major, Op. 67. **Alban Berg Quartet.** Teldec 4509-95503-2 (2/95).

...Four Romantic Pieces, B150. Songs my mother taught me, B104 No. 4 (arr. Kreisler). Slavonic Dances – E minor, B78 No. 8; G minor, B145 No. 2 (both arr. Kreisler); A flat major, B145 No. 8 (arr. Jacobson). Humoresques in G flat major, B187 No. 7 (arr. Jacobson). Rondo in G minor, B171 (arr. Jacobson). Violin Sonatina in G major, B183. **Susanne Stanzeleit** (vn); **Julian Jacobson** (pf). Meridian CDE84281 (3/96).

...Moravian Duets, B50, B60, B62 and B69. **Kühn Mixed Chorus / Pavel Kühn** with **Stanislav Bogunia** (pf). Supraphon CO-72646 (1/90).

...Nine Moravian Duets, B62. *Coupled with works by* **Eben, Smetana** and **Suk** Prague Chamber Choir / **Josef Pancik.** Chandos CHAN9257 (12/95). *See review under Eben; refer to the Index to Reviews.*

...13 Moravian Duets, B107. *Coupled with* **Brahms** Duets – Op. 20: Weg der Liebe I; Weg der Liebe II; Die Meere; Op. 66: Am Strande; Jägerlied. Four Duets, Op. 61. Guter Rat, Op. 75 No. 2. **Reger** Three Duets, Op. 111*a*. **Juliane Banse** (sop); **Brigitte Fassbaender** (mez); **Cord Garben** (pf). Koch Schwann 312592 (8/95).

...Love Songs, B160 – When thy sweet glances; Death reigns; I know that on my love; Never will love lead us. Seven Gipsy Melodies, B104. In Folk Tone, B146. Biblical Songs, B185 – I will sing a new song; By the rivers of Babylon; O sing unto the Lord. *Coupled with* **Janáček** Moravian folk poetry in songs – Nosegay; The Forester; A Letter; Wounded Head. **Martinů** Seven Songs on one page. **Gabriela Beňačková** (sop); **Rudolf Firkušný** (pf). RCA Victor Red Seal 09026 60823-2 (1/94).

...Seven Gipsy Melodies, B104. *Coupled with* **Schumann** Frauenliebe und -leben, Op. 42. **Mendelssohn** Duets, Op. 63[a] – No. 1, Ich woll't meine Lieb; No. 3, Gruss; No. 5, Volkslied. Abendlied[a]. **Marilyn Horne,** [a]**Frederica von Stade** (mezzos); **Martin Katz** (pf). RCA Victor Red Seal 09026 61681-2 (3/93).

...Requiem, B165[a]. *Coupled with* **Kodály** Psalmus Hungaricus, Op. 13[b]. Hymn of Zrinyi[c]. Soloists; [a]Ambrosian Singers; [b]Wandsworth School Boys' Choir; [bc]Brighton Festival Chorus; [ab]London Symphony Orchestra / István Kertész, [c]László Heltay. Decca Ovation 421 810-2DM2 (5/89).

...St Ludmila, B144. Soloists; Prague Children's Choir; Prague Radio Chorus and Symphony Orchestra / Václav Smetáček. Praga PR250 059/60 (7/95).

...Dimitrij. Soloists; Prague Radio Chorus; Czech Philharmonic Chorus and Orchestra / Gerd Albrecht. Supraphon 11 1259-2 (3/93).

...The Cunning Peasant. Soloists; Prague Radio Chorus and Symphony Orchestra / František Vajnar. Supraphon SU0019-2 (2/96).

Sir George Dyson

British 1883-1964

New review

Dyson Violin Concerto in E flat major[a]. Children's Suite, after De la Mare. [a]**Lydia Mordkovitch** (vn); **City of London Sinfonia / Richard Hickox.** Chandos ℗ CHAN9369 (62 minutes: DDD: 9/95). Recorded 1994. *Gramophone Editor's choice.*

Several recordings of Dyson's music in recent years have demonstrated that this public-school music master from a working-class background – finally Director of the Royal College of Music in London – was far more than an academic composer. In many ways this is the most rewarding, most heartwarming Dyson issue yet, certainly the most unexpected. Completed in 1941, his Violin Concerto is a richly inspired, lyrical work that readily sustains its 43-minute span. It was written for Albert Sammons, who gave the first performance, but was then forgotten until its revival for the present recording, largely, one suspects, because it defies what one would expect of a work written at that time and place, with no hint of wartime tensions. Rather this reflects Dyson's contentment in his last position at the Royal College of Music. Not that the extended first movement, *Molto moderato*, which alone lasts 20 minutes, lacks dark undercurrents. The broad theme which opens the orchestral tutti has Elgarian nobility in it as well as melancholy. That launches a movement built largely on seamless melody, not aimless but finely controlled, with bravura passages for the soloist that act as landmarks. The idiom in all four movements is warm and distinctive, with the second movement *Scherzo* and the finale both exhilarating in their rhythmic drive, regularly veering towards swinging waltz-rhythms, with the *Scherzo* starting out like an Irish jig and the finale at times sounding like an English version of *La valse*. The third movement *Andante* for violin and muted strings, divided into variations, brings a hushed beauty, superbly achieved in this dedicated performance. Lydia Mordkovitch, as in so many neglected concertos, not least by British composers, makes light of the formidable technical difficulties to give a reading both passionate and deeply expressive. The

Children's Suite of 1924 has four sharply characterized movements. As in the concerto Dyson reveals a masterly ability to create rich and transparent orchestral textures, beautifully caught in the opulent Chandos recording.

Further listening ...

...Concerto da camera. Concerto da chiesa. Concerto leggiero[a]. [a]**Eric Parkin** (pf); **City of London Sinfonia / Richard Hickox.** Chandos CHAN9076 (8/93).

...Symphony in G major. **City of London Sinfonia / Richard Hickox.** Chandos CHAN9200 (6/94). ⓖ

...Three Rhapsodies. *Coupled with* **Howells** String Quartet No. 3, "In Gloucestershire". **Divertimenti.** Hyperion CDA66139 (6/89).

...Evening Service in D major. *Coupled with works by* **Howells, Leighton, Gibbons, G. Ives, S. Watson** and **Stanford** Lichfield Cathedral Choir / **Andrew Lumsden** with **Mark Shepherd, Nigel Potts** (orgs). Priory PRCD505 (10/95). *See review in the Collections section; refer to the Index to Reviews.*

Petr Eben
Czechoslovakian 1929-

New review

Eben Folk Songs from "About Swallows and Girls" – My lass, my lass, little swallow; The dawn; The cuckoo is calling; A little swallow is flying.

Dvořák Nine Moravian Duets, B62.

Smetana Three Choruses, T119.

Suk 10 Songs, Op. 15[a]. **Prague Chamber Choir / Josef Pancik** with [a]**Marian Lapsansky,** [a]**Daniel Buranovsky** (pf duet). Chandos ⓕ CHAN9257 (59 minutes: DDD: 12/95). Texts and translations included. Recorded 1994.

Dvořák's *Moravian Duets* were among the first of his pieces to attract the interest of Brahms, and so lead to a recommendation to the influential publisher Simrock. It was perceptive of Brahms to see so much in these apparently simple little settings; but, cunning craftsman that he was, and with his own experience of handling folk tunes, he recognized how much went into presenting the naïve material in its ideal light. The duets remain a pleasure: they are part of a Czech tradition that this enjoyable record reflects. Suk can be as openly cheerful; also (as with the touching "Zal", or "Sorrow") he can subtly harmonize or phrase the music so as to tinge it with melancholy, though not with tragic feelings that would weigh too heavily. Smetana contributes only three songs here, including the charming "Má hvězda" ("My star"); and five of a set of nine come from Petr Eben, a distinguished figure now in his mid sixties. He is very much in the same tradition, able to enhance the folk melodies and give them his own creative affection without seeming to interfere too assertively. The skill of the cuckoo song and of the final one about the little swallow is exactly in the spirit of the poems. The songs are delightfully well sung. Few of them are complex, but they need a flexibility of rhythm and rubato to point their fleeting images and emotions; Josef Pancik and the singers give every sign of being comfortable with this material and enjoying themselves. This is hardly a record to listen to straight through with solemn concentration, though getting to know what the songs are about from the texts and translations provided (in Czech, English, French and German) is a worthwhile start; but it makes for easy listening of a kind to freshen the spirits.

Further listening ...

...Chagall Windows. *Coupled with works by* **Arban, Enescu, Fantini, Françaix, Goedicke, Höhne** and **Tartini** John Wallace (tpt/cornet); Meyrick Alexander (bn); Simon Wright (pf/org/hpd). EMI Virtuosi CDC5 55086-2 (11/94).

John Eccles
British *c*1668-1735

Suggested listening ...

...Don Quixote: Scenes from a Musical by Don Taylor after Thomas D'Urfey (Eccles, Purcell et al). **Soloists; The Consort of Musicke; The City Waites; The Purcell Simfony / Anthony Rooley.** Musica Oscura 070973 (10/95). ✍ *See review under Purcell; refer to the Index to Reviews.*

René Eespere
Estonian 1953-

Suggested listening ...

...Trivium. *Coupled with works by* **Põldmäe, Mägi, Kangro, Sumera** and **Vähi** Tallinn **Camerata.** Finlandia 4509-95705-2 (5/95).

Egidius
French/Italian 14th-15th centuries

Suggested listening ...
...Courtois et sages. *Coupled with works by* **Matheus de Sancto Johanne, Philipoctus de Caserta, Anonymous, Ciconia, Bartolomeus da Bologna, Velut, Tapissier, Antonius de Civitate Austrie, Zacharias, Brassart** and **Dufay. Orlando Consort.** Metronome METCD1008 (11/95). *See review in the Collections section; refer to the Index to Reviews.* Ⓖ

Werner Egk
German 1901-1983

Suggested listening ...
...Peer Gynt. **Soloists; Bavarian Radio Chorus; Munich Radio Orchestra / Heinz Wallberg.** Orfeo C005822H (10/89).

Richard Einhorn

New review

Einhorn Voices of Light. **Susan Narucki** (sop); **Corrie Pronk** (alto); **Frank Hameleers** (ten); **Henk van Heijnsbergen** (bass-bar); **Anonymous 4** (Ruth Cunningham, Marsha Genensky, Susan Hellauer, Johanna Rose, sngrs); **Netherlands Radio Choir and Philharmonic Orchestra / Steven Mercurio.** Sony Classical Ⓕ SK62006 (71 minutes: DDD: 6/96). Recorded 1995.

Long fascinated by the enigma of Joan of Arc, Einhorn was moved to compose what he calls a "meditation on the life and personality" of this most uneasy of medieval French icons, inspired by what he thinks of as one of the greatest films ever made, Carl Dreyer's *The Passion of Joan of Arc* (1928). Understandably, he intends the music to transcend its origins and stand on its own away from the film, which immediately brings to mind two questions: is this simply film music in another guise? and does it truly stand on its own? A number of hearings suggests that it more closely approximates a song-cycle on a theme, the sometime presence of a choir notwithstanding, but it is harder to determine whether that collection of 15 parts exists coherently on the story of Joan of Arc once it is shorn of the commentary provided externally by Einhorn himself. The episodic nature of the music and the set texts lend themselves to the idea of a series of meditations on the significance of Joan of Arc, rather than any real attempt at drama or narrative. In this sense the work does hold up, revealing itself as concerned with the religious and social reverberations of Joan's life and death as with her own personal odyssey. The music is a hybrid, drawing on medieval and modern traditions, showing a familiarity with, say, John Adams as well as Hildegard or the Notre Dame school. There is a simplicity of line and a love of sheer sound (especially when it comes to the use of Anonymous 4's voices in seven of the 15 sections) which makes *Voices of Light* readily approachable as any and which places the choral sections, appropriately enough, in a French tradition which includes Duruflé and Fauré. In this sense as well as others, then, it can be termed a backward-looking pastiche, but it contains beauties of its own. It is also undoubtedly sincere and has rich contributions from the performers, with Anonymous 4 being first among equals.

Hanns Eisler
German 1898-1962

New review

Eisler Deutsche Sinfonie, Op. 50. **Hendrikje Wangemann** (sop); **Annette Markert** (contr); **Matthias Görne** (bar); **Peter Lika** (bass); **Gert Gütschow, Volker Schwarz** (spkrs); **Ernst Senff Chorus; Leipzig Gewandhaus Orchestra / Lothar Zagrosek.** Decca Entartete Musik Ⓕ 448 389-2DH (65 minutes: DDD: 12/95). Text and translation included. Recorded 1995. *Gramophone Editor's choice.* Ⓖ

Eisler's *Deutsche Sinfonie*, an avowedly anti-Fascist sequence of mini-cantatas and instrumental movements, is his magnum opus. Why then have so few of us heard it, lazily assuming it to be more dutiful than inspired? The reasons are as much political as musical, an almost inevitable reflection of the curious trajectory of Eisler's career. A Schoenbergian with diatonic leanings, Eisler's Leftist sympathies led him towards a long-term collaboration with Brecht after 1930, marking him down as a poor man's Kurt Weill. In fact, Eisler was adept in any number of genres from Hollywood film scores to simple marching songs, but his serious music is crucially important in that it brings a radical lucidity to the 12-note method of his teachers. While remaining genuinely 'modern' in outlook, he seeks always to communicate. If the *Deutsche Sinfonie* occasionally recalls other figures and other musics (Mahler, Hindemith, Schoenberg, Webern, Weill or even Shostakovich), this is usually because we are insufficiently familiar with the distinguishing features of Eisler's own. Despite what some might view as the outdated ideological posturing of Brecht's texts (there are also passages of great poetic sensitivity), and notwithstanding Eisler's use of deliberately conflicting manners to energize his settings, the composition hangs together without strain and there are no awkward gear changes between sections. The orchestration is always beautifully clear, the sentiments coolly articulated with none of the tub-thumping rhetoric demanded by socialist realism. On the face of it, Eisler's work follows the party line, but it can also be appreciated as a deeply-felt lament for a sophisticated, intelligent and civilized people willing to collaborate with, work for, and, in the end, sacrifice its humanity to sustain the most destructive political regime in history. The soloists are well drilled yet intensely characterful where required, and Zagrosek secures orchestral playing that is not just squeaky clean but genuinely alive and Decca have come up with a recording of rare luminosity and depth. This is an important issue, unexpectedly moving and strongly recommended.

Further listening ...

...Woodbury-Liederbüchlein. *Coupled with* **Rühm** Schöpfung. Foetus. Sprechquartette. **Schwehr** Deutsche Tänze. **Van de Vate** Cocaine Lil. **Bel Canto Ensemble / Dietburg Spohr.** Koch Schwann 314322 (3/95).

...Sechs Hölderlin-Fragmente. *Coupled with works by* **Britten, Cornelius, Fortner, Fröhlich, Hauer, Jarnach, Komma, Pfitzner, Ullmann** and **Reutter** Mitsuko Shirai (mez); Hartmut Höll (pf). Capriccio 10 534 (12/94). *See review in the Collections section; refer to the Index to Reviews.*

Edward Elgar

British 1857-1934

Elgar Cello Concerto in E minor, Op. 85[a]. Sea Pictures, Op. 37[b]. [a]**Jacqueline du Pré** (vc); [b]**Dame Janet Baker** (mez); **London Symphony Orchestra / Sir John Barbirolli.** EMI Ⓕ CDC7 47329-2 (54 minutes: ADD: 5/86). From ASD655 (12/65). Recorded 1965. *Gramophone classical 100.*

Ⓖ Ⓖ Ⓖ

This is a classic recording, offering two performances by soloists at the turning point of their careers. Jacqueline du Pré's performance of the Elgar Concerto is extraordinarily complete: the cello sings, cries almost, with burning force in its upper registers; *pianissimos* barely whisper; pizzicatos ring with muted passion; those moments of palpitating *spiccato* bowing convey more than is almost imaginable. The LSO perform as if inspired; hardly surprising given Barbirolli's magical accompaniment. Dame Janet Baker's *Sea Pictures* are no less masterly. The young voice is gloriously rich but agile, her diction superb whilst some of the exquisite floated high notes simply defy description. The 1965 sound is quite spectacular; its very immediacy and vividness grabs one at the outset and doesn't let go.

Additional recommendations ...

...Cello Concerto[a]. **Haydn** Cello Concerto No. 1 in C major[b]. **Beethoven** Cello Sonata No. 3 in A major, Op. 69[c]. Piano Trio in D major, Op. 70 No. 1, "Ghost"[d]. **Jacqueline du Pré** (vc); [d]**Pinchas Zukerman** (va); [a]**London Symphony Orchestra / Sir John Barbirolli**; [b]**English Chamber Orchestra / Daniel Barenboim** ([cd]pf). EMI Studio Ⓜ CMS7 69707-2 (two discs: 107 minutes: ADD: 3/89). *The Cello Concerto is the same recording as the one reviewed above.*

Ⓖ Ⓖ Ⓖ

...Cello Concerto[a]. Violin Concerto in B minor, Op. 61[b]. [a]**Beatrice Harrison** (vc); [b]**Sir Yehudi Menuhin** (vn); [a]**New Symphony Orchestra**; [b]**London Symphony Orchestra / Sir Edward Elgar.** EMI Great Recordings of the Century mono Ⓜ CDH7 69786-2* (75 minutes: AAD: 11/89). *Gramophone classical 100.*

Ⓖ Ⓖ Ⓖ

...Cello Concerto[a]. **Tchaikovsky** Fantasia on a theme by Thomas Tallis. Fantasia on "Greensleeves" (arr. Greaves). [a]**Felix Schmidt** (vc); **London Symphony Orchestra / Rafael Frühbeck de Burgos.** IMP Classics Ⓜ PCD930 (49 minutes: DDD: 1/90).

...Cello Concerto[a]. The Dream of Gerontius, Op. 38[b]. [a]**Paul Tortelier** (vc); [b]**Soloists**; [b]**Huddersfield Choral Society**; [b]**BBC Symphony Orchestra**; [a]**Liverpool Philharmonic Orchestra / Sir Malcolm Sargent.** Testament mono Ⓕ SBT2025* (two discs: 120 minutes: ADD: 2/94). *See review further on in this section.*

Ⓖ Ⓖ

...Cello Concerto[a]. Violin Concerto[b]. [a]**Lynn Harrell** (vc); [b]**Kyung-Wha Chung** (vn); [a]**Cleveland Orchestra / Lorin Maazel**; [b]**London Philharmonic Orchestra / Sir Georg Solti.** Decca Ⓜ 440 319-2DWO (78 minutes: ADD: 4/94).

...Cello Concerto[a]. **Milhaud** Cello Concerto No. 1, Op. 136[b]. **Respighi** Adagio con variazioni[a]. **Mstislav Rostropovich** (vc); [a]**Moscow Philharmonic Orchestra**; [b]**USSR TV and Radio Large Orchestra / Gennadi Rozhdestvensky.** Russian Disc Ⓕ RDCD11104 (52 minutes: ADD: 7/94).

...Cello Concerto. *Coupled with works by* **Dvořák, Schumann, Saint-Saëns, Delius, Haydn, Monn, Chopin, Franck, Fauré, Bruch, Bach, Handel** and **Beethoven** Jacqueline du Pré (vc) with various artists and orchestras. EMI Ⓑ CZS5 68132-2 (six discs: 437 minutes: ADD: 8/94). *This is the same recording as the one reviewed above. Also see review in the Collections section; refer to the Index to Reviews.*

Ⓖ Ⓖ Ⓖ

...Cello Concerto. **Bloch** Schelomo. **Steven Isserlis** (vc); **London Symphony Orchestra / Richard Hickox.** Virgin Classics Ultraviolet Ⓜ CUV5 61125-2 (51 minutes: DDD: 11/94). *Selected by Sounds in Retrospect.*

Ⓖ

...Cello Concerto[b]. **Dvořák** Cello Concerto in B minor, B191[a]. **Jacqueline du Pré** (vc); [a]**Chicago Symphony Orchestra / Daniel Barenboim**; [b]**London Symphony Orchestra / Sir John Barbirolli.** EMI Ⓕ CDC5 55527-2 (72 minutes: ADD: 11/95). *This is the same recording as the one reviewed above.*

Ⓖ Ⓖ Ⓖ

Elgar Violin Concerto in B minor, Op. 61. **Nigel Kennedy** (vn); **London Philharmonic Orchestra / Vernon Handley.** EMI Eminence Ⓜ CD-EMX2058 (54 minutes: DDD: 12/84). From EMX412058-1 (12/84). Recorded 1984. *Gramophone Award Winner 1985.*　　　ⒼⒼ

Even after the success of his First Symphony, Elgar's self-doubt persisted and caused his creative instincts to look inward. He could identify with his own instrument, the violin, as his own lonely voice pitted against an orchestra which might represent the forces of the outside world. Usually a concerto consisted of a big first movement, then a lyrical slow movement and a lighter finale: Elgar's finale, which balanced the first movement in weight, was unique, and at first the 45-minute-long work daunted all but the bravest soloists. Nigel Kennedy's technique is such that the work's formidable difficulties hold no terrors for him; his playing is first and foremost immaculate in its execution, and it is complemented by Handley's sensitive accompaniment. But it is more than that. He has a pure silvery tone-quality which is a joy to hear; his response to Elgar's vision is unfailingly sympathetic and understanding, and his projection of it is fresh and stimulating. The natural concert-hall sound is excellent in quality, with important orchestral detail always registering clearly.

Additional recommendations ...

...Violin Concerto[a]. Violin Sonata in E minor, Op. 82[b]. **Albert Sammons** (vn); [b]**William Murdoch** (pf); [a]**New Queen's Hall Orchestra / Sir Henry Wood.** Pearl mono Ⓕ GEMMCD9496*.

...Violin Concerto[a]. Cello Concerto[b]. [a]**Sir Yehudi Menuhin** (vn); [b]**Beatrice Harrison** (vc); [a]**London Symphony Orchestra** [b]**New Symphony Orchestra / Sir Edward Elgar.** EMI Great Recordings of the Century mono Ⓜ CDH7 69786-2* (75 minutes: AAD: 11/89).　　　ⒼⒼⒼ

...Violin Concerto. Cockaigne Overture, Op. 40. **Dong-Suk Kang** (vn); **Polish National Radio Symphony Orchestra / Adrian Leaper.** Naxos Ⓢ 8 550489 (61 minutes: DDD: 4/92).

...Violin Concerto. Violin Sonata in E minor, Op. 82[b]. **Hugh Bean** (vn); [b]**David Parkhouse** (pf); **Royal Liverpool Philharmonic Orchestra / Sir Charles Groves.** Classics for Pleasure Ⓑ CD-CFP4632 (75 minutes: ADD: 9/93).

New review

Elgar Falstaff, Op. 68[a]. Introduction and Allegro, Op. 47[b]. Serenade in E minor, Op. 20[b]. [a]**London Symphony Orchestra,** [b]**New Symphony Orchestra / Anthony Collins.** Beulah mono Ⓜ 1PD15* (59 minutes: ADD: 2/96). Item marked [a] from Decca LXT2940 (8/54), [b]LXT2699 (9/52). Recorded 1952-4.

Even among the many recordings of *Falstaff*, few match Collins in the way his timing helps you to visualize the story behind each incident. The reading is strong and purposeful yet not at all rushed, with each section sharply characterized and with linking passages leading the ear on. Though the LSO of 1954 was rather in the doldrums, the crisp ensemble would have done credit to the orchestra as reconstituted later in the decade, not just in the woodwind and brass sections but in the strings too. Plainly Collins inspired the players, who may well have been rediscovering the work, for that was a period when Elgar's music, rather like the orchestra, was also out of favour. The Beulah transfer does not quite capture the full vividness of Decca's recording at the time, but there is a fair body in the sound and the bite of the brass is splendid. What is irritating, however, is that there is only a single track for the 34-minute work, with no sections separately indexed. In the *Serenade* and the *Introduction and Allegro* Collins equally reveals his natural understanding of Elgarian timing and rubato, with spontaneous-sounding results. However, the playing from what was then called the New Symphony Orchestra is not nearly as polished as in *Falstaff* and the string sound tends to be fizzy. None the less, this is an invaluable offering, reminding us of the mastery of a conductor whose achievement was never fully appreciated in his lifetime.

Elgar Falstaff, Op. 68[a]. Cockaigne Overture, Op. 40[a]. Introduction and Allegro, Op. 47[b]. **London Philharmonic Orchestra / Vernon Handley.** Classics for Pleasure Ⓑ CD-CFP4617 (68 minutes: ADD: 6/93). Items marked [a] from CFP403131 (7/79), recorded 1978, [b]EMI Eminence EMX412011 (8/83), recorded 1983.　　　ⒼⒼ

One of the triumphs of the Classics for Pleasure catalogue, Vernon Handley's magnificent account of *Falstaff* is here available at bargain price. Superbly played by the LPO and given ripely resonant sound (if now with just a fraction less body than on the original LP), Handley's achievement is considerable, evincing such a hugely impressive alliance of invincible symphonic thrust and warm-hearted characterization as to make his a version worthy of comparison with the very finest on disc. Barbirolli (reviewed further on), Barenboim, Solti and most notably Elgar himself have all given of their best in this masterpiece: Handley now joins their company. To the original vinyl coupling of *Cockaigne* (another swaggering display, incidentally), Classics for Pleasure have added Handley's disciplined, if somewhat less inspired *Introduction and Allegro*: digitally recorded, this sounds rather less beguiling than its analogue companions. No matter, this is an unmissable prospect overall, and a formidable bargain to boot.

Additional recommendations ...

...Introduction and Allegro[a]. Serenade for Strings in E minor, Op. 20[b]. Pomp and Circumstance Marches Nos. 1 and 4[c]. "Enigma" Variations – Nimrod[d]. The Dream of Gerontius – Praise to the Holiest in the height[ae]. Salut d'amour[f]. There is sweet music[g]. [e]**Yvonne Minton** (sop); [e]**Sir Peter Pears** (ten); [f]**Kyung-Wha Chung** (vn); [f]**Philip Moll** (pf); [g]**Louis Halsey Singers.** [a]**English Chamber**

Orchestra / [ae]Benjamin Britten; [b]Academy of St Martin in the Fields / Sir Neville Marriner; [cde]London Symphony Chorus and Orchestra / Sir Arthur Bliss, [d]Pierre Monteux. Decca Ⓑ 430 094-2DWO (66 minutes: ADD: 6/91).

...Cockaigne Overture. Introduction and Allegro. Serenade for Strings. "Enigma" Variations. **BBC Symphony Orchestra / Andrew Davis.** Teldec British Line Ⓕ 9031-73279-2 (74 minutes: DDD: 3/92).

...Introduction and Allegro. **Barber** Adagio for Strings, Op. 11. Medea's Meditation and Dance of Vengeance, Op. 23. **Tchaikovsky** Serenade in C major, Op. 48. **Boston Symphony Orchestra / Charles Munch.** RCA Victor Gold Seal Ⓜ 09026 61424-2 (61 minutes: ADD: 9/93).   ⒼⒼ

...Introduction and Allegro. **Bridge** Sir Roger de Coverley, H155. **Britten** Simple Symphony, Op. 4. Prelude and Fugue, Op. 29. **Delius** Two Aquarelles. **Purcell** Chacony in G minor for strings, Z730. **English Chamber Orchestra / Benjamin Britten.** Decca The Classic Sound Ⓜ 448 569-2DCS (58 minutes: ADD: 2/96).

Elgar Variations on an Original Theme, Op. 36, "Enigma". Falstaff, Op. 68. Grania and Diarmid – Incidental Music; Funeral March. **City of Birmingham Symphony Orchestra / Sir Simon Rattle.** EMI British Composers Ⓕ CDC5 55001-2 (79 minutes: DDD. 3/95). Recorded 1992-3.   Ⓐ

Rattle gives us perhaps the most meticulously prepared and subtly blended *Falstaff* ever committed to disc. This conductor's keen intellect and almost fanatical fidelity to the letter of the score team up to produce the most invigorating, wittily observant results. It is, however, a bit like viewing a pristinely restored portrait of Shakespeare's fat knight, whereas Barbirolli (reviewed below) presents us with the lovable, vulnerable creature of flesh and blood himself – his epilogue really does touch to the marrow every time. In *Enigma* the results are always enjoyable and refreshing, with myriad details in Elgar's lovingly-woven orchestral canvas adroitly pinpointed (Downes's BBC PO version, too, is especially strong in this regard). The sluggishness that so often blights the opening bars is mercifully absent and Rattle follows it up with a wonderfully transparent and affectionate "C.A.E.". Rattle brings an almost chamber-like intimacy and point to "R.B.T.", "Ysobel" and "W.N.", whilst his "Dorabella" is a veritable miracle of tripping delicacy. Both "Troyte" and "G.R.S." winningly combine athleticism and bluster. "Nimrod", too, is a success, its progress dignified and its noble climax unerringly well graduated (and we really do get a genuine *ppp* at the start). Overall, then, a fine, deeply-felt *Enigma*. The most completely successful item here is the glorious *Grania and Diarmid* incidental music: the magnificent "Funeral March" is one of Elgar's most inspired creations and Rattle gauges its brooding melancholy most eloquently. Both *Enigma* and *Grania* were recorded at Symphony Hall, Birmingham in August 1993, some 16 months after *Falstaff* which emanates from Warwick University's Butterworth Hall. Balance is impeccable (and the transfer level comparatively low) in all three works, though the quality in *Falstaff* isn't quite as rich and glowing as elsewhere. An exceedingly stimulating release.

Additional recommendations ...

..."Enigma" Variations. Pomp and Circumstance Marches. **Royal Philharmonic Orchestra / Norman Del Mar.** DG Galleria Ⓜ 429 713-2GGA (58 minutes: ADD: 9/90).   Ⓖ

..."Enigma" Variations. Cockaigne Overture, Op. 40. Serenade for Strings in E minor, Op. 20. Salut d'amour, Op. 12. **Baltimore Symphony Orchestra / David Zinman.** Telarc Ⓕ CD80192 (62 minutes: DDD: 10/90).

..."Enigma" Variations. Froissart, Op. 19. In the South, Op. 50. **BBC Philharmonic Orchestra / Edward Downes.** Conifer Ⓕ CDCF187 (77 minutes: DDD: 1/91).

..."Enigma" Variations[a]. Falstaff[a]. Cockaigne Overture[a]. The Crown of India[a]. Serenade for Strings[b]. Pomp and Circumstance Marches Nos. 1-5[a]. Imperial March[a]. [a]**London Philharmonic Orchestra;** [b]**English Chamber Orchestra / Daniel Barenboim.** Sony Classical Ⓜ M2YK46465 (two discs: 160 minutes: ADD: 9/91).

..."Enigma" Variations. Cockaigne Overture. Serenade for Strings. Introduction and Allegro, Op. 47. **BBC Symphony Orchestra / Andrew Davis.** Teldec British Line Ⓕ 9031-73279-2 (74 minutes: DDD: 3/92).

..."Enigma" Variations. **R. Strauss** Symphonia domestica, Op. 53. **National Youth Orchestra of Great Britain / Christopher Seaman.** IMP Classics Ⓜ PCD1080 (73 minutes: DDD: 8/94).

..."Enigma" Variations. Froissart, Op. 19. Cello Concerto[a]. [a]**Robert Cohen** (vc); **Royal Philharmonic Orchestra / Sir Charles Mackerras.** Argo Ⓕ 436 545-2ZH (77 minutes: DDD: 6/93).

..."Enigma" Variations. **Debussy** Images. **Berlin Philharmonic Orchestra / James Levine.** Sony Classical Ⓕ SK53284 (67 minutes: DDD: 2/95).

Elgar Variations on an original Theme, Op. 36, "Enigma"[a]. Falstaff, Op. 68[b]. [a]**Philharmonia Orchestra;** [b]**Hallé Orchestra / Sir John Barbirolli.** EMI Studio Ⓜ CDM7 69185-2 (65 minutes: ADD: 11/88). Item marked [a] from ASD548 (11/63), recorded 1962, [b]ASD610-11 (12/64), recorded 1964.   ⒼⒼ

Elgar Variations on an Original Theme, Op. 36, "Enigma"[a]. Pomp and Circumstance Marches, Op. 39[b]. [a]**London Symphony Orchestra,** [b]**London Philharmonic Orchestra / Sir Adrian Boult.** EMI Ⓜ CDM7 64015-2 (55 minutes: ADD: 4/92). Item marked [a] from HMV ASD2750 (11/71), recorded 1970, [b]ASD3388 (10/77), recorded 1976.   ⒼⒼ

The first EMI disc restores to the catalogue at a very reasonable price two key Elgar recordings of works which Sir John Barbirolli made very much his own. Barbirolli brought a flair and ripeness of feeling to the *Enigma* with which Elgar himself would surely have identified. Everything about his performance seems exactly right. The very opening theme is phrased with an appealing combination of warmth and subtlety, and variation after variation has a special kind of individuality, whilst for the finale Barbirolli draws all the threads together most satisfyingly. *Falstaff* is a continuous, closely integrated structure and again Barbirolli's response to the music's scenic characterization is magical while he controls the overall piece, with its many changes of mood, with a naturally understanding flair. The original recordings perhaps sounded more sumptuous but on CD there is more refined detail and greater range and impact to the sound.

As one might expect, Sir Adrian Boult's 1970 recording of the *Enigma* Variations offers similar riches to those of Barbirolli with the additional bonus of a slightly superior recorded sound. Boult's account has authority, freshness and a beautiful sense of spontaneity so that each variation emerges from the preceding one with a natural feeling of flow and progression. There is warmth and affection too coupled with an air of nobility and poise, and at all times the listener is acutely aware that this is a performance by a great conductor who has lived a lifetime with the music. One need only sample the passionate stirrings of Variation One (the composer's wife), the athletic and boisterous "Troyte" variation, or the autumnal, elegiac glow that Boult brings to the famous "Nimrod" variation to realize that this is a very special document indeed. The LSO, on top form, play with superlative skill and poetry and the excellent recording has been exceptionally well transferred to CD. The *Pomp and Circumstance* Marches, recorded six years later with the London Philharmonic Orchestra, are invigoratingly fresh and direct – indeed the performances are so full of energy and good humour that it is hard to believe that Boult was in his late eighties at the time of recording! A classic.

Elgar Symphony No. 1 in A flat major, Op. 55. In the South, Op. 50, "Alassio". **London Philharmonic Orchestra / Leonard Slatkin.** RCA Victor Red Seal Ⓕ RD60380 (74 minutes: DDD: 6/91). Recorded 1989. ⒼⒼⒼ

Elgar's First Symphony was one of those rare pieces of music that seemed to attain full stature and admiration from the very first public hearing. At its première in Manchester in 1908 it caused a sensation, and Elgar was received by the audience very much in the same way that the pop stars of today are. The previous successes of the *Enigma* Variations, *Gerontius* and the masterly *Introduction and Allegro* had created high hopes in the public's mind for what they felt would be the first truly great English Symphony, and they were not disappointed. Its popularity has never waned and it still holds a special place in the affections of the public today. Leonard Slatkin is a conductor whose passion for British music has become something of a crusade, and a listener hearing him play Elgar's First Symphony without knowing the artists could well think that this was a performance under a conductor such as Sir Adrian Boult. But good music knows no bounds (after all, you don't have to be Austrian to play Mozart!) and Slatkin's understanding of this composer is abundantly clear throughout. There is no trace of sentimentality in the mighty first movement, for here is real grandeur and not just grandiose utterance while the noble sadness of the coda has special beauty. The other movements are hardly less fine, for the richly textured *Adagio* is most eloquently done and the finale is thrilling. Elgar's massive though subtle scoring can present problems for engineers; here they are magnificently solved and the sound is rich yet detailed with excellent bass. The Overture *In the South* which begins the disc is brilliantly vivid and dramatic.

Additional recommendations ...

...No. 1. Serenade for Strings. Chanson de nuit, Op. 15 No. 1. Chanson de matin, Op. 15 No. 2. **London Philharmonic Orchestra / Sir Adrian Boult.** EMI British Composers Ⓜ CDM7 64013-2 (69 minutes: ADD). *Gramophone Award Winner 1977*. ⒼⒼⒼ

...No. 1. **London Philharmonic Orchestra / Vernon Handley.** Classics for Pleasure Ⓑ CD-CFP9018 (52 minutes: ADD: 8/88). ⒼⒼ

...No. 1. **London Symphony Orchestra / Sir Charles Mackerras.** Argo Ⓕ 430 835-2ZH (64 minutes: DDD: 8/91).

...Nos. 1 and 2[a]. Falstaff[a]. The Dream of Gerontius[ab] – excerpts. The Music Makers[a] – excerpts. Civic Fanfare[a]. **Anonymous** (arr. Elgar) The National Anthem[a]. [ab]**Soloists;** [a]**London Symphony Orchestra;** [b]**Royal Albert Hall Orchestra / Sir Edward Elgar.** EMI mono Ⓕ CDS7 54560-2* (three discs: 211 minutes: ADD: 6/92). ⒼⒼⒼ

...No. 1. Pomp and Circumstance Marches – No. 1; No. 2 in A minor. **Baltimore Symphony Orchestra / David Zinman.** Telarc Ⓕ CD80310 (62 minutes: DDD: 11/92). Ⓖ

...No. 1. Cockaigne Overture. **London Symphony Orchestra / Jeffrey Tate.** EMI Ⓕ CDC7 54414-2 (72 minutes: DDD: 1/93).

...In the South, Op. 50. **Brahms** Serenade No. 1 in D major, Op. 11. **La Scala Philharmonic Orchestra, Milan / Riccardo Muti.** Sony Classical Ⓕ SK57973 (71 minutes: DDD: 2/95).

...No. 1[a]. Pomp and Circumstance March No. 1 in D major, Op. 39[b]. Introduction and Allegro, Op. 47[c]. [a]**BBC Symphony Orchestra / Sir Colin Davis;** [b]**Boston Pops Orchestra / Arthur Fiedler;**

^c**Boston Symphony Orchestra / Charles Munch.** RCA Victor Classical Navigator Ⓑ 74321 24217-2*
(71 minutes: ADD/DDD: 2/96).

New review

Elgar Symphony No. 1 in A flat major, Op. 55. Introduction and Allegro, Op. 47. **BBC National
Orchestra of Wales / Tadaaki Otaka.** BIS Ⓕ CD727 (69 minutes: DDD: 1/96). *Selected by
Soundings.*
The spacious introduction to the symphony at once proclaims Otaka's considerable Elgarian instincts:
not only is the playing exceptionally refined and responsive but he captures to perfection the mood of
tender strength and nobility in these bars. The ensuing *Allegro* has the right urgency and flexibility:
one notes again the poise and sheen of the strings, the satisfying weight of the lower brass. Otaka's
wistful handling of the two *Poco più mosso* episodes which frame the development section is
particularly appealing, and the same applies to the twilit coda – the big tune now sounding regretful
and resigned Otaka's scherzo is crisp and exciting, the contrasting trio engagingly fresh. With its
expectant opening, purposeful main *Allegro* and trenchant apotheosis, the finale represents another
great success. In fact, the only real quibble concerns the slow movement. For all the sensitivity of the
orchestral response, it is not profoundly moving, whereas tears are never far away when one listens to
the likes of, say, the composer himself, Solti, or Boult. These are, of course, very personal matters, so
do try and hear Otaka for yourself. The coupling is a keen-voiced *Introduction and Allegro*, a
beautifully prepared, hugely committed display, yet ultimately somehow perhaps a little too pristine
and literal. Nevertheless, Otaka's remains an impressive coupling, and BIS's ripe sound adds
considerably to the listener's pleasure.

New review

Elgar Symphonies – No. 1 in A flat major, Op. 55; No. 2 in E flat major, Op. 63. Cockaigne
Overture, Op. 40. In the South, Op. 50, "Alassio". **London Philharmonic Orchestra / Sir Georg
Solti.** Double Decca Ⓜ 443 856-2DF2 (two discs: 135 minutes: ADD: 7/95).
This Double Decca is self-recommending for those who enjoy Solti's highly involving and invigorating
Elgar, with the London Philharmonic's natural understanding and virtuosity. The first disc opens
with an exhilarating account of *Cockaigne* and the second with a rather less successful *In the South*
which is a bit too hard-driven, and not helped by a recording that is slightly top-heavy. However, the
symphonies are a different matter, and are given vintage Decca sound – firm and weighty as well as
brilliant. Before making these 1970s recordings Solti studied Elgar's own closely, so his volatile
urgency is very convincing, the onward flow in each work seemingly totally spontaneous, with both
finales providing a fitting and (in No. 2, especially) thrilling culmination.

Elgar Symphony No. 2 in E flat major, Op. 63. In the South, Op. 50, "Alassio". **BBC Symphony
Orchestra / Andrew Davis.** Teldec Ⓕ 9031-74888-2 (70 minutes: DDD: 11/92). Recorded 1992.
Selected by Sounds in Retrospect.   ⒼⒼⒼ
Elgar Symphony No. 2 in E flat major, Op. 63. Sea Pictures, Op. 37^a. ^a**Della Jones** (mez); **Royal
Philharmonic Orchestra / Sir Charles Mackerras.** Argo Ⓕ 443 321-2ZH (74 minutes: DDD:
12/94). Texts included. Recorded 1993.
In what is unquestionably his finest achievement on record to date, Andrew Davis penetrates right to
the dark inner core of this great symphony. In the opening *Allegro vivace e nobilmente*, for example,
how well he and his acutely responsive players gauge the varying moods of Elgar's glorious
inspiration: be it in the exhilarating surge of that leaping introductory paragraph or the spectral,
twilight world at the heart of this wonderful movement, no one is found wanting. In fact, Davis's
unerring structural sense never once deserts him, and the BBC Symphony Orchestra simply play their
hearts out for their music director. Above all, though, it's in the many more reflective moments that
Davis proves himself an outstandingly perceptive Elgarian, uncovering a vein of intimate anguish that
touches to the very marrow; in this respect, his account of the slow movement is quite heart-rendingly
poignant (just listen to those BBC strings at the final climax!) – undoubtedly the finest since Boult's
incomparable 1944 performance with this very same orchestra – whilst the radiant sunset of the
symphony's coda glows with luminous beauty. Prefaced by an equally idiomatic, stirring *In the South*
(and aided throughout by some sumptuously natural engineering), this is an Elgar Second to set
beside the very greatest. In every way a treasurable release.
    Mackerras's is an Elgar Second of exciting thrust and considerable interpretative flair. His way with
the first movement is charismatically propulsive in the Elgar/Solti manner, yet he allows himself
ample scope for subtlety of expression: in the opening paragraph, for instance, a glance at the score
readily reveals Mackerras's mastery of the music's extraordinary fluidity of pulse. Though a greater
sense of mystery and inwardness during the development section would have been preferable (Elgar's
"malign influence" never really haunts the imagination here), the slow movement goes splendidly,
both deeply felt and infinitely touching, rising to a fine, passionate climax. Indeed, such stirring
application is symptomatic of the RPO strings' contribution as a whole: if hardly the most luxuriantly
full-bodied of sections, they nevertheless respond with unstinting fervour and prove themselves ever
stylish, ideally uncloying advocates for Mackerras's widespread adoption of portamento. Crisp detail
abounds in the sparkling *Rondo*, its pounding central crisis genuinely hair-raising in its physical
power, whilst the finale flows with a supreme confidence and true *nobilmente* swagger that are the

hallmarks of a seasoned Elgarian. Superbly well-lit production serves up a feast for the ears. Della Jones's vividly projected, technically immaculate performance of the *Sea Pictures* is also very enjoyable. In the third and fifth songs especially, her exemplary diction really brings a newly minted freshness to these almost operatic settings, and Mackerras certainly extracts maximum drama from Elgar's masterly, subtly-coloured orchestral backcloth. A fine coupling.

Additional recommendations ...

...No. 2. Cockaigne Overture. **London Philharmonic Orchestra / Sir Adrian Boult.** EMI British Composers Ⓜ CDM7 64014-2 (68 minutes: ADD).

...No. 2. **London Philharmonic Orchestra / Vernon Handley.** Classics for Pleasure Ⓑ CD-CFP4544 (54 minutes: ADD: 10/88).

...No. 2. In the South. **London Philharmonic Orchestra / Sir Georg Solti.** Decca Ⓜ 436 150-2DSP (72 minutes: ADD: 8/89).

...No. 2. Serenade for Strings. **London Philharmonic Orchestra / Leonard Slatkin.** RCA Victor Ⓕ 09026 60072-2 (67 minutes: DDD: 8/89).

...No. 2[a]. Serenade for Strings [b]. [a]**Hallé Orchestra / James Loughran;** [b]**Academy of St Martin in the Fields / Sir Neville Marriner.** ASV Quicksilva Ⓢ CDQS6087 (70 minutes: ADD/DDD: 8/93).

...No. 2[a]. Sospiri[b]. Elegy[b]. [a]**Hallé Orchestra;** [b]**New Philharmonia Orchestra / Sir John Barbirolli.** EMI British Composers Ⓜ CDM7 64724-2 (66 minutes: ADD: 2/94).

...No. 2. **BBC Philharmonic Orchestra / Sir Edward Downes.** Naxos Ⓢ 8 550635 (56 minutes: DDD: 6/94).

Elgar Introduction and Allegro, Op. 47[a]. Chanson de nuit, Op. 15 No. 1 (arr. Fraser). Chanson de matin, Op. 15 No. 2 (arr. Fraser). Three Characteristic Pieces – No. 1, Mazurka, Op. 10. Serenade for Strings in E minor, Op. 20. Salut d'amour, Op. 12 (arr. Fraser). Elegy, Op. 58. [a]**José-Luis Garcia,** [a]**Mary Eade** (vns); [a]**Quentin Ballardie** (va); [a]**Olga Hegedus** (vc); **English Chamber Orchestra / Sir Yehudi Menuhin.** Arabesque Ⓕ Z6563 (45 minutes: DDD: 6/87). From ABQ6563 (1/87). Recorded 1982.

Elgar's pieces for string orchestra contain some of his greatest music and certainly the *Introduction and Allegro, Serenade* and *Elegy* included in this delightful programme embody quintessential Elgar. Sir Yehudi Menuhin's readings dig deep into the hearts of these works, drawing out the nostalgia and inner tragedy that underpins even some of the most seemingly high-spirited of Elgar's music. The lighter pieces allow relief from the intensity of the major works, thus making that intensity all the more effective. The English Chamber Orchestra is more than capable of providing first-rate soloists from its own ranks, and the quartet extracted for the *Introduction and Allegro* is suitably virtuosic. Both performers and engineers have produced an ideal integration of this solo group with the main string body, and the generally effervescent sound suits the celebratory nature of the piece.

Additional recommendations ...

...Violin Sonata in E minor, Op. 82. Six Very Easy Melodious Exercises in the First Position, Op. 22. Salut d'amour (with Steven Isserlis, vc). Mot d'amour, Op. 13. In the South – Canto popolare (In Moonlight). Sospiri, Op. 70. Chanson de nuit. Chanson de matin. **Nigel Kennedy** (vn); **Peter Pettinger** (pf). Chandos Ⓕ CHAN8380 (55 minutes: DDD: 8/85).

...Salut d'amour, Op. 12. Sospiri, Op. 70. *Coupled with works by* **Sibelius, Tchaikovsky, Dvořák** and **Grieg Serenata of London / Barry Wilde.** IMP Classics Ⓜ PCD1108 (69 minutes: DDD: 2/95).

Elgar String Quartet in E minor, Op. 83[a]. Canto popolare[b]. Piano Quintet in A minor, Op. 84[c]. [ab]**Piers Lane** (pf); [ac]**Vellinger Quartet** (Stephanie Gonley, Harvey de Sousa, vns; [b]James Boyd, va; Sally Pendlebury, vc). EMI Eminence Ⓜ CD-EMX2229 (65 minutes: DDD: 3/95). Recorded 1994.

The Vellinger Quartet bring enormous heart, effortless technical accomplishment and (most importantly) genuine freshness of new discovery to the Quartet. In both outer movements their playing ideally combines propulsive excitement with passionate flexibility, yet, at the same time, they do not miss out on the vein of wistfulness and vulnerability coursing through Elgar's glorious inspiration. For the Piano Quintet they are joined by the excellent Piers Lane. Again, the emotional temperature is high, with these young performers extracting maximum drama from the opening movement in particular. The central *Adagio*, stately and very intense, could perhaps do with greater intimacy of feeling; their account of the finale generates all the edge-of-seat thrust of a live concert. Some Elgarians may baulk at the sheer physicality and unrelenting wholeheartedness of it all but their fervour has its place too. As a further appealing bonus, Lane partners the Vellinger's violist, James Boyd, for a generously sung rendering of *In Moonlight*, more familiar as the gloriously long-breathed *Canto popolare* theme from the central portion of *In the South*. Excellent recording.

Additional recommendations ...

...String Quartet. **Delius** String Quartet. **Brodsky Quartet.** ASV Ⓕ CDDCA526 (56 minutes: DDD: 7/89).

...String Quartet. **Walton** String Quartet in A minor. **Britten Quartet.** Collins Classics Ⓕ 1280-2 (56 minutes: DDD: 7/92).

...String Quartet. *Coupled with works by* **Bridge** and **Walton Coull Quartet.** Hyperion Ⓕ CDA66718 (73 minutes: DDD: 10/94). *See review under Bridge; refer to the Index to Reviews.*

New review

Elgar The Black Knight, Op. 25. Scenes from the Bavarian Highlands, Op. 27. **London Symphony Chorus and Orchestra / Richard Hickox.** Chandos Ⓕ CHAN9436 (61 minutes: DDD: 5/96). Texts included. Recorded 1995.

The Black Knight is a large-scale, red-blooded choral setting of Longfellow's translation of a German poem by Ludwig Uhland. Elgar completed it in 1893 and it provided him with his first big success – especially in the Midlands, where it was gratefully taken up by many choral societies. The text tells of a sinister, unnamed "Prince of mighty sway", whose appearance at the King's court during the feast of Pentecost has disastrous consequences. Elgar's score boasts much attractive invention, some of it strikingly eloquent and prescient of greater offerings to come: for example, towards the end of track 8 (the section beginning with "Each the father's breast embraces"), Elgar's touching inspiration momentarily seems to look forward to "Nimrod" and even the First Symphony's sublime slow movement. The choral writing is always effective, the orchestration already vivid and assured. Richard Hickox and his combined London Symphony forces are dab hands at this kind of fare and their performance has great bloom and spaciousness. Similarly, in the tuneful, vernally fresh *Scenes from the Bavarian Highlands* (given here with the orchestral accompaniment Elgar supplied in 1896), Hickox and his colleagues respond with commendable spirit and pleasing polish. Truth to tell, in matters of interpretation there is little to choose between this account and the rival EMI version from Norman Del Mar (see review under Stanford; refer to the Index to Reviews).

Additional recommendations ...

...Scenes from the Bavarian Highlands[a]. O salutaris hostia – three settings[b]. Tantum ergo[b]. Ecce sacerdos magnus[b]. The Light of Life, Op. 29[b] – Doubt not thy Father's care!; Light of the World. **Worcester Cathedral Choir / Christopher Robinson** with [a]**Frank Wibaut** (pf); [b]**Harry Bramma** (org). Chandos Collect Ⓜ CHAN6601 (51 minutes: ADD: 9/94).

...Scenes from the Bavarian Highlands[a]. **Stanford** Symphony No. 3 in F minor, Op. 28[a], "Irish". [a]**Bournemouth Symphony Chorus; Bournemouth Sinfonietta / Norman Del Mar.** EMI British Composers Ⓜ CDM5 65129-2 (70 minutes: ADD: 7/95). *See review under Stanford; refer to the Index to Reviews.*

Elgar The Light of Life (Lux Christi), Op. 29. **Judith Howarth** (sop); **Linda Finnie** (mez); **Arthur Davies** (ten); **John Shirley-Quirk** (bar); **London Symphony Chorus and Orchestra / Richard Hickox.** Chandos Ⓕ CHAN9208 (63 minutes: DDD: 5/94). Text included. Recorded 1993.

Hickox's Elgarian credentials are immediately established in the glorious orchestral "Meditation", where his conducting demonstrates a noble flexibility, sensitivity to dynamic nuance and feeling for climax. Equally the engineering, sumptuous yet detailed, comes close to the ideal. The LSO and Chorus contribute to proceedings in exemplary, disciplined fashion. As The Blind Man, Arthur Davies could hardly be more ardent, but his slightly tremulous timbre will not be to all tastes. John Shirley-Quirk, so eloquent and firm-toned a Jesus for Groves back in 1980 (listed below), now shows signs of unsteadiness in the same part. On the other hand, Linda Finnie and Judith Howarth make a creditable showing. Hickox's reading excels in precisely the areas where the Groves was deficient, and vice versa. If you already have the Groves reissue, hang on to it, for it is by no means outclassed by the Hickox. However, for anyone coming to this underrated score for the first time, Hickox's must now be the preferred version.

Additional recommendations ...

...Soloists; Liverpool Philharmonic Choir; Royal Liverpool Philharmonic Orchestra / Sir Charles Groves. EMI British Composers Ⓜ CDM7 64732-2 (64 minutes: ADD: 5/93).

...The Light of Life – Meditation. The Apostles[a]. [a]**Sheila Armstrong** (sop); [a]**Helen Watts** (contr); [a]**Robert Tear** (ten); [a]**Benjamin Luxon, John Carol Case** (bars); [a]**Clifford Grant** (bass); [a]**London Philharmonic Choir;** [a]**Downe House School Choir; London Philharmonic Orchestra / Sir Adrian Boult.** EMI Ⓜ CMS7 64206-2 (two discs: 127 minutes: ADD).

Elgar The Music Makers, Op. 69[a]. Dream children, Op. 43. Elegy, Op. 58. Sursum corda, Op. 11. Sospiri, Op. 70. Chanson de matin, Op. 15 No. 2. Chanson de nuit, Op. 15 No. 1. Salut d'amour, Op. 12. [a]**Jean Rigby** (mez); [a]**BBC Symphony Chorus and Orchestra / Andrew Davis.** Teldec British Line Ⓕ 4509-92374-2 (76 minutes: DDD: 2/95). Text included. Recorded 1993. *Gramophone Editor's choice.*												ⓆⓆ

Davis strikes right to the heart of *The Music Makers* and the results are profoundly idiomatic and enchanting. Indeed, 'special' moments abound in this performance: note the chilling hush of Elgar's prescribed *ppp* marking at the words "In the buried past of the earth" (7'24"); the ravishing tone Davis draws from his excellent choir for "A breath of our inspiration" (11'43"); and how touching is his handling of that sublime passage beginning at 25'52" ("O men! it must ever be/That we dwell, in our dreaming and singing,/A little apart from ye"), with its poignant intertwining of themes from the *Enigma* Variations and the Violin Concerto. Even more than the admirable Bryden Thomson (listed below), Davis underlines the intensely personal nature of Elgar's inspiration, whilst at the same time doing full justice to this underrated score's dreams and aspirations. The predominantly wistful atmosphere of the main work carries over into the two exquisite miniatures which comprise *Dream children*; Davis and the BBC orchestra capture their nostalgic mood to perfection, and prove to be no less affectionate advocates of the two *Chansons* and *Salut d'amour*. Similarly, both the *Elegy* and *Sospiri* find the BBC strings at their very finest. The sound is sumptuous.

Additional recommendations ...

...The Music Makers[a]. Sea Pictures, Op. 37. **Linda Finnie** (contr); **London Philharmonic** [a]**Choir and Orchestra / Bryden Thomson.** Chandos Ⓕ CHAN9022 (64 minutes: DDD: 3/92).

| New review |

Elgar Sea Pictures, Op. 37. The Music Makers, Op. 69[a]. **Felicity Palmer** (mez); **London Symphony** [a]**Chorus and Orchestra / Richard Hickox.** EMI British Composers Ⓜ CDM5 65126-2 (62 minutes: DDD: 5/96). Texts included. From EL270589-1 (4/87).

These idiomatic Elgar performances from Richard Hickox well merit their mid-price resuscitation within EMI's British Composers series. Strong competition for the coupling of *The Music Makers* and *Sea Pictures* comes in the shape of Bryden Thomson's committed Chandos release. If Thomson has the advantage of more lustrous engineering, Hickox's admirable London Symphony Chorus score over Thomson's London Philharmonic group in matters of intonation and diction. Felicity Palmer (for Hickox) sings commandingly in both works, though her contribution in *The Music Makers* doesn't always generate the necessary tear-laden intensity. However, neither Hickox nor Thomson quite match Andrew Davis's Teldec account (reviewed above) – he in particular evinces a personal identification with Elgar's inspiration that is rather special. In the *Sea Pictures*, however, Hickox and Palmer form an intelligent, distinctive partnership, less endearing, perhaps, than many would like in "In Haven" and "Where corals lie", yet tough and dramatic in "Sabbath morning at sea" and "The swimmer". It is a thrusting, unsentimental view which is most refreshing. Excellent orchestral playing too.

Elgar The Dream of Gerontius, Op. 38[a]. Cello Concerto in E minor, Op. 85[b]. [a]**Gladys Ripley** (contr); [a]**Heddle Nash** (ten); [a]**Dennis Noble** (bar); [a]**Norman Walker** (bass); [b]**Paul Tortelier** (vc); [a]**Huddersfield Choral Society;** [b]**BBC Symphony Orchestra;** [a]**Liverpool Philharmonic Orchestra / Sir Malcolm Sargent.** Testament mono Ⓕ SBT2025* (two discs: 120 minutes: ADD: 2/94). Text included. Item marked [a] from HMV C3435/46 (6/45), [b]HMV BLP1043 (4/54). ⒼⒼ

This pioneering set of *Gerontius* has come up newly minted in these superbly engineered transfers taken from 78rpm masters. That only enhances the incandescence and fervour of the reading itself, in virtually all respects the most convincing the work has received. Sargent's conducting, influenced by Elgar's, is direct, vital and urgently crafted with an inborn feeling for the work's ebb and flow and an overall picture that comprehends the piece's spiritual meaning while realizing its dramatic leanness and force. Heddle Nash's Gerontius is unrivalled in its conviction and inwardness. He was encouraged by Elgar in 1930 to take the part and sang it under the composer's baton in 1932 to his satisfaction. By 1945 the work was in Nash's being; he sang it from memory and had mastered every facet of interpreting it. Such phrases as "Mary pray for me", "Novissima hora est" and "My soul is in my hand, I have no fear" come from and go to the heart. "Take me away" is like a searing cry of pain from the depth of the singer's soul. Gladys Ripley is a natural and communicative Angel throughout, her flexible and appealing tone always a pleasure to hear. The Liverpool Philharmonic lives up to its reputation at the time as the country's leading orchestra (in particular the sonorous string section) and the Huddersfield Choral Society sing as though their lives depended on the outcome. Tortelier's Cello Concerto presents the classical approach as compared with the romantic one of Du Pré, and is the best of Tortelier's readings of the work on disc, with his tone and phrasing at their firmest and most telling. A considered and unaffected reading among the best ever committed to disc.

Additional recommendations ...

...The Dream of Gerontius[a]. **Holst** The Hymn of Jesus, Op. 37[b]. [a]**Yvonne Minton** (mez); [a]**Sir Peter Pears** (ten); [a]**John Shirley-Quirk** (bar); [a]**Choir of King's College, Cambridge;** [a]**London Symphony Chorus and Orchestra / Benjamin Britten;** [b]**BBC Chorus and Symphony Orchestra / Sir Adrian Boult.** Decca London Ⓜ 421 381-2LM2 (two discs: 113 minutes: ADD: 5/89). Ⓖ

...The Dream of Gerontius[a]. Sea Pictures, Op. 37[b]. **Dame Janet Baker** (mez); [a]**Richard Lewis** (ten); [a]**Kim Borg** (bass); [a]**Hallé Choir;** [a]**Sheffield Philharmonic Chorus;** [a]**Ambrosian Singers;** [b]**London Symphony Orchestra;** [a]**Hallé Orchestra / Sir John Barbirolli.** EMI Studio Ⓜ CMS7 63185-2 (two discs: 122 minutes: ADD: 12/89).

...The Dream of Gerontius[a]. Organ Sonata No. 1 in G major, Op. 28 (orch. Jacob). [a]**Soloists;** [a]**Huddersfield Choral Society; Liverpool Philharmonic** [a]**Choir and Orchestra / Vernon Handley.** EMI Eminence Ⓜ CD-EMXD2500 (two discs: 119 minutes: DDD: 10/93).

| New review |

Elgar The Spirit of England, Op. 80[a]. Give unto the Lord, Op. 74. O hearken thou, Op. 64. The Snow, Op. 26 No. 1. Land of Hope and Glory (arr. Fagge). [a]**Felicity Lott** (sop); **London Symphony Chorus; Northern Sinfonia / Richard Hickox.** EMI British Composers Ⓜ CDM5 65586-2 (52 minutes: DDD: 5/96). Texts included. From CDC7 49481-2 (1/89).

Hickox adopts a purposeful approach to the great wartime cantata, *The Spirit of England*. Many collectors got to know this compassionate and moving score through Sir Alexander Gibson's extremely fine 1976 recording (originally made for RCA, now reissued at mid price on Chandos). Gibson's spacious and eloquent interpretation enshrined one of his very finest achievements in the studio, and possibly this EMI rival doesn't match it in sheer depth of feeling. That said, Hickox draws some magnificent singing from the London Symphony Chorus and his mobile reading compensates with a fervour to which many will positively respond. The fillers are all worth having, especially the sublime coronation Offertory from 1911, *O harken thou*. The production lacks nothing in transparency and amplitude, though in *The Spirit of England* especially one ideally craves a more expansive acoustic than that offered by EMI.

Additional recommendation ...

...The Spirit of England[b]. Coronation Ode, Op. 44[a]. [ab]**Teresa Cahill** (sop); [a]**Anne Collins** (contr); [a]**Anthony Rolfe Johnson** (ten); [a]**Gwynne Howell** (bass); **Scottish National Chorus and Orchestra / Sir Alexander Gibson.** Chandos Collect Ⓜ CHAN6574 (67 minutes: ADD: 11/92).

Further listening ...

...The Wand of Youth – Suites Nos. 1 and 2, Opp. 1*a* and 1*b*. Nursery Suite. **Ulster Orchestra / Bryden Thomson.** Chandos CHAN8318 (10/84).

...The Elgar Edition, Volume 2. **Sir Yehudi Menuhin** (vn); **London Symphony Orchestra; Royal Albert Hall Orchestra; New Symphony Orchestra; London Philharmonic Orchestra / Sir Edward Elgar.** EMI Elgar Edition mono CDS7 54564-2* (2/93). ⒼⒼⒼ

...The Elgar Edition, Volume 3. **Sir Edward Elgar** (pf); **London Philharmonic Orchestra; Royal Albert Hall Orchestra; London Symphony Orchestra; New Symphony Orchestra; BBC Symphony Orchestra / Sir Edward Elgar, Lawrence Collingwood, Sir Landon Ronald. New Light Symphony Orchestra / J. Ainslie Murray. Light Symphony Orchestra / Haydn Wood.** EMI Elgar Edition mono CDS7 54568-2* (8/93). *Gramophone* *Editor's choice.* ⒼⒼⒼ

...Organ Sonata No. 1 in G major, Op. 28. *Coupled with* **Bairstow** Organ Sonata in E flat major. **Harris** Organ Sonata in A minor. **John Scott** (org). Priory PRCD401 (8/94).

...Organ Sonata No. 1 in G major. *Coupled with works by* **Hollins, Cocker, Sumsion, Spicer, C.S. Lang, Lemare** and **Wagner Christopher Herrick** (org). Hyperion CDA66778 (3/96). *See review in the Collections section; refer to the Index to Reviews.*

...Partsongs – Opp. 18, 53, 71 and 73. Five Partsongs from the Greek Anthology, Op. 45. Death on the hills, Op. 72. How calmly the evening. Weary Wind of the West. Evening scene. The Prince of Sleep. Go, song of mine, Op. 57. **Finzi Singers / Paul Spicer.** Chandos CHAN9269 (1/95).

...Five Partsongs from the Greek Anthology. The Wanderer. Reveille, Op. 54. *Coupled with works by* **Vaughan Williams, Howells, Bax, Delius, Warlock, Britten** and **Holst London Madrigal Singers / Christopher Bishop; Baccholian Singers of London; Philip Jones Brass Ensemble; English Chamber Orchestra / Ian Humphris.** EMI British Composers CMS5 65123-2 (2/96). *See review in the Collections section; refer to the Index to Reviews.*

...Te Deum and Benedictus, Op. 34 – Te Deum. *Coupled with works by* **Statham, Howells, Moeran, S.S. Wesley, Britten** and **Gladstone Norwich Cathedral Choir / Michael Nicholas** with **Neil Taylor** (org). Priory PRCD470 (10/94).

...Caractacus, Op. 35[a]. Severn Suite, Op. 87*a*. [a]**Judith Howarth** (mez); [a]**Arthur Davies** (ten); [a]**David Wilson-Johnson**, [a]**Stephen Roberts** (bars); [a]**Alistair Miles** (bass); **London Symphony** [a]**Chorus and Orchestra / Richard Hickox.** Chandos CHAN9156/7 (2/93).

...The Apostles. **Soloists; London Symphony Chorus; London Symphony Orchestra / Richard Hickox.** Chandos CHAN8875/6 (12/90). Ⓖ

Manuel de Santo Elias
Spanish 18th century

Suggested listening ...

...Peroration. *Coupled with works by* **Bauld, Connolly, P.P. Nash, Weir, Payne** and **A. Gilbert Jane Manning** (sop); **Jane's Minstrels / Roger Montgomery.** NMC Artists' Series NMCD025 (10/95). *See review in the Collections section; refer to the Index to Reviews.*

Heino Eller
Estonian 1887-1970

Suggested listening ...

...Elegia. Five Pieces for String Orchestra. Dawn. *Coupled with* **Raid** Symphony No. 1 in C minor. **Royal Scottish Orchestra / Neeme Järvi.** Chandos CHAN8525 (11/89).

...Twilight. *Coupled with* **Tormis** Overture No. 2. **Tobias** Julius Caesar. **Lemba** Symphony in C sharp minor. **Pärt** Cantus in memory of Benjamin Britten. **Royal Scottish Orchestra / Neeme Järvi.** Chandos CHAN8656 (8/89).

Duke Ellington
American 1899-1974

Suggested listening ...

...Mainly Black (Black, brown and beige) – Suite. *Coupled with* **Bartók** Solo Violin Sonata. **Nigel Kennedy** (vn); **Alec Dankworth** (db). EMI CDC7 47621-2 (5/87).

...The River – Suite. *Coupled with* **Still** Afro-American Symphony. **Detroit Symphony Orchestra / Neeme Järvi.** Chandos CHAN9154 (4/93).

...Harlem. *Coupled with works by* **Still** and **Dawson** Detroit Symphony Orchestra / **Neeme Järvi**. Chandos CHAN9226 (3/94). *See review under Still; refer to the Index to Reviews.*

Vivian Ellis
British 1903-

Suggested listening ...

...Coronation Scot. *Coupled with works by* **Binge, Williams, Coates, Toye, Collins, Farnon, Baynes, Curzon, Lutz, Gibbs, White, Ketèlbey, Joyce** and **Ancliffe** New London Orchestra / **Ronald Corp.** Hyperion CDA66868 (7/96). *Gramophone Editor's record of the month. See review in the Collections section; refer to the Index to Reviews.* Ⓖ

Maurice Emmanuel
French 1862-1938

Suggested listening ...

...Symphonies[a] – No. 1 in A major, Op. 18; No. 2 in A major, Op. 25, "Bretonne". Le poème du Rhône[b]. **Rhenish Philharmonic Orchestra / [a]James Lockhart, [b]Gilles Nopre.** Marco Polo 8 223507 (3/94).

Juan del Encina
Spanish 1468-1529

Suggested listening ...

...Romances – Una sañosa porfía. Qu'es de ti, desconsolado?. Mortal tristura me dieron (instrumental version). Triste España sin ventura. Villancicos – Levanta, Pascual, levanta. Amor con fortuna. Fata la parte. Ay triste, que vengo. Cucú, cucú, cucucú. A tal perdida tan triste. Quedate, Carillo, adios (instrumental version). Si abrá en este baldres. El que rigue y el regido. Mas vale trocar. Oy comamos y bebamos. Tragedia – Despierta, despierta tus fuerças, Pegaso (recited). **Hespèrion XX / Jordi Savall.** Astrée Auvidis E8707 (2/92) ✒

...Mi libertad en sosiego. Los sospiros no sosiegan. *Coupled with works by* **Peñalosa, Mena, Enrique, Narváez, Fernández Palero, Milán, Segni** and **Anonymous** Gothic Voices / **Christopher Page** with **Christopher Wilson** (vihuela) and **Andrew Lawrence-King** (hp). Hyperion CDA66653 (2/94). *See review in the Collections section; refer to the Index to Reviews.*

...Más vale trocar. Si abrá en este baldrés! Qu'es de ti, desconsolado? Hoy comamos y bevamos. *Coupled with works by* **Anonymous, Narvaez, D. Ortiz, Pisador, Vásquez** and **Mudarra** La **Romanesca / José Miguel Moreno** (vihuela). Glossa GCD920203 (5/96). ✒ *See review in the Collections section; refer to the Index to Reviews.* Ⓖ

George Enescu
Romanian 1881-1955

Enescu Symphonies – No. 1 in E flat major, Op. 13; No. 2 in A major, Op. 17. **Monte-Carlo Philharmonic Orchestra / Lawrence Foster.** EMI Ⓕ CDC7 54763-2 (78 minutes: DDD: 9/93). Recorded 1990-92. *Gramophone Editor's choice.* Ⓖ

Brahmsian in colour the First Symphony may very well be, but the rhythmic vigour of its outer movements is quite unlike Brahms. Wagner? Well, any 24-year-old in 1905 writing a slow movement with moments of romantic yearning to it may be permitted to veer towards *Tristan*. Strauss may be the first name that springs to mind when listening to the Second Symphony, but by then Enescu's orchestration, highly individual and of remarkable refinement, had matured: 'Strauss', here, is merely a metaphor for richness of incident and colour. There is a flavour of Rachmaninov to the Second Symphony's slow movement, and an apparent kinship with Mahler, audible in the tense, martial finale, an apparent reaction to the outbreak of the First World War. Apart from the vividly imaginative orchestration, amazingly assured even in the First Symphony, Enescu's own voice is heard most clearly in his extremely detailed and complex working (which demands close attention from the listener; foreground and background, development and embellishment are in constant flux) of what is often basically bold and clear-cut melodic material. The symphonies are accomplished, immaculately crafted, and add up to distinctly more than the sum of their sometimes only apparent influences. Lawrence Foster's direction is brilliantly successful in ensuring that the wood is not obscured by all its luxuriant foliage; the recording is natural but very clear.

Additional recommendations ...

...No. 1. Overture on popular Romanian themes in A major, Op. 32. Study Symphony No. 4 in E flat major. **Romanian National Radio Orchestra / Horia Andreescu.** Olympia Ⓕ OCD441 (79 minutes: DDD: 11/94).

...No. 2. Romanian Rhapsodies, Op. 11. **Romanian National Radio Orchestra / Horia Andreescu.** Olympia Ⓕ OCD442 (72 minutes: DDD: 11/94).

...No. 3 in C major, Op. 71. Poème roumain, Op. 1[a]. **Romanian National Radio [a]Chorus and Orchestra / Horia Andreescu.** Olympia Ⓕ OCD443 (71 minutes: DDD: 11/94).

New review
Enescu Suites – No. 2 in C major, Op. 20; No. 3 in D major, Op. 27, "Villageoise". Andantino.
Romanian National Radio Orchestra / Horia Andreescu. Olympia Ⓔ OCD495 (62 minutes: DDD:
11/95). Recorded 1995.

Readers whose experience of Enescu extends to *Oedipe*, the symphonies and miscellaneous orchestral
works will already know what rich delights other collectors still have in store. This particular CD
extends the story to a pair of dazzling orchestral Suites, the Second (1915), a busy sequence of
movements reminiscent – at one time or other – of Strauss, Bartók and, most especially, Reger; the
Third (1938), or *Villageoise*, a series of versicoloured tone-poems that spell expertise in virtually every
bar. This Third Suite suggests the sort of freewheeling invention that characterizes Tchaikovsky's
Second Suite, with an opening evocation of "Nature Awakening in Spring" where inspired textural
complexity puts one in mind of Strauss, Korngold, Mahler and even the filigree extravagances of
Canteloube's *Chants d'Auvergne*. Piano and woodwind are employed with considerable imagination,
while the range of sounds that greets the third and fourth movements (distant brass reminiscent of
Don Quixote's sheep, a *Tristan*esque oboe soliloquy, atmospheric percussion, and so on) suggest a
mastery of timbre that equals – in expertise if not in style – Messiaen and Takemitsu. The Second
Suite opens in the bustling manner of Strauss's *Le bourgeois gentilhomme* Overture before recalling
the nature-music of early Bartók and broadening with all the weight and contrapuntal extravagance
of Reger. A gipsy-flavoured "Sarabande" occasionally suggests the Fauré of *Shylock*, while the odd
discursive modulation again brings Reger to mind. There's a "Menuet Grave" that seems to mirror,
albeit from a safe distance, the *Sanctus* from Bach's B minor Mass (of which Enescu was a master
interpreter), then a sultry, Ravelian "Air" and a further Regerian peroration, this time to the closing
"Bourrée". The disc ends with a Brahmsian *Andantino* that Enescu penned when he was just 15 years
old, a certain (and surprisingly skilful) augury of an exceptional talent in the making. Horia
Andreescu attends to each score with obvious affection and a fine sense of aural perspective, while
the Romanian National Radio Orchestra – although not exactly of the front-rank – respond with
obvious commitment. The recordings are spacious.

New review
Enescu String Octet in C major, Op. 7[a]. Wind Decet, Op. 14[b]. [a]**String ensemble** (René Cristian
Popescu, Liviu Morna, Mioara Moroianu, Adriana Winkler, vns; Gabriel Bălă, Florin Matei, vas;
Marin Cazacu, Dan Joitoiu, vcs); [b]**wind ensemble** (Virgil Frâncu, Nicolae Maxim, fls; Adrian
Petrescu, ob; Florin Ionoaia, cor ang; Valeriu Bărbuceanu, Leontin Boantă, cls; Gödri Orban,
Viorica Feher, bns; Simon Jebeleanu, Dan Cinca, hns) / **Horia Andreescu.** Olympia Ⓔ OCD445
(62 minutes: DDD: 11/95). Recorded 1995.

The String Octet of 1900 presents a vertiginous profile which was very much 'of the period'. It is an
almost exact contemporary of Schoenberg's *Verklärte Nacht* (1899 – Enescu's Octet was some 18
months in the making), although it is highly unlikely that either composer influenced the other, at
least not at this stage in their respective careers. There's a further parallel in that both Schoenberg and
Enescu were greatly influenced by Brahms. The Octet's first movement opens to a pulsating
accompaniment and a rich community of interconnected melodic ideas, all of them earnestly argued.
The *Verklärte Nacht* axis strikes home with particular force at 8'44" and then again at 1'33" into the
second movement, a leaping *Très fougueux* replete with Regerian-style modulations and an ethnic
slant to the melodies (noticeable throughout the work). Horia Andreescu directs an ardent, sweetly-
voiced performance, while his equally adept leadership of the Wind Decet (1906) makes a convincing
case for an even stronger work. Here Enescu's more assured style, tighter structures and luminous
instrumentation make for a delightful 23 minutes' listening. Of particular interest is the *Modérément*
second movement, which opens and closes with a plangent, sensitively embellished folk-style melody
and switches half-way to a perky second set that recalls the roughly contemporaneous *Romanian
Rhapsodies*. Both works should give considerable pleasure to lovers of late-romantic chamber music.
The recordings are more than serviceable, although in the Octet some string lines are prone to
edginess.

Additional recommendation ...
...String Octet. **Shostakovich** Two Pieces, Op. 11. **R. Strauss** Capriccio – Sextet. **Academy of St
Martin in the Fields Chamber Ensemble.** Chandos
Ⓔ CHAN9131 (61 minutes: DDD: 5/93).

Further listening ...
...Symphonie concertante, Op. 8[a]. Suite No. 1 in C major, Op. 9. Two Intermezzos, Op. 12. [a]**Marin
Cazacu** (vc); **Romanian National Radio Orchestra / Horia Andreescu.** Olympia OCD444 (6/95).
...Legend. *Coupled with works by* **Arban, Eben, Enescu, Fantini, Françaix, Goedicke,
Höhne** and **Tartini** John Wallace (tpt/cornet); Meyrick Alexander (bn); Simon Wright
(pf/org/hpd). EMI Virtuosi CDC5 55086-2 (11/94).
...String Quartets, Op. 22 – No. 1 in E flat major; No. 2 in G major. **Voces Quartet.** Olympia
Explorer OCD413 (5/92).
...Violin Sonatas – No. 2 in F minor, Op. 6; No. 3 in A minor, Op. 25, "dans le caractère populaire
roumain". Violin Sonata Movement, "Torso". **Adelina Oprean** (vn); **Justin Oprean** (pf). Hyperion
CDA66484 (2/92).

...Violin Sonata No. 3 in A minor, Op. 25, "dans le caractère populaire roumain"[a]. *Coupled with* **Chausson** Poème, Op. 25[b]. *Also includes works*[a] *by* **Beethoven, Corelli, D'Ambrosio, Handel, Kreisler, Pugnani** *and* **Wagner** [a]Sir Yehudi Menuhin, [b]George Enescu (vns); [a]Hepzibah Menuhin, [b]Sanford Schlüssel (pfs). Biddulph mono LAB066* (6/93). ⒼⒼⒼ

Christian Erbach
German 1570/73-1653

Suggested listening ...
...Sacerdotes Dei. Canzona secundi toni. Hic est sacerdos. Fantasia sub Elevatione. Toccata octavi toni. Posuisti Domine. La Paglia. *Coupled with works by* **Hassler** and **Lassus** Westminster Cathedral Choir; His Majesties Sagbutts and Cornetts / James O'Donnell with Timothy Roberts, Iain Simcock, Iris Schöllhorn (orgs). Hyperion CDA66688 (6/94). ✍

Heinrich Ernst
Moravian 1814-1865

New review
Ernst Der Erlkönig, Op. 26.
Liszt Grand duo concertant on Lafont's "Le marin", S128[a]. La lugubre gondola, S134[a]. Soirées de Vienne – Valse caprice d'après Schubert in A minor, S427 (trans. Oistrakh)[a]. Erlkönig, S558 No. 4[a].
Schubert Introduction and Variations in E minor on "Trockne Blumen" from "Die schöne Müllerin", D802[a]. **Gidon Kremer** (vn); [a]**Oleg Maisenberg** (pf). DG Ⓕ 445 820-2GH (57 minutes: DDD: 10/95). Recorded 1993.
Framed either end by dramatic transcriptions of *Der Erlkönig*, and with Schubert's *Die schöne Müllerin* Variations as its centrepiece, this absorbing recital grants maximum musical credibility to a little-known corner of the violinist's repertory. The Liszt pieces are extremely interesting but very rarely heard. Best, musically speaking, is the haunting *La lugubre gondola*, presented here as originally conceived (for violin and piano). Kremer's finely traced tone and judicious phrasing recall his great teacher David Oistrakh, while Heinrich Wilhelm Ernst's shimmering solo violin reworking of *Die Erlkönig* – the disc's opening track – calls on all manner of executive tricks. The sum effect suggests a spidery, coarse-grained witches' sabbath, while Liszt's better-known piano transcription – lavishly served here by Oleg Maisenberg – seems quite sober by comparison. Liszt's *Grand duo concertant on Lafont's "Le marin"* and Schubert's *Introduction and Variations on "Trockne Blumen"* (1824) have a common structural feature in that both start with substantial introductions before moving on to their respective 'theme with variations'. The Schubert was originally composed for flute and piano, and although annotator Volker Scherliess's contention that the transcription is "wholly in accordance with the practices of Schubert's own time" undoubtedly rings true, there's an additional point of interest in being able to trace a more or less straight path from these *Variations* to the great violin *Fantasy* of Schubert's last year. None of this music would register with much force were it not for the combined skills of its interpreters; and in this particular instance, both players employ the full range of their pooled imagination. It's rather like a shadowy soirée, sometimes charming, sometimes searching, but always worth listening to. The recordings are exemplary.

Rudolf Escher
Dutch 1912-1980

Suggested listening ...
...Cello Sonata. *Coupled with* **Crumb** Cello Sonata. **Kodály** Cello Sonata, Op. 8. **Pieter Wispelwey** (vc). Globe GLO5089 (12/94).

Pedro de Escobar
Portuguese c1465-1535

Suggested listening ...
...Clamabat autem mulier. *Coupled with* **Fonseca** Beata viscera. **Trosylho** Circumdederunt me. **Magalhães** Vidi acquam. Missa O soberana luz. Commissa mea pavesco. **Lôbo** Audivi vocem da caelo. Pater peccavi. **Cardoso** Lamentatio. Magnificat secundi toni. **Ars Nova / Bo Holten.** Naxos 8 553310 (3/96).

José Evangelista
Spanish/Canadian 1943-

New review
Evangelista Airs d'Espagne.
Ginastera Concerto for Strings, Op. 33.
Villa-Lobos Suite for Strings. Bachianas Brasileiras No. 9. **I Musici de Montréal / Yuli Turovsky.** Chandos Ⓕ CHAN9434 (65 minutes: DDD: 5/96). Recorded 1995.

Stylistic diversity is a conspicuous feature of this splendidly played (and equally splendidly recorded) disc. The most curious work here is the collection of 15 Spanish folk-tunes of various kinds (more than half lasting less than a minute each) arranged by José Evangelista, now a resident of Canada. He has added no harmony apart from an occasional bass note or drone, but instead treats the melodies with an often out-of-step ornamented heterophony which gives the whole an oddly East European flavour. Villa-Lobos is represented by two works separated by 30 years in his output. The early (1912) *Suite for Strings*, unusually lucid in texture for him, has an endearingly lyrical, nostalgic first movement, a mysterious, heart-searching *Andantino*, and a restless, agitated finale. The Ninth (and last) of the *Bachianas Brasileiras* cycle probably best justifies its Bachian reference: after a brief but beautiful prelude comes a vigorously argued and ingeniously complex fugue, whose syncopated 11-beat rhythm is crisply handled by the Montreal players. It is in Ginastera's masterly 1965 *Concerto for Strings*, however, that they particularly demonstrate their virtuosity. This begins with a series of solo variations for the section leaders (that for double-bass of scarifying difficulty) on a cadenza-like theme, incorporating quarter-tones, expounded by the first violin; a *scherzo fantastico* lives up to its name by all kinds of outlandish effects; an anguished and passionate *Andante* filled with a sense of desolation leads to a violently energetic finale that is an absolute knock-out.

Marco Facoli

Italian 16th century

Suggested listening ...
...Pass'e mezzo moderno.*Coupled with works by* **A. Valente, Giovanni de Macque, A. Mayone, Trabaci, Picchi, Buono, Frescobaldi, Lambardo, Merula, M. Rossi, Salvatore, B. Storace, G. Strozzi, Stradella** and **A. Scarlatti** Rinaldo Alessandrini (hpd). Opus 111 OPS30-118 (4/95). ✒ *See review in the Collections section; refer to the Index to Reviews.*

Manuel de Falla

Spanish 1876-1946

Falla El sombrero de tres picos[a]. Harpsichord Concerto[b]. [a]**Maria Lluisa Muntada** (sop); [b]**Jaime Martin** (fl); [b]**Manuel Angulo** (ob); [b]**Joan-Enric Lluna** (cl); [b]**Santiago Juan** (vn); [b]**Jorge Pozas** (vc); [b]**Tony Millan** (hpd); [a]**Spanish National Youth Orchestra / Edmon Colomer.** Auvidis Valois Ⓕ V4642 (56 minutes: DDD: 9/92). Recorded 1989.

Falla's *El sombrero de tres picos* ("The three-cornered hat") started life as a 'mimed farce', but Diaghilev then persuaded the composer to revise and enlarge it as a one-act ballet for his company which had its première in London in 1919. Besides the orchestra, it features a soprano solo warning wives to resist temptation and cries of "Olé" from men's voices representing a bullring crowd. Much of the score consists of dances such as the fandango and seguidillas, while the finale is a jota. This performance by Maria Lluisa Muntada and the Spanish National Youth Orchestra, playing under the direction of their founder Edmon Colomer, brings to us all the vivid colours, intense melodies and vigorous rhythms that together evoke that southernmost province of Spain which is Andalusia. These artists clearly love and understand this music and they bring tremendous gusto to the famous "Miller's Dance" (the longest single number) with its chunky chords getting louder and faster. The Harpsichord Concerto, completed in 1926, shows us another side of Falla and was among the first twentieth-century compositions for the instrument. It is less obviously Spanish in style and instead more neo-classical – indeed, Stravinsky was probably the chief model – although we may detect an Iberian element in its directness and even toughness. With just five instruments playing alongside the soloist, it is really a chamber work, but the writing is so powerful that the composer's title is doubtless justified. Here, too, the playing is fine and the recording of both these works is full-blooded and atmospheric.

Additional recommendations ...
...El sombrero de tres picos. El amor brujo – ballet[b]. **Colette Boky** (sop); [b]**Huguette Tourangeau** (mez); **Montreal Symphony Orchestra / Charles Dutoit.** Decca Ⓕ 410 008-2DH (62 minutes: DDD: 8/83).
...Siete canciones populares españolas. El amor brujo – Canción del fuego fátuo. Soneto a Córdoba. Harpsichord Concerto. *Coupled with works by* **Granados, Mompou** and **Nin** Maria Barrientos, Ninon Vallin (sops); **Enrique Granados, Federico Mompou, Joaquin Nin** (pfs); **Manuel de Falla** (pf/hpd); **instrumental ensemble.** EMI Composers in Person mono Ⓕ CDC7 54836-2* (78 minutes: ADD: 11/93). *See review in the Collections section; refer to the Index to Reviews.*
...El sombrero de tres picos[a]. Noches en los jardines de España[b]. [a]**Ann Murray** (mez); [b]**Tzimon Barto** (pf); **Academy of St Martin in the Fields / Sir Neville Marriner.** EMI Ⓕ CDC5 55049-2 (63 minutes: DDD: 5/94).

New review

Falla El amor brujo[a]. El sombrero de tres picos[b] – Dance of the Miller's Wife; Neighbours' Dance; Miller's Dance; Final Dance.
Stravinsky The Firebird – Concerto Suite (1919)[c]. [a]**Grace Bumbry** (mez); **Berlin Radio Symphony Orchestra / Lorin Maazel.** DG The Originals Ⓜ 447 414-2GOR (65 minutes: ADD: 10/95). Items marked [ab] from SLPM139115 (4/66), [c]SLPM138006 (12/58). Recorded 1957-65.

Fuss as we may about the glories of vintage Decca, Mercury and RCA recordings (with justification), there can't be many 'golden oldies' of the LP era that are more impressive than Lorin's Maazel's 1957 recording of the *Firebird* Suite, a brilliant reading, spectacularly well engineered and sounding particularly fine in this full-bodied Originals transfer. Of course much of the credit must go to Maazel himself (he was just 27 at the time), whose superb conducting technique facilitates a wealth of colour and dynamic inflexion. The playing of the Berlin Radio Symphony Orchestra is refined, precise and – in Kastchei's "Infernal Dance", especially – extremely high-powered, while the orchestral balance allows for numerous points of scoring that might otherwise (indeed, often do) remain ill-focused. Some eight years later, Maazel revisited the same location (Jesus-Christus Kirche, Berlin) for a Falla programme – and again, the results were remarkable. Here what impresses most is a consistent sense of musical line, especially in *El amor brujo*, where Grace Bumbry's strong, stylish singing serves as an added attraction. The *Three-cornered Hat* Dances could hardly be more idiomatic, as in the opening "Fandango", for example, where Maazel's control of rhythm and rubato is quite masterly; or in the painstakingly articulated "Danza final", a piece which can so often degenerate into mere rowdiness. Everywhere there's evidence of a firm hand at the helm, a genuine moulding influence. Maazel cuts a dash, as they say, and although he has since gone on to make numerous other distinguished recordings, few have proved as inspired as these. Strongly recommended.

Falla El amor brujo – ballet (complete)[a]. Noches en los jardines de España[b].
Rodrigo Concierto de Aranjuez[c]. [c]**Carlos Bonnell** (gtr); [b]**Alicia de Larrocha** (pf); [ac]**Montreal Symphony Orchestra / Charles Dutoit;** [b]**London Philharmonic Orchestra / Rafael Frühbeck de Burgos.** Decca Ovation Ⓜ 430 703-2DM (71 minutes: DDD: 8/91). Item marked [a] from SXDL7560 (7/83), [b]410 289-2DH (10/84), [c]SXDL7525 (7/81). Recorded 1980-83.
Falla El amor brujo – ballet (1915 version)[a]. Siete canciones populares españolas (orch. Berio).
Alicia Nafé (mez); [a]**Silvia Aguilar**, [a]**Antonio Belda Egea** (narrs); **Lausanne Chamber Orchestra / Jesús Lopez-Cobos.** Denon Ⓔ CO-75339 (44 minutes: DDD: 10/93). Notes, texts and translations included. Recorded 1992.

Decca's hugely enjoyable disc of Spanish music includes Rodrigo's most famous work, the *Concierto de Aranjuez* which has never lost its popularity since its Barcelona première in 1940 and here Carlos Bonnell imparts a wistful, intimate feeling to the work, aided by a thoughtful accompaniment from Charles Dutoit's stylish Montreal Orchestra. The famous string tune in the *Adagio* enjoys a fulsome rendition. Dutoit's beautifully played interpretation of *El amor brujo* captures the wide range of emotions that this fiery, mysterious piece requires and his performance of the famous "Ritual Fire Dance" must be among the best in the catalogue. A cooler mood is captured in *Nights in the gardens of Spain* with Alicia de Larrocha as the distinguished soloist. Her smooth, effortless playing matches the mood of the piece exactly and de Burgos's accompaniment with the London Philharmonic is equally sympathetic, with ripe tone colour and careful dynamics. Those unfamiliar with these great Spanish works will be hard pressed to find a better introduction than this superbly recorded disc.

The second disc here provides an opportunity to hear the original 1915 version of *El amor brujo* and the coupling, though stingy, is attractive. Berio's 1978 orchestration of the *Siete canciones* is stylish, the sort of thing that Falla might have done himself had it occurred to him (it uses, in fact, almost exactly the same orchestra that Falla chose for the more familiar 1925 revision of *El amor brujo*). In the *gitaneria* version of *El amor brujo* Nafé must be actress as well as singer, and in the latter role as much folk-singer as concert artist (the central role of Candelas was written for a famous gipsy dancer, Pastora Imperio). She's first-class in all respects, bending notes slightly and expressively, using the quiet and subtle end of her voice as well as its considerable reserves of throaty pungency. Among the alternatives are the Swiss mezzo Martha Senn and the Carme Ensemble, similarly coupled (though Senn uses the original, piano accompanied *Siete canciones*, and there are a couple of minor piano pieces as fill-ups) – excellent though the conductor, Luis Izquierdo is, he has not quite Lopez-Cobos's fire.

Additional recommendations ...

...El amor brujo[ac]. Siete canciones populares españolas[ab]. Serenata[b]. Serenata andaluza[b]. [a]**Martha Senn** (mez); [b]**Maria Rosa Bodini** (pf); [c]**Carme Ensemble / Luis Izquierdo.** Nuova Era Ⓔ 6809 (57 minutes: DDD: 5/90).

...Noches en los jardines de España. *Coupled with works by* **Albéniz** *and* **Turina** Alicia de Larrocha (pf); **London Philharmonic Orchestra / Rafael Frühbeck de Burgos.** Decca Ⓔ 410 289-2DH (52 minutes: DDD: 10/84). *See review under Albéniz; refer to the Index to Reviews.*　　　　　　　　　　　　　　　　　　Ⓖ

...Noches en los jardines de España. **Ravel** Piano Concerto in G major. Piano Concerto for the Left Hand. **Francois-Joël Thiollier** (pf); **Polish National Radio Symphony Orchestra / Antoni Wit.** Naxos Ⓢ 8 550753 (64 minutes: DDD: 3/95).

Falla Quatre pièces espagnoles. Fantasía bética. La vida breve – Spanish dance No. 1. Serenata andaluza. El Retablo de Maese Pedro – Sinfonia.
Montsalvatge Divagación. Three divertimentos on themes of forgotten composers. Si, à Mompou. Berceuse a la memoria de Oscar Esplá. Sonatine pour Yvette. **Alicia de Larrocha** (pf). RCA Victor Red Seal Ⓟ 09026 61389-2 (70 minutes: DDD: 9/94). Recorded 1992. ⒼⒼ

It is odd of RCA to label this disc "Serenata andaluza" when half of it is occupied by music by a Catalan composer with nothing Andalusian about him. The popularity of Montsalvatge's *Canciones negras* has misled some commentators into exaggerating the West Indian calypso influence on his output: a truer perspective on his style is offered by this selection of his piano music. From the *Divertimentos* of 1942 only the habanera, with its echoes of Milhaud's *Saudades do Brasil*, falls into the West Indian category. These pieces were dedicated to Larrocha and the cheerful *Divagación* was a wedding present to her. The *Sonatine* was written in 1962 for his then ten-year-old daughter, obviously not for her to play (unless she was the most extraordinary child super-virtuoso of all time) but as a musical portrait of her vivacious and temperamental moods. Larrocha takes the first movement gently and quietly and the second with impassioned depth: the entertaining finale (which quotes the most famous of nursery tunes) is as brilliant as ever. It then comes as a surprise to find a very different, tougher idiom in the two *in memoriam* pieces (for left hand only) for older contemporaries. In the Falla works Larrocha has surpassed herself. In the austere, penetrating and incisive *Fantasía bética*, so elusive to bring off in performance, she displays great tonal imagination throughout, confirming her status as the foremost interpreter today of Spanish keyboard music.

Falla El retablo de Maese Pedro[a]. **Matthew Best** (bass) Don Quijote; **Adrian Thompson** (ten) Maese Pedro; **Samuel Linay** (treb) El Trujamán; **Maggie Cole** (hpd).
Milhaud Les Malheurs d'Orphée[b]. **Malcolm Walker** (bar) Orphée; **Anna Steiger** (sop) Eurydice; **Paul Harrhy** (ten) Maréchal, Le sanglier; **Patrick Donnelly** (bass) Le charron; **Matthew Best** (bass) Le vannier, L'ours; **Gaynor Morgan** (sop) Le renard, La soeur Jumelle; **Patricia Bardon** (sop) Le loup, La soeur Ainée; **Susan Bickley** (mez) Le soeur Cadette.
Stravinsky Renard[c]. **Hugh Hetherington, Paul Harrhy** (tens); **Patrick Donnelly, Nicolas Cavallier** (basses); **Christopher Bradley** (cimbalom); [abc]**Matrix Ensemble / Robert Ziegler.** ASV Ⓟ CDDCA758 (77 minutes: DDD: 7/91). Texts and translations included.

Three complete operas on one disc lasting 77 minutes must be good value, and especially so when they are important works from the first quarter of this century. One thing they have in common is that all were commissioned by the American-born Princess de Polignac, a patroness of music who exercised considerable flair in her choice of gifted artists in a Paris that was then full of them. The performances here by Robert Ziegler and his Matrix Ensemble are full of flair and his chosen singers for the three works (who include the convincingly Spanish boy treble Samuel Linay as El Trujamán in the Falla) sound at home in Spanish, French and Russian in turn. As presented here, Falla's puppet-opera is full of Iberian colour and verve, and although Milhaud's piece on the Orpheus legend is not so striking or dramatic it still has beauty and is elegantly and expressively sung and played. But the best music is still to come in Stravinsky's magnificently earthy and vivid 'barnyard fable' *Renard*, not a long work but a dazzling one, where this performance of great panache simply bursts out of one's loudspeakers to transport us instantly to a farmyard of old Russia. There's excellent cimbalom playing here from Christopher Bradley. The libretto of all three works is usefully provided in the booklet, together with an English translation. The recording is first class, being both immediate and atmospheric.

Further listening ...
...Homenaje, "Le tombeau de Claude Debussy". *Coupled with works by* **Turina, Sor, Tárrega, Albéniz, Granados, Mudarra, Guerau, Milán, Rodrigo, Moreno Torroba** and **C. Romero** Pepe Romero (gtr). Philips 442 150-2PH (4/95).
...La vida breve   Danses espagnoles. El amor brujo – Ritual Fire Dance. *Coupled with works by* **Lecuona, Albéniz** and **Infante** Katia and Marielle Labèque (pfs). Philips 438 938-2PH (9/94). *See review in the Collections section; refer to the Index to Reviews.*
...La vida breve. **Soloists; Ambrosian Opera Chorus; London Symphony Orchestra / Garcia Navarro.** DG 435 851-2GH (10/92).

Robert Farnon   Canadian/British 1917-

Suggested listening ...
...Portrait of a Flirt. How Beautiful is Night. Melody Fair. A la Claire Fontaine. Peanut Polka. In a Calm. Gateway to the West. Jumping Bean. Pictures in the Fire. Little Miss Molly. Colditz March. A Star Is Born. Westminster Waltz. Manhattan Playboy. Lake in the Woods. Derby Day. State Occasion. **Bratislava Radio Symphony Orchestra / Adrian Leaper.** Marco Polo 8 223401 (9/92).
...Captain Horatio Hornblower – Suite. A la Claire Fontaine. State Occasion. Lake in the Woods. A Promise of Spring. Intermezzo. Rhapsody. **Royal Philharmonic Orchestra / Robert Farnon.** Reference Recordings RR47CD (9/92).
...Jumping Bean. *Coupled with works by* **Binge, Williams, Coates, Toye, Collins, Baynes, Curzon, Lutz, Gibbs, White, Ketèlbey, Joyce, Ellis** and **Ancliffe** New London Orchestra /

Ronald Corp. Hyperion CDA66868 (7/96). *Gramophone Editor's record of the month. See review in the Collections section; refer to the Index to Reviews.* Ⓖ

David Farquhar
New Zealand 1928-

Suggested listening ...

...Ring around the Moon – Short Suite. *Coupled with works by* **C. Blake, A. Ritchie, A. Watson, Lilburn, Whitehead, Jenny McLeod, Pruden** and **Carr** New Zealand Symphony Orchestra / **Kenneth Young.** Continuum (special price) CCD1073 (5/96). *See review in the Collections section; refer to the Index to Reviews.*

Ernest Farrar
British 1885-1918

Suggested listening ...

...O mistress mine!. *Coupled with works by* **Finzi, Milford, Gurney** and **Gill** Ian Partridge (ten); **Stephen Roberts** (bar); **Clifford Benson** (pf). Hyperion CDA66015 (9/91). *See review in the Collections section; refer to the Index to Reviews.*

Carl Friedrich Fasch
German 1688-1758

Suggested listening ...

...Lute Concerto in D minor. *Coupled with works by* **Heinichen, Dieupart, Pisendel, Quantz** and **Veracini** Cologne Musica Antiqua / **Reinhard Goebel.** Archiv Produktion 447 644-2AH (1/96). 🗡

...Concerto for Trumpet, Oboe d'amore, Violin and Strings in E major. *Coupled with works by* **Haydn, Hummel, Neruda** and **F. Weber** John Wallace (tpt); John Anderson (ob d'amore); Peter Thomas (vn); **Philharmonia Orchestra / Christopher Warren-Green, Simon Wright.** Nimbus NI7016 (2/95). *See review in the Collections section; refer to the Index to Reviews.*

...Andantino con Variazioni[a]. *Coupled with* **Benda** Keyboard Sonatinas[a] – Rondeau; Allegro; Allegretto; Allegretto; Allegretto moderato. **Graun** Keyboard Sonata in D minor[a]. **Hasse** Keyboard Sonata in E flat major[a]. **Schulz** Diverses pièces, Op. 1[b] – No. 5, Allegretto; No. 6, Larghetto con Variazioni. **C.P.E. Bach** Pièces Caractéristiques[b] – La Borchward, H79; La Pott, H80; La Gleim, H89; La Bergius, H90; La Stahl, H94; La Boehmer, H81; La Louise, H114. **Christine Schornsheim** ([a]hpd/[b]fp). Capriccio 10 424 (4/95). 🗡

Gabriel Fauré
French 1845-1924

Fauré Pelléas et Mélisande, Op. 80 (with Chanson de Mélisande – orch. Koechlin)[a]. Three Songs, Op. 7 – Après un rêve (arr. vc/orch. Dubenskij)[b]. Pavane, Op. 50[c]. Elégie, Op. 24[b]. Dolly Suite, Op. 56 (orch. Rabaud). [a]**Lorraine Hunt** (sop); [b]**Jules Eskin** (vc); [c]**Tanglewood Festival Chorus; Boston Symphony Orchestra / Seiji Ozawa.** DG Ⓟ 423 089-2GH (56 minutes: DDD: 1/88). Texts and translations included where appropriate. Recorded 1986.

Fauré's music for Maeterlinck's play *Pelléas et Mélisande* was commissioned by Mrs Patrick Campbell and to the usual four movement suite Ozawa has added the "Chanson de Mélisande", superbly sung here by Lorraine Hunt. Ozawa conducts a sensitive, sympathetic account of the score, and Jules Eskin plays beautifully in both the arrangement of the early song, *Après un rêve* and the *Elégie*, which survived from an abandoned cello sonata. The grave *Pavane* is performed here in the choral version of 1901. *Dolly* began life as a piano duet, but was later orchestrated by the composer and conductor Henri Rabaud. Ozawa gives a pleasing account of this delightful score and the recording is excellent.

Additional recommendations ...

...Pelléas et Mélisande. Pavane[a]. **Chausson** Poème de l'amour et de la mer, Op. 19[b]. Poème, Op. 25[c]. [b]**Linda Finnie** (mez); [a]**Renaissance Singers; Ulster Orchestra / Paul Tortelier** ([c]vn). Chandos Ⓕ CHAN8952 (69 minutes: DDD: 12/91).

...(arr. C. Williams): Dolly – Berceuse. *Coupled with works by* **Debussy, Ibert, Françaix, Milhaud, Damase, Pierné** and **Poulenc** Reykjavik Wind Quintet. Chandos Ⓕ CHAN9362 (63 minutes: DDD: 10/95).

New review

Fauré Masques et bergamasques, Op. 112. Ballade, Op. 19[c]. Pavane, Op. 50. Fantaisie, Op. 79[a]. Pénélope – Overture. Elégie, Op. 24[b]. Dolly Suite, Op. 56. [a]**Richard Davis** (fl); [b]**Peter Dixon** (vc); [c]**Kathryn Stott** (pf); **BBC Philharmonic Orchestra / Yan Pascal Tortelier.** Chandos Ⓕ CHAN9416 (72 minutes: DDD: 5/96). Recorded 1995.

Fauré wrote surprisingly few orchestral works, and it was a good idea on the part of Chandos to assemble this selection. However, although the transcription of the celebrated cello *Elégie* is the composer's own, the *Dolly* suite, originally for piano duet, comes here in Henri Rabaud's arrangement and the flute *Fantaisie* is the transcription made by Louis Aubert for Jean-Pierre Rampal. The biggest *concertante* work here, the *Ballade* of 1881, is Fauré's orchestration of his piano piece of the same name; it is gentle music that persuades and cajoles in a very Gallic way. Though not an overtly virtuoso utterance, it makes its own exacting technical demands on the soloist, among them being complete control of touch and pedalling. The highly-regarded Fauréan Kathryn Stott meets these with consistent success. *Masques et bergamasques*, which takes its title from Verlaine's sad, mysterious poem *Clair de lune*, is a late stage work that the composer himself described as melancholy and nostalgic, but it is hardly romantic, being instead pointedly neo-classical in character and shape, recalling Bizet's youthful C major Symphony and Grieg's *Holberg Suite*. The playing here under Tortelier is very satisfying, as are the elegant flute solos of the exquisitely delicate *Pavane*, performed here without the optional chorus, and in *Dolly*. The rarely heard Overture to the opera *Pénélope* is also effectively presented here. There's little rhetoric and no bombast in Fauré's art, but how civilized he was, and what sympathetic interpreters serve him here! Chandos's warm yet delicate recording suits the music well.

Fauré Ballade, Op. 19.
Franck Symphonic Variations, Op. 46.
d'Indy Symphonie sur un chant montagnard français in G major, Op. 25. **François-Joël Thiollier**
(pf); **National Symphony Orchestra of Ireland / Antonio de Almeida.** Naxos Ⓢ 8 550754
(55 minutes: DDD: 1/95). Recorded 1993. *Gramophone Editor's choice.*

This is a disc of French works, all for piano and orchestra, and all from the late 1870s and 1880s. The renamed RTE Symphony Orchestra, a match for its more recorded counterpart in Ulster, taped the programme in their new Dublin concert-hall (acoustically clean, bright and airy, but warm, if this disc's sound is representative). François-Joël Thiollier's playing is individual, often impulsive but always idiomatic, helped by the sensitive, guiding hand of a conductor obviously well acquainted with the music. A more high-profile production would probably have retaken those passages where piano and orchestra co-ordination is occasionally fractionally awry, such as in the last variation of the Franck, but then, it might also have seemed less spontaneous. There isn't quite the sophistication of tone and balance to be found in the (full-price) Thibaudet/Dutoit account of the d'Indy (see review under Franck; refer to the Index to Reviews), but Thiollier's rubato is always distinctive and attractive; the style, particularly and crucially in the Fauré, properly fluid. Both the piano and the orchestra's woodwind are discreetly prominent, but internal balances are generally excellent. There are no budget-price competitors in this repertoire that reproduce with such beauty of tone.

Additional recommendation ...

...Ballade, Op. 19. **Ravel** Piano Concerto in G major. Piano Concerto for the Left Hand. **Louis Lortie** (pf); **London Symphony Orchestra / Rafael Frühbeck de Burgos.** Chandos Ⓕ CHAN8773 (57 minutes: DDD: 1/90).

Fauré Piano Quintets – No. 1 in D minor, Op. 89; No. 2 in C minor, Op. 115. **Domus** (Krysia Ososowicz, vn; Timothy Boulton, va; Richard Lester, vc; Susan Tomes, pf); **Anthony Marwood** (vn). Hyperion Ⓕ CDA66766 (60 minutes: DDD: 7/95). Recorded 1994. *Gramophone Award Winner 1995.*

Having given us exemplary, *Gramophone* Award-winning performances of the two piano quartets (reviewed below), Domus continue with even more inspired recordings of the Quintets. However, not even the most ardent Fauréan or Francophile could admit that such music yields up its secrets easily. Indeed, despite pages pulsing with all of Fauré's sustained radiance and energy the abiding impression is of music of such profound introspection that the listener often feels like an interloper stumbling into an essentially private conversation. But perseverance reaps the richest rewards and moments like the opening of the D minor Quintet where Fauré achieves what is referred to in the insert-notes as a "rapt weightlessness", or the closing pages of the C minor Quintet's *Andante moderato* (starting at 6'25") send out resonances that finally embrace the entire work. The other-worldly dance commencing the finale of the First Quintet, the wild catch-as-catch-can opening and elfin close of the C minor Quintet's *Allegro vivo* or the grave serenity of the following *Andante moderato*; all these are surely at the heart of Fauré's simultaneously conservative and radical genius. Simply as a person Fauré remained conscious of an elusiveness that baffled and tantalized even his closest friends, companions who felt themselves gently but firmly excluded from his complex interior world. Domus fully suggest this enigma yet play with such ardour and *élan* that the composer himself would surely have been delighted ("people play me as if the blinds were down"). The recordings are superb.

Fauré Piano Quartets No. 1 in C minor, Op. 15; No. 2 in G minor, Op. 45. **Domus** (Krysia Ososowicz, vn; Robin Ireland, va; Timothy Hugh, vc; Susan Tomes, pf). Hyperion Ⓕ CDA66166 (62 minutes: DDD: 10/86). From A66166 (10/86). *Gramophone Award Winner 1986.* Ⓠ

The First Piano Quartet reveals Fauré's debt to an earlier generation of composers, particularly Mendelssohn. Yet already it has the refined sensuality, the elegance and the craftsmanship which were always to be hallmarks of his style and it is a thoroughly assured, highly enjoyable work which could come from no other composer's pen. The Second Quartet is a more complex, darker work, but much less ready to yield its secrets. The comparatively agitated, quicksilver scherzo impresses at once, however, and repeated hearings of the complete work reveal it to possess considerable poetry and stature. Just occasionally one could wish that the members of Domus had a slightly more aristocratic, commanding approach to these scores, but overall the achievement is highly impressive, for their playing is both idiomatic and technically impeccable. The recording has an appropriately intimate feel to it and is faithful and well-balanced.

Additional recommendations ...

...Piano Quartets. Piano Quintets. String Quartet in E minor, Op. 121. **Jean-Philippe Collard** (pf); **Augustin Dumay** (vn); **Bruno Pasquier** (va); **Frédéric Lodéon** (vc); **Michel Debost** (fl); **Parrenin Quartet.** EMI Rouge et Noir Ⓜ CMS7 62548-2 (two discs: 157 minutes: ADD: 5/89).

...Piano Quartets. **Isaac Stern** (vn); **Jaime Laredo** (va); **Yo-Yo Ma** (vc) **Emanuel Ax** (pf). Sony Classical Ⓕ SK48066 (67 minutes: DDD: 9/93).

...Piano Quartets. **Los Angeles Piano Quartet.** IMP Masters Ⓕ MCD66 (66 minutes: DDD: 10/93).

New review

Fauré Romance in A major, Op. 69[b]. Elégie, Op. 24[b]. Cello Sonatas – No. 1 in D minor, Op. 109[b]; No. 2 in G minor, Op. 117[b]. Allegretto moderato[a]. Sérénade, Op. 98[b]. Sicilienne, Op. 78[b]. Papillon, Op. 77[b]. Andante[c]. **Steven Isserlis**, [a]**David Waterman** (vcs); [b]**Pascal Devoyon** (pf); [c]**Francis Grier** (org). RCA Victor Red Seal Ⓕ 09026 68049-2 (62 minutes: DDD: 8/95). Recorded 1993-4.   Ⓖ

This, surely, is the most 'complete' of Fauré's complete works for cello yet to appear. Isserlis has unearthed the original version of the *Romance*, Op. 69 (entitled *Andante*, proudly hailed as a "world première recording"), with a sustained, chordal accompaniment for organ in place of the piano's broken chordal semiquavers, and a gracious flourish from the cello itself by way of adieu. Mystically accompanied by Francis Grier at the organ of Eton College Chapel, the cello's song, restored to the church, seems to acquire more depth. But let it be said at once that in the familiar version of this work, as throughout the disc, Pascal Devoyon is a partner in a thousand, keenly aware of Isserlis's respect for the "discretion, reticence and restraint" once hailed as the hallmarks of Fauré's style. In fact only in the noble *Elégie*, earliest of the miniatures, do we discover the full breadth and richness of this cello's (a 1745 Guadagnini) tonal range. A world war, plus the private trauma of incipient deafness, helps to explain the yawning gulf between the miniatures and the two sonatas of 1918 and 1922. Skipping through the score of the First you notice that only once does Fauré use a dynamic marking above a *forte*, relying on the word *espressivo* to elicit just that little extra intensity at moments of climax. This is appreciated by both artists, most movingly in the central *Andante*. In the first movement, however, it is Devoyon's piquant accentuation that brings home the music's menace. The urgency and *Elégie*-evoking heart-throb of the G minor work again benefit from the immediacy of keyboard characterization, and the variety of keyboard colour, underpinning this poetically introspective cellist's fine-spun line.

Fauré Violin Sonatas – No. 1 in A major, Op. 13; No. 2 in E minor, Op. 108. Morceau de concours. Andante in B flat major, Op. 75. Romance in B flat major, Op. 28. Berceuse, Op. 16. **Pierre Amoyal** (vn); **Pascal Rogé** (pf). Decca Ⓕ 436 866-2DH (65 minutes: DDD: 2/95). Recorded 1992. *Gramophone Editor's choice.*   Ⓖ

These radiant early and late masterpieces are unforgettable reflections of Fauré's first romantic ardour and his subsequent, deeply courageous journey through the most remote and interior regions of both soul and mind. Fauré was a 'conservative' only in the richest, most inclusive sense, setting up conventions only to challenge them with his unique mix of audacity and subtlety. Here, in the Second Sonata, are turbulence and hyperactivity on a background of calm (to extend Copland's famous description), the bitter fruit of Fauré's increasing deafness and lack of recognition (his publisher's wife used the scores of his *Nocturnes* and *Barcarolles* as jam-jar covers). Amoyal and Rogé are superbly challenging and authentic at every level. The opening *Allegro molto* from the First Sonata becomes a tumultuous rush of events, a committed alternative to more 'classical' or staid readings, while the *Andante* is kept firmly on the move (a qualifying *con moto*); a reminder, perhaps, of the French fear of all possible sentimentality. Yet how stellar is Rogé's way with the *a tempo* and *dolcissimo* at 2'36", and what an Elysium both players find as the music sinks to its final resting place. The *Allegro vivo*, on the other hand, could hardly be more nimble, a true catch-as-catch-can with a delightful relishing of Fauré's constantly shifting and mischievously altered phrase lengths. Again, in the Second Sonata, both violinist and pianist play with rare individuality and unanimity, Amoyal's sweet and slightly nasal tone complemented by Rogé's greater fullness. Their *Andante* is, again, coolly paced but elsewhere there is a powerful recognition of Fauré's strength and delicacy and the way his ceaseless flow of ideas is so often tinged with irony and unease. For their encores (distinguishing this disc from some stylish alternative recordings of the sonatas) Amoyal and Rogé give us three miniatures where salon clichés are effortlessly and, indeed, magically transformed. Even the *Berceuse*'s passing resemblance to the *Eton Boating Song* seems sublime rather than unfortunate. The recordings are excellent and the entire recital should do much to erase notions (sadly, still current) of Fauré as a poor country cousin of Ravel and Debussy.

Additional recommendations ...

...Nos. 1 and 2. **Krysia Osostowicz** (vc); **Susan Tomes** (pf). Hyperion Ⓕ CDA66277 (50 minutes: DDD: 11/88).

...Nos. 1 and 2[a]. **Franck** Violin Sonata in A major[b]. **Arthur Grumiaux** (vn); [a]**Paul Crossley,**
[b]**György Sebok** (pfs). Philips Musica da Camera Ⓜ 426 384-2PC (73 minutes: ADD: 7/90).   ⒼⒼ
...No. 1. **Debussy** Violin Sonata. **Franck** Violin Sonata in A major. **Pinchas Zukerman** (vn);
Marc Neikrug (pf). RCA Victor Red Seal Ⓕ 09026 62697-2 (68 minutes: DDD: 5/95).
...No. 1. **Debussy** Violin Sonata. **Poulenc** Violin Sonata. **Isabelle van Keulen** (vn); **Ronald
Brautigam** (pf). Koch Schwann Ⓕ 315272 (56 minutes: DDD: 10/95).
...Nos. 1 and 2. Berceuse, Op. 16. Romance. Andante. **Dong-Suk Kang** (vn); **Pascal Devoyon** (pf).
Naxos Ⓢ 8 550906 (62 minutes: DDD: 3/96).

New review

Fauré Five Impromptus. Impromptu, Op. 86. Thème et Variations in C sharp minor, Op. 73.
Romances sans paroles, Op. 17. Four Valses-caprices. 13 Barcarolles. Ballade in F sharp major,
Op. 19. 13 Nocturnes. Souvenirs de Bayreuth (with Martin Roscoe, pf). Pièces brèves, Op. 84.
Dolly, Op. 56 (Roscoe). Nine Préludes, Op. 103. Mazurka in B flat major, Op. 32. **Kathryn Stott**
(pf). Hyperion Ⓜ CDA66911/4 (four discs: 297 minutes: DDD: 5/95). Recorded 1994.
Gramophone Editor's choice.   Ⓖ

Fauré's piano works are among the most subtly daunting in all keyboard literature. Contradicting his
diffidence ("it seems that I repeat myself constantly") they possess on the contrary an astonishing
scope. Encompassing Fauré's entire creative life they range through an early, finely wrought eroticism
via sporting with an aerial virtuosity as teasing and light as the elements themselves (the *Valses-
caprices*) to the final desolation of Fauré's last years. There, in his most powerful works (*Barcarolles*
Nos. 7-11, *Nocturnes* Nos. 11-13) he faithfully mirrors a pain that "scintillates in full consciousness"
a romantic agony prompted by increasing deafness and a lack of recognition that often seemed close
to oblivion. Few compositions have reflected a darker night of the soul and Fauré's anguish, expressed
in both numbing resignation and unbridled anger, could surely only be exorcized by the articulation
of such profound and disturbing emotional complexity. The task for the pianist, then, is immense, but
in Kathryn Stott Fauré has a subtle and fearless champion. Her early Conifer albums were themselves
a vibrant and personal tribute. But, be warned, once your appetite is whetted you will want to move
on to Hyperion's sumptuously recorded, complete offering. Here, on four lavishly packaged CDs, are
the *Ballade* in its original solo version, the sixth *Impromptu* (transcribed from the harp), *Dolly* and
even the *Souvenirs de Bayreuth* where Fauré turns prankster and enjoys a night out with the boys.
How thrilled Fauré would have been by the sheer immediacy of Stott's responses. Time and again she
throws convention to the winds, and although it would be surprising if all her performances were
consistent successes, disappointments are rare. Sometimes her rubato and luxuriant pedalling soften
the outlines of Fauré's starkest, most austere utterances. The Twelfth and Thirteenth *Nocturnes*, for
example, are surely too loosely controlled to achieve their fullest drama and focus, and here, in
particular, Paul Crossley is infinitely more concentrated and dramatic in his brightly lit CRD
recordingss. She hurries rather than lingers over the effusiveness in the third of the *Romances sans
paroles* and the *Variations*, too, are not uniformly poised. A profounder sense of speculation in the
Molto adagio of No. 6 would have been welcome, and an even greater sense of unearthly calm in No.
9. But such quibbles remain quibbles. How Stott relishes a modern Steinway's opulent transformation
of the harp's thin and glittering textures in the Sixth *Impromptu*, and the *Mazurka* has rarely been spun
off with such a truly virtuoso insouciance. The Third *Impromptu*'s missing *Molto meno mosso* (on the
Conifer recording) is reinstated and the First *Impromptu*'s propulsion is even more urgently and richly
inflected. The Fourth *Nocturne* is gloriously supple, and the 13 *Barcarolles* show Stott acutely
responsive to passion and finesse alike. The *Pièces brèves*, too, are played with rare affection. Changes
and developments in the interim period between the Conifer and Hyperion discs make for fascinating
listening. A true and dedicated Francophile (though with an exceptionally wide repertoire), Stott is
among the more stylish and intriguing of the younger generation of pianists. For *Souvenirs de Bayreuth*
and *Dolly* she is robustly partnered by Martin Roscoe, an added bonus in an invaluable issue.

Additional recommendations ...

...Barcarolles Nos. 1-13. **Paul Crossley** (pf). CRD Ⓕ CRD3422 (64 minutes: DDD: 6/88).
...Nocturnes Nos. 1-7. **Paul Crossley** (pf). CRD Ⓕ CRD3406 (52 minutes: ADD: 6/88).
...Nocturnes Nos. 8-13. 8 Pièces brèves, Op. 84. **Paul Crossley** (pf). CRD Ⓕ CRD3407 (51 minutes:
ADD: 6/88).
...Nine Préludes, Op. 103. 13 Nocturnes – No. 1 in E flat minor, Op. 33 No. 1; No. 3 in A flat
major, Op. 33 No. 3; No. 4 in E flat major, Op. 36; No. 6 in D flat major, Op. 63; No. 13 in
B minor, Op. 119. Impromptu No. 3 in A flat major, Op. 34. Eight Pièces brèves – No. 1,
Capriccio; No. 4, Adagietto; No. 5, Improvisation. Romances sans paroles, No. 3. Thème et
Variations. **Albert Ferber** (pf). Saga Classics Ⓜ EC3397-2 (51 minutes: DDD: 3/94).   ⒼⒼ
...Impromptus – No. 1 in E flat major, Op. 25; No. 2 in F minor, Op. 31; No. 3; D flat major,
Op. 86 (arr. pf). Nocturnes – Nos. 1, 4 and 6; No. 8 in D flat major, Op. 84 No. 5; No. 9 in
B minor/major, Op. 97; No. 10 in E minor, Op. 99; No. 11 in F sharp minor, Op. 104 No. 1. Three
Romances sans paroles. Barcarolles – No. 1 in A minor, Op. 26; No. 2 in G, Op. 41; No. 4 in
A flat major, Op. 44; No. 5 in F sharp minor, Op. 66; No. 6 in E flat major, Op. 70; No. 7 in
D minor, Op. 90; No. 11 in G minor, Op. 105; No. 12 in E flat major, Op. 106. Mazurka, Op. 32.
Valse-caprice No. 4 in A flat major, Op. 62. **Kathryn Stott** (pf). Conifer Ⓕ 75605 51751-2
(two discs: 129 minutes: DDD: 5/95).

Fauré Chansons, Volume 2. **Sarah Walker** (mez); **Malcolm Martineau** (pf). CRD Ⓔ CRD3477
(68 minutes: DDD: 8/93). Texts and translations included. Recorded 1991.
La papillon et la fleur, Op. 1 No. 1. Op. 3 – No. 1, Seule!; No. 2, Sérénade toscane. L'absent,
Op. 5 No. 3. Op. 8 – No. 1, Au bord de l'eau; No. 3, Ici-bas. Op. 10 – No. 1, Puisqu'ici-bas;
No. 2, Tarentelle. La fée aux chansons, Op. 27 No. 2. Op. 39 – No. 2, Fleur jetée; No. 3, Le Pays
des rêves; No. 4, Les Roses d'Ispahan. Nocturne, Op. 43 No. 2. Clair de lune, Op. 46 No. 2.
Op. 51 – No. 1, Larmes; No. 2, Au cimetière. Arpège, Op. 76 No. 2. Accompagnement, Op. 85
No. 3. Le plus doux chemin, Op. 87 No. 1. Le don silencieux, Op. 92. Chanson, Op. 94. C'est la
paix!, Op. 114. Vocalise-étude. Pelleas et Mélisande – Chanson de Mélisande.

Starting with an early song, and a charmer, *Le papillon et la fleur* has the young Fauré with (so it
seems) a head full of Schubert, as the piano enters with a ripple of *Die Forelle* and waltzes away
into something more like *Seligkeit*. Here, that rather crusty quality in Sarah Walker's louder tones
is something of a liability. Still, if this is the initial reaction it is not one that prevails for long. It is
hard to imagine the *Nocturne* and *Au bord de l'eau* more beautifully sung, the first entering a very
private world, the second catching perfectly the relaxed, reflective mood, and both benefiting from
the softened, warmed tone of the singer and her excellent accompanist. The programme follows no
chronological order. This has the advantage that the best-known songs can be distributed fairly
evenly, with *Clair de lune*, *Les roses d'Ispahan* and *Aurore* mingled here with some from the 1870s
and others that extend into the twentieth century. These include the frank emotion of the postwar
C'est la paix! and *Le don silencieux* which Sarah Walker sings so affectionately to the haunting
accompaniment of those wistfully unfulfilled harmonies. Most haunting of all, perhaps, is
Mélisande's song, in English, written for Mrs Patrick Campbell and the London production of
1889.

Additional recommendations ...

...Automne, Op. 18 No. 3. Prison, Op. 83 No. 1. Soir, Op. 83 No. 2. Fleur jetée, Op. 39 No. 2. En
sourdine, Op. 58 No. 2. Notre amour, Op. 23 No. 2. Mai, Op. 1 No. 2. La chanson du pêcheur,
Op. 4 No. 1. Clair de lune, Op. 46 No. 2. *Coupled with works by* **Schubert, R. Strauss,
Stanford, Parry, Busch, Warlock, Vaughan Williams, Gurney, Britten, Ireland** and
Quilter Dame Janet Baker (mez); **Gerald Moore** (pf). EMI Ⓜ CDM5 65009-2 (75 minutes: ADD:
11/94). *See review in the Collections section; refer to the Index to Reviews.*

...Op. 18 – No. 2, Le voyageur; No. 3, Automne. Le secret, Op. 23 No. 3. Chanson d'amour, Op. 27
No. 1. Songs, Op. 39 – No. 1, Aurore; No. 2, Fleur jetée. Clair de lune, Op. 46 No. 2. Spleen,
Op. 51 No. 3. Cinq mélodies, Op. 58. Prison, Op. 83 No. 1. *Coupled with works by* **Poulenc** and
Ravel Thomas Allen (bar); **Roger Vignoles** (pf). Virgin Classics Ⓔ VC5 45053-2 (57 minutes:
DDD: 5/95). *See review under Poulenc; refer to the Index to Reviews.*

Fauré Requiem, Op. 48[a]. Messe basse[b]. Cantique de Jean Racine, Op. 11[b].
Vierne Pièces de fantaisie. Suite No. 1, Op. 51 – Andantino[c].
Séverac Tantum ergo[d]. [a]**Lisa Beckley** (sop); [a]**Nicholas Gedge** (bass-bar); [abd]**Oxford Schola
Cantorum;** [a]**Oxford Camerata / Jeremy Summerly** with [abc]**Colm Carey** (org). Naxos Ⓢ 8 550765
(60 minutes: DDD: 9/94). Texts and translations included. Recorded 1993.

One would say at once that this is a highly competitive recording of the Fauré Requiem but in fact it
stands on its own because of the version it presents and the edition it uses. Most of the 30-odd
available recordings are of the final 1901 and now somewhat discredited version; several more recent
ones are of the 1894 score edited either by Nectoux and Delage or by John Rutter. This Naxos
recording is of an edition by Denis Arnold (1983) based on the original version (1887) but
incorporating the two additional movements. On first impulse, the word arising is 'austere'. Certainly
the flashes of gold and scarlet made by the few but highly effective brass entries in the familiar
versions are missed; the harp is notably absent from the *Sanctus*, and that wispy, high solo violin
(1894) is now a less other-worldly presence at normal on-the-stave pitch. The instrumental colours are
dark*ish*, yet not sombre, and are lightened by the sunlight stippling of the organ in the *In Paradisum*.
With the voices added, the effect is of a subtler beauty, still more distinctively itself than even the 1894
score. The performance of this and the *Messe basse* is admirable: excellent playing by Jeremy
Summerly's Oxford Camerata, and fresh-voiced, sensitively attuned choral singing. Authenticity
extends now to French pronunciation of the Latin ("luceat eis" very French indeed). The rather
flaccid organ solo by Vierne, written as a sight-reading exercise for his pupils, is finely played by Colm
Carey. The *Tantum ergo* by Séverac is a haunting, carol-like little piece, beautifully sung, and Fauré's
Cantique de Jean Racine makes a perfect conclusion to this lovely programme.

Additional recommendations ...

...Requiem (original version, ed. Rutter). Motets – Ave verum corpus; Tantum ergo; Ave Maria;
Maria, Mater gratiae. Cantique de Jean Racine, Op. 11 (orch. Rutter). Messe basse. **Soloists;
Cambridge Singers; City of London Sinfonietta / John Rutter.** Collegium Ⓔ COLCD109
(63 minutes: ADD/DDD: 1/89). *Gramophone Award Winner 1985.*

...Requiem (original 1894 version)[a]. **Fauré/Messager** Messe des Pêcheurs de Villerville[b]. [a]**Agnès
Mellon** (sop); [a]**Peter Kooy** (bar); [b]**Jean-Philippe Audoli** (vn); [a]**Leo van Doeselaar** (org); **Petits
Chanteurs de Saint-Louis; Paris Chapelle Royale Chorus; Musique Oblique Ensemble / Philippe
Herreweghe.** Harmonia Mundi Ⓔ HMC90 1292 (56 minutes: DDD: 4/89). Ⓖ

...Requiem (1893 version)[a]. Cantique de Jean Racine, Op. 11[b]. Messe basse[b]. Motets[b] – Ave verum corpus; Tantum ergo. **Corydon Singers; [a]English Chamber Orchestra / Matthew Best** with [b]**John Scott** (org). Hyperion Ⓕ CDA66292 (58 minutes: DDD: 10/89).

...Requiem[a]. **Duruflé** Requiem, Op. 9[b]. [b]**Richard Eteson** (treb); [b]**Ann Murray** (sop); [b]**Olaf Bär** (bar); **King's College Choir, Cambridge; English Chamber Orchestra / Stephen Cleobury.** EMI Ⓕ CDC7 49880-2 (73 minutes: DDD: 12/89).

...Requiem[a]. Cantique de Jean Racine, Op. 11[b]. **Duruflé** Four Motets, Op. 10[c]. Messe cum jubilo, Op. 11[d]. **Messiaen** O sacrum convivium. [a]**Camilla Otaki** (sop); [ad]**Mark Griffiths** (bar); **Trinity College Choir, Cambridge;** [abd]**Richard Pearce** (org); [a]**London Musici / Richard Marlow.** Conifer Ⓕ CDCF176 (73 minutes: DDD: 10/90).

...Requiem (revised version). Cantique de Jean Racine, Op. 11. Messe basse. **Poulenc** Mass in G major. Salve Regina. **Soloists; Academy of St Martin in the Fields; Choir of St John's College, Cambridge / George Guest.** Decca Ovation Ⓜ 430 360-2DM (74 minutes: ADD: 9/91).

...Requiem[a]. Pavane, Op. 50. [a]**Robert Chilcott** (treb); [a]**John Carol Case** (bar); [a]**King's College Choir Cambridge; New Philharmonia Orchestra / Sir David Willcocks.** EMI Ⓜ CDM7 64715-2 (42 minutes: ADD: 7/93).

...Requiem[a]. **Debussy** Chansons de Charles d'Orléans. **Ravel** Chansons[b]. **Saint-Saëns** Deux Choeurs, Op. 68. Deux Choeurs, Op. 141 – Des pas dans l'allée. [a]**Catherine Bott** (sop); [a]**Gilles Cachemaille** (bar); [b]**Sabine Vatin** (pf); [a]**Salisbury Cathedral Boys' Choir; Monteverdi Choir;** [a]**Orchestre Révolutionnaire et Romantique / John Eliot Gardiner.** Philips Ⓕ 438 149-2PH (70 minutes: DDD: 9/94). ✦

...Requiem[a]. Pavane, Op. 50. **Koechlin** Choral sur le nom de Fauré. **Schmitt** In memoriam Gabriel Fauré, Op. 72 – Scherzo. **Ravel** Pavane pour une infante défunte. [a]**Sylvia McNair** (sop); [a]**Thomas Allen** (bar); **Academy of St Martin in the Fields** and [a]**Chorus / Sir Neville Marriner.** Philips Ⓕ 446 084-2PH (54 minutes: DDD: 1/96).

Further listening ...

...Pénélope – drama lyrique. **Soloists; Jean Laforge Vocal Ensemble; Monte-Carlo Philharmonic Orchestra / Charles Dutoit.** Erato Libretto 2292-45405-2 (4/92).

Robert Fayrfax   British 1464-1521

New review

Fayrfax (ed. Skinner) Missa "Tecum principium"[b]. Maria plena virtute[b]. Recorder Works[a] – Mese tenor; O lux beata trinitas; Paramese tenor. [a]**Frideswide Consort** (Caroline Kershaw, Jane Downer, Christine Garratt, Jean McCreery, recs); [b]**The Cardinall's Musick / Andrew Carwood.** ASV Gaudeamus Ⓕ CDGAU145 (71 minutes: DDD: 1/95). ✦ Texts and translations included. Recorded 1995. *Gramophone Editor's choice.*

As regards the authenticity of sound, David Skinner adds to a considerable body of evidence pointing to an ensemble of six or seven choristers supported by four, or possibly slightly more, men, as these are the numbers commonly employed in Tudor choral establishments, although there would inevitably have been variations from one institution to another as well as from one occasion to another. We still need to know a lot more about voice types – falsettists, in particular – and, of course, women's voices are incompatible with 'authenticity', however boyish – that is, like today's boys – they sound. There are only three sopranos on this recording, and their sound has the slightly breathy quality and purity at the centre that we expect from boy singers. If our expectations cannot be those of our forebears, then these singers at least fulfil those we have become accustomed to over the last 20 years; intonation and ensemble are excellent. This recording has as its centrepiece Fayrfax's *Missa Tecum principium*, a setting appropriate to Christmastide. The Cardinall's Musick's fluid, expressive singing works particularly well here, both in full and reduced voice sections, and in the large-scale votive antiphon with which the disc ends, *Maria plena virtute*. Much of the writing is inspired, with Fayrfax employing contrasting vocal scorings to highlight the structure and a rich harmonic language, especially in the build-up in intensity towards cadences to the larger sections – a fine composer indeed. The three brief instrumental pieces attributed to Fayrfax (a fourth survives incomplete) are played here by the Frideswide Consort on recorders and they certainly serve to cleanse the palate pleasingly. The recording, made in the Chapel of the Holy Trinity in Arundel Castle in Sussex, is excellent – warm and vibrant.

Further listening ...

...Missa Albanus. Aeternae laudis lilium. **The Sixteen / Harry Christophers.** Hyperion CDA66073 (12/89).

...Missa O quam Glorifica. Ave Dei patris filia. Somewhat musing. To complayne me, alas. *Coupled with* **Anonymous** That was my joy. **Sarum Chant** Kyrie Orbis factor; O quam Glori fica. **The Cardinall's Musick / Andrew Carwood.** ASV Gaudeamus CDGAU142 (6/95). ✦ *Gramophone Award Winner 1995.*

Philip Feeney

New review
Feeney (arr. Longstaff) Cinderella – ballet suite.
Muldowney The Brontes – ballet suite.
Carl Davis (arr. Longstaff) A Christmas Carol – ballet suite. **Northern Ballet Theatre Orchestra /**
John Pryce-Jones. Naxos Ⓢ 8 553495 (73 minutes: DDD: 3/96). Recorded 1995.
This collection comes as a surprise, and a pleasant one too. A programme such as this, presenting music from three modern British ballets otherwise unavailable on disc, is hardly the sort of fare one expects from a super-bargain label. Anyone wanting a souvenir of a treasured evening in the theatre will thus be doubly delighted to find it here at such a modest price. However, even for someone who has neither seen the ballets concerned nor is a ballet lover, it makes most agreeable listening. It is all richly scored, with modern touches that are never such as to frighten off more timid listeners but, rather, create some marvellously atmospheric sounds to portray the action described in the excellent accompanying notes. It is tuneful stuff, and not just in the Carl Davis suite which quotes Christmas carols but in the other two suites too. These seem much more interesting all round, both using a wide range of effects, including keyboard and more exotic percussion instruments. The Feeney suite is very likeable: try, for instance, the movement in which Cinderella prepares for the ball, with a shimmering gown to wear and white doves helping her to dress. Performance and recording alike are excellent.

Jindřich Feld

Suggested listening ...
...Flute Sonata. *Coupled with works by* **Taktakishvili, Gubaidulina, Amirov** and **Martinů** Leslie
Newman (fl); **Amanda Hurton** (pf). Cala CACD88026 (6/96). *See review in the Collections section;*
refer to the Index to Reviews.

Morton Feldman

New review
M. Feldman Intermission 1. Intermission 2. Intermission 5. Intermission 6. Piano Piece. Four Last
Pieces. Five Pianos[a]. **Steffen Schleiermacher,** [a]**Isabel Mundry,** [a]**Mats Persson,** [a]**Kristine Scholz,**
[a]**Nils Vigeland** (pfs). Hat-Hut Hat Now Series Ⓕ ARTCD6143 (74 minutes: DDD: 12/95).
Recorded 1993.
The major event here is the recording of *Five Pianos*, which was premièred in Berlin in 1972 with Cage, Cardew, Tudor, Rzewski and Feldman himself. No wonder the Germans found it slow, obsessive and unsystematic at that time, but it brings together many of Feldman's very consistent preoccupations in a single 35-minute span based on overlapping waves of the same material from all five players. The unvarying soft texture from the pianos is enriched by humming as a kind of added resonance and the use of the celesta, which announces the work's main motif at 4'27" – a rising nine-note gapped scale echoed by the other players but always unsynchronized. This elegiac motto ends *Five Pianos* on its own, having got rid of its gentle background of chords from the other players interspersed like sticks thrown into a pool. The constantly used sustaining pedals are the resulting ripples and by the end they have all died down. It works beautifully and *Five Pianos* is well recorded, although there are some extraneous noises in *Last Pieces*. The rest of the CD contains solo pieces from the 1950s. The earliest is *Intermission 2* (1950), showing Feldman as pointillist and athematic but with sources in Webern and abstract expressionism. This was a new style, characterized by soft piano sound through chord successions which at first seem aimless but gradually acquire the succulence of Delius. But *Intermission 5* starts with a shockingly loud cluster and is punctuated with other loud attacks later. Unusually the booklet has three different essays (English, French and German) which show different national perspectives on Feldman. Altogether highly recommended.
Further listening ...
...Piano Quintet. **Kronos Quartet; Aki Takahashi** (pf). Elektra Nonesuch 7559-79320-2 (2/94).
...String Quartet. **Group for Contemporary Music.** Koch International Classics 37251-2 (8/94).
...For Philip Guston. **Eberhard Blum** (fls); **Nils Vigeland** (pf/celesta); **Jan Williams** (perc). Hat Hut
Hat Now Series ARTCD4-6104 (four discs: 4/94).
...For Christian Wolff. **Eberhard Blum** (fl); **Nils Vigeland** (pf/celesta). Hat Hut Hat Now Series
ARTCD3-6120 (three discs: 7/94).
...Patterns in a Chromatic Field. **Rohan de Saram** (vc); **Marianne Schroeder** (pf). Hat-Hut Hat Now
Series ART2CD6145 (2/96).

Francesco Feo
Italian 1691-1761

Suggested listening ...

...Salve regina in C minor. *Coupled with* **Pergolesi** Stabat mater[a]. Salve regina in A minor. **Lina Maria Akerlkund** (sop); [a]**Giuseppe Zambon** (alto); **Accademia Bizantina / Carlo Chiarappa.** Denon CO-78904 (2/95). ✒

Barry Ferguson
British 1942-

Suggested listening ...

...South and West Suite. *Coupled with works by* **Langlais, Bonnal, Bach** and **Dupré Roger Sayer** (org). Priory PRCD495 (4/96). *See review in the Collections section; refer to the Index to Reviews.*

Howard Ferguson
British 1908-

Suggested listening ...

...Overture for an Occasion, Op. 16. Partita, Op. 5a. Two Ballads, Op. 1[a]. The Dream of the Rood, Op. 16[b]. [a]**Brian Rayner Cook** (bar); [b]**Anne Dawson** (sop); **London Symphony** [ab]**Chorus and Orchestra / Richard Hickox.** Chandos CHAN9082 (4/93). Ⓖ

...Violin Sonata No. 1, Op. 2. *Coupled with* **Castelnuovo-Tedesco** Violin Concerto No. 2, "I profeti". **Françaix** String Trio in C major; **K. Khachaturian** Violin Sonata in G minor, Op. 1. **Jascha Heifetz** (vn); **Joseph de Pasquale** (va); **Gregor Piatigorsky** (vc); **Lilian Steuber** (pf); **Los Angeles Philharmonic Orchestra / Alfred Wallenstein.** RCA Victor Gold Seal mono GD87872* (9/90).

...Violin Sonatas[a] – No. 1, Op. 2; No. 2, Op. 10. Three Medieval Carols, Op. 3[b]. Five Irish Folk Songs, Op. 17[c]. Discovery, Op. 13[d]. Three Sketches, Op. 14[e]. Four Short Pieces, Op. 6[f]. Love and Reason[g]. [c]**Sally Burgess** (mez); [g]**Reiner Schneider-Waterberg** (alto); [bd]**John Mark Ainsley** (ten); [e]**David Butt** (fl); [f]**Janet Hilton** (cl); [a]**Lydia Mordkovitch** (vn); **Clifford Benson** (pf). Chandos CHAN9316.

...Piano Sonata in F minor, Op. 8. Partita for Two Pianos, Op. 5b[a]. **Howard Shelley,** [a]**Hilary Macnamara** (pfs). Hyperion CDA66130 (1/91). Ⓖ

...Piano Sonata in F minor, Op. 8. *Coupled with works by* **Brahms, D. Scarlatti, Schumann, Matthay** and **Bach Dame Myra Hess** (pf). Biddulph mono LHW025* (3/96). *See review in the Collections section; refer to the Index to Reviews.*

...Amore langueo, Op. 18[a]. Piano Concerto, Op. 12[b]. *Coupled with* **Finzi** Eclogue, Op. 10[b]. [a]**Martyn Hill** (ten); [b]**Howard Shelley** (pf); [a]**London Symphony Chorus; City of London Sinfonia / Richard Hickox.** EMI CDM7 64738-2 (2/88).

Aires Fernandez
Portuguese 16th century

Suggested listening ...

...Posuerunt super caput eius. Circumdederunt me. Nunc dimittis. Te lucis ante terminum. Benedicamus Domino. *Coupled with works by* **P. de Cristo, H. de Paiva, A. Lopez** and **Anonymous A Capela Portuguesa / Owen Rees.** Hyperion CDA66735 (11/94).

John Axel Fernström
Swedish 1897-1961

Suggested listening ...

...Wind Quintet, Op. 59. *Coupled with works by* **Kvandal** and **Nielsen Oslo Wind Ensemble.** Naxos 8 553050 (3/95). *See review under Nielsen; refer to the Index to Reviews.*

Alfonso Ferrabosco II
British before 1578-1628

Suggested listening ...

...Pavan and Alman. *Coupled with works by* **R. Johnson II, Webster, Nau, Notari** and **W. Lawes Parley of Instruments Renaissance Violin Band / Peter Holman.** Hyperion CDA66806 (6/96). ✒ *See review in the Collections section; refer to the Index to Reviews.*

Costanzo Festa
Italian c1490-1545

Suggested listening ...

...Quis dabit oculis. Tribus miraculis. Magnificat septimi toni. Super flumina Babylonis. Missa Se congie pris. Constantia 'l vo' pur dire. E morta la speranza. Quando ritrovo la mia pastorella.

Madonna ohimè. Chi vuol veder. **Huelgas Ensemble / Paul van Nevel.** Sony Classical Vivarte SK53116 (11/94).

Paul Fetler   Irish 1920-

Suggested listening ...
...Contrasts for Orchestra. *Coupled with* **Françaix** Piano Concertino[a] **Auric** Ouverture. **Milhaud** Le boeuf sur le toit. **Satie** Parade. [a]Claude Françaix (pf); **London Symphony Orchestra / Antál Dorati.** Mercury 434 335-2MM.   Ⓖ

Zdeněk Fibich   Bohemian 1850-1900

Fibich Symphonies – No. 2 in E flat major, Op. 38; No. 3 in E minor, Op. 53. **Detroit Symphony Orchestra / Neeme Järvi.** Chandos Ⓕ CHAN9328 (71 minutes: DDD: 12/94). Recorded 1994.
Fibich's symphonies find occasional advocates among his own countrymen, and the Supraphon disc (listed below) likewise couples Nos. 2 and 3 together. Neeme Järvi is the first non-Czech conductor of international standing to put his weight behind them, and these performances with the Detroit Symphony are considerably more forceful, making a much stronger case for No. 2 in particular. The music of both derives much thematic material from the suite of piano pieces known as *Moods, Impressions and Reminiscences* which Fibich wrote on every possible aspect of his romance with his former pupil Anežka Schulzová. The idiom is late-romantic, recognizably Czech in many aspects (such as some delightfully sylvan woodwind writing in No. 2), but also under German influence. The first movement of Symphony No. 2 is strongly written and well-structured. Järvi is excellent at making the most of this, and unfolds the melody of the *Adagio* (to an Englishman's ear almost Elgarian) warmly but without sentimentality. Of all themes it meant the most to Fibich, as it was identified with the moment when he declared himself to Anežka; and it returns in the finale. The Third is also permeated with Anežka music, and very well and originally orchestrated: performers and recording engineers respond enthusiastically to this challenge. There is attractive and interesting material here. Lovers of Czech music who do not know the works will find them well worth exploring.
Additional recommendation ...
...Nos. 2 and 3. **Brno State Philharmonic Orchestra / Jiří Bělohlávek.** Supraphon Ⓕ CO-1256 (70 minutes: DDD: 2/88).

New review
Fibich Moods, Impressions and Reminiscences, Op. 41 – 40 excerpts. **William Howard** (pf).
    Chandos Ⓕ CHAN9381 (71 minutes: DDD: 9/95). Recorded 1993.
Fibich's Op. 41 is the sequence of short piano pieces, most of them lasting somewhere between two and three minutes, written in response to his love for Anežka Schulzová. In all, 376 survive, and an unknown number more of them are thought to have been lost or destroyed, while some were absorbed into other works, including operas, from which clues can be found to their original association. The story has now become quite well known; and though a good many of the pieces are either mysteriously titled or left without allusion, they chart, in music of warmth, charm and emotional delight, Fibich's tenderness for Anežka, his enraptured passion for every aspect of her body, his deep love for a woman who gave him a movingly complete emotional, physical and intellectual devotion. The moods include not only delight but jealousy and regret at having caused her pain; the impressions often have highly erotic associations; the reminiscences refer to shared experiences through which their lives grew and deepened. Their course can be followed from Graham Melville-Mason's helpful note; but once the outline and some of the associations are grasped, it is as a loose suite of short, impressionistic pieces that such a programme is best heard, Schumannesque in nature and sometimes in manner. William Howard plays them with a careful attention to detail, to the deft manner in which a memorable idea can be created in only a page, and with affectionate phrasing of their warm melodies. Fibich is, here, a romantic miniaturist to set beside Schumann and perhaps even more Tchaikovsky, whose short piano pieces can be as apt in their creation of a mood. Touchingly, the sequence of pieces has unity as well as diversity. Anežka must indeed have been a fascinating woman.
Additional recommendation ...
...Moods, Impressions and Reminiscences, Opp. 41, 44, 47 and 57 – excerpts. Studies of Paintings, Op. 56. **Radoslav Kvapil** (pf). Unicorn-Kanchana Ⓕ DKPCD9149 (70 minutes: DDD: 10/94).   Ⓖ
Further listening ...
...Quintet in D major, Op. 42. *Coupled with* **Dohnányi** Sextet in C major, Op. 37. **Endymion Ensemble.** ASV CDDCA943 (2/96). *See review under Dohnányi; refer to the Index to Reviews.*   Ⓖ
...Sonata in B flat major, Op. 28.*Coupled with* **Goetz** Sonata in G minor, Op. 17. **Moscheles** Grande Sonate in E flat major, Op. 47. **Anthony Goldstone, Caroline Clemmow** (pf duet). Meridian CDE84237 (7/93).
...Sarka. **Soloists; Janáček Opera Chorus; Brno State Philharmonic Orchestra / Jan Stych.** Supraphon CO-1746/8 (10/88).

...The Bride of Messina. **Soloists; Prague Radio Chorus; Prague National Theatre Chorus and Orchestra / František Jílek.** Supraphon 11 1492-2 (12/94).

John Field

Irish 1782-1837

Field Piano Concertos – No. 2 in A flat major, H31; No. 3 in E flat major, H32. **John O'Conor (pf); Scottish Chamber Orchestra / Sir Charles Mackerras.** Telarc Ⓕ CD80370 (64 minutes: DDD: 8/94). Recorded 1993.

It must surely delight John Field, in Elysian Fields, to know that it's a fellow Dubliner who now so gallantly champions his concertos. John O'Conor here couples the Second and Third of the seven in effortlessly fluent and faithful performances. As a pianist Field was universally praised (and even Chopin was proud to merit comparison with him) for the way his melody sang, also for "a sweet and tender feeling that few virtuosi were able to achieve". It's this gentleness of style that O'Conor brings to the gracious, albeit ever so slightly bland, A flat work (with a finale so aptly headed *Moderato innocente*), avoiding all danger of the "mere mechanicus" in its streaming semiquavers and phrasing its lyricism with poetic delicacy. In the Third Concerto's more daring opening movement he resists all temptation to take interpretative liberties of his own. Listeners aware that Field wrote no slow movement for this concerto may like to know that O'Conor inserts the composer's fifth *Nocturne* in B flat for solo piano (though the insert-note omits to mention it), here given a slender orchestral accompaniment by some undisclosed hand. Mackerras and his players leave us in no doubt whatsoever of Field's fecund orchestral imagination, and the recording rings true.

Additional recommendation ...

...No. 1 in E flat major, H27; Nos. 2 and 3; No. 4 in E flat major, H28; No. 5 in C major, H39, "L'incendie par l'orage"; No. 6 in C major H49; No. 7 in C minor, H58. **John O'Conor (pf); New Irish Chamber Orchestra / Janos Furst.** Onyx Ⓕ ONYX CD101/3 (three discs: DDD).

Field Nocturnes – No. 1 in E flat major, H24. No. 2 in C minor, H25. No. 3 in A flat major, H26. No. 4 in A major, H36. No. 5 in B flat major, H37. No. 6 in F major, H40. No. 7 in C major, H45. No. 8 in A major, H14E. No. 9 in E flat major, H30. No. 10 in E minor, H46B. No. 11 in E flat major, H56A. No. 12 in G major, H58D. No. 13 in D minor, H59. No. 14 in C major. No. 15 in C major, H61. **Roberto Mamou (pf).** Pavane Ⓕ ADW7110 (64 minutes: DDD: 8/93).

Field Nocturnes – No. 1 in E flat major, H24. No. 2 in C minor, H25. No. 3 in A flat major, H26. No. 4 in A major, H36. No. 5 in B flat major, H37. No. 6 in F major, H40. No. 7 in C major, H45. No. 8 in A major, H14E. No. 9 in E flat major, H30. No. 10 in E minor, H46B. No. 11 in E flat major, H56A. No. 12 in G major, H58D. No. 13 in D minor, H59. No. 14 in C major. No. 15 in C major, H61. No. 16 in F major, H62A. **Joanna Leach (fp).** Athene Ⓕ ATHCD1 (76 minutes: DDD: 10/93). 🎯 Recorded 1990-91.

Liszt was among the first to celebrate Field's quality, finding in the *Nocturnes*, "the morn of life ... before the radiant freshness of emotion was over-clouded by the shadow of reflection", very much a world of innocence rather than experience. Chopin, too, admired Field, locating in his predecessor an ideal foundation for his own *Nocturnes*; works smouldering with an altogether different voltage and range. The Tunisian-born pianist Roberto Mamou achieves an often exemplary middle course between drama and understatement and he stresses Field's closeness to, rather than his remoteness from, Chopin. The recordings are satisfactory and although the last two *Nocturnes* are omitted this is an appealing issue. Joanna Leach forfeits only the last *Nocturne*. She performs on square pianos by Stodart, Broadwood and Thomas D'Almaine dating from 1823 to 1835 and, most persuasively, suggests an intimacy and transparency hard to parallel on more modern, brilliant and forceful instruments. The ear is quickly attuned to the sound, to the radically different pedalling Leach refers to in her excellent notes, and to a cloudy but appropriate and often hypnotic resonance. Melody and accompaniment (at the very heart of this music) are more closely entwined than on today's instruments, offering a greater sense of Field's harmonic subtlety. There are some extraneous noises, inseparable from period instruments, but so far from distracting attention they somehow add to the potent atmosphere of these performances. A fascinating pair of issues.

Additional recommendation ...

...Nocturnes Nos. 1-16. **John O'Conor (pf).** Telarc Ⓕ CD80199 (DDD: 5/90).

Further listening ...

...Piano Sonatas – E flat major, H8 No. 1; A major, H8 No. 2; C minor, H8 No. 3; B major, H17. Nocturnes – No. 3 in A flat major, H26; No. 7 in C major, H45; No. 17 in E major, H54A. **John O'Conor (pf).** Telarc CD80290 (11/92).

...Air du bon roi Henri IV. Irish Dance, "Go to the Devil". Sehnsuchtswalzer. Fantaisie sur l'air de Martini. Rondeau écossois. Andante inédit in E flat major. Variations in D minor on a

Russian song, "My dear bosom friend". Variations in B flat major on a Russian Air,
"Kamarinskaya". Marche triomphale. Nouvelle fantaisie in G major. Nocturne in B flat major.
Polonaise en rondeau. Fantaisie sur un air russe, "In the Garden". Two Album Leaves in
C minor. Rondo in A flat major. **Míceál O'Rourke** (pf). Chandos CHAN9315 (3/95).

Irving Fine
American 1914-1962

Suggested listening ...
...Blue Towers. Diversions for Orchestra. Music for Piano (orch. Spiegelman). Toccata concertante.
Symphony. **Moscow Radio Symphony Orchestra / Joel Spiegelman.** Delos DE3139 (7/94).

Michael Finnissy
British 1946-

Suggested listening ...
...Beuk o' Newcassel Sangs. *Coupled with works by* **N. Hayes, Hallgrimsson, Weir,**
G. Jackson, S. Harrison, Crane, A. Fisher and **Skempton** Tapestry. British Music Label
BML012 (12/95). *See review in the Collections section; refer to the Index to Reviews.*

Gerald Finzi
British 1901-1956

New review
Finzi Eclogue, Op. 10.
Delius Piano Concerto in C minor.
Vaughan Williams Piano Concerto in C major. **Piers Lane** (pf); **Royal Liverpool Philharmonic**
Orchestra / Vernon Handley. EMI Eminence Ⓜ CD-EMX2239 (61 minutes: DDD: 11/95).
Recorded 1994.
Piers Lane brings an exhilarating dash and bravura to Vaughan Williams's craggy concerto and the
results are both clean-cut and refreshing. However, Handley's 1984 Lyrita recording with Howard
Shelley is not outclassed by the newcomer. Not that the balance obtained on Eminence lacks anything
in naturalness, and the dynamic range is certainly satisfyingly wide (that brazen orchestral tutti
towards the end of the *Fuga chromatica* opens out rivetingly), but the overall effect is perhaps just a
little too distant. More importantly, for all Lane's formidable athleticism and technical command, he
doesn't quite match Shelley in terms of sheer commitment or imaginative scope. As it turns out,
Shelley is also a rival for Lane in the lovely Finzi *Eclogue*. Again, although Handley's accompaniment
positively glows, Shelley's limpid touch also pays great dividends. In the Delius Concerto, however,
Lane's big-hearted gusto and genuine poetic insights prove something of a revelation. Not only is his
technique scarcely less prodigious than that of Philip Fowke on Unicorn-Kanchana (reviewed under
Delius; refer to the Index to Reviews), he avoids the latter's tendency to force the tone. A memorable
concentration and flexibility inform every bar of the central *Largo*, where Lane effortlessly sustains
his (almost provocatively) measured initial tempo. Handley and the RLPO are exemplary partners in
all of this (memorable solo contributions throughout); indeed, Handley's wonderfully clear-sighted
conception makes for a glorious sense of home-coming at the close, with the clinching climax
unerringly resolved. The piano sound, too, seems marginally more full-blooded than it was in the VW
Concerto. All in all, the most rewarding version of Delius's endearing work currently available.
Additional recommendations ...
...Eclogue[b]. **Ferguson** Amore langueo, Op. 18[a]. Piano Concerto, Op. 12[b]. [a]**Martyn Hill** (ten);
[b]**Howard Shelley** (pf); [a]**London Symphony Chorus; City of London Sinfonia / Richard Hickox.**
EMI Ⓜ CDM7 64738-2 (66 minutes: DDD: 2/88).
...**Vaughan Williams** Piano Concerto. **Foulds** Dynamic Triptych, Op. 88. **Howard Shelley** (pf);
Royal Philharmonic Orchestra / Vernon Handley. Lyrita Ⓕ SRCD211 (57 minutes: DDD: 3/93). Ⓖ

Finzi. Love's Labour's Lost – Suite, Op. 28. Clarinet Concerto in C minor, Op. 31[a.] Prelude in
F minor, Op. 25. Romance in E flat major, Op. 11. [a]**Alan Hacker** (cl); **English String Orchestra /**
William Boughton. Nimbus Ⓕ NI5101 (65 minutes: DDD: 12/88). Recorded 1987.   Ⓖ
There are several other Finzi issues available which include the Clarinet Concerto. Alan Hacker,
however, encompasses all his colleagues' virtues, providing special insights and revelling in the
brilliant writing. He also adds something extra – an almost mystical realization of the music's poetic
vision which is deeply moving. This is in spite of the fact that the string-playing sometimes lacks
polish and precision. Finzi wrote incidental music for a BBC production of *Love's Labour's Lost* and
expanded it for a later open-air production. It is tuneful, graceful music, but one cannot feel that the
stage was Finzi's world. The disc is completed by two interesting early pieces for strings, the *Prelude*
and *Romance*, both wholly characteristic of the composer and very well played.
Additional recommendations ...
...Clarinet Concerto. **Stanford** Clarinet Concerto in A minor, Op. 80. **Thea King** (cl); **Philharmonia**
Orchestra / Alun Francis. Hyperion Ⓕ CDA66001 (49 minutes: DDD: 6/87).

...Clarinet Concerto[a]. Five Bagatelles, Op. 23[b]. **Stanford** Clarinet Concerto in A minor, Op. 80[a].
Three Intermezzos, Op. 13[b]. **Emma Johnson** (cl); [b]**Malcolm Martineau** (pf); [a]**Royal Philharmonic
Orchestra / Sir Charles Groves.** ASV Ⓕ CDDCA787 (74 minutes: DDD: 6/92).

Finzi Intimations of Immortality, Op. 29[a]. Grand Fantasia and Toccata in D minor, Op. 38[b].
[a]**Philip Langridge** (ten); [b]**Philip Fowke** (pf); [a]**Liverpool Philharmonic Choir and Philharmonic
Orchestra / Richard Hickox.** EMI Digital Classics Ⓜ CDM7 64720-2 (61 minutes: DDD: 10/93).
From CDC7 49913-2 (2/90). Text included. Recorded 1988.

At the beginning of his setting of Wordsworth's *Ode on the Intimations of Immortality*, which is both
eclectic and very Elgarian in feeling, Finzi makes his romantic intentions quite clear in the lovely,
evocative orchestral introduction which sets the scene for the first poem, "There was a time when
meadows, grove and stream". This is definitely in the pastoral tradition of English song setting, yet
with injections of choral passion echoing the dedication of the soloist. Philip Langridge is absolutely
committed, although it must be conceded that his ardour leads to an almost uncontrolled vibrato at
times. However, in moments of repose the lyrical line is very appealing. This involved and involving
performance conducted by Richard Hickox is very rewarding and the choral recording is as spacious
as it is brilliant. The coupling is another fascinatingly eclectic piece, this time for piano and orchestra.
The opening *Grand Fantasia* is more than neo-baroque; it is an unashamed extension of Bach, and
very well written too. The *Toccata* which follows brings a good-natured *vigoroso* fugato idea in a
similar style. It is commandingly played by Philip Fowke and Hickox is again a sympathetic partner.

Finzi All this night, Op. 33. Let us now praise famous men, Op. 35[a]. Lo, the full, final sacrifice,
Op. 26[a]. Magnificat, Op. 36[a]. Seven Part-songs, Op. 17. Though did'st delight my eyes, Op. 32.
Three Anthems, Op. 27[a]. Three Short Elegies, Op. 5[a]. White-flowering days, Op. 37. **Finzi Singers
/ Paul Spicer** with [a]**Harry Bicket** (org). Chandos Ⓕ CHAN8936 (79 minutes: DDD: 9/91).
Texts included. Recorded 1990.

Finzi is no composer to look to for the musical counterpart of a quick fix – and how he would have
abhorred that expression. To the patient spirit of the listener who seeks music in which the fastidious
limitation of its means is itself some guarantee of the depth of its purposes, he will always be
rewarding. This is true of all the works collected here. Some, such as the first and last, *God is gone up*
and *Lo, the full, final sacrifice*, are relatively well-known, which is not to say that they will necessarily
prove the most satisfying. There are some fine shorter pieces including the unaccompanied *Seven
Poems of Bridges* and the *Three Drummond Elegies* that delight as word-settings. "White-flowering
days", to words by Edmund Blunden, comes from *A Garland for the Queen*, the Coronation gift of ten
composers in 1953, none happier than this in catching the fresh hopefulness of the time. Best of all
perhaps is the *Magnificat*, which also had its first British performance in that year. It is heard here in
its original version with organ, beautifully played on this disc and providing a more spiritual
association than is found in the orchestral accompaniment added later. The Finzi Singers are
sensitive, assured and accurate; their tone is uniformly good, and they convey a sense of personal
involvement in the music. The qualities of recorded sound and presentation are well up to the rest.

Further listening ...

...Cello Concerto, Op. 40. *Coupled with* **Leighton** Veris gratia – suite, Op. 9[a]. **Rafael Wallfisch** (vc);
[a]**George Caird** (ob); **Royal Liverpool Philharmonic Orchestra / Vernon Handley.** Chandos
CHAN8471 (10/86).

...The Fall of the Leaf. New Year Music, Op. 7. *Coupled with* **Moeran** Serenade in G major.
Sinfonietta. **Northern Sinfonia / Richard Hickox.** EMI British Composers CDM7 64721-2
(8/94).

...Interlude in A minor, Op. 21 (arr. Ferguson). *Coupled with* **Howells** Oboe Sonata. **Patterson**
Duologue. **Nicholas Daniel** (ob); **Julius Drake** (pf). Léman Classics LC44801 (10/93).

...Let us garlands bring, Op. 18. *Coupled with works by* **Butterworth, Ireland** and **Vaughan
Williams** Bryn Terfel (bass-bar); **Malcolm Martineau** (pf). DG 445 946-2GH (8/95). *See
review under Butterworth; refer to the Index to Reviews.* **Gramophone** *Editor's record of the
month.*   Ⓖ Ⓖ Ⓖ

Gioseffo-Hectore Fiocco   Italian/South Netherlands 1703-1741

Suggested listening ...
...Pièces de clavecin, Op. 1. **Ton Koopman** (hpd). Astrée Auvidis E7731 (3/90). 🖉

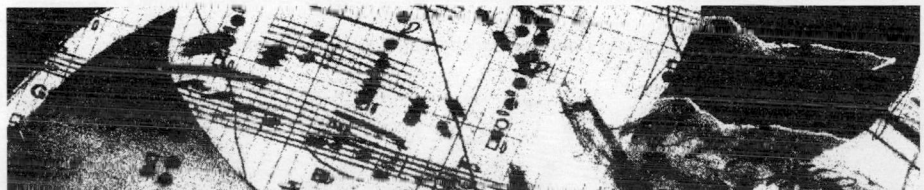

Elena Firsova
USSR 1950-

Suggested listening ...
...Cassandra, Op. 60. *Coupled with* **Gubaidulina** Pro et Contra. **BBC National Orchestra of Wales / Tadaaki Otaka.** BIS CD668 (11/94).

Johann Fischer
German c1670-1746

Suggested listening ...
...Harpsichord Suites – Musicalischer Parnassus: No. 1 in D minor, "Uranie"; No. 2 in F major, "Euterpe". Les pièces de clavecin, Op. 2, Nos. 1-3. **William Christie** (hpd). Harmonia Mundi HMA190 1026 (4/88). ✐

Aidan Fisher
British 1959-

Suggested listening ...
...Leviathan. *Coupled with works by* **N. Hayes, Hallgrimsson, Weir, Finnissy, G. Jackson, S. Harrison, Crane** and **Skempton** Tapestry. British Music Label BML012 (12/95). *See review in the Collections section; refer to the Index to Reviews.*

Graham Fitkin
British 1963-

Suggested listening ...
...Hook[a]. Mesh[b]. Stub[c]. Cud[d]. [a]**Bash Ensemble;** [b]**Icebreaker;** [c]**Delta Saxophone Quartet;** [d]**John Harle Band / Graham Fitkin.** Argo 440 216-2ZH (10/93).

Stephen Flaherty
American 20th century

New review

Flaherty Once On This Island. **Original London Cast / Richard Balcombe.** TER Ⓔ CDTER1224 (76 minutes: DDD: 6/95).

This attractive musical from Broadway, temporarily renamed *Island* for its London run, was themed around the production's setting on a Caribbean island. The show is sung and played without a break, a sensible device for such an atmospheric and comparatively gentle piece, where the cumulative effect of the story is all important. For despite all the colour and dancing suggested by the booklet, this is a chamber musical with no chorus, a small, very good orchestra and some characterful performers. This economy is apparent, too, in Stephen Flaherty's music, where the spare textures are sometimes reminiscent of Sondheim's *Pacific Overtures*. On a first listen you may feel the composer had been bound too much within the strait-jacket of his Caribbean rhythms, but this sensation will not last long, and with "The sad tale of the beauxhommes" and the attractive hymn to the heroine, Ti Moune, his score will hold your attention. This number, led by Shezwae Powell and accompanied notably by the bass clarinet, is one of the highlights of the score. She also memorably leads the lament, "A part of us". Other attractive performances come from Suzanne Packer and Sharon D. Clarke who, like their companions, sing in the story-telling ensembles like "Some say". The recording gives the illusion that the listener is in the theatre enjoying a production that here sounds like undiluted fun.

Mateo Flecha
Spanish 1481-1553

Suggested listening ...
...La negrina. La justa. *Coupled with works by* **Brudieu** and **Alberch Vila** La Colombina Ensemble. Accent ACC94103D (11/95). *See review under Brudieu; refer to the Index to Reviews.*

Friedrich von Flotow
German 1812-1883

Suggested listening ...
...Martha. **Soloists; Bavarian Radio Chorus; Munich Radio Orchestra / Heinz Wallberg.** Eurodisc 352 878 (2/89).

Carlisle Floyd

Suggested listening ...
...Susannah. **Soloists; Chorus and Orchestra of the Opéra de Lyon / Kent Nagano.** Virgin Classics
VCD5 45039-2 (10/94).

Josef Foerster

Suggested listening ...
...From Shakespeare, Op. 76[a]. Cyrano de Bergerac, Op. 55[b]. [a]**Prague Symphony Orchestra;** [b]**Czech
Philharmonic Orchestra / Václav Smetáček.** Campion RRCD1319 (11/93).
...Wind Quintet in D major, Op. 95. *Coupled with* **Haas** Wind Quinet, Op. 10. **Janáček**
Mládí[a]. **Aulos Wind Quintet;** [a]**Kurt Berger** (bass cl). Koch Schwann Musica Mundi 310051
(6/93).

Manuel de Fonseca

Suggested listening ...
...Beata viscera. *Coupled with* **Trosylho** Circumdederunt me. **Magalhães** Vidi acquam. Missa
O soberana luz. Commissa mea pavesco. **Lôbo** Audivi vocem da caelo. Pater peccavi. **Cardoso**
Lamentatio. Magnificat secundi toni. **Escobar** Clamabat autem mulier. **Ars Nova / Bo Holten.**
Naxos 8 553310 (3/96).

Pierre Fontaine

Suggested listening ...
...J'ayme bien celui. *Coupled with works by* **Anonymous, Dunstable, Cardot, Bittering,
Binchois, Fontaine, Johannes de Lymburga, Legrant, Machaut, Power** and **Velut
Gothic Voices / Christopher Page.** Hyperion CDA66783 (1/96). *See review in the Collections
section; refer to the Index to Reviews.*

Arthur Foote

Suggested listening ...
...Suite in E minor, Op. 63. *Coupled with works by* **McDonald, Copland** and **Harris** Boston
Symphony Orchestra / Serge Koussevitzky. Pearl mono GEMMCD9492* (12/91). *See review in the
Collections section; refer to the Index to Reviews.* ⊕⊕⊕

Antoine Forqueray

New review
A. Forqueray (trans. J-B. Forqueray) Pièces de viole. **Jacques Ogg** (hpd). Globe Ⓔ GLO6027
(two discs: 125 minutes: DDD: 2/96). ✒ Recorded 1994.
New review
A. Forqueray (trans. J-B. Forqueray) Pièces de viole – selections from Suite No. 1 in D minor;
Suite No. 3 in D major; Suite No. 5 in C minor. **Luc Beauséjour** (hpd). Naxos Ⓢ 8 553407
(67 minutes: DDD: 1/96). ✒ Recorded 1994.
It used to be thought a remarkable example of filial devotion, not to speak of Christian forgiveness,
that Jean-Baptiste Forqueray should have made harpsichord transcriptions of some of his father
Antoine's pieces for gamba. For Antoine, celebrated as one of the most brilliant viol players of his
day and appointed a chamber musician to Louis XIV, was also crotchety and cruel, and not only had
had Jean-Baptiste thrown into prison but had even tried to have him banished from the kingdom on
charges of debauchery. It now seems, however, that the harpsichord arrangements were very possibly
not by Jean-Baptiste but by his second wife (by all accounts an accomplished player) and that the
pieces were by her husband (also an excellent viol player), not her father-in-law. Whatever the rights
and wrongs of the case, a gamba original may be adduced from the low tessitura which the pieces
favour – strikingly so in *La Bellemont* – though the many graces and virtuoso embellishments are
entirely characteristic of their new medium. (Those readers who would like to sample the viola da
gamba versions can be confidently referred to Jay Bernfeld's recording on Deutsche Harmonia Mundi
– listed on the next page.)
Jacques Ogg has an advantage over his rivals by recording all five suites handed down, whereas
Beauséjour plays only three. Using for alternate suites a fine copy of an anonymous late seventeenth-
century Franco-German instrument and another of a 1638 Ruckers, he also invests these pieces – "so

difficult that only he [Forqueray] and his son can execute them with grace", protested the *Mercure* about the viol originals – with more characterization. These portraits of worthies of the time are frequently as "capricious, whimsical and bizarre" as the composer himself was described as being. Couperin is depicted as magisterial, Leclair as sprightly and flighty, Rameau in highly dramatic fashion, Forqueray himself as delighting in elaboration. The range of affects is indeed startling, from demure (*La Cottine*) or pathetic (*La Sylva*, where Ogg makes the specified non-synchronization of hands convincing) to dignified (*La Du Breuil*), swaggering (*La Boisson*) or vigorously athletic (*La Angrave*); and Ogg brings them all vividly to life. This is a worthy celebration of Forqueray and can be very highly recommended. The Canadian harpsichordist Luc Beauséjour obviously revels in the dramatic fire, the technical challenges and in the sometimes bold harmonies of these pieces. Playing a richly sonorous but unidentified instrument, he immediately captures attention by the dash with which he attacks *La Forqueray* and by his exuberant rhythmic gaiety in *La Portugaise* (both in Suite No. 1); and he fully maintains his hold later on in texturally more complex pieces. His articulation is beautifully crisp and clean throughout. This is a very welcome disc, the more so for being at super-budget price, and excellently recorded.

Additional recommendation ...
...Pièces de viole – Allemande La Laborde[a]. La Cottin. La Portugaise[a]. La Forqueray. La Régente[a]. La Marella. Sarabande La d'Aubonne. La Ferrand[a]. La Couperin. Chaconne La Buisson[a]. Le Leclair. La Rameau. Jupiter[a]. [a]**Jay Bernfield** (va da gamba); **Skip Sempé** (hpd). Deutsche Harmonia Mundi Ⓕ RD77262 (50 minutes: DDD: 5/92). ✒

Wolfgang Fortner   German 1907-1987

Suggested listening ...
...Geh unter, schöne Sonne. *Coupled with works by* **Britten, Cornelius, Eisler, Fröhlich, Hauer, Jarnach, Komma, Pfitzner, Ullmann** and **Reutter** Mitsuko Shirai (mez); **Hartmut Höll** (pf). Capriccio 10 534 (12/94). *See review in the Collections section; refer to the Index to the Reviews.*
...Zum Spielen für dem 70 Geburtstag. *Coupled with works by* **Ginastera, Henze, Beck, Dutilleux, Lutosławski, Berio, C. Halffter, Britten, K. Huber** and **Holliger** Patrick and Thomas Demenga (vcs); **Cello Ensemble / Jürg Wyttenbach.** ECM New Series 445 234-2 (8/95). *See review in the Collections section; refer to the Index to Reviews.*

Lukas Foss   American 1922-

Suggested listening ...
...Three American Pieces. *Coupled with works by* **Barber** and **Bernstein** Itzhak Perlman (vn); **Boston Symphony Orchestra / Seiji Ozawa.** EMI CDC5 55360-2 (6/95). *See review under Barber; refer to the Index to Reviews*   Ⓖ
...American Landscapes. *Coupled with works by* **Corigliano** and **Schwantner** Sharon Isbin (gtr); **Saint Paul Chamber Orchestra / Hugh Wolff.** Virgin Classics CDC5 55083-2 (8/96). *See review under Corigliano; refer to the Index to Reviews.*   Ⓖ
...Song of Songs[c]. *Coupled with* **Ben Haim** The Sweet Psalmist of Israel[b] **Bloch** Sacred Service[a]. [a]**Robert Merrill** (bar); [b]**Sylvia Marlowe** (hpd); [c]**Jennie Tourel** (mez); **New York Metropolitan Synagogue Choir;** [a]**New York Philharmonic Orchestra / Leonard Bernstein.** Sony Classical Bernstein Royal Edition SM2K47533 (11/92).

François de Fossa   French 1775-1849

F. de Fossa Three Trios, Op. 18 – A major; G major; F major. **Simon Wynberg** (gtr); **Martin Beaver** (vn); **Bryan Epperson** (vc). Naxos Ⓢ 8 550760 (78 minutes: DDD: 3/95). Recorded 1993. There are many ways in which history gets things out of focus; one of them concerns the status of François de Fossa. His fame has so far rested mainly on his role as copyist of Boccherini's Guitar Quintets, brought to light by the American musicologist Matanya Ophee, but he was much more than that. De Fossa was a military man who had a distinguished international career, and also a cultured musician with a profound knowledge of the guitar; music brought him only meagre rewards so he wisely remained a professional soldier and an amateur musician. What has been more seriously overlooked is de Fossa's ability as a composer, particularly of chamber music with guitar. This is unfortunate: the guitar's stock of nineteenth-century chamber music of this kind is modest in both size and quality, and de Fossa's works are head and shoulders above the rest. Their superiority lies in both their fuller use of the guitar, an equal partner rather than a subservient accompanist, and the music itself. In their skilful, idiomatic use of the instruments, notably in a variety of textures, they recall Boccherini, with whom they share common ground in spirit and musical content – as they do also with Beethoven and, most of all, Haydn. Recommended even to the general listener, especially when they are as beguilingly played and beautifully recorded as they are here.

John Foulds
British 1880-1939

Suggested listening ...
...Dynamic Triptych, Op. 88. *Coupled with* **Vaughan Williams** Piano Concerto in C major.
Howard Shelley (pf); **Royal Philharmonic Orchestra / Vernon Handley.** Lyrita SRCD211 (3/93). Ⓖ

Jean Françaix
French 1912-

Suggested listening ...
...Piano Concertino[a]. *Coupled with* **Auric** Ouverture. **Milhaud** Le boeuf sur le toit. **Satie** Parade.
Fetler Contrasts for Orchestra, [a]**Claude Françaix** (pf); **London Symphony Orchestra / Antál**
Dorati. Mercury 434 335-2MM.   Ⓖ
...L'Horloge de flore. *Coupled with works by* **R. Strauss, Ibert** and **Satie** John de Lancie (ob);
London Symphony Orchestra / André Previn. RCA Victor Gold Seal GD87989 (12/91). *See review*
in the Collections section; refer to the Index to Reviews.   Ⓖ
...Wind Quintet No. 1. *Coupled with works by* **Ibert, Fauré, Debussy, Milhaud, Damase,**
Pierné and **Poulenc** Reykjavik Wind Quintet. Chandos CHAN9362 (10/95). *See review in the*
Collections section; refer to the Index to Reviews.
...Quartet for Cor anglais and Strings[a]. String Trio[a]. Wind Quintets – Nos. 1 and 2[b]. [a]**The Marwood**
Ensemble; [b]**Huffner Wind Ensemble.** Collins Classics 1438-2 (4/95).
...String Trio in C major. *Coupled with* **Castelnuovo-Tedesco** Violin Concerto No. 2, "I
profeti". **Ferguson** Violin Sonata No. 1, Op. 2. **K. Khachaturian** Violin Sonata in G minor,
Op. 1. **Jascha Heifetz** (vn); **Joseph de Pasquale** (va); **Gregor Piatigorsky** (vc); **Lilian Steuber** (pf);
Los Angeles Philharmonic Orchestra / Alfred Wallenstein. RCA Victor Gold Seal GD87872 (9/90).
...Sonatine. *Coupled with works by* **Arban, Eben, Enescu, Fantini, Goedicke, Höhne** and
Tartini John Wallace (tpt/cornet); **Meyrick Alexander** (bn); **Simon Wright** (pf/org/hpd). EMI
Virtuosi CDC5 55086-2 (11/94). *See review in the Collections section; refer to the Index to*
Reviews.
...Tema con variazioni. *Coupled with* **Honegger** Clarinet Sonatina, H42. **Hindemith** Clarinet
Sonata in B flat major. **Vaughan Williams** Six Studies in English folk song. **Milhaud** Duo
concertante, Op. 351. Caprice, Op. 335a **Bozza** Pulcinella. **Kupferman** Moonflowers, Baby!.
Jonathan Cohler (cl); **Judith Gordon** (pf). Crystal CD733 (5/95).

Petronio Franceschini
Italian c1650-1680

Suggested listening ...
...Sonata for Two Trumpets, Strings and Continuo in D (Friedrich). *Coupled with works by* **Viviani,**
A. Marcello, Torelli, Albinoni, Corelli, Vivaldi and **Baldassare** Håkan Hardenberger (tpt);
I Musici. Philips 442 131-2PH (5/95). *See review in the Collections section; refer to the Index to*
Reviews.

Alberto Franchetti
Italian 1860-1942

Suggested listening ...
...Cristoforo Colombo. **Soloists; Hungarian Radio Chorus; Frankfurt Radio Symphony Orchestra /**
Marcello Viotti. Koch Schwann 310302 (7/92).

Auguste Franchomme
French 1808-1884

Suggested listening ...
...Air auvergnat varié in A minor, Op. 26[d]. Caprices, Op. 7[a] – No. 2 in E minor; No. 4 in A minor;
No. 7 in C major. Nocturne in G major (trans. Chopin)[b]. Grande valse, Op. 34[d]. Nocturne in
A flat minor, Op. 15 No. 3[b]. Air russe varié No. 2 in D minor, Op. 32[d]. *Coupled with* **Chopin**
(trans. Franchomme) Grand Duo concertante in E major on Themes from Meyerbeer's "Robert
le diable"[b]. **Anner Bylsma** (vc); [b]**Lambert Orkis** (fp); [d]**L'Archibudelli** and **Smithsonian Chamber**
Players. Sony Classical Vivarte SK53980 (4/95). 🖊

César Franck
Belgian/French 1822-1890

Franck Symphony in D minor.
d'Indy Symphonie sur un chant montagnard français in G major, Op. 25[a]. [a]**Jean-Yves Thibaudet**
(pf); **Montreal Symphony Orchestra / Charles Dutoit.** Decca Ⓟ 430 278-2DH (67 minutes: DDD:
1/92). Recorded 1989.

These two French masterpieces of the 1880s complement each other perfectly. The Franck is very much in the Austro-German symphonic tradition. Its language calls to mind the vaulted splendours and gothic interiors of many a Bruckner Symphony. d'Indy's Symphony, in reality more of a piano concerto, is based on a folk-song he heard whilst holidaying in the Cévennes mountains. Definitely outdoors music this, and far more recognizably French; indeed, with its echoes of Berlioz to its pre-echoes of Debussy and even 'Les Six', it occupies a central position in a century of French music. Dutoit's elegant, flowing way with the Franck (marvellously refined *espressivo* playing from the Montreal violins, and shining, incisive brass) is ideal for those who shy away from the Brucknerian monumentalism of the work; and Jean-Yves Thibaudet's eloquent solo playing in the d'Indy is matched by exquisitely drawn instrumental solos from within the orchestra. Decca's spacious Montreal sound, too, proves just as apt for the organ-like timbres of the Franck, as for the fresh air and wide horizons of the d'Indy.

Additional recommendations ...

...Symphony in D minor. Grande pièce symphonique in F sharp minor, Op. 17 – Andante. Panis angelicus. **Satie** Gymnopédies – Nos. 1 and 2. **Dukas** L'Apprenti sorcier. **A. Thomas** Mignon – Gavotte. **Berlioz** La damnation de Faust, Op. 24 – Hungarian March. **Philadelphia Orchestra / Leopold Stokowski.** Biddulph mono Ⓜ WHL011* (70 minutes: ADD: 8/95).

...Symphony in D minor. **Roussel** Symphony No. 3 in G minor, Op. 42. **French National Orchestra / Leonard Bernstein.** DG Masters Ⓜ 445 512-2GMA (69 minutes: DDD).

...Symphony in D minor[a]. **Berlioz** Béatrice et Bénédict – Overture[b]. **d'Indy** Symphonie sur un chant montagnard français[c]. [c]**Nicole Henriot-Schweitzer** (pf); [bc]**Boston Symphony Orchestra / Charles Munch;** [a]**Chicago Symphony Orchestra / Pierre Monteux.** RCA Victor Papillon Ⓜ GD86805* (71 minutes: ADD: 3/89).   ⒼⒼⒼ

...Symphony in D minor. Symphonic Variations[a]. [a]**Rudolf Firkušný** (pf); **Royal Philharmonic Orchestra / Claus Peter Flor.** RCA Victor Red Seal Ⓕ RD60146 (60 minutes: DDD: 8/90).

...Symphony in D minor. **Lalo** Symphony in G minor. **French Radio National Orchestra / Sir Thomas Beecham.** EMI Ⓜ CDM7 63396-2* (66 minutes: ADD: 9/92).   Ⓖ

...Symphony in D minor. Symphonic Variations[a]. Prélude, Choral et Fugue[b]. [a]**Philippe Entremont, Pascal Devoyon** (pfs); **French Radio National Orchestra / Jean Martinon.** Erato Bonsai Ⓑ 4509-92871-2 (75 minutes: DDD: 8/94).   Ⓖ

...Symphony in D minor. Grande pièce symphonique in F sharp minor, Op. 17 – Andante. Panis angelicus. **Satie** Gymnopédies – Nos. 1 and 2. **Dukas** L'apprenti sorcier. **A. Thomas** Mignon – Gavotte. **Berlioz** La damnation de Faust, Op. 24 – Hungarian March. **Philadelphia Orchestra / Leopold Stokowski.** Biddulph mono Ⓜ WHL011* (70 minutes: ADD: 8/95).

...Symphony in D minor. **Roussel** Symphony No. 3 in G minor, Op. 42. **French National Orchestra / Leonard Bernstein.** DG Masters Ⓜ 445 512-2GMA (69 minutes: DDD: 10/95). *See review under Roussel; refer to the Index to Reviews.*

...Symphony in D minor. **Haydn** Symphony No. 92, "Oxford". **Dvořák** Symphony No. 8 in G major, B163. **Prokofiev** Symphony No. 1 in D major, Op. 25, "Classical". **Concertgebouw Orchestra / Karel Ančerl.** Tahra Ⓕ TAH124/5 (two discs: 116 minutes: ADD: 3/96).

Franck Psyché[a]. Le Chasseur maudit. [a]**BBC Welsh Chorus; BBC National Orchestra of Wales / Tadaaki Otaka.** Chandos Ⓕ CHAN9342 (65 minutes: DDD: 6/95). Texts and translations included. Recorded 1994.   Ⓖ

The goody-goody 'Pater seraphicus' image of Franck assiduously projected by his devoted pupils has worked to his disadvantage in these more cynical times, as has the common assertion that his orchestral writing is tied to conventions of organ style. The symphonic poem about the Rhenish Count who goes hunting on the Sabbath and is punished for his sacrilege by a curse condemning him to be pursued for all time by the flames and demons of Hell is worthy of Liszt (Franck's model), and as performed by the Welsh orchestra is vividly programmatic. The breadth of dynamic contrasts is a feature of the recording – as it also is of *Psyché*, the opening of which is almost on the edge of sound. Franck's disciple Vincent d'Indy was either grotesquely unperceptive or grossly over-protective in claiming that *Psyché* was devoid of "pagan spirit" and was an ethereal dialogue between the soul and a seraph. In fact the sensual nature of the music can scarcely be missed, particularly in the section depicting the union of Psyche and Eros (in which the cellos here shine) and in the final pardoning of Psyche for disobeying the order not to look at her lover. When, in the first of the choral passages (which are most often omitted from performance), the words run "Do you not feel a sweet desire unfolding in your agitated breast?", this is surely the emotional cry of the composer himself, who was then violently in love with his pupil Augusta Holmès. Tadaaki Otaka shapes the orchestral playing with tenderness and passion, and the chorus contribute sympathetic tone and clear articulation of the words: the women, however, particularly when on their own, are apt to be slightly on the underside of notes.

Additional recommendation ...

...**Belgian Radio and Television Chorus; Liège Orchestra / Paul Strauss.** EMI L'Esprit Français Ⓜ CDM5 65162-2 (47 minutes: ADD: 5/95).

Franck Symphonic Variations, Op. 46[b].
Grieg Piano Concerto in A minor, Op. 16[a].
Schumann Piano Concerto in A minor, Op. 54[c]. [ab]**Sir Clifford Curzon,** [c]**Friedrich Gulda** (pfs); [a]**London Symphony Orchestra / Øivin Fjeldstad;** [b]**London Philharmonic Orchestra / Sir Adrian Boult;** [c]**Vienna Philharmonic Orchestra / Volkmar Andreae.** Decca Headline Classics Ⓑ 433 628-2DSP* (76 minutes: ADD: 1/92). Item marked [a]from LW5350 (7/59), [b]SXL2173 (1/60), [c]LXT5280 (5/57). 😊😊😊

Since the advent of the LP the Grieg and Schumann concertos have been ideally paired and here we have Sir Clifford Curzon's classic account of the Grieg from 1959 where he is sympathetically and idiomatically accompanied by Øivin Fjeldstad and the LSO. Curzon was at his finest in romantic piano concertos, and his playing achieves an exceptional balance between poetry and strength. This is a performance which clearly stakes a claim for the concerto as a work of genius. These same characteristics are also to the fore in the Franck *Symphonic Variations*, this time with Sir Adrian Boult conducting. Probably the finest performance of this popular work, it is imaginative and romantic with a perfect sense of style, and excellent rapport between conductor and soloist. As if these riches were not enough, and at bargain price, it is rounded off with another masterly reading of the Schumann Concerto by Friedrich Gulda, dating from 1956 and with Volkmar Andreae leading the Vienna Philharmonic. This reading is right in the centre of the authentic romantic style: iextremely personal and authoritative. Decca's recorded sound for all three performances is more than acceptable, with true piano tone throughout. This is probably one of the finest bargain issues currently available.

Additional recommendations ...

...Symphonic Variations[a]. Violin Sonata in A major (trans. Delsart)[b]. Piano Quintet in F minor[c].
Pascal Rogé (pf); [c]**Richard Friedman, Steven Smith** (vns); [c]**Christopher Wellington** (va); [a]**London Festival Orchestra / Ross Pople** ([bc]vc). ASV Ⓕ CDDCA769 (79 minutes: DDD: 11/91).

...Symphonic Variations. *Coupled with works by* **Fauré** *and* **d'Indy** François-Joël Thiollier (pf); **National Symphony Orchestra of Ireland / Antonio de Almeida.** Naxos Ⓢ 8 550754 (55 minutes: DDD: 1/95) *Gramophone Editor's choice.*

...Symphonic Variations[b]. **Brahms** Piano Concerto No. 1 in D minor, Op. 15[a]. **Litolff** Concerto symphonique No. 4 in D minor, Op. 102 – Scherzo[b]. **Sir Clifford Curzon** (pf); [a]**London Symphony Orchestra / George Szell;** [b]**London Philharmonic Orchestra / Sir Adrian Boult.** Decca The Classic Sound Ⓜ 425 082-2DCS (74 minutes: ADD: 4/95). *See review under Brahms; refer to the Index to Reviews.* 😊😊😊

...Symphonic Variations[a]. **Grieg** Piano Concerto in A minor, Op. 16. Lyric Pieces[c] – French serenade, Op. 62 No. 3; Cradle song, Op. 68 No. 5. **Liszt** Piano Concerto No. 1 in E flat major, S124[a]. **Walter Gieseking** (pf); [a]**London Philharmonic Orchestra / Sir Henry Wood;** [b]**Berlin State Opera Orchestra / Hans Rosbaud.** APR mono Ⓜ APR5513* (63 minutes: ADD: 3/96).

New review
Franck Violin Sonata in A major.
Fauré Violin Sonata No. 1 in A major, Op. 13.
Debussy Violin Sonata. **Pinchas Zukerman** (vn); **Marc Neikrug** (pf). RCA Victor Red Seal Ⓕ 09026 62697-2 (68 minutes: DDD: 5/95).

These are richly toned, expansive performances. That suits the Franck, and although one might be less sure about the Fauré and Debussy, their sonatas, too, are presented with a degree of mastery that may disarm criticism. The Fauré comes first, a big-boned and strongly projected account of the work which misses the half-lights found by other duos, but on their own terms they are highly effective and arguably their approach could win over those who still find this composer's music pallid. Much the same may be said of the Debussy. Some collectors will revel in the rich beauty of Zukerman's tone in the opening paragraphs; yet some may feel that this performance does not penetrate to the heart of this elusive, essentially melancholy music. The recording also lights everything too closely and brightly for its mystery to survive although the artists handle the finale well. Predictably, Franck's Sonata comes across best in this French triptych. Although the pianist is too solid in the second movement, the performers understand its grandeur and pathos, and give the work real sweep. Although collectors are directed elsewhere for the Fauré and Debussy (see recommendations under these composers; refer to the Index to Reviews), admirers of Zukerman's art need not hesitate if this programme attracts them.

Additional recommendations ...

...Violin Sonata. **Szymanowski** Mythes, Op. 30. King Roger (trans. Kochański). Kurpian Song (trans. Kochanski). **Kaja Danczowska** (vn); **Krystian Zimerman** (pf). DG Galleria Ⓜ 431 469-2GGA (58 minutes: ADD: 8/91).

...Violin Sonata. **Brahms** Horn Trio in E flat major, Op. 40. **Schumann** Adagio and Allegro in A flat major, Op. 70. **Saint-Saëns** Romance in E flat major, Op. 67. **Itzhak Perlman** (vn); **Barry Tuckwell** (hn); **Vladimir Ashkenazy** (pf). Decca Ⓜ 433 695-2DM (73 minutes: ADD: 9/92).

...Violin Sonata (arr. vc/pf). *Coupled with works by* **Dvořák, Schumann, Saint-Saëns, Delius, Elgar, Haydn, Monn, Chopin, Fauré, Bruch, Bach, Handel** and **Beethoven** Jacqueline du Pré (vc) with various artists and orchestras. EMI Ⓑ CZS5 68132-2 (six discs: 437 minutes: ADD: 8/94). *See review in the Collections section; refer to the Index to Reviews.* 😊😊

…Violin Sonata. *Coupled with works by* **Debussy** and **Ravel Augustin Dumay** (vn.); **Maria-João Pires** (pf). DG Ⓕ 445 880-2GH (56 minutes: DDD: 10/95). *See review under Debussy; refer to the Index to Reviews.* Ⓖ

…Violin Sonata. **Szymanowski** Violin Sonata in D minor, Op. 9. **Chee-Yun** (vn); **Akira Eguchi** (pf). Denon Ⓕ CO-78954 (50 minutes: DDD: 1/96). *See review under Szymanowski; refer to the Index to Reviews.*

…Violin Sonata. **Chausson** Concert for Violin, Piano and String Quartet in D major, Op. 21[a]. **Pierre Amoyal** (vn); **Pascal Rogé** (pf); [a]**Ysaÿe Quartet.** Decca Ⓕ 444 172-2DH (70 minutes: DDD: 2/96). *See review under Chausson; refer to the Index to Reviews.*

Franck Prélude, Choral et Fugue[a].
Schumann Etudes symphoniques, Op. 13[b]. Kreisleriana, Op. 16[c]. **Shura Cherkassky** (pf). Nimbus Ⓜ NI7705 (77 minutes: DDD: 3/95). Item marked [a] from NI5090 (recorded 1987), [b]NI5020 (1984), [c]NI5043 (1985). Recorded 1984-7. ⒼⒼ

Cherkassky's performances are infinitely varied, shedding fresh light on even the most familiar cornerstones of the repertoire. These recordings (dating from 1984-87) are living and vital proof of his spontaneity and, in *Kreisleriana* in particular, even the most immovable Beckmesser may well find himself abandoning pencil and paper to listen enchanted to Cherkassky's magical idiosyncrasy. In the *Etudes symphoniques* he is in unusually thoughtful and speculative (though never subdued) mood, with all the repeats offered as a golden opportunity to switch focus and emphasis. Throughout, there is a continuous sense of how Cherkassky's tide of feeling takes him in virtually any direction, a quality of the most life-affirming freedom and generosity. Time and again his playing generates its own ideas and convictions and, even when spinning an arbitrary or, rather, provocative line in the Franck, his playing is so volatile and unpredictable that you take it on its own terms and end haunted and bemused by the richness of his imagination; a quality far above and beyond mere caprice. The recordings (particularly in the Franck) are hardly models of refinement, but the performances are beyond price.

Additional recommendations ...

…Prélude, Choral et Fugue. **Liszt** Mephisto Waltz No. 1, S514. Années de pèlerinage, première année, S160, "Suisse" – Au bord d'une source; deuxième année, S161, "Italie" – Sonetto 104 del Petrarca. Two Concert Studies, S145. Rhapsodie espagnole, S254. **Murray Perahia** (pf). Sony Classical Ⓕ SK47180 (60 minutes: DDD: 10/91). Ⓖ

…Prélude, Chorale et Fugue. Prélude, Aria et Final. Prélude, Fugue et Variation in B minor, Op. 18 (trans. Bauer). Danse lente. Les plaintes d'une poupée. L'Organiste, Volume 1 – Chant de la Creuse; Vieux Noël: Andantino; Vieux Noël: Maestoso; Allegretto; Air béarnais; Chant béarnais; Vieux Noël: Poco lento; Noël angévin: Allegretto; Noël angévin: Quasi allegro. **Robert Silverman** (pf). CBC Records Musica Viva Ⓕ MVCD1061 (70 minutes: DDD: 6/94).

…Prélude, Fugue et Variation in B minor, Op. 18 (trans. Bauer). Prélude, Choral et Fugue. Danse lente. Prélude, Aria et Final. Choral No. 3 in A minor (trans. Crossley). **Paul Crossley** (pf). Sony Classical Ⓕ SK58914 (74 minutes: DDD 2/95).

…Prélude, Choral et Fugue. Les plaintes d'une poupée. Danse lente. Prélude, Aria et Final. **Chausson** Quelques danses, Op. 26. Paysage, Op. 38. **Dukas** Piano Sonata in E flat minor. Prélude élégiaque. La plainte, au loin, du faune ... . Variations, interlude et final sur un thème de Rameau. **Jean Hubeau** (pf). Teldec Ⓑ 4509-96221-2 (two discs: 134 minutes: DDD: 4/96).

New review

Franck Pièce héroique in B minor. Cantabile in B major. Fantaisie in A major. Grande pièce symphonique in F sharp minor, Op. 17. Pastorale in E major, Op. 19. Fantaisie in C major, Op. 16. Prélude, fugue et variation in B minor, Op. 18. Trois chorales (1890). Prière in C sharp minor, Op. 20. Final in B flat major, Op. 21. **Marie-Claire Alain** (org). Erato Ⓕ 0630-12706-2 (two discs: 152 minutes: DDD: 7/96). Played on the Cavaillé-Coll organ, Saint-Etienne, Caen, France. Recorded 1995.

What makes this release exceptional? Why does it stand so imperiously out of the crowd? Many other recordings of Franck's organ works have also taken the trouble to locate a wholly authentic Cavaillé-Coll instrument – Michael Murray's set (listed below) being the most distinguished. If Murray is a great communicator, presenting these large works in an endearingly direct and immediate way, Alain is a completely involved one. More than anyone else she delves into the very soul of these works. Thus we have an intensely prayerful *Prière*, a majestically statuesque *Grande pièce symphonique* while the *Chorales* are delivered with an unexpected degree of fervour; perhaps the Third is a shade overfervent since some of the semiquaver figurations lack absolute clarity – something which after one or two hearings serves to heighten the excitement but which might, after repeated listening, become irritating. This is a highly authoritative release not just in terms of playing but also in Alain's accompanying notes. The Caen organ is a particularly fine specimen of a Cavaillé-Coll, dating from 1884 – 25 years after the St Clotilde organ for which Franck wrote much of this music. The recording captures it, and the church's atmosphere, effectively. A word of warning: anyone seeking out Alain's memorable account of the *Pastorale* will find it on track 10 of the first disc, not track 9 as the tracking details on the box suggest.

Additional recommendations ...

…Fantaisie in A major. Cantabile in B major. Pièce Héroïque in B minor. Fantaisie in C major. Grande Pièce Symphonique. Prélude, fugue et variation. Pastorale. Prière in C sharp minor. Final in B flat major. Chorales – No. 1 in E major; No. 2 in B minor; No. 3 in A minor. **Michael Murray** (org). Telarc Ⓕ CD80234 (two discs: 149 minutes: DDD: 7/90).

...Chorale No. 3. *Coupled with works by* **T. Dubois, Gigout, Langlais , Murrill, Peeters, Reger** and **Vierne Andrew Lucas** (org). Naxos Ⓢ 8 550955 (71 minutes: DDD: 11/94). *See review in the Collections section; refer to the Index to Reviews.*

Franck Rédemption. **Lambert Wilson** (narr); **Béatrice Uria-Monzon** (mez); **Orféon Donostiarra; Toulouse Capitole Orchestra / Michel Plasson.** EMI Ⓕ CDC5 55056-2 (74 minutes: DDD: 5/95). Recorded 1993-4. *Gramophone Editor's choice.*   Ⓖ

This is the first complete recording of Franck's "Poème-Symphonie", *Rédemption.* Most Franckians will know the occasionally recorded orchestral "Morceau symphonique" of the same name (actually, the beginning of the second part of the revised complete work) but its 13 minutes offer few hints of the nature of the surrounding hour's worth – of the opposing and eventually combined terrestrial and heavenly choirs, with the narrator pleading on behalf of the former and the Archangel (mezzo-soprano) showing them the way. This is certainly the kind of performance – one whose insight, preparation and devotion is evident in almost every bar – that will incline many to claim it as a neglected masterpiece (the final chorus is the only part of the work which, most obviously for the sopranos, could have done with extra rehearsal). Lambert Wilson's entreaties are eloquent and involving, Béatrice Uria-Monzon is a radiant Archangel, and chorus and orchestra are ideally agile, responsive and light-toned in the best French tradition. EMI, too, offer their best Toulouse sound to date: a wide dynamic range, a fresh and enlivening clarity and an acute judgement for the placing of the participants, taking into account the need for natural representation and the imagery of the text.

Further listening ...

...Piano Concerto No. 2 in B minor, Op. 11. Variations brillantes sur la ronde favorite de Gustave III, Op. 8. **Jean-Claude Vanden Eynden** (pf); **RTBF New Symphony Orchestra / Edgar Doneux.** Koch Schwann Musica Mundi 311 111 (3/90).

...Piano Quintet in F minor. *Coupled with* **Shostakovich** Piano Quintet in G minor, Op. 57. **Victor Aller** (pf); **Hollywood Quartet.** Testament mono SBT1077* (5/96)

...Les Béatitudes. **Soloists; Stuttgart Gächinger Kantorei and Radio Symphony Orchestra / Helmuth Rilling.** Hänssler Classic 98 964 (7/91).

Benjamin Frankel   American 1906-1973

Frankel Symphonies – No. 1, Op. 33; No. 5, Op. 67. May Day Overture, Op. 22. **Queensland Symphony Orchestra / Werner Andreas Albert.** CPO Ⓕ CPO999 240-2 (53 minutes: DDD: 7/94).   Ⓖ

Here is proof that Benjamin Frankel was a masterly symphonist. The two symphonies on this disc demonstrate that his inexplicable neglect has been our loss. Neglect because of rumours that he was a serialist and therefore probably tuneless and rebarbative (you could well find yourself whistling tunes from these Symphonies for days)? He seems, if the overture *May Day* is anything to go by (it precedes all of his eight symphonies), to have been a natural, indeed an abundantly fertile melodist who felt the need for some sort of discipline on his inventiveness stronger than that of conventional nineteenth-century symphonic form. He found it in a highly personal adaptation of serialism, an adaptation designed to retain a strong sense of key and indeed of melody, but to use the elements of melody with great economy and rigour. Already those very nouns may suggest aridity, but they shouldn't: Haydn, after all, very often did much the same thing. They do not sound like Haydn, these symphonies, nor in the least like Schoenberg. In their openness of texture they are reminiscent of Copland or Martinů, in the rather alfresco geniality of the opening movement of No. 5 of Nielsen, once or twice, fleetingly, of Mahler. The performances are first-class and so are the recordings.

New review

Frankel Symphonies – No. 2, Op. 38; No. 3, Op. 40. **Queensland Symphony Orchestra, Brisbane / Werner Andreas Albert.** CPO Ⓕ CPO999 241-2 (59 minutes: DDD: 8/95). Both works are introduced by the composer. Recorded 1994.

The Second and Third Symphonies are strongly contrasted and they demonstrate Frankel's range as well as his stature. The Second is as grim as Shostakovich at his bleakest, and its austerity is not relieved: a gamelan-like twinkling towards the end of the finale seems to promise a gleam of light but it is transformed instead into the enigmatic twitching of a frozen coda. A mood of poignant resignation is the nearest the symphony gets to a positive resolution. And yet it is not depressing. The composer himself suggested (each symphony is preceded by a brief but illuminating spoken introduction) that it is in some sense a reaction to events in his life but the determination that this experience should be reflected in lucid musical discourse, however sombre, is characteristic. There are no notes wasted here on rhetoric; the rigour of Frankel's thematic working intensifies the music's eloquence. It also seems typical of Frankel that the Third should be so very different from its predecessor. It abandons, or appears to abandon, the Second's strongly personal re-working of serialism, building an extremely cogent single-movement structure from two apparently irreconcilable ideas: a pealing, bell-like figure that seems unable to emerge from the chord that contains it, and an angular but lyrical string melody. The fact that they can be reconciled is beautifully demonstrated not by a single 'development section' but by a series of strongly contrasted ones, and a concluding reversion to quasi-serial practice. Again, the logic of Frankel's argument is all the more compelling for every stage of it being so clearly audible. The performances and recordings are first-rate.

Further listening ...
...The Aftermath, Op. 17[a]. Solemn Speech and Discussion, Op. 11. Three Sketches, Op. 2. Concertante Lirico, Op. 27. Youth Music, Op. 12. [a]**Robert Dan** (ten); **Seattle Northwest Chamber Orchestra / Alun Francis.** CPO CPO999 221-2 (2/95).
...A Kid for Two Farthings – Theme. *Coupled with works by* **Alwyn, Arnold, Vaughan Williams, Addinsell, C. Williams, C. Parker, J. Addison II, Allan Gray, Greenwood, Spoliansky** and **P. Green Various orchestras and conductors.** EMI mono CDGO2059* (9/94). *See review in the Collections section; refer to the Index to Reviews.*

Frederick II, King of Prussia   German 1712-1786

Suggested listening ...
...Flute Concerto No. 3 in C major. *Coupled with works by* **C.P.E. Bach, F. Benda** and **Quantz Patrick Gallois** (fl); **CPE Bach Chamber Orchestra / Peter Schreier.** DG 439 895-2GH (11/94). *See review in the Collections section; refer to the Index to Reviews.*

Girolamo Frescobaldi   Italian 1583-1643

New review
Frescobaldi Il primo libro di Madrigali. **Concerto Italiano / Rinaldo Alessandrini.** Opus 111
Ⓕ OPS30-133 (53 minutes: DDD: 4/96). ✐ Texts and translations included. Recorded 1995.
Gramophone Editor's choice.

This story, which has a happy ending, is a curious one. Frescobaldi, in Antwerp with his Roman patron in 1608, was commissioned by a local printer to produce his first and indeed only book of madrigals. The collection seems to have little impact on contemporaries. It was never reprinted either North or South of the Alps, and in our own times its existence gradually became submerged under the weight of Frescobaldi's reputation as a composer for the keyboard. Those interested in pursuing the matter discovered that the only known surviving copy lacks one of its voice-parts. Frescobaldi's *Primo libro* seemed set fair to remain a footnote in the textbooks rather than a musical reality. All that changed with the discovery of a complete set of partbooks, then in a private library, a challenge that Rinaldo Alessandrini has now taken up by both editing and recording the music. The distinctive sound and approach of his *Gramophone* Award-winning Concerto Italiano will be familiar to all enthusiasts for Italian music of the Monteverdi period (and above all for the music of Monteverdi himself), and their many admirers will not be disappointed with the result. Their instinctive feel for the diction, sound and sense of the Italian language married to a sophisticated and dynamic interpretational approach brings out all the rhetorical subtleties of Frescobaldi's extraordinary music, with its obvious parentage in the madrigals of Gesualdo and Monteverdi. This is virtuoso madrigal singing at its most exhilarating, all the more effective for being sometimes (though not on all tracks) imaginatively underpinned by continuo instruments. The real revelation here is not so much the Concerto Italiano, whose powerfully moving performances we have come to expect, but Frescobaldi's madrigals; no one with a soul should miss them.

Further listening ...
...Toccata. *Coupled with works by* **Lambardo, Buono, Picchi, Trabaci, A. Mayone, Giovanni de Macque, Facoli, A. Valente, Merula, M. Rossi, Salvatore, B. Storace, G. Strozzi, Stradella** and **A. Scarlatti Rinaldo Alessandrini** (hpd). Opus 111 OPS30-118 (4/95). ✐ *See review in the Collections section; refer to the Index to Reviews.*

Hugo Friedhofer   American 1902-1981

Suggested listening ...
...The Young Lions; This Earth is Mine – Original film soundtracks. Varèse Sarabande VSD2-5403 (10/93).

Ignacy Friedman   Polish 1882-1948

Suggested listening ...
...Frühlingsstimmen. *Coupled with works by* **Schulz-Evler, M. Rosenthal, Tausig** and **Godowsky Piers Lane** (pf). Hyperion CDA66785 (2/96).

Johann Froberger   German 1616-1667

Suggested listening ...
...Fantasia II in A minor. *Coupled with* **Palestrina** Coelestis urbs Jerusalem. **Schmelzer** Vesperae sollennes[ab]. Sonata per Chiesa et Camera. Sacro-Profanus Concentus Musicus – Sonata XII. **Biber** Missa alleluja[ab]. **Anonymous** Gregorian Chant for the Dedication of a Church – Mass Propers[a]. Gregorian Chant for Vespers[a].[a]**Vienna Hofburgkapella Schola;** [b]**Concerto Palatino; Gradus ad Parnassum / Konrad Junghänel.** Deutsche Harmonia Mundi 05472 77326-2 (7/95). ✍

Walter Frye   British fl. *c*1450-1475

Suggested listening ...
...Missa "Flos Regalis". Trinitatis dies. Salve virgo mater pya. O florens rosa. Ave regina celorum (two settings). Sospitati dedit. Tout a par moy. So ys emprentid. Myn hertis lust. Alas, alas is my chief song. **The Hilliard Ensemble.** ECM New Series 437 684-2 (6/93).

Robert Fuchs   German 1847-1927

Fuchs Clarinet Quintet in E flat major, Op. 102.
Romberg Quintet in E flat major, Op. 57[a].
Stanford Two Fantasy Pieces. **Thea King** (cl); **Britten Quartet** (Peter Manning, vn; Keith Pascoe, vn/[a]va; Peter Lale, va; Andrew Shulman, vc). Hyperion Ⓔ CDA66479 (80 minutes: DDD: 7/92). Recorded 1991.
Though the clarinet is a beautiful instrument that was admired by several composers from Mozart onwards, its solo repertory is small and we cannot afford to neglect any part of it, particularly as there are many fine players, among whom Thea King stands out as one of the finest. None of these three composers can claim to be among the musical greats, but each wrote sympathetically for the instrument and this sensitively played and well recorded disc makes for pleasing listening. It should win friends for Andreas Romberg (a contemporary of Beethoven and not the Romberg who composed *The Desert Song*), and the turn-of-the-century composers Robert Fuchs and Sir Charles Villiers Stanford – not least if we also gratefully remember two men for teaching, between them, Mahler, Sibelius, Vaughan Williams and Holst. Romberg's Quintet is fluent and unfailingly agreeable, if not more than that: listening to it, and not least the outer sections of the minuet second movement (the trio is more personal), one is reminded of Mozart in a genial yet elegant mood, and Romberg surely knew that composer's Clarinet Quintet and Concerto. Fuchs's work, written in 1917 when he was 70 and first performed at a concert to mark the occasion, is romantic in an almost Schubertian way although it was composed after the radical works of Stravinsky and Schoenberg had shaken the musical world. But we need not disagree with Brahms, who once said, "Fuchs is a splendid musician: all's so refined, skilled and delightfully inventive that we can always enjoy what we hear". The Two *Fantasy Pieces* by Stanford have similar civilized qualities plus occasional attractive touches of Irishness and complete a valuable and very enjoyable programme.

Fuchs Ten Fantasy Pieces, Op. 74[a]. Violin Sonata No. 6 in G minor, Op. 103[a]. Six Fantasy Pieces, Op. 117[b]. **Arnold Steinhardt** ([a]vn/[b]va); **Victor Steinhardt** (pf). Biddulph (special price) LAW012 (two discs: 81 minutes: DDD: 1/95). Recorded 1993.   Ⓖ
This music is deeply Brahmsian though occasionally lightened with Dvořákian sunbeams; the playing, cordial, unforced and with an intimate, sighing tone that particularly suits Robert Fuchs's reflective muse. The Sixth Violin Sonata is a relatively late composition; it was written in 1915, published four years later and dedicated to one of Fuchs's most enthusiastic fans, the young Adolf Busch. It's a strong, beautifully built sonata, with significant developmental incident and plenty of telling counterpoint. The slow movement in particular recalls the later Brahms, although Fuchs's own, somewhat more classical voice emerges as quietly distinctive. One should perhaps remember that Brahms himself had described him as "a young skylark", praising the "intensity and meaning" of his music; and that Fuchs's own pupils included Hugo Wolf, Mahler, Sibelius, Franz Schmidt, Schreker and Zemlinsky. He was, in a limited sense, a sort of missing link, a thoughtful conservative whose very personal sensibilities helped clear a traceable path between the generations. Fuchs's chamber works are rich in allusions and will not be hurried: they demand patient handling, subtle understatement and an acute sense of musical colour. A little like Fauré's chamber music, perhaps. The recording is exemplary. All in all a quiet revelation.

Further listening ...
...20 Duos, Op. 55. *Coupled with* **Bartók** 44 Duos, Sz98. **Eugene Drucker, Philip Setzer** (vns). Biddulph Ⓜ LAW007 (74 minutes: DDD: 3/95).   ⒼⒼ
...Cello Sonatas – No. 1 in D minor, Op. 29; No. 2 in E flat minor, Op. 83. Fantasiestücke, Op. 78. **Nancy Green** (vc); **Caroline Palmer** (pf). Biddulph LAW005 (4/93).
...Piano Sonatas – No. 1 in G flat major, Op. 19; No. 2 in G minor, Op. 88. **Daniel Blumenthal** (pf). Marco Polo 8 223377 (6/93).

Julius Fučik
Bohemian 1872-1916

Suggested listening ...
...Die lustigen Dorfschmiede, Op. 218. Der alte Brummbär, Op. 210. Einzug der Gladiatoren,
Op. 68. *Coupled with works by* **Dvořák, Nedbal** and **Smetana** Malcolm Stewart (vn); **Timothy
Walden** (vc); **Alan Pendlebury** (bn); **Royal Liverpool Philharmonic Orchestra / Libor Pešek.** Virgin
Classics VC7 59285-2 (11/94).

Fulbert de Chartres

New review
Fulbert de Chartres Cantor of the Year 1000. **Venance Fortunat Ensemble / Anne-Marie
Deschamps.** L'Empreinte Digitale Ⓔ ED13036 (63 minutes: DDD: 12/95). Texts included.
Recorded 1989.
Stirps Jesse (six versions). Chorus nove. Benedicamus Domino (two versions). Antiphons and
Responses for Saints' Days – O martyr Domini Christi; Iam super astra poli residens; Vir Dei
Leobinus; Cumque gleba conderetur. Deus, Pater piissime. Aurea personet lyra. Alleluia dies
sanctificatus. Solem justitie (four versions). Ad nutum Domini.
This is an intriguing and fascinating documentary. Fulbert of Chartres can scarcely be more than a
name to the majority of music lovers, and yet there can be few much better-known composers whose
works, like his, have never ceased to be sung for a thousand years and who still maintain their place
in the current repertoire. Indeed, Fulbert's three magnificent responsories – from Matins of the Feast
of the Nativity of the Blessed Virgin Mary – which form the basis of this collection, were reprinted
by Solesmes in a modern edition of their *Processionale monasticum* as recently as 1983. And if few
monastic choirs still have the chance to sing the full night office of Matins, most of their members
will at least be able to hum the tune of *Benedicamus I* – that famous phrase drawn from *Stirps Jesse*
– and innumerable congregations will be familiar with Fulbert's famous Easter hymn *Chorus novae
Jerusalem* – "Ye choirs of new Jerusalem" – though most probably not to its usual Mode 3 chant
melody, nor even to the First Mode one in the *Hymnarius*, as sung here. The interest of this recording
is that it traces the early history of a number of Fulbert's compositions, showing how they came to
be elaborated by the application of successive techniques over the first four centuries of their
existence. We hear each piece first in its original form, often with reference to the rhythmic neumes of
the school of Laon, bringing out the structural notes and skimming over the ornaments with lively
fluidity; and then with numerous subsequent transformations: organum, diaphonia, motet. The few
metrical hymns are sung rather loosely, in a way that is rather attractive and fairly plausible. Michel
Huglo's exemplary insert-notes provide the necessary historic background. Full texts are given, but
only French translations of the Latin.

Dyam Fumet
French 1867-1949

Suggested listening ...
...La nuit. *Coupled with works by* **Honegger** and **d'Indy** Jean-Jacques Wiederker Chamber
Orchestra / Frédéric Bouaniche. Koch Schwann 310652 (6/95). *See review under d'Indy; refer to
the Index to Reviews.*

Wilhelm Furtwängler
German 1886-1954

Suggested listening ...
...Symphony No. 2 in E minor. **Vienna Philharmonic Orchestra / Wilhelm Furtwängler.** Orfeo D'Or
mono C375941B* (4/95).   ⓖⓖⓖ

Johann Fux
Austrian 1660-1741

New review
Fux Concentus musico-instrumentalis – No. 2, Overture (Suite) in B flat major; No. 4, Overture
(Suite) in G minor. Overtures (Suites) – B flat major; D minor. **Il Fondamento / Paul Dombrecht.**
Vanguard Classics Passacaille Collection Ⓜ 99705 (60 minutes: DDD: 3/96). ✐ Recorded 1994.
Fux, chiefly remembered by music students for his theoretical treatise *Gradus ad Parnassum*, was
Kapellmeister at the Vienna Court for over 25 years, between 1715 and his death in 1741. In 1701 he
published seven partitas in the form of dance suites, under the title *Concentus musico-instrumentalis*.
They were his Op. 1 and he dedicated them to the son of Emperor Leopold I who obligingly paid for
the printing of the parts. They are splendid pieces whose character ranges from the noble gestures of
the Lullian French ouverture with its appended suite of dances, to the intimacy of chamber music
trios. Dombrecht has chosen the two works from the set that owe most to their French models, the

Second and Fourth Suites. Both are scored for two oboes, bassoon, strings and continuo. The remaining two pieces on the disc are similarly scored, although they belong to a sizeable miscellany of such works that remained and indeed still remain unpublished. One of the finest movements here is an airy, expansive chaconne which concludes the B flat Suite. Il Fondamento play it gracefully but the performance lacks sharply defined articulation. Overall, however, the performances are excellent, if sometimes lacking in exuberance.

Fuzzy

Denmark 1939-

Suggested listening ...
...Fireplay. *Coupled with works by* **Pape, A. Koppel, Miki** and **Nørgård Safri Duo**. Chandos New Direction CHAN9330 (4/95). *See review in the Collections section; refer to the Index to Reviews.*

Andrea Gabrieli

Italian c1510-1586

Suggested listening ...
...Intonazioni – primo tono (O'Donnell); settimo tono (Timothy Roberts, org). Mass Movements – Kyrie a 5-12; Gloria a 16; Sanctus a 12; Benedictus a 12. O sacrum convivium a 5. Benedictus Dominus Deus sabbaoth. *Coupled with works by* **G. Gabrieli, Bendinelli** and **M. Thomsen Gabrieli Consort and Players / Paul McCreesh**. Virgin Classics Veritas VC7 59006-2 (5/90). *Gramophone Award Winner 1990. See review in the Collections section; refer to the Index to Reviews.* ⓖⓖⓖ

Giovanni Gabrieli

Italian c1553/6-1612

Suggested listening ...
...Symphoniae sacrae – Exaudi me Domine. *Coupled with works by* **Ockeghem, Josquin Desprez, Porta, Tallis, Manchicourt** and **Striggio Huelgas Ensemble / Paul van Nevel**. Sony Classical Vivarte SK66261 (4/96).
...Intonazioni – ottavo tono; terzo e quarto toni, quinto tono alla quarta bassa (James O'Donnell, org solo). Canzonas – XIII a 12; XVI a 15; IX a 10. Sonata VI a 8 pian e forte. Deus qui beatum Marcum a 10. Omnes gentes a 16. *Coupled with works by* **A. Gabrieli, Bendinelli** and **M. Thomsen Gabrieli Consort and Players / Paul McCreesh**. Virgin Classics Veritas VC7 59006-2 (5/90). *Gramophone Award Winner 1990. See review in the Collections section; refer to the Index to Reviews.* ⓖⓖⓖ
...Sacrae symphoniae – Canzon duodecemi toni a 10; Sonata piano e forte alla quarta bassa a 8; Canzon noni toni a 12; Canzon septimi e octavi toni a 12; Canzon primi toni a 8. Canzoni e sonata – Sonata XVIII a 14; Sonata XIX a 15; Canzon VII a 7; Canzon X a 8; Canzon XV a 10; Canzon XVI a 12; Canzon XII a 8; Sonata XX a 22. Canzon La Spiritata a 4. *Coupled with* **A. Gabrieli** Ricercar del duodecimi tono (1589). **Viadana** Sinfonias a 8 – La Bergamasca; La Padovanna. **Frescobaldi** Canzon terzadecima detta la Bianchina a 4. **Wallace Collection / Simon Wright**. Nimbus NI5236 (11/90).

Niels Gade

Danish 1817-1890

New review

Gade Symphony No. 1 in C minor, Op. 5. Hamlet Overture, Op. 37. Echoes from Ossian, Op. 1ª.
Danish National Radio Symphony Orchestra / Dmitri Kitaienko. Chandos ⒻCHAN9422 (61 minutes: DDD: 3/96). Item marked ª from CHAN9075 (11/92), remainder new to UK. Recorded 1992-3.

Gade's First Symphony, which was turned down by the Copenhagen Music Society but accepted and championed in Leipzig by Mendelssohn, launched him on his long and successful career. Its subtitle, *On Sjøland's fair plains* ("Paa Sjølands fagre sletter"), alludes to one of the folk-songs collected and published by his teacher Andreas Peter Berggreen though it is not the only folk-song to figure in the score. The First Symphony comes from 1842 and is exactly contemporaneous with the *Sinfonia sérieuse* of Berwald. Although it may not have as individual a profile, it is eminently civilized, well-schooled music which deserves a place in the repertory. The performance is both vital and sensitive and the recording is splendidly natural, with a good perspective and front-to-back depth and no want of detail or presence. The *Echoes from Ossian* Overture is Gade's first opus, which he composed two years earlier. Like the symphony it is one of his most frequently recorded pieces, and its second group has a charm that is difficult to resist. This performance, incidentally, has appeared before on the Chandos issue of *The Elf-king's daughter* ("Elverskud"). The *Hamlet Overture* was written 21 years later under the influence of what Jens Cornelius calls "Leipzig-inspired ideals". It is beautifully crafted, fresh in its inspiration and well worth its place in the catalogue. The Järvi Symphony set is excellent and those who have it need not feel they are in any way short-changed but readers beginning a Gade collection might well start here.

Additional recommendations ...

...Symphonies – No. 1; No. 8 in B minor, Op. 47. **Stockholm Sinfonietta / Neeme Järvi.** BIS
   Ⓕ CD339 (58 minutes: DDD: 11/87).

...Elf-shot, Op. 30[a]. Echoes from Ossian[b]. Five Songs, Op. 13[c]. Soloists; [a]**Danish National Radio**
   Choir; [c]**Danish National Radio Chamber Choir / Stefan Parkman;** [ab]**Danish National Radio**
   Symphony Orchestra / Dmitri Kitaienko. Chandos Ⓕ CHAN9075 (77 minutes: DDD: 11/92).

...Echoes from Ossian[a]. **Abrahamsen** Symphony[a]. **Horneman** Gurre Suite[b]. **Nørgård** Twilight[b].
   Aarhus Royal Academy of Music Orchestra / [a]**Ole Schmidt,** [b]**Søren K. Hansen.** Kontrapunkt
   Ⓕ 32194 (60 minutes: DDD: 7/95).

New review

Gade String Quartet in F major, "Wilkommen und Abschied". Allegro in A minor. Andante and Allegro molto in F minor[a]. Octet in F major, Op. 17[b]. **Kontra Quartet** (Anton Kontra, Boris Samsing, vns; Peter Fabricius, va; Morten Zeuthen, vc); [b]**Anne Egendal,** [b]**Per Lund Madsen** (vns); [b]**Sune Ranmo** (va); [ab]**Hans Nygaard** (vc). BIS Ⓕ CD545 (76 minutes: DDD: 3/96). Recorded 1992. All these works date from 1836-48; the *Allegro* in A minor for string quartet from 1836, when Gade was 19; the F minor *Andante and Allegro molto* for string quintet from the following year; the F major Quartet, *Wilkommen und Abschied* from 1840 and the Octet from 1848, towards the end of his Leipzig period. All this music is fluent, urbane, civilized and inventive. In some ways its musical ideas are fresher than in Gade's mature pieces. Certainly the Mendelssohnian attire he donned in later life does not radiate the same spontaneity of feeling. The F minor Quintet is particularly delightful. But all this music has charm and is expertly and persuasively played by the Kontra Quartet and their musicianly colleagues. The recording is very acceptable, though there is a slight edge in tuttis. A useful supplement to the three mature Gade quartets already available and in some ways more enjoyable.

Further listening ...

...Symphonies – No. 2 in E major, Op. 10; No. 7 in F major, Op. 45. **Stockholm Sinfonietta / Neeme Järvi.** BIS CD355 (12/87).

...Symphonies – No. 3 in A minor, Op. 15; No. 4 in B flat major, Op. 20. **Stockholm Sinfonietta / Neeme Järvi.** BIS CD338 (7/87).

...Symphonies – No. 4 in B flat major, Op. 20; No. 6 in G minor, Op. 32. **Copenhagen Collegium Musicum / Michael Schønwandt.** Da capo DCCD9202 (5/94).

...Symphonies – No. 5 in D minor, Op. 25[a]; No. 6 in G minor, Op. 32. [a]**Roland Pöntinen** (pf); **Stockholm Sinfonietta / Neeme Järvi.** BIS CD356 (12/87).

...String Quartets – F minor (1851); E minor (1877); D major, Op. 63. **Kontra Quartet.** BIS CD516 (10/92).

Renaud Gagneux

German 1947-

Suggested listening ...

...Triptyque. *Coupled with* **Shchedrin** Sotto voce. **Mstislav Rostropovich** (vc); **London Symphony Orchestra / Seiji Ozawa.** Teldec 4509-94570-2 (6/96). *See review under Shchedrin; refer to the Index to Reviews.*

Cristóbal Gálan

Spanish c1630-1684

Suggested listening ...

...Al espejo que retrata. Humano ardor. *Coupled with works by* **Literes, J. de Torres, F. Valls, F. de Iribarren** and **Anonymous** Al Ayre Español / Eduardo López Banzo. Deutsche Harmonia Mundi 05472 77325-2 (8/95). ✏

Arnaldo Galliera

Italian 1871-1934

Suggested listening ...

...Venerdi Santo dal "Trittico". *Coupled with* **Bossi** Stunde der Wehie, Op. 132 No. 4. Stunde der Freude, Op. 132 No. 5. **Petrali** Messe solennelle – Gloria. **Bettinelli** Toccata Fantasia. **Ambrosi** Messa. **Luigi Benedetti** (org). Priory PRCD427 (4/95).

Jacques Gallot
French c1600-c1690

New review
Gallot Suites – F sharp minor; A minor. Pieces – F major; D minor; C major. Chaconne in C major. **Hopkinson Smith** (lte). Astrée Auvidis Ⓔ E8528 (64 minutes: DDD: 8/95). 🎵 Recorded 1994.

Seventeenth-century Europe abounded in lutenists and guitarists whose name was Gallot, but the one we are concerned with here, Jacques, was known as "le vieux Gallot de Paris", so he is more easily identified than most. He was a distinguished figure in the dying days of the French lute tradition that had enriched the art of ornamentation and given birth to *style brisé* and the genre of the *tombeau*. In one work of the latter type, he mourned the death of the Duchess of Orléans; his own demise was similarly lamented by Robert de Visée – the obituary of a necrologist, as it were! Gallot's music survives in two principal sources, one a manuscript, the other an engraved book of *Pièces de luth* (after 1670) from which (with two small changes) the music on this recording is taken. Many of the pieces fall into 'suites', grouped by common keys, the titles of whose movements recall those of the French harpsichord music of their own and later times, e.g. "Sarabande la Divine" and "Gavotte la Jalousée", the rest are separate pieces. The first of the two chosen Suites is in the unusual key of F sharp minor, known as the *ton de chèvre* because its unsympathetic relationship to the basic tuning of the lute was thought to evoke the bleating of the goat. It is magnificent music, less *brisé* in style than that of Gallot's contemporaries, and played to expressive and technical perfection by Hopkinson Smith; the excellence of the recording *per se* is matched by the quality of the annotation. If you think French baroque lute music to be dully precious, as many performances may have made it seem, this disc could easily change your mind.

Baldassare Galuppi
Italian 1706-1785

Galuppi Confitebor tibi, Domini[a]. Arripe alpestri ad vallem. [a]**Véronique Gens** (sop); [a]**Peter Harvey** (bass); **Il Seminario Musicale / Gérard Lesne** (alto). Virgin Classics Veritas Ⓔ VC5 45030-2 (54 minutes: DDD: 10/94). Texts and translations included. 🎵 Recorded 1992. Ⓖ

Galuppi was almost universally admired during his lifetime. The English musician and historian Charles Burney, visiting him in Venice in 1770, described him as "natural, intelligent and agreeable ... [with] very much the look of a gentleman" and considered him to be one of the best composers of the age. Yet for all his contemporary fame, which included the documented admiration of Salieri, Hasse and C.P.E. Bach, his music was largely forgotten after his death and except for one or two instrumental works has remained so ever since. This recording contains just two of his multi-sectioned motets, a type of music that Galuppi must have often been asked to write in his capacity as both Maestro di cappella at St Mark's Basilica and Maestro di coro at the Ospedale degli Incurabili in Venice. The style is for the most part characterized by mellifluous and apparently unendingly graceful melodies carefully and ingeniously interwoven with string writing, the balance between the two being nicely captured here by Lesne's soloists and the instrumentalists of Il Seminario Musicale. Yet Galuppi's music is not without its moments of drama too; the "genius and fire" which Burney so admired is revealed in a number of moments in both motets, such as the bass solo "Redemptionem misit" from *Confitebor tibi*, whose heroic and virtuosic character is handled with ease and conviction by Peter Harvey. Indeed, the frequent use of contrasts of timbre, texture and 'archaic' and 'modern' styles is one of the principal ways in which the architecture of this music is conveyed. As for Véronique Gens, she is the delight of this disc, with a fresh and open bloom on the voice which radiates the seductive power of Galuppi's vocal lines to perfection. Recommended.

Henry Balfour Gardiner
British 1877-1950

Suggested listening ...
...Shepherd Fennell's Dance. *Coupled with* **Coleridge Taylor** Scenes from "The Song of Hiawatha", Op. 30 – Onaway, awake, beloved[a]. **Harty** A John Field Suite. **Ireland** A London Overture. **Vaughan Williams** The Lark Ascending[b]. **Holst** The Hymn of Jesus, H140[c]. [a]**Webster Booth** (ten); [b]**David Wise** (vn); [c]**Huddersfield Choral Society; Liverpool Philharmonic Orchestra / Sir Malcolm Sargent.** Dutton Laboratories mono CDAX8012* (5/95).

Phillipe Gaubert
French 1879-1941

Suggested listening ...
...Sonata. Madrigal. Deux esquisses. Fantaisie. Romance. Flute Sonatas – No. 2; No. 3. Sicilienne. Berceuse. Suite. Nocturne et Allegro scherzando. Romance. Sonatine. Sur l'eau. Ballade. **Susan Milan** (fl); **Ian Brown** (pf). Chandos CHAN8981/2 (11/91).
...Flute Sonata No. 1. *Coupled with works by* **Caplet, Fauré, Saint-Saëns, Busser, Poulenc, Roussel** and **Ferroud** Peter Lloyd (fl); Rebecca Holt (pf). IMP Classics PCD991 (9/92).

Gauthier de Coincy   French 1177/8-1236

New review

Gautier de Coincy Amours dont sui espris. Entendez tuit ensemble. Ma viele. D'un amour coie et serie. Quant ces floretes florir. Hui matin a l'ajournee. Roine celestre. Esforcier m'estuet ma vois. Pour conforter mon cuer et mon courage. Amours qui bien set enchanter. Puis que voi la flour novele. Qui que face rotruenge novele. Mere Dieu, vierge senee. Pour mon chief reconforter. **Alla Francesca** (Emmanuel Bonnardot, Pierre Hamon, Brigitte Lesne, sngrs/instrs; Catherine Sergent, sngr). Opus 111 Ⓟ OPS30-146 (63 minutes: DDD: 5/96). Texts and translations included. Recorded 1995.

Gautier de Coincy appears to have led a rather retiring existence. None of the wand'ring minstrel about him: he was Prior in two successive monasteries over a 20-year period until his death in 1233. Most of his poetry, though written in praise of the Blessed Virgin Mary, is clearly grounded in the standard tropes and forms of the time. In fact, his output represents something of a crossover between the sacred and the secular. The trick was for the new text to fit the old music as closely as possible – something at which Gautier appears to have been very skilful. Those familiar with this repertory should have little difficulty in tracing the borrowings. Alla Francesca is essentially a triple-act consisting of the singers Brigitte Lesne and Emmanuel Bonnardot, and the irrepressible flautist, Pierre Hamon. All three are distinguished members of the French early music scene, appearing in a number of ensembles. In previous recordings they have augmented their number according to need; here, they are unassisted save on a single track, and they sound all the better for it. The function of instruments in this music is (as always) a delicate matter. There is much to delight in: the rhythmic subtlety of Hamon's bagpiping, the spirituality of Brigitte Lesne's singing in particular, and (on most tracks) the general sense of ensemble. Yet the most satisfying aspect of this disc is the rounded presentation of Gautier's many talents. Those who know this repertory fairly well will appreciate the ways in which this recording fits in with others currently in the catalogue. For those who don't, it's a great place to start.

John Gay   British 1685-1732

Gay (arr. Britten). The Beggar's Opera. **Ann Murray** (mez) Polly; **Philip Langridge** (ten) Macheath; **Yvonne Kenny** (sop) Lucy; **John Rawnsley** (bar) Lockit; **Robert Lloyd** (bass) Peachum; **Anne Collins** (contr) Mrs Peachum; **Nuala Willis** (mez) Mrs Trapes; **Christopher Gillett** (ten) Filch; **Declan Mulholland** (sngr) Beggar; **Aldeburgh Festival Choir and Orchestra / Steuart Bedford.** Argo Ⓟ 436 850-2ZHO2 (two discs: 108 minutes: DDD: 9/93). Notes and text included. Recorded 1992.

"Not a 'sport' among Britten's operas but an integral part of the totality of theatrical work, from *Paul Bunyan* to *Death in Venice*": Donald Mitchell puts the claim well, and this first recording supports it all the way. *The Beggar's Opera* was Britten's new work for the English Opera Group in 1948 but it has had less than its due. Everything here is well set-up to make amends. The 12 players forming the chamber orchestra are excellent individually and they respond sensitively to Steuart Bedford's direction. The singer-actors are expertly assisted, and Michael Woolcock's production is vivid without being obtrusive. At the very least, the speech causes no embarrassment; at best it is spirited, and the full-fathom-five depth of Robert Lloyd's Peachum gives profound pleasure. The singing is probably as good as it should be; in many of the numbers, character matters more than beauty of tone. But it is to Britten's score that one has to return when making a recommendation. *The Beggar's Opera* can also be obtained on records in very different forms. The starry version under Richard Bonynge (listed below) is more entertaining, but the gloss is thick and the enrichment of musical interest, when it occurs, scarcely stretches the imagination. Britten's work is of a different order altogether. It is not mere cleverness, though the sheer ingenuities of rhythm, counterpoint, harmony and orchestration keep the ear fully occupied and delighted. Much more, the process is one of absorption and re-creation, sometimes fierce or poignant, sometimes magical in its loveliness (the use of the chorus in "Cease your funning", for example). The marvel is that the tunes themselves, so far from rejecting Britten's treatment as the body might reject a transplant, seem to find themselves in their element. The recording fills a gap in respect of Gay's masterpiece as surely as it fills another in the Britten *oeuvre*.

Additional recommendations ...

...**Soloists; London Voices; National Philharmonic Orchestra / Richard Bonynge.** Decca Ⓟ 430 066-2DH2 (two discs: 125 minutes: DDD: 5/91).

...(ed. Turner, orch. Pearce-Higgins) **Soloists; 1968 London Cast / Neil Rhoden.** Sony West End Ⓜ SMK66171 (59 minutes: ADD: 10/94).

Francesco Geminiani   Italian 1687-1762

Geminiani Concerti grossi, Op. 2 – No. 1 in C minor; No. 2 in C minor; No. 3 in D minor; No. 4 in D major; No. 5 in D minor; No. 6 in A major. Concerti grossi after Corelli's Op. 5 – No. 3 in C major; No. 5 in G minor. **Tafelmusik / Jeanne Lamon** (vn). Sony Classical Vivarte Ⓟ SK48043 (59 minutes: DDD: 11/92). 🎖 Recorded 1990.   Ⓖ

Imagine the scene. The year is 1715 and Francesco Geminiani is playing his violin for King George I, accompanied on the harpsichord by none other than Handel. But Geminiani had not always enjoyed the absolute favour of his colleagues; it is said that in Italy complaints were voiced regarding his excessive use of rubato – a very unexpected phenomenon, especially when seen in the light of our own attitudes to period performance. So, he left his workplace in Naples (where he was Concert Master), came to London – his new 'base', so to speak – and additionally went on to work in Dublin and Paris. The individual works in Geminiani's concerto-style Op. 2 set are forged in the *sonata da chiesa* (slow-fast-slow-fast) format and contain much beautiful music, especially where, in chordal passages, there is an overlapping of string lines. The faster movements set out on dancing feet – an aspect of the music that Tafelmusik indulges with obvious relish – and the slower ones have a mildly sensuous character. Nowhere, however, will you find as much as a hint of the wayward rubato about which Geminiani's colleagues complained! Similar positive qualities apply to the performances of the two Corelli violin sonata transcriptions, the second of which is particularly appealing. The recordings, too, are warm and immediate, with plenty of space around them and impressive definition.

Roberto Gerhard
Spanish/British 1896-1970

Gerhard Alegrías – suite. Cancionero de Pedrell[a]. Seven Haiku[a]. Pandora – suite. [a]**Josep Benet** (ten); **Teatre Lliure Chamber Orchestra, Barcelona / Josep Pons.** Harmonia Mundi Ⓕ HMC90 1500 (69 minutes: DDD: 11/94). Texts and translations included. Recorded 1993.

There can be little argument that Gerhard was the most important composer that Spain had produced since Falla; but it is frustrating to look at the catalogue and see how inadequately he is represented. There are currently, for example, some 15 recordings of Falla's seven folk-song arrangements – deservedly popular, of course, but Gerhard's equally attractive, if stylistically different, versions of eight folk-songs collected by his (and Falla's) teacher Pedrell have received scant attention. The cycle was designed for a female singer (the much-missed Sophie Wyss), and Josep Benet, who has hitherto been classified as an alto, seems to find the first song too low for him and is happier only in higher-lying numbers like "Laeta" and "Alatá". In the first two songs, moreover, he is disadvantageously placed *vis-à-vis* the microphone: this criticism applies even more strongly in Gerhard's much earlier, exotically expressionist *Seven Haiku*, where the voice (again uneasily low in No. 5) is frequently all but submerged by the handful of wind instruments and the agile, much too closely recorded piano. We are on far surer ground here with suites from the last two of Gerhard's five ballets. *Alegrías*, written for the Ballet Rambert in 1943, is tongue-in-cheek Andalusian in idiom, a high spirited and witty score played here with understandable relish by this excellent chamber orchestra. It hasn't the weight, of course, of the much larger Tenerife Symphony Orchestra performance (listed below), but makes up for it by its crispness, punch and exact dynamic shadings – which are caught to perfection by the recording. The highlight of the disc, however, is *Pandora*, a morality on war, death and hope produced by the Ballets Jooss in 1944. Utterly different and more violent in style, without any of the traditional 'Spanishries', it makes extensive use of the ancient 'dance of death' *Ad mortem festinamus*, and its resonances with recent events in Spain are underlined by the introduction of Catalan folk-songs, a parodied Falangist march and, in one place, a snatch of the composer's own Piano Trio (one of his earliest works) and of a figure associated with Don Quixote in his ballet of that name. Performed with total conviction by Josep Pons and his enterprising chamber orchestra, this is a valuable addition to the Gerhard discography.

Further listening ...
...Symphonies – No. 1; No. 3, "Collages". **Tenerife Symphony Orchestra / Víctor Pablo Pérez.** Auvidis Valois V4728 (9/95).
...Don Quixote. Pedrelliana (En memoria). Albada, Interludi i Dansa. **Tenerife Symphony Orchestra / Victor Pablo Pérez.** Auvidis Valois V4660 (10/92).

Sir Edward German
British 1862-1936

New review
German Richard III – Overture. Theme and Six Diversions. The Seasons. **Radio Telefis Eireann Concert Orchestra / Andrew Penny.** Marco Polo Ⓕ 8 223695 (65 minutes: DDD: 11/95). Recorded 1994.

This is a well planned and impressively executed collection. Of course German could not match the passion or genius of Elgar; but the collection here proves that his music does not deserve the neglect that has been its lot. From the dark, brooding opening of the *Richard III* Overture this is music of real character, meticulously worked out, imaginatively scored, and more than once showing its Elgarian kinship. There may be something a little saccharine about the theme upon which German based the *Theme and Six Diversions* (1919) but the way he builds upon it shows his skills at their best, with some striking contrapuntal writing and a swirling waltz section. Perhaps best of all is the symphonic suite *The Seasons* (1899), in which the restful yearning of the "Autumn" movement is especially striking. Andrew Penny conducts the programme with a fine feel for the music's shape and dynamics, and he coaxes from the RTE Concert Orchestra the impression that this is music they have come to know and love. Listeners may do so too.

Further listening ...

...Nell Gwyn – Overture; Country Dance; Pastoral Dance; Merry-maker's Dance; Gipsy Suite. Henry VIII – Shepherds's Dance; Torch Dance; Morris Dance. The Conqueror – Berceuse. Romeo and Juliet – Pavane; Nocturne; Pastorale. Tom Jones – Waltz Song (arr. Tomlinson). Merrie England – Hornpipe; Minuet; Rustic Dance; Jig. **Bratislava Radio Symphony Orchestra / Adrian Leaper.** Marco Polo British Light Music 8 223419 (6/93).

...Symphony No. 2 in A minor, "Norwich". Symphonic Suite in D minor, "Leeds" – Valse gracieuse. Welsh Rhapsody. **National Symphony Orchestra of Ireland / Andrew Penny.** Marco Polo 8 223726 (1/96).

...Merrie England. **Soloists; Rita Williams Singers; Michael Collins Orchestra / Michael Collins.** Classics for Pleasure Silver Doubles CD-CFPSD4796 (4/96).

George Gershwin
American 1898-1937

New review

Gershwin Piano Concerto in F major[a]. Porgy and Bess – symphonic suite. Second Rhapsody[a]. **Aalborg Symphony Orchestra / Wayne Marshall** ([a]pf). Virgin Classics Ⓜ VM5 61243-2 (72 minutes: DDD: 4/96). Recorded 1995.

Wayne Marshall makes his first entry in the Piano Concerto and, in the space of a bar or two, you hear a quick wit and a cool head, the ability to convey (just as Gershwin strove to do) the jazzman's freewheeling, rhapsodic manner alongside a concert pianist's formality. Where Gershwin sits back in the wee small hours spinning yet another of his blue tunes, Marshall is in no hurry to go anywhere. And yet there's a very real sense of the imperative, too, a 'something's coming' kind of feeling. When it comes, it's a special moment. So, too, is Gershwin's grandiose recapitulation (and Marshall goes all the way with that). Generally speaking, the Aalborg Symphony are well up on the style – no mean achievement when the orchestra can so easily sound like a dead-weight in this piece. But then, Marshall's 'Jack-be-nimble' approach is plainly infectious, encouraging reflexes from his band that are as quick and sparky as his own. The pulse of the Roaring Twenties was racy and capricious. But there was always time to dream. That's the tenor of Marshall's performance. The same is true of his dashing account of the *Second Rhapsody*. Again the contrasts are strong, the manner spontaneous – impulsive, Manhattan-brash to a degree – though Marshall never lets us forget that these are luxury goods. Gershwin's shot-silk climaxes (Hollywood dreams indeed), with all their audacious modulations and fruity horn counterpoints (nobody played with wrong-note harmonies like Gershwin) are played for all they're worth. There's also a spirited account of the Robert Russell Bennett *Porgy and Bess* Suite, as felicitous (real delicacy of atmosphere as "Clara" emerges from the opening street cries) as it is robust (that's quite a hurricane that blows through Catfish Row).

Additional recommendations ...

...Piano Concerto. Rhapsody in Blue[a]. An American in Paris. Variations on "I got rhythm". [a]**Earl Wild** (pf); **Boston Pops Orchestra / Arthur Fiedler.** RCA Victor Papillon Ⓜ GD86519 (70 minutes: ADD: 11/87). Ⓖ

...Piano Concerto. **Ravel** Piano Concerto in G major. **Bournemouth Symphony Orchestra / Andrew Litton** (pf). Virgin Classics Ⓜ VJ7 59693-2 (57 minutes: DDD).

...Piano Concerto[a]. Rhapsody in Blue. An American in Paris. [a]**Joanna MacGregor** (pf); **London Symphony Orchestra / Carl Davis.** Collins Classics Ⓕ 1139-2 (65 minutes: DDD: 11/91).

...An American in Paris. Rhapsody in Blue[a]. **Bernstein** Candide – Overture. West Side Story – symphonic dances. **New York Philharmonic Orchestra / Leonard Bernstein** ([a]pf). Sony Classical Ⓜ SMK47529* (60 minutes: ADD: 11/92). *The first two items recorded here are also on the disc reviewed below.* ⒼⒼⒼ

...Piano Concerto. Rhapsody in Blue. Second Rhapsody. **Howard Shelley** (pf); **Philharmonia Orchestra / Yan Pascal Tortelier.** Chandos Ⓕ CHAN9092 (64 minutes: DDD: 3/93).

Gershwin An American in Paris[a]. Rhapsody in Blue[b]. [a]**Columbia Symphony Orchestra;** [b]**New York Philharmonic Orchestra / Leonard Bernstein** (pf[a]). CBS Maestro Ⓜ MK42611* (35 minutes: ADD: 11/90). From Philips SABL160 (10/60). Recorded 1958. ⒼⒼⒼ

Bernstein conducted and played the music of Gershwin with the same naturalness as he brought to his own music. Here, *An American in Paris* swings by with an instinctive sense of its origins in popular and film music; no stilted rhythms or four-squareness delay the work's progress, and where ripe schmaltz is wanted, ripe schmaltz is what we get, devoid of all embarrassment. *Rhapsody in Blue* is playful and teasing, constantly daring us to try to categorize its style, and then confounding our conclusions. Although the solo passages from individual players are beautifully taken, both orchestras pull together magnificently to capture the authentic flavour of Gershwin's idiom, and Bernstein pushes them to transcend the printed score. His own playing in the *Rhapsody* is tantalizingly unpredictable. The recording is clear and bright, perhaps a touch hard-edged, and a little of the richness of the original LP issue might have been preferred by some, especially as the editing is now made more obvious. The only major criticism would be of the stingy overall timing of the disc – but with these performances quality compensates.

Gershwin Piano Rolls, Volume 2. [a]George Gershwin, [b]Cliff Hess, [c]Rudy Erlebach, [d]Bert Wynn, [e]Fred Murtha (pfs). Nonesuch Ⓔ 7559-79370-2 (42 minutes: DDD: 4/96). Derived from piano rolls cut between 1916 and 1921. Recorded 1992-3.
Gershwin La La Lucille – From now on[a]. Rialto Ripples[a]. **Frey** Havanola[a]. **Conrad** Singin' the Blues ('till My Daddy Comes Home)[a]. **Akst** Jaz-o-mine[a]. **Various** Greenwich Village Follies of 1920 – Just Snap Your Fingers at Care[a]. **Kern** Zip goes a Million – Whip-Poor-Will[a]. **Pinkard** Waitin' for Me[a]. **P. Wendling** Buzzin' the Bee[a]. **Schonberg** Darling[ab]. **Berlin** For Your Country and My Country[ac]. **M. Morris** Kangaroo Hop[a]. **Matthews** Pastime Rag No. 3[e]. **O. Gardner** Chinese Blues[d]. **Schonberger** Whispering[a]. **B. Grant** Arrah go on I'm gonna go Back to Oregon[a].

The first volume of three Gershwin piano rolls (listed under Further listening) was a sensation, bringing his magnificent tunes to life from his own piano rolls, stunningly realized on the Yamaha Disklavier. If that volume was more of a revelation than this one, it is largely because it consisted entirely of Gershwin's own incomparable tunes. Most of his rolls were of popular songs of the day, rushed out to cash in on a hit. But there are some curiosities here and two numbers by Gershwin himself. The first of these is *Rialto Ripples*, a catchy rag Gershwin wrote in collaboration with Will Donaldson and put on to a roll in September 1916. At one time the piece was unknown, but there are now four recordings on CD and it is fascinating to compare Gershwin's own 1916 performance with the sheet music published a year later. The roll has much more of the ragtime idiom in oom-pah left-hand chords and even reveals a few misprints in the score. Another ragtime connection is the 1916 roll, under one of Gershwin's pseudonyms (Fred Murtha), of *Pastime Rag No. 3*, one of only five polished rags in different styles by black composer Artie Matthews. Again there are interesting differences between the sheet music published in the same year and Gershwin's roll – he doesn't play repeats but he returns to the A strain at the end. He doesn't seem to know what to do with the 'stoptime' effect (1'21") in Strain C and just holds the pedal down. The rest of the song arrangements, which sometimes employ two players, show the ragtime background of this piano style, especially in the earlier rolls. These are also good examples of the techniques of the roll arrangers, who hyped it all up by adding notes to create the effect of a whole team of pianists. It is excellent to have more of Gershwin's rolls on CD, but why so few? He recorded over 130, but whereas Vol. 1 was 61 minutes long this one is only 42. This is the only disappointment, however.

Gershwin Of Thee I Sing Prelude[a]; Jilted. Second Rhapsody[a]. The Shocking Miss Pilgrim – For you, for me, for evermore. Cuban Overture[a]. Pardon My English – Isn't it a pity? Variations on "I Got Rhythm"[a]. Catfish Row[a]. Shall we dance? – Let's call the whole thing off[b]; They can't take that away from me[a]. Goldwyn Follies – Our love is here to stay. **Jack Gibbons** (pf). ASV White Line Ⓜ CDWHL2082 (77 minutes: DDD: 3/95). Items marked [a] arr. Gibbons. Recorded 1992-3.

This disc is mostly comprised of Gibbons's own arrangements, based on Gershwin's film music, two-piano pieces, and in the case of the "Catfish Row" *Porgy and Bess* suite, his orchestrations. The longest work is the *Second Rhapsody*, composed for a scene in the Gershwins' first Hollywood movie, *Delicious* (from which the best-known song is "Blah, blah, blah"). The film starred Janet Gaynor and Charles Farrell, and in this sequence the heroine wanders frightened through Manhattan – it might be re-christened *A Scotswoman in New York*. George Gershwin referred to the main tune as his "Brahmsian theme" but today no one would mistake it for anything but Gershwin. "For you, for me", one of the melodies salvaged from their files by Ira Gershwin and used ten years after George's death, emerged in the 1947 film *The Shocking Miss Pilgrim*. Ira and Kay Swift hoped it would be a gold-mine and rated the tune higher than any among Gershwin's unpublished songs. The solo version of the *Cuban Overture* is Gibbons's own adaptation of Gershwin's four-hand arrangement; like the "Catfish Row" suite it makes formidable demands on the pianist and Gibbons gives them both virtuoso performances. The recital ends with three of the standards Gershwin wrote in Hollywood during the last months of his life. "They can't take that away from me" must be a strong contender for the great songs of the twentieth century, and no one hearing "Our love is here to stay" can doubt that a premonition of death lingered somewhere in the composer's heart in the autumn of 1936.

Gershwin Porgy and Bess. **Willard White** (bass) Porgy; **Cynthia Haymon** (sop) Bess; **Harolyn Blackwell** (sop) Clara; **Cynthia Clarey** (sop) Serena; **Damon Evans** (bar) Sportin' Life; **Marietta Simpson** (mez) Maria; **Gregg Baker** (bar) Crown; **Glyndebourne Chorus; London Philharmonic Orchestra / Sir Simon Rattle.** EMI Ⓔ CDS7 49568-2 (three discs: 189 minutes: DDD: 6/89). Notes and text included. Recorded 1988. *Gramophone* classical 100. *Gramophone Award Winner 1989.* ⊙⊙⊙

The company, orchestra and conductor from the outstanding 1986 Glyndebourne production recreate once more a very real sense of Gershwin's 'Catfish Row' community on EMI's complete recording. Such is the atmosphere and theatricality of this recording, we might easily be back on the Glyndebourne stage. From the very first bar it's clear just how instinctively attuned Simon Rattle and this orchestra are to every aspect of a multi-faceted score. The cast, too, are so *right*, so much a part of their roles, and so well integrated into the whole, that one almost takes the excellence of their contributions for granted. Here is one beautiful voice after another, beginning in style with Harolyn

Blackwell's radiant "Summertime", which at Rattle's gorgeously lazy tempo, is just about as beguiling as one could wish. Willard White conveys both the simple honesty and inner-strength of Porgy without milking the sentiment and Haymon's passionately sung Bess will go wherever a little flattery and encouragement take her. As Sportin' Life, Damon Evans not only relishes the burlesque elements of the role but he really *sings* what's written a lot more than is customary. But the entire cast deliver throughout with all the unstinting fervour of a Sunday revivalist meeting. Sample for yourself the final moments of the piece – "Oh Lawd, I'm on my way" – if that doesn't stir you, nothing will.

Additional recommendations ...

...Excerpts. **Soloists; RCA Victor Chorus and Orchestra / Skitch Henderson.** RCA Victor Gold Seal
Ⓜ GD85234 (48 minutes: ADD: 4/89).

...Porgy and Bess – Summertime; I loves you, Porgy. **Barber** Knoxville: Summer of 1915, Op. 24.
Previn Honey and Rue. **Kathleen Battle** (sop); **Orchestra of St Luke's / André Previn.** DG Ⓕ 437
787-2GH (46 minutes: DDD: 1/96). *See review under Previn; refer to the Index to Reviews.*   Ⓖ

Further listening ...

...Lady, Be Good! – Fascinatin' rhythm (arr. Wild); The Man I love (arr. Grainger). Tip-Toes – That
certain feeling (trans. Wodehouse). Oh, Kay! – Clap yo' hands (trans. Wodehouse). *Coupled with
works by* **Waller, Ellington, J.P. Johnson, Gottschalk, Columbia, Rube Bloom, Cowell,
Nancarrow, B. Powell, Beiderbecke, Jelly Roll Morton, Joplin, Cervantes, Grainger**
and **Confrey Alan Feinberg** (pf); **Daniel Druckman** (marimba). Argo 444 457-2ZH (11/95).

...Piano Transcriptions (arr. Wild) – Fantasy on "Porgy and Bess". Improvisation in the form of a
Theme and Three Variations on "Someone to watch over me". Seven Virtuoso Etudes: I got
rhythm; Lady be good; Liza; Embraceable you; Somebody loves me; Fascinatin' rhythm; The
man I love. **Earl Wild** (pf). Chesky CD32 (10/90).

...Piano Rolls: Tip-Toes – Sweet and low-down; That certain feeling[a]. Novelette in Fourths[a]. Lady,
Be Good! – So am I[a]. Rhapsody in Blue[a]. Gershwin Songbook – Swanee[a]. When you want 'em,
you can't get 'em, when you've got 'em, you don't want 'em[a]. Tell me more – Tell me more[a].
George White's Scandals of 1920 – Idle dreams; My lady; On my mind the whole night long;
Scandal walk[a]. An American in Paris (trans. Milne)[b]. [a]**George Gershwin,** [b]**Frank Milne** (pfs).
Elektra Nonersuch 7559-79287-2 (4/94).

...Lady, Be Good!. **Soloists; chorus and orchestra / Eric Stern.** Elektra Nonesuch 7559-79308-2
(7/93). *Gramophone Award Winner 1993.*

...Oh, Kay! **Soloists; chorus; Orchestra of St Luke's / Eric Stern.** Nonesuch 7559-79361-2 (8/95).

...Strike Up the Band. **Soloists; chorus and orchestra / John Mauceri.** Elektra Nonesuch
7559-79273-2 (1/92).

...Girl Crazy. Cast includes **Lorna Luft, David Carroll, Judy Blazer, Frank Gorshin, David Garrison,
Vicki Lewis, chorus and orchestra / John Mauceri.** Elektra Nonesuch 7559-79250-2. Notes and
text included (2/91).

...Pardon My English. **Soloists; chorus and orchestra / Eric Stern.** Elektra Nonesuch
7559-79338-2 (11/94).

Carlo Gesualdo   Italian c1561-1613

Gesualdo Responsoria et alia ad Officium Hebdonadae Sanctae spectantia. Benedictus. Miserere.
The Hilliard Ensemble. ECM New Series Ⓕ 843 867-2 (two discs: 124 minutes: DDD: 3/92). Texts
and translations included. ⌛ Recorded 1990.   Ⓖ

To many, Gesualdo is known above all for the *crime passionnel* which left his wife and her lover
impaled on the same sword, but the notion that his highly-charged music is the product of a tortured
and unstable mind is, no doubt, over-romanticized. The exaggeratedly chromatic melodies and daring
harmonic style of his late music were fully in keeping with the experimental madrigal school of the
late sixteenth century. That said, Gesualdo's setting of the Responds for the Tenebrae of Holy Week
is surely one of the most intense and disturbing works of the entire period. The complex service of
Tenebrae is made up of the two offices, Matins and Lauds. Within Matins come the 27 responsories
that were the inspiration for Gesualdo's music, in addition to which he set the "Miserere" and
"Benedictus" from Lauds. At the beginning of the service the church is illuminated with candles, but
these are extinguished one by one, hence the name *tenebrae* (darkness). It is significant that Gesualdo
chose the most dramatic service of the church year, and one that is concerned with betrayal and death.
The Hilliard Ensemble has not missed one ounce of the profundity of this music, and their
performance is one of those rare artistic achievements that combines a heartfelt emotional response
with faultless technical control. Their phrases are perfectly shaped and directed, and while it is
virtually impossible to single out one particular contribution, David Beaven's ideally focused bass line
should not go unmentioned. The recording is excellent and every detail of the individual voices can
be heard. Texts and translations are included, together with an extract from Hildesheimer's *Tynset*,
but some explanatory notes would have been helpful.

Additional recommendations ...

...Responsoria et alia ad Officium Hebdonadae Sanctae spectantia – excerpts. Marian Motets –
Ave, dulcissima Maria; Precibus et meritis beatae Mariae; Ave, regina coelorum; Maria, mater
gratiae. **The Tallis Scholars / Peter Phillips.** Gimell Ⓕ CDGIM015 (52 minutes: DDD: 12/87).

...Da pacem, Domine. Assumpta est Maria. Illumina nos misericordiarum (all cptd. Stravinsky). Responsoria et alia as Officum Hebdonadae Sanctae spectantia – Sicut ovis; Jerusalem, surge; Plange quasi virgo; Recessit pastor noster; O vos omnes; Ecce quomodo moritur justus; Astiterunt reges terrae; Aestimatus sum; Sepulto Domino. **Stravinsky** Mass[a]. Pater noster. Ave Maria. The dove decending. **Trinity College Choir, Cambridge;** [a]wind players of **London Musici / Richard Marlow.** Conifer Ⓕ 75605-51232-2 (65 minutes: DDD: 6/95).

Further listening ...

...Madrigals – Ahi, disperata vita. Sospirava il mio cor. O malnati messaggi. Non t'amo, o voce ingrata. Luci serene e chiare. Sparge la morte al mio Signor nel viso. Arde il mio cor. Occhi del mio cor vita. Mercè grido piangendo. Asciugate i begli ochi. Se la mia morte brami. Io parto. Ardita Zanzaretta. Ardo per te, mio bene. Instrumental works – Canzon francese. Io tacerò. Corrente, amanti. **Les Arts Florissants Vocal and Instrumental Ensemble / William Christie.** Harmonia Mundi HMC90 1268 (10/88). ✒   Ⓖ

Giorgio Ghedini   Italian 1892-1965

Ghedini Violin Concerto, "Il Belprato".
Respighi Antiche danze ed arie per liuto – Suite No. 3. Trittico botticelliano.
Rota Concerto for Strings. **Accademia Bizantina / Carlo Chiarappa** (vn). Denon Ⓕ CO-78916
   (69 minutes: DDD: 3/95). Recorded 1993. *Gramophone Editor's choice.*

What very intelligent programming. Anyone who enjoys the two Respighi pieces will find that these are performed so beautifully that it would be worth acquiring this disc even if the two rarities by Nino Rota and Giorgio Ghedini were of no interest. In fact both are welcome discoveries. Rota's piece is close to light music – you'll be reminded more than once of his sultry title-music to *The Godfather* – but with an occasional shadow over its gentle, neo-classical melodiousness and an unobtrusively ingenious craftsmanship that make the piece a pleasure to revisit. Ghedini is, on this evidence, a composer well worth investigating. His concerto is neo-classical, too, but often more angular and more bracing than Rota's piece. At times it approaches Stravinsky's neo-baroque works in its sparely elegant line, but with heavy accents and a pounding vigour in the outer movements and touches both of dry wit and of pastoral grace in the central one. Both the unfamiliar works are finely played; it is in the almost hackneyed Respighi pieces that you really notice the qualities of the Accademia Bizantina and realize why Luciano Berio has called them "unique and precious". They are a fairly small string orchestra (19 players on this occasion, supplemented by harp, keyboards, percussion and five wind in the *Trittico*) who make a distinctly Italian sound: richly sonorous (splendidly plangent violas), warmly expressive (lots of fine shading and *rubato*) and exceptionally well-balanced. Although their sound can be sumptuously full, there is no lack of delicacy, a fine sensitivity in very quiet playing and never the slightest impression that they're trying to sound like a symphony orchestra. Their obvious enjoyment of Respighi's gracefully long lines goes together with a soloistic pleasure in the firm bite of bow on string. The recording is excellent: spacious but not cavernous.

Orlando Gibbons   British 1583-1625

New review

Gibbons O clap your hands. Great Lord of Lords. Hosanna to the Son of David. Prelude in
   G major[a]. Out of the deep. See, see, the word is incarnate. Preludes – No. 3 in D minor,
   MBXX/3[a]. Lift up your heads. Almighty and everlasting God. First (Short) Service – No. 6,
   Magnificat; No. 7, Nunc dimittis. Second Service – No. 3, Magnificat; No. 4, Nunc dimittis.
   Fantazia of four parts[a]. O God, the king of glory. O Lord, in Thy wrath rebuke me not.
   [a]**Laurence Cummings** (org); **Oxford Camerata / Jeremy Summerly.** Naxos Ⓢ 8 553130 (65 minutes:
   DDD: 8/96). Texts included. *Gramophone Editor's choice.*

The Oxford Camerata provide us here with a representative selection of choral works by Orlando Gibbons, together with three of his organ pieces. The programme is introduced by a bright and busy performance of the eight-part *O clap your hands*, followed by the noble verse anthem *Great Lord of Lords* – and it is pleasing to hear in this piece, and in the other verse-anthems, the rich timbre of the countertenor Robin Blaze, a welcome acquisition for the Camerata. In fact the group have a great deal of vocal talent in their make-up and are strengthening their reputation all the time. They tackle the gently moving *See, see, the word is incarnate* with great confidence, together with the First and Second Services and the quiet collects with all the knowledge and aplomb of cathedral lay clerks or choral scholars from Oxford and Cambridge. We are obviously unable to tell what King's or Westminster Abbey's choirs would have sounded like in Gibbons's day, but what we have here is very much the sound of an Oxbridge choir today. Laurence Cummings plays two short preludes, the one in G major – a real test of agility – from *Parthenia* and that in D minor from Benjamin Cosyn's *Virginal Book*. The *Fantazia of four parts* is a most extraordinary work, quite hard to steady and control. Nevertheless, it was a welcome addition to the programme. At budget price, this disc is worth every penny.

Additional recommendations ...

...If ye be risen again with Christ. O Lord, in Thy wrath rebuke me not[a]. Almighty God, who by Thy Son. O clap your hands[a]. We praise Thee, O Father. So God loved the world. O God, the king of glory. 10 Fantasias[b]. Four Preludes[b]. [a]**St John's College Choir, Cambridge / Christopher Robinson** with [b]**Robert Woolley** (org). Chandos Chaconne Ⓕ CHAN0559 (79 minutes: DDD: 11/94).

...Hosanna to the Son of David. Almighty and everlasting God. Behold, Thou hast made my days. Blessed are all they that fear the Lord. Deliver us, O Lord, our God. Glorious and powerful God. I am the resurrection. Lift up your heads. O all true faithful hearts. O clap your hands. O Lord, how do my woes increase. O Lord, I lift my heart to thee. O Lord, in Thee is all my trust. O Lord, in Thy wrath rebuke me not. Out of the deep. Praise the Lord, O my soul. See, see, the Word is incarnate. This is the record of John. **Trinity College Choir, Cambridge; Fretwork / Richard Marlow.** Conifer Ⓕ 75605 51231-2 (74 minutes: DDD: 8/95).

Gibbons Pavan and Galliard a 6[d]. Fantasia a 2 No. 1[d]. Go from my window[d]. Fantasias a 6 – Nos. 3 and 5[d]. Fantasia a 4 No. 1 "for the great double bass"[d]. Galliard a 3[d]. In Nomine a 4[d]. Pavan and Galliard in A minor, "Lord Salisbury"[b]. Prelude in G major[b]. Masks – Lincoln's Inn mask; The Fairest Nymph[b]. Alman in G major[b]. Behold, thou hast made my days[cd]. Glorious and powerful God[cd]. The First Set of Madrigals and Mottets[ad] – Daintie fine bird; Faire is the rose; I weigh not fortune's frown; I see ambition never pleased; I feign not friendship where I hate; The silver swanne. [a]**Tessa Bonner** (sop); [b]**Timothy Roberts** (keybds); [c]**Red Byrd;** [d]**Rose Consort of Viols.** Naxos Ⓢ 8 550603 (68 minutes: DDD: 2/95). Recorded 1992. Ⓖ

Beautifully performed and finely recorded, this selection of Gibbons's music is especially attractive on account of the variety of its programme. At its richest it presents writing for voice and viols combined, five parts to each, or for viols alone, sometimes in six parts. In lightest, most transparent texture there is a charming piece for two viols. Three keyboard instruments are used for solos: virginals, harpsichord and organ. A soprano also sings solos to viol accompaniment. Moods and styles vary correspondingly. The *Masks* and *Alman* for virginals have a high-spirited, almost popular manner; the Fifth *Fantasia* includes some unusual chromaticism and harmonic developments that for a while almost anticipate Purcell. Tessa Bonner sings with unvibrant purity; but what will probably be found the most striking feature of the singing here is the pronunciation. It is one of the distinguishing marks of this curiously named group, Red Byrd, that they sing such music with vowel-sounds modified to fit theories about the English in which it would originally have been sung. Thus the "daintie fine bird" tells "oi sing and doy", and the 'u' acquires a sort of umlaut in *I weigh not fortune's frown*, "weigh" and "frown" also having a measure of rusticity. Perhaps it is a good idea, but it does increase the desirability of printed texts in the booklet. The instrumental music is all finely played, the viols avoiding any imputation of belonging to the squeeze-and-scrape school, and Timothy Roberts's keyboard solos are particularly skilful, both in legato and fluent passagework.

Additional recommendation ...

...Prelude in G major. *Coupled with works by* **Draghi** and **Purcell Davitt Moroney** (virg/hpd). Virgin Classics Veritas Ⓕ VC5 45166-2 (67 minutes: DDD: 5/95). 🖅 *See review under Purcell; refer to the Index to Reviews.*

Further listening ...

...Two Fantasias a 4. 9 Fantasias a 3. Galliard a 3. *Coupled with* **Lupo** Fantasy-Airs a 3 – Nos. 16, 17 and 20. Fantasy-Airs a 4 – Nos. 5-7, 11 and 12. Fantasies a 4 – Nos. 4 and 9. **The Parley of Instruments / Peter Holman.** Hyperion CDA66395 (9/91). 🖅

...Fantasia No. 6 in A minor. *Coupled with works by* **Anonymous, Byrd, Tomkins, Aston** and **J. Bull Sophie Yates** (virg). Chandos Chaconne CHAN0574 (12/95). 🖅 *See review under Byrd; refer to the Index to Reviews.*

...Canticles – Magnificat; Nunc dimittis, "Short Service"; Magnificat; Nunc dimittis, "Second Service". Full Anthems – Almighty and Everlasting God; Lift up your heads; Hosanna to the Son of David. Verse Anthems[a] – This is the record of John; See, see, the Word is incarnate; O Thou, the central orb. Hymns and Songs of the Church – Now shall the praises of the Lord be sung; O Lord of Hosts; A song of joy unto the Lord we sing; Come, kiss me with those lips of thine. Organ works – Voluntary; Fantasia for double organ; Fantasia. **King's College Choir, Cambridge / Philip Ledger** with **John Butt** (org) and [a]**London Early Music Group.** ASV Gaudeamus CDGAU123 (4/86). 🖅

...First (Short) Service. *Coupled with works by* **G. Ives, S. Watson, Stanford, Leighton, Howells** and **Dyson Lichfield Cathedral Choir / Andrew Lumsden** with **Mark Shepherd, Nigel Potts** (orgs). Priory PRCD505 (10/95).

...Second Service (ed. Higginbottom) – Te Deum Laudamus; Jubilate Deo; Magnificat; Nunc dimittis. Full Anthems – O clap your hands; O Lord, in Thy wrath rebuke me not. Verse Anthems – O God, the king of glory; Glorious and powerful God; Sing unto the Lord; See, see, the Word is incarnate. Organ works[a] – Fantasia of four parts; A Fancy in A major; Fantasia for double

organ. **New College Choir, Oxford / Edward Higginbottom** with [a]**David Burchell** (org). CRD CRD3451 (12/88). Ⓖ

...Full Anthems – Hosanna to the Son of David; I am the resurrection; O clap your hands; O Lord, how do my woes increase; O Lord, I lift my heart to thee; O Lord, in thy wrath rebuke me not. Verse Anthems – Lord, we beseech thee, pour thy grace; Praise the Lord, O my soul; See, see, the Word is incarnate; Sing unto the Lord, o ye saints. Hymnes and Songs of the Church – Come, kiss me with those lips of thine; How sad and solitary now; Lord, I will sing to Thee; Lord, thy answer I did hear; Now in the Lord my heart doth pleasure take; Now shall the praises of the Lord; O Lord of Hosts and God of Israel; O my love, how comely now; Sing praises Is'rel to the Lord; Song of joy unto the Lord we sing; The beauty, Israel, is gone; When one among the Twelve there was; Who's this, that leaning on her friend. Preces and Psalm 145. **The Clerkes of Oxenford / David Wulstan.** Calliope CAL9611 (12/89).

...Fantasias – D minor, MBXX/5; G major, MBXX/6; D minor, MBBXX/8; A minor, MBXX/11; A minor, MBXX/12; C major, MBXX/14. Preludes – A minor, MBXX/1; A minor, MBXX/4. Galliard, "Lady Hatton", MBXX/20. Ground in A minor, MBXX/26. French Coranto, MBXX/38. Pavan and Galliard in A minor, "Lord Salisbury", MBXX/18-19. The Italian ground, MBXX/27. The Queen's command, MBXX/28. *Coupled with works by* **Byrd Laurent Stewart** (hpd). Pierre Verany PV795051 (3/96). *See review under Byrd; refer to the Index to Reviews.*

Cecil Armstrong Gibbs   British 1889-1960

Suggested listening ...
...Symphonies – No. 1 in E major, Op. 70; No. 3 in B flat major, Op. 104, "Westmorland". **National Symphony Orchestra of Ireland / Andrew Penny.** Marco Polo 8 223553 (5/95).

...Dusk. *Coupled with works by* **Binge, Williams, Coates, Toye, Collins, Farnon, Baynes, Curzon, Lutz, White, Ketèlbey, Joyce, Ellis** and **Ancliffe New London Orchestra / Ronald Corp.** Hyperion CDA66868 (7/96). *Gramophone Editor's record of the month. See review in the Collections section; refer to the Index to Reviews.* Ⓖ

Anthony Gilbert   British 1934-

Suggested listening ...
...Beastly Jingles. *Coupled with works by* **Payne, Elias, Bauld, Connolly, P.P. Nash** and **Weir Jane Manning** (sop); **Jane's Minstrels / Roger Montgomery.** NMC Artists' Series NMCD025 (10/95). *See review in the Collections section; refer to the Index to Reviews.* Ⓖ

Jean Gilles   French 1668-1705

Suggested listening ...
...Three Lamentations. *Coupled with works by* **Carpentras, Bouzignac, Ceppede, Vitré** and **Godolin** Soloists; Boston Schola Cantorum; Boston Camerata / **Joel Cohen.** Erato 4509-98480-2 (11/95). 🖉

Alberto Ginastera   Argentinian 1916-1983

Ginastera Harp Concerto, Op. 25[a].
Glière Harp Concerto, Op. 74[a]. Concerto for Coloratura Soprano and Orchestra, Op. 82[b]. [b]**Eileen Hulse** (sop); [a]**Rachel Masters** (hp); **City of London Sinfonia / Richard Hickox.** Chandos Ⓕ CHAN9094 (65 minutes: DDD: 2/93). Recorded 1992.

Glière was among the comparatively few front-rank Russian composers who stayed on in their homeland after the 1917 Revolution. The music he composed there adopted a middle-of-the-road conservative style which helped him to steer clear of the more viscous controversies of the 1920s and 1930s. The Concertos for harp and coloratura sorano date from 1938 and 1942 respectively and are unashamedly ingratiating, high-grade mood-music, here played and recorded in a manner that those with a sweet tooth should find absolutely irresistible. The Harp Concerto by the Argentinian Alberto Ginastera is made of sterner stuff, but only slightly it's Bartókian acerbities are tempered by an engaging Latin American swing. Once again the performance is crisp and bouncy, although in this instance the reverberant recording takes something of the edge off the rhythmic bite.

Additional recommendations ...
...Harp Concerto[a]. Piano Concerto No. 1, Op. 28[b]. Estancia – concert suite from ballet, Op. 8a. [a]**Nancy Allen** (hp); [b]**Oscar Tarrago** (pf); **Mexico City Philharmonic Orchestra / Enrique Bátiz.** ASV Ⓕ CDDCA654 (64 minutes: DDD: 8/89). Ⓖ

...Harp Concerto. **Mathias** Harp Concerto, Op. 50. **Ann Hobson Pilot** (hp); **English Chamber Orchestra / Isaiah Jackson.** Koch International Classics Ⓕ 37261-2 (49 minutes: DDD: 12/94).

Ginastera Cello Sonata, Op. 49[a]. Pampeana No. 2, Op. 21[a]. Triste, Op. 10 No. 2 (trans. Fournier)[a]. Danzas argentinas, Op. 2. Pequeña danza, Op. 8 No. 1. 12 American Preludes, Op. 12. Piano Sonata No. 1, Op. 22. [a]**Aurora Natola-Ginastera** (vc); **Alberto Portugheis** (pf). ASV Ⓕ CDDCA865 (78 minutes: DDD: 10/93). *Gramophone Editor's choice.*

Ginastera's two cello concertos and fantastically difficult cello sonata were written for his wife Aurora Natola, whom he had first met in 1950 when the young virtuoso had won a Buenos Aires award playing his *Pampeana* No. 2. That is a rhapsodic showpiece with several solo cadenzas (beautifully shaped here), and features strongly rhythmic ostinatos of nationalist colouring: similar violently accented repetitive rhythms characterize most of the earlier works for piano here and Alberto Portugheis is brilliantly fiery in all of these, but equally he brings seductive nuances to the languid second Argentine dance, a sensitivity matched by Natola in the affecting short *Triste*. The principal works on this disc are the two sonatas. That for piano (1952) shows some stylistic development in its ghostly flitting scherzo and desolate *Adagio*. Portugheis's reading is suitably intense and, where required, ferociously rhythmic. He has a splendid duo partner in the much later and exceptionally demanding Cello Sonata(1979), the most remarkable movement of which is the palindromic *Presto*, full of bizarre effects that seem to reflect Ginastera's enthusiasm for the paintings of Paul Klee. Outstandingly good recorded quality.

New review
Ginastera Guitar Sonata, Op. 47.
Villa-Lobos Douze Etudes. Cinq Préludes. **Alexander-Sergei Ramírez** (gtr). Denon Ⓕ CO-78931 (60 minutes: DDD: 12/95). Recorded 1993.

South America is full of guitarists but Ramírez is the first one from Peru to have made a name for himself outside that continent. Quantity is one thing, but quality is another; Ramírez has an abundance of the latter. His teachers included Maritta Kersting and Pepe Romero, and he wisely studied also with a pianist, a violinist and a singer to round out his approach to music. His programme is, by the standards of his instrument, a heavyweight one, providing some of the toughest challenges a guitarist can face. Ramírez's watchword is moderation in both tempo and expression; he is an emotionally charged player but he never 'over-acts'. There are other fine versions available of the Ginastera Sonata but none better than this one, enhanced by an acoustic that captures the percussive sounds with unique vividness. Ramírez has all the technique he needs, with fine sound, and he brings refinement to everything he touches. The Villa-Lobos is remarkably free from left-hand finger squeaks, maybe a result of his work with Pepe Romero. A remarkable recording – one that should put Peru on the international map of the guitar.

Ginastera Dos Canciones, Op. 3[ad]. Canciones populares argentinas, Op. 10[ad]. Las horas de una estancia, Op. 11[ad]. Pampeana No. 1, Op. 16[bc]. Piano Quintet, Op. 29[cd]. [a]**Olivia Blackburn** (sop); [b]**Sherban Lupu** (vn); [c]**Alberto Portugheis** (pf); [d]**Bingham Quartet** (Stephen Bingham, Marina Gillam, vns; Brenda Stewart, va; James Halsey, vc). ASV Ⓕ CDDCA902 (62 minutes: DDD: 3/95). Texts and translations included.

This disc in Alberto Portugheis's admirable conspectus of Ginastera's chamber works offers a clear picture of the composer's stylistic changes, but is also to be welcomed for some outstanding performances. The most spectacular is that of *Pampeana* No. 1, a dazzling rhapsodic violin showpiece that is first cousin to Ravel's *Tzigane* and should equally be in the repertoire of all virtuoso fiddlers; starting meditatively on a single chord, it culminates in an exciting burst of pyrotechnics. It is brilliantly played by Sherban Lupu with a substantial input from Portugheis in the exacting piano part. That work was written in 1947: the Piano Quintet of 1963 is barely recognizable as being by the same composer, though it, too, makes hair-raising demands on the players' virtuosity. By this time, however, Ginastera had progressed to an idiom embracing serialism, aleatoric procedures and other avant-garde technical elements. Interspersed with three long cadenzas, the Quintet is in four main movements, including a scherzo as ghostly as that in Berg's *Lyric Suite*, a *Piccola musica notturna* that is said (improbable as it may appear) to be a tribute to Mozart because the work was commissioned by the Mozarteum Society of Argentina, and a noisily rumbustious finale. The most 'comfortable' listening on the disc is provided by the earlier works, very attractively sung by a pure-toned soprano, Olivia Blackburn, in perfect Spanish and with exemplary enunciation. The 22-year-old composer's Op. 3 songs are both in Argentine dance rhythms; Blackburn treats the well-known first of them, "Song to the tree of oblivion", with a touching simplicity. But the most impressive of the vocal works here is the atmospheric cycle *Times of the day on a farm*, in which, except for the monodic "Midday", Ginastera opts for chordal impressionism.

Further listening ...
...Concerto for Strings, Op. 33. *Coupled with* **Evangelista** Airs d'Espagne. **Villa-Lobos** Suite for Strings. Bachianas Brasileiras No. 9. **I Musici de Montréal / Yuli Turovsky.** Chandos CHAN9434 (5/96). *See review under Evangelista; refer to the Index to Reviews.*
...Punena No. 2, Op. 45[a]. *Coupled with* **Boulez** Messagesquisse[bc]. **Fortner** Zum Spielen für dem 70 Geburtstag[a]. **Henze** Capriccio[a]. **Beck** Drei Epigramme für Paul Sacher[a]. **Dutilleux** Trois strophes sur le nom de Sacher[a]. **Lutosławski** Sacher Variations[b]. **Berio** Les mots sont allés[b]. **C. Halffter** Variations on the theme eSACHERe[b]. **Britten** TemaSacher[b]. **K. Huber**

Transpositio ad infinitum[b]. **Holliger** Chaconne[b]. [a]**Patrick and** [b]**Thomas Demenga** (vcs); [c]**Cello Ensemble / Jürg Wyttenbach.** ECM New Series 445 234-2 (8/95).

Umberto Giordano

Italian 1867-1948

Giordano Andrea Chenier. **Luciano Pavarotti** (ten) Andrea Chenier; **Leo Nucci** (bar) Gerard; **Montserrat Caballé** (sop) Maddalena; **Kathleen Kuhlmann** (mez) Bersi; **Astrid Varnay** (sop) Countess di Coigny; **Christa Ludwig** (mez) Madelon; **Tom Krause** (bar) Roucher; **Hugues Cuénod** (ten) Fleville; **Neil Howlett** (bar) Fouquier-Tinville, Major-domo; **Giorgio Tadeo** (bass) Mathieu; **Piero De Palma** (ten) Incredible; **Florindo Andreolli** (ten) Abate; **Giuseppe Morresi** (bass) Schmidt; **Ralph Hamer** (bass) Dumas; **Welsh National Opera Chorus; National Philharmonic Orchestra / Riccardo Chailly.** Decca Ⓔ 410 117-2DH2 (two discs: 107 minutes: DDD: 2/85). Notes, text and translation included. From 411 117-1DH3 (11/84). Recorded 1982-84.

Andrea Chenier, set at the start of the French Revolution, is a potent blend of the social and the emotional. The three main characters, the aristocratic Maddalena, the idealistic poet Chenier and the fiercely republican Gerard, are caught up in a triangle that pits love against conscience, independence against society. The opera has many well-known set numbers and high on any list of favourites must be Chenier's so-called *Improviso* in Act 1 where he bursts out in a spontaneous poem on the power of love, or Maddalena's glorious and moving "La mamma morta" in the Third Act where she describes how her mother gave up her life to save her. Giordano had a real theatrical flair for the 'big moment' and he paces the work masterfully. The tunes seem to flow endlessly from his pen and the characters have real flesh and blood. The cast is strong, with Caballé and Pavarotti making a powerful central pair. Riccardo Chailly conducts the excellent National Philharmonic with flair and feeling and the whole opera is beautifully recorded.

Additional recommendations ...

...**Soloists; John Alldis Choir; National Philharmonic Orchestra / James Levine.** RCA Victor Gold Seal Ⓜ GD82046 (two discs: 114 minutes: ADD: 9/89).

...**Soloists; Rome Opera Chorus and Orchestra / Gabriele Santini.** EMI Opera Ⓜ CMS5 65287-2 (two discs: 115 minutes: ADD: 7/95).

Giordano Fedora[a]. **Magda Olivero** (sop) Fedora; **Mario del Monaco** (ten) Loris; **Tito Gobbi** (bar) de Siriex; **Leonardo Monreale** (bass) Lorek, Nicola; **Lucia Cappellino** (sop) Olga; **Virgilio Carbonari** (bass) Borov; **Silvio Maionica** (bass) Grech; **Piero de Palma** (ten) Rouvel; **Peter Binder** (bar) Kiril; **Dame Kiri Te Kanawa** (sop) Dmitri; **Riccardo Cassinelli** (ten) Desire; **Athos Cesarini** (ten) Sergio; **Pascal Rogé** (pf) Boleslao Lazinski; **Monte-Carlo Opera Chorus and Orchestra / Lamberto Gardelli.**

Zandonai Francesca da Rimini – excerpts[b]. [c]**Magda Oliviero** (sop) Francesca; [d]**Mario del Monaco** (ten) Paolo; [e]**Annamaria Gasparini** (mez) Biancofiore; [f]**Virgilio Carbonari** (bass) Man-at-arms; [g]**Athos Cesarini** (ten) Archer; **Monte-Carlo Opera Orchestra / Nicola Rescigno.** Decca Grand Opera Ⓜ 433 033-2DM2 (two discs: 132 minutes: ADD: 3/92). Notes, texts and translations included. Item marked [a] from SET435/6 (3/70), [b]SET422 (1/70). Recorded 1969.

Francesca da Rimini: Act 2 – E ancora sgombro il campo del comune? ... Date il segno, Paolo, date ... Un'erba io m'avea, per sanare ... Onta et orrore sopra[cdfg]. Act 3 – No, Smadragedi, no! ... Paolo, datemi pace! ... Ah la parola chi i miei occhi incontrano[cd]. Act 4 – Ora andate ... E così, vada s'è pur mio destino[cde].

Today the name 'Fedora' may suggest a type of hat rather than an opera, but although Giordano was overshadowed by his contemporary Puccini he was a successful composer. *Fedora* is based on a play by Victorien Sardou, the French dramatist whose *La Tosca* provided Puccini with a plot. It is set in the nineteenth century and variously in St Petersburg, Paris and Switzerland, and tells of the tragic love between the Russian Count Loris Ipanov and the Princess Fedora Romazov (Romanov), but to go into further detail of the plot, which disposes of various characters in turn and ends with the heroine herself taking poison, would take up too much space and one admires the booklet writer who has managed to produce a synopsis. *Fedora* has some Trivial Pursuits claim to be the first opera to feature bicycles in the plot! The music is richly textured orchestrally and finely written for the voices, and this recording made in 1969 is notable for the singing of Magda Olivero and Mario del Monaco, who despite being in their mid-fifties bring tremendous verve, vocal resource and dramatic skill to their roles. Tito Gobbi has less to do as the diplomat de Siriex, but gives him character, and another plus is the playing of Pascal Rogé, who performs the non-singing role of the Polish pianist and spy Boleslao Lazinski in Act 2 who, while performing, eavesdrops on a dialogue between Loris and Fedora. This exchange is a marvellous example of verismo writing and singing, and so is their final scene with her death. The set opens with excerpts from another opera, Zandonai's *Francesca da Rimini* with the same two excellent principals. The recordings are as clear and fresh-sounding as they were on the original releases.

Mauro Giuliani

Italian 1781-1829

Giuliani Choix de mes Fleurs chéries, Op. 46 – Le Jasmin; Le Rosmarin; La Rose. Etude in E minor, Op. 100 No. 13. Grande Ouverture, Op. 61. Leçons Progressives, Op. 51 Nos. 3, 7 and 14. Minuetto, Op. 73 No. 9. Preludes, Op. 83 Nos. 5 and 6. Rondeaux Progressives, Op. 14 Nos. 1 and 5. Six Variations, Op. 20. Variazioni sulla Cavatina favorita, Op. 101, "De calma oh ciel". **David Starobin** (gtr). Bridge ⓕ BCD9029 (48 minutes: DDD: 3/92). Recorded 1990.

Giuliani was born and died in Italy, in between which he lived for many years in Vienna, where he achieved great success in salon-music circles with his guitar virtuosity and counted many distinguished musicians amongst his friends and colleagues. He was in a sense the rival of Sor for the guitar's nineteenth-century crown but the two were 'chalk and cheese'. Giuliani the more volatile, ebullient and (as a composer) loquacious – with over 200 works as against Sor's less than 70. Giuliani's incessant desire to please his public (and to make much-needed money in the process) led to the presence of much treadmill dross amongst the gold of his best works, a thing that has contributed to his chronic undervaluation. David Starobin, playing a nineteenth-century guitar, greatly helps to redress the balance in his unfailingly musical and technically fluent playing of a selection of Giuliani's best works. Some testify to Giuliani's contribution to the student literature, the titles of others reflect the salon tastes at which they were aimed; all show that, when he took the trouble, Giuliani could be charming, polished and ingenious, all at the same time. This is a disc to charm the ear without bruising the emotions, in the nicest possible way.

Further listening ...

...Duo concertant in E minor, "Grand Sonata", Op. 25. *Coupled with* **Paganini** Grand Sonata for Violin and Guitar in A major, Op. posth. Sonata concertata in A major, Op. 61. **Monica Huggett** (vn); **Richard Savino** (gtr). Harmonia Mundi HMU90 7116 (5/95). ✍

...*CD411* – Duo for flute and guitar. Gran duetto concertante, Op. 52. Grand duo concertant, Op. 85. 12 Ländler samt Coda, Op. 75. Duetinno facile, Op. 77. *CD413* – Grand Pot-pourri, Op. 126. Grand Potpourri, Op. 53. Pièces faciles et agréables, Op. 74. Potpourri tiré de l'opéra Tancredi, Op. 76. Six Variations, Op. 81. **Mikael Helasvuo** (fl); **Jukka Savijoki** (gtr). BIS CD411 and CD413 (1/91).

...Ariette, Op. 95 – Quando sarà quel di; Le dimore amore non ama; Ad altro laccio. Cavatine, Op. 39 – Confuso, smarrito. Amor, perché m'accendi. Di tanti palpiti, Op. 79. Andantino sostenuto, Op. 71 No. 3. *Coupled with works by* **Carulli, Soler, Sor** and **Mertz.** [a]**Marta Almajano** (sop); **José Miguel Moreno** (gtr). Glossa GCD920202 (2/96). *See review in the Collections section; refer to the Index to Reviews.*

Philip Glass

American 1937-

New review

Glass La Belle et la Bête. **Janice Felty** (mez) La Belle; **Gregory Purnhagen** (bar) La Bête, Avenant, Ardent, Port Official; **John Kuether** (bass) Father, Usurer; **Ana Maria Martinez** (sop) Felicie; **Hallie Neill** (sop) Adelaide; **Zheng Zhou** (bar) Ludovic; **Philip Glass Ensemble / Michael Riesman.** Nonesuch ⓕ 7559-79347-2 (two discs: 89 minutes: DDD: 7/96). Notes, text and translation included. Recorded 1994.

This is one of Philip Glass's most innovative and impressive works. It isn't exactly an opera, nor is it film music; cantata is the nearest term, but even that won't really convey the idea. What Glass has done is to make a setting of the script for Jean Cocteau's 1946 film *La Belle et la Bête*, using every word as it is spoken in the film, but having it sung, the whole thing designed to be performed in concert, with a print of the film being projected silently. Of all Cocteau's movies, *La Belle et la Bête* is visually the most stylized, with its images of the Beast's castle, and the Vermeeresque settings for the family home of the merchant whose search for a rose to give to his youngest daughter sets off the nightmarish story. Cocteau described his film as "the illustration of the border that separates one world from the other". For all its surreal photography and extravagant décor by Christian Bérard (the apparently living, arms-bearing candelabra, poking out from the wall, have influenced hundreds of interior decorators), the dialogue in the film is delivered in a naturalistic way. The words are sung in an ethereal, other-worldly way, and the music trembles with typical Glass motifs. *La Belle et la Bête* hovers somewhere between genteel beat music and Messiaen-influenced *mélodie* and defies categorization. As Beauty, Janice Felty's voice matches the image of Josette Day in the film, but Gregory Purnhagen's light baritone would never suggest Jean Marais, whose smoky tones were such an inspiration to Cocteau. Most people prefer the Beast with his hairy face and claws to the rather effete-looking Prince Charming who emerges at the end, and Glass's music seems to make an ironic commentary on this transformation. Even for those devoted to the film, this is well worth investigating.

Further listening ...

...Itaipú[a]. The Canyon. **Atlanta Symphony** [a]**Chorus and Orchestra / Robert Shaw.** Sony Classical SK46352 (11/93).

...String Quartet No. 1. *Coupled with* **Barber** String Quartet, Op. 11. **Dvořák** String Quartet No. 12 in F major, B179. **Duke Quartet.** Collins Classics 1386-2 (1/94).

..."Low" Symphony. **Brooklyn Philharmonic Orchestra / Dennis Russell Davies.** Point Music
438 150-2PTH (5/93).   ⓖ
...Metamorphosis. Mad rush. Wichita vortex sutra. **Philip Glass** (pf). CBS SMK45576 (3/90).
...Akhnaten. **Soloists; Stuttgart State Opera Chorus and Orchestra / Dennis Russell Davies.**
CBS Masterworks M2K42457 (2/88).   ⓖ
...Anima Mundi. **Jeannie Gagné, Dora Ohrenstein** (sops); **Patricia Dunham, Linda November**
(mezzos); **David Düsing, David Frye** (tens); **Alexander Blachly, Bruce Rodgers** (bars); **orchestra /
Michael Riesman.** Elektra Nonesuch 7559-79329-2 (1/94).
...Einstein on the Beach. **Soloists; Philip Glass Ensemble / Michael Riesman.** CBS M4K38875
(9/86).
...Satyagraha. **NYC Opera Chorus and Orchestra / Christopher Keene.** CBS M3K39672 (9/86).   ⓖ
...Einstein on the Beach – Suite. *Coupled with* **Copland** Duo[a]. **Ornstein** Violin Sonata, Op. 31[b].
Wernick Cadenzas and Variations II. **Gregory Fulkerson** (vn); [a]**Robert Shannon**, [b]**Alan Feinberg**
(pfs). New World 80313-2 (2/96).
...Hydrogen Jukebox. **Allen Ginsberg** (narr); **Vocal Ensemble**; **Carol Wincenc** (fl); **Andrew Sterman**
(sax/bass cl); **Richard Peck** (sax); **Frank Cassara, James Pugliese** (perc); **Philip Glass** (pf) / **Martin
Goldray** (keybds). Elektra Nonesuch 7559-79286-2 (1/94). Texts included.

Alexander Glazunov   USSR 1865-1936

New review

Glazunov Violin Concerto in A minor, Op. 82.
Tchaikovsky Violin Concerto in D major, Op. 35. **Maxim Vengerov** (vn); **Berlin Philharmonic
Orchestra / Claudio Abbado.** Teldec ⓕ 4509-90881-2 (55 minutes: DDD: 11/95). Recorded 1995.
Gramophone Editor's choice.
This seems to be the only disc coupling what might reasonably be counted as the two greatest
romantic Russian violin concertos: if Vengerov's reading of the Tchaikovsky emerges clearly as a
leading contender among many superb versions, in the Glazunov he turns this warhorse concerto
from a display piece into a work of far wider-ranging emotions. This Tchaikovsky immediately
establishes itself as a big performance in the manner and in the range of dynamic of the playing. For
all his power, and his youthfully eager love of brilliance, Vengerov is never reluctant to play really
softly, and how magical that often is. Each theme in turn is sharply characterized, with dynamic
contrasts cleanly established. The central Canzonetta is full of Russian temperament, with Vengerov
freer in his rubato than most rivals, but conveying such natural unforced expressiveness there is
nothing self-conscious about it. The finale is fast, light and sparkling, with articulation breathtakingly
clean to match the transparency of the orchestral textures as controlled by Abbado. Vengerov rounds
the performance off with an explosion of excitement such as one might expect in the concert-hall but
not often in the recording studio. The Glazunov is if anything even more remarkable, with Vengerov
making you appreciate afresh what a wonderful and varied sequence of melodies Glazunov offers. It
is characteristic of Vengerov how he shades and contrasts his tone-colours. He reserves his big,
romantic tone for the third theme, where most rivals let loose sooner with less subtle results. As in the
Tchaikovsky, rubato is free but always spontaneous-sounding, and the lolloping fourth section brings
some delicious portamento. Predictably the dashing final section is spectacular in its brilliance, again
with each episode sharply contrasted and with orchestral textures fresh and clean.
Additional recommendations ...
...Violin Concerto[a]. The Seasons – ballet, Op. 67. [a]**Oscar Shumsky** (vn); **Scottish National Orchestra
/ Neeme Järvi.** Chandos ⓕ CHAN8596 (57 minutes: DDD: 3/89).
...Violin Concerto. **Shostakovich** Violin Concerto No. 1 in A minor, Op. 99. **Itzhak Perlman** (vn);
Israel Philharmonic Orchestra / Zubin Mehta. EMI ⓕ CDC7 49814-2 (55 minutes: DDD: 1/90).
...Violin Concerto[a]. Piano Concerto No. 2 in B major, Op. 100[b]. Saxophone Concerto in E flat
major, Op. 109[c]. [a]**Sergei Stadler** (vn); [b]**Dmitri Alexeev** (pf); [c]**Lev Mikhailov** (sax); [a]**Leningrad
Philharmonic Orchestra / Vladimir Ponkin;** [b]**USSR Radio Symphony Orchestra / Yuri Nikolaevsky;**
[c]**USSR Radio Symphony Orchestra Soloists Ensemble / Alexander Kornelev.** Olympia ⓕ OCD165
(55 minutes: ADD/DDD: 2/90).
...Violin Concerto. **Dvořák** Violin Concerto in A minor, B108. **Frank Peter Zimmermann** (vn);
London Philharmonic Orchestra / Franz Welser-Möst. EMI ⓕ CDC7 54872-2 (52 minutes: DDD:
3/94).   ⓖ
...Violin Concerto. **Dvořák** Violin Concerto in A minor, B108. Romance in F minor, B39. **Ilya
Kaler** (vn); **Polish National Radio Symphony Orchestra / Camilla Kolchinsky.** Naxos ⓢ 8 550758
(63 minutes: DDD: 4/95).

Glazunov The Seasons – ballet, Op. 67.
Tchaikovsky The Nutcracker – ballet, Op. 71[a]. [a]**Finchley Children's Music Group; Royal
Phiharmonic Orchestra / Vladimir Ashkenazy.** Decca ⓕ 433 000-2DH2 (two discs: 131 minutes:
DDD: 4/92). Recorded 1989-90. *Selected by Sounds in Retrospect.*
One cannot think of a happier coupling than Glazunov's complete *Seasons* – perhaps his finest and
most successful score – with Tchaikovsky's *Nutcracker*. Glazunov's delightful ballet, with even the

winter's "Frost", "Hail", "Ice" and "Snow", glamorously presented, and the bitterness of a Russian winter quite forgotten are, like the scenario of the *Nutcracker*, part of a child's fantasy world, for Tchaikovsky too, in Act 2, has a wintry fairy scene and a delectable "Waltz of the snowflakes" (featuring children's wordless chorus). Glazunov's twinklingly dainty scoring of the picturesque snowy characters is contrasted with the glowing summer warmth of the "Waltz of the cornflowers and poppies", and the vigorously thrusting tune (perhaps the most memorable theme he ever wrote) of the Autumn "Bacchanale". Tchaikovsky's ballet opens with a children's Christmas party with the guests arriving, presents distributed and family dancing, in which everyone joins. Ashkenazy captures the atmosphere very engagingly; then night falls, the church clock outside strikes midnight and the magic begins. The drama of the spectacular mock battle between good and evil, the children's journey through the pine forest (to one of Tchaikovsky's most ravishing tunes) and the famous multi-coloured characteristic dances of the Act 2 Divertissement are all beautifully played by the RPO. There is much finesse and sparkle, and the lightest and most graceful rhythmic touch from Ashkenazy: the conductor's affection for the score and his feeling for Tchaikovsky's multi-hued orchestral palette is a constant delight to the ear. Yet the big *Pas de deux* brings a climax of Russian fervour. The recording is properly expansive here; made at Walthamstow, it sets everything within a glowing acoustic ambience. *The seasons* was recorded in Watford Town Hall, and again the ear is seduced by the aural richness and the glowing woodwind detail. The one minor drawback is that in the *Nutcracker* the cueing is not generous and the action not precisely related to the narrative detail. But in every other respect this is marvellous entertainment.

Additional recommendations ...

...The Seasons. Scènes de Ballet in A major, Op. 52. **Minnesota Orchestra / Edo de Waart.** Telarc
Ⓕ CD80347 (66 minutes: DDD: 12/93).

...The Seasons[a]. **Prokofiev** Piano Concerto No. 3 in C major, Op. 26[b]. Visions fugitives, Op. 22[c] – excerpts. Suggestion diabolique, Op. 4 No. 4[d]. Symphony No. 1 in D major, Op. 25, "Classical" – Gavotte[e]. Piano Sonata No. 4 in C minor, Op. 29 – Andante assai[f]. Gavotte, Op. 32 No. 3[f].
[bcdef]**Sergey Prokofiev** (pf); [a]**orchestra / Alexander Glazunov;** [b]**London Symphony Orchestra / Piero Coppola.** EMI Composers in Person mono Ⓕ CDC5 55223-2* (79 minutes: ADD: 5/95).   Ⓖ

New review

Glazunov Raymonda, Op. 57. **Moscow Symphony Orchestra / Alexander Anissimov.** Naxos
Ⓢ 8 553503/4 (two discs: 139 minutes: DDD: 8/96).

If you want to be reminded just how great the three Tchaikovsky ballets really are – and why *The Sleeping Beauty* remains the best three-act ballet score of them all – then listen to the complete *Raymonda*. Not that it's a bad piece of work by any means. Even the bottom line – which is that Tchaikovsky simply has inspired dance-melodies by the yard while Glazunov doesn't – is something turned to good use in *Raymonda*. For while Tchaikovsky finds a new idea or two for each of his characteristic dances, Glazunov forges connections throughout. A waltz melody becomes a pizzicato variation; even a racy coda turns out to be a brilliant transformation of the grand "Pas de deux" with further themes appended. The three principal characters – sweet Raymonda, her chivalrous hero and the lovesick villain (a Saracen, naturally) – have their leitmotifs, but the plot remains uninterestingly confused (still no reason why we shouldn't have been given more details in the booklet – reproducing the scenario that accompanies the printed score would have been enough). It serves only to provide Glazunov with every flavouring in the balletic book: medievalism and moonshine in Act 1, orientalia in Act 2, a Magyar *divertissement* in the last and weakest of the acts. That makes for a feeble sense of unity, but few dull moments; and so welcome to a first-rate complete performance. Alexander Anissimov keeps the Moscow Symphony Orchestra on their toes: the strings are keen of articulation while balances and dynamics are all observed in an end result of greater sophistication than you might expect from this source (with handsome sound to match). Anissimov excels in the grand symphonic unfolding of the first two numbers and the two Entr'actes, over which he takes much time and care. This conductor, orchestra and sound engineers are a team of real distinction. If you really feel unable to wade through the whole score – and it would be a pity to miss the more or less through-composed Act 1 in its entirety – then there's always Järvi's intelligent cross-section: it omits the tedious Magyarisms of the final *divertissement*, and the only casualty of distinction is the jugglers' number. However, the sound is rather murky and Naxos's two CDs still work out cheaper.

Additional recommendation ...

...Raymonda, Op. 57. **Royal Scottish Orchestra / Neeme Järvi.** Chandos Ⓕ CHAN8447 (56 minutes: DDD: 7/86).

Glazunov Symphonies. **USSR Ministry of Culture State Symphony Orchestra / Gennadi Rozhdestvensky.** Olympia Ⓜ OCD100/1 (two discs, oas: 70 and 70 minutes: ADD: 8/86).
OCD100 – No. 1 in E major, Op. 5, "Slavyanskaya"; No. 7 in F major, Op. 77, "Pastoral'naya".   ⒼⒼ

It is always easy to underestimate the Glazunov symphonies. There is no doubt that this set of performances from Rozhdestvensky and the splendid orchestra give them a 'new look'. There is a sophistication in the playing to match the elegance of Glazunov's often highly engaging wind scoring – especially in the scherzos, always Glazunov's best movements – but there is a commitment and vitality too, which makes all the music spring readily to life. In Rozhdestvensky's hands the fine

Adagio of No. 1 sounds remarkably mature while the *Andante* movement of No. 7 is romantically expansive in a very appealing way. The recording is brightly lit without being too brittle, and has plenty of fullness too. For anyone looking for new nineteenth-century symphonies to explore, this would be a good place to start.

Additional recommendations ...

...No. 1; No. 5 in B flat major, Op. 55. **Bavarian Radio Symphony Orchestra / Neeme Järvi.** Orfeo
Ⓕ C093101A (66 minutes: DDD: 9/87).   Ⓖ

...No. 4 in F sharp minor, Op. 16; No. 7. **Bamberg Symphony Orchestra / Neeme Järvi.** Orfeo
Ⓕ C148201A (66 minutes: DDD: 11/90).   Ⓖ

New review

Glazunov Complete Solo Piano Music, Volumes 1 and 2. **Stephen Coombs** (pf). Hyperion
Ⓕ CDA66833, CDA66844 (two discs, oas: 71 and 69 minutes: DDD: 7/96).
CDA66833 – Piano Sonata No. 1 in B flat minor, Op. 74. Suite on the name "Sacha", Op. 2.
Three Miniatures, Op. 42. Valse de salon, Op. 43. Grande valse de concert in E flat major, Op. 41.
Waltzes on the Theme "Sabela", Op. 23. Petite valse, Op. 36. *CDA66844* – Three Etudes, Op. 31.
Two Pieces, Op. 22. Trois morceaux, Op. 49. Nocturne, Op. 37. Miniature in C major. Easy
Sonata. Sonatina. Two Prelude-improvisations. Theme and Variations, Op. 72.

The first two volumes in this admirable Coombs/Hyperion venture seem to be eminently successful: each offers a programme which demands to be heard from start to finish. The grand introduction to the precocious 18-year-old composer's *Suite on the name "Sacha"* melts into four enchanting but none the less fiendishly difficult movements of Schumann-influenced whimsy: he was still a major influence on the Russians at the time, and Liszt approved young Sacha's first flourish when Glazunov visited Weimar in 1883. The Lisztian bravura means pages of more facile alternatives in the score, but Coombs rises to the challenge of the original and admirably keeps his head into the bargain. His finest achievement, however, is in the string of waltzes, cleverly ordered, at the heart of the disc – from simple (Op. 42 No. 3) to dizzyingly involved (the *Grande valse de concert*) and back again. Dazzling harmonic side-slips and pressing melancholy are handled with a masterly spring and a rubato which is obviously second nature to this pianist. Rubato is the chief pleasure of Coombs's playing in Sonata No. 1, too. Here it's back to mainstream romantic sweep, though the theme of the slow movement is admirably simple, and the finale finds Glazunov at his most robustly ceremonial.

Volume 1, then, already suggests the ideal Glazunov piano collection; but the perspectives broaden in Vol. 2 and if one had to pick one work from what Coombs has offered us so far, it would be the *Three Etudes*: a splendid sequence. The Second is a masterpiece, beginning with what sounds like a meditation on Tchaikovsky's "Happiness was once so near us" – from the final meeting of Onegin and Tatyana – before easing the pain with a central E major consolation of which Rachmaninov would have been proud, and which he might have touched upon at the end in much the same way. Several character-pieces, including a "Gavotte" (*Trois morceaux*), of which Prokofiev once made a piano roll, are more like what one might have predicted of Glazunov the miniaturist, and so are the three brief early works which follow; but the dark, almost morbid *Two Prelude-improvisations* of 1918 reveal another facet – a romanticism prompted to move unselfconsciously with the times. It's only at the last minute that what sounds like a real Russian-ness emerges in the *Theme and Variations*; the folk-song turns out to be Finnish. But that's the least of many surprises. Coombs remains an unflappable and imaginative guide throughout; tone and recording both remain unforced.

Additional recommendations ...

...Suite on the name "Sacha", Op. 2. Two Pieces, Op. 22. Waltzes on the Theme "Sabela", Op. 23.
Three Etudes, Op. 31. Petite Valse, Op. 36. Nocturne, Op. 37. Grande valse de concert in E flat
major, Op. 41. Three Miniatures, Op. 42. Prelude and Two Mazurkas, Op. 25. **Tatyana Franová**
(pf). Marco Polo Ⓕ 8 223151 (69 minutes: DDD: 7/93).

...Etudes, Op. 31 – No. 2 in C minor; No. 3 in E minor. Prelude in D major, Op. 25 No. 1. *Coupled
with works by* **Arensky, Liadov, Rachmaninov, Taneyev** and **Tchaikovsky** Margaret
Fingerhut (pf). Chandos Ⓕ CHAN9218 (78 minutes: DDD: 4/94). *See review in the Collections
section; refer to the Index to Reviews.*

Further listening ...

...Piano Concerto No. 1 in F minor, Op. 92. *Coupled with* **Rimsky-Korsakov** Piano Concerto in
C sharp minor, Op. 30. **Prokofiev** Piano Concerto No. 1 in D flat major, Op. 10. **Sviatoslav
Richter** (pf). Moscow Youth Orchestra / Kyrill Kondrashin. Melodiya mono /4321 29468-2* (6/96).

...Saxophone Concerto in E flat major, Op. 109. Out of the Cool. *Coupled with works by* **Debussy,
Ibert, R.R. Bennett** and **Villa-Lobos** John Harle (sax); Academy of St Martin in the Fields /
Sir Neville Marriner. EMI CDC7 54301-2 (1/92). *See review in the Collections section; refer to the
Index to Reviews.*

...Symphony No. 2 in F sharp minor, Op. 16. Concert Waltz No. 1 in D major, Op. 47. **Bamberg
Symphony Orchestra / Neeme Järvi.** Orfeo C148101A (11/90).   Ⓖ

...Symphony No. 3 in D major, Op. 33. Concert Waltz No. 2 in F major, Op. 51. **Bamberg
Symphony Orchestra / Neeme Järvi.** Orfeo C157101A (11/90).

...Symphony No. 3 in D major, Op. 33[a]. Stenka Razin, Op. 13[a]. Serenades[b] – No. 1 in A major,
Op. 7; No. 2 in F major, Op. 11. [a]**London Symphony Orchestra,** [b]**Royal Philharmonic Orchestra /
Yondani Butt.** ASV CDDCA903 (2/95).

...Symphony No. 6 in C minor, Op. 58. Lyric Poem, Op. 12. **Bamberg Symphony Orchestra / Neeme Järvi.** Orfeo C157201A (11/90).

...Symphony No. 8 in E flat major, Op. 83. Ouverture solennelle, Op. 73. Wedding procession, Op. 21. **Bavarian Radio Symphony Orchestra / Neeme Järvi.** Orfeo C093201A (9/87).

...From the middle ages, Op. 79. Scènes de ballet, Op. 52. *Coupled with* **Liadov** A musical snuffbox, Op. 31. **Scottish National Orchestra / Neeme Järvi.** Chandos CHAN8804 (10/90).

...Chant du ménéstrel, Op. 71. *Coupled with* **Kabalevsky** Cello Concerto No. 2. in C major, Op. 77. **Khachaturian** Cello Concerto. **Raphael Wallfisch** (vc); **London Philharmonic Orchestra / Bryden Thomson.** Chandos CHAN8579 (6/88).

...The sea – fantasy, Op. 28. Spring, Op. 34. *Coupled with* **Kalinnikov** Symphony No. 1 in G minor. **Scottish National Orchestra / Neeme Järvi.** Chandos CHAN8611 (10/88).

...Suite in C major, Op. 35. Elegy in D minor, Op. 105. Prelude and Fugue, "Les Vendredis". *Coupled with* **Glazunov, Sokolov** and **Liadov** Les Vendredis. *Also various composers:* Variations on a Russian Folk-song. **Amati Ensemble of Munich / Attila Balogh.** Calig CAL50940 (11/95).

...Suite in C major, Op. 35. Elegy in D minor, Op. 105. String Quintet in A major, Op. 39[a]. **Shostakovich Quartet;** [a]**Alexander Kovalev** (vc). Olympia OCD542 (11/95).

...Mazurka-Oberek in D major. Meditation, Op. 32. *Coupled with works by* **Massenet, Rachmaninov, Sarasate, Rimsky-Korsakov, Tchaikovsky, Wieniawski** and **Kreisler** **Itzhak Perlman** (vn); **Abbey Road Ensemble / Lawrence Foster.** EMI CDC5 55475-2 (1/96).

...Five Novelettes, Op. 15. *Coupled with* **Borodin** String Quartet No. 2 in D major. **Tchaikovsky** String Quartet No. 1 in D major, Op. 11. **Hollywood Quartet.** Testament mono SBT1061* (8/95).

Reyngol'd Glière   USSR 1875-1956

New review

Glière Symphony No. 2 in C minor, Op. 25. The Red Poppy – Ballet Suite, Op. 70. **New Jersey Symphony Orchestra / Zdenek Macal.** Delos Ⓕ DE3178 (73 minutes: DDD: 8/96). Recorded 1995.

Glière's colourful late-romantic Second Symphony is a fine choice for the first issue in the series. Just occasionally the woodwind detail sounds too good to be true, but otherwise the results are extremely satisfying, the blend of transparency and warmth being even finer than on the rival BBC Philharmonic recording on Chandos, who pride themselves on such things. Glière never puts a foot wrong, but that's because he's going along trails blazed for him by others long before 1908. Although the romantic parts of *Firebird* are audibly just round the corner, here the magic is tamed, the fairy-tale domesticated and the amount of repetition can even become slightly irksome. Between the two orchestras the honours are fairly even, though it has to be said that the New Jersey cor anglais plays with peerless refinement in the slow movement. In general Macal takes much the same view of the piece as Sir Edward Downes – the timings are very close indeed – though Macal coaxes slightly more suave phrasing from his musicians. Delos could have made their disc indispensable by choosing something less well-known than the *Red Poppy* suite as a filler; but for newcomers to the composer this is certainly a more necessary work than the uninspired *Zaporozhy Cossacks* tone-poem on Chandos. Delos make a big pitch about their 'Virtual Reality' recording quality. Ultimately destined for Surround Sound Home Theatre reproduction, it involves, amongst other things, a careful choice of venue, slightly more than usual spatial separation of the players in the hall, and a pragmatic approach to multi-miking.

Additional recommendations ...

...No. 2. The Zaporozhy Cossacks, Op. 64. **BBC Philharmonic Orchestra / Sir Edward Downes.** Chandos Ⓕ CHAN9071 (64 minutes: DDD: 7/92).

...Symphony No. 1 in E flat major, Op. 8. The Red Poppy. **BBC Philharmonic Orchestra / Sir Edward Downes.** Chandos Ⓕ CHAN9160 (61 minutes: DDD: 7/93).   Ⓖ

Glière Symphony No. 3 in B minor, Op. 42, "Il'ya Mouromets". **Royal Philharmonic Orchestra / Harold Farberman.** Unicorn-Kanchana Souvenir Ⓜ UKCD2014/5 (two discs: 93 minutes: DDD: 3/89). From PCM500-1 (8/79). Recorded 1978.   Ⓖ

What happened to the Russian symphony between Tchaikovsky and Shostakovich? Scriabin and Rachmaninov were active of course, plus the solidly respectable Glazunov. But there was another distinctive voice, one whose interest lay in blending the heroic-saga tone of Borodin with the orchestral opulence of Wagner. This was Reyngol'd Glière, and his Third Symphony of 1912 is his undoubted masterpiece. It is a supremely late-romantic technicolour score, extreme but never uncontrolled in its excess, and always directed towards vividness of narrative rather than self-display. Now usually performed without the once-standard cuts, its four movements are fairly protracted, the more so when taken at exceptionally spacious tempos as they are here by Harold Farberman (other more recent uncut recordings have clocked in at single-CD duration). But the spaciousness proves the making of the piece, giving the dimensions a truly epic feel and developing an unstoppable slow momentum. The recording quality no longer quite seems to justify the 'demonstration-class' praise originally accorded it, but it is still impressive enough.

Additional recommendations ...

...No. 3. **BBC Philharmonic Orchestra / Sir Edward Downes.** Chandos Ⓕ CHAN9041 (78 minutes: DDD: 5/92). *Selected by Sounds in Retrospect.* Ⓖ

...No. 3. **Czech Radio Symphony Orchestra / Donald Johanos.** Naxos Ⓢ 8 550858 (76 minutes: DDD: 2/94).

...No. 3. **Loeffler** A Pagan Poem, Op. 14[a]. [a]**Houston Symphony Orchestra;** [b]**Leopold Stokowski Symphony Orchestra / Leopold Stokowski.** EMI Matrix Ⓜ CDM5 65074-2* (62 minutes: ADD: 7/94).

...No. 3. The Red Poppy – Ballet Suite, Op. 70 – Russian Sailors' Dance. **Ippolitov-Ivanov** Caucasian Sketches, Op. 10   No. 2, In a village; No. 4, Procession of the Sardar. **Stravinsky** The Firebird – suite (1919 version). **Philadelphia Orchestra / Leopold Stokowski.** Biddulph mono Ⓕ WHL005* (76 minutes: ADD: 7/94).

Further listening ...

...Concerto for Coloratura Soprano, Op. 82[a]. Harp Concerto, Op. 74[b]. *Coupled with* **Ginastera** Harp Concerto, Op. 25[b]. [a]**Eileen Hulse** (sop); [b]**Rachel Masters** (hp); **City of London Sinfonia / Richard Hickox.** Chandos CHAN9094 (2/93). *See review under Ginastera; refer to the Index to Reviews.*

...The Bronze Horseman – Concert Suite. Horn Concerto in B flat major, Op. 91[a]. [a]**Richard Watkins** (hn); **BBC Philharmonic Orchestra / Sir Edward Downes.** Chandos CHAN9379 (12/95).

...Symphony No. 1 in E flat major, Op. 8. The Sirens, Op. 33. **Slovak Philharmonic Orchestra / Stephen Gunzenhauser.** Naxos 8 550898 (10/95).

Mikhail Ivanovich Glinka

USSR 1804-1857

New review

Glinka Songs, Volume 1. A farewell to St Petersburg. Do not tempt me needlessly. The fire of longing burns in my blood. I recall a wonderful moment. Doubt. Mary. How sweet it is to be with you. Say not that it grieves the heart. **Sergei Leiferkus** (bar); **Semion Skigin** (pf). Conifer Ⓕ 75605 51264-2 (63 minutes: DDD: 4/96). Texts and translations included. Recorded 1994.

This volume of Glinka's songs is very welcome indeed. It includes about a quarter of his total output, and encompasses some of his most popular pieces, such as the charming, touching "Cradle song" from *A farewell to St Petersburg* and the marvellous Pushkin setting *I recall a wonderful moment*. Leiferkus sings these with a gentle, lulling tone and the secure grasp of phrasing that saves the former from any hint of sentimentality; he can also summon up a more vigorous tone with a hint of a rasp in it for the "Bolero", and can lighten this without loss of character so as to rattle off the highly entertaining, and very difficult, "Travelling Song". David Brown, author of the standard English-language study of the composer (*Mikhail Glinka*; London: 1974), agreeably suggests in his insert-notes that this song, of 1840, may be the first ever railway music. Apart from the Pushkin setting, these songs are all from the collection of Nestor Kukolnik poems, *A farewell to St Petersburg*. They include "The lark", which Leiferkus sings gracefully: though not the greatest of Glinka's songs, it has been one of his most popular for its early use of Russian local colour. In a good many of the others the Russian element is more latent, though, despite the Italian and especially French manner, they really do possess a Petersburg elegance. There is a great deal to enjoy and admire here.

Further listening ...

...Grand Sextet in E flat major. *Coupled with* **Rimsky-Korsakov** Piano and Wind Quintet in B flat major. **Capricorn.** Hyperion CDA66163 (12/86). Ⓖ

...Jota aragonesa – Spanish Overture No. 1. *Coupled with works by* **Suppé, Thomas, Meyerbeer, Weber, Nicolai, Smetana, J. Strauss I, Brahms, Tchaikovsky** and **Offenbach** London Symphony Orchestra / Sir Charles Mackerras. Mercury Living Presence 434 352-2MM (12/95).

...Ruslan and Ludmilla – Overture. *Coupled with works by* **Kabalevsky, Tchaikovsky, Mussorgsky** and **Borodin** Chicago Symphony Orchestra / Fritz Reiner. RCA Victor Living Stereo 09026 61958-2 (8/94). *See review in the Collections section; refer to the Index to Reviews.* ⒼⒼⒼ

...Ruslan and Ludmilla – Overture. *Coupled with* **Rimsky-Korsakov** Russian Easter Festival Overture, Op. 36. **Ippolitov-Ivanov** Caucasian Sketches, Op. 10. **Tchaikovsky** Francesca da Rimini, Op. 32. Eugene Onegin – Polonaise. **Baltimore Symphony Orchestra / David Zinman.** Telarc CD80378 (12/95).

...A Life for the Tsar. **Soloists; Sofia National Opera Chorus and Festival Orchestra / Emil Tchakarov.** Sony Classical S3K46487 (9/91).

Albert Glinsky

American 1952-

Suggested listening ...

...Toccata-Scherzo. *Coupled with works by* **Corigliano, Pärt, Moravec** and **Messiaen Maria Bachmann** (vn); **Jon Klibonoff** (pf). Catalyst 09026 61824-2 (12/93). *See review under Corigliano; refer to the Index to Reviews.*

Christoph Gluck

New review

Gluck Alessandro.
Rebel Les elémens.
Telemann Sonata (Septett) in E minor. **Cologne Musica Antiqua / Reinhard Goebel.** Archiv
  Produktion Ⓕ 445 824-2AH (63 minutes: DDD: 12/95). ✒ Recorded 1994-5.

Rebel was a contemporary of Couperin and a pupil of Lully, and it was for a revival of the latter's
opera, *Cadmus et Hermione* that *Les elémens* was staged as an afterpiece. *Les Elémens* is a *symphonie
de danse* or choreographed suite with vivid programmatic content. That much is startlingly evident in
the very first bars of the opening section, a representation of Chaos in which all the notes of the
harmonic scale are united in a single cluster of sound. Reinhard Goebel and his Cologne Musica
Antiqua have always revelled in this kind of extrovert gesture and from the moment of their *premier
coup d'archet*, of which these musicians have so often proved latter-day masters, the listener is
captivated by Rebel's often astonishing *charivari*. The remainder of the suite is harmonically plain
sailing though, again, Rebel proves himself well up to maintaining a lively musical interest. What a
contrast exists between the alluring superficial charm of Rebel's suite and the Telemann sonata which
follows. For though the idiom retains a distinctly French bias, the spirit of the piece has a seriousness
of purpose which deeply penetrates the elegant rococo veneer of his trios and quartets. E minor was
a rewarding key for Telemann and so it proves here in some beautifully sustained writing for violin,
oboe, two violas and cello with bassoon, violone and harpsichord. This is the work's first appearance
on disc. Lastly, in a particularly attractive mixed programme, comes ballet music by Gluck. *Alessandro*
or *Les amours d'Alexandre et de Roxane* was first performed in Vienna in 1764 but has evident French
connections and affinities. The music is delightful and was completely new to me. Its eight movements
are effectively varied and deftly orchestrated, with some characteristic Gluckian sounds among the
horns and bassoons. By far the most substantial movement is the concluding Chaconne, an impressive
piece of writing with commanding interventions by trumpets and drums. Altogether, this is a most
appealing release, well equipped to suit a wide variety of tastes. Excellent recorded sound and a
typically animated essay by Goebel add to the enjoyment.

Gluck Orfeo ed Euridice. **Derek Lee Ragin** (alto) Orfeo; **Sylvia McNair** (sop) Euridice; **Cyndia
  Sieden** (sop) Amore; **Monteverdi Choir; English Baroque Soloists / John Eliot Gardiner.** Philips
  Ⓕ 434 093-2PH2 (two discs: 89 minutes: DDD: 2/94). ✒ Notes, text and translation
  included. *Gramophone Editor's choice.*   Ⓖ

This version of *Orfeo*, played on period instruments and following the original text, has a degree of
spiritual force to which other recordings scarcely aspire, and that is to the credit primarily of the
conductor, John Eliot Gardiner. It begins with a taut, almost explosive account of the overture, moves
to a deeply sombre opening chorus and then a *ballo* of intense expressiveness, finely and carefully
moulded phrases (but plenty of air between them) and a lovely translucent orchestral sound. Every
one of the numerous dances in this set, in fact, is the subject of thoughtful musical characterization,
shapely execution and refined timing of detail. Derek Lee Ragin excels himself as Orpheus; the sound
is often very beautiful, the phrasing quite extraordinarily supple and responsive for a countertenor
voice. Eurydice is sung clearly and truly, and with due passion, by Sylvia McNair – she delivers "Che
fiero momento" and some of the recitative, with considerable force – and the casting of Cyndia
Sieden, with her rather pert, forward voice, as Amore is very successful. This is, as a total
interpretation of the work, more penetrating than any other in the catalogue.

Additional recommendations ...

...Orfeo ed Euridice. **Soloists; Ghent Collegium Vocale; La Petite Bande / Sigiswald Kuijken.** Accent
  Ⓕ ACC48223/4D (two discs: 106 minutes: ADD: 1/90). ✒
...Orfeo ed Euridice. Orphée et Eurydice – Air de furies; Ballet des ombres heureuses; Air vif;
  Menuet; Chaconne. **Soloists; Berlin Radio Chorus; CPE Bach Chamber Orchestra / Hartmut
  Haenchen.** Capriccio Ⓕ 60 008-2 (two discs: 114 minutes: DDD: 1/90). ✒
...Orfeo ed Euridice. **Soloists; Stuttgart Chamber Choir; Tafelmusik / Frieder Bernius.** Sony Classical
  Vivarte Ⓕ SX2K48040 (two discs: 83 minutes: DDD: 8/92). ✒
...Orfeo ed Euridice. **Soloists; Robert Blanchard Vocal Ensemble; Lamoureux Orchestra / Hans
  Rosbaud.** Philips Opera Collector mono Ⓜ 434 784-2PM2* (two discs: 115 minutes: ADD: 5/93).
...Orphée et Euridice. **Soloists; Glyndebourne Chorus; London Philharmonic Orchestra / Raymond
  Leppard.** Erato Libretto Ⓜ 2292-45864-2 (two discs: 127 minutes: DDD: 5/93).
...Orphée et Eurydice – abridged recording[a]; J'ai perdu mon Eurydice. **Soloists;** [a]**Alexis Vlassof
  Chorus; Paris Symphony Orchestra / Henri Tomasi.** Pearl mono Ⓜ GEMMCD9169* (66 minutes:
  AAD: 12/95).   Ⓖ

Gluck Iphigénie en Aulide. **Lynne Dawson** (sop) Iphigénie; **José van Dam** (bass) Agamemnon; **Anne
  Sofie von Otter** (mez) Clytemnestre; **John Aler** (ten) Achille; **Bernard Deletré** (bass) Patrocle;
  Gilles Cachemaille (bass) Calchas; **René Schirrer** (bass) Arcas; **Guillemette Laurens** (mez) Diane;
  Ann Monoyios (sop) First Greek woman, Slave; **Isabelle Eschenbrenner** (sop) Second Greek
  woman; **Monteverdi Choir; Lyon Opéra Orchestra / John Eliot Gardiner.** Erato Ⓕ 2292-45003-2
  (two discs: 132 minutes: DDD: 6/90). Notes, text and translation included. Recorded 1987.

Gluck's first reform opera for Paris has tended to be overshadowed by his other *Iphigénie*, the *Tauride* one. But it does contain some superb things, of which perhaps the finest are the great monologues for Agamemnon. On this recording, José van Dam starts a little coolly; but this only adds force to his big moment at the end of the second act where he tussles with himself over the sacrifice of his daughter and – contemplating her death and the screams of the vengeful Eumenides – decides to flout the gods and face the consequences. To this he rises in noble fashion, fully conveying the agonies Agamemnon suffers. The cast in general is strong. Lynne Dawson brings depth of expressive feeling to all she does and her Iphigénie, marked by a slightly grainy sound and much intensity, is very moving. John Aler's Achille too is very fine, touching off the lover and the hero with equal success, singing both with ardour and vitality. There is great force too in the singing of Anne Sofie von Otter as Clytemnestre, especially in her outburst "Ma fille!" as she imagines her daughter on the sacrificial altar. John Eliot Gardiner's Monteverdi Choir sing with polish, perhaps seeming a little genteel for à crowd of angry Greek soldiers baying for Iphigénie's blood. But Gardiner gives a duly urgent account of the score, pressing it forward eagerly and keeping the tension at a high level even in the dance music. A period-instrument orchestra might have added a certain edge and vitality but this performance wants nothing in authority or drama and can be securely recommended.

Additional recommendation ...

…**Soloists; Chorus and Orchestra of La Scala, Milan / Riccardo Muti.** Sony Classical ℗ S2K52492 (two discs: 117 minutes: DDD).

Further listening ...

…Le Cinesi – opera-serenade. **Kaaren Erickson** (sop) Sivene; **Alexandrina Milcheva** (contr) Lisinga; **Marga Schiml** (contr) Tangia; **Thomas Moser** (ten) Silango; **Munich Radio Orchestra / Lamberto Gardelli.** Orfeo C178891A (1/90).

…Don Juan. Semiramis. **Tafelmusik / Bruno Weil.** Sony Classical SK53119 (10/93). ✒

…Paride ed Elena. **Soloists; La Stagione Vocal Ensemble; La Stagione / Michael Schneider.** Capriccio 60 027-2 (6/93). ✒

…Alceste. **Soloists; Bavarian Radio Chorus; Bavarian Radio Symphony Orchestra / Serge Baudo.** Orfeo C027823F (6/87).

…Iphigénie en Tauride. **Soloists; Monteverdi Choir; Lyon Opéra Orchestra / John Eliot Gardiner.** Philips 416 148-2PH2 (6/86). ✒

Pierre Godolin

French c1610

Suggested listening ...

…Sur l'arbre de la Crotz. *Coupled with works by* **Vitré, Ceppede, Gilles, Carpentras** and **Bouzignac** Soloists; Boston Schola Cantorum; Boston Camerata / Joel Cohen. Erato 4509-98480-2 (11/95). ✒

Leopold Godowsky

Polish/American 1870-1938

New review

Godowsky Studies on Chopin Etudes, Volumes 1 and 2. **Carlo Grante** (pf). Altarus ℗ AIR-CD-9092/3 (two discs, oas: 76 and 73 minutes: DDD: 1/96).
AIR-CD9092 – Nos. 1-20. *AIR-CD9093* – Nos. 21-43.

Poetic and pyrotechnical decadence can go no further than in Godowsky's *magnum opus*, his 53 Studies on 26 of Chopin's *Etudes* and it is not difficult to imagine Chopin's rage had he lived to witness Godowsky's fantastic elaborations. Yet in the modest disclaimers contained in his introductory notes to the pieces Godowsky makes it clear that he did not wish to better Chopin. Rather he wanted to draw on possibilities, extending some already formidable technical demands into a realm of polyphonic, polyrhythmic and polydynamic glory and surrealism. Few pianists would or could take on this assignment. The difficulties are outlandish and immense yet Carlo Grante's surpassing ease and aristocratic musicianship remain unruffled. A young Italian pianist, he studied with Ivan Davis, Rudolf Firkušný and Alice Kezeradze. For him the first study, where Chopin's linear texture is transformed into cascading contrary motion arpeggios, complete with counter-melody carillon, becomes the ultimate curtain raiser. The cadenza at the close of No. 12 flashes like so much summer lightning and in No. 13 (based on Op. 10 No. 6) his truly fabulous command creates an unusual sense of the music's darkly glittering tumult. The virtuoso opulence of No. 16 holds no terrors for him and he always prefers the cruellest challenges to the composer's occasionally merciful *ossia* or alternative. His tone throughout the entire range is gloriously rich and full and when Godowsky asks in No. 25 for "a most sensitive and sympathetic touch, extreme delicacy and refinement, independent and even fingers, a perfect *legato* and a poetic soul", Grante fulfils each and every one of these demands to perfection. The recordings are spacious and refined and these performances surpass earlier ones from Geoffrey Douglas Madge, Ian Hobson and Jorge Bolet.

Further listening ...

…Piano Transcriptions: Passacaglia. Triakontameron – Alt Wien. *Coupled with* **Schubert** Die schöne Müllerin, D795 – Das Wandern; Ungeduld. Winterreise, D911 – Gute Nacht. Rosamunde

– Ballet Music. Moment musical in F minor, D780 No. 3. **Weber** Invitation to the dance, J260.
J. Strauss II Kunstlerleben, Op. 316. **Rian De Waal** (pf). Hyperion CDA66496 (3/92).
…Symphonic metamorphosis on "Die Fledermaus". *Coupled with works by* **Schulz-Evler, Friedman, M. Rosenthal** and **Tausig Piers Lane** (pf). Hyperion CDA66785 (2/96).

Alexander Goehr   British 1932-

New review

Goehr Piano Concerto, Op. 33[a]. Symphony in One Movement, Op. 29[b]. [a]**Peter Serkin** (pf);
[a]**London Sinfonietta / Oliver Knussen;** [b]**BBC Scottish Symphony Orchestra / Richard Bernas.**
NMC ℗ NMCD023 (65 minutes: DDD: 8/95). Recorded 1992-3.

Goehr has stressed that the Symphony (1969, revised 1981) is not a four-movements-in-one affair. It is more like an elaborate set of variations on the sinuous solo viola theme heard near the beginning, where this most reticent of instruments already seems as intimidated by the surrounding orchestral fabric as it is spurred on to unusual heights of eloquence by its own unaccustomed prominence. Goehr's search for textural refinements, evident on every one of the score's 117 pages, is not made into an excuse for avoiding imposing, even visionary effects; indeed, the work's symphonic status is ensured by the balance achieved between proliferating lyrical lines and intensifying dramatic assertions. But the score does throw down a considerable challenge to the performers, and this account, despite the power of its climaxes, is in general rather cool and cautious. The performance of the Piano Concerto fully realizes the music's special mixture of incisiveness and allusiveness. Its formal sophistication marks a real advance over the symphony, and even when the musical material leaves listeners in doubt about the appropriate distinctions between more ornamental and more fundamental elements, the work's engagement with its various models (not excluding Beethoven) is absorbing and invigorating. The recordings of both works are to be commended for enabling us to hear so many of the details of these intricate scores, without artificial shifts of focus.

Further listening ...
…Metamorphosis/Dance, Op. 36. Romanza, Op. 24[a]. [a]**Moray Welsh** (vc); **Royal Liverpool Philharmonic Orchestra / David Atherton.** Unicorn-Kanchana Souvenir UKCD2039 (7/91).
...a musical offering (J.S.B. 1985) ..., Op. 46. Behold the Sun, Op. 44*a*[a]. Lyric Pieces, Op. 35. Sinfonia, Op. 42. [a]**Jeanine Thames** (sop); [a]**James Holland** (vib); **London Sinfonietta / Oliver Knussen.** Unicorn-Kanchana DKPCD9102 (11/91).
…Sing, Ariel, Op. 51[a]. The Mouse Metamorphosed into a Maid, Op. 54. **Lucy Shelton,** [a]**Eileen Hulse,** [a]**Sarah Leonard** (sops); [a]**instrumental ensemble / Oliver Knussen.** Unicorn-Kanchana DKPCD9129 (9/93).
…The Death of Moses, Op. 53. **Soloists.** Unicorn-Kanchana DKPCD9146 (9/93).

Hermann Goetz   German 1840-1876

New review

Goetz Nenie, Op. 10[b]. Psalm 137, Op. 14[ab]. Francesca da Rimini Overture. Spring Overture, Op. 15. [a]**Stephanie Stiller** (sop); [b]**North German Radio Choir; North German Radio Philharmonic Orchestra, Hanover / Werner Andreas Albert.** CPO ℗ CPO999 316-2 (55 minutes: DDD: 8/96).
Texts and translations included. Recorded 1990-4.

Goetz's music has never found much of a following in this country, but the present disc includes at least one work which makes this neglect unjustifiable. This is *Nenie*, of 1874, a setting of Schiller's poem which impressed Brahms enough for him to make his own version seven years later. Brahms, characteristically, found out the most sombre side of his invention in his contemplation of the death of Beauty itself; for Goetz, the poem is an occasion for a passionate protest. Though Brahms's setting is admittedly not among his greatest works, it has poignancy and dignity; and yet these qualities do not overshadow the urgency and the lyrical energy of Goetz's treatment. He is closer to Mendelssohn than to any other composer, and here, in a most sympathetic and eloquent performance, the comparison is not invidious. It is, regrettably, more so in Psalm 137, "By the waters of Babylon". The choral society clichés that Mendelssohn mastered, even at his weakest, can here overwhelm a composer with an excellent technique and a fluent idiom but a considerably less distinctive vein of invention. Much the same is true of the prolix *Spring Overture.* The overture to *Francesca da Rimini,* the opera Goetz left unfinished on his early deathbed, includes some potent music, including a fine violin solo, all taken from the opera, but perhaps it was weakness which prevented Goetz from bracing it into a stronger formal structure. Nevertheless, this sympathetic, skilful composer is worth exploring, and *Nenie* is a real discovery.

Further listening ...
…Sonata in G minor, Op. 17. *Coupled with works by* **Fibich** and **Moscheles Anthony Goldstone, Caroline Clemmow** (pf duet). Meridian CDE84237 (7/93).
…Lieder, Op. 12 – No. 1, Geheimnis; No. 2, Schliesse mir die Augen beide; No. 3, Wandervöglein. Lieder, Op. 19 – No. 1, Ein Frühlingstraum; No. 2, Der Frühling kommt!; No. 3, Wandrers Nachtlied, "Der du von dem Himmel bist". *Coupled with works by* **Kreutzer, Nicolai,**

Humperdinck and **Marschner** Olaf Bär (bar); Helmut Deutsch (pf). EMI CDC5 55393-2
(1/96). *See review in the Collections section; refer to the Index to Reviews.*

Elliot Goldenthal
American 1954-

New review

Goldenthal Fire Water Paper: A Vietnam Oratorio. **Ann Panagulias** (sop); **James Maddalena** (bar);
Yo-Yo Ma (vc); **Ngan-Khoi Vietnamese Children's Chorus; Pacific Chorale and Children's Chorus;**
Pacific Symphony Orchestra / Carl St Clair. Sony Classical Ⓔ SK68368 (65 minutes: DDD: 6/96).
Texts and translations included. Recorded 1995.

A pupil of John Corigliano and Aaron Copland, Brooklyn-born Elliot Goldenthal is perhaps best-
known for his highly imaginative, often stunningly effective film music (recent blockbuster projects
have included *Batman Forever, Interview with the Vampire* and *Heat*). Goldenthal has, however,
composed fluently in many other fields. *Fire Water Paper: A Vietnam Oratorio* was commissioned by
the Pacific Symphony Orchestra to commemorate the twentieth anniversary of the end of the
Vietnam War. The first of its three movements, a large-scale "Offertorium" which the composer has
likened to a slowly unfolding passion play, weaves Buddhist and Catholic texts around two more
extended settings: the first comprises a statement left by Nat Chi Mai, a student activist who torched
herself to death in protest against the war; the second is a poem by the Vietnam veteran and Pulitzer
Prize-winning poet Yusef Komunyakaa entitled *You and I Are Disappearing*, which describes the
horror of seeing a young girl's burning body. Fire and self-sacrifice are the twin metaphors here,
whereas in the succeeding *Scherzo* it is paper. This feverish dance of death (which bears the subtitle
giang co or "tug-of-war") utilizes a far-ranging assortment of documents all designed to illustrate the
folly of war. By contrast, the concluding "Hymn" breathes a more conciliatory, though never entirely
comforting air. This time the theme is water. The movement's centrepiece – an affecting setting of a
poem (again by Yusef Komunyakaa) describing the plight of the boat-people – is framed by words
taken from the Book of Jeremiah. The imaginative flair and extraordinary assurance with which
Goldenthal deploys his vast forces will come as no surprise to anyone who has heard his work for the
cinema. The manner of the whole is unashamedly rhetorical, the mood by turns anguished,
compassionate and memorably serene. Stylistic echoes are legion: Mahler, Shostakovich, Bloch,
Britten, Corigliano – yet Goldenthal's own brand of bittersweet lyricism and irresistible orchestral
physicality are everywhere in evidence. Suffice to say, the performance is all one could wish for. Choral
focus could be sharper; otherwise, the sound is spectacular.

Further listening ...
...Interview with the Vampire   original film soundtrack. Geffen GED24719.

Károly Goldmark
Austrian/Hungarian 1830-1915

New review

Goldmark Violin Concerto No. 1 in A minor, Op. 28[a].
Lalo Symphonie espagnole, Op. 21[b]. **Nathan Milstein** (vn); [a]**Philharmonia Orchestra / Harry Blech;**
[b]**St Louis Symphony Orchestra / Vladimir Golschmann.** Testament [a]stereo/[b]mono Ⓔ ① SBT1047*
(71 minutes: ADD: 11/95). Item marked [a] from HMV SXLP30193 (10/75. Recorded 1954-7. Also
includes unpublished session takes.), [b]Capitol CTL7095 (10/55).

The Goldmark A minor Concerto inspired what was surely Nathan Milstein's finest hour in the
recording studio, a reading of the utmost refinement: warm, effortlessly brilliant and displaying that
unmistakably suave, silken tone. The work itself – which is perhaps just a trifle overlong – recalls both
Reger and Dvořák, with wistful melodies, lilting rhythms and much busy counterpoint (principally in
the outer movements). How delightful, therefore, to have – by way of a bonus – a quarter-of-an-
hour's worth of unpublished session takes, where Milstein exhibits the utmost patience (and technical
consistency) in playing and replaying even the most taxing passages. Harry Blech directs a beautifully
turned accompaniment, and one can only echo the sentiments of Hugh Bean who, reminiscing about
these sessions in the context of Testament's excellent booklet, confesses "that if a visitor from an alien
planet asked me, 'What does a violin sound like?', I would want him to hear the second theme of the
first movement – the innocence, the freshness and purity, the sheer simplicity that takes a lifetime to
achieve." That 'innocence, freshness and purity' are equally apparent in the 1954 *Symphonie
espagnole*, in spite of dry, NBC-style sound and an excessively close-up solo image. Vladimir
Golschmann's conducting is every bit as distinctive as Blech's, especially in the *Andante*, where the St
Louis strings exhibit impressive tonal lustre. This was Milstein's second recording of the piece and,
like its predecessor, omits the work's tangy "Intermezzo". As a performance, it cuts a dashing profile,
has real sparkle and provides a worthy companion for the superb Goldmark Concerto.

Additional recommendation ...
...No. 1. **Bruch** Violin Concerto No. 2 in D minor, Op. 44. **Nai-Yuan Hu** (vn); **Seattle Symphony Orchestra / Gerard Schwarz.** Delos Ⓕ DE3156 (60 minutes: DDD: 12/95).

Further listening ...
...Rustic Wedding Symphony, Op. 26. Sakuntula Overture, Op. 13. **Royal Philharmonic Orchestra / Yondani Butt.** ASV CDDCA791 (5/92).

...Rustic Wedding Symphony, Op. 26. Im Frühling, Op. 36. In Italien, Op. 49. **National Symphony Orchestra of Ireland / Stephen Gunzenhauser.** Naxos 8 550745 (12/95).

...Der gefesselte Prometheus, Op. 38. Symphony No. 2 in E flat major, Op. 35. In Italien, Op. 49. **Philharmonia Orchestra / Yondani Butt.** ASV CDDCA934 (11/95).

Berthold Goldschmidt   German 1903-

Goldschmidt Der gewaltige Hahnrei[a]. Mediterranean Songs[b]. [a]**Roberta Alexander** (sop) Stella; [a]**Robert Wörle** (ten) Bruno; [a]**Michael Kraus** (ten) Petrus; [a]**Claudio Otelli** (bar) Ochsenhirt; [a]**Helen Lawrence** (sop) Mémé; [a]**Martin Petzold** (ten) Estrugo; [a]**Erich Wottrich** (ten) Young Man; [a]**Marita Posselt** (sop) Cornelie; [a]**Christiane Berggold** (mez) Florence; [a]**Franz-Josef Kapellmann** (bass) Gendarme; [a]**Berlin Radio Chorus;** [a]**Berlin Deutsches Symphony Orchestra;** [b]**John Mark Ainsley** (ten); [b]**Leipzig Gewandhaus Orchestra / Lothar Zagrosek.** Decca Entartete Musik Ⓕ 440 850-2DHO2 (two discs: 125 minutes: DDD: 3/94). Notes, texts and translations included.
Gramophone Award Winner 1995. Gramophone Editor's choice.   Ⓖ
There are two causes for rejoicing here. Firstly that Berthold Goldschmidt's *Der gewaltige Hahnrei* ("The magnificent cuckold") has been rediscovered at last; after its successful première in Mannheim in 1932, it and its composer's career were victims of the rise of the Nazis. Secondly and more importantly, the opera is masterly. In its vivid characterization, its dramatic use of pungent orchestral colour and sinewy counterpoint and its gripping narrative thrust it is an achievement all the more remarkable for a first opera by a composer then in his twenties. The central character, Bruno, is a man so jealous of his submissive, adoring wife that he compels her to commit adultery and ends by forcing her into the arms of a would-be rapist. Goldschmidt's language is tonal but bony; those who know the music of his teacher Schreker may hear echoes of it; others may detect an occasional kinship (scarcely attributable to influence) with Weill, Shostakovich or Prokofiev. But it is undoubtedly a personal voice, and the assurance of his style is almost as impressive a feature of this opera as its swift-moving, murderously ironic dramaturgy. So often when a work of real quality is rediscovered one has to make a few apologies for the performance. Not in this case. Alexander sings her heart out as the cruelly treated Stella, and as a result quite avoids the risk that she will appear a mere faceless victim. Wörle, very properly a Loge rather than a Siegfried, acts shrewdly as well as singing incisively. It is a tribute as much to Goldschmidt as to the singers to say that even in quite brief roles they all make very positive contributions to the drama. Each of them is there for a purpose, and so is the pithily characterful music given to each of them. The concise economy of this opera is one of the reasons for its power.

The *Mediterranean Songs* date from nearly 30 years later, and for those encountering Goldschmidt's music for the first time they will be an encouraging indication that three decades of neglect had not soured his lyricism. They are rich and delicate, eloquent evocations of the Mediterranean world, scored with great refinement and with vocal lines of a grateful amplitude. Ainsley sings them beautifully, with care for words (Goldschmidt sets English as eloquently as he does German) as well as smoothness of line. Zagrosek is throughout a powerful advocate for Goldschmidt's music, sensitive to its poignancy (the end of the opera is quite haunting) as well as its formidable strength. A major rediscovery, and all those involved seem urgently convinced of it.

Further listening ...
...Cello Concerto[a]. Ciaconna sinfonica. Chronica. [a]**David Geringas** (vc); **Magdeburg Philharmonic Orchestra / Mathias Husmann.** CPO CPO999 277-2 (7/95).

...Retrospectrum[d]. Variations on a Palestinian Shepherd's Song, Op. 32[b]. Capriccio[a]. Capriccio, Op. 11[b]. Little Legend[b]. Scherzo[b]. From the Ballet[b]. Encore[bc]. String Quartet No. 4[e]. **Kolja Lessing** ([a]vn/[b]pf); [c]**Hansheinz Schneeberger** (vn); [d]**Gaede Trio;** [e]**Mandelring Quartet.** Largo 5128 (3/95).   Ⓖ

...String Quartets[a] – No. 2; No. 3. Belsatzar[d]. Letzte Kapitel[bcd]. [a]**Mandelring Quartet;** [b]**Jörg Gottschick** (narr); [c]**Alan Marks** (pf); [d]**Berlin Ars Nova Ensemble / Peter Schwarz.** Largo 5115 (11/91).

...Beatrice Cenci. **Soloists; Berlin Radio Chorus; Deutsches Symphony Orchestra, Berlin / Lothar Zagrosek. Goldschmidt** Clouds. Ein Rosenzweig. Nebelweben. Time. **Iris Vermillion** (mez) **Berthold Goldschmidt** (pf). Sony Classical S2K66836 (7/95). *Gramophone Editor's choice.*   Ⓖ

Jerry Goldsmith   American 1929-

Suggested listening ...
...Legend – original film soundtrack. **National Philharmonic Orchestra / Jerry Goldsmith.** Silva Screen FILMCD045 (5/93).

...Rudy – original film soundtrack. Varèse Sarabande VSD5446 (8/94).
...Lionheart – original film soundtrack. Varèse Sarabande VSD5484 (11/94).
...The Blue Max – original film soundtrack. Columbia Legacy JK57890.
...The Secret of NIMH – original film soundtrack. TER CDTER1026.

Nicolas Gombert

Flanders **c**1495-**c**1560

Suggested listening ...
...Music from the Court of Charles V – Missa Tempore paschali. Regina caeli. In te Domine
speravi. Media vita. Tous les regretz. Je prens congie. Magnificat Sccundi toni. **Huelgas Ensemble
/ Paul van Nevel.** Sony Classical Vivarte SK48249 (4/93).
...Mille regretz; A bien grant tort; Puisqu' ainsi est; Je prens congies. *Coupled with works by*
**Clemens non Papa, Certon, G. Coste, Compère, De Bussy, Fresneau, Guiard,
Hesdin, Josquin Desprez, La Rue, Ninot le Petit, Pipelare, Vermont le Jeune,
Willaert** and **Anonymous** Clément Janequin Ensemble / Dominique Visse. Harmonia Mundi
HMC90 1453 (5/95). *See review in the Collections section; refer to the Index to Reviews.*

Carlos Gomes

Brazilian 1836-1896

Suggested listening ...
...Il Guarany. **Soloists; Bonn Opera Chorus; Orchestra of the Beethovenhalle, Bonn / John Neschling.**
Sony Classical S2K66273 (5/96).

Sir Eugene Goossens

British 1893-1962

New review
Goossens Symphony No. 2, Op. 62[a]. Concertino for Double String Orchestra, Op. 47[a]. Fantasy
for Nine Wind Instruments, Op. 36[b]. [b]**Janet Webb** (fl); [b]**Guy Henderson** (ob); [b]**Lawrence Dobell,**
[b]**Christopher Tingay** (cls); [b]**John Cran,** [b]**Fiona McNamara** (bns); [b]**Robert Johnson,** [b]**Clarence
Mellor** (hns); [b]**Daniel Mendelow** (tpt); [a]**Sydney Symphony Orchestra / Vernon Handley.** ABC
Classics Ⓟ 8 770013 (62 minutes: DDD: 7/96). Items marked [a] recorded live in 1993.
Eugene Goossens was a formidably gifted composer and conductor. His Second Symphony
(completed in 1945) is a teemingly inventive, tightly knit creation, scored with a power, assurance and
imagination that often take the breath away. On first hearing it is the sheer sweep and emotional scope
of Goossens's opulent vision which impress most. Further acquaintance reveals an underlying formal
strength allied to a rugged beauty which proves immensely rewarding. Indeed, the epic grandeur and
turbulent demeanour of Goossens's admirably ambitious inspiration suggest a strong kinship with
another Second Symphony from two decades earlier, that of Sir Arnold Bax (a work whose belated
London première Goossens himself conducted in May 1930). The two remaining pieces are also well
worth getting to know. The splendidly lusty outer sections of the *Concertino for Double String
Orchestra* (1928) frame a central episode of rapt loveliness. Originally conceived for a string octet, the
Concertino is a marvellously crafted affair and an exhilarating addition to the British string-band
works written this century. The *Fantasy for Nine Wind Instruments* dates from 1924 and captivates by
dint of its fluency, consummate blend of colour and engaging, distinctly Gallic wit. Vernon Handley
directs all this material with his customary authority, tireless zeal and unflagging sense of purpose.
Moreover, he draws a strongly committed, utterly sympathetic response from the Sydney Symphony
Orchestra (Goossens was their chief from 1947 to 1956), and the engineering is unobtrusively natural.
The enthusiastic applause at the live performances has been rightly retained.

Michael Gordon

American 20th century

Suggested listening ...
...Industry. *Coupled with works by* **D. Lang, L. Andriessen** and **Wolfe** Bang on a Can All-Stars.
Sony Classical SK66483 (2/96). *See review in the Collections section; refer to the Index to Reviews.*

Henryk Górecki

Polish 1933-

Górecki Symphony No. 3, Op. 36, "Symphony of Sorrowful Songs". **Dawn Upshaw** (sop); **London
Sinfonietta / David Zinman.** Elektra Nonesuch Ⓟ 7559-79282-2 (54 minutes: DDD: 4/93). Recorded
1991. *Gramophone Award Winner 1993.* ⒼⒼ
Górecki's Third Symphony has become legend. Composed over 17 years ago it has always had its
champions and admirers within the contemporary music world, but in 1993 it found a new audience of
undreamt-of proportions. A few weeks after its release, this Elektra Nonesuch release not only entered the

classical top-ten charts, but was also riding high in the UK Pop Album charts. With sales figures exceeding 300,000 it has since become the biggest selling disc of music by a contemporary classical composer. The Symphony, subtitled *Symphony of Sorrowful Songs* was composed during a period when Górecki's musical style was undergoing a radical change from avant-garde serialism to a more accessible style firmly anchored to tonal traditions. The Symphony's three elegiac movements (or 'songs') form a triptych of laments for all the innocent victims of World War Two and are a reflection upon man's inhumanity to man in general, and as such it has become one of the most moving artistic documents of our time. The songs – including a poignant setting of an inscription scratched by a girl prisoner on the wall of her cell in a Gestapo prison – are beautifully and ethereally sung by Dawn Upshaw, and David Zinman and the London Sinfonietta provide an intense and committed performance of the shimmering orchestral writing. The whole venture is supported by an excellent recording.

Additional recommendations ...

...No. 3. **Zofia Kilanowicz** (sop); **Polish State Philharmonic Orchestra / Jerzy Swoboda.** Belart Ⓢ 450 148-2 (56 minutes: DDD).

...No. 3[b]. Three Pieces in Old Style[a]. [b]**Stefania Woytowicz** (sop); [a]**Warsaw Chamber Orchestra / Karol Teutsch;** [b]**Berlin Radio Symphony Orchestra / Wlodzimierz Kamirski.** Koch Schwann Musica Mundi Ⓔ 311041 (55 minutes: ADD: 4/93).

...No. 3[a]. Three Pieces in Old Style. [a]**Zofia Kilanowicz** (sop); **Katowice Radio Symphony Orchestra / Antoni Wit.** Naxos Ⓢ 8 550822 (66 minutes: DDD: 10/94).

New review

Górecki Kleines Requiem für eine Polka, Op. 66[a]. Harpsichord Concerto, Op. 40[b]. Good Night, "In memoriam Michael Vyner", Op. 63[c]. [c]**Dawn Upshaw** (sop); [c]**Sebastian Bell** (fl); [ac]**John Constable** (pf); [b]**Elisabeth Chojnacka** (hpd); [c]**David Hockings** (perc); [ab]**London Sinfonietta /** [a]**David Zinman,** [b]**Markus Stenz.** Nonesuch Ⓔ 7559-79362-2 (59 minutes: DDD: 9/95). Recorded 1993-4. *Gramophone Editor's choice.*

New review

Górecki Kleines Requiem für eine Polka, Op. 66[a]. Lerchenmusik, Op. 53[b]. [b]**Harmen de Boer** (cl); [b]**Larissa Groeneveld** (vc); [a]**Schoenberg Ensemble / Reinbert de Leeuw** ([b]pf). Philips Ⓔ 442 533-2PH (67 minutes: DDD: 5/96). Recorded 1993.

Like a small café huddled within the shadow of some ancient church, Górecki's *Kleines Requiem für eine Polka* (1993) evokes feelings of paradox. The work's ground-springs are inscrutably personal, yet the sum effect is one of overwhelming intensity. The opening movement suggests distracted tranquillity. This is followed by a grating *Allegro* which approximates, at least in overall effect, the sort of vicious 'knees-up' that Shostakovich penned whenever he bared his teeth at empty celebration. Later, we are back within the tranquil interior of Górecki's imagination – and it's there that we stay until the work ends. The *Kleines Requiem für eine Polka* displays a characteristic profundity expressed via the simplest means.

It is therefore a pity that the Harpsichord Concerto breaks the mood so quickly: one's initial impression is of a further violent 'episode' from the first work, although the stylistic contrast breaks the illusion soon enough. This is probably the most famous twentieth-century harpsichord concerto after Falla's, and the most popular of Górecki's pieces after the Third Symphony. Bach served as its creative prime mover (the work grows – or at least seems to – out of the first solo statement in Bach's D minor Harpsichord Concerto), while Elisabeth Chojnacka is both its dedicatee and its most celebrated interpreter. Here she revels in the piece's playful aggression. It's an unrelenting display and in total contrast to *Good Night*, Górecki's deeply felt memorial to one of his staunchest supporters, the late Michael Vyner. Although the language is sombre, it is never merely mournful. Mostly quiet, contemplative and slow moving, *Good Night* is scored for alto flute, piano and tam-tam with Dawn Upshaw intoning Hamlet's "flights of angels" in the closing movement. The work ends in a spirit of veiled ritual with a sequence of quiet gong strokes. Performance and recording standards are consistently high.

In the *Kleines Requiem* Reinbert de Leeuw is less taut than Zinman but rather more free in spirit: the polka itself sounds less convulsively driven than under Zinman, more folksy and madcap, while the recording is both more atmospheric and more comprehensively appreciative of Górecki's brass writing. Either will do nicely. De Leeuw's coupling, *Lerchenmusik*, like the *Kleines Requiem*, conveys an uneasy peace – but with a major difference: this time, strident humour gives way to quiet consolation. Again there are violent interruptions, but the most beautiful movement – the fourth – features a plainchant quotation that melds into a fragment of Beethoven's Fourth Piano Concerto. The whole Philips disc is spontaneously performed, well-recorded and very well-annotated.

Górecki Miserere, Op. 44[ab]. Amen, Op. 35[ab]. Euntes ibant et flebant, Op. 32[ab]. My Vistula, grey Vistula, Op. 46[c]. Broad waters, Op. 39[c]. [a]**Chicago Symphony Chorus;** [b]**Chicago Lyric Opera Chorus / John Nelson;** [c]**Lira Chamber Chorus / Lucy Ding.** Elektra Nonesuch Ⓔ 7559-79348-2 (67 minutes: DDD: 3/95). Texts and translations included. Recorded 1994.

Whether or not the obvious clicking we hear throughout the first six minutes of *Miserere* is the sound of a censer bathing the basses in incense as they embark on their mammoth (32-minute) journey through the five words of text on which the entire work is based, it is entirely appropriate that it should seem so; for this is an intensely spiritual, imploringly prayerful work in which Górecki responds with heartfelt passion to the political events of 1981 (a sit-in by members of Rural Solidarity, the violent breakup of which and General Jaruzelski's subsequent declaration of "a state of war" ultimately led to the democratization of Poland). This is as intellectually demanding and emotionally compelling as anything by Górecki yet released on disc. Lovers of the Third Symphony will fall under its spell straight away, but it should gain respect from those less easily swayed by the opulent orchestral textures of that work, for here Górecki is using what is probably his favourite medium, the unaccompanied choir. The voices enter in a series of layered thirds until, at 26'00", all ten parts commence an electrifying ascent through the word "Domine" to the work's climax which, with the first statement of "Miserere", suddenly bathes us in a quiet chord of A minor – a moment as devastatingly effective as an orchestra full of banging drums and crashing cymbals. John Nelson directs a hypnotic performance which wants for nothing in its impact, his choral forces both emotionally committed and technically excellent. The recording itself is most certainly not technically excellent – that clicking sound is only one of a disturbing number of persistent background rattles, thumps and bangs, not to mention, at 3'42" in *Amen*, something which sounds awfully like gunfire from the Chicago streets surrounding the church where the recording was made. That church suffers from a cloudy acoustic and there is a haze of surface noise. In the end, though, it only serves to reinforce this grainy aural picture of those dark, frightening times in Poland's recent history. Our knowledge of subsequent events does nothing to lessen the terror which must have been in Górecki's heart as he wrote this unforgettable score.

Further listening ...
...Symphony No. 2, Op. 31, "Copernican"[a]. Beatus vir, Op. 38. [a]**Emese Soós** (sop); **Tamás Altorjay** (bar); **Bartók Chorus; Fricsay Symphonic Orchestra / Tamás Pál**. Stradivarius STR33324 (7/94).
...Three Pieces in Old Style[b]. **Baird** Colas Breugnon – suite[b]. **Szymanowski** Violin Concertos[a] No. 1, Op. 35; No. 2, Op. 61. [a]**Konstanty Kulka** (vn); [a]**Polish National Radio Symphony Orchestra,** [b]**Polish Chamber Orchestra / Jerzy Maksymiuk**. EMI Matrix CDM5 65418-2 (3/96).
...Epitafium, Op. 12[ab]. Scontri, Op. 17[b]. Genesis II: Canti strumentali, Op. 19 No. 2[b]. Refrain, Op. 21[b]. Old Polish music, Op. 24[c]. [a]**Polish National Philharmonic Choir;** [b]**Polish National Symphony Orchestra, Katowice / Jan Krenz;** [c]**Polish National Philharmonic Orchestra, Warsaw / Andrzej Markowski**. Olympia OCD385 (4/93).
...Euntes Ibant et Flebant, Op. 32. Totus tuus, Op. 60. Amen, Op. 35. *Coupled with works by* **Pärt** and **Tavener** Oxford Pro Musica Singers / Michael Smedley. Proud Sound PROUCD136 (12/94). *See review under Tavener; refer to the Index to Reviews.*

Sir John Goss
British 1800-1880

Suggested listening
...The Wilderness. If we believe that Jesus died. *Coupled with works by* **Clarke, S.S. Wesley, Mendelssohn, Ouseley, Schubert** and **Parry** Chichester Cathedral Choir / Alan Thurlow with **James Thomas** (org). Priory PRCD539 (5/96).

Ralf Gothóni
Finnish 1946-

Suggested listening
...Der Ochs und sein Hirte. **Soile Isokoski** (sop); **Jorma Hynninen** (bar); **Jan Söderblom** (vn); **Ilari Angervo** (va); **Jan-Erik Gustafsson, Mark Ylönen** (vcs); **Heini Kärkkäinen** (pf) / **Ralf Gothóni**. Ondine ODE832-2 (9/95).

Louis Moreau Gottschalk
American 1829-1869

Suggested listening ...
...*08.4050.71*[a] – Le Banjo, RO22. The Dying Poet, RO75. Souvenir de Porto Rico, RO250. Le Bananier, RO21. Ojos Criollos, RO185. Bamboula, RO20. The maiden's blush, RO141. The last hope, RO133. Suis-moi!, RO253. Pasquinade, RO189. La Savane, RO232. Tournament Galop, RO264. *08.4051.71* – La jota aragonesa, RO130[ab]. Souvenir d'Andalousie, RO242[ac]. La gallina, RO100[ac]. Orfa, RO186[ab]. Marche de nuit, RO151[ac]. Printemps d'amour, RO214[ab]. Radieuse, RO217[ac]. Réponds-moi, RO225[ab]. Tremolo, RO265[ab]. L'etincelle, RO80[ac]. Ses yeux, RO234[ac]. The Union, RO269[ab] (arr. Liszt). Grande tarantelle, RO259[de] (arr. Hershykay). Symphony No. 1, RO255, "La nuit des tropiques"[e]. [a]**Eugene List,** [b]**Cary Lewis,** [c]**Joseph Werner,** [d]**Reid Nibley** (pfs); [e]**Utah Symphony Orchestra / Maurice Abravanel**. Vanguard Classics 08.4050/1.71* (5/93).
...Grande fantaisie triomphale sur l'hymne national brésilien, RO108 (orch. Hazell). *Coupled with works by* **Rachmaninov, Addinsell** and **Litolff** Cristina Ortiz (pf); Royal Philharmonic Orchestra / Moshe Atzmon. Decca 414 348-2DH (9/86). *See review in the Collections section; refer to the Index to Reviews.* Ⓖ
...Suis-moi!, RO253. Berceuse, RO27. La jota aragonesa, RO130. Manchega, RO143. Marche de nuit, RO151. La Savane, RO232. Miserere du Trovatore, RO171. Souvenir d'Andalousie, RO242.

Polkas – A flat major, RO275; B flat major, RO273. Ballade, RO271. Ynes, RO277. Caprice-Polka, RO44. Scherzo-romantique, RO233. Souvenir de Lima, RO247. Grand scherzo, RO114. Pasquinade, RO189. **Philip Martin** (pf). Hyperion CDA66697 (10/94).

...Manchega, RO143. Le Banjo, RO22. *Coupled with* **Barber** Ballade, Op. 46. **Beach** Five Improvisations, Op. 148. **Bernstein** Five Anniversaries. **Cage** Bacchanale for Prepared Piano. **Copland** Four Piano Blues. **Gershwin** Three Preludes. **M. Gould** Boogie Woogie Etude. **Joplin** The Entertainer. Maple Leaf Rag. **MacDowell** New England Idylls, Op. 62. **Nancarrow** Prelude. **Michel Legrand** (pf). Erato 4509-96386-2 (7/95).

Charles François Gounod   French 1818-1893

Gounod Où voulez-vous aller?[a]. Le soir[a]. Venise[a]. Ave Maria[b]. Sérénade[b]. Chanson de printemps[a]. Au rossignol[b]. Ce que je suis sans toi[a]. Envoi de fleurs[a]. La pâquerette[b]. Boléro[b]. Mignon[a]. Rêverie[a]. Ma belle amie est morte[b]. Loin du pays[b]. Clos ta paupière[a]. Prière[b]. L'absent[a]. Le temps des roses[a]. Biondina[c]. The Worker[c]. A lay of the early spring[c]. My true love hath my heart[b]. Oh happy home! Oh blessed flower![c]. The fountain mingles with the river[a]. Maid of Athens[c]. Beware![a]. The Arrow and the Song[b]. Ilala: stances à la mémoire de Livingston[c]. If thou art sleeping, maiden[c]. [a]**Felicity Lott** (sop); [b]**Ann Murray** (mez); [c]**Anthony Rolfe Johnson** (ten); **Graham Johnson** (pf). Hyperion Ⓟ CDA66801/02 (two discs: 136 minutes: DDD: 3/94). Texts and translations included. Recorded 1993.

This well-filled two-CD set is surely the most wide-ranging single issue ever devoted to Gounod's *mélodies*. The first of the discs confirms the commonly held view of Gounod. Almost without exception the songs are pleasing and sentimental, a sweetly-scented posy of hymns to flowers, of reveries and serenades. The selection includes two settings of poems that Berlioz had used in *Les nuits d'été*, plumbing the depths of the poetry, where Gounod is content to skim across the surface. Arranged in chronological order, the songs show how little Gounod's music deepened, but also how evergreen was his inspiration in melody and harmony. To turn to the second disc is to have all one's prejudices overturned. This comprises non-French settings, for which Gounod dons first Italian garb for the song-cycle *Biondina*, and then English for a group of ten songs written during his stay in London in the 1870s. The Italian cycle is a delight. It would be impossible to guess the composer, as Gounod exchanges his customary flowing themes and rippling arpeggios for an ardent, Tosti-like vocal line over dry staccato chords. Anthony Rolfe Johnson catches its mix of sunny lyricism and Gallic sensitivity to perfection. The English songs are even more unusual, ranging from the Victorian ballad style of *The Worker* to a bizarre musical tribute to Livingstone, entitled *Ilala*. All three singers are on their best form here, with Rolfe Johnson bringing an air of intimate seductiveness to Byron's *Maid of Athens*.

New review

Gounod Roméo et Juliette. **Plácido Domingo** (ten) Roméo; **Ruth Ann Swenson** (sop) Juliette; **Alastair Miles** (bass) Frère Laurent; **Kurt Ollmann** (bar) Mercutio; **Susan Graham** (sop) Stephano; **Alain Vernhes** (bar) Capulet; **Sarah Walker** (mez) Gertrude; **Paul Charles Clarke** (ten) Tybalt; **Christopher Maltman** (bar) Paris; **Erik Freulon** (bar) Gregorio; **Toby Spence** (ten) Benvolio; **David Pittman-Jennings** (bar) Duc; **Dankwart Siegele** (bass) Frère Jean; **Bavarian Radio Chorus; Munich Radio Orchestra / Leonard Slatkin**. RCA Victor Red Seal Ⓟ 09026 68440-2 (two discs: 156 minutes: DDD: 6/96). Notes, text and translation included. *Gramophone Editor's choice*. Recorded 1995.

Thanks to the advocacy of Leonard Slatkin and his team, Gounod's romantic work, *Roméo et Juliette*, seems the epitome of the well-made French nineteenth-century opera. Swenson shows a true empathy for the shape and feeling of a Gounod phrase. At the start, in the famous Waltz Song, she announces her gifts. Besides singing this showpiece with technical confidence, a full, rounded tone and refined delicacy in coloratura, she shows an understanding of the girl's youthful vivacity yet tempers that with inner feeling in the "Loin d'hiver" passage. The fear at having to enter the tomb of Tybalt in the solo at the end of Act 4, so often omitted in the opera house, is graphically expressed; as are the last, desperate utterances as she eagerly grasps the *poignard* to join her beloved in Elysium. Her French, though not perfect, is well learnt, quite adequate to support her impressive portrayal. She seems to have inspired Domingo back to almost his best, youthful form. Roméo's famous aria is sung with growing ardour and full resonance. As one would expect from a great Otello and Radames, the outburst against Tybalt when he has killed Mercutio is heroic to a fault. But the golden tenor is still able to soften in the duets in response to this Juliette. Only once or twice the strain on high betrays the advancing years.

Two principals of such calibre deserve and, by and large, get worthy support and all are brought together into a firm ensemble by Slatkin's loving yet never lingering direction. He brings all the bitter-sweetness out of the Entr'actes by which Gounod obviously set so much store, cares for the composer's refined orchestration and shapes the set pieces with an unerring ear for matching tempos. What more can you ask for? Well, a chorus and orchestra that respond with a like mind, and that's what we have here. Most of the original 1873 score is in place, except for the first three movements of the Wedding tableau, often omitted. They are included in the more-or-less complete Plasson set, which in consequence runs to three discs. Their omission can easily be borne. To complete our pleasure the recording is well-nigh faultless. The voices are up-front where they should be but never to the detriment of the orchestra. The Plasson set is by no means outclassed. Catherine Malfitano is almost as appealing a Juliette as Swenson. Alfredo Kraus sometimes manages a finer line than Domingo though he sounds the older singer. The French support and more authentic version are also in its favour. But the recording is too resonant, sounds studio-bound and fails to give the voices a proper presence.

Additional recommendation ...

...Soloists; **Midi-Pyrénées Regional Choir; Toulouse Capitol Chorus and Orchestra / Michel Plasson.** EMI Ⓕ CDS7 47365-8 (three discs: 166 minutes: DDD: 3/87).

Gounod Faust. **Jerry Hadley** (ten) Faust; **Cecilia Gasdia** (sop) Marguerite; **Samuel Ramey** (bass) Méphistophélès; **Alexander Agache** (bar) Valentin; **Susanne Mentzer** (mez) Siébel; **Brigitte Fassbaender** (mez) Marthe; **Philippe Fourcade** (bass) Wagner; **Welsh National Opera Chorus and Orchestra / Carlo Rizzi.** Teldec Ⓕ 4509-90872-2 (three discs: 211 minutes: DDD: 7/94). Notes, text and translation included. Recorded 1993.

Where Gounod is at his most inspired this version of his most popular work is more than commendable. Most notable are the solos for Marguerite and Faust, the Garden scene, the vignette in Marguerite's room that used to be regularly cut, and the Prison scene (considerably extended by the restoration of passages cut – presumably – before the première: we are in controversial Oeser territory). Following the Oeser Edition means unusual variants and an alteration in the placing (later) of the Church scene. These are questionable decisions but not serious enough to cause a problem when making a choice of versions. The ballet music is rightly consigned to an appendix. The tender, sweet-toned and idiomatically French singing and style of Gasdia and Hadley quite exceed expectations in these days of homogenized and uniform interpretation. These two principals step outside those predictable parameters to give us readings of high individuality, favouring their grateful music with delicately etched line, varied dynamics and real involvement in their characters' predicaments – Faust's vain search for the elixir of renewal, Marguerite for the ideal man. Both their happiness and later remorse are eloquently expressed. Gasdia gives a well-nigh faultless performance – light-hearted, elated in the Jewel song, ardent in the Garden duet, ecstatic in the bedtime solo that follows, ineffably sad in her "Il ne revient pas". How can this exquisite solo have ever been omitted, we think, when Gasdia moves us so deeply? She is no less touching when she has lost her reason. Subtle timbres, poised high notes inform all her singing. Hadley, with the ideal weight of voice for Faust, has done nothing better. "Je t'aime" at the first meeting with Marguerite is whispered in wonder. In the love duet he sings to her as a gentle lover, never bawling, caressing his music, and Gasdia replies in kind. The good news continues with Mentzer. She sings both Siébel's regular solos with vibrant, properly virile tone, the quick vibrato attractive. It's a real coup to have Fassbaender as Marthe, making so much of little. Ramey is the one singer to give a standardized performance. His Méphisto is as soundly and resolutely sung as one would expect from this sturdy bass, but it doesn't have the Francophone smoothness and subtlety of other interpretations. The only drawback is the often lax conducting. Rizzi conducts an often alarmingly slow account of the score and in compensation the more exciting passages are given rather too much verve. However, he is always aware of the sensuous nature of Gounod's scoring and the WNO Chorus and Orchestra are excellent. A choice between this and Plasson for a modern recording must rest on one or other singer. Haunted by the plaintive timbre of Gasdia and the artistry of Hadley one is persuaded that this is the version to have. The recording is by and large open, full of presence and well balanced.

Additional recommendations ...

...Soloists; **Paris Opéra Chorus and Orchestra / André Cluytens.** EMI Ⓜ CMS7 69983-2 (three discs: 171 minutes: ADD: 7/89).

...Faust – Ballet Music[a]. **Delibes** Coppélia – Ballet Suite[b]. Sylvia – Ballet Suite[b]. [a]**Budapest Philharmonic Orchestra / János Sándor;** [b]**Berlin Radio Symphony Orchestra / Heinz Fricke.** Capriccio Ⓑ 15 616 (57 minutes: DDD: 5/90).

...Soloists; **French Army Chorus; Toulouse Capitole Choir and Orchestra / Michel Plasson.** EMI Ⓕ CDS7 54228-2 (three discs: 204 minutes: DDD: 12/91).

...Faust (sung in English)[a]. Faust – Ballet Music[b]: Les nubiennes; Adagio (includes an introduction by Beecham). [a]**Soloists;** [a]**BBC Choir;** [a]**symphony orchestra;** [b]**London Philharmonic Orchestra /** [ab]**Sir Thomas Beecham,** [a]**Clarence Raybould.** Dutton Laboratories mono Ⓜ 2CDAX2001* (two discs: 138 minutes: ADD: 5/94).

Further listening ...

...Marche funèbre d'une marionnette. Coupled with works by **Meyerbeer, Saint-Saëns, Rouget de Lisle, Adam, Boieldieu, Offenbach** and **Rossini** Detroit Symphony Orchestra / **Paul Paray.** Mercury Living Presence 434 332-2MM (11/93). See review in the Collections section; refer to the Index to Reviews.   ⒼⒼⒼ

...March funèbre d'une marionette. Coupled with **Grieg** Peer Gynt – Suites Nos. 1 and 2[c]. **Britten** The Young Person's Guide to the Orchestra, Op. 34[b]. **Saint-Saëns** Le carnaval des animaux[a]. **Loesser** Hans Christian Anderson – musical film. [ab]**Hugh Downs** (narr); [a]**Leo Litwin,** [a]**Samuel Lipman** (pfs); [c]**Eileen Farrell** (sop); **Boston Pops Orchestra / Arthur Fiedler.** RCA Victor Living Stereo 09026 68131 2 (12/95).

...Messe solennelle de Sainte Cécile. **Soloists; French Radio National Chorus; Nouvel Philharmonique / Georges Prêtre.** EMI CDC7 47094-2 (5/85).

...Roméo et Juliette – Je veux vivre. *Coupled with works by* **Donizetti, Bellini, G. Charpentier** and **Delibes Mariella Devia** (sop); **Svizzera Italiana Orchestra / Marcello Rota.** Bongiovanni GB2513-2 (10/94).

...Mors et Vita. **Barbara Hendricks** (sop); **Nadine Denize** (mez); **John Aler** (ten); **José van Dam** (bass-bar); **Orféon Donostiarra; Toulouse Capitole Orchestra / Michel Plasson.** EMI CDS7 54459-2 (2/93).

...Sappho. **Soloists; Saint-Etienne Lyric Chorus and Nouvel Orchestra / Patrick Fournillier.** Koch Schwann 313112 (7/94).

Louis Théodore Gouvy
French 1819-1898

Suggested listening ...

...Morceaux, Op. 59 – No. 1, Prelude; No. 2, Caprice. Sonatas – D minor, Op. 36; C minor, Op. 49; F major, Op. 51. Impromptu, Op. 83 No. 5. Scherzo, Op. 77 No. 1. Aubade, Op. 77 No. 2. **Yaara Tal, Andreas Groethuysen** (pf duet). Sony Classical SK53110 (10/93).

Percy Grainger
American/Australian 1882-1961

New review

Grainger The Warriors.
Holst The Planets, H125[a]. [a]women's voices of the **Monteverdi Choir; Philharmonia Orchestra / John Eliot Gardiner.** DG Ⓕ 445 860-2GH (68 minutes: DDD: 8/95). Recorded 1994. Ⓖ

The conductor's great uncle, Henry Balfour Gardiner – composer, patron, promoter *extraordinaire* – is the hidden link here between Holst and Grainger. But who needs an excuse to bring on *The Warriors*? Grainger's *magnum opus*, much admired by Delius among others, was the "music for an imaginary ballet", a commission set up by Sir Thomas Beecham for Diaghilev's Ballets Russes, but one which failed to materialize. Grainger wrote it anyway, of course, his imagination running riot with visions of a great tribal pageant, a "wild sexual concert", the ghostly clans of all humankind spirited together in celebration of life's prime, "an orgy of war-like dances, processions and merry-makings broken or accompanied, by amorous interludes". Grainger bemoaned a world that he believed was "dying of 'good taste'". *The Warriors* was his corrective, a symphony of dissolution. It is excessive, vulgar, as strange as it is beautiful. Above all, it's the rhythmic excitement of the piece that is so totally irresistible. Gardiner's classical and pre-classical explorations have, by necessity of style, set great store by rhythmic matters, and what a boon they are in *The Planets*. It's Gardiner's insistence upon precise articulations that keeps fleet-footed "Mercury" so airborne, that brings the opening of "Jupiter" into such sharp relief, making it shine all the brighter. There are other moments where a little more theatrical rhetoric would not have gone amiss: is the controlled fury of "Mars" perhaps a shade too controlled (the invading 5/4 rhythm doesn't quite blow your socks off on its return)? But the marmoreal beauty of "Venus" and "Neptune" (a ravishing texture descending from the gleam of celeste to an organ pedal sunk too deep to fathom), the sensitivity of the Philharmonia's playing, duly leave their impression. The recorded sound is superb.

Additional recommendation ...

...The Warriors. Hill-Song No. 1. Irish Tune from County Derry, BFMS20. Hill Song No. 2. Danish Folk-Music Suite. Traditional Chinese (harmonized Yasser, arr. Grainger, orch. Sculthorpe): Beautiful fresh flower. **Melbourne Symphony Orchestra / Geoffrey Simon.** Koch International Classics Ⓕ 37003-2 (67 minutes: DDD: 11/90).

Grainger Piano music for four hands, Volumes 2 and 3. **Penelope Thwaites, John Lavender** (pfs). Pearl Ⓕ SHECD9623/31 (two discs, oas: 66 and 78 minutes: DDD: 1/94). Recorded 1989-91. *SHECD9623* – Children's March (Over the hills and far away), RMTB4. Shepherd's Hey, BFMS16. Hill Song No. 1. Handel in the Strand, RMTB2. Harvest Hymn. The Widow's Party, KS7. The Lonely Desert Man Sees the Tents of the Happy Tribes. The Rival Brothers. Warriors II. Two Musical Relics of My Mother. Let's Dance Gay in Green Meadow, FI. Blithe bells. Pritteling, Pratteling, Pretty Poll Parrot. *SHECD9631* – Rondo. Crew of the Long Dragon. Fantasy on George Gershwin's "Porgy and Bess". Ye Banks and Braes, BFMS32. Tiger-Tiger, KS4/JBC9. Walking Tune, RMTB3. **C. Scott** Three Symphonic Dances. **Delius** A Dance Rhapsody No. 1, RTVI/18. **Grieg** Knut Lurasens Halling II. **Addinsell** Festival. **Le Jeune** La Bel'aronde. **Gershwin** Girl Crazy – Embraceable you (all trans. Grainger).

The first volume of this series (listed below) brought many surprising successes. There, as here, Grainger's 'dishings-up' of his music for keyboard is often more satisfying than the better-known orchestral versions. Quite frequently his arrangements for two pianists are his last thoughts about music that has often gone through as many as half a dozen rethinkings already, so Vol. 2 of this highly accomplished series is something more than an anthology of pieces that many Graingerites will already have. *Shepherd's Hey*, for example, is equipped with a particularly exuberant new coda, and the bafflingly titled *Pritteling, Pratteling, Pretty Poll Parrot* turns out to be our old friend the *Gumsuckers' March* with an entirely new middle section and some affectionate sidelong glances at (apparently) Erik Satie. There is literally new music as well, most substantially *Warriors II*, which turns out to have rather little connection with the strange 'imaginary ballet' that we might now call *Warriors I*. Reconstructed from Grainger's sketches by no fewer than four hands it turns out to be one of his stronger pieces: ardently melodious, at times very close to Rachmaninov, big gestured and with more urgency than some of his works of this length. Volume 3 contains shorter original Grainger compositions and a number of his transcriptions. These latter are fascinating in their combination of scrupulous fidelity and creative rethinking for an entirely different medium. You wouldn't think that a transcription, even for *two* pianos, of Delius's First *Dance Rhapsody* could possibly work. In fact, it works so well, revealing in the process quite a few of the constituents of Delius's style, that some may prefer Grainger's version to the original. In the *Porgy and Bess* Fantasy he treats the tunes with loving respect, but as a pianist can't help seeing different ways of presenting them: the very big gestures surrounding "My man's gone now"; a searching little prelude to "It ain't necessarily so" implying all sorts of interesting things Grainger could have done with that slithery little tune if he weren't obliged to play it straight – which he then does, with sparkling enjoyment.

Additional recommendation ...

...Volume 1 – In a Nutshell. Spoon River. When the world was young. Molly on the shore. Hill Song No. 2. Country Gardens. Mowgli's song against people. Eastern Intermezzo. English waltz. The Wraith of Odin. Always bright and merry. The Duke of Marlborough's Fanfare. A Lincolnshire Posy. **Penelope Thwaites, John Lavender** (pfs). Pearl Ⓔ SHECD9611 (77 minutes: DDD: 10/89).

New review

Grainger Jungle Book. Shallow Brown. Good-Bye to Love. Died for Love. The Power of Love. The Rival Brothers. Six Dukes went a fishin'. The Sprig of Thyme. Willow, willow. Recessional. Lord Maxwell's Goodnight. The Three Ravens. The Running of Shindand. Early One Morning. The Love Song of Har Dyal. My Love's in Germanie. **Libby Crabtree** (sop); **John Mark Ainsley** (ten); **David Wilson-Johnson** (bar); **Polyphony; The Polyphony Orchestra / Stephen Layton.** Hyperion Ⓔ CDA66863 (74 minutes: DDD: 7/96). Notes and text included. *Gramophone Editor's choice.*

Grainger's music resembles what one imagines to have been the effect of his physical presence. He opens doors and windows, unleashes sudden bursts of energy, compels a frank response, makes you draw deeper breath and know you're alive; also, he doesn't stay for long. The catalogue of his works is itself a moving and astonishing record, because his life was so teemingly various and his 'works' ("dished up", as he would say, in so many guises) were only a part of it. Only two items are common to this and John Eliot Gardiner's programme on Philips. One is the famous *Shallow Brown*: once heard never forgotten. In this, Stephen Layton and Polyphony secure an immediate advantage over Gardiner by virtue of their soloist. Of course we suppose, as Grainger was told, it is the song of a woman newly parted from the sailor she loves and for whose fidelity she pleads; and it is possible that with a woman singer of genius, a Baker or (think of it!) a Butt, it could be a knockout. But the song is what Grainger called a chanty, a song of men among men, transferring their own emotion in a way that satisfies both it and their masculine vanity. At all events, it sounds better that way. And what a song it is! In Grainger's arrangement it is as mesmeric as the sea itself: play it in the morning and you're still hearing it at night. With Gardiner, the waves swell and crash more inexorably and the chorus suggest a harsh jeer on the face of coarse reality. But it is this new one that goes to the heart. The soloist is David Wilson-Johnson and he sings it with all its due complement of passion. The *Jungle Book* songs also have their own vitality in abundance. Rich in harmonies and sonorities, they date from almost any time between 1898 and 1947, and are wonderfully well performed. In what follows, every item would bear separate comment, and they all deserve something more than our modern listening habits are likely to give them. An attractive (and useful) feature of this production is the helpful layout of the booklet: information about each item is given where you want to find it, with the text.

New review

Grainger I'm seventeen come Sunday, BFMS8. Brigg Fair, BFMS7. Love verses from "The Song of Solomon". The merry wedding. Shallow Brown, SCS3. Father and daughter. My dark-haired maid, "Mo Nighean Dhu". The bride's tragedy. Irish tune from County Derry, BFMS5. Scotch strathspey and reel, BFMS28. The lost lady found, BFMS33. The three ravens, BFMS41. Danny Deever. Tribute to Foster. **Monteverdi Choir; English Country Gardiner Orchestra / John Eliot Gardiner.** Philips Ⓟ 446 657-2PH (75 minutes: DDD: 4/96). Texts included. Recorded 1994-5. ⒼⒶ

The really startling thing about all these settings is the way in which Grainger unlocks the *inner* life of each text, each melody. He'll digest it, understand it, respect it, and then in his response – which is nothing if not personal – he'll elaborate, creating as little or as much subtext as is appropriate. Like Britten, in his folk-song settings, Grainger knew how and when to get out of the way. The plaintive *Brigg Fair* is no more, no less than the tenor solo and chiefly wordless chorus will allow us – a tune so precious to Grainger that even the harmony is almost an intrusion. Then there is the classic

Londonderry Air – no words, just voices – a harmony that is so rich, so expressive, so integrated, that it always shrouds the melody in the imagination. Then what, you may ask, could be more extraordinary (or unlikely) than the *Love verses from "The Song of Solomon"* (inquisitive, oddly erotic, a real Old Testament amplitude to harmony and texture – replete with harmonium)? Well, *Shallow Brown* for a start, which is astounding. A sea shanty with the reach of a spiritual, it is set as the sailors will have yelled it, the vocal line stretching and distorting, straining to be heard over furious oceanic *tremolandos* in guitars and strings. An unexpected upturn (a tiny question mark) in the choral refrain at the close is typical of Grainger. He did so like to keep us guessing. This is a fabulous disc. John Eliot Gardiner may well have inherited some of his joy in this music (though heaven knows, you don't need to inherit it) from his great-uncle, Balfour Gardiner (one of the 'Frankfurt Gang', which included Grainger). He is characteristically hot in his response to its rhythmic zest as are his wonderfully articulate, impeccably tuned, Monteverdi singers and players. The singing is, by turns, fleet, spry, fireside-cosy cathedral-rich – or plain raucous. Brilliant, revealing recorded sound.

New review

Grainger Hill-song No. 1. 14 Songs of the North. Three Scotch Folksongs. Scotch Strathspey and Reel. **Ronald Stevenson** (pf). Altarus Ⓔ AIR-CD-9040 (45 minutes: DDD: 9/95). Recorded 1983.

The *Hill-song No. 1*, regarded by many of Grainger's admirers as a masterpiece, was prompted by "the soul-shaking hill-scapes" that he encountered on a holiday in Argyll in 1900, when he was 18. He took with him a copy of MacLeod and Boulton's *Songs of the North*, and something of the spirit of those folk melodies got into the *Hill-song* as well, so this coupling makes a good deal of sense. *Scotch Strathspey and Reel*, sketched around the same time (1901) but tinkered with for ten years thereafter, is what another sort of Grainger admirer would regard as the best of him, a rollickingly exuberant speculation. Ronald Stevenson's transcription of the *Hill-song* does full justice to it. In other words it sounds as though Grainger had transcribed it himself, and Stevenson's performance, for the 20 minutes the piece lasts, can convince you that the young Grainger, trying to imagine "the hills' own music", and experimenting with dissonance, gapped scales and non-repetitive structures in the effort to find it, genuinely did stumble into a territory whose borders touch Stravinsky-Land and Ives County. Afterwards, 'stumble' seems to be the word: Grainger had the imaginative power for a brilliant *jeu d'esprit* like *Scotch Strathspey* but not for the entirely new, 'democratic' musical language that he thought he was inventing in the *Hill-song*. That is why it so often sounds like Delius without the discipline. But there are wonderful sounds within it, and a recalcitrant boldness to which Stevenson responds with virtuosity and affection. The folksong settings here range from the very simple to the sumptuously lush, but the tune itself is never obscured; you can hear Stevenson's own fondness for them in the way he brings them out. The best of Grainger, in short, is in the most inventive of his transcriptions, and there are few better introductions to the composer at his best than Stevenson's gleeful account of the *Strathspey*. It is a piece that insists that you play it again; like the rest of the programme its recording is ample.

Further listening ...

...Youthful Suite – Rustic dance; Eastern intermezzo. Blithe bells (free ramble on a theme by Bach, "Sheep may safely graze"). Spoon River. My Robin is to the Greenwood Gone. Green Bushes. Country Gardens (orch. Schmid). Mock Morris. Youthful Rapture[a]. Shepherd's Hey. Walking Tune. Molly on the shore. Handel in the Strand (orch. Wood). **Philip Martin** (pf); [a]**Moray Welsh** (vc); **Bournemouth Sinfonietta / Kenneth Montgomery.** Chandos Collect CHAN6542 (2/92).

...Sussex Mummers' Christmas Carol, BFMS17. Arrival Platform Humlet, RMTB1. *Coupled with works by* **Britten, Vaughan Williams, R. Clarke, Bax** and **Bridge** Paul Coletti (va); Leslie Howard (pf). Hyperion CDA66687 (10/94). *See review in the Collections Section; refer to the Index to Reviews.*

...In Dahomey. *Coupled with works by* **Gershwin, Waller, Ellington, J.P. Johnson, Gottschalk, Columbia, Rube Bloom, Cowell, Nancarrow, B. Powell, Beiderbecke, Jelly Roll Morton, Joplin, Cervantes** and **Confrey** Alan Feinberg (pf). Argo 444 457-2ZH (11/95). *See review in the Collections section; refer to the Index to Reviews.*

...Danish Folk-Music Suite – The Power of Love; The Nightingale and the two Sisters; Jutish Medley. One More Day, my John. Knight and Shepherd's Daughter. Near Woodstock Town. Country Gardens. Sussex Mummer's Christmas Carol. Shepherd's Hey. To a Nordic Princess. Love at first sight. Over the hills and far away. Bridal Lullaby. Handel in the Strand. Colonial Song. Paraphrase on the Waltz of the Flowers from Tchaikovsky's "The Nutcracker". **Fauré** (arr. Grainger) Nell, Op. 18 No. 1. *Coupled with* **Dowland** (arr. Grainger) Now, O now, I needs must part. **Penelope Thwaites** (pf). Unicorn-Kanchana DKPCD9127 (3/93).

Enrique Granados   Spanish 1867-1916

New review

Granados 12 Danzas españolas, Op. 37. 7 Valses poéticos. **Alicia de Larrocha** (pf). RCA Victor Red Seal Ⓔ 09026 68184-2 (68 minutes: DDD: 1/96). Recorded 1994.

Alicia de Larrocha, that incomparable interpreter of the Spanish repertoire, is revisiting many of her favourite musical haunts on RCA (this is at least her third recording of Granados's 12 *Danzas*, and her second of the *Valses poéticos*). And if some of her former edge and fire, her tonal and stylistic luxuriance are now replaced by more 'contained' and reflective qualities, her warmth and affection remain undimmed. Her rubato, while less lavishly deployed than before, is potent and alluring, as instantly recognizable as ever, and each and every dance is played with rare naturalness, ease and authority. True, the "Rondella aragonesa" is less thrilling in its dizzying acceleration than on her earlier Decca disc, the swaying rhythms of the "Sardana" less seductive. But if (rather as in Rubinstein's later Chopin) a touch of sobriety occasionally blunts the fullest impact of these fascinating, most aristocratic idealizations of local Spanish life and colour, the actual playing is never less than masterly. The *Valses poéticos* are offered as an engaging encore. The recordings have much less range and reverberance than those on Decca; however, all lovers of this still misunderstood and neglected repertoire, played by one of the great pianists of our time, will want to add this to their collection.

Additional recommendations ...

...12 Danzas españolas. **Alicia de Larrocha** (pf). Decca 414 557-2DH (10/85).

...Valses poéticos (trans. Williams). *Coupled with works by* **Albéniz, Rodrigo** and **Anonymous** **John Williams** (gtr); [a]**London Symphony Orchestra / Paul Daniels.** Sony Classical Ⓕ SK48480 (71 minutes: DDD: 7/92). *See review under Albéniz; refer to the Index to Reviews.* Ⓖ

...12 Danzas españolas. El pelele. Allegro de concierto. **Albéniz** Suite española No. 1, Op. 47. Suite española No. 2. Cantos de España, Op. 232. **Alicia de Larrocha** (pf). Decca Musica Española Ⓜ 433 923-2DM2 (two discs: 119 minutes: ADD/DDD: 9/92).

...12 Danzas españolas. Goyescas, Op. 11 – No. 4, Quejas o la maja y el ruiseñor; No. 7, El pelele. **Angela Hewitt** (pf). CBC Records Ⓕ MVCD1074 (66 minutes: DDD: 11/94).

...12 Danzas españolas – Villanesca; Andaluza (Playera). 7 Valses poéticos. Cuentos de la juventud – Dedicatoria. 15 Tonadillas – El majo Olvidado. *Coupled with works by* **Albéniz** and **Rodrigo** RCA Navigator Ⓢ 74321 17903-2 (77 minutes: DDD: 3/95). *See review under Albéniz; refer to the Index to Reviews.* Ⓖ

...(arr. Breiner) 12 Danzas españolas. Escenas poeticas – Series 2. **Norbert Kraft** (gtr); **Razumovsky Sinfonia / Peter Breiner.** Naxos Ⓢ 8 553037 (72 minutes: DDD: 2/96).

Granados Goyescas. **Alicia de Larrocha** (pf). Decca Ⓕ 411 958-2DH (57 minutes: ADD: 3/89). From SXL6785 (12/77). Recorded 1976. Ⓖ

New review

Granados Goyescas. El pelele. **Eric Parkin** (pf). Chandos Ⓕ CHAN9412 (61 minutes: DDD: 3/96). Recorded 1993.

The Granados *Goyescas* are profoundly Spanish in feeling, but the folk influence is more of court music than of the flamenco or *cante hondo* styles which reflect gipsy and Moorish influence. Alicia de Larrocha's set of seven pieces was given its first performance by the composer in 1911, and his own exceptional ability as a pianist is evident in its consistently elaborate textures. That performance took place in Barcelona, and as Granados's compatriot and a native of that very city de Larrocha fully understands this music in its richly varied moods; a fact which tells in interpretations that have a compelling conviction and drive. Thus, she can dance enchantingly in such a piece as "El Fandango de candil", while in the celebrated "Maiden and the nightingale", No. 4 of the set, we listen to a wonderful outpouring of Mediterranean emotion, all the more moving for its avoidance of excessive rubato and over-pedalling. A splendid disc of one of the twentieth century's piano masterpieces.

A direction in the score at the beginning of the *Goyescas* is *con garbo y donaire* ("with charm and elegance"). The description aptly fits Parkin's performances. His readings have an element of free rubato about them, but this is not allowed to become excessive, and it serves to underline the essentially improvisatory nature of these pieces. Aided by a clean technique in this sometimes complex texture – he is very adept, too, at integrating the numerous small skirls that help to give character to the melodic lines – he gives persuasive performances that also contain much poetry. He captures the dignified flamboyance of the traditional dance in the "Fandango by candlelight", carefully observing the direction *avec beaucoup de rhythme*. Two of the hardest tests for a pianist in this collection of Goyesque studies are the preservation of coherence in the long "Serenata del espectro" and the avoidance of mawkishness in "La maja y el ruiseñor": Parkin emerges successfully from both. A piano with particularly bright top octaves was perhaps not the ideal instrument for this recording, but there is no lack of colour or nuance from the performer. Even measured against the formidable competition of Larrocha, this is a highly recommendable disc.

Additional recommendations ...

...Goyescas – No. 7, El pelele. Danzas españolas, Op. 37 – No. 7, Valenciana; No. 10, Danza triste. *Coupled with works by* **Falla, Mompou** and **Nin** Soloists; instrumental ensemble. EMI Composers in Person mono Ⓕ CDC7 54836-2* (78 minutes: ADD: 11/93). *See review in the Collections section; refer to the Index to Reviews.*

...Goyescas. **Albéniz** Iberia. Navarra. **Alicia de Larrocha** (pf). Double Decca Ⓜ 448 191-2DF2 (two discs: 141 minutes: ADD: 4/96). *See review under Albéniz; refer to the Index to Reviews. This performance is the same as the one reviewed above.* Ⓖ

Carl Heinrich Graun

New review

C.H. Graun Cesare e Cleopatra. **Iris Vermillion** (mez) Cesare; **Janet Williams** (sop) Cleopatra; **Lynne Dawson** (sop) Cornelia; **Robert Gambill** (ten) Tolomeo; **Ralf Popken** (alto) Arsace; **Jeffrey Francis** (ten) Lentulo; **Klaus Häger** (bass) Achilla; **Elisabeth Scholl** (sop) Cneo; **Maria-Cristina Kiehr** (sop) Sesto; **RIAS Chamber Choir, Berlin; Concerto Köln / René Jacobs.** Harmonia Mundi Ⓟ HMC90 1561/3 (three discs: 198 minutes: DDD: 6/96). 🖉 Notes, text and translation included. Recorded 1995.

Within weeks of his accession to the Prussian throne in 1740 Frederick the Great had appointed Carl Heinrich Graun as his court Kapellmeister. Though not Graun's first opera for Berlin, *Cesare e Cleopatra* was that which inaugurated the new Royal Berlin Opera House, the Linden Opera, in 1742. *Cesare e Cleopatra* is loosely based on Corneille's *La mort de Poppée* but, like Handel's *Giulio Cesare* which had first been staged in London 18 years earlier, places emphasis on the love affair between Caesar and Cleopatra rather than on Pompey's death at the hands of Cleopatra's brother Ptolemy. Graun was no Handel, but while there is nothing here to match the older composer's psychological insight and therefore his depth and constancy of character portrayal, there is a wealth of music which, at its best – and it often is – beguiles the senses with its profusion of fine melodies and imaginative instrumental colouring. One of the first of several outstandingly affective arias is given to Cornelia, in the second scene of Act 1. She has just witnessed the treacherous murder of her husband Pompey at Ptolemy's hands and expresses her grief in an F minor aria, noble, tender and deeply sorrowful. Lynne Dawson brings intensity and a tragic presence to the role. Caesar's horror at Pompey's death is genuine if, as here, short-lived. His mind is soon caught up with thoughts of Cleopatra as his aria, "Quel che lontano" (first disc, track 10) reveals. This role was originally a castrato one but is very well sung here by mezzo-soprano Iris Vermillion. Janet Williams's Cleopatra is wonderfully athletic; Graun has given her some exacting coloratura and Williams delivers it with effortless finesse. Her dazzling virtuosity in "Tra la procelle assorto" is not only splendidly dramatic but also musically satisfying. The remaining roles are very well sung. Concerto Köln make the music spring to life from the printed page. And all is directed with energy and dramatic insight by René Jacobs.

Further listening ...

...Keyboard Sonata in D minor[a]. *Coupled with* **Hasse** Keyboard Sonata in E flat major[a]. **Benda** Keyboard Sonatinas[a] – Rondeau; Allegro; Allegretto; Allegretto; Allegretto moderato. **Fasch** Andantino con Variazioni[a]. **Schulz** Diverses pièces, Op. 1[b] – No. 5, Allegretto; No. 6, Larghetto con Variazioni. **C.P.E. Bach** Pièces Caractéristiques[b] – La Borchward, H79; La Pott, H80; La Gleim, H89; La Bergius, H90; La Stahl, H94; La Boehmer, H81; La Louise, H114. **Christine Schornsheim** ([a]hpd/[b]fp). Capriccio 10 424 (4/95). 🖉

...Montezuma. **Soloists; Cantica Nova Chamber Choir; Neuss German Chamber Academy / Johannes Goritzki.** Capriccio 60 032 (7/93).

Christoph Graupner

Suggested listening ...

...Overture-Suites – for Chalumeau, Strings and Continuo in B flat major; Two Chalumeaux, Strings and Continuo in F major[a]; Three Chalumeaux, Strings and Continuo in D minor[b]. **Jean-Claude Veilhan,** [ab]**Yves Tetsu,** [b]**Florence Jacquemart** (chalumeaux); **Ensemble Mensa Sonora / Jean Maillet** (vn). Pierre Verany PV794114 (4/95).

Alexandr Grechaninov

Suggested listening ...

...Symphony No. 1 in B minor, Op. 6[a]. Snowflakes, Op. 47[b]. Missa Sancti Spiritus, Op. 169[c]. [b]**Ludmilla Kuznetsova** (mez); [c]**Tatiana Jeranje** (contr); [c]**Russian State Symphony Cappella and** [ab]**Orchestra / Valery Polyansky.** Chandos New Direction CHAN9397 (12/95).

...String Quartets – No. 2 in D minor, Op. 70; No. 4 in F major, Op. 124. **Moyzes Quartet.** Marco Polo 8 223646 (10/94).

...Piano Trios – No. 1 in C minor, Op. 38; No. 2 in G major, Op. 128. **Viktor Simčisko** (vn); **Jura Alexander** (vc); **Daniela Ruso** (pf). Marco Polo 8 223416 (6/93).

...The Seven Days of the Passion. **Russian State Symphonic Cappella / Valeri Polyansky.** Chandos CHAN9303 (1/95).

...The Liturgy of St John Chrysostom, Op. 13 No. 1. **Cantus Sacred Music Ensemble / Ludmilla Arshavskaya** with **Archdeacon Valeri Shcheglov.** Olympia OCD447 (6/95).

...Liturgy of St John Chrysostom, Op. 177 No. 4. **Cantus Sacred Music Ensemble / Ludmila Arshavskaya.** Olympia OCD480 (9/95).

...Liturgia Domestica, Op. 79. **Victor Radkevich** (ten); **Anatoli Obraztsov** (bass); **Ludmilla Golub** (org); **Russian State Symphonic Cappella; Russian State Symphony Orchestra / Valeri Polyansky.** Chandos New Direction CHAN9365 (8/95).

Maurice Greene

British 1696-1755

Suggested listening ...

...Songs and Keyboard Work. – Bel mirar[aef]. Battillo siediti[aef]. Spenser's Amoretti[af] – The rolling wheele; How long shall this; Sweet smile; The love which me; Faire ye be sure; Like as the Culver. A Cantata and Four English Songs: Book 1 – Orpheus with his Lute[af]; Book 2 – Beauty, an Ode[abcdef]. Farfalletta festosetta[abef]. Quanto contenta godi[abf]. Nell'orror[abef]. The Chaplet[af] – Ye purple-blooming Roses; Sweet Annie; Fair Sally. A Collection of Lessons[f] – Allegro in A minor; Vivace in A minor; Molto allegro in A minor; Aria con Variazioni in A major. Voluntary No. 7 in E flat major[f]. [a]**Emma Kirkby** (sop); [b]**Ursula Weiss,** [c]**Iona Davies** (vns); [d]**Martin Kelly** (va); [e]**Helen Gough** (vc); [f]**Lars Ulrik Mortensen** (hpd). Musica Oscura 070978 (8/95). ✒

Will Gregory

20th century

Suggested listening ...

...Hoe down. *Coupled with works by* **D. Bedford, Nyman, Corea** and **R. Powell** Apollo Saxophone Quartet; **John Harle** (alto sax/keybds); **Roy Powell** (keybds); **Will Gregory** (bar and bass saxes); **Mike Hamnett** (perc). Argo 443 903-2ZH (8/95). *See review in the Collections section; refer to the Index to Reviews.*

Edvard Grieg

Norwegian 1843-1907

New review

Grieg Piano Concerto in A minor, Op. 16[a]. Piano Sonata in E minor, Op. 7[b].
Schumann Piano Concerto in A minor, Op. 54[a]. [a]**Stephen Kovacevich,** [b]**Zoltán Kocsis** (pfs); [a]**BBC Symphony Orchestra / Sir Colin Davis.** Philips Solo Ⓜ 446 192-2PM (78 minutes: [a]ADD/[b]DDD: 6/96). Items marked [a] from 6500 166 (3/72, recorded 1970-71), [b]6514 115 (8/83, recorded 1982). 🄶🄶🄶

Stephen Kovacevich's wholly natural, intimately poetic phrasing, his delicately glistening fingerwork and his bravura and rhythmic virility, too, when required (as in Grieg's finale) must of course be noted first. Yet it is difficult to recall any other performance in which pianist, conductor and orchestra are in closer or more subtly balanced and shaded accord than in this classic account. Each and every participant sounds as personally involved as they would in chamber music-making. The sound quality has not the forward brightness of present-day reproduction: you may need to turn up your volume control a little higher than usual. But its old-world mellowness seems just right for performances as loving as these. For good measure we're even given an encore – though rather curiously there is no mention of it in the accompanying booklet – and from a totally different pianist. But Zoltán Kocsis's account of Grieg's early E minor Sonata is certainly sufficiently incisive and characterful to justify resurgence.

Additional recommendations ...

...Piano Concerto. **Schumann** Piano Concerto in A minor, Op. 54. **Krystian Zimerman** (pf); **Berlin Philharmonic Orchestra / Herbert von Karajan.** DG Karajan Gold Ⓕ 439 015-2GHS (64 minutes: DDD).

...Piano Concerto. **Schumann** Piano Concerto. **Radu Lupu** (pf); **London Symphony Orchestra / André Previn.** Decca Ovation Ⓜ 417 728-2DM (61 minutes: ADD: 12/87). 🄶

...Piano Concerto. **Schumann** Piano Concerto. **Pascal Devoyon** (pf); **London Philharmonic Orchestra / Jerzy Maksymiuk.** Classics for Pleasure Ⓑ CD-CFP4574 (63 minutes: DDD: 2/91).

...Piano Concerto. Lyric Pieces, Book 8, Op. 65. **Liszt** Piano Concerto No. 2 in A major, S125. **Leif Ove Andsnes** (pf); **Bergen Philharmonic Orchestra / Dmitri Kitaienko.** Virgin Classics Ⓕ VC7 59613-2 (78 minutes: DDD: 4/91).

...Piano Concerto. *Coupled with works by* **Schumann** and **Franck** Sir Clifford Curzon, Friedrich Gulda (pfs); **London Symphony Orchestra / Øivin Fjeldstad; London Philharmonic Orchestra / Sir Adrian Boult; Vienna Philharmonic Orchestra / Volkmar Andreae.** Decca Headline Classics Ⓑ 433 628-2DSP (76 minutes: ADD: 1/92). *See review under Franck; refer to the Index to Reviews.* 🄶🄶🄶

...Piano Concerto[b]. Peer Gynt – Suites Nos. 1 and 2[a]. Lyric Suite, Op. 54[c]. Holberg Suite, Op. 40[c]. Lyric Pieces – Book 1, Op. 12; Book 3, Op. 13[d]. Symphonic Dances, Op. 64[e]. [b]**Stephen Kovacevich,** [d]**Zoltán Kocsis** (pfs); [ac]**English Chamber Orchestra;** [e]**Philharmonia Orchestra / Raymond Leppard;** [b]**BBC Symphony Orchestra / Sir Colin Davis.** Philips Duo Ⓜ 438 380-2PM2 (two discs: 155 minutes: ADD: 8/93). *The performance of the Concerto is the same as the one reviewed above.* 🄶

...Piano Concerto. **Schumann** Piano Concerto. **Lars Vogt** (pf); **City of Birmingham Symphony Orchestra / Simon Rattle.** EMI Ⓕ CDC7 54746-2 (62 minutes: DDD: 1/93).

...Piano Concerto *(orig. version)*[a], Larvik's Polka, CW102[a]. 23 Short Pieces, CW105[a]. [a]**Love Derwinger** (pf); **Norrköping Symphony Orchestra / Jun'ichi Hirokami.** BIS Ⓕ CD619 (62 minutes: DDD: 9/93).

...Piano Concerto. **Jean-Marc Luisada** (pf); **London Symphony Orchestra / Michael Tilson Thomas.**
DG Ⓕ 439 913-2GH (65 minutes: DDD: 12/94).

...Piano Concerto[b]. Lyric Pieces – French serenade, Op. 62 No. 3; Cradle song, Op. 68 No. 5.
Franck Symphonic Variations[a]. **Liszt** Piano Concerto No. 1 in E flat major, S124. **Walter
Gieseking** (pf); [a]**London Philharmonic Orchestra / Sir Henry Wood;** [b]**Berlin State Opera Orchestra
/ Hans Rosbaud.** APR mono Ⓜ APR5513* (63 minutes: ADD: 3/96).

Grieg Holberg Suite, Op. 40. Two Elegiac Melodies, Op. 34. Peer Gynt – Suites Nos. 1 and 2,
Opp. 46 and 55. Two Lyric Pieces. **Academy of St Martin in the Fields / Sir Neville Marriner.**
Hänssler Classic Ⓕ 98 995 (66 minutes: DDD: 1/95). Recorded 1994.

The clean ruggedness of Grieg's music comes across well here. Indeed, there is much to praise: the
sheer zest of the opening *Allegro vivace* of the *Holberg Suite* and, in the same five-movement work,
the way Marriner and his players convey the necessary 'period' quality. The *Two Elegiac Melodies* are
also fine; the second of them is the poignant "Last spring" and features some movingly hushed
playing from the violins. The incidental music to *Peer Gynt*, which follows, has a similarly attractive
freshness. One gets the impression that this is the kind of music that the ASMF can play beautifully
at the drop of a hat, but beautiful playing it remains, with nothing routine about it. Even the well-
worn "Morning" in Suite No. 1 sounds as fresh as if it were the morning of the world, and one could
not ask for a more loving account of "Solveig's Song". The two transcriptions of the *Lyric Pieces* are
also evocative, with fine oboe playing in the first, "Evening in the mountains". The recording is richly
reverberant but permits detail to emerge.

Additional recommendation ...

...Peer Gynt – Suites Nos. 1 and 2[c]. **Britten** The Young Person's Guide to the Orchestra,
Op. 34[b]. **Saint-Saëns** Le carnaval des animaux[a]. **Gounod** March funèbre d'une marionette.
Loesser Hans Christian Anderson – musical film. [ab]**Hugh Downs** (narr); [a]**Leo Litwin,** [a]**Samuel
Lipman** (pfs); [c]**Eileen Farrell** (sop); **Boston Pops Orchestra / Arthur Fiedler.** RCA Victor Living
Stereo Ⓜ 09026 68131-2 (76 minutes: ADD: 12/95).

Grieg Norwegian Dances, Op. 35. Lyric Suite, Op. 54. Symphonic Dances, Op. 64. **Gothenburg
Symphony Orchestra / Neeme Järvi.** DG Ⓕ 419 431-2GH (68 minutes: DDD: 1/87).

Grieg's music has that rare quality of eternal youth: however often one hears it, its complexion retains
its bloom, the smile its radiance and the youthful sparkle remains undimmed. Though he is essentially
a miniaturist, who absorbed the speech rhythms and inflections of Norwegian folk melody into his
bloodstream, Grieg's world is well defined. Both the *Norwegian Dances* and the *Symphonic Dances*
were originally piano duets, which Grieg subsequently scored: Järvi conducts both with enthusiasm
and sensitivity. In the *Lyric Suite* he restores "Klokkeklang" ("Bell-ringing"), which Grieg omitted
from the final score: it is remarkably atmospheric and evocative, and serves to show how forward-
looking Grieg became in his late years. The recording is exceptionally fine and of wide dynamic range;
the sound is very natural and the perspective true to life.

Additional recommendations ...

...Norwegian Dances. Old Norwegian Romance with Variations, Op. 51. In Autumn, Op. 11. Lyric
Pieces, Op. 43 – No. 5, "Erotik". **Svendsen** Two Icelandic Melodies. **Iceland Symphony
Orchestra / Petri Sakari.** Chandos Ⓕ CHAN9028 (66 minutes: DDD: 8/92).

...Symphonic Dances. Sigurd Jorsalfar, Op. 56. Peer Gynt – Solveig's Song[a]; Solveig's Cradle Song[a].
Six Romances, Op. 39 – From Monte Pincio[a]. A swan, Op. 25[a]. Spring, Op. 33[a]. Norway, Op. 58
– Henrik Wergeland[a]. [a]**Solveig Kringleborn** (sop); **Royal Stockholm Philharmonic Orchestra /
Gennadi Rozdestvensky.** Chandos Ⓕ CHAN9113 (73 minutes: DDD: 3/93).

Grieg String Quartets – No. 1 in G minor, Op. 27; No. 2 in F major, CW146.
Schumann String Quartet No. 1 in A minor, Op. 41 No. 1. **Petersen Quartet** (Conrad Muck,
Gernot Süssmuth, vns; Friedemann Weigle, va; Hans-Jakob Eschenburg, vc). Capriccio
Ⓕ 10 476 (75 minutes: DDD: 1/94). Recorded 1993.

Grieg String Quartet No. 1 in G minor, Op. 27.
Mendelssohn String Quartet No. 2 in A minor, Op. 13. **Shanghai Quartet** (WeiGang Li,
HongGang Li, vns; Zheng Wang, va; James Wilson, vc). Delos Ⓕ DE3153 (64 minutes:
DDD: 6/94).

Since Grieg owed much to Schumann, coupling their quartets seems a good idea. These G minor and
A minor Quartets were written when the composers were in their thirties, although Grieg was a few
years older. Yet it is his work that sounds more youthfully passionate, while the Schumann is a rather
self-conscious homage to his friend Mendelssohn and classical models. These German players invest
the Grieg G minor Quartet with *gravitas* and are skilful in linking together the disparate sections of
its structure. Their recording has a very natural balance and an impressively wide dynamic range with
real *pianissimo*; it also copes well with Grieg's forceful, semi-orchestral string writing. The whole
performance has vigour and tenderness in good proportion, and a truly Scandinavian feeling. The
unfinished F major Quartet is another sensitively moulded performance and the work sounds no
more incomplete than Schubert's *Unfinished* Symphony. The Schumann is no less enjoyable; the
artists are fully inside his idiom and make a consistently beautiful and meaningful sound. The
youthful Shanghai Quartet's brightly-lit account of the Mendelssohn suggests a rich store of

interpretative potential. Theirs is a sizzling, multicoloured performance. The Grieg coupling is, if anything, even finer, with an *Allegro molto* first movement that truly is *ed agitato*, a warming *Romanze* and a superbly characterized *Intermezzo*. It is arguably the most compelling performance of this endearing score since the original Budapest Quartet's trail-blazing HMV 78s from 1937. It is richly (if rather cavernously) recorded.

Additional recommendations ...

...No. 1. **Schumann** String Quartet No. 1 in A major, Op. 41. **English Quartet.** Unicorn-Kanchana Ⓕ DKPCD9092 (66 minutes: DDD: 3/92).

...No. 1. **Sibelius** String Quartet in D minor, Op. 56, "Voces intimae". **Wolf** Italian Serenade. **Budapest Quartet.** Biddulph mono Ⓜ LAB098* (67 minutes: ADD: 4/95).

| New review |

Grieg Cello Sonata in A minor, Op. 35.
Liszt Romance oubliée, S132. Elégies – No. 1, S130; No. 2, S131. Die Zelle in Nonnenwerth, S382. La lugubre gondola, S134.
Rubinstein Cello Sonata No. 1 in D major, Op. 18. **Steven Isserlis** (vc); **Stephen Hough** (pf). RCA Victor Red Seal Ⓕ 09026 68290-2 (76 minutes: DDD: 4/96). Recorded 1994.

With Steven Isserlis and Stephen Hough an inspired duo, natural recording artists both, it would be a pity if the sentimental title, "Forgotten Romance", a translation of the shortest and least ambitious piece in the collection, deterred any serious listener from investigating it. The logic of the grouping is that the five cello pieces of Liszt, all of them brief and all adapted from earlier works, are used to frame the high romantic cello sonatas, by Grieg and Rubinstein, that are in danger of neglect. With performances like these, as sharply disciplined as they are passionate, all the emotion is very well founded, with sentimentality firmly kept at bay. The magnificent Grieg Sonata was written when he was considering composing a second piano concerto and its material and manner very much reflect the A minor Concerto, with the composer at his most richly distinctive. Compared with, say, Truls Mørk and Jean-Yves Thibaudet, Isserlis and Hough are lighter and more imaginative, choosing speeds that flow easily and naturally. Paradoxically that makes the result more moving than any underlining of expression. One could say the same about all these performances. The two *Elégies* – with Isserlis most persuasive in the improvisation-like passages – lead to the Rubinstein First Sonata. It has the lyrical directness and honest four-square construction which make the Mendelssohn cello sonatas so attractive. The disc is rounded off by two Liszt pieces slightly more substantial than the others – *Die Zelle in Nonnenwerth* ("The Cell in Nonnenwerth") – a late adaptation of an early song, spare in texture, and Liszt's tribute to Wagner after his death, *La lugubre gondola*, one of many different adaptations.

Additional recommendations ...

...Cello Sonata. Intermezzo in A minor, CW118. **Sibelius** Malinconia, Op. 20. Four Pieces, Op. 78. Two Pieces, Op. 77. **Truls Mørk** (vc); **Jean-Yves Thibaudet** (pf). Virgin Classics Ⓕ VC5 45034-2 (69 minutes: DDD: 10/94).

...Cello Sonata[a]. Piano Sonata. Intermezzo in A minor, CW118[a]. [a]**Øystein Birkeland** (vc); **Håvard Gimse** (pf). Naxos Ⓢ 8 550878 (50 minutes: DDD: 11/94).

Grieg Violin Sonatas – No. 1 in F major, Op. 8; No. 2 in G major, Op. 13; No. 3 in C minor, Op. 45. **Augustin Dumay** (vn); **Maria-João Pires** (pf). DG Ⓕ 437 525-2GH (70 minutes: DDD: 9/93). Recorded 1993.   Ⓠ

Grieg's violin sonatas span his creative life, the first two dating from his early twenties, before his Piano Concerto, and the Third Sonata of 1887 belonging to the last decade of his life. Augustin Dumay brings to this music a youthful *seigneur*, manifest in the impetuosity, charm and command of his playing. He and Maria-João Pires are at their considerable best in the G major Sonata, with its vivid first movement, lilting *Allegretto* and triumphant finale – whose conclusion they lift to the skies. The recording does full justice to Dumay's silky and resourceful tone. Pires is rightly an equal partner, and both artists bring an infectiously fresh response to the music. The finale of the C minor Sonata, music that anticipates Sibelius in its urgency and elemental force, is compellingly played.

Additional recommendations ...

...Nos. 1-3. **Lydia Mordkovitch** (vn); **Elena Mordkovitch** (pf). Chandos Ⓕ CHAN9184 (72 minutes: DDD: 9/93).

...Nos. 1-3. **Oscar Shumsky** (vn); **Seymour Lipkin** (pf). Biddulph Ⓕ LAW008 (63 minutes: DDD).

...Nos. 1-3. **Dong-Suk Kang** (vn); **Roland Pöntinen** (pf). BIS Ⓕ CD647 (69 minutes: DDD: 11/94).

| New review |

Grieg Piano Works, Volumes 1-4. **Einar Steen-Nøkleberg** (pf). Naxos Ⓢ 8 550881/4 (four discs, oas: 72, 70, 64 and 71 minutes: DDD: 3/96). Recorded 1993.

8 550881 – Piano Sonata in E minor, Op. 7. Funeral March for Rikard Nordraak, CW117. Melodies of Norway – The sirens' enticement. Stimmungen, Op. 73. Transcriptions of Original Songs I, Op. 41 – No. 3, I love thee. Four Humoresques, Op. 6. Four Piano Pieces, Op. 1.

8 550882 (*Gramophone Editor's choice*) – Two Improvisations on Norwegian Folksongs, Op. 29. Melodies of Norway – A Ballad to Saint Olaf. 25 Norwegian Folksongs and Dances, Op. 17. Transcriptions of Original Songs II, Op. 52 – No. 2, The first meeting. 19 Norwegian Folksongs,

Op. 66. *8 550883* – Four Album Leaves, Op. 28. Six Poetic Tone-pictures, Op. 3. Melodies of Norway – Iceland. Three Pictures from life in the country, Op. 19. Three Pieces from "Sigurd Jorsalfar", Op. 56 – Prelude. Ballade in G minor, Op. 24, "in the form of variations on a Norwegian melody". *8 550884* – Holberg Suite, Op. 40. Melodies of Norway – I went to bed so late. Six Norwegian Mountain Melodies, CW134. Peer Gynt Suite No. 1, Op. 46 – Morning. 17 Norwegian peasant dances, Op. 72.

These are the first four volumes of a complete Grieg cycle which stretches to no fewer than 14 discs. Since all of them are at super-budget price they make a very competitive alternative to other complete or near-complete surveys. Einar Steen-Nøkleberg came into prominence in the 1970s and won numerous Norwegian and other prizes. He was professor of the piano at the Hanover Musikhochschule for some years and is the author of a monograph on Grieg's piano music and its interpretation.

8 550881: The first disc juxtaposes early pieces, the Sonata, Op. 7, the Op. 6 *Humoresques* and the *Funeral March for Rikard Nordraak*, all written in the mid 1890s with his very last piano work, *Stimmungen* (or "Moods"), Op. 73. He plays these bold and original pieces with great flair and understanding. Whatever its limitations there is much greater range in Grieg's piano music than is commonly realized and Steen-Nøkleberg is attuned to the whole spectrum it covers, whether in the Bartókian "Mountaineer's Song" from the Op. 73 to the charm and innocence of the *Allegretto con grazia*, the third of the *Humoresques*, Op. 6.

8 550882: The *19 Norwegian Folksongs* (1896) are remarkable pieces as Grieg himself knew. He wrote to the Dutch composer, Julius Röntgen, of having "put some hair-raising chromatic chords on paper. The excuse is that they originated not on the piano but in my mind. If one has the Vøringfoss beneath one's feet, one feels more independent and daring than down in the valley." Readers will recognize No. 14 as the source of the theme for Delius's *On hearing the first cuckoo in spring*. Steen-Nøkleberg plays them with great tonal finesse and consummate artistry

8 550883: The most substantial work on this disc is the *Ballade* which Grieg wrote on the death of his parents. The catalogue lists a dozen or so recordings, but this newcomer can hold its own with the best – even if there are moments where Steen-Nøkleberg seems too discursive, and one feels the need for some of the variations to be held on a firmer lead. Yet what an imaginative colour he produces in the *Adagio* variation when the music suddenly melts *pianissimo*.

8 550884: The *Norwegian peasant dances* are amazing pieces for their period, and though their audacity and dissonance were later overtaken by Bartók, they still retain their capacity to surprise. Steen-Nøkleberg's playing conveys the extraordinary character and originality of these pieces as do few others. The smaller pieces on this record – and on its companions – are full of rewards. No collector should be without the celebrated Gilels anthology of *Lyric Pieces* and Leif Ove Andsnes's single disc containing the Sonata (both reviewed below), which are more strongly profiled readings. However, the claims of these outstanding discs are strong.

Grieg Piano Sonata in E minor, Op. 7. Six Poetic tone-pictures, Op. 3 – Nos. 4-6. Four Album Leaves, Op. 28 – No. 1 in A flat major; No. 4 in C sharp minor. Agitato. Lyric Pieces – Book 3, Op. 43; Book 5, Op. 54. **Leif Ove Andsnes** (pf). Virgin Classics Ⓔ VC7 59300-2 (72 minutes: DDD: 6/93). Recorded 1992.

Andsnes was 22 when he recorded Grieg's Sonata – exactly the composer's age when he wrote it. Despite the heroic opening, Andsnes does not save the first movement from sounding repetitive. It is the two inner movements that display real character and imagination and the pianist rises to the occasion in both. The finale is stunningly played. He is to be heard at his very best in the *Lyric Pieces*, Op. 43, which is the most familiar set of all. One relishes the glinting colours in "Butterfly", the simple heartfelt yearnings of "Solitary Wanderer" and the delightful twittering energy of the "Little Bird". Here is a pianist with sufficient insight and subtlety not to feel the need to prettify the music. This well-crafted CD has pleasant piano sound, not over-close in impact.

Additional recommendation ...

...Book 1, Op. 12 – No. 3, Watchman's song; No. 5, Folksong; No. 7, Albumleaf; No. 8, National song. Book 2, Op. 38 – No. 1, Berceuse; No. 3, Melody; No. 7, Waltz. Book 4, Op. 47. Book 5, Op. 54. Book 6, Op. 57. Book 7, Op. 62. Book 8, Op. 65. Book 9, Op. 68 – No. 1, Sailor's song; No. 2, Grandmother's minuet; No. 3, At your feet; No. 4, Evening in the mountains; No. 5, Cradle song. **Daniel Adni** (pf). EMI Forte CZS5 68634-2 (two discs: 145 minutes: ADD: 5/96).

Grieg Lyric Pieces – Arietta, Op. 12 No. 1. Berceuse, Op. 38 No. 1. Butterfly, Op. 43 No. 1. Solitary Traveller, Op. 43 No. 2. Album-leaf, Op. 47 No. 2. Melody, Op. 47 No. 3. Norwegian Dance, "Halling", Op. 47 No. 4. Nocturne, Op. 54 No. 4. Scherzo, Op. 54 No. 5. Homesickness, Op. 57 No. 6. Brooklet, Op. 62 No. 4. Homeward, Op. 62 No. 6. In ballad vein, Op. 65 No. 5. Grandmother's minuet, Op. 68 No. 2. At your feet, Op. 68 No. 3. Cradlesong, Op. 68 No. 5. Once upon a time, Op. 71 No. 1. Puck, Op. 71 No. 3. Gone, Op. 71 No. 6. Remembrances, Op. 71 No. 7. **Emil Gilels** (pf). DG The Originals Ⓜ 449 721-GOR (56 minutes: ADD: 10/87). From 2530 476 (3/75).   Ⓔ Ⓔ Ⓔ

This record is something of a gramophone classic. The great Russian pianist Emil Gilels, an artist of staggering technical accomplishment and intellectual power, here turns his attention to Grieg's charming miniatures. He brings the same insight and concentration to these apparent trifles as he did to towering masterpieces of the classic repertoire. The programme proceeds chronologically and one can appreciate the gradual but marked development in Grieg's harmonic and expressive language – from the folk-song inspired early works to the more progressive and adventurous later ones. Gilels's fingerwork is exquisite and the sense of total involvement with the music almost religious in feeling. This is a wonderful recording: pianistic perfection.

Additional recommendation ...

...Complete Works for Solo Piano. **Gerhard Oppitz** (pf). RCA Victor Red Seal Ⓕ 09026 61568/9-2 (two sets of three and four discs: 214 and 305 minutes: DDD: 4/94). *09026 61568-2:* Lyric Pieces – Book 1, Op. 12; Book 2, Op. 38; Book 3, Op. 43; Book 4, Op. 47; Book 5, Op. 54; Book 6, Op. 57; Book 7, Op. 62; Book 8, Op. 65; Book 9, Op. 68; Book 10, Op. 71. *09026 61569-2:* Six Poetic tone-pictures, Op. 3. 25 Norwegian Folksongs and Dances, Op. 17. Three Pictures from life in the country, Op. 19. Ballade in G minor in the Form of Variations on a Norwegian Melody, Op. 24. Four Piano Pieces, Op. 1. Piano Sonata in E minor, Op. 7. Two Improvisations on Norwegian Folksongs, Op. 29. Transcriptions of Original Songs, Opp. 41 and 52. Four Humoresques, Op. 6. Four Album Leaves, Op. 28. Stimmungen, Op. 73. Three Piano Pieces. Holberg Suite, Op. 40. 19 Norwegian Folksongs, Op. 66. Funeral March for Rikard Nordraak, CW117. 17 Norwegian Peasant Dances, Op. 72.

Grieg Bergljot, Op. 42[a]. Olav Trygvason, Op. 50[b]. Funeral March for Rikard Nordraak, CW117.
[a]**Lise Fjeldstad** (narr); [b]**Solveig Kringelborn** (sop); [b]**Randi Stene** (contr); [b]**Per Vollestad** (bar);
Trondheim Symphony [b]**Chorus and Orchestra / Ole Kristian Ruud.** Virgin Classics Ⓕ VC5 45051-2
(59 minutes: DDD: 4/95). Texts and translations included. Recorded 1994.

Olav Trygvason is the nearest that Grieg ever came to opera. Set in the tenth century, Bjørnson's text tells of Olav Trygvason, the first king to convert Norway to Christianity. In the middle of 1873 he sent Grieg the first three scenes, which so fired the composer's enthusiasm that he drafted a short score that summer, but for various reasons the project never got any further, and when the subject resurfaced after his reconciliation with Bjørnson, the poet had lost interest in the idea and Grieg himself had gone off the boil. The three tableaux are closer in musical character to cantata than opera. Grieg adopts a somewhat quasi-Wagnerian declamatory style, but there are no big arias or set-pieces. Neither *Olav Trygvason* nor *Bergljot* is vintage Grieg. In the case of the latter Grieg's aim had been to compose a colourful orchestral piece with spoken narration. The Gothenburg performances under Järvi for DG (listed below) score perhaps in terms of finish and the recordings have slightly greater bloom and tonal refinement but these Trondheim musicians under Ole Kristian Ruud have an appealing freshness of spirit, and are very vividly recorded. If you want this particular combination of pieces, you need not hesitate for a moment.

Grieg Peer Gynt – The Bridal March passes by; Prelude; In the Hall of the Mountain King;
Solveig's Song; Prelude; Arab Dance; Anitra's Dance; Prelude; Solveig's Cradle Song[a].
Symphonic Dances, Op. 64 – Allegretto grazioso[b]. In Autumn, Op. 11[c]. Old Norwegian Romance
with Variations, Op. 51[d]. [a]**Ilse Hollweg** (sop); [a]**Beecham Choral Society; Royal Philharmonic
Orchestra / Sir Thomas Beecham.** EMI Studio Plus Ⓜ CDM7 64751-2* (76 minutes: ADD).
Items marked [a] from HMV ASD258 (1/59), [b]HMV ASD518 (4/63), [cd]Columbia 22CX1363
(9/56). Recorded 1956-57.

Grieg's incidental music was an important integral part of Ibsen's *Peer Gynt* and from this score Grieg later extracted the two familiar suites. This recording of excerpts from *Peer Gynt* goes back to 1957 but still sounds well and is most stylishly played. He included the best known ("Anitra's Dance" is a delicate gem here) together with "Solveig's Song" and "Solveig's Cradle Song". Sir Thomas uses Ilse Hollweg to advantage, her voice suggesting the innocence of the virtuous and faithful peasant heroine. There is also an effective use of the choral voices which are almost inevitably omitted in ordinary performances of the two well-known orchestral suites: the male chorus of trolls in the "Hall of the Mountain King" are thrilling, and the women in the "Arab Dance" are charming. The other two pieces are well worth having too; *Symphonic Dances* is a later, freshly pastoral work, while the overture *In Autumn* is an orchestral second version of an early piece for piano duet. This reissue is further enhanced by the first release in stereo of the *Old Norwegian Romance*.

Additional recommendations ...

...Peer Gynt – complete. Sigurd Jorsalfar – incidental music, Op. 22. **Soloists; Gösta Ohlin's Vocal
Ensemble; Pro Musica Chamber Choir; Gothenburg Symphony Orchestra / Neeme Järvi.** DG
Ⓕ 423 079-2GH2 (two discs: 124 minutes: DDD: 2/88).   Ⓖ

...Peer Gynt – excerpts. **Soloists; San Francisco Symphony Chorus and Orchestra / Herbert
Blomstedt.** Decca Ⓕ 425 448-2DH (73 minutes: DDD: 3/90).

...Peer Gynt Suites – No. 1, Op. 46; No. 2, Op. 55. Land Sighting, Op. 31[a]. Olav Trygvason,
Op. 50[b]. [b]**Randi Stene** (mez); [b]**Anne Gjevang** (contr); [ab]**Håkan Hagegård** (bar); [ab]**Gothenburg
Symphony Chorus; Gothenburg Symphony Orchestra / Neeme Järvi.** DG Grieg Edition Ⓕ 437
523-2GH (73 minutes: DDD: 6/93).

Grieg Songs, Volumes 1 and 2. **Håkan Hagegård** (bar); **Warren Jones** (pf). RCA Victor Red Seal
Ⓟ 09026 61518/61629-2 (two discs, oas: 67 and 68 minutes: DDD: 2/94). Texts and translations
included. Recorded 1992.
09026 61518-2 – Melodies of the Heart, Op. 5. Nine Songs, Op. 18. Six Songs, Op. 25. The
Mountain Thrall, Op. 32. Last Spring, Op. 33 No. 2. Rocking on Gentle Waves, Op. 49 No. 2.
Henrik Wergeland, Op. 58 No. 3. *09026 61629-2* – Four Songs and Ballads, Op. 9. Four Songs,
Op. 21. Five Songs, Op. 26. Six Songs, Op. 39. Reminiscences from Mountain and Fjord, Op. 44.
Håkan Hagegård is the ideal male singer for Grieg's songs, singing with marvellously fresh, firm tone.
Warren Jones is an excellent partner, and the recording keeps voice and piano happily in balance. The
two records are issued separately, and, though the programmes are arranged broadly in chronological
order, each includes early and late compositions so that either of them can offer a fairly representative
conspectus. Volume 1 begins with Op. 5, *Melodies of the Heart*, settings of poems by Hans Andersen.
A crisp rhythm in the piano part of the first, "Two brown eyes", matches the clean, bright focus of
the voice, and in the third song, the famous "I love thee", both artists catch the affectionate
impulsiveness without mawkish indulgence. The *Nine Songs*, Op. 18 are attractive though less striking
than the Op. 25 set of six, which begins with "Fiddlers", an eerie song, almost a Norwegian
"Doppelgänger". It also includes the Ibsen setting, "A swan", which is among the loveliest of all.
"Våren" (better known as the second of the *Elegiac Melodies* for strings) suits the singer beautifully,
a saddened tone colouring the voice till the verse's climax which opens out in superb vocal health.
Then with the second volume we are back to Op. 9, ending with the *Reminiscences from Mountain and
Fjord*, Op. 44, the fine, responsive settings of Holger Drachmann's lyrical ballads about the local girls
and his conviction that "in the hills there is no sin".

Additional recommendation ...
...Six Songs with Orchestra[a]. The First Meeting, Op. 21 No. 1[a]. The Mountain Thrall[b]. Before a
Southern Convent, Op. 20[c]. Bergljot, Op. 42[d]. [ac]**Barbara Bonney** (sop); [ac]**Randi Stene** (mez);
[ab]**Håkan Hagegård** (bar); [d]**Rut Tellefsen** (narr); [c]**Gothenburg Symphony Chorus and Orchestra /
Neeme Järvi**. DG Grieg Edition Ⓟ 437 519-2GH (61 minutes: DDD: 6/93).

Grieg Haugtussa, Op. 67. Two brown eyes, Op. 5 No. 1. I love but thee, Op. 5 No. 3. A swan,
Op. 25 No. 2. With a waterlily, Op. 25 No. 4. Hope, Op. 26 No. 1. Spring, Op. 33 No. 2. Beside
the stream, Op. 33 No. 5. From Monte Pincio, Op. 39 No. 1. Six Songs, Op. 48. Spring showers,
Op. 49 No. 6. While I wait, Op. 60 No. 3. Farmyard song, Op. 61 No. 3. **Anne Sofie von Otter**
(mez); **Bengt Forsberg** (pf). DG Grieg Anniversary Edition Ⓟ 437 521-2GH (68 minutes: DDD:
6/93). Texts and translations included. Recorded 1992. *Gramophone classical 100. Gramophone
Award Winner 1993. Gramophone Editor's choice. Selected by Sounds in Retrospect.*   ⊙⊙⊙
With performances like this, Grieg in his celebratory year emerged as a first-rank composer in this
genre. Anne Sofie von Otter is at the peak of her powers, glorying in this repertoire which she
obviously loves and knows intimately. Take the *Haugtussa* cycle, which Grieg considered his greatest
achievement in this sphere of writing. Von Otter projects her imagination of the visionary herd-girl
with absolute conviction. She is no less successful in the German settings that follow. The sad depths
of *One day, my thought* from Six Songs, Op. 48 also set memorably by Wolf in his *Spanish Songbook*,
the hopelessness of Goethe's *The time of roses* (Op. 48 No. 5), a setting of great beauty are
encompassed with unfettered ease, but so are the lighter pleasures of *Lauf der Welt*. Even the familiar
A dream (Op. 48 No. 6) emerges as new in von Otter's daringly big-boned reading. Throughout, her
readings are immeasurably enhanced by the imaginative playing by Bengt Forsberg. They breathe
fresh life into *A swan* and in the almost as familiar *With a waterlily*, another superb Ibsen setting, the
questing spirit expressed in the music is marvellously captured by the performers. And there are more
pleasures to come. A superb account of *Hope*, a wistful, sweetly voiced and played account of *Spring*,
the charming, teasing *While I wait* and a deeply poetic reading of the justly renowned *From Monte
Pincio* are just three more definitive interpretations. This should be regarded as a 'must' for any
collector of songs, indeed a collector of any kind.

Further listening ...
...Funeral March in memory of Rikard Nordraak. In Autumn, Op. 11. Old Norwegian Romance
with Variations, Op. 51. Symphony in C minor. **Gothenberg Symphony Orchestra / Neeme Järvi**.
DG 427 321-2GH (6/89).   ⊙
...Holberg Suite, Op. 40. *Coupled with* **Barber** Adagio for Strings, Op. 11. **Bloch** Concerto grosso
No. 1[a]. **Puccini** Crisantemi (arr. string orchestra). [a]**Irit Rob** (pf); **Israel Chamber Orchestra /
Yoav Talmi**. Chandos CHAN8593 (8/88).
...Two Melodies, Op. 53. Two Nordic Melodies, Op. 63. Two Elegiac Melodies, Op. 34. *Coupled with
works by* **Elgar, Sibelius, Tchaikovsky** and **Dvořák** **Serenata of London / Barry Wilde**. IMP
Classics PCD1108 (2/95).
...Cello Sonata in A minor, Op. 36. *Coupled with* **Chopin** Cello Sonata in G minor, Op. 65. **Claude
Starck** (vc); **Riccardo Requejo** (pf). Claves CD50-0703 (3/87).
...Lyric Pieces – Book 5, Op. 54; Book 6, Op. 57; Book 7, Op. 62. **Peter Katin** (pf). Unicorn-
Kanchana Souvenir UKCD2034 (11/90).
...Lyric Pieces – Book 8, Op. 65; Book 9, Op. 68; Book 10, Op. 71. **Peter Katin** (pf). Unicorn-
Kanchana Souvenir UKCD2035 (2/91).

Francis Grier

New review

Grier Let us invoke Christ. Three Short Anthems. Day after day[a]. Salve regina[b]. Three Devotions to Christ our Redeemer[b]. The Voice of my Beloved. Dilectus meus mihi. Thou, O God, art praised in Sion[b]. [a]**James Bowman** (alto); **Rodolfus Choir / Ralph Allwood** with [b]**Christopher Hughes** (org). Herald Ⓕ HAVPCD177 (65 minutes: DDD: 7/96). Recorded 1994.

Written as it was for the monumental acoustic of St Paul's Cathedral, it is all too easy to hear *Let us invoke Christ* as a brilliant piece of writing for a specific aural effect. Here in the drier (but still gloriously warm) acoustic of Eton College Chapel the wonderful luminosity of Grier's writing is all the more sharply focused. It is a stunningly effective anthem which finds, in the Rodolfus Choir, sincere and wholly committed advocates. When they first appeared on disc (on the recording listed below) their technical expertise and musical integrity was hugely impressive. For all their relative youth this is a choir who at the hands of a master choir trainer – and Ralph Allwood is indisputably one of the very best – can produce outstanding things. And here they do. Grier's musical language is at once eclectic and, in its devotional intensity, singularly personal. An unusually disparate range of musical and spiritual influences can be identified in these 12 lovely anthems, with the time Grier spent in India studying music, theology and meditation finding expression in the evocative *Day after day*, settings of the Bengali poet Rabindranath Tagore, with James Bowman an intensely moving soloist. But whatever style or tradition Grier celebrates, he does so with unfailing conviction and is magnificently served by these outstanding performances.

Further listening ...

...A Sequence for the Ascension. **Rodolfus Choir / Ralph Allwood** with **Francis Grier** (org). Herald HAVPCD158 (7/93).

Charles Griffes

Griffes Piano Sonata in F sharp minor.
Ives Piano Sonata No. 1.
Sessions Piano Sonata No. 2. **Peter Lawson** (pf). Virgin Classics Ⓕ VC7 59316-2 (72 minutes: DDD: 2/94). Recorded 1991. *Gramophone Editor's choice.*

Critical acclaim greeted Peter Lawson's first volume of American piano sonatas (reviewed in the Collections section; refer to the Index to Reviews) which contains Barber, Carter, Copland and the *Three-page Sonata* by Ives. It says much about the standing of the American piano sonata in the instrument's twentieth-century repertory that there are now so many fine recordings on offer. With this second record, too, Lawson has plenty of competition (some listed below) and, once again, he is well ahead. The Griffes Sonata is the composer's late masterpiece. Landes made an impressive case for this work and, like Lawson, has absolutely no technical problems. However, the way Lawson controls the soft textures which appear like oases between outbursts of passion is preferable; and the passacaglia texture in the final section is admirably paced. There is strong competition in the Ives from Joanna MacGregor. Lawson, too, is outstanding. He manages the same frenzy with greater control and gets the epic moments, such as the last movement, absolutely right. Even in the Sessions there is tough competition – from Barry David Salwen on an all-Sessions CD. Once again, there is not much to choose between two excellent performances with similar qualities of fidelity to the composer's intentions. What a great achievement to record two CDs of major sonatas and come up with virtually the best available performance of every one!

Additional recommendations ...

...Piano Sonata. Fantasy Pieces, Op. 6 – Barcarolle; Notturno; Scherzo. Three Tone-Pictures, Op. 5. **Macdowell** Piano Sonata No. 4 in E minor, Op. 59, "Keltic". **Garah Landes** (pf). Koch International Classics Ⓕ 37045-2 (66 minutes: DDD: 7/91).

...Piano Sonata. **Sessions** Piano Sonatas Nos. 1-3. Pages from a Diary. Five Pieces. Waltz. **Barry David Salwen** (pf). Koch International Classics Ⓕ 37106-2 (74 minutes: DDD: 12/92).

Further listening ...

...Songs – Am Kreuzweg wird begraben. An den Wind. Auf geheimem Waldespfade. Auf ihrem Grab. Das ist ein Brausen und Heulen. Das sterbende Kind. Elfe. Meeres Stille. Mein Herz ist wie die dunkle Nacht. Mit schwarzen Segeln. Des Müden Abendlied. Nachtlied. So halt' ich endlich dich umfangen. Der träumende See. Wo ich bin, mich rings umdunkelt. Wohl lag ich einst in Gram und Schmerz. Zwei Könige sassen auf Orkadal. *Coupled with* **Ives** Du bist wie eine Blume. Feldeinsamkeit. Frühlingslied. Gruss. Ich grolle nicht. Ilmenau. Marie. Minnelied. Rosamunde. Rosenzweige. Ton. Weil' auf mir. Widmung. Wiegenlied; **MacDowell** Drei Lieder, Op. 11. Zwei Leider, Op. 12. **Thomas Hampson** (bar); **Armen Guzelimian** (pf). Teldec 9031-72168-2.

Ferde Grofé

Suggested listening ...

...Grand Canyon Suite. *Coupled with* **Gershwin** Porgy and Bess – A Symphonic Picture. **Detroit Symphony Orchestra / Antál Dorati.** Decca Ovation 430 712-2DM (8/91).

...Grand Canyon Suite. Mississipi. *Coupled with* **Herbert** Cello Concerto No. 2 in E minor, Op. 30[a]. [a]**Georges Miquelle** (vc); **Eastman-Rochester Orchestra / Howard Hanson.** Mercury Living Presence 434 355-2MM (66 minutes: ADD).

Nicolas de Grigny

Suggested listening ...

...Premier Livre d'Orgue[a]. *Coupled with* **Charpentier** O salutaris hostia, H261[b]. **Lully** Domine salvum[b]. [b]**Delphine Collot,** [b]**Emmanuelle Gall,** [b]**Françoise Masset** (sops); [b]**Sophie Vatillon** (bass viol); [a]**Sagittarius Vocal Ensemble;** [a]**André Isoir** (org). Erato 4509-91722-2 (10/93).

Heinz Karl Gruber

Suggested listening ...

...Der rote Teppich wird ausgerollt[c]. Violin Concerto No. 1[ac]. Sechs Episoden (aus einer unterbrochenen Chronik), Op. 20[b]. Four Pieces, Op. 11[a]. Bossa Nova, Op. 21e[ab]. [a]**Ernst Kovacic** (vn); [b]**Paul Crossley** (pf); [c]**London Sinfonietta / Heinz Karl Gruber.** Largo 5124 (9/94).

Carlos Guastavino

New review

Guastavino Santa Fé antiguo. Bailecito. Santa Fé para llorar. Guitar Sonatas Nos. 1-3. Tres Cantos populares[a]. Jeromita Linares[b]. **Maria Isabel Siewers** (gtr); [b]**Stamitz Quartet** ([a]Bohuslav Matoušek, Josef Kekula, vns; Jan Peřuška, va; Vladimír Leixner, vc). ASV Ⓕ CDDCA933 (75 minutes: DDD: 2/96). Recorded 1995.

Carlos Guastavino is one of those composers whose unswerving belief that there are still plenty of good tunes to be written in C major caused him to be brushed aside by the tide of the avant-garde, not least in his own country. This amiable and energetic man lives alone and lives to write only what pleases him. He does not play the guitar but, as a South American, he can scarcely escape from its sounds, or from absorbing a goodly measure of how its music should be – nor does he wish to. Maria Isabel Siewers, also Argentinian, is his friend and collaborator, one who understands well that the music of their country is Hispanic, but 'spoken' with a demonstrative Italian accent. This is just as true in the three formally disciplined sonatas as it is in the overtly folk-musical items and in *Jeromita Linares*, the name of an old lady whom Guastavino remembers fondly from his childhood. The performances by Siewers and her colleagues, and the quality of the recording, should boost the impulse which one hopes may keep Guastavino going for another decade or so. If you're willing to be seduced (in the nicest possible way), open your ears to this love-motivated music.

Guastavino Cuatro Canciones Argentinas. Cuatro Canciones Coloniales. Piececitos. Cita. Se equivicó la paloma. Siete Canciones. La rosa y el sauce. Pueblito, mi pueblo. **Ulises Espaillat** (ten); **Pablo Zinger** (pf). New Albion Ⓕ NA058CD (49 minutes: DDD: 1/94). Texts and translations included. Recorded 1992.

The songs of Guastavino have tunes that can be remembered and hummed, verse structure with beginning and end, and sentiments that are often frankly nostalgic. The writing for voice is that of a composer who sings in imagination as he writes, and so it lies comfortably, encouraging expressiveness without recourse to modernist extremes of vocal range or anti-vocal intervals and dynamics. Ulises Espaillat, a tenor from the Dominican Republic, takes due advantage: we hear a voice which can spend quite a high proportion of the time singing pleasantly at a *mezzo forte* in the upper-middle register where his tone is at its most attractive. He catches the dreamy, midday atmosphere of *Cita*, the affectionate longing of *Pueblito, mi pueblo* and makes a lovely effect in that most haunting of songs, *Se equivicó la paloma*. He is well accompanied by Pablo Zinger, and the recorded sound is clear and well-balanced.

Additional recommendation ...

...Romance del Plata[ab]. Three Romances[ab]. Bailecito[ab]. Gato[ab]. Llanura[ab]. Se equivicó la paloma[ab]. La Siesta[a]. Presencias[b]. [a]**Hector Moreno,** [b]**Norberto Capelli** (pfs). Marco Polo Ⓕ 8 223462 (66 minutes: DDD: 5/94).

Sofia Gubaidulina

Gubaidulina Chaconne. Piano Sonata. Musical Toys. Introitus: Concerto for Piano and Chamber Orchestra[a]. **Andreas Haefliger** (pf); [a]**North German Radio Philharmonic Orchestra / Bernhard Klee.** Sony Classical Ⓕ SK53960 (72 minutes: DDD: 5/95). Recorded 1993.   Ⓖ

This is an ideal disc for listeners who admire Gubaidulina's recent music and wonder where she started from. The earlier works may be less 'polystylistic' than those of her near-contemporary Alfred Schnittke, but there is a distinctive pluralism to be heard which makes her ability to give these compositions an unmistakable coherence all the more remarkable. The *Chaconne* (1962) is a student piece in which coherence is put at risk by a rather episodic form. What compensates is the energy of invention, the presence of a powerful musical imagination which makes the Shostakovich of that vintage seem relatively conventional. The Sonata (1965) has a dangerously diffuse first movement, but a superb, darkly eloquent *Adagio* and an incisive finale rescue the piece and make the overall experience a memorable one. The echoes of Prokofiev do nothing to dilute Gubaidulina's originality. After the collection of delightfully direct and far-from-lightweight pieces for children entitled *Musical Toys* (1969), *Introitus* (1978) offers a characteristically quirky mixture of the ritualistic and the rhapsodic. Scale figures may be made to do more thematic work than a composition of this emotional range can bear without strain, yet the work's striking textures and approachably radical variety of harmonic contexts ensures that, in the end, all the diverse elements balance out. Andreas Haefliger responds wholeheartedly to Gubaidulina's clangorous and frequently demanding piano writing. The solo works are very resonantly recorded, but there is no distortion and the immediacy of the sound seems apt.

New review

Gubaidulina Silenzio[abc]. In Erwartung[de]. De profundis[a]. Classical Accordion Sonata, "Et expecto"[a]. [a]**Geir Draugsvoll** (accordion); [b]**Arne Balk Møller** (vn); [c]**Henrik Brendstrup** (vc); [d]**Rascher Saxophone Quartet;** [e]**Krumata Percussion Ensemble.** BIS Ⓕ CD710 (69 minutes: DDD: 11/95). Recorded 1994.

Silenzio is a Webern-like play on silence rather than a full-frontal assault, with the accordion blocking any fuller articulation from the violin and cello until a long, slow finale which ends alarmingly with the accordion's malignant lower-register heavings. The judderings and note flappings that launch *De profundis* are even more terrifying, and that's only the start; thereafter Geir Draugsvoll takes us on a chastening and never merely virtuosic tour of the accordion's full potential, realized by Gubaidulina in close association with the master of the instrument, Friedrich Lips. The wonder of it is that she could have found, and extracted, fascination enough to stretch to two full scale solos. *Et expecto*, though it begins as an exercise in Schnittke-like polystylism, turns out to be the later composition, proceeds still deeper than *De profundis* and makes a perfect companion-piece; both can be rewardingly absorbed at a single sitting. The most recent work, *In Erwartung*, explores the mysteries of another ensemble rich in potential, namely saxophone quartet and an exotic array of percussion. First impressions are of an all-too-common *lingua franca* in contemporary writing for percussion, but as always there turns out to be an ongoing purpose behind Gubaidulina's increasingly rich mosaic of rhythmic and melodic patterns. The sound quality is as hypnotizingly refined as the performance.

New review

Gubaidulina In croce[a]. Seven Last Words[b]. Five Pieces, "Silenzio"[c]. [bc]**Kathrin Rabus** (vn); [ac]**Maria Kliegel** (vc); [ac]**Elsbeth Moser** (accordion); [b]**Camerata Transsylvanica / György Selmeczi.** Naxos Ⓢ 8 553557 (67 minutes: DDD: 6/96). Recorded 1995.

A CD of music for the Russian push-button accordion by a woman composer in her mid sixties might seem an interesting novelty, a distinctive contribution from an idiosyncratic voice. Yet this disc marks rather the consolidation of a performing tradition in miniature. The Swiss accordion player Elsbeth Moser played in the first Western performance of the best-known piece here – the *Seven Last Words* – and this is at least the third recording of the work. The current catalogue can also boast several versions of *In croce* in its original scoring for cello and organ. Those unfamiliar with Gubaidulina's distinctive sound-world should start with the *Seven Last Words* which has something of the immediacy of appeal of her violin concerto, *Offertorium*. In its revised form, *In croce* is archetypal Gubaidulina in its attempt to create a meaningful narrative from opposing elements: folk music and art music, the human and the divine, Ligeti and Shostakovich. On the one hand a volatile, unstable chromaticism, on the other the reassurance of melody and traditional triadic harmonies. The preoccupation with exploring the character of single notes, whether rich and vibrant or tentative and trembling, makes her music sound different from, and more ascetic than, Schnittke's. Often her invention is spun from threads fined down almost to vanishing point. But however unorthodox the means, there are obvious links with the Soviet past. Behind the stylistic juxtapositions there lurks an authentic Shostakovichian gloom. There is a certain steely cool about the music-making here, a tendency to avoid the disturbing excesses that some might see as Gubaidulina's idiom, but, with Maria Kliegel once again proving herself a cellist of real distinction, the disc would be worth acquiring at twice the price.

Gubaidulina String Quartet No. 2.

Kurtág String Quartet No. 1, Op. 1. Hommage à Milhály András, Op. 13. Officium breve in memoriam Andreae Szervánzky, Op. 28.

Lutosławski String Quartet. **Arditti Quartet** (Irvine Arditti, David Alberman, vns; Levine
Andrade, va; Rohan de Saram, vc). Auvidis Montaigne Ⓕ MO789007 (72 minutes: DDD: 4/92).
Recorded 1990.

Recent political developments ensure that Sofia Gubaidulina's country of birth is given in the notes,
not as Russia, but as the Tatar Autonomous People's Republic. Autonomy – the need for a personal
tone of voice – is a quality all three of these eastern European composers well understand.
Lutosławski's quartet (1964) came at a crucial time in his development, as the first work to relate his
new technique of aleatory counterpoint (in which the pitches but not necessarily the rhythms are
prescribed) to a traditional, abstract genre. Compared to the best of his later works the quartet is
perhaps too long-drawn-out, but this highly expressive and strongly disciplined performance makes
an excellent case for it. Alongside the Lutosławski the three works by György Kurtág sound
remarkably intense and concentrated, yet with a lyricism that prevents their evident austerity from
growing merely arid, and which makes the reference to a tonal melody in the *Officium breve* seem
natural as well as touching. The world of consonant harmony is also evoked by Gubaidulina, not as
an expression of regret for the irretrievable past but as a way of extending her own essentially modern
language. There is a special sense of personal certainty and confidence about all the music on this
well-recorded disc. It needs no special pleading, but the commanding authority of the Arditti
Quartet's performance is still something to marvel at.

New review

Gubaidulina In croce[a]. Ten Preludes (Etudes).
Ustvolskaya Grand (Bolshoi) Duet[b]. **Maya Beiser** (vc); [a]**Dorothy Papadakos** (org); [b]**Christopher
Oldfather** (pf). Koch International Classics Ⓕ 37258-2 (60 minutes: DDD: 11/95). Recorded
1993-4.

Gubaidulina's ambitious *In croce* has the makings of a masterpiece. Few listeners can fail to be riveted
by the progress from an ear-tickling start, with the organ doodling seraphically around a high E and
the cello struggling to break free of the lower register (hints of several later Schnittke works to come),
to a semi-notated central conflict and on to some of the most inspired yet simple pages in
contemporary Russian music – a chromatic weave of newly strengthened cello versus impotent organ
as intense as anything in Tavener's *The Protecting Veil*; characteristically, Gubaidulina can hardly
leave it at that. Beiser's full, rich tone is well to the fore in the recording – it has to be, given the organ's
fortissimo outburst half-way through – and being virtually alongside the cello in the Preludes helps us
to come closer to this emotional, rigorously structured investigation of the instrument's range and
techniques; there is astonishing resonance in the bottom register for the *Legato-Staccato* Prelude
(No. 2), and the ricocheting No. 4 is sensual sound made palpable. Alas that after such near-ideal
performances Gallina Ustvolskaya, Gubaidulina's senior by 12 years, and a tenderly regarded pupil
of Shostakovich, should have such a poor deal: not in terms of the choice of work, for *Grand
(Bolshoi) Duet* can hold its own against the stranger meeting of *In croce*. What Beiser and her pianist,
Christopher Oldfather, have done is to go through the score virtually striking out the more extreme
dynamics; and since the piece depends on its relentless smatterings of *ffff* throughout the first four
movements in order for the (mostly) quiescent finale to make its effect, the point is lost, though Beiser
offers some highly expressive legato playing in the long fifth movement.

Gubaidulina Jetzt immer Schnee[ad]. Perception[bc]. [a]**Stella Kleindienst** (sop); [b]**Siegfried Lorenz** (bar);
[c]**Leonid Stasov** (spkr); [d]**Netherlands Chamber Choir; Schoenberg Ensemble / Reinbert de Leeuw.**
Philips Ⓕ 442 531-2PH (77 minutes: DDD: 4/95). Texts and translations included. Recorded
1992-3.   Ⓖ

Sofia Gubaidulina has an extraordinary gift for dissolving the materials of music into her own spirit-
world and re-shaping them there so that mysteries seem to speak. In some hands her rustling
tremolando strings, hieratic gongs, grumbling double bassoon and whooping solo voice might sound
no better than avant-garde kitsch; in her 1993 song-cycle *Jetzt immer Schnee* ("Now Always Snow")
the same effects are unmistakable tokens of spiritual ecstasy. It's not exactly an uplifting ecstasy. The
verses are by Gennadi Aigi, a poet Gubaidulina has known since student days, and his imagery is
predominantly bleak, with occasional pale beams of redemptive light. Her already familiar
instrumental works are so strongly charged with symbolism you might think the presence of texts
would hem her in. Not a bit of it. She moves around in her spiritually charged Lutosławskian idiom
with complete assurance, and from the shimmering opening to the final dissolving into the ether *Jetzt
immer Schnee* is a compelling experience. Mysteries speak to us too in *Perception*, composed ten years
earlier to German poems by Gubaidulina's friend Francisco Tanzer. This is the source-work for her
symphony *Stimmen ... Verstummen*, and "Voices fall silent" is indeed the final image of the texts. The
13 sections – nine poems and four sound-interludes for the strings – suggest a similar design to the
symphony, and many of the instrumental textures are shared between the two works. Read the texts
in isolation and you might think them about as profound as the musings of John Lennon and Yoko
Ono, and there are times when Gubaidulina's charisma is rather more obvious than her
craftsmanship. But immerse yourself in the music and you will surely doubt neither the poet's nor the
composer's resourcefulness. Soprano Stella Kleindienst and baritone Siegfried Lorenz sing with
marvellous sensitivity and the strings of the Schoenberg Ensemble sound entirely engrossed in the
music. The same can be said of the Netherlands Chamber Choir in *Jetzt immer Schnee*. If these works

feel like the finest of Gubaidulina, that may be because the performances and recording quality are far and away superior to those on other CDs of her work.

Further listening ...

...Symphony "Stimmen ... Verstummen". Stufen. **Royal Stockholm Philharmonic Orchestra / Gennadi Rozhdestvensy.** Chandos CHAN9183 (8/93).

...Concerto for Bassoon and Low Strings[a]. Concordanza. Detto II[b]. [a]**Harri Ahmas** (bn); [b]**Ilkka Pälli** (vc); **Lahti Chamber Ensemble / Osmo Vänskä.** BIS CD636 (6/94).

...Pro et Contra. *Coupled with* **Firsova** Cassandra, Op. 60. **BBC National Orchestra of Wales / Tadaaki Otaka.** BIS CD668 (11/94).

...Allegro rustico. Sounds of the Forest. *Coupled with works by* **Feld, Taktakishvili, Amirov** and **Martinů** Leslie Newman (fl); **Amanda Hurton** (pf). Cala CACD88026 (6/96). *See review in the Collections section; refer to the Index to Reviews.*

...Offertorium[a]. Hommage à T.S. Eliot[b]. [b]**Christine Whittlesey** (sop); [a]**Gidon Kremer,** [b]**Isabelle van Keulen** (vns); [b]**Tabea Zimmermann** (va); [b]**David Geringas** (vc); [b]**Alois Posch** (db); [b]**Eduard Brunner** (cl); [b]**Klaus Thunemann** (bn); [b]**Radovan Vlatkovic**(hn); [a]**Boston Symphony Orchestra / Charles Dutoit.** DG 427 336-2GH (9/89). **Ⓖ**

Francisco Guerau
Spanish mid 17th century-early 18th century

Suggested listening ...

...Poema harmonico – Canario; Marionas[b]. *Coupled with* **Murcia** Cumbés[b]. Giga[b]. **Mudarra** Tres libros de música en cifras para vihuela – Pavana de Alexandre; Fantasia que contrahaze la harpa en la manera de Ludovico[a]. **Milán** El Maestro – Pavana II[a]. **López** Fantasia[a]. **Narváez** Los seys libros del delphin – La canción del Emperador; Diferencias on "Guárdame las vacas"[a]. Paseavase el rey moro[a]. **Sanz** Instruccion de musica sobre la guitarra española – Canarios; Folías; Lantururú; Pavanas al ayre español[b]. **Sor** Thèmes variés et Douze Minuets, Op. 11 – Andante maestoso; Andante expressivo[b]. Introduction and Variations on a theme by Mozart, Op. 9[b]. **José Miguel Moreno** ([a]vihuela/[b]gtr). Glossa GCD920103 (8/95). ✐

Francisco Guerrero
Spanish 1528-1599

Suggested listening ...

...Sacrae Cantiones. **La Capella Reial de Catalunya; Hespèrion XX / Jordi Savall.** Auvidis Astrée E8766 (10/93). ✐

Louis-Gabriel Guillemain
French 1705-1770

Suggested listening ...

...Violin Sonata in A major, Op. 1 No. 4. *Coupled with works by* **Leclair, Mondonville, Duphly** and **J-B. Forqueray** Simon Standage (vn); **Lars Ulrik Mortensen** (hpd). Chandos CHAN0531 (6/93). ✐ *See review under Leclair; refer to the Index to Reviews.*

Jean Guillou
French 1930-

Suggested listening ...

...Toccata. *Coupled with* **P. Pierné** Pastorale. **Peeters** Suite, Op. 71. **Widor** Scherzo in E major, "La Chasse". **Malengreau** Symphonie de la Passion, Op. 20. **John Scott Whiteley** (org). Priory PRCD487 (2/96).

Alexandre Guilmant
French 1837-1911

Guilmant Organ Symphony No. 1 in D minor, Op. 42.
Poulenc Organ Concerto in G minor.
Widor Organ Symphony No. 5 in F minor, Op. 42 No. 1. **Ian Tracey** (org); **BBC Philharmonic Orchestra / Yan Pascal Tortelier.** Chandos Ⓕ CHAN9271 (80 minutes: DDD: 11/94). Played on the organ of Liverpool Cathedral. Recorded 1993. **ⒼⒼ**

As horoscope writers in some magazines might put it, with Yan Pascal Tortelier and the BBC Philharmonic in conjunction with Ian Tracey and the Liverpool Cathedral organ within the orbit of Chandos the earth is bound to move for you. And so it does. The Guilmant is one of those great spectaculars which thrives in just such a steamy acoustic environment, but Tortelier with his incisive, thrusting direction ensures that while there is vivid aural spectacle, musical integrity is preserved with quite remarkable clarity and co-ordination. The BBC Philharmonic are magnificent and Tracey plays this great hulking brute of an organ with a surety of touch which comes not only from years of intimate experience, but from a deep understanding of what is needed. As for the Poulenc, this is a splendid performance, combining high drama with spiritual intensity, but misplaced in these gargantuan Liverpudlian cavities. The sound is just too beefy – the timpani interjections during the *Allegro giocoso* (after 3'18") resound like *émigré* canons from the *1812* – and Poulenc's lightning changes of mood are largely masked by an all-enveloping acoustic. Tracey's true colours are shown off to the full in the Widor – and what an inspired piece of programme planning to include this famous solo organ symphony as the meat in the sandwich between works for organ and orchestra.

Manfred Gurlitt   German 1890-1972

New review

Gurlitt Wozzeck. **Roland Hermann** (bar) Wozzeck; **Celina Lindsley** (sop) Marie; **Anton Scharinger** (bass) Captain; **Jörg Gottschick** (bass) Drum-major; **Robert Wörle** (ten) Doctor; **Erich Wottrich** (ten) Andres; **Christiane Berggold** (mez) First Girl; **Reinhard Ginzel** (ten) Jew; **Regina Schudel** (sop) Solo Soprano; **Gabriele Schreckenbach** (mez) Old Woman, Solo Contralto; **RIAS Chamber Choir; Berlin Radio Children's Choir; Deutsches Symphony Orchestra, Berlin / Gerd Albrecht.** Capriccio Ⓟ 60 052 (74 minutes: DDD: 11/95). Notes, text and translation included. Recorded 1993.

Asked to name a single twentieth-century composition which demonstrates that a radical musical language can convey the full power and pathos of a universal dramatic subject, most of us would probably choose Berg's *Wozzeck*. Any other setting of the same text, and to less radical music, is likely to seem second best by a long way, especially if the composer is otherwise unknown. After all, Leoncavallo, who wrote the 'other' *Bohème*, is celebrated for a quite different theatre piece and, so far, no Gurlitt equivalent to *Pagliacci* has come to light. Manfred Gurlitt wrote his *Wozzeck* before Berg's was performed (in 1925), and the differences are all-pervading. Gurlitt lacked the creative self-confidence that led Berg to pare down the Büchner text to a minimum. In Gurlitt, the key line "Wir arme Leut" is an oft-repeated motto, and his reliance on *espressivo* vocal writing (though there is some speech) casts an aura of refinement around Marie, in particular, that is quite absent from Berg's stark yet heart-rending music. Gurlitt's tendency to grow expansive in relatively incidental episodes and, at the other extreme, his failure to link the 18 scenes together, create real problems of proportion and momentum. So the comparisons could continue. All the more important, then, to declare that even though Gurlitt is not Berg, the result is of great musical (and not just historical) interest. Whatever Gurlitt's other works may be like, Büchner inspired him to a score which, in its own late-romantic terms, is powerful and absorbing. The emotions are genuine, the expression direct and affecting, and this performance – despite a recording that gives too little focus to salient orchestral detail – is highly accomplished. A significant gap in our knowledge of inter-war German music has been filled.

Ivor Gurney   British 1890-1937

Suggested listening ...

...The Western Playland[b]. Ludlow and Teme[a]. *Coupled with* **Vaughan Williams** On Wenlock Edge[a]. [a]**Adrian Thompson** (ten); [b]**Stephen Varcoe** (bar); **Iain Burnside** (pf); **Delmé Quartet.** Hyperion CDA66385 (9/90).

...Sleep. Down by the salley gardens. Hawk and Buckle. *Coupled with works by* **Finzi, Milford, Farrar** and **Gill Ian Partridge** (ten); **Stephen Roberts** (bar); **Clifford Benson** (pf). Hyperion CDA66015 (9/91). *See review in the Collections section; refer to the Index to Reviews.*

Pavel Haas   Czechoslovakian 1899-1944

P. Haas String Quartets – No. 2, Op. 7, "From the Monkey Mountains"; No. 3, Op. 15. **Krása** String Quartet. **Hawthorne Quartet** (Ronan Lefkowitz, Si-Jing Huang, vns; Mark Ludwig, va; Sato Knudsen, vc). Decca Ⓟ 440 853-2DH (76 minutes: DDD: 3/94). Recorded 1993.
Gramophone Award Winner 1995. **Gramophone** *Editor's choice.*   ⒼⒼ

Pavel Haas and Hans Krása were both born in Czechoslovakia in 1899; both were influenced by the modern movement, including neo-classicism, jazz and 'the new tonality', and both entered Theresienstadt in 1941 to travel to their deaths (on the same day) three years later in the gas chambers of Auschwitz. Of all Janáček's pupils it was Haas who absorbed rather than merely imitated his ideas. Something of the master's aphoristic, questing manner remains, but other than that the Quartet represents the mature Haas. An air of tension pervades the three-movements, alternating passages of lyricism with tightly intertwining parts of harmonic complexity. Krása's Quartet also reveals a voice of exceptional talent. As a product of his studies with Zemlinsky its harmonic world leans more towards *fin de siècle* Vienna than his native homeland. The central movement contains a marvellous section of burlesque (very boulevardier in allure) on a theme from the overture to Smetana's *The Bartered Bride*, whilst the slow finale opens up a magical, almost mystical, twilight world that Zemlinsky himself would have been proud to have penned. Excellent performances and superb recording.

Further listening ...
...Wind Quintet, Op. 10. *Coupled with* **Foerster** Wind Quintet in D major, Op. 95. **Janáček**
Mládí[a]. **Aulos Wind Quintet;** [a]**Kurt Berger** (bass cl). Koch Schwann Musica Mundi 310051 (6/93).

Alois Hába   Czechoslovakian 1893-1973

Suggested listening ...
...The Mother. **Soloists; Prague National Theatre Chorus and Orchestra / Jiří Jirouš.** Supraphon
10 8258-2 (1/94).

Patrick Hadley   British 1899-1973

Suggested listening ...
...The Trees so High[a]. *Coupled with* **Sainton** The Island. [a]**David Wilson-Johnson** (bar);
Philharmonia [a]**Chorus and Orchestra / Matthias Bamert.** Chandos CHAN9181 (10/93).

Johann Christian Haeffner   German/Swedish 1759-1833

Suggested listening ...
...Electra. **Soloists; Stockholm Radio Chorus; Drottningholm Baroque Ensemble / Thomas Schuback.**
Caprice CAP22030 (7/94).

Georg Haentzschel   German 1907-1992

Suggested listening ...
...Film Scores: Via Mala. Annelie. Münchhausen. Robinson soll nicht sterben. Emil und die
Detektive. Meine Kinder und ich. Hotel Adlon. **Cologne Radio Orchestra / Emmerich Smola.**
Capriccio 10 400 (8/94).

Reynaldo Hahn   Venezuelan/French 1875-1947

Suggested listening ...
...Le Bal de Béatrice d'Este – ballet suite. *Coupled with* **Poulenc** Sinfonietta. Aubade[a]. [a]**Julian
Evans** (pf); **New London Orchestra / Ronald Corp.** Hyperion CDA66347 (10/89).

Naji Hakim   Lebanese/French 1955-

New review
Hakim The Embrace of Fire. Mariales. Expressions – Nos. 16-18, 20, 23, 25-28. Rhapsody[a]. **Naji
Hakim,** [a]**Marie-Bernadette Dufourcet** (org). Priory Ⓕ PRCD465 (57 minutes: DDD: 6/96). Played
on the Cavaillé-Coll organ of the Sacré-Coeur, Paris. Recorded 1993.
New review
Hakim Saul de Tarse[a]. Vexilla Regis prodeunt[b]. Missa Resurrectionis[c]. Le tombeau d'Olivier
Messiaen[d]. [c]**Kerstin Pettersson** (sop); [a]**Thomas Annmo** (ten); [a]**Morten Ernst Lassen** (bar); [a]**Lars
Hedström** (bass); [a]**Jacques Merienne** (spkr); [bd]**Naji Hakim** (org); [b]**Schola Cantorum Scaniensis,
Malmö / Peter Wallin;** [a]**Lund Academic Choir and Orchestra / Fredrik Malmberg.** Priory
Ⓕ PRCD545 (75 minutes: DDD: 6/96). Texts and translations included. Recorded 1994-5.
Naji Hakim is an international organist whose works have won a plethora of prizes; he succeeded
Messiaen at the Trinité in 1993 and he has become increasingly in demand as a soloist, appearing at
the Proms in 1995. The Messiaen connection is at its most obvious – deliberately so – in *Le tombeau
d'Olivier Messiaen,* but Hakim was a pupil of Langlais, which also shows. He was born in Beirut but
his training was in Paris. This French tradition was clearly the inevitable one for an organist-composer
of such remarkable fluency and natural musicianship. Like Messiaen he uses religious programmes but
in a more spontaneous, often improvisational way. *The Embrace of Fire* contains many original
textures, especially in the second movement which is alarmingly realistic. *Mariales* is a useful set of five
elementary pieces and *Expressions* are for manuals only. *Rhapsody,* based on various popular tunes, is
a rare contribution to the genre of organ duet, played here with the composer's wife, Marie-Bernadette
Dufourcet. Hakim gets so much activity into his solo pieces that it may be hard to hear why two players
are needed. The first and last movements are a comedy of exaggeration driven by sheer physical
exuberance – but the setting of the spiritual *Go, tell it on the Mountain* (track 21) is charming.
      In most of these organ works the French inheritance is ever present, so it is interesting to see what
Hakim does away with the organ, or when he is combining it with other instruments. The half-hour

oratorio, *Saul de Tarse* (sung in French: English text provided), complete with narrator, soloists, chorus and orchestra, is an obviously sincere and resourceful delivery of the main events in the life of St Paul. Hakim's approach is especially vivid in choruses such as the one celebrating the resurrection and overall he makes a surprisingly fresh fusion of influences ranging through Stravinsky, Messiaen, Bernstein and folk music. *Saul* should be quite a discovery for cathedral festivals. Kerstin Pettersson is a splendid advocate of Hakim's *Missa Resurrectionis* for high soprano solo. There is a lot of interest in both these CDs. The Cavaillé-Coll at the Sacré-Coeur in Paris sounds magnificent and the acoustic in the Trinité is flattering for the vocal music; all well recorded.

Fromental Halévy
French 1799-1862

Suggested listening ...
...La Juive. **Soloists; Ambrosian Singers; Philharmonia Orchestra / Antonio de Almeida.** Philips 420 190-2PH3 (11/89).

Cristóbal Halffter
Spanish 1930-

Suggested listening ...
...Variations on the theme eSACHERe. *Coupled with works by* **Berio, Lutosławski, Dutilleux, Beck, Henze, Fortner, Ginastera, Boulez, Britten, K. Huber** and **Holliger** Patrick and Thomas Demenga (vcs); **Cello Ensemble / Jürg Wyttenbach.** ECM New Series 445 234-2 (8/95).

Haflidi Hallgrimsson
Icelandic 1941-

Suggested listening ...
...Syrpa. *Coupled with works by* **N. Hayes, Weir, Finnissy, G. Jackson, S. Harrison, Crane, A. Fisher** and **Skempton** Tapestry. British Music Label BML012 (12/95). *See review in the Collections section; refer to the Index to Reviews.*

Gerre Hancock
American 1934-

Suggested listening ...
...Jessica. *Coupled with works by* **Shemaria, J. Nelson, Babbitt, Van Vliet, Wheeler, Zappa, Stravinsky** and **London** Meridian Arts Ensemble. Channel Classics Channel Crossings CCS8195 (4/96). *See review in the Collections section; refer to the Index to Reviews.* Ⓖ

George Frederic Handel
German-British 1685-1759

New review

Handel Organ Concertos: Op. 4, HWV289-94 – No. 1 in G major; No. 2 in B flat major; No. 3 in G minor; No. 4 in F major; No. 5 in F major; No. 6 in B flat major; Op. 7, HWV306-11 – No. 7 in B flat major; No. 8 in A major; No. 9 in B flat major; No. 10 in D minor; No. 11 in G minor; No. 12 in B flat major; No. 13 in F major, "Cuckoo and the Nightingale", HWV295; No. 14 in A major, HWV296; No. 15 in D minor, HWV304; No. 16 in F major, HWV305*a*. **Rudolf Ewerhart** (org); **Collegium Aureum.** Deutsche Harmonia Mundi Ⓜ 05472 77246-2 (three discs: 208 minutes: ADD: 3/93). 🖉 Recorded 1965-7.

In the 1960s Collegium Aureum embarked on a pioneering series of recordings played on original instruments. Around the same time that these recordings were made Nikolaus Harnoncourt was creating his own ideas of authenticity with the Vienna Concentus Musicus for Telefunken, and the results were wholly different. Harnoncourt sought to produce bright, abrasive sounds, whereas Collegium Aureum's performances are much more like those on modern instruments. Here is a complete set of the organ concertos on three discs, 16 of them, including all six each of Opp. 4 and 7, the *Cuckoo and the Nightingale* and the other three most frequently played works – in A major, F major and D minor. Rudolf Ewerhart is the excellent soloist. He plays four different instruments: the baroque organ at Körbecke, Westfalen, the Gabler in Weingarten, the Rieppe in Ottobeuren and an aurally fascinating cabinet organ in the Geertekerk, Utrecht. It is the organ colouring, vividly recorded, that dominates these performances, although Collegium Aureum, playing freshly yet sonorously, are well in the picture. The 1960s sound is smoothly and realistically transferred to CD, making this set a pleasure to listen to.

...Op. 4 Nos. 1-6. No. 14. **Simon Preston** (org); **The English Concert / Trevor Pinnock.** Archiv
Produktion Ⓕ 413 465-2AH2 (two discs: 90 minutes: DDD: 12/84). 🖉
...Op. 7 Nos. 7-12. Nos. 13 and 15. **Simon Preston** (org); **The English Concert / Trevor Pinnock.**
Archiv Produktion Ⓕ 413 468-2AH2 (two discs: 108 minutes: DDD: 1/85). 🖉 ⒼⒼ
...Op. 4 Nos. 1-6. Op. 7 Nos. 7-12. **chamber orchestra / Karl Richter** (org). Teldec Ⓑ 4509 97900-2
(two discs: 108 minutes: ADD: 5/96). *See review in the Collections section; refer to the Index to
Reviews.*

Handel Concerti grossi, Op. 3. **Tafelmusik / Jeanne Lamon.** Sony Classical Vivarte Ⓕ SK52553
(60 minutes: DDD: 7/93). 🖉 Recorded 1991. *Gramophone Editor's choice.*
This is a fine issue impressive both for its stylistic fluency and its infectious response to Handel's
music which could not conceivably disappoint anyone. Tafelmusik play only the six concertos of
which Handel's authorship is undisputed. Goodman (listed below) further included the Concerto in
F major (No. 4b) which, though not by Handel, is an attractive piece in its own right. Having said
that, it is the Sony version which, in respect of finesse and vitality, has the edge over all the
competition. Where Tafelmusik scores is in the sheer virtuosity of its playing and the easy
gracefulness of its phrasing. Strong accents are not over emphasized and, though vigorous, there is
nothing aggressive in this approach to the music. Tafelmusik include a plucked string instrument
among their continuo colloquium; they have large reinforcements at the top and bottom of the string
texture and the performances have great radiance. The disc is beautifully recorded and lucidly
documented.
...Op. 3. Op. 6. **Academy of St Martin in the Fields / Sir Neville Marriner.** Decca Serenata Ⓜ 444
532-2DM3 (three discs: 221 minutes: ADD).
...Op. 3. Op. 6. **Vienna Concentus Musicus / Nikolaus Harnoncourt.** Teldec Ⓑ 4509 95500-2 (four
discs: 237 minutes: ADD/DDD: 2/96).
...**English Baroque Soloists / John Eliot Gardiner.** Erato Ⓜ 2292-45981-2 (60 minutes: DDD). 🖉
...**The English Concert / Trevor Pinnock** (hpd). Archiv Produktion Ⓕ 413 727-2AH (57 minutes:
DDD: 3/85). 🖉
...**Brandenburg Consort / Roy Goodman.** Hyperion Ⓕ CDA66633 (77 minutes: DDD: 6/93). 🖉

Handel Concerti grossi, Op. 6. **The English Concert / Trevor Pinnock.** Archiv Produktion
Ⓕ 410 897/9-2AH (three discs: Oas. 42, 61 and 58 minutes: DDD: 5/84, 6/85 and 8/85). 🖉
From 2742 002 (11/82). ⒼⒼ
410 897-2AH – No. 1 in G major; No. 2 in F major; No. 3 in E minor; No. 4 in A minor.
410 898-2AH – No. 5 in D major; No. 6 in G minor; No. 7 in B flat major; No. 8 in C minor.
410 899-2AH – No. 9 in F major; No. 10 in D minor; No. 11 in A major; No. 12 in B minor.
Handel's 12 *Concerti grossi*, Op. 6 have from four to six movements and are mostly in *da chiesa* form,
i.e. without dance movements. They were written within one month in the autumn of 1739 (an average
of two movements per day!) and when a great composer is thus carried on the tide of urgent
inspiration it usually shows, as it does here in the flow of felicitous invention and memorable tune-
smithing. The range of musical idioms used throughout is impressive and to them all Handel imparts
his own indelible and unmistakable stamp. Trevor Pinnock's account contains much that is satisfying:
polished ensemble, effectively judged tempos, a natural feeling for phrase, and a buoyancy of spirit
which serves Handel's own robust musical language very well. Crisp attack, a judicious application of
appoggiaturas and tasteful embellishment further enhance these lively performances. Pinnock varies
the continuo colour by using organ and harpsichord and also includes Handel's autograph (though
not printed) oboe parts for Concertos Nos. 1, 2, 5 and 6; where they occur a bassoon is sensibly added
to fulfil the customary three-part wind texture of the period. Recorded sound is clear and captures
well the warm sonorities of the instruments.
...Nos. 1-12. **Montreal I Musici / Yuli Turovsky.** Chandos Ⓕ CHAN9004/6 (three discs: 163 minutes:
DDD: 9/92).
...Nos. 1-6. **Boston Baroque / Martin Pearlman.** Telarc Ⓕ CD80253 (76 minutes: DDD: 10/92). 🖉
...Nos. 1-12. **Handel and Haydn Society Orchestra / Christopher Hogwood.** L'Oiseau-Lyre Ⓕ 436
845-2OH3 (three discs: 157 minutes: DDD: 8/93). 🖉 Ⓖ

Handel The Water Music, HWV348-50. Music for the Royal Fireworks, HWV351. **Le Concert des
Nations / Jordi Savall.** Auvidis Astrée Ⓕ E8512 (74 minutes: DDD: 3/94). 🖉 Recorded 1993.
Gramophone Editor's choice.
New review
Handel Water Music, HWV348-50. Il pastor fido – Suite, HWV8c. **Tafelmusik / Jeanne Lamon**
(vn). Sony Classical Vivarte Ⓕ Ⓘ SK68257 (76 minutes: DDD: 7/96). 🖉 Recorded 1995.
Of the period-instrument couplings of these two 'elemental' suites, Savall's must be placed at or near
the top of the list. It is, however, strange that though the booklet-notes acknowledge that the *Water
Music* falls into "three suites" and that the Suite in G major was probably played during supper, the
recorded performance ends with that in F major (described as "Suite II") preceded by the rest

("Suite I") – neither the published nor the 'logical' order. The 74-minute duration of the disc does not allow the movements from the earlier Concerto in F to be included. There is the familiar re-titling and juggling with the order of movements, so that, *inter alia*, the "Coro" in Suite III becomes "Menuet I" and is followed by the Menuet in G major ("Menuet II"). By now we should be used to such manipulations, and those who like to follow the score will be grateful that they do not extend to the *Music for the Royal Fireworks*. What splendid performances these are though, spirited, clean-edged and elegantly embellished – by a solo trumpet in the *Adagio* of the Ouverture of the *Fireworks Music*, where the preceding section is repeated as marked. The orchestral force is substantial, and the comparatively high-level recording and generous acoustic give a deliberate sense of being close to the performers – just as, on the Thames, King George III may have been in a barge adjacent to the musicians – rather than of hearing them from the riverside. Should the order of play disturb you it will be worth the trouble to programme your player to recognize your preferred one.

The jubilant spirit of the *Water Music* is splendidly captured in Sony's version. This young Canadian group have a good grasp of Handelian style, and lots of energy; there is plenty of vigour to their playing but no roughness. There are many nicely and unobtrusively managed details of timing and accent, yet always perfectly natural and justified from within. Their tempos in the main are on the quick side but not hurried. Their flowing *Andante* for the famous Air, which so readily becomes sticky if done slowly, is particularly likeable; here it sounds just right and no less expressive than usual. Only the D major *Lentement* seems heavy and ponderous, and perhaps the *Bourrée* that follows is also a little clumsily done. The horn playing, recorded well forward, is particularly impressive – clean and clear, with a fine ring; it would have sounded well across the Thames. The movements are done here with the F major music first, then the D major and G major mixed, an unusual arrangement these days but one that probably has Handel's authority: and it works well. Tafelmusik get through the *Water Music* in some 52 minutes, and there is room for a substantial suite of dances from the second version of *Il pastor fido*, when Handel added ballet music for the French dancer Marie Sallé and her troupe. These are charming and lively pieces and the final Chaconne, with its inventive textures, is particularly appealing. The sound is a shade middle- and bottom-heavy, rather more so than in *The Water Music*, but again the playing is splendidly fresh and spirited.

Additional recommendations ...

...Water Music. **Simon Standage, Elizabeth Wilcock** (vns); **The English Concert / Trevor Pinnock** (hpd). Archiv Produktion Ⓕ 410 525-2AH (54 minutes: DDD: 2/84) ✍

...Music for the Royal Fireworks. Concerti a due cori – No. 2 in F major; No. 3 in F major. **The English Concert / Trevor Pinnock.** Archiv Produktion Ⓕ 415 129-2AH (54 minutes: DDD: 8/85). ✍

...Music for the Royal Fireworks. Coronation Anthems[a] – Zadok the priest; The King shall rejoice; My heart is inditing; Let thy hand be strengthened. [a]**New College Choir, Oxford; King's Consort / Robert King.** Hyperion Ⓕ CDA66350 (57 minutes: DDD: 12/89). ✍

...Water Music. Music for the Royal Fireworks. **Orpheus Chamber Orchestra.** DG Ⓕ 435 390-2GH (66 minutes: DDD: 11/92).

...Music for the Royal Fireworks. Solomon – Arrival of the Queen of Sheba. Concerto grosso in C major, "Alexander's Feast". Organ Concerto No. 6 in B flat major, Op. 4. Suite in D major, "Water piece". **La Stravaganza / Andrew Manze.** Denon Aliare Ⓕ CO-79943 (58 minutes: DDD: 3/93). ✍

...Water Music, HWV348-50. **English Baroque Soloists / John Eliot Gardiner.** Philips Ⓕ 434 122-2PH (53 minutes: DDD: 5/93). ✍ *Gramophone Editor's choice.*

...Water Music, HWV348-50. **Amsterdam Baroque Orchestra / Ton Koopman.** Erato Ⓕ 4509-91716-2 (56 minutes: DDD: 10/94). ✍

Handel Trio Sonatas. **London Baroque** (Ingrid Seifert, Richard Gwilt, vns; Charles Medlam, vc; Richard Egarr, hpd). Harmonia Mundi Ⓕ HMC90 1379 and 1389 (two discs, oas: 58 and 69 minutes: DDD: 4/93). ✍ Recorded 1991.
HMC90 1379 – Op. 2: No. 1 in B minor; No. 2 in G minor; No. 3 in B flat major; No. 4 in F major; No. 5 in G minor; No. 6 in G minor. *HMC90 1389* – Op. 5: No. 1 in A major; No. 2 in D major; No. 3 in E minor; No. 4 in G major; No. 5 in G minor; No. 6 in F major; No. 7 in B flat major.   Ⓖ

Handel's publisher, Walsh, printed the six Trio Sonatas, Op. 2 in about 1730, following them up in 1739 with seven further trios which he published as the composer's Op. 5. In each set Handel offered a choice of melody instruments though the writing suggests that he had violins foremost in mind. This is the way in which all 13 sonatas are played on these two separately available discs and the decision is a good one. The performances by London Baroque are poised, well-shaped and susceptible to the subtle nuances of Handel's part-writing. Ingrid Seifert and Richard Gwilt are partners of long standing and their even dialogue, sometimes grave, sometimes lively and at other times playful, serves the music effectively. Tempos are well-judged and phrases are eloquently shaped and articulately spoken. In all this the violinists are sympathetically supported by the continuo players who make their own vital contribution to clear textures and overall balance. Recorded sound is appropriately intimate, serving the sound character of the instruments themselves and evoking a chamber music ambience. The music, it hardly need be said, maintains a high level of craftsmanship and interest which will surely delight listeners.

Handel Sonatas for Recorder and Continuo – No. 1 in G minor, HWV360[ad]; No. 2 in A minor,
HWV362[ac]; No. 3 in C major, HWV365[ac]; No. 5 in F major, HWV369[ad]; No. 6 in B flat major,
HWV377[ad]. Sonata for Flute and Continuo No. 3 in B minor, HWV367b[bc]. **Marion Verbruggen**
([a]rec/[b]fl); **Jaap ter Linden** (vc); **Ton Koopman** ([c]hpd/[d]org). Harmonia Mundi Ⓕ HMU90 7151
(58 minutes: DDD: 3/96). ✍ Recorded 1994.
These are very lively and musically intelligent performances of the Handel recorder sonatas. All six
are played here: the four from the published Op. 1 set, one from a Fitzwilliam manuscript, and also –
a shade perversely – a flute sonata as published in Op. 1, played here on a flute, although it does in
fact exist in a recorder version in a different key (the booklet supposes that the recorder version in D
minor is used, but it is actually the B minor flute one). Well, that's a minor point. The major one is
that this is outstandingly fine recorder playing, sweet in tone, pointed in articulation, perfectly tuned,
technically very fluent, and informed by a really good understanding of the art of ornamentation.
Add to that the fact that Marion Verbruggen has a real command of Handel's language and you will
realize that this CD is out of the ordinary. Some of Ton Koopman's accompaniments are a little busy
(half are on the organ, half on the harpsichord), but it's all part of the sense of lively music-making
that runs through this attractive disc.

Handel Flute Sonatas – No. 1 in E minor, HWV359b; No. 2 in G major, HWV363b; No. 3 in
B minor, HWV367b; No. 4 in A minor, HWV374; No. 5 in E minor, HWV375; No. 6 in B minor,
HWV376; No. 7 in D major, HWV378; No. 8 in E minor, HWV379. **Barthold Kuijken** (fl);
Wieland Kuijken (va da gamba); **Robert Kohnen** (hpd). Accent Ⓕ ACC9180D (73 minutes:
DDD: 11/93). ✍ Recorded 1991.
In this recording of solo flute sonatas Barthold Kuijken plays pieces unquestionably by Handel as well
as others over which doubt concerning his authorship has been cast in varying degrees. Three of the
Sonatas (HWV359b, 363b and 367b) were published as part of Handel's Op. 1 by Walsh in about
1730. Three others (HWV374-6) were published in a collection of pieces by various composers at
about the same time. The remaining two (HWV378 and 379) have been preserved in manuscript form.
HWV378, though attributed to Johann Sigmund Weiss, brother of the celebrated lutenist – his name
appears on the manuscript – is now thought to be the product of Handel's pen. HWV379 is an oddity
in that it consists of a somewhat haphazard compilation and rearrangement of movements from other
of Handel's solo sonatas. Certainly not all of the pieces here were conceived for transverse flute –
there are earlier versions of HWV363b and 367b, for example, for oboe and treble recorder,
respectively; but we can well imagine that in Handel's day most, if not all, of these delightful sonatas
were regarded among instrumentalists as more-or-less common property. Barthold Kuijken, with his
eldest brother Wieland and Robert Kohnen, gives characteristically graceful and stylish performances
of the music. Kuijken is skilful in matters of ornamentation and is often adventurous, though
invariably within the bounds of good taste. Dance movements are brisk and sprightly though he is
careful to preserve their poise, and phrases are crisply articulated. This is of especial benefit to
movements such as the lively *Vivace* of the B minor Sonata (HWV367b) which can proceed rather
aimlessly when too legato an approach is favoured; and the virtuosity of these players pays off in the
Presto (Furioso) movement that follows. In short, a delightful disc which should please both
Handelians and most lovers of baroque chamber music.
Additional recommendation ...
...Nos. 1, 2 and 3. Recorder Sonatas (played on flute) – No. 1 in G minor, HWV360; No. 2 in
A minor, HWV362; No. 3 in C major, HWV365; No. 5 in F major, HWV369. **Robert Stallman**
(fl); **Karl Bennion** (vc); **Edwin Swanborn** (hpd). VAI Audio Ⓕ VAIA1091 (71 minutes: DDD:
7/95).

Handel Alcina – Mi lusinga il dolce affetto; Verdi prati, selve amene; Stà nell'Ircana. Ariodante –
E vivo ancora? ... Scherza infida; Dopa notte. Giulio Cesare – Va tacito e nascosto; Se in fiorito
ameno prato; Piangerò, la sorte mia; Dall' ondoso periglio ... Aure, deh, per pietà. Serse –
Frende tenere e belle ... Ombra mai fù; Se bramate d'amar, chi vi sdegna; Crude furie degl'orrido
abissi. **Ann Murray** (mez); **Orchestra of the Age of Enlightenment / Sir Charles Mackerras.**
Forlane Ⓕ UCD16738 (75 minutes: DDD: 8/95). ✍ Texts and translations included. Recorded
1994.
The cautious tread of the watchful huntsman, with the lovely dialogue of voice and basset-horn in
Caesar's first aria, makes a delightful beginning, and as the recital proceeds one realizes afresh what
variety of mood and manner will be found in almost any collection of arias by Handel. These range
from the simple ease and beneficence of "Verdi prati" to the florid outburst of the frustrated Xerxes in
"Crude furie". In between are Cleopatra's lament, Caesar's love song, Ariodante's sadness and his new-
found joy. The musical interest is unfailing wherever one likes to look for it, in rhythm, in harmonic
poignancy, or in the scoring – the solo violin as woodbird in "Se in fiorito ameno prato" or in the
basset-horn of "Va tacito". Handel and Sir Charles have long been associated, and with the Orchestra
of the Age of Enlightenment he provides the singer with a stylish accompaniment that is never assertive
or doctrinaire but scrupulous in its care for phrasing and texture. Ann Murray responds with singing

which has not only her customary expressiveness and energy but also a generally well-preserved beauty of tone that has not always been so characteristic. Occasionally a harsher, less firmly placed tone threatens to emerge, as at the start and *da capo* of "Stà nell' Ircana", but such moments are short-lived and instead she encourages a mellower, warmer sound which also has the advantage of being precise in its focus. The voice is quite closely recorded.

New review
Handel English Arias. **James Bowman** (alto); [a]**Susan Gritton** (sop); **King's Consort / Robert King.** Hyperion Ⓕ CDA66797 (65 minutes: DDD: 2/96). ✒ Texts included. Recorded 1992-5.
The Choice of Hercules – Yet can I hear that dulcet lay. Esther – Overture; How can I stay. Haman and Mordecai – Tune your harps to cheerful strains. Saul – O Lord, whose mercies; O fairest of ten thousand fair[a]. Belshazzar – Great God! who, yet but darkly known; A Martial Symphony; Destructive War, thy limits know. Theodora – The raptur'd Soul defies the Sword; Kind Heav'n, if Virtue be thy care. Judas Maccabaeus – Father of Heaven! Solomon – Almighty power; What tho' I trace each herb and flower; Welcome as the dawn[a].

If we had to live by Handel alone we would still have world enough. The lulling comfort of "that dulcet lay" in *The Choice of Hercules*, the athletic stride of Assuera's "How can I stay" (*Esther*), the pastoral sweets of the duet in *Saul*: these are just the first three items in the recital, and already the delights range wide in mood and manner. Moreover he never (or never here at least) lets us down. If the "Martial Symphony" in *Belshazzar* had continued in the same vein it might have outstayed its welcome, but it leads straight into Cyrus's aria, where victory and virtuosity go hand in hand. If it is depth we desire, and that without pretentiousness or pomposity, there is the rich, dark orchestration of Solomon's dedication of the Temple; if a lighter, almost Mozartian grace, then the last item of all, the heavenly "Tune your harps" is irresistible. James Bowman and the King's Consort present a programme issued in celebration of the singer's twenty-fifth anniversary as a recording artist. He is still on fine form. His runs are as fluent and clearly defined as ever; his ability to sing loudly or softly throughout the range contrasts with his great predecessor Alfred Deller who became reluctant to sing at a full *forte* above the middle register; and in unaccompanied phrases, as in "The raptur'd Soul" and "Father of Heaven!", the voice is heard to be still pure, firm and of fine quality. In the two duets, Susan Gritton's cool, fresh soprano is like white wine to his red, and they go together remarkably well. In his insert-notes Robert King comments on the "mighty pair of lungs" Handel's oboist must have had for the Overture to *Esther*, and later on the call for "virtuosity and precision of the highest calibre from the violins" in "Kind Heav'n" from *Theodora*, all of which requirements are triumphantly met by his own players here. Engineer and producer also deserve their share of the credit.

Handel The Sorceress. Music from the original soundtrack. [a]**Dame Kiri Te Kanawa** (sop); **Academy of Ancient Music / Christopher Hogwood.** Philips Ⓕ 434 992-2PH (62 minutes: DDD: 8/94). ✒ Recorded 1992.
Rinaldo – Overture; Lascia ch'io pianga[a]. Alcina – Overture; Ah! Ruggiero crudel; Ombre pallide; Ballet[a]. Giulio Cesare – Non disperar, chi sa?; Tu la mia stella sei; V'adoro, pupille; Sinfonia; Piangerò, la sorte mia[a]. Ariodante – Ballet Music. Agrippian – Bel piacere[a]. Admeto – Sinfonia. Giustino – Adagio[a].

Described as "A Handel Celebration", this pasticcio, with items drawn from no fewer than eight of his operas, was devised for a Dutch television programme. The CD is taken from the soundtrack, providing in effect a sequence of seven arias, sung with sumptuous tone by Dame Kiri, spiced with instrumental pieces, mostly brief. Though the plot is broadly based on the situation in *Alcina*, only one aria is taken from that opera, "Ombre pallide", which, preceded by an accompanied recitative, makes up by far the longest item. It is made even longer by Dame Kiri's somewhat languid performance. Otherwise, even with speeds on the slow side, Dame Kiri sings gloriously, not least in the four Cleopatra arias from *Giulio Cesare* – including the seduction aria, "V'adoro, pupille" – which provide the cornerstones of the sequence. Not only Dame Kiri's beauty of tone, but her agility, not least in crisp, tight trills, bears witness to her formidable technique. Hogwood, drawing fresh sounds and clear textures from the Academy, follows his soloist very understandingly without trying to enforce his own period-performance style, which would certainly have required faster speeds. Clear, well-balanced sound.

New review
Handel Apollo e Dafne, HWV122, "La terra e liberata"[a]. Crudel tiranno amor, HWV97. **Nancy Argenta** (sop); [a]**Michael George** (bass); **Collegium Musicum 90 / Simon Standage.** Chandos Chaconne Ⓕ CHAN0583 (58 minutes: DDD: 4/96). ✒ Texts and translations included. Recorded 1994.
Handel's *Apollo e Dafne* is a difficult work to put in context. Completed in Hanover in 1710 but possibly begun in Italy, its purpose is not clear, while as secular cantatas go it is long (40 minutes) and ambitiously scored for two soloists and an orchestra of strings, oboes, flute, bassoon and continuo. But this is not just a chunk of operatic experimentation: it sets its own, faster pace than the leisurely unfolding of a full-length baroque stage-work, yet its simple Ovidian episode, in which Apollo's pursuit of the nymph Dafne results in her transformation into a tree, is drawn with all the subtlety and skill of the instinctive dramatic genius that Handel was. This new recording features the by-now

familiar expert Handelian voices of Nancy Argenta and Michael George, and both convey their roles convincingly. Argenta's hard, clear tone seems just the thing for the nymph, who is not required to be especially alluring but who does have to sound quick to anger and (literally) untouchable; and George strikes the right note as Apollo, bragging loudly at the opening of his superior skill in archery to Cupid before succumbing more gently, and in the end extremely touchingly, to Cupid's arts. The orchestra are bright and efficient (though without ever creating a very big sound), and the pacing of the work seems just right. This is superb Handel then, and as if that were not enough there is a bonus in the form of a shorter cantata for soprano and strings, *Crudel tiranno amor*. Of this no more need be said other than that it is a beautiful piece indeed, and that Nancy Argenta performs it well nigh perfectly.

Handel Dixit Dominus, HWV232[a]. Nisi Dominus, HWV238[b]. Salve Regina, HWV241[c]. [ac]**Arleen Auger,** [a]**Lynne Dawson** (sops); [ab]**Diana Montague** (mez); [a]**Leigh Nixon,** [b]**John Mark Ainsley** (tens); [ab]**Simon Birchall** (bass); **Choir and Orchestra of Westminster Abbey / Simon Preston.** Archiv Produktion Ⓔ 423 594-2AH (56 minutes: DDD: 2/89). Texts and translations included.
Although *Dixit Dominus* is the earliest surviving large scale work by Handel (he was only 22 at the time of its composition in 1707) it displays a remarkable degree of competence and invention and also looks forward to the mature style to come. The vocal writing for both chorus and soloists is extremely ornate and embellished and requires a considerable amount of expertise and flair in order to do full justice to the music. Fortunately, Simon Preston and his team possess all the necessary requirements – indeed, this is one of the most energetic, exhilarating and purposeful performances of this work ever recorded. One need only single out the rhythmically incisive performances of the opening "Dixit Dominus Domineo meo" or the "Judicabit in nationibus" and the superbly crisp and articulate performances from the Orchestra of Westminster Abbey to realize that it is a very special recording indeed. The well thought out coupling of *Nisi Dominus* and *Salve Regina* are no less impressive, with the latter offering the listener another chance to sample the beautiful solo contributions of Arleen Auger. The recorded sound is also outstandingly fine. A delightful disc.
Additional recommendation ...
  Dixit Dominus. Coronation Anthems – Zadok the priest; The King shall rejoice; My heart is inditing; Let thy hand be strengthened. **Soloists; Monteverdi Choir and Orchestra / John Eliot Gardiner.** Erato Ⓔ 2292-45136-2 (ADD). ✒

Handel Acis and Galatea. **Norma Burrowes** (sop) Galatea; **Anthony Rolfe Johnson** (ten) Acis; **Martyn Hill** (ten) Damon; **Willard White** (bass) Polyphemus; **Paul Elliot** (ten); **English Baroque Soloists / John Eliot Gardiner.** Archiv Produktion Ⓔ 423 406-2AH2 (two discs: 95 minutes: ADD: 8/88). ✒ Notes, text and translation included. From 2708 038 (9/78). Recorded 1978.
Gramophone Award Winner 1978.
John Eliot Gardiner made this recording of Handel's masque during the late 1970s when the revival of period instruments was still in a comparatively early stage. Listeners may detect weaknesses both in intonation and in ensemble from time to time but, nevertheless, Gardiner's performance is lively and stylistically assured. He paces the work dramatically revealing nuances both in the text and in the music. The solo team is a strong one and there are especially fine contributions from Norma Burrowes and Anthony Rolfe Johnson. This is an enjoyable performance of an enchanting work.
Additional recommendation ...
  ...Acis and Galatea. **Soloists; St Anthony Singers; Philomusica of London / Sir Adrian Boult.** Decca Ⓜ 436 227-2DM2 (two discs: ADD).

Handel Deborah. **Yvonne Kenny, Susan Gritton** (sops); **Catherine Denley** (mez); **James Bowman** (alto); **Michael George** (bass); **New College Choir, Oxford; Salisbury Cathedral Choristers; King's Consort / Robert King.** Hyperion Ⓔ CDA66841/2 (two discs: 140 minutes: DDD: 2/94).
  Text included. Recorded 1993.
Deborah, written in 1733, occupies an honoured place in the canon of Handel's oratorios as the first composed for the entertainment of London theatre audiences. It is also a compound of numerous earlier works, including the Chandos and Coronation Anthems, the *Brockes Passion* and the *Ode for the Birthday of Queen Anne*, and in putting *Deborah* together in this manner, Handel was less successful than he usually was in creating a unified work – though the librettist and indeed the Bible itself have to be assigned some of the blame. It is, however, eminently worth revival, and this recording, the first on CD, is warmly welcome. It begins with an overture different from the one usually heard: a fine, stirring D major trumpety piece, with a concluding minuet that was to find a place in the *Fireworks* Music. There are some noble choruses, several of which are in five or even eight voices, giving Handel the opportunity for grand effects. In *Deborah*, the chief interest rests with the choruses. Here they are very well sung by forces from Salisbury Cathedral and New College, Oxford, 32 trebles, eight countertenors, six tenors and eight basses, who produce a lot more sound than you might expect. Robert King's control of this group and the polish he imparts to the choral singing, with its clearly projected lines and its firmness of tone is admirable as is Michael George's warm and resonant contribution as Abinoam and Catherine Denley's firm, direct and stylish singing of the music of the unfortunate Sisera. The orchestral playing is polished; the recorded sound is more reverberant than might be ideal.

Handel Alexander's Feast[a]. Concerto grosso in C major, HWV318, "Alexander's Feast". [a]**Donna Brown** (sop); [a]**Carolyn Watkinson** (contr); [a]**Ashley Stafford** (alto); [a]**Nigel Robson** (ten); [a]**Stephen Varcoe** (bar); [a]**Monteverdi Choir; English Baroque Soloists / John Eliot Gardiner.** Philips Ⓕ 422 053-2PH2 (two discs: 98 minutes: DDD: 11/88). 🖊 Text included. Recorded live in 1987.

Alexander's Feast was the first work Handel had set by a major English poet (Dryden) and it was also the first time he allotted the principal male part to a tenor instead of the castrato heroes of his Italian operas. These two factors, combined with much fine music, scored with great brilliance and imagination, ensured the immediate success of *Alexander's Feast*. It is strange that nowadays it is seldom performed so this recording would have been very welcome even had it not been so full of vitality and so stylishly performed (though perhaps with more sophisticated detail than the eighteenth century would have managed). The Monteverdi Choir and the soloists are all Gardiner regulars, though the pure-voiced Canadian soprano Donna Brown is a fairly recent (and welcome) acquisition; and the English Baroque Soloists have ample opportunities to shine – especially the violins, although the natural horns' lusty entry in the bucolic "Bacchus, ever fair and young" is exhilarating.

Additional recommendation ...

...Alexander's Feast. Harp Concerto in B flat major, HWV294. Organ Concerto in G minor/major, HWV289. **Soloists; Tragicomedia; The Sixteen Choir and Orchestra / Harry Christophers.** Collins Classics Ⓕ 7016-2 (two discs: 116 minutes: DDD: 10/91). 🖊

Handel Saul. **Lynne Dawson, Donna Brown** (sops); **Derek Lee Ragin** (alto); **John Mark Ainsley, Neil Mackie, Philip Salmon, Philip Slane** (tens); **Alastair Miles, Richard Savage** (basses); **Monteverdi Choir; English Baroque Soloists / John Eliot Gardiner.** Philips Ⓕ 426 265-2PH3 (three discs: 159 minutes: DDD: 8/91). 🖊 Recorded live in 1989.

Saul is considered by many to be one of the most arresting music dramas in the English language, even though it is officially classed as an oratorio. In it Handel explores in some psychological depth the motivation of his characters, most notably that of the eponymous anti-hero, whose tantrums caused by envy and his searching for supernatural intervention are all vividly delineated; as is the friendship of David and Jonathan and the different characters of Saul's daughters, Merab and Michal. In yet another compelling performance of Handel under his baton, John Eliot Gardiner – in this live recording made at the Göttingen Handel Festival in Germany – fulfils every aspect of this varied and adventurous score, eliciting execution of refined and biting calibre from his choir and orchestra. The young British bass Alastair Miles captures Saul in all his moods. John Mark Ainsley and Derek Lee Ragin are both affecting as Jonathan and David; so are Lynne Dawson and Donna Brown as Michal and Merab. There are a few cuts, but they aren't grievous enough to prevent a firm recommendation.

Handel Israel in Egypt, HWV54. **Nancy Argenta, Emily Van Evera** (sops); **Timothy Wilson** (alto); **Anthony Rolfe Johnson** (ten); **David Thomas, Jeremy White** (basses); **Taverner Choir and Players / Andrew Parrott.** EMI Ⓕ CDS7 54018-2 (two discs: 135 minutes: DDD: 2/91). 🖊 Text included. Recorded 1989.   Ⓖ

If anyone needs to assure themselves as to whether the English choral tradition is alive and well, they need only buy this CD. *Israel in Egypt*, of all Handel's works, is the choral one *par excellence* – so much so, in fact, that it was something of a failure in Handel's own time because solo singing was much preferred to choral by the audiences. Andrew Parrott gives a complete performance of the work, in its original form: that is to say, prefaced by the noble funeral anthem for Queen Caroline, as adapted by Handel to serve as a song of mourning by the captive Israelites. This first part is predominantly slow, grave music, powerfully elegiac; the Taverner Choir show themselves, in what is testing music to sing, to be firm and clean of line, well focused and strongly sustained. The chorus have their chance to be more energetic in the second part, with the famous and vivid Plague choruses – in which the orchestra too play their part in the pictorial effects, with the fiddles illustrating in turn frogs, flies and hailstones. And last, in the third part, there is a generous supply of the stirring C major music in which Handel has the Israelites give their thanks to God, in some degree symbolizing the English giving thanks for the Hanoverian monarchy and the Protestant succession. Be that as it may, the effect is splendid. The solo work is first-rate, too, with Nancy Argenta radiant in Miriam's music in the final scene and distinguished contributions too from David Thomas and Anthony Rolfe Johnson.

Additional recommendation ...

...Israel in Egypt[a]. Chandos Anthem No. 10, HWV255, "The Lord is my light"[b]. [a]**Elizabeth Gale,** [a]**Lilian Watson,** [b]**April Cantelo** (sops); [a]**James Bowman** (alto); **Ian Partridge** (ten); [a]**Tom McDonnell** (bar); [a]**Alan Watt** (bass); [a]**Choir of Christ Church, Oxford;** [b]**Choir of King's College, Cambridge;** [a]**English Chamber Orchestra / Simon Preston;** [b]**Academy of St Martin in the Fields / Sir David Willcocks.** Double Decca Ⓜ 443 470-2DF2 (two discs: 131 minutes: ADD).

Handel Messiah, HWV56. **Barbara Schlick, Sandrine Piau** (sops); **Andreas Scholl** (alto); **Mark Padmore** (ten); **Nathan Berg** (bass); **Les Arts Florissants Chorus and Orchestra / William Christie.** Harmonia Mundi Ⓕ HMC90 1498/9 (two discs: 143 minutes: DDD: 10/94). 🖊 Text included. Recorded 1993. *Gramophone Editor's choice.*   ⒼⒼⒼ

William Christie reaches the heart of Handel's masterpiece with great fluency, sure dramatic pacing and an intuitive feeling for the nobility of the piece. As Donald Burrows remarks in his accompanying essay, one of two included in the booklet, Christie's performance generally follows a pattern of the work close to that which Handel seems to have adhered to from the mid-1740s, thus incorporating the chorus, "Their sound is gone out into all lands" (Part 2). Additionally, Christie uses the later versions of the arias "But who may abide the day of his coming" (Part 1), and "Thou art gone up on high" (Part 2), for alto and soprano, respectively. Christie brings lively characterization to *Messiah*, allowing the text (to which he clearly attaches importance) to determine the prevailing effect of each number. In this he is fully supported by a first-rate team of soloists, a responsive if not always impeccably drilled choir and a body of instrumentalists which sounds particularly strong at the moment. The vocal timbres of the two sopranos, Barbara Schlick and Sandrine Piau are a constant delight, the boy treble, Tommy Williams is as reliable in his intonation as he is clear in declamation. Mark Padmore is impressive, too, for sensitive phrasing and a lyrical approach to the music. However it is perhaps Andreas Scholl who touches the heart most profoundly with his deeply felt singing of "He was despised". The choir of Les Arts Florissants is splendidly alert to the many nuances which Christie discovers in Handel's music. Last, but not least, there is the orchestra, crisp, incisive, warm in timbre and producing one of the most homogeneous sounds yet heard from its strings. In short, this is a triumph. Christie's concept of the oratorio embraces the entirety, enabling him to present a continuous drama in a manner which holds our attention from start to finish.

Additional recommendations ...

...**Soloists; Royal Philhrmonic Chorus and Orchestra / Sir Thomas Beecham.** RCA Victor Red Seal ⓜ 09026-61266-2* (three discs: 161 minutes: ADD).

...**Soloists; Monteverdi Choir; English Baroque Soloists / John Eliot Gardiner.** Philips Ⓕ 434 297-2PH2 (two discs: 137 minutes: ADD: 1/84). ◢

...**Soloists; Christ Church Cathedral Choir, Oxford; Academy of Ancient Music / Christopher Hogwood.** L'Oiseau-Lyre Florilegium Ⓕ 430 488-2OH2 (two discs: 137 minutes: ADD: 7/84). ◢   Ⓖ

...**Soloists; The English Concert Choir; The English Concert / Trevor Pinnock.** Archiv Produktion Ⓕ 423 630-2AH2 (two discs: 150 minutes: DDD: 11/88). ◢   Ⓖ

...**Soloists; Collegium Musicum 90 Chorus; Collegium Musicum 90 / Richard Hickox.** Chandos Chaconne Ⓕ CHAN0522/3 (two discs: 141 minutes: DDD: 3/92). ◢

...**Soloists; The Sixteen; Amsterdam Baroque Orchestra / Ton Koopman.** Erato ⓜ 2292-45960-2 (two discs: 140 minutes: DDD: 3/93). ◢

...**The Scholars Baroque Ensemble / David van Asch** (bass). Naxos ©️ 8 550667/8 (two discs: 161 minutes: DDD: 4/93). ◢

Handel The Occasional Oratorio. **Susan Gritton, Lisa Milne** (sops); **James Bowman** (alto); **John Mark Ainsley** (ten); **Michael George** (bass); **New College Choir, Oxford; The King's Consort / Robert King.** Hyperion Ⓕ CDA66961/2 (two discs: 144 minutes: DDD: 6/95). Text included. Recorded 1994.   Ⓖ

The occasion that called forth this work was the Jacobite rising of 1745 and its impending defeat. The Duke of Cumberland's victory at Culloden was yet to come. Handel, anticipating it, hit off the mood of the moment with a rousing piece full of appeals to patriotic feeling, partly through the traditional identification between the English Protestant culture of Hanoverian times with that of the biblical Hebrews. Much of the music comes from existing works, notably *Israel in Egypt* – the hailstone chorus does not seem to have much relevance to battles between the English and the Scots, but then of course English weather was always rather unpredictable. *The Occasional Oratorio* has usually had a bad press. Its 'plot' pursues the familiar route of Anxiety-Prayer-Victory-Jubilation, but the work lacks the unity of theme and purpose of the great dramatic oratorios; if, however, you value Handel primarily because the music is so splendid you will find a lot to relish here. Many of Robert King's performances excel more through their refinement than their vitality: but here he really rises to the challenge of this sturdier side of Handel's muse and produces playing and singing full of punch and energy, and with that command of the broad Handelian paragraph without which the music lacks its proper stature. The grand eight-part choruses, with the choir properly spaced, antiphonally, over the stereo span, make their due effect. King has a distinguished solo team. John Mark Ainsley's singing is particularly touching in the highly original "Jehovah is my shield", where the rocking figures in the orchestra eventually turn out to symbolize sleep. Also very enjoyable is Susan Gritton's soprano, a sharply focused voice with a fine ring and due agility in the lively music and handled with taste and a keen feeling for the shape of phrases in the contemplative airs. In all this is a very fine set, with a lot of magnificent music, played and sung as well as one could hope for.

New review

Handel Ariodante. **Lorraine Hunt** (sop) Ariodante; **Juliana Gondek** (sop) Ginevra; **Lisa Saffer** (sop) Dalinda; **Jennifer Lane** (mez) Polinesso; **Rufus Müller** (ten) Lurcanio; **Nicolas Cavallier** (bass) King of Scotland; **Jörn Lindemann** (ten) Odoardo; **Wilhelmshaven Vocal Ensemble; Freiburg Baroque Orchestra / Nicholas McGegan.** Harmonia Mundi Ⓕ HMU90 7146/8 (three discs: 202 minutes: DDD: 4/96). ◢ Notes, text and translation included. Recorded 1995. *Gramophone Editor's choice.*

The Leppard performance of 1980 (the reissue of which is listed below) has Dame Janet Baker in superb voice, and for her commanding singing alone that set is more than worth having; but the new version under Nicholas McGegan certainly surpasses it in almost every other way. This recording, made with the cast from the Göttingen Festival last year (largely American singers who have collaborated with McGegan in his Californian performances), seems at least the equal of the best he has done before. The quality of the music is of course a factor: *Ariodante* is one of the richest of the Handel operas. It begins with a flood of fine numbers, just like *Giulio Cesare*, mostly love music for the betrothed pair, Ariodante and the Scottish princess Ginevra – she is introduced in a wonderfully carefree aria, he in a gentle, exquisite slow arietta; then they have a very individual and beautiful love duet, and each goes on to a more jubilant aria. But the plot thickens and the music darkens with Polinesso's machinations, designed to impugn her fidelity: thus Act 2 contains music of vengeance and grief (above all the magnificent "Scherza infida!" for Ariodante, a G minor aria with muted upper and pizzicato lower strings, and soft bassoons), while the final act shows all the characters *in extremis*, until the plot is uncovered and equilibrium is restored. This is also one of Handel's few operas with extensive ballet; each act includes some splendid and ingeniously tuneful dance music. McGegan directs in his usual spirited style. There is a real theatrical sense to his conducting: this is one of those opera sets where, after the overture, you find your spine tingling in expectation of the drama. Lorraine Hunt's soprano seems warm and full for a castrato part, but her line is always well-defined and she has a delightfully musical voice which she uses gracefully and expressively. A fine set.

Additional recommendation ...
...Ariodante. **Soloists; London Voices; English Chamber Orchestra / Raymond Leppard.** Philips
    Ⓜ 442 096-2PM3 (three discs: 139 minutes: ADD: 12/94).

Handel Theodora. **Lorraine Hunt** (sop) Theodora; **Jennifer Lane** (mez) Irene; **Drew Minter** (alto)
    Didymus; **Jeffrey Thomas** (ten) Septimus; **Nigel Rogers** (ten) Messenger; **David Thomas** (bass)
    Valens; **California University, Berkeley Chamber Chorus; Philharmonia Baroque Orchestra /**
    Nicholas McGegan. Harmonia Mundi Ⓕ HMU90 7060/2 (three discs: 170 minutes: DDD: 10/92).
    ✎ Text included. Recorded 1991.   Ⓖ
"The Jews will not come to it ... because it is a Christian story, and the ladies will not come to it because it is a virtuous one" wrote Handel somewhat bitterly after the unfavourable reception of his sublime late oratorio, *Theodora*. If contemporary audiences were put off by its theme of martyrdom, we should be grateful that the self-righteous piety of Morell's libretto inspired some of Handel's finest music, complete for the first time on record with the added bonus of both the original and revised versions of "Symphony of Soft Musick". And at last it has a recording which can be wholeheartedly recommended. David Thomas as Valens, the Roman governor, opens the proceedings with a firm and resolute tone and later gives the bloodthirsty "Racks, gibbets, sword and fire" much menace. Lorraine Hunt was an inspired choice for the taxing title-role: the top notes of "Angels ever bright and fair" are celestially floated, while she finds great intensity in "With darkness deep", the emotional centre of the work. Drew Minter gives a mellifluous and characterful account of Didymus, a Roman officer recently converted to Christianity who attempts to save Theodora. Listen to their duet, "To Thee, Thou glorious Son" to hear how winningly they blend their voices. Praise too for Jeffrey Thomas as Septimius, particularly in his elegant ornamentation in the virtuoso aria "Dread the fruits of Christian folly", only occasionally showing strain in the wide leaps in "From virtue springs". Jennifer Lane is also impressive as Irene (described in the libretto simply as "A Christian") – despite being burdened with some of Morell's most trite utterances: "True Happiness is only found, where Grace and Truth and Love Abound, And pure religion feeds the Flame". This is perhaps Nicholas McGegan's best Handel recording yet. He has at his command a highly skilled orchestra, chooses tempos which are unfailingly apt, supporting and giving weight to the vocal lines. Praise too, for the excellent University of California Chamber Chorus, well schooled by their director John Butt. Harmonia Mundi have provided an informative booklet with a full libretto in three languages and an illuminating introductory essay from McGegan himself.

Additional recommendations ...
...**Soloists; Amor Artis Chorale; English Chamber Orchestra / Johannes Somary.** Vanguard Classics
    Ⓜ 08.4075.72 (two discs: 152 minutes: ADD: 7/93).
...Theodora, HWV68 – Kind Heav'n, if Virtue be thy care; Sweet Rose, and Lilly, flow'ry Form.
    Orlando – Ah Stigie larve!. Jephtha, HWV70 – 'Tis Heaven's all-ruling pow'r. *Coupled with works*
    by **Bach** Alfred Deller (alto); **Handel Festival Orchestra / Sir Anthony Lewis.** Vanguard Classics
    Alfred Deller Edition Ⓜ 08.5069.71* (59 minutes: ADD: 1/95). *See review under J.S. Bach; refer*
    to the Index to Reviews.   ⒼⒼ

Handel Teseo. **Eirian James** (mez) Teseo; **Julia Gooding** (sop) Agilea; **Della Jones** (mez) Medea:
    Derek Lee Ragin (alto) Egeo; **Catherine Napoli** (sop) Clizia; Jeffrey Gall (alto) Arcane; **François**
    Bazola (bar) Sacerdote di Minerva; **Les Musiciens du Louvre / Marc Minkowski.** Erato
    Ⓕ 2292-45806-2 (two discs: 148 minutes: DDD: 3/93). ✎ Texts and translations included.
    Recorded 1992.   Ⓖ
Teseo was Handel's third opera for London, given at the beginning of 1713. Exceptionally, its libretto was based on a French original, written by Quinault for Lully; it is a spectacular piece, in five acts, with Medea (after the events of *Médée*) and Theseus (before the events of *Hippolyte* or the Ariadne

operas) as its central characters. It is Medea who, as slighted lover and jealous sorceress, provides the principal musical thrills; but the score is, in any case, an unusually rich and inventive one, with much colourful orchestral writing even before she turns up at the beginning of Act 2. When she does, she introduces herself with a *Largo* aria. "Dolce riposo", of a kind unique to Handel in its depth of poetic feeling, with a vocal line full of bold leaps above throbbing strings and an oboe obbligato; but, lest we should think her docile, Medea hints at her true colours in the ensuing C minor aria, and by the end of the act she is singing furious recitative and fiery, incisive lines – real sorceress music. Her biggest scene comes at the start of the final act, a *Presto* vengeance aria, packed with raging rapid semiquavers. Handel scored the opera for a more varied orchestra than usual; there are recorders, flutes, oboes, bassoons and trumpets called for. The arias themselves tend to be rather shorter than usual for Handel. The work needs first-rate singing, and by and large receives it here. The role of Medea falls to Della Jones, a singer with a superb technique and a remarkable ability to identify with the role; she truly lives Medea's part and brings to it great resources of spirit and technique. Except when asked, or allowed, to play too fast, too loudly or too coarsely, the Musiciens du Louvre are an impressive group, with an outstanding first oboist and some very capable violinists. Several numbers are accompanied with only a continuo instrument, to good effect. The recitative always moves well, and appoggiaturas are duly observed.

Handel Radamisto. **Ralf Popken** (alto) Radamisto; **Juliana Gondek** (sop) Zenobia; **Lisa Saffer** (sop) Polissena; **Dana Hanchard** (sop) Tigrane; **Monika Frimmer** (sop) Fraarte; **Michael Dean** (bass-bar) Tiridate; **Nicolas Cavallier** (bass) Farasmane; **Freiburg Baroque Orchestra / Nicholas McGegan** (hpd). Harmonia Mundi Ⓔ HMU90 7111/3 (three discs: 190 minutes: DDD: 6/94).
   ✎ Notes, text and translation included. Recorded 1993. *Gramophone Editor's choice.*   ⒼⒼ
Radamisto was Handel's first opera for the Royal Academy of Music, the company set up in 1719 under his musical directorship to put London opera on a secure basis (as optimistic a notion then as now). It is a tale of dynastic doings in post-classical Thrace, with King Tiridate of Armenia forsaking his wife Polissena because he becomes enamoured of Zenobia, Radamisto's queen; Radamisto and Zenobia go through various trials, but "after various Accidents, it comes to pass, that he recovers both Her and his Kingdom". It is easy enough to poke fun at plots such as these, but the score of *Radamisto*, one of Handel's richest, is its justification. Handel certainly knew how to 'wow' the London audiences on these big occasions. In the Second Act particularly, one arresting number follows another; Radamisto's "Ombra cara", which has been claimed (not without justice) as the finest aria Handel ever wrote, falls early in the act, and towards the end there is a wonderful sequence, chiefly of minor-key numbers, as the emotional tensions mount, culminating in a duet for the apparently doomed lovers. The Third Act, although dramatically less powerful, is also full of colourful and characterful music, including a noble quartet which Handel clearly remembered 30 years later when composing *Jephtha*. This performance is the best by far we have had from Nicholas McGegan. Any Handelian will relish the constantly alert playing, the strong dramatic pacing and the weight given to the orchestral textures, and he has the benefit of an excellent cast.

New review
Handel Berenice. **Julianne Baird** (sop) Berenice; **D'Anna Fortunato** (mez) Selene; **Jennifer Lane** (mez) Demetrio; **Andrea Matthews** (sop) Alessandro; **Drew Minter** (alto) Arsace; **John McMaster** (ten) Fabio; **Jan Opalach** (bass) Aristobolo; **Brewer Chamber Orchestra / Rudolph Palmer.**
Newport Classic Ⓔ NPD85620/3 (three discs: 149 minutes: DDD: 4/96). Notes, text and translation included. Recorded 1994.
Commentators have tended to be dismissive of *Berenice*, one of Handel's last operas. It is understandable that it should have failed in 1737 before a London audience, already tiring of conventional Italian *opera seria*, that was faced with yet another stilted complex plot of amorous and political intrigues, and, through financial constraints, with an orchestra largely reduced to strings only and lacking Handel's usual subtleties of instrumental colour. But that it should have remained totally ignored, save for a German version six years later, until the University of Keele revived it in 1985 is rather shameful; so all the more thanks are due to this attractive first recording, by all-American forces, which may help to redress the balance. Though it is true that the level of invention in *Berenice* is uneven, not always equal to Handel at his best, there is a striking final ensemble, virtuoso florid arias (notably Demetrio's "Sù, Megera", Arsace's "Senza nudrisce", Alessandro's "Che sarà?" and Selene's impassioned "Gelo, avvampo") and a fine accompanied recitative for Demetrio. The producer, John Ostendorf has assembled an exceptionally good cast without a single weak member. Recitatives, often the weak point in performances of baroque operas, are handled meaningfully throughout, with intelligent timing and asides given proper perspective; and all the singers decorate *da capo* sections of arias (often with very free final cadenzas). Julianne Baird produces a lovely pure sound and mention must be made of the sterling contributions of Jennifer Lane. Few reservations need to be made: Andrea Matthews, in the castrato part of Alessandro, sounds unmistakably female; and the reverberant acoustic of the church where the opera was recorded sometimes forces itself on the attention. The 30-piece Brewer Chamber Orchestra are heard to good effect here.

Handel Flavio. **Jeffrey Gall** (alto) Flavio; **Derek Lee Ragin** (alto) Guido; **Lena Lootens** (sop) Emilia; **Bernarda Fink** (contr) Teodata; **Christina Högman** (sop) Vitige; **Gianpaolo Fagotto** (ten)

Ugone; **Ulrich Messthaler** (bass) Lotario; **Ensemble 415 / René Jacobs.** Harmonia Mundi
Ⓕ HMC90 1312/3 (two discs: 156 minutes: DDD: 7/90). ✎ Notes, text and translation included.
Recorded 1989.   ⊕⊕

Flavio is one of the most delectable of Handel's operas. Although it comes from his 'heroic' period, it
is not at all in the heroic mould but rather an ironic tragedy with a good many comic elements. Does
that sound confusing? – well, so it is, for you never know quite where you are when King Flavio of
Lombardy starts falling in love with the wrong woman, for although this starts as an amusing idle
fancy it develops into something near-tragic, since he imperils everyone else's happiness, ultimately
causing the death of one counsellor and the dishonour of another. The delicately drawn amorous
feeling is like nothing else in Handel, and in its subtle growth towards real passion and grief is
handled with consummate skill. The opera, in short, is full of fine and exceptionally varied music, and
it is enhanced here by a performance under René Jacobs that, although it takes a number of modest
liberties, catches the moods of the music surely and attractively, with shapely, alert and refined playing
from the admirable Ensemble 415. And the cast is strong. The central roles, composed for two of
Handel's greatest singers, Cuzzoni and Senesino, eighteenth-century superstars, are sung by Lena
Lootens, a delightfully natural and expressive soprano with a firm, clear technique, and the
countertenor Derek Lee Ragin, who dispatches his brilliant music with aplomb and excels in the final
aria, a superb minor-key expression of passion. The singers also include Bernarda Fink as the lightly
amorous Teodata and Christina Högman, both fiery and subtle in the music for her lover, and the
capable Jeffrey Gall as the wayward monarch. Altogether a highly enjoyable set, not flawless but
certainly among the best ever Handel opera recordings.

Handel Giulio Cesare. **Jennifer Larmore** (mez) Giulio Cesare; **Barbara Schlick** (sop) Cleopatra;
  Bernarda Fink (mez) Cornelia; **Marianne Rørholm** (mez) Sextus; **Derek Lee Ragin** (alto) Ptolemy;
  Furio Zanasi (bass) Achillas; **Olivier Lallouette** (bar) Curio; **Dominique Visse** (alto) Nirenus;
  Concerto Cologne / René Jacobs. Harmonia Mundi Ⓕ HMC90 1385/7 (four discs: 244 minutes:
  DDD: 4/92). ✎ Notes, text and translation included. Recorded 1991. **Gramophone** *Award*
  Winner 1992.   ⊕⊕

Handel's greatest heroic opera sports no fewer than eight principal characters and one of the largest
orchestras he ever used. Undoubtedly this, and the singing of Francesca Cuzzoni (Cleopatra) and
Senesino (Caesar), helped to launch *Giulio Cesare* into enduring popularity that it enjoys to this day.
But it is primarily the quality of the music, with barely a weak number in four hours of entertainment,
that has made it such a favourite with musicians and audiences. Surprisingly, this is the only complete
performance on period instruments currently available, an immediate advantage in giving extra 'bite'
to the many moments of high drama without threatening to drown the singers in *forte* passages. This
performance is a particularly fine one with an excellent cast; Caesar, originally sung by a castrato, is
here taken by the young mezzo, Jennifer Larmore. She brings weight and a sense of integrity to the
role (which surely couldn't be matched by a countertenor), seemingly untroubled by the demands of
the final triumphant aria, "Qual torrente". Occasionally her vibrato becomes intrusive, particularly
near the beginning of the opera, but that is a minor quibble in a performance of this stature. Handel
could just as well have called his opera 'Cleopatra' as it is she who is the pivotal element in the drama,
a role taken here by Barbara Schlick. One of Handel's most vividly developed characters, Schlick
represents this many faceted woman with acuity and imagination, ranging from the haunting pathos
of "Piangerò", where she occasionally seems stretched on the top notes, to the exuberant virtuosity
of "Da tempeste" in the final act. If Cleopatra represents strength in a woman, then Cornelia is surely
the tragic figure, at the mercy of events. Her first aria, "Priva son", here taken very slowly, shows
Bernarda Fink to be more than equal to the role, admirable in her steady tone and dignity of
character. Derek Lee Ragin's treacherous Ptolemy is also memorable, venom and fire injected into his
agile voice. A first-rate cast is supported by René Jacobs and Concerto Cologne on fine form, though
the continuo line is sometimes less than ideally clear. The excellent recording completes one's pleasure
in a momentous issue.

Additional recommendations ...

...(sung in German). **Soloists; Stuttgart Radio Chorus; Munich Philharmonia Orchestra / Ferdinand
Leitner.** Orfeo D'Or mono Ⓕ C351943D* (three discs: 215 minutes: ADD: 3/95).

...**Soloists; La Grande Ecurie et La Chambre du Roy / Jean-Claude Malgoire.** Auvidis Astrée
  Ⓕ E8558 (three discs: 221 minutes: DDD: 2/96).

New review

Handel Giustino. **Michael Chance** (alto) Giustino; **Dorothea Röschmann** (sop) Arianna; **Dawn
Kotoski** (sop) Anastasio; **Juliana Gondek** (sop) Fortuna; **Dean Ely** (sngr) Polidarte; **Jennifer Lane**
(mez) Leocasta; **Mark Padmore** (ten) Vitaliano; **Drew Minter** (alto) Amanzio; **Cantamus Chamber
Choir, Halle; Freiburg Baroque Orchestra / Nicholas McGegan.** Harmonia Mundi Ⓕ HMU90
7130/2 (three discs: 173 minutes: DDD: 12/95). ✎ Notes, text and translation included.
Recorded 1994.

Giustino, none too successful in Handel's own day, has had an unjustifiably poor press from Handel
biographers. Taken on its own terms – which are considerably removed from those of traditional
heroic *opera seria* – it is a thoroughly delightful work: consistent in style but very varied in manner,
run through with lively touches of wit and irony, and at its best moments serious and genuinely

moving. First given in 1737, and not revived in Handel's time (indeed not until 1967), it tells a tale based very loosely on history, about the early days of Justin, the country lad who became Byzantine emperor. The shifts of allegiance and the slender motivation sometimes make it hard to be sure where our sympathies are meant to lie, but the story clearly isn't intended to be taken too seriously. The work happens to be particularly well suited to Nicholas McGegan's interpretative approach: the light textures, the faintly quizzical, abrupt phrase-ends, the quickish tempos, the crisp rhythms and the general reluctance to dawdle or luxuriate or aggrandize – all these seem to capture the special qualities of *Giustino* very neatly and make the set highly agreeable entertainment. The singing is stylish and assured though vocally not consistently distinguished. It is slightly regrettable, in a recording, that the voices of the royal couple, Anastasio and Arianna, should sound rather alike. Anastasio was originally a soprano castrato role (it was written for the famous Conti); Dawn Kotoski has the right firmness of focus and concentration of tone, with considerable delicacy and rhythmic life, but her narrow, quick vibrato sometimes makes the intonation seem a shade suspect. The other castrato role is Giustino's, superbly sung here by Michael Chance, who has an unusually generous allocation of arias. His steady and beautiful tone and controlled singing should subdue the objections that many people have to countertenors in castrato roles. Handelians must not miss this.

Further listening ...

...Oboe Concertos – B flat major, HWV301; B flat major, HWV302*a*; G minor, HWV287. Oboe Sonatas – B flat major, HWV357; F, HWV363*a*; G minor, HWV364*a*; C minor, HWV366. Trio Sonata in E minor, HWV404. **London Harpsichord Ensemble / Sarah Francis** (ob). Unicorn-Kanchana DKPCD9153 (8/95).

...Coronation Anthems, HWV258-61[a]. Concerti a due cori[b] – No. 2 in F major; No. 3 in F major. [a]**Westminster Abbey Choir; The English Concert /** [a]**Simon Preston,** [b]**Trevor Pinnock.** Archiv Masters 447 280-2AMA (6/95). ✍ Ⓖ

...Chaconne in G major (arr. Nicholson). Concerto Movement for Organ and Orchestra in D minor. *Coupled with works by* **Roseingrave, Chilcot, Nares, P. Hayes** and **Hook The Parley of Instruments / Paul Nicholson** (hpd/org/fp). Hyperion CDA66700 (8/94). ✍ *See review in the Collections section; refer to the Index to Reviews.*

...20 Sonatas, 'Op. 1'. **Lisa Beznosiuk** (fl); **Rachel Beckett** (rec); **Paul Goodwin** (ob); **Elizabeth Wallfisch** (vn); **Richard Tunnicliffe** (vc); **Paul Nicholson** (hpd). Hyperion CDA66921/3 (3/96). ✍

...Violin Sonatas – G major, HWV358[a]; A major, HWV361[a]; G minor, HWV364*a*[a]; D major, HWV371[a]; A major, HWV372[b]; D minor, HWV359*a*[b]. **Ryo Terakado** (vn); [a]**Hidemi Suzuki** (vc); [b]**Kaori Uemura** (va da gamba); **Christophe Rousset** (hpd). Denon Aliare CO-75858 (12/94). ✍

...Keyboard Suites, HWV426-33 – No. 1 in A major; No. 2 in F major; No. 3 in D minor; No. 4 in E minor; No. 5 in E major; No. 5*a* – Air and Variations, "The Harmonious Blacksmith"; No. 6 in F sharp minor; No. 7 in G minor; No. 8 in F minor. **Scott Ross** (hpd). Erato 2292-45452-2 (2/90). ✍

...Keyboard Suites, HWV426-33 – No. 5 in E major; No. 5*a* – Air and Variations, "The Harmonious Blacksmith"; No. 7 in G minor. *Coupled with* **D. Scarlatti** Keyboard Sonatas – G major, Kk2; D minor, Kk9; C minor, Kk11; G major, Kk14; E minor, Kk15; E major, Kk20; D major, Kk21; D major, Kk23; A major, Kk24. **Martin Souter** (hpd). Isis ISISCD001 (3/93). ✍

...Keyboard Suites, HWV426-33 – No. 1 in A major; No. 2 in F major; No. 3 in D minor; No. 4 in E minor; No. 5 in E major. **Martin Souter** (hpd). Isis ISISCD003 (7/93). ✍

...Keyboard Suites, HWV426-3. **Kenneth Gilbert** (hpd). Harmonia Mundi Musique d'abord HMA190 447/8 (12/95). ✍

...Te Deum in D major, HWV283, "Dettingham". Dettingham Anthem, HWV265, "The King shall rejoice". **Soloists; Westminster Abbey Choir; The English Concert / Simon Preston.** Archiv Produktion 410 647-2AH (9/84). ✍

...Ode for St Cecilia's Day, HWV76. **Felicity Lott** (sop); **Anthony Rolfe Johnson** (ten); **Soloists; The English Concerto Choir; The English Concert / Trevor Pinnock.** Archiv Produktion 419 220-2AH (1/87). ✍

...Aminta e Fillide, HWV83, "Arresta il passo". **Gillian Fisher** (sop); **Patrizia Kwella** (sop); **London Handel Orchestra / Denys Darlow.** Hyperion CDA66118 (7/85). ✍

...Occhi mei, che faceste?[abc]. Udite il mio consiglio[abc]. Quel fior che all'alba ride[abc]. Violin Sonata in G minor, HWV364*b*[bc]. Harpsichord Suite in F minor, HWV433[c]. [a]**Julianne Baird** (sop); [b]**John Dornenburg** (va da gamba); [c]**Malcolm Proud** (hpd). Meridian CDE84189 (12/91). ✍

...Clori, Tirsi e Fileno, HWV96. **Soloists; Philharmonia Baroque Orchestra / Nicholas McGegan.** Harmonia Mundi HMU90 7045 (2/93). ✍

...La Resurrezione. **Soloists; Amsterdam Baroque Orchestra / Ton Koopman.** Erato 2292-45617-2 (7/91). ✍

...Athalia. **Soloists; New College Choir, Oxford; Academy of Ancient Music / Christopher Hogwood.** L'Oiseau-Lyre 417 126-2OH2 (2/87). ✍

...L'Allegro, il Penseroso ed il Moderato. **Soloists; Monteverdi Choir; English Baroque Soloists / John Eliot Gardiner.** Erato 2292 45377-2 (7/85). ✍ *Gramophone Award Winner 1987.*

...Semele. **Soloists; Ambrosian Opera Chorus; English Chamber Orchestra / John Nelson.** DG 435 782-2GH3 (6/93). *Selected by Sounds in Retrospect.*

...Semele. **Soloists; Monteverdi Choir; English Baroque Soloists / John Eliot Gardiner.** Erato Libretto 2292-45982-2 (6/93). ✍ Ⓖ

...Belshazzar. **Soloists; The English Concert Choir; The English Concert / Trevor Pinnock.** Archiv Produktion 431 793-2AH3 (10/91). ✍

...Judas Maccabaeus. **Soloists; New College Choir, Oxford; The King's Consort / Robert King.** Hyperion CDA666412 (12/92). ✍

...Joshua. **Soloists; New College Choir, Oxford; The King's Consort / Robert King.** Hyperion CDA66461/2 (7/91). ✍

...Solomon. **Soloists; Monteverdi Choir; English Baroque Soloists / John Eliot Gardiner.** Philips 412 612-2PH2 (12/85). ✍ Ⓖ

...Susanna. **Soloists; Chamber Chorus of the University of California, Berkeley; Philharmonia Baroque Orchestra / Nicholas McGegan.** Harmonia Mundi HMU90 7030/2 (10/90). ✍ Ⓖ

...Jephtha. **Soloists; Monteverdi Choir; English Baroque Soloists / John Eliot Gardiner.** Philips 422 351-2PH3 (6/89). ✍ *Gramophone Award Winner 1989.* Ⓖ

...Agrippina. **Soloists; Cappella Savaria / Nicholas McGegan.** Harmonia Mundi HMU90 7063/5 (3/93). ✍ Ⓖ

...Amadigi di Gaula. **Soloists; Les Musiciens du Louvre / Marc Minkowski.** Erato 2292-45490-2 (9/91). ✍ Ⓖ

...Floridante (abridged). **Soloists; Tafelmusik Baroque Orchestra / Alan Curtis.** CBC Records SMCD5110 (1/93). ✍

...Muzio Scevola (Act 3). *Coupled with* **Bononcini** Muzio Scevola (Act 2) – Overture; Dolce pensier; E pure in mezzo all'armi; Si, t'ama, o cara; Mutio Scevola – Pupille amate; Come, quando alle mie pene. **Soloists; Brewer Baroque Chamber Orchestra / Rudolph Palmer.** Newport Classic Premier NPD85540 (3/93).✍

...Ottone. **Soloists; Freiburg Baroque Orchestra / Nicholas McGegan.** Harmonia Mundi HMU90 7073/5 (3/93). ✍

...Tamerlano. **Soloists; English Baroque Soloists / John Eliot Gardiner.** Erato 2292-45408-2. ✍

...Rodelina. **Soloists; La Stagione / Michael Schneider.** Deutsche Harmonia Mundi RD77192 (1/93). ✍

...Alessandro. **Soloists; La Petite Bande / Sigiswald Kuijken.** Deutsche Harmonia Mundi Editio Classica GD77110 (2/91). ✍ Ⓖ

...Partenope. **Soloists; La Petite Bande / Sigiswald Kuijken.** Deutsche Harmonia Mundi Editio Classica GD77109 (2/91). ✍ ⒼⒼ

...Poro, Re dell'Indie. **Soloists; L'Europa Galante / Fabio Biondi.** Opus 111 OPS30-113/5 (11/94). ✍

...Orlando. **Soloists; Academy of Ancient Music / Christopher Hogwood.** L'Oiseau-Lyre 430 845-2OH3 (8/91). ✍ Ⓖ

...Alcina. **Soloists; Opera Stage Chorus; City of London Baroque Sinfonia / Richard Hickox.** EMI CDS7 49771-2 (11/88). ✍

...Alceste[a]. Comus[b]. [a]**Emma Kirkby,** [a]**Judith Nelson,** [b]**Patrizia Kwella** (sops); **Margaret Cable** (mez); [a]**Paul Elliott** (ten); **David Thomas** (bass); **Academy of Ancient Music / Christopher Hogwood.** L'Oiseau-Lyre Florilegium 443 183-2OM (11/94). ✍

Howard Hanson

American 1896-1981

Suggested listening ...

...Piano Concerto, Op. 36[a]. Symphonies – No. 5, Op. 43, "Sinfonia Sacra"; No. 7, "A Sea Symphony[b]. Mosaics. [a]**Carol Rosenberger** (pf); [b]**Seattle Symphony Chorale and Orchestra / Gerard Schwarz.** Delos DE3130 (3/93).

...Symphonies – No. 1 in E minor, Op. 21, "Nordic"; No. 2, Op. 30, "Romantic". Song of Democracy[a]. [a]**Eastman School of Music Chorus; Eastman-Rochester Orchestra / Howard Hanson.** Mercury Living Presence 432 008-2MM (2/91).

...Symphony No. 3. Elegy in memory of Serge Koussevitzky. Lament for Beowulf, Op. 25[a]. [a]**Eastman-Rochester Chorus and Orchestra / Howard Hanson.** Mercury Living Presence 434 302-2MM*.

...Dies Natalis I[c]. The Mystic Trumpeter[abc]. Lumen in Christo[bc]. Lux aeterna, Op. 24[c]. [a]**James Earl Jones** (narr); [b]**Seattle Symphony Chorale and** [c]**Orchestra / Gerard Schwarz.** Delos DE3160 (5/95).

John H. Harbison

American 1938-

Suggested listening ...

...Remembering Gatsby. *Coupled with* **Larsen** Collage: Boogie. **Schiff** Stomp. **Kernis** New Era Dance. **J. Adams** The Chairman Dances. **Bernstein** West Side Story – Mambo. **Torke** Black and White – Charcoal. **Moran** Points of Departure. **Agento** The Dream of Valentino – Tango. **Daugherty** Desi. **Rouse** Bonham. **Baltimore Symphony Orchestra / David Zinman.** Argo 444 454-2ZH (7/95).

...Wind Quintet. *Coupled with works by* **Barber, Beach, Fine, Villa-Lobos** and **Schuller** **Reykjavik Wind Quintet**. Chandos CHAN9174 (11/93). *See review in the Collections section; refer to the Index to Reviews.* Ⓖ

Henry Harington
British 1727-1816

Suggested listening ...
...Enchanting harmonist. Ode to the memory of Italian virtuosi. Damon and Clora. The lyre. *Coupled with music by* **Herschel, W.B. Earle, T. Linley I, T. Linley II** *and* **W. Jackson** Hyperion CDA66698 (11/94).

Roy Harris
American 1898-1979

Suggested listening ...
...Symphonies Nos. 1 and 3. *Coupled with works by* **Foote, McDonald** and **Copland** Boston Symphony Orchestra / Serge Koussevitzky. Pearl mono GEMMCD9492* (12/91). *See review in the Collections section; refer to the Index to Reviews.* ⒼⒼⒼ
...American Creed. When Johnny comes marching home. *Coupled with* **Copland** Fanfare for the Common Man. Lincoln Portrait[a]. Canticle of Freedom[b]. An Outdoor Overture. [a]**James Earl Jones** (spkr); **Seattle Chorale and** [b]**Symphony Orchestra / Gerard Schwarz.** Delos DE3140 (5/93).

Sir William Henry Harris
British 1883-1973

Suggested listening ...
...Organ Sonata in A minor. *Coupled with works by* **Bairstow** and **Elgar John Scott** (org). Priory PRCD401 (8/94).

Lou Harrison
American 1917-

L. Harrison Symphony No. 3[a]. Grand Duo[b] [b]**Romuald Tecco** (vn); [a]**Cabrillo Music Festival Orchestra / Dennis Russell Davies** ([b]pf). MusicMasters Ⓕ 7073-2 (68 minutes: DDD: 5/95).
The Third Symphony (1982) is a work of some substance and no little potential for widespread appeal. The boldly striding outer paragraphs of the opening *Allegro moderato* frame a more contemplative, raptly lyrical central section (with some beautiful writing for solo strings). Next follow three linked, nicely contrasted dance episodes, the first of which, a bouncy, good-natured "Reel in Honor of Henry Cowell" (one of Harrison's teachers), is particularly infectious. The slow movement comprises a gently swaying *Largo ostinato* of great dignity and slumbering power, whilst the finale is a joyous, finely-sustained *Allegro* of deceptive rigour and satisfying proportions. The *Grand Duo* for violin and piano from 1988 perhaps makes less consistently compelling listening, though its five movements also contain much characterful invention. Both the "Stampadé" and "Polka" offer plenty of opportunities (gratefully seized here) for vigorous violin double-stopping and piano cluster-chords, whereas a simple, trance-like euphony illuminates the tender central "A Round". Moreover, Harrison's eloquent sense of dialogue similarly distinguishes the thoughtful extended slow movement and more declamatory initial "Prelude". Both works were commissioned by the Cabrillo Music Festival in California, whose eponymous orchestra perform with admirable discipline and total dedication under the ever-sympathetic guidance of Dennis Russell Davies. In the *Grand Duo*, the versatile Davies partners violinist Romuald Tecco with equally idiomatic, wonderfully assured results.
Further listening ...
...Symphony No. 2, "Elegiac". *Coupled with* **Hovhaness** Symphony No. 2, "Mysterious mountain", Op. 132. Lousadzak, Op. 48[a]. [a]**Keith Jarrett** (pf); **American Composers Orchestra / Dennis Russell Davies.** MusicMasters 7021-2 (5/93).
...Suite for Symphonic Strings. *Coupled with* **McPhee** Tabuh-Tabuhan[a]. **Ung** Inner Voices. [a]**Peter Basquin,** [a]**Christopher Oldfather** (pfs); **American Composers Orchestra / Dennis Russell Davies.** Argo 444 560-2ZH (4/96). *See review under McPhee; refer to the Index to Reviews.*
...Harp Suite[a]. Serenade[ac]. Perilous Chapel[cd]. Fugue[ce]. Song of Quetzalcoatl[ce]. May Rain[bc]. [b]**John Duykers** (ten); [a]**David Tanenbaum** (gtr); [b]**Julie Steinberg** (pf); [c]**William Winant** (perc); [d]**San Francisco Contemporary Music Players / Stephen Mosko;** [e]**Percussion Ensemble.** New Albion NA055CD (2/94).

...Mass (to St Anthony). *Coupled with* **Pärt** Berliner Messe[a]. **LeaAnne DenBeste** (sop); **Laura Crockett** (mez); [a]**David Vanderwal** (ten); [a]**Karl Blume** (bass); [a]**Marianne Lewis** (org); **Oregon Repertory Singers / Gilbert Seeley.** Koch International Classics 37177-2 (4/94).

Sadie Harrison   Australian 1965-

Suggested listening ...
...*Nani ka itou. Coupled with works by* **N. Hayes, Hallgrimsson, Weir, Finnissy, G. Jackson, Crane, A. Fisher** and **Skempton** Tapestry. British Music Label BML012 (12/95). *See review in the Collections section; refer to the Index to Reviews.*

Karl Amadeus Hartmann   German 1905-1963

Hartmann Symphonies – No. 1[ac]; No. 2 – Adagio[d]; No. 3[e]; No. 4[d]; No. 5[d]; No. 6[d]; No. 7 (1957-8)[f]; No. 8[d]. Gesangszene (1963)[b]. [a]**Doris Soffel** (contr); [b]**Dietrich Fischer-Dieskau** (bar); **Bavarian Radio Symphony Orchestra /** [c]**Fritz Rieger,** [d]**Rafael Kubelík,** [e]**Ferdinand Leitner,** [f]**Zdenek Macal.** Wergo Ⓕ WER60187-50 (four discs: 225 minutes: ADD: 5/90). From WER60086 (6/81). ⒼⒼⒼ
Stravinsky once remarked that Alban Berg was "synthetic, in the best sense" – the same could perhaps be said about Hartmann. In the 1930s he was beginning to establish a reputation, but was forced to withdraw himself and his works from public musical life as a known opponent of the Nazi regime. During the war he destroyed or radically revised most of his output up till then, and these eight symphonies (five of which are based on, or are revisions of, earlier works) appeared between 1946 and his death in 1963. Together they show his broad sympathies with the twentieth-century masters. As Hartmann chose to write symphonies, he had to be mindful of the enormity of the tradition that preceded him, and you can hear the presence of Bruckner in the monumental sense of structure, of Reger in the densely chromatic counterpoint and an intense, tortured lyricism derived from Berg. There is a tribute to the neo-classical Stravinsky in the Fifth Symphony, and more than a hint of Bartók in the irresistible momentum of the fugues that conclude the Sixth. Mahler is present in the Whitman settings of the First Symphony, significantly entitled *Attempt at a Requiem*; also, in the upheavals of the first movement of the Eighth, the crisis near the end of the *Adagio* of Mahler's Tenth is vividly recalled (sustained high trumpet, screaming violins). The spectral Funeral March in Webern's *Pieces*, Op. 6 haunts sections of the First, Third and Eighth Symphonies. Whether, with Hartmann's synthesis of his models, he managed to forge a demonstrably personal idiom is open to question. What is indisputable is the power of Hartmann's music to communicate, and its capacity to fascinate as sheer sound. On the debit side, not all the vigorously contrapuntal sections of the later works avoid sounding academic. The dates of these live recordings are not given, but they are all naturally balanced, with excellent clarity – Hartmann's torrents of tuned percussion are thrillingly captured. The Bavarian Radio Symphony Orchestra play with polish and evident conviction. Recommended to anyone interested in the development of the symphony in our century.
Additional recommendation ...
...No. 2. Gesangssezene to words from Jean Giraudoux's "Sodom and Gomorrah"[a]. Sinfonia Tragica. [a]**Siegmund Nimsgern** (bar); **Bamberg Symphony Orchestra / Karl Anton Rickenbacher.** Koch Schwann Ⓕ 312952 (64 minutes: DDD: 5/94). *Gramophone Editor's choice.*

| New review |
Hartmann Symphony No. 3.
Ives Robert Browning Overture. **Bamberg Symphony Orchestra / Ingo Metzmacher.** EMI Ⓕ CDC5 55254-2 (52 minutes: DDD: 10/95). Recorded 1994.
All the numbered Hartmann symphonies up to and including the Sixth (1951-3) had complex gestations, none more so than No. 3 (1948-9), which is in fact a conflation of movements from two distinct works composed during the Second World War, the *Sinfonia Tragica* (1940, rev. 1943) and *Klagegesang* (1944-5, rev. 1946-7). The result betrays nothing of the piecemeal construction, being one of Hartmann's deepest and most powerful utterances. One of the most heartening features of this recording is its sheer allure. Metzmacher secures very polished playing and after the raw sound on the rival Wergo disc (reviewed above), the smooth Bamberg sound takes some getting used to, even more so in the case of Ives's volcanic *Robert Browning Overture* (1908-12). As with the music of Villa-Lobos, there is something to be said for the odd rough edge or three in Ives's music (or is it just that we have had to put up with them for so long that they seem natural?), but there is no denying the persuasiveness of the present account. A valuable issue.
Further listening ...
...Concerto funebre. *Coupled with works by* **Berg** and **Janáček** Philharmonia Orchestra / Heinz Holliger; Deutsche Kammerphilharmonie / Thomas Zehetmair (vn/dir). Teldec 4509-97449-2 (6/95). *See review under Berg; refer to the Index to Reviews.*
...String Quartets – No. 1, "Carillon"; No. 2. **Pellegrini Quartet.** CPO CPO999 219-2 (8/94).   Ⓖ
...Simplicius Simplicissimus. **Soloists; Munich Concert Choir; Bavarian Radio Symphony Orchestra / Heinz Fricke.** Wergo WER6259-2 (11/95).

Sir Herbert Hamilton Harty
Irish 1879-1941

Suggested listening ...

...An Irish Symphony. A Comedy Overture. **Ulster Orchestra / Bryden Thomson.** Chandos
   CHAN8314 (9/84).

...A John Field Suite. In Ireland. *Coupled with* **Handel** Water Music (trans. Harty). **Traditional**
   The Londonderry Air – Folksong (trans. Harty). **Ulster Orchestra / Bryden Thomson.** Chandos
   Collect CHAN6583 (11/93).

...A John Field Suite. *Coupled with* **Ireland** A London Overture. **Coleridge Taylor** Scenes from
   "The Song of Hiawatha", Op. 30 – Onaway, awake, beloved[a]. **Gardiner** Shepherd Fennell's
   Dance. **Vaughan Williams** The Lark Ascending[b]. **Holst** The Hymn of Jesus, H140[c]. [a]**Webster
   Booth** (ten); [b]**David Wise** (vn); [c]**Huddersfield Choral Society; Liverpool Philharmonic Orchestra /
   Sir Malcolm Sargent.** Dutton Laboratories mono CDAX8012* (5/95).

Jonathan Harvey
British 1939-

New review

J. Harvey Bhakti. **Nouvel Ensemble Moderne / Lorraine Vaillancourt.** Auvidis Montaigne
   Ⓕ MO782086 (54 minutes: DDD: 7/96). Recorded 1994.

This must rank as one of Jonathan Harvey's most important and approachable works. No one need
feel intimidated by its subtitle – "for 15 instrumentalists and quadrophonic tape". This is a score
whose energy and eloquence appeal as directly as its rich tapestry of (live and recorded) sounds. The
work may have originated in the subterranean caverns of IRCAM in Paris, but the music is full of
light and air. *Bhakti* is also a religious work: the Hindu term which provides its title means "devotion
to a god, as a path to salvation", and most of the movements have quotations from the *Rig Veda*
placed at the end. As with Messiaen, or Stravinsky, however, these theological specifics need not place
constraints on accessibility to those who have different beliefs or concerns. Rather they generate a
musical process which can be appreciated in and for itself – a 'path' that encompasses a brilliantly
realized musical drama of unusual harmoniousness, with the kind of explicit integration around a
central pitch (heard most clearly at the very beginning) which is rare in progressive twentieth-century
music. The recording is excellent and the performance by the Nouvel Ensemble Moderne carries great
conviction and technical sophistication.

J. Harvey I love the Lord. Carols. Lauds (with Paul Watkins, vc). Sobre un éxtasis alte
   contemplación. Come, Holy Ghost. O Jesu, nomen dulce. Two Fragments. The Angels. Forms of
   Emptiness. **The Joyful Company of Singers / Peter Broadbent.** ASV Ⓕ CDDCA917 (63 minutes:
   DDD: 7/95). Texts and translations included. Recorded 1994.

Compare Jonathan Harvey's *Come, Holy Ghost* with one of his large-scale instrumental works and
you might suspect that they are the work of different Jonathan Harveys, one providing short pieces
for cathedral choirs, the other active on the avant-garde concert scene. So it is a particular virtue of
this disc that by providing such a generous cross-section of Harvey's choral music it makes it easier
to hear how the two Harveys are in fact one far-from-inconsistent composer. Since Harvey himself
has progressed from choir school to electronic studio it is not so surprising that his music can relate
to both worlds so effectively, and most of the compositions here take a fresh look at aspects of the
English cathedral tradition without attempting to force those aspects into an unholy alliance with
modernist techniques, and technologies. From the early *Fragments* (1966) to *The Angels* (1994) we can
hear versions of the kind of contemplative intensity that informs some of Harvey's finest concert
works (for example, *Bhakti*, listed below), and these choral pieces are never poor relations. The short
Sobre un éxtasis alte contemplación works within its own essential sounds, and in exploring speech as
well as song develops the more dramatic dialogue to be found in the larger-scale *Forms of Emptiness*
(1986) and *Lauds* (1987). In such compositions, with their highly diverse textures, spiritual and
sensual elements are brought into purposeful conjunction. Though The Joyful Company of Singers
have no boy sopranos, they have the flexibility of tone as well as the strength of sonority to project
all facets of this often challenging music. The recordings are exceptionally atmospheric, and the disc
as a whole can be warmly recommended.

Additional recommendation ...

...I love the Lord. Come, Holy Ghost. *Coupled with works by* **Musgrave, Hoddinott,
   Maconchy, T. Salter** and **Lutyens** Ionian Singers / Timothy Salter; Thalia Myers (pf); Erik
   Jacobsen (perc). Usk Recordings Ⓕ USK1216 (67 minutes: DDD: 3/96).

Further listening ...

...Bhakti for Chamber Ensemble and Quadraphonic Tape. **Spectrum / Guy Protheroe.** NMC
   NMCD001 (9/89).

...From Silence[a]. Natajara[b]. Ritual Melodies[c]. [a]**Karol Bennett** (voc); [b]**Harrie Starreveld** (fl/picc);
   [a]**Lucy Chapman Stoltzman** (vn); [a]**Michael Thompson** (hn); [a]**Dean Anderson** (perc); [b]**René Eckhardt**
   (pf); [a]**Kathleen Supove, [a]John MacDonald, [a]Diana Dabby** (electric keyboards); [ac]**David Atherton**
   (tape op); [ac]**Brent Koeppel, [ac]Ken Malsky, [ac]Philip Sohn** (computer/tape ops) / **Barry Vercoe.**
   Bridge BCD9031 (11/92).

...Song Offerings. *Coupled with* **G. Benjamin** Antara. **Boulez** Dérive. Memoriale. **Penelope Walmsley-Clark** (sop); **Sebastian Bell** (fl); **London Sinfonietta / George Benjamin.** Nimbus NI5167 (10/89).

Basil Harwood
British 1859-1949

Harwood Organ Sonata No. 1 in C sharp minor, Op. 5.
Saint-Saëns Trois Préludes et Fugues, Op. 99. Trois Préludes et Fugues, Op. 109. **Adrian Partington** (org). Priory Ⓕ PRCD384 (66 minutes: DDD: 8/94). Played on the Grove and Milton organs of Tewkesbury Abbey. Recorded 1991.
Adrian Partington has two organs to choose from at Tewkesbury Abbey. The Milton organ goes back to Robert Dallam in 1631 but has been rebuilt and enlarged several times since, including work by Father Willis and latterly J.W. Walker. Partington plays Basil Harwood's Organ Sonata No. 1 on this instrument and it works well. The sonata is an accomplished piece from an Englishman in 1887. The first movement, *Allegro appassionato*, is not quite passionate enough in this performance – the rhythmic figures need to be tighter and more driving to get across the music's striking and urgent character. At 3'17" the chorale enters for the first time and it makes a dramatic reappearance, well paced in this performance, at 4'44" at the end of the fugue in the finale. Harwood knew his Liszt. The Grove organ at Tewkesbury is Victorian and was much admired by W.T. Best. It is particularly suitable for the two sets of Saint-Saëns's Preludes and Fugues, composed in the 1890s. This polished Frenchman can write a catchy fugue subject – No. 1 in E major, for example – and dreams up unexpectedly delicious textures such as the opening of No. 2 in B major. Partington is thoroughly at home in this idiom and his registration is resourcefully varied.

Johann Hasse
German 1699-1783

Hasse Quel vago seno, ò Fille[a]. Fille dolce, mio bene[a]. La conversione di Sant' Agostino – Ah Dio, ritornate[a]. Four Venetian ballads[a]. Trio Sonata in B minor, Op. 2 No. 6. Keyboard Sonata in C minor, Op. 7 No. 6. [a]**Julianne Baird** (sop); **Nancy Hadden** (fl); **Erin Headley** (va da gamba); [b]**Malcolm Proud** (hpd). CRD Ⓕ CRD3488 (75 minutes: DDD: 11/94). Texts and translations included. Recorded 1991. *Gramophone Editor's choice.*   Ⓖ
Though chiefly celebrated now, as in his own day, as an opera composer, Hasse wrote a significant quantity of sacred pieces and much delightful chamber music for voices and instruments of which this disc offers a well-chosen and stylishly performed selection. He was a younger contemporary and compatriot of Bach, Handel and Telemann, whose music by and large reflected the rococo taste for pleasing melodies with lightly textured and graceful accompaniments. The cantatas provide the greatest substance here, consisting of two pairs of alternating recitatives and arias. Hasse seems often to have gone in for unusually extended *da capo* arias. However, they hold our attention with their engaging melodic contours and effective accompaniments. Julianne Baird is one of the most stylish and thoughtful of our present interpreters of baroque and early classical music; and the conjunction of an agile technique with an alluring vocal timbre gives considerable strength to her performances. Malcolm Proud, who provides first-rate continuo realizations throughout, also gives us a favourable impression of Hasse's solo keyboard skill in a fine Sonata in C minor for harpsichord. The outstanding movement here is the third one, a deeply felt, darkly coloured *Adagio* which Proud plays with unhurried and affecting intensity. In short, a delightful disc, well considered, well performed and intimately recorded.
Further listening ...
...Flute Concerto in G major[b]. *Coupled with* **Agrell** Flute Concerto in D major[a]. **Scheibe** Flute Concertos – A major[a]; D major[b]. [a]**Maria Bania,** [b]**Irene Spranger** (fls); **Concerto Cophenhagen / Andrew Manze.** Chandos Chaconne CHAN0535 (6/93). 🖎
...Keyboard Sonata in E flat major[a]. *Coupled with* **Graun** Keyboard Sonata in D minor[a]. **Benda** Keyboard Sonatinas[a] – Rondeau; Allegro; Allegretto; Allegretto; Allegretto moderato. **Fasch** Andantino con Variazioni[a]. **Schulz** Diverses pièces, Op. 1[b] – No. 5, Allegretto; No. 6, Larghetto con Variazioni. **C.P.E. Bach** Pièces Caractéristiques[b] – La Borchward, H79; La Pott, H80; La Gleim, H89; La Bergius, H90; La Stahl, H94; La Boehmer, H81; La Louise, H114. **Christine Schornsheim** ([a]hpd/[b]fp). Capriccio 10 424 (4/95). 🖎
...La conversione di Sant' Agostino. **Soloists; Berlin RIAS Chamber Choir; Berlin Ancient Music Academy / Marcus Creed.** Capriccio 10 389/90 (7/93). 🖎
...Requiem in C major[a]. Miserere in E minor. **Greta de Reyghere** (sop); **Susanna Moncayo von Hase** (contr); [a]**Ian Honeyman** (ten); **Dirk Snellings** (bass); **Il Fondamento Chorus and Orchestra / Paul Dombrecht.** Opus 111 OPS30-80 (11/93). 🖎
...Piramo e Tisbe. **Soloists; Capella Clementina / Helmut Müller-Brühl.** Koch Schwann 310882 (4/94). 🖎

Hans Johann Leo Hassler
German 1564-1612

Suggested listening ...
...Missa I super Dixit Maria. Ad Dominum cum tribularer. O admirabile commercium. Usquequo,
Domine. Domine Deus, Israel. Vater unser in Himmelreich. *Coupled with* **Lechner** Si bona
suscepimus. **Chapelle Royale European Vocal Ensemble / Philippe Herreweghe.** Harmonia Mundi
HMC90 1401 (10/93). ✍

...Canzon duodecimi toni[bcd]. Cantate Domino canticum novum[abcde]. Toccata in G[d]. Canzon noni
toni[bcd]. O sacrum convivium[acd]. Domine Dominus noster[abcde]. *Coupled with works by* **Erbach**
and **Lassus** [a]**Westminster Cathedral Choir;** [b]**His Majesties Sagbutts and Cornetts / James
O'Donnell** with [c]**Timothy Roberts,** [d]**Iain Simcock,** [e]**Iris Schöllhorn** (orgs). Hyperion CDA66688
(6/94). ✍

Joseph Haydn
Austrian 1732-1809

Haydn Cello Concertos – No. 1 in C major, HobVII*b*/1; No. 2 in D major, HobVII*b*/2.
A. Kraft Cello Concerto in C major, Op. 4. **Anner Bylsma** (vc); **Tafelmusik / Jeanne Lamon.**
Deutsche Harmonia Mundi Ⓕ RD77757 (67 minutes: DDD: 9/91). ✍ Recorded 1989.

At best, an 'authentic' performance can only aspire to return to the spirit, rather than the letter of the
period it strives to recreate, and yet the fine Dutch cellist Anner Bylsma comes as near as anyone to
convincing us that this is indeed the way Haydn might have wished these sunny, yet highly
sophisticated concertos to be played. Haydn composed these works for the virtuoso cellist of the
Esterházy court orchestra, Anton Kraft, and the bold and adventurous solo writing reflects his fabled
technical prowess and musical sensitivity. Bylsma offers a lithe, yet scrupulously classical and poised
account of the C major Concerto, with a romantically inflected central *Adagio* followed by a
dashingly brilliant, yet suitably witty finale. His rapid passagework in higher registers is astonishing,
while he reveals the stately dignity of the D major work (long attributed to Kraft) in a cultured and
attractively proportioned reading of rich intensity and variety. Bylsma includes his own revisions of
period cadenzas, which are never less than apposite, and deftly executed. The real discovery here,
though, is the Cello Concerto by Kraft himself, which combines the expected brilliant pyrotechnics
with some effective melodic writing, in a work which anticipates the styles developed during the early
nineteenth century. In fact, Kraft advised Beethoven on the cello part of his Triple Concerto, and his
compositions exercised great influence in the genesis of modern cello technique. Bylsma is superbly
supported by the excellent Canadian ensemble, Tafelmusik, and the recording is first rate. A revealing,
and often stunningly played collection – highly recommended to all cello enthusiasts.

Additional recommendations ...
...*As Haydn*[ab]. Violin Concertos[c] – C major, HobVIIa/1; A major, HobVIIa/3; G major, HobVIIa/4.
Concerto for Violin, Keyboard and Strings in F major, HobXVIII/6[cd]. [a]**Christine Walevska** (vc);
[d]**Bruno Canino** (hpd); **English Chamber Orchestra /** [b]**Edo de Waart,** [c]**Salvatore Accardo** (vn).
Philips Duo Ⓜ 438 797-2PM2 (two discs: 142 minutes: ADD: 4/94).

...*As Haydn.* **Truls Mørk** (vc); **Norwegian Chamber Orchestra / Iona Brown.** Virgin Classics Ⓕ VC5
45014-2 (50 minutes: DDD: 6/94).

...Nos. 1 and 2. *Coupled with works by* **Monn, Dvořák, Schumann, Saint-Saëns, Delius,
Elgar, Chopin, Franck, Fauré, Bruch, Bach, Handel** and **Beethoven** Jacqueline du Pré
(vc); **London Symphony Orchestra /** **Sir John Barbirolli; English Chamber Orchestra /** **Daniel
Barenboim.** EMI Ⓑ CZS5 68132-2 (six discs: 437 minutes: ADD: 8/94). *See review in the
Collections section; refer to the Index to Reviews.* ☻☻

...Nos. 1 and 2. Symphony No. 104 in D major, "London". **Pieter Wispelwey** (vc); **Florilegium.**
Channel Classics Ⓕ CCS7395 (73 minutes: DDD: 7/95).

...No. 2. *Coupled with works by* **Bach, Kodály, Dohnányi, Boccherini, Schumann, Saint-
Saëns, Dvořák, Faure, Milhaud** and **Prokofiev** János Starker (vc); **Gerald Moore** (pf);
Philharmonia Orchestra / Carlo Maria Giulini, Walter Susskind. EMI mono/stereo Ⓜ CZS5
68485-2 (six discs: 398 minutes: ADD: 12/95). *See review in the Collections section; refer to the
Index to Reviews.*

New review
Haydn Horn Concerto No. 1 in D major, HobXVII*d*/3.
Danzi Horn Concerto in E major.
Rosetti Horn Concerto in D minor. **Hermann Baumann** (hn); **Concerto Amsterdam / Jaap
Schröder.** Teldec Das Alte Werk Ⓜ 0630-12324-2 (52 minutes: ADD: 8/96). Recorded 1968.

Hermann Baumann has always been one of the most impressive performers on the eighteenth century
hand horn and in his late 1960s recording of Haydn's splendid First Horn Concerto in D the
characterful smoothness of his playing brings virtually no indications of the problems of hand
'stopping', and his intonation is absolutely true. The *Adagio* soars and there are also some
wonderfully resonant low notes. The coupled Danzi Concerto is also appealing and brings ready
bravura in its flowing opening movement, which is followed by a mellifluous central "Romance" and
a perky finale. The third work here, a fine Bohemian Concerto by Antonio Rosetti, is *galant* in style,

but with hints of high drama. The first movement is slightly reminiscent of Hummel's E major Trumpet Concerto and the slow movement is operatically romantic, the finale jolly. Jaap Schröder and his Concerto Amsterdam provide stylish accompaniments which maintain a firm late-eighteenth-century flavour, and the sound, fresh, warm and clear, is excellent.

Haydn Keyboard Concertos – F major, HobXVIII/3; G major, HobXVIII/4; D major, HobXVIII/11. **Franz Liszt Chamber Orchestra / Emanuel Ax** (pf). Sony Classical Ⓕ SK48383 (59 minutes: DDD: 5/93). Recorded 1992.

Mozart's unique achievement in his 27 piano concertos has tended to overshadow the more modestly scored, less overtly virtuoso works by Haydn and only the D major Concerto is at all well known today. Whilst none of the three works recorded here could claim to add to the development of the form in the way that those of Mozart did, all three possess great charm: take for example the *Largo cantabile* of the early F major work to hear Haydn's melodic gift at its most endearing. The *Presto* finale of the same concerto recalls some of his later piano sonatas in its juxtaposition of knockabout comedy and theatrical minor-key drama. The G major, supposedly written for the blind pianist, composer and singer Maria Theresia von Paradis boasts an extended *Grave* slow movement. But it is the D major with its larger orchestra (horns and oboes added to strings) that works best and the *Rondo all'Ungarese* finale, with its myriad key changes and sparkling good humour, is predictably the highlight of the disc. Emanuel Ax (directing from the keyboard) gives performances of the utmost finesse and affection: if any performance were to help to restore the fortunes of these works then this is surely it. His playing throughout is deeply felt: graceful in the slow movements and dexterous in the outer ones. In addition, he plays his own charming cadenzas in the F and G major works. Sony's sound is spacious, with the piano forwardly placed and the notes are adequate, though no biographical information is included.

Additional recommendation ...
...D major; G major; F major; G major, HobXVIII /9. **Hae-won Chang** (pf); **Camerata Cassovia / Robert Stankovsky.** Naxos Ⓢ 8 550713 (71 minutes: DDD).

Haydn Trumpet Concerto in E flat major, HobVIIe/1[a]. Cello Concerto in D major, HobVIIb/2[b]. Violin Concerto No. 1 in C major, HobVII[c]. [a]**Wynton Marsalis** (tpt); [c]**Cho-Liang Lin** (vn); [b]**Yo-Yo Ma** (vc); [a]**National Philharmonic Orchestra / Raymond Leppard;** [b]**English Chamber Orchestra / José Luis Garcia;** [c]**Minnesota Orchestra / Sir Neville Marriner.** CBS Masterworks Ⓕ MK39310 (59 minutes: DDD: 1/86). From IM39310 (1/85).

This compilation of three Haydn concertos has a different soloist and orchestra for each. The young American trumpeter Wynton Marsalis has all the fluency one could wish for and an instrument allowing a full three octaves to be displayed in his own cadenza to the first movement. Although this is an efficient performance, it in no way approaches the class of the next one. The cellist Yo-Yo Ma is very different as a performer: though equally a master of his instrument, and indeed a virtuoso who seems incapable of producing an ugly sound or playing out of tune, one feels a deep emotional involvement in all he does. In addition, the recording in the D major Cello Concerto is unusually faithful in blending the cello well into the ensemble without ever covering it. Ma is supported by the excellent English Chamber Orchestra and the qualities of integration and ensemble under their leader's direction are all that one could wish for. In the C major Violin Concerto the skilful Cho-Liang Lin has the benefit of a most sympathetic conductor in Sir Neville Marriner, but he cannot match Ma's subtlety and commitment.

Additional recommendations ...
...Trumpet Concerto. **Hummel** Trumpet Concerto in E flat major. **Telemann** Trumpet Concerto in D major. **Neruda** Trumpet Concerto in E flat major. **Tartini** Trumpet Concerto in D major. **Ole Edvard Antonsen** (tpt); **English Chamber Orchestra / Jeffrey Tate.** EMI Ⓕ CDC7 54897-2 (68 minutes: DDD: 2/94).
...Trumpet Concerto. *Coupled with works by* **Neruda, Hummel, F. Weber** and **C.F.C. Fasch** **John Wallace** (tpt); **Philharmonia Orchestra / Christopher Warren-Green.** Nimbus Ⓕ NI7016 (75 minutes: DDD: 2/95). *See review in the Collections section; refer to the Index to Reviews.*
...Trumpet Concerto. *Coupled with works by* **Hertel, Hummel** and **A. Marcello** Maurice André (tpt); **Franz Liszt Chamber Orchestra / János Rolla.** EMI Ⓕ CDC5 55231-2 (61 minutes: DDD: 7/95).

New review

Haydn Six Scherzandos, HobII/33-8. **Vienna Haydn Sinfonietta / Manfred Huss.** Koch Schwann Ⓕ 314432 (52 minutes: DDD: 11/95). Recorded 1993.

The *Six Scherzandos* which Haydn wrote in 1761 to impress his new patron, Prince Paul Anton Esterházy, exhibit all the typical characteristics of the composer's mature style. Each of these miniature symphonies presents the four movements of the classical symphony with a degree of thematic and formal concentration associated with Beethoven's Op. 126 *Bagatelles* and, ultimately, with the works of Anton Webern. Moreover, their sequence here creates a compelling musical cycle. The abounding vitality and subtle sensitivity with which Manfred Huss and the Vienna Haydn Sinfonietta perform this music emphasizes its remarkable formal and instrumental variety, highlighting the startling emotional intensity created by its sudden changes of mood. Sample the vivacious opening *allegros*, the rugged minuets (whose trios feature a solo flute, superbly played here by Reinhard Czasch), the affecting *adagios* – especially the operatic example in the Fourth *Scherzando* – scored for strings alone, and the brief, energetic finales. The set culminates in the Sixth *Scherzando*, in A major, whose opening movement's triadic principal theme, agitated repeated notes and elated interjections from the horns, signal the music's increased dramatic power. The rustic minuet is rhythmically more imaginative and its trio is melodically freer than in the other five works; the *Adagio*'s exquisite pathos is enhanced by tasteful contributions from the *basso continuo*, and the archetypal, witty finale simulates larger forces with its opposition of different instrumental groupings. Ensemble is impeccably balanced throughout, and the recorded sound is vividly clear and natural.

Haydn Symphonies. **Philharmonia Hungarica / Antál Dorati.** Decca Ⓜ 430 100-2DM32
(32 discs: 2191 minutes: ADD: 6/91). Also available as eight four-disc sets. Recorded 1969-73. *425 900-2DM4* (270 minutes) – Nos. 1-16. *425 905-2DM4* (274 minutes) – Nos. 17-33. *425 910-2DM4* (283 minutes) – Nos. 34-47. *425 915-2DM4* (273 minutes) – Nos. 48-59. *425 920-2DM4* (251 minutes) – Nos. 60-71. *425 925-2DM4* (269 minutes) – Nos. 72-83. *425 930-2DM4* (286 minutes) – Nos. 84-95. *425 935-2DM4* (286 minutes) – Nos. 96-104. Symphony "A" in B flat major. Symphony "B" in B flat major. Sinfonia concertante in B flat major, HobI/105. *As we go to press we are informed that this set has been deleted. It is unlikely to remain out of the catalogue for long but will obviously be reinstated under new numbers.* ⓖⓖⓖ

Despite the increasing number of period-instrument performances of Haydn symphonies, this pioneering modern-instrument cycle recorded by Antál Dorati and his band of Hungarian exiles between 1969 and 1973 is always going to be a hard act to follow. When first issued on LP Dorati's performances won almost universal praise for their style and verve, their eager and imaginative engagement with the music's astonishing, protean inventiveness. And in their long overdue CD incarnation, in eight boxes of four discs each, they still have little to fear from most of the competition. Remarkably, for such an extended project, there is hardly a whiff of routine: time and again the orchestra seem to play out of their skin for Dorati, the strings sweet-toned and luminous, the wind deft and resourceful, savouring to the full the wit and whimsy of Haydn's writing. And though one might have reservations about this or that symphony, Dorati's actual interpretations are often exemplary, combining rhythmic resilience and a splendid overall sweep with an unusual care for detail.

Aficionados of period-instrument performances may feel that the strings, especially in the earlier symphonies, are too numerous and too liberal with vibrato. But the buoyancy of Dorati's rhythms and the crispness of the strings' articulation constantly preclude any suggestion of undue opulence. Most of the early symphonies (in which Dorati uses a discreetly balanced harpsichord continuo) are captivatingly done: *Allegros* dance and leap and slow movements are shaped with finesse and affection. Listen, for instance, to the beautiful neo-baroque D minor *Andante* in No. 4, or the grave *Siciliano* in No. 12, a particularly appealing, warm-textured work. And in the second box, containing Nos. 17-33, Dorati brings a characteristic breadth and intensity of line to the opening *Adagios* of No. 21 (a notably mature and eloquent movement, this) and No. 22, the so-called *Philosopher*. The famous *Hornsignal*, No. 31, is also irresistibly done, with rollicking, ripe-toned horns; and practically the only disappointment in the first two boxes is the *Lamentatione*, No. 26, where both the tragic first movement and the quizzical final minuet are too smooth and sluggish.

A number of the minuets in the middle-period symphonies (those written between the late 1760s and the early 1780s) are also distinctly leisurely, lacking Dorati's usual rhythmic spring – cases in point are those in Nos. 43, 52 and 49 (the last funereally slow). And one or two of the passionate minor-key symphonies, especially Nos. 39 and 52, are, like No. 26, wanting in fire and dramatic thrust. But in many of these works of Haydn's first full maturity (several still virtually unknown) Dorati gives penetrating, shrewdly judged performances. Highlights among the rarer symphonies include No. 41, with its pealing trumpets and high horns (stunningly well played), the expansive No. 42, done with real breadth and grandeur, and the subtle, lyrical No. 64, whose sublime *Largo* is sustained at the slowest possible tempo. In one or two works (notably the large-scale D major, No. 61, and the so-called *Laudon*, No. 69), Dorati might seem too frothy and frolicsome. And just occasionally (as in the outrageous six-movement *Il distratto*, No. 60) he can underplay the earthy, rumbustious side of Haydn's complex musical personality.

Two of the most desirable boxes of all are those containing Symphonies Nos. 72-83 and 84-95 – though some collectors may find it inconvenient that both the "Paris" and the "London" sets are split between boxes. Most of the pre-Paris symphonies are still underrated: but works like Nos. 76, 77 and 81 reveal a new, almost Mozartian suavity of manner and a sophistication of thematic development influenced by the Op. 33 String Quartets, while the two minor-key symphonies, Nos. 78 and 80, have notably powerful, concentrated first movements. If Dorati is a shade too comfortable in No. 80 he is superb elsewhere on these discs. Though the competition from rival performances continually hots up, he can more than hold his own in the "Paris" set: listen to the mingled grace and strength he brings to Nos. 85 and 87, with their clear, gleaming textures, or his dramatic urgency in the first movement of the misleadingly named *La poule*, No. 83.

As for the "London" Symphonies, Dorati's readings are as detailed and attentive as any on the market, though at times he can underestimate the music's boldness, grandeur and dangerous wit. This is partly a question of tempos (some distinctly on the slow side) and accent, but also of the variable prominence accorded the brass and timpani – in several works, notably Nos. 94, 96 and, most seriously, the flamboyant, aggressive Nos. 97 and 100, these instruments are too recessed to make their full dramatic effect. Elsewhere, though, the balance is more satisfying: and in symphonies like Nos. 93, 103 and 104 Dorati combines power, incisiveness and symphonic breadth with an unusual sensitivity to the lyrical poignancy which underlies much of Haydn's later music.

The recordings, outstanding in their day, still sound pretty impressive, with a fine spaciousness and bloom, even if the violins can acquire a touch of glare above the stave. All in all, a magnificent, life-enhancing series that has contributed vastly to our deeper understanding of Haydn's genius over the last two decades. Whatever integral cycles may appear in the future, Dorati's will stand as one of the gramophone's grandest achievements.

Additional recommendations ...

...No. 13 in D major; No. 14 in A major; No. 15 in D major; No. 16 in B flat major. **Hanover Band / Roy Goodman.** Hyperion Ⓕ CDA66534 (74 minutes: DDD: 3/94). ✐

...No. 26 in D minor, "Lamentatione"; No. 35 in B flat major; No. 49 in F minor, "La Passione". **Northern Chamber Orchestra / Nicholas Ward.** Naxos Ⓢ 8 550721 (55 minutes: DDD: 1/94).

...No. 26; No. 42 in D major; No. 43 in E flat major, "Mercury"; No. 44 in E minor, "Trauersinfonie"; No. 48 in C major, "Maria Theresia"; No. 49 in F minor, "La Passione". **Academy of Ancient Music / Christopher Hogwood.** L'Oiseau-Lyre Ⓕ 440 222-2OH3 (three discs: 168 minutes: DDD: 11/94). ✐

...No. 44 in E minor, "Trauer". **Mozart** Symphony No. 40 in G minor, K550. **St John's Smith Square Orchestra / John Lubbock.** IMP Red Label Ⓜ PCD820 (55 minutes: DDD: 8/86).

...Nos. 42-44. **Hanover Band / Roy Goodman.** Hyperion Ⓕ CDA66530 (79 minutes: DDD: 2/93). ✐

...Nos. 41-43. **Tafelmusik / Bruno Weil.** Sony Classical Vivarte Ⓕ SK48370 (66 minutes: DDD: 4/93). ✐

...No. 44; No. 51 in B flat major; No. 52 in C minor. **Tafelmusik / Bruno Weil.** Sony Classical Vivarte Ⓕ SK48371 (62 minutes: DDD: 4/93). ✐

...No. 45 in F sharp minor, "Farewell"; No. 48; No. 102 in B flat major. **Capella Istropolitana / Barry Wordsworth.** Naxos Ⓢ 8 550382 (73 minutes: DDD: 9/91).

...No. 48; No. 49 in F minor, "La passione"; No. 50 in C major. **Hanover Band / Roy Goodman.** Hyperion Ⓕ CDA66531 (77 minutes: DDD: 7/93). ✐

...No. 49. **Schubert** Symphony No. 5 in B flat major, D485. **St John's Smith Square Orchestra / John Lubbock.** IMP Classics Ⓑ PCD819 (53 minutes: DDD: 8/86).

...No. 88 in G major, "Letter V". **Schubert** Symphony No. 9 in C major, D944, "Great". **Berlin Philharmonic Orchestra / Wilhelm Furtwängler.** DG The Originals mono Ⓜ 447 439-2GOR* (76 minutes: ADD: 12/95).

...No. 92. **Schubert** Symphony No. 9 in C major, D944, "Great"[b]. Rosamunde, D797[b] – Ballet in B minor; Ballet in G major. [a]**Paris Conservatoire Orchestra,** [b]**London Symphony Orchestra / Bruno Walter.** Dutton Laboratories Essential Archive mono Ⓑ CDEA5003* (79 minutes: ADD: 1/96).

...No. 92. **Franck** Symphony in D minor. **Dvořák** Symphony No. 8 in G major, B163. **Prokofiev** Symphony No. 1 in D major, Op. 25, "Classical". **Concertgebouw Orchestra / Karel Ančerl.** Tahra Ⓕ TAH124/5 (two discs: 116 minutes: ADD: 3/96).

Haydn Early Symphonies – No. 1 in D major; No. 2 in C major; No. 4 in D major; No. 5 in A major; No. 10 in D major; No. 11 in E flat major; No. 18 in G major; No. 27 in G major; No. 32 in C major; No. 37 in C major; No. 107 in B flat major. **Academy of Ancient Music / Christopher Hogwood.** L'Oiseau-Lyre Ⓕ 436 428-2OH3 (three discs: 172 minutes: DDD: 4/94). ✐ Recorded 1990-91.   Ⓖ

These very early symphonies, composed before Haydn moved to the Eszterházy court in 1761, may all too easily blur together in the mind: driving *allegros*, long on physical energy but short on memorable ideas, sparse-textured 'walking' *andantes* and breezy *buffo* finales. Superficially the opening movements of the three D major works, Nos. 1, 4 and 10, and many of the finales throughout this set can seem virtually interchangeable. But even here there is more variety than you might at first suspect; and there is a world of difference between, say, the opening movement of No. 1, all quivering nervous energy, and that of No. 2, with its surprising amplitude and contrapuntal weight. If some of the slow movements are dull and arid, there is a melancholy, neo-baroque D minor *Andante* in No. 4 and a delicately expressive *Adagio, ma non troppo* in No. 32, probably the first in Haydn's long line of ceremonial C major symphonies with trumpets and timpani. But the two richest slow movements, both in texture and expression, stand at the head of works cast in church-sonata form (a sequence of slow, fast, minuet, fast): that in No. 5, with its high-lying *concertante* writing for horns; and the noble, processional *Adagio cantabile* of No. 11, whose eloquent violin writing foreshadows the well-known *Adagio* of No. 44. Hogwood's performances are pretty persuasive: crisp, precise, lightly and elegantly articulated, rhythmically spruce and almost invariably well-tuned. Compared with the rival period-instrument versions from Goodman and the Hanover Band (listed below), Hogwood and the Academy are generally rather broader and more poised in quick movements, with more gracious,

shapely phrasing and in several of the slow movements, Hogwood finds more in the music than Goodman, phrasing more considerately, with greater sensitivity to harmonic flux. Hogwood also has fuller presentation and slightly clearer, less reverberant recorded sound.

Additional recommendations:

…Nos. 1-5. **Hanover Band / Roy Goodman** (hpd). Hyperion Ⓕ CDA66524 (72 minutes: DDD: 3/92). 🖋

…No. 9 in C major; Nos. 10 and 11; No. 12 in E major. **Hanover Band / Roy Goodman.** Hyperion Ⓕ CDA66529 (69 minutes: DDD: 12/92). 🖋

Haydn Symphonies – No. 6 in D major, "Le matin"; No. 7 in C major, "Le midi"; No. 8 in G major, "Le soir". **The English Concert / Trevor Pinnock** (hpd). Archiv Produktion Ⓕ 423 098-2AH (65 minutes: DDD: 1/88). 🖋

These symphonies represent the times of day; *Le matin* portrays the sunrise, and there is a storm in *Le soir*, but otherwise there is not a lot that could be called programmatic. But Haydn did take the opportunity to give his new colleagues in the princely band something interesting to do, for there are numerous solos here, not only for the wind instruments but for the section leaders – listen especially to the *Adagio* of No. 6, with solo violin and prominent flutes and cello, a delectable piece of writing. Inventively, the music is uneven; the concerto-like style was not wholly harmonious with Haydn's symphonic thinking. But there is plenty of spirited and cheerful music here, and that is well caught in these vivacious performances by Trevor Pinnock and his band, with their brisk tempos and light textures; the playing is duly agile, and the period instruments give a bright edge to the sound.

Additional recommendations …

…Nos. 6-8. **Hanover Band / Roy Goodman.** Hyperion Ⓕ CDA66523 (69 minutes: DDD: 12/91). 🖋

…Nos. 6-8; No. 9 in C major; No. 12 in E major; No. 13 in D major; No. 16 in B flat major; No. 40 in F major; No. 72 in D major. **Academy of Ancient Music / Christopher Hogwood.** L'Oiseau-Lyre Ⓕ 433 661-2OH3 (three discs: 189 minutes: DDD: 6/93). 🖋

…Nos. 6-8. **Northern Chamber Orchestra / Nicholas Ward.** Naxos Ⓢ 8 550722 (59 minutes: DDD: 11/94).

Haydn Symphonies – No. 17 in F major; No. 18 in G major; No. 19 in D major; No. 20 in C major; No. 21 in A major. **Hanover Band / Roy Goodman.** Hyperion Ⓕ CDA66533 (79 minutes: DDD: 12/93). 🖋 Recorded 1993.

The symphonies numbered 17-20 were among Haydn's very first; and while none is especially riveting in its invention they are all compact in design, with lean, economical orchestration and a characteristically high quota of nervous energy. The most colourful and ambitious work in this group, and the only one in four movements, is the ceremonial C major, No. 20 with its panoply of trumpets, timpani and horns. Symphony No. 21, the final work on the disc, dates from several years later (1764) and sounds it: the ideas in the fast movements are more striking in themselves and more tautly developed, while the opening *Adagio* is perhaps the most lyrically intense movement in all Haydn's early symphonies. Goodman allows the *Adagio* plenty of space, shaping the music sympathetically, with a firm sense of harmonic direction. Faster movements are rhythmically vital yet never over-driven, with Haydn's contrasts of colour and dynamics vividly realized (thrilling brass sonorities in No. 20). The minuets in Nos. 20 and 21 are neatly phrased, light on their feet (you may initially be thrown by that in No. 21, which opens exactly like the minuet in *Eine kleine Nachtmusik*). Delightful performances, stylish, spirited and deftly executed. Recording, documentation and playing time are all up to the standards set by other issues in the series.

Haydn Symphonies – No. 21 in A major; No. 22 in E flat major, "The Philosopher"; No. 23 in G major; No. 24 in D major; No. 28 in A major; No. 29 in E major; No. 30 in C major, "Alleluja"; No. 31 in D major, "Hornsignal"; No. 34 in D minor. **Academy of Ancient Music / Christopher Hogwood.** L'Oiseau-Lyre Ⓕ 430 082-2OH3 (three discs: 190 minutes: DDD: 12/90). 🖋 Recorded 1988-89.

Haydn Symphonies – No. 22 in E flat major, "Philosopher"; No. 23 in G major; No. 24 in D major; No. 25 in C major. **Hanover Band / Roy Goodman.** Hyperion Ⓕ CDA66536 (75 minutes: DDD: 6/95). 🖋 Recorded 1994.

Haydn Symphonies – No. 22 in E flat major, "Philosopher"; No. 29 in E major; No. 60 in C major, "Il distratto". **Northern Chamber Orchestra / Nicholas Ward.** Naxos Ⓢ 8 550724 (60 minutes: DDD: 6/95). Recorded 1992-3.

As 'the father of the symphony', Haydn had over 100 children! So a complete recorded cycle is a major undertaking for any company, and the L'Oiseau-Lyre one here uses authentic instruments and a slightly lower pitch than modern 'concert' ones. Details of these instruments are listed in the four-language booklet, which has 70 pages including an explanation of the grouping of these works into 15 volumes – the present one, oddly enough, being No. 4 and covering the years 1764-65. The Academy of Ancient Music are usually a small orchestral body, supporting the contention expressed by Joseph Webster that Haydn's orchestra at this time was of about 13 to 16 players and that there was no keyboard continuo. In other words, there is no harpsichord to fill out textures, but although some listeners may miss it initially the playing soon convinces. The music itself cannot be summarized briefly, but as usual with Haydn, even these relatively unfamiliar pieces are inventive and often beautiful. The playing has zest, but however brisk the tempo chosen for quick movements they never degenerate into mere bustle, although other performers may take a less tense view than Christopher Hogwood. There are real discoveries to be made here, beginning with the nervous, dramatic finale to Symphony No. 21, and they also include minuets such as the enigmatic ones to Nos. 28 and 29. Similarly, slow movements have dignity, grace and often a quiet humour too, while phrasing is intelligent and affectionate and textures well balanced. Indeed, Hogwood's wind and string players alike are precise and stylish. Repeats are faithfully observed. Finally, the recording is clear and atmospheric.

Goodman and his orchestra give combustible performances, with pungent, earthy sonorities and terrific rhythmic vigour. They really lash into the repeated *fortissimos* in the development of the first movement of No. 24, the tension increased to breaking point, as Haydn surely intended. And the rollicking triple-time opening movement of No. 23, brilliantly coloured by high-pitched horns, goes with a lusty, infectious swing. In the opening movement of the *Philosopher* the Hanover Band, typically, are rawer, starker and more sharply accented than the rival period-instrument version from Hogwood, with Goodman emphasizing the inexorably tramping bass line. In general Hogwood's readings are more urbane and light-footed; and he is definitely preferable in the slow movements of Nos. 23 and 24, which in Goodman's performances are vitiated by a plodding, graceless bass – the emphatic, upfront harpsichord continuo, sometimes effective in the quicker movements, may also be a problem. But Goodman's rugged, high-voltage readings of, say, the outer movements of Nos. 23 and 24 do lift the music off the page that much more vividly. Physically exciting performances, then, graphically captured in Hyperion's immediate, detailed recording.

In the *Philosopher*, Nicholas Ward and the Northern Chamber Orchestra (using modern instruments) present a spacious, elegantly phrased account of the title-character's personality. The incisive edge of the Hanover Band's period instruments gives the music's inherently austere tone a stronger profile, but Ward's idiomatic feeling for Haydn's style produces a subtly balanced, appealingly smooth-lined performance. The E major Symphony, No. 29 offers Ward and the NCO the opportunity to explore Haydn's attractive variety of instrumental forces and powerful opposition of major and minor. The programme culminates with the C major Symphony, No. 60 (*Il distratto*). Here, Ward controls his orchestra with customary deftness to make the music's overtly descriptive elements especially telling. Haydn's comic depiction of the protagonist's absent-mindedness is vividly portrayed in the two outer movements, and distinctive thematic characterization effectively heightens the dramatic contrasts in the minuet and *Adagio* (*di Lamentatione*), in a winning performance that fully captures the composer's infectious wit.

Additional recommendation ...

...Nos. 31, 59 and 73. **Vienna Concentus Musicus / Nikolaus Harnoncourt.** Teldec Das Alte Werk Ⓔ 4509-90843-2 (78 minutes: DDD: 4/95). ✒

New review

Haydn Symphonies – No. 22 in E flat major, "Philosopher"; No. 86 in D major; No. 102 in B flat major. **City of Birmingham Symphony Orchestra / Sir Simon Rattle.** EMI Ⓔ CDC5 55509-2 (68 minutes: DDD: 1/96). Recorded 1994.

Rattle establishes a middle path between traditional and period styles of performance. In addition, the idea of coupling symphonies from different periods of Haydn's career – not new but relatively rare – is refreshing, and has here produced an issue that one can warmly recommend to anyone simply wanting a representative Haydn symphony disc. The limited vibrato and light phrasing used by the strings throughout these performances set them apart from most others using modern instruments, giving them extra freshness and transparency. So in the *Adagio* of No. 102, elegant at a flowing speed, the solo cello is clearly defined, and the Minuet brings the strongest contrast of all with modern-instrument rivals, exuberantly turned into a scherzo at one-in-a-bar. No. 86, the fifth of the "Paris Symphonies", less appreciated only for lack of a nickname, is similarly refreshing, and here too Rattle refuses to rush his first movement in the name of authenticity. The main *Allegro* is marginally more relaxed than that of Dorati, whose pioneering Decca set still provides a useful yardstick in almost every work. By contrast Rattle's *Presto* for the finale is hectic, and one marvels at the agility of the Birmingham horns in their repeated triplets, though Dorati's tempo is only marginally less urgent. In the square rhythms of the opening *Adagio* of No. 22, Rattle manages to achieve elegance without sacrificing the chunky strength of the chorale on cor anglais, and this symphony, unlike the later ones, finds Rattle using harpsichord continuo. The helpful acoustic of Symphony Hall, Birmingham, sets the seal on the disc's success with warm, clear sound.

Haydn Symphonies – No. 30 in C major, "Alleluia"; No. 53 in D major, "Imperial"; No. 69 in C major, "Loudon". **Vienna Concentus Musicus / Nikolaus Harnoncourt.** Teldec Das Alte Werk Ⓔ 9031-76460-2 (67 minutes: DDD: 6/93). ✒ Recorded 1990.

Three brilliant, extrovert pieces here, with much festive trumpeting and drumming in the two C major symphonies. More, in fact, than Haydn would have expected, since Harnoncourt has added his own trumpet and timpani parts for No. 30 (1765). Whatever the purists might think, the augmented scoring is undeniably effective, enhancing the symphony's celebratory spirit (the nickname, incidentally, comes from the use of the Easter Alleluia plainchant in the first movement); and Harnoncourt and his brilliant period-instrument orchestra give a splendidly vivid, sharp-edged performance. The other symphonies both date from the mid- to late-1770s, and combine ceremonial grandeur with the tuneful, popular manner that Haydn was beginning to cultivate around this time. No. 53, obscurely nicknamed *Imperial* in the early nineteenth century, was among the most spectacular international successes of the composer's career, mainly on account of its *Andante* variations. Harnoncourt is perhaps a touch over-sophisticated here; and the aristocratic minuet is taken at a vehement one-in-a-bar, necessitating a violent deceleration for the trio. But the splendid opening movement is played with verve and flair, while the curious, dullish-looking *Capriccio* which Haydn substituted for the original finale leaps right off the page at Harnoncourt's cracking pace. No. 69, dedicated to the Austrian Field Marshal Laudon (or Loudon), is perhaps one of Haydn's less fetching symphonies, at least until the finale, with its surprisingly violent C minor centrepiece. But Harnoncourt's powerful rhythmic drive and sense of colour (thrilling impact from brass and timpani) make out an unusually strong case for the work. The Teldec recording is spacious and reverberant, but rarely at the expense of clarity.

Additional recommendations ...

...No. 53; No. 73 in D major, "La chasse"; No. 79 in F major. **Orpheus Chamber Orchestra.** DG
Ⓕ 439 779-2GH (63 minutes: DDD: 9/94).

...No. 30; No. 55 in E flat major, "Schoolmaster"; No. 63 in C major, "La Roxelane". **Northern Chamber Orchestra / Nicholas Ward.** Naxos Ⓢ 8 550757 (56 minutes: DDD: 5/95).

Haydn Symphonies. **Tafelmusik / Bruno Weil.** Sony Classical Vivarte Ⓕ SK53985/6 (two discs, oas: 50 and 68 minutes: DDD: 11/94). ✍ Recorded 1993.
SK53985 – No. 50 in C major; No. 64 in A major, "Tempora mutantur"; No. 65 in A major.
SK53986 – No. 45 in F sharp minor, "Farewell"; No. 46 in B major; No. 47 in G major. ⒼⒼ
Whatever the numberings may suggest, the six symphonies on these discs cover a short chronological span. Nos. 45-47 belong to 1772, the climactic year of Haydn's first maturity that also saw the composition of the Op. 20 String Quartets; and the festive C major Symphony, No. 50, whose first two movements probably started life as the overture to a lost marionette opera, bears the date 1773, though the minuet and finale may just have been added later. Neither of the A major symphonies, Nos. 64 and 65, can be precisely dated, though circumstantial evidence suggests 1772-73. As H.C. Robbins Landon points out in his notes, No. 65, with its quirky, disjointed *Andante* and stomping, Brueghelian minuet, may have originally been composed as incidental music. He also proposes a theatrical connection – to my ears less likely – with the enigmatically titled No. 64, an altogether more searching, introspective work, with strange, almost Schubertian harmonic deflexions in the opening movement and a *Largo* of rare gravity and eloquence. The performances by the Toronto-based period-instrument orchestra under Bruno Weil offer playing of verve, flair and finesse is allied to vital, decisive characterization, enhanced by unusually close attention to the composer's markings. In many ways the rival performances from Goodman are similarly conceived – generally spirited tempos, crisp articulation, incisive attack, clear, colourful textures, with pungent contributions from oboes and horns. But there are one or two obvious differences. Weil eschews a harpsichord continuo, which may influence you one way or the other. Goodman's continuo is, as ever, busy and forwardly balanced. As to interpretation, Goodman tends to be earthier and more rugged though his direct, unvarnished manner can sometimes be prosaic in slow movements. But it is Weil, captured in vivid, immediate sound, who has the strongest feeling for long-range symphonic tensions, and conveys most consistently the reach and dramatic power of the sonata allegros, above all in his searing reading of the much-recorded *Farewell*.

Additional recommendations ...

...No. 48 in C major, "Maria Theresia"; No. 49 in F minor; "La Passione"; No. 50. **Hanover Band / Roy Goodman.** Hyperion Ⓕ CDA66531 (77 minutes: DDD: 7/93).

...No. 45. *Coupled with works by* **Bach, Schubert, Litolff, Rachmaninov, Bruckner, Beethoven, Brahms** and **Dvořák** London Symphony Orchestra / Sir Henry Wood. Dutton Laboratories mono Ⓜ 2CDAX2002* (two discs: 138 minutes: ADD: 9/94).

New review

Haydn Symphonies – No. 72 in D major; No. 93 in D major; No. 95 in C minor. **Nicolaus Esterházy Sinfonia / Béla Drahos.** Naxos Ⓢ 8 550797 (64 minutes: DDD: 12/95). Recorded 1994.
The prominent horn writing in Haydn's D major Symphony (No. 72) betrays its earlier chronology (between 1763 and 1765). The addition of the two further horn virtuosos to the Esterházy Orchestra in 1763 offered the composer a technical resource that was unrivalled at the time. In this new recording, the abounding vitality and fluid virtuosity from all sections of the orchestra show the Nicolaus Esterházy Sinfonia and Béla Drahos to be idiomatic Haydn interpreters. The Hanover Band, playing period instruments, present a more exciting timbral brilliance, but the NES's modern-instrument version offers an appealingly elegant, softer-edged alternative. The original *Gramophone* review found Dorati's approach to the C minor Symphony (No. 95, part of the four-disc set reviewed earlier) "simply too tame and pallid". By comparison, Drahos and the NES give a remarkably convincing account that deftly reconciles the music's inherent conflicting expressive messages. There is a compelling sense of organic development in the first movement, the cello solo emerges naturally from the ensemble in both the *Andante cantabile* and the trio to the third movement, and the work resolves emphatically in the ironically cheerful finale, whose stormy interlude (2'45"-3'00") brightens

exultantly into radiant C major. In lively pacing throughout Symphony No. 93 offers great animation. Excellent, spacious recordings.

Additional recommendation ...

...Nos. 70-72. **Hanover Band / Roy Goodman** (hpd). Hyperion Ⓕ CDA66526 (76 minutes: DDD: 9/92). ✍

Haydn Symphonies – No. 82 in C major, "L'ours"; No. 83 in G minor, "La poule"; No. 84 in E flat C major. **Tafelmusik / Bruno Weil.** Sony Classical Vivarte Ⓕ SK66295 (73 minutes: DDD: 7/95). ✍ Recorded 1994. Recorded 1994.
Haydn No. 85 in B flat major, "La reine"; No. 86 in D major; No. 87 in A major. **Tafelmusik / Bruno Weil.** Sony Classical Vivarte Ⓕ SK66296 (71 minutes: DDD: 7/95). ✍ Recorded 1994.
Written in 1785-86 for the ample forces of the Concert de la Loge Olympique, Haydn's *Paris* symphonies were his grandest and most imposing works in the form to date. Bruno Weil and his brilliant period orchestra bring to the "Paris" Symphonies the same flair and finesse that distinguished the previous discs in their ongoing complete cycle. The blazing, far-reaching opening movement of *L'ours*, No. 82, augurs well: an urgent, though never rushed, tempo, keen texturing – some details more tellingly etched than ever heard before on disc – and lithe, vital rhythms. In the *Allegretto*, fleeter and more dapper than from either Goodman or Kuijken (listed below), Weil evokes the spirit of the corresponding movement of Beethoven's Eighth; and the finale, full of razor-sharp instrumental detailing, combines dancing grace with an exhilarating drive. Only in the minuet does one have reservations: Weil's very purposeful tempo here does underestimate the element of *ancien régime* opulence in this music; and as Goodman and Kuijken demonstrate, the trio responds better to a touch more charm and flexibility. In the opening movement of *La poule* Weil brings a real bite and trenchancy to the pervasive dotted rhythms and an exciting dramatic sweep to the development. The *Andante*, more flowingly paced than in the rival versions, is elegantly shaped, with long-breathed lyrical phrasing and beautifully poised woodwind playing. In the finale Weil drives rather fiercely (Kuijken is altogether more genial here). No. 84, the least consistently inspired of the "Paris" set, comes off well in all three versions. But in the opening *Allegro* Weil phrases more graciously than his rivals, and shapes the repeated-note bass lines with a stronger sense of direction. The beautiful *Andante* is ideally paced and full of subtle, delicately placed detail.
   On the second disc Weil and his players are aggressively brisk in the *Adagio* introduction of No. 85. But they shape the main theme of the *Vivace* alluringly and bring plenty of fire to the tuttis, pointing Haydn's nervous, syncopated inner parts and ramming home the *sforzando* offbeat accents. Again, the trio of the minuet is short on wit and affection. But the finale is as spirited and gamesome as you could wish, and works up a fine lather in the central development; and the lightness and elegant ease of the *Allegretto* variations make the Kuijken version, in particular, seem distinctly sober. No. 86, the most imposing of the "Paris" Symphonies, seems less successful. The slow introduction is, again, uncomfortably brisk, while for all the eager athleticism of the playing the *Allegro spiritoso* rather lacks grandeur. In the *Capriccio* second movement Weil plays up Haydn's violent rhetorical outbursts; but at his controversially swift tempo the music's grave, majestic tread and intense, brooding harmonies go for comparatively little. Timings are revealing: Weil takes 5'47" to Kuijken's flowing but not inexpressive 6'30", while Goodman, less poised but more searching, weighs in at 7'44". The finale, on the other hand, combines ample symphonic breadth with terrific *élan*; and Weil brings a nice deadpan wit in the Rossini-ish second theme (0'54"). No. 87 is vividly done in all three recordings, though Weil again scores over his rivals both in his attention to detail and in his control of long-term tensions. In the *Adagio* he encourages warm, gracious phrasing, and shapes the violin sextuplets more eloquently than in the other readings. A final choice among the three period versions of these symphonies, all using an orchestra based on around 25 strings, cannot be clear-cut. Goodman is the least polished of the trio, and his interventionist harpsichord continuo can grow wearisome; but his high-adrenalin music-making is often compelling, especially in his brazen, sabre-rattling reading of No. 82. Honours are pretty evenly divided between the vital, affectionate, occasionally over-leisurely Kuijken and the more tautly controlled Weil. And if Kuijken has the edge in No. 86, these Sony discs come out marginally ahead on points elsewhere, and score decisively in their cleaner, more transparent recorded sound.

Additional recommendations ...

...Nos. 82-84. **Orchestra of the Age of Enlightenment / Sigiswald Kuijken.** Virgin Classics Veritas Ⓕ VC7 59537-2 (78 minutes: DDD: 2/90). ✍

...Nos. 85-87. **Orchestra of the Age of Enlightenment / Sigiswald Kuijken.** Virgin Classics Veritas Ⓕ VC7 59557-2 (79 minutes: DDD: 5/90). ✍

...Nos. 82-84. **Hanover Band / Roy Goodman.** Hyperion Ⓕ CDA66527 (79 minutes: DDD: 10/92). ✍

...Nos. 85-87. **Hanover Band / Roy Goodman.** Hyperion Ⓕ CDA66535 (79 minutes: DDD: 11/94). ✍

...Nos. 64, 84 and 90. **Nicolaus Esterházy Sinfonia / Béla Drahos.** Naxos Ⓢ 8 550770 (68 minutes: DDD: 3/95).

...Nos. 83, 88 and 96. **Hallé Orchestra / Sir John Barbirolli.** Dutton Laboratories mono Ⓕ CDSJB1003* (65 minutes: ADD: 3/96).

...Nos. 80, 87 and 89. **London Mozart Players / Jane Glover.** ASV Quicksilva Ⓢ CDQS6156 (70 minutes: DDD: 4/96).

Haydn Symphonies – No. 82 in C major, "L'ours"; No. 83 in G minor, "La poule"; No. 84 in E flat major; No. 85 in B flat major, "La reine"; No. 86 in D major; No. 87 in A major. **Austro-Hungarian Haydn Orchestra / Adám Fischer.** Nimbus Ⓜ NI5419/20 (two discs: 148 minutes: DDD: 3/95). Recorded 1992.

Adám Fischer's set of the "Paris" Symphonies offers finely sprung readings that steer a well-judged middle course between traditional and period practice. Though modern instruments are used, playing at modern pitch, the scale of the orchestra and the crispness and clarity of the playing reflect some of the lessons learned from the period movement. The weight and warmth of the Austro-Hungarian orchestra's sound readily allows important detail to emerge. The result is full and beefy with plenty of presence, letting one enjoy the geniality of Fischer's readings. Generally Fischer and his players sound more relaxed than Dorati (see above for review of his complete cycle), allowing a degree more affection in the phrasing at similar speeds, with even more spring in the rhythm, as in the witty pointing of the clucking second subject of No. 83, *La poule.* As for the comparisons with Kuijken and Goodman, it is striking that Fischer frequently chooses faster speeds than Kuijken, and is sometimes faster than both, while achieving a comparable elegance, with textures hardly less clear. In the finales of Nos. 83 and 87 Fischer, unlike Kuijken and Goodman but like Dorati, omits the second half repeats. Though there is formidable competition from rival sets of the "Paris" Symphonies, this two-disc box can be warmly recommended to those who appreciate Fischer's intermediate approach to style.

New review

Haydn Symphonies – No. 88 in G major, "Letter V"; No. 89 in F major; No. 90 in C major. **Tafelmusik / Bruno Weil.** Sony Classical Vivarte Ⓕ SK66253 (61 minutes: DDD: 10/95). 🎵 Recorded 1994.

Weil and his responsive players give taut, athletic readings of these three symphonies, crisply paced, sharply accented and full of shrewdly observed instrumental detailing. The *Largo* of No. 88 is swift, the glorious melody phrased with a natural sense of ebb and flow. The first movement, lithe of rhythm, is vividly characterized – a nice conspiratorial air to the opening of the development, and an exciting cumulative tension in the subsequent contrapuntal imbroglio. In the minuet Weil's characteristically smart tempo and spruce rhythms miss something of the music's Bruegelian earthiness, though the mock-rusticity of the trio is well caught, with those buzzy period bassoons splendidly rude in their bagpipe imitations (Haydn's *forte assai* marking here, against the strings' *piano*, for once properly realized). The finale is fast, fiery and brilliantly executed, though other readings have found more wit and grace in the music. In the slighter, more urbane Symphony No. 89 Weil is slightly driven in the opening *Vivace*, with some clipped, peremptory phrasing, though his left-right division of the violins ensures that their rapid sword-play in the development makes its envisaged effect. But Weil's penchant for brisk speeds pays dividends in the *Andante con moto*, which here has the lightness and lilt of a *siciliano* serenade, with delicate, pointed contributions from the woodwind. In the main theme of the finale Weil seems unduly apologetic about Haydn's comic downward portamentos, though he plays the turbulent, syncopated F minor section for all it's worth, with typical care for the precise weighting and rhythmic character of the inner and lower parts. Both Weil and Kuijken opt for Haydn's final version of No. 90, where trumpets and timpani enhance the music's C major grandeur and panache.

Additional recommendation ...

...Nos. 90 and 91. **La Petite Bande / Sigiswald Kuijken.** Virgin Classics Veritas Ⓕ VC5 45068-2 (58 minutes: DDD: 10/95). 🎵

Haydn London Symphonies – No. 93 in D major; No. 94 in G major, "Surprise" (both from 6514 192, 1/83); No. 97 in C major (6514 074); No. 99 in E flat major (9500 139, 4/77); No. 100 in G major, "Military" (9500 510, 3/79); No. 101 in D major, "The Clock" (9500 679, 7/81). **Concertgebouw Orchestra / Sir Colin Davis.** Philips Duo Ⓜ 442 614-2PM2 (two discs: ADD/DDD) . Recorded 1975-81. ⊛⊛⊛

Haydn London Symphonies – No. 95 in C minor (6514 074, 1/82); No. 96 in D major, "Miracle" (6725 010, 6/82); No. 98 in B flat major (9500 678, 12/80); No. 102 in B flat major (9500 679); No. 103 in E flat major, "Drumroll" (9500 303, 7/78); No. 104 in D major, "London" (9500 510). **Concertgebouw Orchestra / Sir Colin Davis.** Philips Duo Ⓜ 442 611-2PM2 (two discs: ADD/DDD) . Recorded 1975-81. ⊛⊛⊛

Haydn Symphonies – No. 99 in E flat major; No. 100 in G major, "Military". Overture in D major to Salomon's opera, "Windsor Castle". **London Classical Players / Roger Norrington.** EMI Ⓕ CDC5 55192-2 (54 minutes: DDD: 12/94). 🎵 Recorded 1993.

Haydn Symphonies – No. 101 in D major, "Clock"; No. 102 in B flat major. **London Classical Players / Roger Norrington.** EMI Ⓕ CDC5 55111-2 (53 minutes: DDD: 12/94). 🎵 Recorded 1993.

A superb achievement all round – indeed, it's nigh on impossible to imagine better 'big-band' Haydn than one encounters here on Sir Colin Davis's four exceedingly well-filled CDs. His direction has exemplary sparkle (try the superb opening movement of the *Miracle* Symphony) and sensitivity (witness his eloquent moulding of No. 98's great *Adagio*). Minuets are never allowed to plod, outer movements have an ideal combination of infectious zip and real poise, and the humour (a commodity, of course, that is never absent for too long in Haydn's music) is always conveyed with a genial twinkle in the eye. Quite marvellous, wonderfully unanimous playing from the great Amsterdam orchestra, too (the woodwind contributions are particularly distinguished), with never a trace of routine to betray the six-year recording span of this critically acclaimed project. The Philips engineering, whether analogue or digital, is of the very highest quality throughout, offering a totally natural perspective, gloriously full-bodied tone and consistently sparkling textures within the sumptuous Concertgebouw acoustic. Invest in this set: it will yield enormous rewards for many years to come.

From Norrington come probing, often charismatic performances that play up the music's drama and rhetorical boldness. Nothing in these familiar works is ever taken for granted. After a swiftish, unsettling *Adagio* introduction (most conductors go for something more monumental here), No. 99's opening *Vivace assai* is unusually taut and urgent, the muscular cross-rhythms powerfully etched, the astringent harmonic clashes rammed home for all they're worth. Norrington's emphasis on the woodwind lines in Haydn's richly scored tuttis (clarinets are featured for the first time in his symphonies) not only makes for vivid, sharply differentiated colours but at salient moments also heightens the music's harmonic tension; and though the timpani are not ideally incisive, the valveless brass bray thrillingly in the movement's closing stages. The *Military* receives one of the most electrifying performances on disc. Both outer movements have a tremendous rhythmic fling, with sharp, precise articulation, not least from the cellos and basses. Haydn's flamboyant contrasts are thrillingly realized, and there is a real sense of abandon in the codas. The coupling of the *Clock* and No. 102 has a direct period rival from the Hanover Band, overseen from the fortepiano by Roy Goodman. Norrington's grander readings are ultimately more exhilarating, subtler in phrasing, more varied in articulation and accent and more commanding in their architectural reach.

Additional recommendations ...
...No. 68 in B flat major. Nos. 93-104. **Royal Concertgebouw Orchestra / Nikolaus Harnoncourt.** Teldec Ⓜ 4509-92628-2 (six discs: 301 minutes: DDD: 4/94).
...No. 92 in G major, "Oxford". No. 104. **English Sinfonia / Sir Charles Groves.** IMP Classics Ⓜ PCD916 (55 minutes: DDD: 6/89).
...Nos. 93, 94, 97, 99, 100 and 101. **Royal Concertgebouw Orchestra / Sir Colin Davis.** Philips Duo Ⓜ 442 614-2PM2.
...Nos. 95, 96, 98, 102, 103 and 104. **Royal Concertgebouw Orchestra, Amsterdam / Sir Colin Davis.** Philips Duo Ⓜ 442 611-2PM2.
...Nos. 93-95. **Hanover Band / Roy Goodman.** Hyperion Ⓕ CDA66532 (66 minutes: DDD: 8/93). 🖋
...Nos. 93-95. **La Petite Bande / Sigiswald Kuijken.** Deutsche Harmonia Mundi Ⓕ 05472 77275-2 (66 minutes: DDD: 10/93). 🖋
...Nos. 93-104. **London Philhrmonic Orchestra / Sir Georg Solti.** Decca Ovation Ⓜ 436 290-2DM6 (six discs: 307 minutes: DDD: 3/93).
...Nos. 93-98. **Royal Philharmonic Orchestra / Sir Thomas Beecham.** EMI Beecham Edition mono Ⓜ CMS7 64389-2* (two discs: 136 minutes: ADD: 9/93).
...Nos. 94, 98 and 104. **Philharmonia Orchestra / Leonard Slatkin.** RCA Victor Red Seal Ⓕ 09026 62549-2 (79 minutes: DDD: 2/95).
...Nos. 97 and 98. **Nicolaus Esterházy Sinfonia / Béla Drahos.** Naxos Ⓢ 8 550780 (59 minutes: DDD: 3/95).
...Nos. 99-104. **Royal Philharmonic Orchestra / Sir Thomas Beecham.** EMI Beecham Edition Ⓜ CMS7 64066-2* (two discs: 156 minutes: ADD: 9/92).
...Nos. 101 and 102. **Hanover Band / Roy Goodman.** Hyperion Ⓕ CDA66528 (52 minutes: DDD: 12/92).
...Nos. 103 and 104. **London Classical Players / Roger Norrington.** EMI Ⓕ CDC5 55002-2 (55 minutes: DDD: 7/94). 🖋
...Nos. 98 and 100. Il mondo della luna – Overture. **Chamber Orchestra of Europe / Claudio Abbado.** DG Ⓕ 439 932-2GH (56 minutes: DDD: 10/95).

Haydn Symphonies – No. 97 in C major; No. 98 in B flat major. **Orchestra of the Eighteenth Century / Frans Brüggen.** Philips Ⓕ 434 921-2PH (53 minutes: DDD: 9/94). 🖋 ⒼⒼ
Haydn Symphonies – No. 96 in D major, "Miracle"; No. 97 in C major; No. 98 in B flat major. **La Petite Bande / Sigiswald Kuijken.** Deutsche Harmonia Mundi Ⓕ 05472-77294-2 (78 minutes: DDD: 10/94). 🖋 Recorded 1993.

Brüggen's recording of the two contrasted symphonies from Haydn's first "London" set, the assertive, martial C major and the more searching, inward-looking B flat benefit from the sharply etched sonorities of his cosmopolitan period orchestra, with its bright, incisive (though never overbearing) valveless horns and trumpets and dry, brittle timpani; and the actual execution is phenomenal in its brilliance, delicacy and precision of articulation and ensemble; the intonation, too, is virtually flawless. Brüggen's interpretations are typically arresting: dramatic, forcefully accented, with exemplary textural clarity (the distinct audibility of the bassoons is a particular delight), and a minute care for rhythmic and dynamic detail. Tempos are well chosen, never hectic, the first movements (especially that of No. 97) quite spacious, the minuet of No. 98 properly *Allegro* but not pressed unforgivingly, as it is by Harnoncourt (listed above). These are more obviously 'conducted' readings than period performances from, say, Hogwood or Goodman. Harnoncourt is that much more abrasive and aggressive than Brüggen, stressing the strange, disturbing aspects of late Haydn (especially in the slow movements). His are provocative, often compelling performances but it is these Brüggen readings which will more often vie with the modern-instrument versions by Davis and Beecham (see above) for these particular works.

By offering a third symphony, Kuijken's recording scores an immediate advantage over Brüggen's. Kuijken's readings of all three works are predictably stylish and sympathetic. His expert period orchestra, including a discreetly balanced harpsichord continuo, is rather smaller than Brüggen's, smaller, too, than the band Haydn directed in London's Hanover Square Rooms. Kuijken is at his most persuasive in the slow movements and the minuets. The 6/8 *Andante* of No. 96 has a chamber-musical finesse and delicacy, while the *Adagio* of No. 98 unfolds with greater breadth and repose than in Brüggen's edgier reading – though Kuijken is fully alive to the tragic implications of the development. In all three minuets tempo and character are shrewdly calculated; and it hardly matters that No. 98's lusty earthiness produces the odd moment of rhythmic instability. In the outer movements Kuijken is invariably lucid and elegant, but sometimes a shade too relaxed. In the opening *Allegro* of No. 98, for instance, Brüggen, at a more urgent tempo, generates a stronger sense of symphonic growth and drama; and in No. 97 he eclipses Kuijken in grandeur and brazen power, with tauter rhythms and sharper accents. If Brüggen's readings of Nos. 97 and 98 are that much bolder and more purposefully controlled, Kuijken's smoother, more genial performances, finely executed and recorded, should appeal to many Haydn collectors, who may in any case be swayed by the inclusion of No. 96.

Haydn Divertimentos – F major, HobII/20; C major, HobII/11, "Der Geburtstag"; G major, HobII/G1; G major, HobII/1. **Linde Consort / Hans-Martin Linde.** Virgin Classics Veritas Ⓜ VER5 61163-2 (73 minutes: DDD: 2/96). From EMI CDC7 47941-2 (4/88). ⟋ Recorded 1986.

Haydn's *Divertimentos* are surprisingly under-represented in the catalogue; yet, besides providing valuable insights into the composer's later symphonic style, these pieces also offer delightful examples of Haydn's open-air music. Flautist Hans-Martin Linde directs his Consort with subtlety and sensitivity in highly engaging performances of four works. The two five-movement *Cassations*, HobII/20 and HobII/G1 are scored for nine instruments, including two horns. Here, the fast, outer movements are projected with lightness and elegance – especially so in the G major *Cassation*'s neat, witty finale – while lithe phrasing, supported by gently pulsating accompaniments in the *Adagio* (scored for strings alone), maximizes the music's expressive impact. The minuets and trios – which fully exploit the horns – show Haydn's potently imaginative instrumentation most vividly, and provide ideal settings for the Linde Consort's accomplished soloist skills and deftly blended ensemble. The two four-movement *Divertimentos*, HobII/1 and HobII/11, use only six instruments, and demonstrate a brilliant synthesis of unity and diversity. The two variation-form finales, in which successive variations present a different instrument as soloist, and the beguilingly comic "Mann und Weib" (HobII/11, second movement), whose bare octaves and opposition of violin and double-bass enchantingly illustrate both the unity of marriage and the difficulties of conjugal life, are particular highlights here. These eloquent expressions of Haydn's characteristically infectious wit, which are attractively presented in excellently balanced recordings, should appeal to a wide audience.

Additional recommendation ...

...Divertimentos – G major, HobII/1; D major, HobII/ D22 Add; G major, HobII/9. **Vienna Haydn Sinfonietta / Manfred Huss.** Koch Schwann Ⓔ 312862 (57 minutes: DDD: 1/96).

Haydn String Quartets, Volumes 1 and 2. **Pro Arte Quartet** (Alphonse Onnou, Laurent Halleux, vns; Germain Prévost, va; Robert Maas, vc). Testament mono Ⓔ SBT3055* and SBT4056* (two sets of three and four discs, oas: 229 and 243 minutes: ADD: 6/95). From HMV Haydn Quartet Society issues; recorded 1931-38.

SBT3055 – B flat major, "La chasse", Op. 1 No. 1. Op. 20: No. 2 in C major; No. 5 in F minor. E flat major, Op. 50 No. 3. Op. 54: No. 1 in G major; No. 2 in C major; No. 3 in E major. Op. 64: No. 3 in B flat major; No. 4 in G major. G minor, "Rider", Op. 74 No. 3. Op. 76: No. 3 in C major, "Emperor"; No. 4 in B flat major, "Sunrise". F major, Op. 77 No. 2. *SBT4056* – C major, Op. 1 No. 6. Op. 20: No. 1 in E flat major; No. 4 in D major. Op. 33: No. 2 in E flat major, "Joke"; No. 3 in C major, "Bird"; No. 6 in D major. D major, "Frog", Op. 50 No. 6. Op. 55: No. 1 in A major; No. 3 in B flat major. E flat major, Op. 64 No. 6. B flat major, Op. 71 No. 1. Op. 74: No. 1 in C major; No. 2 in F major. G major, Op. 77 No. 1. **Hoffstetter** String Quartets, Op. 3 – No. 4 in B flat major; No. 5 in F major. ⒼⒼ

The Pro Arte Quartet's first London appearance in 1925 prompted *The Times* to declare, "One has never heard them surpassed, and rarely equalled, in volume and beauty of tone, in accuracy of intonation and in perfection of balance between the parts" – and that could well be the verdict on these sets. Their tempos invariably seem just right and their phrasing has an inner life that is extraordinarily potent. Alphonse Onnou and Laurent Halleux were superbly matched, and Halleux often led in their early days. Such virtuosity as the quartet exhibits is effortless and totally lacking in ostentation. Of course, the actual sound is dated – the string tone is wanting in bloom and freshness, particularly in some of the earlier recordings – but the ear soon adjusts though one might wish that these transfers could have given us a little more space between movements. Ansermet tells how when the Pro Arte were asked to play his quartet pieces for Stravinsky, the composer, accustomed to scant understanding at that time, asked his visitors to listen first to the pianola transcriptions. After they had done so, modest and a little intimidated, they took up their instruments. From the very first note Stravinsky was won over, and at the end, greatly moved, all he could do was to exclaim, "I have nothing to say! It was perfect! I have never heard my music interpreted with such truth!" Haydn might well have said the same.

Haydn String Quartets, Op. 9. **Kodály Quartet** (Attila Falváy, Tamás Szabó, vns; Gábor Fias, va; János Devich, vc). Naxos Ⓢ 8 550786/7 (two discs, oas: 52 and 58 minutes: DDD: 11/94). Recorded 1993.
8 550786 – No. 1 in C major; No. 3 in G major; No. 4 in D minor. *8 550787* – No. 2 in E flat major; No. 5 in B flat major; No. 6 in A major.

Overshadowed by four dozen later masterpieces, Haydn's Op. 9 has usually received short shrift from both players and commentators. Least neglected of the set is the D minor, No. 4, described by Hans Keller as "the first great string quartet in the history of music". The minor mode at this period (1769-70) invariably drew something special from Haydn, and this work stands apart from the others for its intensity of expression, its mastery of texture and development and the sheer character of its ideas. The opening *Allegro moderato* could well have been at the back of Mozart's mind when he came to write his own great D minor Quartet, K421. "Boring" was Keller's unceremonious dismissal of the remaining five works of Op. 9. It is true that there are *longueurs*, nowhere more so than in the stiff, gawky opening movements of Nos. 1-3, with their neutral thematic material and over-abundance of fussy violin figuration. The routine set of variations that opens No. 5 is also the kind of piece that has one's fingers itching for the fast-forward button. But there are compensations elsewhere: in the terse, resourceful and (especially in No. 3) witty finales; in the varied minuets, ranging from the high-stepping No. 5, with its alfresco octave doublings, to the suave, chromatically subtle No. 2; and in several of the slow movements, notably the tender *siciliano* in No. 1, the sorrowful, rather Gluckian C minor aria in No. 2 and the sensuous, rich-textured *Largo cantabile* in No. 5. The Kodály Quartet are, as ever, sympathetic Haydn exponents, impressing with their slightly old-fashioned warmth of sonority, the natural musicality of their phrasing and their care for blend, balance and intonation, though the rather boomy church acoustic hardly helps. However, in case you hadn't noticed, buying both discs should still leave you change from a tenner.

Haydn String Quartets, Op. 20, "Sun". **Quatuor Mosaïques** (Erich Höbarth, Andrea Bischof, vns; Anita Mitterer, va; Christophe Coin, vc). Auvidis Astrée Ⓕ E8784 (two discs: 147 minutes: DDD: 5/93). ✐ Recorded 1990. *Also available separately as detailed below.* **Gramophone** *Award Winner 1993.* **Gramophone** *Editor's choice.*
E8785 – No. 1 in E flat major; No. 5 in F minor; No. 6 in A major. *E8786* – No. 2 in C major; No. 3 in G major; No. 4 in D major.   ⒼⒼⒼ

Haydn was 40 when he completed his set of Op. 20 String Quartets in 1772. They therefore date from the composer's so-called *Sturm und Drang* period, though Haydn's increasingly frequent use of the more dramatic and 'serious' minor mode in these pieces can perhaps be attributed just as much to the fruitful influence of the three operatic projects he had been working on just a few years previously between 1766 and 1769. Moreover, these quartets also reveal a greater preoccupation with counterpoint than any of his music to that date, and the great fugal finales of Nos. 2, 5 and 6 clearly herald the arrival of the consummate craftsman so overwhelmingly displayed in the mature quartets to come. Incidentally, the Op. 20 set's nickname *Sun* derives from the illustration on the handsome title-page of the Hummel edition of this music, at the top of which peers out the sun-god's head. Admirable though the Salomon Quartet's readings are, they are surpassed by those of the superb Quatuor Mosaïques. These wonderfully flexible performances display an altogether breathtaking refinement, sensitivity and illumination. Indeed, in terms of expressive subtlety, imaginative intensity and sheer depth of feeling, the Mosaïques' achievement in these marvellous works is unmatched in the present catalogue and it is difficult to foresee it being surpassed for some considerable time to come. A stunning set in every way, with vividly realistic engineering to match.

Additional recommendations …
…No. 2. Op. 50: B flat major, Op. 50 No. 1; D minor, Op. 76 No. 2. **Lindsay Quartet.** ASV Ⓕ CDDCA622 (63 minutes: DDD: 9/88).
…Nos. 4-6. **Salomon Quartet.** Hyperion Ⓕ CDA66622 (78 minutes: DDD: 2/93). ✐

New review
Haydn String Quartets, Op. 33 – No. 1 in B minor; No. 2 in E flat major, "Joke"; No. 4 in B flat major. **Lindsay Quartet** (Peter Cropper, Ronald Birks, vns; Robin Ireland, va; Bernard Gregor-Smith, vc). ASV Ⓕ CDDCA937 (62 minutes: DDD: 3/96). Recorded 1994. *Gramophone Editor's choice.*

The Lindsay's is chamber-music-making of unusual recreative flair, untouched by the faintest hint of routine. In their uncommonly grave, inward readings of the slow movements of the E flat and B flat Quartets they sustain a daringly slow tempo magnificently, phrasing in long, arching spans, always acutely sensitive to harmonic movement, as in their subtle colouring of Haydn's breathtaking tonal excursions in No. 4. Beethoven is evoked in the Lindsay's swift, mordant reading of No. 1's epigrammatic *Scherzo*: rarely have the waspish part-writing and the abrupt, disconcerting contrasts in dynamics and articulation been so vividly realized. Typically, they make the most of the complete change of mood and texture in the major-key Trio, finding an almost Viennese sweetness of tone and phrase, complete with touches of portamento. The finale, fast, fierce, utterly un-comical, has a distinct whiff of the Hungarian *puszta* here, both in the wild gipsy figuration from 0'10" and the mounting passion of the sequence in the development. The Lindsay bring an ideal spaciousness and flexibility to the urban, quietly spoken first movement of the E flat Quartet, No. 2, taking due note of Haydn's *cantabile* marking. In the finales of this quartet and No. 4 they enter fully into the music's spirit with vital, inventively varied phrasing, palpably relishing Haydn's exuberance and comic sleight of hand. Here, as occasionally elsewhere, it's easy to overlook the odd moment of rhythmic unsteadiness or impure intonation for the sake of such involved and characterful music-making.

New review
Haydn String Quartets, Op. 33 – No. 2 in E flat major, "Joke"; No. 3 in C major, "Bird"; No. 5 in G major, "How do you do?". **Quatuor Mosaïques** (Erich Höbarth, Andrea Bischof, vns; Anita Mitterer, va; Christophe Coin, vc). Auvidis Astrée Ⓕ E8569 (61 minutes: DDD: 6/96). 🗲 Recorded 1995. *Gramophone Editor's choice.* ⒼⒼ
In the theme-and-variation finale of the G major Quartet, No. 5, the Mosaïques, at a rather slower tempo than usual, find in the music an unsuspected reflective tenderness. The theme itself is played with a characteristic touch of flexibility and a gentle lift to the dotted rhythms; in the first variation Erich Höbarth shapes his decorative semiquaver *fioriture* with apparently spontaneous fantasy; the luminous, high-lying textures of the second are exquisitely realized; and even the *Presto* send-off has a delicacy and whimsy in keeping with what has gone before. In the rival period-instrument reading the Salomon Quartet, with their more austere tonal palette, adopt a typically brisker, straighter manner here. The contrast is even more marked in the quasi-operatic *Largo*, where Simon Standage sounds detached and businesslike alongside Höbarth, with his contained intensity of line and subtle variety of phrase and colour. Nor do the Salomon match the Mosaïques' comic timing in the outrageous rhythmic dislocations of the *Scherzo*. The Mosaïques' readings of the slow movements in the so-called *Joke* and *Bird* Quartets are again outstanding in their grave tenderness, their sensitivity to harmonic flux and the improvisatory freedom Erich Höbarth brings to his ornamental figuration. The Slavonic finale of the *Bird*, one of several movements to benefit from the lighter, more flexible period bows, goes with terrific fire and panache. In the opening *Allegro* of the *Joke* the players take to heart Haydn's *moderato e cantabile* qualification, phrasing fluidly and expansively, with a vital and delicate interplay between the voices. The finale, like that of No. 5, is unusually graceful, with the notorious ending deliciously managed. In sum, this truthfully recorded disc offers playing that marries great style, technical finesse (tuning, blend and balance suffering little by comparison with the finest modern-instrument quartets) and re-creative flair.
Additional recommendations ...
...Nos. 1-3. D major, Op. 1 No. 3. **Weller Quartet.** Decca Ⓜ 433 691-2DM (71 minutes: ADD: 9/92).
...Nos. 4-6. D minor, Op. 42. **Salomon Quartet.** Hyperion Ⓕ CDA66682 (72 minutes: DDD: 9/93). 🗲
...Nos. 1-6. **Appónyi Quartet.** Ars Musici Ⓕ AM1083-2 (two discs: 108 minutes: DDD: 6/95).

Haydn String Quartets, Op. 50. **Salomon Quartet** (Simon Standage, Micaela Comberti, vns; Trevor Jones, va; Jennifer Ward Clarke, vc). Hyperion Ⓕ CDA66821/2 (two discs, oas: 75 and 76 minutes: DDD: 9/94). 🗲
CDA66821 – No. 1 in B flat major; No. 2 in C major; No. 3 in E flat major. *CDA66822* – No. 4 in F sharp minor; No. 5 in F major, "The Dream"; No. 6 in D major, "The Frog".
Commentators have sometimes detected Mozartian influences in Haydn's Op. 50, the first set he completed after the six quartets which Mozart dedicated to him. Perhaps the unusual weight and intensity of several of the minuets and, even more unexpectedly, their trios (especially in Nos. 4-6) can be seen as Haydn's response to the astonishing, subversive anti-minuet in Mozart's K387. But there is little of Mozart's expansive lyrical richness and harmonic sensuousness about Op. 50, which in its musical procedures is arguably Haydn's most ascetic, obsessive and intellectually rigorous set of quartets. There is wit here, of course, in abundance, but of a more subtle, ambivalent kind than the broad comedy of Haydn's previous set, Op. 33 – even in the finale of this set's most famous work, No. 6, whose quick-fire bariolage (repeated notes played alternately on adjacent strings) suggested to early listeners the croaking of a frog. This recording by the Salomon Quartet does ample justice to this masterly, intriguing, sometimes elusive music. Theirs is positive, forthright playing, confidently characterized, with strong, propulsive rhythms and lucid, carefully balanced textures; and despite the less sonorous, gut-strung period instruments and the relative absence of vibrato they can produce a remarkably full-bodied sound where appropriate.

Haydn String Quartets, Op. 54 – No. 1 in G major. No. 2 in C major. No. 3 in E major. **Lindsay Quartet** (Peter Cropper, Robin Ireland, vns; Ronald Birks, va; Bernard Gregor-Smith, vc). ASV Ⓕ CDDCA582 (66 minutes: DDD: 8/87).

All three quartets are in the usual four-movement form but with many surprises: in No. 1, the false recapitulation in the first movement, the dark modulations in the following sonata-form *Allegretto* and the Hungarian gipsy flavour (anticipated in the minuet) and mischievousness of the final rondo. No. 2 has a rhapsodic fiddler in its second movement, a nostalgic minuet with an extraordinarily anguished trio, and an *Adagio* finale in which a *Presto* section turns out to be no more than an episode. A notable feature of No. 3 is its tenary-form *Largo cantabile*, the centre of which is more like a mini-concerto for the first violin; 'Scotch snaps' pervade the minuet, and pedal points the finale. The performances (and the recording) are superb, marked by unanimity, fine tone, suppleness of phrasing, and acute dynamic shaping; in the second movement of No. 1 there are hushed passages whose homogeneity and quality of sound is quite remarkable. Even more remarkable would be the Haydn lover who found this recording resistible.

Additional recommendations ...

...No. 2. D major, Op. 64 No. 5, "The Lark". **Gabrieli Quartet.** Chandos Ⓕ CHAN8531 (39 minutes: DDD: 11/87).

...Nos. 1-3. Op. 55: No. 1 in A major; No. 2 in F minor, "Razor"; No. 3 in B flat major. **Amadeus Quartet.** DG Ⓜ 437 134-2GX2 (two discs: 121 minutes: ADD: 2/93).

...Nos. 1–3. **Salomon Quartet.** Hyperion Ⓕ CDA66971 (71 minutes: DDD: 12/95). ✍

Haydn String Quartets, Op. 55, "Tost II" – No. 1 in A major; No. 2 in F minor; No. 3 in B flat major. **Lindsay Quartet** (Peter Cropper, Ronald Birks, vns; Robin Ireland, va; Bernard Gregor-Smith, vc). ASV Ⓕ CDDCA906 (64 minutes: DDD: 3/95). Recorded 1994. *Gramophone Editor's choice.*

Ⓖ

Most immediately striking of the trilogy is the F minor work, with its searching double variations on related minor and major themes (a favourite form in Haydn's later music), spiky, rebarbative second movement *Allegro* and strangely spare contrapuntal minuet. The A major, No. 1, has much of this key's traditional brilliance, with ample scope for the leader's creative virtuosity in the outer movements and the stratospheric trio of the minuet; in contrast the noble, wonderfully scored *Adagio cantabile* prefigures the profound slow movements of Haydn's final years. The more inward-looking No. 3 in B flat is specially remarkable for the varied recapitulations in the flanking movements, astonishingly free and inventive even for Haydn, and the subtle chromatic colouring in all four movements which may just owe something to the quartets Mozart had dedicated to Haydn three years earlier. Here and there the Lindsay's intonation is less than true, especially from the leader, but as so often with this group, this is a small price to pay for performances of such colour and penetration. The balance, as with many recent quartet recordings, is a shade closer than ideal but the overall sound-picture is very acceptable.

Haydn String Quartets, Op. 64. **Kodály Quartet** (Attila Falvay, Tamás Szabo, vns; Gábor Fias, va; János Devich, vc). Naxos Ⓢ 8 550673/4 (two discs, oas: 64 and 65 minutes: DDD: 1/94). Recorded 1992. *Gramophone Editor's choice.*

8 550673 – No. 1 in C major; No. 2 in B minor; No. 3 in B flat major. *8 550674* – No. 4 in G major; No. 5 in D major, "The Lark"; No. 6 in E flat major.

Like Handel, Haydn remains a victim of his own prodigality. And like most of his 70-odd quartets, Op. 64, are still underexposed both in the concert-hall and on disc. The exception is the so-called *Lark*, whose soaring opening melody and *moto perpetuo* finale have made it perhaps the most immediately fetching of all Haydn's quartets. But No. 6 in E flat (Haydn's homage to Mozart's K428?) is at least as fine, with its intimate and intensely argued opening movement, its poignant, exquisitely textured *Andante* and a finale full of instrumental fooling and insouciant contrapuntal virtuosity. Of the other works, No. 2 in B minor is one of Haydn's most astringent pieces, from its tonally deceptive opening to the mordant, unsettling humour of the finale. Quartets Nos. 3 and 4 return to a more familiar vein of sociable wit. Both are endlessly subtle and surprising in their arguments, with *cantabile* slow movements of peculiar candour and eloquence. Quartet No. 1 in C, is certainly the plainest in its thematic ideas. However, it is an absorbing, immensely sophisticated piece. The Kodaly's wonderfully civilized playing, mellow and lyrical, is far removed from the highly-strung brilliance cultivated by many modern quartets. Ensemble and intonation are first-class, tempos generally spacious with broad, natural and beautifully matched phrasing. The recording, made in a Budapest church, is resonant and less intimate than is ideal in this music. Even so, not even the most casual lover of Haydn's quartets will regret spending a tenner on this pair of discs.

Additional recommendation ...

...**Festetics Quartet.** Harmonia Mundi Musique d'abord Ⓑ HMA190 3040/41 (two discs: 138 minutes: DDD: 12/95).

Haydn String Quartets, Opp. 71 and 74. **Kodály Quartet** (Attila Falvay, Tamás Szabo, vns; Gábor Fias, va; János Devich, vc). Naxos Ⓢ 8 550394 and 8 550396 (two discs, oas: 62 and 63 minutes: DDD: 2/91). Recorded 1989.

8 550394 – Op. 71: No. 1 in B flat major, No. 2 in D major; No. 3 in E flat major. *8 550396* – Op. 74: No. 1 in C major; No. 2 in F major; No. 3 in G minor, "The Rider".

The enterprising Kodály Quartet are working their way through the middle and late Haydn quartets and, rightly, taking their time about it. They rehearse together privately, and then every so often turn up at the Hungaroton Studios in Rottenbiller ready to record a new group. They play with self-evident joy in the music and an easy neatness of ensemble, which comes from familiarity with each other's company. There is never a hint of routine and the intercommunication is matched by enormous care for detail and clean ensemble. In short they play as one, and project this wonderful music with enormous dedication. Just sample the elegant *Andante* with variations which form the slow movement of Op. 71 No. 3, or the witty minuet which follows, or any of the consistently inspired Op. 74 set. The hushed intensity of playing in the *Largo assai* of Op. 74 No. 3 is unforgettable. The recordings are wholly natural and balanced within a well-judged acoustic; the sound is of the highest quality and documentation is excellent. At their modest price this pair of CDs is irresistible.

Additional recommendations ...
...Op. 74: Nos. 2 and 3. **Salomon Quartet.** Hyperion Ⓔ CDA66124 (AAD: 3/87). ✒ *Selected by Sounds in Retrospect.*
...Op. 71 Nos. 1 and 2. **Salomon Quartet.** Hyperion Ⓔ CDA66065 (47 minutes: DDD: 12/87). ✒
...Op. 71 No. 3; Op. 74 No. 1. **Salomon Quartet.** Hyperion Ⓔ CDA66098 (59 minutes: AAD: 12/87). ✒

Haydn String Quartets, Op. 76 – No. 4 in B flat major, "Sunrise". No. 5 in D major, "Fifths". No. 6 in E flat major, "Fantasia". **Takács Quartet** (Gábor Takács-Nagy, Károly Schranz, vns; Gábor Omai, va; András Fejér, vc). Decca Ⓔ 425 467-2DH (68 minutes: DDD: 1/90). Recorded 1988.

In these three quartets from a set of six published in 1797, one can only be delighted by the sheer invention that Haydn showed in his sixties. This youthful Hungarian ensemble bring to this music a freshness that does not inhibit them from the necessary underlining of this or that point. The *Sunrise* Quartet is invigorating in the first movement and lyrically broad in the *Adagio*, and the syncopated minuet and lilting finale are no less delightful. The D major Quartet starts with an *Allegretto* suggesting a set of variations but then moves into a section in new keys before ending with a brisk coda. The slow movement's *cantabile e mesto* marking is fully realized, as is the major-minor contrast of the minuet and the playful *Presto* finale, which begins with an unmistakable joke of six bars that sound more like the end of a movement. The third of these quartets begins with variations that culminate in a fugato; the slow movement (called a fantasia) is another original, and this is followed by a witty scherzo and a finale in which scale fragments participate in a game of dizzy contrapuntal complexity. The recording, made in a London church, is immediate yet atmospheric, although with a touch of glare that tone controls will tame.

Additional recommendation ...
...**Eder Quartet.** Teldec Digital Experience Ⓜ 9031 77602-2 (62 minutes: DDD: 12/92).

Haydn String Quartets – Op. 77: No. 1 in G major; No. 2 in F major. D minor, Op. 103 (unfinished). **Quatuor Mosaïques** (Erich Höbarth, Andrea Bischof, vns; Anita Mitterer, va; Christophe Coin, vc). Auvidis Astrée Ⓔ E8799 (62 minutes: DDD: 2/90). ✒

Anyone who thinks that period-instrument performance means austerity and coolness should listen to this disc. Here is a group of youngish French players, using instruments of the kind Haydn would have heard, played (as far as we can know) in a style he would have been familiar with: the result is a disc full of expressive warmth and vigour. The opening of Op. 77 No. 1 is done duly gracefully, but with a sturdy underlying rhythm and the scherzo is as crisp and alive as one could ask for. Then the first movement of the F major work is very beautifully done, with many sensitive details; and the lovely second movement is ideally leisurely, so that the players have ample room for manoeuvre and the leader makes much of his opportunities for delicate playing in the filigree-like high music. The players show a real grasp of the structure and they know when to illuminate the key moments, with a touch of extra deliberation or a little additional weight of tone. These performances, clearly recorded, are competitive ones not merely within the protected world of 'early music' but in the bigger, 'real' world too!

Additional recommendation ...
...Nos. 1 and 2. **Berio** Notturno. **Alban Berg Quartet.** EMI Ⓔ CDC5 55191-2 (72 minutes: DDD: 10/95). *See review under Berio; refer to the Index to Reviews.*

Haydn Seven Last Words, Op. 51. **Lindsay Quartet** (Peter Cropper, Ronald Birks, vns; Robin Ireland, va; Bernard Gregor-Smith, vc). ASV Ⓔ CDDCA853 (71 minutes: DDD: 6/93).

This performance by the Lindsay Quartet is magical and it confirms them as something a bit more special than just the leading British quartet. There are few groups who could sustain these seven slow movements, each lasting about ten minutes, and yet give them such variety of intensity, colour and mood. Haydn revealed himself as a visionary composer in the way he set about creating these seven miniature tone-poems for string quartet. The work is divided into nine sections comprising the seven slow movements each describing one of the final utterances of Christ on the Cross together with a slow introduction and a final *Presto con tutta la forza* which depicts the earthquake which occurred when "the veil of the temple was rent in twain".

Additional recommendations ...
...Seven Last Words. String Quartet in D minor, Op. 103 (unfinished). **Kodály Quartet.** Naxos Ⓢ 8 550346 (64 minutes: DDD: 2/91).
...Seven Last Words. **Borodin Quartet.** Teldec Ⓔ 4509-92373-2 (73 minutes: DDD: 4/95).

New review

Haydn Flute Trios – No. 15 in G major, HobXV/15; No. 16 in D major, HobXV/16; No. 17 in
· F major, HobXV/17. **Konrad Hünteler** (fl); **Christophe Coin** (vc); **Patrick Cohen** (fp). Harmonia
Mundi Ⓟ HMC90 1521 (62 minutes: DDD: 1/96). ✔ Recorded 1994.

"Nothing very special ... a simple bagatelle to amuse you in moments of extreme boredom", was
Haydn's own offhand description of the F major Flute Trio in a letter to his friend Marianne von
Genzinger. But for all their air of amiable insouciance, these three trios, composed the year before
Haydn's first London visit, are highly sophisticated pieces, worked out with surprising breadth and
harmonic freedom. Patrick Cohen and his partners are sympathetic interpreters, phrasing
imaginatively and responding vividly to, say, the spirited exchanges between flute and keyboard in the
first movement of No. 16, or the delightfully discursive, almost improvisatory progress of No. 17's
opening *Allegro*. Throughout they create an engaging sense of intimacy and spontaneity. Though
balanced a shade too forwardly, Konrad Hünteler's wooden period flute perfectly complements the
delicate sonorities of the Walter fortepiano, with its notably sweet-toned treble; and Christophe Coin's
gutty cello is always a telling presence, adding just the right degree of weight and intensity at climaxes.
This disc can be recommended to anyone who fancies an hour of Haydn at his most relaxed and genial.

Haydn Piano Trios. **Beaux Arts Trio** (Isidore Cohen, vn; Bernard Greenhouse, vc; Menahem
Pressler, pf). Philips Ⓜ 432 061-2PM9 (nine discs: 394 minutes: ADD: 7/92). Recorded 1970-79.
Gramophone classical 100.
G major, HobXV/25. F sharp minor, HobXV/26. C major, HobXV/27 (all from 6500 023, 6/71).
E flat major, HobXV/29. E flat major, HobXV/30. E flat major, HobXV/31 (all from 6500 400,
3/73). C major, HobXV/21. D minor, HobXV/23. D major, HobXV/24. E major, HobXV/28 (all
from 6500 401, 3/73). A major, HobXV/18. G minor, HobXV/19. E flat major, HobXV/22 (all
from 6500 521, 6/74). B flat major, HobXV/20. G major, HobXV/32 (both from 6500 522, 11/73).
G minor, HobXV/1. F major, HobXV/37. F major, HobXV/39. G major, HobXV/41. C major,
HobXV/C1 (all from 6768 077). A flat major, HobXV/14. G major, HobXV/15 (both from 9500
034, 11/76). C minor, HobXV/13, D major, HobXV/16. F major, HobXV/17 (all from 9500 035,
2/77). G major, HobXIV/6. F major, HobXV/6. B flat major, HobXV/8. G major, XVI/6 (all
from 9500 325, 3/78). F major, HobXV/2 (9500 325, 3/78). D major, HobXV/7. A major,
HobXV/9. E minor, HobXV/12 (all from 9500 326, 8/77). G major, HobXV/5. E flat major,
HobXV/10. E flat major, HobXV/f1 (all from 9500 327, 2/78). F minor, HobXV/11. E flat major,
HobXV/36. C major, HobXIV/C1. D major, Hobdeest (all from 9500 472, 7/79). E major,
HobXV/34. A major, HobXV/35. B flat major, HobXV/38. F major, HobXV/40 (all from 9500
473, 6/79). *Gramophone Award Winner 1979.* ⊕⊕⊕

Far more than Mozart's, Haydn's trios are essentially accompanied keyboard sonatas, with the cello
wedded to the keyboard bass almost throughout; this lack of cello independence has deterred many
groups from investigating their undoubted musical riches. Not, fortunately, the Beaux Arts, whose
acclaimed complete cycle accumulated by stealth during the 1970s (when it was finally completed it
received almost universal accolades, including *Gramophone*'s Record of the Year Award) and has
now reappeared on nine mid-price discs. A dozen of the works date from the 1760s, or even earlier
(which for a late developer like Haydn meant pre-puberty), and offer little more than rococo charm,
though the G minor (No. 1 in Hoboken's catalogue), with its neo-baroque severity, is a notable
exception. But the majority of the trios date from the 1780s and 1790s and contain some of Haydn's
most imaginative, lyrical and harmonically adventurous music. Two outstanding works from the
1780s are the E minor, No. 12, with its passionate, closely worked opening *Allegro*, and No. 14 in
A flat, with its exquisitely tender *Adagio* in a remote E major that leads without a break into one of
Haydn's most hilariously quixotic finales.
The 14 magnificent trios of the 1790s range from relaxed, intimate pieces like the E flat, No. 29,
through the sombre, almost tragic F sharp minor, No. 26, to the C major, No. 27, unsurpassed in the
whole series for its intellectual and virtuoso brilliance. Finest of all, perhaps, are the E major, No. 28,
with its radiant outer movements (wonderfully fanciful, delicate textures here) and its astonishing
central E minor *passacaglia*; and the E flat, No. 30, with its noble, lyrically expansive first movement,
its deep-toned, often richly chromatic *Andante* and its glorious German-dance finale. The Beaux
Arts's playing throughout is vital, refined, and sharply responsive to the music's teeming richness and
variety. The early trios were conceived for harpsichord, though such is the deftness and delicacy of
Menahem Pressler's touch here that there is no question of the music being overpowered by the
modern Steinway; and among individual delights in the group's performances of these early works
mention should be made of their gentle, affectionate way with the central minuets, underlining their
dual function as dances and surrogate slow movements. In the later trios they catch beautifully the
leisurely, almost improvisatory feel of many of the opening movements, and bring a ruminative
intensity, and a wonderful quality of soft playing to the great slow movements, while the finales have
immense brio, wit and virtuosity, with ideally clean, crisp articulation from Pressler. Occasionally in
the earlier works the Beaux Arts sound a touch over-sophisticated for this guileless music – the
opening violin solo in No. 2 is a case in point. And there are a few disappointments in the later trios
– the first movement of the great F sharp minor, No. 26, sounds too lightweight, even skittish while,
conversely, in the *passacaglia* of No. 28 they take a surprisingly ponderous view of Haydn's *Allegretto*.

But there's a feast of superlative, little-known music here, most of the playing is extraordinarily felicitous, and the recording has Philips's customary warmth and refinement. £70 or so may seem a lot to fork out all at once, but no one is likely to regret the investment – this is a set that will last a lifetime.

New review

Haydn Piano Trios – E minor, HobXV/12; F sharp minor, HobXV/26;E major, HobXV/28; E flat
major, HobXV/30. **Yuuko Shiokawa** (vn); **Boris Pergamenschikov** (vc); **András Schiff** (pf). Decca
Ⓕ 444 861-2DH (69 minutes: DDD: 6/96). Recorded 1994.

With the outstandingly perceptive period-instrument performances of Haydn's E major Trio (No. 28) by the incisive and bracing Beths/Bylsma/Levin group (reviewed above), András Schiff and his colleagues have to be on their mettle. Their performance of this work is a gentler creature altogether: it may not bite, but it is by no means muzzled. Shiokawa brings bright definition to the first movement with her buoyant violin playing, while the central *Allegretto*, forthright in the striding out of its stark, linear writing, is a match for anyone (and a minute quicker than most). Schiff's trio place this work in the context of an E minor Trio with a deliciously demure *siciliano*; the Trio No. 26 whose F sharp minor pathos is felt more in stern, penetrating accents than in leaning cadences; and finally the E flat Trio. The long and relaxed first movement is as lively with interpretative insight as it is with idea, and the yearning chromaticisms of the slow movement are kept on a taut rein: with short, austere bow strokes, this is an *Andante* with plenty of compelling *moto*. These performances were warmly recorded in the Brahms Saal of the Vienna Musikverein.

New review

Haydn Piano Trios – A flat major, HobXV/14; C major, HobXV/27; E flat major, HobXV/29;
E flat minor, HobXV/31. **Yuuko Shiokawa** (vn); **Boris Pergamenschikov** (vc); **András Schiff** (pf).
Decca Ⓕ 444 862-2DH (69 minutes: DDD: 1/96). Recorded 1994.

This disc gathers together four of Haydn's most inventive late keyboard trios, each one astonishing in its physical and intellectual energy, formal freedom and harmonic vision. The pianist is, of course, the motivating force in these works, above all in the C major Trio, which contains the most virtuosic keyboard writing in all Haydn. Schiff and his colleagues relish the wit, brilliance and sheer speed of Haydn's thoughts in the outer movements, with their comic off-beat accents, sudden changes of register and breathtaking harmonic scope. Rapid keyboard passagework is always imaginatively shaped and directed; and the pellucid, subtly coloured sonorities Schiff draws from his Bösendorfer are a constant source of delight. So, too, is the sharply etched cello of Boris Pergamenschikov, palpably relishing the mobility and vitality of Haydn's bass-lines – so much for the old view that the cello parts in these trios are virtually dispensable. The *Andante*, in the third-related key of A major (a favourite harmonic gambit in late Haydn), is swifter and lighter than the more romantically inflected reading from the Beaux Arts Trio (reviewed above), with more of a *siciliano* lilt – though there is plenty of weight and intensity in the A minor central section which breaks in rudely on Haydn's pastoral idyll. Occasionally, in this movement and elsewhere, Yuuko Shiokawa's tuning is slightly sour. And her phrasing of the soaring solo in the first movement of No. 31 is rather chilly, lacking the eloquence of the Beaux Arts' Isidore Cohen. However, she takes her chances in the German dance-style finale, where keyboard virtuosity is balanced by an unusually elaborate, high lying violin part. Here Shiokawa and Schiff really strike sparks off each other; and sudden moments of poetry are exquisitely handled. The far more riotous German dance that closes No. 29 (shades here of the boozy wine harvest in *The Seasons*) goes with a terrific swing, more abandoned and more pungently accented than the Beaux Arts' version. Decca's recording is intimate and finely balanced, with just the right degree of ambient warmth.

Haydn Piano Trios – C major, HobXV/21. E flat major, HobXV/22. D minor, HobXV/23. **Erich
Höbarth** (vn); **Christophe Coin** (vc); **Patrick Cohen** (fp). Harmonia Mundi Ⓕ HMC90 1400
(62 minutes: DDD: 9/93). 🖎 Recorded 1992.

Of the three works here, No. 21 is a generally lightweight, uncomplicated piece, with bucolic bagpipe effects in the gigue-like opening movement, an *Andante* built on a *Romanze*-type melody such as Mozart often favoured in his later music and a racy final *Presto*, a more compact counterpart to the finales in several of the 'Salomon' symphonies. The D minor, No. 23, opening with a set of variations on Haydn's favourite plan of alternating minor and major themes, has a richly ornamented *Adagio ma non troppo* with a rhapsodic, almost improvisatory feel (a type of Haydn slow movement only found in these late trios) and a wiry, syncopated finale full of teasing cross-rhythms. Finest of the three works, though, is the E flat, No. 22, all of whose movements show Haydn's harmonic thinking at its most subtle and exploratory, above all, the haunting, pre-Schubertian G major *Poco adagio*. The performances from Patrick Cohen and his string colleagues are technically assured (string intonation well-nigh perfect throughout) and strongly characterized, with a wide spectrum of tone colour and dynamics; and the relatively light sonorities of period instruments make for consistently lucid textures. They are vividly recorded.

New review

Haydn Piano Trios – D major, HobXV/24; G major, HobXV/25; F sharp minor, HobXV/26. **Erich Höbarth** (vn); **Christophe Coin** (vc); **Patrick Cohen** (fp). Harmonia Mundi Ⓕ HMC90 1514 (47 minutes: DDD: 9/95). ✎ Recorded 1994.

The Beaux Arts' slick, over-skittish reading of the F sharp minor Trio's opening *Allegro* was one of the chief disappointments in their complete Philips cycle. Here Patrick Cohen and his colleagues realize far more fully the movement's sombre power, with a broader tempo, stronger yet more flexible rhythms and a much sharper response to the mounting harmonic tensions of the development. Cohen has the true measure of the music's emotional and intellectual force, judges rubato subtly and imbues his rapid passagework in the development and recapitulation with a real sense of dramatic urgency. If his fortepiano naturally dominates proceedings, the more egalitarian balance, easier to achieve on period instruments, allows both Erich Höbarth and Christophe Coin to make their mark. As Coin demonstrates, here and elsewhere, Haydn's cello writing is far less dull than it is often held to be. The gipsy rondo of the popular G major Trio can hardly fail to bring the house down; but these players rip into the music with extraordinary flair and abandon, its devilry enhanced by Coin's boldly defined cello line. In the glorious D major Trio they capture beautifully the first movement's lyrical spaciousness and sense of inspired spontaneity, savouring each unexpected twist in harmony and melodic line, and bring an ideal fluidity and delicacy of interplay to the finale, gentlest and most poetic of the German dance movements found in many of Haydn's late trios. The Beaux Arts, with their rather suaver style, are fine in both the D major and the G major Trios, though Cohen and his partners seem to play with that much more fantasy and expressive variety. The recording, if a shade close (and catching a fair amount of sniffing), reproduces truthfully the ensemble's crisp, transparent textures.

Haydn Piano Trios – C major, HobXV/27. E major, HobXV/28. E flat major, HobXV/29. E flat major, HobXV/30. **Vera Beths** (vn); **Anner Bylsma** (vc); **Robert Levin** (fp). Sony Classical Vivarte Ⓕ SK53120 (74 minutes: DDD: 6/94). ✎

These are truly magnificent pieces, full of ideas of startling originality, and conceived on a grand scale – not simply long (though No. 42 certainly is that) but composed with a remarkable spaciousness to their ideas and their working-out. These performances do them ample justice, with their very brilliant and stylish pianism and a beautifully held instrumental balance (which, incidentally, gives the lie to the old notion that Haydn's cello parts are routine stuff: clearly Bylsma doesn't see them that way). Robert Levin, using a McNulty copy of a 1780 piano by J.A. Stein, produces playing of great vitality and delightful crispness, and puts across powerfully the intellectual force and the argumentative character of the music. Outstandingly keen and vital musicianship, excellently recorded.

New review

Haydn Piano works. **John McCabe** (pf). Decca London Ⓑ 443 785-2LC12 (12 discs: 873 minutes: ADD: 12/95). From Decca HDN100/2 (10/75), HDN103/5 (5/76), HDN106/8 (9/76), HDN109/11 (4/77) and HDN112/5 (10/77). Recorded 1974-7.
Sonatas Nos. 1-62. Five Variations in D major, HobXVII/7. Seven Menuets from "Kleine Tänze für die Jugend", HobIX/8. Variations in F minor, HobXVII/6. Fantasia in C major, HobXVII/4. 12 Variations in E flat major, HobXVII/3. Adagio in F major, HobXVII/9. Six Variations in C major, HobXVII/5. 20 Variations in A major, HobXVII/2. Capriccio in G major, HobXVII/1. Seven Last Words.

Together with Schnabel's Beethoven sonatas and Klien's Mozart sonatas, McCabe's recordings of Haydn's piano sonatas represent one of the great recorded monuments of the keyboard repertoire. Sample any one of the discs in this budget-price set and you will immediately become aware of the immense treasures on offer. In addition to being a fine pianist, McCabe is also an accomplished composer, and the special qualities he brings to his performances benefit from his 'insider's' awareness of musical content, pursuing the structural argument in these pieces with the acute perceptions of a composer's ear. Thus, assisted by the rich resonance and tonal subtlety of the modern piano, McCabe provides a consistently stylish view of Haydn's developing musical persona that comprehensively exploits this repertoire's inherent expressive potential. Spare textures and astonishing formal concentration in the earliest works establish a perfect balance between structure and content, and McCabe's crisp, beautifully poised playing enables the music to make its own potently expressive impact. The middle-period sonatas demonstrate Haydn's further experimentation and consolidation of style and technique. Harpsichord textures, reminiscent of Scarlatti, are still apparent in works such as the A flat Sonata (No. 31), but so, too, are new influences. For instance, McCabe luxuriates in the *Sturm und Drang* characteristics of the G minor Sonata (No. 32), penetrating to the core of the musical fabric to release the full power of the score's passionate centre, while, in other pieces, he delights in the music's abundant stylistic diversity.

Haydn's piano sonatas reach a supreme level of refinement in the late works, and McCabe responds with suitably spacious playing, sensitive to the music's richer 'orchestral' colours. He brings a connoisseur's touch to the impressionistic harmonic effects in the first movement of the C major Sonata (No. 60); his sinuous phrasing underlines the Schubertian flavour of the opening *Andante* to the D major Sonata (No. 61); he charmingly points the Beethovenian syncopation in the same work's

Scherzo and ultimately achieves the perfect balance between content and design in the magisterial E flat Sonata (No. 62). McCabe's consummate poise between foreground motivic activity and structural background is equally remarkable in the separate keyboard pieces, which add to the appeal of this set. His outstanding performances of both *Seven Last Words* and the ingeniously constructed F minor Variations are obvious highlights; but try, also, the enchanting *Adagio*, and the charming selection of dances, which provide further evidence of Haydn's mastery of miniature forms. The vividly clear 1970s recordings have retained all the clarity for which they are justly renowned and, as for comparisons, McCabe's performances here set the standards against which others will be judged.

Additional recommendation ...

...Piano Sonatas – C major, HobXVI/21; E major, HobXVI/22; F major, HobXVI/23; D major, HobXVI/24; E flat major, HobXVI/25; A major, HobXVI/26. **Jenö Jandó** (pf). Naxos Ⓢ 8 553127 (67 minutes: DDD: 6/95).

Haydn Piano works. **Alfred Brendel** (pf). Philips Ⓕ 416 643-2PH4 (four discs, oas: 52, 55, 37 and 61 minutes: ADD/DDD: 3/87). Booklet included. *Gramophone classical 100. Gramophone Award Winner 1987.*

Sonatas – C minor, HobXVI/20; E flat major, HobXVI/49 (both from 9500 774, 8/81); E minor, HobXVI/34; B minor, HobXVI/32; D major, Hob XVI/42 (412 228-1PH, 8/85); C major, HobXVI/48; D major, HobXVI/51; C major, Hob XVI/50 (6514 317, 11/83); E flat major, HobXVI/52; G major, HobXVI/40; D major, HobXVI/37 (416 365-1PH, 12/86). Fantasia in C major, HobXVI/4. Adagio in F major, HobXVI/9 (412 228-1PH, 8/85). Variations in F minor, Hob XVI/6 (416 365-1PH, 12/86). ⒼⒼⒼ

The sonatas collected in this set are some magnificent creations, wonderfully well played by Alfred Brendel. Within the order and scale of these works Haydn explores a rich diversity of musical languages, a wit and broadness of expression that quickly repays attentive listening. It is the capriciousness as much as the poetry that Brendel so perfectly attends to; his playing, ever alive to the vitality and subtleties, makes these discs a delight. The sophistication innate in the simple dance rhythms, the rusticity that emerges, but above all, the sheer *joie de vivre* are gladly embraced. Brendel's continual illumination of the musical ideas through intense study pays huge dividends. The recording quality varies enormously between the different works and though the close acoustic on some of the later discs could be faulted for allowing one to hear too much of the keyboard action, it certainly brings one into vivid contact with the music.

Additional recommendations ...

...E minor, HobXVI/34. G major, HobXVI/40. B flat major, HobXVI/41. D major, HobXVI/42. C major, HobXVI/48. Variations in F minor, HobXVII/6. **Jenö Jandó** (pf). Naxos Ⓢ 8 550845 (70 minutes: DDD: 8/94).

...E flat major, HobXVI/49. *Coupled with works by* **Chopin, Liszt** *and* **Wagner/Liszt** Vladimir **Horowitz** (pf). Sony Classical SK45818 (8/90). *See review in the Collections section; refer to the Index to Reviews.* ⒼⒼⒼ

...E flat major, HobXVI/49; C major, HobXVI/50; E flat major, HobXVI/52. Variations in F minor, HobXVII/6. **Mozart** Piano Sonatas – No. 8 in A minor, K310; No. 11 in A major, K331; No. 13 in B flat major, K333; No. 14 in C minor, K457. Fantasia in C minor, K475. Rondo in A minor, K511. Adagio in B minor, K540. Piano Concertos[a] – No. 14 in E flat major, K449; No. 15 in B flat major, K450; No. 19 in F major, K459; No. 21 in C major, K467; E flat major, K365 (with Imogen Cooper, pf); No. 26 in D major, K537, "Coronation"; No. 27 in B flat major, K595. **Alfred Brendel** (pf); [a]**Academy of St Martin in the Fields / Sir Neville Marriner.** Philips Ⓜ 446 921-2PM5 (five discs: 369 minutes: ADD/DDD: 2/96).

New review

Haydn Piano Sonatas – A major, HobXVI/30; E flat major, HobXVI/52.
Schubert Piano Sonata No. 14 in A minor, D784. Marche Militaire No. 1 in D major, D733 (arr. Tausig). **Evgeni Kissin** (pf). Sony Classical Ⓕ SK64538 (62 minutes: DDD: 9/95). *Gramophone Editor's record of the month.* Ⓖ

Enormously enjoyable! This is Haydn playing of high style and verve – also affectionate, articulate, colourful and expressive – and its vitality seems authentic even when Kissin asks you to admire the means with which he achieves it. This is not wilful or eccentric playing. By the end of the A major work, an engaging and (even by Haydn's standards) unconventional Sonata, you feel its stature has been enhanced, which is just as it should be. Kissin meets the greater challenge of Haydn's last Sonata of all (No. 62) equally well. The breadth as well as the brilliance of the first movement is there, and its warmth; his tempo may be a little brisker than usual but it still allows for weight. The last movement *Presto* really is breakneck, at a speed which would be unwise, not to say unrealistic, for most others; once again, the impression is of allure allied to perfectly judged dramatic tension and articulate speech. As someone remarked when we were listening to Kissin with the Boston Symphony at Tanglewood a couple of summers ago, "it's not just that it's all there, but he makes it all happen at the right time". Maybe he sustains the phrases of the *Adagio* with less success: they tend to emerge a bar at a time, as with many players, instead of as an arching span. How difficult this is to do when tone on the piano dies so quickly. But it is precisely this kind of growth and building through sentences and long paragraphs – and through silences – that he manages so well in the first movement of the Schubert sonata. It would be tedious to annotate everything, but admire here what you will: the unforced, perfectly scaled range of dynamics and attacks; the motivating force of the left hand, so often neglected by those who see interest only in the right; the sensitivity to harmonic movement, again, and to the smallest shifts of colour and weight; the infallible timing and marvellous sense of rhythm in all aspects; the voicing and vitality of the texture from top to bottom; a detail such as the way the doubling of a melodic line at the octave produces not just a melody in octaves but an intensification of the single line heard previously. Above all, there is a commanding vision of the whole. The finale is equally fine. The recording balance is not too close and the sound is pleasingly open and natural.

Haydn Piano Sonatas – B minor, HobXVI/32; E minor, HobXVI/34; G minor, HobXVI/44; E flat major, HobXVI/49. **Emanuel Ax** (pf). Sony Classical Ⓕ SK53635 (61 minutes: DDD: 7/95). Recorded 1993.
Emanuel Ax's choice of piano sonatas focuses on the remarkable influence of C.P.E. Bach in this repertoire. Of the three minor-key sonatas recorded here, the two-movement G minor work makes the influences the most poignantly apparent. Ax's performance is finely proportioned, and his elegant, sensitively shaped phrasing creates an arresting expression of the music's homogeneity and dramatic intensity. Ax includes all repeats, which, in the finale of the one in B minor, for example, produces startling results. In the finale of the E minor Sonata, by comparison, Ax's distinctive handling of different textures, which enhances the contrast between sections, vividly reveals the movement's fusion of rondo and variation forms. Ax ends his programme with the E flat major Sonata. Haydn himself was especially proud of the *Adagio*, and Ax's performance of this movement's passionate minor-mode middle section makes a dramatic impact. However, after panache and brilliance in the finale, Ax's breathtakingly beautiful, gentle final cadence leaves the deepest impression. Ax's penetrating insights into the *Sturm und Drang* characteristics of these sonatas make an outstanding contribution to the appreciation of this aspect of the composer's keyboard sonata output.
Additional recommendation ...
...G minor, HobXVI/44. *Coupled with works by* **Debussy, Schumann, Schubert, Bach, Chopin, Scriabin, Rachmaninov** and **Prokofiev** Sviatoslav Richter (pf). DG Double Ⓜ 447 355-2GDB2 (two discs: 150 minutes: ADD: 12/95).

Haydn Piano Sonatas – D major, HobXVI/33; E minor, HobXVI/34. Variations – E flat major, HobXVII/3; F minor, HobXVII/6; G major, on "Gott erhalte den Kaiser". **Andreas Staier** (fp). Deutsche Harmonia Mundi Ⓕ 05472 77285-2 (72 minutes: DDD: 2/94). ✍ Recorded 1992.
Gramophone Editor's choice.
Staier is a player of immense technical and imaginative flair; using a beautiful, even-toned copy of a Walter fortepiano he brings to this shrewdly contrasted programme a rare sense of creative involvement, relishing to the full the music's wit, passion and fantasy. The Variations in E flat based on the minuet from the Quartet Op. 9 No. 2, are of the off-the-peg rococo-decorative type that tends to look pretty unpromising on paper. But the sheer inventiveness of Staier's playing easily overcomes any potential monotony. Of the two sonatas here the earlier is the D major, dating from the early- to mid-1770s. The lightweight outer movements, gaining more than most from the fortepiano's clarity of texture, are spruce and puckish, with Staier palpably savouring every quirk in Haydn's argument. The relatively familiar E minor Sonata of *c*1780 has a magnificent, driving opening movement, which Staier attacks with tigerish energy and a characteristically wide dynamic range. If you still doubt that performances on the fortepiano can rival those on a modern Steinway in colour, excitement and passion, then this is the disc to convert you, although the recording is more closely miked than some might prefer.

Haydn Piano Sonatas – C major, HobXVI/35; C sharp minor, HobXVI/36; D major, HobXVI/37; E flat major, HobXVI/38; G major, HobXVI/39. **Jenö Jandó** (pf). Naxos Ⓢ 8 553128 (62 minutes: DDD: 7/95). Recorded 1993.
The exquisite, classical balance evident in these six keyboard sonatas makes them especially rewarding examples of the composer's exploitation of the piano's broad expressive range and rich textural variety. This latest volume in Jenö Jandó's complete edition presents these pieces in a compelling, modern-instrument version. For example, there is brilliance and sparkle in the opening movements of the D major and E flat Sonatas; warmth and dramatic intensity in the slow movements (most notably in the baroque echoes of the Sonatas in C major and D major), and an appealing blend of wit and elegance in finales such as the third movement of the D major Sonata, or the minuets which conclude the C sharp minor and E flat major Sonatas. Most remarkable, though, is the G major Sonata, where Jandó's customary precision and his sensitive balance of the music's linear and harmonic dimensions powerfully convey the work's concerto character and Haydn's imaginative approach to form. Try Jandó's engaging account of the opening *Allegro*'s mixture of rondo and variation form; his deft balance of the slow movement's effective blend of major and minor, and his exuberant virtuosity in the finale.

Haydn Piano Sonatas – E flat major, HobXVI/49; C major, HobXVI/50; D major, HobXVI/51; E flat major, HobXVI/52. **Jenö Jandó** (pf). Naxos Ⓢ 8 550657 (62 minutes: DDD: 6/94).

The keyboard sonatas which Haydn originally intended for piano, such as the four considered here, show the composer's exploration of the instrument's capacity for greater dynamic variation. Jandó is sensitive to the relationship between motif and dynamics which is particularly evident in the E flat and D major Sonatas respectively. Aided by clear recorded sound, Jandó's satisfying warmth in the lyrical passages provides an effective dramatic contrast to his crisp, positive approach in the livelier music. Jandó's glittering technique has a high profile in the other two sonatas in the programme. Pletnev's recordings of the same pieces are no less impressive technically but, in the C major Sonata, No. 60, he takes more liberties than Jandó does. However, Pletnev's charm lies in the sheer musical personality of his playing and, in matters of articulation and shaping of thematic material, his performances leave a deep and lasting impression. Jandó's stylistically well-turned readings are less controversial, but they lack nothing in excitement. Sample the finale of the E flat Sonata, where the wealth of expressive detail at an extremely fast tempo is breathtaking.

Additional recommendations ...

...C minor, HobXVI/20. HobXVI/50. HobXVI/52. **Mikhail Pletnev** (pf). Virgin Classics
ⓕ VC7 59258-2 (67 minutes: DDD: 11/89).

...D major, HobXVI/24; A major, XVI/26; F major, XVI/29; C major, HobXVI/35; C sharp minor, HobXVI/36. **Julia Cload** (pf). Meridian ⓕ CDE84210 (77 minutes: DDD: 3/93).

New review

Haydn Missa Sancti Bernardi de Offida in B flat major, "Heiligmesse", HobXXII/10[a]. Mare Clausum, HobXXIVa/9[b]. Insanae et vanae curae. Motetti de Venerabili Sacramento, HobXXIIIc/5a-d. Te Deum in C major, HobXXIIIc/2. [a]**Jörg Hering** (ten); [ab]**Harry van der Kamp** (bass); **Tölz Boys' Choir; Tafelmusik / Bruno Weil.** Sony Classical ⓕ SK66260 (63 minutes: DDD: 7/96). ✍ Texts and translations included. Recorded 1994.

A special attraction for Haydn lovers is the first-ever recording of the unfinished ode *Mare Clausum*, commissioned in 1794 by Haydn's colourful English friend Lord Abingdon, and evidently abandoned when the nobleman was imprisoned for libel. The gauche, crudely chauvinistic verses, trumpeting England's sovereignty of the sea, should make the most hardened Europhobe blush. But the two numbers Haydn completed are worthy of his ripest style: a noble F major bass aria with rich, inventive writing for woodwind, authoritatively sung by Harry van der Kamp (despite a hint of rawness on the top notes), and a D major chorus whose verve and contrapuntal power presage the late Masses and oratorios. Under Bruno Weil's spirited direction both the Tölz Boys' Choir, with their bright-edged, slightly breathy tone, and the crack period orchestra, Tafelmusik, are on first-rate form here and throughout this enterprisingly planned disc. It includes the thrilling, majestic late *Te Deum* and the motet *Insanae et vanae curae*, adapted from a 'storm' chorus in the oratorio *Il ritorno di Tobia* and foreshadowing in its D minor apocalyptic grandeur the Mozart of *Don Giovanni* and the Requiem. Weil's reading is eagerly responsive to the music's drama, with taut rhythms, sharp dynamic contrasts and keen instrumental detailing; and he maintains the initial pulse through the tranquil D major section. Between these masterpieces the four little *Motetti de Venerabili* from the 1750s (another recorded first) inevitably sound tame, for all their easy tunefulness and skilful marshalling of rococo cliché. The largest work on the disc is, of course, the so-called *Heiligmesse*, first of the six magnificent Mass settings of Haydn's old age. Like the shorter pieces, this receives an energetic, uplifting reading, with brisk tempos, fresh, incisive choral work and strongly etched orchestral colours. In one or two sections Weil can drive too hard and where Harry van der Kamp sometimes overwhelms the excellent boy soloists. But there is no doubting the vigour and joyfulness of Weil's reading, nor the skill and commitment of his forces. Quite apart from its pioneering value, this is an inspiriting Haydn collection whose appeal is enhanced by vivid sound.

Haydn Mass No. 1[b], Missa Sunt bona mixta malis, HobXXII/2[d] – Kyrie; part of Gloria. Non nobis, Domine, HobXXIIIa/1[d]. Ave regina in A major, HobXXIIIb/3[ac]. Responsoria de Venerabilis, HobXXIIIc/4a-d[c]. Responsorium ad absolutionem in D minor, HobXXIIb/1[c]. Salve regina in E major, HobXXIIIb/1[be]. Mass No. 7 in B flat major, Missa brevis Sancti Johannis de Deo ("Kleine Orgelmesse"), HobXXII/7[e]. [a]**Marie-Claude Vallin**, [b]**Ann Monoyios** (sops); **Tölz Boys' Choir;** [c]**L'Archibudelli** (with [d]**Anner Bylsma**, vc; [d]**Anthony Woodrow**, db; [d]**Bob van Asperen**, org); [e]**Tafelmusik / Bruno Weil.** Sony Classical Vivarte ⓕ SK53368 (60 minutes: DDD: 9/94). ✍ Texts and translations included. Recorded 1992-93.

This is the first appearance on disc of two recent Haydn discoveries, the brief Offertorium *Non nobis, Domine* and fragments (the *Kyrie* and part of the *Gloria*) of a Mass *Sunt bona mixta malis*. But its real charms lie in two works for solo soprano, choir and orchestra composed to mark the entry into convent life of Therese Keller whom Robbins Landon, in his characteristically earthy insert-note, suggests was Haydn's great love: "We must imagine the young Haydn, heartbroken, watching the love of his life taking the veil". Be that as it may, what seeps out of every pore is a warmth and sincerity, something akin to profound inner happiness, which makes one wonder just how deep Haydn's love was for the devout Therese Keller. Marie-Claude Vallin's captivating performance perfectly captures the essential innocence of the *Ave regina*. Her voice has a naïve, almost childlike quality, although in her ethereally soaring high notes and fluent trills there is no doubting her technical command. Ann Monoyios has an altogether fuller, more mature quality as befits the more intense *Salve regina* although, again, if this is Haydn heartbroken, he must have had superhuman powers of recuperation.

Bruno Weil's support for these two delightful singers is as unobtrusive as it is sympathetic. His excellent team of musicians (not forgetting the splendid work from the Vivarte recording team) are allowed to relax in performances which seem almost to float on air, so graceful and effortless does it all sound. Add to this a performance of the *Little Organ* Mass (No. 7) of rare poise and elegance and you have a disc of real beauty.

New review

Haydn Masses – No. 7 in B flat major, HobXXII/7[a], "Missa brevis Sancti Joannis de Deo"; No. 12 in B flat major, HobXXII/12, "Theresienmesse"[b]. **Janice Watson** (sop); [b]**Pamela Helen Stephen** (mez); [b]**Mark Padmore** (ten); [b]**Stephen Varcoe** (bar); **Collegium Musicum 90 Chorus; Collegium Musicum 90 / Richard Hickox.** Chandos Ⓕ CHAN0592 (60 minutes: DDD: 4/96). ✍ Texts and translations included. Recorded 1995. *Gramophone Editor's choice.*

Hickox, with his expert period orchestra and 24-strong professional choir, generates the physical and spiritual elation essential to this music, calling to mind Haydn's own much-quoted remark that whenever he praised God his heart leapt with joy. In the glorious *Theresienmesse* of 1799 his manner is a shade brisker and more athletic than Trevor Pinnock's larger-scaled reading (listed below); but if Pinnock brings rather more breadth and grandeur to, say, the opening of the *Kyrie* or the *Sanctus*, Hickox is particularly fine in the exultant, springing *Gloria* and the rough-hewn vigour of the *Credo*. He understands, too, the Mass's dramatic and symphonic impetus, bringing a powerful cumulative momentum to the sonata-form "Dona nobis pacem" and thrillingly tightening the screws in the closing pages. Where Hickox has a decisive edge over Pinnock is first of all in the more forward placing of his choir (though never at the expense of orchestral detail, keenly observed by Hickox), and secondly in his uncommonly well-integrated solo quartet, who, framed by the sweet-toned Janice Watson and the gentle, mellifluous Stephen Varcoe, sing with a chamber-musical grace and refinement in the "Et incarnatus est" and the *Benedictus*. And their supplicatory tenderness in the "Dona nobis pacem" (where Pinnock's solo quartet is more assertive and less subtle in phrasing) contrasts arrestingly with the choir's urgent demands for peace. Hickox also captures the peculiar serenity and innocence of the much earlier *Missa brevis Sancti Joannis de Deo*, or 'Little Organ Mass', its intimacy enhanced here by the use of solo strings. A disc guaranteed to refresh the spirit.

Additional recommendations ...

...No. 12. **M. Haydn** Ave regina caelorum. **Mozart** Ave verum corpus, K618. **Soloists; Choir of St John's College, Cambridge; Academy of St Martin in the Fields / George Guest.** Decca Ovation Ⓜ 430 159-2DM (56 minutes: ADD: 6/91).

...No. 6 in G major, HobXXII/6, "Missa Sancti Nicolai"; No. 12. **Soloists; The English Concert Choir; The English Concert / Trevor Pinnock.** Archiv Produktion Ⓕ 437 807-2AH (72 minutes: DDD: 1/94). ✍

Haydn Mass No. 11 in D minor, HobXXII/11, "Nelson"[a]. Te Deum in C major, HobXXIIIc/2. [a]**Felicity Lott** (sop); [a]**Carolyn Watkinson** (contr); [a]**Maldwyn Davies** (ten); [a]**David Wilson-Johnson** (bar); **The English Concert and Choir / Trevor Pinnock.** Archiv Produktion Ⓕ 423 097-2AH (50 minutes: ADD: 2/88). ✍ Texts and translations included. *Gramophone Award Winner 1988.* Ⓖ

The British Admiral had ousted the Napoleonic fleet at the Battle of the Nile just as Haydn was in the middle of writing his *Nelson* Mass. Although the news could not have reached him until after its completion, Haydn's awareness of the international situation was expressed in the work's subtitle, "Missa in Augustiis", or "Mass in times of fear". With its rattle of timpani, its pungent trumpet calls, and its highly-strung harmonic structure, there is no work of Haydn's which cries out so loudly for recording on period instruments; and it is the distinctive sonority and highly-charged tempos of this performance which sets it apart from its competitors. The dry, hard timpani and long trumpets bite into the dissonance of the opening *Kyrie*, and the near vibrato-less string playing is mordant and urgent. The fast-slow-fast triptych of the *Gloria* is set out in nervously contrasted speeds, and the *Credo* bounces with affirmation. Just as the choral singing is meticulously balanced with instrumental inflection, so the soloists have been chosen to highlight the colours in Pinnock's palette. This is an unusually exciting recording.

Additional recommendation ...

...No. 11[a]. **Mozart** Mass in C major, K317[b]. **Soloists;** [a]**London Symphony Chorus;** [b]**Choir of King's College, Cambridge;** [a]**City of London Sinfonia / Richard Hickox;** [b]**English Chamber Orchestra / Stephen Cleobury.** Decca Ovation Ⓜ 436 470-2DM (67 minutes: DDD: 5/93).

Haydn Die Jahreszeiten. **Barbara Bonney** (sop); **Anthony Rolfe Johnson** (ten); **Andreas Schmidt** (bar); **Monteverdi Choir; English Baroque Soloists / John Eliot Gardiner.** Archiv Produktion Ⓕ 431 818-2AH2 (two discs: 127 minutes: DDD: 5/92). ✍ Text and translation included. Recorded 1990.

The comparative unpopularity of Haydn's *The Seasons* when considered against his other great oratorio, *Die Schöpfung* ("The Creation"), is understandable perhaps, but it is not really all that well deserved. Less exalted its subject and libretto may be, but its depiction of the progress of the year amid the scenes and occupations of the Austrian countryside drew from its composer – then in his late sixties – music of unfailing invention, benign warmth and constant musical-pictoral delights. It is charming music written with great affection, and as such it is not only quintessentially Haydnesque, but also virtually guaranteed to raise a smile. As usual, John Eliot Gardiner and his forces turn in disciplined, meticulously professional performances. This is not one of those massive readings currently favoured even by period practitioners for Haydn's oratorios, though the orchestra are slightly larger – and consequently a tiny bit less lucid – than the sort you might nowadays find playing a classical symphony. The choir, however, perform with great clarity and accuracy, and brings, too, an enjoyable sense of characterization to its various corporate roles, be they drunken revellers, improbably noisy hunters, homely fireside spinners, or whatever. The soloists all perform with notable poise and intelligence: Barbara Bonney's voice is pure and even, Anthony Rolfe Johnson sounds entirely at ease with the music, and Andreas Schmidt is gentle-voiced but certainly not lacking in substance. Perhaps in the end this is a performance that just lacks that last inch of necessary warmth to make it unbeatable, but it's a first-rate recommendation none the less.

Additional recommendations ...

...**Edith Mathis** (sop); **Siegfried Jerusalem** (ten); **Dietrich Fischer-Dieskau** (bar); **Chorus and Academy of St Martin in the Fields / Sir Neville Marriner.** Philips Duo Ⓜ 438 715-2PM2 (two discs: 134 minutes: ADD: 6/94).

...**Gundula Janowitz** (sop); **Peter Schreier** (ten); **Martti Talvela** (bass); **Vienna Singverein and Symphony Orchestra / Karl Böhm.** DG Double Ⓜ 437 940-2GX2 (two discs: 132 minutes: ADD: 5/95).

Haydn Die Schöpfung, HobXXI/2. **Christine Schäfer** (sop); **Michael Schade** (ten); **Andreas Schmidt** (bar); **Stuttgart Gächinger Kantorei; Stuttgart Bach Collegium / Helmuth Rilling.** Hänssler Classic Ⓒ 98 938 (two discs: 106 minutes: DDD: 12/94). Text and translation included. Recorded 1993.

Here is the fine German performing tradition at its best. Keen scholarship, professional thoroughness and a shared love of music are all shown or felt to be present. And what music it is, its own creativeness the most wonderful testimony to the wonder of Creation itself. Year by year it grows in the mind. Also (and this must have something to do with our own increasing awareness of peril) it is a work that induces a passion of feeling, latent in the score and certainly deep in its Miltonic background, that all this clean, early-morning zest and beauty confronts us with our shame. A primly eighteenth-century *Creation* satisfies no more than does an old-fashioned romantic and weighted one. Rilling has it right: the grace, delicacy and nimbleness of mind and movement are there, and so too are the profundity and reverence. The acoustic is fairly reverberant, but one feels the work to be in a setting that is natural for it. The soloists are recorded close, possibly excessively so, the advantages being a vividness of presence and communication, and, in the numbers where soloists and chorus combine, an additional clarity. All three singers are admirable. Christine Schäfer, sounding like a young Elly Ameling, brings a voice of lovely quality, a well-schooled technique and the simple freshness of approach that is so essential. The biographical note tells that the tenor, Michael Schade, has been compared with Nicolai Gedda, and one can see that too, especially in the trio (No. 18) where his solo has such lively rhythmic impetus. So much is asked of the bass soloist that few succeed in everything, and perhaps in the first of his arias (No. 6) Andreas Schmidt could do with ampler power and depth; but generally he is fine, and particularly impressive in the marvellous solo passage in No. 27. Rilling lets nothing drag, sometimes setting a brisk and risky tempo that keeps everyone on their toes and works well. His players once again exhibit their special distinction in the woodwind department. For many English-speaking listeners, *The Creation* will be a work they want to hear in English; but if that is not a prime requisite then this is a version with a great deal in its favour.

Additional recommendations ...

...(sung in English). **Soloists; Choir of New College, Oxford; Academy of Ancient Music Chorus; Academy of Ancient Music Orchestra / Christopher Hogwood.** L'Oiseau-Lyre Ⓒ 430 397-2OH2 (two discs: 99 minutes: DDD: 3/91). ✐

...**Soloists; Vienna Singverein; Berlin Philharmonic Orchestra / Herbert von Karajan.** DG Galleria Ⓜ 435 077-2GGA2 (two discs: 109 minutes: ADD: 12/91).

...**Soloists; Tafelmusik / Bruno Weil.** Sony Classical Vivarte Ⓒ SX2K57965 (two discs: 91 minutes: DDD: 2/95). ✐

...Die Schöpfung[a]. Salve regina in E major, HobXXIIIb/1[b]. **Soloists; [a]Brighton Festival Chorus; [b]London Chamber Choir; [b]Argo Chamber Orchestra; [a]Royal Philharmonic Orchestra; / [a]Antál Dorati; [b]Laszlo Heltay.** Double Decca Ⓜ 443 027-2DF2 (two discs: 129 minutes: ADD: 5/94).

Haydn Armida. **Jessye Norman** (sop) Armida; **Claes Hakon Ahnsjö** (ten) Rinaldo; **Norma Burrowes** (sop) Zelmira; **Samuel Ramey** (bass) Idreno; **Robin Leggate** (ten) Ubaldo; **Anthony Rolfe Johnson** (ten) Clotarco. **Lausanne Chamber Orchestra / Antál Dorati.** Philips Ⓒ 432 438-2PH2 (two discs: 140 minutes: ADD: 6/93). From 6769 021 (9/79).

Armida, widely considered Haydn's finest opera, is based on a familiar literary classic adopted for opera by numerous other composers: what is surprising is that in his setting Haydn reverted to *opera seria* style, with no *buffo* characters, very few ensembles and extensive *secco* recitatives. Dramatic action is minimal: for three acts Rinaldo lingers under the spell of the enchantress Armida despite all the efforts of fellow-Crusaders to recall him to his mission. The work's static nature, however, casts the emphasis on its musical qualities, and in this regard *Armida* is of the highest standard. The enchantress herself, personified by the redoubtable Jessye Norman, has the widest range of emotions to portray, from tenderness to rage; Ahnsjö as Rinaldo produces a fine legato and very accurate florid passagework, but his low register rather lets him down; Ramey shows laudable firmness and flexibility; and Burrowes's fresh youthful charm is very appealing. Another strength is the alert orchestral playing. The most notable features of the opera are three long through-composed sequences and imaginative scoring: the scene in the magic forest, where Rinaldo at last, to Armida's fury, breaks free from her spell, is masterly, and in itself is sufficient to compel a revision of the too common neglect of Haydn as an operatic composer.

Further listening ...

…Violin Concertos – A major, HobVIIa/3; C major, HobVIIa/1; G major, HobVIIa/4. Concerto for Violin, Keyboard and Strings, HobXVIII/6a. **Rainer Kussmaul** (vn); a**Robert Hill** (hpd); **Amsterdam Bach Soloists.** Olympia OCD428 (6/94). ✍

…Concerto for Violin, Keyboard and Strings in F major, HobXVIII/6. *Coupled with* **Mendelssohn** Concerto for Violin, Piano and Strings in D minor. **Ralf Gothóni** (pf); **Kuhmo Virtuosi / Peter Csaba** (vn). Ondine ODE810-2 (1/95).

…Divertinmentos – G major, HobII/2; C major, HobII/17. Variations in E flat major, HobII/24. **Haydn Sinfonietta, Vienna / Manfred Huss.** Koch Schwann 314812 (4/96).

…String Quartets – Op. 1: No. 5 in E flat major; No. 6 in C major. Op. 2: No. 1 in A major; No. 2 in E major. **Kodály Quartet.** Naxos 8 550399.

…The Seven Last Words. **Soloists; Arnold Schönberg Choir; Vienna Concentus Musicus / Nikolaus Harnoncourt.** Teldec Das Alte Werk 2292-46458-2 (5/92). ✍

…Stabat mater. **Patricia Rozario** (sop); **Catherine Robbin** (mez); **Anthony Rolfe Johnson** (ten); **Cornelius Hauptmann** (bass); **The English Concert and Choir / Trevor Pinnock.** Archiv Produktion 429 733-2AH (9/90). ✍

…Il ritorno di Tobia. **Barbara Hendricks, Linda Zoghby** (sops); **Della Jones** (mez); **Philip Langridge** (ten); **Benjamin Luxon** (bar); **Brighton Festival Chorus; Royal Philharmonic Orchestra / Antál Dorati.** Decca Serenata 440 038-2DM3 (10/94).

…L'anima del filosofo, ossia Orfeo ed Euridice. **Soloists; Bavarian Radio Chorus; Munich Radio Orchestra / Leopold Hager.** Orfeo C262932H (9/95).

…Esterhaza Opera Cycle. – L'infedeltà delusa *(432 413-2PH2)*; L'incontro improvviso – excerpts *(432 416-2PH3)*; Il mondo della luna – excerpts *(432 420-2PH3)*; La vera constanza *(432 424-2PH2)*; L'isola disabitata *(432 427-2PH3)*; La defeltà premiata *(432 430-2PH3)*; Orlando paladino *(432 434-2PH3)*; Armida *(432 438-2PH2)*. **Soloists; Lausanne Chamber Orchestra / Antál Dorati.** Philips (6/93).

Michael Haydn   Austrian 1737-1806

New review

M. Haydn Symphonies – B flat major, MH82 (P9); A major, MH152 (P6); G major, MH334 (P16); E flat major, MH473 (P26); F major, MH507 (P32). **London Mozart Players / Matthias Bamert.** Chandos Ⓟ CHAN9352 (69 minutes: DDD: 4/96). Recorded 1994.

Michael Haydn joined the orchestra of Oradea Cathedral as a violinist in 1757, before becoming Kapellmeister there. The first three movements of his A major Symphony (P6) began life as a ballet, while its finale comes from music previously used in the ballet-pantomime *Hermann*. Nevertheless, this tasteful reading by Bamert and the LMP presents a convincing structural unit. They offer great finesse and precision of ensemble in bright, fresher recordings. Dynamics and instrumental forces are strikingly opposed in the first movement, as are the major/minor contrasts in the minuet. The slow movement has an appropriately mannered stateliness, and the finale is engagingly vivacious. Like the A major Symphony, the B flat work (P9) has as its finale a later addition; but once again, the LMP's stylish playing, in a naturally lit recording, sounds thoroughly satisfying. The spacious acoustic, moreover, effectively highlights the ceremonial character of the G major Symphony, recalling its initial conception as part of the cantata for Nikolaus Hoffmann's installation as Abbot of Michaelbeuern.

M. Haydn String Quintets – Divertimento in B flat major, MH412; Notturno in C major, MH187; Notturno in G major, MH189. **L'Archibudelli** (Vera Beths, Lucy van Dael, vns; Jürgen Kussmaul, Guus Jeukendrup, vas; Anner Bylsma, vc). Sony Classical Vivarte Ⓟ SK53987 (76 minutes: DDD: 8/94). ✍ Recorded 1993.

It is often supposed that the string quintet as a genre was created by Mozart, but in fact there are plenty of examples by other composers before him, both in Salzburg and Vienna. Among the Salzburgers, Michael Haydn was pre-eminent. Two of the Quintets recorded here were written in 1773 – that is, immediately before Mozart wrote his own first Quintet, K174; the date of the third, the B flat work, is uncertain but not likely to be much different. They are really fine pieces, comparable on every level with the music of Michael's Salzburg colleague and his Esterházy brother. The B flat work is full of attractive and amiable invention, and the variation movement carries it to a higher plane, with a slow penultimate variation of real depth and poignancy with almost operatic dialogue between the first viola and first violin. No less fine is the *Adagio cantabile* of the C major work, with a viola melody above pizzicato accompaniments and comments and echoes from the violin (with the roles later reversed): music that is both delectable and profoundly felt. The *perpetuum mobile* finale here, with some nice touches of counterpoint, is another delight, both brilliant and amusing, and it has echoes in Mozart's K174. The last of the works here, in G major, begins just like a mature Joseph Haydn string quartet and is as closely and as wittily argued; its slow movement is again of considerable intensity (hints here of Mozart's much later *Eine kleine Nachtmusik*) and its final *Presto* will strike the listener as distinctly 'Mozartian' with its chromaticisms and its contrapuntal interest. A very appealing disc, finely and sensitively played and full of sympathetic and musicianly touches, especially in the slow movements.

Further listening ...
...Violin Concerto in B flat major, P53[a]. Clarinet Concerto in D major, P54[b]. Concerto for Harpsichord and Viola in C major, P55[c]. Soloists; [ac]**Oradea Philharmonic Orchestra / Ervin Acél;** [b]**Quodlibet Musicum Chamber Orchestra / Aurelian Octav Popa** (cl). Olympia OCD406 (10/90).
...Missa Sancti Aloysii, MH257. Missa sub titulo Sancti Leopoldi, MH837. Vesperae pro festo Sanctissimae innocentium, MH548. **Trinity College Choir, Cambridge; instrumental ensemble / Richard Marlow.** Conifer CDCF220 (2/94).

Philip Hayes
British 1738-1797

Suggested listening ...
...Keyboard Concerto No. 4 in A major. *Coupled with works by* **Nares, Chilcot, Roseingrave, Handel** and **Hook The Parley of Instruments / Paul Nicholson** (fp). Hyperion CDA66700 (8/94). ✐
...The Basket. *Coupled with works by* **Hallgrimsson, Weir, Finnissy, G. Jackson, S. Harrison, Crane, A. Fisher** and **Skempton Tapestry.** British Music Label BML012 (12/95). *See review in the Collections section; refer to the Index to Reviews.*

Christopher Headington
British 1930-1996

Headington Violin Concerto.
R. Strauss Violin Concerto, Op. 8. **Xue-Wei** (vn); **London Philharmonic Orchestra / Jane Glover.** ASV Ⓕ CDDCA780 (63 minutes: DDD: 12/91).   Ⓖ

Xue-Wei's penetrating and intuitive realization of Christopher Headington's Violin Concerto, written in 1959, commands great admiration for this significant modern concerto, dedicated to the late Ralph Holmes, which in many respects inherits the lyric mantle of the great masterworks for the violin composed earlier in the century by Elgar and Walton. Xue-Wei also reminds the listener of the work's darker aspect, especially during the opening paragraphs of the concerto, where an affinity with the Walton Concerto is apparent. The central *Vivace* movement again has something of Walton's caustic wit, but the Headington concerto is searching and original in concept, without being overtly heroic or virtuosic. The lyrical potential of the solo writing is gloriously revealed by Xue-Wei, whose playing is superb, particularly in the lucid six-variation finale, which leads to a hushed and deeply-felt conclusion. The Violin Concerto by Richard Strauss is very much in the traditionally romantic virtuoso vein of Wieniawski and Vieuxtemps, and although an early work it displays great pointers in the direction of Strauss's mature heroism. Xue-Wei's playing is volatile, affectionate and involving, while his rare tonal finesse has an evocative Heifetzian lustre which is always compelling. He is admirably supported throughout by the London Philharmonic, under Jane Glover, and ASV capture every nuance of the performance in the ample acoustic of London's Henry Wood Hall. The interpretation of the Headington concerto alone could well acquire classic status, and this is a disc which deserves to be heard by all who have an affinity with violin music of the twentieth century.

Further listening ...
...Ballade Image. Cinquanta. *Coupled with* **Britten** Holiday Diary. **Delius** Three Preludes. **Elgar** Adieu. In Smyrna. Serenade. **Ireland** The Island Spell. **Moeran** Summer Valley. **Patterson** A Tunnel of Time, Op. 66. **Christopher Headington** (pf). Kingdom KCLCD2017 (11/90).

David Heath
British 1956-

Suggested listening ...
...Soprano Saxophone Concerto, "The Celtic". *Coupled with works by* **I. Wilson, Torke, McGlynn** and **Nyman Gerard McChrystal** (sax); **London Musici / Mark Stephenson.** Silva Classics SILKD6010 (6/96). *See review in the Collections section; refer to the Index to Reviews.*

Johann David Heinichen
German 1683-1729

New review
Heinichen Lamentationes Jeremiae prophetae, S71-3[bcd]. Beatus vir, S26[cd]. Alma mater
redemptoris, S22[b]. Nisi Dominus aedificaverit, S99[c]. De profundis, S35[e]. Nicht das Band, das
dich bestricket, S20[abce]. Warum toben die Heiden, S39[e]. Pastorale in A, "Per la notte della
Nativitate Christi", S242. [a]**Mechthild Georg** (sop); [b]**Axel Köhler** (alto); [c]**Jörg Dürmüller**, [d]**Scot
Weir** (tens); [e]**Raimund Nolte** (bass); **Cologne Musica Antiqua / Reinhard Goebel.** Archiv
Produktion Ⓟ 447 092-2AH2 (two discs: 129 minutes: DDD: 8/96). Text and translations
included.

As a follow-up to their colourful (and *Gramophone* Award-winning) album of concertos by the
Dresden composer Heinichen, Cologne Musica Antiqua have turned their attention to his sacred
vocal music. Heinichen served as Kapellmeister at the Catholic Dresden court of Augustus the Strong
from 1717 until his death. That he himself was a Protestant need not concern us overmuch since, as
Bach was to demonstrate with his B minor Mass, any inner conflict, at least in the creative domain,
was resolvable. Either Reinhard Goebel has chosen judiciously from among Heinichen's significant
surviving body of sacred music, or we need to hear more of it, for much of what is included here is
strikingly effective and of more enduring interest than his concertos. The most spaciously conceived
works in the programme are three *Lamentations of Jeremiah the Prophet,* and a German Oratorio,
Nicht das Band, das dich bestricket, both written for Dresden in 1724. Heinichen's harmonic
vocabulary is fluent – he was a noted theorist whose treatise on the continuo bass prompted Charles
Burney to dub him "The Rameau of Germany" – and his feeling for instrumental colouring often on
a par with that of his contemporary, Telemann. The more prolific and cosmopolitanly inclined
Telemann is often the touchstone, yet it was to be another 30 years before Telemann produced
oratorios such as *Der Tod Jesu,* with which Heinichen's German Oratorio has points in common. On
balance it is the Oratorio which offers the listener the most sustained evidence of Heinichen's skill in
the affective treatment of text by means of telling vocal declamation, graphic rhythms and diverting
instrumental colour. Little of the undeniable drama contained both in the *Lamentations* and the
Oratorio is lost on Goebel, who directs the performances with fervour and expressive intensity. There
are some ravishing arias, too, notably in the second *Lamentation* for bass voice and strings, and in the
Oratorio. The concluding work in the programme is a beguiling *Pastorale* for strings and *colla parte*
oboes which probably belongs to a sacred vocal work. An interesting introductory essay by Goebel
himself and exemplary recorded sound set the seal on a fascinating release.

Further listening ...
...Concertos – C major, S211; G major: S213; S214, "Darmstadt"; S214, "Venezia"; S215; S217;
   F major: S226; S231; S232; S233; S234; S235. Serenata di Moritzburg in F major, S204. Sonata in
   A major, S208. Concerto Movement in C minor, S240. **Cologne Musica Antiqua / Reinhard
   Goebel.** Archiv Produktion 437 549-2AH2 (5/93). ✒ *Gramophone Editor's choice. Gramophone
   Award Winner 1993.*   Ⓖ
...Concerto in F major. Pastorale in A major, "Per la notte della Nativitate Christi". *Coupled with
   works by* **Dieupart, Fasch, Pisendel, Quantz** and **Veracini** Cologne Musica Antiqua /
   Reinhard Goebel. Archiv Produktion 447 644-2AH (1/96). ✒   Ⓖ

Peter Heise
Danish 1830-1879

Suggested listening ...
...Drot og Marsk. **Soloists; Danish National Radio Choir; Danish National Radio Symphony
   Orchestra / Michael Schønwandt.** Chandos CHAN9143/5 (6/93).

Charles d'Helfer
French died after 1664

Suggested listening ...
...Requiem for the Dukes of Lorraine. Missa pro defunctis[bcef]. *Coupled with* **Plainchant** – Procession
   for the funerals of Charles II and Henri II[bcdef]. **L'Estocart** Dun fond de ma pensée[ef]. **Sweelinck** De
   profundis clamavi ad te Domine[ef]. **Du Caurroy** Dixième Fantasie sur Requiem Aeternam (A
   Quatre)[ef]. **M. Lasson** In manibus tuis sortes meae, Domine[bcef]. **Anonymous** Funeral Orations for
   Charles III[a]. [a]**Eugène Green** (spkr); [b]**A Sei Voci;** [c]**La Psallette de Lorraine;** [d]**Jean Chamboux** (tambour);
   [e]**Jay Bernfeld** (va da gamba); [f]**Les Sacqueboutiers de Toulouse / Bernard Fabre-Garrus.** Auvidis Astrée
   E8521 (3/95). ✒

David Heneker/John Taylor
British 1906-

Suggested listening ...
...Charlie Girl. **Original 1986 London revival cast.** First Night OCRCD09.
...Half a Sixpence. **Original London cast.** Decca 820 589-2.

George Martin Adolf von Henselt

Henselt Piano Concerto in F minor, Op. 16. Variations de concert, Op. 11, on "Quand je quittai la Normandie" from Meyerbeer's "Robert le Diable".
Alkan Concerti da camera, Op. 10 – No. 1 in A minor; No. 2 in C sharp minor. **Marc-André Hamelin** (pf); **BBC Scottish Symphony Orchestra / Martyn Brabbins.** Hyperion Ⓟ CDA66717 (70 minutes: DDD: 8/94). *Gramophone Editor's choice.*   ⓖⓖ

Much of the credit for this disc must go to the phenomenal playing and superb musicianship of Marc-André Hamelin (whose account of the staggeringly difficult Henselt Concerto is quite breathtaking) but plaudits must also go to the imaginative programming and excellent booklet-notes. The main work of the disc, both in terms of quality and length, is of course the above-mentioned Henselt F minor Concerto, which, although once an active participant in the repertoire of most top league pianists during the late nineteenth century (at least those sufficiently technically equipped to approach it), dropped out of sight in the early part of this century until revived by those 'champions of the forgotten', Raymond Lewenthal and Michael Ponti. As a concerto it is particularly 'giving' to the listener and very *un*forgiving to the pianist, as the extreme technical difficulties are concealed in such a way that they become almost transparent to the ear – which probably accounts for its disappearance from the repertoire. Rubinstein once recounted that "I procured the concerto and his *études*, but after working on them for a few days I realised it was a waste of time, for they were based on an abnormal formation of the hand. In this respect Henselt, like Paganini, was a freak." Musically the concerto owes allegiance to Chopin (in the *Larghetto*) and Thalberg and Mendelssohn in the outer movements, but generally the overall Henseltian style has its own peculiar flavour which should win many friends through Hamelin's highly persuasive and thoroughly committed performance. The slightly earlier *Variations de concert* (on a theme from Meyerbeer's *Robert le Diable*) is admittedly slighter fare but is nevertheless an attractive and enjoyable work which hails from the same stable as Chopin's *Là ci darem* Variations. The remainder of the disc consists of two 'mini' concertos by Henselt's exact contemporary and fellow 'reticent' Charles-Valentin Alkan (Henselt, like Alkan, gave very few public concerts due to stage-fright that bordered on the pathological). The two early *Concerti da camera* (the only surviving *concertante* pieces by Alkan) are not, it has to be said, 'major' Alkan works, but they are original in invention and full of melodic appeal, with more than a hint or two of the Alkan of later years. Hamelin, who has already proved himself a formidable Alkan exponent with his outstanding recording of the *Concerto for solo piano* (see review under Alkan; refer to the Index to Reviews), delivers them with astonishing dexterity and panache and, as in the Henselt pieces, he is given equally committed support from the BBC Scottish Symphony Orchestra under the direction of Martyn Brabbins. A thoroughly enjoyable disc, well worth exploring.

Further listening ...
...Ballade in B flat major, Op. 31. Grande Valse, Op. 30, "L'aurore boréale". Impromptus – B flat minor, Op. 34; B minor, Op. 37; C minor, Op. 7; F minor, Op. 17. Introduction and Variations on a theme by Donizetti, Op. 1. Pensée fugitive, Op. 8. Rondo serioso. Scherzo in B minor, Op. 9. Toccatina in C minor, Op. 25. Valse mélancolique, Op. 36. **Rudiger Steinfatt** (pf). Koch Schwann 310023.

Hans Werner Henze

Henze Symphony No. 7. Barcarola. **City of Birmingham Symphony Orchestra / Sir Simon Rattle.** EMI Ⓟ CDC7 54762-2 (60 minutes: DDD: 11/93). Recorded live in 1992.   ⓖ

This is a most important and overdue issue. Henze's Seventh adopts a recognizably Beethovenian model, although the music's point of departure may lie more immediately in the symphonies of Karl Amadeus Hartmann. Henze states in the notes that the Seventh is "a German symphony, and it deals with matters German". One of these is the poet Friedrich Hölderlin, whose sufferings in an asylum and late poem *Hälfte des Lebens* ("Half of Life") inspired respectively the scherzo and finale; what lies behind the intense and complex threnody of the towering second – and longest – movement is not divulged. This repertoire is not normally associated with Simon Rattle or the Birmingham orchestra but there is no lack of knowledge or commitment evident in the playing. Particularly impressive are the climaxes to the first and last movements, both superbly prepared and flawless in execution. The many delicate passages in which both the symphony and the earlier *Barcarola* (1979) abound are rendered equally impressively and the excellent recording does full justice to these eruptive scores. All in all, a tremendous achievement.

Henze Requiem. **Ueli Wiget** (pf); **Håkan Hardenberger** (tpt); **Ensemble Modern / Ingo Metzmacher.** Sony Classical Ⓟ SK58972 (63 minutes: DDD: 11/94). Recorded live in 1993.   ⓖⓖ

With its graphic imagery of war and terror, anguish and hope, it is tempting to see in Henze's cycle of nine sacred concertos a memorial for that chapter of German history that closed with the breaching of the Berlin Wall. The temptation must be resisted: the composer has refuted this interpretation absolutely, for the inspiration was both more personal, arising out of the death of his friend, the London Sinfonietta's Artistic Director, Michael Vyner in 1989 (with the Wall as impregnable as ever), and wider than the history of any one nation. Composed between 1990 and 1992, the wholly instrumental, non-liturgical Requiem was premièred in Cologne in February last year by the forces on this first recording, a composite of live performances given seven months later. Playing and interpretation matured during the interval, resulting in a first-class performance every detail of which has been captured with exemplary clarity. The great outbursts of the *Dies irae* and *Rex tremendae*, provoked by events of the Gulf War in 1991, are handled by players and technicians alike with the same assurance as the delicacy and quietude required in the *Lux aeterna* and *Agnus dei*. The Requiem presents a musically varied picture of Henze's latest manner and deserves every success.

Further listening ...

...Capriccio. *Coupled with works by* **Fortner, Ginastera, Boulez, Beck, Dutilleux, Lutosławski, Berio, C. Halffter, Britten, K. Huber** and **Holliger** Patrick and Thomas Demenga (vcs); **Cello Ensemble / Jürg Wyttenbach.** ECM New Series 445 234-2 (8/95). *See review in the Collections section; refer to the Index to Reviews.*

...Capriccio. *Coupled with works by* **Berio, Britten** and **Kodály** Matt Haimovitz (vc). DG 445 834-2GH (12/95).

...El Cimarrón. **Paul Yoder** (bar); **Michael Faust** (fl); **Reinbert Evers** (gtr); **Mircea Ardeleanu** (perc). Koch Schwann Musica Mundi 314030 (1/92).

...Voices. **Roswitha Trexler** (mez); **Joachim Vogt** (ten); **Leipzig Symphony Orchestra / Horst Neumann.** Berlin Classics 0021802BC (12/95).

...Voices – excerpts. **Gudrun Pelker** (mez); **Frieder Lang** (ten); **Musikfabrik NRW / Johannes Kalitzke.** CPO CPO999 192-2 (12/95).

...Die Bassariden. **Soloists; Berlin Radio Chamber Choir; South German Radio Choir; Berlin Radio Symphony Orchestra / Gerd Albrecht.** Koch Schwann Musica Mundi 314006 (10/91).   Ⓖ

...The English Cat. **Soloists; Parnassus Orchestra / Markus Stenz.** Wergo WER6204-2 (12/92).

Victor Herbert   American 1859-1924

New review

Herbert Cello Concerto No. 2 in E minor, Op. 30.
Dvořák Cello Concerto in B minor, B191. **Yo-Yo Ma** (vc); **New York Philharmonic Orchestra / Kurt Masur.** Sony Classical Ⓕ SK67173 (61 minutes: DDD: 4/96). Recorded 1995.   Ⓖ

The Victor Herbert Concerto here receives a high-powered performance, but one which does not overload the romantic element with sentiment, whether in the brilliant and vigorous outer movements or in the warmly lyrical slow movement, with its themes like love-songs translated from Herbert's operettas. Ma's use of rubato is perfectly judged, with the slow movement made the more tender at a flowing speed. The finale is then given a quicksilver performance, both brilliant and urgent. This magnificent performance could not be more welcome, and when Herbert's concerto, first given in 1894, was almost certainly what prompted Dvořák to write his own concerto later that same year, triumphantly demonstrating the viability of the genre, the coupling could not be more apt either. Ma's and Masur's version of the Dvořák is among the very finest, matched by few and outshining most, including Ma's own previous version with Maazel and the Berlin Philharmonic (Sony Classical SK42206, 1/87). It is fascinating to compare Ma's two versions side by side, the new one more readily conveying weight of expression despite the less spotlit placing of the soloist, more disciplined yet more spontaneous-sounding. This time Ma's expressiveness is simpler and more noble, and the recording (made in Avery Fisher Hall, New York), once a trouble-spot for engineers, is fuller and more open than the Berlin one, cleaner in tuttis, with only a touch of unwanted dryness on high violins. Ma and Masur together encompass the work's astonishingly full expressive range, making it the more bitingly dramatic with high dynamic contrasts.

Additional recommendation ...

...No. 2, Op. 30ᵃ. **Grofé** Grand Canyon Suite. Mississipi. ᵃ**Georges Miquelle** (vc); **Eastman-Rochester Orchestra / Howard Hanson.** Mercury Living Presence Ⓜ 434 355-2MM (66 minutes: ADD).

Jerry Herman   American 1933-

Suggested listening ...

...La cage aux folles. **Original Broadway cast.** RCA Victor Red Seal BD84824 (3/87).

...Mack and Mabel. **Original Broadway cast.** MCA MCLD19089.

...Hello, Dolly! – original film soundtrack. Philips 810 368-2PH.

Louis Hérold   French 1791-1833

Hérold (arr. Lanchbery) La fille mal gardée – excerpts. **Orchestra of the Royal Opera House, Covent Garden / John Lanchbery.** Decca Ovation Ⓜ 430 196-2DM (51 minutes: ADD: 1/94). From SXL2313 (8/62). Recorded 1962.   ⒼⒼ

The Royal Ballet's *La fille mal gardée* remains a source of perpetual delight, not least for the music that John Lanchbery arranged largely from Hérold's patchwork score for the 1828 version. The Clog dance is the obvious highlight of the score; but there are felicitous moments throughout, with snatches of Rossini, Donizetti *et al* cropping up all over the place. This recording is the original one that Lanchbery conducted when the ballet proved such a success in the Royal Ballet's repertoire in 1960. More recently he has recorded the score complete (listed below); and ballet lovers will doubtless consider this fuller version essential. However, others will undoubtedly find that the complete score rather outstays its welcome by comparison with this constantly uplifting selection. At medium price and wearing its 30-odd years lightly, it makes a most compelling recommendation.

Additional recommendation ...

...La fille mal gardée – ballet[a]. **Lecocq** (arr. G. Jacob) Mam'zelle Angot – ballet[b]. [a]**Orchestra of the Royal Opera House, Covent Garden / John Lanchbery;** [b]**National Philharmonic Orchestra / Richard Bonynge.** Decca Ovation Ⓜ 430 849-2DM2 (two discs: 134 minutes: DDD: 12/91).

Henry Heron
British 1730-1795

Suggested listening ...

...Voluntary in G major. *Coupled with works by* **Boyce, Handel, Hook, Russell, Stanley, Stubley** and **S. Wesley** Jennifer Bate (org). Unicorn-Kanchana DKPCD9106 (11/91). *See review in the Collections section; refer to the Index to Reviews. Selected by Sounds in Retrospect.* Ⓖ

Bernard Herrmann
American 1911-1975

Herrmann The Devil and Daniel Webster – Suite. Silent Noon. For the Fallen. Currier and Ives Suite. **New Zealand Symphony Orchestra / James Sedares.** Koch International Classics Ⓕ 37224-2 (51 minutes: DDD: 6/94).

The popular 20-minute suite from *The Devil and Daniel Webster* was assembled shortly after the film's score won its Oscar in 1942, and throughout the five movements Herrmann treats several New England folk-tunes to his own special brand of orchestral wizardry. The score is both a gentle, sepia-tinted portrait of rustic Americana and a wickedly endearing account of Mr Scratch's devilish interventions. *Silent Noon* is a warm if rather meandering romantic idyll clearly influenced by Delius. Far more characteristic is the 1943 berceuse *For the Fallen*, a brief, but poignant lament for the soldiers killed in action. The star items on the disc, though, are the five vibrant dance episodes that make up the *Currier and Ives Suite* (1935). As well as bringing to life the painter's beautifully detailed engravings with a sparkling, generous humour that would rarely surface in Herrmann's later works, the Suite also possesses the elegant period flavour that would colour the scores for *Citizen Kane*, *The Magnificent Ambersons* as well as *Daniel Webster*. James Sedares and the NZSO are on top form and the sound is pleasantly warm and full-bodied.

Further listening ...

...Symphony No. 1. The Fantasticks[a]. [a]**Gillian Humphreys** (sop); [a]**Meriel Dickinson** (mez); [a]**John Amis** (ten); [a]**Michael Rippon** (bass); [a]**Thames Chamber Choir; National Philharmonic Orchestra / Bernard Herrmann.** Unicorn-Kanchana Souvenir UKCD2063 (1/94).

...Symphony No. 1. *Coupled with* **Schuman** New England Triptych. **Phoenix Symphony Orchestra / James Sedares.** Koch International Classics 37135-2 (9/92).

...Film Scores – On Dangerous Ground – The death hunt. Citizen Kane – Suite[a]. Beneath the 12-Mile Reef – Suite. Hangover Square – Concerto macabre[b]. White Witch Doctor – Suite. [a]**Dame Kiri Te Kanawa** (sop); [b]**Joaquin Achucarro** (pf); **National Philharmonic Orchestra / Charles Gerhardt.** RCA Victor Gold Seal GD80707 (11/91).

...Welles Raises Kane – Suite[a]. The Devil and Daniel Webster – Suite[a]. Obsession – film score[b]. [a]**London Philharmonic Orchestra;** [b]**National Philharmonic Orchestra / Bernard Herrmann.** Unicorn-Kanchana Souvenir UKCD2065 (1/94).

...Wuthering Heights. **Soloists; Elizabethan Singers; Pro Arte Orchestra / Bernard Herrmann.** Unicorn-Kanchana Souvenir UKCD2050/2 (8/93).

...Souvenirs de voyage[a]. Echoes[b]. [a]**Robert Hill** (cl); [a]**Ariel Quartet;** [b]**Amici Quartet.** Unicorn-Kanchana Souvenir UKCD2069 (5/95).

William Herschel
German/British 1738-1822

Suggested listening ...

...Sonata for Harpsichord with Violin and Cello, Op. 4 No. 4. *Coupled with music by* **T. Linley I, T. Linley II, Jackson, Harington** and **Herschel** Various artists. Hyperion CDA66698 (11/94).

Johann Hertel

German 1727-1789

Suggested listening ...
...Trumpet Concerto in D major. *Coupled with works by* **Hummel, J. Stamitz** and **Haydn** Håkan
Hardenberger (tpt); **Academy of St Martin in the Fields / Sir Neville Marriner.** Philips 420 203-
2PH (12/87). *See review in the Collections section; refer to the Index to Reviews.*
...Trumpet Concerto in E flat major. *Coupled with works by* **Haydn, Hummel** and **A. Marcello**
Maurice André (tpt); **Franz Liszt Chamber Orchestra / János Rolla.** EMI CDC5 55231-2 (7/95).

Juan Hidalgo

Spanish *c*1612/16-1685

Suggested listening ...
...El templo de Palas – Ay que si, ay que no. Los celos hacen estrellas – De los luces que en el mar;
Peynándose estaba un olmo. Ay, que me río de Amor. La Estatua de Prometeo – Tonante Dios!
Cuydado, pastor. *Coupled with works by* **Sanz, Martín y Coll, Marín, Selma y Salaverde,**
Ruiz de Ribayaz, Guerau, Durón La Romanesca / José Miguel Moreno (gtr/vihuela). Glossa
GCD920201 (11/94). *See review in the Collections section; refer to the Index to Reviews.*

Hildegard of Bingen

German 1098-1179

New review
Hildegard of Bingen O Euchari, in leta vita. O virga mediatrix. Ave generosa. Laus Trinitati.
Kyrie eleison. O presul vere civitatis. O ignis Spiritus Paracliti. Ordo Virtutum – Procession.
O pastor animarum. O viridissima virga. O virga ac diadema. **Oxford Camerata / Jeremy**
Summerly. Naxos Ⓢ 8 550998 (59 minutes: DDD: 9/95). Texts and translations included.
Recorded 1993.
Here is music by that astonishing, ever-popular twelfth-century abbess. Some of the pieces will already
be familiar to listeners who have heard "A Feather on the Breath of God" and either of the two
Deutsche Harmonia Mundi recordings by Sequentia, *Ordo virtutum* and, more recently – high in the
classical charts – "Canticles of Ecstasy" (all listed below). Jeremy Summerly approaches Hildegard's
outpourings in a thoughtful and mature manner. He seems to be more concerned with the actual sound
of the music than with its female monastic setting and possible liturgical use. The high and low voices
have separate items – don't be misled by an obvious printing error in the track listing for No. 8 – well
in character with male or female singers. Out of 11 pieces eight receive a strictly metrical interpretation
(three beats in a bar) and this appears to work fairly well. There is no intrusive instrumental
accompaniment, but some of the music sung by the high voices has an occasional discreet hint of a
drone. It is all very restrained: there is a total absence of ostentation and indeed very little 'ecstasy', yet
the whole peaceful recital is never dull or monotonous. Full texts with English translations are given
and also concise insert-notes in English, German and French. However, to profit from the information
supplied, one needs some knowledge of all three languages, since each one, like the three Synoptic
Gospels, offers its own special details. This is an interesting and thought-provoking disc.
Additional recommendations ...
...Ordo Virtutum. **Sequentia Medieval Music Ensemble.** Deutsche Harmonia Mundi Editio Classica
Ⓜ GD77051 (1/84).   Ⓖ
...Columba aspexit. Ave, generosa. O ignis spiritus Paracliti. O Jerusalem. O Euchari, in leta vita.
O viridissima virga. O presul vere civitatis. O Ecclesia. **Gothic Voices / Christopher Page** with
Doreen Muskett (symphony); **Robert White** (reed drones). Hyperion Ⓕ CDA66039 (44 minutes:
DDD: 7/85). *Gramophone classical 100. Gramophone Award Winner 1982-83.*   ⒼⒼⒼ
...O vis aeternitatis. Nunc aperuit nobis. Quia ergo femina. Cum processit factura. Ave Maria, o
auctrix vitae. Spiritus Sanctus vivificans vite. O ignis Spiritus Paracliti. Caritas abundat in omnia.
O virga mediatrix. O viridissima virga. O pastor animarum. O tu suavissima virga. O choruscans
stellarum. O nobilissima viriditas. **Anonymous** Alma Redemptoris mater. Instrumental Piece.
Sequentia. Deutsche Harmonia Mundi Ⓕ 05472 77320-2 (73 minutes: DDD: 5/95). *Gramophone*
Editor's choice.   Ⓖ

New review
Hildegard of Bingen O rubor sanguinis. Favus distillans. Laus Trinitati. In Matutinis Laudibus.
O ecclesia oculi tui. O viridissima virga. O aeterne Deus. O dulcissime amator. Rex noster
promptus est. O cruor sanguinis. Cum vox sanguinis. Instrumental Piece based on D modes of
antiphon cycle. O virgo ecclesia. Nunc gaudeant materna. O orzchis ecclesia. **Sequentia.** Deutsche
Harmonia Mundi Ⓕ 05472 77346-2 (77 minutes: DDD: 3/96). Texts and translations included.
Recorded 1994.
Vox sanguinis, the term used by Hildegard herself, occurs in an antiphon recalling the massacre of
St Ursula and her legendary following of 11,000 virgin companions. This new collection assumes
roughly the shape of a proper office, honouring Ursula with antiphons, responsories, hymns and
sequences that reflect, with colourful imagery, upon the virtues of consecrated virginity combined

with martyrdom. In the concluding items the focus turns away from Ursula towards Ecclesia, seen as both virgin and mother. We can only hazard a guess as to the manner in which Hildegard intended these pieces to be performed. Could they really have been sung in a liturgical context? Perhaps not. The female section of Sequentia divides them up, very sensibly, between soloists and a distant ensemble, adding the occasional drone, and also some freely composed instrumental interludes based on melodic snatches from Hildegard's music. The singing is splendid: full-bodied, well-sustained, displaying *gravitas* as well as exuberance. Towards the end, in the antiphon *Nunc gaudeant*, the voices rise to a top C in an unexpectedly wild burst of ecstasy. But this is a rare occurrence: usually the singers manage to capture the spirit of Hildegard's vision and fervour without ever going over the top – even when she indulges in her strange *lingua ignota*. What we have here is a thoughtful account, sung with care and warmth, a worthy addition to Sequentia's well-planned series of recordings of the whole of Hildegard's musical output.

Additional recommendation ...

...O magne Pater. O aeterne Deus. Ave generosa. O frondens virga. O felix anima. Ave Maria, o auctrix vitae. O quam mirabilis. O virtus sapientiae. O vis aeternitatis. *Coupled with* **Abélard** Planctus David. O quanta qualia **Anonymous** Promat chorus hodie. Annus novus in gaudio. Fulget dies celebris. **Augsburg Early Music Ensemble.** Christophorus Musica Practica Ⓟ CIIR74584 (65 minutes: DDD: 3/93).

Paul Hindemith

German 1895-1963

Hindemith Cello Concerto[a]. The Four Temperaments[b]. [a]**Raphael Wallfisch** (vc); [b]**Howard Shelley** (pf); **BBC Philharmonic Orchestra / Yan Pascal Tortelier.** Chandos Ⓟ CHAN9124 (52 minutes: DDD: 3/93). Recorded 1992.

These two concertos, both from Hindemith's maturity (1940), make a good pairing. The outwardly conventional Cello Concerto contrasts a relatively small voice (the cello) which carries the work's lyrical message, with a large orchestra used initially for active statements delivered with great power. Hindemith's plan would seem to be gradually to reconcile these apparently contradictory modes of address. *The Four Temperaments* is a concerto for piano and string orchestra, a much more evenly balanced combination, using theme and variations form to integrate and relate the contrasted 'humours'; the old jibe that Hindemith's variations should have been called "Four Equal Temperaments" is not too wide of the mark, and Hindemith's treatment of his material would appear to argue that all temperaments, whatever the dominant disposition, are closely related. His portraiture, in fact, reveals characterization of great depth and dimension. Performances are superbly accomplished, indeed this is the finest of many currently available recordings of *The Four Temperaments*. And Chandos have resisted the temptation, which must be considerable, to move in on the soloist in the Cello Concerto. The sound is open and spacious.

Additional recommendations ...

...The Four Temperaments[a]. Symphony in B flat major. **Berg** Chamber Concerto for Piano, Violin and 13 Wind Instruments[b]. [a]**Clara Haskil,** [b]**Carl Seemann** (pfs); [b]**Wolfgang Marschner** (vn); **Bavarian Radio Symphony Orchestra / Paul Hindemith.** Orfeo Ⓟ C197891A (76 minutes: ADD: 8/90).

...The Four Temperaments. Piano Concerto. **Siegfried Mauser** (pf); **Frankfurt Radio Symphony Orchestra / Andreas Werner Albert.** CPO Ⓟ CPO999 078-2 (62 minutes: DDD: 12/91).

New review

Hindemith Clarinet Concerto[a]. Horn Concerto[b]. Concerto for Trumpet, Bassoon and Strings[c]. Concerto for Flute, Oboe, Clarinet, Bassoon, Harp and Orchestra[d]. [d]**Walter Buchsel** (fl); [d]**Liviu Varcol** (ob); [ad]**Ulrich Mehlhart** (cl); [cd]**Carsten Wilkening** (bn); [c]**Reinhold Friedrich** (tpt); [b]**Marie Luise Neunecker** (hn); [d]**Charlotte Cassedanne** (hp); [b]**Brigitte Goebel** (spkr); **Frankfurt Radio Symphony Orchestra / Werner Andreas Albert.** CPO Ⓟ CPO999 142-2 (70 minutes: DDD: 11/95). Recorded 1990-93.

Hindemith's four wind concertos (1947-9) have never enjoyed the success of the *Kammermusik* concertos (with which they have much in common). That for clarinet came first, to a commission from Benny Goodman. As was noted in *Music Survey* in 1950, it is "a musician's rather than a showman's piece", and the lack of overt display may have militated against its popularity. Ulrich Mehlhart's performance more than bears comparison with any rivals, and is served by the best sound. With the 1949 Horn Concerto, competition is concentrated in the definitive recording by composer and dedicatee (Dennis Brain, reviewed below), which has rarely been out of the catalogue for long. If not quite in Brain's class, Marie Luise Neunecker's is a fine, highly musical account. The declamation of Hindemith's poem in praise of the horn, inscribed over its wordless setting, may be thought intrusive. The other two concertos (both 1949) are rarities indeed, not until now commercially available in the UK. In them, Hindemith most nearly approaches his 1920s manner, for instance in the woodwinds and harp Concerto with the finale's quotations from Mendelssohn's *Wedding March* (and perhaps fleeting allusions to Wagner's in the opening movement), occasioned by his silver anniversary. In the Clarinet and Horn Concertos, Albert's tempos are brisker than the composer's own; in all four works the soloists and Frankfurt orchestra prove committed advocates. A delightful issue.

Additional recommendations ...
...Clarinet Concerto. **Milhaud** Clarinet Concerto, Op. 230. Scaramouche, Op. 165c. **Copland**
Clarinet Concerto. **Eduard Brunner** (cl); **Bavarian Radio Symphony Orchestra / Urs Schneider.**
Koch Schwann Ⓕ 310352 (DDD: 62 minutes).
...Clarinet Concerto[a]. Cello Concerto[b]. [a]**George Pieterson** (cl); [b]**Tibor de Machula** (vc); **Royal
Concertgebouw Orchestra / Kyrill Kondrashin.** Etcetera Ⓕ KTC1006 (46 minutes: ADD: 6/88).

Hindemith Violin Concerto[a]. Symphonic Metamorphosis on Themes of Carl Maria von Weber[b].
Mathis der Maler[c]. [a]**David Oistrakh** (vn); [ab]**London Symphony Orchestra / **[a]**Paul Hindemith,**
[b]**Claudio Abbado;** [c]**Suisse Romande Orchestra / Paul Kletzki.** Decca Enterprise Ⓜ 433 081-2DM
(77 minutes: ADD: 9/92). Item marked [a] from SXL6035 (2/63), recorded 1962, [b]SXL6398 (5/69),
[c]SXL6445 (12/70), both recorded 1968.   ⒼⒼⒼ
Hindemithians who can afford to be choosy about the *Mathis der Maler* Symphony and the
Symphonic Metamorphosis will immediately recognize the superiority of the full-price Blomstedt
readings (reviewed below). Consistently spectacular 1960s Decca sound adds allure to the merely
proficient performances on offer here. What makes this medium-price disc indispensable is the 30
minute Violin Concerto with Oistrakh at his legendary best and the composer conducting. The late
Deryck Cooke, in his original *Gramophone* review, wrote of Oistrakh as "superbly poised and
eloquent ... and as performed here the Concerto shows that behind Hindemith's stony neo-classical
facade beats a romantic German heart". Listening to this recording it's hard to understand the
concerto's relative neglect – strange indeed are the tides of fashion – but easy to imagine current star
violinists finding Oistrakh's an impossible act to follow. The 1962 sound gives Oistrakh a discreet
dominance, and the engineers flatten out the slow movement's central climax, but thankfully no other
allowances need be made for this preservation of a classic recording.

Additional recommendations ...
...Violin Concerto. Cello Concerto. **K.A. Hartmann** Concerto funèbre. **André Gertler** (vn); **Paul
Tortelier** (vc); **Czech Philharmonic Orchestra / Karel Ančerl.** Supraphon Ⓕ 11 1955-2 (76 minutes:
ADD).
...Symphonic Metamorphosis. **Reger** Variations and Fugue on a Theme of Mozart, Op. 132.
Bavarian Radio Symphony Orchestra / Sir Colin Davis. Philips Ⓕ 422 347-2PH (55 minutes:
DDD: 9/90).
...Mathis der Maler[a]. Symphonic Metamorphosis[b]. **Walton** Variations on a Theme by Hindemith[b].
[a]**Philadelphia Orchestra / Eugene Ormandy;** [b]**Cleveland Orchestra / George Szell.** Sony Classical
Essential Classics Ⓑ SBK53258 (69 minutes: ADD: 4/94).
...Mathis der Maler[a]. String Trio No. 2[b]. String Quartet No. 3, Op. 22[c]. [b]**Szymon Goldberg** (vn);
[b]**Emanuel Feuermann** (vc); [c]**Amar Quartet;** [a]**Berlin Philharmonic Orchestra / Paul Hindemith** ([b]va).
Koch Schwann mono Ⓕ 311342* (70 minutes: ADD: 5/94).
...Violin Concerto[a]. Symphony in E flat major[b]. [a]**Joseph Fuchs** (vn); [a]**London Symphony Orchestra /
Sir Eugene Goossens;** [b]**London Philharmonic Orchestra / Sir Adrian Boult.** Everest Ⓕ EVC9009
(57 minutes: ADD: 4/95).
...Violin Concerto[a]. Concerto for Orchestra, Op. 38. Kammermusik No. 4, Op. 36 No. 3[a]. Suite of
French Dances. Rag Time (well-tempered). [a]**Michael Guttman** (vn); **Philharmonia Orchestra / José
Serebrier.** ASV Ⓕ CDDCA945 (78 minutes: DDD: 3/96).

Hindemith Der Dämon.
Schreker Der Geburtstag der Infantin – Suite.
Schulhoff Die Mondsüchtige. **Leipzig Gewandhaus Orchestra / Lothar Zagrosek.** Decca Entartete
Musik Ⓕ 444 182-2DH (78 minutes: DDD: 5/95). Recorded 1994.   Ⓖ
Schreker's *The Birthday of the Infanta* is a 'dance pantomime', first performed at the opening of the
Vienna Kunstschau in 1908: it had choreography by Max Reinhardt's colleague Grete Wiesenthal and
was performed in a huge temporary exhibition building by Otto Wagner, in which a large number of
paintings by Gustav Klimt (including *The Kiss*) and Oskar Kokoschka were exhibited for the first
time. That is the context in which to listen to it: it is *Jugendstil* music, all the more so in the lavish
orchestral suite that Schreker prepared 15 years later for Willem Mengelberg: charmingly lyrical,
fluent melody, scored with rich but fresh colour in a way that sometimes recalls Respighi, sometimes
Korngold. At times it is very close to light music, at others its melodies have a tender, poised and
balletic quality that is quite memorable. The suite continued to be performed, in Austria and
elsewhere, after the Nazi ban on Schreker's music, from the effect of which his later music is only now
emerging. The abruptness of the ban and his dismissal from public office, together no doubt with
terror at what might follow, undoubtedly contributed to his early death, from a stroke, in 1934. *Die
Mondsüchtige*, Erwin Schulhoff's 'dance grotesque', was denied production in Germany or his native
Czechoslovakia; it achieved only a concert performance (in Oxford) in 1931 and then followed its
composer into oblivion: as a Communist as well as a Jew, Schulhoff ended his life in a concentration
camp. It is a jazz ballet rather in Krenek's manner, complete with a "Valse Boston" (which in fact
sounds distinctly Viennese, though thinned down to a disquieting ghostliness), a shimmy and a tango
(another oddly bony, quiet piece). Throughout Schulhoff is at least as open to contemporary
influences from Paris and elsewhere as to a genuinely popular idiom: a curious, adventurous
personality peers out from behind the modish use of ragtime rhythms. Hindemith's *Der Dämon* is an

expressionist ballet from the same laboratory as his notorious *Nusch-Nuschi*. Alongside the expected toccata manner, heavily pounding or angular, a characteristic lyrical idiom is also present, an almost gracious element which must have increased the shock value of the piece, as does his use of a grave passacaglia to represent the Demon himself. From the one-line plot summary provided it would seem that Hindemith was already working the disturbing trick of his opera *Cardillac*: presenting a monster with a detachment close to sympathy. It is an inventive, colourful, fiercely aggressive piece, aided in its impact by Lothar Zagrosek's decision to use a small string orchestra instead of the solo quintet that Hindemith asked for. In fact, as ever in this area of the repertoire, Zagrosek is an outstandingly sympathetic conductor, turning this collection into an absorbing essay on the various alternatives to classical or even modern ballet that were in the air in the earlier years of the century. Another issue in the Entartete Musik series that does more than repay a posthumous debt.

Hindemith Mathis der Maler[a]. Symphonic Metamorphosis on Themes of Carl Maria von Weber.
[a]**Geraldine Walther** (va); **San Francisco Symphony Orchestra / Herbert Blomstedt.** Decca Ⓕ 421 523-2DH (55 minutes: DDD: 10/88). Recorded 1987. ⒼⒼ
Hindemith Symphonic Metamorphoses on Themes of Carl Maria von Weber. Mathis der Maler.
Nobilissima Visione. **Philadelphia Orchestra / Wolfgang Sawallisch.** EMI Ⓔ CDC5 55230-2
(71 minutes: DDD: 6/95). Recorded 1994. Ⓖ

The charge sometimes levelled against Hindemith of being dry and cerebral utterly collapses in the face of Blomstedt's disc. Masterly craftsmanship and virtuosity there is in plenty; but the powerful emotions of *Mathis der Maler* and the festive high spirits of the *Symphonic Metamorphosis* could not be denied except by those who wilfully close their ears. Each of the three movements of the *Mathis* Symphony is based on a panel of Grünewald's great Isenheim altar. The eventual glorious illumination of "The angels" folk-tune, the poignant slow movement and the blazing triumphant Alleluias after the desperate struggle with the demons in the finale have a searing intensity in Blomstedt's performance, which also presents Hindemith's elaborate web of counterpoints with the utmost lucidity. For brilliant and joyously ebullient orchestral writing few works can match that based on Weber's piano duets and his *Turandot* overture: here the San Francisco woodwind and brass have a field day. In addition, this warmly recommended disc contains a heartfelt performance of the touching elegy on the death of King George V which Hindemith wrote overnight in 1936.

The Philadelphia players for Sawallisch give taut performances that simply outclass most of the competition. Another by no means inconsiderable plus point is the unusual running order that achieves a better musical balance, starting with the most brilliant piece, the *Symphonic Metamorphoses*, and increasing in weight to the resounding brass Alleluias at the climax of the *Mathis* Symphony. Sawallisch's interpretations rank with Blomstedt in the *Mathis* Symphony and *Symphonic Metamorphoses*. Though many will prefer the leaner sound of the San Francisco Orchestra, EMI's sound for Sawallisch is relatively recessed. Given the spacious acoustic of Memorial Hall and the conductor's largeness of vision this is entirely apposite, there is no loss of detail.

Additional recommendations ...
...Mathis der Maler. **Stravinsky** Jeu de cartes. **Berlin Philharmonic Orchestra / Paul Hindemith.**
Teldec Ⓕ 9031-76440-2* (46 minutes: ADD). Ⓖ
...Mathis der Maler. Symphonic Metamorphosis. Konzertmusik for Strings and Brass, Op. 50.
Israel Philharmonic Orchestra / Leonard Bernstein. DG Ⓕ 429 404-2GH (67 minutes: DDD: 5/91). ⒼⒼ
...Symphony in E flat major. Nobilissima Visione. Neues vom Tage – overture. **BBC Philharmonic Orchestra / Yan Pascal Tortelier.** Chandos Ⓕ CHAN9060 (60 minutes: DDD: 10/92).
...Symphonic Metamorphosis. Symphony in E flat major. Konzertmusik for Strings and Brass, Op. 50. **New York Philharmonic Orchestra / Leonard Bernstein.** Sony Classical Bernstein Royal Edition Ⓜ SMK47566 (70 minutes: ADD: 5/93). Ⓖ

Hindemith Hindemith plays and conducts Hindemith. [a]**Louis Cahuzac** (cl); [b]**Dennis Brain** (hn); [c]**Szymon Goldberg** (vn); [d]**Emanuel Feuermann** (vc); [e]**Philharmonia Orchestra / Paul Hindemith** ([f]va). EMI Composers in Person mono/[e]stereo Ⓕ CDS5 55032-2* (two discs: 157 minutes: ADD: 5/94). Recorded 1934-56.
Solo Viola Sonata, Op. 25 No. 1[f] (from German Columbia LW10/12). Scherzo for Viola and Cello[df] (LW12. Both recorded 1934). String Trio No. 2[cdf] (Columbia LX311/13, 8/34). Nobilissima Visione[e] (EG291173-2, 4/87). Clarinet Concerto[ae] (Columbia 33CX1533, 5/58). Symphonia serena[e] (33CX1676, 12/59; both stereo, appears for first time). Horn Concerto[be] (HMV HLS7001, 3/72). Concert Music, Op. 50[e] (EG291173-2). ⒼⒼ

As a young man Hindemith played the viola professionally and is an excellent advocate of his own Solo Viola Sonata, a work of considerable emotional depth. The orchestral items (all from 1956 sessions) include the Clarinet Concerto, with the veteran Louis Cahuzac a beautifully clear-toned soloist, the *Symphonia serena*, Dennis Brain's unique, unmatchable account of the Horn Concerto, and superlatively played performances of the masterly *Nobilissima Visione* suite and the *Concert Music* for brass and strings, all in excellent stereo for the era. Common to all the interpretations here is that very special directness of expression which is a unique feature of composer recordings. Hindemith's clear, practical approach as a performer in a way reflects the symmetry and logic of his own music. What is striking, however, is the degree of emotion that he also finds in it.

...Symphonia serena. Symphony, "Die Harmonie der Welt". **BBC Philharmonic Orchestra / Yan Pascal Tortelier.** Chandos Ⓕ CHAN9217 (64 minutes: DDD: 11/94).   Ⓖ

Hindemith Kammermusik – No. 1, Op. 24 No. 1; No. 2[a]; No. 3, Op. 36 No. 2[b]; No. 4, Op. 36 No. 3[c]; No. 5, Op. 36 No. 4[d]; No. 6, Op. 46 No. 1[e]; No. 7, Op. 46 No. 2[f] Kleine Kammermusik No. 1 for Wind Quintet, Op. 24 No. 2. [c]**Konstanty Kulka** (vn); [d]**Kim Kashkashian** (va); [e]**Norbert Blume** (va d'amore); [b]**Lynn Harrell** (vc); [a]**Ronald Brautigam** (pf); [f]**Leo van Doeselaar** (org); **Royal Concertgebouw Orchestra / Riccardo Chailly.** Decca Ⓕ 433 816-2DH2 (two discs: 138 minutes: DDD: 11/92). Recorded 1990. *Gramophone Award Winner 1993.*   Ⓖ

Even were the performances and recordings not outstanding (and they most certainly are) this would be an extremely valuable set. Hindemith's series of *Kammermusik* ("Chamber Music") began in 1921 as an iconoclastic response to the hyper-intense emotionalism of German music over the previous 15 years (somewhat loosely termed Expressionism). It continued until 1927, at which point he began to rationalize both the harmonic and the expressive foundations of his style (and arguably lost as much as he gained). This, then, is neo-classicism with a German accent and as such it was to be a vital force in sweeping away the cobwebs of musty late romanticism; Walton, Prokofiev, Shostakovich and Britten were among those who, however indirectly, would feel the benefit. The music is also immensely enjoyable in its own right. Hindemith cheekily throws together disparate idioms, ideas spiral off with unselfconscious abandon, and sheer force of personality is all that guards against total anarchy. All this is done with more than half an eye on the performers' own enjoyment of recreation, and the fine array of artists assembled by Chailly savour every detail. Recording quality is exemplary.

...Der Schwanendreher. Konzertmusik, Op. 48. Kammermusik No. 5. **Paul Cortese** (va); **Philharmonia Orchestra / Martyn Brabbins.** ASV Ⓕ CDDCA931 (73 minutes: DDD: 9/95).

Hindemith Octet.
Prokofiev Overture on Hebrew Themes in C minor, Op. 34[a]. Quintet in G minor, Op. 39. **Berlin Soloists;** [a]**Elena Bashkirova** (pf). Teldec Ⓕ 9031-73400-2 (58 minutes: DDD: 6/93).   Ⓖ

This intriguing disc brings together two of Prokofiev's early chamber works and Hindemith's last. The earlier of the two Prokofiev pieces, the *Overture on Hebrew Themes* for piano, string quartet and clarinet (1919), is an attractive, rather sad little work (he made a version for small orchestra in 1934). The Quintet for oboe, clarinet, violin, viola and double-bass (1924) has six well-contrasted movements, whose often spikey (but by no means unmelodic) character owes much to Stravinsky and Les Six. Hindemith wrote his Octet for clarinet, bassoon, horn, violin, two violas, cello and double-bass in 1957-58 for the Berlin Philharmonic Octet, for whose benefit he quoted, in the fourth of its five movements, a popular tune from Berlin. There are allusions to classical models, a compact set of variations, and in the finale, a fugue and three dances (waltz, polka and galop). It is not, perhaps, one of his most immediately ingratiating works, but it will repay closer acquaintance. The Berlin Soloists play all three works marvellously, and are beautifully recorded.

...Octet. **Beethoven** Septet in E flat major, Op. 20. **Berlin Philharmonic Octet.** Nimbus Ⓕ NI5461 (69 minutes: DDD: 4/96).

Hindemith String Quartet No. 3, Op. 22[a].
Prokofiev String Quartet No. 2 in F major, Op. 92[a].
Walton String Quartet in A minor[b]. **Hollywood Quartet** (Felix Slatkin, Paul Shure, vns; Paul Robyn, va; Eleanor Aller, vc). Testament mono Ⓕ SBT1052* (74 minutes: ADD: 3/95). Items marked [a] from Capitol CTL7016 (4/52), [b]CTL7004 (6/51). Recorded 1951.   ⒼⒼ

Although numerous accounts of the Prokofiev have appeared over the years, none has approached, let alone surpassed, the Hollywood version of the Second Quartet. The same would no doubt apply to the Hindemith but for the fact that there have been fewer challengers. What a wonderful feeling for line these players had, what an incredible, perfectly matched and blended ensemble they produced – and how well these transfers sound! That goes for the Walton, too: there is no other account of the piece that makes so positive a case for it.

...String Quartet. **Schulhoff** String Quartet No. 1. **Weill** String Quartet. **Brandis Quartet.** Nimbus Ⓕ NI5410 (60 minutes: DDD: 3/95).

New review

Hindemith Violin Sonatas – E flat major, Op. 11 No. 1; D major, Op. 11 No. 2; E major (1935); C major (1939). **Ulf Wallin** (vn); **Roland Pöntinen** (pf). BIS Ⓕ CD761 (56 minutes: DDD: 8/96).

It seems odd to think that, with several complete cycles on the market of Hindemith's sonatas for viola with and without piano, there are none of those for violin and piano. Only the E major of 1935 – the third of four that he composed – appears in recital or on disc, and then only fitfully. This is due to its brevity (under 10 minutes long – as is Op. 11 No. 1) and lack of complication (it is more of a *sonatina*), yet it is familiar Hindemith from first note to last. The C major work (1939) is more complex and grave, and probably the finest of them. The longest sonata – and most conservative in idiom is that in D major. Both Op. 11 works were written in 1918 while Hindemith was on active service, and are remarkable for bearing few traces of either the grimness of the Great War or Hindemith's personal voice. Both deserve wider currency. This issue is also welcome in including the fragmentary abandoned finale of Op. 11 No. 1, a rustic dance not in keeping with the symmetry of the whole. Hindemith was right to omit it. The sweet-toned Ulf Wallin is fully attuned to Hindemith's wavelength and Roland Pöntinen as ever provides exemplary support. The recording is typical BIS (i.e. excellent). A splendid disc.

Hindemith Viola Sonatas – F major, Op. 11 No. 4; Op. 25 No. 4; C major (1939). Nobilissima Visione – Meditation. **Nobuko Imai** (va); **Roland Pöntinen** (pf). BIS Ⓕ CD651 (60 minutes: DDD: 9/94). Recorded 1993. Ⓖ

Hindemith's three sonatas for viola with piano accompaniment date from the 21-year period between the two world wars. The differences in style between the First (1918) and Second (1922) are rather more marked than the short gap might suggest, the still slightly gauche romanticism of the former (written during the catastrophic collapse and revolution in Germany that followed military defeat) replaced by the aggressive astringency of its successor. That notwithstanding, the First's finale (marked "with bizarre ungainliness") clearly prefigures the burlesque attitude of the early 1920s and both works are full of vitality and invention. The Third (1939) is on a much larger scale. This four-movement work is one of the finest ever penned for the viola, fully worthy of comparison with the sonatas of Brahms and Reger, and one of Hindemith's best instrumental compositions. Imai and Pöntinen are at their best in these works, the stylistic variances (more pronounced than with the unaccompanied sonatas) interpreted with equal conviction. Fine as Pöntinen's support is, with her quite beautiful playing Imai is undeniably the star of the show, her tone rich and mellow, her technique assured.

Additional recommendation ...

...Viola Sonatas – C major (1939)[a]; Op. 25 No. 1; Op. 25 No. 4[a]; Op. 11 No. 4[a]; Op. 11 No. 5; Viola Sonata (1937). **Kim Kashkashian** (va); [a]**Robert Levin** (pf). ECM New Series Ⓕ 833 309-2 (two discs: 128 minutes: DDD: 10/88).

Hindemith Ludus tonalis.
Prokofiev Visions fugitives, Op. 22. **Olli Mustonen** (pf). Decca Ⓕ 444 803-2DH (68 minutes: DDD: 5/96). Recorded 1994.

For a work that was once regarded as a landmark in twentieth-century piano music, Hindemith's *Ludus tonalis* has received scant attention in the way of recent studio recordings from pianists of note. To be fair, it is not an easy work for either audience or artist: its contrapuntal, angular and unforgiving textures pose demanding interpretative problems for the pianist, and at 50 minutes' duration its knotty sound-world can be difficult to digest for even the most enthusiastic of listeners. From an interpretative standpoint John McCabe and Olli Mustonen give very different performances. McCabe's strong points are structure, contrapuntal clarity (to the point of dryness at times) and a clear sense of something monumental unfolding. When compared with Mustonen he can seem a little impersonal and distant. In Mustonen's reading there is a real sense of journey as he traverses the 25 studies and there is greater tonal variation, expressive range and playfulness in his playing, which helps the listener to feel more involved in this music. Die-hard Hindemith enthusiasts may find McCabe's approach the more authoritative, but Mustonen is extremely persuasive in the way he sheds new light on this music, making it more accessible – ideal for winning new admirers to the work. Mustonen adds Prokofiev's *Visions fugitives* which makes an effective contrast. There's strong competition here but Mustonen acquits himself well, giving a fluid and beautifully shaped account of these "fleeting thoughts", and the recordings for both works are excellent.

Additional recommendation ...

...Ludus tonalis. Suite "1922", Op. 26. **John McCabe** (pf). Hyperion Ⓕ CDA66824 (69 minutes: DDD: 5/96).

Hindemith Mass. Six Chansons. Eine lichte Mitternacht. Du musst dir Alles geben. Der Tod. Nun da der Tag. Zwölf Madrigale – Mitwelt; Tauche deine Furcht in schwarzen Wein; Trink aus!; Frühling; Judaskuss; Du Zweifel an dem Sinn der Welt. **Netherlands Chamber Choir / Uwe Gronostay.** Globe Ⓕ GLO5125 (57 minutes: DDD: 5/96). Texts and translations included. Recorded 1994.

Hindemith Mass. Zwölf Madrigale – Eines Narren, eines Künstlers Leben; An eine Tote; An einen Schmetterling; Magisches Rezept; Es bleibt wohl, was gesagt wird; Kraft fand zu Form. Lieder nach alten Texten, Op. 33. **Danish National Radio Choir / Uwe Gronostay.** Chandos Ⓕ CHAN9413 (52 minutes: DDD: 5/96). Texts and translations included. Recorded 1995.

Given Hindemith's awareness of sometimes centuries-old traditions when writing his own music, it was almost inevitable that he should compose a Mass. The wonder is that it took him so long to get round to doing so, and he barely made it in time – dying in 1963, just six weeks after the first performance, having begun sketching a second. His tardiness can partly be explained by his view that

Palestrina had had the last word with the Mass as a musical form. What is more important is the quality of the music, irrespective of why he wrote it. If not quite capturing the spirit of the missal, the Mass is still an evocative, exploratory setting, proving that he was far from being a spent force. Uwe Gronostay obviously has an affection for this work in particular, given that he has recorded it twice in as many years for two separate companies. There is little to choose between the performances, both being beautifully sung and shaped, qualities that are evident in the rest of each programme. Nor, indeed, are the couplings much help in the selection process, since the Mass is the sole duplication. Both discs contain six of the 12 deeply felt Madrigals Hindemith composed in 1958. The early *Lieder nach alten Texten* (1923) on Chandos are not really a sufficient makeweight, delightful though they are. Globe offer more in the lovely Rilke *Chansons* (1939) and the four male choruses, written between 1929 and 1939 to words by Whitman, Gottfried Benn, Hölderlin and Nietzsche. Chandos's sound is fuller, but Globe's is still very good. If you want just one disc of Hindemith's *a cappella* choral music, then go for Globe; but the Mass is worth having twice for its own sake, let alone in completing the Madrigal set.

Additional recommendation ...

...Mass. Zwölf Madrigale – Eines Narren, eines Künstlers Leben; An eine Tote; An einen Schmetterling; Magisches Rezept; Es bleibt wohl, was gesagt Wird; Kraft fand zu Form. Lieder nach alten Texten, Op. 33. **Danish National Radio Choir / Uwe Gronostay.** Chandos Ⓟ CHAN9413 (52 minutes: DDD: 5/96).

Hindemith Mathis der Maler. **Roland Hermann** (bar) Mathis; **Josef Protschka** (ten) Albrecht von Brandenburg; **Gabriele Rossmanith** (sop) Regina; **Sabine Hass** (sop) Ursula; **Harald Stamm** (bass) Riedinger; **Heinz Kruse** (ten) Hans Schwalb; **Victor von Halem** (bass) Lorenz von Pommersfelden; **Hermann Winkler** (ten) Wolfgang Capito; **Ulrich Hielscher** (bass) Truchsess von Waldberg; **Ulrich Ress** (ten) Sylvester von Schaumberg; **John Cogram** (ten) Der Pfeifer des Grafen von Helfenstein; **Marilyn Schmiege** (mez) Gräfin Helfenstein; **North German Radio Chorus; Cologne Radio Chorus and Symphony Orchestra / Gerd Albrecht.** Wergo Ⓟ WER6255-2 (three discs: 166 minutes: DDD: 9/94). Notes and text included. Recorded 1990.

Hindemith Mathis der Maler. **Dietrich Fischer-Dieskau** (bar) Mathis; **James King** (ten) Albrecht; **Gerd Feldhoff** (bass) Lorenz von Pommersfelden; **Manfred Schmidt** (ten) Capito; **Peter Meven** (bass) Riedinger; **William Cochran** (ten) Schwalb; **Alexander Malta** (bass) Truchsess von Waldburg; **Donald Grobe** (ten) Sylvester von Schaumberg; **Rose Wagmann** (mez) Ursula; **Urszula Koszut** (sop) Regina; **Trudeliese Schmidt** (mez) Countess Helfenstein; **Bavarian Radio Chorus and Symphony Orchestra / Rafael Kubelík.** EMI Ⓟ CDS5 55237-2 (three discs: 183 minutes: ADD: 7/95). Notes, text and translation included. From SLS5182 (12/79). Recorded 1977.

The masterpiece, *Mathis der Maler,* is one of the pinnacles of twentieth-century German opera. It has become axiomatic to see in it a parable of the times, with Hindemith using the turbulent world of sixteenth-century Germany to mirror the Nazi Reich and his place in it. But in reality *Mathis* is a spiritual and historical opera, not a political one, even in the handling of the artist's relationship to the society around him. Hindemith was at first equivocal in his feelings towards the regime, being by nature apolitical, even when his brother-in-law was despatched to Oranienburg. The Nazi's antagonism towards Hindemith rested on a few iconoclastic works from the 1920s and the prudish outrage of Hitler and Goebbels at *Neues vom Tage.* Later, both Goebbels and Rosenberg tried to secure Hindemith's remaining in Germany by hinting at a staging of *Mathis* if its composer played their game. So full marks to Rudolf Stephan in his essay for Wergo for playing down the political angle; if Hitler had not risen to power until, say, 1936, one doubts that *Mathis* would have turned out much different. As his brief note declares, Gerd Albrecht's acquaintance with Hindemith's music, particularly the operas, goes back to the early 1960s, before the composer's death. Hindemith even sanctioned some retouching of the orchestration in *Mathis* made by Albrecht for a festival performance, though it is not made clear whether Albrecht has applied this here, nor to what extent. Rarely have Hindemith's often heavy textures sounded so clear. As to the music, is not the brief concluding "Alleluia" duet that crowns the sixth tableau one of *the* great moments in twentieth-century opera? You will be convinced from your very first hearing of it and any doubters on this point – or to the quality of the score as a whole – are urged to sample either of these accounts.

There are fine moments aplenty in Albrecht's reading, not least where familiar passages from the *Mathis* Symphony surface and precipitate some of the most intense music of the opera. Roland Hermann is, perhaps, a shade stolid in places as the painter (though his world-weariness in the final scene is just right); Josef Protschka makes a most authoritative Cardinal, acting as a perfect foil to Hermann's Mathis. They head a fine cast, supported by some lusty singing and playing from the combined forces of Cologne and North German Radios. Comparing the newer set with Kubelík's reissued version shows that honours are fairly even; choosing between them would depend largely on one's keenness for individual names. There is little to choose between the two versions; neither is perfect, but both are very fine. Albrecht, who makes one or two minor but noticeable cuts, has the benefit of more modern sound, but EMI's for Kubelík has transferred well. The choruses in particular are excellent, although Albrecht's seem tame in the famous "Temptation of St Antony" scene when set next to Kubelík's devilish-sounding Bavarians. Comparison of the casts yields a mixed picture; many readers will prefer Fischer-Dieskau as Mathis to the rather raw-voiced Hermann (except, as mentioned above, in the final tableau); for many this will be the crucial criterion, but Wergo do have the better of some other principals. The roles of Schwalb and his daughter encapsulate the predicament: for EMI, William Cochran is more imposing than Heinz Kruse as the peasant leader but Wergo's Gabriele Rossmanith is sweeter and younger-toned as Regina. For Albrecht, their first appearance seems to be a mid-afternoon stroll and not the convincing escape from pursuit that Kubelík effects here (first disc, track 4). Despite the urgings of sentiment, neither set outclasses the other. For most, choice will rest on preferences for specific cast members. Those who love this score will want both.

Further listening ...

...Trauermusik[a]. *Coupled with* **Schoenberg** Verklärte Nacht. **Bartók** Divertimento, Sz113. [a]**Cecil Aronowitz** (va); **English Chamber Orchestra / Daniel Barenboim.** EMI CDM5 65079-2 (3/94). **Ⓖ**

...*999 005-2*[a] – Lustige Sinfonietta, Op. 4. Rag Time ("well-tempered"). Symphonische Tänze. *999 006-2*[a] – Das Nusch-Nuschi – dance suite, Op. 20. Konzertmusik for strings and brass, Op. 50. Symphony, "Die Harmonie der Welt". CPO999 005-2, 999 006-2 (12/91).

...Der Schwanendreher. *Coupled with* **Bartók** Viola Concerto, Sz120. **Tabea Zimmermann** (va); **Bavarian Radio Symphony Orchestra / David Shallon.** EMI CDC7 54101-2 (3/93).

...Wind Septet. *Coupled with* **Toch** Five Pieces for Wind and Percussion, Op. 83. **Weill** Violin Concerto, Op. 12[a]. [a]**Christian Tetzlaff** (vn); **Deutsche Kammerphilharmonie.** Virgin Classics VC5 45056-2 (7/95).

...Clarinet Sonata in B flat major. *Coupled with* **Honegger** Clarinet Sonatina, H42. **Françaix** Tema con variazioni. **Vaughan Williams** Six Studies in English folk song. **Milhaud** Duo concertante, Op. 351. Caprice, Op. 335a. **Bozza** Pulcinella. **Kupferman** Moonflowers, Baby!. **Jonathan Cohler** (cl); **Judith Gordon** (pf). Crystal CD733 (5/95).

...Organ Sonatas Nos. 1-3. *Coupled with* **Pepping** Three Fugues on BACH. **Schoenberg** Variations on a Recitative, Op. 40. Two Fragments of an Organ Sonata. **Kevin Bowyer** (org). Nimbus NI5411 (1/95).

...When Lilacs Last in the Door-yard Bloom'd (Requiem for those we love). **Jan DeGaetani** (mez); **William Stone** (bar); **Atlanta Symphony Chorus and Orchestra / Robert Shaw.** Telarc CD80132 (7/87).

Alun Hoddinott

British 1929-

Suggested listening ...

...Passagio, Op. 94. The Heaventree of Stars, Op. 102[a]. Doubles, Op. 106[b]. Start Children, Op. 135. [a]**Hu Kun** (vn); [b]**David Cowley** (ob); [b]**Rosalie Armstrong** (hpd); **BBC Welsh Symphony Orchestra / Tadaaki Otaka.** Nimbus NI5357 (7/93).

...Quodlibet on Welsh Nursery Tunes. Chorales, Variants and Fanfares[a]. Ritornelli 2, Op. 100 No. 2. *Coupled with* **Mathias** Summer Dances. Soundings. [a]**Kevin Bowyer** (org); **Fine Arts Brass Ensemble.** Nimbus NI5466 (5/96).

...Piano Sonatas – No. 1, Op. 17; No. 2, Op. 27, No. 3, Op. 40; No. 4, Op. 49; No. 5, Op. 57. **Martin Jones** (pf). Nimbus NI5369 (12/93).

...Piano Sonatas – No. 6, Op. 78 No. 3; No. 7, Op. 114; No. 8, Op. 125; No. 9, Op. 134; No. 10, Op. 136. **Martin Jones** (pf). Nimbus NI5370 (5/95).

...The Lady and the Unicorn, Op. 110. *Coupled with works by* **J. Harvey, Musgrave, Maconchy, T. Salter** and **Lutyens Ionian Singers / Timothy Salter; Thalia Myers** (pf); **Erik Jacobsen** (perc).Usk Recordings USK1216 (3/96).

Ernst Theodor Amadeus Hoffmann

German 1776-1822

Suggested listening ...

...Undine. **Soloists; St Hedwig's Cathedral Choir, Berlin; Berlin Radio Symphony Orchestra / Roland Bader.** Koch Schwann 31092-2 (10/93).

Carl Höhne

Suggested listening ...

...Slavonic Fantasy. *Coupled with works by* **Arban, Eben, Enescu, Fantini, Françaix, Goedicke** and **Tartini John Wallace** (tpt/cornet); **Meyrick Alexander** (bn); **Simon Wright** (pf/org/hpd). EMI Virtuosi CDC5 55086-2 (11/94). *See review in the Collections section; refer to the Index to Reviews.*

Antony Holborne
British fl. 1584-1602

Suggested listening ...
...Pavans, Galliards, Almaines and other Short Aeirs – The Choise. The widowes myte. Heres paternus. Muy linda. Infernum. Pardizo. The Sighes. The night watch. As it fell on a holie Eve. Heigh ho holiday. Spero. Last will and testament. Posthuma. The Honie-suckle. The Fairie-round. Almayne. Three Pavans. Seven Galliards. Solo Pieces – Almaine. Fantasia. Prelude. Quadro Pavan. Lullaby. The maydens of the Countrey. The Spanish Pavane. A Jyg. **Dowland Consort / Jakob Lindberg**. BIS CD469 (4/92). ✍

Joseph Holbrooke
British 1878-1958

Suggested listening ...
...Ulalume, Op. 35. Bronwen – Overture. The Bells, Op. 50 – Prelude. The Raven, Op. 25. Byron, Op. 39[a]. [a]**Slovak Philharmonic Choir; Bratislava Radio Symphony Orchestra / Adrian Leaper.** Marco Polo 8 223446 (11/93). *Gramophone Editor's choice.*

Trevor Hold
British 20th Century

Suggested listening ...
...Kemp's Nine Daies Wonder. The Lilford Owl. Kaleidoscopes. **Peter Jacobs** (pf). Continuum CCD1066 (10/93).

Heinz Holliger
Swiss 1939-

New review
Holliger Beiseit[a]. Alb-Chehr[b]. [a]**David James** (alto); [b]**Oswald Bumann** (bass); [b]**Franziskus Abgottspon** (spkr); [b]**Elmar Schmid**, [b]**Klaus Schmid** (cls); [b]**Paul Locher** (vn); [a]**Teodoro Anzellotti**, [b]**Marcel Volken**, [b]**Markus Tenisch** (accordions); [b]**Sabine Gertschen**, [b]**Edmund Volken** (dulcimers); [a]**Johannes Nied** (db) **/ Heinz Holliger.** ECM New Series Ⓟ 447 391-2 (61 minutes: DDD: 8/95). Texts and translations included. Recorded 1992-4.
These two works, both dating from the early 1990s, reinforce Heinz Holliger's claim to be considered one of our leading contemporary composers. *Beiseit* is dedicated to György Kurtág (like Holliger, he was a pupil of Sándor Veress) and it shares something of the unsparing spirit of Kurtág's own song collections. "Beiseit", meaning "aside" or "apart", has connotations of separation and neglect, reflecting the poet Robert Walser's descent into madness and silence, and Holliger responds with a haunting sound-world, clarinet, accordion and double-bass accompanying a vocalist whose singing (countertenor) and speaking voices occupy quite different registers. What in the end makes this harrowing portrait of spiritual suffering artistically worthwhile is the lyric beauty and dramatic intensity of Holliger's economical, imaginative designs; the performance is quite riveting from start to finish. *Alb-Chehr* (in one sense, "piece of music about a ghost") has its sinister moments too, but its character is that of a folk entertainment, the music accompanying the telling, in fruity Swiss-German dialect, of a tale about how an Alpine cheesemaker comes to a sticky end. The ensemble includes several folk instruments, like washboard and 'Gutteruspil' (tuned bottles), and there are some delightfully pointed dance movements, including a *Ländler* and a Polka. Listeners with ears tuned to the way Sir Peter Maxwell Davies can sour and scarify the most innocent musical material may feel that Holliger's ghostly transformations risk blandness, but there are enough shivers and shocks to counterbalance the sprightliness of the dances, and the instrumental effects are fascinating and never overdone in a performance which is all the better for avoiding any hint of playing to the gallery. The recordings are excellent and the set is accompanied by a well-documented and informative booklet.
Further listening ...
...Chaconne. *Coupled with works by* **K. Huber, Britten , C. Halffter, Berio, Lutosławski, Dutilleux, Beck, Henze, Fortner, Ginastera** and **Boulez Patrick and Thomas Demenga** (vcs); **Cello Ensemblc / Jürg Wyttenbach**. ECM New Series 445 234-2 (8/95).
...Siebengesang[a]. Der magische Tänzer[b]. [a]**Soloists;** [b]**Basle Theatre Choir;** [a]**Stuttgart Schola Cantorum; Basle Symphony Orchestra /** [a]**Francis Travis,** [b]**Hans Zender.** DG 20th Century Classics 445 251-2GC (10/94).
...Scardanelli-Zyklus – Die Jahreszeiten[a]. Ubungen zu Scardanelli[b]. (t)air(e)[c]. Turm-Musik – excerpts[d]. Ostinato funebre[e]. [cd]**Aurèle Nicolet** (fl); [a]**London Voices / Terry Edwards;** [bde]**Ensemble Modern / Heinz Holliger.** ECM New Series 437 441-2 (7/93).

Alfred Hollins
British 1865-1942

Suggested listening ...
... A Trumpet Minuet. *Coupled with works by* **Elgar, Cocker, Sumsion, Spicer, C.S. Lang, Lemare** and **Wagner** **Christopher Herrick** (org). Hyperion CDA66778 (3/96). *See review in the Collections section; refer to the Index to Reviews.*

Robin Holloway
British 1943-

Holloway Second Concerto for Orchestra, Op. 40. **BBC Symphony Orchestra / Oliver Knussen.** NMC (Special price) NMCD015 (34 minutes: DDD: 5/94). Recorded 1993. *Gramophone Award Winner 1994. Gramophone Editor's choice.* **ⒼⒼ**

It was a visit to North Africa during 1977-78 that launched Robin Holloway on his *Second Concerto for Orchestra*. The extremes of contrast, he tells us, haunted him and were soon demanding to be turned into music. At the same time, the experience seems to have set him off on a more enigmatic, private voyage through his, and our musical past. We hear a few particularly aching bars from Act 2 of *Tristan* and rather more of Chopin's F sharp major *Barcarolle*; *Arrivederci Roma* reaches a breathtaking, brash Honegger/Messiaen apotheosis, while a strange, broken tune on muted trombone metamorphoses neatly into Parry's *Jerusalem*. It's bewildering, but gripping at the same time. Holloway doesn't just quote – his allusions or clear references emerge from the musical fabric, and then return to fertilize it again. And what gorgeous, vibrant, bewitching fabric it is. Holloway can swerve from lush, late romanticism to strident modernism and back again with the alarming quickness of an opium dream; but as with any really revelatory dream, the more you probe it, the more lucid it seems. Oliver Knussen's triumph in pulling it all together, and then shaping and shading it so lovingly, is just one of the technically miraculous aspects of this disc; another is that the production team have somehow turned BBC Maida Vale Studio No. 1 into a fine, spacious acoustic, with teeming details beautifully focused. It adds up to a fascinating disc that deserves the widest possible hearing.

Further listening ...
...Sea Surface Full of Clouds, Op. 28[a]. Romanza, Op. 31[b]. [a]**Penelope Walmsley-Clark** (sop); [a]**Margaret Cable** (mez); [a]**Charles Brett** (alto); [a]**Martyn Hill** (ten); [b]**Erich Gruenberg** (vn); [a]**Richard Hickox Singers; City of London Sinfonia / Richard Hickox.** Chandos CHAN9228 (9/94). **Ⓖ**

Vagn Holmboe
Danish 1909-

Holmboe Symphonies – No. 1, Op. 4; No. 3, Op. 25, "Sinfonia rustica"; No. 10, Op. 105. **Aarhus Symphony Orchestra / Owain Arwel Hughes.** BIS Ⓕ CD605 (70 minutes: DDD: 11/94). Recorded 1993.

The First Symphony is strongly modal and neo-classical in outlook, its invention guided by that vital forward current that distinguishes so much of Holmboe's music. Its dimensions are modest (it takes just over 15 minutes), its argument lucid and its textures open. The Third, subtitled *Sinfonia rustica*, is the first of his three wartime symphonies: its first movement is distinctly folk-like, based on Jutt folk material (in the two outer movements) and a medieval Danish song in the middle movement, which strikes a defiant note. The finale has a wonderfully exhilarating spirit. The most important of the three works recorded here is the Tenth Symphony (1970-71). This inhabits a completely different sound-world, its vision more cosmic as the Whitman quotation that prefaces the score shows. Indeed, it aptly illustrates the principle of metamorphosis underlying Holmboe's musical thinking: "All space, all time/The stars, the terrible perturbations of the suns,/Swelling, collapsing, ending, serving their longer, shorter use/Fill'd with eidolons only./Ever the mutable,/Ever materials, changing, crumbling, re cohering." The Tenth is a work of great power whose stature has yet to be recognized. The Aarhus orchestra give excellent and dedicated performances of all three symphonies under Owain Arwel Hughes who conducts with an evident feeling for this music, and the recording is eminently satisfactory.

New review

Holmboe Symphonies – No. 8, Op. 56, "Sinfonia boreale"; No. 9, Op. 95. **Aarhus Symphony Orchestra / Owain Arwel Hughes.** BIS Ⓕ CD618 (65 minutes: DDD: 8/95). Recorded 1993. **Ⓖ**

In autumn 1984 *The New York Times* devoted a long article to Vagn Holmboe by Richard Taruskin (well known for his illuminating and scholarly writings on Russian opera in general and Mussorgsky in particular), in which he described the Danish composer as "possibly the greatest living traditional symphonist". His words are worth quoting since he describes Holmboe's "virtuosic metamorphosis technique" in the Sixth and Seventh Symphonies so well – and what he says applies equally to the Eighth and Ninth. "In these works, traditionally 'symphonic' in the purest, truest sense, the entire multi-movement span is generated out of a single network of motives under perpetual transformation. Remotely placed variants no longer resemble one another directly but depend for their intelligibility on the listener's tracking a beautifully shaped and directed chain of intermediate relationships that in turn describes an overall chain of moods." He speaks of form and expressive content as being one, "every symphonic composer's ideal but very few achieve it so fully", and goes on to compare it to "academic discourse of a thrillingly high order ... if you have ever left a lecture hall haunted and altered, this may offer a comparable cognitive adventure". Of course, there is nothing academic in the perjorative sense about this music: it is vital and living in the same way as a Sibelius or Nielsen symphony. Owain Arwel Hughes has a real feeling for Holmboe's music and realizes its stature. If he is meticulous in his observance of the letter of the score in matters of dynamic nuances and agogic markings, he penetrates its spirit, too. There is a gap of some 17 years between the Eighth and its successor. After its première in 1968 it was revised and this is its first recording. A dark, powerful work, the Ninth is among the finest Holmboe has given us. The recording is the best so far in BIS's cycle.

New review

Holmboe String Quartets – No. 2, Op. 47; No. 5, Op. 66; No. 6, Op. 78. **Kontra Quartet** (Anton Kontra, Boris Samsing, vns; Peter Fabricius, va; Morten Zeuthen, vc). Da capo Ⓔ 8 224026 (66 minutes: DDD: 7/96). Recorded 1995.

This disc is hardly less impressive than the first in this series (listed below). Those who know the Holmboe quartets well will know that the claims made on their behalf are not a whit exaggerated. True, they have a certain reticence and rely on their cumulative effect rather than on beauty of incident. There is no more attempt to cultivate a popular appeal than there is in the quartets of Sir Michael Tippett or Robert Simpson. And, like Simpson, Holmboe is perhaps more at home with the string quartet than any other medium. He had written ten between 1926 and 1944 before actually publishing his first numbered quartet, and was only relatively recently finishing No. 20. The Second Quartet comes from 1949, between the Sixth and Seventh Symphonies, and like its two immediate neighbours, speaks with a distinctive voice. It has freshness and an immediate lyrical appeal. The Fifth came in 1955, after the Eighth Symphony, and the Sixth from 1961. Both are challenging, highly concentrated pieces of an elevating and compelling eloquence. The Kontra Quartet play them with total commitment and conviction and readers need not hesitate to buy. The only reservation concerns the Sixth Quartet, which is recorded in a less flattering acoustic than its companions with the result that the sound is harder and edgy. Nos. 2 and 5 are exemplary in every way.

Further listening ...

...Symphony No. 2. Sinfonia in Memoriam. **Aarhus Symphony Orchestra / Owain Arwel Hughes.** BIS CD695 (6/96). *Gramophone Editor's choice.*

...Symphonies – No. 4, Op. 29, "Sinfonia sacra"[a]; No. 5, Op. 35. [a]**Jutland Opera Choir; Aarhus Symphony Orchestra / Owain Arwel Hughes.** BIS CD572 (6/93).

...Symphonies – No. 6, Op. 43; No. 7, Op. 50. **Aarhus Symphony Orchestra / Owain Arwel Hughes.** BIS CD573 (6/93).

...String Quartets – No. 1, Op. 46; No. 3, Op. 48; No. 4, Op. 63. **Kontra Quartet.** Marco Polo Da capo DCCD9203 (6/94).

Augusta Holmès   French 1847-1903

Suggested listening ...

...Andromède[a]. Irlande[a]. Ouverture pour une comédie[a]. Ludus pro Patria – La nuit et l'amour[b]. Pologne[a]. **Rheinland-Pfalz State Philharmonic Orchestra /** [a]**Samuel Friedmann,** [b]**Patrick Davin.** Marco Polo 8 223449 (10/94).

Gustav Holst   British 1874-1934

Holst Beni Mora, H107[a]. A Fugal Overture, H151[b]. Hammersmith, H178[a]. Japanese Suite, H126[c]. Scherzo, H192[a]. A Somerset Rhapsody, H87[a]. [ab]**London Philharmonic Orchestra;** [c]**London Symphony Orchestra / Sir Adrian Boult.** Lyrita Ⓕ SRCD222 (62 minutes: ADD: 7/92). Items marked [a] from SRCS56 (5/72), [b]SRCS37 (10/68), [c]SRCS50 (6/71). Ⓖ

Here's another classic Boult anthology from Lyrita, and unquestionably one of this enterprising company's finest CDs to date. Opening in fine style with a roistering account of the *Fugal Overture*, this indispensable all-Holst concert also includes the haunting *Somerset Rhapsody* (framed by a ravishingly atmospheric oboe d'amore contribution), the riotously colourful 'Oriental Suite' entitled *Beni Mora*, the engaging *Japanese Suite*, as well as the very late, bracing *Scherzo* (all that the composer left us of a projected symphony). But the highlight of the collection has to be that utterly magical nocturnal evocation *Hammersmith*: heard here in its full orchestral dress, it's one of Holst's most sublimely personal utterances and an undoubted masterpiece. These uniquely authoritative, radiantly played performances all show Sir Adrian at the height of his considerable powers, and the remastered Lyrita recordings continue to sound, for the most part, quite superb. In a word: unmissable.

Additional recommendation ...

...St Paul's Suite, H118. A Fugal Concerto, H152[a]. Brook Green Suite, H190. A Somerset Rhapsody. The Perfect Fool – ballet music. [a]**Jonathan Snowden** (fl); [a]**David Theodore** (ob); **English**

Chamber Orchestra / Sir Yehudi Menuhin. EMI Eminence Ⓜ CD-EMX2227 (48 minutes: DDD: 12/94).

Holst The Planets, H125. Women's voices of the **Montreal Symphony Chorus and Orchestra / Charles Dutoit.** Decca Ⓕ 417 553-2DH (53 minutes: DDD: 4/87). Recorded 1986. *Gramophone Award Winner 1987.* ⒼⒼⒼ

Holst's brilliantly coloured orchestral suite, *The Planets*, is undoubtedly his most famous work and its success is surely deserved. The musical characterization is as striking as its originality of conception: the association of "Saturn" with old age, for instance, is as unexpected as it is perceptive. Bax introduced Holst to astrology and while he wrote the music he became fascinated with horoscopes, so it is the astrological associations that are paramount, although the linking of "Mars" (with its enormously powerful 5/4 rhythms) and war also reflects the time of composition. Throughout, the work's invention is as memorable as its vivid orchestration is full of infinite detail. No recording can reveal it all but this one comes the closest to doing so. Dutoit's individual performance is in a long line of outstanding recordings.

Additional recommendations ...

...The Planets. **Berlin RIAS Chamber Choir; Berlin Philharmonic Orchestra / Herbert von Karajan.** DG Karajan Gold Ⓕ 439 011-2GHS (52 minutes: DDD). ⒼⒼ

...The Planets. **Geoffrey Mitchell Choir; London Philharmonic Orchestra / Sir Adrian Boult.** EMI Studio Ⓜ CDM7 64748-2 (49 minutes: ADD: 5/88). Ⓖ

...The Planets. The Perfect Fool – ballet music. **Royal Liverpool Philharmonic Chorus and Orchestra / Sir Charles Mackerras.** Virgin Classics Ⓕ CUV5 61257-2 (60 minutes: DDD: 12/91).

...The Planets. **King's College Choir, Cambridge; Royal Philharmonic Orchestra / James Judd.** Denon Ⓕ CO-75076 (50 minutes: DDD: 3/93).

...The Planets[a]. Egdon Heath[b]. The Perfect Fool – ballet music[b]. **London Philharmonic Orchestra / [a]Sir Georg Solti, [b]Sir Adrian Boult.** Decca Ⓜ 440 318-2DWO (73 minutes: ADD: 4/94).

...The Planets[a]. St Paul's Suite, H118. [a]**Ambrosian Singers; Royal Philharmonic Orchestra / Vernon Handley.** Tring International Ⓢ TRP007 (62 minutes: DDD: 6/94).

...The Planets[a]. Egdon Heath, H172. **BBC Symphony [a]Chorus and Orchestra / Andrew Davis.** Teldec British Line Ⓕ 4509-94541-2 (64 minutes: DDD: 12/94). *Selected by Sounds in Retrospect.*

...The Planets[a]. **Grainger** The Warriors. [a]women's voices of the **Monteverdi Choir; Philharmonia Orchestra / John Eliot Gardiner.** DG Ⓕ 445 860-2GH (68 minutes: DDD: 8/95). *See review under Grainger, refer to the Index to Reviews.* Ⓖ

New review

Holst The Hymn of Jesus, H140[a]. First Choral Symphony, H155[b]. [b]**Felicity Palmer** (sop); [a]**St Paul's Cathedral Choir;** [a]**London Symphony Chorus; London Philharmonic** [b]**Choir and Orchestra /** [a]**Sir Charles Groves,** [b]**Sir Adrian Boult.** EMI British Composers Ⓜ CDM5 65128-2 (72 minutes: ADD: 7/96). Texts included. Item marked [a] from HMV ASD3435 (2/78), [b]HMV SAN354 (10/74).

The really good news here is the return of Boult's powerful 1974 première recording of the awesome *Choral Symphony*. This was originally coupled (at full price) with the same composer's *Choral Fantasia*, but it didn't last long in the catalogue, so make sure you don't miss out this time for it is an admirably searching interpretation. When it first appeared in 1978, Groves's account of *The Hymn of Jesus* was generally rated a finer effort than Boult's 1961 Decca recording. The authority and honesty of Sir Charles's direction is impressive. True, orchestral discipline could at times be tighter (witness those rather ragged wind and brass chords at the outset), but the choral singing is never less than very commendable. It should, however, be pointed out that Groves's achievement has since been outshone by Richard Hickox (reviewed further on), who in turn cannot quite match the extraordinary fervour and intensity of Sir Malcolm Sargent in his pioneering 1944 account. The Kingsway Hall sound in both items remains satisfyingly full and immediate.

Additional recommendations ...

...The Hymn of Jesus[a]. **Elgar** The Dream of Gerontius[b]. [b]**Yvonne Minton** (mez); [b]**Sir Peter Pears** (ten); [b]**John Shirley-Quirk** (bar); [b]**Choir of King's College, Cambridge;** [b]**London Symphony Chorus and Orchestra / Benjamin Britten;** [a]**BBC Chorus and Symphony Orchestra / Sir Adrian Boult.** Decca London Ⓜ 421 381-2LM2 (two discs: 113 minutes: ADD: 5/89).

...The Hymn of Jesus[c]. **Vaughan Williams** The Lark Ascending[b]. **Gardiner** Shepherd Fennell's Dance. **Coleridge Taylor** Scenes from "The Song of Hiawatha", Op. 30 – Onaway, awake, beloved[a]. **Harty** A John Field Suite. **Ireland** A London Overture. [a]**Webster Booth** (ten); [b]**David Wise** (vn); [c]**Huddersfield Choral Society; Liverpool Philharmonic Orchestra / Sir Malcolm Sargent.** Dutton Laboratories mono Ⓜ CDAX8012* (75 minutes: ADD: 5/95).

Holst Partsongs – Ave Maria, H49. Of one that is so fair, H130. Lullay my liking, H129. Bring us in good ale, H131. Diverus and Lazarus, H137. This have I done for my true love, H128. Songs from The Princess, H80-81. O Spiritual Pilgrim, H188. Welsh Folk Songs, H183 – No. 9, My sweetheart's like Venus. Eastern Pictures, H112[c]. Light Leaves Whisper, H20. In Youth is Pleasure, H76. Choral Folk Songs, H136. Carols, H91[ab]. Jesu, thou the Virgin-born, H82. [a]**David Theodore** (ob); [b]**Robert Truman** (vc); [a]**Sioned Williams** (hp); **Holst Singers / Stephen Layton.** Hyperion Ⓕ CDA66705 (71 minutes: DDD: 6/94).

For an object lesson in economy of means look no further than the magical setting of "Terly Terlow" accompanied by oboe and cello. The richness of this music belies such meagre resources. Part-songs, of which this single disc can only offer a representative selection, were in many ways central to Holst's output. The earliest dates from 1896, the latest (Holst's last choral composition *O Spiritual Pilgrim*) from 1933. During this period he passed from being a student, a touring orchestral musician and a girls' school teacher into the realms of international acclaim as the composer of *The Planets*. The styles and influences are as multifarious as were the choirs and singers for whom the songs were written. The Holst Singers' beautifully pure sound easily moulds itself to the character of each song, while Stephen Layton's unfussy, tightly controlled direction keeps everything perfectly in proportion.

New review

Holst Seven Partsongs, H162[a]. A Choral Fantasia, H177[b]. A Dirge for Two Veterans, H121[c]. Ode to Death, H144[d]. [ab]**Patricia Rozario** (sop); [d]**London Symphony Chorus;** [abc]**Joyful Company of Singers; City of London Sinfonia / Richard Hickox.** Chandos Ⓟ CHAN9437 (59 minutes: DDD: 6/96). Texts included. Recorded 1994.

It is the First World War that is the unnamed, ever-felt presence here. "I float this carol with joy, with joy to thee O Death" chants Walt Whitman with that willed mystical intoxication that proved so surprisingly attractive to both Holst and Vaughan Williams, composers who could face reality soberly enough and in Holst's case often with a bleak, spare beauty of sound that takes and bestows only a hard-won comfort. Listening even to the relatively 'light' and partially happy Bridges settings (the *Seven Partsongs*), one becomes aware of a hollow, half-anxious feeling, located in that mysterious area of midriff wherein these undefined apprehensions take their dwelling. With it comes (as in the third of them, "Angel spirits of sleep") a musician's cherishing of silence, as though the music which intrudes upon it ("threading dances light") must be most finely attuned if it is to justify the presumption. Death emerges from its temporary hiding place in the seventh ("Assemble, all ye maidens") and then, for the rest of the recital, comes into its kingdom. Most explicitly, the *Dirge for Two Veterans* takes up the "full-keyed bugles" of war, and that was written in the last months of 1914. In the *Ode to Death* (1931) and even the partsongs for women's voices, it is surely the dreadful sadness of that war which fills the hollow places and so, for comfort, enhances the apprehension of beauty in music. The programme has a very special value, and the performances are worthy of it. Comparisons work pretty regularly in favour of Hickox and his forces: in the *Partsongs*, for instance, the admirable Holst Singers are recorded with less sense of presence. With the *Dirge for Two Veterans* the Baccholian Singers with the Philip Jones Brass Ensemble from 1969 have the greater rhythmic vitality. Generally, however, this new issue is the one to have.

Additional recommendations ...

...Two psalms, H117[a]. Six choruses, H186[a]. The evening watch, H159. Seven Partsongs, H162[a]. Nunc dimittis, H127. **Holst Singers and** [a]**Orchestra / Hilary Davan Wetton.** Hyperion Ⓟ CDA66329 (65 minutes: DDD: 1/90).

...The Homecoming, H120. Choral Hymns from the Rig Veda (Group 4), H100 – No. 3, Hymn to Manas. Canons, H187 – No. 3, The fields of sorrow; No. 4, David's lament for Jonathan; No. 6, Truth of all truth. Choral Folk Songs, H136 – No. 1, I sowed the seeds of love; No. 3, Matthew, Mark, Luke and John; No. 4, The song of the blacksmith; No. 5, I love my love; No. 6, Swansea Town. Male Choruses, H186 – No. 1, Intercession; No. 2, Good Friday; No. 3, Drinking song; No. 4, A love song; No. 6, Before sleep. A Dirge for Two Veterans. *Coupled with works by* **Bax, Elgar, Vaughan Williams, Howells, Delius, Britten** and **Warlock London Madrigal Singers / Christopher Bishop; Baccholian Singers of London; Philip Jones Brass Ensemble; English Chamber Orchestra / Ian Humphris.** EMI British Composers Ⓜ CMS5 65123-2 (two discs: 149 minutes: ADD: 2/96). *See review in the Collections section; refer to the Index to Reviews.*

Holst The Cloud Messenger, Op. 30[a]. The Hymn of Jesus, Op. 37. [a]**Della Jones** (mez); **London Symphony Chorus and Orchestra / Richard Hickox.** Chandos Ⓟ CHAN8901 (66 minutes: DDD: 5/91). Texts included. Recorded 1990.

When this CD was first released, the great talking point was *The Cloud Messenger*, a 43-minute work of considerable imaginative power, virtually forgotten since its disastrous première under the baton of Holst himself in 1913. It shows the composer already working on an epic scale – something which casts light on the subsequent eruption of *The Planets*. It is marvellous to have the work on disc, though it is, as you might expect, uneven. Those who admire the ascetic rigour of Holst's later music may share the reservations of Imogen Holst and find the score disappointingly 'backward'. There are certainly echoes of Vaughan Williams's *A Sea Symphony* and several older models. On the other hand, the glittering approach to the sacred city on Mount Kailasa and the stylized orientalism of the climactic dance are new to British music; another world, the world of "Venus", is foreshadowed in the closing pages. The text is Holst's own translation from the Sanskrit. Hickox's expansive account of the familiar *Hymn of Jesus* is more than a mere filler. One of the few incontrovertible masterpieces in Holst's output, it has seldom received a better performance on disc, although the impressively grand

acoustics of London's St Jude's impart a certain warm imprecision – the choral singing itself is splendidly crisp – which can blunt the impact of Holst's acerbic harmonies.

Further listening ...

...Invocation, Op. 19/2. *Coupled with* **Delius** Cello Concerto. **Vaughan Williams** Fantasia on Sussex Folk Tunes. **Philharmonia Orchestra / Vernon Handley.** RCA Victor Red Seal RD70800 (7/87).

...Two songs without words, H88[a]. Double Violin Concerto, H175[b]. The Golden Goose, H163 – ballet music[a]. Capriccio for Orchestra, H185[a] (ed. I. Holst). A Fugal Concerto, H152[c]. A Moorside Suite, H173 – Nocturne[c]. Lyric Movement, H191[d]. Brook Green Suite, H190[d]. [c]**William Bennett** (fl); [c]**Peter Graeme** (ob); [b]**Emanuel Hurwitz,** [b]**Kenneth Sillito** (vns); [d]**Cecil Aronowitz** (va); **English Chamber Orchestra / Imogen Holst.** Lyrita SRCD223 (4/93).

...A Winter Idyll, H31[c]. The Cotswolds, Symphony in F major, H47 – Elegy in memoriam William Morris[c]. A Song of the Night, H74[ac]. Indra, H66[c]. Invocation for Cello and Orchestra, H75[bc]. Sita – Act 3, Interlude (ed. C. Matthews)[c]. Dances from "The Morning of the Year", H164 (ed. C. Matthews)[c]. The Lure, H149 (ed. C. Matthews and I. Holst)[d]. [a]**Lorraine McAslan** (vn); [b]**Alexander Baillie** (vc); [c]**London Philharmonic Orchestra;** [d]**London Symphony Orchestra / David Atherton.** Lyrita SRCD209 (6/93).

...A Fugal Concerto. St Paul's Suite. Morris Dance Tunes. Lyric movement, H191. Brook Green Suite. **Soloists; New Zealand Chamber Orchestra / Nicholas Braithwaite.** Koch International Classics 370582 (4/92).

...A Fugal Concerto. St Paul's Suite. Song without words, H88. Lyric movement, H191. Brook Green Suite. **Soloists; City of London Sinfonia / Richard Hickox.** Chandos CHAN9270 (7/94).

...Piano Quintet in A minor H11[b]. Wind Quintet in A flat major, H67[a]. *Coupled with* **Jacob** Sextet, Op. 3[ab]. **Elysian Wind Quintet;** [b]**Anthony Goldstone** (pf). Chandos CHAN9077 (10/92).

...Short Piano Trio in E major. *Coupled with works by* **Bax** and **Stanford** Pirasti Trio. ASV CDDCA925 (9/95). *See review under Bax; refer to the Index to Reviews.*

...Toccata on the Northumbrian Pipe Tune, "Newburn Lads". Chrissemas Day in the Morning, on a tune from "North Country Ballads", Op. 46 No. 1. Two Folk Song Arrangements, Op. 46 No. 2. Nocturne. Jig. Arpeggio Study. Two Pieces. A Piece for Yvonne. Dances (with Caroline Clemmow, pf). *Coupled with* **C. Lambert** Piano Sonata. Elegiac Blues. Elegy. **Anthony Goldstone** (pf). Chandos CHAN9382 (10/95).

...Songs, H174 – Persephone; Now in these fairylands; A little music; The Floral Bandit; The Dream-city; Journey's End. *Coupled with songs by* **Warlock, Ireland, Howells** *and* **Bridge** **Sarah Leonard** (sop); **Malcolm Martineau** (pf). Cala United 88016-2 (3/95).

...Sávitri, H96. **Soloists; Richard Hickox Singers; City of London Sinfonia / Richard Hickox.** Hyperion CDA66099 (2/88).

...The Golden Goose, H163. The Morning of the Year, H164. King Estmere, H70. **Guildford Choral Society; Philharmonia Orchestra / Hilary Davan Wetton.** Hyperion CDA66784 (4/96).

...At the Boar's Head[a]. The Wandering Scholar[b]. **Soloists;** [a]**Royal Liverpool Philharmonic Orchestra / David Atherton;** [b]**English Chamber Orchestra / Steuart Bedford.** EMI British Composers CDM5 65127-2 (4/96).

Simon Holt

British 1958-

Suggested listening ...

...Era madrugada. Canciones[a]. Shadow realm. Sparrow night[b]. [a]**Fiona Kimm** (mez); [b]**Gareth Hulse** (ob); **Nash Ensemble / Lionel Friend.** NMC NMCD008 (5/93).

Ignaz Holzbauer

Austrian 1711-1820

New review

Holzbauer Günther von Schwarzburg. **Robert Wörle** (ten) Günther; **Michael Schopper** (bass) Rudolf, Palsgrave; **Claron McFadden** (sop) Anna; **Clarry Bartha** (sop) Asberta; **Christoph Prégardien** (ten) Karl; **La Stagione Vocal Ensemble; La Stagione / Michael Schneider.** CPO Ⓔ CPO999 265-2 (three discs: 178 minutes. DDD: 7/96). Text and translation included. Recorded 1994.

"The music is incomparably fine", wrote Mozart of Ignaz Holzbauer's *Günther von Schwarzburg* – and he was just about the severest music critic of all time. He went on to add that it was not only very beautiful but had remarkable fire: better than the text deserved. Mozart heard it in Mannheim in 1777, where Holzbauer was Kapellmeister, and surely had it in his ears when, three years later, he was composing *Idomeneo* for the same orchestra and the same court (now transposed to Munich). The end of the opening recitative there has a precise precedent in Holzbauer's opera, for example, and so too do the repeated chords in the overture of *Die Zauberflöte*. Those are not the only echoes, but more significant is the general influence in style and feeling. *Günther* was a novel opera, an early attempt to compose serious German opera along broadly similar lines to Italian *opera seria*. Holzbauer had composed Italian opera up to this point, and resumed it afterwards, but *Günther* came at a time of

German nationalist feeling and is patriotic not only in its language but also in its theme. The story relates events around the election of the Holy Roman Emperor in 1349, when the German hero Günther is named but dies as a result of a plot by Asberta, mother of another candidate for the office: it's a feeble story, with little variety of situation or character development but plenty of opportunity for the expression of pious sentiment, especially about German heroism. The scoring is rich, colourful and frequently intricate with an abundance of accompanied recitative, with numbers often interlinked to avoid the traditional breaks. There are many lengthy sections of dramatically declaimed text, some of them run through with thematic reference but for the most part just highly illustrative of the expression of the words. The ideas themselves are often rewarding and there is some fine, stormy music as well as several beautiful arias, most of all graceful ones in which his fluent melodic gift serves well.

The opera is quite strongly cast. Much of the most appealing music goes to Anna, betrothed of Karl (King of Bohemia, the aspirant Emperor); Claron McFadden sings the role in a suitably elevated manner, with a pure, bright tone for her arias, which include a remarkable coloratura one with obbligato oboe, a stormy outburst in Act 2 and an appealing expression of joy in the final act. Clarry Bartha, who sings Asberta, mother of Karl, has an elaborate, richly scored aria in Act 1, which she copes with very adequately. Karl himself is gracefully sung by Christoph Prégardien, in the best traditions of German lyric tenors, true and focused; he and Anna have an ecstatic duet in Act 3 when Asberta's plot is exposed and they are united. Günther himself, who dies as the opera ends, disappointed in his imperial hopes yet nobly magnanimous, is gently and sympathetically sung by Robert Wörle. His dying aria, with rich textures on muted strings, is a very beautiful piece. As Rudolf, the Elector and Palsgrave, Anna's father, Michael Schopper shows a warm, forward bass-baritone, though his intonation in his final aria, a touching minor-key lament, is not quite secure. There are only two ensembles, the duet and a trio, besides some choruses, but the presence of so much orchestral recitative rescues the work from the pattern of alternating recitative and aria that modern listeners find so hard to take. It is difficult to tell whether Michael Schneider paces it all ideally, or manages the level of intensity effectively: however, it has an atmosphere very much its own: very Germanic, self-consciously serious and exalted. It is likely that many readers will find it fascinating and edifying.

Arthur Honegger   French/Swiss 1892-1955

Honegger Symphony No. 1. Pastorale d'été. Three symphonic movements – No. 1, "Pacific 231"; No. 2, "Rugby"; No. 3. **Bavarian Radio Symphony Orchestra / Charles Dutoit.** Erato Ⓔ 2292-45242-2 (55 minutes: DDD: 12/86). From NUM75254 (4/86). Recorded 1985. *Selected by Sounds in Retrospect.*

Honegger's First Symphony is a highly impressive work, concisely and effectively constructed in what might be generally described as a neoclassical style; and the scoring is attractive and skilful. His evocation of dawn on a summer's day in *Pastorale d'été*, scored for small orchestra with exquisite, quiet beauty, is surely a miniature masterpiece, and both *Pacific 231* (1924) and *Rugby* (1928) are brilliantly contrived essays in imaginative scoring and the use of cross-rhythms. Honegger was distressed by a critical notion that he was trying to imitate the sound of a steam locomotive and specific moves in a game of rugby: he insisted that the two scores conveyed only a general impression of a train journey and the atmosphere of Colombes stadium. So offended was he that he called the third companion piece merely *Mouvement symphonique No. 3*, but it is a little less effective than its two bedfellows. These vigorous performances are excellent.

Additional recommendations ...

...Symphonies Nos. 1-5. La tempête. Three symphonic movements – Nos. 1 and 3. **Czech Philharmonic Orchestra / Serge Baudo.** Supraphon Ⓔ 11 1566-2 (two discs: 146 minutes: ADD: 9/92).

...Le tempête – Prélude. Pastorale d'été. Horace victorieux. Pacific 231; Rugby. La traversée des Andes. Le vol sur l'Atlantique. **Toulouse Capitole Orchestra / Michel Plasson.** DG Ⓔ 435 438-2GH (65 minutes: DDD: 9/93).   Ⓖ

...Pastorale d'été[a]. Cello Concerto[b]. **Poulenc** Trois mouvements perpétuels[c]. Trio for Oboe, Bassoon and Piano[d]. Deux novelettes[c]. Nocturnes[f] – No. 1 in C major; No. 2 in A major; No. 4 in C minor. Improvisations[g] – No. 2 in A flat major; No. 5 in A minor; No. 9 in D major; No. 10 in F major. Aubade for Piano and 18 Instruments[h]. [d]**Roger Lamorlette** (ob); [d]**Gustave Dhérin** (bn); [b]**Maurice Maréchal** (vc); [cdefgh]**Francis Poulenc** (pf); [b]**Paris Conservatoire Orchestra**; [a]**symphony orchestra / Arthur Honegger;** [h]**Walther Straram Concerts Orchestra / Walther Straram.** EMI Composers in Person mono Ⓔ CDC5 55036-2* (76 minutes: ADD: 6/94).

New review

Honegger Symphonies[a] – No. 2 for Strings and Trumpet obbligato, H153; No. 3, H186, "Liturgique".

Stravinsky Concerto in D[b]. **Berlin Philharmonic Orchestra / Herbert von Karajan.** DG The Originals Ⓜ 447 435-2GOR (72 minutes: ADD: 12/95). Items marked [a] from 2530 068 (7/73), [b]2530 267 (8/72). Recorded 1969. *Gramophone classical 100.*   ⓖⓖⓖ

Honegger Symphonies – No. 2; No. 3, "Liturgique". Three symphonic movements – No. 1, "Pacific 231". **Oslo Philharmonic Orchestra / Mariss Jansons.** EMI Ⓔ CDC5 55122-2 (66 minutes: DDD: 7/94). *Gramophone Editor's record of the month.*   Ⓖ

Karajan's performances of these Honegger symphonies enjoy legendary status – and rightly so. Both the Second Symphony and the *Symphonie Liturgique* are well represented in the current catalogue by a dozen or so versions, but there is no point in mentioning any of them individually as this recording remains in a class of its own for sheer beauty of sound and flawless ensemble. Only one exception need be made: Mariss Jansons and the Oslo Philharmonic, one of the best records of 1994 and arguably the Oslo's best disc to date. The French critic Bernard Gavoty once spoke rather flightily of Karajan "transcending emotions and imparting to them that furnace heat that makes a work of genius give off light if brought to the desired temperature" – but it's true! There is a luminous quality and an incandescence about these performances. The Stravinsky Concerto in D was written within a year of the *Symphonie Liturgique* and may perhaps be a little too 'cultured' and not spiky enough for some tastes. The lightness of touch, sprightliness of rhythm and flawless ensemble of the Berlin Philharmonic are a joy in themselves. Self-recommending this disc may be, but its claims on every music lover cannot be too strongly pressed.

Additional recommendations ...

...No. 2; No. 5, "di tre re". **Milhaud** Suite Provençale, Op. 152[b]. La création du monde, Op. 81[b]. **Boston Symphony Orchestra / Charles Munch**. RCA Victor Gold Seal Ⓜ GD60685* (77 minutes: ADD).

...Nos. 3 and 5. **Danish National Radio Symphony Orchestra / Neeme Järvi**. Chandos Ⓕ CHAN9176 (57 minutes: DDD: 9/93). ⒼⒼ

...No. 2. **R. Strauss** Metamorphosen. **Webern** (trans. Schwarz) Langsamer Satz. **Seattle Symphony Orchestra Strings / Gerard Schwarz**. Delos Ⓕ DE3121 (71 minutes: DDD: 4/94).

...Nos. 3 and 5. Pastorale d'été. Chant de joie. Pacific 231. **Czech Philharmonic Orchestra / Serge Baudo**. Supraphon Ⓜ 11 0667-2* (71 minutes: ADD).

Honegger Jeanne d'Arc au bûcher. **Françoise Pollet, Michèle Command** (sops); **Nathalie Stutzman** (contr); **John Aler** (ten); **Marthe Keller, Georges Wilson, Pierre-Marie Escourrou, Paola Lenzi** (narrs); **Chorus and Children's Voices of French Radio; French National Orchestra / Seiji Ozawa**. DG Ⓕ 429 412-2GH (69 minutes: DDD: 4/91). Text and translations included. Recorded live in 1989. *Selected by Sounds in Retrospect.* Ⓖ

Honegger described *Joan of Arc at the stake* as a "dramatic oratorio", but it is a work almost impossible to categorize, the two chief characters – Joan and Brother Dominc – being speaking parts, but with a chorus, a children's chorus, and a curiously constituted orchestra including saxophones instead of horns, two pianos and, most notably, an ondes martenot which, with its banshee shriek, bloodcurdlingly reinforces the climax as Joan breaks her earthly chains. The action is partly realistic, partly symbolic, unfolding in quasi-cinematic flashbacks. The musical techniques and styles employed by Honegger are extraordinarily varied, with humming and shouting besides singing, and with elements of polyphony, folk-song, baroque dances and jazz rhythms; yet all is fused together in a remarkable way to produce a work of gripping power and, in the final scenes, almost intolerable emotional intensity: the beatific *envoi* "Greater love hath no man ..." is a passage that catches the throat and haunts the mind. Ozawa fully captured the work's dramatic forces in this public performance, which has been skilfully served by the recording engineers; Marthe Keller vividly portrays Joan's bewilderment, fervour and agony, John Aler makes a swaggering Procus, and Françoise Pollet is radiant-voiced as the Virgin. Even more than *Le Roi David*, this is Honegger's masterpiece.

Further listening ...

...Concerto da camera. *Coupled with works by* **Ibert, Nielsen** *and* **Poulenc** Jennifer Stinton (fl); Geoffrey Browne (cor ang); **Scottish Chamber Orchestra / Steuart Bedford**. Collins Classics 1210-2 (8/91). *See review in the Collections section; refer to the Index to Reviews.*

...Crime et Châtiment – Suite[a]. Le Déserteur ou Je t'attendrai. Farinet ou L'Or dans la Montagne – Suite. le Grand Barrage. L'Idée. [a]**Jacques Tchamkerten** (ondes martenot); **Bratislava Radio Symphony Orchestra / Adriano**. Marco Polo 8 223466 (6/94).

...Les misérables – film score. **Bratislava Radio Symphony Orchestra / Adriano**. Marco Polo 8 223181 (3/91).

...Le dit des jeux du monde. *Coupled with works by* **Fumet** *and* **d'Indy** Jean Ferrandis (fl); Hervé Noël (tpt); **Jean-Jacques Wiederker Chamber Orchestra / Frédéric Bouaniche**. Koch Schwann 310652 (6/95). *See review under d'Indy; refer to the Index to Reviews.*

...Le Roi David. **Soloists; Philippe Cailard Chorale; instrumental ensemble / Charles Dutoit**. Erato 2292-45800-2.

...Clarinet Sonatina, H42. *Coupled with* **Hindemith** Clarinet Sonata in B flat major. **Françaix** Tema con variazioni. **Vaughan Williams** Six Studies in English folk song. **Milhaud** Duo concertante, Op. 351. Caprice, Op. 335*a*. **Bozza** Pulcinella. **Kupferman** Moonflowers, Baby!. **Jonathan Cohler** (cl); **Judith Gordon** (pf). Crystal CD733 (5/95).

...Fugue and Chorale. *Coupled with works by* **Dupré, Roussel, d'Indy, R. Vierne, Barié, Langlais** *and* **L. Vierne** Marie-Bernadette Dufourcet (org). Priory PRCD422 (6/95). *See review in the Collections section; refer to the Index to Reviews.*

...Petit cours de morale, H148. *Coupled with* **Messiaen** Pourquoi? Le sourire. La fiancée perdue. **Poulenc** La courte paille. Banalités – Hôtel; Voyage à Paris. Métamorphoses – C'est ainsi que tu es. Poèmes – Fêtes galantes. A sa guitare. **Satie** Trois mélodies. **Debussy** Ariettes oubliées.

Fêtes galantes, Set 1. **Ravel** Cinq mélodies populaires grecques. **Frederica von Stade** (mez); **Martin Katz** (pf). RCA Victor Red Seal 09026 62711-2 (4/95).

…Les aventures du roi Pausole. **Soloists; Basle Madrigalists; Swiss Youth Philharmonic Orchestra / Mario Venzago.** MGB Musiques Suisses CD6115 (9/94).

James Hook
British 1746-1827

Suggested listening ...

…Concerto for Harpsichord or Forte-Piano and Orchestra in D major, Op. 1 No. 5 (recons. Holman). *Coupled with works by* **P. Hayes, Nares, Chilcot, Roseingrave** and **Handel The Parley of Instruments / Paul Nicholson** (fp). Hyperion CDA66700 (8/94). ✐

…Voluntary in C minor. *Coupled with works by* **Boyce, Handel, Heron, Russell, Stanley, Stubley** and **S. Wesley Jennifer Bate** (org). Unicorn-Kanchana DKPCD9106 (11/91). *Selected by Sounds in Retrospect. See review in the Collections section; refer to the Index to Reviews.*

Mervyn Horder
1910-

Suggested listening ...

…White in the moon. *Coupled with works by* **Butterworth, L. Berkeley, Barber, Ireland, Moeran** and **C.W. Orr** Anthony Rolfe Johnson (ten); **Graham Johnson** (pf). Hyperion CDA66471/2 (8/95). Includes various poems from Housman's "A Shrophire Lad" read by Alan Bates. *See review in the Collections section; refer to the Index to Reviews.*

Emil Horneman
Danish 1840-1906

New review

Horneman Gurre[a]. Ouverture héroïque. Aladdin Overture. [a]**Guido Päevatalu** (bar); **Danish National Radio** [a]**Choir and Symphony Orchestra / Michael Schønwandt.** Chandos Ⓔ CHAN9373 (57 minutes: DDD: 2/96). Texts and translations included. Recorded 1992-4.

"He was the clear flame, the separating fire of Danish music that melted all that was false and consumed the artificial." Such was Nielsen's judgement, quoted by Jens Cornelius in the booklet, of Christian Frederik Emil Horneman. For a variety of reasons Horneman was able to compose rather less music than he wished, but what he did write makes him, with Peter Heise, the vital link between Gade and J.P.E. Hartmann on the one hand and Nielsen on the other. The music Horneman wrote in 1900-01 for Holger Drachmann's play *Gurre* (on the same subject as Schoenberg's *Gurrelieder*) is finely crafted, and at its best (which is much of the time) worthy of comparison with Sibelius's better incidental music – which in places it seems to foreshadow. The two fill-ups (Horneman's sole purely orchestral concert works) are much earlier, the *Ouverture héroïque* dating from 1867 and the delightful *Aladdin* (to which Horneman eventually added an opera) from three years earlier. Both are rather Mendelssohnian in tone but the earlier piece is the better proportioned piece. Michael Schønwandt proves himself yet again the perfect exponent of this repertoire.

Additional recommendation ...

…Gurre[b]. *Coupled with* **Gade** Echoes from Ossian, Op. 1[a]. **Abrahamsen** Symphony[a]. **Nørgård** Twilight[b]. **Aarhus Royal Academy of Music Orchestra /** [a]**Ole Schmidt,** [b]**Søren K. Hansen.** Kontrapunkt Ⓕ 32194 (60 minutes: DDD: 7/95).

Jacques Hotteterre
French 1674-1763

Suggested listening ...

…Airs et Brunettes. *Coupled with works by* **Leclair, Blavet, Rameau** and **M. La Barre Rachel Brown** (fl); **Mark Caudle** (viol); **James Johnstone** (hpd). Chandos Chaconne CHAN0544 (2/94). ✐

Alan Hovhaness
American 1911-

New review

Hovhaness Symphony No. 2, Op. 132[a], "Mysterious Mountain".
Prokofiev Lieutenant Kijé – Suite, Op. 60[b].
Stravinsky Divertimento from "La baiser de la fée"[a]. **Chicago Symphony Orchestra / Fritz Reiner.** RCA Victor Living Stereo Ⓜ 09026 61957-2 (64 minutes: ADD: 9/95). Items marked [a] new to UK, [b]VICS1280 (2/68). Recorded 1957-8.

Reiner's mastery is everywhere in evidence, from the hymn-like cadences of Hovhaness's wholesome though skilfully crafted Symphony to the fairy-tale excitement of *Kijé*'s "Troika". The Chicago

Symphony play like a generously augmented chamber ensemble, with delicately tapered strings, sweet-toned woodwinds, impeccable brass (surely the most subtly voiced horns on disc) and a rhythmically alert but never over-zealous percussion section. Reiner's Straussian credentials are particularly telling wherever musical lines converge – in Hovhaness's discursive celesta/harp embellishments, for example, or the dreamlike review in *Kijé*'s "Burial" – while the *Fairy's Kiss* "Divertimento" has a positively Mozartian elegance. Try, by way of sampling-points, Stravinsky's "Scherzo" and "Pas de Deux"; or, if you've ever doubted Reiner's capacity for tenderness, put on the closing half-minute of *Kijé*'s "Romance". There's impressive virtuosity, too – especially in the Nielsenesque string flurries that open Hovhaness's hectic *Allegro vivo*. Musically, this is a superb programme and the performance of *Mysterious Mountain* an American 'classic' – is unmissable. Similarly, the Stravinsky is in a class of its own and *Lieutenant Kijé* is superbly executed. This RCA Living Stereo transfer is fairly good, save for a momentary tape glitch 0'47" into Hovhaness's opening *Andante* and a fair degree of tape noise. The overall sound is more hollow than one remembers from the old LPs, but there's ample clarity and impressive channel separation. All in all, in a priceless CD – certainly from a musical stand-point.

Additional recommendations ...

..."Mysterious mountain". Lousadzak, Op. 48[a]. **L. Harrison** Symphony No. 2, "Elegiac". [a]**Keith Jarrett** (pf); **American Composers Orchestra / Dennis Russell Davies.** MusicMasters Ⓕ 7021-2 (67 minutes: DDD: 5/93).

..."Mysterious mountain". Prayer of St Gregory, Op. 62*b*. Prelude and Quadruple Fugue, Op. 128. And God Created Great Whales, Op. 229 No. 1. Alleluia and Fugue, Op. 40*b*. Celestial Fantasy, Op. 44. **Seattle Symphony Orchestra / Gerard Schwarz.** Delos Ⓕ DE3157 (63 minutes: DDD: 7/94).

Hovhaness Mountains and Rivers without End, Op. 225. Symphony No. 6, Op. 173, "The Celestial Gate". Prayer of St Gregory, Op. 62*b*[a]. Haroutiun, Op. 71 – Aria[a]. Return and Rebuild the Desolate Places, Op. 213[a]. [a]**Chris Gekker** (tpt); **Manhattan Chamber Orchestra / Richard Auldon Clark.** Koch International Classics Ⓕ 37221-2 (63 minutes: DDD: 7/94).

In *Mountains and Rivers without End* (1968), sliding solo trombone writing alternates with passages of canonic woodwind bird-song and exotic, percussion-laden promises of the Orient (the work was, in fact, originally inspired by a Korean landscape painting). Quite what it all adds up to is anybody's guess, but presumably that is all part of the intrigue. Hovhaness's beautifully judged string-writing lends an enchanting serenity to both the *Prayer of St Gregory* and *Haroutiun* ("Resurrection"), whilst the Sixth Symphony contains perhaps the most consistently memorable melodic material of all the works gathered here; certainly, it possesses a spiritual glow and sense of enchantment to which many will readily warm. The disc concludes with *Return and Rebuild the Desolate Places*, a ten-minute concerto for trumpet and wind band. Again, the scoring is deceptively assured, with some hauntingly luminous woodwind sonorities. These are all immaculately-turned, highly responsive performances from the Manhattan Chamber Orchestra, Richard Auldon Clark and Chris Gekker (with his astonishingly poised solo trumpet contributions). The recording is beautifully transparent.

Hovhaness Four Bagatelles, Op. 30. String Quartets – No. 1, Op. 8, "Jupiter"; No. 3, Op. 208 No. 1, "Reflections on my Childhood"; No. 4, Op. 208 No. 2, "The Ancient Tree". Suite from String Quartet No. 2 – Gamelan in Sosi Style; Spirit Murmur; Hymn.

Z. Long Song of the Ch'in. **Shanghai Quartet** (WeiGang Li, HongGang Li, vns; Zheng Wang, va; James Wilson, vc). Delos Ⓕ DE3162 (69 minutes: DDD: 3/95). Recorded 1994.　　ⒼⒼ

The likeable First Quartet of 1936 boasts, like Mozart's *Jupiter* Symphony, a four-part fugue of impressive rigour (hence the work's subtitle). In fact, this movement, along with the opening "Prelude", was later reworked for full orchestra into the *Prelude and Quadruple Fugue*, whilst the vigorous fugue with which the quartet closes also crops up again in the latter half of the middle movement of the Second Symphony, *Mysterious mountain*. Next come three out of the seven pithy movements that comprise the Second Quartet from 1952: the concluding "Hymn" is a particularly affecting creation. Both the Third and Fourth Quartets share the same opus number (208) and were inspired by childhood memories. The former basks in a soothing, supplicatory glow, with occasional touches of Eastern promise (aural reminders of the composer's Armenian roots), whereas its more nostalgic companion is a sweetly lyrical essay of beguiling euphony and striking resonance. Delos's collection begins with the haunting, perfectly crafted *Four Bagatelles* (delightful miniatures, these) and ends with *Song of the Ch'in* by the Chinese composer, Zhou Long: the 'ch'in' is a traditional Chinese zither and this imaginative, fastidiously conceived piece from 1985 attempts to convey the piquant sounds of that ancient instrument through the 'modern' medium of the string quartet. These are consistently pure-toned, beautifully rapt performances from the talented young Shanghai Quartet, and Delos's sound is warm and true to match.

Further listening ...

...Symphonies – No. 22, Op. 236, "City of Light"[a]; No. 50, Op. 360, "Mount St Helens"[b]. **Seattle Symphony Orchestra /** [a]**Alan Hovhaness;** [b]**Gerard Schwarz.** Delos DE3137 (12/93). *Gramophone Editor's choice. Selected by Sounds in Retrospect.*

...Symphonies – No. 39, Op. 321[a]; No. 46, Op. 347, "To the Green Mountains". *Coupled with* **Traditional** (arr. Kim Hee-jo) Milyang Arirang. [a]**Michael Long** (gtr); **KBS Symphony Orchestra / Vakhtang Jordania.** Koch International Classics 37208-2.

...Requiem and Resurrection, Op. 224[a]. Symphony No. 19, Op. 217, "Vishnu"[b]. [a]**North Jersey Wind Symphony Orchestra;** [b]**Sevan Philharmonic Orchestra / Alan Hovhaness.** Crystal CD805 (4/95).
...And God Created Great Whales, Op. 229 No. 1. Concerto No. 8, Op. 117. Elibris, Op. 50[a]. Alleluia and Fugue, Op. 40*b*. Anahid, Op. 57. [a]**Christine Messiter** (fl); **Philharmonia Orchestra / David Amos.** Crystal CD810 (4/95).

Elgar Howarth
British 1935-

Suggested listening ...
...Trombone Concerto. *Coupled with concertos by* **D. Bourgeois** and **Jacob Christian Lindberg** (tbn); **BBC National Orchestra of Wales / Grant Llewellyn.** BIS CD658 (10/95). *See review under D. Bourgeois; refer to the Index to Reviews.*

Herbert Howells
British 1892-1983

New review
Howells King's Herald. Paradise Rondel. Fantasia[a]. Threnody[a]. Pastoral Rhapsody. Procession. [a]**Moray Welsh** (vc); **London Symphony Orchestra / Richard Hickox.** Chandos Ⓕ CHAN9410 (58 minutes: DDD: 3/96). Recorded 1995. *Gramophone Editor's choice.*
This delightful and moving disc offers a whole sequence of orchestral works which, for whatever reason, Howells hid from the world. One reason he was shy about offering such music for performance was that it often involved such deeply personal feelings. One remembers his reluctance even to allow the most ambitious of his works, the *Hymnus Paradisi*, to be performed, and here the two *concertante* works for cello similarly reflect Howells's anguish over the death of his ten-year-old son. He wrote the longer and more complex of the two, the *Fantasia*, in 1936-7, when he was still in deep mourning, and though the predominant mood is elegiac, with occasional echoes of the Elgar Cello Concerto, there are understandable flashes of violence and anger. The *Threnody* was sketched rather earlier, and is given here in the orchestration made by Christopher Palmer for the Howells centenary concert in 1992. More direct in style and structure, it is an effective pendant to the *Fantasia*, with the two movements together forming a rhapsodic concerto lasting almost half an hour. The other major piece is the *Pastoral Rhapsody* (1923), more conventionally English except for a radiant climax with anglicized echoes of *Daphnis* and *Petrushka*. In his note Lewis Foreman speculates that Howells may have allowed the piece to be forgotten after a couple of performances, feeling that Vaughan Williams's *Pastoral Symphony* was too close a model. In fact the *Rhapsody* is totally distinct, and so is the *Paradise Rondel*, named after a Cotswold village, a generally vigorous movement dating from 1925, which over a shorter span is full of sharp contrasts, including one passage which in its addition of a piano offers clear echoes of the "Russian Dance" from *Petrushka*. Helped by rich, atmospheric sound, Richard Hickox draws performances both brilliant and warmly persuasive from the LSO, with Moray Welsh a movingly expressive soloist in the *concertante* works.

Howells Piano Quartet in A minor, Op. 21[a]. Phantasy Quartet, Op. 25. Rhapsodic Quintet, Op. 31[b]. [b]**Michael Collins** (cl); **Lyric Quartet** (Patricia Calnan, Harriet Davies, vns; Nick Barr, va; David Daniels, vc); [a]**Andrew West** (pf). Metier Ⓕ MSVCD92003 (52 minutes: DDD: 10/93). Recorded 1992.
Herbert Howells wrote a brief note about his Piano Quartet, slightly defensively justifying his having written such an effusion of untroubled lyricism in 1916, when many of his contemporaries and friends were facing death. However, the abiding impression of the work is not of evanescent nature poetry, still less a redolence of cowpats, but a wonderfully sturdy and forthright lyricism. The slightly later *Phantasy Quartet* has rather more of elegy to it, and a further development is heard in the immediately post-war *Rhapsodic Quintet*. The lyricism here is more subdued, the energy more angular, as though Howells were deliberately taming the fecundity of his invention and making his ideas really work for their living; the variety of their development is all the more striking for this. The performances have just the qualities one hopes for: the sense of a group of young performers delightedly discovering that these neglected works are not in the least dusty or faded, but strong, urgent and brilliantly crafted is palpable throughout. Good sound, too, despite a very slightly boxy piano.

Howells Three Psalm-Preludes, Set 1, Op. 32. Three Psalm-Preludes, Set 2. Three Rhapsodies, Op. 17. Rhapsody No. 4 in C major. **Stephen Cleobury** (org). Priory Ⓕ PRCD480 (75 minutes: DDD: 6/95). Played on the organ of King's College, Cambridge. Recorded 1993.
There is certainly some logic behind Priory's decision to record these pieces at King's – Howells knew the building well, having written highly effectively for its warm resonance – and Stephen Cleobury's archetypally English background (formative years, like Howells, in that Golden Triangle of Cathedral music – Gloucester/Hereford/Worcester – and organ scholar at St John's College, Cambridge, where Howells served as organist during the war years) seems to have given him a natural empathy for this music. It calls for a subtle balance of emotional introspection and undemonstrative technical fluency to capture effectively this curiously English combination of genuine heartfelt emotions masked by a

veneer of tight-lipped restraint. Cleobury's vaguely dispassionate approach, letting the music speak for itself – not to mention his absolute faithfulness to the letter of the score and his adept handling of this lovely instrument – pays handsome dividends in remarkably compelling performances of what can so often sound like mere mood music.

New review

Howells Behold, O God our defender[a]. Three Carol-Anthems. Te Deum[a]. The Scribe. Thee will I love[a]. Blessed are the dead. Even such is time. Inheritance. Haec dies. God is gone up[a]. **Finzi Singers / Paul Spicer** with [a]**Andrew Lumsden** (org). Chandos Ⓔ CHAN9458 (60 minutes: DDD: 7/96). Texts included. Recorded 1996.

The earliest offerings here comprise *Even such is time*, an unpublished effort from 1913 (labelled on the manuscript as "Student Homework for Dr Charles Wood", Howells's professor of harmony and counterpoint at the Royal College of Music), and *Haec dies*, the latter the last of eight memorable *a cappella* pieces written for Richard Terry and his Westminster Cathedral Choir during the period 1912-18. (Spicer and his admirable group have already recorded all the other surviving examples – including the amazingly assured *Mass in the Dorian Mode* – listed further on.) The ravishing *Three Carol-Anthems* (1918-20) are products of Howells's early maturity and include that much-loved gem "A spotless rose" with its breathtakingly beautiful close ("Oh Herbert! That cadence!" as Patrick Hadley used to inscribe his annual Christmas card to the composer). The motet *Blessed are the dead* dates from April 1920 and bears a dedication to the memory of Howells's father, Oliver, who had died the previous year; it is heard here in a completion by Patrick Russill (who also supplies the authoritative booklet-notes). Moving on three decades, we encounter the 1953 Coronation anthem *Behold, O God our defender*, the rousing 1958 motet *God is gone up*, as well as the two part-songs after Walter de la Mare: *Inheritance* was Howells's contribution to *A Garland for the Queen* (along with Bliss's *Aubade* and Tippett's *Dance, Clarion Air* one of the more technically demanding items in that particular collection), while *The Scribe* – an especially beguiling creation – was conceived as an eighty-fifth birthday tribute to Vaughan Williams. Finally, we have the big *Te Deum* written in 1965 for the Church of St Mary, Redcliffe, Bristol, and *Thee will I love*, a heartfelt setting from 1970 of words by Robert Bridges, "commemorating the massacre of the monks of the Abbey of Medehamstede – now Peterborough Cathedral – in AD 870". These are splendidly fervent, finely disciplined performances (one readily forgives the occasional raw sonority from the sopranos). Excellent Chandos engineering, too. A hearty recommendation.

Howells Songs. [a]**Lynne Dawson**, [b]**Catherine Pierard** (sops); [c]**John Mark Ainsley** (ten); [d]**Benjamin Luxon** (bar), **Julius Drake** (pf). Chandos Ⓔ CHAN9185/6 (two discs: 157 minutes: DDD: 8/94). Texts included.   Ⓖ

An Old Man's Lullaby[c]. Here she lies[c]. O Garlands, hanging by the doors[c]. Two South African Settings[b]. Upon a Summer's Day[b]. By the Hearth-stone[b]. Blaweary[b]. Three Folksongs[ad]. Sweet Content[a]. A Garland for De la Mare[bcd]. Peacock Pie, Op. 33[d]. Four French Chansons, Op. 29[a]. In Green Ways, Op. 43[a]. Old Meg[a]. Three Children's Songs[a]. Four Songs, Op. 22[b]. Lost love[b]. O my deir hert[b]. Come sing and dance[b]. A Mugger's Song[d]. The little boy lost[d]. The restful branches[d]. Mally O![d]. Old Skinflint[d]. King David[d]. Gavotte[c]. Flood[c]. Goddess of the Night[c].

This is an important issue and, in all ways but one, every bit as delightful as it is important. That 'but one', however, had better be faced immediately. These songs have all been recorded in a church, which would not matter if it did not *sound* like a church: but it very instantly and reverberantly does. In the quietest of the songs, such as *Sweet Content*, the effect is not unpleasant; in two of the *French Chansons* ("Sainte Catharine" and "Angèle au couvent") it is even appropriate; elsewhere it is a nuisance. The songs are all worth knowing, and together they create a strong feeling for the composer's individuality. It is not so much the confirmation of impressions already established (the moments of ecstasy, the dreamy and melancholy moods, the feeling for a soaring vocal line, especially for the soprano): it is rather the affinity with certain poets, particularly De la Mare, with all that that tells, the purposeful, well-disciplined vigour and resourcefulness of much of the writing, and (what perhaps should not come as any surprise) the thoroughly pianistic character of the piano parts. Among the 'new' songs, the long poem of James Stephens, "The Goat Path", is a marvellous setting, and so is the "Wanderer's Night Song", where the hilltops of Goethe's original take, musically, the shape of the Malverns. Lynne Dawson, with something of Isobel Baillie in her tone, sings these beautifully, as she does the French songs. Catherine Pierard has a voice very apt for many, if a little less pure in the climax of *Come sing and dance*. John Mark Ainsley phrases with fine breadth, and lets his voice ring out exultantly when the occasion arises; and it is good to have Benjamin Luxon, for there is no one like him for boldly catching at a song's character. Julian Drake plays admirably throughout, and the notes are first-rate.

Additional recommendation ...

...Gavotte. Come sing and dance. King David. Girl's Song, Op. 22 No. 4. *Coupled with songs by* **Warlock, Ireland Bridge** *and* **Holst Sarah Leonard** (sop); **Malcolm Martineau** (pf). United Recordings 88016-2 (61 minutes: DDD: 3/95).

Howells Stabat mater. **Neill Archer** (ten); **London Symphony Chorus and Orchestra / Gennadi Rozhdestvensky.** Chandos Ⓕ CHAN9314 (52 minutes: DDD: 1/95). Text and translation included. Recorded 1994. Ⓖ

Those who feel that the visionary, but definitely Anglican radiance of *Hymnus Paradisi* (1938) encapsulates the essential Howells may well wish to reconsider on hearing this first recording of the *Stabat mater*, his last large-scale work, finished and first performed in 1965 when he was 73. It is unquestionably a remarkable and distinctive piece, totally characteristic of this composer in his late maturity and owing nothing at all to earlier settings. It is hard to think of a more passionate setting of the text, or (surprisingly for a composer *par excellence* of church music) one which removes it further from its ritual roots. *The Times* review of the 1965 première commented that "this is not at all music in the contemplative pastoral vein such as Howells has been associated with ... Howells' choir and orchestra fix on the element of ecstasy through physical pain that the music suggests". The vocal writing is extremely melismatic with searingly sustained climaxes, the harmony deeply coloured (on occasion even saturated) with chromaticisms and added notes, the orchestration purple-hued but flecked with copper and gold. The London Symphony Chorus are not always as buoyant, technically, as they can be, especially in matters of pitch in soft music. The sopranos sound under-balanced by the engineers, or else they simply lack attack and projection. However, Rozhdestvensky's impulsive direction (even when not entirely judicious) always sounds spontaneous, and he makes sure that Howells's beautiful mixing of orchestral pastel shades makes as great an impression as the sustained incandescence of the tuttis. His approach to the fractured funeral marches, which are such a feature of the work's progress, is shadowy and nightmarish rather than plainly ominous. He allows himself plenty of elbow-room to uncover many moments of tender delicacy as well as delivering towering climaxes (to which, it should be granted, the chorus always rise). Neill Archer dominates the performance with singing of real ardour, compassion and poetry. The general character of the recording is full-blooded – a warm concert-hall acoustic – with the wind solos (relished by the LSO principals) given plenty of presence.

Howells Requiem[a]. Take him, earth, for cherishing.
Martin Mass for Double Chorus. [a]**Sally Barber** (sop); [a]**Julia Field** (mez); [a]**Mark Johnstone** (ten); [a]**Andrew Angus** (bass); **Vasari / Jeremy Backhouse.** Cala United Ⓕ 88033 (56 minutes: DDD: 12/94). Recorded 1994. Ⓖ

There is no shortage of recordings of either of the major pieces here, but why has no one else thought of coupling them together? Both are private works, not really intended for performance. Howells wrote the Requiem to exorcize his grief at the death of his son, and only at the very end of his life allowed it to be published. Martin described his Mass as "something between God and myself, and of no concern to anyone else". It should ideally be premièred, he thought, in a liturgical context and anonymously, though he wryly reflected that any such mystification would merely draw unsuitable attention to it; so he kept it to himself for close on 40 years. Both now look like crucial works in each composer's development. Howells's Requiem is not only the source of his masterpiece, the *Hymnus Paradisi*, but also of much that is characteristic in his later music, its radiance (sometimes shadowed) and its long expressive lines. Martin's Mass is not only a research laboratory into the problems of setting religious texts (how he enjoys 'dramatizing' the various sections of the *Credo*, using elaborate choral coloratura in the *Gloria*, inventing a surprising but effective staccato imagery to convey a heaven and earth filled with dazzling glory in the *Sanctus*!) but also into the neo-classical element that seasoned his later serialism. Although they make a fascinating coupling, they demand quite different types of singing; so again does Howells's much later motet, with its more public gestures and its broader span. Vasari succeed admirably. The difficulties of the Howells Requiem are exemplified in the image of light (a wonderful Howells chord, needing absolutely precise pitching and balance) and the expressive intensification of line that follows it in the fifth movement. It is beautifully done, but the singers also have the athletic virtuosity for Martin's twining melismas, the hurtling excitement of his "et resurrexit". This is choral singing of a high order, in short, and it gains from a very spacious and natural recording.

Additional recommendations ...

...Requiem[a]. Take him, earth, for cherishing. **Vaughan Williams** Mass in G minor[b]. Te Deum in G major (1928)[c]. [a]**Mary Seers** (sop); [ab]**Michael Chance** (alto); [ab]**Philip Salmon** (ten); [ab]**Jonathan Best** (bass); **Corydon Singers / Matthew Best** with [c]**Thomas Trotter** (org). Hyperion Ⓕ CDA66076 (60 minutes: ADD: 10/87). *See review under Vaughan Williams; refer to the Index to Reviews.* ⒼⒼ

...Requiem. A Sequence for St Michael. The House of the Mind. **Vaughan Williams** Prayer to the Father of Heaven. A Vision of Aeroplanes. Lord, Thou has been our Refuge. **Finzi Singers / Paul Spicer** with **Harry Bickett** (org). Chandos Ⓕ CHAN9019 (67 minutes: DDD: 5/92).

Further listening ...

...Piano Concerto No. 2 in C minor[a]. Three Dances, Op. 7[b]. Concerto for Strings. [a]**Kathryn Stott** (pf); [b]**Malcolm Stewart** (vn); **Royal Liverpool Philharmonic Orchestra / Vernon Handley.** Hyperion CDA66610 (3/93). Ⓖ

...Violin Sonatas – No. 1, Op. 18; No. 2, Op. 26; No. 3, Op. 38. Cradle Song, Op. 9 No. 1. Three Pieces, Op. 28. **Paul Barritt** (vn); **Catherine Edwards** (pf). Hyperion Ⓕ CDA66665 (3/94).

...Oboe Sonata. *Coupled with works by* **Finzi** *and* **Patterson** **Nicholas Daniel** (ob); **Julius Drake** (pf). Léman Classics LC44801 (10/93).

...Collegium regale – canticles. Six Pieces for Organ – No. 3, Master Tallis's Testament[a]. Like as the hart. Behold, O God our defender. Psalm-Preludes, Set 2 – No. 1, De profundis[a]. Take him, earth, for cherishing. St Paul's – Canticles. [a]**Christopher Dearnley** (org); **St Paul's Cathedral Choir, London / John Scott.** Hyperion CDA66260 (9/88).

...Gadabout. Sarum sketches. Three Pieces, Op. 14. Slow Dance (Double the Cape). Cobler's Hornpipe. Snapshots, Op. 30. Chosen Tune. Lambert's Clavichord, Op. 41 – Lambert's Fireside; Hughes' Ballet; De la Mare's Pavane; Sir Hugh's Galliard. Musica sine Nomine. Sonatina. **Margaret Fingerhut** (pf). Chandos CHAN9273 (9/94).

...Lambert's Clavichord, Op. 41. Howells' Clavichord, Books 1 and 2. **John McCabe** (pf). Hyperion CDA66689 (8/94). *Gramophone Editor's choice.*

...Mass in the Dorian Mode. Salve regina. O salutaris Hostia. Sweetest of sweets. Come, my soul. Let all the world in every corner sing. Nunc dimittis. Regina caeli. *Coupled with* **Stevens** Mass for double choir. **Finzi Singers / Paul Spicer.** Chandos CHAN9021 (12/92).

...Missa Sabrinensis. **Janice Watson** (sop); **Della Jones** (mez); **Martyn Hill** (ten); **Donald Maxwell** (bar); **London Symphony Chorus and Orchestra / Gennadi Rozhdestvensky.** Chandos CHAN9348 (6/95). *Gramophone Editor's choice.*

...Hymnus Paradisi[a]. An English Mass. [a]**Julie Kennard** (sop); [a]**John Mark Ainsley** (ten); **Royal Liverpool Philharmonic Choir and Orchestra / Vernon Handley.** Hyperion CDA66488 (5/92).

...Collegium Regale – Te Deum; Jubilate. *Coupled with works by* **Moeran, Elgar, Statham, S.S. Wesley, Britten** and **Gladstone** Norwich Cathedral Choir / **Michael Nicholas** with **Neil Taylor** (org). Priory PRCD470 (10/94).

...Evening Service in G major. *Coupled with works by* **Leighton, Gibbons, G. Ives, S. Watson, Stanford** and **Dyson** Lichfield Cathedral Choir / **Andrew Lumsden** with **Mark Shepherd, Nigel Potts** (orgs). Priory PRCD505 (10/95). *See review in the Collections section; refer to the Index to Reviews.*

...A Dirge. *Coupled with works by* **Elgar, Vaughan Williams, Bax, Delius, Warlock, Britten** and **Holst** London Madrigal Singers / **Christopher Bishop**; Baccholian Singers of London; Philip Jones Brass Ensemble; English Chamber Orchestra / **Ian Humphris.** EMI British Composers CMS5 65123-2 (2/96). *See review in the Collections section; refer to the Index to Reviews.*

Klaus Huber   Swiss 1924-

Suggested listening ...

...Transpositio ad infinitum. *Coupled with works by* **Britten, C. Halffter, Berio, Lutosławski, Dutilleux, Beck, Henze, Fortner, Ginastera, Boulez** and **Holliger** Patrick and Thomas Demenga (vcs); Cello Ensemble / **Jürg Wyttenbach.** ECM New Series 445 234-2 (8/95).

Johann Hummel   Austrian 1778-1837

Hummel Piano Concertos – A minor, Op. 85; B minor, Op. 89. **Stephen Hough** (pf); **English Chamber Orchestra / Bryden Thomson.** Chandos Ⓔ CHAN8507 (66 minutes: DDD: 4/87). *Gramophone Award Winner 1987.*   ⒼⒼ

This is a staggering disc of Hummel's piano concertos played by Stephen Hough. The most obvious comparison is with the piano concertos of Chopin, but whereas those works rely on the grace and panache of the piano line to redeem an often lacklustre orchestral role, the Hummel works have finely conceived orchestral writing and certainly no shortage of original ideas. The piano part is formidable, combining virtuosity of a very high order indeed with a vigour and athleticism that does much to redress Hummel's somewhat tarnished reputation. The A minor is probably the better known of the two works here, with a thrilling rondo finale, but the B minor is no less inventive with some breathtaking writing in the piano's upper registers. This disc makes strong demands to be heard: inventive and exciting music, a masterly contribution from Stephen Hough, fine orchestral support from the ever sympathetic ECO under Bryden Thomson and, last but not least, a magnificent Chandos recording.

Further listening ...

...Trumpet Concerto in E flat major. *Coupled with works by* **Jolivet, Tomasi** and **Haydn** Sergei Nakariakov (tpt); Lausanne Chamber Orchestra / Jésus López-Cobos. Teldec 4509-90846-2 (10/93). *See review in the Collections section; refer to the Index to Reviews.*

...Trumpet Concerto in E flat major. *Coupled with works by* **A. Sandoval, L. Mozart** and **Arutiunian** Arturo Sandoval (tpt); **London Symphony Orchestra / Luis Haza.** GRP Classical GRK75002 (1/95).

...Trumpet Concerto in E flat major. *Coupled with works by* **Haydn, Neruda, F. Weber** and **C.F.C. Fasch** John Wallace (tpt); **Philharmonia Orchestra / Christopher Warren-Green.** Nimbus NI7016 (2/95). *See review in the Collections section; refer to the Index to Reviews.*

... Trumpet Concerto in E flat major. *Coupled with works by* **Haydn, Hertel** and **A. Marcello** Maurice André (tpt); **Franz Liszt Chamber Orchestra / János Rolla.** EMI CDC5 55231-2 (7/95).

...Septet in D minor, Op. 74. *Coupled with* **Berwald** Septet in B flat major. **Nash Ensemble.** CRD CRD3344 (6/89).

...Clarinet Quintet in E flat major. *Coupled with* **Reicha** Clarinet Quintet in B flat major, Op. 89.
Weber Clarinet Quintet in B flat major, J182. **Charles Neidich** (cl); **L'Archibudelli.** Sony Classical
SK57968 (9/95). ✐

...Piano Quintet in E flat major, Op. 87. *Coupled with* **Schubert** Piano Quintet in A major, D667,
"Trout". **Schubert Ensemble of London.** Helios CDH88010 (6/90).

...Violin/Flute Sonata in D major, Op. 50 (trans. Eichler). Viola Sonata E flat major, Op. 5 No. 3
(trans. Eichler). **Ralph Holmes** (vn); **Richard Burnett** (fp); Amon Ra CD-SAR12 (7/87).

...Viola Sonata in E flat major, Op. 5 No. 3. *Coupled with* **C. Stamitz** Viola Sonata in B flat major.
Dittersdorf Viola Sonata in E flat major. **Vanhal** Viola Sonata in E flat major. **Anna Barbara
Duetschler** (va); **Ursula Duetschler** (fp). Claves CD50-9502 (11/95). ✐

Englebert Humperdinck
German 1854-1921

Humperdinck Hänsel und Gretel. **Jennifer Larmore** (mez) Hänsel; **Ruth Ziesak** (sop) Gretel;
Hildegard Behrens (sop) Mother; **Bernd Weikl** (bar) Father; **Rosemary Joshua** (sop) Sandman;
Christine Schäfer (sop) Dew Fairy; **Hanna Schwarz** (mez) Witch; **Tölz Boys' Choir; Bavarian
Radio Symphony Orchestra / Donald Runnicles.** Teldec Ⓕ 4509-94549-2 (two discs: 103 minutes:
DDD: 1/95). Notes, text and translation included. Recorded 1994.

Donald Runnicles here makes a very impressive recording début in a major opera set. Like EMI's
version with Tate, this one was recorded by the Bavarian Radio Symphony Orchestra in the
Herkulessaal in Munich, and with the Tölz Boys' Choir, yet thanks to Runnicles as well as to the
engineers, the sound is noticeably different. In place of Tate's Brucknerian glow – as in the very
opening – Runnicles has a lighter touch, regularly favouring faster speeds than do any of those
conductors listed below. The lightness and refinement of the playing brings transparent textures and
the most delicate *pianissimos*, with gentler markings observed more closely than usual, a point that
comes out at the very start of the Overture. Far from reducing the impact of the performance, the
lightness goes with an element of fantasy delightfully in keeping with the fairy-tale atmosphere.
Though the choice of singers for the two title-roles in all the sets listed has been inspired, the
emphasis here is more than ever on fresh, youthful voices. So it was too with Barbara Bonney and
Anne Sofie von Otter on the Tate set, but here the distinction between boy and girl is if anything
even more sharply drawn. Ruth Ziesak as Gretel and Jennifer Larmore as Hänsel are, above all,
natural-sounding, with little or no feeling of mature opera-singers pretending to be children, yet
with no sense of strain and none of the edginess which occasionally afflicted the otherwise delightful
partnership of Edita Gruberová and Ann Murray in the Davis/Philips set. Hanna Schwarz's Witch
is sharply sinister without being too frightening. Schwarz was the Mother on the Tate set and here
Hildegard Behrens is comparably strong and characterful, with Bernd Weikl firm and dark as the
Father, while young voices are chosen for the two incidental roles of the Sandman and Dew Fairy.
All the rival versions have points in their favour, with Davis more glowing than any, though with a
less winning cast, and with Karajan subtler than the others in his rhythmic and tonal shading. Yet,
this Teldec set for many will be a first recommendation. It brings, incidentally, a fascinating
supplement in a brief orchestral coda, just over a minute long, which Humperdinck wrote in 1894
for a production of the opera in Dessau with Cosima Wagner as director. Ingeniously he has the
Dessau national anthem set in counterpoint against various themes from the work, with toy
trumpets providing a commentary.

Additional recommendations ...

...**Soloists; Tölz Boys' Choir; Bavarian Radio Symphony Orchestra / Jeffrey Tate.** EMI Ⓕ CDS7
54022-2 (two discs: 103 minutes: DDD).

...**Soloists; Loughton High School for Girls and Bancroft's School Choirs; Philharmonia Orchestra /
Herbert von Karajan.** EMI mono Ⓜ CMS7 69293-2* (two discs: 108 minutes: ADD: 4/88).

...**Soloists; Cologne Opera Children's Chorus; Cologne Gurzenich Orchestra / Sir John Pritchard.**
CBS Masterworks Ⓜ M2K79217 (two discs: 108 minutes: ADD: 11/88).

...**Soloists; Dresden Staatskapelle / Sir Colin Davis.** Philips Ⓕ 438 013-2PH2 (two discs:
103 minutes: DDD: 10/93). *Selected by Sounds in Retrospect.*

...Hänsel und Gretel[a]. **Weber** Abu Hassan[b]. **Soloists;** [a]**Mozart Chorus;** [a]women's voices of the
Deutsche Oper Chorus, Berlin; [b]**chorus; Berlin Radio Symphony Orchestra /** [a]**Artur Rother,**
[b]**Leopold Ludwig.** Preiser mono Ⓕ 90209* (two discs: 145 minutes: ADD: 3/96).

Further listening ...

...Shakespeare Suite Nos. 1 and 2. Overture No. 2 from "Die Heirat wider Willen". Humoresque in
E major. **Bamberg Symphony Orchestra / Karl Anton Rickenbacher.** Koch Schwann 311972
(4/95).   Ⓖ

William Yeates Hurlstone
British 1876-1906

Suggested listening ...

...Variations on an original theme. The Magic Mirror Suite. Variations on a Hungarian air. **London
Philharmonic Orchestra / Nicholas Braithwaite.** Lyrita SRCD208 (4/93).

Karel Husa

Czechoslovakian/American 1921-

Suggested listening ...
...Fresque. Reflections, "Symphony No. 2". Music for Prague 1968. **Slovak Radio Symphony Orchestra / Barry Kolman.** Marco Polo 8 223640 (5/95).

Jacques Ibert

French 1890-1962

Ibert Divertissement.
Milhaud Le boeuf sur le toit, Op. 58. La création du monde, Op. 81.
Poulenc Les biches – Suite. **Ulster Orchestra / Yan Pascal Tortelier.** Chandos Ⓕ CHAN9023
(68 minutes: DDD: 9/92). Recorded 1991.
Here is 1920s French music directed by a conductor who is completely in the spirit of it, and plenty of spirit there is, too. Except for Ibert's *Divertissement*, this is ballet music, and that work too originated in the theatre as incidental music for Eugène Labiche's farce *The Italian Straw Hat*. Poulenc's suite from *Les biches*, written for Diaghilev's ballet company and first heard in Monte Carlo, is unfailingly fresh and bouncy and stylishly played here although Chandos's warm recording, good though it is, takes some edge off the trumpet tone; the genial nature of it all makes us forget that it is a unique mix of eighteenth-century *galanterie*, Tchaikovskian lilt and Poulenc's own inimitable street-Parisian sophistication and charm. As for Ibert's piece, this is uproariously funny in an unbuttoned way, and the gorgeously vulgar trombone in the Waltz and frantic police whistle in the finale are calculated to make you laugh out loud. Milhaud's *Le boeuf sur le toit* also has Parisian chic and was originally a kind of music-hall piece, composed to a scenario by Cocteau. It was while attending a performance of it in London in 1920 that the composer first heard the American jazz orchestra that, together with a later experience of new Orleans jazzmen playing "from the darkest corners of the Negro soul" (as he later expressed it) that prompted him to compose his masterly ballet, *La création du monde*, in which a deep-rooted African voice seems to speak through western instruments. Tortelier and his orchestra understand this strangely powerful music no less than the other pieces. This is a most desirable disc.
Additional recommendations ...
...Divertissement. **Ravel** Le tombeau de Couperin. **Debussy** Danse sacrée et danse profane[a].
Fauré Dolly Suite, Op. 56. [a]**Osian Ellis** (hp); **Academy of St Martin in the Fields / Sir Neville Marriner.** ASV Ⓕ CDDCA517 (60 minutes: ADD: 2/85)
...Divertissement. **Saint-Saëns** Danse macabre, Op. 40. Le rouet d'Omphale, Op. 31. **Bizet** Jeux d'enfants. **Berlioz** Le carnaval romain, Op. 9. Le corsaire, Op. 21. **Paris Conservatoire Orchestra / Jean Martinon.** Decca The Classic Sound Ⓜ 448 571-2DCS (64 minutes: ADD: 2/96).
Further listening ...
...Flute Concerto. *Coupled with works by* **Honegger, Nielsen** and **Poulenc** Jennifer Stinton (fl); **Scottish Chamber Orchestra / Steuart Bedford.** Collins Classics 1210-2 (8/91).
...Flute Concerto. *Coupled with works by* **Martin, Nielsen** and **Bernstein** Michael Faust (fl); **Cologne Radio Symphony Orchestra / Serge Baudo.** Capriccio 10 495 (12/94). *See review in the Collections section; refer to the Index to Reviews.*
...Bacchanale. Bostoniana. Escales. Flute Concerto[a]. Louisville Concerto. Suite Symphonique, "Paris". Hommage à Mozart. [a]**Timothy Hutchins** (fl); **Montreal Symphony Orchestra / Charles Dutoit.** Decca 440 332-2DH (6/94).
...Symphonie Concertante. *Coupled with works by* **Françaix, Satie** and **R. Strauss** John de Lancie (ob); **London Symphony Orchestra / André Previn.** RCA Victor Gold Seal GD87989 (12/91). *See review in the Collections section; refer to the Index to Reviews.* Ⓖ
...Concertino da camera. *Coupled with works by* **Debussy, Glazunov, R.R. Bennett** and **Villa-Lobos** John Harle (sax), **Academy of St Martin in the Fields / Sir Neville Marriner.** EMI CDC7 54301-2 (1/92). *See review in the Collections section; refer to the Index to Reviews.*
...Aria[a]. Entr'acte[a]. Histoires[a]. Two interludes from "Le burlador"[a]. Jeux[a]. Deux mouvements[a]. Trois pièces brèves[a]. Pièce pour flûte seule. Le jardinier de Samos[a]. **Toke Lund Christiansen** (fl); [a]**Collegium Musicum Soloists.** Kontrapunkt 32202 (12/95).
...Film Suites – Macbeth; Golgotha[b]. Don Quichotte – Chanson de Sancho[a]. Chanson de Don Quichotte[a]. [a]**Henry Kiichli** (bass); [b]**Jacques Tchamkerten** (ondes martenot); **Bratislava Radio Symphony Orchestra / Adriano.** Marco Polo 8 223287 (3/91).
...Trois pièces brèves. *Coupled with works by* **Françaix, Fauré, Damase, Pierné** and **Poulenc** **Reykjavik Wind Quintet.** Chandos CHAN9362 (10/95).

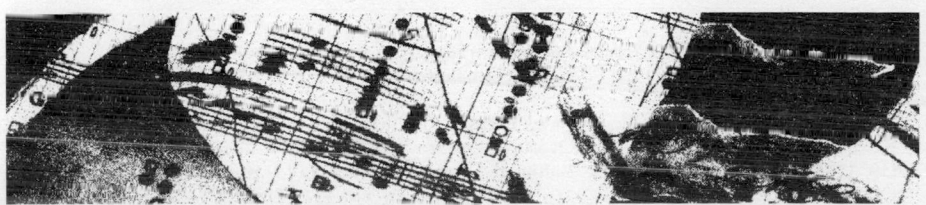

Vincent d'Indy
French 1851-1931

d'Indy Concerto for Piano, Flute, Cello and Strings, Op. 89[abde].
Fumet La nuit[e].
Honegger Le dit des jeux du monde[bce]. [a]**Patrick Dechorgnat** (pf); [b]**Jean Ferrandis** (fl); [c]**Hervé Noël** (tpt); [d]**Jean-Jacques Wiederker** (vc); [e]**Jean-Jacques Wiederker Chamber Orchestra / Frédéric Bouaniche.** Koch Schwann Ⓟ 310652 (56 minutes: DDD: 6/95).

Many collectors can remember when it was impossible to buy recordings of all Mahler's symphonies or Debussy's *Préludes*, so one cannot fail to wonder at the enterprise and perhaps financial boldness of today's smaller record companies. Each work offered here by Koch Schwann is new to the catalogue, indeed, the name of Fumet is probably unfamiliar to most people. A pupil of Franck, his radical politics seem to have hindered his career, although d'Indy supported his work. His symphonic poem for strings, *La nuit*, is atmospheric and the performance sensitive, although the rich textures are not fully served by the relatively small sound of this orchestra. Fumet reflects the more hothouse fervour of his teacher, and there is also some affinity with Szymanowski; if ultimately this music offers more sensuality than substance or shape, it has some interest and receives a committed performance. D'Indy's Concerto is surprisingly neo-classical, with little of the Franckian richness that one might expect, and this work of 1927 was his last orchestral piece. This again receives a sympathetic performance, although the music lacks weight and fails to make a strong impression. But admirers of this composer should snap up this disc while they can. The same applies to *aficionados* of Honegger, whose early (1918) incidental music to a mystery play called *Le dit des jeux du monde* receives its first recording in the form of a suite of six pieces. They are scored for 14 instruments including a bouteillophone (tuned bottles), and the third piece, "Mountain and Stones", is for percussion only. This suite is the most interesting music here and the performance is a strong one. The recording is clear, though not very atmospheric.

---

d'Indy Symphony No. 3, Op. 70, "de bello gallico". Saugefleurie, Op. 21. Souvenirs, Op. 62.
Strasbourg Philharmonic Orchestra / Theodore Guschlbauer. Auvidis Valois Ⓟ V4686 (72 minutes: DDD: 9/93). Recorded 1992.   Ⓖ

The real find here is *Souvenirs* (1906), a haunting, imaginatively scored tone-poem that starts with what sounds like a ghostly premonition of Shostakovich's Eleventh Symphony, then proceeds to varieties of chromatic lyricism that recall the Debussy of *Pelléas* and the lone Symphony of Ernest Chausson. The Third Symphony, a highly inventive commentary on aspects of the Great War, suggests a specific programme and is an ambiguous, loosely constructed piece that effectively extends one's limited experience of its composer. Theodore Guschlbauer's broadly sympathetic readings are more appreciative of the music's *lent et calm* than its *vif et agité*. Still, it's a gripping programme and essential listening for all incurable romantics.

Further listening ...
...L'étranger – Prélude, Act 2[a]. Six tableaux de voyage, Op. 36[a]. Fantaisie sur des thèmes populaires français, Op. 31[b]. Fervaal – Prélude[a]. Saugefleurie, Op. 21[a]. [b]**Philippe Cousu** (ob); **Württemberg Philharmonic Orchestra / [a]Gilles Nopre, [b]Jean-Marc Burfin.** Marco Polo 8 223659 (1/95).
...Symphonie sur un chant montagnard français in G major, Op. 25. *Coupled with works by* **Franck** Symphony in D minor. **Jean-Yves Thibaudet** (pf); **Montreal Symphony Orchestra / Charles Dutoit.** Decca 430 278-2DH (1/92). *See review under Franck; refer to the Index to Reviews.*   Ⓖ
...Symphonie sur un chant montagnard français in G major, Op. 25. *Coupled with works by* **Fauré** and **Franck** François-Joël Thiollier (pf); **National Symphony Orchestra of Ireland / Antonio de Almeida.** Naxos 8 550754 (1/95). *See review under Fauré; refer to the Index to Reviews.*
...Symphonie sur un chant montagnard français in G major, Op. 25[b]. *Coupled with* **Berlioz** Harold in Italy, Op. 16[a]. [a]**William Primrose** (va); [b]**Nicole Henriot-Schweitzer** (pf); **Boston Symphony Orchestra / Charles Munch.** RCA Victor Gold Seal 09026 62582-2 (5/95).
...String Quartets – No. 1 in D major, Op. 35; No. 2 in E major, Op. 45. **Kodály Quartet.** Marco Polo 8 223140 (10/91).
...Prélude in E flat minor, Op. 66. *Coupled with works by* **R. Vierne, Barié, Roussel, Honegger, Dupré, Langlais** and **L. Vierne** Marie-Bernadette Dufourcet (org). Priory PRCD422 (6/95). *See review in the Collections section; refer to the Index to Reviews.*

Mikhail Ippolitov-Ivanov
USSR/American 1859-1935

Suggested listening ...
...Caucasian Sketches, Op. 10. *Coupled with* **Khachaturian** Symphony No. 3 in C major, "Simfoniya-poema". Triumphal Poem. **BBC Philharmonic Orchestra / Fedor Glushchenko.** Chandos CHAN9321 (5/95).
...Caucasian Sketches, Op. 10. *Coupled with* **Glinka** Ruslan and Ludmilla – Overture. **Rimsky-Korsakov** Russian Easter Festival Overture, Op. 36. **Tchaikovsky** Francesca da Rimini, Op. 32. Eugene Onegin – Polonaise. **Baltimore Symphony Orchestra / David Zinman.** Telarc CD80378 (12/95).

...Yar-khmel', Op. 1, "Spring Overture". Symphonic Scherzo, Op. 2. From Ossian's songs, Op. 56.
Jubilee March. Armenian Rhapsody on National Themes, Op. 48[b]. An Episode from the Life of
Schubert, Op. 61[a]. [a]Miroslav Dvorský (ten); [b]Viktor Simčisko (vn); Bratislava Radio Symphony
Orchestra / Donald Johanos. Marco Polo 8 223629 (10/94).

John Ireland   British 1879-1962

New review

Ireland A Downland Suite (arr. Ireland and Bush). Orchestral Poem in A minor. Concertino
pastorale. Two Symphonic Studies (arr. Bush). City of London Sinfonia / Richard Hickox.
Chandos Ⓕ CHAN9376 (64 minutes: DDD: 11/95). Recorded 1994.

There is little to choose between David Garforth's excellent 1983 version of the fresh-faced *Downland
Suite* and Hickox's new account, though it is the latter who extracts the slightly greater expressive
intensity from the glorious second movement "Elegy". The *Concertino pastorale* is another fine work,
boasting a most eloquent opening "Eclogue" and tenderly poignant "Threnody", towards the end of
which Ireland seems to allow himself a momentary recollection of the haunting opening phrase of his
much earlier orchestral prelude, *The Forgotten Rite*. In 1969 Ireland's pupil, Geoffrey Bush, arranged
two sections of the score for the 1946 film *The Overlanders* which were not incorporated into the 1971
concert suite compiled by Sir Charles Mackerras. The resulting, finely wrought *Two Symphonic Studies*
were recorded many years ago by Sir Adrian Boult for Lyrita – no longer available – and Hickox
proves just as sympathetic an interpreter, whereas the *Orchestral Poem* in A minor is here receiving its
recorded début. This is a youthful essay, completed in 1904, some three years after Ireland's studies
with Stanford. It is a worthy rather than especially inspiring effort, with hardly a glimpse of the mature
manner to come, save for some particularly beautiful string writing. Hickox makes out a decent enough
case for it. However, with rich, refined Chandos sound, this remains a most enjoyable collection overall.

Additional recommendation ...

A Downland Suite. The Holy Boy. Meditation on Keble's Rogotation Hymn. Bridge Suite, H93.
English Chamber Orchestra / David Garforth. Chandos Ⓕ CHAN8390 (47 minutes: DDD: 5/87).

New review

Ireland Violin Sonatas – No. 1 in D minor[ad]; No. 2 in A minor[ad]. Fantasy-Sonata in E flat
major[ae]. Cello Sonata in G minor[cd]. The Holy Boy[cd]. Phantasie Trio in A minor[bcd]. Trio No. 2 in
E major[bcd]. Trio No. 3 in E major[bcd]. [a]Gervase de Peyer (cl); [b]Lydia Mordkovitch (vn); [c]Karine
Georgian (vc); [d]Ian Brown, [a] Gwenneth Pryor (pfs). Chandos Ⓕ CHAN9377/8 (two discs:
147 minutes: DDD: 12/95). Item marked [ae] from ABRD1237 (11/87). Recorded 1982-3 and 1993.

This valuable two-disc collection from Chandos usefully fills several gaps in the current John Ireland
discography. Especially welcome here is the red-blooded rendering of the superb Second Violin
Sonata. Premièred in 1917 to enormous acclaim by Albert Sammons and William Murdoch, the
sonata secured the composer's reputation virtually overnight, not surprisingly, given its striking
confidence, powerful sweep and wealth of memorable ideas. The passionate opening *Allegro* is
especially compelling, its dark-hued turbulence grippingly conveyed. The second disc opens with the
fine Cello Sonata of 1923. These admirable artists capture well this music's wistful, brooding
atmosphere and are especially sensitive in the slow movement, a haunting evocation inspired by the
landscape of the composer's beloved Sussex Downs. The early single-movement *Phantasie Trio* is a
most likeable piece: fluent, resourceful and brimming with self-confidence. By contrast, the Second
Trio of 1917 inhabits a far more troubled world. The appalling carnage of the First World War deeply
distressed Ireland and it is surely not too fanciful to hear the relentless march of troops in the grim
tread of the *Allegro giusto* section. These whole-hearted, affectionate performances receive
characteristically ripe, realistic Chandos engineering. A very rewarding set.

Further listening ...

...Piano Concerto in E flat major[a]. Legend[a]. Mai-Dun. [a]Eric Parkin (pf); London Philharmonic
Orchestra / Bryden Thomson. Chandos CHAN8461 (1/87).

...Piano Concerto in E flat major. *Coupled with* Bridge Phantasm. Walton Sinfonia concertante
(original version). Kathryn Stott (pf); Royal Philharmonic Orchestra / Vernon Handley. Conifer
CDCF175 (1/90).   Ⓖ

...Piano Concerto in E flat major. *Coupled with* Moeran Symphony in G minor. Eileen Joyce (pf);
Hallé Orchestra / Leslie Heward. Dutton Laboratories mono CDAX8001* (5/93).   ⒼⒼⒼ

...Scherzo and Cortège (arr. G. Bush). Tritons – Symphonic Prelude. The Forgotten Rite – Prelude.
Satyricon – Overture. The Overlanders – Suite from the film (arr. Mackerras). London Symphony
Orchestra / Richard Hickox. Chandos CHAN8994 (2/92).

...A London Overture. *Coupled with* Harty A John Field Suite. Coleridge Taylor Scenes from
"The Song of Hiawatha", Op. 30 Onaway, awake, beloved[a]. Gardiner Shepherd Fennell's
Dance. Vaughan Williams The Lark Ascending[b]. Holst The Hymn of Jesus, H140[c]. [a]Webster
Booth (ten); [b]David Wise (vn); [c]Huddersfield Choral Society; Liverpool Philharmonic Orchestra /
Sir Malcolm Sargent. Dutton Laboratories mono CDAX8012* (5/95).

...Cello Sonata in G minor. *Coupled with* Bridge Elegy, H47. Scherzetto, H19. Stanford Cello Sonata
No. 2 in D minor, Op. 39. Julian Lloyd Webber (vc); John McCabe (pf). ASV CDDCA807 (2/93).

...Cello Sonata in G minor. *Coupled with* **Moeran** and **Rubbra Raphael Wallfisch** (vc); **John York** (pf). Marco Polo 8 223718 (8/95). *See review under Moeran; refer to the Index to Reviews.*

...The salley gardens. The Trellis. Her song. My true love hath my heart. *Coupled with songs by* **Warlock, Howells, Bridge** *and* **Holst Sarah Leonard** (sop); **Malcolm Martineau** (pf). Cala United 88016-2 (3/95).

...Sea Fever. The Vagabond. The Bells of San Marie. *Coupled with works by* **Butterworth, Finzi** *and* **Vaughan Williams Bryn Terfel** (bass-bar); **Malcolm Martineau** (pf). DG 445 946-2GH (8/95). *Gramophone* Editor's record of the month. *See review under Butterworth; refer to the Index to Reviews.* ⓖⓖⓖ

...A Sea Idyll. On a Birthday Morning. Soliloquy. April. Bergomask. Spring will not wait. February's Child. Aubade. Ballade of London Nights. Month's Mind. Three Pastels. Columbine. Sarnia. **Eric Parkin** (pf). Chandos CHAN9250 (1/95). ⓖ

...Hawthorn time. The heart's desire. The lent lily. Goal and wicket. The vain desire. The encounter. Epilogue. *Coupled with works by* **Horder, Butterworth, L. Berkeley, Barber, Moeran** *and* **C.W. Orr Anthony Rolfe Johnson** (ten); **Graham Johnson** (pf). Hyperion CDA66471/2 (8/95). Includes various poems from Housman's "A Shrophire Lad" read by Alan Bates. *See review in the Collections section; refer to the Index to Reviews.*

...Decorations. The Almond Tree. Four Preludes. Rhapsody. The Towing-Path. Merry Andrew. Summer Evening. Piano Sonata in E minor. **Eric Parkin** (pf). Chandos CHAN9056 (8/92).

...In Those Days. London Pieces. Leaves from a Child's Sketchbook. The darkened valley. Two Pieces. Equinox. Sonatina. Prelude in E flat major. Ballade. Greenways. **Eric Parkin** (pf). Chandos CHAN9140 (6/93).

Juan Francés de Iribarren
Spanish

Suggested listening ...

...Quién nos dira de una flor. Viendo que Jil, hizo raya. *Coupled with works by* **F. Valls, J. de Torres, C. Galán, Literes** *and* **Anonymous Al Ayre Español / Eduardo López Banzo.** Deutsche Harmonia Mundi 05472 77325-2 (8/95). *See review in the Collections section; refer to the Index to Reviews.* 🖋 ⓖ

Heinrich Isaac
Flanders *c*1450-1517

Suggested listening ...

...Carmen. In meinem Sinn (three versions). Greiner, zancker, schnöpffitzer. Mein Freud allein. Ich stund an einem Morgen. La mi la sol. Las rauschen. *Coupled with works by* **Obrecht, Senfl Hofhaimer, Heinrich Finck, Ammerbach, A. Bruck, Küffer, G. Meyer** *and* **Rhau Convivium Musicum; Villanella Ensemble / Sven Berger.** Naxos 8 553352 (1/96). *See review in the Collections section; refer to the Index to Reviews.*

...Missa de Apostolis a 6. Optime pastor. Regina caeli laetare. Resurexi et adhuc tecum sum. Tota pulchra es. Virgo prudentissima a 6. **The Tallis Scholars / Peter Phillips.** Gimell CDGIM023 (10/91).

...Angeli, Archangeli. *Coupled with works by* **Ockeghem, Busnois** *and* **Obrecht The Clerks' Group / Edward Wickham.** ASV Gaudeamus CDGAU139 (3/95). *See review under Ockeghem; refer to the Index to Reviews.*

Charles Ives
American 1874-1954

New review

Ives Holidays – Symphony[a]. Orchestral Set No. 1, "A New England Symphony" – Three Places in New England. They are there![a]. **Baltimore Symphony** [a]**Chorus and Orchestra / David Zinman.** Argo Ⓔ 444 860-2ZH (64 minutes: DDD: 6/96). Recorded 1994.

Distinctive and enjoyable. Aided by some wonderfully sensitive playing from the excellent Baltimore orchestra (plus a superbly refined sound-picture from Argo), Zinman directs an evocative, sweetly expressive account of *Three Places in New England*. Both outer tableaux receive raptly beautiful treatment, with *pianissimos* so hushed as to have you gasping for breath; perhaps Tilson Thomas and the Boston SO distil just that touch more spine-tingling atmosphere. But it's the centrepiece, the riotous "Putnam's Camp", which finds Zinman's interpretation at its most freshly illuminating. Whereas rivals like Tilson Thomas combine bullish extroversion with considerable textural mastery in this giddy essay, Zinman's more consciously moulded manner imparts an infectiously sprung, almost balletic elegance to Ives's multi-layered writing. The results are certainly engaging – by contrast, Dohnányi's Cleveland performance sounds a little lacking in sheer swagger and fun. In the case of the four colourful and evocative tone-poems which comprise the *Holidays* Symphony, Zinman has again a formidable rival in Tilson Thomas. The latter's authoritative 1986 Chicago SO recording remains a remarkable achievement and its revelatory lucidity and extraordinary sense of dedication are not quite equalled in Baltimore. Not that Zinman's performance is anything other than admirable, you understand: how beautifully, for instance, these newcomers conjure "the dismal, bleak, cold weather of a February night" at the start of "Washington's Birthday". As captured by the Argo engineers, tuttis in "The Fourth of July" register with an almost frightening physical impact, yet Tilson Thomas's remains perhaps the more dazzlingly poised, charismatic rendering. On the other hand, the concluding tableau, "Thanksgiving and Forefathers' Day", is altogether magnificently realized by Zinman and his colleagues. The ravishingly sweet string melody at its soft heart is delivered with exactly the right charm and wide-eyed innocence, while the Baltimore Symphony Chorus make an ardent showing both at the big choral climax and in the rousing curtain-raiser, *They are there!*, a "War Song March" dating from 1942 (itself converted from an earlier First World War march song entitled *He is there!*). Overall, a most desirable Ives collection.

Additional recommendations ...

...The Unanswered Question (orig. and rev. versions)[a]. Central Park in the Dark. Holidays[b].
[a]**Adolph Herseth** (tpt); **Chicago Symphony** [b]**Chorus and Orchestra / Michael Tilson Thomas.** Sony Classical Ⓕ SK42381 (63 minutes: DDD: 10/88).

...Orchestral Set No. 1[a]. Symphony No. 4[b]. Central Park in the Dark[c]. [b]**Tanglewood Festival Chorus; Boston Symphony Orchestra /** [a]**Michael Tilson Thomas,** [bc]**Seiji Ozawa.** DG 20th Century Classics Ⓜ 423 243-2GC (57 minutes: ADD: 10/88).

...Orchestral Set No. 1. **Schuman** New England Triptych. **Mennin** Symphony No. 5. **Eastman-Rochester Orchestra / Howard Hanson.** Mercury Living Presence Ⓜ 432 755-2MM (77 minutes: ADD).

Ives Symphony No. 2. The Gong on the Hook and Ladder. Tone Roads – No. 1. A set of Three Short Pieces – Largo cantabile, Hymn. Hallowe'en. Central Park in the Dark. The Unanswered Question. **New York Philharmonic Orchestra / Leonard Bernstein.** DG Ⓕ 429 220-2GH (68 minutes: DDD: 8/90). Recorded 1987-88.　　　ⒼⒼⒼ

Although Bernstein thought of Ives as a primitive composer, these recordings reveal that he had an undeniably deep affinity for, and understanding of, his music. The Second Symphony (written in 1902 and first performed in 1951) is a glorious work, still strongly rooted in the nineteenth century yet showing those clear signs of Ives's individual voice that are largely missing from the charming but lightweight First Symphony. Bernstein brings out all its richness and warmth without wallowing in its romantic elements, and he handles with utter conviction the multi-textures and the allusions to popular tunes and snatches from Bach, Brahms and Dvořák, to name but a few. The standard of playing he exacts from the NYPO, both here and in the disc's series of technically demanding shorter pieces, is remarkably high with the depth of string tone at a premium – and the engineers retain this to a degree unusual in a live recording. Altogether an essential disc for any collection.

Additional recommendations ...

...Central Park in the Dark. The Unanswered Question. Orchestral Set No. 1 – Three Places in New England. March No. 3, with My Old Kentucky Home. Fugue in four keys, on The Shining Shore. Symphony No. 3, "The Camp Meeting". **St Louis Symphony Orchestra / Leonard Slatkin.** RCA Victor Red Seal Ⓕ 09026 61222-2 (63 minutes: DDD: 4/93).

...Orchestral Set No. 1, "A New England Symphony" – Three Places in New England. The Unanswered Question. Set for Theatre or Chamber Orchestra[a]. Symphony No. 3, "The Camp Meeting". Set No. 1[a]. [a]**Gilbert Kalish** (pf); **Orpheus Chamber Orchestra.** DG Ⓕ 439 869-2GH (66 minutes: DDD: 10/94).

...Universe Symphony (realized L. Austin)[a]. Orchestral Set No. 2[b]. The Unanswered Question. [b]**C.C.M. Chamber Choir;** [a]**C.C.M. Percussion Ensemble; Cincinnati Philharmonia / Gerhard Samuel.** Centaur Ⓕ CRC2205 (62 minutes: DDD: 5/95). *Gramophone Editor's choice.*

Ives Piano Sonata No. 1.
Barber Piano Sonata in E flat major, Op. 26. Excursions, Op. 20. **Joanna MacGregor** (pf). Collins Classics Ⓕ 1107-2 (68 minutes: DDD: 3/92). Recorded 1990.

There are many fine recordings of the Barber Sonata since it is a work which has attracted well-equipped players right from the start. MacGregor stands up well, but the greater attraction is her Ives Sonata No. 1. The work, which waited 45 years for a first performance, is just as characteristic of Ives as the Second Sonata, and in some ways its mixture of hymn-tunes and ragtime makes a more coherent impact. The ragtime aspects are based on what Ives heard improvised or played that way himself: he went to a lot of trouble to catch the difference between playing the dots and swinging away. This informality is superbly caught by MacGregor, who risks all in truly Ivesian fashion in one or two places. She thoroughly understands the driving rhythms as well as the transcendental calm. By comparison anything by Barber is more polite. But the four *Excursions* come off well and show a different approach to popular idioms – more that of a tourist than an insider. But both composers know how to make use of sonata structure in these two American classics, vividly played and recorded.

Further listening ...

...Symphony No. 1. *Coupled with* **Barber** Essays for Orchestra – No. 1, Op. 12; No. 2, Op. 17; No. 3, Op. 47. **Detroit Symphony Orchestra / Neeme Järvi.** Chandos CHAN9053 (3/92).

...Symphonies – No. 1; No. 4 (including original hymn settings). **Chicago Symphony Orchestra / Michael Tilson Thomas.** Sony Classical SK44939 (2/91).

...Symphony No. 2. Symphony No. 3, "The camp meeting". **Royal Concertgebouw Orchestra /
Michael Tilson Thomas.** Sony Classical SK46440 (61 minutes: DDD: 5/91).   ⊙

...Robert Browning Overture. *Coupled with* **Hartmann** Symphony No. 3. **Bamberg Symphony
Orchestra / Ingo Metzmacher.** EMI CDC5 55254-2 (10/95) *See review under Hartmann; refer to
the Index to Reviews.*.

...Trio for Violin, Clarinet and Piano. *Coupled with works by* **Bernstein, Gershwin** and
Kirchner Yo-Yo Ma (vc); **Ronan Lefkowitz** (vn); **Gilbert Kalish** (pf). Sony Classical SK53126
(4/94). *See review in the Collections section; refer to the Index to Reviews.*   ⊙

...Violin Sonata No. 4, "Children's Day at the Camp Meeting". *Coupled with works by* **Bartók,
Bloch, Debussy, Schubert, Bach, Brahms, Corelli, Debussy, Dvořák, Falla, Hubay,
Kodály, Lalo, Milhaud, Mussorgsky** and **Schubert** Joseph Szigeti (vn); **Andor Foldes** (pf).
Biddulph mono LAB070/71*. *See review in the Collections section; refer to the Index to
Reviews.*   ⊙⊙

...Piano Sonata No. 2, "Concord Mass: 1840-60". *Coupled with* **M. Wright** Piano Sonata.
Marc-André Hamelin (pf). New World NW378-2 (9/89).

...Three-page Sonata, Op. 14. *Coupled with* **Cage** Works for Prepared Piano – Bacchanale; The
Perilous Night; Music for Marcel Duchamp. **Sessions** Piano Sonata No. 3, "Kennedy Sonata".
William Grant Naboré (pf). Doron Music DRC3002.

...Three-page Sonata, Op. 14 (ed. Cowell). *Coupled with works by* **Copland, Carter** and **Barber**
Peter Lawson (pf). Virgin Classics VC7 59008-2 (5/91). *See review in the Collections section; refer
to the Index to Reviews.*   ⊙⊙

Grayston Ives   British 1948-

Suggested listening ...

...Evening (Edington) Service. *Coupled with works by* **S. Watson, Stanford, Gibbons,
Leighton, Howells** and **Dyson** Lichfield Cathedral Choir / Andrew Lumsden with **Mark
Shepherd, Nigel Potts** (orgs). Priory PRCD505 (10/95). *See review in the Collections section; refer
to the Index to Reviews.*

Gabriel Jackson   Bermuda 1962-

Suggested listening ...

...French Song. *Coupled with works by* **N. Hayes, Hallgrimsson, Weir, Finnissy, S. Harrison,
Crane, A. Fisher** and **Skempton** Tapestry. British Music Label BML012 (12/95). *See review in
the Collections section; refer to the Index to Reviews.*

William Jackson   British 1730-1803

Suggested listening ...

...Sonata for Harpsichord with violin obbligato in A minor, Op. 2. A Second Set of 12 Canzonets,
Op. 13 – Love in thine eyes for ever plays. Elegy, Op. 3 No. 3, Could he whom my dissembled
rigour grieves. Quartet, Op. 11, Where the bee sucks. *Coupled with music by* **Harington,
Herschel, W.B. Earle, T. Linley I** and **T. Linley II** Various artists. Hyperion CDA66698
(11/94).

Gordon Jacob   British 1895-1984

Further listening ...

...Concerto for Bassoon, Strings and Percussion[b]. *Coupled with* **J. Andriessen** Concerto for
Bassoon and Wind Ensemble[c]. **Downey** Edge of Space[a]. **Robert Thompson** (bn); [a]**London
Symphony Orchestra;** [b]**English Chamber Orchestra;** [c]**English Chamber Orchestra Wind Ensemble /
Geoffrey Simon.** Chandos CHAN9278 (10/94).

...Mini-Concerto. *Coupled with* **Rawsthorne** Clarinet Concerto. **Cooke** Clarinet Concerto. **Thea
King** (cl); **Seattle Northwest Chamber Orchestra / Alun Francis.** Hyperion CDA66031 (10/89).

...Trombone Concerto. *Coupled with concertos by* **Howarth** and **D. Bourgeois** Christian Lindberg
(tbn); **BBC National Orchestra of Wales / Grant Llewellyn.** BIS CD658 (10/95). *See review under
D. Bourgeois; refer to the Index to Review*

Hyacinthe Jadin

Suggested listening ...
...String Quartets – E flat major, Op. 2 No. 1; C major, Op. 3 No. 1. *Coupled with* **L-E. Jadin**
String Quartet No. 2 in F minor. **Quatuor Mosaïques.** Auvidis Valois V4738 (3/96).

Louis Emanuel Jadin

Suggested listening ...
...String Quartet No. 2 in F minor. *Coupled with* **H. Jadin** String Quartets – E flat major, Op. 2
No. 1; C major, Op. 3 No. 1. **Quatuor Mosaïques.** Auvidis Valois V4738 (3/96).

Leos Janáček

Janáček Sinfonietta, Op. 60[a]. Taras Bulba[a].
Shostakovich The Age of Gold – Suite, Op. 22a[b]. [a]**Vienna Philharmonic Orchestra / Sir Charles
Mackerras;** [b]**London Philharmonic Orchestra / Bernard Haitink.** Decca Ovation Ⓜ 430 727-2DM
(66 minutes: DDD: 12/91). Item marked [a] from 410 138-2DH (11/83), recorded 1980, [b]D213D2
(11/80), recorded 1979.   ⒼⒼ
The Janáček items have long been a favourite coupling and in these thoroughly idiomatic
performances the effect is spectacular. Of course these are far more than just orchestral show-pieces.
Both works were fired by patriotic fervour – *Taras Bulba* by Czechoslovakia's struggle towards
independence, the *Sinfonietta* by the city of Brno, the composer's adopted home town. Both works
display a deep-seated passion for the basic elements of music and yield unprecedented levels of
excitement. To get the most out of *Taras Bulba* you really need all its gory programmatic details (of
battles, betrayal, torture and murder) to hand. The *Sinfonietta* needs no such props; its impact is as
irresistible and physically direct as a massive adrenalin injection. If the listener is to revel in this music
a corresponding sense of abandon in the playing is even more important than precision. The Vienna
Philharmonic supply a good measure of both and Sir Charles Mackerras's commitment and
understanding are second to none, while the high-level recording captures every detail in vivid close-
up. Bernard Haitink's highly disciplined if somewhat straitlaced LPO account of Shostakovich's *Age
of Gold* suite is the coupling.

Additional recommendations ...
...Sinfonietta. Taras Bulba. Concertino[a]. [a]**Rudolf Firkušný** (pf); **Bavarian Radio Symphony
Orchestra / Rafael Kubelík.** DG Ⓑ 439 437-2GCL (61 minutes: ADD).   ⒼⒼ
...Sinfonietta. The Danube[a]. Violin Concerto, "Pilgrimage of the Soul"[b]. Schluk und Jau. [a]**Karolina
Dvořáková** (sop); [b]**Ivan Zenaty** (vn); **Brno State Philharmonic Orchestra / František Jílek.**
Supraphon Ⓕ 11 1522-2 (63 minutes: DDD: 9/93).   Ⓖ
...Taras Bulba. The Cunning Little Vixen – Suite. **Novák** Slovak Suite, Op. 32. **Czech Philharmonic
Orchestra / Václav Talich.** Supraphon Historical mono Ⓜ 11 1905-2* (71 minutes: AAD:
1/94).   ⒼⒼ
...Sinfonietta[a]. **Bartók** The Miraculous Mandarin[b]. Two Portraits, Sz37[c]. [c]**Shlomo Mintz** (vn);
[b]**Ambrosian Singers,** [a]**Berlin Philharmonic Orchestra,** [b]**London Symphony Orchestra / Claudio
Abbado.** DG Masters Ⓜ 445 501-2GMA (66 minutes: DDD: 12/94). *See review under Bartók;
refer to the Index to Reviews.*   Ⓖ
...Taras Bulba. **Rachmaninov** Symphonic Dances. **North German Radio Symphony Orchestra /
John Eliot Gardiner.** DG Ⓕ 445 838-2GH (56 minutes: DDD: 1/96).

Janáček String Quartets[a] – No. 1, "Kreutzer Sonata"; No. 2, "Intimate Letters". Along an
overgrown path – Suite No. 1[b]. [b]**Radoslav Kvapil** (pf); [a]**Talich Quartet** (Petr Messiereur, Jan
Kvapil, vns; Jan Talich, va; Evzen Rattai, vc). Calliope Ⓕ CAL9699 (73 minutes: DDD: 4/89).
Items marked [a] from CAL1699 (1/86), [b]CAL9206 (8/88).   ⒼⒼ
Janáček's two string quartets stand with those of Bartók, Debussy and Ravel among the supreme
masterpieces of the medium, composed during the first half of this century. Both are relatively late
works: the *Kreutzer Sonata* dates from 1923 and was inspired by Tolstoy's tragic short story of the
same title, depicting a women's disappointment in love both inside and outside marriage. Janáček
translates the emotions of Tolstoy's story into music of intense passion. Even more immediate and
personal is the Second Quartet entitled *Intimate Letters*, inspired by Janáček's infatuation at the age
of 64 for his young pupil Kamila Slösslova. He poured into this quartet all his feelings for her: doubt,
release, joy and despair are all graphically portrayed in Janáček's elliptical music. Inference and
statement paradoxically give the quartet a wholeness which eludes other more forthright works. The
Talich Quartet portray these two similar psycho-dramas with total commitment and devotion. The
immense technical difficulties with which Janáček confronts his performers are set aside by the white
heat of emotion clearly felt both by performers and composer. The insight of these readings
fortunately even overcomes a recording perhaps too dry for Janáček's highly exposed string writing.
As a bonus, Radoslav Kvapil gives an idiomatic reading of the first suite from *Along an overgrown*

path, written between 1901 and 1908, and marked by the death of his daughter Olga in 1903. These short piano pieces display in embryo many of the stylistic features which were later to reappear in the two quartets. Again the performance is wholly authentic and committed, allowing Janáček's exceptional creativity to shine through without compromise. Again a rather dry recording.

Additional recommendations ...

...Quartets. **Bartók** String Quartets – No. 1, Sz40; No. 2, Sz67; No. 3, Sz85; No. 4, S91; No. 5, Sz102; No. 6, Sz114. **Tokyo Quartet.** RCA Victor Red Seal Ⓕ 09026 68286-2 (three discs: 199 minutes: DDD)

...Quartets. **Dvořák** Cypresses, B152. **Lindsay Quartet.** ASV Ⓕ CDDCA749 (75 minutes: DDD: 11/91). Ⓖ

...Quartets. **Dvořák** String Quartet No. 10 in E flat major, B92. **Vanbrugh Quartet.** Collins Classics Ⓕ 1381-2 (73 minutes: DDD: 4/94). Ⓖ

...Quartet No. 1. **Dvořák** String Quartet No. 12 in F major, B179, "American". Piano Quintet in A major, B155[a]. [a]**Pavel Stěpán** (pf); **Smetana Quartet.** Testament Ⓕ SBT1074 (79 minutes: ADD: 3/96). *See review in the Collections section; refer to the Index to Reviews.* ⒼⒼ

...Quartet No. 2. **Dvořák** Terzetto in C major, B148. String Quartet No. 14 in A flat major, B193. **Smetana Quartet.** Testament Ⓕ SBT1075 (77 minutes: ADD: 3/96). *See review in the Collections section; refer to the Index to Reviews.* ⒼⒼ

New review

Janáček Pohádka.
Kodály Cello Sonata, Op. 4.
Liszt Elégies – No. 1, S130; No. 2, S131. La lugubre gondola, S134. **Anne Gastinel** (vc); **Pierre-Laurent Aimard** (pf). Auvidis Valois Ⓕ V4748 (50 minutes: DDD: 9/95).
This is an imaginative piece of programme planning, with arrangements of Liszt's *Elégies* and *La lugubre gondola* separated by Kodály's Sonata and Janáček's *Pohádka*. Liszt, writing in the 1870s and early 1880s, sounds as modern as either of the two composers writing in 1910; and indeed there is much in his augmented-chord harmony and his fondness for unusual scales that influenced Kodály, while Janáček also admired him and used his religious music for teaching purposes. This is romantic music outside the mainstream of European musical romanticism. Gastinel and Aimard give performances as intelligent as these juxtapositions suggest, oblique and dark in the linking figure of Liszt, especially with *La lugubre gondola*, one of the most extraordinary late piano pieces. Kodály's sonata is played with a quiet intensity, rhapsodic in manner but in fact strongly held together by the clarity of emphasis on the motto theme and its musical implications. Janáček's pieces can sound sharper and quirkier than here, and in such performances make their point more strongly; but this playing is of a piece with the whole approach in this recital. Anne Gastinel has a clean, resinous tone, and a strong sense of line; she is well partnered by Pierre-Laurent Aimard, and the recording is clear and well-balanced.

Janáček Piano Sonata 1.X.1905, "From the street". Along an overgrown path. In the mists. Thema con variazioni, "Zdenka". **Rudolf Firkušný** (pf). DG 20th Century Classics Ⓜ 429 857-2GC (79 minutes: ADD: 3/91). From 2707 055 (6/72). Recorded 1971. ⒼⒼⒼ
Janáček's only piano sonata has a history almost as dramatic as the events which inspired it. Its subtitle, *From the street* commemorates a student demonstration in which a 20-year-old worker was killed, an event which so outraged Janáček that he wrote a three movement sonata as an expression of his feelings. Before the première in 1906 he burnt the third movement and after a private performance in Prague he threw the remaining movements into a river. It is only thanks to the pianist, Ludmil Tučkova, who had copied out the first two movements, that the work survives. The underlying theme of Firkušný's approach to this work (who may claim historical authenticity as he studied with Janáček) is anger, turning the first movement into a defiant roar of fury whilst the slow movement has an inherent restlessness, bitterness never far below the surface. Much of the same characteristics can be found in the other works – *Along an overgrown path* and the masterly *In the mists* although he occasionally overloads these delicate little pieces with dramatic power. The early Theme and Variations are conventionally romantic but impeccably played. This disc represents playing of the highest class with full notes and tracking details.

Additional recommendations ...

...Piano Sonata. In the mists. Along an overgrown path. **Leif Ove Andsnes** (pf). Virgin Classics Ⓕ VC7 59639-2 (71 minutes: DDD: 10/91).

...Piano Sonata. Along an overgrown path – Suite No. 1. In the mists. **Josef Páleníček** (pf). Supraphon Ⓕ 10 1481-2 (54 minutes: ADD: 3/92).

...Piano Sonata. In the mists. Presto[a]. From a Fairy Tale[a]. Capriccio[b]. **András Schiff** (pf); [a]**Boris Pergamenschikov** (vc); [b]**Wolfgang Schulz** (fl); [b]**Hans Gansch**, [b]**Konrad Monsberger** (tpts); [b]**Erik Hainzl**, [b]**William McElheney**, [b]**Hans Stroecker** (trebs); [b]**Rudolf Josel** (tuba). Decca Ⓕ 440 312-2DH (64 minutes: DDD: 1/94).

Janáček Folk-songs. **Dagmar Pecková** (mez); **Iván Kusnjer** (bar); **Marián Lapšanský** (pf) [b]**Prague Philharmonic Chorus / Pavel Kuhn.** Supraphon Ⓕ 11 2214/25-2 (two-disc set and single disc: 154 and 77 minutes: DDD: 11/95). Recorded 1994.
11 2214-2: Moravian folk poetry in songs (1892-1901). Hukvaldy folk poetry in songs (1898). 10 Silesian songs from Helena Salichová's Collection (1918). *11 2225-2*[b]: Six Folk-songs which Eva Gabel sang (1909). Seven Folk Nocturnes (1906). Detvan Brigand Songs (1916). Five Folk-songs (1916-17). Four Ballads (1908-12).

The performers are a mezzo-soprano and a baritone chosen for voices that are strong and unaffected. Some of the ensemble between baritone and piano is less than wholly polished, but it scarcely matters. Anyone who loves Janáček's music must be drawn into delight in these songs. Sometimes he provides quite elaborate accompaniments; sometimes his intervention is token; in a few cases there is something close to an act of composition. And this is where complications arise. In Janáček's second opera, *The Beginning of a Romance*, folk-tunes are inserted into the score of what is actually rather a feeble piece. By *Jenůfa*, these were entering his imagination at a much deeper level, though it is interesting to hear one tune, "Na horách, na dol'ách", from the *Detvan Brigand Songs*, which plays a more direct part in *Jenůfa*. He was (like Bartók) already discovering in his national resources a mature, modern idiom of international eloquence. The grouping of the songs reflects various differences – of region, of technique, of treatment, of function and much else. Among the most fascinating are the *Folk Nocturnes*, arrangements of material Janáček collected himself. He was particularly taken with them and their strange harmony, as he described in a magazine article quoted in Jaroslav Vogel's study *Leoš Janáček* (London: 1962): "In the evening, after sunset, the girls meet at the back of the cottages and one of them, the best singer, stands in front of the others leading the singing. She sings the first line and the others join in, holding hands, with an unusual melody which carries away over the hilltops, falls into the valleys and dies away in the distant dark forest." They are lovingly performed here by the Prague chorus. There are several kinds of listener who might enjoy these songs, over 100 of which are included here. The folklorist has fascinating material, and so does the admirer of Janáček who can perceive where much in his musical language began. But a wider audience could take much pleasure in, at any rate, the single disc that includes the *Folk Nocturnes*. These well-springs of a great composer's art have refreshment for all.

Janáček Diary of one who disappeared (two versions). [a]**Nicolai Gedda**, [b]**Beno Blachut** (tens), [a]**Věra Soukupová**, [b]**Stěpánka Stěpánová** (mezzos); [a]**Prague Radio Chamber Chorus**; [b]**Czech Singers Chamber Chorus**; [ab]**Josef Páleniček** (pf). Supraphon [a]stereo/[b]mono Ⓜ SU0022-2* (73 minutes: DDD/AAD: 2/96). Item marked [a] new to UK (recorded 1984), [b]from LPV319 (3/59, recorded 1956). Text and translation included.

Here is a highly interesting enterprise: two parallel performances of Janáček's song-cycle, both recorded in Prague, but one being the classic version with Beno Blachut made in 1956, the other hitherto unknown in this country and made in 1984 by Nicolai Gedda. Blachut, who despite his heroic use of his voice kept it in good order throughout a long career, was then in his early forties, and in his prime; Gedda, another singer who preserved his voice carefully, was in his sixtieth year. Any lover of Janáček's music is strongly urged to acquire this striking record. The commentary, by the distinguished scholar Jiří Vysloužil, makes no bones about preferring Blachut, observing that, "what may have displeased some critics, including even those abroad, was the operatic style of Gedda's interpretation". It is easy enough to see what he means: for instance, in No. 6, translated as "Hey there my tawny oxen", as the young man ploughing has his head set afire by a glimpse of the gipsy girl in the bushes, Gedda gives the climactic phrase "v jednom je plameni" an Italianate fervour where Blachut develops the song's passion more steadily towards the phrase, which can therefore be less strenuously emphasized. Nevertheless, Gedda's vocal elegance and eloquence have their own appeal; and his Russian background has long helped him towards a deep understanding of music in the Slavonic repertory. His is a superb performance of a work that can well sustain a new approach, whatever loyalties there may be to Blachut's identification with the work. Listeners have a unique opportunity here for getting, literally, two for the price of one and enjoying the comparisons. A linchpin of both performances, as he so often was, is Josef Páleniček.

Janáček Glagolitic Mass[a]. Sinfonietta, Op. 60[b]. [a]**Felicity Palmer** (sop); [a]**Ameral Gunson** (mez); [a]**John Mitchinson** (ten); [a]**Malcolm King** (bass); [a]**Jane Parker-Smith** (org); [a]**City of Birmingham Chorus and Orchestra**; [b]**Philharmonia Orchestra / Sir Simon Rattle.** EMI Ⓔ CDC7 47504-2 (62 minutes: DDD: 10/88). Text and translation included. Item marked [a] from ASD4066 (5/82), recorded 1981, [b]ASD143522-1 (10/83), recorded 1982.   Ⓖ

"I am not an old man, and I am not a believer – until I see for myself." Thus Janáček replied angrily to a critic after the première of his *Glagolitic Mass*. This is a gritty, masterful performance of a jagged, uncomfortable masterpiece. Its unusual title stems from the script of the ancient Slavonic text (Glagol) which Janáček set to music. Rattle's is a full-blooded, urgent view of the work, with particularly fine solo contributions from Felicity Palmer and John Mitchinson. That the language is an unfamiliar one is occasionally evident in the chorus, though they, like the orchestra, give totally committed performances under Rattle's inspired leadership. Also included on this disc is the *Sinfonietta* (originally entitled "Military Sinfonietta", reflecting in the brass-heavy scoring of the work). It is as much a study in orchestration as form with the melody of the fourth movement appearing unaltered no less than 14 times, changed only in orchestral colour. It is brilliantly played here, with the 12 trumpets coming up gleaming in the final climax. An enticing proposition!

Additional recommendation ...

...Glagolitic Mass. **Poulenc** Gloria. **Soloists; Westminster Choir; New York Philharmonic Orchestra / Leonard Bernstein.** Sony Classical Bernstein Royal Edition Ⓜ SMK47569 (65 minutes: ADD: 5/93).

Janáček (ed. Wingfield) Glagolitic Mass (original version)[a].
Kodály Psalmus Hungaricus, Op. 13[b]. [a]**Tina Kiberg** (sop); [a]**Randi Stene** (contr); **Peter Svensson** (ten); [a]**Ulrik Cold** (bass); [a]**Per Salo** (org); [b]**Copenhagen Boys' Choir; Danish National Radio Choir and Symphony Orchestra / Sir Charles Mackerras.** Chandos Ⓕ CHAN9310 (63 minutes: DDD: 12/94). Texts and translations included. Recorded 1994.

Mackerras's version of the *Glagolitic Mass* is of particular interest as it embodies one of the reconstructions that have been painstakingly made of Janáček's original intentions in different works as his stature has drawn greater scholarly interest. This one has been made by Paul Wingfield. He has gone into the nature of his restorations in great detail in his excellent monograph on the work in the Cambridge Music Handbooks series (CUP: 1992), and summarizes them in his note to this recording. Briefly, they involve the playing of the Intrada at the beginning and the end, in the Introduction a very complex rhythmic pattern and in the "Gospodi pomiluj" ("Kyrie") use of quintuple metre instead of the familiar four-in-a-bar (both far more effectively), and fierce timpani interjections in the wild organ solo. There are other points; but in any case, most interested listeners will care less for them in detail than for the heightened force and impact of the music. This it certainly now (or once again) has. These matters make it the more regrettable that, despite marvellous handling of the work by Mackerras, there are problems with a quartet of soloists that is less than exciting, and a recording that even with the most modern techniques can obscure the detail of the music and the clarity of the words. This should not detract from the interest of the disc, which every lover of the work must want to hear. Those who acquire it will have the additional benefit of a fine performance of Kodály's *Psalmus Hungaricus*, though the restored Mass is naturally the occasion for recommendation and choice.

New review

Janáček The wild duck. The dove. Our birch tree. The wandering madman. Schoolmaster Halfar. Elegy on the death of his daughter Olga. The wolf's trail. Songs of Hradčany. Nursery Rhymes. **Netherlands Chamber Choir; Schoenberg Ensemble / Reinbert de Leeuw.** Philips Ⓕ 442 534-2PH (60 minutes: DDD: 12/95). Texts and translations included.

Some of Janáček's most characteristic invention is to be found in the many choruses he wrote for local choirs who were moved by both a love of singing together and a demonstration of their national identity. There is a good selection here. Even the earliest, a touching little lament for a duck, has a quirkiness which saves it from sentimentality; the latest, the *Nursery Rhymes*, are marvellous little inventions from the dazzling evening of Janáček's life. One must resist any temptation to say that they take Stravinsky on at his own game: Janáček is his own man. In between comes a varied diet here. *Schoolmaster Halfar* (or *Cantor Halfar*) is set with a dazzling range of little musical ironies as the story unfolds of the teacher who ruined his life by insisting on speaking Czech. The *Elegy on the death of his daughter Olga* goes some way toward dignifying a conventional text with some heartfelt music, but the pressure of grief has not drawn the greatest of his music from him: perhaps more time was needed, and indeed the piano pieces he entitled *Along an Overgrown Path* re-enter ancient griefs more expressively. The performances are fluent and smooth; and perhaps this is not always a recommendation. Czech group brought to this music a sharpness, an oddity, a tang in the rhythms and phrasing that responded better to the music than these well-ironed performances. Nevertheless, for the best here there is enjoyment, and a most pleasurable reminder of Janáček's unquenchable individuality in whatever he set out to do.

Janáček Jenůfa. **Elisabeth Söderström** (sop) Jenůfa; **Wieslaw Ochman** (ten) Laca; **Eva Randová** (mez) Kostelnička; **Petr Dvorský** (ten) Steva; **Lucia Popp** (sop) Karolka; **Marie Mrazová** (contr) Stařenka; **Václav Zitek** (bar) Stárek; **Dalibor Jedlička** (bass) Rychtar; **Ivana Mixová** (mez) Rychtarka; **Vera Soukopová** (mez) Pastuchyňa, Tetka; **Jindra Pokorná** (mez) Barena; **Jana Janasová** (sop) Jano; **Vienna State Opera Chorus; Vienna Philharmonic Orchestra / Sir Charles Mackerras.** Decca Ⓕ 414 483-2DH2 (two discs: 130 minutes: DDD: 12/85). From D276D3 (9/83). Recorded 1982. *Gramophone Award Winner 1984.*   ⓖⓖⓖ

Janáček's first operatic masterpiece is a towering work which blends searing intensity with heart-stopping lyricism. It tells of Jenůfa and the appalling treatment she receives as she is caught between the man she loves and one who eventually comes to love her. But dominating the story is the Kostelnička, a figure of huge strength, pride and inner resource who rules Jenůfa's life and ultimately kills her baby. Eva Randová's characterization of the role of the Kostelnička is frightening in its intensity but also has a very human core. The two men are well cast and act as fine foils to Elisabeth Söderström's deeply impressive Jenůfa. The Vienna Philharmonic play beautifully and Mackerras directs magnificently. The recording is all one could wish for and the booklet is a mine of informed scholarship.

Janáček Kátá Kabanová[a]. Capriccio[b]. Concertino[b]. **Elisabeth Söderström** (sop) Kátá; **Petr Dvorský** (ten) Boris; **Naděžda Kniplová** (contr) Kabanicha; **Vladimír Krejčík** (ten) Tichon; **Libuše Márová** (mez) Varvara; **Dalibor Jedlička** (bass) Dikoj; **Zdeněk Svehla** (ten) Kudrjáš; **Jaroslav Souček** (bar) Kuligin; **Jitka Pavlová** (sop) Glaša; **Gertrude Jahn** (mez) Fekluša; **Vienna State Opera Chorus; Vienna Philharmonic Orchestra / Sir Charles Mackerras;** [b]**Paul Crossley** (pf); [b]**London Sinfonietta / David Atherton.** Decca Ⓟ 421 852-2DH2 (two discs: 140 minutes: ADD: 10/89). Notes, text and translation included. Item marked [a] from D51D2 (10/77), recorded 1976, [b]D223D5 (4/81), recorded 1978. *Gramophone classical 100. Gramophone Award Winner 1977.* ⓖⓐⓦ

With *Kátá Kabanová* in 1919, Janáček embarked on the four operatic masterpieces that would occupy him for the remaining nine years of his life, and Decca in 1976 on their now classic series of Janáček opera recordings with Sir Charles Mackerras. Unlike the other three late operas, *Kátá Kabanová*'s story *is* one you would expect to see on the opera stage: Kátá, a free spirit, is imprisoned by marriage into, and domicile with, a family in a provincial Russian town on the Volga. The family is manipulated by her mother-in-law, a widow whose sole, obsessive concern is her status (familial and social). The only son (Kátá's husband) is understandably spineless, and Kátá looks for escape in love. She finds the love, but true escape only in suicide. Janáček focuses on his heroine, giving her at least two of the most moving scenes in opera: the first where, to music of shimmering, seraphic beauty she describes her childhood imagination given free rein by pillars of sunlight streaming through the dome in church; and the second in the last scene where, after her confession of adultery, she concludes that "not even God's own sunlight" gives her pleasure any more. Söderström has the intelligence and a voice which guarantees *total* credibility (how often can you claim that of an operatic portrayal?); and of the superb all-Czech supporting cast one might only have wished for a slightly younger-sounding sister-in-law. Mackerras persuades from the Vienna Philharmonic their very finest ensemble and tone; and Decca, true to their best operatic traditions, reproduce the whole with clarity, atmosphere, ideal perspectives and discernible stage movement – only a detectable levelling of the score's few extreme *fortissimos* points to the recording's vintage. As a bonus, Decca add the late chamber concertos, both excellently performed and engineered, and equally essential Janáček.

Additional recommendations ...

...Capriccio. Concertino. **Dvořák** Piano Concerto in G minor, Op. 33. **Rudolf Firkušný** (pf); **Czech Philharmonic Orchestra / Václav Neumann.** RCA Victor Red Seal Ⓟ RD60781 (73 minutes: ADD: 7/92).

...Kátá Kabanová. **Soloists; Prague National Theatre Chorus and Orchestra / Jaroslav Krombholc.** Supraphon Ⓟ 10 8016-2* (two discs: 90 minutes: ADD: 11/93).

...Capriccio[a]. **Bartók** Music for Strings, Percussion and Celesta, Sz106. **Martinů** Concerto for String Quartet and Orchestra. [a]**Joela Jones** (pf); **Cleveland Orchestra / Christoph von Dohnányi.** Decca Ⓟ 443 173-2DH (70 minutes: DDD: 4/95).

Janáček The Cunning Little Vixen. The Cunning Little Vixen – orchestral suite (arr. V. Talich)[a]. **Lucia Popp** (sop) Vixen, Young vixen; **Dalibor Jedlička** (bass) Forester; **Eva Randová** (mez) Fox; **Eva Zikmundová** (mez) Forester's wife, Owl; **Vladimir Krejčik** (ten) Schoolmaster, Gnat; **Richard Novák** (ten) Priest, Badger **Václav Zítek** (bar) Harašta; **Beno Blachut** (ten) Pásek; **Ivana Mixová** (mez) Pásek's wife, Woodpecker, Hen; **Libuše Marová** (contr) Dog; **Gertrude Jahn** (mez) Cock, Jay; **Eva Hríbiková** (sop) Frantik; **Zuzana Hudecová** (sop) Pepik; **Peter Saray** (treb) Frog, Grasshopper; **Miriam Ondrášková** (sop) Cricket; **Vienna State Opera Chorus; Bratislava Children's Choir; Vienna Philharmonic Orchestra / Sir Charles Mackerras.** Decca Ⓟ 417 129-2DH2 (two discs: 109 minutes: DDD: 11/86). Notes, text and translation included. From D257D2 (5/82). Item marked [a] new to UK. Recorded 1981. *Gramophone Award Winner 1983.* ⓖⓐⓦ

Janáček used the most unlikely material for his operas. For *The Cunning Little Vixen* his source was a newspaper series of drawings, with accompanying text, about the adventures of a vixen cub and her escape from the gamekeeper who raised her. The music is a fascinating blend of vocal and orchestral sound – at times ludicrously romantic, at others raw and violent. Sir Charles Mackerras's Czech training has given him a rare insight into Janáček's music and he presents a version faithful to the composer's individual requirements. In the title-role, Lucia Popp gives full weight to the text while displaying all the richness and beauty of her voice. There is a well-chosen supporting cast of largely Czech singers, with the Vienna Philharmonic to add the ultimate touch of orchestral refinement.

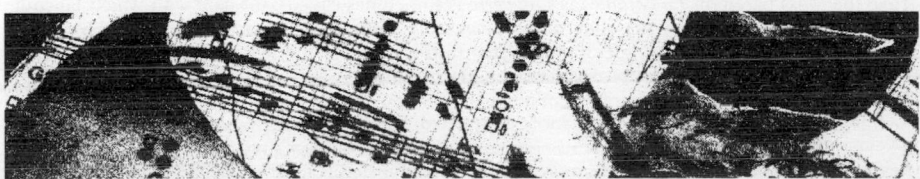

Decca's sound is of demonstration quality, bringing out all the violent detail of Janáček's exciting vocal and orchestral effects.

Additional recommendation ...

...The Cunning Little Vixen (sung in English)[a]. Taras Bulba[b]. **Soloists;** [a]**Chorus and Orchestra of the Royal Opera House, Covent Garden;** [b]**Philharmonic Orchestra / Simon Rattle.** EMI
Ⓕ CDS7 54212-2 (two discs: 120 minutes: DDD: 3/92).

Further listening ...

...Violin Concerto, "Pilgrimage of the soul". *Coupled with works by* **Berg** *and* **Hartmann** **Thomas Zehetmair** (vn/dir); **Philharmonia Orchestra / Heinz Holliger; Deutsche Kammerphilharmonie.** Teldec 4509-97449-2 (6/95). *See review under Berg; refer to the Index to Reviews.*

...Violin Sonata. *Coupled with* **Foerster** Sonata quasi fantasia, Op. 77. **Novak** Violin Sonata in A minor. **Josef Suk** (vn); **Jan Panenka** (pf). Supraphon 11 0705-2 (5/90).

...Nine Male-voice choruses[a]. Nursery Rhymes[b]. [a]**Moravian Teachers' Choir / Antonín Tučapský;** [b]**Czech Philharmonic Chorus and Orchestra / Jan Kühn** with **Alfred Holeček** (pf). Somm Recordings SOMMCD201 (2/96).

...Moravian folk poetry in songs. **Zdena Kloubová** (sop); **Leo Marián Vodička** (ten); **Radoslav Kvapil** (pf). Unicorn-Kanchana DKPCD9154 (4/95).   ⒼⒼ

...The Lord's Prayer[jghk]. Hail Mary[cehjk]. Mass in E flat major (ed. Wingfield)[abcdjik]. Adagios (ed. Reinberger)[j]. Exaudi Deus[jk]. Regnum mundi[jk]. Graduale in festo purificationis (Suscepimus Deus)[jk]. In nomine Jesu[jk]. *Coupled with* **Puccini** Requiem[jfhk]. Salve del ciel regina[ahk]. Vexilla regis[cdhk]. [a]**Shelley Everall** (sop); [b]**Lynette Alcantara** (contr); [c]**William Kendall** (ten); [d]**Peter Harvey** (bar); **Douglas Paterson** ([e]vn/[f]va); [g]**Helen Cole** (hp); [h]**Christopher Monks,** [i]**Michael Phillips** (orgs); [j]**Gonville and Caius College Choir, Cambridge /** [k]**Geoffrey Webber** ([l]org). ASV CDDCA914 (6/95).

...I'm waiting for you (two versions). War Song (first version). War Song (second version), "Blessing the flag". Fanfares – A major; D minor. Festival Chorus. Along an Overgrown Path – Our evenings; A blown-away leaf; The Madonna of Frýdek; Good night!; The barn owl has not flown away. Jealousy. Jenufa – And that's how we would go ... Ah, he was so strong. Taras Bulba – original opening. The Excursions of Mr Brouček – postlude to Part 1. The Living Corpse – fragment. March of the Blue Boys. **Soloists** (vocalists and instrumentalists); **Prague Philharmonic Chorus; Brno State Philharmonic Orchestra / Leoš Svárovský.** Supraphon 11 1878-2 (3/95).

...The Excursions of Mr Brouček. **Soloists; Czech Philharmonic Chorus and Orchestra / František Jílek.** Supraphon 11 2153-2 (2/95)

...Sárka. **Soloists; Brno Radio Symphony Chorus and Orchestra / Břetislav Bakala.** Multisonic mono 310154-2* (6/94).   Ⓖ

...The Makropoulos Affair. Lachian Dances[a]. **Soloists; Vienna State Opera Chorus; Vienna Philharmonic Orchestra / Sir Charles Mackerras;** [a]**London Philharmonic Orchestra / François Huybrechts.** Decca 430 372-2DH2 (10/91).   Ⓖ

...The Makropulos Affair. **Soloists; Prague National Theatre Chorus and Orchestra / Bohumil Gregor.** Supraphon 10 8351-2 (5/95).

...From the House of the Dead[a]. Mládi[b]. Nursery rhymes[c]. [b]**Soloists;** [bc]**Vienna State Opera Chorus;** [a]**Vienna Philharmonic Orchestra / Sir Charles Mackerras;** [b]**London Sinfonietta Chorus;** [ab]**London Sinfonietta / David Atherton.** Decca 430 375-2DH2 (10/91).   Ⓖ

...Fate (sung in English). **Soloists; Welsh National Opera Chorus and Orchestra / Sir Charles Mackerras.** EMI CDC7 49993-2 (9/90).

...Osud. **Soloists; Brno Janáček Opera Chorus and Orchestra / František Jílek.** Supraphon SU0045-2 (1/96).

Clément Janequin   French c1485-1558

New review

Janequin Missa super "La bataille". Missa super "L'aveuglé dieu". Congregati sunt. **Clément Janequin Ensemble; Les Sacqueboutiers de Toulouse / Dominique Visse.** Harmonia Mundi
Ⓕ HMC90 1536 (50 minutes: DDD: 1/96). 🎵 Texts and translations included. Recorded 1994.
Gramophone Editor's choice.

Janequin's reputation rests squarely on his secular music, in particular the fame of such descriptive compositions as *Le chant des oiseaux* and *La guerre*. His sacred output – all of two Masses, a single motet and a few psalms – seems pretty slim in comparison, but that is more likely to reflect Janequin's inability to secure any permanent ecclesiastical appointment than any lack of interest. Nevertheless, so little is his name associated with the sacred that this disc will cme as a revelation to quite a few. Take the Mass based on *La bataille* (as *La guerre* is sometimes called): the care with which Janequin doses his borrowings from the song, introducing something new in each movement, bespeaks a masterly sense of pacing, even of drama. Listen to the way that the first appearance of the 'battle sequence' energizes those most problematic, lengthy expanses of text in the *Credo*: this is an inspired move, witty, bold and original. The coupling of the two Masses has more than an anthological justification, for they could hardly be more contrasted. The Mass on *L'aveuglé dieu* appears to have been composed about 20 years after its companion, in the composer's old age. Its rich melodic vein bears the unmistakable stamp of his more serious, sophisticated Ronsard song-settings, though many will find *La bataille* the more immediately compelling of the two. The Janequin Ensemble's customary panache is here reinforced by a judicious coupling of organ, cornet and sackbuts, but they also manage to communicate the considerable dignity emanating from both Masses. This ensemble's forays into sacred music are rare, but always memorable. In revealing an unsuspected facet of Janequin's genius, they yet again do their standard-bearer.

Further listening ...
...Chansons – Le chant des oiseaux. Toutes les nuictz. J'atens le temps. Il estoit une fillette. Ung jour Colin. O doulx regard, o parler. Or sus vous dormez trop (L'alouette). Quand contrement verras. Hellas mon Dieu, ton ire. Ma peine n'est pas grande. O mal d'aymer. Herbes et fleurs. A ce joly moys. Assouvy suis. Quelqu'un me disoit l'aultre jour. M'y levay par ung matin. M'ayme a eu de Dieu. Le chant du rossignol. Las on peult juger (arr. Morlaye). L'aveuglé dieu qui partout vole (arr. Alberto da Ripa). **Ensemble Clément Janequin.** Harmonia Mundi HMC90 1099 (8/85).   Ⓖ

Philipp Jarnach   German 1892-

Suggested listening ...
...An eine Rose. *Coupled with works by* **Britten, Cornelius, Eisler, Fortner, Fröhlich, Hauer, Komma, Pfitzner, Ullmann** and **Reutter** Mitsuko Shirai (mez); **Hartmut Höll** (pf). Capriccio 10 534 (12/94). *See review in the Collections section; refer to the Index to Reviews.*

John Jenkins   British 1592-1678

Suggested listening ...
...Pavan in F major in six parts. Fantasia in C minor in five parts. Divisions in C major. Fantasia in C minor in four parts. Fantasia in F major, "All in a Garden Green". Pavan and Galliard, "Newarke Seidge". Ayre, Almaine and Coranto in D minor. Fantasia-Suite in A minor in two parts. Fantasias in three parts – C minor; D major; E minor. In Nomine in six parts in G minor. **Rose Consort of Viols.** Naxos 8 550687 (8/94). ✒
...Two Pavans. 11 Fantasias. Two In Nomines. **Hespèrion XX; Michel Behringer** (org). Auvidis Astrée E8724 (2/92). ✒
...Fantasia-Suites in four parts – F major; C major; E minor; A minor; F major, D major. Airs for lyra consort – C major, "The Six Bells"; G major. **The Parley of Instruments / Peter Holman.** Hyperion CDA66604 (12/92). ✒

Jongen Jersild   Danish 1913-

Suggested listening ...
...Three Romantic Songs. *Coupled with* **Rautavaara** Suite de Lorca, Op. 72. **Sandström** A Cradle Song/The Tyger. **Nørgård** And time shall be no more. **Tormis** The Curse of Iron. **Danish National Radio Choir / Stefan Parkman.** Chandos CHAN9264 (4/95).

Ignacio de Jerúsalem   Italian/Mexican c1710-1769

Jerúsalem Responsorio Segundo de S. S. José: "Esuriente terra Aegypti". Dixit Dominus. Polychoral Mass in D major.
Zumaya Sol fa de Pedro. Hieremiae Prophetae Lamentationes. Celebren, publiquen. **Chanticleer Chorus and Sinfonia / Joseph Jennings.** Teldec Das Alte Werk Ⓟ 4509-93333-2 (58 minutes: DDD: 12/94). Texts and translations included. Recorded 1993.

This is a very exciting disc indeed. We are hardly well supplied with recordings of baroque music from Spain and Portugal, let alone South America. Chanticleer have selected two of the most significant Mexican composers active in the first half of the eighteenth century and, in performances of outstanding quality, show that they are not merely pale imitations of their European counterparts, but have something original to say and the craftsmanship with which to say it. The border between *stile antico* and *stile moderno* in Latin American countries is almost imperceptible, and the former continued to be an important aspect of the latter. Zumaya's *Lamentationes*, recorded here, show just how thorough was the contrapuntal training he received and what effective use he could make of it. The delightful *Sol-fa de Pedro*, on the other hand, is entirely lost to the baroque at its most chromatic, and the stunning *Celebren, publiquen* shows what he could do with two choirs. The sonorous blocks of Jerúsalem's music, which one might describe as rococo, are quite different from the contrapuntal edifices of Zumaya, though there is no doubting the baroqueness of *Esuriente terra Aegypti*. Both composers are very well served by this fine recording, a breath of fresh air to anyone with the slightest interest in the baroque and just as much to those who consider the baroque of little interest – how strange it is that we continue to need these labels.

Jan Jirásek

Czechoslovakian 1955-

Suggested listening ...
...Missa Propria[a]. Katharsis[b]. *Coupled with* **Pärt** Variations for the healing of Arinushka[c].
Hildegard of Bingen (arr. Ivanoff) O Euchari, in leta vita[d]. **Traditional** Georgian Kartl-
k'akhetian Songs – Shen Khar Venakhi; Romelni Kerubinta[e]. **Eespere** Trivium[f]. [c]**Kalle Randalu**
(pf); [a]**Boni Pueri Boys' Choir / Jiri Skopal;** [d]**Vox / Vladimir Ivanoff;** [e]**Georgika Ensemble;**
[b]**Quartetto con Flauto;** [f]**Tallinn Camerata.** Catalyst 09026 68331-2 (2/96).

Joseph Joachim

Austrian/Hungarian 1831-1907

Suggested listening ...
...Violin Concerto in Hungarian Style, Op. 11[a]. Overtures – Hamlet, Op. 4; Henry IV, Op. 7. [a]**Elmar**
Oliveira (vn); **London Philharmonic Orchestra / Leon Botstein.** IMP Masters MCD27 (8/91).
...Variations on an Original Theme in E major, Op. 10. *Coupled with* **Brahms** Viola Sonatas,
Op. 120 – No. 1 in F minor; No. 2 in E flat major. **Rivka Golani** (va); **Konstantin Bogino** (pf).
Conifer CDCF199 (9/92). *See review under Brahms; refer to the Index to Reviews.*
...Andantino in A minor. Romance in B flat major. *Coupled with* **Brahms** (arr. Joachim)
21 Hungarian Dances. **Marat Bisengaliev** (vn); **John Lenehan** (pf). Naxos 8 553026 (3/96).

Robert Johnson II

British c1583-1633

R. Johnson Shakespeare's Lutenist – Where the bee sucks[ab]. Hark, hark! the lark[a]. Come hither,
you that love[a]. As I walked forth[a]. Woods, rocks and mountains[a]. 'Tis late and cold[b]. O let us
howl[b]. Arm, arm![b]. Come away, Hecate[ab]. Charon, oh Charon[a]. Away delights[a]. Come, heavy
sleep[a]. Care-charming sleep[a]. Full fathom five[b]. Have you seen the bright lily grow?[b]. Adieu, fond
love[b]. Come away, thou lady gay[ab]. Tell me dearest[ab]. Lute solo: Fantasia. Pavan. Galliard. Three
almans. Corant. [a]**Emma Kirkby** (sop); [b]**David Thomas** (bass); **Anthony Rooley** (lte). Virgin
Classics Veritas Ⓕ VC7 59321-2 (67 minutes: DDD: 4/94). Texts included. Recorded 1991. Ⓖ
Gramophone Editor's choice.
Robert Johnson's reputation in his own time was comparable with that of Dowland, but though his
also rested heavily on his songs and lute works he wrote far fewer of either. With this recording about
80 per cent of Johnson's songs are now available, and we are unlikely to be disturbed by their removal
from their original contexts. Kirkby is superbly expressive in her solo items, effortlessly agile in *Hark,*
hark! the lark, and contemptuously mocking in *Come away, thou lady gay*, giving her seducer a hard
time. Thomas snarls with mock menace in *Come away, Hecate* – Kirkby, the 'airy spirit', calls from a
microphonic distance – and is as stentorian in *Arm, arm!*, as he is sensitive in *Full fathom five* and
Have you seen the bright lily grow?. Rooley delivers the lute solos confidently. In short, a magnificent
(and clearly recorded) tribute to a composer who has received rather less attention than he deserves.
Further listening ...
...The Prince's Alman and Coranto. Air in G minor. The Temporiser a 4. The Witty Wanton.
Fantasia in G minor. *Coupled with works by* **A. Ferrabosco, II Webster, Nau, Notari** and
W. Lawes Parley of Instruments Renaissance Violin Band / Peter Holman. Hyperion CDA66806
(6/96). ✒ *See review in the Collections section; refer to the Index to Reviews.* Ⓖ

André Jolivet

French 1905-1974

New review
Jolivet Petite Suite[a]. Fantaisie-Caprice[b]. Flute Sonata[c]. Sonatine for Flute and Clarinet[d]. Alla
Rustica[e]. Suite en concert[f]. **Anna Noakes** (fl); [d]**Leslie Craven** (cl); [a]**Jonathan Barritt** (va); [ae]**Gillian**
Tingay (hp); [bc]**Kathron Sturrock** (pf); [f]**Graham Cole,** [f]**Kate Eyre,** [f]**Rachel Gledhill,** [f]**Gary Kettel**
(perc) / [f]**Martin Yates.** ASV Ⓔ CDDCA948 (66 minutes: DDD: 8/96). Recorded 1994.
Despite an accompaniment from just four percussionists, the *Suite en concert* (1965) counts as André
Jolivet's Second Flute Concerto (the First, with string orchestra, dates from 1949). For what is
effectively a Quintet, the Suite docs possess a remarkably orchestral feel, and one can understand why
its composer thought of it as a true concerto. Here it receives a splendid performance from Anna
Noakes. Jolivet loved the flute, and it is a tribute to his powers of invention that he was able to
produce such varied textures for these pieces, from the impressionist delicacy of the *Alla Rustica* and
Petite Suite (the latter scored for flute, viola and harp – surely the most euphonious of trios) to the
angular severity of the Sonata (1958 – the major item here after the Suite) and *Sonatina* (for flute and
clarinet, 1961). Anna Noakes proves a most committed and persuasive advocate in all these works, as
do her colleagues. ASV's recording is beautifully clear and well-balanced.
Additional recommendation ...
...Chant de Linos[a]. Flute Sonata[b]. *Coupled with* **Koechlin** Flute Sonata, Op. 52[c]. Quintet, Op. 156,
"Primavera"[d]. **Philippe Racine** (fl); [ad]**Robert Zimansky** (vn); [ad]**Monika Clemann** (va); [ad]**Curdin**

Coray (vc); [ad]**Xenia Schindler** (hp); [bc]**Daniel Cholette** (pf). Claves Ⓕ CD50-9003 (56 minutes: ADD: 10/90).

Further listening ...

...Concertino for Trumpet, Piano and Strings. *Coupled with works by* **Hummel, Tomasi** and **Haydn Sergei Nakariakov** (tpt); **Alexander Markovich** (pf); **Lausanne Chamber Orchestra / Jésus López-Cobos**. Teldec 4509-90846-2 (10/93). *See review in the Collections section; refer to the Index to Reviews.*

...Poèmes pour l'enfant[a]. Chant de Linos[b]. Pastorales de Noël. Suite liturgique[a]. [a]**Barbara Rearick** (mez); [b]**Karen Jones** (fl); **Britten-Pears Ensemble.** ASV CDDCA918 (8/95).

...Ascèses. *Coupled with* **Stravinsky** Three Pieces for Solo Clarinet. **Berio** Lied per clarinetto solo. Sequenza IX. **Stockhausen** In Freundschaft. **Messiaen** Quatuor pour la fin du temps – Abîme des oiseaux. **Boulez** Domaines. **Paul Meyer** (cl). Denon CO-78917 (7/95).

...Hymne à l'Univers. *Coupled with works by* **Dubois, Batiste, Bossi, Dupré, Lefébure-Wély, Lemare** and **Saint-Saëns Christopher Herrick** (org). Hyperion CDA66457 (9/91). *See review in the Collections section; refer to the Index to Reviews.* ⒼⒼⒼ

Joseph Jongen
Belgian 1873-1953

Jongen Symphonie concertante, Op. 81[a]. Suite, Op. 48[b]. Allegro appassionato, Op. 79[b] [a]**Hubert Schoonbroodt** (org); [b]**Therese-Marie Gilissen** (va); [a]**Liège Symphony Orchestra / René Defossez;** [b]**RTBF Symphony Orchestra / Brian Priestman.** Koch Schwann Ⓕ 315 012 (70 minutes: DDD: 8/92). Recorded 1975-85.

Jongen's *Symphonie concertante* is a spectacular showpiece for organ and large orchestra, full of thrilling effects, unforgettable tunes, spine-tingling climaxes and flashes of great beauty. Written in 1926 its rare performances today belie its sheer crowd-pulling potential, so it's very good to have the work readily available on CD. Having said that it should be pointed out that while this is a perfectly acceptable recording, it's neither the only one nor the best (see below for details of the Telarc recording which is very much in the demonstration class). No, what makes this a "Good CD" are the two works for viola and orchestra. The viola has little worthwhile concert repertory yet here is some wonderful music (especially the ravishing "Poème élégiaque" from the *Suite*) which has been allowed to wallow in obscurity for the best part of a century. Hopefully this disc will change all that. Therese-Marie Gilissen puts her all into this music, summoning up a vast array of emotions in the *Suite* and producing the kind of virtuoso playing in the *Allegro appassionato* more usually associated with the violin.

Additional recommendation ...

...Symphonie concertante. **Franck** Fantaisie in A major. Pastorale, Op. 19. **Michael Murray** (org); **San Francisco Symphony Orchestra / Edo de Waart.** Telarc Ⓕ CD80096 (56 minutes: DDD. 3/85).

Further listening ...

...Pièce pour Grand Orgue. Two Pieces, Op. 53. Pieces, Op. 5 – No. 1, Andante cantabile; No. 2, Pastorale; No. 4, Offertoire; No. 5, Communion. Prélude et Fugue, Op. 121. Elégie. Cantilene. Papillons noirs, Op. 69 No. 11. Two Pieces, Op. 47. Petite Pièce. Petit Prélude. Toccata, Op. 104. **John Scott Whiteley** (org). Priory PRCD324 (7/93).

Scott Joplin
American 1868-1917

Suggested listening ...

...The Entertainer. Maple Leaf Rag. *Coupled with* **Barber** Ballade, Op. 46. **Beach** Five Improvisations, Op. 148. **Bernstein** Five Anniversaries. **Cage** Bacchanale for Prepared Piano. **Copland** Four Piano Blues. **Gershwin** Three Preludes. **Gottschalk** Manchega, RO143. Le Banjo, RO22. **M. Gould** Boogie Woogie Etude. **MacDowell** New England Idylls, Op. 62. **Nancarrow** Prelude. **Michel Legrand** (pf). Erato 4509-96386-2 (7/95).

Josquin Desprez
French c1440-1521

New review

Josquin Desprez Missa de beata virgine.
Mouton Nesciens mater. Ave Maria virgo serena. Ave sanctissima Maria. O Maria piissima. Ave Maria gemma virginum. **Theatre of Voices / Paul Hillier.** Harmonia Mundi Ⓕ HMU90 7136 (53 minutes: DDD: 11/95). Texts and translations included. Recorded 1993.

Among the group of glorious composers who make the years around 1500 one of the richest eras in the history of music, it is too easy to forget Jean Mouton. However, he was one of the most successful; and he was the one who, in the eyes of sixteenth-century musicians, most successfully challenged the peerless Josquin Desprez. So it was a good idea to assemble a programme that juxtaposes the two composers: for Josquin it is his most successful Mass; and for Mouton a group of motets on the same theme – varied but all of them luscious and exhilarating. Effectively Paul Hillier divides up the Mass, as it would have been divided in a celebration, and puts Mouton's motets into the gaps. This works particularly well, because the constant juxtaposition of the two similar yet contrasting styles manages to clarify one's perception of both composers. The music is also superbly performed. The 15 singers of the Theatre of Voices are effortlessly clear, wonderfully in tune and beautifully balanced. You hear the lines and spaces of Josquin just as you hear the immaculately modulated colours of Mouton; and that is partly because the singers have such good control of a range of vocal timbre, from the sweetest to something really quite direct. But beyond that there is an energy in the performances that keeps everything marvellously alive: even for the listener who may occasionally feel that Hillier takes the music a touch briskly, there is constant delight in the shapes that result. Briefly, this is an issue of enormous distinction.

Josquin Desprez Missa Ave maris stella. Motets – Illibata Dei virgo nutrix. Gaude virgo, mater Christi. Salve regina. In te Domine speravi (with Andrew Lawrence-King, hp). Plaine de dueil. Que vous madame. Regretz sans fin. Adieu mes amours. Je n'ose plus (both with Andrew Lawrence-King).
Anonymous Ave maris stella. **Taverner Consort and Choir / Andrew Parrott.** EMI Reflexe
Ⓟ CDC7 54659-2 (77 minutes: DDD: 5/93). Texts and translations included. Recorded 1992.
Gramophone Editor's choice.　　　　　　　　　　　　　　　　　　　　　　　　　　Ⓖ
The customary glittering, steely sound of the Taverner Consort and Choir is here altered by the unexpected presence of countertenors, in an impressive programme of seldom-heard and seldom-recorded Josquin. The panorama it gives of Josquin's mastery of various techniques is fascinating: nobody could miss the contrast between *Illibata Dei virgo nutrix* and *Gaude virgo, mater Christi*. They are equally impressive, perfect examples of Josquin's contrapuntal and harmonic skill, and yet significantly different in their technical procedures and utterly different in the impression they make. Similarly, the *Missa Ave maris stella*, which stands midway between the earlier Mass settings and later works such as the *Missa Pange lingua*, offers points of comparison and contrast both because of its musical magnificence and because of its relative unfamiliarity. The performances are commensurate with the music, and though it is often a risk for an English group to record French-texted works (especially when experiments in pronunciation are involved), the *chansons* recorded here are also delightful. Altogether a provocative collection.
Additional recommendation ...
...Missa Ave maris stella. Monstra te esse matrem (Ave maris stella). Salve regina. Gaude virgo, mater Christi. Alma Redemptoris mater. Ave regina celorum. Vultum tuum deprecabuntur. **A Sei Voci / Bernard Fabre-Garrus.** Auvidis Astrée Ⓟ E8507 (63 minutes: DDD: 2/94).

New review
Josquin Desprez Missa de beata virgine. O virgo prudentissima. Stabat mater dolorosa/Comme femme desconfortee. Ave Maria ... virgo serena (six-voice version). Inviolata integra et castra es, Maria. Tu solus qui facis mirabilia. **A Sei Voci / Bernard Fabre-Garrus.** Auvidis Astrée Ⓟ E8560 (59 minutes: DDD: 5/96). Recorded 1995.
A Sei Voci have learned much from the British ensembles in recent years, but here they profit from that experience without losing their own distinctively French sound and attitude to musical lines. Their performances on this disc are perhaps faster than any others currently available; and with that speed comes a particular approach to musical details, a way of allowing a certain freedom of line to highlight some things and let others take care of themselves. It is a remarkably attractive sound; and lovers of this music will surely want it as representing a fresh approach to Josquin's most successful Mass. Bernard Fabre-Garrus takes the Mass *De beata virgine* at a low pitch – singing the low-clef *Credo* at modern concert pitch and transposing the rest down a fourth to match its ranges; strangely, he seems to be the first to take account of the ranges in this way, and his approach is entirely convincing. There is the occasional moment of muddy texture, but it makes for ease of tone-production and is the clue to the apparently effortless sound the singers produce. The result is very soothing but never lacking in verve. For the motets, this approach works particularly well. The *Stabat mater* sounds wonderfully moulded in this brisk performance, coming across better as a musical design than in any other recording. And the matching of voices to lines results in a beautifully clear and expressive reading of *Inviolata*. They also give a remarkably persuasive reading of the *Ave Maria ... virgo serena* in the expanded six-voice version that is highly unlikely to be Josquin's work but is nevertheless eminently worth hearing. This is Josquin to wallow in.

Josquin Desprez Missa L'homme armé super voces musicales. Missa L'homme armé sexti toni.
Anonymous L'homme armé. **The Tallis Scholars / Peter Phillips.** Gimell Ⓟ CDGIM019
(74 minutes: DDD: 7/89). 🖉 Text and translation included.
Towards the end of the Middle Ages it became customary to use popular secular melodies instead of the usual plainchant themes as the basis for composing polyphonic Masses. One such was the fifteenth-century melody *L'homme armé* ("Beware of the armed man"), a melody that may have originated as a crusader song. These settings would provide endless opportunities for a composer to demonstrate his contrapuntal skills. In the first of Josquin's two settings, *Super voces musicales*, he

uses the tune over and over again, beginning each time on successive ascending degrees of the six-note scale *Ut Re Mi Fa Sol La*, so that it rises higher and higher as the Mass progresses. Sometimes the melody appears back to front from halfway through the piece on to the end. In the *Sexti toni* Mass the tune is transposed so that F rather than G is the final note. The listener's enjoyment is in no way lessened by all this contrapuntal ingenuity. The music flows along with unsurpassed ease and beauty, displaying that unique quality of seeming inevitability which characterizes all great music. It is well matched by the expertise and enthusiasm of The Tallis Scholars and their first-class recording engineers.

Further listening ...

...Missa L'homme armé super voces musicales. *Coupled with* **Ockeghem** Missa Pro defunctis. **Pro Cantione Antiqua / Bruno Turner.** Archiv Produktion 415 293-2AH (4/86).

...Missa Pange lingua. Missa La sol fa re mi. **The Tallis Scholars / Peter Phillips.** Gimell CDGIM009 (3/87). *Gramophone classical 100.*   ⊙⊙⊙

...Missa Hercules dux Ferrarie. La déploration de Johannes Ockeghem, "Nymphes des bois". *Coupled with* **La Rue** Missa pro defunctis. **New London Chamber Choir / James Wood.** Amon Ra CDSAR24 (3/87).

...Missa Pange Lingua. Vultum tuum deprecabuntur. Planxit autem David. **Westminster Cathedral Choir / James O'Donnell.** Hyperion CDA66614 (4/93).

...Illibata Dei Virgo nutrix. *Coupled with* **Pullois** Flos de spina. **Busnois** Gaude coelestis Domina. In hydraulis. **Obrecht** (attrib.): Humilium decus. **Ockeghem** Missa prolationum. **The Clerks' Group / Edward Wickham.** ASV Gaudeamus CDGAU143 (3/96).

...(attrib.) Qui habitat in adjutorio Altissimi. *Coupled with works by* **Porta, Tallis, Ockeghem, Manchicourt, G. Gabrieli** and **Striggio** Huelgas Ensemble / Paul van Nevel. Sony Classical Vivarte SK66261 (4/96). *See review in the Collections section; refer to the Index to Reviews.*

Archibald Joyce   British 1873-1963

Suggested listening ...

...Dreaming. Prince of Wales. Songe d'automne. Frou-Frou. A thousand kisses. Caravan Suite. Dreams of you. Iris. Passing of Salome. Toto – suite. Acushla. Bohemia. Brighton hike. Song of the river. **Radio Telefis Eireann Concert Orchestra / Andrew Penny.** Marco Polo British Light Music 8 223694 (2/96).

...Dreaming. *Coupled with works by* **Binge, Williams, Coates, Toye, Collins, Farnon, Baynes, Curzon, Lutz, Gibbs, White, Ketèlbey, Ellis** and **Ancliffe** New London Orchestra / Ronald Corp. Hyperion CDA66868 (7/96). *Gramophone Editor's record of the month. See review in the Collections section; refer to the Index to Reviews.*   ⊙

Jurgis Juozapaitis   USSR/Lithuanian 1942-

Suggested listening ...

...Perpetuum mobile. *Coupled with* **Vasks** Cantabile. **Kutavičius** Northern Gates. **Urbaitis** Lithuanian Folk Music. **Tüür** Insular Deserta. **Rekašius** Music for Strings. **Ostrobothnian Chamber Orchestra / Juha Kangas.** Finlandia 4509-97893-2 (11/95).

Dmitry Kabalevsky   USSR 1904-1987

New review

Kabalevsky Cello Concerto No. 2 in G major, Op. 77[a].
Khachaturian Cello Concerto[a].
Rachmaninov (trans. Rose) Vocalise, Op. 34 No. 14[b]. **Mats Lidström** (vc); [a]**Gothenburg Symphony Orchestra / Vladimir Ashkenazy** ([b]pf). BIS Ⓔ CD719 (65 minutes: DDD: 7/96). Recorded live in 1995.

The cello does not have available too many twentieth-century concertos of real thematic memorability and so this BIS coupling is welcome in providing performances of two works which, if not masterpieces of the calibre of the Elgar or Dvořák concertos, are still sufficiently rewarding to be in the regular concert repertory. It certainly enables Ashkenazy (who proves an admirable accompanist throughout) to create an evocative opening atmosphere for the first movement of the Kabalevsky, when after mysterious string pizzicatos the soloist steals in with a gentle, singing tone. The soliloquy continues, for the work's unusual structure, with its three unbroken sections linked by cadenzas, invites an improvisational approach well understood by Mats Lidström. The *Allegro molto* centrepiece of the first movement brings unforced, yet exciting, virtuosity and then the opening mood is tenderly re-evoked. The *Poco marcato* scherzo features blazes of orchestral colour while the soloist swings along with splendid verve. Like the opening section, the third begins with another tender soliloquy, which continues with relatively minor interruptions from the wind and a burst of energetic passion shared by soloist and orchestra; then the mood again becomes tranquil. How differently the

Khachaturian Concerto opens, with a flamboyantly coloured orchestral declamation before the cello sails off with vigorous animation. This is followed by a sinuous Armenian theme from the wind which the cello takes up ruminatively, with well-judged *espressivo*. Yet it is the energetic main theme that dominates and the soloist is carried along on its impetus, while ardently recalling the secondary material, finally leading to an exciting sequential coda. Khachaturian produces a memorably long-breathed Slavic theme for the *Andante* to which Mats Lidström responds very affectingly while the finale again offers the busy, rumbustious Khachaturian we know so well from the Violin Concerto. This composer's major works (with the exception of the Violin Concerto) can seem rather inflated, but it must be said that here the combined concentration of Lidström and Ashkenazy minimizes this impression. As an encore we are given a beautiful, restrained account of Rachmaninov's *Vocalise*. The recording is of high quality and well balanced, but it is a shade over-resonant, although the ear adjusts.

Additional recommendation ...

...Cello Concerto. **Glazunov** Chant du ménéstrel, Op. 71; **Khachaturian** Cello Concerto. **Raphael Wallfisch** (vc); **London Philharmonic Orchestra / Bryden Thomson.** Chandos Ⓕ CHAN8579 (69 minutes: DDD: 6/88). Ⓖ

Kabalevsky Symphony No. 2 in C minor, Op. 19[a].
Miaskovsky Symphony No. 21, Op. 51, "Fantasy in F sharp minor"[a].
Shostakovich Hamlet suite, Op. 116a[b] – Introduction; Ball at the palace; The ghost; The poisoning; The players; Duel and death of Hamlet. [a]**New Philharmonia Orchestra / David Measham;** [b]**National Philharmonic Orchestra / Bernard Herrmann.** Unicorn-Kanchana Souvenir Ⓜ UKCD2066 (64 minutes: ADD: 2/95). Items marked [a] from RHS346 (4/78), [b]Decca PFS4315 (8/75). Recorded 1973-5.

Miaskovsky's twenty-first was for a long time the one symphony which kept his name alive in the West. The subtitle 'Fantasy' is rather a misnomer; nor is there any conspicuous sign of the times in which it was composed. But the themes are attractive in their friendly, neo-romantic-Waltonian way, and for the most part they are capable of standing up to the extensive repetition to which they are subjected – altogether an audience-friendly and rewarding piece. Kabalevsky's Second is no less indebted to the Rimsky-Korsakov academic line of symphonism – Russian romantic but without the emotional pressure. There is much sensitive phrasing from the New Philharmonia and the outer movements of the Kabalevsky go at a fine lick, while the hushed conclusion of his slow movement is beautifully handled. The only signs of short acquaintance are some scrabbly passages in the violins, which are also a drawback in the National Philharmonic Orchestra's playing of the Palace Ball movement in the Shostakovich *Hamlet* Suite. But never mind. This, too, is an idiomatic performance in its gritty determination, and rival versions certainly show no superior understanding of this bleak score. The recordings still sound first-rate.

Further listening ...

...Colas Breugnon – Overture. *Coupled with works by* **Glinka, Tchaikovsky, Mussorgsky** and **Borodin Chicago Symphony Orchestra / Fritz Reiner.** RCA Victor Living Stereo 09026 61958-2 (8/94). *See review in the Collections section; refer to the Index to Reviews.* ⒼⒼⒼ
...Piano Sonatas – No. 1 in F major, Op. 6; No. 2 in E flat major, Op. 45; No. 3 in F major, Op. 46. Four Preludes, Op. 5. Recitative and Rondo, Op. 84. **Artur Pizarro** (pf). Collins Classics 1418-2 (12/94).
...Piano Sonata No. 3 in F major. *Coupled with works by* **Prokofiev, Poulenc, Barber** and **Fauré** Vladimir Horowitz (pf). RCA Victor Gold Seal mono/[a]stereo GD60377* (6/92). *See review in the Collections section; refer to the Index to Reviews.*

Mauricio Kagel
Argentinian 1931-

New review

Kagel Sankt-Bach-Passion. **Anne Sofie von Otter** (mez); **Hans-Peter Blochwitz** (ten); **Roland Hermann** (bar); **Peter Roggisch** (narr); **Gerd Zacher** (org); **Limberg Cathedral Children's Choir; Hamburg Radio Choir; Stuttgart Radio Chorus and Symphony Orchestra / Mauricio Kagel.** Auvidis Montaigne Ⓕ MO782044 (two discs: 100 minutes: ADD: 6/96). Text and translation included. Recorded 1985.

If your immediate response to Kagel's title is to suspect an elaborate joke, study of his text, with lines like "Ein feste Burg ist uns'rer Bach", might suggest (at least to sensitive souls) a subversiveness bordering on blasphemy. So the easily shocked should be reassured that the one thing Kagel does not do is to send up large chunks of Bach's Passions. This is a respectful, even reverent, tribute from one composer to a great predecessor, and there is no direct quotation or parody of Bach's own music. As for the purely verbal parody, it is difficult to find such understated humour in any way offensive. Written for performance during the tricentennial year of 1985, the work traces Bach's life through a narration which draws on contemporary documents. The most obvious difference between its structure and that of Bach's Passions is that the commentaries on that narration – arias, choruses – are a good deal less substantial. Kagel seems well aware that his own idiom is not primarily a lyrical one, and the story of Bach's long and (fairly) eventful life is told through very direct, uncluttered music. From time to time the music taps a more expressionistic, even surrealistic vein, yet its prevailing restraint reflects the constructivist methods which Kagel employed in putting it together. Such restraint does not make for dull listening, even though the emphasis on narration, and the use of a speaker for certain passages, undoubtedly reduces the purely musical interest of the work in places. Fortunately there is a lively spontaneity to compensate, which is well caught in an excellent performance recorded soon after the Berlin première in 1985. The recording is fine, the documentation excellent.

Further listening ...

...Exotica[a]. Tactil[b]. **Wilhelm Bruck, Theodor Ross** ([a]instrs/[b]gtr and harm); [a]**Michel Portal,** [a]**Vinko Globokar,** [a]**Christoph Caskel,** [a]**Siegfried Palm** (instrs) / **Mauricio Kagel** ([b]pf/harm). DG 20th Century Classics 445 252-2GC (10/94).

Jouni Kaipainen

Finnish 1956-

New review

Kaipainen Symphony No. 2, Op. 44. Oboe Concerto, Op. 46[a]. Sisyphus Dreams, Op. 47. [a]**Helén Jahren** (ob); **Finnish Radio Symphony Orchestra / Sakari Oramo.** Ondine Ⓕ ODE855-2 (64 minutes: DDD: 3/96). Recorded 1995.

Jouni Kaipainen is one of the finest amongst the younger generations of Finnish composers. His music characteristically displays an engaging and remarkable fusion of diatonicism within a sound-world of serial complexity, reflecting the impact of the two principal mentors from his youth: Aulis Sallinen and Paavo Heininen. But Kaipainen has steadily developed away from both of them to forge his own style. This can be already heard in his First Symphony (1980-85) and Clarinet Concerto, *Carpe diem!* (1990). The single-span structure of Symphony No. 1 retained remarkable spontaneity despite taking six years to perfect. Its successor, outwardly more conventional in three movements, had less protracted birth pangs and is an even more impressive achievement, perhaps the finest Finnish symphony since Rautavaara's Fifth (1986). Admirers of Sibelius's architectonic instinct will find much to their liking here, even if at times Kaipainen sounds rather closer in spirit to Karl Amadeus Hartmann. The other two pieces also date from 1994. *Sisyphus Dreams* is basically a tone-poem, alternating black moods with hopeful quietude. The splendid Oboe Concerto is outwardly of a lighter disposition than the symphony but highly virtuosic, delivered with breathtaking aplomb by its dedicatee, Helén Jahren. The orchestral playing in all three items is of a high order.

Vaasily Sergeyevich Kalinnikov

USSR 1866-1901

Suggested listening ...

...Symphony No. 1 in G minor. *Coupled with* **Glazunov** The sea – Fantasy, Op. 28. Spring, Op. 34. **Scottish National Orchestra / Neeme Järvi.** Chandos CHAN8611 (10/88).

...Symphony No. 2 in A major. Tsar Boris – Overture. The cedar and the palm. **Scottish National Orchestra / Neeme Järvi.** Chandos CHAN8805 (6/90).

Imre Kalmán

Hungarian/American 1882-1953

Suggested listening ...

...Gräfin Mariza – operetta: excerpts. **Soloists; New Sadlers Wells Opera Chorus and Orchestra / Barry Wordsworth.** TER Classics CDTEO1007.

Giya Kancheli

Georgian 1935-

New review

Kancheli Symphony No. 3[a].

Pärt Symphony No. 3. Fratres. [a]**David James** (alto); **London Philharmonic Orchestra / Franz Welser-Möst** EMI Ⓕ CDC5 55619-2 (55 minutes: DDD: 8/96). *Gramophone Editor's choice.*

This is a natural and effective coupling of spiritual-minimalist pieces from the Baltic and the Balkans. The benefits are clear in Kancheli's Third Symphony, with its extreme contrasts of solo vocal keening and Stravinskian outbursts. Here the spaciousness of EMI's recording and the refinement of the LPO's playing are clear gains over the rival Georgian performance (which comes with the added drawback of having been transferred a whole tone too high by the original Melodiya team). The mesmeric folk-derived lament which punctuates the structure was sung on the earlier recording by Rustavi choir-member Gamlet Gonashvili, for whose unearthly tenor Kancheli conceived it. On the new issue David James's ethereal countertenor, familiar from his work with the Hilliard Ensemble, is a valid alternative and one sanctioned by the composer. Franz Welser-Möst's basic tempo for the piece is less extreme than Kakhidze's; however, by the same token the impression of hypnotically sustained timelessness is slightly diminished. So for the fullest appreciation of this extraordinary music, both versions are needed. Pärt's Third Symphony, composed in 1971, two years before Kancheli's, is something of a half-way house in the composer's journey towards his now famous ascetic minimalism. Its chant-based archaisms sit rather oddly beside reminders of the twentieth-century mainstream, like a meditation annoyingly distracted by the outside world. Pärt's real breakthrough came with pieces like *Fratres*, which first appeared six years later, where the technical means are even slighter but the contemplative end is the more fully realized. *Fratres* is beautifully shaded and sustained by Welser-Möst and his players.

Additional recommendation ...
...Symphonies Nos. 3[a] and 6[b]. [a]**Gamlet Gonashvili** (ten); [b]**Archil Kharadze**, [b]**Giya Chaduneli** (vas); **Georgia State Symphony Orchestra / Dzansug Kakhidze.** Olympia Explorer OCD401 (9/90). Ⓖ

New review
Kancheli Exil. **Maacha Deubner** (sop); **Natalia Pschenitschnikova** (fl); **Catrin Demenga** (vn); **Ruth Killius** (va); **Rebecca Firth** (vc); **Christian Sutter** (db) / **Wladimir Jurowski.** ECM New Series Ⓕ 447 808-2 (48 minutes: DDD: 12/95). Texts and translations included. Recorded 1994.
Exil is a five-movement song-cycle, wholly contemporary in spirit, yet not excluding any listener with ears to hear and a soul to suffer. Some might counter by saying that music like Kancheli's, which increasingly wears its spirituality on its sleeve, is in danger of creating its own clique of New Age compassion-obsessed fellow-travellers. Certainly there is a danger that a concept such as that of *Exil*, so resonant in a world of multiple ethnic conflagrations, emotionally blackmails us into uncritical approval. But that would only be so if the music itself were deficient. One is immediately drawn in by the hovering, flute-timbred lines which make up the very discreet taped background to the first movement, a setting of Psalm 23. They are like melancholy calls over bleak mountains, and they return to punctuate and haunt the rest of the cycle. The very first chord which joins in, so familiar yet so elusive, has Kancheli's signature all over it. Exemplary performances and recording make this a valuable addition to the discography of one of the more notable voices in the music of our time.

Further listening ...
...Symphonies – No. 2, "Songs"; No. 7, "Epilogue". **Berlin Radio Symphony Orchestra / Michail Jurowski.** CPO CPO999 263-2 (8/95).
...Symphonies – No. 4, "In Commemoration of Michaelangelo" (1975); No. 5 (1976). **Georgia State Symphony Orchestra / Dzansug Kakhidze.** Olympia OCD403 (4/91).
...Symphonies – No. 6; No. 7, "Epilogue". **Tbilisi Symphony Orchestra / Jansug Kakhidze.** Sony Classical St Petersburg Classics SMK66590 (5/95).
...Liturgy for Viola and Orchestra, "Mourned by the Wind"[a]. *Coupled with* **Schnittke** Viola Concerto[b]. **Kim Kashkashian** (va); [a]**Bonn Beethovenhalle Orchestra;** [b]**Saarbrücken Radio Symphony Orchestra / Dennis Russell Davies.** ECM New Series 437 199-2 (4/93). Ⓖ
...Morning Prayers[a]. Evening Prayers[b]. Abii ne viderem[c]. [a]**Vasiko Tevdorashvili** (voc); [a]**Natalia Pschenitschnikova** (fl); [c]**Kim Kashkashian** (va); [b]**Hilliard Ensemble; Stuttgart Chamber Orchestra / Dennis Russell Davies.** ECM New Series 445 941-2 (4/95).   ⒼⒼ

Raimo Kangro
Estonian 1949-

Suggested listening ...
...Idioms, Op. 43a. *Coupled with works by* **Mägi, Põldmäe, Eespere, Sumera** and **Vähi Tallinn Camerata.** Finlandia 4509-95705-2 (5/95).
...Suite, Op. 1. *Coupled with works by* **Mägi, Rääts, Sumera, Tüür, Vähi** and **Pärt Lauri Väinmaa** (pf). Finlandia 4509-95704-2 (7/95).

Johann Kapsberger
German/Italian c1580-1651

Kapsberger Libro IV d'intavolatura di chitarrone. Libro I d'intavolatura di chitarrone – Toccata arpeggiata. **Rolf Lislevand** (theorbo); **Eduardo Eguez** (gtr); **Brian Feehan** (chitarrone); **Guido Morini** (org/hpd); **Lorentz Duftschmid** (violone); **Pedro Estevan** (perc). Auvidis Astrée Ⓕ E8515 (60 minutes: DDD: 4/95). Recorded 1993. ⒼⒼ
Rolf Lislevand is one of the most interesting lutenists active today. He has dazzling technique (listen to the last track), an extraordinarily wide dynamic range, an effortlessly infectious rhythmic style, and he grasps hold of the music in a way that makes each piece very much his own. Briefly, he projects with uncanny ease. That is also to say that he is a thoroughly idiosyncratic musician, and it may be that in the longer term his pure showiness could wear thin. But for the moment one can unhesitatingly recommend this as a disc for those who normally find lute music tedious and introverted: everything here sizzles with life. Kapsberger generally has a reputation as an extremely interesting bad composer – a reputation enthusiastically endorsed in Lislevand's quirky insert-note. But the performances here bring the music very much to life. Taking his lead from Agazzari's treatise, Lislevand uses a five-man continuo group to back the solos: a wonderfully flexible and exciting group. And, drawing hints from some of the titles and styles as well as from the international ambience of Kapsberger's Venice, he makes much use of oriental sources, not least in the colourful percussion playing of the virtuosic

Pedro Estevan: there is very sophisticated drumming here, and for the "Canario" he creates an uncanny imitation of a canary. The only faint criticism is that there could have been a little more documentation. Details of who is playing in which piece would have helped the ear to understand the myriad sounds.

Nikolai Karetnikov
USSR 1930-

Suggested listening ...
...Till Eulenspiegel. **Soloists; Chorus; Soviet Cinema Orchestra / Emin Khatchaturian, Valery Poliansky.** CdM Russian Season LDC288 029/30 (7/92).

Sigfrid Karg-Elert
German 1877-1933

Suggested listening ...
...Stimmen der Nacht, Op. 142 No. 1. Four diverse Pieces, Op. 75. *Coupled with* **Bach** Trio Sonata No. 5 in C major, BWV529. **Reger** Chorale Fantasia, "Wie schön leucht' uns der Morgenstern", Op. 40 No. 1. **Graham Barber** (org). Priory PRCD315 (11/93).

Udo Kasemets
Estonian/Canadian 1919-

Suggested listening ...
...Requiem Renga. Palestrina on Devil's Staircase. The Eight Houses of the I Ching. **Lyra Borealis Ensemble / Paavo Järvi.** Koch International Classics 37165-2 (4/95).

Alexandr Kastal'sky
USSR 1856-1926

New review
Kastal'sky Liturgy of St John Chrysostom. *(Coupled with works detailed below.)* **Bolshoi Theatre Children's Choir / Andrey Zaboronok.** Collins Classics Ⓕ 1443-2 (68 minutes: DDD: 7/95). Recorded 1994.
Anonymous Russian Orthodox Chant: Easter Stikhiras. From my youth. Stikhira to the Russian Holymen. **Chesnokov** Come, let us entreat Joseph, Op. 9 No. 9. Bless the Lord, o my soul, Op. 27 No. 1. Joyous light, Op. 9 No. 21. Let us, mystically representing the Cherubim. Praise ye the name of the Lord in heaven. **Sariyev** The Lord, our God. **Bortnyansky** Many years.

Kastal'sky is certainly under-represented in the record catalogues, so this disc is particularly welcome, though one should not come away with the impression that all the music on it was specially written for children's choir, the art of transposing up or down an octave being an important part of Russian choral practice. The Bolshoi Theatre Children's Choir (originally the children's choir of the famous Synodal School of Moscow) are outstanding, singing with perfect blend and tuning and a bell-like clarity reminiscent of choirs in Finland and Estonia. In the supple melodic writing of Kastal'sky's *Liturgy* they contrast very well with the baritone voice of Father Alexey Godunov, who sings the priest's sections (they can hardly be called "solo responds" as the booklet has it, since the choir are responding to the priest). The highlight of the *Liturgy* is undoubtedly *Miloserdiya dveri otverzi nam* ("The doors of mercy"), though it does not have quite the impact of the mixed-choir version, which shows Kastal'sky's formidable choral technique at its best. Equally impressive are the pieces by Chesnokov and the three Easter *stikhira* written in what was for Russia the Middle Ages (that is, up to the eighteenth century). These are superb examples of this astringent style, and immaculately sung. They all sound considerably more modern than the piece by Valery Sariyev (b.1950), which relies rather heavily on the lush sound and melodic style typical of nineteenth-century repertoire. An excellent disc, then, though presentation is sketchy: translations would be useful to those without specialist knowledge of this repertoire.

Reinhard Keiser
German 1674-1739

Suggested listening ...
...Masagniello furioso. **Soloists; Bremen Vocal Ensemble for Ancient Music; Fiori Musicali / Thomas Albert.** CPO CPO999 110-2 (11/93). 🎵
...St Mark Passion. **Soloists; Parthenia Vocal; Parthenia Baroque / Christian Brembeck.** Christophorus CHR77143 (3/95).

David Kellner

German c1670-1748

Suggested listening ...
...Auserlesene Lauten-Stücke. **Stephen Stubbs** (lte). CPO CPO999 097-2 (9/93). ✐

Jerome Kern

American 1885-1945

Kern Jerome Kern Treasury. [a]**Rebecca Luker** (sngr); [b]**Jeanne Lehman** (sop); [c]**Lydia Mila** (sngr); [d]**Hugh Panaro** (sngr); [e]**George Dvorsky** (ten); [f]**Thomas Hampson** (bar); [g]**London Sinfonietta Chorus; London Sinfonietta / John McGlinn.** EMI Ⓕ CDC7 54883-2 (79 minutes: DDD: 4/94). Texts included. Recorded 1992.　　　　　　　　　　　　　　　　　　　　　Ⓖ
The Red Petticoat – The Ragtime Restaurant[adg]. Very Good Eddie – Babes in the Wood[ad]. Love o' Mike – Drift with me[ae]. Have a Heart – I'm so busy[ae]. Oh Boy! – Till the clouds roll by[ad]. Zip Goes a Million – Whip-poor-will[be]. She's a Good Fellow – The Bullfrog Patrol[abg]. Dear Sir – I want to be there[ae]; Wishing-well scene[ae]. The Cat and the Fiddle – She didn't say "Yes"[b]; Every little while[be]. Music in the Air – In Egern of the Tegern See[b]; The song is you[f]. Roberta – Smoke gets in your eyes[b]. High, Wide and Handsome – The folks who live on the hill[f]. Very Warm for May – Harlem Boogie-Woogie; Heaven in my arms[abcdeg]. The last time I saw Paris[f].
A quick glance at these titles points up the familiarity of the post-*Show Boat* songs of the 1930s in comparison with those recorded here from 1912 to 1924, of which "Till the clouds roll by" alone has found popularity. With the exception of "The Ragtime Restaurant", a timely reminder that Berlin didn't have the monopoly on that craze, these early songs inhabit a world of expression that Kern made peculiarly his own both in the sentiments they express and in his musical settings. Included here is the "Wishing-well scene" from *Dear Sir* that foreshadows the composition of *Show Boat* three years later. In the later songs, it is instructive to be reminded that a song like "The folks who live on the hill" was composed with a lolloping rhythmic background not at all like the popular version by Peggy Lee. Thomas Hampson brings his powerful baritone to this ballad and gives a sensitive account of *Last time I saw Paris*, and the other soloists have never given better of themselves than here. In common with their conductor, they have an instinct and a rapport for Kern's infectious musical world that is matched by the warmth of this recording that enables all the many varied touches in the orchestrations to gleam brightly. This treasury deserves to become a classic of the music-theatre discography.
Additional recommendation ...
...High, Wide and Handsome – The folks who live on the hill. You Were Never Lovelier – I'm old fashioned. Swing Time – The way you look tonight; A fine romance. Music in the Air – The song is you. Roberta – Yesterdays; Smoke gets in your eyes. Lady be good. The last time I saw Paris. Very Warm for May – All the things you are. Show Boat – Can't help lovin' dat man; Bill. Cover Girl – Long ago and far away. Centennial Summer – All through the day. Sally – Look for the silver lining. **Dame Kiri Te Kanawa** (sop); **London Sinfonietta / Jonathan Tunick.** EMI Ⓕ CDC7 54527-2 (45 minutes: DDD: 7/93).

Kern Show Boat. Cast includes **Teresa Stratas, Frederica von Stade, Jerry Hadley, Bruce Hubbard, Karla Burns; Ambrosian Chorus; London Sinfonietta / John McGlinn.** EMI Ⓕ CDS7 49108-2 (three discs: 222 minutes: DDD: 11/88). Notes and text included. Recorded 1987. *Gramophone classical 100*. *Gramophone Award Winner 1989.*　　　　　　　　　　　　　　ⒼⒼⒼ
This three-CD *Show Boat* is a remarkable, inspired achievement that is far from being an example of a musical swamped by the misguided use of operatic voices. *Show Boat* was composed on a large scale for singers of accomplishments far above those we often hear in the theatre today, and here it is given its due. "Make believe", "Ol' man river", "Can't help lovin' dat man", "Why do I love you?" and "You are love" have been sung by countless singers over the years, but in beauty and style the performances here can surely never have been rivalled. The love duets between Frederica von Stade and Jerry Hadley are stunningly beautiful and Bruce Hubbard's firm, honeyed baritone has absolutely nothing to fear from comparisons with Paul Robeson. Teresa Stratas's "Can't help lovin' dat man" is quite ravishing. But the success of this set is due above all to the enthusiasm and dedication of its conductor, John McGlinn. His avowed aim has been to include all the music Kern wrote for the piece over the years for various stage and film productions. Much of this appears in a lengthy and fascinating appendix; but the main text itself includes not only full-length versions of numbers traditionally much shortened but other magnificent items dropped during try-outs and only rediscovered in a Warner Brothers warehouse in 1982. Not least he has restored the original orchestrations of Robert Russell Bennett. The London Sinfonietta clearly revel in them, not least the jazz-flavoured elements of the final Act. The Ambrosian Chorus, too, have a field day in the rousing choral numbers. Bright, spacious recorded sound helps to make this a quite magnificent, quite irresistibly enjoyable achievement.
Additional recommendation ...
...(1946 version) **Soloists; National Symphony Orchestra / John Owen Edwards.** TER Classics Ⓕ CDTER21199 (two discs: 95 minutes: DDD: 6/94).
Further listening ...
...Swing Time – Pick yourself up; The way you look tonight; Waltz in Swing Time. Roberta – You're devastating; Smoke gets in your eyes; Let's begin; I won't dance. High, Wide and

Handsome – The folks who live on the hill. Show Boat – I have the room above her. Music in the Air – Medley. Cover Girl – Sure thing. I Dream Too Much – I dream too much. Can't help singing – Can't help singing. The Cabaret Girl – Dancing time. The Cat and the Fiddle – She didn't say "Yes". Night Boat – Left all alone again blues. Miss 1917 – Go little boat. Very Warm for May – All the things you are; In the heart of the dark. Leave it to Jane – There it is again. Oh Boy! – Till the clouds roll by. The Girl from Utah – They didn't believe me. **Eric Parkin** (pf). Silva Treasury SILVAD3006 (3/95). All items arr. Parkin.

Aaron Kernis

American 1960-

Suggested listening ...

...New Era Dance. *Coupled with* **J. Adams** The Chairman Dances. **Bernstein** West Side Story – Mambo. **Schiff** Stomp. **Larsen** Collage: Boogie. **Harbison** Remembering Gatsby. **Torke** Black and White – Charcoal. **Moran** Points of Departure. **Agento** The Dream of Valentino – Tango. **Daugherty** Desi. **Rouse** Bonham. **Baltimore Symphony Orchestra / David Zinman.** Argo 444 454-2ZH (7/95).

Albert Ketèlbey

British 1875-1959

Ketèlbey Bells across the meadows[b]. Chal Romano[b]. The Clock and the Dresden Figures[bf]. In a Chinese Temple Garden[ab]. In a Monastery Garden[ab]. In a Persian Market[ab]. In the Moonlight (Sous la lune)[b]. In the Mystic Land of Egypt[abe]. Sanctuary of the Heart[abd].
Luigini Ballet égyptien, Op. 12 – Suite[c]. [d]**Jean Temperley** (mez); [e]**Vernon Midgley** (ten); [f]**Leslie Pearson** (pf); [a]**Ambrosian Singers;** [b]**Philharmonia Orchestra / John Lanchbery;** [c]**Royal Philharmonic Orchestra / Anatole Fistoulari.** Classics for Pleasure ® CD-CFP4637 (69 minutes: ADD: 3/94). Items marked [abdef] recorded in 1977, [c]1958.
The favourites are played with grace and sensitivity on the Marco Polo disc but we also get the opportunity to hear some of Ketèlbey's unjustly overshadowed compositions. And what delights there are! Over-exposure to Ketèlbey's more stereotyped, highly perfumed compositions has disguised what varied and inventive music he composed. We know the charms of *The Clock and the Dresden Figures* and *In the Moonlight*, the invigorating open-air spirit of *Chal Romano* from the Lanchbery collection. However, surely nobody would want to be without the equally invigorating overture *The Adventurers*, the elegant *Suite romantique*, the sparkling *Caprice pianistique* and the jaunty *Wedgwood Blue* – and what a pity we are restricted to just two movements of the *Cockney Suite*. With playing, conducting and recording of a high standard, this is a collection that demands to be heard. The Classics for Pleasure reissue gives us a captivating and indispensable budget-price Ketèlbey collection with the Philharmonia Orchestra playing with great style and hugely enjoying themselves. The Ambrosian Singers provide additional atmosphere in *In a Monastery Garden, In a Persian Market, In a Chinese Temple Garden* and *In the Mystic Land of Egypt*, and ensure the sentimental opulence of *Sanctuary of the Heart*. Ketèlbey programmes don't come much better than this. To make it even more enticing, CfP have added the superb 1958 RPO/Anatole Fistoulari recording of Luigini's *Ballet égyptien*. Like the Ketèlbey pieces it is a tuneful suite and has been in and out of the catalogue seemingly since the dawn of time, but has certainly never been better played than it is here. This CD also benefits from exceptionally informative notes.

Additional recommendations ...

...In a Monastery Garden. Wedgewood Blue. In the Mystic Land of Egypt. Bells across the meadows. In a Chinese Temple Garden. Sanctuary of the Heart. Cockney Suite – No. 5, Bank Holiday. Phantom melody. In a Persian Market. *Coupled with works by* **Hubay, Godard, Tchaikovsky, Sternhold, Massenet, Heuberger, Korngold** and **Monti** Royal Philharmonic Choir and Orchestra / Eric Rogers. Decca London Phase 4 ⓜ 444 786-2LPF (77 minutes. ADD. 8/96).

...In a Monastery Garden[a]. The Adventurers. Chal Romano – Descriptive Overture. Suite romantique. Caprice pianistique. The Clock and the Dresden Figures. Cockney Suite – No. 3, At the Palais de Danse; No. 5, Bank Holiday. In the Moonlight. Wedgwood Blue. Bells across the meadows. Phantom melody. In a Persian Market[a]. [a]**Slovak Philharmonic Male Chorus; Bratislava Radio Symphony Orchestra / Adrian Leaper.** Marco Polo ⓕ 8 223442 (74 minutes: DDD: 4/94).

...Bells across the meadows. *Coupled with works by* **Binge, Williams, Coates, Toye, Collins, Farnon, Baynes, Curzon, Lutz, Gibbs, White, Joyce, Ellis** and **Ancliffe** New London Orchestra / Ronald Corp. Hyperion ⓕ CDA66868 (78 minutes: DDD: 7/96). *Gramophone Editor's record of the month. See review in the Collections section; refer to the Index to Reviews.* ⓖ

Aram Khachaturian

New review
Khachaturian Violin Concerto in D minor.
Tchaikovsky (arr. Glazunov) Méditation, Op. 42 No. 1. **Itzhak Perlman** (vn); **Israel Philharmonic Orchestra / Zubin Mehta.** EMI Ⓔ CDC7 47087-2 (46 minutes: DDD: 7/85). From EL270108-1 (3/85).

The twentieth century has had its share of great violin concertos. Khachaturian's is not quite that, in the sense that it never attempts the heights and depths we find in his Soviet colleagues, Prokofiev and Shostakovich; but is a work of considerable charm, beautifully written. Shostakovich once pointed out that a "natural and folk idiom" was evident in everything his friend wrote, and Khachaturian's Armenian origin is agreeably evident in the melodic and harmonic contours of the lilting second theme in the first movement and the *Andante sostenuto* that follows. It goes without saying that Itzhak Perlman plays this work with total technical command and persuasive feeling, and the result is most enjoyable, even if one feels in some places, such as the first movement's long cadenza, that musical inspiration is being spread rather thin. The finale, however, is predictably exciting. The Tchaikovsky *Méditation* coupling is well worth having, both for its intrinsic quality and also because it was originally planned as the slow movement of his own Violin Concerto. There is good accompaniment from Mehta and the Israel Philharmonic Orchestra and a bright recording.

Additional recommendation ...
...Violin Concerto in D minor. *Coupled with* **Kabalevsky** Violin Concerto in C major, Op. 48.
 Lydia Mordkovitch (vn); **Royal Scottish National Orchestra / Neeme Järvi.** Chandos
 Ⓔ CHAN8918 (53 minutes: DDD: 3/91).

New review
Khachaturian Piano Concerto[a]. Dance Suite. Five Pieces for Wind Band – Waltz; Polka.
[a]**Dora Serviarian-Kuhn** (pf); **Armenian Philharmonic Orchestra / Loris Tjeknavorian.** ASV
 Ⓔ CDDCA964 (59 minutes: DDD: 6/96). Recorded 1995.

In the Piano Concerto Dora Serviarian-Kuhn and her Armenian compatriot, Loris Tjeknavorian are in every way first-class: both identify naturally with the sinuous oriental flavour of the melodic lines and understand that the outer movements need above all to convey thrusting vitality. Here there is plenty of drive and rhythmic lift in the outer movements. But what primarily makes this performance memorable is Serviarian-Kuhn's sense of fantasy, so that her various cadential passages, for all their brilliance, are charismatically quixotic rather than merely bravura displays. The other works are very small beer. The "Waltz" for wind band has an engaging carousel flavour; the somewhat vulgar "Polka" which follows roisterously suggests the circus. The *Dance Suite* goes through the usual Khachaturian routines with which he likes to clothe his agreeable but at times rather insubstantial Armenian folk ideas. Easily the most memorable movement is the first and much the longer of the two Uzbek dances, which opens gently and touchingly: the reprise, with its haunting cor anglais solo, has a genial Nordic feeling. The closing "Lezghinka", too, is rather jolly, but repetitive. Excellent performances, vividly recorded.

Additional recommendations ...
...Piano Concerto. *Coupled with works by* **Prokofiev** and **Liszt** William Kapell (pf); **Boston Symphony Orchestra / Serge Koussevitzky.** RCA Victor Gold Seal mono Ⓜ GD60921* (71 minutes: ADD: 5/95).   Ⓖ
...Symphony No. 2 in E minor, "The Bell"[a]. Piano Concerto[b]. Violin Concerto in D minor[c].
 Masquerade – Suite[d]. [c]**Ruggiero Ricci** (vn); [b]**Alicia de Larrocha** (pf); [a]**Vienna Philharmonic Orchestra / Aram Khachaturian;** [bc]**London Philharmonic Orchestra /** [b]**Raphael Frühbeck de Burgos,** [c]**Anatole Fistoulari;** [d]**London Symphony Orchestra / Stanley Black.** Double Decca
 Ⓜ 448 252-2DF2 (two discs: 146 minutes: ADD: 6/96).

New review
Khachaturian Masquerade[a] – Waltz; Nocturne; Mazurka. Violin Concerto in D minor[b].
 Gayaneh[c] – Sabre Dance; Ayesha's Dance; Dance of the Rose Maidens; Lullaby; Lezghinka;
 Gayaneh's Adagio; Lyrical duo; Dance of the old people. [b]**David Oistrakh** (vn); **Philharmonia Orchestra / Aram Khachaturian.** EMI Composers in Person mono Ⓔ CDC5 55035-2*
 (79 minutes: ADD: 7/94). Item marked [a] from Columbia 33C1043 (11/55), [b]Columbia 33CX1303 (12/55), [c]33C1041 (10/55).

From the 1950s onwards Khachaturian made records quite regularly in the Soviet Union. There were also sessions in Vienna and London in 1954, 1961 and 1977. All the fruits of the 1954 sessions are here, with the exception of a short essay, *In memoriam*, for which there was no room on a very well-filled disc. The 1954 mono sound is not exactly state-of-the-art for its time, despite the expert attention of the remastering engineer, but it is more than good enough to convey the superb quality of the Philharmonia's playing at a vintage period in their existence. Khachaturian was a vigorous, effective conductor and the players respond to his uncomplicated, outgoing style as a composer with obvious enthusiasm. The recordings were sandwiched between Beethoven sessions with Klemperer and must have made a pleasant contrast. The Violin Concerto was written for Oistrakh in 1940 and he plays it with effortless, cheerful virtuosity in the outer movements and responds to the warmth of the central *Andante* in a particularly expressive, eloquent fashion. The three attractively romantic

Masquerade pieces are very charmingly played, while in the seven numbers from *Gayaneh* the Philharmonia tear into the faster items with great gusto, and produce a particularly beautiful quality of string tone in the *Adagio*. None of the music on this disc is exactly first-rate, but it all comes to life very vividly and enjoyably through being played with such expertise and authority.

Khachaturian The Widow of Valencia – Suite. Gayaneh – Suite No. 2.
Tjeknavorian Danses fantastiques. **Armenian Philharmonic Orchestra / Loris Tjeknavorian.** ASV
Ⓟ CDDCA884 (65 minutes: DDD: 3/94). Ⓖ

Khachaturian's *The Widow of Valencia* is an early work (1940), yet already reveals the composer's fund of good tunes. He admitted its lack of authentic Spanishness and while the "Introduction" opens with flashing southern Mediterranean gusto, it soon makes way for a sultry Armenian melody of best local vintage. However, why worry? Altogether this is a most winning suite, without a dull bar, piquantly scored and brilliantly presented by an orchestra who are completely at home and clearly enjoying themselves. They also give us another suite, comprising six indelible numbers – for the most part little known from Khachaturian's masterpiece, *Gayaneh*. Tjeknavorian's own *Danses fantastiques* frequently burst with energy and the gentler dances have that Armenian flavour so familiar in *Gayaneh*. Brilliant playing in glittering yet spacious sound.

New review

Khachaturian Spartacus – Ballet suites Nos. 1-3. **Royal Scottish National Orchestra / Neeme Järvi.**
Chandos Ⓟ CHAN8927 (63 minutes: DDD: 5/91).

Khachaturian's ballet, *Spartacus*, first produced in 1956, was a judicious, and in the event a highly successful artistic response to the demands of Soviet populist realism. For its dramatic narrative of a Roman slave rebelling against his captors, eventually to be betrayed and killed, the composer created a score of striking vitality, at once full-blooded and crude, passionate and tuneful, and yet undoubtedly individual. The ballet's most famous number, the "Adagio of Phrygia and Spartacus", with its sweeping string tune, is justly popular and the theme returns nostalgically at the end in Phrygia's parting scene. Elsewhere there are many expressions of joyous extroversion and scenes of wild revelry, in which the music erupts with great physical energy, for example the "Entrance of the Merchants" and the wild "Dance of the Pirates", both in Suite No. 2. The scene of "The Market" which opens Suite No. 3 has enormous bustle. The romantic side of the score is full of languid sensuality: the Gaditanian Maidens (in the First Suite) are deliciously and decadently alluring, and the "Dance of the Egyptian Girl" is hardly less seductive in its sentient atmosphere. Those who enjoy the "Sabre Dance" from *Gayaneh* will respond to the vigorous "Dance of a Greek Slave" with its fiery rhythmic bite. Järvi and his Scottish players respond exuberantly to the near vulgarity of the unbuttoned animation and obviously revel in the lusher evocations. The resonant acoustics of the Henry Wood Hall, Glasgow, cast a rich ambient glow over Khachaturian's vivid primary colours and prevent the cruder climaxes from sounding too aggressive.

Further listening ...

…Cello Concerto. *Coupled with* **Kabalevsky** Cello Concerto No. 2 in G major, Op. 77. **Glazunov** Chant du ménestrel, Op. 71. **Raphael Wallfisch** (vc); **London Philharmonic Orchestra / Bryden Thomson.** Chandos CHAN8579 (6/88).

…Cello Concerto. *Coupled with works by* **Kabalevsky** and **Rachmaninov** Mats Lidström (vc); **Gothenburg Symphony Orchestra / Vladimir Ashkenazy** (pf). BIS CD719 (7/96). *See review under Kabalevsky; refer to the Index to Reviews.*

…Symphonies – No. 1 in E minor; No. 3 in C major, "Simfoniya-poema". **Armenian Philharmonic Orchestra / Loris Tjeknavorian.** ASV CDDCA858 (6/93).

…Symphony No. 3 in C major, "Simfoniya-poema". Triumphal Poem. *Coupled with* **Ippolitov-Ivanov** Caucasian Sketches, Op. 10. **BBC Philharmonic Orchestra / Fedor Glushchenko.** Chandos CHAN9321 (5/95).

…Trio for Clarinet, Violin and Piano. *Coupled with* **Kokai.** Quartettino. **Prokofiev** Overture on Hebrew Themes in C minor, Op. 34. Quintet in G minor, Op. 39. **Walter Boeykens Ensemble.** Harmonia Mundi HMC90 1419 (6/93).

Karen Khachaturian
USSR 1920-

Suggested listening ...

…Violin Sonata in G minor, Op. 1. *Coupled with* **Castelnuovo-Tedesco** Violin Concerto No. 2, "I profeti". **Ferguson** Violin Sonata No. 1, Op. 2. **Françaix** String Trio in C major. **Jascha Heifetz** (vn); **Joseph de Pasquale** (va); **Gregor Piatigorsky** (vc); **Lilian Steuber** (pf); **Los Angeles Philharmonic Orchestra / Alfred Wallenstein.** RCA Victor Gold Seal GD87872 (9/90). Ⓖ Ⓔ Ⓖ

John Kinsella
Irish 1932-

Suggested listening ...

…String Quartet No. 3. *Coupled with* **I. Wilson** Winter's Edge. **Beckett** String Quartet No. 1. **Boydell** String Quartet No. 2, Op. 44. **Vanbrugh Quartet.** Chandos CHAN9295 (10/94).

Theodor Kirchner

German 1823-1903-

Suggested listening ...
...Triptych. *Coupled with works by* **Ives, Bernstein** and **Gershwin** Yo-Yo Ma (vc); **Lynn Chang** (vn). Sony Classical SK53126 (4/94). *See review in the Collections section; refer to the Index to Reviews.*   ⓖ

Uuno Klami

Finnish 1900-1961

Suggested listening ...
...Symphony No. 1, Op. 26. King Lear Overture, Op. 33. **Tampere Philharmonic Orchestra / Tuomas Ollila.** Ondine ODE854-2 (3/96).
...Lemminkäinen's Island Adventures. Song of Lake Kuujärvi[a]. Whirls – Suites Nos. 1 and 2. [a]**Esa Ruuttunen** (bar); **Lahti Symphony Orchestra / Osmo Vänskä.** BIS CD656 (12/94).

Gideon Klein

Czechoslovakian 1919-1945

Klein String Trio. Fantasie à Fuga. Piano Sonata[a]. String Quartet, Op. 2.
Ullmann String Quartet No. 3, Op. 43. **Hawthorne Quartet** (Roman Lefkowitz, Si Jing Huang, vns; Mark Ludwig, va; Sato Knudsen, vc); [a]**Virginia Eskin** (pf). Channel Classics Ⓕ CCS1691 (68 minutes: DDD: 12/91). Recorded 1991.   ⓖⓖ
This CD is devoted to music by two Jewish musicians incarcerated in the Theresienstadt ghetto camp established by the Nazis in November 1941. On the evidence of the works recorded here, Gideon Klein and Viktor Ullmann were substantial figures whose music needs no special pleading. In stylistic terms, Ullman is perhaps the more predictable of the two. His Third Quartet shows him remaining true to Schoenbergian expressionism within a tonal context. Klein, deported to the camp at the age of 21, was by all accounts an astonishingly accomplished musician. His own music shows unmistakable signs of potential greatness even if the major influences – including Schoenberg, Janáček and Bartók – are not fully assimilated within a definitive creative profile. The bravely invigorating String Trio, completed only nine days before Klein's disappearance, receives a magnificent performance from members of the Hawthorne Quartet, a group drawn from the Boston Symphony Orchestra. Virginia Eskin gives a powerful account of the hard-hitting Piano Sonata, humming along discreetly as she plays. Channel Classics deserve high praise for these ideally balanced recordings which document a form of spiritual resistance of an isolated and terrorized community which we can barely begin to comprehend.
Further listening ...
...Fantasie a Fuga[a]. String Trio[b]. Piano Sonata[c]. First Sin[d]. Two Madrigals[e]. Czech and Russian Folksongs[f]. [d]**Karel Kožušnik** (ten); [c]**Allan Sternfield** (pf); [ab]**The Group for New Music;** [ef]**Prague Philharmonic Choir / Pavel Kühn.** Koch International Classics 37230-2 (8/94).

Oliver Knussen

British 1952-

Knussen Songs without Voices, Op. 26[d]. Whitman Settings, Op. 25[bc]. Hums and songs of Winnie-the-Pooh, Op. 6[ad]. Piano Variations, Op. 24[c]. Four Late Poems and an Epigram of Rainer Maria Rilke, Op. 23[a]. Sonya's Lullaby, Op. 16[c]. Océan de terre, Op. 10[bd]. [a]**Lisa Saffer,** [b]**Lucy Shelton** (sops); [c]**Peter Serkin** (pf); [d]**Lincoln Center Chamber Music Society / Oliver Knussen.** Virgin Classics Ⓕ VC7 59308-2 (76 minutes: DDD: 10/93). Texts and translations included. Recorded 1992.
If Ravel had been an expressionist, living now, this is the music he might have been writing. The early *Océan de terre*, a setting of Apollinaire, still has traces of the strenuousness which Knussen needed to exorcize in order to free his personal voice. But all the rest is sheer delight. Even the potential whimsy of *Hums and songs* is transcended by the quality of the musical thought, summed up in the poignant concluding "Cloud Piece". If the later works suggest that Knussen might be a miniaturist from now on, there can be little sense of loss when so much richness results. The boldly sculpted Piano Variations, the tellingly concentrated Rilke monodies, the Whitman settings that brilliantly elucidate the poet's tricky rhetoric, the *Songs without Voices* whose pulsating inventiveness is matched by cool formal discipline – all are realized with uncommon finesse and conviction. The recordings have both clarity and character, while the performances are as exuberant and polished as one would expect with the composer at hand.
Further listening ...
...Symphonies – No. 2, Op. 7[a]; No. 3, Op. 18[b]. Trumpets, Op. 12[c]. Coursing, Op. 17[e]. Cantata, Op. 15[d]. Ophelia Dances, Book 1, Op. 18[b]. [a]**Elaine Barry,** [c]**Linda Hirst** (sops); [c]**Michael Collins,** [c]**Edward Pillinger,** [c]**Ian Mitchell** (clarinets); [d]**Nash Ensemble;** [b]**Philharmonia Orchestra / Michael Tilson Thomas;** [ae]**London Sinfonietta / Oliver Knussen.** Unicorn-Kanchana Souvenir UKCD2010 (9/88).   ⓖ

Erland von Koch

Suggested listening ...
...Exotic Songs – No. 1, In the month of Tjaitra; No. 3, Of lotus scent and moonlight. The wild swans – Spring night's rain; Mankind's lot; The wild swans. *Coupled with works by* **Peterson-Berger, Sigurd von Koch, Stenhammar, Rangström, Alfvén** and **Sjögren** Anne Sofie von Otter (mez); **Bengt Forsberg** (pf). DG 449 189-2GH (5/96). *See review in the Collections section; refer to the Index to Reviews.*

Zoltán Kodály

New review
Kodály Symphony in C major. Summer Evening. Magyar Rondo[a]. [a]**Christopher Warren-Green** (vn); **Philharmonia Orchestra / Yondani Butt.** ASV Ⓕ CDDCA924 (54 minutes: DDD: 9/95). Recorded 1994.
Kodály's only Symphony has an engagingly pastoral quality, with mild but memorable thematic material, lively – even somewhat over-wrought – musical arguments (probably the symphony's main weakness) and notably scenic orchestration. Yondani Butt presents a volatile view of the piece, with weighty textures and a fairly intense delivery, especially in the first movement's emphatic development section. The slow movement, an elegiac *Andante* based on folk-style motives, is appealingly atmospheric, while the fresh-faced finale (which starts out rather like the last section of Bartók's *Dance Suite*) generates plenty of rustic excitement. As to available alternatives, the most obvious comparison has been issued as part of a mid-price Double Decca album which features two of the works programmed here – the Symphony and *Summer Evening* – in 1973 recordings by the Philharmonia Hungarica under Antál Dorati. The differences between the performances of the Symphony are quite significant, with Butt offering the broader paced, more momentous reading set within an imposing sound-frame, and Dorati (who is clearly, if less dynamically, recorded) scoring both in terms of superior orchestral execution and greater overall refinement. Both versions of *Summer Evening* underline the music's alternation of dance and reverie, whereas Butt's invigorating performance of the rarely heard but strangely moreish *Magyar Rondo* (shades of Bartók's *Romanian Folk Dances*, especially at the beginning) has the Philharmonia playing like a generously augmented gipsy band, with stylish solo work from Christopher Warren-Green. Enthusiasm and sincerity are much in evidence throughout this well-recorded concert, while the odd spot of executive ruggedness is fairly appropriate to the music's outdoor character. A cordial recommendation.
Additional recommendation ...
...Symphony in C major. Háry János – concert suite. Dances from Galánta. Variations on a Hungarian folksong. Dances of Marosszék. Theatre Overture. Concerto for Orchestra. Summer Evening. **Philharmonia Hungarica / Antál Dorati.** Double Decca Ⓜ 443 006-2DF2 (two discs: 150 minutes: ADD).

New review
Kodály Magyar Rondo. Summer Evening.
Suk Serenade in E flat major, Op. 6. **Orpheus Chamber Orchestra.** DG Ⓕ 447 109-2GH (52 minutes: DDD: 7/96).
The programme is winning, the playing spruce and the sound remarkably lifelike. Kodály's *Magyar Rondo* opens as if in imitation of Bartók's *Romanian Folkdances* (of two years earlier), though what actually emerges is a sequence of original Hungarian folk tunes – the recurring principal piece slow, the others fast – scored for strings, two clarinets and bassoons. It's a delightful work and a remarkable performance, not least for the way the Orpheus Chamber Orchestra cope with gipsy slides and teasing rubato: once the action hots up, you could as well be listening to a top-class Hungarian folk band. *Summer Evening* also incorporates folk-style material, albeit with a certain formal ingenuity; the overall tone suggests an affectionate though unsentimental pastoral soundscape. Again, the scoring is relatively light (although the wind line-up is heavier than in the *Rondo*), which of course suits the Orpheus well. In Suk's *Serenade*, the playing itself is extremely well drilled, the tone silken, the phrasing effectively attenuated but the overall effect might have benefited from rather more in the way of dynamic shading and phrasal individuality. However, this is an enjoyable programme and the *Rondo* in particular is a real delight.

New review
Kodály Háry János – concert suite. Dances of Marosszék. Variations on a Hungarian folksong, "The Peacock". Dances from Galánta. **Montreal Symphony Orchestra / Charles Dutoit.** Decca Ⓕ 444 322-2DH (77 minutes: DDD: 4/96). Recorded 1994.
The Dorati disc (listed above), compiled from analogue recordings made in Marl in 1973, still sounds very impressive, though the CD transfer brings brightness that next to the Dutoit versions seems rather aggressive, almost glaring. The obvious merit of the Dorati reading of each piece is that, with Hungarian players as well as Hungarian conductor, they convey an extra idiomatic flair in the rhythms. So in the fifth movement "Intermezzo" of *Háry János* the big *tenutos* in this very

nationalistic piece are even more winningly timed than with Dutoit, warmly persuasive though he is. Against that, the instrumental solos are often more imaginatively played by the Montreal principals, as for example the saxophone in the final Funeral March section of the fourth movement, the "Battle and Defeat of Napoleon". The *Peacock* Variations benefit even more than *Háry János* from the opulence of the Montreal sound, most of all in the glorious climax of the finale, which with Dutoit has tremendous panache. In the Dorati version there may be a degree more wildness, but that climax is not nearly so rich. In the two sets of *Dances* Dutoit is not only warmly sympathetic in his springing of rhythms and moulding of phrases, he is more purposeful even than Dorati. For this apt and generous coupling of Kodály's four most popular orchestral pieces Dutoit stands as a clear first choice, though at mid price, with keenly idiomatic performances, the Dorati disc is still a strong contender.

Additional recommendations ...

...Háry János. Theatre Overture. **Liszt** Mazeppa, S100. Mephisto Waltz No. 1, S110, "Der Tanz in der Dorfschenke". **New York Philharmonic Orchestra / Kurt Masur.** Teldec Ⓕ 9031-77547-2 (66 minutes: DDD).

...Dances of Marosszék. Dances from Galánta. *Coupled with* **Bartók** Divertimento, Sz113. Romanian folk dances, Sz68. **Saint Paul Chamber Orchestra / Hugh Wolff.** Teldec 9031-73134-2 (5/94).

...Dances of Marosszék[a]. Symphony in C major[b]. Psalmus Hungaricus[c]. [c]**Ernst Haefliger** (ten); [c]**St Hedwig's Cathedral Choir, Berlin;** [a]**Berlin RIAS Orchestra;** [bc]**Berlin Radio Symphony Orchestra / Ferenc Fricsay.** DG Dokumente mono/stereo Ⓜ 445 410-2GDO* (73 minutes: ADD: 11/94).

...Háry János. Variations on a Hungarian folksong. **Ravel** Daphnis et Chloé – Suite No. 2. **Concertgebouw Orchestra / Willem Mengelberg.** Archive Documents Mengelberg Edition mono Ⓕ ADCD115* (70 minutes: AAD: 3/96).

New review

Kodály Duo, Op. 7[ab]. Solo Cello Sonata, Op. 8[b].
Veress Solo Violin Sonata[a]. [a]**Sergiu Luca** (vn); [b]**Roel Dieltiens** (vc). Harmonia Mundi Ⓕ HMC90 1560 (70 minutes: DDD: 3/96). Recorded 1995.

A significant precursor of Ravel's duo sonata (1920-22) and hardly less memorable, Kodály's earthy Op. 7 (1914) has a searingly intense *Adagio* at its core, flanked either side by a wealth of Hungarian-flavoured dialogue. Harmonia Mundi's programming context is particularly useful in that it extends the folk element to a major Solo Cello Sonata (also by Kodály) and a concise but powerfully expressive Solo Violin Sonata by the Hungarian-born Swiss composer Sándor Veress (1907-92). Again, the *Adagio* holds the deepest secrets, whereas both outer movements are rich in harmonic and rhythmic incident, much of it reminiscent of Romanian folk music. The most riveting item on the disc, however, is the highly unusual account of Kodály's epic Solo Cello Sonata, where Dieltiens employs a wide range of slides, vibrato and dynamics, inflecting the notes gipsy-fashion and retaining some arpeggiated writing in the finale that János Starker – surely the work's most fêted living interpreter – habitually cut. Listening to Op. 8 played in this manner is rather like encountering a one-man folk band, what with copious instances of strumming *pizzicato*, *pizzicato-glissando*, *arco* and *pizzicato* combined, crunchy chords accompanying folk-song-style melodies and wild recitative. It really is a fabulous piece and Dieltiens's colourful, loose-wristed account resembles a spontaneous improvisation. Not that Starker is upstaged, just that Dieltiens offers a fascinating new slant on the work. The recordings are excellent.

Additional recommendations ...

...Solo Cello Sonata. *Coupled with works by* **Crumb** and **Escher** Pieter Wispelwey (vc). Globe Ⓕ GLO5089 (68 minutes: DDD: 12/94).

...Solo Cello Sonata. *Coupled with works by* **Britten, Berio** and **Henze** Matt Haimovitz (vc). DG Ⓕ 445 834-2GH (69 minutes: DDD: 12/95).

...Solo Cello Sonata. *Coupled with works by* **Bach, Dohnányi, Boccherini, Haydn, Schumann, Saint-Saëns, Dvořák, Fauré, Milhaud** and **Prokofiev** János Starker (vc); **Gerald Moore** (pf); **Philharmonia Orchestra / Carlo Maria Giulini, Walter Susskind.** EMI mono/stereo Ⓜ CZS5 68485-2 (six discs: 398 minutes: ADD: 12/95). *See review in the Collections section; refer to the Index to Reviews.*

...Solo Cello Sonata. Cello Sonata, Op. 4[a]. **Lluis Claret** (vc); [a]**Rose-Marie Cabestany** (pf). Harmonia Mundi Musique d'abord Ⓑ HMA190 1325 (50 minutes: DDD: 2/96).

Kodály Háry János, Op. 15[a]. **Erzsébet Komlóssy** (contr) Orzse; **László Palócz** (bass-bar) Marczi; **György Melis** (bar) Háry János, Napoleon; **Zsolt Bende** (bar) Bombazine; **Olga Szönyi** (sop) Marie-Louise; **Margit László** (sop) Empress; **Sir Peter Ustinov** (narr).
Kodály Variations on a Hungarian folksong, "The peacock"[b]. The peacock[c]. Psalmus Hungaricus, Op. 13[d]. [d]**Lajos Kozma** (ten); [a]**Edinburgh Festival Chorus;** [d]**Brighton Festival Chorus;** [ad]**Wandsworth School Boys' Choir; London Symphony** [c]**Chorus and** [abd]**Orchestra / István Kertész.** Double Decca Ⓜ 443 488-2DF2 (two discs: 153 minutes: ADD: 10/95). Item marked [a] from SET399/400 (11/69), [bcd]SXL6497 (4/71).

An absolute must for children young and old, and certainly for all lovers of the Suite that Kodály extracted from his delightful musical-cum-opera-cum-pantomime. Peter Ustinov's dazzling, occasionally Goon-like characterizations of the entire speaking cast are inexhaustibly entertaining, and yet the kindly moral theme that underpins the libretto of *Háry János* – Hungarian nationalism benevolently respected by the Austrians – emerges intact. And if you're wondering whether the complete score harbours much in the way of worthwhile music that lovers of the Suite don't already know, then the answer is a resounding 'yes' – gipsy tunes, Hussar songs, colourful extensions of familiar material (the "Intermezzo", especially) and a substantial finale based on the Suite's "Song". Kertész's extrovert conducting is quite beyond criticism and Decca's 1968 recording is an experience in itself, with sundry sound effects (galloping steeds, gurgling liquids, crowd scenes, and so on) and a thrillingly aggressive presentation of brass and percussion. Decca's transfer is admirably up-front, and the odd audible edit or spot of rumble (tape or traffic, or both) hardly amount to adequate grounds for complaint. The fill-ups are both welcome and musically substantial. It was a good idea to preface the *Peacock* Variations with Kodály's choral arrangement of the original folk-song (a fine performance by the London Symphony Chorus), while the Variations themselves are given with considerable gusto and feeling for atmosphere. The *Psalmus Hungaricus* (arguably Kodály's masterpiece) receives a bright and forceful performance under Kertész, dramatically sung by tenor Lajos Kozma. This is a remarkably well-filled and well-planned set, although readers are warned that the otherwise excellent annotation includes neither texts nor translations.

Additional recommendations ...

...Psalmus Hungaricus[a]. Hymn of Zrinyi[b]. **Dvořák** Requiem, B165[c]. **Soloists;** [c]**Ambrosian Singers;** [a]**Wandsworth School Boys' Choir;** [ab]**Brighton Festival Chorus;** [ac]**London Symphony Orchestra /** **István Kertész,** [b]**László Heltay.** Decca Ovation Ⓜ 421 810-2DM2 (two discs: 137 minutes: ADD: 5/89).

...Psalmus Hungaricus[a]. Missa Brevis[b]. Pange Lingua[c]. Psalm 114[d]. [ab]**Elizabeth Gale,** [b]**Sally Le Sage,** [b]**Hannah Francis** (sops); [b]**Alfreda Hodgson** (contr); [a]**Lajos Kozma,** [b]**Ian Caley** (tens); [b]**Michael Rippon** (bass); [bc]**Christopher Bowers-Broadbent,** [d]**Gillian Weir** (orgs); [abcd]**Brighton Festival Chorus /** László Heltay; [a]**London Symphony Orchestra /** István Kertész. Decca Enterprise Ⓜ 433 080-2DM (70 minutes: ADD: 8/92). Ⓖ

Further listening ...

...String Quartet No. 2, Op. 10. *Coupled with* **Dvořák** String Quartet No. 12 in F major, B179, "American". Cypresses, B152 – Nos. 1, 2, 5, 9 and 11. **Hagen Quartet.** DG 419 601-2GH (5/87).

...String Quartets – No. 1, Op. 2; No. 2, Op. 10. Gavotte. **Kontra Quartet.** BIS CD564 (1/95). Ⓖ

...String Quartet No. 2, Op. 10. *Coupled with works by* **Dvořák** *and* **Smetana Hollywood Quartet.** Testament mono/stereo SBT1072* (5/96).

...Laudes organi. Missa brevis **Netherlands Chamber Choir /** Uwe Gronostay with **Edgar Krapp** (org). Globe GLO5115 (1/95).

...Seven Pieces, Op. 11. *Coupled with works by* **Liszt, Dohnányi, Bartók, Weiner, Kurtág** and **Szöllösy Peter Frankl** (pf). ASV CDDCA860 (6/93). *See review in the Collections section; refer to the Index to Reviews.* ⒼⒼⒼ

...Cello Sonata, Op. 4. *Coupled with works by* **Janáček** *and* **Liszt** Anne Gastinel (vc); Pierre-Laurent Aimard (pf). Auvidis Valois V4748 (9/95). *See review under Janáček; refer to the Index to Reviews.*

Charles Koechlin
French 1867-1950

New review

Koechlin Au loin, Op. 20 No. 2. Sur les flots lointains, Op. 130 (two versions). Le buisson ardent, Op. 203/171. **Rheinland-Pfalz State Philharmonic Orchestra / Leif Segerstam.** Marco Polo Ⓕ 8 223704 (56 minutes: DDD: 8/95). Recorded 1985-7.

Distance, for Koechlin, certainly added enchantment to the view, as is attested not only by his titles – here *Au loin* and *Sur les flots lointains*, elsewhere *Vers la plage lointaine* – but by his constant yearning for distant horizons (*Le livre de la jungle*) or idealized heights (*Vers la cime, Vers la voûte étoilée*). This, it is suggested in an admirable note by Michael Fleury, reflects a common fascination of impressionist painters and composers, which is borne out by the contemplative mysticism of the two shorter works here, separated though they were by more than 30 years. That the composer should have considered the rapt meditation *Au loin* (originally a piece for cor anglais and piano) not worth keeping is baffling; both it and the later, coolly lovely *Sur les flots lointains* (here played in two versions, for string orchestra and for small orchestra with extensive woodwind writing) are minor treasures. Also a paean to Nature, in a very different way, is the major work on this disc – *Le buisson ardent*, a large-scale symphonic poem (Koechlin's last) for a huge orchestra (including ondes martenot, five saxophones, piano and organ) based on an episode in Romain Rolland's novel *Jean-Christophe*. Written in two parts (1938 and 1945) whose order was later reversed, it illustrates an artist's renewal from the depths of despair to hope, serenity and, finally, confidence by the coming of spring. With impressive mastery Koechlin builds a structure that, despite a great diversity of techniques and textures – polytonality, atonality, modality, pentatonicism, fugue – retains cohesion. (This is disturbed only by a built-in silent pause that lasts 44 seconds – surely far too long – in the first part.) The chaotic violence unleashed in the depiction of the *foehn* wind heralding spring would test any orchestra to the limit, but Segerstam's forces acquit themselves honourably; and the recorded quality is exemplary.

Koechlin Le livre de la jungle – Poèmes, Op. 18[a]. La course de printemps, Op. 95. La méditation de Purun Bhagat, Op. 159. La loi de la Jungle, Op. 175. Les Bandar-Log, Op. 176. [a]**Iris Vermillion** (mez); [a]**Johan Botha** (ten); [a]**Ralf Lukas** (bass); [a]**Berlin Radio Chamber Choir; Berlin Radio Symphony Orchestra / David Zinman.** RCA Victor Red Seal (Special price) 09026 61955-2 (two discs: 90 minutes: DDD: 6/94). Texts and translations included. Recorded 1993. *Gramophone Award Winner 1994.*   ⊙⊙

For 40 years, from his mid-thirties onwards, Koechlin, when he wasn't day-dreaming about goddesses of the cinema screen, was obsessed with Kipling's two *Jungle Books*. This eventually materialized in a large canvas of four symphonic poems, preceded by three songs (with chorus) that he then orchestrated. The complete sequence, called *The Jungle Book*, appears for the first time on the present disc; the Marco Polo disc (listed below) contains only the orchestral works. RCA's inclusion of the Op. 18 songs necessitates spreading to two discs, (though priced as a single disc): nevertheless the first song, the lushly scored "Seal lullaby" (the only movement not sited in the Indian rain forest) is so seductively beautiful that it would be a pity to miss it, especially as well sung as it is by Iris Vermillion. Of the symphonic poems, only *The Bandar-Log* is at all known here. The title refers to the noisy, empty-headed race of monkeys – "self-satisfied mimics whose only goal is to follow the fashions of the day" – which gives Koechlin an opportunity to pillory parallelism, dodecaphony and the sterile 'Back to Bach' movement then topical (in a fugato with each voice in a different key), all in a dazzlingly virtuoso piece of scoring for a huge orchestra. Much the longest of the orchestral pieces is *The spring running*, another virtuoso score, which falls into four sections – mysticism as spring slowly stirs in the forest, Mowgli's urge finally to leave the animal companions with whom he has lived and return to mankind, the painful following of unsettling "new trails" and "time of new talk" (another metaphor for the world of musical composition), and night falling again (mainly an immensely long monodic line over a pedal-note). Do not miss these remarkable scores, which reveal a distinctly individual and boldly forward-looking mind with a wide stylistic vocabulary (generally atonal), great dramatic sense and a stunning technical command. The orchestra rise fully to the occasion and the sound is clear and vivid.

Additional recommendation ...

...**Rheinland-Pfalz Philharmonic Orchestra / Leif Segerstam.** Marco Polo Ⓕ 8 223484 (73 minutes: DDD: 6/94).   ⓖ

Further listening ...

...The Seven Stars Symphony[a], Op. 132. Ballade, Op. 50[b]. [a]**Françoise Pellié** (ondes martenot); [b]**Bruno Rigutto** (pf); **Monte Carlo Philharmonic Orchestra / Alexandre Myrat.** EMI CDM7 64369-2 (3/93).

...Les Heures Persanes, Op. 65. **Rhineland-Pfalz State Philharmonic Orchestra / Leif Segerstam.** Marco Polo 8 223504 (7/94).

...14 Chants, Op. 157/2[c]. Premier album de Lilian, Op. 139[ac]. Second album de Lilian, Op. 149[c] – Sérénade à l'étoile errante; Swimming; Les jeux du clown; Le voyage chimérique. Morceau de lecture, Op. 218[c]. Flute Sonata, Op. 52[c]. Sonata for two flutes, Op. 75[b]. [a]**Jayne West** (sop); **Fenwick Smith,** [b]**Leone Buyse** (fls); [c]**Martin Amlin** (pf). Hyperion CDA66414 (10/90).

...Flute Sonata, Op. 52[c]. Quintet, Op. 156, "Primavera"[d]. *Coupled with* **Jolivet** Chant de Linos[a]. Flute Sonata[b]. **Philippe Racine** (fl); [ad]**Robert Zimansky** (vn); [ad]**Monika Clemann** (va); [ad]**Curdin Coray** (vc); [ad]**Xenia Schindler** (hp); [bc]**Daniel Cholette** (pf). Claves CD50-9003 (10/90).

...Choral sur le nom de Fauré. *Coupled with* **Ravel** Pavane pour une infante défunte. **Fauré** Requiem, Op. 48[a]. Pavane, Op. 50. **Schmitt** In memoriam Gabriel Fauré, Op. 72 – Scherzo. [a]**Sylvia McNair** (sop); [a]**Thomas Allen** (bar); **Academy of St Martin in the Fields** and [a]**Chorus / Sir Neville Marriner.** Philips 446 084-2PH (1/96).

Joonas Kokkonen   Finnish 1921-

Suggested listening ...

...Cello Concerto[a]. Symphonic Sketches. Symphony No. 4. [a]**Torleif Thedéen** (vc); **Lahti Symphony Orchestra / Osmo Vänskä.** BIS CD468 (12/91).

...Symphony No. 1. The Hades of the Birds[a]. Music for Strings. [a]**Monica Groop** (mez); **Lahti Symphony Orchestra / Ulf Söderblom.** BIS CD485 (4/92).

Kolessa Mykola   USSR 1903-

Suggested listening ...

...Symphony No. 1. *Coupled with* **Skoryk** Hutsul Triptych. Carpathian Concerto. **Odessa Philharmonic Orchestra / Hobart Earle.** ASV CDDCA963 (2/96).

Karl Komma

German 1913-

Suggested listening ...
...Fünf Hölderlin Fragmente. *Coupled with works by* **Britten, Cornelius, Eisler, Fortner, Fröhlich, Hauer, Jarnach, Pfitzner, Ullmann** and **Reutter** Mitsuko Shirai (mez); **Hartmut Höll** (pf). Capriccio 10 534 (12/94). *See review in the Collections section; refer to the Index to Reviews.*

Anders Koppel

Danish 1947-

Suggested listening ...
...Toccata. *Coupled with works by* **Fuzzy, Pape, Miki** and **Nørgård** Safri Duo. Chandos New Direction CHAN9330 (4/95). *See review in the Collections section; refer to the Index to Reviews.*

Nikolai Korndorf

Russian 1947-

New review
Korndorf Hymn II. Hymn III (in honour of Gustav Mahler)[a]. [a]**Catherine Bott** (sop); **BBC Symphony Orchestra / Alexander Lazarev.** Sony Classical Ⓔ SK66824 (57 minutes: DDD: 6/96). Recorded 1994.

Nikolai Korndorf started out as an avant-garde composer, but (and here he has similarities with Górecki, Pärt, Schnittke and Tavener) he suddenly changed to a more tonal, simple and above all spiritual style in the early 1980s. In 1991 he moved to Vancouver, Canada, and since then his music has been steadily gaining admirers and exponents in the West. Sharing the same title, and possibly general sentiments, Korndorf's three orchestral *Hymns* would appear to constitute a cycle but, as Korndorf himself has said, he prefers that they should not be performed or considered as such. In terms of musical style the works presented on this disc share much in common with Górecki's Third Symphony – slow moving, seamless textures, minimal material, peaking climaxes and, in *Hymn III*, an ethereal, wordless soprano part. If anything Korndorf's music is even more static than either Górecki or Pärt, and generally the impression is of vertical rather than linear movement – walls of 'bell-like' pulsating chords dominate and seem to suggest a kind of 'summoning prelude' to a great event – Korndorf himself would suggest perhaps the dawning of a new spiritual age. *Hymn III* was composed in response to a commission by the Kohler-Osbahr Foundation for a piece in honour of Gustav Mahler, and there are certainly Mahlerian echoes to be found here – not least the off-stage trumpets heard at the beginning and the high sustained string texture which recall the First Symphony. Generally speaking, if you have enjoyed the sound world of Górecki and Pärt then you will probably enjoy discovering Korndorf too. As for the performances, the BBC Symphony Orchestra play this music with great conviction and the soprano solo in *Hymn III* is beautifully delivered by Catherine Bott.

Erich Wolfgang Korngold

Austrian/Hungarian 1897-1957

Korngold Violin Concerto, Op. 35[a].
Rózsa Violin Concerto, Op. 24[b]. Tema con variazioni, Op. 29a[c].
Waxman Fantasy on Bizet's "Carmen"[d]. Jascha Heifetz (vn); [c]**Gregor Piatigorsky** (vc); [c]**Chamber Orchestra**; [a]**Los Angeles Philharmonic Orchestra / Alfred Wallenstein**; [b]**Dallas Symphony Orchestra / Walter Hendl**; [d]**RCA Victor Symphony Orchestra / Donald Voorhees.** RCA Victor Gold Seal [ad]mono/[bc]stereo Ⓜ GD87963* (70 minutes: ADD: 4/89). Item marked [a] from HMV ALP1233 (12/55), [b]SB6605 (4/65), [cd]new to UK. Recorded 1946-63. ⒼⒼⒼ

Heifetz's legendary recording of the Korngold Concerto serves a double purpose: as an effective introduction to Korngold's seductive musical style, and as the best possible example of Heifetz's violin artistry. The work itself was written at the suggestion of Bronislaw Huberman, but it was Heifetz who gave the première in 1947. It calls on material that Korngold had also used in three of his film scores (he was at the time composing for Hollywood), although the way he welds the themes into a three-movement structure is masterly enough to suggest that the concerto came to him 'of a piece'. The very opening would be enough to seduce most listeners, unless – that is – they have an aversion to the film music of the period. Miklós Rózsa's Concerto has its roots in the composer's Hungarian soil, and echoes of Bartók are rarely absent. But whereas Korngold's score is taken from movie music, Rózsa's (or parts of it) became a film score – namely, *The Private Life of Sherlock Holmes*. Rózsa's self-possessed, skilfully written *Tema con variazoni* was taken, in 1962, from a much larger work then in progress, but Heifetz and Piatigorsky play it in a reduced orchestration. As to the *Carmen Fantasy* by Franz Waxman (another notable film composer), its luscious tunes and frightening technical challenges were written with the great violinist very much in mind. It's a stunning piece of playing, and wears its 48 years lightly. The other recordings sound far better, and the Rózsa items are in stereo. Marvellous stuff!

...Violin Concerto[a]. Much ado about nothing, Op. 11[b] – The maiden in the bridal chamber; Dogberry and Verges; Intermezzo; Hornpipe. **Barber** Violin Concerto, Op. 14[a]. **Gil Shaham** (vn); [a]**London Symphony Orchestra / André Previn** ([b]pf). DG Ⓕ 439 886-2GH (71 minutes: DDD: 9/94). *Gramophone Editor's choice. See review under Barber; refer to the Index to Reviews.* Ⓖ

Korngold Sinfonietta, Op. 5. Sursum corda, Op. 13. **BBC Philharmonic Orchestra / Matthias Bamert.** Chandos Ⓕ CHAN9317 (63 minutes: DDD: 5/95). Recorded 1994. *Gramophone Editor's choice.* ⒼⒼ

Erich Korngold's *Sinfonietta* must surely rank as one of the most invigorating and uplifting large-scale works ever produced by a 14-year-old. However, to enjoy fully this glorious piece one must put aside thoughts of precocious youngsters and simply luxuriate in the gorgeous outpourings of this remarkable work. If the likes of Richard Strauss, Zemlinsky and Schreker are to your taste and you have not yet discovered this work then it should go straight to the top of your 'investigate next' list. Not only does Bamert coax a performance that sounds as if it has been in his repertoire for years (remarkable when one learns that he took on this recording at short notice due to the indisposition of Sir Edward Downes) but the recorded sound is exemplary. Add to that a thoroughly ebullient and spirit-raising account of the symphonic poem *Sursum corda* and this disc becomes a real must for all Korngold admirers. *Sursum corda* ("Lift up your hearts") is a glorious extravaganza of a piece, with wonderful orchestration, even by Korngold's standards! The composer must have known a good thing when he saw one, for although the music was considered 'difficult' and 'too modern' when first performed in 1920 (it was even booed!) he later made extensive use of material from it in his 1938 film score to *The Adventures of Robin Hood* – and that won him his second Academy Award!

Korngold Symphony in F sharp major, Op. 40. Abschiedlieder, Op. 14[a]. [a]**Linda Finnie** (mez); **BBC Philharmonic Orchestra / Sir Edward Downes.** Chandos Ⓕ CHAN9171 (68 minutes: DDD: 9/93). Ⓖ

Newcomers to Korngold's music who have dipped their toes into the waters of *Das Wunder der Heliane* and found the temperature a little too hot and headily intoxicating might do well to explore the orchestral version of the beautiful *Abschiedlieder* songs. Though there is much that is operatic here, musically they fall more within the gravitational orbit of Mahler than the opulent excesses of his operas. Linda Finnie gives rapt and majestic performances of considerable insight and conviction. The sparse, percussive opening of the F sharp major Symphony and the stridently defiant stance of the material seem a world apart from the warmth and chromatic richness of the songs, despite the fact that Mahlerian undertones can be heard here too. It is one of Korngold's most crucial compositions – an exposé of the man if you like, and an exposé which, despite a tragically nostalgic slow movement, reveals a bold and powerfully optimistic spirit. Downes and the BBC Philharmonic's performance is all one could wish for. In their hands the sombre, tragic *Adagio* becomes pure melt-down as climax upon inexorable climax culminate in a passage of almost unbearable intensity. Chandos have complemented inspirational music-making with inspirational recorded sound.

...Symphony. Theme and Variations, Op. 42. Straussiana. **North West German Philharmonic Orchestra / Werner Andreas Albert.** CPO Ⓕ 999 146-2 (68 minutes: DDD/ADD: 10/91).

New review
Korngold Piano Sonatas – No. 1 in D minor; No. 2 in E major, Op. 2; No. 3 in C major, Op. 25. **Geoffrey Tozer** (pf). Chandos Ⓕ CHAN9389 (70 minutes: DDD: 3/96). Recorded 1995.

The Third Sonata is a beautifully crafted and glowingly elegant performance full of memorable incident and sharply contrasted moods. The second movement is given an exceptionally poetic and moving reading and should in itself persuade any listener of the desirability of this disc. The Second Sonata (dedicated to Korngold's teacher Zemlinsky and premièred by Artur Schnabel in 1911) is a more imposing and grandly designed sonata and Tozer tackles it accordingly, producing a very 'orchestral' and full-bodied reading. The finale is given an especially characterful performance. Only in the First Sonata might one prefer Verschoor's reading, where in terms of breadth and dramatic sweep (most notably in the first movement) he certainly seems to have the edge over Tozer. It is perhaps worth mentioning, too, that only here are Verschoor's and Tozer's timings for individual movements more or less identical; elsewhere Tozer tends to be marginally faster which contributes to his success in projecting these sonatas. To crown Tozer's achievement, the piano sound has been beautifully captured and engineered.

...**Matthijs Verschoor** (pf). Etcetera Ⓕ KTC1042 (71 minutes: DDD: 7/87).

Korngold Das Wunder der Heliane. **Anna Tomowa-Sintow** (sop) Heliane; **Hartmut Welker** (bar) Ruler; **John David de Haan** (ten) Stranger; **Reinhild Runkel** (contr) Messenger; **René Pape** (bass) Porter; **Nicolai Gedda** (ten) Blind Judge; **Martin Petzold** (ten) Young Man; **Berlin Radio Chorus; Berlin Radio Symphony Orchestra / John Mauceri.** Decca Entartete Musik Ⓕ 436 636-2DH3 (three discs: 168 minutes: DDD: 4/93). Notes, text and translation included. *Gramophone Award Winner 1995.* ⒼⒼ

This recording – part of Decca's ongoing Entartete Musik series – marks the rediscovery of a major operatic masterpiece of the 1920s, and certainly the rediscovery of one of the most ravishing, opulently orchestrated and complex scores of the period. *Das Wunder der Heliane* was the fourth of Korngold's five magnificent contributions to the genre, and was considered by the composer to be his finest achievement. The plot, based on the play *Die Heilige* by Hans Kaltneker, concerns the strange mystical – non-physical – union between Heliane (wife of the tyrant Ruler) and a character known only as The Stranger who has been imprisoned and condemned to death by Ruler. When their love is discovered, Heliane and The Stranger are put on trial, during which Heliane sings the memorable aria "Ich ging zu ihm" ("I went to him who is to die tomorrow") in her own defence. After an ecstatic duet The Stranger stabs himself. Heliane proves her innocence by miraculously bringing him back to life, but she is stabbed to death by her husband in a fit of jealousy. Heliane is brought to life by The Stranger, and after a tender duet the lovers finally depart this life into the realm of Eternal Love. The opera was premièred in 1927, but despite enjoying a certain success with its audiences it failed to establish itself in the repertoire and disappeared completely after 1930. Reasons for its neglect are numerous and complex (it was labelled 'degenerate' by the Nazis and banned, and it also became embroiled in a musical and artistic battle with Krenek's opera *Jonny spielt auf* which was premièred in the same year) and these are discussed in depth in the excellent booklet-notes. The orchestral writing is lush and harmonically complex (almost bitonal in places) and plays throughout the opera like a vast symphonic poem, and indeed the enormous orchestral and vocal forces required for performance may well have been a contributing factor in its demise. *Das Wunder der Heliane*, however, could not have wished for a more persuasive and triumphant reappraisal than this recording. Anna Tomowa-Sintow is a moving, compassionate Heliane, John David de Haan an ardent and suitably mysterious Stranger, and Hartmut Welker a strong and menacing Ruler. John Mauceri conducts the RSO Berlin with passion, commitment and bravura, and the recording, made in Jesus-Christus-Kirche, Dahlem is excellent. *Heliane* may turn out to be one of the most important and significant opera recordings this decade.

Further listening ...

...Cello Concerto in C major, Op. 37[a]. Film scores – The Private Lives of Elizabeth and Essex – Overture; The Prince and the Pauper – Suite; Anthony Adverse – In the forest; The Sea Wolf – Suite; Deception. Another Dawn – Night scene; Of Human Bondage – Suite. [a]**Francisco Gabarro** (vc); **National Philharmonic Orchestra / Charles Gerhardt.** RCA Victor Gold Seal GD80185 (11/91). Ⓖ

...Baby Serenade, Op. 24[a]. Cello Concerto in C major, Op. 37[b]. Symphonic Serenade, Op. 39[c]. [b]**Julius Berger** (vc); **North West German Philharmonic Orchestra / Werner Andreas Albert.** CPO 999 077-2 (10/91).

...The Adventures of Robin Hood – film score. **Utah Symphony Orchestra / Varujan Kojian.** That's Entertainment CDTER1066 (3/87).

...String Sextet in D major, Op. 10. *Coupled with* **Schoenberg** Verklärte Nacht. **Raphael Ensemble.** Hyperion CDA66425 (1/91). Ⓖ

...Piano Trio in D major, Op. 1[a]. Violin Sonata in D major, Op. 6. **Glenn Dicterow** (vn); [a]**Alan Stepansky** (vc); **Israela Margalit** (pf). EMI Anglo-American Chamber Music Series CDC5 55401-2 (7/95). *Gramophone Editor's choice.*

...Einfache Lieder, Op. 9 No. 1, Schneeglöckchen; No. 2, Nachtwander; No. 3, Ständchen. Der Kranke, Op. 38 No. 2. *Coupled with works by* **Wolf** Boje Skovhus (bar); **Helmut Deutsch** (pf). Sony Classical SK57969 (1/95). *See review under Wolf; refer to the Index to Reviews.*

...Unver-gänglichkeit, Op. 27. Lieder, Op. 38 – No. 1, Glückwunsch; No. 2, Der Kranke. *Coupled with works by* **Schreker, Schoenberg** and **Weigl** Steven Kimbrough (bar); **Dalton Baldwin** (pf). Koch Schwann 310942 (2/95). *See review under Schoenberg; refer to the Index to Reviews.*

...Kings Row – excerpts. **National Philharmonic Orchestra / Charles Gerhardt.** Varèse Sarabande VCD47203.

...Die tote Stadt – Mein Sehnen, mein Wähnen. *Coupled with works by* **Lortzing, Marschner, Weber, Spohr, Kreutzer, Schreker, Humperdinck** and **Wagner** Thomas Hampson (bar); **Pestalozzi Gymnasium Children's Choir; Munich Radio Orchestra / Fabio Luisi.** EMI CDC5 55233-2 (9/95). *See review in the Collections section; refer to the Index to Reviews.*

...Die Tote Stadt. **Soloists; Tolz Boys' Choir; Bavarian Radio Chorus; Munich Radio Orchestra / Erich Leinsdorf.** RCA Opera Series GD87767 (11/89). ⒼⒼ

...Violanta. **Soloists; Bavarian Radio Chorus; Munich Radio Orchestra / Marek Janowski.** CBS MK79229 (9/89).

Leopold Koželuch

Bohemian/Austrian 1747-1818

Suggested listening ...

...Clarinet Concerto in E flat major. *Coupled with works by* **Crusell** and **Krommer** Emma Johnson (cl); **Royal Philharmonic Orchestra / Günther Herbig.** ASV CDDCA763 (9/91). *See review under Crusell; refer to the Index to Reviews.*

Anton Kraft

Bohemian 1749-1820

Suggested listening ...
...Cello Concerto in C major, Op. 4. *Coupled with* **Haydn** Cello Concertos – C major, HobVII*b*/1; D major, HobVII*b*/2. **Anner Bylsma** (bar vc); **Tafelmusik / Jeanne Lamon.** Deutsche Harmonia Mundi RD77757 (9/91). ✒ *See review under Haydn; refer to the Index to Reviews.*

William Kraft

American 1923-

Suggested listening ...
...Timpani Concerto[a]. Piano Concerto[b]. Veils and Variations[c]. Evening Voluntaries[d]. [cd]**Jeff von der Schmidt** (hn); [b]**Mona Golabek** (pf); [a]**Thomas Akins** (timp); [ab]**Alabama Symphony Orchestra / Paul Polivnick;** [c]**Berkeley Symphony Orchestra / Kent Nagano.** Harmonia Mundi HMU90 7106 (2/94).

Hans Krása

Czechoslovakian 1899-1944

Suggested listening ...
...String Quartet. *Coupled with* **Haas** String Quartets – No. 2, Op. 7, "From the Monkey Mountain"; No. 3, Op. 15. **Hawthorne Quartet.** Decca 440 853-2DH (3/94). *See review under Haas; refer to the Index to Reviews. Gramophone Editor's choice.* 🅖🅖
...Brundibár[a]. *Coupled with* **Domazlicky** Eight Czech Songs, Op. 17[b]. [a]**Soloists;** [b]**Disman Radio Children's Choir and Orchestra / Joža Karas.** Channel Classics CCS5193 (8/93).

Joseph Martin Kraus

Swedish 1756-1792

Suggested listening ...
...Sinfonia con fugato per la chiesa. Symphony in C major. Symphonie funèbre in C minor. Sinfonia in C sharp minor. **Concerto Cologne.** Capriccio 10 430 (9/93). ✒
...Symphonies – C major; C minor; D major; E flat major. **Concerto Cologne.** Capriccio 10 396 (8/92).

Johann Krebs

German 1713-1780

Suggested listening ...
Fantasia à giusto Italiano. Fantasia sopra Wer nur den lieben Gott lässt walten. Fugue in B flat major on B-A-C-H. Herr Gott disch loben alle wir. Herzlich lieb hab ich dich, o Herr. Preludes and Fugues – C major; D major. Trios – D minor; E flat major. Wir glauben all an einen Gott. Zeuch ein zu deinen Toren. **Graham Barber** (org). ASV Gaudeamus CDGAU125 (10/91).

Fritz Kreisler

Austrian 1875-1962

New review

Kreisler Praeludium and Allegro in the style of Pugnani. Schön Rosmarin. Tambourin chinois, Op. 3. Caprice viennois, Op. 2. Précieuse in the style of Couperin. Liebesfreud. Liebesleid. La Gitana. Berceuse romantique, Op. 9. Polichinelle. Rondino on a theme by Beethoven. Tempo di Menuetto in the style of Pugnani. Toy Soldier's March. Allegretto in the style of Boccherini. Marche miniature viennoise. Aucassin and Nicolette, "Canzonetta medievale". Menuet in the style of Porpora. Siciliano and Rigaudon in the style of Francoeur. Syncopation. **Joshua Bell** (vn); **Paul Coker** (pf). Decca Ⓕ 444 409-2DH (63 minutes: DDD: 4/96). Recorded 1995.
The music of Fritz Kreisler has become something of a repertory rarity, even though years of 'encore' employment have guaranteed its cult longevity – certainly among violinists. And as light music goes, make no mistake that Kreisler's finest work vies with the best of Eric Coates, Leroy Anderson or even Johann Strauss. Joshua Bell learned Kreisler from his teacher, the late Josef Gingold, and yet his approach is anything but 'old school'. He habitually avoids the pitfalls of imitation, flashiness and patronizing overkill, preferring instead to revisit the music with modern ears. His *Caprice viennois* is light years removed from the composer's own (whichever version you choose), a fresh-faced, strongly characterized reading that trades sentimentality for just a hint of jazz. And of course there's that inseparable twosome, *Liebesfreud* and *Liebesleid*, the latter in particular displaying Bell's tone at its most alluring. The longest piece on the disc is the *Praeludium and Allegro in the style of Pugnani* which Bell gives 'the full treatment', deftly pointing the *Allegro*, relishing passagework and double-stopping with impressive accuracy. This of course is one of numerous spoof baroque pieces that Kreisler passed off as edited originals but that were in fact his own compositions. Some pieces seem indivisible from Kreisler's own very individual tone and phrasing, *Polichinelle*, for example, and *Marche miniature viennoise*, both of which paraded the sort of personalized rubato, timing and tone-

production that have for so long seemed part of the music's very essence. Here and in a few other instances, Bell's brighter, more overtly virtuosic approach doesn't quite catch the music's period charm and yet a mini-masterpiece like the rarely heard *Berceuse romantique* (a sort of Fauré-Korngold synthesis) displays ample style, subtlety and affection of phrasing. Joshua Bell's smooth, witty and keenly inflected readings make for elevated entertainment: they may not replace the composer's own, but they do provide a youthful and in many ways illuminating alternative. The recordings are excellent, save that Paul Coker's excellent accompaniments occasionally seem a mite overprominent.

Further listening ...
...Violin Concerto in C major, "in the style of Vivaldi". *Coupled with* **Vivaldi** The Four Seasons, Op. 8 Nos. 1-4. **Gil Shaham** (vn); **Orpheus Chamber Orchestra**. DG 439 933-2GH (3/95).
...Schön Rosmarin. Tambourin chinois. Caprice viennois. *Coupled with works by* **Wieniawski, Paganini, Bloch, Tchaikovsky, Messiaen, Sarasate** and **Bazzini** Maxim Vengerov (vn); **Itamar Golan** (pf). Teldec 9031-77351-2 (4/94). *See review in the Collections section; refer to the Index to Reviews.*
...Schön Rosmarin. Liebeslied. Liebesfreud. *Coupled with works by* **Tchaikovsky, Dvořák** and **Schubert** Vera Vaidman (vn); **Emanuel Krasovsky** (pf). IMP CDI PWK1137 (6/90). *See review in the Collections section; refer to the Index to Reviews.*
...Liebesfreud[a]. *Coupled with* **Mendelssohn** Violin Concerto in E minor, Op. 64[b]. **Bruch** Violin Concerto No. 1 in G minor, Op. 26[c]. **Sarasate** Introduction et Tarantelle, Op. 43. **Cho-Liang Lin** (vn); [a]**Sandra Rivers** (pf); [b]**Philharmonia Orchestra / Michael Tilson Thomas**; [c]**Chicago Symphony Orchestra / Leonard Slatkin.** CBS Masterworks CD44902 (3/91). Ⓖ
...Tempo di Menuetto in the style of Pugnani. *Coupled with works by* **Sarasate, Elgar, Khachaturian, Paganini, Chopin, Shostakovich, Gershwin, Liszt, Tchaikovsky** and **Prokofiev** (Sarah Chang (vn); Sandra Rivers (pf). EMI CDC7 54352-2 (1/93). *See review in the Collections section; refer to the Index to Reviews.*
...Original Compositions and Arrangements – works by **Kreisler** and arrangements of works by **Bach, Brandl, Dvořák, Falla, Glazunov, Heuberger, Poldini, Rimsky-Korsakov, Schubert, Scott Tchaikovsky** and **Weber** Fritz Kreisler (vn) with various artists. EMI Références mono CDH7 64701-2* (12/93). ⒼⒼⒼ

Ernst Krenek

Austrian/American 1900-1991

New review

Krenek O Lacrymosa, Op. 48. Stella's Monolog, Op. 57. Die Nachtigall, Op. 68. Fünf Lieder, Op. 82. Four Songs, Op. 112. The Flea, Op. 175. Wechselrahmen, Op. 189. **Christine Schäfer** (sop); **Axel Bauni** (pf). Orfeo Musica Rediviva Ⓕ C373951A (67 minutes: DDD: 2/96). Texts and translations included. Recorded 1994.

In this entertaining recital, the chronological arrangement of the songs affords a fair view of Krenek's stylistic development across nearly 40 years (1926-65). And quite a development it was, too, from the radiant *O Lacrymosa*, three further musings by Rilke on the Virgin Mary, to the near-volcanic *Wechselrahmen* ("Changing Settings"), to poems by Emil Barth. Date of composition and subject alone would point to Hindemith's *Das Marienleben* as the example for *O Lacrymosa*, even if the musical language were not so suggestive of it. More individual in execution is *Stella's Monolog* (1928), on lines from Goethe's play *Stella*. Cast as a dramatic scena, this compositional *tour de force* (Krenek had seven stage works under his belt by this time) has a wide range of moods, some of *buffa*-like airiness at odds with the text's romantic ardour, suggesting a send-up. When in 1937 Krenek came to set five brief stanzas by Kafka, he had finally embraced Schoenberg's 12-note method. The Kafka songs, Op. 82, as well as those of Op. 112 (1946-7, setting Gerard Manley Hopkins) show a concomitant spareness of texture, but his setting of Donne's *The Flea* (1960) is wonderfully exuberant, while *Wechselrahmen*'s extremity of expression is entirely apposite given Krenek's tirelessly adventurous spirit. Christine Schäfer is nothing if not a sympathetic interpreter; a touch shrill in the topmost registers, her voice is big enough to cope with these songs' widely varying demands. Axel Bauni gives first-class support and the recording sounds bright and truthful. A must for anyone remotely interested in Lieder, of the twentieth century or any other.

Further listening ...
...Symphony No. 2, Op. 12. **Hanover Radio Philharmonic Orchestra / Takao Ukigaya.** CPO CPO999 255-2 (1/96).
...Piano Sonatas – No. 2, Op. 59; No. 3, Op. 92; No. 4. *Coupled with* **Berg** Piano Sonata, Op. 1. **Webern** Piano Variations, Op. 27. **Marcelo Bratke** (pf). Olympia OCD431 (4/94).
...Lamentatio Jeremiae prophetae, Op. 93. **Berlin RIAS Chamber Choir / Marcus Creed.** Harmonia Mundi HMC90 1551 (7/95).
...Jonny spielt auf. **Soloists; Leipzig Opera Chorus; Chinchilla; Leipzig Gewandhaus Orchestra / Lothar Zagrosek.** Decca 436 631-2DH2 (4/93). *Gramophone Award Winner 1995.*

Conradin Kreutzer   German 1780-1849

Suggested listening ...
...Frühlingsglaube. Die Post. Nähe des Geliebten. Die Kapelle, Op. 64 No. 1. Nachtreise. Entschluss,
   Op. 64 No. 2. *Coupled with works by* **Nicolai, Goetz, Humperdinck** and **Marschner** Olaf
   Bär (bar); **Helmut Deutsch** (pf). EMI CDC5 55393-2 (1/96). *See review in the Collections section;*
   refer to the Index to Reviews.
...Das Nachtlager in Granada. **Soloists; Cologne Radio Chorus and Symphony Orchestra / Helmuth**
   Froschauer. Capriccio 60 029 (1/94).

Franz Krommer   Bohemian 1759-1831

New review
Krommer Clarinet Concerto in E flat major, Op. 36. Double Clarinet Concertos – E flat major,
   Op. 35[a]; E flat major, Op. 91[b]. [a]**Kaori Tsutsui**, [b]**Tomoko Takashima** (cls); **Nicolaus Esterházy**
   Sinfonia / Kálmán Berkes (cl). Naxos Ⓢ 8 553178 (66 minutes: DDD: 8/95). Recorded 1994.
Two of the works on this record, Opp. 35 and 36, have been recorded several times, and their elegant
charm well merits it. Both were written in about 1802-3. The solo concerto is a beautiful piece, with
a melodic grace tinged with a faint melancholy in the *Adagio* and, in the finale, a wry, lilting humour
that anticipates Weber. The Double Concerto is more extrovert, and great fun: as one would expect,
it deals much in scales in thirds, burbling accompaniments to a serene melody, imitations handed
courteously to and fro, plunging sequences as the ball is rapidly thrown backwards and forwards, and
so on; but expectations are sometimes amusingly confounded, and the general atmosphere is of a
civilized conversation that does not go much beyond cheerful banter. The later Double Concerto,
probably dating from 1815, is a more searching piece, written with a fuller awareness of the romantic
tensions that were coming into music and especially into German opera (1815 was the year of Spohr's
Faust and Hoffmann's *Undine*). The *Adagio* is virtually an operatic duet, but one conducted between
warmly contrasting personalities. The Polacca pays scarcely more than lip service to this popular
romantic manner, but is a very attractive movement that begins in original fashion with a tripping
pizzicato figure over which the clarinets discourse nimbly. The performances are fresh and appealing,
as is the recording. Well worth a try for those who enjoy the music of this period.
Additional recommendation ...
...Clarinet Concerto, Op. 36. *Coupled with works by* **Crusell** and **Koželuch** Emma Johnson (cl);
   Royal Philharmonic Orchestra / Günther Herbig. ASV Ⓔ CDDCA763 (67 minutes: DDD: 9/91).
   See review under Crusell; refer to the Index to Reviews.
Further listening ...
...Symphonies – No. 2 in D major, Op. 40; No. 4 in C minor, Op. 102. **London Mozart Players /**
   Matthias Bamert. Chandos CHAN9275 (7/94).

Nikolaus von Krufft   Austrian 1779-1818

Suggested listening ...
...Horn Sonata in F major. *Coupled with* **Brahms** Horn Trio in E flat major, Op. 40[a]. **Beethoven**
   Horn Sonata in F major, Op. 17. **Lowell Greer** (hn); [a]**Stephanie Chase** (vn); **Steven Lubin** (fp).
   Harmonia Mundi HMU90 7037 (9/92). ✍

Rafael Kubelík   Czechoslovakian/Swiss 1914-

Suggested listening ...
...Orphikon[a]. Cantata without Words[b]. Inventions and Interludes[c]. [c]**Kühn Children's Chorus;**
   Bavarian Radio [b]**Chorus and** [ab]**Symphony Orchestra;** [c]**instrumental ensemble / Rafael Kubelík.**
   Panton 81 1264-2 (2/95).   Ⓖ

Friedrich Kuhlau   German/Danish 1786-1832

New review
Kuhlau Three Flute Quintets, Op. 51. **Eyvind Rafn** (fl); **Kim Sjøgren** (vn); **Bjarne Boye Rasmussen,**
   Georg Svendsen Andersen (vas); **Lars Holm Johansen** (vc). Naxos Ⓢ 8 553303 (79 minutes: DDD:
   10/95). Recorded 1985.
When the German-born composer, Friedrich Kuhlau, wrote his Op. 51 Flute Quintets in 1823, he was
already installed as a court musician for the Danish Royal Family. Kuhlau had taken Danish
citizenship in 1813, and later established himself as Denmark's national composer with operas such
as *Elverhøj* (1828). However, aside from his theatrical compositions, Kuhlau was a prolific
instrumental composer, earning the reputation among his contemporaries as the Beethoven of the

flute. The three flute quintets on this disc demonstrate Kuhlau's fluent style and dramatic flair. Flautist Eyvind Rafn and his Danish group present an alert, well-balanced ensemble, with clear textures and stylish phrasing that demonstrate their evident enthusiasm for this music. Sample the open-air exuberance in the outer movements of the D major Quintet (No. 1), its charmingly rugged minuet or its expressive slow movement. Most impressive, though, is the passionately romantic, E major Quintet (No. 2). Here Rafn and his team give a persuasive performance, highlighting the music's effective blend of major/minor colours, and flamboyant opposition of flute and strings in concerto-like exchanges that culminate in an infectious, spirited finale. Eyvind Rafn was also the producer and engineer of this disc, and both his flute playing – sensitively supported by his colleagues – and his 1980s recordings remain fresh and appealing.

Further listening ...

...The elf's hill   Suite[a]. Overtures – Lulu; The triplet brothers from Damascus; The robber's castle; William Shakespeare. **Odense Symphony Orchestra / [a]Othmar Maga, Eduard Serov.** Unicorn-Kanchana DKPCD9132 (5/93).

Johann Kuhnau

German 1660-1722

New review

Kuhnau Biblical Sonatas – No. 1, Fight between David and Goliath[a]; No. 2, Saul cured by David through music[b]; No. 3, Jacob's wedding[c]; No. 4, The healing of Hezekiah[a]; No. 5, Gideon, the Saviour of Israel[b]; No. 6, Jacob's death and burial[c]. **John Butt** ([a]org/[b]clav/[c]hpd). Harmonia Mundi Ⓕ HMU90 7133 (72 minutes: DDD: 3/96). Recorded 1994.

Johann Kuhnau was Bach's predecessor at Leipzig and one of the most imaginative of the Lutheran organist-composers of the generation before Bach. He seems to have been the composer of the earliest German keyboard 'sonata' which he included among the pieces of his *Neue Clavier Ubung* (1692); but of far greater interest are the later sonatas contained in the *Frische Clavier Früchte* ("Fresh Keyboard Fruits") of 1696 and the *Musicalische Vorstellung einiger biblischer Historien* ("Musical Representation of Several Biblical Stories") of 1700. The *Musicalische Vorstellung* was not, of course, by any means the earliest excursion into the field of keyboard programme music but it was, as John Butt remarks in his introductory note, the first collection to present a detailed narrative commentary. Thankfully Harmonia Mundi have resisted any temptation to have the narrations read aloud on disc between every individual section. That was once tried on an elderly Teldec recording with Gustav Leonhardt, and very tedious it was, too. What Harmonia Mundi have done is to provide the original texts in translation under each Sonata heading. It isn't quite like seeing the text written into the notation as Kuhnau arranged it, but on balance it seems the least intrusive solution. Butt plays the sonatas on three instruments: organ, harpsichord and clavichord. The notion is a good one, for not only does the character and form of the music often lend itself more readily to one of these than to another, but it also provides effective variety of colour for the listener. The instruments, all modern ones built after suitable models, sound very well. Butt's playing is fluent, rhetorical and virtuosic and he makes more sense of these extraordinary, often theatrical pieces than anyone previously. The music is full of fantasy, symbol and gesture and Kuhnau requires more than cursory aural reception on the part of his audience. A stimulating release.

Friedrich Kunzen

German 1761-1817

New review

Kunzen Holger Danske. **Inga Nielsen** (sop) Oberon; **Henriette Bonde-Hansen** (sop) Titania, Echo; **Gert Henning-Jensen** (ten) Holger Danske; **Johannes Mannov** (bar) Kerasmin; **Johan Reuter** (bass) Buurman, Bobul; **Inger Dam-Jensen** (sop) Rezia; **Guido Paëvatalu** (bar) Mufti, Herald; **Marianne Rørholm** (mez) Almansaris; **Danish National Radio Choir and Symphony Orchestra / Thomas Dausgaard.** Da capo Ⓕ 8 224036/7 (two discs: 142 minutes: DDD: 8/96). Notes, text and translation included. Recorded 1995.

Why is *Holger Danske* ("Ogier the Dane") all but unknown, even in Denmark itself? The première was a great success, but at the time Denmark was in the grip of anti-German sentiment. Librettist Jens Baggesen was attacked as being too pro-German and a heated debate ensued. Baggesen asked for the opera to be withdrawn and it was not heard again in full until 1941 – when Denmark was under German occupation. If the name on the cover were Mozart or Weber, then it would be a familiar operatic standard, not a novelty exhumed after a gap of two centuries. It is not unworthy of comparison with, say, *The Magic Flute* or *Oberon*, and indeed features both a magic instrument (here a horn) like the former and the Fairy King himself. But *Holger* pre-dates these works, having been written in 1789. The score is remarkable, each scene through-composed to form a coherent, unified whole; there are plenty of good tunes and the orchestration sparkles, with Turkish percussion for exotic colour in the middle act and anticipations elsewhere of Mendelssohn and nineteenth-century French opera. The plot, set during the early ninth century, has strong resonances of *A Midsummer Night's Dream*. Oberon and Titania have had a particularly acrimonious quarrel and can only be reconciled through the constancy of a human couple: Holger, a Danish knight in the service of

Charlemagne, and Rezia, daughter of the Sultan of Baghdad. In expiation for killing one of the King's sons, Holger has been charged to cut off a lock of the Sultan's beard and kiss his daughter in public, which he achieves thanks to Oberon's help. The debt to Charlemagne paid, the lovers then redeem Oberon and Titania by proving their fidelity despite the direst perils. The two couples are reunited in an unequivocally happy ending. *Holger Danske* is a joy, especially when as lovingly re-created and captured as it is here.

György Kurtág

Romanian 1926-

Kurtág Messages of the late Miss R.V. Troussova, Op. 17[a]. ... Quasi una Fantasia ..., Op. 27[b]. Scenes from a Novel, Op. 19[c]. [a]**Rosemary Hardy**, [c]**Christine Whittlesey** (sops); [c]**Mathias Tacke** (vn); [c]**Thomas Fichter** (db); [c]**Márta Fábián** (cimbalom); [b]**Hermann Kretzschmar** (pf); [ab]**Ensemble Modern / Peter Eötvös**. Sony Classical Ⓕ SK53290 (55 minutes: DDD: 12/93). Texts and translations included. Recorded 1990-92.   Ⓖ

At last – an all-Kurtág CD that celebrates the full substance and power of his music. The *Troussova* cycle, still Kurtág's most familiar score, is well performed by a vibrant Rosemary Hardy, with Peter Eötvös and his players bringing out the score's varied colours and imaginative instrumental effects. Kurtág is at his most expressionistic and also his most lyrical here. The later *Scenes from a Novel* has a comparable obsessiveness in its exploration of feminine frustration and resignation but, with only violin, double-bass and cimbalom supporting the voice, the emotional range is more restricted, the music often more personal, yet also more explicitly allusive, not least to Kurtág's Bartókian heritage. The performance grips from start to finish. ... *Quasi una Fantasia* ... (1987-88) is the most recent work included. Its four short movements for piano and assorted instruments, including prominent mouth organs and an extraordinary timpani part, turn its (apparently accidental) Beethovenian connection into a remarkable exploration of extremes. Caliban and Prospero are mentioned in the insert-notes, but no extra-musical props are needed to mediate the impact of this absorbing score, which can veer from simple, sustained scale figures to extreme fragmentation without loss of coherence. The recordings are appropriately vivid.

New review

Kurtág Neun Stücke[a]. Jelek, Op. 5[a]. Hommage à R. Sch, Op. 15*d*[abc].
Schumann Märchenbilder, Op. 113[bc]. Fantasie-stücke, Op. 73[ab]. Märchenerzählungen, Op. 132[abc]. [c]**Eduard Brunner** (cl); [a]**Kim Kashkashian** (va); [b]**Robert Levin** (pf). ECM New Series Ⓕ 437 957-2 (76 minutes: DDD: 1/96).

It's logical enough: three works by György Kurtág, one of which is called *Hommage à R. Sch*, placed alongside three works by Schumann himself. It's not as if the two composers had nothing whatsoever in common. Both place their most concentrated, poetic utterances in groups of miniatures, both are intensely allusive. Such extreme contrasts – since Kurtág never really sounds remotely like Schumann – always have their attractions. The Kurtág works are excellently done. The violist Kim Kashkashian has all the control and refinement necessary to make the extremely brief movements of *Jelek* ("Signs") and the *Neun Stücke* tell to maximum effect, and despite the emphasis on miniature forms (only the last movement of *Hommage à R. Sch* runs for more than three minutes), a tremendously wide range of moods and textures is encompassed. While Kurtág's discography is still modest, these Schumann pieces have been much recorded, and at least one of them, the late *Märchenerzählungen*, finds him well below his best. These are good performances, nevertheless. The 'large hall' acoustic of the recording attaches considerable resonance to the piano, but the balance with the other instruments is perfectly acceptable.

Further listening ...

...String Quartet No. 1, Op. 1. Hommage à Milhály András, Op. 13. Officium breve in memoriam Andreae Szervánzky, Op. 28. *Coupled with works by* **Gubaidulina** and **Lutosławski** Arditti **Quartet**. Auvidis Montaigne MO789007 (4/92). *See review under Gubaidulina; refer to the Index to Reviews.*

...Plays and Games for Piano, Book 3 – excerpts. *Coupled with works by* **Liszt, Dohnányi, Kodály, Bartók, Weiner** and **Szöllösy** Peter Frankl (pf). ASV CDDCA860 (6/93). *See review in the Collections section; refer to the Index to Reviews.*   ⒼⒼⒼ

Johan Kvandal

Norwegian 1919-

Suggested listening ...

...Wind Quintet, Op. 34. Three Sacred Folktunes, Op. 23*b*. *Coupled with works by* **Fernström** and **Nielsen** **Oslo Wind Ensemble**. Naxos 8 553050 (3/95). *See review under Nielsen; refer to the Index to Reviews.*

Joseph La Barre

Suggested listening ...
...Sonate l'inconnuë in G major, Book 2 No. 9. *Coupled with works by* **Leclair, Blavet, Rameau**
and **Hotteterre** Rachel Brown (fl); **Mark Caudle** (viol); **James Johnstone** (hpd). Chandos
Chaconne CHAN0544 (2/94). 🖉

Pierre de La Rue
French c1460-1518

Suggested listening ...
...Missa L'homme armé. Missa pro defunctis. **Ensemble Clément Jancquin** with **Yvon Repérant** (org).
Harmonia Mundi HMC90 1296 (9/89).
...Missa pro defunctis. *Coupled with* **Josquin Desprez** Missa Hercules dux Ferraric. La
déploration de Johannes Ockeghem, "Nymphes des bois". **New London Chamber Choir / James
Wood.** Amon Ra CDSAR24 (3/87).

Franz Lachner
German 1803-1890

Suggested listening ...
...Symphony No. 8 in G minor, Op. 100[a]. Ball-Suite in D major, Op. 170[b]. **Košice State
Philharmonic Orchestra /** [a]**Paul Robinson,** [b]**Alfred Walter.** Marco Polo 8 223594 (3/95).

Edouard Lalo
French 1823-1892

Lalo Cello Concerto in D minor.
Massenet Fantaisie.
Saint-Saëns Cello Concerto No. 1 in A minor, Op. 33. **Sophie Rolland** (vc); **BBC Philharmonic
Orchestra / Gilbert Varga.** ASV Ⓕ CDDCA867 (65 minutes: DDD: 12/93). Recorded 1993.
Gramophone Editor's choice.   Ⓖ
Sophie Rolland's performance of the Lalo Concerto is surely as fine as any recorded. It opens with
great character, thanks to Gilbert Varga's strong accompaniment, and the solo playing is wonderfully
songful. But Rolland is heard at her very finest as she plays her introduction to the finale with
commanding improvisatory spontaneity. The orchestra burst in splendidly and she shows her
technical mettle with some lovely bouncing bowing in the attractive closing Rondo. The Saint-Saëns
Concerto brings similar felicities. Massenet's *Fantaisie* opens dramatically and is rhythmically vital,
flowing onwards boldly to produce a winningly sentimental yearning melody which the soloist clearly
relishes. A cadenza then leads to a charming, very French Gavotte (which has a flavour of *Manon*)
and the piece ends jubilantly. It really is a find, and it could hardly be presented more persuasively.
The balance is as near perfect as one could wish, the orchestral sound detailed, yet attractively full
and resonant, and the cello placed in excellent perspective.

Additional recommendations ...
...Cello Concerto. **Bruch** Kol Nidrei, Op. 47. **Saint-Saëns** Cello Concerto. Matt Haimovitz (vc);
Chicago Symphony Orchestra / James Levine. DG Ⓕ 427 323-2GH (59 minutes: DDD: 6/89).
...Cello Concerto. **Fauré** Elégie, Op. 24. **Saint-Saëns** Cello Concerto No. 1 in A minor, Op. 33.
Heinrich Schiff (vc); **New Philharmonia Orchestra / Sir Charles Mackerras.** DG Ⓑ 431 166-2GR
(53 minutes: DDD: 8/91).
...Cello Concerto. **Saint-Saëns** Cello Concerto[b]. **Schumann** Cello Concerto No. 1 in A minor,
Op. 129[a]. **János Starker** (vc); **London Symphony Orchestra /** [a]**Stanislaw Skrowaczewski,** [b]**Antál
Dorati.** Mercury Ⓜ 432 010-2MM (65 minutes: ADD: 4/92).   ⒼⒼ
...Cello Concerto[a]. **R. Strauss** Don Quixote, Op. 35[b]. **Jacqueline du Pré** (vc); [b]**Herbert Downes**
(va); [a]**Cleveland Orchestra / Daniel Barenboim;** [b]**New Philharmonia Orchestra / Sir Adrian Boult.**
EMI Ⓕ CDC5 55528-2 (73 minutes: ADD: 11/95).

| New review |
Lalo Symphonie espagnole, Op. 21[a].
Vieuxtemps Violin Concerto No. 5 in A minor, Op. 37[b]. **Sarah Chang** (vn); [a]**Royal Concertgebouw
Orchestra,** [b]**Philharmonia Orchestra / Charles Dutoit.** EMI Ⓕ CDC5 55292-2 (52 minutes: DDD:
5/96). Item marked [a]recorded live in 1995, [b]1994. *Gramophone Editor's choice.*   Ⓖ
Vieuxtemps's Fifth Violin Concerto opens disarmingly, but the tutti gathers strength in Dutoit's hands
before Chang steals in silkily and proceeds to dominate the performance with her warm lyricism and
natural, flowing rubato. In a performance like this it remains a small-scale work to cherish, for it hasn't
a dull bar in it. The recording is warm and full, the balance treating the relationship between the violin
and the excellent Philharmonia Orchestra as an equal partnership. The *Symphonie espagnole* is
altogether more ambitious, as befitting its portentous title, but the Lalo's inventive Spanishry holds up
well throughout the five movements. How attractive is the Concertgebouw acoustic for the fanfare-like

opening – giving it weight as well as point. Again Dutoit's approach is full of impetus so that when the malagueña secondary theme arrives, presented with a special feminine allure, it makes a shimmering contrast. The delicious piping woodwind crescendo and decrescendo which begins the finale sets the scene for scintillating salterello fireworks from the soloist, with Dutoit's spirited orchestral interjections adding to the fun, and the solo lyrical interludes as seductive as ever. The dash into the home straight brings vociferous applause, which makes one realize that the concentration and spontaneity of the performance has been helped by the presence of an audience, who aren't apparent until this point. Certainly the splendidly resonant Concertgebouw sound and nigh perfect balance would never have given the game away that this was not a recording made under studio conditions.

Additional recommendations ...

...Symphonie espagnole. **Saint-Saëns** Violin Concerto No. 3 in B minor, Op. 61. **Itzhak Perlman** (vn). **Orchestre de Paris / Daniel Barenboim.** DG Ⓜ 445 549-2GMA (61 minutes: DDD).

...Symphonie espagnole. **Saint-Saëns** Introduction and Rondo capriccioso, Op. 28. **Vieuxtemps** Violin Concerto No. 5 in A minor, Op. 37. **Shlomo Mintz** (vn); **Israel Philharmonic Orchestra / Zubin Mehta.** DG Ⓕ 427 676-2GH (60 minutes: DDD: 3/92).

...Symphonie espagnole. **Bruch** Scottish Fantasy, Op. 46. **Anne Akiko Meyers** (vn); **Royal Philharmonic Orchestra / Jesús López-Cobos.** RCA Victor Red Seal Ⓕ RD60942 (60 minutes: DDD: 9/92). Ⓖ

...Symphonie espagnole[a]. **Ravel** Tzigane[a]. **Sibelius** Violin Concerto in D minor, Op. 47[b]. **Itzhak Perlman** (vn); [a]**London Symphony Orchestra / André Previn;** [b]**Boston Symphony Orchestra / Erich Leinsdorf.** RCA Gold Seal Masters Collection Ⓜ 07863 56520-2 (72 minutes: ADD: 7/93).

...Symphonie espagnole[a]. Cello Concerto[b]. **Saint-Saëns** Violin Concerto No. 1[a]. [a]**Kyung-Wha Chung** (vn); [b]**Lynn Harrell** (vc); [a]**Montreal Symphony Orchestra / Charles Dutoit;** [b]**Berlin Radio Symphony Orchestra / Riccardo Chailly.** Decca Ⓜ 436 483-2DM (74 minutes: DDD: 2/94).

...Symphonie espagnole[a]. **Berlioz** Rêverie et caprice, Op. 8[a]. **Saint-Saëns** Violin Concerto No. 3 in B minor, Op. 61[b]. **Itzhak Perlman** (vn); **Orchestre de Paris / Daniel Barenboim.** DG Digital Masters Ⓜ 445 549-2GMA (69 minutes: DDD: 7/95).

...Symphonie espagnole[a]. **Goldmark** Violin Concerto No. 1 in A minor, Op. 28[b]. **Nathan Milstein** (vn); [a]**Philharmonia Orchestra / Harry Blech;** [b]**St Louis Symphony Orchestra / Vladimir Golschmann.** Testament [a]stereo/[b]mono Ⓕ SBT1047* (71 minutes: ADD: 11/95). *See review under Goldmark; refer to the Index to Reviews.*

Lalo Symphonie espagnole, Op. 21.
Dvořák Violin Concerto in A minor, B108. **Christian Tetzlaff** (vn); **Czech Philharmonic Orchestra / Libor Pešek.** Virgin Classics Ⓕ VC5 45022-2 (63 minutes: DDD: 7/94). Recorded 1992-3.

This is a unique and generous coupling and if Virgin Classics' decision to record Tetzlaff in Prague was dictated by the obvious advantage in having Dvořák's compatriots accompanying in his Violin Concerto, the Czech Philharmonic's playing under Pešek proves just as idiomatic in the Spanish dance rhythms of Lalo as in Czech dances, with crisp ensemble and rhythm deliciously sprung. What is especially remarkable about Tetzlaff's performances of the *Symphonie espagnole* as well as the Violin Concerto, is the quicksilver lightness of the passagework, which brings out the element of fantasy; in that he is helped by a recording balance which does not spotlight the soloist as sharply as in most other versions. In both works, each more episodic than most and hard to hold together, Tetzlaff's concentration makes for a sense of spontaneity, leading one on just as magnetically as, for example, Perlman in his more obviously weighty, more vibrato-laden readings of both pieces. Tetzlaff's sense of fantasy consistently marks him out, so that with delectable pointing of rhythm and phrase he makes the Lalo more subtly winning than it often is, less of a mere barnstorming showpiece, helped by the extra transparency of textures.

Further listening ...

...Piano Trios – No. 1 in C minor, Op. 7; No. 2 in B minor; No. 3 in A minor, Op. 26. **Henry Trio.** Pierre Verany PV794031 (8/94). Ⓖ

...Symphony in G minor. *Coupled with* **Franck** Symphony in D minor. **French Radio National Orchestra / Sir Thomas Beecham.** EMI CDM7 63396-2* (9/92).

...Symphony in G minor. Rapsodie. Scherzo. Divertissement. **Basle Symphony Orchestra / Giancarlo Andretta.** CPO CPO999 296-2 (3/96).

...Piano Trios – No. 1 in C minor, Op. 7; No. 2 in B minor; No. 3 in A minor, Op. 26. **Barbican Piano Trio.** ASV CDDCA899 (11/94).

Francesco Lambardi

Italian c1587-1642

Suggested listening ...

...Gagliarda. Partite sopra "Fidele". *Coupled with works by* **Buono, Picchi, Trabaci, A. Mayone, Giovanni de Macque, Facoli, A. Valente, Frescobaldi, Merula, M. Rossi, Salvatore, B. Storace, G. Strozzi, Stradella** and **A. Scarlatti** Rinaldo Alessandrini (hpd). Opus 111 OPS30-118 (4/95). ✐ *See review in the Collections section; refer to the Index to Reviews.*

Walter Lambe
British c1450-c1499

Suggested listening ...
...Nesciens mater. *Coupled with works by* **Davy** and **Nesbet** Eton College Chapel Choir / Ralph
   Allwood. Chatsworth FCM1004 (5/95). *See review under Davy; refer to the Index to Reviews.*
...Salve regina. *Coupled with works by* **Davy, Plummer** and **William, Monk of Stratford**
   Magnificat. **The Sixteen / Harry Christophers.** Collins Classics 1462-2 (3/96). *See review in the
   Collections section; refer to the Index to Reviews.*

Constant Lambert
British 1905-1951

Lambert Concerto for Piano and Nine Players[a]. Eight Poems[b]. Piano Sonata[c]. Mr Bear Squash-
you-all-flat[d]. [b]**Philip Langridge** (ten); [d]**Nigel Hawthorne** (narr); [ac]**Ian Brown** (pf); [abd]**Nash
Ensemble / Lionel Friend.** Hyperion Ⓔ CDA66754 (80 minutes: DDD: 7/95). Texts included.
Recorded 1994. *Gramophone Editor's choice.*   Ⓖ
The performance of the Piano Concerto is a rounded and deeply felt experience with the performers
scrupulously attentive to dynamic nuance; their playing also possesses immaculate polish,
irrepressible rhythmic vigour and heaps of panache – witness the exhilaratingly racy close to the first
movement. More crucially, this perceptive reading probes the unnerving strain of bleak melancholy
coursing through this poignant score. Nowhere is this more evident than in the elegiac finale, a tragic,
world-weary utterance which here attains an anguished climax of truly heartbreaking proportions.
Moreover, the ensuing coda is no less numbing in its inconsolable grief. Pianist Ian Brown acquits
himself as admirably in the Sonata as he does in the Concerto. This big-boned, daunting work calls
for a really strong technique which it duly receives. The tenderly affecting *Eight Poems* of Li-Po find
Philip Langridge in exquisite voice. These ravishing settings, given here with their rarely heard
accompaniment for flute, oboe, clarinet and string quintet, occupied Lambert on and off for a period
of four years (1926-29). In June 1924 Lambert completed his 'ballet' *Mr Bear Squash-you-all-flat*, the
earliest of his compositions currently known to us. This wittily anarchic entertainment, colourfully
and confidently scored for chamber ensemble, more than likely also incorporated a part for narrator.
Based on "a Russian children's tale" (a bedtime story from Lambert's St Petersburg-born father,
perhaps, or just a leg-pulling piece of fiction?), the music reveals the influence of such contemporary
continental figures as Satie, Milhaud, Honegger and, above all, Stravinsky. Assuming the voices and
characters of Lambert's assorted menagerie (Mr Frog, Mr Mouse *et al*), Nigel Hawthorne enters into
the fray with altogether infectious humour and enthusiasm. Featuring immaculate sound and
excellent insert-notes, this anthology deserves the widest possible currency.

Additional recommendation ...
...Piano Sonata. Elegiac Blues. Elegy. **Holst** Toccata on the Northumbrian Pipe Tune, "Newburn
   Lads". Chrissemas Day in the Morning, on a tune from "North Country Ballads", Op. 46 No. 1.
   Two Folk Song Arrangements, Op. 46 No. 2. Nocturne. Jig. Arpeggio Study. Two Pieces. A Piece
   for Yvonne. Dances (with Caroline Clemmow, pf). **Anthony Goldstone** (pf). Chandos
   Ⓔ CHAN9382 (67 minutes: DDD: 10/95).

Further listening ...
...Horoscope. *Coupled with* **Bliss** Checkmate. **Walton** Façade – Suites Nos. 1 and 2. **English
   Northern Philharmonia / David Lloyd-Jones.** Hyperion CDA66436 (3/91).
...Rio Grande[a]. Summer's Last Will and Testament[b]. Aubade héroïque. [a]**Sally Burgess** (mez);
   [b]**William Shimell** (bar); [a]**Jack Gibbons** (pf); [a]**Opera North Chorus**; [b]**Leeds Festival Chorus; English
   Northern Philharmonia / David Lloyd-Jones.** Hyperion CDA66565 (6/92).   ⒼⒼ

John Lambert
British 1926-1995

New review
J. Lambert Tread softly[a]. Slide[b]. Meditations[c]. Toccata[d]. Family Affairs – excerpts[e]. String
Quartet No. 2[f]. [b]**Anthony Aarons** (tpt); [d]**Charles Ramirez** (gtr); [a]**Albion Guitar Quartet** (Helen
Sanderson, Abigail James, Maureen Maratzzi, Jane Phillips, gtrs); [f]**Bingham Quartet** (Stephen
Bingham, Mark Messenger, vns; Brenda Stewart, va; Miriam Lowbury, vc); [ce]**Sounds Positive**
(Simon Desorgher, fl; Edwin Roxburgh, cor ang; Linda Merrick, cl; Sally Mays, pf) / **David
Sutton-Anderson.** NMC Ⓔ NMCD026 (59 minutes: DDD: 3/96).
John Lambert is best known as the teacher of several prominent British composers, including Oliver
Knussen and Mark-Anthony Turnage. A pupil of Nadia Boulanger, Lambert was a dedicated
composer himself, yet performances in his lifetime were relatively rare. This disc can only hint at an
explanation for his neglect, and can barely begin to redress it, since none of the larger-scale works is
included. Yet it is still possible to gain a clear impression of Lambert's distinctive musical personality.
The most recent work is arguably the most successful. *Meditations* (1991) requires an unusual
ensemble – bass flute, cor anglais, clarinet and piano – and the way it traverses a textural spectrum
from simple to complex, reflecting a fascination with the exotic, yet making that fascination seem
natural and inevitable, is completely convincing. The Second String Quartet (1986) is less original, its

scurrying figurations redolent of Ligeti or Lutosławski, yet there is a true feeling of fulfilment in the final section's incorporation of more sustained material. Where style is concerned, Lambert could always avoid simplistic typecasting, and his writing for guitar, whether solo (*Toccata*) or ensemble (*Tread softly*), is especially skilful in balancing unexpected effects against more predictable pattern-making. *Slide* (1989) is rather routine in its treatment of the trumpet's limited resources. Far more rewarding are the tantalizingly brief extracts from the chamber opera *Family Affairs* (1987-8), in which Lambert's concern with the nature of sound itself, electronically analysed and expanded, interacts absorbingly with the opera's allusive, evocative subject matter (including nursery rhymes). It is indeed a pity that so little of this intriguing work could be included here. Performances and recordings, supervised by Lambert himself two years before his death, are ideal.

John Lampe
British c1703-1751

New review
Lampe Pyramus and Thisbe[a]. Concerto for Flute and Orchestra in G major, "The Cuckoo"[b]. [a]**Mark Padmore** (ten) Pyramus; [a]**Susan Bisatt** (sop) Thisbe; [a]**Michael Sanderson** (ten) Wall, Master; [a]**Arwel Treharne** (ten) Moon, Prompter; [a]**Andrew Knight** (bass) Lion, Prologue; [a]**Peter Milne** (spkr) Mr Semibrief; [a]**Alan McMahon** (spkr) First Gentleman; [a]**Jack Edwards** (spkr) Second Gentleman; [a]**Philippa Hyde** (sop); [a]**Colin Baldy** (bar); [b]**Rachel Brown** (fl); **Opera Restor'd / Peter Holman.** Hyperion Ⓔ CDA66759 (64 minutes: DDD: 12/95). 🖉 Notes and text included.

John Frederick Lampe, born in Saxony, settled in England in the 1720s. For a time he played the bassoon in Handel's opera orchestra; then in the early 1730s he was one of the group of musicians who put on English operas at the theatre opposite Handel's in the Haymarket and he wrote several pieces for the company before turning to burlesque, enjoying particular success with *The Dragon of Wantley* (1737). *Pyramus and Thisbe* (1745) was his last opera; later he went to Dublin and to Edinburgh, where he died in 1751. None of his operas survives complete; publications of the time usually reproduced the airs but not the recitatives or choruses, and the scores of most operas perished in the numerous theatre fires of the time. For *Pyramus* Peter Holman has had to supply recitatives, which he does with style and probably a touch more imagination than Lampe himself might have managed. Yet Lampe's airs are deftly written. The text is based on Shakespeare's 'lamentable play' in *A Midsummer Night's Dream*, with Wall, Moon and Lion among the characters as well as Pyramus and Thisbe. Lampe's music has a good deal of wit – listen for example to the Wall's Song, with the lovers' groans and moans represented by harsh open violin Gs, its pseudo-pathetic G minor tonality, its amusing setting of "whisp'ring whisp'ring [17 times] hole"; or the duet as the lovers depart 'without delay', in typical operatic haste, with much repetition and many pauses; or the Lion's Song with its rhythmic growls. No one would suggest that it is high quality music, but it is resourceful and entertaining. And it is excellently presented here, in unpretentious style – this kind of music fares far better with modest-sized voices and careful diction than if more self-consciously sung. The two principals sing with due charm and tenderness: Mark Padmore offers a pleasantly relaxed and fresh-sounding tenor and Susan Bisatt some shapely lines and well-focused tone. Peter Holman's direction is direct and idiomatic.

Further listening ...
...Britannia – Welcome Mars[a]. Dione – Pretty warblers. *Coupled with works by* **Arne** and **Handel** **Emma Kirkby** (sop); **Academy of Ancient Music / Christopher Hogwood.** L'Oiseau-Lyre 436 132-2OH (7/93). *See review under Arne; refer to the Index to Reviews.* Ⓖ

John Lanchbery
British 1923-

Suggested listening ...
...Tales of Beatrix Potter – film score. **Royal Opera House Orchestra, Covent Garden / John Lanchbery.** EMI CDC7 54537-2 (11/94).

Burton Lane
American 1912-

The Burton Lane Songbook, Volume 2. **Michael Feinstein** (bar); **Burton Lane** (pf). Elektra Nonesuch Ⓔ 7559-79285-2 (66 minutes: DDD: 8/94).
Carmelina – It's time for a love song. Hold on to your hats – The world is in my arms; Don't let it get you down. Love on Toast – I want a new romance. Dancing Lady – Everything I have is yours. Kid Millions – Your head on my shoulders. Ship Ahoy – Poor you. Royal Wedding – Open your eyes; The happiest day of my life. Dancing on a Dime – I hear music. Some like it Hot – The lady's in love with you. Where have I seen your face before? Give a Girl a Break – It happens every time. Look who's here. On a clear day you can see forever – medley.
Only dedicated film buffs know the 1939 Bob Hope comedy *Some like it Hot*. It has left us with one of Burton Lane's most charming songs, "The lady's in love with you", with lyrics by Frank Loesser.

Michael Feinstein sings it with his accustomed delicate charm, words balanced skilfully within a smooth vocal line. With the composer at the piano, this second volume of Lane numbers makes the strongest case for his work to be better known. The chosen songs are divided between rarities from movies and standards such as "Everything I have is yours" from *Dancing Lady*, which Feinstein and Lane perform in tandem with "Your head on my shoulders" from *Kid Millions*. Lane spent a decade in Hollywood before returning to Broadway, where his career had begun in 1930 with songs for *Three's a Crowd*. E.Y. Harburg supplied the lyrics for *Hold on to your hats* in 1940 from which we hear two songs as well as a couple of other Harburg-penned items ("Poor you" and "Where have I seen your face before?"). Alan Jay Lerner was Lane's most successful collaborator with *On a clear day you can see forever* and the disc ends with a ten-song sequence from this show. "The happiest day of my life" has a gentle, pleasant tune and Lane plays a solo piano reprise of it; the disc opens with another Lerner lyric, "It's time for a love song" from *Carmelina*, their 1979 Broadway show based on *Buona Sera, Mrs Campbell*. This disc is highly recommended as an unhackneyed survey of Lane's output.

Craig Sellar Lang   British 1891-1971

Suggested listening ...
...Tuba tune. *Coupled with works by* **Whitlock, Howells, Elgar, Vaughan Williams** and **Cocker** Gareth Green (org). Naxos 8 550582 (3/93). *See review in the Collections section; refer to the Index to Reviews.*

David Lang   American 1957-

Suggested listening ...
...Are you experienced?[c] Under Orpheus[d]. *Coupled with* **J. Adams** Short ride in a fast machine (arr. L.T. Odorn)[a]. Grand Pianola Music[b]. [c]**David Lang** (narr); [b]**Lindsay Wagstaff**, [b]**Kym Amps**, [b]**Ruth Holton** (sops); [bd]**Ellen Corver**, [bd]**Sepp Grotenhuis** (pfs); **Netherlands Wind Ensemble / Stephen Mosko**. Chandos New Direction CHAN9363 (10/95). *See review under J. Adams; refer to the Index to Reviews.*
...The Anvil Chorus. *Coupled with works by* **L. Andriessen, Wolfe** and **Gordon** Bang on a Can All-Stars. Sony Classical SK66483 (2/96). *Selected by Sounds in Retrospect. See review in the Collections section; refer to the Index to Reviews.*

Rued Langgaard   Danish 1893-1952

Langgaard Symphonies – No. 4, "Fall of the Leaf"; No. 5, "Steppelands"; No. 6, "Heavens Asunder". **Danish National Radio Symphony Orchestra / Neeme Järvi.** Chandos Ⓕ CHAN9064 (63 minutes: DDD: 12/92). Recorded 1991.
This reclusive Dane (pronounced Ruth Langor, should you want to rave about him to your friends) was either a visionary mystic or wildly nutty, depending on your point of view. Unfortunately for Langgaard, the Danes had already embraced Carl Nielsen as their country's answer to Sibelius; and in any case these three Langgaard symphonies seldom display the much valued Scandinavian symphonic virtues of coherence and far-sighted evolution. Indeed Robert Layton, in his original **Gramophone** review, referred to the effect of the Fifth and Sixth as "overwhelmingly episodic". But what astonishing episodes! The Fourth Symphony's "Leaf-fall" is a Danish, foreshortened but distinctly apocalyptic, *Alpine Symphony* with quite as much Wagner along the way as Richard Strauss (it opens with exactly the same brass chord as *Götterdämmerung*); it is thrilling nature music, with moments of wild, flying energy contrasted with episodes of almost Delian contemplation and atmosphere. The Fifth is more ordered and shows that, for all Langgaard's jealousy of Nielsen, in his Rondo theme for the work, he was quite content to powerfully imitate him. And the Sixth's cosmic conflicts recall Bruckner and Charles Ives. That's enough influences to be going on with; you can enjoy spotting many more for yourself. None of them detract from these communications of an extraordinary imagination. As to the performances, suffice it to say that the Danish orchestra sound entirely at home, and Järvi has never been more in his element. And Chandos, even by their own standards, have never produced more spectacular sound.
Further listening ...
...Symphony No. 1, "Klippepastoraler". Fra Dybet[a]. [a]**Danish National Radio Choir; Danish National Radio Orchestra / Leif Segerstam.** Chandos CHAN9249.

Jean Langlais
French 1907-1991

Langlais Symphonies – No. 1; No. 2, "Alla Webern". Suite française – Nazard; Arabesque sur les flûtes. Suite brève. Poem of Happiness. **Kevin Bowyer** (org). Nimbus Ⓕ NI5408 (68 minutes: DDD: 1/95). Played on the 1987 Carthy Organ of the Calgary Centre for the Performing Arts, Canada. Recorded 1992.

Langlais's First Symphony is an angry work, born out of the frustrations and horrors of the Nazi occupation of Paris. Bowyer has clearly gone for the emotive approach, venting his spleen at the microphones and uncompromisingly emphasizing Langlais's frequent outbursts of almost incoherent rage. It doesn't make for comfortable listening, but certainly underlines the starkness of the work. The most immediately obvious *alla Webern* aspects of the Second Symphony are its brevity – four movements totalling five minutes compared with 33 minutes for the First – and its desiccated, highly concentrated musical language. The profound Christian faith which was the driving force behind so much of Langlais's music finds an outlet here in the first nine notes, which spell out the words 'Dieu' and 'Marie'. The classical French organ composers of the seventeenth and eighteenth centuries seem poles apart from Webern, but Langlais absorbed their influence in equally distinctive ways, the most obvious results being the *Suite française* and the *Suite brève*. What all these works have in common is a restrained language almost devoid of emotional involvement. The crisp, sharp colours of this large but surprisingly intimate-sounding Canadian instrument, coupled with Bowyer's precise and fluent delivery, allow the music to speak with perfect clarity and impressive conviction.

Further listening ...

...Trois Paraphrases Grégoriennes, Op. 5. *Coupled with works by* **Alain** and **Messiaen Catharine Crozier** (org). Delos DE3147 (2/95).

...Poèmes évangéliques, Op. 2 – No. 2, La Nativité. Paraphrases grégoriennes, Op. 5 – Hymne d'actions de grâce. *Coupled with works by* **T. Dubois, Franck, Gigout, Murrill, Peeters, Reger** and **Vierne Andrew Lucas** (org). Naxos 8 550955 (11/94). *See review in the Collections section; refer to the Index to Reviews.*

...Prelude and Fugue, Op. 1. *Coupled with works by* **Honegger, Dupré, Roussel, d'Indy, R. Vierne, Barié** and **L. Vierne Marie-Bernadette Dufourcet** (org). Priory PRCD422 (6/95). *See review in the Collections section; refer to the Index to Reviews.*

...Triptyque. *Coupled with works by* **Bonnal, Bach, B. Ferguson** and **Dupré Roger Sayer** (org). Priory PRCD495 (4/96). *See review in the Collections section; refer to the Index to Reviews.*

Libby Larsen
American 1950-

Suggested listening ...

...Six Sonnets from the Portuguese. *Coupled with works by* **Purcell, Schumann** and **Mozart Arleen Auger** (sop); members of the **Saint Paul Chamber Orchestra** and the **Minnesota Orchestra / Joel Revzen** (pf). Koch International Classics 37248-2 (4/94). *See review in the Collections section; refer to the Index to Reviews.*

...Collage: Boogie. *Coupled with* **Schiff** Stomp. **Kernis** New Era Dance. **J. Adams** The Chairman Dances. **Bernstein** West Side Story – Mambo. **Harbison** Remembering Gatsby. **Torke** Black and White – Charcoal. **Moran** Points of Departure. **Agento** The Dream of Valentino – Tango. **Daugherty** Desi. **Rouse** Bonham. **Baltimore Symphony Orchestra / David Zinman.** Argo 444 454-2ZH (7/95).

Lars-Erik Larsson
Swedish 1908-1986

Suggested listening ...

...Concerto, Op. 42[a]. God in Disguise (Förklädd gud), Op. 24[b]. Pastoral Suite, Op. 19. [a]**Arve Tellefsen** (vn); [b]**Hillevi Martinpelto** (sop); [b]**Håkan Hagegård** (bar); [b]**Erland Josephson** (narr); [b]**Swedish Radio Choir and Symphony Orchestra / Esa-Pekka Salonen.** Sony Classical SK64140.

Orlando Lassus
Franco/Flemish 1532-1594

New review

Lassus Libro de villanelle, moresche, e altre canzoni. Madrigals – Tutto 'l dì piango; Sol'e pensoso i più deserti campi; O Lucia miau; Madonna mia pietà. **Concerto Italiano / Rinaldo Alessandrini.** Opus 111 Ⓕ OPS30-94 (59 minutes: DDD: 10/95). Texts and translations included. Recorded 1994.

This wickedly funny disc was released to coincide with the commemoration of the quincentenary of Lassus's death. Hitherto, Concerto Italiano have concentrated on the highbrow end of Italian secular music. They have done so with style, and as much wit as the aesthetic of the late madrigal allows. Here at last they get a chance to let their hair down: the result is as hilarious as one could have hoped. Concerto Italiano do for Lassus's Italian secular music what the Clément Janequin Ensemble have done for his *chansons*: they get inside both the meaning *and* the sound of the words, transfiguring musical texts that are (at times) purposefully naïve. They also capture the incipient, slightly worrying hysteria that pervades many of these pieces, and of which the French songs usually steer clear. Psychologically, this is well judged: as Lassus's letters show, Italian is the language of his manic phases, just as French corresponds to his depressive ones. This disc, then, completes the picture of the composer in his more unbuttoned moments. Apart from some indispensable anthology numbers such as "Matona mia cara" from the *Libro de villanelle* (performed with all the parody that the text demands), the most convincing performances are those of the *moresche*, which have already appeared on the above-mentioned disc by the French group. If the Italians have the edge here, it isn't merely a matter of language: they make a clearer case for the form and pace of these pieces than the Janequin do, and are even freer than the Janequin Ensemble with the musical text itself, adding effective glosses of their own. A few more serious items are thrown in for the sake of contrast. These are the only disappointing pieces in the set, too slow for comfort by some margin – but then again, the rather archaic madrigal, *Madonna mia pietà* is delivered with real passion. Finally, a word about that packaging gimmick – a red banner that proclaims, "Everything you ever wanted to know about sex on CD!" A note of reassurance for those who might need it: the humour here is more often allusive than explicit, and as often lavatorial as genuinely bawdy. Those familiar with French *chanson* texts will probably have seen worse. Besides, one cannot help but respond to Lassus's evident relish at setting these dubious gems. Do follow the composer's and the singers' example, and let your hair down as well.

Additional recommendation ...
...Libro de villanelle, moresche, e altre canzoni – excerpts. Chansons. Chansons (arr. for lute). **Eric Belloq** (lte); **Ensemble Clément Janequin.** Harmonia Mundi Ⓒ HMC90 1391 (54 minutes: DDD: 2/93).　　　Ⓖ

Lassus Lagrime di San Pietro. **Ensemble Vocal Européen / Philippe Herreweghe.** Harmonia Mundi Ⓕ HMC90 1483 (60 minutes: DDD: 8/94). Texts and translations included. Recorded 1993.　　Ⓖ
Lassus Lagrime di San Pietro. **Huelgas Ensemble / Paul van Nevel.** Sony Classical Ⓕ SK53373 (63 minutes. DDD: 8/94). Texts and translations included. Recorded 1993.
Lassus completed his swan-song days before his death in 1594. The decision to set 20 stanzas from Luigi Tansillo's unfinished meditation on "the tears of St Peter" must have been a highly personal one. The poet's portrayal of a man driven nearly insane with remorse allowed Lassus to exorcize the mental illness that engulfed him in his last years. The result is perhaps his most moving work, for there is in these *madrigali spirituali* a sense of distilled mannerism that calls to mind the understated passion of late-period Brahms. Philippe Herreweghe captures the detached expression of pain that makes this music so haunting. This is partly a matter of vocal timbre: individually the singers' tone is a shade cooler than that of the Huelgas Ensemble's members, but collectively they sound every bit as full-bodied as their rivals. However, it is in their interpretative acuteness that Herreweghe's singers gain a decisive edge. This is best illustrated by the groups' differing approaches to rubato: van Nevel uses *accelerandos* or straightforward shifts (usually to emphasize a textual illustration), but Herreweghe ever so slightly *stretches* the pulse when the voices achieve a poignant inflexion or come to a standstill. Such moments acquire an intensity that clearly identifies them as the key moments in a psychological drama, making the cycle as a whole compulsive listening. This is not to understate the many virtues of van Nevel's approach, but simply to say that Herreweghe's singers achieve something very, very special indeed.

Additional recommendation ...
...**Ars Nova / Bo Holten.** Naxos Ⓢ 8 553311 (55 minutes: DDD: 1/96).

New review
Lassus Missa Vinum bonum. Missa Triste depart. Missa Quand'io pens'al martire. Vinum bonum et suave.
Arcadelt Quand'io pens'al martire.
Gombert Triste depart m'avoit. **King's College Choir, Cambridge / Stephen Cleobury.** Decca London Ⓕ 444 335-2LH (70 minutes: DDD: 7/96). Texts and translations included.

New review
Lassus Musica Dei donum optimi. Bicinia – Nos. 3, 9 and 14. Vinum bonum et suave. Missa Vinum bonum. Salve regina mater. Laudent Deum cythara. Justorum animae. Quam pulchra es. Agimus tibi gratias. Christus resurgens ex mortuis. Tristis est anima mea. Ave verum corpus, Bone Jesu verbum patris. Tui sunt coeli. Vide homo, quae pro te patior. **Ex Cathedra / Jeffrey Skidmore; His Majesties Sagbutts and Cornetts / Jeremy West** (cornett). ASV Gaudeamus Ⓕ CDGAU150 (69 minutes: DDD: 7/96). Texts and translations included.
Lassus's *Vinum bonum* Mass is one of a group of three double-choir cycles composed in the 1580s (the others being *Osculetur me* and the *Bell'amphitrit'altera*). Lassus's Masses have generally had a rather bad press, for reasons that have never really been spelt out. Nearly all are of the so-called 'parody' variety, that is, based on previously composed polyphonic pieces (by Lassus or by others), and it is fascinating to observe the skill with which he reworks his models, chosen most commonly from among Italian madrigals, French chansons and Latin motets; Stephen Cleobury's generous selection gives us one of each (the Masses on *Quand'io pens'al martire* and *Triste depart* are not to be found elsewhere). All three are sung immediately before the corresponding Mass, allowing the listener to

explore the correspondences at leisure. These are fine performances, typical of the English treble tradition at its best; and if the four-voice Mass on *Quand'io pens'al martire* is a touch disappointing after the glorious promise of Arcadelt's madrigal, the two other cycles show Lassus on his best form. The King's College disc is (by definition) *a cappella*.

Ex Cathedra is a mixed choir and they are here joined for the *Vinum bonum* Mass by His Majesties Sagbutts and Cornetts. In that respect, they offer a clear alternative to King's. Their account of the motet *Vinum bonum* itself is more involving that that of King's, and for the Mass theirs is the more dynamic reading, and yet King's solemn account is not without grandeur. However, the balance in the mixed version favours the instruments ever so slightly more than than one might wish, sometimes to the detriment of the choral effect. Ex Cathedra present a contrasting series of motets for three to eight voices, and the wind ensemble round out the disc with a few *bicinia*, two-part pieces excerpted from his vocal music; so the two programmes are different enough for duplication scarcely to be an issue. In the final analysis, the choice largely depends on how you like your Lassus.

Lassus Missa Entre vous filles. Missa Susanne un jour. Infelix ego. **Oxford Camerata / Jeremy Summerly.** Naxos Ⓢ 8 550842 (68 minutes: DDD: 8/94). Text and translation of *Infelix ego* included. Recorded 1993.

The only Mass from this composer's considerable output to have found favour with record companies has been the eight-part *Bell'amfitrit altera*. This disc helps to dispel the still-current myth that Lassus's other Masses are of little interest. Both *Entre vous filles* and *Susanne un jour* show Lassus at his best, full of variety and invention, music of an immediate impact; in fact, they display exactly the same qualities as the better-known motets. The Oxford Camerata have understood this well, taking considerable care with the nuances of the text and really enjoying the music's rich sonorities. Sometimes a slight imprecision in the playing of chords is detectable, but this is more than outweighed by the sense of melodic contour and the powerful, somewhat dark and austere sound which conveys so well the spirit of the music. With over 68 minutes of some of the finest sixteenth-century polyphony available at such a low price, no one should hesitate to buy this disc.

Further listening ...

...Lamentationes Hieremiae a 5. **La Chapelle Royale European Ensemble / Philippe Herreweghe.** Harmonia Mundi HMC90 1299 (12/89).

...Missa Osculetur me. Motets – Osculetur me; Hodie completi sunt; Timor et tremor; Alma Redemptoris mater a 8; Salve regina mater a 8; Ave regina caelorum II a 6; Regina coeli a 7. **The Tallis Scholars / Peter Phillips.** Gimell CDGIM018 (7/89).

...Motets – Regina coeli laetare (five versions). Laetentur coeli. Alma Redemptoris mater. Resonet in laudibus. Tui sunt coeli. Quem vidistis pastores. Omnes de Saba Venient. Peccantem me quotidie. Timor et tremor. Popule meus. Aurora lucis rutilat. Christus resurgens ex mortuis. Jesu nostra redemptio. Jam non dicam vos. Hodie completi sunt. Alleluja laus et gloria. Benedictio et claritas. Justorum animae. Exultate justi. **Trinity College Choir, Cambridge / Richard Marlow.** Conifer CDCF230 (10/94).　　　　　　　　　　　　　　　　　　　　　　　　　　Ⓖ

...Missa Bell'Amfitrit altera. Tui sunt coeli. *Coupled with works by* **Caldara, A. Gabrieli, Frescobaldi, Cavalli, Monteverdi** and **G. Gabrieli The Sixteen / Harry Christophers** with [a]**Laurence Cummings** (org). Collins Classics 1360-2 (10/93). *See review in the Collections section; refer to the Index to Reviews.*

...Missa Bell'Amfitrit' altera[abcd]. *Coupled with* **Erbach** Sacerdotes Dei[acd]. Canzona secundi toni[c]. Hic est sacerdos[acd]. Fantasia sub Elevatione[c]. Toccata octavi toni[d]. Posuisti Domine[acd]. La Paglia[bc]. **Hassler** Canzon duodecimi toni[bcd]. Cantate Domino canticum novum[abcde]. Toccata in G major[d]. Canzon noni toni[bcd]. O sacrum convivium[acd]. Domine Dominus noster[abcde]. [a]**Westminster Cathedral Choir;** [b]**His Majesties Sagbutts and Cornetts / James O'Donnell** with [c]**Timothy Roberts,** [d]**Iain Simcock** [e]**Iris Schöllhorn** (orgs). Hyperion CDA66688 (6/94).　　Ⓖ

...Missa Qual donna attende à gloriosa fama. Tristis est anima mea. Exaltabo te Domine a 4. Psalmi Davidis poenitentiales – De profundis. Missa Venatorum. *Coupled with* **de Rore** Qual donna à gloriosa fama. **Christ Church Cathedral Choir, Oxford / Stephen Darlington.** Nimbus NI5150 (4/89).

...Prophetiae Sibyllarum. **Cantus Cölln / Konrad Junghänel.** Deutsche Harmonia Mundi 05472 77304-2 (7/94).

Henry Lawes　　　　　　　　　　　　　　　　　　　　　British 1596-1662

Further listening ...

...Cease you jolly shepherds. *Coupled with works by* **W. Lawes, J. Wilson, J. Cobb, S. Ives, Jenkins** and **Hilton II The Consort of Musicke / Anthony Rooley.** Musica Oscura 070972 (3/96). *See the review which follows.*

William Lawes

New review

W. Lawes Royall Consorts – No. 1 in D minor; No. 3 in D minor; No. 6 in D major; No. 7 in A minor; No. 9 in F major. **The Greate Consort** (Anne Schumann, vn; Emilia Benjamin, Reiko Ichise, viols; Elizabeth Kenny, William Carter, ltes) / **Monica Huggett** (vn). ASV Gaudeamus Ⓔ CDGAU146 (70 minutes: DDD: 3/96). ✦ Recorded 1995.

These works, if not as profoundly romantic in spirit as the more lavishly scored *Fantasias*, are courtly chamber works of supreme quality. Lawes is a master of line; what logic and textural finesse we detect, for instance, in the Corant of Suite No. 6 in D: true refinement (in its proper meaning of human dignity reflected in acute perceptions – not merely self-conscious daintiness) and a graciousness which, unlike many later baroque courtly styles, still has the rough grain of an honest composer writing as much for artistic self-discovery as to satisfy royal obligations. The Purcell Quartet (listed below) communicate above all a warmth and openness of expression and a compelling familiarity with the genre. The Greate Consort, on the other hand, are less hale and hearty but instead bring a greater spectrum of possibilities in the ebb and flow of the music. These are less obvious in the more energetic dances in the Third and Sixth Suites than in the noble pavans and fantazies, where the slightly recessed and transparent ensemble can almost imperceptibly keep you on tenterhooks as the music probes away at its own intrinsic propriety. This idea is expanded upon in the glorious Suite No. 9 where the group play with a strong sense of an overall 'complaint'. That is not to say that all the movements of this sort tease the listener with such studied and controlled panache. The Fantazy of Suite No. 6 builds up from its quizzical opening and grows into a more involved legato, subtly pulling up at the half-way stage with the bass viols energetically taking up the fibrous counterpoint before sensually releasing the tension at the cadence: a sublime conception. How spoilt for choice we are but perhaps it is Huggett's group who tell us that little bit more about Lawes's extraordinary temperament.

Additional recommendation ...

...The Royall Consort. **Purcell Quartet; Nigel North, Paul O'Dette** (theorbos). Chandos Chaconne Ⓔ CHAN0584/5 (two discs: 127 minutes: DDD: 11/95). ✦

New review

W. Lawes Consort Setts a 6^d – G minor; C major; B flat major. Consort Setts a 5^d – A minor; G minor. Dances for Lyra Viol[b] – The Countrey Coll, VdGS421; Jigg, VdGS422; Almaine, VdGS430; Corant, VdGS431; Saraband, VdGS432. Aires for Lyra Viol[b] – VdGS462; VdGS463. To Pansies, "Ah cruel love"[abc]. Gather ye rosebuds while you may[abc]. To the sycamore, "I'm sick of love"[abc]. On the Lillyes, "White though yee be"[abc]. [a]**Catherine Bott** (sop); [b]**Richard Boothby** (lyra viol); [c]**Paul Nicholson** (org); [d]**Fretwork** (Wendy Gillespie, Richard Campbell, William Hunt, Julia Hodgson, Susanna Pell, Richard Boothby, viols). Virgin Classics Veritas Ⓔ VC5 45147-2 (67 minutes: DDD: 10/95). ✦ Texts included. Recorded 1991.

Lawes's Consort Setts are richer in melodic invention than most of their kind. The first *Fantazy* of the A minor Sett begins with exquisite points of imitation, delicately doubled on the organ by Paul Nicholson; the ravishing sighs that follow contrast with the second *Fantazy*'s upward chromatic motif. In both Setts, the concluding light-hearted *Aires*, with their clear tunes and bouncy rhythms fit to dance to, serve as welcome contrast to the richly-textured fantasias. The opening movements of the G minor and B flat major six-part Consort Setts carry the listener effortlessly off on voyages through liquid, linear abstract music, the likes of which surely had never been heard in their day. Fretwork play with remarkable delicacy, especially in the opening *Fantazy* of the C major Sett and in the *Aire* of the G minor Sett where the inner parts carry on intense little conversations among themselves while the outer parts propel the movement forward towards an exciting chromatic pile-up at the end of the second section. Catherine Bott joins Richard Boothby in four songs on texts by Herrick. She knows just how much weight to give the words, dallying ever so slightly on the final lines so that the listener has a moment to reflect before each song ends. Boothby plays his lyra viol like an archlute, providing harmony and a second, wordless voice as required. Interspersed between the setts and songs are four pieces for lyra viol which Boothby performs with great panache. He plays with great presence of mind and sense of fun, successfully creating the illusion of multiple parts with a single instrument. *The Countrey Coll* and *Jigg* are very jolly while the second *Aire for Lyra* positively muses. This is definitely a recording that you will want to listen to again and again, hoping to unravel its many intricacies and metaphorically bathe in the charm of the performances: a fitting tribute to a man who gave his life for his king.

New review

W. Lawes Psalms – Lord, as the hart imbost with heat; Out of the horrour of the deep; Praise the Lord enthron'd on high; How like a widow; How long wilt thou forget me, O Lord; Ne irascaris Domine!; Gloria Patri et filio. Songs – Perfect and endless circles; Amarillis, teare thy haire; Come Adonis, come away; He that will not love; Aglaura – Why soe pall and wan, fond lover; Yee feinds and furies, come along; Gather ye rosebuds while ye may. Elegies – Musick, the master of thy art is dead. **The Consort of Musicke / Anthony Rooley.** Musica Oscura Ⓔ 070972 (56 minutes: DDD: 3/96). Texts included. Recorded 1995.

H. Lawes Cease you jolly shepherds. **J. Wilson** O doe not now lament and cry. **J. Cobb** Dear Will is dead. **S. Ives** Lament and mourne. **Jenkins** Why in this shade of night? **Hilton II** Bound by the neere conjunction of our souls.

If brother Henry Lawes is the more polished song composer, William has the reddest blood, as his extraordinarily angular and dissonant elegy to John Tomkins, *Musick, the master of thy art is dead* shows. Indeed, this disc is deftly arranged to include a selection of songs and works from *Choice Psalms*, an anthology published posthumously by Henry in 1648, including heartfelt, if not always inspired, elegies on William's death. However esoteric this music, there is much to enjoy here. The Psalms at their best are particularly effective, the three-part texture belying a dramatic ambition heard in *Ne irascaris Domine!*, where angular declamation and pungent dissonance combine at "Jerusalem desolat"; as with Byrd's setting in *Cantiones sacrae*, a sure reference to political unrest. No singer stands out more than any other in this imaginative recital: The Consort of Musicke capture all the salient sentiments in the text from the charm and wit of "Why soe pall and wan" to the considerable poignancy of the elegies. Whilst those of friend John Jenkins and brother Henry have polish and an intimate nobility – the rougher-hewn dedications by Wilson and Ives are just as touching in their own way. There are odd lapses in intonation but the dry, honest acoustic gives us readings which bring us close to Lawes's dying world and the memory of an eminent Englishman.

Further listening ...

...Alman in D major "for the Violins of Two Trebles". Airs for Consort. *Coupled with works by* **Notari, Webster, A. Ferrabosco II, R. Johnson II** and **Nau** Parley of Instruments Renaissance Violin Band / Peter Holman. Hyperion CDA66806 (6/96). ✍ *See review in the Collections section; refer to the Index to Reviews.*   Ⓖ

Gaspard Le Roux   French fl. second half of 17th Century-1705/7

Suggested listening ...

...Pièces de clavessin. **Christophe Rousset** (hpd). L'Oiseau-Lyre 443 329-2OH (7/95). ✍ *Gramophone Editor's choice.*

Leonhard Lechner   Austrian/German 1553-1606

Suggested listening ...

...Si bona suscepimus. *Coupled with* **Hassler** Missa I super Dixit Maria. Ad Dominum cum tribularer. O admirabile commercium. Usquequo, Domine. Domine Deus, Israel. Vater unser in Himmelreich. **Chapelle Royale European Vocal Ensemble / Philippe Herreweghe.** Harmonia Mundi HMC90 1401 (10/93).

Jean-Marie Leclair   French 1697-1764

Leclair Flute Concerto No. 3 in C major, Op. 7[a]. Violin Concertos[b] – Op. 7: No. 4 in F major; No. 6 in A major. No. 2 in A major, Op. 10. [a]**Rachel Brown** (fl); **Collegium Musicum 90 / Simon Standage** ([b]vn). Chandos Chaconne Ⓕ CHAN0564 (65 minutes: DDD: 2/95). ✍ Recorded 1994.   ⒼⒼ

Of the violin concertos here, Op. 10 No. 2 is the richest harmonically. The solo instrument in Op. 7 No. 3 is Leclair's stated alternative of flute, the only one of his 12 violin concertos to be so designed. Accordingly, it lacks the double-stopping so much favoured by this greatly admired violinist-composer; but otherwise it exploits the graceful sequential passagework found in the other concertos, though here with a fuller accompanying texture, with more movement in inner parts. Rachel Brown's playing throughout is deliciously cool and poised. Virtuoso violin fireworks abound in the vigorous first movements of the other two Op. 7 concertos here and the ebullient finale of the A major (the start of whose first movement has a Vivaldian resonance): as expected, Simon Standage throws off their difficulties with panache and an apparent ease that allows him also to add stylish embellishments of his own. The extensive multiple-stopping on which the elegant minuet-like Aria of Op. 7 No. 6 relies is performed with well-nigh impeccable intonation.

New review

Leclair Violin Concertos – Op. 7: No. 1 in D minor; Op. 10: No. 3 in D major; No. 4 in F major; No. 6 in G minor. **Collegium Musicum 90 / Simon Standage** (vn). Chandos Chaconne Ⓕ CHAN0589 (59 minutes: DDD: 11/95). ✍ Recorded 1995. *Gramophone Editor's choice.* ⒼⒼ

This disc contains Leclair's most vivacious and attractive works, played with great *élan*, sensitivity and neatness, and recorded with exemplary clarity and balance. The concertos represent a high-water mark in eighteenth-century violin technique, with extensive double-stopping (quite spectacular in the first *Allegro* of the F major Concerto and the *Andante* of the G minor), an extended range that soars up to heights scarcely ventured previously, rapid scales and flying arpeggios, and elaborate figurations of all kinds. To all of this Standage brings a seasoned virtuosity which he places completely at the service of the music's grace: his bowing in particular commands admiration. He shows an occasional urge to hurry, but the only movement that brings unease is the finale of the G minor, where his sudden changes of pace are unconvincing. From the stylistic viewpoint these concertos are interesting for their mingling of French and Italian elements. There are Vivaldian unisons, but French dance forms for the middle movements – a pair of minuets in the D minor, minuets *en rondeau* in the G minor, a pair of gavottes with unusual interplay between solo and tutti in the F major, and an ornate solo line over supporting reiterated chords in the D major. (Standage adds spontaneous embellishments of his own on repeats.) The first movements of Op. 10 Nos. 3 and 4 are more substantial than the others, with freer harmonic progressions, and the dotted rhythms of No. 6 impart a new dramatic flavour. A strongly recommended disc.

Additional recommendations ...

...Op. 7: No. 2 in D major; No. 5 in A minor. Op. 10: No. 1 in B flat major; No. 5 in E minor.
Collegium Musicum 90 / Simon Standage (vn). Chandos Chaconne Ⓕ CHAN0551 (62 minutes: DDD: 8/94). 🎶 ⓖⓖ

...Op. 7[a]: No. 3 in C major; No. 5. Op. 10[a]: No. 6. **Naudot** Recorder Concerto in G major, Op. 17 No. 5[b]. [b]**Frans Brüggen** (rec); [a]**Concerto Amsterdam / Jaap Schröder** (vn); [b]**Vienna Concentus Musicus / Nikolaus Harnoncourt.** Teldec Ⓜ 4509-92180-2 (59 minutes: ADD: 2/94). 🎶

New review

Leclair Ouverture in A major, Op. 13 No. 3. Deuxième Recréation de musique d'une execution facile in G minor, Op. 8.
Boismortier Sonata in G minor, Op. 34 No. 1[b].
Corrette Concerto comique No. 25, "Les Sauvages et la Furstemberg"[ab]. **Florilegium Ensemble** (Ashley Solomon, traverso; Rachel Podger, Anna McDonald, vns; Daniel Yeadon, vc; Elizabeth Kenny, theorbo/gtr; Neal Peres Da Costa, hpd); [a]**Jane Rogers** (va); [b]**Scott Pauley** (theorbo). Channel Classics Ⓕ CCS7595 (58 minutes: DDD: 12/95). 🎶 Recorded 1994.

By far the greatest musical substance here lies in the two fine compositions by Leclair, the *Deuxième Recréation de musique* (Op. 8) and an *Ouverture* in A major (Op. 13 No. 3). In the *Ouverture*, above all, there is a pleasing *rapprochement* of Italian with French idioms – sequences, held under tighter rein than those typical of his Italian models, jostling with essentially French gestures such as those characterizing the distinctive *ouverture Française* itself. The *Recréation*, a suite of dances in all but name, is more consistently French while the pieces by Boismortier and Corrette reveal a marked bias towards the Italian sonata and concerto. Florilegium imbue all this music with a vitality which, at least in part, emanates from the players' effective application of appropriate ornament and their evident savouring of delicately wrought colours and textures. Perhaps there is occasionally a degree of self-consciousness or, at least, study in their playing which detracts from the light-hearted spirit which reigns, for example, in the "Forlane" of the *Recréation*, and the captivating first movement of the Corrette, based on Rameau's beguiling dance rondeau *Les sauvages*. But such reservations are the slightest of details when so much else here is endowed with graceful gesture, transparent textures and an evident affection for the music. Throughout, the continuo is imaginatively realized, with the constant presence of at least one theorbo or a baroque guitar in all but the Boismortier, where two theorbos are preferred. The recording itself is clear and resonant, though perhaps a little lacking in intimacy.

Additional recommendation ...

...Première Récréation de musique, Op. 6. Deuxième Récréation de musique, Op. 8. **Les Nièces de Rameau.** Pierre Verany Ⓕ PV794011 (57 minutes: DDD: 9/94).

Leclair Violin Sonatas[a] – A minor, Op. 5 No. 7; A major, Op. 9 No. 4. [a]**Simon Standage** (vn); **Lars Ulrik Mortensen** (hpd). Chandos Chaconne Ⓕ CHAN0531 (68 minutes: DDD: 6/93). 🎶 Recorded 1992.
Mondonville Violin Sonata in G major, Op. 3 No. 5[a]. **Guillemain** Violin Sonata in A major, Op. 1 No. 4. Harpsichord solos – **Duphly** La de Redemond. La du Buq. **J-B. Forqueray** La Morangis ou La Plissay.

From the beginning of the eighteenth century and during the minority of Louis XV, there was a great flowering of chamber music and, in particular, violin sonatas and harpsichord suites. These are not, however, works for amateurs. They are fiendishly demanding and all the more exciting for being so. Simon Standage has never been diffident, but as the years pass he plays more beautifully. The sonatas of Leclair and Guillemain admirably suit Standage. The Leclair sonatas are packed with wonderful arching phrases, intricately wrought ornamentation and unexpected chromatic twists. They are essentially happy works. Lars Ulrik Mortensen's performance is no less impressive, weaving exquisite textures beneath and, as in the Mondonville sonata, around the violin part, subtly picking up on all the composers' nuances and tricks, all the while offering just the right support to the violin. As a soloist, Mortensen delivers equally fascinating performances by developing a rich palette of instrumental colour on the Blanchet copy made by David Rubio.

Further listening ...

...Flute Sonatas: *ACC58435D* – Op. 1: No. 2 in C major. Op. 2: No. 1 in E minor; No. 3 in C major; No. 5 in G major. *ACC58436D* – Op. 1: No. 6 in E minor. Op. 2: No. 8 in D minor; No. 11 in B minor. Op. 9: No. 2 in E minor; No. 7 in G major. **Barthold Kuijken** (fl); **Wieland Kuijken** (va da gamba); **Robert Kohnen** (hpd). Accent ACC58435/6D (2/86). 🎶 ⓖⓖ

...Trio Sonatas – No. 1 in E minor, Op. 2; No. 7 in G major, Op. 9. *Coupled with works by* **Blavet, Rameau , M. La Barre** and **Hotteterre** Rachel Brown (fl); **Mark Caudle** (viol); **James Johnstone** (hpd). Chandos Chaconne CHAN0544 (2/94).

...Trio Sonatas, Op. 4 – No. 1 in D minor; No. 2 in B flat major; No. 3 in D minor; No. 4 in F major; No. 5 in G minor; No. 6 in A major. **Purcell Quartet.** Chandos Chaconne CHAN0536 (7/93). 🖎

Alexandre Charles Lecocq
French 1832-1918

Suggested listening ...

...Mam'zelle Angot[a]. *Coupled with* **Hérold** La fille mal gardée (arr. Lanchbery)[b]. [a]**National Philharmonic Orchestra / Richard Bonynge;** [b]**Orchestra of the Royal Opera House, Covent Garden / John Lanchbery.** Decca Ovation 430 849-2DM2 (12/91).

Nicola LeFanu
British 1947-

Suggested listening ...

...Lullaby. Nocturne. *Coupled with works by* **Powers, Lutyens, G. Williams** and **R. Marsh Mühlfeld Ensemble.** Clarinet Classics CC0007 (10/94). *See review in the Collections section; refer to the Index to Reviews.*

Louis Lefébure-Wély
French 1817-1869

Suggested listening ...

...Marche in F major, Op. 122 No. 4. *Coupled with works by* **Dubois, Batiste, Bossi, Dupré, Jolivet, Lemare** and **Saint-Saëns** Christopher Herrick (org). Hyperion CDA66457 (9/91). *See review in the Collections section; refer to the Index to Reviews.* ⓔⓔⓔ

Charles Lefebvre
French 1843-1917

Suggested listening ...

...Suite, Op. 57. *Coupled with works by* **Briccialdi, Rossini** and **Taffanel** Aulos Quintet. Koch Schwann Musica Mundi 310087 (10/91).

Michel Legrand
French 1932-

New review

Legrand Magic – The Music of Michel Legrand. **Dame Kiri Te Kanawa** (sop); **Ambrosian Singers; London Studio Orchestra / Michel Legrand.** Teldec Ⓟ 9031-73285-2 (64 minutes: DDD: 11/92).
Songs include His eyes, her eyes; I will say goodbye; Magic; The windmills of your eyes; Little boy lost; What are you doing the rest of your life?

The "Magic" album consists entirely of songs by Michel Legrand, whose career as a songwriter took off after the international success of *Les parapluies de Cherbourg*, released in 1964. This disc avoids those songs and other much recorded ones in favour of the less well-known, a commendable idea provided the alternatives are worth it. Most of them are. On the positive side there are happy memories of *The Thomas Crown Affair*, its intimate chess scene between Steve McQueen and Faye Dunaway providing the cue for *His eyes, her eyes (his move, her move)* as well as the Oscar-winning *The windmills of your eyes*. There is also the rarely heard *After the rain*, a pretty ballad , and what for many is Legrand's finest song, *What are you doing the rest of your life?* However, there are a few other songs which could, arguably, be considered to be either too cute or just a little dull. Dame Kiri, moving closer to a more contemporary 'pop' style than we've heard from her before, receives excellent support from a superb band that can really swing, and there's at least one succinct and tightly harmonized contribution from the Ambrosian singers. The recording benefits from the venue of Petersham Church in Surrey which adds a lovely warm sheen.

Johannes Legrant
French 15th century

Suggested listening ...

...Se liesse. *Coupled with works by* **Anonymous, Johannes de Lymburga, Fontaine, Dunstable, Cardot, Bittering, Binchois, Machaut, Power** and **Velut** Gothic Voices / **Christopher Page.** Hyperion CDA66783 (1/96). *See review in the Collections section; refer to the Index to Reviews.*

Franz Lehár

Lehár Die lustige Witwe. **Cheryl Studer** (sop) Hanna; **Boje Skovhus** (bar) Danilo; **Bryn Terfel** (bass-bar) Zeta; **Rainer Trost** (ten) Camille; **Barbara Bonney** (sop) Valencienne; **Uwe Peper** (ten) Raoul; **Karl-Magnus Fredriksson** (bar) Cascada; **Heinz Zednik** (ten) Njegus; **Richard Savage** (bar) Bogdanowitsch; **Lynette Alcantara** (sop) Sylviane; **Philip Salmon** (ten) Kromow; **Constanze Backes** (mez) Olga; **Julian Clarkson** (bass) Pritschitsch; **Angela Kazimierczuk** (sop) Praškowia; **Wiener Tschuschenkapelle; Vienna Philharmonic Orchestra / John Eliot Gardiner.** DG Ⓕ 439 911-2GH (80 minutes: DDD: 2/95). Notes, text and translation included. Recorded 1994. 🅶🅶
Gramophone Editor's record of the month.

This is one of those great operetta interpretations that is committed to record once in a generation if one is lucky. Gardiner's approach is on an altogether more inspired plane than his rivals. In the Viennese rhythms, he shows himself utterly at home – as in the Act 2 Dance scene, where he eases the orchestra irresistibly into the famous waltz. But there are also countless instances where Gardiner provides a deliciously fresh inflexion to the score. The cast of singers is uniformly impressive. If Cheryl Studer's "Vilja" isn't quite as assured as some others, her captivatingly playful "Dummer, dummer Reitersmann" is typical of a well-characterized performance. As Danilo, Boje Skovhus acquits himself well with a polished performance and he offers a natural, more human characterization than his rivals, while Barbara Bonney is superb. Not the least inspired piece of casting comes with Bryn Terfel, who transforms himself outstandingly well into the bluff Pontevedran ambassador. As for Gardiner's personally selected chorus, they make Monteverdi to Montenegro and Pontevedra seem the most natural transition in the world. DG's recorded sound has an astonishing clarity and immediacy, as in the way the piccolos shriek out at the Widow's Act 1 entrance or in the beautiful *pianissimo* accompaniment to the "Vilja-Lied".

Additional recommendations ...
...**Soloists; Philharmonia Chorus and Orchestra / Lovro von Matačic.** EMI Ⓕ CDS7 47178-8 (two discs: 80 minutes: AAD: 4/86). 🅶
...**Soloists; BBC Chorus; Philharmonia / Otto Ackermann.** EMI mono Ⓜ CDH7 69520-2* (72 minutes: ADD: 11/88).

Lehár Das Land des Lächelns. **Anneliese Rothenberger** (sop) Lisa; **Harry Friedauer** (ten) Gustl; **Nicolai Gedda** (ten) Sou-Chong; **Renate Holm** (sop) Mi; **Jobst Moeller** (bar) Tschang; **Bavarian Radio Chorus; Graunke Symphony Orchestra / Willy Mattes.** EMI Ⓜ CMS5 65372-2 (two discs: 87 minutes: ADD: 2/95). From World Record Club SOC242/3 (8/71). Recorded 1967.

The great glory of this *Das Land des Lächelns*, Lehár's portrayal of the clash of western and eastern cultures, is the singing of Nicolai Gedda, who brings off "Dein ist mein ganzes Herz" and the other Richard Tauber favourites to splendid effect. Anneliese Rothenberger is on excellent form vocally and full of charm, and she and Gedda make an excellent partnership. Renate Holm is a smiling Mi and the other principals, chorus and orchestra all play their full parts. Willy Mattes is an experienced and sympathetic conductor of operetta. The score here is, of course, not identical with that given in London when the operetta was first produced there in 1931. Apparently, Tauber was in and out of the cast every other day, providing his understudy, Robert Naylor, with plenty of opportunities. The show only had a short run in London on its first appearance. It seems that it was Tauber rather than Lehár that people wanted to hear. It's a recording to savour and it should be in every Viennese operetta collection as a reissue to be welcomed and snapped up.

Further listening ...
...**Die Zarewitsch** – excerpts. **Berlin Deutsche Opera Chorus; Berlin Symphony Orchestra / Robert Stolz.** Eurodisc 258 357 (4/88).
...**Zigeunerliebe** – Hör' ich Cymbalklänge. **Friederike** – Warum hast du mich wachgeküsst? Die lustige Witwe – Es lebt eine Vilja, ein Waldmägdelein. *Coupled with works by* **Offenbach, J. Strauss II, Romberg, Novello, Coward, Chabrier, Heuberger** and **Sullivan. Lesley Garrett** (sop); **Crouch End Festival Chorus; Royal Philharmonic Concert Orchestra / James Holmes.** Silva Screen Classics SILKTVCD1 (2/96). *See review in the Collections section; refer to the Index to Reviews.*

Jón Leifs

New review

Leifs Symphony No. 1, Op. 26, "Saga Symphony". **Iceland Symphony Orchestra / Osmo Vänskä.** BIS Ⓕ CD730 (54 minutes: DDD: 3/96). Recorded 1995.

Jón Leifs once averred "Wagner ... misunderstood the essence and artistic tradition of the North in ... a detestable manner". Many of his works – not least this First Symphony – were conceived as a protest against that misunderstanding. Leifs's stance was derided in his lifetime after isolated and uncomprehending performances. The symphony typically has an uncompromising, primitivistic sound-world, employing tuned anvils, specially made wooden drums (without skins, hammered by huge mallets), iron and wooden shields, rocks of differing sizes approximating different pitches, and replica Bronze Age horns (or lurs). Nearly 30 years after his death, enough of his output has received sufficient exposure for a tradition to evolve, at least in Iceland. This is the first complete recording of the *Saga Symphony*. The Iceland Symphony Orchestra are a fine body of players and their reading under Osmo Vänskä, in a recording of astonishing clarity, is nothing short of revelatory. It must be conceded that there is little conventional development or counterpoint, but however brusque or awkward it all seems (echoes of critical misperceptions of Havergal Brian or Ives here), *Saga Symphony* is extremely effective, as the scherzo, "Björn behind Kari", or the nightmarish intermezzo, "Glamr og Grettir", manifestly confirm. This issue is a massive act of restitution, both for its much-maligned composer and the culture – which is not nearly so remote as it might seem – that produced him.

New review

Leifs Icelandic Overture, Op. 9[a]. Iceland Cantata, Op. 13[b]. Elegy, Op. 53. Fine I, Op. 55. Fine II,
    Op. 56. [ab]**Chorus of the Icelandic Opera;** [b]**Graduale Choir of Langholts Church; Iceland**
    Symphony Orchestra / Petri Sakari. Chandos New Direction Ⓕ CHAN9433 (54 minutes:
    DDD: 5/96).

The *Icelandic Overture* opens with "Island farsaelda frón", a melody which rises from Iceland's deepest consciousness. With seven other tunes, characteristically coexisting and overlapping without development, it is whirled into a resounding choral climax in the voices of the Langholts Church Choir. Seven patriotic poems are heard in stark choral settings, sung by the Icelandic Opera Chorus, in the *Iceland Cantata*, written to celebrate the millennium of the Althing, or parliament, in 1930. Words are compacted in chords, punctuated by percussion and brass, and ripple over each other as tales break, wave-like, through one generation after another. The Iceland Symphony Orchestra, who completed their first tour of the States in 1986, are fervent accompanists here, and give finely drawn performances of the ten-minute *Elegy* for strings, written in response to the death of Leifs's mother, and recalling the Second String Quartet, *Vita et Mors* in its quiet inhalation and exhalation of open-textured, modal writing. *Fine I* and *II* are short, late orchestral pieces written just five years before Leifs's own death, and vibrant with tone clusters and straining chords inhabiting that totally isolated tone-world which conveyed Leifs's "greetings to earthly life".

Further listening ...
...String Quartets – No. 1, "Mors et vita", Op. 21; No. 2, "Vita et mors", Op. 36; No. 3, "El
    Greco", Op. 64. **Yggdrasil Quartet.** BIS CD691 (7/95).

Kenneth Leighton   British 1929-1988

Leighton Second Service, Op. 62[a]. Give me wings of faith[a]. O sacrum convivium. Solus ad
    victimam[a]. Crucifixus pro nobis, Op. 38[a].
Howells Chichester Service[a]. A Hymn for St Cecilia[a]. Salve regina. O salutaris hostia. My eyes for
    beauty pine[a]. Like as the hart[a]. **Queen's College Choir, Oxford / Matthew Owens** with [a]**David
    Went** (org). ASV Ⓕ CDDCA851 (74 minutes: DDD: 5/93). Texts included.

Herbert Howells was at Queen's College, Oxford, in 1916, and Kenneth Leighton read Classics there in 1947, so it is appropriate that they should be brought together by their college choir. A quality they had in common was their sure instinct for choral sound, and at the take-over point in this recital (the opening of Leighton's *Second Evening Service*) the succession is felt to be a very close and natural one. Both are well represented. An extraordinary amount of Howells's choral work has been recorded recently (refer to the Index to Reviews), but the selection here overlaps very little with other desirable records: *Like as the hart* is the principal exception, and as this is a particularly lovely performance the duplication is easily justified. The Chichester Service has its first recording here: it is a fine work, rising in characteristic ecstasy. Leighton's Second Service is also impressive, the *Magnificat*'s "Gloria" swaying slowly, while that of the *Nunc Dimittis* ends in subdued fashion, beautiful in its quietness. The other major work, the *Crucifixus pro nobis*, is probably better served by a tenor soloist, but this is a fine, urgent performance with excellent work by the choir, as indeed they provide throughout the recital.

Additional recommendation ...
...Crucifixus pro nobis[a]. Second Service. Te Deum laudamus. Missa brevis, Op. 5. An Evening
    Hymn. Let all the world in every corner sing. **Traditional** (arr. Leighton) Lully, lulla (Coventry
    carol). [a]**Neil Mackie** (ten); **St Paul's Cathedral Choir / John Scott** with **Andrew Lucas** (org).
    Hyperion Ⓕ CDA66489 (74 minutes: DDD: 12/92).

Further listening ...
...Cello Concerto, Op. 31[a]. Symphony No. 3[b]. [a]**Raphael Wallfisch** (vc); [b]**Neil Mackie** (ten); **Royal
    Scottish Orchestra / Bryden Thomson.** Chandos CHAN8741 (10/89).
...Fantasy on an American Hymn Tune, Op. 70[a]. Alleluia Pascha Nostrum, Op. 85[b]. Piano
    Variations, Op. 30. Piano Sonata, Op. 64. [a]**Janet Hilton** (cl); [ab]**Raphael Wallfisch** (vc); **Peter
    Wallfisch** (pf). Chandos CHAN9132 (5/93).
...Evening (Magdalen) Service. *Coupled with works by* **Gibbons, G. Ives, S. Watson, Stanford,
    Howells** and **Dyson** Lichfield Cathedral Choir / Andrew Lumsden with Mark Shepherd, Nigel
    Potts (orgs). Priory PRCD505 (10/95). *See review in the Collections section; refer to the Index to
    Reviews.*

Guillaume Lekeu
Belgian 1870-1894

Suggested listening ...
...Molto adagio. Piano Quartet. Larghetto[b]. Adagio, Op. 3. Trois poèmes[a]. [a]**Rachel Yakar** (sop);
[b]**Isabelle Veyrier** (vc); **Musique Oblique Ensemble.** Harmonia Mundi HMC90 1455 (4/95).

Edwin Lemare
British/American 1865-1934

Suggested listening ...
...Concert Fantasy on "Hanover", Op. 4. Marche héroïque in D major, Op. 74. *Coupled with works
by* **Batiste, Bossi, Dubois, Dupré, Jolivet, Lefébure-Wély** and **Saint-Saëns** Christopher
Herrick (org). Hyperion CDA66457 (9/91). *See review in the Collections section; refer to the Index
to Reviews.* 🅖🅖🅖
...Concertstück in the form of a Polonaise, Op. 80. *Coupled with works by* **Elgar, Hollins,
Sumsion, Cocker, Spicer, C.S. Lang** and **Wagner** Christopher Herrick (org). Hyperion
CDA66778 (3/96). *See review in the Collections section; refer to the Index to Reviews.*

Artur Lemba
Estonian 1885-1963

Suggested listening ...
...Symphony in C sharp minor. *Coupled with* **Tobias** Julius Caesar. **Eller** Twilight. **Tormis**
Overture No. 2. **Pärt** Cantus in memory of Benjamin Britten. **Royal Scottish Orchestra / Neeme
Järvi.** Chandos CHAN8656 (8/89).

Leonardo Leo
Italian 1694-1744

Suggested listening ...
...Concerto in D major for Four Violins and Strings. *Coupled with works by* **Torelli, Mossi,
Valentini** and **Locatelli Cologne Musica Antiqua / Reinhard Goebel.** Archiv Produktion
435 393-2AH (9/92). ✒ *See review in the Collections section; refer to the Index to Reviews.*

Ruggero Leoncavallo
Italian 1858-1919

Leoncavallo Pagliacci[a]. **Carlo Bergonzi** (ten) Canio; **Joan Carlyle** (sop) Nedda; **Giuseppe Taddei**
(bar) Tonio; **Rolando Panerai** (bar) Silvio; **Ugo Benelli** (ten) Beppe.
Mascagni Cavalleria Rusticana[a]. **Fiorenza Cossotto** (mez) Santuzza; **Adriane Martino** (mez) Lola;
Carlo Bergonzi (ten) Turiddu; **Giangiacomo Guelfi** (bar) Alfio; **Maria Gracia Allegri** (contr)
Lucia; **Chorus and Orchestra of La Scala, Milan / Herbert von Karajan.**
Opera Intermezzos[b]. **Berlin Philharmonic Orchestra / Herbert von Karajan.** DG Ⓔ 419
257-2GH3 (three discs: 198 minutes: ADD: 10/87). Notes, texts and translations included.
Items marked [a] from SLPM139205/07 (10/66), [b]SLPM139031 (6/69), both recorded 1965.
Verdi La traviata – Prelude, Act 3. **Puccini** Manon Lescaut – Intermezzo. Suor Angelica –
Intermezzo. **Schmidt** Notre Dame – Intermezzo. **Massenet** Thaïs – Méditation (with
Michel Schwalbé, vn). **Giordano** Fedora – Intermezzo. **Cilea** Adriana Lecouvreur –
Intermezzo. **Wolf-Ferrari** I gioiello della Madonna – Intermezzo. **Mascagni** L'amico
Fritz – Intermezzo.
Cav and Pag, as they are usually known, have been bedfellows for many years. Lasting for about 75
minutes each, both operas have certain similarities. Each work concerns the passions, jealousies and
hatred of two tightly knit communities – the inhabitants of a Sicilian town and the players in a
travelling troupe of actors. *Cavalleria rusticana* ("Rustic chivalry") concerns the triangular
relationship of mother, son and his rejected lover. Played against a rich musical tapestry, sumptuously
orchestrated, the action is played out during the course of an Easter day. Bergonzi is a stylish, ardent
Turiddu whose virile charms glitter in his every phrase and Fiorenza Cossotto makes a thrilling
Santuzza motivated and driven by a palpable conviction; her contribution to the well-known Easter
hymn scene is gripping. But the real hero of the opera is Karajan, whose direction of this powerful
work is magnificent. Conviction and insight also instil *Pagliacci* with excitement and real drama. A
troupe of actors arrive to give a performance of a *commedia dell'arte* play. The illustration of real
love, life and hatred is portrayed in the interplay of Tonio, Silvio, Nedda and her husband Canio. As
the two rivals, Caro Bergonzi and Giuseppe Taddei are superb. Taddei's sinister, hunch-backed
clown, gently forcing the play-within-the-play closer to reality until it finally bursts out violently is a
masterly assumption, and Karajan controls the slow build-up of tension with a grasp that few
conductors could hope to equal. The Milan La Scala forces respond wholeheartedly and the 1965
recording sounds well. The third disc is filled by a selection of very rich, very soft-centred opera
intermezzos.

Additional recommendations ...

...Pagliacci[a]. Cavalleria[b]. **Soloists;** [a]**London Voices;** [a]**Finchley Children's Music Group;** [b]**London Opera Chorus;** [ab]**National Philharmonic Orchestra /** [a]**Giuseppe Patanè,** [b]**Gianandrea Gavazzeni.** Decca Ⓕ 414 590-2DH2 (two discs: 143 minutes: ADD: 1/89).

...Pagliacci. Cavalleria. **Soloists; Ambrosian Opera Chorus; Philharmonia Orchestra / Riccardo Muti.** EMI Ⓜ CMS7 63650-2 (two discs: 150 minutes: ADD: 3/91).

...Pagliacci. **Soloists; Slovak Philharmonic Chorus; Bratislava Radio Symphony Orchestra / Alexander Ráhbari.** Naxos Ⓢ 8 660021 (70 minutes: DDD: 4/93).

Franciszek Lessel   Polish c1780-1838

Suggested listening...

...Piano Concerto in C major, Op. 14[a]. Adagio et rondeau à la polonaise, Op. 9. Variations, Op. 15 – No. 1, on a Ukrainian song, "Jichaw kozak zza Dunaju"; No 2, in A minor. **Jerzy Sterczynski** (pf); [a]**Silesian Philharmonic Orchestra / Jerzy Salwarowski.** Le Chant du Monde LDC278 1092 (10/93).

Anatoli Liadov   USSR 1855-1914

New review

Liadov The Enchanted Lake, Op. 62.
Mussorgsky Boris Godunov – I am sick at heart[a].
Tchaikovsky Marche slave, Op. 31. Capriccio italien, Op. 45. Eugene Onegin – Waltz; Polonaise. **Kirov Theatre** [a]**Chorus and Orchestra / Valery Gergiev.** Philips Ⓕ 442 775-2PH (54 minutes: DDD: 7/95). This set includes a bonus sampler CD of previous previous recordings from the Kirov Theatre forces conducted by Gergiev.

Liadov's orchestral pieces have always had a tenuous hold on the repertory, and afford glimpses of an exceptional talent. His failure to realize more of this was partly due to a peculiarly Russian compulsive idleness. But he was also highly self-critical, and essentially a miniaturist who could probably never have achieved the full length ballet, *The Firebird*, commissioned from him by Diaghilev. Stravinsky always felt that Liadov was more relieved than hurt when the comission fell through, and would have defended the score that was the outcome. In the shifting harmonies and dissolving textures of *The Enchanted Lake*, which shimmers atmospherically, there is not only acknowledgement of *Siegfried's* Forest Murmurs but anticipation of Scriabin and even Schoenberg. It was a novel idea to have the Kirov orchestra's "Russian Spectacular", the title of this disc, open to the rich aural canvas of *Boris Godunov's* "Coronation Scene" as refashioned by Shostakovich, complete with tolling bells, weighty brass and generous cymbal spray. The sound is big and generalized, the conducting more majestic than excitable – which usefully serves to minimize the contrast with *Marche slave*, a comparatively lyrical statement with a notably sad-eyed account of the principal theme and lightweight, almost balletic sequences thereafter. Gergiev never drives too hard, while his artful shaping of *Eugene Onegin's* "Polonaise" incorporates particularly sensitive handling of the central section. Likewise in the Waltz, where the cello line is affectionately moulded. *Capriccio italien* is thoughtfully held together, with much deft passagework in the closing tarantella. There's a bonus CD too, made up of snippets from Gergiev's various Russian stage work recordings for Philips – nothing earth-shattering, but a nice cross-section to whet the appetite for more. This is a good, well-planned (if hardly generous) programme, warmly recorded and fairly representative of Gergiev's sympathetic and often dramatic conducting style.

Additional recommendation ...

...The enchanted lake. Baba-Yaga, Op. 56. Kikimora, Op. 63. Musical snuffbox, Op. 32. **Khachaturian** Masquerade – Waltz; Galop. **Rimsky-Korsakov** The Snow Maiden – Suite. Dubinushka, Op. 62. The Golden Cockerel – Suite. **Kabalevsky** The Comedians, Op. 26. **Shostakovich** Symphony No. 1 in F minor, Op. 10. **Prokofiev** Symphony No. 1 in D major, Op. 25, "Classical". **Glinka** A Life for the Tsar – Ballet music. **Philharmonia Orchestra; Royal Philharmonic Orchestra / Efrem Kurtz.** EMI Profile Ⓑ CZS7 67729-2 (two discs: 147 minutes: ADD: 9/93).

Further listening ...

...Kikimora, Op. 63[c]. *Coupled with* **Borodin** Prince Igor – Overture[a]. Symphony No. 2 in B minor[b]. **Shostakovich** Concerto for Piano, Trumpet and Strings in C minor, Op. 35[d]. **Tchaikovsky** The Sleeping Beauty – Valse[e]. [d]**Eileen Joyce** (pf); [d]**Arthur Lockwood** (tpt); **Hallé Orchestra /** [b]**Constant Lambert,** [ad]**Leslie Heward,** [c]**Sir Adrian Boult,** [e]**Sir Malcolm Sargent.** Dutton Laboratories mono CDAX8010* (2/95).

...Atmosphères. *Coupled with works by* **Boulez, Nono** and **Rihm** Vienna Jeunesse Choir; Vienna Philharmonic Orchestra / Claudio Abbado. DG 429 260-2GH (4/90).   Ⓖ

...Two Bagatelles, Op. 17. Prelude in B minor, Op. 11 No. 1. Prelude in F sharp minor, Op. 39 No. 4. *Coupled with works by* **Arensky, Glazunov, Rachmaninov, Taneyev** and **Tchaikovsky** Margaret Fingerhut (pf). Chandos CHAN9218 (4/94). .

...Preludes – C major, Op. 39 No. 4; F sharp minor, Op. 40 No. 2; D flat major, Op. 57 No. 1. *Coupled with works by* **Mussorgsky, Rachmaninov, Medtner** and **Balakirev** Boris Berezovsky (pf). Teldec 4509-96516-2 (7/96).

Ingvar Lidholm

Swedish 1921-

Lidholm Greetings from an Old World. Toccata e Canto. Kontakion. Ritornell. **Royal Stockholm Philharmonic Orchestra / Gennadi Rozhdestvensky.** Chandos Ⓔ CHAN9231 (63 minutes: DDD: 3/94). Recorded 1991-93.

Since the death in 1985 of his former teacher, Hilding Rosenberg, Ingvar Lidholm (b. 1921) has been the dominant figure amongst Swedish composers. The programme ranges across four decades of his career, covering a diversity of styles: early neo-classicism (*Toccata e Canto*), aggressive modernism (*Ritornell*) and the mature synthesis of the lyrical with the radical (*Greetings, Kontakion*). In *Greetings from an Old World* (1976) and *Kontakion,* Lidholm gradually unveils the pre-existing melodies, that serve as the musical basis for each work. In *Kontakion* the source is the Byzantine/Orthodox hymn for the dead. Unsurprisingly, *Kontakion* struck a deep and emotive chord in Russian audiences, but non-Orthodox listeners have also responded keenly, especially to the moving closing pages, as passionate and fervent as Pärt but without the numbing repetition. The opening of *Toccata e Canto* has an invigorating, American brashness to it, but British listeners may be struck more by uncanny pre-echoes of Rubbra and Simpson in the elegiac *Canto.* The disc concludes in exuberant – and heavily percussive – fashion with *Ritornell* (1954), a tribute to the virtuosity of composer and performers. Excellent recordings.

Further listening ...
...A Dream Play. **Soloists; Adolf Frederik Boys' and Girls' Choirs; Stockholm Royal Choir and Orchestra / Kjell Ingebretsen.** Caprice CAP22029 (9/93).

Juan de Lienas

?Spanish/Mexican fl. *c*1620-1650

Suggested listening ...
...Coenantibus autem. *Coupled with* **Victoria** Et egressus est. Ecce vidimus eum. Amicus meus. Unus ex discipulis. Eram quasi agnus. Seniores populi. Benedictus Deus Dominus Israel. Vere languores nostros. **attrib. Morales** Vigilate et orate. **Brito** Lamentations of Jeremiah – Incipit lamentatio Jeremiae. **F. Vásquez** In te, Domine, speravi. **Cardoso** Magnificat Primi Toni. **La Colombina.** Accent ACC9394D (8/94).

Gyorgy Ligeti

Hungarian 1923-

Ligeti Violin Concerto[a]. Cello Concerto[b]. Piano Concerto[c]. [a]**Saschko Gawriloff** (vn); [b]**Jean-Guihen Queyras** (vc); [c]**Pierre-Laurent Aimard** (pf); **Ensemble InterContemporain / Pierre Boulez.** DG Ⓔ 439 808-2GH (67 minutes: DDD: 1/95). Recorded 1992-3. *Gramophone Award Winner 1995.* ⓖⓖ

The Violin Concerto (1992) is music by a composer fascinated with Shakespeare's *The Tempest:* indeed, it might even prove to be a substitute for Ligeti's long-mooted operatic version of the play. There are plenty of "strange noises", the result not just of Ligeti's latter-day predilection for ocarinas, but of his remarkable ability to play off natural and artificial tunings against each other. This work is superior to the Piano Concerto because the solo violin is so much more volatile and poetic as a protagonist, an animator who 'fires up' the orchestra while functioning, in places at least, as an alien presence, a leader at odds with the led. Saschko Gawriloff is a brilliantly effective soloist, and well served by a sharply defined yet expressive accompaniment – Boulez at his most incisive – and a totally convincing recording. The other works are played and recorded with similar success. The Cello Concerto (1966) is a particularly powerful reminder of the strengths of the earlier Ligeti, where elementally simple, basic elements generate anything but minimal consequences. Despite the virtues of the Sony Classical versions of the Cello and Piano Concertos (listed below), the Violin Concerto gives DG the advantage: it's a major work, and a marvellous demonstration of Ligeti's unique, and uniquely persuasive, angle on modern musical discourse.

Additional recommendation ...
...Cello Concerto[a]. Piano Concerto[b]. Chamber Concerto. [a]**Miklós Perényi** (vc); [b]**Ueli Wiget** (pf); **Ensemble Modern / Peter Eötvös.** Sony Classical Ⓔ SK58945 (57 minutes: DDD: 6/94). ⓖ

Further listening ...
...Continuum[a]. Ten Pieces for Wind Quintet[d]. Artikulation[e]. Glissandi[f]. Two Studies for Organ[b]. Volumina[c]. [a]**Antoinette Vischer** (hpd); [b]**Zsigmond Sathmáry**, [c]**Karl-Erik Welin** (orgs); [d]**South-West German Radio Wind Quintet;** [ef]**Cologne Radio Studio for Electronic Music.** Wergo WER60161-50 (11/89).

508 Ligeti

...Chamber Concerto[b]. Ramifications (versions for string orchestra[d] and solo strings[c]). Lux aeterna[a]. Atmosphères[d]. [a]Stuttgart Schola Cantorum / Clytus Gottwald; [b]Vienna Die Reihe Ensemble / Friedrich Cerha; [c]Saar Radio Chamber Orchestra / Antonio Janigro; [d]South West German Radio Symphony Orchestra / Ernest Bour. Wergo WER60162-50 (10/89).
...Le Grand Macabre. Soloists; Austrian Radio Chorus; Arnold Schönberg Choir; Gumpoldskirchner Spartzen; Austrian Radio Symphony Orchestra / Elgar Howarth. Wergo WER6170-2 (12/91). **Ⓖ**

Douglas Lilburn
New Zealand 1915-

New review
Lilburn Drysdale Overture[a]. A Song of Islands[a]. Suite for Orchestra[a]. A Birthday Offering[a]. Prodigal Country[b]. [b]**David Griffiths** (bar); [b]**Wellington Orpheus Choir; New Zealand Symphony Orchestra /** [a]**John Hopkins,** [b]**Sir Charles Groves.** Kiwi Pacific Records Ⓔ CDSLD-100 (68 minutes: ADD: 5/96). Text included.
The two earliest works on this CD – the *Drysdale Overture* (1937) and *Prodigal Country* (1939) – were both prize-winners in the music competition organized by the New Zealand Government as part of its 1940 Centennial Celebrations. The overture is a fluent, polished piece – hardly earth-shatteringly memorable, it's true, but at the same time not devoid of a certain fresh-faced eagerness. *Prodigal Country* is a much more substantial achievement, a stirring, highly accomplished setting of texts by Walt Whitman and two New Zealand poets, Allen Curnow and Robin Hyde. It possesses a breadth of vision and affirmative ardour which communicate vividly. Amazingly, *Prodigal Country* lay in a drawer for nearly half a century, until it was revived by the present team under the leadership of Sir Charles Groves. *A Song of Islands*, which dates from 1946, is an eloquent, richly lyrical and often passionate orchestral essay, employing a satisfying arch form. Composed in 1955 for the Auckland Junior Symphony Orchestra, the five-movement *Suite for Orchestra* is a real charmer, brimful of sparkling invention and gratifying instrumental resource. *A Birthday Offering* was written in 1956 for the National (later New Zealand) Symphony Orchestra on the occasion of its tenth anniversary. It, too, makes very rewarding listening and offers plenty of opportunities for individual members of the orchestra to shine. Splendid performances and very good sound throughout. This enjoyable issue very usefully expands our knowledge and appreciation of Lilburn, New Zealand's distinguished elder statesman of music.
Further listening ...
...Symphonies – No. 1[a]; No. 2[b]; No. 3[a]. **New Zealand Symphony Orchestra /** [a]**John Hopkins,** [b]**Ashley Heenan.** Kiwi-Pacific Records CDSLD-90 (3/94).
...Symphonies Nos. 1-3. **New Zealand Symphony Orchestra / John Hopkins.** Continuum CCD1069 (8/94).
...Aotearoa Overture. *Coupled with works by* **A. Watson, A. Ritchie, C. Blake, Whitehead, Jenny McLeod, Farquhar, Pruden** and **Carr** New Zealand Symphony Orchestra / Kenneth Young. Continuum CCD1073 (5/96). *See review in the Collections section; refer to the Index to Reviews.*
...Diversions. Landfall in unknown seas[a]. Allegro. *Coupled with* **Pruden** Soliloquy. **A. Watson** Prelude and Allegro. [a]**Sir Edmund Hillary** (narr); **New Zealand Chamber Orchestra.** Koch International Classics 37260-2 (12/95).

Thomas Linley
British 1756-1778

Suggested listening ...
...Ode on the Spirits of Shakespeare. **Lorna Anderson, Julia Gooding** (sops); **Richard Wistreich** (bass); **The Parley of Instruments Choir; The Parley of Instruments / Paul Nicholson.** Hyperion CDA66613 (5/93). ✐ *Gramophone Editor's choice.*
...Awake, my lyre. Six Elegies and an Invocation – No. 1, Ah, what avails the spritely morn of life; No. 2, Ye sportive loves, that round me wait; No. 5, He who could first two gentle hearts unbind; No. 6, In thousand thoughts of love and thee; Invocation (Fly to my aid, O mighty Love). Alas, from the day my poor hearth. **T. Linley II** To heal the wound a bee had made. *Coupled with works by* **Harington, Herschel, W.B. Earle** and **W. Jackson Various soloists.** Hyperion CDA66698 (11/94).

Dinu Lipatti
Romanian 1917-1950

New review
Lipatti Concertino en style classique, Op. 3[ae]. Three Romanian Dances[ac]. Symphonie concertante[bc]. Tziganes[c].
Liszt Piano Concerto No. 1 in E flat major, S124[c]. [a]**Dinu Lipatti,** [b]**Madeleine Lipatti,** [b]**Béla Siki** (pfs); [c]**Suisse Romande Orchestra / Ernest Ansermet;** [d]**South-West German Radio Orchestra / Paul Sacher;** [e]**orchestra.** Archiphon mono Ⓔ ARC112/13* (two discs: 139 minutes: ADD: 10/95). From private and test recordings and public performances; recorded 1936-51. The discs also include

works (some with various artists) by Bach, Bartók[d], Brahms, Chopin, Enescu, Fauré, Liszt, Ravel, Rimsky-Korsakov, D. Scarlatti and Schumann.

The originators of this anthology make no secret of their problems in transferring imperfect and predominately private recordings to CD, or of their awareness when the odds go against them. But never mind the 'surface noise' and all that. The second disc, invaluable for its reminders of the lure of composition for the younger Lipatti, "reunites for the first time all his symphonic work", as the informative booklet-notes put it. The collector's piece (despite inferior reproduction) is surely the Geneva world première of his *Three Romanian Dances* with himself as customarily close-knit soloist with Ansermet and the Suisse Romande. Here, irrepressible love of his own country's folk heritage emerges with near Bartók-like voltage – thanks to an intellectual discipline and compression notably absent from his, none the less, exuberantly imaginative, colourfully scored gipsy suite, *Tziganes*. This, understandably, won him an honorary Enescu prize when still only 17. His overflowing romantic imagination is clearly revealed in his Bach-cum-Haydn-inspired *Concertino en style classique* of 1936, with himself as a lithe and light-hearted soloist (*c*1948, though no one knows with whom). The fuller impact of the then eclectic Paris is even more potently revealed in his *Symphonie concertante* for two pianos and string orchestra (1938), here with his wife and Béla Siki alongside Ansermet in 1951. Its central *Molto adagio* has the same haunting nocturnal mystery of many of Bartók's slow movements. Nothing more than this brings home our loss in December 1950, when he died prematurely of leukaemia, not only of a pianist blessed by the gods, but of a potentially spellbinding post-impressionist Romanian composer.

Solos on the first disc range from Lipatti's first Parisian recordings of 1936 to extracts from a Zurich concert given only ten months before he died. Even as a 19-year-old student, in the *Presto vivace* of an F sharp minor Sonata by his godfather, Enescu, you recognize the pinpoint clarity of articulation and the rhythmic alacrity and precision that were to remain hallmarks of his style for life. The simplicity with which he conveys the aching nostalgia of the central melody in Chopin's E minor *Etude* (Op. 25 No. 5) is also somehow uniquely his own. Three cello and piano miniatures in an acutely sensitive partnership with his friend, Antonio Janigro, come as a welcome reminder of his great love of chamber music. The main discoveries on the first disc are the two concertos, notably Lipatti's only known recording of Liszt's in E flat (a lifelong favourite) with Ansermet and the Suisse Romande, embodying his maturer 'rethoughts' after hearing a recording by Liszt's pupil, Emil von Sauer. The expansive grandeur of his bolder gestures, the exquisitely intimate poetry of his lyricism, and the delicately tingling scintillation of his technique are unforgettable. So, too, are the intensity underpinning his purity and his fingertip atmospheric evocation in the central *Adagio religioso* of Bartók's Third Concerto (also a work very close to his heart) in a much cleaner and truer recording than the Liszt – superior enough, in fact, to make it hard to forgive the conductor, Paul Sacher, for forbidding the issue of this 1948 Baden-Baden performance in its entirety.

Franz Liszt
Hungarian 1811-1886

New review

Liszt Piano Concertos – No. 1 in E flat major, S124[a]; No. 2 in A major, S125[a]. Piano Sonata in B minor, S178[b]. **Sviatoslav Richter** (pf); [a]**London Symphony Orchestra / Kyrill Kondrashin.** Philips Solo Ⓜ 446 200-2PM (69 minutes: ADD: 11/95). Items marked [a] from SABL207 (5/62, recorded 1961), [b]438 620-2PH3 (8/94). *Gramophone classical 100*. ⊙⊙⊙

A bargain in a million, albeit one that reflects two very different aspects of Richter's art. The concertos are strong, clear-headed, brilliantly executed and superbly accompanied. Philips confess Mercury engineering, and Wilma Cozart-Fine has herself remastered the original three-track tapes – which means that what started out as a clean-cut, judiciously balanced production, now sounds fuller, brighter and keener-edged than ever. The improvements are particularly telling where Kondrashin and the LSO are concerned: everything tells with more presence than before which, given the lofty standard of orchestral playing, is a real boon. As to Richter, his *pianissimos* are rapt, his running passages crystal-clear and the stormier elements in both concertos are given with immense force. The Sonata, a concert performance, was recorded almost 30 years later on a somewhat less well-tuned instrument. However, the mind behind the notes has lost none of its grip and the notes themselves, although occasionally blurred or botched, spring to life as in no other performance. The *Allegro energico* and final peroration rage mercilessly, while the closing *Lento assai* can rarely have sounded so calmly inevitable. In terms of sound, things aren't as well managed as in the concertos: there's the odd thump or cough and the piano tone is a mite shallow, but the performance is so compelling that you soon forget any sonic inadequacies.

Additional recommendations ...

...Nos. 1 and 2. Totentanz. **Krystian Zimerman** (pf); **Boston Symphony Orchestra / Seiji Ozawa.** DG Ⓟ 423 571-2GH (56 minutes: DDD: 11/88). ⊙⊙

...Nos. 1 and 2. Totentanz, S126. **Alfred Brendel** (pf); **London Philharmonic Orchestra / Bernard Haitink.** Philips Silver Line Ⓜ 426 637-2PSL (56 minutes: ADD: 11/90). ⊙⊙

...No. 2. **Grieg** Piano Concerto. Lyric Pieces, Book 8, Op. 65. **Leif Ove Andsnes** (pf); **Bergen Philharmonic Orchestra / Dmitri Kitaienko.** Virgin Classics Ⓔ VC7 59613-2 (78 minutes: DDD: 4/91)

...Nos. 1[a] and 2[b]. Hungarian Rhapsody in D flat major, S244 No. 6. Valse oubliée, S215 No. 1.
Années de pèlerinage – Deuxième année, S160, "Italie" – No. 5, Sonetto 104 del Petrarca.
Coupled with works by **Schumann, Falla** and **Guion** Byron Janis (pf); [a]**Moscow Philharmonic
Orchestra / Kyrill Kondrashin;** [b]**Moscow Radio Symphony Orchestra / Gennadi Rozhdestvensky.**
Mercury Living Presence Ⓜ 432 002-2MM (63 minutes: ADD: 9/91).
...No. 1[a]. Piano Sonata in B minor, B178[a]. Hungarian Rhapsody No. 6[a]. Les jeux d'eau à la Villa
d'Este[b]. Vallée d'Oberman. [a]**Martha Argerich,** [b]**Lazar Berman** (pfs); [a]**London Symphony
Orchestra / Claudio Abbado.** DG Ⓜ 439 409-2GCL (72 minutes: ADD: 1/94).
...No. 1[a]. Liebestraum in A flat major, S541 No. 3. Réminiscences de Don Juan (Mozart), S418.
Hungarian Rhapsody No. 13 in A minor, S244. Faust (Gounod) – Waltz, S407. **Saint-Saëns** Le
carnaval des animaux – Le cygne. **Liadov** A musical snuffbox, Op. 32. **Shura Cherkassky** (pf);
[a]**Philharmonia Orchestra / Anatole Fistoulari.** Testament mono Ⓕ SBT1033* (62 minutes: ADD:
9/94). *See review in the Collections section; refer to the Index to Reviews.*   Ⓖ
...Nos. 1 and 2. Mazeppa, S100. Les Préludes, S97. [a]**Geoffrey Tozer** (pf); **Suisse Romande Orchestra
/ Neeme Järvi.** Chandos Ⓕ CHAN9360 (72 minutes: DDD: 9/95).
...Nos. 1 and 2. Danse macabre, Paraphrase on "Dies irae"[a]. Piano Sonata in B minor. Csárdás
macabre. Valse oubliée No. 1. Années de pèlerinage – Première année:; Deuxième année;
Troisième année. Weinachtsbaum-Suite – No. 7, Schlummerlied. Nuages gris. Klavierstück in
F sharp major, S192 No. 3. En rêve. R.W. – Venezia. Vexilla regis prodeunt. Mosonyis Grabgeleit.
Schlaflos, Frage und Antwort. Unstern: Sinistre, distastro. La lugubre gondola – No. 1; No. 2 .
Légendes. Harmonies poétiques et religieuses – No. 7, Funérailles. Fantasia and Fugue on the
Theme B-A-C-H. Harmonies poétiques et religieuses – No. 1, Invocations; No. 3, Bénédiction de
Dieu dans la solitude; Pensée des morts. Weinen, Klagen, Sorgen, Zagen. Isoldens Liebestod.
Alfred Brendel (pf); [a]**London Philharmonic Orchestra / Bernard Haitink.** Philips Ⓜ 446 924-2PM5
(five discs: 361 minutes: ADD: 2/96).
...No. 1[a]. **Grieg** Piano Concerto in A minor, Op. 16[b]. Lyric Pieces – French serenade, Op. 62 No. 3;
Cradle song, Op. 68 No. 5. **Franck** Symphonic Variations[a]. **Walter Gieseking** (pf); [a]**London
Philharmonic Orchestra / Sir Henry Wood;** [b]**Berlin State Opera Orchestra / Hans Rosbaud.** APR
mono Ⓜ APR5513* (63 minutes: ADD: 3/96).

Liszt A Dante Symphony, S109[a]. Années de pèlerinage – deuxième année, S161, "Italie" – No. 7,
Après une lecture du Dante – Fantasia quasi sonata[b]. [a]**Berlin Radio Women's Chorus;** [a]**Berlin
Philharmonic Orchestra / Daniel Barenboim** ([b]pf). Teldec Ⓕ 9031-77340-2 (67 minutes: DDD:
7/94). Item marked [a] recorded at a performance in the Schauspielhaus, Berlin in 1992.
Gramophone Editor's choice.   Ⓖ
This disc proves conclusively that the *Dante Symphony* (a contemporary of the *Faust Symphony*) is no
longer one that needs its apologists. Tone, full and rounded, firm and true, and rock-steady pacing
elevate the symphony's opening ("Abandon all hope, ye who enter here") beyond its all too familiar
resemblance to a third-rate horror-film soundtrack. As the symphony progresses, together with the
countless examples of Berlin tone and artistry filling out, refining or shaping gestures in often
revelatory ways, you become aware of Barenboim's skill in maintaining the large-scale tension he has
created. And that is a very real achievement. As for the final choral Magnificat, if Liszt owed Wagner
a debt of gratitude for persuading him to conclude the symphony with the "noble and softly soaring"
bars that precede a more noisily affirmative appended coda, in Barenboim's Magnificat (and much else
in the symphony), it is Wagner's debt to Liszt that is more readily apparent; the *Parsifal*ian radiance of
these final pages is unmistakable. More importantly, for once they sound convincingly conclusive. The
Dante Sonata was recorded with the kind of risk-taking abandon and occasionally less than perfect
execution that you might expect from a live event. Improvisatory, impulsive and full of extreme
contrasts, Barenboim's Dante Sonata is vividly pictorial (with almost orchestral colourings). In the best
Lisztian tradition, the instrument itself (closely miked and widely spaced) sounds larger than life. This
is, in a word, riveting. The recording of the symphony is spacious, focused and expertly balanced.

New review
Liszt A Faust Symphony, S108. **Vinson Cole** (ten); **Dresden State Opera Chorus; Staatskapelle
Dresden / Giuseppe Sinopoli.** DG Ⓕ 449 137-2GH (67 minutes: DDD: 7/96). Recorded live in
1995.   Ⓖ
New review
Liszt A Faust Symphony, S108. **Kenneth Riegel** (ten); **Tanglewood Festival Chorus; Boston
Symphony Orchestra / Leonard Bernstein.** DG The Originals Ⓜ 447 449-2GOR (77 minutes:
ADD: 7/96). Text included. From 2707 100 (4/78).   Ⓖ
Giuseppe Sinopoli projects Liszt's "Mephistopheles" with such unrelenting urgency that he could as
well be fighting the devil in person. True, the recorded balance keeps the strings fairly close at hand,
but the playing itself has real drive and panache, frequently throwing caution to the winds in pursuit
of maximum spontaneity (as regards tempo, Sinopoli beats Bernstein to the finishing post by no less
than ten minutes). He convinces you that this is absolutely the right way to approach Liszt's orchestral
music, although sticklers for executive precision will no doubt quibble over the odd patch of scrappy
ensemble. Not that Sinopoli is inattentive to the subtler aspects of Liszt's greatest orchestral work: he
effects superb control at the soulful passage where the opening theme (played on lower strings) is

merged with the second subject (on woodwinds). Both here and throughout the following two or three minutes he keeps the argument moving. Gretchen is both responsive and transparent, especially at 8'54" where cellos and violins call to each other above a fluid woodwind accompaniment. The symphony's brief choral finale, where "woman's eternal soul leads us on high" and Vinson Cole is in good voice, finds Sinopoli favouring Wagnerian drama rather than pre-Mahlerian expansiveness. The chorus are excellent, the sound forward, forceful and prone to highlight whoever plays loudest (in that respect, it is very much a live production). Also, some may find certain extraneous noises – including Sinopoli's low-key vocal contributions and energetic footwork – a mite distracting.

The absorbing booklet-note for the Leonard Bernstein release informs us that at a particular Tanglewood concert in 1941 (August 8th) Bernstein scored a triumph in modern American repertoire and Serge Koussevitzky conducted the first two movements of *A Faust Symphony*. Some 20 years later Bernstein himself made a distinguished recording of the work, faster than this superb 1976 Boston remake by almost five minutes yet ultimately less involving. The passage of time witnessed not only an easing of tempo but a heightened response to individual characters, be it Faust's swings in mood and attitude, Gretchen's tender entreaties or the unpredictable shadow-play of "Mephistopheles". Orchestral execution is first-rate, the strings in particular really showing their mettle (such biting incisiveness), while Bernstein's pacing, although often slower than average, invariably fits the mood. The sound too is far warmer and more lifelike than its rather opaque New York predecessor, although when it comes to the tenor soloist in the closing chorus, both Sinopoli's Vinson Cole and Sony's sweet-toned Charles Bressler to DG's more strident Kenneth Riegel. There are many other recommendable versions but, arguably, Sinopoli in Dresden and Bernstein in Boston offer the most compelling available reportage of an endlessly fascinating score.

Additional recommendations ...

...**Charles Bressler** (ten); **New York Choral Art Society; New York Philharmonic Orchestra / Leonard Bernstein.** Sony Classical Bernstein Royal Edition Ⓜ SMK47570 (72 minutes: ADD: 5/93). Ⓠ
...**Peter Seiffert** (ten); **Ernst-Senff Chorus; Prague Philharmonic Chorus; Berlin Philharmonic Orchestra / Sir Simon Rattle.** EMI Ⓔ CDC5 55220-2 (69 minutes: DDD: 1/95). Ⓖ
...**András Molnár** (ten); **Hungarian State Choir; Orchestra of the Franz Liszt Academy / András Ligeti.** Naxos Ⓢ 8 553304 (73 minutes: DDD: 10/95).

Liszt Complete Symphonic Poems, Volumes 1 and 2. **London Philharmonic Orchestra / Bernard Haitink.** Philips Ⓜ 438 751/4-2PM2 (two sets of two discs: 127 and 131 minutes: ADD: 10/94). Recorded 1968-71.
438 751-2PM2 – Ce qu'on entend sur la montagne, S95 (from 6500 189, 1/72). Tasso, S96. Les Préludes, S97. Orpheus, S98 (SAL3750, 12/69). Prometheus, S99. Festklänge, S101 (6709 005, 9/72). Mazeppa, S100 (6500 046, 8/71). *438 754-2PM2* – Héroïde funèbre, S102. Die Ideale, S106. Mephisto Waltz No. 1, S514, "Der Tanz in der Dorfschenke"; No. 2, S110 (from 6709 005, 9/72). Hungaria, S103. Hamlet, S104 (6500 046, 8/71). Hunnenschlacht, S105. Von der Wiege bis zum Grabe, S107 (6500 189, 1/72). ⒼⒼⒼ
The 12 'numbered' symphonic poems date from Liszt's rich maturity (the first, *Ce qu'on entend sur la montagne*, was composed during the late 1840s) with the lean, near-expressionist *Von der Wiege bis zum Grabe* ("From the Cradle to the Grave") following on after a period of some 25 years. Initial orchestration was invariably undertaken by Joachim Raff, although the composer himself always had the final say. When, in the early 1970s, Bernard Haitink galvanized the LPO into re-enacting these symphonic dramas, he had the field more or less to himself. Haitink's readings have an abundance of personality. In *Héroïde funèbre*, for example, his dangerously slow tempo exceeds Liszt's prescribed timing by some seven minutes: it is a terrifying vision, superbly sustained and beautifully played. He also copes manfully with the more explosive aspects of *Hamlet, Prometheus* and *Hunnenschlacht* (which he paces more securely than any other rival, past or present), and his way with the scores' many reflective episodes is entirely winning. Elsewhere, he sorts through the complexities of Liszt's colourful orchestration with a cool head and a warm heart, etching the frequent examples of 'nature music' much as he does Wagner's and keeping abreast of each tone-poem's narrative trail. True, some of Liszt's *marcatos, impetuosos, appassionatos* and *agitatos* are occasionally brought to heel, but then others aren't – and we have Liszt's blessing for flexibility in what he himself terms "the degree of sympathy" that conductors employ for his work. What matters is that Haitink has us enter Liszt's world direct, rather than through the distorting mirror of the conductor's own ego. It is a volatile sequence, yes, and not without its *longueurs*, but it remains an essential musical confrontation for all students of the romantic orchestra and an accurate pointer to where Tchaikovsky, Smetana and countless others found significant musical sustenance. With excellent sound and commonsense documentation, these two sets will provide hours of aural adventure.

Additional recommendations ...

...**Prometheus, S99.** *Coupled with works by* **Beethoven, Scriabin** and **Nono** Soloists; **Berlin Singakademie; Freiburg Soloists Choir; Berlin Philharmonic Orchestra / Claudio Abbado.** Sony Classical Ⓔ SK53978 (75 minutes: DDD: 1/95). *See review in the Collections section; refer to the Index to Reviews* ⒼⒼⒼ
...**Mazeppa. Mephisto Waltz No. 1, S110, "Der Tanz in der Dorfschenke".** **Kodály** Háry János – concert suite. Theatre Overture. **New York Philharmonic Orchestra / Kurt Masur.** Teldec Ⓕ 9031 77547-2 (66 minutes. DDD).

New review

Liszt Piano Sonata in B minor, S178. Funeral Odes – No. 2, La notte, S699. Harmonies poétiques et réligieuses, S173 – Funérailles. Nuages gris, S199. La Lugubre gondola II, S200. **Krystian Zimerman** (pf). DG Ⓕ 431 780-2GH (66 minutes: DDD: 10/91). Ⓖ

It is to be expected that an artist who has made one of the outstanding recordings of the Liszt concertos should also give us one of the finest ever B minor Sonatas. Whether you think it is *the* finest ever may depend on your priorities (and on whether you think it is sensible to venture such opinions). What can surely be said is that Zimerman brings to bear a combination of ardour, forcefulness, drive and sheer technical grasp which are tremendously exciting and for which it is difficult to think of a direct rival. However, others have achieved a subtler pacing and shading of climaxes, or a more philosophical inwardness, that make their readings equally, if not more rewarding. Pollini is perhaps the most nearly comparable in approach, but he is less overtly rhetorical from moment to moment and more concerned with long arcs of dramatic tension. DG have given Zimerman a very bright, close sound-image, as the very opening demonstrates. The release of tension at the first *fortissimo* has an almost startling vehemence. Zimerman's dramatic timing in the opening pages is wonderful, and the sternness which regulates the emotional pressure is close to ideal for the whole of the long *allegro energico*. This is playing in the grand manner, and if you automatically dislike 'conventional' hesitations and surges you will probably resist many of Zimerman's initiatives. It is with the *Andante sostenuto* slow movement that the inspiration wavers a little, not so much in the lyrical playing as in the building of the central climax. This comes to the boil too soon to clinch the crucial moment at 15'14" and it is the overall profile of climaxes which is the Achilles heel of the performance. Blame the music if you like but others have shown that a more convincing overall trajectory is possible. Richter and Brendel are two such. Although Zimerman's performance of "Funérailles" is curiously clinical, the central section emerging as a block-like episode rather than an integrated accumulation, memories from the rest of his recital linger in the mind. There is the magical evaporation at the end of *Nuages gris*, the passionate igniting towards the highpoint of *La notte* (a late reworking of "Il pensiero" from the second volume of *Années di pèlerinage*) and the subtle tonal shadings and high rhetorical charge of *La lugubre gondola II*. The instrument is superb and the sound quality, though not lacking impact, can be slightly tiring in the long run.

Additional recommendations ...

...Piano Sonata. Three Concert Studies, S144. **Louis Lortie** (pf). Chandos Ⓕ CHAN8548 (52 minutes: DDD: 5/87).

...Piano Sonata. Mephisto Waltz No. 1, S514. Années de pèlerinage – Troisième année, S163: No. 4, Les jeux d'eau à la Villa d'Este; Deuxième année, S161, "Italie": No. 2, Il penseroso. Hungarian Rhapsody No. 15 in A minor, S244. **Mikhail Pletnev** (pf). Olympia Ⓑ OCD172 (67 minutes: ADD: 12/87). Ⓖ

...Piano Sonata. Piano Concerto No. 1 in E flat major (with orchestra / David Brockman). Années de pèlerinage, Deuxième année – Sonnetto 104 del Petrarca. Rapsodie espagnole. Two Concert Studies – No. 2, Gnomenreigen (two performances). Harmonies poétiques et religieuses – No. 7, Funérailles. Hungarian Rhapsody No. 12 in C sharp minor. **Gounod** (trans. Liszt) Faust – Waltz. **Simon Barere** (pf). APR Ⓜ APR7007* (two discs: 93 minutes: ADD: 11/89). ⓖⓖⓖ

...Piano Sonata. Nuages gris, S199. Unstern: sinistre, disastro, S208. La lugubre gondola No. 1. R.W. – Venezia, S201. **Maurizio Pollini** (pf). DG Ⓕ 427 322-2GH (46 minutes: DDD: 7/90). ⓖⓖ

...Piano Sonata. Two Légendes, S175. Scherzo and March, S177. **Nikolai Demidenko** (pf). Hyperion Ⓕ CDA66616 (67 minutes: DDD: 2/93). Ⓖ

...Piano Sonata. Hungarian Rhapsody No. 6 in D flat major, S244. **Brahms** Two Rhapsodies, Op. 79. **Schumann** Piano Sonata No. 2 in G minor, Op. 22. **Martha Argerich** (pf). DG Galleria Ⓜ 437 252-2GGA (64 minutes: ADD: 2/93). ⓖⓖ

...Piano Sonata. **Schubert** Piano Sonata in D major, D850. **Emil Gilels** (pf). RCA Victor Living Stereo Ⓜ 09026 61614-2 (71 minutes: ADD: 4/94). ⓖⓖ

...Piano Sonata. Polonaise in E major, S223 No. 2. Scherzo in G minor, S153. Nuages gris, S199. Consolations, S172 – No. 6, Allegretto sempre cantabile. Hungarian Rhapsody in A minor, S242 No. 17. Klavierstück in F sharp major, S193. Mephisto Polka, S217. Etudes d'exécution transcendante, S139 – No. 1, Preludio; No. 2, Molto vivace; No. 3, Paysage; No. 5, Feux follets; No. 7, Eroica; No. 8, Wilde Jagd; No. 10, Appassionata; No. 11, Harmonies du soir. Un sospiro, S144 No. 3. Gnomenreigen, S145 No. 2. *Coupled with works by* **Chopin** Sviatoslav Richter (pf). Philips Ⓕ 438 620-2PH3 (three discs: 202 minutes: DDD: 8/94). ⓖⓖ

...Piano Sonata. Fantasia and Fugue in G minor (Bach), S463. Hungarian Rhapsodies, S244 – No. 2 in C sharp minor; No. 12 in C sharp minor; No. 13 in A minor; No. 15 in A minor, "Rákóczy march". Liebesträum No. 3 in A flat major, "O lieb, so lang du lieben kannst", S541. **Shura Cherkassky** (pf). Decca Ⓕ 433 656-2DH (79 minutes: ADD: 1/95). ⓖⓖ

...Piano Sonata. Hungarian Rhapsody No. 6 in D flat major. *Coupled with works by* **Ravel, Prokofiev, Brahms** and **Chopin** Martha Argerich (pf). DG The Originals Ⓜ 447 430-2GOR (71 minutes: ADD: 6/95). *See review in the Collections section; refer to the Index to Reviews.* ⓖⓖ

...Piano Sonata. Mephisto Waltz No. 1, S514. Un sospiro, S144 No. 3. Etudes d'exécution transcendante d'après Paganini, S140 – No. 3, La campanella. *Coupled with works by* **Bartók** and **Delibes/Dohnányi** Géza Anda (pf). Testament mono Ⓕ SBT1067* (63 minutes: ADD: 10/95). *See review in the Collections section; refer to the Index to Reviews.*   Ⓖ

...Piano Sonata. Mephisto Waltz No. 1, S514. Harmonies poétiques et religieuses, S173 – Funérailles. Réminiscences de Don Juan (Mozart), S418. Etudes d'exécution transcendante d'apres Paganini, S140 – La campanella. Hungarian Rhapsody No. 12 in C sharp minor, S244. Consolations, S172 – No. 3, Lento placido. Années de pèlerinage – Première année, S160, "Suisse"; Au bord d'une source; Deuxième année, S161: Sonetto 104 del Petrarca; Troisième année, S163: Les jeux d'eau à la Villa d'Este. Concert Studies – Gnomenreigen, S145 No. 2; Un sospiro, S144 No. 3. Rigoletto Paraphrase, S434. **Schubert/Liszt** Die Forelle, S564. Erlkönig, S557a. **Jorge Bolet** (pf). Double Decca Ⓜ 444 851-2DF2 (two discs 140 minutes: ADD/DDD: 1/96).

...Etudes d'exécution transcendante, S139 – No. 1, Preludio; No. 2, Etude; No. 3, Paysage; No. 5, Feux follets; No. 11, Harmonies du soir. **Ravel** Miroirs. Valses nobles et sentimentales. **Sviatoslav Richter** (pf). Praga mono/stereo Ⓑ CMX354009* (65 minutes: ADD: 6/96).   Ⓖ

New review

Liszt Piano Sonata in B minor, S178[a]. La leggierezza, S144 No. 2[a]. Consolations, S172 – No. 3, Lento placido[b]. Hungarian Rhapsody No. 12 in C sharp minor, S244[b]. Années de pèlerinage, deuxième année, S161   No. 5, Sonetto 104 del Petrarca; No. 6, Sonetto 123 del Petrarca[b]. Rigoletto (Verdi) – Paraphrase, S434[b]. Il trovatore (Verdi) – Miserere, S433[b]. Réminiscences de Norma (Bellini), S394[b]. Tannhäuser (Wagner) – Overture, S442[b]. Die Meistersinger von Nürnberg (Wagner) – Am stillen Herd, S448[b]. Tristan und Isolde (Wagner) – Liebestod, S447[b]. [a]**Bernard d'Ascoli**, [b]**Craig Sheppard** (pfs). Classics for Pleasure Silver Doubles Ⓢ CD-CFPSD4745 (two discs: 126 minutes: ADD/DDD: 2/96). Items marked [a] from CFP40380 (10/82), [b]CFP40051 (8/73). Recorded 1973-82.

True virtuosity is an elusive elixir. Far transcending mere accuracy or 'correctness' it sets the pulse racing and the scalp tingling. Many will experience a similar twinge when they listen to Craig Sheppard's recordings made in the early 1970s at the start of his meteoric, dangerously hectic career. True, he can alternate passion and inwardness to memorable effect in the *Petrarch Sonnets*, or spin the most delicate of lines in the D flat *Consolation*. But in page after page of the operatic paraphrases he flaunts his hypnotic temperamental brio and brilliance. Listen to his concluding octaves in *Rigoletto* (from him a burst of thunderous applause) or the final pages of *Tannhäuser* and you will witness an astounding force and charisma; playing which rides on a knife edge between abandon and control. In total contrast Bernard d'Ascoli, the blind French pianist, tempers Liszt's heroics with dignity and poetic restraint. Those who yearn for a more swashbuckling B minor Sonata will find plenty of alternatives, but for inner strength and refinement d'Ascoli is exceptional, particularly in the *Andante sostenuto* where he so lucidly locates Liszt's mystical, still centre. *La leggierezza*, too, is spun off with rare elegance, with a light, corruscating and *détaché* touch. But it is Craig Sheppard who has the lion's share of the proceedings. You won't easily find more exciting or, indeed, more leonine Liszt playing. The recordings cope superbly with his instantly recognizable lean and biting sonority – and all this can be heard at CfP's super-bargain price!

Additional recommendation ...

...Deuxième année – No. 4, Sonetto 47 del Petrarca; Nos. 5 and 6. Three Concert Studies, S144. Liebestraüme, S541. **Kathryn Stott** (pf). Conifer Ⓕ CDCF180 (63 minutes: DDD: 8/90).

New review

Liszt Fantasia on two themes from Mozart's "Le nozze di Figaro", S697. Réminiscences de Don Juan (Mozart), S418. Réminiscences de Norma (Bellini), S394. Rigoletto (Verdi) – paraphrase, S434. Faust (Gounod) – Waltz, S407.

Rossini/Ginsburg Il barbiere di Siviglia – Largo al factotum **Grigory Ginsburg** (pf). Melodiya mono Ⓜ 74321 33210-2* (70 minutes: ADD: 8/96). Recorded 1948-58.

What can be said of Grigory Ginsburg's Liszt transcriptions? They are already well-known to piano buffs, if only by reputation, since the LP versions have long been like gold-dust. From the stable of Goldenweiser, and a long-time colleague of his at the Moscow Conservatoire, Ginsburg possessed a jaw-dropping facility and lightness of touch which recall the piano rolls of Lhevinne and Rosenthal. It's the kind of playing that sets you wondering if he was equally phenomenal in live performance and whether such playing could perhaps only be achieved on light-touch instruments. Whatever the case, his seemingly spontaneous eloquence and wit, heard at their most breathtaking in his own *Barber of Seville* transcription, shine through the very shabby sound quality. This is about as 'must-have' as a must-have can be for collectors of great piano recordings.

Liszt Hungarian Rhapsodies, S244. Rhapsodie espagnole, S254[a]. **György Cziffra** (pf). EMI Rouge et Noir Ⓜ CZS7 67888-2* (two discs: 131 minutes: ADD: 11/94). Rhapsodies Nos. 2, 6, 12 and 15 from HMV ALP1446 (3/58); Nos. 8 and 11 from HMV 7ER5199 (9/61); Nos. 9, 10 and 13 from ALP1915/6 (11/62); No. 14 from 7ER5206 (11/61). Item marked [a] from ALP1534 (12/57).
                                                                      ⒼⒼⒼ

These recordings were made at a time when Cziffra's star shone with a unique, unsurpassed brilliance. Here is all his death-defying bravura: the dizzying changes of pace and direction, the hair-raising crescendos within the bar (almost as if a grenade had been tossed into the piano), the steam-drill left-hand accentuation, and the sky-rocketing flights that leave a trail of sparks in their wake. Cziffra's characterization can be subtle as well as bold, and the continuous sense of improvisation (almost as if the music were being composed on the spot, with several added ornaments and flourishes Liszt forgot), wit and relish is breathtaking. How jaunty the "Friska" from the Second *Rhapsody* sounds after that truly lugubrious *Lento a capriccio* introduction, and listen to the final *Vivace* of No. 11, the last word in glistening *perlé* pianism. However, pride of place should surely go to the *Rhapsodie espagnole*, where Cziffra's alternation of languorous poetry and the most tightly coiled virtuosity makes the mind reel. The split octave ascent at 9'52" is one of several instances where the effect is like rapidly applied centrifugal force. The recordings, when you notice them, vary from the uncomfortably close and airless to a greater sense of ambience. Yet they do nothing to dim one's overall impression. Cziffra is, quite simply, unique in this repertoire.

Additional recommendations ...

...Rhapsodie espagnole. Etudes de Concert, S145 – Gnomenreigen. Etudes de Concert, S144 – La leggierezza. Années de pèlerinage, Deuxième année, S161, "Italie" – Sonetto 104 del Petrarca. Réminiscences de Don Juan, S418. Valse oubliée, S215 No. 1. *Coupled with works by* **Chopin, Balakirev, Blumenfeld, Glazunov, Scriabin, Lully, Rameau** and **Schumann** Simon Barere (pf). APR mono Ⓕ CDAPR7001* (two discs: 126 minutes: ADD: 5/91). *See review in the Collections section; refer to the Index to Reviews.* ⒼⒼⒼ

...Hungarian Rhapsody No. 12. **Brahms** Piano Concerto No. 2 in B flat major, Op. 83[a]. Variations on a Theme by Paganini, Op. 35 – Book 2. **Beethoven** Piano Sonata No. 9 in E major, Op. 14 No. 1. **Gina Bachauer** (pf); [a]**London Symphony Orchestra / Stanislaw Skrowaczewski.** Mercury Living Presence Ⓜ 434 340-2MM (77 minutes: ADD: 9/95).

Liszt Années de pèlerinage – Première année, S160, "Suisse"; Deuxième année, S161, "Italie"; Troisième année, S163. Venezia e Napoli, S162. **Lazar Berman** (pf). DG Ⓜ 437 206-2GX3 (three discs: 176 minutes: ADD: 11/93). Recorded 1977. ⒼⒼ

Liszt's three volumes of *Années de pèlerinage* are rarely recorded complete, largely because many pianists remain baffled by the dark-hued prophecy and romanticism of the third and final book. So it is particularly gratifying to welcome Lazar Berman's superb DG recordings back into the catalogue. Berman's resource here is remarkable and his performance of the entire book is hauntingly inward and sympathetic to both the radiance of "Les jeux d'eau à la Villa d'Este" and to Liszt's truly dark night of the soul (*lamentoso, doloroso* and so on), and to his desolate lack of spiritual solace elsewhere. He is hardly less persuasive in the first two books. "Chapelle de Guillaume Tell" is a true celebration of Switzerland's republican hero with alpine horns ringing through the mountains, while in "Au lac de Wallenstadt" Berman's gently undulating traversal is truly *pianissimo* and *dolcissimo egualamente*. His "Orage" is predictably breathtaking, and in the gloomy Byronic "Vallée d'Obermann" the severest critic will find himself mesmerized by Berman's free-wheeling eloquence. The 1977 recordings have been finely remastered.

Additional recommendations ...

...Première année. **Jorge Bolet** (pf). Decca Ⓕ 410 160-2DH (50 minutes: DDD: 12/84). ⒼⒼ

...Deuxième année. **Jorge Bolet** (pf). Decca Ⓕ 410 161-2DH (51 minutes: DDD: 7/85). ⒼⒼ

...Troisième année – No. 4, Les jeux d'eaux à la Villa d'Este. Harmonies poétiques et religieuses. Venezia e Napoli. Ballade No. 2 in B minor, S171. **Jorge Bolet** (pf). Decca Ⓕ 411 803-2DH (58 minutes: DDD: 12/85). Ⓖ

...Deuxième année – No. 4, Sonetto 47 del Petrarca; No. 5, Sonetto 104 del Petrarca. Six Consolations, S172. Liebestraüme, S541. Rigoletto (Verdi) Paraphrase, S434. **Daniel Barenboim** (pf). DG Galleria Ⓜ 435 591-2GGA (61 minutes: DDD: 9/92).

...Deuxième année. **Michael Dalberto** (pf). Denon Ⓕ CO-75500 (71 minutes: DDD: 2/94).

New review

Liszt Années de pèlerinage – Deuxième année, S161, "Italie". Venezia e Napoli, S162 – Gondoliera. Deux Légendes, S175. **William Kempff** (pf). DG Galleria Ⓜ 449 093-2GGA (57 minutes: ADD: 7/96). Recorded 1974. Ⓖ

In the very early days of the mono LP era Wilhelm Kempff made a famous recording of Liszt's piano music for the Decca label. He re-recorded much of the same programme for DG in the Hannover Beethovensaal in 1974, adding "Sposalizio" to the other excerpts from the Deuxième année of the *Années de pèlerinage* – which included "Il penseroso" (a particularly haunting rendition), the "Canzonetta del Salvator Rosa" – and the three Petrarch Sonnets plus "Gondoliera" from *Venezia e Napoli*. But perhaps most famous of all were the *Deux Légendes* – wonderfully evocative and poetic readings. The opening bird-song of "St Francis of Assisi" is quite magical, and then the solemn tread of "St Francis de Paule walking on the water" is slowly built to an overwhelming climax. These are masterly and unforgettable performances and one finds oneself wondering why DG chose to reissue this outstanding recital – which is most realistically recorded – on their mid-price Galleria label rather than as an Original. However, this is a quite outstanding release and is certainly not to be missed.

Liszt Complete Solo Piano Music, Volume 15 – Song transcriptions. **Leslie Howard** (pf). Hyperion
Ⓔ CDA66481/2 (two discs: 147 minutes: DDD: 4/92). Recorded 1990.
  Beethoven Adelaïde, S466. Sechs geistliche Lieder, S467. An die ferne Geliebte, S469. Lieder
  von Goethe, S468. **Mendelssohn** Lieder, S547. **Dessauer** Lieder, S485. **Franz** Er ist
  gekommen in Sturm und Regen, S488. Lieder, S489. **Rubinstein** Two songs, S554. **Schumann**
  Lieder von Robert und Clara Schumann, S569. Provenzalisches Lied, S570. Two songs, S567.
  Frühlingsnacht, S568. Widmung, S566.

Few composers have ever shown a more insatiable interest in the music of others than Liszt, or
devoted more time to transcribing it for the piano. In this radio-cum-gramophonic age, such activity
might even be deemed time wasted. But in Liszt's day it was a godsend for music-lovers and
composers alike, and all praise to Leslie Howard for including it in his mammoth pilgrimage through
the composer's complete keyboard works. Here, he plays 60 of Liszt's 100 or so song transcriptions,
including several by the lesser-known Dessauer, Franz and (as composers) Anton Rubinstein and
Clara Schumann, alongside Beethoven, Mendelssohn and Robert Schumann. The selection at once
reveals Liszt's variety of approach as a transcriber no less than his unpredictability of choice.
Sometimes, as most notably in Beethoven's concert aria, *Adelaïde*, the keyboard virtuoso takes over:
he links its two sections with a concerto-like cadenza as well as carrying bravura into an amplified
coda. Mendelssohn's *On wings of song* brings imitative subtleties all his own, while the fullness of
heart of Schumann's *Dedication* and *Spring Night* is likewise allowed to expand and overflow. But
after the dazzling pyrotechnics of many of his operatic arrangements, the surprise here is the self-
effacing simplicity of so much included. The five songs from Schumann's *Liederalbum für die Jugend*
are literal enough to be played by young children. Even his later (1880) fantasy-type transcriptions
of Rubinstein's exotic *The Asra* has the same potent economy of means, characterizing his own
original keyboard music in advancing years. Howard responds keenly to mood and atmosphere,
and never fails, pianistically, to emphasize the 'singer' in each song – in response to the actual
verbal text that Liszt was nearly always conscientious enough to write into his scores. The recording
is clean and true.

Liszt Complete Solo Piano Music, Volume 18 – Capriccio alla turca from "Die Ruinen von
Athen", S388. March from "Die Ruinen von Athen", S388*a*. Fantasie über "Die Ruinen von
Athen", S389. Wedding March and Dance of the Elves from "A Midsummer Night's Dream",
S410. Einsam bin ich, nicht alleine from "La Preciosa", S453. Incidental music to Hebbel's
"Nibelungen" and Goethe's "Faust", S496. Symphonisches Zwischensiel zu Calderons schauspiel
"Uber allen Zauber Liebe", S497. Pastorale from choruses to Herder's "Prometheus Bound",
S508. **Leslie Howard** (pf). Hyperion Ⓔ CDA66575 (78 minutes: DDD: 3/93). Recorded 1991.

After two volumes of "Liszt at the Opera" in his mammoth cycle, Leslie Howard now introduces us
to "Liszt at the Theatre", i.e. as transcriber-paraphraser of incidental music written for various stage
productions by Beethoven, Weber, Mendelssohn, Lassen – and even an excerpt from what he himself
produced for Herder's *Prometheus Bound*. Best-known, of course, is Mendelssohn's *Midsummer
Night's Dream*-inspired "Wedding March" and "Dance of the Elves", miraculously merged in the
course of Liszt's transcription. The "Turkish March" from Beethoven's *The Ruins of Athens* is
familiar enough too, though it's not every day of the week that we can compare Liszt's first, succinctly
piquant transcription with his two extended and elaborated later versions, as Howard allows us to do
here. The 'mystery' composer of the five is Liszt's protégé (and ultimately his successor at Weimar),
the Danish-born, Belgian-naturalized Eduard Lassen, at his best in his Wagner-influenced music for
Hebbel and Calderon, but on this showing no match for Goethe's *Faust*. As always Howard meets
diabolical technical challenges with commendable sang-froid, and the recording maintains Hyperion's
customary fidelity.

Liszt Complete Solo Piano Music, Volume 21 – Soirées musicales, S424. Soirées italiennes, S411.
Nuits d'été à Pausilippe, S399. Tre sonetti del Petrarca, S158. Venezia e Napoli, S159. La serenata
e L'orgia (Grande fantaisie sur des motifs des Soirées musicales), S422. La pastorella dell'Alpi e
Li marinari (Deuxième fantaisie sur des motifs des Soirées musicales), S423. **Leslie Howard** (pf).
Hyperion Ⓔ CDA66661/2 (two discs: 157 minutes: DDD: 7/93). Recorded 1991-92.

The two discs comprising Vol. 21 of Howard's enormous cycle remind us of the young Liszt's love
affair with Italy, the spotlight now falling primarily – though not exclusively – on frolics with Rossini,
Mercadante and Donizetti in lighter, lyrical vein. The special interest of the two original sets of pieces
included, i.e. the three *Sonetti del Petrarca* and the four *Venezia e Napoli*, is that Howard introduces
them as first written (c1839 and 1840 respectively) before Liszt's characteristically painstaking later
revisions. There is much to enjoy in the playing itself, especially in simpler contexts when gondolas
glide through calm waters, or lovers dream, or shepherds dance. Melody, so important throughout, is
nicely sung. And whether in filigree delicacy or exuberant zest (as in excitable Venetian regattas)
Howard invariably relishes Liszt's ear-catching ornamentation.

Additional recommendations ...
...Complete Solo Piano Music, Volume 25 – Cantico di San Francesco – Preludio per il Cantico del
Sol, S499*a*. Cantico del sol di San Francesco, S499. Von der Wiege bis zum Grabe, S512.
O sacrum convivium, S674*a* (two versions). Salve Regina, S669 No. 1. Ave maris stella, S669
No. 2. Gebet, S265. Ora pro nobis, S262. Resignazione, S187*b*. Il m'aimait tant, S533. Romance,
"O pourquoi donc", S169. Ich liebe dich, S546*a*. Die Zelle in Nonnenswerth, S534. **Leslie Howard**
(pf). Hyperion Ⓕ CDA66694 (77 minutes: DDD: 5/94).
...Complete Solo Piano Music, Volume 27 – Szózat und Ungarischer Hymnus, S486. God Save the
Queen, S235. Canzone napolitana, S248. Ungarische Nationalmelodien, S243. Hussitenlied on a
melody by J. Krov, S234. Glanes de Woronince, S249. La Marseillaise, S237. Vive Henri IV, S239.
La cloche sonne, S238. Rákóczy March, S242*a*/1. **Leslie Howard** (pf). Hyperion Ⓕ CDA66787
(73 minutes: DDD: 9/94).

Liszt Complete Solo Piano Music, Volume 28 – Dances and Marches: Scherzo and March, S177;
Petite valse favorite, S212*a*; Mazurka brillante, S221; Grand galop chromatique, S219; Galop in
A minor, S218; Festpolonaise, S230*a*; Csárdás, S225; Csárdás macabre, S224; Mephisto Polka,
S217; Festvorspiel, S226; Heroischer Marsch im ungarischen Styl, S231; Ungarischer
Sturmmarsch, S524; Festmarsch zur Goethejubiläumsfeier, S521; Festmarsch nach Motiven von
E. H. zu S-C-G, S522; Marche heroïque, S510; Huldigungsmarsch, S228; Ungarischer Marsch
zur Krönungsfeier in Ofen-Pest, S523; Siegesmarsch, S233*a*; Ungarischer Geschwindmarsch,
S233; Vom Fels zum Meer, S229; Bülow-Marsch, S230; Kunstlerfestzug zur Schillerfeier, S520;
Rákóczy March, S244*b*/1. **Leslie Howard** (pf). Hyperion Ⓕ CDA66811/2 (two discs: 146 minutes:
DDD: 1/95). Recorded 1993.
"Liszt's Marches have not so much had an unfair press as no press at all." So Howard affirms in his
(as always) invaluable insert-notes. Ten of the 12 'first recordings' included in these 14 pieces are in
fact marches conspicuous by their absence (save for the well-known *Rákóczy*, played here in a
dazzling transcription of the orchestral version) from most recital programmes. Some, as Howard
admits, are just "extrovert stuff", as jolly and four-square as Sousa. But several of the shorter ones
are spiced by unmistakable Hungarianisms. And one or two others make an indelible impression –
not least the Weimar-domiciled Liszt's tributes to this lovely town's two great literary sons, Goethe
and Schiller, on the occasion of their respective centenaries in 1849 and 1859: how tellingly, too, they
bear witness to the composer's own stylistic evolution in the course of that decade. Save for an
exquisitely tender, quasi-Wagnerian subsidiary subject, the much later tribute to his erstwhile
son-in-law, Hans von Bülow, nevertheless proves the disappointment Howard warns us to expect – in
part he attributes its failure to the two daily bottles of Cognac with which the ageing Liszt tried to
counter depression. The most haunting march of all is surely that enclosed like a trio in the
diabolically demanding *Scherzo and March* of 1851-54, which, with the menacing A minor *Galop* and
the two late *Csárdás* and *Mephisto Polka*, testifies to the lifelong inspiration he found in the macabre
– even on the dance-floor. But its brighter side is remembered too on this first of Vol. 28's two
generously filled discs. Howard surmounts innumerable hurdles with only the very occasional betrayal
of strain or loss of finesse, complementing clear-cut, sparkling fingers with powerful wrists. As
sometimes before, the piano emerges close, with just a touch of pluminess in tone quality. But it's
plainly what he wants.

Liszt Complete Solo Piano Music, Volume 29. Hungarian Themes and Rhapsodies, S242. **Leslie
Howard** (pf). Hyperion Ⓕ CDA66851/2 (two discs: 159 minutes: DDD: 4/95). Recorded 1993.
When listening to these 22 pieces, officially entitled *Magyar Dalok* and *Magyar Rapszódiák*, you at once
realize you've heard many a snatch of them before. And not surprisingly, for they are in fact the source
of most of what eventually emerged as Liszt's world-wide best-sellers, the *Hungarian Rhapsodies*. Liszt
revels in the lavishly decorative, cimbalom-coloured, improvisational style of the gipsies, in the process
making demands on the pianist variously described by Howard in his insert-notes as "devil-may-care,
frighteningly difficult, frenetic, hand-splitting" and so on. Whether due to Liszt's own waning interest
in platform pyrotechnics, or the fact that only he could really bring them off, simplification and formal
condensation seem to have been primary aims when recasting these first flings as *Hungarian Rhapsodies*.
But as Howard reveals, there are losses as well as gains in the maturer Liszt. Despite moments of
protracted rodomontade there is a vast amount to enjoy in the vibrant warmth and spontaneity of the
earlier set no less than in Howard's own generously open-hearted response to it.

Liszt Complete Solo Piano Music, Volume 30. **Leslie Howard** (pf). Hyperion Ⓕ CDA66861/2
(two discs: 153 minutes: DDD: 4/95). Recorded 1993.
Weber/Liszt Oberon – Overture, S574. **Mozart/Liszt** Fantasia on themes from Le nozze di
Figaro and Don Giovanni, S697. **Verdi/Liszt** Ernani Paraphrase, S432. Miserere du Trovatore,
S433. Rigoletto Paraphrase, S434. Réminiscences de Boccanegra, S438. **Donizetti/Liszt** Valse
de concert sur deux motifs du Lucia et Parisina, S214/3. **Meyerbeer/Liszt** Réminiscences de
Robert le diable – Cavatine; Valse infernale, S413. **Gounod/Liszt** Les Adieux – Reverie sur un
motif de Roméo et Juliette, S409. **Erkel/Liszt** Schwanengesang and Marsch from Hunyadi
László, S405. **Wagner/Liszt** Lohengrin – Elsa's Bridal Procession, S445/2; Three Pieces, S446.
Fantasy on themes from Rienzi, S439.

Liszt's operatic outings, ranging from literal transcriptions, such as the opening *Oberon* Overture, to the most free fantasias, like that on motives from *Rienzi* at the end of the disc. The sequence is artfully planned to provide the maximum contrast between Liszt as lion and dove, with four of the 16 items earmarked as "first recordings". Of these, the Gounod *Roméo et Juliette* Reverie is a tender, nocturne-like idyll that not for a second outstays its welcome. Liszt scholars may nevertheless be still more grateful for Howard's rescue of the other three, and first and foremost the nearly 22-minute long Fantasia on themes from *Le nozze di Figaro and Don Giovanni*, the "almost-complete" manuscript of which Howard has now himself completed for performance and publication. Though self-indulgently protracted (as Busoni surely realized when preparing his own shortened version), its thematic interweavings *en route* still take your breath away. With Verdi and Wagner we are on more familiar ground, where it goes without saying that Howard has formidable CD rivals. But throughout the disc there is a spaciousness in his characterization that far more often than not compensates for momentary technical strain or loss of finesse. His tonal range is certainly wide, ranging from the deep, dark, brooding intensity he finds for the *Ernani* and *Il trovatore* excerpts to his translucent delicacy in the upper reaches of Gounod's Reverie. Apart from a slight touch of metal above a certain dynamic level in the treble, the recorded sound quality can best be described in a nutshell as ripe.

New review

Liszt Complete Solo Piano Music, Volumes 32 and 33. The Schubert Transcriptions, Volumes 2 and 3. **Leslie Howard** (pf). Hyperion Ⓕ CDA66954/9 (two sets of three discs: 220 and 225 minutes: DDD: 10/95). Recorded 1994.
CDA66954/6 – Vier geistliche Lieder, S562. Mélodies hongroises after Schubert, S425a. Sechs Müllerlieder, S565. Meeresstille, S557b. Die Forelle, S564. Ständchen, S560/7a. Schwanengesang, S560. Frühlingsglaube, S557c. Winterreise, S561. Sechs Melodien, S563. Marche hongroise, S425/2iii.
CDA66957/9 – 12 Lieder, S558. Sechs Müllerlieder, S565bis. Die Nebensonnen, S561/2a. Schwanengesang, S560bis. Die Gestirne, S562/3bis. Meeresstille, S557b/6bis. Die Forelle, S563/6bis. Die Rose, S556ii. Lob der Thränen, S557. Lieder, S558bis. Meerestille, S558/5bis. Winterreise, S561bis. Marche hongroise, S425/2vi. Valse caprice No. 6, S427/6iii.

The Schubert transcriptions recorded here vary a great deal in style. Some, though not many, have the failures of taste that could afflict Liszt. The second version of *Die Forelle* becomes self-indulgent, and "Abschied" (from *Schwanengesang*) allows piano decoration to dazzle, rather than illuminate, the listener's appreciation. But such idiosyncrasies (to put it no more strongly) were part of Liszt's wide-ranging personality, one that kindled his century and bequeathed a wonderful legacy to ours. Time and again in these transcriptions he uses his musical understanding to re-interpret the musical invention, and to do so with perception and – a quality not always associated with Liszt – humility. *Die junge Nonne* is a devoted re-interpretation of a song that had a deep appeal for the Abbé in him; "Der Atlas" (from *Schwanengesang*) clearly spoke to a man who had known his share of the world's burdens; and one might even say that this enthusiastic lover had wry cause to be sympathetic to Gretchen's plight as she sits at her spinning-wheel grieving the loss of Faust. Many of the transcriptions, about which Leslie Howard writes in his notes with scholarly perception, take up a hint in the song, perhaps different hints for different versions, and use it to enhance the musical idea. Such is "Auf dem Wasser zu singen", which nearly goes over the top at the end. The second "Gretchen" setting does so at the start, by beginning with the breakdown that interrupts the song at the memory of Faust's kiss; but this can be seen in the context of nineteenth-century practice, when pianists would 'prelude' inventively before settling down to a performance. Among the many merits of the performances is the lack of showiness. Howard has the technical mastery to enable him to avoid over-emphasis. He seems to take the intelligent view that what he is playing is Liszt's response to a Schubert song, not the Schubert song itself. Hence some of the rubato, which would be unacceptable in the original song but can be a sensitive response to what Liszt has done. It is a fascinating anthology and it tells us much about one of the composers who, of any in history, knew the most about the actual making of music.

New review

Liszt Complete Solo Piano Works, Volume 34. Douze Grandes Etudes, S137. Morceau de salon, S142. **Leslie Howard** (pf). Hyperion Ⓕ CDA66973 (76 minutes: DDD: 10/95). Recorded 1994.
In this first recording of the concert version of the *Douze Grandes Etudes* (1837), Leslie Howard brings his customary technical wizardry to bear on this outrageously difficult music in an arresting virtuoso display that demonstrates Liszt's consummate skill at transforming musical material. Moreover, despite Liszt's exhortation that only the later revisions of the studies should be played, there is a great deal to recommend the 1837 set, as these performances attest. The extreme technical demands of these pieces have led to critical scorn, but the challenges they contain are not designed merely for display, but are the result of the composer's comprehensive exploitation of the piano's expressive capabilities. Saint-Saëns said that "in Art a difficulty overcome is a thing of beauty" and, in the present instance, Howard's triumph over the monumental difficulties posed by these pieces

compellingly reveals the astonishing beauty of Liszt's 'orchestral' use of tone colour and sparkling virtuosity.

Liszt Opera Transcriptions – Rigoletto (Verdi) – Paraphrase, S434. Lucia et Parisina (Donizetti) – Valse à capriccio, S401. Faust (Gounod) – Waltz, S407. Eugene Onegin (Tchaikovsky) – Polonaise, S429. Der Fliegende Holländer (Wagner) – Spinning Chorus, S440. Tannhäuser (Wagner) – Rezitativ und Romanze, S444. Lohengrin (Wagner) – Verweis an Elsa, S446. Tristan und Isolde (Wagner) – Liebestod, S447. Le nozze di Figaro (Mozart) – Fantasia, S697. **Jean-Yves Thibaudet** (pf). Decca Ⓕ 436 736-2DH (69 minutes: DDD: 2/94). Recorded 1992.

Surely no major composer ever did more to propagate the music of others than Liszt. But he was also a legendary virtuoso, not easily allowing himself to forget his own dazzling fingers in his innumerable transcriptions. In this operatic selection Jean-Yves Thibaudet artfully contrasts five of the more demonstrative kind with four in which faithfulness to the original text was Liszt's main concern – these latter, significantly, drawn from the music of his formidable son-in-law to be, Richard Wagner. The filigree delicacy of Thibaudet's effortlessly brilliant finger-work is very impressive, not least in the decorative flights of the first three Verdi, Donizetti and Gounod items. Sometimes it suggests the trickles of scintillating fairy lights in the sky after the bursting of a rocket, sometimes the liquidity of water itself though still with each note retaining its own pinpoint glisten. In the earlier Wagner items Thibaudet matches Wagner's comparative simplicity with a similar concern for the unadorned truth, again, with his light pedalling, drawing sounds of ear-catching translucency from the keyboard's upper reaches. He finds the full, close-woven intensity of the "Liebestod" harder to sustain but the piece is finely shaped as a whole. The recital ends heartily with the less frequently heard *Figaro* Fantasia completed in 1912 by no less a man than Busoni.

New review

Liszt Excelsior!, S666. Am Grabe Richard Wagners, S267. Harmonies poétiques et réligieuses, S173 – Funérailles (trans. Kynaston). Two Recital Pieces, S268 – No. 2, Trauerode. Orpheus, S98. Fantasia and Fugue, S259, "Ad nos, ad salutarem undam". **Nicolas Kynaston** (org). IMP Masters Ⓕ 30366 0003-2 (75 minutes: DDD: 7/96). Played on the Klais organ of Ingolstadt, Münster, Germany. Recorded 1994. *Gramophone Editor's choice.*   Ⓖ

As one of the wonders of the organ world the Ingolstadt Klais has frequently been the focus of record producers' attention. Similarly Liszt's organ music is no stranger to the catalogues, while Nicolas Kynaston has an impressive discography to his credit. Certainly we have here all the ingredients of a splendid release. It's not merely splendid, though: this disc is a true colossus among organ recordings. The instrument's vast dynamic range positively luxuriates in a sumptuous acoustic, vividly captured by a recording of true demonstration quality. Here's one to impress neighbours and friends with, whether or not they (or you, for that matter) enjoy organ music. Sometimes the Liszt of seemingly endless transcriptions and small programmatic organ pieces can pall, but it's in these very pieces – not least Kynaston's own perceptive transcription of "Funérailles" – that the real strengths of this disc lie and there is a thrilling account of the great *Ad nos*. Kynaston handles the organ with matchless sensitivity, continually conjuring up ravishing sounds and making these performances intensely pleasurable. His astute interpretative insight reveals every bar of music with utter conviction.

Liszt Fantasia and Fugue, "Ad nos, ad salutarem undam", S259. Variations on "Weinen, Klagen, Sorgen, Zagen", S673. Evocation à la Chapelle Sixtine, S658. Prelude and Fugue on the name B-A-C-H, S260. **Thomas Trotter** (org). Decca Ⓕ 440 283-2DH (72 minutes: DDD: 10/94). Played on the Ladegast organ of the Dom Merseburg, Germany. ✒ Recorded 1992.

Trotter's earlier recording of the Liszt *B-A-C-H* was the 1870 revision, for over a century regarded as the definitive version of the work. In fact there are two organ versions and two piano versions of this piece: Trotter's new recording is of the 1855 original version for organ played on the instrument much admired by Liszt where it was first heard, coupled with the *Ad nos* which was also premièred there. Anyone who is familiar with the 1870 revision of the *Prelude and Fugue on the name B-A-C-H* is in for some surprises – pedal cadenzas at 0'50" and 2'40" followed by a longer *maestoso* section (weaker) leading to the fugue (indistinct here in the low register opening). Cuts made for the 1870 revision around 6'57" surely improved it. Trotter is a compelling advocate and the organ of the Dom Merseburg is authentic right down to the clatter from the mechanical action and some wobble in the wind supply as the instrument copes with Liszt's piano writing at 8'42". Liszt's *Variations on "Weinen, Klagen"*, stemming from his reverence for the chromatic aspects of Bach, are often admired. In practice the work is difficult to sustain and sags even in Trotter's performance. The *Ad nos* is the big test and here Trotter is consistently reliable, and musical, with a fine sense of timbre, if slightly lacking in flair. Breaking the flow in the fugue (at 3'30", 4'53" and 6'34") holds up what one has come to regard as the work's final ineluctable sweep. Trotter as usual has absolutely no technical problems and he (and the engineers) make the organ sound truly magnificent. No wonder Liszt was impressed!

New review

Liszt Ihr Glocken von Marling, S328. Im Rhein, im schönen Strome, S272. Bist du!, S277. Vergiftet sind meine Lieder, S289. Jugendglück, S323. Freudvoll und leidvoll, S280. Wilhelm Tell, S292 – Der Fischerknabe; Der Hirt, Der Alpenjäger. Die drei Zigeuner, S320. Der Glückliche, S334.

Kling leise, mein Lied, S301. Die Macht der Musik, S302. Wer nie sein Brot mit Tranen ass, S297. Ich möchte hingehn, S296. Die Vätergruft, S281. Ich scheide, S319. Uber allen Gipfeln ist Ruh, S306 (Wanderers Nachtlied II). **Philip Langridge** (ten); **John Constable** (pf). Unicorn-Kanchana Ⓕ DKPCD9162 (71 minutes: DDD: 2/96). Recorded 1995.

Liszt's songs, a much underrated part of his output, find a most sympathetic interpreter in Philip Langridge. He has the intelligence and poetic sensibility to appreciate their very varied nature, and indeed without such qualities no singer is likely to make very much of them. He even comes close to persuading this listener that the setting of Goethe's *Wanderers Nachtlied* is a fair response to one of the most famous and exquisite lyrics in the German language, but not even his elegance of line can justify the interminable repetitions of the ending. Never mind: there is much here that is well chosen from quite a long list, and Langridge shows a striking ability to enter the world of each song and think it through with real perception. He can colour the graceful melodies of *Bist du!* and *Kling leise* with a sweetness of tone that is exactly judged to match his smooth line; he can, appropriately, seem to poison this for *Vergiftet sind meine Lieder* and darken it for *Die Vätergruft*; he can characterize the three gipsies colourfully (with Constable strutting out the proud Hungarian cadences); he can produce a remarkable burst of power for *Jugendglück*. Only in *Der Alpenjäger* does he seem rather overwhelmed, careful as John Constable is at all times to do justice to Liszt's piano sonorities without unleashing too much sheer volume. Theirs is a sensitive partnership, and Constable is scrupulous in judging when the piano is supportive, when almost contradictory, when independent and when the soloist.

Additional recommendations ...

...Die Vätergruft, S281. Go not, happy day, S335. Es rauschen die Winde, S294. Ihr Auge, S310. Uber allen Gipfeln ist Ruh, S306. Am Rhein, in schönen Strome, S272. Es muss ein Wunderbares sein, S314. Vergiftet sind meine Lieder, S289. La Tombe et la rose, S285. Comment, dissaient-ils, S276. Oh! quand je dors, S282. **Wagner** Mignonne. Tout n'est qu'images fugitives. Les Deux grenadiers. Faust Lieder, Op. 5 – No. 4, Es war einmal ein König; No. 5, Was machst du mir. Der Tannenbaum. **Berlioz** Mélodies Irlande, Op. 2 – No. 1, Le Coucher du soleil, revêrie; No. 4, La Belle voyageuse; No. 7, L'origine de la harpe; No. 8, Adieu, Bessy; No. 9, Elégie en prose. **Thomas Hampson** (bar); **Geoffrey Parsons** (pf). EMI Ⓕ CDC5 55047-2 (77 minutes: DDD: 5/94).

...Freudvoll und leidvoll, S280. Uber allen Gipfeln ist Ruh. Mignons Lied I, S275. Der du von dem Himmel bist, S279. *Coupled with works by* **Wolf, Cornelius** *and* **Wagner** Dame Margaret Price (sop); **Graham Johnson** (pf). Forlane UCD16728 (71 minutes: DDD: 2/95). *See review in the Collections section; refer to the Index to Reviews.*

Further listening ...

...Totentanz. **Weber** Invitation to the Dance. **Rachmaninov** The isle of the dead, Op. 29. **Ravel** Pavane pour une infante défunte. Rapsodie espagnole. **Chicago Symphony Orchestra / Fritz Reiner.** RCA Victor Living Stereo 09026 61250-2 (4/93).

...Mephisto Waltz No. 1, S514, "Der Tanz in der Dorfschenke". *Coupled with works by* **Prokofiev** *and* **Khachaturian** William Kapell (pf). RCA Victor Gold Seal mono GD60921* (5/95). Ⓖ

...Grand duo concertant on Lafont's "Le marin", S128[a]. La lugubre gondola, S134[a]. Soirées de Vienne – Valse caprice d'après Schubert in A minor, S427 (trans. Oistrakh)[a]. Erlkönig, S558 No. 4[a]. *Coupled with works by* **Ernst** *and* **Schubert** Gidon Kremer (vn); [a]**Oleg Maisenberg** (pf). DG 445 820-2GH (10/95). *See review under Ernst; refer to the Index to Reviews.*

...Romance oubliée, S132. Elégies – No. 1, S130; No. 2, S131. Die Zelle in Nonnenwerth, S382. La lugubre gondola, S134. *Coupled with works by* **Grieg** *and* **Rubinstein** Steven Isserlis (vc); **Stephen Hough** (pf). RCA Victor Red Seal 09026 68290-2 (4/96). *See review under Grieg; refer to the Index to Reviews.*

...Elégies – No. 1, S130; No. 2, S131. La lugubre gondola, S134. *Coupled with works by* **Janáček** *and* **Kodály** Anne Gastinel (vc); Pierre-Laurent Aimard (pf). Auvidis Valois V4748 (9/95). *See review under Janáček; refer to the Index to Reviews.*

...Harmonies poétiques et religieuses, S173. **Hugh Tinney** (pf). Meridian CDE84240 (7/93).

...Beethoven Symphonies, S464. **Leslie Howard** (pf). Hyperion CDA66671/5 (9/93).

...Romance oubliée, S132[a]. *Coupled with* **Berlioz.** Harold in Italy[a]. **Gounod** Hymne à Sainte Cécile, S491. **Meyerbeer** Le Moine, S416. Festmarsch zu Schillers Jähriger Geburtsfeier, S549. **Leslie Howard** (pf); [a]**Paul Coletti** (va). Hyperion CDA66683 (11/93).

...Variations on a Waltz by Diabelli, S147. Waltz in A major, S208[a]. Variations on a Theme from Méhul's "Joseph", S147a. Eight Variations, S148. Variations brillantes on a Theme by Rossini, S149. Impromptu brillant on themes by Rossini and Spontini, S150. Allegro di bravura, S151. Rondi di bravura, S152. Etude en douze exercices, S136. Scherzo in G minor, S153. Hungarian Recruiting Dances (Zum Andenken), S241. Waltz in E flat major, S209a. Galop de bal, S220. Marche hongroise in E flat minor, S233b. Klavierstücke in A flat major, S189a. Liebesträume No. 2, "Gestorben war ich", S192a. Berceuse, S174. Feuille d'Album (Albumblatt) in E major, S164. Feuille d'Album in A minor, S167. Feuilles d'Album in A flat major, S165. Apparitions, S155. **Leslie Howard** (pf). Hyperion CDA66771/2 (7/94).

...Complete Solo Piano Music, Volume 30 – **Weber/Liszt** Oberon – Overture, S574. **Mozart/Liszt** Fantasia on themes from Le nozze di Figaro and Don Giovanni, S697. **Verdi/Liszt** Ernani Paraphrase, S432. Miserere del Trovatore, S433. Rigoletto Paraphrase, S434. Réminiscences de Boccanegra, S438. **Donizetti/Liszt** Valse de concert sur deux motifs du Lucia et Parisina, S214/3. **Meyerbeer/Liszt** Réminiscences de Robert le diable – Cavatine; Valse infernale, S413. **Gounod/Liszt** Les Adieux – Reverie sur un motif de Roméo et Juliette, S409. **Erkel/Liszt** Schwanengesang and Marsch from Hunyadi László, S405. **Wagner/Liszt** Lohengrin – Elsa's Bridal Procession, S445 No. 2; Three Pieces, S446. Fantasy on themes from Rienzi, S439. **Leslie Howard** (pf). Hyperion CDA66861/2 (4/95).

...Complete Solo Piano Music, Volume 31. The Schubert Transcriptions – Soirées de Vienne: Valses caprices, S427. Mélodies hongroises (Divertissement à l'hongroise), S425. Two Transcriptions for Sophie Menter. Three Marches, S426. Marche militaire, S426*a*. Ave Maria, S557*d*. La sérénade, S559*a*. Erlkönig, S557*a*. Die Rose, S556*i*. Der Gondelfahrer, S559. **Leslie Howard** (pf). Hyperion CDA66951/3 (8/95).

..."Weinen, Klagen, Sorgen, Zagen", Präludium, S179. *Coupled with works by* **Wagner/Liszt, Haydn** and **Chopin** Vladimir Horowitz (pf). Sony Classical SK45818 (8/90). *See review in the Collections section; refer to the Index to Reviews.* ⒼⒼⒼ

...Liebestraum No. 3. *Coupled with works by* **Busoni, Liszt, Debussy, Mendelssohn, Schumann, Chopin, Scriabin, Rachmaninov** and **Weber** Anatol Ugorski (pf). DG 447 105-2GH (3/96). *See review in the Collections section; refer to the Index to Reviews.*

Antonio Literes
Spanish 1673-1747

Suggested listening ...

...Ah del rustico pastor. *Coupled with works by* **C. Galán, J. de Torres, F. de Iribarren, F. Valls,** and **Anonymous** Al Ayre Español / Eduardo López Banzo. Deutsche Harmonia Mundi 05472 77325-2 (8/95). ✒ *See review in the Collections section; refer to the Index to Reviews.* Ⓖ

...Azis y Galatea – Seguidillas; Confiado gilguerillo; Monstruo, en quien ha sobrado; Pues del culto mi peidad; Coplas. Los elementos – Deydades que en el monte; Ay amor; Mas si fuese la planta fugitiva. El estrago en la fineza, o Jupiter y Semele – Pues soy abejuela; Yo he de enmudecer; Ven dulcissimo bien. *Coupled with works by* **Durón** and **Martín y Coll** Al Ayre Español / Eduardo López Banzo. Deutsche Harmonia Mundi 05472 77336-2 (62 minutes: DDD: 1/96). ✒ *See review under Durón; refer to the Index to Reviews.* Ⓖ

Henry Litolff
British/French 1818-1891

Suggested listening ...

...Concerto symphonique No. 4 in D minor, Op. 102 – Scherzo. *Coupled with works by* **Rachmaninov, Addinsell** and **Gottschalk** Cristina Ortiz (pf); **Royal Philharmonic Orchestra / Moshe Atzmon.** Decca 414 348-2DH (9/86). *See review in the Collections section; refer to the Index to Reviews.* Ⓖ

...Concerto symphonique No. 4 in D minor, Op. 102 – Scherzo[ab]. *Coupled with* **Bruckner** Overture in G minor[d]. **Haydn** Symphony No. 45 in F sharp minor, "Farewell"[b]. **Bach** Brandenburg Concerto No. 3 in G major, BWV1048[c]. **Schubert** Symphony No. 8 in B minor, D759[b], "Unfinished". **Rachmaninov** (arr. Wood) Prelude in C sharp minor, Op. 3 No. 2[e] . **Beethoven** Symphony No. 5 in C minor, Op. 67[d]. **Brahms** Variations on a Theme by Haydn, Op. 56*a*, "St Antoni"[d]. **Dvořák** Symphonic Variations, B70[d]. [a]**Irene Scharrer** (pf); [b]**London Symphony Orchestra;** [c]**British Symphony Orchestra;** [d]**Queen's Hall Orchestra;** [e]**symphony orchestra / Sir Henry Wood.** Dutton Laboratories mono 2CDAX2002* (9/94).

...Concerto symphonique No. 4 in D minor, Op. 102 – Scherzo[b]. *Coupled with* **Brahms** Piano Concerto No. 1 in D minor, Op. 15[a]. **Franck** Symphonic Variations[b]. **Sir Clifford Curzon** (pf); [a]**London Symphony Orchestra / George Szell;** [b]**London Philharmonic Orchestra / Sir Adrian Boult.** Decca The Classic Sound 425 082-2DCS (4/95). *See review under Brahms; refer to the Index to Reviews. Gramophone classical 100.* ⒼⒼⒼ

George Lloyd
British 1913-

Lloyd Iernin. **Marilyn Hill Smith** (sop) Iernin; **Geoffrey Pogson** (ten) Gerent; **Henry Herford** (bar) Edryn; **Malcolm Rivers** (bass-bar) Bedwyr; **Jonathon Robarts** (bass) Priest; **Jeremy White** (bass) Saxon Thane; **Stephen Jackson** (bar) Huntsman; **Claire Powell** (mez) Cunaide; **BBC Singers and Concert Orchestra / George Lloyd.** Albany Ⓜ TROY121/3 (three discs: 173 minutes: ADD: 9/94). Notes and text included. Also includes an interview with George Lloyd. Recorded 1985.

The heart goes out to this opera. Some of the causes may be suspect. Perhaps it is sentimental to allow knowledge of the composer's age at the time of writing (George Lloyd was 21) to influence one's response, but it does. Then there is the pleasure of seeing the work which enjoyed so much success followed by such complete neglect convincingly revived, with the composer, now as conductor, renewing acquaintance with his own music half a century later. At the London première in 1935 *The Times* found the opera "spontaneous in invention and almost consistently effective ... the only exception [being] the choral writing which, conceived along unusual lines and largely unisonous, does not quite achieve the composer's intentions and might well be revised". Whether the hint was taken we are not told, but the score has not been revised for this performance, and most of the choral writing (not all that "unisonous") works well. More important is the writing for soloists, and on the whole this seems instinctively expert: for instance, the high notes are sparingly required, so that when they occur they have maximum effect. The heroine's role wants a coloratura soprano who also has a substantial middle and lower-middle register. That should not be too much to ask, but one can only guess at the kind of Italianate full-bodied sound that was probably in the composer's ear when he wrote the work. Marilyn Hill-Smith is more successful with the higher, more agile and less dramatic parts of the role. All the male principals have splendidly singable music, but the best performance comes from Claire Powell, sumptuous of voice and noble of manner.

Further listening ...

...Piano Concerto No. 3. **Kathryn Stott** (pf); **BBC Philharmonic Orchestra / George Lloyd.** Albany TROY019-2 (3/90).

...Symphonies – No. 2; No. 9. **BBC Philharmonic Orchestra / George Lloyd.** Albany TROY055-2 (6/87).

...Symphonies – No. 6[a]; No. 10, "November Journeys"[b]. John Socman – Overture[a]. [b]**BBC Philharmonic Brass**; [a]**BBC Philharmonic Orchestra / George Lloyd.** Albany TROY015-2 (8/89).

...A Symphonic Mass. **Brighton Festival Chorus; Bournemouth Symphony Orchestra / George Lloyd.** Albany TROY100-2 (12/93). *Gramophone Editor's choice.*

...The Vigil of Venus. **Carolyn James** (sop); **Thomas Booth** (ten); **Welsh National Opera Chorus and Orchestra / George Lloyd.** Albany TROY170-2 (1/96).

...John Socman – Act 1 scenes 1 and 2; Act 2 scene 1; Act 3. **Soloists; London Voices; Trinity Boys' Choir; Philharmonia Orchestra / George Lloyd.** Albany TROY131-2 (1/95).

Sir Andrew Lloyd Webber
British 1948-

Suggested listening ...

...Sunset Boulevard. **Original London cast.** Polydor 519 767-2.

Duarte Lôbo
Portuguese c1565-1646

Suggested listening ...

...Missa pro defunctis a 8. Audivi vocem de caelo. Pater peccavi. *Coupled with* **M. Cardoso** Missa Regina caeli. Sitivit anima mea. Tulerunt lapides. Non mortui. **The Sixteen / Harry Christophers.** Collins Classics Ⓕ 1407-2 (63 minutes: DDD: 8/94).

...Missa Pro defunctis a 6. Missa Vox clamantis. **The Tallis Scholars / Peter Phillips.** Gimell CDGIM028 (3/93).

...Audivi vocem da caelo. Pater peccavi. *Coupled with* **Cardoso** Lamentatio. Magnificat secundi toni. **Magalhães** Vidi acquam. Missa O soberana luz. Commissa mea pavesco. **Fonseca** Beata viscera. **Trosylho** Circumdederunt me. **Escobar** Clamabat autem mulier. **Ars Nova / Bo Holten.** Naxos 8 553310 (3/96).

Pietro Locatelli
Italian 1695-1764

New review

Locatelli 10 Sonatas, Op. 8. **Locatelli Trio** (Elizabeth Wallfisch, vn; Richard Tunnicliffe, vc, Paul Nicholson, hpd); **Rachel Isserlis** (vn). Hyperion Ⓕ CDA67021/2 (two discs: 116 minutes: DDD: 8/96). ✏

There is a sense of the decadent about the music of Locatelli. His style is essentially post-Corellian, but with the broad lines fragmented into shorter ones, an excess of sequences and cadences, an almost mechanical handling of forms, and the element of virtuosity hugely inflated with a great deal of violinistic cliché. But decadence, we all know, can be quite fun, and it would be an austere spirit that took little pleasure in these sonatas and especially the playing of them here. This two-disc set of his Op. 8 (published in 1744) contains six violin sonatas and four trio sonatas, three for two violins and continuo and one using the much less common combination of violin, cello and continuo. The violin sonatas each begin with a slow movement, mostly very elaborate in line (though some, Nos. 2 and 6 for example, have hints of Corellian nobility). The second movements are all rapid and energetic pieces, binary in form, full of very busy figurative writing, often with lots of double-stopping (try No. 3 for some high-level virtuoso playing) and occasionally very tortuous in manner. A number of them then have a slowish movement and most end with a quick triple-metre piece, again in brilliant violinistic style (some with a slower *minore* middle section). The most attractive was No. 5, with its interesting gestures and hints of wit in the second movement. The most demanding is No. 6 with its final minuet with variations, quite breathtaking (and improbably set in E flat, a perverse gesture): here

Elizabeth Wallfisch clambers unruffled through the technical thickets, which include an extraordinary variation with trills on one string and moving parts on another and dashes from one end of the compass to the other and back again, and much more besides. This is amazing violin playing of a kind of virtuosity rarely heard from a period instrument player: there is not a note out of tune on this disc, and there is a sustained musical intensity, partly arising from the technical pressure, which is quite remarkable. The three trio sonatas for two violins are not of course virtuoso music in quite the same way, and musically not generally very inventive. The Third, in F minor, is quite a sombre piece, and the finales of all three are little gems of wit and inventiveness, with unpredictable gestures and the instruments chasing one another and dashing around amusingly. The Sonata for violin and cello is distinct from the rest, with a much more *galant* style in the opening movement and a set of variations in which different kinds of echoing phrases between the instruments are imaginatively used. The performances are altogether admirable; no one who admires good violin playing will want to miss Elizabeth Wallfisch's crisp, rhythmic playing, her precise articulation or her impeccable intonation or indeed her general command of the style and expressive content of this music.

New review

Locatelli Sonata a tre, Op. 5 – No. 1 in G major[a]; No. 2 in E minor[b]; No. 3 in E major[c]; No. 4 in C major[d]; No. 5 in D minor[e]; No. 6 in G major[f]. **Musica ad Rhenum** (Jed Wentz, [bce]Marion Moonen, fls; Norbert Kunst, bn; [adf]Manfred Kraemer, vn; Balázs Máté, vc; Marcelo Bussi, [f]Ulrike Wild, hpds). Vanguard Classics Ⓜ 99087 (63 minutes: DDD: 7/96).

Founded in 1991, Musica ad Rhenum are making a name for themselves by recording, stylishly and with panache, music of mainstream baroque composers. Rehearsing in a Utrecht canal house on the Old Rhine, they have developed a lively, serious, if occasionally controversial and self-consciously musicological approach to music that others have rather taken for granted. Here, then, is an entire CD devoted to Locatelli's trio sonatas, performed with alternating ensembles, of two flutes and flute with violin, and continuo. The forms Locatelli employed vary from *chiesa* and *camera* movements to rondos and a pastorale complete with nasal drone. The antiphonal final sonata is performed with two delightfully contrasted ensembles (accompanied by two matching harpsichords) of flute with bassoon and violin with cello. So what is particularly interesting about these performances? They are fresh and warm and expressively articulated. They wear their scholarship lightly. There is a clarity about everything these players do in terms of texture, rhythm – Locatelli provides them with lots of Lombard snaps and hemiolas – and metre: Musica ad Rhenum exercise particular pride in the liberties they take with the latter, bending phrases, stretching cadences and revelling in silence. With the exception of the unusually extended, pulsing final appoggiatura of the E major *Largo* (No. 3), they bring them off with conviction. They are an ensemble of spirited virtuosos who play together sympathetically and with precision.

Further listening ...

...12 Concerti grossi, Op. 1. **Raglan Baroque Players / Elizabeth Wallfisch** (vn), **Nicholas Kraemer** (hpd/org). Hyperion CDA66981/2 (1/96).

...Concerti grossi – Op. 1: C minor; D major; G minor; Op. 7: E flat major, "Il pianto d'Arianna". Sinfonia in F minor, "Composta per le esequie della sua Donna che si celebrarono in Roma". **Europa Galante / Fabio Biondi** (vn). Opus 111 OPS30-104 (1/96).

...12 Concertos, Op. 3, "L'Arte del Violino". **Elizabeth Wallfisch** (vn); **Raglan Baroque Players / Nicholas Kraemer.** Hyperion CDA66721/3 (1/95). 🖉

...Introduttioni Teatrali and Concerti, Op. 4 – No. 12 in F major. *Coupled with works by* **Leo, Torelli, Mossi** and **Valentini Cologne Musica Antiqua / Reinhard Goebel.** Archiv Produktion 435 393-2AH (9/92). 🖉 *See review in the Collections section; refer to the Index to Reviews.*

Matthew Locke
British 1621-1677

New review

Locke Consort of Fower Parts[d] – Suite in D minor/major; Suite in F major. Consort "ffor seaverall ffriends" – A minor[d]. The Flatt Consort, "for my cousin Kemble" – Six Dances in B flat major[d]. Voluntaries[b] – F major; A minor; A minor. Harpsichord Suite in C major[c]. Prelude in C major[c]. Urania to Parthenissa, "In a soft vision of the night"[ad]. Divinest syren, cruel fair[ad]. Lucinda winke, or vaile those eyes[ad]. Bone Jesu verbum Patris[ad]. [a]**Rachel Platt** (sop); [d]**John Holloway** (vn); **Gary Cooper** ([b]org/[c]hpd); [d]**Concordia / Mark Levy.** Dervorguilla Ⓟ DRVCD108 (68 minutes: DDD: 3/96). 🖉 Texts included. Recorded 1993.

Mark Levy, director of Concordia, makes a point of inviting distinguished artists such as Laurence Dreyfus, and now John Holloway and Gary Cooper, to appear with his consort of viols. Certainly John Holloway brings eloquence and spirit to these performances, but Gary Cooper is the hero of the CD, perfectly shadowing Rachel Platt's narrative singing in *Urania to Parthenissa* and enriching her interpretations of the other Locke songs, and then emerging as the accomplished, poised soloist in the harpsichord and organ pieces. Pride of place in this disc must go jointly to Cooper's virtuoso performance of the Harpsichord Suite in C, for the colours, resonance and command of complex textures, rhythms and ornamentation, and Concordia's of the sixth suite *ffor seaverall ffriends* which is framed by the rhetorical Pavan and the cryptic Jigg with its closing benediction, enhanced as elsewhere by Cooper. A number of Locke's works appear uniquely on this CD, which will lend it interest for those with a passion for seventeenth-century English music.

New review

Locke Psyche. **Catherine Bott** (sop) Venus, Prosperine; **Christopher Robson** (alto) Pyracmon, River God, Apollo; **Andrew King** (ten) Chief Priest, Praesul; **Paul Agnew** (ten) Vulcan, Mars; **Michael George** (bass) Pan, Brontes, Pluto; **Simon Grant** (bass) Envy, Steropes, Bacchus; **Julia Gooding, Helen Parker** (sops); **Julian Podger** (ten); **New London Consort Chorus; New London Consort / Philip Pickett.** L'Oiseau-Lyre Ⓟ 444 336-2OH (77 minutes: DDD: 2/96). ✒ Notes and text included. Recorded 1994. *Gramophone Editor's choice.* Ⓖ

This is an important recording of a major landmark in the brief but kaleidoscopic history of early English 'opera'. Philip Pickett and Peter Holman have reconstituted the dances by arranging a selection of Draghi's keyboard works and the results are stunning. Pickett is in his element when there is a code to crack and when his eager imagination can be exercised alongside a keen knowledge of seventeenth-century performance practices. His colourful choice of instruments (very little specific information is found in the score) seems so appropriate to the proceedings, and he skilfully manipulates that paradoxical blend of intimate declamation and grand gesture. Much of *Psyche* is surprisingly atmospheric, despite the fact that the music is less harmonically daring or melodically interesting than some of Locke's earlier works, and Pickett's solo singers are superb advocates in their efforts to get to the heart of the text. Catherine Bott is the equal of the exquisite symphony which marks Venus's descent in Act 1, and Michael George, Christopher Robson and Paul Agnew are all expert and memorable in their multifarious guises. Particularly enjoyable is Vulcan's leading of the Cyclopes in song at the forge, involving the majority of the troupe complete with clanking anvils. Indeed, the Chorus of the New London Consort have a field-day. Singing in their typically glowing and homogeneous fashion (only once or twice is intonation less than perfect), they are given some charming music, not least the "Nymphs' Chorus" at the outset, where the gentle lilt provides the perfect contrast for great Psyche's entrance. There are many details to admire here but the greatest achievement is the overall conception which, even when the music is less than inspired, maintains its shape and celebrates the unique spirit of English opera. An enterprising project of the very highest order.

Further listening ...

...Sacred Choral Music – Descende caelo cincta sororibus (The Oxford Ode). How doth the city sit solitary. Super flumina Babylonis. O be joyful in the Lord, all ye lands. Audi, Domine, clamantes ad te. Lord let me know mine end. Jesu auctor clementie. Be Thou exalted, Lord. **New College Choir, Oxford; The Parley of Instruments / Edward Higginbottom** with **Peter Holman** (org). Hyperion CDA66373 (9/91). ✒

Charles Martin Loeffler
French/American 1861-1935

Suggested listening ...

...Two Rhapsodies. *Coupled with* **Nielsen** Wind Quintet, FS100. **Prokofiev** Quintet in G minor, Op. 39. **Chamber Music Northwest / David Shifrin** (cl). Delos DE3136 (12/93).

...Quatre poèmes, Op. 5. *Coupled with works by* **A. Busch, Brahms, R. Strauss, Marx, Dargomïzhsky, Reutter** and **Gounod** Mitsuko Shirai (mez); Tabea Zimmermann (va); Hartmut Höll (pf). Capriccio 10 462 (9/95). *See review in the Collections section; refer to the Index to Reviews.* Ⓖ

Frank Loesser
American 1910-1969

Suggested listening ...

...Guys and Dolls. **Original 1992 Broadway revival cast.** RCA Victor 09026-61317-2 (10/92).

... Hans Christian Anderson – musical film. *Coupled with works by* **Gounod, Grieg, Britten** and **Saint-Saëns** Soloists; Boston Pops Orchestra / Arthur Fiedler. RCA Victor Living Stereo 09026 68131-2 (12/95).

Carl Loewe
German 1796-1869

New review

Loewe Der Asra, Op. 133. Der Wirthin Töchterlein, Op. 1 No. 2. Die Überfahrt, Op. 94 No. 1. Der seltne Beter, Op. 141. Gesammelte Lieder, Gesänge, Romanzen und Balladen, Op. 9 – Bauernregel; Graf Eberstein; Der alte Goethe. Fridericus Rex, Op. 61 No. 1. Der gefangene Admiral, Op. 115. Gruss vom Meere, Op. 103 No. 1. Mein Geist ist trüb, Op. 5 No. 5, Hebräische Gesänge, Op. 13 – No. 4, Jordans Ufer; No. 6, Die Sonne der Schlaflosen. Legenden, Op.75 – No. 2, Der Weichdorn;

No. 4, Das Wunder auf der Flucht. Ich bin ein guter Hirte. Das dunkle Auge. **Dietrich Fischer-Dieskau** (bar); **Hartmut Höll** (pf). Teldec Ⓜ 4509-97458-2 (52 minutes: DDD: 12/95). Texts and translations included. From 8 43753 (12/88). Recorded 1987.

Until his retirement Fischer-Dieskau remained a remarkable explorer. Happily, this recording was made in the late 1980s, just in time to catch his voice still in a good state of preservation. Though not a second Schubert, Loewe is an underrated song-writer, as each disc of his music that comes along predictably reminds us. Fischer-Dieskau starts with *Der seltne Beter*, a typical Loewe ballad about old warriors and castles, but how powerfully the story is told, punching home the climax just as effectively as Schubert did in his *Erlkönig*. From there the programme moves on to a well-chosen mixture of shorter ballads and genuine Lieder, extremes of mood and style sitting side by side. (Fischer-Dieskau often planned his live recitals for maximum contrast and Hartmut Höll, his accompanist here, fully lives up to the challenge.) The baritone brings a splendid panache to the story-telling of the ballads, but there is also some touchingly gentle singing, as in *Der Weichdorn*, the tale of Mary and the hawthorn – pure charm, from Loewe and Fischer-Dieskau alike. The disc lasts 52 minutes, not 70 as stated on the jewel-box.

Further listening ...

...Archibald Douglas, Op. 128. Der heilige Franziskus, Op. 75 No. 3. Herr Oluf, Op. 2 No. 2. Kaiser Ottos Weihnachtsfeier, Op. 121 No. 1. Lieder, Op. 145 – Meeresleuchten; Der Feind; Im Sturme; Heimlichkeit; Reiterlied. Der Mönch zu Pisa, Op. 114. Odins Meeresritt, Op. 118. Der Pilgrim vor St Just, Op. 99 No. 3. Der Räuber, Op. 34 No. 2. Traumlicht. Die Uhr, Op. 123 No. 3. **Cornelius Hauptmann** (bass); **Klaus Melber** (pf). Bayer BR100038 (5/90).

Frederick Loewe
German/American 1901-1988

Suggested listening ...

...Brigadoon. **Soloists; Ambrosian Chorus; London Sinfonietta / John McGlinn.** EMI CDC7 54481-2 (1/93).

...My Fair Lady – original film soundtrack. Sony SK66711 (5/95).

Simon Lole
British 1957-

Suggested listening ...

...This is the Day. The St David's Service. Angels. Vesper Responsory. The St Nicholas Service. An Evening Hymn. I will lift up mine eyes. O God the Holy Spirit. The Father's Love. Shall we not love thee, Mother dear?. I got me Flowers. The St Mary's Service. Love Eternal. **Traditional** (arr. Lole) Mary's Child. Morning Star. Child of the Manger. The Journey. Jesus, good above all other. **St Mary Collegiate Church Choir, Warwick / Simon Lole** with **Kevin Bowyer** (org). Regent REGCD107 (3/94).

Frank London
American 1958-

Suggested listening ...

...(arr. Stewart) Shvitz Suite. *Coupled with works by* **H. Hancock, Shemaria, J. Nelson, Babbitt, Van Vliet, Wheeler, Zappa** and **Stravinsky Meridian Arts Ensemble.** Channel Classics Channel Crossings CCS8195 (4/96). *See review in the Collections section; refer to the Index to Reviews.*
Ⓖ

Zhou Long
20th Century Chinese

Suggested listening ...

...Song of the Ch'in. *Coupled with* **Hovhaness** Four Bagatelles, Op. 30. String Quartets – No. 1, Op. 8, "Jupiter"; No. 3, Op. 208 No. 1, "Reflections on my Childhood"; No. 4, Op. 208 No. 2, "The Ancient Tree". Suite from String Quartet No. 2 – Gamelan in Sosi Style; Spirit Murmur; Hymn. **Shanghai Quartet.** Delos Ⓕ DE3162 (69 minutes: DDD: 3/95). *See review under Hovhaness; refer to the Index to Reviews.*
ⓇⓇ

López
Spanish 16th century

Suggested listening ...

...Fantasia[a]. *Coupled with* **Narváez** Los seys libros del delphin – La canción del Emperador; Diferencias on "Guárdame las vacas"[a]. Paseavase el rey moro[a]. **Milán** El Maestro – Pavana II[a]. **Mudarra** Tres libros de musica en Cifras para vihuela – Pavana de Alexandre; Fantasia que contrahaze la harpa en la manera de Ludovico[a]. **Murcia** Cumbés[b]. Giga[b]. **Guerau** Poema harmonico – Canario; Marionas[b]. **Sanz** Instruccion de musica sobre la guitarra española – Canarios; Folías; Lantururú; Pavanas al ayre español[b]. **Sor** Thèmes variés et Douze Minuets, Op. 11 – Andante maestoso; Andante expressivo[b]. Introduction and Variations on a theme by Mozart, Op. 9[b]. **José Miguel Moreno** ([a]vihuela/[b]gtr). Glossa GCD920103 (8/95). ✎

Albert Lortzing
German 1801-1851

New review

Lortzing Der Wildschütz. **Gottfried Hornik** (bar) Count Eberbach; **Doris Soffel** (mez) Countess Eberbach; **Peter Schreier** (ten) Baron Kronthal; **Edith Mathis** (sop) Baroness Kronthal; **Gertrud von Ottenthal** (mez) Nanette; **Hans Sotin** (bass) Baculus; **Georgine Resick** (sop) Gretchen; **Reiner Süss** (bar) Pancratius; **Bernd Riedel** (bar) Guest; **Berlin Radio Chorus and Children's Choir; Berlin Staatskapelle / Bernhard Klee**. Berlin Classics Ⓔ 0011 432BC (two discs: 152 minutes: ADD: 12/95). Notes and text included. From DG 2740 271 (11/82).

How does Berlin Classics suppose that those without German are going to enjoy this amusingly written comedy? The German original is complete, but the English and French translations of the libretto have been removed. A synopsis is no substitute. That said, it is good to have this cheerful little opera, for many years Lortzing's most popular, back in the British catalogue, especially in so well sung a performance. Casting has never been much of a problem with Lortzing in Germany, since this most practical of theatre composers wrote not so much for subtleties of character as for the voice types that were the staple of the average opera company of the day. This is not to say that plenty cannot be made of them. Hans Sotin does splendidly by the hearty Baculus, delivering "Fünftausend Taler" with great gusto, but also making the pompous old schoolmaster a figure of considerable warmth and one with a touch of pathos in his character. Peter Schreier and Edith Mathis also have the manner in their bones, but are artists of sufficient stature to make the Baron and Baroness human beings, and sympathetic ones, without confusing the uncomplicated directness that is part of the idiom. Doris Soffel enjoys herself in the role of the Sophocles-besotted Countess, and Georgine Resick sings a charming but not over sweet Gretchen. There is a good sense of company enjoyment in the set, which is part of Lortzing's whole style, and this is encouraged by Bernhard Klee with his lively and sympathetic direction.

Further listening ...

...Undine. **Soloists; Cologne Radio Chorus and Orchestra / Kurt Eichhorn**. Capriccio 60 017-2 (3/91).

Antonio Lotti
Italian c1667-1740

Suggested listening ...

...Crucifixus. *Coupled with works by* **Allegri, Palestrina, Byrd, Parsons, Viadana, Tallis, Philips, G. Gabrieli, Tye, Victoria** and **Monteverdi** Soloists; Westminster Cathedral Choir / **James O'Donnell**. Hyperion CDA66850 (5/96). *See review in the Collections section; refer to the Index to Reviews.*

Hermann Løvenskjold
Danish 1815-1870

Suggested listening ...

...La Sylphide. **Royal Danish Orchestra / David Garforth**. Chandos Collect CHAN6546 (4/92)

Donato Lovreglio
Italian 1841-1907

Suggested listening ...

...Fantasia on Verdi's "La traviata", Op. 45. *Coupled with works by* **Schumann, Debussy, Poulenc, Weber** and **Messager** Michael Collins (cl); Kathryn Stott (pf). EMI Virtuosi CDC7 54419-2 (9/92). *See review in the Collections section; refer to the Index to Reviews.*

Nicholas Ludford
British c1485-1557

Ludford Missa Lapidaverunt Stephanum. Ave Maria ancilla trinitatis. **The Cardinall's Musick / Andrew Carwood**. ASV Gaudeamus Ⓔ CDGAU140 (69 minutes: DDD: 1/95). Texts and translations included. Also contains Plainsong Propers for the Feast of St Stephen's Day. Ⓠ

This is the fourth and final instalment of the Ludford series from The Cardinall's Musick under Andrew Carwood on ASV Gaudeamus. The whole project has been so smoothly and efficiently realized by all concerned – and the result is so very fine – that much praise is deserved. As David Skinner points out in his insert-notes, the four recordings have not embraced the complete works attributed to Nicholas Ludford, but they have given us an unprecedented view of a large part of the compositional output of this excellent composer. This latest disc has as its centrepiece the *Missa Lapidaverunt Stephanum*, a work firmly in the English tradition as represented by the Eton Choirbook. Meandering duets and trios are contrasted with more declamatory tutti sections and The Cardinall's Musick emphasize these contrasts of sonority with appropriately distinctive approaches, at times more contemplative, at others more forceful and declamatory. The Mass, which boasts a magical setting of the *Agnus Dei*, is, as on the other Ludford discs, embedded in chant, this time the Propers for the Feast of St Stephen. The chant takes up rather less than a quarter of the playing time and again The Cardinall's Musick respond to the different texts with conviction. This series, already noted for its high standards of performance and scholarship, has succeeded brilliantly in bringing back to life the inspirational sacred polyphony of early sixteenth-century England.

Further listening ...
...Missa Videte miraculum. Ave cuius conceptio. **The Cardinall's Musick / Andrew Carwood**. ASV Gaudeamus CDGAU131 (7/93). *Gramophone Editor's choice*.

Alexandre Luigini   French 1850-1906

Suggested listening ...
...Ballet égyptien, Op. 12 – Suite. *Coupled with* **Ketèlbey** Bells across the meadows. Chal Romano. The Clock and the Dresden Figures. In a Chinese Temple Garden. In a Monastery Garden. In a Persian Market. In the Moonlight (Sous la lune). In the Mystic Land of Egypt. Sanctuary of the Heart. **Soloists; Ambrosian Singers; Philharmonia Orchestra / John Lanchbery; Royal Philharmonic Orchestra / Anatole Fistoulari.** Classics for Pleasure CD-CFP4637 (3/94). *See review under Ketèlbey; refer to the Index to Reviews.*

Jean-Baptiste Lully   Italian/French 1632-1687

Lully Phaëton. **Howard Crook** (ten) Phaëton; **Rachel Yakar** (sop) Clymène; **Jennifer Smith** (sop) Théone; **Véronique Gens** (sop) Libye; **Gérard Thervel** (bar) Epaphus; **Jean-Paul Fouchécourt** (ten) Triton, Sun, Earth, Goddess; **Philippe Huttenlocher** (bar) Mérops; **Laurent Naouri** (bar) Saturn, Protée; **Virginie Pochon** (mez) Astrée, Hour of the Day; **Jérôme Varnier** (sop) Autumn, Jupiter; **Florence Couderc** (sop) Shepherdess, Hour of the Day; **Sagittarius Vocal Ensemble; Les Musiciens du Louvre / Marc Minkowski.** Erato Ⓔ 4509-91737-2 (two discs: 144 minutes: DDD: 8/94). ✍ Notes, text and translation included. Recorded 1993. ⒼⒼ

In 1688 *Phaëton* was chosen to inaugurate the new Royal Academy of Music at Lyon where, as Jérôme de la Gorce remarks in his excellent introduction, it was so successful "that people came to see it from forty leagues around". The libretto is based on the famous legend in Ovid's *Metamorphoses* and afforded composer and librettist ample opportunity for evocative and colourful writing. The score is generously endowed with *divertissements*, an invigorating overture and a supple swiftly moving chaconne. The casting is effective, by and large, and notably for the stylish, alluring and impassioned singing of Véronique Gens. Jennifer Smith is authoritative as the hapless princess Théone; her diction is excellent and her careful placing of notes comparably so. The exchanges with Phaëton are passionately sung, with Howard Crook in the title-role engaging vigorously in the dialogue. Third in this impressive triumvirate of princesses is Rachel Yakar who, as Clymène, Phaëton's mother, is affectionate yet forceful. Her Act 1 air, "D'une amoureuse ardeur un grand Coeur peut brûler" ("A mighty heart can burn with amorous ardour"), with its fleeting resemblance to Henry Lawes's "Sufferance", is beautifully done with the dual emphasis on heroism and love skilfully balanced. There are fine contributions from the remaining dramatis personae, too. Last, but in French opera certainly not least, are the choral and instrumental contributions; both make a strong impression, the orchestra especially so with a resonant basso continuo team affording constant pleasure. Minkowski sets a cracking pace for the drama and there are few if any flagging moments. In short, all this is engaging music, imaginatively performed and thoroughly entertaining. Recorded sound is excellent and the booklet, give or take a few small errors, all that one could wish for. Strongly recommended; the cover illustration alone, one of a group of seventeenth-century wooden panels depicting Phaëton, horses and chariot plunging headlong to earth invites further investigation.

Lully Armide. **Guillemette Laurens** (mez) Armide; **Howard Crook** (ten) Renaud; **Véronique Gens** (sop) Fame, Phenice, Melisse, Shepherdess; **Noémi Rime** (sop) Wisdom, Sidonie, Lucinde, Naiad; **Bernard Delétré** (bass) Hidraot, Ubalde; **Gilles Ragon** (ten) Danish Knight, Fortunate Lover; **John Hancock** (bar) Artemidore, Hate; **Luc Coadou** (bass) Aronte; **Collegium Vocale; La Chapelle Royale Chorus and Orchestra / Philippe Herreweghe.** Harmonia Mundi Ⓔ HMC90 1456/7 (two discs: 156 minutes: DDD: 8/93). ✍ Notes, text and translation included. Recorded 1992.

Armide was the last of the *tragédies en musique* in which Lully and his trusty Quinault collaborated – Gluck was to use the same *livret* some 90 years later. Armide, a sorceress and a warrior, has won a victory over the Crusaders; but one of the Christian knights, Renaud (Rinaldo) – the bravest of them all – though held captive, remains unconquered in spirit and impervious to her charms. At last two knights rescue Renaud by breaking Armide's spell with a magic shield. Her palace collapses and she flies away in a winged chariot. Herreweghe and his expert groups of singers and players give a pleasingly rounded account of Lully's accomplished and often strikingly beautiful score. The casting of Guillemette Laurens in the title-role was an inspired choice. She is notably skilful in the art of declamation, is gifted with a sharp ear for detail and has a lively feeling for musical gesture. Howard Crook's Renaud is lightly articulated and tonally well-focused and the remaining soloists make a very impressive showing, too. A must for opera-lovers and Francophiles.

Further listening ...

...Divertissements. **Guillemette Laurens** (mez); **Capriccio Stravagante / Skip Sempé.** Deutsche Harmonia Mundi RD77218 (1/91). ☞

...Le bourgeois gentilhomme – incidental music. *Coupled with* **Campra** L'Europe galante – ballet suite. **Soloists; Tölz Boys' Choir; La Petite Bande / Gustav Leonhardt.** Deutsche Harmonia Mundi Editio Classica GD77059 (2/91). ☞

...Le bourgeois gentilhomme. Cadmus et Hermione. Les noces de village. *Coupled with* **A. Philidor** Le mariage de la grosse Cathos. **Marie-Ange Petit** (perc); **London Oboe Band / Paul Goodwin.** Harmonia Mundi HMU90 7122 (4/95).

...Dies irae. Miserere. *Coupled with* **Du Mont** Memorare **Soloists; Parish Chappelle Royale Chorus and Orchestra / Philippe Herreweghe.** Harmonia Mundi HMC90 1167 (5/86). ☞

...Alceste. **Soloists; Sagittarius Vocal Ensemble; La Grande Ecurie et La Chambre du Roy / Jean-Claude Malgoire.** Auvidis Astrée E8527 (4/93). ☞

...Atys. *Prologue. Tragédie-lyrique.* **Soloists; Les Arts Florissants Chorus and Orchestra / William Christie.** Harmonia Mundi HMC90 1257/9 (7/87). ☞

Hans Christian Lumbye

Danish 1810-1874

Suggested listening ...

...Amélie. Britta. Champagne, Op. 14. Columbine. Concert. Copenhagen Steam Railway Galop. The Guard of Amager – Final Galop. Mon salut à Petersburg. Napoli – Final Galop. Petersburg Champagne. Petersburg. Pictures from a Dream. Polonaise with cornet solo. Queen Louise's Waltz. Salute to August Bournonville. **Danish National Radio Symphony Orchestra / Gennadi Rozhdestvensky.** Chandos CHAN9209 (2/94).

David Lumsdaine

Australian 1931-

Suggested listening ...

...Aria for Edward John Eyre[a]. What shall I sing[b]. [a]**Jane Manning**, [b]**Mary Wiegold** (sops); [a]**John Buddeley**, [a]**John Rye** (narrs); **Gemini /** [a]**Elgar Howarth.** NMC NMC 007 (6/93).

Thomas Lupo

British c1598-1628

Suggested listening ...

...Fantasy-Airs a 3 – Nos. 16, 17 and 20. Fantasy-Airs a 4 – Nos. 5-7, 11 and 12. Fantasies a 4 – Nos. 4 and 9. *Coupled with* **Gibbons** Two Fantasias a 4. 9 Fantasias a 3. Galliard a 3. **The Parley of Instruments / Peter Holman.** Hyperion CDA66395 (9/91). ☞

John Lurie

American 1952-

Suggested listening ...

...Stranger than Paradise. *Coupled with works by* **Byrne, Moran** and **Torke Balanescu Quartet.** Argo 436 565-2ZH (3/93). *See review in the Collections section; refer to the Index to Reviews.*

Witold Lutosławski

Polish 1913-1994

New review

Lutosławski Concerto for Orchestra. Funeral Music. Mi-parti. **BBC Philharmonic Orchestra / Yan Pascal Tortelier.** Chandos ℗ CHAN9421 (55 minutes: DDD: 4/96). Recorded 1993. *Selected by Soundings.*

All three phases of Lutosławski are here, with two of his finest orchestral works flanking a 'transitional' score whose historical importance outweighs its purely musical interest. Tortelier's virtues as a conductor – expressive warmth allied to a special rhythmic buoyancy – are generously apparent in a sizzling account of the *Concerto for Orchestra.* The musical flow is firmly controlled, yet the effect is never inflexible, and the technical precision and alertness of the playing throughout is something for the listener to revel in. The sound is bright, well-differentiated dynamically, and even if the BBC's Manchester studio lacks some of the depth and atmosphere of Chicago's Orchestra Hall, as caught in Barenboim's rival version on Erato, the Chandos recording is generally more vivid, in keeping with a performance which has precisely the kind of bite and energy that the score demands. It is good that Chandos and Tortelier chose *Mi-parti* to complete the disc, since of all Lutosławski's later instrumental works this one makes out the best possible case for his radical change of technique around 1960. Although the composer's own Polish recordings of *Mi-parti* (and of the *Concerto*) remain in the catalogue, and are naturally of some historical interest, the music-making on this Chandos release is superior, making this the primary recommendation of these works.

Lutosławski Concerto for Orchestra. Symphony No. 3. **Chicago Symphony Orchestra / Daniel Barenboim.** Erato Ⓕ 4509-91711-2 (58 minutes: DDD: 8/93). Recorded live in 1992. *Gramophone Editor's choice.*   ⒼⒼ

Lutosławski's Third Symphony was commissioned by the Chicago SO and first performed by them under Sir Georg Solti in 1983, but only nine years later did the orchestra record the work. None of the versions made in the interim can equal Barenboim's blend of refined detail and cumulative power, and the Erato recording is also more faithful to the dynamics marked in the score. The *Concerto for Orchestra*, completed almost 30 years before the symphony, is comparatively conservative in style, but it has ample substance to match its panache. It also remains a formidable challenge to an orchestra. As with the symphony, Barenboim's strength is the large-scale creation and sustaining of tension, and the Erato recording contains the heavy climaxes without draining them of clarity or impact.

Additional recommendations ...

...Symphonies Nos. 3 and 4. Les espaces du sommeil[a]. [a]**John Shirley-Quirk** (bar); **Los Angeles Philharmonic Orchestra / Esa-Pekka Salonen.** Sony Classical Ⓕ SK66280 (68 minutes: DDD: 11/94).

...Concerto for Orchestra. Jeux vénitiens. Livre pour Orchestre. Mi-Parti. **Polish National Radio Symphony Orchestra / Witold Lutosławski.** EMI Matrix Ⓜ CDM5 65305-2 (78 minutes: ADD: 7/95).

Lutosławski Symphonies – No. 1; No. 2. Symphonic Variations. Funeral music. **Polish National Radio Symphony Orchestra / Witold Lutosławski.** EMI Matrix Ⓜ CDM5 65076-2 (71 minutes: ADD: 2/95). From 1C 165 03231/6 (7/79). Recorded 1976-77.   ⒼⒼ

All four works included on this superbly refurbished CD share an acute sense of texture, with the *Symphonic Variations* (1938) serving as a sort of changing room where the composer busily experiments with all manner of musical dress. The *Funeral music* for Bartók (1956-58) is a powerful synthesis of original thought and active homage, with plentiful reminders of the master himself – especially of his *Divertimento* for strings. The real ground-breaker, however, is the Second Symphony, a seething, structured mass in two parts: the first, nervous and diffuse (with strikingly original passagework for piano and percussion), the second – which arrives without a break – initially dense, but ultimately ethereal. All in all, this must surely count as *the* introduction to Lutosławski's symphonic world, and helpful notes offer the uninitiated plenty of useful musical signposts.

New review

Lutosławski Symphony No. 2. Piano Concerto[a]. Chantefleurs et Chantefables[b]. Fanfare for Los Angeles Philharmonic. [b]**Dawn Upshaw** (sop); [a]**Paul Crossley** (pf); **Los Angeles Philharmonic Orchestra / Esa-Pekka Salonen.** Sony Classical Ⓕ SK67189 (74 minutes: DDD: 6/96). Text and translation included. Recorded 1994.

It is Lutosławski's last completed work, the Fourth Symphony (1993), which most fully embodies his highly personal reinterpretation of Polish music's romantic past. But another late piece, *Chantefleurs et Chantefables* (1990), offers clear evidence of how satisfying that reinterpretation could be. These 'songflowers and songfables' represent a refinement rather than a dilution of Lutosławski's hard-won modernity, and they are all the more effective for their brevity – the longest lasts less than three minutes. That 'hard-won modernity' did not imply a total rejection of such traditional genres as symphony and concerto – though some would say that it should have done. Certainly Lutosławski's Symphony No. 2 (1966-7) remains a problem piece, mainly because the material of its first movement seems designed precisely not to generate a traditional kind of symphonic argument. The second movement has far greater breadth, but it can hardly serve to 'explain' the first movement in retrospect; it would be better on its own. Twenty years later, in his Piano Concerto, Lutosławski was more alert to the possibilities of creating a viable symphonic style out of the interaction rather than separation of lyric and dramatic materials, and although the concerto's range of stylistic allusions can be disconcerting, a good performance can turn such ambiguities to positive ends. This is certainly a good performance. If the recording by Krystian Zimerman, the work's dedicatee, summons up shades of Rachmaninov, Paul Crossley's less forceful but no less well-characterized reading seems closer to Ravel. Esa-Pekka Salonen is a sensitive accompanist, and the Sony sound has spacious clarity as well as spatial depth, even if it may not bring the orchestra sufficiently far forward for some tastes. This recording of Symphony No. 2 must rank as superior to either of the composer's, and although Dawn Upshaw is occasionally rather shrill in *Chantefleurs et Chantefables* the performance as a whole is well judged. As for the brief *Fanfare*, it has a splendidly brassy exuberance.

Additional recommendation ...
...Piano Concerto[a]. Chain 3. Novelette. [a]**Krystian Zimerman** (pf); **BBC Symphony Orchestra / Witold Lutosławski.** DG Ⓔ 431 664-2GH (55 minutes: DDD: 4/92).

New review

Lutosławski Symphony No. 3. Chantefleurs et Chantefables[a]. [a]**Valdine Anderson** (sop); **BBC National Orchestra of Wales / Tadaaki Otaka.** BIS Ⓔ CD743 (54 minutes: DDD: 8/96). Text and translation included.

A great deal of care has been taken over this recording. BIS have achieved an extremely satisfying sound-balance, so that Lutosławski's finely-blended, imaginatively varied instrumental colours can be heard with commendable naturalness and clarity. The question is whether too much care, not to say caution, has been lavished on the performances themselves. At 34$^1/_2$ minutes, Tadaaki Otaka's timing for the symphony is a substantial 6$^1/_2$ minutes slower – or broader – than Daniel Barenboim's (reviewed above), which comes close to the "c28 mins." indicated in the score. Otaka's deliberation is evident from the start, but the main problem with his performance is not so much its overall duration as the relative lack of contrast between the faster and slower tempos indicated by the composer. Otaka evidently sees the work in a more romantic light than Barenboim, whose spontaneous, even impetuous approach risks sounding too brusque and casual at times. Nevertheless, it seems to project the symphony's shape and character more effectively than any other current version. The leaner Erato sound is also an advantage in this respect, though Otaka's BBC forces are as alert and technically assured as Barenboim's Chicago players. In *Chantefleurs et Chantefables* full focus is given to the composer's subtle, often magical orchestral fabric. Valdine Anderson gives an engaging performance and her account of this delightful work is convincing in context.

Further listening ...
...Paroles tissées[a]. Cello Concerto[b]. Postlude I[bc]. Livre pour Orchestre[d]. [a]**Louis Devos** (ten); [b]**Roman Jablónski** (vc); [b]**Katowice Radio Symphony Orchestra;** [ad]**Warsaw National Philharmonic Orchestra / [cd]Jan Krenz, [ab]Witold Lutosławski.** Polskie Nagrania Muza PNCD042 (9/90).
...Partita for Violin, Orchestra and Obbligato Solo Piano[a]. Chain 2[b]. *Coupled with* **Stravinsky** Violin Concerto in D major[c]. **Anne-Sophie Mutter** (vn); [a]**Phillip Moll** (pf); [ab]**BBC Symphony Orchestra / Witold Lutosławski;** [c]**Philharmonia Orchestra / Paul Sacher.** DG 423 696-2GH (2/89). *See review under Stravinsky; refer to the Index to Reviews.*   Ⓖ
...Preludes and Fugues for 13 Solo Strings[a]. Mi-parti[a]. Novelette[b]. [a]**Polish Chamber Orchestra / Witold Lutosławski;** [b]**Junge Deutsche Philharmonie / Heinz Holliger.** Polskie Nagrania Muza PNCD043 (9/90).
...Chain 2[a]. *Coupled with* **Schnittke** Viola Concerto[b]. **Isabelle van Keulen** ([a]vn/[b]va); **Philharmonia Orchestra / Heinrich Schiff.** Koch Schwann 31523-2 (11/95).
...Dances Preludes. *Coupled with* **Copland** Clarinet Concerto. **Nielsen** Clarinet Concerto, FS129. **Janet Hilton** (cl); **Royal Scottish Orchestra / Mattias Bamert.** Chandos CHAN8618 (10/88).
...Sacher Variations. *Coupled with works by* **Dutilleux, Beck, Henze, Fortner, Ginastera, Boulez, Berio, C. Halffter, Britten, K. Huber** and **Holliger** Patrick and Thomas Demenga (vcs); **Cello Ensemble / Jürg Wyttenbach.** ECM New Series 445 234-2 (8/95).

Agnes Elisabeth Lutyens   British 1906-1983

Lutyens Chamber Concerto No. 1, Op. 8 No. 1[b]. The Valley of Hatsu-Se, Op. 62[ab]. Six Tempi, Op. 42[b] Lament of Isis on the Death of Osiris[a]. Triolet I, Op. 160a[b]. Triolet II, Op. 160b[b]. Requiescat, "in memoriam Igor Stravinsky"[ab]. [a]**Jane Manning** (sop); [b]**Jane's Minstrels / Roger Montgomery.** NMC Ⓔ NMCD011 (66 minutes: DDD: 10/93). Notes, texts and translations included. Recorded 1992. *Gramophone Editor's choice.*

Serialism for Elizabeth Lutyens was no dogma or easy route to 'modernity' but a refining process, and with it she distilled a very individual voice. It is salutary and in a way thrilling to set her First Chamber Concerto of 1940 in the context of its age: who else in Britain at that time was capable of such elegant rigour, channelling such an intense lyricism? It is – or should be – a landmark of recent British music. The *Six Tempi* are its lineal descendant of nearly 20 years later: still more pared-down, 'late serial' in their bare economy but all of them radiating out from the tenderly haunting funeral march at their centre and all rooted in a lyricism which we can now recognize as Lutyens's own: no wonder this piece prompted, at an unexpected meeting with Stravinsky, an embrace and a cry of "This is the sort of music that I like!". Moving in another way are the two late *Triolets*, each composed when the pain of arthritis made writing an ordeal: 'miniatures' in which the craft of a lifetime is used to draw big images with the fewest possible notes. The performances are eloquently phrased, amply expressive and refined of sound: the recording is clean and natural. One can think of a dozen other Lutyens compositions that would be welcome on CD, but this collection has been very shrewdly compiled to represent her at her best.

Further listening ...
...Trio, Op. 135. *Coupled with works by* **Powers, LeFanu, G. Williams** and **R. Marsh** Mühlfeld Ensemble. Clarinet Classics CC0007 (10/94). *See review in the Collections section; refer to the Index to Reviews.*

...Verses of Love. *Coupled with works by* **T. Salter, Maconchy, Hoddinott, J. Harvey** and **Musgrave Ionian Singers / Timothy Salter; Thalia Myers** (pf); **Erik Jacobsen** (perc). Usk Recordings USK1216 (3/96).

Meyer Lutz
British

Suggested listening ...
...Pas de quatre. *Coupled with works by* **Binge, Williams, Coates, Toye, Collins, Farnon, Baynes, Curzon, Gibbs, White, Ketèlbey, Joyce, Ellis** and **Ancliffe New London Orchestra / Ronald Corp.** Hyperion CDA66868 (7/96). *Gramophone Editor's record of the month. See review in the Collections section; refer to the Index to Reviews.* Ⓖ

Sergey Lyapunov
USSR 1859-1924

Suggested listening ...
...Symphony No. 1 in B minor, Op. 12. Ballada in C sharp minor, Op. 2. **Moscow State Symphony Orchestra / Fedor Glushchenko.** Olympia OCD519 (11/93).
...Transcendental Studies – No. 1 in F sharp major, "Berceuse"; No. 2 in D sharp minor, "Rondes des fantômes"; No. 3 in B major, "Carillon"; No. 4 in G sharp minor, "Terek"; No. 5 in E major, "Nuit d'été"; No. 6 in C sharp minor, "Tempête"; No. 7 in A major, "Idylle"; No. 8 in F sharp minor, "Chant épique"; No. 9 in D major, "Harpes éoliennes"; No. 10 in B minor, "Lesghinka"; No. 11 in G major, "Rondes des Sylphes"; No. 12 in E minor, "Elégie en mémoire de François Liszt". **Malcolm Binns** (pf). Pearl SHECD9624 (5/92).

Boris Lyatoshinsky
Ukrainian 1895-1968

Lyatoshinsky Symphonies – No. 2, Op. 26; No. 3 in B minor, Op. 50. **Ukrainian State Symphony Orchestra / Theodore Kuchar.** Marco Polo Ⓕ 8 223540 (77 minutes: DDD: 11/94). Recorded 1993. Boris Lyatoshinsky, who died aged 73 in 1968, was one of the most distinguished Ukrainian composers of his time, and did much to establish a flourishing musical life in Kiev. This did not, of course, exempt him from trouble. Most of his five symphonies were forced to go through various revisions. No. 2, of 1936, suffered the fate of a bad review in advance of its scheduled première, which did not take place until 1964 in a revised version; No. 3 managed a première in 1951, but was subjected to compulsory revision before further performance. Russian sources speak of the early influence of Borodin, later of Scriabin (which does not seem very marked in these works). Lyatoshinsky also experimented with atonality, but was evidently brought into Socialist Realist line at the time of the victory of the repressives over the progressives in official Soviet circles at the end of the 1920s. Not surprisingly, then, both these works show a number of different elements in his style. Particularly in No. 2, there is the use of a good deal of folk material and what sounds like a version of Orthodox chant. There is a gift for the sweeping melody of the breadth we might associate with Elgar. However, behind such themes often goes a more troubling counterpoint in another key, and there may also be counter-rhythms or contrasting musics to disturb the atmosphere. These are committed and authoritative performances.

Additional recommendation ...
...No. 3[a]. Romeo and Juliet – Suite[b]. [a]**Ukrainian State Symphony Orchestra,** [b]**Ukrainian Radio and TV Symphony Orchestra / Vladimir Gnedash.** Russian Disc Ⓜ RDCD11060 (68 minutes: AAD: 7/95).

Further listening ...
...Symphonies – No. 4 in B flat minor, Op. 63; No. 5 in C major, Op. 67, "Slavonic". **Ukrainian State Symphony Orchestra / Theodore Kuchar.** Marco Polo 8 223541 (1/95).
...Symphonies – No. 4 in B flat minor, Op. 63; No. 5 in C major, Op. 67, "Slavonic". **Cracow Philharmonic Orchestra / Roland Bader.** CPO CPO999 183-2 (4/95).
...Polish Suite, Op. 60. Overture on four Ukrainian themes, Op. 20. Intermezzo. Lyric Poem. Op. 66. Fantastic March, Op. 3. **Young Russia State Symphony Orchestra, Moscow / Virko Baley.** CdM Russian Season RUS288 085 (1/95).

Hamish MacCunn
British 1868-1916

New review
MacCunn Jeanie Deans – Introduction; I love a lass; What can it be?; Why com'st thou thus?; O God, whose eyes; O friends, I said but now; Nay, neighbour; O father, father, shame indeed; Thou has shamed; Oh!, would that I again; Sleep for the day is done; O Effie, darling; That shout!. **Janice Watson** (sop) Jeanie; **Lisa Milne** (sop) Effie; **Jamie MacDougall** (ten) Staunton; **Peter Sidhom** (bar) Deans; **Stephen Gadd** (bass) Dumbiedykes; **Graeme Danby** (bass) Constable.

MacCunn The Land of the mountain and the flood, Op. 3. The Dowie Dens o' Yarrow. The Ship o' the Fiend. The Lay of the Last Minstrel[a] – Breathes there the man; O Caledonia! stern and wild. [a]**Stephen Cadd** (bass); **Scottish Opera Chorus; BBC Scottish Symphony Orchestra / Martyn Brabbins.** Hyperion Ⓔ CDA66815 (70 minutes: DDD: 2/96). Texts included.

Hamish MacCunn belonged to the first generation of students at the Royal College of Music, from which he promptly withdrew, not liking it there. His studies nevertheless equipped him to write a highly successful concert overture (*The Land of the mountain and the flood*) at the age of 18, and to pursue a vigorous career as composer and conductor, in which capacity he took the Carl Rosa opera company through the first performances in English of *Siegfried* and *Tristan und Isolde*. His opera *Jeanie Deans*, an adaptation of Scott's *The Heart of Midlothian*, was acclaimed at its première in 1894 and held its place in the repertoire till around 1920. The opera is represented here in extracts that are just about impressive enough to encourage a hearing of the whole. Effie's lullaby is a touchingly beautiful song, and the duet with Staunton, sung while the Porteous Riots are in progress off-stage, has genuine dramatic tension and pathos. The three concert overtures which introduce the programme command admiration for their effective scoring and some warmer response to the surge of melody charged with a strong rhythmic impulse. The performances here are keen and incisive, as is the recorded sound. In *Jeanie Deans* the soloists do well enough for this kind of sampler, which on the whole prompts interest rather than dismissal, despite some melodrama of the stagiest kind.

Further listening ...
...The land of the mountain and the flood, Op. 3. *Coupled with works by* **Butterworth** and **Coleridge-Taylor** Royal Liverpool Philharmonic Orchestra / Grant Llewellyn. Argo 436 401-2ZH (6/93). *See review under Butterworth; refer to the Index to Reviews.*

Edward MacDowell
American 1860-1908

New review
MacDowell Piano Sonata No. 4 in E minor, Op. 59, "Keltic". Forgotten Fairy Tales, Op. 4. Six Poems after Heine, Op. 31. 12 Virtuoso Etudes, Op. 46. **James Barbagallo** (pf). Marco Polo Ⓔ 8 223633 (65 minutes: DDD: 2/96).

Edward MacDowell's star may have faded to near oblivion over the years. Yet even when his very personal and oddly touching voice seems stifled by deference to outmoded European ideals he provides enough poetic and psychological interest to make James Barbagallo's affectionate tribute more than worthwhile. The rough-and-tumble of academic life, with its hard-nosed jockeying for position, was ill-suited to MacDowell's gentle nature and his professorship at Columbia was short-lived. A romantic escapist, he retreated to his "House o' Dreams" in idyllic New Hampshire, where he indulged his passion for "the Gaelic world ... of bards and heroes of great adventure", a "love of other times". Significantly, the gems of this disc in this ongoing and excellently recorded series are surely the six Op. 31 *Poems after Heine*, their charm and piquancy evoking Scottish castles, nightingales and a shepherd boy "crowned with golden sunshine", The *Forgotten Fairy Tales*, too, have their moments but the 12 *Virtuoso Etudes* are less interesting than their title implies: the "Polonaise" is truly awful and the "Valse triste" an unengaging mixture of whimsy and complacency. But "Wilde Jagd", with its sinister chromatic undertow, is effective and there is much homely lyricism elsewhere. The larger forms, however, surely defeated a composer who was essentially a miniaturist. And although the *Keltic* Sonata urges us on with instructions such as "with tragic pathos", the music is overwhelmed by Grieg's influence and by too many tub-thumping, inflated gestures. Overall, Barbagallo is more persuasive in intimacy than in brilliance. However, if he is hard-pressed by some of MacDowell's more hectoring demands he is unfailingly warm-hearted in his approach.

Further listening ...
...Piano Concertos – No. 1 in A minor, Op. 15; No. 2 in D minor, Op. 23. **Donna Amato** (pf); **London Philharmonic Orchestra / Paul Freeman.** Olympia OCD353. Ⓖ
...New England Idylls. *Coupled with* **Barber** Ballade, Op. 46. **Beach** Five Improvisations, Op. 148. **Bernstein** Five Anniversaries. **Cage** Bacchanale for Prepared Piano. **Copland** Four Piano Blues. **Gershwin** Three Preludes. **Gottschalk** Manchega, RO143. Le Banjo, RO22. **M. Gould** Boogie Woogie Etude. **Joplin** The Entertainer. Maple Leaf Rag. **Nancarrow** Prelude. **Michel Legrand** (pf). Erato 4509-96386-2 (7/95).
...Woodland Sketches, Op. 51. Sea Pieces, Op. 55. Fireside Tales, Op. 61. New England Idylls, Op. 62. **James Barbagallo** (pf). Marco Polo 8 223631 (4/95).

Sir Alexander MacKenzie
British 1847-1935

Suggested listening ...
...The Cricket on the Hearth, Op. 62 – Overture. Twelfth Night, Op. 40. Benedictus, Op. 37 No. 3. Scottish Rhapsody No. 2, Op. 24, "Burns". Coriolanus, Op. 61. **BBC Scottish Symphony Orchestra / Martyn Brabbins** Hyperion CDA66764 (5/95).

James MacMillan   British 1959-

MacMillan Seven Last Words from the Cross[a]. Cantos Sagrados[b]. **Polyphony;** [b]**Christopher Bowers-Broadbent** (org); [a]**London Chamber Orchestra / James MacMillan.** Catalyst Ⓕ 09026 68125-2 (68 minutes: DDD: 5/95). Texts included. Recorded 1994. *Gramophone Editor's choice.*   Ⓖ

Seven Last Words from the Cross is a modern choral counterpart of Haydn's masterpiece. On one level this is just another of the slow-moving, easily mellifluous expressions of religious devotion that have had such spectacular success on disc. But where works by Górecki or Pärt can so readily be treated as aural wallpaper (wrongly so of course), MacMillan in a performance like this compels immediate and close attention. The second movement illustrates the way that MacMillan uses traditional musical associations, often elided with one another, to intensify the meaning of the words from the Cross. So after the sharp impact of the opening a choral ostinato to the words "Woman, behold thy Son!" brings conscious echoes of Bach's Passion chorales, with a moment of triumph emerging when a major triad is firmly established, before the final agonized disintegration on "Behold thy Mother!". He often superimposes liturgical texts, often chanted quickly in monotone whether in Latin or English, over the main words from the Cross. The result is both complex and clean-cut, strikingly dramatic, and the other work on the disc, *Cantos Sagrados*, illustrates the device again. This is a work inspired by Liberation theology, bringing together MacMillan's left-wing views and his devout Catholicism. The idiom is clear and approachable but hardly conventional. The performances, vividly recorded, are electrifying, with the players of the London Chamber Orchestra and the organist Christopher Bowers-Broadbent (in *Cantos Sagrados*), as well as the fine singers of Stephen Layton's group, Polyphony, consistently inspired by the music and its composer-conductor. Characteristically, MacMillan's notes are terse, clear and helpful.

| New review |

MacMillan The Berserking[a]. Sowetan Spring[b]. Britannia[b]. Sinfonietta[b]. [a]**Peter Donohoe** (pf); **Royal Scottish National Orchestra /** [a]**Markus Stenz,** [b]**James MacMillan.** RCA Victor Red Seal Ⓕ 09026 68328-2 (77 minutes: DDD: 7/96). Recorded 1995. *Gramophone Editor's choice.*   Ⓖ

Today's New Music scene is said to be pluralistic: everything is permitted; style is no longer a moral issue. But that supposedly 'pluralistic' scene is still full of people pursuing narrowly exclusive paths. Sometimes MacMillan's style-contrasts do take on a moral/political dimension, as in *Britannia*, in which Celtic modality and folk-elements and a moment of radiant protest from his own *Confession of Isobel Gowdie* are submitted to crude onslaughts from drunken versions of *Knees up Mother Brown*, *God save the Queen* (particularly the line "send her victorious") and a yobbishly strutting version of the first theme from Elgar's *Cockaigne*. The militaristic violence at the heart of *Sinfonietta* derives in part from an Ulster Loyalist song, *The Sash*. The message seems clear enough. But, says MacMillan, the underlying "serious" purpose of *Britannia* is "to hold up a mirror to xenophobia" and the "negative, unsavoury brand of nationalism", not to demonize the English *per se*. Macmillan is a Catholic who can sympathize with the American Indian victims of Catholicism, a Scot who can make an entire piano concerto – *The Beserking* – out of the notion of "the Scots' seeming facility for shooting themselves in the foot". His folksiness is not without irony, even when it can seem to offer a haven of peace after a great deal of 'misdirected' energy. Charles Ives is clearly one of MacMillan's synthesizer-heroes. In fact there are moments in *Britannia* that actually sound like Ives, with something too of the American composer's robust delight in musical oil-and-vinegar mixes. Each of these pieces tells its story with a directness and warm empathy that may remind the listener of Mahler or Tchaikovsky. The hocketting-dominated *Sowetan Spring* is an impressive technical exercise but perhaps focused a little too narrowly. It is strikingly well performed though, as are all the other works on this disc, and beautifully recorded too. It would be difficult to think of a better introduction to MacMillan's music.

MacMillan The Confession of Isobel Gowdie. Tryst. **BBC Scottish Symphony Orchestra / Jerzy Maksymiuk.** Koch Schwann Ⓕ 310502 (54 minutes: DDD: 10/92). *Gramophone Award Winner 1993.*   Ⓖ

This time the publicity doesn't exaggerate. The première of *The Confession of Isobel Gowdie* at the 1990 Proms was a "spectacular triumph" – nothing less – and this with an audience drawn largely (one presumes) by Beethoven's Fourth Symphony and Sibelius's Violin Concerto. But success can fade with alarming rapidity. What matters now is that several years later, away from the uplift of that extraordinary reception, *The Confession of Isobel Gowdie* tells its story as stirringly as ever. If MacMillan's programme (the martyrdom of a Scottish Catholic 'witch') seems over-pictorial, no problem; the progression from rapt modal string threnody (complete with keening *glissandos*) through mounting violence to the re-emergence and transformation of the modal lament is as easy to follow as the 'narrative' of a Mahler symphony – and the after-effect isn't all that dissimilar. Others may be bothered by undisguised echoes of other composers: Copland, Messiaen, Stravinsky, Ives, the famous single-note crescendo from Berg's *Wozzeck* ... but the fact that they are undisguised is part of their strength – that and the way they are so obviously drawn into the argument. Of course the quality of the performance matters, and Maksymiuk and his orchestra give the kind of penetrating performance which (usually) only comes from long involvement. *Tryst* also emerges well: the forces may be smaller, but the head-on confrontation of violence with calmer, more humane sounds again generates a compelling musical drama, and the ending, though less spectacular than Isobel Gowdie's final one-tone immolation, works both as an imaginative conclusion and a challenge to go back and dig deeper. Away with caution! Give this a try.

Further listening ...

...Veni, veni, Emmanuel[a]. After the tryst[b]. "...as others see us..."[c]. Three Dawn Rituals[c]. Untold[c]. [a]**Evelyn Glennie** (perc); [b]**Ruth Crouch** (vn); [b]**Peter Evans** (pf); [ac]**Scottish Chamber Orchestra /** [a]**Jukka-Pekka Saraste,** [c]**James MacMillan.** Catalyst 09026 61916-2 (9/93). *Gramophone Editor's choice.* Ⓖ

...Kiss on Wood. *Coupled with works by* **Bolcom, Copland, Schnittke** and **Dresher Maria Bachmann** (vn); **Jon Klibonoff** (pf); **James Saporito** (perc). Catalyst 09026 62668-2 (5/95). *See review in the Collections section; refer to the Index to Reviews.* Ⓖ

...Visitatio Sepulchri[a]. Búsqueda[b]. **Soloists; Scottish Chamber Orchestra /** [a]**Ivor Bolton,** [b]**James MacMillan.** Catalyst 09026 62669-2 (4/95).

John McCabe
British 1939-

New review

McCabe Salamander. Cloudcatcher Fells. Desert II: Horizon. Images. Northern Lights. **Britannia Building Society Band / Howard Snell.** Doyen Ⓕ DOYCD030 (70 minutes: DDD: 2/96). Recorded 1994.

Here is a collection of all five (to date) of McCabe's brass band compositions. The programming is not chronological, but starts and ends with the two most recent, from 1992: *Salamander* and the rather Waltonian *Northern Lights*. In between come *Cloudcatcher, Desert II: Horizon* (1985) and *Images*. This last, written as long ago as 1967, caused a considerable furore in the then sedate brass-band world (before Henze, Birtwistle or Simpson contributed their ground-breaking works) with its use of serial techniques, though the music is still tonally based. The Britannia Building Society Band under Howard Snell have the measure of all these works. Mention of Robert Simpson provides some interesting parallels between McCabe's and Simpson's brass band careers: both wrote an isolated work to start with (Simpson's *Energy* dates from 1971), before striking gold with their second one (Simpson's *Volcano* was written in 1978), which led to three further pieces. Simpson has perhaps the edge in contrapuntal rigour, McCabe a wider textural palette.

Harl McDonald
American 1899-1955

Suggested listening ...

...San Juan Capistrano. *Coupled with works by* **Foote, Copland** and **Harris Boston Symphony Orchestra / Serge Koussevitzky.** Pearl mono GEMMCD9492* (12/91). *See review in the Collections section; refer to the Index to Reviews.* ⒼⒼⒼ

Sir John McEwen
Scottish 1868-1948

McEwen Solway Symphony. Hills o'Heather[a]. Where the Wild Thyme blows. [a]**Moray Welsh** (vc); **London Philharmonic Orchestra / Alasdair Mitchell.** Chandos Ⓕ CHAN9345 (61 minutes: DDD: 6/95). Recorded 1994. Ⓖ

This sumptuous recording of the *Solway Symphony* (1911) should help win it many new admirers. The *Solway* is cast in three movements. The opening *Allegro moderato*, entitled "Spring Tide", is a passionate, invigorating essay, richly evocative, colourfully scored (McEwen's heady orchestral palette owes a considerable debt to Rimsky-Korsakov, Debussy and Sibelius) and boasting a second subject of memorable sweep and uncommon lyrical beauty. No less beguiling is the ensuing *Molto tranquillo* slow movement ("Moonlight"): built around a simple recurring eight-note idea, it distils a haunting, fragrant atmosphere that lingers in the mind long afterwards. *Hills o'Heather* is a delightful miniature for cello and orchestra from 1918. McEwen's ravishingly judged solo writing is lent exquisite advocacy here by Moray Welsh, whilst Mitchell and the LPO tender loving support. Lastly, we are offered McEwen's final orchestral work, *Where the Wild Thyme blows*. This bleakly beautiful, highly atmospheric nature-poem dates from 1936, the year McEwen retired from his position as Principal of the Royal Academy of Music, and again reveals a considerable, subtle mastery of texture and harmony. Suffice to report, Mitchell obtains a most sensitive rendering. Nor can there be any complaints about the spacious Chandos sound, which possesses fine bloom and transparency throughout.

Further listening ...

...Three Border Ballads. **London Philharmonic Orchestra / Alasdair Mitchell.** Chandos CHAN9241 (3/94).

Michael McGlynn   Ireland 1958-

Suggested listening ...
...From Nowhere to Nowhere. *Coupled with works by* **Torke, I. Wilson, D. Heath** and **Nyman**
   Gerard McChrystal (sax); **London Musici / Mark Stephenson.** Silva Classics SILKD6010 (6/96).
   See review in the Collections section; refer to the Index to Reviews.

William McKinley   American 1938-

Suggested listening ...
...Four Text Settings. *Coupled with* **Amlin** Time's Caravan. **Carter** Emblems. The harmony of
   morning. Heart not so heavy as mine. Musicians wrestle everywhere. **Sheng** Two folksongs from
   Chinhai. **John Oliver Chorale / John Oliver.** Koch International Classics 37178-2 (5/95).

Jenny McLeod   New Zealand 1941-

Suggested listening ...
...Little Symphony. *Coupled with works by* **C. Blake, A. Ritchie, A. Watson, Lilburn,**
   Whitehead, Farquhar, Pruden and **Carr** New Zealand Symphony Orchestra / Kenneth Young.
   Continuum CCD1073 (5/96). *See review in the Collections section; refer to the Index to Reviews.*

Colin McPhee   Canadian/American 1901-1964

New review
McPhee Tabuh-Tabuhan[a].
L. Harrison Suite for Symphonic Strings.
Ung Inner Voices. [a]**Peter Basquin,** [b]**Christopher Oldfather** (pfs); **American Composers Orchestra /**
   Dennis Russell Davies. Argo Ⓔ 444 560-2ZH (68 minutes: DDD). Recorded 1994.
The major landmark here is the first modern recording of *Tabuh-Tabuhan* by the Canadian-born
composer, writer and ethnomusicologist, Colin McPhee. This sparkling toccata for two pianos and
orchestra is one of the earliest examples of mid-Pacific music since it adapts the musical traditions of
Bali, where McPhee lived for eight years, to western instruments – the first performance was
conducted by Carlos Chávez in Mexico City in 1936, but New York had to wait until 1953. If the
sound-world feels up-to-the-minute this is because the opening movement, "Ostinatos", might almost
have been written by John Adams. Much of the central "Nocturne" prolongs oriental scales into a
static trance with celebratory outbreaks of a kind which are more developed in the finale. The
freshness and individuality are extraordinary. The Cambodian-American, Chinary Ung settled in the
USA in his early twenties and has won several prestigious awards. Without quite the easy access of
Takemitsu, *Inner Voices* has a sumptuous orchestral sound, finely heard. This time western instruments
are being adapted to an oriental imagination – haunting microtones on woodwind and an eerie role for
the contra-bassoon. The Lou Harrison orchestral work is a bonus. This *Suite* was a 1956 Louisville
Orchestra commission including ideas going back 20 years. The slower movements have some of the
rapt stillness of Ives: charming but overextended. All the performances are convincing.
Further listening ...
...Balinese Ceremonial Music[e]. *Coupled with* **Britten** Seven Sonnets of Michelangelo, Op. 22[a].
   Folk Song Arrangements[b] – The Salley Gardens; Little Sir William; The ash grove; Oliver
   Cromwell. Introduction and Rondo alla burlesca, Op. 23 No. 1[c]. Mazurka elegiaca, Op. 23 No.
   2[c]. Serenade for Tenor, Horn and Strings, Op. 31[d]. [abd]**Sir Peter Pears** (ten); [d]**Dennis Brain** (hn);
   [e]**Colin McPhee,** [c]**Sir Clifford Curzon** (pfs); [d]**Boyd Neel String Orchestra / Benjamin Britten** ([abce]pf).
   Pearl mono GEMMCD9177* (10/95).

Guillaume de Machaut   French c1300-1377

Machaut Messe de Nostre Dame. Je ne cesse de prier (Lai "de la fonteinne"). Ma fin est mon
   commencement. **Hilliard Ensemble / Paul Hillier.** Hyperion Ⓔ CDA66358 (54 minutes: DDD:
   2/90). Texts and translations included.   Ⓖ
Machaut's *Messe de Nostre Dame* is the earliest known setting of the Ordinary Mass by a single
composer though we cannot be certain either that Machaut wrote it at one time or even that he
initially intended to bring its six movements together. Paul Hillier avoids a full reconstruction: his
deference to 'authenticity' restricts itself to the usage of fourteenth-century French pronunciation of
the Latin. His ensemble sing two to a part, with prominent countertenors. It is arguable whether the
group sing the chant at too fast a tempo but they are smooth and flexible and the performance as a
whole is fluid and light in texture. Also included are two of Machaut's French compositions. The
wonderful *Lai "de la fonteinne"* is admirably sung by three tenors and is pure delight – food for the

heart as well as the intellect. The more familiar *Ma fin est mon commencement,* with its retrograde canon, is a final happy addition to this admirable disc.

Further listening ...

...Songs – Dame, de qui toute ma joie vient. Foy porter, honneur garder. Dame, je sui cilz/Fins cuers doulz. Tuit mi penser. Dame, mon cuer en vous temaint. Dame a qui m'ottri. Biauté qui toutes autres pere. Je vivroie liement. Rose, liz. Dame, a vous sans retollir. Amours me fait desirer. Douce dame jolie. Felix virgo/Inviolata/Ad te suspiramus. **Gothic Voices / Christopher Page.** Hyperion CDA66087 (1/84). ⓖ

...French Songs and Motets – Dame, je suis cilz/Fins cuer. Trop plus/Biauté paree/Je ne suis. Tres bonne et belle. Se mesdisans. Dame, je vueil endurer. *Coupled with works by* **Pycard, Solage** and **Anonymous** Gothic Voices / Christopher Page. Hyperion CDA66619 (6/93). *See review in the Collections section; refer to the Index to Reviews.*

Elizabeth Maconchy
British 1907-

Suggested listening ...

...Concertinos – Nos. 1 and 2. *Coupled with works by* **Arnold** and **Britten Thea King** (cl); **English Chamber Orchestra / Barry Wordsworth.** Hyperion CDA66634 (12/93). *See review under Arnold; refer to the Index to Reviews.*

...String Quartets – Nos. 1-4. **Hanson Quartet.** Unicorn-Kanchana DKPCD9080 (11/89).

...String Quartets – Nos. 5-8. **Bingham Quartet.** Unicorn-Kanchana DKPCD9081 (6/90).

...String Quartets – Nos. 9-12; No. 13, "Quartetto Corto". **Mistry Quartet.** Unicorn-Kanchana DKPCD9082 (2/91).

...Sirens' Song. *Coupled with works by* **Hoddinott, J. Harvey, Musgrave, T. Salter** and **Lutyens.** Ionian Singers / Timothy Salter; Thalia Myers (pf); Erik Jacobsen (perc). Usk Recordings USK1216 (3/96).

Bruno Maderna
Italian 1920-1973

Maderna Oboe Concertos Nos. 1-3. **Heinz Holliger** (ob); **Cologne Radio Symphony Orchestra / Gary Bertini.** Philips Ⓟ 442 015-2PH (69 minutes: DDD: 9/94). Recorded 1993.

The oboe was a special instrument for Bruno Maderna, and he filled these three concertos (composed in 1962-63, 1967 and 1973) with solo lines in which sharply fragmented and fluently rhapsodic materials constantly interact. Heinz Holliger, in turn, pours all his unrivalled dexterity and capacity for infinitely varied expressive nuance into the performances here. Yet the music remains problematic. Perhaps it would be better to say that the concerto form remained problematic for Maderna. Though he relished ringing the changes in the ways in which the oboe and its various close relatives – musette, oboe d'amore, cor anglais – could be played, and devised a host of imaginative orchestral contexts which set off the soloist to best advantage, the forms as such never seem to advance beyond a rather primitive succession of improvisatory episodes. Neither large-scale contrast nor steadily accumulating expressive tension are high priorities. The First Concerto finds Maderna fascinated by the possibilities of translating electronic sounds into purely orchestral textures, while the Second and Third reflect the impact of those mobile structures, and graphic notations, which a range of European composers from Lutosławski to Boulez employed to such memorable avant-garde purpose in the 1960s. Maderna was responding to important innovations without, at least in these works, adding very much of his own to them. The recordings are technically excellent, giving natural prominence to the soloist while still conveying the full range of the often exotic colours to be heard in the orchestral accompaniments. Maderna could not have wished for more distinguished advocacy.

Further listening ...

...Satyricon. **Soloists; Divertimento Ensemble / Sandro Gorli.** Salabert Actuels SCD9101 (9/93).

...Hyperion. **Soloists; Les Jeunes Soloists Vocal Ensemble; Asko Ensemble / Peter Eötvös.** Auvidis Montaigne MO782014 (9/93).

Leevi Madetoja
Finnish 1897-1947

Madetoja Comedy Overture, Op. 53. Symphony No. 3 in A major, Op. 55. Okon Fuoko – ballet suite, Op. 58. The Ostrobothnians – suite, Op. 52. **Iceland Symphony Orchestra / Petri Sakari.** Chandos Ⓟ CHAN9036 (71 minutes: DDD: 8/92). Recorded 1991.

Madetoja belongs to the generation immediately after Sibelius and his music inhabits much the same landscape. This issue brings recordings from the excellent Iceland Symphony Orchestra, including the Third Symphony, the finest of Madetoja's works. It comes from the period 1925-26 which he spent in Houilles not far from Paris. Its outlook is both Gallic in its clarity of line and elegance of orchestration, and Finnish in its modality and sense of melancholy. Its invention is well sustained and only in the finale does the inspiration appear to sag. The *Comedy Overture* is a delightful piece, which gets better at each hearing, and the ballet suite, *Okon Fuoko,* is inventive and atmospheric. Of course, though he has a distinctive voice, Madetoja does not possess the extraordinary intuitive grasp of form that Sibelius had at his command but as readers who invest in this disc will discover, he is a rewarding composer who does not deserve to be passed over. The Chandos disc has very natural recorded sound.

Additional recommendation ...

...The Ostrobothnians – Suite, Op. 52. Symphony No. 3. Okon Fuoko – ballet suite. **Finnish Radio Symphony Orchestra / Jukka-Pekka Saraste.** Finlandia Ⓕ 4509-96867-2 (58 minutes: DDD: 4/95).

Further listening ...

...Symphonies – No. 1 in F major, Op. 29; No. 2 in E flat major, Op. 35. **Iceland Symphony Orchestra / Petri Sakari.** Chandos CHAN9115 (1/93).

Jef Maes
Dutch 1905-

New review

Maes Symphony No. 2 in A major. Viola Concerto[a]. Ouverture concertante. Arabesque and Scherzo[b]. [b]**Frank Vanhove** (fl); [a]**Leo DeNeve** (va); **Royal Flanders Philharmonic Orchestra / Gerard Oskamp.** Marco Polo Ⓕ 8 223741 (55 minutes: DDD: 11/95). Recorded 1994.

There is always a temptation to label lushly scored neo-romantic symphonies as 'potential film music', and yet a minute or two spent in the company of Jef Maes's emotionally candid Second Symphony inevitably suggests – at least to this listener – passionate happenings on the big screen. Maes calls himself a "modern romantic". The symphony's orchestration and melodic complexion seem to acknowledge both Richard Strauss and Korngold, while the alternation of sultry romance (very much a 1920-30s vintage) and energetic action music could have hailed from the pen of many a 'second league' symphonist. Maes's harmonic writing is occasionally reminiscent of Gershwin, although the second movement's foggy impressionism (dark brass and woodwinds, rhapsodizing strings) strikes far nearer our own shores (Bax, maybe). The finale is distinguished by colourful brass writing *à la* Hindemith and the symphony ends in a mood of martial exuberance. As an orchestral, chamber and solo violist, Maes was well equipped to compose a viola concerto and indeed his lively contribution to the genre (dating from 1956) deserves an occasional airing. Again, reverie alternates with busyness, although here Maes seems to take himself rather less seriously and the concerto is notably good-humoured. The other works in the programme are both lighter in tone. All the performances are lusty and enthusiastic; the recordings are excellent, and the documentation informative. Recommended to all post-romantics who possess a musically sweet tooth.

Filipe de Magalhaes
Portuguese c1571-1652

Suggested listening ...

...Asperges me[a]. Missa O soberana luz[a]. Commissa mea pavesco[a]. *Coupled with* **Carreira** Tento[b]. **Coelho** Verso sobre Ave maris stella Deo gratias[b]. **F. Guerrero** Ave virgo sanctissima[a]. La luz de vuestros ojos[a]. **Alvarado** Obre sobra el Pange lingua[b]. **Brito** Salve regina[a]. **Anonymous** Obra de sexto tom para o Levantar o Deus[b]. Gregorian Chant for the Festival of the Virgin Mary – Nativity of the BVM Mass[a]. [a]**A Capella Portuguesa / Owen Rees** with [b]**Stephen Farr** (org). Hyperion CDA66725 (11/94).

...Vidi acquam. Missa O soberana luz. Commissa mea pavesco. *Coupled with* **Lôbo** Audivi vocem da caelo. Pater peccavi. **Cardoso** Lamentatio. Magnificat secundi toni. **Fonseca** Beata viscera. **Trosylho** Circumdederunt me. **Escobar** Clamabat autem mulier. **Ars Nova / Bo Holten.** Naxos 8 553310 (3/96).

Ester Mägi
Estonian 1922-

Suggested listening ...

...The Ancient Kannel. *Coupled with* **Kangro** Suite, Op. 1. **Rääts** Toccata. **Sumera** Piece from the Year 1981. **Tüür** Sonata. **Vähi** Fata Morgana. **Pärt** Partita. **Lauri Väinmaa** (pf). Finlandia 4509-95704-2 (7/95).

Gustav Mahler
Austrian 1860-1911

New review

Mahler Symphonies. [bh]**Cheryl Studer**, [c]**Jessye Norman**, [h]**Sylvia McNair**, [h]**Andrea Rost** (sops); [b]**Waltraud Meier**, [d]**Frederica von Stade**, [h]**Anne Sofie von Otter** (mezzos); [h]**Rosemarie Lang** (contr); [h]**Peter Seiffert** (ten); [h]**Bryn Terfel** (bass-bar); [h]**Jan-Hendrik Rootering** (bass); [c]**Vienna Boys' Choir;** [h]**Tölz Boys' Choir;** [b]**Arnold Schoenberg Choir;** [c]**Vienna State Opera Chorus;** [h]**Berlin Radio Chorus;** [h]**Prague Philharmonic Chorus;** [aeh]**Berlin Philharmonic Orchestra;** [bcdij]**Vienna Philharmonic Orchestra;** [fg]**Chicago Symphony Orchestra / Claudio Abbado.** DG Ⓜ 447 023-2GX12 (12 discs: 718 minutes: ADD/DDD: 12/95). Texts and translations included. Item marked [a] from 431 769-

2GH (10/91), [b]439 953-2GH2 (5/94), [c]2741 010 (7/82), [d]2530 966 (6/78), [e]437 789-2GH (12/93), [f]2707 117 (11/80), [g]413 773-2GH2 (3/85), [h]445 843-2GH2 (6/95), [ij]423 564-2GH2 (8/88). Recorded 1977-94.

No. 1 in D major[a] (recorded live in 1989); No. 2 in C minor, "Resurrection"[b] (1992); No. 3 in D minor[c]; No. 4 in G major[d]; No. 5 in C sharp minor[e] (1993 – *Gramophone Editor's choice.*); No. 6 in A minor[f]; No. 7 in E minor[g]; No. 8 in E flat major, "Symphony of a Thousand"[h] (1994); No. 9 in D major[i] (1987); No. 10 in F sharp minor – Adagio[j] (1985).

The current pre-eminence of Gustav Mahler in the concert-hall and on disc is not something that could have been anticipated – other than by the composer himself. Hard now to believe that his revival had to wait until the centenary celebrations of his birth in 1960. And yet by 1980 he was more widely esteemed than his longer-lived contemporaries Sibelius and Strauss and could suddenly be seen to tower over twentieth-century music much as Beethoven must have done in a previous age. (Not that he hadn't been there all along: the music of Berg, Shostakovich, Britten and even Copland bears witness to this, disparately but resonantly Mahlerian.) By this time too, a new generation of conductors had come to the fore, further transforming our perceptions of the composer. Claudio Abbado is arguably the most distinguished of this group and, while his interpretations will not satisfy every listener on every occasion, they make an excellent choice for the library shelves, when the price is reasonably competitive and the performances so emblematic (and arguably central to our understanding) of Mahler's place in contemporary musical life.

Of the alternatives listed below, Haitink's package has the fewest expressive distortions while Bernstein's is of course the most ceaselessly emotive of them all; neither has Abbado's particular combination of qualities. It is probably no accident that Donald Mitchell's notes for the new set are focused on the nature of Mahler's 'modernity'. For it is that ironic, inquisitive, preternaturally aware young composer who haunts this conductor's performances. Not for Abbado the heavy, saturated textures of nineteenth-century romanticism, nor the chilly rigidity of some of his own 'modernist' peers. Instead an unaffected warmth and elegance of sound allows everything to come through naturally – in so far as the different venues and DG's somewhat variable technology will permit – even in the most searingly intense of climaxes. Increasingly these days, Abbado is presenting Mahler as a fluent classicist, less concerned to characterize the surface battle of conflicting emotions than to elucidate the underlying symphonic structure. The lack of Solti's brand of forthright theatricality can bring a feeling of disappointment, as in his recent live versions of Nos. 2 and 8. But even where he underplays the drama of the moment, sufficient sense of urgency is sustained by a combination of well-judged tempos, marvellously graduated dynamics and precisely balanced, ceaselessly changing textures. The propulsion comes from within. For those still put off by Mahler's supposed vulgarity the unhurried classicism of these readings may well be the most convincing demonstration of the composer's absolute integrity.

It was in November 1907 that Mahler famously told Sibelius that "the symphony must be like the world. It must embrace everything." And perhaps it is only today that we see this as a strength rather than a weakness in his music. He wrote music that is 'about' its own past while at the same time probing into all our futures, music that is so all-embracing and communicates with such directness that we can make it 'mean' whatever we want it to, confident that we alone have really understood the code. Abbado lacks Bernstein's desire to explore these limitless possibilities every time he mounts the podium, but some will count that a blessing. These are committed and authoritative performances.

Additional recommendations ...

...Nos. 1-9. No. 10 – Adagio. **Soloists; Bavarian Radio Chorus; Tölz Boys' Choir; Regensburg Cathedral Boys' Choir; Munich Motet Choir; North German Radio Chorus; West German Radio Chorus; Bavarian Radio Symphony Orchestra / Rafael Kubelík.** DG ℗ 429 042-2GX10 (ten discs: 651 minutes: ADD: 5/90). 🅖🅖

...Nos. 1-9. No. 10 – Adagio. **Soloists; Brooklyn Boys' Choir; Vienna Boys' Choir; Westminster Choir; New York Choral Artists; Vienna Singverein; Vienna State Opera Chorus; New York Philharmonic Orchestra; Royal Concertgebouw Orchestra; Vienna Philharmonic Orchestra / Leonard Bernstein.** DG Ⓜ 435 162-2GX13 (13 discs: 764 minutes: ADD/DDD: 2/92). 🅖🅖

...Nos. 1-9. **Soloists; Chicago Chorus and Symphony Orchestra / Sir Georg Solti.** Decca ℗ 430 804-2DC10 (ten discs: 672 minutes: DDD/ADD: 4/92). 🅖

...Nos. 1-9. No. 10 – Adagio. **Soloists; Southend Boys's Choir; Tiffin Boys' School Choir; London Philharmonic Choir and Orchestra / Klaus Tennstedt.** EMI Mahler Edition available as follows: Nos. 1-4: Ⓜ CMS7 64471-2 (four discs: 295 minutes: ADD/DDD: 4/93). Nos. 6-8: Ⓜ CMS7 64476-2 (four discs: 254 minutes: ADD/DDD: 4/93). Nos. 5, 9 and 10 – Adagio: Ⓜ CMS7 64481-2 (189 minutes: ADD/DDD: 4/93). 🅖

...Nos. 1-9. **Concertgebouw Orchestra / Bernard Haitink.** Philips Bernard Haitink Symphony Edition Ⓜ 442 050-2PB10 (ten discs: 692 minutes: ADD: 11/94). 🅖🅖

Mahler Symphony No. 1 in D major. Berlin Philharmonic Orchestra / Claudio Abbado. DG ℗ 431 769-2GH (55 minutes: DDD: 10/91). Recorded live in 1989. 🅖🅖

While Bernstein's vision of this symphony is intense, with every corner of the work stamped with his personality, Abbado directs a technically immaculate account. Combined with his own particular insight this performance conveys more a sense of Mahler's sound world rather than, as previously, Mahler and Bernstein's. The playing of the BPO combined with the extraordinarily vivid and well balanced recording takes the performance of this work into a new league. Perhaps orchestras are only now fully able to realize Mahler's music in the way that they have been able to with, for instance, Beethoven's for years. There is here a confidence, familiarity and precision that is most unusual and deeply impressive. Added to its technical perfection is Abbado's assured control of tempos, phrasing and dynamics. These define very strongly both the character and atmosphere of each movement which are much more clearly delineated than has usually been the case in the past. The overall result is a major symphonic work at last coming into true focus: both weaknesses, such as its episodic nature, and strengths, its tremendous originality and character, stand fully revealed. Warts and all, this is an outburst of young musical genius fully realized by another, interpretative, genius.

Additional recommendations ...

...No. 1. Lieder eines fahrenden Gesellen. **Bavarian Radio Symphony Orchestra / Rafael Kubelík.** DG Classikon Ⓑ 439 410-2GCL (66 minutes: ADD: 2/90). ⒼⒼⒼ

...No. 1. **London Symphony Orchestra / Sir Georg Solti.** Decca Ⓜ 417 701-2DM (ADD). ⒼⒼ

...No. 1. **Frankfurt Radio Symphony Orchestra / Eliahu Inbal.** Denon Ⓕ C37-7537 (55 minutes: DDD: 12/85). ⒼⒼ

...No. 1. **Berlin Philharmonic Orchestra / Bernard Haitink.** Philips Ⓕ 420 936-2PH (57 minutes: DDD: 10/88). ⒼⒼ

...No. 1. **Royal Concertgebouw Orchestra / Leonard Bernstein.** DG Ⓕ 427 303-2GH (56 minutes: DDD: 3/89). ⒼⒼ

...No. 1. **London Symphony Orchestra / Jascha Horenstein.** Unicorn-Kanchana Souvenir Ⓜ UKCD2012 (57 minutes: ADD: 4/89). Ⓖ

...No. 1. No. 2[a]. [a]**Emilia Cundari** (sop); [a]**Maureen Forrester** (mez); **Columbia Symphony Orchestra / Bruno Walter.** CBS Masterworks Ⓜ CD45674 (two discs: 132 minutes: ADD: 7/90). Ⓖ

...No. 1. **Chicago Symphony Orchestra / Klaus Tennstedt.** EMI Ⓕ CDC7 54217-2 (61 minutes: DDD: 11/91). Ⓖ

...No. 1. **Royal Liverpool Philharmonic Orchestra / Sir Charles Mackerras.** EMI Eminence Ⓜ CD-EMX2197 (54 minutes: DDD: 12/92). Ⓖ

...No. 1. Blumine. **City of Birmingham Symphony Orchestra / Simon Rattle.** EMI Ⓕ CDC7 54647-2 (65 minutes: DDD: 12/92). Ⓖ

...Nos. 1[a] and 2[b]. [b]**Sheila Armstrong** (sop); [b]**Dame Janet Baker** (mez); [b]**Edinburgh Festival Chorus;** [a]**New York Philharmonic Orchestra,** [b]**London Symphony Orchestra / Leonard Bernstein.** Sony Classical Bernstein Royal Edition Ⓜ SM2K47573 (two discs 142 minutes: ADD: 5/93). Ⓖ

...No. 1. Blumine. **Danish National Radio Symphony Orchestra / Leif Segerstam.** Chandos Ⓕ CHAN9242 (67 minutes: DDD: 3/94). Ⓖ

...No. 1. Blumine. **Florida Philharmonic Orchestra / James Judd.** Harmonia Mundi Ⓕ HMU90 7118 (66 minutes: DDD: 9/94). Ⓖ

Mahler Symphony No. 2 in C minor, "Resurrection". **Arleen Auger** (sop); **Dame Janet Baker** (mez); **City of Birmingham Symphony Chorus and Orchestra / Sir Simon Rattle.** EMI Ⓕ CDS7 47962-8 (two discs: 86 minutes: DDD: 12/87). Text and translation included. From EX270598-3 (10/87). *Gramophone Award Winner 1988.* ⒼⒼⒼ

Mahler Symphony No. 2 in C minor, "Resurrection". **Cheryl Studer** (sop); **Waltraud Meier** (mez); **Arnold Schoenberg Choir; Vienna Philharmonic Orchestra / Claudio Abbado.** DG Ⓕ 439 953-2GH2 (two discs: 87 minutes: DDD: 5/94). Recorded live in the Musikverein, Vienna in 1992. *Selected by Sounds in Retrospect.* ⒼⒼ

The folk-poems from *Des Knaben Wunderhorn*, with their complex mixture of moods and strong ironic edge, formed the basis of Mahler's inspiration for the Second Symphony. It is a work of huge scope, emotionally as well as physically taxing, and from Rattle it receives a performance that remarkably rekindles the feeling of a live performance with a quite breathtaking immediacy. The CBSO play magnificently and Rattle's attention to the letter of the score never hinders his overall vision of this masterpiece. The recording is superb. As has often been suggested in these pages, a live performance should have a headstart in tapping the vital component of spiritual uplift. Abbado presents the score directly with the maximum clarity and precision. In this he is assisted by playing of astounding accuracy and beauty of tone, captured in a recording of (impractically?) wide dynamic range and exquisite detail. Rattle's more radical rethink is not on the agenda; neither is his slow and deliberate treatment of the curious staccato nose-dive at the end of the first movement. Abbado's funeral march is relatively contained, the quiet passages very atmospheric. The deft, restrained manner works well enough in the inner movements, especially the *Andante moderato*. He launches into the third movement *Scherzo* with the audience restive (elsewhere they are pleasingly inaudible); there follows charm but perhaps insufficient sense of threat. The "Urlicht" is again on the cool side, though Waltraud Meier, beautifully controlling her legato while conscientiously projecting to a real public in a large hall, is suddenly impassioned at "Ich bin von Gott". The massive finale, conceived here on the very grandest scale, goes well but not quite well enough: the choir are backwardly balanced and do not efface memories of the Philharmonia Chorus for Klemperer or the City of

Birmingham chorus for Rattle. More seriously, there are some agogic touches which impede the natural flow. However, as a document of a great occasion, the Abbado set stands up very well indeed.

Additional recommendations ...

...**Barbara Hendricks** (sop); **Christa Ludwig** (mez); **Westminster Choir; New York Philharmonic Orchestra / Leonard Bernstein.** DG Ⓕ 423 395-2GH2 (two discs: 94 minutes: DDD: 7/88). ⒼⒼ

...**Benita Valente** (sop); **Maureen Forrester** (mez); **Ardwyn Singers; BBC Welsh Chorus; Cardiff Polyphonic Choir; Dyfed Choir; London Symphony Chorus and Orchestra / Gilbert Kaplan.** IMP Classics Ⓜ DPCD910 (two discs: 83 minutes: DDD: 1/89). ⒼⒼ

...**Elisabeth Schwarzkopf** (sop); **Hilde Rössl-Majdan** (mez); **Philharmonia Chorus and Orchestra / Otto Klemperer.** EMI Studio Ⓜ CDM7 69662-2 (79 minutes: ADD: 1/90). ⒼⒼⒼ

...**Sylvia McNair** (sop); **Jard van Nes** (contr); **Ernst-Senff Chorus; Berlin Philharmonic Orchestra / Bernard Haitink.** Philips Ⓕ 438 935-2PH2 (two discs: 86 minutes: DDD: 11/94). ⒼⒼ

...**Ruth Ziesak** (sop); **Charlotte Hellekant** (mez); **San Francisco Symphony Chorus and Orchestra / Herbert Blomstedt.** Decca Ⓜ 443 350-2DX2 (two discs: 80 minutes: DDD: 12/94). *Selected by Sounds in Retrospect.* Ⓖ

...No. 2[a]. **Beethoven** (arr. Mahler) String Quartet No. 11 in F minor, Op. 95, "Serioso". [a]**Tina Kilberg** (sop); [a]**Kirsten Dolberg** (mez); [a]**Danish National Radio Choir; Danish National Radio Symphony Orchestra / Leif Segerstam.** Chandos Ⓕ CHAN9266/7 (two discs: 116 minutes: DDD: 10/95).

Mahler Symphony No. 3 in D minor. **Norma Procter** (contr); **Wandsworth School Boys' Choir; Ambrosian Singers; London Symphony Orchestra / Jascha Horenstein.** Unicorn-Kanchana Souvenir Ⓜ UKCD2006/7 (two discs: 97 minutes: ADD: 11/88). Text and translation included. From RHS302/03 (12/70). Ⓖ

Every now and again, along comes a Mahler *performance* that no serious collector can afford to be without. Horenstein's interpretation of the Third Symphony is an outstanding example and its reissue on CD at mid price is a major addition to the Mahler discography. No other conductor has surpassed Horenstein in his total grasp of every facet of the enormous score. Even though the LSO strings of the day were not as powerful as they later became, they play with suppleness and a really tense sound, especially appropriate in the kaleidoscopic first movement, where changes of tempo and mood reflect the ever-changing face of nature. Horenstein gives the posthorn solo to a flügelhorn, a successful experiment. His light touch in the middle movements is admirable, and Norma Procter is a steady soloist in "O Mensch! Gib acht!", with the Wandsworth School Boys' Choir bimm-bamming as if they were all Austrian-born! Then comes the *Adagio* finale, its intensity and ecstasy sustained by Horenstein without dragging the tempo. The recording is not as full or rich in dynamic range as some made more recently, but it is still a classic.

Additional recommendations ...

...No. 3[a]. Four Rückert Lieder[b]. Seven Lieder und Gesänge aus dre Jugendzeit[b]. [a]**Martha Lipton** (mez); [b]**Dietrich Fischer-Dieskau** (bar); [a]womens' chorus of the **Schola Cantorum**; [a]**Boys' Choir of the Transfiguration**; [a]**New York Philharmonic Orchestra / Leonard Bernstein** (pf[b]). Sony Classical Ⓕ SM2K47576 (two discs: 142 minutes: ADD: 12/86). ⒼⒼ

...**Jessye Norman** (sop); **Vienna Boys' Choir; Vienna State Opera Concert Choir; Vienna Philharmonic Orchestra / Claudio Abbado.** DG Ⓕ 410 715-2GH2 (two discs: 103 minutes: DDD: 11/88). ⒼⒼ

...**Christa Ludwig** (mez); **Brooklyn Boys' Chorus; New York Choral Artists; New York Philharmonic Orchestra / Leonard Bernstein.** DG Ⓕ 427 328-2GH2 (two discs: 106 minutes: DDD: 6/89). Ⓖ

...**Jard van Nes** (contr); **Tölz Boys' Choir; women's voices of the Ernst-Senff Choir; Berlin Philharmonic Orchestra / Bernard Haitink.** Philips Ⓕ 432 162-2PH2 (two discs: 103 minutes: DDD: 4/92). ⒼⒼ

Mahler Symphony No. 4 in G major. **Dawn Upshaw** (sop); **Cleveland Orchestra / Christoph von Dohnányi.** Decca Ⓕ 440 315-2DH (57 minutes: DDD: 4/94). Text and translation included. Recorded 1992. Ⓖ

New review

Mahler Symphony No. 4 in G major. **Angela Maria Blasi** (sop); **Bavarian Radio Symphony Orchestra / Sir Colin Davis.** RCA Victor Red Seal Ⓕ 09026 62521-2 (61 minutes: DDD: 7/96). Text and translation included.

Rarely has this work been recorded with such cool precision but Decca's sound, effective enough in its unremitting brightness, is not exactly state-of-the-art. It is slightly constricted and there is, perhaps, too much minutely observed instrumental detail. That said, this is probably the best yet in Dohnányi's Mahler series. His first movement is much less heavily inflected than Leonard Bernstein's. But, for once, the more objective manner is not unsympathetic. It was after all the music's apparent simplicity, the stylized brightness of mood, which so confounded Mahler's contemporaries. There is no profound *Weltschmerz* here, neither a titanic struggle with, nor a resigned acceptance of, Death. Dohnányi obtains excellent results by setting a sensible tempo, the jingle player rigidly in step as the first subject creeps in. Only the horns are not quite as disciplined as you might expect from this source. In the second movement, the menacing timbre of Freund Hein's fiddle is consciously emulated by Daniel Majeske; his 'ugly' nuances are not always well integrated into the line, and the trio sections, though full of detailed pointing, seem rather lacking in charm. But Dohnányi's finale almost restores the balance. This is an extremely alert reading, with both conductor and soloist responsive to every nuance of the text. Though the orchestral accompaniment is not always as light and delicate as it might be, woodwind tone is wonderfully well matched at the start. After Sylvia McNair's more generalized rendition for Haitink, Dawn Upshaw is a demonstrative, almost unruly child; her intonation and enunciation are, moreover, flawless, with just the right hint of boyish vulnerability. However you rate Dohnányi's performance in its entirety, this is another triumph for Upshaw.

Sir Colin Davis's Fourth is enormously enjoyable. Maybe his Mahler is too restless, too blatantly 'conducted' for some tastes, but his occasionally heavy-handed manipulations of tempo are at least symptomatic of a desire to communicate a personal vision of and affection for Mahler's score. Both playing and recording are of exceptional standard, even if the lack of ironic edge to the sound lends the music-making a somewhat old-fashioned air (strikingly at odds with RCA's strident, pop-inspired packaging). Davis's scherzo is warm and characterful in a rather cumbersome sort of way, but his slow movement is a marvel – elevated in feeling and blessedly free of the intrusive inflexions which mar an otherwise refreshing account of the opening movement. No more affecting account has appeared for a decade. After this, the finale disappoints just a little. The 'operatic' soloist does not really point her words with sufficient poignancy – nor does she seem willing or able to sing quietly in her upper register – and Sir Colin again insists on playing up the composer's expressive hesitations, adding one or two of his own. This may not be wholly idiomatic Mahler and yet, like so many recent discs from this source, it has abundant humanity and an extraordinary lack of artifice. The sympathetic acoustic of the Herkulessaal, well caught, is a great asset.

Additional recommendations ...

...No. 4. Lieder eines fahrenden Gesellen. **Judith Raskin** (sop); **Cleveland Orchestra / George Szell.** Sony Classical Essential Classics Ⓕ SBK46535 (75 minutes: ADD: 11/88). ⒼⒼ

...No. 4. **Helen Donath** (sop); **Frankfurt Radio Symphony Orchestra / Eliahu Inbal.** Denon Ⓕ C37-7952 (57 minutes: DDD: 2/87).

...No. 4. **Helmut Wittek** (treb); **Concertgebouw Orchestra / Leonard Bernstein.** DG Ⓕ 423 607-2GH (57 minutes: DDD: 8/88). ⒼⒼ

...No. 4. **Felicity Lott** (sop); **London Philharmonic Orchestra / Franz Welser-Möst.** EMI Eminence Ⓜ CD-EMX2139 (63 minutes: DDD: 12/88). Ⓖ

...No. 4. **Barbara Hendricks** (sop); **Los Angeles Philharmonic Orchestra / Esa-Pekka Salonen.** Sony Classical Ⓕ SK48380 (58 minutes: DDD: 8/92). Ⓖ

Mahler Symphony No. 5 in C sharp minor. **Berlin Philharmonic Orchestra / Claudio Abbado.** DG Ⓕ 437 789-2GH (69 minutes: DDD: 12/93). Recorded live in the Philharmonie, Berlin in 1993. Ⓖ
The *Adagietto* is suddenly, almost imperceptibly, there. It is the hallmark of any great performance of the symphony, and Abbado is in amongst the very select few as these magical bars materialize. It might even be the most beautiful, the most subtly inflected account of the movement we have yet heard on disc; the breathless *pianopianissimo* to a barely grazed *glissando* towards the close is out of this world. So too is the huge central *Scherzo*, another of those testing movements separating natural Mahlerians from the would-bes. The key here is patience – respect for space, silence, atmosphere. Not even Bernstein (also DG) quite matches Abbado's relish of the finale's airborne fantasy (how commonly this movement is driven to distraction): it's that delicate balance between tip-toeing sweetness and light and inherently rugged, foot-stomping good humour. He is right inside the spirit and sound of this score, much freer and less calculating over detail than he can sometimes be. In the eye of the second movement storm is an extraordinary passage for shell-shocked cellos over rolling timpani: it's rather like the *Adagietto*; only a select few get through to the subtext. Abbado is one.

Additional recommendations ...

...No. 5. **Frankfurt Radio Symphony Orchestra / Eliahu Inbal.** Denon Ⓕ CO-1088 (73 minutes: DDD: 1/87).

...**Vienna Philharmonic Orchestra / Leonard Bernstein.** DG Ⓕ 423 608-2GH (75 minutes: DDD: 8/88). ⒼⒼ

...**New Philharmonia Orchestra / Sir John Barbirolli.** EMI Ⓜ CDM7 64749-2 (74 minutes: ADD: 11/88). *Gramophone* classical 100. ⒼⒼⒼ

Mahler Symphony No. 6 in A minor. Kindertotenlieder[a]. [a]**Thomas Hampson** (bar); **Vienna Philharmonic Orchestra / Leonard Bernstein.** DG Ⓕ 427 697-2GH2 (two discs: 115 minutes: DDD: 1/90). Recorded live in 1988. ⒼⒼ
Mahler's tragic Sixth Symphony digs more profoundly into the nature of man and Fate than any of his earlier works, closing in desolation, a beat on the bass drum, a coffin lid closing. Bernstein's reading was a live recording at a concert, with all the electricity of such an occasion, and the Vienna Philharmonic Orchestra respond to the conductor's dark vision of Mahler's score with tremendous bravura. Fortunately, the achingly tender slow movement brings some relief, but with the enormous finale lasting over 30 minutes we must witness a resumption of a battle to the death and the final outcome. The coupling is a logical one, for the *Kindertotenlieder* takes up the theme of death yet again. But it is in a totally different, quieter way: these beautiful songs express a parent's grief over the loss of a child, and although some prefer a woman's voice, the sensitive Thomas Hampson makes

a good case here for a male singer. The recording of both works is so good that one would not know it was made 'live', particularly as the applause is omitted.

Additional recommendations ...

...No. 6. Five Rückert-Lieder[a]. [a]**Christa Ludwig** (mez); **Berlin Philharmonic Orchestra / Herbert von Karajan.** DG Ⓕ 415 099-2GH2 (two discs: 102 minutes: ADD: 4/85). 🅖🅖

...No. 6. Five Rückert-Lieder[a]. [a]**Hanna Schwarz** (mez); **Chicago Symphony Orchestra / Claudio Abbado.** DG Galleria Ⓜ 423 928-2GGA2 (two discs: 104 minutes: ADD/DDD: 3/89). 🅖

...No. 6. **City of Birmingham Symphony Orchestra / Simon Rattle.** EMI Ⓕ CDS7 54047-2 (two discs: 86 minutes: DDD: 11/90).

...Nos. 6[a] and 8[b]. [b]**Soloists;** [b]**Leeds Festival Chorus;** [b]**London Symphony Chorus;** [b]**Orpington Junior Singers;** [b]**Highgate School Choir;** [b]**Finchley Children's Music Group;** [a]**New York Philharmonic Orchestra,** [b]**London Symphony Orchestra / Leonard Bernstein.** Sony Classical Bernstein Royal Edition Ⓜ SM3K47581 (three discs: 157 minutes: ADD: 5/93). *Gramophone classical 100.* 🅖🅖🅖

...No. 6. **Vienna Philharmonic Orchestra / Pierre Boulez.** DG Ⓕ 445 835-2GH (79 minutes: DDD: 6/95).

...No. 6. **R. Strauss** Metamorphosen. **New Philharmonia Orchestra / Sir John Barbirolli.** EMI Rouge et Noir Ⓜ CZS7 67816-2 (two discs: 111 minutes: ADD: 9/95).

New review

Mahler Symphonies – No. 6 in A minor[a]; No. 7 in E minor[b]. **London Philharmonic Orchestra / Klaus Tennstedt.** EMI Ⓕ CDS5 55294-2 (three discs: 180 minutes: DDD: 9/95). Recorded live in [a]1991 and [b]1993.

In spite of the difficulties, Klaus Tennstedt always thrived on the tensions of live performance and this disc receives a particularly warm welcome in the wake of his retirement from the podium. They present the conductor at his most single-minded in music that always brought out the best in him. Not that the results will be to all tastes. This is not all-embracing, world-view Mahler. The sight-lines are too limited for that, the outlook sometimes constrictingly bleak. Despite Tennstedt's inspirational approach there is a lack of tonal variety and the London Philharmonic can sound penny plain for all the dour strength of the brass. This is partly because the conductor is indifferent to the finer points of stylization. You won't find Bernstein's flexibility and emotional range: Tennstedt's rubato, similarly extreme, has a coarser grain and is intended neither to console nor to play up Mahler's sticky Viennese lyricism. What Tennstedt brings to these scores is an aura of integrity and a fierce intensity of expression finally unencumbered by the technical flaws that have sometimes detracted from his achievement. In both works, EMI have obtained good results from the tapes given the acoustic attributes of the venue. The Sixth is the more impressive of the two readings, executed with splenetic zeal at broader tempos than Tennstedt at one time favoured in this music. The Seventh sounds a little less confident. The main body of the movement has the grittily determined demeanour of the Sixth, its second section most obviously emotive, dripping with rubato. In music so reliant on colour and texture there isn't really enough gradation of dynamic: the more sparsely orchestrated passages sound insufficiently hushed and the sluggish alpine reveries offer no refuge from anxious monochrome. The rest of the performance is not uninteresting – the central *Scherzo* incisive, the second *Nachtmusik* carefully prepared and notable for the dusky veiled tone of the strings, the vigorous finale solid rather than crisp. And yet, in attempting to push home every nuance, Tennstedt could in the end be destroying what it is he is trying to create, rocking the boat so much that forward momentum is lost. If you take the Seventh to be an inherently contradictory search for an unrealized ideal of expression, you might find Tennstedt's disruptive manner just the ticket – he never seems quite sure which way to turn. Go elsewhere – to Bernstein above all – if you want the music to make more conventional sense. What we have here are two expertly captured performances by a Mahlerian with a singular vision – ungainly and uncomfortable perhaps, but for many unforgettable.

Mahler Symphony No. 7 in E minor.
Diepenbrock Im grossen Schweigen[a]. [a]**Håkan Hagegård** (bar); **Royal Concertgebouw Orchestra / Riccardo Chailly.** Decca Ⓕ 444 446-2DH2 (two discs: 108 minutes: DDD: 5/95). Text and translation included. 🅖🅖

With Rattle complete on one disc, Chailly's two-CD coupling looks ungenerous but is by no means ill-chosen. Diepenbrock's original version of *Im grossen Schweigen* was premièred in May 1906, making it a close contemporary of Mahler's Seventh, a composition whose 'meaning' is at least as elusive as that of the Nietzsche prose poem set by Diepenbrock. Where some commentators hear Mahler anatomizing a musical language on the brink of collapse, others note parallels with Strauss's Nietzsche-inspired *Also sprach Zarathustra* in the first movement, followed thereafter by "music embodying a romanticism that we thought we had overcome" (Bruno Walter). The raucous finale has everyone foxed. Be it a strength or a weakness, Chailly is not one to dwell on the darker side. His account is an opulent, positive, comfortably Straussian affair in which every detail is wonderfully articulated by the players, mostly without the brittle edges one might think implicit in those self-conscious stylistic allusions and precisely imagined sonorities. As for the recording, Decca have surpassed themselves.

Additional recommendations ...

...No. 7. **Chicago Symphony Orchestra / Sir Georg Solti.** Decca Ovation Ⓜ 425 041-2DM (78 minutes: ADD).

...No. 7. **New York Philharmonic Orchestra / Leonard Bernstein.** DG Ⓕ 419 211-2GH2 (two discs:
83 minutes: DDD: 12/86). ⒼⒼ
...No. 7. **Frankfurt Radio Symphony Orchestra / Eliahu Inbal.** Denon Ⓕ CO-1553/4 (two discs:
78 minutes: DDD: 8/87). Ⓖ
...No. 7. **City of Birmingham Symphony Orchestra / Simon Rattle.** EMI Ⓕ CDC7 54344-2
(77 minutes: DDD: 9/92). Ⓖ
...Nos. 7 and 9; 10 – Adagio. **New York Philharmonic Orchestra / Leonard Bernstein.** Sony Classical
Bernstein Royal Edition Ⓜ SM3K47585 (three discs: 185 minutes: ADD: 5/93).
...No. 7; No. 10 – Adagio. **Russian State Symphony Orchestra / Evgeni Svetlanov.** CdM Russian
Season Ⓕ RUS288 117/8 (two discs: 117 minutes: DDD: 3/96).

Mahler Symphony No. 8 in E flat major. **Elizabeth Connell, Edith Wiens, Felicity Lott** (sops);
Trudeliese Schmidt, Nadine Denize (contrs); **Richard Versalle** (ten); **Jorma Hynninen** (bar); **Hans
Sotin** (bass); **Tiffin Boys' School Choir; London Philharmonic Choir and Orchestra / Klaus
Tennstedt.** EMI Ⓕ CDS7 47625-8 (two discs: 82 minutes: DDD: 5/87). Notes, text and translation
included. From EX270474-3 (3/87). Recorded 1986. *Gramophone Award Winner 1987. Selected
by Sounds in Retrospect.* ⒼⒼ

New review

Mahler Symphony No. 8 in E flat major. **Heather Harper, Lucia Popp, Arleen Auger** (sops); **Yvonne
Minton** (mez); **Helen Watts** (contr); **René Kollo** (ten); **John Shirley-Quirk** (bar); **Martti Talvela**
(bass); **Vienna Boys' Choir; Vienna State Opera Chorus; Vienna Singverein; Chicago Symphony
Orchestra / Sir Georg Solti.** Decca Ⓕ 448 293-2DH (80 minutes: ADD: 5/96). Text and
translation included. From SET534/5 (10/72). Recorded 1971. ⒼⒼ
Mahler's extravagantly monumental Eighth Symphony, often known as the *Symphony of a Thousand*,
is the work that raises doubts in even his most devoted admirers. Its epic dimensions, staggering vision
and sheer profligacy of forces required make it a 'difficult work'. Given a great live performance it
will sway even the hardest of hearts; given a performance like Tennstedt's, reproduced with all the
advantages of CD, home-listeners, too, can be mightily impressed (and so, given the forces involved,
will most of the neighbourhood!) – the sheer volume of sound at the climax is quite overwhelming.
The work seeks to parallel the Christian's faith in the power of the Holy Spirit with the redeeming
power of love for mankind and Tennstedt's performance leaves no doubt that he believes totally in
Mahler's creation. It has a rapt, almost intimate, quality that makes his reading all the more moving.
The soloists are excellent and the choruses sing with great conviction.
    Of the so-called classic accounts, it is Solti's which most conscientiously sets out to convey an
impression of large forces in a big performance space, this despite the obvious resort to compression
and other forms of gerrymandering. Whatever the inconsistencies of Decca's multi-miking and
overdubbing, the overall effect remains powerful even today. The remastering has not eradicated all
trace of distortion at the very end, despite some cautious clipping of levels and, given the impressive
flood of choral tone at the start of the "Veni creator spiritus", it still seems a shame that the soloists
and the Chicago brass are quite so prominent in its closing stages: the chorus tend to recede into the
background. As for the performance itself, Solti's extrovert way with Part 1 works tremendously
without quite erasing memories of Bernstein's ecstatic fervour. In Part 2, it may be the patient
Wagnerian mysticism of Tennstedt that sticks in the mind. Less inclined to delay, Solti makes the
material sound more conventionally operatic. And yet for its combination of gut-wrenching
theatricality and great solo singing, Solti's version makes a plausible first choice – now more than ever.
Also, it has been squeezed onto a single CD, albeit at premium price.
Additional recommendations ...
...Nos. 6-8. **Soloists; Tiffin Boys' School Choir; London Philharmonic Choir and Orchestra / Klaus
Tennstedt.** EMI Mahler Edition Ⓜ CMS7 64476-2 (four discs: 254 minutes: ADD/DDD: 4/93).
No. 8 is the same recording as the one reviewed above. ⒼⒼ
...No. 8. **Soloists; Tölz Boys' Choir; Berlin Radio Chorus; Prague Philharmonic Chorus; Berlin
Philharmonic Orchestra / Claudio Abbado.** DG Ⓕ 445 843-2GH2 (two discs: 81 minutes: DDD:
6/95). Ⓖ

Mahler Symphony No. 9 in D major[a]. Kindertotenlieder[b]. Five Rückert-Lieder[c]. [bc]**Christa Ludwig**
(mez); **Berlin Philharmonic Orchestra / Herbert von Karajan.** DG Double Ⓜ 439 678-2GX2
(two discs: 131 minutes: ADD: 4/95). Items marked [a] from 2707 125 (5/81), [b]2707 081 (6/75),
[c]2707 082 (12/75). Recorded 1979-80. *Gramophone Award Winner 1981.* ⒼⒼ
Mahler's Ninth is a death-haunted work, but is filled, as Bruno Walter remarked, "with a sanctified
feeling of departure". Rarely has this symphony been shaped with such understanding and played
with such selfless virtuosity as it was by Herbert von Karajan and the Berlin Philharmonic in a
legendary series of concerts in 1982. Karajan came late to Mahler and yet, until the release of his
(rather more fiercely recorded) 1982 concert relay (happily, this has now been reissued on DG's
Karajan Gold label – see the listing below), he seemed content to regard this studio performance as
perhaps his finest achievement on disc (both incidentally won *Gramophone* Awards). Incidentally,
Richard Osborne, the original reviewer in *Gramophone* in 1984 described the Gold reissue as one of
the seven wonders of the modern musical world!. The attractions of the disc under review are greatly
enhanced by Christa Ludwig's carefully considered Mahler performances of the mid-1970s. The voice

may not be as fresh as it was when she recorded the songs in the late 1950s, but there are few readings of comparable nobility. Dame Janet Baker and Brigitte Fassbaender (both of whom are reviewed further on) are perhaps more responsive to the mood of each song, the one intimate, almost self-communing, the other more bitingly dramatic. Nevertheless, Ludwig articulates the text with unrivalled clarity and "In diesem Wetter" at least is positively operatic. How much of the grand scale should be attributed to Karajan? It is difficult to say; the voice *is* sometimes strained by the tempos. Despite the absence of texts, this collection is not to be missed. One-disc Ninths are not exactly commonplace but, with both Walter's celebrated 1938 recording and Barbirolli's 1964 Berlin version also in the running, the field is not short of distinguished contenders.

Additional recommendations ...

...No. 9; No. 10 – Adagio. **Frankfurt Radio Symphony Orchestra / Eliahu Inbal.** Denon
Ⓕ CO-1566/7 (two discs: 104 minutes: DDD: 1/88). Ⓖ

...No. 9. **Vienna Philharmonic Orchestra / Bruno Walter.** EMI Références mono Ⓜ CDH7 63029-2*
(70 minutes: ADD: 8/89). *Gramophone Award Winner 1989.* ⒼⒼⒼ

...No. 9. **Berlin Philharmonic Orchestra / Sir John Barbirolli.** EMI Studio Ⓜ CDM7 63115-2
(78 minutes: ADD: 11/89). Ⓖ

...No. 9[a.] **Wagner** Siegfried Idyll[b]. [a]**New Philharmonia Orchestra;** [b]**Philharmonia Orchestra / Otto Klemperer.** EMI Studio Ⓜ CMS7 63277-2 (two discs: 105 minutes: ADD: 1/90).

...No. 9. **Berlin Philharmonic Orchestra / Leonard Bernstein.** DG Ⓕ 435 378-2GH2 (two discs:
82 minutes: ADD: 5/92).

...No. 9. **Chicago Symphony Orchestra / Carlo Maria Giulini.** DG Double Ⓜ 437 467-2GX2
(two discs: 88 minutes: ADD: 12/94).

...No. 9. **Philharmonia Orchestra / Giuseppe Sinopoli.** DG Ⓕ 445 817-2GH2 (two discs: 83 minutes:
DDD: 3/95).

...No. 9. **Berlin Philharmonic Orchestra / Herbert von Karajan.** DG Karajan Gold Ⓕ 439 024-
2GHS2 (two discs: 85 minutes: DDD: 4/96). *Gramophone classical 100.* ⒼⒼⒼ

New review

Mahler Symphony No. 9 in D major. **Vienna Philharmonic Orchestra / Bruno Walter.** Dutton
Laboratories Essential Archive mono Ⓑ CDEA5005* (70 minutes: ADD: 8/96). Recorded live in
1938. From HMV DB3613/22 (1/39). ⒼⒼⒼ

Of course, there is no such thing as a 'definitive' performance but this is as near as one can get to it. Bruno Walter conducted the first performance of the Ninth Symphony in 1912 (it is dedicated to him) as well as this, its first commercial recording. It bestrode no fewer than ten 78rpm discs and consumed many fibre needles! Although later performances (including Walter's) have offered more polished orchestral playing and more vivid recording, none brings one closer to its world of feeling or takes one more deeply into its spirit. For all its blemishes, it has a unique authority and atmosphere. Its fires are white-hot and there is a blazing intensity that has never been surpassed on the gramophone. There is a demonic passion to the *Rondo-Burlesque* (the orchestra play as if their corporate life is at stake) and the final *Adagio* has a poignancy that once heard is not easily forgotten. Even younger readers unencumbered by nostalgia will recognize the authenticity of feeling here, and everyone who cares about Mahler is urged to listen to it. Although this has appeared in various manifestations (this is the same performance as the EMI Références set listed below), the superiority in every respect of the present transfer is in no doubt. The image is better defined and has both body and presence: the sonority is closer to the original 78s than the EMI set.

Additional recommendation ...

...No. 9. **Vienna Philharmonic Orchestra / Bruno Walter.** EMI Références mono Ⓜ CDH7 63029-2*
(70 minutes: ADD: 8/89). *Gramophone Award Winner 1989.* ⒼⒼⒼ

Mahler (ed. Cooke) Symphony No. 10 in F sharp minor. **Bournemouth Symphony Orchestra /
Sir Simon Rattle.** EMI Ⓕ CDC7 54406-2 (76 minutes: DDD: 5/92). From HMV SLS5206
(12/80). ⒼⒼ

Rattle's superb interpretation of Cooke's performing version of the Tenth Symphony now sweeps the board. His achievement is in a special class, empowering the music with such emotional clout that you forget the scholarly debates. There are in fact several adjustments to Schirmer's published score which Rattle explained in the splendid booklet which accompanied the original LP issue. Unfortunately, this has not been included with this CD reissue. One example of his innovatory approach is his merging of the drum stroke which ends the fourth movement with the one which triggers the fifth; furthermore the opening pages of the finale are truly awesome here. Tempos are unfailingly appropriate and the Bournemouth orchestra are second to none. This is music-making of extraordinary fervour, with excellent sound. It is altogether an essential purchase.

Additional recommendations ...

...(ed. Cooke). **Schoenberg** Verklärte Nacht, Op. 4. **Berlin Radio Symphony Orchestra / Riccardo
Chailly.** Decca Ⓕ 444 872-2DX2 (two discs: 110 minutes: DDD: 3/88). Ⓖ

...(ed. Cooke). **Frankfurt Radio Symphony Orchestra / Eliahu Inbal.** Denon Ⓕ CO-75129
(71 minutes: DDD: 4/93). Ⓖ

...(recons. R. Mazzetti Jnr). **St Louis Symphony Orchestra / Leonard Slatkin.** RCA Victor Red Seal
Ⓕ 09026 68190-2 (75 minutes: DDD: 4/96).

Mahler Das Lied von der Erde. **Agnes Baltsa** (mez); **Klaus König** (ten); **London Philharmonic Orchestra / Klaus Tennstedt.** EMI Ⓕ CDC7 54603-2 (67 minutes: DDD: 2/93). Text and translation included. Recorded 1982-84.

New review

Mahler Das Lied von der Erde. **Ruxandra Donose** (mez); **Thomas Harper** (ten); **National Symphony Orchestra of Ireland / Michael Halász.** Naxos Ⓢ 8 550933 (59 minutes: DDD: 11/95). Text and translation included. Recorded 1994.

Mahler (trans. Schoenberg and Riehn) Das Lied von der Erde. **Birgit Remmert** (contr); **Hans Peter Blochwitz** (ten); **Ensemble Musique Oblique / Philippe Herreweghe.** Harmonia Mundi Ⓕ HMC90 1477 (63 minutes: DDD: 12/94). Texts and translations included. Recorded 1993.   Ⓖ

Mahler (trans. Schoenberg and Riehn) Das Lied von der Erde. **Monica Groop** (mez); **Jorma Silvasti** (ten); **Lahti Chamber Ensemble / Osmo Vänskä.** BIS Ⓕ CD681 (61 minutes: DDD: 7/95). Texts and translations included. Recorded 1994.   ⒼⒼ

For some unaccountable reason, Tennstedt's version of Mahler's masterpiece was left to languish in EMI's vaults for almost ten years. When it finally saw the light of day, it was revealed as by far the most convincing version of recent times, given by one of the most committed Mahler exponents ever. Tennstedt penetrates to the heart of every aspect of the soul-searching work. Without any sign of self-indulgence he gives it a searing, emotionally-draining performance faithfully supported by the superb work of the London Philharmonic which rivals and, in most cases, surpasses the readings of the work by other great orchestras. Their work would be set at naught were it not for the lifelike and wide-ranging recording. Baltsa might seem an unlikely candidate for this piece but her clean line, her nourishing overtones, her direct but eloquent phrasing fulfil almost all of its demands. König, a true Heldentenor but one with the lightness and sensitivity needed for the middle of his three songs, makes an honest and positive soloist. The alternative recommendations listed below all have much to offer, especially the classic Walter, a truly inspired and dedicated interpretation by one of Mahler's earliest advocates. Walter and Klemperer have, by a small margin, the better soloist but neither is recorded or played with more conviction than Tennstedt's disc. At mid price Fritz Reiner's interpretation presents a fitting alternative and Barenboim's version is also compelling and spontaneous. Although Meier and Jerusalem give the impression of not having lived quite long enough with this music, the sheer beauty of the sound is outstanding.

The Naxos recording has a clarity, bloom, depth and truthfulness not often found even at the top of the price range, and is particularly notable for placing the singers in a prominent position yet in exactly the right relationship with the orchestra. Above all it has *presence*. The musical performance seems just right for someone coming new to the work. It is plain, unadorned, presenting the score, if that is possible, as it is, with little in the way of 'deliberate' interpretation. Which is not to say that Halász is in any way dull: he realizes the import of the great work but doesn't impose himself on it as so many Mahler conductors are inclined to. By the same token the pacing is on the fast side, thus avoiding overt sentimentality and at the same time allowing Mahler's masterpiece, played as well as it is here, to speak for itself. The soloists perform in the same vein. Donose, who is something of a find, sings her contributions with inherent beauty, her tone refulgent and with a slight, not unattractive edge to it in the manner of Eastern European mezzos (she hails from Romania). There are few of the personal *aperçus* or the intensity of expression of Baker in the bargain issue listed below, but the essence of the song's meaning is conveyed in secure, long-breathed phrasing, particularly so in the finale. Only those averse to her type of voice are likely to be disappointed. Thomas Harper possesses a serviceable, compact voice that realizes the tenor songs with the minimum of fuss and a good deal of artistry. All in all this is an amazing bargain.

In 1920 Schoenberg began a chamber version of the work but left it unfinished. It wasn't until 1983 that his ideas were brought to fruition by Reiner Riehn, who scrupulously followed the indications left in the score by his famous predecessor to good effect. The results are fascinating, not to say enchanting. An already delicate orchestration becomes even more translucent and sensuous in its new attire for 13 instruments, and the much more transparent accompaniment allows for lighter singers. Blochwitz's silvery tenor makes the third and fifth songs sound airy and exhilarating, while the opening number no longer finds the singer struggling to be heard in the mêlée of the middle section. In consequence, Blochwitz can concentrate on pointing the words, which he does with appreciable finesse. However, here and in the final song, the upper reaches of the part still tax him, even against this more lightly scored background. Birgit Remmert is a discovery. She sings with as fine a line as any contralto soloist in this work, and conveys all the inner meaning of the text without exaggeration. Of course, she too never has to worry that her voice won't carry over the orchestra, yet the sound, as at "Ich sehne mich" in the finale, lacks nothing of the warmth and overtones necessary to fulfil Mahler's emotional demands. Herreweghe predictably conducts a reading of grace combined with directness and strength. His tempo is a shade laboured in the third song, and the fifth could do with a little more *élan*. Nevertheless, by and large he makes a strong case for this version as an alternative to what we usually hear, assisted by playing of the utmost refinement and feeling from his chamber ensemble. The sound is clear and spacious.

Osmo Vänskä's reading is nothing short of superb in every respect. A recording of demonstration quality, it lets us hear every strand of the translucent scoring; its range and focus are quite remarkable and the balance ideal. All this displays Vänskä's dedicated interpretation and the finely chiselled playing of his ensemble to the greatest advantage. The Swedish team are superior even to

Herreweghe's excellent group, each individual executing his or her part with the utmost refinement
and sensibility; the oboe/cor anglais player Jukka Hirvikangas distinguishes himself in particular.
Vänskä takes an even brisker view of tempo than Herreweghe, and the work, especially the final
movement, is all the more cohesive and forward-moving as a result, avoiding any hint of
sentimentality; nor can one imagine the third movement sounding more effervescent or the fourth
more heady. The soloists just about surpass the achievements of their counterparts for Herreweghe.
Silvasti has the ideal tenor for this version of the work: it has a silvery sheen yet with a touch of metal
in it. As long as you don't mind the occasional use of a fast vibrato, Silvasti is sure to please because
he has the words and the music at his command, projecting everything with great aplomb. Groop,
better known than her tenor colleague, further enhances her growing reputation with an impassioned
performance of the alto's songs, quite a match for the also excellent Remmert (Herreweghe), and
perhaps just that bit richer in timbre. She rises magnificently to all the challenges of the "Abschied",
declaiming with extraordinary Baker-like urgency.

Additional recommendations ...
...**Dame Janet Baker** (mez); **James King** (ten); **Royal Concertgebouw Orchestra / Bernard Haitink.**
Philips Silver Line Ⓜ 432 279-2PSL (66 minutes: ADD).   Ⓖ
...**Kathleen Ferrier** (contr); **Julius Patzak** (ten); **Vienna Philharmonic Orchestra / Bruno Walter.**
Decca Ⓕ 414 194-2DH* (ADD: 1/85). *Gramophone classical 100.*   ⒼⒼⒼ
...**Christa Ludwig** (mez); **Fritz Wunderlich** (ten); **Philharmonia Orchestra; New Philharmonia**
Orchestra / Otto Klemperer. EMI Ⓕ CDC7 47231-2 (64 minutes: ADD: 12/85).   Ⓖ
...**Christa Ludwig** (mez); **René Kollo** (ten); **Berlin Philharmonic Orchestra / Herbert von Karajan.**
DG Galleria Ⓜ 419 058-2GGA (66 minutes: ADD: 4/88).
...**Maureen Forrester** (contr); **Richard Lewis** (ten); **Chicago Symphony Orchestra / Fritz Reiner.** RCA
Victor Gold Seal Ⓜ GD60178 (63 minutes: ADD: 10/91).   ⒼⒼ
...**Waltraud Meier** (mez); **Siegfried Jerusalem** (ten); **Chicago Symphony Orchestra / Daniel**
Barenboim. Erato Ⓕ 2292-45624-2 (60 minutes: DDD: 4/92). *Selected by Sounds in Retrospect.*
...**Dame Janet Baker** (mez); **John Mitchinson** (ten); **BBC Northern Symphony Orchestra / Raymond**
Leppard. BBC Radio Classics Ⓑ BBCRD9120 (64 minutes: ADD: 3/95). *Gramophone Editor's*
choice.

Mahler Lieder aus "Des Knaben Wunderhorn". **Jard van Nes** (contr); **John Bröcheler** (bass);
Arnhem Philharmonic Orchestra / Roberto Benzi. Ottavo Ⓕ OTRC79238 (55 minutes: DDD:
2/94). Texts included. Recorded 1992.
Jard van Nes is a natural for Mahler, both from the vocal and interpretative point of view. Particularly
admirable is the fresh, spontaneous way in which she approaches her contributions, free from both the
long shadow of past performance or awe before such familiar songs. She catches ideally the folk-like
charm of "Rheinlegendchen" and "Wer hat dies Liedlein erdacht?". She is also appropriately earthy in
"Das irdische Leben", then marvellously tender as the distant lover in "Des Schildwache Nachtlied".
Her unadorned mastery of word and tone cannot be praised too highly – listen to the *keck* delivery
of "Verlor'ne Muh": just right – and she crowns her performance with her grave utterance in
"Urlicht". Bröcheler is among the best, characterizing "Lob des hohen Verstandes" with enthusiastic
vivacity and revelling in St Antony's sermon. Benzi and his orchestra never make the mistake of some
more noted performers of over-egging the pudding. Although the detail is all clearly projected and
keenly played, in a perfectly balanced recording, the music is kept on the move, never sentimentalized.

Additional recommendations ...
...**Dame Elisabeth Schwarzkopf** (sop); **Dietrich Fischer-Dieskau** (bar); **London Symphony Orchestra /**
George Szell. EMI Ⓕ CDC7 47277-2 (48 minutes: ADD: 11/88).   Ⓖ
...No. 2, Verlorne Müh; No. 7, Rheinlegendchen; No. 9, Wo die schönen Trompeten blasen; No. 10,
Lob des hohen Verstands. Lieder und Gesang – No. 1, Frühlingsmorgen. No. 2, Erinnerung.
No. 4, Serenade aus Don Juan. No. 5, Phantasie aus Don Juan No. 7, Ich ging mit Lust durch
einen grünen Wald. No. 8, Aus! Aus!. *Coupled with* **Wolf** Heiss mich nicht reden (Mignon I). Nur
wer die Sehnsucht (Mignon II). So lasst mich scheinen (Mignon III). Kennst du das Land
(Mignon) Frühling übers Jahr. Frage nicht. Die Spröde. Der Schäfer. Gesang Weylas. **Anne Sofie**
von Otter (mez); **Ralf Gothóni** (pf). DG Ⓕ 423 666-2GH (59 minutes: DDD: 6/89).

Mahler Das klagende Lied (complete version including "Waldmärchen"). **Susan Dunn** (sop);
Markus Baur (alto); **Brigitte Fassbaender** (mez); **Werner Hollweg** (ten); **Andreas Schmidt** (bar);
Städtischer Musikverein Düsseldorf; Berlin Radio Symphony Orchestra / Riccardo Chailly. Decca
Ⓕ 425 719-2DH (64 minutes: DDD: 2/92). Text and translation included. Recorded 1989.   ⒼⒼ
Even the musically acute listener would be unlikely to realize that *Das klagende Lied* is the work of a
teenager. Mahler's first significant work is as self-assured as anything he was to write in later life.
Indeed enthusiastic Mahlerians will recognize here passages which crop up in other works, most
notably the Second Symphony. Those same enthusiastic Mahlerians might not recognize much of this
recording, however, since only two movements of *Klagende Lied* are usually performed: the 30-minute
first movement is considered too rambling. But no one could possibly arrive at that conclusion from
this tautly directed, electrifying performance, and it contains some wonderfully imaginative music,
including some delightful forest murmurs, which it seems tragic to miss out. For this movement alone
this CD is a must for any Mahler fan, but more than that this is a spectacular recording of a once-in-

a-million performance. The soloists, choir and orchestra achieve near perfection under Chailly's inspired direction, and the decision to substitute for the marvellous Brigitte Fassbaender a boy alto (Markus Baur) to represent the disembodied voice of the dead brother is a stroke of pure genius. His weird, unnatural voice provides a moment of sheer spine-tingling drama.

Additional recommendations ...

...**Soloists; Shin-Yuh Kai Chorus; Philharmonia Orchestra / Giuseppe Sinopoli.** DG Ⓕ 435 382-2GH (65 minutes: DDD: 8/92).

...**Soloists; Bath Festival Chorus; Waynflete Singers; Bournemouth Symphony Orchestra / Richard Hickox.** Chandos Ⓕ CHAN9247 (71 minutes: DDD: 5/94).

Mahler Kindertotenlieder[a]. Rückert-Lieder[b]. Lieder eines fahrenden Gesellen[a]. **Dame Janet Baker** (mez); [a]**Hallé Orchestra;** [b]**New Philharmonia Orchestra / Sir John Barbirolli.** EMI Ⓕ CDC7 47793-2 (three discs: ADD: 12/87). Texts and translations included. Items marked [a] from ASD2338 (2/68), [b]ASD2518/19 (12/69).   Ⓖ Ⓖ Ⓖ

Mahler Kindertotenlieder. Rückert-Lieder. Lieder eines fahrenden Gesellen. Lieder aus Des Knaben Wunderhorn – Das irdische Leben; Des Antonius von Padua Fischpredigt; Urlicht. **Brigitte Fassbaender** (mez); **Deutsches Symphony Orchestra, Berlin / Riccardo Chailly.** Ⓕ 425 790-2DH (71 minutes: DDD: 4/94). Texts and translations included. Recorded 1988-89. Ⓖ

The songs of the *Lieder eines fahrenden Gesellen* ("Songs of a Wayfarer") are directly quoted from Mahler's First Symphony and the same fresh, springtime atmosphere is shared by both works. The orchestration has great textural clarity and lightness of touch. The *Kindertotenlieder*, more chromatically expressive than the earlier work, tap into a darker, more psychologically complex vein in Mahler's spiritual and emotional make-up. The *Rückert Lieder* are not a song-cycle as such but gather in their romantic awareness and response to the beauties of the poetry a unity and shape that acts to bind them. Together, Baker and Barbirolli reach a transcendental awareness of Mahler's inner musings. Barbirolli draws from the Hallé playing of great delicacy and precision and establishes a clear case for having this CD in your collection.

Fassbaender's emotionally charged way of singing is ideally matched to Mahler yet she is just as able – as in St Anthony's Sermon from the *Knaben Wunderhorn* – to smile and sing gently, wittily. It is the dramatic declamation, however, as at "Herr über Tod und Leben" in "Um Mitternacht" from the *Rückert-Lieder*, that the true flavour of her singing is caught. Throughout the *Fahrenden Gesellen* it is the immediacy, fearlessness of attack and her particular intensity, that makes these readings so arresting. The swiftish speeds throughout ensure that sentimentality is kept at bay; so does Chailly's and the orchestra's biting precision and light touch. Similar characteristics inform a deeply eloquent interpretation of *Kindertotenlieder*. Right from the start the world-weary tone and verbal illumination in the first song catch at the heart and suggest palpably the sense of personal responsibility for the children's deaths on the part of the protagonist. Baker/Barbirolli, still surprisingly at full price, with the singer in lovely voice, must be a 'safer' recommendation than the more daring Fassbaender, but with up-to-date recording and even more songs included the new disc is an inviting proposition – and a searing experience.

Additional recommendations ...

...Lieder eines fahrenden Gesellen[a]. Kindertotenlieder[b]. Rückert-Lieder[b]. **Dietrich Fischer-Dieskau** (bar); [a]**Bavarian Radio Symphony Orchestra / Rafael Kubelík;** [b]**Berlin Philharmonic Orchestra / Karl Böhm.** DG Ⓕ 415 191-2GH (60 minutes: ADD: 9/85).

...Lieder eines fahrenden Gesellen. Lieder und Gesange. Im Lenz (1880). Winterlied (1880). **Dame Janet Baker** (mez); **Geoffrey Parsons** (pf). Hyperion Ⓕ CDA66100 (58 minutes: DDD: 4/87).   Ⓖ

...**Catherine Robbin** (mez); **Kitchener-Waterloo Symphony Orchestra / Raffi Armenian.** CBC Records Ⓕ SMCD5098 (55 minutes: DDD: 5/92).

...Das Lied von der Erde[a]. Lieder eines fahrenden Gesellen[b]. Kindertotenlieder[b]. Rückert-Lieder[c]. Lieder aus Des Knaben Wunderhorn – Wer hat dies Liedlein erdacht?[d]; Des Antonius von Padua Fischpredigt[e]; Wo die schönen Trompeten blasen[d]; Revelge[e]; Der Tambourg'sell[e]. [d]**Lucia Popp** (sop); [bc]**Dame Janet Baker** (mez); [a]**Murray Dickie** (ten); [a]**Dietrich Fischer-Dieskau,** [e]**Bernd Weikl** (bars); [a]**Philharmonia Orchestra / Paul Kletzki;** [b]**Hallé Orchestra;** [c]**New Philharmonia Orchestra / Sir John Barbirolli;** [de]**London Philharmonic Orchestra / Klaus Tennstedt.** EMI Rouge et Noir Ⓜ CZS7 62707-2 (two discs: 155 minutes: ADD/DDD: 8/92). *The recordings cross referenced to Dame Jane Baker are the same as those reviewed above.*

...**Andreas Schmidt** (bar); **Cincinnati Symphony Orchestra / Jésus López-Cobos.** Tclarc Ⓕ CD80269 (56 minutes: DDD: 5/93).

...Lieder eines fahrenden Gesellen[a]. Im Lenz. Winterlied[a]. Maitanz im Grünen. Lieder und Gesänge[a] – Serenade aus Don Juan; Aus! Aus!' Starke Einbildungskraft; Selbstgefühl. Lieder und Gesänge[a] – Erinnerung; Um schlimme Kinder artig zu machen; Zu Strassburg auf der Schanz; Ablösung im sommer; Nicht wiedersehen!. Lieder und Gesänge (orch. Berio)[b] – Frühlingsmorgen; Erinnerung; Hans und Grethe; Phantasie aus Don Juan; Ich ging mit Lust durch einen grünedn Wald; Scheiden und Meiden. **Thomas Hampson** (bar); [a]**David Lutz** (pf); [b]**Philharmonia Orchestra / Luciano Berio.** Teldec Ⓕ 9031-74002-2 (68 minutes: DDD: 8/94).

Further listening ...

...The 1905 Welte-Mignon Piano Rolls: Symphonies – No. 4 in G major: Fourth movement (two versions: with and without Yvonne Kenny, sop); No. 5 in C sharp minor: Trauermarsch. Lieder eines fahrenden Gesellen – Ging heut' Morgen übers Feld (two versions: with and without Claudine Carlson, mez). Lieder und Gesänge – No. 7, Ich ging mit Lust durch einen grünen Wald (two versions: with and without Carlson). Also includes "Remembering Mahler", an oral history with the voices of Alfred Sendry, Victor Fuchs, Richard Lert, Klaus Pringsheim, Herman Martonne, Franz Kuchynka, Alois Reiser, Benjamin Kohon, Herbert Borodkin and Anna Mahler. IMP Golden Legacy of Recorded Sound GLRS101 (12/93). 🔴🔴

...Quartet in A minor. *Coupled with works by* **Webern, Schoenberg** and **Berg Gidon Kremer** (vn); **Veronika Hagen** (va); **Clemens Hagen** (vc); **Oleg Maisenberg** (pf). DG 447 112-2GH (4/96). *See review in the Collections section; refer to the Index to Reviews.*

George Malcolm
British 1917-

Suggested listening ...

...Bach Before the Mast. *Coupled with works by* **Templeton, F. Couperin, Rameau, Rimsky-Korsakov, Daquin, Paradis** and **Bach George Malcolm** (hpd). Decca 444 390-2DWO (11/95). ✒

Paul Malengreau
Belgian 1887-1959

Suggested listening ...

...Symphonie de la Passion, Op. 20. *Coupled with* **Widor** Scherzo in E major, "La Chasse". **Peeters** Suite, Op. 71. **P. Pierné** Pastorale. **Guillou** Toccata. **John Scott Whiteley** (org). Priory PRCD487 (2/96).

Gian Francesco Malipiero
Italian 1882-1973

New review

Malipiero Symphony No. 6, "degli archi".
Morricone Essercizi per dieci archi.
Porena Vivaldi.
Rota Concerto for Strings. **I Solisti Italiani.** Denon Ⓔ CO-78949 (63 minutes: DDD: 10/95). Recorded 1994.

Four Italian neo-classical string orchestra pieces, but 'neo-classical' needs re-defining for each of them. Nino Rota's charming little concerto is civilized, tuneful, urbane, neatly turned: all those things that the word used to mean. Malipiero's symphony digs deeper: deeper into the past (into the renaissance, where he can join hands with both Respighi and Tippett) and into fruitful conflicts between past and present, finding some unease, some tension, and occasionally an element that one can only label *nobilmente*. It is a modern *concerto grosso*, and a fine one at that. What Boris Porena and Ennio Morricone do with the past is stranger. Porena takes Vivaldi (the first movement of the Concerto for four violins, Op. 3 No. 10 – the one that Bach transcribed for four harpsichords) and gradually transforms him into himself, rather like those word-puzzles in which, by changing a letter at a time, 'fish' is transmuted into 'fowl': the two species are linked by a kindred liking for idiomatic string figuration. Morricone, no less disconcertingly, takes a famous Verdian image (the six-note descending "Amami, Alfredo!" from *La traviata*) and by inverting its intervals gradually disguises it entirely as a virtuoso toccata for ten solo strings. Still more oddly, the end product of this disguise, the second of the two *Essercizi*, sounds distinctly like Vivaldi (or like Malipiero meditating on Vivaldi), with the ghost of Verdi clearly present throughout. Rota's piece is a little too simple for I Solisti Italiani: they lavish rather too much artful rubato on it, and some of its charm evaporates. But in the other music here their virtuosity is both needed and sensitively used. The recording is sumptuously rich but admirably clear.

Further listening ...

...String Quartets – No. 1, "Rispetti e strambotti"; No. 2, "Stornelli e ballate"; No. 3, "Cantari alla madrigalesca"; No. 4; No. 5, "dei capricci"; No. 6, "L'arca di Noè"; No. 7; No. 8, "per Elisabetta". **Orpheus Quartet.** ASV CDDCD457 (2/92).

...Sette Invenzioni. Quattro Invenzioni, "La festa degli indolenti". Il Finto Arlecchino – Symphonic fragments. Vivaldiana. **Veneto Philharmonic Orchestra / Peter Maag.** Marco Polo 8 223397 (9/93).

...Symphonies – No. 1, "in quattro tempi, come le quattro stagioni"; No. 2, "elegiaca". Sinfonia del silenzio e de la morte. **Moscow Symphony Orchestra / Antonio de Almeida.** Marco Polo 8 223603 (4/94).

...Symphonies – No. 3, "delle campane"; No. 4, "in memoriam". Sinfonia del mare. **Moscow Symphony Orchestra / Antonio de Almeida.** Marco Polo 8 223602 (4/94).

...Symphonies – No. 5, "Concertante, in eco"; No. 6; No. 8, "Symphonia brevis"; No. 11, "delle cornamuse". **Moscow Symphony Orchestra / Antonio de Almeida.** Marco Polo 8 223696 (2/95).

...Symphonies – No. 7, "delle canzoni". Sinfonia in un tempo. Sinfonia per Antigenida. **Moscow Symphony Orchestra / Antonio de Almeida.** Marco Polo 8 223604 (4/94).

...Symphonies – No. 9, "dell'ahime"; No. 10, "atropo". Sinfonia dello Zodiaco. **Moscow Symphony Orchestra / Antonio de Almeida.** Marco Polo 8 223697 (2/95).

Pierre de Manchicourt
French c1510-1564

Suggested listening ...
...Laudate Dominum. *Coupled with works by* **Ockeghem, Josquin Desprez, Porta, Tallis, G. Gabrieli** and **Striggio** Huelgas Ensemble / **Paul van Nevel.** Sony Classical Vivarte SK66261 (4/96). *See review in the Collections section; refer to the Index to Reviews.*

Francesco Mancini
Italian 1672-1737

Suggested listening ...
...Sonata for Recorder, two Violins and Continuo in D minor. *Coupled with works by* **Sarri, D. Scarlatti, Durante** and **A. Scarlatti** Il Giardino Armonico / **Giovanni Antonini** (rec). Teldec Das Alte Werk 4509-93157-2 (11/94). ✍ *See review in the Collections section; refer to the Index to Reviews.*   ⓖⓖ

Henry Mancini
American 1924-1994

Suggested listening ...
...Film Scores – The Pink Panther; Charade; Hatari!; Breakfast at Tiffany's. **Henry Mancini and his Orchestra.** RCA Victor Red Seal RD85938.
...Mancini in Surround – Film Scores: The White Dawn – Arctic whale hunt. Mommie Dearest. Frenzy. Monster Movie Music Suite. Fear – Casey's theme. The Man Who Loved Women – Little boys. The Prisoner of Zenda – Suite. Nightwing. Without a clue – excerpts. Sunset – Suite. **The Mancini Pops Orchestra / Henry Mancini.** RCA Victor RD60471 (5/91).

Carl Mangold
German 1813-1889

New review
Mangold Abraham. **Michael Ruhr** (treb); **Monika Frimmer** (sop); **Mechthild Georg** (contr); **Bernhard Gärtner, Gerd Türk, Thomas Essmann** (tens); **Gilles Cachemaille** (bar); **Thomas Sehrbrock** (bass); **Darmstadt Chorus and Philharmonic Orchestra / Wolfgang Seeliger.** Christophorus Ⓟ CHR77172 (two discs: 98 minutes: DDD: 11/95). Texts and translations included. Recorded 1986.

Once highly regarded in his native Germany, Carl Mangold is little performed today. He was born the same year as Verdi and Wagner, and wrote operas on national themes (including a Tannhäuser setting that ends with the hero getting married) as well as concert dramas and oratorios in which a patriotic element interacts with biblical themes. Something of this marks his text for *Abraham*. It covers most of Abraham's life, from the departure of Lot, the war with hostile tribes, Hagar's rejection by Sarah, and the destruction of Sodom and Gomorrah, to the birth of Isaac and his near-sacrifice. There is a lot of action and detail to fit into a work of just over an hour-and-a-half, and the strain tells. Mangold rarely gives himself time to take lyrical flight; and the melodic plainness of the few arias kindles the suspicion that he was protecting himself from his weaknesses. The strengths include a skill in binding the work together motivically (the techniques are quite close to Mendelssohn), and a beautiful feeling for the orchestra, especially for subtle and original string combinations. For the most part, the action is carried on in recitative or a kind of free arioso. Abraham occasionally settles into a brief aria, when Gilles Cachemaille takes his opportunities well. Mangold writes expertly for the chorus, and the recording keeps matters clear, even in a violent fugue for the destruction of Sodom and Gomorrah. But repeatedly he turns aside from what might seem an ideal opportunity for a big aria, for instance with Abraham's prayer of gratitude to Jehovah for promising him a son. The words of the Twenty-third Psalm are addressed to Abraham and put into the mouth of an Angel (freshly sung by Monika Frimmer) addressing Hagar, the girl whose child Abraham previously fathered. She has quite a pleasant duet with him; hers is not a very grateful part, and Mechthild Georg does her best with it. The small part of Isaac goes to a boy treble. A full text, with English and French translations, is provided. There are also excellent introductory essays. *Abraham* is no masterpiece, but it has its interest and Wolfgang Seeliger's enthusiastic advocacy does well for it.

Giovanni de Maque

Suggested listening ...
...Due Gagliarde. Seconde Stravaganze. *Coupled with works by* **Facoli, A. Valente, A. Mayone, Trabaci, Picchi, Buono, Frescobaldi, Lambardo, Merula, M. Rossi, Salvatore, B. Storace, G. Strozzi, Stradella** and **A. Scarlatti** Rinaldo Alessandrini (hpd). Opus 111 OPS30-118 (4/95). *See review in the Collections section; refer to the Index to Reviews.*

Dumisani Maraire

Suggested listening ...
...Mai Nozipo. *Coupled with works by* **Piazzolla, B. Johnston, Reich, Górecki, Riley, Crumb, Glass, Tahmizyan, Barber, Pärt, R. Scott, S. Johnson, Daugherty** and **Hendrix** Dumisani Maraire (ngoma/hosho); **Astor Piazzolla** (bandoneon); **Patty Manning, John Taylor, Larry Caballero** (vocs); **Djivan Gasparian** (duduk); **Kronos Quartet.** Nonesuch 7559-79394-2 (2/96). *See review in the Collections section; refer to the Index to Reviews.*

Marin Marais

Marais Alcyone – Suites. **Le Concert des Nations / Jordi Savall.** Auvidis Astrée Ⓟ E8525 (53 minutes: DDD: 2/95). 🎵 Recorded 1993.   Ⓖ
As one of the greatest exponents of the solo viol tradition perfected by Marais, Savall focuses his insights upon this music and interprets the scoring as Marais might have done. He experiments with all the chamber-music combinations of the day and, typically, hazards some of his own, particularly in the Chaconne. Occasionally, Savall uses winds where Marc Minkowski (his recording of the complete opera is reviewed below) used strings and occasionally miscalculates his effects, as in the "Bourrée pour les Bergers et Bergères". His command of Maraisian ornamentation is, however, everywhere evident and indeed very welcome because of the constant melodic echoes of the solo repertoire in the opera score. With chamber music come more transparent textures, revealing the harmonic and textural richness of the post-Lullian style; cross-rhythms, syncopations and sequences have more impact. By contrast, the opera performances can often sound sluggish and four-square. Savall also includes music that was left out of the opera recording, including the delicately syncopated "Air pour les Faunes et les Driades" from the Prologue, the exquisitely scored Sarabande, with its beautifully shaded cadences, and the Gigue from Act 1 as well as the "Sarabande pour les Prêtresses de Junon" from Act 2. In the "Menuets pour les Bergers et Bergères" in the Prologue and the March and Air "pour les Matelots" in Act 3, Savall orchestrates passages that were once vocal solos to maintain the proportions of the movements.

Marais Alcyone. **Jennifer Smith** (sop) Alcyone; **Gilles Ragon** (ten) Ceyx; **Philippe Huttenlocher** (bar) Pélée; **Vincent Le Texier** (bass-bar) Pan, Phorbas; **Sophie Boulin** (sop) Ismène, First Sailor; **Bernard Deletré** (bass) Tmole, High Priest, Neptune; **Jean-Paul Fouchécourt** (alto) Morpheus; **Véronique Gens** (sop) Second Sailor, Priestess; **Les Musiciens du Louvre / Marc Minkowski.** Erato MusiFrance Ⓟ 2292-45522-2 (two discs: 154 minutes: DDD: 4/92). 🎵 Notes, text and translation included. Recorded 1990.   ⒼⒼ
Today, Marin Marais is remembered almost entirely for his legacy of music for the bass viol. But in his own day Marais was recognized as a talented opera composer, too. *Alcyone*, first performed in 1706, was his dramatic *chef d'oeuvre* and held the stage at intervals for more than half a century. Though he followed in Lully's footsteps, Marais spoke with a voice of his own and nowhere is this more apparent than in *Alcyone*, which contains in its Fourth Act one of the great moments in French opera – a tempest, judged so successful by his contemporaries that not only was it performed as a separate item at court, at the express command of the king, but also found its way into a revival of a Lully opera early in the eighteenth century. The plot centres on the thwarted love of Alcyone for Ceyx, a *tragédie* which moves, however, to a happy ending. Marais's music explores a wide range of emotions. Catchy instrumental pieces – the sailors' dance in Act 3 is especially captivating – supple choruses and touching airs abound, several foreshadowing Rameau in their colourful orchestration. The mainly strong cast is headed by the soprano, Jennifer Smith, in the title-role, with lively performances by Sophie Boulin as Ismène, Phorbas's partner in crime, and Gilles Ragon as Ceyx. Minkowski directs with stylish conviction and a good sense of pace. A few rough edges count for little where so much else is enlightened. The vivid recording comes with full texts and translations.

Further listening ...
...Pièces en trio – Suites: C major; B flat major; G minor; F major; E minor; G minor. **Quadro Hotteterre.** Teldec 9031-77617-2. 🎵
...Pièces en Trio – Suites: B flat major; C minor; E minor. Suite d'un goût étranger – La rêveuse; Le badinage. **Ensemble Fitzwilliam.** Auvidis Valois V4638 (11/92).
...Pièces de Viole, Troisième Livre – Suites: E minor; D major; G major. **Jordi Savall** (va da gamba); **Hopkinson Smith** (theorbo); **Ton Koopman** (hpd). Auvidis Astrée E8761 (12/92). 🎵   Ⓖ

...Pièces de Viole, Quatrième Livre: Suite d'un goût étranger – Marche Tartare; La Tartarine and Double; Les festes champêtre; Le toubillon; Le labyrinthe; L'arabesque; Allemande la superbe; La rêveuse; Marche; Gigue; Le badinage. **Jordi Savall** (va da gamba); **Ton Koopman** (hpd); **Hopkinson Smith** (baroque gtr; theorbo). Auvidis Astrée E7727 (9/88). 🎵   ⓖ

...Pièces de Viole, Cinquième Livre – Suites: G minor; E minor/major. Le tableau de l'opération de la taille. Le tombeau pour Marais le cadet. **Jordi Savall** (bass viol); **Hopkinson Smith** (theorbo); **Ton Koopman** (hpd) with **Jean-Michael Damian** (spkr). Auvidis Astrée E7708 (2/88). 🎵   ⓖ

...La gamme et autres Morceaux de Simphonies – La gamme en forme d'un petit opéra; Sonate à la mariesienne; Saint-Geneviève du Mont. **Boston Musum Trio**. Centaur CRC2129.   ⓖ

Marco Marazzolli   Italian c1602-1662

Suggested listening ...

...San Tomaso. Per il giorno della resurrezione. *Coupled with* **Carissimi** Jephte. **Cantus Cölln**. Deutsche Harmonia Mundi 05472 77322-2 (64 minutes: DDD: 10/95). 🎵 *See review under Carissimi; refer to the Index to Reviews.*

...Ogni nostro piacer, quanto. *Coupled with works by* **Carissimi, Mazzocchi, Rossi, V. Mazzocchi, Landi** and **Anonymous** Tragicomedia / Stephen Stubbs. Teldec Das Alte Werk 4509-98410-2 (3/96). *See review in the Collections section; refer to the Index to Reviews.* 🎵

Alessandro Marcello   Italian 1684-1750

Suggested listening ...

...Six Oboe Concertos, "La cetra" – No. 1 in D major; No. 2 in E major; No. 3 in B minor; No. 4 in E minor; No. 5 in B flat major; No. 6 in G major. **Heinz Holliger** (ob); **Berne Camerata / Thomas Furi**. Archiv Produktion 427 137-2AGA.

...Six Oboe Concertos, "La cetra" – No. 1 in D major; No. 2 in E major; No. 3 in B minor; No. 4 in E minor; No. 5 in B flat major; No. 6 in G major. Concerto in B flat major. **Collegium Musicum 90 / Simon Standage**. Chandos CHAN0563 (5/95).

...Oboe Concerto in D minor. *Coupled with* **Vivaldi** Trio Sonata in D minor, RV63, "La folia". Flautino Concerto in C major, RV443. Amor hai vinto, RV651. Nulla in mundo pax, RV630. **Soloists; Academy of Ancient Music / Christopher Hogwood**. L'Oiseau-Lyre 421 655-2OH (9/89). 🎵

...Oboe Concerto in D minor. *Coupled with works by* **Torelli, Albinoni, Corelli, Vivaldi, Viviani, Franceschini** and **Baldassare** Håkan Hardenberger (tpt); **I Musici**. Philips 442 131-2PH (5/95). *See review in the Collections section; refer to the Index to Reviews.*   ⓖ

Louis Marchand   French 1669-1732

Suggested listening ...

...Pièces Choisies pour l'Orgue – Premier Livre. *Coupled with* **Guilain** Pièces d'Orgue pour le Magnificat. **François Espinasse** (org). Sony Classical SK57489 (7/94).

Tomas Marco   Spanish 1942-

Suggested listening ...

...Concierto Guadiana. *Coupled with* **Benguerel** Tempo. **Cruz de Castro** Guitar Concerto. **Wolfgang Weigel** (gtr); **European Masters Orchestra / Peter Schmelzer**. Koch Schwann ⓕ 312362 (63 minutes: DDD: 5/95).

Luca Marenzio   Italian 1553/4-1599

Marenzio Madrigali a 4vv ... libro primo. **Concerto Italiano** (Rossana Bertini, sop; Claudio Cavina, alto; Giuseppe Maletto, ten; Sergio Foresti, bass; Mara Galassi, hp; Andrea Damiani, lte) **/ Rinaldo Alessandrini**. Opus 111 ⓕ OPS30-117 (62 minutes: DDD: 10/94). Texts and translations included. Recorded 1994.   ⓖ

What Concerto Italiano reveal to us is that four-part writing in this expressive and varied milieu makes a virtue out of its limitations: Marenzio capitalizes on exposed dialogues between voices and textural brittleness. Classicism (in the broadest musical sense synonymous with four-part writing long before Bach chorales or Haydn quartets) is what Alessandrini is seeking to impart in this clear juxtaposition of fluent canzonets with intimate rhetoric. The music is so subtly shaded, both by Marenzio and the singers, that unless you are a reincarnated madrigalist this should be experienced in small doses. There is just the same commitment and concentration to the extensive detail in the music. Just observe how much care has gone into *Chi vol udire i miei sospiri in rime* with its beautifully paced crescendo on the word "sospiri" (sighs), the almost imperceptible sketching of the pulse and other wonderful liberties with rhythmic inflexion. So much of this innate understanding is of course expressed through the singers' native tongue (what life those watery vowels bring to Petrarch's later-to-be-famous *Zefiro torna*) and a warm changeable Mediterranean breeze which unselfconsciously manipulates the temperature. None of this would count for much were the ensemble not highly refined in purely abstract terms and this is perhaps the best yet in that respect. Only rarely does the soprano's rich and penetrating tone cause one to worry and when it does this is usually because of a slight tendency to flatness. A small concern in a very fine release.

Further listening ...
...Il primo libro de madrigali (5vv) – Dolorosi martir, fieri tormenti; Liquide perle Amor da gli occhi sparse. Il secondo libro de madrigali (5vv) – O voi che sospirate a miglior note. Il quinto libro de madrigali (5vv) – Due rose fresche, e colte in Paradiso. Madrigali ... libro primo (4-6vv) – O fere stelle homai datemi pace; Piango che Amor con disusato oltraggio. Il quinto libro de madrigali (6vv) – Baci soavi e cari. Il sesto libro de madrigali (6vv) – Se quel dolor che va inanzi al morire. **The Consort of Musicke / Anthony Rooley.** Musica Oscura 070992 (1/94).

Biagio Marini

Italian c1587-1685

Suggested listening ...
...Concerto terzo delle musiche da camera, Op. 16. **The Consort of Musicke / Anthony Rooley.** Musica Oscura 070994 (3/94). ✒

Igor Markevitch

USSR/Italian 1912-1983

New review
Markevitch Galop[a]. Noces[b]. Serenade[c]. L'Envol d'Icare[d]. [c]**Wolfgang Meyer** (cl); [c]**Dag Jensen** (bn); **Kolja Lessing** ([e]vn/[bd]pf), [d]**Christopher Lyndon-Gee** (pf); [d]**Franz Lang**, [d]**Jens Gagelmann**, [d]**Raphael Haeger** (perc); [a]**Markevitch Ensemble, Cologne.** Largo Ⓕ Largo5127 (47 minutes: DDD: 10/95). Recorded 1993.

Igor Markevitch is far more than a 'mid-price' conductor. In fact, he is actually an unsung hero of the pre-war European musical scene. The trouble is that he stopped composing, and although he did set down some of his own music on 78s (including *L'Envol d'Icare*), posterity – being notoriously slothful – has yet to act in his interests. This selection is dominated by one extraordinary work, *L'Envol d'Icare* (of which, more later), but it also includes a madcap *Galop*, a wedding present for Swiss family friends and an 11-minute *Serenade*. The disc opens with the *Galop*, a two-minute *jeu d'esprit* that was premièred in front of Aldous Huxley, Giacometti, Cocteau, Dali and Luis Buñuel (some house-party!). The second, *Noces* for solo piano, is a three-movement charmer that recalls Satie and (occasionally) Fauré, whereas the third – the *Serenade* of 1930 for violin, clarinet and bassoon – marries Hindemith-style busyness with considerable wit and a certain sense of foreboding. However, the real *pièce de résistance* is placed fourth. The tale of Icarus, whose flight to the sun spelled his undoing, fascinated Markevitch, though more as a symbol of all-consuming creativity than as a cautionary tale. His original score was born under the influence of opium. However, although Markevitch battled against his addiction (and won), his 'heightened perception' found expression in a work that is still virtually unknown except in a simplified version. Now we have access to this brilliant transcription (Markevitch's own, albeit 'completed' by Christopher Lyndon-Gee) for two pianos and percussion – conceived, incidentally, some years before Bartók's Sonata for the same forces. Musically, the work seethes with textural and rhythmic invention, from the multi-perspectival "Games of the Adolescents", through a motoric "Flight" (with distant echoes of Prokofiev's 1920s phase), an eerie "Fall" and "Icarus's Death" which favours a Franco-Russian musical axis with hints of Colin McPhee and Messiaen. Recordings and performance standards are uniformly excellent (the sound is suitably dry and punchy) and the annotation is extremely comprehensive.

Heinrich Marschner

German 1795-1861

Suggested listening ...
...Overtures – Kaiser Adolph von Nassau; Des Falkners Braut; Prinz Friedrich von Homburg; Lukretia; Der Bäbu; Der Goldschmied von Ulm. Der Templer und die Jüdin. Grande Ouverture solenne on "God save the King", Op. 78. **Košice State Philharmonic Orchestra / Alfred Walter.** Marco Polo 8 223342.
...Rheinromanzen, Op. 128 – No. 1, Die sieben Freier. Gesänge und Balladen, Op. 160 – No. 1, Der König von Thule; No. 2, Die Rache. Das Flämmchen auf der Heide, Op. 80 No. 12. Die Monduhr, Op. 102 No. 2. Das Lied von alten König, Op. 82 No. 2. Der betrogene Teufel, Op. 87 No. 1. *Coupled with works by* **Kreutzer, Nicolai, Goetz** *and* **Humperdinck** Olaf Bär (bar); **Helmut Deutsch** (pf). EMI CDC5 55393-2 (1/96). *See review in the Collections section; refer to the Index to Reviews.*

...Hans Heiling – An jenam Tag. Der Vampyr – Ha! Noch einen ganzen Tag. *Coupled with works by* **Korngold, Lortzing, Weber, Spohr, Kreutzer, Schreker, Humperdinck** and **Wagner** **Thomas Hampson** (bar); [a]**Pestalozzi Gymnasium Children's Choir; Munich Radio Orchestra / Fabio Luisi.** EMI CDC5 55233-2 (9/95). *See review in the Collections section; refer to the Index to Reviews.*

Istvan Marta

Hungarian 1952-

Suggested listening ...
...Doom. A sigh. *Coupled with works by* **Crumb, Tallis, Ives** and **Shostakovich Kronos Quartet.** Elektra Nonesuch 7559-79242-2 (4/91). *See review in the Collections section; refer to the Index to Reviews.*

John March

British 1752-1828

Suggested listening ...
...Quartetto in B flat major in imitation of the Stile of Haydn's Opera Prima. *Coupled with works by* **Shield, Abel, Webbe** and **S. Wesley Salomon Quartet.** Hyperion CDA66780 (3/96). *See review in the Collections section; refer to the Index to Reviews.*

Roger Marsh

British 1949-

Suggested listening ...
...Ferry Music. *Coupled with works by* **Powers, Lutyens, LeFanu** and **G. Williams Mühlfeld Ensemble** Clarinet Classics CC0007 (10/94). *See review in the Collections section; refer to the Index to Reviews.*

Frank Martin

Swiss 1890-1974

New review

Martin Concerto for Seven Wind Instruments, Timpani, Percussion and Strings[a]. Etudes for String Orchestra[a]. Petite Symphonie concertante[b]. Passacaglia for String Orchestra[c]. Violin Concerto[d]. In terra pax[e]. [e]**Ursula Buckel** (sop); [e]**Marga Höffgen** (contr); [e]**Ernst Haefliger** (ten); [e]**Pierre Mollet** (bar); [e]**Jakob Stämpfli** (bass); [d]**Wolfgang Schneiderhan** (vn); [b]**Pierre Jamet** (hp); [b]**Germaine Vaucher-Clerc** (hpd); [b]**Doris Rossiaud** (pf); [c]**Lausanne Choral Union;** [c]**Stuttgart Chamber Orchestra / Karl Münchinger;** [abde]**Suisse Romande Orchestra / Ernest Ansermet.** Double Decca [bcd]mono/[ae]stereo Ⓜ 448 264-2DF2 (two discs: 147 minutes: ADD: 8/96). Items marked [a] from SXL2311 (6/62), [b]LXT2631 (12/51), [c]LXT5153 (8/57), [d]LX3146 (2/56), [e]SXL6098 (6/64).

This invaluable issue restores not only the pioneering recording of Martin's masterpiece, the *Petite Symphonie concertante* for harp, harpsichord, piano and double string orchestra, but also that of the Violin Concerto. They have great authority and a sense of atmosphere that is very special. The Violin Concerto is an inspired and noble piece, and Schneiderhan's mono recording makes its first appearance since the mid-1950s. In reviewing the original Vox LP the reviewer spoke of the work's "clarity, restraint and dignity". Anyone who responds to the Prokofiev D major Concerto or the Bartók and Walton will feel at home here. The *Concerto for seven wind instruments* and the *Etudes* for string orchestra were recorded in the early 1960s and the sound is very fresh. The performances do not match the wonderful accounts, coupled with the *Polyptique*, by Thierry Fischer (reviewed below). *In terra pax* is a strong work but is here showing its age (see the Chandos review further on). In any event this package is well worth having for the sake of the Violin Concerto.

Martin Symphonie concertante. Symphonie. Passacaglia. **London Philharmonic Orchestra / Matthias Bamert.** Chandos Ⓟ CHAN9312 (67 minutes: DDD: 1/95). Recorded 1993.
Gramophone Editor's choice.
Frank Martin's *Symphonie concertante* is a transcription of the *Petite symphonie concertante* for harp, harpsichord, piano and double string orchestras, made in 1945-6, a year after the original. As one would expect from so imaginative a master, the orchestration is characteristically resourceful and intelligent. Melodic ideas, previously associated with the three soloists, are generally assigned to the wind and effective use is made of muted trumpets. Successful though it is, one can understand why it has not supplanted its predecessor, whose sonorities are so subtle and original. The *Symphonie* (1936-37) is a great rarity. Although scored for large orchestra, the instrumentation is of consistent lightness and delicacy, almost chamber-like in its subtlety. The slow movement, suffused with the muted colours and moonlit landscapes of some shadowy *Pelléas* country, is the most haunting movement of the four. At first the overall structure of the symphony seems somewhat amorphous, but the logic of Martin's thought processes emerges as one immerses oneself in the piece. This luminous and beautiful

score deserves a warm welcome and is well served by the LPO under Matthias Bamert, and the Chandos team. The recording is truthfully balanced and has a natural concert-hall perspective. Both these are first recordings and the *Passacaglia*, too, is a first modern recording. An invaluable and rewarding issue.

Martin Concerto for Seven Wind Instruments, Percussion and String Orchestra. Polyptique[a].
   Etudes. [a]**Marieke Blankestijn** (vn); **Chamber Orchestra of Europe / Thierry Fischer.** DG
   Ⓕ 435 383-2GH (66 minutes: DDD: 6/92).

This is a disc of exceptional excellence. These three pieces have all been recorded before but never as well – and they have certainly never been better played! In the concerto the virtuosity and sophistication of the wind of the Chamber Orchestra of Europe is so effortless and their accents far lighter in touch than their rivals. Their playing has real delicacy and clarity of articulation and the slow movement for once really sounds as it is marked, mysterious and yet elegant, while the muted strings have a lightness of sonority and colour which greatly enhances the atmosphere. The artistry of the strings is everywhere in evidence in the Etudes and they quite outclass other performances in their sensitivity of response and range of colour. The *Polyptique* for violin and two string orchestras dates from the last year of Martin's life, when he was 83. It was inspired by a polyptych, a set of very small panels that Martin saw in Sienna representing various episodes in the Passion. The work is inward-looking and powerfully searching, and is played with great beauty and purity of tone, and rapt concentration by Marieke Blankestijn and the Chamber Orchestra of Europe. The recording is one of the best from this (or any other) source. It is completely natural, truthful in timbre and has remarkable clarity and presence. The perspective is very musically judged and both producer and engineer deserve a special mention for the refinement and quality of the sound they have captured.

Additional recommendation ...

...Concerto for Seven Wind Instruments. Erasmi Monumentum. Etudes for String Orchestra.
   London Philharmonic Orchestra / Matthias Bamert. Chandos Ⓕ CHAN9283 (67 minutes: DDD: 7/94).

New review

Martin Der Sturm – Overture; Mein Ariel, hast du, der Luft nur ist; Ein feierliches Lied; Hin sind meine Zauberei'n[a]. Maria-Triptychon[b]. Sechs Monologe aus Jedermann[c]. [b]**Linda Russell** (sop); [ac]**David Wilson-Johnson** (bar); [c]**Duncan Riddell** (vn); **London Philharmonic Orchestra / Matthias Bamert.** Chandos Ⓕ CHAN9411 (68 minutes: DDD: 3/96). Recorded 1994. *Gramophone Editor's choice*

The *Maria-Triptychon* was written in the late 1960s in response to a request from Wolfgang Schneiderhan for a work for violin, soprano and orchestra that he could perform with his wife, Irmgard Seefried. Although the alternative recording with Seefried and Schneiderhan under the composer himself emanating from a Swiss Radio tape is authoritative, it does not match this Chandos recording in sheer beauty of sound. Linda Russell sings the solo part with great sympathy and intelligence, and Duncan Riddell assumes the mantle of Schneiderhan with no mean success. The transparency of texture that the Chandos team achieve shows this visionary score in the most favourable light. It makes a stronger impression than in any earlier performance and much of its success is due to the dedication of the LPO and their conductor Matthias Bamert. He distils a strong atmosphere and sense of mystery in all these scores. David Wilson-Johnson is on impressive form in the *Jedermann* Monologues (one of the great song-cycles of the century). His is as perceptive and moving an account as any – and he is no less impressive in *Der Sturm*, and what a magical score that is! The recording is well balanced.

Additional recommendation ...

...Petite symphonie concertante[a]. Maria-Triptychon[b]. Passacaglia (transc. comp.)[c]. [b]**Irmgaard Seefried** (sop); [b]**Wolfgang Schneiderhan** (vn); [a]**Eva Hunziker** (hp); [a]**Germaine Vaucher-Clerc** (clavecin); [a]**Doris Rossiaud** (pf); [ab]**Suisse Romande Orchestra;** [c]**Berlin Philharmonic Orchestra / Frank Martin.** Jecklin Disco mono Ⓕ JD645-2* (57 minutes: ADD: 10/91).

New review

Martin Der Cornet. **Jard van Nes** (contr); **Nieuw Sinfonietta Amsterdam / Reinbert de Leeuw.** Philips Ⓕ 442 535-2PH (61 minutes: DDD: 11/95). Text and translation included. Recorded 1993.   Ⓖ

Der Cornet is among Martin's greatest compositions and one of the most powerful works of its kind that our war-torn century has produced. *Der Cornet*, or to give it its full title, *Die Weise von Liebe und Tod des Cornets Christoph Rilke* ("The Song of the Love and Death of Cornet Christoph Rilke"), to Rainer Maria Rilke's celebrated text, strikes chilling resonances today. Briefly speaking it tells of a youthful ensign who fell in 1660 under "the sabres of the Turks into an ocean of flowers", and at times of war – and in particular Balkan wars – the story inevitably makes poignant reading. Later in life Rilke thought the poem "highly second-rate" though second-rate is the last thing one could say about Frank Martin's setting. The work is a rarity, which is understandable considering that *Der Cornet* takes nearly an hour, and makes great demands not only on the contralto but on the emotional tranquillity of the listener. This very fact, as well as the concentration of the piece, has militated against its wider dissemination. The setting comprises all but four of the 27 stanzas and the conductor and patron, Paul Sacher, encouraged Martin to score them for small chamber orchestral resources. The narrative is very much in command and the orchestral colouring is economical. Martin's responsiveness to the rhythm and music of the words is almost Debussian in its subtlety (German was not his first tongue). Each of the songs encapsulates a different aspect of the drama that unfolds in the prose poems, and in each the composer sought a musical form as close as possible to its literary form. The chamber forces involved are used with the utmost economy and to maximum effect. In addition to the strings, there are some winds, harp, piano and percussion but the textures have the lucidity and transparency that mark the Hofmannsthal *Everyman* settings which were composed in the same year (1943). Jard van Nes gives a dedicated and moving account of the cycle and Reinbert de Leeuw and the Nieuw Sinfonietta Amsterdam are sensitive and supportive. The sound is clean and well-focused. Readers who have the Lipovšek recording need not feel impelled to change. Both performances cast so strong a spell that it is difficult to choose between them. If you find one not in stock, you can safely acquire the other. Buy neither and you will be missing a powerful musical experience.

Additional recommendation ...

...Der Cornet (Die Weisse von Liebe und Tod des Cornets C. Rilke). **Marjana Lipovšek** (mez); **Austrian Radio Symphony Orchestra / Lothar Zagrosek.** Orfeo Ⓔ C164881A (59 minutes: DDD: 10/88). ⒼⒼ

New review

Martin In terra pax[a]. Les quatre éléments. [a]**Judith Howarth** (sop); [a]**Della Jones** (contr); [a]**Martyn Hill** (ten); [a]**Roderick Williams** (bar); [a]**Stephen Roberts** (bass); [a]**Brighton Festival Chorus; London Philharmonic Orchestra / Matthias Bamert.** Chandos Ⓔ CHAN9465 (67 minutes: DDD: 8/96). Text and translations included.

Sometime in 1944, towards the end of the Second World War, Swiss Radio approached Frank Martin with a commission for a work to be performed at the conclusion of the hostilities. The result was *In terra pax*, which Ernest Ansermet conducted in 1945 and which he eventually recorded in the 1960s. (this is the reissue reviewed at the beginning of this section). Matthias Bamert has now put us in his debt with his impressive ongoing survey of Martin's output, to which this disc is a distinguished addition. *In terra pax* is an eloquent and noble work, in every way characteristic of the master. The singers are not always quite as impressive as in the Ansermet set, but in every other respect the new recording is superior. Ansermet was a lifelong and loyal champion of Martin's music and the composer paid him a handsome tribute with *Les quatre éléments*, written in 1963 to celebrate the great conductor's eightieth birthday the following year. It is a work of keen and vibrant imaginative force. As usual the textures are pale but luminous, translucent and subtle; the invention is highly personal and distinctive. As with most of Martin's music, the rewards are richer on each occasion one returns to it. As this series continues Martin emerges as a figure of far greater substance than he was given credit for by the arbiters of taste in the 1960s and 1970s.

Further listening ...

...Ballade for Piano and Orchestra. Piano Concertos Nos. 2 and 4. **Jean-François Antonioli** (pf); **Turin Philharmonic Orchestra / Marcello Viotti.** Claves CD50-8509 (3/87).

...Three Danses[bcf]. Petite complainte[be]. Pièce brève[abd]. *Coupled with* **Martinů** Concerto for Oboe and Small Orchestra[bf]. **Honegger** Concerto da camera[acf]. Petite Suite, H89[ace]. Antigone[bcd]. [a]**Aurèle Nicolet** (fl); **Heinz Holliger** ([b]ob/[c]cor ang); [d]**Ursula Holliger** (hp); [e]**John Constable** (pf); [f]**Academy of St Martin in the Fields / Sir Neville Marriner.** Philips 434 105-2PH (9/93).

...Ballade for Piano and Orchestra[a]. Ballade for Trombone and Orchestra[b]. Concerto for Harpsichord and Small Orchestra[c]. [a]**Sebastian Benda** (pf); [b]**Armin Rosin** (tbn); [c]**Christiane Jaccottet** (hpd). Jecklin Disco JD5292 (9/89).

...Pavane couleur du temps[a]. Piano Quintet[b]. String Trio[c]. Trio sur des mélodies populaires irlandaises[d]. **Zurich Chamber Ensemble** (Brenton Langbein, [ab]Andreas Pfenninger, vns; [a]Cornel Anderes, [bc]Jürg Dähler, vas; Raffaele Altwegg, [a]Luciano Pezzani, vcs); [bd]**Hanni Schmid-Wyss** (pf). Jecklin Disco JD646-2 (10/91).

...Mass for Double Chorus. *Coupled with* **Poulenc** Mass in G major. Quatre petites prières de Saint François d'Assise. Salve regina. **Christ Church Cathedral Choir, Oxford / Stephen Darlington.** Nimbus NI5197 (12/89).

...Mass for Double Chorus. *Coupled with* **Howells** Requiem[a]. Take him, earth, for cherishing. [a]**Sally Barber** (sop); [a]**Julia Field** (mez); [a]**Mark Johnstone** (ten); [a]**Andrew Angus** (bass); **Vasari / Jeremy Backhouse.** Cala United 88033 (12/94). *See review under Howells; refer to the Index to Reviews.* Ⓖ

...Requiem. **Elisabeth Speiser** (sop); **Ria Bollen** (contr); **Eric Tappy** (ten); **Peter Lagger** (bass); **Lausanne Women's Chorus; Union Chorale; Ars Laeta Vocal Ensemble; Suisse Romande Orchestra / Frank Martin.** Jecklin Disco JD631-2 (1/90).

...Ballade (arr. Ansermet). *Coupled with works by* **Nielsen, Bernstein** and **Ibert** Michael Faust (fl); **Cologne Radio Symphony Orchestra / Alun Francis, Serge Baudo.** Capriccio 10 495 (12/94). *See review in the Collections section; refer to the Index to Reviews.*

Philip Martin   Irish 20th century

New review

Philip Martin Piano Trio No. 1, "Serendipity"[a]. Two Elegies[b]. Songs for the Four Parts of the Night[c]. Light Music[d]. The Rainbow Comes and Goes[e]. [cd]**Penelope Price Jones** (sop); [bc]**Ruxandra Colan** (vn); [bde]**Philip Martin** (pf); [a]**Crawford Piano Trio** (Adrian Petcu, vn; Iosef Calef, vc; Jan Cáp, pf). Altarus Ⓕ AIR-CD-9011 (70 minutes: DDD: 12/95). Recorded 1995.

Philip Martin is an Irish composer in his forties, a pupil of Franz Reizenstein and Sir Lennox Berkeley. His music is lyrical and economical, tonal and melodious. He is also a fine pianist, and writes gratefully for voices and instruments. His Piano Trio, the most substantial work here, was commissioned by the Crawford Trio for performance in the art gallery in Cork from which they take their name. It is Martin's 'Pictures at an Exhibition', illustrating seven of the paintings in that collection, linking them not with 'promenades', as in Mussorgsky, but with brief interludes in which we sense the composer saying "Where next? Good heavens, is that a Jack Yeats in the next room?" Sober lyricism, then, and close, expert counterpoint for a melancholy "Goose Girl" by Edith Somerville (author as well as painter: one half of Somerville and Ross), evocations of Irish folk music for Diarmuid O'Ceallacháin's "The Fiddler" (though this fiddler knows his Bartók as well), a fine surge of waves for indeed a splendid Jack Yeats, "Off the Donegal Coast". It must have been a delightful evening in the Crawford Gallery, an experience which the CD listener can recapture since all seven pictures are excellently reproduced in colour in the accompanying booklet, giving an extra dimension to this attractive work. *Light Music* is curious: a cycle of songs to poems by Derek Mahon so epigrammatically brief that 25 of them occupy only 24 minutes. They are not light in weight but rather are about light, and here Martin's lyricism is thinned down, sometimes to a striking bareness and once or twice to blandness. There is bareness without blandness to the songs with violin (an effective series of also epigrammatic settings of American Indian verses) and to the *Elegies* for violin and piano. *The Rainbow Comes and Goes* is ampler, serenely lyrical (it is in part a portrait of the composer's children), ending with a brilliant and quite difficult scherzo. The performances here are excellent throughout, and the recordings are first-class.

Antonio Martín y Coll   Spanish d. after 1743

Suggested listening ...

...Flores de musica – Ruede la Vola; Cancion Franzesa; Diferencias sobre la gayta. *Coupled with works by* **Durón** and **Literes** Al Ayre Español / **Eduardo López Banzo**. Deutsche Harmonia Mundi 05472 77326-2. ✒   Ⓖ

Vicente Martín y Soler   Spanish 1754-1806

Suggested listening ...

...Una cosa rara. **Soloists; La Capella Reial de Catalunya; Le Concert des Nations / Jordi Savall.** Auvidis Astrée E8760 (2/92). ✒

Manuel Martinez-Sobral   Guatemalian 1879-1946

Suggested listening ...

...Acuarelas Chapinas. *Coupled with* **Castillo** Sinfonieta para Orquesta. Xibalbá. Guatemala I and II. **Moscow Symphony Orchestra / Antonio de Almeida.** Marco Polo 8 223710 (5/95).

Bohuslav Martinů   Czech 1890-1959

Martinů Cello Concertos – No. 1; No. 2. Cello Concertino. **Raphael Wallfisch** (vc); **Czech Philharmonic Orchestra / Jiří Bělohlávek.** Chandos Ⓕ CHAN9015 (76 minutes: DDD: 4/92). Recorded 1991.

Following his centenary year in 1990, Bohuslav Martinů has been returning to favour, although, as the composer of almost 30 concerto-type works, he cannot always escape the charge of flatulent note-spinning that attaches itself to such fertility. On the present disc, his unique imaginative vision is most obvious in the Cello Concerto No. 1. The central slow movement in particular finds Martinů at his best, a deeply moving threnody with a potent nostalgic quality which will be instantly recognizable to admirers of the later symphonics. There is an improvisatory freedom about the Second Concerto which makes it harder to grasp and the thematic material has rather too much in common with other, better scores. The much earlier *Concertino* is in Martinů's playful, more overtly neoclassical vein. You may notice some vamp-until-ready eighteenth-century scrubbing in the concertos, but here the younger composer is preoccupied with the lighter aspects of the style. There's a Stravinskian wit and elegance about the writing and the chamber scoring reflects both the fashionable trends and the

economic constraints of life in 1920s Paris. In the First Concerto, Raphael Wallfisch is rather
backwardly balanced *vis-à-vis* the Czech Philharmonic, whose regular conductor, Jiří Bělohlávek, is
of course totally inside this music. At the same time, the resonant Spanish Hall of Prague Castle
provides an agreeable ambient glow which does not mask too much detail. Make no mistake: this is
a most attractive proposition for those already familiar with the idiom. Adventurous beginners should
perhaps start elsewhere.

Martinů Piano Concertos – No. 2; No. 3; No. 4, "Incantation". **Rudolf Firkušný** (pf); **Czech
Philharmonic Orchestra / Libor Pešek.** RCA Victor Red Seal Ⓕ 09026 61934-2 (67 minutes:
DDD: 4/95). Recorded 1993. *Gramophone Editor's choice.*   Ⓖ
These performances not only have special authority but are in a class of their own. Although the five
piano concertos are not of comparable importance to the Martinů symphonies, they are not of
negligible interest. Martinů returned to the medium throughout his career: the First and weakest
dates from 1925 and the last, the *Fantasia concertante* in B flat, from 1957, two years before his
death. The disc bears the title "Tribute to Rudolf Firkušný" and the jewel-case reminds us that he
gave the first performance of all three concertos. The Fourth. *Incantation* is undoubtedly the finest
of them all, highly imaginative in its exotic sound-world, with what sound like wild Aztec bird calls
and war cries, and full of extraordinarily luminous and subtle sonorities. Firkušný's account is a
revelation to those who have heard only the Páleníček, Leichner or Havliková recordings. There is
the right sense of pace – and space: phrases have time to breathe and make their point. The Czech
Philharmonic under Libor Pešek give Firkušný dedicated and sympathetic support. The recording is
very good and allows one to hear more orchestral detail than ever before. In Firkušný's hands the
Second Concerto has a real sense of warmth and delight, and like all good music makes one feel
better. The Third, too, emerges in fresher and more vivid colours than ever before. What is also
astonishing is that at no time does Firkušný's playing betray an inkling of his years: he was 81 when
these performances were given! He was an aristocrat among pianists and this is a worthy memorial
to him.

Martinů Symphonies. **Bamberg Symphony Orchestra / Neeme Järvi.** BIS Ⓕ CD362, CD363
(Selected by Sounds in Retrospect) and CD402 (three discs, oas: 61, 63 and 59 minutes: DDD:
9/87, 12/88).
  CD362 – Nos. 1 and 2. *CD363* – Nos. 3 and 4. *CD402* – Nos. 5 and 6.   Ⓖ
Martinů began composing at the age of ten and later studied and lived in Paris, America and
Switzerland. Despite his travels he remained a quintessentially Czech composer and his music is
imbued with the melodic shapes and rhythms of the folk-music of his native homeland. The six
symphonies were written during Martinů's years in America and in all of them he uses a large
orchestra with distinctive groupings of instruments which give them a very personal and
unmistakable timbre. The rhythmic verve of his highly syncopated fast movements is very infectious,
indeed unforgettable, and his slow movements are often deeply expressive, most potently, perhaps, in
that of the Third Symphony which is imbued with the tragedy of war. The Bamberg orchestra play
marvellously and with great verve for Järvi, whose excellently judged tempos help propel the music
forward most effectively. His understanding of the basic thrust of Martinů's structures is very
impressive and he projects the music with great clarity. The BIS recordings are beautifully clear, with
plenty of ambience surrounding the orchestra, a fine sense of scale and effortless handling of the wide
dynamic range Martinů calls for. Enthusiastically recommended.

Additional recommendations ...

...Nos. 1 and 2. **Berlin Symphony Orchestra / Claus Peter Flor.** RCA Victor Red Seal Ⓕ RD60154
  (62 minutes: DDD: 11/90).
...No. 6. **Janáček** Sinfonietta. **Suk** Fantasticke scherzo, Op. 25. Czech Philharmonic Orchestra /
  Jiří Bělohlávek. Chandos Ⓕ CHAN8897 (65 minutes: DDD: 1/91).
...Nos. 1-6. **Czech Philharmonic Orchestra / Václav Neumann.** Supraphon Ⓕ 11 03822 (three discs:
  181 minutes: DDD: 4/91).
...Nos. 3 and 4. **Royal Scottish National Orchestra / Bryden Thomson.** Chandos Ⓕ CHAN8917
  (60 minutes: DDD: 6/91).
...Nos. 1-6. **Czech Philharmonic Orchestra / Václav Neumann.** Supraphon Ⓕ 110382-2 (three discs:
  181 minutes: AAD: 1/92).
...No. 5. Memorial to Lidice. Les fresques de Piero della Francesca[a]. **Czech Philharmonic
  Orchestra / Karel Ančerl.** Supraphon Historical mono/[a]stereo Ⓕ 11 1931-2* (77 minutes:
  AAD: 3/93).   Ⓖ
...No. 4. Field Mass[a]. Memorial to Lidice. [a]**Ivan Kusnjer** (bar); **Czech Philharmonic** [a]**Chorus and
  Orchestra / Jirí Bělohlávek.** Chandos Ⓕ CHAN9138 (65 minutes: DDD: 5/93).   ⒼⒼⒼ

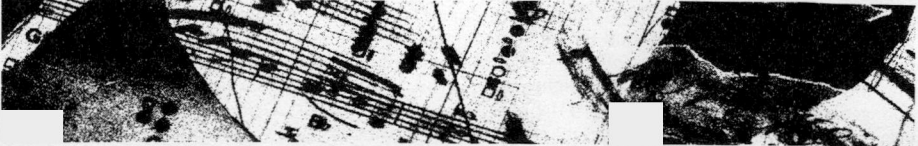

...Nos. 3 and 4. **Czech Philharmonic Orchestra / Václav Neumann.** Supraphon Ⓜ 11 1967-2 (62 minutes: DDD: 12/95).

Further listening ...
...Double Concerto for Two String Orchestras, Piano and Timpani[a]. Sinfonietta giocosa[b]. Rhapsody-Concerto for Viola and Orchestra[c]. [c]**Rivka Golani** (va); [a]**Jírí Skovajska,** [b]**Dennis Hennig** (pfs); [a]**Brno State Philharmonic Orchestra,** [b]**Australian Chamber Orchestra / Sir Charles Mackerras;** [c]**Berne Symphony Orchestra / Peter Maag.** Conifer CDCF210 (9/92).
...Violin Concertos Nos. 1 and 2. Rhapsody-Concerto for Viola and Orchestra. **Josef Suk** ([a]vn/[b]va); **Czech Philharmonic Orchestra / Václav Neumann.** Supraphon 11 1969-2 (11/95).
...Concerto for String Quartet and Orchestra. *Coupled with* **Janáček** Capriccio[a]. **Bartók** Music for Strings, Percussion and Celesta, Sz106. [a]**Joela Jones** (pf); **Cleveland Orchestra / Christoph von Dohnányi.** Decca 443 173-2DH (4/95).
...The parables. Estampes. Overture. La rhapsodie, "Allegro symphonique". **Czech Philharmonic Orchestra / Jiří Bělohlávek.** Supraphon 10 4140-2 (6/91).
...String Sextet. Three Madrigals. *Coupled with* **Schulhoff** String Sextet. **Raphael Ensemble.** Hyperion CDA66516 (7/92).
...Nonet. Trio in F major. La Rêvue de Cuisine. **The Dartington Ensemble.** Hyperion CDA66084 (1/84).
...String Quartets Nos. 1–7. **Panocha Quartet.** Supraphon 11 0994-2 (9/95).
...Cello Sonatas Nos. 1-3. **Steven Isserlis** (vc); **Peter Evans** (pf). Hyperion CDA66296 (7/89).
...Flute Sonata. *Coupled with works by* **Handel, Purcell, Rameau, Saint-Saëns, Roussel, Obradors, Head** *and* **Bishop** **Jean-Pierre Rampal** (fl); **John Steele Ritter** (pf). Sony Classical SK53106 (9/94).
...Flute Sonata No. 1. *Coupled with works by* **Gubaidulina, Feld, Taktakishvili** and **Amirov** **Leslie Newman** (fl); **Amanda Hurton** (pf). Cala United CACD88026 (6/96). *See review in the Collections section; refer to the Index to Reviews.*
...Three Czech Dances. Borová. 12 Esquisses. Four Mouvements. Les ritournelles. Windows on the garden. **Radoslav Kvapil** (pf). Unicorn-Kanchana DKPCD9140 (12/93).
...The Butterfly that stamped. Women's voices of the **Kühn Chorus; Prague Symphony Orchestra / Jiří Bělohlávek.** Supraphon 11 0380-2 (9/95).
...The Epic of Gilgamesh. **Eva Depoltová** (sop); **Stefan Margita** (ten); **Ivan Kusnjer** (bar); **Ludek Vele** (bass); **Milan Karpíšek** (spkr); **Slovak Philharmonic Choir; Slovak Philharmonic Orchestra / Zdeněk Košler.** Marco Polo 8 223316 (4/91).
...The Opening of the Wells. Legend of the Smoke from Potato Fires. Mikeš of the Mountains. **Soloists; Kühn Chorus / Pavel Kühn.** Supraphon 11 0767-2 (5/94).
...Echec au Roi[a]. The Revolt. [a]**Vladimír Olexa** (spkr); [a]**Kateřina Kachlíková** (contr); **Prague Symphony Orchestra / Jiří Bělohlávek.** Supraphon 11 1415-2 (5/94).
...Spalíček. The Romance of the Dandelions. Primrose. **Soloists; Kantilena Children's Chorus; Kuhn Chorus; Brno State Philharmonic Orchestra / František Jílek.** Supraphon 11 07522 (4/93).
...Julietta. **Soloists; Prague National Theatre Chorus and Orchestra / Jaroslav Krombholc.** Supraphon 10 8176-2 (6/93). Ⓠ
...The Greek Passion. **Soloists; Kuhn Children's Chorus; Czech Philharmonic Chorus; Brno State Philharmonic Orchestra / Sir Charles Mackerras.** Supraphon 10 36112 (3/91).

Giuseppe Martucci
Italian 1856-1909

Suggested listening ...
...Piano Concerto No. 2 in B flat minor, Op. 66[a]. Canzonetta, Op. 55 No. 1. Tempo di gavotta, Op. 55 No. 2. Giga, Op. 61 No. 3. Serenata, Op. 57 No. 1. Minuetto, Op. 57 No. 2. Momento musicale, Op. 57 No. 3. [a]**Francesco Caramiello** (pf); **Philharmonia Orchestra / Francesco d'Avalos.** ASV CDDCA691 (7/90).
...Symphony No. 1 in D minor, Op. 75. Novelletta, Op. 82 No. 2. Notturno in G flat major, Op. 70 No. 1. Tarantella, Op. 44 No. 6. **Philharmonia Orchestra / Francesco d'Avalos.** ASV CDDCA675 (12/89).
...Symphony No. 2 in F major, Op. 81. Andante in B flat major, Op. 69 No. 2[a]. Colore orientale, Op. 44 No. 3. [a]**George Ives** (vc); **Philharmonia Orchestra / Francesco d'Avalos.** ASV CDDCA689 (5/90).
...Canzone dei Ricordi[a]. Nocturne, Op. 70 No. 1. *Coupled with* **Respighi** Il tramonto[a]. [a]**Carol Madalin** (mez); **English Chamber Orchestra / Alfredo Bonavera.** Hyperion CDA66290 (7/88).
...Notturno in G flat major, Op. 70 No. 1. Novelletta, Op. 82 No. 2. Giga, Op. 61 No. 3. *Coupled with* **Busoni** Turandot – Suite, Op. 41. **Casella** Paganiniana, Op. 65. **La Scala Philharmonic Orchestra, Milan / Riccardo Muti.** Sony Classical SK53280 (4/94). *See review under Busoni; refer to the Index to Reviews.* Ⓖ Ⓠ

Joseph Marx
Austrian 1882-1964

Suggested listening ...
...Durch Einsamkeiten. *Coupled with works by* **Dargomïzhsky, Loeffler, A. Busch, Brahms,
R. Strauss, Reutter** and **Gounod** Mitsuko Shirai (mez); Tabea Zimmermann (va); Hartmut
Höll (pf). Capriccio 10 462 (9/95). *See review in the Collections section; refer to the Index to
Reviews.* **ⓖ**

Pietro Mascagni
Italian 1863-1945

Suggested listening ...
...Cavalleria Rusticana. *See review and listings under Leoncavallo; refer to the Index to Reviews.*

Benedict Mason
British 1954-

Suggested listening ...
...String Quartet No. 1[a]. Double Concerto[b]. Self-referential Songs and Realistic Virelais[c]. [c]**Christine
Whittlesey** (sop); [b]**Michael Thompson** (hn); [b]**David Purser** (tbn); [a]**Arditti Quartet;** [b]**London
Sinfonietta / Diego Masson;** [c]**Ensemble Modern / Ingo Metzmacher.** Bridge BCD9045 (10/94).
...Lighthouses of England and Wales. **BBC Symphony Orchestra / Lothar Zagrosek.** Collins
Classics 2004-2 (3/92). *See review in the Collections section; refer to the Index to Reviews.*

Jules Massenet
French 1842-1912

New review

Massenet Hérodiade. **Nadine Denize** (mez) Hérodiade; **Cheryl Studer** (sop) Salomé; **Ben Heppner**
(ten) Jean; **Thomas Hampson** (bar) Hérode; **José van Dam** (bass-bar) Phanuel; **Marcel Vanaud**
(bar) Vitellius; **Jean-Philippe Courtis** (bass) High Priest; **Martine Olmeda** (mez) Young
Babylonian; **Jean-Paul Fouchécourt** (ten) Voice in the Temple; **Toulouse Capitole Chorus and
Orchestra / Michel Plasson.** EMI Ⓟ CDS5 55378-2 (three discs: 166 minutes: DDD: 2/96). Notes,
text and translation included. Recorded 1994. *Gramophone Editor's choice.*   **ⓖ**
Written in 1880, *Hérodiade* is typical of the early grand operas with which Massenet courted
popularity. In its final version, which is the one used for this recording, it offers five magnificent roles
to singers who have the wherewithal to make the most of them. It is no wonder that Studer and
Heppner want to sing the opera, when their solo scenes are such glorious show-pieces and – as always
with Massenet – gratefully written for the voice. There is little point in making biblical comparisons.
Forget Strauss's *Salome* for a moment and think instead of Verdi and *Aida*. It is impossible to say
whether Massenet consciously took Verdi's masterpiece as a model, but we do know that he put in his
request for tickets to see the first performance of *Aida* at the Palais Garnier while he was orchestrating
Hérodiade. The similarities are inevitable, as both operas are descendants of Meyerbeer. There are
copious ballets, mystic off-stage chanting, grand choral finales and exotic settings of Eastern promise.
Michel Plasson conducts the opera uncut and has the advantage of a good studio recording. He is not
one for taking an objective view of the music and there are times when he rushes frenetically ahead,
as if he is as possessed by the lurid goings-on in the drama as the characters on stage. The sense of
atmosphere is palpable. In Plasson's hands the heavy chords at the opening of Act 3 resound with a
potent mysticism that presages Klingsor's castle (Massenet knew his Wagner too). In fact, we are at
the dwelling of Phanuel the sorcerer, a less threatening proposition. José van Dam is marvellous in
this big solo, leaning on the opening words of "Dors, ô cité perverse" with a sinister gleam in his voice
that sends shivers down one's back. Silvery pure in tone, Studer's Salomé throws herself into the
drama with lustful abandon and Heppner phrases the music with remarkable breadth and seems to
have heroic top notes to spare.

Massenet Don Quichotte[a]. Scènes alsaciennes[b]. **Nicolai Ghiaurov** (bass) Don Quichotte; **Régine
Crespin** (sop) Dulcinée; **Gabriel Bacquier** (bar) Sancho Panza; **Michèle Command** (sop) Pedro;
Annick Duterte (sop) Garcias; **Peyo Garazzi** (ten) Rodriguez; **Jean-Marie Fremeau** (ten) Juan;
[a]**Suisse Romande Chorus and Orchestra / Kazimierz Kord;** [b]**National Philharmonic Orchestra /
Richard Bonynge.** Decca Ⓜ 430 636-2DM2 (two discs: 133 minutes: ADD: 4/92). Notes, text and
translation included. Item marked [a] from D156D3 (11/79), [b]SXL6827 (12/77). Recorded 1978.
Massenet's operas are patchily represented in the catalogue, and this heroic comedy, which was his last
big success (in 1910, when he was 68), is most welcome. People who think of him as only a salon
composer, lacking the vigour and depth of a Berlioz or a Debussy, should listen to the start of Act 1,
set in a Spanish town square at fiesta time; the opening music bursts out of the loudspeakers like that
of Verdi's *Otello*, although here the mood is joyous, with tremendous rhythmic verve and gusto. In
fact, this opera is closer to Verdi's *Falstaff*, with the same admixture of gentler serious moments
amidst the comic bustle and intrigue, and of course, here again the central character is a comic yet

lovable figure. The recording, made by a British team in Geneva in 1978, still sounds well although orchestral detail could be clearer. As for the performance by mainly Swiss forces under Kazimierz Kord, and with a Bulgarian bass in the title role (written for Chaliapin), one can only praise it for its idiomatic realization of a 'Spanish' opera by a gifted French composer for the theatre. Though Régine Crespin may be too mature vocally for Dulcinée, the object of the elderly Don Quixote's adoration, she sings splendidly and few will find this a serious weakness. Nicolai Ghiaurov rightly makes Quixote himself a real person, touching and dignified as well as comic, and Gabriel Bacquier gives a rounded portrayal of his servant Sancho Panza, so that Quixote's death scene in the company of his old friend is particularly strong. The booklet provides a synopsis plus the French text and a translation. This is a fine mid-price issue, and the lively and tuneful *Scènes alsaciennes* with a British orchestra under Richard Bonynge make a fine fill-up.

Additional recommendation ...

...**Soloists; Toulouse Capitole Chorus and Orchestra / Michel Plasson.** EMI Ⓕ CDS7 54767-2 (two discs: 115 minutes: DDD: 12/93).

Further listening ...

...Fantaisie. *Coupled with* **Lalo** Cello Concerto in D minor. **Saint-Saëns** Cello Concerto No. 1 in A minor, Op. 33. **Sophie Rolland** (vc); **BBC Philharmonic Orchestra / Gilbert Varga.** ASV CDDCA867 (12/93). *See review under Lalo; refer to the Index to Reviews. Gramophone Editor's choice.* Ⓖ

...Orchestral Suites – *2292-45858-2:* No. 3, "Scènes dramatiques"; No. 6, "Scènes de féerie". La Vierge – Le dernier sommeil de la Vierge. *2292-45859-2:* No. 4, "Scènes pittoresques"; No. 7, "Scènes alsaciennes". Don Quichotte – Interludes. **Monte-Carlo Opera Orchestra / John Eliot Gardiner.** Erato 2292-45858/9-2 (2/93).

...Hérodiade – Ballet music. Orchestral Suites – No. 1, Op. 13. No. 2, "Scènes hongroises"; Suite No. 3, "Scènes dramatiques". **New Zealand Symphony Orchestra / Jean-Yves Ossonce.** Naxos 8 553124 (9/95).

...Orchestral Suites – No. 4, "Scènes pittoresques"; No. 5, "Scènes napolitaines"; No. 6, "Scènes de féerie"; No. 7, "Scènes alsaciennes". **New Zealand Symphony Orchestra / Jean-Yves Ossonce.** Naxos 8 553125 (9/95).

...Le Roi de Lahore. **Soloists; London Voices; National Philharmonic Orchestra / Richard Bonynge.** Decca Grand Opera 433 851-2DMO2 (2/93).

...Werther. **Soloists; Cantoria Children's Choir; Chorus and Orchestra of the Opéra-Comique, paris / Elie Cohen.** EMI Références mono CHS7 63195-2 (3/90). *Gramophone classical 100.* ⒼⒼⒼ

...Werther. **Soloists; Children's Choir; Royal Opera House Orchestra, Covent Garden / Sir Colin Davis.** Philips 416 654-2PH2 (2/87).

...Le Cid. **Soloists; Byrne Camp Chorale; New York Opera Orchestra / Eve Queler.** CBS M2K79300 (2/90).

...Grisélidis. **Soloists; Lyon National Choir; Lyon Opéra Chorus; Franz Liszt Symphony Orchestra, Budapest / Patrick Fournillier.** Koch Schwann 312702 (12/94).

...Le Carillon[a]. **Delibes** Coppelia[b]. [a]**National Philharmonic Orchestra;** [b]**Suisse Romande Orchestra / Richard Bonynge.** Decca 425 472-2DM2 (1/90).

...Esclarmonde. **Soloists; Finchley Children's Music Group; John Alldis Choir; National Philharmonic Orchestra / Richard Bonynge.** Decca 425 651-2DM3 (8/90).

...Chérubin. **Soloists; Bavarian State Opera Chorus; Munich Radio Orchestra / Pinchas Steinberg.** RCA Victor Red Seal 09026-60593-2 (12/92).

...Thaïs – Méditation. *Coupled with works by* **Glazunov, Rachmaninov, Sarasate, Rimsky-Korsakov, Tchaikovsky, Wieniawski** and **Kreisler** Itzhak Perlman (vn); **Abbey Road Ensemble / Lawrence Foster.** EMI CDC5 55475-2 (1/96).

Matheus de Sancto Johanne
French *fl.* 1365-?1389

Suggested listening ...

...Inclite flos orti Gebenensis. *Coupled with works by* **Johanne Egidius, Philipoctus de Caserta, Ciconia, Bartolomeus da Bologna, Velut, Anonymous, Tapissier, Antonius de Civitate Austrie, Zacharias, Brassart** and **Dufay** Orlando Consort. Metronome METCD1008 (11/95). *See review in the Collections section; refer to the Index to Reviews.* Ⓖ

William Mathias
British 1934-1992

New review

Mathias String Quartets – No. 1, Op. 38; No. 2, Op. 84; No. 3, Op. 97. **Medea Quartet** (Morven Bryce, Andrew Storey, vns; Duncan Ferguson, va; Judith Rees, vc). Metier Ⓕ MSVCD92005 (63 minutes: DDD: 10/95). Recorded 1993.

William Mathias's three string quartets, written between 1967 and 1986, could hardly make a more powerful impression. In many ways the first of the three is the most ambitious, direct and pithy in its arguments over a single-movement span lasting a full 20 minutes. Mathias was in his mid-thirties when he wrote it, and had already established his distinctive idiom, but here he adopted a less traditional structure, using sharply conceived motifs rather as Stravinsky does in his *Symphonies of Wind Instruments*. With occasional passing echoes of the quartets of Britten and Tippett, one might describe this as music by a composer who has lived with and thoroughly digested the Bartók quartets. Direct echoes are only incidental but as in Bartók there is a consistent tautness, with disparate ideas compellingly drawn together. The Second Quartet, dating from 1980-81, was written as a BBC commission for the Gabrieli Quartet. In each of its four compact movements, Mathias echoes medieval music in different ways, using drone basses and pedal points in support of material with a modal tinge. Echoes of Chanson and Minnelied are heard, as he put it himself, "through an aural prism". The result is stylistically as individual as the First Quartet, never sounding merely derivative. The Third Quartet, dating from 1986, brings together elements of both the earlier works. That the three quartets in sequence make such an involving experience is in fair measure due to the quality of the playing by the young Medea Quartet, a very accomplished group, both technically brilliant and deeply expressive. The Metier sound is first-rate too, with superb presence and atmosphere.

Mathias Ave Rex, Op. 45[a]. Elegy for a Prince, Op. 59[b]. This Worlde's Joie, Op. 67[c]. [c]**Janet Price** (sop); [c]**Kenneth Bowen** (ten); [b]**Sir Geraint Evans** (bar); [c]**Michael Rippon** (bass); [a]**Welsh National Opera Chorus;** [c]**Bach Choir;** [c]**St George's Chapel Choir, Windsor Castle;** [ab]**London Symphony Orchestra / David Atherton;** [c]**New Philharmonia Orchestra / Sir David Willcocks.** Lyrita Ⓟ SRCD324 (79 minutes: ADD: 2/95). Texts included. Item marked [a] from Decca SXL6607 (12/73), [b]Argo ZRG882 (6/78), [c]HMV ASD301 (12/76). Recorded 1973.

Here are three works for voice and orchestra, two choral, one for soloist, written between 1969 and 1974. They have a good deal in common yet enough separate identity for them to comprise an acceptably varied programme, the *Elegy for a Prince* forming a relatively tough and tangy item to be sandwiched in between the choral collections. Of these, *Ave Rex* is a set of carols, "Sir Christmas" being now by far the best known, and *This Worlde's Joie* a cantata in four movements, nearly 50 minutes long, employing a boys' choir as well as the usual forces of soloists, mixed choir and orchestra. This, of course, makes us think of Britten, and indeed it is difficult not to think of him, and to a lesser extent Tippett, throughout the disc. In his useful booklet-note, Geraint Lewis acknowledges this but expresses it in terms of "occasional points of contact and homage", which is probably excessively diplomatic. *This Worlde's Joie* moves delightfully from one good setting to another, always contriving to unify the structure and work effectively towards climax and contrast. The Prince of the *Elegy* is Llywelyn ap Gruffudd, killed by English soldiers in 1282: a stern mood prevails, the orchestral writing harder and more austere than the composer's usual style, though it yields to some tender expression in the last section. Sir Geraint Evans sings with authority and dark coloration. The soloists in the cantata are excellent and one cannot help wondering why more was not heard on record of Janet Price. Willcocks and Atherton conduct with vigour and care for detail, and the recordings are admirably clean.

Additional recommendation ...

...Ave Rex. I will celebrate. O how amiable, Op. 90 No. 3. Rex Gloriae – Four Latin Motets, Op. 83. Missa Aedis Christi, Op. 92. Jesus College Service, Op. 53. A Grace, Op. 89 No. 3. As truly as God is our Father. Let the people praise Thee, O God, Op. 87. Organ Fantasy, Op. 78 – No. 2, Canzonetta. **Simon Lawford** (org); **Christ Church Cathedral Choir / Stephen Darlington.** Nimbus Ⓟ NI5243 (76 minutes: DDD: 9/90).

Further listening ...

...Harp Concerto, Op. 50. *Coupled with* **Ginastera** Harp Concerto, Op. 25. **Ann Hobson Pilot** (hp); **English Chamber Orchestra / Isaiah Jackson.** Koch International 37261-2 (12/94).

...Clarinet Concerto, Op. 68; Harp Concerto, Op. 50. **Gervase de Peyer** (cl); **Osian Ellis** (hp); Piano Concerto No. 3, Op. 40. **Peter Katin** (pf); **London Symphony Orchestra; New Philharmonia Orchestra / David Atherton.** Lyrita SRCD325 (7/95).

...Summer Dances. Soundings. *Coupled with* **Hoddinott** Quodlibet on Welsh Nursery Tunes. Chorales, Variants and Fanfares[a]. Ritornelli 2, Op. 100 No. 2. [a]**Kevin Bowyer** (org); **Fine Arts Brass Ensemble.** Nimbus NI5466 (5/96).

...Fanfare. Processional. Invocations, Op. 35. Fantasy, Op. 78. Berceuse, Op. 95 No. 3. Jubilate, Op. 67 No. 2. Antiphonies, Op. 88 No. 2. Fenestra. Recessional, Op. 96 No. 4. Chorale. **John Scott** (org). Nimbus NI5367 (6/93).

Nicola Matteis

Italian/British died 1707 or later

Suggested listening ...

...Setts of Ayres – Book 2: No. 10, Preludio in ostinatione; No. 12, Andamento malincolico; Book 3: No. 7, Preludio-Prestissimo; No. 8, Sarabanda-Adagio; No. 9, Gavotta con divisioni; Book 4: No. 27, Bizzararrie sopra un basso malinconico; No. 28, Aria amorosa-Adagio. *Coupled with works by* **Locke, Baltzar, Weldon, Blow, Butler** *and* **J. Banister.** Palladian Ensemble. Linn Records CKD041 (5/96). *☞ See review in the Collections section; refer to the Index to Reviews.*

...Ayres for the Violin – Book 1: Sonata in C minor. Book 2: Suite in G minor. Book 4: Suites – A major; D minor; E minor. Sonata in C major. **Arcadian Academy / Nicholas McGegan** (hpd/org). Harmonia Mundi HMU90 7067 (9/92). *☞*

Ⓖ

...Ayres for the Violin: Book 2 – Sonatas: B flat major; E major. Suite in A minor.
Book 3 – Sonata in F major. Suites: G minor; C minor. Book 4 – Suites: D major; F major.
Almand's by Mr Nicola Matteis. **Arcadian Academy / Nicholas McGegan** (hpd/org). Harmonia
Mundi HMU90 7108 (3/95). ✒   Ⓖ

Colin Matthews   British 1946-

New review
C. Matthews Fourth Sonata. Suns Dance. Broken Symmetry. **London Sinfonietta / Oliver Knussen.**
DG Ⓕ 447 067-2GH (65 minutes: DDD: 1/96). Recorded 1992-4.   Ⓖ
Here are three major works by Colin Matthews, from the mid 1970s (Fourth Sonata), mid 1980s (*Suns Dance*) and early 1990s (*Broken Symmetry*). They make an intriguing sequence – no, let's drop the pretence of intellectual detachment: the word is devastating. The Fourth Sonata shows Matthews in his late twenties reacting to American minimalism, but coming up with something utterly personal: angrily pulsating rhythms, textures full of jagged edges, anguished string harmonies – music that looks forward to Adams's *The Chairman Dances* and backward to the Mahlerian nightmare scherzo. But Matthews does allow himself a vision of what you might call qualified hope at the end – a radiantly scored dawn in a sort of D major. The same dark urgency dominates *Suns Dance* – a ballet for ten instruments with a power out of all proportion to its instrumental means – and *Broken Symmetry*, a kind of extended scherzo for very large orchestra. But now there are no images of consolation. *Suns Dance* sounds like a piece possessed by its own energy: it's dance till you drop – or until the music lets you drop. Formal outlines are more obvious in *Broken Symmetry* (especially if you follow DG's helpful tracking), but the scherzo-trio sequence seems increasingly challenged by forces from within. The ending finally fulfils the promise of the title: a fabulously scored pulsating crescendo swells, then breaks apart – a few fragmentary sounds, then silence. Matthews's language is very different from that of Robert Simpson, but there is more than a passing resemblance to the end of Simpson's Fifth Symphony. It's a similar sequence: elemental violence, explosion, collapse. In both works the effect is grim, but at the same time tremendously exhilarating – like surviving a musical white-knuckle ride. Of course, the effect depends partly on the performances. Whether reduced to ten players or amplified to nearer 100, the London Sinfonietta play with breathtaking energy and precision for Oliver Knussen. The recordings help, too: clarity of focus without dryness. Few contemporary music discs get it right as thoroughly as this one has.

New review
C. Matthews Hidden Variables. Memorial. Quatrain. Machines & Dreams[a]. **London Symphony Orchestra / Michael Tilson Thomas.** Collins Classics Ⓕ 1470-2 (51 minutes: DDD: 5/96). Item marked [a] recorded live in 1991. *Selected by Soundings.*
"A battle for the soul of modern music" is how Antony Bye's booklet-note aptly describes Colin Matthews's *Hidden Variables*. Gritty and scintillating modernism contends with unmistakably transatlantic brands of minimalism and post-minimalism. It isn't easy to say who wins – or, categorically, where Matthews's sympathies lie (you can't imitate something so brilliantly if you don't have *any* inclination towards it); but as a musical representation of current musical politics it will take some beating – few battle symphonies are as concise, as musically ingenious, or as wickedly funny. There's less ambiguous evidence of Matthews's sense of fun in *Machines & Dreams*, a toy symphony this time, for orchestra and a virtuoso children's ensemble playing toy pianos, claxons, sirens, fishing reels, metronomes, football rattles, bird-calls, whistles and assorted computer-game horrors. Messiaen-like bird-song blends with nursery imitations of the real thing in the slow movement, until two of the toy birds meet sticky ends, though the cuckoo seems to have the last laugh in the riotous last movement. *Quatrain* and *Memorial* are more purely serious exercises – darker, more troubled perhaps, but less bleak and hectically active than *Suns Dance* and *Broken Symmetry* on the superbly performed and recorded Knussen/London Sinfonietta disc (reviewed above). Luckily for Matthews, Michael Tilson Thomas, the LSO and the Collins recording team have served him just as well here – composers are rarely so fortunate. As a result, Matthews now has excellent, up-to-date representation in the catalogue – a tribute to the courage of Collins and DG in these worryingly conservative times.
Further listening ...
...11 Studies in Velocity. *Coupled with works by* **Tippett, Saxton** and **C. Lambert** Nicholas **Unwin** (pf). Metier MSVCD92009 (1/96). *See review in the Collections section; refer to the Index to Reviews.*

David Matthews   British 1943-

Further listening ...
...Symphony No. 4, Op. 52. **East of England Orchestra / Malcolm Nabarro.** Collins Classics 20th
Century Plus 2008-2 (8/94). *Gramophone Editor's choice.*   Ⓖ
...A little threnody[a]. String Quartets[b] – No. 3; No. 6. The flaying of Marsyas[c]. **Nicholas Daniel**
([c]ob/[a]cor ang); [bc]**Brindisi Quartet.** Metronome METCD1005 (2/95).

Nicholas Maw

New review

Maw Life Studies. Sonata notturna[a]. [a]**Raphael Wallfisch** (vc); **English String Orchestra / William Boughton.** Nimbus Ⓕ NI5471 (65 minutes: DDD: 8/96).

Elgar's *Introduction and Allegro*, Vaughan Williams's *Tallis* Fantasia, Britten's *Bridge* Variations, Tippett's Double Concerto and *Corelli* Fantasia – what is it about string orchestras that seems so often to bring out the best in English composers? It is impossible to say whether posterity will place Nicholas Maw's *Sonata notturna* or *Life Studies* squarely in the same rank; but it's hard to think of any better modern British candidates, and *Life Studies* in particular shows an originality in its string writing, plus a lyrical expressive intensity, that puts it at the forefront of Maw's own output. 'Originality' here doesn't mean the piling up of novel effects, rather that Maw's use of the antiphonally divided 15-strong string ensemble creates textures, colours, moods that are rarely quite like anything else. The opening double-bass solo is compelling enough, quiet and gesturally economical though it is; the sounds that grow from it live up to that initial promise magnificently. One could pick out highlights but *Life Studies* isn't just a sequence of highlights; it's a musical quest, with a powerful sense of culmination (if not quite full resolution) at the end. Boughton's version seems richer in detail and more powerful in its final impact than an old, now unavailable, Marriner recording with the Academy of St Martin in the Field, and more atmospherically recorded. *Sonata notturna* initially seems less arrestingly original than *Life Studies*, though the growth of the argument from the simple but striking opening idea is palpable enough, and there's an exciting sense of fulfilment in the final *Capriccio* section. Raphael Wallfisch's eloquent playing shows how much he enjoys Maw's generously lyrical writing. However, it will probably be *Life Studies* that will lure you repeatedly back to this disc. It becomes more impressive the more one hears it. Strongly recommended to anyone whose interest in contemporary British music goes further than George Lloyd.

New review

Maw Odyssey (1972-85, rev. 1989-90). **City of Birmingham Symphony Orchestra / Sir Simon Rattle.** EMI Ⓕ CDS7 54277-2 (two discs: 95 minutes: DDD: 9/91). Recorded live in 1990. *Gramophone classical 100.*   ⓖⓖⓖ

Nicholas Maw's *Odyssey* is a musical voyage of extraordinary emotional conviction. Given its well-nigh 20-year gestation, it is also a composition of remarkable coherence, a super-symphony in a single span which sustains its forward movement and sense of direction over an hour and a half with formidable skill. The listener is undoubtedly helped by a formal design that sets up plentiful associations with the grand symphonic structures of the late romantic era, particularly Mahler and Strauss. But Maw is no parodist: he is a late twentieth-century affirmation of belief in certain fundamental musical truths, especially the abiding need for contrast between consonance and dissonance, and the consequently inescapable relevance of tonality. The whole enterprise, like the title itself, could have yielded an embarrassing pretentiousness. Yet the actual effect is rather to reinforce awareness of the difficulties the composer had to surmount in bringing *Odyssey* to a convincing conclusion – a conclusion that seems to express fulfilment and apprehension in equal measure. Simon Rattle, the CBSO and the EMI recording team are all equal to the composer's imaginative vision. A studio recording might have managed an even richer sound, but the impact of this live event is overwhelming in a very special way.   ⓖⓖⓖ

New review

Maw Dance Scenes. **Philharmonia Orchestra / Daniel Harding.** EMI British Composers (special price) MDS8 82648-2 (19 minutes: DDD: 7/96). Recorded 1995.   ⓖ

There's still some disagreement about whether Maw has ever quite risen to the level of his cantata *Scenes and Arias* (1962), a voluptuous, very late-romantic synthesis of Strauss and Viennese expressionism. It was a hard act to follow. However, here we find him trying something utterly different in *Dance Scenes* (1995) – this is unashamedly 'light' music, but of the most resourceful, invigorating kind, dodging clichés with the skill of a star centre forward. Where *Scenes and Arias* courted Schoenberg and Berg, *Dance Scenes* is daylight and fresh air, with the robust orchestral brilliance of Walton. If there's one chief guiding spirit, it's the American Hindemith. Harmonies, short phrases and long lines are steeped in Hindemith – no bad thing, since it seems to have breathed new life into Maw's melodic invention. If your idea of a 'big tune' stretches to include the lovely long melody Walton made the basis of his *Variations on a theme of Hindemith*, then you shouldn't be disappointed here: the oboe tune introduced in the third dance is very beguiling, and its apotheosis should appeal to all but the most thickly insulated hearts. The Philharmonia Orchestra, who commissioned *Dance Scenes*, play as though it had thoroughly won them over, and the recording does performance and music justice.

Further listening ...
...Flute Quartet. Piano Trio. **Judith Pearce** (fl); **Paul Coletti** (va); **Monticello Trio.** ASV CDDCA920 (6/95). *Gramophone Editor's choice.* ⓖ

Sir Peter Maxwell Davies
British 1934-

New review

Maxwell Davies Symphony No. 1. **BBC Philharmonic Orchestra / Sir Peter Maxwell Davies.**
  Collins Classics Ⓕ 1435-2 (55 minutes: DDD: 12/95). Recorded 1994.

Analysis isn't much use. No, the only thing is to leap straight in and don't worry greatly about any commentator's assurances that vestigial sonata structures are to be perceived in the outer movements, or even the composer's avowal of debts to Dante and St Thomas Aquinas. Listened to with as little such luggage as possible the Symphony's sheer splendour of sound is gripping from beginning to end, and after its seascapes and cliffscapes, its surging and breaking waves, its palette of blues and silvers, white and deep green, its sense of powerful undercurrents as well as iridescent surface, it would almost spoil the magnificent string theme that emerges near the end, repeated by pealing brass, to be told in advance that it is derived by the use of 'magic square' techniques from the plainchant *Ave maris stella*. Time enough, when you've experienced the long opening cello melody of the slow movement (a Mahlerian or a Schoenbergian cantilena, according to taste) and savoured its colouring with high flutes and piccolo, a susurration of muted violas and quiet marimba, timpani and violin pizzicato, to work out (if you can) on later hearings whether that theme is developed, transformed or merely superseded by what follows and thus brings about the movement's eloquent climax. The performance has rhythmic precision and precision of accent especially, which between them account for a large part of the work's urgent forward thrust. In some ways the First Symphony is the toughest of the five, but Maxwell Davies's exhilaration is audible throughout: at writing a symphony at last, at his now mature orchestral mastery, and at finding a means of fusing both these with his feelings about the sea and the Orkney landscape. Hence the exuberant grandeur of its sound, which the recording captures admirably.

Maxwell Davies Symphony No. 4. Trumpet Concerto[a]. [a]**John Wallace** (tpt); [a]**Scottish Chamber Orchestra / Sir Peter Maxwell Davies.** Collins Classics Ⓕ 1181-2 (73 minutes: DDD: 6/91).

Sir Peter Maxwell Davies has survived the transition from *enfant terrible* to *éminence grise* with equanimity – perhaps because he was always less 'terrible' than he seemed, and is still far from seriously 'grise'. From his earliest works to his most recent – the Trumpet Concerto and Fourth Symphony date from the late 1980s – he has used his delight in system-building to generate ambitious and complex structures that vibrate with no less complex but utterly uninhibited emotions. The concerto is the more immediately accessible of the two: the nature of the solo instrument, and Maxwell Davies's willingness not to jettison all the conventions of the concerto genre see to that. The work was written for John Wallace, and while it would be wrong to say that he makes light of its difficulties – at times you could swear that only a flautist could get round such florid writing – he succeeds brilliantly in demonstrating that the difficulties serve musical ends. The symphony has less immediately arresting ideas, but when the music is savoured, returned to, and allowed time to weave its spells, its rewards become progressively more apparent. These recordings capture the composer's own highly-charged readings with commendable fidelity.

Maxwell Davies Strathclyde Concertos – No. 3[a]; No. 4[b]. [a]**Randall Cook** (hn); [b]**Lewis Morrison** (cl); [a]**Peter Franks** (tpt); **Scottish Chamber Orchestra / Sir Peter Maxwell Davies.** Collins Classics Ⓕ 1239-2 (61 minutes: DDD: 10/92). Recorded 1991.

Sir Peter Maxwell Davies's plan to write a sequence of no fewer than ten *Strathclyde* Concertos for the principals of the Scottish Chamber Orchestra is turning into a research project into the nature of the concerto, the relationship between soloist and orchestra. His solo parts are always satisfying, even virtuoso, but the orchestra seldom adopt an accompanying or antagonistic role. In the double concerto for trumpet and horn, for example, the flutes and strings also play a very important part, with material of their own that the soloists hardly touch, but the effect is to emphasize the 'flute-ness' of the flutes and the 'string-ness' of the strings: they become, in effect, co-soloists themselves. Maxwell Davies is also interested of course, in this concerto, in the 'trumpet-ness' and 'horn-ness' of his two principal soloists, and in the beautiful slow movement they dramatize this by eventually exchanging functions, the trumpet becoming lyrical, the horn martial. One of the functions of the clarinet, in its concerto, is to point up the sober beauty, the 'un-clarinet-ness', of the textures against which its cool solo line moves; it has an especially fruitful relationship with that section of the orchestra with which it is in greatest contrast, the low strings. Both works require intent listening; both reward it with readily perceptible formal ingenuity (the way in which the clarinet concerto's main theme is only gradually revealed as a haunting folk-song is especially absorbing) and a fascinating interplay of instrumental character. Both concertos are vividly performed and very cleanly recorded.

New review
Maxwell Davies Corpus Christi, with Cat and Mouse. House of Winter. Sea Runes. Lullabye for Lucy. Apple-Basket; Apple-Blossom. One star, at last. A Hoy Calendar. Westerlings. **BBC Singers**

/ **Simon Joly.** Collins Classics Ⓕ 1463-2 (71 minutes: DDD: 2/96). Texts and translation included. Recorded 1995.

You might think unaccompanied voices would cramp Maxwell Davies's style. Far from it: the range of colour and texture here is remarkable, all the more so since, with a single exception, all these pieces sound challenging but grateful to sing. The exception is *Westerlings*, which calls for a chorus of virtuosos. Like all this music, save *Corpus Christi*, it uses poems by the late George Mackay Brown, in this case a narrative of the Norse settlement of Orkney, interspersed with magical wordless 'seascapes' and concluding with a setting of the Lord's Prayer in the Orkney dialect of Old Norse: a solemn thanksgiving for a safe landfall. It is closely related to the sea music of Maxwell Davies's symphonies, but the texts and a brilliantly resourceful use of vocal effect and vocal 'scoring' (the illusion of flutes, strings, even an organ, is consummate) make it both dramatic and pictorially evocative. *House of Winter* portrays both the frozen stillness and the violent storms of an Orkney winter, but with poetry and luminous colour rather than onomatopoeia; like its companion piece, *Sea Runes*, its lines are kind to voices. Some of the smaller works here – the very pure melody over rocking "lullays" of *Lullabye for Lucy*, *A Hoy Calendar* – would not tax a good amateur choir, though some pages of *Corpus Christi* most certainly would. The choral singing, as one would expect of this ensemble and this conductor, is superfine; the recording is both clean and pleasingly spacious.

New review

Maxwell Davies The Beltane Fire. Caroline Mathilde – suite from Act 2. [a]**Carys Lane,** [a]**Carolyn Sampson** (sops); [a]**Deborah Miles-Johnson,** [a]**Sally Bruce-Payne** (mezzos); **BBC Philharmonic Orchestra / Sir Peter Maxwell Davies.** Collins Classics Ⓕ Ⓘ 1464-2 (70 minutes: DDD: 6/96). Recorded 1995.

You would expect a pronounced Scottish element in the ballet score that is actually set in Scotland; in fact a touching and distinctly Scottish melody, associated with the unfortunate princess, recurs throughout the *Caroline Mathilde* suite as well, though it isn't heard in its 'pure' form until the very end when Caroline is sent into exile. Elsewhere Maxwell Davies shows a remarkable ability to adapt his style – one of his styles, at all events – to the needs of ballet, writing what any ballet-goer will recognize as a real *pas-de-deux* in the form of a passacaglia which rises to impassioned lyricism and then sombre gravity. Elements of paraphrase rather than pastiche are present in a menacing courtly gavotte and a dance of grotesque violence in which the people mock Caroline's doomed affair with a court doctor. No less sinister, there is a scene in which a conspiracy against the hated foreign princess is represented in quiet, rather hymn-like music with conventional harmonies (it is also rather like – can this be a coincidence? – one of Carl Nielsen's patriotic songs): consonance itself curdles and becomes nightmarish. At one time Maxwell Davies would have raucously parodied this; here he no longer needs to. Similar elements are present in *Beltane Fire*, and again the destructive elements are not mocked: the music of the minister and the elders whose influence eventually destroys a folk fiddle-player is quiet, often sinisterly so, but it is never caricatured. The folk music references here are overt. Maxwell Davies writes Orkney fiddle tunes of total authenticity, but also expands their expressive range, in this instance to a wild pagan vigour for the fertility dance around the Beltane flames and to the pathos of the fiddler's son remembering a destroyed way of life as the curtain falls. As Maxwell Davies's major concert works move closer towards tonal reference so the pieces in his other style take on deeper seriousness and eloquence. Could the two be moving towards each other? Excellent performances, as by now we would expect, from the Maxwell Davies/BBC Philharmonic partnership; the recordings are clean and vivid.

Further listening ...

…Miss Donnithorne's Maggot[a]. Eight Songs for a Mad King[b]. [a]**Mary Thomas** (sop); [b]**Julius Eastman** (bar); **The Fires of London / Sir Peter Maxwell Davies.** Unicorn-Kanchana DKPCD9052 (3/88).
…Ave maris stella. Image, Reflection, Shadow[a]. Runes from a Holy Island[b]. [a]**Gregory Knowles** (cimbalom); **The Fires of London /** [b]**Sir Peter Maxwell Davies.** Unicorn-Kanchana Souvenir UKCD2038 (3/91). Ⓖ
…The Martyrdom of St Magnus. **Soloists; Scottish Chamber Opera Ensemble / Michael Rafferty.** Unicorn-Kanchana DKPCD9100 (3/91).
…Black Pentecost[a]. Stone Litany. **Della Jones** (mez); [a]**David Wilson-Johnson** (bar); **BBC Philharmonic Orchestra / Sir Peter Maxwell Davies.** Collins Classics 1366-2 (8/93).
…Resurrection. **Soloists; BBC Philharmonic Orchestra / Sir Peter Maxwell Davies.** Collins Classics 7034-2 (8/95).
…The Lighthouse. **Soloists; BBC Philharmonic Orchestra / Sir Peter Maxwell Davies.** Collins Classics 1415-2 (1/95).

John Mayer
Indian/British 1930-

New review
Mayer Prabhanda[a]. Calcutta-Nagar.
Britten Cello Sonata, Op. 65[a].
Rubbra Cello Sonata in G minor, Op. 60[a]. [a]**Timothy Gill** (vc); **Fali Pavri** (pf). Guild Ⓔ GMCD7114 (79 minutes: DDD: 4/96). Recorded 1994.
This enterprising concert is performed with sensitivity and much quiet insight. Perhaps the highlight is Edmund Rubbra's ruminative and beautifully crafted Cello Sonata of 1946, here given a reading which strikes a perfect balance between formal elegance and gentle passion. In the Britten Sonata, Timothy Gill and his pianist Fali Pavri adopt a more restrained, less commandingly articulate approach than either Rostropovich and the composer on Decca (still peerlessly eloquent and sounding full-bodied 35 years on) or Moray Welsh and John Lenehan on EMI (listed and reviewed under Britten; refer to the Index to Reviews). That said, these gifted young artists undoubtedly have the full measure of this work's considerable technical demands, and their playing exhibits unfailing musicality and dedication. This set also contains two offerings by the Calcutta-born figure, John Mayer (a composition pupil of Mátyás Seiber). Prabhanda for cello and piano dates from 1982. It is an approachable piece in eight movements which manages to combine Indian and Western musical elements to colourful and emotionally diverse effect (the title is an ancient Indian musical form not dissimilar to our own Suite). Gill and Pavri lend exemplary advocacy to this attractive creation. Inspired by "the incredibly contrasting sights and sounds" (to quote the excellent, uncredited booklet-notes) of Mayer's home city, the suite for solo piano from 1993 entitled Calcutta-Nagar ("City of Calcutta") consists of 18 vignettes, most of them pithy in the extreme, yet all exquisitely chiselled and often highly evocative: try the soothing "Kali Temple" (track 29) or bustling "Hooghley River" (track 30). Suffice to report, the composer's fellow countryman, Fali Pavri, is an outstandingly sympathetic interpreter. Sound and balance are good. Background traffic rumble also intrudes from time to time, but not enough to spoil the listener's pleasure.

Billy Mayerl
British 1902-1959

New review
Mayerl Piano Transcriptions, Volume 3 – There's a small hotel; The mood that I'm in; So rare; I'm always in the mood for you; Turkey in the straw; For only you; Thanks for the memory; The Highland Swing; I got love; Amoresque; There's rain in my eyes; Patty cake, patty cake, baker man; Blame it on my last affair; I have eyes; Like a cat with a mouse; Phil the Fluter's Ball; Fools rush in; Peg o' my heart; All the things you are; The Musical Earwig; Transatlantic Lullaby; Tell me I'm forgiven; Japanese Juggler; Poor little rich girl. **Eric Parkin** (pf). Priory Ⓕ PRCD468 (63 minutes: DDD: 7/95). Recorded 1993. *Gramophone Editor's choice.* ⒼⒼ
This is pure 1930s music. The period that Auden, in *1st September 1939*, called "a low, dishonest decade" and went on, "The lights must never go out,/The music must always play". This is the music – popular songs of the period arranged in Mayerl's inimitable English accent. This is not Mayerl as the lightning-fingered whizz-kid of the 1920s, although many of the transcriptions are tricky enough: it's the style he taught through the Billy Mayerl School of Music, a success story here and abroad until the war. The war killed nostalgia and well before Mayerl died in 1959 a teenage pop culture was on the rampage. But these transcriptions are a wonderful encapsulation of an era and they transcend it – as long as they are played like this. The demands on the performer are similar to studying the style of the period at any time. Classically trained pianists have to work hard to play Joplin, Gershwin and Mayerl. But Mayerl belongs to them, as long as their left hand is strong enough, because this is basically a notated tradition rather than an improvised one. Parkin understands it all – the effortless lilt, the light touch, not too much pedal, nothing overdone (not even the periodic pre Addinsell rhetoric), everything speaking for itself.

Further listening ...

...Marigold[a]. A Lily Pond. Four Aces[a]. From a Spanish lattice[a]. Minuet by Candlelight. Aquarium
Suite[a]. Autumn Crocus[a]. Bats in the Belfry[a]. Pastoral Sketches. Fireside Fusiliers[a]. The Parade of
the Sandwich-Board Men[a]. Waltz for a lonely heart. Busybody. [a]**Andrew Ball** (pf); **Bratislava
Radio Symphony Orchestra / Gary Carpenter.** Marco Polo 8 223514 (12/94).
...Piano Works, Volume 2 – Four Aces Suite – No. 1, Ace of Clubs; No. 4, Ace of Spades.
Mistletoe. Autumn crocus. Hollyhock. White heather. Three Dances in Syncopation, Op. 73.
Sweet William. Parade of the Sandwich-Board Men. Hop-O'-My-Thumb. Jill all alone.
Aquarium Suite. *Coupled with* **Mayerl/Croom-Johnson** Bats in the Belfry. Green tulips. **Eric
Parkin** (pf). Chandos CHAN8848 (11/90).
...Piano works, Volume 3 – Filigree. Three Miniatures in syncopation, Op. 76. Siberian lament. In
my Garden: Summertime. Three Japanese Pictures, Op. 25 – A Temple in Kyoto; The Cherry
Dance. Beguine Impromptu. The Big Top. The Legends of King Arthur – The Sword Excalibur;
Guinevere. Honky-tonk. In my Garden: Autumntime. Romanesque. Four insect Oddities.
Leprechaun's Leap. **Eric Parkin** (pf). Chandos CHAN9141 (9/93).   Ⓖ
...Piano Transcriptions, Volume 1 – Did you ever see a dream walking?; Thanks; Love locked out;
On the other side of Lovers' Lane; I cover the waterfront; Weep no more my baby; We belong
together; Close your eyes; Masquerading in the name of love; Two cigarettes in the dark; Oceans
of time; April in Paris; Arlene; Love thy neighbour; Say it. Balloons; Other people's babies; June
in January; Imaginary Foxtrot; The Continental; With my eyes wide open I'm dreaming; Chasing
shadows; The girl with the dreamy eyes; Cheek to cheek. **Eric Parkin** (pf). Priory Ⓔ PRCD466
(67 minutes: DDD: 1/95).
...Piano Transcriptions, Volume 2 – Smoke gets in your eyes; You hit the spot; Anything goes; I feel
like a feather in the breeze; Love me forever; Please believe me; Evr'thing's been done before; I
breathe on windows; Without a word of warning; There's a star in the sky; Fatal fascination;
Limehouse Blues; Will I ever know?; A penny in my pocket; Turn on the taps; The dance goes
on; I'm in a dancing mood; Without rhythm; My first thrill; Stranger in a cup of tea; You're not
too bad yourself; Lambeth Walk; At the Balalaika; Everything's in rhythm with my heart. **Eric
Parkin** (pf). Priory PRCD467 (5/95).

Ascanio Mayone
Italian c1565-1627

Suggested listening ...

...Partite sopra "Fidele". *Coupled with works by* **Giovanni de Macque, Facoli, A. Valente,
Trabaci, Picchi, Buono, Frescobaldi, Lambardo, Merula, M. Rossi, Salvatore,
B. Storace, G. Strozzi, Stradella** and **A. Scarlatti** Rinaldo Alessandrini (hpd). Opus 111
OPS30-118 (4/95). ✍ *See review in the Collections section; refer to the Index to Reviews.*

Simon Mayr
German 1763-1845

Suggested listening ...

...Medea in Corinto. **Soloists; Geoffrey Mitchell Choir; Philharmonia Orchestra / David Parry.**
Opera Rara OROC11 (11/94).

Domenico Mazzocchi
Italian 1592-1665

Suggested listening ...

...Misereris omnium, Domine[ac]. Gaudebunt labia mea[ade]. Peccantem me quotidie[abe]. Jesu, dulcis
memoria[ade]. Dialogo della Cantica. Vide, Domine, afflictionem nostram. Dialogo di Lazaro.
Dialogo della Maddalena. Dialogo dell'Apocalisse. Lamento di David. Concilio de' Farisei.
[a]**Maria Cristina Kiehr,** [b]**Barbara Borden** (sops); [c]**Andreas Scholl** (alto); [d]**Gerd Türk** (ten); [e]**Ulrich
Messthaler** (bass); **Netherlands Chamber Choir; Lucia Swarts** (vc); **Karl-Ernst Schröder** (theorbo);
Christophe Rousset (org/hpd) **/ René Jacobs.** Harmonia Mundi HMC40 1357 (2/92). ✍
...Musiche sacre e morali – Da tutti gli horologi si cava moralità. *Coupled with works by*
Carissimi, Marazzoli, Rossi, V. Mazzocchi, Landi and **Anonymous** Tragicomedia **/
Stephen Stubbs.** Teldec Das Alte Werk 4509-98410-2 (3/96). ✍ *See review in the Collections
section; refer to the Index to Reviews.*

Nikolay Medtner
USSR 1880-1951

Medtner Piano Concerto No. 1 in C minor, Op. 33[a]. Piano Quintet in C major, Op. posth[b]. **Dmitri
Alexeev** (pf); [b]**New Budapest Quartet** (András Kiss, Ferenc Balogh, vns; Laszlo Barsony, va;
Karoly Botvay, vc); [a]**BBC Symphony Orchestra / Alexander Lazarev.** Hyperion Ⓔ CDA66744
(59 minutes: DDD: 3/95). Recorded 1994.

Medtner would have been both grateful and astonished by his present and ever-increasing recognition. Once dismissed as an unsatisfactory betwixt-and-between composer, one without a convincing personal voice who was overshadowed by Rachmaninov's greater glamour and accessibility, his time has truly come. For Dmitri Alexeev the First Concerto is Medtner's masterpiece, an argument he sustains in a performance of superb eloquence and discretion. Even the sort of gestures later vulgarized and traduced by Tinseltown are given with an aristocratic quality, a feel for a love of musical intricacy that takes on an almost symbolic force and potency, but also for Medtner's dislike of display. You may occasionally miss Igor Zhukov's more blustering, devil-may-care virtuosity (listed below), yet time and again Alexeev makes you pause to reconsider Medtner's quality, and his reserve brings its own distinctive reward. The early *Abbandonamente ma non troppo* has a haunting improvisatory inwardness and later, as the storm clouds gather ominously at 11'55", his playing generates all the necessary electricity. How thankful one is, too, for Alexeev's advocacy of the Piano Quintet where, together with his fully committed colleagues, he recreates music of the strangest, most unworldly exultance and introspection. Instructions such as *poco tranquillo (sereno)* and *Quasi Hymn* take us far away from the turbulence of the First Concerto (composed in the shadow of the First World War) and the finale's conclusion with *glissando,* and *tremolo,* for added effect, is wonderfully uplifting. The recordings are judiciously balanced in both works, and the BBC Symphony Orchestra under Lazarev are as alert as they are sympathetic.

Additional recommendations ...

...Piano Concertos Nos. 1-3[a]. Sonata-Ballade in F sharp major, Op. 27. **Geoffrey Tozer** (pf); [a]**London Philharmonic Orchestra / Neeme Järvi.** Chandos Ⓟ CHAN9040 (two discs: 127 minutes: DDD: 4/92).

...Piano Concerto No. 1[a]. **Balakirev** Piano Concerto No. 1 in F sharp major, Op. 1[a]. **Rimsky-Korsakov** Piano Concerto in C sharp minor, Op. 30[b]. **Igor Zhukov** (pf); USSR TV and Radio Large Orchestra / [a]**Alexander Dmitriev,** [b]**Gennadi Rozhdestvensky.** Mezhdunarodnaya Kniga Ⓟ MK417087 (62 minutes: ADD: 2/94).

Medtner Piano Concertos – No. 2 in C minor, Op. 50; No. 3 in E minor, Op. 60. **Nikolai Demidenko** (pf); **BBC Scottish Symphony Orchestra / Jerzy Maksymiuk.** Hyperion Ⓟ CDA66580 (74 minutes: DDD: 4/92). Recorded 1991. *Gramophone Award Winner 1992.*   ⊕⊕

Medtner Piano Concertos – No. 2 in C minor, Op. 50[a]; No. 3 in E minor, Op. 60[b]. Arabesque in A minor, Op. 7 No. 2[c]. Fairy Tale in F minor, Op. 26 No. 3[d]. **Nikolay Medtner** (pf); [ab]**Philharmonia Orchestra / Issay Dobrowen.** Testament mono Ⓟ SBT1027* (77 minutes: ADD: 4/94). Item marked [a] from HMV DB6559/63 (7/48), [b]DB6718/22 (8/48), [c]DB6563, [d]DB6564 (both 2/48). Recorded 1947.   ⊕⊕

Hyperion's splendid disc is given a fine recording, good orchestral playing from a Scottish orchestra under a Polish conductor and, above all, truly coruscating and poetic playing from the brilliant young Russian pianist Nikolai Demidenko. It also did a splendid rehabilitation job for Nikolay Medtner who is steadily coming in from the cold after half a century of neglect. He was a contemporary and friend of Rachmaninov who settled in Britain in the 1930s, and like Rachmaninov (to whom the Second Concerto is dedicated and who returned the compliment with his own Fourth) he was an excellent pianist. But while the other composer became immensely popular, Medtner languished in obscurity, regarded (if thought about at all) as an inferior imitation of Rachmaninov who wrote gushing music that was strong on gestures but weak on substance. The fact is that he can be diffuse (not to say long-winded) and grandiose, and memorable tunes are in short supply, so that his music needs to be played well to come off. But when it is there's much to enjoy and the strong Russian flavour of the ornate writing is evident, as is the composer's masterly understanding of the piano. Listening to the composer himself in the Second's first *molto cantabile a tempo, ma expressivo* or the Third's *dolce cantabile* is to be made doubly aware of his haunting and bittersweet lyricism. The streaming figuration in the Second Concerto's *Romanza* is spun off with deceptive ease, a reminder that while Medtner despised obvious pyrotechnics he was a superlative pianist. So here, surely, is an ideal complement to Demidenko's hypnotically fiery and articulate accounts. Two exquisitely played encores are included (the ambiguous poetry of the A minor *Arabesque* could be by no other composer), and the 1947 recordings have been superbly remastered.

Medtner Violin Sonatas – No. 1 in B minor, Op. 21; No. 2 in G major, Op. 44. **Lydia Mordkovitch** (vn); **Geoffrey Tozer** (pf). Chandos Ⓟ CHAN9293 (60 minutes: DDD: 11/94).

Lydia Mordkovitch and Geoffrey Tozer face stiff competition in this repertoire from Alexander Shirinsky and Dmitri Galynin (listed below), not only because they offer exceptionally fine performances, but also because their two-CD set offers all three violin sonatas plus the remaining (very attractive) shorter works that make up Medtner's total output for violin and piano. In general, Mordkovitch's readings emphasize a more lyrical and relaxed approach (as opposed to Galynin's more intense and passionate readings), and this is particularly so in the lyrical first movement of the short, attractive First Sonata – a little too relaxed perhaps in the outer sections of the lilting second movement "Danza". Elsewhere (for instance the *Allegro appassionato* and Finale-Rondo of the Second Sonata), Mordkovitch has a more intuitive grasp of structure, allowing the music to unfold with a degree more ease and direction. Nevertheless, in their own way, both artists are persuasive interpreters of these works and can be strongly recommended to the first-time explorer. The Chandos recorded sound is warm and well balanced.

...Nos. 1 and No. 2; No. 3 in E minor, Op. 57, "Epica". Three Nocturnes, Op. 16. Canzonas and Danzas, Op. 43. **Alexander Shirinsky** (vn); **Dmitri Galynin** (pf). Mezhdunarodnaya Kniga Ⓕ MK417109 (two discs: 81 minutes: DDD: 11/93).

Medtner The Angel, Op. 1*a*. Winter Evening, Op. 13 No. 1. Songs, Op. 28 – No. 2, I cannot hear that bird; No. 3, Butterfly; No. 4, In the Churchyard; No. 5, Spring Calm. The Rose, Op. 29 No. 6. I loved thee well, Op. 32 No. 4. Night, Op. 36 No. 5. Sleepless, Op. 37 No. 1. Songs, Op. 52 – No. 2, The Raven; No. 3, Elegy; No. 5, Spanish Romance; No. 6, Serenade. Noon, Op. 59 No. 1. Eight Songs, Op. 24. **Ludmilla Andrew** (sop); **Geoffrey Tozer** (pf). Chandos Ⓕ CHAN9327 (60 minutes: DDD: 12/95). Texts and translations included.

Musical Opinion, reviewing the newly published Op. 52 in 1931, concluded that, "very accomplished musician" as he undoubtedly was, Medtner could hardly be considered "a born song writer": "These restless, feverish compositions with their incessant chromaticism and modulations are essentially unvocal, though they are dramatic and rhapsodical enough." It says something for the achievement of Ludmilla Andrew that the 'unvocal' character of Medtner's writing is hardly evident at all, though, to be fair, the first three songs from Op. 52 are perhaps the very ones in which the voice is most hard-pressed and in which it is even possible to feel that they might do very well as piano solos. In the fourth, the "Serenade" (No. 6 in the set), the piano part *is* an accompaniment, and the singer brings to it a charm and delicacy worthy of its dedicatee, Nina Koshetz. Geoffrey Tozer is an excellent accompanist (he is in any case a highly experienced Medtner pianist). His playing of "Winter Evening", with its evocative rustling start, is superb; but always, along with the sheer virtuosity, there is a responsive feeling for mood and coloration. In his written notes he mentions critics who complain that Medtner's songs are "sonatas in disguise", and the balance of recording might have helped to stifle such objections if it had allowed the singer more presence. Certainly there are songs in which the piano takes over (the fifth of Op. 24, for instance). Yet in many the interest is evenly distributed, and these – the last three of the present recital – are among the most delightful in the repertoire.

Further listening ...

...Russian Round Dance (A Tale), Op. 58 No. 1. Knight Errant, Op. 58 No. 2. *Coupled with* **Rachmaninov** Suite No. 2, Op. 17. Russian Rhapsody, Op. posth. Symphonic Dances, Op. 45. **Dmitri Alexeev, Nikolai Demidenko** (pfs). Hyperion CDA66654 (10/94). *Gramophone Editor's choice.*

...Forgotten Melodies, Op. 38 – Sonata reminiscenza; Canzona serenata. Sonaten-Triade, Op. 11 – Sonata elegia. Forgotten Melodies, Op. 39 – Canzona matinata; Sonata tragica. Scazka (Fairy Tale) in B flat minor, Op. 20 No. 1. Theme and Variations in C sharp minor, Op. 55. Dithyramb in E flat major, Op. 10 No. 2. **Nikolai Demidenko** (pf). Hyperion CDA66636 (9/93). *Gramophone Editor's choice. Selected by Sounds in Retrospect.*

...Danza festiva, Op. 38 No. 3. *Coupled with* **Alkan** Transcription de Concert (Beethoven Piano Concerto No. 3 in C minor, Op. 37 – first movement). Three Etudes, Op. 76. **Chopin/Alkan** Piano Concerto No. 1 in E minor, Op. 11 – Romanza. **Busoni** Sonatina No. 6 super Carmen (Kammerfantasie). **Marc-André Hamelin** (pf). Hyperion CDA66765 (3/95). *See review under Alkan; refer to the Index to Reviews. Gramophone Editor's choice.* Ⓖ Ⓖ

...Fairy Tales – F sharp minor, Op. 26 No. 4; G sharp minor, Op. 31 No. 3; A minor, Op. 34 No. 3, "Wood-Goblin". *Coupled with* **Schumann** Papillons, Op. 2. **Bach** Overture in the French style in B minor, BWV831. **Scriabin** Mazurkas, Op. 3 – C sharp minor; E minor; G sharp minor. **Konstantin Lifschitz** (pf). Denon CO-78907 (12/94). *Gramophone Editor's choice.* Ⓖ Ⓖ

Nicholas Méhul
French 1763-1817

Suggested listening ...

...Symphonies – No. 1 in G minor; No. 2 in D major; No. 3 in C major; No. 4 in E major. La Chasse de jeune Henri – Overture. Le Trésor supposé – Overture. **Lisbon Gulbenkian Foundation Orchestra / Michel Swerczewski.** Nimbus NI5184/5 (7/89).

Erkki Melartin
Finnish 1875-1937

Suggested listening ...

...Symphonies – No. 2; No. 4, Op. 80, "Summer"[a]. [a]**Pia Freund** (sop); [a]**Lilli Paasikivi** (mez); [a]**Laura Nykänen** (contr); **Tampere Phiharmonic Orchestra / Leonid Grin.** Ondine ODE822-2 (12/94).

...Symphonies – No. 5, Op. 90, "Sinfonia brevis"; No. 6, Op. 100. **Tampere Phiharmonic Orchestra / Leonid Grin.** Ondine ODE799-2 (12/94).

Henryk Melcer-Szczawinski

Polish 1869-1928

Suggested listening ...

...Piano Concerto No. 1 in E minor[b]. *Coupled with* **Paderewski** Piano Concerto in A minor, Op. 17[a]. [a]**Piotr Paleczny,** [b]**Michael Ponti (pfs);** [a]**Polish National Radio Symphony Orchestra;** [b]**Warsaw National Philharmonic Orchestra / Tadeusz Strugala.** Olympia OCD398 (7/94).

Diogo Melgas

Portuguese 1638-1700

Suggested listening ...

...Lamentationes. In Monte Oliveti. O vos omnes. Pia et dolorosa Mater. In ieiunio et fletu. Memento homo. Ecce ascendimus. Adiuva nos. Ille homo. Ego sum resurrectio. Magister volumus. Rex tremendae maiestatis. Recordare Virgo Mater. Salve Regina. *Coupled with* **Morago** De profundis. Versa est in luctum. Oculi mei. Laetentur caeli. Commissa mea. Montes Israel. Parce Domine. Revelabitur gloria Domini. Esto mihi. Exsurge. **Pro Cantione Antiqua / Mark Brown** with **Robert Aldwinckle** (org), **Celia Harper** (hp), **Andrew Watts** (dulcian). Hyperion CDA66715 (11/94).

Felix Mendelssohn

German 1809-1847

Mendelssohn Piano Concertos – No. 1 in G minor, Op. 25; No. 2 in D minor, Op. 40. Capriccio brillant in B minor, Op. 22. **London Mozart Players / Howard Shelley** (pf). Chandos (F) CHAN9215 (55 minutes: DDD: 4/94). (G)

Mendelssohn Piano Concertos – No. 1 in G minor, Op. 25; No. 2 in D minor, Op. 40. Capriccio brillant in B minor, Op. 22. Rondo brillant in E flat, Op. 29. **Benjamin Frith** (pf); **Košice State Philharmonic Orchestra / Robert Stankovsky.** Naxos (S) 8 550681 (70 minutes: DDD: 4/94). Recorded 1992. (G)

The piano concertos were composed when Mendelssohn was still in his twenties. Benjamin Frith, playing with a full symphony orchestra under Robert Stankovsky, includes two of the composer's three single-movement works for piano and orchestra as bonus on his super-bargain-price disc. Howard Shelley contents himself with just the familiar *Capriccio brillant* as an extra, and prefers to direct the London Mozart Players himself on a full-price issue some 15 minutes shorter. The difference in playing time is not just due to Shelley's omission of the *Rondo brillant*. Always he prefers a livelier tempo for the flanking movements of both concertos, particularly their scintillating finales. Mendelssohn himself liked to play that of the G minor work "as fast as possible provided that the notes can be heard", and that's exactly what Shelley does – quickening an already electrifying introductory *presto* into a *molto allegro e vivace* of irrepressible youthful *joie de vivre*. Both here and in this concerto's opening *Molto allegro con fuoco*, Frith and his Slovakian colleagues emerge just a little more middle-aged in their caution. Nor do they arrest attention with Shelley's immediacy and urgency in the opening *Allegro appassionato* of the D minor work. In the finale, however, their refusal to rush allows fuller appreciation of its craftsmanly cunning. While in its way a virtuoso *tour de force*, Shelley's tempo here is fast enough to sound gabbled. As for the slow movements, both pianists open one's ears anew to their beauties. From both of them the *Andante* of the earlier work, in particular, would melt the heart of the proverbial stone. But if forced to make a choice it would have to be the slightly older, maturer Shelley for the effortless continuity of his shapely phrasing and the closeness of the orchestral response. With his slower spread chords and more expansive melodic line in the introduction, plus springier rhythms in the ensuing fun and games, Shelley does just that little bit more for the engaging *Capriccio brillant* too. But that said, Frith is willing to challenge metronome tyranny with an occasional touch of caprice. He is also keenly aware of the music as well as the notes in the less often heard *Rondo brillant*. As for recording, the Chandos disc brings you better balance between keyboard and orchestra, and by and large a more truthful quality of sound. But at its modest price the Naxos disc remains a bargain on every count.

Additional recommendations ...

...Nos. 1 and 2. Prelude and Fugue in E major/minor, Op. 35 No. 1. Variations sérieuses in D minor, Op. 54. Andante and Rondo capriccioso, Op. 14. **Murray Perahia** (pf); [a]**Academy of St Martin in the Fields / Sir Neville Marriner.** CBS Masterworks (F) MK42401 (70 minutes: ADD/DDD: 11/87). (G)

...Nos. 1 and 2[a]. Piano Concerto in A minor[b]. **Cyprien Katsaris** (pf); [a]**Leipzig Gewandhaus Orchestra / Kurt Masur;** [b]**Liszt Chamber Orchestra / János Rolla.** Teldec Digital Experience (M) 9031 75860-2 (70 minutes: DDD: 6/92). (G)

Mendelssohn Violin Concertos – E minor, Op. 64; D minor. **Kyoko Takezawa** (vn); **Bamberg Symphony Orchestra / Claus Peter Flor.** RCA Victor Red Seal (F) 09026 62512-2 (53 minutes: DDD: 2/95). Recorded 1994.

Takezawa and Flor offer performances which consistently reflect the joy of the performers in the music. Mullova (listed below) is faster in all but one of the six movements but Takezawa uses that additional elbow-room to give the music an extra sense of fantasy, often of fun, entirely apt for this composer. In the central *Andante* Takezawa, at her relatively slow speed, is just as fresh and unsentimental as Mullova and a degree more tender. Rather than power and weight, Takezawa in the outer movements finds a muscular resilience which in context is just as compelling. In the D minor Concerto such qualities are if anything even more striking, and though Mullova's performance remains impressive, the Takezawa is the one in which one keeps registering moments of delight, whether in the Mozartian lightness of the first movement, full of fantasy, the Schubertian lyricism of the second, raptly done, with its musing little cadenzas for the soloist, or the Hungarian point of the finale. Highly recommendable as the Philips disc is, the RCA issue, given refined sound, must now take precedence.

Additional recommendations ...

...E minor. **Tchaikovsky** Violin Concerto in D major, Op. 35. **Takako Nishizaki** (vn); **Slovak Philharmonic Orchestra / Kenneth Jean.** Naxos Ⓢ 8 550153 (67 minutes: DDD).

...E minor. **Bruch** Violin Concerto No. 1 in G minor, Op. 26. **Anne-Sophie Mutter** (vn); **Berlin Philharmonic Orchestra / Herbert von Karajan.** DG Ⓕ 400 031-2GH (57 minutes: DDD: 3/83).

...E minor. **Tchaikovsky** Violin Concerto in D major, Op. 35. **Nathan Milstein** (vn); **Vienna Philharmonic Orchestra / Claudio Abbado.** DG Galleria Ⓜ 419 067-2GGA (DDD: 8/87).

...E minor. **Bruch** Violin Concerto. **Schubert** Rondo in A major, D438. **Nigel Kennedy** (vn); **English Chamber Orchestra / Jeffrey Tate.** EMI Ⓕ CDC7 49663-2 (71 minutes: DDD: 1/89).

...D minor. Violin and Piano Concerto in D minor. **Gidon Kremer** (vn); **Martha Argerich** (pf). DG Ⓕ 427 338-2GH (59 minutes: DDD: 9/89). ⒼⒼ

...E minor[a]. **Beethoven** Violin Concerto in D major, Op. 61[b]. **Yehudi Menuhin** (vn); [a]**Berlin Philharmonic Orchestra;** [b]**Philharmonia Orchestra / Wilhelm Furtwängler.** EMI Références mono Ⓜ CDH7 69799-2* (71 minutes: ADD: 10/89). ⒼⒼ

...E minor[b]. **Bruch** Violin Concerto[c]. **Kreisler** Liebesfreud[a]. **Sarasate** Introduction et Tarantelle, Op. 43[a]. **Cho-Liang Lin** (vn); [a]**Sandra Rivers** (pf); [b]**Philharmonia Orchestra / Michael Tilson Thomas;** [c]**Chicago Symphony Orchestra / Leonard Slatkin.** CBS Masterworks Ⓜ MK44902 (61 minutes: DDD: 3/91).

...E minor[a]. **Bruch** Violin Concerto[b]. [a]**Miklós Szenthelý,** [b]**Emmy Verhey** (vns); [a]**Budapest Philharmonic Orchestra / János Sándor;** [b]**Budapest Symphony Orchestra / Arpád Joó.** LaserLight Ⓑ 15 615 (52 minutes: DDD: 3/91).

...E minor. **Brahms** Violin Concerto in D major, Op. 77. **Xue-Wei** (vn); **London Philharmonic Orchestra / Ivor Bolton.** ASV Ⓕ CDDCA748 (67 minutes: DDD: 4/91).

...E minor; D minor. **Viktoria Mullova** (vn); **Academy of St Martin in the Fields / Sir Neville Marriner.** Philips Ⓕ 432 077-2PH (50 minutes: DDD: 5/91).

...E minor. **Beethoven** Violin Concerto in D major, Op. 61. **Kyung-Wha Chung** (vn); **Vienna Philharmonic Orchestra / Kyrill Kondrashin.** Decca Ⓜ 430 752-2DM (71 minutes: DDD: 2/93).

...E minor[a]. Symphony No. 4 in A major, Op. 90, "Italian". The Hebrides, Op. 26. [a]**Pinchas Zukerman** (vn); **New York Philharmonic Orchestra / Leonard Bernstein.** Sony Classical Bernstein The Royal Edition Ⓜ SMK47592 (73 minutes: DDD: 8/93). Ⓖ

...E minor. **Prokofiev** Violin Concerto No. 2 in G minor, Op. 63. **Itzhak Perlman** (vn); **Chicago Symphony Orchestra / Daniel Barenboim.** Erato Ⓕ 4509-91732-2 (53 minutes: DDD: 1/94).

...E minor[b]. **Elgar** Violin Concerto in B minor, Op. 61[a.] **Alfredo Campoli** (vn); **London Philharmonic Orchestra / Sir Adrian Boult.** Beulah [a]mono/[b]stereo Ⓜ 1PD10* (73 minutes: ADD 10/94).

...E minor[a]. **Mozart** Violin Concerto in A major, K219[b]. **Vieuxtemps** Violin Concerto No. 5 in A minor, Op. 37[c]. **Jascha Heifetz** (vn); [a]**Royal Philharmonic Orchestra / Sir Thomas Beecham;** [b]**London Philharmonic Orchestra / Sir John Barbirolli;** [c]**London Symphony Orchestra / Sir Malcolm Sargent.** EMI Références mono Ⓜ CDH5 65191-2* (69 minutes: ADD: 10/94).

...E minor. **Vieuxtemps** Violin Concerto No. 5 in A minor, Op. 37. **Chee-Yun** (vn); **London Philharmonic Orchestra / Jésus Lopez-Cóbos.** Denon Ⓕ CO-78913 (50 minutes: DDD: 1/95). *See review under Vieuxtemps; refer to the Index to Reviews.*

New review

Mendelssohn Symphonies for Strings – No. 1 in C major; No. 2 in D major; No. 3 in E minor; No. 4 in C minor; No. 5 in B flat major; No. 6 in E flat major; No. 7 in D minor; No. 8 in D major; No. 9 in C major; No. 10 in B minor; No. 11 in F major; No. 12 in G minor; No. 13 in C minor, "Sinfoniesatz". **Hanover Band / Roy Goodman.** RCA Victor Red Seal Ⓕ 09026 68069-2 (three discs: 225 minutes: DDD: 1/96). Recorded 1992-3.

Mendelssohn's extraordinary precocity is nowhere more comprehensively shown than in the 13 early string symphonies, and though it is extraordinary that these were unknown until 1960, it is scarcely less so that there are still works in Berlin awaiting editing and performance. The symphonies are exceptional, though, in that the range of their invention far exceeds what might be expected of even so prodigiously talented a boy. The inventiveness remains dazzling, as with (to take only two examples) the chorale idea in the Minuet of the Sixth Symphony or the brilliant contrapuntal writing in the Eighth Symphony, in which the more immediate inspiration was Mozart, and in particular the *Jupiter* Symphony. Roy Goodman makes use of the version with wind instruments for this symphony, which Mendelssohn made within three days of having written the original, and (with one reservation) accepts Mendelssohn's astonishingly fast tempo markings. He brings them off brilliantly, even the helter-skelter bass pizzicatos in the Trio of the Minuet. He also shows, with the use of period string techniques, how quick Mendelssohn's ear was for novel sonorities. An affection for the still underprivileged viola may have come from Mozart, but Mendelssohn would also have heard these sounds pioneered by Weber (who otherwise barely influenced him in these works). There are beautiful string sonorities even in the very earliest works, especially in the often darkly-hued slow movements; and the finales have all the pace and wit of the more mature Mendelssohn (that is to say, when he was in his teens). Goodman judges tempo well, which is to say he has a shrewd sense of weight as well as of pace. He also directs from the keyboard, which it is certain Mendelssohn himself would have done at those famous Sunday morning concerts in his parents' Berlin house, and he permits himself the occasional contribution: both in theory and in practice, this is entirely in style. This is an excellent set, intelligently assembled, scrupulously prepared, lucidly recorded, played with a freshness and wit that serve these delightful pieces well.

Additional recommendations ...

...Nos. 1-6. **English String Orchestra / William Boughton.** Nimbus Ⓕ NI5141 (60 minutes: DDD: 3/89).

...Nos. 7, 8 and 10. **English String Orchestra / William Boughton.** Nimbus Ⓕ NI5142 (52 minutes: DDD: 3/89).

...Nos. 9, 11 and 12. **English String Orchestra / William Boughton.** Nimbus Ⓕ NI5143 (71 minutes: DDD: 3/89).

...Nos. 1-12. **London Festival Orchestra / Ross Pople.** Hyperion Ⓕ CDA66561/3 (three discs: 203 minutes: DDD: 12/91). Ⓖ

...No. 12. Double Piano Concerto in E major[a]. Concerto for Piano and Strings in A minor. **John Ogdon, [a]Brenda Lucas** (pfs); **Academy of St Martin in the Fields / Sir Neville Marriner.** Decca Ⓕ 433 729-2DM (56 minutes: DDD: 5/93).

...Nos. 8-10. **Orpheus Chamber Orchestra.** DG Ⓕ 437 528-2GH (58 minutes: DDD: 8/93). *Gramophone Editor's choice.* ⒼⒼ

...Nos. 2, 3, 9 and 10. **Nieuw Sinfonietta, Amsterdam / Lev Markiz.** BIS Ⓕ CD643 (60 minutes: DDD: 6/94).

...Nos. 8-10. **Concerto Cologne.** Teldec Das Alte Werk Ⓕ 4509-94565-2 (67 minutes: DDD: 12/94). 🖉

New review

Mendelssohn String Symphonies – No. 1 in C major; No. 4 in C minor; No. 6 in E flat major; No. 7 in D minor; No. 12 in G minor. **Concerto Cologne.** Teldec Das Alte Werk Ⓕ 4509-98435-2 (68 minutes: DDD. 7/96).

Concerto Cologne gave delightful performances of three of Mendelssohn's early string symphonies, Nos. 8-10, on Teldec (listed above). The same qualities are displayed on this disc, including a lively sense of chamber music playing which derives, no doubt, from their practice of performing without a conductor after there has been rehearsal under the guidance of their leader, Werner Ehrhardt. The most remarkable work here is No. 7 in D minor, in which Mendelssohn broke through into new and more expansive territory with what were never meant to be more than youthful exercises in imagination flowering out of good technique. The brusque alternations of the opening are strongly handled; so is the fiery, even threatening manner of the Minuet. The final *Allegro molto* comes close to pressing tempo too hard for clear articulation, a habit which also marks the *Allegro* of No. 1, but the fugato is well paced and beautifully clear, as is that in No. 12. The players have a strong sense of string colour, and respond to the care for the viola which marks these works, as in the *Andante* of No. 12. All in all, some admirable performances, filled with character and vivacity.

New review

Mendelssohn String Symphonies – No. 1 in C major; No. 6 in E flat major; No. 7 in D minor; No. 12 in G minor. **Nieuw Sinfonietta Amsterdam / Lev Markiz.** BIS Ⓕ CD683 (70 minutes: DDD: 9/95). Recorded 1994.

Amazing stuff, brilliantly performed. The first of the symphonies fair bursts from the staves, with a chuckling finale that would surely have delighted Rossini. And although the Sixth Symphony's finale harbours hints of miracles to come, Mendelssohn's mature personality is more comprehensively anticipated in the Seventh. Again, the finale (and its opening in particular) suggests the ebullient, life-affirming manner of the orchestral symphonies, albeit sobered by a spot of fugally formal writing later on. The Twelfth Symphony – the last that Mendelssohn completed in the genre – opens with a Handelian sense of ceremony, goes on to incorporate a characteristically tender *Andante* and ends with a finale that, to quote Stig Jacobsson's enthusiastic notes, "dies away to *pizzicato* and a subsequent *accelerando* which recalls Rossini". This is truly delightful music, a product of natural genius and destined to remain unique (at least in terms of youthful precocity) until Wolfgang Korngold penned his *Sinfonietta* and Piano Trio some 90 years later. Competing claims of versions from other performers (many of whom are excellent) are unlikely to upstage this latest volume of Nieuw Sinfonietta Amsterdam's ongoing cycle. The playing is both sensitive and exciting (No. 6's finale is despatched with maniacal zeal), while BIS's sound is impressively full-bodied. Lev Markiz was the first leader of Rudolf Barshai's magnificent Moscow Chamber Orchestra and readers who recall that group's greatest recordings can anticipate a parallel level of distinction here.

Mendelssohn Symphonies – No. 1 in C minor, Op. 11; No. 5 in D major, Op. 107, "Reformation". **Deutsches Symphony Orchestra, Berlin / Vladimir Ashkenazy.** Decca Ⓕ 444 428-2DH (60 minutes: DDD: 6/95). Recorded 1994.   Ⓖ

Ashkenazy conducts the former Radio Symphony Orchestra in fresh, finely moulded readings of Symphonies Nos. 1 and 5. The performances can best be characterized in direct comparison with Masur's outstanding Teldec versions, similarly coupled. Where Masur typically keeps *andantes* flowing very freely, faster than with most interpreters, Ashkenazy allows himself a much more spacious approach, phrasing more affectionately in slow movements marked by *pianissimos* consistently gentler than Masur's, not just a question of recording balance. So the second movement *Andante* of No. 1 is more tender with Ashkenazy, and the slow introductions of the *Reformation* Symphony have more mystery. The *pianissimo* statements of the Dresden Amen introduction to the first movement have you catching your breath, and the initial statement of the *Ein' feste Burg* in the finale, on unaccompanied flute, in its warmth makes Masur sound matter-of-fact by comparison. By contrast Ashkenazy's *allegros* are often faster than Masur's, with the Minuet of No. 1 becoming almost a scherzo, as does the second movement of the *Reformation*. There are moments in the first movements of both symphonies, where Ashkenazy comes near to sounding too hectic, but he compensates in springing rhythms more infectiously than Masur. What is slightly disappointing is the relative thinness of the string sound, not as sweet as that of the Gewandhaus Orchestra, and recorded with less bloom. It is a minor reservation, and anyone to whom the coupling and Ashkenazy's approach appeal can safely go ahead.

Additional recommendations ...

...No. 1; No. 2 in B flat major, Op. 52, "Hymn of Praise" (with Elizabeth Connell, Karita Mattila, sops; Hans-Peter Blochwitz, ten); No. 3 in A minor, Op. 56, "Scottish"; No. 4 in A major, Op. 90, "Italian"; No. 5. Overtures – The Hebrides, Op. 26; A Midsummer Night's Dream, Op. 21. The Fair Melusina, Op. 32. Octet in E flat major, Op. 20 – Scherzo. **London Symphony Orchestra / Claudio Abbado.** DG Ⓕ 415 353-2GH4 (four discs: 245 minutes: DDD: 1/86).   ⒼⒼ

...Nos. 1 and 5. **Leipzig Gewandhaus Orchestra / Kurt Masur.** Teldec Ⓕ 2292-44933-2 (55 minutes: DDD: 6/90).   Ⓖ

...Nos. 1-5. **New Philharmonia Orchestra / Wolfgang Sawallisch.** Philips Ⓑ 432 598-2PB3 (three discs: 194 minutes: ADD: 8/91).   Ⓖ

...Nos. 1-5. **Berlin Philharmonic Orchestra / Herbert von Karajan.** DG Ⓜ 429 664-2GSE3 (three discs: 202 minutes: ADD: 8/91).

...Nos. 1 and 5. **Bamberg Symphony Orchestra / Claus Peter Flor.** RCA Victor Red Seal Ⓕ 09026-60391-2 (58 minutes: DDD).   Ⓖ

...Nos. 1 and 5. **Milton Keynes Chamber Orchestra / Hilary Davan Wetton.** Unicorn-Kanchana Ⓕ DKPCD9117 (63 minutes: DDD: 2/93).

...Nos. 1 and 5. The Hebrides. **Philharmonia Orchestra / Walter Weller.** Chandos Ⓕ CHAN9099 (75 minutes: DDD: 2/93).

...No. 5. Die erste Walpurgisnacht, Op. 60[a]. [a]**Jean Rigby** (mez); [a]**Robert Tear** (ten); [a]**Anthony Michaels-Moore** (bar); [a]**Richard Van Allan** (bass); **Philharmonia** [a]**Chorus and Orchestra / Francesco d'Avalos.** IMP Masters Ⓕ MCD68 (61 minutes: DDD: 3/94).

Mendelssohn Symphony No. 2 in B flat major, Op. 52, "Hymn of Praise". **Soile Isokoski** (sop); **Mechthild Bach** (sop); **Frieder Lang** (ten); **Cologne Chorus Musicus; Das Neue Orchester / Christoph Spering.** Opus 111 Ⓕ OPS30-98 (65 minutes: DDD: 9/94). 🖝 Text and translation included. Recorded 1993.

This is one of Mendelssohn's lesser-known but highly rewarding symphonies. The *Hymn of Praise* stands under the shade of Beethoven's *Choral* Symphony, with its considerable length and choral and solo contributions, but it does not reach similar heights of sublimity. What it does possess is an unassuming lyricism, vitality and elegance throughout that is highly attractive. Popular with choral societies during the last century, this is an interesting part of Mendelssohn's symphonic canon. Christoph Spering is relaxed in his choice of tempos. In no way, however, does he let the music drag or become sentimental. With clean, crisp textures this is a most refreshing performance, full of incidental beauties. In the main *Allegro* of the first movement as well as in the opening section of the big choral cantata-finale, Spering's speeds are fast but refreshing. The rest is different, not just slower in its speeds, but often more affectionate. The duet for the two soprano soloists, "Ich harrete des Herrn" ("I waited on the Lord"), is especially beautiful, with Soile Isokoski and Mechthild Bach both angelically sweet yet nicely contrasted. The tenor soloist too, Frieder Lang, is exceptionally sweet-toned. The chorus, as recorded in a warm acoustic, are not always ideally clear in inner definition, but the freshness of their singing matches that of the whole performance. Anyone attracted by the advance of period performance into nineteenth-century repertory should certainly not miss this issue.

Additional recommendation ...

...**Cynthia Haymon, Alison Hagley** (sops); **Peter Straka** (ten); **Philharmonia Chorus and Orchestra / Walter Weller.** Chandos Ⓕ CHAN8995 (73 minutes: DDD: 5/92).

Mendelssohn Symphonies – No. 3 in A minor, Op. 56, "Scottish"[a]; No. 4 in A major, Op. 90, "Italian"[b]. **San Francisco Symphony Orchestra / Herbert Blomstedt.** Decca Ⓕ 433 811-2DH (67 minutes: DDD: 4/93). Item marked [a] recorded 1989, [b]1991.   ⒼⒼ

Recent years have seen a number of competitive releases of this popular coupling, not least a treasurable Teldec CD featuring Nikolaus Harnoncourt at the helm of the remarkably responsive Chamber Orchestra of Europe, full of that conductor's special brand of re-creative insight (listed below). Enter Herbert Blomstedt and his splendid San Francisco orchestra, in matters of interpretation more traditionally solid and less daring than that Teldec partnership, perhaps, but with considerable virtues of their own. Blomstedt's *Scottish* impresses most by dint of its joyous vigour (outer movements go with a will), rhythmic bounce (perky, personable winds and razor-sharp strings in the *Scherzo*) and unaffected eloquence (as in his affectionately flowing yet never short-winded conception of the third movement *Adagio*). This new *Italian*, too, is first-rate. Under Blomstedt the opening *Allegro vivace* positively fizzes along, aided by some quite beautifully sprung string playing, whilst the *Saltarello* finale is articulated with real panache. The middle movements are perhaps marginally less memorable, though again the irreproachably stylish orchestral response yields much pleasure. Although the symphonies were actually set down some 17 months apart, Decca's admirably consistent sound-picture possesses the exemplary clarity and sheen we have now come to expect from this particular source. No one can go far wrong with this disc.

Additional recommendations ...

...Nos. 4 and 5. **London Symphony Orchestra / Claudio Abbado.** DG Ⓕ 415 974-2GH (DDD: 9/86).   ⒼⒼ

...Nos. 3 and 4. **Orchestra of St John's, Smith Square / John Lubbock.** ASV Quicksilva Ⓢ CDQS6004 (71 minutes: ADD: 12/87).

...No. 3. Die erste Walpurgisnacht[a]. [a]**Christine Cairns** (mez); [a]**Jon Garrison** (ten); [a]**Tom Krause** (bar); **Cleveland Orchestra and** [a]**Chorus / Christoph von Dohnányi.** Telarc Ⓕ CD80184 (67 minutes: DDD: 3/89).

...Nos. 3 and 4. **London Symphony Orchestra / Claudio Abbado.** DG 3-D Classics Ⓑ 427 810-2GDC (71 minutes: DDD: 2/90).   ⒼⒼ

...Nos. 3 and 4. **Chamber Orchestra of Europe / Nikolaus Harnoncourt.** Teldec Ⓕ 9031-72308-2 (69 minutes: DDD: 5/92).   ⒼⒼⒼ

...Nos. 4 and 5. A Midsummer Night's Dream[b] – Scherzo. Octet in E flat major, Op. 20 – Scherzo. **NBC Symphony Orchestra / Arturo Toscanini.** RCA Victor Gold Seal mono Ⓜ GD60284* (64 minutes: ADD: 6/92).   ⒼⒼ

...No. 4[a]. Overture – The Hebrides, Op. 26[a]. A Midsummer Night's Dream[b] – Overture; Scherzo; Nocturne; Wedding March. [a]**Israel Philharmonic Orchestra;** [b]**Bavarian Radio Symphony Orchestra / Leonard Bernstein.** DG Classikon Ⓑ 439 411-2GCL (67 minutes: DDD: 3/94).   Ⓖ

...Nos. 3 and 4. **Leipzig Gewandhaus Orchestra / Kurt Masur.** Teldec Digital Experience Ⓜ 4509-92148-2 (67 minutes: DDD: 4/94).   ⒼⒼⒼ

...Nos. 3 and 4. **Academy of St Martin in the Fields / Sir Neville Marriner.** Philips Ⓕ 442 130-2PH (69 minutes: DDD: 10/94).

...No. 4. **Shostakovich** Symphony No. 5 in D minor, Op. 47. **Vienna Philharmonic Orchestra / Sir Georg Solti.** Decca Ⓕ 440 476-2DH (71 minutes: DDD: 10/94).

Mendelssohn Symphony No. 3 in A minor, Op. 56, "Scottish"[a]. The Hebrides, Op. 26[a]. A Midsummer Night's Dream[b] – Overture and incidental music, Opp. 21 and 61: Scherzo; Nocturne; Wedding March. **London Symphony Orchestra / Peter Maag.** Decca The Classic Sound Ⓜ 443 578-2DCS* (76 minutes: ADD: 7/95). Items marked [a] from SXL2246 (12/60), [b]SXL2060 (3/59). Recorded 1957-60. *Gramophone* classical 100.   ⒼⒼⒼ

The Hebrides and the *Scottish* Symphony offer 'Classic' Decca engineering at its best: airy 1960 Kingsway Hall sound with a real sense of perspective drawing the ear in (woodwind set behind strings but without loss of clarity – how flat is the layout of many a modern recording), pin-point instrumental positioning yet no impression of instruments sealed off from each other, and, for the pre-Dolby period, a remarkable dynamic range, accomplished with low hiss levels and no audible overloading. There is, perhaps, a slight thinness of tone in the middle register, a characteristic that is far more pronounced in the 1957 *Midsummer Night's Dream* excerpts (calling to mind, if memory serves correctly, one critic's charge, decades ago, that Decca were recording in "zinc tanks"), but the high-key clarity and fizzing presence readily compensate. At the time, Maag would probably have earned the description of a classically oriented Mendelssohnian, but his intelligent balancing of the orchestra and gauging of the work's proportions and rhetoric do not preclude imaginative handling of their illustrative poetry; in other words, he is a superb Mendelssohnian stylist. Personal rhythmic and dynamic inflexions abound (no doubt eyebrows will rise at such things as his sudden broad delivery of the Mechanicals' clowning in the *Midsummer Night's Dream* Overture). Singing lines are all beautifully wrought, especially that of the symphony's *Adagio* (rather more leisurely than we are used to nowadays), and its 'martial' sections benefit from discreetly balanced timpani. In *The Hebrides*, the balance and range of the sound allow all those swells (superbly observed) to register in proper proportion – here is both delicate impressionism and all the stormy drive and drama that you could want, putting many more recent rivals in the shade. At the heart of this disc's success is, of course, the playing of the revitalized LSO, responding to some challenging tempos with mainly knife-edge precision of ensemble and superb attack, producing heart-easing warmth in the symphony's *Adagio*, and shining in all solo opportunities – truly vintage LSO champagne.

Additional recommendation ...

...The Hebrides, Op. 26. **Brahms** Symphony No. 3 in F major, Op. 90. **Schubert** Symphony No. 5 in B flat major, D485. **Chicago Symphony Orchestra / Fritz Reiner.** RCA Victor Gold Seal Ⓜ 09026 61793-2 (69 minutes: ADD: 9/95). *See review under Brahms; refer to the Index to Reviews.*

Mendelssohn Overtures – Die Hochzeit des Camacho, Op. 10; A Midsummer Night's Dream, Op. 21 (from RD87764, 10/88); Meeresstille und glückliche Fahrt, Op. 27; Ruy Blas, Op. 95; Athalie, Op. 74; The Hebrides, Op. 26. **Bamberg Symphony Orchestra / Claus Peter Flor.** RCA Victor Red Seal Ⓕ RD87905 (59 minutes: DDD: 1/89). Recorded 1987-8. Ⓖ

Die Hochzeit des Camacho ("The Marriage of Camacho") Overture was written in 1825, two years before the masterly evocation of *A Midsummer Night's Dream*, with its gossamer fairies, robust mortals and pervading romanticism, and already demonstrates the teenage composer's enormous musical facility and organizational skills, together with the high quality of his invention. *Meeresstille und glückliche Fahrt* ("Calm sea and prosperous voyage" of 1828) anticipates *The Hebrides* of a year later, and celebrates an ocean voyage on a sailing ship. *Ruy Blas* is a jolly, slightly melodramatic, but agreeably tuneful piece and *Athalie* is also attractive in its melodic ideas. *Fingal's Cave* with its beauty and dramatic portrayal of Scottish seascapes matches the Shakespearian overture in its melodic inspiration (the opening phrase is hauntingly unforgettable) and shows comparable skill in its vivid orchestration. Flor directs wonderfully sympathetic and spontaneous performances, with the Bamberg Symphony Orchestra playing gloriously. There is abundant energy and radiant lyrical beauty in the playing and each piece is unerringly paced and shaped. The glowing recording gives a wonderful bloom to the orchestral textures without preventing a realistic definition. There has never been a collection of Mendelssohn's overtures to match this and it will give enormous pleasure in every respect.

Mendelssohn A Midsummer Night's Dream, Opp. 21 and 61. **Kathleen Battle** (sop); **Frederica von Stade** (mez); **Dame Judi Dench** (narr); **Tanglewood Festival Chorus; Boston Symphony Orchestra / Seiji Ozawa.** DG Ⓕ 439 897-2GH (56 minutes: DDD: 10/94). Text and translation included. Ⓖ

Ozawa strikes an ideal balance between conveying the underlying strength of Mendelssohn's writing and bringing out the music's wide-eyed freshness, its delicacy and its gentle, slightly teasing sense of humour. The Overture is played in quite a strong, clear-cut fashion, but there is a smile in the conducting too, and carefully observed detail. Some listeners might find the *Scherzo* a little too slow in tempo, but the playing (as throughout the disc) is of the highest quality, and Ozawa points the music very neatly and effectively. All the orchestral items are beautifully brought off, and the two famous soloists perform with great distinction, as does the chorus. If Ozawa is the disc's hero then its heroine is Dame Judi Dench, who brings great character and wit to her spoken excerpts from Shakespeare's text. Her first entry comes unexpectedly and indeed somewhat jarringly over the end of the *Scherzo*, but in every other respect it is her contribution, and the setting of the music in its dramatic context, which finally lifts the issue above all other competition. The engineering throughout the disc is first-class.

Additional recommendations ...

...A Midsummer Night's Dream. **Lillian Watson** (sop); **Delia Wallis** (mez); **Finchley Childrens' Music Group; London Symphony Orchestra / André Previn.** EMI Ⓕ CDC7 47163-2 (58 minutes: DDD: 9/86).

...A Midsummer Night's Dream. **Lucia Popp** (sop); **Marjana Lipovšek** (mez); **Bamberg Symphony Chorus and Orchestra / Claus Peter Flor.** RCA Victor Red Seal Ⓕ RD87764 (47 minutes: DDD: 10/88).

...A Midsummer Night's Dream. **Edith Wiens** (sop); **Sarah Walker** (mez); **London Philharmonic Choir and Orchestra / Andrew Litton.** Classics for Pleasure Ⓑ CD-CFP4593 (50 minutes: DDD: 9/92).

...A Midsummer Night's Dream[a]. Die erste Walpurgisnacht, Op. 60[b]. [a]**Pamela Coburn** (sop); [a]**Elisabeth von Magnus** (contr/narr); [b]**Birgit Remmert** (contr); [b]**Uwe Heilmann** (ten); [b]**Thomas Hampson** (bar); [b]**René Pape** (bass); [a]**Christoph Bantzer** (narr); [b]**Arnold Schoenberg Choir; Chamber Orchestra of Europe / Nikolas Harnoncourt.** Teldec Ⓕ 9031-74882-2 (78 minutes: DDD: 2/94).

...A Midsummer Night's Dream[a]. Die schöne Melusine – Overture, Op. 32. [a]**Judith Howarth** (sop); [a]**Jean Rigby** (mez); [a]**Bach Choir; Philharmonia Orchestra / Francesco d'Avalos.** IMP Masters Ⓕ MCD78 (63 minutes: DDD: 7/94).

...A Midsummer Night's Dream[a]. The Hebrides, Op. 26. [a]**Sandrine Piau**, [a]**Delphine Collot** (sops); [a]**La Chapelle Royale Choir;** [a]**Collegium Vocale; Champs Elysées Orchestra / Philippe Herreweghe.** Harmonia Mundi Ⓕ HMC90 1502 (55 minutes: DDD: 4/95).

Mendelssohn A Midsummer Night's Dream – incidental music, Opp. 21 and 61: Overture; Scherzo; Intermezzo; Dance of the clowns. The Hebrides, Op. 26. Die schöne Melusine, Op. 32. **Suisse Romande Orchestra / Armin Jordan.** Erato Ⓕ 4509-91734-2 (52 minutes: DDD: 5/94). Recorded 1993. ⊖⊖⊖

Armin Jordan is a Mendelssohn conductor of exceptional sensitivity and insight. In the six numbers from *A Midsummer Night's Dream* he gets delicate, alert playing, and the way in which he allows the music to express its own very particular qualities of innocence, joy and exuberance is very appealing. *The Hebrides* is given a leisurely, warm, very romantic and highly expressive reading. Still more in *Die schöne Melusine* Jordan shows that he is not afraid to indulge in old-fashioned fluctuations of tempo, reminiscent of Furtwängler, and there is an almost Beecham like quality in the elegance of Jordan's phrasing.

Mendelssohn Octet in E flat major, Op. 20. String Quintet No. 2 in B flat major, Op. 87. **Academy of St Martin in the Fields Chamber Ensemble.** Philips Ⓕ 420 400-2PH (63 minutes: ADD: 11/87). From 9500 616 (3/80). Recorded 1978. ⊖

Mendelssohn was as remarkable a prodigy as Mozart and one can only speculate with sadness what marvels he might have left us had he lived longer. Had death claimed him at 20 we would still have this glorious Octet, a work of unforced lyricism and a seemingly endless stream of melody. The Academy Chamber Ensemble, all fine soloists in their own right, admirably illustrate the benefits of working regularly as an ensemble for they play with uncommon sympathy. The string quintet is a work of greater fervour and passion than the Octet but it is characterized by the same melodiousness and unfettered lyricism with plenty of opportunities for virtuoso playing, which are well taken. The recordings, made in 1978, give a pleasant and warm sheen to the string colour of the ensemble.

Additional recommendations ...

...Octet. String Symphonies – No. 6 in E flat major; No. 10 in B minor. **I Solisti Italiani.** Denon Ⓕ CO-73185 (58 minutes: DDD: 4/90).

...Octet. **Bargiel** Octet in C minor, Op. 15*a*. **Divertimento.** Hyperion CDA66356 (67 minutes: DDD: 4/90).

...Octet. String Quintet No. 1 in A major, Op. 18ᵃ. **Hausmusik.** EMI Ⓕ CDC7 49958-2 (63 minutes: DDD: 9/90). ✍

Mendelssohn String Quintet No. 2 in B flat major, Op. 87. String Quartet No. 2 in A minor, Op. 13. **Hausmusik** (Monica Huggett, Pavlo Besnoziuk, vns; Roger Chase, Simon Whistler, vas; Richard Lester, vc). Virgin Classics Veritas Ⓕ VC5 45104-2 (60 minutes: DDD: 5/95). ✍

Mendelssohn's A minor Quartet, Op. 13, is an uncharacteristically serious work. Its quotation from Mendelssohn's song *Ist es wahr*, and the music's Beethovenian tone convey a prevailing mood of stress and anxiety. In a finely judged, excellently recorded version of the work, the Coull Quartet reveal a wealth of detail, through deftly controlled ensemble and perceptive structural observation. Nevertheless, the keener edge of Hausmusik's period instruments gives the quartet's dramatic contrasts more bite and makes the emotional content more potent. Resonant, sensitively blended harmonies and closely argued counterpoint in the first movement evolve into subtly balanced oppositions of minor (fugato) and major (lyrical calm) in the second movement, and delicate, gossamer textures in the *Intermezzo* (evocative of the fairy music in *A Midsummer Night's Dream*), emphasize the finale's expressive intensity, with its poignant echoes of the quartet's opening. By contrast, Mendelssohn's Second Quintet, Op. 87, is a gloriously exultant piece that still remains sadly neglected. Written in 1845, only a few months after the Violin Concerto, the quintet has suffered from accusations that it shows a decline in Mendelssohn's creative powers. However, the engaging freshness of Hausmusik's vividly recorded, period-instrument account powerfully brings out the work's instrumental brilliance and *joie de vivre*. The exuberance of the outer movements is expressed with boundless energy; crisp precision highlights the second movement's contrapuntal detail, and Hausmusik's attentive playing in the slow movement arrestingly conveys the music's ardently impassioned mood.

Mendelssohn String Quartets – E flat major (1823); No. 1 in E flat major, Op. 12; No. 2 in A minor, Op. 13; No. 3 in D major, Op. 44 No. 1; No. 4 in E minor, Op. 44 No. 2; No. 5 in E flat major, Op. 44 No. 3; No. 6 in F minor, Op. 80. Andante, Scherzo, Capriccio and Fugue, Op. 81 Nos. 1-2. **Melos Quartet** (Wilhelm Melcher, Gerhard Voss, vns; Hermann Voss, va; Peter Buck, vc). DG Ⓜ 415 883-2GCM3 (three discs: 199 minutes: ADD: 12/87). From 2740 267 (11/82). Recorded 1976-81. ⊖⊖⊖

The familiar and misleading cliché of Mendelssohn as the cheerful chappie of early romanticism vanishes at the sound of the F minor Quartet, Op. 80. Here is the intensity, anguish and anger that everyone thought Mendelssohn incapable of. His beloved sister Fanny died in May 1847 (his own death was merely months away), and the ensuing summer saw him leave Berlin for Switzerland, where he began to "write music very industriously". And what remarkable music it is. Right from the opening *Allegro assai* one senses trouble afoot, an unfamiliar restlessness mixed in with the more familiar busyness. Furthermore the second movement is surely the most fervent and punishing that Mendelssohn ever wrote – wild, insistent and unmistakably tragic in tone. This gradual intensification and darkening that occurs throughout Mendelssohn's quartet cycle makes it a most revealing guide to his creative development. But of course much of the earlier music is in fact profoundly 'Mendelssohnian' in the accepted sense of that term: fresh, dynamic, light-textured, beautifully crafted and full of amiable melodic invention. The very early E flat Quartet, Op. posth (composed when Mendelssohn was only 14), although fashioned very much in the style of Haydn and Mozart, points towards imminent developments – a song-like A minor Quartet, already taking its lead from late Beethoven in the same key, the E flat, Op. 12, with its delightful Canzonetta (once popular as a separate 'encore') and the eventful Op. 44 set, three of Mendelssohn's most concentrated full-scale works. And DG also add the four separate pieces, Op. 81, thus treating us to the entire Mendelssohn string quartet canon (the chronology of which, incidentally, is very much at odds with that suggested by the published opus numbers). The Melos Quartet come up trumps with a really superb set of performances – technically immaculate, transparent in tone and full of enthusiasm. The recordings, too, although analogue, report their playing with great presence and clarity.

Additional recommendations ...
...Nos. 1 and 2. **Gabrieli Quartet.** Chandos Ⓕ CHAN8827 (59 minutes: DDD: 1/92).
...Nos. 1 and 2. Andante in E major, Op. 81 No. 1. Scherzo in A minor, Op. 81 No. 2. **Coull Quartet.** Hyperion Ⓕ CDA66397 (62 minutes: DDD: 1/92).
...Nos. 2 and 6. **Carmina Quartet.** Denon Ⓕ CO-79527 (53 minutes: DDD: 3/92).
...Nos. 4 and 6. E flat major (1823). **Coull Quartet.** Hyperion Ⓕ CDA66579 (80 minutes: DDD: 11/92).
...Nos. 1-6. **Cherubini Quartet.** EMI Ⓕ CDS7 54514-2 (three discs: 125 minutes: DDD: 8/93).   Ⓖ
...Nos. 1-6. Four Pieces for String Quartet, Op. 81 – Andante in E major; Scherzo in A minor; Capriccio in E minor; Fugue in A flat major. **Coull Quartet.** Hyperion Ⓜ CDS44051/3 (three discs: 222 minutes: DDD: 6/94).
...Nos. 2 and 5. Andante in E major, Op. 81 No. 1. Scherzo in A minor, Op. 81 No. 2. **Aurora Quartet.** Naxos Ⓢ 8 550861 (70 minutes: DDD: 12/94).
...Nos. 3 and 6. Capriccio in E minor, Op. 81 No. 3. Fugue in A flat major, Op. 81 No. 4. **Aurora Quartet.** Naxos Ⓢ 8 550861 (65 minutes: DDD: 12/94).

Mendelssohn Cello Sonatas – No. 1 in B flat major, Op. 45; No. 2 in D major, Op. 58. Variations concertantes, Op. 17. Assai tranquillo. Song without words, Op. 109. **Steven Isserlis** (vc); **Melvyn Tan** (fp). RCA Victor Red Seal Ⓕ 09026 62553-2 (62 minutes: DDD: 3/95). 🎯 Recorded 1994.
Gramophone Editor's choice.
Isserlis and Tan offer idiomatic, well-turned performances full of freshness and vigour. In the First Sonata in B flat major (which Mendelssohn wrote for his brother, Paul, in 1838), where the second movement's dual function as scherzo and slow movement is convincingly characterized, and the music's passionate outbursts sound arrestingly potent. The *Variations concertantes*, Op. 17, were also written for Paul Mendelssohn and here, too, Isserlis's and Tan's fine blend of subtlety and panache (enhanced by the fortepiano's relatively delicate timbre) affectingly conveys the music's nostalgic mood, and culminates powerfully in the work's conclusion. In the D major Second Sonata, Isserlis's and Tan's spontaneity and energy in the outer movements, skilfully controlled variety of timbre and touch in the scherzo, and dramatic opposition of chorale (piano) and recitative (cello) in the third movement – with its striking resolution in the piano's own recitative statement – sound immensely compelling. The *Assai tranquillo*, written during a journey from Dusseldorf to Leipzig in 1835, bears a touching dedication from the composer to his friend, Julius Rietz. Here, as in the charming *Song without words*, Op. 109, sympathetic tonal balance between cello and fortepiano in the softly lit recording poignantly brings out the music's sentiment. Isserlis and Tan effectively draw out the work's inconclusive ending to create a telling analogy of the eternal nature of friendship. Excellent balance and crisp, restrained recording helps vividly to evoke this music's romantic atmosphere.

Additional recommendation ...
...Nos. 1 and 2. Variations concertantes. Song without words – Op. 19 No. 1; Op. 109. **Lynn Harrell** (vc); **Bruno Canino** (pf). Decca Ⓕ 430 198-2DH (67 minutes: DDD: 10/92).

New review
Mendelssohn Piano Sonata in E major, Op. 6. Variations sérieuses in D minor, Op. 54. Three Preludes, Op. 104*a*. Three Studies, Op. 104*b*. Kinderstücke, Op. 72, "Christmas Pieces". Gondellied in A major. Scherzo in B minor. **Benjamin Frith** (pf). Naxos Ⓢ 8 550940 (65 minutes: DDD: 5/96). Recorded 1994-5.
The multiplicity of notes in Mendelssohn's piano music sometimes lays him open to the charge of 'note-spinning'. So what higher praise for Frith than to say that thanks to his fluency, tact and fancy, not a single work in this second volume seems to outstay its welcome. The unchallengeable masterpiece, of course, is the *Variations sérieuses*, so enthusiastically taken up by Clara Schumann, and still a repertory work today. Frith characterizes each variation with telling contrasts of tempo and touch without sacrificing the continuity and unity of the whole. Equally importantly, never for a moment does he allow us to forget the *sérieuses* of the title. No less impressive is his sensitively varied palette in the early E major Sonata (unmistakable homage to Beethoven's Op. 101) so often helped by subtle pedalling. But surely the recitative of the *Adagio* at times needs just a little more intensity and underlying urgency. Of the miniatures the six *Kinderstücke* ("Christmas Pieces" – written for the

children of a friend) emerge with an unforced charm. As music they lack the romance of Schumann's ventures into a child's world, just as the *Three Studies* do of Chopin's magical revelations in this sphere. However, Frith's fingers never let him down. In the first B flat Study he even seems to acquire a third hand to sustain its middle melody. For sheer seductive grace, the independent *Gondellied* haunts the memory most of all, here with its melody so gracefully floated over a gently gliding bass. With pleasantly natural sound in its favour, too, this disc could surely sell at more than its modest price.

Additional recommendations ...

...Six Preludes and Fugues, Op. 35. Rondo capriccioso in E major, Op. 14. Variations sérieuses. String Quartet No. 1 in E flat major, Op. 12 – Canzonetta (trans. F. Le Couppey). **Danielle Laval** (pf). Auvidis Valois Ⓕ V4729 (68 minutes: DDD: 7/95). Ⓖ

...Piano Sonatas – Op. 6; G minor, Op. 105; B flat major, Op. 106. Andante and Rondo capriccioso in E minor, Op. 14. **Frederic Chiu** (pf). Harmonia Mundi Ⓕ HMU90 7117 (67 minutes: DDD: 5/94).

Mendelssohn Lieder – Op. 8: No. 4, Erntelied; No. 8, And'res Maienlied. Op. 9: No. 6, Scheidend. Op. 19*a*: No. 1, Frühlingslied; No. 2, Das erste Veilchen; No. 3, Winterlied; No. 4, Neue Liebe; No. 5, Gruss; No. 6, Reiselied. Op. 34: No. 1, Minnelied; No. 2, Auf Flügeln des Gesanges; No. 3, Frühlingslied; No. 6, Reiselied. Op. 47: No. 1, Minnelied; No. 2, Morgengrüss; No. 3, Frühlingslied; No. 4, Volkslied; No. 6, Bei der Wiege. Op. 57: No. 1, Altdeutsches Lied; No. 2, Hirtenlied; No. 4, O Jugend; No. 5, Venetianisches Gondellied; No. 6, Wanderlied. Op. 71: No. 1, Tröstung; No. 3, An die Entfernte; No. 4, Schilflied; No. 5, Auf der Wanderschaft; No. 6, Nachtlied. Op. 84: No. 1, Da lieg' ich unter den Bäumen; No. 3, Jagdlied. Op. 86: No. 1, Es lauschte das Laub; No. 4, Allnächtlich im Traume; No. 5, Der Mond. Op. 99: No. 1, Erster Verlust; No. 5, Wenn sich zwei Herzen Scheiden. Op. posth.: Das Waldschloss; Pagenlied; Der Blumenkranz; Warnung vor dem Rhein; Schlafloser Augen Leuchte. **Dietrich Fischer-Dieskau** (bar); **Wolfgang Sawallisch** (pf). EMI Ⓜ CMS7 64827-2 (two discs: 95 minutes: ADD: 12/93). Texts included. From HMV SLS805 (7/72). Recorded 1970. Ⓖ Ⓖ

Mendelssohn's Lieder offer a challenge all their own, and Fischer-Dieskau takes it up with characteristic alacrity. As the majority of these songs are primarily accompanied melody, with little inherent teasing out or biting on the words, the singer is presented with a comparatively empty stage for his recreative imagination to design and pace. There are passing moments (in the Op. 47 *Morgengrüss*, for example) when the simplicity and ingenuousness of Mendelssohn's settings seems to frustrate Fischer-Dieskau. These moments, though, are rare. His voice, here in its prime, can draw on an extraordinarily wide palette of colour within the legato of the most timeworn strophic song. Both Fischer-Dieskau and Sawallisch, whose light-filled piano playing shows his real sympathy and understanding for this composer, know just when to move into the salon with Mendelssohn. The four Lenau settings and the little drama of mortality offered in *Das erste Veilchen* are recreated with a perfectly-scaled sense of fleeting ardour and melancholy. Best of all, perhaps, are those little vignettes of the dark mythology of the German folk-soul, those diabolic night rides into the forest which find Mendelssohn at his witchy best, and Fischer-Dieskau at his most virtuosic. This revelatory boxed set comes with gracefully detailed notes by Philip Radcliffe, full song texts but no translations.

Additional recommendations ...

...Scheidend. Frühlingslied. Winterlied. Neue liebe. Gruss. Auf Flügeln des Gesanges. Reiselied. Das Waldschloss. Pagenlied. Morgengrüss. Frühlingslied. Volkslied. Bei der Wiege. Venetianisches Gondellied. An die Entfernte. Schilflied. Herbstlied, Op. 84 No. 2. Allnächtlich im Traume. Der Mond. Lieblingsplätzchen, Op. 99 No. 3. **Wolfgang Holzmair** (bar); **Anna Wagner** (pf). Preiser Ⓕ 93368 (53 minutes: ADD: 7/91).

...Op. 19*a* – No. 4, Neue Liebe; No. 5, Gruss. Lieder, Op. 34 – No.2, Auf Flügeln des Gesanges; No. 6, Reiselied. Morgengruss, Op. 47 No. 2. Allnächtlich im Träume, Op. 86 No. 4. **Schubert** Schwanengesang, D957 – Der Atlas; Ihr Bild; Das Fischermädchen; Die Stadt; Am Meer; Der Doppelgänger. **Schumann** Dichterliebe, Op. 48. **Christoph Prégardien** (ten); **Andreas Staier** (fp). Deutsche Harmonia Mundi Ⓕ 05472 77319-2 (57 minutes: DDD: 12/94). *✐ See review under Schumann; refer to the Index to Reviews.*

Mendelssohn Lieder – Op. 8: No. 8, And'res Maienlied; No. 10, Romanze. Op. 9: No. 1, Frage; No. 5, Im Herbst; No. 7, Sehnsucht; No. 8, Frühlingsglaube; No. 9, Ferne; No. 10, Verlust; No. 12, Die Nonne. Op. 19*a*: No. 3, Winterlied; No. 4, Neue Liebe. Op. 34: No. 2, Auf Flügeln des Gesanges; No. 3, Frühlingslied; No. 4, Suleika; No. 5, Sonntagslied. Op. 47: No. 3, Frühlingslied; No. 5, Der Blumenstrauss; No. 6, Bei der Wiege. Op. 57 No. 3, Suleika. Op. 71: No. 2, Frühlingslied; No. 6, Nachtlied. Op. 86: No. 3, Die Liebende schreibt; No. 5, Der Mond. Op. 99: No. 1, Erster Verlust; No. 5, Wenn sich zwei Herzen Scheiden; No. 6, Es weiss und rät es doch keiner. Pagenlied, Op. posth. **Barbara Bonney** (sop), **Geoffrey Parsons** (pf). Teldec Ⓕ 2292-44946-2 (60 minutes: DDD: 2/93). Texts and translations included. Recorded 1991.

The charm of these songs lies in their simple style and almost endless stream of delightful melody. Unlike other Lieder composers Mendelssohn avoided blatant word-painting or vivid characterizations and certainly the most satisfying songs here tend to be settings of texts which do not on the surface of it offer much scope for musical expression. But while this disc may not give us the very best of Mendelssohn, or indeed the finest examples of nineteenth-century Lied, the singing of

Barbara Bonney makes this a CD not to be missed. Here is a rare example of a singer caught on record at the very height of her technical and artistic powers, able to exercise seemingly effortless vocal control in portraying the subtle colours and understated moods of each songs. The partnership with that ever-sensitive accompanist Geoffrey Parsons is inspired. Listen to how Bonney seems to float ethereally above the rippling piano figures in that most famous of all Mendelssohn songs, *Auf Flügeln des Gesanges* ("On wings of song") – a performance which can surely never have been bettered on record. An interesting footnote is that three of these songs are by Fanny Mendelssohn but have by convention always been ascribed to her brother.

Mendelssohn Lieder – Op. 8: No. 7, Maienlied; No. 8, And'res Maienlied; Op. 9: No. 1, Frage; No. 2, Geständnis; No. 8, Frühlingsglaube; Op 19*a*: No. 4, Neue Liebe; No. 5, Gruss; Op. 34: No. 2, Auf Flügeln des Gesanges; No. 3, Frühlingslied; No. 4, Suleika; Op. 47: No. 1, Minnelied; No. 4, Volkslied; Op. 57: No. 3, Suleika; No. 6, Wanderlied; Op. 71: No. 4, Schilflied; No. 6, Nachtlied; Op. 86: No. 3, Die Liebende schreibt; No. 5, Der Mond; Op. 99: No. 1, Erster Verlust; No. 6, Es weiss und rät es doch keiner. Op. posth.: Mädchens Klage; Das Waldschloss. Romances (Byron) – There be none of beauty's daughters; Sun of the sleepless. **Dame Margaret Price** (sop); **Graham Johnson** (pf). Hyperion Ⓟ CDA66666 (59 minutes: DDD: 3/94). Texts and translations included. Recorded 1993. *Gramophone Editor's choice.*

This recital wholly dispels any lingering doubts there may be about Mendelssohn as a composer of Lieder. He surpassed even Schubert and Brahms in his understanding of Heine's *Die Liebende schreibt.* At the heart of the recital are the settings of Goethe. Besides *Die Liebende schreibt* the pair include the poignant *Erster Verlust* and the two Suleika settings, neither quite a match for Schubert's inspired versions but valid in their own right, particularly when sung with Price's uninhibited, Lehmannesque ardour. Another facet of the performances, a free-ranging *Schwung*, can be heard in *Frühlingslied* and the familiar *Neue Liebe.* The real discoveries here are the two Byron settings uncovered by Johnson. Mendelssohn understood and knew how to set English and the accentuations here are wholly idiomatic. The recording has great presence. Both singer and pianist are in the room with us, anxious and able to please.

New review

Mendelssohn Paulus, Op. 36. **Juliane Banse** (sop); **Ingeborg Danz** (mez); **Michael Schade** (ten); **Andreas Schmidt** (bar); **Stuttgart Gächinger Kantorei; Prague Chamber Choir; Czech Philharmonic Orchestra / Helmuth Rilling.** Hänssler Classic Ⓟ 98 926 (two discs: 131 minutes: DDD: 6/96). Text and translation included. Recorded 1994.

Rilling gives dramatic life to a work that can all too easily ramble episodically. His own Stuttgart choir, such a revered group, and the Czech forces partnering them make certain that their conviction comes across to us boldly. Each section is firmly integrated into the whole and offers great clarity. Schmidt is excellent with his steady, warm voice and he is completely inside the role. His singing of "Gott sei gnädig" is both firmly phrased and movingly interpreted. Young Juliane Banse sings her recitatives and solos, especially "Jerusalem", with notable beauty of tone. The youthful German-Canadian tenor Michael Schade is an artist of the utmost refinement and intelligence. If you already have the Kurt Masur version on Philips (now deleted) you need not feel you have second-best but if you're a newcomer to the work Schmidt will probably win you over to Rilling.

New review

Mendelssohn Elijah (sung in German). **Christine Schäfer** (sop); **Cornelia Kallisch** (contr); **Michael Schade** (ten); **Wolfgang Schöne** (bass-bar); **Stuttgart Gächinger Kantorei; Stuttgart Bach Collegium / Helmuth Rilling.** Hänssler Classic Ⓟ 98 928 (two discs: 128 minutes: DDD: 9/95). Text and translation included. Recorded 1994. *Gramophone Editor's choice.*

Rilling has recorded *Elijah* before with his Stuttgart forces, a 1981 account not without merits but wholly superseded by this one. Above all he brings out arrestingly the drama of the piece, turning it into a well-varied, exciting quasi-opera, a far from traditional view of the oratorio and rivalling, in that respect, Sawallisch and even more Masur. The vicissitudes of the prophet's eventful life, his reaction to events, the challenge to Baal, the encounter with Jezebel, have never sounded so electrifying. For that we have to thank Rilling's disciplined chorus, as biting in diction, precise and convincing in attack, and firm in tone as Sawallisch's, as involving as Masur's. Yet they can also provide the most sensitive, ethereal tone, as in Nos. 28 and 29, trio and chorus, "Siehe, der Hüter Israels". In general, every strand of the complex writing for chorus is made clear yet the overall effect is one of spontaneous combustion. The orchestral playing is no less arresting. Furthermore no Elijah since Theo Adam has so unerringly or authoritatively captured his many moods than Schöne. Here is the courageous man of action as he confronts Baal's followers and ironically taunts them, the sense of fiery conviction in "Ist's nichts des Herrn Wort", of doubt in "Es ist genug", and finally the wonderful Bachian serenity in "Ja, es sollen wohl Berge weichen", all evoked in the most positive and imaginative delivery of the text. The voice itself, a firm, expressive bass-baritone, is ideal for the role, one on which the singer has obviously lavished much time and consideration – to excellent effect. The same can be said for Schäfer, the soprano sensation from Germany, who brings a Silja-like conviction to all her work, nowhere more so than in "Höre Israel". Anyone hearing her declaim "Weiche nicht" would never be afraid again. The voice itself is interesting, gleaming yet not without warmth in the tone. Kallisch is almost as convincing in the mezzo solos and gives us a wonderfully malign portrayal of Jezebel. Schade is a fresh-voiced, communicative Obadiah, not quite in the Schreier class (Sawallisch) but close to it and he's another who is vivid with his words, especially so in the juniper tree recitative. Drawbacks? Just two. The recording is slightly too reverberant, but on this occasion the added space around the voices doesn't preclude immediacy of impact. Then the booklet has an incredibly pretentious and impenetrable note plus a confusing layout for the text.

Additional recommendations ...

...**Soloists; London Symphony Chorus; London Symphony Orchestra / Richard Hickox.** Chandos ℗ CHAN8774/5 (two discs: 131 minutes: DDD: 2/90).

...(Sung in English). **Soloists; Academy of St Martin in the Fields Chorus and Orchestra / Sir Neville Marriner.** Philips ℗ 432 984-2PH2 (two discs: 127 minutes: DDD: 10/92). Ⓖ

...**Soloists; Leipzig Radio Chorus; Israel Philharmonic Orchestra / Kurt Masur.** Teldec ℗ 9031-73131-2 (two discs: 110 minutes: DDD: 5/93). *Gramophone Award Winner 1993. Selected by Sounds in Retrospect.* ⒼⒼ

...**Soloists; Leipzig Radio Chorus; Leipzig Gewandhaus Orchestra / Wolfgang Sawallisch.** Philips Duo Ⓜ 438 368-2PM2 (two discs: 131 minutes: ADD: 8/93). ⒼⒼ

...**Soloists; Collegium Vocale; La Chapelle Royale Choir and Orchestra; Champs Elysées Orchestra / Philippe Herreweghe.** Harmonia Mundi ℗ HMC90 1463/4 (two discs: 127 minutes: DDD: 11/93). Ⓖ

...(Sung in English). **Soloists; Wandsworth School Boys' Choir; New Philharmonia Chorus; New Philharmonia Orchestra / Rafael Frühbeck de Burgos.** EMI Forte ® CZS5 68634-2 (two discs: 139 minutes: ADD: 5/96).

Further listening ...

...Double Piano Concertos – E major; A flat major. **Stephen Coombes, Ian Munro** (pfs); **BBC Symphony Orchestra / Jerzy Maksymiuk.** Hyperion CDA66567 (9/92). Ⓖ

...Concerto for Violin, Piano and Strings in D minor. *Coupled with* **Haydn** Concerto for Violin, Keyboard and Strings in F major, HobXVIII/6. **Ralf Gothóni** (pf); **Kuhmo Virtuosi / Peter Csaba** (vn/dir). Ondine ℗ ODE810-2 (58 minutes: DDD: 1/95).

...Sextet in D major, Op. 110[a], Piano Quartet No. 1 in C minor, Op. 1. **Bartholdy Piano Quartet.** Naxos 8 550966 (10/94).

...Piano Quartets – No. 1 in C minor, Op. 1; No. 2 in F minor, Op. 2; No. 3 in B minor, Op. 3. **Domus.** Virgin Classics VC7 59628-2 (6/91).

...Piano Quartets – No. 2 in F minor, Op. 2; No. 3 in B minor, Op. 3.[a]**Andra Darzins** (va); [a]**Wolfgang Wagner** (db); **Bartholdy Piano Quartet.** Naxos 8 550967 (10/94).

...Piano Duets – Piano Trio No. 2 in C minor, Op. 66. Variations in B flat major, Op. 83a. Andante and Allegro brillant in A major, Op. 92. *Coupled with* **Mendelssohn-Hensel** Three pieces for Piano Duet. **Yaara Tal, Andreas Groethuysen** (pf duet). Sony Classical SK48494 (6/93). ⒼⒼ

...Piano Trios – No. 1 in D minor, Op. 49; No. 2 in C minor, Op. 66. **Solomon Trio.** IMP Masters MCD46 (12/92).

...Piano Trio No. 1 in D minor, Op. 49. *Coupled with* **Brahms** Piano Trio No. 1 in B major, Op. 8. **Chung Trio.** Decca ℗ 421 425-2DH (65 minutes: DDD: 4/95). *See review under Brahms; refer to the Index to Reviews.* Ⓖ

...Clarinet Sonata in E flat major. *Coupled with* **Danzi** Clarinet Sonata in B flat major. **Weber** Grand duo concertant, J204. **Charles Neidich** (cl); **Robert Levin** (fp). Sony Classical SK64302 (9/95). 🎵

...Organ works, Volume 1 – Sonatas, Op. 65: No. 1 in F minor; No. 2 in C minor. Fugue in D minor. Chorale variations on "Wie gross ist des Allmächt'gen Güte". Andante in D major. Trio in F major. Prelude and Fugue in G major. Andante with variations. Allegro in D minor/major. **Peter Planyavsky** (org). Motette CD11271 (10/92).

...Violin Sonata in F minor, Op. 4. *Coupled with* **Schubert** Violin Sonatas – D major, D384; A minor, D385; G minor, D408. **Jaap Schröder** (vn), **Christopher Hogwood** (fp). L'Oiseau-Lyre Florilegium 443 196-2OM (9/94). 🎵 *See review under Schubert; refer to the Index to Reviews.*

...Songs without Words. Kinderstücke, Op. 72. **Daniel Barenboim** (pf). DG 2CD Serie 453 061-2GTA2. Ⓖ

...Six Preludes and Fugues, Op. 35. Three Caprices, Op. 33. Perpetuum mobile in C major, Op. 119. **Benjamin Frith** (pf). Naxos 8 550939 (11/95).

...Christus, Op. 97 – Say where is He born; There shall a Star. *Coupled with works by* **Clarke, Goss, S.S. Wesley, Ouseley, Schubert** and **Parry** Chichester Cathedral Choir / Alan Thurlow with James Thomas (org). Priory PRCD539 (5/96).

...Oedipus at Colonos, Op. 93. **Soloists; Berlin Radio Chorus; Carl Maria von Weber Men's Choir; Bavarian Radio Symphony Orchestra / Stefan Soltesz.** Capriccio 10 393 (1/95). Ⓖ

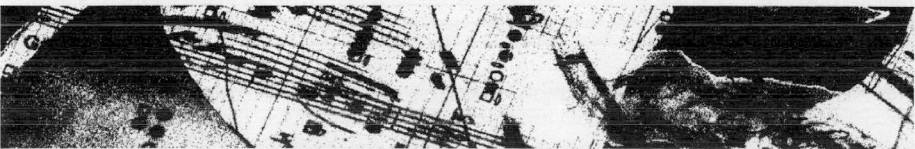

Fanny Mendelssohn-Hensel

German 1805-1847

Suggested listening ...
...Piano Trio in G minor, Op. 11. *Coupled with works by* **Beach, Carreño, C. Schumann , Tailleferre, Boulanger** and **Chaminade** Macalester Trio; Joseph Roche, Robert Zelnick (vns); Tamas Strasser (va); Camilla Heller (vc); Paul Freed (pf). Vox Box 115845-2 (10/94. *See review in the Collections section; refer to the Index to Reviews.*
...Piano Trio in G minor, Op. 11. *Coupled with* **C. Schumann** Piano Trio in G minor, Op. 17. **Dartington Trio.** Hyperion CDA66331 (3/90).

Alan Menken

American 20th Century

Suggested listening ...
...Beauty and the Beast – original film soundtrack. IMP/Disney DSTCD458.

Peter Mennin

American 1923-1983

Suggested listening ...
...Symphony No. 5. *Coupled with* **Schuman** New England Triptych. **Ives** Orchestral Set No. 1, "A New England Symphony". **Eastman-Rochester Orchestra / Howard Hanson.** Mercury 432 755-2MM.

Gian Carlo Menotti

Italian/American 1911-

Suggested listening ...
...Amahl and the Night Visitors. **Soloists; Royal Opera House Chorus and Orchestra, Covent Garden / David Syrus.** TER Classics CDTER1124 (7/88).

Pierre Menu

French 1896-1919

Suggested listening ...
...Sonatine. *Coupled with* **Ravel** String Quartet in F major. **Debussy** String Quartet in G minor, Op. 10. **Parisii Quartet.** Auvidis Valois V4730 (10/95).

Saverio Mercadante

Italian 1795-1870

Suggested listening ...
...Flute Concertos – D major; E minor; E major. **James Galway** (fl); **I Solisti Veneti / Claudio Scimone.** RCA Victor Red Seal 09026 61447-2 (4/94).
...(ed. Spada) Decimino I. Decimino II^a. La Poesia. **Philharmonia Soloists / Pietro Spada** (^{a}pf). ASV CDDCA936 (3/96).
...Orazi e Curiazi. **Soloists; Geoffrey Mitchell Choir; Philharmonia Orchestra / David Parry.** Opera Rara ORC12 (12/95).

Aarre Merikanto

Finnish 1893-1958

New review
A. Merikanto Juha. **Jorma Hynninen** (bar) Juha; **Eeva-Liisa Saarinen** (sop) Marja; **Raimo Sirkiä** (ten) Shemeikka; **Ritva-Liisa Korhonen** (sop) Anja; **Päivi Nisula** (contr) Mother-in-law; **Merja Wirkkala** (sop) Kaisa; **Matti Lehtinen** (bar) Kalamatti; **Hannu Ilmolahti** (bar) First Tar Maker; **Hannu Forsberg** (bass) Second Tar Maker; **Mia Huhta** (sop) First Girl; **Elina Laakkonen** (sop) Second Girl; **Tapiola Chamber Choir; Finnish Chamber Singers; Finnish Radio Symphony Orchestra / Jukka-Pekka Saraste.** Ondine Ⓟ ODE872-2D (two discs: 148 minutes: DDD: 8/96). Notes, text and translation included.
The Finnish soprano Aino Ackté, an enthusiastic promoter of her country's music, was so struck by Juhani Aho's novel *Juha* that she wrote a libretto based on it and offered it first to Sibelius, who after long consideration rejected it, and then to Aarre Merikanto. It was an imaginative choice: in 1920 he was a promising young composer, from an operatic background (his father Oskar Merikanto was the most successful Finnish opera composer of the period), and had already written one opera himself. However, the Finnish Opera demanded various changes to *Juha* and then, without actually rejecting the piece, shelved it. With remarkable insensitivity Ackté later offered the libretto to yet another composer, Leevi Madetoja, thus making it even less likely that Merikanto's work, with its rumoured

reputation as a difficult modern piece, would ever be performed. It was not heard until a broadcast performance three months after the composer's death, and did not reach the stage until five years after that. Since then, however, Merikanto's work has come to be seen as something of a classic in the Finnish operatic repertoire. It is late- or post-romantic in style, the richly sonorous orchestration owing something to the nineteenth-century Russians, Scriabin and Debussy. The vocal lines recall Janáček but the melodic lines have a strength that is Merikanto's own. The plot concerns an eternal triangle of a loving but elderly, crippled husband, dissatisfied young wife and glamorous but brutal stranger. Marja leaves Juha for the wealthy merchant Shemeikka (in fact much of his income is from robbery and extortion) but soon discovers that she is but the latest of his annual 'summer girls', who become unpaid servants once he has finished with them. She returns to Juha, who forgives her, forgives even the child she has had by Shemeikka, but on learning that she was not abducted by him but followed him of her own free will he despairs and kills himself. The music is at its strongest when it touches the rawest emotions: Juha's passive suffering and his blind animal rage when he at last confronts Shemeikka and cripples him; Marja's adoration of Shemeikka and her pain at his abandonment of her; the moving sincerity of Juha's forgiveness; perhaps most of all the touching lyricism of Anja, an earlier 'summer girl' who still loves Shemeikka despite everything. The music is saved from austerity by its often rich colour and the use of folk (or folk-like) music. The performance is splendid, Hynninen dark-voiced and vehemently eloquent, Saarinen capable both of long-lined lyricism and a touch of edgy shrewishness, Sirkiä suggesting Shemeikka's allure in broad lyrical lines delivered with a heroic ring. There are no weak links in the supporting cast, and Saraste obviously loves the score's opulence and its big gestures. The recording is first-rate, giving an excellent impression of how stageworthy *Juha* is.

Johann Mertz   Hungarian 1806-1856

Suggested listening ...
...Bardenklänge, Books 1-8 – excerpts. **Richard Savino** (gtr). Harmonia Mundi HMU90 7115 (10/94).
...Six Schubertian Songs. *Coupled with* **Paganini** Grand Sonata in A major – second and third movements. Ghiribizzi, MS43 – No. 20, Andante in C major on Mozart's "Là ci darem la mano"; No. 37, Adagietto con espressione in A major. Sonatina No. 1 in C major. **Regondi** Introduction and Caprice, Op. 23. **Schubert** (arr. Tárrega) Piano Sonata in G major, D894 – Menuetto. Moment musical in F minor, Op. 94 No. 3. **Chopin** (arr. Tárrega) Preludes – No. 7 in A major; No 15 in D flat major; No. 20 in C minor. **Tárrega** Preludes – Endecha; Oremus; Allegro; Andante sostenuto; Lágrima. Capricho árabe. Mazurkas – Adelita; Marieta; Sueño. Pavana. Alborada. **Tom Kerstens** (gtr). Conifer CDCF518 (9/94).

Tarquinio Merula   Italian 1594/5-1665

Merula Madrigali, libro secondo, Op. 10 – Aria di Ciaccona, "Su la cetra amorosa". Curtio precipitato, libro secondo, Op. 13 – Folle è ben che si crede; Chi vuol ch'io m'inamori; Un bambin chi va alla scola; Quando gli uccelli portaranno i zoccoli; Sentirete una canzonetta; Menti lingua bugiarda; Ho ch'è tempo di dormire. Capriccio cromatico[a]. Toccata del secondo tono[b]. **Montserrat Figueras** (sop); **Jean-Pierre Canihac** (cornet); **Lorenz Duftschmid** (vn); [b]**Andrew Lawrence-King** (hp); **Rolf Lislevand** (theorbo/baroque gtr); **Jordi Savall** (va da gamba); [a]**Ton Koopman** (hpd). Auvidis Astrée Ⓟ E8503 (56 minutes: DDD: 1/94). 🖅 Texts and translations included. Recorded 1992.
Tarquinio Merula is barely represented in the catalogue except as a composer of distinctive instrumental music. This release shows that Merula's secular vocal style is if anything even more interesting. The 1638 book of solo songs, from which most of this disc is taken, is an expressive and ingenious collection which displays amongst other things Merula's mature handling of Monteverdi's *stile concitato* and a highly attractive treatment of popular songs. Figueras's approach in the intricate and colourful melodic strands of the 'concerted' pieces is impetuous but effectively paced too. The result is at times little short of spellbinding: *Su la cetra amorosa* is executed with all the considerable virtuosity, energy and emotional intensity it deserves, complemented moreover by an exciting and fluent dialogue with a solo cornett. Also impressive is her ability to judge the fine line between comedy and despair in *Quando gli uccelli portaranno i zoccoli* ("When birds wear clogs"), where Merula's slightly bizarre sense of humour and a proven sense of irony are exhibited to the full. Ensemble can be a little ropey, but the overall richness of musical timbre and freedom of expression is what ultimately prevails. Well worth investigating.

André Charles Messager   French 1853-1929

Suggested listening ...
...Solo de concours. *Coupled with works by* **Schumann, Debussy, Poulenc, Lovreglio** and. **Weber Michael Collins** (cl); **Kathryn Stott** (pf). EMI Virtuosi CDC7 54419-2 (9/92). *See review in the Collections section; refer to the Index to Reviews.*

...Les deux pigeons. **Orchestra of Welsh National Opera / Richard Bonynge.** Decca 433 700-2DH
(10/93).

...Fortunio. **Soloists; Lyon Opera Chorus and Orchestra / John Eliot Gardiner.** Erato 2292-45983-2.

Ⓖ

Olivier Messiaen   French 1908-1992

New review
Messiaen Concert à quatre[a]. Les offrandes oubliées. Un sourire. Le tombeau resplendissant.
[a]**Catherine Cantin** (fl); [a]**Heinz Holliger** (ob); [a]**Mstislav Rostropovich** (vc); [a]**Yvonne Loriod** (pf);
Orchestra of the Opéra-Bastille, Paris / Myung-Whun Chung. DG Ⓕ 445 947-2GH (66 minutes:
DDD: 8/95). Recorded 1994.

Messiaen's musical testament is the great hour-long orchestral cycle *Eclairs sur l'au-delà*. If the late
works on this disc, *Un sourire* and the *Concert à quatre*, lack the visionary grandeur, still strong in
Eclairs, which made Messiaen one of the most powerful forces in twentieth-century music, they both
embody that spirit of joyous serenity which sets the composer apart from virtually all his
contemporaries. *Un sourire*, inspired by what Messiaen felt to be the 'smiling' quality of Mozart's
music, involves the familiar contrast between other-worldly meditation and more mundane
exuberance (birdsong), with a well-balanced formal design in which contrast matters more than
continuity. *Concert à quatre* similarly juxtaposes reflective and lively materials, but the stylistic range
is unusually wide, since Messiaen based the delightful second movement on a *Vocalise* of 1935. The
pianist tends to dominate, especially in the finale (in whose completion Yvonne Loriod was actively
involved) but the three other soloists also make their presence felt in a vivid and affectionate
performance. The two early orchestral scores that complete the disc belong to Messiaen's pre-birdsong
world. Contrasts are already extreme, but here the celestial meditations are offset by explosive
episodes whose provenance reaches back to the Witches Sabbaths of Berlioz, Liszt and Franck. The
youthful composer can even be forgiven his excessive use of the bass drum in *Le tombeau
resplendissant* when the total effect of the piece is so absorbing and original. These are state-of-the-
art recordings of performances given in the fraught days of Chung's final appearances with the
orchestra. The atmosphere is suitably apocalyptic, but the playing remains superbly disciplined.

Messiaen Un sourire[c]. Et exspecto resurrectionem mortuorum[c]. Oiseaux exotiques[ab]. La ville
d'en-haut[ac]. Un Vitrail et des oiseaux[ac]. [a]**Yvonne Loriod** (pf); [b]**Bavarian Radio Symphony
Orchestra;** [c]**Berlin Radio Symphony Orchestra / Karl Anton Rickenbacher.** Koch Schwann
Ⓕ 311232 (70 minutes: DDD: 12/94). Recorded 1993.

This performance of *Oiseaux exotiques* was recorded by Bavarian Radio in 1985; Messiaen admired
it and apparently suggested the four other works on this CD as a coupling. Very shrewd. In *Oiseaux
exotiques* Messiaen creates a bower-bird's nest of extravagant, endearingly ramshackle ornateness. *Et
exspecto resurrectionem mortuorum*, on the other hand, is one of his grandest and simplest structures,
with its litany-like repetitions and responses. Placed between these, the three shorter pieces can be seen
both as a useful way of programming works that fit awkwardly in concerts or as a series of further
illustrations of Messiaen's use of what one might call 'strophic form'. *Un Vitrail et des oiseaux* ("A
stained-glass window and birds"), for example, splits a typical chorale-like theme into four strophes,
follows each with a varied 'antistrophe' of birdsong, and each of those with a progressively
embellished cadenza, ending with a coda and a solemn re-statement of all four strophes of the
chorale. It is disarmingly simple and yet audibly related to the cumulative nobility of *Et exspecto*.
That tiny but lovely homage to Mozart, *Un sourire*, is a miniature example of the same process; so is
La ville d'en-haut, which can now be heard as a sort of sketch for Messiaen's last vision of eternity,
Eclairs sur l'Au-Delà (reviewed further on). He was right, in short: these five disparate pieces do make
a satisfying and illuminating programme. *Oiseaux exotiques* (what a cheerful racket of a piece it is, by
the way) is rather drily recorded; there's more space around the other pieces in the collection. All are
very well played, with proper regard to Messiaen's all-important silences and near-silences as well as
his precisely judged juxtapositions.

Additional recommendation ...
...Oiseaux exotiques[a]. Sept Haïkaï[b]. Couleurs de la cité céleste[c]. La ville d'en Haut[d]. Un vitrail et
des oiseaux[e]. Et exspecto resurrectionem mortuorum[f]. [abc]**Peter Donohoe** (pf); **Nether-lands Wind
Ensemble / Reinbert de Leeuw.** Chandos New Direction Ⓕ CHAN9301/02 (two discs:
102 minutes: DDD: 1/95).

Messiaen Des canyons aux étoiles. **Marja Bon** (pf); **Hans Dullaert** (hn); **Ger de Zeeuw**
(xylorimba); **Wim Vos** (glockenspiel); **Asko Ensemble; Schoenberg Ensemble; The Hague
Percussion Ensemble / Reinbert de Leeuw.** Auvidis Montaigne Ⓕ MO782035 (two discs:
91 minutes: DDD: 4/95). Recorded 1990.

This is one of Messiaen's most vivid scores, new and magnificent landscapes, as so often with him,
drawing his imagination to further extremes of instrumental sonority. In this case the landscapes were
the cliffs and towers of red, orange and violet rock that he marvelled at in Bryce Canyon, Utah ("the
most beautiful thing that exists in the United States"), the huge natural amphitheatre of Cedar Breaks

and, endearing itself to Messiaen by its name as well as its "limpid waters", its "rock walls of pink, white, mauve, red, black", the river gorge of Zion Park. (A steep rock pinnacle in the area was later named Mount Messiaen.) The orchestra to evoke all this is modest in size (44 players, including solo piano, horn, xylorimba and glockenspiel), with only 13 solo strings set against quadruple woodwind, triple brass and much percussion. But within this already dazzlingly bright ensemble Messiaen calls for such extra effects as wind machine and géophone (a shallow drum with lead shot inside), cellos and double-bass playing on the wrong side of the bridge, a trumpeter using the mouthpiece of his instrument only, a high clarinet with the reed restrained by the player's teeth, and so on. Although extreme, these sounds are calculated with great care. After an invocation of Bryce Canyon has twice led to a contemplation of "chasms of darkness, terror of the abyss" (rasping trombones and pounding drums) the third cycle achieves a brazen splendour over which the song of the white-winged dove, played by solo horn, piano and strings, hovers just as Messiaen describes it. And in the ensuing eighth movement one of his hushed, motionless string melodies has each of its phrases embellished at the end with *glissandos* in harmonics from a solo violin and with the double-bass quietly bouncing the bow stick on the strings: "droplets of water and silken rustlings", said Messiaen, and the effect is magically precise. This performance exults in such details and in the fearsome scale of many of the score's gestures. It was recorded live (though apparently without an audience) and is fully worthy of the work, and the excellent recording (the instruments are audibly arranged according to the layout printed in the score) gives the music space to resound in.

Messiaen Chronochromie. La ville d'en haut. Et exspecto resurrectionem mortuorum. **Cleveland Orchestra / Pierre Boulez.** DG Ⓕ 445 827-2GH (58 minutes: DDD: 4/95). Recorded 1993.   Ⓖ
Boulez has spoken of his pleasure at performing Messiaen with an orchestra relatively unfamiliar with his music. It sounds as though the Cleveland Orchestra must have enjoyed it too. You would expect them to, perhaps, in such a passage as that in the fourth movement of *Et exspecto*, where the two superimposed plainchant melodies return together with the noble "theme of the depths" – it has great splendour, as does the chorale melody of the finale, rising at the end to a satisfyingly palpable *fffff*. And in this performance of *Chronochromie* you can hear why Messiaen said that certain pages of it were "a double homage to Berlioz and Pierre Schaeffer [the French pioneer of electronic music]". Absolute rhythmic precision and the clarity of colour that comes from meticulous balance are among the other pleasures of these performances. They make a most satisfying coupling, too. The recordings are excellent: clean but not clinical and ample in dynamic range.

Messiaen Turangalîla-symphonie[a]. Quatuor pour la fin du temps[b]. [b]**Saschko Gawriloff** (vn); [b]**Siegfried Palm** (vc); [b]**Hans Deinzer** (cl); [b]**Aloys Kontarsky**, [a]**Peter Donohoe** (pfs); [a]**Tristan Murail** (ondes martenot); [a]**City of Birmingham Symphony Orchestra / Simon Rattle.** EMI Ⓕ CDS7 47463-8 (two discs: 130 minutes: DDD/ADD: 12/87). Item marked [b] from Deutsche Harmonia Mundi 065 99711 (8/79).   Ⓖ
No longer a rarity in the concert-hall, Messiaen's epic hymn to life and love has been lucky on record too, with Rattle's performance staying just ahead of the pack. Messiaen's luxuriant scoring presents a challenge for the engineers as much as the players and the EMI team come through with flying colours. Tristan Murail's ondes martenot is carefully balanced here – evocative and velvety, neither reduced to inaudibility nor over-miked to produce an ear-rending screech. Peter Donohoe's piano obbligato is similarly integrated into the orchestral tapestry yet provides just the right kind of decorative intervention. Rattle is at his best in the work's more robust moments like the jazzy fifth movement and the many rhythmic passages which recall Stravinsky's *Le Sacre*. But those unfamiliar with Messiaen's extraordinary score should perhaps start with the central slow movement, the beautiful *Jardin du sommeil d'amour*, exquisitely done by the Birmingham team. Unlike at least one rival account, this *Turangalîla* spills on to a second CD, which leaves room for a distinguished *Quatuor pour la fin du temps* as a makeweight. The music-making here lacks the youthful spontaneity of the main work, but is notable for an unusually slow and sustained performance of the movement with cello solo.

Additional recommendations ...
...Turangalîla-symphonie. **Soloists; Royal Concertgebouw Orchestra / Riccardo Chailly.** Decca Ⓕ 436 626-2DH (77 minutes: DDD: 11/93).   Ⓖ
...Quatuor pour la fin du temps. **Bartók** Contrasts, Sz111. **Chamber Music Northwest.** Delos Ⓕ DE3043 (63 minutes: ADD: 6/87).
...Quatuor pour la fin du temps. **Eduard Brunner** (cl); **Trio Fontenay.** Teldec Ⓕ 9031-73239-2 (44 minutes: DDD: 12/92).
...Quatuor pour la fin du temps. **Krauze** Quatuor pour la Naissance. **David Campbell** (cl); **Madeline Mitchell** (vn); **Christopher van Kampen** (vc); **Joanna MacGregor** (pf). Collins Classics Ⓕ 1393-2 (65 minutes: DDD: 6/94).

Messiaen Eclairs sur L'Au-Delà. **Polish Radio National Symphony Orchestra, Katowice / Antoni Wit.** Jade Ⓕ JADC099 (63 minutes: DDD: 6/94). Recorded live in 1993.
Messiaen Eclairs sur l'Au-Delà. **Orchestra of the Opéra-Bastille, Paris / Myung-Whun Chung.** DG Ⓕ 439 929-2GH (66 minutes: DDD: 12/94).   ⒼⒼ
Eclairs sur L'Au-Delà ("Illuminations of the Beyond") was Olivier Messiaen's last major work. It is almost a summary, musical and spiritual, of the preoccupations of his preceding 60 years but,

inspiritingly enough, shows him delightedly discovering not only new birds but also entrancingly new sounds: he has not made such startling use before of the contrabass clarinet (in the huge and complex eighth movement, which culminates in a Great Messiaen Tune of sonorous nobility), nor employed (to evoke the Lyrebird) such vertiginous leaps between sections of the orchestra. In one way, then, it is a series of nostalgic revisits. In the fourth movement, for example, there's a sort of two-minute summary of the extremely dense counterpoint of *Chronochromie*; the sixth recalls the "Dance of fury for the seven trumpets" in the *Quartet for the end of time*. But there's also a touching sense of Messiaen in his eighties preparing to contemplate the beyond. In the ninth of the 11 movements he writes his last birdsong piece, no fewer that 25 birds impersonated simultaneously by 18 woodwind instruments: the image is of Christ as the Tree of Life, the birds are the souls of the blessed, and of course they are all singing at once. He then considers "The path to the invisible", and if we were expecting a rapt meditation we do not know Messiaen: it is a clamorous and insistent piece, one of his great angular toccatas, expressing the very difficulty of keeping to that path. And finally, most movingly, one of his almost motionless, beginningless and endless string chorales, "Christ, Light of Paradise". The live Jade recording has remarkably few signs of how very difficult a piece it is to play. The recording is pleasantly spacious, the audience only makes its presence felt by a certain amount of coughing between movements; it is, in short, the sort of 'première recording' in which one can safely concentrate on the music.

Chung has distinct advantages, mark you, including an arguably finer orchestra and the comparative leisure of a studio recording; in fact it was made in the Opéra-Bastille itself, and impressively spacious it sounds. Where these advantages show is in small but quite important details of balance and sheer finesse. In the very opening wind chorale, for example, Chung's chording is a touch more precise, and on many pages he has obviously worked very hard to ensure clarity of texture and polished playing. Yet the sense that the Polish orchestra is excitedly discovering this score is no less absorbing than the Parisians' meticulous and loving care of it. Chung takes a little more time over the piece, most noticeably in the way that he allows silences their full measure. He also explores a finer range of very quiet sounds than Wit (perhaps a studio and the absence of an audience helped). These together might tip the balance in Chung's direction but then, listening again to Messiaen's discovery of a (to him) new and vociferous bird in the third movement, you sense the Polish players sharing his pleasure and seasoning that emotion with relief that this frighteningly difficult music is coming off without a hitch. In short, Chung's is an obvious first choice: it's beautifully played, immaculately recorded and vividly expressive. But once in a while a live recording of a difficult score gets pretty well everything right and manages as well to communicate the excitement of a first performance.

New review

Messiaen Six Petites Esquisses d'Oiseaux. Cantéyodjayâ. Quatre Etudes de rythme. Pièce pour le Tombeau de Paul Dukas. **Gloria Cheng** (pf). Koch International Classics Ⓕ 37267-2 (49 minutes: DDD: 9/95).

Gloria Cheng is a pianist much in demand as a specialist in taxing contemporary scores, and you can easily hear why: she is technically fearless and meticulously attentive to complex rhythms, she can sustain a bold melodic line splendidly, and her playing has powerful attack. She is just what the exhilarating but exhausting *Cantéyodjayâ* needs, in fact, and she gives it a performance of great *élan* and exciting drama. Similar qualities are needed, of course, in the outer sections of the *Quatre Etudes*, which have all the ferocity that Messiaen asks for. If there is any criticism it is that she tends to mark up Messiaen's quieter dynamics. Thus the famous "Mode de valeurs et d'intensités", which has a 'mode' of seven degrees of intensity, from *ppp* to *fff*, seems to lack a couple of degrees at the bottom end. However, rarely does one hear this piece sound quite so coherent, and Cheng's concentration in the austere "Neumes rythmiques" is remarkable. There is admirable precision in the *Petites Esquisses*, but again a slight lack of dynamic range at the quieter end of the spectrum means that each bird does not quite, as Messiaen insists, "have its own aesthetic". Still, an enjoyable if rather short recital, ending with an impressively austere account of Messiaen's elegy for his teacher; for once it really does sound "like an enormous block of stone".

Additional recommendation ...

...Pièce pour le Tombeau de Paul Dukas. Fantaisie burlesque. Rondeau. Six Petites Esquisses d'Oiseaux. Visions de l'Amen[a]. **Peter Hill**, [a]**Benjamin Frith** (pfs). Unicorn-Kanchana Ⓕ DKPCD9144 (79 minutes: DDD: 6/94).

Messiaen Préludes – No. 1, La colombe; No. 3, Le nombre léger; No. 6, Cloches d'angoisse et larmes d'adieu. Etudes de rythme – Ile de feu II. Cantéyodjayâ. Catalogue d'oiseaux – La traquet rieur; Le courlis cendré. Vingt regards sur l'enfant Jésus – Regard du Père; Par Lui a été fait; Regard des prophètes, des bergers et des Mages. **Rolf Hind** (pf). Cala United Ⓕ 88019 (69 minutes: DDD: 12/94). Recorded 1994.

Most pianists these days seem to prefer to record Messiaen's great piano cycles complete or not at all. Hopefully, Rolf Hind's judicious selection may set a trend. He's good at big gestures and steely attack, and the way he launches into *Le courlis cendré* ("The curlew") conjures up an image of a large and fearsomely beaked bird, dangerously close. He soon gets over this, however, and characterizes the other birds on this wild rocky shore quite vividly. Later the fog descends tangibly and the lighthouse siren is precisely as Messiaen describes it: "a powerful and lugubrious howl". Hind is splendid at the craggy grandeur and almost lurid colour of *Ile de feu II*, no less effective in the more limpid colours of the *Préludes* and the brighter ones of *La traquet rieur* (literally "the laughing pursuer", though we prosaically call it "the black wheatear"). He is best of all in the three pieces from *Vingt Regards*, grandly and excitingly pianistic, and at maintaining a firm line through the virtuoso thickets of *Cantéyodjayâ*, that extraordinary pair of interlocked rondos that can easily fall to pieces in the hands of a pianist who is too scared of its huge difficulties to characterize its juxtaposed blocks with maximum character and brilliance. Once or twice the ample acoustic (Conway Hall in London) muddies the colour a little; much more often Hind uses it most intelligently, enabling for example his powerful account of *Par Lui a été fait* to emerge concert-sized rather than studio-sized. A very welcome coupling, especially for those who have glumly concluded that the only way to get to know a fair cross-section of Messiaen's piano music is to buy at least six CDs.

Additional recommendation ...

...Etudes de rythme – Ile de feu I and II. *Coupled with works by* **Berg, Ravel, Stravinsky, Scriabin, Britten** and **Copland** Shura Cherkassky (pf). Decca Ⓕ 433 657-2DH (79 minutes: ADD: 2/96). *See review in the Collections section; refer to the Index to Reviews.* Ⓖ

New review

Messiaen Vingt regards sur l'enfant Jésus. **Joanna MacGregor** (pf). Collins Classics Ⓕ 7033-2 (two discs: 128 minutes: DDD: 5/96). Recorded 1995.

Joanna MacGregor is a pianist who combines fearless technique with great intelligence and imagination. When these qualities are matched by stunningly beautiful piano sound the likelihood of a distinguished account of the *Vingt regards sur l'enfant Jésus* is strong, and so it proves. Sheer beauty of colour is the outstanding virtue of this reading. MacGregor knows very well that some of these pieces require exquisitely vivid colour while others need a narrower chromatic range but one of absolute clarity (the crystalline glistening of the first variation in No. 15, "La baiser de l'Enfant-Jésus", the cycle's 'slow movement'). But she has few problems with the sheer strength needed elsewhere and only a couple of times do you get a slight impression that either she or the piano had reached its limits (at the height of No. 6, the tumultuous "Par Lui tout a été fait") or that a little more dynamic variation would have aided her brilliant colour contrasts (in the second development section of No. 10, "Regard de l'esprit de joie"). Elsewhere, not least in the huge finale, her playing has commanding power and grandeur. Her precision, too, is admirable: all those passages where Messiaen requires the two hands to be doing quite different things are splendidly clear. Above all, perhaps, she communicates a real love for the sound-world of this cycle, which is just as often sensuous and pianistic as it is mystical. We are not short of good recordings of the *Vingt regards*, but MacGregor's is probably the most sheerly beautiful of them all. Yvonne Loriod has great authority and a tireless strength that MacGregor cannot match on one or two pages, but she also has an occasional tendency to hurry, and the recorded sound is a touch hard. Peter Hill finds at times subtler shadings and occasionally allows silences to register more magically, but his instrument is not quite as superb nor so finely recorded as MacGregor's. The same is true of Håkon Austbø's performance, otherwise exceptionally good and exceptionally cheap. MacGregor's version was made in the concert-hall at Snape on an extremely fine Steinway but the central achievement here is her perception of Messiaen's prodigal invention of sonorities.

Additional recommendations ...

...Vingt regards. **Peter Hill** (pf). Unicorn-Kanchana Ⓕ DKPCD9122/3 (two discs: 142 minutes: DDD: 9/92).   ⒼⒼ

...Vingt regards. **Mélisande Chauveau** (pf). Forlane Ⓕ UCD16709/10 (two discs: 140 minutes: DDD: 7/94).

...Vingt regards. **Håkon Austbø** (pf). Naxos Ⓢ 8 550829/30 (two discs: 133 minutes: DDD: 12/94). *Gramophone Editor's choice.* Ⓖ

...Vingt regards. Petites esquisses d'oiseaux. Préludes. Etudes de rythme – Ile de feu I and II. **Yvonne Loriod** (pf). Erato Ⓜ 4509-96222-2 (three discs: 185 minutes: ADD: 12/94). ⒼⒼ

Messiaen La nativité du Seigneur[a]. Le banquet céleste[b]. **Jennifer Bate** (org). Unicorn-Kanchana Ⓕ DKPCD9005 (62 minutes: DDD: 2/88). Played on the organ of Beauvais Cathedral. Item marked [a] from DKP9005 (6/82), [b]DKP9018 (2/83). ⒼⒼⒼ

La nativité du Seigneur comprises nine meditations on themes associated with the birth of the Lord. Messiaen's unique use of registration gives these pieces an extraordinarily wide range of colour and emotional potency and in Jennifer Bate's hands (and feet) it finds one of its most persuasive and capable advocates. Bate was much admired by the composer and is so far the only organist to have recorded his complete works for the instrument. *Le banquet céleste* was Messiaen's first published work for the organ and is a magical, very slow-moving meditation on a verse from St John's Gospel (VI, 56). The very faithful recording captures both the organ and the large acoustic of Beauvais Cathedral to marvellous effect.

Additional recommendation ...

...La nativité du Seigneur. Diptyque. Les corps glorieux. Verset pour la fête de la dédicace. Le banquet céleste. Apparition de l'église eternelle. Livre d'orgue. Nine Méditations sur le mystère de la Sainte Trinité. L'ascension. Messe de la Pentecôte. Livre du Saint Sacrement. **Gillian Weir** (org). Collins Classics Ⓜ 7031-2 (seven discs: 418 minutes: DDD: 12/94). Ⓖ

Messiaen Apparition de l'église éternelle[a]. La nativité du Seigneur[b]. **Olivier Messiaen** (org). EMI
Composers in Person mono Ⓕ CDC5 55222-2* (72 minutes: ADD: 6/95). Item marked [a] from
Ducretet-Thomson DUC4/5, [b]DUC2/3 (both recorded 1956). Played on the organ of Sainte-
Trinité, Paris.   Ⓖ

During 1956 Messiaen recorded what was up to that date his complete organ *oeuvre* at Sainte-Trinité
– the church where he had been organist since 1931. This pairing of two famous works, written
shortly after his appointment to Sainte-Trinité, is more than a simple reissue, for it has been newly
edited and digitally remastered by Simon Gibson and Andrew Walter. The most obvious benefit is
the vivid aural picture it gives of the instrument which so inspired Messiaen – listen to the sense of
utter calm created by the voix céleste in "Desseins éternels", or that peculiar luminosity which bathes
"Les mages" (both from *La nativité*) as they trudge along following the night star. No recording
process yet invented could recapture that hypnotic mixture of vision, utter conviction and virtuosity
which were the hallmarks of Messiaen's playing in the flesh, but this CD does come very close and
coupled with Felix Aprahamian's fascinating notes, makes an issue of considerable musical as well
as historic value.

Messiaen Livre du Saint Sacrement. **Jennifer Bate** (org). Unicorn-Kanchana Ⓕ DKPCD9067/8
(two discs: 129 minutes: DDD: 10/87). Recorded on the organ of L'Eglise de la Sainte-Trinité,
Paris. *Selected by Sounds in Retrospect*.   ⒼⒼ

The crowning achievement of Messiaen's unique cycle of music for the organ, the *Livre du Saint
Sacrement* is also his largest work for the instrument. It is an intensely personal score based on the
cornerstone of his faith, the Blessed Sacrament, and spans a wide range of emotions from hushed,
private communion to the truly apocalyptic. Jennifer Bate gave the British première of the work in
1986, following which Messiaen invited her to record it using his own organ at the Trinity Church in
Paris. He was on hand throughout the sessions as he so often was. The recording is a model of clarity
and it is hard to imagine the complex and often very subtle textures of this music being better
conveyed. This is a magnificent achievement and should be heard by all who profess an interest in the
music of our time.

Messiaen L'ascension. Apparition de l'église éternelle. Diptyque. Messe de la Pentecôte.
Thomas Trotter (org). Decca Ⓕ 436 400-2DH (75 minutes: DDD: 9/93). Played on the organ
of the Eglise-Collégiale Saint-Pierre de Douai, France. Recorded 1991. *Gramophone Editor's
choice*.   ⒼⒼ

Even if the shelf is buckling under the weight of Messiaen recordings this one just has to be included.
Trotter proves to be in the top rank of Messiaen interpreters. Both the vision and language of *Messe
de la Pentecôte* are remote and too often performers fight shy of such musical intensity by
concentrating on dazzling registration or displays of technical bravado. Not so Trotter whose
sensitivity and self-control are never in doubt, not least at the spiritual and emotional climax of the
work, "Communion". There's nothing remotely silly or contrived about the birdsong element here –
it seems a natural and musical expression of joy and peace: which is what we all know Messiaen
intended but which so rarely works in performance. The choice of instrument is inspired. Its warm
colours glow like sunlight seen through a stained glass window down the length of a dark, incense-
laden nave. Perhaps the action noise can be a little distracting at first but this is quickly forgotten in
these intense and deeply-moving performances.

Additional recommendations ...

...Méditations. L'ascension. Messe de la Pentecôte. **Jennifer Bate** (org). Unicorn-Kanchana
Ⓕ DKPCD9024/5 (two discs: 134 minutes: DDD: 5/89).

...L'ascension. Le banquet céleste. Apparition de l'église éternelle. Diptyque. **Hans-Ola Ericsson**
(org). BIS Ⓕ CD409 (64 minutes: DDD: 9/89).

Messiaen Trois petites liturgies de la Présence Divine[a]. Cinq Rechants[b]. O sacrum convivium[c].
[a]**Cynthia Miller** (ondes martenot); [a]**Rolf Hind** (pf); [a]**London Sinfonietta** [a]**Chorus and** [bc]**Voices**;
[a]**London Sinfonietta / Terry Edwards**. Virgin Classics Ⓕ VC7 59051-2 (60 minutes: DDD: 11/91).
Notes, texts and translations included.

Even if, as Messiaen himself insisted, he was pre-eminently a 'theological' composer, dedicated to
celebrating the divine presence in his music, that music often seems to embrace the sensuous as
wholeheartedly as the spiritual. Indeed, one suspects that anyone listening to the *Trois petites liturgies
de la Présence Divine* in ignorance of the content of the text would assume that the chanted phrases
and opulent consonances of the all-female chorus, coupled with the swooning tonal quality of the
ondes martenot, which is so prominent in the instrumental accompaniment, were hymning an
essentially physical union after the manner of Stravinsky's *Les noces*. In *Cinq Rechants* the secularity
is more explicit, though hidden to a degree within Messiaen's own rather surrealistic texts. Here the
musical focus is even more directly on the voices, now unaccompanied, and the panache and polish
of the London Sinfonietta Chorus are remarkably well sustained. For the ultimate in refined control
of a slow moving, quiet choral texture, the short motet *O sacrum convivium* is the ideal foil to the
larger, more dramatic compositions, and the recordings are exemplary in ensuring that each vocal
strand is clear without any artificial spotlighting.

Additional recommendations ...

...O sacrum convivium. **Duruflé** Four Motets, Op. 10. Messe cum jubilo, Op. 11[b]. **Fauré** Requiem[a]. Cantique de Jean Racine, Op. 11[c]. [a]**Camilla Otaki** (sop); [ab]**Mark Griffiths** (bar); **Trinity College Choir, Cambridge;** [abc]**Richard Pearce** (org); [a]**London Musici / Richard Marlow.** Conifer Ⓕ CDCF176 (73 minutes: DDD: 10/90).

...O sacrum convivium[ab]. **Daniel-Lesur** Le cantique des cantiques[a]. Messe du Jubilé[ab]. In paradisum[b]. La vie intérieure[b]. [a]**BBC Symphony Chorus / Stephen Jackson** with [b]**Jeremy Filsell** (org). ASV Ⓕ CDDCA900 (70 minutes: DDD: 1/95).

Further listening ...

...Catalogue d'oiseaux, Books 1-3. **Peter Hill** (pf). Unicorn-Kanchana DKPCD9062 (5/88).
...Catalogue d'oiseaux – Books 4-6. **Peter Hill** (pf). Unicorn-Kanchana DKPCD9075 (9/89).
...Catalogue d'oiseaux – Book 7. La Fauvette des jardins. **Peter Hill** (pf). Unicorn-Kanchana DKPCD9090 (8/90).
...Méditations sur le mystère de la Sainte Trinité. **Hans-Ola Ericsson** (org). BIS CD464 (3/92).
...Pourquoi? Le sourire. La fiancée perdue. *Coupled with* **Poulenc** La courte paille. Banalités – Hôtel; Voyage à Paris. Métamorphoses – C'est ainsi que tu es. Poèmes – Fêtes galantes. A sa guitare. **Satie** Trois mélodies. **Debussy** Ariettes oubliées. Fêtes galantes, Set 1. **Honegger** Petit cours de morale, H148. **Ravel** Cinq mélodies populaires grecques. **Frederica von Stade** (mez); **Martin Katz** (pf). RCA Victor Red Seal 09026 62711-2 (4/95).

Giacomo **Meyerbeer**   German 1791-1864

Meyerbeer Dinorah. **Deborah Cook** (sop) Dinorah; **Christian du Plessis** (bar) Hoël; **Alexander Oliver** (ten) Corentin; **Della Jones** (mez) Goatherd; **Marilyn Hill Smith** (sop) Goatgirl; **Roderick Earle** (bass) Huntsman; **Ian Caley** (ten) Reaper; **Geoffrey Mitchell Choir; Philharmonia Orchestra / James Judd.** Opera Rara Ⓕ ORC005 (three discs: 151 minutes: ADD: 4/94). Notes, text and translation included. From OR5 (8/80). Recorded 1979.

The day after its première at the Opéra-Comique, Meyerbeer wrote to his wife to say that everybody, including the Emperor and Empress, seemed to have liked his opera but that with a Paris first-night you could never really be sure. In the event, success pursued it till the taste for such things lapsed. There is nothing second-rate about the singing here, simply that it lacks star-quality (which does not necessarily mean big names). Deborah Cook is fluent and likeable in the title-role; Christian du Plessis competent in his (the grief-stricken ending of his aria having fine effect), and Alexander Oliver, an excellent comedian, brings a happy touch to the simple but not entirely witless Corentin. Della Jones does admirably in her supporting role, and the Geoffrey Mitchell Choir sing as well as ever. The orchestral playing is of a quality that makes appreciation of Meyerbeer's scoring no problem at all, and James Judd conducts without too much of the modern maestro's rigidity. As always in Opera Rara's record productions, the presentation is exemplary, and recorded sound, if afflicted in this outdoor opera with distinctly indoor resonance, is clear and well-balanced. The opera itself is hampered by an awkward plot (involving, for one thing, almost as much retrospective narration as *The Ring*), but the music has a genuine lyric charm. More than that, its strands are skilfully interwoven, with a delightful ending. Meyerbeer and his librettists planned originally a short opera in three scenes; if they had had their way it might have been a masterpiece.

Further listening ...

...Komm!. Der Garten des Herzens. Lied des venezianischen Gondoliers. Hör' ich das Liedchen klingen. Die Rose, die Lilie, die Taube. Sie und ich. Menschenfeindlich. Chant des moissonneurs vendéens. La barque légère. La chanson de Maître Floh. Sicilienne. La poète mourant. *Coupled with* **Rossini** Au chevet d'un mourant. La lazzarone. La chanson du bébé. La gita in gondola. Il rimprovero. Ave Maria. L'ultimo ricordo. **Thomas Hampson** (bar); **Geoffrey Parsons** (pf). EMI CDC7 54436-2 (4/92).
...Les Huguenots. **Soloists; Ambrosian Opera Chorus; New Philharmonic Orchestra / Richard Bonynge.** Decca 430 549-2DM4.

Nikolay **Miaskovsky**   USSR 1881-1950

New review

Miaskovsky Sinfonietta No. 1 in B minor, Op. 32 No. 2. Theme and Variations. Two Pieces, Op. 46 No. 1. Napeve. **St Petersburg Chamber Ensemble / Roland Melia.** ASV Ⓕ CDDCA928 (56 minutes: DDD: 10/95). Recorded 1994.

The dignity and solid craftsmanship of Nikolay Miaskovsky make him a likeable figure, and the circumstances in which he maintained those values make him rather more than likeable. The Variations are consistently attractive, as are the shorter works, despite disconcerting reminiscences of the *Skye Boat Song* in the first of the Op. 46 Pieces. That's not to say that the music 'holds' you in the way that Stravinsky, Martinů, Honegger or Tippett do. And, as so often with Miaskovsky, there are slack moments where ideas seem to be coming back for no better reason than to fill out a pre-allocated space. The fact remains that if you have got the Miaskovsky bug, or if you want the fullest possible picture of middle-of-the-road Soviet music, you will find confident, full-bodied performances here which are the equal of the excellent Kremlin Chamber Orchestra on Claves and rather more warmly recorded.

Additional recommendation ...

...Sinfoniettas – No. 1; No. 2 in A minor, Op. 58. Two Pieces, Op. 46. **Kremlin Chamber Orchestra / Misha Rachlevsky.** Claves Ⓕ CD50-9415 (68 minutes: DDD: 2/95).

Miaskovsky Symphony No. 6 in E flat minor, Op. 23, "Revolutionary". **Yurlov Russian Choir; USSR Symphony Orchestra / Kyrill Kondrashin.** Russian Disc mono Ⓕ RDCD15008* (65 minutes: ADD: 10/94). Recorded 1959.

Ⓖ

This is not a flawless performance and the sound is on the thinnish side. But then no other recording of this work has anything approaching the fire, the expressive ebb and flow, or the sheer dramatic sweep of Kondrashin. When it first appeared in the early 1920s Miaskovsky's Sixth was hailed as the first Soviet symphony – not the first composed on Soviet soil, but the first to embody the cataclysmic experiences, the conflicts and aspirations of Revolution. Of course that begs all sorts of questions. For instance, does the finale's turn from heroic optimism to funereal tragedy represent solidarity with past martyrdom or present betrayal of ideals? And what, apart from the emblematic tunes in that finale, distinguishes the essential message of this music from, say, Rachmaninov's Second or Glière's Third, to mention two comparable pre-revolutionary Russian symphonies? Not that it is really necessary to agonize over such things. This is a musically self-sufficient symphonic drama of aspiration, yearning, frustration and wistfulness, all held in a tense state of becoming by a squared-off but masterly Wagnerian chromaticism and lit up from time to time by moments of immensely touching poetic inwardness. If you are sufficiently curious to give Miaskovsky a try and are unsure where to start with the 13 out of 27 symphonies currently available on CD, do go for this one in this recording.

Further listening ...

...Cello Concerto in C minor, Op. 66. *Coupled with* **Shostakovich** The Limpid Stream, Op. 39 – Adagio. **Tchaikovsky** Variations on a Rococo Theme in A minor, Op. 33. Nocturne, Op. 19 No. 4. **Julian Lloyd Webber** (vc); **London Symphony Orchestra / Maxim Shostakovich.** Philips 434 106-2PH (5/92).

...Symphonies – No. 1 in C minor, Op. 3[a]; No. 19 in E flat major, Op. 46[b]. [a]**USSR Ministry of Culture Symphony Orchestra / Gennadi Rozhdestvensky;** [b]**Russian State Brass Orchestra / Nikolai Sergeyev.** Russian Disc RDCD11007 (3/94).

...Symphonies – No. 5 in D major, Op. 18; No. 9 in E minor, Op. 28. **BBC Philharmonic Orchestra / Sir Edward Downes.** Marco Polo 8 223499 (7/94).

...Symphony No. 21, Op. 51, "Fantasy in F sharp minor". *Coupled with works by* **Kabalevsky** and **Shostakovich** New Philharmonia Orchestra / David Measham; National Philharmonic Orchestra / Bernard Herrmann. Unicorn-Kanchana Souvenir UKCD2066 (2/95). *See review under Kabalevsky; refer to the Index to Reviews.*

...Serenade in E flat major, Op. 32 No. 1. Sinfonietta in B minor, Op. 32 No. 2. Lyric Concertino in G major, Op. 32 No. 3. Salutation Overture in D major, Op. 48. **Moscow New Opera Orchestra / Yevgeny Samoilov.** Olympia OCD528 (7/94).

...Piano Sonatas – No. 1 in D minor, Op. 6; No. 2 in F sharp minor, Op. 13; No. 3 in C minor, Op. 19; No. 6 in A flat major, Op. 64 No. 2. **Murray McLachlan** (pf). Olympia OCD214 (12/88).

...Piano Sonata No. 3 in C minor, Op. 19. *Coupled with* **Scriabin** No. 6. Etudes – C sharp minor, Op. 2 No. 1; Op. 8: No. 5 in E major; No. 11 in B flat minor; Op. 42: No. 2 in F sharp minor; No. 3 in F sharp major; No. 4 in F sharp major; No. 5 in C sharp minor; No. 6 in D flat major; No. 8 in E flat major; Trois Etudes, Op. 65. **Prokofiev** Piano Sonata No. 7 in B flat major, Op. 83. **Sviatoslav Richter** (pf). Melodiya mono 74321 29470-2* (6/96).

...Piano Sonatas – No. 4 in C minor, Op. 27; No. 5 in B major, Op. 64 No. 1. Sonatine in E minor, Op. 57. Prelude, Op. 58. **Murray McLachlan** (pf). Olympia OCD217 (3/89).

...Cello Sonatas[a] – No. 1 in D major, Op. 12; No. 2 in A minor, Op. 81. Cello Concerto in C minor, Op. 66[b]. **Marina Tarasova** (vc); [a]**Alexander Polezhaev** (pf); [b]**Moscow New Opera Orchestra / Yevgeny Samoilov.** Olympia OCD530 (12/94).

Minoru Miki

Japanese 1930-

Suggested listening ...

...Marimba Spiritual II. *Coupled with works by* **Pape, Fuzzy, A. Koppel** and **Nørgård Safri Duo.** Chandos New Direction CHAN9330 (4/95). *See review in the Collections section; refer to the Index to Reviews.*

finale are typical of this uneven but nearly always fascinating composer who
25 concertos in all.

ons ...

Satie Parade. **Auric** Ouverture. **Françaix** Piano Concertino[a]. **Fetler**
estra. [a]**Claude Françaix** (pf); **London Symphony Orchestra / Antál Dorati.**
35-2MM (67 minutes: ADD).

oit. Le carnaval d'Aix, Op. 83b[a]. Le carnaval de Londres, Op. 172. L'Apothéose
286. [a]**Jack Gibbons** (pf); **New London Orchestra / Ronald Corp.** Hyperion
(77 minutes: DDD: 12/92).

le toit. La création du monde. Scaramouche, Op. 165b. Saudades do Brasil,
provençale, Op. 152b. **Marcelle Meyer** (pf); **Concerts Arts Orchestra; Champs
atre Orchestra / Darius Milhaud.** EMI Composers in Person [a]mono Ⓕ CDC7
77 minutes" ADD: 4/93).

sur le toit. La création du monde. Trois opéras-minute. Piano Concerto No. 1[a]. La fête
sique, Op. 159. [a]**Marguerite Long** (pf); **Darius Milhaud** (pf/cond); various artists.
Collector mono Ⓕ 150 122* (three discs: 256 minutes: ADD: 9/93).

ation du monde[b]. **Poulenc** Sextet for Piano and Wind Quintet[a]. **Saint-Saëns** Septet in
major, Op. 65[c]. [a]**Elizabeth Mann** (fl); [a]**Stephen Taylor** (ob); [a]**David Shifrin** (cl); [a]**Dennis**
urn (bn); [a]**Richard Todd** (hn); [c]**Thomas Stevens** (tpt); [bc]**Ani Kavafian,** [bc]**Julie Rosenfeld** (vns);
by **Hoffman** (va); [bc]**Carter Brey** (vc); [c]**Jack Kulowitsch** (db); André Previn (pf). RCA Victor
d Seal Ⓕ 09026 68181-2 (50 minutes: DDD: 11/95).

---

w review

lhaud Symphony No. 3, Op. 271, "Te Deum". Les cloches – Symphonic Suite, Op. 259.
Saudades do Brasil, Op. 67 – Botafogo; Leme; Tijuca; Laranjeiras. **Russian State Symphony
Cappella / Gennadi Rozhdestvensky.** Olympia Ⓜ OCD452 (61 minutes: DDD: 6/96). Recorded live
in 1993.

A couple of first recordings here are useful in filling gaps in the discography of the compulsively
productive Milhaud (who once said that he "had to continue writing as long as there was ink in the
pen"). Don't let the existence of Rachmaninov's famous choral setting of *The Bells*, or the fact that
Russian forces are involved here, mislead you into false expectations: this is not a setting of Poe's
poem but a ballet score based on it. Written in 1946, it was well received at its première in Chicago
but was a disaster when performed in New York by an ill-prepared Ballets Russes de Monte-Carlo:
Milhaud was obliged to substitute a simpler finale for subsequent performances, but restored the
original for the Symphonic Suite now recorded. The work, about a young bride and her groom, begins
joyously and melodiously, but at the "Bronze bells" section the atmosphere becomes heavy with
menace, and the hysterical final bacchanale depicts the King of the Ghouls spiriting the bridegroom
away. The resonance of the hall in which this live recording was made creates a slightly thick sound,
though detail is mostly clear. Rozhdestvensky adopts slower speeds for the "Silver" and "Golden"
sections than the composer indicates and makes heavy cuts in the finale. The Third Symphony (the
only one of Milhaud's first ten not hitherto recorded) was commissioned by French radio to celebrate
the ending of the Second World War. Starting with a vigorous, tough movement that could be
interpreted as symbolizing wartime struggles, it passes to a meditative, prayerfully intense slow
movement (in which a wordless chorus is imaginatively used): a jubilant *Pastorale* suggests the coming
of peace, which is finally hailed in a choral *Te Deum*. Again there are marked divergences from
Milhaud's printed timings (a couple of minutes shorter in both the second and the last movements),
but e performance is persuasive and exudes great confidence – more so than in *The Bells* – and the
twiddle movements, at least, represent Milhaud at his best.

F listening ...

inet Concerto, Op. 230. Scaramouche, Op. 165c. *Coupled with* **Copland** Clarinet Concerto.
demith Clarinet Concerto. **Eduard Brunner** (cl); **Bavarian Radio Symphony Orchestra / Urs
eider.** Koch Schwann 310352.

Concerto No. 1, Op. 136[b]. *Coupled with* **Elgar** Cello Concerto in E minor, Op. 85[a].
ighi Adagio con variazioni[a]. [a]**Mstislav Rostropovich** (vc); [a]**Moscow Philharmonic Orchestra;
R TV and Radio Large Orchestra / Gennadi Rozhdestvensky.** Russian Disc RDCD11104

Concerto No. 1, Op. 136. *Coupled with works by* **Bach, Kodály, Dohnányi, Boccherini,
n, Schumann, Saint-Saëns, Dvořák** and **Fauré, Prokofiev.** János Starker (vc); [a]**Gerald**
(pf); **Philharmonia Orchestra / Carlo Maria Giulini, Walter Susskind.** EMI mono/stereo
68485-2* (12/95). *See review in the Collections section; refer to the Index to Reviews.*

onies – No. 1, Op. 210; No. 2, Op. 247. Suite provençale, Op. 152b. **Toulouse Capitole
ra / Michel Plasson.** DG 435 437-2GH (7/92).

nies – No. 4, Op. 281; No. 8, Op. 362, "Rhodanienne". **French Radio National Orchestra /
ilhaud.** Erato 2292-45841-2.

nies – No. 6, Op. 343; No. 7, Op. 344. Overture méditerranéenne, Op. 330. **Toulouse
Orchestra / Michel Plasson.** DG 439 939-2GH (6/95).

ies – No. 7, Op. 344; No. 8, Op. 362, "Rhodanienne"; No. 9, Op. 380. **Basle Radio
Orchestra / Alun Francis.** CPO CPO999 166-2 (6/95).

Luis de Milán

New review

Milán El Maestro – Fantasias, Pavanas, Galliarda
(hp/psaltery); **Jordi Savall, Sergi Casademun**
gamba). Auvidis Astrée Ⓔ E8535 (63 min
El Maestro was both a collection of pieces an
information on the music of the time and on th
indicated which passages are to be played 'broadly
quickly. Very little consort music from sixteenth-centu
it is a valid exercise to add to it by adaptation, which it is
Milán's book contains 40 contrapuntal *fantasias*, four *ten*
(in both duple and triple time, and both slow and fast); a
galliardas from elsewhere, are here converted with great skill in
are fleshed out by judicious beefing-up of chords and, enh
individual lines. Seven items are given as solos on either the harp o
the vihuela at the time. The chosen instrumentation gives scope for an
showing this wonderfully pure and noble music in a less 'private' and un
on a solitary vihuela. This record is revelatory and compelling.

Further listening ...
...Libro de musica de vihuela de mano, "El maestro" – excerpts. **Hopkinson S**
Astrée E7748 (5/91). ✐
...El Maestro – Pavana IIª. *Coupled with* **López** Fantasiaª. **Narváez** Los seys lib
La canción del Emperador; Diferencias on "Guárdame las vacas"ª. Paseavase el re
Mudarra Tres libros de musica en Cifras para vihuela – Pavana de Alexandre; Fan
contrahaze la harpa en la manera de Ludovicoª. **Murcia** Cumbésᵇ. Gigaᵇ. **Guerau** Po
harmonico – Canario; Marionasᵇ. **Sanz** Instruccion de musica sobre la guitarra españo
Canarios; Folías; Lantururú; Pavanas al ayre españolᵇ. **Sor** Thèmes variés et Douze Minue
Op. 11 – Andante maestoso; Andante expressivoᵇ. Introduction and Variations on a theme b
Mozart, Op. 9ᵇ. **José Miguel Moreno** (ªvihuela/ᵇgtr). Glossa GCD920103 (8/95). ✐

Francesco Milano
Italian 1497-1543

Suggested listening ...
...Fantasias – Castelfranco MS; Dolcissima et amorosa; Nos. 8, 26, 39, 56 and 83. Ricercar No. 13.
Coupled with works by **Borrono da Milano, Ripa** *and* **Dall'Aquila** Paul O'Dette (lte).
Harmonia Mundi HMU90 7043 (10/95). ✐ *See review in the Collections section; refer to the
Index to Reviews.*

Robin Milford
British 1903-195

Suggested listening ...
...If it's ever spring again. The colour. *Coupled with works by* **Finzi, Farrar, Gurney** *and* **Gill** I
Partridge (ten); **Stephen Roberts** (bar); **Clifford Benson** (pf). Hyperion CDA66015 (9/91). *Se*
review in the Collections section; refer to the Index to Reviews.

Darius Milhaud
French

Milhaud Harp Concerto, Op. 323ª. Le boeuf sur le toit, Op. 58. La création du mond
ªFrédérique Cambreling (hp); **Lyon Opéra Orchestra / Kent Nagano**. Erato MusiFr
45820-2 (59 minutes: DDD: 2/93). Recorded 1992.
Here is music to delight, with performances to match. Milhaud's ballet *Le boeuf su*
for Jean Cocteau in 1919 and is set in an American bar during the Prohibition pe
manufacture and sale of alcohol) that was then just beginning. Some perfo
French score lay the humour on too thick, but this one under Kent Nagano ha
sophistication and the playing is above all musicianly, while the more uproari
all the more effectively for this very reason. The playing by the accom
excellent, not least the wind players who have plenty to do. Written four
monde was one of the first works by a European composer to take
folklore and the raw black jazz that Milhaud heard in New Orleans. Th
ends with a mating dance and the whole work is powerfully and da
French orchestra bring out all the character of this music and take
urgently than usual, to excellent effect. The Harp Concerto dates fro
into Milhaud's career, and inevitably it has a brighter character, th
influence, though of a far gentler kind. Frédérique Cambreling is a

...Little Symphonies and Little Operas – No. 1, Op. 43, "Le printemps"; No. 2, Op. 49, "Pastorale"; No. 3, Op. 71, "Serenade"; No. 4, Op. 74, "Dixtuour"; No. 5, Op. 75; No. 6, Op. 79. L'enlèvement d'Europe. L'abandon d'Ariane. La deliverance de Thésée. **Capella Cracoviensis / Karl Anton Rickenbacher.** Koch Schwann 311392 (5/93).

...Le carnaval d'Aix, Op. 83*b*. Piano Concertos – No. 1, Op. 127; No. 4, Op. 294. Five Etudes, Op. 63. Ballade, Op. 61. **Claude Helffer** (pf); **French National Orchestra / David Robertson.** Erato MusiFrance 2292-45992-2 (6/93).

...String Quartets[a] – No. 1, Op. 5; No. 2, Op. 16. Quatre poèmes de Léo Latil, Op. 20[b]. Trois poèmes de Jean Cocteau, Op. 59[b]. [b]**Ulrike Sonntag** (sop); [b]**Rudolf Jansen** (pf); [a]**Fanny Mendelssohn Quartet.** Troubadisc TRO-CD01409 (5/95).

...String Quartets – No. 3, Op. 32[a], "Latil"; No. 4, Op. 46[b]; No. 5, Op. 64[b]. Machines agricoles, Op. 56[c]. Catalogue de fleurs, Op. 60[d]. [acd]**Ulrike Sonntag** (sop); [cd]**Irmela Nolte** (fl); [cd]**Deborah Marshall** (ob); [cd]**Michael Weigel** (bn); [cd]**Arpat György** (db); [ab]**Fanny Mendelssohn Quartet** ([cd]Renate Eggebrecht, Mario Korunić, vns; [cd]Stefan Berg, va; [cd]Friedemann Kupsa, vc) / [d]**Linda Horowitz.** Troubadisc TRO-CD01410 (6/96).

...Sonatine, Op. 100. Duo Concertant, Op. 351. *Coupled with* **Copland** Clarinet Sonata. **Tailleferre** Arabesque. Sonata for Solo Clarinet. **Honegger** Sonatine. **Poulenc** Clarinet Sonata. **Victoria Soames** (cl); **Julius Drake** (pf). Clarinet Classics CC0001 (9/92).

...Pacem in terris, Op. 404[a]. L'homme et son désir[b]. [ab]**Soloists;** [a]**Utah University Chorus; Utah Symphony Orchestra / Maurice Abravanel.** Vanguard Classics 08.9070.71 (11/93).

...Duo concertante, Op. 351. Caprice, Op. 335*a. Coupled with* **Françaix** Tema con variazioni. **Honegger** Clarinet Sonatina, H42. **Hindemith** Clarinet Sonata in B flat major. **Vaughan Williams** Six Studies in English folk song. **Bozza** Pulcinella. **Kupferman** Moonflowers, Baby!. **Jonathan Cohler** (cl); **Judith Gordon** (pf). Crystal CD733 (5/95).

...Quatre esquisses, Op. 227. Madame Bovary, Op. 128. Three Rag Caprices, Op. 78. Saudades do Brasil, Op. 67. Les charmes de la vie, Op. 360. Polka, Op. 95. Tango des Fratellini, Op. 58*c. Coupled with* **Satie** (arr. Milhaud) Cinq grimaces. **Boaz Sharon** (pf). Unicorn-Kanchana DKPCD9155 (5/95).

...Saudades do Brasil, Op. 67. La muse ménagère, Op. 245[a]. Madame Bovary, Op. 128[a]. **Alexandre Tharaud** (pf); [a]**Madeleine Milhaud** (spkr). Naxos 8 553443 (65 minutes: DDD: 5/96).

Carl Millöcker
Austrian 1842-1899

Suggested listening ...
...Der Bettelstudent. **Soloists; Bavarian Radio Chorus; Graunke Symphony Orchestra / Franz Allers.** EMI CMS5 65387-2 (2/95).

Léon Minkus
Czechoslovakian or Polish 1826-1917

New review

Minkus La bayadère – excerpts. Paquita. **Sofia National Opera Orchestra / Boris Spassov.** Capriccio ℗ 10 544 (69 minutes: DDD: 12/95).

Minkus may not have been a Delibes or a Tchaikovsky, but he does not deserve the disparaging comments that have often been his lot. His music is easy on the ear, always tuneful and often stirring. *La bayadère* (1877) was his major success after *Don Quixote* (1869), and its final act ("The Kingdom of the Shades") has often since been danced as a separate ballet. For *Paquita* (1881) he merely supplemented an existing score by Deldevez, but again Minkus's contribution has subsequently been danced as a separate ballet. Using as reference the complete recording under Richard Bonynge, what is described here as excerpts from *La bayadère* turns out to be just Act 2 minus the introduction. What is then presented as Minkus's complete *Paquita* music also includes contributions attributed to Delibes, Pugni and Tcherepnin. It is *Paquita* which contains the more exciting and memorable music – above all the *Grand Pas*. Although there is no doubt that, for the purposes of home listening, Bonynge manages to inject more variation and excitement into *La bayadère*, Boris Spassov has the greater experience of conducting ballet in the theatre, and his recording is on any count excellently performed and recorded. It should make rewarding listening for anyone wishing to hear Minkus's music for *Paquita* complete.

Additional recommendation ...

...La Bayadère. **English Chamber Orchestra / Richard Bonynge.** Decca ℗ 436 917-2DH2 (two discs: 114 minutes: DDD: 7/94).

Further listening ...

...Don Quixote. **Sofia National Opera Orchestra / Boris Spassov.** Capriccio 10 540/1 (5/95).

Edward Mirzoyan   USSR 1921-

Suggested listening ...
...Symphony for Timpani and Strings. Theme and Variations. Poem Epitaph (in memory of Aram
  Khachaturian). **St Petersburg Chamber Ensemble / Roland Melia.** ASV CDDCA916 (7/95).

Ernest Moeran   British 1894-1950

New review
Moeran Cello Sonata.
Ireland Cello Sonata in G minor.
Rubbra Cello Sonata in G minor, Op. 60. **Raphael Wallfisch** (vc); **John York** (pf). Marco Polo
  Ⓕ 8 223718 (59 minutes: DDD: 8/95). Recorded 1994.
Unlike the concerto, examples of the English cello sonata are not particularly thick on the ground
(one thinks also of those by Britten, Rawsthorne, Bax and Truscott) but one would be hard put to it
to select a finer trio than the three recorded here. All are products of full maturity, each composer
being in his forties or fifties at the time. Moeran's solitary Sonata is arguably his finest and most
satisfying work. The music has a dramatic and passionate demeanour – Moeran composed it for his
wife of two years, Peers Coetmore, in 1947 – yet its three movements are very diverse, the vigorous
finale even seeming to glance towards Bartók. Rubbra's, composed the previous year, bears a more
thoughtful aspect, not least in the fast-faster-slow disposition of its three movements. None the less,
for all the work's serenity it too possesses an inner steel. Ireland's Sonata (1923) has not perhaps the
same intellectual rigour but is still an object lesson in musical construction and balance. Raphael
Wallfisch has an appealing warmth of tone and his playing is always deeply musical. He also wears
his technique rather more lightly than some of his more abrasive, higher-profile rivals, though he does
sound a shade raw in the uppermost register. Pianist John York provides able support, and Gary
Cole's recording is clean and natural. Well worth investigating.

Moeran Songs of Springtime. Phyllida and Corydon.
Warlock A Cornish Carol. I saw a fair maiden. Benedicamus Domino. The full heart. The rich
  cavalcade. Corpus Christi. All the flowers of the Spring. As dew in Aprylle. Bethlehem Down.
  A Cornish Christmas Carol. **Finzi Singers / Paul Spicer.** Chandos Ⓕ CHAN9182 (76 minutes:
  DDD: 10/93). Texts included. Recorded 1992. *Gramophone Editor's choice.*   Ⓖ
The Peter Warlock we all know and love from the evergreen *Capriol Suite* and the boisterous songs
seems a world away from the introverted and intense artist of these unaccompanied choral carols.
Perhaps Warlock's real genius was an ability to create profound expression in short musical structures,
but even the more outgoing pieces – the joyful *Benedicamus Domino* and the Cornish Christmas Carol
with its gentle hint at "The First Nowell" – have an artistic integrity which raises them high above the
level of the syrup of modern day carol settings. Given performances as openly sincere and sensitive as
these few could remain unmoved. In the two Moeran madrigal suites there is an indefinable Englishness
– the result of a deep awareness of tradition and love of the countryside. The Finzi Singers' warm-toned,
richly expressive voices seem to capture the very essence of this uniquely lovely music.

New review
Moeran Three Piano Pieces. On a May Morning. Three Fancies. Two Legends. Theme and
  Variations. Stalham River. Toccata. Irish Love Song. Summer Valley. The White Mountain.
  Two Pieces. Bank Holiday. **Eric Parkin** (pf). J. Martin Stafford Ⓕ JMSCD2 (79 minutes: DDD:
  5/96). Recorded 1994.
The frequently held view that Moeran was at his best as a miniaturist is a rather sweeping statement
considering the stature of the Symphony in G minor, the *Sinfonietta* or the gorgeous Violin Concerto.
However, when confronted with a disc of consistently delightful, small-scale gems as here, one can
certainly understand why that view has persisted. Devotees of the composer will need little
encouragement to explore this disc, but for those unfamiliar with his music this recording would make
a superb introduction, because contained in these 18 pieces are all the elements that make up
Moeran's highly individual style. In the two most well-known pieces, *Stalham River* and the *Toccata*,
Moeran can be heard drawing inspiration from his beloved Norfolk landscape, whilst his abiding
passion for the south-west coast of Ireland can be heard in *Irish Love Song*, *The White Mountain* and
at times in the *Theme and Variations* of 1920 – his most substantial work for the piano. Eric Parkin
plays this repertoire – the first time all the piano music has been brought together on one disc – with
authority and affection and the piano sound is very natural.

Further listening ...
...Cello Concerto[a]. Sinfonietta. [a]**Raphael Wallfisch** (vc); **Bournemouth Sinfonietta / Norman Del
  Mar.** Chandos CHAN8456 (9/87).
...Violin Concerto[a]. Lonely Waters. Whythorne's Shadow. [a]**Lydia Mordkovitch** (vn); **Ulster
  Orchestra / Vernon Handley.** Chandos CHAN8807 (9/90).
...Serenade in G major. Sinfonietta. *Coupled with* **Finzi** The Fall of the Leaf. New Year Music,
  Op. 7. **Northern Sinfonia / Richard Hickox.** EMI British Composers CDM7 64721-2 (8/94).

...Serenade in G major. Nocturne[a]. **Warlock** Serenade for Strings. Capriol Suite. [a]**Hugh Mackey** (bar); [a]**Renaissance Singers; Ulster Orchestra / Vernon Handley.** Chandos CHAN8808 (3/91).

...Symphony in G minor. Overture to a Masque. **Ulster Orchestra / Vernon Handley.** Chandos CHAN8577 (4/88).

...Symphony in G minor. *Coupled with* **Ireland** Piano Concerto in E flat major[a]. [a]**Eileen Joyce** (pf); **Hallé Orchestra / Leslie Heward.** Dutton Laboratories mono CDAX8001* (5/93). ⊙⊙⊙

...Te Deum and Jubilate in E flat major. *Coupled with works by* **Elgar, Statham, Howells, S.S. Wesley, Britten** and **Gladstone** Norwich Cathedral Choir / **Michael Nicholas** with **Neil Taylor** (org). Priory PRCD470 (10/94).

...Far in a western brookland. O fair enough are sky and plain. *Coupled with works by* **Ireland, Horder, Butterworth, L. Berkeley, Barber** and **C.W. Orr** Anthony Rolfe Johnson (ten); **Graham Johnson** (pf). Hyperion CDA66471/2 (8/95). Includes various poems from Housman's "A Shropshire Lad" read by Alan Bates. *See review in the Collections section; refer to the Index to Reviews.*

Johann Molter
German 1696-1765

Suggested listening ...
...Trumpet Concertos Nos. 1-3. Double Trumpet Concertos Nos. 1, 2, 4 and 5. **Guy Touvron, Guy Messler** (tpts); **Württemberg Chamber Orchestra / Jörg Faerber.** RCA Victor Red Seal 09026 61200-2 (5/93).

Federico Mompou
Spanish 1893-1987

New review
Mompou Música callada. **Herbert Henck** (pf). ECM New Series Ⓕ 445 699-2 (63 minutes: DDD: 9/95). Recorded 1993. *Gramophone Editor's choice.*
Listening to this disc is rather like entering a retreat. There is a rapt, contemplative atmosphere around these 28 miniatures (only two run for as long as three minutes) written between 1959 and 1967 as an attempt to express St John of the Cross's mystic ideal of "the music of silence". Practically all slow-moving, using repetition as a structural device but avoiding anything like keyboard virtuosity, and rarely rising even to a *forte*, they seem to acknowledge descent from Erik Satie via the impressionists, though harmonically much freer and sometimes harsher (as in Nos. 12, 14, 21 and 23) – even, occasionally, stepping inside the area of atonality (for example in Nos. 25 and 26). No. 3 has a childlike innocence in its folkloric theme: Mompou's fascination with bell-sounds finds echoes in Nos. 5, 17 and 22. Overall there is a sense of tranquil, private self-communion which, paradoxically, exerts a strange spell on the listener. Herbert Henck, a specialist in twentieth-century music, plays this collection with a tender sensitivity and an ideally suited luminosity of tone, and he is finely recorded. An exceptional and haunting issue, whose sounds seem to hang in the air, as it were.

Mompou Cançons i danses. Preludes – Nos. 5, 6, 7, "Fireworks" and 11. **Alicia de Larrocha** (pf). RCA Victor Red Seal Ⓕ 09026 62554-2 (60 minutes: DDD: 11/94). Recorded 1992. ⊙⊙
Each of the elegantly salon-like series of 13 *Songs and dances*, with only very few exceptions, consists of a coupling of two traditional Catalan melodies, freely arranged with artfully expressive harmonies. The earlier pieces, from the 1920s, reveal influences of the Parisian composers with whom Mompou was friendly (the piled-up fourths of No. 3 unmistakably point to Milhaud), but the idiom becomes rather more personal later (and No. 6, which *is* entirely original, goes to Latin America for its inspiration). More individual than this series, however, are the Preludes: No. 6, the longest piece here, is somewhat Scriabinesque (apart from the similarity of its being for the left hand alone) and No. 7 by far the most impressionist and virtuosic. As one who knew Mompou well and is the dedicatee of some of his pieces, Alicia de Larrocha is in an almost unique position as an interpreter of his music, of which she again shows herself here a splendid champion. Larrocha's performances and the warm, natural recorded piano sound are both in the highest class.

Additional recommendation ...
...Scènes d'enfants – No. 5, Jeunes filles au jardin. Suburbis – No. 1, El carrer, el guitarrista i el vell cavall. Cançons i dansas – Nos. 5-8. Paisajes – No. 1, La fuente y la campana. *Coupled with works by* **Falla, Granados** and **Nin** Maria Barrientos, Ninon Vallin (sops); **Enrique Granados, Federico Mompou, Joaquin Nin** (pfs); **Manuel de Falla** (pf/hpd); **instrumental ensemble.** EMI Composers in Person mono Ⓕ CDC7 54836-2* (78 minutes: ADD: 11/93). *See review in the Collections section; refer to the Index to Reviews.*

Mompou Los Improperios[a]. Combat del somni[b]. Suburbis (orch. Rosenthal). Scènes d'enfants (orch. Tansman). [ab]**Virgínia Parramon** (sop); [a]**Jerzy Artysz** (bar); [a]**Valencia Choir; Teatre Lliure Chamber Orchestra, Barcelona / Josep Pons.** Harmonia Mundi Ⓕ HMC90 1482 (58 minutes: DDD: 4/94). Texts included. Recorded 1993.
The usual image (a true one) of Mompou is of a quiet, retiring composer of exquisite miniatures for piano or for voice. Not until he had reached the age of 70 did he write for the orchestra, and then only

in the present *Los Improperios* (from the liturgy for Good Friday). This issue has a very good solo baritone, a well-trained and fresh-sounding choir and clean orchestral sound. It is a moving performance of a work of deep commitment, exhibiting more passion and drama than is usually associated with Mompou. Harmonically it is, at times, reminiscent of Poulenc (who was an admirer of his), especially in the curiously jaunty ritornello in "Ego propter te" and in the beatific close-harmony female chorus in the final antiphon, which after an exultant climax dies away with repeated calls of "Domine!". The orchestrations by other hands of two of his early piano suites are undeniably effective, but they decidedly change the music's character.

Jean-Joseph de Mondonville   French 1711-1772

Suggested listening ...
...Violin Sonata in G major, Op. 3 No. 5. *Coupled with works by* **Leclair, Guillemain, Duphly** and **J-B. Forqueray** **Simon Standage** (vn); **Lars Ulrik Mortensen** (hpd). Chandos Chaconne CHAN0531 (6/93). *See review under Leclair; refer to the Index to Reviews.*
...Titon et Aurore. **Soloists; Françoise Herr Vocal Ensemble; Les Musiciens du Louvre / Marc Minkowski.** Erato MusiFrance 2292-45715-2 (10/92).

Stanislaw Moniuszko   Polish 1819-1872

Suggested listening ...
...Overtures – Paria[a]. The Countess[b]. Verbum nobile[c]. Halka[d] – Overture; Mazur. The Raftsman[d]. The fairy tale[d]. Polonaise de concert in A major[d]. [abc]**Polish National Radio Symphony Orchestra, Katowice /** [ac]**Grzegorz Fitelberg,** [b]**Jan Krenz;** [d]**National Philharmonic Orchestra, Warsaw / Witold Rowicki.** Olympia OCD386 (8/93).

Meredith Monk   American 1943-

Suggested listening ...
...Atlas. **Soloists; orchestra / Wayne Hankin.** ECM New Series 437 773-2 (10/93).

Matthias Monn   Austrian 1717-1750

Suggested listening ...
...Cello Concerto in G minor (arr. Schoenberg). *Coupled with works by* **Dvořák, Schumann, Saint-Saëns, Delius, Elgar, Haydn, Chopin, Franck, Fauré, Bruch, Bach, Handel** and **Beethoven** **Jacqueline du Pré** (vc); **Gerald Moore, Ernest Lush, Stephen Kovacevich** (pfs); **London Symphony Orchestra / Sir John Barbirolli; Royal Philharmonic Orchestra / Sir Malcolm Sargent; New Philharmonia Orchestra; Chicago Symphony Orchestra; English Chamber Orchestra / Daniel Barenboim** (pf). EMI CZS5 68132-2 (six discs: 8/94). *See review in the Collections section; refer to the Index to Reviews.*

James Moody   British 1907-

Suggested listening ...
...Toledo, A Spanish fantasy[c]. *Coupled with* **Spivakovsky** Harmonica Concerto[c]. **Villa-Lobos** Harmonica Concerto in A minor[d]. **Arnold** Harmonica Concerto, Op. 46[a]. **Farnon** Prelude and Dance[b]. **Tommy Reilly** (harmonica); [a]**Basle Radio Symphony Orchestra / Cedric Dumont;** [b]**orchestra / Robert Farnon;** [c]**Munich Radio Orchestra / Charles Gerhardt;** [d]**South West German Radio Orchestra / Emmerich Smola.** Chandos CHAN9248 (5/94).

Stephen Montague   American 1943-

Suggested listening ...
...From the White Edge of Phrygia[a]. String Quartet No. 1, "in memoriam Barry Anderson and Tomasz Sikorski"[b]. Haiku[c]. Tigida Pipa[d]. [bcd]**Stephen Montague** (electronics); [c]**Philip Mead** (pf); [b]**Smith Quartet;** [d]**Singcircle / Gregory Rose;** [a]**Florida Orchestra / Jahja Ling.** Continuum CCD1061 (4/95).

Phillippus de Monte
Dutch 1521-1603

Suggested listening ...
...Quand de ta lèvre. Si trop souvent. Le premier jour du mois de mai. *Coupled with works by*
Regnard, Boni, J. de Castro and **Rippe** Clément Janequin Ensemble / Dominique Visse
(alto). Harmonia Mundi HMC90 1491 (2/95). *See review in the Collections section; refer to the Index to Reviews.*

Michel Pignolet de Montéclair
French 1667-1737

Montéclair Jephté. **Jacques Bona** (bass-bar) Jephté; **Sophie Daneman** (sop) Iphise; **Claire Brua** (sop) Almaise, Vénus; **Nicolas Rivenq** (bass) Phinée, Apollon; **Mark Padmore** (ten) Ammon; **Bernard Loonen** (ten) Abdon; **Jean-Claude Sarragosse** (bass) Abner; **Sylviane Pitour** (sop) Polhymnie, Israelite; **Sylvie Colas** (sop) Terpsichore; **Mary Saint-Palais** (sop) Woman of Maspha, Shepherdess, Truth. **François Bazola** (bass) Man of Maspha; **Patrick Foucher** (ten) A Hebrew; **Anne Pichard** (sop) Elise; **Les Arts Florissants Chorus and Orchestra / William Christie.** Harmonia Mundi Ⓟ HMC90 1424/5 (two discs: 150 minutes: DDD: 1/93). ✍ Notes, text and translation included. Recorded 1992.   Ⓖ

Growing acquaintance with the operas of Lully, Charpentier and Rameau has led to an increasing curiosity about the works of fellow compatriots: composers whom we have long suspected might have something more to say than we have been led to believe. It is clear from the opening bars of *Jephté* that Montéclair's dramatic instincts are embedded in the finest French traditions of opera. Writing at a time when the 'giants' were either dead or yet to influence the stage (Rameau's *Hippolyte et Aricie* was performed a year after *Jephté,* in 1733), Montéclair has been historically judged as an operatic footnote between Lully and Rameau. On the evidence of this fine *tragédie lyrique* opinions of French opera in the early eighteenth century need to be seriously revised. *Jephté* is a full-scale work which deservedly had a considerable following in its day. The plot is an entertaining conflation of a fiery, action-packed Old Testament story with a tale of romance running simultaneously. Jephté returns from exile to defend Israel from Ammon, vowing that he will not permit himself to see his wife or daughter until he has defeated him, and that he will sacrifice the first person he sees after conquering the enemy. Ammon is spared but falls in love with Iphisa, Jephté's daughter. Iphisa is the unfortunate soul whom her father first notices, her grief compounded by the guilt of loving Jephté's enemy. A thunderbolt removes Ammon permanently and Iphisa's life is spared. Far-fetched certainly, but like Handel, Montéclair has the resource to elevate standard emotions in a convincing and inventive manner. William Christie is as alert to the possibilities of colour as the composer himself, pacing the narrative with momentum and extreme sensitivity to nuance. All the singers, without exception, are well-groomed for the delicacies of the style and vocally they make a pleasantly contrasting team. The choir are not as exact as the outstanding instrumental group but they are exciting and always alive to theatricality. Many moments to savour then: try Iphisa's haunting and sensual scene at the beginning of Act 4 evoking memories of Charpentier's *Médée* (and Christie's recording too) or instrumental vignettes, such as the enchanting *Air* in Act 2, which anticipates Rameau. Every effort should be made to get acquainted with this spellbinding masterpiece.

Further listening ...
...Cantatas – La mort de Didon. Il dispetto in amor. Le triomphe de l'amour. Morte di Lucretia. Pyrame et Thisbé. **Soloists; Les Arts Florissants Instrumental Ensemble / William Christie** (hpd). Harmonia Mundi HMC90 1280 (6/89). ✍

Claudio Monteverdi
Italian 1567-1643

New review
Monteverdi Vespro della Beata Virgine – Domine ad adiuvandum; Dixit Dominus; Laudate pueri; Laetatus sum; Nisi Dominus; Lauda Jerusalem (with plainchant antiphons). Magnificat II. Motets – O quam pulchra es. Domine, ne in furore. Ego flos campi. Adoramus te, Christe. Laudate Dominum omnes gentes. Ego dormio, et cor meum vigilat. Christe, adoramus te. Cantate Domino. **Concerto Italiano / Rinaldo Alessandrini.** Opus 111 Ⓟ OPS30-150 (75 minutes: DDD: 7/96). ✍ Texts and translations included. *Gramophone Editor's choice.*   Ⓖ

During the last few years Rinaldo Alessandrini and the Concerto Italiano have acquired a formidable reputation, above all for their records of Monteverdi madrigals. The kind of knowledge and detailed understanding of the subtleties of both meaning and pronunciation of the Italian language which in the end only a native speaker can possess, and an impressive command of seventeenth-century vocal styles and techniques that is all too rare in a country where the baleful influences of the opera-house and the conservatoire still cast long shadows over the performance of early repertoires, are two of the important elements that characterize their distinctive approach. Allied to a profound sense of drama and a lively musicality, these skills have been expertly shaped by Alessandrini to produce some of the finest recordings ever made of this repertory. This makes their recent foray into Monteverdi's church music all the more intriguing. The first half of the disc is made up of a complete vespers setting assembled from individual pieces published throughout the composer's career. Sung by one voice to a part and richly underpinned by a varied continuo group including theorbo, double harp and contrabass, there is a clarity and intimacy about the result. Details that often disappear in performances with larger forces here speak clearly (the performance of "Dixit Dominus" from the *Vespers* of 1610 is notable in this respect). The attention to textual detail, the careful shaping of phrases, the dramatically contrasted readings of opposing images – in short, all the features that are familiar from the group's madrigal records – are here used to the full in a sequence of powerfully rhetorical accounts that instructively dissolve the boundaries between secular and sacred styles. The disc is completed by a series of motets including three for solo voice; particular mention must be made of Rossana Bertini's breathtakingly audacious performance of *Laudate Dominum*, invigorated by a good deal of ornamentation, which is executed with great flair and élan. This recording brims with revelations and surprises – no serious Monteverdian can afford to be without it.

Monteverdi Il Combattimento di Tancredi e Clorinda[a]. Il ballo della ingrate[b]. Tempro la cetra[c]. Tirsi e Clori[d]. [ab]**Barbara Borden,** [bd]**Suzie LeBlanc** (sops); [b]**Päivi Järviö** (mez); [cd]**John Potter,** [a]**Douglas Naswari** (tens); [a]**Cesare Righetti** (bar); [b]**Harry van der Kamp** (bass); **Tragicomedia / Stephen Stubbs** (lte). Teldec Das Alte Werk Ⓕ 4509-90798-2 (76 minutes: DDD: 10/93). 🎵 Texts and translations included. Recorded 1992. ⓖ

The *Combattimento* was premièred at the Venice Carnival of 1624. It is a crucial work in Monteverdi's output, partly because it is virtually the only clue we have of his approach to music for dramatic performance between the two Mantuan operas and the two late Venetian ones. Moreover, the style that he so comprehensively introduces, the *genere concitato*, was closely bound up with his general thinking on the subject of musical rhythm, merely one aspect of his lifelong concern with the ability of music to portray the full range of human experience. In other words, it is something of an oddity. As if to emphasize the narrative element, Monteverdi uses a deliberately narrow vocal range, leaving all expressiveness, even pictorial effects, to the accompaniment. Tragicomedia, directed by Stephen Stubbs, offers a rich and at times rather fussy interpretation of the unprecedentedly full orchestral palate, but in Cesare Righetti Stubbs has the advantage of a native-singing Italian narrator with a full, clear, firm and at times operatic voice. The disc is interestingly completed with Monteverdi's surviving *balli* including the *Ballo delle ingrate*. The latter is superbly done; nicely resonant accompaniment, a good sense of the theatrical nature of the piece, and some fine singing particularly from Harry van der Kamp's plummy and agile Pluto. This is without doubt the best version available of this work.

Additional recommendations ...

...Il Combattimento di Tancredi e Clorinda. Il ballo della ingrate. Altri canti d'amor. Volgendo il ciel. **Red Byrd; The Parley of Instruments / Peter Holman.** Hyperion Ⓕ CDA66475 (69 minutes: DDD: 9/92). 🎵

...Il Combattimento di Tancredi e Clorinda. Madrigals – Ardo, avvampo, mi struggo; Mentre vaga Angioletta ogn'anima; Con che soavita; O come sei gentile, caro augellino; Tu dormi? Ah crudo core; Eri già tutta mia; Quel sguardo sdegnosetto; Zefiro torna; Presso un fiume tranquillo. **Les Arts Florissants / William Christie.** Harmonia Mundi Ⓕ HMC90 1426 (59 minutes: DDD: 10/93).

...Il Combattimento di Tancredi e Clorinda. Madrigali guerrieri et amorosi[a] – Ogni amante e guerrier; Lamento della ninfa, "Non havea Febo ancora"; Mentre vaga Angioletta ogn'anima. [a]**Soloists; Vienna Concentus Musicus / Nikolaus Harnoncourt.** Teldec Das Alte Werk Ⓜ 4509-92181-2 (53 minutes: DDD: 2/94). 🎵

...Il ballo del ingrate. Lamento d'Arianna. **Soloists; Alfred Deller Consort.** Vanguard Classics Ⓜ 08.2030.71 (61 minutes: ADD: 4/94).

...Il Combattimento di Tancredi e Clorinda[a]. Il ballo delle ingrate[b]. Tirsi e Clori[c]. **Catherine Bott,** [b]**Tessa Bonner** (sops); [ac]**Andrew King,** [a]**John Mark Ainsley** (tens); [b]**Michael George** (bass); **New London Consort / Philip Pickett.** L'Oiseau-Lyre Ⓕ 440 637-2OH (70 minutes: DDD: 6/95). 🎵

New review

Monteverdi Il primo libro de madrigali. Settimo libro de madrigali – Tempro la cetra; Tirsi e Clori. **The Consort of Musicke / Anthony Rooley.** Virgin Classics Veritas Ⓕ VC5 45143-2 (57 minutes: DDD: 8/96). Texts and translations included.

This is a 'first' in more ways than one. To begin with, Monteverdi's *Primo libro* of 1587 is, even by the standards of the sixteenth century, a youthful publication. The composer was then just 19 years old. This collection, preceded by the precocious *Sacrae cantiunculae* of five years earlier, and the *Canzonette* of 1584, presents a detailed map of his absorption of contemporary madrigalian styles, and above all of his command of the lighter repertories that had become so popular in Italy during the 1580s. At the same time, there is a bittersweet quality about these pieces, for all that they are so episodically structured. This presages the later books when Monteverdi had moved to the Gonzaga court at Mantua, and had become acquainted with the more adventurous music then being written by composers both there and at Ferrara, inspired by the poetry of Guarini and Tasso. This is a 'first' also in the sense that it is the first recording to treat the book in its entirety. Few madrigals from the *Primo libro* have attracted other ensembles who, inevitably, have been drawn to the later madrigals, and above all to the contents of the last two books. Here The Consort of Musicke are on fine form, turning in sensitively wrought and carefully considered accounts, with perfect ensemble and tuning, and the textual details sensitively registered. The disc is rounded off with a number of pieces from the

Settimo libro, clearly more dramatic in conception and effect, which provide an instructive and dramatic contrast with the madrigals from the first book. The continuo grouping here provides a sturdy and richly textured accompaniment to the soloists, and both instrumentalists and vocalists apply discreet and appropriate ornamentation with style.

Monteverdi Il secondo libro de madrigali. **Concerto Italiano** (Rossana Bertini, sop; Rosa Dominguez, mez; Claudio Cavina, alto; Giuseppe Maletto, Sandro Naglia, tens; Marco Radaelli, bar; Daniele Carnovich, bass) / **Rinaldo Alessandrini.** Opus 111 ℗ OPS30-111 (58 minutes: DDD: 8/95). Texts and translations included. ✏ *Gramophone Editor's choice.* ⒼⒼ
Captivation begins with the very opening of the first piece on the disc, *Non si levav'anchor l'alba novella*, whose gently growing sense of the awakening dawn is itself a delicately drawn metaphor for transition from the urgent desire of the lovers' final embrace after a night of lovemaking to the gentle pain of their parting. The exquisite bittersweet pathos of the scene, whose every nuance and ambiguity is superbly caught in Alessandrini's vision of Monteverdi's music, sets both the standard and the tone for much of what follows in a number of important ways. First, with the exception of *S'andasse amor a caccia* and *Non giacinto o narcisi*, there are no examples here of the lighter *canzonetta*, such a prominent feature of the musical picture in Italy during the 1580s and a strong presence in the composer's own *Primo libro* of 1587. Secondly, and crucially, almost half the contents of the *Secondo libro* of three years later are settings of poetry by Torquato Tasso, whose *Gerusalemme liberata* was the most significant and influential epic to have been written in Italy since Ariosto's *Orlando furioso*, first published in the early decades of the century. Packed with strong images and bright colours, Tasso's verse was much drawn upon by many composers, including Monteverdi who continued to set it throughout his career. In Rinaldo Alessandrini and the Concerto Italiano, the intimate fusion of words and music which the composer embarks upon in this Second Book, and which was to remain a lifelong preoccupation, is delineated with charm, skill and profound understanding. More than any other musicians performing this repertory, the Concerto Italiano have already raised the interpretational stakes to a new level of subtlety and textual sophistication. For those already familiar with their considerable achievements this new record will not disappoint; for those yet to discover them it will be a revelation.

Monteverdi Il quarto libro de madrigali. **Concerto Italiano** / **Rinaldo Alessandrini.** Opus 111 ℗ OPS30-81 (62 minutes: DDD: 12/93). ✏ Texts and translations included. Recorded 1993. *Gramophone Award Winner 1994 Gramophono Editor's choice.* ⒼⒼ
Monteverdi's Fourth Book of Madrigals, first published in 1603, is a wide-ranging collection of pieces written during the previous ten years. Originally written for performance before a select audience by an ensemble of professional virtuoso singers, these madrigals, many of which are set to the sensuous, emotional and epigrammatic verses of Guarini and Tasso, demonstrate Monteverdi's seemingly inexhaustible ability to unite words and music in expressively effective ways. A complete and profound understanding of textual nuance is, then, central to any successful performance and here the Concerto Italiano begins with an obvious and considerable advantage over any group of non-Italians. Some of the finest madrigals in the Fourth Book are those involving direct speech, which allowed Monteverdi to make full use of the court virtuosi, famed for their abilities to combine clear declamation with dramatic gestures and subtle shadings of dynamics and speed. In general the Concerto Italiano have taken the combined messages of music and history to heart; these are performances infused with a flexible approach to tempo and strong projection of text geared to a determination to allow each detail of the words to speak with due force. The singing style itself is muscular without losing its ability to move into a gentler mood, the vocal balance good, the overall sound rich in its lower registers and bright and clear in the upper ones. At its best this record is simply without equal.

New review
Monteverdi L'Orfeo. **Laurence Dale** (ten) Orfeo; **Efrat Ben-Nun** (sop) Euridice, Music; **Jennifer Larmore** (mez) Messenger; **Andreas Scholl** (alto) Hope; **Paul Gérimon** (bass) Charon; **Bernarda Fink** (contr) Proserpina; **Harry Peeters** (bass) Pluto; **Nicolas Rivenq** (bar) Apollo; **Concerto Vocale** / **René Jacobs.** Harmonia Mundi ℗ HMC90 1553/4 (two discs: 120 minutes: DDD: 12/95). ✏ Notes, text and translation included. Recorded 1995.
It is clear right from the start, with the almost aggressive snarling brass and thudding drums of the opening Toccata, that René Jacobs's reading of *L'Orfeo* is a full-blooded one. The tone is set almost immediately by Efrat Ben-Nun, whose approach to the two roles that she sings is refreshingly direct and dramatic; her lines are sensitively shaped and phrased, and only the improvised embellishments to the part of Music, at times quite elaborate, could possibly cause any controversy. Among the other soloists Bernarda Fink delivers a convincingly urgent account of Proserpina's appeal at the opening of the Fourth Act, while Harry Peeters's Pluto presents his measured responses with an attractively lyrical authority. Charon's strangely angular lines, with their air of menace appropriate to one who spends time in contact with the Underworld, are expertly managed by Paul Gérimon, who shows himself to be a true Monteverdi bass. René Jacobs's approach to the thorny question of orchestration is robust. The score is notoriously difficult to interpret in this respect, often contradictory in its indications and in the end any solution can only be judged against some notion of what Monteverdi's

sound-world might have been. Jacobs's version was originally given at the Salzburg Festival in 1993, and his instrumental resources, based around three continuo instruments spatially separated, are more a reflection of the acoustical properties of a modern pit rather than those of the sort of room in the Ducal Palace in which *L'Orfeo* was first performed. There is nothing necessarily wrong with that, and it has to be said that the result is successful, discriminating and only rarely over-elaborate. In Laurence Dale in the title-role, Jacobs has found a powerful protagonist, a singer capable of negotiating convincingly the sudden changes of emotional state that characterize the part at some of its most critical moments. More to the point, "Possente spirto" is something of a *tour de force*, conveying the central conception of the power of song with true rhetorical understanding. This is a version of *L'Orfeo* to be reckoned with.

Additional recommendations ...

...**Soloists; Munich Capella Antiqua; Vienna Concentus Musicus / Nikolaus Harnoncourt.** Teldec Das Alte Werk Ⓜ 2292-42494-2 (two discs: 108 minutes: ADD: 7/85). ✍

...**Soloists; New London Consort / Philip Pickett.** L'Oiseau-Lyre Ⓕ 433 545-2OH2 (two discs: 108 minutes: DDD: 2/93). ✍

...**Soloists; Chiaroscuro; London Cornett and Sackbutt Ensemble / Theresa Caudle; London Baroque / Charles Medlam.** EMI Ⓜ CMS7 64947-2 (two discs: 104 minutes: DDD: 4/94). ✍   Ⓖ

Monteverdi Il Ritorno d'Ulisse in Patria. **Christoph Prégardien** (ten) Ulisse; **Bernarda Fink** (contr) Penelope; **Christina Högmann** (sop) Telemaco, Siren; **Martyn Hill** (ten) Eumete; **Jocelyne Taillon** (mez) Ericlea; **Dominique Visse** (alto) Pisandro, Human Fragility; **Mark Tucker** (ten) Anfinomo; **David Thomas** (bass) Antinoo; **Guy de Mey** (ten) Iro; **Faridah Subrata** (mez) Melanto; **Jörg Dürmüller** (ten) Eurimaco; **Lorraine Hunt** (sop) Minerva, Fortune; **Michael Schopper** (bass) Nettuno, Time; **Olivier Lallouette** (bass) Giove; **Claron McFadden** (sop) Giunone; **Martina Bovet** (sop) Siren, Love; **Concerto Vocale / René Jacobs.** Harmonia Mundi Ⓕ HMC90 1427/9 (three discs: 179 minutes: DDD: 3/93). ✍ Notes, text and translation included. Recorded 1992.

The only surviving manuscript score of this major musical drama, preserved in Vienna, presents an incomplete version of three acts. For this recording, René Jacobs has, within the spirit of seventeeth-century music-making, added more music by Monteverdi and others to expand the work to a satisfying five-act structure suggested by some surviving libretto. He has also considerably expanded the scoring, very much enlivening the instrumental palette that Monteverdi would have had available to him for his original production in Vienna in 1641. For some, this will rule this recording out of consideration. However, the result, even though weakly argued for in the insert-notes, is so powerful and effective that it is to be hoped that most would not be prey to such reservations. The extensive cast, led by Christoph Prégardien in the title role, is excellently chosen, not only for vocal quality but also for a convincing awareness of Monteverdi's idiom. Without that, the performance could have seemed tame, and that is nowhere better exemplified than in Act 1, Scene 7 where Ulysses awakes, wondering where he is and what is to happen to him. Prégardien here manages to convey as much depth of feeling as a Pagliaccio yet stays clearly within the bounds of Monteverdi's expressive style. The result is a *tour de force*, one of the many within this production. The adept instrumental contribution certainly helps to maintain variety throughout the work, and an accompaniment suited to the sentiments expressed by the vocalists is always possible with these resources. Ultimately, this production is very much one for our time. It presents a practical solution to the problems of performing music of another age – this realization was, in fact, for a 1992 Montpellier production – and one that turns out to be inspired, moving and totally compelling.

Additional recommendation ...

...**Soloists; Vienna Concentus Musicus / Nikolaus Harnoncourt.** Teldec Das Alte Werk Ⓜ 2292-42496-2 (three discs: 193 minutes: ADD). ✍

Further listening ...

...Vespro della Beata Vergine (ed. Parrott/Keyte). **Taverner Consort; Taverner Choir; Taverner Players / Andrew Parrott.** EMI CDS7 47078-8 (10/85). ✍   Ⓖ

...Vespro della Beata Vergine. *Coupled with* **Palestrina** Gaude, Barbara. **Soloists; The Sixteen; The Sixteen Orchestra / Harry Christophers.** Hyperion CDA66311/2 (4/89). ✍

...Vespro della Beata Vergine. Magnificat II a 6. **Soloists; Monteverdi Choir; London Oratory Junior Choir; His Majesties Sagbutts and Cornetts; English Baroque Soloists / John Eliot Gardiner.** Archiv Produktion 429 565-2AH2 (1/91). ✍   Ⓖ

...Vespro della Beata Vergine. Missa in illo tempore. **Soloists; Regensburg Cathedral Choir; Hamburg Wind Ensemble for Early Music / Hans-Martin Schneidt.** Archiv Produktion 447 719-2AX2 (4/96).

...Altri canti d'amor. Il Combattimento di Tancredi e Clorinda[abc]. Volgendo il ciel. Il ballo delle ingrate. **Red Byrd; The Parley of Instruments / Peter Holman.** Hyperion CDA66475 (9/92). ✍

...Madrigals, Book 5. **The Consort of Musicke / Anthony Rooley.** L'Oiseau-Lyre 410 291-2OH (11/89). ✍

...Su le penne de' venti[a]. Selva morale e spirituale – Nos. 1, 6, 7, 10, 16 and 21[b]. Messa et salmi, concertati, e parte da capella – Nos. 4 and 13[c]. [bc]**Emma Kirkby** (sop); [bc]**Ian Partridge** (ten); [ab]**David Thomas** (bass); **Parley of Instruments.** Hyperion CDA66021 (11/87). ✍   Ⓖ

...Selva morale e spirituale. **Lausanne Vocal and Instrumental Ensemble / Michel Corboz.** Erato 4509 98530-2.

…Motets – Dixit Dominus a 8; Confitebor tibi, Domine a 3; Beatus vir a 6; Laudate pueri a 5; Laudate Dominum a 5; Deus tuorum militum a 3; Magnificat a 8 (ed. Parrott); Jubilet tota civitas a 1; Salve Regina a 3. **Soloists; Taverner Consort Choir and Players / Andrew Parrott.** EMI CDC7 47016-2 (3/85). *

…Motets – Gloria in excelsis Deo a 7; Chi vol che m'innamori; O ciechi il tanto affaticar; Confitebor tibi, Domine a 5; E questa vita un lampo; Beatus vir a 6; Adoramus te, Christe a 6; Confitebor tibi, Domine a 1; Laudate Dominum a 1. **Les Arts Florissants / William Christie.** Harmonia Mundi HMC90 1250 (7/87). * Ⓖ

…Motets – Dixit Dominus; Laetanie della beata vergine; Laetatus sum; Lauda, Jerusalem; Laudate pueri, Dominum; Nisi Dominus; Beatus vir; Memento et omnis mansuetudinis; Adoramus te, Christe; Christe, adoramus te; Cantate Domino; Domine, ne in furore. **Trinity College Choir, Cambridge / Richard Marlow.** Conifer CDCF212 (11/92).

…L'Incoronazione di Poppea. **Soloists; Vienna Concentus Musicus / Nikolaus Harnoncourt.** Teldec Das Alte Werk 2292-42547-2 (9/86). *

…L'incoronazione di Poppea. **Soloists; English Baroque Soloists / John Eliot Gardiner.** Archiv Produktion 447 088-2AH3 (7/96).

Xavier Montsalvatge

Spanish 1912-

…Concierto breve[b]. Sinfonía de réquiem[a]. *Coupled with* **Rodrigo** Zarabanda lejana y villancico. [a]**Catalina Moncloa** (sop); [b]**Leonel Morales** (pf); **Madrid Symphony Orchestra / Antoni Ros Marbà.** Marco Polo 8 223753.

…Divagación. Three divertimentos on themes of forgotten composers. Si, à Mompou. Berceuse a la memoria de Oscar Esplá. Sonatine pour Yvette. *Coupled with* **Falla** Quatre pièces espagnoles. Fantasía bética. La vida breve – Spanish dance No. 1. Serenata andaluza. El Retablo de Maese Pedro – Sinfonia. **Alicia de Larrocha** (pf). RCA Victor Red Seal 09026 61389-2 (9/94). *See review under Falla; refer to the Index to Reviews.* Ⓖ Ⓖ

Thomas Moore

Irish 1779-1852

New review
T. Moore Irish Melodies – selections.
Bunting The Ancient Music of Ireland – selections. **Invocation** (Julia Gooding, Ana-María Rincón, sops; Rufus Müller, ten; Christopher Purves, bass; Frances Kelly, hp) **/ Timothy Roberts** (fp); **Giles Lewin** (vn); **Paula Chateauneuf** (gtr). Hyperion Ⓕ CDA66774 (70 minutes: DDD: 7/96). Texts included. Recorded 1995.

Immensely popular in the mid-nineteenth century, the ten volumes of Moore's *Irish Melodies* consisted of poems written to suit traditional airs collected and provided with simple accompaniments by Sir John Stevenson, on whose death in 1833 the task fell to Sir Henry Bishop. Some of the tunes (most famously "The Last Rose of Summer") remain part of common knowledge. Some may be more familiar in other connections: for instance, "The Pretty Girl Milking the Cows", also used in "The Song of O'Ruark", has been adapted for "Terence's Farewell to Kathleen", and Stanford used "Bob and Joan" (the air to "Fill the Bumper Fair") in his song "Trotting to the Fair". All have a simple, wholesome appeal, uncontrived and unmawkish. The performances admirably match the spirit of the originals. The voices are used in a good drawing-room style, with Rufus Müller's tenor particularly mellifluous in tone and easy in usage. The instruments do most to give the recital its special flavour. The bell-like sound of the metal-strung harp is most distinctive, and Giles Lewin's fiddle solos are delightful. Timothy Roberts, as pianist and director, earns gratitude, and recording and presentation are up to the company's customary high standard.

Estâvâo Morago

Portuguese c1575-after 1630

…De profundis. Versa est in luctum. Oculi mei. Laetentur caeli. Commissa mea. Montes Israel. Parce Domine. Revelabitur gloria Domini. Esto mihi. Exsurge. *Coupled with* **Melgás** Lamentationes. In Monte Oliveti. O vos omnes. Pia et dolorosa Mater. In ieiunio et fletu. Memento homo. Ecce ascendimus. Adiuva nos. Ille homo. Ego sum resurrectio. Magister volumus. Rex tremendae maiestatis. Recordare Virgo Mater. Salve Regina. **Pro Cantione Antiqua / Mark Brown** with **Robert Aldwinckle** (org), **Celia Harper** (hp), **Andrew Watts** (dulcian). Hyperion CDA66715 (11/94). *

Cristóbal de Morales

New review

Morales Mass for the feast of St Isidore of Seville. **Gabrieli Consort and Players / Paul McCreesh.**
Archiv Produktion Ⓕ 449 143-2AH (76 minutes: DDD: 8/96). Texts and translations included.
Gramophone Editor's record of the month.   ⒼⒼ
Morales Missa "Mille regretz". Emendemus in melius. **Guerrero** O Doctor optime.
Instrumental and organ works by Cabézon, Rogier, Guerrero, Gombert and Santa María.

It must have been difficult to find a suitable programme to follow the Gabrieli Consort's triumphant
recording of Victoria's Requiem (refer to the Index to Reviews), but with this disc of Morales's *Missa
Mille regretz* this has certainly been achieved, and with a logical connection to the previous release.
To begin at the beginning, expecting that the instrumental *canciones* by Guerrero and Rogier
(transcribed from the Lerma manuscript by Douglas Kirk) which open the disc would be merely
padding, it is delightful to hear playing of such sensitivity: one can understand why instrumentalists
were so prized in Spanish cathedrals at this time if they played like this. Morales's Mass itself
(performed, like the Victoria, by an all-male consort) is sung splendidly. There is a real feeling for the
work's direction (not easily discerned in music so seamlessly polyphonic as Morales) which, in
combination with the seductively rich sonority of the choir, make it a performance of genuine stature.
The only reservations concern the stodgy singing of the "Hosanna" which would surely benefit from
a lighter, more rhythmic approach. The plainchant is for the feast of St Isidore of Seville, taken from
unspecified sixteenth- and seventeenth-century sources by Robert Snow. It is sung (again as on the
Victoria disc) accompanied by a dulcian, as indeed is the polyphony, common Spanish practice of the
time. Instruments and choir come together only in Guerrero's motet, *O Doctor optime*, sung at the
Offertory, which is an object lesson in how to achieve blend and balance. Another *canción* by Rogier
acts as a recessional, and the disc closes with a short piece by Tomás de Santa María followed by a
magnificent performance of Morales's motet *Emendemus in melius*. This disc is a must!

Morales Missa "Queramus cum pastoribus". Andreas Christi famulus. Sancta Maria, succurre
miseris. Clamabat autem mulier. O sacrum convivium. Regina coeli.
Mouton Queramus cum pastoribus. **Westminster Cathedral Choir / James O'Donnell.** Hyperion
Ⓕ CDA66635 (65 minutes: DDD: 1/96). Texts and translations included. Recorded 1992.

In the *Missa Queramus cum pastoribus* the *divisi* basses of Westminster provide the ideal
counterweight to the warm forthright tone of the boys. James O'Donnell adopts generally unhurried
tempos that allow the counterpoint to unfold with seamless ease, but the choral sound is of such
intensity and focus that the ear is constantly arrested. At its most punchy, as in the "Osannas", this
could become wearing, but in the more sustained movements it is just what is needed to bring the
music alive. Parts of this recording have an almost tactile quality and these occur precisely where the
tactus is at its most spacious. Westminster Cathedral Choir supplement their Mass, preceded by the
Mouton motet on which it is based, with five marvellous motets by Morales, of which the simplest
but perhaps the most effective is *Sancta Maria, succurre miseris*. The *Regina coeli*, with its running
quaver figures, could have done with a little more lightness of touch, but what a thrilling sound this
choir makes when in full cry.

Further listening ...
...Missa Pro defunctis a 5. Officium defunctorum a 5. **La Capella Reial de Catalunya; Hespèrion XX
/ Jordi Savall.** Auvidis Astrée E8765. ✒   Ⓖ

Robert Moran

Suggested listening ...
...Points of Departure. *Coupled with* **Torke** Black and White – Charcoal. **Harbison** Remembering
Gatsby. **Larsen** Collage: Boogie. **Schiff** Stomp. **Kernis** New Era Dance. **J. Adams** The
Chairman Dances. **Bernstein** West Side Story – Mambo. **Agento** The Dream of Valentino –
Tango. **Daugherty** Desi. **Rouse** Bonham. **Baltimore Symphony Orchestra / David Zinman.** Argo
444 454-2ZH (7/95).
...Three Dances. *Coupled with* **D. Lang** Face so pale. **Volans** Kneeling Dance. **Reich** Four
Organs. **Piano Circus.** Argo 440 294-2ZH (1/94).
...Music from the Towers of the Moon. *Coupled with works by* **Byrne, Lurie** and **Torke** Balanescu
Quartet. Argo 436 565-2ZH (3/93). *See review in the Collections section; refer to the Index to
Reviews.*   Ⓖ

Paul Moravec

Suggested listening ...
...Violin Sonata. *Coupled with works by* **Corigliano, Glinsky, Pärt** and **Messiaen** Maria
Bachmann (vn); **Jon Klibonoff** (pf). Catalyst 09026 61824-2 (12/93). *See review under Corigliano;
refer to the Index to Reviews.*   Ⓖ

Federico Moreno Torroba

New review

Moreno Torroba Luisa Fernanda. **Verónica Villarroel** (sop) Luisa Fernanda; **Ana Rodrigo** (sop) Carolina; **Juan Pons** (bar) Vidal; **Plácido Domingo** (ten) Javier; **Isabel Monar** (mez) Rosita; **Rosa Maria Ysàs** (contr) Mariana; **Pedro Farrés** (bass-bar) Nogales; **Enrique R. del Portal** (ten) Aníbal; **Santiago S. Jericó** (bar) Savoyard; **Chorus of the Polytechnic University, Madrid; Madrid Symphony Orchestra / Antoni Ros Marbà.** Auvidis Valois Ⓟ V4759 (two discs: 81 minutes: DDD: 4/96). Notes, text and translation included. Recorded 1995.

Plácido Domingo (who is in splendid voice) confides that he had known every note of the score since childhood and that his parents, whom he heard over 100 times in the work, were regarded by Moreno Torroba as its ideal interpreters. He is in excellent company. Outstanding is the dark-voiced Juan Pons as the solid Extremaduran landowner Vidal, who is Javier's rival for the hand of the eponymous heroine. Wounded by Javier's flirtation with the Duchess Carolina (delightfully sung by Ana Rodrigo), Luisa Fernanda agrees to marry Vidal, who however, realizing her true feelings, magnanimously cedes her to the handsome officer. There is a sense of involvement by all in this performance, both in its gaiety and its pathos, and it is well produced – with a single exception; in the quarrel scene in Act 2, Vidal's demand that Javier and Luisa speak out instead of in asides to each other makes no sense if they have both in fact been singing at full voice. This is a fine score, exceptional in the zarzuela repertory for the freshness of its invention and the notable sophistication of its orchestration: several of its numbers, such as the "parasols' mazurka", have won a secure place in the hearts of the Spanish public. Especially in this extremely good performance, it can be cordially recommended – particularly to those who have yet to make the acquaintance of this special genre.

Further listening ...

...Aires de la Mancha. *Coupled with* **Rodrigo** Por tierras de Jerez. **Falla** Homenaje, "Le tombeau de Claude Debussy". **Turina** Guitar Sonata, Op. 61. **Sor** (ed. P. Romero) Fantasía in D minor. **Tárrega** (arr. P. Romero) Gran Jota. **Albéniz** (arr. C. Romero) Torre Bermeja, Op. 92 No. 12. **Granados** Tonadillas al estilo antiguo – No. 7, La maja de Goya[a]. **Mudarra** Tres libros – Fantasía que contrahaze la harpa en la manera de Ludovico[a]. **Guerau** Canarios. **Milán** El Maestro – Fantasia XVI. **C. Romero** Los Maestros. **Pepe Romero** (gtr). Philips 442 150-2PH (4/95).

Guillaume Morlaye

Suggested listening ...

...Works for Guitar and Lute – Livres de tabulature de leut[a]: Premier livre – Fantasie; Sans liberté. Deuxième livre – Fantasie; Gaillarde des Dieux. Troisième livre – Fantasie. Lute Pieces – Gaillarde piemontoise; Romaine. Livres de tabulature de Guiterne[b]: Premier livre – Gaillarde "Les cinq pas"; Bransle. Deuxième livre – Fantasie; Tin que tin tin. Quatrième livre – Si iay du bien; Bransle "Scaramella". **Federico Marincola** ([a]lte/[b]gtr). Pierre Verany PV794052 (2/95).

Thomas Morley

Suggested listening ...

...Funeral Sentences[gh] – I am the resurrection and the life; I know that my Redeemer liveth; We brought nothing into this world; Man that is born of a woman; In the midst of life. I heard a voice from Heaven[gh]. *Coupled with* **Tollett** The Queen's Farewell[h]. **Purcell** I was glad when they said unto me, Z19[gh]. Praise the Lord, O Jerusalem, Z46[gh]. Birthday Ode, "Now does the glorious day appear", Z332[cdefgh]. Stript of their green our groves appear, Z444[b]. Thou know'st Lord, Z58c[gh]. O dive custos Auriacae domus, Z504[abh]. The Queen's Epicedium, "Incassum, Lesbia, rogas", Z383[ah]. March and canzona in C minor, Z860[h]. **Blow** Whilst he abroad does like the sun[a]. The sullen years are past[d]. **Paisible** The Queen's Farewell[h]. [a]**Emma Kirkby**, [b]**Evelyn Tubb** (sops); [c]**Michael Chance** (alto); [d]**Ian Bostridge** (ten); [e]**Stephen Richardson** (bar); [f]**Simon Birchall** (bass); [g]**Westminster Abbey Choir**; [h]**New London Consort / Martin Neary.** Sony Classical Arc of Light SK66243 (3/95).

Jerome Moross

Suggested listening ...

...Symphony No. 1. The Last Judgement. Variations on a Waltz. **London Symphony Orchestra / JoAnn Falletta.** Koch International Classics 37188-2 (10/93).
...The Big Country – film score. **Philharmonia Orchestra / Tony Bremner.** Silva Screen FILMCD030 (5/89).
...The War Lord – original film soundtrack. Varèse Sarabande VSD5536.

Ennio Morricone
Italian 1928-

Suggested listening ...
...Essercizi per dieci archi. *Coupled with works by* **Rota, Malipiero** and **Porena** I Solisti Italiani.
Denon CO-78949 (10/95). *See review under Malipiero; refer to the Index to Reviews.*

Ignaz Moscheles
Bohemian 1794-1870

Suggested listening ...
...Grande Sonate in E flat major, Op. 47. *Coupled with* **Fibich** Sonata in B flat major, Op. 28.
Goetz Sonata in G minor, Op. 17. **Anthony Goldstone, Caroline Clemmow** (pf duet). Meridian
CDE84237 (7/93).

Alexandr Mosolov
USSR 1900-1973

New review
Mosolov Piano Sonatas – No. 2 in B minor, Op. 4, "From old notebooks"; No. 5 in D minor,
Op. 12. Two Nocturnes, Op. 15. **Herbert Henck** (pf). ECM New Series Ⓕ 449 460-2 (52 minutes:
DDD: 8/96).

The two best-known things about Alexandr Mosolov are that he composed *The Iron Foundry* in 1928,
a Russian-futurist equivalent of Honegger's *Pacific 231*, and that he fell from grace spectacularly in
the mid 1930s. Forced to abandon his modernist compositional style, he cooled his heels documenting
folk-song traditions in Turkmenistan, Kirgizia and the southern republics of Russia until his death in
total obscurity in 1973. His music was rediscovered shortly afterwards, and his name now carries the
resonance of a martyr. Prokofiev heard Mosolov's music on his visit to Russia in 1927 and declared
its composer the most interesting of the young talents he encountered, Shostakovich included. Sure
enough, echoes of Mosolov's intransigent chromaticism can be heard as late as Prokofiev's famous
wartime sonata trilogy, as they can too in both of Shostakovich's piano sonatas. The slow movement
of the Fifth Sonata even brings some extraordinary premonitions of Messiaen. Mosolov's piano
works from the 1920s are typical of the hothouse Scriabinism which several of his contemporaries
cultivated as a progressive line against the forces of proletarian and academic conformism. As so
often, mention of paths to and from a composer immediately suggests his limitations. There is
something constraining about the mystical vapours and contrived angularities of Mosolov's style;
certainly no whiff of humour or surprise or transcendence dispels them, as it does with Prokofiev or
Shostakovich. It's difficult to pass such judgements without sounding like a henchman of the Soviet
cultural thought-police; but it would simply be wishful thinking to claim that the interest of
Mosolov's creative powers is equal to that of his aesthetic stance and his political fate. Herbert Henck
offers imposing yet subtly shaded performances, doing ample justice to the intensity of the music. His
instrument is rich in tone and his touch is varied, without lacking an ounce of conviction.

Mihaly Mosonyi
Hungarian 1815-1870

Suggested listening ...
...Piano Concerto in E minor[a]. Symphony No. 1 in D major[b]. [a]**Klára Körmendi** (pf); [a]**Košice State
Philharmonic Orchestra;** [b]**Bratislava Radio Symphony Orchestra / Robert Stankovsky.** Marco Polo
8 223539 (4/95).
...Hungarian Children's World. 20 Studies for Development in the Performance of Hungarian
Music. **István Kassai** (pf). Marco Polo 8 223557 (9/94).
...Grand Duo in F minor. Three Colours of Burning Love. Festival Music. *Coupled with* **Liszt** (arr.
Mosonyi) Missa solemnis, S9. **István Kassai, Klära Körmendi** (pfs). Marco Polo 8.223558 (12/94).

Moritz Moszkowski
German 1854-1925

New review
Moszkowski Tarantella, Op. 27 No. 2. Barcarolle aus Hoffmans Erzählungen. Valse mignonne.
Characteristic Pieces, Op. 36 – No. 2, Reverie; No. 3, Expansion; No. 4, En Automne; No. 5, Air
de Ballet. Albumblatt, Op. 2. Four Pieces, Op. 68. Poème de Mai, Op. 67 No. 1. Serenata, Op. 15
No. 1. La Jongleuse, Op. 52 No. 4. Près de Berceau, Op. 58 No. 3. Chanson bohème de l'opéra
"Carmen" de Georges Bizet. **Seta Tanyel** (pf). Collins Classics Ⓕ 1412-2 (69 minutes: DDD:
10/95). Recorded 1993.

When Paderewski claimed "after Chopin he best understands how to write for the piano" he paid
Moszkowski a shrewd and ingenuous compliment. For although Moszkowski could be limited and
facile he wrote superbly for his chosen instrument, decking out one charming melody after another
with the most grateful and scintillating virtuosity. The opening *Tarantella*, with its bunny-hopping

tune, is gloriously raffish, "Expansion" beautifully illustrates its intriguing title and "Au Crepuscule" (from Op. 68) shows how Moszkowski often achieves not only a genuine pianistic sophistication but also rises above picture-postcard evocation. "Air de Ballet" summons its dancers smartly to the floor while *Albumblatt* contains roseate memories of both Field and Chopin. Seta Tanyel, a pianist with an unerring sense of keyboard graciousness, is perfectly attuned to her task, weaving her way through every intricacy with nonchalant expertise. She is hardly the sort to throw her hat to the winds, yet her virtues are as natural as they are affectionate and fluent. The recordings are of demonstration quality.

Further listening ...
...Piano Concerto in E major, Op. 59. *Coupled with* **Paderewski** Piano Concerto in A minor,
   Op. 17. **Piers Lane** (pf); **BBC Scottish Symphony Orchestra / Jerzy Maksymiuk.** Hyperion
   CDA66452 (2/92).

Jean-Joseph Mouret
French 1682-1738

Suggested listening ...
...Les amours de Ragonde. **Soloists; Les Musiciens du Louvre / Marc Minkowski.** Erato MusiFrance
   2292-45823-2 (12/92). ✐   Ⓖ
...Trumpet Concerto in D major. *Coupled with* **Hummel** Trumpet Concerto in E flat major.
   Arutiunian Trumpet Concerto. **A. Sandoval** (orch. Zelanti) Trumpet Concerto. **Arturo
   Sandoval** (tpt); **London Symphony Orchestra / Luis Haza.** GRP Classical GRK75002 (1/95).

Jean Mouton
French c1459-1522

Suggested listening ...
...Nesciens mater. Ave Maria virgo serena. Ave sanctissima Maria. O Maria piissima. Ave Maria
   gemma virginum. *Coupled with* **Josquin Desprez** Missa de beata virgine. **Theatre of Voices /
   Paul Hillier.** Harmonia Mundi HMU90 7136 (11/95). *See review under Josquin Desprez; refer to
   the Index to Reviews.*
...Queramus cum pastoribus. *Coupled with* **Morales** Missa "Queramus cum pastoribus". Andreas
   Christi famulus. Sancta Maria, succurre miseris. Clamabat autem mulier. O sacrum convivium.
   Regina cœli. **Westminster Cathedral Choir / James O'Donnell.** Hyperion CDA66635 (1/96). *See
   review under Morales; refer to the Index to Reviews.*

Leopold Mozart
German/Austrian 1719-1787

Suggested listening ...
...Trumpet Concerto in D major. *Coupled with* **Hummel** Trumpet Concerto in E flat major.
   M. Haydn Concertos for Trumpet and Strings – C major; D major. **J. Haydn** Trumpet
   Concerto in E flat major, HobVIIe/1. **Reinhold Friedrich** (tpt); **Academy of St Martin in the Fields
   / Sir Neville Marriner.** Capriccio 10 436 (6/93).

Wolfgang Amadeus Mozart
Austrian 1756-1791

Mozart Sinfonia concertante in E flat major, K364/K320*d*[a]. Concertone in C major for Two
   Violins, Oboe, Cello and Orchestra, K190/K186*E*[b]. **Cho-Liang Lin** (vn); **Jaime Laredo** ([b]vn/[a]va);
   English Chamber Orchestra / Raymond Leppard. Sony Classical Ⓕ SK47693 (60 minutes: DDD:
   6/92), Recorded 1991.
Cho-Liang Lin's Mozart concerto cycle has been one of the best to have appeared in recent years: he possesses great beauty of tone and purity of style. His accounts of the *Sinfonia concertante* in E flat and the *Concertone* in C, with Jaime Laredo and the English Chamber Orchestra under Raymond Leppard are performances of great quality. They possess all the spontaneity and warmth of live music-making with the perfection of the studio. Both Lin and Laredo bring to this music an aristocratic finesse and a magic that put the listener wholly under their spell. The slow movement of the *Sinfonia concertante* shows a marvellous interplay between these distinguished artists and has both depth and eloquence. Excellent, well-balanced recordings too.

Additional recommendations ...
...*As above.* **Itzhak Perlman** (vn); **Pinchas Zukerman** (va/vn); **Chaim Jouval** (ob); **Marcel Bergman**
   (vc); **Israel Philharmonic Orchestra / Zubin Mehta.** DG Ⓕ 415 486-2GH (60 minutes: DDD;
   12/85).
...Sinfonias concertante – K364/K320*d*; E flat major, KAnh9/C14.01/K297*b*[a]. **Todd Phillips** (vn);
   Maureen Gallagher (va); [a]**Stephen Taylor** (ob); [a]**David Singer** (cl); [a]**Steven Dibner** (bn); [a]**William
   Purvis** (hn); **Orpheus Chamber Orchestra.** DG Ⓕ 429 784-2GH (63 minutes: DDD; 4/91).
...Sinfonia concertante[c]. **Casadesus** Viola Concerto in B minor[a]. **Handel** Trio Sonata in E,
   HWV394 – Adagio[b] **Beethoven** Duo in E flat, WoO32[d]. [bc]**Albert Spalding** (vn); **William Primrose**

(va); [d]Emanuel Feuermann (vc); [b]André Benoist (pf); [a]chamber orchestra / Walter Goehr; [c]New Friends of Music Orchestra / Fritz Stiedry. Biddulph mono Ⓜ LAB088* (58 minutes: ADD: 9/94).

New review

Mozart Flute Concertos – No. 1 in G major, K313/K285c; No. 2 in C major, K314/K285d. Andante in C major, K315/K285e. Flute and Harp Concerto in C major, K299/K297c[a]. **Konrad Hünteler** (fl); [a]**Helga Storck** (hp); **Orchestra of the Eighteenth Century / Frans Brüggen.** Philips Ⓕ 442 148-2PH (78 minutes: DDD: 8/96).

Mozart's splendid flute music provides the strongest proof that his supposed dislike for the instrument was only to justify his failure to complete the famous commission from the Dutch amateur musician DeJean. In this issue, Konrad Hünteler and the Orchestra of the Eighteenth Century, directed by Frans Brüggen, shape the elegant lines of the G major Concerto with appropriate finesse, enhanced by an exceptionally attractive blend between Hünteler's c1720 Denner flute and the orchestra's pleasingly fine-grained sound. Susan Palma's eloquent alternative with the Orpheus Chamber Orchestra is one of the finest versions of this piece played on modern instruments; however, Hünteler's softer flute sound (atmospherically evoking the human voice) and the orchestra's more distinctive period instruments bring added dramatic intensity to this music. Likewise, Hünteler and the orchestra capture the direct charm of the C major *Andante*. To appease DeJean, Mozart offered an arrangement for flute of his Oboe Concerto. For this recording, the eighteenth-century flute parts have been compared with those for oboe for a more 'authentic' text, and the resulting exquisitely balanced account makes a wholly convincing masterpiece for the flute. Mozart was prompt with the commission for a flute and harp concerto for Comte de Guines, who "played the flute matchlessly" and whose daughter "played the harp magnificently". Hünteler and Storck, aided by the orchestra's subtle playing, highlight vividly the music's perfect match of technical and instrumental resources.

Additional recommendations ...

...No. 1. Andante. Flute and Harp Concerto. Bassoon Concerto. **Soloists; Academy of Ancient Music / Christopher Hogwood.** L'Oiseau-Lyre Ⓕ 417 622-2OH (74 minutes: DDD: 5/88).

...No. 1. Andante. Flute and Harp Concerto. **Irena Grafenauer** (fl); **Maria Graf** (hp); **Academy of St Martin in the Fields / Sir Neville Marriner.** Philips Ⓕ 422 339-2PH (58 minutes: DDD: 7/89).

...Nos. 1 and 2. Flute and Harp Concerto. Andante. Rondo in D major for Flute and Orchestra, K373 (arr. Galway). Divertimento in D major, K334 – Menuetto (arr. Galway). Serenade No. 13 in G major, K525, "Eine kleine Nachtmusik". **Marisa Robles** (hp); **Chamber Orchestra of Europe / James Galway** (fl). RCA Victor Red Seal Ⓕ RD87861 (two discs: 109 minutes: DDD: 7/89).

...No. 1. Andante. Flute and Harp Concerto[a]. **Susan Palma** (fl); [a]**Nancy Allen** (hp); **Orpheus Chamber Orchestra.** DG Ⓕ 427 677-2GH (58 minutes: DDD: 3/90).

Mozart Clarinet Concerto in A major, K622[a]. Clarinet Quintet in A major, K581[b]. **Thea King** (basset cl); [b]**Gabrieli String Quartet** (Kenneth Sillito, Brendan O'Reilly, vns; Ian Jewel, va; Keith Harvey, vc); [a]**English Chamber Orchestra / Jeffrey Tate.** Hyperion Ⓕ CDA66199 (64 minutes: DDD: 9/86). From A66199 (3/86).
Mozart Clarinet Concerto in A major, K622[a].
Spohr Clarinet Concerto No. 1 in C minor, Op. 26.
Weber Clarinet Concerto No. 2 in E flat major, J118. **Ernst Ottensamer** (cl/[a]basset cl); **Vienna Philharmonic Orchestra / Sir Colin Davis.** Philips Ⓕ 438 868-2PH (72 minutes: DDD: 6/94). Recorded 1992.

The two works on the Hyperion disc are representative of Mozart's clarinet writing at its most inspired; however, the instrument for which they were written differed in several respects from the modern clarinet, the most important being its extended bass range. Modern editions of both the Clarinet Concerto and the Quintet have adjusted the solo part to suit today's clarinets, but Thea King reverts as far as possible to the original texts, and her playing is both sensitive and intelligent. Jeffrey Tate and the ECO accompany with subtlety and discretion in the concerto, and the Gabrielli Quartet achieve a fine sense of rapport with King in the Quintet. Both recordings are clear and naturally balanced, with just enough distance between soloist and listener.

Ernst Ottensamer is a virtuoso with a real sense of style, that is to say a musician with an instinct for the difference between the contained romanticism of Mozart's concerto and the overt but differing romanticism of Spohr and Weber. His tone is rich and warm, with a beautiful depth in the lower registers of the basset clarinet in the Mozart, but also a brilliance that has a bit of a wicked glint to it in Weber's finale compared to the dancing ease of Mozart's. Mozart's *Adagio* is beautifully judged in tempo, a song with a seamless line, while Weber's *Romanza* is taken quite differently, like a wordless operatic aria. Spohr's short *Adagio,* a touchingly simple, direct piece, is charmingly delivered, and elsewhere Ottensamer listens with a careful ear to the woodwind and other lines which in this work intermingle so subtly: he is an old Philharmoniker who shows a proper attention to his colleagues. He is given close, sympathetic support by orchestra and conductor. One of Davis's particular qualities is his ear for the telling simplicities in Mozart, so that here a plain arpeggio springs to life with the clarinet's melody, or a set of repeated notes has a sense of direction towards a cadence. Anyone acquiring this record should enjoy taking special note of just how musically the 'accompaniment' is all done. The Vienna Philharmonic respond with complete understanding, and the recording engineers have missed nothing. Ottensamer's beautiful performances deserve no less.

Additional recommendations ...

...Clarinet Concerto[a]. Flute and Harp Concerto in C major, K299/K297*c*[b]. [a]**Emma Johnson** (cl); [b]**William Bennett** (fl); [b]**Osian Ellis** (hp); **English Chamber Orchestra / Raymond Leppard.** ASV Ⓕ CDDCA532 (54 minutes: DDD).

...Clarinet Concerto. Oboe Concerto in C major, K314/K285. **Antony Pay** (basset cl); **Michael Piguet** (ob); **Academy of Ancient Music / Christopher Hogwood** (fp/hpd). L'Oiseau-Lyre Ⓕ 414 339-2OH (47 minutes: DDD: 5/86). 🗲

...Clarinet Concerto. Oboe Concerto. **Jack Brymer** (cl); **Neil Black** (ob); **Academy of St Martin in the Fields / Sir Neville Marriner.** Philips Ⓕ 416 483-2PH (50 minutes: ADD: 10/88). Ⓖ

...Clarinet Quintet. Oboe Quartet. Horn Quintet. **Anthony Pay** (cl); **Neil Black** (ob); **Timothy Brown** (hn); **Academy of St Martin in the Fields Chamber Ensemble.** Philips Musica da Camera Ⓜ 422 833-2PC (69 minutes: ADD: 10/89).

...Clarinet Concerto[b]. Oboe Concerto[c]. Bassoon Concerto in B flat major, K191/[g]. Flute and Harp Concerto[ah]. Flute Concerto in G major, K313[a]. Horn Concertos – No. 1 in D major, K412/K386*b*[e]; No. 2 in E flat major, K417[f]; No. 3 in E flat major, K447[f]; No. 4 in E flat major, K495[e]. Andante for Flute and Orchestra in C major, K315/K284*e*. Sinfonia concertante in E flat major, KAnh9/K297*B*[bf]. [b]**Susan Palma** (fl); [b]**Stephen Taylor**, [c]**Randall Wolfgang** (obs); [b]**David Singer** (cl); [d]**Charles Neidich** (basset cl); [b]**Steven Dibner**, [g]**Frank Morelli** (bns); [c]**David Jolley**, [f]**William Purvis** (hns); [h]**Nancy Allen** (hp); **Orpheus Chamber Orchestra.** DG Ⓑ 431 665-2GX3 (three discs: 113 minutes: DDD: 7/91).

...Clarinet Concerto[a]. Oboe Concerto[b]. Bassoon Concerto[c]. [a]**Jacques Lancelot** (cl); [b]**Pierre Pierlot** (ob); [c]**Paul Hongne** (bn); [a]**English Chamber Orchestra / Jean-Pierre Rampal**; [b]**Jean-François Paillard Chamber Orchestra / Jean-François Paillard**; [c]**Bamberg Symphony Orchestra / Theodore Guschlbauer.** Erato Bonsai Ⓑ 2292-45937-2 (67 minutes: ADD: 6/93).

...Clarinet Concerto[a]. **Spohr** Clarinet Concerto No. 1[b]. **Weber** Clarinet Concerto No. 2[b]. **Gervase de Peyer** (cl); **London Symphony Orchestra /** [a]**Peter Maag**, [b]**Sir Colin Davis.** Decca Serenata Ⓜ 433 727-2DM (72 minutes: ADD: 7/93).

...Clarinet Concerto[a]. Bassoon Concerto[b]. Oboe Concerto[c]. [a]**Michele Carulli** (cl); [b]**Sergio Azzolini** (bn); [c]**Alessandro Baccini** (ob); **European Community Chamber Orchestra / Eivind Aadland.** IMP Classics Ⓜ PCD1054 (67 minutes: DDD: 12/93).

...Clarinet Quintet. Divertimento in D major, K136. **Thea King** (cl); **Aeolian Quartet.** Saga Classics Ⓜ EC3387-2 (51 minutes: ADD: 3/94).

...Clarinet Quintet. **Brahms** Clarinet Quintet in B minor, Op. 155. **Harold Wright** (cl); **Boston Symphony Chamber Players.** Philips Ⓕ 442 149-2PH (72 minutes: DDD: 9/94). *See review under Brahms; refer to the Index to Reviews.*

...Clarinet Concerto[a]; Oboe Concerto in C major, K314/K271*k*[b]; Bassoon Concerto[c]. [b]**John Mack** (ob); [a]**Franklin Cohen** (cl); [c]**David McGill** (bn); **Cleveland Orchestra / Christoph von Dohnányi.** Decca Ⓕ 443 176-2DH (69 minutes: DDD: 2/96).

New review

Mozart Horn Concertos – No. 1 in D major, K412, No. 2 in E flat major, K417; No. 3 in E flat major, K447; No. 4 in E flat major, K495. Rondos for Horn and Orchestra – D major, K514; E flat major, K371, "Concert Rondo". **Anthony Halstead** (hn); **Academy of Ancient Music / Christopher Hogwood.** L'Oiseau-Lyre Ⓕ 443 216-2OH (60 minutes: DDD: 8/95). 🗲 Recorded 1993. Ⓖ

Jokes, we all know, are best told with a straight face. These horn concertos, mostly written for Mozart's family friend Joseph Leutgeb, are full of humour: phrases turning in unexpected directions, surprising exploitations of the horn's special capacities and incapacities, and so on. A particular charm of this CD lies in Anthony Halstead's cool, understated performances, which are in the best traditions of British horn playing and in the variety in his approach to the different concertos: the broader phrasing and longer lines he brings to the more consciously expansive and symphonic K495, for example, the chamber musical playing in K447 (easily the finest of the concertos), and the gentle lyricism in K417. Everywhere, however, he excels with his shapely moulding of the music and his natural, musical way of rounding off phrases. Playing a period horn, valveless, of course, he 'makes' the notes that are not natural harmonics by deft movements of his hand in the bell. Sometimes this technique can lead to the chromatic notes differing sharply in quality from the open ones, but Halstead seems to have more control over tone quality than most natural horn players: the stopped notes sometimes slip in unobtrusively, but where he wants to use colour to stress them or pick them out, he does so very effectively, with the occasional touch of brassiness or muffling. Clearly his special skill allows him extra options. Some of the soft playing (the first movement development of K417, the lovely *Romance* of K447) is particularly appealing; and the rhythm of the hunting finales has a splendid spring – that of K495 is taken pretty speedily, almost, I should think, at the limit of safety. For the D major Concerto, the last of the four (the correct chronological order is K417, K495, K447, K412), we are given here both the Süssmayr version of the finale (the familiar one, written during the Easter after Mozart's death and including a Lamentation plainsong) and a very capable filling-out of Mozart's incomplete autograph version by John Humphries, who also supplies the skilful completion of the skeletal K371 *Rondo*. With the Academy of Ancient Music under Christopher Hogwood on lively form, with well pointed ritornellos and attentive accompaniments, this is a thoroughly enjoyable and musicianly account of these endearing works.

Additional recommendations ...

...Horn Concertos. Piano Quintet, K452. **Dennis Brain** (hn); **Philharmonia Orchestra / Herbert von Karajan.** EMI mono Ⓕ CDC5 55087-2* (77 minutes: ADD: 2/88). *Gramophone classical 100.*   ⒼⒼⒼ

...Horn Concertos. **English Chamber Orchestra / Barry Tuckwell** (hn). Decca Ⓕ 410 284-2DH (52 minutes: DDD: 9/85).

...Horn Concertos. Fragment for Horn and Orchestra in E major, K494*a*. **Anthony Halstead** (natural hn); **Hanover Band / Roy Goodman.** Nimbus Ⓕ NI5104 (55 minutes: DDD: 8/88). ✍

...Horn Concertos. Rondo (cptd. Tuckwell). **Barry Tuckwell** (hn); **Academy of St Martin in the Fields / Sir Neville Marriner.** EMI Studio Ⓜ CDM7 69569-2 (60 minutes: ADD: 1/89).

...Horn Concertos. Rondos – K371 (cptd. Greer); K514 (cptd. Jeurissen). **Lowell Greer** (natural hn); **Philharmonia Baroque Orchestra / Nicholas McGegan.** Harmonia Mundi Ⓕ HMU90 7012 (62 minutes: ADD: 3/89). ✍

...Horn Concertos. Rondo, K371 (rev. Levin). **Ab Koster** (hn); **Tafelmusik / Bruno Weil.** Sony Classical Vivarte Ⓕ SK53369 (64 minutes: DDD: 2/94). ✍   Ⓖ

...Nos. 1-4. Rondo, K371 (cptd. Tuckwell). **R. Strauss** Horn Concerto No. 1 in E flat major, Op. 11. **Radovan Vlatković** (hn); **English Chamber Orchestra / Jeffrey Tate.** EMI Studio Plus Ⓜ CDM7 64851-2 (76 minutes: DDD: 10/94).

...Nos. 1-4. Fragment for Horn and Orchestra in E major, K494*a* (ed. Humphries). Rondo, K371 (cptd. Humphries). **Swann** Ill wind[a]. **Eric Ruske** (hn); [a]**Richard Suart** (bass); **Scottish Chamber Orchestra / Sir Charles Mackerras.** Telarc Ⓕ CD80367 (64 minutes: DDD: 10/94).

Mozart Oboe Concerto in C major, K314/K285.
R. Strauss Oboe Concerto in D major. **Douglas Boyd** (ob); **Chamber Orchestra of Europe / Paavo Berglund.** ASV Ⓕ CDCOE808 (44 minutes: DDD: 11/87). From COE808 (7/87).
This coupling links two of the most delightful oboe concertos ever written. Mozart's sprightly and buoyant work invests the instrument with a chirpy, bird-like fleetness encouraging the interplay of lively rhythm and elegant poise. Boyd's reading of this evergreen work captures its freshness and spontaneity beautifully. If the Mozart portrays the sprightly side of the instrument's make-up the Strauss illustrates its languorous ease and tonal voluptuousness. Again Boyd allows himself the freedom and breadth he needs for his glowing interpretation; he handles the arching melodies of the opening movement and the witty staccato of the last with equal skill. Nicely recorded.

Additional recommendations ...

...Oboe Concerto. Clarinet Concerto in A major, K622. **Michael Piguet** (ob); **Antony Pay** (basset cl); **Academy of Ancient Music / Christopher Hogwood** (fp/hpd). L'Oiseau-Lyre Ⓕ 414 339-2OH (DDD: 5/86). ✍

...Oboe Concerto. Clarinet Concerto. **Neil Black** (ob); **Jack Brymer** (cl); **Academy of St Martin in the Fields / Sir Neville Marriner.** Philips Ⓕ 416 483-2PH (50 minutes: ADD: 10/88).

Mozart Piano Concertos – No. 1 in F major, K37; No. 2 in B flat major, K39; No. 3 in D major, K40; No. 4 in G major, K41 (all from SLS5031, 1/76); No. 5 in D major, K175 (ASD2484, 11/69); No. 6 in B flat major, K238 (ASD3032, 11/74); No. 8 in C major, K246 (ASD3033, 1/75); No. 9 in E flat major, K271, "Jeunehomme" (ASD2484); No. 11 in F major, K413/K387*a* (ASD2999, 9/74); No. 12 in A major, K414/K385*p* (ASD2956, 2/74); No. 13 in C major, K415/K387*b* (ASD2357, 4/68); No. 14 in E flat major, K449; No. 15 in B flat major, K450 (both ASD2434, 11/68); No. 16 in D major, K451 (ASD2999); No. 17 in G major, K453 (ASD2357); No. 18 in B flat major, K456 (ASD2887, 7/73); No. 19 in F major, K459 (ASD2956); No. 20 in D minor, K466 (ASD2318, 7/67); No. 21 in C major, K467 (ASD2465, 2/69); No. 22 in E flat major, K482 (ASD2838, 11/72); No. 23 in A major, K488 (ASD2318); No. 24 in C minor, K491 (ASD2887); No. 25 in C major, K503 (ASD3033); No. 26 in D major, K537, "Coronation" (ASD3032); No. 27 in B flat major, K595 (ASD2465). Rondo in D major, K382 (ASD2838).
English Chamber Orchestra / Daniel Barenboim (pf). EMI Ⓜ CZS7 62825-2 (ten discs: 661 minutes: ADD: 6/90). Recorded 1967-74.
Here are all 27 of Mozart's piano concertos plus the D major Rondo, K382, on ten medium-priced discs giving a total of 11 hours' listening. The skills of Daniel Barenboim and the English Chamber Orchestra in this repertory are well proven, and his account of these concertos, directed from the keyboard, is spacious and satisfying. This artist has always been a master of clean exposition and structure, and from the early concertos to the late masterpieces such as Nos. 21, 24 and 27 he is a sure guide with a full awareness of Mozart's inventive and expressive range. Sometimes one may feel that he allows a rather romantic self-indulgence to creep in, and in the more dramatic music (e.g. in the D minor and C minor Concertos) he may be thought to be too powerfully Beethovenian and, incidentally, he uses a Beethoven cadenza, as arranged by Edwin Fischer, in the first movement of the

first of these. Ideally, too, we might prefer a smaller body of strings than was used in these performances from the late 1960s and early 1970s. But these are only small reservations, given the high overall standard, and certainly this is a major achievement. The recordings sound well, with mellow piano tone and good balance.

Additional recommendations ...

...Nos. 1-27. **English Chamber Orchestra / Murray Perahia** (pf). Sony Classical Ⓜ SX12K46441 (12 discs: 608 minutes: ADD/DDD). *Gramophone classical 100.* ⊙⊙⊙

...Nos. 1-27. **Salzburg Mozarteum Orchestra / Géza Anda** (pf). DG Ⓜ 429 001-2GX10 (ten discs: 670 minutes: ADD: 6/90).

...Nos. 1-27. Concertos after J.C. Bach, K107 – D major; G major; E flat major. Double Piano Concertos – K242; K365/K316a. Concerto in F major for Three Pianos, K242, "Lodron". Rondos – K382; A major, K386. **Alfred Brendel, Imogen Cooper, Katia** and **Marielle Labèque** (pfs); **Ingrid Haebler** (fp); **Academy of St Martin in the Fields / Sir Neville Marriner; Berlin Philharmonic Orchestra / Semyon Bychkov** (pf); **Vienna Capella Academica / Eduard Melkus; Amsterdam Baroque Orchestra / Ton Koopman** (hpd). Philips Mozart Edition Ⓜ 422 507-2PME12 (12 discs: 755 minutes: ADD/DDD: 5/91).

...No. 13 in C major, K415/K387b; No. 24 in C minor, K491. **London Mozart Players / Howard Shelley** (pf). Chandos Ⓜ CHAN9326 (57 minutes: DDD: 1/95).

...Nos. 21-24, 26 and 27. Double Piano Concerto in E flat major, K365. **Robert Casadesus, Gaby Casadesus** (pfs); **Cleveland Orchestra, Columbia Symphony Orchestra / George Szell;** [a]**Philadelphia Orchestra / Eugene Ormandy.** Sony Legendary Interpretations Ⓜ SM3K46519* (three discs: 195 minutes: ADD: 9/91). ⊙⊙

...Nos. 21 and 25. **Stephen Kovacevich** (pf); **London Symphony Orchestra / Sir Colin Davis.** Philips Concert Classics Ⓑ 426 077-2PC (59 minutes: ADD: 2/90).

...No. 21. **Tchaikovsky** Piano Concerto No. 2 in G major, Op. 44. **Emil Gilels** (pf); **USSR Symphony Orchestra / Kyrill Kondrashin.** Mezhdunarodnaya Kniga Ⓕ MK417106* (63 minutes: AAD: 5/93).

...Nos. 21 and 26. **Robert Casadesus** (pf); **Cleveland Orchestra / George Szell.** Sony Classical Essential Classics Ⓑ SBK67178 (66 minutes: ADD: 5/96).

...Nos. 22 and 23. **Mitsuko Uchida** (pf); **English Chamber Orchestra / Jeffrey Tate.** Philips Insignia Ⓜ 434 164-2PM (60 minutes: DDD).

...Nos. 22 and 23. **Berlin Philharmonic Orchestra / Daniel Barenboim** (pf). Teldec Ⓕ 9031-75711-2 (63 minutes: DDD: 11/92).

...Nos. 22 and 24. **English Chamber Orchestra / Murray Perahia** (pf). CBS Masterworks Ⓕ SK42242 (67 minutes: DDD: 8/87). ⊙⊙⊙

...Nos. 23 and 24. **Wilhelm Kempff** (pf); **Bamberg Symphony Orchestra / Ferdinand Leitner.** DG Galleria Ⓜ 423 885-2GGA (56 minutes: ADD: 12/88). ⊙

...Nos. 23 and 24. **Jenö Jandó** (pf); **Concentus Hungaricus / Mátyás Antal.** Naxos Ⓢ 8 550204 (63 minutes: DDD: 10/90).

...Nos. 23 and 24. **Mitsuko Uchida** (pf); **English Chamber Orchestra / Jeffrey Tate.** Philips Solo Ⓜ 442 648-2PM (58 minutes: DDD: 7/95).

Mozart Piano Concertos – No. 9 in E flat major, K271, "Jeunehomme"; No. 12 in A major, K414/K385p. **Robert Levin** (fp); **Academy of Ancient Music / Christopher Hogwood.** L'Oiseau-Lyre Ⓕ 443 328-2OH (56 minutes: DDD: 7/94). 🗡

Mozart Piano Concertos – No. 9 in E flat major, K271, "Jeunehomme"; No. 12 in A major, K414/K385p. **Polish Chamber Orchestra / Fou Ts'ong** (pf). IMP Masters Ⓕ MCD84 (56 minutes: DDD: 9/94). Recorded 1986.

As Robert Levin starts with the one concerto in which the piano enters at once, K271, you don't have long to wait before you hear his crisp tone, precise articulation and spruce rhythms. His pianism is athletic, alert and very neatly pointed. He makes much of the quicksilver changes of mood in the music, emphasizing them by rhythmic means rather than stressing continuity of line. In the slow movement of K271 he shows a keen sensitivity to the ebb and flow of tension in the music; he has, and he conveys, a strong sense of the direction each phrase is taking, its destiny implicit from its beginning. The articulation in the finale is delightfully clear. The cadenzas are improvised, and (in the best sense) sound it. Levin's accompanying note argues that using new cadenzas preserves the spirit of spontaneity, especially as we all know the old ones backwards by now; that is true, although anyone who plays this disc repeatedly will soon know the new ones too. But the policy seems an intelligent one, and there is indeed a sense of something fresh and exciting about the performances. In K414, too, there is the same emphasis on characterizing the music strongly, even at the cost of rhythmic flow from time to time. In the slow movement he draws a beautifully clear line, with his very precise fingerwork; in the finale too the detail is carefully placed. Again, the cadenzas here follow Mozart's design but are his own. Levin's instrument is bright-toned and exceptionally even in quality, and he stands out sharply from the orchestra. The support offered by Christopher Hogwood and the AAM is lively and rhythmically alert, with some nicely shaped detail and a proper touch of swagger to the tuttis. Altogether a very impressive and enjoyable disc, with a happy air of adventure.

Fou Ts'ong, who directs the Polish Chamber Orchestra from the keyboard, gives an appealing and dramatically poised performance of the K271, in which careful phrasing, and balance between piano and orchestra are sensitively controlled. Felicitous observation of the score, and the dramatically effective contrast of nimble passagework and stylish elegance in the finale, in particular, compellingly achieve the music's remarkable expressive variety. In the A major Concerto, K414 Fou Ts'ong's purity of tone and clarity of style (sample the beautifully floated *cantabile* melody in the *Andante*) sound immensely attractive. Levin's readings, which benefit from delicate, transparent orchestral textures and greater emphasis on improvisation, are powerfully convincing. However, Fou Ts'ong's performances, which have plenty of vitality, will undoubtedly have a wide appeal for their dazzling brilliance and polished refinement.

Additional recommendations ...

...No. 9[a]. Piano Sonata No. 17 in B flat major, K570. **Beethoven** Piano Concerto No. 1 in C major, Op. 15[a]. **Walter Gieseking** (pf); [a]**Berlin State Opera Orchestra / Hans Rosbaud.** APR mono Ⓜ APR5511* (75 minutes: ADD).

...Nos. 9 and 21. **English Chamber Orchestra / Murray Perahia** (pf). CBS Masterworks Ⓕ SK34562 (59 minutes: DDD: 6/87).   ⓖⓖⓖ

...Nos. 9 and 17. **London Mozart Players / Howard Shelley** (pf). Chandos Ⓕ CHAN9068 (61 minutes: DDD: 11/92).

New review

Mozart Piano Concertos – No. 9 in E flat major, K271, "Jeunehomme"; No. 17 in G major, K453. **Cologne Concerto / Andreas Staier** (fp). Teldec Das Alte Werk Ⓕ 4509-98412-2 (61 minutes: DDD: 3/96). Recorded 1995. *Gramophone Editor's choice.*

Andreas Staier, speaking of the use of period instruments in his new and outstanding recording of Mozart's G major Concerto, K453, declares the piece has "more of the farmyard about it" that way – and he's absolutely right. From the braying and bellowing of the mid-phrase crescendos, the snuffling and snorting of the bassoons and the hee-hawing of the alternating loud and soft chords, Staier appears throughout it all the delighted child with a favourite picturebook. Conductorless, the string playing in the outer movements of both this and the E flat Concerto is buoyant with daring. The impetus and excitement of both dialogue and modulations in the slow movement of K453 is thrilling – and so is the dialogue within the orchestral writing itself in the finale. In K271 the music-making has a bracing immediacy as the almost percussive string playing cuts into the fortepiano's rhetoric, so imaginatively developed in Staier's fingers.

Additional recommendations ...

...Nos. 8 and 9. **Mitsuko Uchida** (pf); **English Chamber Orchestra / Jeffrey Tate.** Philips Ⓕ 432 086-2PH (55 minutes: DDD: 7/92).

...Nos. 9 and 17. **Berlin Philharmonic Orchestra / Daniel Barenboim** (pf). Teldec Ⓕ 9031-73128-2 (63 minutes: DDD: 11/92).

...Nos. 9 and 27. **Jenö Jandó** (pf); **Concentus Hungaricus / András Ligeti.** Naxos Ⓢ 8 550203 (58 minutes: DDD: 10/90).

...Nos. 17 and 18. **Jenö Jandó** (pf); **Concentus Hungaricus / Mátyás Antal.** Naxos Ⓢ 8 550205 (57 minutes: DDD: 10/90).

New review

Mozart Piano Concertos – No. 9 in E flat major, K271; No. 20 in D minor, K466. **Deutsche Kammerphilharmonie / Mikhail Pletnev.** Virgin Classics Ⓕ VC5 45130-2 (66 minutes: DDD: 6/96). Recorded 1995.

Pletnev's K271 raises no alarms, though he certainly enjoys the piano's early entry into some high-stepping *staccato* which draws a *marcato* string riposte. There's a degree of audacity, too, in the interplay of one hand with another, and both with the woodwind soloists in the development. The strings of the Deutsche Kammerphilharmonie play with restrained vibrato which makes the slow movement even darker, more austere; and Pletnev's probing rubato makes it more of a debate than an aria. The finale is a true *Presto*, made lucid by the rigour of its rhythmic definition, and constantly unpredictable in Pletnev's pacing of its cadenzas and of the perverse little minuet. The K466 is not too quick off the mark to deprive the snarling upbeats of their full fury, the syncopations from tugging hard, and the descending chords from digging deep. The deliberation of Pletnev's own playing can verge on the ponderous (especially when the recorded sound is on the constricted side); but then this is a deeply pondered performance of real *gravitas*, using Beethoven's cadenzas and making a weighty argument out of the *Rondo* right until its final return.

New review

Mozart Piano Concertos – No. 11 in F major, K413/K387*a*; No. 13 in C major, K415/K387*b*. Rondo in A major, K386. **Robert Levin** (fp); **Academy of Ancient Music / Christopher Hogwood.** L'Oiseau-Lyre Ⓕ 444 571-2OH (57 minutes: DDD: 9/95). ✐ Recorded 1994.

The first impression, at the beginning of the F major Concerto, is of a performance very much in chamber-music style: a neat, compact body of strings, playing attentively in crisp and springy rhythms, with the faint clang of the fortepiano continuo in the background adding sharpness and definition. Robert Levin performs this concerto, one of the less familiar among Mozart's, most beautifully and unassumingly. He draws very precise articulation and sweet tone from the instrument; there is a delightful sense of the brilliance arising naturally and spontaneously rather than as self-conscious virtuosity. Although chamber musical in approach, the performance has its moments of drama too, with hints of the opera house in its characterization and its surprises. Mozart wrote cadenzas for these concertos, but Levin, true to the practice of the time, improvises his own. The music of K415 is thematically less interesting than the other two in the set and possibly the ideas cannot quite support the larger canvas on which Mozart was evidently trying to work. Some of the bravura material seems just a shade empty. Still, this is a very sympathetic reading, with a really splendid improvised cadenza, and again there is some lovely melodic shaping in the slow movement. Mozart used material from his original slow movement draft within the finale, and these sections are handled here with considerable drama. Levin, of course, adds a certain amount of decoration to the lines throughout both concertos, especially in repeated material, and does so with impeccable taste and style and at exactly the points where it seems to be needed. The lone *Rondo*, K386, a charming piece, completes this distinguished disc.

Mozart Piano Concertos – No. 12 in A major, K414/K385*p*; No. 19 in F major, K459. **London Mozart Players / Howard Shelley** (pf). Chandos Ⓕ CHAN9256 (52 minutes: DDD: 6/94). Recorded 1993.

These are clear and stylish readings. The playing of both the Shelley and the London Mozart Players is assured, relaxed and unfailingly enjoyable, allowing the music to unfold very naturally. Shelley demonstrates his fine judgement of tempo, and textures are also well served; the recording gives quite a bold sound to his modern piano, but its overall immediacy and warmth are not excessive and the balance is just right. Phrasing is another area deserving praise: Shelley and his expert team manage to shape the music gracefully without falling into the slightly mannered delivery which can affect other artists in this repertory. Finally, cadenzas have the right balance of freedom and formality. Perhaps the two 'slow' movements here – the quotes are because that of K414 is an *Andante* and K459's is an *Allegretto* – are richer in style than will suit some tastes: they do not sound authentic in period-performance terms, but then this is another kind of performance and perfectly convincing. The recordings are of the high quality we have come to expect from the Chandos team.

Additional recommendations ...

...Nos. 12 and 14. **Louis Lortie** (pf); **I Musici de Monteal / Yuli Turovsky.** Chandos Ⓕ CHAN8455 (48 minutes: DDD: 1/87).

...Nos. 12 and 15. **Mozartian Players / Steven Lubin** (fp). Arabesque Ⓕ Z6552 (48 minutes: DDD: 3/87). ✒

...Nos. 19 and 27. **András Schiff** (pf); **Salzburg Mozarteum Camerata Academica / Sándor Végh.** Decca Ⓕ 421 259-2DH (59 minutes: DDD: 3/89).

...Nos. 14, 15, 19, 21, 26 and 27. Double Piano Concerto in E flat major, K365 (with Imogen Cooper, pf). Piano Sonatas – No. 8 in A minor, K310; No. 11 in A major, K331; No. 13 in B flat major, K333; No. 14 in C minor, K457. Fantasia in C minor, K475. Rondo in A minor, K511. Adagio in B minor, K540. **Haydn** Piano Sonatas – E flat major, HobXVI/49; C major, HobXVI/50; E flat major, HobXVI/52. Variations in F minor, HobXVII/6. **Alfred Brendel** (pf); **Academy of St Martin in the Fields / Sir Neville Marriner.** Philips Ⓜ 446 921-2PM5 (five discs: 369 minutes: ADD/DDD: 2/96).

New review

Mozart Piano Concertos – No. 15 in B flat major, K450; No. 16 in D major, K451. **English Chamber Orchestra / Murray Perahia** (pf). Sony Classical Ⓕ SK37824 (50 minutes: DDD). *Gramophone Award Winner 1984.*   ⒼⒼⒼ

It is difficult to do justice to interpretations of this calibre in a short review: Perahia's delicious shaping of even the longest and most elaborate phrases, his unfailingly clear and arresting articulation, and his delicacy and refinement of tone are without parallel. Perahia's attention is, moreover, by no means restricted to the solo parts: even the tiniest details of the orchestral writing are subtly characterized, and the piano and orchestra take on the character of a dialogue sometimes poignant, often witty or sparklingly humorous. The two works are admirably contrasted: the Fifteenth is on the whole light and high-spirited, while the first movement of the Sixteenth is almost Beethovenian in its grandeur and purposefulness, and both concertos have typically beautiful slow movements. Recordings are superb: an overly attentive microphone could have done irreparable damage to Perahia's legato, but here the distance is expertly judged and the soloist/orchestra balance is exemplary.

New review

Mozart Piano Concertos – No. 17 in G major, K453[a]; No. 21 in C major, K467. **Maria-João Pires** (pf); **Chamber Orchestra of Europe / Claudio Abbado.** DG Ⓕ 439 941-2GH (58 minutes: DDD: 2/96). Recorded [a]live in 1993. *Gramophone Editor's choice.*

It is clear from the opening of the G major Concerto that Claudio Abbado and the Chamber Orchestra of Europe were on good form at this concert in Italy. It springs along, yet unhastily, and the orchestral sound, while full-bodied, has none of the heaviness that detracts from good Mozartian style. Playing what sounds like a modern piano of unusual tonal crispness, Maria-João Pires also satisfies, with shapely phrasing and lovely sonorities, and this whole first movement proceeds with both a keen sense of purpose and unmannered grace, the exchanges of the development section being delightfully done. The cadenza here is Mozart's own and, of course, a model of what cadenzas in his concertos should be but often are not, in other words suiting the music and not overlong. After these unalloyed pleasures, the touching *Andante* is no less satisfying, elegantly sculptured and with marvellous woodwind playing. The playful, variation-form finale is again perfectly judged, and indeed the performance of the whole concerto offers truly outstanding Mozart playing, among the best on disc and unquestionably in the Perahia class. The recording is worthy of it: beautifully balanced and clear for one taken live while also being refreshingly free of audience noise and applause. The C major Concerto is also excellent, the first movement strong yet not pompous, with all concerned thankfully never forgetting that this is Mozart and not Beethoven. The famous 'Elvira Madigan' slow movement is not at all romanticized but admirably poised, and the finale springs along.

Mozart Piano Concertos. **English Chamber Orchestra / Murray Perahia** (pf). CBS Masterworks
Ⓕ SK42241 and SK42243 (two discs, oas: 63 and 70 minutes: ADD/DDD: 9/87). Items marked [a]
from 76651 (4/78), [b] 76731 (5/80), [c] 76481 (5/76).
SK42241 – No. 20 in D minor, K466[a]; No. 27 in B flat major, K595[b]. *SK42243* – No. 11 in
F major, K413[a]; No. 12 in A major, K414/K385p[b]; No. 14 in E flat major, K449[c].   ⒼⒼⒼ
These discs happily epitomize some of the best qualities of the complete Perahia/ECO set. Always intelligent, always sensitive to both the overt and less obvious nuances of this music, Perahia is firstly a true pianist, never forcing the instrument beyond its limits in order to express the ideas, always maintaining a well-projected singing touch. The superb ECO reflect his integrity and empathy without having to follow slavishly every detail of his articulation or phrasing. K414 and K413 are charming and typically novel for their time, but do not break new ground in quite the way that K449 does. Here, Mozart's success in the theatre may have suggested a more dramatic presentation and working of ideas for this instrumental genre. K595 is a work pervaded by a serenity of acceptance that underlies its wistfulness. Mozart had less than a year to live, and the mounting depression of his life had already worn him down, yet there is still a sort of quiet joy in this music. The vast range of styles, emotions, and forms that these few works encompass are evocatively celebrated in these performances, and admirably captured in civilized recordings.

Additional recommendations ...

...Nos. 12 and 20. Rondo in D major, K382. **Evgeni Kissin** (pf); **Moscow Virtuosi / Vladimir
Spivakov.** RCA Victor Red Seal Ⓕ 09026 60400-2 (67 minutes: DDD: 2/93).
...Nos. 13 and 20. **Jenö Jandó** (pf); **Concentus Hungaricus / András Ligeti.** Naxos Ⓢ 8 550201
(56 minutes: DDD: 10/90).
...Nos. 12, 14 and 21. **Jenö Jandó** (pf); **Concentus Hungaricus / András Ligeti.** Naxos Ⓢ 8 550202
(71 minutes: DDD: 10/90).
...Nos. 14 and 27. **London Mozart Players / Howard Shelley** (pf). Chandos Ⓕ CHAN9137
(55 minutes: DDD: 6/93).
...Nos. 14-16. **English Chamber Orchestra / Daniel Barenboim** (pf). EMI Studio Ⓜ CDM7 69124-2
(74 minutes: ADD: 12/88).
...Nos. 20, 21, 23 and 27. Piano Sonata No. 18 in D major, K576. Rondo in A minor, K511.
Philharmonia Orchestra / Vladimir Ashkenazy (pf). Double Decca Ⓜ 436 383-2DF2 (two discs:
149 minutes: ADD).   Ⓖ
...Nos. 20 and 21. **Mitsuko Uchida** (pf); **English Chamber Orchestra / Jeffrey Tate.** Philips Ⓕ 416
381-2PH (62 minutes: DDD: 7/86).
...Nos. 20 and 27. **Sir Clifford Curzon** (pf); **English Chamber Orchestra / Benjamin Britten.** Decca
Ⓕ 417 288-2DH (65 minutes: ADD: 10/86).
...Nos. 20 and 21. **Berlin Philharmonic Orchestra / Daniel Barenboim** (pf). Teldec Ⓕ 9031-75710-2
(61 minutes: DDD: 11/92).
...Nos. 26 and 27. **Mitsuko Uchida** (pf); **English Chamber Orchestra / Jeffrey Tate.** Philips
Ⓕ 420 951-2PH (65 minutes: DDD: 11/88).
...No. 27. Double Piano Concerto in E flat major, K365/K316a[a]. **Emil Gilels, [a]Elena Gilels** (pfs);
Vienna Philharmonic Orchestra / Karl Böhm. DG Galleria Ⓜ 419 059-2GGA (59 minutes: ADD:
1/87).   Ⓖ

Mozart Piano Concerto No. 20 in D minor, K466[a]. Symphony No. 38 in D major, K504,
"Prague"[b]. Serenade No. 13 in G major, K525, "Eine kleine Nachtmusik"[c]. Three German
Dances, K605[d]. **Vienna Philharmonic Orchestra / Bruno Walter** ([a]pf). Pearl mono
Ⓜ GEMMCD9940* (72 minutes: AAD: 3/94). Item marked [a] from HMV DB3273/6 (10/38),
[b]DB3112/14, [c]DB3075/6, [d]HMV DA1570, 9/37).
Bruno Walter was an accomplished pianist, and his solo work in Mozart's D minor Concerto is full of personality. The first movement cadenza by Reinecke is boring, but otherwise there's much to enjoy in this romantic and subjective interpretation. The VPO plays beautifully both here and in the other Mozart works. The *Prague* Symphony has lots of muscle as well as grace and elegance. If a romantic approach to *Eine kleine Nachtmusik* is sought by the listener then Walter's affectionate interpretations will surely give great pleasure, and the little *German Dances* are charmingly played. Pearl have used commercial pressings for their issue, and a certain amount of surface noise is present. Colin Attwell has reproduced the original sound-quality very faithfully and straightforwardly, and his transfers are much kinder to the ears than most others from this period.

Additional recommendation ...
...Eine kleine Nachtmusik. *Coupled with works by* **Bach, Schubert, Berlioz** and **Borodin**. Louis Zimmerman, Ferdinand Hellmann (vns); Concertgebouw Orchestra / Willem Mengelberg. Pearl mono Ⓜ GEMMCD9154* (76 minutes: ADD: 3/96).

Mozart Piano Concerto No. 22 in E flat major, K482[a]. Rondo in A minor, K511.
Beethoven Piano Sonata No. 5 in C minor, Op. 10 No. 1. **Till Fellner** (pf); [a]**Lausanne Chamber Orchestra / Uri Segal.** Claves Ⓕ CD50-9328 (62 minutes: DDD: 9/94). Recorded live in 1993.
This is an impressive musical curriculum vitae for the young Viennese pianist, Till Fellner, first prize-winner at the Clara Haskil Competition in Vevey in 1993, where this was recorded. His Mozart Piano Concerto No. 22 shows open-faced, boyish playing, with a clarity of articulation and imaginative vigour reminiscent of the young Murray Perahia. Phrasing is songful, delicately shaded, and the second movement's variations are quietly but fearlessly explorative. The sudden pools of dark sobriety which appear among the gleeful episodes of the *Rondo* finale become, in Fellner's hands, potent echoes of the Countess's music in *Figaro*, a close contemporary of this work. Fellner plays a sturdy A minor Rondo, the left hand deliberate and robust – possibly an imprint of his lessons with Brendel? Beethoven's C minor Sonata (Op. 10 No. 1) is no less strong-fingered, its first movement quick to ignite, but just as ready to stand back and reflect. The *Andante* is expansive and clear-sighted, with a wonderfully warm *pianissimo* ending, and the finale shows Fellner's quicksilver responses of both mind and muscle.

Additional recommendations ...
...Rondo, K511. **Chopin** Nocturnes, Op. 37 – No. 1 in G minor; No. 2 in G major. Polonaise in F sharp minor, Op. 44. Berceuse in D flat major, Op. 57. Etude in G flat major, Op. 10 No. 5. **Ravel** Gaspard de la nuit. **Konstantin Lifschitz** (pf). Denon Ⓕ CO-78908 (66 minutes: DDD: 12/94).
...Nos. 21 and 22. **Homero Francesch** (pf); **Nice Philharmonic Orchestra / Klaus Weise.** Kontrapunkt Ⓕ 32189 (60 minutes: DDD: 2/95).
...Nos. 21 and 22. **London Mozart Players / Howard Shelley** (pf). Chandos Ⓕ CHAN9404 (63 minutes: DDD: 2/96).

Mozart Violin Concertos[b] – No. 1 in B flat major, K207; No. 2 in D major, K211; No. 3 in G major, K216; No. 4 in D major, K218 (all from 6706 011-1/4, 10/70); No. 5 in A major, K219; D major, K271a/K271i (both from SAL3588, 2/67). Rondos[b] – B flat major, K269/K261a; C major, K373 (0707 011-1/4). Concertone in C major, K190/K186E (6707 011-1/4)[abce]. Adagio in E major, K261 (6500 036, 1/72)[b]. Sinfonia concertante in E flat major, K364/K320d[dh]. Piano and Violin Concerto in D major, KAnh56/K315f[gh]. Sinfonia concertante in A major, KAnh104 /K320e[dfh] (all new to UK). [a]**Richard Morgan** (ob); [b]**Henryk Szeryng**, [c]**Gérard Poulet** (vns); [d]**Nobuko Imai** (va); [e]**Norman Jones**, [f]**Stephen Orton** (vcs); [g]**Howard Shelley** (pf); [b]**New Philharmonia / Sir Alexander Gibson;** [h]**Academy of St Martin in the Fields / Iona Brown** (vn). Philips Mozart Edition Ⓜ 422 508-2PME4 (four discs: 265 minutes: ADD/DDD: 6/91). Recorded 1966-70.   ⒼⒼ
Leaving aside works of doubtful authenticity, there are five Mozart violin concertos. They belong to his late teenage years in Salzburg and were composed in 1775. They have always been overshadowed by the piano concertos which, of course, are not only five times as numerous but also span the composer's whole career and include many mature masterpieces. While this is understandable, it would be a pity to miss out on these violin works which are surprisingly refreshing, youthful works of great charm. They agreeably reflect their creator's love and understanding of an instrument which he himself played more than capably. It is believed that his father Leopold, who was an authority on violin playing as well as a performer, may have encouraged him to compose them and then play them himself. It seems likely that Mozart did play them, at least for his own pleasure. The concertos have much in common with Mozart's cassations, divertimentos and serenades, which also highlight the solo violin and have other concerto-like elements in them. But their lightweight means of expression in no way diminishes their long-term appeal, for Mozart filled them to the brim with wonderful ideas. Henryk Szeryng has a relaxed way with these works and the orchestral contribution from the New Philharmonia under Sir Alexander Gibson is alert yet sensitive. Szeryng's tone is unfailingly beautiful with a sweetness that is greatly appealing. His evident affection for these works makes for pleasing listening and the vivid and witty 'Turkish' episode in the finale of No. 5 has great spirit. This disc also includes the 'doubtful' but agreeable solo Concerto in D major, K271a, together with a rather laid-back account of the *Sinfonia concertante* with Iona Brown and Nobuko Imai as the soloists (beautifully matched and well blended). In addition we have the reconstructions of the incomplete projected Concerto for piano and violin and the single-movement *Sinfonia concertante* in A major for string trio and orchestra. The quality of the recordings is quite satisfying and at mid-price this compilation is very good value indeed.

Additional recommendations ...
...Nos. 1 and 2. Rondo, K269/K261a. **Jean-Jacques Kantorow** (vn); **Netherlands Chamber Orchestra / Leopold Hager.** Denon Ⓕ C37-7506 (47 minutes: DDD: 12/86).
...Nos. 3 and 5. Adagio, K261. **Cho-Liang Lin** (vn); **English Chamber Orchestra / Raymond Leppard.** CBS Masterworks Ⓕ SK42364 (62 minutes: DDD: 12/87). *Selected by Sounds in Retrospect.*

…Nos. 3-5. **Christian Altenburger** (vn); **German Bach Soloists / Helmut Winscherman.** LaserLight
Ⓑ 15 525 (75 minutes: DDD: 5/90).

…No. 1. Adagio, K261. Sinfonia concertante in E flat major, K364/K320d[a]. **Anne-Sophie Mutter**
(vn); [a]**Bruno Giuranna** (va); **Academy of St Martin in the Fields / Sir Neville Marriner.** EMI
Ⓕ CDC7 54302-2 (59 minutes: DDD: 1/92).

…Nos. 1-5. **Andrea Cappelletti** (vn); **European Community Chamber Orchestra / Eivind Aaland.**
Koch Schwann Musica Mundi Ⓕ 311164 (two discs: 123 minutes: DDD: 5/92).

…Nos. 2 and 4. Sinfonia concertante, K364/K320d[a]. [a]**Josef Suk** (vn); **Academy of St Martin in the
Fields / Iona Brown** (vn). Argo Ⓜ 433 171-2DM (74 minutes: ADD/DDD: 5/92).

…Nos. 1-5[a]. Rondo, K373[b]. Adagio, K261[b]. Sinfonia concertante, K364/K320d[c]. **Arthur Grumiaux**
(vn). [c]**Arrigo Pelliccia** (va); [a]**London Symphony Orchestra / Sir Colin Davis;** [b]**New Philharmonia
Orchestra / Raymond Leppard.** Philips Duo Ⓜ 438 323-2PM2 (two discs: 153 minutes: ADD: 9/93).

…Nos. 3 and 5. Sinfonia concertante, K364/K320d[a]. **Stephanie Chase** (vn); [a]**Roger Chase** (va);
Hanover Band / Roy Goodman. Cala Ⓜ CACD1014 (two discs: 82 minutes: DDD: 12/93). ✐

…Violin Concerto No. 5[b]. **Mendelssohn** Violin Concerto in E minor, Op. 64[a]. **Vieuxtemps**
Violin Concerto No. 5 in A minor, Op. 37[c]. **Jascha Heifetz** (vn); [a]**Royal Philharmonic Orchestra /
Sir Thomas Beecham;** [b]**London Philharmonic Orchestra / Sir John Barbirolli;** [c]**London Symphony
Orchestra / Sir Malcolm Sargent.** EMI Références mono Ⓜ CDH5 65191-2* (69 minutes: ADD:
10/94).

…Nos. 1-5. Sinfonia concertante in E flat major, K364/K320d[a]. [a]**Rudolf Barshai** (va); **Bath Festival
Orchestra / Yehudi Menuhin** (vn). EMI Seraphim Ⓢ CES5 68530-2 (two discs: 172 minutes: ADD:
1/96).

Mozart Violin Concertos – No. 1 in B flat major, K207; No. 2 in D major, K211; No. 5 in A major,
K219. **Orchestra of the Age of Enlightenment / Monica Huggett** (vn). Virgin Classics Veritas
Ⓕ VC5 45010-2 (77 minutes: DDD: 9/94). ✐ Recorded 1991.

These fresh, appealing performances stand up well in an awesomely crowded field. With her gut-
strung Amati, Monica Huggett does not, of course, rival modern-instrument virtuosos like
Grumiaux, Szeryng and Perlman in brilliance and dynamic range. But these concertos gain much
from her sweet, slender tone, her light, buoyant articulation and her beautiful control of colour in
piano dynamics. The passagework in the opening movements of the first two concertos can often seem
tedious in high-powered traditional performances; but the lighter period bow and Huggett's deft
touches of timing and shading invariably lend wit and point to Mozart's sequences of triplets and
semiquavers. The finales of both these concertos are delightfully lithe and airy, while the closing minuet
of No. 5 is unusually delicate – though there is plenty of gusto in the A minor 'Turkish' episode (from
3'59"). In the three slow movements other performances may be more overtly expressive, freer with
rubato; but Huggett's purity and poise, her subtle graduations of vibrato and her gentle eloquence of
phrase are very persuasive. These performances share with the rival period readings from Simon
Standage (listed below) a keen feeling for the music's dance rhythms and a sure sense of style in
cadenzas (aptly brief) and ornamentation. The orchestral contribution in both versions, too, is crisp,
transparent and nicely detailed. Standage is generally the more assertive player, brighter of tone,
sharper of attack but lacking Huggett's tenderness and imagination. Huggett, too, has the edge in
purity of intonation. Clear, warm sound, with a natural balance between soloist and orchestra.

Additional recommendation ...

…Nos. 1-5. Adagio, K261. Rondos – K269/K261a; K373. **Simon Standage** (vn); **Academy of Ancient
Music / Christopher Hogwood.** L'Oiseau-Lyre Ⓕ 433 045-2OH2 (two discs: 128 minutes: DDD:
4/92). ✐

New review
Mozart Violin Concerto No. 3 in G major, K216.
Brahms Violin Concerto in D major, Op. 77[a]. **Frank Peter Zimmermann** (vn); **Berlin Philharmonic
Orchestra / Wolfgang Sawallisch.** EMI Ⓕ CDC5 55426-2 (60 minutes: DDD: 5/96). Item marked [a]
recorded live in 1995.

With the string complement of the Berlin Philharmonic reduced, and Sawallisch at his most
sparkling, the Mozart is a delight throughout, with a quicksilver lightness in the outer movements
very different from the big bow-wow approach that virtuoso violinists used to adopt. More than in
the Brahms Zimmermann finds a vein of fantasy, and in the central *Adagio* he plays with a repose and
concentration markedly greater than in his live account of the Brahms slow movement. Curiously, it
is not until the finale of the Brahms, where Zimmermann seems to acquire an extra degree of daring,
that the advantages of live recording come home at all clearly. Till then, his performance seems just a
little too well-mannered, with his silvery tone pointing a lack of bravura, however brilliant the playing
is technically. Yet in the finale not only does the performance take wing, but Zimmermann becomes
more individual, less plain in his manners, as in the little commas of expression he inserts each time
in the main Hungarian dance theme.

Mozart Violin Concertos – No. 3 in G major, K216; No. 4 in D major, K218. Adagio in E major,
K261. Rondo in B flat major, K269/K261a. **Orchestra of the Age of Enlightenment / Monica
Huggett** (vn). Virgin Classics Veritas Ⓕ VC5 45060-2 (57 minutes: DDD: 3/95). ✐

Huggett, with her freshness, imagination of phrase and beautiful range of soft colouring fully captures the exuberance, impishness and tenderness of the 19-year-old Mozart. Immediately in the opening movement of K216 she captivates with her sweet, subtly coloured tone, her delicately articulated passagework and her vivid feeling both for the music's youthful exhilaration and its moments of lyrical repose. If you favour the kind of luscious vibrato and seamless *sostenuto* that, say, Perlman, Zukerman or Stern bring to the *Adagio*, you may be disappointed by Huggett's reading. For many, though, it is all the more moving for its intimacy, tonal purity (as throughout, vibrato is sparingly but tellingly applied) and natural flexibility of phrase, with Huggett's minute care for detail balanced by an eloquent command of the longer line. The D major is equally successful. The *Andante*, so often indulged, has a natural, easy flow with Huggett deftly pointing the coquettish grace of the second subject; and the finale is done with a delightful feeling for the dance – in the tiptoeing elegance of the opening or the eager spring of the jig-like episodes, with their quick-witted interplay between soloist and orchestra. There is crisp orchestral support and a lucid, well-balanced sound-picture.

Mozart Serenade No. 3 in D major, K185/K167*a*[a]. March in D major, K189/K167*b*. Five Contredanses, K609. Notturno in D major, K286/K269*a*. [a]**Arvid Engegard** (vn); **Salzburg Mozarteum Camerata Academica / Sándor Végh.** Capriccio Ⓟ 10 302 (66 minutes: DDD: 10/91). Recorded 1988-89.

The main work here is the big *Serenade*, K185, commissioned by the Antretter family of Salzburg and first performed in August 1773 to celebrate the end of the university year. Like other works of its kind it incorporates a miniature two-movement violin concerto within a loose symphonic framework: an *Andante* designed to display the instrument's powers of cantilena, and a brisk *contredanse* with plenty of opportunities for ear-catching virtuosity There is also a violin solo in the glum D minor trio of the second minuet. But perhaps the finest movements are the sensuous A major *Andante grazioso*, with its *concertante* writing for flutes and horns, and the rollicking 6/8 finale, preceded by an unexpectedly searching *Adagio* introduction. The performance by Végh and his hand-picked Salzburg players is affectionate, rhythmically alive and beautifully detailed, with an imaginative, subtly coloured solo violin contribution from Arvid Engegard. The tempo and specific character of each movement is shrewdly judged: the two minuets, for example, are vividly differentiated, the first properly swaggering, with a nice lilt in the trio, the second spruce and quick-witted. Only in the finale is Végh arguably too leisurely, though here too the style and rhythmic lift of the playing are infectious. Végh follows the serenade with deft, colourful readings of five contredanses from Mozart's last year and a beguiling performance of the *Notturno* for four orchestras, exquisitely imagined open-air music, with its multiple echoes fading into the summer night. All in all a delectable disc, offering a varied concert of Mozart's lighter music performed with exceptional flair and finesse. The recording, too, is outstandingly vivid, with the spatial effects in the *Notturno* beautifully managed.

New review
Mozart Serenade No. 10 in B flat major, K361/K370, "Gran Partita"[a]. **Berlin Philharmonic Orchestra Wind Ensemble / Zubin Mehta.** Sony Classical Ⓟ SK58950 (50 minutes: DDD: 9/95). Recorded 1993.

A big work, this, written for the kind of wind ensemble that became popular during the 1780s at the Austrian imperial court and its aristocratic imitators. In fact, the usual combination was of pairs of oboes, clarinets, horns and bassoons, but here Mozart adds two more horns, a pair of bassett horns and a double-bass; the effect is thus even more massive, although his mastery of texture is such that it never feels overblown and a contemporary described this piece as "herrlich und gross, trefflich und her", which the insert-note here translates as "glorious and grand, excellent and sublime". Since the 13 players here are of the highest quality and Mehta is a sympathetic conductor, everything unfolds impressively, and there is a sense of joy in the music-making, the playing natural, easy without slickness and expressive (sometimes even passionate) without mannerism. To experience the blend of weight and grace that the music and performance offer, listen to the first Minuet, the second of the five movements. The tempo is just right and the shaping of phrases (not least in the delicately scored first trio and the bouncy second one) elegant. Altogether, this is playing of distinction. As for the sound of the *Adagio* which follows, the music which awed Salieri in Shaffer's play *Amadeus*, this is no less poised. Indeed, here is an excellent performance that is complemented by a clear and atmospheric recording made in the Berlin Philharmonie. Strongly recommended and earning first place among current versions.

Additional recommendations ...
...No. 10. **Chamber Orchestra of Europe Wind Soloists / Alexander Schneider.** ASV Ⓟ CDCOE804 (52 minutes: DDD: 4/87).
...No. 10. **Academy of St Martin in the Fields Wind Ensemble / Sir Neville Marriner.** Philips Ⓟ 412 726-2PH (49 minutes: DDD: 5/87).
...Complete Edition, Volume 3 – Serenades, Marches and Cassations for Orchestra. Serenades: No. 3 in D major, K185/K167*a*; No. 4 in D major, K203/K189*b*; No. 5 in D major, K204/K231*a*; No. 6 in D major, K239, "Serenata notturna"; No. 7 in D major, K250/K248*b*, "Haffner"; No. 9 in D major, K320, "Posthorn"; No. 13 in G major, K525, "Eine kleine Nachtmusik". Marches: D major, K62; D major, K189/K167*b*; D major, K215/K213*b*; D major, K237/K189*c*; K249; D major, K335/K320*a* No. 1; D major, K335/K320*a* No. 2. Cassations: G major, K63; B flat major,

K99/K63*a*; D major, K100/K62*a*. Divertimento in D major, K131. Notturno in D major,
K286/K269*a*. Galimathias musicum, K32. **Soloists; Academy of St Martin in the Fields / Sir Neville
Marriner.** Philips Mozart Edition Ⓜ 422 503-2PME7 (seven discs: 404 minutes: DDD: 12/90).
…No. 10. **St Luke's Orchestra / Sir Charles Mackerras.** Telarc Ⓕ CD80359 (51 minutes: DDD:
8/94).
…No. 10. Divertimento No. 12 in E flat major, K252/K240*a*. **Linos Ensemble.** Capriccio Ⓕ 10 472
(60 minutes: DDD: 7/95).

| New review |

Mozart Serenade No. 11 in E flat major, K375. Sextet in E flat major, KAnh183.
Pleyel Sextet in E flat major. **Mozzafiato** (Ayako Oshima, cl; William Purvis, Stewart Rose, hns;
Dennis Godburn, Michael O'Donovan, bns; Marji Danilow, db) **/ Charles Neidich** (cl). Sony
Classical Ⓕ SK64306 (73 minutes: DDD: 9/95). ✍

Mozart's K375 Wind Serenade has been recorded before in its original form, for six instruments
rather than eight, but all the other currently available versions prefer the later, fuller form. That is
understandable: Mozart not only made it richer and more varied in colour when he revised it, adding
the oboe parts, but also made some little improvements to the musical content (and incidentally took
out a singularly awkward clarinet passage in the finale). Yet in its original form the work does have a
kind of integrity of colour and invention that the familiar text lacks: the ideas are perfectly keyed to
the sextet, and – with knowledge of the original version – one can see that the 'better' version isn't
really what Mozart would have composed from the start for eight instruments. So this disc is of
considerable interest to the Mozartian who knows only the final version, and it is very decently if
rather soberly performed. Tempos are steady, and the first movement – Mozart later took out both
the repeats, which here are diligently observed – seems hugely long for the thematic material. Further,
these players add a double-bass, which in some contexts may be authentic, but it does overweigh the
bass and soften the crispness of texture that a true wind ensemble can attain. There is some expressive
playing from the clarinets in the slow movement, the ensemble playing and corporate thinking is of a
high standard, and here and there some modest and apt touches of ornamentation are added. The
second work is a serenade version of the Horn Quintet K407, with a minuet from the K563 String
Trio. It goes surprisingly well: the ideas are of course already well suited to wind instruments and the
reviser has exercised a good deal of ingenuity in his adaptation (the horn music by no means
corresponds exactly with what Mozart wrote in K407). The Pleyel Sextet is a very respectable piece
though there aren't many ideas that set the pulse racing. Some of the virtuosity does, however –
though for the horns it is occasionally extremely testing.

Additional recommendation …
…No. 11. No. 12 in C minor, K388/K384*a*. Wind soloists of the **Chamber Orchestra of Europe /
Alexander Schneider.** ASV Ⓕ CDCOE802 (47 minutes: DDD: 5/88).
…**Orpheus Chamber Orchestra.** DG Ⓕ 431 683-2GH (48 minutes: DDD: 9/91).

Mozart Serenade No. 13 in G major, K525, "Eine kleine Nachtmusik". Divertimentos – E flat
major, K252/K240*a*; D major, K131. **Orpheus Chamber Orchestra.** DG Ⓕ 419 192-2GH
(64 minutes: DDD: 12/86).

There are many worthy recorded performances of Mozart's most famous *Serenade*, the one that is
now universally called *Eine kleine Nachtmusik,* but this one by the string section of the Orpheus
Chamber Orchestra has qualities of refinement and alertness, even enthusiasm, that make it rather
special. These players clearly enjoy the music, but bring to it a delightful precision as well as the
necessary *joie de vivre* and spontaneity, and each of the four movements is beautifully shaped and
characterized, so that this very familiar music comes up as fresh as anyone could wish for. The two
early *divertimentos* which accompany the serenade provide a pleasing complement and contrast. Each
has a different instrumentation, the one in D (written when Mozart was 16, but sounding more
mature) being for flute, oboe, bassoon, four horns and strings while the one in E flat is for just six
instruments, these being pairs of oboes, bassoons and horns. Here, too, the Orpheus players are of the
highest calibre both technically and artistically and their sound is well captured, as is that of the
strings in *Eine kleine Nachtmusik.*

Additional recommendations …
…Eine kleine Nachtmusik. Serenade No. 6 in D major, K239, "Serenata notturna". **Elgar** Serenade
for Strings in E minor, Op. 20. **Grieg** Holberg Suite, Op. 40. **Serenata of London.** IMP Classics
Ⓜ PCD861 (65 minutes: DDD: 11/87).
…Eine kleine Nachtmusik. Overtures – Idomeneo; Die Entführung aus dem Serail; Der
Schauspieldirektor; Le nozze di Figaro; Don Giovanni; Così fan tutte; La clemenza di Tito;
Die Zauberflöte. **Tafelmusik / Bruno Weil.** Sony Classical Vivarte Ⓕ SK46695 (60 minutes: DDD:
5/92). ✍
…Eine kleine Nachtmusik. **Tchaikovsky** Symphony No. 5 in E minor, Op. 64. **Vienna
Philharmonic Orchestra / David Oistrakh.** Orfeo Ⓕ C302921B (67 minutes: ADD: 6/93).
…Eine kleine Nachtmusik. Divertimentos for Strings – D major, K136; B flat major, K137; F
major, K138. [a]**Alois Posch** (db); **Hagen Quartet.** DG Ⓕ 439 940-2GH (58 minutes: DDD: 4/95).
…Eine kleine Nachtmusik. Divertimentos for Strings, K136-138. Adagio and Fugue in C minor,
K546. **Sinfonia Varsovia / Emmanuel Krivine.** Denon Ⓕ CO-75597 (67 minutes: DDD: 3/95).

...Eine kleine Nachtmusik. **Bach** Orchestral Suite No. 2 in B minor, BWV1067. Harpsichord Concerto in F minor, BWV1056. **Vivaldi** Violin Concerto, Op. 8 No. 3, "Autumn". **J.C. Bach** Keyboard Concerto in B flat major, Op. 13 No. 4. **Agi Jambor, Marinus Flipse** (pfs); **Concertgebouw Orchestra / Willem Mengelberg.** Archive Documents Mengelberg Edition mono Ⓕ ADCD112* (69 minutes: AAD: 5/95).

Mozart Divertimentos – B flat major, K287/K271*h*; D major, K205/K167*a*. **Salzburg Mozarteum Camerata Academica / Sándor Végh.** Capriccio Ⓕ 10 271 (59 minutes: DDD: 11/89).　　ⒼⒼⒼ
Mozart's Divertimento, K287 is a six-movement work cast on quite a large scale, and is scored for two violins, viola, two horns and bass, a combination which presents some difficulties of balance. One solution is to use a full orchestral string section, but this can bring its own problems, for Mozart demands playing of virtuoso standard in this score, and anything less than this is ruthlessly exposed. Sandor Végh's smallish string band is of high quality, and has a pleasantly rounded tone quality. The engineers have managed to contrive a satisfactory balance which sounds not at all unnatural, and the sound quality itself is very good. Végh directs an attractive, neatly-pointed performance of the work, one which steers a middle course between objective classicism and expressive warmth. The Divertimento, K205, has five movements, but none lasts longer than five minutes, and the work is much shorter and more modest than K287. Scoring in this case is for violin, viola, two horns, bassoon and bass, to provide another difficult but well resolved problem for the engineers. Végh directs another characterful, delightful performance, to round off a very desirable disc.

Additional recommendations ...
...Complete Edition, Volume 4 – Divertimentos and Marches. Divertimentos: E flat major, K113; D major, K136/K125*a*; B flat major, K137/K125*b*; F major, K138/K125*c*; K205/167*a*; F major, K247; D major, K251; K287/K271h; D major, K334/K320*b*. Marches: F major, K248; D major, K290/K167*ab;* D major, K445/K320*c*. Eine kleine Nachtmusik. Ein musikalischer Spass, K522. **Academy of St Martin in the Fields / Sir Neville Marriner.** Philips Mozart Edition Ⓜ 422 504-2PME5 (five discs: 271 minutes: DDD: 12/90).
...D major, K131; K287/K271*h*. **Capella Istropolitana / Harald Nerat.** Naxos Ⓢ 8 550996 (73 minutes: DDD: 6/95).

Mozart Ein musikalischer Spass, K522. Contredanses – C major, K587, "Der Sieg vom Helden Koburg"; D major, K534, "Das Donnerwetter"; C major, K535, "La Bataille"; G major, K610, "Les filles malicieuses"; F flat major, K607/K605*a*, "Il trionfo delle donne". Gallimathias musicum, K32. German Dances – K567; K605; C major, K611, "Die Leyerer". March in D major, K335 No. 1. **Orpheus Chamber Orchestra.** DG Ⓕ 429 783-2GH (69 minutes: DDD: 4/91). Recorded 1989.
After all the Mozart with which we were bombarded during his bicentenary year, it is a mark of his greatness that an issue such as this comes up with an incomparably engaging freshness. The celebrated *Musikalischer Spass* ("Musical Joke") which begins the disc is never so crudely funny that it wears thin, but make no mistake, the jokes are there in just about every passage, whether they are parodying third-rate music or wobbly playing, and oddly enough sound still more amusing when the performance is as stylishly flexible as this one by the conductorless Orpheus Chamber Orchestra. One of the tunes here (that of the finale on track four) is that of the BBC's *Horse of the Year* programme – and what a good tune it is, even at the umpteenth repetition as the hapless composer finds himself unable to stop. The rest of this programme is no less delightful and includes miniature pieces supposedly describing a thunderstorm, a battle, a hurdy-gurdy man and a sleigh-ride (with piccolo and sleigh-bells). There is also a *Gallimathias musicum*, a ballet suite of dainty little dances averaging less than a minute in length, which Mozart is supposed to have written at the age of ten. Whatever the case this CD, subtitled "A Little Light Music", provides proof of his genius, though differently from his acknowledged masterpieces. The recording is as refined as anyone could wish yet has plenty of impact.

Mozart Symphonies　No. 1 in E flat major, K16; No. 4 in D major, K19; No. 5 in B flat major, K22; No. 6 in F major, K43; No. 7 in D major, K45; No. 7*a* in G major, K45*a*/KAnh221, "Alte Lambach"; No. 8 in D major, K48; No. 9 in C major, K73; No. 10 in G major, K74; No. 11 in D major, K84/K73*q*; No. 12 in G major, K110/K75*b*; No. 13 in F major, K112; No. 14 in A major, K114; No. 15 in G major, K124; No. 42 in F major, K75; No. 43 in F major, K76/K42*a*; No. 44 in D major, K81/K731; No. 45 in D major, K95/K73*n*; No. 46 in C major, K96/K111*h*; No. 47 in D major, K97/K73*m*; No. 55 in B flat major, K45*b*; F major, KAnh223/K19*a*; B flat major, K74*g*/KAnh216/C11.03. **The English Concert / Trevor Pinnock.** Archiv Produktion Ⓕ 437 792-2AH4 (four discs: 297 minutes: DDD: 11/93). 🎜 Recorded 1992. *Gramophone Editor's choice.*
Pinnock's Mozart symphony cycle is only the second to use period instruments, and the performances on these four discs are outstandingly vital and stylish, making the most persuasive case for this music. Hogwood's pioneering period cycle from the early 1980s, with its revelations of articulation and sonority, is often exciting, but suffers from intermittent roughness of execution and an often stiff, austere approach to the slow movements. In both these respects Pinnock and The English Concert are far preferable, reflecting the advance in all facets of period performance in the intervening decade.

The string sound is recognizably 'authentic' in its bright edge and restrained use of vibrato, but is altogether smoother, sweeter and more subtly coloured than on the Hogwood discs. Ensemble is more polished, tuning (especially of the oboes) far more precise. And Pinnock is not only more elegant and affectionate in the slow movements, but often shapes the *Allegros* more purposefully, with more considered phrasing and surer long-term control. The first contains six works (Köchel Nos. 16, 19, 19a, 22, 43 and 45a) written between 1764, when Mozart was eight, and late 1767, just before his twelfth birthday. Though the invention here is often rudimentary, Mozart already reveals himself as a precocious musical mimic, adeptly manipulating the clichés of the contemporary *galant* style. Textures are, as always, ideally transparent, and violins divided on opposite sides so that the many antiphonal passages make their proper effect. The second disc covers the years 1768-70, and begins with Mozart's first symphony with trumpets and drums, K45, unremarkable in its actual ideas but shrewdly laid out for maximum orchestral brilliance. Most of the works on the third disc were written on Mozart's first two Italian journeys, in the spring and summer of 1770 and the autumn of 1771; and they are distinctly Italianate in their harmonic and textural simplicity and easy *buffo* brilliance. Not surprisingly, the final disc, with five symphonies from 1771 and early 1772, contains the most consistently memorable music in this set. Finest of all these symphonies is the very Viennese K114 in A major, a key that invariably drew something out of the ordinary from Mozart. The first movement, with its luminous textures (high horns complemented by flutes rather than oboes), has a particularly expressive second theme in imitation, shaped by Pinnock with a vocal eloquence. This superb set, recorded with truthful immediacy, becomes the prime recommendation for these juvenile symphonies.

Additional recommendations ...

...Complete Edition, Volume 1 – Early Symphonies: No. 1 in E flat major, K16; No. 4 in D major, K19; F major, KAnh223/K19a; No. 5 in B flat major, K22; No. 6 in F major, K43; No. 7 in D major, K45; G major, Kdeest, "Neue Lambacher" (attrib. L. Mozart); No. 7a in G major, K45a/KAnh221, "Alte Lambacher"; (No. 55) in B flat major, K45b/KAnh214; No. 8 in D major, K48; No. 9 in C major, K73; No. 10 in G major, K74; (No. 42) in F major, K75; (No. 43) in F major, K76/K42a; (No. 44) in D major, K81/K73l; No. 11 in D major, K84/K73q; (No. 45) in D major, K95/K73n; (No. 46) in C major, K96/K111b; (No. 47) in D major, K97/K73m; No. 12 in G major, K110/K75b; No. 13 in F major, K112; No. 14 in A major, K114 (with additional alternative minuet); No. 15 in G major, K124; No. 16 in C major, K128; No. 17 in G major, K129; No. 18 in F major, K130; No. 19 in E flat major, K132 (with additional alternative slow movement); No. 20 in D major, K133; (No. 50) in D major, K141a (K161 and K163); (No. 48) in D major, K111a (K111 and K120); (No. 51) in D major, K207a (K196 and K121); (No. 52) in C major, K213c (K208 and K102). Minuet in A major, K61g No. 1. **Academy of St Martin in the Fields / Sir Neville Marriner.** Philips Mozart Edition Ⓜ 422 501-2PME6 (six discs: 399 minutes: ADD/DDD: 12/90).

...Complete Edition, Volume 2 – Middle and Late Symphonies: No. 21 in A major, K134; No. 22 in C major, K162; No. 23 in D major, K181/K162b; No. 24 in B flat major, K182/K173dA; No. 25 in G minor, K183/K173dB; No. 26 in E flat major, K184/K161a; No. 27 in G major, K199/K161b; No. 28 in C major, K200/K189k; No. 29 in A major, K201/K186a; No. 30 in D major, K202/K186b; No. 31 in D major, K297/K300a, "Paris" (with additional alternative slow movement); No. 32 in G major, K318; No. 33 in B flat major, K319; No. 34 in C major, K338; No. 35 in D major, K385, "Haffner"; No. 36 in C major, K425, "Linz"; No. 38 in D major, K504, "Prague"; No. 39 in E flat major, K453; No. 40 in G minor, K550; No. 41 in C major, K551, "Jupiter". Minuet in C major, K409/K383f. Adagio maestoso in G major, K444/K425a. **Academy of St Martin in the Fields / Sir Neville Marriner.** Philips Mozart Edition Ⓜ 422 502-2PME6 (six discs: 402 minutes: ADD: 12/90).

...CD80256 – No. 1 in E flat major, K16; F major, K19a; No. 4 in D major, K19; No. 5 in B flat major, K22; No. 6 in F major, K43; B flat major, K45b/KAhn214; No. 7 in D major, K45. CD80272 – No. 8 in D major, K48; No. 9 in C major, K73/K75a; D major, K731/K81; D major, K73m/K97; D major, K75n/K95; D major, K73n/K95; D major, K73q/K84. CD80273 – No. 10 in G major, K74/K73p; C major, K111b/K96; F major, K75; G major, K75b/K110; No. 13 in F major, K112. **Prague Chamber Orchestra / Sir Charles Mackerras.** Telarc Ⓕ CD80256, CD80272/3 (three discs, oas: 83, 61 and 58 minutes: DDD: 11/91).

...8 550113 (65 minutes): No. 25 in G minor, K183/K173dB; No. 32 in G major, K318; No. 41 in C major, K551, "Jupiter". 8 550119 (69 minutes): No. 29 in A major, K201/K186a; No. 30 in D major, K202/K186b; No. 38 in D major, K504, "Prague". 8 550164 (61 minutes): No. 28 in C major, K200/K189k; No. 31 in D major, K297/K300a, "Paris"; No. 40 in G minor, K550. 8 550186 (62 minutes): No. 34 in C major, K338; No. 35 in D major, K385, "Haffner"; No. 39 in E flat major, K543. 8 550264 (65 minutes): No. 27 in G major, K199/K161b; No. 33 in B flat major, K319; No. 36 in C major, K425, "Linz". 8 550299 (62 minutes): No. 40 in G minor, K550; No. 41 in C major, K551, "Jupiter". **Capella Istropolitana / Barry Wordsworth.** Naxos Ⓢ (six discs, oas: 384 minutes: DDD: 4/91).

...Nos. 31, 33 and 34. **Prague Chamber Orchestra / Sir Charles Mackerras.** Telarc Ⓕ CD80190 (65 minutes: DDD: 3/90).

...Nos. 31–41. **The English Concert / Trevor Pinnock.** Archiv Produktion Ⓕ 447 043-2AH4 (four discs: 256 minutes: DDD: 12/95). ✍

...Nos. 13–24. D major (No. 48), K120/K111a; D major (No. 50), K141a/K161, K163; D major (No. 51), K121/K207a; C major (No. 52), K102/K213c. **English Chamber Orchestra / Jeffrey Tate.** EMI Ⓔ CDS5 55480-2 (three discs: 201 minutes: DDD: 1/96).

New review

Mozart Symphonies. **Northern Chamber Orchestra / Nicholas Ward.** Naxos Ⓢ 8 550871/2 (59 and 56 minutes, oas: DDD: 12/95).
  8 550871 – No. 1 in E flat major, K16; No. 2 in B flat major, K17 (attrib. L. Mozart); No. 4 in D major, K19; No. 5 in B flat major, K22. **Abel** (formerly attrib. Mozart) Symphony, Op. 7 No. 3. *8 550872* – No. 6 in F major, K43; No. 7 in D major, K45; No. 8 in D major, K48; No. 9 in C major, K73; No. 10 in G major, K74.
These two discs of Mozart's first ten symphonies offer a unique view of the composer's earliest years of apprenticeship as a symphonist. Ward and his orchestra demonstrate a sensitive response to the wealth of stylistic influences apparent in these works. Purists may question the inclusion of two of the symphonies, Nos. 2 and 3, since neither work is actually by Mozart. The former is attributed to the composer's father, Leopold, while the latter is Mozart's orchestration of C.F. Abel's E flat Symphony, Op. 7 No. 3. However, when they are played with such engaging style and elegance as here, these two works add a further important dimension to Mozart's early symphonic output. Where J.C. Bach's influence is most powerful (Symphonies Nos. 1, 4, 5 and 6), the NCO present the music's contrasting thematic characters with fine clarity, balancing the music's beautifully transparent textures with appropriate lightness of touch. The inclusion of trumpets and drums in the next three symphonies (Nos. 7, 8 and 9) announces the young composer's growing brilliance and stature. In these pieces, the NCO move into a suitably higher gear, revealing Mozart's new and potent originality, with powerfully dramatic tuttis and expressively sung *andantes*. Mozart made his first trip to Italy in 1770, and the symphony he wrote in Milan that year (No. 10) shows his enthusiastic incorporation of Italian stylistic models. Here the NCO's deliciously spacious orchestral playing demonstrates Mozart's ravishing originality, with dramatic opposition of gesture and instrumentation in the exuberant *allegros* and a beguilingly graceful slow movement that winningly displays a keen awareness of the composer's innovative touches. These are indeed splendid performances, admirably complemented by vivid recordings (made in the spacious acoustic of the Concert Hall, New Broadcasting House, Manchester).

New review

Mozart Symphonies – No. 15 in G major, K124; No. 16 in C major, K128; No. 17 in G major, K129; No. 18 in F major, K130. **Northern Chamber Orchestra / Nicholas Ward.** Naxos Ⓢ 8 550874 (58 minutes: DDD: 12/95). Recorded 1994.
After Mozart returned from his first extended tour of Italy in 1771, he embarked on a number of symphonic projects that show his astonishing assimilation and transformation of the Italian overture, with crisp, transparent orchestration and suppleness of expression. The influence of Sammartini and J.C. Bach – whose music could be heard at concerts in Salzburg during 1772 when these pieces were written – is especially apparent in the bold thematic gestures and civilized discourse between wind and strings. Nicholas Ward and the NCO bring their customary style and eloquence to this music in performances that evocatively portray its blend of formal unity, radiant vitality and occasionally – as in the rhythmically imaginative finale of the C major Symphony – rustic charm. Opening *allegros* are suitably vivacious, *andantes* are graceful and poignant and the vigorous finales bristle with energy. The first movement of the C major Symphony offers a more potent dramatic formula, with subtly poetic triplets and tense tremolos; however, the highlight of the programme is the F major Symphony (No. 18), which Saint-Foix described as "the first of [Mozart's] great symphonies". Here, Ward's and the NCO's dramatically compelling account, beautifully presented in a natural, spacious recording, brilliantly highlights the music's operatic qualities.

Mozart Salzburg Symphonies – No. 16 in C major, K128; No. 17 in G major, K129; No. 18 in F major, K130; No. 19 in E flat major, K132; No. 20 in D major, K133; No. 21 in A major, K134; No. 22 in C major, K162; No. 23 in D major, K181/K162b; No. 24 in B flat major, K182/K173dA; No. 25 in G minor, K183/K173dB; No. 26 in E flat major, K184/K161a; No. 27 in G major, K199/K161b; No. 28 in C major, K200/K189k; No. 29 in A major, K201/K186a; No. 30 in D major, K202/K186b. **The English Concert / Trevor Pinnock.** Archiv Produktion Ⓔ 439 915-2AH4 (four discs: 264 minutes: DDD: 1/95). 🎵　　　　Ⓖ
This is the second of the projected three boxes making up Trevor Pinnock's more or less comprehensive cycle of the Mozart symphonies and includes all the symphonies Mozart wrote between the spring of 1772 and the end of 1774, his most prolific period of symphony composition. Trevor Pinnock's are the first period-instrument performances of most of these works since Christopher Hogwood's pioneering recordings of the late 1970s and early 1980s. Techniques of handling these instruments have improved greatly over the last decade, and what is exciting about this set is the sweetness of the sound (not at all the same as the sweetness of a modern chamber orchestra) and the suppleness and flexibility The English Concert bring to the music. They play, much of the time, as if it were chamber music, particularly in second subjects – the lyrical passages, that is, where they shape the phrases with a warmth and refinement you hardly expect in orchestral music. Timing

is quietly witty, yet not at all contrived or artificial: it is the sort of expressive refinement that depends on listening to one another, not on the presence of a conductor. There is large-scale playing too. The opening of the brilliant D major work, K133 has a splendid swing, with its prominent trumpets, and a real sense of a big, symphonic piece. K184 is duly fiery and its accents are neatly judged. The two final symphonies are both very impressively done: an eloquent rather than a fiery account (though something of that too) of the opening movement of K201, with a particularly euphonious and shapely *Andante*, and the finales of both are done with exceptional vitality and the rhythmic resilience that is characteristic of these performances. In short, quite outstanding performances, unfailingly musical, wholly natural and unaffected, often warmly expressive in the slow music and always falling very happily on the ear, with no trace of the harshness that some people think is inevitable with period instruments. They are excellently recorded, with the properly prominent wind balance helping to characterize the sound-world of each work.

Additional recommendations ...

...No. 23. March in D major, K237/K189c. Serenade No. 4 in D major, K203/K189b. **Vienna Concentus Musicus / Nikolaus Harnoncourt.** Teldec Das Alte Werk Ⓕ 4509-90842-2 (61 minutes: DDD: 10/94).

...No. 29. **Bach** Orchestral Suite No. 3 in D major, BWV1068. **Haydn** Symphonies – No. 88 in G major, "Letter V"; No. 96 in D major, "Miracle". **Handel** Concerto grosso in G minor, Op. 6 No. 6. **Schumann** Manfred – Overture. **Schubert** Symphony No. 3 in D major, D200. **Brahms** Tragic Overture, Op. 81. **Leipzig Gewandhaus Orchestra / Hermann Abendroth.** Tahra mono Ⓕ TAH106/07* (two discs: 154 minutes: AAD: 9/94).

...Nos. 24, 26, 27 and 30. **Prague Chamber Orchestra / Sir Charles Mackerras.** Telarc Ⓕ CD80186 (58 minutes: DDD: 8/89).

New review

Mozart Symphonies – No. 21 in A major, K134; No. 22 in C major, K162; No. 23 in D major, K181/K162b; No. 24 in B flat major, K182/K173dA; No. 26 in E flat major, K184/K161a. **Northern Chamber Orchestra / Nicholas Ward.** Naxos Ⓢ 8 550876 (53 minutes: DDD: 1/96). Recorded 1993.

This is an opportunity to enjoy Mozart's inexhaustibly imaginative assimilation and transformation of Italian operatic models. To begin, Ward's sensitively balanced orchestral textures reveal Mozart's fragrant orchestration with great clarity in the A major Symphony. Sample the second movement's deftly handled interplay of strings, woodwind and horns, and buoyantly stately Menuetto that culminates effectively in the finale's restless drive. The complete musical satisfaction provided by the four Italian-overture symphonies that comprise the remainder of the programme is due both to the fullness and vigour of the orchestration itself, and to the NCO's lively performances. The opening *allegros* and cheerfully effervescent finales bubble with infectious vitality, while the slow movements provide the opportunity for more intimate instrumental ensembles. Most impressive, however, is the E flat major work, which originated as the overture to the play *Lanassa*. Here, Ward and the NCO compellingly portray the dramatic violence of the opening *Presto*, the profound despair of its minor-key *Andante* and the exuberant rhythms of its finale. The recording is atmospheric.

Mozart Symphonies – No. 25 in G minor, K183/K173d; No. 31 in D major, K297/K300a, "Paris"; D major, K320. Maurerische Trauermusik in C minor, K477/K479a. **Berlin Philharmonic Orchestra / Claudio Abbado.** Sony Classical Ⓕ SK48385 (75 minutes: DDD: 5/95). Recorded 1992.   Ⓖ

These are exhilarating accounts of Mozart using modern instruments in performances which marry sweetness and purity to crisp rhythms and dramatic bite. What the title above fails to underline is the fact that the third of the three symphonies, K320 in D major, on the disc is the one which Mozart adapted from that same *Posthorn Serenade*, selecting just the first, fifth and seventh movements. It is astonishing that though the three-movement symphony is so much briefer than the seven-movement Serenade, it seems much bolder and more powerful in its arguments. This version of the *Paris* Symphony has the alternative, earlier slow movement as a supplement, as well as the later one in its usual place. No. 29 is presented, as most recent versions have been, as a large-scale structure, with both halves of the outer movements repeated. Anyone wanting performances on modern instruments is unlikely to find the approach too massive for Mozart, for although the string band is substantial, the purity and clarity of the playing aerates textures. Woodwind doubling is always clearly audible, as with the bassoons in the second movement of No. 29. Abbado's underlining of light and shade regularly makes for delectable moments, for example in the woodwind trio for the Minuet where the descending scales are made to sound like laughter. The recording also captures very tellingly the lugubrious timbres of the *Masonic Funeral Music*, made dark with extra weight of wind set against a string section without cellos.

Mozart Symphonies – No. 25 in G minor, K183/K173dB; No. 28 in C major, K200/K189k; No. 29 in A major, K201/K186a. **Prague Chamber Orchestra / Sir Charles Mackerras.** Telarc Ⓕ CD80165 (78 minutes: DDD: 9/88).

Here are three symphonies from Mozart's late teens, written in his native Salzburg, in crisply articulated performances. The first of them is a *Sturm und Drang* piece in a key that the composer reserved for moods of agitation. Mackerras takes the orchestra through the big opening *Allegro con brio* of No. 25 with drive and passion, although it is unlikely that Mozart would have expected a Salzburg orchestra in the 1770s to play as fast as this skilful body of Czech players. The gentle *Andante* comes therefore as a relief, though here too Mackerras keeps a firm rhythmic grasp on the music, and indeed a taut metrical aspect is a feature of all three symphonies as played here, so that minuets dance briskly and purposefully and finales bustle. However, the sunlit warmth of the beautiful A major Symphony, No. 29, comes through and the bracing view of the other two symphonies is a legitimate one, though giving little or nothing in the direction of expressive lingering, much less towards sentimental indulgence. The Prague Chamber Orchestra are an expert ensemble, not over-large for this style of music and the recording is admirably clear although a little reverberant. A well-filled disc.

Additional recommendation ...

...Nos. 28 and 29. No. 35 in D major, K385, "Haffner". **Berlin Philharmonic Orchestra / Claudio Abbado.** Sony Classical Ⓕ SK48063 (74 minutes: DDD: 3/92).

Mozart Symphonies – No. 29 in A major, K201/K186a[a]; No. 31 in D major, K297/K300a, "Paris"[b]; No. 32 in G major, K318[c]; No. 33 in B flat major, K319[a]; No. 34 in C major, K338[b]; No. 35 in D major, K385, "Haffner"[c]; No. 36 in C major, K425, "Linz"[c]; No. 38 in D major, K504, "Prague"[d]; No. 39 in E flat major, K543[d]; No. 40 in G minor, K550[e]; No. 41 in C major, K551, "Jupiter"[e]. **English Baroque Soloists / John Eliot Gardiner.** Philips Ⓜ 442 604-2PH5 (five discs: 309 minutes: DDD: 3/95). Items marked [a] from 420 736-2PH (8/86), [b]420 937-2PH (7/88), [c]422 419-2PH (9/89), [d]426 283-2PH (2/91), [e]426 315-2PH (11/92). ✄   ⓖⓖ

Gardiner took his pilgrimage through the late Mozart symphonies more or less in chronological order over a span of six years. The first disc contains appealing performances of Nos. 29 and 33, the former particularly lyrical and shapely, with an eloquent account of the *Andante*, the latter distinguished for its refinement of line and the properly spirited opening movement. Then comes the *Paris*, No. 31, a piece designed to show off a virtuoso orchestra, which it duly does in this alert and shapely reading, coupled with No. 34, another large-scale piece, in which Gardiner again provides a specially graceful slow movement. In the *Haffner, Linz* and *Prague* Symphonies Gardiner is possibly more concerned with classical grandeur than with strong characterization of the ideas. The G minor is the outstanding achievement of the set: the first movement performed with great drive and spaciousness, the second shapely and intense in expression, the finale done with immense vitality, the strings' arpeggios leaping vividly through the texture. The *Jupiter* is almost equally splendid, if slightly flawed by some *piano* effects in the first movement tuttis (this happens too in No. 39) where they do not belong, but the crowning glory, the finale, contains many thrilling things. In all, this is probably the version to choose, under any single conductor, of these symphonies on period instruments – indeed perhaps on any instruments.

Additional recommendations ...

...No. 40. **Haydn** No. 44 in E minor, "Trauer". **St John's Smith Square Orchestra / John Lubbock.** IMP Red Label Ⓜ PCD820 (DDD: 8/86).

...Nos. 40 and 41. **Prague Chamber Orchestra / Sir Charles Mackerras.** Telarc Ⓕ CD80139 (71 minutes: DDD: 5/87).

...Nos. 34, 35 and 39. **London Mozart Players / Jane Glover.** ASV Ⓕ CDDCA615 (74 minutes: DDD: 7/88).

...Nos. 40 and 41. **English Baroque Soloists / John Eliot Gardiner.** Philips Ⓔ 426 315-2PH (75 minutes: DDD: 11/92). ✄

...No. 40. **Tchaikovsky** Symphony No. 5 in E minor, Op. 64. **North German Radio Symphony Orchestra / Günter Wand.** RCA Victor Red Seal Ⓕ 09026 68032-2 (73 minutes: DDD: 6/95).

...Nos. 40 and 41. **The English Concert / Trevor Pinnock.** Archiv Produktion Ⓕ 447 048-2AH (73 minutes: DDD: 12/95). ✄

...Nos. 35, 36 and 38. **London Philharmonic Orchestra / Sir Thomas Beecham.** Dutton Laboratories Essential Archive mono Ⓑ CDEA5001* (71 minutes: ADD: 1/96).

...Nos. 35, 36, 38-41. **Berlin Philharmonic Orchestra / Karl Böhm.** DG The Originals Ⓜ 447 416-2GOR2 (two discs: 146 minutes: ADD: 11/95).

Mozart Symphonies – No. 36 in C major, K425, "Linz"; No. 38 in D major, K504, "Prague". **Prague Chamber Orchestra / Sir Charles Mackerras.** Telarc Ⓕ CD80148 (66 minutes: DDD: 10/87).

Mozart wrote his *Linz* Symphony in great haste (five days to be precise), but needless to say there is little evidence of haste in the music itself, except perhaps that the first movement has all the exuberance of a composer writing on the wing of inspiration. The slow movement with its siciliano rhythm certainly has no lack of serenity, although it has drama too. The *Prague* Symphony was written only three years later, yet Mozart's symphonic style had matured and the work is altogether more ambitious and substantial. A glorious spaciousness surrounds Sir Charles's performances. The recording venue is reverberant, yet there is no loss of detail, and the fullness of the sound helps to add weight to climaxes without going beyond the bounds of volume that Mozart might have expected. Sir Charles captures the joy and high spirits that these symphonies embody without in any way undermining their greatness. This vivacity is emphasized by the East European sound of the Prague

Chamber Orchestra, with the out-of-doors timbre of its winds which provides a pleasing contrast both with those of the standard British and Germanic orchestras and specialist, authentic ensembles. Mackerras does, however, adopt some aspects of the modern approach to Mozart performance: he includes harpsichord continuo, his minuets are taken trippingly, one-to-a-bar, and he prefers bowing that is crisper, more detached, and pointed. Phrasing and articulation are taken with a natural grace and without overemphasis, dynamics being graded to provide drama at the right moments. The very rightness of the result is recommendation enough.

Additional recommendation ...

...Nos. 38 and 39. **English Baroque Soloists / John Eliot Gardiner.** Philips Ⓕ 426 283-2PH (66 minutes: DDD: 2/91). ✒

Mozart Complete Edition, Volume 14 – Piano Quintet in E flat major, K452[a] (from 420 182-2PH, 8/87). Clarinet Trio in E flat major, K498, "Kegelstatt"[b] (6500 073, 2/71). Adagio and Rondo in C minor, K617[c] (9500 397, 5/78). Adagio in C major, K356/K617a[d]. Piano Quartets[e] – No. 1 in G minor, K478; No. 2 in E flat major, K493 (both from 410 391-1PH, 10/84). Piano Trios[f] – B flat major, K254; D minor, K442 (cptd. Stadler and Marguerre); G major, K496; B flat major, K502; E major, K542; C major, K548; G major, K564 (all from 422 079-2PH3, 11/88). [a]**Aurèle Nicolet** (fl); [ac]**Heinz Holliger** (ob); [a]**Eduard Brunner,** [b]**Jack Brymer** (cls); [a]**Hermann Baumann** (hn); [a]**Klaus Thunemann** (bn); [cd]**Bruno Hoffmann** (glass harmonica); [b]**Patrick Ireland,** [c]**Karl Schouten,** [e]**Bruno Giuranna** (vas); [c]**Jean Decroos** (vc); [ef]**Beaux Arts Trio** (Isidore Cohen, vn; Bernard Greenhouse, vc; Menahem Pressler, pf); [a]**Alfred Brendel,** [b]**Stephen Kovacevich** (pfs). Philips Mozart Edition Ⓜ 422 514-2PME5 (five discs: 274 minutes: ADD/DDD: 9/91). *Gramophone Award Winner 1991.*   Ⓖ

These recordings come from different locations and dates, ranging from 1969 to 1987. Four discs out of the five offer the two piano quartets and seven piano trios, played by the Beaux Arts Trio who are joined in the quartets by the viola player Bruno Giuranna; these are clearly the centrepiece of the issue and the playing of this fine ensemble is strongly characterful yet thoughtful. These are alert, direct and yet refined performances and earn only praise, although the recording in Philips's favoured Swiss location of La-Chaux-de-Fonds could have placed a little more distance between the players and the listener (we also hear the odd intake of breath). But otherwise this clear sound suits the music, and Menahem Pressler's piano tone is well captured. The D minor Trio which ends the series is not wholly authentic, being mainly Maximilian Stadler's compilation from existing material found by Mozart's widow Constanze after his death. Before we come to the piano quartets and piano trios, the first disc also has important works in fine performances in which Alfred Brendel and Heinz Holliger are just two of the artists involved (the Quintet for piano and wind was among the composer's favourite works). The first disc also offers two pieces featuring the ravishing sound of the glass harmonica (musical glasses), which is played by its leading exponent, Bruno Hoffmann, and the solo *Adagio* in C major is quite ethereally beautiful, if rather closely recorded. This unique instrument is usefully described and illustrated in the booklet.

Additional recommendations ...

...Piano Quartets Nos. 1 and 2[a]. Horn Quintet in E flat major, K407[b]. [a]**Sir Clifford Curzon** (pf); [a]members of the **Amadeus Quartet;** [b]**Dennis Brain** (hn); [b]**Max Gilbert** (va); [b]members of the **Griller Quartet.** Decca Historic mono Ⓜ 425 960-2DM* (62 minutes: ADD: 4/90).   Ⓖ

...Piano Quartets Nos. 1 and 2. **Mozartean Players.** Harmonia Mundi Ⓕ HMU90 7018 (64 minutes: DDD: 3/91).

...Piano Trios – K496, K502, K542, K548, K564. Divertimento, K254. **Mozartean Players.** Harmonia Mundi Ⓕ HMU90 7033/4 (two discs: 136 minutes: DDD: 8/93). ✒

...Piano Quintet, K452. **Beethoven** Piano and Wind Quintet in E flat major, Op. 16. **Hansjörg Schellenberger** (ob); **Larry Combs** (cl); **Dale Clevenger** (hn); **Daniele Damiano** (bn); **Daniel Barenboim** (pf). Erato Ⓕ 4509-96359-2 (49 minutes: DDD: 12/94).

...Piano Quintet, K452[b]. Piano Concerto No. 26 in D major, K537, "Coronation"[a]. [b]**Heinz Holliger** (ob); [b]**Elmar Schmid** (cl); [b]**Klaus Thunemann** (bn); [b]**Radovan Vlatkovic** (hn); **András Schiff** (pf); [a]**Salzburg Mozarteum Camerata Academica / Sándor Végh.** Decca Ⓕ 443 877-2DH (56 minutes: DDD: 4/95).

...Piano Quartet No. 1. **Schubert** Piano Quintet in A major, D667, "Trout"[a]. **Thomas Zehetmair** (vn); **Tabea Zimmermann** (va); **Richard Duven** (vc); [a]**Peter Riegelbauer** (db); **Alfred Brendel** (pf). Philips Ⓕ 446 001-2PH (75 minutes: DDD: 1/96). *See review under Schubert; refer to the Index to Reviews.*

Mozart Complete Edition, Volume 11 – String Quintets: No. 1 in B flat major, K174; No. 2 in C minor, K406/K516b; No. 3 in C major, K515; No. 4 in G minor, K516; No. 5 in D major, K593; No. 6 in E flat major, K614. **Arthur Grumiaux, Arpad Gérecz** (vns); **Georges Janzer, Max Lesueur** (vas); **Eva Czako** (vc). Philips Mozart Edition Ⓜ 422 511-2PME3 (three discs: 170 minutes: ADD: 9/91). From 6747 107 (1/76). Recorded 1973. *Gramophone classical 100. Gramophone Award Winner 1991.*   ⒼⒼⒼ

Of the six works which comprise Mozart's complete *oeuvre* for string quintet, that in B flat major, K174, is an early composition, written at the age of 17. It is a well-made, enjoyable work, but not a great deal more than that. The C minor work, K406, is an arrangement by Mozart of his Serenade for six wind instruments, K398. It is difficult not to feel that the original is more effective, since the music seems to sit a little uncomfortably on string instruments. But the remaining four works, written in the last four years of Mozart's life, are a different matter. The last string quintets from Mozart's pen were extraordinary works, and the addition of the second viola seems to have encouraged him to still greater heights. It has been suggested that Mozart wrote K515 and K516 to show King Friedrich Wilhelm II of Prussia that he was a better composer of string quintets than Boccherini, whom the King had retained as chamber music composer to his court. There was no response, so he offered these two quintets for sale with the K406 arrangement to make up the usual set of three. K593 and K614 were written in the last year of his life. Arthur Grumiaux and his colleagues recorded their survey in 1973. Refinement is perhaps the word that first comes to mind in discussing these performances, which are affectionate yet controlled by a cool, intelligent sensitivity. The recordings have been well transferred, the quality is warm and expansive and Grumiaux's tone, in particular, is a delight to the ear but all the playing is alert and stylish. In all, this Philips release is one to earn a strong recommendation, offering as it does Mozart playing of fine quality allied to very decent sound.

Additional recommendations ...

...K515. K593. **Simon Whistler** (va); **Salomon Quartet.** Hyperion Ⓕ CDA66431 (66 minutes: DDD: 11/91). ✍

...K516. K614. **Simon Whistler** (va); **Salomon Quartet.** Hyperion Ⓕ CDA66432 (64 minutes: DDD: 11/91). ✍

...K406/K516*b*. **R. Strauss** Capriccio – Prelude[a]. Metamorphosen, AV142 (arr. Leopold)[ab].
   Vienna String Sextet with [b]**Alois Posch** (db). EMI Ⓕ CDC5 55108-2 (61 minutes: DDD: 2/95).

...K174 (including two rejected movements); K515. **Eder Quartet; János Fehérvári** (va). Naxos Ⓢ 8 553103 (67 minutes: DDD: 4/95).

...K515. K516. **L'Archibudelli.** Sony Classical Vivarte Ⓕ SK66259 (63 minutes: DDD: 9/95). ✍

New review

Mozart String Quintets – No. 2 in C minor, K406/K516*b*; No. 4 in G minor, K516. **Eder Quartet** (György Selmeczy, Péter Szüts, vns; Sándor Papp, va; György Eder, vc); **János Fehérvári** (va). Naxos Ⓢ 8 553104 (56 minutes: DDD: 1/96). Recorded 1994.

Despite its initial conception for wind instruments (K388), the C minor Quintet, K406, retains much of its emotional power and dramatic intensity, particularly when played with as much warmth and affection as here. The second movement is especially impressive, with first violinist, György Selmeczy's heavenly phrasing vividly recalling the oboe of the original scoring. Mozart wrote the G minor Quintet, K516, during the period of his father's final illness in 1787, and the music's sustained high emotional intensity makes it one of the most dramatically powerful of all the composer's works. The Eder Quartet give a performance of profound sensitivity and depth and the recording is excellent

---

Mozart String Quintet No. 4 in G minor, K516[a]. String Quartet No. 14 in G major, K387. **Lindsay Quartet** (Peter Cropper, Ronald Birks, vns; Robin Ireland, va; Bernard Gregor-Smith, vc); [a]**Patrick Ireland** (va). ASV Ⓕ CDDCA923 (73 minutes: DDD: 6/95). ✍   Ⓖ

This is distinguished Mozart playing, effectively blending sweetness, energy, high intelligence and poignant sadness. Its quality is at once evident in the monumental first movement of the G minor Quintet, played with tension yet not 'pushed' tonally or tempo-wise. The recording, made in the well-tried venue of All Saints' Church, Petersham, is close but of high quality, and its revealing detail exposes no weakness among the players, whose unanimity throughout is impressive. The *Adagio ma non troppo* is, of course, the wounded heart of this masterwork, and the Lindsays and Patrick Ireland are equal to its challenge: indeed, this is beautiful and eloquent playing which makes every point without exaggeration. The G major Quartet, the first of the six dedicated to Haydn, is no less effective. The Lindsays have a refreshing spring in their step in the first movement and finale, rightly observing the markings *Allegro vivace assai* and *Molto allegro*, though here again they also give us finesse and the development of the first movement has an apt spontaneity. The strange rhythmic patterns of the minuet are well realized.

Mozart Complete Edition, Volume 12   String Quartets: No. 1 in G major, K80/K73*f*; No. 2 in D major, K155/K134*a*; No. 3 in G major, K156/K134*b* (with additional original Adagio); No. 4 in C major, K157 (all from 6500 142, 12/71); No. 5 in F major, K158; No. 6 in B flat major, K159; No. 7 in E flat major, K160/K159*a*; No. 8 in F major, K168 (6500 172, 12/72); No. 9 in A major, K169; No. 10 in C major, K170; No. 11 in E flat major, K171; No. 12 in B flat major, K172; No. 13 in D minor, K173 (6747 097, 9/74); No. 14 in G major, K387; No. 15 in D minor, K421/K417*b* (SAL3632, 10/67); No. 16 in E flat major, K428/K421*b*; No. 17 in B flat major, K458, "Hunt" (SAL3633, 10/67); No. 18 in A major, K464; No. 19 in C major, K465, "Dissonance" (SAL3634, 10/67); No. 20 in D major, K499, "Hoffmeister"; No. 21 in D major, K575 (6500 241, 7/72); No. 22 in B flat major, K589; No. 23 in F major, K590 (6500 225, 7/73). **Quartetto Italiano** (Paolo Borciani, Elisa Pegreffi, vns; Piero Farulli, va; Franco Rossi, vc). Philips Mozart Edition Ⓜ 422 512-2PME8 (eight discs: 474 minutes: ADD: 8/91). Recorded 1966-73. *Gramophone Award Winner 1991.*   Ⓖ

These are classic performances which have won praise ever since they began to appear back in 1967. Admittedly, a little allowance has to be made for the sound since the recordings date from between

1966 and 1973. For example, it is a touch heavy and close in the 1966 recording of the D minor Quartet that is one of the wonderful set of six that Mozart dedicated to Haydn. In a way, this accords to some extent with the playing of the Quartetto Italiano, which is at times rather earnest – and in the first movement of this work, rather deliberate in its pace. But these are really the only criticisms of a generally splendid issue, and the innate seriousness of these fine Italian artists is almost always a plus feature: indeed, they bring an overall intelligence, refinement and, above all, range of interpretative values to this often superb and always attractive music. As for quality of ensemble, they are impeccable. This is undeniably still the best general survey of Mozart's string quartets available, and at mid-price the eight discs represent a safe investment that should yield many years of pleasure.

Additional recommendations ...

...Nos. 1-13. Divertimentos – D major, K136/K125*a*; B flat major, K137/K125*b*; F major, K138/K125*c*. **Hagen Quartet**. DG Ⓕ 431 645-2GH3 (three discs: 116 minutes: DDD: 6/91).

...Nos. 7, 8, 9 and 22. **Eder Quartet**. Naxos Ⓢ 8 550544 (67 minutes: DDD: 9/93).

...Nos. 10, 11 and 15. **Eder Quartet**. Naxos Ⓢ 8 550546 (62 minutes: DDD: 2/95).

...Nos. 12, 13 and 21. **Eder Quartet**. Naxos Ⓢ 8 550545 (57 DDD: 2/95).

New review

Mozart String Quartets – No. 15 in D minor, K421/K417*b*; No. 16 in E flat major, K428/K421*b*; No. 17 in B flat major, K458, "Hunt"; No. 20 in D major, K499, "Hoffmeister". **Franz Schubert Quartet** (Florian Zwiauer, Helge Rosenkranz, vns; Hartmut Pascher, va; Vincent Stadlmair, vc). Nimbus Ⓕ NI5455/6 (two discs: 115 minutes: DDD: 3/96). Recorded 1994.

Mozart's profound debt to Haydn in the six string quartets he dedicated to the composer (of which the Franz Schubert Quartet here play K421 and K428) is most evident in their innovative approach to texture. Moreover, the true equality between the four parts – demonstrating a critical relationship between instrumentation and musical substance – has inspired startlingly different interpretative approaches. The Chilingirian Quartet's elegantly refined, charmingly understated accounts of the D minor and E flat Quartets convincingly present the music in an intimate, private context. By contrast, like the Alban Berg Quartet, the Franz Schubert Quartet offer more dramatic readings, whose wider dynamic range projects the music in a more public manner. Nimbus's impressively truthful recording reveals the music's varied textures with pellucid clarity in the opening *allegros*, and relatively fast *andantes* imbue the performers' lush ensemble with appropriately increased animation. The minuets are more passionate than those of the Chilingirian, and the finales are likewise bold and dramatic, with the variation finale of the D minor work, in particular, confirming a satisfying sense of overall unity. Despite their striking contrasts, though, the Franz Schubert Quartet do not quite achieve the extremes of the Alban Berg, whose powerfully arresting 1979 recording of the *Hunt* Quartet (K458) still sounds exceptionally fresh. The Franz Schubert Quartet's comparatively relaxed approach to the first movement, for example, fails to match the Berg's exhilarating evocation of the chase. Nevertheless, for those who find the latter too highly charged, the Franz Schubert Quartet here offer an alternative whose beautiful textural clarity and vivid thematic detail many will find irresistible. The Eder Quartet's remarkably robust, fluent version of the *Hoffmeister* Quartet, whose greater formal and expressive scope is everywhere apparent, represents excellent value. However, the Franz Schubert Quartet bring greater delicacy and finesse to their performance, most notably in their dynamic control and contrapuntal clarity. Try them in the first movement's development section, their lucid counterpoint in the second movement's introspective trio (in the tonic minor), their heartfelt expression in the *Adagio*, and their enthralling, symphonic conception of the finale. These distinguished accounts by the Franz Schubert Quartet deserve an assured place among the very best alternatives.

Additional recommendations ...

...Nos. 14-23. **Alban Berg Quartet**. Teldec Ⓜ 4509-95495-2 (four discs: 265 minutes: ADD).

...Nos. 14-17 and 19. **Kuijken Quartet**. Denon Aliare Ⓕ CO-75850/2 (three discs: 206 minutes: DDD). ✒

...Nos. 17 and 19. **Alban Berg Quartet**. Teldec Ⓕ 2292-43037-2 (57 minutes: ADD: 7/86).

...Nos. 20 and 21. **Chilingirian Quartet**. CRD Ⓕ CRD3427 (53 minutes: DDD: 2/87).

...Nos. 15 and 19. **Salomon Quartet**. Hyperion Ⓕ CDA66170 (63 minutes: DDD: 4/87). ✒

...Nos. 14 and 15. **Chilingirian Quartet**. CRD Ⓕ CRD3362 (59 minutes: ADD: 9/90).

...Nos. 16 and 17. **Chilingirian Quartet**. CRD Ⓕ CRD3363 (56 minutes: ADD: 9/90).

...Nos. 18 and 19. **Chilingirian Quartet**. CRD Ⓕ CRD3364 (68 minutes: ADD: 9/90).

...Nos. 21 and 23. **Salomon Quartet**. Hyperion Ⓕ CDA66355 (61 minutes: DDD: 4/91). ✒

...Nos. 18 and 19. **Quatuor Mosaïques**. Auvidis Astrée Ⓕ E8748 (76 minutes: DDD: 8/92). ✒   Ⓖ

...No. 19. Divertimentos – K136-8. **Eder Quartet**. Naxos Ⓢ 8 550543 (66 minutes: DDD: 9/93).

...Nos. 20 and 23. Adagio and Fugue in C minor, K546. **Eder Quartet**. Naxos Ⓢ 8 550547 (62 minutes: DDD: 4/95).

...No. 19. **Beethoven** String Quartet No. 12 in E flat major, Op. 127. **Amadeus Quartet**. Orfeo mono Ⓕ C358941B* (63 minutes: ADD: 10/95)

...Nos. 20 and 23. Adagio and Fugue in C major, K546. **Eder Quartet**. Naxos Ⓢ 8 550547 (62 minutes: DDD: 5/95).

...Nos. 14-19. **Kuijken Quartet**. Denon Aliare Ⓕ CO-75850/2 (three discs: 206 minutes: DDD: 10/95). ✒

Mozart Flute Quartets – No. 1 in D major, K285; No. 2 in G major, K285*a*; No. 3 in
C major, K285*b*/KAnh171; No. 4 in A major, K298. Oboe Quartet in F major, K370/K368*b*.
 Australia Ensemble (Geoffrey Collins, fl; David Nuttall, ob; Dene Olding, vn; Irina Morozova,
va; Julian Smiles, vc). Tall Poppies Ⓟ TP029 (65 minutes: DDD: 7/94). Recorded 1992.

Despite the composer's open declarations of dislike for the flute which appear in his correspondence,
there is no evidence that they affected the music. In this new issue of the flute quartets, the Australia
Ensemble embrace the music's carefree, buoyant mood wholeheartedly. Their mix of youthful
enthusiasm and disciplined ensemble is particularly well suited to this music, and an incisively edged
tone-quality gives their performances added impact. They are at their best in the exuberant, faster
music, as in the light-hearted expression of, say, the finale of K285, the first movement of K285*b*, or
the wittily parodic finale of K298. However, in slower, lyrical passages, such as the slow movement of
the D major Quartet, K285, or the second movement of the C major Quartet, K285*b*, they deny some
of the music's possibilities for contrast. Here, the extremely sensuous melodiousness of Galway and
the Tokyo Quartet seem more successful. Galway's disc includes his own version for flute of the Oboe
Quartet, K370; here it is played in its original scoring. Galway's arrangement is wholly convincing,
but Nuttall's fine oboe playing makes an eloquent case for Mozart's original scoring. These bold,
forthright performances from the Australia Ensemble will have a wide appeal.

Additional recommendations ...

...Flute Quartets. Oboe Quartet (arr. Galway)[a]. [a]**James Galway** (fl); **Tokyo Quartet.** RCA Victor
Red Seal Ⓟ 09026 60442-2 (69 minutes: DDD: 6/93).

...Flute Quartets. **Irena Grafenauer** (fl); **Gidon Kremer** (vn); **Veronika Hagen** (va); **Clemens Hagen**
(vc). Sony Classical Ⓓ SK66240 (55 minutes: DDD: 6/96)

...Oboe Quartet[a]. Oboe Quintet in C minor, K406/K516*b*[b]. Adagio in F major, KAnh94/K580*a*[c].
String Quartet No. 22. [abc]**Lajos Lencsés** (ob/[c]cor ang); **Stamitz Quartet.** Capriccio Ⓟ 10 525
(68 minutes: DDD: 6/96).

Mozart Complete Edition, Volume 18 – Piano Variations: G major, K24[a]; D major, K25[a]; C major,
K179/K189*a*[a]; G major, K180/K173*a*[a]; C major, K264/K315*d*[a]; C major, K265/K300*e*[a]; F major,
K352/K374*ca*[a]; E flat major, K353K/300*f*[a]; E flat major, K354/K299*u*[a]; F major, K398/K416*e*[a];
G major, K455[a] (all from 6747 380, 6/79); A major, K460/K454*a*[c] (new to UK); B flat major,
K500[a]; D major, K573[a]; F major, K613[a] (6747 380). Minuets – F major, K1*d*[c]; G major/C major,
K1/K1*e*/K1*f*[c]; F major, K2[c]; F major, K4[c]; F major, K5[c]; D major, K94/K73*h*[c]; D major,
K355/K576*b*[b] (all new to UK). Fantasia in D minor, K397/K385*g*[b] (412 123-1PH, 7/84). Rondos
– D major, K485[b] (420 185-2PH, 7/87); A minor, K511[b] (412 122-1PH, 11/84). Adagio in
B minor, K540[b]. Gigue in G major, K574[b] (both from 412 616-1PH, 4/85). Klavierstück in
F major, K33*B*[c]. Capriccio in C major, K395/K300*g*[c]. March No. 1 in C major, K408/K383*c*[c].
Prelude and Fugue in C major, K394/K383*a*[c]. Allegros – C major, K1*b*[c]; F major, K1*c*[c], B flat
major, K3[c]; C major, K5*a*[c]; G minor, K312/K590*d*[c]; B flat major, K400/K372*a* (cpted Stadler)[c].
Suite in C major, K399/K385*i*[c]. Kleine Trauermarsch in C minor, K453*a*[c]. Andante in C major,
K1*a*[c]. Fugue in G minor, K401/K375*c*[c] (with Tini Mathot, hpd. All new to UK). [a]**Ingrid Haebler,**
[b]**Mitsuko Uchida** (pfs); [c]**Ton Koopman** (hpd). Philips Mozart Edition Ⓜ 422 518-2PME5
(five discs: 274 minutes: ADD/DDD: 10/91). 🎵 *Gramophone Award Winner 1991.* ⒼⒶⒼ

These five mid-price discs offer music of fine and often superb quality in a convenient format. The
piano was Mozart's own instrument (though he also played the violin) and he composed much music
for it besides the sonatas and concertos. Of the three artists here, two are generally fine and satisfying,
though the third is more controversial. Ingrid Haebler was recorded back in 1975, but the piano
sound is good and little tape background remains, and her performances of the variation sets, which
take up the first three discs, are delicate without cuteness, effortlessly encompassing the music's wide
range of moods. Mitsuko Uchida, on the fourth disc, performs individual pieces including the two
rondos and the beautiful *Adagio* in B minor (the only piece Mozart wrote in this key) in a highly
refined manner, a touch over-sophisticated perhaps but still beautiful and expressive and taking full,
unashamed advantage of the sound of a modern grand. By contrast, Ton Koopman's disc of minuets
and other miscellaneous things is played on a harpsichord at a semitone below modern concert pitch
and offers a recording of such immediacy that some listeners will regard it as too bright. Koopman
puts gusto into everything he does, but not always to good effect. However, even if grace is in short
supply in his performances, they undeniably offer ample personality and such reservations as one may
have about his playing should not affect the desirability of the set as a whole.

Mozart (arr. Grieg) Keyboard Sonatas – No. 15 in F major, K533/K494; No. 16 in C major, K545.
Fantasia in C minor, K475. **Sviatoslav Richter, Elisabeth Leonskaja** (pfs). Teldec Ⓟ 4509-90825-2
(62 minutes: DDD: 2/96). Recorded 1993.

Now this really is something to tickle the fancy of transcription-fanciers. When Grieg added an
accompaniment for a second piano to Mozart's keyboard sonatas, he did it primarily with teaching
in mind. It was apparently common practice in the 1880s for teachers to accompany their pupils on a
second piano. But the resulting compositions soon found their way into the concert-hall where,
according to Grieg, "the whole thing sounded surprisingly good". And so it does today. In trying to

"impart to several of Mozart's sonatas a tonal effect appealing to our modern ears" Grieg left a telling little document or two on just what those late nineteenth-century Norwegian ears expected. If the C major 'Sonata facile' seems to sit even more sedately in the drawing-room, then it soon becomes clear that the light glinting through its windows is not a million miles away from that bouncing off the fjord waters which lap around Troldhaugen. The C minor *Fantasia* becomes a dark salon melodrama (shades of *Bergljot*) which moves from conversation with not a little chromatic prevarication to the hanging of whimsical icicles of figuration around the major-key section. Gently exuberant harmonies cross-weave their way through the sparse trio-sonata-like textures of the opening F major before a trotting bass makes a high-stepping mountain horse of the rondo-finale. These are Mozart-Kugeln with a *bonne bouche* or two of the finest Gravadlax on the side. And if these fond tributes are good enough for Elisabeth Leonskaja and Sviatoslav Richter, who could resist tasting them?

Mozart Violin Sonatas – No. 1 in C major, K6. No. 2 in D major, K7. No. 3 in B flat major, K8. No. 4 in G major, K9. No. 5 in B flat major, K10. No. 6 in G major, K11. No. 7 in A major, K12. No. 8 in F major, K13. No. 9 in C major, K14. No. 10 in B flat major, K15. No. 11 in E flat major, K26. No. 12 in G major, K27. No. 13 in C major, K28. No. 14 in D major, K29. No. 15 in F major, K30. No. 16 in B flat major, K31. **Gérard Poulet** (vn); **Blandine Verlet** (hpd). Philips Duo Ⓜ 438 803-2PM2 (two discs: 135 minutes: ADD: 4/94). ✇ From 422 515-2PME7 (9/91). Recorded 1975.

The early keyboard and violin sonatas include the boy composer's first works to appear in print: K6-9 were composed during his five-month Paris stay of 1763-4; K10-15 followed in 1765, when the Mozarts resided in London's Belgravia for over a year. The Sonatas, K26-31 appeared a month or two later when the family moved to The Hague. The precociously lively invention is consistently ear-catching, especially in the spunky violin part in the *allegros* and the often graceful lyrical writing. Even if the keyboard dominates the musical partnership, the violinist is always contributing attractive comments. The performances here are very well played, being vital and fresh, and very spontaneous sounding; moreover, they are well balanced and naturally recorded. There is much to intrigue here and many of these miniature works are extremely rewarding in their simplicity and direct melodic appeal.

Additional recommendation ...
...Nos. 4, 11, 16, 17 and 36. **Pinchas Zukerman** (vn); **Marc Neikrug** (pf). RCA Victor Red Seal Ⓕ 09026 60744-2 (71 minutes: DDD: 10/94).

Mozart Violin Sonatas – No. 18 in G major, K301/K293*a*; No. 19 in E flat major, K302/K293*b*; No. 20 in C major, K303/K293*c*; No. 21 in E minor, K304/K300*c*; No. 22 in A major, K305/K293*d*; No. 23 in D major, K306/K300*l*. Variations in G on "La bergère Célimène", K359/K374*a*. Variations in G minor on "Hélas, j'ai perdu mon amant", K360/K374*b*. **Chiara Banchini** (vn); **Temenuschka Vesselinova** (fp). Harmonia Mundi Ⓕ HMC90 1466/7 (two discs: 110 minutes: DDD: 5/94). ✇ Recorded 1993.

The performances here are not quite the kind you might expect from period specialists. They are not at all 'objective', careful, small-scale or self-conscious but, on the contrary, full-blooded, spirited, eager to make the most of the music. They bring out the variety in this group of sonatas as strongly as any performance available. The appealing E flat work, K302, is tellingly done, its *Andante grazioso* second movement in particular, with the melancholy tone of its principal theme accentuated by the deliberate tempo, the intensity, and the care with which the varying textures are characterized. The last sonata, K306, is the only one in three movements, and these players make it clear that they regard it as a bigger piece in every sense, the opening movement done with glitter and spirit, the *Andante cantabile* taken slowly and allowed considerable weight and the finale not so much elegant and humorous, as it is apt to be, but again duly serious and substantial. The recording is excellent.

Additional recommendations ...
...Nos. 17, 32 and 35. **Isaac Stern** (vn); **Yefim Bronfman** (pf). Sony Classical SK53972 (70 minutes: DDD: 9/94).
...Nos. 19, 20, 22, 24 and 28. **Isaac Stern** (vn); **Yefim Bronfman** (pf). Sony Classical Ⓕ SK64309 (72 minutes: DDD: 11/95).

Mozart Violin Sonatas – No. 17 in C major, K296; No. 24 in F major, K376/K374*d*; No. 25 in F major, K377/K374*e*; No. 26 in B flat major, K378/K317*d*; No. 27 in G major, K379/K373*a*; No. 28 in E flat major, K380/K374*f*; No. 33 in E flat major, K481. **Chiara Banchini** (vn); **Temenuschka Vesselinova** (fp). Harmonia Mundi Ⓕ HMC90 1468/9 (two discs: 146 minutes: DDD: 10/94). ✇ Recorded 1993.

These are performances of intense conviction, informed by some very interesting and original musical insights. The first six of these seven sonatas are the group Mozart published shortly after he settled in Vienna; they are supplemented by a later work. Take the first sonata played here, K376: the opening movement is treated not as a lively and showy piece but rather as a pensive one, with little touches of passing rubato (the kind Mozart favoured, time borrowed and repaid rather than actually stolen) to illuminate the shape or the meaning of a phrase or to add point to the instrumental dialogue. In the *Andante* too the selective and musicianly use of small-scale rhythmic inflexion is extraordinarily telling, heightening many moments and lending much extra expressive weight to the whole; and the finale is done duly gracefully, with proper significance assigned to its chromatic harmonies and its contrasts of texture. So it continues. There is a splendidly exuberant reading of the opening movement of K377, with many happy details of shaping, and the variation movement, with the breadth of their view of its structure, becomes much more than merely decorative. They seem to have a special feeling for Mozart's variation movements and a capacity to bring to them a real cumulative sense rather than being content to read them as a series of ornamental episodes. There are one or two places where you might fault the ensemble or find some small technical detail awry; but clearly Vesselinova and Banchini truly think the music together, and the result is a quite exceptional pair of discs.

Mozart Violin Sonatas – No. 32 in B flat major, K454; No. 35 in A major, K526; No. 36 in
   F major, K547. **Chiara Banchini** (vn); **Temenuschka Vesselinova** (fp). Harmonia Mundi
   Ⓔ HMC90 1470 (63 minutes: DDD: 2/95). ✒ Recorded 1993.
If you want a nice, polished, civilized performance of Mozart's late sonatas for piano and violin, don't buy the CD from Chiara Banchini and Temenuschka Vesselinova. These are vivid, adventurous readings, which take nothing for granted and say a lot of new things about familiar music, often in a very exciting way. Nowhere more so than at the beginning of K454, with its very slow and grandly performed introduction: a startlingly dramatic opening, which Mozart could well have intended (it was after all written to catch the ear of the emperor, when Mozart was giving a concert with a visiting *virtuosa*). In the *Andante* the expressive articulation of the principal theme and the impeccable timing of the detail – a delightful sense of the players perfectly capturing the logic of the music – helps give rise to an extraordinarily intense reading; the finale is no less individual, with its precise timing and placing of accents and many a phrase interpreted in novel fashion. K526 is equally daring and equally persuasive. The large-scale architecture is particularly appealing and so forcefully conveyed, in the finale, which is passionate and yet still has a sense of fun. In the first movement there is some very brilliant dialogue between the instruments, as well as eloquence from the violin in the lyrical music and much resourceful management of dynamic detail. In K547, however, they are less successful, trying, it seems, to impose on a slender work ("A little sonata for beginners", Mozart called it) an intensity that it cannot support. Still, overall these are performances of distinction, originality and real vision.

New review
Mozart Suite in the style of Handel in C major, K399 – Overture. Adagio and Allegro in F minor,
   K594 (ed. Trotter). Londoner Notenskizzenbuch, KAnh109b – Allegro in F major, K15a;
   Andante in E major, K15o; Andante in B flat major, K15q. Andante in B flat major, K15ii.
   Adagio in B minor, K540. Allegro in G major, K72a. Fugue in G minor, K401/K375e. Gigue in
   G major, K574. Prelude and Fugue in C major, K394/K383a. Andantino in E flat major, K236.
   Andante für eine Walze in eine kleine Örgel in F major, K616. Adagio in C major, K356/K617a.
   Fantasia für eine Uhr, K608 (ed. Trotter). **Thomas Trotter** (org). Decca London Ⓔ 443 451-2LH
   (66 minutes: DDD: 10/95). Played on the organ of the Nederlandse Hervormde Kerk, Farmsum,
   The Netherlands. Recorded 1993.
It takes much scratching around in the dirt to find enough Mozart organ music to fill a CD. It wasn't that Mozart was unfamiliar with the organ: far from it – Robin Langley's absorbing insert-notes quote a conversation between Vincent Novello and Mozart's widow in which she says "Mozart's favourite instrument was the organ – upon which he played with incomparable skill". It was this "incomparable skill" which meant Mozart left so little organ music for posterity; he was such a fluent improviser that he never really needed to write anything down. So what we have here, apart from pieces for other instruments which probably wouldn't get much of an airing if they weren't played on the organ (K594 and K608, originally for mechanical clock, are, ironically, generally considered to be the greatest organ works between Bach and Mendelssohn), are fragments and miniatures, tantalizing crumbs from the table of a genius, which in the hands of most players would seem little more than worthwhile curiosities. Thomas Trotter is an openly communicative player and while his discography to date centres around the extensive romantic repertoire, he proves himself here to be equally compelling in both classical repertoire and in short musical structures. Helped by a ravishing instrument which he handles with admirable fluency (although the action noise is horribly obtrusive), Trotter's Mozart truly comes to life. The big pieces (including a breathtakingly virtuosic account of K608) sit comfortably alongside the miniatures and the whole disc presents a thoroughly rewarding musical experience – required listening to anyone who would dismiss the classical era as anti-organ.

Mozart Complete Edition, Volume 17 – Complete Piano Sonatas: No. 1 in C major, K279/K189d
   (from 412 617-1PH, 1/86); No. 2 in F major, K280/K189e; No. 3 in B flat major, K281/K189f;
   No. 4 in E flat major, K282/K189g; No. 5 in G major, K283/K189h (all from 420 186-2PH, 4/88);
   No. 6 in D major, K284/K205b (420 185-1PH, 7/87); No. 7 in C major, K309/K284b; No. 8 in
   A minor, K310/K300d; No. 9 in D major, K311/K284c (412 174-1PH, 4/86); No. 10 in C major,
   K330/K300h (412 616-1PH, 4/85); No. 11 in A major, K331/K300i; No. 12 in F major,
   K332/K300k (412 123-1PH, 7/84); No. 13 in B flat major, K333/K315c (412 616-1PH); No. 14 in
   C minor, K457 (412 617-1PH); No. 15 in F major, K533/K494; No. 16 in C major, K545 (412
   122-1PH, 11/84); No. 17 in B flat major, K570 (420 185-1PH); No. 18 in D major, K576 (420 617-

1PH). Fantasia in C minor, K475 (412 617-1PH). **Mitsuko Uchida** (pf). Philips Mozart Edition Ⓜ 422 517-2PME5 (five discs: 325 minutes: DDD: 9/91). *Gramophone Award Winner 1989.*

By common consent, Mitsuko Uchida is among the leading Mozart pianists of today, and her recorded series of the piano sonatas won critical acclaim as it appeared and finally *Gramophone* Awards in 1989 and 1991. Here are all the sonatas, plus the *Fantasia* in C minor, K475, which is in some ways a companion piece to the sonata in the same key, K457. This is unfailingly clean, crisp and elegant playing, that avoids anything like a romanticized view of the early sonatas such as the delightfully fresh G major, K283. On the other hand, Uchida responds with the necessary passion to the forceful, not to say *Angst*-ridden, A minor Sonata, K310. Indeed, her complete series is a remarkably fine achievement, comparable with her account of the piano concertos. The recordings were produced by Erik Smith in the Henry Wood Hall in London and offer excellent piano sound; thus an unqualified recommendation is in order for what must be one of the most valuable volumes in Philips's Complete Mozart Edition. Do not be put off by critics who suggest that these sonatas are less interesting than some other Mozart compositions, for they are fine pieces written for an instrument that he himself played and loved.

Additional recommendations ...

...Complete Sonatas. Fantasia, K475. **Maria João Pires** (pf). DG Ⓕ 431 760-2GH6 (six discs: 397 minutes: DDD: 2/92).

...Complete Sonatas. Fantasia, K475. **Christoph Eschenbach** (pf). DG Ⓜ 419 445-2GX5 (five discs: 339 minutes: ADD: 3/94).

...Nos. 1-10. **Walter Klien** (pf). Vox Ⓜ 115842-2 (two discs: 142 minutes: ADD).

...Nos. 2-5. **Mitsuko Uchida** (pf). Philips Ⓕ 420 186-2PH (54 minutes: DDD: 4/88). *Part of the five-disc set reviewed above.*

...Nos. 8, 11 and 15. **Murray Perahia** (pf). Sony Classical Ⓕ SK48233 (64 minutes: DDD: 12/92).

...Nos. 3, 4 and 15. **Maria-João Pires** (pf). DG Ⓕ 437 546-2GH (62 minutes: DDD: 7/93).

...Nos. 2, 5, 13, 14 and 15. Fantasia in C minor, K475. **Sviatoslav Richter** (pf). Philips Ⓕ 438 480-2PH2 (two discs: 138 minutes: 8/94).

...No. 8. *Coupled with works by* **Bach, Schubert** *and* **Chopin Dinu Lipatti** (pf). EMI Références mono Ⓜ CDH5 65166-2* (73 minutes: ADD: 12/94). *See review in the Collections section; refer to the Index to Reviews.*

...No. 10. *Coupled with works by* **Bach, Schoenberg** *and* **Sweelinck Glenn Gould** (pf). Sony Classical mono Ⓜ SMK53474* (76 minutes: ADD: 9/95). *See review under Bach; refer to the Index to Reviews.*

Mozart Piano Sonatas – No. 5 in G major, K283/K189*h*; No. 6 in D major, K284/K205*b*; No. 10 in C major, K330/K300*h*. **Maria-João Pires** (pf). DG Ⓕ 437 791-2GH (73 minutes: DDD: 3/94).

Maria-João Pires presents these sonatas with clear yet lightly pedalled textures and an overall directness that still allows room for tonal and rhythmic flexibility – which, generally speaking, is not overdone. Largely, her playing seems to let the music speak for itself, although of course just offering the notes is not enough and what we here appreciate is the art that conceals art. However, one might question the occasional detail: for example, less than a minute into the G major Sonata, Pires's longish trill on the D preceding the second subject is questionable, which gives us a bar with four beats in it instead of three. The *Andante* of the same work begins with repeated Cs that seem too emphatically staccato, and its central section is a little over-dramatized. The dance movement called *Rondeau en Polonaise* in K284 is on the slow side, though it still holds together, and the variation-form finale varies considerably in pace. Pires consistently observes repeats, including the second halves of movements (thus we get virtually every note of K283 twice), as is indicated. These are clear, commendable performances that give pleasure, and the kind of grace that Pires brings to this music, in which other pianists can sound a touch severe, is most appealing. The recording is pleasing and admirably faithful.

Additional recommendation ...

...Nos. 5 and 11. Fantasia in D minor, K397/K385*g*. **Ivo Pogorelich** (pf). DG Ⓕ 437 763-2GH (48 minutes: DDD: 8/95).

New review

Mozart Concert Arias – Ah! se in ciel, benigne stelle, K538; Vorrei spiegarvi, oh Dio!, K418; No, no che non sei capace, K419; Se tutti i mali miei, K83/K73*p*; Popoli di Tessaglia! ... Io non chiedo, eterni Dei, K316/K300*b*; Mia speranza adorata ... Ah, non sai qual pena sia, K416; Alcandro, lo confesso ... Non so d'onde viene, K294; Ma che vi fece, o stelle ... Sperai vicino il lido, K368. **Natalie Dessay** (sop); **Orchestra of the Opéra de Lyon / Theodor Guschlbauer.** EMI Ⓕ CDC5 55386-2 (64 minutes: DDD: 8/96). Texts and translations included.

Natalie Dessay is a charming singer, with almost all the endowments of art and nature which these arias so exactly require. Her range extends upward far into the leger lines yet without incurring breathiness of a pallid coloration in the lower notes. She has a sylph's grace and lightness, and yet the timbre or character of her voice is thoroughly human. The profusion of scales and more intricate passagework common in some degree to all these pieces finds in her an unostentatious virtuoso, mind and breath giving well-regulated support, and a sensitive feeling for phrase and line making good musical sense throughout. Where vehemence and a dramatic quality of voice are in demand, as in the opening of *Popoli di Tessaglia*, we can find some reassurance in their absence because at least the young singer does not try to force an effect. In less strenuous attack, as in *No, no che non sei capace*, she conveys the energy of a determined spirit yet still has some way to develop as an expressive artist. The more sorrowful and tender phrases of *Se tutti i mali miei*, for example, evoke only a mild response in her. Occasionally, too, Dessay's purity forfeits normal resonance and for what seems to be an involuntary note or two the voice flutes with a kind of disembodied hollowness. An instance occurs just before the second part of *Vorrei spiegarvi*, yet this is such a lovely performance, so graceful in its leisurely interplay of voice and instruments, that grumbling really is out of order. Orchestra, conductor and recorded sound all make their contributions. In all of these marvellous incidental compositions the listener has one essential occupation, which is the discovery of delight.

Mozart Mass in C major, K257, "Credo". Litaniae de venerabili altaris sacramento, K243. **Angela Maria Blasi** (sop); **Elisabeth von Magnus** (contr); **Deon van der Walt** (ten); **Alistair Miles** (bass); **Arnold Schoenberg Choir; Vienna Concentus Musicus / Nikolaus Harnoncourt.** Teldec Das Alte Werk Ⓟ 9031-72304-2 (61 minutes: DDD: 6/93). ✍ Notes, texts and translations included. Recorded 1991. ⒼⒼⒼ

The *Litaniae de venerabili altaris sacramento* of 1775 has powerful claims to be reckoned the finest of Mozart's church works before the C minor Mass and Requiem; but it has never quite had the recognition it deserves. Or the performance: until now, that is. It is clearly a deeply felt work, from the grave, warm opening of the "Kyrie", through the imposing "Verbum caro factum" and the graceful "Hostia" that succeeds it, the "Tremendum" with its almost Verdian menace and the appealing "Dulcissum convivium" (a soprano aria with soft textures supplied by flutes and bassoons), the highly original "Viaticum" and the resourcefully and lengthily developed "Pignus" to the "Agnus", a beautiful soprano aria with solo writing for flute, oboe and cello. The performance here under Nikolaus Harnoncourt rightly sees no need to apologize for the stylistic diversity of the work. The issue is made still more attractive by the inclusion of a Mass setting of the same year, one of Mozart's most inventive and original in its textures and its treatment of words. Altogether a very attractive record.

Mozart Mass in C major, K317, "Coronation". Vesperae solennes de confessore in C major, K339. Epistle Sonata in C major, K278/K271e[a]. **Emma Kirkby** (sop); **Catherine Robbin** (mez); **John Mark Ainsley** (ten); **Michael George** (bass); **Winchester Cathedral Choir; Winchester Quiristers; Academy of Ancient Music / Christopher Hogwood** with [a]**Alastair Ross** (org). L'Oiseau-Lyre Ⓟ 436 585-2OH (54 minutes: DDD: 4/93). ✍ Texts and translations included. Recorded 1990.
Mozart Mass in C major, K317[a], "Coronation"[a]. Vesperae solennes de confessore in C major, K339[b]. Ave verum corpus in D major, K618[c]. [ab]**Marinella Pennicchi** (sop); [ab]**Catherine Patriasz** (contr); [ab]**Zeger Vandersteene** (ten); [ab]**Jelle Draijer** (bass); **Netherlands Chamber Choir; Orchestra of the Eighteenth Century / Frans Brüggen.** Philips Ⓟ 434 799-2PH (51 minutes: DDD: 6/95). ✍ Recorded 1991. ⒼⒼ

It is difficult to think of many recordings of Mozart's church music that so happily captures its character – the particular mixture of confidence, jubilation and contemplation – as Hogwood's. His unfussy direction, his broad phrasing, his lively but generally unhurried tempos and his happy details of timing serve splendidly in the *Coronation* Mass, the finest of Mozart's completed mass settings; the solemnity of the *Kyrie*, the fine swing of the *Gloria* and the energy of the *Credo*, with due pause for its rapt moment at the "Et incarnatus", all these come over with due effect. Arguably the "Osanna" is rather quick, but its jubilation is splendid. And the sweetness of the *Benedictus* is ravishing. Not more so, however, than the *Agnus*, for there, at a decidedly slow tempo, Hogwood allows Emma Kirkby to make the most of this very sensuous music, which she duly most beautifully does. The soloists are altogether an excellent team, with two refined voices in the middle and Michael George a firm and sturdy bass. The inclusion of the K278 Epistle Sonata is a happy notion. The *Vesperae solennes de confessore* is a setting of the five vesper psalms and the *Magnificat*, made in 1780, a year after the Mass, for some church feast in Salzburg. With admirable singing from the choir, a fresh-voiced group whose boys have a fine bright ring, and a spacious recording with exceptionally good stereo separation that properly conveys the ecclesiastical ambience, this is a disc to treasure.

The coupling on the Philips disc is becoming increasingly popular, and Frans Brüggen's version is as appealing as Hogwood's. The performances are direct and spirited, mostly at lively tempos, and, in feeling, very much in tune with how this music was regarded in its time – part of a straightforward act of worship, essentially a joyous one. The playing and singing are attractively shapely, as the elegant solos for soprano and tenor, and for the orchestral oboe, in the *Kyrie* of K317, show at the outset. In the *Gloria*, and elsewhere, some of the accents are perhaps overdone, but there is a good, flowing rhythm and a sense of jubilation about it, and much the same goes for the *Credo*; both are taken decidedly on the quick side, with the result that the contrast in the latter with a distinctly slow "Et incarnatus" is perhaps too marked. The *Sanctus* is duly imposing, the *Benedictus* very light and delicate, almost a little sugary; then in the *Agnus Dei* there is particularly warm and graceful singing from Marinella Pennicchi, accompanied with much refinement. The *Vesperae solennes de confessore* is predominantly a choral work and the Netherlands Chamber Choir produce plenty of strong, forthright singing for Brüggen, especially in the affirmative music of the two outer movements, done in very spirited fashion. A gentle and finely controlled account of the *Ave verum corpus* rounds off a very pleasing disc.

Additional recommendations ...
...K317[a]. C minor, K427/K417*a*, "Great"[b]. D minor, K626[c], "Requiem". **Soloists;** [ac]**John Alldis Choir; London Symphony** [b]**Chorus and** [ab]**Orchestra,** [c]**BBC Symphony Orchestra / Sir Colin Davis.** Philips Duo Ⓜ 438 800-2PM2 (two discs: 135 minutes: ADD: 3/94).   Ⓖ
...K317. Exsultate, jubilate, K165/K158*a*. Vesperae solennes de confessore. **Soloists; The English Concert and** [a]**Choir / Trevor Pinnock.** Archiv Produktion Ⓕ 445 353-2AH (68 minutes: DDD: 10/94). ✍
...K317[a]. Ave verum corpus[b]. Vesperae solennes de confessore[a]. Exsultate, jubilate, K165/K158*a*[c]. [ac]**Barbara Schlick** (sop); [a]**Elisabeth von Magnus** (contr); [a]**Paul Agnew** (ten); [a]**Matthijs Mesdag** (bass); **Amsterdam Baroque** [ab]**Choir and Orchestra / Ton Koopman.** Erato Ⓕ 0630-10705-2 (72 minutes: DDD: 2/96).

Mozart (ed. Maunder) Mass in C minor, K427/K417*a*, "Great". **Arleen Auger, Lynne Dawson** (sops); **John Mark Ainsley** (ten); **David Thomas** (bass); **Winchester Cathedral Choir; Winchester College Quiristers; Academy of Ancient Music / Christopher Hogwood.** L'Oiseau-Lyre Florilegium Ⓜ 425 528-2OH (51 minutes: DDD: 7/90). ✍ Text and translation included. Recorded 1988.
Mozart left unfinished the work that ought to have been the choral masterpiece of his early Viennese years but there is enough of it to make up nearly an hour's music – music that is sometimes sombre, sometimes florid, sometimes jubilant. Christopher Hogwood avoids any charge of emotional detachment in his steady and powerful opening *Kyrie*, monumental in feeling, dark in tone; and he brings ample energy to the big, bustling choruses of the *Gloria* – and its long closing fugue is finely sustained. The clarity and ring of the boys' voices serve him well in these numbers. There is a strong solo team, headed by the late Arleen Auger in radiant, glowing voice and, as usual, singing with refined taste; Lynne Dawson joins her in the duets, John Mark Ainsley too in the trio. But this is essentially a "soprano mass" – Mozart wrote it, after all, with the voice of his new wife (and perhaps thoughts of the much superior one of her sister Aloysia) in his mind – and Auger, her voice happily stealing in for the first time in the lovely "Christe", excels in the florid and expressive music of the "Et incarnatus" (where Richard Maunder has supplied fuller string parts than usual, perhaps fuller than Mozart would have done had he finished the work). Hogwood directs with his usual spirit and clarity.

Additional recommendations ...
...Mass in C minor. **Soloists; Monteverdi Choir; English Baroque Soloists / John Eliot Gardiner.** Philips Ⓕ 420 210-2PH (54 minutes: DDD: 5/88). ✍
...Mass in C minor. **Beethoven** Missa solemnis. **Soloists; Atlanta Symphony Chorus and Orchestra / Robert Shaw.** Telarc Ⓕ CD80150 (two discs: 139 minutes: DDD: 11/88).
...Mass in C minor. **Soloists; Berlin Radio Chorus; Berlin Philharmonic Orchestra / Claudio Abbado.** Sony Classical Ⓕ SK46671 (53 minutes: DDD: 10/91).
...Mass in C minor. Masonic Funeral Music, K477. **Soloists; Collegium Vocale; La Chapelle Royale Choir; Champs Elysées Orchestra / Philip Herreweghe.** Harmonia Mundi Ⓕ HMC90 1393 (60 minutes: DDD: 9/92). ✍
...Mass in C minor. Ave verum corpus in D major, K618. **Soloists; Academy of St Martin in the Fields Chorus and Orchestra / Sir Neville Marriner.** Philips Ⓕ 438 999-2PH (55 minutes: DDD: 12/94).

Mozart (cptd. Süssmayr) Mass in D minor, K626, "Requiem". **Sylvia McNair** (sop); **Carolyn Watkinson** (contr); **Francisco Araiza** (ten); **Robert Lloyd** (bass); **Chorus and Academy of St Martin in the Fields / Sir Neville Marriner.** Philips Ⓕ 432 087-2PH (50 minutes: DDD: 12/91). Text and translation included. Recorded 1990.

New review
Mozart Mass in D minor, K626, "Requiem" (cptd. Süssmayr)[a]. Ave verum corpus in D major, K618. [a]**Anna Maria Panzarella** (sop); [a]**Nathalie Stutzmann** (contr); [a]**Christoph Prégardien** (ten); [a]**Nathan Berg** (bass); **Les Arts Florissants / William Christie.** Erato Ⓕ 0630-10697-2 (54 minutes: DDD: 11/95). ✍ Texts and translations included. Recorded 1994.
Alongside those old musical teasers, "Who wrote Haydn's *Toy* Symphony?" (Leopold Mozart) and "Who wrote Purcell's Trumpet Voluntary?" (Jeremiah Clarke) can be added "Who wrote Mozart's Requiem?". Mozart's pupil Süssmayr was responsible for much of the work as most modern audiences would recognize it, but exactly how much was Mozart's, how much Süssmayr's, and how much anybody else's is anyone's guess. But performers don't seem unduly perturbed by this masterpiece's less than certain provenance, and there is no shortage of first-rate CD versions. Sir Neville Marriner's interpretation stands out as one of towering authority with a nobility and emotional impact few performances outside the concert-hall could expect to muster. From the stately opening "Requiem aeternam" to the Requiem's emotional climax, the "Agnus Dei", Marriner's musicians produce superlative performances. The chorus is remarkably well disciplined (just listen to the beautifully incisive singing with its dramatic dynamic contrasts in the "Domine Jesu"), and from the soloists Robert Lloyd's resonant "Tuba mirum" is a stunning contribution to a disc of exceptional quality.

Les Arts Florissants provide a substantial, dramatic reading: the tempo for the "Requiem aeternam" is slow, but malleable, and Christie is ready to make the most of the changes in orchestral colour or choral texture and indeed to dramatize the music to the utmost. Clearly he has little truck with any notion that this is an austere piece: he sees it as operatic, almost romantic – and the result is very compelling. There are surprising things: "Quantus tremor", in a very weighty account of the "Dies irae", for example, is hushed rather than terrifying; the "Recordare" is slow to the point of stickiness; there are rather mannered crescendos in the *Sanctus*; and often cadences are drawn out, for example in the "Hostias". The powerful choruses of the Sequence are imposingly done, and the grave "Lacrimosa" wonderfully catches the special significance not only of the music itself but also of the fact that this is the moment where Mozart's last autograph trails off. The choral singing is sharply etched and generally distinguished: the choir give a vigorous yet finely dovetailed *Kyrie* fugue and the "Quam olim Abrahae" is splendidly sturdy. Although the solo singing is not uniformly outstanding the soprano's melting tone is sometimes very appealing, and Prégardien is an excellent stylist; the *Benedictus* is particularly impressive, very shapely and refined. In short, this is a reading full of character and ideas, very much a conscious modern interpretation of the work and very finely executed. The disc is completed by perhaps the only piece which can reasonably follow the Requiem, the *Ave verum corpus*, in a slow, hushed, rather romantic reading that is undeniably moving.

Additional recommendations ...

...Requiem. Kyrie in D minor, K341. **Soloists; Monteverdi Choir; English Baroque Soloists / John Eliot Gardiner.** Philips Ⓕ 420 197-2PH (54 minutes: DDD: 11/87). ✍

...Requiem. **Soloists; St John's College Choir, Cambridge; English Chamber Orchestra / George Guest.** Chandos Ⓕ CHAN8574 (54 minutes: DDD: 2/88).

...Requiem. **Soloists; John Alldis Choir; BBC Symphony Orchestra / Sir Colin Davis.** Philips Silver Line Ⓜ 420 353-2PM (54 minutes: ADD: 2/88).

...Requiem (ed. Druce). Ave verum corpus, K618. Maurerische Trauermusik, K477/K479. **Soloists; Schütz Choir of London; Schütz Consort; London Classical Players / Roger Norrington.** EMI Ⓕ CDC7 54525-2 (58 minutes: DDD: 11/92). ✍

...Requiem[a]. Ave verum corpus in D major, K618. [a]**Anna Maria Panzarella** (sop); [a]**Nathalie Stutzmann** (contr); [a]**Christoph Prégardien** (ten); [a]**Nathan Berg** (bass); **Les Arts Florissants / William Christie.** Erato Ⓕ 0630-10697-2 (54 minutes: DDD: 11/95). ✍

Mozart Così fan tutte – In uomini, in soldati; Temerari! ... Come scoglio; Ei parte ... Per pietà, ben mio. Le nozze di Figaro – E Susanna non vien! ... Dove sono; Giunse alfin il momento ... Al desio (K577a). Don Giovanni – Batti, batti; In quali eccessi ... Mi tradì quell' alma ingrata. Davidde penitente, K469 – Lunghi le cure ingrate. Exsultate, jubilate, K165/K158a. **Cecilia Bartoli** (mez); **Vienna Chamber Orchestra / György Fischer.** Decca Ⓕ 443 452-2DH (61 minutes: DDD: 11/94). Texts and translations included. Recorded 1993.

On disc anything is possible: taking this selection of arias together with her other Mozart/da Ponte recordings, we can now hear Bartoli in all three female roles in *Così fan tutte*, three in *Le nozze di Figaro* and two in *Don Giovanni* – versatility unbounded. There are relatively few Italian mezzos, or sopranos for that matter, who sing a lot of Mozart and Bartoli's very Italian characteristics are immediately identifiable: brilliance of execution, vitality of words, sharpness of mind. She tears into the recitative before Donna Elvira's "Mi tradì" with a blistering fury that leaves most interpreters of the role standing and has no problems with the *fioriture* of the aria itself. Her Fiordiligi has the bite for "Come scoglio", but comparisons with a variety of lyric sopranos show up a want of depth to the tone, both here and in "Per pietà". Her Countess delivers her lines with appropriately aristocratic weight, though one senses her natural temperament being suppressed with difficulty. However much she tries to disguise herself, the real Bartoli is likely to pop her head out. There are unlikely to be any complaints about her effervescent Despina or Zerlina, both portrayals for which she has stage experience. In the concert-hall she is also a spirited interpreter of *Exsultate, jubilate*. From the opening line Bartoli makes other singers seem bland by comparison, getting the Latin words to tingle with a sense of elation that only an Italian-speaker would dare. The orchestral sound might be more firmly focused (the sound picture in "Batti, batti" has the solo cello close, while the wind struggle to be heard from some deep recess) but Fischer accompanies his soloist with energy and tact.

Additional recommendation ...

...Die Entführung aus dem Serail[a]. Exsultate, jubilate[b]. **Soloists;** [a]**Berlin RIAS Chamber Choir and Orchestra;** [b]**Berlin Radio Symphony Orchestra / Ferenc Fricsay.** DG Dokumente [a]mono/[b]stereo Ⓜ 445 412-2GDO2* (two discs: 125 minutes: ADD 7/95).

Margaret Price sings Mozart Dame Margaret Price (sop); [a]**English Chamber Orchestra;** [b]**London Philharmonic Orchestra / James Lockhart** ([c]pf). RCA Victor Gold Seal Ⓜ 09026 61635-2 (two discs: 151 minutes: ADD: 5/95). Items marked [a] from SER5675 (10/73), [b]LRL1 5077 (10/75), [c]LSB5001 (4/71). Texts and translations included.

Mozart La clemenza di Tito – Parto, parto (with Thea King, cl)[a]. Le nozze di Figaro – Voi che sapete[a]; E Susanna non vien! ... Dove sono[a]; Giunse alfin il momento ... Deh vieni, non tardar[a]. Die Entführung aus dem Serail – Martern aller Arten[a]. Il rè pastore – L'amerò, sarò costantea (Jose-Luis Garcia, vn)[a]. Don Giovanni – In quali eccessi ... Mi tradì quell' alma ingrata[a]; Crudele! Ah no mio bene ... Non mi dir[a]. Idomeneo – Parto, e l'unico ... Idol mio, se ritroso[b].

Concert arias – Vado, ma dove? oh Dei!, K583[b]; Vorrei spiegarvi, oh Dio, K418[b]; Ch'io me scordi di te ... Non temer, amato bene, K490 (Dennis Simons, vn)[b]; Al desio, K577[b]; Bella mia fiamma ... Resta, oh cara, K528[b]. Ch'io mi scordi di te ... Non temer, amato bene, K505[b]; Nehmt meinen Dank, ihr holden Gönner, K383[b]. Eine kleine deutsche Kantate, K619[c]. **Mussorgsky** The Nursery[c]. **Liszt** Sonetti di Petrarca, S270[c].   Ⓖ

Margaret Price's early recordings announced to the world a unique singer: nobody could mistake that purity of tone or the way she has of moving from note to note, as though each is a separate gem in a row of pearls. Although complete recordings followed of some of the Mozart operas, this disc of individual arias holds its own. "Idol mio" from *Idomeneo* has never been more ravishing; the Countess's "Dove sono" is an example of the purest classical poise, despite some plummy Italian vowels. A touch of breathiness intrudes in fast passages where the voice is asked to move around, but even mentioning it seems unfair, when there is so much beauty on all sides. At this stage of her career Margaret Price was not the kind of artist to inject drama into Mozart's more formal concert arias, but that disc also contains some favourite tracks. Her *Nehmt meinen Dank* lights upon an unexpectedly sweet tone and *Vorrei spiegarvi* seems even more spectacular today than it did at the time, given that the young Mozartian soprano has subsequently gone on to sing Aida. The fillers are taken from Price's "Wigmore Hall" song recital. There is no room for the Italian songs, but we do get her fearless singing of Liszt's Petrarch Sonnets, accompanied in a drily unromantic fashion by James Lockhart. The verdict is clear-cut: not to be missed.

Mozart Le nozze di Figaro – Non so più; Voi che sapete; Giunse alfin il momento ... Deh vieni. Così fan tutte – E'amore un ladroncello. Don Giovanni – Vedrai, carino. La clemenza di Tito – Parto, parto[b]; Deh, per questo; Ecco il punto, o Vitellia ... Non piu di fiori[c]. Concert Arias – Chi sa, chi sa, qual sia, K582; Alma grande e nobil core, K578; Ch'io mi scordi di te?, K505[a]. **Cecilia Bartoli** (mez); [a]**András Schiff** (pf); **Peter Schmidtl** ([b]basset cl and [c]basset hn); **Vienna Chamber Orchestra / György Fischer.** Decca Ⓕ 430 513-2DH (58 minutes: DDD: 12/91). Texts and translations included. Recorded 1989-90.

Mozart wrote some of his most appealing music for the mezzo-soprano voice with the roles of Cherubino and Susanna in *Le nozze di Figaro*, Dorabella in *Così fan tutte* and Zerlina in *Don Giovanni* each boasting at least one memorable aria. Alongside these this disc includes a handful of concert arias including *Ch'io mi scordi di te?* which was written for the farewell performance of the great mezzo Nancy Storace with Mozart himself playing the concertante piano role. Here with as innate an interpreter of Mozart's piano writing as András Schiff and a voice so remarkably self-assured as Cecilia Bartoli's the electricity of that first, historic performance seems almost to be recreated. And, here as elsewhere, György Fischer directs the splendid Vienna Chamber Orchestra with disarming sensitivity while the recording is wonderfully warm and vibrant. Cecilia Bartoli boasts a voice of quite extraordinary charm and unassuming virtuosity: her vocal characterizations would be the envy of the finest actresses and her intuitive singing is in itself a sheer delight. But she also brings to these arias a conviction and understanding of the subtleties of the language which only a native Italian could. Listen to the subtle nuances of "Voi che sapete", the depth of understanding behind Dorabella's seemingly frivolous "E'amore un ladroncello"; these are not mere performances, but interpretations which penetrate to the very soul of the music. No Mozart lover should be without this CD.

Additional recommendation ...

...Alma grande e nobil core, K578. Ah, lo previdi ... Ah, t'invola, K272. A questo seno ... Or, che il chielo, K374. Vado, ma dove? oh Dei!, K583. Bella mia fiamma ... Resta, oh cara, K528. Misera! dove son ... Ah! non son io, K369. *Coupled with works by* **Wagner, Weber** and **Schubert** **Gundula Janowitz** (sop); **Irwin Gage** (pf); **Vienna Symphony Orchestra / Wilfried Boettcher; Orchestra of the Deutsche Staatsoper, Berlin / Ferdinand Leitner.** DG Double Ⓜ 447 352-2GDB2 (two discs: 152 minutes: ADD: 12/95).

Mozart Le nozze di Figaro. **Bryn Terfel** (bass-bar) Figaro; **Alison Hagley** (sop) Susanna; **Rodney Gilfry** (bar) Count Almaviva; **Hillevi Martinpelto** (sop) Countess Almaviva; **Pamela Helen Stephen** (mez) Cherubino; **Susan McCulloch** (sop) Marcellina; **Carlos Feller** (bass) Bartolo; **Francis Egerton** (ten) Don Basilio, Don Curzio; **Julian Clarkson** (bass) Antonio; **Constanze Backes** (sop) Barbarina; **Monteverdi Choir; English Baroque Soloists / John Eliot Gardiner.** Archiv Produktion Ⓕ 439 871-2AH3 (three discs: 179 minutes: DDD: 8/94). Notes, text and translation included. Recorded live in 1993. ✍   Ⓖ

The catalogue of *Figaro* recordings is a long one, and the cast lists are full of famous names. In this version there is only one principal with more than a half-dozen recordings behind him, and some have none at all. It is a commentary on the times, on the astuteness of the casting here and on the capacity of a strong conductor to make the whole so much more than the sum of its parts that this version can stand comparison with any, not only for its grasp of the drama but also for the quality of its singing. It is, of course, a period-instrument recording, more evidently so than many under Gardiner. The string tone is pared down and makes quite modest use of vibrato, the woodwind is soft-toned (but happily prominent). The voices are generally lighter and fresher-sounding than those on most recordings of the opera and the balance permits more than usual to be heard of Mozart's instrumental commentary on the action and the characters. The recitative is done with quite exceptional life and feeling for its meaning and dramatic import, with a real sense, during much of it, of lively and urgent conversation, especially in the first half of the work. Bryn Terfel and Alison Hagley make an outstanding Figaro and Susanna. Terfel is quite a deep bass-baritone with enough darkness in his voice to sound pretty menacing in "Se vuol ballare" as well as bitter in "Aprite un po' quegli occhi"; it is an alert, mettlesome performance – and he also brings off a superlative "Non più andrai", done with tremendous spirit to its rhythms and richly and pointedly coloured. Hagley offers a reading of spirit and allure. The interplay between her and the woodwind in "Venite inginocchiatevi" is a delight, and her cool but heartfelt "Deh vieni" is very beautiful. Once or twice her intonation seems marginally under stress but that is the price one pays for singing with so little vibrato, and it's worth it. Hillevi Martinpelto's unaffected, youthful-sounding Countess is enjoyable; both arias are quite lightly done, with a very lovely, warm, natural sound in "Dove sono" especially. Some may prefer a more polished, sophisticated reading, of the traditional kind, but this is closer to what Mozart would have wanted and expected. Rodney Gilfry provides a Count with plenty of fire and authority, firmly focused in tone; the outburst at the *Allegro assai* in "Vedrò mentr'io sospiro" is formidable. Pamela Helen Stephen's Cherubino sounds charmingly youthful and impetuous; "Voi che sapete" is taken a good deal quicker than usual, and with a touch of comedy, and benefits from it. There is no want of dramatic life in Gardiner's direction. His tempos are marginally quicker than most, and the orchestra often speaks eloquently of the drama. Gardiner adopts the Moberly/Raeburn order of events in Act 3. This involves placing "Dove sono" before, instead of after, the sextet and in the last Act he places Susanna's aria before, instead of after, Figaro's. Tempos are marginally faster on the Oestman version, which also offers a valuable appendix of alternative numbers. It is a very difficult choice: Gardiner's is the more dramatic, Oestman's the livlier and the more Italianate and giving a remarkable sense of everyone enjoying themselves.

Additional recommendations ...

...**Soloists; London Opera Chorus; London Philharmonic Orchestra / Sir Georg Solti.** Decca Ⓕ 410 150-2DH3 (three discs: 169 minutes: 4/84).

...**Soloists; Glyndebourne Chorus; London Philharmonic Orchestra / Bernard Haitink** with **Martin Isepp** (hpd). EMI Ⓕ CDS7 49753-2 (three discs: 178 minutes: DDD: 7/88).

...**Soloists; Chorus and Orchestra of the Drottningholm Court Theatre / Arnold Oestman** with **Mark Tatlow** (hpd cont). L'Oiseau-Lyre Ⓕ 421 333-2OH3 (three discs: 186 minutes: DDD: 12/88). ✍

...**Soloists; Vienna State Opera Chorus; Vienna Philharmonic Orchestra / Erich Kleiber.** Decca Grand Opera Series Ⓜ 417 315-2DM3* (three discs: 172 minutes: ADD: 2/90). *Gramophone classical 100.*   ⊙⊙⊙

...**Soloists; Glyndebourne Festival Chorus and Orchestra / Vittorio Gui.** Classics for Pleasure Ⓑ CD-CFPD4724* (two discs: 158 minutes: ADD. 9/91).

...**Soloists; Netherlands Opera Chorus; Royal Concertgebouw Orchestra / Nikolaus Harnoncourt.** Teldec Ⓕ 4509-90861-2 (three discs: 185 minutes: DDD: 10/94). ✍

...**Soloists;Vienna State Opera Chorus; Vienna Symphony Orchestra / Karl Böhm.** Philips Opera Collector mono Ⓜ 438 670-2PM3* (three discs: 167 minutes: ADD: 10/94).

...**Overtures – Le nozze di Figaro. Don Giovanni. Die Zauberflöte.** *Coupled with works by* **Weber, Brahms, Wagner, Berlioz** and **Rossini** London Philharmonic Orchestra; Berlin Philharmonic Orchestra **/ Sir Thomas Beecham.** Dutton Laboratories mono Ⓜ CDLX7009* (75 minutes: ADD: 10/94). *See review in the Collections section; refer to the Index to Reviews.*

...**Soloists; Scottish Chamber Chorus and Orchestra / Sir Charles Mackerras.** Telarc Ⓕ CD80388 (three discs: 209 minutes: DDD: 8/95).

...**Soloists; Vienna State Opera Chorus; Vienna Philharmonic Orchestra / Claudio Abbado.** DG Ⓕ 445 903-2GH3 (three discs: 170 minutes: DDD: 10/95).

Mozart Don Giovanni. **Eberhard Waechter** (bar) Don Giovanni; **Dame Joan Sutherland** (sop) Donna Anna; **Dame Elisabeth Schwarzkopf** (sop) Donna Elvira; **Graziella Sciutti** (sop) Zerlina; **Luigi Alva** (ten) Don Ottavio; **Giuseppe Taddei** (bar) Leporello; **Piero Cappuccilli** (bar) Masetto; **Gottlob Frick** (bass) Commendatore; **Philharmonia Chorus and Orchestra / Carlo Maria Giulini.** EMI Ⓕ CDS7 47260-8* (three discs: 162 minutes: ADD: 12/87). Notes, text and translation included. From Columbia SAX2369/72 (2/61). *Gramophone classical 100.*   ⊙⊙⊙

New review

Mozart Don Giovanni. **Rodney Gilfry** (bar) Don Giovanni; **Luba Orgonasova** (sop) Donna Anna; **Charlotte Margiono** (sop) Donna Elvira; **Eirian James** (mez) Zerlina; **Christoph Prégardien** (ten) Don Ottavio; **Ildebrando d'Arcangelo** (bass) Leporello; **Julian Clarkson** (bass) Masetto; **Andrea Silvestrelli** (bass) Commendatore; **Monteverdi Choir; English Baroque Soloists / John Eliot Gardiner.** Archiv Produktion Ⓕ 445 870-2AH3 (three discs: 176 minutes: DDD: 8/95). ✍ Notes, text and translation included. Recorded 1994.

Although the EMI set is over 35 years old, none of its successors is as skilled in capturing the piece's drama so unerringly. It has always been most recommendable and Giulini captures all the work's most dramatic characteristics, faithfully supported by the superb Philharmonia forces of that time. At this stage of Giulini's career, he was a direct, lithe conductor, alert to every turn in the story and he projects the nervous tension of the piece ideally while never forcing the pace, as can so easily happen. Then he had one of the most apt casts ever assembled for the piece. Waechter's Giovanni combines the demonic with the seductive in just the right proportions, Taddei is a high-profile Leporello, who relishes the text and sings with lots of 'face'. Elvira was always one of Schwarzkopf's most successful roles: here she delivers the role with tremendous intensity. Sutherland's Anna isn't quite so full of character but it is magnificently sung. Alva is a graceful Ottavio. Sciutti's charming Zerlina, Cappuccilli's strong and Italianate Masetto and Frick's granite Commendatore are all very much in the picture. The recording still sounds well.

The Gardiner set has a great deal to commend it. The recitative is sung with exemplary care over pacing so that it sounds as it should, like heightened and vivid conversation, often to electrifying effect. As an adjunct, ensembles, particularly the Act 1 quartet, are also treated conversationally, as if one were overhearing four people giving their opinions on a situation in the street. The orchestra, perfectly balanced with the singers in a very immediate acoustic, supports them, as it were 'sings' with them. That contrasts with, and complements, Gardiner's expected ability to empathize with the demonic aspects of the score, as in Giovanni's drinking song and the final moments of Act 1, which fairly bristle with rhythmic energy without becoming rushed. The arrival of the statue at Giovanni's dinner-table is tremendous, the period trombones and timpani achieving an appropriately brusque, fearsome attack. Throughout this scene, Gardiner's familiar penchant for sharp accents is wholly appropriate; elsewhere he is sometimes too insistent. As a whole, tempos not only seem right on their own account but also, all-importantly, carry conviction in relation to each other. Where so many conductors today, including Norrington on EMI, rush "Mi tradì", Gardiner prefers a more meditative, inward approach, allowing his soft-grained Elvira to make the most of the aria's expressive possibilities.

As in his other Mozart opera recordings, Gardiner benefits from working with singers whom he knows well. Gilfry's Giovanni is lithe, ebullient, keen to exert his sexual prowess; an obvious charmer, at times surprisingly tender yet with the iron will only just below the surface. Suave and appealing, delivered in a real baritone timbre, his Giovanni is as accomplished as any on disc. Ildebrando d'Arcangelo was the discovery of these performances: this young bass is a lively foil to his master and on his own a real showman, as "Madamina" indicates, a number all the better for a brisk speed. Orgonasova once more reveals herself a paragon as regards steady tone and deft technique – no need here to slow down for the coloratura at the end of "Non mi dir" – and she brings to her recounting of the attempted seduction a real feeling of immediacy. In "Or sai chi l'onore" she manages just the right kind of supple urgency. As Anna, Margiono sometimes sounds a shade stretched technically, but consoles us with the luminous, inward quality of her voice and her reading of the role, something innate that cannot be learnt. Nobody in their right senses is ever going to suggest that there is one, ideal version of *Don Giovanni*; the work has far too many facets for that, but for sheer theatrical *élan* complemented by the live recording, Gardiner is among the best, particularly when one also takes into account a recording that is wonderfully truthful and lifelike.

Additional recommendations ...

...**Soloists; Glyndebourne Festival Chorus; London Philharmonic Orchestra / Bernard Haitink.** EMI
Ⓕ CDS7 47037-8 (three discs: 172 minutes: DDD: 12/84). Ⓖ

...**Soloists; Vienna State Opera Chorus; Vienna Philharmonic Orchestra / Joseph Krips.** Decca Ⓜ 411 626-2DM3 (three discs: 166 minutes: ADD: 9/89).

...**Soloists; Drottningholm Theatre Chorus and Orchestra / Arnold Oestman.** L'Oiseau-Lyre Ⓕ 425 943-2OH3 (three discs: 171 minutes: DDD: 12/90). ✍

...**Soloists; Vienna State Opera Chorus; Vienna Philharmonic Orchestra / Wilhelm Furtwängler.** EMI Références mono Ⓜ CHS7 63860-2* (three discs: 182 minutes: ADD: 7/91).

...**Soloists; Chorus and Orchestra of the Royal Opera House, Covent Garden / Sir Colin Davis.** Philips Mozart Edition Ⓜ 422 541-2PME3 (three discs: 164 minutes: ADD: 1/92).

...**Soloists; Schütz Choir of London; London Classical Players / Roger Norrington.** EMI Ⓕ CDS7 54859-2 (three discs: 195 minutes: DDD: 10/93). ✍

...**Soloists; Vienna State Opera Chorus; Vienna Philharmonic Orchestra / Dimitri Mitropoulos.** Sony Classical mono Ⓕ SM3K64263* (three discs: 154 minutes: ADD: 11/94). ⒼⒼ

Mozart Così fan tutte. **Dame Elisabeth Schwarzkopf** (sop) Fiordiligi; **Christa Ludwig** (mez) Dorabella; **Hanny Steffek** (sop) Despina; **Alfredo Kraus** (ten) Ferrando; **Giuseppe Taddei** (bar) Guglielmo; **Walter Berry** (bass) Don Alfonso; **Philharmonia Chorus and Orchestra / Karl Böhm.** EMI Ⓜ CMS7 69330-2 (three discs: 165 minutes: ADD: 11/88). Notes, text and translation included. From SAN103/6 (5/63). Recorded 1962. Ⓖ

Mozart Così fan tutte. **Amanda Roocroft** (sop) Fiordiligi; **Rosa Mannion** (sop) Dorabella; **Eirian James** (mez) Despina; **Rainer Trost** (ten) Ferrando; **Rodney Gilfry** (bar) Guglielmo; **Carlos Feller** (bass) Don Alfonso; **Monteverdi Choir; English Baroque Soloists / John Eliot Gardiner.** Archiv Produktion Ⓕ 437 829-2AH3 (three discs: 134 minutes: DDD: 2/94). ✍ Recorded live in 1992.

Mozart Così fan tutte. **Soile Isokoski** (sop) Fiordiligi; **Monica Groop** (mez) Dorabella; **Nancy Argenta** (sop) Despina; **Markus Schäfer** (ten) Ferrando; **Per Vollestad** (bar) Guglielmo; **Huub Claessens** (bass) Don Alfonso; **La Petite Bande and Chorus / Sigiswald Kuijken.** Accent Ⓕ ACC9296/8D (three discs: 181 minutes: DDD: 2/94). ✍ Notes, text and translation included. Recorded live in 1992.

Così fan tutte is the most balanced and probing of all Mozart's operas, formally faultless, musically inspired from start to finish, emotionally a matter of endless fascination and, in the second act, profoundly moving. It has been very lucky on disc, and besides this delightful set there have been several other memorable recordings. However, Böhm's cast could hardly be bettered, even in one's dreams. The two sisters are gloriously sung – Schwarzkopf and Ludwig bring their immeasurable talents as Lieder singers to this sparkling score and overlay them with a rare comic touch. Add to that the stylish singing of Alfredo Kraus and Giuseppe Taddei and the central quartet is unimpeachable. Walter Berry's Don Alfonso is characterful and Hanny Steffek is quite superb as Despina. The pacing of this endlessly intriguing work is immaculate. The emotional control of the characterization is masterly and Böhm's totally idiomatic response to the music is arguably without peer. However, two modern recordings, using period instruments, do offer stimulating alternative views.

Gardiner's is a *Così* with a heart, and a heart in the right place. It comes from a stage performance given in the Teatro Comunale at Ferrara – the city from which, of course, the sisters in the story hail – in 1992. The vitality and the communicativeness of the recitative is one result of recording a live performance; it is flexible, conversational and lively, as it ought to be, and the Italian pronunciation is remarkably good considering there isn't a single Italian in the cast. Amanda Roocroft makes a capable Fiordiligi, with a big, spacious "Come scoglio", and shows real depth of feeling in what is a very beautiful account of "Per pietà"; her tone is bright and forward. Rosa Mannion, as Dorabella, acts effectively with her voice in "Smanie implacabili" and is full of life in her Act 2 aria. The Guglielmo, Rodney Gilfry, is quite outstanding for his light, warm and flexible baritone, gently seductive in Act 1, showing real brilliance and precision of articulation in "Donne mie". Eirian James's Despina is another delight, spirited, sexy and rich-toned, and full of charm without any of the silliness some Despinas show. Period instruments notwithstanding, this is a fairly traditional performance. Gardiner often uses quite generous rubato to highlight the shape of a phrase, and he is alert, as always, to how the orchestral writing can underline the sense.

The Kuijken, another live recording, is lighter in mood than Gardiner's. Nearly all the tempos are quicker and there is more sense of spontaneity. Mozart very rarely wrote dynamic or accentuation marks into his singers' parts; the singers were expected to learn their music from a repetiteur (or Mozart himself) and take their cues from what they heard in performance. Gardiner has his singers follow, meticulously, the orchestral dynamics; Kuijken leaves them, more or less, to sing with what they hear. This is a symptomatic difference: one performance is highly wrought, the other freer and more natural. The sisters in the Kuijken version are excellently done by Soile Isokoski, even in voice and with an attractive ring, and Monica Groop, again a pleasing and even voice intelligently and musically used. Their duets are both very appealing, with a happy sense in "Prenderò quel brunettino" that they might be getting up to a little mischief. The Alfonso here, Huub Claessens, more baritone than bass, is particularly successful in the recitative, which here again is done with much care for its meaning. A pleasing and lively *Così*, it would be a good recording with which to get to know the opera, whereas the Gardiner is a connoisseur's performance, subtle and sophisticated, and communicating important things about the opera.

Additional recommendations ...

...**Soloists; Glyndebourne Chorus; London Philharmonic Orchestra / Bernard Haitink** with **Martin Isepp** (hpd). EMI Ⓕ CDS7 47727-8 (three discs: 186 minutes. DDD: 7/87).

...**Soloists; Philharmonia Chorus and Orchestra / Herbert von Karajan.** EMI Références mono Ⓜ CHS7 69635-2* (three discs: 157 minutes: ADD: 12/88).

...**Soloists; Ambrosian Opera Chorus; Academy of St Martin in the Fields / Sir Neville Marriner.** Philips Ⓕ 422 381-2PH3 (three discs: 191 minutes: DDD: 11/90).

...**Soloists; Royal Concertgebouw Orchestra / Nikolaus Harnoncourt.** Teldec Ⓕ 9031-71381-2 (three discs: 197 minutes: DDD; 11/91).

...**Soloists; Chorus and Orchestra of the Royal Opera House, Covent Garden / Sir Colin Davis.** Philips Mozart Edition Ⓜ 422 542-2PME3 (three discs: 183 minutes: ADD: 1/92).

...**Soloists; Edinburgh Festival Chorus; Scottish Chamber Orchestra / Sir Charles Mackerras.** Telarc Ⓕ CD80360 (three discs: 188 minutes: DDD: 4/94). *Gramophone Editor's choice.*

...**Excerpts. Soloists; Glyndebourne Festival Orchestra / Fritz Busch; Philharmonia Orchestra / Walter Susskind.** Testament mono Ⓕ SBT1040* (73 minutes: ADD: 6/94).

...**Soloists; Vienna State Opera Chorus; Vienna Philharmonic Orchestra / Karl Böhm.** Orfeo mono Ⓕ C357942I* (two discs: 137 minutes: ADD: 2/95).

...**Soloists; London Voices; Chamber Orchestra of Europe / Sir Georg Solti.** Decca Ⓕ 444 174-2DHO3 (three discs: 179 minutes: DDD: 3/96).

New review

Mozart Die Entführung aus dem Serail[a]. **Wilma Lipp** (sop) Constanze; **Emmy Loose** (sop) Blonde; **Walther Ludwig** (ten) Belmonte; **Peter Klein** (ten) Pedrillo; **Endre Koréh** (bass) Osmin; **Heinz Woester** (spkr) Bassa Selim; **Vienna State Opera Chorus; Vienna Philharmonic Orchestra / Josef Krips.**

Mozart Overtures[b] – Die Zauberflöte; Così fan tutte; Le nozze di Figaro; Don Giovanni; Der Schauspieldirektor. [b]**London Symphony Orchestra / Josef Krips.** Double Decca mono Ⓜ 443 530-2LF2* (two discs; 137 minutes: ADD: 7/95). Items marked [a] from LXT2536/8 (1/51), [b]LXT2684 (6/52).

New review

Mozart Die Entführung aus dem Serail[a]. Exsultate, jubilate, K165/K158a[b]. [ab]**Maria Stader** (sop) Constanze (Beate Guttmann); **Rita Streich** (sop) Blonde; **Ernst Haefliger** (ten) Belmonte (Sebastian Fischer); **Martin Vantin** (ten) Pedrillo (Wolfgang Spier); **Josef Greindl** (bass) Osmin;

Walter Franck (spkr) Bassa Selim; [a]**Berlin RIAS Chamber Choir and Orchestra,** [b]**Berlin Radio Symphony Orchestra / Ferenc Fricsay.** DG Dokumente [a]mono/[b]stereo Ⓜ 445 412-2GDO2* (two discs: 125 minutes: ADD: 7/95). Notes, texts and translations included. Item marked [a] from DGM18184/5 (7/55), [b]SLPEM136291 (11/62).

The Decca set was the first-ever opera to appear on LP in the UK, and in consequence it caused quite a stir. We have travelled far since then, but the old favourite still has its charms, not least the vivacious, prompt and, where needed, tender conducting of Krips, a notable Mozartian perhaps not as much appreciated today as he should be. Krips conducted the same cast at the 1948 Salzburg Festival which may have prompted the recording. Ludwig, also Belmonte at Glyndebourne in 1935, remains one of the most attractive interpreters of the role on disc, his voice poised between the lyrical and heroic and happily more substantial than those encountered for the most part in the role today. He sings ardently off his words. Klein is a lively Pedrillo, whose "Frisch zum Kampfe" is one of the set's highlights. Their women aren't quite as happily cast. Lipp is lightweight for Constanze. Pleasing and accurate, she isn't sufficiently differentiated from Loose's very Viennese and pert Blonde. Neither they nor Koréh, a reasonably characterful Osmin, are as precise in their runs as some of their successors and indeed predecessors (in the days of 78s). Cuts then traditional are made. Belmonte's Act 2 aria replaces his difficult Act 3 piece and excisions are made in Constanze's G minor "Traurigkeit" and her duet with Belmonte in Act 3. Some dialogue is included. The orchestra is too backwardly placed in relation to the singers but the recording is in other respects remarkable for its day. As a whole, the set has plenty of life, not surprising when the singers were all familiar with each other's performances. Before the complete opera, we have Krips's early LP of Mozart overtures, which only confirms his Mozartian credentials.

In spite of the pleasures of the Krips, the 1954 Fricsay, at mid price, is probably the better buy. Fricsay was an advocate of crisp, zestful, pared-down Mozart *avant la lettre*. This was the first in his distinguished series of Mozart opera recordings, throughout which he used Berlin Radio forces and singers familiar with his work. They prove formidable advocates. The orchestra, recorded in resonant, honest mono, play superbly throughout for their conductor. Stader was a particular favourite with Fricsay. If not the most refulgent of sopranos, she had both the consistency of voice and thoroughness of technique to cope with almost all the demands of Constanze's music. Although one ideally wants a more dramatic singer in the part, her feeling for the shape of a Mozart phrase is always admirable. She is suitably partnered by the fluent, lyrical Haefliger, who also sang Belmonte at Glyndebourne in the 1950s. Although his voice hasn't quite the bite and positive characteristics of other Belmontes, it is used with consummate style. Rita Streich is one's ideal Blonde, singing with pure tone and spirited attack: she has the individuality of voice, the hint of vibrato most attractive, to please the most fastidious listener. Vantin is a more than adequate Pedrillo, who sings his Serenade in an appropriate *mezza voce*. Greindl brings a fully fledged bass to bear on Osmin's music and fills it with a nice combination of vicious sadism leavened by comedy. Although his singing is occasionally marred by intrusive aspirates, he is among the most enjoyable Osmins on disc. Happily he and Streich are allowed to speak their own dialogue so that their Act 2 encounter goes particularly well. As was a dubious custom with DG at the time, the other singers are doubled by speaking voices that hardly match their own. Those who have come to appreciate Fricsay's many attributes as a conductor will not be disappointed by this latest reissue, and will gain as a generous bonus Stader's delightful account of *Exsultate, jubilate*. In absolute terms those without *Die Entführung* in their collection should hear this one. If they are not wedded to stereo sound, it may be the answer, as evenly cast and well conducted as any.

Additional recommendations ...

...**Soloists; Zurich Opera House Chorus and Orchestra / Nikolaus Harnoncourt.** Teldec
Ⓕ 2292-42643-2 (three discs: 135 minutes: DDD: 5/88).

...**Soloists; Leipzig Radio Choir; Dresden Staatskapellle / Karl Böhm.** DG Ⓜ 429 868-2GX2
(two discs: 131 minutes: ADD: 12/90).

...**Soloists; Vienna State Opera Chorus; Vienna Symphony Orchestra / Bruno Weil.** Sony Classical
Ⓕ SK48053 (two discs: 123 minutes: DDD: 5/92).

Mozart Idomeneo. **Anthony Rolfe Johnson** (ten) Idomeneo; **Anne Sofie von Otter** (mez) Idamante; **Sylvia McNair** (sop) Ilia; **Hillevi Martinpelto** (sop) Elettra; **Nigel Robson** (ten) Arbace; **Glenn Winslade** (ten) High Priest; **Cornelius Hauptmann** (bass) Oracle; **Monteverdi Choir; English Baroque Soloists / John Eliot Gardiner.** Archiv Produktion Ⓕ 431 674-2AH3 (three discs: 211 minutes: DDD: 6/91). 🖉 Notes, text and translation included. Recorded 1990.
Gramophone classical 100. *Gramophone* Award Winner 1991.   🅖🅖🅖

This is unquestionably the most vital and authentic account of the opera to date on disc. We have here what was given at the work's first performance in Munich plus, in appendices, what Mozart wanted, or was forced, to cut before that première and the alternative versions of certain passages, so that various combinations of the piece can be programmed by the listener. Gardiner's direct, dramatic conducting catches ideally the agony of Idomeneo's terrible predicament – forced to sacrifice his son because of an unwise row. This torment of the soul is also entirely conveyed by Anthony Rolfe Johnson in the title role to which Anne Sofie von Otter's moving Idamante is an apt foil. Sylvia McNair is a diaphanous, pure-voiced Ilia, Hillevi Martinpelto a properly fiery, sharp-edged Elettra. With dedicated support from his own choir and orchestra, who have obviously benefited from a long

period of preparation, Gardiner matches the stature of this noble *opera seria*. The recording catches
the excitement which all who heard the live performances will recall.

Additional recommendations ...

...**Soloists; Zurich Opera House Chorus and Mozart Orchestra / Nikolaus Harnoncourt.** Teldec
Ⓕ 2292-42600-2 (three discs: ADD: 3/86).

...**Soloists; Leipzig Radio Choir; Dresden Staatskapelle / Karl Böhm.** DG Ⓜ 429 864-2GX3
(three discs: 170 minutes: ADD: 12/90).

...**Soloists; Vienna State Opera Chorus; Vienna Philharmonic Orchestra / Ferenc Fricsay.** DG mono
Ⓜ 447 662-2GX3* (three discs: 155 minutes: ADD: 9/95).

Mozart La clemenza di Tito. **Uwe Heilmann** (ten) Tito; **Della Jones** (mez) Vitellia; **Cecilia Bartoli**
(mez) Sesto; **Diana Montague** (mez) Annio; **Barbara Bonney** (sop) Servillia; **Gilles Cachemaille**
(bar) Publio; **Academy of Ancient Music Chorus; Academy of Ancient Music / Christopher
Hogwood.** L'Oiseau-Lyre Ⓕ 444 131-2OHO2 (two discs: 137 minutes: DDD: 3/95). ✒ Notes,
text and translation included.Recorded 1993. *Gramophone Editor's choice.*

New review

Mozart La clemenza di Tito. **Gösta Winbergh** (ten) Tito; **Carol Vaness** (sop) Vitellia; **Delores
Ziegler** (mez) Sesto; **Martha Senn** (mez) Anno; **Christine Barbaux** (sop) Servilia; **László Polgár**
(bass) Publio; **Vienna State Opera Chorus; Vienna Philharmonic Orchestra / Riccardo Muti.** EMI
Ⓕ CDS5 55489-2 (two discs: 136 minutes: ADD: 10/95). Notes, texts and translation included.
Recorded live in 1988. *Gramophone Editor's choice.*

The appeal of *La clemenza di Tito*, if less immediate and less obvious than that of the other operas of
Mozart's maturity, is still very powerful and very individual. Hogwood has assembled a quite
remarkable cast, with certainly two, perhaps three, outstanding readings. First among them must be
Cecilia Bartoli, who rightly establishes Sextus as the central character, the one whose actions and whose
feelings are the focal point of the drama. The opening number is the duet "Come ti piace, imponi",
where the firm and pure sound of Bartoli's voice, in contrast with the contained hysteria of Vitellia's, at
once defines the opera's basis. It is clear from her singing that she reads Sextus, for all his weakness in
giving way to Vitellia, as a man of integrity, one of the noblest Romans of them all. Then there is Della
Jones's remarkable Vitellia. There are lots of interesting and emotionally suggestive touches in her
singing, which is very committed and very passionate, if not perhaps immaculately tidy – but then,
tidiness is no part of Vitellia's persona. Her rich bottom register is magnificent and the top Bs have no
fears for her. Uwe Heilmann's Titus is marked by much subtle and finely shaped singing and a keen
awareness of how phrasing conveys sense. Occasionally the tone is inclined to be nasal, but that does not
interfere with a very sympathetic and often moving reading. Hogwood's keen awareness of what,
expressively speaking, is going on in the music, and his refusal to be tied to a rigid rhythmic pulse in
order to make it manifest, is one of the strengths of this recording. The recitatives are sung with a great
deal of life and awareness of meaning, not simply gabbled through at maximum speed. These, of course,
are not Mozart's own work and are usually heavily cut; Gardiner (listed below) cuts them extensively.
While some may feel that the inclusion of every note, as in the present version, is an advantage, others
may not unreasonably take the opposite view. At any rate, a new track begins for each aria, which
enables the listener to cut without difficulty. There are now two very fine recordings of this opera with
period instruments. On balance, the Hogwood is better sung, whereas Gardiner has the advantage of a
stronger sense of continuity, derived no doubt from the fact of its having been recorded more or less live.

Muti, oblivious to or at least putting aside attempts at period practice, interprets the work
unashamedly as a grand, incisive near-tragedy. Nor is he averse to the players of the Vienna
Philharmonic drawing the most sensuous sounds from the score, something that Gardiner, even more
Hogwood, eschew, yet he never indulges Mozart, favouring swiftish, though flexible tempos and sharp
rhythms. Muti is also notable for catching the *tinta*, the individual colour, of this work. Listen to the
trio of contrasted feeling, "Quello di Tito", in Act 2 and you'll divine the calibre of this reading, or
a little earlier to the way Muti persuades the chorus into the most mellifluous sounds in "Ah, grazie
si rendamo". Muti's approach is admirably seconded by the generous voices taking the three central
roles: Vaness is in her element as Vitellia, alternately amorous, vindictive, scheming and forgiving.
Hers is not as verbally detailed nor so keenly vituperative an account as Varady's for Gardiner and
Böhm, or indeed Baker's for Davis, but it is boldly and confidently sung throughout a longish evening.
As Sextus, Ziegler is fully the equal of her/his loved one, encompassing both her arias with richly
contoured tone and courageously delivered coloratura, all tending to convey Sesto's torture of the
mind. The only drawback is a certain similarity in the two singers' refulgent tone. At the centre of the
emotional chasm stands Winbergh's commanding, concerned Tito, perhaps the most heroically sung
on any version yet sufficiently flexible for his arias' runs (given a few unwanted aspirates). If the other
singers aren't quite in the same category, they are all well in the vocal and dramatic picture. It is good
to hear the true sound of a theatre acoustic. On the other hand you have to cope with applause at the
end of many numbers and one intrusion, happily only in dry recitative, of an audible jet. So, a
formidable addition to the work's discography, totally engrossing on its own terms and
recommendable as a contender to any newcomer to the piece on disc.

Additional recommendations ...

...**Soloists; Leipzig Radio Choir; Dresden Staatskapelle / Karl Böhm.** DG Ⓜ 429 878-2GX2
(two discs: 140 minutes: ADD: 12/90).

...**Soloists; Monteverdi Choir; English Baroque Soloists / John Eliot Gardiner.** Archiv Produktion
Ⓕ 431 806-2AH2 (two discs: 118 minutes: DDD: 12/91). ✐

...**Soloists; Chorus and Orchestra of the Royal Opera House, Covent Garden / Sir Colin Davis.**
Philips Mozart Edition Ⓜ 422 544-2PME2 (two discs: 128 minutes: ADD: 4/92).

New review

Mozart Die Zauberflöte. **Rosa Mannion** (sop) Pamina; **Nathalie Dessay** (sop) Queen of Night;
Hans-Peter Blochwitz (ten) Tamino; **Anton Scharinger** (bass) Papageno; **Reinhard Hagen** (bass)
Sarastro; **Willard White** (bass) Speaker; **Steven Cole** (ten) Monostatos; **Linda Kitchen** (sop)
Papagena; **Anna Maria Panzarella** (sop) First Lady; **Doris Lamprecht** (mez) Second Lady;
Delphine Haidan (contr) Third Lady; **Damien Colin** (treb) First Boy; **Patrick Olivier Croset** (treb)
Second Boy; **Stéphane Dutournier** (treb) Third Boy; **Christopher Josey** (ten) First Armed Man,
First Priest; **Laurent Naouri** (bass) Second Armed Man, Second Priest; **Les Arts Florissants /
William Christie.** Erato Ⓕ 0630-12705-2 (two discs: 150 minutes: DDD: 5/96). ✐ Notes, text
and translation included. Recorded 1995.

With a background primarily in the French baroque, William Christie comes to *Die Zauberflöte* from
an angle quite unlike anyone else's; yet nobody need be put off for this is as idiomatic and as deeply
Mozartian a reading of the work as any in the catalogue. Interviewed in the accompanying booklet,
Christie says wise things about the work and ways of performing it, and in particular remarks on the
unforced singing that is one of his objectives and which, of course, is much more readily manageable
with the gentler sound of period instruments. All of this is borne out by the performance itself, which
is euphonious to a degree and falls more sweetly and lovingly on the ear than any. All this gives
Christie opportunities to shape the work subtly and sensitively, with finer levels of nuance than are
available to most modern performances. Mozartians will relish it, and they will find other reasons in
it to think freshly about the work. His tempos, for example, often set tradition aside, and not always
in the same direction. Many are quickish, but not all: "Der Hölle Rache" is distinctly slower than
usual, deliberate rather than fiery; so in particular is the union of Pamina and Tamino in the second
finale, which gives it a weight, a *gravitas*, that establishes it as the true emotional climax of the work.
Yet taken overall, the performance is quick and light-textured – and often quite dramatic. These light
and soft textures and graceful phrasing are what above all characterize this recording. Some may find
Christie less readily responsive than many more traditional interpreters to the music's quicksilver
changes in mood, yet this is a part of his broad and essentially gentle view of *Die Zauberflöte*.

His cast has few famous names. There is of course Hans-Peter Blochwitz, probably the finest
Tamino around these days. As Pamina, Rosa Mannion, has much charm and a hint of girlish vivacity
but blossoms into maturity and indeed passion in "Ach, ich fühl's" – the final phrases, as the wind
instruments fall away and leave her alone and desolate, are very moving. Natalie Dessay's Queen of
Night is forthright, clean and well tuned, with ample weight and tonal glitter. The orchestral playing
from Les Arts Florissants is as polished as always, and the translucent sound is a joy on the ear. You
may find the Oestman particularly appealing for its exceptional pointedness and vivacity; Christie is
quite different in character and offers a very satisfying and acutely musical view of the work.

Additional recommendations ...

...**Soloists; Bavarian Radio Chorus and Symphony Orchestra / Bernard Haitink.** EMI Ⓕ CDS7
47951-8 (three discs: 159 minutes: DDD: 3/88).

...**Soloists; Favres Solisten Vereinigung; Berlin Philharmonic Orchestra / Sir Thomas Beecham.** Pearl
mono Ⓕ GEMMCDS9371* (130 minutes: AAD: 3/90). *Gramophone classical 100.* ⒼⒼⒼ

...**Soloists; Vienna Boys' Choir; Vienna State Opera Concert Choir; Vienna Philharmonic Orchestra /
Sir Georg Solti.** Decca Ⓕ 433 210-2DH2 (two discs: 152 minutes: DDD: 10/91).

...**Soloists; Schütz Choir of London; London Classical Players / Roger Norrington.** EMI Reflexe
Ⓕ CDS7 54287-2 (two discs: 139 minutes: DDD: 11/91). ✐

...**Soloists; Scottish Chamber Chorus and Orchestra / Sir Charles Mackerras.** Telarc Ⓕ CD80302
(two discs: 153 minutes: DDD: 12/91).

...**Soloists; Dresden Kreuzchor; Leipzig Radio Chorus; Dresden Staatskapelle / Sir Colin Davis.**
Philips Mozart Edition Ⓜ 422 543-2PME3 (three discs: 162 minutes: DDD: 4/92).

...**Soloists; Drottningholm Court Theatre Chorus and Orchestra / Arnold Oestman.** L'Oiseau-Lyre
Ⓕ 440 085-2OHO2 (two discs: 156 minutes: DDD: 2/94). ✐ *Gramophone Editor's choice.*
Selected by Sounds in Retrospect. Ⓖ

...**Soloists; Hungarian Festival Chorus; Budapest Failoni Orchestra / Michael Halász.** Naxos Opera
Classics Ⓢ 8 660030/31 (two discs: 149 minutes: DDD: 7/94). *Gramophone Editor's choice.*

...**Soloists; Stuttgart Radio Chorus and Orchestra / Joseph Keilberth.** Preiser mono Ⓕ 90254*
(two discs: 151 minutes: AAD: 1/96).

...**Soloists; Vienna State Opera Chorus; Vienna Philharmonic Orchestra / Wilhelm Furtwängler.**
EMI Salzburg Festival Edition mono Ⓜ CHS5 65356-2* (three discs: 176 minutes: ADD: 1/96).

Further listening ...

...Bassoon Concerto in B flat major, K191/K186*a*. Serenade No. 9 in D major, K320, "Posthorn".
ᵃ**Eberhard Marschall** (bn); **Bavarian Radio Symphony Orchestra / Sir Colin Davis.** RCA Victor
Red Seal 09026 61927-2 (9/94).

...Cassations – G major, K63, "Final-Musik"; B flat major, K99/K63*a*. Adagio and Fugue in C minor,
K546. **Salzburg Mozarteum Camerata Academica / Sándor Végh.** Capriccio 10 192 (3/88). ⒼⒼ

...Cassations – G major, K63, "Final-Musik"; B flat major, K99/K63*a*; D major, K100/K62*a*.
Salzburg Chamber Orchestra / Harald Nerat. Naxos 8 550609 (4/93).

...Dances, Marches and Overtures – Five Minuets, K461K/K448*a*[b]. Contredanses[b] – Six,
K462/K448*b*; D major, K534, "Das Donnerwetter"; C major, K535, "La Bataille"; C major,
K587, "Der Sieg vom Helden Koburg"; Two, K603. Two Minuets with Contredanses
(Quadrilles), K463[b]. German Dances[b] – Six, K509; Six, K600; Three, K605. Marches[b] – D major,
K52; D major, K189/K167*b*; C major, K214; D major, K215/K213*b*; D major, K237/K189*c*;
F major, K248; D major, K249; Two in D major, K335/K320*a*; C major, K408 No. 1/K383*e*;
D major, K408 No. 2/K385*a*; C major, K408 No. 3/K383*F*; D major, K445/K320*c*. Overtures[a] –
Die Zauberflöte; Le nozze di Figaro; Ascanio in Alba; Idomeneo; Der Schauspieldirektor; Così
fan tutte; Die Entführung aus dem Serail; La Finta Giardiniera; Lucio Silla; La clemenza di Tito;
Don Giovanni. Idomeneo – Marches[b]: Nos. 8, 14 and 25. Le nozze di Figaro: March[b]: No. 23.
[a]**Dresden Staatskapelle / Hans Vonk;** [b]**Salzburg Mozarteum Orchestra / Hans Graf.** Capriccio
10 809 (three discs: 10/91).

...Serenade No. 7 in D major, K250/K248*b*, "Haffner". March in D major, K249, "Haffner". **Pavlo
Beznosiuk** (vn); **Amsterdam Baroque / Ton Koopman.** Erato 2292-45436-2 (2/90). 🗡 🅖🅖

...Symphonies after Serenades – D major: K100/K62*a*; K185/K167*a*; K203/K198*b*; K204/K213*a*;
K250/K248*b*; K320. **Tafelmusik / Bruno Weil.** Sony Classical S2K47260 (12/92). 🗡

...17 Church Sonatas. **Ian Watson** (org); **Classical Orchestra of the King's Consort / Robert King**
(org). Hyperion CDA66377 (11/90). 🗡

...Divertimento in E flat major for String Trio, K563. Six Preludes and Fugues (after Bach), K404*a*
– No. 1 in D minor; No. 2 in G minor; No. 3 in F major; No. 6 in F minor. **L'Archibudelli Trio.**
Sony Classical Vivarte SK46497. 🗡

...Double Piano Sonata in D major, K448/K375*a*. Andante and Variations in G major, K501.
Coupled with **Schubert** Fantasie in F minor, D940. **Louis Lortie, Hélène Mercier** (pf duet).
Chandos CHAN9162 (7/93).

...Masonic music – Lobegesang auf die feierliche Johannisloge, K148[ae]. Dir, Seele des Weltalls,
K429/K468*a*[cf]. Lied zur Gesellenreise, K468[ae]. Die Maurerfreude, K471[acf]. Maurerische
Trauermusik, K477[f]. Zerfliesset heut', geliebte Brüder, K483[acd]. Ihr unsre neuen Leiter, K484[acd].
Die ihr des unermesslichen Weltalls, K619[ae]. Laut verkünde unsre Freude, K623[abcf]. Lasst uns
mit geschlungnen Händen, K623*a*[cd]. [a]**Werner Krenn** (ten); [b]**Tom Krause** (bar); [c]**Edinburgh Festival
Chorus;** György Fischer ([d]org/[e]pf); [f]**London Symphony Orchestra / István Kertész.** Decca Serenata
425 722-2DM (11/90).

...La Betulia liberata, K118. **Soloists; Padua Centro Musica Antica Choir; Venice and Padua
Chamber Orchestra / Peter Maag.** Denon CO-79945/6 (5/94).

...Thamos, König in Aegypten. **Alastair Miles** (bass); **Monteverdi Choir; English Baroque Soloists /
John Eliot Gardiner.** Archiv Produktion 437 556-2AH (2/94). 🗡

...Apollo et Hyacinthus. **Soloists; Salzburg Chamber Choir; Salzburg Mozarteum Orchestra /
Leopold Hager.** Philips Mozart Edition 422 526-2PME2 (11/91).

...La finta semplice. **Soloists; C.P.E. Bach Chamber Orchestra / Peter Schreier.** Philips Mozart
Edition 422 528-2PME2 (11/91).

...Mitridate. **Soloists; Salzburg Mozarteum Orchestra / Leopold Hager.** Philips Mozart Edition
422 529-2PME3 (2/92).

...Ascanio in Alba. **Soloists; Choir of the Sorbonne, Paris; Concerto Armonico / Jacques Grimbert.**
Naxos 8 660040/41 (12/95).

...Lucio Silla. **Soloists; Arnold Schönberg Choir; Vienna Concentus Musicus / Nikolaus Harnoncourt.**
Teldec 2292-44928-2 (3/91).

...La finta giardiniera. **Soloists; Salzburg Mozarteum Orchestra / Leopold Hager.** Philips Mozart
Edition 422 533-2PME3 (5/92).

...Il rè pastore. **Soloists; Academy of St Martin in the Fields / Sir Neville Marriner.** Philips Mozart
Edition 422 535-2PME2 (4/92).

Alonso Mudarra
Spanish c1510-1580

Mudarra Libro tercero de música en cifras y canto. **Montserrat Figueras** (sop); **Hopkinson Smith**
(vihuela). Auvidis Astrée Ⓔ E8533 (53 minutes: DDD: 5/95). 🗡 Texts and translations included.
Recorded 1994.

In renaissance Spain the four-course renaissance guitar was used to provide strummed
accompaniments to popular songs, but the vihuela – to which it was related – was a courtly instrument
with a large corpus of contrapuntal art music, for the most part *fantasias* and sets of *diferencias*
(variations) but few dances. It also included a number of songs, with sophisticated accompaniments,
which have received far less attention than the works for solo vihuela. Figueras's pure voice and clear
diction (in all three languages: Spanish, Italian and Latin) are excellently suited to the emotional
range of the selected *villancicos*, *romances*, *canciónes* and *sonetos*; a considerable amount of
lamentation is offset by lighter moments such as in *Isabel, perdiste la tu faxa*, where the eponym's
beauty is revealed when her girdle floats downstream. The vihuela, like the lute, was made in different
sizes (at different pitches) and Smith uses four, all necessarily modern 'notional' reproductions. The

accompaniments, like those in Elizabethan lute-song, are halves of genuine partnerships, but differ in that they contain introductory and connective solo passages. If these songs can be better presented than this, it is difficult to imagine by whom. This is a deeply rewarding recording, supported by excellent annotation and the texts of the songs, complete with English translations.

Further listening ...

...Tres libros de música en cifras para vihuela – Pavana de Alexandre; Fantasia que contrahaze la harpa en la manera de Ludovico[a]. *Coupled with* **Milán** El Maestro – Pavana II[a]. **López** Fantasia[a]. **Narváez** Los seys libros del delphin – La canción del Emperador; Diferencias on "Guárdame las vacas"[a]. Paseavase el rey moro[a]. **Murcia** Cumbés[b]. Giga[b]. **Guerau** Poema harmonico – Canario; Marionas[b]. **Sanz** Instruccion de musica sobre la guitarra española – Canarios; Folías; Lantururú; Pavanas al ayre español[b]. **Sor** Thèmes variés et Douze Minuets, Op. 11 – Andante maestoso; Andante expressivo[b]. Introduction and Variations on a theme by Mozart, Op. 9[b]. **José Miguel Moreno** ([a]vihuela/[b]gtr). Glossa GCD920103 (8/95).

...Tres libros de musica en cifras para vihuela – Si me llaman a mi; Ysabel, perdiste la tu faxa; Guárdame las vacas. *Coupled with works by* **Vásquez, Anonymous, Pisador, D. Ortiz, Encina** and **Narváez** La Romanesca / José Miguel Moreno (vihuela). Glossa GCD920203 (5/96). ✐ *See review in the Collections section; refer to the Index to Reviews.*   Ⓖ

Georg Muffat   German 1653-1704

Suggested listening ...

...Armonico tributo – No. 2 in G minor; No. 5 in G major. *Coupled with* **Biber** Sonatae tam aris quam aulis servientes – No. 2 in D major; No. 3 in G minor; No. 5 in E minor; No. 9 in B flat major. **Freiburg Baroque Orchestra Consort.** Deutsche Harmonia Mundi Ⓟ 05472 77303-2 (59 minutes: DDD: 10/94). *See review under Biber; refer to the Index to Reviews.*   ⒼⒼ

Dominic Muldowney   British 1952

Suggested listening ...

...The Brontes – ballet suite. *Coupled with works by* **Feeney** and **Carl Davis** Northern Ballet Theatre Orchestra / John Pryce-Jones. Naxos 8 553495 (3/96). *See review under Feeney; refer to the Index to Reviews.*

Henri Mulet   French 1878-1967

Suggested listening ...

...Carillon-sortie in D major. *Coupled with works by* **Alain, Sibelius, Sløgedal, Lindberg, Mozart, Lefébure-Wély, Nielsen** and **Elgar** Christopher Herrick (org). Hyperion CDA66676. *See review in the Collections section; refer to the Index to Reviews.*

Iwan Müller   Estonian 1786-1854

Suggested listening ...

...Quartet No. 2 in F sharp minor[b]. *Coupled with* **Mozart** La clemenza di Tito – Parto, parto (arr. Bergmann)[a]. **Paer** Sargino, ossia l'allievo dell'amore – Una voca al cor mi parla (arr. Weston and Voxman)[c]. **Spohr** Sechs Lieder, Op. 103[d]. Faust – Ich bin allein[e]. Variations in B flat major on a Theme from "Alruna"[f]. [acde]**Elizabeth Ritchie** (sop); **Victoria Soames** (cl); [b]**Anna Coleman** (vn); [b]**Matthew Souter** (va); [b]**Alastair Blayden** (vc); [acdef]**Jennifer Purvis** (pf). Clarinet Classics CC0006 (3/94).

William Mundy   British c1529-1591

Suggested listening ...

...Kyrie. Magnificat. *Coupled with* **Tye** Mass, "Euge Bone". Omnes gentes, plaudite. Peccavimus cum patribus. **Oxford Camerata / Jeremy Summerly.** Naxos 8 550937 (2/95). *Gramophone Editor's choice.*

Santiago di Murcia   Spanish 16th-17th centuries

Suggested listening ...

...Cumbés[b]. Giga[b]. *Coupled with* **Mudarra** Tres libros de musica en Cifras para vihuela – Pavana de Alexandre; Fantasia que contrahaze la harpa en la manera de Ludovico[a]. **Milán** El Maestro –

Pavana II^a. **López** Fantasia^a. **Narváez** Los seys libros del delphin – La canción del Emperador; Diferencias on "Guárdame las vacas"^a. Paseavase el rey moro^a. **Guerau** Poema harmonico – Canario; Marionas^b. **Sanz** Instruccion de musica sobre la guitarra española – Canarios; Folías; Lantururú; Pavanas al ayre español^b. **Sor** Thèmes variés et Douze Minuets, Op. 11 – Andante maestoso; Andante expressivo^b. Introduction and Variations on a theme by Mozart, Op. 9^b. **José Miguel Moreno** (^avihuela/^bgtr). Glossa GCD920103 (8/95).

Thea Musgrave

British 1928-

Suggested listening ...

...Rorate cocli. *Coupled with works by* **J. Harvey, Hoddinott, Maconchy, T. Salter** and **Lutyens** Ionian Singers / Timothy Salter; Thalia Myers (pf); Erik Jacobsen (perc). Usk Recordings USK1216 (3/96).

Modest Mussorgsky

USSR 1839-1881

Mussorgsky Pictures at an Exhibition (orch. Ravel). A Night on the Bare Mountain (arr. Rimsky-Korsakov).
Ravel Valses nobles et sentimentales. **New York Philharmonic Orchestra / Giuseppe Sinopoli.** DG Ⓔ 429 785-2GH (67 minutes: DDD: 5/91).

Sinopoli's recording of *Pictures at an Exhibition* has great panache and is full of subtle detail and sharply characterized performances. Of course none of this would be possible without the marvellous virtuosity of the New York Philharmonic, whose brass section play with a wonderful larger-than-life sonority (just what's needed in this colourful extravaganza) and whose woodwind section produce playing of considerable delicacy and finesse, as for example in "Tuileries" and the "Ballet of the Unhatched Chicks". Sinopoli clearly revels in the drama of this work and this is nowhere more noticeable than in his sinister readings of "Catacombs" and "Baba-Yaga". *A Night on the Bare Mountain* is no less impressive, where again the flair and dazzling virtuosity of the NYPO have an almost overwhelming impact. Less successful are Ravel's *Valses nobles et sentimentales* which are perhaps a little too idiosyncratic for an individual recommendation despite some superb performances and moments of great beauty. The sound is beautifully balanced and engineered

Additional recommendations ...

...Pictures at an Exhibition. A Night on the Bare Mountain. **Cleveland Orchestra / Lorin Maazel.** Telarc Ⓔ CD80042 (41 minutes: DDD: 11/84).

...Pictures at an Exhibition (orig. piano version)^a. Pictures at an Exhibition (orch. Ashkenazy)^b. ^b**Philharmonia Orchestra / Vladimir Ashkenazy** (^apf). Decca Ⓔ 414 386-2DH (67 minutes: DDD: 5/86).

...Pictures at an Exhibition (orch. Funtek). Songs and Dances of Death (arr. Aho)^a. ^a**Martti Talvela** (bass); **Finnish Radio Symphony Orchestra / Neeme Järvi.** BIS Ⓕ CD325 (67 minutes: DDD: 6/87).

...Pictures at an Exhibition (orig. piano version). Gopaks. Souvenirs d'enfance – No. 2. First punishment (Nurse shuts me in a dark room). Intermezzo in modo classico. Ein Kinderscherz. Une larme. Au village. **Mario Papadopoulos** (pf). Helicon Ⓕ CDHLR143-2 (59 minutes: DDD: 1/89).

...Pictures at an Exhibition. **Stravinsky** Petrushka^a. ^a**Leslie Howard** (pf); **London Symphony Orchestra / Claudio Abbado.** DG Ⓔ 423 901-2GH (68 minutes: DDD: 3/89).

...Pictures at an Exhibition. A Night on the Bare Mountain. Khovanshchina – Prelude. **Oslo Philharmonic Orchestra / Mariss Jansons.** EMI Ⓒ CDC7 49797-2 (49 minutes: DDD: 1/90).

...Pictures at an Exhibition. **Stravinsky** The Firebird – concert suite. **Royal Concertgebouw Orchestra / Carlo Maria Giulini.** Sony Classical Ⓔ SK45935 (61 minutes: DDD: 12/90).

...A Night on the Bare Mountain^a. **Prokofiev** Romeo and Juliet – concert suites^b. ^a**London Symphony Orchestra / Antál Dorati;** ^b**Minneapolis Symphony Orchestra / Stanislaw Skrowaczewski.** Mercury Ⓜ 432 004-2MM (67 minutes: ADD: 3/91).

...Pictures at an Exhibition (orig. piano version). **Tchaikovsky** (arr. Pletnev). The Sleeping Beauty, Op. 66 – excerpts. **Mikhail Pletnev** (pf). Virgin Classics Ⓔ VC7 59611-2 (64 minutes: DDD: 4/91). Ⓖ

...Pictures at an Exhibition. A Night on the Bare Mountain. **Borodin** In central Asia. Prince Igor – Polovtsian Dances. **Slovak Philharmonic Orchestra / Daniel Nazareth.** Naxos Ⓢ 8 550051 (68 minutes: DDD: 7/91).

...Pictures at an Exhibition. Khovanshchina – symphonic excerpts. **Rotterdam Philharmonic Orchestra / James Conlon.** Erato Ⓕ 2292-45596-2 (49 minutes: DDD: 8/91).

...Pictures at an Exhibition. **Stravinsky** The Rite of Spring. **Philadelphia Orchestra / Riccardo Muti.** EMI Ⓜ CDM7 64516-2 (64 minutes: DDD: 11/92).

...Pictures at an Exhibition. A Night on the Bare Mountain. Khovanshchina – Prelude. **Atlanta Symphony Orchestra / Yoel Levi.** Telarc Ⓕ CD80296 (50 minutes: DDD: 4/92).

...Pictures at an Exhibition. **Respighi** The Pines of Rome. The Fountains of Rome. **Chicago Symphony Orchestra / Fritz Reiner.** RCA Victor Gold Seal Ⓜ 09026 61401-2 (70 minutes: ADD: 8/93).   ⒼⒼ

...Pictures at an Exhibition. **Tchaikovsky** Piano Concerto No. 1 in B flat minor, Op. 23[a]. **Vladimir Horowitz** (pf); [a]**NBC Symphony Orchestra / Arturo Toscanini.** RCA Victor Gold Seal Ⓜ GD60321* (61 minutes: ADD: 9/93).   Ⓖ

...Pictures at an Exhibition (arr. Leonard)[a]. A Night on the Bare Mountain (orch. Rimsky-Korsakov). Sorochinsky Fair – Gopak (orch. Liadov). Pictures from the Crimea (orch. Goehr). Khovanshchina – Prelude (orch. Stokowski). From my tears (orch. Kindler). Scherzo in B flat major (orch. Rimsky-Korsakov). [a]**Tamás Ungár** (pf). **Philharmonia Orchestra / Geoffrey Simon.** Cala Ⓕ CACD1012 (77 minutes: DDD: 11/93).

...Pictures at an Exhibition. A Night on the Bare Mountain. *Coupled with works by* **Tchaikovsky, Borodin, Kabalevsky** and **Glinka** **Chicago Symphony Orchestra / Fritz Reiner.** RCA Victor Living Stereo Ⓜ 09026 61958-2 (71 minutes: ADD: 8/94). *See review in the Collections section; refer to the Index to Reviews.*   ⒼⒼⒼ

...A Night on the Bare Mountain (arr. Rimsky-Korsakov and Stokowski). Boris Godunov – Symphonic Synthesis (arr. Stokowski). Pictures at an Exhibition (omitting Nos. 3 and 7; orch. Stokowski). Khovanshchina – Prelude, Act 4 (orch. Stokowski). Borodin Prince Igor – Dance of the Polovtsi Maidens (orch. Glazunov, Rimsky-Korsakov and Stokowski). **Philadelphia Orchestra / Leopold Stokowski.** Dutton Laboratories mono Ⓜ CDAX8009* (79 minutes: ADD: 11/94).

...Pictures at an Exhibition. **Debussy** La mer. **Ravel** Boléro. **Berlin Philharmonic Orchestra / Herbert von Karajan.** DG The Originals Ⓜ 447 426-2GOR (75 minutes: ADD: 12/95).

...Pictures at an Exhibition (piano version[a]; orch. Ravel[b]). **Chopin** Etude in F major, Op. 25 No. 3[c]. Waltz in A minor, Op. 34 No. 2[d]. [acd]**Byron Janis** (pf); [b]**Minneapolis Symphony Orchestra / Antál Dorati.** Mercury Living Presence Ⓜ 434 346-2MM (66 minutes: ADD: 2/96). *See review under Chopin; refer to the Index to Reviews.*   Ⓖ

...Pictures at an Exhibition (piano version[a]; orch. Ravel[b]). [a]**Alfred Brendel** (pf); [b]**Vienna Philharmonic Orchestra / André Previn.** Philips Solo Ⓜ 442 650-2PM (67 minutes: DDD: 2/96).

...A Night on the Bare Mountain (arr. Tchernov). *Coupled with works by* **Rachmaninov, Liadov, Medtner** and **Balakirev** **Boris Berezovsky** (pf). Teldec Ⓕ 4509-96516-2 (61 minutes: DDD: 7/96). *See review in the Collections section; refer to the Index to Reviews.*

New review

Mussorgsky Pictures at an Exhibition[a].
Tchaikovsky Piano Sonata in G major, Op. 37[b]. **Sviatoslav Richter** (pf). Melodiya mono Ⓜ74321 29469-2* (61 minutes: ADD: 6/96). Item marked [a] recorded 1958, [b]1956.

The blend of German and Russian backgrounds must have something to do with the unique power of Richter at his best. Certainly that comes across in the tempering of rhetoric with structural insight which elevates the Tchaikovsky Sonata beyond any other performance of this unwieldy piece; again Richter's sweeping panache and volcanic sense of flow make for a colossal Mussorgsky *Pictures* (Moscow, 1958), far better recorded than the famous, though currently unavailable, live Sofia account. Richter's interpretations in these years had an elemental power and unselfconscious abandon that was refined and tempered in later life. The mono sound is acceptable.

Mussorgsky Songs and Dances of Death. The Nursery. The Peep-show. Forgotten. The Seminarist. Darling Savishna. The he-goat: A worldly story. Mephistopheles' song of the flea. **Sergei Leiferkus** (bar); **Semeon Skigin** (pf). Conifer Ⓕ CDCF229 (66 minutes: DDD: 2/95). Texts and translations included. Recorded 1993. *Gramophone Editor's choice.*   ⒼⒼ

Few have interpreted Mussorgsky with the kind of confidence, understanding and sheer vocal bravura that Leiferkus shows here. He has all the necessary *gravitas*, vocal presence and tonal nuance. Leiferkus has recorded *Songs and Dances of Death* before with orchestra but the version with piano is to be preferred because their very intimacy in this form makes the pieces that much more frightening. At present there is no version with piano in the catalogue to rival Leiferkus's for intensity of expression or breadth of characterization. Here Death in all its terrifying guises as so arrestingly depicted by the composer, comes starkly into your home, courtesy of the singer, his vivid partner and an ideal recording. The accomplishment in *The Nursery* cycle is, if possible, even more astonishing as the baritone completely changes the character of his tone for impersonating the child. Usually assigned to a soprano, it has been attempted in the past on disc, and successfully so, by Christoff (listed below). Leiferkus at once emulates his great predecessor's achievement yet manages to give these delightful songs his own, very definite profile. More delights follow. The satire of *The Peep-show* is brilliantly realized. In the rest of the songs Mussorgsky's gift for strongly flavoured story-telling and figure-painting is conveyed in abundance through Leiferkus's ebullient delivery, closing with a rollicking but never overdone *Song of the flea.*

Additional recommendations ...

...The Complete Songs. **Boris Christoff** (bass); **Various accompanists and orchestras.** EMI Ⓜ CHS7 63025-2* (three discs: 192 minutes: ADD: 8/89). *Gramophone classical 100.*   ⒼⒼⒼ

...Songs and Dances of Death. *Coupled with works by* **Rimsky-Korsakov, Borodin, Rubinstein** and **Rachmaninov** Dmitri Hvorostovsky (bar); **Kirov Theatre Orchestra / Valery Gergiev.** Philips

Ⓕ 438 872-2PH (62 minutes: DDD: 5/94). *See review in the Collections section; refer to the Index to Reviews.*

...Songs and Dances of Death[a]. **Tchaikovsky** Symphony No. 5 in E minor, Op. 64. [a]**Anatoly Kotscherga** (bass); **Berlin Philharmonic Orchestra / Claudio Abbado.** Sony Classical Ⓕ SK66276 (65 minutes: DDD: 3/95). *See review under Tchaikovsky; refer to the Index to Reviews.*

...The Nursery. Songs and Dances of Death. *Coupled with works by* **Rachmaninov** and **Tchaikovsky Ewa Podles** (contr); **Graham Johnson** (pf). Forlane UCD16683 (5/95). *See review in the Collections section; refer to the Index to Reviews.*

...Songs and Dances of Death (orch. Shostakovich)[a]. **Shostakovich** Symphony No. 10 in E minor, Op. 93. [a]**Robert Lloyd** (bass); **Philadelphia Orchestra / Mariss Jansons.** EMI Ⓕ CDC5 55232-2 (72 minutes: DDD: 6/95). *See review under Shostakovich; refer to the Index to Reviews.*

New review

Mussorgsky Epitaph. The sphinx. Not like thunder, trouble struck. Softly the spirit flew up to heaven. Pride. Is spinning man's work?. The vision. It scatters and breaks. On the Dnieper. Eremushka's lullaby. The feast. The classicist. From my tears. Sunless. **Sergei Leiferkus** (bar); **Semion Skigin** (pf). Conifer Ⓕ 75605 51248-2 (59 minutes: DDD: 12/95). Texts and translations included. Recorded 1995. *Gramophone Editor's choice.*

Leiferkus so much *enjoys* singing. That's evident from first to last on this, the second instalment of his absolutely riveting account of Mussorgsky's songs. His success here, even more than in Vol. 1 (reviewed above), is based on his amazing variety of tone colour and textual inflexion. The singer who is so embittered, so biting in a big, baritonal manner for projecting the harshness in *Not like thunder* dissolves into the warm, all-enveloping, bass-like interpreter of *Softly the spirit flew up to heaven*, one of the composer's most melodically inspired songs. Then in the next song, another voice, another character is met as Leiferkus catches to perfection the heroic irony of *Pride*. In *The vision*, and again in the Schumannesque *From my tears*, we hear a lyrically vibrant baritone, dispensing an appropriately erotic charge so strongly contrasting with the deliberately light, almost mincing tone employed to convey the sharp satire of *The classicist*. The grand passion of that Cossack lament, *On the Dnieper*, and the extrovert good cheer of *The feast* are further triumphs – and all that is before we reach his reading of the *Sunless* cycle, where Leiferkus sounds suitably world-weary as he plumbs the depths of this profoundly depressing work. In everything his confident and pointed delivery of the text is exemplary yet verbal histrionics never get in the way of good singing. With Skigin once again a wonderfully responsive partner and a recording that improves, in terms of intimacy, on that of Vol. 1, no more need be said except to recommend this disc unreservedly and urge you to acquire it.

Mussorgsky St John's Night on the Bare Mountain. Pictures at an Exhibition (orch. Ravel). The destruction of Sennacherib[a]. Salammbô – Chorus of priestesses[a]. Oedipus in Athens Chorus of people in the temple[a]. Joshua[b]. [b]**Elena Zaremba** (mez); [a]**Prague Philharmonic Chorus; Berlin Philharmonic Orchestra / Claudio Abbado.** DG Ⓕ 445 238-2GH (65 minutes: DDD: 2/95). Texts and translations included. Recorded live in 1993. ⒼⒼ

St John's Night on the Bare Mountain is the original version of *A Night on the Bare Mountain*. Abbado obviously relishes the odd grotesque spurts of colour from the woodwind, and the Mussorgskian ruggedness. The composer's structural clumsiness is not shirked and the lack of the smooth continuity found in the Rimsky arrangement does not impede the sense of forward momentum; indeed at the close the Russian dance element is emphasized, rather than the sinister pictorialism. (Of course the luscious slow ending is not here at all – that was added by Rimsky.) The choral pieces are gloriously sung and again Abbado brings out their Russian colour, especially in the glowing yet sinuous "Chorus of priestesses". *Joshua* is made to seem a minor masterpiece with its lusty opening (hints of Borodin's Polovtsians) and its touching central solo ("The Amorite women weep"). This is most eloquently sung by Elena Zaremba and the theme is then movingly taken up first by the women of the chorus and then the men, before the exultant music returns. The performance of *Pictures at an Exhibition*, like the choral items, gains from the spacious ambience and sumptuous overall textures. It is not, perhaps, an electrifying performance, but it is dramatic in its contrasts and very beautifully played.

Additional recommendation ...

...Joshua[ab]. St John's Night on the Bare Mountain. Salammbô – Chorus of priestesses[b]. The destruction of Sennacherib[b]. Oedipus in Athens – Chorus of people in the temple[b]. Khovanshchina – Prelude; Galitsin's journey (Introduction, Act 4). Scherzo in B flat major. Triumphal march, "The capture of Kars". [a]**Zehava Gal** (contr); **London Symphony** [b]**Chorus and Orchestra / Claudio Abbado.** RCA Gold Seal Master Series Ⓜ 09026 61354-2 (54 minutes: ADD: 6/93).

Mussorgsky Khovanshchina. **Aage Haugland** (bass) Ivan Khovansky; **Vladimir Atlantov** (ten) Andrey Khovansky; **Vladimir Popov** (ten) Golitsin; **Anatolij Kotscherga** (bar) Shaklovity; **Paata Burchuladze** (bass) Dosifey; **Marjana Lipovsk** (contr) Marfa; **Brigitte Poschner-Klebel** (sop) Susanna; **Heinz Zednik** (ten) Scribe; **Joanna Borowska** (sop) Emma; **Wilfried Gahmlich** (ten) Kouzka; **Vienna Boys' Choir; Slovak Philharmonic Choir; Vienna State Opera Chorus and Orchestra / Claudio Abbado.** DG Ⓕ 429 758-2GH3 (three discs: 171 minutes: DDD: 11/90). Notes, text and translation included. Recorded live in 1989. Ⓖ

The booklet-essay suggests that Mussorgsky's music constantly poses a question to his Russian compatriots: "What are the causes of our country's continuing calamities, and why does the state crush all that is good?". Anyone who follows today's news from Russia and then experiences this opera will understand what is meant, and while we observe with sympathy we seem no nearer than the citizens of that great, tormented country to finding solutions for its endemic problems. However, Mussorgsky was not the least of those Russian musicians who found lasting beauty in her history and he expressed it in a powerfully dramatic idiom that drew on folk-music and had both epic qualities and deep humanity as well as an occasional gentleness. There is also an element here of Russian church music, since *Khovanshchina* has a political and religious theme and is set in the 1680s at the time of Peter the Great's accession. Since the work was unfinished when Mussorgsky died, performances always involve conjectural work, and the version here – which works convincingly – is mostly that of Shostakovich with the choral ending that Stravinsky devised using Mussorgsky's music. The cast in this live recording is not one of star opera singers, but they are fully inside the drama and the music, as is the chorus and the orchestra under Abbado, and the result is deeply atmospheric. The booklet has the Russian text and a translation as well as informative essays on the music.

Additional recommendation ...

...**Soloists; Kirov Theatre Chorus and Orchestra / Valery Gergiev.** Philips Ⓕ 432 147-2PH3 (three discs: 196 minutes: DDD: 6/92).

Mussorgsky Boris Godunov. **Anatoly Kotcherga** (bass) Boris; **Sergei Larin** (ten) Grigory; **Marjana Lipovšek** (mez) Marina; **Samuel Ramey** (bass) Pimen; **Gleb Nikolsky** (bass) Varlaam; **Philip Langridge** (ten) Shuisky; **Helmut Wildhaber** (ten) Missail; **Sergei Leiferkus** (bar) Rangoni; **Liliana Nichiteanu** (mez) Feodor; **Valentina Valente** (sop) Xenia; **Yevgenia Gorokhovskaya** (mez) Nurse; **Eléna Zaremba** (mez) Hostess; **Alexander Fedin** (ten) Simpleton; **Albert Shagidullin** (bar) Shchelkolov; **Wojciech Drabowicz** (ten) Mitukha, Krushchov; **Slovak Philharmonic Chorus; Berlin Radio Chorus; Tölz Boys' Choir; Berlin Philharmonic Orchestra / Claudio Abbado.** Sony Classical Ⓕ S3K58977 (three discs: 200 minutes: DDD: 5/94). Notes, text and translation included. Ⓖ Ⓖ

Mussorgsky (arr. Rimsky-Korsakov) Boris Godunov. **Boris Christoff** (bass) Boris, Pimen, Varlaam; **Nicolai Gedda** (ten) Grigory; **Eugenia Zareska** (mez) Marina, Feodor; **André Bielecki** (ten) Shuisky, Missail, Krushchov; **Kim Borg** (bass) Rangoni, Shchelkalov; **Ludmila Lebedeva** (sop) Xenia; **Lydia Romanova** (mez) Nurse, Hostess; **Wassili Pasternak** (ten) Simpleton; **Raymond Bonte** (ten) Lavitsky; **Eugène Bousquet** (bass) Chernikovsky; **Choeurs Russes de Paris; French Radio National Orchestra / Issay Dobrowen.** EMI Références mono Ⓜ CHS5 65192-2* (three discs: 178 minutes: ADD: 12/94). From HMV ALP1044/7 (4/53). Recorded 1952.

Nobody has been more diligent than Abbado in seeking the truth about this vast canvas. Here we have the latest fruits of his efforts. He chooses the definitive 1872-74 version, adding scenes, including the complete one in Pimen's cell and the St Basil's scene from 1869. His is a taut, tense reading, grand, virtuosic, at times hard-driven, favouring extremes of speed and dynamics. The orchestra is very much in the foreground, sounding more emphatic than would ever be the case in the opera house. Kotcherga has a superb voice, firmly produced throughout an extensive register. His is a Boris avoiding conventional melodrama and concerned to show the loving father. The ambitious lovers are well represented. Indeed, Larin is quite the best Grigory yet on disc, sounding at once youthful, heroic and ardent, and quite free of tenor mannerisms. Lipovšek characterizes Marina forcefully: we are well aware of the scheming Princess's powers of wheeler-dealing and of erotic persuasion. The recording is of demonstration standard: most potent in the way it captures the incisive and pointed singing of the combined choruses in their various guises. Here all is vividly brought before us by conductor and producer in the wide panorama predicated by Mussorgsky's all-enveloping vision.

Dobrowen's lean, vivid, acutely shaped direction, benefiting from taut rhythms and fastish tempos, is as vital as that on any version since, certainly making this set the recommendation for the Rimsky recension. Its other main attribute is, of course, Christoff's first complete reading on disc of the tortured Tsar, whose role he sings with an enviable combination of firm tone, vital diction and concentrated histrionics, never overstepping the mark. His assumption of two other parts has always been frowned on, but he so subtly varies his tone – softer, greyer for Pimen, rotundly rollicking for Varlaam – that the tripling only worries in the final scene when Pimen comes face to face with the dying ruler. The contrast of his finely shaded Pimen with Ramey's one-dimensional singing on the Abbado version is most marked. If that were not enough, there is the beauty and ardour of the young Gedda as Grigory to please the ear and Zareska's seductive, vocally appealing Marina. She also sings a likeable Feodor. Kim Borg doubles successfully as Shchelkalov and an oily Rangoni. The choral singing is good. We have heard much better on disc since, but few orchestras, in the West at least, have sounded so Russian as these French players but then few have had the benefit of being tutored by Dobrowen. The digital transfers bring out the excellence of the original engineering.

Additional recommendation ...

...**Soloists; Bodra Smyana Representative Children's Choir; Sofia National Opera and Festival Orchestra / Emil Tchakarov.** Sony Classical Ⓕ S3K45763 (three discs: 210 minutes: DDD: 4/92).

Further listening ...

...What are words of love to you?. Night. *Coupled with* **Borodin** The false note. The sea princess. **Rimsky-Korsakov** The octave, Op. 45 No. 3. The clouds begin to scatter, Op. 42 No. 3. Of what I dream in the quiet sky, Op. 40 No. 3. Enslaved by the rose, the nightingale, Op. 2 No. 2. In spring, Op. 43 – No. 1, The lark sings louder; No. 2, Not the wind, blowing from the heights. **Balakirev** 20 Songs – The bright moon; My heart is torn; Song of Selim; When I hear thy voice. Three Forgotten Songs – Thou art so captivating; Spanish song. 10 Songs – Over the lake; I loved him. **Cui** I remember the evening. 25 Songs, Op. 57 – No. 11, "You" and "Thou"; No. 17, The statue of Tsarskoie Selo; No. 25, Desire. Ici-bas. I touched the bloom lightly, Op. 49 No. 1. It's over. **Olga Borodina** (mez); **Larissa Gergieva** (pf). Philips 442 780-2PH (8/95).

…The Marriage (orch. Rozhdestvensky). **Soloists; USSR Ministry of Culture Symphony Orchestra / Gennadi Rozhdestvensky.** *Coupled with* **Rimsky-Korsakov** Mozart and Salieri. **Soloists; Bolshoi Theatre Orchestra / Mark Ermler.** Olympia OCD145 (9/93).

Stanley Myers
British 1934-1993

Suggested listening ...
…Concerto for Soprano Saxophone and Orchestra[a]. *Coupled with* **R.R. Bennett** Concerto for Stan Getz[b]. **Torke** Concerto for Soprano Saxophone and Orchestra[c]. **John Harle** (sax); [a]**Argo Symphony Orchestra / James Judd;** [b]**BBC Concert Orchestra / Barry Wordsworth;** [c]**Albany Symphony Orchestra / David Alan Miller.** Argo 443 529-2ZH (7/95).

Josef Mysliveček
Bohemian 1737-1781

Suggested listening ...
…Il bellerofonte. **Soloists; Czech Philharmonic Chorus; Prague Chamber Orchestra / Zoltán Peskó.** Supraphon 11 0006-2 (3/92).

Conlon Nancarrow
Mexican 1912-

Suggested listening ...
…Studies for Player Piano (arr. Mikhashoff) – Nos. 1, 2, 3*c*, 5, 6, 7, 9, 12, 14, 18, 19. Tango? (arr. Mikhashoff). Toccata (arr. Mikhashoff). Piece No. 2. Trio. Sarabande and Scherzo. **Ensemble Modern / Ingo Metzmacher.** RCA Victor Red Seal 09026 61180-2 (11/93). Ⓖ
…Studies for Player Piano – Nos. 42, 45*a*, 45*b*, 45*c*, 48*a*, 48*b*, 48*c*, 49*a*, 49*b*, 49*c*. **Conlon Nancarrow.** Wergo WER60165-50 (8/89).

Onute Narbutaite
USSR/Lithuanian 1956-

New review
Narbutaite Opus lugubre.
Balakauskas Ostrobothnian Symphony.
Vasks Symphony for Strings, "Stimmen". **Ostrobothnian Chamber Orchestra / Juha Kangas.** Finlandia Ⓕ 4509-97892-2 (65 minutes: DDD: 11/95).
These pieces demonstrate the independence and vibrancy of the cultures at the eastern end of the Baltic Sea; they have also evaded Russification. The prevalence of minimalism probably derives from Pärt, Górecki and Scandinavian models but is of an audibly different cast to these. Not all the pieces are uniformly successful: if you accept the definition of a symphony as the "large-scale integration of contrasts", then that by Osvaldas Balakauskas will not pass muster. Its 20-odd event-packed minutes are impressively atmospheric but with little sense of symphonic thrust. Its harmonic stasis is fortunately absent from Vasks's *Stimmen* Symphony (1990-91, inspired in part by the desperate Soviet attempts to rein in the separatist Baltic states) which has something of the immediacy of appeal of his popular *Cantabile* (1979). *Opus lugubre* (1991) by Onute Narbutaite is more radical and compelling, suggesting she shares with Kaija Saariaho (b.1952) a compositional persona fusing delicacy with resilience. The Ostrobothnian band, one of the finest of its kind in Europe, play magnificently throughout, making this disc well worth investigating.

James Nares
British 1715-1783

Suggested listening ...
…Sonata for Harpsichord, Two Violins and Continuo, Op. 2 No. 6[a]. *Coupled with* **Chilcot** Harpsichord Concerto in A major, Op. 2 No. 2[a] (recons. R. Langley). **Roseingrave** Concerto for Harpsichord, Trumpets, Timpani and Strings in D major[b] (recons. P. Holman). **Handel** Chaconne in G major[a] (arr. Nicholson). Concerto Movement for Organ and Orchestra in D minor[b]. **P. Hayes** Keyboard Concerto No. 4 in A major[c]. **Hook** Keyboard Concerto in D major, Op. 1 No. 5[c] (recons. Holman). **The Parley of Instruments / Paul Nicholson** ([a]hpd/[b]org, [c]fp). Hyperion CDA66700 (8/94). ✎

Luys de Narváez

Spanish fl1530-1550

Suggested listening ...

...Paseavase el rey moro. Lós Seys libros del delphin – Diferencias de Guardame las vacas. *Coupled with works by* **Encina, D. Ortiz, Pisador, Anonymous, Vásquez** and **Mudarra La Romanesca / José Miguel Moreno** (vihuela). Glossa GCD920203 (5/96). ✒ *See review in the Collections section; refer to the Index to Reviews.* Ⓖ

...Los seys libros del delphin – La canción del Emperador; Diferencias on "Guárdame las vacas"[a]. Paseavase el rey moro[a]. *Coupled with* **López** Fantasia[a]. **Milán** El Maestro – Pavana II[a]. **Mudarra** Tres libros de musica en Cifras para vihuela – Pavana de Alexandre; Fantasia que contrahaze la harpa en la manera de Ludovico[a]. **Murcia** Cumbés[b]. Giga[b]. **Guerau** Poema harmonico – Canario; Marionas[b]. **Sanz** Instruccion de musica sobre la guitarra española – Canarios; Folías; Lantururú; Pavanas al ayre español[b]. **Sor** Thèmes variés et Douze Minuets, Op. 11 – Andante maestoso; Andante expressivo[b]. Introduction and Variations on a theme by Mozart, Op. 9[b]. **José Miguel Moreno** ([a]vihuela/[b]gtr). Glossa GCD920103 (8/95).

Peter Paul Nash

British 1950-

Suggested listening ...

...In a walled garden[ab]. *Coupled with works by* **Weir, Connolly, Bauld, Elias, Payne** and **A. Gilbert Jane Manning** (sop); [a]**Jane's Minstrels /** [b]**Roger Montgomery**. NMC Artists' Series NMCD025 (10/95). *See review in the Collections section; refer to the Index to Reviews.* Ⓖ

Stephen Nau

French/British ?-1647

Suggested listening ...

...Suite in F major. Ballet in F major. Pavan and Galliard in D minor. *Coupled with works by* **Webster, A. Ferrabosco II, R. Johnson II, Notari** and **W. Lawes Parley of Instruments Renaissance Violin Band / Peter Holman**. Hyperion CDA66806 (6/96). ✒ *See review in the Collections section; refer to the Index to Reviews.* Ⓖ

Naudot, Jacques-Christophe

French c1690-1762

Suggested listening ...

...Recorder Concerto in G major, Op. 17 No. 5. *Coupled with* **Leclair** Violin Concertos – Op. 7: No. 3 in C major; No. 5 in A minor. G minor, Op. 10 No. 6. **Frans Brüggen** (rec); **Vienna Concentus Musicus / Nikolaus Harnoncourt**. Teldec 4509-92180-2 (2/94). ✒

Johann Naumann

German 1741-1801

New review

Naumann Gustaf Wasa. **Anders Andersson** (ten) Gustaf Wasa; **Nicolai Gedda** (ten) Christjern II; **Tord Wallström** (bass) Severin Norrby; **Lena Nordin** (sop) Christina Gyllenstierna; **Dorrit Kleimert** (sop) Cecilia af Eka; **Eva Pilat** (sop) Margaretha Wasa; **Inger Blom** (contr) Anna Bielke; **Staffan Sandlund** (bass) Lars Sparre; **Henrik Westberg** (bar) Danish Herald; **Marie Dimpker** (sngr) Sweden's Guardian Angel; **Chorus and Orchestra of the Royal Opera, Stockholm / Philip Brunelle**. Virgin Classics Ⓟ VCD5 45148-2 (two discs: 136 minutes: DDD: 3/96). Notes, text and translation included. Recorded 1992.

Johann Gottlieb Naumann was a Dresden composer who spent several years in Scandinavia. While there, he wrote what is in effect regarded as the Swedish national opera, *Gustaf Wasa*; composed in 1783 and produced in 1786, it treats of an episode in sixteenth-century Swedish history when Wasa freed the country from Danish domination, in spite of the cruel threats (at least according to this libretto) of the Danish king, Christjern. He called it, with Gluck's recent operas in mind, a *lyrisk tragedi*, and although the music itself is Italian-influenced, the structure and general approach do have strong resemblances to those of Gluck's mature, French-style operas or *tragédies lyriques*, and the actual language is often markedly Gluckian. There are few expansive or formal arias, much recitative (most of it orchestrally accompanied) and several ensembles, forming a more or less continuous texture, as well as a good deal of work for the chorus and several ballet sequences, including (like *Idomeneo*, two years earlier) a final chaconne. The overture, astonishingly, starts like a Handel operatic French overture, barely updated in style, though the fugue doesn't stay fugal very long. It effectively, *à la* Gluck, sets the mood for what is an intense and dramatic opera.

Simply in terms of quality and originality, the music is unexceptional; but it is extremely well written, with the touch of an experienced professional and man of the theatre, and the actual invention is always very apt – there are several stirring arias for Gustaf and a number of ensembles of a tragic or mournful cast. Naumann is good at setting atmosphere, with his solemn choruses, his richly accompanied monologues, his colourful ballets; there is a particularly fine ballet or mime sequence forming the second half of Act 2. The present recording is based on a production of the opera given in 1991 by the Royal Swedish Opera. The principals, with one notable exception, are little known, but they give a remarkably good account of the piece in their confident and persuasive singing. Nicolai Gedda, if he cannot quite escape sounding slightly older than King Christjern seems likely to be, brings to the role great clarity of diction and precision of line, and passion too, and is a great pleasure to listen to. The admirable chorus and orchestra of the Royal Swedish Opera perform with vitality and enthusiasm under Philip Brunelle. This is a fascinating issue and enthusiasts of eighteenth-century opera will find much to enjoy in it.

José Melchor de Nebra
Spanish 1702-1768

New review

Nebra Viento es la dicha de Amor. **Maite Arruabarrena** (mez) Zefiro; **Marta Almajano** (sop) Liriope; **Raquel Pierotti** (mez) Amor; **Pilar Jurado** (sop) Delfa; **Maria del Mar Doval** (sop) Marsias; **Coro Capilla Peñaflorida; Limoges Baroque Ensemble / Christophe Coin.** Auvidis Valois
Ⓟ V4752 (two discs: 98 minutes: DDD: 8/96). Notes, text and translation included. *Gramophone Editor's choice.*

To most people the term 'zarzuela' implies (if anything at all) the Spanish form of light operetta that enjoyed a huge vogue in the latter part of the nineteenth century; but in fact its history goes back another couple of hundred years, when it was all but indistinguishable from baroque Italian opera except by being in the vernacular and including spoken dialogue and some folk-dance elements. Auvidis have done us a considerable service by issuing this early zarzuela by one of the most famous and prolific eighteenth-century Spanish composers (with 68 stage works to his credit), teacher of Padre Soler and uncle of the keyboard writer Blasco de Nebra. The two-act *Wind is the happiness of love* was first produced in 1743 and revised nine years later: the present recording is of the version produced in Madrid in 1992 from the careful reconstruction by Alicia Lázaro, who provides a useful introduction (whose scholarshiip, unfortunately, is undermined by a musically ignorant and often inaccurate translator who renders, for example, "the continuo" as "the whole thing"). Without the dialogue, replaced here by sketchy printed resumés, you will probably find the complex and apparently inconsequential action incomprehensible; but it centres on the reluctance of the nymph Liriope to accept the love of Zephyr, since (prophetically) she fears giving birth to Narcissus, for the love of whom Echo will die. Musically the score is a treasure-house of fresh and appealing melodiousness, with inventive instrumentation, revealing Nebra (a composer all but unknown today) as a baroque master of outstanding quality, fully justifying the encomiums showered on him in his lifetime. From the striking opening, with its chorus cries of "Fire!" (the initial sung *jácara* is lost), there is not a dull moment. Highlights are two arias for Amor, one with *soli* horns, the other martial, with trumpets; a brilliantly bravura coloratura aria in Act 2 for Liriope (splendidly sung by Marta Almajano); a "turtle-dove" lament for Zephyr (inevitably with flutes); and a vigorous comic quarrel for two minor characters. There is an unusual number of duets, and even a trio; the accompanied recitatives have vitality; and the folk element is provided by a lively *seguidilla* just before the end of Act 1 and by a final *contradanza*. Christophe Coin directs a distinguished performance by a remarkably fine all-female cast that does not have a single weak member and is admirably supported by a neatly stylish orchestra. The whole issue is a delight.

Jon Nelson
American 1966-

Suggested listening ...

...Song for a dead king. Paterson 2:35. *Coupled with works by* **Babbitt, Van Vliet, Wheeler, Zappa, Stravinsky, Shemaria, H. Hancock** and **London** Meridian Arts Ensemble. Channel Classics Channel Crossings CCS8195 (4/96). *See review in the Collections section; refer to the Index to Reviews.*

Alberto Nepomuneco
Brazilian 1864-1920

Suggested listening ...

...Suíte antiga, Op. 11. Two Nocturnes. Improviso, Op. 27 No. 2. Piano Sonata in F minor, Op. 9. Nocturne, Op. 33. Galhofeira, Op. 13 No. 4. Cinco pequenas peças. **Maria Inês Guimarães** (pf). Marco Polo 8 223548 (2/95).

Johann Neruda
Czechoslovakian/German c1707-c1780

Suggested listening ...

...Trumpet Concerto in E flat major. *Coupled with works by* **Haydn, Hummel, F. Weber** and **C.F.C. Fasch John Wallace** (tpt); **John Anderson** (ob d'amore); **Peter Thomas** (vn); **Philharmonia Orchestra / Christopher Warren-Green, Simon Wright.** Nimbus NI7016 (2/95). *See review in the Collections section; refer to the Index to Reviews.*

John Nesbet
British died ?1488

Suggested listening ...

...Magnificat. *Coupled with* **Lambe** Nesciens mater. **Davy** The Passion according to St Matthew. **Eton College Chapel Choir / Ralph Allwood.** Chatsworth FCM1004 (5/95). *See review under Davy; refer to the Index to Reviews.*

Alfred Newman
American 1900-1970

Suggested listening ...

...Airport – original film soundtrack. Varèse Sarabande VSD5436 (8/94).
...Anastasia – original film soundtrack. Varèse Sarabande VSD5422 (8/94).
...How Green Was My Valley – original film soundtrack. Fox 07822 11008-2 (11/94).
...The Robe – original film soundtrack. Fox 07822 11011-2 (11/94).

Otto Nicolai
German 1810-1849

Suggested listening ...

...Die Lustigen Weiber von Windsor – Nun eilt herbei. *Coupled with works by* **Bishop, Handel, Donizetti, Rossini, Verdi, Chopin, Meyerbeer, Schubert, J. Strauss II, Kreisler** and **Anonymous Maria Ivogün** (sop) with various artists. Nimbus Prima Voce NI7832* (8/92). *See review in the Collections section; refer to the Index to Reviews.*

Carl Nielsen
Danish 1865-1931

Nielsen Clarinet Concerto, FS129[a]. Pan and Syrinx, FS87. Love and the Poet – Allegretto con brio. Little Suite in A minor, FS6. [a]**Walter Boeykens** (cl); **Beethoven Academy / Jan Caeyers.** Harmonia Mundi Ⓕ HMC90 1489 (54 minutes: DDD: 6/94). Recorded 1985-f9.

There have been plenty of recommendable recordings of Nielsen's concerto masterpiece in recent years, but this one is something special. You sense it in the opening theme on the lower strings, which strikes that paradoxical and immensely appealing Nielsenesque balance between grace and clumsiness, something that often eludes conductors. And you find it confirmed in the lyricism and poetry with which Walter Boeykens invests the solo part. This is above all a dignified, caring and musicianly performance. For some tastes that may mean that it fractionally underplays the bellicose outbursts to which the main protagonist is prone. Yet there is no shortage of boisterous *élan* and virtuosity, and the regretful returns to even-temperedness are properly touching. *Pan and Syrinx* (1918) is an intriguing curiosity – a compelling instance of the experimental idiom Nielsen favoured in his comparatively rare forays into programme music, and shot through with Sibelian influences. The overture from *Love and the Poet* is a late piece – four-and-a-half minutes of intense musings on musical images from Nielsen's last and most far-out symphony, the *Sinfonia semplice*. Like these, the genial *Little Suite*, from the other end of Nielsen's career, has immense care lavished on every detail of articulation, phrasing and balance. The acoustic may be on the borders of over-reverberant; but for most ears, it will surely be an entirely positive feature of an outstandingly rewarding disc.

Additional recommendations ...

...Clarinet Concerto. **Copland** Clarinet Concerto. **Lutosławski** Dances Preludes. **Janet Hilton** (cl); **Royal Scottish Orchestra / Matthias Bamert.** Chandos Ⓜ CHAN8618 (51 minutes: DDD: 10/88).

...Concertos – Clarinet, FS129[b]; Flute, FS119[a]; Violin, FS61[c]. [a]**Patrick Gallois** (fl); [b]**Olle Schill** (cl); [c]**Dong-Suk Kang** (vn); **Gothenburg Symphony Orchestra / Myung-Whun Chung.** BIS Ⓕ CD616 (79 minutes: DDD: 7/93).   Ⓖ

...Flute Concerto[a]. Clarinet Concerto[b]. Rhapsody Overture: an imaginary trip to the Faroe Islands, FS123. Saul and David – Prelude to Act 2. Springtime in Funen (Fynsk Forår), FS96[c]. [c]**Asa Bäverstam**, [c]**Linnéa Ekdahl** (sops); [c]**Andreas Thors** (treb); [c]**Kjell Magnus Sandvé** (ten); [c]**Per Høyer** (bar); [a]**Per Flemström** (fl); [b]**Håken Rosengren** (cl); [c]**Swedish Boys' Choir;** [c]**Swedish Radio Choir; Swedish Radio Symphony Orchestra / Esa-Pekka Salonen.** Sony Classical Ⓕ SK53276 (75 minutes: DDD: 4/94).   Ⓖ

Nielsen Flute Concerto, FS119[a]; Clarinet Concerto, FS129[b]. Maskarade[c] – Overture; Magdalone's dance scene; Prelude, Act 2; Dance of the cockerels. [a]**Holger Gilbert-Jespersen** (fl); [b]**Ib Erikson** (cl); **Danish State Radio Symphony Orchestra / [ac]Thomas Jensen, [b]Mogens Wöldike.** Dutton Laboratories mono Ⓕ CDLXT2505* (62 minutes: ADD: 2/96). Items marked [ab] from Decca LXT2979 (12/54), [c]Decca LW5132 (12/54). ⒼⒼ

In the early 1920s Nielsen heard the Copenhagen Wind Quintet rehearsing some works by Mozart and was moved to compose his enchanting Wind Quintet. He subsequently planned to write each of its members a concerto but only lived long enough to compose the two recorded here – the Flute Concerto of 1926 and the Clarinet Concerto of two years later. The soloist at the former's première was Holger Gilbert-Jespersen and it was he who made its first recording over a quarter of a century later. Gilbert-Jespersen was by all accounts an artist of refined taste and strong Gallic sympathies, and much of the piece was inspired by his temperament. The burlesque gestures of the trombone at the end are a joke which Nielsen made at his expense. Unless it is discreetly handled, the affectionate little jest can itself sound crude; but here all is perfection, particularly in such a superb CD transfer as this. These concertos and the four excepts from *Maskarade* were all recorded in April 1954, albeit with Mogens Wöldike conducting the Clarinet Concerto. Aage Oxenvad, who was the original dedicatee, was to have recorded it but died shortly before the sessions were due to take place. At the time, Ib Erikson was Principal Clarinet of the Danish State Radio Symphony Orchestra, which throughout the 1950s was without question the finest orchestra in Scandinavia. This version conveys better than so many more modern ones the unearthly quality of the Concerto, its rarefied and bracing air. These performances carry a special authority and cannot be too strongly recommended.

Nielsen Violin Concerto, FS61[a].
Sibelius Violin Concerto in D minor, Op. 47[b]. **Cho-Liang Lin** (vn); [a]**Swedish Radio Symphony Orchestra, [b]Philharmonia Orchestra / Esa-Pekka Salonen.** CBS Masterworks Ⓕ CD44548 (69 minutes: DDD: 1/89). Recorded 1987-8. *Gramophone Award Winner 1989.* ⒼⒼ
Nielsen Violin Concerto, FS61[a]. Flute Concerto, FS119[b]. Clarinet Concerto, FS129[c]. [d]**Toke Lund Christiansen** (fl); **Niels Thomsen** (cl); [a]**Kim Sjøgren** (vn); **Danish National Radio Symphony Orchestra / Michael Schønwandt.** Chandos Ⓕ CHAN8894 (80 minutes: DDD: 4/91). Recorded 1990. Ⓖ

Oddly enough no one has previously recorded the two greatest Nordic violin concertos on one CD and the result on the CBS disc is a triumphant success. This was the best recording of the Sibelius Concerto to have appeared for more than a decade and probably the best ever of the Nielsen. Cho-Liang Lin brings an apparently effortless virtuosity to both concertos. He produces a wonderfully clean and silvery sonority and there is no lack of aristocratic finesse. Only half-a-dozen years separate the two concertos, yet they breathe a totally different air. Lin's perfect intonation and tonal purity excite admiration and throughout them both there is a strong sense of line from beginning to end. Esa-Pekka Salonen gets excellent playing from the Philharmonia Orchestra in the Sibelius and almost equally good results from the Swedish Radio Symphony Orchestra. This should take its place among the classic concerto recordings of the century. The well-filled Chandos CD brings all three concertos together: the Violin Concerto comes from the period of the Third Symphony and the two wind concertos were written after the Sixth during the last years of his life. Nielsen planned to write five concertos, one for each member of the Copenhagen Wind Quintet. Kim Sjøgren may not command the purity of tone of Cho-Liang Lin but he has the inestimable advantage of totally idiomatic orchestral support: Michael Schønwandt has an instinctive feeling for this music – and this shows throughout the whole disc. The perspective between soloist and orchestra is well-judged (Sjøgren is never larger than life) and so is the internal balance. In the Flute Concerto, which veers from Gallic wit to moments of great poetic feeling, Toke Lund Christiansen is an excellent soloist. He has no want of brilliance or authority and his performance also has plenty of character. Niels Thomsen's account of the Clarinet Concerto is one of the very finest now before the public. If there is any music from another planet, this is it! There is no attempt to beautify the score nor to overstate it: every dynamic nuance and expressive marking is observed by both the soloist and conductor. Thomsen plays as if his very being is at stake and Michael Schønwandt secures playing of great imaginative intensity from the Danish Radio Orchestra.

Additional recommendations ...
...Flute Concerto. **Honegger** Concerto da camera[a]. **Ibert** Flute Concerto. **Poulenc** (orch. L. Berkeley) Flute Sonata. **Jennifer Stinton** (fl); [a]**Geoffrey Browne** (cor ang); **Scottish Chamber Orchestra / Steuart Bedford.** Collins Classics Ⓓ 1210-2 (66 minutes: DDD: 8/91). *See review in the Collections section; refer to the Index to Reviews.*
...Flute Concerto[a]. Clarinet Concerto[b]. **Hindemith** Violin Concerto[c]. [a]**Julius Baker** (fl); [b]**Stanley Drucker** (cl); [c]**Isaac Stern** (vn); **New York Philharmonic Orchestra / Leonard Bernstein.** Sony Classical Bernstein Royal Edition Ⓜ SMK47599 (73 minutes: ADD: 7/93). ⒼⒼ
...Flute Concerto[a]. **Bernstein** Halil[a]. **Ibert** Flute Concerto[b]. **Martin** (arr. Ansermet) Ballade[a]. **Michael Faust** (fl); **Cologne Radio Symphony Orchestra / [a]Alun Francis, [b]Serge Baudo.** Capriccio Ⓓ 10 405 (64 minutes; DDD 12/95).

Nielsen Symphonies – No. 1 in G minor, FS16; No. 6, FS116, "Sinfonia semplice". **San Francisco Symphony Orchestra / Herbert Blomstedt.** Decca Ⓕ 425 607-2DH (67 minutes: DDD: 2/90). Recorded 1989.   ⒼⒼⒼ

Nielsen always nurtured a special affection for his First Symphony – and rightly so, for its language is natural and unaffected. It has great spontaneity of feeling and a Dvořákian warmth and freshness. Blomstedt's recording is one of the best to have appeared for some years. It is vital, beautifully shaped and generally faithful to both the spirit and the letter of the score. The recording, too, is very fine: the sound has plenty of room to expand, there is a very good relationship between the various sections of the orchestra and a realistic perspective. Blomstedt gives a powerful account of the Sixth, too, with plenty of intensity and an appreciation of its extraordinary vision. It is by far the most challenging of the cycle and inhabits a very different world from early Nielsen. The intervening years had seen the cataclysmic events of the First World War and Nielsen himself was suffering increasingly from ill health. Blomstedt and the fine San Fransisco orchestra convey the powerful nervous tension of the first movement and the depth of the third, the *Proposta seria*. He is splendidly served by Decca's recording team.

Additional recommendations ...

...No. 1. Flute Concerto[a]. An imaginary journey to the Faroe Islands, FS123. [a]**Patrick Gallois** (fl); **Gothenburg Symphony Orchestra / Myung-Whun Chung.** BIS Ⓕ CD454 (63 minutes: DDD: 8/90).   ⒼⒼ

...No. 1. No. 2 in B minor, FS29, "The four temperaments", FS29. **Royal Scottish Orchestra / Bryden Thomson.** Chandos Ⓕ CHAN8880 (63 minutes: DDD: 6/92).

...Nos. 1-6. **Gothenburg Symphony Orchestra / Neeme Järvi.** DG Ⓕ 437 507-2GH3 (three discs: 202 minutes: DDD: 12/93).

...No. 1[a]; No. 2[b]; No. 3, FS60, "Sinfonia espansiva"[c]; No. 4, FS76, "The inextinguishable"[c]; No. 5, FS97[a]; No. 6, FS116, "Sinfonia semplice"[c]. **Danish Radio Symphony Orchestra / [a]Erik Tuxen, [b]Launy Grøndahl, [c]Thomas Jensen.** Danacord mono Ⓕ DACOCD351/3* (three discs: 203 minutes: ADD: 4/95).

...Nos. 1 and 5. Helios Overture[a]. **Danish State Radio Symphony Orchestra / Thomas Jensen, [a]Erik Tuxen.** Dutton Laboratories mono Ⓜ CDLXT2502* (79 minutes: ADD: 7/95).   Ⓖ

New review

Nielsen Symphonies – No. 1 in G minor, FS16; No. 6, FS116"Sinfonia semplice". **National Symphony Orchestra of Ireland / Adrian Leaper.** Naxos Ⓢ 8 550826 (68 minutes: DDD: 12/95).

Adrian Leaper's well-judged and sensible tempos in the First Symphony show his obvious feeling for Nielsen, and although there may perhaps be performances of greater eloquence and finesse, all of them are far more expensive. To go briefly into hypercritical mode one would have to say that the last few bars of the finale, at the *Allegro molto* marking, are just a bit too *molto* for comfort: the spurt to the final double bar-line feels a bit headlong. The Sixth Symphony is very good indeed: it sounds very well prepared, with finely shaped phrasing and is immaculate in its observance of dynamic nuance. Perhaps the climax of the first movement could be more intense but Leaper makes such good sense of everything, including the "Humoreske" movement which is so difficult to bring off. The recording team deserve special mention for the excellence of the sound: the perspective is natural and the orchestral texture beautifully transparent. The timpani could, perhaps, have been more savage at the climax of the first movement but the closing pages of the movement, or the beautiful eighth variation in the last, could hardly be bettered. This is well worth the money even if Blomstedt's version of this coupling (reviewed above) is not displaced.

Nielsen Symphonies – No. 2, FS29, "The Four Temperaments"; No. 3, FS60, "Sinfonia espansiva"[a]. [a]**Nancy Wait Fromm** (sop); [a]**Kevin McMillan** (bar); **San Francisco Symphony Orchestra / Herbert Blomstedt.** Decca Ⓕ 430 280-2DH (67 minutes: DDD: 8/90). *Gramophone Award Winner 1991.*   ⒼⒼⒼ

This disc couples two of Nielsen's most genial symphonies, both of which come from the earliest part of the century, in performances of the very first order. The Second (1902), inspired by the portrayal of *The Four Temperaments* (Choleric, Phlegmatic, Melancholic, Sanguine) that he had seen in a country inn, has splendid concentration and fire and, as always, from the right pace stems the right character. Moreover the orchestra sounds inspired, for there is a genuine excitement about their playing. Indeed Blomstedt's accounts are by far the most satisfying to have appeared for some time. The Third *Espansiva*, is even more personal in utterance than *The Four Temperaments*, for during the intervening years Nielsen had come much further along the road of self-discovery. His melodic lines are bolder, the musical paragraphs longer and his handling of form more assured. It is a glorious and richly inventive score whose pastoral slow movement includes a part for two wordless voices. Blomstedt gives us an affirmative, powerful reading and in the slow movement, the soprano produces the required ethereal effect. The Decca sound is very detailed and full-bodied, and in the best traditions of the company. Blomstedt's *Espansiva* has greater depth than most rival accounts; the actual sound has that glowing radiance that characterizes Nielsen, and the tempo, the underlying current on which this music is borne, is expertly judged – and nowhere better than in the finale. Blomstedt is an experienced guide in this repertoire and this shows, while his orchestra play with refreshing enthusiasm.

...No. 2. Aladdin – Orchestral Suite, Op. 34. **Gothenburg Symphony Orchestra / Myung-Whun Chung.** BIS Ⓕ CD247 (56 minutes: DDD: 5/84).

New review

Nielsen Symphonies – No. 2, FS29, "The Four Temperaments"; No. 3, FS60, "Sinfonia espansiva". **National Symphony Orchestra of Ireland / Adrian Leaper.** Naxos Ⓢ 8 550825 (68 minutes: DDD: 11/95).

The vital current on which every phrase must be borne in Nielsen needs to flow at higher voltage. This is music which needs to be played at white heat. Well, there is no lack of electricity in Leaper's reading of the Second. He sets a cracking pace for the first movement, the choleric temperament, and hardly puts a foot wrong in its three companions. His tempos in the *Sinfonia espansiva* are well-judged and sensible throughout all four movements. The finale, where many conductors get it wrong, seems to be just right. These are more than just serviceable performances: they are very good indeed and the Irish orchestra sound well rehearsed and inside the idiom. You can pay more and do worse although some collectors will be inclined to think the additional polish one gets from Blomstedt or Myung-Whun Chung is worth the extra outlay. These latter performances continue to grow in stature, and it is no mean compliment to the Naxos versions to say that they give them a very good run for their money. Naxos do not identify the singers in the slow movement of the *Espansiva*. No one investing in this new issue and then going on to either of the Blomstedt accounts is going to feel that they have been let down. The recording team secure a very decent balance: well laid-back wind and brass, with good front-to-back perspective and transparency of texture.

Nielsen Symphonies – No. 3, FS60, "Sinfonia espansiva"[a]; No. 5, FS97. [a]**Catherine Bott** (sop); [a]**Stephen Roberts** (bar); **Royal Scottish Orchestra / Bryden Thomson.** Chandos Ⓕ CHAN9067 (71 minutes: DDD: 2/93). Recorded 1991.

Bryden Thomson and the Royal Scottish Orchestra give fresh and direct readings of the *Espansiva* and the Fifth which are eminently satisfying. At no point are we aware of the conductor interposing himself between composer and listener, and one can sense an evident enthusiasm on the part of the players. This is Nielsen plain and unadorned without any frills. Thomson has a very good feeling for Nielsen's tempos and his account of the finale feels just right. All in all, a splendidly sane performance with good singing from the fine soloists in the slow movement. The Fifth Symphony is another unaffected and straightforward performance that has a great deal going for it – not least the beautiful clarinet playing in the coda, and the thoroughly committed second movement. One is, perhaps, more aware of the beat in the first movement than in Blomstedt's Decca account (reviewed above) and it rarely seems to float or sound disembodied as it does with him. However, Thomson gets very spirited playing from all departments of the orchestra and the recordings are very good and present, even if the sound lacks the transparency Decca achieved for Blomstedt. These are eminently enjoyable, ardent performances that can hold their head high amongst any competition.

...No. 3. Clarinet Concerto, FS129[a]. Maskarade – Overture. **Pia Raanoja** (sop); **Knut Skram** (bar); [a]**Olle Schill** (cl); **Gothenburg Symphony Orchestra / Myung-Whun Chung.** BIS Ⓕ CD321 (68 minutes: DDD: 8/86).

...Nos. 3 and 5. **New York Philharmonic Orchestra / Leonard Bernstein.** Sony Classical Bernstein Royal Edition Ⓜ SMK47598 (71 minutes: ADD: 7/93).

...Nos. 3[a] and 4. At the bier of a young artist, FS58. [a]**Kirsten Schultz** (sop); [a]**Peter Rasmussen** (bar); **Danish Radio Symphony Orchestra / Herbert Blomstedt.** EMI Matrix Ⓜ CDM5 65415-2 (75 minutes: ADD: 12/95).

Nielsen Symphonies – No. 4, FS76, "The inextinguishable"; No. 5, FS97. **San Francisco Symphony Orchestra / Herbert Blomstedt.** Decca Ⓕ 421 524-2DH (72 minutes: DDD: 10/88).

Nielsen Symphonies – No. 4, FS76, "The inextinguishable"; No. 6, FS116, "Sinfonia semplice". **Royal Scottish National Orchestra / Bryden Thomson.** Chandos Ⓕ CHAN9047 (70 minutes: DDD: 3/93). Recorded 1991.

These are two of Nielsen's most popular and deeply characteristic symphonies. Blomstedt's are good performances that can hold their own with any in the current catalogue, and as recordings they surpass the competition. The Fourth Symphony occupied Nielsen between 1914 and early 1916 and reveals a level of violence new to his art. The landscape is harsher; the melodic lines soar in a more anguished and intense fashion (in the case of the remarkable slow movement, "like the eagle riding on the wind", to use the composer's own graphic simile). Blomstedt's opening has splendid fire: this must sound as if galaxies are forming and he is not frightened of letting things rip. The finale with its exhilarating dialogue between the two timpanists comes off splendidly. The Fifth Symphony of 1922 is impressive, too: it starts perfectly and has just the right glacial atmosphere. The climax and the desolate clarinet peroration into which it dissolves are well handled. The recording balance could not be improved upon: the woodwind are decently recessed (though clarinet keys are audible at times), there is an almost ideal relationship between the various sections of the orchestra and a thoroughly realistic overall perspective. Blomstedt has a good rapport with his players who sound in excellent shape and respond to these scores as to the manner born.

Bryden Thomson's accounts of the Fourth and Sixth calls to mind the ardent intensity of the pioneering Danish recordings (no longer available) by Launy Gróndahl and Thomas Jensen such are their fire. The orchestra play as if their lives depend on it and the underlying violence of No. 4 makes a powerful impact, both at the opening and in the finale. But his Sixth is arguably the very finest version of the work on disc, notwithstanding the cultured and splendidly recorded account by Herbert Blomstedt (reviewed above with the First Symphony). Thomson strikes exactly the right tempo for the first movement nor has the problematic "Humoreske" ever made better sense. He takes it at a steadier pace than most rival conductors, so that its questioning spirit registers. The third movement, the "Proposta seria", is both eloquent and searching. Even in a strongly competitive field this splendidly recorded Chandos account brings one closer to this extraordinary work than any other.

Additional recommendations ...

...No. 5. Violin Concerto, Op. 33[a]. [a]**Dong-Suk Kang** (vn); **Gothenburg Symphony Orchestra / Myung-Whun Chung.** BIS Ⓕ CD370 (68 minutes: DDD: 12/87).

...Nos. 3 and 6. **Royal Danish Orchestra / Paavo Berglund.** RCA Victor Red Seal Ⓕ RD60427 (68 minutes: DDD: 4/92).   ⒼⒼ

...No. 4[a]. Pan and Syrinx, FS87[a]. **Sibelius** Symphony No. 5 in E flat major, Op. 82[b]. [a]**City of Birmingham Symphony Orchestra;** [b]**Philharmonia Orchestra / Simon Rattle.** EMI Ⓜ CDM7 64737-2 (78 minutes: DDD: 11/93).

...Nos. 4 and 5. **National Symphony Orchestra of Ireland / Adrian Leaper.** Naxos Ⓢ 8 550/43 (74 minutes: DDD: 10/94).

...No. 5[a]. Sibelius Luonnotar, Op. 70[b]. Night Ride and Sunrise, Op. 55[c]. The Oceanides, Op. 73[c]. [b]**Dame Gwyneth Jones** (sop); [a]**Danish National Radio Symphony Orchestra / Rafael Kubelik;** [bc]**London Symphony Orchestra / Antál Dorati.** EMI Studio Plus Ⓜ CDM5 65182-2) (73 minutes: ADD: 10/94).

...Nos. 4 and 6. **Gothenburg Symphony Orchestra / Neeme Järvi.** BIS Ⓕ CD600 (67 minutes: DDD: 7/93).

Nielsen Wind Quintet, FS100.
Fernström Wind Quintet, Op. 59.
Kvandal Wind Quintet, Op. 34. Three Sacred Folktunes, Op. 23b. **Wind Ensemble** (Tom Ottar Andreasson, fl; Lars Peter Berg, ob; Arild Stav, cl; Jan Olav Marthinsen, hn; Hans Peter Aasen, bn). Naxos Ⓢ 8 553050 (70 minutes: DDD: 3/95). Recorded 1993.

This is a thoroughly entertaining CD, combining three very different and unfamiliar works with what is probably the finest wind quintet ever penned. The major item here, of course, is the Nielsen: a glorious work which achieves the rare combination of seriousness of expression as well as being utterly relaxed in tone. The Oslo Ensemble are a little slower than usual, but their measured tempos are most convincing; indeed, in the finale they highlight musical connections with Nielsen's Fifth and Sixth Symphonies in ways rarely heard elsewhere. The Swede John Axel Fernström was undeniably a minor composer; his Twelfth Symphony has been available briefly in this country (conducted by Vernon Handley, no less). If his music does not possess many visionary qualities it is certainly well-crafted and his 1943 Quintet is an engaging and worthwhile concert opener. Johan Kvandal from Norway is a weightier proposition and better-known outside of his native country than is Fernström. Kvandal's Quintet, Op. 34 (1971), was written for the Oslo ensemble (apparently for a couple of cases of wine!) and is serious and high-minded in tone, contrasting effectively with both the Fernström and Kvandal's own *Sacred Folktunes* of 1963. In the Quintet's fast second movement Kvandal adopts a rather Shostakovichian manner, even alluding to the Soviet master's Twelfth Symphony, though to what purpose (if deliberate at all) is unexplained. The idiomatic playing is reproduced in a slightly flat recording (made in the studios of Norwegian Radio), although the Naxos sound has great immediacy. The Bergen Quintet on BIS must remain the first choice but this disc, with its welcome couplings, makes a fine alternative.

Additional recommendations ...

...Wind Quintet. **Holst** Wind Quintet in A flat major, H67. **Zemlinsky** Humoreske. **Jolivet** Sérénade for Oboe, Piano and Wind Quintet. **P. Pierné** Suite pittoresque. **Aulos Wind Quintet.** Koch Schwann Musica Mundi Ⓕ 310100 (71 minutes: DDD).   Ⓖ

...Wind Quintet[a]. Fantasy Piece for Clarinet and Piano, FS3h[b]. Fantasy Pieces for Oboe and Piano, FS8[c]. Canto serioso for Horn and Piano, FS132[d]. Serenata in vano, FS68[e]. The Mother, FS94 – The fog is lifting[f]; The children are playing[g]; Faith and Hope are playing[h]. Allegretto for Two Recorders, FS157[i]. [a]**Bergen Wind Quintet** (Gro Sandvik, fl[fgh], rec[i]; [c]Steinar Hannevold, ob; [be]Lars Kristian Holm Brynildsen, cl; [de]Vidar Olsen, hn; Per Hannevold, bn[e], rec[i]); [f]**Turid Kniejski** (hp); [h]**Lars Anders Tomter** (va); [e]**Sally Guenther** (vc); [e]**Torbjorn Eide** (db); [bcd]**Leif Ove Andsnes** (pf). BIS Ⓕ CD428 (56 minutes: DDD: 9/89).

...Wind Quintet. **Loeffler** Two Rhapsodies. **Prokofiev** Quintet in G minor, Op. 39. **Chamber Music Northwest.** Delos Ⓕ DE3136 (71 minutes: DDD: 12/93).

Nielsen String Quartets – No. 1 in G minor, FS4; No. 2 in F minor, FS11; No. 3 in E flat major, FS23 (Op. 14); No. 4 in F major, FS36. Movements for String Quartet, FS3c. **Danish Quartet** (Tim Frederiksen, Arne Balk-Møller, vns; Claus Myrup, va; H. Brendstrup, vc). Kontrapunkt Ⓕ 32150/1 (two discs: 138 minutes: DDD: 10/93).   Ⓖ

Nielsen composed two quartets and a string quintet during his student years. There was a gap of eight years between the F minor Quartet and the Third, in E flat, Op. 14 (FS23) during which Nielsen had written his First Symphony, and another eight before the F major, Op. 44 (FS36) saw the light of day. By this time he had written his opera, *Saul and David* and the best part of *Maskarade* as well as the Second Symphony. The Danish Quartet do not have the thrust or, perhaps, the finish of the Kontra Quartet on BIS (listed below), but they are very sensitive to dynamic nuance, phrase more imaginatively, and are generally speaking more involving. Of course, the F major Quartet goes deeper than the Third. There is a grace, an effortless fluency and a marvellous control of pace. Ideas come and go just when you feel they should; yet its learning and mastery is worn lightly. Though the earlier quartets are not such perfect works of art, they are nevertheless always endearing. The Danish Quartet is completely inside this music and is totally persuasive. In spite of the closely balanced recording this set gives real pleasure and can be recommended with enthusiasm.

Additional recommendation ...
...Nos. 1-4. String Quintet in G major, FS5[a]. At the bier of a young artist, FS58[b]. **Kontra Quartet**; [a]**Philipp Naegele** (va); [b]**Jan Johannsson** (db). BIS Ⓕ CD503/04 (two discs: 150 minutes: DDD: 4/92).

New review

Nielsen Five Pieces, FS10. Humoresque Bagatelles, FS22. Chaconne, FS79. Suite, FS91. Three Pieces, FS131. **Leif Ove Andsnes** (pf). Virgin Classics Ⓕ VC5 45129-2 (54 minutes: DDD: 8/96).
Gramophone Editor's choice.

This music is quite wonderful and deserves the widest dissemination. Although the *Suite* (*Suite luciferique*) was dedicated to Schnabel, the great pianist never played it in public. On record the finest advocate of the piano music was Arne Skjold Rasmussen, whose three-LP set appeared fleetingly in this country in a Vox box during the 1960s. Without the slightest disrespect to him, it now has to be said that this music has at last found its true interpreter in the Norwegian Leif Ove Andsnes. He has the measure both of the fresh and charming early pieces, FS10 and 22, and the later more searching, other-worldly *Suite* and the *Three Pieces*. The *luciferique* of the former alludes, incidentally, to the messenger of light, not the prince of darkness, and Nielsen subsequently withdrew the title. This is music of great substance and a deep and powerful originality. Andsnes has such a natural feeling for it that you will probably never find yourself questioning his interpretative judgements. He brings wit and subtlety to pieces like the "Spinning Top" and "Jumping Jack" from FS10, and there is always a splendid rhythmic grip, tonal sensitivity and variety of keyboard colour. He communicates real conviction to the listener, a feeling that this is the only way this music can sound. There is an impressive eloquence and nobility here, and the recorded sound is in every respect exemplary. It is 'present', natural and lifelike. Because this music is unfamiliar, collectors may be cautious or slow in exploring it. To judge from his BBC Proms performance in 1995, Andsnes has quite a following and it is to be hoped that he will lead his admirers on to this music which he has here served so well.

Nielsen Aladdin. Mette Ejsing (contr); **Guido Paevatalu** (bar); **Danish National Radio Chamber Choir; Danish National Radio Symphony Orchestra / Gennadi Rozhdestvensky.** Chandos Ⓕ CHAN9135 (79 minutes: DDD: 5/93). Text and translation included. Recorded 1992.
Gramophone Editor's choice.   Ⓖ

So far Nielsen's music to Adam Oehlenschläger's *Aladdin* has been known only from the seven-movement suite. However, the suite only comprises about 20 minutes of music, which is little more than a quarter of Nielsen's original score. *Aladdin* comes from 1917-18, and was commissioned for a particularly lavish production of the play at the Royal Theatre in Copenhagen. More than half the music consists of orchestral interludes to accompany processions and dances, most of which come in the Third Act. Many are delightful and endearing, and once heard difficult to get out of one's head. Robert Simpson summed the work up in his Nielsen monograph: "The market-square in Isfahan where four orchestras play in four different tempos suggesting marvellously the clashing colours, movements and sounds of an eastern market-place in undoubtedly the most striking and original part of the music. Some of it is not very interesting (the rather commonplace Blackamoors' Dance, for instance) but most is intensely perceptive and colourful." It is full of characteristic Nielsenesque touches, and although it is not the composer at his very best, it offers many irresistible delights. Performance and recording are superb.

Further listening ...
...Helios Overture, FS32. Symphonic Rhapsody, FS7. Saga-drøm, FS46. An evening on Giske, FS9. Paraphrase on "Nearer my God to Thee", FS63. Bohemian-Danish Folk tune. FS130. Rhapsody Overture: An imaginary journey to the Faroe Islands, FS123. Pan and Syrinx, FS87. **Danish National Radio Symphony Orchestra / Gennadi Rozhdestvensky.** Chandos CHAN9287 (9/94)
...String Quintet in G major, FS5. *Coupled with* **Svendsen** Octet in A major, Op. 3. Romance in G major, Op. 26[a]. [a]**Kenneth Sillito** (vn); **Academy of St Martin in the Fields Chamber Ensemble.** Chandos CHAN9258 (5/94).   Ⓖ

…Violin Sonatas – No. 1 in A major, FS20; No. 2, FS64. **Lydia Mordkovitch** (vn); **Clifford Benson** (pf). Chandos CHAN8598 (9/89).

…Commotio, FS155. *Coupled with works by* **Alain, Mulet, Sibelius, Sløgedal, Lindberg, Mozart, Lefébure-Wély** and **Elgar Christopher Herrick** (org). Hyperion CDA66676. *See review in the Collections section; refer to the Index to Reviews.*

…Saul and David. **Soloists; Danish National Radio Choir and Symphony Orchestra / Neeme Järvi.** Chandos CHAN8911/12 (3/91).

Joaquín Nin
Cuban 1879-1949

Suggested listening …

…Cantos populares españolas – No. 3, Tonada de la niña perdida; No. 4, Montañesa; No. 6, Malagueña; No. 7, Granadina; No. 19, Canto Andaluz; No. 20, Polo. *Coupled with works by* **Granados, Falla** and **Mompou Maria Barrientos, Ninon Vallin** (sops); **Enrique Granados, Federico Mompou, Joaquin Nin** (pfs); **Manuel de Falla** (pf/hpd); **instrumental ensemble.** EMI Composers in Person mono CDC7 54836-2* (11/93). *See review in the Collections section; refer to the Index to Reviews.*

Guillaume Nivers
French c1632-1714

Suggested listening …

…Antiphonarium Monasticum, Antiennes I-VI. *Coupled with works by* **Charpentier Le Concert Spirituel / Hervé Niquet.** Naxos 8 553174 (3/96). *See review under Charpentier; refer to the Index to Reviews.* ⒢

Luigi Nono
Italian 1924-1990

Nono Il canto sospeso[a].
Mahler Kindertotenlieder[b]. Rückert-Lieder – Ich bin der Welt abhanden gekommen[b]. [a]**Susanne Lothar**, [a]**Bruno Ganz** (spkrs); [a]**Barbara Bonney** (sop); [a]**Susanne Otto** (mez); [b]**Marjana Lipovšek** (contr); [a]**Marek Torzewski** (ten); [a]**Berlin Radio Chorus**; **Berlin Philharmonic Orchestra / Claudio Abbado.** Sony Classical Ⓕ SK53360 (70 minutes: DDD: 10/93). Recorded live in 1992.

Three years on from the re-unification of Berlin, the promise of *Freiheit* looks distinctly hollow, undermined by resurgent nationalism, rampant consumerism, xenophobia, racism and fear. The mood of the present programme (edited together from individual concerts) is therefore very different. Nono's *Il canto sospeso* is a key work of the European avant-garde, one in which serial processes and Communist ideology are brought together in a dramatically compelling memorial to the victims of Fascism and this performance is unlikely to be bettered for a long time. Under Abbado, the playing is as tight and stylish as might be expected from these forces: choral singing is unprecedentedly secure and Barbara Bonney is especially radiant. Less welcome for repeated listening are the interpolated readings, by Bruno Ganz and Susanne Lothar, of the letters from which Nono builds his cantata, the last dispatches of members of the Resistance condemned to death. Nono's texts include many painful messages from children to parents – they too might have been subtitled *Kindertotenlieder* – and Mahler's familiar Rückert verses are lent a new resonance from the very first. Marjana Lipovšek sings with long, resonant and well-balanced phrases and a dark, solemn manner. The 20-bit technology does not entirely offset the drawbacks of live recording in the Philharmonie, but the results are perfectly acceptable. Despite reservations, strongly recommended.

New review

Nono Prometeo. **Ingrid Ade-Jesemann, Monika Bair-Ivenz** (sops); **Peter Hall** (ten); **Freiburg Soloists Choir; Ensemble Modern / Ingo Metzmacher.** EMI Ⓕ CDS5 55209-2 (two discs: 134 minutes: DDD: 12/95). Notes, text and translation included. Recorded live in 1993.

Prometeo is a challenge to the faculty of listening; at least part of the meaning of its subtitle, "tragedia dell'ascolto", is that it is a tragedy to be perceived through the hearing only. It is a two-and-a-quarter-hour opera without staging or action, in which few if any of the words are intended to be distinguishable and whose dynamic level is often at the very limit of audibility. You could add "and proceeds at a tempo of *adagissimo* almost throughout", but even when, as often happens, the basic tempo is very slow indeed there are often two or more musics of different degrees of slowness going on at once, thus colour, texture and harmony change more rapidly than pulse. The effect, even so, is of a very long piece of very slow, very quiet music. It is in nine sections; two of them give a clear indication of Nono's intentions. The fourth, *Interludio primo*, is for solo contralto, flute, clarinet and tuba, the instruments mostly doubling the voice, so that the whole piece can be heard as a monody in which the function of the instruments is to 'colour' the voice expressively. The text hints, with the aid of a single line from Hesiod's *Theogony*, at a vision of a new Prometheus. It was Nono's intention, one suspects, that having previously read the text (it is very short) we should perceive its meaning through the music alone. It is like a sort of ritual 'still centre' to the entire work, inviting you to suspend your sense of time and listen to every change of pitch and timbre with an unaccustomed intensity: the musicians are instructed never to rise above *ppppp*, and in this performance they are admirably faithful to that instruction.

A different kind of challenge is posed by the sixth section, in which three very fragmentary 'movements', each for a different vocal and instrumental combination, are played simultaneously, punctuated by a separate chorus intoning six 'distant memories' from the Prologue. This time you will need the texts in front of you, since there are not three but seven of them and here they have fused with the music, as the voice and the instruments fused in *Intermedio primo*. The effort of hearing and making sense of three different, intermittent musical strands is great but one is aware of a strange poetry, a grave beauty. One of the reasons for this is the extraordinary care with which Nono planned every aspect of what he called his 'acoustic dramaturgy', including its complex yet subtle electronic transformations. The performance maintains a remarkable control over this huge span of hushed concentration. The recording, too, is exceptional, revealing gradations of quietness that you will rarely before have been asked to perceive. A challenging redefinition of how music may encompass myth and drama (oh yes: you are aware of a compelling drama taking place, one which only your ears can interpret).

Further listening ...

...Promoteo – suite. *Coupled with works by* **Scriabin, Liszt** and **Beethoven** Soloists; Berlin Singakademie; Freiburg Soloists Choir; Berlin Philharmonic Orchestra / Claudio Abbado. Sony Classical SK53978 (1/95). *See review in the Collections section; refer to the Index to Reviews.* 🅖🅖🅖

...Liebeslied [a]. *Coupled with* **Boulez** Notations I-IV. **Ligeti** Atmosphères. Lontano. **Rihm** Départ[a]. [a]Vienna Jeunesse Choir; Vienna Philharmonic Orchestra / Claudio Abbado. DG 429 260-2GH (4/90).

Per Nørgård
Danish 1932-

New review

Nørgård Trio, Op. 15[a]. Spell[a]. Cao Shu. Lin[a]. **LINensemble** (Jens Schou, cl; [a]John Ehde, vc; Erik Kaltoft, pf). Kontrapunkt Ⓔ 32211 (78 minutes: DDD: 3/96). Recorded 1994-5.

There is something here for everyone interested in twentieth-century repertoire, the most ardent of serialists aside. In the course of a very distinguished career Per Nørgård has encountered most of the styles and 'isms' this century has produced – and invented one or two himself – and the four works for clarinet and/or cello with piano collected on this CD reflect his diversity of experience. The Trio was written in 1955 during his final year in Holmboe's composition class. Already one can hear hints of the composer's mature concerns, as in the second movement's initial Philip Glass-like pattern a full decade before minimalism appeared. This style would be explored more fully – perhaps too much so for the minimalist label to stick – in his second trio, *Spell* (1973). Here different types of motion were fused together in the course of 16 minutes, a process reversed in the more recent *Lin* ("Approach", 1986). *Cao Shu* ("Letters of grass", 1992 3), a beautiful, rather meditative duet written for Jens Schou and Erik Kaltoft, shares with *Lin* the oriental connection common to much of Nørgård's recent output. Nørgård's journeys have always been interesting, even when they needed time to be fully appreciated. These are committed and persuasive performances and the recordings are very clear.

Further listening ...

...Echo Zone I-III. *Coupled with works by* **Miki, Pape, Fuzzy** and **A. Koppel** Safri Duo. Chandos New Direction CHAN9330 (4/95). *See review in the Collections section; refer to the Index to Reviews.*

...Twilight[b]. *Coupled with* **Gade** Echoes from Ossian, Op. 1[a]. **Abrahamsen** Symphony[a]. **Horneman** Gurre Suite[b]. Aarhus Royal Academy of Music Orchestra / [a]Ole Schmidt, [b]Søren K. Hansen. Kontrapunkt 32194 (7/95).

...And time shall be no more. *Coupled with* **Tormis** The Curse of Iron. **Rautavaara** Suite de Lorca, Op. 72. **Sandström** A Cradle Song/The Tyger. **Jersild** Three Romantic Songs. **Danish National Radio Choir** / Stefan Parkman. Chandos CHAN9264 (4/95).

...Siddharta[a]. Percussion Concerto, "For a Change"[b]. [a]Soloists; [b]Gert Mortensen (perc); Danish National Radio [a]Choir; [a]Childrens' Choir and Symphony Orchestra / Jan Latham-Konig. Da Capo 8 224031/2 (12/95).

Ib Nørholm
Danish 1931-

New review

Nørholm Symphonies – No. 4, Op. 76[a], "De-creation"; No. 5, Op. 80, "The Elements". [a]Nina Pavlovski (sop); [a]Stefan Dahlberg (ten); [a]Per Høyer (bar); [a]Ib Nørholm (narr); [a]Danish National Radio Choir; Odense Symphony Orchestra / Eduard Serov. Kontrapunkt Ⓔ 32212 (74 minutes: DDD: 10/95). Recorded 1995.

Like Per Nørgård, Ib Nørholm was a pupil of Vagn Holmboe and is currently Professor of Composition in Copenhagen. His early music was in what can best be described as a lyrical Nordic style very much in the tradition of Nielsen and Holmboe. But unlike his master, who "without glancing to left or right, without regard to fashions or trends, goes his own way" (as Klemperer said of Sibelius), Nørholm has looked very much to left and right, and has been keenly responsive to the European avant-garde and has, perhaps, embraced "the new internationalism" too eagerly. The very titles of some of his works betray their self-consciousness: the Sixth Symphony is called "Moralities, or There may be many miles to the nearest spider" – doubtless reassuring news if you are arachnophobic. Nørholm possesses a sophisticated aural imagination and a fine ear for texture. Both symphonies offer us moments of considerable beauty and many others that are not. Basically the Fourth Symphony is deficient in thematic vitality and although there is a great deal of activity, there is little real musical movement. The Fifth Symphony is the more interesting of the two pieces. The opening of its third movement, *Poco fluente*, is quite beautiful but there is, arguably, too much neo-expressionistic hysteria and too little sense of momentum. The performances are dedicated and the recording copes admirably with the complex textures and reproduces them with lucidity.

Further listening ...

...Violin Concerto, Op. 60[a]. Cello Concerto, Op. 108[b]. [a]**Kishiko Suzumi** (vn); [b]**Erling Blöndal Bengtsson** (vc); **Aalborg Symphony Orchestra / Tamás Vetö.** Kontrapunkt 32099 (9/93). Ⓖ

...Symphonies – No. 1, Op. 10; No. 3, Op. 57, "Day's Nightmare". **Odense Symphony Orchestra / Eduard Serov.** Kontrapunkt 32132 (9/93). Ⓖ

...Symphonies – No. 6, Op. 85, "Moralities, or There may be many miles to the nearest spider"[a]. No. 8, Op. 114, "Faith and Longing"[b]. [a]**Majken Bjerno** (sop); [ab]**Per Høyer** (bar); [a]**Uffe Henriksen**, [a]**Ulla Seel** (narrs); **Odense Symphony Orchestra / Edward Serov.** Kontrapunkt 32162 (2/94). Ⓖ

...Symphonies – No. 7, Op. 88, "Ecliptic Instincts"; No. 9, Op. 116, "The Sun Garden in Three Shades of Light". **Odense Symphony Orchestra / Eduard Serov.** Kontrapunkt 32112 (9/93). Ⓖ

Katherine Norman

British 1960-

New review

Norman London[a] – In her own time; London E17; People underground. Trilling Wire[b]. [a]**Rita Norman** (voc); [b]**Jonathan Cooper** (cl); **Katherine Norman** (tape op). NMC Ⓟ NMCD034 (69 minutes: DDD: 8/96).

Katherine Norman has strong views about the purpose of her work. Aiming "to create a sonic equivalent to montage film", she believes that our sensibilities can be expanded by making "the familiar" – the cries of market traders, even the disembodied voice at underground stations urging customers to "mind the gap" – more poignant and more intense. The aim is not to pursue the composer's traditional role of transcending "the familiar", and Norman's work does indeed appear to have more in common with the documentary ethos of television programmes like *Yesterday's Witness* than with the explicit transformations and contextualizations of "the familiar" found in a work like Steve Reich's *Different Trains*. Judged by the standards of 'High Art', Norman's soundscapes and soundtracks might well appear simplistic, yet it would be pointless to expect the kind of elaborately abstract exploitation of the electro-acoustic medium that emanates, in particular, from IRCAM. Norman tends to use unchallenging musical sounds to provide a pleasing context for her quotation, and occasional manipulation, of non-musical sounds – most strikingly, here, in her mother's vivid reminiscences of life in the wartime East End. And while in the third part of *London* – "People underground" – many of the 'concrete' noises, like clanging gates and echoing footsteps, begin to acquire a purely musical resonance, Norman still resists the lure of abstraction. Even in the short final piece on the disc, *Trilling Wire*, it is flow rather than argument that comes across, an unthreatening liveliness as approachable as it is unassuming. The technical quality of the disc is impressive, and the whole enterprise provides food for thought for anyone who believes that 'art' can only prosper when it keeps "the familiar" at arm's length.

Alex North

American 1910-1991

Suggested listening ...

...2001 – film score. **National Philharmonic Orchestra / Jerry Goldsmith.** Varèse Sarabande VSD5400 (3/94).

Angelo Notari

Italian 1556-1663

Suggested listening ...

...Prime musiche nuove. **The Consort of Musicke / Anthony Rooley.** Musica Oscura 070983 (8/95). ✐

...Variations on the "Ruggiero". *Coupled with works by* **Webster, A. Ferrabosco II, R. Johnson II, Nau** and **W. Lawes Parley of Instruments Renaissance Violin Band / Peter Holman.** Hyperion CDA66806 (6/96). ✐ *See review in the Collections section; refer to the Index to Reviews.* Ⓖ

Vítezslav Novák

Suggested listening ...
...Slovak Suite, Op. 32. *Coupled with* **Janáček** Taras Bulba. The Cunning Little Vixen – Suite. **Czech Philharmonic Orchestra / Václav Talich.** Supraphon Historical mono 11 1905-2* (1/94).
...Slovak Suite, Op. 32[a]. Eternal Longing, Op. 33[b]. In the Tatra Mountains, Op. 26[a]. [a]**Brno State Philharmonic Orchestra;** [b]**Czech Philharmonic Orchestra / Karel Sejna.** Supraphon Crystal Collection 11 0682-2 (6/93).
...Pan, Op. 43. **Slovak Philharmonic Orchestra / Zdenek Bílek.** Marco Polo 8 223325 (10/91).
...Serenades – F major, Op. 9; D major, Op. 36. **Ukrainian Chamber Orchestra / Andrew Mogrelia.** Marco Polo 8 223649 (3/96).

Michael Nyman
British 1944-

Nyman The Piano Concerto[a]. MGV (Musique à Grande Vitesse)[b]. [a]**Kathryn Stott** (pf); [a]**Royal Liverpool Philharmonic Orchestra;** [b]**Michael Nyman Band; orchestra / Michael Nyman.** Argo Ⓕ 443 382-2ZH (59 minutes: DDD: 9/94). Recorded 1994.
Considering the international success of Jane Campion's film *The Piano*, it seems quite logical that Nyman should adapt his celebrated score into a concert piece. Though performed uninterrupted, the 32-minute concerto is divided into four clear-cut sections. The Scottish folk-songs on which much of the score is based imbue the piece with a yearning, heartfelt quality not usually associated with this composer. Indeed, the whole concerto, as so convincingly advocated by Kathryn Stott and the RLPO, throbs with an unbridled romantic fervency (the second movement and the end of the third almost Rózsa-like in their ardour) that may come as something of a shock to hardened Nymanites or those who appreciate the less grandiose scoring for the film. More recognizably Nymanesque is *MGV*, a sort of *Pacific 231* for the 1990s, composed for the inauguration of the TGV North-European line in France. Here the composer's abstract style is eminently suited to describing a non-stop, imaginary railway journey through five regions between Paris and Lille; his repeated phrases and chugging, insistently propulsive rhythms create an effect that is totally spellbinding, with the strings adding an especially effective sense of speed and visual sweep. A rewarding disc that will appeal to Nyman fans old and new.

Nyman Noises, Sounds and Sweet Airs. **Catherine Bott** (sop); **Hilary Summers** (contr); **Ian Bostridge** (ten); **Basse-Normandie Instrumental Ensemble / Dominique Debart.** Argo Ⓕ 440 842-2ZH (73 minutes: DDD: 4/95). Text included. Recorded 1993.
Nymanites will rejoice. The pulse, the raunchy textures and the restless alternation of metre (either between 'numbers' or within them) all hail from a familiar work-bench: this is miniaturist minimalism taken to epic extremes. The sound is unmistakable: hear it at your local record store and you'll either be reaching for your wallet, or racing for the door. A 'Prospero Express', with 20 carriages (musical sections), each housing a different slice of the action – hyperactive, restless, moody (the score is far darker than various of its concert or film-based predecessors) and featuring some imaginative word-painting. Not that Shakespeare's *The Tempest* could possibly serve you as a libretto – not unless you have scissors and paste handy. "Very heavily and idiosyncratically edited", admits the composer. And how! *Prospero's Books*, incidentally, is a totally separate score. The performance itself seems fairly expert, save for one or two instances where the soprano's relatively high tessitura gives Catherine Bott cause for some strain. The recording is excellent.

Further listening ...
...Where the Bee Dances[a]. *Coupled with works by* **McGlynn, Torke, I. Wilson** and **D. Heath** Gerard McChrystal (sax); [a]**London Musici / Mark Stephenson.** Silva Classics SILKD6010 (6/96). *See review in the Collections section; refer to the Index to Reviews.*
...String Quartets Nos. 1-3. **Balanescu Quartet.** Argo 433 093-2ZH (8/91).
...Prospero's Books (music from the film by Peter Greenaway). **Sarah Leonard, Ute Lemper, Marie Angel** (sops); **Deborah Conway** (sngr); **Michael Nyman Band / Michael Nyman.** Decca 425 224-2DH (11/91).
...Four Songs for Tony. *Coupled with works by* **Corea, D. Bedford, W. Gregory** and **R. Powell** Apollo Saxophone Quartet. Argo 443 903-2ZH (8/95). *See review in the Collections section; refer to the Index to Reviews.*

Gösta Nystroem
Swedish 1890-1966

Suggested listening ...
...The Arctic Ocean. Viola Concerto, "Hommage à la France"[a]. Sinfonia concertante[b]. [a]**Nobuko Imai** (va); [b]**Niels Ullner** (vc); **Malmö Symphony Orchestra / Paavo Järvi.** BIS CD682 (4/95).

Jacob Obrecht

New review

Obrecht Missa Maria Zart. **The Tallis Scholars / Peter Phillips.** Gimell Ⓕ CDGIM032 (69 minutes: DDD: 3/96). Text and translations included. Recorded 1994. *Gramophone Editor's choice.*

This is a bizarre and fascinating piece: normally a Renaissance Mass cycle lasts from 20 to 30 minutes; in the present performance, this one lasts 69 minutes. No 'liturgical reconstruction' with chants or anything to flesh out the disc: just solid polyphony the whole way. It seems, in fact, to be the longest known Renaissance Mass. Most critics agree that this is one of Obrecht's last and most glorious works, even if it leaves them tongue-tied. Rob C. Wegman's recent masterly study of Obrecht's Masses put it in a nutshell: "Forget the imitation, it seems to tell us, be still, and listen". There is room for wondering whether all of it needs to be quite so slow: there may be ways of making the music run a little more fluidly, so that the irrational dissonances do not come across as clearly as they do here. But in most ways it is hard to fault Peter Phillips's reading of this massive work. With only eight singers on the four voices, he takes every detail seriously. And they sing with such conviction and skill that there is hardly a moment when the ear is inclined to wander. As we have come to expect, The Tallis Scholars are technically flawless and constantly alive. Briefly, the disc is a triumph. But, more than that, it is a major contribution to the catalogue, unflinchingly presenting both the beauties and the apparent flaws of this extraordinary work. Phew!

Further listening ...

...Quod Chorus Vatum/Haec Deum Caeli. *Coupled with* **Ockeghem** Missa, "Mi-Mi" (quarti toni). Salve regina I. Alma redemptoris mater. **Busnois** Victimae Paschali laudes. **Isaac** Angeli, Archangeli. **The Clerks' Group / Edward Wickham.** ASV Gaudeamus CDGAU139 (3/95). *See review which follows.*

...Salve regina. *Coupled with* **Ockeghem** Missa Ecce ancilla Domini. Intemerata Dei mater. Ave Maria. **Josquin Desprez** Déploration sur la mort de Johannes Ockeghem, "Nymphes des bois". **The Clerks' Group / Edward Wickham.** Proud Sound PROUCD133 (10/93). *See review which follows.* Ⓖ

...(attrib.) Humilium decus. *Coupled with* **Ockeghem** Missa prolationum. **Busnois** Gaude coelestis Domina. In hydraulis. **Pullois** Flos de spina. **Josquin Desprez** Illibata Dei Virgo nutrix. **The Clerks' Group / Edward Wickham.** ASV Gaudeamus CDGAU143 (3/96). *See review which follows. Gramophone Editor's choice.*

Johannes Ockeghem

New review

Ockeghem Missa prolationum.
Fifteenth-Century Choral Works The Clerks' Group / Edward Wickham. ASV Gaudeamus Ⓕ CDGAU143 (65 minutes: DDD: 3/96). Recorded 1995. *Gramophone Editor's choice.*
    Obrecht (attrib.) Humilium decus. **Busnois** Gaude coelestis Domina. In hydraulis. **Pullois** Flos de spina. **Josquin Desprez** Illibata Dei Virgo nutrix.

This recording focuses on one of the most astonishing compositional feats of the second half of the fifteenth century: Ockeghem's *Missa prolationum*. The successive movements of the Ordinary of the Mass are based on double canons that progress from the unison to the octave, while at the same time the composer also exploits the inherent ambiguity of the mensural system (hence the work's title) of the later Middle Ages so that the rhythmic relationships between the voices are constantly being transformed. The astonishing thing is how effortlessly Ockeghem weaves his complex polyphonic web, and this is reinforced here by the unfettered, direct way in which The Clerks' Group approach the music. Although there are only eight singers in the group (so a maximum of two voices to a part), they bring a very satisfactory mix of the vocal agility one might expect from a small ensemble and the ability to sing through the long-breathed lines favoured by Ockeghem, without ever sounding strained or thin. The overall sound is immediate, crystal clear and closely recorded, but it never lacks for richness or blend – much credit to the ASV production team, too, in this respect. Although at first sight the five motets on the disc seem only loosely related to each other and to the Mass (the works date variously from the 1460s through to the 1490s), there are potentially illuminating links: several of the composers appear to pay homage, whether directly or indirectly, to one another's pieces and in general they all opt for quite self-consciously complex structures yet create a musical idiom that is lucid and full of emotional responses to the texts (mostly Marian) they chose to set. This recording allows the listener fully to appreciate the Franco-Netherlandish school at its best.

Ockeghem Missa Ecce ancilla Domini. Intemerata Dei mater. Ave Maria.
Josquin Desprez Déploration sur la mort de Johannes Ockeghem, "Nymphes des bois".
Obrecht Salve regina. **The Clerks' Group / Edward Wickham.** Proud Sound Ⓕ PROUCD133 (64 minutes: DDD: 10/93). Texts and translations included. Recorded 1993.
This is the finest Ockeghem disc available, and there are very few recordings of fifteenth-century polyphony to match it. This astonishing music poses a considerable challenge in performance. With formal and stylistic conventions being flouted at every turn, matters of phrasing and pacing acquire

a crucial importance, and much depends on the performers' ability to render local details intelligently. That is what makes this recording so special. *Missa Ecce ancilla*, though one of Ockeghem's most impressive Mass-cycles, is hardly an obvious choice for an ensemble making its recording début, but the Clerks' Group have absorbed Ockeghem's idiom to an extent that has scarcely been achieved hitherto, and command the technical means to match: balance and richness of tone, registral security and dynamic flexibility are all spot on. As a result, one makes sense of details which seemed baffling in previous recordings. Better still, such moments acquire the dramatic impact that is their ultimate justification. It is a joy to hear such an intelligent reading delivered with such confidence.

Ockeghem Missa, "Mi-Mi" (quarti toni). Salve regina I. Alma redemptoris mater.
Busnois Victimae Paschali laudes.
Obrecht Quod Chorus Vatum/Haec Deum Caeli.
Isaac Angeli, Archangeli. **The Clerks' Group / Edward Wickham.** ASV Gaudeamus Ⓔ CDGAU139
    (63 minutes: DDD: 3/95). Recorded 1994.
Over the next few years it is anticipated that a further four discs on ASV will each present one of Ockeghem's Masses alongside a selection of motets by his contemporaries. If the first of the new set is any indication, The Clerks are set to strike a powerful chord in favour of a shamefully under-recorded figure. In the *Mi-Mi* Mass, which includes only men's voices, the dark sonorities achieved by The Clerks seem just right for this most mysterious of Ockeghem's Masses. Also, the accompanying motets find The Clerks on their strongest form. These are crisp, clever, truly imaginative performances, delivered with a confidence bordering on arrogance. The sopranos' robust delivery is a welcome contrast to the brooding abstraction of Ockeghem's Mass. Listen to the hint of bells in Isaac's *Angeli, Archangeli*: this is an astonishing piece that you won't find recorded elsewhere. Why mince words? This is superb.

Ockeghem Requiem. **Les Pages de la Chapelle; Organum Ensemble / Marcel Pérès.** Harmonia
    Mundi Ⓔ HMC90 1441 (55 minutes: DDD: 2/94). ✍ Text and translation included.
    Recorded 1992.
Marcel Pérès brings his own colour to what will always remain the strangest piece by one of music's most puzzling composers. Mainly he works at about a fourth below modern pitch, keeps all the singing unusually quiet and chooses fairly sprightly tempos. In general this works extremely well, with the cheerful and occasionally slap-happy voices of the Ensemble Organum bringing an attractive dash of *élan* to what would otherwise be intolerably lugubrious. Pérès makes the occasional strange decision: he returns to the manuscript with some bizarre results; he also changes pitch standard by a fourth for the middle section of the Tract. There is also his decision to add on a couple of movements from the much later Requiem of Divitis at the end, so entirely different in sound as to startle the ear and adds boy trebles for the first of the Divitis movements. Most of the intervening chants are sung by Pérès himself in a kind of muezzin style (big upward *glissandos* on the consonants and oriental ornaments on various notes), which adds to the solemnity of the event. In all, this is a fascinating and challenging record.
Further listening ...
...Complete Secular Music – Ma bouche rit. La despourveue. D'un autre amer. Quant ce viendra.
    Il ne m'en chault plus. Presque trainsi. Ma maistresse. Les desleaux. Mort tu as navre. Quant de
    vous. Au travail suis. Prenez sur moi. Fors seulement l'actente. L'autre d'antan. S'elle m'amera.
    O rosa bella. Tant fuz gentement. Je n'ay dueil. Malheur me bat. Se vostre cuer. Qu'es mi vida.
    Qu'es mi vida (original version by Johannes Cornago). Je n'ay dueil. Ce n'est pas jeu. Resjois toy.
    Departez vous. Ung aultre l'a. Autre Venus. Baissiez moi. Fors seulement contre ce. **The Medieval
    Ensemble of London / Peter Davies, Timothy Davies.** L'Oiseau-Lyre 436 194-2OH2 (9/93).   Ⓖ
...Intemerata Dei mater. *Coupled with* **Anonymous** (attrib. Josquin) Nunc Dimittis. **Morales**
    Magnificat octavi toni. **Lhéritier** Surrexit pastor bonus. **Rogier** Laboravi in gemitu meo.
    Clemens non Papa Ego flos campi. **Palestrina** Si ignoras te. **Lassus** Lauda mater ecclesia.
    Victoria Vadam, et circumibo civitatem. **Byrd** Laudibus in sanctis. **João IV** Crux fidelis.
    Oxford Camerata / Jeremy Summerly. Naxos 8 550843 (3/95).
...(attrib.) Deo gratias. *Coupled with works by* **Josquin Desprez, Porta, Tallis, Manchicourt,
    G. Gabrieli** and **Striggio** Huelgas Ensemble / Paul van Nevel. Sony Classical Vivarte SK66261
    (4/96). *See review in the Collections section; refer to the Index to Reviews.*

Jacques Offenbach
German/French 1819-1880

Offenbach (arr. M. Rosenthal) Gaîté parisienne.
Rossini (arr./orch. Respighi) La boutique fantasque. **Boston Pops Orchestra / Arthur Fiedler.** RCA
    Victor Living Stereo Ⓜ 09026 61847-2* (64 minutes: ADD: 2/94). Recorded 1954-56.   Ⓖ
Arthur Fiedler and the Boston Pops, for so long the guardians of traditional concert-hall light music in America, never made a better stereo recording than the amazing early (1954) complete Offenbach/Rosenthal *Gaîté parisienne* ballet score. It scintillates with effervescence and vitality, has just the right degree of brash vulgarity, yet the richly embracing acoustics of Symphony Hall ensure that the entry of the great "Barcarolle" has warmth as well as allure. This transfer makes the very

most of the outstanding mastertape. The coupling comprises some 27 minutes (almost all the best music) from the hardly less delectable Rossini/Respighi *La boutique fantasque* also brightly and atmospherically played and again given first-class sound from two years later. A real collector's item, not to be missed by anyone who cares about the history of stereo reproduction and also for the sheer *joie de vivre* of the music.

Additional recommendation ...

...Gaîté parisienne. *Coupled with* **Gounod** Faust – ballet music. **Montreal Symphony Orchestra / Charles Dutoit.** Decca Ovation Ⓜ 430 718-2DM (59 minutes: DDD: 8/91).

Further listening ...

...Concerto-rondo[a]. *Coupled with* **Saint-Säens** Cello Concerto No. 1 in A minor, Op. 33. **Tchaikovsky** Variations on a Rococo Theme in A major, Op. 33. **Ofra Harnoy** (vc); [a]**Cincinnati Symphony Orchestra / Erich Kunzel; Victoria Symphony Orchestra / Paul Freeman.** RCA Victor Red Seal RD71003 (11/86).

...Orphée aux enfers – Overture. *Coupled with works by* **Suppé, Thomas, Meyerbeer, Weber, Nicolai, Smetana, J. Strauss I, Brahms, Tchaikovsky** and **Glinka** London Symphony Orchestra / Sir Charles Mackerras. Mercury Living Presence 434 352-2MM (12/95).

...La belle Hélène – On me nomme Hélène la Blonde. Orphée aux enfers – J'ai vu le Dieu Bacchus; Ce bal est original. *Coupled with works by* **J. Strauss II, Romberg, Novello, Lehár, Coward, Chabrier, Heuberger** and **Sullivan** Lesley Garrett (sop); [a]**Crouch End Festival Chorus; Royal Philharmonic Concert Orchestra / James Holmes.** Silva Screen Classics SILKTVCD1 (2/96). *See review in the Collections section; refer to the Index to Reviews.*

...La belle Hélène. **Soloists; Toulouse Capitol Chorus and Orchestra / Michel Plasson.** EMI CDS7 47157-8 (9/86).

...Orphée aux enfers – operetta. **Soloists; Les Petits Chanteurs à la Croix Potencée; Toulouse Capitole Chorus and Orchestra / Michel Plasson.** EMI CDS7 49647-2 (1/89).

...Orphée aux enfers (sung in English). **Soloists; D'Oyly Carte Opera Chorus; D'Oyly Carte Opera Orchestra / John Owen Edwards.** Sony Classical SM2K66616 (2/95). *Selected by Sounds in Retrospect.*

...La Périchole. **Soloists; Rhine Opera Chorus; Strasbourg Philharmonic Orchestra / Alain Lombard.** Erato Libretto 2292-45686-2 (5/92).

...Les contes d'Hoffmann. **Soloists; Lausanne Pro Arte Chorus; Du Brassus Chorus; Suisse Romande Chorus and Orchestra / Richard Bonynge.** Decca 417 363-2DH2 (11/86).

...Robinson Crusoe (sung in English). **Soloists; Geoffrey Mitchell Choir; Royal Philharmonic Orchestra / Alun Francis.** Opera Rara ORC007 (8/94).

...Christopher Columbus. **Soloists; Geoffrey Mitchell Choir; London Mozart Players / Alun Francis.** Opera Rara ORC002 (4/93).

Georges Onslow

British/French 1784-1853

New review

Onslow String Quintets – C minor, Op. 38, "The Bullet"; E major, Op. 39; B minor, Op. 40. **Vera Beths, Lisa Rautenberg** (vns); **Steven Dann** (va); **Anner Bylsma, Kenneth Slowik** (vcs). Sony Classical Ⓕ SK64308 (77 minutes: DDD: 6/96). Recorded 1994.

If you happened to pick up this music on, say, the car radio, it would be quite a challenge to identify it. Georges Onslow was Anglo-French (English ancestry, French birth and principal domicile). Beethoven and Schubert are very distant as reference points, Mendelssohn and Spohr perhaps rather closer. The music, however, is richly worked, vivid and passionate. Its textures are very full and very busy, much more egalitarian than most in the chamber repertory – undoubtedly great fun to play – with much interchange between the voices, and involving elaborate accompaniment figures. It would be easy to say that sometimes there is a lot going on and plenty of excitement, but not much actually happening; however that would be slightly unfair. The C minor work in particular, which has a programme derived from a shooting accident during a hunt when Onslow nearly lost his life, is quite remarkable: a first movement of great intensity, with some passionate music in the development section, a minuet (*Dolore, febbre e delirio*) with ferocious accents, vast chromatic slithers and diminished sevenths galore, portraying his desperation, then an *Andante* representing convalescence (not quite on the ethereal spiritual level of Beethoven's Op. 132, but hymn-like and dark-textured), and then a brilliant C major finale. The other two works are not programmatic but also have plenty of strongly imagined music. Onslow may not be a great composer, but he is certainly an extremely interesting one, with ideas of some originality and a considerable technique. These musicians, using the famous Stradivari instruments in the Smithsonian Institute in Washington DC, play with great spirit, warmth and skill and convey the full measure of the passion behind the music.

Carl Orff   German 1895-1982

Orff Carmina Burana. **Gundula Janowitz** (sop); **Gerhard Stolze** (ten); **Dietrich Fischer-Dieskau**
(bar); **Schönberg Boys' Choir; Chorus and Orchestra of the Deutsche Oper, Berlin / Eugen Jochum.**
DG The Originals Ⓜ 447 437-2GOR (56 minutes: ADD: 12/95). Text and translation included.
From SLPM139362 (7/68). Recorded 1967.   ⒼⒼ
Since its original release, Jochum's performance has consistently been a prime recommendation for
this much-recorded piece. Listening to it again in the superbly remastered sound, one can easily hear
why. He pays great attention to detail – particularly with regard to tempo and articulation – yet the
performance as a whole has a tremendous cogent sweep and the choruses have terrific power. The
more reflective sections are not neglected, however, and movements such as "Stetit Puella", with
Janowitz sounding alluring and fey, have surely never been more sensitively handled. Stolze is ideal as
the roasted swan and Fischer-Dieskau encompasses the very varied requirements of the baritone's
music with ease. In spite of the presence of more than 30 rivals in the catalogue, this distinguished
performance, authorized by the composer and now sounding better than ever, easily retains its place
at the head of the queue. For those who insist on digital sound, the modern versions listed below,
particularly Slatkin's, are viable alternatives.
Additional recommendations ...
...**Soloists; Rutgers University Choir; Philadelphia Orchestra / Eugene Ormandy.** Sony Classical
Ⓜ SBK47668* (58 minutes: ADD).
...**Soloists; St Clement Danes Grammar School Boys' Choir; London Symphony Chorus and
Orchestra / André Previn.** EMI Ⓔ CDC7 47411-2 (63 minutes: DDD: 12/86).
...**Soloists; Shinyukai Choir; Berlin Cathedral Boys' Choir; Berlin Philharmonic Orchestra / Seiji
Ozawa.** Philips Ⓕ 422 363-2PH (60 minutes: DDD: 7/89).
...**Soloists; San Francisco Girls' Chorus; San Francisco Boys' Chorus; San Francisco Symphony
Chorus and Orchestra / Herbert Blomstedt.** Decca Ⓕ 430 509-2DH (59 minutes: DDD: 12/91).
...**Soloists; Southend Boys' Choir; London Philharmonic Choir and Orchestra / Zubin Mehta.** Teldec
Ⓕ 9031-74886-2 (60 minutes: DDD: 2/94).
...**Soloists; St Louis Symphony Chorus and Orchestra / Leonard Slatkin.** RCA Victor Red Seal
Ⓕ 09026 61673-2 (60 minutes: DDD: 4/95).

Orff Trionfi – Carmina Burana[a]; Catulli Carmina[b]; Trionfo di Afrodite[c]. [a]**Barbara Hendricks,**
[bc]**Dagmar Schellenberger,** [c]**Lisa Larson,** [c]**Eva Maria Nobauer** (sops); [c]**Barbara Reiter** (contr);
[a]**Michael Chance** (alto); [bc]**Lothar Odinius,** [c]**Robert Swensen** (tens); [c]**Klaus Kuttler,** [a]**Jeffrey Black**
(bars); [c]**Alfred Reiter** (bass); [a]**St Albans Abbey Choir;** [a]**London Philharmonic Choir;** [bc]**Linz Mozart
Choir;** [a]**London Philharmonic Orchestra;** [bc]**Munich Radio Orchestra / Franz Welser-Möst.** EMI
Ⓕ CDS5 55519-2 (two discs: 137 minutes: DDD: 5/96). Texts and translations included. Item
marked [a] from CDC7 54054-2 (11/90). Items marked [b] and [c] are also available on CDC5 55517-2
(79 minutes: DDD). Recorded 1989.
This is a most welcome issue, since *Catulli Carmina* and *Trionfo di Afrodite* are under-represented
in the current catalogue, unlike *Carmina Burana* which is here given a lithe and vigorous reading
with spectacular playing from the LPO and fine singing from the choruses. Barbara Hendricks's
vibrato may not be to all tastes and Jeffrey Black is too genial, lacking the requisite *slancio* quality
his part demands, whilst Michael Chance's beautiful tone is not what was intended by the composer
since a tenor singing in his highest register is specified. Nevertheless, this performance is more than
the sum of its parts and Welser-Möst's attention to detail is evidence of his careful and considered
approach. In the central section of *Catulli Carmina*, the unaccompanied settings of Catullus are
well realized with secure intonation and variety of expression and the prologue, with its insistent
ostinatos for four pianos and percussion, is quite electrifying. (Unfortunately, there is half a bar
missing – 3'41" of track one – but we understand from EMI that this fault will be corrected.)
Trionfo di Afrodite receives a thrilling and compelling performance and the final, orgiastic shouts
of the chorus greeting the appearance of the goddess, make it the climax of the whole triptych. As
bride and bridegroom, Dagmar Schellenberger and Lothar Odinius rise to the challenges of their
parts with their wide-ranging and melismatic melodic lines, although the soprano eschews the top
E which concludes the duet representing their wedding-night. A pity, too, that the voices were not
placed off-stage as the score requires at this point. The other soloists and chorus sing with
conviction and enthusiasm, supported by colourful and confident orchestral playing. Just
occasionally, Welser-Möst presses ahead when Orff directs otherwise, but he draws out the
dramatic qualities inherent in these works which were conceived for the theatre and despite
blemishes, this set is now the preferred version of *Trionfo*. The single disc, pairing the less familiar
pieces, with excellent notes and translations, is highly recommended to those willing to discover that
Orff was by no means a 'one work' composer.

Orff Orff-Schulwerk. **Godela Orff-Büchtemann** (spkr); **Tolz Boys' Choir / Gerhard Schmidt-Gaden;
Munich Hochschule Chamber Choir / Fritz Schieri; Stuttgart Sprechchor / Heinz Mende;**

instrumental ensemble / Carl Orff. RCA Victor Red Seal Ⓟ 09026 68031-2 (six discs: 365 minutes: ADD: 8/95). Recorded 1963-71.

Six discs of Orff's *Music for Children* might seem a daunting prospect, but this set contains some fascinating insights into Orff's techniques as a composer as well as providing model performances of most of the pieces which comprise the *Schulwerk*. The philosophy behind this method of music education lies in the unity between music, speech and movement. Thus many of the pieces are derived from dances and all have a strong rhythmical foundation, as do all of Orff's large-scale compositions. Several of the early pieces are very short and consist of speech exercises and word games but music is soon introduced in the form of rhythm patterns and ostinatos. There are a number of songs which are adapted from the folk traditions and nursery rhymes of different countries, but transformed through the use of very varied instrumentation. Apart from pitched and unpitched percussion, wind, brass and strings are employed in addition to instruments such as the krummhorn and gamba. The musical language is appropriately direct, with modal melodies and harmonies which often conjure up the atmosphere of medieval or even earlier music. Some of the later pieces are more complex and extended including declaimed verses from Hölderlin's versions of *Antigonae* and *Oedipus*, later adapted and incorporated into Orff's dramatic settings of the complete texts, as well as settings of Goethe and Schiller and poems from the *Knaben Wunderhorn* collection. There is also St Francis's Hymn to the Sun (which begins with a most vividly expressive phrase depicting sunrise) together with a number of sacred texts and prayers, the music for which suggests a kinship with the spirit of the medieval mystery play. Whilst these pieces are, ultimately, intended for didactic purposes and were never conceived as a purely aural experience, there is, nevertheless, a rich variety of music in this collection which will be of interest to Orff enthusiasts and to anyone wishing to discover more about this influential method of teaching music. The notes accompanying the set are exemplary but not all the texts and translations are given and some pieces are grouped together where it would have been preferable to have allocated a separate track for each. However, all in all, a most welcome issue.

Further listening ...

...Catulli carmina. *Coupled with* **Stravinsky** Les noces. **Soloists / Wolfgang Schäfer.** Koch Schwann Musica Mundi 314021 (7/91).

...De temporum fine comoedia – symbolic drama. **Soloists; Cologne Radio Chorus; Tölz Boys' Choir; Berlin RIAS Chamber Chorus; Cologne Radio Symphony Orchestra / Herbert von Karajan.** DG 20th Century Classics 429 859-2GC.

...Die Kluge. Der Mond. **Soloists; Rudolf Kiermeyer Children's Choir; Bavarian Radio Chorus; Munich Radio Orchestra / Kurt Eichhorn.** Eurodisc GD69069 (3/91).

...Antigone. **Soloists; Bavarian Radio Chorus and Symphony Orchestra / Ferdinand Leitner.** DG 20th Century Classics 437 721-2GC3 (8/93).

Leo Ornstein

USSR/American 1892-

Suggested listening ...

...Cello Sonata, Op. 52. *Coupled with* **Foss** Capriccio. **Barber** Cello Sonata, Op. 6. **Yehuda Hanani** (vc); **Michelle Levin** (pf). Koch International Classics 37070-2 (10/93).

...Violin Sonata, Op. 31[b]. *Coupled with* **Glass** Einstein on the Beach – Suite. **Copland** Duo[a]. **Wernick** Cadenzas and Variations II. **Gregory Fulkerson** (vn); [a]**Robert Shannon,** [b]**Alan Feinberg** (pfs). New World 80313-2 (2/96).

C.W. Orr

British 1893-1976

Suggested listening ...

...When I watch the living meet. Hughley steeple. Into my heart. O see how thick the goldcup flowers. The Isle of Portland. This time of year. *Coupled with works by* **Moeran, Ireland, Horder, Butterworth, L. Berkeley** and **Barber** Anthony Rolfe Johnson (ten); **Graham Johnson** (pf). Hyperion CDA66471/2 (8/95). Includes various poems from Housman's .
"A Shrophire Lad" read by Alan Bates. *See review in the Collections section; refer to the Index to Reviews.*

Diego Ortiz

Spanish c1510-c1570

Suggested listening ...

...Trattado de glosas – Recercarda segunda sobre el passamezzo moderno; Recercada tercera para viola de gamba sola; Recercada quarta sobre la folia; Recercada quinta sobre el passamezzo antiguo; Recercada settima sobre la Romanesca. *Coupled with works by* **Encina, Narváez, Anonymous, Pisador, Vásquez** and **Mudarra** La Romanesca / José Miguel Moreno (vihuela). Glossa GCD920203 (5/96). 🖉 *See review in the Collections section; refer to the Index to Reviews.*

Ⓖ

James Oswald

Suggested listening ...
...Feuilles d'album, Op. 20. Seis Peças, Op. 14. Três Peças, Op. 23. Two Nocturnes, Op. 6. Il neige. Valse lente. **Maria Inês Guimarães** (pf). Marco Polo 8 223639
...A Collection of Scot's Tunes with Variations – Rory Dall's port. *Coupled with works by* **Gow, Haydn, Beethoven, Weber, Hummel, L. Koželuch** and **Traditional** Scottish Early Music Consort. Chandos Chaconne CHAN0581 (10/95). 🖊

Johann Pachelbel

Pachelbel Musicalische Ergötzung. **Les Cyclopes** (Manfred Kraemer, Laura Johnson, vns; Nina Diehl, vc; Bibiane Lapointe, hpd; Thierry Maeder, org). Pierre Verany Ⓔ PV794111 (53 minutes: DDD: 7/95). 🖊 Recorded 1994.

If the celebration of Biber's music in the 350th anniversary of his birth last year has distracted us from other fine instrumental collections of the period, this recording is a sobering reminder that the likes of Pachelbel and Muffat from the German-speaking world are on the same level and sometimes even better. Indeed, it is most likely that Biber published his partitas for *scordatura* violins, *Harmonia artificioso–ariosa*, as a direct consequence of this very set, which Pachelbel sent to the press in 1691. One can quite believe it, judging by the way Biber articulates and circumnavigates the contours of the sarabande as Pachelbel does equally well in the third *Partie*. But there is more to it than that: it is the freedom of the polyphonic textures and coloration achieved through the special *scordatura* tuning of the violins (an elaborate system to facilitate double- and triple-stopping and diversify the tonal properties of the instrument) which both composers share. The relatively restricted structure of the dance, the chaconne and the suite as a whole gives the spirit of free invention and variation a context in which Pachelbel would seem to have set a trend for his Moravian colleague to contemplate. Pachelbel's *scordatura* music is arguably more instantly appealing (as the title, "musical entertainment", suggests) than Biber's more arcane examples, though less intricate and rhetorically concentrated. Pachelbel was, after all, a more cosmopolitan figure by the very nature of his geographical situation, a world of less maverick virtuosity than Biber's though one which exhibits a greater range of up-to-date sonata techniques from Italy and mature dance movements from France. As with Muffat, and so many other Germans, the marriage is fortuitous and, as the sonata *allegro* of the third *Partie* shows, the rigours of indigenous counterpoint blend effortlessly into the merry hybrid. In all the six suites – each one for two violins and basso continuo – Les Cyclopes are admirably forthright, yet capable, too, of portraying with a rich palette an intensity of feeling and immediacy which few baroque chamber ensembles achieve so effortlessly. The character of the dances is clearly and often humorously communicated and the passagework is always executed with precision and a sleight of hand, even if the tuning is occasionally a touch wayward (especially in the fourth *Partie* where the group appear less relaxed than elsewhere). These committed performances can be safely recommended to those searching for attractive and finely wrought music of the pre-Bach period.

Additional recommendation ...
...Musicalische Ergötzung – Suite No. 4 in E minor. Suite in G major. Aria con variazoni in A major. Canon and Gigue in D major. *Coupled with* **Buxtehude** Trio Sonatas – C major, BuxWV266; G major, BuxWV271; B flat major, BuxWV273. **Cologne Musica Antiqua / Reinhard Goebel.** Archiv Produktion Galleria Ⓜ 427 118-2AGA (63 minutes: ADD: 6/89). 🖊
Further listening ...
...Jauchzet dem Herrn. Nun Danket alle Gott. Exsurgat Deus. Tröste uns Gott. Magnificat. Der Herr ist König und herrlich geschmückt. Gott ist unser Zuversicht. Paratum cor meum Deus. Der Herr ist König. Singet dem Herrn. Jauchzet Gott, alle Lände. *Coupled with* **J.C. Bach** Fürchte dich nicht. Der Gerechte, ob er gleich zu zeitlich stirbt. Ich lasse dich nicht. **J.M. Bach** Halt, was du hast. Fürchtet euch nicht. **Cantus Cölln / Konrad Junghänel.** Deutsche Harmonia Mundi 05472 77305-2 (7/94). 🖊   Ⓖ
...Hexachordum Apollinis. Ciacconas – D major; F minor. **John Butt** (org). Harmonia Mundi HMU90 7029 (5/91).

Ignacy Paderewski

Suggested listening ...
...Piano Concerto in A minor, Op. 17[a]. *Coupled with* **Melcer-Szczawinski** Piano Concerto No. 1 in E minor[b]. [a]**Piotr Paleczny**, [b]**Michael Ponti** (pfs); [a]**Polish National Radio Symphony Orchestra;** [b]**Warsaw National Philharmonic Orchestra / Tadeusz Strugala.** Olympia OCD398 (7/84).
...Piano Concerto in A minor, Op. 17. *Coupled with works by* **Balakirev** and **F.X. Scharwenka** **Earl Wild** (pf); **Boston Symphony Orchestra / Erich Leinsdorf; London Symphony Orchestra / Arthur Fiedler.** Elan CD82266 (7/96). *See review under Balakirev; refer to the Index to Reviews.*   Ⓖ

Ferdinando Paer

Italian 1771-1839

Suggested listening ...

... Sargino, ossia l'allievo dell'amore – Una voca al cor mi parla (arr. Weston and Voxman)[c]. *Coupled with* **Mozart** La clemenza di Tito – Parto, parto (arr. Bergmann)[a]. **Müller** Quartet No. 2 in F sharp minor[b]. **Spohr** Sechs Lieder, Op. 103[d]. Faust – Ich bin allein[e]. Variations in B flat major on a Theme from "Alruna"[f]. [acde]**Elizabeth Ritchie** (sop); **Victoria Soames** (cl); [b]**Anna Coleman** (vn); [b]**Matthew Souter** (va); [b]**Alastair Blayden** (vc); [acdef]**Jennifer Purvis** (pf). Clarinet Classics CC0006 (3/94).

Nicolò Paganini

Italian 1782-1840

Paganini Violin Concertos – No. 1 in E flat major, Op. 6; No. 2 in B minor, Op. 7, "La campanella". **Salvatore Accardo** (vn); **London Philharmonic Orchestra / Charles Dutoit**. DG Ⓕ 415 378-2GH (69 minutes: ADD: 2/87). From 2740 121 (11/75).
Paganini Violin Concerto No. 1 in E flat major, Op. 6.
Saint-Saëns Havanaise in E major, Op. 83. Introduction and Rondo capriccioso in A minor, Op. 28. **Sarah Chang** (vn); **Philadelphia Orchestra / Wolfgang Sawallisch**. EMI Ⓕ CDC5 55026-2 (55 minutes: DDD: 1/95). Recorded 1993-4.

Paganini's violin music was at one time thought quite inaccessible to lesser mortals among the violin-playing fraternity, but as standards of technique have improved master technicians are now able to do justice to such works as these concertos. Salvatore Accardo is certainly among them, and we can judge his skill as early as the opening violin solo of the First Concerto. This is typical of the style, with its authoritative and rhetorical gestures and use of the whole instrumental compass, but so is the second theme which in its refinement and songlike nature demands (and here receives) another kind of virtuosity expressed through a command of tone, texture and articulation. Dutoit and the London Philharmonic Orchestra have a mainly subordinate role, certainly when the soloist is playing, but they fulfil it well and follow Accardo through the kind of rhythmic flexibilities which are accepted performing style in this music and which for all we know were used by the virtuoso performer-composer himself. The 1975 recording is faithful and does justice to the all-important soloist.

Paganini would surely have been utterly astonished at Sarah Chang's version of his No. 1. She made her début with the piece in the Avery Fisher Hall at the age of eight(!), but had reached more advanced years (12) when she recorded it in Philadelphia for EMI. The performance is dazzling, particularly the finale where her light rhythmic touch and deliciously pert sliding "harmonized harmonics" are a wonder of technical assurance. Note too, in the first movement, the relaxed ease of the decorated bouncing bow passages and the gently tender reprise of the second subject. The slow movement is not overtly romantic, but the freshness is never in doubt. One does not expect her to sound maturely sophisticated like Perlman (who remains unsurpassed in this repertoire) and she slightly understates the sultry atmosphere of the Saint-Saëns *Havanaise* to pleasing effect, yet manages the coda with spruce flexibility of phrase and the most subtle graduations of timbre. The *Introduction and Rondo capriccioso* has plenty of dash and she catches the Spanish sunlight in the *Introduction* without an overtly sensuous response. She is not flattered by the recording: balanced close. Sawallisch directs with plenty of verve and he supports his soloist admirably.

Additional recommendations ...

...No. 1. **Wieniawski** Violin Concerto No. 2 in D minor, Op. 22. **Mark Kaplan** (vn); **London Symphony Orchestra / Mitch Miller**. Arabesque Ⓕ Z6597 (57 minutes: DDD: 7/89).
...No. 1. **Saint-Saëns** Violin Concerto No. 3 in B minor, Op. 61[a]. **Zino Francescatti** (vn); **Philadelphia Orchestra / Eugene Ormandy**. CBS Masterworks Portrait mono Ⓜ CD46728* (51 minutes: ADD: 12/91).
...Nos. 1 and 2. **Auvergne Orchestra / Jean-Jacques Kantorow** (vn). Denon Ⓕ CO-77611 (60 minutes: DDD: 4/92).
...Nos. 1 and 2. **Ilya Kaler** (vn); **Polish National Radio Symphony Orchestra / Stephen Gunzenhauser**. Naxos Ⓢ 8 550649 (67inutes: DDD: 12/93).
...No. 1[d]. **Beethoven** Violin Concerto in D major, Op. 61[a]. **Brahms** Violin Concerto in D major, Op. 77[b]. **Bruch** Violin Concerto No. 1 in G minor, Op. 26[c]. **Mendelssohn** Violin Concerto in E minor, Op. 64[c]. **Tchaikovsky** Violin Concerto in D major, Op. 35[e]. **Itzhak Perlman** (vn); [a]**Philharmonia Orchestra**; [b]**Chicago Symphony Orchestra / Carlo Maria Giulini**; [c]**Concertgebouw Orchestra / Bernard Haitink**; [d]**Royal Philharmonic Orchestra / Lawrence Foster**; [e]**Philadelphia Orchestra / Eugene Ormandy**. EMI Ⓜ CMS7 64922-2 (three discs: 211 minutes: ADD/DDD: 4/94).

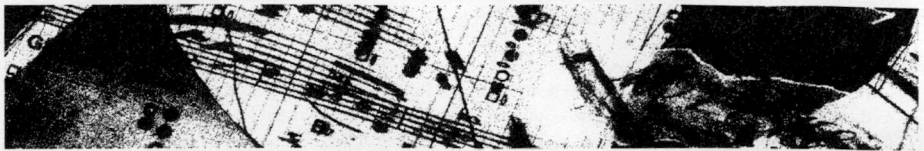

Paganini Centone di sonate – Nos. 7-12. **Moshe Hammer** (vn); **Norbert Kraft** (gtr). Naxos
Ⓢ 8 553142 (72 minutes: DDD: 2/96).
The *Centone di sonate* (a "hotchpotch of sonatas") consists of 18 'sonatas' which are really salon
works with a variety of movements – none of them in sonata form. Whether Paganini, who wrote
them sometime after 1828, intended these pieces for public performance or merely for the use of the
then abundant amateur musicians is not known. As usual in his works of this genre, it is the violin
which hogs the limelight while the guitar remains a humble bag-carrier. The guitar parts are indeed
so simple that they would have been within the reach of any amateur who was capable of keeping his
end up with another musician; Segovia considered them beneath his dignity and refused many
invitations to play them with famous partners! Nothing is harder than to be 'simple': Mozart
managed it whilst at the same time being deceptively complex; Paganini did it at a far less sublime
level, with sentimental, cheerful and pert tunes. Truth to tell, they are not the kind of works which
impel one to listen to them at one sitting except for the most devoted *aficionado* of Paganini's violinistic
voice or of hearing the guitar in an unremittingly subservient though genuinely complementary role.
These splendid performances on modern instruments make no claim to 'authentic' status, but they are
no less appealing for that. They squeeze every last drop from the music with (inauthentically) full
sound, and a Siamese-twin tightness of ensemble that was probably rare amongst those who played
these works in Paganini's own time. In the end, these works have a charm that is hard for any but the
most straitlaced to resist. It is unlikely that the *Centone* will ever be better played and/or recorded.

Paganini Music for Violin and Guitar, Volumes 1 and 2. **Scott St John** (vn); **Simon Wynberg** (gtr).
Naxos Ⓢ 8 550690/759 (two discs, oas: 54 and 59 minutes: DDD: 12/94). Recorded 1993.
8 550690 – Six Sonatas for Guitar and Violin, Op. 3. Sonata concertata in A major, Op. 61.
60 Variations on "Barucabà", Op. 14. Cantabile in D major, Op. 17. *8 550759* – Six Sonatas for
Guitar and Violin, Op. 2. Cantabile e Valtz, Op. 19. Variazioni di bravura on Caprice No. 24.
Duetto amoroso. Sonata per le gran viola e chitarra.
Many legends were attached (and they still are) to the life of Paganini. Those concerning his alleged
relationships with the devil and with women (more probable) would have made rich pickings for
today's tabloids. Several of the violin/guitar duos testify to Paganini's amorous inclinations: the
sections of the *Duetto amoroso* spell out the course of an affair, from beginning to separation, and
may have been aimed (unsuccessfully, one imagines) at the Princess Elisa Baciocchi in Lucca. His
conservative harmonic vocabulary springs few surprises and his melodies sometimes verge on
banality, but by dint of sheer charm and technical ingenuity he somehow gets away with it; only the
po-faced could resist an admiring smile at his effrontery. Collectively, these works present the full
range of Paganini's technical armoury – the left-hand pizzicatos, high harmonics, double-stopping,
'sneaky' chromatic runs and the rest, and Scott St John betrays no difficulty in dealing with every
googly that comes his way. More than that, in the daunting *Sonata per le gran viola e chitarra*
(celebrating Paganini's acquisition of a Stradivarius instrument) cocks a snook at every viola joke that
ever was. The guitar's role in the action varies from purely supportive subservience to more equal
(though at a lower acrobatic level) partnership, as in the *Sonata concertata* and from time to time in
the Op. 3 Sonatas. Wynberg proves as well matched a partner as St John could have wished for.
Violinists, guitarists and lovers of winsomeness for its own sake should revel in these very well
recorded discs and will find much information in the booklet.
Additional recommendations ...
...Sonata concertata. Six Sonatas for Guitar and Violin, Op. 3 – No. 1 in A major; No. 4 in
A minor; No. 6 in E minor. Grand Sonata for Violin and Guitar in A major, Op. posth. Centone
di Sonate, Op. 64 – No. 2 in D major; No. 4 in A major. Cantabile. Sonata a preghiera (arr.
Hannibal). Moto perpetuo in C major (Allegro di concert), Op. 11. **Gil Shaham** (vn); **Göran
Söllscher** (gtr). DG Ⓔ 437 837-2GH (61 minutes: DDD: 4/94).
...Grand Sonata for Violin and Guitar in A major, Op. posth. Sonata concertata, Op. 61. **Giuliani**
Duo concertant in E minor, Op. 25, "Grand Sonata". **Monica Huggett** (vn); **Richard Savino** (gtr).
Harmonia Mundi Ⓕ HMU90 7116 (69 minutes: DDD: 5/95). ☛

Paganini 24 Caprices, Op. 1. **Itzhak Perlman** (vn). EMI Ⓕ CDC7 47171-2 (72 minutes: ADD:
7/88). From SLS832 (6/72).   ⓖⓖ
This electrifying music with its dare-devil virtuosity has long remained the pinnacle of violin
technique, and they encapsulate the essence of the composer's style. For a long time it was considered
virtually unthinkable that a violinist should be able to play the complete set; even in recent years only
a handful have produced truly successful results. Itzhak Perlman has one strength in this music that
is all-important, other than a sovereign technique – he is incapable of playing with an ugly tone. He
has such variety in his bowing that the timbre of the instrument is never monotonous. The notes of
the music are despatched with a forthright confidence and fearless abandon that are ideal. The
frequent double-stopping passages hold no fear for him. Listen to the fire of No. 5 in A minor and
the way in which Perlman copes with the extremely difficult turns in No. 14 in E flat; this is a master
at work. The set rounds off with the famous A minor Caprice, which inspired Liszt, Brahms and
Rachmaninov, amongst others, to adapt it in various guises for the piano.

Additional recommendations ...

...**Salvatore Accardo** (vn). DG Galleria Ⓜ 429 714-2GGA (75 minutes: DDD: 9/90).

...**Leonidas Kavacos** (vn). Dynamic Ⓕ CDS66 (77 minutes: DDD: 9/93).

...**Michael Rabin** (vn). EMI Ⓜ CDM7 64560-2 (69 minutes: ADD: 9/93).   ⒼⒼ

...**Ilya Kaler** (vn). Naxos Ⓢ 8 550717 (79 minutes: DDD: 9/93).

Further listening ...

...Grand Sonata in A major – second and third movements. Ghiribizzi, MS43 – No. 20, Andante in C major on Mozart's "Là ci darem la mano"; No. 37, Adagietto con espressione in A major. Sonatina No. 1 in C. *Coupled with* **Mertz** Six Schubertian Songs. **Regondi** Introduction and Caprice, Op. 23. **Schubert** (arr. Tárrega) Piano Sonata in G major, D894 – Menuetto. Moment musical in F minor, Op. 94 No. 3. **Chopin** (arr. Tárrega) Preludes – No. 7 in A major; No 15 in D flat major; No. 20 in C minor. **Tárrega** Preludes – Endecha; Oremus; Allegro; Andante sostenuto; Lágrima. Capricho árabe. Mazurkas – Adelita; Marieta; Sueño. Pavana. Alborada. **Tom Kerstens** (gtr). Conifer CDCF518 (9/94).

...Centone di sonate Nos. 1-6. **Moshe Hammer** (vn); **Norbert Kraft** (gtr). Naxos 8 553141 (5/95).

John Paine

American 1839-1906

Suggested listening ...

...Symphony No. 1 in C minor, Op. 23. As You Like It, Op. 28. **New York Philharmonic Orchestra / Zubin Mehta.** New World NW374-2.

...Symphony No. 2 in A major, Op. 34, "In the Spring". **New York Philharmonic Orchestra / Zubin Mehta.** New World NW350-2 (5/88).

Giovanni Paisiello

Italian 1740-1816

Suggested listening ...

...Piano Concertos – No. 1 in C major; No. 5 in D major; No. 7 in A major; No. 8 in C major. **Mariaclara Monetti** (pf); **English Chamber Orchestra / Stephanie Gonley.** ASV CDDCA873 (8/94).

...Piano Concertos – No. 2 in F major; No. 3 in A major; No. 4 in G minor; No. 6 in B flat major. **Mariaclara Monetti** (pf); **English Chamber Orchestra / Stephanie Gonley.** ASV CDDCA872 (2/94).

Giovanni Palestrina

Italian *c*1525/6-1594

Palestrina The Palestrina 400 Collection. **The Tallis Scholars / Peter Phillips.** Gimell Ⓜ CDGIMB400 (four discs: 249 minutes: ADD/DDD: 1/94). Items marked [a] from 1585-01 (11/81), [b]1585-03 (4/83), [c]CfP CFP40339 (10/80), [d]CDGIM008 (1/87), [e]CDGIM020 (9/90). Recorded 1980-89. *Gramophone Award Winner 1991. Selected by Sounds in Retrospect.*
Palestrina Missa Benedicta es[a]. Missa Nigra sum[b]. Missa Papae Marcelli[c]. Missa brevis[d]. Missa Nasce la gioia mia[d]. Missa Assumpta est Maria[e]. Missa Sicut lilium inter spinas[e]. Nigra sum[b]. Assumpta est Maria[e]. Sicut lilium inter spinas I[e]. **Anonymous** Benedicta es[a]. Assumpta est Maria in caelum[e]. **Josquin Desprez** Benedicta es, celorum regina[a]. **Lheritier** Nigra sum[b]. **Primavera** Nasce la gioia mia[d].
From the 100-plus Masses that he could have recorded, Peter Phillips has chosen so shrewdly that the selection here offered appears as comprehensive a cross-section of Palestrina's achievement as you could possibly wish in the space of four hours. The Palestrina enthusiast, converted perhaps by The Tallis Scholars' recording of the *Missa Papae Marcelli* (reviewed below) will very likely have bought all these performances as they appeared. But does the non-specialist need more than a couple of Palestrina Masses to represent the composer? Would not seven of them prove ... well, not to put too fine a point upon it, a bit same-y? The answers are an emphatic 'yes' and a firm 'no' respectively. The variety of texture and audible technique among these Mass settings is quite remarkable. Among the seven Masses collected here, a profound development takes place between the massive sonority of the *Missa Benedicta es*, audibly both Palestrina's homage to, and his measuring of himself against, his great predecessor Josquin Desprez (Josquin's motet and its plainchant base are included, to make the point crystal-clear), and the division of the voices in the *Missa Assumpta est Maria* into two dissimilar, antiphonal choirs, projecting and dramatizing the text with urgent force as well as beauty. The music is most beautifully but not too beautifully sung. Balance, intonation, chording and clarity of texture are all immaculate, but the performances respond to the changes of emotional temperature between the Masses also; they are expressively sung, in the best sense of that word. The recordings, in ample but not obscuring acoustics, are very fine.

Additional recommendation ...

...Missa Assumpta est Maria. Missa Sicut lilium inter spinas. Motets – Assumpta est Maria a 6; Sicut lilium inter spinas I. **Plainchant** Assumpta est Maria. **The Tallis Scholars / Peter Phillips.** Gimell Ⓕ CDGIM020 (72 minutes: DDD: 9/90).

Palestrina Surge, illuminare Jerusalem. Missa Papae Marcelli. Stabat mater. Alma Redemptoris mater. Magnificat Primi Toni. Nunc dimittis.
Allegri Miserere mei. **The Tallis Scholars / Peter Phillips.** Gimell Ⓕ CDGIM994 (73 minutes: DDD: 9/94). Texts and translations included. Recorded live in 1994.

The sense of a memorable occasion is quite tangible here. The largely Italian audience, assembled in Palestrina's own great Basilica of Santa Maria Maggiore to mark the 400th anniversary of his death, is clearly impressed by The Tallis Scholars' virtuosity. The *Missa Papae Marcelli* is in fact a good four minutes faster than in their previous recording, made in 1980 (listed below). No doubt they know the piece even better now, and no doubt Phillips has changed his view of it. But it really seems as though the building and its acoustic both had an effect, firstly in encouraging the singers really to sing out (the *Sanctus* has an extraordinary full-throated fervour), but perhaps also the knowledge that this was the very spot where Palestrina worked with his choir prompted an even greater awareness of the music's eloquence. The Allegri *Miserere* doesn't really belong in this collection, of course; it was written for another building entirely (the Sistine Chapel) decades after Palestrina's death. It may have been included because Peter Phillips, alongside his scholarship and his gifts as a choir-trainer, has a feeling for drama and the spatial effects of this music could not be rendered nearly so spectacularly in the Sistine. It is stunning, with Deborah Roberts in the florid solo soprano part floating high Cs and roulades up into the vast space with luminous clarity. The Palestrina pieces have their own drama, and they are shrewdly programmed. It was good to begin with the almost rollicking jubilation of *Surge, illuminare*, wise to follow the showy *Miserere* with Palestrina at his most sublime in the *Stabat mater*. To follow that with the hymn-like, homophonic *Alma Redemptoris mater*, and that with the joyous *Magnificat* (for two choirs, but sounding like at least six, of quite different colours) is programme-building of a high order. To add the eight-part *Nunc dimittis* as an encore with its wonderful arching lines and a firework-display of counterpoint at the end, has a touch of genius to it. The sound is splendid, the acoustic always perceptible but the singers never lost in it.

Additional recommendations ...

...Missa Aeterna Christi munera. Sicut cervus. Super flumina Babylonis a 4. Vidi turbam magnam. Quae est ista. Duo ubera tua. Nigra sum, sed formosa. Surge, amica mea. Magnificat Primi Toni. **Anonymous** Aeterna Christi munera. **Westminster Cathedral Choir / James O'Donnell.** Hyperion Ⓕ CDA66490 (67 minutes: DDD).

...Missa Papae Marcelli. Tu es Petrus. **Allegri** Miserere. **Anerio** Venite ad me omnes. **Nanino** Haec dies. **Giovannelli** Jubilate Deo. **Westminster Abbey Choir / Simon Preston.** Archiv Produktion Ⓕ 415 517-2AH (59 minutes: DDD: 5/86). ◪

...Missa Papae Marcelli. **Allegri** Miserere[a]. **W. Mundy** Vox patris caelestis. [a]**Alison Stamp** (sop); **The Tallis Scholars / Peter Phillips.** Gimell Ⓕ CDGIM339 (69 minutes: ADD: 7/86). ◪

Palestrina Vergine bella. Motets – Ave Maria; Salve regina; Sub tuum praesidium; Ave regina coelorum; Salve regina; Ave mundi spes; Alma Redemptoris mater; Regina coeli. Magnificat.
Akademia / Françoise Lasserre with **Laurent Stewart** (org). Pierre Verany Ⓕ PV794041 (56 minutes: DDD: 9/94). Texts and translations included. Recorded 1994. ◪

Akademia have a clean, incisive sound, bright and well-tuned, and is capable of changing received opinions of how French choirs sound. The ensemble has a real feel for Palestrina's polyphony, shaping lines with great intelligence and with an excellent choral blend. Only occasionally are there frayed entries, and the constant *forte* in the opening group of motets is a little monotonous, though this latter is a result of enthusiasm rather than insensitivity. The second group is Marian, like the first, but this time polychoral. All these pieces, far too rarely heard, are sung with a greater variety of dynamics and a real enjoyment of the antiphonal writing. The splendid *Ave regina caelorum* in particular receives a truly inspired performance. The Petrarch madrigal cycle *Vergine bella* is beautifully performed, this time by a smaller ensemble, with the voices more individually 'expressive' in that they are allowed more scope for vibrato and shaping. The sense of ensemble is still excellent, and their understanding of the subtleties of Palestrina's superb settings is evident in every phrase. A well-planned, excellently-sung recital of some of Palestrina's best music.

Palestrina Masses – Viri Galilaei; O Rex gloriae. Motets – Viri Galilaei; O Rex gloriae.
Westminster Cathedral Choir / James O'Donnell. Hyperion Ⓕ CDA66316 (68 minutes: DDD: 1/90). Texts and translations included. Recorded 1988.

This is music in which Westminster Cathedral Choir excel: their response to the richly reverberant acoustic is warm and generous; they perform with the ease and freedom of kinship – a far cry from the studied perfection of many other choirs. Each motet is heard before its reworking as a Mass. The six-part scoring of *Viri Galilaei* (two trebles, alto, two tenors and bass) invites a variety of combinations and textures, culminating in the joyful cascading Alleluias at the end of Part I and the jubilant ascending series in Part II. In the Mass the mood changes from triumph to quiet pleading – a change partly due to revised scoring: the two alto parts beneath the single treble produce a more subdued sound. The Choir clearly relishes this exploration of the deeper sonorities: in the *Creed* one entire section is entrusted to the four lowest voices. The four-part motet *O Rex gloriae* is lithe and fast-moving. The corresponding Mass, largely syllabic in style, gives the Choir the chance to demonstrate their superb command of phrasing and accentuation: the Latin comes over with intelligibility and subtlety. Listen, also, to the wonderful solo boys' trio in the "Crucifixus", and for the carefully crafted canons in the *Benedictus* and the *Agnus Dei*.

Further listening ...

...Gaude, Barbara. *Coupled with* **Monteverdi** Vespro della Beata Vergine. **Soloists; The Sixteen; The Sixteen Orchestra / Harry Christophers.** Hyperion CDA66311/2 (4/89). ✍

...Motets – Stabat mater a 8. Hodie beata virgo. Senex puerum portabat. Magnificat a 8. Litaniae de Beata Vergine Mariae I a 8. *Coupled with* **Allegri** Miserere mei. **Roy Goodman** (treb); **King's College Choir, Cambridge / Sir David Willcocks.** Decca Ovation 421 147-2DM (5/89). Ⓖ

...Coelestis urbs Jerusalem. *Coupled with* **Schmelzer** Vesperae sollennes[ab]. Sonata per Chiesa et Camera. Sacro-Profanus Concentus Musicus – Sonata XII. **Biber** Missa alleluja[ab]. **Froberger** Fantasia II in A minor. **Anonymous** Gregorian Chant for the Dedication of a Church – Mass Propers[a]. Gregorian Chant for Vespers[a].[a]**Vienna Hofburgkapelle Schola;** [b]**Concerto Palatino; Gradus ad Parnassum / Konrad Junghänel.** Deutsche Harmonia Mundi 05472˙77326-2 (7/95). ✍

...Missa in festis Apostolorum I and II. Missa sine nomine. Missa in Semiduplicibus Maioribus I and II. **Soloists of San Petronio Cappella Musicale Nova Schola Gregoriana / Sergio Vartolo** with **Liuwe Tamminga** (org). Bongiovanni GB5544/5-2 (5/95).

...Missa brevis. Missa Nasce la gioia mia. **Primavera** Nasce la gioia mia. **Tallis Scholars / Peter Philips.** Gimell CDGIM008 (1/87).

...Missa Dum complerentur. Motets – Super flumina Babylonis; Exsultate Deo; Sicut cervus; O bone Jesu, exaudi me a 8; Dum complerentur a 6. **Christ Church Cathedral Choir, Oxford / Stephen Darlington.** Nimbus NI5100 (11/88).

...Exsultate Deo. Sicut cervus desiderat. *Coupled with works by* **Byrd, Parsons, Viadana, Tallis, Philips, Allegri, G. Gabrieli, Lotti, Tye, Victoria** and **Monteverdi** Soloists; **Westminster Cathedral Choir / James O'Donnell.** Hyperion CDA66850 (5/96). *See review in the Collections section; refer to the Index to Reviews.*

Zakhari Paliashvili   USSR 1871-1933

New review
Paliashvili Liturgy of St John Chrysostom. **Cantus Sacred Music Ensemble / Ludmilla Arshavskaya.** Olympia Ⓕ OCD483 (75 minutes: DDD: 5/96). English text included. Recorded 1995. *Gramophone Editor's choice.*

No other liturgical music of this century – this work was published in 1909 – sounds quite like this. It has (like Tchaikovsky's Liturgy, though achieved by quite different musical means) an internal unity of considerable force, and an overwhelming spiritual power and beauty. The musical surprises are endless: though the Georgian Orthodox Church, like the Russian, celebrates in Church Slavonic rather than Georgian, Paliashvili consciously based himself on Georgian national style and technique; specifically, he employed chants written down by Ippolitov-Ivanov, who had long been resident in Tbilisi. The score states that the work is composed "in the Kartli-kakheti singing style", and to anyone who has heard the currently fashionable Georgian folk-singing this will sound familiar. It involves that typically dense harmonic vocabulary full of dissonant parallel intervals, seemingly meandering polyphonic lines, and a dark, strong vocal colour. The opening litany hints at all this, but it is with track 5, a magnificent setting of *Priidite poklanimsya*, that the Georgian influence really begins to show through. Other noteworthy settings include the Cherubic Hymn, with wandering internal lines deftly subverting any traditional harmonic sense, and a tremendous Creed – a mixture of Georgian folk dissonance with the traditional Russian recitative style. It would not be true to say that Paliashvili's music springs out of the blue – his opera reveals how much he learned from Tchaikovsky and Taneyev, for example, and in the Liturgy one can hear elements of these two composers and even such Russian pioneers as Kastalsky, but this synthesis of a dexterity of compositional technique learned via Russia, and a genuine feeling for the idiosyncratic power of the traditions of his own country, is unique indeed. Its nearest musical relations seem to me to be, aside from Georgian folk polyphony, some of the Russian medieval repertoires, and – odd though this might at first sight seem – some of Stravinsky's liturgical and para-liturgical works such as the Mass and *Canticum sacrum* (and, indeed, *Les noces*). The Cantus Sacred Music Ensemble project the text with great clarity, and are a model of tuning and vocal blend: a better performance would be hard to imagine.

Giovanni Pandolfi   Italian fl. 1660-1669

Suggested listening ...

...Sonatas per chiesa e camera, Op. 3 – No. 2, La Cesta in A minor; No. 4, La Castella in D major; No. 5, La Clemente in E minor; No. 6, La Sabbatina in C major. Sonatas for Violin and Continuo, Op. 4 – No. 1, La Bernabea in E minor; No. 4, La Biancuccia in D minor; No. 6, La Vinciolina in D minor. *Coupled with* **Anonymous** Harpsichord Suites[a] – C major; D minor; A major. **Andrew Manze** (vn); [a]**Richard Egarr** (hpd); **Fred Jacobs** (theorbo). Channel Classics CCS5894 (7/94). ✍

Sir Andrzej Panufnik

Polish/British 1914-1991

Panufnik Sinfonia concertante[a]. Concerto for Timpani, Percussion and Strings[b]. Harmony.
[a]**Karen Jones** (fl); [a]**Rachel Masters** (hp); [b]**Richard Benjafield** (perc); [b]**Graham Cole** (timp);
London Musici / Mark Stephenson. Conifer Ⓕ CDCF217 (55 minutes: DDD: 8/94). Recorded
1993.

All of the works recorded here, as with most of Andrzej's Panufnik's later music, are quite
rigorously built from spare basic resources (*Harmony* and the *Sinfonia concertante* from two three-
note cells, the *Concertino* from a single motif of four notes). They ought to sound 'same-y', and in
a sense they do, in that all three have a certain serenity at their core, with frequent recourse to
quietness, and all three are harmonically transparent. That is Panufnik's idiom, and one wouldn't
complain of two Mozart symphonies that they both sound Mozartian. But all three pieces are also
'about' the unification of dissimilarity. The basic material of the *Sinfonia concertante* is put to
lyrical, meditative, tranquil use in the first of its main movements but is shown in the second to be
just as capable of generating abrupt discontinuity, swift movement and vigorous rhythm; the brief
concluding "Postscriptum" reflects on how very simple the raw material for such contrast can be.
The 'method' is tested more severely in the five-movement *Concertino*, which was written as a test-
piece, and, since the two soloists are percussionists, as something of a display vehicle as well.
Harmony takes the unifying of dualities a step further: here we have two instrumental groups (wind
octet and a small string ensemble without double-basses) that engage in serene dialogue until they
eventually merge and the music intensifies through angular stress to passionate but austere
tenderness. It is a memorable image, surely not coincidentally dedicated to Panufnik's wife on the
occasion of their silver wedding; it is subtitled "Poem", and is indeed poetic, but the poetry and
severity of the technique are inseparable. All three works are beautifully played and very cleanly
recorded.

Additional recommendation ...
...Concerto festivo[a]. Landscape[a]. Katyń Epitaph[a]. Concerto for Timpani, Percussion and Strings[ab].
Sinfonia sacra[c]. [b]**Kurt-Hans Goedicke** (timp); [b]**Michael Frye** (perc); [a]**London Symphony Orchestra;**
[c]**Monte Carlo Opera Orchestra / Andrzej Panufnik.** Unicorn-Kanchana Souvenir Ⓜ UKCD2020
(69 minutes: DDD/ADD: 8/89).

Panufnik String Quartets – No. 1; No. 2, "Messages"; No. 3. Song to the Virgin Mary[a]. String
Sextet[a]. **Chilingirian Quartet** (Levon Chilingirian, Charles Stewart, vns; Simon Rowland, va;
Philip de Groote, vc); [a]**Roger Chase** (va), [a]**Stephen Orton** (vc). Conifer Ⓕ CDCF218 (72 minutes:
DDD: 12/93). Recorded 1993.
While the Second Quartet (1980) recalls the outdoor nocturnals of Bartók and Szymanowski, the
First (1976) – opens with urgent, strongly differentiated chatter and then switches to luminous, long-
breathed lines; subdued, shifting and rising to an ethereal height. The Third Quartet (1991) serves as
a concentrated résumé of Panufnik's quartet style. The *Song to the Virgin Mary* was transcribed from
an *a cappella* choral piece of the same name and conjures up something of Dvořák's steadfast, simple
piety. "Trains of Thought" was inspired by the hypnotic rhythm of wheels on a track and the thoughts
suggested by them; it is based on a three note cell, "constantly rotated and frequently transposed and
reflected". But the effect is more like a dream one might have of the train floating off the tracks and
careering up into the firmament: the rhythm remains gently insistent, the harmonic language subtle
and suggestive. The Chilingirian Quartet perform well, the sound is excellent and the notes are both
appetizing and informative. A most engaging release.

Further listening ...
...Symphony No. 8, "Sinfonia Votiva". *Coupled with* **Sessions** Concerto for Orchestra. **Boston
Symphony Orchestra / Seiji Ozawa.** Hyperion CDA66050 (7/89).
...Symphony No. 8, "Sinfonia Votiva"[a]. **Szymanowski** Symphonies – No. 3, Op. 27, "The Song of
the Night"[b]; No. 4, Op. 60, "Symphonie concertante"[c]. [b]**Philip Langridge** (ten); [c]**Piotr Paleczny**
(pf); [b]**BBC Singers;** [b]**BBC Symphony Chorus and Orchestra /** [a]**Andrzej Panufnik,** [b]**Norman Del
Mar,** [c]**Mark Elder.** BBC Radio Classics BBCRD9124 (12/95).
...Symphony No. 9, "Sinfonia della Speranza". Piano Concerto[a]. [a]**Ewa Poblocka** (pf); **London
Symphony Orchestra / Sir Andrzej Panufnik.** Conifer CDCF206 (5/92).
...Sinfonia sacra[a]. Arbor cosmica[b]. [a]**Royal Concertgebouw Orchestra;** [b]**New York Chamber
Symphony / Sir Andrzej Panufnik.** Elektra Nonesuch 7559-79228-2 (5/91).
...Tragic Overture[a]. Autumn Music[a]. Heroic Overture[a]. Nocturne[a]. Sinfonia rustica[b]. [a]**London
Symphony Orchestra / Jascha Horenstein;** [b]**Monte Carlo Opera Orchestra / Andrzej Panufnik.**
Unicorn-Kanchana Souvenir UKCD2016 (4/89).

Andy Pape

Danish 1955-

Suggested listening ...
...CaDance 4 2. *Coupled with works by* **Fuzzy, A. Koppel, Miki** and **Nørgård** Safri Duo.
Chandos New Direction CHAN9330 (4/95). *See review in the Collections section; refer to the
Index to Reviews.*

Pietro Paradis

Italian 1707-1791

Suggested listening ...
...12 Sonate di gravicembalo – No. 6a, Toccata. *Coupled with works by* **Bach, Daquin, Rimsky-Korsakov, Rameau, F. Couperin, Templeton** and **Malcolm** George Malcolm (hpd). Decca 444 390-2DWO (11/95). ✎

Elias Parish Alvars

Brtiish 1808-1849

Suggested listening ...
...Harp Concerto in G minor, Op. 81. *Coupled with works by* **Boieldieu** and **Viotti** Marielle Nordmann (hp); **Franz Liszt Chamber Orchestra / Jean-Pierre Rampal.** Sony Classical SK58919 (10/95). *See review under Boieldieu; refer to the Index to Reviews.*

Sir Hubert Parry

British 1848-1918

New review
Parry Piano Concerto in F sharp major.
Stanford Piano Concerto No. 1 in G major, Op. 59. **Piers Lane** (pf); **BBC Scottish Symphony Orchestra / Martyn Brabbins.** Hyperion Ⓔ CDA66820 (73 minutes: DDD: 2/96). Recorded 1995.
Parry's Piano Concerto (1879) is a resourceful, imposing creation, stylistically most obviously indebted to Brahms's D minor Concerto (there's also an endearing crib from the Tchaikovsky B flat minor Concerto in the coruscating solo writing towards the very close of the work). The writing is assured, fluent and harmonically often quite daring: within 50 seconds of the piece's F sharp major opening, for instance, we find ourselves plunged into an amazingly distant G major! By contrast, Stanford's First Concerto in G, composed 14 years after its companion here, has an altogether less weighty demeanour. This tuneful, unpretentious and beautifully crafted essay, which Stanford intended to be "of a bright and butterfly nature", though longer than the Parry, actually feels shorter, so charming are Stanford's melodic gifts and felicitous sense of colour. The limpid central *Adagio molto* is especially appealing. Piers Lane proves a fearlessly secure, eloquent exponent of all this material, whilst Martyn Brabbins elicits polished and responsive playing from the BBC Scottish SO. The sound is clean and true.

Parry Orchestral works. **London Philharmonic Orchestra / Matthias Bamert.** Chandos Ⓜ (four discs, oas: 53, 52, 76 and 57 minutes: DDD: 7/92, 10/91, 1/91 and 9/91). Recorded 1990-92. *CHAN9062* – Symphony No. 1 in G minor. Concertstück in G minor. *CHAN8961* – Symphony No. 2 in F major, "Cambridge". Symphonic Variations. *CHAN8896* – Symphonies: No. 3 in C major, "English"; No. 4 in E minor (*Selected by Sounds in Retrospect*). *CHAN8955* – Symphony No. 5 in B minor, "Symphonic Fantasia 1912". From Death to Life. Elegy for Brahms.   Ⓖ
Written in its composer's thirty-second year, Parry's First Symphony witnessed the realization of several decades of aspiration and dedication toward this grandest of musical objectives. Despite its obvious Germanic, and more specifically Brahmsian affiliations, the symphony reflects much of the comfortable optimism of the Victorian era. Even so, there's little in the way of Gothic excess, and not a trace of inflated jingoism here. The symphony is ably constructed and tastefully orchestrated, with several of its most powerful statements returning in the finale. Matthias Bamert's performance is assured and totally committed, as he makes out the strongest possible case for the work from its very opening bars. He also includes an ardently reasoned account of Parry's *Concertstück* in G minor, hardly music of the calibre of the symphony, but worth hearing, none the less. This is a revelatory issue and it is difficult to imagine these triumphant offerings being superseded for a very long time to come. The same forces score another important first with their fine recordings of the *Cambridge* Symphony and the *Symphonic Variations*. This disc also offers some surprises, for it seems incredible that this music has remained virtually unknown for the best part of a century! The Second Symphony has no particular link with Cambridge, save for the fact that it received its première there in 1883. Bamert and the LPO offer a revelatory performance here in which the real qualities of the music are allowed to shine through any reverential backward glances at the works of Brahms, Dvořák and Schumann. Parry was enthusiastic, however, about Dvořák's *Symphonic Variations* and Brahms's *Haydn* Variations, and followed the example of both in his own set for orchestra. The London Philharmonic are captured here on vibrant form and the Chandos sound is especially full-bodied and resonant.
The discovery on the third disc is the Fourth Symphony, first performed (conducted by Hans Richter) in 1889, revised in 1910, performed twice in its new version and then forgotten for nearly 80 years. It is a deeply personal work, almost confessional in its repressed passion. The first movement (16 minutes) is on an immense scale, covering an emotional range comparable with Elgar's Second (which it preceded). The Third Symphony is more conventional, an English equivalent of Schumann's *Rhenish*. Its sunny exuberance and the lightness of the scoring make it highly attractive. Performance

and recording are both admirable. Parry's Fifth Symphony dates from 1912 and like so much of his output this substantial work reveals the composer's enduring devotion to the music of Brahms. However, Parry was fascinated by the idea of writing a programmatic symphony, in the Lisztian mould, and thus each of the four linked movements have titles which relate strongly to his personal ethical outlook. The finale, entitled "Now" culminates with an expansive review of material from earlier in the work, and here it is clearly a sense of confidence and affirmation, expressed in grandiose Edwardian musical rhetoric, which concludes Parry's symphonic cycle. The remaining movements, "Stress", "Love" and "Play" also serve to remind us of the clear romantic origins of this splendid and inexplicably neglected British symphony. Also included on this disc are two shorter, although no less weighty Parry rarities, and the Symphonic Poem *From Death to Life* shares much common ground with the Fifth Symphony, at least in terms of its general subject matter. The London Philharmonic again respond with tremendous conviction and brilliance. In conclusion, all these recordings are highly recommended.

Additional recommendations ...

...No. 1. From Death to Life. **English Symphony Orchestra / William Boughton.** Nimbus Ⓕ NI5296 (64 minutes: DDD: 5/92).

...No. 5. Symphonic Variations. Elegy for Brahms. Ode at a Solemn Music, "Blest Pair of Sirens"[a].
[a]**London Philharmonic Choir; London Philharmonic Orchestra / Sir Adrian Boult.** EMI Ⓜ CDM5 65107-2 (58 minutes: ADD).

New review

Parry Shulbrede Tunes. Theme and 19 Variations in D minor. Hands across the Centuries. **Peter Jacobs** (pf). Priory Ⓕ PRCD451 (73 minutes: DDD: 10/95). Recorded 1992.

This likeable anthology usefully expands our appreciation of a figure best known for his choral and symphonic offerings. The three works gathered here span some 38 years. Nearly three decades separate the publication dates of the *Theme and 19 Variations* and Parry's next piano work, the charming ten-movement suite of 1914 entitled *Shulbrede Tunes*. The twelfth-century Shulbrede Priory in Sussex was the home of Parry's elder daughter, Dorothea, her husband, Arthur Ponsonby, and their two children, Elizabeth and Matthew. Each family member, as well as the house and grounds, is lovingly evoked by Parry in this winsome, nicely contrasted series of character pieces. Indeed, Dorothea (or "Dolly", as she is named here) is represented by two portraits, the second of which comprises the emotional core of the series. Parry's seven-movement suite from 1916, *Hands across the Centuries*, instantly recalls his earlier *Lady Radnor's Suite* (and the *English Suite* to come) in its easy tunefulness and reliance on baroque dance forms. Peter Jacobs's playing here betokens total commitment and idiomatic warmth. The engineering, too, is eminently truthful (if just a touch hissy). Lovely stuff.

Further listening ...

...Nonet in B flat major (ed J. Dibble). *Coupled with* **Stanford** Serenade (Nonet) in F major, Op. 95. Capricorn. Hyperion CDA66291 (9/89).

...Violin Sonata in D major. 12 Short Pieces. Fantasie-sonata in B minor. **Erich Gruenberg** (vn); **Roger Vignoles** (pf). Hyperion CDA66157 (9/91).

...The Soul's Ransom – Sinfonia Sacra[a]. Choric song from Tennyson's "The Lotos Eaters". **Della Jones** (mez); [a]**David Wilson-Johnson** (bar); **London Philharmonic Choir and Orchestra / Matthias Bamert.** Chandos CHAN8990 (1/92).

...Blest Pair of sirens. I was glad (orch. Jacob). Jerusalem (orch. Elgar). Judith – Long since in Egypt's plenteous land. *Coupled with* **Bairstow** Blessed city, heavenly Salem. **Elgar** Give unto the Lord, Op. 74. Great is the Lord, Op. 67. O hearken Thou. **Hadley** My beloved spake. **Stanford** Evening Service in B flat major, Op. 10. Te Deum in B flat major. **Winchester Cathedral Choir; Waynflete Singers; Bournemouth Symphony Orchestra / David Hill** with **Timothy Byram-Wigfield** (org). Argo 430 836-2ZH (4/92).

...Sunset. *Coupled with works by* **Schubert, Clarke, Goss, S.S. Wesley, Ouseley** and **Mendelssohn** Chichester Cathedral Choir / Alan Thurlow with James Thomas (org). Priory PRCD539 (5/96).

Arvo Pärt

Estonian 1935-

Pärt Fratres (seven versions). Festina Lente. Cantus in Memory of Benjamin Britten. Summa. **Peter Manning** (vn); **France Springuel** (vc); **Mireille Gleizes** (pf); **I Fiamminghi.** Telarc Ⓕ CD80387 (79 minutes: DDD: 6/95). Recorded 1994. Ⓖ

Telarc's *Fratres-Fest* proves beyond doubt that good basic material can be re-worked almost *ad infinitum* – if the manner of its arrangement is sufficiently colourful. The present sequence is particularly imaginative in that it alternates two varied pairs of *Fratres* with atmospheric original string pieces, then separates the last two versions with the sombre pealing of *Festina Lente*. The first *Fratres* opens to a low bass drone and chaste, ethereal strings: the suggested image is of a slow oncoming processional – mourners, perhaps, or members of some ancient religious sect – with drum and xylophone gradually intensifying until the percussive element is so loud that it resembles Copland's *Fanfare for the Common Man*. One envisages aged protagonists who have been treading the same ground since time immemorial, whereas the frantically propelled, arpeggiated opening to the version for violin, strings and percussion leaves a quite different impression. Still, even here the music does eventually calm and Peter Manning provides an expressive solo commentary. All six arrangements share a common 'approach-and-retreat' formula, with ideas that arrive from – and subsequently retreat to – some distant horizon. Next comes the gentle cascading of Pärt's *Cantus in Memory of Benjamin Britten*, with its weeping sequences and lone, tolling bell. The eight-cello *Fratres* uses eerie harmonics (as does the cello and piano version that ends the programme), whereas *Fratres* for wind octet and percussion is cold, baleful, notably Slavonic-sounding and occasionally reminiscent of Stravinsky. The alternation of *Summa* (for strings) and the quartet version of *Fratres* works nicely, the former more animated than anything else on the disc; the latter, more intimate. The performances are consistently sympathetic, and the recordings are excellent.

Additional recommendations ...

...Cantus in Memory of Benjamin Britten. **Eller** Twilight. **Tormis** Overture No. 2. **Tobais** Julius Caesar – overture. **Lemba** Symphony in C sharp minor. **Royal Scottish Orchestra / Neeme Järvi.** Chandos Ⓕ CHAN8656 (74 minutes: DDD: 11/89).

...Fratres. *Coupled with works by* **Corigliano, Moravec, Glinsky** and **Messiaen** Maria **Bachmann** (vn); **Jon Klibonoff** (pf). Catalyst Ⓕ 09026 61824-2 (69 minutes: DDD: 12/93). *See review under Corigliano; refer to the Index to Reviews.* Ⓖ

...Fratres. **Tubin** String Quartet. Piano Quartet in C sharp minor[a]. Elegy. **Tüür** String Quartet. **Tallinn Quartet;** [a]**Love Derwinger** (pf). BIS Ⓕ CD574 (67 minutes: DDD: 1/94).

...Fratres[ab]. Cantus in Memory of Benjamin Britten[c]. Summa[c]. Spiegel im Spiegel[ab]. Festina lente[c]. Tabula Rasa[abcd]. [a]**Tasmin Little** (vn); [b]**Martin Roscoe** (pf); [c]**Bournemouth Sinfonietta / Richard Studt** ([d]vn). EMI Eminence Ⓜ CD-EMX2221 (64 minutes: DDD: 6/94). Ⓔ

...Fratres. Spiegel im Spiegel. *Coupled with works by* **Balakauskas, Barkauskas** and **Schnittke** Rusné Mataityté (vn); Margrit-Julia Zimmermann (pf). Proud Sound Ⓕ PROUCD139 (57 minutes: DDD: 7/96). *See review under Balakauskas; refer to the Index to Reviews.*

...Fratres. Symphony No. 3. **Kancheli** Symphony No. 3[a]. [a]**David James** (alto); **London Philharmonic Orchestra / Franz Welser-Möst.** EMI Ⓕ CDC5 55619-2 (55 minutes: DDD: 8/96). *Gramophone Editor's choice. See review under Kancheli; refer to the Index to Reviews.*

Pärt Te Deum[a]. Silouans Song, "My soul yearns after the Lord ... "[a]. Magnificat. Berliner Messe[a]. **Estonian Philharmonic Chamber Choir;** [a]**Tallinn Chamber Orchestra / Tonu Kaljuste.** ECM New Series Ⓕ 439 162-2 (66 minutes: DDD: 11/93). Texts and translations included. Recorded 1993. *Gramophone Editor's choice.* Ⓖ Ⓖ

Pärt's *Te Deum* sets the standard liturgical text to a wide range of nuances, shades and dynamics; brief string interludes provide heart-rending wordless commentaries, and the work's closing pages provide a serenely moving affirmation of holiness. Although relatively static in its musical narrative, Pärt's *Te Deum* is both mesmerizing and enriching. *Silouans Song* (1991), an eloquent study for strings, is as reliant on silence as on sonority. It is again austere and chant-like, although its dramatic interpolations approximate a sort of sacral protest. The brief *Magnificat* for *a cappella* choir (1989) positively showers multi-coloured resonances. However, the *Te Deum's* closest rival – in terms of substance and appeal – is surely the 25-minute *Berliner Messe* (1990-92). Here again Pärt employs the simplest means to achieve the most magical ends: "Veni Sancte Spiritus" weaves a luminous thread of melodic activity either side of a constant, mid-voice drone, while the weighted phrases of the *Sanctus* take breath amid seraphic string chords. And how wonderful the gradual darkening of the closing *Agnus Dei*, where tenors initially answer sopranos and an almost imperceptible mellowing softens the work's final moments. Beautiful sounds, these – gripping yet remote, communicative yet deeply personal in their contemplative aura, while the all-round standard of presentation – performance, engineering, documentation – serves Pärt as devotedly as Pärt serves the Divine Image.

Additional recommendation ...

...Magnificat. Summa. *Coupled with works by* **Górecki** and **Tavener** Oxford Pro Musica Singers / **Michael Smedley.** Proud Sound Ⓕ PROUCD136 (77 minutes: DDD: 12/94). *See review under Tavener; refer to the Index to Reviews.*

New review

Pärt Annum per annum[a]. Pari intervalli[a]. Mein Weg hat Gipfel und Wellentäler[a]. Trivium I-III[a]. **Cage** Souvenir[a]. **Scelsi** In nomine lucis[b]. **Christoph Maria Moosmann** (org). New Albion Ⓕ NA074CD (64 minutes: DDD: 2/96). Items marked [a] played on the organ in St Martin's Cathedral, Rottenburg, [b]Collegiate Church of St Hippolyte, Poligny, France.

The pieces by Pärt constitute his complete organ output to date. *Pari intervalli*, originally written for woodwind as a memorial tribute, and *Trivium I-III* are the earliest, dating from 1976 when Pärt broke a three-year composing silence. Then came *Annum per annum* (1980) where five movements representing sections of the Mass are framed by one long sustained chord of D – loud going down to soft in the prelude and the opposite in the postlude. The latest piece, *Mein Weg* (1989), is closely based on a poem about the spiritual journey through life. Most of the Pärt works have a veritable fixation on D, which comes up resplendently in the loud second piece of *Trivium* which, like the first one, is on a pedal. This is the organ music of spiritual minimalism, restrained but powerful if you are on the right wavelength. The Cage and Scelsi are first recordings. Cage's *Souvenir* (1984), commissioned by the American Guild of Organists, at times sounds like an improvisation on a recurrent theme suggesting plainsong. But, being Cage, the piece contains irreverent squawks and eruptions of clusters to put things into perspective. The interaction between textures is – for Cage – unusually structured and satisfying. *In nomine lucis* (1974) by the eccentric Italian Giacinto Scelsi, who died in 1988, is in memory of his younger colleague Franco Evangelisti. This is a most unusual, atmospheric piece, where Moosmann uses assistants to operate the mechanical stops very precisely to obtain microtones. *In nomine lucis* seems to be Scelsi's only organ work and there is nothing quite like it. The organ of St Martin's Cathedral at Rottenburg (on which everything is performed except the Scelsi), although modern, sounds exactly right for the neo-medievalism of Pärt's timeless message, and the recording is outstanding.

Further listening ...

...Cello Concerto, "Pro et contra"[a]. Perpetuum mobile, Op. 10. Symphonies – No. 1, "Polyphonic"; No. 2; No. 3. [a]**Frans Helmerson** (vc); **Bamberg Symphony Orchestra / Neeme Järvi.** BIS CD434 (9/89).   ⓖ

...Partita. *Coupled with* **Vähi** Fata Morgana. **Tüür** Sonata. **Sumera** Piece from the Year 1981. **Rääts** Toccata. **Kangro** Suite, Op. 1. **Mägi** The Ancient Kannel. **Lauri Väinmaa** (pf). Finlandia 4509-95704-2 (7/95).

...Passio Domini nostri Jesu Christi secundum Johannem. **Michael George** (bass); **John Potter** (ten); **Hilliard Ensemble; Western Wind Chamber Choir / Paul Hillier.** ECM New Series 837 109-2 (2/89).   ⓖⓖⓖ

...Miserere[a]. Festina lente[b]. Sarah was ninety years old[c]. [a]**Western Wind Choir;** [ac]**Hilliard Ensemble / Paul Hillier;** [b]**Bonn Beethovenhalle Orchestra / Dennis Russell Davies.** ECM New Series 847 539-2 (1/92).   ⓖⓖ

...Variations for the healing of Arinushka[c]. *Coupled with* **Jirásek** Missa Propria[a]. Katharsis[b]. **Hildegard of Bingen** (arr. Ivanoff): O Euchari, in leta vita[d]. **Traditional** Georgian Kartl-k'akhetian Songs – Shen Khar Venakhi; Romelni Kerubinta[e]. **Eespere** Trivium[f]. [c]**Kalle Randalu** (pf); [a]**Boni Pueri Boys' Choir / Jiri Skopal;** [d]**Vox / Vladimir Ivanoff;** [e]**Georgika Ensemble;** [b]**Quartetto con Flauto;** [f]**Tallinn Camerata.** Catalyst 09026 68331-2 (2/96).

Paul Patterson   British 1947-

Suggested listening ...

...Duologue. *Coupled with* **Finzi** (arr. Ferguson) Interlude in A minor, Op. 21. **Howells** Oboe Sonata. **Nicholas Daniel** (ob); **Julius Drake** (pf). Léman Classics LC44801 (10/93). *See review under Finzi; refer to the Index to Reviews.*

Anthony Payne   British 1936-

Suggested listening ...

...Adlestrop[ab]. *Coupled with works by* **Elias, Bauld, Connolly, P.P. Nash, Weir** and **A. Gilbert** Jane Manning (sop); [a]**Jane's Minstrels /** [b]**Roger Montgomery.** NMC Artists' Series NMCD025 (10/95).   ⓖ

Flor Peeters   Belgian 1903-1986

Suggested listening ...

...Aria, Op. 51. Concert Piece, Op. 52a. Elégie, Op. 38. Preludium, Canzona e Ciacona, Op. 83. *Coupled with* **Bonnet** Pièces nouvelles, Op. 7 – No. 1, Clair de lune; No. 2, Etude de concert; No. 3, Pastorale; No. 4, Caprice héroique. **Dupré** Three Preludes and Fugues, Op. 36. **Jane Watts** (org). Priory PRCD377 (8/94).

...Suite, Op. 71. *Coupled with* **Widor** Scherzo in F major, "La Chasse". **Malengreau** Symphonic de la Passion, Op. 20. **P. Pierné** Pastorale. **Guillou** Toccata. **John Scott Whiteley** (org). Priory PRCD487 (2/96).

Francisco de Peñalosa   Spanish c1470-1528

Peñalosa Missa Ave Maria peregrina. Missa nunca fue pena mayor. Sacris solemnüs. **Westminster Cathedral Choir / James O'Donnell.** Hyperion Ⓟ CDA66629 (67 minutes: DDD: 6/93). Texts and translations included.

Francisco de Peñalosa was the best composer of his generation at the courts of Ferdinand and Isabella, and the nearest the Iberian peninsula came to rivalling Josquin in his own lifetime. On this disc we have one of the best choirs in the world for this kind of polyphony, Richard Runciman Terry (director of the choir, 1902-24) having established a tradition for performing the works of sixteenth-century Spanish composers that has been preserved ever since. Their many more recent recordings of this repertory have been much and justly acclaimed, and this is another feather in their cap. Maybe Peñalosa's polyphony was intended to flow a little more freely, especially in the *Kyrie* and *Sanctus* of the Marian Mass. This apart, there are some marvellous moments: the excitement of the triple section at "Cum sancto spiritu" in the *Gloria* of the *Missa Ave Maria*, with its upward leaping basses; the intensity of the sustained passages in the *Credos* of both Masses; the contemplative tone of the *Agnus Dei* movements and so on. Unmissable.

Further listening ...

...Por las sierras de Madrid. Ne reminiscaris, Domine. Precor te, Domine. Sancta Maria. *Coupled with works by* **Encina, Mena, Enrique, Anonymous, Narváez, Fernández Palero, Milán, Segni** and **Anonymous Gothic Voices / Christopher Page** with **Christopher Wilson** (vihuela) and **Andrew Lawrence-King** (hp). Hyperion CDA66653 (2/94). *See review in the Collections section; refer to the Index to Reviews.* **G**

...Motets – Inter vestibulum et altare. Tribularer, si nescirem. Ne reminiscaris, Domine. Versa est in luctum. Domine, secundum actum meum. Adore te, Domine Jesus Christe. Ave, verum corpus natum. Nigra sum, sed formosa. Sancta Maria. Unica est colomba mea. Ave, vera caro Christi. Ave, vere sanguis Domini. In passione positus. Precor te, Domine Jesu Christe. Pater noster. Ave Regina caelorum. Sancta Mater, istud agas. O Domina sanctissima. Emendemus in melius. Deus, qui manus tuas. Domine Iesu Christe, qui neminem. Transeunte Domino Jesu. **Pro Cantione Antiqua / Bruno Turner.** Hyperion CDA66574 (7/92).

Krzysztof Penderecki
Polish 1933-

New review

Penderecki St Luke Passion – Stabat mater; Miserere; In pulverem mortis. Magnificat – Sicut locutus est. Agnus Dei. Song of Cherubim. Veni creator. Benedicamus Domino. Benedictus. **Tapiola Chamber Choir / Juha Kuivanen.** Finlandia Ⓕ 4509-98999-2 (52 minutes: DDD: 3/96). Texts and translations included.

There is a neat correspondence in the way the earliest and most recent pieces included here – *Stabat mater* (1962) and *Benedictus* (1992) – both move to resolutions on simple major triads. So far, so consistent: the difference is in the extent to which the triads in later work govern the musical fabric throughout. In the 1960s such common chords had to be fought for, and could even seem tacked on rather arbitrarily; an effect without a sufficient cause. In general, however, it is another kind of consistency that makes this disc musically worthwhile. Although all the works tend to be reflective and devotional in character, the contrapuntal medium of the unaccompanied chorus inspires the composer to an economical intensity all too often absent from his later instrumental works. Indeed, it is as part of that intensity that elements of his early, much more dissonant style, so powerfully represented in the three extracts from the *St Luke Passion* and the fragment from the *Magnificat*, re-emerge within the more traditional harmonic world of the later pieces – especially the *Veni creator*. Yet it should also be said that Penderecki's austere response to this celebratory text seems more than a little strange. Of the later works *Song of Cherubim* is the most powerful, ending as it does with remarkably rapt "Alleluias". A note tells us that the composer regards the *Benedictus* as a draft to be reworked at a later stage. These performances are on the whole models of pure-toned clarity, although the sound of the Tapiola Chamber Choir can harden into harshness at higher dynamic levels. The recordings, made in the Olari Church, Espoo, Finland, are full of atmosphere but well-balanced and not excessively resonant.

Penderecki Anaklasis[a]. Threnody for the victims of Hiroshima[b]. Fonogrammi[c]. De natura sonoris I[d]. Capriccio[e]. Canticum canticorum Salomonis[f]. De natura sonoris II[g]. Dream of Jacob[h]. [e]**Wanda Wilkomirska** (vn); [f]**Cracow Philharmonic Chorus;** [bcdefgh]**Polish National Radio Symphony Orchestra;** [a]**London Symphony Orchestra / Krzysztof Penderecki.** EMI Matrix Ⓜ CDM5 65077-2 (75 minutes: ADD: 10/94). Items marked [a] from HMV EMD5507 (1/74), [bdfh] EMD5529 (6/76), [ceg] HMV SLS850 (8/74). Recorded 1972-75. **GG**

Krzysztof Penderecki's creative heyday (1950s-1970s) prompted a release of dramatic aural ingenuity the like of which had not been heard before and has rarely been heard since. Works such as the *St Luke Passion*, the *Dies irae* and, most especially, the *Threnody for the victims of Hiroshima* featured on this CD, delve deep within the recesses of collective memory, often triggering disturbing nightmare images. Even that master musical psychologist Alban Berg could hardly have approximated the *Threnody*'s chamber of horror – the blinding light of its opening bars, the aural swerve as trees bend and houses shatter, the jittery aftermath as fall-out spreads its poisonous message, and the myriad gestures and effects that amount to a terrifying experience. No other twentieth-century instrumental work quite equals the *Threnody* for graphic impact and no other composer has provided the victims of Hiroshima and Nagasaki with such a dramatic or telling memorial. The trouble is that the *Threnody* accounts for just 9'55" on a 75'25" CD – so what of the rest? Penderecki's invariable preference for slow motion, dense tonal clusters, roaring sonorities (*De natura sonoris II* rises to a deafening primeval groan), wailing vocalizations and sundry instrumental effects (tapping and screeching), not to mention a virtual absence of melody and definable rhythm, make for a pretty draining listening session. One wonders whether the musical metaphors that Penderecki used during this phase of his career are actually capable of expressing anything brighter than *Angst*, terror, fear, disorientation and – very occasionally – black humour. If they do it is difficult to discern, and yet it is a fascinating sound-world for all that, and the *Threnody* is surely its most profound justification. The recordings report all with merciless clarity.

Further listening ...

...String Quartets Nos. 1[b] and 2[b]. Prelude[a]. Der unterbrochene Gedanke[b]. String Trio[cef]. Clarinet Quartet[acdf]. [a]**Martin Fröst** (cl); [b]**Tale Quartet** (Tale Olsson[c], Patrick Swedrup[d], vns; Ingegerd Kierkegaard, va[e]; Helena Nilsson, vc[f]). BIS CD652 (5/95).

...St Luke Passion (Passio et mors Domini nostri Jesu Christi secundum Lucam). **Soloists; Cracow Boys' Choir; Warsaw National Philharmonic Chorus; Polish Radio National Symphony Orchestra / Krzysztof Penderecki.** Argo 430 328-2ZH (3/91).　　　　　　　　　　　　　🅖🅖

Ernst Pepping
German 1901-1981

Suggested listening ...

...Concerto No. 2. Four Fugues. Partita No. 1, "Ach wie flüchtig". Wie schön leuchtet der Morgenstern. **Wolfgang Stockmeier** (org). CPO CPO999 039-2 (7/91).

...Three Fugues on BACH. *Coupled with* **Hindemith** Organ Sonatas Nos. 1-3. **Schoenberg** Variations on a Recitative, Op. 40. Two Fragments of an Organ Sonata. **Kevin Bowyer** (org). Nimbus NI5411 (1/95).

Giovanni Pergolesi
Italian 1710-1736

Pergolesi Stabat mater[a]. Salve regina in C minor. **Emma Kirkby** (sop); [a]**James Bowman** (alto); **Academy of Ancient Music / Christopher Hogwood.** L'Oiseau-Lyre Florilegium 🅟 425 692-2OH (52 minutes: DDD: 2/90). 🖉 Texts and translations included. Recorded 1988.

Pergolesi's *Stabat mater*, written in the last few months of his brief life, enjoyed a huge popularity throughout the eighteenth century. But modern performances often misrepresent its nature, either through over-romanticizing it or by transforming it into a choral work. None of these are qualities overlooked in this affecting performance, for Emma Kirkby and James Bowman are well-versed in the stylistic conventions of baroque and early classical music – and their voices afford a pleasing partnership. Both revel in Pergolesi's sensuous vocal writing, phrasing the music effectively and executing the ornaments with an easy grace. Singers and instrumentalists alike attach importance to sonority, discovering a wealth of beguiling effects in Pergolesi's part writing. In the *Salve regina* in C minor Emma Kirkby gives a compelling performance, pure in tone, expressive and poignant, and she is sympathetically supported by the string ensemble. The recording is pleasantly resonant and does justice to Pergolesi's translucent textures. Full texts are included.

Additional recommendations ...

...Stabat mater. **Margaret Marshall** (sop); **Lucia Valentini Terrani** (mez); **London Symphony Orchestra / Claudio Abbado.** DG 🅟 415 103-2GH (43 minutes: DDD: 4/85).

...Stabat mater[ab]. Salve regina[a]. In coelestibus regnis[b]. [a]**Gillian Fisher** (sop); [b]**Michael Chance** (alto); **King's Consort / Robert King.** Hyperion 🅟 CDA66294 (54 minutes: DDD: 11/88). 🖉

...Salve regina in A minor[a]. Salve regina in C minor[a]. **Leo** Salve regina in F major[a]. **Gallo** Trio Sonatas – G major; B flat major. [a]**Barbara Schlick** (sop); **Europa Galante / Fabio Biondi** (vn). Opus 111 🅟 OPS30-88 (59 minutes: DDD: 4/94). 🖉

...Stabat mater[a]. Orfeo. **Regina Klepper** (sop); [a]**Martina Borst** (mez); **Bamberg Quartet; Stefan Adelmann** (db); **Berthold Höps** (hpd/org). Capriccio 🅟 10 517 (52 minutes: DDD: 7/95).

New review

Pergolesi La Serva Padrona[a]. L'Olimpiade – Overture (arr. anon). [a]**Isabelle Poulenard** (sop) Serpina; [a]**Philippe Cantor** (bass) Uberto; **Nice Baroque Ensemble / Gilbert Bezzina.** Pierre Verany 🅟 PV795111 (52 minutes: DDD: 4/96). 🖉 Notes, text and translation included.

As *La Serva Padrona* was originally merely an intermezzo played between the acts of an *opera seria* by Pergolesi, no overture exists; for this performance one has been borrowed from another *opera seria* of his written two years later. The original duet ending has also been replaced by a longer one used in later productions; but the original has usefully been added in an appendix (not an "epilogue", as the booklet-note calls it). The work's appeal lies in its vivacity and its unpretentious, well-characterized treatment of a familiar *commedia dell'arte* plot. Gilbert Bezzina, with a vigorous, slightly rough-toned but tidy period string ensemble, certainly keeps things moving well and a pleasing feature here is the flexible timing of the recitatives, whose words are given real point. Full advantage of this isn't equally taken in arias, however. Isabelle Poulenard rightly represents Serpina as pert and volatile though not as a termagant; but there are further subtle nuances of colour she could have introduced into her sly mock-penitent aria, where she is content to be merely sweet-voiced. The image of a perplexed Uberto torn between frustration, indignation and fondness is a difficult one to project: Philippe Cantor does his utmost with this, but is somewhat hampered by too close a recorded balance that makes him sound overloud and over-vehement. Since there is a mute third character in this playlet who is essential to the action, it is certainly justifiable, in a non-visual performance, that he should be permitted to add guffaws, gulps and grunts in response to events around him. Altogether, this is an enjoyable recording.

George Perle
American 1915-

Suggested listening ...
...Piano Concerto No. 2[a]. Six Etudes. *Coupled with* **Danielpour** Metamorphosis[a]. **Michael Boriskin** (pf); [a]**Utah Symphony Orchestra / Joseph Silverstein**. Harmonia Mundi HMU90 7124 (5/95).
...Wind Quintets – No. 1, Op. 37; No. 2, Op. 41; Nos. 3 and 4. **Dorian Quintet; Julie Landsman** (hn). New World NW359-2 (10/88).

Pérotin
French c1160-c1225

Suggested listening ...
...Viderunt omnes. Alleluia, Posui adiutorium. Dum sigillum summi Patris. Alleluia, Nativitas. Beata viscera. Sederunt principes. *Coupled with* **Anonymous Twelfth Century** Veni creator spiritus. O Maria virginei. Isias cecinit. **Hilliard Ensemble / Paul Hillier** (bar). ECM New Series 837 751-2 (2/90). Ⓖ

Vincent Persichetti
American 1915-1987

Suggested listening ...
...Divertimento for Band, Op. 42. Psalm for Band, Op. 53. Choral Prelude: O God Unseen, Op. 160. Pageant, Op. 59. Masquerade for Band, Op. 102. O Cool is the Valley, Op. 118. Parable for Band, Op. 121. **Winds of the London Symphony Orchestra / David Amos**. Harmonia Mundi HMU90 7092 (10/94).
...The Hollow Men. *Coupled with works by* **Cowell** and **MacDowell** **Manhattan Chamber Orchestra / Richard Auldon Clark**. Koch International Classics 37282-2 (7/95). *See review under Cowell; refer to the Index to Reviews.*

Wilhelm Peterson-Berger
Swedish 1867-1942

Suggested listening ...
...Nothing is like the time of waiting. Swedish folk ballads, Op. 5 – No. 1, When I go myself in the dark forest; No. 3, Like stars in the heavens. Three Marit's Songs, Op. 12. Böljeby Waltz. Return. Aspåkers Polka. *Coupled with works by* **Sigurd von Koch, Stenhammar, Rangström, Alfvén** and **Sjögren** Anne Sofie von Otter (mez); **Bengt Forsberg** (pf). DG 449 189-2GH (5/96). *See review in the Collections section; refer to the Index to Reviews.* ⒼⒼ

Vincenzo Petrali
Italian 1832-1889

Suggested listening ...
...Messe solennelle – Gloria. *Coupled with* **Bossi** Stunde der Wehie, Op. 132 No. 4. Stunde der Freude, Op. 132 No. 5. **Galliera** Venerdi Santo dal "Trittico". **Bettinelli** Toccata Fantasia. **Ambrosi** Messa. **Luigi Benedetti** (org). Priory PRCD427 (4/95).

Allan Pettersson
Swedish 1911-1980

New review
Pettersson Symphony No. 2. Symphonic Movement. **BBC Scottish Symphony Orchestra / Alun Francis**. CPO Ⓕ CPO999 281-2 (57 minutes: DDD: 9/95). Recorded 1994.
In his essay on Pettersson, and this work in particular, in *Opus est: six composers from Northern Europe* (Kahn & Averill; London: 1978), Paul Rapoport describes the Second Symphony as "a work of extreme tension and extreme contrasts, a work of unrest, grotesquerie, despair, turbulence, terror". In his notes to the present recording, Andreas Meyer highlights the composer's "joy of experimentation and treatment of the orchestra" which "have no real parallels in his later works". Certainly this symphony, written in 1952-53 follows a more variegated course than the vast majority of Pettersson's symphonies, a feature this excellent recording underlines. The BBC Scottish players also turn in a splendid account of the short (for Pettersson) *Symphonic Movement* from 1973: at 11 minutes in length, it provides an ideal encapsulation of the salient features of this composer's style.

Pettersson Symphonies – No. 3; No. 15. **Norrköping Symphony Orchestra / Leif Segerstam.** BIS
Ⓕ CD680 (71 minutes: DDD: 1/96). Recorded 1993-4.
The first difference that strikes the casual ear when comparing Leif Segerstam's account of
Pettersson's Fifteenth Symphony (1978) with that by Peter Ruzicka on CPO is tempo; so pronounced
is it, that Segerstam takes six minutes less (at 32'20") than his rival. In CPO's notes, Andreas Meyer
and Ruzicka make a virtue of their more relaxed paces (the work is built around three principal and
interacting speeds), which arose from the alleged impracticality of certain passages. Segerstam and his
Swedish forces take these in their stride to come much closer to the composer's timing of 31'00" (he
never heard the work performed). Repeated hearings reinforce Segerstam's superiority. His vision of
the work is more clearly focused, the interpretation tauter and more compelling than Ruzicka's, and
the excellent BIS sound ensures that the orchestral detail comes through still more clearly. Yet Ruzicka
knows Pettersson's music probably better than anyone; perhaps it is just that Segerstam is able to
translate his own understanding into actual sound rather better. The BIS coupling, of No. 3 (1954-5),
is a further advantage, though here competition is somewhat stiffer. Again, Segerstam is quicker,
though only by two minutes, largely accounted for by the treatment of the introduction to the first
movement. There is little to choose between the two versions (Francis's coupling of No. 4 is a fine
one), but in the final analysis BIS and Segerstam must be first choice for both symphonies.
Additional recommendations ...
...Symphonies Nos. 3 and 4. **Saarbrücken Radio Symphony Orchestra / Alun Francis.** CPO
Ⓕ CPO999 223-2 (78 minutes: DDD: 12/95).
...Symphony No. 15. **Ruzicka** "... das Gesegnete, das Verfluchte". **Berlin Radio Symphony
Orchestra / Peter Ruzicka.** CPO Ⓕ CPO999 095-2 (52 minutes: DDD: 12/95).

Pettersson Symphonies Nos. 7 and 11. **Norrköping Symphony Orchestra / Leif Segerstam.** BIS
Ⓕ CD580 (70 minutes: DDD: 4/94). Recorded 1992.
Most of Pettersson's major works are constructed as large, unified movements (although he was an
accomplished miniaturist) and Nos. 7 and 11, respectively 46 and 24 minutes in length, are no
exceptions. The former in some ways is unrepresentative of the composer; the obsessiveness of mood
and hectoring tone are present, especially in the *Angst*-ridden first and third spans, but the range of
expression is much wider than in most of his other works. Composed in 1967-68, it has a unique
atmosphere, both haunting and haunted, which will stay with you for a long time. His melodic genius
is confirmed in the long and heartfelt central threnody, as well as by the beautiful quiet coda, truly
music to "soften the crying of a child"; its delivery by the Norrköping players has just the right
amount of detachment. Segerstam's tempos permit the work to breathe and resonate not unlike
Mahler. The Eleventh Symphony (1974) is less combative in tone, although it has its moments, and
is not on the same elevated plane as the Seventh. As usual from BIS, the recording quality is first-
rate, allowing both the devastating power and delicate fine detail of these scores to emerge equally
well.
Additional recommendation ...
...No. 7. **Hamburg Philharmonic Orchestra / Gerd Albrecht.** CPO CPO999 190-2 (45 minutes: DDD:
10/94).

Pettersson Symphony No. 9. **Deutsches Symphony Orchestra / Alun Francis.** CPO Ⓕ CPO999
231-2 (70 minutes: DDD: 9/95). Recorded 1993.
This is the biggest of Pettersson's symphonies and in this performance much of it is more genuinely
fast-paced than is usual for this composer. The Ninth (1969-70) was the climactic composition of
Pettersson's 'middle phase', a huge work of synthesis drawing together the experiences communicated
so compellingly in Nos. 5-8 (written over the previous decade) and reworked on an even broader
canvas. It feels like a piece that Pettersson needed to write, to get out of his system, before moving on
to the different concerns of Nos. 10, 11 *et al.*, and its completion coincided with the start of
protracted hospitalization for the rheumatoid arthritis that crippled and eventually killed him. (The
Fifth had been the last work he was able to write out in his normal, legible hand.) If the music lacks
the direct melodic appeal of the better-known Seventh (reviewed above), No. 9 is the more gripping
score. All the familiar Pettersson fingerprints that people either love or loathe are here: the insistent
stridency of tone, long, anguished lines and near-unrelenting tension, though there are points of
repose where less intense writing comes to the surface, at times reminiscent of Shostakovich. The
Deutsches Symphony Orchestra play with commitment, but cannot disguise their lack of familiarity
with the style. However, any other version will need to be special to surpass this one.

Pettersson Concerto for Violin and String Quartet No. 1[a]. Four Improvisations[b]. Fuga in
E major[c]. Fantasy[d]. Lamento[e]. [c]**Christiane Dimigen** (ob); [c]**Johannes Peitz** (cl); [e]**Eckart Hübner**
(bn); [a]**Ulf Hoelscher** (vn); [e]**Volker Banfield** (pf); [ab]**Mandelring Quartet** (Sebastian Schmidt,
Nanette Schmidt, vns; [d]**Michael Scheitzbach**, va; Bernhard Schmidt, vc). CPO Ⓕ CPO999
169-2 (60 minutes: DDD: 1/96).
This is a revelatory issue. Readers of a nervous disposition regarding Pettersson's music should start

this disc with the *Four Improvisations* (1936). The opening's rusticity will come as a surprise; the remainder oscillates between Bartók in folk-mode and Hindemith. Like the other shorter items, the *Improvisations* are stylistically anonymous, unrecognizable when set against the monumental, *Angst*-driven output of the composer's maturity, and strangely patchy in quality. When vast symphonic canvases could later be erected from the sparest of material, the two-and-a-half-minute *Fantasy* (1936) seems prodigal by comparison in achieving so little with so much. On a similar scale, *Lamento* (1945) – Pettersson's only surviving piano work – is quite forgettable. At over 14 minutes in duration, the 1948 wind *Fuga* is certainly no trifle; its obsessive reliance on pure counterpoint is suggestive of the later symphonist. Yet it just does not *sound* like Pettersson, making the vibrancy of personality evident in every bar of the Concerto of a year later all the more extraordinary. This really is a masterpiece, albeit a discomfiting one, written by a composer who was also a master string player. Hoelscher and the Mandelring Quartet give a fine performance and CPO's sound has very little glare, softening edges that are unnaturally severe with no loss of impact.

Further listening ...
...Symphony No. 8. **Berlin Radio Symphony Orchestra / Thomas Sanderling.** CPO CPO999 085-2 (10/94).
...Symphony No. 14. **Berlin Radio Symphony Orchestra / Johan M. Arnell.** CPO CPO999 191-2 (10/94).

Hans Pfitzner

German 1869-1949

Pfitzner Palestrina. **Nicolai Gedda** (ten) Palestrina; **Dietrich Fischer-Dieskau** (bar) Borromeo; **Gerd Nienstedt** (bass) Master of Ceremonies; **Karl Ridderbusch** (bass) Christoph Madrusch, Pope Pius IV; **Bernd Weikl** (bar) Morone; **Herbert Steinbach** (ten) Novagerio; **Helen Donath** (sop) Ighino; **Brigitte Fassbaender** (mez) Silla; **Renate Freyer** (contr) Lukrezia; **Victor von Halem** (bass) Cardinal of Lorraine; **John van Kesteren** (ten) Abdisu; **Peter Meven** (bass) Anton Brus; **Hermann Prey** (bar) Count Luna; **Friedrich Lenz** (ten) Bishop of Budoja; **Adalbert Kraus** (ten) Theophilus; **Franz Mazura** (bass) Avosmediano; **Tölz Boys' Choir; Bavarian Radio Chorus and Symphony Orchestra / Rafael Kubelík.** DG 20th Century Classics Ⓜ 427 417-2GC3 (three discs: 206 minutes: ADD: 7/89). Notes, text and translation included. From 2711 013 (2/74).   ⓖⓖⓖ
Rafael Kubelík's magnificent, sumptuously cast DG recording of *Palestrina* is an almost impossible act to follow, indeed it's hard to imagine such an extravagance of vocal riches being encountered in a German opera recording nowadays: Brigitte Fassbaender ardently impulsive in the brief role of Palestrina's pupil Silla, Helen Donath pure-voiced and touching as his son Ighino, and an absolute constellation of superb basses and baritones, often doubling quite small parts: Karl Ridderbusch, Bernd Weikl, Hermann Prey, Franz Mazura, with at their head Dietrich Fischer-Dieskau as a surely unsurpassable Borromeo: dangerously powerful, intensely concerned and in magnificent voice. And those are just the 'secondary' roles! Pfitzner's text is one of the finest librettos ever written, and Gedda's singing gives the impression that the beauty of the words and their portrayal of Palestrina's dignity and suffering are more important to him than concern for his own voice. It is a beautiful reading. Kubelík's urgent conducting has a visionary quality and he has a marvellous ear for the lucid radiance of this wonderful score.

Further listening ...
...Cello Concertos – G major, Op. 42; A minor, Op. 52; A minor, Op. posth. **David Geringas** (vc); **Bamberg Symphony Orchestra / Werner Andreas Albert.** CPO CPO999 135-2 (4/94).
...Piano Concerto in E flat major, Op. 31. **Volker Banfield** (pf); **Munich Philharmonic Orchestra / Werner Andreas Albert.** CPO CPO999 045-2.
...Violin Concerto in B minor, Op. 34. Duo for Violin, Cello and small orchestra, Op. 43. Scherzo in C minor. **Saschko Gawriloff** (vn); **Julius Berger** (vc); **Bamberg Symphony Orchestra / Werner Andreas Albert.** CPO CPO999 079-2 (5/91).
...Das Fest auf Solhaug – Three Preludes. Kleine Symphonie in G major, Op. 44. Symphony in C major, Op. 46. **Bamberg Symphony Orchestra / Werner Andreas Albert.** CPO CPO999 080-2 (5/91).
...Abbitte, Op. 29 No. 1. *Coupled with music by* **Britten, Cornelius, Eisler, Fortner, Fröhlich, Hauer, Jarnach, Komma, Ullmann** *and* **Reutter** Mitsuko Shirai (mez); Hartmut Höll (pf). Capriccio 10 534 (12/94). *See review in the Collections section; refer to the Index to Reviews.*
...Das dunkle Reich, Op. 38[a]. Der Blumen Rache[b]. Fons salutifer, Op. 48[c]. [a]**Yvonne Wiedstruck** (sop); [b]**Yvi Jänicke** (contr); [a]**Yaron Windmüller** (bar); [ac]**Sigurd Bruns** (org); **Berlin Radio** [bc]**Chorus and Symphony Orchestra / Rolf Reuter.** CPO CPO999 158-2 (4/95).
...Das Christ-Elflein – Overture[c]. Palestrina – Preludes, Acts 1, 2 and 3[c]. Duo for Violin, Cello and Small Orchestra, Op. 43[bc]. 1938). Lieder[a] – Hast du von den Fischerkindern, Op. 7 No. 1; Der Gärtner, Op. 9 No. 1; Die Einsame, Op. 9 No. 2; Zum Abschied meiner Tochter, Op. 10 No. 3; Michaelskirchplatz, Op. 19 No. 2; In Danzig, Op. 22 No. 1; Nachts, Op. 26 No. 2; Abbitte, Op. 29 No. 1; Hussens Kerker, Op. 32 No. 1; Säerspruch, Op. 32 No. 2 (originally unpublished); Leuchtende Tage, Op. 40 No. 1; Herbstgefühl, Op. 40 No. 4. [a]**Gerhard Hüsch** (bar); [b]**Max Strub** (vn); [b]**Ludwig Hoelscher** (vc); [c]**Berlin State Opera Orchestra / Hans Pfitzner** ([a]pf). EMI Composers in Person mono Ⓔ CDC5 55225-2* (5/94).

François-André Philidor

Suggested listening ...
...Le mariage de la grosse Cathos. *Coupled with* **Lully** Le bourgeois gentilhomme. Cadmus et Hermione. Les noces de village. **Marie-Ange Petit** (perc); **London Oboe Band / Paul Goodwin.** Harmonia Mundi HMU90 7122 (4/95).

Peter Philips

Suggested listening ...
...Consort Music – Pavan and Galliard Pavan. Paget Pavan and Galliard. Aria del Gran Duca. Galliard. Bassano Galliard. Morley Pavan and Galliard. Bassano Pavan and Galliard. Dolorosa Pavan and Galliard. Alman Tregian. Balla d'Amore. Pavan and Galliard in F major. Aria. Passamezzo Pavan. **The Parley of Instruments.** Hyperion CDA66240 (1/89). ✄

Astor Piazzolla

Suggested listening ...
...Five Tango Sensations for String Quartet and Bandoneon. **Astor Piazzolla** (bandoneon); **Kronos Quartet.** Elektra Nonesuch 7559-79254-2.
...Histoire du Tango[ab]. Five Pieces[b]. Six Etudes tanguistiques[a]. [a]**Mikael Helasvuo** (fl); [b]**Jukka Savijoki** (gtr). Ondine ODE781-2 (12/92).
...Asleep. *Coupled with works by* **Maraire, B. Johnston, Reich, Górecki, Riley, Crumb, Glass, Tahmizyan, Barber, Pärt, R. Scott, S. Johnson, Daugherty** and **Hendrix Dumisani Maraire** (ngoma/hosho); **Astor Piazzolla** (bandoneon); **Patty Manning, John Taylor, Larry Caballero** (vocs); **Djivan Gasparian** (duduk). **Kronos Quartet.** Nonesuch 7559-79394-2 (2/96). *See review in the Collections section; refer to the Index to Reviews.*

Giovanni Picchi

Suggested listening ...
...Balli – Ballo ongaro, Ballo alla polacha, Ballo ditto il Picchi. *Coupled with works by* **Trabaci, A. Mayone, Giovanni de Macque, Facoli, A. Valente, Buono, Frescobaldi, Lambardo, Merula, M. Rossi, Salvatore, B. Storace, G. Strozzi, Stradella** and **A. Scarlatti Rinaldo Alessandrini** (hpd). Opus 111 OPS30-118 (4/95). ✄ *See review in the Collections section; refer to the Index to Reviews.*

Niccolò Piccinni

New review
Piccinini Intavolutura di liuto et di chitarrone libro primo. **Nigel North** (lte/theorbo). Arcana Ⓟ A06 (75 minutes: DDD: 8/95). Recorded 1994.
The nomenclature of early instruments being littered with false trails, the chitarrone in fact has nothing to do with the guitar. It is a large lute with an extended headstock to handle its many strings, and is taller than most of those who play it and looks like something made for transmitting radio or television signals; unwisely used, it is also a short cut to backache or a dislocated shoulder. It is possible to see one 'walking' on-stage, yet be unable to see the player! The instrument was first developed for the purpose of accompanying songs (it was so used by Caccini among others), but later acquired a small solo repertory of its own, similar in style and genre to that of the keyboard music of the time – toccatas, canzonas, dances and sets of variations. The archlute, whose repertory was similar, was rather shorter – but still potentially hazardous! For all practical purposes we can regard them both as very large lutes. Alessandro Piccinini (1566-c1638) played an important role in the development of both instruments and their repertory; his published book of 1623 is both a tutor, with explicit directives concerning style, and the source of many fine pieces, including some for two or three lutes. The music on this recording is most rewarding, not least the varied toccatas, of which the *Toccata cromatica* is particularly adventurous. North, aided by commanding technique (and superb recording), brings it vividly to life. Strongly recommended to all lovers of the lute family and/or the music of the period.

Wenzel Pichl

Bohemian 1741-1805

...Symphonies – D major, "Mars"; B flat major, Op. 1 No. 5; D major, Op. 17. Symphonie concertante in D major, "Apollo", Op. 6. **Oradea Philharmonic Orchestra / Romeo Rimbu.** Olympia Explorer Series OCD434 (5/94).

Gabriel Pierné

French 1863-1937

Suggested listening ...
...Violin Sonata, Op. 36. *Coupled with* **Ravel** Violin Sonatas. **Debussy** Violin Sonata. **Gérard Poulet** (vn); **Noël Lee** (pf). Arion Ⓕ ARN68228 (9/94). *Gramophone Editor's choice. See review under Ravel; refer to the Index to Reviews.*
...Pastorale, Op. 41 No. 1 (original version). *Coupled with works by* **Damase, Milhaud, Françaix, Ibert, Fauré, Debussy** and **Poulenc** Reykjavik Wind Quintet. Chandos CHAN9362 (10/95).
...Pastorale. *Coupled with* **Peeters** Suite, Op. 71. **Widor** Scherzo in E major, "La Chasse". **Malengreau** Symphonie de la Passion, Op. 20. **Guillou** Toccata. **John Scott Whiteley** (org). Priory PRCD487 (2/96).

Willem Pijper

Dutch 1894-1947

Pijper String Quartets – No. 1 in F minor (1914); No. 2 (1920); No. 3 (1923); No. 4 (1928); No. 5 (1946). **Schoenberg Quartet** (Janneke van der Meer, Wim de Jong, vns; Henk Guittart, va; Viola de Hoog, vc). Olympia Ⓕ OCD457 (67 minutes: DDD: 2/95). Recorded 1994.

Quartets by Willem Pijper have been available before, but the Olympia disc is the first complete recording; indeed, it may well be the first at all of No. 1. Roughly twice the length of any of its successors, the latter was written during Pijper's studies with Wagenaar. Prophetic as its muted scherzo is, the contrast between the late romanticism of this apprentice piece and its polytonal successors could scarcely be wider. Pijper's mature voice was never very distinctive, but there is no denying the quality of his impeccably crafted, compact designs. Although he was alive to most of the progressive trends current in 1920s Europe, impressionism proved the most durable for him. Debussian harmonies form the backdrop to the Third Quartet (1923), an engaging suite of dance fantasies, while Ravel was the inspiration for the Fourth (1928). The latter is Pijper's finest quartet, though the two completed movements of the unfinished Fifth, begun but set aside in 1946, show that he was still developing stylistically. The Schoenberg Quartet prove near ideal advocates for Pijper's cause.

Daniel Pinkham

American 1923

New review

Pinkham Serenades[a]. Symphonies Nos. 3 and 4. Sonata for Organ and Strings No. 3[b]. [a]**Maurice Murphy** (tpt); [b]**James David Christie** (org); **London Symphony Orchestra / James Sedares.** Koch International Classics Ⓕ 37179-2 (49 minutes: DDD: 8/95). Recorded 1994.

Daniel Pinkham's teachers amount to quite a roll-call: among them, Piston, Copland, Honegger, Barber; harpsichord with Wanda Landowska, organ with E. Power Biggs – and Nadia Boulanger. There's that name again, that presence. It's there in the music's very particular sensibilities – an unassuming craftsmanship, an underlying reserve, a Frenchness. There is little that one could characterize as specifically American about Pinkham's music. He does not sell his material wholesale. Even at its most extrovert, concision and discretion are the watchwords here. And yet, there is still a sense in which Pinkham is a playful personality. Within its carefully prescribed framework, *Serenades* for solo trumpet and wind ensemble is the music of inconsequential banter. Even the title is gently ironic. Maurice Murphy's trumpet (listen to his lovely relaxed manner and that unmistakable Black Dyke cornet-like timbre) is the life and soul of this party, loud and skittish, one of those voices with an exclamatory leap in every phrase. The symphonies are intricately plotted and deftly scored. Symphony No. 4 lives up to its subtitles – "Purling", "Pining", "Prancing" – and they in themselves tell you a great deal about the composer. He's a man who likes order, symmetry. He's fastidious by nature, even about his jokes – you could say he's a classicist at heart. His music is full of allusion to the same: a 'pining' aria whose underlying pulse is the very essense of *bel canto accompagnamento*; a 'prancing' finale which has everything to do with 'the dance'. Sonata No. 3 for organ and strings (originally organ and string quintet) is baroque through and through, the spirit of one age glimpsed from another, the spare, almost skeletal, registrations of the organ melding dream-like into the string texture. Only in the full-throated, Gothic gesture of the last bars does it appear to loom menacingly into our times. The case for Daniel Pinkham is well made in these vital, crisply recorded performances.

Further listening ...
...Christmas Cantata[a]. Advent Cantata[b]. Wedding Cantata[c]. Introduction, Nocturne and Rondo[d].
String Quartet[e]. [d]**William Buonocore** (mandolin); [d]**John Curtis** (gtr); [b]**Carol Baum** (hp); [c]**Barbara
Bruns** (pf); [b]**Ariel Wind Quintet**; [e]**Boston Composers Quartet** (Clayton Hoener, Mark Beaulieu,
vns; Scott Woolweaver, va; Andrew Mark, vc); [a]**Lennox Brass**; [abc]**Boston Cecilia / Donald Teeters**
with [a]**James David Christie** (org). Koch International Classics 37180-2 (1/94).

George Pinto   British 1785-1806

Suggested listening ...
...Three Scenes from Childhood. *Coupled with* **Prokofiev** Piano Concerto No. 3 in C major,
Op. 26. Toccata in C major, Op. 11. **Rachmaninov** Piano Concerto No. 1 in F sharp minor,
Op. 1. **Byron Janis** (pf); **Moscow Philharmonic Orchestra / Kyrill Kondrashin**. Mercury 434
333-2MM (7/94).   ⓖⓖ
...Piano Sonatas, Op. 3 – No. 1 in E flat minor; No. 2 in A major. Grand Sonata in C minor (1803).
Fantasia and Sonata in C minor, Op. posth. **Riko Fukuda** (fp). Olympia Explorer Series OCD494
(4/96). ✏

Diego Pisador   Spanish 1509/10-after 1557

Suggested listening ...
...Libro de música – En la fuente del rosel; La manana de Sant Juan. *Coupled with works by*
D. Ortiz, Encina, Anonymous, Narváez, Vásquez and **Mudarra** La Romanesca / José
Miguel Moreno (vihuela). Glossa GCD920203 (5/96). ✏ *See review in the Collections section;
refer to the Index to Reviews.*   ⓖ

Johann Pisendel   Bohemian 1687-1755

New review
Pisendel Violin Concerto in D major. Sonata in C minor.
Zelenka Hipocondrie a 7 in A major. Concerto a 8 in G major. Sinfonia a 8 in A minor. Freiburg
Baroque Orchestra / Gottfried von der Goltz (vn). Deutsche Harmonia Mundi ⓑ 05472 77339-2
(64 minutes: DDD: 10/95). ✏ Recorded 1994.
The Freiburg Baroque Orchestra have here chosen several fascinating pieces by Pisendel and
Zelenka. Both composers were closely associated with the Dresden court during the first half of the
eighteenth century, Pisendel eventually becoming leader of the excellent court orchestra in 1730.
Pisendel's surviving compositions are few – hardly a dozen concertos by him are known, but these
show him to have been a skilled orchestrator and an imaginative composer for his own instrument,
the violin. Zelenka's instrumental music will be much more familiar to readers. Like Pisendel, his
legacy is modest, the greater part by far of what survives being sacred vocal music. Of the two styles,
Zelenka's is much the more quirky and distinctive. He was a master of the *Gruppenkonzert* or
concerto with two or more concertino instruments, often dissimilar. The three works included in this
programme demonstrate that mastery, with colourful writing for pairs of oboes, bassoon and violin.
These Freiburgers seem to revel in the resonant sounds, eccentricities and often surprising harmonic
caprices which characterize these works. The playing has a spontaneous enthusiasm and a refreshing
exuberance tempered only by the observance of stylistic good taste. After the whimsical flourishes
of Zelenka, Pisendel's music sounds decidedly conventional; yet it may well be that on developing
acquaintance with the two styles that of Pisendel yields the greater satisfaction. His Violin Concerto
in D major, with two oboes, two horns, bassoon and strings, betrays his illustrious Italian
connections, above all in the tuttis, and possesses, furthermore, a slow movement of affecting beauty.
The violinist and director here gives a wonderfully virtuoso performance. The remaining Pisendel
composition, a Sonata for two oboes and strings in two short movements, is altogether slighter. A
captivating disc.
Additional recommendation ...
...Sonata. *Coupled with works by* **Heinichen, Dieupart, Fasch, Quantz** and **Veracini**
Cologne Musica Antiqua / Reinhard Goebel. Archiv Produktion ⓑ 447 644-2AH (70 minutes:
DDD: 1/96). ✏ *See review in the Collections section; refer to the Index to Reviews.*   ⓖ

Walter Piston   American 1894-1976

Piston The Incredible Flutist – Suite[a]. Fantasy for English Horn, Harp and Strings[b]. Suite for
Orchestra. Concerto for String Quartet, Wind Instruments and Percussion[c]. Psalm and Prayer of
David[d]. [a]**Scott Goff** (fl); [b]**Glen Danielson** (hn); [b]**Theresa Elder Wunrow** (hp); [c]**Juilliard Quartet**
(Robert Mann, Joel Smirnoff, vns; Samuel Rhodes, va; Joel Krosnick, vc); **Seattle Symphony**

^d**Chorale and Orchestra / Gerard Schwarz.** Delos Ⓔ DE3126 (68 minutes: DDD: 2/94). Recorded 1991-2.

Piston's most lovable score is heard in very fine fettle here. The circus comes and goes with panache, cheering crowds and obbligato dog right on cue. Gerard Schwarz's flutist fixes you with his limpid tone. However, it will always be known as the score with the Tango. Schwarz goes with the flow, the sway of the melody, but it can never linger long enough. The *Fantasy* enters darkened Elysian fields – Piston's lyricism sits well with this distinctive voice of sorrow and regret. We can trace their kinship right back to the composer's first published work – the orchestral *Suite* of 1929. At its heart is a long and intense pastorale: the cor anglais is there at the inception. Framing it, motoric syncopations carry us first to a kind of drive-by the blues with bar-room piano and Grappelli violin. The finale is essentially a fugal work-out: high-tech Hindemith. Cut to 1976 and Piston's very last work, the *Concerto*. Ten eventful minutes in which the imperative is once again pitted against the contemplative. The mixing of timbres is masterly, a fleck of woodwind or a brush of tambourine or antique cymbal speaking volumes. But at the centre of gravity is the Juilliard Quartet, moving in mysterious ways, leading on to a closing viola solo – another dark voice posing both unanswered question and valediction. In fact, the last words uttered here are those of the *Psalm and Prayer of David* – a rare vocal setting for Piston, and as such, refreshingly open, unhackneyed, unhieratical. Performance and recording values make the strongest possible case for the musical goods.

Piston Symphony No. 6. The Incredible Flutist – Suite. Three New England Sketches. **St Louis Symphony Orchestra / Leonard Slatkin.** RCA Victor Red Seal Ⓔ RD60798 (57 minutes: DDD: 1/92). Recorded 1989-90.   Ⓐ

The Incredible Flutist's title is perhaps misleading, for there is no solo flute part, and in fact the score consists of a series of short, attractive dance movements. The original music was written for a 1938 ballet: two years later Piston used about half the material for a concert suite which soon became quite popular. The *Three New England Sketches* date from 1959. They comprise "Seaside", a mostly peaceful, evocative essay, "Summer Evening", a wispy, delicate scherzo and "Mountains", whose very grand, portentous outer sections surround a central episode of busy counterpoint. Piston's Sixth Symphony is generally regarded as his best. Written in 1955, it is typically direct in expression, and has no programme. The first movement is very American in its suggestion of wide-open space and in its rhythmic irregularities. A quicksilver scherzo forms the second movement, and then a serene *Adagio* is followed by a cheerful finale, with strident brass, rushing strings, and bubbling woodwind. Leonard Slatkin always conducts music of his own country with great sympathy and insight, as he does here. His orchestra has exactly the right timbre, which is important in American repertoire of this kind, and the engineering is very good.

Ildebrando Pizzetti   Italian 1880-1968

Suggested listening ...
...String Quartets – A major; D major. **Lajtha Quartet.** Marco Polo 8 223722 (4/96).
...Messa di Requiem. Two Composizione corali. Three Composizione corali. **Danish National Radio Chamber Choir / Stefan Parkman.** Chandos CHAN8964 (5/92).

John Playford I   British 1623-1686

Suggested listening ...
...The English Dancing Master – Country Dance Collection. Musick's Delight on the Cithren, Restored and Refined – Collection for the Cithren. Musick's Recreation on the Lyra Viol. **Broadside Band / Jeremy Barlow.** Amon Ra CD-SAR28 (3/88).

Ignace Pleyel   Austrian/French 1757-1831

Suggested listening ...
...Sextet in E flat major. *Coupled with* **Mozart** Serenade No. 11 in E flat major, K375. Sextet in E flat major, KAnh183. **Mozzafiato / Charles Neidich** (cl). Sony Classical SK64306 (9/95). 🖎 *See review under Mozart; refer to the Index to Reviews.*

John Plummer   British c1418-c1484

Suggested listening ...
...Tota pulchra es. Anna mater matris Christi. *Coupled with works by* **Lambe, Davy** and **William, Monk of Stratford** The Sixteen / Harry Christophers. Collins Classics 1462-2 (3/96). *See review in the Collections section; refer to the Index to Reviews.*

Alo Põldmäe

Suggested listening ...
...Sonatina, Op. 9. *Coupled with* **Eespere** Trivium. **Mägi** Cantus and Processus. **Kangro** Idioms,
Op. 43*a*. **Sumera** For B.B.B. and his Friend. **Vähi** To His Highness Salvador D. **Tallinn
Camerata.** Finlandia 4509-95705-2 (5/95).

Manuel Ponce

New review
Ponce Piano Concerto[a]. Violin Concerto[b]. Concierto del sur[c]. [b]**Henryk Szeryng** (vn), [c]**Alfonso
Moreno** (gtr); [a]**Jorge Federico Osorio** (pf); [b]**Royal Philharmonic Orchestra,** [ac]**State of Mexico
Symphony Orchestra / Enrique Bátiz.** ASV Ⓔ CDDCA952 (78 minutes: DDD: 8/96). Item
marked [a] from CDDCA916 (1/96), [b]HMV EL270151-1 (8/85), [c]HMV ESD165105-1 (8/83).
Manuel Ponce has been called the "father of Mexican musical nationalism"; but in his Piano
Concerto (his first sizeable work) there is little, if any, trace of local colour. This is a showy,
conventional late-romantic work of the barnstorming variety, and despite a great deal of bravura
piano writing – Ponce himself was the soloist in its first performance in 1912 – its sound and fury
do not amount to much musically. Osorio (who made an agreeable record of Ponce's solo piano music
for ASV, listed below) is suitably exhibitionist: the orchestral sound is a bit shrill. By 1941, the year
of the *Concierto del sur*, Ponce's style had changed and matured, he having meanwhile studied in Paris
with Dukas; and this is one of the best guitar concertos in the repertory; its Mexican character is
evident in the festive finale. Moreno's performance is strong in urgency and intensity though it could
have had a greater sense of poetry in the *Andante*. Ponce's only other concerto, that for violin two
years later, is his best-known thanks to the championship of Szeryng, its dedicatee, and through the
inclusion in its melancholy second movement of references to his famous song *Estrellita* (whose rights
he had unwittingly surrendered to an astute publisher). Szeryng plays the virtuoso solo part – which
includes a lengthy cadenza, as does the guitar concerto – brilliantly, but in the acoustic of the
Mexican hall used for this mid-1980s recording the tuttis are somewhat thick and rowdy.

Further listening ...
...Sonatina meridional. Thème varié et finale. Sonata III. Variations and Fugue on "La Folia de
España". **Timo Korhonen** (gtr). Ondine ODE770-2 (7/92).
...Balada mexicana. Arrulladora. Tema mexicano variado. Romanza de amor. Preludio y Fuga
sobre un tema de Handel. Mazurkas Nos. 1, 2, 4-7 and 10. Scherzino mexicano. Gavota.
Intermezzo No. 1. Rapsodia cubana No. 1. **Jorge Federico Osorio** (pf). ASV CDDCA874 (5/95).
...Prelude y Fuga sobre un tema de Handel. Suite Cubana – Plenilunio. Cuatro danzas Mexicanas.
Intermezzo No. 1. Introduccíon, Preludio y Fuga sobre un tema de J.S. Bach. Malgré tout.
Scherzino Mexicano. Preludio y Fuga para la mano izquierda sola. Dos Estudios de Concierto.
Notturno. Balada Mexicana. **David Witten** (pf). Marco Polo 8 223609 (5/96).

Amilcare Ponchielli

Ponchielli La Gioconda. **Maria Callas** (sop) La Gioconda; **Fiorenza Cossotto** (mez) Laure
Adorno; **Pier Miranda Ferraro** (ten) Enzo Grimaldo; **Piero Cappuccilli** (bar) Barnaba; **Ivo Vinco**
(bass) Alvise Badoero; **Irene Companeez** (contr) La Cieca; **Leonardo Monreale** (bass) Zuane;
Carlo Forte (bass) A Singer, Pilot; **Renato Ercolani** (ten) Isepo, First Distant Voice; **Aldo Biffi**
(bass) Second Distant Voice; **Bonaldo Giaiotti** (bass) Barnabotto; **Chorus and Orchestra of La
Scala, Milan / Antonio Votto.** EMI mono Ⓜ CDS7 49518-2* (three discs: 167 minutes:
DDD: 2/88). Notes, text and translation included. From Columbia SAX2359/61 (11/60).
Recorded 1959.
Ponchielli's old warhorse has had a bad press in recent times, which seems strange in view of its
melodic profusion, his unerring adumbration of Gioconda's unhappy predicament and of the sensual
relationship between Enzo and Laura. But it does need large-scale and involved singing – just what it
receives here on this now historic set. Nobody could fail to be caught up in its conviction. Callas was
in good and fearless voice when it was made, with the role's emotions perhaps enhanced by the traumas
of her own life at the time. Here her strengths in declaiming recitative, her moulding of line, her response
to the text are all at their most arresting. Indeed she turns what can be a maudlin act into true tragedy.
Ferraro's stentorian ebullience is most welcome. Cossotto is a vital, seductive Laura. Cappuccilli gives
the odious spy and lecher Barnaba a threatening, sinister profile, whilst Vinco is a suitably implacable
Alvise. Votto did nothing better than this set, bringing out the subtlety of the Verdi-inspired scoring
and the charm of the "Dance of the Hours" ballet. The recording sounds excellent for its age.

Additional recommendations ...
...Soloists; **London Opera Chorus; Finchley Children's Music Group; National Philharmonic
Orchestra / Bruno Bartoletti.** Decca Ⓔ 414 349-2DH3 (three discs: 151 minutes: ADD: 7/85).
...Soloists; **Chorus and Orchestra of the Accademia di Santa Cecilia, Rome / Lamberto Gardelli.**
Decca Grand Opera Ⓜ 430 042-2DM3 (three discs: 155 minutes: ADD).

Gavriil Popov

New review

Popov Symphonies – No. 1, Op. 7[a]; No. 2, Op. 39, "Motherland[b]. [a]**Moscow State Symphony Orchestra;** [b]**USSR TV and Radio Symphony Orchestra / Gennadi Provatorov.** Olympia
Ⓔ OCD576 (78 minutes: [a]DDD/[b]ADD: 2/96). Item marked [a] recorded 1989, [b]1961. *Gramophone Editor's choice.*

Gavriil Popov is something of a mystery man of twentieth-century Russian music. His First Symphony was much admired by musicians including Shostakovich, to whose youthful, rebellious vigour it owes something in manner if not a great deal in idiom. The opening *Allegro energico* must rank as one of the most powerful symphonic movements to come out of Russia in the twentieth century, well able to hold its place beside Shostakovich and Prokofiev. The harmony is bitter, the rhythmic impetus relentless, the orchestration violent, the sense of form brilliant in its control of this harsh, compelling music. The *Largo* is a tormented piece of introspection, beautifully scored and enigmatic in mood; the finale is a scherzo and coda, balancing what has gone before with some passages that seem sardonic but which are genuinely absorbed into a glowing conclusion. The Soviet authorities, already in a state of muddle when he played it to them in 1932, were thrown into disarray. It *was* played, however, and was taken up in the West by conductors including Malko, Klemperer, Scherchen and Kleiber. We have heard too little of it since, and this fine performance should do much to awaken interest. Then came a Second Symphony, simpler in mood and written out of a deep sense of patriotism in the middle of the war. It is also excellently composed, and genuinely symphonic despite its fashioning out of film music. The first movement excludes wind and brass in a long, powerful exordium for strings and timpani. There follow a lively *Presto*, somewhat in *Petrushka* vein, a beautifully sustained *Largo*, and a cheerfully optimistic finale. No doubt with some relief, the authorities gave it a Stalin Prize in 1946. Two years later came Zhdanov and rejection. Popov's later career never really recovered. He drank himself to death, eventually, in 1972. It is only just that there should be so much passion and conviction in these performances, by a conductor who has clearly taken great trouble to master difficult music and convey his belief in it to his two orchestras.

David Popper

Suggested listening ...

...Fantasy on Little Russian songs, Op. 43. Serenade, Op. 54 No. 2. *Coupled with* **Cassadó** Dance of the Green Devil. **Bach** (trans. Rose) Suite in D major, BWV1068 – Air. **Schubert** Schwanengesang, D957 – Ständchen. **F. Schubert II** Bagatelle, Op. 13 No. 9. Die Biene. **Granados** Goyescas – Intermezzo. **Shostakovich** The gadfly, Op. 97 —Tarantella. **Ravel** Sites auriculaires – Habanera. **Debussy** Préludes, Book 1 – La fille aux cheveux de lin. **Senaillé** Violin Sonata No. 5 in D minor – Allegro spirituoso. **Vieuxtemps** 36 Etudes, Op. 48 – No. 24, Cantilena. **Barchet** Images de Menton – Boulevard de Garavan. **Offenbach** Danse bohémienne, Op. 28. **Rachmaninov** Vocalise, Op. 34 No. 14. **Gershwin** Short Story. **Maria Kliegel** (vc); **Raimund Havenith** (pf). Marco Polo 8 223403 (9/92). .

Boris Porena

Suggested listening ...

...Vivaldi. *Coupled with works by* **Morricone, Rota** and **Malipiero** I Solisti Italiani. Denon CO-78949 (10/95). *See review under Malipiero; refer to the Index to Reviews.*

Constanza Porta

Suggested listening ...

...Missa Ducalis – Sanctus; Agnus Dei. *Coupled with works by* **Tallis, Josquin, Desprez, Ockeghem, Manchicourt, G. Gabrieli** and **Striggio** Huelgas Ensemble / Paul van Nevel. Sony Classical Vivarte SK66261 (4/96). *See review in the Collections section; refer to the Index to Reviews.*

Cole Porter

Suggested listening ...

...Paris – Let's do it. Gay Divorce – Night and Day. Leave it to Me – My heart belongs to daddy. Miss Otis Regrets. Nymph Errant – The Physician. *Coupled with* **Britten** Four Cabaret songs[a]. When you're feeling like expressing your affection[a]. On this Island – As it is, plenty[a]. Blues (arr. Runswick)[b] – The Spider and the Fly; Blues; The clock on the wall; Boogie-Woogie. [a]**Jill Gomez** (sop); [a]**Martin Jones** (pf); [b]**instrumental ensemble**. Unicorn-Kanchana DKPCD9138 (9/93). *Gramophone Editor's choice. See review under Britten; refer to the Index to Reviews.*

Ⓖ

...Born to Dance – I've got you under my skin. Broadway Melody of 1940 – I concentrate on you. Can-Can – I love Paris; It's all right with me. Gay Divorce – Night and Day; After you. High Society – True Love. Jubilee – Just one of those things. Kiss me, Kate – So in Love am I. Paris – Let's Misbehave; Don't look at me that way. Red, Hot and Blue – Ridin' high. Rosalie – In the still of the night. Seven Lively Arts – Ev'ry time we say goodbye. Something to shout about – You'd be so nice to come to. **Dame Kiri Te Kanawa** (sop); **New World Philharmonic / Peter Matz.** EMI CDC5 55050-2 (7/94).

...Anything Goes. **Soloists; Ambrosian Chorus; London Symphony Orchestra / John McGlinn.** EMI CDC7 49848-2 (12/89). *Gramophone Award Winner 1990.*

...High Society – original film soundtrack. Capitol CDP793787-2.

Quincy Porter
American 1907-1966

Suggested listening ...
...Ukrainian Suite. *Coupled with* **Bloch** Concerti grossi Nos. 1 and 2. **San Diego Chamber Orchestra / Donald Barra.** Koch International Classics 37196-2 (12/94).

Francis Poulenc
French 1899-1963

Poulenc Les Biches[a]. Bucolique[b]. Pastourelle[b]. Matelote provençale[b] (all from ASD4067, 9/81). Les Mariés de la Tour Eiffel[c] – Discours; La baigneuse de Trouville. Suite française, d'après Claude Gervaise[c] (all from ASD2450, 6/69). Les animaux modèles[d] (ASD2316, 7/67). Sinfonietta[c]. Marches et un intermède[c] (both from ASD2450, 6/69). Concert champêtre[de]. Double Piano Concerto in D minor[df] (both from ASD517, 4/63). [e]**Aimée van de Wiele** (hpd); [f]**Francis Poulenc,** [f]**Jacques Février** (pfs); [a]**Ambrosian Singers;** [ab]**Philharmonia Orchestra,** [c]**Orchestre de Paris;** [d]**Paris Conservatoire Orchestra / Georges Prêtre.** EMI Rouge et Noir Ⓜ CZS7 62690-2 (two discs: 156 minutes: ADD/DDD: 3/92). Recorded 1962-80.

Now here's a bargain not to be missed – over two-and-a-half hours of the inimitably frothy art of Francis Poulenc crammed on to just two CDs. The highlight has to be Georges Prêtre's marvellous 1980 recording of the complete *Les Biches* ballet music: with the Philharmonia on sparkling form and a suitably lusty contribution from the Ambrosian Singers, it makes for deliciously inconsequential entertainment. This item, as well as a trio of shorter purely orchestral offerings (the graceful *Pastourelle*, cheeky *Matelote provençale* and sublimely haunting *Bucolique: Hommage à Marguerite Long*), are captured here in a stunningly vivid Abbey Road recording – unquestionably one of EMI's very finest early digital efforts. In fact, Prêtre directs proceedings with no little flair throughout, though the robust response of the two Paris-based groups may come as something of a shock after the silky refinement of our own Philharmonia. Vintage accounts of the winsomely skittish *Concert champêtre* (with harpsichordist Aimée van de Wiele) and elegant Concerto for two pianos (featuring Jacques Février and the composer himself) are joined by lively readings of the engagingly anachronistic *Suite française, Sinfonietta* and the rarely-heard wartime ballet *Les Animaux modèles.* This last item suffers most from orchestral imprecision (and is rather dully engineered into the bargain), though Poulenc's actual music is well worthy of further investigation: both outer tableaux ("Le petit jour" and "Le repos de midi") are supremely touching in their wistful nobility In sum, an irresistible package – and it's at mid price, too!

Additional recommendations ...
...Gloria[a]. Piano Concerto[b]. Les Biches – Ballet suite[c]. [a]**Norma Burrowes** (sop); [b]**Cristina Ortiz** (pf); **City of Birmingham Symphony Orchestra and** [a]**Chorus / Louis Frémaux.** EMI Ⓜ CDM7 69644-2 (62 minutes: ADD: 1/89).

...Sinfonietta. Aubade[a]. **Hahn** Le Bal de Béatrice d'Este – ballet suite. [a]**Julian Evans** (pf); **New London Orchestra / Ronald Corp.** Hyperion Ⓔ CDA66347 (64 minutes: DDD: 10/89).

Poulenc Piano Concerto[a]. Double Piano Concerto in D minor[b]. Organ Concerto in G minor[c]. [ab]**Pascal Rogé,** [b]**Sylviane Deferne** (pfs); [c]**Peter Hurford** (org); **Philharmonia Orchestra / Charles Dutoit.** Decca Ⓔ 436 546-2DH (60 minutes: DDD: 12/93). Recorded 1992.　　　Ⓖ

The Piano Concerto has the right blend of melodic and textural richness, wit and warmth in the hands of performers who understand the music well enough to bring out all its felicitous detail without exaggeration. The mood of its expansive first movement is more tender than usual here, with its incisive wit and spiky Stravinskian instrumentation being correspondingly less in evidence. But the music can take this approach, and the climaxes are not underplayed, while the ecstatically chorale-like music towards the end of the movement is done to perfection. In the gentle *Andante con moto,* Rogé and Dutoit are in their element, but here again the powerful passages also make their impact, while the romp of a finale has the right *joie de vivre.* The Double Piano Concerto comes over with great vivacity, with Deferne and Rogé (playing second piano) skilfully unanimous and crisply recorded. The Organ Concerto, recorded in St Alban's Cathedral, is also successful; Peter Hurford's mastery in Bach serves him well in its more darkly baroque aspects, but he is equally idiomatic in the uninhibitedly bouncy passages.

Additional recommendations ...

...Organ Concerto[a]. Concert champêtre[b]. Double Piano Concerto[c]. Piano Concerto[d]. Aubade[e].
[a]**Marie-Claire Alain** (org); [b]**Ton Koopman** (hpd); [cde]**François-René Duchable**, [c]**Jean-Philippe
Collard** (pfs); **Rotterdam Philharmonic Orchestra / James Conlon.** Erato Ⓑ 4509-95303-2
(two discs: 105 minutes: DDD).   Ⓖ

...Organ Concerto[a]. Concert champêtre[b]. Gloria[c]. **George Malcolm** ([a]org/[b]hpd); [ab]**Academy of St
Martin in the Fields / Iona Brown**; [c]**Sylvia Greenberg** (sop); [c]**Lausanne Pro Arte Chorus**; [c]**Suisse
Romande Chorus and Orchestra / Jesús López-Cobos.** Decca Enterprise Ⓜ 425 627-2DM
(73 minutes: ADD/DDD: 7/90).

...Double Piano Concerto[a]. Sonata for Piano Duet. Capriccio. L'embarquement pour Cythère.
Elégie. **Milhaud** Scaramouche. **Katia and Marielle Labèque** (pfs); [a]**Boston Symphony Orchestra /
Seiji Ozawa.** Philips Ⓕ 426 284-2PH (50 minutes: DDD: 8/91).

...Organ Concerto. *Coupled with works by* **Guilmant** and **Widor** Ian Tracey (org); BBC
Philharmonic Orchestra / Yan Pascal Tortelier. Chandos Ⓕ CHAN9271 (80 minutes: DDD:
11/94). *See review under Guilmant; refer to the index to Reviews.*   ⒼⒼ

...Double Piano Concerto. **Saint-Saëns** Le carnaval des animaux. **Güher and Süher Pekinel** (pfs);
French Radio Philharmonic Orchestra / Marek Janowski. Teldec Ⓜ 4509-97445-2 (38 minutes:
DDD: 2/96).

New review

Poulenc Sextet for Piano and Wind Quintet[a].
Milhaud La création du monde[b].
Saint-Saëns Septet in E flat major, Op. 65[c]. [a]**Elizabeth Mann** (fl); [a]**Stephen Taylor** (ob); [a]**David
Shifrin** (cl); [a]**Dennis Godburn** (bn); [a]**Richard Todd** (hn); [c]**Thomas Stevens** (tpt); [bc]**Ani Kavafian**,
[bc]**Julie Rosenfeld** (vns); [bc]**Toby Hoffman** (va); [bc]**Carter Brey** (vc); [c]**Jack Kulowitsch** (db); **André
Previn** (pf). RCA Victor Red Seal Ⓕ 09026 68181-2 (50 minutes: DDD: 11/95). Recorded 1993.
Predictably, one feels that Previn is the moving spirit behind these performances of three vivid French
pieces for biggish chamber ensembles, and that it is especially his *joie de vivre* that informs Poulenc's
sextet, where his charming solo at 2'13" in the first movement is just the first of many delights that
help us to forget that its construction is not of the tightest. His colleagues also deserve every credit,
and this crisply recorded account of the work is admirable, sparkling without glare. This version of
Milhaud's ballet score, *La création du monde*, is a five-movement suite for piano plus string quartet
that the composer made at his publisher's request. This is hard on its primitive elements, and indeed
is no substitute for the original, but the performers offer all the vigour and sexiness that they can and
it comes across well enough. After the uninhibited Poulenc and Milhaud, the programming of Saint-
Saëns makes one fear a let-down in musical temperature, but the composer of the *Carnival of the
Animals* had five years before already penned a jolly, witty and busy score in his Septet of 1881, whose
scoring includes a trumpet and double-bass. This is another sparkling performance and rounds off an
excellent, enterprising disc.

New review

Poulenc Capriccio[c]. Sonata for Two Pianos[c]. Elégie[c]. Sonata for Piano Duet[c]. L'embarquement
pour Cythère[c]. Violin Sonata[a]. Elégie[b]. [a]**Chantal Juillet** (vn); [b]**André Cazalet** (hn); **Pascal Rogé**,
[c]**Jean-Philippe Collard** (pfs). Decca Ⓕ 443-968-2DH (70 minutes: DDD: 10/95). Recorded
1989-94.   ⒼⒼ
Few records could be more haunting or thought-provoking than this. For the lasting and predominant
impression is of how Poulenc's music (generally celebrated for its café aplomb and insouciance) is so
frequently clouded by a sense of elegy, by an uneasy if richly fruitful truce between levity and despair.
The presence of two *Elégies*, and by implication, a third, is therefore hardly insignificant. Yet how
typical of Poulenc, given so sombre a setting, to ring the changes with infinite elegance and poetry.
The *Elégie* for horn and piano, composed in memory of Dennis Brain's tragic death in 1957, sounds
the darkest note, the *Elégie* for two pianos, on the other hand, is intended to evoke the aroma of
cognac and Gauloises, while the Violin and Piano Sonata's central "Intermezzo" and "Presto tragico"
luxuriantly and tersely recall the death of Federico Garcia Lorca, murdered by Franco's minions in
1936 for his combined liberalism and homosexuality. Elsewhere the light shines through.
L'embarquement pour Cythère is classic Poulenc, mischievously linking Watteau's painting of idealized
love and the comforting world of seaside chips, accordions and cheap perfume (both Watteau and
Poulenc were frequent holiday visitors to Nogent-sur-Marne). Here is witty and dazzling relief
indeed. Both performances and recording are superb. Pascal Rogé, who has the lion's share of the
proceedings, could hardly sound more authentically Gallic, more stylishly aware of the composer's
tears and laughter. Jean-Philippe Collard, Chantal Juillet and André Cazalet are distinguished
partners.

...Violin Sonata. *Coupled with* **Fauré** Violin Sonata No. 1 in A major, Op. 13. **Debussy** Violin
Sonata. **Isabelle van Keulen** (vn); **Ronald Brautigam** (pf). Koch Schwann Ⓕ 315272 (56 minutes:
DDD: 10/95).

...Violin Sonata. *Coupled with works by* **Debussy** and **Ravel** Tasmin Little (vn); **Piers Lane**
(pf). EMI Eminence Ⓜ CD-EMX2244 (61 minutes: DDD: 12/95). *Gramophone Editor's
choice.*   ⒼⒼ

Poulenc Les soirées de Nazelles. Deux Novelettes – No. 1 in C major; No. 2 in B flat minor. Novelette "sur un thème de M de Falla". Pastourelle (arr. pf). Trois mouvements perpétuels. Valse. 15 Improvisations – No. 1 in B minor; No. 2 in A flat major; No. 3 in B minor; No. 6 in B flat major; No. 7 in C major; No. 8 in A minor; No. 12 in E flat major, "Hommage à Schubert"; No. 13 in A minor; No. 15 in C minor, "Hommage à Edith Piaf". Trois Pièces. **Pascal Rogé** (pf). Decca Ⓕ 417 438-2DH (67 minutes: DDD: 7/87). Recorded 1986. *Gramophone Award Winner 1988. Selected by Sounds in Retrospect.*   ⒼⒼ

Poulenc Humoresque. Nocturnes. Suite in C major. Thème varié. 15 Improvisations – No. 4 in A flat major; No. 5 in A minor; No. 9 in D major; No. 10 in F major, "Eloge des gammes"; No. 11 in G minor; No. 14 in D flat major. Two Intermezzos. Intermezzo in A flat major. Villageoises. Presto in B flat major. **Pascal Rogé** (pf). Decca Ⓕ 425 862-2DH (63 minutes: DDD: 4/91). Recorded 1989.   Ⓐ

These beautifully recorded and generously filled discs offer a rich diversity of Poulenc's output. On the first disc, the masterly *Soirées de Nazelles* were improvised during the early 1930s at a country house in Nazelles as a memento of convivial evenings spent together with friends. It paints a series of charming portraits – elegant, witty and refined. The *Trois mouvements perpétuels* are, like so many of the works represented here, lighthearted and brief, improvisatory in flavour and executed with a rippling vitality. The *Improvisations* constantly offer up echoes of the piano concertos with their infectious rhythmic drive – the "Hommage à Schubert" is a tartly classical miniature in three-time played with just the right amount of nonchalant ease by Pascal Rogé. The "Hommage à Edith Piaf" is a lyrical and touching tribute – obviously deeply felt. The *Humoresque* which opens the second recital is open-air and open-hearted in style, yet songlike too in its melodic richness. The simplicity of this music is deceptive, as is that of the warmly caressing C major Nocturne that follows, for both pieces need subtle phrasing, rubato and the kind of textures only obtainable through the most refined use of the sustaining pedal. Rogé has these skills, and he is also fortunate in having an excellent piano at his disposal as well as a location (the Salle Wagram in Paris) that gives the sound the right amount of reverberation. There are many delights in this music and the way it is played here: to mention just one, listen to the masterly way that the composer and pianist together gradually bring around the flowing freshness of the C major Nocturne towards the deeply poignant feeling of the close. Both discs hold the listener's attention effortlessly from one piece to the next, and though suitable for any time of day they make perfect late-night listening. They should especially delight, and to some extent reassure, anyone who deplores the absence of charm and sheer romantic feeling in much of our century's music.

Additional recommendations ...

...Suite in C major. Les Biches – Adagietto. Trois mouvements perpétuels. Les soirées de Nazelles. Intermezzo No. 3 in A flat major. Valse-improvisation sur le nom de Bach. Trois Pièces. Badinage. Napoli. **Eric Parkin** (pf). Chandos Ⓕ CHAN8637 (59 minutes: DDD: 10/88).

...Humoresque. Deux Novelettes. Novelette "sur un thème de M de Falla". Villageoises. 15 Improvisations. Intermezzos – No. 1 in C major; No. 2 in D flat major. Suite française. Presto. Mélancolie. Thème varié. **Eric Parkin** (pf). Chandos Ⓕ CHAN8847 (72 minutes: DDD: 12/90).

New review

Poulenc Un soir de neige. Chansons françaises. Sept chansons. Chanson à boire. Petites voix. Figure humaine. **New London Chamber Choir / James Wood.** Hyperion Ⓕ CDA66798 (67 minutes: DDD: 12/95). Texts and translations included. Recorded 1995.

Except for the charming miniature *Petites voix*, all the works here exist in recordings by The Sixteen, whose performances have rightly been much praised. But the versatile James Wood and his choir have never shrunk from challenges, and they give The Sixteen a good run for their money. Poulenc's unaccompanied secular choral works, which demand virtuoso choirs, evidently hold no terrors for them. The major work here is the wartime *Figure humaine*, whose finale, "Liberté", became an inspiration to the Resistance movement. The choir at once impresses by the vividness with which it treats words and by its intelligent verbal phrasing (though some vowels, especially nasal ones, are not entirely native-sounding): it commands a wide dynamic range, thrilling at climaxes, with perceptive tonal nuances; and the chording of the difficult chromaticisms is commendably assured. The most characteristic movement of the cantata, "Toi ma patiente", is beautifully shaped, and the final cadence of "En chantant" is perfectly 'placed', thanks to the bright-voiced sopranos. In faster-moving pieces The Sixteen are rather neater, but the New London's accelerating passion in "Liberté" is scarifying, and the final cry (complete with a blood-curdling top E) is overwhelming. The other wartime work, *Un soir de neige*, is finely moulded throughout, with a movingly deep appreciation of its melancholy contemplation. These all illustrate the serious side of Poulenc. In the earlier *Sept chansons* there is a mixture of moods, which are well caught, though the nimble "Marie" could have been cleaner. There is energy in plenty and obvious enjoyment in the performance of the eight folk-song arrangements, especially "Les tisserands", but also quiet pathos in "La belle se sied au pied de la tour".

Poulenc Le travail du peintre.
Fauré Songs, Op. 18 – No. 2, Le voyageur; No. 3, Automne. Le secret, Op. 23 No. 3. Chanson
d'amour, Op. 27 No. 1. Songs, Op. 39 – No. 1, Aurore; No. 2, Fleur jetée. Clair de lune, Op. 46
No. 2. Spleen, Op. 51 No. 3. Cinq mélodies, Op. 58. Prison, Op. 83 No. 1.
Ravel Cinq mélodies populaires grecques. Don Quichotte à Dulcinée. **Thomas Allen** (bar); **Roger
Vignoles** (pf). Virgin Classics Ⓕ VC5 45053-2 (57 minutes: DDD: 5/95). Texts and translations
included. Recorded 1993.

The glory of this CD is Allen and Vignoles's performance of Poulenc's *Le travail du peintre*. This is a
very difficult cycle to bring off with success – to begin with, as Pierre Bernac who first sang it notes
in his book on Poulenc's songs, it is *ff* or *f* nearly all the way through – of course this makes the
occasional soft phrase all the more heart-stopping. In the opening "Picasso", Allen is marvellous at
the words "Et des murs innombrables croulent" ("And numberless walls crumble"). The swift
"Chagall", the charmingly lyrical "Braque" – Poulenc thought this was the most subtle – the slow and
mysterious "Gris", with its pre-echo of Mère Marie's theme from *Carmélites* (this was the first of the
songs Poulenc sketched, before work on the opera was complete) all work perfectly. Poulenc wrote
that *Le travail du peintre* is "more than ever a duo where the material for voice and piano is closely
integrated", and he added that there is "no question of 'an accompaniment'". So, a duet it is, and
Vignoles provides his half to the full. What a subtle wit and extraordinary mind Poulenc had – who
else can one imagine evoking modern paintings in such a way? The gentle melancholy of Fauré's "En
sourdine", the dance-like "Mandoline" and especially the ardent "Green" all bring out the most
lyrical qualities in Allen's voice. These songs seem to suit him better than the preceding group of
Fauré settings of three other Verlaine poems, contrasted with five by Armand Silvestre. In particular
"Fleur jetée" calls for more red-blooded passion. The exception is the *Winterreise*-like "Le voyageur"
which Allen does splendidly, with its opening question, "Voyageur, où vas-tu?". In Ravel's five settings
of traditional Greek songs, Allen is very successful in the fourth, the song of the Lentisk gatherers,
but like other baritones who have recorded this group, the quicksilver quality eludes him in "Réveille-
toi" and "Tout gai". Ravel composed these settings for soprano voice. Conversely, his personality is
perfect for *Don Quichotte* and in this, Ravel's final work, Roger Vignoles provides the most
wonderfully playful accompaniment to the opening "Chanson romanesque".

Additional recommendation ...
...Le travail du peintre. Chansons gaillardes. Tel jour, telle nuit. Cinq Poèmes d'Eluard. **Bernard
Kruysen** (bar); **Noël Lee** (pf). Arion ARN68258 (45 minutes: ADD: 3/94).

Poulenc Le Bestiaire ou Cortège d'Orphée. Cocardes. Poèmes de Louise Lalanne. A sa guitare. Tel
jour, telle nuit. Miroirs brûlants – Tu vois le feu du soir. Banalités. Métamorphoses. Voyage. Le
Souris. La Dame de Monte-Carlo. **Felicity Lott** (sop); **Graham Johnson** (pf). Forlane
Ⓕ UCD16730 (64 minutes: DDD: 8/94). Texts and translations included. Recorded 1994.

This programme of Poulenc *mélodies* is perfectly chosen and balanced. Juxtaposing song cycles and
single numbers from the whole of Poulenc's career, putting them in chronological order, it highlights
the extreme modernity of Poulenc's choice of poetry with his universal appeal as a songwriter. *Le
Bestiaire* from 1918, to Apollinaire's verses, is his earliest substantial group and it is remarkable how
vivid and strong the Poulenc sound already was, when he was just 19. Of the three early Cocteau
settings, *Cocardes*, Poulenc said he wanted "the smell of French fried, the accordion, Piver perfume"
– once one has that in mind, both pianist and singer do splendidly, with lines such as "Lionoléum en
trompe-l'oeil. Merci. Cinéma, nouvelle muse". *Tel jour, telle nuit* was, of course, one of the great cycles
composed for Pierre Bernac but the brighter colours of Lott's voice make it more romantic than, for
instance, Souzay's interpretation. Graham Johnson as accompanist is the worthy successor to Dalton
Baldwin and the composer himself as the perfect interpreter of Poulenc's *mélodies*.

Additional recommendations ...
...Le bal masqué[a]. Le Bestiaire ou Cortège d'Orphée[a]. Trio for Oboe, Bassoon and Piano. Piano
and Wind Sextet. [a]**Thomas Allen** (bar); **Nash Ensemble**. CRD CRD3437 Ⓕ (55 minutes: DDD:
10/86).
...La courte paille. Banalités – Hôtel; Voyage à Paris. Métamorphoses – C'est ainsi que tu es.
Poèmes – Fêtes galantes. A sa guitare. *Coupled with* **Satie** Trois mélodies. **Debussy** Ariettes
oubliées. Fêtes galantes, Set 1. **Honegger** Petit cours de morale, H148. **Ravel** Cinq mélodies
populaires grecques. **Messiaen** Pourquoi? Le sourire. La fiancée perdue. **Frederica von Stade**
(mez); **Martin Katz** (pf). RCA Victor Red Seal Ⓔ 09026 62711-2 (70 minutes: DDD: 4/95).

New review
Poulenc Gloria. Stabat mater. **Janice Watson** (sop); **BBC Singers; BBC Philharmonic Orchestra /
Yan Pascal Tortelier**. Chandos Ⓕ CHAN9341 (56 minutes: DDD: 8/95). Texts and translations
included. Recorded 1994.

We are immediately struck, at the start of the *Gloria*, by the radiantly warm but clean orchestral
sonority: only later does an uneasy suspicion arise that, apparently seduced by the sound, the
recording engineers may be favouring it at the expense of the chorus, especially at orchestral *fortes*
(this is more evident in the *Gloria* than the *Stabat mater*, for example at the burst of joy of "Domine
Fili unigenite"). But it is committed and thoroughly secure choral singing, perhaps most easily

appreciated in some of the unaccompanied passages – tender in the almost mystic "O quam tristis" and firm-toned at "Fac ut ardeat" (both in the *Stabat mater*); it gives real attack at "Quis est homo" (just holding its own against the orchestra); the sopranos can produce a bright, ringing tone; and only the very first line of the *Stabat mater*, lying low in the basses, needed to be a bit stronger (as in most performances). Janice Watson is a sweet-voiced soloist with very pure intonation; but she could with advantage have strengthened her consonants throughout. Tortelier gives intensely felt readings of both works – the murmurous ending of the *Stabat mater* and the thrilling *fortissimo* chords at "Quoniam" in the *Gloria* spring to mind – and fortunately he keeps the vocal "Domine Deus" entry moving at the same pace as at its introduction (a debatable moment in the Hickox version). He takes the Stravinskian "Laudamus te" fast and lightly; the only questionable speed is of "Quae moerebat", which sounds too cheerful for the words ("mourning and lamenting"). Taken all in all, these are performances of undoubted quality.

Additional recommendations ...

...Gloria[a]. Stabat mater[a]. Litanies à Vierge noire. [a]**Catherine Dubosc** (sop); **Westminster Singers; City of London Sinfonia / Richard Hickox.** Virgin Classics Ⓕ VC7 59286-2 (68 minutes: DDD: 2/93).

...Gloria[a]. Stabat mater[a]. Litanies à la vierge noire[b]. [a]**Françoise Pollet** (sop); [a]**French Radio Choir;** [b]**Maîtrise de Radio France; French National Orchestra / Charles Dutoit.** Decca Ⓕ 448 139-2DH (62 minutes: DDD: 4/96).

Poulenc Mass in G major. Quatre motets pour le temps de Noël. Quatre petites prières de Saint François d'Assise. Quatre motets pour un temps de pénitence. Laudes de Saint Antoine de Padoue. Salve regina. Ave verum corpus. Exultate Deo. **Trinity College Choir, Cambridge / Richard Marlow.** Conifer Ⓕ CDCF151 (70 minutes: DDD: 10/88). Texts and translations included. ⒼⒼ

The lusciously chromatic harmony of the Mass in G major can easily cloy but the bright, radiant textures of the singing of the Trinity College Choir avoids this entirely. Readers unfamiliar with this work will be surprised how potent it is. The *Ave verum corpus* for high high voices is quite exquisite and in the St Francis *Prières* Marlow is assured and musically aware. The choir does, however, produce occasional curious French pronunciation, with some very odd mute "e"s. An interesting personal sidelight on these graceful and expressive pieces for male voices is revealed by the dedication to Frère Jérome of Champfleury "in memory of his grandfather, my uncle Camille Poulenc". The interpretation of the Penitential Motets is very dramatic and the short motet *Salve regina* is graceful and serene. Caution needs to be taken not to listen to too many of these works – virtually entirely homophonic, and nearly all characterized by Poulenc's special brand of tartly sweet harmonies – one after the other. The performances, with fine balance, expressive dynamic shadings, pure intonation, intelligent phrasing and excellent enunciation, are very impressive. Marlow, of course, is operating on home ground, in the almost ideal acoustics of Trinity College Chapel in Cambridge. The accompanying notes are interesting and informative.

Additional recommendations ...

...Gloria[ab]. Salve regina. Ave verum corpus. Exultate Deo. Litanies à la Vierge Noire[b]. Quatre motets pour un temps de pénitence[c]. Quatre motets pour le temps de Noël. [a]**Donna Deam,** [c]**Mary Seers** (sops); **Cambridge Singers;** [b]**City of London Sinfonia / John Rutter.** Collegium Ⓕ COLCD108 (67 minutes: DDD: 10/88).

...Figure humaine. Quatre motets pour un temps de pénitence. Laudes de Saint Antoine de Padoue. Quatre motets pour le temps de Noël. Quatre petites prières de Saint François d'Assise. **The Sixteen / Harry Christophers.** Virgin Classics Ⓕ VC7 59192-2 (62 minutes: DDD: 3/90).

...Mass. Quatre petites prières. Salve regina. **Martin** Mass for double chorus. **Christ Church Cathedral Choir, Oxford / Stephen Darlington.** Nimbus Ⓕ NI5197 (59 minutes: DDD: 12/89).

...Mass[d]. Salve regina. **Fauré** Requiem (revised version)[a]. Cantique de Jean Racine, Op. 11[b]. Messe basse[c]. [ad]**Jonathon Bond,** [c]**Andrew Brunt** (trebs); [a]**Benjamin Luxon** (bar); [abc]**Stephen Cleobury** (org); [a]**Academy of St Martin in the Fields; Choir of St John's College, Cambridge / George Guest.** Decca Ovation Ⓜ 430 360-2DM (74 minutes: ADD: 9/91).

...Mass. Salve regina. Ave verum corpus. Exultate Deo. Un soir de neige. Chansons françaises. Chanson à boire. Sept Chansons. **The Sixteen / Harry Christophers.** Virgin Classics Ⓕ VC7 59311-2 (69 minutes: DDD: 12/93).

...Mass in G major. Salve regina. Exultate Deo. Litanies à la vierge noire. *Coupled with works by* **Duruflé** and **Fauré** Soloists; **St John's College Choir, Cambridge; Academy of St Martin in the Fields / George Guest** with **Stephen Cleobury** (org). Double Decca Ⓜ 436 486-2DF2 (two discs: 149 minutes: ADD: 7/94). *See review under Duruflé; refer to the Index to Reviews.* Ⓖ

New review

Poulenc Mass in G major. Quatre motets pour un temps de pénitence. Quatre motets pour le temps de Noël. Exultate Deo. Salve regina. **Berlin RIAS Chamber Choir / Marcus Creed.** Harmonia Mundi Ⓕ HMC90 1588 (52 minutes: DDD: 8/96). Texts and translations included. ⒼⒼ

We seem to be in danger of becoming spoilt by the number of fine recordings of Poulenc's *a cappella* religious works; but this latest disc bids fair to go to the top of the list of contenders. There has never been a more beautiful performance of the *Salve regina*. And elsewhere this virtuoso choir display, beyond impeccably pure intonation and chording (chorus-masters everywhere will note with envy the sopranos' clean, dead-sure attacks on high notes), a sensitivity to verbal meaning, dynamics and vocal colour that argues not only skilful direction but a complete ease and absorption into the music's often chromatic nature by all the singers. They bring a bright-eyed tone to the *Exultate Deo*, awe to "O magnum mysterium" (in the Christmas motets), and a striking diversity of timbre to "Tristis est anima mea" (in the penitential motets); in the Mass they interpret to perfection the *doucement joyeux* indication of the *Sanctus*. Like the Shaw Singers listed below, they appear to have been recorded in some large church, but without the problems of resonance occasionally found in that earlier issue: words are extremely clear throughout. (If one were to be ultra-critical, one might feel, in the Christmas motets, that words were being separated rather too much.) The excellent Westminster Cathedral disc contains the *Litanies à la vierge noire* and the *Petites prières* in addition to the same programme as here; but it has something of a preponderance of the treble voices, and here the use of women rather than boys results in a more sophisticated tone and a truer internal balance. A first-class disc.

Additional recommendations ...

...Mass[a]. Quatre motets pour le temps de Noël. Quatre motets pour un temps de pénitence. Quatre petites prières[b]. [a]**Donna Carter** (sop); [b]**Christopher Cock** (ten); **Robert Shaw Festival Singers / Robert Shaw.** Telarc Ⓕ CD80236 (52 minutes: DDD: 10/90).

...Mass[a]. Quatre petites prières. Quatre motets pour un temps de pénitence[b]. Quatre motets pour le temps de Noël. Salve regina. Exultate Deo. Litanies à la vierge noire[c]. [a]**Mark Kennedy,** [b]**Eamonn O'Dwyer** (trebs); **Westminster Cathedral Choir / James O'Donnell,** with [c]**Ian Simcock** (org). Hyperion Ⓕ CDA66664 (70 minutes: DDD: 6/94).

Poulenc Dialogues des Carmelites. **Catherine Dubosc** (sop) Blanche de la Force; **Rachel Yakar** (sop) Madame Lidoine; **Rita Gorr** (mez) Madame de Croissy; **Brigitte Fournier** (sop) Soeur Constance; **Martine Dupuy** (mez) Mère Marie; **José van Dam** (bass-bar) Marquis de la Force; **Jean-Luc Viala** (ten) Chevalier de la Force; **Michel Sénéchal** (ten) L'Aumônier; **François Le Roux** (bar) Le geôlier; **Lyon Opéra Chorus and Orchestra / Kent Nagano.** Virgin Classics Ⓕ VCD7 59227-2 (two discs: 152 minutes: DDD: 9/92). Notes, text and translation included. *Gramophone Award Winner 1993.*   ⓖⓖ

Once more in a work out of the ordinary (following that given to them in 1990 for Prokofiev's *Love for Three Oranges*) the dedication of Kent Nagano and his Opéra de Lyon forces resulted in the 1993 *Gramophone* Record Award for best opera recording. Poulenc's chef d'oeuvre is one of the few operas written since *Wozzeck* that has survived in the repertory – and deservedly so. It is written from, and goes to, the heart, not in any extrovert or openly histrionic way but by virtue of its ability to explore the world of a troubled band of Carmelite nuns at the height of the terrors caused by the French Revolution, and do so in an utterly individual manner. Poulenc unerringly enters into their psyches as they face their fatal destiny. Nagano responds keenly to the sombre, elevated mood and intensity of Poulenc's writing and unfailingly delineates the characters of the principals as they face their everyday martyrdom. The magisterial authority of Martine Dupuy's Mère Marie, the agony of Rita Gorr's Old Prioress, the inner torment of Catherine Dubosc's Sister Blanche, the restraint of Rachel Yakar's Madame Lidoine, the eager charm of Brigitte Fournier's Sister Constance are only the leading players in a distribution that is admirable in almost every respect. The score is for once given complete. The recording is atmospheric and suggests stage action without exaggeration.

Poulenc La voix humaine[a].
Cocteau Le bel indifférent[b]. [a]**Denise Duval** (sop) La Femme; [b]**Edith Piaf** (spkr); [a]**Paris Opéra-Comique Orchestra / Georges Prêtre;** [b]**instrumental ensemble.** EMI L'Esprit Français Ⓜ CDM5 65156-2* (69 minutes: ADD: 10/94). Item marked [a] from Vox OPL160 (8/63), recorded 1959, [b]recorded 1953, new to UK.

Auteuil 04 virgule 7 is on the line again. But one shouldn't make jokes. Poor woman, the situation is real and dreadful, with Cocteau's script never betraying itself into the cheapness which lies waiting, available at the drop of a word or a receiver, and with the music capturing mood, pace and development in such sympathy with the text that one marvels both were not written by the same man. It conjures up the image of her agonized one-sided conversation, over a maddeningly frustrating telephone line, as a woman driven suicidal by her lover's desertion for another woman. Imagination, of course, can do much on its own, as it certainly did with the original singer, Denise Duval, for whom the role was written, whose performance, skilfully judged and varied, provides a genuine dramatic experience. She is incomparably sure in her feeling for the idiom, and Prêtre, who conducted the première, is a strong ally, never over-indulgent in the sickly-sweet torments of memory and desire, but keeping the piece moving and rightly tense. The recording took full advantage of the then recent advent of stereo, so that the singer carries the telephone across from (perhaps) table to bed, in a way that might now be found disconcerting or too self-conscious a feature of production. It is coupled here with another Cocteau monologue-play, but this time in its original form. *Le bel indifférent* was a *tour de force* for Edith Piaf, and the recording magnificently catches her in all her moods, sardonic, murderous or tearful. EMI may be congratulated on the issue; not, however, on its presentation, which is quite inadequate. In both pieces it is essential that the listener should be able to understand the French text and no printed texts are given.

...La voix humaine. **Françoise Pollet** (sop) La Femme; **Lille National Orchestra / Jean-Claude Casadesus.** Harmonia Mundi Ⓔ HMC90 1474 (46 minutes: DDD: 7/94).

New review

Poulenc Les mamelles de Tirésias[a]. **Denise Duval** (sop) Thérèse, Fortune-teller; **Marguérite Legouhy** (mez) Marchande de journaux, Grosse Dame; **Jean Giraudeau** (ten) Husband; **Emile Rousseau** (bar) Policeman; **Robert Jeantet** (bar) Director; **Julien Thirache** (bar) Presto; **Frédéric Leprin** (ten) Lacouf; **Serge Rallier** (ten) Journalist; **Jacques Hivert** (sngr) Son; **Gilbert Jullia** (sngr) Monsieur Barbu; **Chorus and Orchestra of the Opéra-Comique, Paris / André Cluytens.**
Poulenc Le bal masqué[b]. **Jean-Christoph Benoit** (bar); **Maryse Charpentier** (pf); **Paris Conservatoire Orchestra / Georges Prêtre.** EMI L'Esprit Français [a]mono/[b]stereo Ⓜ CDM5 65565-2* (70 minutes: ADD: 12/95). Item marked [a] from Columbia 33CX1218 (2/55, recorded 1953), [b]HMV ASD2296 (1/67, recorded 1965).

If you have never hunted elephants "the Zanzibar way", now could be the time to start. Apollinaire's play, written in the 1900s, did not reach the stage until 1917. Poulenc was at the first performance – which gave the word "sur-réaliste" to the language – but he did not compose the opera until 25 years later, during the Second World War. *Les mamelles de Tirésias* is Poulenc's *Così fan tutte*; the story is absurd, naïve, although the puns and rhymes of Apollinaire's poetry are a constant delight. (Mostly untranslatable, Thérèse-française-fraises-Zanzibaraise, it goes on throughout the piece.) What Poulenc has done is to express a whole range of deep emotion in the music, the homesickness of the exile, the longing for children, the mystery of masculine/feminine desires. He described the music as "producing laughter while still allowing tenderness and real lyricism". Poulenc found his ideal interpreter in Denise Duval, who created the role of Thérèse in 1947, and went on to sing it wherever the opera was given right up until the time of its first American (concert) performance in 1960. Duval combines the "wild touch of vaudeville", as Ned Rorem put it, with her typically forward, slightly nasal, French soprano. "The work that is dearest to me" was how Poulenc described *Mamelles* at the time of this recording in 1953, and he judged Cluytens's conducting "sensational" and wrote, "it is one of the greatest joys of my life". What can one add? It is one of the greatest recordings of French opera, unchallenged and unsurpassed for 40 years. The filler, Poulenc's early cantata *Le bal masqué* is an ephemeral work, but it is done with style and vigour by Jean-Christoph Benoit and Prêtre. No libretto, nor even a synopsis, is included with this CD, which seems an even greater shame than usual, since the text is of such a complicated pattern. Highly recommended, nevertheless.

...Oboe Sonata. L'invitation au château. Villanelle[e]. Sonata for Two Clarinets. Trio for Oboe, Bassoon and Piano. Sextet for Piano and Wind Quintet. Clarinet and Bassoon Sonata. Rapsodie nègre. Clarinet Sonata. Mouvements perpétuels. Flute Sonata. *Coupled with* **Ravel** Introduction and Allegro for Flute, Clarinet, Harp and String Quartet. Pièce en forme de habanera. **Various soloists.** Cala CACD1018 (2/95).
...Oboe Sonata[d]. Trio for Oboe, Bassoon and Piano[c]. *Coupled with* **Britten** Temporal Variations[a]. Six Metamorphoses after Ovid, Op. 49. Two Insect Pieces[b]. Phantasy, Op. 2[c]. **François Leleux** (ob); [e]**Jean-François Duquesnoy** (bn); [c]**Guillaume Sutre** (vn); [c]**Miguel da Silva** (va); [c]**Marc Coppey** (vc); [abde]**Emmanuel Strosser** (pf). Harmonia Mundi Les Nouveaux Interprètes HMN91 1556 (2/96). *See review under Britten; refer to the Index to Reviews.*   Ⓖ
...Gloria. *Coupled with* **Janáček** Glagolitic Mass. **Soloists; Westminster Choir; New York Philharmonic Orchestra / Leonard Bernstein.** Sony Classical Bernstein Royal Edition SMK47569 (5/93).
...Banalités – Chanson d'Orkenise; Hôtel. La courte paille – Le carafon; La reine de coeur. Chansons villageoises – Les gars qui vont à la fête. Deux poèmes de Louis Aragon. *Coupled with works by* **Berlioz, Ravel** and **Debussy** John Wustman (pf). Decca 417 813-2DH (11/88). *See review in the Collections section; refer to the Index to Reviews.*

Roy Powell   20th century

...Bow out. *Coupled with works by* **W. Gregory, D. Bedford, Nyman** and **Corea** Apollo Saxophone Quartet; **Roy Powell** (keybds). Argo 443 903-2ZH (8/95). *See review in the Collections section; refer to the Index to Reviews.*

Leonel Power   British c1370-1445

...Gloria. *Coupled with works by* **Anonymous, Legrant, Johannes de Lymburga, Fontaine, Dunstable, Cardot, Bittering, Binchois, Machaut** and **Velut** Gothic Voices / **Christopher Page.** Hyperion CDA66783 (1/96). *See review in the Collections section; refer to the Index to Reviews.*

Anthony Powers

Suggested listening ...
...Trio. *Coupled with works by* **Lutyens, LeFanu, G. Williams** and **R. Marsh** Mühlfeld
  Ensemble. Clarinet Classics CC0007 (10/94). *See review in the Collections section; refer to the
  Index to Reviews.*
...The Memory Room. *Coupled with* **D. Matthews** Piano Sonata, Op. 47. **William Howard** (pf).
  NMC Artists Series NMCD021S (3/95).

Michael Praetorius

New review
Praetorius Wachet auf, ruft uns die Stimme. Nun kommt der Heiden Heiland. In dulci jubilo.
  Vom Himmel hoch. Resonet in laudibus. Wie schön leuchtet der Morgenstern. Puer natus in
  Bethlehem. **Trinity College Choir, Cambridge / Richard Marlow.** Conifer Ⓕ 75605 51256-2
  (70 minutes: ADD: 3/96). Texts and translations included.
Praetorius was the first great musical commentator and elaborator of the Lutheran chorale. Prolific
he certainly was, with over 1,000 chorale settings (quite apart from a mass of other work in
compositional and theoretical fields), but his level of invention is remarkable too. This disc presents
32 settings and one of its great merits is that in choosing chorales from the Advent, Christmas and
Epiphany seasons the tunes are likely to be familiar to many listeners. So one can follow, for example,
the orderly six-voice unfolding of *Nun kommt der Heiden Heiland*, appreciating not just Praetorius's
pliable working of the familiar melodic material, but also sensing the simple, strong theological
substance the chorale bears. Rhythmic wit and textural variety abound, from the catch-as-catch-can
soprano duet of *Wachet auf* to the veritable compositional playground he creates out of *Puer natus
in Bethlehem* for double choir. It is affectionate music of great intellect and charm. As for the
performances, perhaps the most significant issue is that Richard Marlow has opted for
unaccompanied performance throughout. Praetorius himself offered exhaustive and famous advice
in his *Syntagma musicum* (1614-19) on the use of instruments together with voices, and though *a
cappella* performance is certainly valid, to devote a 70-minute CD to this one option out of a whole
range of possibilities is rather risky. In truth, the choir's German is really rather anglican, especially
in the matter of vowel colour, and lacks the native textual accentuation that would bring the words
themselves to life, yet the musical properties inherent in the settings are so nimbly and euphoniously
realized that the performances (luminously recorded) are enjoyable and command attention,
particularly if this CD is dipped into, rather than heard at one sitting.

Praetorius Lutheran Christmas Mass. **Roskilde Cathedral Boys' Choir and Congregation; Gabrieli
  Consort; Gabrieli Players / Paul McCreesh.** Archiv Produktion Ⓕ 439 250-2AH (79 minutes:
  DDD: 12/94). 🔊 Text and translation included.   🅖🅖
The aesthetic of contrast, so central to early baroque spectacle (sacred or profane), is inspired here by
the traditional part played by the congregation in Lutheran worship. Praetorius's music for the
figuraliter (the vocal/instrumental choirs) is greatly influenced by fashionable Venetian techniques.
But what is striking is the way the old *alternatim* practices of the Protestant church blend so naturally
with the intricate textures and scorings of a colourful Italian-style canvas, ranging from intimate
dialogues—though rarely reflecting the sensual imagery of Grandi or Monteverdi – to full
grandiloquent sonority. What is more, the centrality of the chorale is never compromised. Despite all
these ingredients, it is McCreesh's research and imagination that make this service such a powerful
testament to the faith expressed by Lutherans of Praetorius's generation, and indeed by subsequent
generations to which Bach was so indebted. The service follows, to all intents and purposes, the Mass
of the Roman rite (sung with distinction by the Gabrieli Consort though the sopranos seem a little
unsure in the *Kyrie*) interspersed with a versatile array of motets, hymns, prayers, intoned readings, a
superbly conceived and suitably mysterious Pavan by Schein for the approach to Communion and
several rhetorically positioned organ preludes. For a congregation, the Gabrieli Consort and players
are joined by the boys of Roskilde Cathedral, Denmark and a congregation of local amateur choirs.
The massed sound, so to speak, is remarkable for its fervour in the hymns; now one can see why *Von
Himmel hoch da komm ich her* inspired so many settings in the seventeenth century from Praetorius to
Zachow. Other familiar tunes predominate including *Quem pastores, Wie schon leuchtet der
Morgenstern* in a shimmering prelude by Scheidt followed by a delicately nuanced motet on the same
tune. *In dulci jubilo* is treated to a flamboyant setting by Praetorius with six trumpets on top of
everything else. The spacious acoustic of the cathedral exhibits McCreesh's acute timbral sense; with
the galleries fully employed, definition is not ideally sharp but this is a small price to pay for a natural
perspective which embraces the sense of community worship essential for this project.

Further listening ...

...Terpsichore – excerpts. **New London Consort / Philip Pickett.** L'Oiseau-Lyre Florilegium 414 633-2OH (11/86). ✒

...Magnificat per omnes versus. Aus tiefer Not à 4. Der Tag vertreibt die finster Nacht. Venite exultemus Domino. Maria Magdalena. Peccavi fateor. Psalm 116. **Huelgas Ensemble / Paul van Nevel.** Sony Classical Vivarte SK48039. ✒

André Previn

German/American 1929-

New review

Previn Honey and Rue.
Barber Knoxville: Summer of 1915, Op. 24.
Gershwin Porgy and Bess – Summertime; I loves you, Porgy. **Kathleen Battle** (sop); **Orchestra of St Luke's / André Previn.** DG Ⓕ 437 787-2GH (46 minutes: DDD: 1/96). Texts included. Recorded 1992.   Ⓖ

"Honey and Rue". It's a nice title, an intriguing title. And Toni Morrison's words and André Previn's music sound as if they found each other a long time ago. The other factor will have been Kathleen Battle. The six settings of *Honey and Rue* are custom-made to go where the Battle voice takes them. So, some detail. "First I'll try love" locks into the bittersweetness of the title – a 'title-song' in all but name. Its bouncy, open countenance takes a wistful turn with the line "So when winter comes ...", the dark centre of the song – Previn identifies it beautifully. "Whose house is this?" deals in feelings of not belonging, Previn in his moodiest Shostakovich mode. "The town is lit" depicts the respectable face of (sub)urban living, middle America keeping up appearances. But "Do you know him?" is the way things really are – unaccompanied, unharmonized, one voice, one truth, one faith. A classic blues invocation. "I am not seaworthy" is an unlikely kind of sea picture, a dreamlike meditation cast around a long and very beautiful oboe cantilena. Consonant string harmonies and salon-like piano chordings lend it an air of reassuring homeliness which resonates into the final song, "Take my mother home". You might call it 'Recitative and Spiritual'. And Previn has again caught the uplift of the genre in a way that has nothing to do with pastiche and everything to do with understanding. The excellent Orchestra of St Luke's sound as if they've recruited soloists from uptown Harlem, so convincing is the inflexion: instrumentation is artfully tailored to the characters, the kith and kin of the text, *Honey and Rue* repays repetition.

It says a lot for *Honey and Rue* that it can stand up in the company of a real masterpiece: Barber's perennially affecting *Knoxville: Summer of 1915*. This, too, might have been written for Battle. And as she soars ecstatically to that key phrase "Now is the night one blue dew" it's hard to think of another voice whose timbre so naturally embraces the line of this beautiful score. Yet something in her manner keeps it, and us, at arm's length: an air of formality, a little too rounded, too well enunciated to be true, especially after Dawn Upshaw's plainer, reedier, more homespun quality in her altogether more involving account for Nonesuch. Two numbers from *Porgy and Bess* make up the ungenerous playing time – short measure if you're concerned about quantity. The quality of "Honey and Rue" must suffice.

Sergey Prokofiev

USSR 1891-1953

New review

Prokofiev Symphony-Concerto (Sinfonia concertante) for Cello and Orchestra in E minor, Op. 125.
Tchaikovsky Variations on a Rococo Theme for Cello and Orchestra, Op. 33. Andante cantabile for Cello and Strings. **Yo-Yo Ma** (vc); **Pittsburgh Symphony Orchestra / Lorin Maazel.** Sony Classical Ⓕ SK48382 (68 minutes: DDD: 11/92).

The *Symphony-Concerto* – a re-working of Prokofiev's earlier Cello Concerto – states that "the title was prompted by the enhanced role of the orchestra which sounds at par in the ensemble with the solo cello". It is sometimes called *Sinfonia concertante* (as it is on this disc). This revision, like that of the Fourth Symphony, has its detractors; those who feel Prokofiev's second (even third) thoughts were not necessarily an improvement. However, you are likely to come away from this performance less aware of patchwork and padding and more excited about what this music is capable of expressing. Take the last half of the finale: the theme rings out slowly and majestically on full brass, then, in an instant, confidence withers at the icy *sul ponticello* from orchestral cellos, and we are transported to the nursery accompanied by a funereal tread from timpani and basses. The solo cello rises from this to fix on the home key with a fast and furious ostinato while the brass intone an outline of the theme – menacing, like the *Dies Irae*. At the end we are left with the cello hanging on to his ostinato for grim life and a final peremptory chord from the orchestra – "grim life"? Yes, if the cello is any more forwardly placed the notion of a single voice at the mercy of ... well, at the mercy of whatever, is upset; and when this work was substantially recast, for Prokofiev (both body and soul) in his final years, times were pretty grim. It's tempting to say that Ma and Maazel emphasize the lyrical and elegiac elements at the expense of the dramatic and sardonic ones, but their reading is not that easily pigeonholed. In the second movement there is a marvellous wit, fantasy and playfulness from Ma, and refined tone of great beauty for the *cantabile* at 3'13", without a doubt one of Prokofiev's loveliest melodies. Mindful of the work's dedicatee, Rostropovich's special authority in this work, Ma's is the version to be recommended as a basic library choice. Was there restricted session time for the *Rococo* Variations? The woodwind seem too loud for their *piano* markings in the fifth bar, and at 1'53" the oboist thinks there's no repeat of the second half of the theme. The slower woodwind refrain isn't too convincing, which prior to the second variation, draws attention to the fact that Ma and Maazel race off here 50 per cent faster (the marking is *tempo della thema*). Despite all of this, Ma lends his playing a blend of aristocratic finesse, caprice and elevated lyricism. The *Andante cantabile* is slow, almost a lullaby and quite hypnotic – even the silences soothe. As to the recording, quite apart from the truthful perspectives which allow the listener to perceive details of orchestration normally obscured, the soundstage has openness and coherence.

Additional recommendation ...

...Symphony-Concerto. **Borodin** Symphony No. 2 in B minor. **Mstislav Rostropovich** (vc);
  Leningrad Philharmonic Orchestra / Kurt Sanderling. Multisonic Russian Treasure Ⓜ 310188-2
  (67 minutes: ADD).

Prokofiev Piano Concertos – No. 1 in D flat major, Op. 10; No. 2 in G minor, Op. 16; No. 3 in
  C major, Op. 26; No. 4 in B flat major, Op. 53 (left-hand); No. 5 in G major, Op. 55. **Vladimir
  Ashkenazy** (pf); **London Symphony Orchestra / André Previn.** Decca Ⓜ 425 570-2DM2 (two discs:
  126 minutes: ADD: 3/90). From 15BB 218 (10/75). Recorded 1974-75.   ⒼⒼ

While it's true that the Prokofiev piano concertos are an uneven body of work, there's enough imaginative fire and pianistic brilliance to hold the attention even in the weakest of them; the best, by common consent, Nos. 1, 3 and 4 have stood the test of time very well. As indeed have these Decca recordings. The set first appeared in 1975, but the sound is fresher than many contemporary digital issues, and Ashkenazy has rarely played better. Other pianists have matched his brilliance and energy in, say, the Third Concerto, but very few have kept up such a sure balance of fire and poetry. The astonishingly inflated bravura of the Second Concerto's opening movement is kept shapely and purposeful and even the out-of-tune piano doesn't spoil the effect too much. And the youthful First has the insouciance and zest its 22-year-old composer plainly intended. Newcomers to the concertos should start with No. 3: so many facets of Prokofiev's genius (including that wonderfully piquant lyricism) are here, and Ashkenazy shows how they all take their place as part of a kind of fantastic story. But there are rewards everywhere, and the effort involved in finding them is small. Why hesitate?

Additional recommendations ...

...Nos. 1-5. Overture on Hebrew themes, Op. 34[a]. Visions fugitives, Op. 22. **Michel Béroff** (pf);
  [a]**Michel Portal** (cl); [a]**Parrenin Quartet; Leipzig Gewandhaus Orchestra / Kurt Masur.** EMI
  Ⓜ CMS7 62542-2 (two discs: 148 minutes: ADD: 7/89).   Ⓖ
...Nos. 1, 3 and 4. **Kun Woo Paik** (pf); **Polish National Radio Symphony Orchestra / Antoni Wit.**
  Naxos Ⓢ 8 550566 (72 minutes: DDD: 11/92).   Ⓖ
...No. 1[b]. Suggestion diabolique, Op. 4 No. 4. **Tchaikovsky** Piano Concerto No. 1 in B flat minor,
  Op. 23[a]. Morceau, Op. 19 No. 6. **Balakirev** Islamey. **Andrei Gavrilov** (pf); [a]**Philharmonia
  Orchestra / Riccardo Muti;** [b]**London Symphony Orchestra / Sir Simon Rattle.** EMI Studio Ⓜ
  CDM7 64329-2 (74 minutes: DDD: 11/92).   Ⓖ
...Nos. 2 and 5. **Kun Woo Paik** (pf); **Polish National Radio Symphony Orchestra / Antoni Wit.** Naxos
  Ⓢ 8 550565 (57 minutes: DDD: 11/92).
...Nos. 1-5. **Vladimir Krainev** (pf); **Frankfurt Radio Symphony Orchestra / Dmitri Kitaienko.** Teldec
  Ⓕ 9031-73257-2 (two discs: 123 minutes: DDD: 7/93).   ⒼⒼ
...No. 1. **Glazunov** Piano Concerto No. 1 in F minor, Op. 92. **Rimsky-Korsakov** Piano
  Concerto in C sharp minor, Op. 30. **Sviatoslav Richter** (pf). **Moscow Youth Orchestra / Kyrill
  Kondrashin.** Melodiya mono Ⓜ 74321 29468-2* (57 minutes: ADD: 6/96).

Prokofiev Piano Concertos – No. 1 in D flat major, Op. 10; No. 3 in C major, Op. 26[a]. **Evgeni
  Kissin** (pf); **Berlin Philharmonic Orchestra / Claudio Abbado.** DG Ⓕ 439 898-2GH (42 minutes:
  DDD: 12/94). Item marked [a] recorded live in 1993.   Ⓖ

Kissin always seems to have time to acknowledge the implications of Prokofiev's harmony, to allow the left hand to converse with the right (always naturally, never tricksily), and to gauge the relationship of his part to the orchestra. He is also scrupulous with dynamics. At the first entry in the C major Concerto he manages, as few pianists do, the *piano* contrast after the first three notes without losing soloistic presence. And he resists the temptation to shout out *forte* passages, so that Prokofiev's *fortissimos* stand in proper relief, as do his carefully placed accents (hear the opening theme of the same concerto's finale). Perhaps none of that strikes you as exceptional, but it is so in Prokofiev, where the sheer athletic demands are extreme and refinement seems like too much to ask. With a technique like his and an orchestra as responsive as the Berlin Philharmonic there are just a few places in the C major Concerto, such as the final pages, where Kissin might have allowed himself to be a bit more carried away. But there is no shortage of exhilaration in the youthful D flat Concerto, which is a model blend of attack, wit, poetry and drive. In fact there is little discernible difference between this studio recording and the live C major, either in accuracy of in excitement. It would be wrong to say that Kissin surpasses Ashkenazy (reviewed above), whose performances of all five concertos on a two-disc, mid-price Decca set still sound breathtakingly vivid. Bronfman (listed below) on Sony Classical is virtually a match for him and offers the Fifth Concerto in addition. But DG's recording is clearer than the 20-year-old Decca set, and Abbado and the Berliners are far superior to Mehta and the Israel Philharmonic. Full price for 42 minutes of music may seem a bit steep; but what Kissin and Abbado have to offer is certainly in the luxury class.

Additional recommendations ...

...Nos. 1, 4 and 5. **Boris Berman** (pf); **Royal Concertgebouw Orchestra / Neeme Järvi.** Chandos
Ⓕ CHAN8791 (64 minutes: DDD: 10/90).

...No. 3[a]. Visions fugitives, Op. 22 – Nos. 3, 5, 6, 9-11 and 16-18. Suggestion diaboloque, Op. 4
No. 4. Tales of an old grandmother, Op. 31 – Nos. 2 and 3. Three Pieces, Op. 59 – Nos. 2 and 3.
Gavotte. Piano Piece, Op. 52 No. 3. Sonata No. 4 in C minor, Op. 29 – Andante. Four Pieces,
Op. 32 – No. 3. **Sergey Prokofiev** (pf); [a]**London Symphony Orchestra / Piero Coppola.** Pearl
Ⓕ GEMMCD9470* (57 minutes: ADD: 11/91).

...Nos. 1 and 3. Piano Sonata No. 7 in B flat major, Op. 83. **Mari Kodama** (pf); **Philharmonia
Orchestra / Kent Nagano.** ASV Ⓕ CDDCA786 (64 minutes: DDD: 4/92).

...Nos. 1, 3 and 5. **Yefim Bronfman** (pf); **Israel Philharmonic Orchestra / Zubin Mehta.** Sony
Classical Ⓕ SK52483 (66 minutes: DDD: 12/93).   Ⓖ

...No. 3[a]. Violin Concerto No. 1 in D major, Op. 19[b]. Lieutenant Kijé – Suite, Op. 60[b]. [a]**Martha
Argerich** (pf); [b]**Shlomo Mintz** (vn); [a]**Berlin Philharmonic Orchestra;** [b]**Chicago Symphony Orchestra
/ Claudio Abbado.** DG Classikon Ⓑ 439 413-2GCL (69 minutes: ADD/DDD: 1/94).   ⒼⒼ

...No. 3[b]. Visions fugitives, Op. 22[c] Nos. 3, 5, 6, 9-11 and 16-18. Suggestion diabolique, Op. 4 No.
4[d]. Symphony No. 1 in D major, Op. 25, "Classical" – Gavotte[e]. Piano Sonata No. 4 in C minor,
Op. 29 – Andante assai[f]. Gavotte, Op. 32 No. 3[f]. **Glazunov** The Seasons[a]. [bcdef]**Sergey Prokofiev**
(pf); [a]**orchestra / Alexander Glazunov;** [b]**London Symphony Orchestra / Piero Coppola.** EMI
Composers in Person mono Ⓕ CDC5 55223-2* (79 minutes: ADD: 5/95).   Ⓖ

...No. 3. **Schumann** Piano Concerto in A minor, Op. 54. Van Cliburn (pf); Chicago
Symphony Orchestra / [a]Walter Hendl, [b]Fritz Reiner. RCA Victor Living
Stereo 09026 62691-2 (61 minutes: ADD).

Prokofiev Piano Concertos[a] – No. 2 in G minor, Op. 16; No. 4 in B flat major, Op. 53 (left-hand).
Overture on Hebrew Themes in C minor, Op. 34[b]. **Yefim Bronfman** (pf); [b]**Giora Feidman** (cl);
[b]**Juilliard Quartet** (Robert Mann, Joel Smirnoff, vns; Samuel Rhodes, va; Joel Krosnick, vc);
[a]**Israel Philharmonic Orchestra / Zubin Mehta.** Sony Classical Ⓕ SK58966 (65 minutes: DDD:
5/95). Recorded 1993-4. ***Gramophone** Editor's choice.*   ⒼⒼ

Bronfman's technical facility makes light of the Second Concerto's massive first movement cadenza, and when the Israeli brass break through at 9'45" – all brawn and thunder – the effect is quite overwhelming. The *Scherzo* is neat and mechanized, the *Intermezzo*'s initial 'fee-fi-fo-fum' brisk but grimly intimidating, while the long, dizzyingly eventful finale is effectively held in check. As to the Fourth (left-hand) Concerto, this is, perhaps, the work's finest recording to date. The first movement has an appropriately cool demeanour, with nimble pianism and precise orchestral support. Then there is the *Andante*, one of Prokofiev's most introspective narratives, here given with just the right balance of mobility and restraint. The *Moderato*, too, has great charisma, its quick-fire mood changes (from menace to laughter, and back again) inspiring from these players a combination of energy, poise and finesse. It is a beautifully recorded, trim, dapper and above all stylish account of Prokofiev's most underrated concerto. As if that were not enough, Sony throw in an extraordinary rendition of the tangy *Overture on Hebrew Themes*, where the Juilliard Quartet mimic and humour Giora Feidman's saucy, Klezmer-style clarinet playing, an authentic flashback to old-time Yiddish theatre or street song: caustic, lovable and primary-coloured in the manner of Chagall. It makes a wonderful encore.

Additional recommendations ...

...No. 4. **Britten** Diversions for Piano (left-hand) and Orchestra. **Ravel** Piano Concerto for the
Left Hand. **Leon Fleisher** (pf); **Boston Symphony Orchestra / Seiji Ozawa.** Sony Classical
Ⓕ SK47188 (68 minutes: DDD: 4/93).

...Overture on Hebrew Themes[a]. Quintet in G minor, Op. 39. **Hindemith** Octet. **Berlin Soloists;**
[a]**Elena Bashkirova** (pf). Teldec Ⓕ 9031-73400-2 (58 minutes: DDD: 6/93). *See review under
Hindemith; refer to the Index to Reviews.*   Ⓖ

Prokofiev Piano Concerto No. 3 in C major, Op. 26. Toccata in C major, Op. 11.
Rachmaninov Piano Concerto No. 1 in F sharp minor, Op. 1.
Pinto Three Scenes from Childhood. **Byron Janis** (pf); **Moscow Philharmonic Orchestra / Kyrill
Kondrashin.** Mercury Ⓜ 434 333-2MM (69 minutes: ADD: 7/94). Recorded 1962.   ⒼⒼ

Many would consider this Mercury reissue to be the finest record to emerge from that company's visit to Moscow in 1962, where they went to make the first Western-engineered recordings of the Soviet era. Byron Janis accompanied the American team to join Kyrill Kondrashin and the Moscow Philharmonic in two quite remarkable concerto performances, in which soloist, conductor and orchestra consistently strike sparks off each other. The Prokofiev Third Piano Concerto is an unforgettable mix of Russian lyricism, in which powerful pianistic bravura is spiced with wit – especially in the slow movement theme and variations. In the coupled Rachmaninov Concerto No. 1 the solo playing is of Horowitz calibre; scintillating in the finale, the work's warmth fully conveyed.

Don't miss this, even if it involves duplication. To fill out the disc some solo piano 'encores' have been added, including the Prokofiev *Toccata*, Op. 11 and an engaging suite called *Three scenes from Childhood* by the virtually unknown Octavio Pinto (1890-1950). The recording, crystal clear, yet full and never clinical, is another brilliant example of Mercury's engineering expertise.

Additional recommendation ...

...No. 3[a]. **Khachaturian** Piano Concerto[b]. **Liszt** Mephisto Waltz No. 1, S514, "Der Tanz in der Dorfschenke". **William Kapell** (pf); [a]**Dallas Symphony Orchestra / Antál Dorati;** [b]**Boston Symphony Orchestra / Serge Koussevitzky.** RCA Victor Gold Seal mono Ⓜ GD60921* (71 minutes: ADD: 5/95).   Ⓖ

New review

Prokofiev Piano Concerto No. 3 in C major, Op. 26[a].
Ravel Piano Concerto in G major[a]. Gaspard de la nuit[b]. **Martha Argerich** (pf); [a]**Berlin Philharmonic Orchestra / Claudio Abbado.** DG The Originals Ⓜ 447 438-2GOR (71 minutes: ADD: 12/95). Items marked [a] from SLPM139349 (2/68, recorded 1967), [b]2530 540 (8/75, recorded 1974).

There have been others to match the bustle and brilliance of Argerich's Prokofiev, her coloristic range, her drive, her flashiness, her straining at the leash. But none who has so satisfyingly combined all those qualities, who has given us such a rocket-launched recapitulation in the first movement, such circus-routine vividness in the following variations (Prokofiev grew up in a Russia where 'circusization of the arts' was one of the 'in' concepts), or such monstrous, hyperbolic fairy-tale imagery in the finale, and all done with the most engaging reckless abandon. The Ravel Concerto is another bundle of energy. Yet how miraculous is the blend and interplay of piano and orchestra, and how ecstatically Argerich weaves around the cor anglais restatement in the slow movement. *Embarras de richesses* indeed: Argerich's *Gaspard* is a version of Ravel's devilish triptych which is unusually faithful to his subdued dynamic markings, quite apart from its breathtaking agility. The results ring poetically true at the same time as defying criticism in pianistic terms.

Prokofiev Piano Concerto No. 5 in G major, Op. 55[a].
Rachmaninov Piano Concerto No. 2 in C minor, Op. 18[b]. **Sviatoslav Richter** (pf); **Warsaw Philharmonic Orchestra /** [a]**Witold Rowicki,** [b]**Stanislaw Wislocki.** DG Ⓟ 415 119-2GH* (58 minutes: ADD: 6/85). Item marked [a] from 138075 (3/60), [b] 138076 (1/60). Recorded 1959.

ⒼⒼⒼ

Prokofiev was to find no more dedicated an advocate for his keyboard works than Richter. So how good that this artist's now legendary account of the Fifth Piano Concerto has been granted a new lease of life on CD. Although it has never enjoyed the popularity of Prokofiev's Nos. 1 and 3, here, however, attention is riveted from first note to last. Richter delights in the music's rhythmic vitality and bite, its melodic and harmonic unpredictability. Both piano and orchestra are so clearly and vividly reproduced that it is difficult to believe that the recording is 35 years old. Though betraying its age slightly more, notably in the sound of the keyboard itself, Rachmaninov's No. 2 is no less gripping. Not all of Richter's tempos conform to the score's suggested metronome markings, but his intensity is rivalled only by his breathtaking virtuosity. Never could the work's opening theme sound more laden, more deeply and darkly Russian.

New review

Prokofiev Violin Concertos[a] – No. 1 in D major, Op. 19; No. 2 in G minor, Op. 63. Solo Violin Sonata in D major, Op. 115. **Gil Shaham** (vn); [a]**London Symphony Orchestra / André Previn.** DG Ⓟ 447 758-2GH (60 minutes: DDD: 6/96). *Gramophone* Editor's choice.   Ⓖ

Rarely, if ever, have there been performances where soloist, orchestra and conductor connect with such unerring intuition, where the music – rather than its superficial display potential – is treated so naturally. Previn ushers in the First Concerto's crystalline opening with gentle intensity, raising the curtain for Gil Shaham's warmly tended first entry. Both make great play with the march theme that follows. The effect is like spicy gossip shared between friends while the *Scherzo* is equally rich in dialogue. Shaham's tone is at its most expressive at the beginning of the third movement, and at its most delicate, just prior to the last big climax. This natural exegesis extends to the darker Second Concerto, even where Shaham or Previn linger about a particular phrase (as Shaham does in his very first entry, or Previn does when he pauses before the final bars of the second movement). The recording, too, is extremely impressive, with well defined string lines and a fine body of winds, brass and percussion (the all-important bass drum especially). Note how, beyond the raucous happenings of the second movement's central episode, the violins waft back with the principal theme (at 6'56"). Similar felicities occur regularly throughout both concertos, while the Second's finale – a riotous, slightly tongue-in-cheek *danse macabre* – is here sensibly paced and very well articulated. And as if all that weren't enough, Shaham treats us to a substantial encore in the lively Solo Sonata that Prokofiev intended to be performed in unison by a group of young players. Although hardly on the level of the concertos, the voice is unmistakable and this particular performance as bright as a button.

Additional recommendations ...

...Nos. 1 and 2. **Shlomo Mintz** (vn); **Chicago Symphony Orchestra / Claudio Abbado.** DG Ⓟ 410 524-2GH (DDD: 4/84).   Ⓖ

...Nos. 1 and 2. **Itzhak Perlman** (vn); **BBC Symphony Orchestra / Gennadi Rozhdestvensky.** EMI Ⓕ CDC7 47025-2 (DDD: 9/84).

...No. 2. **Shostakovich** Violin Concerto No. 1 in A minor, Op. 99. **Viktoria Mullova** (vn); **Royal Philharmonic Orchestra / André Previn.** Philips Ⓕ 422 364-2PH (60 minutes: DDD: 6/89). ⒼⒼ

...Nos. 1 and 2. **Stravinsky** Violin Concerto in D major. **Kyung-Wha Chung** (vn); **London Symphony Orchestra / André Previn.** Decca Ovation Ⓜ 425 003-2DM (72 minutes: ADD: 7/90). Ⓖ

...No. 1[a]. Violin Sonata No. 1 in F minor, Op. 80[b]. Five Melodies, Op. 35[b]. **David Oistrakh** (vn); [b]**Frida Bauer** (pf); [a]**Moscow Philharmonic Orchestra / Yuri Temirkanov.** Praga Ⓕ PR250 041 (61 minutes: ADD: 9/93).

...No. 1[a]. Piano Concerto No. 3 in C major, Op. 26[b]. [a]**Shlomo Mintz** (vn); [b]**Martha Argerich** (pf); [a]**Chicago Symphony Orchestra;** [b]**Berlin Philharmonic Orchestra / Claudio Abbado.** DG Classikon Ⓑ 439 413-2GCL (69 minutes: ADD/DDD: 1/94). ⒼⒼ

...Nos. 1 and 2[a]. The Love for Three Oranges – Les ridicules; Scène infernale; Marche; Scherzo; Le Prince et la Princesse; La fruite. [a]**Joshua Bell** (vn); **Montreal Symphony Orchestra / Charles Dutoit.** Decca Ⓕ 440 331-2DH (65 minutes: DDD: 1/94).

...No. 1. **Shostakovich** Violin Concerto No. 1 in A minor, Op. 99. **Maxim Vengerov** (vn); **London Symphony Orchestra / Mstislav Rostropovich.** Teldec Ⓕ 4509-92256-2 (62 minutes: DDD: 2/95). Includes bonus sampler disc. *Gramophone Award Winner 1995. Gramophone Editor's choice. See review under Shostakovich; refer to the Index to Reviews.* ⒼⒼⒼ

...Nos. 1 and 2. **Boris Belkin** (vn); **Zurich Tonhalle Orchestra / Michael Stern.** Denon Ⓕ CO-75891 (48 minutes: DDD: 3/95).

...Nos. 1 and 2. **Stravinsky** Violin Concerto in D major. **Cho-Liang Lin** (vn); **Los Angeles Philharmonic Orchestra / Esa-Pekka Salonen.** Sony Classical Ⓕ SK53969 (70 minutes: DDD: 3/95). Ⓖ

...No. 1. **Tchaikovsky** Violin Concerto in D major, Op. 35. **Julian Rachlin** (vn); **Moscow Radio Symphony Orchestra / Vladimir Fedoseyev.** Sony Classical Ⓕ SK66567 (58 minutes: DDD: 8/95).

...No. 2. *Coupled with works by* **Brahms, Saint-Saëns, Vieuxtemps, Wieniawski, Sarasate and Walton** Jascha Heifetz (vn); **Boston Symphony Orchestra / Serge Koussevitzky.** Pearl Ⓜ GEMMCDS9167* (two discs: 157 minutes: ADD: 11/95).

...No. 2. **Shostakovich** Violin Concerto No. 1 in A minor, Op. 99. **Vadim Repin** (vn); **Hallé Orchestra / Kent Nagano.** Erato Ⓕ 0630-10696-2 (59 minutes: DDD: 1/96). *See review under Shostakovich; refer to the Index to Reviews.*

Prokofiev Peter and the wolf, Op. 67[a]. Symphony No. 1 in D major, Op. 25, "Classical". March in B flat minor, Op. 99. Overture on Hebrew Themes, Op. 34*bis*[b]. [a]**Sting** (narr); [b]**Stefan Vladar** (pf); **Chamber Orchestra of Europe / Claudio Abbado.** DG Ⓕ 429 396-2GH (50 minutes: DDD: 4/91). Recorded 1986-90. Ⓖ

Abbado and the multi-talented Sting offer a lively and beautifully crafted account of Prokofiev's ever popular *Peter and the wolf.* Any fears that the original freshness of Prokofiev's creation may be lost in favour of a less formal approach are soon dispelled – Sting is an effective and intelligent storyteller capable of capturing the imagination of adults and children alike, and there is never a feeling of contrivance or mere gimmickry. The orchestral playing is a real delight too; sharply characterized and performed with great affection. The *Overture on Hebrew Themes* is more commonly heard in its drier, more acerbic version for clarinet, piano and string quartet, but makes a welcome and refreshing appearance on this disc in Prokofiev's own arrangement for small orchestra. Abbado's elegant and graceful reading of the *Classical* Symphony is one of the finest in the catalogue, and is particularly notable for its beautifully shaped phrasing, clarity of inner detail and crisp articulation.

Additional recommendations ...

...Peter and the wolf[a]. **Britten** The Young Person's Guide to the Orchestra, Op. 34. Gloriana – Courtly dances. **Royal Philharmonic Orchestra / André Previn** ([a]narr). Telarc Ⓕ CD80126 (55 minutes: DDD: 10/87).

...Peter and the wolf[a]. Symphony No. 1 in D major, Op. 25, "Classical"[b]. Lieutenant Kijé-Suite, Op. 60[c]. The Love for Three Oranges – Suite[d]. [a]**Sir Ralph Richardson** (narr); [b]**London Symphony Orchestra / Sir Malcolm Sargent;** [c]**Paris Conservatoire Orchestra / Sir Adrian Boult;** [d]**London Philharmonic Orchestra / Walter Weller** Decca Headline Classics Ⓑ 433 612-2DSP (76 minutes: ADD: 1/92).

...Peter and the wolf[a]. **Bizet** Jeux d'enfants. **Saint-Saëns** Le carnaval des animaux. [a]**Sir John Gielgud** (narr); **Royal Philharmonic Orchestra / Andrea Licata.** Tring International Royal Philharmonic Collection Ⓢ TRP046 (69 minutes: DDD: 11/95).

New review

Prokofiev Peter and the Wolf, Op. 67[a].

Debussy La boîte à joujoux. [a]**Patrick Stewart** (narr); **Orchestra of Opéra de Lyon / Kent Nagano.** Erato Ⓕ 4509-97418-2 (61 minutes: DDD: 8/95). Text included.

Choosing the 'right' *Peter and the Wolf* is particularly difficult in that the versions that most please young children tend to drive parents mad, while the more urbane productions can challenge a child's concentration span, *Star Trek* veteran Patrick Stewart manages to straddle the borders with a narration that is both involving and restrained, an intimate yet lively reading, beautifully integrated into the orchestral score – which is itself superbly played by the Orchestra of Opéra de Lyon. Kent Nagano's roster of insights is far too substantial to itemize individually, so suffice to say that anyone in search of a stylishly tailored, tastefully phrased account is unlikely to complain. The recording, too, is exceptionally well balanced, albeit in the slightly cavernous acoustic of the Opéra de Lyon; whereas the location chosen for *La boîte à joujoux* – Lyon's Auditorium Maurice Ravel – is near ideal. This, too, is a performance of rare refinement and poise – a keenly inflected, tender and texturally luminous reading, with graphic characterization and phrasing that suggests lightning reflexes all round. However, as each of the four movements is positively crammed with dramatic incident, anyone interested in following the storyline will need some sort of synopsis – either as prescribed by the composer (if such a thing exists) or as imagined by a skilful annotator. Regrettably, all Erato give us is the bare text for *Peter and the Wolf*, plus essential recording details. There are no notes on Prokofiev's music and absolutely nothing whatsoever about the Debussy. This is ridiculous, especially as the disc is aimed primarily at youngsters. After all, here was a golden opportunity to realize, via tracking or indexing, the power of words in relation to music – the sort of educational adventure that labels such as Denon and Delos embark on almost as a matter of course. Kent Nagano's conducting is superb, the recordings are generally excellent, Patrick Stewart tells a mean tale – it's just a shame that Erato's presentation is inadequate.

Prokofiev Cinderella, Op. 87. Summer Night – Suite, Op. 123. **Russian National Orchestra /**
   Mikhail Pletnev. DG Ⓕ 445 830-2GH2 (two discs: 138 minutes: DDD: 6/95). *Gramophone*
   Editor's record of the month.   ⒼⒼ
This is an outstanding release. If Pletnev launches *Summer Night* somewhat brusquely, what follows is beyond reproach. Most striking of all is the radical clarity of texture which makes Prokofiev's modest suite seem at once unprecedentedly modern and that much more shrewdly realized in terms of colour. The score was extrapolated from the opera *The Duenna* (or *Betrothal in a Monastery*) in 1950 and its neglect, as Pletnev shows, is unaccountable. It is curious that a ballet as familiar as *Cinderella* should be so seldom heard in its entirety. Like *Romeo and Juliet*, *Cinderella* gives an impression of immense assurance, belying the obvious hazards of cultural production under Stalin. It is strong without being daring, colourful without being extravagant, and once again exhibits an emotional involvement often hidden in the past. This sounds reassuringly Tchaikovskian and yet there is also something pale and elusive in its make-up, perhaps designed to reflect the character of its main protagonist. The motif of Cinderella repressed, first heard at the very start of the ballet, is given a heavy tread, the orchestra dragging their metaphorical feet to intensify the pensive mood. As for the second motto theme, anticipating her eventual happiness with her dream prince, it is not so much broad and impassioned as achingly beautiful. Nor is the conducting without humour. The sisters' "dancing lesson" has never been more vividly evoked, their unruly behaviour and slow learning curve precisely delineated in the truculent attack of the two solo violins. "The Prince's first galop" (thrice he rushes off impetuously in search of his beloved) is as light as a feather, executed with matchless finesse by the Russian strings. The sound is good, the orchestral playing superb.

Prokofiev Romeo and Juliet, Op. 64 – Suites Nos. 1-3: excerpts. Chout, Op. 21 – ballet suite.
   London Symphony Orchestra / Claudio Abbado. Decca Ovation Ⓜ 425 027-2DM (54 minutes:
   ADD: 6/91). From SXL6286 (5/67). Recorded 1966.   Ⓖ
It was an excellent idea to couple nine items from the familiar *Romeo and Juliet* ballet score with a similar sequence from the unjustly neglected *Chout* – the blackly comic tale of a village trickster, the Buffoon of the alternative title. *Romeo and Juliet* is more popular than ever these days, but Abbado's mid-1960s selection – less predictable than most – retains its freshness and appeal; only his sluggish *Dance of the girls with lilies* lacks something in charm. The sound is pretty good, the brass very immediate. While *Chout* has that rather sadistic plot – and the audiences of 1921 had ultra-modern cubist sets, costumes and choreography to object to – its neglect seems unaccountable today, given the quality of the music. Here, Prokofiev was clearly inspired by Stravinsky's *Petrushka*. Even if there remains some loosely-written connective tissue, there is also a fund of melodic invention that could only have come from the younger man. The orchestration glitters throughout, sharp-edged and totally distinctive. Decca's analogue recording remains impressive with the scintillating textures clearly defined.

Additional recommendations ...
...Romeo and Juliet – excerpts. **Phiharmonia Orchestra / Claus Peter Flor.** RCA Victor Red Seal
   Ⓕ 09026 61388-2 (58 minutes: DDD: 10/93).
...Romeo and Juliet – excerpts. **Royal Liverpool Philharmonic Orchestra / Libor Pešek.** Virgin
   Classics Ⓕ VC7 59278-2 (71 minutes: DDD: 10/93). *Gramophone Editor's choice.*
...Romeo and Juliet[b]. **Rimsky-Korsakov** Scheherazade, Op. 35[a]. [a]**Berlin Radio Symphony**
   Orchestra, [b]**Leipzig Gewandhaus Orchestra / Karel Ančerl.** Tahra mono Ⓕ TAH119* (68 minutes:
   DDD: 11/95).

Prokofiev Romeo and Juliet, Op. 64 – Introduction; Romeo; The street awakens; Morning Dance;
   The Quarrel; The Fight; The Prince gives his order; Juliet, as a young girl; Arrival of the guests;
   Mask; Dance of the Knights; Romeo and Juliet; Folk Dance; Friar Laurence; Dance; Tybalt and

Mercutio fight; Mercutio dies; Romeo decides to avenge Mercutio's death; Romeo fights Tybalt; Introduction to Act 3; The last farewell; Dance of the girls with the lilies; Juliet's funeral, Death of Juliet. **Montreal Symphony Orchestra / Charles Dutoit.** Decca Ⓕ 430 279-2DH (75 minutes: DDD: 9/91). Recorded 1989.

The melodic invention, always consistently inspired, the harmonic flavour, often pungent, and the individual and brilliantly colourful orchestration of *Romeo and Juliet* bring the ear constant diversity and stimulation. Charles Dutoit's 1991 recording is extremely attractive: by judicious selection he compresses the epic span of the ballet into 24 separate items from the original score. The playing of the Montreal Symphony Orchestra is spectacular with very fleet strings and brass playing of imposing weight and tragic pungency. Dutoit's interpretation is highly theatrical: the lighter excerpts from the score are pointed and witty, while the more romantic elements are given full expression and the variety of Shakespeare's and Prokofiev's dramatic vision is most expertly recreated by Dutoit. The recording is top class, not only expertly balanced but capturing the wide dynamic range and finesse of the splendidly virtuoso Montreal orchestra.

Additional recommendations ...

...Romeo and Juliet. **Cleveland Orchestra / Lorin Maazel.** Decca Ⓕ 417 510-2DH2 (two discs: 141 minutes: ADD: 2/87). ⒼⒼ

...Romeo and Juliet. **Orchestra of the Royal Opera House, Covent Garden / Mark Ermler.** Royal Opera House Records Ⓕ ROH309/10 (two discs: 145 minutes: DDD: 11/94).

...Romeo and Juliet – excerpts. **Royal Liverpool Philharmonic Orchestra / Libor Pešek.** Virgin Classics Ⓕ VC7 59278-2 (71 minutes: DDD: 10/93).

...Romeo and Juliet – excerpts. **Royal Concertgebouw Orchestra / Myung-Whun Chung.** DG Ⓕ 439 870-2GH (63 minutes: DDD: 10/94).

...Romeo and Juliet – Suites Nos. 1 and 2: excerpts. **Cleveland Orchestra / Yoel Levi.** Telarc Ⓕ CD80089 (50 minutes: DDD: 2/87).

...Romeo and Juliet – Suites Nos. 1 and 2. **Oslo Philharmonic Orchestra / Mariss Jansons.** EMI Ⓕ CDC7 49289-2 (59 minutes: DDD: 5/89).

...Romeo and Juliet – Suites Nos. 1-3[a]. **Mussorgsky** A Night on the Bare Mountain[b]. [a]**Minneapolis Symphony Orchestra / Stanislav Skrowaczewski;** [b]**London Symphony Orchestra / Antál Dorati.** Mercury Living Presence Ⓜ 432 004-2MM (67 minutes: ADD: 3/91). Ⓖ

...Romeo and Juliet – Suites Nos. 1-3. **Royal Scottish National Orchestra / Neeme Järvi.** Chandos Ⓕ CHAN8940 (78 minutes: DDD: 9/91).

...Romeo and Juliet – Suites Nos. 1-3: excerpts. **Czecho-Slovak State Philharmonic Orchestra, Košice / Andrew Mogrelia.** Naxos Ⓢ 8 550380 (55 minutes: DDD: 9/91).

...Romeo and Juliet – Suites Nos. 1-3. **Suisse Romande Orchestra / Armin Jordan.** Erato Ⓕ 2292-45817-2 (76 minutes: DDD: 7/93). Ⓖ

...Romeo and Juliet – excerpts. **San Francisco Symphony Orchestra / Michael Tilson Thomas.** RCA Victor Red Seal Ⓕ 09026 68288-2 (78 minutes: DDD: 5/96).

New review
Prokofiev Romeo and Juliet, Op. 64. **London Symphony Orchestra / André Previn.** EMI Forte Ⓜ CZS5 68607-2 (two discs: 149 minutes: ADD: 7/96). Notes included. From HMV SLS864 (12/73).

New review
Prokofiev Cinderella, Op. 87[a]. Symphony No. 1 in D, Op. 25[b]. "Classical". **London Symphony Orchestra / André Previn.** EMI Forte Ⓜ CZS5 68604-2 (two discs: 127 minutes: [a]DDD/[b]ADD: 7/96). Synopsis included. Item marked [a] from SLS143595-3 (12/83), [b] HMV ASD3556 (11/78).

It is good to have André Previn's 1973 set of *Romeo and Juliet* restored to circulation at such a reasonable price. The EMI recording still sounds pretty sumptuous and the legendary Kingsway bloom remains mercifully intact on CD. Compared with some other versions, Previn's hard-working LSO can sound just a touch cautious and technically fallible. Yet his affectionate, wittily pointed reading has its place: many will rightly respond to its sense of easy spontaneity, tender restraint and unaffected honesty. It is, in sum, a more relaxed, less relentlessly high-powered affair than his rivals, but no less compelling for that. His admirable *Cinderella* appeared originally on LP in 1983 but was never transferred to CD in its entirety, EMI opting for a single-disc 'highlights' compilation instead. It has come up quite beautifully in this new transfer, the Abbey Road production possessing a most appealing warmth and lustre. Previn's imaginative, highly sympathetic direction combines both warmhearted affection as well as a seductive theatrical flair (the whole of Act 2 is particularly memorable in this regard). Throughout, the LSO respond with considerable dash and character: just occasionally, the strings are wanting in the last ounce of finesse and absolute technical security, and the woodwind contribution is especially felicitous. Unfortunately, the 'bonus' item – an enthusiastic, but distractingly scrappy *Classical* Symphony – is far from ideal (this isn't a patch on Previn's own supremely stylish Los Angeles remake for Philips – listed further on). No matter, a bargain all the same.

Prokofiev Symphonies – No. 1 in D major, Op. 25, "Classical" (from CHAN8400, 3/86); No. 2 in D minor, Op. 40 (CHAN8368, 10/85. *Selected by Sounds in Retrospect*); No. 3 in C minor, Op. 44; No. 4 in C major, Op. 47 (original 1930 version, both from CHAN8401, 5/86); No. 4 in C major, Op. 112 (revised 1947 version, from CHAN8400, 3/86); No. 5 in B flat major, Op. 100

(CHAN8450, 7/86); No. 6 in E flat minor, Op. 111 (CHAN8359, 7/85); No. 7 in C sharp minor, Op. 131 (CHAN8442, 7/86). **Royal Scottish National Orchestra / Neeme Järvi.** Chandos Ⓕ CHAN8931/4 (four discs: 260 minutes: DDD). *Gramophone Award Winner 1985.*   Ⓖ

Prokofiev was not a natural symphonist. Albeit successful in emulating Haydn in the *Classical Symphony*, the Sixth Symphony is his only undisputed integrated symphonic structure (and an epic-tragic utterance as intense as any by Shostakovich). It has been suggested that his symphonies all have a sense of some unstaged scenario, and the Third and Fourth (and to a lesser extent, the Seventh) Symphonies actually rework material from his music for the stage. The Fourth (in both versions) in particular fails to convince as a symphony owing to the profusion and individuality of its often strikingly beautiful thematic ideas – it's a real patchwork quilt of a piece. Enter Neeme Järvi, nothing if not a man of the theatre, to give maximum dramatic intensity and character to all Prokofiev's ideas, whether they add up symphonically or not; capable of overawing his Scottish forces into playing of aerial lightness and easeful lyricism in the *Classical* Symphony, and pulling no punches where Prokofiev's inspiration (as in the Second and Third Symphonies) is at is most strident, violent and hysterical. Make no mistake, though, these are also readings of real stature: where there is symphonic 'line', Järvi unerringly finds it. Drawbacks? Some may feel the need for a deeper pile of string sound, particularly in the Fifth Symphony; and these typically spacious Chandos productions do not always ensure adequate projection for the woodwind (e.g. some of the quiet, lyrical woodwind lines in the Fourth Symphony), but more often than not one cannot faile to be impressed by the coherence and co-ordination, both musically and technically, of some of this century's most fabulous and fraught orchestral essays. As a cycle, this is unlikely to be challenged for some time.

Additional recommendations ...

...Nos. 1 and 7. The Love for Three Oranges – suite, Op. 33*a*[b]. **Philharmonia Orchestra / Nicolai Malko.** Classics for Pleasure Ⓑ CD-CFP4523* (57 minutes: ADD).   Ⓖ

...Nos. 5 and 7. **London Symphony Orchestra / André Previn.** EMI Ⓜ CDM5 65181-2 (77 minutes: ADD).

...No. 6. Waltz Suite, Op. 110 – Nos. 1, 5 and 6. **Scottish National Orchestra / Neeme Järvi.** Chandos Ⓕ CHAN8359 (57 minutes: DDD: 7/85).

...No. 2. Romeo and Juliet – Suite No. 1. **Scottish National Orchestra / Neeme Järvi.** Chandos Ⓕ CHAN8368(61 minutes: DDD: 10/85).

...No. 1. No. 4 (revised 1947 version). **Scottish National Orchestra / Neeme Järvi.** Chandos Ⓕ CHAN8400 (52 minutes: DDD: 3/86). *Selected by Sounds in Retrospect.*

...No. 3; No. 4 (original 1930 version). **Scottish National Orchestra / Neeme Järvi.** Chandos Ⓕ CHAN8401 (59 minutes: DDD: 5/86).

...No. 7. Sinfonietta in A major, Op. 48. **Scottish National Orchestra / Neeme Järvi.** Chandos Ⓕ CHAN8442 (51 minutes: DDD: 7/86).

...No. 1. **Bizet** Symphony in C major. **Britten** Simple Symphony, Op. 4. **Orpheus Chamber Orchestra.** DG Ⓕ 423 624-2GH (64 minutes: DDD: 1/89).

...No. 1. Peter and the wolf, Op. 67[a]. March in B flat major, Op. 99. Overture on Hebrew Themes,
...Op. 34*bis*[b]. [a]**Sting** (narr); [b]**Stefan Vladar** (pf); **Chamber Orchestra of Europe / Claudio Abbado.** DG Ⓕ 429 396-2GH (50 minutes: DDD: 4/91). *Reviewed earlier in this section.*

...Nos. 1 and 3. **Philadelphia Orchestra / Riccardo Muti.** Philips Ⓕ 432 992-2PH (49 minutes: DDD: 2/93).

...Nos. 1[a] and 5[b]. [a]**London Philharmonic Orchestra;** [b]**Saint Louis Symphony Orchestra / Leonard Slatkin** RCA Masters Collection Ⓜ 09026 61350-2 (57 minutes: DDD: 3/93).

...No. 6. **Stravinsky** Petrushka (1911 version). **Leningrad Philharmonic Orchestra / Evgeny Mravinsky.** Multisonic Russian Treasure mono Ⓜ 310189-2* (76 minutes: ADD: 8/94).

...Nos. 1 and 5. **Los Angeles Philharmonic Orchestra / André Previn.** Philips Solo Ⓜ 442 399-2PM (57 minutes: DDD: 9/94).

...No. 6. Waltz Suite, Op. 110. **National Symphony Orchestra of Ukraine / Theodore Kuchar.** Naxos Ⓢ 8 553069 (70 minutes: DDD: 1/96).

New review

Prokofiev Symphonies – No. 3 in C minor, Op. 44; No. 4 in C major, Opp. 47/112. **Berlin Philharmonic Orchestra / Seiji Ozawa.** DG Ⓕ 437 838-2GH (78 minutes: DDD: 9/95). Recorded 1990-92.

A mere glance at the full score of Prokofiev's Third Symphony is enough to induce a migraine. It really is a brute of a piece, a rowdy eruption pushed to the very limits of propriety. Which, in a sense, makes Seiji Ozawa's attempts at musical riot control especially rewarding: one is almost grateful for his careful charting of significant counterpoint, his way of stalking the anguished first movement development and keeping the ensuing revolution tidily under control. Turn to Kondrashin, and the shields are down, the violent aggressors given full reign, yet Ozawa's acknowledgement of the score's more *espressivo* elements makes for some tender revelations. His handling of the first movement's gently rocking triplets (11'02") is beautifully even, the *Andante* second movement, cool and eerie; and the *Scherzo* (with its slithery 12-part string writing) as shockingly reptilian as any. The Third is of course a re-working of music from Prokofiev's opera *The Fiery Angel*, whereas the 1947 revision (and expansion) of the Fourth is a second symphonic exploitation of music from his ballet, *The Prodigal Son*. Here Ozawa's warmth, energy and relative decorum pay high dividends. The first movement's

Allegro eroica has great cut and vigour and the huge, almost desperate central climax is truly its crowning glory. The movement's frequent spells of tranquillity are beautifully realized and Ozawa again brings a sense of cultured ease to the *Andante*. The one disappointment is a third movement that sounds sluggish and uninvolving. The last movement, though, is excellent, with a deft, punchy coda and plenty of power for the concluding *Moderato, brioso*. The recordings are generally more refined – but less spontaneous – than Järvi's. Ozawa's Fourth is top of the league, but the Third is marginally better served by Muti and Kondrashin, the latter being live and an essential purchase for anyone wishing to understand this provocative but endlessly fascinating phase in Prokofiev's creative development.

Prokofiev Symphony No. 5 in B flat major, Op. 100. Scythian Suite, Op. 20. **City of Birmingham Symphony Orchestra / Sir Simon Rattle.** EMI Ⓔ CDC7 54577-2 (64 minutes: DDD: 6/93). Recorded 1992. Ⓖ

A Prokofiev Fifth as vibrant, intelligent and meticulously prepared as you'd expect from this partnership. In the mighty opening movement, there's real mystery about those fairy-tale slumberings at the start of the development, and how naturally Rattle quickens the pulse during the pages which follow, the sense of expectancy and adventure palpably conveyed. Come the coda, and Rattle's expertly-graduated dynamics ensure a riveting succession of spectacular climaxes. Here, too, EMI's impressive Birmingham Symphony Hall production opens out magnificently. Rattle's scherzo is a marvellously quick-witted conception, the slow movement etched with genuine tenderness and bustling good humour reigns supreme in the admirably spirited finale. The coupling is a stunning *Scythian Suite*, combining foundation-threatening pagan spectacle and heart-stopping beauty in ideal equilibrium. A terrific display, excitingly engineered.

Additional recommendations ...

...Alexander Nevsky, Op. 78[a]. Scythian Suite, Op. 20. [a]**Linda Finnie** (sop); **Scottish National** [a]**Chorus and Orchestra / Neeme Järvi.** Chandos Ⓔ CHAN8584 (60 minutes: DDD: 5/88).

...Alexander Nevsky, Op. 78[a]. Lieutenant Kijé – Suite, Op. 60[b]. Scythian Suite, Op. 20[b]. [a]**Elena Obraztsova** (mez); [a]**London Symphony Chorus and Orchestra;** [b]**Chicago Symphony Orchestra / Claudio Abbado.** DG The Originals Ⓜ 447 419-2GOR (79 minutes: ADD: 6/95).

...No. 5[a]. Scythian Suite, Op. 20[b]. Dreams, Op. 6[c]. The white swan, Op. 7 No. 2[d]. [d]**Alan Civil** (hn); [d]women's voices of the **BBC Symphony Chorus;** [a]**Leningrad Philharmonic Orchestra;** [b]**London Symphony Orchestra;** [cd]**BBC Symphony Orchestra / Gennadi Rozhdestvensky.** BBC Radio Classics Ⓑ 15656 9146-2 (76 minutes: ADD: 3/96).

Prokofiev Symphonies – No. 5 in B flat major, Op. 100[b;] No. 1 in D major, Op. 25, "Classical"[a]. Romeo and Juliet – Suite No. 2[c]. The Tale of the Buffoon (Chout) – Danse finale[a]. **Boston Symphony Orchestra / Serge Koussevitzky.** RCA Victor Gold Seal mono Ⓜ 09026 61657-2* (73 minutes: ADD: 4/95). Items marked [a] recorded 1947, [bc]from VL71077, 7/77, recorded 1945-7. *Gramophone classical 100.* ⒼⒼⒼ

Although there have been many fine and some thrilling performances of Prokofiev's Fifth Symphony since it first appeared on record, this is one of the best. Another is the perfectly proportioned and beautifully played Karajan (listed below). Of course, there are many more modern and better recorded versions that can be recommended but (to put an unwelcome scenario) were the bomb about to drop, and one had only time to play one version of the Fifth, for many people it would be this one. Not even the Berlin Philharmonic under Karajan can match the strings of the Boston Symphony in sheer power and eloquence under Koussevitzky. They possess a lyrical intensity matched by few others. Above the stave they sing with unerring purity of intonation: the sound is marvellously clean and their tone can only be called luminous. The wind and brass are of comparable excellence. This account dates from February 6th and 7th, 1946, yet the musicians sound as if they have known this music all their lives. The *Classical* is both vivacious and enchanting. Superb performances, then, in a class of their own, which produce even better results now than they did on vinyl.

Additional recommendation ...

...Nos. 1 and 5. **Berlin Philharmonic Orchestra / Herbert von Karajan.** DG Galleria Ⓜ 437 253-2GGA (71 minutes: ADD: 1/93). ⒼⒼ

Prokofiev String Quartets – No. 1 in B minor, Op. 50; No. 2 in F major, Op. 92. **American Quartet** (Mitchell Stern, Laurie Carney, vns; Daniel Avshalomov, va; David Geber, vc). Olympia Ⓜ OCD340 (50 minutes: ADD: 2/90). Recorded 1982. ⒼⒼ

Prokofiev's wider popularity has never extended to his chamber music. Of his two quartets, the Second is by far the better-known and comes from the war years when Prokofiev was evacuated to the Caucasus, where he made a study of the musical folklore of Kabarda – indeed, it is sometimes known as the "Kabardinian" Quartet. Although the material is folk-derived, it is completely absorbed into Prokofiev's own melodic bloodstream and doesn't sound in the least bit 'folksy'. The second movement quotes a Kabardinian love song of great lyrical beauty, and at one point in the slow movement, the accompaniment imitates a Caucasian stringed instrument, the kamancha. It is a work of real quality which has the astringent flavouring and poetic flair that characterizes Prokofiev at his best. Although the First Quartet, written at the behest of the Library of Congress in 1930, is not so immediately appealing it, too, is a work of substance which grows on the listener. Prokofiev's friend and colleague, Nikolay Miaskovsky, who composed 13 string quartets and more than twice as many symphonies, particularly admired the last movement, and encouraged Prokofiev to score it for full strings. The American Quartet communicate conviction and belief in this music: theirs is a persuasive account, sensitive and yet full-blooded, and they are very well recorded.

Additional recommendations ...

...Nos. 1 and 2. Sonata in C major for Two Violins, Op. 56. **Emerson Quartet.** DG Ⓕ 431 772-2GH (59 minutes: DDD: 10/91).   Ⓖ

...Nos. 1 and 2. Overture on Hebrew Themes in C minor, Op. 34[a]. **Coull Quartet;** [a]**Angela Malsbury** (cl); [a]**David Petitt** (pf). Hyperion Ⓕ CDA66573 (57 minutes: DDD: 9/92).

...No. 2. **Hindemith** String Quartet No. 3, Op. 22. **Walton** String Quartet in A minor. **Hollywood Quartet.** Testament mono Ⓕ SBT1052* (74 minutes: ADD: 3/95). *See review under Hindemith; refer to the Index to Reviews.*   ⒼⒼ

...Nos. 1[a] and 2[a]. Cello Sonata in C major, Op. 119[b]. [a]**Aurora Quartet;** [b]**Michael Grebanier** (vc); [b]**Janet Guggenheim** (pf). Naxos Ⓢ 8 553136 (69 minutes: DDD: 6/95).

Prokofiev Piano Sonatas – No. 1 in F minor, Op. 1; No. 4 in C minor, Op. 29; No. 6 in A major, Op. 82. **Yefim Bronfman** (pf). Sony Classical Ⓕ SK52484 (52 minutes: DDD: 11/94). Recorded 1991. *Gramophone Editor's choice.*   Ⓖ

These are performances which are highly considered, thoroughly idiomatic, possessed of exceptionally clean fingerwork and articulation and rich in subtleties and expressive nuance. Bronfman opens the disc with a particularly impressive and bold-hearted account of the Sixth Sonata; one of those interpretations that seizes and holds the listener's attention from the first to last bar. There's a real sense of dramatic narration about this performance, as opposed to the sometimes overtly (and exclusively) virtuosic readings of some pianists. That's not to deny the virtuosic elements of Bronfman's performance, of which there are plenty, though more impressive is the deceptive ease and finesse with which he traverses some of Prokofiev's excessive demands. In the Fourth Sonata every mood change and transition are superbly caught, and Bronfman's lyricism and delicacy in the tender, probing central section of the slow movement is particularly memorable. The short, youthful First Sonata, always a difficult work to bring off successfully, is played with great verve and panache. Good recorded sound.

Additional recommendations ...

...No. 1; No. 4; No. 5 in C major (revised version), Op. 135; No. 9 in C major, Op. 103; No. 10 in E minor, Op. 137. **Murray McLachlan** (pf). Olympia Ⓜ OCD255 (70 minutes: DDD: 3/90).

...No. 4. Music for Children, Op. 65. Six Pieces, Op. 52. **Boris Berman** (pf). Chandos Ⓕ CHAN8926 (65 minutes: DDD: 6/91).   Ⓖ

...No. 1. Gavotte No. 4 from "Hamlet", Op. 77*bis*. Three Pieces, Op. 96. Sonatinas, Op. 54 – No. 1 in E minor; No. 2 in G major. Four Pieces, Op. 4. **Buxtehude** (arr. Prokofiev) Organ Prelude and Fugue in D minor. **Boris Berman** (pf). Chandos Ⓕ CHAN9017 (57 minutes: DDD: 11/92).

...Piano Sonata No. 3 in A minor, Op. 28. Three Pensées, Op. 62. Three Pieces from "Cinderella", Op. 95. Ten Pieces, Op. 12. **Boris Berman** (pf). Chandos Ⓕ CHAN9069 (56 minutes: DDD: 11/92).

...No. 1. No. 8 in B flat major, Op. 84. Four Pieces, Op. 3. Three Pieces, Op. 59. The tales of an old grandmother, Op. 31. **Oleg Marshev** (pf). Danacord Ⓕ DACOCD392 (64 minutes: DDD: 1/94).

...Nos. 4 and 6. Legend, Op. 12 No. 6. Visions fugitives, Op. 22 Nos. 3-6, 8, 9, 11, 14, 15 and 18. Pieces, Op. 32 – No. 1, Danse; No. 4, Waltz. Pieces from "Cinderella" – Op. 95: No. 2, Gavotte; Op. 97: No. 3, Autumn fairy, No. 6, Oriental dance; Op. 102: No. 1, Grand waltz, No. 3, Quarrel. **Scriabin** Poème-nocturne, Op. 61. Two Danses, Op. 73. Vers la flamme, Op. 72. Fantasie in B minor, Op. 28. **Shostakovich** 24 Preludes and Fugues, Op. 87 – No. 4 in E minor; No. 12 in G sharp minor; No. 14 in E flat major; No. 15 in D flat major; No. 17 in A flat major; No. 23 in F major. **Sviatoslav Richter** (pf). Philips Ⓕ 438 627-2PH2 (two discs: 152 minutes: DDD: 8/94).   ⒼⒼ

Prokofiev Piano Sonatas – No. 2 in D minor, Op. 14; No. 7 in B flat major, Op. 83. The Love for Three Oranges, Op. 33*ter* – March. Ten Pieces from "Cinderella", Op. 97 – No. 10, Waltz. Six Pieces from "Cinderella", Op. 102 – No. 4, Amoroso. Three Pieces, Op. 96 – No. 1, Waltz from "War and Peace". **Barry Douglas** (pf). RCA Victor Red Seal Ⓕ RD60779 (56 minutes: DDD: 3/92). Recorded 1991.   Ⓖ

Prokofiev Ten Pieces from "Romeo and Juliet", Op. 75. Ten Pieces from "Cinderella", Op. 97. The Love for Three Oranges, Op. 33*ter* – March; Scherzo. **Tedd Joselson** (pf). Olympia Ⓕ OCD453 (62 minutes: DDD: 10/92). Recorded 1991.

There has often been a tendency with Prokofiev's piano music for pianists to overplay the percussive, steely qualities of the piano writing at the expense of the lyrical aspects. Barry Douglas, however, attains the perfect blend – muscular and athletic where power and agility are called for, but ever alert to the lyricism which lies beneath the surface. The Second Sonata is a prime example. Douglas has the full measure of this youthful, energetic masterpiece, and one feels that he has fully assimilated this piece before committing it to disc. The first movement with its restless oscillation between expressive melody and ruminative figuration is thoughtfully fashioned, and the knockabout scherzo and fleet-footed energetic finale are delivered with much vigour and flair. The Seventh Sonata (the central work of Prokofiev's "War Trilogy") is impressive too, with Douglas fully in command of its bristling difficulties. As for the rest of the disc, Douglas offers some of the less frequently heard piano transcriptions, of which the delirious 'love' Waltz from *Cinderella* and the March from *The Love for Three Oranges* crave particular attention. The recording is beautifully engineered and balanced.

Crisp, clean finger-work and a fine sense of rhythmic buoyancy can also be found on the very recommendable Olympia disc featuring the American pianist Tedd Joselson. Joselson made a considerable impact in 1976 with his recording of Prokofiev's Sonatas Nos. 2 and 8 (no longer available), and his special empathy with this composer can be heard further in his readings of Prokofiev's own transcriptions from the ballets *Cinderella* and *Romeo and Juliet*. Both collections contain some of the composer's most delightful and engaging numbers: from the charming character portrait "Juliet as a young girl" (brilliantly characterized here by Joselson) and the famous "Montagues and "Capulets" found in *Romeo and Juliet*, to the capricious "Grasshoppers and Dragonflies" and miniature "Four Seasons" suite from *Cinderella*. Joselson displays a keen talent for story-telling and atmosphere throughout, and has been exceptionally well served with a clear and vivid recording.

Additional recommendations ...

...No. 5. Ten Pieces from "Romeo and Juliet", Op. 75. Four Pieces, Op. 32. March and Scherzo from "The Love for Three Oranges", Op. 33*ter*. **Boris Berman** (pf). Chandos Ⓕ CHAN8851 (65 minutes: DDD: 2/91).

...No. 7. Toccata, Op. 11. *Coupled with works by* **Poulenc, Barber, Kabalevsky** and **Fauré** **Vladimir Horowitz** (pf). RCA Victor Gold Seal mono/stereo Ⓜ GD60377* (65 minutes: ADD: 6/92). *See review in the Collections section; refer to the Index to Reviews.* ⒼⒼⒼ

...No. 2. Dumka. Three Pieces, Op. 59. Six Pieces from "Cinderella", Op. 102. Waltzes Suite (Schubert). **Boris Berman** (pf). Chandos Ⓕ CHAN9119 (65 minutes: DDD: 4/93).

...Nos. 2 and 7. Visions fugitives, Op. 22. **Laurent Cabasso** (pf). Auvidis Valois Ⓕ V4655 (58 minutes: DDD: 11/92).

...No. 7. **Stravinsky** Three movements from "Petrushka". **Webern** Piano Variations, Op. 27. **Boulez** Piano Sonata No. 2. **Maurizio Pollini** (pf). DG The Originals Ⓜ 447 431-2GOR (68 minutes: ADD: 6/95). *See review in the Collections section; refer to the Index to Reviews.* ⒼⒼ

...No. 7. **Scriabin** No. 6. Etudes – C sharp minor, Op. 2 No. 1; Op. 8: No. 5 in E major; No. 11 in B flat minor; Op. 42: No. 2 in F sharp minor; No. 3 in F sharp major; No. 4 in F sharp major; No. 5 in C sharp minor; No. 6 in D flat major; No. 8 in E flat major. Trois Etudes, Op. 65. **Miaskovsky** Piano Sonata No. 3 in C minor, Op. 19. **Sviatoslav Richter** (pf); Melodiya mono Ⓜ 74321 29470-2* (68 minutes: ADD: 6/96).

Prokofiev Piano Sonatas – No. 6 in A major, Op. 82; No. 7 in B flat major, Op. 83. Dumka. Visions fugitives, Op. 22. **Oleg Marshev** (pf). Danacord Ⓕ DACOCD391 (74 minutes: DDD: 1/94). Recorded 1991. Ⓖ

Oleg Marshev is a charismatic performer whose dynamic, full-throated volcanic approach (though he is certainly not afraid to allow lyricism into the music when called upon to do so), provides great involvement for the listener. This, Volume One of his complete survey, opens with a commanding, virtuosic performance of the Sixth Sonata which simply teems with detail and subtle nuance. The second movement *Allegretto* is delivered with tremendous flair and *élan* in the outer sections, and the phlegmatic third movement is beautifully paced and crafted. Marshev unleashes the full power of his formidable armoury in the tumultuous finale, where in the closing bars he almost hits boiling-point in terms of sheer virtuosity; his performance may not quite reach those of Kissin or Pogorelich (listed below) but it is certainly a recording that anyone would be happy to live with. In contrast, the early *Dumka* is given a beautifully poised and effortless reading, and the same can be said of Marshev's extremely fine account of the *Visions fugitives*, which can be added to the growing throng of commendable recordings in the catalogue. Marshev concludes the first volume with a stunning account of the Seventh Sonata, which approaches Pollini's classic recording (listed below) for its breadth of vision, dynamic control and sheer virtuosity; pianistically it has all one could wish for – superb rhythmic impetus, tremendous force, wonderful phrasing and in the slower, more reflective moments beautiful tonal control and expressive nuance. The fearsome, toccata finale can only be compared to Pollini's scorching reading for its accuracy and heart-pounding excitement. The recording is full bodied.

Additional recommendations ...

...No. 6. **Ravel** Gaspard de la nuit. **Ivo Pogorelich** (pf). DG Ⓕ 413 363-2GH (52 minutes: DDD: 11/84). ⒼⒼ

...No. 6. *Coupled with works by* **Rachmaninov, Liszt, Chopin, Scriabin** and **Anonymous** **Evgeni Kissin** (pf). Sony Classical Ⓕ SK45931 (73 minutes: DDD: 11/90). *See review in the Collections section; refer to the Index to Reviews.* ⒼⒼ

...No. 6. Etude in C minor, Op. 2 No. 3. **Chopin** Waltz in C sharp minor, Op. 64 No. 2. **Liszt** Etude d'exécution transcendante in F minor, S139 No. 10, "Appassionata". Liebestraum No. 3, S541. Rhapsodie espagnole, S254. **Schumann** Etudes symphoniques, Op. 13. Theme and Variations on the name "Abegg", Op. 1. **Schumann/Liszt** Widmung, S566. **Evgeni Kissin** (pf). RCA Victor Red Seal Ⓕ RD60443 (two discs: 103 minutes: DDD: 3/91). ⒼⒼ

...Visions fugitives – Nos. 1, 2, 3, 6, 7, 9, 10, 11, 12, 13, 14, 16. *Coupled with works by* **Debussy, Szymanowski, Villa-Lobos, Schumann** and **Albéniz** Artur Rubinstein (pf). RCA Victor

Gold Seal Ⓜ 09026 61445-2 (64 minutes: ADD: 10/93). *See review in the Collections section; refer to the Index to Reviews.* ⒼⒼⒼ

…No. 7. *Coupled with works by* **Boulez, Stravinsky** and **Webern** Maurizio Pollini (pf). DG Ⓜ 447 431-2GOR (69 minutes: ADD: 6/95). *See review in the Collections section; refer to the Index to Reviews.* ⒼⒼ

…Visions fugitives. **Hindemith** Ludus tonalis. **Olli Mustonen** (pf). Decca Ⓕ 444 803-2DH (68 minutes: DDD: 5/96).

Prokofiev Piano Sonata No. 8 in B flat major, Op. 84[a]. Visions fugitives, Op. 22 – Nos. 3, 6 and 9[a].
Debussy Estampes[b]. Préludes, Book 1[b] – Voiles; Le vent dans la plaine; Les collines d'Anacapri.
Scriabin Piano Sonata No. 5 in F sharp major, Op. 53[b]. **Sviatoslav Richter** (pf). DG Dokumente Ⓜ 423 573-2GDO (67 minutes: ADD: 9/88). Items marked [a] from SLPM138950 (8/65), [b]SLPM138849 (4/63). Recorded 1963. ⒼⒼ

Richter has long been acclaimed as one of the most dedicated champions of Prokofiev's keyboard music, with the Eighth Sonata always particularly close to his heart. It would certainly be hard to imagine a more profoundly and intensely experienced performance than the one we get here, or one of greater keyboard mastery. After the yearning introspection of the temperamental opening movement and the *Andante*'s evocation of a more gracious past, the rhythmic tension and sheer might of sonority he conjures in the finale make it easy to understand why the composer's biographer, I.V. Nestyev, suspected some underlying programme culminating in "heroic troops resolutely marching ahead, ready to crush anything in their path". In the uniquely Prokofievian fantasy of the three brief *Visions fugitives* he is wholly bewitching. As for the Fifth Sonata of Scriabin, his impetuous start at once reveals his understanding of its manic extremities of mood. For just these Russian performances alone, this excellently refurbished disc can be hailed as a collector's piece. And as a bonus there is Debussy too, with infinite subtleties of tonal shading to heighten atmospheric evocation.

Additional recommendation …

…Visions fugitives. **Scriabin.** Piano Sonatas – No. 2 in G sharp minor, Op. 19, "Sonata-fantasy"; No. 9 in F major, Op. 68, "Messe noire". Etudes – F sharp minor, Op. 8 No. 2; B major, Op. 8 No. 4; E major, Op. 8 No. 5; F sharp major, Op. 42 No. 3; F sharp major, Op. 42 No. 4; F minor, Op. 42 No. 7. Four Pieces, Op. 51. Vers la flamme, Op. 72. **Nikolai Demidenko** (pf). Conifer Ⓕ CDCF204 (73 minutes: DDD: 8/91). Ⓖ

New review

Prokofiev Violin Sonatas – No. 1 in F minor, Op. 80; No. 2 in D major, Op. 94*a*. Five Melodies, Op. 35*b*. **Vadim Repin** (vn); **Boris Berezovsky** (pf). Erato Ⓕ 0630-10698-2 (63 minutes: DDD: 1/96). Recorded 1995. *Gramophone Editor's choice.* Ⓖ

A clear first choice in this repertoire and heartening confirmation of the young Vadim Repin's considerable violinistic skills. Tension sets in right from the First Sonata's opening bars: the tone is bright, sweet, tremulous and warmly expressive, while the music's sombre mood is precisely gauged. Repin phrases with considerable sensitivity and his attack in the work's faster episodes – the *Allegro brusco*'s outer sections and most of the finale – has a Heifetzian 'edge'. Nervous energy is also much in evidence, while the *Andante* – one of Prokofiev's most haunting creations – has a wistfully distracted air that Boris Berezovsky matches with some notably perceptive piano playing. The *Allegrissimo* finale, too, is arresting: deftly fingered, percussively insistent and with a truly heartfelt projection of the work's tender closing phrase. One of Repin's leading qualities is his obvious interpretative sincerity; nowhere does one sense the suave affectation that afflicts some of his contemporaries, a fact that registers with particular force in the Second Sonata's opening *Moderato*. Here lesser artists often sound either matter-of-fact or uninterested, and even superior ones (in particular Mullova and Milstein) opt for relative coolness. Repin and Berezovsky, on the other hand, are both tender and relaxed; phrasal 'crossfire' and keen inflexion keep sparks flying in the *Scherzo*, the *Allegretto leggiero e scherzando* is appropriately limpid, and although the finale could have swaggered rather more freely, there are magical moments to spare. Both players achieve an impressive range of colour throughout and the five delightful *Melodies* make for a welcome sequence of encores. A first-rate programme, very well recorded.

Additional recommendations …

…Violin Sonata No. 2. **Ravel** Violin Sonata (1927). **Stravinsky** Divertimento. **Viktoria Mullova** (vn); **Bruno Canino** (pf). Philips Ⓕ 426 254-2PH (61 minutes: DDD: 8/90).

…Violin Sonatas. Five Melodies, Op. 35*b*. **Gidon Kremer** (vn); **Martha Argerich** (pf). DG Ⓕ 431 803-2GH (66 minutes: DDD: 10/92). Ⓖ

…Violin Sonatas[b]. Violin Concerto No. 2 in G minor, Op. 63[a]. **Itzhak Perlman** (vn); [b]**Vladimir Ashkenazy** (pf); [a]**Boston Symphony Orchestra / Erich Leinsdorf**. RCA Victor Gold Seal Ⓜ 09026 61454-2 (78 minutes: ADD: 9/94). Ⓖ

…Violin Sonatas. Five Melodies. **Nikolai Madojan** (vn); **Elisabeth Westenholz** (pf). Kontrapunkt Ⓕ 32185 (68 minutes: DDD: 9/94).

...Violin Sonatas. **Ravel** Violin Sonata in G major. **Shlomo Mintz** (vn); **Yefim Bronfman** (pf).
DG Masters Ⓜ 445 557-2GMA (74 minutes: DDD: 11/95).

Prokofiev The Love for Three Oranges (sung in French). **Gabriel Bacquier** (bar) King of Clubs;
Jean-Luc Viala (ten) Prince; **Hélène Perraguin** (mez) Princess Clarissa; **Vincent Le Texier** (bass-
bar) Leandro; **Georges Gautier** (ten) Truffaldino; **Didier Henry** (bar) Pantaloon, Farfarello,
Master of Ceremonies; **Gregory Reinhart** (bass) Tchelio; **Michèle Lagrange** (sop) Fata Morgana;
Consuelo Caroli (mez) Linetta; **Brigitte Fournier** (sop) Nicoletta; **Catherine Dubosc** (sop) Ninetta;
Jules Bastin (bass) Cook; **Béatrice Uria Monzon** (mez) Smeraldina; **Chorus and Orchestra of Lyon
Opéra / Kent Nagano.** Virgin Classics Ⓕ VCD7 59566-2 (two discs: 102 minutes: DDD: 12/89).
Notes, text and translation included. *Gramophone Award Winner 1990.*   Ⓖ
This is a wonderfully zany story about a prince whose hypochondriac melancholy is lifted only at the
sight of a malevolent witch tumbling over, in revenge for which she casts on him a love-spell for three
oranges: in the ensuing complications he encounters an ogre's gigantic cook who goes all gooey at the
sight of a pretty ribbon, princesses inside two of the oranges die of oppressive desert heat, and the
third is saved only by the intervention of various groups of 'spectators' who argue with each other on
the stage. The music's brittle vivacity matches that of the plot, and though there are no set-pieces for
the singers and there is practically no thematic development – the famous orchestral March and
Scherzo are the only passages that reappear – the effervescent score is most engaging. The
performance, conducted by the musical director of the Lyon Opéra, is full of zest, with lively
orchestral playing and a cast that contains several outstanding members and not a single weak one;
and the recording is extremely good. Those desirous of so doing can delve into the work's symbolism
and identify the objects of its satire – principally Stanislavsky's naturalistic Moscow Arts Theatre;
others can simply accept this as a thoroughly enjoyable romp.

Prokofiev War and Peace. **Lajos Miller** (bar) Prince Andrei Bolkonsky; **Galina Vishnevskaya** (sop)
Natasha Rostova; **Katherine Ciesinski** (mez) Sonya; **Maria Paunova** (mez) Maria Akhrosimova;
Dimiter Petkov (bass) Count Ilya Rostov; **Wieslaw Ochman** (ten) Count Pytor Bezukhov; **Stefania
Toczyska** (mez) Helena Bezukhova; **Nicolai Gedda** (ten) Anatol Kuragin; **Vladimir de Kanel** (bass-
bar) Dolokhov; **Mira Zakai** (contr); Princess Maria Bolkonsky; **Malcolm Smith** (bass) Colonel
Vasska Denisov; **Nicola Ghiuselev** (bass) Marshal Mikhail Kutuzov; **Eduard Tumagian** (bar)
Napoleon Bonaparte; **Radio France Chorus; French National Orchestra / Mstislav Rostropovich.**
Erato Libretto Ⓜ 2292-45331-2 (four discs: 247 minutes: DDD: 4/92). Notes, text and translation
included. From ECD75480 (1/89). Recorded 1986.   Ⓖ
Over four hours long, 72 characters, 13 scene changes: is it any wonder that Prokofiev's *War and
Peace*, adapted from Tolstoy's famously epic novel, has had few performances and even fewer forays
into the recording studio? At the front of the booklet Rostropovich recalls how, as Prokofiev lay
dying, he reiterated one wish, that Rostropovich should make this opera known to the world. It comes
as no surprise, then, to find a deeply committed performance from both soloists (only 45 of them due
to some adroit doubling), chorus and orchestra. Prokofiev adapted the novel into seven 'peace' and
six 'war' tableaux, thus sustaining drama through contrast throughout its Wagnerian length. With few
exceptions the multinational cast sing in good Russian and among them Lajos Miller is particularly
affecting as Prince Andrei, pleasingly ardent in his opening moonlit aria. The central female role of
Natasha is taken by Galina Vishnevskaya. She sang the role in the 1959 première and inevitably no
longer sounds like an innocent 16 year old. Unfortunately, problems are compounded by a hardness
in her tone and a lack of attention to detail in some of the quieter sections – particularly in her
exchanges with Helena where the asides sound like part of the normal conversation. Stefania
Toczyska as the treacherous Helena makes a great impression, as does Katherine Ciesinski as
Natasha's confidante, Sonya. Of the men, Nicolai Gedda as Prince Anatol sings with character and
great style and Eduard Tumagian is a suitably heroic and steadfast Napoleon. An added attraction of
the recording are the sound effects, particularly in the war scenes, convincing but never overly
obtrusive. Good translations are provided in three languages, crowning a laudable achievement.

New review
Prokofiev The Fiery Angel. **Galina Gorchakova** (sop) Renata; **Sergei Leiferkus** (bar) Ruprecht;
Vladimir Galusin (ten) Agrippa; **Konstantin Pluzhnikov** (ten) Mephistopheles; **Sergei Alexashkin**
(bass) Faust; **Vladimir Ognovanko** (bass) Inquisitor; **Evgeni Boitsov** (ten) Jakob Glock; **Valery
Lebed** (bass) Doctor; Yuri Laptev (ten) Mathias; **Mikhail Kit** (bar) Servant; **Evgenia Perlasova**
(mez) Landlady; **Larissa Diadkova** (mez) Fortune teller; **Olga Markova-Mikhailenko** (contr)
Mother Superior; **Yevgeny Fedotov** (bass) Innkeeper; **Mikhail Chernozhukov** (bass) First
Neighbour; **Andrei Karabanov** (bar) Second Neighbour; **Gennadi Bezzubenkov** (bass) Third
Neighbour; **Tatiana Kravtsova** (sop) First Nun; **Tatiana Filimoniva** (sop) Second Nun; **Chorus and
Orchestra of the Kirov Opera / Valery Gergiev.** Philips Ⓕ 446 078-2PH2 (two discs: 119 minutes:
DDD: 1/96). Recorded live in 1993. Notes, text and translation included. Recorded 1993.
Gramophone Editor's choice.   ⒼⒼ
At last we have something close to the music's full potential revealed. The opera is no blameless
masterpiece – Prokofiev's indulgence in lurid sensationalism sometimes gets the better of his artistic
judgement. But that sounds a pretty po-faced judgement in the face of the overwhelming power which

so much of this score exudes. This Maryinsky performance comes live from what is clearly a highly-charged occasion in one of the world's great opera houses. That brings with it the disadvantage of a constrained opera-pit acoustic, which makes some of Prokofiev's over-the-top scoring seem pretty congested. But the immediacy and clarity of the sound, plus the orchestra's rhythmic grasp, ensures that the effect is still properly blood-curdling. If Leiferkus's distinctive rich baritone at first sounds a touch microphoney, the ear can soon adjust to that too, and Gorchakova brings intense beauty as well as intensity to Renata's hysterics, taking us right inside the psychological drama. The supporting roles are filled with distinction and this makes a huge difference to the sustaining of dramatic tension, the crescendo which Prokofiev aimed to build through his five acts. Considering the extent of the stage goings-on there is remarkably little audience distraction on the recording.

Further listening ...

...Eugene Onegin. **Timothy West, Samuel West, Niamh Cusack** (narrs); **New Company; Sinfonia 21 / Sir Edward Downes.** Chandos CHAN9318/9 (11/94).

...War and Peace – Symphonic Suite (arr. Palmer). Summer Night – Suite, Op. 123. Russian Overture, Op. 72. **Philharmonia Orchestra / Neeme Järvi.** Chandos CHAN9096 (3/93).

...Semyon Kotko – symphonic suite, Op. 81*bis*. Four Portraits and Denoument from "The Gambler", Op. 49. **Royal Scottish Orchestra / Neeme Järvi.** Chandos CHAN8803 (9/90).

...Lieutenant Kijé – Suite, Op. 60. *Coupled with* **Rimsky-Korsakov** Scheherazade, Op. 35. **London Philharmonic Orchestra / Takuo Yuasa.** EMI Eminence CD-EMX2214 (12/93).

...Lieutenant Kijé – Suite, Op. 60. *Coupled with works by* **Hovhaness** and **Stravinsky** Chicago Symphony Orchestra / Fritz Reiner. RCA Victor Living Stereo 09026 61957-2 (9/95). *See review under Hovaness; refer to the Index to Reviews.*

...Cantata for the 20th Anniversary of the October Revolution, Op. 74[a]. The tale of the stone flower – excerpts. [a]**Gennadi Rozhdestvensky** (spkr); **Philharmonia** [a]**Chorus and Orchestra / Neeme Järvi.** Chandos CHAN9095 (3/93).

...Flute Sonata in D major, Op. 94. *Coupled with* **Poulenc** Flute Sonata. **E. Burton** Flute Sonatina. **Fauré** Morceau de lecture. **Martinů** Flute Sonata No. 1. **Jennifer Stinton** (fl); **Scott Mitchell** (pf). Collins Classics 1103-2 (12/91).

...Toccata in C major, Op. 11. *Coupled with works by* **Brahms, Chopin, Ravel** and **Liszt** Martha **Argerich** (pf). DG The Originals 447 430-2GOR (6/95). *See review in the Collections section; refer to the Index to Reviews.*   ⓖⓖ

...Alexander Nevsky, Op. 78. Ivan the Terrible, Op. 116 (ed. Lankester). **Soloists; New London Children's Choir; London Symphony Chorus and Orchestra / Mstislav Rostropovich.** Sony Classical S2K48387 (4/93).

...Alexander Nevsky, Op. 78[a]. **Rachmaninov** The Bells, Op. 35[b]. [b]**Sheila Armstrong** (sop); [a]**Anna Reynolds** (mez); [b]**Robert Tear** (ten); [b]**John Shirley-Quirk** (bar); **London Symphony Chorus and Orchestra / André Previn.** EMI Studio Ⓜ CDM7 63114-2 (78 minutes: ADD: 10/89). *See review under Rachmaninov; refer to the Index to Reviews.*   ⓖⓖ

Giacomo Puccini   Italian 1858-1924

Puccini Opera Arias: La rondine – Chi il bel sogno di Doretta. La bohème – Sì, mi chiamano Mimì; Donde lieta uscì. Gianni Schicchi – O mio babbino caro. Manon Lescaut – In quelle trine morbide; Sola, perduta, abbandonata. Suor Angelica – Senza mamma, O bimbo. Tosca – Vissi d'arte. Madama Butterfly – Un bel di vedremo; Che tua madre; Tu, tu, piccolo iddio. Turandot – Signore, ascolta!; In questa reggia; Tu, che di gel sei cinta. **Julia Varady** (sop); **Berlin Radio Symphony Orchestra / Marcello Viotti.** Orfeo Ⓕ C323941A (52 minutes: DDD: 5/95). Recorded 1993.

A lovely and somewhat surprising record by the most fascinating and patrician lyric soprano of the present age: 'surprising' because, though Varady is associated closely enough with Verdi, the Puccini connection is less readily made, 'lovely' because the voice is still so pure, the style so musical and (above all) the response so intelligent, immediate and full-hearted. She adjusts wonderfully well to the Italian idiom, lightening the vowels, freeing the upper range, allowing more portamento than she would probably do in other music, yet employing in its use the finest technical skill and artistic judgement. Her singing of Magda's song in *La rondine* opens the record and introduces a singer who sounds (give or take a little) half her actual age: Varady's début dates back to 1962, and these recordings were made in 1993. In Mimi's narrative she sings with so fine a perception of the character – the hesitancies, the joy in "mi piaccion quelle cose" – that Schwarzkopf's exquisite recording came to mind, just as, from time to time, and especially in the *Madama Butterfly* excerpts, the finely concentrated, tragic restraint of Meta Seinemeyer was recalled. It is good to hear, too, how sensitively Varady differentiates between characters, Manon Lescaut having that essential degree of additional sophistication in tone and manner. What runs as a thread through all of these characterizations is a feeling for their dignity. Mimì does not simper. Sister Angelica does not sob. Lauretta has resolution in her pleading. Butterfly, Liù and Tosca are what they should be: women whose pathos lies not in their weakness but in a passionate, single-minded fidelity. That leaves Turandot which is a mistake. That is, she is outside the singer's scope and should remain so: it is not merely a matter of vocal thrust, weight and stamina, but also of voice-character. The performance of her aria has clear merits (the imperiousness of "Mai nessun m'avrà" for instance), but a little more of Manon ("L'ora, o Tirsi") or Tosca ("Non lo sospiri la nostra casetta") or the solos from *Le Villi* and *Edgar* would have been more welcome. Welcome too would have been printed texts, though it is true the excerpts are all pretty well known. None of that should deter purchase; this is singing to treasure.

Puccini Manon Lescaut. **Mirella Freni** (sop) Manon Lescaut; **Luciano Pavarotti** (ten) Des Grieux; **Dwayne Croft** (bar) Lescaut; **Giuseppe Taddei** (bar) Geronte; **Ramon Vargas** (ten) Edmondo; **Cecilia Bartoli** (mez) Singer; **Federico Davia** (bass) Innkeeper, Captain; **Anthony Laciura** (ten) Dancing Master; **Paul Groves** (ten) Lamplighter; **James Courtney** (bass) Sergeant; **Chorus and Orchestra of the Metropolitan Opera / James Levine.** Decca Ⓕ 440 200-2DHO2 (two discs: 120 minutes: DDD: 11/93). Notes, text and translation included. Recorded 1992.

With Luciano Pavarotti as a powerful Des Grieux, James Levine conducts a comparably big-boned performance of *Manon Lescaut*, bringing out the red-blooded drama of Puccini's first big success, while not ignoring its warmth and tender poetry in exceptionally full, vivid sound with the voices well in front of the orchestra. In the title-role Freni's performance culminates in an account of the big Act 4 aria, more involving and passionate than any of the others on the versions listed below with the voice showing no signs of wear, and with her sudden change of face at the words "terra di pace" ("a land of peace") bringing a magical lightening of tone. That aria makes a thrilling climax, when too often this act can seem a letdown. In this as in so much else, Levine conveys the tensions and atmosphere of a stage performance in a way that owes much to his experience at the Metropolitan. More completely than the other versions, each with very great merits, it avoids the feeling of a studio performance. Reactions to Pavarotti as Des Grieux will differ widely. The closeness of balance means that in volume his singing rarely drops below *mezzo forte*, but there is little harm in having so passionate a portrait of Des Grieux as Pavarotti's. Needless to say, the hero's big emotional climaxes in each of the first three acts come over at full force. The rest of the cast is strong too, with Dwayne Croft a magnificent Lescaut who, as well as singing with rich, firm tone, brings out the character's wry humour. Many collectors will count this a clear first choice among current versions. For the sheer power of Puccinian drama, vividly conveyed, it will be hard to beat.

Additional recommendations ...

...**Soloists; Chorus of the Royal Opera House, Covent Garden; Philharmonia Orchestra / Giuseppe Sinopoli.** DG Ⓕ 413 893-2GH2 (two discs: DDD: 3/85).

...**Soloists; Chorus and Orchestra of La Scala, Milan / Tullio Serafin.** EMI mono Ⓔ CDS7 47393-8* (two discs: 120 minutes: 9/86).

...**Soloists; Jack Gregoor Choir; Belgian Radio and TV Philharmonic Chorus and Orchestra / Alexander Rahbari.** Naxos Ⓢ 8 660019/20 (two discs: 126 minutes: DDD: 12/92).

Puccini La bohème. **Jussi Björling** (ten) Rodolfo; **Victoria de los Angeles** (sop) Mimì; **Robert Merrill** (bar) Marcello; **Lucine Amara** (sop) Musetta; **John Reardon** (bar) Schaunard; **Giorgio Tozzi** (bass) Colline; **Fernando Corena** (bass) Benoit, Alcindoro; **William Nahr** (ten) Parpignol; **Thomas Powell** (bar) Customs Official; **George del Monte** (bar) Sergeant; **Columbus Boychoir; RCA Victor Chorus and Orchestra / Sir Thomas Beecham.** EMI mono Ⓕ CDS7 47235-8* (two discs: 108 minutes: ADD: 6/87). Notes, text and translation included. From ALP1409/10 (1/57). *Gramophone classical 100.* ⒼⒼⒼ

To recommend a 37-year-old mono recording of *La bohème* over all the more glamorously star-studded and sumptuously recorded versions that have appeared since may seem perverse, but the Beecham version is a true classic which has never been surpassed. This intimate opera is not about two superstars showing off how loudly they can sing their top Cs, but about a poverty-stricken poet's love for a mortally-ill seamstress. De los Angeles's infinitely-touching Mimì and Björling's poetic, ardent Rodolfo are backed by consistently fine and characterful ensemble work making this the most realistic version ever recorded. The recording of course shows its age, but this is scarcely noticeable as page after page of the score come freshly alive again: not a *tour de force* of vocalism, not a sequence of famous arias with bits of dialogue between but a lyric tragedy of wrenching pathos and truth.

Additional recommendations ...

...**Soloists; Sainta Cecilia Academy Chorus, Rome; Santa Cecilia Academy Orchestra, Rome / Alberto Erede.** Decca mono Ⓜ 440 233-2LF2* (two discs: 105 minutes: ADD). Ⓖ

...**Soloists; Chorus and Orchestra of La Scala, Milan / Antonino Votto.** EMI mono Ⓜ CDS7 47475-2* (two discs: 106 minutes: ADD: 11/87).

...**Soloists; Schöneberger Boys' Choir; Berlin German Opera Chorus; Berlin Philharmonic Orchestra / Herbert von Karajan.** Decca Ⓕ 421 049-2DH2 (two discs: 110 minutes: ADD: 11/87).

...Act 4. **Heddle Nash** (ten) with various artists. **London Philharmonic Orchestra / Sir Thomas Beecham.** Dutton Laboratories mono Ⓜ CDLX7012* (69 minutes: ADD: 2/95). *See review in the Collections section; refer to the Index to Reviews.* Ⓖ

...**Soloists; Chorus and Orchestra of La Scala, Milan / Carlo Sabajno.** VAI mono Ⓕ VAIA1078* (two discs: 104 minutes: ADD: 3/95).

...**Soloists; Chorus and Orchestra of La Scala, Milan / Umberto Berrettoni.** Nimbus mono Ⓜ NI7862/3* (two discs: 102 minutes: ADD: 3/95).

Puccini Tosca. **Maria Callas** (sop) Floria Tosca; **Giuseppe di Stefano** (ten) Mario Cavaradossi;
Tito Gobbi (bar) Baron Scarpia; **Franco Calabrese** (bass) Cesare Angelotti; **Angelo Mercuriali**
(ten) Spoletta; **Melchiorre Luise** (bass) Sacristan; **Dario Caselli** (bass) Sciarrone, Gaoler; **Alvaro
Cordova** (treb) Shepherd Boy; **Chorus and Orchestra of La Scala, Milan / Victor de Sabata.**
EMI mono Ⓕ CDS7 47175-8* (two discs: 108 minutes: ADD: 9/85). Notes, text and translation
included. From Columbia 33CX1094/5 (12/53). Recorded 1953. *Gramophone classical
100.*   ⓖⓖⓖ
In the course of *Tosca*'s history there have been many notable interpreters, but few have been able to
encompass so unerringly the love, jealousy and eventual courage of Tosca as well as Maria Callas. Her
resinous, sensuous tone, her wonderful diction, and her inborn passion filled every phrase of the score
with special and individual meaning. In 1953 she was in her early prime, the tone seldom prey to those
uneasy moments on high that marred her later recordings, and with the vital, vivid conducting of
Victor de Sabata, her performance has rightly attained classic status. Giuseppe di Stefano is the ardent
Cavaradossi, his tone forward and vibrant in that way peculiar to Italians. Tito Gobbi's cynical,
snarling Scarpia, aristocratic in manner, vicious in meaning, remains unique in that part on record.
The mono recording stands up well to the test of time.
Additional recommendations ...
...**Soloists; Vienna State Opera Chorus; Vienna Philharmonic Orchestra / Herbert von Karajan.**
Decca Grand Opera Ⓜ 421 670-2DM2 (two discs: 114 minutes: ADD: 1/89).
...**Soloists; Paris Opéra Chorus and Conservatoire Orchestra / Georges Prêtre.** EMI Ⓜ CMS7
69974-2 (two discs: 112 minutes: DDD: 8/89).
...**Soloists; Slovak Philharmonic Chorus; Czecho-Slovak Radio Symphony Orchestra, Bratislava /
Alexander Rahbari.** Naxos Ⓢ 8 660001/2 (two discs: 116 minutes: DDD: 10/91).
...**Soloists; Chorus and Orchestra of the Royal Opera House, Covent Garden / Sir Colin Davis.**
Philips Duo Ⓜ 438 359-2PM2 (two discs: 118 minutes: ADD: 8/93).

New review

Puccini Tosca (sung in English). **Jane Eaglen** (sop) Tosca; **Dennis O'Neill** (ten) Cavaradossi;
Gregory Yurisich (bar) Scarpia; **Peter Rose** (bass) Angelotti; **John Daszak** (ten) Spoletta; **Andrew
Shore** (bass) Sacristan; **Christopher Booth-Jones** (bass) Sciarrone; **Ashley Holland** (bass) Gaoler;
Charbel Michael (mez) Shepherd Boy; **Peter Kay Children's Choir; Geoffrey Mitchell Choir;
Philharmonia Orchestra / David Parry.** Chandos Ⓕ CHAN3000 (two discs: 118 minutes: DDD:
6/96). Notes and text included. Recorded 1995.
This is an issue to delight far more than devotees of opera in English, a gripping account of Puccini's
red-blooded drama. Above all, it offers the first major recording to demonstrate the powers of Jane
Eaglen at full stretch in one of the most formidable, vocally satisfying portrayals of the role of Tosca
in years. David Parry here demonstrates his full understanding of Puccini and the bite and energy in
the playing of the Philharmonia, not to mention the expressive warmth in the love music, will have
you riveted as though hearing the music for the first time. The opulent Chandos sound, cleanly
focused with plenty of atmosphere and presence, adds to the impact, whether in the power of the big
tuttis or in the subtlety of whispered string *pianissimos*. Off-stage effects are nicely evocative, though
the sequence of bell-sounds at the start of Act 3 is so clear it suggests an orchestra rather than a
Roman landscape. Otherwise, the slightly forward balance of voices against orchestra is very well
judged for a set in which the audibility of words is paramount. The translation is Edmund Tracey's
as used by ENO at the Coliseum and generally very good because unobtrusive, even if you get
occasional awkwardnesses. Eaglen is well matched by Dennis O'Neill as Cavaradossi, aptly Italianate
in every register, and betraying only a slight unevenness occasionally, not a wobble, on high notes
under pressure. Gregory Yurisich makes a powerful Scarpia, younger-sounding than most, and
therefore a more plausible lover. The others are well-cast too, notably Peter Rose as an outstanding,
fresh-voiced Angelotti.

Puccini Madama Butterfly. **Renata Scotto** (sop) Madama Butterfly; **Carlo Bergonzi** (ten)
Pinkerton; **Rolando Panerai** (bar) Sharpless; **Anna di Stasio** (mez) Suzuki; **Piero De Palma** (ten)
Goro; **Giuseppe Morresi** (ten) Prince Yamadori; **Silvana Padoan** (mez) Kate Pinkerton; **Paolo
Montarsolo** (bass) The Bonze; **Mario Rinaudo** (bass) Commissioner; **Rome Opera House Chorus
and Orchestra / Sir John Barbirolli.** EMI Ⓜ CMS7 69654-2 (two discs: 142 minutes: ADD: 5/89).
Notes, text and translation included. From SAN184/6 (9/67). Recorded 1966.
This is not quite the best sung *Butterfly* available but Barbirolli ensures that it is the most richly and
enjoyably Italianate. Italian opera was in his blood and as a cellist at Covent Garden, playing under
Puccini's direction, and as a conductor whose formative years were spent in the theatre (his Covent
Garden début was in this very opera), Barbirolli's pleasure in returning to the world of opera is
audible throughout this recording. The rapport between him and the Italian orchestra is close and
affectionate; it is a heartwarming performance, subtle and supple in the pacing of the love duet,
urgently passionate in the great outbursts. Scotto is a touching Butterfly, with all the tiny and crucial
details of characterization delicately moulded. There have been more dashing Pinkertons than
Bergonzi, but not many who have so effectively combined suavity of sound with neatness of phrasing
and good taste. Panerai is a first-class Sharpless and di Stasio a sympathetic Suzuki; there are no weak

links elsewhere, and the recording is decent enough for its date, if a bit narrow in perspective and with the singers rather forwardly placed. Barbirolli's *Butterfly* has several distinguished rivals on CD, but for a performance that will remind you of the first time you fell in love with this opera it has permanent value and great eloquence.

Additional recommendations ...

...Soloists; **Vienna State Opera Chorus; Vienna Philharmonic Orchestra / Herbert von Karajan.** Decca Ⓔ 417 577-2DH3 (three discs: 145 minutes: ADD: 6/87).

...Soloists; **Chorus and Orchestra of La Scala, Milan / Herbert von Karajan.** EMI mono Ⓜ CDS7 47959-8* (two discs: 139 minutes: ADD: 10/87).

...Soloists; **Ambrosian Opera Chorus; Philharmonia Orchestra / Giuseppe Sinopoli.** DG 423 567-2GH3 (three discs: 154 minutes: DDD: 12/88).

...Soloists; **Rome Opera Chorus and Orchestra / Gabriele Santini.** EMI Studio Ⓜ CMS7 63634-2 (two discs: 137 minutes: ADD: 3/91).

...Soloists; **Slovak Philharmonic Chorus; Czecho-Slovak Radio Symphony Orchestra, Bratislava / Alexander Rahbari.** Naxos Ⓢ 8 660015/6 (two discs: 141 minutes: DDD: 5/92). ⒺⒺ

Puccini La Fanciulla del West. **Carol Neblett** (sop) Minnie; **Plácido Domingo** (ten) Dick Johnson; **Sherrill Milnes** (bar) Jack Rance; **Francis Egerton** (ten) Nick; **Robert Lloyd** (bass) Ashby; **Gwynne Howell** (bass) Jake Wallace; **Paul Hudson** (bass) Billy Jackrabbit; **Anne Wilkens** (sop) Wowkle; **Chorus and Orchestra of the Royal Opera House, Covent Garden / Zubin Mehta.** DG Ⓔ 419 640-2GH2 (two discs: 130 minutes: ADD: 11/87). Notes, text and translation included. From 2709 078 (9/78). Recorded 1977. *Gramophone Award Winner in 1978.*

This opera depicts the triangular relationship between Minnie, the saloon owner and 'mother' to the entire town of gold miners, Jack Rance, the sheriff and Dick Johnson (alias Ramerrez), a bandit leader. The music is highly developed in Puccini's seamless lyrical style, the arias for the main characters emerge from the texture and return to it effortlessly. The vocal colours are strongly polarized with the cast being all male except for one travesti role and Minnie herself. The score bristles with robust melody as well as delicate scoring, betraying a masterly hand at work. Carol Neblett is a strong Minnie, vocally distinctive and well characterized, whilst Plácido Domingo and Sherrill Milnes make a good pair of suitors for the spunky little lady. Zubin Mehta conducts with real sympathy for the idiom and the orchestra respond well.

Additional recommendation ...

...Soloists; **Hungarian Radio Chorus; Frankfurt Radio Symphony Orchestra / Marcello Viotti.** Sine Qua Non Ⓔ 39820212 (two discs: 125 minutes: DDD: 1/94).

Puccini Il Tabarro[a]. **Tito Gobbi** (bar) Michele; **Margaret Mas** (sop) Giorgetta, **Giacinto Prandelli** (ten) Luigi; **Piero De Palma** (ten) Tinca; **Plinio Clabassi** (bas) Talpa; **Miriam Pirazzini** (mez) Frugola.

Puccini Suor Angelica[b]. **Victoria de los Angeles** (sop) Suor Angelica; **Fedora Barbieri** (mez) Princess; **Mina Doro** (mez) Abbess, Mistress of the novices; **Corinna Vozza** (mez) Sister Monitor; **Lidia Marimpietri** (sop) Suor Genovieffa, Almoner Sister I; **Santa Chissari** (sop) Suor Osmina, Almoner Sister II, Novice; **Anna Marcangeli** (sop) Suor Dolcina; **Teresa Cantarini** (mez) Infirmary Sister, **Silvia Bertona** (sop) Lay Sister I; **Maria Huder** (mez) Lay Sister II.

Puccini Gianni Schicchi[c]. **Tito Gobbi** (bar) Gianni Schicchi; **Victoria de los Angeles** (sop) Lauretta; **Carlo del Monte** (ten) Rinuccio; **Anna Maria Canali** (Zita); **Adelio Zagonara** (ten) Gherardo; **Lidia Marimpietri** (sop) Nella; **Claudio Cornoldi** (ten) Gherardino; **Saturno Meletti** (bass) Betto di Signa; **Paolo Montarsolo** (bass) Simone; **Fernando Valentini** (bar) Marco; **Giuliana Raymondi** (sop) La Cieca; **Rome Opera Chorus; Rome Opera Orchestra /** [a]**Vincenzo Bellezza,** [b]**Tullio Serafin,** [c]**Gabriele Santini.** EMI mono/[c]stereo Ⓜ CMS7 64165-2* (three discs: 161 minutes: ADD: 6/93). Texts and translations included. Item marked [a] from HMV ALP1355 (5/56), [b] ALP1577 (6/58), [c] ASD295 (12/59).

Unless you insist on the most up-to-date recorded sound, or on buying the individual operas of Puccini's trilogy separately (and that, regrettably, is becoming harder to do these days; most available recordings come as indivisible boxed sets) this is the classic *Trittico*, and the obvious first recommendation. Gobbi's blackly authoritative but pitiful Michele in *Il Tabarro* and his genially authoritative Schicchi (the two outer panels of the triptych *do* match, in an odd sort of way) have seldom been equalled, let alone surpassed. De los Angeles's Angelica is more purely and movingly sung than any other on record, and her Lauretta in *Gianni Schicchi* is enchanting. Could it be said, even so, that *Il Tabarro* is the weak link in this trilogy? It is a three-hander, surely, and neither the soprano nor the tenor are quite in Gobbi's league? Mas is a bit plummy and mezzoish, true, but the slight implication this gives that Giorgetta's liaison with the young stevedore Luigi is her last chance at escape from a hateful life and a marriage that has soured adds an extra twinge of pain to a plot in which all three principals are victims. And in this context Prandelli's slightly strenuous rawness of tone characterizes Luigi rather well. In *Gianni Schicchi*, Carlo del Monte as Rinuccio also looks like under-casting but in fact he's one of the few tenors who've recorded the part who sounds convincingly young, and his ardent praise of Florence and the 'new men' who are reinvigorating the city is proudly sung. Here, too, Gobbi is surrounded by a constellation of pungent character actors, and de los Angeles in *Suor Angelica* is teamed with a charmingly girlish, impulsive Genovieffa and with Fedora

Barbieri's rigidly implacable Princess (is there another parallel here, with the stiff-necked Zita, 'La Vecchia', in *Gianni Schicchi*?). With generally very stylish conducting throughout (only Belezza in *Il Tabarro* is a touch staid, and he omits nearly all of Puccini's off-stage sound effects) only the rather elderly recordings might be seen as a drawback. EMI boldly label the whole set 'stereo', but both *Il Tabarro* and *Suor Angelica* sound like minimally 'processed' mono: a touch congested in fuller pasages, a hint of fizzy brightness here and there but nothing that's not abundantly worth putting up with for such performances as these.

Additional recommendation ...
...**Soloists; Jaak Gregoor Choir; Belgian Radio and TV Philharmonic Chorus and Orchestra, Brussels / Alexander Rahbari.** Koch International Classics Ⓢ DICD920209 (48 minutes: DDD: 4/95).

Puccini Turandot. **Dame Joan Sutherland** (sop) Princess Turandot; **Luciano Pavarotti** (ten) Calaf; **Montserrat Caballé** (sop) Liù; **Tom Krause** (bar) Ping; **Pier Francesco Poli** (ten) Pang, Prince of Persia; **Piero De Palma** (ten) Pong; **Sir Peter Pears** (ten) Emperor Altoum; **Nicolai Ghiaurov** (bass) Timur; **Sabin Markov** (bar) Mandarin; **Wandsworth School Boys' Choir; John Alldis Choir; London Philharmonic Orchestra / Zubin Mehta.** Decca Ⓕ 414 274-2DH2 (two discs: 117 minutes: ADD: 5/85). From SET561 (9/73). Notes, text and translation included. Recorded 1972. ⓖⓖⓖ
Turandot is a psychologically complex work fusing appalling sadism with self-sacrificing devotion. The icy Princess of China has agreed to marry any man of royal blood who can solve three riddles she has posed. If he fails his head will roll. Calaf, the son of the exiled Tartar king Timur, answers all the questions easily and when Turandot hesitates to accept him, magnanimously offers her a riddle in return – "What is his name?". Liù, Calaf's faithful slave-girl, is tortured but rather than reveal his identity kills herself. Turandot finally capitulates, announcing that his name is Love. Dame Joan Sutherland's assumption of the title role is statuesque, combining regal poise with a more human warmth, whilst Montserrat Caballé is a touchingly sympathetic Liù, skilfully steering the character away from any hint of the mawkish. Pavarotti's Calaf is a heroic figure in splendid voice and the chorus is handled with great power, baying for blood at one minute, enraptured with Liù's nobility at the next. Mehta conducts with great passion and a natural feel for Puccini's wonderfully tempestuous drama. Well recorded.

Additional recommendations ...
...**Soloists; Chorus and Orchestra of La Scala, Milan / Tullio Serafin.** EMI Ⓜ CDS7 47971-2* (two discs: 118 minutes: ADD: 11/87).
...**Soloists; Rome Opera Chorus and Orchestra / Francesco Molinari-Pradelli.** EMI Ⓜ CMS7 69327-2* (two discs: 112 minutes: ADD).

Further listening ...
...*Crisantemi. Coupled with* **Donizetti** String Quartet No. 13 in E minor. **Verdi** String Quartet in E minor. **Alberni Quartet** CRD CRD3366 (5/89).
...Requiem[jfhk]. Salve del ciel regina[ahk]. Vexilla regis[cdhk]. *Coupled with* **Janáček** The Lord's Prayer[jghk]. Hail Mary[cehjk]. Glagolitic Mass in E flat major (ed. Wingfield)[abcdjik]. Adagios (ed. Reinberger)[i]. Exaudi Deus[jk]. Regnum mundi[jk]. Graduale in festo purificationis (Suscepimus Deus)[jk]. In nomine Jesu[jk]. [a]**Shelley Everall** (sop); [b]**Lynette Alcantara** (contr); [c]**William Kendall** (ten); [d]**Peter Harvey** (bar); **Douglas Paterson** ([e]vn/[f]va); [g]**Helen Cole** (hp); [h]**Christopher Monks,** [i]**Michael Phillips** (orgs); [j]**Gonville and Caius College Choir, Cambridge /** [k]**Geoffrey Webber** ([l]org). ASV CDDCA914 (6/95).
...Messe di Gloria in A flat major[a]. *Coupled with* **Mozart** Vesperae solennes de confessore – Laudate Dominum[b]. [a]**Soloists;** [b]**Dame Kiri Te Kanawa** (sop); [a]**West German Radio Chorus;** [b]**London Symphony Chorus;** [a]**Frankfurt Radio Symphony Orchestra / Eliahu Inbal;** [b]**London Symphony Orchestra / Sir Colin Davis.** Philips 434 170-2PM (1/93).
...Tosca – Recondita armonia; E lucevan le stelle. Turandot – Nessun dorma!. *Coupled with* **Verdi** I vespri siciliani – Overture. Luisa Miller – Oh! fede negar potessi ... Quando le sere al placido. **Donizetti** Lucia di Lammermoor – Fra poco a me ricovero. **Cilea** L'Arlesiana – E la solita storia. **Leoncavallo** Mattinata (L'aurora di bianco vestita). **Mascagni** Serenata. **Bixio** La mia canzone al vento. **Ellington** It don't mean a thing (if it ain't got that swing)[b]. **Traditional** I can go to God in prayer[b]. **Di Lazzaro** Chitarra romana. **Sibella** La Girometta. **Denza** Occhi di fata. **Borne** Fantasia brillante sur "Carmen"[a]. **Crescenzo** Rondine al nido. **De Curtis** Non ti scordar di me. **Massenet** Werther – Pourquoi me reveiller?. **Di Capua** 'O sole mio. **Luciano Pavarotti** (ten); [a]**Andrea Griminelli** (fl); [b]**Harlem Boys' Choir; New York Philharmonic Orchestra / Leone Magiera.** Decca 444 450-2DH (2/95).
...Le Villi. **Soloists; Ambrosian Opera Chorus; National Philharmonic Orchestra / Lorin Maazel.** CBS Masterworks MK76890 (5/88).
...Edgar. **Soloists; New York Schola Cantorum; New York City Opera Children's Chorus; New York Opera Orchestra / Eve Queler.** CBS M2K79213 (10/89).
...La Rondine. **Soloists; Ambrosian Opera Chorus; London Symphony Orchestra / Lorin Maazel.** CBS M2K37852 (10/85).

Maximo Diego Pujol
Argentinian 1957-

Suggested listening ...
...Tristango en vos. Preludio tristón. Candombe en mi. *Coupled with* **Tippett** The blue guitar.
Villa-Lobos Five Preludes. **Delerue** Mosaïque. **Giorginakis** Four Greek images. **Fampas**
Greek Dances Nos. 1 and 3. **Eleftheria Kotzia** (gtr). Pearl SHECD9609 (6/89).

Jean Pullois
died 1478

Suggested listening ...
...Flos de spina. *Coupled with* **Busnois** Gaude coelestis Domina. In hydraulis. **Obrecht** (attrib.)
Humilium decus. **Ockeghem** Missa prolationum. **Josquin Desprez** Illibata Dei Virgo nutrix.
The Clerks' Group / Edward Wickham. ASV Gaudeamus CDGAU143 (3/96).

Henry Purcell
British 1659-1695

New review
Purcell Complete Ayres for the Theatre – The History of Dioclesian, or The Prophetess, Z627[b].
King Arthur, Z628[b]. The Fairy Queen, Z629[b]. The Indian Queen, Z630[b]. The Married Beau,
Z603[a]. The Old Bachelor, Z607[b] Amphitryon, Z572[a]. The Double Dealer, Z592[a]. Distressed
Innocence, Z577[a]. The Gordian Knot Unty'd, Z597[a]. Abdelazer, Z570[a]. Bonduca, Z574[a]. The
Virtuous Wife, Z611[a]. Sonata While the Sun Rises in "The Indian Queen"[b]. Overture in
G minor[a]. Sir Anthony Love, Z588 – Overture[a]. Timon of Athens, Z632[a]. The Indian Queen,
Z630 – Symphony[b]. [a]**The Parley of Instruments;** [b]**The Parley of Instruments Baroque Orchestra /
Roy Goodman.** Hyperion Ⓕ CDA67001/3 (three discs: 209 minutes: DDD: 10/95). Recorded 1994.
Gramophone Editor's choice.   Ⓖ
The difference between this latest 'completist' project and the others is that all these works were
published within 18 months of Purcell's death. The 13 suites of choice movements from plays and
semi-operas, entitled *A Collection of Ayres, compos'd for the Theatre, and upon other occasions*, may
well have been the editing work of Purcell's brother, Daniel. Whoever it was had a rare combination
of musical integrity and commercial flair: the pieces lifted from Purcell's interpolations to plays are
often re-ordered and arranged with a deftness and charm which conveys the spirit of the theatre as
well as heightening – in the way that only abstract music can – the loss and poignancy of Purcell's
passing. How moving the Rondeau Minuet from *The Gordian Knot Unty'd* must have seemed to those
who knew and loved Purcell. As a major retrospective of Purcell's life in the theatre, the *Ayres for the
Theatre* mainly comprise instrumental dances from their original sources, though there are several
movements re-adapted from sung airs, such as "Fairest isle" from *King Arthur* and "If love's a sweet
passion" from *The Fairy Queen* – some possibly arranged by Purcell himself.
By and large, such a recording project cannot fail. The tunes are wonderful and varied, the inner
part-writing as skilful as Muffat and Rameau (to name two other composers who bring fine
counterpoint to slight forms) and the rhythmic imagination knows no bounds. Even so, this is not
music where more than a suite at a time can be recommended for ultimate satisfaction: stop while you
still want more. And more you will most certainly want with Roy Goodman's alert and distinctive
direction. About a decade ago, Goodman and Peter Holman recorded this music in a series of
programmes for the BBC alongside suites by Purcell's peers. There is a greater aplomb and colour
nowadays, a far keener sense of shape and understanding to Purcell's blend of elusive side-glances and
uninhibited bravura. If a few of the movements sound a touch mundane and lack dynamism as one
follows on from another (the *Dioclesian* music, using the full 'four and twenty fiddlers' here, is
strangely subdued), the positive side is that the performances are never forced and rarely mannered.
For the semi-opera 'suites', Goodman employs a full orchestra. What The Parley of Instruments have
in abundance, especially in the incidental music from the plays, is a cordiality of expression which
seems so absolutely right, especially in the slower airs. A most welcome release.

New review
Purcell Ayres for the Theatre – Suites: Dioclesian; King Arthur; The Fairy Queen; The Indian
Queen. **Tafelmusik / Jeanne Lamon.** Sony Classical Vivarte Ⓕ SK66169 (71 minutes: DDD:
2/96). 🎶 Recorded 1994.
The various Purcell releases of the last few years have come in many guises, from the wildly
entertaining to the merely informative. This disc, containing instrumental theatre music, need only be
enjoyed for what it is, which is an exhilarating reminder that, whatever Purcell was, he was simply one
of the greatest tune-writers Britain has ever produced. That would be beyond doubt, of course, even
if all we knew were the show-stopping song-tunes contained here, such as "Fairest isle" from *King
Arthur* or "If love's a sweet passion" from *The Fairy Queen*. But when practically every Trumpet Tune
and Rondeau has you tapping your feet and wanting to sing along, you know you are in the presence
of genius. The four suites which Tafelmusik have selected from the *Ayres for the Theatre*, published
by Purcell's widow a few months after his death, are each taken from one of the composer's great

semi-operas of the 1690s, and the end result is a succession of 50 short, catchy numbers, mainly for strings but sometimes also featuring oboes and trumpets. Unlike a number of collections of this sort, it is never in any danger of outstaying its welcome. Tafelmusik are surely one of the best-equipped baroque orchestras in the world to perform this music. They have an unparalleled ability to play straightforwardly well with uncomplicated energy and high polish, and given that performing this kind of music in suite form necessarily banishes all considerations of theatrical context, perhaps that is all that is needed. True, these performances probably reek more of the studio than the playhouse, but if all you want to do is sit back, relax and enjoy the music, then this is certainly a disc to do it with.

Purcell Fantasias – three part, Z732-34; four part, Z735-43; five part, "upon one note", Z745; A minor (incomplete). In Nomines – G minor, Z746; G minor, "Dorian", Z747[a]. **Fretwork** (Wendy Gillespie, Richard Campbell, William Hunt, Julia Hodgson, Susanna Pell, Richard Boothby, viols); [a]**Imogen Seth-Smith** (viol). Virgin Classics Veritas Ⓔ VC5 45062-2 (55 minutes: DDD: 5/95). ✐ Recorded 1994. *Gramophone* *Editor's record of the month.*

Purcell's music for viols represents the final flowering of the English consort tradition. While we know when many of them were composed (the four-part *fantasias* date from the summer of 1680 when Purcell was in residence with the court at Windsor Castle) no one has yet satisfactorily explained why they exist and for whom they were composed. Viol consorts had been out of fashion for at least 20 years, ousted by the Italian violin sonatas and French ballet music. Purcell's polished essays in this antique form were neither published nor, apparently, widely circulated. Nevertheless, we cherish them today for their sublime expressiveness and craftsmanship. Having worked their way through many of Purcell's most skilled predecessors in this genre, Fretwork were exceptionally well placed to articulate the subtleties of form, texture, rhythm, harmony and counterpoint embodied in these works. No two *fantasias* are quite alike, providing a succession of contrasting sections to delight the listener – linear, rhetorical, imitative, syncopated, homophonic, chromatic, sustained, sprightly or a combination of these elements. Fretwork's performances leave little to be desired: they are in turn organic or translucent as befits the texture, enhanced by precise articulation and poise reminiscent of a less frenetic era which allowed for contemplation. Fretwork are joined by Imogen Seth-Smith in the final seven-part *In Nomine*. Although the excellent note by Bruce Wood and Andrew Pinnock will inform your listening, this mysteriously conceived music speaks eloquently for itself.

Purcell A Choice Collection of Lessons – Suites: No. 1 in G major, Z660; No. 2 in G minor, Z661; No. 3 in G major, Z662; No. 4 in A minor, Z663; No. 5 in C major, Z666; No. 6 in D major, Z667; No. 7 in D minor, Z668; No. 8 in F major, Z669. Ground in C minor, T D221. The Second Part of Musick's Hand-maid – A New Scotch Tune in G major, Z655; A New Ground in E minor, Z T682. Hornpipe in E minor, Z T685. **Kenneth Gilbert** (hpd). Harmonia Mundi Ⓔ HMC90 1496 (67 minutes: DDD: 5/95). ✐ Recorded 1993.

For many, this music is little more than a series of diverting miniatures with the slight advantage over others of being by a genius whose real greatness lies elsewhere. But there is still plenty that is unmistakably Purcellian about it. In the selection offered here French and Italian influences sit side by side, rubbing shoulders with the occasionally more homely English atmosphere provided by a hornpipe or two. And in the grounds and chaconnes among the various extra items inserted into four of the suites (a practice common enough in the composer's own day) we see plenty of evidence of Purcell's unrivalled resourcefulness in the use of ground bass technique. Undoubtedly, though, it is the broken-chord figuration, improvisatory preludes and dotted rhythms of the French taste whose influence is most striking in this music, even if it is less grandly conceived than that of a Chambonnières or Louis Couperin. So it comes as no surprise to find Kenneth Gilbert – long a master of the French style – making the most of its presence here. He uses a vibrant Couchet-Taskin instrument from 1671, and pays these little pieces the compliment of treating them as seriously as they seem able to take. The results are convincing. Add to that the crisply eloquent playing of which Gilbert has always been capable, and what you have are discs that give real pleasure.

Additional recommendation ...

...A Choice Collection of Lessons[a] – Nos. 4 and 5. 12 Keyboard Pieces[a]. **Draghi** Suites[b] – A major; G minor; C minor; G major. **Gibbons** Prelude in G major[a]. **Davitt Moroney** ([a]virg/[b]hpd). Virgin Classics Veritas Ⓔ VC5 45166-2 (67 minutes: DDD: 5/95). ✐

New review

Purcell 12 Sonatas of Three Parts, Z790-801 – No. 1 in G minor; No. 2 in B flat major; No. 3 in D minor; No. 4 in F major; No. 5 in A minor; No. 6 in C minor; No. 7 in E minor; No. 8 in G major; No. 9 in C minor; No. 10 in A minor; No. 11 in F minor; No. 12 in D major. **Pavlo Beznosiuk, Rachel Podger** (vns); **Christophe Coin** (bass viol); **Christopher Hogwood** (org). L'Oiseau-Lyre Ⓔ 444 449-2OH (72 minutes: DDD: 4/96). Recorded 1994.

If the lyrical refinement and other-worldliness of the *Fantasias* is largely absent, Purcell manipulates the flighty drama of the Italian spirit with a seasoned individuality. For a start he never entirely rejects the Englishness of the *Fantasias*, both in terms of harmonic unpredictability and the contrapuntal texture which forced Roger North to describe the sonatas as "clog'd with somewhat of an English vein". Sonata No. 5 is a case in point and one which the performers here relish with an imploring legato and doleful accentuation, plentifully endowed with rhetorical detail. Indeed, characterization – and just how far one goes in music whose gestures are mapped out with great clarity – is what makes this such an interesting recording. There is a grandeur and interpretational scope which gives each sonata its own measure of distinction. The violin playing of Pavlo Beznosiuk and Rachel Podger is beautifully matched and coloured, warm-toned in the opening of the Corellian Sixth Sonata but 'just and quick', crisp and precise in the canzona-style *allegros* of Sonatas Nos. 2 and 12. Hogwood performs on a chamber organ throughout (often in tandem – when Purcell decrees it – with Christophe Coin's eloquent if slightly restrained gamba), unlike Richard Egarr in London Baroque's polished and finely-crafted accounts who varies the texture with a harpsichord. However, youthful abandon and effervescent personality are what makes this new disc such an infectious addition to the catalogue. We have distinguished performances from the Purcell Quartet and London Baroque but this is chamber music playing which seeks out new territory.

Additional recommendations ...

...Nos. 1-7. Pavans – G minor, Z752[a]; B flat major, Z750; A minor, Z749. [a]**Risa Browder** (vn); **Purcell Quartet.** Chandos Ⓕ CHAN8591 (51 minutes: DDD: 1/89). 🖉

...Nos. 8-12. Ten Sonatas in Four Parts, Z802-11 – No. 1 in B minor; No. 2 in E flat major. Fantasia upon a Ground in D and F major[a]. Pavans – A major, Z748; G minor, Z751. Chacony in G minor, Z730[a]. [a]**Risa Browder** (vn); **Purcell Quartet.** Chandos Ⓕ CHAN8663 (53 minutes: DDD: 10/89). 🖉

...Nos. 1-12. **London Baroque.** Harmonia Mundi Ⓕ HMC90 1439 (71 minutes: DDD: 8/94). 🖉 Ⓖ

New review

Purcell A Choice Collection of Lessons – Suites: No. 1 in G major, Z660; No. 2 in G minor, Z661; No. 3 in G major, Z662; No. 4 in A minor, Z663; No. 5 in C major, Z666; No. 6 in D major, Z667; No. 7 in D minor, Z668; No. 8 in F major, Z669; Chaconne in G minor, Z T680. Ground in Gamut in G major, Z645. Ground in C minor, Z D221. Ground in D minor, Z D222. Prelude in G minor. The Second Part of Musick's Hand-maid – A New Ground in E minor, Z T682; Suite in C major, Z665. Sarabande with Division, Z654. Hornpipe in D minor, "Round O", Z T684. **Sophie Yates** (hpd). Chandos Chaconne Ⓕ CHAN0587 (70 minutes: DDD: 3/96). 🖉 Recorded 1994.

Purcell A Choice Collection of Lessons – Suites: No. 1 in G major, Z660; No. 2 in G minor, Z661; No. 3 in G major, Z662; No. 4 in A minor, Z663; No. 5 in C major, Z666; No. 6 in D major, Z667; No. 7 in D minor, Z668; No. 8 in F major, Z669. The Second Part of Musick's Hand-maid – March in C major, Z647; Minuet in A minor, Z649; A New Scotch Tune in G major, Z655, A New Ground in E minor, Z T682; A New Irish Tune in G major, Z646; Sefauchi's Farewell in D minor, Z656. Ground in Gamut in G major, Z645. Ground in C minor, Z T681. Ground in D minor, Z D222. Air in G major, Z641. Air in D minor, Z T675. Hornpipe in D minor, "Round O", Z T684. Hornpipe in E minor, Z T685. **Olivier Baumont** (hpd). Erato Ⓕ 0630-10695-2 (64 minutes: DDD: 3/96). 🖉 Recorded 1995.

Considering Purcell's long involvement with keyboard instruments, it is curious, and certainly disappointing, that he wrote so little of any substance for them. So far, they have attracted little attention, but these two recommendable discs go far to redress the balance. Not many are likely to echo the late Professor Westrup's claim that the eight three- or four-movement suites (published posthumously by the composer's widow, and revealing influences from Froberger and contemporary French musicians) are "worthy predecessors of Bach's"; but they do contain fine individual movements, such as the Almands of Nos. 8 and, particularly, 7. Other than the suites, the harpsichord works consist of brief dance movements, popular tunes (including the satiric anti-English Irish *Lillibullero*, unaccountably adopted by the BBC for their World Service news bulletins), grounds (of which Purcell was a supreme master) and transcriptions from his theatre music. There is a good deal of overlap between these two discs – the suites, three grounds and the *Round O* Hornpipe which Britten used as the basis for his virtuosic orchestral *tour d'horizon*. This last forms a good starting-point for comparisons here.

Sophie Yates, playing on a copy of a 1681 Vaudry harpsichord, takes it at Britten's sturdily stately pace; Olivier Baumont, on the 1664 Hatley virginals at Fenton House in London (though employing that collection's 1752 Kirckman harpsichord for the suites) takes it up-tempo as a real hornpipe, to startling effect. Features of Yates's playing, throughout, are its freshness and neatness (especially of ornaments), and she is always stylish – her unmeasured preludes convey a true improvisatory feeling – but overall her readings are more sober than Baumont's and have less sense of fantasy. He shows more boldness, more dash in the energetic Preludes to Suites Nos. 2, 3 and 5, is more springy in all the corants (and makes more of No. 3's syncopations), and almost everywhere adopts faster speeds which tend to give the miniature movements more character. In two of the grounds, particularly the moving E minor "Here the deities approve", he also makes the melody line stand out better. (Incidentally, there is a confusion in Chandos's notes, which state that a C minor ground from the ode *Ye tuneful Muses* – given a mixed-up catalogue number too! – is included, though in fact it isn't.) Baumont extends the Fifth Suite with a skippety Jigg taken from the 1689 volume which was the only one to be printed in Purcell's lifetime, and is daring enough to precede the Seventh Suite (which has no prelude) with a Prelude from a seventeenth-century manuscript now in Oxford which he has transposed for the occasion.

Purcell Complete Anthems and Services, Volume 7 – I was glad when they said unto me[a]. I was glad when they said unto me, Z19[b]. O consider my adversity, Z32[c]. Beati omnes qui timent Dominum, Z131[d]. In the black dismal dungeon of despair, Z190[e]. Save me, O God, Z51[f]. Morning and Evening Service in B flat major, Z230 – Te Deum; Jubilate[g]. Thy Way, O God, is Holy, Z60[h]. Funeral Sentences for the death of Queen Mary II[i] – Drum Processional; March and Canzona in C minor, Z860; Man that is born of Woman, Z27; In the midst of Life, Z17b; Thou know'st Lord, Z58b; Thou know'st Lord, Z58c. [dfgi]**Mark Kennedy**, [dg]**Eamonn O'Dwyer**, [fg]**James Goodman** (trebs); [e]**Susan Gritton** (sop); [fg]**James Bowman**, [g]**Nigel Short** (altos); [bcdi]**Rogers Covey-Crump**, [bcfghi]**Charles Daniels**, [g]**Mark Milhofer** (tens); [bcdfghi]**Michael George**, [g]**Robert Evans** (basses); [b]**New College Choir, Oxford**; [acfi]**King's Consort Choir; King's Consort / Robert King.** Hyperion Ⓕ CDA66677 (70 minutes: DDD: 6/94). 🎵 Recorded 1993.

This recording is made up predominantly of anthems, devotional songs and a morning service (a functional, though not perfunctory, setting of the *Te Deum* and *Jubilate*) most of which disclose the range and quality of the composer's sacred *oeuvre* near its best. Of the two settings of *I was glad*, the first was, until not long ago, thought to be the work of John Blow. This full anthem more than whets our appetite with its agreeable tonal and melodic twists; when the *Gloria* arrives, we are assured that this is vintage Purcell by the sensitive pacing as much as an exquisite contrapuntal denouement. The earlier setting is more poignant. Opening with a string symphony in the spirit of a Locke consort, the music blossoms into a deliciously Elysian melodic fabric. Good sense is made of the overall shape and the soloists are, as ever, excellent. *Beati omnes* is a positive gem; this may well have been written for the composer's wedding. Of the small-scale pieces, *In the black dismal dungeon* is the real masterpiece and it is delivered astutely by the secure and musicianly voice of Susan Gritton. Finally to the funeral pieces. Here we have an ominous procession from the Guild of Ancient Fifes and Drums and the first appearance of four 'flatt' trumpets – as opposed to two plus two sackbuts; the effect of this subtle timbral change makes extraordinary sense of the music, engendering a new grandeur and uncompromising clarity as would have befitted such an occasion. The vocal performances are earthy and impassioned.

Additional recommendations ...

...Complete Anthems and Services, Volume 3 – Blow up the trumpet in Sion, Z10. The Lord is king, be the people never so impatient, Z53. Begin the song, and strike the living lyre, Z183. Thy word is a lantern unto my feet, Z61. Tell me, some pitying Angel, Z196. Hear my prayer, O Lord, Z15. Lord, I can suffer Thy rebukes, Z136. O Lord our governor, Z39. Remember not, Lord, our offences, Z50. Hosanna to the highest, Z187. O God, thou hast cast us out, Z36. **Soloists; King's Consort Choir; King's Consort / Robert King.** Hyperion Ⓕ CDA66623 (DDD: 4/93). 🎵

...Complete Anthems and Services, Volume 5 – Lord, rebuke me not, Z40. With sick and famish'd eyes, Z200. How long, great God, Z189. Awake, and with attention hear, Z181. O God, thou art my God, Z35. We sing to him whose wisdom form'd the ear, Z199. Praise the Lord, O my soul and all that is within me, Z47. O, I'm sick of life, Z140. O God, the King of glory, Z34. Job's Curse, "Let the night perish", Z191. When on my sick bed I languish, Z144. The Bell Anthem, "Rejoice in the Lord alway", Z49. **Soloists; New College Choir, Oxford; King's Consort Choir; King's Consort / Robert King.** Hyperion Ⓕ CDA66656 (71 minutes: DDD: 2/94). 🎵

...Complete Anthems and Services, Volume 8 – In thee, O Lord, do I put my trust, Z16. Blessed is the man that feareth the Lord, Z9. Morning and Evening Service in B flat major, Z230 – Benedicite. Jehova, quam multi sunt hostes mei, Z135. Full of wrath, his threatening breath, Z185. Bow down thine ear, O Lord, Z11. Evening Service in G minor, Z231. Be merciful unto me, Z4. They that go down to the sea in ships, Z57. **Soloists; King's Consort and [i]Choir / Robert King.** Hyperion CDA66686 (65 minutes: DDD: 10/94). 🎵 Ⓖ

...Te Deum in D major, Z232. Funeral Sentences – Man that is born of Woman; In the midst of life. Thou know'st Lord. March and Canzona, Z860, The Bell Anthem, "Rejoice in the Lord alway". Z49. Remember not, Lord, our offences, Z50. Blow up the trumpet in Sion, Z10. Hear my prayer, O Lord, Z15. My heart is inditing, Z30. O Lord God of hosts, Z37. **Soloists; Ghent Collegium Vocale / Philippe Herreweghe.** Harmonia Mundi Ⓕ HMC90 1462 (68 minutes: DDD: 2/94). 🎵

...Harmonia Sacra –Lord, what is man?, Z192. O Solitude! my sweetest choice, Z406. In the black dismal dungeon of despair, Z190. Lord, I can suffer Thy rebukes, Z136. Saul and the Witch of Endor, "In guilty night", Z134. Plung'd in the confines of despair, Z142. Awake, ye dead, Z182. The Earth trembled, Z197. My op'ning eyes are purg'd, ZD72. With sick and famish'd eyes, Z200. O, I'm sick of life, Z140. Close thine eyes and sleep secure, Z184. Funeral Sentences for the death of Queen Mary II – Man that is born of woman, Z27. Voluntaries – C major, Z717; G major, Z720[a]. Ground in C minor, T D221[b]. **Gabrieli Consort and Players / Paul McCreesh; Timothy Roberts** ([a]org/[b]hpd). Archiv Produktion Ⓕ 445 829-2AH (70 minutes: DDD: 7/95). 🎵 *Gramophone Editor's choice.*

...Morning and Evening Service in B flat major, Z230 – Benedicite; Evening Service: Te Deum and Jubilate in D major, Z232. Evening Service in G minor, Z231. O God, thou hast cast us out, Z36. O Lord God of hosts, Z37. Remember not, Lord, our offences, Z50. Lord, how long wilt thou be angry?, Z25. O God, thou art my God, Z35. Funeral Sentences for the death of Queen Mary II – Man that is born of Woman, Z27; Thou know'st Lord, Z58. Jehova, quam multi sunt hostes mei,

Z135. My heart is inditing, Z30. O sing unto the Lord, Z44. My beloved spake, Z28. They that go down to the sea in ships, Z57. Praise the Lord, O Jerusalem, Z46. **Various soloists; The English Concert / Simon Preston.** Archiv Produktion The Purcell Collection Ⓜ 447 150-2AP2 (two discs: 157 minutes: DDD: 7/95). ✍

Purcell Complete Anthems and Services, Volume 9 – The Lord is my light, Z55[a]. The Lord is King, the earth may be glad thereof, Z54[b]. Blessed is he whose unrighteousness is forgiven, Z8[c]. O Lord God of hosts, Z37[d]. Let God arise, Z23[e]. Morning and Evening Service in B flat major, Z230 – Cantate Domino; Deus misereatur[f]. Blessed be the Lord my strength, Z6[g]. O Lord our governor, Z141[h]. In guilty night (Saul and the Witch of Endor), Z134[i]. [i]**Susan Gritton** (sop); [c]**Connor Burrowes,** [cdfh]**Eamonn O'Dwyer,** [dh]**Mark Kennedy,** [f]**Aaron Webber** (trebs); [cdf]**James Bowman** (alto); [afgi]**Rogers Covey-Crump,** [acdefg]**Charles Daniels,** [ceh]**Mark Padmore,** [d]**Mark Milhofer** (tens); [abcdfghi]**Michael George** (bass); **King's Consort Choir; King's Consort / Robert King.** Hyperion Ⓟ CDA66693 (65 minutes: DDD: 12/94). Texts included. Recorded 1993-94. ✍ ⓖ

This volume of Robert King's survey of Purcell's sacred music introduces four more works receiving first recordings, and six more of which only two are currently available in the catalogue. None of the newcomers is universally top-notch but there are moments of great individual beauty in each which warrant repeated listening. *The Lord is my light* is a distinctive work, tautly constructed with satisfying alternations between solo exclamations and fetching instrumental commentaries. If the subdued and melancholic effect is a touch unyielding vocally, Purcell's magisterial command of the string symphony and ritornello makes for a satisfying introduction to the disc, all the more so for the understated and genial shaping of lines. John Gostling's astonishing bass voice with its spectacular range was a source of some admiration at court (Charles II is said to have given him a silver egg of guineas since "eggs were good for the voice") and if we can assume that *The Lord is King* was written for him, Purcell found a noble medium to set the lucid imagery of Psalm 97. The expressive range of the music requires sustained artistry and Michael George, who must feel by now that he is a reincarnation of Gostling, gives a committed account of the work. Most of the remaining works have found their way into the studio and they are headed by *O Lord God of hosts*, a beautifully moulded work in eight parts; Purcell is in his element here with a meaningful but economical text (a desolate one, of course), set with subtly interchanging textures and producing a harmonic fabric of the composer at his most elusively grand. Two more early works precede the jewel in the crown of the volume, if not the series. *Saul and the Witch of Endor*, these days more often called *In guilty night*, is as King points out in the booklet, an unclassifiable work of mesmerizing proportions. This dramatic scena is given a profound and impassioned reading and caps another distinguished release.

Additional recommendations ...

...Complete Anthems and Services, Volume 10 – I will give thanks unto the Lord, Z21. I will sing unto the Lord, Z22. How have I stray'd, Z188. Morning and Evening Service in B flat, Z230 – Benedictus; Kyrie; Credo. Hear my prayer, O God, Z14. Out of the deep have I called, Z45. Blessed is he that considereth the poor, Z7. The Lord is King, and hath put on glorious apparel, Z69. Unto Thee will I cry, Z63. **Soloists; King's Consort Choir; King's Consort / Robert King.** Hyperion CDA66707 (3/95). ✍

...Complete Anthems and Services, Volume 11 – Praise the Lord, O my soul, O Lord my God, Z48. Close thine eyes and sleep secure, Z184. Lord, how long wilt thou be angry?, Z25. Hear me, O Lord, and that soon, Z13a/Z13b. Morning and Evening Service in B flat, Z230 – Magnificat; Nunc dimittis. Turn thou us, O good Lord, Z62. O Lord, thou art my God, Z41. An Evening Hymn on a Ground, "Now that the sun hath veiled his light", Z193. Awake, awake, put on thy strength, Z1. **Soloists; King's Consort Choir; King's Consort / Robert King.** Hyperion CDA66716 (3/95). ✍

New review

Purcell The Second Part of Musick's Handmaid – Suite in C major, Z665. A Choice Collection of Lessons, Suites – G major, Z660; G minor, Z661; A minor, Z663; D minor, Z668. **The Harp Consort** (Ellen Hargis, sop; Douglas Nasrawi, alto; Rodrigo Del Pozo, ten; Harry van der Kamp, bass; David Douglass, vn; Nancy Hadden, fls; Hille Perl, lira/bass viol; Jane Achtman, bass viol; Paul O'Dette, lte/gtr; Pat O'Brien, banduria/gtr; Thomas Ihlenfeldt, theorbo/gtr; Steve Player, gtr; Lee Santana, chitarrone/theorbo) / **Andrew Lawrence-King** (hp/org/hpd/perc). Astrée Auvidis Ⓟ E8564 (75 minutes: DDD: 1/96). Texts and translations included. Recorded 1995.

Andrew Lawrence-King's name is synonymous with many of the most exotic and beguiling recorded sounds of the pre-classical harp, whether as soloist or within a continuo battery. On this occasion he directs a delightful programme of Purcell's songs and instrumental music drawn from the second part of *Musick's Hand-maid* (1687), Playford's attractively titled publication, and the later *Choice Collection of Lessons* (1696). Self-made suites of sung and non-sung airs are indeed an ingenious way of relieving the beautifully opaque but fairly uncompromising sound of the harp, though Lawrence-King's instinctive control of line and delicate embellishment – heard most poignantly in "A New Ground" (a transcription of "Here the deities approve") – makes a very strong case for an extended recital. He does not chance his arm (except in the delightful way the improvisatory spirit raises its head above the parapet, as in the "Round-O") and breaks up the solo numbers with his own succinct playing on a selection of keyboards, as well as agreeable contributions from a small band of obbligato instrumentalists and four solo singers. Each of the latter is adequate for the task without taking the breath away, although Ellen Hargis's atmospheric "Evening Hymn" comes closer than any with its supple phrasing and crystalline accompaniment on the harp. The longest piece, "Begin the song and strike the living lyre", demonstrates the prowess, in purely vocal terms, of Harry van der Kamp. None of the instrumental music was written specifically for the harp, though Lawrence-King explains in his note how harpists were ever-present at court and one can easily imagine how this instrument could add exotic spice to an evening entertainment; the D minor *Suite* is especially atmospheric, capped only by a wonderfully intimate and finite, "Thou knowest, Lord, the secrets of our hearts". A colourful and inventive Purcell recital, then, quite unlike anything else we have heard in these days of inexhaustible Purcelliana.

Purcell Funeral Sentences for the death of Queen Mary II – Man that is born of woman, Z27; In the midst of life, Z17 (first version); Thou knows't Lord, Z58 (second and third settings). The Queen's Epicedium, "Incassum, Lesbia, rogas", Z383 (with Carys-Anne Lane, sop). March and Canzona in C minor, Z860. Jehova, quam multi sunt hostes mei, Z135 (Andrew Carwood, ten; Michael MCarthy, bass). Remember not, Lord, our offences, Z50. I will sing unto the Lord, Z22. O God, thou art my God, Z35. O God, the King of Glory, Z34. Lord, how long wilt thou be angry?, Z25. Hear my prayer, O Lord, Z15. Blow up the trumpet in Sion, Z10. O God, thou hast cast us out, Z36. Organ Music[a] – Three Voluntaries: C major, Z717, D minor, Z718; G major, Z720. **Oxford Camerata / Jeremy Summerly** with [a]**Laurence Cummings** (org). Naxos Ⓢ 8 553129 (72 minutes: DDD: 2/95). Recorded 1994.

This release enters a growing field with a mouthwatering selection of the best of the anthems with just organ accompaniment. However, some of them are gathered together into a little sequence misleadingly titled "Funeral Music for Queen Mary", for which extra flavour is provided by the *March and Canzona* (Z860) and, in this case, one of the solo elegies, *Incassum, Lesbia*. It's great stuff, but not much of it was actually composed for Queen Mary. Put the Queen from your mind, however, and there are few obstacles to enjoyment. The Oxford Camerata are a young-sounding group, sharply defined and clear if not always as expertly balanced as some of today's chamber choirs. Jeremy Summerly extracts loving and, in the main, convincing performances from them. There are plenty of good things, including an impressive general crescendo in *Hear my prayer*, and indeed it is in longer-range effects such as this that the main successes are scored; smaller details, by contrast – the first dissonance in *Jehova, quam multi sunt hostes mei* for instance, or the odd moment where a little more time is needed – tend to disappoint. But these are small worries; any disc which offered such a 24-carat Purcell selection in performances even half as good as these would be hard to resist.

Additional recommendations ...

...Jehova, quam multi sunt hostes mei, Z135. Miserere mei, Z109. Funeral Sentences for the death of Queen Mary II – Man that is born of woman, Z27; In the midst of life, Z17; Thou know'st Lord, Z58 (first and second settings). The Queen's Epicedium, "Incassum, Lesbia, rogas", Z383. Birthday Ode, "Love's goddess sure was blind', Z331. O dive custos Auriacae domus, Z504. March and Canzona in C minor, Z860. **Paisible** The Queen's Farewell. **Tollet** The Queen's Farewell. **Morley** I am the resurrection and the life. I know that my Redeemer liveth. In the midst of life. Man that is born of woman. We brought nothing into this world. I heard a voice from Heaven. **The Sixteen Choir and Orchestra / Harry Christophers.** Collins Classics Ⓕ 1425-2 (80 minutes: DDD: 1/95). ✍

...Funeral Sentences for the death of Queen Mary II[b]. Ode for St Cecilia's Day, 1683, "Welcome to all the pleasures", Z339[a]. Come ye sons of art away, Z323[c]. March and Canzona in C minor, Z860[d]. Funeral Music for the death of Queen Mary[b]. [c]**Emily Van Evera** (sop); [c]**Timothy Wilson** (alto); [ac]**John Mark Ainsley**, [ac]**Charles Daniels** (tens); [c]**David Thomas** (bass); [abc]**Taverner Consort,** [abc]**Choir and Players / Andrew Parrott.** Virgin Classics Veritas Ⓕ VC5 45159-2 (55 minutes: DDD: 12/95). ✍

Purcell Music for the Funeral of Queen Mary – March and Canzona in C minor, Z860[c]. Funeral Sentences for the death of Queen Mary II[a]. The Bell Anthem, "Rejoice in the Lord alway", Z49[ad]. Remember not, Lord, our offences, Z50[a]. Give sentence with me, O Lord, Z12[a]. Jehova, quam multi sunt hostes mei, Z135[ab]. O, I'm sick of life, Z140[a]. My beloved spake, Z28[ad]. Hear my prayer, O Lord, Z15[a]. O God, thou art my God, Z35[ab]. Voluntaries[e] – No. 1 in C minor, Z717; No. 4 in G major, Z720. [a]**Winchester Cathedral Choir;** [b]**Hilary Brooks** (vc); [c]**Baroque Brass of London;** [d]**The Brandenburg Consort / David Hill** ([e]org) with **David Dunnett** (org). Argo Ⓕ 436 833-2ZH (66 minutes: DDD: 6/94). ✍ Texts included. Recorded 1992.

David Hill is a master of long-breathed melody and sustained intensity and he brings to Purcell's anthems a breadth of vision inspired by the time-span of earlier genres. Indeed, it is the range of anthems skilfully chosen from amongst Purcell's finest church music which distinguishes this disc as much as the funeral pieces. *Jehova, quam multi sunt hostes mei* is particularly effective, exemplifying not only Hill's astute pacing but also his vigorous sense of the dramatic declamatory style which Purcell must have gleaned from continental sources. The open-throated treble sound is equally appropriate and characterizes the vocal colouring of almost all the works. The soloists for the verse anthems are drawn both from the ranks of the choir and a pool of professional soloists. Between them they shape the music with spirit and eloquence as can be relished in the abundant fruits of *My beloved spake*. The strings of The Brandenburg Consort balance the buoyant vocal style here with sparkling rhythmic exchanges. Winchester benefits from that fragility and loneliness which a solo treble can give to "In the midst of life", especially in a gothic acoustic. The Baroque Brass of London capture the doleful strains with finesse and make wonderful musical sense of the Canzona. The same players on 'flat' trumpets reappear on all current versions. There is good reason for this: only the truly dedicated are prepared to spend hours practising an instrument which splits notes as soon as you look at it, for a complete repertoire lasting no more than ten minutes.

Additiona lrecommendation ...

...Four Voluntaries, Z717-20. Verse in F major, Z716. A Choice Collection of Lessons – March in C major, Z T687; Chaconne in G minor, Z T680; Trumpet Tune in C major, Z T678, "Cibell". Grounds – Gamut in G major, Z645; C minor, T D221. Voluntary in A major (on the Old 100th), Z721. Trumpet Voluntary in D major. O Solitude! my sweetest choice, Z406. If music be the food of love, Z379 No. 1. **Blow** Six Organ Voluntaries. **Locke** Seven Voluntaries. **John Butt** (org). Harmonia Mundi Ⓜ HMX290 1528/33 (65 minutes: DDD: 7/95).

New review

Purcell Ode for St Cecilia's Day, 1692, Hail, bright Cecilia, Z328. My beloved spake, Z28. O sing unto the Lord, Z44. **Gabrieli Consort and Players / Paul McCreesh.** Archiv Produktion Ⓕ 445 882-2AH (70 minutes: DDD: 10/95). Texts included. Recorded 1994. *Gramophone Editor's record of the month.*

New review

Purcell Ode for St Cecilia's Day, 1683, Z339, "Welcome to all the pleasures"[a]. Funeral Sentences for the death of Queen Mary[b]. Birthday Ode, Z323, "Come ye sons of art away"[c]. March and Canzona in C minor, Z860[d]. Funeral Music for the death of Queen Mary[b]. [c]**Emily Van Evera** (sop); [c]**Timothy Wilson** (alto); [ac]**John Mark Ainsley**, [ac]**Charles Daniels** (tens); [c]**David Thomas** (bass); [abc]**Taverner Consort**, [abc]**Choir and Players / Andrew Parrott.** Virgin Classics Veritas Ⓕ VC5 45159-2 (55 minutes: DDD: 12/95). From EMI CDC7 49635-2 (2/90).

The Archiv performance of the 1692 Ode for St Cecilia's Day is exceptionally receptive to the brilliance of the score. The trumpets are bold and brassy (only occasionally overblown) and the ensemble as a whole moves effortlessly from discretion and intimacy to the imposing timbral homogeneity of McCreesh's most extrovert Venetian exploits. His tempos – especially in the grand opening instrumental sinfonia – are irrepressible and invigorating; there is a danger that this eight-section introduction can seem too much of a good thing, if not briskly negotiated. The solo singing is almost uniformly outstanding: Peter Harvey is the busiest of the basses and he delivers his splendid music, including "Wondrous machine!", with authority and variety of colour. Charles Daniels must, by now, have sung almost everything by Purcell but there is no sign of flagging: "'Tis Nature's voice" has a magical sense of unfolding as the music's captivating charms are gradually exposed. His duet with Mark le Brocq, "In vain the am'rous flute" has its moments, though the intonation of the recorders is languorous to say the least. Susan Hemington Jones sounds bright and alert though she seems just a touch unsettled and she is guilty of the occasional rather ugly 'early-musicy' swell, though to pick out a couple of bars there should certainly not detract attention from some notable singing in the verse anthem, *O sing unto the Lord*, especially in an extraordinarily moving close where the Gabrieli Consort's warmth of tone is exquisitely caught. *My beloved spake* is the other filler: a wonderful work and again very well performed. It is the Ode, above all, which takes the plaudits here. Whilst McCreesh makes the score sparkle with his energetic view of tempos, Andrew Parrott (listed below) parades his smooth and integrated forces with less instant theatricality. Instead we have a typically homogeneous and unfolding scenario which complements McCreesh's more effervescent and lush reading.

The reappearance of Parrott's recordings of Purcell's earlier Cecilian ode, *Welcome to all the pleasures* and the time-honoured and particularly accessible *Come ye sons of art away* is also received with open arms. Some may distrust the low pitch (A=392) but the high tenor of Charles Daniels and the satisfying registral blend of Timothy Wilson and John Mark Ainsley in "Sound the trumpet" are more than adequate recompense and the former's mellifluous rendering of "Here the deities approve" is a real gem to be savoured. King has much to say about all these odes too. Blessed on almost all fronts.

Additional recommendation ...

...Hail, bright Cecilia, Z328. **Taverner Consort, Choir and Players / Andrew Parrott.** Virgin Classics Veritas Ⓕ VC5 45160-2 (57 minutes: DDD: 12/95).

Purcell Secular Solo Songs, Volume 3. [a]**Barbara Bonney**, [b]**Susan Gritton** (sops); [c]**James Bowman** (alto); [d]**Rogers Covey-Crump**, [e]**Charles Daniels** (tens); [f]**Michael George** (bass); [g]**Mark Caudle**, [h]**Susanna Pell** (vas da gamba); **David Miller** (lte/theorbo) / **Robert King** (org/hpd). Hyperion Ⓕ CDA66730 (76 minutes: DDD: 1/95). 🎵 Texts included. Recorded 1993-94.

She loves, and she confesses, Z413[bh]. Amintas, to my grief I see, Z356[dh]. Corinna is divinely fair, Z365[ag]. Amintor, heedless of his flocks, Z357[cg]. He himself courts his own ruin, Z372[cg]. No, to what purpose, Z468[bfg]. Sylvia, 'tis true you're fair, Z512[cfg]. Lovely Albina's come ashore, Z394[ag]. Spite of the godhead, pow'rful love, Z417[dg]. If music be the food of love, Z379/3[ag]. Phyllis, I can ne'er forgive it, Z408[eg]. Bacchus is a pow'r divine, Z360[fg]. Bess of Bedlam, "From silent shades",

Z370[bh]. Let formal lovers still pursue, Z391[cg]. I came, I saw, and was undone, Z375[ag]. Who can behold Florella's charms?, Z441[eg]. Cupid, the slyest rogue alive, Z367[dh]. If prayers and tears, Z380[bh]. In Chloris all soft charms agree, Z384[dg]. Let us, kind Lesbia, give away, Z466[afg]. Love is now become a trade, Z393[cg]. Ask me to love no more, Z358[cg]. O Solitude! my sweetest choice, Z406[bg]. Olinda in the shades unseen, Z404[ag]. Pious Celinda goes to prayers, Z410[dg]. When Strephon found his passion vain, Z435[afg]. The fatal hour comes on apace, Z421[bh]. Sawney is a bonny lad, Z412[dh]. Young Thirsis' fate, ye hills and groves, deplore, Z473[fg].   ⓖ

This third and last volume of Purcell's non-theatrical secular songs consummates a most rewarding survey of 87 songs with more of the same: a vocal palette of six singers who are by now so steeped in the nuances of Purcell's strains that even the slightest offering sparkles with something memorable. The treasure is shared between Barbara Bonney and Susan Gritton who complement each other superbly. Gritton, becoming more refined in characterization and tonal colour by the day, is allotted the free-style and dramatic pieces whilst to Bonney's fluid and sensual melisma is designated the more strophic or *cantabile* settings. *Lovely Albina's come ashore*, at one time thought to be "the last song that Mr. Henry Purcell sett before he Dy'd", is at any rate one of the composer's most mature creations, tantalizingly hinting at a new, tautly designed and classically balanced type of song. This work, *If music be the food of love* (the best of the three versions) and *I came, I saw* are striking examples of how exceptionally Bonney negotiates Purcell's skipping and curling contours and makes these songs sound even finer creations than we previously thought. *From silent shades* ("Bess of Bedlam") is Purcell's quintessential mad-song and Gritton has the measure of it all the way; packed full of incident, imagery and musical detail, her narration is clear and finely judged, reporting the tale with irony and change of colour, thereby never resorting to the more usual over-exaggeration which tends to lessen the impact of Bess's condition. Nancy Argenta's account (reviewed further on) is also persuasive but not as subtly shaded as here. There are four other songs common to both discs; the quietude of Argenta's *The fatal hour* and *O Solitude!* are hard to rival. Another scalp, then, for Purcellians. Seven really fine pieces, a few charming *bonnes bouches* and some for the specialist collector only. The CD is beautifully and thoroughly documented but prepare to rip the booklet to shreds getting it back in the jewel-case.

Additional recommendations ...

...Secular Solo Songs, Volume 1 – Draw near, you lovers, Z462[af]. While Thyrsis, wrapt in downy sleep, Z437[c]. Love thou can'st hear, tho' thou art blind, Z396[e]. I lov'd fair Celia, Z381[d]. What hope for us remains now he is gone?, Z472[bf]. Pastora's beauties when unblown, Z407[a]. A thousand sev'ral ways I tried, Z359[d]. Urge me no more, Z426[b]. Farewell, all joys, Z368[c]. If music be the food of love, Z379a[d]. Amidst the shades and cool refreshing streams, Z355[a]. They say you're angry, Z422[e]. Let each gallant heart, Z390[e]. Anacreon's Defeat, "This poet sings the Trojan wars", Z423[f]. Ah! how pleasant 'tis to love, Z353[a]. My heart, whenever you appear, Z399[d]. On the brow of Richmond Hill, Z405[c]. Rashly I swore I would disown, Z411[e]. Since the pox or the plague, Z471[ef]. Beneath a dark and melancholy grove, Z461[bf]. Musing on cares of human fate, Z467[af]. Whilst Cynthia sung, all angry winds lay still, Z438[d]. How I sigh when I think of the charms, Z374[b]. Ye happy swains, whose nymphs are kind, Z443[a]. Beware, poor shepherds, Z361[e]. See how the fading glories of the year, Z470[af]. Cease, anxious world, your fruitless pain, Z362[b]. O! fair Cedaria, hide those eyes, Z402[e]. [a]**Barbara Bonney**, [b]**Susan Gritton** (sops); [c]**James Bowman** (alto); [d]**Rogers Covey-Crump**, [e]**Charles Daniels** (tens); [f]**Michael George** (bass); **Mark Caudle** (viol); **David Miller** (lte/theorbo); **Robert King** (org/hpd). Hyperion ℗ CDA66710 (70 minutes: DDD: 9/94). ✍   ⓖ

...Secular Solo Songs, Volume 2 – I love and I must, "Bell Barr", Z382[a]. When her languishing eyes said "love", Z432[e]. Not all my torments can your pity move, Z400[b]. Ah! cruel nymph, you give despair, Z352[d]. Sylvia, now your scorn give over, Z420[c]. Since one poor view has drawn my heart, Z416[a]. I resolve against cringing and whining, Z386[e]. Gentle shepherds, you that know, Z464[bf]. If grief has any power to kill, Z378[d]. She that would gain a faithful lover, Z414[a]. Fly swift, ye hours, Z369[e]. The Knotting Song: "Hears not my Phyllis", Z371[b]. Phyllis, talk no more of passion, Z409[d]. Celia's fond, too long I've loved her, Z364[a]. In vain we dissemble, Z385[a]. When my Aemelia smiles, Z434[d]. Farewell, ye rocks, Z463[ef]. What a sad fate is mine, Z428[b]. I take no pleasure in the sun's bright beams, Z388[a]. Love's power in my heart shall find no compliance, Z395[d]. How delightful's the life of an innocent swain, Z373[bf]. She who my heart possesses, Z415[c]. Love arms himself in Celia's eyes, Z392[a]. When first my shepherdess and I, Z431[e]. Through mournful shades and solitary groves, Z424[a]. If music be the food of love, Z379 No. 2[a]. Scarce had the rising sun appear'd, Z469[af]. Who but a slave can well express, Z440[b]. High on a throne of glitt'ring ore, Z465[af]. The Queen's Epicedium: "Incassum, Lesbia, rogas", Z383[b]. [a]**Barbara Bonney**, [b]**Susan Gritton** (sops); [c]**James Bowman** (alto); [d]**Rogers Covey-Crump**, [e]**Charles Daniels** (tens); [f]**Michael George** (bass); **King's Consort** (Mark Caudle, Susanna Pell, bass viols; David Miller, theorbo/lte; Robert King, org/hpd). Hyperion ℗ CDA66720 (77 minutes: DDD: 10/94). ✍

New review

Purcell Welcome, viceregent of the mighty king, Z340[a]. O dive custos Auriacae domus, Z504[b]. Raise, raise the voice, Z334[c]. The Fairy Queen – O let me weep[d]. The Queen's Epicedium, "Incassum, Lesbia, rogas", Z383[e]. Why, why are all the Muses mute?, Z343[f]. Young Thirsis' fate, ye hills and groves, deplore, Z473[g]. [abdf]**Suzette Leblanc,** [abcfg]**Barbara Borden** (sops); [af]**Steve Dugardin** (alto); [acef]**Douglas Nasrawi** (ten); [af]**Harry van der Kamp,** [acfg]**Simon Grant** (basses); **Tragicomedia / Stephen Stubbs, Erin Headley.** Teldec Das Alte Werk Ⓕ 4509-95068-2 (76 minutes: DDD: 7/95). Texts included. Recorded 1994.

The music chosen here is all out of Purcell's top drawer, with Tragicomedia combining works with ravishing string ritornellos and extrovert paeans to the King, such as the gloriously crystalline and breezy *Welcome, viceregent*, with the more intimate elegies on the death of Queen Mary which have the capacity to melt marble. The ensemble in the larger works is always fresh and immediate and how Tragicomedia relish the rich glowing textures of this first Welcome Song. The solo singing of Suzette Leblanc and Barbara Borden is particularly striking: bright though never uniformly, they produce a glistening yet suitably threnodizing reading of the deliciously poignant *O dive custos*. Douglas Nasrawi is a naturally dramatic and effective singer though apart from favouring a soprano in *Incassum, Lesbia*, his tone is rather wearingly projected. The most significant work to be included is the unjustly little-known but outstanding Ode, *Why, why are all the Muses mute?*. This was the first Welcome Ode which Purcell composed for King James II in 1685. The usual array of solos, duets, choruses and so on is framed by an unusually rhetorical opening in a declamatory quasi-recitative where the musicians have to be awakened from their slumber and, at the close, by a harmonically devastating (and emotionally draining) setting of the words, "His fame shall endure till all things decay, His fame and the world together shall die, Shall vanish together away". In between, we are blessed with one of Purcell's most affecting ground bass arias, "Britain, thou now art great", which is sung acceptably by Steve Dugardin, though there is really no touching James Bowman on Hyperion in this song as the latter curls himself with such effortless nobility around the seamless melodic strand. Elsewhere, Tragicomedia provide an altogether different approach to Robert King, a tighter, more shapely consort with an attractive vibrancy and immediacy throughout. The recorded sound is spacious.

Purcell Odes and Welcome Songs, Volumes 6-8. **Gillian Fisher, Mary Seers, Susan Hamilton, Tessa Bonner** (sops); **James Bowman, Nigel Short, Michael Chance** (altos); **Mark Padmore, Andrew Tusa, Rogers Covey-Crump, Charles Daniels, John Mark Ainsley** (tens); **Michael George, Robert Evans** (basses); **New College Choir, Oxford; King's Consort / Robert King.** Hyperion Ⓕ CDA66494, CDA66587 and CDA66598 (three discs, oas: 68, 66 and 68 minutes: DDD: 3/93). Texts included. Recorded 1991.

CDA66494 – Love's goddess sure was blind, Z331, Raise, raise the voice, Z334. Laudate Ceciliam, Z329. From those serene and rapturous joys, Z326. *CDA66587* – Of old, when heroes thought it base, Z333. Swifter, Isis, swifter flow, Z336. What, what shall be done on behalf of the man?, Z341. *CDA66598* – Come ye sons of art, away, Z323. Welcome, viceregent of the mighty king, Z340. Why, why are all the Muses mute?, Z343.

These three CDs represent the final instalments in Hyperion's complete recording of Purcell's Odes and Welcome Songs. Purcell composed a number of these celebratory works between 1680 and 1695, and 24 survive. They were written for a considerable range of events: most of them for royal birthdays, of King James II and Queen Mary, but also for a royal wedding, educational celebrations, and the 'Yorkshire Feast' of 1689. This cornucopia of wonderful music has largely been ignored, and Hyperion's edition is to be warmly welcomed, not only for bringing to the catalogue such magnificent music, but also for the extremely sympathetic and musical performances by the King's Consort under the direction of Robert King. Of all the works on these discs, probably the most well-known is *Come ye sons of art, away* written for Queen Mary in 1694 (Volume 8). This joyous work contains some of Purcell's most ebullient music, typified by the duet for two countertenors, "Sound the trumpet". Like all of the works in the set this is surrounded by a well contrasted group of solos and duets for individual voices, instrumental interludes, and the occasional chorus. Less famous, but equally full of Restoration pomp and ceremony is the Yorkshire Feast song (Volume 7). Like many of the odes, the text for this is second-rate, ostensibly telling the story of York from the Roman occupation to the seventeenth century. However, this is merely the pretext for a splendidly varied set of vocal and instrumental items, the climax of which might be more fitting for a coronation than for a dinner of Yorkshire worthies! Volume 6 contains four of the least well-known if no less rich and varied odes, two of which are dedicated to the patron saint of music, St Cecilia. While composed for slightly smaller forces than the more ceremonial odes, these contain music which is equally jaunty and exhilarating. Throughout all three volumes the most striking fact is Purcell's extraordinary inventiveness, and his incredible facility at word setting: even the most lame texts come alive in his hands, and the variety of expression throughout is astonishing. That such fine music should have lain unrecognized and unplayed for so long is cause for some amazement, but no less rejoicing that at last it has been restored in such understanding performances. Robert King's direction is always sensitive to both the broad span and individual nuances of Purcell's kaleidoscopic writing for voice and instruments. The King's Consort play with great understanding throughout and has clearly wholly absorbed the often elusive style of this music, in which many influences, most notably those from France, are combined. The vocal soloists are uniformly excellent, but special mention must be made of the ravishing soprano Gillian Fisher, and the versatile countertenor James Bowman. Hyperion's recordings throughout are without fault, achieving both excellent internal balance and appropriate atmosphere and perspective.

...Come ye sons of art away. Funeral Sentences for the death of Queen Mary II. **Soloists; English Baroque Soloists / John Eliot Gardiner.** Erato Ⓜ 4509-96553-2 (44 minutes: ADD/DDD: 7/95). ✍

Purcell O Solitude! my sweetest choice, Z406[a]. Not all my torments can your pity move, Z400[ac]. Stript of their green our groves appear, Z444[abc]. The Blessed Virgin's Expostulation – Tell me, some pitying Angel, Z196[abc]. If music be the food of love, Z379/1[bc]. The fatal hour comes on apace, Z421[a]. The Queen's Epicedium – Incassum, Lesbia, rogas, Z383[ac]. Cupid, the slyest rogue alive, Z367[abc]. Bess of Bedlam – From silent shades, Z370[abc]. An Evening Hymn on a Ground – Now that the sun hath veiled his light, Z193[c]. O Solitude! my sweetest choice, Z406[b]. Tyrannic Love – Ah! how sweet it is to love[bc]. The Fairy Queen – Hark! the echoing air[abc]. Pausanias – Sweeter than roses[ab]. The Tempest – Dear pretty youth[ab]. The Comical History of Don Quixote – From rosy bow'rs[abc]. Sophonisba – Beneath the poplar's shadow[ab]. The Indian Queen – I attempt from love's sickness[c]. The History of Dioclesian – Let us dance, let us sing[abc]. King Arthur – Fairest isle[a]. **Nancy Argenta** (sop); [a]**Nigel North** (lte/gtr); [b]**Richard Boothby** (va da gamba); [c]**Paul Nicholson** (hpd/org). Virgin Classics Veritas Ⓕ VC7 59324-2 (74 minutes: DDD: 6/94). ✍ Texts included. Recorded 1992. *Gramophone Editor's choice.*   ⒼⒼ

Here we can delight in one of the best recordings of Purcell's songs (mainly taken from *Orpheus Britannicus*) to have emerged in recent times and arguably the most literary-sensitive accounts since Alfred Deller. Nancy Argenta proves that declamatory and strophic songs (and many sub-genres in between) can be negotiated in the same recital with supreme technical finesse, profound understanding of the texts and the type of inventive nuances which enhance the implied conceits of an extraordinary range of songs. Moreover, she has the technical and temperamental control to explore the expressive gamut, from impish and deliberately impersonal no-nonsense texts (such as "Stript of their green", where the singer's rolling spontaneity is just what is called for) to the impulsive gestures and psychological tensions in "Tell me, some pitying Angel" and "From rosy bow'rs". The former is an especially fine portrayal with its sustained organ continuo commentating alongside sundry plucks (always astutely gauged by Nigel North, Richard Boothby and Paul Nicholson) whilst Argenta delivers the Virgin's touching and anxious expostulation with a rare understanding and empathy. Sheer technical bravura, however, is what performances of these songs too frequently lack and the quality of pitching (notoriously awkward leaps abound) and tuning sets this disc in a class of its own; only very occasionally does shrillness or a rather lifeless vibrato detract from an otherwise exquisite release – one which should sit on the shelves of all those who need convincing that Purcell's solo vocal music of this ilk is anything but a glorious testament to the human voice.

...Harmonia – Sacra Lord, what is man?, Z192. O Solitude! my sweetest choice, Z406; In the black dismal dungeon of despair, Z190; Lord, I can suffer Thy rebukes, Z136; Saul and the Witch of Endor, "In guilty night", Z134; Plung'd in the confines of despair, Z142; Awake, ye dead, Z182; The Earth trembled, Z197; My op'ning eyes are purg'd, ZD72; With sick and famish'd eyes, Z200; O, I'm sick of life, Z140; Close thine eyes and sleep secure, Z184. Funeral Sentences for the death of Queen Mary II – Man that is born of Woman, Z27. Voluntaries – C major, Z717; G major, Z720[a]. Ground in C minor, T D221[b]. **Gabrieli Consort and Players / Paul McCreesh; Timothy Roberts** ([a]org/[b]hpd). Archiv Produktion Ⓕ 445 829-2AH (70 minutes: DDD: 7/95). ✍
...The Fairy Queen – Thrice happy lovers; O let me weep ("The Plaint"). The History of King Richard II – Retir'd from any mortal's sight. King Arthur – Fairest isle. Sir Anthony Love – Pursuing Beauty. Oedipus – Music for a while. Henry the Second, King of England – In vain 'gainst love I strove. Rule a Wife and Have a Wife – There's not a swain. The Married Beau – See where repenting Celia lies. Timon of Athens – The cares of lovers. Tyrannic Love – Ah! how sweet it is to love. The Tempest – Dear pretty youth. Bonduca – O lead me to some peaceful gloom. Pausanias – Sweeter than roses. *Coupled with works by* **Locke, Blow, Draghi, Courteville, J. Eccles** and **Weldon. Catherine Bott** (sop); **Pamela Thorby** (rec); **Anthony Robson** (ob); **Pavlo Beznosiuk, Rachel Podger** (vns); **Paula Chateauneuf** (theorbo/gtr); **Richard Egarr** (hpd); **Mark Levy** (bass viol). L'Oiseau-Lyre Ⓕ 443 699-2OH (58 minutes: DDD: 4/96). ✍ *See review in the Collections section; refer to the Index to Reviews.*

Purcell The Echoing Air. [a]**Sylvia McNair** (sop); **Academy of Ancient Music / Christopher Hogwood.** Philips Ⓕ 446 081-2PH (63 minutes: DDD: 9/95). Texts included. Recorded 1994. The Staircase Overture. Suite of Instrumental Pieces (arr. Hogwood) – Cebell; Slow Air; We Come to Sing; Trumpet Tune; Jig; Hear, mighty Love. If music be the food of love, Z379C[a]. The Libertine – To arms, heroic prince[a]. Tell me, some pitying Angel, Z196[a]. Bonduca – O lead me to some peaceful gloom[a]. O Solitude! my sweetest choice, Z406[a]. The Fairy Queen[a] – Hark! the echoing air; O let me weep. Pausanias – Sweeter than roses[a]. King Arthur – Fairest isle[a]. She that would gain a faithful lover, Z414[a]. Cupid, the slyest rogue alive, Z367[a]. The Indian Queen – I attempt from love's sickness[a]. Oedipus – Music for a while[a]. The fatal hour comes on apace, Z431[a]. Chaconne in G minor, Z730.

Though the vocal items outlast the purely instrumental in a proportion of roughly three-to-one, the short pieces which are played by the orchestra in between some of Sylvia McNair's solos probably have prior claim on our attention because they are not only recorded for the first time but, according to Richard Luckett's notes, "receive their first modern performances here". They come from the Magdalene Partbooks (c1706) and are arranged by Christopher Hogwood. All are attractive, delightfully played and well chosen to set the mood or provide a transition for the next song; and, frankly one would like the notes to have given more information. The *Staircase Overture* is probably so-called on account of the 'step', scale-like, figures, rather as the first symphony of *Rejoice in the Lord* explains its title as the "Bell" Anthem. But is it Purcell's title or somebody else's? Why are *We Come to Sing* and *Hear, mighty Love* so called? There may even be listeners who would appreciate information on the *Cebell* (a dance movement, as composed also by Thomas Mace who dedicated his *Cebell* to his wife, its subsequent neglect being, according to Percy Scholes, "perhaps due to lack of matrimonial inspiration"). From the singer we have nothing but the sweetest tone and manner, which after a while leaves one slightly wishing for something more robust. In *The fatal hour comes on apace*, for example, the singer tells "It wracks me in each vital part" but evidently the vocal organ does not come within that category. *Cupid, the slyest rogue alive* surely wants a touch of the not quite maidenly in its delivery; even *I attempt from love's sickness to fly in vain* calls for a more substantial toughness in the lower notes. But the voice is extremely beautiful and in many of the songs entirely apt. *If music be the food of love* (third setting) suits particularly well, the runs sung with exemplary evenness and clarity, the invitation to "save me in your arms" meltingly irresistible. *The Blessed Virgin's Expostulation* (*Tell me, some pitying Angel*), too, has a freshness and spontaneity about it, the repetition of "Was it, was it a waking dream?" suggesting the hesitancy of anxious private thought. The balance of voice and instruments is fine, and the programme (along the lines of the concerts in 1704 of music "by the late Mr Purcell") is a thoroughly happy conception.

New review

Purcell Dioclesian Acts 1-4. **Catherine Pierard** (sop); **James Bowman** (alto); **John Mark Ainsley, Mark Padmore** (tens); **Michael George** (bass); **Collegium Musicum 90 Chorus; Collegium Musicum 90 / Richard Hickox.** Chandos Chaconne Ⓟ CHAN0568 (54 minutes: DDD: 7/95). ✍ Text included.

It was *Dioclesian*, the least known of the four semi-opera masterpieces of Purcell, for which the composer initially earned a reputation for writing stage music. The 'opera' was by all accounts a roaring success, though music played a less important part in the stage works of the 1690s than it did in the masque-related works of the previous decades – ironically just at the time when England could at last boast a dramatic master who could stand tall amongst the 'greats' of France and Italy. If the paucity of tableaux means a less atmospheric scenic context, such as we experience in *The Fairy Queen* or *King Arthur*, there is still much fine music which deserves to be highly regarded. Hickox is evidently committed to this score: the instrumental movements are all disciplined and yet display the buoyancy and variety of expression of one who senses the freshness and special flavour of Purcell's first foray into the theatre. His soloists are authoritative Purcellians and they never disappoint. What fine music this is. Hickox manages to sustain the tension and climate he sets from the start which is arguably what Gardiner never quite manages.

Purcell Dido and Aeneas. **Catherine Bott** (sop) Dido; **John Mark Ainsley** (ten) Aeneas; **Emma Kirkby** (sop) Belinda; **David Thomas** (bass) Sorceress; **Elizabeth Priday** (sop) First Witch; **Sara Stowe** (sop) Second Witch; **Julianne Baird** (sop) Second Woman; **Daniel Lochmann** (treb) First Sailor; **Michael Chance** (alto) Spirit; **Academy of Ancient Music Chorus and Orchestra / Christopher Hogwood.** L'Oiseau-Lyre Ⓟ 436 992-2OH (52 minutes: DDD: 7/94). ✍ Notes and text included. Recorded 1992. ⒼⒼ

Purcell Dido and Aeneas. **Véronique Gens** (sop) Dido; **Nathan Berg** (bass-bar) Aeneas; **Sophie Marin-Degor** (sop) Belinda; **Claire Brua** (sop) Sorceress; **Sophie Daneman** (sop) Second Woman, First Witch; **Gaëlle Mechaly** (sop) Second Witch; **Jean-Paul Fouchécourt** (ten) Spirit, Sailor; **Les Arts Florissants / William Christie.** Erato Ⓟ 4509-98477-2 (52 minutes: DDD: 6/95). ✍ Notes and text included. Recorded 1994. Ⓖ

Emma Kirkby (whose Dido, for Parrott, remains one of the finest on record) sings Belinda for Hogwood; David Thomas (whose Aeneas, on the same recording, was outstanding) sings the Sorceress; Michael Chance takes the tiny part of the Spirit, thereby putting its moment into centre stage as the gloriously conceived turning-point of the story. A few innovations, too. We have had all kinds of Sorceress on record but following the arguments that the Sorceress could be a man, Hogwood opts for David Thomas, who offers perhaps the most eloquent version so far. He gives full value to the words and the music. Less convincing, perhaps, is the use of a boy for the sailor's song; despite direct and spirited singing, its text is so inappropriate for a boy as to make the decision seem quite wrong. Much more successful is the use of the Drottningholm wind-machines, in all their wonderful variety, to interpret the various stage-instructions and give the entire performance a real sense of verisimilitude. Catherine Bott is a fine Dido, even-voiced across the range and powerfully expressive if occasionally a touch free with the rhythms. John Mark Ainsley easily stands as the finest Aeneas since David Thomas. This is a very difficult role to handle dramatically, because its moods change so fast; and Ainsley handles all this with heartbreaking ease. This is a classic interpretation. So too is Hogwood's reading of the score, with his faultless sense of the right speed and the right rhythm as well as his ability to see the moment when everything must be interrupted to give space to the drama.

William Christie's reading of *Dido* is very much in terms of the reputed French influence on Purcell. Over-dotting, reverse dotting and *inégalité* are used throughout; the lines are often heavily embellished in the manner of Lully. This is a perfectly justifiable approach to the music, since there is little direct evidence to say exactly how much the French style dominated in England. But it is entirely different from the other available recordings. This version – with single strings, an excellent small choir and a slightly obtrusive harpsichord – stands well alongside what is otherwise available: if you prefer *Dido* in the French manner this is the record you will want; if not, you will probably still want it as a different view of a major work. Apart from a few moments' inattention in Belinda's "Haste, haste to town", you would hardly notice that most of the cast are Francophone, except in that Nathan Berg's imposing bass-baritone finds it slightly easier to exploit the colour and the meaning of Aeneas's words. Véronique Gens is a lucid and sensible Dido (which is to say not stunningly individual but consistently admirable), partnered by a sprightly Belinda from Sophie Marin-Degor and a good Second Woman from Sophie Daneman. Claire Brua's Sorceress is a splendidly insinuating conception, with a slithering melodic style that neatly characterizes her evil. Perhaps the main musical distinction of this version is the way Christie presents the final paragraphs. Up to this point he has taken generally quick speeds, and he runs the final confrontation of Dido and Aeneas at a headlong tempo, which works very well. Then he comes almost to a standstill at the moment when Aeneas leaves the stage, choosing an unusually slow speed for the chorus "Great minds against themselves conspire". This makes way for a dangerously slow Lament, which is heart-stopping and the final chorus, which is not.

Additional recommendations ...

...**Soloists; St Anthony Singers; English Chamber Orchestra / Anthony Lewis.** Decca Serenata
　Ⓜ 425 720-2DM* (53 minutes: ADD: 12/90).

...**Soloists; English Chamber Choir and Orchestra / Raymond Leppard.** Erato Libretto
　Ⓜ 2292-45263-2 (56 minutes: ADD: 11/91).

...**Soloists; Taverner Choir and Players / Andrew Parrott.** Chandos Chaconne Ⓕ CHAN0521
　(56 minutes: DDD: 11/91). ⤳

...**Soloists; St James's Singers and Baroque Players / Ivor Bolton.** Teldec Das Alte Werk
　Ⓕ 4509-91191-2 (58 minutes: DDD: 9/93). ⤳

...**Soloists; Hamburg Monteverdi Choir; Hamburg NDR Chamber Orchestra / Sir Charles Mackerras.**
　Archiv Produktion The Purcell Collection Ⓜ 447 148-2AP (63 minutes: DDD: 7/95).

New review

Eccles, Purcell et al Don Quixote: Scenes from a Musical by Don Taylor after Thomas
D'Urfey. **Paul Scofield** (spkr) Don Quixote; **Roy Hudd** (spkr/bar) Sancho Panza; **Emma Kirkby**
(sop) Altisdora; **Evelyn Tubb** (sop) Marcella; **David Thomas** (bass) Cardenio; **The Consort of
Musicke; The City Waites; The Purcell Simfony / Anthony Rooley.** Musica Oscura Ⓕ 070973
(two discs: 128 minutes: DDD: 10/95). Notes and text included. Recorded 1995.

Very justifiably, Anthony Rooley felt it was a terrible waste that, because Thomas D'Urfey's three Restoration plays on *Don Quixote* had not only fallen into oblivion but were unlikely ever to be revived, all the splendid music for them by Purcell and John Eccles, except for a handful of admittedly great songs, has remained almost unknown. So Rooley, convinced that it was only in a dramatic setting that the music would make its full impact, persuaded Don Taylor, an experienced playwright and producer, to write a play for Radio 3 after – a long way after – D'Urfey (in fact returning more to Cervantes) which would incorporate that music. With considerable ingenuity and a good deal of wit, Taylor has created this new structure, not necessarily placing the musical pieces in their original order, for the same situations or for the same characters, and re-writing not a few of the lyrics (though leaving untouched the well-known splendid set pieces). He has taken other liberties too: he has added a finale from *The Indian Queen* (with a new lyric), and not all the Eccles movements were originally for this play. But it works convincingly, and purists need not throw up their hands in horror. The point is well made that the songs gain in effect from being placed in a dramatic framework, and performance throughout is not only 'authentic' in style but of the highest quality. We have already heard David Thomas's wild frenzy in "Let the dreadful engines" and Emma Kirkby's seductive characterization of "From rosy bowers" in a previous Musica Oscura disc ("The Mantle of Orpheus") by The Consort of Musicke, but equally outstanding is Evelyn Tubb's interpretation of yet another 'mad song' in the play, *I burn, I burn*, by Eccles (which in the seventeenth century was greeted with the greatest acclaim of all); and other highlights are Eccles's "Dirge", the varied scena "With this sacred charming wand", and some vulgar low-life ditties sung with obvious relish (in appropriate accents) by Lucie Skeaping and Doug Wootton (the latter including some hilariously xenophobic verses by Don Taylor as a prelude to the rousing "Genius of England", with its virtuoso trumpet part). Paul Scofield makes a bewildered but dignified Don Quixote, and Roy Hudd is in his element as his squire Sancho Panza (he also sings two patter-songs very creditably, though it is perhaps too much to list him as "baritone") – first-class casting both; but there are also a number of other good actors, of whom Roger Allam in particular deserves mention. To have recorded the whole play-with-music, or latter-day 'musical', would have spread on to considerably more than two discs; and the compromise to limit this recording by completely cutting out some scenes and concentrating on sections in which music occurs is understandable but results in discontinuities in the action – the only real criticism to be made here; but fortunately the booklet includes the full text, so it can be seen how the sections join up. The boldness of Rooley and Taylor's experiment wins our admiration, and if it succeeds in focusing general attention on Purcell's (and Eccles's) instinct for the theatre it will have done valuable service.

Purcell King Arthur. **Véronique Gens, Claron McFadden, Sandrine Piau, Susannah Waters** (sops); **Mark Padmore, Iain Paton** (tens); **Jonathan Best, Petteri Salomaa, François Bazola-Minori** (basses); **Les Arts Florissants Chorus and Orchestra / William Christie.** Erato Ⓕ 4509-98535-2 (two discs: 90 minutes: DDD: 6/95). ✒ Notes and text included. *Gramophone Award Winner 1995. Gramophone Editor's choice.*   ⓖⓖⓖ

If the co-operation with John Dryden led to a unity of vision in terms of music's expressive role in the overall drama, Purcell was limited to a historical patriotic fantasy with little room for the magic and pathos of, say, the superior *Fairy Queen*. Yet in the context of a stage presentation, Purcell's music shines through strongly. On disc though, with just the music, not even the dramatic powers of William Christie can restore its place in the overall scheme. But never mind, this is a score with some magnificent creations and Christie is evidently enchanted by it. The choral singing is richly textured, sensual and long-breathed, yet always alert to a nuance which can irradiate a passage at a stroke, as Christie does in the bittersweet close of "Honour prizing" – easily the best moment in Act 1. The instrumental movements are finely moulded so that sinewy counterpoint and rhythmic profile are always strongly relayed. The songs, too, have been acutely prepared and are keenly characterized without resorting to excess. All the basses deliver their fine music with aplomb. If there is one drawback to extracting the musical numbers from the 'opera' when they have so clearly been delivered within a theatrical context, it is that the highly contextual characterizations lend themselves less well to the musical continuity of a CD. But *King Arthur* without the play is dramatically a nonsense so why try to pretend? Christie does not but makes the strongest case for this music to date.

Additional recommendation ...

...**Soloists; Monteverdi Choir; English Baroque Soloists / John Eliot Gardiner.** Erato Ⓕ 4509-96552-2 (two discs: 90 minutes: DDD: 7/95). ✒

New review

Purcell The Indian Queen. **Tessa Bonner, Catherine Bott** (sops); **Rogers Covey-Crump** (ten); **Peter Harvey** (bass); **Purcell Simfony Voices; Purcell Simfony / Catherine Mackintosh** (vn). Linn Records Ⓕ CKD035 (60 minutes: DDD: 9/95). Recorded 1994.

New review

Purcell The Indian Queen. **Emma Kirkby, Catherine Bott** (sops), **John Mark Ainsley** (ten); **Gerald Finley** (bar); **David Thomas** (bass); **Tommy Williams** (sngr); **Chorus and Orchestra of the Academy of Ancient Music / Christopher Hogwood.** Also includes additional Act by Daniel Purcell. L'Oiseau-Lyre Ⓕ 444 339-2OHO (73 minutes: DDD: 1/96). Notes and text included. Recorded 1994.

Although until the Linn disc, there had been no new version of *The Indian Queen* since Gardiner's (now unavailable) 1979 recording, this is no reflection on the quality of the work. If *The Indian Queen* is less ambitious than the other three 'operas' there is the sure touch here of the composer at his most mature and adept (as his last great work for the theatre, there is a strong possibility that Purcell may never have lived to hear it). The Prologue, in which he had the rare opportunity to set an extended dialogue, is beautifully balanced, the humour in Act 2 delicate and inimitably charming, and the music in Act 3 – when Zempoalla's ill-fated love is prophesied by Ismeron the magician in "Ye twice ten hundred deities" – ranks alongside the finest moments in Purcell's output and was praised by Dr Burney nearly 100 years later. The small-scale character of the work, compared to its siblings, is taken a stage further by the Purcell Simfony, who employ a minute chamber-size group of four strings, doubling oboe and recorder, single trumpet and drums. The soloists sing with airy restraint but each responds to these Hilliardesque proportions with a rhythmic buoyancy and direct intimacy which projects a finely gauged overall conception of the work. If the expressive power of the music is at times rather glazed, there is a sure atmosphere which is captured by a delightful perspective on the recorded sound, ensuring that the light puff-pastry of "I come to sing great Zempoalla's story" and "I attempt from love's sickness" is both warm and yet never imposing. The ensemble is not always first-rate but there is nothing too worrisome and the instrumental numbers are elegantly shaped. Tessa Bonner gets the lion's share of the solo soprano numbers, ahead of the more colourful Catherine Bott, though the former's comparatively brittle sound has a crystalline quality which suits director Catherine Mackintosh's consistent, if austere strategy. To sum up, the Linn release is consistently touching, one which in a paradoxical way gets under the skin despite the recessed emotional climate it conveys.

The difference between the Purcell Simfony's graceful and intimate performance and the account from Christopher Hogwood is that the latter makes us realize that for all the constraints, the score is not inherently small-scale and that it warrants all the subtlety of colour that can be achieved using 12 soloists and a decent sized choir and orchestra. Needless to say, Hogwood conveys a consistent, logical and meticulous understanding of the score. The orchestral playing is crisp and transparent, the Academy of Ancient Music's articulation allowing the integrity of the inner parts to be heard to the full without compromising blend. Amongst a distinguished line-up of singers, John Mark Ainsley gets the lion's share and is perhaps marginally more effective as the Indian Boy than as Fame, but such gloriously mellifluous and controlled singing can only enhance the reputation of this work. Emma Kirkby is in fine fettle and she executes the justly celebrated song "I attempt from love's sickness" with her usual communicative panache. Then comes the pleasurably contrasted voice of Catherine Bott: "They tell us that your mighty powers" could not be in better hands. David Thomas as Envy, with his two followers in the Act 2 masque, highlights this brilliant scene as the work of a true connoisseur of the theatre. Mature Purcell is most strongly felt in the deftly ironic invocation by the conjurer, Ismeron, whose "Ye twice ten thousand deities" is delivered authoritatively by Gerald Finley, though the lulling to sleep, before the God of Dream's gloomy non-prediction, is strangely unconvincing. Taken as a whole, the quality of music shines very brightly in Hogwood's reading. It is perhaps a touch calculated in places. The Purcell Simfony's melting chorus "While thus we bow before your shrine" is preferable; but Hogwood's new version has to stand as the current favourite. His inclusion of Daniel Purcell's Act 5 masque is interesting but not much more than that.

Additional recommendation ...
...**Soloists; Deller Choir; The King's Music / Alfred Deller.** Harmonia Mundi Ⓕ HMC90 243
    (61 minutes: ADD: 8/87).

Purcell The Fairy Queen. **Gillian Fisher, Lorna Anderson** (sops); **Ann Murray** (mez); **Michael Chance** (alto); **John Mark Ainsley, Ian Partridge** (tens); **Richard Suart, Michael George** (basses); **The Sixteen Choir and Orchestra / Harry Christophers.** Collins Classics Ⓕ 7013-2 (two discs: 133 minutes: DDD: 4/92). 🖉 Text included. Recorded 1990.   Ⓖ

Purcell The Fairy Queen. **Lorraine Hunt, Catherine Pierard** (sops); **Susan Bickley** (mez); **Howard Crook, Mark Padmore** (tens); **David Wilson-Johnson** (bar); **Richard Wistreich** (bass); **Schütz Choir of London; London Classical Players / Roger Norrington.** EMI Ⓕ CDS5 55234-2 (two discs: 122 minutes: DDD: 2/95). 🖉 Notes and text included.Recorded 1993.

Of Purcell's four semi-operas in which extended musical set pieces or masques are mixed with substantial dialogue, it is *The Fairy Queen* that stands the best chance of catching the public's imagination, not only because of its superb music but also on account of its foundation in such a well-loved part of England's literary heritage as *A Midsummer Night's Dream*. Much has been made of the liberties taken by Purcell's anonymous librettist for this work, but no one who has heard the music could deny that the composer conjures just as truthfully as Shakespeare the pains and pleasures of love, the interludes of low comedy, and the magical atmosphere of the fairy wood. Harry Christophers has assembled a strong cast for his recording. With singers like Gillian Fisher, Michael Chance, John Mark Ainsley and Ian Partridge aboard, things are hardly likely to go far astray, while the contribution of the always excellent Sixteen Choir means, too, that this is a performance without any serious weakness. The orchestra, it's true, could sound more committed at times, while Ann Murray seems a little out of place in this particular company (though there's certainly nothing wrong with her singing as such); but in general there is a refreshing lightness, an authentic Englishness, to this recording that serves the music well. Perhaps the highlight is the gentle Second Act Masque which lulls the eponymous Titania to sleep, but also highly enjoyable are the comic scenes, such as the one in which a drunken poet suffers an uncomfortable encounter with some fairies. This is not a recording which has everything – it lacks sheer splendour for one thing – but of those available it is among the best.

Roger Norrington clearly identifies with Purcell's refined characterization. There is a great sense throughout that each gesture in the music has been thoroughly absorbed and filtered. This makes for an extraordinarily tidy, persuasively articulated and lean account: the instrumental dances contain a textural luminosity which is at times revelatory and the attention to detail gives the marvellously fleeting nuance of Purcell's part-writing the chance to be noticed; no one has produced such a mesmerically crafted evocation in "A Dance for the Followers" of Oberon sprinkling magic flower juice into Titania's eyes. The vocal numbers boast a skilfully chosen array of singers, each of whom evidently suits Norrington's highly focused view of the music. Unlike Christophers's if not more celebrated then more recognizably diverse group of soloists, we have here an easy and pleasing contrast between different voices. Norrington's is 'state of the art' Purcell and the price for such intricate and poised expression is that the whole feels rather studio-made, each scene a graceful vignette of layered perceptions. On a less fundamental level, the keen edge of his vision denies a more yielding approach at some moments. For all that, this is a splendid achievement.

Additional recommendations ...
...**Soloists; Monteverdi Choir; English Baroque Soloists / John Eliot Gardiner.** Archiv Produktion
    Ⓕ 419 221-2AH2 (two discs: 138 minutes: DDD: 8/87). 🖉
...**Soloists; Les Arts Florissants / William Christie.** Harmonia Mundi Ⓕ HMC90 1308/9 (two discs:
    128 minutes: DDD: 1/90). 🖉
...**Soloists; Ambrosian Opera Chorus; English Chamber Orchestra / Benjamin Britten.** Decca
    Serenata Ⓜ 433 163-2DM2 (two discs: 96 minutes: ADD: 5/92).
...**The Scholars Baroque Ensemble.** Naxos Ⓢ 8 550660/1 (two discs: 129 minutes: DDD: 7/94).
...**Soloists; Arnold Schoenberg Choir; Vienna Concentus Musicus / Nikolaus Harnoncourt.** Teldec
    Ⓕ 4509-97684-2 (two discs: 119 minutes: DDD: 2/96).

Further listening ...
...Chacony in G minor for strings, Z730. *Coupled with* **Delius** Two Aquarelles. **Elgar** Introduction and Allegro, Op. 47. **Bridge** Sir Roger de Coverley, H155. **Britten** Simple Symphony, Op. 4.

Prelude and Fugue, Op. 29. **English Chamber Orchestra / Benjamin Britten.** Decca The Classic Sound 448 569-2DCS (2/96).

...The History of Dioclesian – orchestral suite; Let the soldiers rejoice[b]. If music be the food of love, Z379 No. 1[a]. O! how happy's he, Z403[a]. Lost is my quiet for ever, Z502[ab]. *Coupled with* **Handel** Concerto grosso in G minor, Op. 6 No. 8. Il duello amoroso, HWV82[ab]. [a]**Nancy Argenta** (sop); [b]**Michael Chance** (alto); **Freiburg Baroque Orchestra / Gottfried von der Goltz.** Deutsche Harmonia Mundi 05472 77295-2 (10/94).

...Suites – The Fairy Queen; Dido and Aeneas; King Arthur; Abdelazer; Chaconne in G minor, Z730. **Freiburg Baroque Orchestra / Thomas Hengelbrock.** Deutsche Harmonia Mundi RD77231 (3/92). ✏

...Fantasia upon a Ground in D major/F major/Z731. Ten Sonatas in Four Parts – No. 6 in G minor, Z801. Pavans – Z748; Z749; Z750; Z751; Z752. Chaconne. 12 Sonnatas of Three Parts – E minor, Z796; D major, Z801. Overtures – Z771; Z772. Swiftere Isis, swifter flow, Z336 – Overture in G major. Suite in G major, Z770. **London Baroque.** Harmonia Mundi HMC90 1327 (10/90). ✏

...Ten Sonatas in Four Parts, Z802-11 – No. 3 in A minor; No. 4 in D minor; No. 5 in G minor; No. 6 in G minor; No. 7 in G major; No. 8 in G minor (with two variant movements); No. 9 in F major; No. 10 in D major. Organ Voluntaries, Z717-20 – No. 2 in D minor; No. 4 in G major. Prelude for Solo Violin in G minor, ZN773. **Purcell Quartet.** Chandos CHAN8763 (12/89).

...Organ Works – Four Voluntaries, Z717-20. Verse in F major, Z716. A Choice Collection of Lessons: March in C major, ZT687; Chaconne in G minor, ZT680; Trumpet Tune in C major, "Cibell", ZT678; Trumpet Tune in C major, ZT698. Ground in Gamut in G major, Z645. Ground in C minor, TD221. Voluntary in A major on the Old Hundredth, Z721. Trumpet Voluntary in D major. *Coupled with* **Blow** Six Voluntaries. **Locke** Seven Voluntaries from Melothesia. **John Butt** (org). Harmonia Mundi HMU90 7103 (6/94). ✏

...Songs from Orpheus Britannicus: The Rival Sisters, Z609 – Calia has a thousand charms. Fly swift, ye hours, Z369. Gentle shepherds, you that know, Z464. Aureng-Zebe, Z573 – I see, she flies me. Pausanias, Z585 – Sweeter than roses. I came, I saw, and was undone, Z375. If music be the food of love, Z379/3. Bess of Bedlam, "From silent shades", Z370. Timon of Athens, Z632 – Love in their little veins. The Comical History of Don Quioxte, Z578 – From rosy bow'rs. King Arthur, Z628 – Fairest isle. Tyrannic Love, Z613 – Ah! how sweet it is to love. The Fatal hour comes on apace, Z421. O Solitude! my sweetest choice, Z406. The history of Dioclesian, Z627 – Since from my dear Astrea's sight. Bonduca, Z574 – O lead me to some peaceful gloom. The Fairy Queen, Z629 – Thrice happy lovers. Solo Harpsichord: The Second Part of Musick's Handmaid – A New Ground in E minor, Z T682. Ground in D minor, Z D222. Hornpipe in D minor, "Round O", Z T684. A Choice Collection of Lessons – Chaconne in G minor, Z T680. **Agnès Mellon** (sop); **Wieland Kuijken** (va da gamba); **Christophe Rousset** (hpd). Auvidis Astrée E8757 (9/93). ✏

...Anthems, Instrumental Music and Songs. **Soloists; King's College Choir, Cambridge / Sir David Willcocks; Leonhardt Consort / Gustav Leonhardt; Brüggen Consort / Frans Brüggen.** Teldec 9031-77608-2 (9/93). ✏

...The Symphony Songs – Hark, Damon, hark, Z541. How pleasant is this flowery plain, Z543. We reap all the pleasures, Z547. Hark how the wild musicians sing, Z542. Weeping, "See where she sits", Z508. Oh! what a scene does entertain my sight, Z506. A Serenading Song, "Soft notes and gently raised", Z510. If ever I more riches did desire, Z544. Four Pavans, Z748-51. **Red Byrd** (Suzie Le Blanc, Julia Gooding, sops; John Potter, Angus Smith, tens; Richard Wistreich, bass); **The Parley of Instruments / Peter Holman.** Hyperion CDA66750 (8/95). ✏

...Hail, bright Cecilia, Z328. **Equale Brass; Monteverdi Choir and Orchestra / John Eliot Gardiner.** Erato 4509 96554-2 (7/95). ✏

...Timon of Athens – Masque. The History of Dioclesian – Masque. **Soloists; Collegium Musicum 90 / Richard Hickox.** Chandos Chaconne CHAN0558 (11/94). ✏

...Timon of Athens. The History of Dioclesian. **Soloists; English Baroque Soloists / John Eliot Gardiner.** Erato 4509 96556-2 (7/95). ✏

...The Tempest. **Soloists; English Baroque Soloists / John Eliot Gardiner.** Erato 4509-96555-2 (7/95). ✏

Johann Quantz

German 1697-1773

Suggested listening ...

...Flute Concertos – C major; D major, "pour Potsdam"; G major; G minor. **James Galway** (fl); **Württemberg Chamber Orchestra / Jörg Faerber.** RCA Victor Red Seal RD60247 (11/91).

...Flute Concerto in G major. *Coupled with works by* **C.P.E. Bach, F. Benda** and **Frederick the Great** Patrick Gallois (fl); CPE Bach Chamber Orchestra / Peter Schreier. DG 439 895-2GH (2/95). *See review in the Collections section; refer to the Index to Reviews.*

...Double Flute Concerto in G major. *Coupled with works by* **Heinichen, Dieupart, Fasch, Pisendel** and **Veracini. Cologne Musica Antiqua / Reinhard Goebel.** Archiv Produktion 447 644-2AH (1/96). ✏ *See review in the Collections section; refer to the Index to Reviews.* Ⓖ

Jean-Baptiste Quentin

French fl. 1718-c1750

Suggested listening ...
...Flute Sonata in D major. Violin Concerto in A major. *Coupled with* **Corrette** Concerto comique
25. **Boismortier** Five Sonatas for Cello, Viol, Bassoon and Continuo, Op. 26 – No. 6 in
D major. **Blavet** Flute Concerto in A minor. **Buffardin** Flute Concerto in E minor. **Cologne
Musica Antiqua / Reinhard Goebel.** Archiv Produktion 447 286-2AMA. ✍

Roger Quilter

British 1877-1953

Suggested listening ...
...A Children's Overture, Op. 17. Where the Rainbow Ends – Suite. As you like it – Suite,
Op. 21. Country Pieces. The Rake – Suite. Three English Dances, Op. 11. Julia – Concert Waltz
from "Rosmé". **Bratislava Radio Symphony Orchestra / Adrian Leaper.** Marco Polo British Light
Music 8 223444 (8/94).
...Three Songs, Op. 3 – No. 1, Love's Philosophy; No. 2, Now Sleeps the Crimson Petal. At Close of
Day. Three Shakespeare Songs, Op. 6. To Julia, Op. 8. Four Songs, Op. 14. Seven Elizabethan
Lyrics, Op. 12. Three Songs of William Blake, Op. 20. Go, Lovely Rose, Op. 24 No. 3. Arab Love
Song, Op. 25 No. 4. Music, When Soft Voices Die, Op. 25 No. 5. In the Bud of the Morning-o,
Op. 25 No. 6. I Arise from Dreams of Thee, Op. 29. **Benjamin Luxon** (bar); **David Willison** (pf).
Chandos CHAN8782 (3/90).

Jaan Rääts

Estonian 1932-

Suggested listening ...
...Toccata. *Coupled with* **Kangro** Suite, Op. 1. **Mägi** The Ancient Kannel. **Sumera** Piece from the
Year 1981. **Tüür** Sonata. **Vähi** Fata Morgana. **Pärt** Partita. **Lauri Väinmaa** (pf). Finlandia
4509-95704-2 (7/95).

Henri Rabaud

French 1873-1949

Suggested listening ...
...Mârouf, savetier du Caire – Dances. Procession nocturne, Op. 6. Suites anglaises – No. 2; No. 3.
Eglogue, Op. 7. Divertissement on Russian songs, Op. 2. **Rhineland-Pfalz State Philharmonic
Orchestra / Leif Segerstam.** Marco Polo 8 223503 (1/95).

Sergey Rachmaninov

USSR/American 1873-1943

Rachmaninov The Complete Recordings. [a]**Fritz Kreisler** (vn); [b]**Sergey Rachmaninov** (pf);
Philadelphia Orchestra / [c]**Leopold Stokowski,** [d]**Eugene Ormandy,** [e]**Sergey Rachmaninov.** RCA
Victor Gold Seal mono Ⓜ 09026 61265-2* (ten discs: 640 minutes: ADD: 3/93). *Gramophone
classical 100. Gramophone Award Winner 1993.*
Rachmaninov Piano Concertos[b] – No. 1 in F sharp minor, Op. 1[d]; No. 2 in C minor, Op. 18[c];
No. 3 in D minor, Op. 30[d]; No. 4 in G minor, Op. 40[d]. Rhapsody on a Theme of Paganini,
Op. 43[bc]. The isle of the dead, Op. 29[e]. Vocalise, Op. 34 No. 14[e]. Symphony No. 3 in A minor,
Op. 44[e]. Solo Piano works[b] – Daisies. Nine Etudes tableaux, Op. 33 – No. 2 in C major; No. 7 in
E flat major. Nine Etudes tableaux, Op. 39 – No. 6 in A minor. Lilacs (two versions, recorded in
1923 and 1942). Six Moments musicaux, Op. 16 – Allegretto. Five Morceaux de fantaisie, Op. 3 –
No. 5, Sérénade in B flat minor. Seven Morceaux de salon, Op. 10 – No. 5, Humoresque in
G major. Oriental Sketch in B flat major. Polka de W.R. (three versions, recorded in 1919, 1921
and 1928). Preludes – C sharp minor, Op. 3 No. 2 (three versions, recorded in 1919, 1921 and
1928); G minor, Op. 23 No. 5; G flat major, Op. 23 No. 10; E major, Op. 32 No. 3; G major,
Op. 32 No. 5; F minor, Op. 32 No. 6; G sharp minor, Op. 32 No. 12. **Beethoven** Violin Sonata
No. 8 in G major, Op. 30 No. 3[ab]. 32 Variations on an original theme in C minor, WoO80[b].
Schubert Violin Sonata in A major (Duo), D574[ab]. **Grieg** Violin Sonata No. 3 in C minor,
Op. 45[ab]. **Schumann** Carnaval, Op. 9[b]. **Chopin** Piano Sonata No. 2 in B flat minor, Op. 35[b].
Also includes solo piano works by **Bach, Beethoven, Bizet, Borodin, Chopin, Daquin,
Debussy, Dohnányi, Gluck, Grieg, Handel, Henselt, Kreisler, Liszt, Mendelssohn,
Moszkowski, Mozart, Mussorgsky, Paderewski, Rimsky-Korsakov, Saint-Saëns,
D. Scarlatti, Schubert, Schumann, Scriabin, J. Strauss II** and **Tchaikovsky.** ⓖⓖⓖ
Here, on RCA's superbly remastered ten-disc set, is awe-inspiring and scintillating confirmation of
Rachmaninov's greatness; as composer, pianist, chamber musician and conductor. Controversy over
his stature as a composer may live on in the dustier corners of academia, but today once confident
assertions that his music would never last, that it lacked the regenerative force of true tragedy or that

it was, in essence, little more than a precursor of Hollywood, have been triumphantly erased. Works such as the Second Symphony, the Third Piano Concerto and the Second Piano Sonata are played without the once acceptable and debilitating cuts so sadly sanctioned by the composer, and innovative as well as traditional elements in Rachmaninov's writing are celebrated. What is indisputable, however, is Rachmaninov's quality as a pianist. Alternatively teasing and granitic in other composer's music (his way with Schumann's *Carnaval* and Chopin's Second Sonata, to name but two, will always incite argument) his performances of his own works are, quite simply, inimitable, imbued with a brio and aristocracy entirely his own. The most immediately appealing include all four concertos and the Paganini *Rhapsody*, Handel's *Harmonious Blacksmith* Variations (pure pianistic sorcery) and Rachmaninov's own second *Moment musical* and *Mélodie*, Op. 3 No. 2; the former of a mind-bending virtuosity, the latter aglow with the *cantabile* and rubato of another, far-off age. But everything is absorbing, nothing without interest. These recordings blazen out Rachmaninov's stature both as creator and re-creator in every golden bar.

Additional recommendations ...

...Nos. 1-4. Rhapsody on a Theme of Paganini. **Rafael Orozco** (pf); **Royal Philharmonic Orchestra / Edo de Waart.** Philips Ⓜ 438 326-2PM2 (two discs: 150 minutes: ADD).

...Nos. 1-4. Rhapsody on a Theme of Paganini. **Earl Wild** (pf); **Royal Philharmonic Orchestra / Jascha Horenstein.** Chandos Ⓕ CHAN8521/2 (two discs: 134 minutes: ADD: 9/87). ⒼⒼⒼ

...No. 4. **Ravel** Piano Concerto in G major. **Arturo Benedetti Michelangeli** (pf); **Philharmonia Orchestra / Ettore Gracis.** EMI Ⓕ CDC7 49326-2* (47 minutes: ADD: 9/88). *Gramophone classical 100.* ⒼⒼⒼ

...Nos. 1-4. **Vladimir Ashkenazy** (pf); **Concertgebouw Orchestra / Bernard Haitink.** Decca Ⓕ 421 590-2DH2 (two discs: 134 minutes: DDD: 4/89).

...Nos. 1 and 4. **Vladimir Ashkenazy** (pf); **London Symphony Orchestra / André Previn.** Decca Ⓜ 425 004-2DM (55 minutes: ADD: 7/90). Ⓖ

...Nos. 1-4. Rhapsody on a Theme of Paganini. **Howard Shelley** (pf); **Royal Scottish National Orchestra / Bryden Thomson.** Chandos Ⓕ CHAN8882/3 (two discs: 154 minutes: DDD: 4/91).

...Lilacs, Op. 21 No. 5. Etudes tableaux, Op. 39 – No. 1 in C minor; No. 5 in E flat minor. **Prokofiev** Piano Sonata No. 6 in A major, Op. 82. **Liszt** Concert Studies, S144 – La leggierezza; Waldestauschen. **Chopin** Nocturne in A flat major, Op. 32 No. 2. Polonaise in F sharp minor, Op. 44. **Scriabin** Mazurka in E minor, Op. 25 No. 3. Etude in C sharp minor, Op. 42 No. 5. **Anonymous** (arr. Saegusa) Natu – Wa Kinu. Todai – Mori. Usagi. **Evgeni Kissin** (pf). Sony Classical Ⓕ SK45931 (73 minutes: DDD. 11/90). *See review in the Collections section; refer to the Index to Reviews.* ⒼⒼ

Rachmaninov Piano Concerto No. 1 in F sharp minor, Op. 1[a]. Rhapsody on a Theme of Paganini, Op. 43[b]. **Vladimir Ashkenazy** (pf); [a]**Concertgebouw Orchestra;** [b]**Philharmonia Orchestra / Bernard Haitink.** Decca Ⓕ 417 613-2DH (52 minutes: DDD: 12/87). Ⓖ

Showpiece that it is, with its lush romantic harmonies and contrasting vigorous panache, the First Concerto has much to commend it in purely musical terms and although its debts are clear enough (most notably perhaps to Rimsky-Korsakov), it stands on its own two feet as far as invention, overall design and musical construction are concerned. The *Paganini* Rhapsody is one of the composer's finest works and arguably the most purely inventive set of variations to be based on Paganini's catchy tune ever written. The wealth of musical invention it suggested to Rachmaninov is truly bewildering and his control over what can in lesser hands become a rather laboured formal scheme is masterly indeed. Ashkenazy gives superb performances of both works and the Concertgebouw and the Philharmonia are in every way the perfect foils under Bernard Haitink's sympathetic direction. There is weight, delicacy, colour, energy and repose in equal measure here and it is all conveyed by a full-bodied and detailed recording.

Additional recommendations ...

....*As above.* **Mikhail Pletnev** (pf); **Philharmonia Orchestra / Libor Pešek.** Virgin Classics Ⓜ VC7 59506-2 (51 minutes: DDD: 12/88).

...No. 1. **Prokofiev** Piano Concerto No. 3 in C major, Op. 26. Toccata in C major, Op. 11. **Pinto** Three Scenes from Childhood. **Byron Janis** (pf); **Moscow Philharmonic Orchestra / Kyrill Kondrashin.** Mercury Ⓜ 434 333-2MM (69 minutes: ADD: 7/94). *See review under Prokofiev; refer to the Index to Reviews.* ⒼⒼ

...Nos. 1 and 3. **Jean-Yves Thibaudet** (pf); **Cleveland Orchestra / Vladimir Ashkenazy.** Decca Ⓕ 448 219-2DH (71 minutes: DDD: 10/95).

...Nos. 1[a] and No. 2[b]. **Sviatoslav Richter** (pf). [a]**USSR Radio Symphony Orchestra,** [b]**Leningrad Philharmonic Orchestra / Kurt Sanderling.** Melodiya mono Ⓜ 74321 29467-2* (62 minutes: ADD: 6/96).

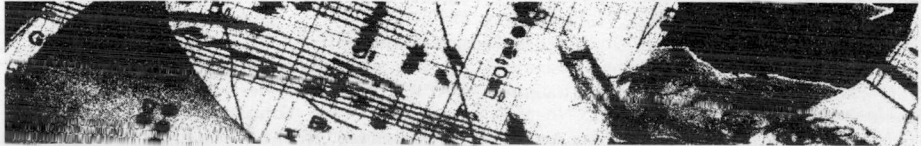

Rachmaninov Piano Concertos – No. 1 in F sharp minor, Op. 1; No. 2 in C minor, Op. 18; No. 3 in D minor, Op. 30; No. 4 in G minor, Op. 40. **Vladimir Ashkenazy** (pf); **London Symphony Orchestra / André Previn.** Double Decca Ⓜ 444 839-2DF2 (two discs: 135 minutes: ADD: 2/96). From SXLF6565/7 (9/72). Recorded 1990-1. Ⓖ

This reissue dates from 1972 yet the sound and balance are superb and there is nothing to cloud or impede one's sense of Ashkenazy's greatness in all these works. From him every page declares Rachmaninov's nationality, his indelibly Russian nature. What nobility of feeling and what dark regions of the imagination he relishes and explores in page after page of the Third Concerto in particular. Significantly his opening is a very moderate *Allegro ma non tanto*, later allowing him an expansiveness and imaginative scope hard to find in other more 'driven' or hectic performances. His rubato, his sense of the music's emotional ebb and flow, is as natural as it is distinctive and his way of easing from one idea to another shows him at his most intimately and romantically responsive. There are no cuts, and his choice of the bigger of the two cadenzas is entirely apt, given the breadth of his conception. Even the skittering figurations and volleys of repeated notes just before the close of the central *Intermezzo* cannot tempt Ashkenazy into display and he is quicker than any other pianist to find a touch of wistfulness beneath Rachmaninov's occasional outer playfulness (the *scherzando* episode in the finale).

Such imaginative fervour and delicacy are just as central to Ashkenazy's other performances. His steep unmarked *decrescendo* at the close of the First Concerto's opening rhetorical gesture is symptomatic of his romantic bias, his love of the music's interior glow. And despite his prodigious command in, say, the final pages of both the First and Fourth Concertos, there is never a hint of bombast or a more superficial brand of fire-and-brimstone virtuosity. Previn works hand in glove with his soloist. Clearly, this is no one-night partnership but the product of the greatest musical sympathy, of a mutual skill and affection. The opening of the Third Concerto's *Intermezzo* (where the orchestra momentarily step into the limelight) could hardly be given with a more idiomatic, brooding melancholy, a perfect introduction for all that is to follow. Naturally, you will have your own favourite individual performances but if you want playing which captures Rachmaninov's always elusive, opalescent centre then Ashkenazy is hard to beat. No more personal or deeply felt performances exist.

Additional recommendations ...

...No. 2[a]. **Prokofiev** Piano Concerto No. 5 in G major, Op. 55[b]. **Sviatoslav Richter** (pf); **Warsaw Philharmonic Orchestra / [a]Stanislaw Wislocki, [b]Witold Rowicki.** DG Ⓕ 415 119-2GH* (58 minutes: ADD: 6/85). *See review under Prokofiev; refer to the Index to Reviews.* ⒼⒼⒼ

...No. 2. *Coupled with works by* **Addinsell, Litolff** *and* **Gottschalk** Cristina Ortiz (pf); **Royal Philharmonic Orchestra / Moshe Atzmon.** Decca Ⓕ 414 348-2DH (58 minutes: DDD: 9/86). *See review in the Collections section; refer to the Index to Reviews.* Ⓖ

...No. 2. Rhapsody on a Theme of Paganini, Op. 43. **Vladimir Ashkenazy** (pf); **London Symphony Orchestra / André Previn.** Decca Ovation Ⓜ 417 702-2DM (58 minutes: ADD: 7/87). *This is the same recording as the one reviewed above.* Ⓖ

...No. 2. Rhapsody on a Theme of Paganini. **Philip Fowke** (pf); **Royal Philharmonic Orchestra / Yuri Temirkanov.** EMI Eminence Ⓜ CD-EMX9509 (59 minutes: DDD: 10/87).

...Nos. 2[a] and 3[b]. **Sergei Rachmaninov** (pf); **Philadelphia Orchestra / [a]Leopold Stokowski, [b]Eugene Ormandy.** RCA Red Seal mono Ⓕ RD85997* (66 minutes: ADD: 10/88). ⒼⒼⒼ

...No. 3[a]. Preludes[b] – C sharp minor, Op. 3 No. 2; B flat major, Op. 23 No. 2; G minor, Op. 23 No. 5; B minor, Op. 32 No. 10; D flat major, Op. 32 No. 13. **Vladimir Ashkenazy** (pf); [a]**London Symphony Orchestra / André Previn.** Decca Ovation Ⓜ 417 764-2DM (70 minutes: ADD: 10/88). *This is the same recording as the one reviewed above* Ⓖ

...No. 2. Rhapsody on a Theme of Paganini. **Jenö Jandó** (pf); **Budapest Symphony Orchestra / György Lehel.** Naxos Ⓢ 8 550117 (58 minutes: DDD: 10/90).

...Nos. 2 and 3. **Earl Wild** (pf); **Royal Philharmonic Orchestra / Jascha Horenstein.** Chandos Collect Ⓜ CHAN6507 (66 minutes: ADD: 2/91). ⒼⒼ

...No. 3. *Coupled with works by* **Saint-Saëns** *and* **Shostakovich** Emil Gilels (pf); **Paris Conservatoire Orchestra / André Cluytens.** Testament mono Ⓕ SBT1029* (65 minutes: ADD: 2/94). *See review under Saint-Saëns; refer to the Index to Reviews.* ⒼⒼ

...Nos. 2 and 3. **Lilya Zilberstein** (pf); **Berlin Philharmonic Orchestra / Claudio Abbado.** DG Ⓕ 439 930-2GH (76 minutes: DDD: 2/95).

...No. 2[a]. **Tchaikovsky** Piano Concerto No. 1 in B flat minor, Op. 23[b]. **Sviatoslav Richter** (pf); [a]**Warsaw Philharmonic Orchestra / Stanislaw Wislocki;** [b]**Vienna Symphony Orchestra / Herbert von Karajan.** DG The Originals Ⓜ 447 420-2GOR (71 minutes: ADD: 7/95). ⒼⒼ

...No. 2[a]. Rhapsody on a Theme of Paganini[b]. Preludes – C sharp minor, Op. 3 No. 2; G minor, Op. 23 No. 5; G major, Op. 32 No. 5; B minor, Op. 32 No. 10; G sharp minor, Op. 32 No. 12. Moment musical in E minor, Op. 16 No. 4. **Mendelssohn** (arr. Rachmaninov) A Midsummer Night's Dream – Scherzo. **Benno Moiseiwitsch** (pf); **London Philharmonic Orchestra / [a]Walter Goehr, [b]Basil Cameron.** APR Signature mono Ⓜ APR5505* (78 minutes: ADD: 10/95).

...No. 2[a]. Preludes – G minor, Op. 23 No. 5; G major, Op. 32 No. 5. **Tchaikovsky** Piano Concerto No. 1 in B flat minor, Op. 23[a]. **Géza Anda** (pf); [a]**Philharmonia Orchestra / Alceo Galliera.**

Testament mono Ⓟ SBT1064* (76 minutes: ADD: 10/95). *See review in the Collections section; refer to the Index to Reviews.*

Rachmaninov Piano Concertos[a] – No. 1 in F sharp minor, Op. 1; No. 4 in G minor, Op. 40. Rhapsody on a Theme of Paganini, Op. 43[b]. **Zoltán Kocsis** (pf); **San Francisco Symphony Orchestra / Edo de Waart.** Philips Solo Ⓜ 446 582-2PM (72 minutes: DDD: 7/96). Items marked [a] from 6514 377 (2/84), [b]412 738-1PH. Recorded 1982.

Rachmaninov Piano Concertos – No. 2 in C minor, Op. 18[a]; No. 3 in D minor, Op. 30[b]. Vocalise, Op. 34 No. 14 (arr. Kocsis)[c]. **Zoltán Kocsis** (pf); [ab]**San Francisco Symphony Orchestra / Edo de Waart.** Philips Solo Ⓜ 446 199-2PM (75 minutes: DDD: 7/96). Item marked [a] from 412 738-1PH (5/86), [b]411 475-2PH (8/85), [c]412 213-1PH (1/86). Recorded 1978-84.

Few if any readings of the piano concertos and the *Paganini* Rhapsody spark or scintillate with such daredevilry, are of such unapologetic virtuoso voltage, as these. True, Kocsis can sometimes be more voluble than poised, breezing through the Third Concerto's haunting opening theme at the fastest flowing tempo and – for lovers of the ever-romantic Variation No. 18 from the *Paganini* Rhapsody, in particular – sometimes sacrificing heart's-ease for high-octane bravura. Again, you may question his near *allegretto* spin through the Second Concerto's central *Adagio*, eagerly glimpsing so many dazzling athletic opportunities ahead. Even so, try him in the Third Concerto's cadenza (the slimmer and better of the two) and you will hear it topped and tailed with a ferocious and almost palpable aplomb. Listen to him snapping off phrase ends in the intricate reel of the *Paganini* Rhapsody's Variation No. 15 or flashing fire in the *Allegro leggiero* from the First Concerto's finale and you may well wonder when you last encountered such fearless brilliance, pace and relish. Even those attuned to the darker, more introspective Rachmaninov of Ashkenazy (reviewed above) will surely pause to wonder. Edo de Waart and the San Francisco Symphony Orchestra are no match for the LSO for Previn; yet, overall, this is the most propulsive and exciting set of the complete concertos. Kocsis's whirlwind tempos even allow him time for an encore – his own ardent elaboration of the *Vocalise*, a performance sufficiently ecstatic to set even the least susceptible heart a-flutter.

Additional recommendations ...

...No. 3. Rhapsody on a theme of Paganini. **Mikhail Rudy** (pf); **St Petersburg Philharmonic Orchestra / Mariss Jansons.** EMI Ⓔ CDC7 54880-2 (66 minutes: DDD: 11/93).

...No. 3[a]. Piano Sonata No. 2 in B flat minor, Op. 36. **John Lill** (pf); [a]**BBC National Orchestra of Wales / Tadaaki Otaka.** Nimbus Ⓔ NI5348 (72 minutes: DDD: 10/94).

...Vocalise, Op. 34 No. 14 (trans. Rose). *Coupled with works by* **Kabalevsky** and **Khachaturian Mats Lidström** (vc); **Gothenburg Symphony Orchestra / Vladimir Ashkenazy** (pf). BIS Ⓔ CD719 (65 minutes: DDD: 7/96). *See review under Kabalevsky; refer to the Index to Reviews.*

Rachmaninov Piano Concerto No. 3 in D minor, Op. 30[a].

Tchaikovsky Piano Concerto No. 1 in B flat minor, Op. 23[b]. **Martha Argerich** (pf); [a]**Berlin Radio Symphony Orchestra / Riccardo Chailly;** [b]**Bavarian Radio Symphony Orchestra / Kyrill Kondrashin.** Philips Ⓔ 446 673-2PH (73 minutes: DDD: 8/95). Item marked [a] recorded live in 1982, new to UK; [b]1980, from 6514 118 (7/82). *Gramophone Editor's choice.* ⊙⊙⊙

Here, at long last, is Martha Argerich's legendary 1982 Rachmaninov Third Concerto with Chailly coupled with a reissue of her famously volatile 1980 Tchaikovsky First with Kondrashin. To describe both performances as 'live' is to deal in understatement, for rarely in her entire and extraordinary career has Argerich sounded more exhaustingly restless and quixotic, her mind and fingers flashing with reflexes merely dreamt of by other less phenomenally endowed pianists. Yet her Rachmaninov is full of surprises, her opening *Allegro* almost convivial until she meets directions such as *più vivo* or *veloce*, where the tigress in her shows her claws and the music is made to seethe and boil at a white-hot temperature. The cadenza (the finer and more transparent of the two) rises to the sort of climax that will make all pianists' hearts beat faster and her first entry in the "Intermezzo" interrupts the orchestra's musing with the impatience of a hurricane. But throughout these pages it is almost as if she is searching for music that will allow her virtuosity its fullest scope. In the finale she finds it, accelerating out of the second movement with a sky-rocketing propulsion. Here the music races like wildfire, with a truly death-defying turn of speed at 7'21" and an explosive energy throughout that must have left audience, conductor and orchestra feeling as if hit by some seismic shock-wave. The Tchaikovsky, too, finds Argerich at her most inflammatory. Those of a nervous disposition or, more precisely, those who like their Tchaikovsky to be more magisterial and composed will, of course, look elsewhere but who would miss volleys of octave spun off like single notes, or a second movement central *Prestissimo* dispatched at a scarcely credible tempo? A performance, then, for those who like life in the fast lane, though it has to be said that such incandescence is hardly flaunted, more a "spontaneous overflow of powerful feelings" of emotion recollected not so much in tranquillity as in a cloud of fire and fury. The recordings, given the tricky circumstances, are remarkably successful.

Additional recommendations ...

...No. 3[a]. **Tchaikovsky** Piano Concerto No. 1 in B flat minor, Op. 23[b]. **Martha Argerich** (pf); [a]**Berlin Radio Symphony Orchestra / Riccardo Chailly;** [b]**Bavarian Radio Symphony Orchestra / Kyrill Kondrashin.** Philips Ⓔ 446 673-2PH (73 minutes: DDD: 8/95). Ⓖ

Rachmaninov Symphonies – No. 1 in D minor, Op. 13; No. 2 in E minor, Op. 27; No. 3 in
A minor, Op. 44[c]. Symphonic Dances, Op. 45[a]. The isle of the dead, Op. 29[a]. Vocalise, Op. 34
No. 14[b] (arr. composer). Aleko[c] – Intermezzo; Gipsy Girls' Dance. **London Symphony Orchestra /
André Previn.** EMI ® CMS7 64530-2 (three discs: 227 minutes: ADD: 10/93). Items marked
[a] from ASD3259 (9/76), [b] ASD3284 (12/76), [c] ASD3369 (8/77). Recorded 1974-76.   ⊕⊕
Rachmaninov's three symphonies reflect three very different phases in his creative development: the
first (1895) is a stormy synthesis of contemporary trends in Russian symphonic music, the Second
(1906-07), an epic study in Tchaikovskian opulence, and the third (1935-36) a seemingly unstoppable
stream of original ideas and impressions. The Second was the first to gain wide acceptance, and with
good reason. It shares both the key and general mood of Tchaikovsky's Fifth. Cast in E minor, its
initial gloom ultimately turns to triumph, and the symphony includes enough glorious melodies to
keep Hollywood happy for decades. The First Symphony had a difficult birth, largely through the
incompetent musical midwifery of Alexander Glazunov whose conducting of the work's première
apparently left much to be desired. It is, however, an immensely promising piece and although
undeniably the product of its times, prophetic not only of the mature Rachmaninov, but of other
Northern voices, including – occasionally – the mature Sibelius. Both the Third Symphony and its
near-contemporary, the *Symphonic Dances* find Rachmaninov indulging a fruitful stream of musical
consciousness, recalling motives and ideas from earlier compositions, yet allowing gusts of fresh air
to enliven and rejuvenate his style. Both works have yet to receive their full due in the concert-hall,
although the strongly evocative *Isle of the dead* is more securely embedded in the repertory. What with
these and a trio of warming shorter pieces, André Previn's mid-1970s LSO package makes for an
excellent mid-price bargain package. The performances are entirely sympathetic, avoiding familiar
interpretative extremes such as slickness, bombast and emotional indulgence. Previn shows particular
understanding of the Third Symphony, the *Symphonic Dances* and *The isle of the dead,* works that
represent Rachmaninov at his most innovative and assured. The Second Symphony is played without
cuts (not invariably the case, even today) and Christopher Bishop's recordings are generous in tone
and revealing of detail, especially among the woodwinds.
Additional recommendations ...
...Nos. 1-3. Vocalise. **Philadelphia Orchestra / Eugene Ormandy.** CBS Maestro Ⓜ M2YK45678
(two discs: 137 minutes: ADD: 8/90).
...Symphonic Dances[c]. **Smetana** The Bartered Bride – Polka; Furiant; Dance of the Comedians[a].
Offenbach Gaîté Parisienne – excerpts[b]. [a]**Cleveland Orchestra / George Szell;** [bc]**Philadelphia
Orchestra / Eugene Ormandy.** Sony Classical Essential Classics ® SBK48279 (76 minutes: ADD:
6/93).
...Nos. 1-3. The isle of the dead. Symphonic Dances. Vocalise. **Royal Philharmonic Orchestra /
Andrew Litton.** Virgin Classics Ⓜ VMT7 59279-2 (three discs: 214 minutes: DDD: 10/93).   ⊕⊕
...No. 1. The isle of the dead. **Concertgebouw Orchestra / Vladimir Ashkenazy.** Decca Ovation
Ⓜ 436 479-2DM (63 minutes: DDD: 2/94).   ⊕⊕

Rachmaninov Symphony No. 2 in E minor, Op. 27. The Rock, Op. 7. **Russian National Orchestra
/ Mikhail Pletnev.** DG ℗ 439 888-2GH (64 minutes: DDD: 6/94). Recorded 1993. *Gramophone
Editor's choice. Selected by Sounds in Retrospect.*   ⊕⊕
Mikhail Pletnev's achievement is to make us hear the music afresh: a performance characterized by
relatively discreet emotionalism, strong forward momentum and a fanatical preoccupation with
clarity of articulation. When there is no Slavic wobble, it scarcely matters that his winds display an
individuality which once or twice fails to transcend mere rawness – so much the better in this music!
The strings, forceful and husky (with separated violin desks) are beyond reproach. The most
remarkable playing comes in the finale. The lyrical effusions are superbly characterized without
undermining the sense of inexorability, the climaxes not just powerful but affecting too. The closing
pages bring a rush of adrenalin of the kind rarely experienced live, let alone in the studio. This is great
music-making, the rubato always there when required, the long phrases immaculately tailored yet
always sounding spontaneous. DG's unexpected coupling is *The Rock*, an early, rather bitty piece
which is however very deftly scored and intriguingly Scriabinesque in places. In Pletnev's hands, the
central climax is surprisingly powerful, with just a hint of the buzz-saw in the brass playing. The
fabulous delicacy elsewhere is alone worth the price of admission.
Additional recommendations ...
...No. 2. **London Symphony Orchestra / Gennadi Rozhdestvensky.** IMP Classics Ⓜ PCD904
(66 minutes: DDD: 1/89).   ⊕
...No. 2. Vocalise. **BBC Welsh Symphony Orchestra / Tadaaki Otaka.** Nimbus ℗ NI5322
(66 minutes: DDD: 5/92).
...No. 2. Vocalise[a]. [a]**Sylvia McNair** (sop); **Baltimore Symphony Orchestra / David Zinman.** Telarc
℗ CD80312 (68 minutes: DDD: 10/92). *Selected by Sounds in Retrospect.*
...No. 2. The Rock, Op. 7. **St Petersburg Philharmonia Academic Symphony Orchestra /
Alexander Dmitriev.** Sony Classical St Petersburg Classics Ⓜ SMK57650 (63 minutes: DDD:
2/95).
...No. 2. The Rock, Op. 7. **Philadelphia Orchestra / Charles Dutoit.** Decca ℗ 440 604-2DH
(72 minutes: DDD: 6/95).

Rachmaninov Symphony No. 3 in A minor, Op. 44. Symphonic Dances, Op. 45. **St Petersburg Philharmonic Orchestra / Mariss Jansons.** EMI Ⓕ CDC7 54877-2 (72 minutes: DDD: 12/93). Recorded 1992. *Gramophone Editor's choice.* ⓖⓖ

This is one of the more distinguished Rachmaninov issues of recent years. While no Rachmaninov Third unfolds as inexorably as Previn's (reviewed above), it is refreshing to hear the opening 'motto' theme played perfectly in tune by an orchestra on even more dazzling form than the LSO, and Jansons unearths such exquisite details of sonority and texture that criticism is all but silenced. There have been more haunting, more fundamentally pessimistic accounts, but none with such an ear for Rachmaninov's sometimes risky orchestral effects. The *Symphonic Dances* are even more impressive. The insinuating waltz movement is irresistible, very free with idiomatic-sounding rubato, while the dynamic outer portions of the finale are superbly articulated, dazzling in the closing stages. EMI's close-miking of instrumental lines may inhibit the sort of tonal blend implied by Rachmaninov's scoring, but the distinctive heft and huskiness of Mravinsky's string section is not betrayed. In its lush, extrovert way, this disc is unbeatable.

Additional recommendations ...

...No. 3. **Shostakovich** Symphony No. 6 in B minor, Op. 54[b]. **London Symphony Orchestra / André Previn.** EMI Studio Ⓜ CDM7 69564-2 (75 minutes: ADD: 12/88). ⓖⓖ

...No. 3. The isle of the dead, Op. 29. Vocalise (arr. composer). **Philadelphia Orchestra / Sergey Rachmaninov.** Pearl Ⓕ GEMMCD9414* (59 minutes: AAD). ⓖⓖ

...No. 3. The isle of the dead. **BBC Welsh Symphony Orchestra / Tadaaki Otaka.** Nimbus Ⓕ NI5344 (64 minutes: DDD: 4/93).

...No. 3. Symphonic Dances, Op. 45. **Concertgebouw Orchestra / Vladimir Ashkenazy.** Decca Ovation Ⓜ 436 481-2DM (76 minutes: DDD: 2/94). ⓖⓖ

...No. 3. Symphonic Dances, Op. 45. **Baltimore Symphony Orchestra / David Zinman.** Telarc Ⓕ CD80331 (74 minutes: DDD: 1/95).

New review

Rachmaninov Symphonic Dances, Op. 45[a].
Janáček Taras Bulba[b]. **North German Radio Symphony Orchestra / John Eliot Gardiner.** DG Ⓕ 445 838-2GH (56 minutes: DDD: 1/96). Recorded live in 1993.

Rachmaninov's *Symphonic Dances* are played with great sharpness here, emphasizing the extraordinary originality of his last completed work and serving as a reminder that the original title was *Fantastic Dances*: this might be more suitable for a performance that, though not lacking in lyrical grace, sets some familiar characteristics in a novel, strange and even somewhat disquieting context. The waltz of the central movement (once to have been called "Twilight") has a rhythmic fluency that suggests not so much elegance as a faintly uncertain atmosphere; and there are shadows lying across the urgency of the finale. A fascinating score, intelligently and imaginatively read. *Taras Bulba* is also very well played. Here, the problems include unusual instrumental balance but, still more, getting the relationships between the many tempo changes into the right perspective. Gardiner is sensitive to these, without always following the instructions in the score to the letter. For the most part, his reading justifies this, though in the first movement, "The Death of Andri", the move into the *Allegro vivo* is not done *accelerando* but abruptly, three bars early, which seems to go against the nature of the melodic phrases. But this is a small point, and for the rest the performance is admirably detailed and well-judged; and in both works the orchestral playing is of individual virtuosity and clarity.

Additional recommendation ...

...Symphonic Dances. 14 Songs, Op. 34 – Vocalise (rev. 1915)[a]. **Stravinsky** Jeu de cartes. [a]**Nelli Lee** (sop); **Novosibirsk Philharmonic Orchestra / Arnold Kaz.** Sony Classical St Petersburg Classics Ⓜ SMK57660 (65 minutes: DDD: 2/95).

Rachmaninov Trios élégiaques – G minor; D minor, Op. 9. **Copenhagen Trio** (Søren Elbaek, vn; Troels Svane Hermansen, vc; Morten Mogensen, pf). Kontrapunkt Ⓕ 32187 (65 minutes: DDD: 12/94). Recorded 1994.

The shade of Tchaikovsky haunts both these works. In the first, there are turns of phrase from his Trio, and much of the style and the textural approach to the problems derive from his example – not always a very good one, when it came to dealing with a virtuoso piano part against the weaker sound of the strings. Rachmaninov is ingenious, and handles his material expertly in a long, shapely movement. Tchaikovsky is more consciously the exemplar of the second trio. Deeply impressed by the younger composer's *The Rock*, he had agreed to conduct the first performance in January 1894, a rare gesture of appreciation. On Tchaikovsky's death in October, the shocked Rachmaninov wrote his Trio "in memory of a great artist", just as Tchaikovsky had once written a Trio in memory of another great artist, Nikolay Rubinstein. And here, too, there is a substantial variation movement, on a theme from *The Rock*. It is lyrically varied, not with conscious allusions after the manner of Tchaikovsky's elegy but with a sense of indebtedness that is unmistakable. Rachmaninov initially intended to have the opening statement of the theme played on the harmonium; he later revised the work, removing this appalling idea, and it is the second version which is recorded here, and well recorded in a fine performance that does full justice to a lengthy but affecting piece.

Additional recommendation ...
...**Borodin Trio.** Chandos Ⓕ CHAN8341 (60 minutes: DDD: 3/85).

Rachmaninov Complete Solo Piano Music. **Howard Shelley** (pf). Hyperion Ⓜ CDS44041/8
(eight discs: 449 minutes: DDD: 3/94). From CDA66081, CDA66082, CDA66184, CDA66047,
CDA66009 (all 10/88), CDA66198 (9/87), CDA66091 (8/88) and CDA66486 (3/92).
Variations on a Theme of Chopin, Op. 22. Variations on a Theme of Corelli, Op. 42. Mélodie in
E major, Op. 3 No. 3. Piano Sonatas – No. 1 in D minor, Op. 28; No. 2 in B flat minor, Op. 36
(orig. version); No. 2 in B flat minor, Op. 36 (rev. version). Ten Preludes, Op. 23. 13 Preludes,
Op. 32. Prelude in D minor. Prelude in F major. Morceaux de fantaisie, Op. 3. Morceau de
fantaisie in G minor. Song without words in D minor. Pièce in D minor. Fughetta in F major.
Fragments in A flat major. Oriental Sketch in B flat major. Three Nocturnes – No. 1 in F sharp
minor; No. 2 in F major; No. 3 in C minor. Quatre Pièces – Romance in F sharp minor; Prélude
in E flat minor; Mélodie in E major; Gavotte in D major. 17 Etudes-tableaux, Opp. 33 and 39.
Transcriptions – **Rimsky-Korsakov** The Tale of Tsar Saltan – The flight of the bumble-bee.
Kreisler Liebesleid. Liebesfreud. **Bizet** L'Arlésienne Suite No. 1 – Menuet. **Schubert** Die
schöne Müllerin, D957 – Wohin? **Mussorgsky** Sorochinsky Fair – Gopak. **Bach** Solo Violin
Partita No. 3 in E major, BWV1006 – Preludio, Gavotte, Gigue. **Rachmaninov** Daisies, Op. 38
No. 3. Lilacs, Op. 21 No. 5. Vocalise, Op. 34 No. 14 (arr. Kocsis). **Mendelssohn** A Midsummer
Night's Dream, Op. 61 – Scherzo. **Behr** Lachtäubchen, Op. 303 (pubd. as Polka de VR).
Tchaikovsky Cradle Song, Op. 16 No. 1. Recorded 1978-91.   Ⓖ
This Hyperion set is a significant testament to Howard Shelley's artistry. Pianistically impeccable, he
understands what Rachmaninov was about. The original piano works span some 45 years of the
composer's life. The earliest pieces here, the *Nocturnes*, strangely owe allegiance neither to Field nor
Chopin, but are very much in the mid-to-late nineteenth-century Russian salon style. The Third, in
C minor, has nothing whatever to do with its title. Nicely written too, but still uncharacteristic, are
four pieces from 1888, which amply demonstrate that from his early teens the composer had
something individual to say. The *Mélodie* in E (not to be confused with that from Op. 3) is memorable
for its hypnotic use of piano tone. Hyperion's recording quality can be heard at its very best here;
there is real bloom and colour. Written shortly after his First Piano Concerto in the early 1890s, the
Morceaux de fantaisie, Op. 3 bring us to familiar Rachmaninov. The ubiquitous Prelude in C sharp
minor is the second number but Shelley tries to do too much with it; he is more effective in the
Sérénade with its Spanish overtones. In the E flat minor *Moments musicaux*, Op. 16 one feels that he
is able to master Rachmaninov's swirling accompaniments idiomatically. In Variation No. 15 of the
seldom-heard *Variations on a Theme of Chopin* (the theme is the Prelude in C minor from Op. 28)
Shelley succeeds in bringing the notes to life, getting his fingers around the fleet *scherzando* writing.
The first set of Preludes is, of course, mainstream repertoire and, as such, easier to assess. In the
warmly expressive D major Prelude he lends the piece a strong Brahmsian feel and it emerges as very
well focused, especially since the voices are so subtly separated. He manages to transform the C minor
into a restless mood picture. Moving on to the First Sonata Shelley achieves a symphonic stature. This
is a piece that is conventionally dismissed as being unwieldy; he convinces one otherwise and allows
it to be seen in conjunction more with the composer's orchestral writing. Within a couple of years
Rachmaninov was at the height of his powers and shortly after the Third Concerto he wrote the
Op. 32 Preludes. Shelley is able to conjure up an exquisite, shimmering moonlit scene for the G major,
but he is not as monumentally impressive in the B minor. However, with him it is always the music
that dictates the course of the interpretation. In the two sets of *Etudes-tableaux* he excels as he does
too in the Second Sonata. He draws together the disparate elements of the finale with terrific
mastery and shows himself entirely the equal of the 'Horowitz clones' in matters of technique. In the
Corelli Variations he is not quite in tune with the scope of the work but is outstanding in the
transcriptions, if a little straight-faced. The recorded sound is never less than serviceable and is
sometimes excellent.

Additional recommendations ...
...Preludes – B flat major, Op. 23 No. 2; G minor, Op. 23 No. 5; C minor, Op. 23 No. 7; C major,
Op. 32 No. 1; B flat major, Op. 32 No. 2. **Tchaikovsky** Piano Concerto No. 1 in B flat minor[a].
Sviatoslav Richter (pf); [a]**Vienna Symphony Orchestra / Herbert von Karajan.** DG Galleria Ⓜ 419
068-2GGA (50 minutes: ADD: 8/87).
...Piano Sonata No. 2. Morceau de fantaisie. Song without words. Pièce in D minor. Fughetta.
Fragments. Oriental Sketch. Three Nocturnes. Quatre Pièces – Romance; Prélude; Mélodie;
Gavotte. **Howard Shelley** (pf). Hyperion Ⓕ CDA66198 (59 minutes: DDD: 9/87). *This is the same
recording as the one reviewed above.*
...Preludes – C sharp minor, Op. 3 No. 2; B flat major, Op. 23 No. 2; G minor, Op. 23 No. 5;
B minor, Op. 32 No. 10; D flat major, Op. 32 No. 13. Piano Concerto No. 3 in D minor, Op. 30[a].
Vladimir Ashkenazy (pf); [a]**London Symphony Orchestra / André Previn.** Decca Ovation Ⓜ 417
764-2DM (70 minutes: ADD: 10/88).
...Preludes, Op. 23. Morceaux de fantaisie. **Howard Shelley** (pf). Hyperion Ⓕ CDA66081
(60 minutes: ADD: 10/88). *This is the same recording as the one reviewed above.*
...Preludes, Op. 32. Preludes – F major; D minor. **Howard Shelley** (pf). Hyperion Ⓕ CDA66082
(48 minutes: ADD: 10/88).

...Piano Sonatas – No. 1; No. 2 (original version). **Gordon Fergus-Thompson** (pf). Kingdom
Ⓕ KCLCD2007 (73 minutes: DDD: 6/89).
...Variations on a Theme of Chopin. Piano Sonata No. 1. **Boris Berezovsky** (pf). Teldec
Ⓕ 4509-90890-2 (66 minutes: DDD: 7/94).
...24 Preludes. **Peter Katin** (pf). IMP Classics Ⓜ PCD1081 (80 minutes: ADD: 1/95).
...Variations on a Theme of Corelli. *Coupled with works by* **Brahms, Mendelssohn, Bach** and
Tchaikovsky Shura Cherkassky (pf). Decca Ⓕ 433 655-2DH (68 minutes: ADD: 2/96). *See
review in the Collections section; refer to the Index to Reviews.*
...Flight of the bumble-bee (arr. Malcolm). *Coupled with works by* **Daquin, Paradis, Bach,
Rameau, F. Couperin, Templeton** and **Malcolm** George Malcolm (hpd). Decca Ⓜ 444 390-
2DWO (75 minutes: ADD: 11/95). ✔

New review

Rachmaninov Piano Works. **Santiago Rodriguez** (pf). Elan Ⓕ 82244, 82248 (two discs, oas: 73 and
73 minutes: DDD: 3/96). Recorded 1993.
82244 – Piano Sonata No. 1 in D minor, Op. 28. 13 Preludes, Op. 32. *82248* – Piano Sonata No. 2
in B flat minor, Op. 36. Morceaux de fantaisie, Op. 3. Variations on a theme of Chopin, Op. 22.
Santiago Rodriguez, the Cuban-American virtuoso, is born for Rachmaninov, and it is doubtful
whether any of the works on these two discs have often been played with such a spellbinding mix of
high-born virtuosity and poetic glamour. In the case of the Second Sonata this is saying a great deal,
for this romantic maelstrom is now in the repertoire of many pianists. Rodriguez opens in a positive
fire-storm of brilliance yet his playing is no less alive to the music's innermost character, its dark,
introspective undertow. Unlike Kocsis (reviewed below) he plays the 1931 revision of this sonata. The
First Sonata is far less familiar, though, given Rodriguez's overwhelming advocacy, it could well come
to equal the Second in popularity. Listen to the first movement's development section – among the
most heart-stopping in all Rachmaninov – as, in this pianist's hands, it roars into the straight as if
nothing can impede its frenzied brio and propulsion. How Rodriguez revels, too, in Rachmaninov's
romantic polyphony, voicing and inflecting the central *Lento* with a sumptuous sense of the
composer's luxury and elaboration. Then there are the *Variations on a theme of Chopin*, where
Rodriguez is as sensitive in the funereal trend of Var. 13 as he is suave and beguiling in Var. 21. His
final *maestoso* has an imposing breadth and character and, in the more dizzying pages (of which there
are many), the listener is swept along in a whirl of intricacy. Yet no less significantly Rodriguez omits
the composer's tacked-on and flamboyant coda, preferring the more authentic, all-passion-spent
conclusion. Rodriguez once confessed to a sunny, Cuban disposition, yet few pianists have relished
more subtly or audaciously Rachmaninov's darkest imaginings. The recordings are excellent: warm,
and with an exciting ring and breadth.

New review

Rachmaninov Piano Sonata No. 2 in B flat minor, Op. 36 (original version). Preludes – Op. 23:
No. 1 in F sharp minor; No. 7 in C minor; Op. 32: No. 2 in B flat minor; No. 6 in F minor; No. 9
in A major; No. 10 in B minor. Etudes-tableaux – Op. 39: No. 2 in B minor; No. 7 in C minor;
F minor, Op. 33 No. 1. Morceaux de fantaisie, Op. 3 – No. 3 in E major, "Mélodie"; No. 5 in
B flat minor, "Sérénade". **Zoltán Kocsis** (pf). Philips Ⓕ 446 220-2PH (61 minutes: DDD: 2/96).
Recorded 1994. *Gramophone Editor's choice.*   ⒢⒢
This richly exploratory recital – far removed from a popular or commercial programme – contradicts
at every turn stale, still prevailing notions concerning Rachmaninov. For not only is the Second
Sonata played in its original 1913 version rather than the stitched-together 1931 revision, but the
shorter items include many of the composer's finest works. The seventh rather than the first C minor
Etude-tableau, Op. 39, for example, is an elegy of the most startling modernity with its *lamentoso*
outcries, its memory of the Russian liturgy and its massive central carillon. How refreshing, too, to
open with the Brahmsian syncopation and expressive richness of the A major Prelude, Op 32 No. 9
and to mix mood and key to such kaleidoscopic and dazzling effect. Throughout, Kocsis's
performances are as bold and stimulating as his choice of works, gloriously free-spirited and of an
immense pianistic brio and command. Indeed his performance of the Second Sonata is as fulminating
and rhapsodic as any on record. Action-packed in an exhausting and enthralling way, his reading
never sounds arch or contrived in a way that so often disfigures Horowitz's famous account. Kocsis
possesses a stupendous technique, stepping out in dazzling style in the ultra-Russian *Etude-tableau*,
Op. 33 No. 1 and clarifying the Siberian whirlwind of the F minor Prelude, Op. 32 No. 6 with a
breathtaking clarity and focus. Kocsis's accompanying essay is no less stimulating and astringent than
his playing (he is unsparing over the 1931 revision of the Sonata) and he has been magnificently
recorded.

Rachmaninov 24 Preludes, Opp. 23 and 32. Prelude in D minor. Morceaux de fantaisie, Op. 3.
Lilacs. Daisies. Mélodie in E major. Oriental Sketch in B flat major. Moments musicaux, Op. 16.
Dmitri Alexeev (pf). Virgin Classics Ⓕ VCD7 59289-2 (two discs: 138 minutes: DDD: 5/94).
Recorded 1987-89.
Rachmaninov 24 Preludes, Opp. 23 and 32. **Peter Donohoe** (pf). EMI Ⓜ CMS7 64787-2
(two discs: 84 minutes: DDD: 10/94). *Gramophone Editor's choice.*

Alexeev's all-Russian mastery has seldom been heard to such advantage and his technical force and authority throughout are unarguable. True, he hardly wears his heart on his sleeve in the quixotic minuet of Op. 23 No. 3, is less than poetically yielding in the Chopinesque tracery of Op. 23 No. 4. He does, however, capture the Slavonic malaise of No. 1 with rare insight and his punishing weight and rhetoric in Op. 23 Nos. 2 or 7 will make even the most sanguine listener's pulse beat faster. He unleashes the central build-up of Op. 32 No. 7 with the impact of a Siberian whirlwind and time and again his icy, determinedly unsentimental approach gives added strength and focus to the composer's brilliant fury. Alexeev is more convincing in the more vertiginous numbers from the *Moments musicaux*, in Nos. 2, 4 and 6 rather than in the opening rhythmic play of No. 1 where he sounds altogether too literal and austere. Yet you only have to hear his way of making even *Polichinelle*'s well-worn phrases come up as fresh as paint or his trenchancy in *Oriental Sketch* to realize that you are in the presence of a master pianist. The recordings are of demonstration quality and the accompanying essay mirrors the rare toughness and integrity of these performances; the essential nobility of Rachmaninov's genius.

Listening to the Preludes straight through is not really the best way of appreciating the range and subtlety of Rachmaninov's art, even in Peter Donohoe's highly intelligent and appreciative performances. He has the virtuosity: that is a *sine qua non* for what is sometimes fearfully demanding music technically. But he also has the understanding of what Rachmaninov consciously owed to Chopin, acknowledging this in his touching performance of Op. 23 No. 4 but also in the pieces where Rachmaninov matches, but by no means overtakes, some of Chopin's astonishing harmonic explorations. Again, he takes note of how close Rachmaninov comes to the kind of witty piano writing which Debussy was exploring in some of his own preludes. The great B minor Prelude (Op. 32 No. 10), which Rachmaninov himself preferred above all of them, is superbly delivered, with a carefully controlled progress towards the majestic delivery of the opening idea. Many of the preludes open upon just a simple, strong idea, and use it to explore different aspects of romantic piano writing; many of them also end on mysterious, laconic chords (another feature they owe to Chopin). Donohoe has clearly thought deeply about the music, and taken trouble to understand the various sources of Rachmaninov's inspiration. The result is a set that does ample justice to some superb and still underrated music. The only factor which mitigates against this set is its short playing time, compensated in part by its mid-price status.

Additional recommendation ...

...Preludes – Op. 23: No. 1 in F sharp minor; No. 2 in B flat; No. 5 in G minor; No. 6 in E flat major; Op. 32: No. 12 in G sharp minor. Etudes-tableaux, Op. 39 – No. 3 in F sharp minor; No. 5 in E flat minor. Moments musicaux, Op. 16 – No. 3 in B minor; No. 4 in E minor; No. 5 in D flat major; No. 6 in C major. Elégie in E flat minor, Op. 3 No. 1. **Scriabin** Preludes, Op. 11 – No. 2 in A minor; No. 4 in E minor; No. 5 in D major; No. 6 in B minor; No. 8 in F sharp minor; No. 9 in E major; No. 10 in C sharp minor; No. 11 in B major; No. 12 in G flat minor; No. 13 in G flat major; No. 14 in E flat minor; No. 16 in B flat minor; No. 18 in F minor; No. 20 in C minor; No. 22 in G minor; No. 24 in D minor. **Andrei Gavrilov** (pf). EMI Eminence Ⓜ CD-EMX2237 (72 minutes: DDD: 12/95).

Rachmaninov Etudes-tableaux: Op. 33[a] – No. 5 in D minor (new to UK. 1983); No. 6 in E flat minor; No. 9 in C sharp minor (610 075, 10/84); Op. 39 – No. 1 in C minor; No. 2 in A minor; No. 3 in F sharp minor; No. 4 in B minor; No. 7 in C minor; No. 9 in D major (all 610 075). Preludes: Op. 23 – No. 1 in F sharp minor; No. 2 in B flat major; No. 4 in D major; No. 5 in G minor; No. 7 in C minor; No. 8 in A flat major; Op. 32 – No. 1 in C major; No. 2 in B flat minor; No. 6 in F minor; No. 7 in F major; No. 9 in A major; No. 10 in B minor; No. 12 in G sharp minor (all new to UK. 1971). **Sviatoslav Richter** (pf). Olympia Ⓔ OCD334/7 (74 minutes: DDD/ADD: 1/94). Items marked [a] recorded 1983, others 1971. ⊖⊖

As in previous volumes in this valuable series, sound quality is on the dry side. But Richter's is the sort of playing which positively benefits from close analytical scrutiny, and serious collectors of piano recordings should need no further encouragement. Recorded between 1971 and 1983 they show a Richter in transition. Still in evidence is the prime-of-life virtuoso who burst on to the Western scene in the 1960s; but increasingly taking over is the uncompromising, ascetic philosopher-pianist of the 1980s. Metaphysics in Rachmaninov? Certainly. And not just the apparently superhuman fingerwork in the E flat minor *Etude-tableau* or the first C minor of Op. 39. What comes across is something beyond expression. It is an overriding fatalism, a sense of the immense sadness of Russia, broken only by moments of heroic resistance. The Preludes are more resonantly recorded, with a rather disappointing tubby bass. If you can live with that there is a quite unique Rachmaninov to be heard here – a brave, noble spirit, expressed in piano writing of an unquenchable fervour and orchestral solidity.

New review

Rachmaninov Etudes-tableaux, Opp. 33 and 39. **John Lill** (pf). Nimbus Ⓔ NI5439 (64 minutes: DDD: 9/95). Recorded 1995.

The *Etudes-tableaux* are known to be musical evocations of various pictorial or perhaps narrative ideas, though quite rightly Rachmaninov did not let on where the stimuli came from. If the A minor piece really derives from Little Red Riding Hood, one does not need to be thinking of grandmother's big teeth as Rachmaninov develops a fine piece out of the contrast between two keyboard textures; and there is certainly no sign that John Lill is much preoccupied with such matters. He is a powerful keyboard technician, which is the first necessity in approaching these virtuoso studies, and this puts him in a strong position for dealing with the bold assertiveness of some of them, for instance the first piece of all. He also has a very vivid sense of tempo (balancing speed and texture sympathetically), and equally a sense for the slight lifting of pressure as well as slowing up, or the reverse, which is the essence of true romantic rubato. Where he can seem less responsive than some of his colleagues is with the more delicate pieces, whose fantasy he perhaps underrates. But if he also loses something in introspection, he can command admiration with his magisterial delivery. In sum, a very strong set of performances of some fascinating music.

Additional recommendation ...

...Etudes-tableaux, Op. 39 – No. 3 in F sharp minor; No. 4 in B minor; No. 7 in C minor; No. 9 in D major. *Coupled with works by* **Mussorgsky, Liadov, Medtner** and **Balakirev Boris Berezovsky** (pf). Teldec Ⓕ 4509-96516-2 (61 minutes: DDD: 7/96). *See review in the Collections section; refer to the Index to Reviews.*

Rachmaninov Etudes-tableaux: Op. 33 – No. 2 in C major; No. 8 in G minor. Op. 39 – No. 3 in F sharp minor; No. 4 in B minor; No. 5 in E flat minor. Preludes: Op. 23 – No. 1 in F sharp minor; No. 3 in D minor; No. 5 in G minor; No. 7 in C minor; No. 10 in G flat major. Preludes: Op. 32 – No. 6 in F minor; No. 8 in A minor; No. 10 in B minor; No. 12 in G sharp minor. Five Morceaux de fantaisie, Op. 3. **Nikolai Demidenko** (pf). Hyperion Ⓕ CDA66713 (70 minutes: DDD: 10/94). Recorded 1994

Nikolai Demidenko's performances couple immense pianistic tact and skill, though the rushes of adrenalin, when they come (the searing central climax of the Op. 3 "Elégie" or the A minor Prelude, Op. 32 where a tiny motif is tempest-tossed seemingly in all directions at the same time) are almost palpable. The C major *Etude-tableau*, Op. 23 No. 2 rises and falls with supreme naturalness and impetus and the absence of all lushness or luxuriance in the G minor *Etude-tableau*, Op. 32 No. 8 is a pointed reminder of Rachmaninov's serious, religious inspiration. Demidenko creates a magnificent carillon of Moscow bells in the great B minor Prelude and his E flat minor *Etude-tableau*, Op. 39 is arrestingly sombre and dry-eyed, its conclusion articulated with a rare sense of ebbing drama, of all passion spent. If you prefer Rachmaninov's emotional storms viewed acutely but from a distance then Demidenko is your man. The recordings faithfully mirror this pianist's very distinctive sound-world.

New review

Rachmaninov The Bells, Op. 35[a].
Prokofiev Alexander Nevsky, Op. 78[b]. [a]**Sheila Armstrong** (sop); [b]**Anna Reynolds** (mez); [a]**Robert Tear** (ten); [a]**John Shirley-Quirk** (bar); **London Symphony Chorus and Orchestra / André Previn.** EMI Studio Ⓜ CDM7 63114-2 (78 minutes: ADD: 10/89). Item marked [a] from ASD3284 (12/76), [b]ASD2800 (7/72). ⒼⒼ

This is an ideal coupling with first-rate soloists in both works. Sheila Armstrong is especially fine in *The Bells* and Anna Reynolds provides genuine Slavonic intensity in her contribution to the Prokofiev. The chorals singing too, if without the special vocal timbre and enunciation of a Russian group, has undoubted fervour, while in the famous "The Battle on the Ice" sequence in *Alexander Nevsky*, the orchestral playing has thrilling pungency and bite. The orginal analogue recordings, made in London's Kingsway Hall, were exceptionally well balanced and on LP the combination of ambient effect and sharpness of detail was ideally judged. Undoubtedly the remastering increases the clarity and projection of the sound with, perhaps, a slight loss of warmth and atmosphere. However, the ovrall effect is certainly vividly spectacular and compulsively dramatic. This disc is a very real bargain for the performances are both very fine indeed.

Additional recommendations ...

...The Bells[a]. Vocalise[b]. **Tchaikovsky** Romeo and Juliet (orch. Taneyev) – duet[ac]. Festival Coronation March in D major. [abc]**Suzanne Murphy** (sop); [ab]**Keith Lewis** (ten); [a]**David Wilson-Johnson** (bar); **Scottish National** [a]**Chorus and Orchestra / Neeme Järvi.** Chandos Ⓕ CHAN8476 (63 minutes: DDD: 2/87). *Selected by Sounds in Retrospect.*

...The Bells[a]. Three Russian Songs. [a]**Natalia Troitskaya** (sop); [a]**Ryszard Karczykowski** (ten); [a]**Tom Krause** (bar); **Concertgebouw Chorus and Orchestra / Vladimir Ashkenazy.** Decca Ovation Ⓜ 436 482-2DM (50 minutes: DDD: 2/94).

Rachmaninov Vespers, Op. 37. **Olga Borodina** (mez); **Vladimir Mostowoy** (ten); **St Petersburg Chamber Choir / Nikolai Korniev.** Philips Ⓕ 442 344-2PH (56 minutes: DDD: 11/94). Texts and translations included. Recorded 1993.

The St Petersburg Chamber Choir sing the *Vespers*, or *All-Night Vigil*, dramatically. Korniev follows the composer's markings carefully, but he is evidently concerned to give a concert performance of vivid immediacy, and there are places where this departs from the reflective or celebratory nature of music that is so strongly grounded in Orthodox tradition. This is most marked with Olga Borodina, who is not the first fine singer to bring too operatic a note to her solo in "Blagoslovi, dushe moya" ("Bless the Lord, O my soul"); Vladimir Mostowoy is more discreet in "Blagosloven esi" ("Blessed art Thou"). The choir itself is excellent, with particularly fine sopranos who can chant high above the others in beautifully pitched thirds; while there is, as ever in Russian church choirs, a splendid bass section that can underpin the textures with effortlessly rich low Cs, and find no difficulty with the famous descending scale down to a sonorous bottom B flat at the end of "Nyne otpushchayeshi" (the *Nunc dimittis*). The recording is not always as clear as it could be with the textures and especially the words. A strength of the issue, which distinguishes it from almost all others available, is the booklet, which includes not only the full text in transliteration (with English, German and French translations), but also excellent essays.

Additional recommendation ...

...Vespers. **Corydon Singers / Matthew Best.** Hyperion CDA66460 (66 minutes: DDD: 7/91).   ⓖ

...Vespers. **St Petersburg Cappella / Vladislav Chernushenko.** CDM Russian Season ⓕ LDC288 050 (62 minutes: DDD: 5/93).

...Vespers. **Swedish Radio Choir / Tönu Kaljuste.** Virgin Classics ⓕ VC5 45124-2 (54 minutes: DDD: 9/95).

New review

Rachmaninov At the gate of the holy abode[d]. I shall tell you nothing[d]. Again you leapt, my heart[a]. April! A festive Spring[c]. Twilight has fallen[c]. Song of the disillusioned[d]. The flower has faded[b]. Do you remember the evening[b]. Six Songs, Op. 4[abcd]. Six Songs, Op. 8[abcd]. 12 Songs, Op. 14[abcd]. [a]**Joan Rodgers** (sop); [b]**Maria Popescu** (mez); [c]**Alexander Naoumenko** (ten); [d]**Sergei Leiferkus** (bar); **Howard Shelley** (pf). Chandos ⓕ CHAN9405 (76 minutes: DDD: 4/96). Texts and translations included. Recorded 1994-5.

This first volume in Chandos's three-disc anthology of all Rachmaninov's songs is laid out for four voices, an intelligent plan intelligently carried out. The strongly prevailing atmosphere of the melancholy or the pensive means that to have some vocal contrast helps to make a proper recital of what might otherwise come to sound too much of a sequence in chronological order; but thought has also gone into choosing the singers for the various songs. The very first two songs Rachmaninov ever wrote (heading the above list) are firmly delivered by Sergei Leiferkus, who sings them with the touch of grit in the voice they need to lend them as much character as possible; later, with the stronger ones, such as the last on this record, "'Tis time" (from Op. 14), he allows himself a deeper warmth of tone. Joan Rodgers (singing, as far as it is fair for a foreigner to judge, in beautiful Russian) is at her best in the more intimate songs, and she gives a lovely performance of the Shelley setting (in Balmont's translation) "The isle". She can also rise to the extremely demanding occasion of "Spring waters", and others in the Op. 14 songs where Rachmaninov's new-found virtuosity as a pianist can threaten to seize the expressive initiative from the singer and even prove overwhelming. Howard Shelley, a fine Rachmaninov pianist, is scrupulous in judging these proportions, which vary a great deal from song to song in Op. 14 as well as throughout the record, and is a guiding figure in the whole enterprise. Maria Popescu is particularly strong on some of the more inward and reflective songs, as with the fine Shevchenko setting "I have grown fond of sorrow" (Op. 8 No. 4), the lament of the lonely girl for her absent soldier. A certain amount of strain is put upon Alexander Naoumenko's tenor at the most strenuous moments, but he can soar in heroic phrases and in quieter passages produce the authentic Russian tenor sound, a touch French in influence, that is needed for the song to the Georgian beauty, "Sing not to me, beautiful maiden" and the subtly folk-influenced "Oh thou, my field" (both from Op. 4). Transliterations and translations into English, French and German are included.

Further listening ...

...Cello Sonata in G minor, Op. 19. *Coupled with* **R. Strauss** Cello Sonata in F major, Op. 6. **Anne Gastinel** (vc); **Pierre-Laurent Aimard** (pf). Auvidis Valois V4692 (12/93).

...Suite No. 2, Op. 17. Russian Rhapsody, Op. posth. Symphonic Dances, Op. 45. *Coupled with* **Medtner** Russian Round Dance (A Tale), Op. 58 No. 1. Knight Errant, Op. 58 No. 2. **Dmitri Alexeev, Nikolai Demidenko** (pfs). Hyperion CDA66654 (10/94). *Gramophone Editor's choice.*

...Six Songs, Op. 4 – No. 1, Oh no, I beg you, forsake me not; No. 3, In the silence of the secret night; No. 4, Sing not to me, beautiful maiden. Six Songs, Op. 8 – No. 5, The dream. 12 Songs, Op. 14 – No. 9, She is as lovely as the noon. 12 Songs, Op. 21 – No. 6, Fragment from Musset. 15 Songs, Op. 26 – No. 2, He took all from me; No. 6, Christ is risen; No. 13, When yesterday we met. *Coupled with* **Tchaikovsky** Six Songs, Op. 6 – No. 4, A tear trembles; No. 6, None but the lonely heart. Six Songs, Op. 25 – No. 1, Reconciliation. Six Songs, Op. 28 – No. 6, The fearful minute. Six Songs, Op. 38 – No. 1, Don Juan's Serenade. 12 Songs, Op. 60 – No. 4, The nightingale; No. 11, Exploit. Six Songs, Op. 63 – No. 2, I opened the window. Six Songs, Op. 73 – No. 6, Again, as before, alone. **Dmitri Hvorostovsky** (bar); **Oleg Boshniakovich** (pf). Philips 432 119-2PH (10/91).

...Six Songs, Op. 4[a]. Six Songs, Op. 8[a]. 12 Songs, Op. 14[a]. 12 Songs, Op. 21[a]. 15 Songs, Op. 26[a]. 14 Songs, Op. 34[a]. Six Songs, Op. 38[a]. At the gate of the holy abode[a]. Song of the disillusioned[a]. The flower has faded[a]. Do you remember the evening?[a]. Were you hiccoughing?[a]. I shall tell you nothing[a]. Again you leapt, my heart[a]. April! A festive Spring[a]. Twilight has fallen[a]. Powdered paint[a]. Night[a]. Letter to K. S. Stanislavsky[a]. From the Gospel of St John[a]. Daisies. Lilacs. [a]**Elisabeth Söderström** (sop); **Vladimir Ashkenazy** (pf). London 436 920-2LM3 (5/94).

...Six Songs, Op. 4 – No. 2, Morning; No. 3, In the silence of the secret night. Op. 14 – No. 1, I wait for thee; No. 8, Oh, do not grieve; No. 9, She is as lovely as the moon; No. 11, Spring waters. Op. 26 No. 6, Christ is risen. *Coupled with works by* **Mussorgsky** and **Tchaikovsky** Ewa Podleś (contr); **Graham Johnson** (pf). Forlane UCD16683 (5/95). *See review in the Collections section; refer to the Index to Reviews.*

...At the gate of the holy abode. Do you remember the evening. From the Gospel of St John. I shall tell you nothing. Letter to K.S. Stanislavsky. Song of the disillusioned. Were you hiccoughing? Songs, Op. 4 – Oh no, I beg you, forsake me not; Morning; In the silence of the secret night; Sing not to me, beautiful maiden. Songs, Op. 8 – Child, thou art as beautiful as a flower; Brooding. Songs, Op. 14 – I was with her; How everyone loves thee; She is as lovely as the moon; Spring waters; 'Tis time. Songs, Op. 21 – Fate; By the fresh grave; Lilacs; Before the icon; No prophet I. Songs, Op. 26 – He took all from me; Let us rest; Christ is risen; When yesterday we met; All things pass by. Songs, Op. 34 – In the soul of each of us; The raising of Lazarus; You knew him; The peasant. **Sergei Leiferkus** (bar); **Howard Shelley** (pf). Chandos CHAN9374 (10/95).

...Liturgy of St John Chrysostom, Op. 31. **Soloists; Bulgarian National Radio Chorus / Mikhail Milkov.** EMI Forte CZS5 68664-2 (5/96).

...The Miserly Knight. **Soloists; Bolshoi Theatre Orchestra / Andrey Chistiakov.** CdM Russian Season LDC288 080 (10/94).

Joseph Raff
Swiss/German 1822-1882

Suggested listening ...

...Symphony No. 5 in E major, Op. 77, "Lenore". **London Philharmonic Orchestra / Bernard Herrmann.** Unicorn-Kanchana Souvenir UKCD2031 (10/90).

...Symphony No. 7 in B flat major, Op. 201, "In den Alpen". Concert Overture in F major, Op. 123. **Košice State Philharmonic Orchestra / Urs Schneider.** Marco Polo 8 223506 (8/94).

...Symphonies – No. 8 in A major, Op. 205, "Frühlingsklänge"; No. 9 in E minor, Op. 208, "Im Sommer". **Košice State Philharmonic Orchestra / Urs Schneider.** Marco Polo 8 223362 (11/92).

Kaljo Raid
Estonian 1922-

New review

Raid Symphony No. 2, "Stockholm".
Tubin Elegy for Strings (arr. Raid). Symphony No. 11 (orch. Raid). **Estonian State Symphony Orchestra / Arvo Volmer.** Koch International Classics Ⓟ 37291-2 (48 minutes: DDD; 1/96).

The packaging of this disc is very misleading. From the front and spine of the box one would be forgiven for assuming this was a CD single, since only the two Tubin pieces are listed, amounting to less than 12 minutes (Tubin only left one movement of Symphony No. 11). Granted, Tubin is a higher octane composer than Kaljo Raid but his symphonic *Allegro*, while a typical creation, hardly adds much to our knowledge of him and the latter's Second Symphony is undoubtedly the major offering. To add insult to injury, Raid is respectively arranger and orchestrator of the Tubin works – the 1945 *Elegy* being a trifle scored originally for pairs of violins and cellos. In the second of his two symphonies, Raid for the most part exchanged the stylistic influences of Borodin and early Sibelius that infused its predecessor for Shostakovich and a more definitively Nordic sound. Surprisingly, some of the themes – particularly in the slow movements – bear a Petterssonesque tang (bereft of the Swede's habitual hysteria): a fascinating anticipation by several years. The *Stockholm* Symphony (it was completed in that city in 1946) is an engaging work, by turns pastoral and sober, lyrical and epic. It marks a definite advance on the First (listed below). Arvo Volmer and the Estonian State Symphony Orchestra deliver a very decent performance, well recorded. The disc is still short measure even including the Raid, but well worth investigating for all that.

Further listening ...

...Symphony No. 1 in C minor. *Coupled with* **Eller** Elegia. Five Pieces for String Orchestra. Dawn. **Royal Scottish Orchestra / Neeme Järvi.** Chandos CHAN8525 (11/89).

Priaulx Rainier
South African 1903-1986

Suggested listening ...

...String Quartet[a]. Quanta[b]. String Trio[b]. Ploërmel[c]. [a]**Edinburgh Quartet** (Miles Baster, Peter Markham, vns; Michael Beeston, va; Mark Bailey, vc); [b]**Redcliffe Ensemble;** [c]**Royal Northern College of Music Wind Ensemble / Timothy Reynish.** Redcliffe Recordings RR007 (11/92).

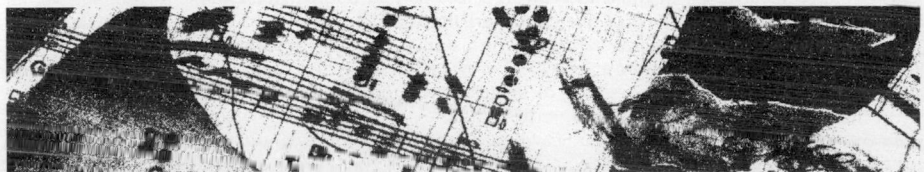

Thomas Rajna Hungarian/South African 1928-

Suggested listening ...
...Harp Concerto[a]. Piano Concerto No. 2[b]. [a]**Moya Wright** (hp); [b]**Thomas Rajna** (pf); **South African National Symphony Orchestra / Allan Stephenson**. Claremont CDGSE1526 (11/93).

Jean-Philippe Rameau French 1683-1764

Rameau Premier livre de pièces de clavecin. Pièces de clavecin en concerts. Nouvelles suites de pièces de clavecin. Les petits marteaux de M Rameau. La Dauphine. **Christophe Rousset** (hpds). L'Oiseau-Lyre Ⓕ 425 886-2OH2 (two discs: 129 minutes: DDD: 12/91). ✒ Recorded 1989. *Gramophone Award Winner 1992.*
This recording of Rameau's solo harpsichord music outdistances most of the competition. Rousset does not include everything that Rameau wrote for the instrument but he does play all the music contained in the principal collections of 1706, 1724 and c1728 as well as *La Dauphine*. Rousset's phrasing is graceful and clearly articulated, the inflexions gently spoken and the rhythmic pulse all that one might wish for. Tempos are, for the most part, well-judged and the playing admirably attentive to detail and delightfully animated. Only occasionally does Rousset perhaps just miss the mark with speeds that are uncomfortably brisk and lacking that choreographic poise which is such a vital ingredient in French baroque music. But he is at his strongest is irresistible and this is how we find him in "Les niais de Sologne" and its variations, the reflective "L'entretien des Muses", the animated "Les cyclopes", "La poule", "L'enharmonique" and the dazzling A minor Gavotte and variations. In these and in many other of the pieces, too, Rousset's impeccable taste and seemingly effortless virtuosity provide the listener with constant and intense delight. The quality of the recording is ideal as are the two instruments which Rousset has chosen to play.
Additional recommendations ...
...Pièces de clavecin en concerts. **Robert Kohnen** (hpd); **Barthold Kuijken** (fl); **Sigiswald Kuijken** (vn); **Wieland Kuijken** (va da gamba). Accent Ⓕ ACC9493D (61 minutes: DDD: 8/95). ✒ Ⓖ
...Nouvelles suites de pièces de clavecin – A minor. Pièces de clavecin – Suite in E minor. **Trevor Pinnock** (hpd). CRD Ⓕ CRD3310 (52 minutes: ADD: 8/88). ✒
...Premier livre de pièces de clavecin – Suite in A minor. La Dauphine. Cinq pièces pour clavecin seull. Pièces de clavecin en concerts. La pantomime. **Trevor Pinnock** (hpd). CRD Ⓕ CRD3320 (43 minutes: ADD: 8/88). ✒
...Pièces de clavecin – Suite in D minor/major. Nouvelles suites de pièces de clavecin – G major/minor. **Trevor Pinnock** (hpd). CRD Ⓕ CRD3330 (52 minutes: ADD: 8/88). ✒
...Pièces de clavecin en concerts. **Ryo Terakado** (vn); **Kaori Uemura** (va da gamba); **Christophe Rousset** (hpd). Harmonia Mundi Ⓕ HMC90 1418 (74 minutes: DDD: 4/93). ✒
...Pièces de clavecin en concerts – Cinquième concert. **Leclair** Sonatas – E minor, Op. 2 No. 1; G major, Op. 9 No. 7. **Blavet** Sonata in D minor, Op. 2 No. 2, "La Vibray". **M. La Barre** Sonate l'inconnuë in G major, Book 2 No. 9. **Hotteterre** Airs et Brunettes. **Rachel Brown** (fl); **Mark Caudle** (viol); **James Johnstone** (hpd). Chandos Chaconne Ⓕ CHAN0544 (71 minutes: DDD: 2/94). ✒
...L'enharmonique. L'Egyptienne. La Dauphine. *Coupled with works by* **D'Anglebert, F. Couperin** and **Forqueray Sophie Yates** (hpd). Chandos Chaconne Ⓕ CHAN0545 (71 minutes: DDD: 11/93). ✒ *See review in the Collections section; refer to the Index to Reviews.*
...Pièces de clavecin en concerts. **Catherine Mackintosh** (vn); **Laurence Dreyfus** (va da gamba); **Ketil Haugsand** (hpd). Simax Ⓕ PSC1095 (69 minutes: DDD: 6/94). ✒ *Gramophone Editor's choice.*

New review
Rameau Deus noster refugium. In convertendo. Quam dilecta. **Sophie Daneman, Noémi Rime** (sops); **Paul Agnew** (ten); **Nicolas Rivenq** (bar); **Nicolas Cavallier** (bass); **Les Arts Florissants / William Christie**. Erato Ⓕ 4509-96967-2 (70 minutes: DDD). ✒ Texts and translations included. Recorded 1994. *Gramophone Award Winner 1995.*
Rameau's three examples of the *grand motet* form were not much respected in his own day, and that was in the 1750s, when his reputation as a composer, built on the success of his operas, could hardly have been higher. Today, it is that very reputation which inclines us more towards Rameau's church music than that of his contemporaries. This recording was an auspicious start to William Christie's association with Erato. Erato have considerably improved their insert-note information and presentation in general, and they've been repaid with bright, eventful performances. All three motets date from relatively early in Rameau's career, before he had really made a name for himself, yet all show to a certain extent some of the characteristics that 20 years or so later would so thrillingly illuminate his operas. *Deus noster refugium*, for instance, features impressive depictions of nature in turmoil that would not sound out of place in *Hippolyte et Aricie*, and all three begin with long, expressive solos not unlike the opening of an act from a *tragédie-lyrique*. *Quam dilecta* does sound a little more 'churchy' than the others, with its impressive, rather Handelian double fugue, but *In convertendo* – a work which Rameau heavily revised well into his operatic Indian summer in 1751 – absolutely reeks of the theatre. Drop anyone familiar with the composer's operas into the middle of

this piece, and surely only its Latin text would give away that this is church music. It comes as no surprise to find Christie going to town on this dramatic element. The slightly dry acoustic of the Radio France studio is a help, as are the forceful, penetrating qualities of the solo and choral singers. But it is Christie's command of gesture, pacing and contrast which really gives these performances such an invigorating character.

Rameau Castor et Pollux. **Howard Crook** (ten) Castor; **Jérôme Corréas** (bass) Pollux; **Agnès Mellon** (sop) Télaïre; **Véronique Gens** (sop) Phebe; **René Schirrer** (bar) Mars; Jupiter; **Sandrine Piau** (sop) Venus, Happy Spirit, Planet; **Mark Padmore** (ten) Love, High Priest; **Claire Brua** (sop) Minerve; **Sophie Daneman** (sop) Follower of Hebe; Celestial Pleasure; **Adrian Brand** (ten) Athlete I; **Jean-Claude Sarragosse** (bass) Athlete II; **Les Arts Florissants and Orchestra / William Christie.** Harmonia Mundi Ⓕ HMC90 1435/7 (three discs: 173 minutes: DDD: 7/93). ✒ Notes, text and translation included. Recorded 1992. ⒼⒼ

Castor et Pollux was Rameau's second *tragédie en musique*. Its first performance took place in October 1737 but the opera was greeted with only moderate enthusiasm. It was only with the composer's thoroughly revised version of 1754 that the opera enjoyed the popularity that it unquestionably deserved. The revision tautened a drama which had never been weak but it dispensed with a very beautiful Prologue. Christie and Les Arts Florissants perform Rameau's first version complete with its Prologue. The librettist, Pierre-Joseph Bernard, was one of the ablest writers with whom Rameau collaborated and his text for *Castor et Pollux* has been regarded by some as the best in the history of eighteenth-century French opera. Bernard focuses on the fraternal love of the 'heavenly twins' and specifically on the generosity with which Pollux renounces his immortality so that Castor may be restored to life. Christie's production was staged at Aix-en-Provence in the summer of 1991 and recorded by Harmonia Mundi a year later. This performance, more than that of Nikolaus Harnoncourt on Teldec (listed below), realizes the element of tragedy, above all in the First Act, and Christie's singers sound altogether more at home with French declamation than Harnoncourt's cast. A very beautiful score, affectionately and perceptively interpreted that will afford deep and lasting pleasure.

Additional recommendations ...

...Soloists; **Stockholm Chamber Choir; Vienna Concentus Musicus / Nikolaus Harnoncourt.** Teldec Das Alte Werk Ⓕ 2292-42510-2 (three discs: 166 minutes: ADD: 7/87). ✒

...Soloists; **English Bach Festival Chorus and Baroque Orchestra / Charles Farncombe.** Erato Ⓜ 4509-95311-2 (two discs: 137 minutes: DDD: 5/95). Ⓖ

New review

Rameau Naïs. **Linda Russell** (sop) Naïs; **Ian Caley** (ten) Neptune; **Ian Caddy** (bass) Jupiter, Telenus; **John Tomlinson** (bass) Pluton; **Richard Jackson** (bass) Tiresic; **Brian Parsons** (ten) Asterion; **Antony Ransome** (bar) Palemon; **Ann Mackay** (sop) Flore, Second Shepherdess; **Jennifer Smith** (sop) First Shepherdess; **English Bach Festival Chorus and Orchestra / Nicholas McGegan.** Erato Ⓓ 4509-98532-2 (two discs: 106 minutes: ADD: 11/95). Notes, text and translation included. From STU71439 (10/81). Recorded 1980.

Naïs was commissioned to celebrate the Treaty of Aix-la-Chapelle in 1748, and first performed the following year. Thus it was a vocal counterpart to Handel's *Music for the Royal Fireworks*, both pieces marking the conclusion of the War of the Austrian Succession. The present recording was made in 1980 following performances at London's Old Vic Theatre and at Versailles under the auspices of Lina Lalandi's enterprising English Bach Festival. Though, dramatically, *Naïs* is unremarkable, Rameau and his librettist, Louis de Cahusac, with whom he collaborated on many occasions, made a special point of establishing a strong relationship between dance and action. As Graham Sadler, editor of the edition and author of an informative introduction points out, Cahusac himself provided detailed choreographic outlines for the dances which feature so prominently in this piece. And Rameau responded with music which, of its kind, is much closer to the spirit of *opéra-ballet* than heroic opera, and is representative of his finest.

Nicholas McGegan has an effective understanding of French baroque style and brings out much that is graceful and enlivening in Rameau's score. Only the Prologue bears any relevance to the Treaty which occasioned the work, and this in strictly allegorical terms. Here, John Tomlinson and Ian Caddy are especially effective. In the opera itself Linda Russell is appealing in the title-role with Ian Caley an ardent Neptune in love with her. But, as so often with Rameau's vocal music in the tenor register, the uppermost notes sometimes betray a hint of strain. For the most part in the purely instrumental numbers the participants seem to revel in Rameau's uniquely colourful orchestral palette. Who wouldn't? From the moment that we hear the superbly inventive overture, through to the sparkling tambourins which occur towards the end of Acts 1 and 3, Rameau never for a second lets us down; there is nothing like hearing the wonderful dances in their dramatic context so carefully considered by composer and librettist. Only the choral singing occasionally fails to measure up to the solo and instrumental contributions. But this is, notwithstanding, a welcome reappearance of an exhilarating score.

Additional recommendation ...

...Naïs – Suite. Le temple de la gloire – Suite. **Philharmonia Baroque Orchestra / Nicholas McGegan.** Harmonia Mundi Ⓕ HMU90 7121 (71 minutes: DDD: 7/95). ✒ ⒼⒼ

Rameau Les Indes galantes – Prologue: **Claron McFadden** (sop) Hébé; **Jérôme Corréas** (bar)
Bellone; **Isabelle Poulenard** (sop) L'Amour. Le Turc généreux: **Nicolas Rivenq** (bass) Osman;
Miriam Ruggieri (sop) Emilie; **Howard Crook** (ten) Valère. Les Incas du Pérou: **Bernard Deletré**
(bass) Huascar; **Poulenard** (Phanie); **Jean-Paul Fouchécourt** (ten) Carlos. Les fleurs: **Fouchécourt**
(Tacmas); **Corréas** (Ali); **Sandrine Piau** (sop) Zaïre; **Noémi Rime** (sop) Fatime. Les sauvages:
Rivenq (Adario); **Crook** (Damon); **Deletré** (Don Alvar); **McFadden** (Zima); **Les Arts Florissants /
William Christie.** Harmonia Mundi Ⓔ HMC90 1367/9 (three discs: 203 minutes: DDD: 2/91).
    ✒ Notes, text and translation included.

Les Indes galantes was Rameau's first *opéra-ballet*. He completed it in 1735 when it was performed at
the Académie Royale in Paris. *Opéra-ballet* usually consisted of a prologue and anything between
three and five entrées or acts. There was no continuously developing plot but instead various sections
might be linked by a general theme, often hinted at in the title. Such is the case with *Les indes galantes*
whose linking themes derives from a contemporary taste for the exotic and the unknown. Following
a prologue come four entrées, "Le Turc généreux", "Les Incas du Pérou", "Les fleurs" and "Les
sauvages". William Christie and Les Arts Florissants give a characteristically warm-blooded
performance of one of Rameau's most approachable and endearing stage works. Christie's control of
diverse forces – his orchestra consists of some 46 players – his dramatic pacing of the music, his
recognition of Rameau's uniquely distinctive instrumental palette and his feeling for gesture and
rhythm contribute towards making this a lively and satisfying performance. The choir are alert and
well-disciplined and the orchestra a worthy partner in respect of clear textures and technical finesse;
this can be readily appreciated in the splendid, spaciously laid out and tautly constructed orchestral
Chaconne which concludes the work. The booklet contains full texts in French, English and German
and the music is recorded in a sympathetic acoustic.
Additional recommendations ...
...Soloists; **Valencia Vocal Ensemble; Jean-François Paillard Chamber Orchestra / Jean-François
Paillard.** Erato Ⓜ 4509-95310-2 (three discs: 205 minutes: ADD: 5/95).
...Les Indes galantes – Suite. **Orchestra of the Eighteenth Century / Frans Brüggen.** Philips Ⓔ 438
946-2PH (44 minutes: DDD: 8/94). ✒   ⒼⒼ
...Les Indes galantes – Suite[a]. Dardanus – Suite[b]. **Collegium Aureum / [a]Gustav Leonhardt,
[b]Reinhard Peters.** Deutsche Harmonia Mundi Editio Classica Ⓜ 05472 77269-2 (70 minutes:
ADD: 8/93). ✒

| New review |

Rameau Hippolyte et Aricie. **Jean-Paul Fouchécourt** (ten) Hippolyte; **Véronique Gens** (sop) Aricie;
Bernarda Fink (contr) Phèdre; **Russell Smythe** (bar) Thésée; **Thérèse Feighan** (sop) Diane; **Annick
Massis** (sop) L'Amour, Shepherdess, Female Sailor; **Laurent Naouri** (bar); Pluton, Neptune,
Jupiter; **Florence Katz** (sop) Oenone; **Jean-Louis Georgel** (ten) Mercure, Arcas; **Luc Coadau** (ten)
Tisiphone; **Jean-Louis Meunier** (ten) Fate I; **Jacques-François Loiseleur des Longchamps** (ten)
Fate II; **Jerome Varnier** (bar) Fate III; **Monique Simon** (sop) High Priestess; **Stephan Van Dyck**
(ten) Follower of Cupid; **Kiyoko Okada** (sop) Priestess; **Meredith Hall** (sop) Huntress; **Sagittarius
Vocal Ensemble; Les Musiciens du Louvre / Marc Minkowski.** Archiv Produktion Ⓔ 445 853-
2AH3 (three discs: 167 minutes: DDD: 9/95). Notes, text and translation included. Recorded
1994.

Rameau's older contemporary, Campra, in a subsequently oft-quoted remark to the Prince of Conti,
observed of *Hippolyte et Aricie*, "My Lord, there is enough music in that opera to eclipse us all".
Notwithstanding the opera's title, or the fact that the love of Hippolytus and Aricia for one another
acts as a mainspring for Rameau's opera, the drama focuses chiefly upon the personalities of Theseus
and Phaedra and their tragic destinies, determined by Phaedra's incestuous love for her stepson,
Hippolytus. In the reissued mid-1960s recording with Janet Baker as Phaedra and John Shirley-Quirk
as Theseus, Sir Anthony Lewis omitted the Prologue as well as making smaller cuts, too. But in using
Vincent d'Indy's edition he also incorporated scoring which had more to do with d'Indy than with
Rameau. It is Minkowski who first brings us on disc a complete *Hippolyte et Aricie* in a version closely
adhering to one that we know met with the composer's approval. The performance is strongly cast,
with Bernarda Fink as an outstandingly impressive Phaedra. She is at least a worthy successor to
Baker's fine portrayal of the role under Lewis, clear-toned and deeply affecting in her passionate
monologues. Russell Smythe makes a plausible Theseus and his voice is both resonant and pleasing
in quality. Yet perhaps he underplays the role – readers acquainted with Shirley-Quirk's interpretation
on the Lewis set are likely to think so – and a decided tendency towards sharpness in pitch, detracts
from his otherwise clear and forthright declamation.
    The lovers, Hippolytus and Aricia are affectionately portrayed and very well sung by Jean-Paul
Fouchécourt and Véronique Gens. Rameau gave them some alluring music in the first two scenes of
the Fourth Act and these two artists do it full justice. Fouchécourt's celebrated "Ah! faut il, en un jour,
perdre tout ce que j'aime" is heart-rending. Most of the remaining roles come across authoritatively
and the Sagittarius Vocal Ensemble enlivens and brings character to the many fine choruses; "Que ce
rivage retentisse", the most famous of them, sounds splendid but "Dans ce paisible séjour" for upper
voices is ragged and not always at one with the instrumental support. The orchestral playing of Les
Musiciens du Louvre is mostly assured and sensible to the requirements of the voices, though

woodwind, above all oboes, are variable in tuning and upper strings sometimes sound thin and edgy. If we make allowances for the fact that the recording was made from live performances then the sound is perhaps not too bad; but readers may be bothered by frequent extraneous noises, some of which would appear to emanate from an insecure rostrum. However, in general, Minkowski's *Hippolyte et Aricie*, well paced dramatically, is a considerable achievement. The reissued Lewis cannot, indeed should not, take precedence over Minkowski's complete and stylistically more authoritative reading but it will be for ever treasured by those who recognize in the contributions of Baker and Shirley-Quirk a profound and moving account of their tragic predicament.

Additional recommendations ...

...Soloists; **St Anthony Singers; English Chamber Orchestra / Sir Anthony Lewis.** Decca Serenata Ⓜ 444 526-2DMO2 (two discs: 146 minutes: ADD: 5/96).

...Hippolyte et Aricie – Orchestral Suite. **La Petite Bande / Sigiswald Kuijken.** Deutsche Harmonia Mundi Editio Classica Ⓜ GD77009 (52 minutes: 7/90). ✔

Rameau Pygmalion. **John Elwes** (ten) Pygmalion; **Mieke van der Sluis** (sop) Céphise; **Françoise Vanhecke** (sop) Statue; **Rachel Yakar** (sop) Amour; **Paris Chapelle Royale Chorus; La Petite Bande / Gustav Leonhardt.** Deutsche Harmonia Mundi Editio Classica Ⓜ GD77143 (47 minutes: ADD: 7/90). ✔ Text and translation included. From 1C 065 99914 (2/82). Recorded 1980. Ⓖ
This is amongst the most invigorating excursions into Rameau's music currently available. *Pygmalion* dates from 1748 when Rameau's creative energy was at its peak. It consists of a continuous plot confined within a single act. The score contains music that is at times vigorous and at others tenderly affecting. The action takes place in Pygmalion's studio; captivated by the appearance of the statue he has just created, Pygmalion becomes oblivious to the love shown towards him by the very human Céphise. Then the statue comes to life and falls for Pygmalion. It is a beautifully balanced and well-constructed work and, in this stylish and sympathetic performance, many of its subtleties are revealed. John Elwes is convincing and lyrical in the title-role though occasionally the exceptional demands of the role almost get the better of him. Mieke van der Sluis as Céphise makes considerable appeal; her voice is warm in timbre and she has a firm grasp of style. The playing of La Petite Bande under the direction of Gustav Leonhardt is lively in spirit and tidy in ensemble. However, the choir are rather weak but since they are allotted only two sections in the ballet that need not trouble us too much. The recorded sound is clear and effective.

Additional recommendation ...

...Pygmalion. Nélée et Myrthis. **Soloists; Les Arts Florissants Chorus and Orchestra / William Christie.** Harmonia Mundi Ⓔ HMC90 1381 (78 minutes: DDD: 7/92). ✔

Further listening ....

...Grand Motets: Deus noster refugium; In convertendo[b]; Quam dilecta. **Soloists; Les Arts Florissants Chorus and Orchestra / William Christie.** Erato 4509-96967-2. ✔ ⒼⒼⒼ

...Pièces de clavecin – Suites: A minor (1706); E minor (1724); D major (1724); A minor (c1729); G major (c1729). Quatre Pièces en concert. *Coupled with works by* **F. Couperin, D. Scarlatti** and **Rossini** Marcelle Meyer (pf). EMI mono CZS5 68092-2* (6/95). *See review in the Collections section; refer to the Index to Reviews.* ⒼⒼⒼ

...Platée. **Soloists; Françoise Herr Vocal Ensemble; Musiciens du Louvre / Marc Minkowski.** Erato MusiFrance 2292-45028-2 (9/90). ✔ ⒼⒼ

...Zoroastre. **Soloists; Ghent Collegium Vocale; La Petite Bande / Sigiswald Kuijken.** Deutsche Harmonia Mundi Editio Classica GD77144 (7/90). ✔

...Les Paladins – Suite. **Orchestra of the Age of Enlightenment / Gustav Leonhardt.** Philips 432 968-2PH (9/92). ✔ ⒼⒼ

...La rappel des oiseaux. Tambourin. La poule. *Coupled with works by* **Rimsky-Korsakov, Daquin, Paradis, Bach, F. Couperin, Templeton** and **Malcolm** George Malcolm (hpd). Decca 444 390-2DWO (11/95). ✔

...Hippolyte et Aricie. **Soloists; Sagittarius Vocal Ensemble; Les Musiciens du Louvre / Marc Minkowski.** Archiv Produktion 445 853-2AH3 (9/95). ✔

Robert Ramsey

British c1612-1644

New review

Ramsey How are the mighty fallen. Almighty and everlasting God, we humbly beseech. When David heard. O come, let us sing unto the Lord. Magnificat and Nunc dimittis. In guilty night. Sleep, fleshly birth. Thou maist be proud. Go perjured man. What tears, dear Prince. Inclina, Domine. O Sapientia. In Monte Oliveti. O vos omnes. Te Deum and Jubilate. **Magnificat Choir and Players / Philip Cave.** ASV Gaudeamus Ⓔ CDGAU138 (65 minutes: DDD: 7/95). ✔
This disc is unlikely to change the current view of Ramsey's status as a minor composer to that of a major one, but it argues convincingly for his reinstatement from time to time in concert programmes and liturgical performances. The most familiar piece here is undoubtedly *How are the mighty fallen*, quite frequently sung by Anglican church and cathedral choirs. It is an impressive work in many ways, but somewhat undistinguished melodically. This seems, in fact, to be the chief problem with Ramsey's work as a whole; he has little of the long-breathed melodic distinctiveness of previous generations, or

the idiosyncratic imagination of a Byrd or a Gibbons, and is not quite a fully-fledged dramatic baroque composer in the mould of Purcell, as one may tell from the rather staid dialogue, *In guilty night*. As Timothy Symonds points out in his note, Ramsey's music is transitional in character, and with that we must be content. The performances by Magnificat are in general first-class, very much in the English choral tradition (they sound closer to a cathedral or collegiate choir than they do to The Tallis Scholars or The Sixteen). A taste of what Ramsey might have been is given by *Thou maist be proud*, sung here most sensitively by Robin Blaze and probably the highlight of the disc. Among the choral works, *In Monte Oliveti* impresses the most with its startling harmonies and varied textures. Recommended for enthusiasts of the period.

Ture Rangström Swedish 1884-1947

Suggested listening ....

...Poems by Bo Bergman – No. 1, Wings in the night; No. 3, Melody. The Dark Flower – No. 2, Prayer to the night; No. 4, Farewell. Pan. Old Swedish. *Coupled with works by* **Stenhammar, Peterson-Berger, Sigurd von Koch, Alfvén** and **Sjögren** Anne Sofie von Otter (mez); Bengt Forsberg (pf). DG 449 189-2GH (5/96). *See review in the Collections section; refer to the Index to Reviews.* ⒼⒼ

Einojuhani Rautavaara Finnish 1928-

New review

Rautavaara Symphony No. 7, "Angel of Light". Annunciations[a]. [a]Kari Jussila (org); Helsinki Philharmonic Orchestra / Leif Segerstam. Ondine Ⓟ ODE869-2 (65 minutes: DDD: 6/96). Recorded 1995. *Gramophone Editor's choice. Selected by Soundings.* Ⓖ

The Seventh Symphony's opening *Tranquillo* evokes a calm though powerful atmosphere, with many Sibelian points of reference – most especially in recognizable echoes of the *Largo* fourth movement from Sibelius's Fourth Symphony, whereas the closing *Pesante-cantabile* is more in line with the symphonic world of Alan Hovhaness. The Angel idea originates in a series that already includes a number of other works (*Angels and Visitations* and *Angel of Dusk*, for instance), the reference being (as the composer himself explains) to "an archetype, one of mankind's oldest traditions and perennial companions". This Jungian axis is reflected in monolithic chords, ethereal harmonic computations (invariably broad and high-reaching) and an unselfconscious mode of musical development. Readers schooled in the more contemplative works of Górecki, Pärt and Tavener will likely respond to this spatially generous essay, though Rautavaara's language is more a celebration of nature and her works than of any specific religious ritual. Comparisons with the *Annunciations* (for organ, brass quintet, wind orchestra and percussion) find the earlier work far harsher in tone, much more demanding technically (it calls for a formidable organ virtuoso) and more radical in its musical language. Here the style ranges from the primeval drone that opens the work through canon, 'bird forest' activity (a recurring strategy in Rautavaara's music) and the novel effect of having the "notes of a dense chord weirdly circulating in the room" when the organ motor is switched off. Kari Jussila rises to the various challenges set for him with what sounds like genuine enthusiasm (his fast fingerwork is amazing) while Leif Segerstam and the Helsinki Philharmonic fully exploit the tonal drama of both works. The recordings are warm and spacious.

New review

Rautavaara Departure. The bride. Praktisch Deutsch. With joy we go dancing. Summer night. The cathedral. Suite de Lorca, Op. 72. Ludus verbalis, Op. 10. Nirvana Dharma[a]. Die erste Elegie. [a]Petri Alanko (fl); Finnish Radio Chamber Choir / Eric-Olof Söderström. Ondine Ⓟ ODE851-2 (61 minutes: DDD: 6/96). Texts and translations included. Ⓖ

Rautavaara's compositional career has been one of exploration rather than outright experimentation, its goal the evolution (achieved in the mid 1980s) of his personal fusion of the serial and the tonal. The impressive quality and diversity of Rautavaara's output for mixed chorus, leaving aside the huge cantata *The Myth of Sampo*, are laid out for close inspection on this disc, ranging from the folk-based partsongs *Departure*, *The bride* and *Summer night* (all 1975), to the collage-like absurdism of *Praktisch Deutsch* ("Practical German", 1969; the text derives from a dictionary and phrase book), to the grand canvas of *The cathedral* (1983) which is in fact a tone-poem for unaccompanied voices rather than a large-scale motet. Tone-painting is used again in the 1979 *Nirvana Dharma*, with its enchanting flute solo depicting the god Krishna. This, *The cathedral* and the concluding *Die erste Elegie* (1993, setting the first of Rilke's *Duino* elegies) are major compositions by any standard. The most familiar work here is the exuberant *Suite de Lorca* (1973). Söderström's performances are fine. A cracking disc.

Further listening ....
...Cantus arcticus, Op. 61[a]. Symphony No. 5[a]. String Quartet No. 4, Op. 87[b]. [b]**Sirius Quartet;**
[a]**Leipzig Radio Symphony Orchestra / Max Pommer.** Catalyst 09026 62671-2.
...Suite de Lorca, Op. 72. *Coupled with* **Sandström** A Cradle Song/The Tyger. **Nørgård** And time
shall be no more. **Tormis** The Curse of Iron. **Jersild** Three Romantic Songs. **Danish National
Radio Choir / Stefan Parkman.** Chandos CHAN9264 (4/95).
...The Myth of Sampo. **Tom Nyman** (ten); **Sauli Tiilikainen** (bar); **Antti Suhonen** (bass); **Helsinki
University Chorus / Matti Hyökki.** Ondine ODE842-2 (12/95).

Oreste Ravanello

Italian 19th Century

Suggested listening ....
...Theme and Variations in B minor. *Coupled with* **Stanford** Fantasia and Toccata in D minor,
Op. 57. **Reger** Five Easy Preludes and Fugues, Op. 56 – No. 1 in E major. **Shostakovich** Lady
Macbeth of the Mtsensk district – Passacaglia. **Schmidt** Chaconne in C sharp minor. **Keith John**
(org). Priory PRCD370 (11/92). *Selected by Sounds in Retrospect. See review in the Collections
section; refer to the Index to Reviews.*   ⓖⓖⓖ

Maurice Ravel

French 1875-1937

Ravel Boléro. Alborada del gracioso. Rapsodie espagnole. La valse (all from SXDL7559, 9/82). Ma
mère l'oye. Pavane pour une infante défunte. Le tombeau de Couperin. Valses nobles et
sentimentales (all from 410 254-1DH, 8/84). Piano Concerto in G major[a]. Piano Concerto for the
Left Hand[a]. Menuet antique. Une barque sur l'océan. Fanfare pour "L'Eventail de Jeanne" (all
from SXDL7592, 8/83). Daphnis et Chloé (from SXDL7526, 6/81). [a]**Pascal Rogé** (pf); **Montreal
Symphony Chorus and Orchestra / Charles Dutoit.** Decca Ovation Ⓜ 421 458-2DM4 (four discs:
230 minutes: DDD).   ⓖ
Ravel's orchestral music, during the ten-year span of this *Guide*, has had more than its fair share of
claimants for an entry. Yet in every edition, three of these four discs have consistently remained top
recommendations (the fourth disc was, and still is, equally worthy of inclusion, and is listed below),
and Decca have conveniently gathered together their four discs (in their original format) into this mid-
price box. The survey turns out to be not absolutely complete, as Dutoit omitted the early
Shéhérazade Overture (not a serious loss) and the violin work *Tzigane*, but there is, to date, no
comparably comprehensive set of Ravel's orchestral music. It is, of course, possible to build a
satisfying Ravel library from different sources, but that would bring unavoidable duplication of
repertoire. Yet collections like this one, however convenient and financially attractive, are rarely
consistent in quality. This is that rare case: not one of these recordings is seriously outclassed, either
interpretatively or sonically. Dutoit and his Montreal orchestra are superb stylists; Ravel was just as
much of a musical magpie as Stravinsky, with few historical, contemporary, or popular styles
remaining exempt from a sophisticated Ravelian transformation (in some works they rub shoulders,
for example, the *Valses nobles et sentimentales*). Dutoit ensures that the styles register, but without
labouring the point – the result is always pure Ravel. There is also a consistent elegance, both of
execution and expression, though Dutoit has a cunning (or sixth sense) in knowing when to let the
players off the leash, and by how much (the G major Piano Concerto abounds in examples). A
balletic stance goes hand in hand with rare departures from Ravel's suggestions of pace; for example,
the languorous *Rapsodie espagnole* "Prélude" is kept on its toes (even this atmospheric nocturne is a
slow dance), and the virtuosity of his orchestra allows him to take the mercurial "Prélude" to *Le
tombeau de Couperin* at Ravel's marking, without loss of composure. One radical departure from the
score is his slow tempo for the strings' melody as we enter the "Jardin féerique" in *Ma mère l'oye*, but
even the most fastidious Ravelian will surely succumb to the rapt beauty of the result. Ravel, the time
traveller, from the childhood, fairy-tale world of *Ma mère l'oye* to *Le tombeau de Couperin*'s homage
to the French baroque, also benefits from an acoustic setting where space can add an extra dimension,
a depth for, say, the horn fanfares at the "once upon a time" start of *Ma mère l'oye* or the last post
resonances that the trumpet imparts in the Trio of *Le tombeau*'s Minuet. St Eustache in Montreal has
just such an acoustic, and nowhere is it put to better use than in *Daphnis*, where the perspective laid
out by the different planes draws you in and envelops you. Unlike so many recordings made in
churches these days, there's no blurring of detail, or ungainly weight in *fortissimos*; and microphone
placement gives a discreet presence to all that glitters. The only possible causes for concern may be the
gremlin in the machine that brings some momentary (and hardly serious) distortion near the end of
Boléro; and there is a general, prudent tailoring of extreme *fortissimos* (compared to Rattle's
recordings, for example), but many will regard that as an attribute. No, even after all this time,
Dutoit's Ravel firmly remains *the* reference.

Additional recommendations ...
...Piano Concerto in G major[a]. Piano Concerto for the Left Hand[a]. Menuet antique. Une barque
sur l'océan. Fanfare pour "L'éventail de Jeanne". [a]**Pascal Rogé** (pf); **Montreal Symphony
Orchestra / Charles Dutoit.** Decca Ⓔ 410 230-2DH (57 minutes: DDD: 3/84).

...Piano Concerto in G major. Gaspard de la nuit. Sonatine. **Martha Argerich** (pf); **Berlin Philharmonic Orchestra / Claudio Abbado.** DG Galleria Ⓜ 419 062-2GGA (54 minutes: ADD: 12/87).   Ⓖ

...Piano Concerto in G major. **Rachmaninov** Piano Concerto No. 4 in G minor, Op. 40. **Arturo Benedetti Michelangeli** (pf); **Philharmonia Orchestra / Ettore Gracis.** EMI Ⓕ CDC7 49326-2* (47 minutes: ADD: 9/88). *Gramophone classical 100.*   ⒼⒼⒼ

...Piano Concerto in G major[a]. Piano Concerto for the Left Hand[b]. Fanfare pour "L'éventail de Jeanne". Menuet antique. Le tombeau de Couperin. [a]**Martha Argerich,** [b]**Michel Béroff** (pfs); **London Symphony Orchestra / Claudio Abbado.** DG Ⓕ 423 665-2GH (65 minutes: DDD: 2/89).

...Piano Concerto in G major. Piano Concerto for the Left Hand. **Louis Lortie** (pf); **London Symphony Orchestra / Rafael Frühbeck de Burgos.** Chandos Ⓕ CHAN8773 (57 minutes: DDD: 1/90).

...Piano Concerto for the Left Hand[ab]. Menuet antique[c]. La valse[c]. Ma mère l'oye[c]. Daphnis et Chloé[c]. Shéherazade – fairy overture[c]. Valses nobles et sentimentales[c]. Le tombeau de Couperin[c]. Une barque sur l'océan[c]. Alborada del gracioso[b]. Pavane pour une unfante défunte[b]. Rapsodie espagnole[b]. Fanfare pour "L'éventail de Jeanne"[c]. Boléro[c]. [a]**Philippe Entremont** (pf); [b]**Cleveland Orchestra,** [c]**New York Philharmonic Orchestra / Pierre Boulez.** Sony Classical Ⓜ SM3K45842 (three discs: 223 minutes: ADD: 2/91).

...Boléro. Le tombeau de Couperin. Shéhérazade[a]. Tzigane[b]. [a]**Dame Margaret Price** (sop); [b]**Salvatore Accardo** (vn); **London Symphony Orchestra / Claudio Abbado.** DG Classikon Ⓑ 439 414-2GCL (58 minutes: ADD/DDD: 6/94).

...Boléro. Ma mère l'oye. Rapsodie espagnole. Une barque sur l'océan. Alborada del gracioso. **Berlin Philharmonic Orchestra / Pierre Boulez.** DG Ⓕ 439 859-2GH (76 minutes: DDD: 9/94).   Ⓖ

...Boléro. La valse. Ma mère l'oye. *Coupled with works by* **Beethoven, Brahms, Ravel, Schubert** *and* **Tchaikovsky.** London Symphony Orchestra / Pierre Monteux. Philips The Early Years Ⓜ 442 544-2PM5 (five discs: 311 minutes: ADD: 12/94). *See review in the Collections section; refer to the Index to Reviews.*   ⒼⒼⒼ

...Boléro. La valse. Rapsodie espagnole. **Debussy** Images. **Boston Symphony Orchestra / Charles Munch.** RCA Victor Living Stereo Ⓜ 09026 61956-2* (74 minutes: ADD: 12/94). *See review under Debussy; refer to the Index to Reviews.*   Ⓖ

...Rapsodie espagnole. *Coupled with works by* **Brahms, Klemperer** and **Vaughan Williams** New Philharmonia Orchestra / Leopold Stokowski. BBC Radio Classics Ⓑ BBCRD9107 (74 minutes: ADD: 3/95). *See review in the Collections section; refer to the Index to Reviews.*   Ⓖ

...Piano Concerto in G major[a]. Piano Conferto for the left hand[a]. **Falla** Noches en los jardines de España. [a]**François-Joël Thiollier** (pf); **Polish National Radio Symphony Orchestra / Antoni Wit.** Naxos Ⓢ 8 550753 (64 minutes: DDD: 3/95).

...Rapsodie espagnole. **Debussy** Nocturnes. Prélude à l'après-midi d'un faune. Danse sacrée et danse profane. Préludes, Book 1 – No. 10, La cathédrale engloutie. Estampes – Soirée dans Grenade (both orch. Stokowski). **Philadelphia Orchestra / Leopold Stokowski.** Biddulph mono Ⓜ WHL013* (77 minutes: ADD: 8/95).

...Boléro. **Mussorgsky** Pictures at an Exhibition. **Debussy** La mer. **Berlin Philharmonic Orchestra / Herbert von Karajan.** DG The Originals Ⓜ 447 426-2GOR (75 minutes: ADD: 12/95).

...La valse (arr. cpsr). *Coupled with works by* **Dukas** and **R. Strauss** Martha Argerich, Alexandre Rabinovitch (pfs). Teldec 4509-96435-2 (7/96). *See review under Dukas; refer to the Index to Reviews.*   Ⓖ

Ravel Fanfare pour "L'éventail de Jeanne". Shéhérazade[a]. Alborada del gracioso. Miroirs – La vallée des cloches (arr. Grainger). Ma mère l'oye. La valse. [a]**Maria Ewing** (mez); **City of Birmingham Symphony Orchestra / Simon Rattle.** EMI Ⓕ CDC7 54204-2 (75 minutes: DDD: 8/91). Text and translation included. Recorded 1989.   ⒼⒼ

A paean of British critical praise greets almost every new issue from this team with monotonous regularity, so it is gratifying, in this instance, to note *Diapason*'s reviewer (the French contemporary to *Gramophone*) finding Rattle's *Ma mère l'oye* of a "striking delicacy" and "releasing an indescribable emotion" (apologies to Rémy Louis for a wholly inadequate translation). In the past there have been instances of Rattle's intensive preparation for setting down a much loved masterpiece precluding spontaneity in the end result. Not here. Along with the customary refinement and revelation of texture, there is a sense of Rattle gauging the very individual fantasy worlds of this varied programme with uncanny precision: an aptly childlike wonder for *Ma mère l'oye*'s fairy tale illustrations; the decadence and decay that drive *La valse* to its inevitable doom; and the sensual allure of the Orient in *Shéhérazade* providing a vibrant backdrop for soprano Maria Ewing's intimate confessions. Space does not permit enthusing about the three shorter items that make up this indispensable (and generously filled) disc, recorded with stunning realism. Try it for yourself and marvel at the astonishing range of Ravel's imagination.

Additional recommendations ...

...Ma mère l'oye. Pavane pour une infante défunte. Le tombeau de Couperin. Valses nobles et sentimentales. **Montreal Symphony Orchestra / Charles Dutoit.** Decca Ⓕ 410 254-2DH (67 minutes: DDD: 11/84). *Gramophone Award Winner 1985.*

...Shéhérazade. *Coupled with works by* **Berlioz, Debussy** and **Poulenc** Régine Crespin (sop);
  John Wustman (pf); **Suisse Romande Orchestra / Ernest Ansermet.** Decca Ⓕ 417 813-2DH
  (68 minutes: ADD: 11/88). *See review in the Collections section; refer to the Index to Reviews.*
...Ma mère l'oye. **Bizet** Symphony in C major. **Scottish Chamber Orchestra / Jukka-Pekka Saraste.**
  Virgin Classics Virgo Ⓑ VJ7 59657-2 (64 minutes: DDD: 12/91).
...La valse. **Bartók** Dance Suite, Sz77. **Satie** Parade. **Busoni** Tanzwalzer, Op. 53. **Liadov**
  Kikimora, Op. 63. **Chabrier** Le roi malgré lui – Fête polonaise. **Liszt** Mephisto Waltz No. 2,
  S111. **Philharmonia Orchestra / Igor Markevitch.** Testament mono Ⓕ SBT1060* (77 minutes:
  ADD: 2/96).

| New review |

Ravel Daphnis et Chloé[a]. La valse. [a]**Berlin Radio Chorus; Berlin Philharmonic Orchestra / Pierre
  Boulez.** DG Ⓕ 447 057-2GH (71 minutes: DDD: 12/95). Recorded 1993-4. *Gramophone Editor's
  choice. Selected by Soundings.*   Ⓔ

Increasingly, for considering modern recordings of *Daphnis*, it seems you must banish memories of
1959 Monteux; put behind you the most playful, mobile, texturally diaphanous, rhythmically supple
account of the score ever recorded; one that is uniquely informed by history and self-less conductorial
wisdom (and one that perhaps presents the work as a 'choreographic chamber symphony'). For some,
Monteux's view may remain a rather moderate one – certainly in terms of basic tempo and basic
dynamic range; and Ravel's score suggests tempos and dynamics which modern performances, and
especially recordings, have more faithfully reproduced (not necessarily to its advantage). Boulez has,
of course, acquired 20 years of conductorial wisdom (not least in subtle accommodations of pace and
general phrasing) since his first New York recording of *Daphnis* (now on Sony). And here he has the
Berlin Philharmonic Orchestra – on top form – to sustain and shape melody within some of his
strikingly slow tempos (such as the opening, and Part 3's famous "Daybreak"), and who remain
'composed' in his daringly fast ones (the "Dance of the young girls around Daphnis" and the "Danse
guerrière" – one of the most exciting on disc). Just occasionally, you feel that there are parts of the
work that interest him less than others (Chloé's "Danse suppliante", and the 'amours' of the
"Pantomime"). But anyone who doubts Boulez's ability to achieve, first, a sense of ecstasy should
hear this "Daybreak"; secondly, a refined radiance (rather than ripe refulgence), should try the first
embrace (track 5, 2'49"; at this point, this is also one of the very few recordings where you can hear
the chorus); or, thirdly, to characterize properly the supernatural, listen to the 'flickering' accents he
gives the start of the string *tremolo* chords in the "Nocturne".

The chorus work, not least in the so-called "Interlude", is outstanding; the harmonic boldness of
this passage was just as startling in New York, but the Berlin chorus, unlike the New York one, are
here properly set back. Vowel sounds are varied; the dynamics are just as powerfully graded and the
passage builds superbly to the "Danse guerrière", with off-stage brass perfectly placed and timed. In
general, DG's recording – a sumptuous Jesus-Christus Kirche production – strikes exactly the right
compromise between clarity and spaciousness, much as Decca's did for Dutoit. Finer details, dynamic
extremes and internal balances aren't quite as consistently observed as in the Rattle, either from the
podium or from the mixing desk, but that production sounds comparably studio-bound. With the
added lure of an expansive and often massively powerful *La valse* (spectacular timpani), this is now
the most recommendable modern *Daphnis* available.

Ravel Daphnis et Chloé[a]. Rapsodie espagnole[b]. Pavane pour une infante défunte[b]. [a]**Chorus of the
  Royal Opera House, Covent Garden; London Symphony Orchestra / Pierre Monteux.** Decca
  Historic Ⓜ 425 956-2DM* (74 minutes: ADD: 5/90). Item marked [a] from SXL2164 (12/59),
  recorded 1959, [b]SXL2312 (7/62), recorded 1961. *Gramophone classical 100.*   ⒺⒺⒺ
Ravel Daphnis et Chloé. **New England Conservatory Choir; Boston Symphony Orchestra / Charles
  Munch.** RCA Victor Living Stereo Ⓜ 09026 61846-2* (54 minutes: ADD: 3/94). From VICS1297
  (12/70). Recorded 1955.   ⒺⒺ

Diaghilev's ballet *Daphnis et Chloé*, based on a pastoral romance by the ancient Greek poet Longus,
was first produced in June 1912, with Nijinsky and Karsavina in the title roles and choreography by
Mikhail Fokine. Pierre Monteux conducted the first performance, and 47 years later he recorded his
peerless interpretation for Decca. Though the Second Suite from the ballet is familiar to concert-goers
and makes an effective piece in its own right, the full score, with wordless chorus, conveys still greater
atmosphere and magic. No work of more sheer sensual beauty exists in the entire orchestral
repertoire, and Monteux was its perfect interpreter. He conducts with a wonderful sense of clarity and
balance: every important detail tells, and there is refinement of expression, yet inner strength too. The
LSO play with superlative poetry and skill, and the chorus is magnificent in its tonal blend and colour.
The *Rapsodie espagnole* and *Pavane* are also given ideal performances, and the recordings show off
Decca's exceedingly high standards during the late 1950s and early 1960s. Another landmark *Daphnis*,
Munch's with the Boston Symphony Orchestra made in stereo, sounds equally astonishing in RCA's
transfer (available with or without the mono Roussel coupling, listed below). Robert Layton, writing
in *Gramophone*, and comparing Monteux with Munch "succumbed more readily to the heady
intoxication, the dazzling richness of colour and virtuosity" of the Munch. Both Monteux and
Munch (along with Ansermet and more recently Dutoit) understood the dangers of extremes and
excessive lingering in this score; of sentiment turning into syrup and Ravel's "Choreographic

Symphony" (his own term) falling apart. It should be noted that, though their recordings balance Ravel's complex score more skilfully and imaginatively than most modern contenders, the score's huge range of dynamics (almost overwhelming in the recent recordings from Rattle and Nagano, listed below) could not be fully realized by the technology of the time.

Additional recommendations ...

...Daphnis et Chloé. **Montreal Symphony Chorus and Orchestra / Charles Dutoit.** Decca ⒡ 400 055-2DH (56 minutes: DDD: 3/83).   ⒢

...Daphnis et Chloé – Suite No. 2. Boléro. **Debussy** La mer. Prélude à l'après-midi d'un faune. **Berlin Philharmonic Orchestra / Herbert von Karajan.** DG Galleria Ⓜ 427 250-2GGA (64 minutes: ADD: 7/89).   ⒢⒢

...Alborada del gracioso. Rapsodie espagnole. Valses nobles et sentimentales. Pavane pour une infante défunte. **Debussy** Images. **Chicago Symphony Orchestra / Fritz Reiner.** RCA Victor Gold Seal Ⓜ GD60179* (68 minutes: ADD: 1/90).   ⒢⒢

...Alborada del gracioso. Rapsodie espagnole. La valse. Pavane pour une infante défunte. Le tombeau de Couperin. **Ibert** Escales. **Detroit Symphony Orchestra / Paul Paray.** Mercury Living Presence Ⓜ 432 003-2MM* (67 minutes: ADD: 4/91).   ⒢

...Daphnis et Chloé[a]. **Roussel** Bacchus et Ariane – Ballet Suite No. 2[b]. [a]**New England Conservatory Choir;** [a]**Alumni Chorus; Boston Symphony Orchestra / Charles Munch.** RCA Victor Gold Seal [a]stereo/[b]mono Ⓜ GD60469* (71 minutes: ADD: 12/91).   ⒢⒢

...Daphnis et Chloé. Boléro. **City of Birmingham Symphony Orchestra / Sir Simon Rattle.** EMI ⒡ CDC7 54303-2 (74 minutes: DDD: 6/92).

...Daphnis et Chloé – Suite No. 2. Rapsodie espagnole. Pavane pour une infante défunte. Alborada del gracioso. Boléro. **Chicago Symphony Orchestra / Daniel Barenboim.** Erato ⒡ 2292-45766-2 (63 minutes: DDD: 12/92).

...Daphnis et Chloé. **London Symphony Chorus and Orchestra / Kent Nagano.** Erato ⒡ 4509-91712-2 (58 minutes: DDD: 7/93).   ⒢⒢⒢

...Daphnis et Chloé[a]. **Debussy** Khamma.[a]**Het Groot Omroepkoor; Royal Concertgebouw Orchestra / Riccardo Chailly.** Decca ⒡ 443 934-2DH (74 minutes: DDD: 10/95). *See review under Debussy; refer to the Index to Reviews.*

...Pavane pour une infante défunte. **Koechlin** Choral sur le nom de Fauré. **Fauré** Requiem, Op. 48[a]. Pavane, Op. 50. **Schmitt** In memoriam Gabriel Fauré, Op. 72 – Scherzo. [a]**Sylvia McNair** (sop); [a]**Thomas Allen** (bar); **Academy of St Martin in the Fields** and [a]**Chorus / Sir Neville Marriner.** Philips ⒡ 446 084-2PH (54 minutes: DDD: 1/96).

...Daphnis et Chloé – Suite No. 2. **Kodály** Háry János – Suite. Variations on a Hungarian folksong, "The Peacock". **Concertgebouw Orchestra / Willem Mengelberg.** Archive Documents Mengelberg Edition mono ⒡ ADCD115* (70 minutes: AAD: 3/96).

...Pavane pour une infante défunte. Ma mère l'oye – Suite. **Debussy** La mer. Prélude à l'après-midi d'un faune. **Royal Concertgebouw Orchestra / Carlo Maria Giulini.** Sony Classical ⒡ SK66832 (64 minutes: DDD: 11/95).

Ravel String Quartet in F major.
Vaughan Williams On Wenlock Edge[ab]. String Quartet No. 1 in G minor. [a]**Philip Langridge** (ten); [b]**Howard Shelley** (pf); **Britten Quartet** (Peter Manning, Keith Pascoe, vns; Peter Lale, va; Andrew Shulman, vc). EMI ⒡ CDC7 54346-2 (78 minutes: DDD: 2/92). Recorded 1990-91.

This outstanding disc from the Britten Quartet brings together several works which have far more in common than one might at first imagine. Vaughan Williams spent a short study vacation in Paris during 1908 hoping, on his own admission, to acquire "a little French polish" from Ravel, who himself took part in the French première of his student's song cycle, *On Wenlock Edge*. Ravel's String Quartet receives a provocative, and yet totally convincing reading from the Britten Quartet, who choose to dwell upon the polarization of tonal and melodic content in this work to a greater degree than any of their rivals on disc, all of whom offer the more usual coupling in the shape of the Debussy Quartet. *On Wenlock Edge*, a setting of six poems selected from A.E. Housman's set of 63 poems, *A Shropshire Lad*, is heard here in a quite exceptional performance from the tenor, Philip Langridge, joined by pianist Howard Shelley and the Britten Quartet. Langridge recognizes the irony and understatement of Housman's verse, whilst exploiting its more sinister undertones with searching skill, as he does in the uncanny dialogue between the living and the dead, in "Is my team ploughing", bringing chilly pallor to his delivery of the opening stanza in particular. It would be difficult to match the communicative power of this performance even in the concert-hall. The Brittens also excel in a crystalline and devoted account of Vaughan Williams's underrated G minor Quartet, which sounds more than usually weighty and musically coherent in this fluid and sharply perceived reading. The technical aspects of the playing are second to none, while its added sensitivity contributes to an involving and frequently moving musical experience. The recorded sound is brilliant and immediate, and this disc is a clear triumph from every conceivable viewpoint.

Additional recommendations ...

...String Quartet. **Debussy** String Quartet. **Quartetto Italiano.** Philips Silver Line Ⓜ 420 894-2PSL (57 minutes: ADD: 10/88).   ⒢

...String Quartet. **Debussy** String Quartet in G minor, Op. 10. **Carmina Quartet.** Denon ⒡ CO-75164 (62 minutes: DDD: 3/93).

...String Quartet. **Beethoven** String Quartet No. 10 in E flat major, Op. 74, "Harp". **Mozart** String Quartet No. 1 in G major, K80, "Lodi". **Sharon Quartet.** Koch International Classics Ⓢ DICD920171 (74 minutes: DDD: 10/94).

...String Quartet. **Debussy** String Quartet. **Menu** Sonatine. **Parisii Quartet.** Auvidis Valois Ⓕ V4730 (68 minutes: DDD: 10/95).

...String Quartet. **Debussy** String Quartet. **Stravinsky** Three Pieces for String Quartet. **Lindsay Quartet.** ASV Ⓕ CDDCA930 (61 minutes: DDD: 12/95).

New review

Ravel Piano Trio in A minor.
Debussy Premier trio in G major. **Julie Rosenfeld** (vn); **Gary Hoffman** (vc); **André Previn** (pf). RCA Victor Red Seal Ⓕ 09026 68062-2 (48 minutes: DDD: 11/95).

There was an old HMV LP with a youthful looking André Previn on the sleeve (no longer available) and coupling the Ravel Trio and Shostakovich E minor Trio, and very good it was too. Now an older Previn returns to the Ravel, and with his colleagues brings to it the same affection, together with a chaste quality wholly appropriate to this composer who evinced an honourable bashfulness yet whose passion is unfailingly genuine and moving – surely one reason for his immense popularity today. The Trio is one of the largest and grandest of chamber works, yet its rhetoric is without hollowness (and how rare that is in French music!) and it somehow just stays within the bounds of chamber music: oddly enough, one of the most shattering climaxes comes in the slow movement. A rich yet un-glitzy recording helps this intensely felt yet refined performance, and altogether the artists offer a memorable musical experience. Debussy's long lost piano trio is a youthful work that he probably would have hated to have played at all, but scholars don't always mind about that sort of thing. Having come to light fairly recently, this jejune piece now has several performances on disc. Undoubtedly it needs skilful playing to avoid seeming embarrassingly weak alongside the Ravel, and the present artists do a very decent job, presenting its naïvety without apology. Their disc is not generous at 48 minutes, but the performance of the Ravel above all makes it value for money.

Additional recommendations ...

...Piano Trio. **Chausson** Piano Trio in G minor, Op. 3. **Beaux Arts Trio.** Philips Ⓕ 411 141-2PH (4/85).

...Piano Trio. **Chausson** Concert for Violin, Piano and String Quartet in D major, Op. 21. **Joshua Bell** (vn); **Steven Isserlis** (vc); **Jean-Yves Thibaudet** (pf); **Takács Quartet.** Decca Ⓕ 425 860-2DH (62 minutes: DDD: 1/91). *See review under Chausson; refer to the Index to Reviews.*

...Piano Trio. **Debussy** Premier Trio in G major. **Fauré** Piano Trio in D minor, Op. 120. **Solomon Trio.** IMP Ⓕ Masters MCD41 (68 minutes: DDD: 7/92).

...Piano Trio. **Debussy** Premier Trio in G major. **Schmitt** Très lent. **Joachim Trio.** Naxos ③ 8 550934 (57 minutes: DDD: 8/95).

Ravel Violin Sonatas – 1897; 1927.
Debussy Violin Sonata.
Pierné Violin Sonata, Op. 36. **Gérard Poulet** (vn); **Noël Lee** (pf). Arion Ⓕ ARN68228 (65 minutes: DDD: 9/94). Recorded 1993. *Gramophone Editor's choice.*

The special significance of this performance of Debussy's Sonata – his last work – is that it was written for the violinist's father Gaston Poulet, who gave the première in 1917 with the composer at the piano; a second performance by the same artists in September was Debussy's last public appearance. Gérard Poulet is very impressive in this beautiful, mercurial and ultimately melancholy piece – which, he says, his father taught him "in every detail". This performance, therefore, is probably as close as we can get to the authentic preservation of the composer's intentions. His tone is warm yet delicate, and the lilt and fantasy of the sonata emerge strikingly, with an idiomatic flexibility of tempo and dynamics. The recording, too, is a good one, with just the right amount of atmosphere, although the piano could have been placed a bit more forwardly, not least because Lee is such a fine artist: Nadia Boulanger called him "one of the finest musicians I have ever met". Ravel's Violin Sonata of 1927 also gets a strong performance. Rightly, the playing style is quite different here, and the edgy lyricism of the first movement is perfectly caught, as is the bittersweet quality of the Blues and the barely suppressed hysteria of the *Perpetuum mobile*. As for Ravel's one-movement Sonata of 1897, which remained unplayed until 1975, this performance brings out its naïve charm, though it reveals little of the composer we know. Pierné's Sonata (1900) is a welcome addition to the current catalogue, passionate and brilliant and in every way rewarding. Altogether, an outstanding disc.

Additional recommendations ...

...Violin Sonata (1927). **Prokofiev** Violin Sonata No. 2 in D major, Op. 94a. **Stravinsky** Divertimento. **Viktoria Mullova** (vn); **Bruno Canino** (pf). Philips Ⓕ 426 254-2PH (61 minutes: DDD: 8/90).

...Violin Sonata (1927)[a]. Trois poèmes de Stéphane Mallarmé[b]. Chansons madécasses[c]. Piano Trio[d]. [bc]**Sarah Walker** (mez); [ad]**Marcia Crayford** (vn); [ad]**Christopher van Kampen** (vc); [d]**Ian Brown** (pf); [bc]**Nash Ensemble / Lionel Friend.** Virgin Classics Ⓕ VC5 45016-2 (70 minutes: DDD: 6/94).

...Violin Sonata (1927). **Prokofiev** Violin Sonatas – No. 1 in F minor, Op. 80; No. 2 in D major, Op. 94a. **Shlomo Mintz** (vn); **Yefim Bronfman** (pf). DG Masters Ⓜ 445 557-2GMA (74 minutes: DDD: 11/95).

Ravel Gaspard de la nuit[a]. Valses nobles et sentimentales[b]. Jeux d'eau[c]. Miroirs[c]. Sonatine[b]. Le tombeau de Couperin[b]. Prélude[a]. Menuet sur le nom de Haydn[a]. A la manière de Borodine[a]. Menuet antique[a]. Pavane pour une infante défunte[a]. A la manière de Chabrier[a]. Ma mère l'oye[d]. **Pascal Rogé,** [d]**Denise-Françoise Rogé** (pfs). Double Decca Ⓜ 440 836-2DF2 (two discs: 142 minutes: ADD: 10/94). Items marked [a] from SXL6700 (3/75), [b]SXL6674 (11/74), [cd]SXL6715 (11/75). Recorded 1973-4.   ⒼⒼ

Everything is expressed with a classic restraint, elegance and economy, an ideal absence of artifice or idiosyncrasy. Rogé, exemplifying the finest French pianism, knows precisely where to allow asperity to relax into lyricism and vice versa, and time and again he finds that elusive, cool centre at the heart of Ravel's teeming and luxuriant vision. True, those used to more Lisztian but less authentic Ravel may occasionally find Rogé diffident or *laissez-faire*. But lovers of subtlety will invariably see him as illuminating and enchanting. How often do you hear *Ma mère l'oye* given without a trace of brittleness or archness, or find *Jeux d'eau* presented with such stylish ease and tonal radiance? Rogé may lack something of Thibaudet's menace and high-flying virtuosity in "Scarbo" (listed below) but how memorably he recreates Ravel's nocturnal mystery. Even if one misses a touch of cruelty behind Ondine's entreaty (her menace viewed, as it were, from a safe distance) few pianists can have evoked her watery realm with greater transparency. Overall, this is arguably the finest recording available of Ravel's piano works.

Additional recommendations ...

...Gaspard de la nuit. **Prokofiev** Piano Sonata No. 6 in A major, Op. 82. **Ivo Pogorelich** (pf). DG Ⓔ 413 363-2GH (52 minutes: DDD: 11/84).   ⒼⒼ

...Ma mère l'oye. **Fauré** Dolly Suite, Op. 56. **Bizet** Jeux d'enfants. **Katia and Marielle Labèque** (pfs). Philips Ⓔ 420 159-2PH (56 minutes: DDD: 11/87).

...Gaspard de la nuit. Sonatine. Piano Concerto in G major[a]. **Martha Argerich** (pf); [a]**Berlin Philharmonic Orchestra / Claudio Abbado.** DG Galleria Ⓜ 419 062-2GGA (54 minutes: ADD: 12/87).   ⒼⒼ

...Pavane. Le tombeau de Couperin. Sérénade. Jeux. Valses nobles et sentimentales. La valse. **Louis Lortie** (pf). Chandos Ⓔ CHAN8620 (66 minutes: DDD: 5/89).

...Gaspard de la nuit. Menuet antique. Menuet sur le nom de Haydn. A la manière de Borodine. A la manière de Chabrier. Prélude. Miroirs. Sonatine. **Louis Lortie** (pf). Chandos Ⓔ CHAN8647 (74 minutes: DDD: 10/89).

...Miroirs – Alborada del gracioso. *Coupled with works by* **Brahms, Chopin, Enescu** and **Liszt Dinu Lipatti** (pf). EMI Références mono Ⓜ CDH7 63038-2* (66 minutes: ADD: 11/89).   ⒼⒼⒼ

...Boléro. Introduction and Allegro. La valse. Ma mère l'oye. Rapsodie espagnole. **Louis Lortie, Hélène Mercier** (pfs). Chandos CHAN8905 (65 minutes: DDD: 3/91).

...Sérénade grotesque. Menuet antique. Pavane pour une infante défunte. Jeux d'eau. Sonatine. Miroirs. Gaspard de la nuit. Menuet sur le nom de Haydn. Valses nobles et sentimentales. Prélude. A la manière de Borodine. A la manière de Chabrier. Le tombeau de Couperin. **Jean-Yves Thibaudet** (pf). Decca Ⓔ 433 515-2DH2 (two discs: 130 minutes: DDD: 11/92).

...Gaspard de la nuit. Jeux. Le tombeau de Couperin. Valses nobles. **Gordon Fergus-Thompson** (pf). ASV Ⓔ CDDCA805 (72 minutes: DDD: 12/92).

...A la manière de Borodine. A la manière de Chabrier. Menuet antique. Menuet sur le nom de Haydn. Miroirs. Pavane pour une infante défunte. Prélude. Sérénade grotesque. Sonatine. **Gordon Fergus-Thompson** (pf). ASV Ⓔ CDDCA809 (68 minutes: DDD: 10/93).

...(arr. Sadlo) Ma mère l'oye – Pavane de la Belle au bois dormant; Les·entretiens de la belle et la bête; Petit Poucet; Laideronette, Imperatrice des Pagodes; Le jardin féerique. Rapsodie espagnole. **Bartók** Sonata for Two Pianos and Percussion, Sz110. **Martha Argerich, Nelson Freire** (pfs); **Peter Sadlo, Edgar Guggeis** (perc). DG Ⓔ 439 867-2GH (56 minutes: DDD: 10/94). *Gramophone Editor's choice. See review under Bartók; refer to the Index to Reviews.*   ⒼⒼⒼ

...Gaspard de la nuit. **Chopin** Nocturnes, Op. 37 – No. 1 in G minor; No. 2 in G major. Polonaise in F sharp minor, Op. 44. Berceuse in D flat major, Op. 57. Etude in G flat major, Op. 10 No. 5. **Mozart** Rondo in A minor, K511. **Konstantin Lifschitz** (pf). Denon Ⓔ CO-78908 (66 minutes: DDD: 12/94). .   ⒼⒼ

...La parade. Pavane pour une infante défunte. Sérénade grotesque. A la manière de Chabrier. A la manière de Borodine. Menuet antique. Jeux d'eau. Menuet sur le nom de Haydn. Prélude. Sonatine. Miroirs. **François-Joël Thiollier** (pf). Naxos Ⓢ 8 550683 (75 minutes: DDD: 2/95).

...Miroirs. Sonatine. Jeux d'eau. **Debussy** Pour le piano. Estampes. **Lilya Zilberstein** (pf). DG Ⓔ 439 927-2GH (74 minutes: DDD: 2/95).

...Gaspard de la nuit. Sonatine. Valses nobles et sentimentales. La valse. **Boris Berezovsky** (pf). Teldec Ⓔ 4509-94539-2 (57 minutes: DDD: 3/95).

...Jeux d'eau. *Coupled with works by* **Prokofiev, Brahms, Chopin** and **Liszt Martha Argerich** (pf). DG The Originals Ⓜ 447 430-2GOR (71 minutes: ADD: 6/95). *See review in the Collections section; refer to the Index to Reviews.*   ⒼⒼ

...Sonatine. *Coupled with works by* **Stravinsky, Scriabin, Berg, Messiaen, Britten** and **Copland Shura Cherkassky** (pf). Decca Ⓟ 433 657-2DH (79 minutes; ADD: 2/96). *See review in the Collections section; refer to the Index to Reviews.* Ⓖ

...Miroirs. Valses nobles et sentimentales. **Liszt** Etudes d'exécution transcendante, S139 – No. 1, Preludio; No. 2, Etude; No. 3, Paysage; No. 5, Feux follets; No. 11, Harmonies du soir. **Sviatoslav Richter** (pf). Praga mono/stereo Ⓑ CMX354009* (65 minutes: ADD: 6/96).

New review

Ravel Gaspard de la nuit. Prélude. Menuet sur le nom de Haydn. Jeux d'eau. Le tombeau de Couperin. **Huseyin Sermet** (pf). Auvidis Valois Ⓕ V4755 (59 minutes: DDD: 7/96).

Here is not only a subtle and distinguished reassessment of *Gaspard de la nuit*, a score in danger of being blunted by overfamiliarity, but a romantic reaction to the sort of stiffness and rigidity that too often passes for an authentic Gallic style. "Ondine" shimmers with seductive rubato and stylish turns of phrase, making her entreaty hard to resist, while "Le gibet" is a true and macabre nocturne, teeming with nuance and variety. "Scarbo", too, is given a superb performance, yielding to few in terms of whirlwind virtuosity and excelling many in characterization. In such imaginative and re-creative hands we encounter a multi-faceted tone-poem rather than a brittle and colourless concert *étude*. A missing bass note in the penultimate bar is a small price to pay for such dark and opalescent magic and throughout this cycle one is grateful for infinite shades of *pianissimo* rather than a more familiar, generalized and impersonal *forte*. The *Prélude* is given with a special ease and translucency and the *Menuet sur le nom de Haydn* is more serene than acerbic. However, in *Jeux d'eau* Sermet's freedom or leeway comes close to laxness and, later, his gracefully flowing "Forlane" from *Le tombeau de Couperin* softens too much of this antique dance's piquancy. However, there are some elegant compensations for such occasional looseness, notably in a light-fingered, *détaché* spin through the opening "Prelude", and an enviably fleet and mercurial "Toccata". The recordings are warm and luminous and this is the first volume in a complete set of Ravel's solo piano works.

Ravel L'enfant et les sortilèges. **Françoise Ogéas** (sop) Child; **Jeanine Collard** (contr) Mother, Chinese cup, Dragonfly; **Jane Berbié** (sop) Sofa, She Cat, Squirrel, Shepherd; **Sylvaine Gilma** (sop) Fire, Princess, Nightingale; **Colette Herzog** (sop) Bat, Little Owl, Shepherdess; **Heinz Rehfuss** (bar) Armchair, Tree; **Camille Maurane** (bar) Grandfather Clock, Tom Cat; **Michel Sénéchal** (ten) Teapot, Little Old Man (Mr Arithmetic), Frog; **Chorus and Children's Voices of French Radio; French Radio National Orchestra / Lorin Maazel.** DG Ⓕ 423 718-2GH* (43 minutes; ADD: 3/89). Notes, text and translation included. From SLPM138675 (6/61). Recorded 1960. *Gramophone Award Winner 1989. Selected by Sounds in Retrospect.* ⓐⓖⓢ

This is a Desert Island Disc if ever there was one. Every musical and verbal point in Ravel's brilliantly ingenious, deliciously witty and entirely enchanting score is brought out by a well-nigh perfect cast, backed by first class orchestral playing; and the recording is as vivid as anyone could wish. The story is that of a petulant brat who breaks the china, pulls the cat's tail, pricks the pet squirrel with a pen-nib, puts the fire out by upsetting the kettle on it, tears the wallpaper and his books and snaps off the pendulum of the grandfather clock – only to find that all these come to life and turn on him. Their anger is appeased only when he tends the squirrel's paw; and finally the naughty child, having seen the error of his ways, falls tearfully into his mother's arms. Everyone will have their own favourite passages but the last pages of the opera, in particular, are hauntingly beautiful. An absolute gem of a disc.

Additional recommendation ...

...L'enfant et les sortilèges. **Soloists; Maîtrise, Chorus and National Orchestra of French Radio / Ernest Bour.** Testament mono SBT1044* (43 minutes: ADD: 2/95). *Gramophone Award Winner 1995.* Ⓖ

New review

Ravel L'enfant et les sortilèges[a]. Shéhérazade[b]. Shéhérazade – fairy overture. [a]**Colette Alliot-Lugaz** (sop) Child; [a][b]**Catherine Dubosc** (sop) Sofa, Bat, Owl, Princess; [a]**Marie-Françoise Lefort** (sop) Shepherdess, Fire, Nightingale; [a]**Odette Beaupré** (mez) Squirrel, Dragon-fly, She-cat; [a]**Claudine Carlson** (mez) Mother, Chinese cup, Shepherd; [a]**Georges Gautier** (ten) Teapot, Little Old Man, Frog; [a]**Didier Henry** (bar) Clock, Tom-cat; [a]**Lionel Sarrazin** (bass) Armchair, Tree; **Montreal Symphony Orchestra / Charles Dutoit.** Decca Ⓕ 440 333-2DH (73 minutes: DDD: 10/95). Notes, texts and translations included. Recorded 1992.

The sound quality of this fine Decca recording of Ravel's intoxicating opera is of such splendid clarity that every nuance of this witty and highly emotional score can be heard, without any sacrifice where the voices and text are concerned. Dutoit and the Montreal forces play with obvious care and affection. Of all operas, this is one where orchestral texture and balance is of the utmost importance. Among the soloists, Odette Beaupré is a sensual and characterful Dragon-fly and Squirrel. Marie-Françoise Lefort is lively as the Fire and contributes to the ensemble of the Shepherds and Shepherdesses – perhaps the saddest, most typical Colette-Ravel moment, it seems to describe in music all the mixed grief and joy at the loss of innocence and childhood. Catherine Dubosc is better as the Sofa, Bat and Owl than she is in the song of the Princess – how one longs for the security of the old-time French singers on the three classic versions (Martha Angelici for Bour, Sylvaine Gilma for Maazel and, the best of all, Suzanne Danco for Ansermet). Colette Alliot-Lugaz does what she can with the role of the Child – it is, of course, mostly an acting, not singing, part but she gets the little solo about the heart of the rose, and deals with it gently. Only the Maazel set – incredibly, nearly 34 years old – comes anywhere near the sound quality of this recording. However, the Dutoit must now be the standard recommendation, with either the Bour or Ansermet as a reminder of the past glories of the French style. The fill-up is generous, with a sumptuous account of the early *Shéhérazade* Overture, contrasting with the better-known song-cycle. Dubosc performs this, making a strong impression, but of course it is a work that has attracted every possible great singer, including Suzanne Danco herself.

Further listening ...

...Tzigane[b]. **Berg** Violin Concerto[a]. **Stravinsky** Violin Concerto in D major[a]. **Itzhak Perlman** (vn); [a]**Boston Symphony Orchestra / Seiji Ozawa;** [b]**New York Philharmonic Orchestra / Zubin Mehta.** DG The Originals 447 445-2GOR.

...Berceuse sur le nom de Gabriel Fauré. Pièce en forme de habanera. Tzigane. *Coupled with works by* **Franck** *and* **Debussy** Violin Sonata. **Augustin Dumay** (vn); **Maria-João Pires** (pf). DG 445 880-2GH (10/95). *See review under Debussy; refer to the Index to Reviews..*   Ⓖ

...Introduction and Allegro. Pièce en forme habanera. *Coupled with* **Poulenc** Oboe Sonata. L'invitation au château. Villanelle[e]. Sonata for Two Clarinets. Trio for Oboe, Bassoon and Piano. Sextet for Piano and Wind Quintet. Sonata for Clarinet and Bassoon. Rapsodie nègre. Clarinet Sonata. Mouvements perpétuels. Flute Sonata. **Soloists.** Cala CACD1018 (2/95).

...Introduction and Allegro. *Coupled with works by* **Debussy, Turina, Villa-Lobos** and **Creston** **Arthur Gleghorn** (fl); **Mitchell Lurie** (cl); **Ann Mason Stockton** (hp); **Hollywood Quartet; Concert Arts Strings / Felix Slatkin.** Testament mono SBT1053* (3/95). *See review in the Collections section; refer to the Index to Reviews.*   ⒼⒼ

...Cinq mélodies populaires grecques. Don Quichotte à Dulcinée. *Coupled with works by* **Poulenc** and **Fauré** Thomas Allen (bar); **Roger Vignoles** (pf). Virgin Classics VC5 45053-2 (5/95). *See review under Poulenc; refer to the Index to Reviews.*

...L'aurore[d]. Matinée de Provence[b]. Tout est lumière[c]. Les bayadères[b]. La nuit[c]. *Coupled with* **Debussy** Printemps[b]. **Caplet** Myrrha[ade]. Tout est lumière[b]. [a]**Sharon Coste,** [b]**Brigitte Desnoues,** [c]**Gaële Le Roi** (sops); [d]**Marc Duguay** (ten); [e]**Jean-François Lapointe** (bar); **Chorus and Orchestra of the Sorbonne, Paris / Jacques Grimbert.** Marco Polo 8 223755 (10/95).

...L'heure espagnole. **Soloists; French Radio National Orchestra / Lorin Maazel.** DG 423 719-2GH (3/89).

...L'heure espagnole. **Soloists; Orchestra of the Opéra-Comique, Paris / André Cluytens.** EMI mono CDM5 65269-2* (9/95).

Thomas Ravenscroft   British *c*1582-*c*1635

Suggested listening ...

...A Round of three Country dances in one. A wooing Song of a Yeoman of Kents Sonne. Browning Madame. The crowning of Belphebe. The Cryers Song of Cheape-Side. Laboravi in gemitu meo. The Marriage of the Frogge and the Mouse. Martin said to his man. Musing mine owne selfe all alone. Ne laeteris inimica mea. Of all the birds that ever I see. There were three ravens. Three blinde Mice. To morrow the Fox will come to towne. Wee be Souldiers three. The wooing of Hodge and Malkyn. Yonder comes a courteous knight. Instrumental works – Fancy No. 1. Fantasia No. 4. Viol Fancy a 5. **The Consort of Musicke / Anthony Rooley.** Virgin Classics Veritas VC7 59035-2 (8/91). ✎

Alan Rawsthorne   British 1905-1971

New review

Rawsthorne Symphonies – No. 1[a]; No. 2, "Pastoral"[b]; No. 3[c]. [b]**Tracey Chadwell** (sop); [ab]**London Philharmonic Orchestra /** [a]**Sir John Pritchard,** [b]**Nicholas Braithwaite;** [c]**BBC Symphony Orchestra / Norman Del Mar.** Lyrita Ⓕ SRCD291 (75 minutes: ADD/DDD: 2/96). Text included. Item marked [a] recorded 1975, [b]1993, [c]1967.

The two vintage recordings have come up as fresh as new paint in these admirable transfers – turn up the volume just a little and the Third Symphony in particular sounds astonishingly fresh nearly 30 years on. The Second Symphony, entrusted to the London Philharmonic under Lyrita stalwart Nicholas Braithwaite, is of more recent origin. Rawsthorne's three symphonies form a powerful triptych. The First (1950) impresses with its urgency and polish. It is a substantial utterance, turbulent and serene by turns, rich in strong ideas, and passionately essayed here by Pritchard and the LPO. The Second, of nine years later (*A Pastoral Symphony*) inhabits an altogether more relaxed and delicate landscape than its moody predecessor, yet with no diminution in terms of concentration or proportional elegance. In the *Andante* finale, Rawsthorne incorporates a radiant setting (pleasingly delivered on this occasion by soprano Tracey Chadwell) of a poem in praise of summer by Henry Howard, Earl of Surrey (1516-47): it exhibits a grace and gentle melancholy which are entirely characteristic of its creator. Braithwaite and the London Philharmonic have the measure of this likeable score, and the sound is full and airy to match. Del Mar and the BBC SO prove themselves to be no less eloquent protagonists of the Third Symphony (1964). This is at once the darkest, most extended and profound of the three. Ambitious in scope and evincing a fastidious craftsmanship, its emotional kernel comprises the second movement "Alla Sarabanda", a noble, deeply felt processional, which contains some of Rawsthorne's most intense, anguished inspiration. A hearty welcome for another Lyrita winner.

Further listening ...

...Clarinet Concerto. *Coupled with* **Jacob** Mini-Concerto. **Cooke** Clarinet Concerto. **Thea King** (cl); **Seattle Northwest Chamber Orchestra / Alun Francis.** Hyperion CDA66031 (10/89).

...Piano Concerto No. 2. Concerto for Piano, Strings and Percussion No. 1. Double Piano Concerto[a]. **Geoffrey Tozer,** [a]**Tamara-Anna Cislowski** (pfs); **London Philharmonic Orchestra / Matthias Bamert.** Chandos CHAN9125 (4/93).

Jean-Féry Rebel
French 1661-1747

Rebel Les élémens. Les caractères de la danse. Le tombeau de Monsieur de Lully. **Les Musiciens du Louvre / Marc Minkowski.** Erato Ⓕ 2292-45974-2 (48 minutes: DDD: 11/93). 🎵 Recorded 1992.
ⒼⒼ

Jean-Féry Rebel, a contemporary of Couperin, was among those composers who lent real distinction to the comparatively unsung period of French baroque music between Lully's death and the full flowering of Rameau's genius. In *Les élémens* (1737) the composer, in accordance with intellectual trends of the time, evokes Nature in many of its movements; and at times it is quite startlingly vivid as you will hear at once in the harmonically confused opening measures of the overture. Each element is allotted its own distinctive character, Earth recognizable by its tied bass notes, Water by upward and downward scale passages on the flutes, Air by reiterated piccolo trills and Fire by brilliant upper string passagework. The second of the suites on this delightful disc, like *Les élémens*, has both a programmatic and choreographic purpose. *Les caractères de la danse* (1715) consists of a compendium of some of the most popular dances of the time, skilfully interlocked to form a single unit. Third on the disc is a touching and beautifully written three-part sonata *Le tombeau de Monsieur de Lully*. Italian and French manners interweave rewardingly in this heartfelt lament for Louis XIV's redoubtable "surintendant de la musique". Here and throughout the programme the performances are first-rate. All is well documented and superbly recorded. A splendid achievement and a 'must' for all who love music of this period.

Additional recommendation ...

...Les élémens. **Gluck** Alessandro. **Telemann** Sonata (Septett) in E minor. **Cologne Musica Antiqua / Reinhard Goebel.** Archiv Produktion Ⓕ 445 824-2AH (63 minutes: DDD: 12/95). 🎵 *Gramophone* Editor's choice. See review under Gluck; refer to the Index to Reviews.

Max Reger
German 1873-1916

New review

Reger Piano Concerto, Op. 114[a]. Suite im alten Stil, Op. 93. [a]**Love Derwinger** (pf); **Norrköping Symphony Orchestra / Leif Segerstam.** BIS Ⓕ CD711 (67 minutes: DDD: 5/96). Recorded 1994.

Leif Segerstam may occasionally be wilful or unpredictable, but he is never boring and this Reger CD makes an extremely strong case for some fine but relatively unfamiliar music. Reger's Piano Concerto is comfort food for all lovers of chromaticism and counterpoint, a vast canvas (44 minutes at this showing) sized up with the help of Brahms's B flat and rich in interpretative potential. Comparing Derwinger and Segerstam with Gerhard Oppitz and Horst Stein finds the latter consistently faster (by nearly five minutes overall), more sharply focused, less prone to rhetorical exaggeration and less sensitive to key transitions. Segerstam's creative credentials (he has a number of works to his credit, including over 30 string quartets) guarantee a minimum of 'inside information': one senses that he knows precisely where Reger is coming from. Both pianists give excellent accounts of the beautiful *Largo* but Oppitz is preferable at the start of the closing *Allegretto* where Derwinger more suggests an effortful *Giocoso* than the prescribed *con spirito*. The only other version currently in the catalogue is a fine 1959 performance by Serkin and Ormandy (on Sony, MPK46452, 12/91); however, the transfer leaves a good deal to be desired and could only really be recommended to those collectors who are specifically interested in 'historic' recordings. As to the *Suite im alten Stil*, this is by far the best recording available – a light, affectionate and warmly played affair in excellent sound. The first movement is something of a Third *Brandenburg* sound-alike; there's a haunting *Largo* and a delightful, *echt*-Regerian fugue that takes seven-and-a-half minutes to broaden from a sprightly *Allegro con spirito* to a monumental *Quasi largo*.

Additional recommendation ...

...Piano Concerto. **Gerhard Oppitz** (pf); **Bamberg Symphony Orchestra / Horst Stein.** Koch Schwann 311058.
ⒼⒼ

Reger Four Symphonic Poems after Arnold Böcklin, Op. 128. Variations and Fugue on a Theme of J.A. Hiller, Op. 100. **Royal Concertgebouw Orchestra / Neeme Järvi.** Chandos Ⓕ CHAN8794 (67 minutes: DDD: 3/90). Recorded 1989.
ⒼⒼ

Reger Variations and Fugue on a Theme of Beethoven, Op. 86. Eine Ballettsuite in D major, Op. 130. Four Symphonic Poems after Arnold Böcklin, Op. 128. **Norrköping Symphony Orchestra / Leif Segerstam.** BIS Ⓕ CD601 (72 minutes: DDD: 6/94). Recorded 1993.   Ⓖ

Mention of Reger's name in 'informed' circles is likely to produce a conditioned reflex: "Fugue!". In his day he was the central figure of the 'Back to Bach' movement, but he was also a romantic who relished all the expressive potential of the enormous post-Wagnerian orchestra. Then came the slender acerbities of the next generation of neo-classicists, and Reger's backward glances were deemed inflated and in shocking taste. Until relatively recently he has proved largely unexportable from his native Germany. Chandos, not surprisingly, exploit the open spaces of the Amsterdam Concertgebouw, forsaking some of the healthy transparency of the Davis disc (listed below) for an extra spatial dimension; a more sumptuous glow. With Järvi's instinct for pacing in late romantic music, and his great orchestra's evident delight in the copious riches of the discovery, for the *Hiller* Variations, this disc is very tempting. Anyone who warms to Vaughan Williams's *Tallis Fantasia* will immediately respond to the "Hermit playing the violin", the first of the four *Böcklin* tone-poems; Debussy's "Jeux de vagues" from *La mer* was obviously in Reger's mind for the second poem "At play in the waves"; and the "Isle of the dead" is Reger's no less doom- and gloom-laden response to the painting that so captured Rachmaninov's imagination. The final painting, "Bacchanal", was described as a Munich beer festival in Roman costume – an entirely fitting description for Reger's setting of it!

Segerstam's disc is well programmed to show off the contrasting sides of orchestral Reger: firstly, the familiar champion of absolute music and the German tradition in the Variations; secondly, in *Eine Ballettsuite*, the unlikely purveyor of a relatively lightly scored *divertissement* of six dance or character portraits "for musical epicures"; and finally, in the *Böcklin* Poems, one who succumbed to the lure of programme music and 'impressionist' colour and timbre. Maybe the epicurean pleasures of *Eine Ballettsuite* are savoured by Sir Colin Davis with a little more humour, and, as recorded, brighter timbres, but Segerstam's Swedish orchestra in every way match Davis's Bavarians' evident love for the music (the oboe and cello solos in Segerstam's "Pierrot et Pierette" are exquisite). In both the first and third *Böcklin* Poems Segerstam is closer to Reger's metronome markings than the faster, more freewheeling Järvi. Segerstam is also, throughout the Poems, more acutely responsive to the extremes – and the minutest gradations in between – of both pace and dynamics. For the first and third poems (and parts of the second) this means that you are now aware just how much of this music dwells in the regions of *pianissimo* and beyond, and also how fine an impressionist Reger was. In the Poems, Järvi, it has to be said, has the advantage of a great orchestra, rather than a very good one, and a more accommodating acoustic. BIS give Segerstam another of their textbook recordings, that is to say: an ears only, halfway back in an average size, modern concert-hall experience (levels are lower for the *Böcklin* Poems).

Additional recommendations ...

...Hiller Variations. Eine Ballettsuite, Op. 130. **Bavarian Radio Symphony Orchestra / Sir Colin Davis.** Orfeo Ⓕ C090841A (59 minutes: DDD; 4/87).   Ⓖ

...Hiller Variations. **Zemlinsky** Gesänge nach Maeterlinck, Op. 13ᵃ. [a]**Hedwig Fassbender** (mez); **Czech Philharmonic Orchestra / Václav Neumann.** Supraphon Ⓕ 11 1811-2 (60 minutes: DDD: 7/93).

...Hiller Variations. Mozart Variations, Op. 32. **New Zealand Symphony Orchestra / Franz-Paul Decker.** Naxos Ⓢ 8 553079 (72 minutes: DDD: 7/95).

New review
Reger Six Morceaux, Op. 24. Silhouetten, Op. 53. Blätter und Blüten, Op. 58. **Jean Martin** (pf). Naxos Ⓢ 8 550932 (79 minutes: DDD: 10/95). Recorded 1994.

A valuable treat for all inquisitive piano buffs and dedicated Regerians, even if some of the music is of variable quality. Least impressive, perhaps, are the *Six Morceaux*, Op. 24 (1898) – all of them fairly derivative, especially of Chopin (No. 2), Schubert (No. 4) and Brahms (No. 5, especially the sprawling 14-minute "Rhapsodie" that serves as No. 6). Whether they quite repay their taxing demands is open to some doubt, whereas the *Silhouetten* Op. 53 (1900) and *Blätter und Blüten* Op. 58 (1900-02) are quite another matter. Both sets are rich in playful modulations and lyrical ideas. Op. 53's opening "Ausserst lebhaft" anticipates the mischievous Reger of the *Hiller* Variations; the Ninth recalls the Grieg of the *Lyric Pieces*, the Tenth, Reger's own *Ballettsuite* (of some 13 years later), and the Twelfth, Brahms's late *Intermezzos*. All could enrich any programme of late-romantic piano music, while the more aphoristic (and technically simpler) *Blätter und Blüten* are lighter in tone, their high-points being (at least on first acquaintance) a charming "Frühlingslied" and a thoughtful pair of "Romanzen", the second of which recalls Smetana's piano music at its finest. Seventy-nine minutes constitute a fair chunk out of anyone's leisure timetable but, with the present context, 44 of them (that is, Op. 53 and 58) could be very happily spent listening. And certainly Jean Martin plays well and is realistically recorded.

Reger Six Preludes and Fugues, Op. 131*a*. Preludes and Fugues, Op. 117 – No. 1 in B minor; No. 2 in G minor; No. 3 in E minor; No. 5 in G major; No. 6 in D minor; No. 7 in A minor; No. 8 in E minor. **Mateja Marinković** (vn). ASV Ⓜ CDDCA876 (two discs: 82 minutes: DDD: 9/94). Recorded 1993.

Reger's knowledge of, and feeling for, the violin were all-embracing, and although his winding melodic lines can sometimes prove maddeningly discursive, there is much beauty in the writing – the A minor Prelude, or the E minor Prelude, Op. 131*a* providing particularly good sampling points. Bach is of course an overwhelming presence: quite apart from direct quotations there is the all-pervasive influence of the unaccompanied Sonatas and Partitas, especially with regard to Reger's fugues, which invariably start with a hint of Bachian *déjà-vu* before modulating way beyond the baroque's customary orbit. All 13 works here are surprisingly varied in theme and tone, although even the most enthusiastic listener is advised not to take in more than a few at a time. The prize-winning violinist Mateja Marinković is professor at both the Royal Academy of Music and the Guildhall School of Music, and his warm-centred, tonally true performances serve Reger handsomely. A major addition to the solo violin repertory on CD, and a must for all Regerians.

Reger Drei geistliche Gesänge, Op. 110. Drei Gesänge, Op. 39. **Danish National Radio Choir / Stefan Parkman.** Chandos Ⓕ CHAN9298 (56 minutes: DDD: 10/94). Texts and translations included. Recorded 1993-4.   Ⓖ

Visions of myriad notes covering the page would frighten most choirs away, but these singers are made of sterner stuff. For them complex contrapuntal structures, devious chromatic harmonies and textures so thick you need a forage knife to get through them, hold no terrors. Rather they not only weave their way through Reger's characteristically tangled scores without a moment's doubt, but illuminate the paths so clearly one hardly notices the dense musical undergrowth all around. Parkman has a clear-sighted view of what is wanted and, aided by singers whose pure, perfectly blended tone is in itself a joy to hear, he follows his vision unfalteringly: everything falls neatly into place making real musical sense. The hefty Op. 110 Motets (ostensibly in five, but often diverging into as many as nine independent parts) can, and usually do, sound oppressively heavy, but here offer some of the most sublimely beautiful moments yet captured on CD. A triumph of skill over adversity if ever there was one.

Further listening ...

...Variations and Fugue on a Theme of Mozart, Op. 132. *Coupled with* **Hindemith** Symphonic Metamorphosis on Themes of Carl Maria von Weber. **Bavarian Radio Symphony Orchestra / Sir Colin Davis.** Philips 422 347-2PH (9/90).   ⒼⒼ

...Konzert im alten Stil, Op. 123[a]. Sinfonietta in A major, Op. 90. **Peter Rosenberg,** [a]**Harold Orlovsky** (vns); **Bamberg Symphony Orchestra / Horst Stein.** Koch Schwann 313542 (8/94).

...Latin Requiem, Op. 145*a*. Requiem, Op. 144*b*. **Soloists; North German Radio Chorus and Symphony Orchestra / Roland Bader.** Koch Schwann 313004.

...Serenades[a] – D major, Op. 77*a*; G major, Op. 141*a*. Three Suites for Viola, Op. 131*d* – G minor; D major, E minor. [a]**Anna Noakes** (fl); [a]**Barry Wilde** (vn); **George Robertson** (va). ASV CDDCA875 (9/94).   Ⓖ

...An die Hoffnung, Op. 124[b]. *Coupled with* **Brahms** Schicksalslied, Op. 54[a]. **Rihm** Hölderlin-Fragmente[c]. **R. Strauss** Drei Hymnen, Op. 71[b]. [b]**Karita Mattila** (sop); [c]**Johannes M. Kosters** (bar); [a]**Leipzig Radio Chorus; Berlin Philharmonic Orchestra / Claudio Abbado.** Sony Classical SK53975 (3/95).

...Three Duets, Op. 111*a*. *Coupled with* **Dvořák** 13 Moravian Duets, B107. **Brahms** Duets – Op. 20: Weg der Liebe I; Weg der Liebe II; Die Meere; Op. 66: Am Strande; Jägerlied. Four Duets, Op. 61. Guter Rat, Op. 75 No. 2. **Juliane Banse** (sop); **Brigitte Fassbaender** (mez); **Cord Garben** (pf). Koch Schwann 312592 (8/95).

...Pieces, Op. 59 – No. 5, Toccata in D minor; No. 6, Fugue in D major; No. 9, Benedictus. *Coupled with works by* **T. Dubois, Franck, Gigout, Langlais, Murrill** Carillon. **Peeters** Aria, Op. 51. **Vierne** Pièces de fantaisie, Op. 54 – No. 6, Carillon de Westminster. **Andrew Lucas** (org). Naxos 8 550955 (11/94). *See review in the Collections section; refer to the Index to Reviews.*

Giulio Regondi   Italian 1822-1872

New review

The Great Regondi, Volumes 1 and 2. [a]**D'Anna Fortunato** (mez); [b]**David Starobin** (gtr); [c]**Douglas Rogers** (concertina); [d]**Julie Lustman** (pf). Bridge Ⓕ BCD9039 and BCD9055 (two discs, oas: 63 and 57 minutes: DDD: 12/95). ✍ Texts included.

    BCD9039 – Morceau de concert in B flat major, Op. 12, "Les oiseaux"[cd]. Serenade in A major[cd]. 10 Etudes[b]. *BCD9055* – As slowly part the shades of night[ad]. L'avviso[ad]. Absence[ad]. Tell me heart! Why so desponding?[ad]. Leisure moments[c] – Nos. 2-4, 5, 7 and 8. Introduction and Caprice, Op. 23[b]. Remembrance[c]. Rêverie, Op. 19[b].

Our hero's mother died in giving birth to him in 1822, probably in Geneva, after which he was brought up by a man whose name was Regondi, whose relationship to him is uncertain, and whose exploitation of him was inhuman. Giulio was forced to practise the guitar for five hours a day and by the time he was eight he had been 'exhibited' in most European courts. A contemporary portrait shows him with long fair hair, velvet-clad like Little Lord Fauntleroy, having never known a normal childhood. In 1830 he met Sor and Carcassi in Paris; both were so impressed that they dedicated substantial works to him. One year later he toured England, with such success that he settled here where, apart from triumphant visits to Europe in the 1840s, he remained for the rest of his days.

Unusually for a guitarist, his name was coupled in programmes with those of Mendelssohn, Clara Schumann, Moscheles and others. Sometime in the early 1830s Regondi senior absconded with the considerable profits, leaving Giulio with a £5 note. Friends and admirers helped him to come to terms with his situation and to learn how to make his own way; he resumed his career. He was hailed everywhere as a genius and, though contemporary reports contain a good deal of purple prose, the virtuosic nature and high compositional quality of his known works (there is reason to believe that many others have been lost) suggest that they were not far wrong. As if this were not enough, Regondi enthusiastically embraced the recently invented concertina (c1833), achieving equal fame with it as both performer and composer. After his death, the popularity of both the guitar and the concertina declined rapidly! The natural home of Regondi's music, overtly romantic and punctuated with demonstrative flourishes, is the salon, where the passionate nature of his performances was directly communicated to his close-at-hand audiences. We cannot recapture that personal immediacy (any more than any violinist can bring Paganini back to life), but these discs, made by the cream of the specialists (using period instruments), come as close to it as anyone is likely to get. Regondi's obituary in *The Musical World* stated that "All he did has died with him", but its writer could not have foreseen these discs. Their excellence extends to the quality of their recording and the accompanying annotation.

Further listening ...
...Introduction and Caprice, Op. 23. *Coupled with* **Mertz** Six Schubertian Songs. **Paganini** Grand Sonata in A major – second and third movements. Ghiribizzi, MS43 – No. 20, Andante in C major on Mozart's "Là ci darem la mano"; No. 37, Adagietto con espressione in A major. Sonatina No. 1 in C major. **Schubert** (arr. Tárrega) Piano Sonata in G major, D894 – Menuetto. Moment musical in F minor, Op. 94 No. 3. **Chopin** (arr. Tárrega) Preludes – No. 7 in A major; No 15 in D flat major; No. 20 in C minor. **Tárrega** Preludes – Endecha; Oremus; Allegro; Andante sostenuto; Lágrima. Capricho árabe. Mazurkas – Adelita; Marieta; Sueño. Pavana. Alborada. **Tom Kerstens** (gtr). Conifer CDCF518 (9/94).

Steve Reich   American 1936-

Suggested listening ...
...Drumming. Six Pianos. Music for Mallet Instruments, Voices and Organ. **Steve Reich and Musicians.** DG 20th Century Classics 427 428-2GC2 (9/89).   ⓖⓖ
...Four Organs. *Coupled with* **Moran** Three Dances. **D. Lang** Face so pale. **Volans** Kneeling Dance. **Piano Circus.** Argo 440 294-2ZH (1/94).   ⓖ
...Six Pianos. *Coupled with* **Riley** In C. **Piano Circus.** Argo 430 380-2ZH (6/91).
...The Four Sections[a]. Music for Mallet Instruments, Voices and Organ[b]. [b]**Steve Reich and Musicians;** [a]**London Symphony Orchestra / Michael Tilson Thomas.** Elektra Nonesuch 7559-79220-2 (6/91).   ⓖⓖ
...Tehillim (Psalms) for Women's Voices and Instruments. **Vocal ensemble; instrumental ensemble / George Manahan.** ECM New Series 827 411-2.   ⓖ
...The Cave. **The Steve Reich Ensemble / Paul Hillier.** Nonesuch 7559-79327-2 (3/96).

Antoine-Joseph Reicha   Bohemian/French 1770-1836

Suggested listening ...
...Cello Quintets – No. 1 in A major; No. 2 in F major; No. 3 in E major. **Anner Bylsma** (vc); **L'Archibudelli.** Sony Classical Vivarte SK53118 (10/93). ✒
...Clarinet Quintet in B flat major, Op. 89. *Coupled with* **Hummel** Clarinet Quintet in E flat major. **Weber** Clarinet Quintet in B flat major, J182. **Charles Neidich** (cl); **L'Archibudelli.** Sony Classical SK57968 (9/95). ✒

Antanas Rekašius   Lithuanian/USSR 1928-

Suggested listening ...
...Music for Strings. *Coupled with* **Tüür** Insular Deserta. **Urbaitis** Lithuanian Folk Music. **Juozapaitis** Perpetuum mobile. **Vasks** Cantabile. **Kutavičius** Northern Gates. **Ostrobothnian Chamber Orchestra / Juha Kangas.** Finlandia 4509-97893-2 (11/95).

Henriette Renié   French 1875-1956

Suggested listening ...
...Contemplation. *Coupled with works by* **Casella, Rosetti, Spohr, Debussy, Damase, Tournier, Prokofiev** and **Fauré** Naoko Yoshino (hp). Philips 446 064-2PH (2/96). *See review in the Collections section; refer to the Index to Reviews.*

Ottorino Respighi

New review

Respighi Piano Concerto in A minor. Toccata. Fantasia slava. **Konstantin Scherbakov** (pf); **Slovak Radio Symphony Orchestra / Howard Griffiths.** Naxos ⑤ 8 553207 (51 minutes: DDD: 11/95). Recorded 1994.

All these pieces are otherwise available in decent performances, but at this price how could anyone with the slightest weakness for Respighi hesitate? Scherbakov and Griffiths do a good deal more than dutifully go through the motions, the soloist in particular playing with delicacy and affection, grateful for the (quite frequent) opportunities to demonstrate how well he would play Liszt or Rachmaninov, but in the *Toccata* he is interested as well in Respighi's more characteristic modal vein; as a Russian, he demonstrates that this too, like so much in Respighi, was influenced by the time he spent in Russia. Russian soloist, English conductor and Slovak orchestra all enjoy the moment in the *Fantasia slava* where Respighi presents a morsel of Smetana in the evident belief that it's a Russian folk-dance, but the Concerto and the *Fantasia*, both very early Respighi, are not patronized in the slightest. The central slow section of the Concerto, indeed, achieves something like nobility, and although there is a risk of the pianism in this work seeming overblown and rhetorical, Scherbakov's fondness for Respighi's more fleet-footed manner doesn't let this happen often. The *Toccata* is not so much an exercise in the neo-baroque, often though its dotted and florid figures promise it, more of an essay on how far one can be neo-baroque without giving up a post-Lisztian keyboard style and comfortable orchestral upholstery. But in a slow and florid central section, a rather melancholy aria that passes from the soloist to the oboe, to the strings and back again, there is a real quality of Bachian utterance translated not unrecognizably into a late romantic language (you may be momentarily reminded of Gerald Finzi). Scherbakov sounds touched by it, and obviously wants us to like it. Indeed these are likeable performances of music that needs that sort of help, but repays it. The recordings are more than serviceable, but each work is given only a single track.

Additional recommendations ...

...Piano Concerto. Concerto in modo misolidio. **Geoffrey Tozer** (pf); **BBC Philharmonic Orchestra / Sir Edward Downes.** Chandos Ⓕ CHAN9285 (65 minutes: DDD: 8/94).

...Toccata[a]. Tre corali. Fantasia slava[a]. Belfagor – overture. [a]**Geoffrey Tozer** (pf); **BBC Philharmonic Orchestra / Sir Edward Downes.** Chandos Ⓕ CHAN9311 (60 minutes: DDD: 1/95).

Respighi Concerto gregoriano. Poema autunnale.
Saint-Saëns Violin Concerto No. 3 in B minor, Op. 61. **Pierre Amoyal** (vn); **French National Orchestra / Charles Dutoit.** Decca Ⓕ 443 324-2DH (69 minutes: DDD: 7/95). Recorded 1993. ❷❸

This is big, bold, romantic violin playing, just what both concertos need. The Respighi especially, perhaps: he had recently discovered Gregorian chant and modality, and the *Concerto gregoriano* was the first big work to exploit these. But Respighi was a violinist long before he discovered plainchant, and the noun of the work's title is at least as important as its adjective. Moreover in numerous of his compositions he shows himself well acquainted with Saint-Saëns, who also knew about chant and the modes, as the 'third subject' of his Third Concerto's finale demonstrates. The two concertos make a good coupling, in short, and an excellent demonstration that the manner appropriate to Saint-Saëns's work, conceived for a great virtuoso (Sarasate), pays dividends in the Respighi as well. The *Concerto gregoriano*'s problem is that its first two movements are both rhapsodic and relatively slow. A performance that reticently takes the description 'Gregorian' too seriously risks differentiating them inadeqately. "Quelques longueurs en ce Concerto?" asks the author of the French notes on this coupling. Not in a performance as sumptuous as this, one which finds strength and drama in what can seem dulcet meandering; and when the finale arrives and is given suitable vigour we seem to be hearing another of Respighi's Roman pictures, a jubilant and richly coloured one. The Saint-Saëns is just as good: Amoyal's tone is sweetly seductive in legato playing, opening out admirably to the more flamboyant gestures, never becoming hectic in the virtuoso passages. That 'third subject' in the finale is not played ethereally, as some violinists take it: Amoyal knows very well that its function is to return triumphantly in the brass (Saint-Saëns might well have subtitled it, as Respighi did his finale, "Alleluia") and he plays it firmly and brightly. Both Amoyal and Dutoit seem to be enjoying Respighi's richly coloured, warmly elegaic *Poema autunnale*, discovering maybe that a work dutifully chosen as an appropriate filler is perhaps the best music here. The recording manages both to place Amoyal in a flatteringly forward perspective and to allow a satisfying fullness to orchestral tuttis.

Additional recommendations ...

...Concerto gregoriano[a]. Poema autunnale. Ballata delle gnomidi. [a]**Lydia Mordkovitch** (vn); **BBC Philharmonic Orchestra / Sir Edward Downes.** Chandos Ⓕ CHAN9232 (64 minutes: DDD: 4/94).

...Concerto gregoriano. Concerto all'antica. **Andrea Cappelletti** (vn); **Philharmonia Orchestra / Matthias Bamert.** Koch Schwann Ⓕ 311242 (63 minutes: DDD: 8/94).

Respighi The Pines of Rome. The Fountains of Rome. Roman Festivals. **Montreal Symphony Orchestra / Charles Dutoit.** Decca Ovation Ⓜ 430 729-2DM (60 minutes: DDD: 8/94). From 410 145-2DH (11/83). Recorded 1982. *Selected by Sounds in Retrospect.* ❷❸

Respighi's three orchestral showpieces inspired by Rome have often been dismissed as merely musical picture postcards, but in ripely committed performances like Dutoit's, stunningly recorded, there are few works to match them in showing off the glories of a modern orchestra in full cry. Dutoit's performance is as brilliant as any, but he also finds a vein of warm expressiveness in the writing as well as rhythmic point, so adding to the vividness of atmosphere. The atmospheric central movements of *Pines* have such a lovely radiance that one is not a bit surprised the nightingale feels the need to respond to the beauty of the evening. Similarly, the picturesque *Fountains* all spring to watery life, with detail beautifully observed and naturally revealed by the recording. In *Roman Festival*s, which can often merely sound noisy, there is a nice balance between pictorial vividness and brashness. There is an unsurpassed edge of brilliance in this recording, emphasized by the microphone placing of the Decca engineers, and the acoustics of St Eustache, Montreal combine glitter and translucence. This was always one of the most reliable couplings of Respighi's trilogy of tetralogies; it's now good value as well.

Additional recommendations ...

...Pines of Rome. Fountains of Rome. Roman Festivals. **Philadelphia Orchestra / Riccardo Muti.** EMI Ⓕ CDC7 47316-2 (3/86).   Ⓖ

...Pines of Rome. Fountains of Rome. Roman Festivals. **NBC Symphony Orchestra / Arturo Toscanini.** RCA Victor Gold Seal mono Ⓜ GD60262* (60 minutes: ADD: 1/91).   Ⓖ

...Pines of Rome. Fountains of Rome. Roman Festivals. **Philadelphia Orchestra / Eugene Ormandy.** RCA Victor Silver Seal Ⓑ VD60486 (62 minutes: ADD: 2/91).

...Pines of Rome. Fountains of Rome. Roman Festivals. **Academy of St Martin in the Fields / Sir Neville Marriner.** Philips Ⓕ 432 133-2PH (64 minutes: DDD: 4/92).

...Pines of Rome; Fountains of Rome; Roman Festivals. **Royal Philharmonic Orchestra / Enrique Bátiz.** Naxos Ⓢ 8 550539 (61 minutes: DDD: 8/92).

...Pines of Rome. Fountains of Rome. **Mussorgsky** Pictures at an Exhibition. **Fritz Reiner.** RCA Victor Ⓑ 09026 61401-2* (70 minutes: ADD: 8/93).   ⒼⒼ

...Pines of Rome. Roman Festivals. **Verdi** The Four Seasons. **Cleveland Orchestra / Lorin Maazel.** Decca Ⓜ 425 052-2DM (76 minutes: ADD: 11/93).

...Fountains of Rome[b]. **Verdi** Messa da Requiem[a]. La traviata[b] – Preludes, Act 1 and 3. I vespri siciliani – Overture[b] . **Wolf-Ferrari** I quattro rusteghi – Intermezzo[b]. Il segreto di Susanna – Overture[b]. **Rossini** Guillaume Tell – Overture[b]. [a]**Dame Elisabeth Schwarzkopf** (sop); [a]**Oralia Dominguez** (mez); [a]**Giuseppe di Stefano** (ten); [a]**Cesare Siepi** (bass); [a]**Chorus and Orchestra of La Scala, Milan,** [b]**Santa Cecilia Academy Orchestra, Rome / Victor de Sabata.** EMI Références mono Ⓜ CHS5 65506-2* (two discs: 148 minutes: ADD: 9/95).

...Pines of Rome. Fountains of Rome. **Debussy** La mer. **Chicago Symphony Orchestra / Fritz Reiner.** RCA Victor Living Stereo Ⓜ 09026 68079-2 (62 minutes: ADD: 9/95).

Respighi Church Windows. Brazilian Impressions. Roman Festivals. **Cincinnati Symphony Orchestra / Jesús López-Cobos.** Telarc Ⓕ CD80356 (71 minutes: DDD: 7/94). Recorded 1993. *Gramophone Editor's choice.*

The conventional coupling of *Pines, Fountains* and *Festivals* makes sense, of course. They are seen as the 'essential' Respighi, and one could easily argue that neither *Church Windows* nor *Brazilian Impressions* is quite as successful (and that *Festivals* is the weakest of the Roman trilogy anyway). The only answer to that, López-Cobos seems to suggest, is to take the music perfectly seriously and pay scrupulous attention not just to its potential for sonorous spectacle but to its wealth of beautifully crafted detail. The gong at the end of the second movement of *Church Windows* is magnificently resonant, as is the organ in the finale, and the work is given an extra inch or two of stature by sensitive handling of those moments that need but don't always get delicacy. He pays such care to character and detail in "Butantan", that creepy depiction of a snake-farm in *Brazilian Impressions*, that you can not only recapture the real, crawling horror that Respighi experienced there, but discover in the music also a queer sort of Debussian grace as well. And as for *Roman Festivals*, well, what's wrong with 20-odd minutes of wide-screen spectacular once in a while? But if every colour is precisely rendered, the quiet passages as affectionately turned as they are here (and it's surprising how much of this score is quiet), what skill there is to be found in it, what a gift for immaculately precise instrumental detail. With that sort of handling all three pieces sound quite worthy of sharing shelf space with *Pines* and *Fountains*. The recording is spectacular and the orchestral playing is in the luxury class.

Additional recommendation ...

...Church Windows. Brazilian Impressions. **Philharmonia Orchestra / Geoffrey Simon.** Chandos Ⓕ CHAN8317 (45 minutes: DDD: 8/84).

New review

Respighi Antiche danze ed arie per liuto. Aria. Berceuse. **Sinfonia 21 / Richard Hickox.** Chandos Ⓕ CHAN9415 (63 minutes: DDD: 2/96). Recorded 1995.

There is no shortage of recordings of these three suites of *Ancient Airs and Dances*, but Hickox's are among the very best available, ideally combining chamber-orchestra delicacy of detail (and very beautiful playing) with full-orchestra richness where required. Not an opaque, stodgy richness, mark you: one of the most appealing qualities of these performances is that the purity of the original melodies is always perceptible: thus *Campanae Parisiennses* (from the Second Suite) eventually becomes very full, but never heavy, and the slow tempo Hickox chooses is ideal for its touching solemnity. There is a wide range of dynamic and texture, especially valuable in the Third Suite where you really do seem to be hearing a chamber group and an ample string orchestra simultaneously, or rather in alternation. The clean colours of Respighi's scoring are precisely rendered, never muddied or coarsened, and the dance rhythms are crisp and exuberant. There is a little confusion over the two additional items, prominently labelled "premier recordings". Both are from a set of Six Pieces for violin and piano which Respighi wrote around 1901, soon afterwards arranging the *Aria* for strings and organ, and the *Berceuse* for strings alone. The *Aria* also appears in the Suite in G for strings and organ of 1905 but not, as the booklet alleges, in the Suite for flute and strings of the same year, nor in the "2nd Suite" for that combination, which does not exist. Both the Six Pieces and the Suite in G have been recorded before. The *Aria*, here transcribed for strings alone by Potito Pedarra, is in Respighi's richest 'neo-Bach' manner, but the charming *Berceuse* is an indication that he could write suave, long-limbed melodies without any need to be 'neo-' anything in particular. The recordings are very fine indeed.

Respighi Gli uccelli. Antiche danze ed arie per liuto – Suites Nos. 1 and 3. Trittico botticelliano.
    Orpheus Chamber Orchestra. DG Ⓕ 437 533-2GH (69 minutes: DDD: 7/93). Recorded 1991.

ⒼⒼⒼ

This is astonishing playing. To do without a conductor when performing Respighi might seem an easier task than in an authentic masterpiece, but these suites require so much care over details of phrasing, colour, balance and articulation that not a few skilled conductors have failed to distil their freshness and charm unalloyed. But there are no conducted performances that excel these in their immaculate care over texture, delicacy of nuance and precision of tuning. Nor do they lack character, by any means: the orchestra's method of rehearsal, democracy tempered by the authority of a leader elected for each work, seems to have ensured a pretty well ideal balance between unanimity and soloistic individuality. If you add an infectious sense of enjoyment (not least, in these purist times, the not quite respectable enjoyment of Respighi's hand-colouring of his monochrome originals) and solo playing of great refinement, it becomes hard to imagine how these readings could be improved on. The recording is as transparent as one could wish.

Additional recommendations ...

...Gli uccelli. Trittico botticelliano. Il tramonto[a]. Adagio con variazioni[b]. [a]**Linda Finnie** (contr);
    [b]**Raphael Wallfisch** (vc); **Bournemouth Sinfonietta / Tamás Vásáry.** Chandos Ⓕ CHAN8913
    (65 minutes: DDD: 3/92).

... Ballata delle gnomidi. Adagio con variazioni[a]. Trittico botticelliano. Suite in G major for Strings
    and Organ[b]. [a]**Alexander Baillie** (vc); [b]**Leslie Pearson** (org); **Philharmonia Orchestra / Geoffrey
    Simon.** Cala Ⓕ CACD1007 (69 minutes: DDD: 3/93).

...Gli uccelli. Antiche danze ed arie per liuto – Suites Nos. 1 and 3. Trittico botticelliano. **Saint Paul
    Chamber Orchestra / Hugh Wolff.** Teldec Ⓕ 4509-91729-2 (70 minutes: DDD: 1/95).   Ⓖ

...Antiche danze ed arie per liuto – Suite No. 3. Trittico botticelliano. **Ghedini** Violin Concerto, "Il
    Belprato". **Rota** Concerto for Strings. **Accademia Bizantina / Carlo Chiarappa** (vn). Denon
    Ⓕ CO-78916 (69 minutes: DDD: 3/95). *Gramophone Editor's choice. See review under Ghedini;
    refer to the Index to Reviews.*

Respighi Violin Sonata in B minor.
R. Strauss Violin Sonata in E flat major, Op. 18. **Kyung-Wha Chung** (vn); **Krystian Zimerman** (pf).
    DG Ⓕ 427 617-2GH (52 minutes: DDD: 2/90). Recorded 1988. *Gramophone* Award Winner
    1990.   Ⓖ

This is wonderful violin playing, as richly romantic as both works often demand, but with a wide range of colour to underline the subtleties and the varying tones of voice that both employ. To add to the coupling's appeal, Kyung-Wha Chung's pianist is a musician of exceptional subtlety who is clearly as intent as she is to demonstrate that both sonatas deserve a position much closer to the centre of the repertory than they have so far been given. In the Strauss in particular they succeed eloquently. It is often described as the last work of his apprentice years, but in this performance the mature Strauss steps out from the shadow of Brahms so often and so proudly that its stature as his 'real' Op. 1 seems confirmed. The Respighi is a lesser piece, no doubt, but its melodies and its rhapsodic manner are attractive, and Chung's warm response to Respighi's idiomatic way with the instrument (he was a violinist himself) is infectious. Good and natural-sounding balance between violin and piano is not easy to achieve, but the recording here, significantly helped by Zimerman's combination of poetry and alert responsiveness, is outstandingly successful.

Additional recommendations ...

...Violin Sonata. **Franck** Violin Sonata. **Poulenc** Violin Sonata. **Josef Suk** (vn); **Josef Hála** (pf).
    Supraphon Ⓕ 11 0710-2 (70 minutes: ADD: 5/90).

Respighi Aretusa[a]. Il tramonto[a]. Lauda per la natività del Signore[b]. Trittico botticelliano.
    [b]**Patricia Rozario** (sop); [a]**Dame Janet Baker,** [b]**Louise Winter** (mezzos); [b]**Lynton Atkinson** (ten);
    [b]**Richard Hickox Singers; City of London Sinfonia / Richard Hickox.** Collins Classics Ⓕ 1349-2
    (72 minutes: DDD: 9/92). Texts and translations included. Recorded 1991.

Attention is probably attracted towards this disc in the first place by Dame Janet Baker's presence on it. *Aretusa* and *Il tramonto* are also set to translations of poems by Shelley: colourful works with a wide range of expression, stimulating just that kind of boldness and generosity of utterance in which

Dame Janet is expert. She is in fine voice here, and at the end of *Il tramonto* ("the tomb of the dead self") her tone is stern, strong and dark, intensely personal. Even so, going to the disc initially for these tone-poems for solo voice and orchestra, one may still eventually be most glad of the purchase for its introduction to the choral *Lauda per la natività del Signore.* This was written in the late 1920s and is a most lovely work. It has solo parts for Mary, the Angel and a shepherd (all well taken), but the great joy lies in the choral and orchestral writing, rich and imaginative, its medievalism shot through with delight in the idiom. The better-known *Trittico botticelliano* is highly enjoyable too, and all are fine in performance and recorded sound.

Additional recommendations ...

...Il tramonto[a]. **Martucci** Canzone dei Ricordi[a]. Nocturne, Op. 70 No. 1. [a]**Carol Madalin** (mez); **English Chamber Orchestra / Alfredo Bonavera.** Hyperion Ⓔ CDA66290 (56 minutes: DDD: 7/88).

...Poema autunnale[a]. Suite in G major[b]. Il tramonto[c]. **Menotti** Cantilena e scherzo[d]. [c]**Christopher Trakas** (bar); [a]**Igor Gruppman** (vn); [b]**Hollace C. Koman** (org); [d]**Marian Rian Hays** (hp); [c]**Quartetto di Venezia;** [abd]**San Diego Chamber Orchestra / Donald Barra.** Koch International Classics Ⓔ 37215-2 (63 minutes: DDD: 8/94).

New review

Respighi La bella dormente nel bosco. **Richard Haan** (bar) King, Woodcutter; **Denisa Slepkovská** (mez) Queen, Duchess; **Jana Valásková** (sop) Princess; **Guillermo Dominguez** (ten) Prince April; **Adriana Kohútková** (sop) Blue Fairy, Nightingale; **Ivana Czaková** (sop) Old Woman, Green Fairy; **Dagmar Pecková** (mez) Cuckoo, Cat; **Henrietta Lednárová** (sop) Frog, Spindle; **Igor Pasek** (ten) Jester; **Ján Durčo** (bar) Ambassador; **Adriano** (narr) Mr Dollar Cheques; **Karol Bernáth** (ten) First Doctor; **Márian Smolárik** (bass) Second Doctor; **Stanislav Beňačka** (bass) Third Doctor; **Anton Kúrňava** (bass) Fourth Doctor; **Slovak Philharmonic Chorus; Slovak Radio Symphony Orchestra (Bratislava) / Adriano.** Marco Polo Ⓔ 8 223742 (77 minutes: DDD: 7/96). Italian text included.

Respighi's *La bella dormente nel bosco* ("Sleeping Beauty"), a "musical fairy-tale in three acts", is one of his most unassumingly charming pieces. It was originally written in 1922 for Vittorio Podrecca's famous puppet company, I Piccoli, and was apparently so popular that it stayed in their repertory for over 20 years. Respighi revised it in 1934 as a mime play for children (as with the puppet original, adult singers and actors are placed in the orchestra pit). It tells the familiar Perrault story, in quick-fire doggerel verse, with the difference that 300 years elapse between the evil fairy's magic spell and the arrival of the handsome prince. Thus Act 3 takes place in 1940, still some way in the future when even the revised score was prepared, but it provides Respighi and his librettist with the opportunity to introduce a party of American tourists to the plot, led by Mr Dollar Cheques, bizarrely portrayed here by the conductor of this performance. He and his party arrive to the sound of a cakewalk, and the happy ending is celebrated with a foxtrot. Otherwise the music is characteristically colourful, despite the use of a modest orchestra, and its lyricism is genial and relaxed. It is toy music at times, quoting or distancing emotion rather than expressing it ardently, quite appropriately to a fairy story much of whose action is danced. With the arrival of Prince April (Guillermo Dominguez, a capable lyric tenor), the music no less appropriately grows warmer. The scene of the Princess's awakening (to bird-song in the woodwind, and then an amply lyrical love duet) is effective. So is the very simple but striking slumber music earlier on, the excitably girlish music of the Princess herself, and the delightful humming chorus of spiders, weaving cobwebs to enshroud the sleeping castle. It is, in short, a very pretty miniature opera, giving Respighi more opportunities than most of his other opera plots to demonstrate a neat sense of humour and a rather touching, childlike fantasy. It is admirably performed (the sparkly coloratura of Adriana Kohútková especially effective) and cleanly recorded.

Further listening ...

...Sinfonia drammatica. **BBC Philharmonic Orchestra / Sir Edward Downes.** Chandos CHAN9213 (1/94). Ⓖ

...Belkis, Queen of Sheba – orchestral suite. Metamorphosen modi XII. **Philharmonia Orchestra / Geoffrey Simon.** Chandos CHAN8405 (5/86). Ⓖ

...Adagio con variazioni[a]. *Coupled with* **Elgar** Cello Concerto in E minor, Op. 85[a]. **Milhaud** Cello Concerto No. 1, Op. 136[b]. [a]**Mstislav Rostropovich** (vc); [a]**Moscow Philharmonic Orchestra;** [b]**USSR TV and Radio Large Orchestra / Gennadi Rozhdestvensky.** Russian Disc RDCD11104 (7/94).

...La primavera[a]. Quattro Liriche su poesie popolari armene[ab]. [ab]**Soloists;** [a]**Slovak Philharmonic Chorus;** [a]**Bratislava Radio Symphony Orchestra /** [ab]**Adriano.** Marco Polo 8 223595 (5/95).

...Semirama. **Soloists; Hungarian Radio and Television Chorus; Hungarian State Orchestra / Lamberto Gardelli.** Hungaroton HCD31197/8 (7/93).

Julius Reubke

German 1834-1858

Suggested listening ...

...Sonata on the 94th Psalm in C minor. *Coupled with* **Schumann** Six Fugues on B-A-C-H, Op. 60. **Kevin Bowyer** (org). Nimbus NI5361 (2/94).

Herman Reutter
German 1900-1985

Suggested listening ...
...Fünf antike Oden, Op. 57. *Coupled with works by* **Marx, Dargomïzhsky, Loeffler, A. Busch, Brahms, R. Strauss** and **Gounod** Mitsuko Shirai (mez); Tabea Zimmermann (va); Hartmut Höll (pf). Capriccio 10 462 (9/95). *See review in the Collections section; refer to the Index to Reviews.* Ⓖ

Silvestre Revueltas
Mexican 1899-1940

Revueltas Homenaje a Federico Garcia Lorca[a]. Sensemayá[a]. Ocho x rondo[b]. Toccata[b]. Alcancías[b]. Planos[b]. La noche de los Mayas[c]. [a]**New Philharmonia Orchestra / Eduardo Mata;** [b]**London Sinfonietta / David Atherton;** [c]**Jalapa Symphony Orchestra / Luis Herrera de la Fuente.** Catalyst ℗ 09026 62672-2 (69 minutes: ADD: 2/95). Items marked [a] recorded 1975, [b]1979, [c]1980. *Gramophone Editor's choice.*

If *Gramophone*'s Record Awards included a category for Presentation, this would almost certainly win hands down. To prepare us for the pulsatingly barbaric music of this half-crazed Mexican composer who, after an appallingly stressful life, drank himself to death at an early age, an image of a grisly death's-head is stamped on the disc itself; and the admirably complete documentation and eloquent notes (in interlined English and Spanish, which is unusual) are printed on the back of an 18 by 14 inch reproduction of the picture from which the skull is taken by Mexico's greatest painter, Revueltas's slightly older contemporary, Diego Rivera. The compilation on this disc covers the greater part of the composer's all too brief creative career, and well conveys his "colourful, convulsive, astonishingly powerful and unfailingly original" style, heavily influenced by, but never quoting, folk sources. The *Homenaje* to the murdered poet Lorca was one of his most significant achievements – a long trumpet-led lament curiously interspersed with vivid dance-like episodes. The latter pieces are brilliantly played by the London Sinfonietta, who then sober up for the austere *Planos*, which the composer described as "functional architecture". *Ocho x rondo* is a scherzo (with a gentler central section) for octet; perhaps more immediately striking is a *Toccata* from the same year (1933), which demands (and gets) virtuoso playing from a chamber group. Revueltas's best-known work, the snake-killing ritual *Sensemayá*, is taken by Mata at a deliberate pace which makes it sound quite decorous. There is, however, nothing sedate, except, very properly, in the evocative and beautiful third movement ("Night in Yucatán"), about the performance by the Jalapa (or Xalapa) Symphony under Fuente of the four-movement suite drawn from the music for the film *La noche de los Mayas*: its finale, with an orgy of manic percussion and brass, would almost rouse the dead (which presumably was the scene it accompanied). A fascinating disc.

Further listening ...
String Quartets – No. 1; No. 2, "Agaves"; No. 3; No. 4, "Musica de Feria". **Latin-American Quartet.** New Albion NA062CD (6/94). ⒼⒼ
...Caminos[b]. Musica para charlar[b]. Ventanas[b]. *Coupled with* **Chávez** Sinfonia de Antigona[a]. Symphony No. 4, "Sinfonia romantica"[a]. [a]**Royal Philharmonic Orchestra;** [b]**Mexican State Philharmonic Orchestra / Enrique Bátiz.** ASV CDDCA653 (8/89). ⒼⒼ

Emil Nikolaus von Rezniček
Austrian 1860-1945

Suggested listening ...
...Symphonies – No. 3 in D major; No. 4 in F minor. **Philharmonia Hungarica / Gordon Wright.** Koch Schwann 312032.

Joseph Rheinberger
German 1839-1901

Suggested listening ...
...Organ Concertos – No. 1 in F major, Op. 137; No. 2 in G minor, Op. 177. **Andreas Juffinger** (org); **Berlin Radio Symphony Orchestra / Hartmut Haenchen.** Capriccio 10 336. Ⓖ
...Organ Concerto No. 1 in F major, Op. 137. *Coupled with* **Dupré** Symphony for Organ and Orchestra in G minor, Op. 25. **Michael Murray** (org); **Royal Philharmonic Orchestra / Jahja Ling.** Telarc CD80136 (6/87).

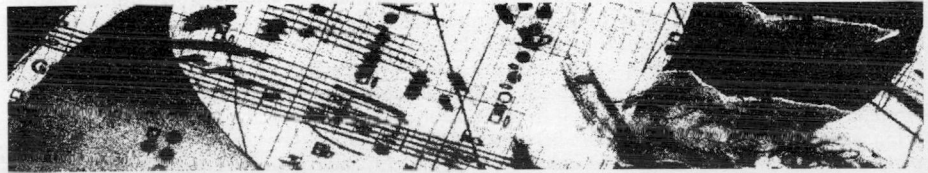

Wolfgang Rihm
German 1952-

Suggested listening ...
...Gesungene Zeit. *Coupled with* **Berg** Violin Concerto. **Anne-Sophie Mutter** (vn); **Chicago
Symphony Orchestra / James Levine.** DG 437 093-2GH (1/93). *Selected by Sounds in Retrospect.
See review under Berg; refer to the Index to Reviews.*   ⓖⓖ
...Hölderlin-Fragmente[c]. *Coupled with* **Reger** An die Hoffnung, Op. 124[b]. **Brahms** Schicksalslied,
Op. 54[a]. **R. Strauss** Drei Hymnen, Op. 71[b]. [b]**Karita Mattila** (sop); [c]**Johannes M. Kösters** (bar);
[a]**Leipzig Radio Chorus; Berlin Philharmonic Orchestra / Claudio Abbado.** Sony Classical SK 53975
(3/95).
...Départ[a]. *Coupled with* **Boulez** Notations I-IV. **Ligeti** Atmosphères. Lontano. **Nono** Liebeslied[a].
[a]**Vienna Jeunesse Choir; Vienna Philharmonic Orchestra / Claudio Abbado.** DG 429 260-2GH
(4/90).   ⓖ

Terry Riley
American 1935-

New review
Riley In C. New Music Theatre; Life on the Water / Terry Riley, Loren Rush. New Albion
ⓕ NA071CD (76 minutes: DDD: 11/95). Recorded live in 1990.
In C (1964), that great classic of early minimalism came of age some years ago. The original recording
(not available in the UK) had the air of an easygoing improvisation, unfolding at leisurely pace during
the course of 40 minutes, whilst Piano Circus on Argo took about half that time. By those standards
this New Albion performance at over 76 minutes, plus applause, has made a meal of things – but you
could say that the history of minimalism since then fully justifies such triumphalism! The ensemble
for *In C* is never specified, but this performance has 30 players plus the percussion beat on marimba.
The line-up is five saxophones, four voices, two synthesizers, two xylophones and a second marimba,
string quartet, flute, two clarinets, two guitars, two trombones, accordion, piano, glockenspiel, drums
and somebody who plays "various instruments". Riley said that he was conscious of the fact that *In
C* was "very democratic, no one had a lead part, everyone supposedly contributing an equal part".
After real excitement, built up and sustained over long stretches, *In C* tails off at the end to leave a
prolonged silence before one person breaks the ritual with applause. The whole conception is utterly
West Coast, beguilingly nostalgic for those who remember the 1960s, and *In C* invigoratingly towers
above its imitators as such a classic should.
Additional recommendation ...
...In C. *Coupled with* **Reich** Six Pianos. **Piano Circus.** Argo 430 380-2ZH (6/91).

Nicolay Rimsky-Korsakov
USSR 1844-1908

Rimsky-Korsakov Scheherazade, Op. 35. Capriccio espagnol, Op. 34. **London Symphony Orchestra /
Sir Charles Mackerras.** Telarc ⓕ CD80208 (60 minutes: DDD: 10/90). Recorded 1990.
Rimsky-Korsakov Scheherazade, Op. 35[a]. Capriccio espagnol, Op. 34[b]. Russian Easter Festival
Overture, Op. 36[b]. [a]**Herman Krebbers** (vn); [ac]**Concertgebouw Orchestra /** [a]**Kyrill Kondrashin;**
[b]**London Symphony Orchestra /** [bc]**Igor Markevitch.** Philips Solo Ⓜ 442 643-2PM (74 minutes:
ADD: 6/95). Item marked [a] recorded in 1980, [b]1963, [c]1965.   ⓖⓖ
Sir Charles Mackerras throws himself into this music with expressive abandon, but allies it to control
so that every effect is realized and the London Symphony Orchestra play these familiar works as if
they were discovering them afresh. Together they produce performances that are both vivid and
thoughtful, while the solo violin in *Scheherazade*, who represents the young queen whose storytelling
skills prolong and finally save her life in the court of the cruel Sultan Shahriar (portrayed by powerful
brass), is seductively and elegantly played by Kees Hulsmann, not least at the wonderfully peaceful
end to the whole work. The finale featuring a storm and shipwreck is superbly done, the wind and
brass bringing one to the edge of one's seat and reminding us that Rimsky-Korsakov served in the
Russian Navy and well knew the beauty and danger of the sea. This sensuous and thrilling work needs
spectacular yet detailed sound, and that is what it gets here, the 1990 recording in Walthamstow Town
Hall being highly successful and giving us a CD that many collectors will choose to use as a
demonstration disc to impress their friends. The performance and recording of the *Capriccio espagnol*
is no less of a success, and this issue is worth every penny of its price.
    Kondrashin's performance of *Scheherazade* is one of the very finest made of Russian music in the
Concertgebouw; it has glamour and brilliance, and the resonance brings a wonderful feeling of
spaciousness in the first movement and adds a thrill to the spectacle of the finale. Kondrashin has the
full measure of this colourful score, while the finale builds up to a feeling of excitement which leads
to a riveting climax at "The Shipwreck". Of course, any performance of this masterpiece stands or
falls by the portrayal of Scheherazade herself by the solo violin, and here the Concertgebouw's leader,
Herman Krebbers dominates the action from the gentle, beguiling opening to his exquisite closing
solo, suggesting that all is well at last between the Sultan and his bewitching Sultana. A brilliant
performance of Rimsky's *Capriccio espagnole* follows, very well played by the LSO under Igor

Markevitch; indeed, the 1963 recording sounds far more lustrous than it did on LP. It is upstaged, however, by Markevitch's performance of the composer's *Russian Easter Festival Overture*, made two years later, when again the aura of the Concertgebouw ambience adds a glow to more remarkable playing from this great orchestra. Altogether a superb disc, and generously full.

Additional recommendations ...

...Scheherazade. **Debussy** La mer. **Chicago Symphony Orchestra / Fritz Reiner.** RCA Victor Gold Seal Ⓜ GD60875* (69 minutes: ADD). ⒼⒼ

...Scheherazade. **Tchaikovsky** Capriccio italien. **Philharmonia Orchestra / Paul Kletzki.** Classics for Pleasure Ⓑ CD-CFP4341 (60 minutes: ADD). Ⓖ

...Scheherazade. **Borodin** Prince Igor – Polovtsian Dances[a]. [a]**Beecham Choral Society; Royal Philharmonic Orchestra / Sir Thomas Beecham.** EMI Ⓕ CDC7 47717-2* (58 minutes: ADD: 9/87). ⒼⒼ

...Scheherazade. **Ravel** Boléro. **London Philharmonic Orchestra / Andrew Litton.** Virgin Classics Virgo Ⓑ VJ7 59658 (64 minutes: DDD: 12/91).

...Scheherazade. **Prokofiev** Lieutenant Kijé – Suite, Op. 60. **London Philharmonic Orchestra / Takuo Yuasa.** EMI Eminence Ⓜ CD-EMX2214 (68 minutes: DDD: 12/93).

...Scheherazade. Russian Easter Festival Overture, Op. 36. **Vienna Philharmonic Orchestra / Seiji Ozawa.** Philips Ⓕ 438 941-2PH (58 minutes: DDD: 6/94).

...Scheherazade. The tale of Tsar Saltan, Op. 57 – Tsar's farewell and departure; Tsarina in a barrel at sea; The three wonders. **Philharmonia Orchestra / Enrique Bátiz.** Naxos Ⓢ 8 550726 (61 minutes: DDD: 6/94).

...Capriccio espagnol. Russian Easter Festival Overture. The Tsar's Bride – Overture. May Night – Overture. The Golden Cockerel – Introduction and Dodon's sleep; Wedding Feast; Death of King Dodon; Finale. **Bolshoi Symphony Orchestra / Alexander Lazarev.** Erato Ⓕ 4509-94808-2 (72 minutes: DDD: 8/94).

...Scheherazade. **Stravinsky** Scherzo fantastique, Op. 3. **Royal Concertgebouw Orchestra / Riccardo Chailly.** Decca Ⓕ 443 703-2DH (59 minutes: DDD: 10/94). Ⓖ

...Scheherazade[a]. **Prokofiev** Romeo and Juliet[b]. [a]**Berlin Radio Symphony Orchestra,** [b]**Leipzig Gewandhaus Orchestra / Karel Ančerl.** Tahra mono Ⓕ TAH119* (68 minutes: DDD: 11/95).

New review

Rimsky-Korsakov Scheherazade, Op. 35. Capriccio espagnol, Op. 34. **London Philharmonic Orchestra / Mariss Jansons.** EMI Ⓕ CDC5 55227-2 (62 minutes: DDD: 7/95). Ⓖ

The first point to distinguish this powerful coupling of *Scheherazade* and *Capriccio espagnol*, from Jansons and the LPO, is the weight and richness of the recording. It has got to be one of EMI's finest, not as analytically transparent as some but vivid and immediate with a thrillingly wide dynamic range. Not that detail is lacking: it is fascinating to register the castanets very clearly at the end of the final "Fandango" of the *Capriccio*, normally obscured in the general hubbub. As to Jansons's interpretation of the main work, he follows up the big bold, brassy opening with a surprisingly restrained account of the main theme as it develops, keeping power in reserve, building up more slowly than usual. What then is consistently striking in all four movements is Jansons's pointing of rhythm, lilting, bouncy and affectionate in a way that distinguishes this from most other versions. This is a *Scheherazade* that dances winningly, less earnest than usual, often suggesting a smile on the face. That is very welcome in a work that, for all its exotic colour and memorable themes, needs persuasive handling if it is not to seem like a lot of introductions leading to introductions, and codas leading to codas, with little meat in the middle. Jansons's control of structure leads to a masterly sense of resolution at the great climax towards the end of the finale, as the main theme returns *fortissimo*. Nowhere does this seem like a virtuoso exercise, brilliant as the playing of the LPO is, not least that of the warmly expressive violin soloist, Joakim Svenheden. Rather, emotionally involved, Jansons finds a rare exuberance in Rimsky-Korsakov's stream of ideas and colours, leading compellingly from one to another. The *Capriccio espagnol* brings a similar combination of expressive warmth and exuberance. In the brilliant "Alborada" at the beginning of the *Capriccio* Jansons's speed is less hectic than some, and with springy rhythms it is made to sound relaxed, jolly rather than fierce. Not that in either work is there any shortage of biting excitement. Particularly in *Scheherazade* choice between versions leaves many options open, but this warmly distinctive account with its opulent sound clearly stands among the strongest contenders.

Rimsky-Korsakov Symphonies – No. 1 in E minor, Op. 1; No. 2 (Symphonic Suite), Op. 9, "Antar"; No. 3 in C major, Op. 32. Russian Easter Festival Overture, Op. 36. Capriccio espagnol, Op. 34. **Gothenburg Symphony Orchestra / Neeme Järvi.** DG Ⓕ 423 604-2GH2 (two discs: 125 minutes: DDD: 2/89). ⒼⒼ

No one is going to claim Rimsky's First and Third Symphonies to be neglected masterpieces. He came to refer to his First (partly written whilst the young naval officer was on duty!) as a "disgraceful composition", and along with the other two symphonies, it was subjected to extensive revision by the later learned master of musical technique. As the equally learned, entertaining and informative essay accompanying this set points out, the opening of the symphony could have been a trial run for the opening of Schumann's Fourth (and a very fine one, too!). It's the beautifully lyrical second theme which reminds us that Rimsky was reared in the country and had the early advantage of a good soaking in folk-song. Though the debt to Glinka is obvious, to our ears classical concerns seem uppermost throughout, and the music is free from anything that could be called exoticism. Not so the Second. Rimsky was a member of the 'Mighty Five', a group of composers (including Mussorgsky, Balakirev and Borodin) sworn to the nationalist cause, professing horror at anything tinged with German academicism and ever searching for subjects on which they could lavish a preference for orchestral colour above form. Rimsky's *Antar* combined these ideals, and more. Our hero of the title is allocated a Berliozian *idée fixe*, an oriental location (the desert of Sham) and the joys of vengeance, power and love from the grateful fairy Gul-Nazar as a gift for saving her from a winged monster. It is, in every way, an antecedent of *Sheherazade* and, after hearing Järvi's rich and eloquently descriptive account, one wonders why it has never attained anything like the same popularity. His Third Symphony reverts to a more academic manner. In 1871 he was invited to join the theory and composition faculty at the St Petersburg Conservatory and, in Tchaikovsky's words, "from contempt of schooling he had turned all at once to the cult of musical technique". Despite a paucity of truly memorable ideas, it is a symphony to admire for its construction and light-as-air orchestration. The set is completed with urgent, vibrant accounts of the *Capriccio espagnol* and the *Russian Easter Festival Overture*, quite the most colourful and exciting versions on disc, and they confirm that the less familiar symphonies could not be in better hands. DG's engineers resist the temptation to glamorize the music and offer a lucid and spacious panorama of sound.

Additional recommendations ...

...Russian Easter Festival Overture. Capriccio espagnol. **Borodin** In Central Asia. Prince Igor – Polovtsian Dances[ab]. **Tchaikovsky** 1812 – overture, Op. 49[bc]. Marche slave, Op. 31. [a]**Torgny Sporsén** (bass); [b]**Gothenburg Symphony Brass Band; Gothenburg Symphony** [b]**Chorus and Orchestra / Neeme Järvi.** DG Ⓕ 429 984-2GH (76 minutes: DDD: 3/91).

...Russian Easter Festival Overture. **Glinka** Ruslan and Ludmilla – Overture. **Ippolitov-Ivanov** Caucasian Sketches, Op. 10. **Tchaikovsky** Francesca da Rimini, Op. 32. Eugene Onegin – Polonaise. **Baltimore Symphony Orchestra / David Zinman.** Telarc Ⓕ CD80378 (69 minutes: DDD: 12/95).

Rimsky-Korsakov Symphonies – No. 1, Op. 1; No. 2, Op. 9, "Antar". **Russian State Symphony Orchestra / Evgeni Svetlanov.** RCA Victor Red Seal Ⓕ 09026 62558-2 (67 minutes: DDD: 11/94). Recorded 1993.   Ⓖ

Rimsky-Korsakov was an inveterate reviser of his own work but in the case of the First Symphony, the 1884 version serves as more or less definitive (the original dates from 1861-65). However, even there, Rimsky's stylistic antecedents are fairly conspicuous, with Schumann prominent among their ranks, especially in the symphony's very opening and the trio section of the third movement. It's an engaging piece, classical in design and reminiscent now of Glinka, now of Balakirev, but full of specifically Rimskian tensions, especially in the first two movements. Svetlanov's recording is a fresh, relatively easygoing affair, while Järvi's (reviewed above) is all bluster and bustle, less incisive than Svetlanov's but very enjoyable none the less. In the case of *Antar*, textual complications are both rife and hopelessly confusing. Rimsky completed his very first version of the score in 1868, then revised it in 1875 and again in 1897. Until quite recently, conductors have tended to favour a 1903 re-working of the 1875 version. The 1875 'original' is more dramatically focused, especially as presented in Svetlanov's latest account. It's a strong, powerfully argued performance, nicely pointed in the first movement's more delicate passages and generally very well recorded.

Additional recommendation ...

...Nos. 1 and 2. Capriccio espagnole, Op. 34. **Bergen Philharmonic Orchestra / Dmitri Kitaienko.** Chandos CHAN9178 (11/93).

New review

Rimsky-Korsakov Symphony No. 3 in C major, Op. 32. Sadko, Op. 5. Mlada – Procession of the Nobles. The Maid of Pskov – Overture. The Tale of Tsar Saltan – The three wonders. The Tsar's Bride – Overture. **Russian State Symphony Orchestra / Evgeni Svetlanov.** RCA Victor Red Seal Ⓕ 09026 62684-2 (76 minutes: DDD: 10/95). Recorded 1993.

Borodin and Tchaikovsky were both hostile to Rimsky-Korsakov's Third Symphony when they heard it in its first version, but not as critical as the composer himself. What we have here is its third and final revision, purged of the excesses of technique that, he wrote in his memoirs, made it all too dry. In this version, which has had several recordings, it is enjoyable less as the solemn exercise to which Borodin objected than as a piece of vivid orchestral writing with some attractive ideas guiding it. It therefore fits easily into a programme of Korsakov orchestral show-pieces, of which the most substantial is the musical picture *Sadko*. Svetlanov is an old hand with this music, and he draws properly colourful performances from the orchestra, clearly and brightly recorded. Serious collectors of Rimsky-Korsakov's symphonies will no doubt have acquired the fine set by Neeme Järvi with the Gothenburg Symphony Orchestra on DG (reviewed above). For those following Svetlanov's series or for what might be called a Rimsky-Korsakov taster, even if not of his best music, the present disc is very acceptable.

Rimsky-Korsakov Sadko. **Vladimir Galusin** (ten) Sadko; **Valentina Tsidipova** (sop) Volkhova; **Sergei Alexashkin** (bass) Okean-More; **Marianna Tarassova** (mez) Lyubava Buslayevna; **Larissa Diadkova** (contr) Nezhata; **Bulat Minjelkiev** (bass) Viking Merchant; **Gegam Grigorian** (ten)

Indian Merchant; **Alexander Gergalov** (bar) Venetian Merchant; **Vladimir Ognovenko** (bass) Duda; **Nikolai Gassiev** (ten) Sopel; **Nikolai Putilin** (bar) Apparition; **Yevgeny Boitsov** (ten) Foma Nazarich; **Gennadi Bezzubenkov** (bass) Luka Zinovich; **Kirov Opera Orchestra / Valery Gergiev.** Philips Ⓟ 442 138-2PH3 (three discs: 173 minutes: DDD: 1/95). Notes, text and translation included. Recorded live in 1993.

Rimsky-Korsakov's operas are not so well represented in the catalogue that one can afford to give anything but a welcome to this complete version from the Maryinsky company, for all its drawbacks. *Sadko* is a panoramic work, packed with numbers, rather less packed with event or with character. The various characters delivering themselves of a song or a ballad or an address are reasonably well contrasted, partly because of Rimsky-Korsakov's skills in drawing on different Russian influences and in differentiating between a simple tonal language for the real world and a more chromatic idiom for the seductive realm of the Sea King (Okean-More) and his daughter Volkhova. It needs a numerous and strong cast who can make the most of its opportunities. Sadko himself is sung by Vladimir Galusin pretty steadily at full volume. He settles down a little as the opera proceeds, and by Act 3 is finding a somewhat more pacific manner. Valentina Tsidipova returns his advances, and makes her own, with a good feeling for line, if one can overcome resistance to the steady vibrato. The Sea King is strongly sung by Sergei Alexashkin, truculent at first but warming his tone somewhat as he comes to accept Sadko. But it is a pity that the best-known number from the opera, the song of the Indian Merchant, should be sung as half-heartedly as it is by Gegam Grigorian. Valery Gergiev leads his forces well, and draws some vigorous, colourful singing from the choruses in their various manifestations. There is, however, a good deal of noise occasioned by the many stage comings and goings, with clumpings and hoarse whisperings as well as tunings-up and applause. The recording has difficulty in catching all the singers equally in their various peregrinations across the stage, but for the most part this is a fair representation of a score that is nothing if not colourful.

Rimsky-Korsakov The Tsar's Bride. **Pyotr Gluboky** (bass) Sobakin; **Ekaterina Kudriavchenko** (sop) Marfa; **Vladislav Verestnikov** (bar) Grigory Gryaznoy; **Nikolai Nizinenko** (bass) Skuratov; **Arkady Mishenkin** (ten) Ivan Lykov; **Nina Terentieva** (mez) Lyubasha; **Vladimir Kudriashov** (ten) Bomelius; **Irina Udalova** (sop) Saburova; **Elena Okolycheva** (contr) Duniasha; **Tatiana Pechuria** (mez) Petrovna; **Vladislav Pashinsky** (bass) Driver; **Nina Larionova** (mez) Servant; **Yury Markelov** (ten) Boy; **Sveshnikov Russian Academy Choir; Bolshoi Theatre Orchestra / Andrey Tchistiakov.** CdM Russian Season Ⓟ LDC288 056/7 (two discs: 146 minutes: DDD: 8/93). Notes and English text included. Recorded 1992.

The Tsar's Bride comes roughly half way in the list of Rimsky-Korsakov's operas (a complicated list, due to various revisions and differing versions). Though there have been Russian-language productions in America and Britain, it has not really caught on in the West. Though there should be a welcome for this new recording (there have been at least two others), one can see why. The story is awkward, turning on the search by the Tsar in question, Ivan the Terrible, for a wife. He chooses Marfa, betrothed to Ivan Lykov but also loved by Grigory Gryaznoy, who in turn is trying to discard his impassioned lover Lyubasha in favour of Marfa. There is a sinister German doctor, Bomelius, who supplies poisons and also love potions: confusion and substitution here lead to Marfa's madness and her final eerie song. Tchaikovsky is the most potent influence on the work. It is cast in separate but linked numbers, and draws in part on the kind of elegant, song-like melodic line of which Tchaikovsky was such a great master. Some of the duets are quite close in manner to those in *Eugene Onegin*. Yet there is also a strong folk influence: Marfa's beautiful aria in Act 2 scene 2 owes much to the Russian predilection for developing a melody out of varied repetition of a single idea. Rimsky-Korsakov was very familiar with the manner, as his own collection of national songs alone goes to show. The aria is tenderly sung by Ekaterina Kudriavchenko, who handles with great sensitivity this portrayal of a figure familiar from many Russian novels and operas, the suffering heroine. Lyubasha is potently sung by Nina Terentieva, somewhat in the charged manner of another Marfa, that of Mussorgsky's *Khovanshchina*. She suggests banked fires of passion, sings her unaccompanied song caressingly, and rounds with both dignity and rage on the slimy Bomelius (Vladimir Kudriashov) even as she consents to his advances for the sake of his potions, snarling at him the word "nemets": translated by the libretto as "monster", it is the ordinary Russian word for "German", but carries with it the older, contemptuous meaning, "dumb". Arkady Mishenkin tenorizes fluently as Ivan Lykov, not a very grateful part. Gryaznoy's opening aria is also a difficult one, for Rimsky-Korsakov gives him a melodic line that presents him as a character of some sympathy, if we do not know that he is regretting that he is now getting too old for the rapes he used to enjoy so much and is casting his eyes on the innocent Marfa instead of his mistress Lyubasha. Vladislav Verestnikov rightly handles this with a kind of blunt strength that does not give away too much. Later, he suggests an increasing and destructive tension, while also a certain magnificence. The chorus consist chiefly of oprichniks, Ivan the Terrible's dreaded private army which was, really, the ancestors of the KGB. They might have been characterized more menacingly, with more sense of the brutalizing effect of their comradeship; and the orchestral playing, too, while graceful and responsive, is a little lacking in character and is not always ideally synchronized with the singers. Andrey Tchistiakov is better in the more lyrical sections, but he paces the music well and does not over-discipline the work. It is one very well worth hearing, especially as recordings of Rimsky-Korsakov's operas, apart from the most famous, are not that easy to come by. The booklet provides essays and synopses in French, German and English, the text only in French and English.

Further listening ...

...Piano Concerto in C sharp minor, Op. 30. *Coupled with* **Balakirev** Piano Concertos – No. 1 in F sharp major, Op. 1; No. 2 in E flat major, Op. posth. **Malcolm Binns** (pf); **English Northern Philharmonia / David Lloyd-Jones.** Hyperion CDA66640 (7/93). *See review under Balakirev; refer to the Index to Reviews.* ⓖⓖ

...Piano Concerto in C sharp minor, Op. 30[b]. *Coupled with* **Balakirev** Piano Concerto No. 1 in F sharp major, Op. 1[a]. **Medtner** Piano Concerto No. 1 in C minor, Op. 33[a]. **Igor Zhukov** (pf); **USSR TV and Radio Large Orchestra /** [a]**Alexander Dmitriev,** [b]**Gennadi Rozhdestvensky.** Mezhdunarodnaya Kniga MK417087 (2/94).

...Piano Concerto in C sharp minor, Op. 30. *Coupled with* **Glazunov** Piano Concerto No. 1 in F minor, Op. 92. **Prokofiev** Piano Concerto No. 1 in D flat major, Op. 10. **Sviatoslav Richter** (pf). **Moscow Youth Orchestra / Kyrill Kondrashin.** Melodiya mono 74321 29468-2* (6/96).

...May Night – Overture. Orchestral Suites – Snow Maiden; Christmas Eve; Mlada; Invisible City of Kitezh; The Golden Cockerel. The Tale of Tsar Saltan. **Royal Scottish Orchestra / Neeme Järvi.** Chandos CHAN8327/9. ⓖ

...(arr. Kreisler) Fantasia on Two Russian Themes, Op. 33. *Coupled with works by* **Massenet, Glazunov, Rachmaninov, Sarasate, Tchaikovsky, Wieniawski** and **Kreisler.** Itzhak Perlman (vn); **Abbey Road Ensemble / Lawrence Foster.** EMI CDC5 55475-2 (1/96).

...Piano Quintet in B flat major. *Coupled with* **Glinka** Grand Sextet in E flat major. **Capricorn.** Hyperion CDA66163 (12/86). ⓖ

...Orchestral Suites – The Golden Cockerel; The Tale of Tsar Saltan; Christmas Eve. **Armenian Philharmonic Orchestra / Loris Tjeknavorian.** ASV CDDCA772 (9/92). ⓖ

...The octave, Op. 45 No. 3. The clouds begin to scatter, Op. 42 No. 3. Of what I dream in the quiet sky, Op. 40 No. 3. Enslaved by the rose, the nightingale, Op. 2 No. 2. In spring, Op. 43 – No. 1, The lark sings louder; No. 2, Not the wind, blowing from the heights. *Coupled with* **Borodin** The false note. The sea princess. **Mussorgsky** What are words of love to you?. Night. **Balakirev** 20 Songs – The bright moon; My heart is torn; Song of Selim; When I hear thy voice. Three Forgotten Songs – Thou art so captivating; Spanish song. 10 songs – Over the lake; I loved him. **Cui** I remember the evening. 25 Songs, Op. 57 – No. 11, "You" and "Thou"; No. 17, The statue of Tsarskoie Selo; No. 25, Desire. Ici-bas. I touched the bloom lightly, Op. 49 No. 1. It's over. **Olga Borodina** (mez); **Larissa Gergieva** (pf). Philips 442 780-2PH (8/95).

...Christ is risen, Op. 26 No. 6. How fair this spot, Op. 21 No. 7. Aleko – Young Gipsy's song. *Coupled with works by* **Handel, Schubert, R. Strauss, Duparc, Poulenc, Miaskovsky, Khachaturian, Napravnik, Massenet** *and* **Malawski** Russian Song. Nicolai Gedda (ten); **Erik Werba** (pf). EMI Salzburg Festival Edition mono ⓜ CDH5 65352-2* (69 minutes: ADD) *See review in the Collections section; refer to the Index to Reviews..*

...Sadko – The paragon of cities; Beautiful city! Kashchey the Immortal – In this, night's darkest hour. Snow Maiden (second version) – Under the warm blue sea. The Tsar's Bride – Still the beauty haunts my mind. *Coupled with* **Mussorgsky** Songs and Dances of Death. **Borodin** Prince Igor – No sleep, no rest. **Rubinstein** The Demon – Do not weep, my child; On the airy ocean; I am whom you called. Nero – Vindex's Epithalamium: I sing to you, Hymen divine! **Rachmaninov** Aleko – Aleko's cavatina. **Dmitri Hvorostovsky** (bar); **Kirov Theatre Orchestra / Valery Gergiev.** Philips 438 872-2PH (5/94). *See review in the Collections section; refer to the Index to Reviews.*

...Mozart and Salieri. **Soloists; Bolshoi Theatre Orchestra / Mark Ermler.** *Coupled with* **Mussorgsky** (orch. Rozhdestvensky) The Marriage. **Soloists; USSR Ministry of Culture Symphony Orchestra / Gennadi Rozhdestvensky.** Olympia OCD145 (9/93).

Alberto da Ripa
Italian c1500-1551

Suggested listening ...

...Fantasias Nos. 8 and 22. L'Eccho. *Coupled with works by* **Borrono da Milano, Francesco da Milano** and **Dall'Aquila** Paul O'Dette (lte). Harmonia Mundi HMU90 7043 (10/95). ✏ *See review in the Collections section; refer to the Index to Reviews.*

Richard Rodgers
American 1902-1979

Suggested listening ...

...Victory at Sea – television score. **RCA Victor Symphony Orchestra / Robert Russell Bennett.** RCA Victor 09026 60963-2.

...Carousel – original film soundtrack. EMI Angel ZDM7 64692-2. ⓖⓖⓖ

...Oklahoma! – original film soundtrack. EMI Angel ZDM7 64691-2. ⓖⓖⓖ

...South Pacific – original film soundtrack. RCA Victor ND83681 (12/89). ⓖ

...The Rodgers and Hammerstein Songbook – Oklahoma!. Carousel. South Pacific. The King and I. Cinderella. Flower Drum Song. The Sound of Music. **Original Broadway casts, etc.** Sony Broadway SK53331.

...The Boys from Syracuse. **Soloists; orchestra / Lehman Engel.** Sony Broadway SK53329.
...The King and I. **Soloists; Hollywood Bowl Orchestra / John Mauceri.** Philips 438 007-2PH (10/92).
...On your toes. **Original 1983 Broadway revival cast.** That's Entertainment CDTER1063 (10/83).
...Carousel. **Original 1993 London cast.** First Night CASTCD40 (5/94).

Joaquin Rodrigo

Spanish 1901-

Rodrigo Concierto de Aranjuez[ac]. Fantasía para un gentilhombre[ac]. Cançoneta[bc]. Invocacíon y Danza[a]. Tres Pequeñas piezas[a]. [a]**Pepe Romero** (gtr); [b]**Augustín Léo Ara** (vn); [c]**Academy of St Martin in the Fields / Sir Neville Marriner.** Philips Ⓕ 438 016-2PH (64 minutes: DDD: 8/94). Recorded 1992. Ⓖ

For *Aranjuez* and the *Fantasía* an outright first choice is no longer realistically possible. There are 35 versions of the former in the current *Classical Catalogue*, many of which are reviewed elsewhere in this guide (see below). What we have here is simply one of the best: Pepe Romero, a close friend of Rodrigo, has the technique to do whatever he pleases, though his capacity for high speed does not tempt him to display it for its own sake. There is elegance and a certain nobility in his interpretations, though he lacks the warmth of Bream (listed below), for instance, and the 'flamenco steeliness' of his *rasgueados* does perhaps stand in uncomfortable contrast with the rest. The ASMF must by now know these scores by heart but, perhaps stimulated by the presence of a soloist who is so completely in command of his material, their immaculate support bears no trace of staleness. The *Cançoneta* (1923) is one of Rodrigo's earliest works, a small (2'50") island of peaceful romantic dreams in a sea of guitar music, sweetly played by Ara (Rodrigo's son-in-law) and ignored in the annotation. There is no better recording of the *Invocacíon y Danza*, and no other at all of the *Tres Pequeñas piezas*, in the last of which the steely *rasgueados* are entirely in character. If you are not already liberally provided with recordings of the two main items you may rightly be tempted by this outstanding recording.

Additional recommendations ...

...Concierto serenata[a]. Concierto de Aranjuez[b]. **Casteldnuovo-Tedesco** Guitar Concerto No. 1[c]. [a]**Nicanor Zabaleta** (hp); [bc]**S. Behrend** (gtr); [a]**Berlin Radio Symphony Orchestra / Ernst Märzendorfer;** [bc]**Berlin Philharmonic Orchestra / Reinhard Peters.** DG Privilege Ⓑ 427 214-2GR (62 minutes: ADD).

...Concierto de Aranjuez. Fantasía para un gentilhombre. **John Williams** (gtr); **Philharmonia Orchestra / Louis Frémaux.** CBS Masterworks Ⓕ SK37848 (53 minutes: DDD: 7/85).

...Concierto de Aranjuez. Fantasía para un gentilhombre. **Villa-Lobos** Guitar Concerto. **Göran Söllscher** (gtr); **Orpheus Chamber Orchestra.** DG Ⓕ 429 232-2GH (65 minutes: DDD: 6/90).

...Concierto de Aranjuez[a]. **Falla** El amor brujo[b]. Noches en los jardines de España[c]. [a]**Carlos Bonnell** (gtr); [c]**Alicia de Larrocha** (pf); [ab]**Montreal Symphony Orchestra / Charles Dutoit;** [c]**London Philharmonic Orchestra / Rafael Frühbeck de Burgos.** Decca Ovation Ⓜ 430 703-2DM (71 minutes: DDD: 8/91). *See review under Falla; refer to the Index to Reviews.*

...Invocación y Danza. En los trigales. **Albéniz** Iberia[a] (arr. Gray) – El Albaicín; Triana; Rondeña. **Granados** Valses poéticos (trans. Williams). **Anonymous** (arr. Llobet) Ten Catalan Folk-songs. **John Williams** (gtr); [a]**London Symphony Orchestra / Paul Daniels.** Sony Classical Ⓕ SK48480 (71 minutes: DDD: 7/92). *See review under Albéniz; refer to the Index to Reviews.* Ⓖ

...Concierto de Aranjuez. **Arnold** Guitar Concerto, Op. 67. **Takemitsu** To the Edge of Dream. **Julian Bream** (gtr); **City of Birmingham Symphony Orchestra / Sir Simon Rattle.** EMI Ⓕ CDC7 54661-2 (58 minutes: DDD: 7/93). Ⓖ

...Concierto de Aranjuez[a]. Fantasia para un gentilhombre[b]. Tres piezas españolas. Invocacíon y danza. **Julian Bream** (gtr); [a]**Chamber Orchestra of Europe / John Eliot Gardiner;** [b]**RCA Victor Chamber Orchestra / Leo Brouwer.** RCA Victor Gold Seal Ⓜ 09026 61611-2 (69 minutes: DDD: 2/94).

...Concierto de Aranjuez. **Castelnuovo-Tedesco** Guitar Concerto No. 1 in D major, Op. 99. **Villa-Lobos** Guitar Concerto. **Norbert Kraft** (gtr); **Northern Chamber Orchestra / Nicholas Ward.** Naxos Ⓢ 8 550729 (60 minutes: DDD: 4/94). *See review under Castelnuovo-Tedesco; refer to the Index to Reviews.*

...Concierto de Aranjuez[a]. **Bennett** Guitar Concerto. **Arnold** Guitar Concerto, Op. 67. **Julian Bream** (gtr); **Melos Ensemble /** [a]**Sir Colin Davis.** RCA Victor Julian Bream Edition Ⓕ 09026 61598-2 (62 minutes: ADD: 6/94). *See review under Bennett; refer to the Index to Reviews.*

Further listening ...

...Concierto pastoral. *Coupled with* **Khachaturian** (arr. Gallois) Flute Concerto in D minor. **Patrick Gallois** (fl); **Philharmonia Orchestra / Ion Marin.** DG 435 767-2GH (10/92).

...Suite. Preludio al gallo mañanero. Zarabanda lejana. Pastorale. Bagatela. Serenata española. Sonada de adiós (Hommage à Paul Dukas). Tres Danzas de España. Danza de la Amapola. Tres Evocaciones. Preludio de Añoranza. Cinco Sonatas de Castilla con Toccata a modo de pregón. Berceuse de printemps. Berceuse d'automne. Air de Ballet sur le nom d'une Jeune Fille. El Album de Cecilia (Seis Piezas para manos pequeñas). A l'ombre de Torre Bermeja. Cuatro Piezas. Cuatro Estampas andaluzas. Cinco Piezas infantiles[a]. Sonatiuna para dos Munecas[a]. Gran Marcha de los Subsecretarios[a]. Atardecer[a]. **Gregory Allen,** [a]**Anton Nel** (pfs). Bridge BCD9027 (7/92).

...Tres Piezas españolas. *Coupled with* **Albéniz** Mallorca, Op. 202. Suite española, Op. 47. Cantos de España, Op. 232 – Córdoba. **Granados** Cuentos de la juventud – Dedicatoria. 15 Tonadillas – El majo Olvidado. 12 Danzas españolas, Op. 37 – Villanesca; Andaluza (Playera). Seven Valses poéticos. **Julian Bream** (gtr). RCA Navigator 74321 17903-2 (3/95). *See review under Albéniz; refer to the Index to Reviews.* Ⓖ

...Por tierras de Jerez. *Coupled with* **Falla** Homenaje, "Le tombeau de Claude Debussy". **Turina** Guitar Sonata, Op. 61. **Sor** (ed. P. Romero) Fantasía in D minor. **Tárrega** (arr. P. Romero) Gran Jota. **Albéniz** (arr. C. Romero) Torre Bermeja, Op. 92 No. 12. **Granados** Tonadillas al estilo antiguo – No. 7, La maja de Goya[a]. **Mudarra** Tres libros – Fantasía que contrahaze la harpa en la manera de Ludovico[a]. **Guerau** Canarios[a]. **Milán** El Maestro – Fantasia XVI[a]. **Moreno Torroba** Aires de la Mancha. **C. Romero** Los Maestros. **Pepe Romero** (gtr). Philips 442 150-2PH (4/95). Items marked [a] trans. P. Romero.

...Zarabanda lejana y villancico. *Coupled with* **Montsalvatge** Concierto breve[b]. Sinfonía de réquiem[a]. [a]**Catalina Moncloa** (sop); [b]**Leonel Morales** (pf); **Madrid Symphony Orchestra / Antoni Ros Marbà**. Marco Polo 8 223753.

Alessandro Rolla

Italian 1757-1841

New review

Rolla Viola Concerto in E flat major, Op. 3. Divertimento for Viola and Strings in F major. Concertino for Viola and Strings in E flat major. Rondo for Viola and Orchestra in G major.
Massimo Paris (va); **I Musici**. Philips Ⓔ 442 154-2PH (62 minutes: DDD: 11/95). Recorded 1993.
The music of Alessandro Rolla is quite conventional in tone and idiom but by no means empty or cliché-ridden, as is so much music of this period. The Op. 3 Concerto is a big, expansive piece; its style is quite austere, it has a number of unexpected if not deeply original ideas, while its handling of the viola (Rolla's own instrument, though he was also a violinist and for many years leader at La Scala) is highly effective – its darker colours tellingly used, the emotional appeal of its reedy, readily plaintive upper register well exploited. There is no want of eloquence in the *Largo* and the finale is a cheerful, spirited *polacca*. The *Concertino* is more intent on virtuosity and expression, with a shortish first movement leading directly into the quite intense *Andante* and this time a *polonese* finale. Clearly, Rolla relished these Polish rhythms: the second section of the *Divertimento* here is once again a *polacca*, after an *Andante* of considerable depth of expression and with some appealing ideas. The *Rondo*, seemingly earlier, is quite a brilliant piece, with a spirited main theme and also some *cantabile* writing. Massimo Paris is an extremely accomplished player who clearly has the measure, technically and musically, of these pieces; he also composed the cadenzas, allowing himself perhaps more space, and wider scope, than Rolla himself might have done. But nothing but praise is due for his performance, his handling of the instrument's colours, his command of the idiom and his management of the virtuoso music. The accompaniments, too, are prompt and efficient. The adventurous listener might well like to try this unusual disc.

Johan Helmich Roman

Swedish 1694-1758

Suggested listening ...
...Suites – D major, "Lilla Drottningholmsmusiquen"; G minor, "Sjukmans musiquen". Piante amiche[a]. [a]**Pia-Maria Nilsson** (sop); **Stockholm Nationalmuseum Chamber Orchestra / Claude Génetay**. Musica Sveciae MSCD417 (1/93).
...12 Harpsichord Suites. **Joseph Payne** (hpd). BIS CD669/70 (2/95). ✐

Andreas Romberg

German 1767-1821

Suggested listening ...
...Quintet in E flat major, Op. 57[a]. *Coupled with* **Fuchs** Clarinet Quintet in E flat major, Op. 102. **Stanford** Two Fantasy Pieces. **Thea King** (cl); **Britten Quartet**. Hyperion CDA66479 (7/92). *See review under Fuchs; refer to the Index to Reviews.*

Sigmund Romberg

Hungarian/American 1887-1951

Suggested listening ...
...The Student Prince (Romberg/Donelly). **Soloists; Ambrosian Chorus; Philharmonia Orchestra / John Owen Edwards**. TER Classics CDTER2 1172 (3/91).
...The New Moon – Softly, as in a morning sunrise; Lover, come back to me. *Coupled with works by* **J. Strauss II, Offenbach, Novello, Lehár, Coward, Chabrier, Heuberger** and **Sullivan** **Lesley Garrett** (sop); **Crouch End Festival Chorus; Royal Philharmonic Concert Orchestra / James Holmes**. Silva Screen Classics SILKTVCD1 (2/96). *See review in the Collections section; refer to the Index to Reviews.*

Cipriano de Rore

Italian 1515/16-1565

Rore Il quinto libro de madrigali. Le vive fiamme – Alma real, se come fida stella; Alma Susanna; Amor che t'ho fatt'io; Di l'estrem' orizonte; Fera gentil; Vaghi pensieri. O voi che sotto. **The Consort of Musicke** (Emma Kirkby, Evelyn Tubb, sops; Mary Nichols, mez; Andrew King, Paul Agnew, tens; Alan Ewing, bass) / **Anthony Rooley.** Musica Oscura Ⓔ 070991 (56 minutes: DDD: 1/94). Texts and translations included. Recorded 1991.

Cipriano de Rore's understanding of the emotional potential of the madrigal was explored in both four- and five-part scorings. The four-part pieces are generally lighter-veined but the imagery and expressive range is no less detailed than the intensely wrought five-part madrigals, and in many ways they are more representative of the compendium of skills which were to blossom with Monteverdi and his contemporaries. This is an imaginative first step in The Consort of Musicke's latest departure of 'encircling' Monteverdi with music by his predecessors and contemporaries, and they have rightly considered it irrelevant that Monteverdi was not born until two years after Rore died, since it is clear that Monteverdi sought much inspiration from his rich musical inheritance. Impressive as ever is the uniform breathing, the purring ensemble, even in works with speech rhythms which require extreme discipline to make them sound spontaneous. The mock piety of the darker-scored works is greatly assisted by the singers' subtlety of accentuation. Less persuasive is the way The Consort imposes rhetorical formulae on Rore's relatively abstract style (in this book anyway). That said, there are, as you would expect, many fine things here, including a stunning *Vaghi pensieri* and *O santo fior felice*, the latter all but releasing the sweet scent of Rore's blest and happy flower.

Rore Missa Praeter rerum seriem. Motets – Infelix ego; Parce mihi; Ave regina; Descendi in hortum meum.
Josquin Desprez Praeter rerum seriem. **The Tallis Scholars / Peter Phillips.** Gimell Ⓔ CDGIM029 (72 minutes: DDD: 6/94). Texts and translations included. *Gramophone Award Winner 1994.* Ⓖ

This record begins with a magisterially concentrated and evocative account of one of Josquin's most inspired and tightly-constructed motets, the six-voice *Praeter rerum seriem*. This in turn is the starting-point for Rore's Mass – which takes as its cue Josquin's antiphonal approach – wherein the song on which the Mass is based is passed from the upper to the lower voices in succession. Rore, whose piece is in one sense an act of homage to Josquin was, if briefly, Josquin's successor at the d'Este court at Ferrara. It is in this context that Rore's work is an act of homage in a second sense, since to Josquin's already rich texture Rore adds an additional soprano part, while the first alto voice carries throughout a *cantus firmus* to the text "Hercules secundus dux Ferrarie quartus vivit et vivet". Around this structural scaffolding the remaining voices weave an endlessly inventive sequence of carefully-worked motives reminiscent of Josquin's original. This performance is characterized by great sensitivity to textual inflexion and to the many moments of exquisite bonding of words and music. Nevertheless, in the end it is Peter Phillips's ability to control the overall architecture of the music, as well as its detail, that provides the basis for a reading of such conviction; his direction, combined with The Tallis Scholars's strongly-focused singing and well-balanced ensemble, results in a gripping performance of rare beauty, intelligence and power. No less fine is the group of four motets that completes the recording, and which reveals Rore as one of the greatest and last exponents of the Franco-Flemish tradition.

Ned Rorem

American 1923-

Rorem Piano Concerto for the Left Hand[a]. Eleven Studies for Eleven Players[b]. [b]**Kathy Lord** (ob); [b]**Gregory Raden** (cl); [b]**Elizabeth Ostling** (fl); [b]**Katerina Englichova** (hp); [b]**Jack Sutte** (tpt); [b]**Anthony Lafargue,** [b]**Ryan Leveille** (perc); [b]**Steven Copes** (vn); [b]**Choong-Jin Chang** (va); [b]**Jeffrey Lastrapes** (vc); [a]**Gary Graffman,** [b]**Reiko Uchida** (pfs) / **Rossen Milanov;** [a]**Curtis Institute Student Orchestra / André Previn.** New World Ⓔ 80445-2 (62 minutes: DDD: 2/95). Recorded 1993.

In an appealingly candid booklet-essay, Ned Rorem describes his Left-Hand Concerto (his fourth for piano so far) as an "entertainment" – an entirely apt epithet, as it turns out, but one even more well-suited to the earlier companion work on this valuable New World offering, namely the austerely titled *Eleven Studies for Eleven Players*. Dating from 1959-60, this charming suite is full of sparkling invention, nostalgic and witty by turns, and everywhere Rorem's scoring displays a very Gallic refinement. The Left-Hand Concerto of 1991 is another multi-movement work, eight in all, spread across three varying sections. Again, Rorem's inspiration impresses by dint of its appealing lyrical fervour and colourful, assured instrumentation, nowhere more so than in the strikingly beautiful "Hymn" and "Duet" which together form the emotional core of the concerto. The *Eleven Studies* receive a thoroughly sensitive, nicely polished rendering from New World's *ad hoc* ensemble. In the concerto, Gary Graffman is a committed exponent (though his chosen instrument is not in the best of health) and André Previn draws an enthusiastic orchestral response from the students of the Curtis Institute.

Rorem Miss Julie. **Theodora Fried** (sop) Miss Julie; **Philip Torre** (bar) John; **Heather Sarris** (mez) Christine; **David Blackburn** (bar) Mr Niels; **Mark Mulligan** (ten) Young Boy; **Laurelyn Watson** (sop) Young Girl; **Judd Ernster** (bass) Bass Soloist; **Manhattan School of Music Opera Chorus and Orchestra / David Gilbert.** Newport Classic Ⓟ Ⓓ NPD85605 (two discs: 88 minutes: DDD: 5/96). Notes and text included. Recorded live in 1994.

Newport Classic have already brought out two earlier one-acters by Rorem (listed below) and now his only full-length opera, *Miss Julie*, based on Strindberg and premièred in 1965, adds considerably to the picture of his operatic output. *Miss Julie* took a long time to settle down at the planning stage and has been much revised since then. Rorem admits that he is a song composer, never "comfortable with the opera medium, much less a buff". *Miss Julie* is an anguished story about a count's daughter who rejects her fiancé and then insists on being seduced by her father's valet during the servants' Midsummer's Eve revels. The play was attacked as immoral when it was published in 1888 and in the next year was not successful in the theatre in Denmark. Rorem delivers most of the opera in a kind of *parlando* which is too bland to reflect the growing infatuation of Act 1 but gets nearer to the nastiness and tortured remorse of Act 2, where Miss Julie and her lover plan futile expedients to escape. Nothing works and in the end Miss Julie kills herself: it all proceeds in slow motion, as in the play itself, but without access to the Strindbergian hysteria *en route*. However, there are plenty of well-focused moments when the music is allowed to expand – the innocent duet between the boy and girl in Act 1 (track 9); Julie's aria on returning with stolen money in Act 2 (track 6); a confusion ensemble (track 7); and the drama is finally engaged when feelings turns to desperation between Miss Julie, the valet and his fiancée, the cook Christine. Recorded live, this remains a good conservatoire production with some fine solo voices, that at last allows this corner of the American operatic repertoire to be explored.

Further listening ...

...Winter pages[a]. Bright music[b]. [b]**Marya Martin** (fl); [a]**Todd Palmer** (cl); [a]**Frank Morelli** (bn); **Ida and** [b]**Ani Kavafian** (vns); **Fred Sherry** (vc); [a]**Charles Wadsworth**, [b]**André-Michel Schub** (pfs). New World 80416-2 (10/92).

...Day Music[a]. Night Music[b]. [a]**Jaime Laredo**, [b]**Earl Carlyss** (vns); [a]**Ruth Laredo**, [b]**Ann Schein** (pfs). Phoenix PHCD123 (9/94).

...A Childhood Miracle[a]. Three Sisters Who Are Not Sisters[b]. **Singers**; [b]**John van Buskirk** (pf); [a]**Magic Circle Chamber Orchestra / Ray Evans Harrell.** Newport Classic NPD85594 (10/95).

Thomas Roseingrave
British 1688-1766

Suggested listening ...

...Concerto for Harpsichord, Trumpets, Timpani and Strings in D major[b] (recons. P. Holman). *Coupled with* **Handel** Chaconne in G major[a] (arr. Nicholson). Concerto Movement for Organ and Orchestra in D minor[b]. **Chilcot** Harpsichord Concerto in A major, Op. 2 No. 2[a] (recons. R. Langley). **Nares** Sonata for Harpsichord, Two Violins and Continuo, Op. 2 No. 6[a]. **P. Hayes** Keyboard Concerto No. 4 in A major[c]. **Hook** Keyboard Concerto in D major, Op. 1 No. 5[c] (recons. Holman). **The Parley of Instruments / Paul Nicholson** ([a]hpd/[b]org/[c]fp). Hyperion CDA66700 (8/94). ✍

Hilding Rosenberg
Swedish 1892-1985

Suggested listening ...

...Symphony No. 4, "The Revelation of St John". **Håkan Hagegård** (bar); **Swedish Radio Choir; Pro Musica Choir; Rilke Ensembe; Gothenburg Symphony Orchestra / Sixten Ehrling.** Caprice CAP21429 (5/93).

...Orpheus in Town. Sinfonia concertante. Violin Concerto No. 1, Op. 22. Suite in D major, Op. 13 – Pastorale. Symphonies – No. 3; No. 4, "The Revelation of St John": Fragments; No. 5, "Ortågardsmästern". The Holy Night. **Soloists; Swedish Radio Choir; Stockholm Chamber Choir; Radiojänst Symphony Orchestra; Stockholm Concert Society Orchestra; Radiotjänst Entertainment Orchestra; Swedish Radio Orchestra / Hilding Rosenberg.** Caprice Collector's Classics mono CAP21510* (three discs, recorded from broadcast performances between 1940-49: 5/93).

Johann Rosenmüller
German 1619-1684

Suggested listening ...

...Sacri Concerti – Beatus vir qui timet Dominum. Magnificat. Benedicam Dominum. De profundis clamavi. Confitebor. Gloria in excelsis Deo. **Cantus Cölln / Konrad Junghänel** (lte). Deutsche Harmonia Mundi 05472 77181-2 (6/93).   Ⓖ

...12 Sonate a 2, 3, 4 e 5 stromenti da arco e altri e Basso continuo – Nos. 2, 7, 9 and 11. Sonate da Camera – Nos. 1, 2 and 4. Student-Music – Suite in C major. **Hespèrion XX / Jordi Savall.** Auvidis Astrée E8709. ✎

Manuel Rosenthal   French 1904-

New review

M. Rosenthal Les petits métiers. Trois poèmes de Marie Roustan[a]. Deux sonnets de Jean Cassou[a]. Trois pièces liturgiques[a]. Musique de table. [a]**Catherine Dubosc** (sop); **Nancy Symphony Orchestra / Jérôme Kaltenbach.** Marco Polo ℗ 8 223768 (59 minutes: DDD: 6/96). Texts and translations included.

Manuel Rosenthal's name is well known as a conductor, and as arranger of the high-spirited Offenbach caper *Gaîté Parisienne*, to all record collectors; but his compositions have remained almost virgin territory. Record companies have now shown some stirrings of curiosity about the output of someone, now in his ninety-second year, who for so many years has been a distinguished figure in French musical life. A favourite pupil of Ravel, among his compositions are a handful of operettas, a couple of ballets, cantatas, orchestral, chamber and instrumental works and songs; this disc, however, presents him only in miniatures. Even the lavish *Musique de table*, a "concerto for orchestra", consists of eight musically unrelated movements depicting, with humour, the courses of a banquet, incidentally offering considerable challenges to all the players: indeed, if the insert-note is to be believed, both the BBC Symphony Orchestra and the New York Philharmonic initially jibbed at its difficulties. The Nancy orchestra, which we have scarcely heard before, rises admirably to the occasion and, well supported by a very good recording, proves itself a body of quality. Rosenthal's light-hearted set of ten character pieces about Parisian artisans and small tradesmen (*Les petits métiers*) is not only vastly entertaining, but also a dazzling display of virtuosity in orchestral scoring. There is exquisite orchestral colour too in "Rêverie", the first of the Marie Roustan songs; but Catherine Dubosc is unfortunately not ideally placed in relation to the microphone; her high notes impinge too strongly, marring her line. The three religious pieces are more restrained in style, and the wartime sonnets display a more advanced idiom, distancing itself from the composer's Ravelian roots and, in the second, venturing into atonality.

Moritz Rosenthal   Polish 1862-1946

Suggested listening ...

...Carnaval de Vienne. Fantasia on Themes by Johann Strauss II. *Coupled with works by* **Schulz-Evler, Friedman, Tausig** and **Godowsky Piers Lane** (pf). Hyperion CDA66785 (2/96).

Antonio Rosetti   Bohemian *c*1750-1792

Suggested listening ...

...Horn Concerto in D minor. *Coupled with works by* **Haydn** and **Danzi Hermann Baumann** (hn); **Concerto Amsterdam / Jaap Schröder.** Teldec Das Alter Werk 0630-12324-2 (8/96). *See review under Haydn; refer to the Index to Reviews.*

...Sinfonias – G minor, K1:27; E flat major, K1:23; B flat major, K1:25; E flat major, K1:32. **Concerto Köln.** Teldec Das Alte Werk 4509-98420-2 (12/95). ✎

...Piano Sonata No. 2 in E flat major. *Coupled with works by* **Spohr, Debussy, Casella, Damase, Tournier, Prokofiev, Renié** and **Fauré Naoko Yoshino** (hp). Philips 446 064-2PH (2/96). *See review in the Collections section; refer to the Index to Reviews.*

Luigi Rossi   Italian *c*1597-1653

Suggested listening ...

...Le Canterine Romane. **Tragicomedia.** Teldec Das Alte Werke 4509-90799-2 (10/93). ✎

...Ergi la mente al sole. O si quis daret concentum. *Coupled with works by* **Carissimi, Marazzoli, Mazzocchi, V. Mazzocchi, Landi** and **Anonymous Tragicomedia / Stephen Stubbs.** Teldec Das Alte Werk 4509-98410-2 (3/96). ✎ *See review in the Collections section; refer to the Index to Reviews.*

Gioachino Rossini   Italian 1792-1868

New review

Rossini Overtures – Armida; Il barbiere di Siviglia; Bianca e Falliero; Demetrio e Polibio; La gazza ladra; Guillaume Tell; L'inganno felice; Matilde di Shabran; Semiramide; Il Signor

Bruschino. **Orchestra of La Scala, Milan / Riccardo Chailly.** Decca Ⓕ 448 218-2DH (75 minutes: DDD: 5/96). Recorded 1995. *Gramophone Editor's choice.*   Ⓖ
This collection is a truly memorable day out at the Rossini fair. Musically everything is top notch. Chailly's conducting is characteristically full-blooded, but stylish and witty too. Milan's La Scala orchestra respond to his masterly direction with playing of tremendous colour, verve and corporate virtuosity. And Decca's engineers have done that near impossible thing, found a venue (the Chiesa della Pace in Milan) and set up their microphones in such a way as to achieve a sound whose mixture of warmth, brilliance and immediacy ensures that all the overtures, big and small, come up in a razor-sharp focus. For the most part, the collection juxtaposes the familiar with the rather less familiar. Nor are the less familiar pieces of lesser interest. The overture to *Armida*, with its solemn drum-beats and vertiginous warbling horns, is a case in point. And it was a very clever move indeed to include the overture to *Bianca e Falliero* which is itself a kind of guided tour of the later Neapolitan operas, containing as it does themes for *La donna del lago, Ricciardo e Zoraide* and *Ermione*. This is one of those records when everything goes right. It offers an hour-and-a-quarter of untrammelled pleasure.

Rossini Overtures – Guillaume Tell; La scala di seta; Il Signor Bruschino; Il barbiere di Siviglia; La gazza ladra; La Cenerentola. **Chicago Symphony Orchestra / Fritz Reiner.** RCA Victor Gold Seal Ⓜ GD60387* (47 minutes: ADD: 9/90). From SB2075 (7/60). Recorded 1958.   ⒼⒼⒼ
This is one of the most famous of all collections featuring this sparkling repertoire. By the time of this recording, Fritz Reiner had built the Chicago Symphony into one of the world's greatest ensembles, and their swaggering yet supremely flexible virtuosity is heard to superb effect on this survey. Not that these accounts are in any sense over-driven or that Rossini's music is used merely as an excuse for high-powered orchestral display; far from it: Reiner's direction possesses elegance, genial high-spirits and (at times) an almost Beechamesque wit – sample, say, the pointed woodwind dialogue in the scintillating reading of *La Cenerentola* to hear this. In fact, the only regret one could possibly have about this simply marvellous music-making is that, with a total duration of just under 47 minutes there isn't more of it! Despite some (inevitable) residual hiss, the RCA transfer engineers have worked wonders with these elderly tapes, producing a far more full-blooded, transparent sound-picture than one would have thought possible. At mid-price, this is unmissable. Buy it!

Additional recommendations ...
...Il barbiere di Siviglia. La Cenerentola. La gazza ladra. L'italiana in Algeri. Il Signor Bruschino. Le siège de Corinthe. **London Symphony Orchestra / Claudio Abbado.** DG Galleria Ⓜ 419 869-2GGA (47 minutes: DDD: 5/88).
...La scala di seta; Il Signor Bruschino; L'italiana in Algeri; Il barbiere di Siviglia; La gazza ladra; Semiramide; Guillaume Tell. **London Classical Players / Roger Norrington.** EMI CDC7 54091-2 (60 minutes: DDD: 4/91). ✍   Ⓖ
...Complete Overtures – La cambiale di matrimonio. La scala di seta. Il barbiere di Siviglia. Tancredi. L'italiana in Algeri. Il Signor Bruschino. Il turco in Italia. L'inganno felice. Guillaume Tell. Semiramide. Le siège de Corinthe. La Cenerentola. La gazza ladra. Il viaggio a Reims. Maometto II. Ricciardo e Zoraide. Otello. Armida. Ermione. Torvaldo e Dorliska. Bianca e Falliero. Demetrio e Polibio. Eduardo e Cristina. Edipo a Colono. Sinfonia al Conventello. Sinfonia di Bologna. **Academy of St Martin in the Fields / Sir Neville Marriner.** Philips Ⓜ 434 016-2PM3 (three discs: 209 minutes: ADD: 10/92).   ⒼⒼ
...La scala di seta. *Coupled with works by* **Berlioz, Weber, Brahms, Mozart** and **Wagner London Philharmonic Orchestra; Berlin Philharmonic Orchestra / Sir Thomas Beecham.** Dutton Laboratories mono Ⓜ CDLX7009* (75 minutes: ADD: 10/94). *See review in the Collections section; refer to the Index to Reviews.*
...Guillaume Tell[b]. **Wolf-Ferrari** I quattro rusteghi – Intermezzo[b]. Il segreto di Susanna – Overture[b]. **Respighi** Fountains of Rome[b]. **Verdi** Messa da Requiem[a]. La traviata[b] – Preludes, Act 1 and 3. I vespri siciliani – Overture[b]. [a]**Dame Elisabeth Schwarzkopf** (sop); [a]**Oralia Dominguez** (mez); [a]**Giuseppe di Stefano** (ten); [a]**Cesare Siepi** (bass); [a]**Chorus and Orchestra of La Scala, Milan,** [b]**Santa Cecilia Academy Orchestra, Rome / Victor de Sabata.** EMI Références mono Ⓜ CHS5 65506-2* (two discs: 148 minutes: ADD: 9/95).
...Il barbiere di Siviglia; Guillaume Tell; La Cenerentola; L'italiana in Algeri; La scala di seta; La gazza ladra; Semiramide; Il Signor Bruschino; Il turco in Italia. **Academy of St Martin in the Fields / Sir Neville Marriner.** Philips Ⓜ 446 196-2PM (76 minutes: ADD: 12/95).
...Guillaume Tell. *Coupled with works by* **Bartók** and **Beethoven** Soloists; [a]**London Voices; World Orchestra for Peace / Sir Georg Solti.** Decca Ⓕ 448 901-2DH (62 minutes: DDD: 3/96). *See review in the Collections section; refer to the Index to Reviews.*

New review
Rossini Sonate a quattro – No. 1 in G major; No. 2 in A major; No. 3 in C major; No. 4 in B flat major; No. 5 in E flat major; No. 6 in D major.
Bellini Oboe Concerto in E flat major[a].
Cherubini Horn Sonata in F major[b].
Donizetti String Quartet in D major (1828). [a]**Roger Lord** (ob); [b]**Barry Tuckwell** (hn); **Academy of St Martin in the Fields / Sir Neville Marriner.** Double Decca Ⓜ 443 838-2DF2 (two discs: 112 minutes: ADD: 7/95). Recorded 1964-8.

Rossini's six string sonatas are usually heard performed by a string orchestra, although they were in fact composed for a quartet of two violins, cello and double bass. The sonatas, which display amazing musical dexterity and assurance, may date from as early as 1804. The world of eighteenth-century opera is never far away, with the first violin frequently taking the role of soprano soloists, particularly in the slow movements. Written for Rossini's friend Agostino Triosso, who was a keen double bass player, the sonata's bass parts are full of wit and suavity. There are other thoroughly recommendable modern digital versions, including the Hyperion issue using original instruments, and the performances by the Serenata of London, full of elegance and polish, which give us for the first time on CD the original instrumentation. Yet there is something very special about Marriner's Academy set, made for Argo in the late 1960s. The playing has an elegance and finesse, a sparkle and touch of humour that catches the full character and charm of these miraculous examples of the precocity of the 12-year-old composer. The Double Decca format here is ideal because of the substantial bonuses. Donizetti's String Quartet sounds elegant in its string-orchestra version, Bellini's Oboe Concerto is played stylishly by Roger Lord and Cherubini's mini-concerto for horn and strings is dispatched with aplomb by by Barry Tuckwell. Highly recommendable.

Additional recommendations ...

...Nos. 1-6. **Serenata of London.** ASV Ⓕ CDDCA767 (78 minutes: DDD: 10/91).

...Nos. 1-6. **Elizabeth Wallfisch, Marshall Marcus** (vns); **Richard Tunnicliffe** (vc); **Chi-Chi Nwanoku** (db). Hyperion Ⓕ CDA66595 (80 minutes: DDD: 10/92). 🖈

...Nos. 1-6. **Kremlin Chamber Orchestra / Mischa Rachlevsky.** Claves Ⓕ CD50-9222 (79 minutes: DDD: 11/93).

Rossini Péchés de vieillesse – Book 2, "Album français"; Book 3, "Morceaux réservés" – Chant funèbre à Meyerbeer; Les amants de Séville; Ave Maria; Le chant des titans. **Maryse Castets** (sop); **Mechthild Georg** (mez); **Jean-Luc Maurette** (ten); **Michel Brodard** (bar); **Raimund Nolte** (bass); **Elzbieta Kalvelage** (pf); **Marcel Jorand** (perc); **Chorus Musicus / Christoph Spering** (harm). Opus 111 Ⓕ OPS30-70 (74 minutes: DDD: 7/93). Text and translations included. Recorded 1992.

This is a very collectable CD. In the first place, it gives us not some arbitrary and ill-matched selection from Rossini's *Péchés de vieillesse*, but a charming gallimaufry of pieces that make up the *Album français*, plus four striking items from Rossini's *Morceaux réservés*. For the most part, it is Gallic music played and sung with in an authentic Gallic style. And that includes a splendid period Erard piano, expertly played by Elzbieta Kalvelage. There is also an Alexandre harmonium joining the piano in Rossini's exquisite *pastorale* "La Nuit de Noël" and in a spirited orchestra-less rendering of his strangely belligerent "Le chant des titans". The disc begins with the firefly brilliance of the *a cappella* "Toast pour le nouvel an" and ends with an exquisite short "Requiem". On the way, we have the desperate brilliance of "Roméo", a musical soliloquy Berlioz might have been proud to own. Flirtatiousness and pathos sit side by side in "La grande Coquette" and the famous tenor and baritone duo "Un sou". And if that seems too lachrymose, relief is at hand in the form of a charming musical sorbet, "Chanson de Zora". Each of the soloists seems to be a natural Rossinian and Christoph Spering's Chorus Musicus are stylish and disciplined in the five choral pieces.

Rossini Stabat mater. **Helen Field** (sop); **Della Jones** (mez); **Arthur Davies** (ten); **Roderick Earle** (bass); **London Symphony Chorus; City of London Sinfonia / Richard Hickox.** Chandos Ⓕ CHAN8780 (59 minutes: DDD: 3/90). Text and translation included. Recorded 1989.

This used to be a ripe nineteenth-century favourite, and many a proudly-bound vocal score at present languishing in a pile of second-hand music would testify to a time when its owner felt enabled, with its help, to combine the pleasure of church-going with the duty of attendance at the opera. The words are those of Jacopone da Todi's sacred poem, but Rossini's music is dramatic, exciting and sometimes almost indecently tuneful. Certainly the soloists have to be recruited from the opera company; the soprano who launches out into the "Inflammatus" must be generously supplied with high Cs as well as the power to shoot them over the heads of full choir and orchestra, while the tenor at one alarming moment is asked for a top D flat and has to ring out the melody of his "Cujus animam" with tone to match the trumpets which introduce it. In all four soloists, grace and technical accomplishment are as important as range and power; they must also have the taste and discipline to work harmoniously as a quartet. In this recording they certainly do that, and neither are they lacking in range or technique, if there is a limitation it is rather in richness of tone and in the heroic quality which the solos mentioned above ideally need. Even so, individually and collectively, they compare well with most of their competitors on record, and the choral and orchestral work under Hickox is outstanding.

Additional recommendations ...

...**Soloists; Philharmonia Chorus and Orchestra / Carlo Maria Giulini.** DG Ⓕ 410 034-2GH (65 minutes: DDD: 9/83).

...**Soloists; London Symphony Chorus and Orchestra / István Kertész.** Decca Ovation Ⓜ 417 766-2DM (54 minutes: ADD: 7/89).

...**Soloists; Bavarian Radio Chorus and Symphony Orchestra / Semyon Bychkov.** Philips Ⓕ 426 312-2PH (65 minutes: DDD: 3/91).

Rossini Petite messe solennelle. **Helen Field** (sop); **Anne-Marie Owens** (mez), **Edmund Barham** (ten); **John Tomlinson** (bass); **David Nettle, Richard Markham** (pfs); **Peter King** (harm); **City of**

Birmingham Symphony Orchestra Chorus / Simon Halsey. Conifer Ⓕ CDCF184 (78 minutes: DDD: 10/90). Text and translation included. Recorded 1989. *Selected by Sounds in Retrospect.*

Rossini Petite messe solennelle. **Daniella Dessì** (sop); **Gloria Scalchi** (mez); **Giuseppe Sabbatini** (ten); **Michele Pertusi** (bass); **Chorus and Orchestra of the Teatro Comunale, Bologna / Riccardo Chailly.** Decca Ⓜ 444 134-2DX2 (two discs: 82 minutes: DDD: 2/95). Text and translation included. *Gramophone Editor's choice.*

Of Rossini's later works, none has won such affection from the general listening public as the *Petite messe solennelle*. He called it "the final sin of my old age" and, as with the other of his *péchés de vieillesse*, he declined to have it published. Editions issued in 1869, the year after his death, failed to retain his original scoring and contained numerous inaccuracies, yet there have been the basis of most subsequent recordings of the work. This disc presents the mass in a revelatory new Oxford University Press edition by Nancy Fleming, using two pianos in addition to a fine, French harmonium. That alone would mark it out for prime consideration, even if the reading were only passable, but here we have the bonus of dedicated, heartfelt performances from all involved. Above all, the scale of the work is finely captured – it was intended for chamber performance and both writing and scoring reflect the intimacy of Rossini's ideas. Much praise must go to Simon Halsey for so clearly establishing the parameters for this performance, and to the recording engineers for making it all seem so convincing. The whole issue establishes a benchmark for assessing recordings of this work.

Whatever misgivings one might have about the orchestrated version, a properly representative recording has been long overdue. Happily, the wait is over. Chailly's performance is a glorious heart-warming affair. Not that you are likely to be convinced right away. To ears accustomed to the *Kyrie* in its original form, the texturing here is pure suet. Nor does the sound of the largish and here rather distantly placed choir seem especially well focused in the *Christe eleison*. Gradually, though, the ear adjusts, the musicians warm to their task, the performance gets into its stride. By the time we reach the "Domine Deus", Chailly really has worked out the pace of the wicket. A century before lunch is clearly in the offing, followed by an afternoon of gloriously relaxed strokeplay. And so it proves. The Bologna Chorus sing the *Gloria* and *Credo* with passion, clarity and love. The tenor is adequate, the bass superb, the two girls absolutely fabulous. (The *Qui tollis* is sung with near-shameless allure.) If the *Crucifixus* can never be as painful as it is in the sparer original version, this is amply offset by the sheer beauty of Daniella Dessì's singing and by the hair-raising force of the "Et resurrexit" (superbly recorded) as Chailly and his choir realize it. By the end, after Gloria Scalchi's deeply affecting account of the *Agnus Dei*, you begin to wonder whether the orchestral version wasn't more than a match for the original. It isn't, but it is an indication of the cumulative eloquence of this utterly inspired performance that it comes to seem so.

Additional recommendation ...

...Petite messe solennelle[a]. Stabat mater[b]. **Soloists;** [a]**Choir of King's College, Cambridge / Stephen Cleobury;** [b]**Chorus and Orchestra of the Maggio Musicale, Florence / Riccardo Muti.** EMI Forte Ⓜ CZS5 68658-2 (two discs: 147 minutes: DDD: 7/96).

New review

Rossini Otello – Che ascolto? ... Ah come mai non senti pietà. Guillaume Tell – Ne m'abandonne pas ... Asile héréditaire. Stabat mater – Cujus animam gementem. L'italiana in Algeri – Languir per una bella; Ah, come il cor di giubilo. Le siège de Corinthe – Avançons, oui ces murs ... Grand Dieu faut-il qu'un peuple qui t'adore.

Donizetti La favorite – Un ange, une femme inconnue; Je ne méritais pas ... Qui ta voix m'inspire; La maîtresse du roi? ... Ange si pur. Messa da Requiem – Ingemisco. Gabriella di Vergy – Si compia il sacrificio ... Io l'amai. **Justin Lavender** (ten); **Bournemouth Symphony Orchestra / Howard Williams.** IMP Classics Ⓢ 30367 0010-2 (73 minutes: DDD: 3/96). Recorded 1994.

Rodrigo's long and incredibly difficult aria from Rossini's *Otello* announces Lavender's ability both to spin a secure legato and negotiate divisions with facility. But it is the second item that places him in the forefront of Rossini singing today. Every note of Arnold's strenuous outpouring is hit dead centre; up to the high C near the aria's close, the runs are cleanly delivered, the tone is clear and unfettered. Lavender's kind of tenor with its keen, pointed head voice may well be very much the sound Rossini had in mind for that part – and for Néocles in *Siège*, whose Act 3 scena is interpreted with the involvement possible only to an artist who has already sung the part on stage. In both these pieces Lavender's French is idiomatic. *La favorite* is at last being restored to the original language and Lavender demonstrates how much smoother Fernand's arias sound in French. Note also his long breath and his feeling for the shape of a Donizettian phrase. His Italian is no less excellent than his French. Perhaps there isn't enough light and shade in Lindoro's pieces from *L'italiana* but Raoul's romantic outpouring from *Gabriella* goes well. One piece in Latin from each composer finds Lavender full of the right conviction, the top D flat in "Cuius animam" taken fearlessly. Howard Williams is the ideal partner, breathing life into every bar of the orchestration, especially notable in the Rossini pieces. The only reservations concern the recording – too much air around the voice – and the insert-notes which are inadequate. Let neither prevent you hearing a notable and fascinating début recital – and one available at a very reasonable price.

Rossini Zelmira – Riedi al soglio[a]. Le nozze di Teti e di Peleo – Ah, non potrian reistere.
Maometto II – Ah! che invan su questo ciglio; Giusto ciel, in tal periglio[a]. La donna del lago –

Tanti affetti in tal momento[a]. Elisabetta, Regina d'Inghilterra – Quant' è grato all'alma mia[a]; Fellon, la penna avrai[a]. Semiramide – Serenai vaghirai ... Bel raggio lusinghier[a]. **Cecilia Bartoli** (mez); [a]**Chorus and Orchestra of the Teatro La Fenice, Venice / Ion Martin.** Decca Ⓕ 436 075-2DH (59 minutes: DDD: 2/92). Recorded 1991. Texts and translations included.

This sparkling disc brings together a collection of arias composed by Rossini for one of the great prima donnas of the nineteenth century, who was also his wife, Isabella Colbran. It is tempting to wonder whether even she had a voice to match that of Cecilia Bartoli, one of the most luscious, most exciting voices in opera. All those dazzling chromatic runs, leaps, cadenzas and cascading coloraturas are handled with consummate ease. Throughout, Bartoli sounds as if she's enjoying the music; there is always an engaging smile in the voice, although she is properly imperious in the extracts from *Elisabetta* and disarmingly simple in the prayerful "Giusto ciel, in tal periglio" ("Righteous heaven in such danger") from *Maometto II*. The orchestral and choral forces bring a delightful intimacy to the proceedings, with some cheeky woodwind solos and fruity brass passages. The recording, produced at the Teatro La Fenice by Decca veteran Christopher Raeburn, favours the voices but gives it just enough distance to accommodate high Cs and astounding A flats at the bottom of the range. The orchestral perspective is changeable but satisfactory. For Rossini and Bartoli fans alike, this disc is a must.

Rossini Il Signor Bruschino. **Samuel Ramey** (bass) Gaudenzio; **Claudio Desderi** (bar) Bruschino padre; **Kathleen Battle** (sop) Sofia; **Frank Lopardo** (ten) Florville; **Michele Pertusi** (bass) Filiberto; **Jennifer Larmore** (mez) Marianna; **Octavio Arévalo** (ten) Bruschino figlio, Commissario; **English Chamber Orchestra / Ion Marin.** DG Ⓕ 435 865-2GH (76 minutes: DDD: 12/93). Notes, text and translation included. Recorded 1991.

Witty and sentimental but also at times hair-raisingly cruel, *Il Signor Bruschino* is the last, and arguably the best, of the one-acters Rossini wrote for the tiny Teatro San Moisè in Venice between 1810 and January 1813. These early *farse* can get by on tolerably good singing. What they absolutely can't do without is first-rate conducting – and, on record, clear, sharply defined orchestral sound. Choosing between the conducting of DG's Ion Marin and Claves's Marcello Viotti isn't all that difficult. Marin is far more vital; and what a cast there is on DG – a cast so expert and experienced they can't fail to bring the score wonderfully to life. Central to the whole enterprise is the Bruschino of Desderi, a superbly rounded portrait of a man who, despite the sweltering heat and the machinations of everyone around him, finally gives as good as he gets. Ramey's portrait of Gaudenzio is masterly, acted with relish and richly sung. Battle gives a ravishing account of Sofia's aria "Ah!, donate il caro sposo" with its cor anglais colourings. This *Bruschino* is probably the one to have. Whatever reservations one may occasionally have about the conducting and the focus of the recording, it is difficult to imagine a better-cast account.

Additional recommendations:

...Soloists; **Turin Philharmonic Orchestra / Marcello Viotti.** Claves Ⓕ CD50-8904/5 (two discs: 84 minutes: DDD: 10/89).

...Soloists; **Warsaw Chamber Opera Orchestra / Jacek Kaspszyk.** Pavane Ⓕ ADW7158 (72 minutes: DDD: 5/93).

New review

Rossini Tancredi. **Ewa Podles** (contr) Tancredi; **Sumi Jo** (sop) Amenaide; **Stanford Olsen** (ten) Argirio; **Pietro Spagnoli** (bar) Orbazzano; **Anna Maria di Micco** (sop) Isaura; **Lucretia Lendi** (mez) Roggiero; **Capella Brugensis; Collegium Instrumentale Brugense / Alberto Zedda.** Naxos Ⓢ 8 660037/8 (two discs: 147 minutes: DDD: 11/95). Notes and Italian text included. Recorded 1994. *Gramophone Editor's choice.* Ⓖ

Tancredi is a seminal work in the Rossini canon, a work which mingles a new-found reach in the musical architecture with vocal and instrumental writing of rare wonderment and beauty. Yet until now, and the appearance of this exceptionally fine recording, it has never been available on record in anything other than live theatre or concert performances. Philip Gossett's new Critical Edition of the score. is the one used here, albeit somewhat pragmatically, by Alberto Zedda. The singing is splendid throughout, with a cast that is unusually starry. Podles herself has sung the role of Tancredi (to acclaim) at La Scala, Milan; and the Amenaide, Sumi Jo, is a touch cool at first, too much the pert coloratura but this is not an impression that persists. Hers is a performance of wonderful vocal control and flowering sensibility. Podles, a smoky-voiced Pole, likes to go her own way at times. In recitatives, rests are ignored and emphases freely redistributed. In arias, it is not unusual to find the pulse beating faster or slower as the musical temperature rises or falls. In the event, though, she and Sumi Jo work well together, and they sound marvellous. Podles also manages, chameleon-like, to adjust to the purer, more obviously stylish Rossini manner of a singer who is very unlike herself, the young American tenor Stanford Olsen. His portrait of the conscience-stricken father Argirio matches singing of grace and impetus with great fineness of dramatic sensibility. As a result, something like the scene of the signing of his daughter's death-warrant emerges here as the remarkable thing it is. Zedda is lucky to have at his disposal another of those wonderfully stylish chamber orchestras and chamber choirs that Naxos seem able to conjure at will. The aqueously lovely preface to Tancredi's first entrance is a fairly representative example of the players' ear for Rossini's delicately-limned tone-painting. And the recording itself is beautifully scaled. As usual with Naxos, you get a multilingual synopsis plus an original-language libretto without translation; but in the case of an opera like

Tancredi, where it is very much a case of 'Prima la musica', this is not a great disincentive to buy. All in all, then, this is a fine set; the first-ever studio recording of *Tancredi*, and a palpable hit.

Rossini Il turco in Italia. **Simone Alaimo** (bar) Selim; **Sumi Jo** (sop) Fiorilla; **Enrico Fissore** (bar) Geronio; **Raúl Giménez** (ten) Narciso; **Susanne Mentzer** (mez) Zaida; **Peter Bronder** (ten) Albazar; **Alessandro Corbelli** (bar) Prosdocimo; **Ambrosian Opera Chorus; Academy of St Martin in the Fields / Sir Neville Marriner.** Philips Ⓕ 434 128-2PH2 (two discs: 154 minutes: DDD: 12/92). Notes, text and translation included. Recorded 1991.

The audience at the première of *Il turco in Italia*, given in 1814 at La Scala in Milan, presumed (wrongly) that Rossini was recycling material for what was essentially *L'italiana in Algeri* in another guise. The notion has stuck with the opera, and its reputation has not been helped by the fact that Rossini delegated much of the work on the *secco* recitative and arias. In fact, and in contrast to *L'italiana*, *Il turco* is a surprisingly searching piece of psychological drama, given the seemingly trivial and prejudiced nature of its subject matter, and it very much benefits from the insight that repeated listening on CD, with commentary and translation, can supply. It depends for its effect on ensembles, rather than finding its dramatic and emotional heart in the solo arias and so, inevitably, the chief star of this performance must be Sir Neville Marriner, as the skilful development of the drama rests chiefly in his hands. The soloists are generally first rate. Although Sumi Jo is not perhaps as forceful or acerbic a Fiorilla as Caballé or Callas in their recordings of this work, she is nevertheless a highly skilled performer who makes her entrance with delicate phrasing and sweet tone. Alaimo, Corbelli and Fissore bring a particularly distinguished solidity to the casting. Captured in a clean, unfussy recording, the result is enthralling. Typically for a Rossini opera, recording *Il turco* has not been without its problems of deciding which version of the text to use. This issue scores heavily because it finds a happy balance of theatrical necessity and authenticity. The opera's music that is not by Rossini has been pruned and the result added to in order to develop the dramatic pacing. But in the end it is the overall quality of this performance that carries the day.

Additional recommendations ...

...**Soloists; Chorus and Orchestra of La Scala, Milan / Gianandrea Gavazzeni.** EMI mono Ⓜ CDS7 49344-2* (two discs: 113 minutes: ADD: 12/87).

...**Soloists; Ambrosian Opera Chorus; National Philharmonia Orchestra / Riccardo Chailly.** CBS Masterworks Ⓕ S2K37859 (two discs: 146 minutes: DDD: 9/89).

Rossini Il barbiere di Siviglia. **Roberto Servile** (bar) Figaro; **Sonia Ganassi** (mez) Rosina; **Ramon Vargas** (ten) Almaviva; **Angelo Romero** (bar) Doctor Bartolo; **Franco de Grandis** (bass) Don Basilio; **Ingrid Kertesi** (sop) Berta; **Kázmér Sarkany** (bass) Fiorello; **Hungarian Radio Chorus; Failoni Chamber Orchestra, Budapest / Will Humburg.** Naxos Ⓢ 8 660027/9 (three discs: 158 minutes: DDD: 3/94). Notes and text included. *Gramophone Editor's choice.* ⓖⓖ

Not everyone will approve, but there are ways in which this super-budget recording of *Il barbiere di Siviglia* puts to shame just about every other version of the opera there has yet been. Those it may not please are specialist vocal collectors for whom *Il barbiere* is primarily a repository of vocal test pieces, a kind of musical Badminton. If, on the other hand, you regard *Il barbiere* (Rossini, ex-Beaumarchais) as a gloriously subversive music drama – vibrant, scurrilous, unstoppably vital – then the new set is guaranteed to give a great deal of pleasure. 'Performance' is the key word here. Humburg is described in the Naxos booklet as "Conductor and Recitative Director"; and for once the recitatives really are part of the larger drama. The result is a meticulously produced, often very funny, brilliantly integrated performance that you will almost certainly find yourself listening to as a stage play – rather than an opera with eminently missable (often arbitrarily abbreviated) recitatives. With a virtually all-Italian cast, the results are a revelation. The erotic allure of the duet "Dunque io son" is striking, arising as it does here out of the brilliantly played teasing of Rosina by Figaro about her new admirer. Similarly, Don Basilio's Calumny aria, superbly sung by Franco de Grandis, a black-browed bass from Turin who was singing for Karajan, Muti and Abbado while still in his twenties. This takes on added character and colour from the massive sense of panic created by de Grandis and the admirable Dr Bartolo of Angelo Romero when Basilio comes in with news of Almaviva's arrival in town. The Overture is done with evident relish, the playing of the Failoni Chamber Orchestra (a group from within the Hungarian State Opera Orchestra) nothing if not articulate. Aided by a clear, forward recording, a *sine qua non* with musical comedy, the cast communicates the Rossini/ Sterbini text – solo arias, ensembles, recitatives – with tremendous relish. They are never hustled by Humburg, nor are they spared: the *stretta* of the Act 1 finale is a model of hypertension and clarity. It would have been nice to have an English version of the libretto, but you can't have everything at rock-bottom prices and Naxos do provide an excellent track-by-track synopsis. Super-Scrooges might complain that 158 minutes of music could have been shoe-horned on to two CDs, but three CDs is a fair deal for a complete *Il barbiere*, and the layout is first-rate. This *Il barbiere* jumps to the top of the pile in a single leap. As operatic pole-vaulters, this puts Naxos in the Olympic class

Additional recommendations ...

...**Soloists; Ambrosian Opera Chorus; Academy of St Martin in the Fields / Sir Neville Marriner** with **Nicholas Kraemer** (fp). Philips Ⓕ 446 448-2PH2 (three discs: 147 minutes: DDD: 4/84).

...**Soloists; Philharmonia Chorus and Orchestra / Alceo Galliera.** EMI Ⓜ CDS7 47634-8* (two discs: 130 minutes: ADD: 6/87).

...**Soloists; Chorus and Orchestra of La Scala, Milan / Riccardo Chailly.** CBS Masterworks
Ⓕ S3K37862 (three discs: 155 minutes: DDD: 9/88).
...**Soloists; Chorus and Orchestra of the Teatro Communale, Bologna / Giuseppe Patanè.** Decca
Ⓕ 425 520-2DH3 (three discs: 161 minutes: DDD: 9/89).
...**Soloists; Glyndebourne Festival Chorus; Royal Philharmonic Orchestra / Vittorio Gui.** EMI Rossini
Edition Ⓜ CMS7 64162-2 (two discs: 141 minutes: ADD: 5/92).
...**Soloists; Chorus of the Teatro La Fenice, Venice; Chamber Orchestra of Europe / Claudio Abbado.**
DG Ⓕ 435 763-2GH2 (two discs: 155 minutes: DDD: 12/92).
...**Soloists; Chorus; Orchestra della Toscana / Gianluigi Gelmetti.** EMI Ⓕ CDS7 54863-2 (three discs:
140 minutes: DDD: 11/93).

Rossini L'italiana in Algeri. **Marilyn Horne** (mez) Isabella; **Ernesto Palacio** (ten) Lindoro;
Domenico Trimarchi (bar) Taddeo; **Samuel Ramey** (bass) Mustafà; **Kathleen Battle** (sop) Elvira;
Clara Foti (mez) Zulma; **Nicola Zaccaria** (bass) Haly; **Prague Philharmonic Chorus; I Solisti
Veneti / Claudio Scimone.** Erato Libretto Ⓜ 2292-45404-2 (two discs: 140 minutes: ADD: 1/92).
Notes and text included. From STU7 1394 (3/81). Recorded 1980.

Written within the space of a month during the spring of 1813, and with help from another
anonymous hand, Rossini's *L'italiana in Algeri* was an early success, and one which went on to receive
many performances during the nineteenth century, with an increasingly corrupt text. A complete
reconstruction was undertaken by Azio Corghi and published in 1981; this recording uses this new
edition which corresponds most closely to what was actually performed in Venice in 1813. *L'italiana*
is one of Rossini's wittiest operas, featuring as did a number of his most successful works a bewitching
central character, in this case Isabella, who makes fun of her various suitors, with the opera ending
with a happy escape with her beloved, Lindoro, a typical *tenorino* role. This fine recording on Erato
has plenty of vocal polish. Scimone's biggest asset is Marilyn Horne as Isabella: possibly the finest
Rossini singer of her generation and a veteran in this particular role, she sings Rossini's demanding
music with great virtuosity and polish. Her liquid tone and artful phrasing ensure that she is a
continuous pleasure to listen to. She is strongly supported by the rest of the cast: Kathleen Battle is a
beguiling Elvira, Domenico Trimarchi a most humorous Taddeo, and Samuel Ramey a sonorous Bey
of Algiers – Isabella's opponent and pursuer. Ernesto Palacio's Lindoro, however, has patches of
white tone and is correct rather than inspiring. Scimone's conducting is likewise efficient if at times
slightly lacking in sparkle. It is, however, guaranteed to give considerable pleasure.

Additional recommendation ...

Soloists; Vienna State Opera Chorus; Vienna Philharmonic Orchestra / Claudio Abbado. DG Ⓕ
427 331-2GH2 (two discs: 127 minutes: DDD: 10/89).

Rossini La Cenerentola. **Teresa Berganza** (mez) Angelina; **Luigi Alva** (ten) Don Ramiro; **Renato
Capecchi** (bar) Dandini; **Paolo Montarsolo** (bar) Don Magnifico; **Margherita Guglielmi** (sop)
Clorinda; **Laura Zannini** (contr) Tisbe; **Ugo Trama** (bass) Alidoro; **Scottish Opera Chorus;
London Symphony Orchestra / Claudio Abbado.** DG Ⓕ 423 861-2GH2 (two discs: 144 minutes:
ADD: 9/86). Notes, text and translation included. From 2709 039 (6/72). Recorded 1971. Ⓖ

Rossini's Cinderella is a fairy-tale without a fairy, but no less bewitching for the absence of a magic
wand. In fact the replacement of the winged godmother with the philanthropic Alidoro, a close friend
and adviser of our prince, Don Ramiro, plus the lack of any glass slippers and the presence of a
particularly unsympathetic father character, makes the whole story more plausible. *La Cenerentola*,
Angelina, is more spunky than the average pantomime Cinders, not too meek to complain about her
treatment or to beg to be allowed to go to the ball. She herself gives Don Ramiro one of her pair of
bracelets, charging him to find the owner of the matching ornament and thus taking in hand the
control of her own destiny. Along the way, Don Ramiro and his valet Dandini change places, leading
to plenty of satisfyingly operatic confusion and difficult situations. This recording, when originally
transferred to CD, was spread across three discs, but it has now been comfortably fitted into two. It
gives a sparkling rendition of the score with a lovely light touch and well-judged tempos from Abbado
and the London Symphony Orchestra and virtuoso vocal requirements are fully met by the cast. The
chief delight is Teresa Berganza's Angelina, gloriously creamy in tone and as warm as she is precise.
The supporting cast is full of character, with Luigi Alva a princely Don Ramiro, Margherita
Guglielmi and Laura Zannini an affected and fussy pair of sisters, and Renato Capecchi as Dandini,
gleeful and mischievous as he takes on being prince for a day. Although the recording was made in
1972 it has survived its technological transfers more than usually well.

Additional recommendations ...

...**Soloists; West German Radio Choir; Cappella Coloniensis / Gabriele Ferro.** Sony Classical
Ⓕ S2K46433 (two discs: 148 minutes: ADD: 6/91).
...**Soloists; Glyndebourne Festival Chorus and Orchestra / Vittorio Gui.** EMI Rossini Edition mono
Ⓜ CMS7 64183-2* (two discs: 117 minutes: ADD: 5/92).
...**Soloists; Bologna Teatro Communale Chorus and Orchestra / Riccardo Chailly.** Decca Ⓕ 436 902-
2DHO2 (two discs: 148 minutes: DDD: 11/93).

Rossini La donna del lago. **June Anderson** (sop) Elena; **Martine Dupuy** (mez) Malcolm; **Rockwell
Blake** (ten) Uberto/Giacomo; **Chris Merritt** (ten) Rodrigo di Dhu; **Giorgio Surjan** (bar) Douglas

d'Angus; **Marilena Laurenza** (sop) Albina; **Ernesto Gavazzi** (ten) Serano; **Ferrero Poggi** (ten) Bertram; **Chorus and Orchestra of La Scala, Milan / Riccardo Muti.** Philips Ⓕ 438 211-2PH2 (two discs: 156 minutes: DDD: 2/95). Recorded live in 1992. Text and translation included.
Although *La donna del lago* was written in 1819, towards the end of Rossini's time in Naples, it has little of the monumentalism or ferocity of *Maometto II* or *Ermione*. For much of the time it is more a watercolour than a painting in oils. It is also a relatively intimate piece extolling (as *Guillaume Tell* will later do among not dissimilar mountain peoples) the abiding virtues of hearth and home. Muti's reading of the score is masterly: pacey yet affectionate. His ear for countervailing lyric voices in the orchestra is especially acute. It is a darker-browed – more proto-Verdian – reading than the one Maurizio Pollini gave us in the studio in the wake of performances at the 1983 Pesaro Festival. Muti and his La Scala players find rich autumnal colourings in Rossini's score where Pollini and the Chamber Orchestra of Europe emphasize its vernal charm, its buoyancy and brilliance. Pollini's cast had the luxury of post-production studio sessions. Or is it a luxury? The studio can chill passions and it does sound a shade prim in the wake of the new La Scala version. Player for player for player, Pollini has slightly the better cast, yet the Muti is a real *performance*, and a good one too.
Additional recommendation ...
...**Soloists; Prague Philharmonic Chorus; Chamber Orchestra of Europe / Maurizo Pollini.** CBS Masterworks Ⓜ S2K39311 (three discs: 138 minutes: DDD: 8/88).

Rossini Semiramide. **Dame Joan Sutherland** (sop) Semiramide; **Marilyn Horne** (mez) Arsace; **Joseph Rouleau** (bass) Assur; **John Serge** (ten) Idreno; **Patricia Clark** (sop) Azema; **Spiro Malas** (bass) Oroe; **Michael Langdon** (bass) Ghost of Nino; **Leslie Fryson** (ten) Mitrane; **Ambrosian Opera Chorus; London Symphony Orchestra / Richard Bonynge.** Decca Ⓜ 425 481-2DM3 (three discs: 168 minutes: ADD: 2/90). Notes, text and translation included. From SET317/19 (10/66). Recorded 1966. ⒼⒼ
Wagner thought it represented all that was bad about Italian opera and Kobbe's *Complete Opera Book* proclaimed that it had had its day – but then added what looked like second thoughts, saying that "were a soprano and contralto to appear in conjunction in the firmament the opera might be successfully revived". That was exactly what happened in the 1960s, when both Sutherland and Horne were in superlative voice and, with Richard Bonynge, were taking a prominent part in the reintroduction of so many nineteenth-century operas which the world thought it had outgrown. This recording brought a good deal of enlightenment in its time. For one thing, here was vocal music of such 'impossible' difficulty being sung with brilliance by the two principal women and with considerable skill by the men, less well-known as they were. Then it brought to many listeners the discovery that, so far from being a mere show-piece, the opera contained ensembles that possessed quite compelling dramatic intensity. People who had heard of the duet "Giorno d'orroré" (invariably encored in Victorian times) were surprised to find it remarkably unshowy and even expressive of the ambiguous feelings of mother and son in their extraordinary predicament. It will probably be a long time before this recording is superseded, admirably vivid as it is in sound, finely conducted and magnificently sung.

Rossini Il viaggio a Reims. **Sylvia McNair** (sop) Corinna; **Cheryl Studer** (sop) Madama Cortese; **Luciana Serra** (sop) Contessa di Folleville; **Lucia Valentini Terrani** (mez) Marchesa Melibea; **Raúl Giménez** (ten) Cavalier Belfiore; **William Matteuzzi** (ten) Conte di Libenskof; **Samuel Ramey** (bass) Lord Sidney; **Ruggero Raimondi** (bass) Don Profondo; **Enzo Dara** (bar) Barone di Trombonok; **Giorgio Surian** (bar) Don Prudenzio; **Lucio Gallo** (bar) Don Alvaro; **Berlin Radio Chorus; Berlin Philharmonic Orchestra / Claudio Abbado.** Sony Classical Ⓕ S2K53336 (two discs: 135 minutes: DDD: 12/93). Notes, text and translation included. Recorded in 1992. ⒼⒼ
The rediscovery of Rossini's dazzling, sophisticated coronation entertainment *Il viaggio a Reims* was one of the musical highlights of the 1980s; and it was Abbado's DG recording that brought the work to the public at large (it was voted *Gramophone*'s Record of the Year in 1986). No one who already has the DG recording need feel compelled to go out and buy the Sony. After all, the music is the same, and so are no fewer than six of the 11 principal singers. Of the singers who are repeating their roles, both Ramey and Dara now surpass their already superb earlier performances. Dara has transformed the aria in which Baron Trombonok catalogues national foibles. What was previously more or less a straight recitation is now a miracle of subversive inflexion, with Abbado and the Berlin players adding wonderful new colours that seem to lie dormant in the earlier recording. When it comes to new singers, the Sony set has its weaknesses. Not Gallo. His Don Alvaro is less cumbersome than Nucci's on DG. Nor perhaps Serra as the fashion-crazed young French widow. But for Count Libenskof DG's Francisco Araiza is far more in command of the role than William Matteuzzi. On balance, though, new collectors will be better off with the new Sony, and it is better recorded.
Additional recommendation ...
...**Soloists; Prague Philharmonic Chorus; Chamber Orchestra of Europe / Claudio Abbado.** DG Ⓕ 415 498-2GH2 (two discs: 136 minutes: DDD: 1/86). *Gramophone classical 100. Gramophone Award Winner 1986.* ⒼⒼⒼ
Further listening ...
...Introduction, Theme and Variations in B flat major. *Coupled with* **Weber** Clarinet Concertino in E flat major, Op. 26. **Crusell** Clarinet Concerto No. 2 in F minor, Op. 5. **Baermann** Quintet

(Septet) in E flat major, Op. 23 – Adagio. **Emma Johnson** (cl); **English Chamber Orchestra / Sir Charles Groves.** ASV CDDCA559 (11/86). 🅖🅖

...Wind Quartet No. 6. *Coupled with* **Briccialdi** Wind Quintet, Op. 124. **Lefebvre** Suite, Op. 57. **Taffanel** Wind Quintet. **Aulos Quintet.** Koch Schwann Musica Mundi 310087 (10/91).

...Péchés de Vieillesse – excerpts. Book 5 – Première Communion; La lagune de Venise à l'expiration de l'année 1861. Book 8 – Prélude rococo; Un regret; Un espoir. Book 9 – Chansonette; La savoie aimante; Impromptu tarantellisé in F major; Marche et reminiscences pour mon dernier voyage. Book 12 – Un rien Nos. 3, 5 and 12; Douces reminiscences offertes à mon ami Carafa; Un rien sur le Mode Enharmonique. Book 14 – Une réjouissance. **Alberto Portugheis** (pf). ASV CDDCA901 (11/94).

...Péchés de Vieillesse, Book 5, "Album pour les enfants adolescents" – Ouf! les petits pois; Un sauté; Book 8, "Album de château" – Un regret, un espoir; Prélude prétentieux; Book 9 – La savoie aimante. *Coupled with works by* **D. Scarlatti, F. Couperin** and **Rameau** Marcelle Meyer (pf). EMI mono CZS5 68092-2* (6/95). *See review in the Collections section; refer to the Index to Reviews.* 🅖🅖🅖

...Messa di gloria. **Sumi Jo** (sop); **Ann Murray** (mez); **Raúl Giménez, Francisco Araiza** (tens); **Samuel Ramey** (bass); **Academy of St Martin in the Fields Chorus and Orchestra / Sir Neville Marriner.** Philips 434 132-2PH (12/92).

...Giovanna d'Arco. Songs – Ariette à l'ancienne. Beltà crudele. Canzonetta spagnuola. Il risentimento. Il trovatore. L'âme délaissée. L'Orpheline du Tyrol. La Grande Coquette. La légende de Marguerite. La pastorella. La regate veneziana. Mi lagnerò. Nizza. **Cecilia Bartoli** (mez); **Charles Spencer** (pf). Decca 430 518-2DH (4/91).

...L'occasione fa il ladro. **Soloists; English Chamber Orchestra / Marcello Viotti.** Claves CD50-9208/9 (5/93).

...La pietra del paragone. **Soloists; New York Clarion Concerts Chorus and Orchestra / Newell Jenkins.** Vanguard Classics 08.9031.73 (12/92).

...Tancredi. **Soloists; Venice La Fenice Chorus; Venice La Fenice Orchestra / Ralf Weikert.** Sony Classical S3K39073 (8/88).

...Elisabetta, Regina d'Inghilterra. **Soloists; Ambrosian Singers; London Symphony Orchestra / Gian-Franco Masini.** Philips 432 453-2PM2 (12/92).

...Otello. **Soloists; Ambrosian Opera Chorus; Philharmonia Orchestra / Jesús López-Cobos.** Philips 432 456-2PM2 (12/92).

...Adelaide di Borgogna. **Soloists; New Cambridge Chorus; Martina Franca Festival Orchestra / Alberto Zedda.** Fonitcetra Italia Ⓟ CDC64 (4/95).

...La gazza ladra. **Soloists; Prague Philharmonic Choir; Turin Radio Symphony Orchestra / Gianluigi Gelmetti.** Sony Classical S3K45850 (10/90).

...Mosè in Egitto. **Soloists; Ambrosian Opera Chorus; Philharmonia Orchestra / Claudio Scimone.** Philips 420 109-2PM2 (12/92).

...Ermione. **Soloists; Prague Philharmonic Chorus; Monte Carlo Philharmonic Orchestra / Claudio Scimone.** Erato 2292-45790-2.

...Le Comte Ory. **Soloists; Chorus and Orchestra of Lyon Opera / John Eliot Gardiner.** Philips 422 406-2PH2 (10/89).

...Le Comte Ory. **Soloists; Glyndebourne Festival Chorus; Glyndebourne Festival Orchestra / Vittorio Gui.** EMI mono CMS7 64180-2* (5/92).

...Guillaume Tell. **Soloists; Ambrosian Opera Chorus; National Philharmonic Orchestra / Riccardo Chailly.** Decca 417 154-2DH4 (2/87).

Nino Rota
Italian 1911-1979

Rota La strada – ballet suite. Il Gattopardo – dances. Concerto for Strings. **La Scala Philharmonic Orchestra / Riccardo Muti.** Sony Classical Ⓟ SK66279 (62 minutes: DDD: 8/95). Recorded 1994. *Gramophone Editor's choice.* 🅖

The sumptuous sound propels one into the opening of Rota's ballet score for *La strada* – inspired by Fellini's film; has there ever been a more exhilarating opening to a modern ballet? First given at La Scala in 1966, with Carla Fracci in the main role, it is still in the repertory there. Muti conducts with the tension and dramatic flair with which one associates him, and the Scala orchestra seem to have the music in their bones. The ballroom scene from Visconti's *Il Gattopardo* must be one of the most complex and, in its way, daring passages in any film. Lasting over an hour in its full version, it is so gripping and dramatically satisfying, that the audience feels no sense of boredom, even though the story is over and the action complete. Rota's music contributes to the extraordinary energy of the sequence, including his orchestration of a previously unpublished waltz by Verdi, which at the time was in Visconti's private collection. On the film soundtrack, Visconti used Rota's improvised orchestrations to give the impression of "a modest ensemble hired for the occasion". Needless to say the Scala orchestra under Muti play the seven dances with irresistible *élan*. The Concerto for strings makes a pleasant interlude between the two big dramatic scores. If you do not already know *La strada*, this CD is the best possible introduction to Rota's music; for Rota enthusiasts it is a must.

...Concerto for Strings. *Coupled with works by* **Respighi** and **Ghedini** Accademia Bizantina /
   Carlo Chiarappa (vn). Denon Ⓕ CO-78916 (69 minutes: DDD: 3/95). *See review under Ghedini;*
   refer to the Index to Reviews.
...Concerto for Strings. *Coupled with works by* **Morricone, Malipiero** and **Porena** I Solisti
   Italiani. Denon Ⓕ CO-78949 (63 minutes: DDD: 10/95). *See review under Malipiero; refer to the*
   Index to Reviews.

Further listening ...
...The Symphonic Fellini/Rota – Lo Sceicco Bianco. I Vitelloni. La Strada. Il Bidone. Le Notte di
   Cabiria. La Dolce Vita. Boccaccio '70. Otto e Mezzo. Giulietta degli Spiriti. Fellini Satyricon. I
   Clowns. Roma. Amarcord. Casanova. Prova d'orchestra. **Czech Symphony Orchestra / Derek**
   Wadsworth. Silva Screen FILMCD129 (10/93).

Hans Rott   Austrian 1858-1884

Suggested listening ...
...Symphony in E major. **Cincinnati Philharmonic Orchestra / Gerhard Samuel.** Hyperion
   CDA66366 (12/89).   Ⓖ

Christopher Rouse   American 1949-

Suggested listening ...
...Bonham. *Coupled with* **Daugherty** Desi. **Agento** The Dream of Valentino – Tango. **Moran**
   Points of Departure. **Torke** Black and White – Charcoal. **Harbison** Remembering Gatsby.
   Larsen Collage: Boogie. **Schiff** Stomp. **Kernis** New Era Dance. **J. Adams** The Chairman
   Dances. **Bernstein** West Side Story – Mambo. **Baltimore Symphony Orchestra / David Zinman.**
   Argo 444 454-2ZH (7/95).

Albert Roussel   French 1869-1937

New review
Roussel Bacchus et Ariane, Op. 43. Le festin de l'araignée, Op. 17. **BBC Philharmonic Orchestra /**
   Yan Pascal Tortelier. Chandos Ⓕ CHAN9494 (68 minutes: DDD: 8/96). *Gramophone Editor's*
   choice.   ⒼⒼ
As compared to his contemporary Dukas, Roussel has been somewhat sidelined as a "connoisseur's
composer". That presumably means that he did not write fat, lush tunes that could be exploited in
television commercials, but produced works of vigorous ideas and more subtle quality. Record
companies used to fight shy of his music – the Third and Fourth Symphonies have indeed maintained
a foothold, but with the ballet *Bacchus et Ariane*, which is closely linked with the Third, we have
mostly been given only its second half. Here are alert, rhythmically vital performances of Roussel's
two most famous ballets, which even at the most exuberantly excited moments (like the "Bacchanale"
in *Bacchus*) preserve a truly Gallic lucidity, and which Tortelier marks by a captivating lightness of
touch; and when it comes to quiet passages one could not ask for greater tenderness than in the
beautiful end of Act 1 of *Bacchus* (shame on those conductors who neglect this for the more extrovert
Act 2), when Bacchus puts Ariadne to sleep. *Le festin de l'araignée*, written 18 years earlier, is in a
quite different style. Where *Bacchus*'s trenchant idiom at times makes one think of Stravinsky's
Apollon Musagète, *Le festin* (which had the misfortune to be overshadowed by *The Rite of Spring*,
produced only eight weeks later) is atmospheric and more impressionistic (in the same vein as
Roussel's First Symphony). It is a score full of delicate invention, whose one weakness is that for its
full appreciation a knowledge of its detailed programme is needed – and that is provided here in the
booklet. The BBC Philharmonic play it beautifully. If this is 'connoisseur's music', then be happy to
be called a connoisseur: you will find it delectable.

Additional recommendation ...
...Bacchus et Ariane – ballet suite No. 2[b]. *Coupled with* **Ravel** Daphnis et Chloé[a]. [a]**New England**
   Conservatory Chorus; [a]**Alumni Chorus; Boston Symphony Orchestra / Charles Munch.** RCA Victor
   Gold Seal [a]stereo/[b]mono Ⓜ GD60469* (72 minutes: ADD: 12/91).   ⒼⒼ

New review
Roussel Symphony No. 3 in G minor, Op. 42[b].
Franck Symphony in D minor[a]. **French National Orchestra / Leonard Bernstein.** DG Masters
   Ⓜ 445 512-2GMA (69 minutes: DDD: 10/95). Recorded live in 1981. Item marked [a] from 2532
   050 (12/82), [b]previously unpublished.
This 1981 Roussel Third is recognizably via Bernstein, and is more kaleidoscopic and meaningful than
you are likely to have heard it, unless you possess his first New York account (CBS, 11/67 – never
reissued on CD). The *Rite of Spring*-cum-*Age of Steel* stamping rhythms of the first movement are

now a little slower, the effect possibly a little relaxed until you arrive at the central climax (astonishing 'whooping' horns and crashing metal) and the coda (now superbly emphatic with ringing trumpets and lots more crashing metal). The slow movement's songful yearning is, as it was before, slow, sublime and intensely searching in the manner of its counterpart in Mahler's Sixth, though the contrasting *più mosso* is not now fast enough and has its limp moments. That said, the general control is superior, particularly at and around the movement's now awesome final climax. Bernstein's New Yorkers were uninhibitedly rowdy and brash in the finale; the finale's moments of brashness are now offset by rather more sophistication (at, again, a slower tempo). The recording, which has a less than ideally full and focused bass drum, is both spacious and present, with an appropriate touch of astringency on top. Bernstein's Franck is atmospheric, big on rhetoric, extreme in its range of tempo and dynamics and typically intense. Bernstein's control is again superb, with the orchestra's winds mellifluous in tone.

Additional recommendations ...

...No. 3. Bacchus et Ariane – ballet suite No. 2. **Detroit Symphony Orchestra / Neeme Järvi.** Chandos Ⓕ CHAN8996 (68 minutes: DDD: 10/95).

...No. 1, Op. 7, "Le poème de la forêt"; No. 2 in B flat major, Op. 23; No. 3; No. 4 in A major, Op. 53. **French Radio Philharmonic Orchestra / Marek Janowski.** RCA Victor Red Seal Ⓕ 09026 62511-2 (two discs: 119 minutes: 6/96).

New review

Roussel Impromptu, Op. 21[a]. Deux Poèmes de Ronsard, Op. 26[b]. Joueurs de flûte, Op. 27[c]. Violin Sonata No. 2 in A major[d]. Segovia, Op. 29[e]. Sérénade, Op. 30[f]. Duo[g]. Vocalises – Aria No. 2[h]. [b]**Irene Maessen** (sop); [bcf]**Paul Verhey** (fl); [h]**Hans Roerade** (ob); [gh]**Jos de Lange** (bn); [d]**Jean-Jacques Kantorow** (vn); [a]**Erika Waardenburg** (hp); [e]**Jan Goudswaard** (gtr); [g]**Quirijn van Regteren Altena** (db); [cdh]**Jet Röling** (pf); [f]**Schoenberg Quartet** (Janneke van der Meer, Wim de Jong, vns; Henk Guittart, va; Viola de Hoog, vc). Olympia Ⓕ OCD459 (65 minutes: DDD: 9/95). Recorded 1994.

While Roussel's orchestral music has won a following in this country, his chamber music still, for the most part, enjoys only cult status here. This excellent second volume covers the period from 1919 to 1928, when Roussel, firmly rejecting the impressionism of his contemporary Ravel, had adopted what is often (though loosely) referred to as neo-classical style. Try as one may, it is difficult to avoid the use of the adjective "astringent" commonly applied to his music; but along with its clean-cut clarity (like that of a good dry wine) and a rhythmic alertness often manifested in unusual time-signatures and changeable tempos goes a dry humour – as in the comic *Duo* for bassoon and double-bass, the fourth piece of the *Joueurs de flûte* (in the vein of Debussy's *Prélude*, "General Lavine, eccentric") or the angular finale (mostly in 10/8) of the Second Violin Sonata. What is in short supply, however, except in the *Aria* played here on the oboe, is lyricism: Roussel can be seductive (the charmingly sung Ronsard songs, with their elaborate flute arabesques) or exotic ("Krishna", the third of the "flute players"), he can even indulge in pastiche, as in the guitar *Segovia*, but – even if this sounds like heresy – his themes remain obstinately unmemorable and he lacks purely melodic invention. Throughout the disc the present performances merit the highest praise but special mention must be made of Erika Waardenburg's beautiful playing, with superfine tonal gradations, of the *Impromptu* for harp.

Further listening ...

...Piano Concerto in G major, Op. 36[a]. Concertino, Op. 57[b]. Pour une fête de printemps, Op. 22. Suite in F major, Op. 33. [b]**Albert Tétard** (vc); [a]**Danielle Laval** (pf); **Orchestre de Paris / Jean-Pierre Jacquillat.** EMI L'Esprit Français CDM5 65154-2 (7/95).

...Symphony No. 4 in A major, Op. 53. Sinfonietta, Op. 52. *Coupled with* **Debussy** La mer. **Milhaud** Suite provençale, Op. 152h. **Detroit Symphony Orchestra / Neeme Järvi.** Chandos CHAN9072 (12/92).

...Suite in F major, Op. 33. *Coupled with* **Chabrier** España. Suite pastorale. Joyeuse marche. Bourrée fantasque. Le Roi malgré lui – Fête polonaise; Danse slave. Gwendoline – Overture. **Detroit Symphony Orchestra / Paul Paray.** Mercury 434 303-2MM*. *See review under Chabrier; refer to the Index to Reviews.* ⊚⊚⊚

...Trio, Op. 40[afg]. String Quartet in D major, Op. 45[g]. Andante and Scherzo, Op. 51[ae]. Pipe in D major[ae]. Trio, Op. 58[g]. Elpénor, Op. 59[ag]. Andante[bcd]. [a]**Paul Verhey** (fl); [b]**Hans Roerade** (ob); [c]**Frank van den Brink** (cl); [d]**Jos de Lange** (bn); [e]**Jet Röling** (pf); [f]**Herre-Jan Stegenga** (vc); [g]**Schoenberg Quartet.** Olympia OCD460 (11/95).

...Divertissement, Op. 6. *Coupled with works by* **Saint-Saëns, d'Indy, Tansman, Françaix, Poulenc** and **Milhaud** Various soloists; Pascal Rogé (pf). Decca 425 861-2DH (5/91). *See review in the Collections section; refer to the Index to Reviews.*

...Andante and Scherzo, Op. 51[a]. *Coupled with* **Gaubert** Flute Sonata No. 1[a]. **Caplet** Rêverie et petite valse[a]. **Fauré** Fantaisie, Op. 79[a]. **Saint-Saëns** Romance in D flat major, Op. 37[a]. **Busser** Prélude et Scherzo[a]. **Poulenc** Flute Sonata[a]. **Ferroud** Trois Pièces. Peter Lloyd (fl); [a]**Rebecca Holt** (pf). IMP Classics PCD991 (9/92).

...Prelude and Fughetta, Op. 41. *Coupled with* **d'Indy** Prélude in E flat minor, Op. 66. **R. Vierne** Six pièces de différents caractères. **Barié** Trois Pièces, Op. 7. **Honegger** Fugue and Chorale. **Dupré** Scherzo, Op. 16. **Langlais** Prelude and Fugue, Op. 1. **L. Vierne** Les cloches de Hinckley, Op. 55 No. 6. **Marie-Bernadette Dufourcet** (org). Priory PRCD422 (6/95). *See review in the Collections section; refer to the Index to Reviews.*

Joseph-Nicolas-Pancrace Royer

French c1705-1755

Royer Pièces de clavecin. La Chasse de Zaïde. **Christophe Rousset** (hpd). L'Oiseau-Lyre Ⓕ 436
127-2OH (59 minutes: DDD: 9/93). ✐ Recorded 1991.   ⊚⊚

Pancrace Royer was a more prominent figure in French musical life than the comparative
unfamiliarity of his name nowadays would suggest. He was an imaginative director of the Concert
Spirituel, leader for several years of the Opéra orchestra, and a successful composer for the stage. His
ballet-héroïque, *Zaïde* (1739) was especially popular and was still being performed in the 1760s. *La
Chasse de Zaïde* is the composer's own harpsichord arrangement of a "symphonie" in the opera and,
in this new recital, Christophe Rousset appends it to the pieces of the 1746 publication. Royer's music
is not on a level with that of Rameau, his illustrious older contemporary, but it is neither dull or
predictable; and it sometimes recalls Rameau's idiom, especially in the more delicately wrought pieces
such as the wistful "La Zaïde" which hints at the latter's "Les Tendres Plaintes". Royer could be quite
an adventurous harmonist – another quality which he shared with Rameau – and he proves this in a
wild piece, "Le Vertigo", full of extravagant gestures and excitement generated by vigorously repeated
chordal passages, *tirades*, rhythmic interruptions and so forth. Indeed, its distinctly improvisatory
character foreshadows C.P.E. Bach. Rousset responds to these extremes of temperament with passion
on the one hand and sensibility on the other. The beautifully recorded, fine sounding harpsichord is
a 1751 instrument by the Parisian maker, Hemsch.

Miklós Rózsa

Hungarian/American 1907-

Rózsa Theme, Variations and Finale, Op. 13*a*. Hungarian Nocturne, Op. 28. Three Hungarian
Sketches, Op. 14. Overture to a Symphony Concert, Op. 26*a*. **New Zealand Symphony Orchestra /
James Sedares**. Koch International Classics Ⓕ 37191-2 (57 minutes: DDD: 9/93). Recorded 1992.
Gramophone Editor's choice.

The fervent Magyar rhythms that captivated Rózsa during his upbringing in Hungary spice almost
every bar of his music for both concert-hall and screen, but strikingly so in his early non-film work.
The *Theme, Variations and Finale* from 1933 was inspired by a wistful melody that came to him after
leaving his family and homeland for Paris. Tightly structured and bustling with youthful energy, it
illustrates perfectly how Rózsa's rhapsodic intensity and flair for dramatic shading would soon lead
to a remarkable career in Hollywood (Variation No. 4 could have come straight from one of the many
films noirs he later scored during the 1940s). Similarly flavourful and just as vigorously rhythmic are
the *Three Hungarian Sketches* (1938), whilst the balmy, moonlit *Hungarian Nocturne* (1964),
reminiscent of his impressionistic score for *Lust for Life*, is the composer's attempt "to recapture the
rare beauty of the nights on our estate in rural Hungary". The composition of the turbulent Overture
coincided with the Hungarian revolution in 1957. Sedares and the NZSO are remarkably intuitive
and, in the composer's own words "combine passion with discipline in exactly the way my music
demands". Add to this a clean, full-bodied recording and no further endorsement is required.

Rózsa Symphony in Three Movements, Op. 6*a*. The Vintner's Daughter, Op. 23*a*. **New Zealand
Symphony Orchestra / James Sedares.** Koch International Classics Ⓕ 37244-2 (56 minutes: DDD:
6/94). Recorded 1993.

Written in 1930, when the composer was 23, Rózsa deemed the Symphony in Three Movements a
failure, and after several attempts to pare down its length he eventually cast it aside completely.
However, in 1993 with the aid of Christopher Palmer, the surviving portions of his manuscript were
dusted off once again and edited into the 39-minute work premièred here. The ambitious structure
and expansive canvas used for the volatile 19-minute opening movement is particularly impressive,
with Rózsa fusing two memorable themes (one vigorously heroic, the other strongly nostalgic) into a
compelling, well-argued piece that possesses the direct intensity and emotion of his film scores, and
could well stand on its own. The second movement is a misty, reflective *Andante* for strings, whilst the
energetic finale is charged with the furious dancing rhythms so redolent of Rózsa's beloved Hungary.
The Vintner's Daughter (1953) makes a lovely and revealing companion. Here the youthful zeal and
bold, dramatic gestures that define the symphony have matured into a sensitive command of
orchestral colour. Through 12 enchanting variations, each one more beguiling than the last, Rózsa
illuminates Juste Olivier's nineteenth-century poem in delicate, sun-bleached shades, crowning the
piece with a nocturne liberally sprinkled with stardust. James Sedares and the NZSO prove exemplary
interpreters of this composer's music. Rózsa himself endorses the "fire and passion" they
undoubtedly bring to the Symphony (aided by warm and beefy sound), but their eloquent shading of
the 12 variations also deserves the highest praise.

New review

Rózsa Variations on a Hungarian Peasant Song, Op. 4[a]. North Hungarian Peasant Songs and
Dances, Op. 5[a]. Duo, Op. 7[a]. Solo Violin Sonata, Op. 40. **Isabella Lippi** (vn); [a]**John Novacek** (pf).
Koch International Classics Ⓕ 37256-2 (62 minutes: DDD: 11/95). Recorded 1994.

In his autobiography, *A Double Life* (Midas Books: 1982) Rózsa proudly declares that "the music of
Hungary is stamped indelibly ... on virtually every bar I have ever put on paper", and nowhere are the

fervent, rustic rhythms of the composer's beloved homeland more vividly assimilated than in his music for solo violin. This is especially true of Opp. 4 and 5, two early successes from 1929, both of which blaze with potent memories of the Magyar peasant music that Rózsa felt was all around him, and which he would jot down "in a kind of delirium" during his youth on the family estate. Op. 7 was written two years later and marked the end of his term as a student in Leipzig. Though evoking once again the gipsy fiddlers of his boyhood, the themes here are actually Rózsa's own and reveal some of the surging romanticism that would later characterize his film scores. Following his memorable career in Hollywood, Rózsa made a satisfying return to 'pure' music with the Solo Violin Sonata of 1986. Dedicated to his friend Manuel Compinsky, this passionate, energetic piece pays another loving tribute to the mother country that provided Rózsa with a "living source of inspiration". Isabella Lippi is a highly expressive soloist. She tackles the many fiendishly animated passages with great panache but also displays a keen understanding of the music's pastoral colouring and darkly romantic fervour. Sympathetic support from her accompanist and clear, warm sound.

New review

Rózsa El Cid. **Tamra Saylor Fine** (org); **New Zealand Youth Choir; New Zealand Symphony Orchestra / James Sedares.** Koch International Classics Ⓔ 37340-2 (66 minutes: DDD: 6/96). Recorded 1995.

When it came to the musical swashing of bucklers there were few to equal, and none to surpass, Miklós Rózsa. His 95 film scores encompassed a great variety of subjects and styles, but it was above all in epics that he was pre-eminent; and he himself considered the 1961 *El Cid*, about the real-life Castilian eleventh-century military hero, "my last important film, with the exception of *Providence* ... the climax and watershed of my film career". Steeping himself, as usual, in the historical and musical background of the time, he produced a brilliantly rich score in which are incorporated Moorish influences and medieval elements (one of the *cantigas* of Alfonso the Wise is elaborated in one of the music cues) but which also reveals his own brand of luscious romanticism. (The theme of the Love scene here would rival that of Rodrigo's famous slow movement and is vastly superior in its treatment.) The test for listeners to any film score without the images it was intended to support is whether it can stand on its own, purely as music. In this case Rózsa's music cues – several connected up for the purpose of this recording – rise above their evocation of dramatic atmosphere and, through his powers of invention, skill in construction and mastery of orchestral coloration, make satisfying independent entities. Intense playing from the New Zealand SO and vivid recording further enhance this disc.

Further listening ...

...Violin Concerto, Op. 24[b]. Tema con variazioni, Op. 29a[c]. *Coupled with* **Korngold** Violin Concerto, Op. 35[a]. **Waxman** Fantasy on Bizet's "Carmen"[d]. **Jascha Heifetz** (vn); [c]**Gregor Piatigorsky** (vc); [c]**Chamber Orchestra;** [a]**Los Angeles Philharmonic Orchestra / Alfred Wallenstein;** [b]**Dallas Symphony Orchestra / Walter Hendl;** [d]**RCA Victor Symphony Orchestra / Donald Voorhees.** RCA Victor Gold Seal [ad]mono/[bc]stereo GD87963* (4/89). *See review under Korngold; refer to the Index to Reviews.* ⒼⒼⒼ

...Film Scores – The Red House – Suite[a]; The Thief of Bagdad – The love of the princess; The Lost Weekend – Suite; The Four Feathers – Sunstroke/River journey; Double Indemnity – Mrs Dietrichson/ The conspiracy; Knights of the Round Table – Hawks in flight; The Jungle Book – Song of the jungle[a]; Spellbound – The dream sequence, The mountain lodge; Ivanhoe – Overture. [a]**Ambrosian Singers; National Philharmonic Orchestra / Charles Gerhardt.** RCA Victor GD80911 (5/91).

...Lust for Life – Suite. Background to Violence – Suite. **Frankenland State Symphony Orchestra / Miklós Rózsa.** Varèse Sarabande VSD5405 (10/93).

...Ivanhoe (reconstructed Robbins). **Sinfonia of London / Bruce Broughton.** Intrada Excalibur MAF7055D (5/95). Ⓖ

Edmund Rubbra

British 1901-1986

Rubbra Violin Concerto, Op. 103[a]. Viola Concerto, Op. 75[b]. [a]**Tasmin Little** (vn); [a]**Rivka Golani** (va); **Royal Philharmonic Orchestra / Vernon Handley.** Conifer Ⓔ CDCF225 (54 minutes: DDD: 10/94). Recorded 1994. ⒼⒼ

The Viola Concerto, a première recording, is a work of striking euphony and depth. There are none of the piquant dissonances of, say, the Bartók or Walton concertos; the Rubbra concentrates on linear development; the satisfaction this concerto gives resides primarily in the subtlety with which its lines evolve and grow. The pensive, rhapsodic opening puts one immediately under its spell. The most poetic of the three movements is the finale, subtitled *Collana musicale* or "musical necklace", nine linked sections, each of them self-contained and offering thoughts on the theme rather than conventional variations. Rivka Golani gives a fine account of the solo part, her playing committed and intelligent even though her tone could at times do with greater opulence. The Violin Concerto, too, is a three-movement piece, though here it is the middle movement, *Poema,* that is the emotional centre of gravity; it has both depth and serenity. The invention unfolds seemlessly and organically, each idea growing out of and developing from the preceding one. Tasmin Little's playing is thoughtful and eloquent and her virtuosity conveys a sense of effortless ease. Moreover, in Vernon Handley she is supported by a conductor who both knows what this music is about, and has its measure.

New review

Rubbra Symphonies – No. 4, Op. 53; No. 10, Op. 145, "Sinfonia da camera"; No. 11, Op. 153.
BBC National Orchestra of Wales / Richard Hickox. Chandos Ⓕ CHAN9401 (58 minutes: DDD: 1/96). Recorded 1993-4.

Rubbra's music lacks the kind of surface allure that captivates the ear at first acquaintance. Nor does he possess the dramatic power of Vaughan Williams or his immediate contemporary Walton, but he does have a sense of organic continuity that is both highly developed and immediately evident to the listener. Wilfrid Mellers put it in a nutshell when he said of the symphonies, there is "nothing abstruse about their tonality and harmony, which is basically diatonic", but they are difficult because "the continuity of their melodic and polyphonic growth is logical and unremitting. The orchestration shows scarcely any concern for the possibilities of colour, nothing on which the senses can linger and the nerves relax. Second subjects are hardly ever contrasting ideas but rather evolutions from or transfigurations of the old." The opening of the Fourth Symphony is one of the most beautiful things not just in Rubbra but in the English music of our time. These pages are free from any kind of artifice, and their serenity and quietude remain with the listener for a long time. The Fourth (1940-42) was a wartime work, though no one would ever guess so. The Tenth and Eleventh Symphonies are late works from 1974 and 1979 respectively. Both symphonies are highly concentrated one-movement affairs which unfold with the seeming inevitability and naturalness so characteristic of the composer. To sum up, this is music made to last. Richard Hickox has the measure of its breadth and serenity, and secures a sense of total commitment and dedication from his excellent players. The Chandos recording is in the best traditions of the house.

…No. 10. Improvisations on Virginal Pieces by Giles Farnaby, Op. 50. A Tribute, Op. 56.
Bournemouth Sinfonietta / Hans-Hubert Schönzeler. Chandos Collect Ⓜ CHAN6599 (40 minutes: ADD: 11/93).

New review

Rubbra Symphony No. 9, Op. 140, "Sinfonia sacra"[a]. The Morning Watch, Op. 55. [a]**Lynne Dawson** (sop); [a]**Della Jones** (mez); [a]**Stephen Roberts** (bar); **BBC National Chorus and Orchestra of Wales / Richard Hickox.** Chandos Ⓕ CHAN9441 (57 minutes: DDD: 6/96). Texts included. Item marked [a] recorded 1993, [b]1994. *Gramophone Editor's choice.*   Ⓖ

The Ninth is Rubbra's most visionary utterance and its subtitle, *Sinfonia sacra*, gives a good idea of its character. It tells the story of the Resurrection very much as do the Bach Passions. There are three soloists: the contralto narrates from the New Testament while the soprano takes the part of Mary Magdalen and the baritone that of Jesus. Other parts – those of disciples and angels – are taken by the chorus who also function outside the action, in four settings of meditative Latin texts from the Roman liturgy or in Lutheran chorales to which Rubbra has put verses by Bernard de Nevers. The symphonic dimension is reinforced by the opening motive, which pretty well dominates the work or, as the composer puts it, casts its shadow over everything. Its argument unfolds with a seeming inevitability and naturalness that is the hallmark of a great symphony. Its depth and beauty call to mind only the most exalted of comparisons and it should be heard as often as *Gerontius* or the *War Requiem*. This is music of an inspired breadth and serenity and everyone connected with this magnificent performance conveys a sense of profound conviction. *The Morning Watch*, one of Rubbra's most eloquent choral pieces (1946) comes roughly half-way between the Fourth and Fifth Symphonies. A setting of the seventeenth-century metaphysical poet, Henry Vaughan, it too is music of substance and its long and moving orchestral introduction is of the highest order of inspiration. Richard Hickox and his fine team of singers and players deserve thanks and congratulations, as indeed do Chandos for giving it such excellent sound.

New review

Rubbra String Quartets – No. 1 in F minor, Op. 35; No. 2 in E flat major; No. 3, Op. 112; No. 4, Op. 150. **Sterling Quartet** (Megan Pound, Rebecca Jones, vns; John Rayson, va; Brian Mullan, vc). Conifer Classics Ⓕ 75605 51260-2 (two discs: 81 minutes: DDD: 5/96). Recorded 1995.

Rubbra's four quartets cover an even longer period of his creative career than the symphonies: the first version of the F minor Quartet goes back to 1933, before the First Symphony, while the Fourth dates from 1977 just before the last, one-movement Eleventh. The First pays tributes to Vaughan Williams, "whose persistent interest" in the original 1933 version led to a revision of the score in 1946, while the Fourth is dedicated to a younger master of the medium, Robert Simpson. The late Harold Truscott went so far as to call the Second "a key work in [Rubbra's] output, and in the revised version of 1946, one of the greatest string quartets I know". The Third, written in 1963, moves with a tremendous sense of purpose, and is a work of great nobility and expressive substance, and the same holds for the elegiac Fourth. It almost beggars belief that three of these quartets are appearing on CD for the first time. Gratitude is in order for the advocacy of the Sterling Quartet, whose playing has splendid commitment. They have evident feeling for this music. Generally speaking intonation and ensemble are very good, though dynamic contrasts could be made more telling. Much of the blame must rest with the forward balance which does not flatter the musicians tonally. However, readers need not hold back on this count. This is music of depth and eloquence and needs to resonate in the world. As Sir Adrian Boult once wrote, Rubbra has never made any concession to popularity, but "he goes on creating masterpieces, which I am convinced will survive their composer and most of those who are his contemporaries".

Additional recommendation ...
...No. 2 in E flat major. **Tate** String Quartet in F major. **P. Wishart** String Quartet No. 3 in A major. **English Quartet.** Tremula Ⓕ TREM102-2 (69 minutes: DDD: 12/93).

Further listening ...
...Symphonies – No. 2 in D major, Op. 45[a]; No. 7 in C major, Op. 88[b]. Festival Overture, Op. 62[c]. [ac]**New Philharmonia Orchestra / Vernon Handley;** [b]**London Philharmonic Orchestra / Sir Adrian Boult.** Lyrita SRCD235 (12/92).
...Symphonies – No. 3, Op. 49; No. 4, Op. 53. A Tribute, Op. 56. Resurgam – Overture, Op. 149. **Philharmonia Orchestra / Norman Del Mar.** Lyrita SRCD202 (11/90). *Selected by Sounds in Retrospect.*
...Symphony No. 5 in B flat major, Op. 63[a]. *Coupled with* **Bliss** Checkmate – excerpts[b]. **Tippett** Little Music for Strings (1946)[c]. [a]**Melbourne Symphony Orchestra;** [b]**West Australian Symphony Orchestra;** [c]**Soloists of Australia /** [c]**Ronald Thomas,** [ab]**Hans-Hubert Schönzeler.** Chandos Collect CHAN6576 (6/92).
...Symphonies – No. 6, Op. 80[a]; No. 8, Op. 132, "Hommage à Teilhard de Chardin". Soliloquy, Op. 57[b]. [b]**Rohan de Saram** (vc); [b]**London Symphony Orchestra / Vernon Handley;** [a]**Philharmonia Orchestra / Norman Del Mar.** Lyrita SRCD234 (10/92).
...Cello Sonata in G minor, Op. 60. *Coupled with works by* **Moeran** *and* **Ireland** Raphael Wallfisch (vc); **John York** (pf). Marco Polo 8 223718 (8/95). *See review under Moeran; refer to the Index to Reviews.*
...Cello Sonata in G minor, Op. 60. *Coupled with works by* **Britten** *and* **Mayer** Timothy Gill (vc); **Fali Pavri** (pf). Guild GMCD7114 (4/96). *See review under Mayer; refer to the Index to Reviews.*

Anton Rubinstein

USSR 1829-1894

New review
Rubinstein Piano Concerto No. 4 in D minor, Op. 70[a].
Encores Shura Cherkassky (pf); [a]**Royal Philharmonic Orchestra / Vladimir Ashkenazy.** Decca Ⓕ 448 063-2DH (76 minutes: [a]DDD/[b]ADD: 3/96). Items marked [b] from L'Oiseau Lyre DSLO7 (6/75). Items marked [a]recorded 1994, [b]1974.
Encores[b]: **Rubinstein** Melody in F major, Op. 3 No. 1. **J. Strauss II/Godowsky** Wein, Weib und Gesang. **Godowsky** Waltz-poem No. 4 (for left hand). Triakontameron – Alt Wien. **Saint-Saëns/Godowsky** Le carnaval des animaux – No. 13, The swan. **Schubert/Godowsky** Moment musical in F minor, D780 No. 3. **Tchaikovsky** Nocturne in C sharp minor, Op. 19 No. 4. **Glazunov** Valse in D major, Op. 42 No. 3. **Chaminade** Autrefois, Op. 87 No. 4. **Moszkowski** Caprice espagnole, Op. 37.
All these performances now achieve an added poignancy given Cherkassky's demise and make one ask, what other pianist possessed so succulent or teasing a sense of sophistication? Every glistening strand of Godowsky's *Wein, Weib und Gesang*, his polyphonic, poly-rhythmic maze, is highlighted with uncanny virtuoso resource, and even Sir Clifford Curzon – that incomparable Schubertian – would surely have smiled rather than frowned over Cherkassky's Schubert-Godowsky, an arrangement he abhorred. Glazunov's *Valse* in D is spun off with a delicate, vertiginous brilliance entirely Cherkassky's own and Chaminade's *Autrefois*, a charming pastiche, repeats an early and legendary success on an HMV 78. Then there is Rubinstein's Fourth Concerto, another work for long at the centre of Cherkassky's affections. That august publication, *The Record Guide* (Collins: 1951) may have offered a sniping estimate ("the swelling introduction promises great things, but what emerges is perhaps only a rather large mouse") but played with Cherkassky's musical commitment even the most outwardly conventional gestures take wing. A passing sense of frailty is instantly erased by Cherkassky's tip-toe delicacy in the whirlwind finale, by a shot-silk tonal finesse in the central *Andante*, and by a capacity to take all the time in the world to make his points, whether piquantly or expressively. Ashkenazy's partnership with his quicksilver soloist could hardly be more sympathetic and the recordings capture Cherkassky's tonal bloom and colour to perfection.

Additional recommendation ...
...Piano Concertos – No. 3 in G major, Op. 45; No. 4. **Joseph Banowetz** (pf); **Košice State Philharmonic Orchestra / Robert Stankovsky.** Marco Polo 8 223382.

Rubinstein Piano Concerto No. 5 in E flat major, Op. 94. Caprice russe, Op. 102. **Joseph Banowetz** (pf); **Bratislava Radio Symphony Orchestra / Robert Stankovsky.** Marco Polo Ⓕ 8 223489 (67 minutes: DDD: 2/95). Recorded 1993.
This disc brings to a conclusion Joseph Banowetz's admirable survey of Rubinstein's complete music for piano and orchestra for Marco Polo. The Fifth Concerto (dating from 1874) is by far the most monumental, both in terms of duration – it spans some 46 minutes – and in the virtuosic demands that it places on any pianist brave enough to undertake a performance. Although it certainly has its

flaws (its length being one) there is still a great deal to admire, not least its abundance of warmly lyrical melodies. The technical difficulties of the solo part may largely account for the concerto's absence from the repertoire (the work is dedicated to the high priest of super-virtuosity, Alkan, and contains chordal spans of gigantic proportions); but there is certainly more to this work than mere showy virtuosity. The *Caprice russe* was composed four years after the Fifth Concerto and is a single movement *concertante* work based on three Russian folk-songs whose origins, as Banowetz writes, are somewhat dubious. Judging by his brilliant and engaging performance Banowetz clearly has a good deal of faith in the piece.

New review

Rubinstein The Demon. **Anatoly Lochak** (bar) Demon; **Alison Browner** (mez) Angel; **Marina Mescheriakova** (sop) Tamara; **Leonid Zimnenko** (bass) Gudal; **Valery Serkin** (ten) Sinodal; **Richard Robson** (bass) Servant; **Ludmilla Andrew** (sop) Nanny; **Wjacheslav Weinorowski** (ten) Messenger; **Wexford Festival Chorus; National Symphony Orchestra of Ireland / Alexander Anissimov.** Marco Polo Ⓔ 8 223781/2 (two discs: 127 minutes: DDD: 3/96). Notes, text and translation included. Recorded live in 1994.

It was an excellent idea to record Wexford's 1994 production of *The Demon*, Rubinstein's most popular opera (it was given more times in nineteenth-century Russia than any other opera except the regular season-opening *Life for the Tsar*), the first Russian opera to be given in England (Covent Garden, 1881), and a work which has since fallen into comparative neglect. If the result has its flaws, they are superficial and are well worth ignoring: the recording tends to come and go a bit, there is a good deal of stage clumping, and the oddly arranged booklet separates transliteration from translation instead of having them face to face, rendering the exercise pretty pointless. No matter (or not much matter): *The Demon* is a fascinating work. Lermontov's immensely popular poem tells of the Demon (a fallen angel) pursuing Tamara to a monastery where she is mourning the bridegroom he has killed; she is also trying to escape the Demon's seductive lurings (which provide the work with some of its finest music). She accepts his kiss and dies, but her soul is redeemed while the Demon is denied his hoped-for redemption through her love. There is, in fact, a note of the Flying Dutchman about him, as well as that of the Byronic *âme damnée* so much admired in Russia. Rubinstein's opera certainly influenced his pupil Tchaikovsky's *Eugene Onegin*. The cast is excellent. Anatoly Lochak delivers his siren lures to Tamara with just the right mixture of the sinister, the melancholy and the impassioned. She, Marina Mescheriakova, is a bright-voiced soprano with a touching sense of phrasing. Valery Serkin, her soon-murdered bridegroom, sings lightly and truly, and Alison Browner hovers gleaming as the Angel. The chorus sound a little ill-served by the recording, but the orchestra, under Alexander Anissimov, do good justice to Rubinstein's colourful and lyrically expressive score. There is one sizeable cut, the ballet, and a number of smaller ones.

Further listening ...

...Piano Concertos – No. 1 in E major, Op. 25; No. 2 in F major, Op. 35. **Joseph Banowetz** (pf); **Košicee State Philharmonic Orchestra / Alfred Walter.** Marco Polo 8 223456 (7/93).

...Symphony No. 4 in D minor, Op. 95, "Dramatic". **Russian State Symphony Orchestra / Igor Golovchin.** Russian Disc RDCD11357 (6/95).

...Don Quixote, Op. 87. Ivan the Terrible, Op. 79. **Russian State Symphony Orchestra / Igor Golovchin.** Russian Disc RDCD11397 (9/95).

...Cello Sonata No. 1 in D major, Op. 18. *Coupled with works by* **Liszt** and **Grieg** Steven Isserlis (vc); **Stephen Hough** (pf). RCA Victor Red Seal 09026 68290-2 (4/96). *See review under Grieg; refer to the Index to Reviews.*

...Piano Sonatas – No. 1 in E minor, Op. 12; No. 3 in F major, Op. 41. **Leslie Howard** (pf). Hyperion CDA66017 (5/90).

...Piano Sonatas – No. 2 in C minor, Op. 20; No. 4 in A minor, Op. 100. **Leslie Howard** (pf). Hyperion CDA66105 (5/90).

...Barcarolles – No. 3 in G minor; No. 4 in G major. Valse-caprice in E flat major. *Coupled with* **Liszt** Harmonies poétiques et réligieuses, S173 – Funérailles. Valses impromptu, S213. Valses oubliées, S215 – No. 1, Mephisto Waltz No. 1, "Der Tanz in der Dorfschenke", S514. Liebesträume, S541 – No. 2. Hungarian Rhapsodies, S244 – No. 10 in E major; No. 12 in C sharp minor. Consolations, S172 – No. 3, Lento placido. **Artur Rubinstein** (pf). RCA Victor Gold Seal mono 09026 61860-2* (1/94).

...The Demon – Do not weep, my child; On the airy ocean; I am he whom you called. Nero – Vindex's Epithalamium: I sing to you, Hymen divine! *Coupled with works by* **Rimsky-Korsakov, Mussorgsky, Borodin** and **Rachmaninov** Dmitri Hvorostovsky (bar); **Kirov Theatre Orchestra / Valery Gergiev.** Philips 438 872-2PH (5/94). *See review in the Collections section; refer to the Index to Reviews.*

...*See also the* **Great Singers at the Maryinsky Theatre** *review in the Collections section; refer to the Index to Reviews.* Nimbus Prima Voce mono NI7865* (3/95).

Poul Ruders

New review
Ruders Violin Concerto No. 1[a]. Etude and Ricercare[b]. The Bells[c]. The Christmas Gospel[d]. [c]**Lucy Shelton** (sop); [a]**Rolf Schulte** (vn); [c]**Speculum Musicae / David Starobin** ([b]gtr); [a]**Riverside Symphony Orchestra / George Rothman;** [d]**Malmö Symphony Orchestra / Ola Rudner.** Bridge Ⓕ BCD9057 (62 minutes: DDD: 2/96). Texts included. Recorded 1994-5. *Gramophone Editor's choice.*　Ⓖ

Ruders's First Violin Concerto (from 1981) begins as routine minimalist auto-hypnosis. But it develops some wonderfully inventive ways of disrupting and reassembling itself. Admittedly the last movement, with its chaconne based on Vivaldi and Schubert, tiptoes on the border of sensationalism. Otherwise the work could join Schnittke's Fourth as one of the few contemporary violin concertos with a strong claim to standard-repertoire status. The previous performance by Rebecca Hirsch on Unicorn-Kanchana was superb; now Rolf Schulte gives an even more intense account of the solo part, the Riverside orchestra are even tighter in discipline, and the recording is a fraction closer. All these factors help to make the overall musical impression even more vivid. Less persuasive is Ruders's vocal writing in *The Bells* (the same Edgar Allen Poe texts as set by Rachmaninov), and there is something not quite convincing about the instrumental setting too – perhaps too uniform an intensity, too much frantic heterophony (Messiaen's "Danse de la Fureur" from the *Quatuor pour la fin du temps* has a lot to answer for). Oliver Knussen has done this sort of thing rather more successfully. *The Christmas Gospel*, tossed off in two weeks for a mixed animation and live-action film, is darkly impressive – necessarily simple and direct, but still rewarding, even when divorced from the visual images. Superb performances and recordings, as throughout the disc.

Ruders Violin Concerto No. 2[a]. Dramaphonia[b]. [a]**Rebecca Hirsch** (vn); [b]**Poul Rosenbaum** (pf); [a]**Copenhagen Collegium Musicum / Michael Schønwandt;** [b]**Lontano / Odaline de la Martinez.** Da capo Ⓕ DCCD9308 (61 minutes: DDD: 9/84). Recorded 1992.

The Second Violin Concerto was composed in 1990-91. It opens with two contrasting but tranquil movements, the first inspired by the sight of an Andean eagle, seen by the composer whilst on holiday in Chile. The imagery of a bird in flight, soaring, wheeling, diving, now still, permeates the music, the last two movements of which are more impassioned. *Dramaphonia* (1987), played here by the ensemble for whom it was composed (Lontano and Odaline de la Martinez), is of a more radical cast, having no particular programme. The music charts a cumulatively compelling course through three movements (played without a break) depicting a wide range of emotional states and atmospheres, such as "Sinister", "Nervous", "Bleak", "Frantic" and so on. Both works receive committed and well-prepared performances and the disc has been well-engineered.

Ruders Gong. Symphony "Himmelhoch Jauchzend – zum Tode Betrübt". Thus saw Saint John. Tundra. **Danish National Radio Symphony Orchestra / Leif Segerstam.** Chandos Ⓕ CHAN9179 (75 minutes: DDD: 10/93). Recorded 1993.　Ⓖ

Imagine, if you can, a music with the visceral impact of a Xenakis, the celebratory energy of a Tippett and the subtlety of a Dutilleux; a music of volcanic pulsation and of undreamt-of sound-colours, hurled around orchestral space with sure-footed abandon; a music which, at its best, seems to hail from a triumphant future. Such are the first impressions of these orchestral works by Poul Ruders. Over the last ten years or so Ruders has vaulted to prominence over the backs of such estimable senior colleagues as his fellow-Dane Per Nørgaard. The style is extrovert and international, direct in its appeal, especially its sonic appeal, yet at the same time always searching, never complacent or opportunistic – a thinking person's John Adams, perhaps. From the opening explosion of *Gong*, and the descending shards of sound which result, it is instantly clear that Ruders has been conducting a passionate love-affair with the resources of the symphony orchestra. Even a rather crude conclusion does little to detract from the sheer excitement generated by this piece. If reservations must be entered, one is not always convinced by his attempts to generate interest from slender material. *Tundra,* a 1990 tribute for the 125th anniversary of Sibelius's birth, is an example of this and the second movement of the Symphony overestimates the potential of its two alternating, overlapping and inter-penetrating chords. Still, most of this Goethe-inspired symphony exerts an enthralling power, and renewed acquaintance will not dull its impact. That already says much for the orchestral playing under the dynamic direction of Leif Segerstam, not to mention the spacious perspectives of yet another first-rate Chandos recording. It is arguable that the kind of apocalyptic extremism of a piece such as *Thus saw Saint John* does not exactly represent the greatest of compositional challenges. However, if you are prepared to believe that virtuosic energy and beauty are self-justifying virtues, the chances are you will revel in this music.

Further listening ...

…String Quartets – No. 2; No. 3, "Motet". *Coupled with* **Abrahamsen** String Quartets Nos. 1 and 2. **Kontra Quartet.** Da capo DCCD9006.

…Violin Concerto No. 1[a]. Concerto for Clarinet and Twin-orchestra[b]. Drama-Trilogy – Cello Concerto, "Polydrama"[c]. [a]**Rebecca Hirsch** (vn); [b]**Niels Thomsen** (cl); [c]**Morten Zeuthen** (vc); **Odense Symphony Orchestra / Tamás Vetö.** Unicorn-Kanchana DKPCD9114 (4/92).

…Psalmodies[a]. Vox in Rama[b]. Nightshade[c]. [a]**David Starobin** (gtr), [a]**Speculum Musicae / David Palma;** [bc]**Capricorn / **[c]**Oliver Knussen.** Bridge BCD9037 (5/93).

Carl Ruggles

New review

Ruggles Sun-treader. Men and Mountains.
Ives Orchestral Sets – No. 1, "A New England Symphony"; No. 2[a].
Crawford Seeger Andante for Strings. **Cleveland** [a]**Chorus and Orchestra / Christoph von**
Dohnányi. Decca Ⓕ 443 776-2DH (62 minutes: DDD: 12/95). Recorded 1993-4.

The policy of linking Ives with other American heroic pioneers is the basis of this release. The
complete novelty here is the *Andante* from Crawford's pioneering 1931 String Quartet in its string
orchestra version. As an exploratory use of texture, it has a strong atmosphere but will never reach
the public in the way that Barber's heart-throb *Adagio*, taken from his string quartet, has done. In
concentration she's a kind of American Webern. Ruggles, too, was far from prolific. At the 1974 Ives
Centenary Conference in New York badges were handed out declaring "Ives thrives". He certainly
does in the CD catalogue today and, conversely, the best you could claim for his friend is that
"Ruggles struggles", and both *Sun-treader* and *Men and Mountains* are Ruggles classics needed on
CD. The choice about Ives depends on coupling. The *Orchestral Set* No. 2, long unavailable, is now
in competition with the Cincinnati Orchestra under Samuel on Centaur, the release that launched the
controversial Ives/Austin *Universe Symphony*. Both performances are effective, but perhaps the
Cincinnati players swing better in "The Rockstrewn Hills". The Cleveland release gives us both the
First and Second *Orchestral Sets*, the First best known as *Three Places in New England*, of which this
is the seventh recording in the British catalogue. It is always interesting to compare different recorded
versions of Ives's denser canvases. *Three Places* comes off well, but the bass is too remote at the start
of No. 1. Strongly recommended for the Ruggles.

Gerhard Rühm

Suggested listening ...
...Schöpfung. Foetus. Sprechquartette. *Coupled with* **Eisler** Woodburry-Liederbüchlein. **Schwehr**
Deutsche Tänze. **Van de Vate** Cocaine Lil. **Bel Canto Ensemble / Dietburg Spohr.** Koch
Schwann 314322 (3/95).

Lucas Ruiz de Ribayaz

New review

Ruiz de Ribayaz Luz y norte. **The Harp Consort** (Paul O'Dette, gtr/lte/banduria/theorbo; Pat
O'Brien, gtr/banduria; Thomas Ihlenfeldt, gtr/theorbo; Steve Player, gtr/dncr; Hille Perl, va da
gamba/lira; Jane Achtman, va da gamba; Pedro Estevan, perc) / **Andrew Lawrence-King** (hp/
psaltery/org/hpd). Deutsche Harmonia Mundi Ⓕ 05472 77340-2 (72 minutes: DDD: 1/96).
Recorded 1994.

Ruiz de Ribayaz was a seventeenth-century Spanish priest whose only surviving work is the *Luz y*
norte ("A Lantern and guiding star"), published in 1677 in Madrid when he was 51 years old. The
book includes tutors for the five-course guitar and two-course chromatic harp, and musical
instruction – an instrumental coupling mirrored in the reprinting of some items from Mudarra's
vihuela book of 1546 by Henestrosa, also "for keyboard and harp". A supplement contains many
pieces in dance form for both instruments, of which some were based on works by other composers.
The dances, representative of both court and popular (even 'punk') cultures, came mainly from Spain
and Italy but a few crossed the Atlantic from Ibero-America and are to be found also in an undated
manuscript by Santiago de Murcia, found in Mexico; this raises teasing questions to which we lack
answers. The music is presented in both solo-instrumental and various ensemble settings, several of
the latter according with the structure of dance bands of the time – with a veritable shop-full of
instruments. All is explained in the excellent annotation, which reveals that the chromatic notes (on a
diatonic harp) in the Mexican *Zarambeques* are produced by pressing the tuning hammer against the
strings, but does not mention that those in Mudarra's *Fantasia* were probably made by pressing with
the fingers – as folk harpists still do in Ibero-America. This was a period of experiment and adventure,
and the music reflects it in all its happier aspects; in turn, The Harp Consort convey it in the most
fascinatingly vivid and imaginatively varied way one might wish for. Here is a joyous experience, not
to be missed.

William Russell

Suggested listening ...
...Voluntary in F major. *Coupled with works by* **Boyce, Handel, Heron, Hook, Stanley,**
Stubley and **S. Wesley** Jennifer Bate (org). Unicorn-Kanchana DKPCD9106 (11/91).
Selected by Sounds in Retrospect. See review in the Collections section; refer to the Index
to Reviews.   Ⓖ

John Rutter

Rutter Five Traditional Songs.
Vaughan Williams Five English Folksongs.
Traditional (arr. Rutter) I know where I'm going. Down by the sally gardens. The bold grenadier.
The keel row. The cuckoo. She's like the swallow. Willow song. The willow tree. The miller of
Dee. O can ye sew cushions? Afton water. The sprig of thyme. She moved through the fair (arr.
Runswick). The lark in the clear air (arr. Carter). **Cambridge Singers; City of London Sinfonia /
John Rutter.** Collegium Ⓟ COLCD120 (66 minutes: DDD: 11/93). Texts included.   Ⓖ

Pleasure in singing is almost the *raison d'être* of this disc. John Rutter not only provides those of us
over 30 with a healthy dollop of nostalgia, but gives these songs a whole new lease of life in some
characteristically scrumptious arrangements. He is not attempting to follow in the footsteps of the
great folk-song arrangers (he pays tribute to this tradition by including Vaughan Williams's *Five
English Folksongs*). His arrangements belong more to the light music tradition; what Messrs Binge,
Coates and Tomlinson achieved with orchestral colours Rutter finds primarily through vocal ones –
and it's significant that the very finest arrangements here (including a ravishing "Golden Slumbers")
are unaccompanied. To this end he is supported beyond all dreams by this outstanding group of
singers. This is a lovely disc.

Further listening ...

...Fancies[a]. Suite antique[b]. Five Childhood Lyrics[c]. When icicles hang[a]. [b]**Duke Dobing** (fl); [b]**Wayne
Marshall** (hpd); [ac]**Cambridge Singers;** [ab]**City of London Sinfonia / John Rutter.** Collegium
COLCD117 (3/93).

...Gloria for chorus and orchestra. Anthems – All things bright and beautiful; The Lord bless you
and keep you; The Lord is my shepherd; O clap your hands; Open thou mine eyes; Praise ye the
Lord; A Prayer of St Patrick. **Cambridge Singers; Philip Jones Brass Ensemble / John Rutter.**
Collegium COLCD100 (6/87).

...Requiem. I will lift up mine eyes – Psalm 121. **Caroline Ashton, Donna Deam** (sops); **Cambridge
Singers; City of London Sinfonia / John Rutter.** Collegium COLCD103 (11/86).

Peter Ruzicka

Suggested listening ...

..."... das Gesegnete, das Verfluchte", *Coupled with* **Pettersson** Symphony No. 15. **Berlin Radio
Symphony Orchestra / Peter Ruzicka.** CPO CPO999 095-2 (12/95).

Terje Rypdal

Suggested listening ...

...Q.E.D., Op. 52. Largo, Op. 55. **Terje Rypdal** (electric gtr); **Borealis Ensemble / Christian Eggen.**
ECM 513 374-2 (8/93).

Kaija Saariaho

Suggested listening ...

...Du cristal[a]. ... à la fumée[b]. Nymphea, "Jardin secret III"[c]. [b]**Petri Alanko** (alto fl); [b]**Anssi
Karttunen** (vc); [c]**Kronos Quartet;** [ab]**Los Angeles Philharmonic Orchestra / Esa-Pekka Salonen.**
Ondine ODE804-2 (10/93).

Antonio Sacchini

Suggested listening ...

...La contadina in corte. **Soloists; Sassari Symphony Orchestra / Gabrielle Catalucci.** Bongiovanni
GB2145/6-2 (1/95).

Nicholas Sackman

New review

Sackman Hawthorn. **BBC Symphony Orchestra / Andrew Davis.** NMC (special price) NMCD027S
(27 minutes: DDD: 7/96).

Nicholas Sackman composed *Hawthorn* for the 1993 Henry Wood Promenade Concerts. The work
brought a strong impression of what Sackman terms "the physicality of the Yorkshire countryside"
into the Albert Hall, but it is not simply a piece of musical landscape painting. Late-eighteenth-century
Yorkshire, as depicted in Glyn Hughes's novel *The Hawthorn Goddess*, was a "bigoted and superstitious

world" in which the aptly named Anne Wylde lived and rebelled. Sackman's music responds to the atmosphere of this story rather than to its sequence of events, and it does so with considerable strength of character. From the outset fragments knit together to hold the attention, and periodic surges of energy set the reflective passages into appropriate relief. Sackman's idiom owes something to the pungent intensity of his mentor Alexander Goehr, as well as suggesting the panache and neo-romantic turbulence of Colin Matthews – another, earlier product of Nottingham University, where Sackman studied and now teaches. Yet Sackman is no mere imitator, and this landscape is very much his own. He writes of the way "long-limbed melodies push their way through the undergrowth of ornate musical detail", and in places the pushing may seem rather protractedly effortful; but the work as a whole is well integrated, assured and approachable without patently playing to the gallery. This performance is no less assured, and the recording brings every detail of the score into clear and colourful focus.

Further listening ...

...Piano Sonata. *Coupled with works by* **Tippett, Saxton** and **Connolly** Steven Neugarten (pf). Metier MSVCD92008 (1/96). *See review in the Collections section; refer to the Index to Reviews.* Ⓖ

Camille Saint-Saëns

French 1835-1921

New review
Saint-Saëns Cello Concerto No. 1 in D minor[a].
Lalo Cello Concerto[b].
Schumann Cello Concerto No. 1 in A minor, Op. 129[b]. **János Starker** (vc); **London Symphony Orchestra** / [a]**Antál Dorati,** [b]**Stanislaw Skrowaczewski.** Mercury Ⓜ 432 010-2MM (65 minutes: ADD: 4/92). Item marked [a] from Philips SAL3482 (3/65), [b]SAL3559 (7/66). ⒼⒼ

János Starker recorded for the Mercury label on several occasions during the 1960s, and the results provide a vivid document of an extraordinary artist heard at the peak of his career. The First Cello Concerto – which the composer completed in 1872 - is possibly Saint-Saëns's most fluent of all his concertos. However, he found the technical means of the instrument so restrictive that he vowed never to write another one, a vow he failed to keep. It has a pleasing, symmetrical design, full of engaging music. Starker succeeds in making it sound a good deal more substantial than it really is, in a reading of exemplary mastery coupled with scrupulous attention to every requirement of the score. His outward intensity belies a formidable intellectual mastery of Schumann's Cello Concerto, a work whose tangible mood of paranoia and mingled heroism has perplexed generations of players and listeners alike. Interpretations as zealous and charismatic as this are certainly to be treasured, as much for a clarification of the composer's intention, as for the valiant heroism of Starker's playing. He brings a similar clear-sighted gravity of purpose to the Lalo concerto, with a suitably massive opening movement contrasted effectively by a charmingly realized intermezzo and a finale of quicksilver brilliance. The sheer dynamism and drama of this reading has never been bettered. Mercury's original masters traditionally set new standards of fidelity and dynamic range, but in their refurbished form it seems scarcely possible that these classic performances are over 30 years old, whilst from a musical standpoint, these individual and occasionally provocative readings remain as enthralling as ever.

Additional recommendations ...

...Cello Concerto. **Bruch** Kol Nidrei, Op. 47. **Lalo** Cello Concerto in D minor. **Matt Haimovitz** (vc); **Chicago Symphony Orchestra / James Levine.** DG Ⓕ 427 323-2GH (59 minutes: DDD: 6/89).

...Cello Concerto. **Fauré** Elégie in C minor, Op. 24. **Lalo** Cello Concerto. **Heinrich Schiff** (vc); **New Philharmonia Orchestra / Sir Charles Mackerras.** DG Privilege Ⓑ 431 166-2GR (53 minutes: ADD: 8/91).

...Cello Concerto. **Lalo** Cello Concerto. **Massenet** Fantaisie. **Sophie Rolland** (vc); **BBC Philharmonic Orchestra / Gilbert Varga.** ASV Ⓕ CDDCA867 (65 minutes: DDD: 12/93). *See review under Lalo; refer to the Index to Reviews.* Ⓖ

...Cello Concerto. Le carnaval des animaux – The swan[a]. Romance in F major, Op. 36[b]. Romance in D major, Op. 51[b]. Cello Sonata No. 1 in C minor, Op. 32[b]. Chant saphique in D major, Op. 91[b]. Gavotte in G minor, Op. posth[b]. Allegro appassionato in B minor, Op. 43[b]. Prière, Op. 158[c]. **Steven Isserlis** (vc); **Dudley Moore,** [b]**Pascal Devoyon** (pfs); [c]**Francis Grier** (org); **London Symphony Orchestra / Michael Tilson Thomas.** RCA Victor Red Seal Ⓕ 09026 61678-2 (59 minutes: DDD: 12/93). Ⓖ

...Cello Concerto. *Coupled with works by* **Dvořák, Schumann, Delius, Elgar, Haydn, Monn, Chopin, Franck, Fauré, Bruch, Bach, Handel** *and* **Beethoven** Jacqueline du Pré (vc) with various artists and orchestras. EMI Ⓑ CZS5 68132-2 (six discs: 437 minutes: ADD: 8/94). *See review in the Collections section; refer to the Index to Reviews.* ⒼⒼ

Saint-Saëns Piano Concertos – No. 1 in D major, Op. 17[a]; No. 2 in G minor, Op. 22[b]; No. 3 in E flat major, Op. 29[c]; No. 4 in C minor, Op. 44[a]; No. 5 in F major, Op. 103, "Egyptian"[b]. **Pascal Rogé** (pf); [a]**Philharmonia Orchestra;** [b]**Royal Philharmonic Orchestra;** [c]**London Philharmonic Orchestra / Charles Dutoit.** Double Decca Ⓜ 443 865-2DF2 (two discs: 140 minutes: ADD: 7/95). From D244D3 (10/81). ⒼⒼ

Saint-Saëns's First Concerto was written when the composer was 23 years old, and it is a sunny, youthful, happy work conventionally cast in the traditional three-movement form. A decade later he wrote the Second Concerto in a period of only three weeks. This concerto begins in a mood of high seriousness rather in the style of a Bach organ prelude; then this stern mood gives way to a jolly fleet-footed scherzo and a *presto* finale: it is an uneven work, though the most popular of the five concertos. The Third Concerto is perhaps the least interesting work, whilst the Fourth is the best of the five. It is in effect a one-movement work cast in three ingeniously crafted sections. Saint-Saëns wrote his last, the *Egyptian*, in 1896 to mark his 50 years as a concert artist. Mirroring the sights and sounds of a country he loved, this is another brilliant work. Pascal Rogé has a very secure, exuberant sense of rhythm, which is vital in these works, as is his immaculate, pearly technique. Dutoit is a particularly sensitive accompanist and persuades all three orchestras to play with that lean brilliance which the concertos demand. The recordings are true and well-balanced.

Additional recommendations ...

...No. 2[a]. **Falla** Nights in the gardens of Spain[a]. El amor brujo. Ritual Fire Dance (arr. Rubinstein). **Franck** Symphonic Variations, Op. 46[b]. **Prokofiev** The Love for Three Oranges – March. **Artur Rubinstein** (pf); [a]**Philadelphia Orchestra / Eugene Ormandy;** [b]**Symphony Orchestra of the Air / Alfred Wallenstein.** RCA Digital Red Seal Ⓜ RD85666 (63 minutes: ADD: 10/87). Ⓖ

...Nos. 2 and 4. **Idil Biret** (pf); **Philharmonia Orchestra / James Loughran.** Naxos Ⓢ 8 550334 (55 minutes: DDD: 12/90).

...Nos. 1-5. **Aldo Ciccolini** (pf); **Orchestre de Paris / Serge Baudo.** EMI Rouge et Noir Ⓜ CMS7 69443-2 (two discs: 138 minutes: ADD: 3/92). ⒼⒼ

Saint-Saëns Piano Concerto No. 2 in G minor, Op. 22[b].
Rachmaninov Piano Concerto No. 3 in D minor, Op. 30[a].
Shostakovich Prelude and Fugue in D major, Op. 87 No. 5[c]. **Emil Gilels** (pf); [ab]**Paris Conservatoire Orchestra / André Cluytens.** Testament mono Ⓕ SBT1029* (65 minutes: ADD: 2/94). Item marked [a] from Columbia 33CX1323 (1/56), [b]33CX1217 (3/55), [c]33CX1364 (9/56). Recorded 1954-56. ⒼⒼ

Gilels was a true king of pianists and these Paris and New York based recordings can only strengthen and confirm his legendary status. Here, once more, is that superlative musicianship, that magisterial technique and, above all, that unforgettable sonority; rich and sumptuous at every level. What breadth and distinction he brings to the first movement of the Saint-Saëns, from his fulmination in the central octave uproar to his uncanny stillness in the final pages. High jinks are reserved for the second and third movements, the former tossed off with a teasing lightness, the latter's whirling measures with infinite brio. An approximate swipe at the *Scherzo*'s flashing double-note flourish, a false entry and a wrong turning five minutes into the finale offer amusing evidence of Gilels's high-wire act; this performance was, after all, recorded before today's obsession with a gleaming and artificial perfection. No performance of this concerto is more 'live', and it is small wonder that Claudio Arrau included it among his desert island favourites. Gilels's Rachmaninov is altogether more temperate yet, once more, this is among the few truly great performances of this work. His tempo is cool and rapid, and maintained with scintillating ease through even the most formidable intricacy. The cadenza – the finer and more transparent of the two billows and recedes in superbly musical style and the climax is of awe-inspiring grandeur and the central *scherzando* in the finale is as luminous as it is vivacious. The finale's *meno mosso* variation is excluded (a beautiful passage that Gilels would doubtless have reinstated in our more enlightened times) and, it has to be said, Cluytens's partnership is distant and run of the mill. But the recordings hardly show their age in such admirably smooth transfers. Gilels's 'encore', Shostakovich's piquant Prelude and Fugue No. 5 shines like a brilliant shaft of light after the Rachmaninov. The performance is perfection, entirely justifying Artur Rubinstein's comment after hearing him play in Russia: "If that boy comes to the West, I shall have to shut up shop".

Saint-Saëns Violin Concerto No. 3 in B minor, Op. 61.
Wieniawski Violin Concerto No. 2 in D minor, Op. 22. **Julian Rachlin** (vn); **Israel Philharmonic Orchestra / Zubin Mehta.** Sony Classical Ⓕ SK48373 (52 minutes: DDD: 12/92). Recorded 1991.

Saint-Saëns's expansive Third Violin Concerto has the rare distinction of providing a showcase for virtuosos without compromising purely musical values. In terms of thematic material and orchestration, it has all the gracefulness and restraint of a classical concerto (as well it might, given its composer's admiration for Beethoven), but, additionally, it manages to find space for passion (first movement) and tenderness (second), as well as encourage a highly musical brand of technical display (third). Written for Sarasate in the early 1880s, the Concerto has long attracted the attention of leading players, yet has still to achieve the popularity of Saint-Saëns's more celebrated shorter works for violin and orchestra, his *Havanaise* and *Introduction and Rondo capriccioso*. Tchaikovsky was much taken with Henryk Wieniawski's Second Concerto (1862), a less ambitious piece than the Saint-Saëns but one that, over the years, has proved more popular. A great violinist himself, Wieniawski knew how to challenge his interpreters with devilishly difficult passagework and gorgeous melodies (such as we encounter at the heart of this D minor Concerto), and it is a pleasure to encounter a young player who so fully understands its idiom. Lithuanian-born Julian Rachlin has a smooth, velvety tone and a lightning left hand; his playing has something of the cultured refinement of the late Nathan Milstein, yet it has its own personality and on this particular CD enjoys the added advantage of superb accompaniments, beautifully recorded. Incidentally, in the Wieniawski, the orchestral tutti passages are played complete – a bonus that you won't find on either of Jascha Heifetz's classic recordings!

Additional recommendations ...

...Violin Concerto No. 3. **Lalo** Symphonie espagnole, Op. 21. **Itzak Perlman** (vn). **Orchestre de Paris / Daniel Barenboim**. DG Masters Ⓜ 445 549-2GMA (61 minutes: DDD).

...Violin Concerto No. 3. Caprice andalous in G major, Op. 122. Introduction and Rondo capriccioso in A minor, Op. 28. Morceau de concert in G major, Op. 62. Romance in C major, Op. 48. **Dong-Suk Kang** (vn); **Katowice Radio Symphony Orchestra / Antoni Wit**. Naxos Ⓢ 8 550752 (64 minutes: DDD: 10/94).

...Violin Concerto No. 3[b]. **Lalo** Symphonie espagnole, Op. 21[a]. **Berlioz** Rêverie et caprice, Op. 8[a]. **Itzhak Perlman** (vn); **Orchestre de Paris / Daniel Barenboim**. DG Digital Masters Ⓜ 445 549-2GMA (69 minutes: DDD: 7/95).

...Violin Concerto No. 3. **Respighi** Concerto gregoriano. Poema autunnale. **Pierre Amoyal** (vn); **French National Orchestra / Charles Dutoit**. Decca Ⓕ 443 324-2DH (69 minutes: DDD: 7/95). *See review under Respighi; refer to the Index to Reviews.*   ⒼⒼ

Saint-Saëns Danse macabre in G minor, Op. 40. Phaéton in C major, Op. 39. Le rouet d'Omphale in A major, Op. 31. La Jeunesse d'Hercule in E flat major, Op. 50. Marche héroïque in E flat major, Op. 34. Introduction and Rondo capriccioso in A minor, Op. 28[a]. Havanaise in E major, Op. 83[a]. [a]**Kyung-Wha Chung** (vn); [a]**Royal Philharmonic Orchestra; Philharmonia Orchestra / Charles Dutoit**. Decca Ⓜ 425 021-2DM (66 minutes: ADD).   Ⓖ

It's enough to make you weep – at the age of three, Saint-Saëns wrote his first tune, analysed Mozart's *Don Giovanni* from the full score when he was five, and at ten claimed he could play all of Beethoven's 32 piano sonatas from memory. There is some consolation in the fact that, according to a contemporary, physically "he strangely resembled a parrot", and perhaps even his early brilliance was a curse rather than a blessing, as he regressed from being a bold innovator to becoming a dusty reactionary. In his thirties (in the 1870s) he was at the forefront of Lisztian avant-garde. To Liszt's invention, the 'symphonic poem' (Saint-Saëns was the first Frenchman to attempt the genre, with César Franck hard on his heels), he brought a typically French concision, elegance and grace. Charles Dutoit currently has few peers in this kind of music; here is playing of dramatic flair and classical refinement that exactly matches Saint-Saëns intention and invention. Decca's sound has depth, brilliance and richness.

Additional recommendations ...

...Introduction and Rondo capriccioso. Havanaise. **Paganini** Violin Concerto No. 1 in D major, Op. 6. **Waxman** Carmen Fantasy. **Maxim Vengerov** (vn); **Israel Philharmonic Orchestra / Zubin Mehta**. Teldec Ⓕ 9031-73266-2 (63 minutes: DDD: 5/92).

...Marche héroïque. Suite algérienne in C major, Op. 60 – March militaire française. *Coupled with works by* **Meyerbeer, Gounod, Rouget de Lisle, Adam, Boieldieu, Offenbach** and **Rossini Detroit Symphony Orchestra / Paul Paray**. Mercury Living Presence Ⓜ 434 332-2MM* (66 minutes: ADD: 11/93). *See review in the Collections section; refer to the Index to Reviews.*   ⒼⒼⒼ

...Introduction and Rondo capriccioso. Havanaise. **Paganini** Violin Concerto No. 1 in E flat major, Op. 6. **Sarah Chang** (vn); **Philadelphia Orchestra / Wolfgang Sawallisch**. EMI Ⓕ CDC5 55026-2 (55 minutes: DDD: 1/95). *See review under Paganini; refer to the Index to Reviews.*

...Danse macabre. Le rouet d'Omphale. **Ibert** Divertissement. **Bizet** Jeux d'enfants. **Berlioz** Le carnaval romain, Op. 9. Le corsaire, Op. 21. **Paris Conservatoire Orchestra / Jean Martinon**. Decca The Classic Sound Ⓜ 448 571-2DCS (64 minutes: ADD: 2/96).

Saint-Saëns Symphonies – A major; F major, "Urbs Roma"; No. 1 in E flat major, Op. 2; No. 2 in A minor, Op. 55; No. 3 in C minor, Op. 78, "Organ"[a]. [a]**Bernard Gavoty** (org); **French Radio National Orchestra / Jean Martinon**. EMI Ⓜ CZS7 62643-2 (two discs: 156 minutes: ADD: 5/91). Recorded 1972-75.   Ⓖ

Saint-Saëns's four early symphonies have rather tended to be eclipsed by the popularity of his much later *Organ* Symphony. It's easy to see why the latter, with its rich invention, its colour and its immediate melodic appeal has managed to cast an enduring spell over its audiences, but there is much to be enjoyed in the earlier symphonies too. The A major dates from 1850 when Saint-Saëns was just 15 years old and is a particularly attractive and charming work despite its debt to Mendelssohn and Mozart. The Symphony in F major of 1856 was the winning entry in a competition organized by the Societé Sainte-Cécile of Bordeaux but was immediately suppressed by the composer after its second performance. The pressures of writing for a competition no doubt contribute to its more mannered style but it nevertheless contains some impressive moments, not least the enjoyable set of variations that form the final movement. The Symphony No. 1 proper was in fact written three years before the *Urbs Roma* and shares the same youthful freshness of the A major, only here the influences are closer to Schumann and Berlioz. The Second Symphony reveals the fully mature voice of Saint-Saëns and in recent years has achieved a certain amount of popularity which is almost certainly due in part to this particularly fine recording. Inevitably we arrive at the *Organ* Symphony, and if you don't already have a recording then you could do a lot worse than this marvellously colourful and flamboyant performance. Indeed, the performances throughout this generous set are persuasive and exemplary. A real bargain and well worth investigating.

Additional recommendations ...

...No. 2. Suite algérienne in C major, Op. 60. Phaéton in C major, Op. 39. **London Symphony Orchestra / Yondani Butt.** ASV Ⓕ CDDCA599 (54 minutes: DDD: 5/88).

...Nos. 2 and 3[a]. [a]**Gillian Weir** (org); **Ulster Orchestra / Yan Pascal Tortelier.** Chandos Ⓕ CHAN8822 (56 minutes: DDD: 7/90).

New review

Saint-Saëns Symphony No. 3 in C minor, Op. 78[a], "Organ". Le carnaval des animaux[b]. Cyprès et Lauriers, Op. 156[c]. [ab]**Youngho Kim,** [ab]**Jinho Kim** (pfs); [ac]**Nicolas Kynaston** (org); **Philharmonia Orchestra / Djong Victorin Yu.** IMP Masters Ⓕ 30366 0001-2 (74 minutes: DDD: 3/96). Recorded 1994.

In this IMP recording of Saint-Saëns's Third Symphony there is none of the aural opulence of the others – the infamously dry acoustic of the recording venue – London's Royal Festival Hall – is no match for either Boston Symphony Hall or Belfast's Ulster Hall (for the RCA and Chandos discs respectively) – while Djong Victorin Yu's painstaking attention to every last detail of the score leaves little room for the lovingly nurtured melodies which characterized Charles Munch's 1959 recording or the great displays of Gallic fire ignited by Yan Pascal Tortelier. Indeed, at first hearing this seems rather a cold, clinical reading. However, this is a recording which not only deserves repeated listening but positively demands it. Yu reveals just what a magnificent piece of music this is; shorn of its customary sonic spectacle the brilliant craftsmanship of Saint-Saëns's writing is displayed in unimpeded glory. That we hear everything in such detail is due to Jonathan Wearn's fine recording. The sound, from three microphones positioned in the stalls, will be instantly familiar to all RFH *habitués* and is unquestionably 'real'. Nowhere is this more vividly demonstrated than in *The carnival of the animals* where ten double-basses ranged along the back of the platform create a striking impression of lumbering elephants. Yu opts for the version for large orchestra complete with glass harmonica (adeptly played by Alasdair Malloy), and while it is again characterized by meticulous attention to detail, it is also a performance full of buoyant wit. *Cyprès et Lauriers* has to be the oddest thing Saint-Saëns ever wrote. After an eight-minute dirge for organ solo (enlivened only by Nicolas Kynaston's impish sense of melodrama) the orchestra burst into an astonishingly vulgar display of French jingoism. Perhaps if this had been given wider currency at the time of the Treaty of Versailles (it was composed to celebrate its signing) the more musically sensitive of Europe's politicians might have held back from plunging into another war for fear of a similar musical exercise rising out of that conflict.

Saint-Saëns Symphony No. 3 in C minor, Op. 78, "Organ"[a]. Le carnaval des animaux[b]. [a]**Peter Hurford** (org); [b]**Pascal Rogé,** [b]**Christina Ortiz** (pfs); [a]**Montreal Symphony Orchestra;** [b]**London Sinfonietta / Charles Dutoit.** Decca Ovation Ⓜ 430 720-2DM (58 minutes: DDD: 12/91). Ⓖ

Saint-Saëns Symphony No. 3 in C minor, Op. 78, "Organ"[a].
Debussy La mer[b].
Ibert Escales[b]. [a]**Berj Zamkochian** (org); **Boston Symphony Orchestra / Charles Munch.** RCA Living Stereo Ⓜ 09026 61500-2* (73 minutes: ADD: 4/93). Item marked [a] recorded 1959, [b]1956. ⒼⒼ

Let's face it, 'motto' themes and their transformations rarely produce good singable tunes. This Symphony uses a unifying motto theme, but it is fertile enough to produce two unforgettable melodies; the sensuous, arching string cantilena in the slow movement, and the grandly striding theme of the finale (so singable it was even borrowed for a pop chart-topping hit in the 1970s). In 1886 Saint-Saëns poured his considerable experience as an unequalled virtuoso of the organ, piano and practitioner of Lisztian unifying techniques into his *Organ* Symphony; it instantly put the French Symphony on the map, and provided a model for Franck and many others. With its capacity for grand spectacle (aside from the organ and a large orchestra, its scoring includes two pianos) it has suffered inflationary tendencies from both conductors and recording engineers. Dutoit's (and Decca's) achievement is the restoration of its energy and vitality. The private and affectionate portraits in the 'zoological fantasy', *The carnival of the animals*, benefit from more intimate though no less spectacular sound, and a direct approach that avoids obvious clowning.

The famous Charles Munch recording of this Symphony was made in Symphony Hall, Boston. To get round the problems of the hall resonance the RCA engineers moved many of the seats from the body of the hall so that the orchestra could spread out, while the organ (situated behind the stage) was miked separately. The result was a wonderfully rich, sumptuous sound which at the same time achieved internal clarity – one notices that in the *Scherzo* and the filigree passages for piano in the introduction to the finale. However, it is the spectacular moments that one remembrs: the rich bonding of organ and strings in the *Poco adagio* and the full-blooded organ entry from Berj Zamkochian in the finale. Munch's superb reading moves forward with a powerful lyrical impulse in a single sweep from the first note to the last. To make this issue even more enticing Munch's 1956 versions of Debussy's *La mer* and Ibert's *Escales* ("Port of call") have been included. There is some marvellous playing in both, especially from the lustrous Boston violins. Here, however, the original recordings were more closely balanced and the effect is less rich, the dynamic range less wide. Yet the adrenalin runs high in both performances and the picturesque imagery of *Escales* is vividly conveyed.

Additional recommendations ...

...Le carnaval des animaux[a]. **Ravel** Ma mère l'oye. [a]**Joseph Villa, Patricia Jennings** (pfs); **Pittsburgh Symphony Orchestra / Andró Previn.** Philips Ⓕ 400 016-2PH (49 minutes: 4/83).

…No. 3. **Daniel Chorzempa** (org); **Berne Symphony Orchestra / Peter Maag.** IMP Red Label
Ⓜ PCD847 (37 minutes: DDD: 4/87).

…No. 3[a]. Samson et Dalila – Bacchanale[b]. Le déluge – Prélude[b]. Danse macabre[b]. [a]**Gaston Litaize**
(org); [a]**Chicago Symphony Orchestra;** [b]**Orchestre de Paris / Daniel Barenboim.** DG Galleria
Ⓜ 415 847-2GGA (56 minutes: DDD: 4/87). ⒼⒼ

…No. 3. **Dukas** L'apprenti sorcier. **Simon Preston** (org); **Berlin Philharmonic Orchestra / James
Levine.** DG Ⓕ 419 617-2GH (47 minutes: DDD: 8/87). *See review under Dukas; refer to the Index
to Reviews.* Ⓖ

…No. 3[a]. Phaéton, Op. 39. [a]**Michael Murray** (org); **Royal Philharmonic Orchestra / Christian Badea.**
Telarc Ⓕ CD80274 (46 minutes: DDD: 12/91).

…No. 3[a]. **Paray** Mass for the 500th Anniversary of the Death of Joan of Arc[b]. [a]**Marcel Dupré**
(org); [b]**Soloists;** [b]**Rackham Symphony Choir; Detroit Symphony Orchestra / Paul Paray.** Mercury
Living Presence Ⓜ 432 719-2MM (73 minutes: ADD: 9/92).

…Le carnaval des animaux (with Olga Barabini, Mary Binney Montgomery, pfs). Danse macabre,
Op. 40. Samson et Dalila – Bacchanale. **Bizet** Carmen – suite. L'Arlésienne – Suite No. 1.
Philadelphia Orchestra / Leopold Stokowski. Biddulph mono Ⓜ WHL012* (72 minutes:
ADD: 8/95).

…No. 3[c]. Le carnaval des animaux[d]. **Berlioz** Symphonie fantastique, Op. 14[a]. Le carnaval romain,
Op. 9[b]. **John Ogden, Brenda Lucas** (pfs); [c]**C. Robinson** (org); [a]**Berlin Philharmonic Orchestra,**
[b]**Vienna Philharmonic Orchestra /** [ab]**Rudolf Kempe;** [cd]**City of Birmingham Symphony Orchestra /
Louis Fremaux.** EMI Seraphim Ⓜ CES5 68525-2 (two discs: 120 minutes: ADD: 11/95).

…Le carnaval des animaux. **Bizet** Jeux d'enfants. **Prokofiev** Peter and the wolf, Op. 67[a]. [a]**Sir John
Gielgud** (narr); **Royal Philharmonic Orchestra / Andrea Licata.** Tring International Royal
Philharmonic Collection Ⓢ TRP046 (69 minutes: DDD: 11/95).

…Le carnaval des animaux[a]. **Britten** The Young Person's Guide to the Orchestra, Op. 34[b]. **Grieg**
Peer Gynt – Suites Nos. 1 and 2[c]. **Gounod** March funèbre d'une marionette. **Loesser** Hans
Christian Anderson – musical film. [ab]**Hugh Downs** (narr); [a]**Leo Litwin,** [a]**Samuel Lipman** (pfs);
[c]**Eileen Farrell** (sop); **Boston Pops Orchestra / Arthur Fiedler.** RCA Victor Living Stereo Ⓜ 09026
68131-2 (76 minutes: ADD: 12/95).

…Le carnaval des animaux. **Poulenc** Double Piano Concerto in D minor. **Güher and Süher Pekinel**
(pfs); **French Radio Philharmonic Orchestra / Marek Janowski.** Teldec Ⓜ 4509-97445-2
(38 minutes: DDD: 2/96).

New review

Saint-Saëns Piano Trios – No. 1 in F major, Op. 18; No. 2 in E minor, Op. 92. **Joachim Trio**
(Rebecca Hirsch, vn; Caroline Dearnley, vc; John Lenehan, pf). Naxos Ⓢ 8 550935 (65 minutes:
DDD: 12/95). Recorded 1993. *Gramophone* Editor's choice.
1863 and 1892 are the dates of these trios, of which No. 1 was written by a composer not yet 30 but
already a confident master of his craft. Bland his voice may be, but it is intelligent and agreeable: a
French Brahms without genius, one dares suggest, although Mendelssohn also comes to mind. At the
same time, there are passages unlike either of these composers, such as the bare and angular main
theme of the A minor slow movement in No. 1, though Grieg might have written it. Such music needs
sympathetic, unfussy interpretation and the skilful and sensitive Joachim Trio give it just that; as for
the First Trio as a whole, the work is charming (try the fleet scherzo for a sample) and the booklet-
essay rightly notes the "delicate brilliance" of the piano writing by a composer who was also an expert
player. The E minor Trio, a more dramatic five-movement piece is played here with fine judgement
and thus warmly expressive without sentimentality or mannerism. The recording is excellent.

New review

Saint-Saëns Samson et Dalila. **Carlo Cossutta** (ten) Samson; **Marjana Lipovšek** (mez) Dalila;
Alain Fondary (bar) Priest; **Yves Bisson** (bar) Abimelech; **Harald Stamm** (bass) Old Hebrew;
Constantin Zaharia (ten) Messenger; **Jerôme Engramer** (ten) First Philistine; **Ionel Pantea** (bass)
Second Philistine; **Sofia Chamber Choir; Bregenz Festival Chorus; Vienna Volksoper Chorus;
Vienna Symphony Orchestra / Sylvain Cambreling.** Koch Schwann Ⓕ 317742 (two discs:
127 minutes: DDD: 4/96). Notes, text and translation included. Recorded live in 1988.
One distinguished German critic claimed this was the finest performance in the 40 years' existence of
the Bregenz Festival. Cambreling draws as much sensuousness and delicacy from the score as any, and
also attends to its pagan element with suitable brio. Though like some of his predecessors, such as
Barenboim and Davis, he is inclined to linger unduly against the composer's express wishes, as in the
marginally too slow tempo for "Mon coeur s'ouvre à ta voix", he uses the gained time to underline
the refinement of the scoring, helped by some lovely playing from his orchestra, which is in true
theatrical balance with the singers. Although by rights the polyglot cast should tell against the set, the
French is in fact as idiomatic as any apart from that on the recently reissued Fourestier. While
Lipovšek sometimes, like Baltsa (Davis) and Meier (Chung), indulges in dramatic gestures strictly
outside the realm of style appropriate to the piece, she sings for the most part with a more luscious
tone than either of those rivals, is certainly more pleasing to listen to than Meier and instils the whole
role, by vocal means alone, with a sense of Dalila's dangerous powers of seduction. Working in a live
performance she has an advantage over all her rivals in creating theatrical intensity.

She is matched in that by Cossutta. The then 56-year-old tenor has just the kind of *élan* in his attack that sometimes eludes Domingo (Barenboim and Chung). In that he comes close to matching Luccioni on the old Fourestier version. Some may find the vibrato that is part and parcel of Cossutta's timbre disturbing. Once that is taken on board, Cossutta's is as vigorous, pliable and musically attentive a Samson as any. Vickers, *chez* Prêtre, is something else again, highly individual, but occasionally exaggerated in expression in a way Cossutta avoids. Cossutta matches Luccioni and Vickers in the concentrated pathos of "Vois ma misère" and the declamatory attack called for at "Et! je proclame ta justice!", which has an Otello-like power to it. Fondary was Chung's High Priest, and here he repeats his formidable assumption, matched on disc only by Blanc (Prêtre) and Cabanel (Fourestier). The smaller roles are adequately taken and the choral singing equals the excellence of that on the other recent sets. Stage noises are minimally distracting even during the dances; applause is confined to ends of acts. As a whole the recording has more presence than the backwardly recorded Chung set. The work has been reasonably fortunate on disc. For all its merits as regards solo singing (and do try to hear Bouvier), the Fourestier is too dimly recorded for a first recommendation. The Barenboim is out of court for its poor Dalila, and Davis's Baltsa is something of an acquired taste. Choice really lies among the still highly competitive Prêtre (with Gorr almost in the Bouvier class as Dalila), and the two most recent versions. Chung is undoubtedly the safer recommendation, Cambreling the more exciting both because it is taken live and because of the special frisson the two principals give to their music. Do hear one or other version of what is a carefully crafted and superbly integrated score.

Additional recommendations ...

...**Soloists; Bavarian Radio Symphony Chorus and Orchestra / Sir Colin Davis.** Philips Ⓟ 426 243-2PH2 (two discs: 123 minutes: DDD: 1/91).

...**Soloists; Chorus and Orchestra de Paris / Daniel Barenboim.** DG Ⓜ 413 297-2GX2 (two discs: 126 minutes: ADD: 11/91).

...**Soloists; Chorus and Orchestra of the Bastille Opera, Paris / Myung-Whun Chung.** EMI Ⓔ CDS7 54470-2 (two discs: 124 minutes: DDD: 2/93). Ⓠ

Further listening ...

...Septet in E flat major, Op. 65[c]. *Coupled with* **Milhaud** La création du monde[b]. **Poulenc** Sextet for Piano and Wind Quintet[a]. [a]**Elizabeth Mann** (fl); [a]**Stephen Taylor** (ob); [a]**David Shifrin** (cl); [a]**Dennis Godburn** (bn); [a]**Richard Todd** (hn); [c]**Thomas Stevens** (tpt); [bc]**Ani Kavafian**, [bc]**Julie Rosenfeld** (vns); [bc]**Toby Hoffman** (va); [bc]**Carter Brey** (vc); [c]**Jack Kulowitsch** (db); **André Previn** (pf). RCA Victor Red Seal 09026 68181-2 (11/95).

...Odelette, Op. 162. Clarinet Sonata in E flat major, Op. 167. Feuillet d'album, Op. 81. Bassoon Sonata in G major, Op. 168. Caprice sur des airs danois et russes, Op. 79. Oboe Sonata in D major, Op. 166. Romance in D flat major, Op. 37. Tarantelle in A minor, Op. 6. *Coupled with* **Debussy** Rapsodie. Syrinx. Première rapsodie. Sonata for Flute, Viola and Harp. Le petit nègre[e]. Petite pièce. Rapsodie. **Various soloists.** Cala CACD1017 (2/95).

...Allegro appassionato in B minor, Op. 43. *Coupled with works by* **Debussy, Bach, Handel, Boccherini, Schubert, Schumann, Chopin** and **Bloch** Mischa Maisky (vc); Daria Hovora (pf). DG 439 863-2GH (9/94). *See review in the Collections section; refer to the Index to Reviews* Ⓠ

...Trois Prélude et Fugues, Op. 99. Trois Préludes et Fugues, Op. 109. *Coupled with* **Harwood** Organ Sonata No. 1 in C sharp minor, Op. 5. **Adrian Partington** (org). Priory PRCD384 (8/94). *See review under Harwood; refer to the Index to Reviews.*

...Henry VIII – Ballet-divertissement. *Coupled with* **Delibes** Sylvia. **Razumovsky Sinfonia / Andrew Mogrelia.** Naxos 8 553338/9 (6/96). *See review under Delibes; refer to the Index to Reviews.*

...Henry VIII. Soloists; Rouen Théâtre des Arts Chorus; French Lyrique Orchestra / Alain Guingal. Le Chant du Monde LDC278 1083/5 (4/93).

Sieur de Sainte-Colombe

French died c1691-1701

Suggested listening ...

...Concerts a Deux Violes Esgales, Volumes 1 and 2. **Jordi Savall, Wieland Kuijken** (bass viols). Auvidis Astrée E7729/8743 (11/93). ✎

Philip Sainton

British 1891-1967

Suggested listening ...

...The Island. *Coupled with* **Hadley** The Trees so High[a]. [a]**David Wilson-Johnson** (bar); **Philharmonia** [a]**Chorus and Orchestra / Matthias Bamert.** Chandos CHAN9181 (10/93).

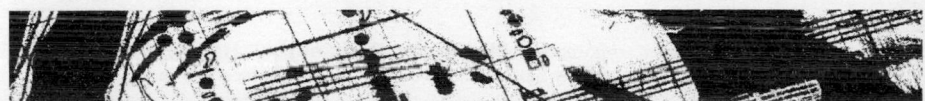

Antonio Salieri   Italian 1750-1825

Suggested listening ...
...Keyboard Concerto in B flat major[a]. Concerto for Flute, Oboe and Orchestra in C major[b].
Coupled with **F. Salieri** Sinfonia in B flat major, "La tempesta di mare". [a]**Paul Badura-Skoda**
(fp); [b]**Clementine Hoogendoorn** (fl); [b]**Pietro Borgovono** (ob); **I Solisti Veneti / Claudio Scimone.**
Erato 0630-12987-2 (6/96).
...Axur, Re d'Ormus. **Soloists; Guido d'Arezzo Choir; Russian Philharmonic Orchestra / René
Clemencic.** Nuova Era 6852/4 (12/90).

Aulis Sallinen   Finnish 1935-

Sallinen Variations for Orchestra, Op. 8. Violin Concerto, Op. 18[a]. Some aspects of Peltoniemi
Hintrik's funeral march, Op. 19[b]. The nocturnal dances of Don Juanquixote, Op. 58. [a]**Eeva
Koskinen** (vn); [b]**Torleif Thedéen** (vc); **Tapiola Sinfonietta / Osmo Vänskä.** BIS Ⓕ CD560
(63 minutes: DDD: 6/93). Recorded 1992.
Sallinen's operas and symphonies have stolen the limelight in recent years at the expense of other
works fully worthy of attention as this well-played and well-recorded disc proves. Whereas the
Variations (1963) are somewhat anonymous if deftly written, the Violin Concerto (1968) is an
altogether maturer work, unusually sombre for so bright a solo instrument. The Third String Quartet
(1969), subtitled *Some aspects of Peltoniemi Hintrik's funeral march* has, thanks to the Kronos
Quartet's advocacy, become one of Sallinen's most heard works. This arrangement for string orchestra
dates from 1981. *The nocturnal dances of Don Juanquixote* is an extended fantasia for cello and
strings, the title being the only parody of Strauss (although a solo violin enters late as Sancho Panza-
leporello!). Sallinen is fond of playing games and all is never as it seems: one can almost hear the
collective thud of critics' jaws falling open at this Arnold-like spoof, yet there are darker moments too:
bravo to Sallinen and BIS for this intriguing issue.

New review
Sallinen Songs of Life and Death, Op. 69[a]. The Iron Age – Suite, Op. 55b[b]. [b]**Margit Papunen**
(sop); [a]**Jorma Hynninen** (bar); **Opera Festival Chorus;** [b]**East Helsinki Music Institute Choir;
Helsinki Philharmonic Orchestra / Okko Kamu.** Ondine Ⓕ ODE844-2 (75 minutes: DDD: 12/95).
Texts and translations included. Recorded 1995.
Listening to these two works by Aulis Sallinen is a bit like looking at two different photographs of the
composer: the face is undeniably the same but not the perspective. *Songs of Life and Death* (1993-4)
arose, rather by mischance, from a failed effort to compose a Requiem on verses by Lassi Nummi.
Although title and outward form suggest Mahlerian associations, the conservative musical language
rather brings Verdi to mind, and in a very real sense this cycle is a twentieth-century equivalent of the
latter's Requiem: both are symphonic in construction and operatic in idiom, composed from spiritual
rather than religious standpoints, and make use of secular elements. There are differences, of course,
not least in scale and conception, which serve to underline a similarity of purpose and stature relative
to their epochs. And while Sallinen's songs are also very much songs of *life*, death is not here perceived
as a grim or tragic end, and this imparts to the whole a peculiarly late twentieth-century aspect. Here
at last is the choral-and-orchestral masterpiece Sibelius should have written, Finnish to the core yet
international in appeal. It is one of the very finest compositions Sallinen has yet produced. Where in
the *Songs of Life and Death* voices are the principal element, in the *Iron Age* Suite (1978-82) the focus
is rather on the orchestra, the chorus being an important but more colouristic extra. The suite
originated in music written for a series of prize-winning Finnish TV documentaries and in it the more
familiar Sallinen of the symphonies and early operas is on display. Both works receive terrific
performances. There is no one better in this repertoire than Sallinen's long-standing champion Okko
Kamu, underused by a recording industry often in favour of younger, less talented rivals.
Further listening ...
...Symphonies – No. 4, Op. 49; No. 5, Op. 57, "Washington Mosaics". Shadows, Op. 52. **Malmö
Symphony Orchestra / James DePreist.** BIS CD607 (12/94).
...String Quartets – No. 1, Op. 14; No. 2, "Canzona"; No. 3, "Aspects of Peltoniemi Hintrik's
Funeral March", Op. 19; No. 4, "Silent Songs"; No. 5, "Pieces of Mosaic". **Jean Sibelius
Quartet.** Ondine ODE831-2 (12/95).
...Kullervo. **Soloists; Finnish National Opera Chorus; Finnish National Opera Orchestra / Ulf
Söderblom.** Ondine ODE780-2 (8/92).

Timothy Salter   British 1942-

Suggested listening ...
...Katharsios. Eternity. *Coupled with works by* **Maconchy, Hoddinott, J. Harvey, Musgrave**
and **Lutyens** Ionian Singers / Timothy Salter; Thalia Myers (pf); Erik Jacobsen (perc). Usk
Recordings USK1216 (3/96).

Giovanni Salvatore

Suggested listening ...
...Toccata prima. Canzon Francese terza. Due Correnti. *Coupled with works by* **Frescobaldi,**
Lambardo, Buono, Picchi, A. Mayone, Giovanni de Macque, Facoli, A. Valente,
Merula, M. Rossi, B. Storace, G. Strozzi, Stradella and **A. Scarlatti** Rinaldo
Alessandrini (hpd). Opus 111 OPS30-118 (4/95). ✔ *See review in the Collections section; refer to*
the Index to Reviews.   �

Giuseppe Sammartini

Giovanni Battista Sammartini

New review

G. Sammartini Recorder Concerto in F major. Oboe Concerto in E flat major. Concerto for
Piccolo Cello, Strings and Continuo in C major. Trio for Two Recorders and Continuo in
F major.
G.B. Sammartini Trio for Two Flutes and Continuo in D major. Sonata for Flute, Two Violins
and Continuo in D major. **Cologne Camerata.** Deutsche Harmonia Mundi ℗ 05472 77323-2
(59 minutes: DDD: 8/95). Recorded 1992-4.   ⊙

An earlier recording by Cologne Camerata (reviewedbelow) sets small-scale instrumental works by
the brothers Giuseppe and Giovanni Battista Sammartini side by side; this new one continues the
exercise, introducing a few works that call for larger forces. It is a pity, however, that when it comes
to the running order of the items the booklet is unhelpful; the track times are in the right order
overall, but they do not correspond to the stated movements. The rot sets in right at the outset: the
Concerto in C for violoncello piccolo and strings ("for piccolo and cello" according to the
annotation) is given as the third item, whereas it comes first. If you don't mind the hassle of putting
all this right, you will be rewarded with a programme of most attractive music, beautifully played
and recorded. It isn't hard to hear echoes of some of the giants of baroque music (Vivaldi, Handel,
Telemann *et al*) in that of Giuseppe, which is not to underrate what is pleasantly inventive in its own
right. He was a 'man of the baroque' whereas his younger brother, who survived him by 24 years,
lived to breathe the air of the *galant* and beyond, as the two works on this disc show. As on the
previous disc, there are little surprises around many corners, and much in between to charm the
senses.

G. Sammartini Sonata for Flute and Continuo in E minor. Solos for Flute, Violin or Oboe and
Continuo, Op. 13 – No. 1 in G major; No. 4 in G major. Sonatas for Recorder and Continuo –
F minor; G major.
G.B. Sammartini Sonata for Cello and Continuo in B flat major, Op. 4 No. 2. Harpsichord
Sonata in A major. Organ Sonata No. 6 in C major. **Cologne Camerata** (Michel Schneider, rec;
Karl Kaiser, fl; Hans-Peter Westermann, ob; Rainer Zipperling, Nicholas Selo, vcs; Sabine Bauer,
hpd/org). Deutsche Harmonia Mundi ℗ 05472 77283-2 (64 minutes: DDD: 10/93). ✔ Recorded
in 1992.

Giuseppe, the elder of the two brothers, was a celebrated oboist who came to London in the 1720s
and who played in many of Handel's opera productions. He is represented here by two recorder
sonatas, two flute sonatas and an oboe sonata. Giovanni Battista Sammartini's contribution consists
of two keyboard sonatas, one for organ, the other for harpsichord and a Sonata in B flat for cello and
continuo. The younger brother was the more forward-looking of the two in matters of style and his
music reflects the changes in musical idiom taking place on the continent in the second quarter of the
eighteenth century. New and old, so to speak, are clearly differentiated in the juxtaposition of the
entirely 'baroque' oboe sonata of Giuseppe, on the one hand, and the 'galant' cello sonata of
Giovanni Battista, on the other. These are the strongest pieces in a programme which contains little
that is either routine or predictable. An entertaining recital, thoughtfully constructed and
imaginatively performed. Fine recorded sound.

Further listening ...
...**G. Sammartini** Recorder Concerto in F major[a]. Concerti grossi – No. 6 in E minor; No. 8 in
G minor. *Coupled with* **G.B. Sammartini** Symphonies – G major; D major. String Quintet in
E major. [a]**Conrad Steinmann** (rec); **Ensemble 415 / Chiara Banchini** (vn). Harmonia Mundi
HMA190 1245. ✔   ⊙⊙⊙

Arturo Sandoval

Suggested listening ...
...(orch. Zelanti) Trumpet Concerto. *Coupled with* **L. Mozart** Trumpet Concerto in D major.
Hummel Trumpet Concerto in E flat major. **Arutiunian** Trumpet Concerto. **Arturo Sandoval**
(tpt); **London Symphony Orchestra / Luis Haza.** GRP Classical GRK75002 (1/95).

Sven Sandström
Swedish 1942-

Suggested listening ...
...A Cradle Song/The Tyger. *Coupled with* **Nørgård** And time shall be no more. **Tormis** The Curse
of Iron. **Rautavaara** Suite de Lorca, Op. 72. **Jersild** Three Romantic Songs. **Danish National
Radio Choir / Stefan Parkman.** Chandos CHAN9264 (4/95).

Gaspar Sanz
Spanish 1640-1710

New review
Sanz Instrucción de música sobre la guitarra española (excerpts). **Hopkinson Smith** (gtr). Auvidis
Astrée Ⓔ E8576 (64 minutes: DDD: 8/96). 🖋
Book 1 – Canarios. Fuga I, por Primer Tono al Ayre Español. Jiga al Ayre ingles. Preludio o
Capricho, arpendo por la. Preludio y Fantasía. Zarabanda Francesca. *Book 2* – Canciónes. Clarín
de los Mosqueteros de Francia. Clarines y Trompetas. Folías. Jácaras I and II. La Tarantela. La
Coquina Francesca. Zarabanda. La Esfachata de Nápoles. La Miñona de Portugal. La Miñona
de Cataluña. Lantururú. Marizápolos. Matachin. Pavanas por la D con Partidas al Aire Español.
Book 3 – Passacalles por la I. Passacalles por la K2.
The five-course baroque guitar was smaller than today's instrument and had a variety of re-entrant
tunings, in all of which it lacked a true bass. Arrangements of baroque guitar music for the modern
instrument routinely add bass notes that, 'right' though they may sound, are not in the original texts;
the new simply cannot reproduce the idiosyncratic sonorities and sound-world of the old. Sanz's
Instrucción de música sobre la guitarra española was published in two volumes (1674), to which a third
was added in 1697. In addition to instruction in music theory and guitar technique, it contains a
considerable number of pieces written in tablature. Some had associated academic purposes, for
example *passacalles* with *diferencias* (variations), some were settings of popular and courtly dances of
the time, others were character pieces. It is on themes taken from this source that Rodrigo based his
Fantasía para un gentil-hombre. Both styles of playing are involved: *punteado* (plucking separate notes,
as on a lute or guitar) and *rasgueado* (strumming, as better suits the more earthy dances). Hopkinson
Smith's splendid and freely expressive performances are rewarding in themselves, but they also
provide a means of letting us know how the music was meant to sound compared with how we are
more accustomed to hearing it today. Recording and annotation are of a high standard.
Additional recommendation...
...Instruccion de musica sobre la guitarra española – Canarios; Folías; Lantururú; Pavanas al ayre
español[b]. *Coupled with* **Guerau** Poema harmonico – Canario; Marionas[b]. **Murcia** Cumbés[b].
Giga[b]. **Mudarra** Tres libros de música en cifras para vihuela – Pavana de Alexandre; Fantasia
que contrahaze la harpa en la manera de Ludovico[a]. **Milán** El Maestro – Pavana II[a]. **López**
Fantasia[a]. **Narváez** Los seys libros del delphin – La canción del Emperador; Diferencias on
"Guárdame las vacas"[a]. Paseavase el rey moro[a]. **Sor** Thèmes variés et Douze Minuets, Op. 11 –
Andante maestoso; Andante expressivo[b]. Introduction and Variations on a theme by Mozart,
Op. 9[b]. **José Miguel Moreno** ([a]vihuela/[b]gtr). Glossa Ⓔ GCD920103 (73 minutes: DDD: 8/95).

Pablo Sarasate
Spanish 1844-1908

Suggested listening ...
...Zigeunerweisen, Op. 20. *Coupled with works by* **Saint-Saëns, Massenet, Chausson, Ysaÿe**
and **Ravel** Joshua Bell (vn); Royal Philharmonic Orchestra / Andrew Litton. Decca 433 519-2DH
(1/92). *See review in the Collections section; refer to the Index to Reviews.*
...Zigeunerweisen, Op. 20[c].*Coupled with works by* **Waxman, Arban, Falla, Saint-Saëns,
Paganini, Tchaikovsky, Fauré** and **W. Brandt** Sergei Nakariakov (tpt); Alexander Markovich
(pf). Teldec 4509-94554-2 (6/95). *See review in the Collections section; refer to the Index to
Reviews.*   ⓖⓖ
...Zigeunerweisen, Op. 20. Introduction and Tarantella, Op. 43. *Coupled with works by* **Massenet,
Glazunov, Rachmaninov, Rimsky-Korsakov, Tchaikovsky, Wieniawski** and **Kreisler**
Itzhak Perlman (vn); **Abbey Road Ensemble / Lawrence Foster.** EMI CDC5 55475-2 (1/96).

Valery Sariyev
USSR 1950-

Suggested listening ...
...The Lord, our God. *Coupled with* **Chesnokov** Come, let us entreat Joseph, Op. 9 No. 9. Bless
the Lord, o my soul, Op. 27 No. 1. Joyous light, Op. 9 No. 21. Let us, mystically representing the
Cherubim. Praise ye the name of the Lord in heaven. **Bortnyansky** Many years. **Kastal'sky**
Liturgy of St John Chrysostom. **Anonymous** Russian Orthodox Chant: Easter Stikhiras. From
my youth. Stikhira to the Russian Holymen. **Bolshoi Theatre Children's Choir / Andrey
Zaboronok.** Collins Classics 1443-2 (7/95).

Erik Satie

Satie Parade. Trois Gymnopédies – Nos. 1 and 3 (orch. Debussy); No. 2 (orch. Corp). Mercure. Three Gnossiennes (orch. Corp). Rêlache. **New London Orchestra / Ronald Corp.** Hyperion Ⓕ CDA66365 (66 minutes: DDD: 2/90). Recorded 1989.

In 1918, the year after Diaghilev's Russian Ballet staged Satie's *Parade* in Paris, Poulenc wrote that "to me, Satie's *Parade* is to Paris what *Petrushka* is to St Petersburg" (André Gide, however, commented on its poverty-stricken pretentiousness). Satie was thenceforth adopted as the spiritual father of "Les Six", whose ideal was the marriage of serious music with jazz, vaudeville, and the circus. Those who only know Satie from his early *Gymnopédies* and *Gnossiennes* – take heed: *Parade* shuffles along its apparently aimless, deadpan and wicked way with interjections from typewriters, lottery wheels, pistols and sirens. What does it all mean? Ronald Corp could be accused of retaining a slightly stiff upper lip, but there may well be a seriousness of purpose behind Satie's balletic miniatures. Certainly, there is little here of the uproarious debunking of some of "Les Six". His orchestrations of the *Gnossiennes* and the remaining *Gymnopédie* are idiomatic, and his performances of all six have the requisite cool beauty. Hyperion's sound is spacious and natural.

Additional recommendations ...

...Parade. **Milhaud** Le boeuf sur le toit. **Auric** Ouverture. **Françaix** Piano Concertino[a]. **Fetler** Contrasts for Orchestra. [a]**Claude Françaix** (pf); **London Symphony Orchestra / Antál Dorati.** Mercury Ⓜ 434 335-2MM (67 minutes: ADD).　　　　　　　　　　　　　　　Ⓖ

...Parade. **Ravel** La valse. **Bartók** Dance Suite, Sz77. **Busoni** Tanzwalzer, Op. 53. **Liadov** Kikimora, Op. 63. **Chabrier** Le roi malgré lui – Fête polonaise. **Liszt** Mephisto Waltz No. 2, S111. **Philharmonia Orchestra / Igor Markevitch.** Testament mono Ⓕ SBT1060* (77 minutes: ADD: 2/96).

New review

Satie Six Gnossiennes. Ogives. Petite ouverture à danser. Sarabandes. Trois Gymnopédies. **Reinbert de Leeuw** (pf). Philips Ⓕ 446 672-2PH (67 minutes: DDD: 2/96). Recorded 1992.

Tender, solemn, droll, silly and occasionally plain boring, Satie's piano music has certainly proved its appeal for performers and record collectors, judging from the number of recitals devoted to it. But this one is out of the ordinary, for unlike the majority of artists, who offer a mixed bag of pieces, Reinbert de Leeuw has chosen music that is entirely solemn and even hieratic in utterance. He begins with the archaically beautiful *Gnossiennes*, taking the first of them unusually slowly but with compelling concentration. The composer's devotees will be thrilled, though you have to surrender completely to get the message of this repetitive, proto-minimalist music. The four *Ogives* derive their name from church architecture and their unbarred, diatonically simple music has clear affinities with plainchant although unlike chant it is richly harmonized. Monotonous it may be, but that is part of its charm, if that term can apply to such a contemplative style. The very brief *Petite ouverture à danser* is a mere meandering sketch in lazy waltz-time, but all Satie is sacred to the converted and the writer of the booklet-essay accords it four lines, finding in it (as translated here) "a suggestion of indifference, vacillating between a melancholy melody and indecisive harmony". (Not exactly Beethoven, one might say.) The two pensively sad triptychs of *Sarabandes* and *Gymnopédies* – here very slow yet tonally most refined – complete this finely played and recorded disc, which offers nothing whatsoever of the bouncier *café-concert* Satie.

Satie Avant-dernières pensées. Caresse. Chapitres tournés en tous sens. Trois Gymnopédies. Jack-in-the-box. Six Pieces. Trois Préludes flasques. Deux Rêveries nocturnes. Sonatine bureaucratique. Sports et divertissements. **Michel Legrand** (pf). Erato Ⓕ 4509-92857-2 (54 minutes: DDD: 12/93). Recorded 1993.

Satie is a composer who defies description. His piano music has the same quirky originality as his life and his love of flying in the face of convention are crystallized in these fascinating miniatures. As a musician who has released over 100 albums and whose many film scores include *The Umbrellas of Cherbourg*, Legrand needs little introduction, but this seems to be his début as a solo pianist in classical repertoire, and his arrival is welcome. He is not just an adroit pianist but also a sensitive one, with the kind of tonal control that needs a fine ear even more than deft fingers, and his response to the music is summed up in his own description of discovering "things that overwhelmed me, they were so beautiful, so profound, so funny, so irritating and so boring ... altogether fascinating" This enthusiasm comes across in vividly recorded performances that are a shade larger than life but none the worse for that. The first *Gymnopédie* is taken more slowly than usual but has the right hushed tenderness, while the *Sonatine bureaucratique* that follows has all the bustle of a Parisian office in a Feydeau farce. From this you may deduce that Legrand separates the *Gymnopédies*, understandably perhaps, since they are so alike. They come on tracks 1, 5 and 27 of a total of 49. Tracks 6 to 26 are taken up with the 21 *Sports et divertissements*, the longest of which lasts a mere 74 seconds and the shortest just 14. Bitty though they are, they are enjoyable, for Legrand unfailingly conveys their varied wit and their derivation from popular songs. The beautifully written manuscript score of one of them, "Le Water-Chute", is reproduced as page 5 of the booklet, and in colour – evidently Satie used manuscript paper with the staves drawn in red. This issue is a model of presentation, with excellent notes

Satie Trois Gymnopédies. Six Gnossiennes. Cinq Nocturnes. Trois Embryons desséchés. Trois avant-dernières pensées. Valsc-ballet. Fantaisie-valse. Je te veux. **Ronan O'Hora** (pf). Tring International ⑤ TRP069 (61 minutes: DDD: 7/96).

Ronan O'Hora is a sensitive pianist in this repertory, where there are now many recorded contenders and a fair range of interpretative styles, and the sad tenderness of the *Gymnopédies* comes across, although he is brisker than some artists with the meltingly beautiful flow of Nos. 1 and 3. If O'Hora is justifiably concerned to eschew an inappropriately romantic approach, this is not at the expense of the occasional discreet rubato (as towards the end of No. 2) without which the music would lack humanity. Not all this music has the gravity of this triptych, or the *Gnossiennes*. Elsewhere Satie gives us his characteristic caperings and banalities, and O'Hora responds neatly and wittily, doing the best he can with the silly repetitive endings of at least two pieces. Indeed, his programme is well played and planned. As suggested, there are many rival Satie pianists on disc but there is so much of Satie's piano music now available that you can purchase several discs without duplicating repertory, save perhaps for the ubiquitous *Gymnopédies*. O'Hora's disc offers a pleasingly intimate, atmospheric recording.

Additional recommendations ...

...Trois Gymnopédies. Je te veux valse. Quatre préludes flasques. Prélude en tapisserie. Nocturne No. 4. Vieux séquins et vieilles cuirasses. Embryons desséchés. Six Gnossiennes. Sonatine bureaucratique. Le Piccadilly. **Pascal Rogé** (pf). Decca Ⓕ 410 220-2DH (61 minutes: DDD: 5/89).

...Six Gnossiennes. Véritables préludes flasques (pour un chien). Vieux séquins et vieilles cuirasses. Chapitres tournés en tous sens. Trois Gymnopédies. Embryons desséchés. Je te veux valse. Sonatine bureaucratique. Heures séculaires et instantanées. Le Picadilly. Avant-dernières pensées. Sports et divertissements. **Anne Queffélec** (pf). Virgin Classics Ⓕ VC7 59515-2 (76 minutes: DDD: 5/89).

...Chapitres tournés en tous sens. Croquis et agaceries d'un gros bonhomme en bois. Je te veux valse. Le Picadilly. Pièces froides. Le piège de Méduse. Poudre d'or. Trois préludes du fils des étoiles. Prélude en tapisserie. Sonatine bureaucratique. Sports et divertissements. Trois Gymnopédies. Véritables préludes flasques (pour un chien). Vexations. **Peter Dickinson** (pf). Conifer Ⓜ CDCF512 (77 minutes: DDD: 5/93).

...Six Gnossiennes. Avant-dernières pensées. Première pensée Rose + Croix. Trois préludes du fils des étoiles. Chapitres tournés en tous sens. Trois Gymnopédies. Le Piège de Méduse. Rêverie du pauvre. Je te veux valse. Prélude de la Porte héroïque du ciel. **John Lenehan** (pf). Earthsounds Ⓕ CDEASM003 (63 minutes: DDD: 5/93).

...Croquis et agaceries d'un gros bonhomme en bois. Trois descriptions automatiques. Trois valses du précieux dégoûté. Petite ouverture à danser. Valse-ballet. Fantaisie-valse. Les pantins dansent. Caresse. Danse de travers. Deux pièces froides. Première pensée Rosé + Croix. Prélude de la Porte heroique du ciel. Passacaille. Prélude en tapisserie. Poudre d'or. Trois morceaux en forme de poire[a]. La belle excentrique. **Anne Queffélec**, [a]**Cathérine Collard** (pfs). Virgin Classics Ⓕ VC7 59296-2 (72 minutes: DDD: 8/93).

Further listening ...

...(arr. Milhaud) Cinq grimaces. *Coupled with* **Milhaud** Quatre esquisses, Op. 227. Madame Bovary, Op. 128. Three Rag Caprices, Op. 78. Saudades do Brasil, Op. 67. Les charmes de la vie, Op. 360. Polka, Op. 95. Tango des Fratellini, Op. 58*c*. **Boaz Sharon** (pf). Unicorn-Kanchana DKPCD9155 (5/95).

Emil von Sauer

German 1862-1942

Sauer Piano Concerto No. 1 in E minor.

Scharwenka Piano Concerto No. 4 in F minor, Op. 82. **Stephen Hough** (pf); **City of Birmingham Symphony Orchestra / Lawrence Foster.** Hyperion Ⓕ CDA66790 (70 minutes: DDD: 11/95). Recorded 1994. *Gramophone Editor's record of the month.*   Ⓖ

In Scharwenka's Fourth Piano Concerto grand, Lisztian ambitions are fulfilled and embellished in writing of the most ferocious intricacy and the tarantella finale throws everything at the pianist, seemingly simultaneously. It is therefore hardly surprising that after early triumphs the Fourth Concerto fell into neglect. At its second performance, given in 1910 with Scharwenka as soloist and Mahler as conductor, it was described as being of a "truly Dionysian and bewildering brilliancy", a phrase that, lifted into our own times, encapsulates Stephen Hough's astonishing performance. Then there is Sauer's First Concerto, its key a warm, over-the-shoulder memory of Chopin's E minor Concerto, yet with a style and content to make even the least susceptible listeners' heads nod and feet tap. The *Cavatina* is as luscious and enchanting as the finale is teasingly brief and light-hearted. Throughout, haunting melodies are embroidered with the finest pianistic tracery and, once again, the performance is bewitching. In the *Cavatina* Hough's caressing, fine-spun tone and long-breathed phrasing are a model for singers as well as pianists, and in the finale there is a lightly deployed virtuosity that epitomizes his aristocratic style. Naturally, the spotlight falls unashamedly on the soloist in such music, but the orchestra have no small part in the proceedings, and Lawrence Foster and the City of Birmingham Symphony Orchestra are superbly resilient and enthusiastic, with strings that sing their hearts out, notably in the third movement of the Sauer. These are both première recordings, and the sound and balance are exemplary.

Robert Saxton

British 1953-

Suggested listening ...

...Piano Sonata. *Coupled with works by* **Tippett, C. Matthews** and **C. Lambert** Nicholas Unwin (pf). Metier MSVCD92009 (1/96). *See review in the Collections section; refer to the Index to Reviews.*

...Chacony. *Coupled with works by* **Tippett, Sackman** and **Connolly** Steven Neugarten (pf). Metier MSVCD92008 (1/96). *See review in the Collections section; refer to the Index to Reviews.*

...Violin Concerto[a]. I will awake the dawn[b]. In the beginning[c]. [a]**Tasmin Little** (vn); [b]**BBC Singers / John Poole**; [ac]**BBC Symphony Orchestra / Matthias Bamert.** Collins Classics 1283-2 (4/92).

...Caritas. **Soloists; English Northern Philharmonia / Diego Masson.** Collins Classics 1350-2 (7/92).

Alessandro Scarlatti

Italian 1660-1725

New review

A. Scarlatti Humanità e Lucifero[a].

Corelli Trio Sonatas – B flat major, Op. 3 No. 3; C major, Op. 4 No. 1. [a]**Rossana Bertini** (sop); [a]**Massimo Crispi** (ten); **Europa Galante / Fabio Biondi** (vn). Opus 111 Ⓔ OPS30-129 (61 minutes: DDD: 3/96). Text and translation included. ✍

Alessandro Scarlatti's oratorio, *Humanità e Lucifero*, here receives its first recording. It dates from 1704 when it was first performed at the Collegio Nazareno in Rome on the Feast of the Blessed Virgin Mary. The text is written in the Italian vernacular, more widely understood than Latin. It takes the form of a dispute between Humanity – who celebrates the birth of the Virgin – and Lucifer, who struggles with her for supremacy. Eventually, Lucifer recognizes that in Humanity he has more than met his match and he returns to Lake Avernus and the nether regions "neither prince nor king". The imagery evoked by the unidentified librettist is charmingly naïve and sometimes colourful, both aspects of which are characteristically capitalized upon by Scarlatti. This is a vibrant score of instant melodic and harmonic appeal, very well sung by Rossana Bertini (Humanity) and marginally less so by Massimo Crispi (Lucifer). Bertini has a particularly bright vocal timbre which suits her role admirably. Her intonation is deadly accurate and her performance radiates light throughout. Crispi is more variable in the success with which he negotiates some of Scarlatti's exacting passagework. The voice is less refined in tone quality than Bertini's and, while this is appropriate to his Stygian role, there is a tendency towards bluster which adversely affects tonal focus. The music itself holds the attention throughout and, as so often with Scarlatti, there are moments of outstanding beauty, enhanced by delicate scoring perhaps for solo violin, cello or sopranino recorder. In contrast with these delicate touches are passages of resonant scoring for solo trumpet. The insertion of two trio sonatas by Scarlatti's contemporary, Corelli, from Opp. 3 and 4 are also very affecting in context. They are sensitively played by Biondi and his instrumentalists who bring a rare sense of poetry to the slow movements. In summary, this is a rewarding issue and one which readers so far unacquainted with Scarlatti's vocal music are likely to find a very enjoyable introduction. Recorded sound is excellent and full texts with translations are included.

Further listening ...

...Sinfonie di concerto grosso Nos. 7-12. Concerti grossi Nos. 1-3. **I Musici.** Philips 434 160-2PM.

...Sonata for Recorder, Two Violins and Continuo in A minor. *Coupled with works by* **Sarri, D. Scarlatti, Durante** and **Mancini Il Giardino Armonico / Giovanni Antonini** (rec). Teldec Das Alte Werk 4509-93157-2 (11/94). *See review in the Collections section; refer to the Index to Reviews.* ⒼⒼ

...Toccata per il cembalo. *Coupled with works by* **G. Strozzi, Salvatore, Frescobaldi, Lambardo, Buono, Picchi, Trabaci, A. Mayone, Giovanni de Macque, Facoli, A. Valente, Merula, M. Rossi, B. Storace** and **Stradella** Rinaldo Alessandrini (hpd). Opus 111 OPS30-118 (4/95). ✍ *See review in the Collections section; refer to the Index to Reviews.* ⒼⒼ

...Dixit Dominus II. *Coupled with* **Vivaldi** Gloria in D major. **Soloists; The English Concert Choir; The English Concert / Trevor Pinnock.** Archiv Produktion 423 386-2AH (5/88). ✍

...Cain overo Il Primo Omicidio. **Concerto Italiano; L'Europa Galante / Fabio Biondi.** Opus 111 OPS30-75/6. ✍ Ⓖ

...Lamentazioni per la Settimana Santa. **Noémi Rime, Martina Lins** (sops); **Le Parlement de Musique / Martin Gester.** Opus 111 OPS30-66 (8/93). ✍

...Abramo, il tuo semblante, "Cinque profeti". *Coupled with* **Corelli** String Sonata No. 1 in G minor, WoO2. **Soloists; Stagione / Michael Schneider.** Deutsche Harmonia Mundi 05472 77291-2. ✍

...Variations on "La folia"[a]. Cantatas[b] – Correa nel seno amato; Già lusingato appieno. [b]**Lynne Dawson** (sop); **Purcell Quartet.** Hyperion CDA66254 (3/90). ✍

...Infirmata, vulnerata. De tenebroso lacu. Salve regina in F minor[a]. Totus amore languens.
[a]**Véronique Gens** (sop); **Gérard Lesne** (alto); **Il Seminario Musicale.** Virgin Classics Veritas
VC5 45103-2 (6/95).

...Agar et Ismaele esiliati (Ishmael). Sonatas for Recorder and Strings – C minor; A minor[a].
Soloists; [a]**Elissa Berardi** (rec); **Brewer Chamber Orchestra / Rudolph Palmer.** Newport Classic
Premier NPD85558 (7/94).

...Il trionfo della grazia (La Maddalena). **Silvia Piccollo** (sop); **Rossana Bertini** (sop); **Gloria
Banditelli** (contr); **L'Europa Galante / Fabio Biondi.** Opus 111 OPS30-96 (10/94).

Domenico Scarlatti

Italian 1685-1757

D. Scarlatti Keyboard Sonatas – C major (manuscript – Yale University); G major; D major;
C major (all three ed. Henle); G major (ed. Sociedad Española de Musicología, Madrid);
D minor; A major; G major (all ed. Unión Musical Española, Madrid); A major (ed. Musica
Antiqua, Lisbon); A major; E major (both MS – Biblioteca de Catalunya, Barcelona); A major
(MS – British Library, London); A major (MS – Real Conservatorio de Música, Madrid).
Fandango in D minor. **Mayako Soné** (hpd). Erato Ⓕ 4509-94806-2 (51 minutes: DDD: 10/94).

It's a bit silly of Erato to label this disc "Unpublished sonatas" when the publishers of eight of the
present 14 are actually listed: if they meant 'recently discovered sonatas', why not say so? Apart from
this, however, a certain scepticism is called for by the claim that these are by Scarlatti. A few may well
be by him; the majority, to differing extents, are of doubtful authenticity. The most convincing
'possibles' are the robustly exuberant Yale C major and three sonatas (two of them longer than usual)
found in Valladolid and published by UME in Madrid. The *Fandango* has been worked up by the
player here from a sketch (an impression of Scarlatti's improvisation?) in a private collection in
Tenerife: shorter than the famous example attributed to Soler but closely resembling it in style. It is
played with tremendous gusto – like everything else on this disc – on a Blanchet copy by Mayako
Soné, a young harpsichordist who is making quite a name for herself. Her experience as a continuo
player has doubtless been a contributory factor in her splendidly strong rhythmic sense; and her crisp
articulation is a pleasure to hear. Regardless of the authenticity or otherwise of these pieces, this is a
very attractive disc.

New review
D. Scarlatti Keyboard Sonatas – D minor, Kk1; A minor, Kk3; G minor, Kk8; D minor, Kk9;
C minor, Kk11; F major, Kk17; A major, Kk24; F sharp minor, Kk25; B minor, Kk27; D major,
Kk29; B minor, Kk87; D major, Kk96; A major, Kk113; D minor, Kk141; G major, Kk146;
B minor, Kk173; D minor, Kk213; D major, Kk214; C sharp minor, Kk247; G major, Kk259;
A major, Kk268; G minor, Kk283; G major, Kk284; E major, Kk380; F minor, Kk386; F minor,
Kk387; A major, Kk404; D major, Kk443; F minor, Kk519; G major, Kk520; G major, Kk523.
Mikhail Pletnev (pf). Virgin Classics Ⓕ VCD5 45123-2 (two discs: 140 minutes: DDD: 3/96).
Recorded 1994. *Gramophone Editor's choice.*

Every so often a major pianist reclaims Scarlatti for the piano with an outstanding recording and this
is certainly such an occasion. As Ralph Kirkpatrick put it, Scarlatti's harpsichord, while supremely
itself, is continually menacing a transformation into something else. True, the relation of the music to
harpsichord sound could hardly be closer – you can't argue on that point! – and of course it wouldn't
have been composed the way it is for a different instrument. Enter Mikhail Pletnev. A two-CD album
seems hardly sufficient to contain the feast of thrilling and imaginative playing he offers here. But let's
put the music first; 140 minutes of Scarlatti is hardly enough to display the full range of this
inexhaustibly surprising composer. He is marvellous at suggesting imaginary orchestrations and
stimulating our own imagination. He makes us aware of the different vantage points as the music
passes before us, of the different tones of voice and rhetorical inflexions – as various in these sonatas
as the events in them are unpredictable. There are dances and fiestas and processions here, serenades
and laments, and evocations of everything from the rudest folk music to courtly entertainments and
churchly polyphony; and as the kaleidoscope turns you marvel at the composer who could embrace
such diversity and shape it and put it all on to the keyboard. No wonder Chopin found Scarlatti a
kindred spirit.

This is strongly individual playing, be warned. Pletnev's free-ranging poetic licence may not be to
your taste, and admittedly it does beg a few questions. Not that his spectacular virtuosity is likely to be
controversial: this really is *hors de catégorie* and enormously enjoyable. And the evocations of the
harpsichord are often very witty – only a fool would play Scarlatti on the piano as if the harpsichord
had never existed. But Pletnev doesn't shrink from using the full resources of the piano, sustaining
pedal included, and if you baulk at the prospect of that as the means to an end he will probably not be
for you. The sustaining pedal is indeed dangerous in music which is almost wholly to do with lines, not
washes of colour; its effect is to make us see Scarlatti as if through Mendelssohn's eyes. Yet moments
of such falsification are rare. As often as not when Pletnev appears to be on the verge of stepping
outside Scarlatti's world, or reinventing a little bit of it, it's because of some shaft of insight vouchsafed
to his extraordinary musical mind that is well worth having. Characterization is everything, and though

he can be a mite coy in the reflective sonatas he generally goes straight to the heart of the matter. The vigorous, full tone in the quick numbers is a joy to have, and most admirable of all is the way he makes sound immediately command character. That is something only the best artists are able to do. There are no doubts about the recorded sound: this is one of the best piano recordings available.

New review

D. Scarlatti Keyboard Sonatas – Kk69; Kk113; Kk114; Kk115; Kk116; Kk208; Kk209; Kk215; Kk216; Kk246; Kk247; Kk394; Kk395; Kk414; Kk415; Kk426; Kk427; Kk513. **Andreas Staier** (hpd). Teldec Das Alte Werk Ⓔ 0630-12601-2 (74 minutes: DDD: 7/96). ✍

Staier's previous Scarlatti records aroused a keen anticipation for more, which at long last has been fulfilled. He is adept at capturing the mercurial changes of mood and still surprising harmonic quirks of that unpredictable genius, and even when we disagree with his readings they always hold the interest. In particular, he manages to convey the spirit of Scarlatti's spur-of-the-moment inventive powers, not merely by adding spontaneous extra ornaments or inserting buckshee pauses-for-thought, but by his very flexible pace – which may take some getting used to. Kk427, which is marked "as fast as possible", has never been played faster than here, but Kk114 – one of two sonatas including the direction *Tremulo* to indicate a continuous trill – sounds rushed, and Kk208 is preternaturally slow, drawing attention to a left-hand-before-right mannerism that also affects the pensive Kk69. Staier makes big variations within Kk394 and Kk395, for example, and starts the second half of the bright Kk414 at a new tempo. Yet he only does it to tease, and he can, when he wants to, maintain an admirably direct forward impulse, as in the C sharp minor Sonata, Kk246, his wonderfully springy Kk209, or in Kk113, with its exhilarating cross-hand leaps. Scarlatti styles exemplified here range from the Neapolitan three-section Pastorale, Kk513 to the savage Spanish scrunches of Kk215, and from continuity – even isorhythm in Kk415 – to constant stop-and-start tactics, as in Kk426 (which, together with its companion Kk427, calls for an instrument with a top G, which this Keith Hill copy of a mid-eighteenth-century German harpsichord evidently has). For some unfathomable reason Teldec's booklet totally ignores the programme and instead prints a completely irrelevant short story.

Additional recommendations ...

...555 Keyboard Sonatas. **Scott Ross** (hpd) with **Monica Huggett** (vn); **Christophe Coin** (vc); **Michael Henry** (ob); **Marc Vellon** (bn). Erato Ⓔ 2292-45309-2 (34 discs: DDD: 6/88). ✍

...Kk7; Kk84; Kk185; Kk187; Kk193; Kk208; Kk491; Kk492. *Coupled with works by* **Soler** **Virginia Black** (hpd). Cala United Ⓔ 88005-2 (58 minutes: DDD: 8/94). ✍ *See review under Soler; refer to the Index to Reviews.*

...Kk30, "Cat's Fugue"; Kk46; Kk87; Kk119; Kk132; Kk133; Kk208; Kk213; Kk215; Kk259; Kk260; Kk278; Kk380; Kk429; Kk517; Kk544; Kk545. **Colin Booth** (hpd). Olympia Ⓜ OCD251 (74 minutes: DDD: 3/95).

...Kk32; Kk109; Kk234; Kk296; Kk259; Kk440; Kk490; Kk515. **Wanda Landowska** (hpd). EMI Références mono Ⓜ CDH7 64934-2* (69 minutes: ADD: 8/94).

...Kk52; Kk211; Kk212; Kk248; Kk249; Kk261; Kk262; Kk263; Kk264; Kk318; Kk319; Kk347; Kk348; Kk416; kk417; kk490; Kk491; Kk492. **Elaine Thornburgh** (hpd). Koch International Classics Ⓔ 37014-2 (72 minutes: DDD: 10/91). ✍ ⒼⒼ

...Kk64; Kk87; Kk96; Kk132; Kk133; Kk175; Kk202; Kk213; Kk214; Kk263; Kk264; Kk277; Kk278; Kk420; Kk421; Kk460; Kk461. **Andreas Staier** (hpd). Deutsche Harmonia Mundi Ⓔ 05472-77274-2 (71 minutes: DDD: 3/93). ✍ ⒼⒼⒼ

...Kk108; Kk118; Kk119; Kk141; Kk198; Kk203; Kk454; Kk455; Kk490; Kk491; Kk492; Kk501; Kk502; Kk516; Kk517; Kk518; Kk519. **Andreas Staier** (hpd). Deutsche Harmonia Mundi Ⓔ RD77224 (70 minutes: DDD: 2/92). ✍ ⒼⒼⒼ

...Kk113; Kk380; Kk381; Kk213; Kk119; Kk120; Kk501; Kk502; Kk466; Kk146; Kk318; Kk319; Kk24. **Virginia Black** (hpd). CRD Ⓔ CRD3442 (60 minutes: DDD: 6/87). ✍ Ⓖ

...Kk124; Kk99; Kk201; Kk87; Kk46; Kk95; Kk204a; Kk490; Kk491; Kk492; Kk520; Kk521; Kk513. **Trevor Pinnock** (hpd). CRD Ⓔ CRD3368 (61 minutes: ADD. 12/86). ✍ Ⓖ

...Kk213; Kk214; Kk318; Kk319; Kk347; Kk348; Kk356; Kk357; Kk380; Kk381; Kk454; Kk455; Kk478; Kk479; Kk524; Kk525; Kk526. **Ralph Kirkpatrick** (hpd). DG Classikon Ⓜ 439 438-2GCL (52 minutes: ADD).

...Kk1; Kk8; Kk9; Kk11; Kk13; Kk20; Kk87; Kk98; Kk119; Kk135; Kk159; Kk380; Kk450; Kk487; Kk529. **Ivo Pogorelich** (pf). DG Ⓔ 435 855-2GH (60 minutes: DDD: 1/93).

...Kk9; Kk13; Kk17; Kk27; Kk29; Kk30; Kk32; Kk64; Kk69; Kk87; Kk96; Kk114; Kk119; Kk125; Kk159; Kk175; Kk202; Kk245; Kk279; Kk377; Kk380; Kk427; Kk430; Kk432; Kk446; Kk450; Kk474; Kk478; Kk492; Kk519; Kk523; Kk533. *Coupled with works by* **F. Couperin, Rameau** *and* **Rossini** Marcelle Meyer (pf). EMI mono Ⓜ CZS5 68092-2* (four discs: 275 minutes: ADD: 6/95). *See review in the Collections section; refer to the Index to Reviews.* ⒼⒼⒼ

...Kk9; Kk27; Kk30; Kk33; Kk69; Kk87; Kk96; Kk159; Kk193; Kk247; Kk492; Kk531. **Anne Queffélec** (pf). Erato Ⓜ 4509-96960-2 (51 minutes: ADD: 3/95). ⒼⒼ

...Kk14. *Coupled with works by* **Schumann, Matthay, Brahms** *and* **Ferguson** Dame Myra Hess (pf). Biddulph mono Ⓜ LHW025* (76 minutes: ADD: 3/96). *See review in the Collections section; refer to the Index to Reviews.* Ⓖ

...Kk33; Kk54; Kk96; Kk146; Kk162; Kk198; Kk391; Kk466; Kk474; Kk481; Kk491; Kk525. **Vladimir Horowitz** (pf). Sony Classical Ⓔ SK53460 (72 minutes: ADD: 7/94).

Further listening ...

...Sonata for Mandolin and Continuo in D minor, Kk90. *Coupled with* **Sarri** Concerto for
Recorder, Two Violins, Viola and Continuo in A minor. **Durante** Concerto for Two Violins,
Viola and Continuo in G minor. **A. Scarlatti** Sonata for Recorder, Two Violins and Continuo in
A minor. **Mancini** Sonata for Recorder, Two Violins and Continuo in D minor. **Il Giardino
Armonico / Giovanni Antonini** (rec). Teldec Das Alte Werk 4509-93157-2 (11/94). *See review in the
Collections section; refer to the Index to Reviews.*   ⓖⓖ

...Stabat mater[a]. *Coupled with* **Esteves** Mass for Eight Voices. [a]**Elisabeth Hermans** (sop); [a]**Jan Van
Elsaker** (ten); **Currende Vocal Ensemble / Erik Van Nevel** with **Jacques Van Der Meer** (va da
gamba); **Lidewij Scheifes** (vc); **Herman Stinders** (org). Accent ACC9069D (5/92). ✒

...Cantatas – Scritte con falso inganno. Tinte a note di sangue. O qual meco Nice cangiata.
Dir vorrei. **Kate Eckersley** (sop); **Fiori Musicali / Penelope Rapson** (hpd). Unicorn-Kanchana
DKPCD9119 (5/92).

Anthony Scarmolin   1890-1969

Suggested listening ...

...Symphonies[a] – No. 1 in E minor; No. 2. Sinfonia breve[b]. [a]**Slovak Radio Symphony Orchestra;**
[b]**Polish Radio National Symphony Orchestra / Joel Eric Suben.** New World Records 80502-2
(8/96).

Giacinto Scelsi   Italian 1905-1988

Suggested listening ...

...In nomine lucis. *Coupled with works by* **Pärt** and **Cage** **Christoph Maria Moosmann** (org). New
Albion NA074CD (2/96). *See review under Pärt; refer to the Index to Reviews.*

Franz Xaver Scharwenka   Polish 1850-1924

Scharwenka Piano Quartet in F major, Op. 37. Piano Trio in A minor, Op. 45. **Levon Chilingirian**
(vn); **Ivo-Jan van der Werff** (va); **Garbis Atmacayan** (vc); **Seta Tanyel** (pf). Collins Classics
Ⓕ 1419-2 (76 minutes: DDD: 3/95). Recorded 1994.
These are world première recordings of two sadly neglected works (one is inclined to say masterpieces,
even on a first hearing), superbly performed and recorded. Those who only know Scharwenka from
his piano concertos and the odd solo piece will be astonished and deeply gratified, for even when the
shadows of both Mendelssohn and Brahms flit across the surface, his music is full of surprises and
often real breadth and vibrancy. The Quartet's *Adagio* is notably rich, and who can resist the trio's
second movement, its solace shadowed by a near-Franckian chromaticism and malaise? The final
pages, too, have a beguiling intimacy, particularly when spun off by all three players with such
enviable ease and tonal radiance. Then there is the *Molto allegro*, as lightly tripping (a memory of
Mendelssohn's fairy world?) as the work's very opening is questioning and rhythmically ambiguous.
Seta Tanyel is beautifully balanced with her colleagues and, as always, she makes light of every
difficulty, bringing all of her tonal translucency and charm to even the most awkward and
strenuous moments. All lovers of worthwhile byways of music of both depth and novelty will surely
snap this up.

New review

Scharwenka Piano Trio No. 1 in F sharp minor, Op. 1[ab]. Violin Sonata in D minor, Op. 2[a]. Cello
Sonata in E minor, Op. 46[ab]. Serenade, Op. 70[a]. [a]**Lydia Mordkovitch** (vn); [b]**Colin Carr** (vc); **Seta
Tanyel** (pf). Collins Classics Ⓕ 1448-2 (76 minutes: DDD: 10/95). Recorded 1995. *Gramophone
Editor's choice.*
The sixth volume in Seta Tanyel's invaluable Scharwenka series takes us on an intriguing journey
through innocence to experience. The Piano Trio owes a heavy debt to both Mendelssohn and
Schumann, yet there is already so much to enjoy that one feels churlish for mentioning such
influences. Even here familiar conventions are quickly discarded in favour of adventure (this is
particularly true of the second movement, which happily foils a witty "March of the toys" with the
most assuaging lyricism). Op. 2 gets off to an already more restless, exploratory start before whirling
us away with true *Allegro appassionato* energy. The fire-spitting finale, too, is a surprise, particularly
after the central "Romanze" or idyll. Then there is the Cello Sonata, a dark and weighty work with a
finale most oddly related in its angularity to Fauré's G minor Cello Sonata (Scharwenka and Fauré
were almost exact contemporaries). Finally, the *Serenade*, played by Lydia Mordkovitch with great
affection, returns us to an early salon melancholy. Here, then, is music for perfect late summer
listening; accessible but piquant and easy to underestimate. However, the piano writing can be fiercely
demanding and Seta Tanyel's performances are beyond praise. Few pianists have worn their virtuosity
and musicianship with such enviable lightness. The recordings are, once again, superb.

Further listening ...

...Piano Concerto No. 1 in B flat minor, Op. 32. *Coupled with* **Chopin** Piano Concerto No. 1 in E minor, Op. 11. **Seta Tanyel** (pf); **Philharmonia Orchestra / Yuri Simonov.** Collins Classics 1263-2. Ⓖ

...Piano Concerto No. 1 in B flat minor, Op. 32. *Coupled with works by* **Balakirev** and **Paderewski Earl Wild** (pf); **Boston Symphony Orchestra / Erich Leinsdorf.** Elan CD82266 (7/96). *See review under Balakirev; refer to the Index to Reviews.*

...Piano Concerto No. 4 in F minor, Op. 82. *Coupled with* **Sauer** Piano Concerto No. 1 in E minor. **Stephen Hough** (pf); **City of Birmingham Symphony Orchestra / Lawrence Foster.** Hyperion CDA66790 (11/95). *See review under Sauer; refer to the Index to Reviews. Gramophone Editor's record of the month.* Ⓖ

...Five Polish Dances, Op. 3. Piano Sonata No. 1 in C sharp minor, Op. 6. First Polonaise, Op. 12. Impromptu, Op. 17. Valse-Caprice, Op. 31. Polonaise, Op. 42. Eglantine Waltz, Op. 84. **Seta Tanyel** (pf). Collins Classics 1325-2 (9/92).

Peter Schat   Dutch 1935-

Suggested listening ...

...The Heavens, Op. 37. **Royal Concertgebouw Orchestra / Riccardo Chailly.** NM Classics NM92033 (7/94).

Johann Scheibe   German 1708-1776

Suggested listening ...

...Flute Concertos – A major[a]; D major[b]. *Coupled with* **Agrell** Flute Concerto in D major[a]. **Hasse** Flute Concerto in G major[b]. [a]**Maria Bania,** [b]**Irene Spranger** (fls); **Concerto Cophenhagen / Andrew Manze.** Chandos Chaconne CHAN0535 (6/93). ✎

Samuel Scheidt   German 1587-1654

Suggested listening ...

...Ich glaub und weiss. Paduan a 4. Lobet, ihr Himmel, den Herren. *Coupled with works by* **Zachow** and **Handel Stadtsingechor, Halle; Berolina Quartet.** Berlin Classics 0011 312BC (6/96).

Johann Hermann Schein   German 1586-1630

Suggested listening ...

...Vocal Works – O Amarilli zart. Aurora schön mit ihrem Haar. Frischauf, ihr Klosterbrüder mein. Ringstum mich schwebet Trauerigkeit. Als Filli schön und fromm. In Filli schönen Augelein. O Scheiden, o bitter Scheiden. Unlängst dem blinden Gröttelein. Wie kommst's, o zarte Filli mein. Kickehihi, kakakanei. Cupido blind, das Venuskind. Wenn Filli ihre Liebesstrahl. O Amarilli, schönste Zier. Heulen und schmerzlichs Weinen. All wilden Tier im grünen Wald. O Venus und Cupido blind. Amor, das liebe Räuberlein. O seidene Härelein. Ihr Brüder, lieben Brüder mein. Mirtillo hat ein Schäfelein. Die Vöglein singen. Mein Schifflein lief im wilden Meer. **Cantus Cölln / Konrad Junghänel.** Deutsche Harmonia Mundi RD77088 (10/90). ✎

Johann Schelle   German 1648-1701

Suggested listening ...

...Actus musicus auf Weyh-Nachten[a]. Vom Himmel kam der Engel Schar[a]. Uns ist ein Kind geboren[a]. Ach mein herzliebes Jesulein[a]. Machet die Tore weit[a]. Nun komm der Heiden Heiland. [a]**La Capella Ducale; Musica Fiata, Cologne / Roland Wilson.** Deutsche Harmonia Mundi 05472 77298-2 (5/94). Ⓖ

David Schiff   American 1945

Suggested listening ...

...Stomp. *Coupled with* **Kernis** New Era Dance. **J. Adams** The Chairman Dances. **Bernstein** West Side Story – Mambo. **Larsen** Collage: Boogie. **Harbison** Remembering Gatsby. **Torke** Black and White – Charcoal. **Moran** Points of Departure. **Agento** The Dream of Valentino – Tango. **Daugherty** Desi. **Rouse** Bonham. **Baltimore Symphony Orchestra / David Zinman.** Argo 444 454-2ZH (7/95).

Max Schillings
German 1868-1933

Suggested listening ...

...Violin Concerto, Op. 25[a]. Moloch – Harvest Festival. Symphonic Prologue to Oedipus Tyrannus of Sophocles, Op. 11. [a]**Ernö Rozsa** (vn); **Košice State Philharmonic Orchestra / Alfred Walter.** Marco Polo 8 223324 (4/92).

...Mona Lisa. **Soloists; Kiel Opera Chorus; Kiel Philharmonic Orchestra / Klauspeter Seibel.** CPO CPO999 303-2 (8/95).

Johann Heinrich Schmelzer
Austrian c1620/23-1680

Suggested listening ...

...Sonata a 3 in B minor, "Lamento. Duodena selectarum sonatarum – No. 2 in A minor; No. 8 in B flat major. Sonata sopra la morte Ferdinand III. Lamento a 3 in B flat major. Harmonia a 5 in B flat major. *Coupled with works by* **Biber Freiburg Baroque Orchestra Consort.** Deutsche Harmonia Mundi 05472 77348-2 (7/96). *See review under Biber, refer to the Index to Reviews.*

...Sonatas – Lamento sopra la morte Ferdinandi III; Sonata a tre violini. Sonata a tre; Sonata a tre "Lanterly"; Duodena selectarum sonatarum – No. 9. *Coupled with* **Muffat** Violin Sonata. Armonico tributo – Five Sonatas: No. 5. **London Baroque / Charles Medlam.** Harmonia Mundi HMA190 1220 (11/87). ✎

...Vesperae sollennes[ab]. Sonata per Chiesa et Camera. Sacro-Profanus Concentus Musicus – Sonata XII. *Coupled with* **Biber** Missa alleluja[ab]. **Palestrina** Coelestis urbs Jerusalem. **Froberger** Fantasia II in A minor. **Anonymous** Gregorian Chant for the Dedication of a Church – Mass Propers[a]. Gregorian Chant for Vespers[a]. [a]**Vienna Hofburgkapella Schola;** [b]**Concerto Palatino; Gradus ad Parnassum / Konrad Junghänel.** Deutsche Harmonia Mundi 05472 77326-2 (7/95). ✎

Franz Schmidt
Czechoslovakian/Austrian 1874-1939

New review

Schmidt Symphony No. 1 in E major.
R. Strauss Intermezzo – symphonic interludes. **Detroit Symphony Orchestra / Neeme Järvi.**
Chandos Ⓕ CHAN9357 (68 minutes: DDD: 4/96). Recorded 1994.

Franz Schmidt's First Symphony is the rarity here and it is more easily, and misleadingly, described by its influences than their sum total. There is a lot of Strauss, Wagner, a little Bruckner, a general suggestion of Brahmsian expansiveness and, arguably, Dvořák in some of the writing for wind. Yet while these comparisons may help place the idiom for a newcomer to the repertoire, the music is a good deal more difficult to describe. Schmidt was only in his mid-twenties when he wrote it but although it is derivative, it is full of vitality, and coherently argued. Indeed it is held together in a fashion that leaves no doubt that a master symphonist was in the making. (The trumpet theme in the first movement is perhaps a hint of what was to come in the Fourth Symphony.) Small wonder that the work won the *Gesellschaft der Musikfreunde* Prize in Vienna when Schmidt conducted its first performance in 1902. (The otherwise excellent note tells us that he wrote the symphony at the age of 38 when in fact he was 22 when he started it and only 25 when it was finished.) Its invention is fresh, and its orchestration marvellously accomplished. It is very well played by the Detroit orchestra, who manage to produce a really Viennese sonority for Neeme Järvi, both here and in the delightful symphonic interludes Strauss extracted from his opera, *Intermezzo*. There are several rival performances of the *Intermezzo* interludes but this warmly recorded version can hold its own against any of them. The recording team produce truthful and well-detailed sound.

New review

Schmidt Symphony No. 4 in C major. Variations on a Hussar's Song. **London Philharmonic Orchestra / Franz Welser-Möst.** EMI Ⓕ CDC5 55518-2 (72 minutes: DDD: 1/96). Recorded 1994.
Gramophone Editor's choice. 🅖🅖🅖

Writing in *The Symphony* (ed. Robert Simpson, Penguin Books: 1967) the late Harold Truscott made out a strong case for Franz Schmidt. He robustly dismissed the notion that his music does not travel. "It 'travels' very well, when allowed to do so, and I will go so far as to say that anyone who claims a love and understanding of Beethoven, Brahms or Sibelius, should have no difficulty with Schmidt. There could," he went on, "scarcely be a more positive work than No. 4, whose confidence is complete and without bombast" and it is obvious that Schmidt's mastery of the art of symphonic thinking and of the orchestra is everywhere in evidence. The symphony is in one unbroken span whose material derives from the haunting opening 21-bar theme on solo trumpet – in itself an idea of remarkable originality. Unlike Reger, whose influence can at times be clearly heard, Schmidt was a late developer and far from prolific. Indeed apart from the four symphonies, there is only one other orchestral work, the *Variations on a Hussar's Song* recorded here. For those who have never encountered his music, it is perhaps best if loosely described as rich in palette, in much the same way as Elgar, chromatic in its harmonic language yet never cloying, and above all it has an innate nobility, an elegiac dignity of utterance and a sense of vision. Not without reason did Truscott call Schmidt the "only real successor to Bruckner – in so far as there is one at all". Welser-Möst shows great feeling for and sympathy with this music and carries his fine players with him. Theirs is playing of eloquence and dedication, and the recording team produce truthful and well-detailed sound.

New review

Schmidt String Quartets – No. 1 in A major; No. 2 in G major. **Franz Schubert Quartet of Vienna** (Florian Zwiauer, Helge Rosenkranz, vns; Hartmut Pascher, va; Vincent Stadlmair, vc). Nimbus Ⓔ NI5467 (78 minutes: DDD: 6/96). Recorded 1995.

Schmidt was not a prolific composer but nearly all his music is of quality, and radiates a mastery and nobility that recalls the likes of Elgar, Stenhammar and Suk. In both quartets there is a strong affinity with or indebtedness to his immediate contemporary, Reger. Indeed, like Reger's quartets, these are unlikely to enjoy as wide a following as they deserve. The Franz Schubert Quartet of Vienna play this music with a conviction, beauty of tone and wide dynamic range that eluded their predecessors. The slow movement of the A major Quartet, for example, is beautifully played and even the dense chromaticism of the G major is well elucidated. Moreover the recording is well balanced with plenty of air around the aural image. In short, these performances are unlikely to be surpassed for a long time, and can be warmly recommended. Both quartets take just under 40 minutes each so that Nimbus offer good value in giving us both on one CD.

New review

Schmidt Das Buch mit sieben Siegeln. **Hilde Gueden** (sop); **Ira Malaniuk** (contr); **Anton Dermota, Fritz Wunderlich** (tens); **Walter Berry** (bass-bar); **Vienna Singverein; Vienna Philharmonic Orchestra / Dimitri Mitropoulos.** Sony Classical Festspieldokumente mono Ⓜ SM2K68442* (two discs: 111 minutes: ADD: 3/96). Text included. Recorded live in 1959.

Franz Schmidt's oratorio combines learned, Bruckner-like contrapuntal artifice with a vivid sense of drama that at times recalls the naïve peasant baroque of some Austrian and South German carved altarpieces, at others the horrific realism of Matthias Grünewald. As a composer himself and a man of deep religious conviction Mitropoulos responded to both these aspects, and such haunting passages as the duet for two survivors of the pestilence and death spread by the horsemen of the Apocalypse, or the tremendous earthquake chorus that follows the breaking of the seventh seal have a powerful sense of drama which is emphasized by Mitropoulos's precise care for contrapuntal and instrumental detail. Yes, in this live performance there are a few untidinesses but the impact and the devout urgency of the reading are not in the least diminished by them. In the hugely taxing central role of St John, Dermota is deeply impressive. Although the part is often given to a dramatic tenor it responds to a lyric voice that is capable at times of ringing fullness. Dermota matches Mitropoulos's urgency, and clearly means every word of the role. At one point, where a descending vocal line illustrates the text's reference to the four beasts and the elders falling down before the Lamb, it is obvious that the bottom note of the phrase is not within his range. Instead, quietly and reverently, he speaks it, and the expressive effect of this is characteristic of his whole performance. The other soloists, Gueden and Berry especially, are distinguished, and both chorus and orchestra audibly respond to Mitropoulos's conviction. The mono recording is a little constricted at times, with patches of acid string tone, but it improves and gains impact as it proceeds. *Das Buch mit sieben Siegeln* still has the reputation of a piece that the Austrians regard as a classic but which doesn't travel. This recording refutes that view with inspiriting eloquence.

Further listening ...

...Drei Phantasiestücke nach ungarischen Nationalmelodien. *Coupled with* **Brahms** (arr. Piatti) 21 Hungarian Dances. **Nancy Green** (vc); **Frederick Moyer** (pf). Biddulph LAW010 (5/95). *See review under Brahms; refer to the Index to Reviews.*

...Chaconne in C sharp minor. *Coupled with works by* **Stanford, Reger, Shostakovich** and **Ravanello** Keith John (org). Priory PRCD370 (11/92). *Selected by Sounds in Retrospect. See review in the Collections section; refer to the Index to Reviews.* ⒼⒼⒼ

...Symphony No. 2 in E flat major. **Chicago Symphony Orchestra / Neeme Järvi.** Chandos CHAN8779 (3/90).

...Symphony No. 4 in C major. *Coupled with* **Mahler** Symphony No. 2, "Resurrection". **Vienna Philharmonic Orchestra / Zubin Mehta.** Double Decca 440 615-2DF2 (5/94).

...Notre Dame. **Soloists; Choir of St Hedwig's Cathedral, Berlin; Berlin RIAS Chamber Choir; Berlin Radio Symphony Orchestra / Christof Perick.** Capriccio 10 248/9 (5/89).

Florent Schmitt

French 1870-1958

Schmitt La tragédie de Salomé. **Marie-Paule Fayt** (sop); **Rhineland-Pfalz State Philharmonic Orchestra / Patrick Davin.** Marco Polo Ⓔ 8 223448 (59 minutes: DDD: 12/93). Recorded 1991.

This is a real rarity. We have had recordings of the large-orchestra suite from *La tragédie de Salomé* before but here, apparently for the first time, is the complete ballet which runs to twice the length of the suite and calls for only a chamber orchestra (the theatre couldn't accommodate more). Schmitt's virtuosity in drawing rich sonorities and a voluptuous, barbaric atmosphere from it is astonishing.

Unlike the treatments of the biblical story by Strauss or Massenet, in the scenario here there is no question of Salome being in love with John the Baptist. Schmitt composed a well-structured score of exotic and sensual colour that includes broad lyrical episodes as well as vividly orgiastic sections. Compared to the suite for full orchestra, these lose nothing in impact or impressiveness by the smaller forces employed – indeed, the music gains in clarity and pungency thereby. It is not surprising that Stravinsky, to whom the work was dedicated, described it as "one of the greatest masterpieces of modern music". The performance, and the recording, are deserving of the highest commendation. A notable issue.

Further listening ...

...Symphonie concertante, Op. 82[a]. Rêves, Op. 65. Soirs, Op. 5. [a]**Huseyin Sermet** (pf); **Monte-Carlo Philharmonic Orchestra / David Robertson.** Auvidis Valois V4687 (9/94).

...La danse d'Abisag, Op. 75. Habeyssée, Op. 110[a]. Rêves, Op. 65. Symphony No. 2, Op. 137. [a]**Hannele Segerstam** (vn); **Rheinland-Pfalz State Philharmonic Orchestra / Leif Segerstam.** Marco Polo 8 223689 (3/95).

...In memoriam Gabriel Fauré, Op. 72 – Scherzo. *Coupled with* **Koechlin** Choral sur le nom de Fauré. **Ravel** Pavane pour une infante défunte. **Fauré** Requiem, Op. 48[a]. Pavane, Op. 50. [a]**Sylvia McNair** (sop); [a]**Thomas Allen** (bar); **Academy of St Martin in the Fields** and [a]**Chorus / Sir Neville Marriner.** Philips 446 084-2PH (1/96).

Alfred Schnittke   USSR 1934-

Schnittke Concerto grosso No. 1[a]. Quasi una sonata[b]. Moz-Art à la Haydn[c]. [ac]**Tatiana Grindenko** (vn); **Yuri Smirnov** ([a]hpd/[a]prep pf/[b]pf); **Chamber Orchestra of Europe /** [a]**Heinrich Schiff,** [bc]**Gidon Kremer** ([a]vn). DG Ⓜ 439 452-2GCL (62 minutes: DDD: 9/90). Recorded live in 1988.

For a single representative of Alfred Schnittke's work you could choose nothing better than the first *Concerto grosso* of 1977. Here are the psychedelic mélanges of baroque and modern, the drastic juxtapositions of pseudo-Vivaldi with pseudo-Berg, producing an effect at once aurally exciting and spiritually disturbing. The piece has been recorded several times over, but never with the panache of Gidon Kremer and friends and never with the vivid immediacy of this live DG recording (in fact the solo violins are rather too closely miked for comfort, but that's only a tiny drawback). *Quasi una sonata* was originally composed in 1968 for violin and piano and it was something of a breakthrough piece for Schnittke as he emerged from what he called "the puberty rites of serialism", letting his imagination run riot for the first time. No one could call it a disciplined piece, but if that worries you, you should leave Schnittke alone anyway. The transcription for solo violin and string orchestra is an ingenious one and Kremer again supplies all the requisite agonized intensity. *Moz-Art à la Haydn* is a very slight piece of work, and it really depends on visual theatricality to make its effect. Still, it complements the other two pieces well enough, and this disc makes another excellent introduction to this composer.

Additional recommendation ...

...Concerto grosso No. 1[a]. Viola Concerto[b]. Concerto for Piano and Strings[c]. Monologue[d]. Praeludium in memoriam Dmitri Shostakovich[e]. Suite in the Old Style[f]. [a]**Gidon Kremer,** [a]**Tatjana Grindenko,** [e]**Sasha Rozhdestvensky** (vns); [c]**Vladimir Krainev,** [e]**Sergei Bezrodny** (pfs); [ab]**London Symphony Orchestra /** [a]**Gennadi Rozhdestvensky,** [b]**Mstislav Rostropovich;** [cf]**Moscow Virtuosi /** **Vladimir Spivakov** ([e]vn); [d]**Moscow Soloists /** [d]**Yuri Bashmet** ([b]va). RCA Victor Ⓜ 74321 24894-2 (two discs: 127 minutes: ADD/DDD: 5/95).   Ⓖ

Schnittke Violin Concertos[a] – No. 2; No. 3. Stille Nacht[b]. Gratulations rondo[b]. **Gidon Kremer** (vn); [a]**Chamber Orchestra of Europe / Christoph Eschenbach** ([b]pf). Teldec Ⓕ 4509-94540-2 (61 minutes: DDD: 2/95). Recorded 1994.   ⒼⒼ

Schnittke's Second Violin Concerto opens with the kind of jagged, convulsive, Webern-crossed-with-Shostakovich cadenza that is a trademark of his string writing. Does the rest of the concerto live up to this opening? And what is all the curious writing for the solo double-bass supposed to mean? Jürgen Köchel's accompanying note reveals all – or at least something startling. It turns out that the structure is based on Christ's life, death and resurrection, and that the double-bass is a Judas figure, an anti-soloist (shades of Liszt's Faust/Mephistopheles perhaps). That may or may not affect one's reactions to the music. Do Berg's Violin Concerto and Chamber Concerto, for instance, stand by their hidden programmes or by the notes composed as a result of them? And the Third Concerto is certainly not a piece to be trifled with. Its unusual scoring for 13 winds and four strings is partly modelled on Berg's Chamber Concerto, and at one stage the composer was toying with another Biblical subtitle, *The Song of Songs*. But the musical invention seems more self-sufficient, more concentrated and more finished than that of the Second Concerto. The violin's trills convey the alarm of a whole psychic world tottering, and all three movements have their nerve-endings exposed. The Mahlerian chorale of the finale carries bittersweetness to the *n*th degree. Throughout the disc Kremer's personality is a compelling presence, and the Chamber Orchestra of Europe are terrific in their support. Eschenbach's contribution is perhaps less overt but certainly no less vital, and in the two contrasted miniatures (in many ways the outstanding compositions in the programme) his discretion is the ideal foil for his charismatic partner. Recording quality is of the very finest.

Additional recommendation ...

...Violin Concertos Nos. 1 and 2. **Mark Lubotsky** (vn); **Malmö Symphony Orchestra / Eri Klas.** BIS CD487 (4/91).

New review

Schnittke Symphony No. 1. **Russian State Symphony Orchestra / Gennadi Rozhdestvensky.**
Chandos Ⓕ CHAN9417 (68 minutes: DDD: 8/96). Recorded live in 1988.

Sporadic aggressive bravos and mild applause greet this performance of Schnittke's First Symphony, given in the Great Hall of the Moscow Conservatory in 1988. Which seems about right. The bravos salute the courage it took to produce such an iconoclastic piece from the depths of Brezhnevian stagnation around 1970, and all that meant to Russian composers at the time. The muted applause reflects the obvious fact that the symphony's intrinsic merits are slight, plus perhaps the realization that its symbolic value as a kind of musical dissidence was nullified by the freedoms instituted under Gorbachov. It had already become non-contemporary, in other words. That does not prevent Rozhdestvensky from motivating his orchestra to a performance of considerably more immediacy than Segerstam's Stockholmers (who were no shrinking violets themselves). That's hardly surprising, given Rozhdestvensky's involvement with the work – as dedicatee and as the man responsible for the rewrite of its conclusion, for its notorious première in Gorky and for its first recording on Melodiya (never made widely available). As with that Melodiya version, the recording quality on the new disc makes up in directness and impact what it loses to BIS in warmth and clarity. At times you fancy you can hear the audience discussing the show – a not inappropriate addition, given the deliberately provocative nature of Schnittke's collage techniques. The main point is that coarseness and blatancy are the manner to which interpretations of this symphony need to be born, and this is what the new issue offers.

Additional recommendation ...

...Symphony No. 1. **Ben Kallenberg** (vn); **Ake Lännerholm** (tbn); **Carl-Axel Dominique** (pf); **Royal Stockholm Philharmonic Orchestra / Leif Segerstam.** BIS Ⓕ CD577 (72 minutes: DDD: 11/93).

Schnittke Quasi una sonata[a]. Piano Trio[b]. Piano Sonata No. 2[c]. [ab]**Mark Lubotsky** (vn); [bc]**Irina Schnittke** (pf); [a]**English Chamber Orchestra / Mstislav Rostropovich** ([b]vc). Sony Classical Ⓕ SK53271 (63 minutes: DDD: 4/94). Recorded 1992. *Gramophone Editor's choice.*   Ⓖ

The opening bars of Schnittke's *Quasi una sonata* grab you by the throat here and the rest of the piece never lets go. It is one of the earliest examples of Schnittke's polystylistic manner and its raw, agonized inspiration and marvellous sense of dramatic timing make it one of his most durable works. Mark Lubotsky's playing is spellbinding. The orchestration of the piano part, dating from 1986, also works extremely well. The Second Piano Sonata (1990) was written for, and is here marvellously played by, the composer's wife. Like so many of Schnittke's recent works it largely avoids the Gothic horror effects which made so much of his earlier output immediately appealing. In purging his reliance on them he occasionally flounders in search of a comparable intenity of communication through the notes alone. All the same, the fake-Brahms-cum-Franck siciliano which underpins the last of the three movements is a haunting idea. The 1992 Piano Trio is another reworking, this time of the String Trio of 1985. The chilling eruptions and dumbstruck responses come across well enough in the piano trio medium, and like everything on the disc it is played with intensity and dedication. Beautiful recorded sound, too.

Schnittke String Quartet No. 3. Piano Quintet[a].
Mahler/Schnittke Piano Quartet[a]. **Borodin Quartet** (Mikhail Kopelman, Andrei Abramenkov, vns; Dmitri Shebalin, va; Valentin Berlinsky, vc); [a]**Ludmilla Berlinsky** (pf). Virgin Classics Ⓕ VC7 59040-2 (66 minutes: DDD: 12/91). Recorded 1990.

Schnittke's chamber music does not have the high public profile of some of his symphonies and concertos, but in many ways it is more fastidiously composed and it certainly makes for equally rewarding listening at home. The Piano Quintet is the outstanding feature of this disc. Predominantly slow and mournful (it is dedicated to the memory of the composer's mother) and with a haunting waltz on the notes of the BACH monogram, it is here played with compelling intensity, especially by the pianist Ludmilla Berlinsky, daughter of the Borodin Quartet's cellist. The Piano Quartet is a conflation of the 16-year-old Mahler's first movement with his incomplete second movement in Schnittke's own paraphrase – another haunting experience, beautifully played and recorded. Less satisfying as a performance, because slightly glossed over, is the Third Quartet; but this is perhaps the finest and undoubtedly the most often performed of Schnittke's chamber works, and as a whole the disc can be warmly recommended to those looking for a representative sample of Schnittke rather than a comprehensive library.

Additional recommendation ...

...String Quartets Nos. 1-3. **Tale Quartet.** BIS Ⓕ CD467 (62 minutes: DDD: 7/90).

New review

Schnittke String Trio (1985). Concerto for Three (1995)[a]. Minuet (1995).
Berg (trans. Schnittke) Four-part Canon[a]. **Gidon Kremer** (vn); **Yuri Bashmet** (va); **Mstislav Rostropovich** (vc); [a]**Moscow Soloists.** EMI Ⓕ CDC5 55627-2 (55 minutes: DDD: 5/96). Recorded live in 1995.

It is hard work keeping up with Alfred Schnittke's changes of style, or apparent changes of style, but this disc satisfyingly couples one of his most perplexing works with one of his richest and most absorbing. The String Trio is a fascinating piece, revealing more and more of itself on repeated hearings. It was commissioned to commemorate Alban Berg's centenary, and one of its recurring ideas is based on the rhythm (though not the notes) of *Happy birthday to you*. This is not, however, one of Schnittke's jokes. There is much poignancy and anxiety in the piece, and some Shostakovich-like fury and despair, but the melody that remains at the end, rising eerily above the drama but certainly not exorcizing it, is a close relative of the *Happy birthday* idea in a nostalgically lyrical form. If the work is 'about' anything it may be how far genuine rather than false simplicity is accessible to a modern composer, especially one overtly celebrating one of modernism's heroes. It is a passionate, at times anguished piece, and a strangely moving one. Another sort of simplicity is the puzzling element in the *Concerto for Three*. The soloists are not heard together until the very short fourth movement. Instead they have a movement apiece, gruffly restless for the cello, eloquently lyrical for the viola, still more intense for the violin. The finale, a furious *moto perpetuo* for all the players, is abruptly snuffed out by a single chord on the piano. It is weirdly disconcerting, but the initially lyrically expressive, then tongue-in-cheek Minuet was designed by Schnittke to be played as an encore to the concerto and, perhaps, as its true or 'alternative' finale. All three of the dedicatees play with passionate urgency, and the recording is close but not airless. Berg's soberly beautiful canon is amplified and coloured by Schnittke's transcription.

Schnittke String Trio[a]. Violin Sonatas[b] – No. 1; No. 2, "Quasi una sonata". **Mateja Marinković** (vn); [a]**Paul Silverthorne** (va); [a]**Timothy Hugh** (vc); [b]**Linn Hendry** (pf). ASV Ⓕ CDDCA868 (65 minutes: DDD: 8/94).

This performance is extremely satisfying. It is atmospherically recorded, and convincingly reinforces the Trio's claims to be considered one of Schnittke's major works. The music is surely to be preferred in this original version, rather than as the 'Trio Sonata' of Yuri Bashmet's orchestral arrangement. Dating from 1985, and written in response to a commission from the Alban Berg Society of Vienna, the Trio is notable for the extent to which its reminiscences and re-creations are far less contrived and self-indulgent than is often the case with this composer. They are not merely backward-looking, nostalgic gestures, but suggest a blueprint for a new, romantically tinged post-modernism. Whether or not you go along with this analysis, it is difficult to deny that the Trio puts the pair of early violin sonatas into the shade. They are not negligible pieces, even so, and these performances have much to commend them. True, Mark Lubotsky's version on Ondine (listed below) have particular authority – he is the dedicatee of both sonatas – and Lubotsky is an arrestingly muscular player, but the dry, close sound on the Ondine disc is inferior to the more spacious, better balanced ASV. Mateja Marinković and Linn Hendry make a first-rate duo: even the most turbulent, piano-bashing bits of the Second Sonata are not deprived of all musical sense, and the urgent interplay between the instruments has an authentic intensity.

Additional recommendations ...

...Violin Sonatas. Suite in the Old Style. **Mark Lubotsky** (vn); **Ralf Gothóni** (pf). Ondine Ⓔ ODE800-2 (53 minutes: DDD: 4/94).

...Violin Sonata No. 1. *Coupled with works by* **Copland, Bolcom, MacMillan** and **Dresher Maria Bachmann** (vn); **Jon Klibonoff** (pf); **James Saporito** (perc). Catalyst Ⓔ 09026 62668-2 (67 minutes: DDD: 5/95). *See review in the Collections section; refer to the Index to Reviews.*   Ⓖ

...Violin Sonata No. 1. *Coupled with works by* **Balakauskas, Barkauskas** and **Pärt** Rusné Mataityté (vn); **Margrit-Julia Zimmermann** (pf). Proud Sound Ⓔ PROUCD139 (57 minutes: DDD: 7/96). *See review under Balakauskas; refer to the Index to Reviews.*

Schnittke Suite in the Old Style[c]. Moz-Art à la Haydn[a]. Praeludium in memoriam Dmitri Shostakovich[a]. A Paganini. Stille Musik[b]. Stille Nacht[c]. Madrigal in Memoriam Oleg Kagan. Gratulations rondo[c]. **Mateja Marinković**, [a]**Thomas Bowes** (vns); [b]**Timothy Hugh** (vc); [c]**Linn Hendry** (pf). ASV Ⓕ CDDCA877 (68 minutes: DDD: 4/95).

At first glance, this disc presents a rather scrappy impression. It contains no large-scale pieces, and the largest work – the early *Suite in the Old Style* – is for the most part an uneventful exercise in dutiful imitation. It is what the *Suite* only hints at that the other works realize more fully. In the *Gratulations rondo* Schnittke again wears the mask of conformity to an old, easygoing classicism. When the mask begins to slip, we wonder what to think. Is this a serious lesson about the potential banality of classicism's familiar formulas? Are the distortions of those formulas expressive of affection or hostility? These issues come most fully into focus in *Stille Nacht*, as Gruber's sweet little tune, with its obediently basic harmony, is subjected to quiet but ruthlessly dissonant deconstruction. "Silent Night" acquires the connotations of Rachel Carson's *Silent Spring*, suggesting an environmental disaster rather than a cosy spirituality. Schnittke's ability to create memorable musical laments is well displayed here, in the Shostakovich and Kagan memorial pieces, in *Stille Musik* and even in *A Paganini*, which traces an absorbing contest between an apparent distaste for virtuosity and a celebration of it. The impact of these compositions is the greater for their relative concentration – not an invariable virtue in Schnittke – and Mateja Marinković is a player of admirable technical refinement. The recording is first-class, and the disc can serve as an ideal introduction to Schnittke for listeners who may have doubts about his larger-scale works. 'Scrappy' it is not.

Additional recommendation ...

...Moz-Art[ab]. Praeludium[ab]. A Paganini[a]. Stille Musik[ac]. Madrigal – violin version[a]; cello version[c]. Trio[acd]. [a]**Oleh Krysa,** [b]**Alexander Fischer** (vns); [c]**Torleif Thedéen** (vc); [d]**Tatiana Tchekina** (pf). BIS Ⓕ CD697 (78 minutes: DDD: 11/95).

Further listening ...

...Cello Concerto No. 2[a]. In memoriam. [a]**Mstislav Rostropovich** (vc); **London Symphony Orchestra / Seiji Ozawa.** Sony Classical SK48241 (7/92).

...Minnesang. Choir Concerto. **Danish National Radio Choir / Stefan Parkman.** Chandos CHAN9126 (2/93).

...Choir Concerto. **Russian State Symphonic Cappella / Valéry Polyansky.** Chandos New Direction CHAN9332 (3/95).

...Viola Concerto[b]. **Lutosławski** Chain 2[a]. **Isabelle van Keulen** ([a]vn/[b]va); **Philharmonia Orchestra / Heinrich Schiff.** Koch Schwann Ⓕ 31523-2 (54 minutes: DDD: 11/95).

...Concerti grossi – No. 3; No. 4/Symphony No. 5. **Royal Concertgebouw Orchestra / Riccardo Chailly.** Decca 430 698-2DH (2/92).

...Concerto grosso No. 5[a]. *Coupled with* **Glass** Violin Concerto. **Gidon Kremer** (vn); [a]**Rainer Keuschnig** (invisible pf); **Vienna Philharmonic Orchestra / Christoph von Dohnányi.** DG 437 091-2GH (10/93).

...Concerto grosso No. 6[a]. Symphony No. 8. [a]**Sasha Rozhdestvensky** (vn); [a]**Viktoria Postnikova** (pf); **Royal Stockholm Philharmonic Orchestra / Gennadi Rozhdestvensky.** Chandos CHAN9359 (7/95).

...Symphony No. 4[a]. Three Sacred Hymns. [a]**Iaroslav Zdorov** (alto); [a]**Dmitri Pianov** (ten); **Russian State Symphony Cappella;** [a]**Russian State Symphony Orchestra / Valéry Polyansky.** Chandos CHAN9463 (7/96).

...Peer Gynt. **Stockholm Royal Opera Orchestra / Eri Klas.** BIS CD677/8 (4/95).

...String Quartet No. 2. *Coupled with works by* **Shostakovich** and **Tchaikovsky** Duke Quartet. Collins Classics 1450-2 (2/96). *See review under Shostakovich; refer to the Index to Reviews.*

...Piano Sonata (1987). *Coupled with* **Stravinsky** Piano Sonata. Serenade in A. Piano-rag-music. **Boris Berman** (pf). Chandos CHAN8962 (10/91).

Johann Schobert   Silesian c1735-1767

Schobert Four Trio Sonatas for Harpsichord, Violin and Cello, Op. 16. **Concerto Rococo** (Alice Piérot, vn; Paul Carlioz, vc; Jean-Patrice Brosse, hpd). Pierre Verany Ⓕ PV791042 (57 minutes: DDD: 6/94). ✍ Recorded 1990.

The main appeal of Schobert's music lies in its wide emotional range and the rich variety of its forms and textures. Mozart warmly admired his work and the skilled musical invention in the four trios on this disc makes it easy to see why. These are period instrument performances, using lower pitch, and the matching of mood and theme to the characteristics of the keys in which they are written makes an immediate impact. Contrast the deeply felt *Andante poco adagio* first movement of the second Trio in C minor with the much brighter opening *Andante* of the third Trio in D major. Alert phrasing combined with freshness and spontaneity from the Concerto Rococo contributes effectively to interpretations which capture the individual character of each piece. They respond with appropriate robustness to the bold, direct expression of the First Trio, while the greater emotional intensity of the C minor Trio's opening movement is engagingly contrasted with cheerfulness and wit in both its Minuet and final *Allegro*. In addition to their vivid characterization, this group also exploits the textural variety of these pieces. In the finale of the D major Trio, for example, they produce a remarkably full, orchestral sound, while they achieve an affecting intimacy in the fluid expression of the F major Trio's opening *Andante*. With clear, naturally balanced recorded sound this issue offers music which deserves to be better known.

Othmar Schoeck   Swiss 1886-1957

Schoeck Penthesilea. **Helga Dernesch** (sop) Penthesilea; **Jane Marsh** (sop) Prothoe; **Mechtild Gessendorf** (sop) Meroe; **Marjana Lipovšek** (mez) High Priestess; **Gabriele Sima** (sop) Priestess; **Theo Adam** (bass-bar) Achilles; **Horst Hiestermann** (ten) Diomede; **Peter Weber** (bass) Herold; **Austrian Radio Chorus and Symphony Orchestra / Gerd Albrecht.** Orfeo Ⓕ C364941B (80 minutes: ADD: 3/95). Notes and text included. Recorded live in 1982. *Gramophone Editor's choice.*   Ⓖ

Schoeck's one-act opera, *Penthesilea* is an astonishing and masterly score. It seems barely credible that a work so gripping in its dramatic intensity, and so powerful in atmosphere, should be so little known. It has the listener on the edge of the seat throughout its 80 short minutes and, like any great opera, it continues to cast a spell long after the music has ended. In the *Grove Dictionary of Opera*, Ronald Crichton wrote that "at its most intense, the language of *Penthesilea* surpasses in ferocity Strauss's *Elektra*, a work with which it invites comparison". In so far as it is a one-act work, set in the Ancient World, highly concentrated in feeling and with strongly delineated characters, it is difficult not to think of Strauss's masterpiece. Yet its sound-world is quite distinctive. Though he is a lesser figure, Schoeck similarly renders the familiar language of Straussian opera entirely his own. The vocabulary is not dissimilar yet the world is different. We are immediately plunged into a vivid and completely individual world, packed with dramatic incident: off-stage war cries and exciting, dissonant trumpet calls. There is an almost symphonic handling of pace, but the sonorities are unusual: for example, there is a strong wind section, some ten clarinets at various pitches, while there are only a handful of violins; much use is made of two pianos in a way that at times almost anticipates Britten. The present performance emanates from the 1982 Salzburg Festival; Helga Dernesch in the title-role commands the appropriate range of emotions as Penthesilea and the remainder of the cast, including the Achilles of Theo Adam, rise to the occasion. The important choral role and the orchestral playing under Gerd Albrecht are eminently committed and the recording is good without being state-of-the-art. There is a useful essay and libretto, though in German, not English or French.

Further listening ...

...Cello Concerto in A major/minor, Op. 61[a]. Sommernacht, Op. 58. **Neuss German Chamber Academy / Johannes Goritzki** ([a]vc). Claves CD50-8502 (10/89).

...Concerto quasi una fantasia, Op. 21[a]. Penthesilea – Suite (arr. Delfs). [a]**Bettina Boller** (vn); **Swiss Youth Symphony Orchestra / Andras Delfs.** Claves CD50-9201 (2/93).

...Der Sänger, Op. 57. **Frieder Lang** (ten); **Ruth Lang-Oester** (pf). Koch Schwann 310912 (10/94).

...Venus. **Soloists; Heidelberg Chamber Choir; Basle Boys' Choir; Swiss Youth Philharmonic Orchestra / Mario Venzago.** MGB Musikszene Schweiz CD6112 (10/94).

Arnold Schoenberg   Austrian/Hungarian 1874-1951

Schoenberg Verklärte Nacht, Op. 4 (arr. string orch). Variations for Orchestra, Op. 31. **Berlin Philharmonic Orchestra / Herbert von Karajan.** DG Ⓕ 415 326-2GH (52 minutes: ADD: 3/86). From 2711 014 (3/75).   ⒼⒼ

Schoenberg Verklärte Nacht, Op. 4 (arr. string orch).
R. Strauss Metamorphosen for 23 solo strings, AV142.
Wagner Siegfried Idyll. **Sinfonia Varsovia / Emmanuel Krivine.** Denon Ⓕ CO-79442 (74 minutes: DDD: 10/92). Recorded 1990.

The decadence of German culture in the 1920s and 1930s is already very apparent in the saturated romanticism of *Verklärte Nacht* (1899), the most lusciously sentient work ever conceived for a string group. By comparison the *Variations for Orchestra* comes at the peak of the composer's atonal period and is perhaps the most impressive and imaginative demonstration of the possibilities of this compositional method. Thus the two works on this CD are pivotal in Schoenberg's career and Karajan and the Berlin Philharmonic make the very best case for both works. It is impossible not to respond to the sensuality of *Verklärte Nacht* in their hands, while the challenging *Variations* also make a profound impression. The recording matches the intensity of the playing brilliantly. The stimulating Denon issue embraces three works which are as ideally matched as one could wish for. The performances verge on the miraculous; Krivine's visionary direction summons up playing of exultant intensity from the Polish orchestra. *Verklärte Nacht* has seldom sounded so moving; with Krivine, the transformation from aspiration to absolution is magical. His nobly compelling *Metamorphosen* charges each strand of Strauss's valedictory essay with tangible dismay and regret, as quotations from *Tristan* and Beethoven's *Eroica* lament the passing of a once great culture. An ardent yet naturally paced account of Wagner's *Siegfried Idyll* recalls that sense of sanctified joy which filled the Villa Triebschen on Christmas morning in 1870, as this musical birthday offering was heard for the first time. Krivine's spiritual empathy with these works combined with the outstanding orchestral playing and exemplary recorded sound make this a disc to covet.

Additional recommendations ...

...Verklärte Nacht. **Mahler** Symphony No. 10. **Berlin Radio Symphony Orchestra / Riccardo Chailly.** Decca Ⓜ 444 872-2DX2 (two discs: 110 minutes: DDD: 3/88).

...Verklärte Nacht. Variations for Orchestra. Pelleas und Melisande, Op. 5. **Berg** Three Pieces for String Orchestra. **Webern** Passacaglia, Op. 1. Five Movements, Op. 5. Six Pieces for Orchestra, Op. 6. Symphony, Op. 21. **Berlin Philharmonic Orchestra / Herbert von Karajan.** DG Ⓜ 427 424-2GC3 (three discs: 181 minutes: ADD: 9/89).   ⒼⒼ

...Variations for Orchestra. Cello Concerto in D major. Five Orchestral Pieces, Op. 16. Modern Psalm. **Soloists / Bratislava Philharmonic Choir; South-West German Radio Symphony Orchestra / Michael Gielen.** Wergo Ⓕ WER60185-50 (60 minutes: DDD: 10/90).

...Verklärte Nacht. Suite in E flat major, Op. 29. Three Pieces. **Ensemble InterContemporain / Pierre Boulez.** Sony Classical Ⓜ SMK48465 (61 minutes: ADD: 12/93).

The original version of Verklärte Nacht is reviewed further on in this section.

| **New review** |

Schoenberg Verklärte Nacht[a]. Five Orchestral Pieces, Op. 16[a]. Three Piano Pieces, Op. 11[b]. Six Piano Pieces, Op. 19[b]. Piano Piece, Op. 11 No. 2 (arr. Busoni)[b]. [a]**Chicago Symphony Orchestra / Daniel Barenboim** ([b]pf). Teldec Ⓕ 4509-98256-2 (77 minutes: DDD: 8/95). Recorded in 1995.

Like Barenboim's 1967 EMI Matrix reissue of *Verklärte Nacht* with the English Chamber Orchestra, this version begins with the evident belief that Schoenberg's initial marking of *Sehr langsam* is not an invitation to linger lovingly over every last semiquaver. The newer performance is far from a mere re-run, however. The verdict on the 1967 account was that "weight of expression tends to impede rather than further the musical flow". In 1995 the expressive trajectory of the whole is magnificently natural and persuasive, as one might expect from the experienced Wagnerian that Barenboim has now become. Only at the very end does he risk too weighty an articulation and too broad a tempo, a tendency confirming that his reading is still stronger in passion than it is in tenderness. The recorded sound is also spacious in the extreme, so many collectors will prefer the more intimate effect of the kind achieved by the Sinfonia Varsovia or the Orpheus Chamber Orchestra. Barenboim's superbly played account is nevertheless a superior example of the kind of 'wide screen' approach to Schoenberg's early masterwork favoured by conductors like Karajan and Sinopoli. The appeal of this disc is greatly enhanced by the other items. There is a marvellously vivid performance of the Op. 16 *Pieces* which, for clarity of texture and depth of expression, counts – along with Robert Craft's – as one of the most convincing of current versions. And we also hear Barenboim as pianist in the Op. 11 and Op. 19 *Pieces*. There are minor idiosyncracies in Op. 19 – for example, a rather brisk tempo for No. 6 – but Op. 11 is excellent. As a bonus Barenboim also plays Busoni's 'amplification' (perhaps 'dilution' is a better term) of Op. 11 No. 2. This is one of the more pointless attempts by one talent to render another, very different talent more 'comprehensible', but it provides a distinctive and far from insignificant footnote to a Schoenberg disc of unusual substance and distinction.

Additional recommendations ...

...Verklärte Nacht. **Hindemith** Trauermusik for Viola and Strings[a]. **Bartók** Divertimento for Strings, Sz113. [a]**Cecil Aronowitz** (va); **English Chamber Orchestra / Daniel Barenboim.** EMI Matrix Ⓜ CDM5 65079-2 (65 minutes: DDD: 12/94). Ⓖ

...Verklärte Nacht. Pelleas und Melisande, Op. 5. **Philharmonia Orchestra / Giuseppe Sinopoli.** DG Ⓔ 439 942-2GH (79 minutes: DDD: 6/95).

Schoenberg Variations for Orchestra, Op. 31. Pelleas und Melisande, Op. 5. **Chicago Symphony Orchestra / Pierre Boulez.** Erato Ⓔ 2292-45827-2 (62 minutes: DDD: 4/93). Recorded 1991. Ⓖ

The two faces of Schoenberg could scarcely be more starkly juxtaposed than they are on this superbly performed and magnificently recorded disc – Boulez and the CSO at their formidable best. *Pelleas und Melisande* can be taken not only as Schoenberg's 'answer' to Debussy's opera (also based on Maeterlinck's play) but as his challenge to Richard Strauss's supremacy as a composer of symphonic poems. It is indeed an intensely symphonic score in Schoenberg's early, late-romantic vein, with an elaborate single-movement structure and a subtle network of thematic cross-references. Yet none of this is an end in itself, and the music is as gripping and immediate a representation of a tragic love story as anything in the German romantic tradition. To move from this to the abstraction of the 12-note Variations, Op. 31 may threaten extreme anticlimax. Yet from the delicate introduction of the work's shapely theme to the turbulent good humour of the extended finale Schoenberg proves that his new compositional method did not drain his musical language of expressive vitality. The elaborate counterpoint may not make for easy listening, but the combination of exuberance and emotion is irresistible – at least in a performance like this.

Additional recommendations ...

...Pelleas und Melisande. **Webern** Passacaglia for Orchestra, Op. 1. **Scottish National Orchestra / Matthias Bamert.** Chandos Ⓔ CHAN8619 (54 minutes: DDD: 10/88).

...Pelleas und Melisande, Op. 5. Verklärte Nacht. **Philharmonia Orchestra / Giuseppe Sinopoli.** DG Ⓟ 439 942-2GH (79 minutes: DDD: 6/95).

Schoenberg Chamber Symphony No. 1, Op. 9[a]. Erwartung[b]. Variations for Orchestra, Op. 31[c]. [b]**Phyllis Bryn-Julson** (sop); [a]**Birmingham Contemporary Music Group;** [bc]**City of Birmingham Symphony Orchestra / Sir Simon Rattle.** EMI Ⓜ CDC5 55212-2 (75 minutes: DDD: 4/95). Text and translation included. Recorded 1993. *Gramophone Award Winner 1995*. **Gramophone** *Editor's choice.* ⒼⒼ

This well-filled disc offers an unusually comprehensive survey of the essential Schoenberg – the irascible late-romantic of the *Chamber Symphony* (1906), the radical expressionist of *Erwartung* (1909) and, in the *Variations* (1928), the synthesizer of expressionist moods with techniques that set up neo-classical associations. Rattle's account of the *Chamber Symphony* may well come to displace that of the Orpheus Chamber Orchestra (reviewed below) from its favoured position, if only for the demonstration quality of the sound, which has remarkable depth and realism. Rattle ensures a superbly well-characterized and integrated performance, which only veers towards over-emphasis at the very end. There is also ample refinement where that is called for, and this quality is no less abundant in *Erwartung*. Here the almost impressionistic sheen of the orchestral sound fits well with Phyllis Bryn-Julson's generally restrained approach to the vocal line. When it comes to the *Variations for Orchestra*, Rattle and the CBSO are supreme. This recording may well be the first to convey the full, astonishing range of the work's textures, from the most delicate chamber music to dense tuttis, without a hint of artificiality. But it is the interpretation which counts for most. Rattle brings all these textures to rhythmic and expressive life, avoiding the lumpiness and stridency which occasionally afflict other conductors. He has evidently taken enormous care to follow Schoenberg's detailed markings, yet the result has a sovereign spontaneity. Despite strong competition from Boulez this performance is a triumph.

Additional recommendation ...

...Chamber Symphony No. 1, Op. 9[b]. Die Jakobsleiter[a]. Begleitmusik zu einer Lichtspielszene, Op. 34[c]. [a]**Soloists.** [a]**BBC Singers;** [b]**Ensemble InterContemporain;** [ac]**BBC Symphony Orchestra / Pierre Boulez.** Sony Classical Ⓜ SMK48462 (76 minutes: ADD: 12/93). Ⓖ

Schoenberg Chamber Symphonies – No. 1, Op. 9; No. 2, Op. 38. Verklärte Nacht, Op. 4 (arr. string orch). **Orpheus Chamber Orchestra.** DG Ⓕ 429 233-2GH (69 minutes: DDD: 7/90). Recorded 1989. ⒼⒼ

In the late twentieth century there's increasing evidence that the early twentieth century's most radical music is becoming so easy to perform that it may at last be losing its terrors for listeners as well as players. This can only be welcomed, provided that performances do not become bland and mechanical, and the conductorless Orpheus Chamber Orchestra triumphantly demonstrate how to combine fluency with intensity. If you like your Schoenberg effortful – to feel that the players are conquering almost insuperable odds – these recordings may not be for you. But if you like spontaneity of expression that is never an end in itself, and communicates Schoenberg's powerfully coherent forms and textures as well as his abundant emotionalism, you should not hesitate. The DG disc is the first to place Schoenberg's two Chamber Symphonies alongside *Verklärte Nacht*. The First Chamber Symphony shows Schoenberg transforming himself from late-romantic into expressionist, while in the Second the recent American immigrant, in the 1930s, looks back to his romantic roots and forges a new, almost classical style. With superb sound, this is a landmark in recordings of twentieth-century music.

Additional recommendations ...

...Symphony No. 1. Pierrot lunaire, Op. 21[a]. [a]**Marianne Pousseur** (sop); **Musique Oblique Ensemble / Philippe Herreweghe.** Harmonia Mundi Ⓕ HMC90 1390 (58 minutes: DDD: 8/92).

...Symphony No. 2[a]. **Busoni** Berceuse élégiaque, Op. 42[a]. **Weill** Symphonies[b] – No. 1; No. 2. [a]**New Philharmonia Orchestra / Frederick Prausnitz;** [b]**BBC Symphony Orchestra / Gary Bertini.** EMI Matrix Ⓜ CDM5 65869-2 (79 minutes: ADD: 4/96).

Schoenberg String Quartets – No. 1, Op. 7; No. 2 in F sharp minor, Op. 10[a]; No. 3, Op. 30; No. 4, Op. 37. [a]**Dawn Upshaw** (sop); **Arditti Quartet** (Irvine Arditti, David Alberman, vns; Garth Knox, va; Rohan de Saram, vc). Auvidis Montaigne Ⓕ MO782024 (two discs: 139 minutes: DDD: 1/95). Recorded 1993. ⒼⒼ

These recordings were made in London, in collaboration with the BBC, and the sound is consistently spacious, with a natural clarity and an even balance; the details of Schoenberg's complex counterpoint, as evident in No. 1 as in No. 4, can be heard with a minimum of stress and strain. Although one occasionally gets the impression that the Arditti are relatively cool in their response to this often fervent music, the overall mood they create is far from anti-romantic, and they call on a remarkably wide range of dynamics and tone-colours. Even if every nuance in Schoenberg's markings is not followed, this is warmly expressive playing. Dawn Upshaw's contribution to the Second Quartet also helps to heighten the sense of drama although she misses some of that mysterious, ecstatic quality which makes this music so haunting. In fact, for an unambiguously romantic reading of the two early quartets you need to brave the grinding surface noise of the marvellously vibrant Kolisch performances (recorded in 1936). It is in the Third and Fourth Quartets that the superior sound-quality of the Auvidis Montaigne issue pays the greatest dividends. Textural clarity is vital here, and although even the Arditti struggle to sustain the necessary lightness in the long second movement of No. 4, their wider dynamic range brings you consistently close to the toughly argued, emotionally expansive essence of this music. Yet the performance of No. 3 is the finest achievement of the set: clarity of form and emotional conviction combine to create an absorbing account of a modern masterwork. It sets the seal on a most distinguished enterprise.

Additional recommendations ...

...Nos. 1-4. **Clemence Gifford** (sop); **Kolisch Quartet.** Archiphon mono Ⓕ ARC103/04* (two discs: 140 minutes: ADD: 1/94). Ⓖ

...No. 2[a]. **Berg** String Quartet, Op. 3. **Webern** Five Movements, Op. 5. Langsamer Satz. [a]**Christiane Oelze** (sop); **Brindisi Quartet.** Metronome Ⓕ METCD1007 (70 minutes: DDD: 6/95).

...No. 2[a]. **Schubert** String Quartet No. 13 in A minor, D804. [a]**Amanda Roocroft** (sop); **Britten Quartet.** EMI Ⓕ CDC5 55289-2 (67 minutes: DDD: 7/95).

Schoenberg Verklärte Nacht, Op. 4[a] (orig. version).
Schubert String Quintet in C major, D956[b]. [a]**Alvin Dinkin** (va); **Kurt Reher** (vc); **Hollywood Quartet** (Felix Slatkin, Paul Shure, vns; Paul Robyn, va; Eleanor Aller, vc). Testament mono Ⓕ SBT1031* (73 minutes: ADD: 4/94). Item marked [a] from Capitol CCL7507 (4/51), [b]Capitol CTL7011 (1/52). Item marked [a] recorded 1950, [b]1951. *Gramophone Award Winner 1994.* ⒼⒼⒼ

This was the first ever recording of *Verklärte Nacht* in its original sextet form and it remains unsurpassed. When it was first reviewed in *Gramophone*, Lionel Salter wrote of it as being "beautifully played with the most careful attention to details of dynamics and phrasing, with unfailing finesse, with consistently sympathetic tone, and, most important, with a firm sense of the basic structure". The Schubert too fully deserves its classic status. The tranquillity of the slow movement has never been conveyed with greater nobility or more perfect control. The Hollywood

Quartet made music for the sheer love of it and as a relaxation from their duties in the film-studio orchestras, for which they were conspicuously overqualified. They have incomparable ensemble and blend; and their impeccable technical address and consummate tonal refinement silence criticism. The transfers could not be better.

New review

Schoenberg Five Orchestral Pieces, Op. 16[a]. A Survivor from Warsaw, Op. 46[b]. Begleitmusik zu einer Lichtspielszene, Op. 34[a]. Herzgewächse, Op. 20[c]. Serenade, Op. 24[d]. [c]**Eileen Hulse** (sop); [d]**Stephen Varcoe** (bar); [b]**Simon Callow** (narr); [b]**London Voices**; [d]**Twentieth Century Classics Ensemble**; [abc]**London Symphony Orchestra / Robert Craft.** Koch International Classics Ⓕ 37263-2 (69 minutes: DDD: 6/95). Recorded 1994.

This is an absorbing issue, not least for the sheer variety of works that it contains. The two largest compositions, Op. 16 and Op. 24, define the disc's range. The *Five Orchestral Pieces*, in which expressionism can be heard emerging from the chrysalis of late romanticism, are played with supreme finesse by the LSO, and Robert Craft probes the richly diverse textures with exemplary concentration and precision. The downside is some loss of immediacy, a general feeling of caution. There are also slight reservations about the balance in *A Survivor from Warsaw*, where Simon Callow is, one imagines, placed behind the orchestra, depriving this harrowing work of its visceral impact. Since Callow's style can veer in a flash from the conversational to the melodramatic, a closer focus would have been preferable. *Herzgewächse* and *Begleitmusik zu einer Lichtspielszene* are both well performed, the latter with a recessed perspective, similar to that in Op. 16, which ensures an extremely well-blended texture without loss of detail. Nevertheless, there is no doubt that the finest performance here is that of the *Serenade*, Op. 24, where the sound (recorded in New York, not in London) is cleaner, and the characterization is superb from beginning to end. Stephen Varcoe is a rather breathy singer in the dauntingly angular and wide-ranging "Sonnet", but the performance as a whole makes a convincing case for the work's high level of musical thought and purely technical mastery. With this outstanding account, Craft's latest Schoenberg series is well and truly launched.

Additional recommendation ...

...Serenade[a]. Five Orchestral Pieces[b]. Ode to Napoleon, Op. 41[c]. [a]**John Shirley-Quirk** (bar); [bc]**David Wilson-Johnson** (bar); [ac]**Ensemble InterContemporain; BBC Symphony Orchestra / Pierre Boulez.** Sony Classical Ⓜ SMK48463 (66 minutes: ADD: 12/93).

Schoenberg Cabaret Songs – No. 1, Galathea; No. 2, Gigerlette; No. 3, Der genügsame Liebhaber. Drüben geht die Sonne scheiden. Vier Lieder, Op. 2. Die Aufgeregten, Op. 3 No. 2. Lieder, Op. 6 – No. 1, Traumleben; No. 4, Verlassen; No. 8, Der Wanderer. Gedenken. Jane Grey, Op. 12 No. 1. Zwei Lieder, Op. 14. Folksong arrangements – Der Mai tritt ein mit Freuden; Es gingen zwei Gespielen gut; Mein Herz ist mir gemenget; Mein Herz in steten Treuen. **Mitsuko Shirai** (mez); **Hartmut Höll** (pf). Capriccio Ⓕ 10 514 (63 minutes: DDD: 5/95). Texts and translations included. Recorded 1993.

Mitsuko Shirai has pretty well the ideal voice for these songs. It's not large, but her subtle control of dynamics enables her to encompass surprisingly big gestures. Her vehemence, though, and her dramatic gestures are always Lieder-scaled. Her intimacy and deft way with words bring great rewards, too. Most of these songs are early Schoenberg, still within hailing distance of Brahms or Wolf (who would not have been ashamed of the long, lyrical line of "Traumleben", with its overt quotation from Wagner's *Tristan*). Even in Op. 14, where atonality is in sight, close motivic working and, in "In diesen Wintertagen", a graceful vocal line, retain a close kinship to the nineteenth-century Lied, and Shirai's easy negotiation of awkward intervals prevents them from ever sounding ungrateful. The strangest pieces here, but oddly attractive, are Schoenberg's folk-song arrangements (who would ever have thought he had much time for such things?). Much later than any of the original songs in this collection, in their close and sometimes busy counterpoint they are a touching homage to Brahms (who loved, collected and arranged such songs himself) and even to Bach: they are 'chorale preludes' in all but name. Shirai, very properly, sings them beautifully but plainly. Her husband is an ideally responsive and supportive partner; the recording is satisfactory, if a bit too close.

Schoenberg Gurrelieder. **Susan Dunn** (sop); **Brigitte Fassbaender** (mez); **Siegfried Jerusalem, Peter Haage** (tens); **Hermann Becht** (bass); **Hans Hotter** (narr); **St Hedwig's Cathedral Choir, Berlin; Düsseldorf Musikverein Chorus; Berlin Radio Symphony Orchestra / Riccardo Chailly.** Decca Ⓕ 430 321-2DH2 (two discs: 101 minutes: DDD: 3/91). Text and translation included. Recorded 1985. *Selected by Sounds in Retrospect.* Ⓖ

"Every morning after sunrise, King Waldemar would have a realization of the renewing power of nature, and would feel the love of Tove within the outward beauty of Nature's colour and form" (thus said Leopold Stokowski, who made the first-ever recording of *Gurrelieder*). This vast cantata, here more than ever experienced as a direct descendant of Wagnerian music-drama, was for the turn-of-the-century musical scene in general, more the ultimate gorgeous sunset. Schoenberg started work on it in 1899, the same year as his *Verklärte Nacht*, but delayed its completion for over a decade, by which time some of his more innovatory masterpieces were already behind him. Schoenberg's forces are, to put it mildly, extravagant. As well as the six soloists and two choruses, the orchestra sports such luxuries as four piccolos, ten horns and a percussion battery that includes iron chains; and so complex are some of the textures that, to achieve a satisfactory balance, a near miracle is required of conductor and recording engineers. Decca have never been mean with miracles where large scale forces are concerned and this set is no exception. Chailly and Decca's give us a superbly theatrical presentation of the score. The casting of the soloists is near ideal. Susan Dunn's Tove has youth, freshness and purity on her side. So exquisitely does she float her lines that you readily sympathize with King Waldemar's rage at her demise. Siegfried Jerusalem has the occasional rough moment but few previous Waldemars on disc have possessed his heroic ringing tones and range of expression. And Decca make sure that their trump card, the inimitable Hans Hotter as the speaker in "The wild hunt of the summer wind", is so tangibly projected that we miss not one single vowel or consonant of his increasing animation and excitement at that final approaching sunrise.

Additional recommendation ...

...Gurrelieder. Four Lieder, Op. 11. **Soloists; BBC Singers; BBC Choral Society; Goldsmith's Choral Union; London Philharmonic Choir; BBC Symphony Orchestra / Pierre Boulez.** Sony Classical Ⓜ SM2K48459 (two discs: 129 minutes: ADD: 12/93).

Further listening ...

...Piano Concerto, Op. 42. *Coupled with* **Schumann** Piano Concerto in A minor, Op. 54. **Maurizio Pollini** (pf); **Berlin Philharmonic Orchestra / Claudio Abbado.** DG 427 771-2GH (7/90). Ⓖ

...Piano Concerto, Op. 42[a]. Drei Klavierstücke, Op. 11. Suite, Op. 25. *Coupled with* **Berg** Piano Sonata, Op. 1. **Webern** Piano Variations, Op. 27. **Glenn Gould** (pf). [a]**CBC Symphony Orchestra / Jean-Marie Beaudet.** CBC Records Perspective Series mono PSCD2008* (1/96).

...Drei Klavierstücke, Op. 11. Sechs Klavierstücke, Op. 19. Funf Klavierstücke, Op. 23. Suite, Op. 25. Klavierstück, Op. 33[a]. Klavierstück, Op. 33[b]. Piano Concerto, Op. 42[a]. Phantasy, Op. 47[b]. Ode to Napoleon, Op. 41[c]. Pierrot lunaire, Op. 21[d]. [d]**Patricia Rideout** (spkr); [c]**John Horton** (narr); [b]**Israel Baker** (vn); **Glenn Gould** (pf); [c]**Juilliard Quartet;** [a]**CBC Symphony Orchestra / Robert Craft.** Sony Classical Glenn Gould Edition SM2K52664 (4/95).

...Sechs Klavierstücke, Op. 19[c]. Ode to Napoleon, Op. 41[d]. *Coupled with* **Ullmann** Die Weise von Liebe und Tod des Cornets Christoph Rilke[a]. Variationen und Doppelfuge über ein Theme von Arnold Schoenberg, Op. 3[ab]. [a]**Gert Westphal,** [d]**Roland Hermann** (spkrs); [d]**Tim Vogler,** [d]**Frank Reinecke** (vns); [d]**Stefan Fehlandt** (va); [d]**Michael Sanderling** (vc); [a]**Michael Allan,** [bc]**Günther Herzfeld,** [d]**Frank-Immo Zichner** (pfs). Edition Abseits EDA008-2 (11/95). *See review under Ullmann; refer to the Index to Reviews.*

...String Quartets – No. 1, Op. 7; No. 2 in F sharp minor, Op. 10; No. 3, Op. 30; No. 4, Op. 37. **Kolisch Quartet.** Archiphon ARC103/4* (1/94).

...Piece in D minor. String Trio, Op. 45. Phantasy, Op. 47. *Coupled with works by* **Mahler, Webern** and **Berg Gidon Kremer** (vn); **Veronika Hagen** (va); **Clemens Hagen** (vc); **Oleg Maisenberg** (pf). DG 447 112-2GH (4/96). *See review in the Collections section; refer to the Index to Reviews.*

...Variations on a Recitative, Op. 40. Two Fragments of an Organ Sonata. *Coupled with* **Pepping.** Three Fugues on BACH. **Hindemith** Organ Sonatas Nos. 1-3. **Kevin Bowyer** (org). Nimbus NI5411 (1/95).

...Three Piano Pieces, Op. 11. Six Little Piano Pieces, Op. 19. Five Piano Pieces, Op. 23. Piano Suite, Op. 25. Piano Pieces, Opp. 33*a* and 33*b*. **Maurizio Pollini** (pf). DG 20th Century Classics 423 249-2GC (6/88). ⒼⒼ

...Suite, Op. 25. *Coupled with works by* **Mozart, Bach** and **Sweelinck** Glenn Gould (pf). Sony Classical mono SMK53474* (9/95). *See review under Bach; refer to the Index to Reviews.*

...Choral Works – Friede auf Erden, Op. 13; Kol nidre, Op. 39; Drei Volkslieder, Op. 49. Zwei Kanons – Wenn der schwer Gedrückte klagt; O dass der Sinnen doch so viele sind!. Drei Volkslieder – Es gingen zwei Gespielen gut; Herzlieblich Lieb, durch Scheiden; Schein uns, du liebe Sonne. Vier Stücke, Op. 27. Drei Satiren, Op. 28. Sechs Stücke, Op. 35. Dreimal tausen Jahre, Op. 50*a*. De profundis (Psalm 130), Op. 50*b*. Modern Psalm (Der erste Psalm), Op. 50*c*. A Survivor from Warsaw, Op. 46. **John Shirley-Quirk, Günter Reich** (narrs); **BBC Singers; BBC Chorus and Symphony Orchestra; London Sinfonietta / Pierre Boulez.** Sony Classical SM2K44571 (8/90).

...Pierrot lunaire, Op. 21[a]. *Coupled with* **Webern** Concerto, Op. 24. [a]**Jane Manning** (sop); **Nash Ensemble / Sir Simon Rattle.** Chandos Collect CHAN6534 (8/92).

...Moses und Aron. **Soloists; BBC Singers; Orpheus Boys' Choir; BBC Symphony Orchestra / Pierre Boulez.** Sony Classical Ⓜ SM2K48456 (two discs: 121 minutes: ADD: 12/93). Ⓖ

Paul Schoenfield   American 1947-

Schoenfield Four Parables[a]. Vaudeville[b]. Klezmer Rondos[c]. [c]**Carol Wincenc** (fl); [b]**Wolfgang Basch** (piccolo tpt); [a]**Jeffrey Kahane** (pf); **New World Symphony / John Nelson.** Argo Ⓕ 440 212-2ZH (72 minutes: DDD: 6/94). Recorded 1992. *Gramophone Editor's choice.* ⒼⒼ

Paul Schoenfield's existentialist response to a 70-year-old murderer's release from prison prompts a wildly diverting, madcap tone-poem that opens amongst pensive, dank shadows and suddenly flies into dizzy, high spirited confusion – a sort of Gershwin-cum-Shostakovich, complete with sliding brass, high-hat cymbals and tam-tam. This is the first of Schoenfield's hugely enjoyable *Four Parables*: 'slices of life' etched with a combination of wry humour and pathos. *Vaudeville* takes its cue from

Schumann's versicoloured brand of thematic transformation (as displayed in *Carnaval*), with piccolo trumpet and clarinet taking centre stage. As in the *Klezmer Rondos*, Jewish folk-style music has a spot to itself, whereas elsewhere, Schoenfield's roll-call of effects includes the sentimental ballad, hectic dancing and a hilarious send-up of Mahler's Second Symphony as the "Sketches" swing into "Carmen Rivera". The *Rondos* themselves are perhaps the most 'mainstream' items on the CD, with telling but well-integrated side-glances at Bartók, Stravinsky, Weill and Bernstein. Here, as elsewhere, you leave his work with a party-bag full of good tunes and the meaningful recollection of his own guiding aphorism, that "Life is tantamount to a burlesque show". So, sit back – and *enjoy*, as they say. Which barely leaves enough room to pay adequate tribute to the performers, all of them first-rate. The sound, by the way, is superb. A real tonic!

Claude-Michel Schönberg

French 20th century

Suggested listening ...
...Les Miserables. **Original London cast.** First Night ENCORECD1 (3/87).
...Miss Saigon. **Original London cast.** First Night ENCORECD5.

Franz Schreker

Austrian 1878-1934

New review

Schreker Irrelohe. **Michael Pabst** (ten) Count Heinrich; **Luana DeVol** (sop) Eva; **Goran Simic** (bass) Forester, Anselmus; **Eva Randová** (mez) Lola; **Monte Pederson** (bar) Peter; **Heinz Zednik** (ten) Christobald; **Neven Belamaric** (sngr) Parson, Strahlbusch; **Sebastian Holecek** (sngr) Miller, Ratzekahl; **Helmut Wildhaber** (ten) Fünkchen, A Lackey; **Vienna Singverein; Vienna Symphony Orchestra / Peter Gülke.** Sony Classical Ⓟ S2K66850 (two discs: 127 minutes: DDD: 12/95).
Notes, text and translation included. Recorded live in 1989.

Immediately after the First World War Schreker was hailed as the most significant musical-dramatist after Wagner. But his star began to wane after the critical mauling *Irrelohe* received, and against a background of resentment at his success, and growing anti-Semitism. He later enjoyed the venom of that self-appointed pontiff of modernism, Adorno (as indeed did Sibelius – so he was in good company). *Irrelohe*, to the composer's own libretto, is set in the eighteenth century. Count Heinrich lives as a recluse in Irrelohe castle, fearing hereditary madness should he give way to sexual passion. His love for Eva inspires the jealousy of her suitor, Peter, as well as the enmity of Christobald, whose own fiancée had been raped by Heinrich's father. Peter attempts to prevent their wedding but is killed in the ensuing struggle, and in the meantime Christobald sets fire to Irrelohe. Echoes of Valhalla's fate in *Götterdämmerung*! Eva finally sings of the redemptive power of love. While Schreker's mastery of dramatic and psychological effects is not in question, many critics have felt that his music is too close to the wilder shores of Hollywood for comfort (the booklet note speaks of it having "quite an inventory of horror-film clichés") but we do not condemn, say, Ravel or Prokofiev, because others have pillaged and polluted their harmonic vocabulary; nor should we Schreker. While recognizably indebted, mainly to Strauss and Puccini, *Irrelohe* as drama with music holds you almost from start to finish. The characters and the vocal lines are drawn with care and the orchestral textures are sumptuous. The performance under Peter Gülke is thoroughly committed and the cast is a strong one. Although the recording favours the singers there is excellent, well-balanced orchestral detail. Those who know *Der ferne Klang* or *Der Schatzgräber* will probably need no prompting to investigate this set; for those who don't, *Irrelohe* is for the most part a gripping and imaginative score, well served by all involved in this production.

Schreker Die Gezeichneten. **Heinz Kruse** (ten) Alviano Salvago; **Elizabeth Connell** (sop) Carlotta; **Monte Pederson** (bar) Count Vitelozzo Tamare; **Alfred Muff** (bass) Duke Adorno/Capitaneo di Giustizia; **László Polgar** (bass) Lodovico Nardi, Podesta; **Christiane Berggold** (mez) Martuccia; **Martin Petzold** (ten) Pietro; **Robert Wörle** (ten) Guidobald Usodimare; **Endrik Wottrich** (ten) Menaldo Negroni; **Oliver Widmer** (bar) Michelotto Cibo; **Matthias Görne** (bass-bar) Gonsalvo Fieschi; **Kristin Sigmundsson** (bass) Julian Pinelli; **Petteri Salomaa** (bass) Paolo Calvi; **Marita Posselt** (sop) Ginevra Scotti; **Reinhard Ginzel** (ten) First Senator; **Jörg Gottschick** (bass) Second Senator; **Friedrich Molsberger** (bass) Third Senator; **Herbert Lippert** (ten) A youth; **Berlin Radio Chorus; Deutsches Symphony Orchestra, Berlin / Lothar Zagrosek.** Decca Entartete Musik Ⓟ 444 442-2DHO3 (three discs: 171 minutes: DDD: 6/95). Notes, text and translation included.
Recorded 1993-94. *Gramophone Award Winner 1995.* *Gramophone Editor's choice.* ⒼⒼ

The mingling in *Die Gezeichneten* of post-*Salome* opulence (Strauss with rich admixtures of Scriabin, Szymanowski, Korngold and Puccini) with post-*Salome* gaminess of subject matter is indeed strong stuff. Carlotta, a beautiful but gravely ill painter knows that her health would never withstand physical love. She is loved, he believes hopelessly, by the monstrously ugly nobleman Alviano; she is desired by the licentious Count Tamare. Drawn by the beauty of Alviano's soul she at first declares her love for him, but then deserts him for Tamare. On learning that she gave herself to Tamare voluntarily, knowing the fatal consequences, Alviano first kills his rival, then goes mad. Schreker's sheer resourcefulness is breathtaking. Each character seems to have not merely an identifying theme but a whole sound-world. Scenes of extreme complexity are handled with total assurance. The score is melodious, fabulously multi-coloured and has great cumulative power. One reservation was hinted at by Alban Berg's reaction to the libretto: he found it superb but "a bit kitschy". It is, and this quality is intensified in the music by a curious impassivity, as though Schreker were observing his characters from outside. Carlotta's 'conversion' from spiritual to physical love is not accompanied by much change in her alluringly mysterious music; her characterization is fantastically detailed but has no depth. She, Alviano and Tamare are ideas, not people. It is an opera in which richness of detail, complexity of texture and sheer glamour replace humanity. The end is 'effective' but not tragic. Nevertheless, as a document of its time (1918) and as a score of unprecedented richness it abundantly deserves recording. Edo de Waart's performance (listed below) was a splendid achievement, all the more so for being recorded live. Indeed choice between his version and the newcomer would be tricker were it not for the fact that de Waart makes several lengthy cuts (about 20 minutes of music in all) in the last act and his tenor is under painfully audible strain. Zagrosek's reading is superb, his cast almost without flaw. Connell has all Carlotta's glamour, together with a purity of tone and a subtle response to words and phrasing that come close to giving her a soul. Kruse is less imaginative, one or two of Alviano's high notes give him trouble, but he sings strongly and lyrically; Pederson makes a grippingly formidable, physical opponent. The precision and detail of the subsidiary characters are praiseworthy throughout; even very small roles have been cast from strength. The recording is remarkably fine, spacious and sumptuous, with not a single detail out of focus.

Additional recommendation ...

...**Soloists; Dutch Radio Philharmonic Chorus and Orchestra / Edo de Waart.** Marco Polo 8 223328/30 (three discs: 147 minutes: DDD: 12/91).

Further listening ...

...Chamber Symphony[a]. Prelude to a Drama[a]. Valse lente[b]. Die Ferne Klang – Night Interlude[b]. **Berlin Radio Symphony Orchestra / [a]Michael Gielen, [b]Karl Anton Rickenbacher.** Koch Schwann 311078 (11/88).   Ⓖ

...Der Geburtstag der Infantin – Suite. *Coupled with* **Hindemith** Der Dämon. **Schulhoff** Die Mondsüchtige. **Leipzig Gewandhaus Orchestra / Lothar Zagrosek.** Decca Entartete Musik Ⓕ 444 182-2DH (5/95). *See review under Hindemith; refer to the Index to Reviews.*   Ⓖ

...Entführung. Und wie mag die Liebe dir kommen sein?. Lieder, Op. 4 – No. 1, Unendliche Liebe; No. 2, Frühling; No. 3, Wohl fühl' ich wie das Leben rinnt; No. 4, Die Liebe als Rezensenten. Wiegenliedchen, Op. 7 No. 1. Ein Rosenblatt. *Coupled with* **Schoenberg** In hellen Träumen. Warum bist du aufgewacht. Mannesbangen. Mailied. Gruss in die Ferne. **Weigl** Sieben Gesänge, Op. 1. Liebeslied. **Korngold** Unver-gänglichkeit, Op: 27. Lieder, Op. 38 – No. 1, Glückwunsch; No. 2, Der Kranke. **Steven Kimbrough** (bar); **Dalton Baldwin** (pf). Koch Schwann 310942 (2/95).

...Der Ferne Klang. **Soloists; Berlin RIAS Chamber Chorus; Berlin Radio Chorus and Symphony Orchestra / Gerd Albrecht.** Capriccio 60 024-2 (12/91).

...Der ferne Klang – In einem Lande ein bleicher König. *Coupled with works by* **Korngold, Lortzing, Marschner, Weber, Spohr, Kreutzer, Humperdinck** and **Wagner** Thomas Hampson (bar); Pestalozzi Gymnasium Children's Choir; Munich Radio Orchestra / Fabio Luisi. EMI CDC5 55233-2 (9/95). *See review in the Collections section; refer to the Index to Reviews.*

Franz Schubert   Austrian 1797-1828

Schubert Symphonies – No. 1 in D major, D82; No. 2 in B flat major, D125; No. 3 in D major, D200; No. 4 in C minor, D417, "Tragic"; No. 5 in B flat major, D485; No. 6 in C major, D589; No. 8 in B minor, D759, "Unfinished". No. 9 in C major, D944, "Great". **Royal Concertgebouw Orchestra / Nikolaus Harnoncourt.** Teldec Ⓕ 4509-91184-2 (four discs: 284 minutes: DDD: 12/93). Recorded live in 1992. *Gramophone Editor's choice.*   ⒼⒼⒼ

Harnoncourt, like Abbado on DG, has researched Schubert's own manuscripts, and corrected many unauthentic amendments that found their way into the printed editions of the symphonies, such as the eight bars later added to the Fourth Symphony's first movement exposition; but the differences between Harnoncourt's interpretative Schubert and Abbado's are startling. The Ninth's finale, unlike Abbado's, a whirling, spinning *vivace* – is borne aloft on astonishingly precise articulation of its rhythms and accents, and a springy delivery of the triplets. Characteristics, of course, one has come to expect from an Harnoncourt performance. Still, what a joy to hear this *Allegro*, and those of most of the earlier symphonies, seized with such bright and light-toned enthusiasm. Here is urgent, virile and vehement playing, never over-forceful, over-emphatic or burdened with excessive weight. What came as a surprise was the consistent drawing out of these scores' potential for sadness and restlessness. Harnoncourt does not set apart the first six symphonies as merely diverting, unlike Abbado (out-and-out charm is seldom part of Harnoncourt's Schubertian vocabulary): their bittersweet ambiguities and apparent affectations of anxiety here acquire a greater significance, and the cycle, as a whole, a greater continuity. Up to a point, the darker, more serious Schubert that emerges here, derives from the type of sound Harnoncourt fashions from his orchestra; not least, the lean string tone and incisive brass. And maybe, up to a point, from the corrections: Harnoncourt refers to the manuscripts as often being "harsher and more abrupt in tone [than the printed editions], juxtaposing extreme dynamic contrasts", though you can't help feeling that contrasts in general have been given a helping hand. Trios are mostly much slower than the urgent minuets/scherzos that frame them (with pauses in between the two). And Schubert's less vigorous moments are very noticeable as such, and are inflected with varying degrees of melancholy – it is uncanny how the string playing, in particular, often suggests a feeling of isolation (along with the sparing vibrato is an equally sparing use of that enlivening facility: *staccato*). The *Unfinished* Symphony's first movement is a stark, harrowing experience (yet it remains a well-tempered musical one: gestures are never exaggerated); the opening is as cold as the grave itself; the second subject knows its song is short-lived. In both movements, the elucidation and balance of texture can only be described as masterly: just listen to the trombones casting shadows in both codas. This, then, is as seriously pondered, coherent and penetrating a view of the complete cycle as we have had. Whether or not you feel Harnoncourt focuses too much on Schubert's darker side, you have to marvel at his ability to realize his vision. The recorded sound offers that inimitable Concertgebouw blend of the utmost clarity and wide open spaces.

Additional recommendations ...

...Nos. 1-6. No. 7 in E major, D729. Nos. 8 and 9. No. 10 in D major, D936A (realized Newbould). Symphonic fragments – D major, D615 (orch. Newbould); D major, D708A (completed and orch. Newbould). **Academy of St Martin in the Fields / Sir Neville Marriner.** Philips Ⓕ 412 176-2PH6 (six discs: DDD: 3/85).

...Nos. 1-6, 8 and 9. Rosamunde – incidental music, D797. Entr'acte No. 3 in B flat major. Ballet Music – No. 1 in B minor; No. 2 in G major. **Cologne Radio Symphony Orchestra / Günter Wand.** RCA Victor Gold Seal Ⓜ GD60096 (five discs: 267 minutes: ADD/DDD: 2/89).

...Nos. 1-6, 8 and 9. **Chamber Orchestra of Europe / Claudio Abbado.** DG Ⓕ 423 651-2GH5 (five discs: 320 minutes: DDD: 2/89). 😀😀😀

...Nos. 1 and 2. **Chamber Orchestra of Europe / Claudio Abbado.** DG Ⓕ 423 652-2GH (59 minutes: DDD: 9/89).

...No. 2. **Voříšek** Symphony in D major, Op. 24. **West German Sinfonia / Dirk Joeres.** IMP Classics Ⓜ PCD1052 (57 minutes: DDD: 8/94). *See review under Voříšek; refer to the Index to Reviews.* 😀

...No. 4. **Debussy** Images – Ibéria. **Tchaikovsky** Francesca da Rimini, Op. 32. **New York Philharmonic Symphony Orchestra / Sir John Barbirolli.** Dutton Laboratories Essential Archive mono Ⓑ CDEA5000* (69 minutes: ADD: 1/96).

Schubert Symphony – No. 3 in D major, D200[a]; No. 5 in B flat major, D485[a]; No. 6 in C major, D589[b]. **Royal Philharmonic Orchestra / Sir Thomas Beecham.** EMI Studio Ⓜ CDM7 69750-2* (78 minutes: ADD: 8/90). Items marked [a] from HMV ASD345 (6/60), [b]Columbia 33CX1363 (9/56). *Gramophone classical 100.* 😀😀😀

Beecham was well into his seventies when he made these recordings with the Royal Philharmonic, the orchestra he had founded in 1946. His lightness of touch, his delight in the beauty of the sound he was summoning, the directness of his approach to melody, and his general high spirits will all dominate our memory of these performances. But listening again, we may be reminded that Beecham could equally well dig deep into the darker moments of these works. Schubert's elation was rarely untroubled and the joy is often compounded by its contrast with pathos – Beecham had that balance off to a tee. It should be noted that he does not take all the marked repeats and he doctored some passages he considered over-repetitive. However, these recordings may also serve as a reminder of the wonderful heights of musicianship that his players achieved, as in the trio of the Third Symphony's minuet, where a simple waltz-like duet between oboe and bassoon attains greatness by the shapeliness, ease and poignancy of its execution. Despite some signs of age, these recordings still preserve the brilliance of their readings and the tonal quality of this orchestra. Altogether, a disc to lift the heaviest of spirits.

Additional recommendations ...

...Nos. 3 and 4. **Chamber Orchestra of Europe / Claudio Abbado.** DG Ⓕ 423 653-2GH (58 minutes: DDD: 9/89). 😀😀😀

...Nos. 3 and 5. **Hanover Band / Roy Goodman.** Nimbus Ⓕ NI5172 (58 minutes: DDD: 7/89). 🖊

...No. 3. **Schumann** Symphony No. 3 in E flat major, Op. 97, "Rhenish". **North German Radio Symphony Orchestra / Günter Wand.** RCA Victor Red Seal Ⓕ 09026 61876-2 (56 minutes: DDD: 2/94). 😀😀

...Nos. 5 and 6. Overture in C major in the Italian style, D591. **Stockholm Sinfonietta / Neeme Järvi.** BIS Ⓕ CD387 (72 minutes: DDD: 9/88).

...Nos. 5 and 6. **Chamber Orchestra of Europe / Claudio Abbado.** DG Ⓕ 423 654-2GH (61 minutes: DDD: 9/89).

...Nos. 5 and 8. **Royal Concertgebouw Orchestra / Leonard Bernstein.** DG Ⓕ 427 645-2GH (57 minutes: DDD: 1/90).

...No. 5. **Brahms** Symphony No. 3 in F major, Op. 90. **Mendelssohn** The Hebrides, Op. 26.
Chicago Symphony Orchestra / Fritz Reiner. RCA Victor Gold Seal Ⓜ 09026 61793-2 (69 minutes:
ADD: 9/95). *See review under Brahms; refer to the Index to Reviews.*
...**Beethoven** Symphony No. 6 in F major, Op. 68, Pastoral". **Schubert** Symphony No. 5 in B
flat major, D485. **Vienna Philharmonic Orchestra / Karl Böhm.** DG The Originals Ⓜ 447 433-
2GOR (74 minutes: ADD: 1/96). *Gramophone classical 100. See review under Beethoven; refer to
the Index to Reviews.*   ⓖⓖⓖ
...Nos. 2, 3 and 5. **Orchestra of the Eighteenth Century / Frans Brüggen.** Philips Ⓕ 446 100-2PH
(78 minutes: DDD: 7/96). ✍

New review

Schubert Symphonies – No. 8 in B minor, D759, "Unfinished"; No. 9 in C major, D944, "Great".
Berlin Philharmonic Orchestra / Günter Wand. RCA Victor Red Seal Ⓜ 09026 68314-2 (two discs:
85 minutes: DDD: 1/96). Recorded live in 1995.
The advantages of these Berlin readings over Wand's 1991 Hamburg Musikhalle/North German RSO
recordings (also live) are, often, as you might expect: greater facility (in, say, the infamous string
triplets in the Ninth's last movement), generally richer string sonority (a proper 'heft' for those
stamping C major chords also in the Ninth's finale), sweeter, more vibrant and more focused
woodwind (wonderful solos in the Eighth's second movement second subject), a generally wider
(though far from excessive) range of dynamics in the Eighth, more expansive phrasing, and accents
more consistently placed (and recorded sound with marginally greater presence). The ground-plans
remain the same, in other words, the basic tempo and its modification (and what ingenious and
effective plans they are, and how marvellous it has been to re-encounter Wand's sublimely wrought
rubato); as does the conductor's views on repeats (taken in the Eighth's first movement, but not in the
Ninth's outer movements). It is pointless to speculate whether the small details that *have* changed (for
example, the now truly *pianissimo* second subject of the Eighth's first movement) are due to Wand's
further four years' thoughts on the works, or changes brought about by the Berlin orchestra's own
musical collective, or just 'another time, another place'. Probably a bit of all three. If you already own
the Hamburg recordings, there is no need to rush out and buy this package (and, of course, you will
also be the proud owner of the finest Schumann Fourth of the last two decades – the Hamburg
Schubert Eighth's coupling). But if you don't, this set is an obvious choice. Wand's Schubert is
informed by a very special devotion, wisdom and insight, and a very individual spirit of adventure.
Additional recommendations ...
...No. 8. Sonata for Piano Duet in C major, D812, "Grand Duo" (orch. Joachim). **Chamber
Orchestra of Europe / Claudio Abbado.** DG Ⓕ 423 655-2GH (71 minutes: DDD).
...No. 8 in B minor, D759, "Unfinished". **Schumann** Symphony No. 4 in D minor, Op. 120. **North
German Radio Symphony Orchestra / Günter Wand.** RCA Victor Red Seal Ⓕ RD60826
(57 minutes: DDD: 5/92). *See review under Schumann; refer to the Index to Reviews.*   ⓖⓖ
...No. 8. *Coupled with music by* **Beethoven, Brahms, Debussy, Ravel** *and* **Tchaikovsky.**
Concertgebouw Orchestra / Pierre Monteux. Philips The Early Years Ⓜ 442 544-2PM5 (five discs:
311 minutes: ADD: 12/94). *See review in the Collections section; refer to the Index to Reviews.*
                                                                                            ⓖⓖⓖ
...No. 8. Marche militaire in D major, D733 No. 1. *Coupled with works by* **Bach, Mozart, Berlioz**
and **Borodin Louis Zimmerman, Ferdinand Hellmann** (vns); **Concertgebouw Orchestra / Willem
Mengelberg.** Pearl mono Ⓜ GEMMCD9154* (76 minutes: ADD: 3/96).
...No. 9. **Vienna Philharmonic Orchestra / Sir Georg Solti.** Decca Ⓕ 430 747-2DM (55 minutes:
DDD: 3/83).   ⓖ
...No. 9. **Royal Concertgebouw Orchestra / Leonard Bernstein.** DG Ⓕ 427 646-2GH (50 minutes:
DDD: 1/90).
...No. 9. **North German Radio Symphony Orchestra / Günter Wand.** RCA Victor Red Seal
Ⓕ RD60978 (53 minutes: DDD: 1/92).
...No. 9. **Bavarian Radio Symphony Orchestra / Carlo Maria Giulini.** Sony Classical Ⓕ SK53971
(57 minutes: DDD: 8/95).
...No. 9. **Haydn** Symphony No. 88 in G major, "Letter V". **Berlin Philharmonic Orchestra /
Wilhelm Furtwängler.** DG The Originals mono Ⓜ 447 439-2GOR* (76 minutes: ADD: 12/95).
...No. 9. Rosamunde, D797ᵇ – Ballet in B minor; Ballet in G major. **Haydn** Symphony No. 92 in
G major, "Oxford"ᵃ. ᵃ**Paris Conservatoire Orchestra,** ᵇ**London Symphony Orchestra / Bruno
Walter.** Dutton Laboratories Essential Archive mono Ⓑ CDEA5003* (79 minutes: ADD: 1/96).
...No. 9. **Orchestra of the Age of Enlightenment / Sir Charles Mackerras.** Virgin Classics Veritas
Ⓜ VER5 61245-2 (60 minutes: DDD: 1/96). ✍

New review

Schubert Octet in F major, D803. Minuet and Finale in F major, D72ᵃ. **Vienna Octet;** ᵃ**Vienna
Wind Soloists.** Decca Eclipse Ⓑ 448 715-2DEC (72 minutes: DDD: 8/96). From 430 516-2DH
(2/93).
Over the years Decca have made a speciality of recording the Schubert Octet in Vienna, and this
budget-priced reissue of their latest version by the Vienna Octet, captured within the glowing acoustics
of the Mozartsaal of the Vienna Konzerthaus, and ideally balanced by Christopher Raeburn, is the

most winning of all. The enticing warmth of the opening *Adagio* catches the listener's attention at once, and the central movements – the *Scherzo* bustling with vitality and the deliciously played *Andante con variazioni* – are unforgettable. Then comes the lovingly Schubertian *Menuetto*, and after an arresting *tremolando* introduction, the joyfully bucolic finale rounds things off in sparkling fashion. At its price, this Vienna version is now in a class of its own. As a bonus we are offered the *Minuet and Finale*, D72, two engaging miniatures from the composer's youth, nicely elegant in the hands of the Vienna Wind Soloists. The demonstration-standard recording makes this a bargain not to be passed by.

Additional recommendations ...

...Octet. **Gaudier Ensemble.** ASV Ⓕ CDDCA694 (64 minutes: DDD: 5/90).

...Octet. **Walter Boeykens Ensemble.** Harmonia Mundi Ⓕ HMC90 1440 (64 minutes: DDD: 8/93).

...Octet. **Budapest Schubert Ensemble.** Naxos Ⓢ 8 550389 (68 minutes: DDD: 8/93).

...Octet. **Berlin Soloists.** Teldec Digital Experience Ⓜ 4509-91448-2 (63 minutes: DDD: 11/93).

Schubert String Quintet in C major, D956. **Melos Quartet** (Wilhelm Melcher, Ida Bieler, vns; Hermann Voss, va; Peter Buck, vc); **Wolfgang Boettcher** (vc). Harmonia Mundi Ⓕ HMC90 1494 (57 minutes: DDD: 8/94). Includes free sampler disc of other Melos Quartet recordings. Recorded 1993.

Schubert String Quintet in C major, D956. **Borodin Quartet** (Mikhail Kopelman, Andrei Abramenkov, vns; Dmitri Shebalin, va; Valentin Berlinsky, vc); **Mikhail Milman** (vc). Teldec Ⓕ 4509-94564-2 (52 minutes: DDD: 4/95). Recorded 1994.

In his programme notes, Christian Girardin compares Schubert's String Quintet with the composer's *Great* C major Symphony: both works share the same key, involve a profound investigation of tone-colour and exhibit a kind of transcendency which derives not from the quantity, but from the quality of musical time. The Melos Quartet's playing is broad and expansive, and their sensational string tone sounds extraordinarily resonant in their rich recording. Relaxed speeds and sensitively balanced textures allow internal voices to make their full impact. However, it is the dramatic intensity which this group achieves in the music's silences that is most remarkable. Prospective buyers are further enticed by a free sampler of other Melos recordings which, aside from music by Janáček, Bruckner and Brahms, includes a fine performance of Schubert's *Quartettsatz*.

Dying swans don't only sing: they get angry too. There is plenty of wing-beating and lashing out in the Borodin Quartet's performance: 50 years (nearly half of them spent with the current membership intact) have taught the Borodin Quartet that there is more to late Schubert than resignation and dream. In each movement, it is harmonic instability, suddenness of dynamic contrast, harshness of rhythm and texture which are emphasized – and all caught faithfully in the outstanding engineering and production. Comparison in the case of this work, and this performance, really is odious. But surely there are few other accounts with a longer, more intense inner crescendo at the very core of those opening chords, or a more starkly rhythmic cut-off? The fierceness of those ever-tautening sequences and imitations at the start do away with any need for over-sweetness in the second, lyrical subject: it simply becomes set into gentle, natural relief. The great slow movement convinces entirely in its pulse rate and pacing, with great dignity drawn from the full, sustained dotted note values in the violin parts. The *presto* of the *Scherzo* is restrained by a certain heavy-heeled ballast, so that the velocity of every note counts, and this most sober of Trios is given a frame of fitting substance. Few quartets capture so movingly the anxious tremor in the heart of the finale, as it lunges savagely between major and minor. But then few quartets have learned to look so far away from themselves and so deep into the very centre of the music.

Additional recommendations ...

...String Quintet. **Aeolian Quartet; Bruno Schrecker** (vc). Saga Classics Ⓜ EC3368-2* (54 minutes: ADD: 4/92).

...String Quintet. **Emerson Quartet; Mstislav Rostropovich** (vc). DG Ⓕ 431 792-2GH (53 minutes: DDD: 9/92). ⓆⒼ

...String Quintet[a]. String Quartet No. 12 in C minor, D703, "Quartettsatz". **Takács Quartet;** [a]**Miklos Perényi** (vc). Decca Ⓕ 436 324-2DH (64 minutes: DDD: 6/93).

...String Quintet. **Brandis Quartet; Wenn-Sinn Yang** (vc). Nimbus Ⓕ NI5313 (54 minutes: DDD: 6/93).

...String Quintet. **Schoenberg** Verklärte Nacht, Op. 4[a] (orig. version). **Hollywood Quartet;** [a]**Alvin Dinkin** (va); **Kurt Reher** (vc). Testament mono Ⓕ SBT1031* (73 minutes: ADD: 4/94). *See review under Schoenberg; refer to the Index to Reviews. Gramophone Award Winner 1994.* ⓆⒼⓆ

...String Quintet[a]. Symphony No. 5 in B flat major, D485[b]. [a]**Isaac Stern,** [a]**Alexander Schneider** (vns); [a]**Milton Katims** (va); [a]**Paul Tortelier** (vc); [b]**Prades Festival Orchestra / Pablo Casals** ([a]vc). Sony Classical Casals Edition mono Ⓜ SMK58992* (76 minutes: ADD: 5/94). ⓆⒼⓆ

...String Quintet[a]. **Beethoven** Grosse Fuge in B flat major, Op. 133. **Hagen Quartet;** [a]**Heinrich Schiff** (vc). DG Ⓕ 439 774-2GH (68 minutes: DDD: 11/94).

...String Quintet. String Trio in B flat major, D471. **Raphael Ensemble.** Hyperion Ⓕ CDA66724 (65 minutes: DDD: 12/95).

Schubert Piano Quintet in A major, D667, "Trout"[a]. String Quartet No. 14 in D minor, D810, "Death and the Maiden"[b]. [a]**Sir Clifford Curzon** (pf); [a]members of the **Vienna Octet** (Willi Boskovsky, vn; Gunther Breitenbach, va, Nikolaus Hübner, vc; Johann Krump, db); [b]**Vienna**

Philharmonic Quartet (Willi Boskovsky, Otto Strasser, vns; Rudolf Streng, va; Robert Scheiwein, vc). Decca Ⓜ 417 459-2DM* (71 minutes: ADD: 6/88). Item marked [a] from SXL2110 (6/59), recorded 1957, [b]SXL6092 (5/64), recorded 1963. Ⓖ

Schubert composed the *Trout* Quintet in his early twenties for a group of amateur musicians in the town of Steyr in Upper Austria, which lies upon the River Enns which was then noted for its fine fishing and keen fishermen. The Quintet was certainly tailored for special circumstances, but like all great occasional music it stands as strongly as ever today, with its freshly bubbling invention and sunny melodiousness. Willi Boskovsky's gentle and cultured mind is very much responsible for the success of these performances of Schubert's two best-known chamber works. In the delectable *Trout* Quintet there is real unanimity of vision between the players, as well as an immaculate attention to the details of the scoring. Clifford Curzon's part in the performance is memorable especially for his quiet playing – the atmosphere is magical in such moments. Everywhere there is a great awareness of the delicacy and refinement of Schubert's inventiveness. The *Death and the Maiden* Quartet is no less successful. Schubert's strikingly powerful harmonies, together with a sustained feeling of intensity, all go to heighten the urgency of the first movement. Despite this, string textures are generally kept light and feathery. In the *Andante* all is subtly understated and although a mood of tragedy is always lurking in the background, never is it thrown at the listener. Boskovsky's understanding of the music is very acute and the performance cannot fail to satisfy even the most demanding. These are two vintage recordings and in the quartet the quality of sound is quite remarkable.

Additional recommendations ...

...Piano Quintet. **Clemens Hagen** (vn); **Veronika Hagen** (va); **Lukas Hagen** (vc); **Alois Posch** (db); **András Schiff** (pf). Decca Ⓕ 411 975-2DH (44 minutes: DDD: 4/85).

...Piano Quintet. Der Hirt auf dem Felsen, D965[b]. [b]**Felicity Lott** (sop); **Nash Ensemble.** IMP Classics Ⓜ PCD868 (57 minutes: DDD: 12/87).

...Piano Quintet. String Trios[a] – B flat major, D471; B flat major, D581. [a]**Grumiaux Trio; Jacques Cazauran** (db); **Ingrid Haebler** (pf); Philips Musica da Camera Ⓜ 422 838-2PC (63 minutes: ADD: 10/89).

...Piano Quintet. **Hummel** Piano Quintet in E flat major, Op. 87. **Schubert Ensemble of London.** Hyperion Helios Ⓜ CDH88010 (61 minutes: DDD: 6/90).

...Piano Quintet[a]. Adagio and Rondo concertante in F major, D487. **Kodály Quartet;** [a]**István Tóth** (db); **Jenő Jandó** (pf). Naxos Ⓢ 8 550658 (53 minutes: DDD: 4/93).

...Piano Quintet[b]. Lieder[a] – Die Forelle, D550; Am Strome, D539; Auf dem see, D543; Erlafsee, D586; An eine Quelle, D530; Der Jüngling am Bache, D192; Der Schiffer, D536. [a]**John Mark Ainsley** (ten); [b]**Steven Lubin** (fp); [b]**Academy of Ancient Music Chamber Ensemble.** L'Oiseau-Lyre Ⓕ 433 848-2OH (60 minutes: DDD: 9/93). ✐

...Piano Quintet[a]. Quartet in G major for Guitar, Flute, Viola and Cello, D96[b]. [b]**Wolfgang Schulz** (fl); [a]**Georg Hetzel** (vn); [ab]**Wolfram Christ** (va); [ab]**Georg Faust** (vc); [a]**Alois Posch** (db); [b]**Göran Söllscher** (gtr); [a]**James Levine** (pf). DG Ⓕ 431 783-2GH (65 minutes: DDD: 1/94). *Gramophone Editor's choice.*

New review

Schubert Piano Quintet in A major, D667, "Trout"[a].
Mozart Piano Quartet in G minor, K478. **Thomas Zehetmair** (vn); **Tabea Zimmermann** (va); **Richard Duven** (vc); [a]**Peter Riegelbauer** (db); **Alfred Brendel** (pf). Philips Ⓕ 446 001-2PH (75 minutes: DDD: 1/96). Recorded 1994.

"The Schubert of this quintet is not the great Schubert, but the one whom we cannot help but love." Pertinent sentiments (Alfred Einstein quoted by William Kinderman) although listening to this particular performance of the *Trout* suggests something of a compromise between 'lovable' and 'great'. Brendel is of course the lynchpin and, as ever, balances heart and mind with innate good taste. Time and again you find yourself overhearing detail that might otherwise have passed for nothing: every modulation tells (needless to say, this *Andante* probes deeper than most); every phrase of dialogue has been polished, pondered and carefully considered. And yet it *is* a dialogue, with the loose-limbed Thomas Zehetmair leading his supremely accomplished colleagues through Schubert's delightful five-tier structure. The *Scherzo* and *Allegro giusto* frolic within the bounds of propriety (some will favour an extra shot of animal vigour), whereas the first, second and fourth movements are rich in subtle – as opposed to fussy – observations. The recording, too, is exceedingly warm, with only the occasional want of inner detail to bar unqualified enthusiasm. As ever, Philips achieve a well-rounded, almost tangible piano tone. Mozart's G minor Quartet makes for an unexpected, though instructive, coupling, treading as it does on the *Trout*'s playful tail. Here again there is much to learn and enjoy, especially in terms of phrasal dovetailing and elegant articulation (Brendel's opening flourish is a model of Mozartian phrase-shaping). Still, you may sometimes crave rather more in the way of *Sturm und Drang* – a fiercer, more muscular attack, most especially in the first movement. And yet there will be times when the conceptual unity and executive refinement of this performance – its articulate musicality – will more than fit the bill. Both works include their respective first movement repeats.

Schubert String Quartets – No. 12 in C minor, D703, "Quartettsatz"[b]; No. 13 in A minor, D804[a]; No. 14 in D minor, D810, "Death and the Maiden"[a]; No. 15 in G major, D887[b]. **Melos Quartet**

(Wilhelm Melcher, Gerhard Voss, vns; Hermann Voss, va; Peter Buck, vc). Harmonia Mundi
Ⓕ HMC90 1408/9 (two discs: 134 minutes: DDD: 12/92). Items marked [a] recorded 1989, [b]1991.

😊😊

These quartets belong to the years 1820-26 and thus the last decade of Schubert's short life. As the violent *fortissimo* attack of the D minor reminds us right away, they don't make for comfortable listening: there's plenty of passion and tension here, and even an occasional alarming outburst such as occurs in the *Andante un poco moto* of the G major Quartet. Yet since this is still Schubert's music, there's also melodic richness. In fact one often senses a dramatic contrast between Viennese *Gemütlichkeit* and something like terror or pain, maybe even the thought of approaching death which we know haunted the already ill composer. The Melos Quartet have played this music in public over a period of years and bring authority as well as insight to the performance of the three late quartets and the earlier but no less compelling *Quartettsatz* in C minor. Thus, the big first movement of *Death and the Maiden* has both vigour in the fiery first subject and gentleness in the lilting second, while the coda smoulders impressively before bursting into flames. There is a hushed beauty in the famous slow movement, based on the song which gave its name to the work, while the final *Presto* has all the urgency of an Erl King-like pursuit. The Melos are equally at home in the radiantly melodious yet sorrowful A minor Quartet and the dramatic and enigmatic G major Quartet. These are performances of distinction, and the recording is truthful, with a natural degree of resonance.

Additional recommendations ...

...Nos. 13 and 14. **Alban Berg Quartet.** EMI Ⓕ CDC7 47333-2 (72 minutes: DDD: 7/86).

...Nos. 12 and 14. **Lindsay Quartet.** ASV Ⓕ CDDCA560 (52 minutes: DDD: 3/87).

... No. 8 in in B flat major, D112; No. 13. **Lindsay Quartet.** ASV Ⓕ CDDCA593 (65 minutes: ADD: 4/88).

...Nos. 14 and 15. **Busch Quartet.** EMI Références mono Ⓜ CDH7 69795-2* (73 minutes: ADD: 5/89). *Gramophone classical 100.*

😊😊😊

...No. 2 in C major, D32. No. 14. **Artis Quartet.** Sony Classical Ⓕ SK52582 (59 minutes: DDD: 6/93).

...Nos. 13 and 14. **Takács Quartet.** Decca Ⓕ 436 843-2DH (75 minutes: DDD: 12/93).

...No. 8 in B flat major, D112[a]; Nos. 14[a] and 15[a]. Fantasy in C major, D934[ab]. Piano Trio No. 2[ab]. [b]**Rudolf Serkin** (pf); [a]**Busch Quartet.** Pearl mono Ⓜ GEMMCDS9141* (two discs: 158 minutes: AAD: 7/95).

...No. 13. **Schoenberg** String Quartet No. 2 in F sharp minor, Op. 10[a]. [a]**Amanda Roocroft** (sop); **Britten Quartet.** EMI Ⓕ CDC5 55289-2 (67 minutes: DDD: 7/95).

New review

Schubert String Quartets – No. 13 in A minor, D804; No. 14 in D minor, D810, "Death and the Maiden". **Brandis Quartet** (Thomas Brandis, Peter Brem, vns; Wilfried Strehle, va; Wolfgang Boettcher, vc). Nimbus Ⓕ NI5438 (79 minutes: DDD: 12/95). Recorded 1994-5.

The three major chamber works that followed Schubert's initial discovery of his serious illness in 1823 – the Octet, D803 and the two string quartets in A minor and D minor, D804 and D810 – all look backwards with significant quotations from earlier works. This new version of Schubert's two 1824 string quartets by the Brandis poignantly highlights the composer's tragic predicament. Yearning lyricism, chillingly underscored by bare fifths in the lower strings, gives way to boldly defiant gestures in the first movement of the A minor Quartet. Meanwhile the movingly nostalgic *Rosamunde* music in the work's second movement reaches a tragic climax in the bleak reminiscence from *Der Götter Griechenlands* in the scherzo, recalling Schubert's despairing letter to Schober ("whether I shall ever quite recover I am inclined to doubt"). The trio offers a momentary period of brightness, but a *moderato* pace in the finale tellingly tinges the music's optimism with sinister unease. The vigorous virtuosity of the Alban Berg Quartet's account of the *Death and the Maiden* Quartet vividly portrays Schubert's struggle against his fate, but the Brandis here offer an immensely powerful alternative. The first movement's startlingly violent central motif is made more intense by an agogic accent on the long note preceding the triplet, and the high emotional temperature is maintained by a wealth of textural detail and the inclusion of the exposition repeat. In the second movement, the Brandis's miraculous resolution of the rhythmically climactic third variation into the radiant major fourth one, culminates in the *Scherzo*'s and finale's triumphant mood.

Schubert Piano Trios[a] – B flat major, D28 (Sonata in one movement); No. 1 in B flat major, D898; No. 2 in E flat major, D929. Notturno in E flat major, D897[a]. String Trios[b] – B flat major, D471; B flat major, D581. [a]**Beaux Arts Trio** (Menahem Pressler, pf; Daniel Guilet, vn; Bernard Greenhouse, vc); [b]**Grumiaux Trio** (Arthur Grumiaux, vn; Georges Janzer, va, Eva Czako, vc). Philips Duo Ⓜ 438 700-2PM2 (two discs: 127 minutes: ADD: 4/94). Items marked [a] recorded 1966, [b]1969.

😊😊

These performances are polished, yet the many solo contributions from each of the players emerge with a strong personality. The Beaux Arts cellist brings lovely phrasing and a true simplicity of line, so right for Schubert – memorably in the lovely slow movement melody of the Trio No. 2 in E flat. In addition to the great piano trios (B flat, D898 and E flat, D929) the set includes the extremely personable, very early Sonata in B flat, D28, where the lyrical line already has the unmistakable character of its young composer. Also included is the *Notturno*, D897, a raptly emotive short piece played here with a remarkable depth of feeling that recalls the gentle intensity of the glorious slow movement of the String Quintet. The recording is naturally balanced, although a little dry in the treble. Of the two rarer string trios, also early works, the four-movement Trio, D581 is totally infectious, with that quality of innocence that makes Schubert's music stand apart. Given such persuasive advocacy, and vivid recording, both pieces cannot fail to give the listener great pleasure.

Additional recommendations ...

...No. 1. **Borodin Trio.** Chandos Ⓕ CHAN8308 (43 minutes: DDD: 3/84).

...No. 2 in E flat major, D929. **Borodin Trio.** Chandos Ⓕ CHAN8324 (DDD: 11/84).

Schubert Piano Music for Four Hands, Volume 1. Overture in F major, D675. Eight Variations on a theme from Hérold's "Marie", D908. Rondo in D major, D608. Marches héroïques, D602. Fantasie in F minor, D940. Variations in B flat major, D603/D968a. Divertissement à la hongroise, D818. Six Polonaises, D824. **Yaara Tal, Andreas Groethuysen** (pf duet). Sony Classical Ⓕ S2K58955 (two discs: 137 minutes: DDD: 9/94). Recorded 1993.

The first thing one notices about this issue is the very clear and firm sound; Tal and Groethuysen explain that they have used a Fazioli Model 308 piano and thank their recording team for its "exceptional abilities". Indeed, an impressive sound comes from this big instrument, which the artists consider necessary to re-create the "symphonic ambitions" and "extremes" of the music, although it is unlike anything Schubert could have heard, and they play with a fine tonal and dynamic range which allows intimacy as well as power. The treble is bright yet not glaring, as we hear in the closing page of the *Overture*. The recording is fairly reverberant but produces a satisfying aural picture. The performances are strong and compelling, with plenty of momentum, yet flexible. The *Rondo* has a winning *galanterie*, and the players know that *Allegretto* marking here applies to style as well as tempo. The F minor *Fantasie* is Schubert's best-known keyboard duet and, of course, inhabits a more private world in which despair features strongly. Tal and Groethuysen's basic tempo is a genuine *Allegro molto moderato*, and they know how to make transitions from one mood to the next, as when approaching the doom-laden F sharp minor section at 4'55". Furthermore, they rightly bring out the 'smiles through tears' aspect of the more lyrical music, do not hurry the scherzo (which is consequently all the stronger) and shape the fugue finely. They are very impressive and one is reminded of the performance by Louis Lortie and Hélène Mercier (listed below) which is equally magisterial.

Additional recommendations ...

...Fantasie. **Mozart** Sonata in D major, K448/K375a. Andante and Variations in G major, K501. **Louis Lortie, Hélène Mercier** (pfs). Chandos Ⓕ CHAN9162 (50 minutes: DDD: 7/93).

...Divertissement à la Hongroise. Trois Marches Militaires, D733. Grandes marches, D819 – No. 2 in G minor; No. 3 in B minor. **Isabel Beyer, Harvey Dagul** (pf duet). Four Hands Music Ⓕ FHMD894 (69 minutes: DDD: 4/95).

...Polonaises. Divertissement, D823. **Isabel Beyer, Harvey Dagul** (pf duet). Four Hands Music Ⓕ FHMD895 (70 minutes: DDD: 12/95).

New review

Schubert Piano Music for Four Hands, Volume 2. Allegro in A minor, D947, "Lebensstürme". Four Polonaises, D599. Variations in E minor on a French song, D624. Divertissement, D823. Grandes marches, D819. Rondo in A major, D951. **Yaara Tal, Andreas Groethuysen** (pf duet). Sony Classical Ⓕ S2K66256 (two discs: 153 minutes: DDD: 4/96). Recorded 1994.

The first discs in the Schubert series from Tal and Groethuysen is reviewed above. This pair of discs features the same Fazioli Model 308 grand piano, its big modern sound clearly unauthentic but surprisingly effective in conveying what the artists call the 'symphonic' aspects of the music. The recording is splendidly clear yet atmospheric, with a fine dynamic range. As for the playing, it is wonderfully controlled, affectionate while subtly poised and textured, with flexible tone and tempo – a model of Schubert duet style and ultimately surpassing the recent Isabel Beyer/Harvey Dagul series, good though that is, because of the younger artists' greater responsiveness and refinement. With Beyer and Dagul one cannot quite forget that some of this music is the lesser Schubert: Tal and Groethuysen are just that bit more persuasive, and winningly so. However, the little-known "Lebensstürme" *Allegro* that opens the first disc here is of a higher quality than that, a vivid and intense piece in Schubert's tragic key of A minor that is not unworthy of comparison with the *Fantasie* and was composed a month after that masterpiece of the composer's final year. The *Four Polonaises* of 1818 are more ordinary, but still delightful when played as elegantly as this, and the same may be said of the E minor *Variations on a French song* (the theme apparently penned by Napoleon's sister-in-law) – a work from the same year that the young Schubert dedicated to Beethoven. The later *Divertissement* ("sur des motifs originaux françaix"), a three-movement suite in all but name, is in the same key of E minor but more striking: its central variation-form *Andantino* is among the best and most personal music that Schubert wrote, with subtleties of every kind that Tal and Groethuysen respond to consistently.All this music is on the first disc. The second offers the same mixed bag: medium to highest quality in the music but outstanding playing. Thus the six *Grandes marches* are frankly conventional despite their occasional Hungarian flavour; they also last far too long, occupying well over an hour in all and with No. 5 alone lasting nearly 20 minutes – though the latter, funeral and in the unusual key of F flat minor, is rather special and was later transcribed for orchestra by Liszt. However, the very late *Rondo* in A is rich in invention and emotionally deep.

Schubert Violin Sonatas[a] – D major, D384; A minor, D385; G minor, D408.
Mendelssohn Violin Sonata in F minor, Op. 4[b]. **Jaap Schröder** (vn); **Christopher Hogwood** (fp).
L'Oiseau-Lyre Florilegium Ⓜ 443 196-2OM (76 minutes: ADD: 9/94). Items marked [a] from
DSLO565 (11/80), [b]DSLO571 (4/81). ✏

In the first of Schubert's three violin sonatas of 1816, the violin and piano are deployed on equal
terms and, in this recording, the instruments themselves (a Stradivarius violin of 1709 and a c1825
Haschka fortepiano) sound ideally matched. The Second Sonata's more introspective character offers
the opportunity for the artists to demonstrate more comprehensively the special abilities of their
instruments. In the first movement, subtle pedal effects produce a textural variety which amply
compensates for any lack of power compared with the modern piano, while the second movement
shows most vividly the violin's astonishing tonal variety in different registers. Despite this duo's
remarkably robust sound at times, the Third Sonata's defiant opening achieves a vehemence which
modern instruments are possibly better able to express. Nevertheless, Schröder and Hogwood's true
Schubertian feeling makes theirs an arresting and valuable period-instrument alternative. A sensitive
and intelligent performance of Mendelssohn's F minor Sonata, Op. 4 completes this excellent reissue's
thoroughly satisfying programme.

Additional recommendations ...

...D384; D385; D408; A major, D574. **Raphaël Oleg** (vn); **Théodore Paraskivesco** (pf). Denon
Ⓕ CO-75027 (71 minutes: DDD: 3/93).

...D384; D385; D408; D574. **Gidon Kremer** (vn); **Oleg Maisenberg** (pf). DG Ⓕ 437 092-2GH
(62 minutes: DDD: 4/93).   ⒼⒼⒼ

...D384. *Coupled with works by* **Bartók, Bloch, Debussy, Ives, Bach, Brahms, Corelli,
Debussy, Dvořák, Falla, Hubay, Kodály, Lalo, Milhaud, Mussorgsky** and **Schubert**
Joseph Szigeti (vn); **Andor Foldes, Béla Bartók** (pfs). Biddulph mono Ⓜ LAB070/71* (two discs:
129 minutes: ADD: 7/94). *See review in the Collections section; refer to the Index to Reviews.* ⒼⒼ

...D384; D385; D408; A major, D574. **Fabio Biondi** (vn); **Olga Tverskaya** (fp). Opus 111 Ⓕ OPS30-
126 (79 minutes: DDD: 10/95). ✏

Schubert Violin Sonata in A major (Duo), D574. Rondo brillant in B minor, D895. Fantasy in
C major, D934. **Gidon Kremer** (vn); **Valery Afanassiev** (pf). DG Ⓕ 431 654-2GH (67 minutes:
DDD: 3/92). Recorded 1990.   ⒼⒼⒼ

Few recitals can offer the listener such unalloyed pleasure as this gloriously played and generously
conceived Schubert recording from Gidon Kremer and Valery Afanassiev. Rarer yet by far, though,
are releases capable of generating the kind of communicative ambience more normally revealed by
the intimacy of live music making. The very opening bars of the *Duo* in A major, D574, with its restrained yet expectant dignity of utterance would
mesmerize the heart of the sternest critic, whilst Kremer exhibits charm, wit, understatement and
sheer delight in this work. The B minor Rondo and the magnificent Fantasy in C major were written
a decade after the *Duo* and were both intended to display the talents of the composer's friend, the
Czech violinist, Josef Slavic, who had settled in Vienna during 1826. Neither work found favour at the
time, and quite possibly the dark premonitions of the Rondo, whose emotional sympathies recalled
those of the *Unfinished* Symphony, were unsuited to Viennese popular tastes. However, although
Kremer's approach avoids mere rhetoric here, this superb recording is surely crowned by a magisterial
performance of the *Fantasy*. It combines bravura, elegance and a deep affinity with the Schubertian
genre, captured with splendid realism by a recording which is technically beyond criticism.

Additional recommendation ...

...Fantasy in C major, D934[a]. Rondo brillant[b]. **Raphael Oleg** ([a]vn/[b]va); **Gerard Wyss** (pf). Denon
Ⓕ CO-75636 (66 minutes: DDD: 7/94).

Schubert Sonata in A minor, D821, "Arpeggione".
Schumann Märchenbilder, Op. 113. Adagio and Allegro in A flat major, Op. 70.
Bruch Kol nidrei, Op. 47.
Enescu Konzertstück. **Yuri Bashmet** (va); **Mikhail Muntian** (pf). RCA Victor Red Seal
Ⓕ RD60112 (73 minutes: DDD: 12/90). Recorded 1989.

The booklet tells us that Yuri Bashmet, aged 38 at the time of this recording, had already 30 new
works for the viola dedicated to him. Perhaps thanks should go to this Russian artist, with his glorious
tone, and his closely attuned pianist, Mikhail Muntian, for enriching the CD catalogue with Georges
Enescu's rarely heard *Konzertstück*, written in Paris in the composer's impressionable early twenties,
and played here with intuitive understanding of its fantasy and lyrical rapture. Like that work, the
four miniatures of Schumann's *Märchenbilder* of 1851 were also inspired by the viola itself, whereas
Schumann's *Adagio and Allegro*, Bruch's *Kol nidrei* (based on one of the oldest and best-known
synagogue melodies) and Schubert's charming A minor Sonata were originally written for valve-horn,
cello and the now obsolete arpeggione respectively. But with his wide range of colour and his
"speaking" phrasing Bashmet makes them all entirely his own, only causing the occasional raised
eyebrow with slower tempos for slow numbers (such as Schumann's lullaby-like Op. 113, No. 4 and
the *Adagio* of Schubert's Sonata) than could be enjoyed from players without his own fine spun,
intimately nuanced line. Strongly recommended.

Additional recommendations ...

...Sonata, D821. **Debussy** Cello Sonata. **Schumann** Fünf Stücke im Volkston, Op. 102. **Mstislav Rostropovich** (vc); **Benjamin Britten** (pf). Decca Ⓕ 417 833-2DH (59 minutes: ADD: 9/88). *See review under Debussy; refer to the Index to Reviews.* ⊖⊖⊖

...Sonata, D821. **Schumann** Fantasiestücke, Op. 73. Fünf Stücke im Volkston. Adagio and Allegro, Op. 70. **Mendelssohn** Variations concertantes, Op. 17. Song without words in D major, Op. 109. **Friedrich-Jürgen Sellheim** (vc); **Eckart Sellheim** (pf). Sony Classical Essential Classics Ⓑ SBK48171 (72 minutes: ADD: 10/92).

...Sonata, D821. **Schumann** Fantasiestücke, Op. 73. Funf Stücke im Volkston. Op. 102. **Maria Kliegel** (vc); **Kristin Merscher** (pf). Naxos Ⓢ 8 550654 (68 minutes: DDD: 7/93).

...Sonata, D821. **Bridge** Cello Sonata in D minor, H125. **Mstislav Rostropovich** (vc); **Benjamin Britten** (pf). Decca The Classic Sound Ⓜ 443 575-2DCS (52 minutes: ADD: 4/95). ⊖⊖

New review

Schubert Andante in C major, D29. Minuet in A minor, D277a. Minuet in A major, D334. 13 Variations in A minor on a theme by Anselm Hüttenbrenner, D576. Andante in A major, D604. Fantasy in C major, D605a, "Grazer Fantasie". Three Impromptus, D946. **James Lisney** (pf). Olympia Ⓕ OCD479 (65 minutes: DDD: 2/96). Recorded 1995.

James Lisney's unusual Schubert recital offers an illuminating programme of lesser-known works, demonstrating the composer's exploitation of tonal colour and keyboard sonority. After a sensitive performance of the enchanting C major *Andante*, D29, Lisney plays a group of pieces that exploit the expressive potential of A major/minor tonality. Two minuets establish the emotional contrast between these tonal colours: the A minor one is bold and defiant, with a tranquil F major trio, while the carefree, amiable A major work is balanced by a poignantly lyrical trio in E major. The *Variations on a theme by Anselm Hüttenbrenner* demonstrates a more complex and dramatic A major/minor dichotomy, which Lisney here presents beautifully with subtle control of the theme's different transformations and telling modal shifts. In addition, Lisney offers a thoroughly absorbing, searching account of the brooding, introspective A major *Andante* and a poetically romantic, finely conceived performance of the *Grazer Fantasie*. To conclude, carefully observed interpretations of the three *Impromptus*, D946, whilst perhaps lacking the spontaneity of Brendel's reissued versions (on a two-disc set), nevertheless confirm Lisney as a thoughtful and perceptive Schubertian. This fascinating concert, which benefits from satisfyingly faithful recorded sound, should attract a wide audience.

New review

Schubert Impromptus – D899; D935. **Krystian Zimerman** (pf). DG Ⓕ 423 612-2GH (65 minutes: DDD: 5/91).

Krystian Zimerman, with these performances, banishes all thoughts of Schubert as a domestic composer. Partly because of a full-bodied, fairly close recording, and no less because of Zimerman's strong climaxes, the music comes over boldly. In fact, with his wide dynamic range and clearly delineated texture, he makes you think of how these pieces might have sounded if Schubert had scored them for orchestra. *Ritenutos* in the leading theme's phrase-ends on its first solo appearance in D899 No. 1 in C minor initially rouses fears that we might find ourselves made too aware of an interpreter at work. However, one is soon won over by the immediacy of Zimerman's response to the narrative quality of this piece. Impromptu No. 2 in E flat brings a dramatically defiant second subject and an uncommonly desperate, headlong home-coming; No. 3 in G flat has a purposeful yet wholly natural melodic flow while No. 4 in A flat brings an eloquently expressive central trio where Zimerman's deep savouring of the magical switch from minor to major in his repeat of the second half is most enjoyable. In the D935 set the textural clarity underlying his strongly characterfull story-telling in No. 1 in F minor is admirable, as is his directness of expression and poise in No. 2 in A flat. The *Rosamunde* theme itself is beautifully played both at the start and end of No. 3 in B flat. His ardour in the third is as arresting as his 'orchestration' of the fourth. As for the last F minor Impromptu, he flings it off with all the right temperamental caprice and sheer keyboard *élan*. There are many other first-rate recordings of these eight pieces but these expansive performances will enhance any record library – despite what now and again sounds like a ghostly vocal obbligato from the artist himself.

Additional recommendations ...

...D899. D935. **Radu Lupu** (pf). Decca Ⓕ 411 711-2DH (DDD: 10/84).

D899 – No. 2 in E flat major; No. 3 in G flat major. *Coupled with works by* **Bach, Mozart** and **Chopin Dinu Lipatti** (pf). EMI Références mono Ⓜ CDH5 65166-2* (73 minutes: ADD: 12/94). *See review in the Collections section; refer to the Index to Reviews.* ⊖⊖⊖

...D899. D935. **Alfred Brendel** (pf). Philips Ⓕ 422 237-2PH (61 minutes: DDD: 10/89).

...D899; D935. **Peter Katin** (fp). Athene Ⓕ ATHCD5 (64 minutes: DDD: 1/95). ✍

...D899; D935. Allegretto in C minor, D915. 11 Ecossaises, D781. Ungarische Melodie in B minor, D817. **Alfred Brendel** (pf). Philips Solo Ⓜ 442 543-2PM (74 minutes: ADD: 1/96).

New review

Schubert Fantasy in C major, D760, "Wandererfantasie"[a].
Schumann Fantasie in C major, Op. 17[b]. **Maurizio Pollini** (pf). DG The Originals Ⓜ 447 451-2GOR (52 minutes: ADD: 6/96). Item marked [a] from 2530 473 (1/75), [b] 2530 379 (5/74). Recorded 1973.

The cover shows Caspar David Friedrich's familiar *The Wanderer above the Sea of Fog*. Pollini, on the other hand, is a wanderer in a transparent ether or crystalline light and both of these legendary performances, recorded in 1973 and beautifully remastered, are of a transcendental vision and integrity. In the Schubert his magisterial, resolutely un-virtuoso approach allows everything its time and place. Listen to his flawlessly graded triple *piano* approach to the central *Adagio*, to his rock-steady octaves at 5'23" (where Schubert's merciless demand is so often the cause of confusion) or to the way the decorations in the *Adagio* are spun off with such rare finesse, and you may well wonder when you have heard playing of such an unadorned, unalloyed glory. Pollini's Schumann is no less memorable. Doubting Thomases on the alert for alternating touches of imperiousness and sobriety will be disappointed, for again, Pollini's poise is unfaltering. The opening *Moderato* is *sempre energico*, indeed, its central *Etwas langsamer* is so sensitively and precisely gauged that all possible criticism is silenced. The coda of the central march (that *locus classicus* of the wrong note) is immaculate and in what someone once called the finale's "shifting sunset vapour" Pollini takes us gently but firmly to the shores of Elysium. Here is a record that should grace every musician's shelf.

Additional recommendation ...

...Fantasy. **Dvořák** Piano Concerto in G minor, B63. **Sviatoslav Richter** (pf); **Bavarian State Orchestra / Carlos Kleiber.** EMI Ⓔ CDC7 47967-2 (59 minutes: ADD: 11/87).

New review

Schubert Fantasy in C major, D760, "Wandererfantasie". Piano Sonata in C major, D613.
16 Deutsche Tänze und Zwei Ecossaises, D783. Waltz in G major, AI/14, "Kupelwieser-Waltzer".
March in E major, D606. **Michel Dalberto** (pf). Denon Ⓔ CO-78955 (55 minutes: DDD: 10/95).
Recorded 1993-4.

Michel Dalberto presents an attractive programme of well-known and less familiar works that show different aspects of the composer's creative output and personality. The *16 Deutsche Tänze und Zwei Ecossaises*, D783, the delightful E major March, D606, and the touching little G major Waltz (which Schubert composed in 1826 as a wedding gift for his friend Leopold Kupelwieser) are all enchanting examples of the composer's social music, which Dalberto plays with an abundance of elegance and idiomatic charm. The first movement of the incomplete C major Sonata, D613, offers a curious foretaste of Chopin and, despite Dalberto's doubts about its authenticity, his stylishly phrased performance – in which he confines himself to Schubert's fragmentary score – provides a fascinating insight into the composer's developing instrumental style and approach to form. By contrast, the *Wanderer* Fantasy is one of Schubert's most striking architectural achievements, and Perahia's intellectually rewarding account of it offers a vivid portrayal of the music's constantly evolving thematic structure. Dalberto, on the other hand, presents a searching account of the music's discontinuities, effectively highlighting the opposition between Schubert's lyricism and startling volcanic outbursts in a dramatic reading. Listen, in particular, to the overt tempestuousness of the first movement which, after serene calm in the *Adagio* and buoyant optimism in the *Scherzo*, erupts violently in the work's exciting finale.

Additional recommendation ...

...Fantasy. **Schumann** Fantasie in C major, Op. 17. **Murray Perahia** (pf). CBS Masterworks Ⓔ CD42124 (52 minutes: DDD: 12/86).

New review

Schubert Piano Sonatas – No. 1 in E major, D157; No. 3 in E major, D459; No. 13 in A major, D664. **András Schiff** (pf). Decca Ⓔ 440 311-2DH (71 minutes: DDD: 11/95). Recorded 1992-3.

This seventh volume in Schiff's Schubert sonata cycle spotlights the young composer, starting with the E major work (D157) which, at the age of 18, he chose as his official No. 1. Schiff plays it with a delectable, springlike freshness and tonal charm – banishing every vestige of the "impersonality" the insert-note writer warns us to expect in the opening *Allegro ma non troppo*. His delicate keyboard 'orchestration' is no less a delight in the slow movement, with its plaintive reminders of Mozart's Barbarina and her lost pin. It is easy to understand why the E major Sonata (D459) of the following year first appeared in print, posthumously, as *Fünf Klavierstücke*. Each of the five movements inhabits a world of its own. And each is as unpredictable in sequence of ideas and modulation as in actual keyboard texture. Schiff himself revels in the music's romantic pre-echoes, not least in the demonstrative finale unusually headed *Allegro patetico*. The disc is completed by the A major Sonata of 1819, the last of Schubert's youthful essays in the genre before a four-year break, but the first of these early works to find a regular place in the repertory. Its gracious, lyrical charm is caught by Schiff in a reading of winning simplicity. No detail is overlooked (there are endless subtleties to enjoy just from his left hand) but never does his point-making intrude. Even in the spirited final *Allegro* his relaxed approach suggests not a hard-working concert pianist but a Schubert playing at home for the delectation of his friends.

Additional recommendations ...

...Nos. 17, 20 and 21. March in E major, D606. Six Moments musicaux, D780. **Artur Schnabel** (pf). EMI Références Ⓜ CHS7 64259-2* (two discs: 138 minutes: ADD: 5/92).

...No. 13. Fantasy in C major, D760, "Wanderer", *Works by* **Beethoven, Berg, Schumann** and **Prokofiev** Sviatoslav Richter (pf). EMI Ⓜ CMS7 64429-2 (four discs: 273 minutes: ADD: 3/93).

...No. 13; No. 20. **Elisabeth Leonskaja** (pf). Teldec Ⓔ 9031-74865-2 (71 minutes: DDD: 10/93).

...Nos. 13 and 21. **Radu Lupu** (pf). Decca Ⓕ 440 295-2DH (59 minutes: DDD: 11/94).

...Nos. 13 and 14. Ungarische Melodie in B minor, D817. 12 Waltzes, D145. **Vladimir Ashkenazy** (pf). Decca The Classic Sound Ⓜ 443 579-2DCS (57 minutes: ADD: 4/95).

Schubert Piano Sonatas – No. 2 in C major, D279; No. 11 in F minor, D625; No. 21 in B flat major, D960. **András Schiff** (pf). Decca Ⓕ 440 310-2DH (78 minutes: DDD: 6/95). Recorded 1992.

In his own contribution to the insert-notes, Schiff writes, "[Schubert's] music is most sensitive to tonal quality, especially in soft and softest dynamics. He's also a quintessentially Viennese composer, and for this reason a Bösendorfer Imperial has been chosen." The C major Sonata, D279, eloquently reinforces Schiff's argument. Despite its strong Beethovenian flavour, most notably in the first two movements, Schiff is undemonstrative with the music's overt virtuosity, preferring to allow his sensitive *cantabile*, attractively enhanced by the Bösendorfer's delicate edge, to express Schubert's radiant lyricism. Schubert left the first movement of the F minor Sonata, D625, incomplete and Schiff poignantly breaks off where the composer did. His graceful, elegant playing charmingly conveys the music's Biedermeier character in the second movement, and he shows a profound sympathy for Schubert's musical and expressive language through effective opposition of the finale's dramatic forces in a performance that matches Richter's affectionately attentive account. Brendel's omission, on his two-disc set (listed further on), of the exposition repeat in the first movement of the B flat major Sonata, D960, conveys a fluid sense of organic development within a prevailing mood of calm and serenity. By contrast, Schiff's inclusion of the exposition repeat emphasizes the music's discontinuities for a more potent expression of the underlying unease, first apparent in the bass trills. Subtle shifts of key and colour are powerfully effective in both the slow movement and the finale, and deft control in the *Scherzo* yields much revelatory detail – further evidence of the appropriateness of the Bösendorfer sound.

Additional recommendations ...

...Complete Piano Sonatas. **Wilhelm Kempff** (pf). DG Ⓜ 423 496-2GX7 (seven discs: 461 minutes: ADD).

...Nos. 11 and 17. Galopp and Eight Ecossaises, D735. **Michel Dalberto** (pf). Denon Ⓕ CO-78803 (65 minutes: DDD: 4/96).

New review

Schubert Piano Sonatas – No. 4 in A minor, D537; No. 20 in A major, D959. **Malcolm Bilson** (fp). Hungaroton Ⓕ HCD31587 (59 minutes: DDD: 8/96). ✐

Bilson's is not the first disc to highlight the close affinity between Schubert's A minor Piano Sonata, composed in March 1817, and the great A major Sonata from the composer's final year. In a recording of the same two works, Schiff – aided by the modern Bösendorfer piano's capacity for sustained serene tone – perceptively reveals the A minor Sonata's voice-leading threads in a compelling blend of romantic, dance-like grace and lyrical warmth. With judicious use of the moderator pedal, Bilson here effectively exploits the 1815 Lagrassa fortepiano's robust tone in a reading which, though less dramatic than Schiff's, atmospherically opposes different tonal regions. Schubert miraculously transformed the duple-metre theme of the A minor Sonata's slow movement into the flowing lines of the A major Sonata's rondo finale. Schiff's concentration on detail throughout this later work could be seen to be impeding the music's natural impetus. However, the spaciousness of his account does successfully convey the music's broad landscape. Bilson's blend of spontaneity and distinctive contrasts of tonal colour in all movements winningly conveys both the music's potently dramatic use of motivic material and its large-scale psychological spans.

Additional recommendation ...

...Nos. 4 and 20. **Andras Schiff** (pf). Decca Ⓕ 440 309-2DH (65 minutes: DDD: 1/95).

Schubert Piano Sonatas – No. 4 in A minor, D537; No. 15 in C major, D840, "Relique". **Ralf Gothóni** (pf). Ondine Ⓕ ODE797-2 (56 minutes: DDD: 1/95). Recorded 1991.

When Schubert's C major Piano Sonata, D840 was first published in 1861, it was given the title *Relique* in the mistaken belief that it was the composer's last work. In fact, it was composed in April 1825, around the same time as Schubert began work on the *Great* C major Symphony. Usually, only the first two completed movements are played, but like Richter (reviewed further on), Gothóni also includes the fragmentary third and fourth ones. Gothóni's is a thoughtful performance that shows a sympathetic response to Schubert's harmonic language and the various tonal colours associated with it. Richter's characteristically profound concentration creates an exceptionally broad landscape – especially in the first movement – but Gothóni's account, though less challenging intellectually, offers a comparable technical and expressive range and he gives a vivid and powerful performance of the work's dramatic extremes. The reverberant recording given to Gothóni adds powerful emphasis to the music's volcanic outbursts.

Additional recommendations ...

...Nos. 4 and 13. **Alfred Brendel** (pf). Philips Ⓕ 410 605-2PH (11/83).

...Nos. 15 and 20. **Imogen Cooper** (pf). Ottavo Ⓕ OTRC58714 (65 minutes: DDD: 12/88).

...Nos. 15 and 18. **Alfred Brendel** (pf). Philips Ⓕ 422 340-2PH (64 minutes: DDD: 10/89).

...Nos. 4, 13 and 14. Impromptus, D899 – No. 2 in E flat major; **Sviatoslav Richter** (pf). Olympia Ⓕ OCD288 (50 minutes: DDD: 10/92).

...Nos. 4 and 13. Fantasy in C major, D760, "Wanderer". **Jenö Jandó** (pf). Naxos Ⓢ 8 550846
(59 minutes: DDD: 3/95).

...Nos. 5, 6, 9 and 13. **Michael Endres** (pf). Capriccio Ⓕ 10 553 (74 minutes: DDD: 9/95).

...Nos. 4, 7 and 15. **Michael Endres** (pf). Capriccio Ⓕ 10 717 (78 minutes: DDD: 5/96).

Schubert Piano Sonatas – No. 5 in A flat major, D557; No. 9 in B major, D575; No. 18 in
G major, D894. **András Schiff** (pf). Decca Ⓕ 440 307-2DH (76 minutes: DDD: 6/94). Recorded
1992.

Schubert's piano music from András Schiff always lifts the spirits, and this time quite a bit higher than
most comparable available versions. Typically, he chooses his favourite Bösendorfer Imperial with its
Viennese accent and writes in an introduction to the notes of its Schubertian sensitivity to tone-
quality, particularly in the softest dynamics. Schiff cites the opening of the G major Sonata, D894 as
an example and, indeed, this movement, which the composer originally called a Fantasy, has a gentle
luminosity about it. Schiff's approach to the vast first movement more closely resembles Lupu's
(reviewed further on) in its meditative, long-sighted qualities; but Schiff again triumphs, in coaxing
both a wider and a more finely controlled tone palette out of his instrument. Schiff's greatest
achievement here, though, is his organic view of the inner and outer worlds of this sonata. As in the
song, "Der Lindenbaum" (from *Winterreise*), images of both tender dream and harsh reality seem to
shape the piece. Schiff makes them seem simply different sides of the same persona. One flows into
and out of another, with the dark concentration of rhythm in the eye of the storm never
compromising the original impulse of the music. In the last movement, Schiff outdoes Lupu in the
dance of constantly shifting weights and measures, lights and half-lights which dapple the rondo's
returns. Schiff seems to play through the childlike ears and eyes of Schubert himself. This outstanding
performance of D894 is nicely balanced by a deliciously understated D557, the most classically
conceived of all Schubert's sonatas, and by the more adventurous D575. Here, Schiff continues to
exploit the qualifying *ma non troppo* of the opening *Allegro* to create a sense of a plethora of ideas
and energies being held back within an unquiet serenity. If the slow movement is a little over-
deliberate, the finale again seems to be constantly surprising itself with the new ideas which sing out
as if they had only just been imagined.

Additional recommendation ...

...Nos. 9 and 11. Six Moments musicaux, D780 – No. 1 in C major; No. 3 in F minor; No. 6 in
A flat major. **Sviatoslav Richter** (pf). Olympia Ⓕ OCD286 (65 minutes: DDD: 10/92).   Ⓖ

Schubert Piano Sonatas – No. 7 in E flat major, D568, No. 19 in C minor, D958. **András Schiff**
(pf). Decca Ⓕ 440 308-2DH (61 minutes: DDD: 10/94).

Those who like their C minor Sonata bulging with Byronic sentiment or exploding with theatrical
sparks will no doubt find Schiff's unshowy approach intolerably ascetic though the absorption, the
inner penetration of his playing here is worth the loss of a few histrionic thrills. His understanding is
revealed in tiny, delicate touches – the way the C minor's first movement eases gently into the second
subject, or the nicely timed silences in the Menuetto, with the *Allegro* finale arising after another short
but pregnant pause. At the same time there's a profound grasp of the Schubertian pulse: the tension
between subtle rubato and what Theodor Adorno called the "somnambulistic" forward tread. It's
beautifully judged, whether in minute details (the slight holding back in the running quavers near the
start of the E flat Sonata is a perfect example) or in the longer term – the way D568's Minuet resumes
the first movement's basic pulse. Schiff is emphatically not one of those pianists that wants to show
you at every stage what a fabulously rich palette he possesses, but the sound he coaxes from his
Bösendorfer is hauntingly lovely, and the Decca recording captures it, and the Vienna Musikverein
Brahms-Saal's intimate warmth, superbly.

Additional recommendation ...

...Nos. 7 and 17. **Malcolm Bilson** (fp). Hungaroton Ⓕ HCD31586 (64 minutes: DDD: 5/96). ✍

New review

Schubert Piano Sonatas – No. 9 in B major, D575; No. 13 in A major, D664. Adagio in G major,
D178. Six Ecossaises, D421. Waltzes, D365 – No. 1 in A flat major; No. 2 in A flat major;
No. 14 in D flat major; No. 20 in G major; No. 22 in B major; No. 26 in E major; No. 29 in
D major; No. 30 in A major; No. 31 in C major; No. 32 in F major; No. 33 in F major; No. 34 in
F major; No. 35 in F major; No. 36 in F major. Cotillon in E flat major, D976. **Michel Dalberto**
(pf). Denon Ⓕ CO-78914 (70 minutes: DDD: 7/95). Recorded 1994.

Dalberto's Schubert cycle has the added virtue of mixing the sonatas with other, smaller piano pieces.
This volume couples two sonatas with a selection of rarely recorded dance miniatures. Dalberto
highlights Schubert's thematic diversity and adventurous approach to tonality in the B major Sonata,
D575, with tautly sprung rhythms and broad, smooth lines. András Schiff's faster speed in the
Scherzo may bring out the music's inherent dance qualities better, but Dalberto's careful approach
offers an appealing, poetic contrast both to the trio's charming rusticity, and to the disarmingly
simple finale. Brendel's sensitivity to colour in the delightful A major Sonata, D664, makes his
revelations of this work's unifying motivic threads especially vivid. Dalberto's deftly shaded
performance shows a similar alertness to the first movement's registral variety and subtle alternations
of mood. The G major *Adagio*, D178, six *Ecossaises*, D421, and *Cotillon*, D976, present lively

illustrations of Schubert's contribution to Biedermeier Vienna's thirst for dancing; a judiciously chosen group of dances from D365 shows how he elevated these unassuming pieces to great art. Clear, naturally lit recording.

Schubert Piano Sonatas – No. 9 in B major, D575; No. 15 in C major, D840, "Relique"; No. 18 in G major, D894. **Sviatoslav Richter** (pf). Philips Ⓕ 438 483-2PH2 (two discs: 117 minutes: ADD: 8/94). Recorded 1979.   ⒢⒢⒢
These sonatas are audibly live performances, made in Germany, and they have compelling presence. Facts first. The G major Sonata, D894 takes up an entire CD, in comparison with the average 16 or 17 minutes. Richter's first movement is no less than 26'51" long. Then the C major, D840 appears not *unvollendet* at all, but with its little unfinished Menuetto and Rondo taking their own eye- and ear-opening place. Behind these facts lie the concepts which set these performances apart. The heavenly length of the first movement of D894 is created out of Richter's relationship with time itself. The more one listens to his late Schubert, the more one realizes that movement and momentum are not conceived as linear. Rather they are cyclical, very much in the spirit of the final song of *Winterreise* in which the Leiermann's turning melody could be eternal. No wonder that it is to Richter that singers like Peter Schreier turn when working out the when and the how of their Schubert. The opening *Molto moderato* is read as extremely slow: the ear begins by being on tenterhooks for what might come next – then shocked by the sudden, harsh brightening of tone as the first temporary modulation is prepared. As the movement progresses, the opening motif becomes like a mantra in an extended meditation in which the listener must go through the same discipline of private pacing as the performer. At a practical level, Richter's tempo allows the mood of *Molto moderato e cantabile* to be unbroken by busy-ness even as the theme metamorphoses into quaver figuration. The *Andante*, when at last it arrives, moves with a contrastingly lithe, blithe ease, more songlike, more forceful at its centre. The simplicity and clarity of movement created by Richter's fingers in the bright dance of weight and measure which is the final *Allegretto* (and which makes for an archaic, hymn-like *Andante* in D575) is Schubert's sweetness and light. His dark side, in both these sonatas, is explored uncompromisingly by Richter in modulations of key and dynamics abrupt enough to hurt. Richter's complete incomplete Sonata, D840 is another extraordinary journey. Another endless *Moderato* (22 minutes) is this time relentless in the bare, unbeautiful resonance of its repeated figures which, all the more miraculously, become song accompaniment. It is followed by a strange, minimalist Menuetto and an almost surreal sense of bleakness as the pirouetting Rondo melts into thin air.

Schubert Piano Sonatas – No. 14 in A minor, D784; No. 17 in D major, D850. **Alfred Brendel** (pf). Philips Ⓕ 422 063-2PH (63 minutes: DDD: 11/88).   ⒢⒢
There is an extraordinary amount of highly experimental writing in Schubert's piano sonatas. The essence of their structure is the contrasting of big heroic ideas with tender and inner thoughts; the first impresses the listener, the second woos him. The two works on this CD are in some ways on a varying scale. The D major lasts for 40 minutes, the A minor for around 23. However, it is the latter that contains the most symphonically inspired writing – it sounds as if it could easily be transposed for orchestra. Alfred Brendel presents the composer not so much as the master of Lieder-writing, but more as a man thinking in large forms. Although there are wonderful quiet moments when intimate asides are conveyed with an imaginative sensitivity one remembers more the urgency and the power behind the notes. The A minor, with its frequently recurring themes, is almost obsessive in character whilst the big D major Sonata is rather lighter in mood, especially in the outer movements. The recorded sound is very faithful to the pianist's tone, whilst generally avoiding that insistent quality that can mar his loudest playing.

Additional recommendations ...
...No. 14. Six Moments musicaux, D780. Scherzos, D593. **Maria João Pires** (pf). DG Ⓕ 427 769-2GH (63 minutes: DDD: 2/90).
...Nos. 14, 16, 18 and 20. **Trudelies Leonhardt** (fp). Jecklin Ⓕ J4420/1-2 (two discs: 141 minutes: ADD: 11/91). ✐
...Nos. 1, 14 and 20. **Radu Lupu** (pf). Decca Ovation Ⓜ 425 033-2DM (73 minutes: ADD: 2/92).
...Nos. 6, 14 and 17. **András Schiff** (pf). Decca Ⓕ 440 306-2DH (75 minutes: DDD: 12/93).
...No. 17[a]. Impromptus, D899[a] – No. 3 in G flat major; No. 4 in A flat major. Six Moments musicaux, D780[b]. **Sir Clifford Curzon** (pf). Decca The Classic Sound Ⓜ 443 570-2DCS (77 minutes: ADD: 4/95).
...No. 14 . Marche Militaire No. 1 in D major, D733 (arr. Tausig). **Haydn** Piano Sonatas – A major, HobXVI/30; E flat major, HobXVI/52. **Evgeni Kissin** (pf). Sony Classical Ⓕ SK64538 (62 minutes: DDD: 9/95). *Gramophone Editor's record of the month. See review under Haydn; refer to the Index to Reviews.*

Schubert Piano Sonata No. 16 in A minor, D845. Impromptus, D946. **Alfred Brendel** (pf). Philips
Ⓕ 422 075-2PH (61 minutes: DDD: 10/89).

Schubert Piano Sonatas – No. 16 in A minor, D845[a]; No. 18 in G major, D894[b]. **Radu Lupu** (pf).
Decca Ⓕ 417 640-2DH (74 minutes: ADD: 6/87). Item marked [a] from SXL6931 (12/79),
[b]SXL6741 (5/76).

Though love of the music alone, as pianists know, is not enough to master these pieces, it is essential,
and in this big A minor Sonata (a key that was somehow especially important to Schubert) Brendel
presents us with a drama that is no less tense for being predominantly expressed in terms of shapely
melody. There is a flexibility in this playing that reminds us of the pianist's own comment that in such
music "we feel not masters but victims of the situation": he allows us plenty of time to savour detail
without ever losing sight of the overall shape of the music, and the long first movement and finale
carry us compellingly forwards, as does the scherzo with its urgent energy, while the *Andante* second
movement, too, has the right kind of spaciousness. In the *Impromptus* which date from the composer's
last months, Brendel is no less responsive or imaginative. Richly sonorous digital recording in a
German location complements the distinction of the playing on this fine disc. Radu Lupu also
understands Schubert's style as do few others and the way in which he is able to project this essentially
private world is outstanding. His tone is unfailingly clear, and this adds substantially to the lucidity
of the readings. The simplicity of the opening themes of the A minor Sonata is a marvel of eloquence
and when it is reset in the development section of the first movement one is amazed to hear Lupu
transforming it into something far more urgent and full of pathos. The G major Sonata again fires
Lupu's imagination and in the Minuet third movement he uses a considerable amount of rubato for
the dance; its solid rhythmic pulse is an ideal foil to offset the extraordinary transitions of the finale
that follows. The recorded sound does full justice to the colour of the pianist's tone.

Additional recommendations ...

...No. 16. Fantasy in C major, D760, "Wanderer". **Maurizio Pollini** (pf). DG Ⓕ 419 672-2GH
(58 minutes: DDD: 8/87). ⒼⒼ

...Nos. 1 and 16. Valses sentimentales, D779 – No. 1 in C major; No. 3 in G major; No. 5 in B flat
major; No. 7 in G minor; No. 13 in A major; No. 14 in D major; No. 19 in A flat major; No. 21
in E flat major; No. 24 in G minor; No. 28 in E flat major; No. 30 in C major; No. 34 in A flat
major. Waltz in A flat major, D978. **Michel Dalberto** (pf). Denon Ⓕ CO-73787 (67 minutes:
DDD: 4/90).

...Nos. 8, 15 and 16. **András Schiff** (pf). Decca Ⓕ 440 305-2DH (71 minutes: DDD: 12/93).

...No. 16. Impromptus, D899. **Jan Vermeulen** (pf). Vanguard Classics Ⓜ 99704 (68 minutes:
DDD: 2/96).

<hr>

New review

Schubert Piano Sonata No. 16 in A minor, D845. Impromptus, D946. **Andreas Staier** (fp). ✎
Teldec Das Alte Werk Ⓕ 0630-11084-2 (62 minutes: DDD: 7/96).

Once again, it is Andreas Staier's imagination and insight as a musician, rather than Staier-as-
fortepianist, which comes to the fore in this rich recital. In the Sonata, for instance, Staier sets up a
wide gulf between the two poles of Schubert's musical material – the sustained and lyrical, and the
percussive and propulsive – in metaphysical terms, if you like, between the inner and outer, the
contemplative and active life of this movement. Then he starts to paint with the pedal: there is a
choice of four on this 1825 Viennese Johann Fritz fortepiano, and his changing use of them as the
hands wander through the development creates a wide landscape for the journey, reminiscent of some
of the piano writing in *Winterreise*. Here, and in the even more far-reaching expressive palette of the
E flat major *Impromptu*, Staier really does realize the truth of his own statement that this – unlike the
multi-purpose modern concert grand – is truly a "specifically Romantic instrument". In the slow
movement's variations, the shifting balance between the hands are uniquely tailored to the resonating
scale of the instrument, to uniquely revelatory effect. None of this could happen, of course, without
Staier's own exceptionally sensitive imagination. At the start of the E flat minor *Impromptu* he creates
a wide area of open space for the *Andante*, with the little, high, cadenza-like scalic figure appearing,
as a sudden and wonderful bright light, as time is momentarily suspended.

<hr>

Schubert Piano Sonata No. 19 in C minor, D958. Impromptus, D899. Deutsche Tänze, D783.
Imogen Cooper (pf). Ottavo Ⓕ OTRC78923 (70 minutes: DDD: 2/92). Recorded 1989. ⒼⒼ

This is in fact the last of Imogen Cooper's six-disc cycle of the piano music of Schubert's last six years,
a cycle launched in 1988 hard on the heels of similar cycles given on the concert platform in both
London and Amsterdam. Like its predecessors, it confirms her as a Schubert player of exceptional
style and finesse. Intuitively perceptive phrasing and a willingness to let the music sing within a wholly
Schubertian sound-world are prime virtues. And though (like her erstwhile mentor, Alfred Brendel)
she is no slave to the metronome when contrasting first and second subjects in sonata expositions, she
still makes the music her own without the self-consciously mannered kind of interpretation heard
from one or two more recent rivals in this strongly competitive field. Her urgent yet poised
performance of the late C minor Sonata certainly confirms her admission (in a 1988 *Gramophone*
interview) that the comparatively clinical atmosphere of an audience-less recording venue worries her
not at all. In London's Henry Wood Hall her Yamaha is as clearly and truthfully reproduced (save for

a slight suspicion of pedal-haze in the sonata's demonically driven finale) as most else in the series. The *Impromptus* reveal an acutely sensitive response to Schubert's dynamic subtleties and surprises of key, while the 16 *German Dances* tell their own simple Viennese tale without any suggestion of applied make-up.

Additional recommendation ...

...Nos. 19-21. Impromptus, D946. Allegretto in C minor, D915. **Maurizio Pollini** (pf). DG Ⓕ 419 229-2GH2 (two discs: 142 minutes: DDD: 4/88).

New review

Schubert Piano Sonata No. 20 in A major, D959. Moments musicaux, D780. **Stephen Kovacevich** (pf). EMI Ⓕ CDC5 55219-2 (66 minutes: DDD: 1/96). Recorded 1994. Ⓖ

Here is Schubert playing as compulsive and single-minded as any on record. Formidably serious and concentrated this is not for lovers of 'lilac time' or of softly focused, lyrical options. Indeed, it is often as if the Grim Reaper himself had cut a swathe through Schubert, forbidding at a glance even a touch of solace, let alone *Gemütlichkeit*. Yet the force and authenticity of such an outwardly controversial view is made unarguable and few pianists have penetrated more deeply to the dark, restlessly beating heart beneath Schubert's outwardly genial surface. The ferocity of Kovacevich's *fortissimo* chording in the development section of the sonata's first movement is wholly typical of his refusal of all polite circumspection, and rarely can the *Andantino*, with its central elemental uproar, have sounded more spare or disconsolate. Even the *Scherzo* becomes both a memory of Beethoven's fierce whimsy and a presage of Chopin's irony, and more than touch of unease erases much chance of a conventionally meandering or leisurely view of the finale. For Kovacevich, then, this is surely Schubert's sonata equivalent of *Winterreise*; a savage journey into oblivion. Many will look for light relief in the *Moments musicaux*, but once again Kovacevich refuses all obvious sentiment or enticement. His tone remains lean and acidulous, and he possesses a rare ability to drain his sonority of all colour substance, accentuating the hectic flush of No. 5 and achieving an extreme sense of desolation in No. 6. This record, then, is for those who concede that Schubert could be "full of sorrow/And leaden eyed despair", a composer who had more than his share of life's vicissitudes. Competition from other great Schubertians (Schnabel, Brendel, Pollini, Lupu and Imogen Cooper, to name but five!) is intense, yet Kovacevich's Schubert surely inhabits a world of its own and is in a sense beyond compare; an extraordinary achievement. The recordings are spectacularly bold and the full force of a modern Steinway comes at you in an often volcanic blaze of sound.

Additional recommendations ...

...Nos. 19 and 21. **Jenö Jandó** (pf). Naxos Ⓢ 8 550475 (69 minutes: DDD).

...No. 20. Ungarische Melodie in B minor, D817. 16 Deutsche Tanze and Two Ecossaises, D783. Allegretto in C minor, D915. **Alfred Brendel** (pf). Philips Ⓕ 422 229-2PH (56 minutes: DDD: 2/89).

...Nos. 19-21. Three Impromptus, D946. **Alfred Brendel** (pf). Philips Duo Ⓜ 438 703-2PM2 (two discs: 128 minutes: ADD: 5/94).

...Nos. 4 and 20. **Laurent Cabasso** (pf). Auvidis Valois Ⓕ V4630 (64 minutes: DDD: 4/91).

...No. 20. Six Moments musicaux, D780. **Olga Tverskaya** (fp). Opus 111 Ⓕ OPS30-139 (74 minutes: DDD: 3/96). ✍

New review

Schubert Piano Sonata No. 21 in B flat major, D960. Allegretto in C minor, D915. 12 Ländler, D790. **Stephen Kovacevich** (pf). EMI Ⓕ CDC5 55359-2 (58 minutes: DDD: 7/95). Recorded 1994.
Gramophone Editor's choice. Ⓖ

Kovacevich creates his own ambience with such force and fidelity that he achieves an ultimate musical illusion: a definitive and unarguable statement indelibly and disturbingly true to Schubert's always ambiguous genius. Of course, those wedded to a less savage sense of experience, to a lightness and civility that are part of Schubert's appeal, will look elsewhere. For even in his selection of encores, Kovacevich retreats at every opportunity into a crepuscular, near hallucinatory world, his sense of elegy all pervasive. In the sonata's first-movement repeat (the nine bars despised by Brendel but, clearly, relished by Kovacevich) the distant thunder of the opening erupts in a violent upheaval. The outwardly innocent quaver flourish at 4'03" flashes with sudden anger, a startling gesture, yet one wholly in keeping with a work where desperation so easily surfaces through autumnal sadness and resignation. The *Andante*, too, is a marvel of the most concentrated musical thinking, there are some swingeing *sforzandos* in the finale to remind us, once more, of underlying menace and even the *Scherzo*'s brightly tripping outer sections are shadowed by an unusually dark-hued way with the central trio. Throughout, the effort of interpretation is immense and so although you will doubtless return to deeply cherished recordings by Pollini (magisterially detached), Kempff, with his more whimsical poetry or Brendel with his intellectual rigour and refinement on Philips you will probably find a special place for Stephen Kovacevich. No more darkly questing performance exists on disc. The recordings – when you stop to notice them – faithfully capture Kovacevich's awe-inspiring dynamic range, from the merest whisper to an elemental uproar.

Additional recommendations ...

...No. 21. Fantasy in C major, D760, "Wanderer". **Alfred Brendel** (pf). Philips Silver Line Ⓜ 420 644-2PM (57 minutes: ADD: 8/87).

...No. 21. Allegretto in C minor, D915. Impromptus, D946. **Maurizio Pollini** (pf). DG Ⓕ 427 326-2GH (71 minutes: DDD: 5/89).

...No. 21. Fantasy. **Alfred Brendel** (pf). Philips Ⓕ 422 062-2PH (58 minutes: DDD: 1/90).

...No. 21. Allegretto in C minor, D915. 12 Deutsche Ländler, D790. **Stephen Kovacevich** (pf). EMI Ⓕ CDC5 55359-2 (58 minutes: DDD: 7/95).

...No. 21. **Schumann** Fantasie in C major, Op. 17. **Sir Clifford Curzon** (pf). Orfeo D'Or Ⓜ C401951B (66 minutes: ADD: 4/96).

New review

Schubert Drei Klavierstücke, D946. 12 Waltzes, D969. Six Moments musicaux, D780. **Peter Katin** (fp). Athene Ⓕ ATHCD7 (74 minutes: DDD: 6/96). ✒ Recorded 1995.

One of the most attractive features of Katin's Schubert disc is its comfortable intimacy, conjuring images of the composer's own domestic music-making. The Clementi square piano sounds wholly appropriate in the *Waltzes*, highlighting Schubert's magical blend of Viennese gaiety and warmer harmonic shades. In the *Drei Klavierstücke*, Katin further underlines his relaxed approach with some beautifully atmospheric effects and the inclusion of all repeats. Witness the timeless quality in the slower sections of the first piece; the menacing tremolos of the C minor music and the ethereal upper register of the A flat minor music in the second piece, and the subtly coloured textures and boldly projected voice-leading in the third one.

Schubert Stabat mater – oratorio, D383[a]. Magnificat in C major, D486[b]. Offertorium in B flat major, D963[c]. [ab]**Sheila Armstrong** (sop); [ab]**Hanna Schaer** (mez); [ac]**Alejandro Ramirez** (ten); [ab]**Philippe Huttenlocher** (bar); Lausanne Vocal Ensemble; Lausanne Chamber Orchestra / **Michel Corboz**. Erato Ⓜ 4509 96961-2 (59 minutes: ADD: 3/95). Recorded 1979.

Schubert's strikingly fresh setting of the *Stabat mater* (in a German translation) was written in the composer's nineteenth year, yet it displays clear anticipations of his later music, especially in the terzetto (No. 11) for soprano, tenor, baritone and chorus and the striking chorus "Wer wird Zähren sanften Mitleids" (No. 5) with its superb horn writing. There is a beautiful tenor aria with oboe obbligato, in which Alejandro Ramirez is very stylish, while the bass aria "Sohn des Vaters" is dark and strong. Here Philippe Huttenlocher may not be quite sombre enough, yet his contribution is still most enjoyable. The singing of the Lausanne Vocal Ensemble, with the Lausanne CO under Corboz, combines clarity of focus with a firm sonority, and Schubert's lively, if somewhat uncharacteristic, fugues certainly have plenty of vigour. The two shorter Schubert pieces that make up the rest of the disc, the Magnificat (again with a fine contribution from Ramirez) and the Offertorium, are also given strong performances from Corboz. The recording, although not crystal clear, has transferred vividly.

Schubert Mass No. 5 in A flat major, D678[a]. Deutsche Messe, D872[b]. [a]**Stefan Preyer** (treb); [a]**Thomas Weinhappel** (alto); [a]**Jörg Hering** (ten); [a]**Harry van der Kamp** (bass); [b]**Arno Hartmann** (org); **Vienna Boys' Choir; Chorus Viennensis; Orchestra of the Age of Enlightenment / Bruno Weil**. Sony Classical Vivarte Ⓕ SK53984 (60 minutes: DDD: 8/94). ✒ Texts and translations included. Ⓖ

In the *Deutsche Messe* Bruno Weil makes no attempt to impose interpretative individuality on music designed purely for liturgical use: he is content merely to oversee neat ensemble and balance. The orchestra, consisting mainly of wind instruments, double the chorus parts and while their role might seem largely superfluous they do provide a comfortable cushion on which the choir can relax while making their way effortlessly through such unchallenging music. It's a different story with the sparkling A flat major Mass, but again Bruno Weil's understated direction results in an immensely satisfying performance. There is a youthful vigour and infectious enthusiasm here. Of course, much of that comes from the superb singing of the Vienna Boys' Choir. Their exuberant 'Hosanna's in the *Sanctus* and *Benedictus* are more unashamedly joyful than such music has a right to be. The two boy soloists sing with a musical maturity way beyond their years. That is not to belittle the splendid contribution from the adult voices nor the exquisite playing of the Orchestra of the Age of Enlightenment. Weil achieves the perfect tonal blend: nothing disturbs the open-hearted honesty of this genuinely sincere performance.

Additional recommendations ...

...No. 6 in E flat major, D950. **Soloists; Vienna State Opera Concerto Choir; Vienna Philharmonic Orchestra / Claudio Abbado**. DG Ⓕ 423 088-2GH (57 minutes: DDD: 8/88).

...No. 2 in G major, D167. Salve regina in A major, D676. **Haydn** Missa brevis Sancti Joannis de Deo, "Kleine Orgelmesse". Flute-clock pieces, HobXIX – Nos. 6, 9, 15, 20 and 32. **Soloists; Haydn Society Chorus and Orchestra / Denis McCaldin**. Meridian Duo Ⓜ DUOCD89003 (55 minutes: ADD: 2/90).

...No. 2[a]; No. 6[b]. [a]**Dawn Upshaw**, [b]**Benita Valente** (sops); [b]**Marietta Simpson** (mez); [a]**David Gordon**, [b]**Jon Humphrey**, [b]**Glenn Siebert** (tens); [a]**William Stone** [b]**Myron Myers** (bars); **Atlanta Symphony Chamber Chorus; Atlanta Symphony Chorus and Orchestra / Robert Shaw**. Telarc Ⓕ CD80212 (78 minutes. DDD: 9/90)

...CMS7 64778-2 – Masses: No. 1 in F major, D105[a]; No. 2[b]; No. 3 in B flat major, D324[c]; No. 4 in C major, D452[d]; No. 5[e]; No. 6[f]. Stabat mater, D383[g]. Also contains six other short works. *CMS7 64783-2* Lazarus, D689[h]. Deutsche Messe. Also contains 20 other short works. [abcdh]**Lucia Popp**,

[abefgh]Helen Donath, [h]Maria Venuti (sops); [acdef]Brigitte Fassbaender (mez); [abcd]Adolf Dallapozza,
[a]Peter Schreier, [ef]Francisco Araiza, [gh]Josef Protschka, [h]Robert Tear (tens); Dietrich Fischer-
Dieskau (bar); Bavarian Radio Chorus; Bavarian Radio Symphony Orchestra / Wolfgang
Sawallisch. EMI Sawallisch Edition Ⓜ CMS7 64778-2 and CMS7 64783-2 (two sets of four and
three discs: 297 and 217 minutes: ADD/DDD: 8/94).   Ⓖ

New review

Schubert Mass No. 6 in E flat major, D950. **Benjamin Schmidinger** (treb); **Albin Lenzer** (alto); **Jörg
Hering** (ten); **Kurt Azesberger** (ten); **Harry van der Kamp** (bass); **Vienna Boys' Choir; Chorus
Viennensis; Orchestra of the Age of Enlightenment / Bruno Weil.** Sony Classical Vivarte
Ⓕ SK66255 (48 minutes: DDD: 8/95). ✍ Text and translation included. Recorded 1994.
The most striking thing about this disc is the recording balance. It is as if there's a microphone behind
every music-stand. The effect is of a group of disparate musicians more than a conglomerate whole
but, with individual playing as good as this, it does provide a real listening treat, although it won't be
to everyone's taste. To even fewer tastes will be the unequivocal bias towards orchestral playing. After
all, what is a Schubert Mass if not primarily a choral work? There is some lovely singing here, not
least from the quintet of soloists; yet all the voices are relegated to play second fiddle to the orchestra.
Of all his Masses the E flat work (Schubert's last) is the least concerned with expressing a belief or in
presenting fundamental Christian texts (although it wasn't the only Mass from which he unilaterally
omitted unpalatable sections of the *Credo*) and its intricate orchestral textures and delightful
instrumental writing are worthy of the closest inspection. Bruno Weil has already proved himself to
be a deeply sympathetic Schubertian with a clear sense of what works, and what on first hearing
comes as something of a shock is shown on repeated listening to make perfectly good musical sense.
This view of Schubert may be from an unusual angle, but it is an infinitely rewarding approach to this
unutterably beautiful music.

Schubert Lieder, Volumes 1-3. **Dietrich Fischer-Dieskau** (bar); **Gerald Moore** (pf). DG
Ⓑ 437 214-2GX21 (21 discs: 1463 minutes: ADD: 3/93). Volumes also available separately, as
detailed below. Recorded 1966-72. *Gramophone classical 100.*
437 215-2GX9 (Volume 1: nine discs: 404 minutes): 234 Lieder, written between 1811 and 1817
(from 2720 022, 12/70). *437 225-2GX9* (Volume 2: nine discs: 395 minutes): 171 Lieder, written
between 1817 and 1828 (from 643547/58, 1/70). *437 235-2GX3* (Volume 3: three discs:
184 minutes): Die schöne Müllerin, D795. Winterreise, D911. Schwanengesang, D957 (2720 059,
1/73).   ⒼⒼⒼ
Twenty-one discs at under £100 bringing together two of this century's greatest Lieder interpreters –
it sounds like a recipe for success, as indeed it is, fulfilling the highest expectations. The recordings
were made when Dietrich Fischer-Dieskau was at his peak and Gerald Moore could draw on a
lifetime's experience and love of this repertoire. Though the set makes no claims to completeness (in
the way that Graham Johnson's ongoing Schubert series on Hyperion does), most of the songs for
male voice are included here. The use of a single singer and pianist gives the set a unity that allows
the listener to gasp anew at the composer's wide-ranging inspiration and imagination. Fischer-
Dieskau brings a unique understanding, an elegant line and a diction that renders the text clear
without resort to the written texts. If occasionally he imparts an unnecessary weightiness to the lighter
songs, this quibble is as nothing when his historic achievement is taken as a whole. And though he
made many recordings of the song cycles these are perhaps the finest, with Moore the ideal partner.
Try for example, the bleakness of "Ihr Bild" from *Schwanengesang* or the hallucinatory happiness of
"Der Lindenbaum" from *Winterreise*. The songs themselves are basically in chronological order (but
with the three song cycles collected together in the final box). It is unfortunate there is no index –
trying to find individual songs can be frustrating. It should also be added that the translations are
distinctly quirky in places; better to use Richard Wigmore's excellent book *Schubert: The Complete
Song Texts* (Gollancz: 1988) if you have a copy to hand. This is undoubtedly one of the greatest
bargains in the *Guide*. Buy, without fear of disappointment.

Additional recommendations ...
...Heimliches Lieben, D922. Minnelied, D429. Die abgeblühte Linde, D514. Der Musensohn, D764.
Coupled with works by **Schumann** and **Brahms** Dame Janet Baker (mez); Martin Isepp (pf).
Saga Classics Ⓜ EC3361-2 (47 minutes: AAD: 3/92). *See review in the Collections section; refer to
the Index to Reviews.*
...Seligkeit, D433. Frühlingsglaube, D686. Das Lied im Grunen, D917. Lachen und Weinen, D777.
Der Jüngling an der Quelle, D300. Auf dem Wasser zu singen, D774. Die junge Nonne, D828.
Die Verschworenen (Der häusliche Krieg) – Ich schleiche bang und stilla. Claudine von Villa
Bella – Liebe schwarmt auf allen Wegen. Der Einsame, D800. Nacht und Träume, D827. Die
Mutter Erde, D788. Der Hirt auf dem Felsen, D965a. Fischerweise, D881. Heidenröslein, D257.
An Silvia, D891. Liebhaber in allen Gestalten, D558. An die Musik, D547. **Edith Wiens** (sop);
[a]**Joaquin Valdepeñas** (cl); **Rudolf Jansen** (pf). CBC Records Musica Viva Ⓕ MVCD1053
(66 minutes: DDD: 5/93).
...Suleika I, D720. Suleika II, D717. Heidenröslein, D257 (includes a false start). Der König in
Thule, D367. Ganymed, D544. Gretchen am Spinnrade, D118. Im Frühling, D882. Ave Maria,
D839. *Coupled with works by* **Mozart, Beethoven, Schumann** and **Wolf** Irmgard Seefried

(sop); **Erik Werba** (pf). Orfeo D'Or mono ℗ C297921B* (71 minutes: ADD: 9/93). *See review in the Collections section; refer to the Index to Reviews.* ⓖⓖ

...Gretchen am Spinnrade, D118. An die Sonne, D270. Der König in Thule, D367. Wiegenlied, D498. Die Forelle, D550. Berthas Lied in der Nacht, D653. Die gefangenen Sänger, D712. Suleika II, D717. Suleika I, D720. Die Rose, D745. Schwestergruss, D762. Du bist die Ruh, D776. Vergissmeinnicht, D792. Die junge Nonne, D828. Lied der Anne Lyle, D830. Gesang der Norna, D831. Raste Krieger!, Krieg ist uns, D837. Jäger, ruhe von der Jagd!, D838. Ave Maria, D839. Lied der Delphine, D857/1. Die Männer sind méchant, D866 No. 3. Wiegenlied, D867. Heiss mich nicht reden, D877/2. So lasst mich scheinen, D877/3. Nur wer die Sehnsucht kennt, D877/4. Im Freien, D880. Fischerweise, D881. Im Frühling, D882. Heimliches Lieben, D922. Der Hirt auf dem Felsen, D965ᵃ. **Gundula Janowitz** (sop); ᵃ**Ulf Rodenhäuser** (cl); **Irwin Gage** (pf). DG Double Ⓜ 437 943-2GX2 (two discs: 144 minutes: ADD: 1/94).

...Rastlose Liebe, D138. Gretchen am Spinnrade, D118. Mignons Gesang, D877 No. 4. Suleika I, D720. Versunken, D715. Wanderers Nachtlied II, D768. Ganymed, D544. An den Mond, D296. *Coupled with works by* **Schumann, Wolf** and **Mozart Dawn Upshaw** (sop); **Richard Goode** (pf). Elektra-Nonesuch ℗ 7559-79317-2 (53 minutes: DDD: 8/94). *See review in the Collections section; refer to the Index to Reviews.* ⓖ

...Am Grabe Anselmos, D504. Abendstern, D806. Die Vögel, D691. Die Götter Griechenlands, D677. Gondelfahrer, D808. Auflösung, D807. *Coupled with works by* **Fauré, R. Strauss, Stanford, Parry, Busch, Warlock, Vaughan Williams, Gurney, Britten, Ireland** and **Quilter Dame Janet Baker** (mez); **Gerald Moore** (pf). EMI Ⓜ CDM5 65009-2 (75 minutes: ADD: 11/94). *See review in the Collections section; refer to the Index to Reviews.*

...Myrthen, Op. 25 - No. 2, Freisinn; No. 5, Lied aus dem Schenkenbuch im Divan I; No. 6, Lied aus dem Schenkenbuch im Divan II. *Coupled with works by* **Amalia, Reichardt, Zelter, Beethoven, Schubert, Brahms, R. Strauss, Schoeck, Reger, Busoni** and **Wolf Dietrich Fischer-Dieskau** (bar); **Karl Engel** (pf). Orfeo D'Or mono ℗ C389951B (72 minutes: ADD: 2/96).

Schubert Der Musensohn, D764*b*. Schwanengesang, D957 - Liebesbotschaft; Abschied; Die Stadt; Die Taubenpost. Der Schiffer, D536. Die Forelle, D550*e*. An eine Quelle, D530. Auf der Bruck, D853. Das Rosenband, D280. Rastlose Liebe, D138. Winterreise, D911 - Der Lindenbaum. Auf dem Wasser zu singen, D774. Im Freien, D880. Im Abendrot, D799. Wandrers Nachtlied II, D768. Im Frühling, D882. An den Mond, D296. Auf dem Strom, D943ᵃ. **Hans-Peter Blochwitz** (ten); ᵃ**Marie-Luise Neunecker** (hn); **Rudolf Jansen** (pf). Philips ℗ 438 932-2PH (64 minutes: DDD: 3/95). Texts and translations included. Recorded 1992.

You are a young, eager, inquisitive collector with, as yet, no Schubert Lieder in your library. Provided that you don't mind the disc being at full price, this one would surely be the answer for you. The choice of songs gives a true and rewarding conspectus of Schubert's genius as a writer of Lieder. Here is Schubert's world, its emotions and mysteries, encapsulated in miniature. On the other hand, even if you are a collector well-versed in Schubert and perhaps investing in the Hyperion Edition, and/or with Fischer-Dieskau by your side, you could still profit by the purchase of this one-off CD, simply because Blochwitz's voice, is exactly right for this repertoire: a silvery, easily produced tenor, owned by an artist who sings German as a natural speaker and as an unaffected musician. Every piece makes its point yet with the kind of innate art that conceals art. As he has the ever-perceptive and musically faultless Jansen, so pellucid in his playing, as his partner this is a delight from start to finish; and that finish, a fitting climax to an intelligently planned programme, is the grandly romantic *Auf dem Strom*, beautifully balanced and clear recording completes one's pleasure in this CD.

Schubert Ave Maria (Ellens Gesang III), D839. Ganymed, D544. Kennst du das Land, D321; Heiss mich nicht reden, D877 No. 2; So lasst mich scheinen, D877 No. 3; Nur wer die Sehnsucht kennt, D877 No. 4. Liebhaber in allen Gestalten, D558. Heidenröslein, D257. Nahe des Geliebten, D162. Die Forelle, D550. Auf dem Wasser zu singen, D774. Im Abendrot, D799. Ständchen, D889. Du bist die Ruh, D776. Gretchen am Spinnrade, D118. Gretchens Bitte, D564. Der Hirt auf dem Felsen, D965ᵃ. **Barbara Bonney** (sop); ᵃ**Sharon Kam** (cl); **Geoffrey Parsons** (pf). Teldec ℗ 4509-90873-2 (73 minutes: DDD: 3/95). Texts and translations included. Recorded 1994. ⓖ

This rewarding recital forms an apt complement to that by Blochwitz (reviewed above) with only two overlaps. Indeed if you are a new collector and can afford both discs you would have as rounded and satisfying a conspectus of Schubert's song-writing, bar maybe the big ballad settings, as could be wished. Bonney's programme is as carefully planned as that of her tenor colleague. She begins with a substantial selection of Goethe settings, going to the heart of the matter in all the Mignon songs, singing *Ganymed* with exemplary legato and breath control. Then she makes a well-varied selection from many of the better-known pieces. She crosses paths with Blochwitz only in *Die Forelle* and *Auf dem Wasser zu singen*. Both take the same time over each, but it is worth noting that Jansen, for Blochwitz, finds more variety and lift in the barcarolle-like accompaniment of the latter song that does Parsons. Vocally speaking, both versions are enjoyable in their natural accomplishments. Bonney's line and breath are again remarkable in *Du bist die Ruh*, which also demonstrates, as do all the other offerings, the purity of her tone – more North American clear-aired than Viennese creamy – yet that is never allowed to exclude depth of feeling. Indeed when she returns to the Goethe settings with *Gretchen am Spinnrade* she shows particular eloquence in the way that, at a deliberate pace, she builds the song unerringly to its climaxes and also catches the inwardness of Gretchen's state of mind. The Teldec recording is faultless throughout.

Additional recommendation ...

...Der Hirt auf dem Felsen, D965. Seligkeit, D433. Gretchen am Spinnrade, D118. Du liebst mich nicht, D756. Heimliches Lieben, D922. Im Frühling, D882. Die Vögel, D691. Der Jüngling an der Quelle, D300. Der Musensohn, D764. *Coupled with works by* **Brahms, Telemann, C.P.E. Bach, J.S. Bach, Handel** and **Schumann** Elly Ameling (sop); **Various soloists.** Deutsche Harmonia Mundi Ⓟ 74321 26617-2 (four discs: 239 minutes: ADD: 12/95). *See review in the Collections section; refer to the Index to Reviews.*

Schubert Schiller Lieder – Die Bürgschaft, D246; Hoffnung, D637; Hektors Abschied, D312; An Emma, D113; Des Mädchens Klage, D191; Gruppe aus dem Tartarus, D583; Der Pilgrim, D794; Der Alpenjäger, D588; Leichenfantasie, D7; Die Götter Griechenlands, D677; Sehnsucht, D636. **Christoph Prégardien** (ten); **Andreas Staier** (fp). Deutsche Harmonia Mundi Ⓟ 05472 77296-2 (74 minutes: DDD: 1/94). Texts and translations included. Recorded 1993. *Gramophone Editor's choice.*   Ⓖ

In *Die Götter Griechenlands,* Prégardien encompasses all the most compelling aspects of such notable tenor interpreters of Lieder as Patzak, Pears and Schreier. The plangent timbre is perfect for this elegiac lament, the legato ideal, the phraseology touching. Because this is perhaps Schubert's most telling setting of Schiller, to whose poetry the disc is devoted, it heads the many reasons for buying it. The performance of a quite different song, the ballad *Die Bürgschaft,* is another as here Prégardien brings to bear quite different attributes – a darker tone, a powerful sense of the song's drama and an innate feeling for the pulse of this long but ultimately rewarding piece. Over and above that the singer makes every word tell. The same is true of the jejune but entertaining *Leichenfantasie.* All the other songs, even the more intractable ones, are interpreted with the high intelligence and sense of style one would expect. Staier is both an alert and persuasive player, but once or twice, such as in *Der Pilgrim,* one longs for the softer timbre of a modern instrument, in preference to the fortepiano. The recording is first-rate.

New review

Schubert Lieder, Volume 23 – Der Tod Oscars, D375. Das Grab, D377a. Der Entfernten, D350. Pflügerlied, D392. Abschied von der Harfe, D406. Der Jüngling an der Quelle, D300. Abendlied, D382. Stimme der Liebe, D412. Romanze, D144. Geist der Liebe, D414. Klage, D415. Julius an Theone, D419. Der Leidende, D432. Der Leidende (second version), D432b. Die frühe Liebe, D430. Die Knabenzeit, D400. Edone, D445. Die Liebes-götter, D446. An Chloen, D363. Freude der Kinderjahre, D455. Wer sich der Einsamkeit ergibt, D478. Wer nie sein Brot mit Tränen ass, D480. An die Türen, D479. Der Hirt, D490. Am ersten Maimorgen, D344. Bei dem Grabe meines Vaters, D496. Mailied, D503. Zufriedenheit, D362. Skolie, D507. **Christoph Prégardien** (ten); a**London Schubert Chorale; Graham Johnson** (pf). Hyperion Ⓟ CDJ33023 (78 minutes: DDD: 7/95). Texts and translations included. Recorded 1994.

When the Hyperion Schubert Edition is completed, this latest wondrous offering, singer and pianist perfectly suited to the music in hand, will rank among its most precious jewels. Prégardien is a prince among tenor interpreters of Lieder at present, on a par with Blochwitz in instinctive, natural and inevitably phrased readings. Johnson, besides of course finding exactly the right horse for this chosen course, surpasses even his own high standard of playing in this series. Then there is Schubert himself, the Schubert of 1816 by and large, as Johnson tentatively suggests in his notes, going through a phase of "bringing himself under control". That means, largely but far from entirely, writing gently lyrical strophic songs, most of them of ineffable beauty and simplicity, starkly contrasting with the Harfenspieler settings from *Wilhelm Meister,* two written in 1816, the other in 1822. In such an outright masterpiece as *Der Jüngling an der Quelle,* Prégardien and Johnson confirm the latter's view that this piece "makes time stand still". They emphasize, in *Stimme der Liebe,* how Schubert uses shifting harmonies to indicate romantic obsession. They show in the two similar but subtly different versions of *Der Leidende* ("The suffering one") what Johnson calls "two sides of the same coin", with the tenor's plangent, tender singing, line and text held in perfect balance, an unalloyed delight. The two Hölty songs that follow, *Die frühe Liebe* and *Die Knabenzeit,* evince a wonderful affinity with thoughts of childhood on the part of poet and composer, again ideally captured here. So is the "chaste and wistful" mood of Klopstock's *Edone.* These are just a few in a basket of discoveries on a disc lasting a generous 78 minutes. Ideally balanced recording.

Additional recommendations ...

...Volume 1. Der Jüngling am Bache, D30. Thekla, D73. Schäfers Klagelied, D121 (first version). Nähe des Geliebten, D162 (second version). Meerestille, D216. Amalia, D195. Die Erwartung, D159 (second version). Wandrers Nachtlied, D224. Der Fischer, D225 (second version). Erster Verlust, D226. Wonne der Wehmut, D260. An den Mond, D296. Das Geheimnis, D250. Lied, D284. Der Flüchtling, D402. An den Frühling, D587 (second version). Der Alpenjäger, D588 (second version). Der Pilgrim, D794. Sehnsucht, D636 (second version). **Dame Janet Baker** (mez); **Graham Johnson** (pf). Hyperion Ⓟ CDJ33001 (70 minutes: DDD: 10/88).   Ⓖ

...Volume 6. Die Nacht, D534 (completed by Anton Diabelli). Jagdlied, D521 (with chorus). Abendstern, D806. Abends unter der Linde, D235. Abends unter der Linde, D237. Der Knabe in der Wiege, D579. Abendlied für die Entfernte, D856. Willkommen und Abschied, D767. Vor meiner Wiege, D927. Der Vater mit dem Kind, D906. Des Fischers Liebesglück, D933. Die Sterne, D939. Alinde, D904. An die Laute, D905. Zur guten Nacht, D903 (chorus). **Anthony Rolfe Johnson** (ten); **Graham Johnson** (pf). Hyperion Ⓔ CDJ33006 (73 minutes: DDD: 6/90).

...Volume 7. Minona, D152. Der Jüngling am Bache, D192. Stimme der Liebe, D187. Naturgenuss, D188. Des Mädchens Klage, D191. Die Sterbende, D186. An den Mond, D193. An die Nachtigall, D196. Die Liebe (Klärchens Lied), D210. Meeresstille, D215a. Idens Nachtgesang, D227. Von Ida, D228. Das Sehnen, D231. Die Spinnerin, D247. Wer kauft Liebesgötter?, D261. An den Frühling, D283. Das Rosenband, D280. Liane, D298. Idens Schwanenlied, D317. Luisens Antwort, D319. Mein Gruss an den Mai, D305. Mignon, D321. Sehnsucht, D310 (two versions). **Elly Ameling** (sop); **Graham Johnson** (pf). Hyperion Ⓔ CDJ33007 (71 minutes: DDD: 8/90).

...Volume 8. An den Mond, D259. Romanze, D114. Stimme der Liebe, D418. Die Sommernacht, D289. Die frühen Gräber, D290. Die Mondnacht, D238. An den Mond in einer Herbstnacht, D614. Die Nonne, D208. An Chloen, D462. Hochzeit-Lied, D463. In der Mitternacht, D464. Trauer der Liebe, D465. Die Perle, D466. Abendlied der Fürstin, D495. Wiegenlied, D498. Ständchen, D920 (with chorus). Bertas Lied in der Nacht, D653. Der Erlkönig, D328. **Sarah Walker** (mez); **Graham Johnson** (pf). Hyperion Ⓔ CDJ33008 (72 minutes: DDD: 10/90).

...Volume 10. Der Sänger, D149. Auf einen Kirchhof, D151. Am Flusse, D160. An Mignon, D161. Vergebliche Liebe, D177. An die Apfelbäume, wo ich Julien erblickte, D197. Seufzer, D198. Auf den Tod einer Nachtigall, D201. Der Liebende, D207. Adelwold und Emma, D211. Der Traum, D213. Die Laube, D214. Der Weiberfreund, D271. Labetrank der Liebe, D302. An die Geliebte, D303. Harfenspieler I, D325. **Martyn Hill** (ten); **Graham Johnson** (pf). Hyperion Ⓔ CDJ33010 (74 minutes: DDD: 5/91).

...Volume 11. An den Tod, D518. Auf dem Wasser zu singen, D774. Auflösung, D807. Aus Heliopolis I, D753. Aus Heliopolis II, D754. Dithyrambe, D801. Elysium, D584. Der Geistertanz, D116. Der König in Thule, D367. Lied des Orpheus, D474. Nachtstück, D672. Schwanengesang, D744. Seligkeit, D433. So lasst mich scheinen, D727. Thekla, D595. Der Tod und das Mädchen, D531. Verklärung, D59. Vollendung, D989. Das Zügenglöcklein, D871. **Brigitte Fassbaender** (mez); **Graham Johnson** (pf). Hyperion Ⓔ CDJ33011 (65 minutes: DDD: 8/91).

...Volume 14. An die Leier, D737. Amphiaraos, D166. Gruppe aus dem Tartarus, D396. Gruppe aus dem Tartarus, D583. Hippolits Lied, D890. Memnon, D541. Fragment aus dem Aeschylus, D450. Philoktet, D540. Uraniens Flucht, D554. Hektors Abschied, D312. Antigone und Oedip, D542 (both with Marie McLaughlin, sop). Lied eines Schiffers an die Dioskuren, D360. Orest auf Tauris, D548. Der entsühnte Orest, D699. Der zürnenden Diana, D707. Freiwilliges Versinken, D700. Die Götter Griechenlands, D677. **Thomas Hampson** (bar); **Graham Johnson** (pf). Hyperion Ⓔ CDJ33014 (80 minutes: DDD: 4/92).

...Volume 15. An die untergehende Sonne, D457. Der Mondabend, D141. Klage an den Mond, D436. Die Mainacht, D194. Der Unglückliche, D713. An die Sonne, D270. Der Morgenkuss, D264. Kolmas Klage, D217. Ins stille Land, D403. Gondelfahrer, D808. Der Winterabend, D938. Der Wanderer an den Mond, D870. Im Freien, D880. Am Fenster, D878. Der blinde Knabe, D833. Die junge Nonne, D828. **Dame Margaret Price** (sop); **Graham Johnson** (pf). Hyperion Ⓔ CDJ33015 (72 minutes: DDD: 2/93).

...Volume 16. Leichenfantasie, D7. Laura am Klavier, D388. Die Entzückung an Laura – first version, D390, second version (completed van Hoorickx), D577. An die Freude, D189. An Emma, D113. Das Mädchen aus der Fremde, D117. Das Geheimnis, D793. Die Bürgschaft, D246. Der Jüngling am Bache, D638. Die vier Weltalter, D391. Sehnsucht, D52. Der Pilgrim, D794. **Thomas Allen** (bar); **Graham Johnson** (pf). Hyperion Ⓔ CDJ33016 (78 minutes: DDD: 3/93).

...Volume 17. Lied (Mutter geht durch ihre kammern), D373. Lodas Gespenst, D150. Klage, D371. Lorma, D376. Der Herbstabend, D405. Die Einsiedelei, D393. Der Herbstnacht, D404. Lied in der Abwesenheit, D416. Frühlingslied, D398. Winterlied, D401. Minnelied, D429. Aus Diego Manazares (Ilmerine), D458. Pflicht und Liebe, D467. An den Mond, D468. Litanei auf das Fest aller Seelen, D343. Geheimnis (An Franz Schubert), D491. Am Grabe Anselmos, D504. An die Nachtigall, D497. Klage um Ali Bey, D496a. Phidile, D500. Herbstlied, D502. Lebenslied, D508. Lieden der Trennung, D509. An mein Klavier, D342. **Lucia Popp** (sop); **Graham Johnson** (pf). Hyperion Ⓔ CDJ33017 (71 minutes: DDD: 6/93).

...Volume 18. Das Finden, D219. Die Nacht, D358. An den Schlaf, D477. Blumenlied, D431. Auf den Tod einer Nachtigall, D399. Erntelied, D434. An die Harmonie, D394. Das Heimweh, D456. Abendlied, D499. An die Entfernte, D765. Drang in die Ferne, D770. Das Heimweh, D851. Auf der Bruck, D853. Um Mitternacht, D862. Die Blume und der Quell, D874 (cpted. R. Van Hoorickx). Der liebliche Stern, D861. Tiefes Lied (Im Jänner 1817), D876. Im Walde, D834. Im Frühling, D882. Lebensmut, D883. Über Wildemann, D884. Am mein Herz, D860. **Peter Schreier** (ten); **Graham Johnson** (pf). Hyperion Ⓔ CDJ33018 (76 minutes: DDD: 7/93). *Gramophone Editor's choice.* Ⓖ

...Volume 21. Schlaflied D527. Sehnsucht, D516. Liebe, D522. Die Forelle, D550. Nur wer die Liebe kennt, D513a. Flug der Zeit, D515. Trost, D523. Die Abgeblühte Linde, D514. Das Lied vom Reifen, D532. An eine Quelle, D530. An die Musik, D547. Der Schäfer und der Reiter, D517. Hänflings Liebeswerbung, D552. Schweizerlied, D559. Liebhaber in allen Gestalten, D558. Abschied, D578. Erlafsee, D586. Lied eines Kindes, D596. Evangelium Johannis, D607. Lob der Tränen, D711. Grablied für die Mutter, D616. Der Blumenbrief, D622. Blondel zu Marien, D626. Vom Mitleiden Mariä, D632. **Edith Mathis** (sop); **Graham Johnson** (pf). Hyperion Ⓕ CDJ33021 (65 minutes: DDD: 8/94). *Gramophone Editor's choice.*   ⒼⒼ

...Volume 22. Trinklied, D148[efgh]. Morgenlied, D266[a]. An Sie, D288[e]. Das Mädchen aus der Fremde, D252[g]. Der Abend, D221[d]. Punschlied, D277[efgh]. An die Sonne, D272[a]. Das Leben ist ein Traum, D269[abd]. Die drei Sänger, D329 (cpted Hoorickx)[d]. Erinnerung: Die Erscheinung, D229[e]. Das Abendroth, D236[ach]. Genüg-samkeit, D143[d]. An Rosa I, D315[e]. An Rosa II, D316[e]. Das Bild, D155[e]. Furcht der Geliebten, D285[g]. Skolie, D306[e]. Cora an die Sonne, D263[d]. Die Sterne, D313[e]. Lob des Tokayers, D248[efgh]. Vaterlandslied, D287[a]. Gebet während der Schlacht, D171[g]. Hermann und Thusnelda, D322[ag]. Selma und Selmar, D286[ae]. Lorma, D327 (cpted Hoorickx)[d]. Cronnan, D282[ag]. Hymne an den Unendlichen, D232[bceh]. Das Grab, D330[efgh]. [a]**Lorna Anderson,** [a]**Patricia Rozario** (sops); [c]**Catherine Denley** (mez); [d]**Catherine Wyn-Rogers** (contr); [e]**Jamie MacDougall,** [f]**John Mark Ainsley** (tens); [g]**Simon Keenlyside** (bar); [h]**Michael George** (bass); **Graham Johnson** (pf). Hyperion Ⓕ CDJ33022 (78 minutes: DDD: 1/94).

New review

Schubert Lieder, Volume 24 – Schäfers Klagelied, D121[be]. An Mignon, D161[ae]. Geistes-Gruss, D142 (two versions)[de]. Rastlose Liebe, D138[be]. Der Gott und die Bajadere, D254[abde]. Tischlied, D234[ce]. Der Schatzgräber, D256[de]. Der Rattenfänger, D255[ce]. Bundeslied, D258[bcde]. Erlkönig, D328[abde]. Jägers Abendlied, D215[ce]. Jägers Abendlied, D368[ce]. Wer nie sein Brot mit Tränen ass, D480 (two versions)[be]. Nur wer die Sehnsucht kennt, D359[ae]. So lasst mich scheinen, D469a and D469b (two fragments)[ae]. Nur wer die Sehnsucht kennt, D481[ae]. Nur wer die Sehnsucht kennt, D656[f]. An Schwager Kronos, D369[ce]. Hoffnung, D295[de]. Mahomets Gesang, D549 (cptd. R. Van Hoorickx)[be]. Ganymed, D544[ae]. Der Goldschmiedsgesell, D560[ce]. Gesang der Geister über den Wassern, D484 (cptd. R. Van Hoorickx)[de]. Gesang der Geister über den Wassern, D705 (cptd. E. Asti)[ef]. [a]**Christine Schäfer** (sop); [b]**John Mark Ainsley** (ten); [c]**Simon Keenlyside** (bar); [d]**Michael George** (bass); [e]**Graham Johnson** (pf); [f]**London Schubert Chorale / Stephen Layton.** Hyperion Ⓕ CDJ33024 (79 minutes: DDD: 1/96). Texts and translations included. Recorded 1993-4.

Renewed praise first of all for Graham Johnson. This volume is as cogent an example as any of his method, a masterly exposition, in written words and musical performance, of the crucial relationship between Goethe and Schubert upon which Johnson throws a good deal of new light. As ever here the familiar happily rubs shoulders with the unfamiliar. Not all is notable Schubert, but the lesser songs, among them one or two hearty occasional pieces, merely serve to place in perspective the greater ones. The CD begins with one of the latter, *Schäfers Klagelied*, in a finely honed, dramatic performance by Ainsley, who is heard later on the disc always to advantage. Track 2 introduces Christine Schäfer, a kind of amalgam of Popp and Silja, if you can imagine such a singer. Good as she is in this first version of *An Mignon* she is better in the sadly neglected *Der Gott und die Bajadere*, as Johnson avers. This is the only song in the genre about prostitution, and a haunting one, even though, throughout its appreciable length, it relies on just one melody. Schäfer precisely catches its haunting atmosphere. But the climax of her contribution comes in *Ganymed*. With Johnson providing exactly the right rhythmic lilt at the piano, her voice conveys all the elation of poem and music. Schäfer is the child in a three-voice rendering of *Erlkönig*, a manner of performing the piece that has the composer's blessing. Johnson has surely never surpassed his account here of the hair-raisingly difficult piano part. Then he is just as accomplished with Keenlyside in a thrilling account of another masterpiece engendered by response to Goethe's genius, *An Schwager Kronos*. George, who perhaps has the least ingratiating songs to perform, sings with feeling and style but sometimes an excess of vibrato. A short review can only touch on the most significant delights in what is an engrossing and invaluable addition to this series.

Schubert Lieder – Gruppe aus dem Tartarus, D583. Litanei auf das Fest Allerseelen, D343. Die Forelle, D550. An die Leier, D737. Lachen und Weinen, D777. Schwanengesang, D957 – No. 4, Ständchen; No. 10, Das Fischermädchen; No. 14, Die Taubenpost. Meerestille, D216. Der Wanderer, D489 (formerly D493). Erlkönig, D328. Der Tod und das Mädchen, D531. Heidenröslein, D257. Wandrers Nachtlied II, D768. An die Musik, D547. Auf der Bruck, D853. Schäfers Klagelied, D121. An Silvia, D891. Du bist die Ruh', D776. An die Laute, D905. Rastlose Liebe, D138. Ganymed, D544. Der Musensohn, D764. **Bryn Terfel** (bass-bar); **Malcolm Martineau** (pf). DG Ⓕ 445 294-2GH (69 minutes: DDD: 10/94). Texts and translations included. Recorded 1994. *Gramophone* Award Winner 1995. *Gramophone Editor's choice.*   ⒼⒼ

Terfel's gift, now well-known, is a generous, individual voice, a natural feeling for German and an inborn ability to go to the heart of what he attempts. His singing here is grand in scale – listen to any of the dramatic songs and the point is made – but like Hotter, whom he so often resembles, he is able to reduce his large voice to the needs of a sustained, quiet line, as in *Meerestille*. When the two come together as in *Der Wanderer*, the effect can be truly electrifying, even more so, perhaps, in *Erlkönig* where the four participants are superbly contrasted. Yet this is a voice that can also smile, as in *An die Laute* and "Die Taubenpost" or express wonder, as in *Ganymed*, a most exhilarating interpretation, or again explode in sheer anger as in the very first song, the strenuous *Gruppe aus dem Tartarus*. Terfel is not afraid to employ rubato and vibrato to make his points and above all to take us right into his interpretations rather than leave us admiring them, as it were, from afar. Throughout, Martineau's at once vigorous and subtle playing is an apt support: his accompaniment in *Erlkönig* is arrestingly clear and precise.

Additional recommendation ...

...An den Mond, D259. An Schwager Kronos, D369. Meeres Stille, D216. Erlkönig, D328. Geheimes, D719. Der Musensohn, D764. *Coupled with works by* **Amalia, Reichardt, Zelter, Beethoven, Schumann, Brahms, R. Strauss, Schoeck, Reger, Busoni** and **Wolf Dietrich Fischer-Dieskau** (bar); **Karl Engel** (pf). Orfeo D'Or mono Ⓔ C389951B* (72 minutes: ADD: 2/96).

Schubert Im Abendrot, D799. Die Sterne, D939. Nacht und Träume, D827. Der liebliche Stern, D861. Der Vollmond strahlt, D797 No. 3b. Der Einsame, D800. Schlaflied, D527. An Silvia, D891. Das Mädchen, D652. Minnelied, D429. Die Liebe hat gelogen, D751. Du liebst mich nicht, D756. An die Laute, D905. Der Blumenbrief, D622. Die Männer sind méchant, D866 No. 3. Seligkeit, D433 (all from ᵃ6500 704, 1/76). Nachtviolen, D752. Du bist die Ruh, D776 (both from ᵃ9500 350, 6/78). Das Lied im Grünen, D917. Der Schmetterling, D633. An die Nachtigall, D497. An die Nachtigall, D196. Der Wachtelschlag, D742. Im Freien, D880. Die Vögel, D691. Fischerweise, D881. Die Gebüsche, D646. Im Haine, D738 (ᵃ6500 706, 10/75). Kennst du das Land, D321. Nur wer die Sehnsucht kennt, D877 No. 4. Heiss mich nicht reden, D877 No. 2. So lasst mich scheinen, D877 No. 3. Die Liebende schreibt, D673. Nähe des Geliebten, D162. Heidenröslein, D257. Liebhaber in allen Gestalten, D558 (6500 515, 7/74). Die junge Nonne, D828. Der König in Thule, D367. Gretchen am Spinnrade, D118. Gretchens Bitte, D564. Szene aus Goethes Faust, D126 (with Meinard Kraak, ten; chorus and org). Suleika I, D720. Suleika II, D717. Raste Kreiger!, D837. Jäger, ruhe von der Jagd, D838. Ave Maria, D839 (ᵃ9500 169, 4/78). An die Musik, D547. Schwestergrüss, D762. Sei mir gegrüsst, D741. Die Blumensprache, D519. An den Mond, D296. Abendbilder, D650. Frühlingssehnsucht, D957 No. 3. Erster Verlust, D226. Nachthymne, D687. Die Sterne, D684. Der Knabe, D692. Wiegenlied, D498. Berthas Lied in der Nacht, D653 (ᵃ6514 298, 6/83). Ganymed, D544. Die Götter Griechenlands, D677. Der Musensohn, D764. Fülle der Liebe, D854. Sprache der Liebe, D410. Schwanengesang, D744. An den Tod, D518. Die Forelle, D550. Am Bach im Frühling, D361. Auf dem Wasser zu singen, D774. Der Schiffer, D694. An die Entfernte, D765. Sehnsucht, D516. An die untergehende Sonne, D457. Abendröte, D690 (ᵇ416 294-2PH, 8/87). **Elly Ameling** (sop); ᵃ**Dalton Baldwin**, ᵇ**Rudolf Jansen** (pfs). Philips The Early Years Ⓜ 438 528-2PM4 (four discs: 260 minutes: ADD/DDD: 4/94). Texts included. Recorded 1972-84.

The first *Im Abendrot* (the Lappe setting) introduces the smiling Ameling of 1973, her voice basking in the images of golden shafts of light, and rapt in an easeful legato. In the shorter vowels and pulsing pianistic light of *Die Sterne*, she still finds serenity, just as in *Der Einsame* the poet's solitude is sensed at the heart of a tingling, sentient world. The expressive subtlety of these performances comes from an unique fusion of response between Ameling and Baldwin during this period. In the second disc, their creative empathy is turned to Schubert's settings of Goethe. Ameling focuses on the vulnerability and childlike eagerness of Mignon, missing, perhaps, the nervous feverishness which lies just below the surface of these songs, and which Wolf was to exploit to the full. After one of the most perfectly scaled performances of *Heidenröslein* on disc, Ameling and Baldwin turn to Goethe's Gretchen and Suleika, and to Scott's Ellen. Gretchen's searing vision at the spinning-wheel is answered by the rarely heard *Szene aus Goethes Faust* in which Ameling finds herself in the company of an anonymous and very spooky *Böser Geist*, as well as a ghostly choir who seem piped in from another planet. Seven years later, Ameling turns to a still stranger spirit world. The third disc, recorded in 1982, includes the lunar beauty of Schubert's Bruchmann setting, *Schwestergrüss*, articulated by a voice bleached of any colour. It is almost impossible to detect any sense of ageing in the voice here. Characterized by songs which search out the most elusive of soul moods, this third recital reveals Ameling's soprano at its most finely nuanced, in songs such as *Abendbilder* and the Novalis *Nachthymne*. In the final disc, at the age of 50, Ameling took on the challenge of some of Schubert's most visionary songs: facing Schiller's Greek gods, Goethe's Ganymed, Schlegel's *Der Schiffer* and moving through Mayrhofer's longing to Schlegel's final sunset. These songs stretch the voice and the mind to its very limits, yet Ameling's artistry seems to grow with the music itself. Collectors should probably be warned that the set includes full texts but no translations. In the end, though, Ameling's singing renders them all but redundant.

Additional recommendations ...

...Der Hirt auf dem Felsen, D965 (with Hans Deinzer, cl). Seligkeit, D433. Gretchen am Spinnrade, D118. Du liebst mich nicht, D756. Heimliches Lieben, D922. Im Frühling, D882. Die Vögel, D691. Der Jüngling an der Quelle, D300. Der Musensohn, D764. **Schumann** Myrthen, Op. 25 Widmung; Der Nussbaum. Aufträge, Op. 77 No. 5. Sehnsucht, Op. 51 No. 1. Frage, Op. 35 No. 9. Mein schöner Stern, Op. 101 No. 4. Lieder Album für die Jugend, Op. 79 – Schmetterling; Käuzlein; Der Sandmann; Marienwürmchen; Er ists's; Schneeglöckchen. Erstes Grün, Op. 35 No. 4. Die Sennin, Op. 90 No. 4. Sehnsucht nach der Waldgegend, Op. 35 No. 5. Jasminenstrauch, Op. 27 No. 4. Liederkreis, Op. 39 – Waldesgespräch. Loreley, Op. 53 No. 2.

Die Meerfee, Op. 125 No. 1. **Elly Ameling** (sop); **Jörg Demus** (fp). Deutsche Harmonia Mundi
Editio Classica Ⓜ GD77085 (69 minutes: ADD: 5/90). 🖅
…Suleika I, D720. Suleika II, D717. Du bist die Ruh, D776. Schwestergrüss, D762. Die Forelle,
D550. Raste Kriege!, D837. Jager, rühe von der Jagd, D838. Ave Maria, D839. *Coupled with
works by* **Wagner, Mozart** and **Weber Gundula Janowitz** (sop); **Irwin Gage** (pf); **Vienna
Symphony Orchestra / Wilfried Boettcher; Orchestra of the Deutsche Staatsoper, Berlin /
Ferdinand Leitner.** DG Double Ⓜ 447 352-2GDB2 (two discs: 152 minutes: ADD: 12/95).

New review

Schubert Songs to poems by Goethe. Am Flusse, D160. Trost in Tränen, D120. Schäfers
Klagelied, D121. Meeres Stille, D216. Heidenröslein, D257. Jägers Abendlied, D368. Sehnsucht,
D123. Die Liebe, D210. Rastlose Liebe, D138. Nähe des Geliebten, D162. Der Fischer, D225.
Erster Verlust, D226. Der König in Thule, D367. Wer sich der Einsamkeit ergibt, D478. An die
Türen, D479. Wer nie sein Brot mit Tränen ass, D480. An Schwager Kronos, D369. An Mignon,
D161. Ganymed, D544. An die Entfernte, D765. Versunken, D715. An den Mond, D259. Der
Musensohn, D764. Auf dem See, D543. Geistes-Gruss, D142. **Christoph Prégardien** (ten);
Andreas Staier (fp). Deutsche Harmonia Mundi Ⓟ 05472 77342-2 (70 minutes: DDD: 6/96).
Texts and translations included. Recorded 1994.

Prégardien proves himself just as adept at such a light piece as *Heidenröslein* as in the still, solemn
thoughts of *Meeres Stille*, or the forceful challenge of *An Schwager Kronos*; the eager striving of
Ganymed, or the spring-like joy of *Der Musensohn*, adapting his flexible tone to the varying
requirements of each. The reading of the *Harfenspieler Lieder* forms the centrepiece of the recital, the
singer catching the melancholy and mystery so unerringly suggested by the composer himself. The
books speak unkindly of *Sehnsucht*, but Prégardien, a superb Bach interpreter, brings out the
connection with the older composer in the recitative of this cantata-like song. Staier again seems the
ideal partner for this singer. His luminous playing of his fortepiano, notably in such a piece as *An den
Mond*, exactly matches the ethereal beauty of the tenor's performance. Once or twice we may wish for
the more substantial tones of a Fischer-Dieskau or a Schreier with their attendant 'modern' pianists,
but the older interpreters' gifts are, in a sense, complementary to and different from the younger
artists. The natural, well-balanced recording allows us to hear all the subtleties to be found in these
performances, which pay homage, in their verbal detailing, as much to poet as to composer.

Schubert Der Einsame, D800. Ständchen, D889. An Silvia, D891. Der Jüngling an der Quelle,
D300. Lied eines Schiffers, D360. Gruppe aus dem Tartarus, D583. Die Götter Griechenlands,
D677. Im Walde, D708. Der Wanderer an den Mond, D870. Freiwilliges Versinken, D700.
Himmelsfunken, D651. Prometheus, D674. Gondelfahrer, D808. Die Sterne, D939. Auf der
Bruck, D853. Heidenröslein, D257. Im Haine, D738. Nachtviolen, D752. Bei dir allein, D866/2.
Du bist die Ruh, D776. **Simon Keenlyside** (bar); **Malcolm Martineau** (pf). EMI Eminence
Ⓜ CD-EMX2224 (71 minutes: DDD: 8/94). Texts and translations included. *Gramophone
Editor's choice.*   Ⓖ

Simon Keenlyside is the best baritone singer and interpreter of Schubert this country has ever had
and is fully the equal of such Austro-German coevals as Holzmair and Schmidt. Hyperbole? Anyone
who hears this enriching recital will not think so. Keenlyside has just about all the attributes needed
by a Schubert interpreter: a magnificent tone, firm and natural, rounded throughout an extensive
register, an inborn sense of line, perfect German, and in addition to all that an instinctive intelligence
that carries him confidently through his long and taxing programme with hardly a phrase that could
be bettered in terms of colour or word-painting. You can sit back without a qualm knowing that he
will have the reserves and the trenchancy of purpose to conquer such Everests of the Schubert
repertory as *Prometheus* and *Gruppe aus dem Tartarus* where his vocal means are fully equal to the
defiance the songs proclaim. *Auf der Bruck* is filled with the ongoing energy Schubert calls for. Then
there's the thoughtfulness to fulfil the demands of such a philosophical and forward-looking song as
Freiwilliges Versinken, the sense of questing romanticism for *Im Walde*. Among the reflective pieces,
Die Götter Griechenlands is notable for plangent feeling and tone – just right. *Gondelfahrer*, that
marvellous evocation of bells heard at night, is full of nocturnal mystery. *Heidenröslein* is delicate in its
subtle timbres and smiling tone; so is *Die Sterne* while *Bei dir allein* has a Fischer-Dieskau enthusiasm.
And the recital is crowned by the final offering, *Du bist die Ruh*, where the voice opens out in its full
beauty. These successes make the one or two failures mystifying. They come at the start of the disc so
perhaps the performers weren't yet into their stride. *Der Einsame* plods at an unduly slow tempo.
Ständchen lacks airiness, Martineau's foursquare accompanying thereabouts doesn't help. Later he
provides many inspired moments (try *Im Haine*, where he so charmingly supports the baritone's *mezzo
voce*), and he never over-eggs the pudding in the heavier songs. The recording is ideally balanced and
judged but the texts and translations have been carelessly read. However, any trifling drawbacks don't
prevent an outright recommendation for this well chosen and absorbing mid-price disc.

Schubert Schwanengesang, D957. Herbst, D945. Der Wanderer an den Mond, D870. Am Fenster,
D878. Bei dir allein, D866 No. 2. **Peter Schreier** (ten); **András Schiff** (pf). Decca Ⓟ 425 612-2DH
(63 minutes: DDD: 6/90). Texts and translations included. Recorded 1989. *Gramophone Award
Winner 1990.*   ⒼⒼⒼ

Schubert Schwanengesang, D957. Sehnsucht, D879. Der Wanderer an den Mond, D870.
  Wiegenlied, D867. Am Fenster, D878. Herbst, D945. **Brigitte Fassbaender** (mez); **Aribert Reimann**
  (pf). DG Ⓕ 429 766-2GH (68 minutes: DDD: 6/92). Texts and translations included.
  Recorded 1989-91. *Gramophone Award Winner 1992.*   Ⓖ

Though *Schwanengesang* is not a song-cycle but a collection of Schubert's last (or 'swan') songs by their
first publisher, it is generally felt to form a satisfying sequence, with a unity of style if not of theme or
mood. This is certainly not weakened by the addition on the Decca disc of the four last songs which
were originally omitted, all of them settings of poems by Johann Seidl. Seidl is one of the three poets
whose work Schubert used in these frequently sombre songs and it is strange to think that all concerned
in their creation were young men, none of the poets being older than Schubert. The listener can
scarcely be unaware of a shadow or sometimes an almost unearthly radiance over even the happiest
(such as "Die Taubenpost", the last of all) and that is particularly true when the performers themselves
have such sensitive awareness as here. Peter Schreier is responsive to every shade of meaning in music
and text; graceful and charming in "Das Fischermädchen", flawlessly lyrical in "Am Meer", he will
sometimes risk an almost frightening raw-boned cry as in the anguish of "Der Atlas" and "Der
Doppelgänger". András Schiff's playing is a miracle of combined strength and delicacy, specific insight
and general rightness. One of the great Lieder recordings, and not merely of recent years.

Fassbaender and Reimann offer something equally compelling but rather different in their account
of *Schwanengesang*. Fassbaender's interpretation, idiosyncratic in every respect, pierces to the heart
of the bleak songs with performances as daring and challenging as the playing of her partner. More
than anyone, these two artists catch the fleeting moods of these mini-dramas, and their searing
originality of concept. Even the lighter songs have a special individuality of utterance. This is a
starkly immediate interpretation that leaves the listener shattered. The extra Seidl settings, rarely
performed, are all worth hearing. The true lover of Lieder will need to have both these notable
partnerships, superb in their own, searching ways.

Additional recommendations ...

...Schwanengesang. **Bryn Terfel** (bass-bar); **Malcolm Martineau** (pf). Sain Ⓕ SCDC4035
  (57 minutes: DDD: 5/92).
...Schwanengesang. Die schöne Müllerin, D795. Winterreise, D911. **Dietrich Fischer-Dieskau** (bar);
  Gerald Moore (pf). DG Ⓑ 437 235-2GX3 (three discs: 184 minutes: ADD: 3/93). *Part of the set
  reviewed above.*
...Schwanengesang, D957[a]. An die Musik, D547[b]. Meeres Stille, D216[b]. Im Frühling, D882[b]. Am
  Bach im Frühling, D361[c]. Gruppe aus dem Tartarus, D583[d]. Geheimes, D719[e]. Sei mir gegrüsst,
  D741[c]. Im Abendrot, D799[e]. Wandrers Nachtlied I, D224[c]. Wandrers Nachtlied II, D768[c]. **Hans
  Hotter** (bass-bar), **Gerald Moore** (pf). EMI Références mono Ⓜ CDH5 65196-2* (78 minutes:
  ADD: 10/94).
...Schwanengesang, D957 – Der Atlas; Ihr Bild; Das Fischermädchen; Die Stadt; Am Meer; Der
  Doppelgänger. **Mendelssohn** Lieder, Op. 19*a* – No. 4, Neue Liebe; No. 5, Gruss. Lieder, Op. 34
  – No.2, Auf Flügeln des Gesanges; No. 6, Reiselied. Morgengruss, Op. 47 No. 2. Allnächtlich im
  Träume, Op. 86 No. 4. **Schumann** Dichterliebe, Op. 48. **Christoph Prégardien** (ten); **Andreas
  Staier** (fp). Deutsche Harmonia Mundi Ⓕ 05472 77319-2 (57 minutes: DDD: 12/94). ☞ *See
  review under Schumann; refer to the Index to Reviews.*   Ⓠ
...An Schwager Kronos, D369. Hoffnung, D295. Auf der Donau, D553. Der Strom, D565. Der
  Wanderer, D649. Die Götter Griechenlands, D677. Freiwilliges Versinken, D700. Der Zwerg,
  D771. Wehmut, D772. Totengräbers Heimwehe, D842. Auf der Brück, D853. Des Sängers Habe,
  D832. Am Fenster, D878. Fischerweise, D881. Das Zügenglöcklein, D871. Der Kreuzzug, D932.
  Des Fischers Liebesglück, D933. Die Sterne, D939. Der Einsame, D800. Im Abendrot, D799.
  Schwanengesang, D957 – Abschied. **Dietrich Fischer-Dieskau** (bar); **Hartmut Höll** (pf). Erato Ⓕ
  4509-98493-2 (77 minutes: DDD: 9/95).

New review

Schubert Lieder, Volume 25. Die schöne Müllerin, D795, with a reading of six poems not set by
  Schubert. **Ian Bostridge** (ten); **Dietrich Fischer-Dieskau** (narr); **Graham Johnson** (pf). Hyperion
  Ⓕ CDJ33025 (73 minutes: DDD). Text and translation included. Recorded 1994-5. *Gramophone
  Editor's choice*   Ⓖ Ⓖ Ⓠ
Schubert Die schöne Müllerin, D795. **Wolfgang Holzmair** (bar); **Jörg Demus** (pf). Preiser
  Ⓕ 93337 (68 minutes: ADD: 3/89). Recorded 1984.
Schubert Die schöne Müllerin, D795. **Håkan Hagegård** (bar); **Emanuel Ax** (pf). RCA Victor Red
  Seal Ⓕ 09026 61705-2 (61 minutes: DDD: 2/95). Texts and translations included. Recorded 1987.

The 20 songs of *Die schöne Müllerin* portray a Wordsworthian world of heightened emotion in the
pantheistic riverside setting of the miller. The poet, Wilhelm Müller, tells of solitary longings,
jealousies, fears and hopes as the river rushes by, driving the mill-wheel and refreshing the natural
world. Bostridge and Johnson go to the heart of the matter, the young tenor in his aching tones and
naturally affecting interpretation, the pianist in his perceptive, wholly apposite playing – and, of
course, in his extensive notes. The sum of their joint efforts is a deeply satisfying experience. Bostridge
shares with Partridge the right timbre for the protagonist and a straightforward approach, with
Schreier a deeper journey into the meaning of each song, with Prégardien a liquid, refined line, and
with all three an instinctive rightness of phrasing. Bostridge's peculiarly beseeching voice enshrines

the vulnerability, tender feeling and obsessive love of the youthful miller, projecting in turn the young lover's thwarted passions, self-delusions and, finally, inner tragedy. Nowhere does he stretch beyond the bounds of the possible, as even Schreier just occasionally does, everything expressed in eager then doleful tones. Johnson suggests that "Ungeduld" mustn't be "masterful and insistent" or the youth would have won the girl, so that even in this superficially buoyant song the sense of a sensitive, sad, introverted youth is maintained. The daydreaming strophic songs have the smiling, innocent, intimate sound that suits them to perfection, the angry ones the touch of stronger metal that Bostridge can now add to his silver, the tragic ones before the neutral "Baches Wiegenlied" an inner intensity that rends the heart as it should. An occasional moment of faulty German accenting matters not at all when the sense of every word is perceived.

As a bonus we have here, as on the Fassbaender recording, a recitation of the Prologue and Epilogue and of the Müller poems not set by Schubert: Fischer-Dieskau, who for various reasons set out by Johnson, didn't, regretfully, have a part in this series as a singer now graces it with his speaking voice. The ideal Hyperion recording catches everything in very present terms, as it does Johnson's own adumbration in his playing of what he writes in his notes. In all musical matters, everything Johnson writes only enhances one's enjoyment, if that is the right word, of a soul-searching interpretation which now ranks with those tenor versions listed below as a recommendation.

Simply as a voice Hagegård is perhaps superior to that of any of those singers reviewed and listed here. It is, paradoxically, a light yet heroic sound, typically Swedish in timbre, flexible throughout its range and – relevant to the work in hand – tenor-like in tone. Its owner uses it with marked attention to vocal verities, never disturbing a sure legato, placing his words firmly and naturally on it. The eager youth of the early songs is unerringly enacted, perhaps without quite the sense of vulnerability suggested by Holzmair and other tenor interpreters, although by the same token he suggests an appropriately open-air, fresh youth. When sorrow, jealousy and eventually heartbreak enter the lad's life, Hagegård projects these with as much conviction yet without a hint of exaggeration or sentimentality. He, and the sensitive but never obtrusive Ax, allow Schubert to speak for himself in sensible, moderate speeds and discreet phrasing: in the context of frequent repetitions, this has undoubted advantages. Holzmair and Demus, Schmidt and Jansen do much the same. It would be hard to choose among these three versions if you wanted a straightforward reading, but the sheerly beautiful sound of Hagegård's voice places him marginally in front. Bär and, most of all, Fischer-Dieskau peer deeper into the songs and the youth's psychology – but Hagegård and his partner probably come closer to a truly Schubertian ideal. The recording is ideally balanced.

Additional recommendations ...

...Die schöne Müllerin. **Dietrich Fischer-Dieskau** (bar); **Gerald Moore** (pf). DG Ⓔ 415 186-2GH (62 minutes: ADD: 9/85).   Ⓖ

...Die schöne Müllerin. **Josef Protschka** (ten); **Helmut Deutsch** (pf). Capriccio Ⓔ 10 082 (66 minutes: DDD: 6/87).

...Die schöne Müllerin. **Olaf Bär** (bar); **Geoffrey Parsons** (pf). EMI Ⓔ CDC7 47947-2 (65 minutes: DDD: 8/87).

...Die schöne Müllerin. **Siegfried Lorenz** (bar); **Norman Shetler** (pf). Capriccio Ⓔ 10 220 (68 minutes: DDD: 5/90).

...Die schöne Müllerin. **Peter Schreier** (ten); **András Schiff** (pf). Decca Ⓕ 430 414-2DH (63 minutes: DDD: 5/91). *Selected by Sounds in Retrospect.*   ⒼⒼ

...Die schöne Müllerin. **Christoph Prégardien** (ten); **Andreas Staier** (fp). Deutsche Harmonia Mundi Ⓕ 05472 77273-2 (60 minutes: DDD: 12/92). 🖉

...Die schöne Müllerin. **Beethoven** An die ferne Geliebte, Op. 98. **Gerhard Hüsch** (bar); **Hanns Udo Müller** (pf). Preiser Lebendige Vergangenheit mono Ⓔ 89202* (two discs: 137 minutes: AAD: 12/92).

...Die schöne Müllerin. Schwanengesang, D957 – Die Taubenpost. Der Einsame, D800. An die Laute, D905. **Sir Peter Pears** (ten); **Benjamin Britten** (pf). Decca Ⓜ 436 201-2DM (73 minutes: ADD: 8/93).

...Die schöne Müllerin. **Ian Partridge** (ten); **Jennifer Partridge** (pf). Classics for Pleasure Ⓑ CD-CFP4672 (63 minutes: ADD: 9/95).   Ⓖ

...Die schöne Müllerin. **Peter Schreier** (ten); **Konrad Ragossnig** (gtr). Berlin Classics Ⓔ 0011 232BC (65 minutes: ADD: 3/96).

Schubert Winterreise, D911. **Peter Schreier** (ten); **András Schiff** (pf). Decca Ⓕ 436 122-2DH (72 minutes: DDD: 5/94). Text and translation included. Recorded 1991. *Gramophone Editor's choice.*   ⒼⒼ

Schubert Winterreise, D911. **Bernd Weikl** (bar); **Helmut Deutsch** (pf). Nightingale Classics Ⓕ NC070960-2 (70 minutes: DDD: 5/95). Text and translation included. Recorded 1993.

New review

Schubert Winterreise, D911. **Dietrich Fischer-Dieskau** (bar); **Jörg Demus** (pf). DG The Originals Ⓜ 447 421-2GOR (71 minutes: ADD: 8/95). Text and translation included. From SLPM139201/2 (6/66). Recorded 1965.

New review

Schubert Winterreise, D911. **Wolfgang Holzmair** (bar); **Imogen Cooper** (pf). Philips Ⓕ 446 407-2PH (70 minutes: DDD: 5/96). Text and translation included. Recorded 1994.

Winterreise can lay claim to be the greatest song cycle ever written. It chronicles the sad, numbing journey of a forsaken lover, recalling past happiness, anguishing over his present plight, commenting on how the snow-clad scenery reflects or enhances his mood. Schreier himself, in his note in the booklet accompanying his recording, refers to the unique density and spiritual concentration of the songs; that, and their hallucinatory nature, inform this riveting performance from start to finish, nowhere more so than in "Wasserflut" and "Einsamkeit". The latter is a paradigm of the whole searing, almost unbearable experience. If you can tolerate it you will be engaged and surely moved by the whole. In this song, Schreier leans into the words and notes of "Ach, das die Luft so ruhig!" suggesting the cry of a desperate, tormented soul – as does the emphatic enunciation of the single word "Bergstroms" earlier, in "Irricht". Also arresting is the curiously daring way Schreier asks the question at the end of "Die Post", as if it were a spontaneous afterthought. These make the moments of calm and repose all the more eerie. The sad delicacy of Schiff's playing at the start of "Frühlingstraum" sets the scene of the imagined May to perfection, and the flowing lift of his left hand in "Täuschung" is as deceptively friendly as the light described by the singer. "Das Wirtshaus" is all false resignation: voice and piano tell us of the man's tired emptiness. Anger and defiance, as in the earlier performance, are registered in raw, chilling tone and phraseology. Then, in the pair's revelatory way, they draw attention anew to the originality of concept of "Letzte Hoffnung". The final songs taken simply, speak beautifully of acceptance. The disc further benefits from the warm yet clear acoustic of the recording. Viewing the whole scene, it matches Fassbaender in its unbridled involvement. Fischer-Dieskau is still there as another kind of benchmark for those who prefer a lower, more amenable voice in this cycle.

For those who prefer a baritone Weikl seriously challenges the hegemony, among lower-voiced singers, of the versions listed below. Indeed it is the absolute vocal security and evenness of Weikl's actual singing that so impresses even before one considers his view of the work, and in that he recalls Schmidt on DG. Nowhere is there any sign of strain, overemphasis, faltering in pitch, or failure of nerve in executing a phrase with a long breath, and as the singer has such a strong voice one feels throughout that there is always something held in reserve. As a reading the Weikl unerringly keeps that balance between detachment and subjectivity. Tempos are in every case perfectly judged – and here Deutsch's well-observed and well-balanced playing makes a significant contribution – a wonderful frozen feeling in "Auf dem Flusse", for instance. Weikl displays many gradations of tone to enhance his thought-through reading – "Gefrorne Tränen" is a good example – but he uses vocal emphases more sparingly, reserving his most pointed verbal accents for such things as "Gras" in "Erstarrung", "Hähne" in "Frühlingstraum" and "Hunde" in "Im Dorfe", but even these never upset the verities of line and firm tone, and the sheer beauty of the singing, as in "Der Lindenbaum", is balm to the ear. For those who find Fischer-Dieskau's more agonized, psychological readings too much to bear, or find his style too interventionist, Weikl is the obvious choice. A superb recording.

The issue in the DG Originals series of Fischer-Dieskau's *Winterreise* was recorded in 1965. On the verge of his fifth decade, the singer was in his absolute prime – and it shows. Indeed listening to his interpretation is like coming home to base after many interesting encounters away from the familiar. Indeed, it is possibly the finest of all in terms of beauty of tone and ease of technique – and how beautiful, how smooth and velvety was the baritone's voice at that time. That this is the most interior, unadorned and undemonstrative of Fischer-Dieskau's readings perhaps arises from the fact that Demus, a discerning musician and sure accompanist, is the most reflective of all the singer's many partners in the cycle. Demus never strikes out on his own, is always there unobtrusively and subtly supportive, with the right colour and phrasing, literally in hand. Given an intimate, slightly dry recording, finely remastered, the whole effect is of a pair communing with each other and stating the sad, distraught message of Schubert's bleak work in terms of a personal message to the listener in the home. A deeply rewarding performance. Certainly if you want Fischer-Dieskau in the cycle you need look no further.

As far as Holzmair is concerned, we are at the opposite extreme from Fischer-Dieskau's big-scale approach with its huge variety of tonal colour and expression, much nearer to Schmidt, who has a more rounded tone than Holzmair but doesn't match the Austrian's personal involvement. Bär and Weikl lie somewhere in between Holzmair and Fischer-Dieskau, their readings bigger in scale than Holzmair's but not as overtly dramatic as the older baritone's. Among the pianists, Demus and Jansen come closest to Cooper's penetrating *aperçus*. Absolute recommendations are simply not possible. Yet Holzmair and Cooper give us such a natural, unvarnished view of the great work, that their CD deserves to stand as recommendation, among baritone interpretations, with the others.

Additional recommendations ...

...Winterreise. **Peter Schreier** (ten); **Sviatoslav Richter** (pf). Philips Ⓕ 442 360-2PH (77 minutes: DDD: 9/94).

...Winterreise. **Dietrich Fischer-Dieskau** (bar); **Alfred Brendel** (pf). Philips Ⓕ 411 463-2PH (70 minutes: DDD: 12/86).

...Winterreise. **Robert Holl** (bass-bar); **Konrad Richter** (pf). Preiser Ⓕ 93317 (72 minutes: ADD: 8/89).

...Winterreise. **Olaf Bär** (bar); **Geoffrey Parsons** (pf). EMI Ⓔ CDC7 49334-2 (75 minutes: DDD: 11/89).

...Winterreise. **Brigitte Fassbaender** (mez); **Aribert Reimann** (pf). EMI Ⓔ CDC7 49846-2 (70 minutes: DDD: 7/90).

…Winterreise. **Sir Peter Pears** (ten); **Benjamin Britten** (pf). Decca Ⓜ 417 473-2DM (73 minutes: ADD: 10/91).

…Winterreise. **Max van Egmond** (bar); **Jos van Immerseel** (fp). Channel Classics Ⓕ CCS0190 (67 minutes: DDD: 3/92). ✍

…Winterreise. **Dietrich Fischer-Dieskau** (bar); **Daniel Barenboim** (pf). DG Classikon Ⓑ 439 432-2GGL (73 minutes: ADD: 9/94).

Further listening …

…Sonata for Piano Duet in C major, D812, "Grand Duo". Eight Variations in A flat major, D813. Grande Marche in E flat major, D819 No. 1. **Isabel Beyer, Harvey Dagul** (pf duet). Four Hands Music FHMD893 (6/94).

…Introduction and Variations in E minor on "Trockne Blumen" from "Die schöne Müllerin", D802. *Coupled with works by* **Liszt** *and* **Ernst** Gidon Kremer (vn); Oleg Maisenberg (pf). DG 445 820-2GH (10/95). *See review under Ernst; refer to the Index to Reviews.*

…Fierrabras. **Soloists; Arnold Schönberg Choir; Chamber Orchestra of Europe / Claudio Abbado.** DG 427 341-2GH2 (10/90).

Ervin Schulhoff
Bohemian 1894-1942

New review

Schulhoff Concerto for String Quartet and Orchestra[a]. Symphonies – No. 2; No. 3. [a]**Kyncl Quartet** (Pavel Kyncl, Eduard Krivý, vns; Vladimir Kovár, va; Václav Horák, vc); **Czech State Philharmonic Orchestra, Brno / Israel Yinon.** Koch Schwann Ⓕ 315432 (62 minutes: DDD: 2/96). Recorded 1993-4.

This compilation is valuable in showing us how the *provocateur* of the 1920s sought to transform himself into a purveyor of music for the masses. With no Schulhoff performance tradition to speak of and a wide range of interpretative options, Yinon's solutions seem more deeply considered than those of his peers. Music that can seem to be running on empty is here always carefully shaped and relatively continuous. The Brno State Philharmonic play well for him and the recording quality is good. Schulhoff's Second Symphony (1932) represents a partial return to the priorities of his student days, juggling with the traditional Austro-German archetypes to fabricate a more easily accessible, if still ambivalent, form of new music. It was supposed to be a new start; instead it was the last of his compositions to be publicly performed. Although you might agree with the conductor that the piece sits somewhat uncomfortably between the antic posture of No. 1 and the full-blown socialist realism of No. 3, it has been recorded several times. As in his reading of the First Symphony, Yinon is comparatively weighty and intense in the slower music, tauter and springier elsewhere. The Concerto is, for Schulhoff, an uncharacteristically austere utterance. The Third Symphony (1935) will always be a problem piece, more interesting as a historical artefact than as pure music. Yinon's treatment suggests that he at least is unembarrassed by it.

New review

Schulhoff Symphony No. 1. Suite for Chamber Orchestra. Flammen – festive overture. **Brno State Philharmonic Orchestra / Israel Yinon.** Koch Schwann Ⓕ 314372 (56 minutes: DDD: 8/95). Recorded 1993-4.

Ⓖ

This is the finest all-Schulhoff orchestral CD in the catalogue, deeply pondered and carefully prepared. The First Symphony's folk colouring is of the sophisticated urban variety complete with pseudo-orientalism and jazz. The form retains its loose-knit, woolly jumper feel, but, since Schulhoff's music sometimes seems to exist for no other purpose than to poke fun at other people's, it is difficult to gauge what might be the 'correct' degree of integration. This is music of continuous incident rather than inexorable logic, the composer being at pains to distance his own 'varied unity' from the 'pathos' and 'heroism' characteristic of Austro-German symphonic processes. The *Festliches Vorspiel*, written as an overture for the Second Act of the opera *Flammen* ("Flames") in 1929, was also designated by the composer as an independent piece. It finds him feeling towards a new, more overtly expressive, 'mass' idiom, sacrificing some of his textural refinement in the process. The combination of compositional overkill and cloudy recording is not altogether persuasive. The *Suite for Chamber Orchestra*, originally entitled "Suite in the New Style", comes from earlier in the decade when Schulhoff had just discovered the liberating potential of jazz. Koch's disc is helpfully annotated and deserves to reach a wide public. Both orchestra and venue sometimes seem a little big for the idiom but the music-making has personality and is not easily swamped.

New review

Schulhoff Sextet[a]. String Quartet in G major, Op. 25[b]. Duo[c]. Solo Violin Sonata[d]. [a]**Rainer Johannes Kimstedt** (va); [a]**Michael Sanderling** (vc); [ab]**Petersen Quartet** ([d]Conrad Muck, [c]Gernot Sussmuth, vns; Friedemann Weigle, va; [c]Hans-Jakob Eschenburg, vc). Capriccio Ⓕ 10 539 (77 minutes: DDD: 11/95). Recorded 1994.

As Schulhoff enthusiasts will have come to expect, the works represented are not at all uniform in style. The early quartet is prematurely neo-classical (or is it just cod Beethoven?). It was conceived in 1918 when the composer was still serving in the Austrian Army. The German group certainly give it their all. Taut and tough, they seem intent on radicalizing the discourse whether through a heightened response to its finer points or a profound understanding of the Beethovenian models that lurk beneath the surface invention. As a result, the Quartet emerges as a witty, substantial piece. The string Sextet was completed six years later but sounds quite different, its Schoenbergian first movement well-integrated with the more eclectic idiom of the rest. Whatever the outward manner, Schulhoff's rhythmic phraseology is metrically conceived. Even if you already know the Sextet the Petersen make a plausible first choice. The aggressive communication of their playing is emphasized by the bright, not quite top-heavy sound balance. The Janáček-Bartók-Ravel axis of the *Duo* is equally well served. The Sonata for solo violin (1927) is at least as interesting as similar works by Hindemith, less emotionally wrenching than the Bartók. That work was composed a couple of years after Schulhoff's premature death as a victim of Nazi persecution in 1942. A thoroughly distinguished issue by an ensemble seemingly incapable of giving a dull performance.

Schulhoff String Quartet No. 1.
Hindemith String Quartet No. 3, Op. 22.
Weill String Quartet. **Brandis Quartet** (Thomas Brandis, Peter Brem, vns; Wilfried Strehle, va;
    Wolfgang Boettcher, vc). Nimbus Ⓕ NI5410 (60 minutes: DDD: 3/95). Recorded 1992.   Ⓖ
All three works bear witness to a culture that, in terms of tempo and sensation, was in the process of excited transformation. The period covered is 1923-24, the time of rocketing German inflation, the establishment of the USSR, Rilke's *Duino Elegies* as well as major Kafka (who died in 1924), Mann, Musil, Cocteau and Bréton (his Surrealist manifesto). This music is full of it all. Hindemith's bold Third Quartet – one of the composer's most arresting and accessible pieces – launches its explorations within a relatively formal framework, certainly in comparison with Schulhoff and Weill. Rich invention is tempered by a sense of outward propriety. Weill's Quartet opens with considerable expressive warmth, although it soon busies itself with a whole range of interesting ideas (the finale is particularly rich in incident), with a hoot of a *Scherzo* that suddenly swerves to a Reger-like March, then waltzes gently forth in a manner that suggests Shostakovich before embarking on further discursive episodes and scurrying off to a cheeky *diminuendo*. Granted, one feels that Weill is in search of something he never quite finds, but the very act of searching makes for an absorbing adventure. Even more compelling, however, is Schulhoff's dazzling First Quartet, the last piece in the programme and a highly dramatic musical mystery tour. Urgency rules right from the opening bars, while Schulhoff's tonal palette is both wide-ranging and ingeniously employed: pizzicato, *col legno*, *sul ponticello*, harmonics (wonderfully effective in the finale), dense harmonic computations and a rhythmic vitality that recalls Bartók at full cry (most especially in the third movement). The work's pale, equivocal coda recalls the parallel quartet mysteries of Schulhoff's fellow Holocaust victims Krása and Haas, while the work as a whole is far more than the sum of its restless and endlessly fascinating parts. A fine programme, then, very well executed and lustrously recorded.

Additional recommendation ...
...String Quartets Nos. 1 and 2. Five Pieces for String Quartet. **Petersen Quartet.** Capriccio
    Ⓕ 10463 (47 minutes: DDD: 5/93).

Further listening ...
...Piano Concerto No. 2[a]. Concerto for Flute and Piano[b]. Concertino for String Quartet and
    Orchestra[c]. Jazz Etudes – Blues; Chanson; Tango[d]. Esquisses de jazz – Blues; Charleston[d].
    Partita – Tango-Rag; Tempo di Fox à la Hawai; Tango; Shimmy-Jazz[d]. [b]**Bettina Wild** (fl);
    [ab]**Aleksandar Madzar**, [d]**Erwin Schulhoff** (pfs); [c]**Hawthorne Quartet;** [abc]**Deutsche
    Kammerphilharmonie / Andreas Delfs.** Decca Entartete Musik [d]mono/stereo 444 819-2DH
    (12/95).
...Symphonies Nos. 1-3. **Philharmonia Hungarica / George Alexander Albrecht.** CPO CPO999 251-2
    (1/95).
...Concertino[a]. Divertissement[b]. Flute Sonata[c]. Hot Sonata[d]. [ac]**Hans-Udo Heinzmann** (fl); [b]**Malte
    Lammers** (ob); [b]**Walter Hermann** (cl); [d]**Detlef Bensmann** (sax); [b]**Björn Groth** (bn); [a]**Thomas Oepen**
    (va); [a]**Volker Donandt** (db); [c]**Jürgen Lamke**, [d]**Michael Rische** (pfs). Koch Schwann 312322 (9/95).
...Duo for Violin and Cello[a]. Violin Sonata No. 2[b]. Cello Sonata[c]. [ab]**Stefan Wagner** (vn); [ac]**Bernhard
    Gmelin** (vc); [bc]**Jürgen Lamke** (pf). Koch Schwann 311672 (9/95).
...Die Mondsüchtige. *Coupled with* **Schreker** Der Geburtstag der Infantin – Suite. **Hindemith**
    Der Dämon. **Leipzig Gewandhaus Orchestra / Lothar Zagrosek.** Decca Entartete Musik Ⓕ 444
    182-2DH (5/95). *See review under Hindemith; refer to the Index to Reviews.*   Ⓖ
...Flammen. **Soloists; Berlin RIAS Chamber Choir; Berlin Deutsches Symphony Orchestra / John
    Mauceri.** Decca Entartete Musik 444 630-2DHO2 (1/95).   Ⓖ

Gunther Schuller   American 1925-

Suggested listening ...
...Suite. *Coupled with works by* **Barber, Beach, Fine, Harbison** and **Villa-Lobos** Reykjavik
    Wind Quintet. Chandos CHAN9174 (11/93). *See review in the Collections section; refer to the
    Index to Reviews.*

Johann Schulz

German 1747-1800

Suggested listening ...
...Diverses pièces, Op. 1[b] – No. 5, Allegretto; No. 6, Larghetto con Variazioni. *Coupled with* **Fasch** Andantino con Variazioni[a]. **Benda** Keyboard Sonatinas[a] – Rondeau; Allegro; Allegretto; Allegretto; Allegretto moderato. **Graun** Keyboard Sonata in D minor[a]. **Hasse** Keyboard Sonata in E flat major[a]. **C.P.E. Bach** Pièces Caractéristiques[b] – Là Borchward, H79; La Pott, H80; La Gleim, H89; La Bergius, H90; La Stahl, H94; La Boehmer, H81; La Louise, H114. **Christine Schornsheim** ([a]hpd/[b]fp). Capriccio 10 424 (4/95). ✎

Andrey Schulz-Evler

Polish 1854-1905

Suggested listening ...
...An der schönen, blauen Donau. *Coupled with works by* **Friedman, M. Rosenthal, Tausig** and **Godowsky** **Piers Lane** (pf). Hyperion CDA66785 (2/96).

William Schuman

American 1910-1992

Schuman New England Triptych. Symphony for Strings. (Symphony No. 5). Judith.
Ives (orch. Schuman) Variations on "America". **Seattle Symphony Orchestra / Gerard Schwarz.**
   Delos Ⓔ DE3115 (64 minutes: DDD: 7/93).
This record was completed before Schuman died and when he heard some of it on a cassette he wrote: "The performance has so many superlative elements that I would do the overall excellence of the rendition an injustice by citing the special places that appeal particularly to this composer's soul ...". This may seem to disarm criticism but one can see what Schuman meant. He must have been particularly pleased to have a modern performance of his ballet *Judith*. Its bloodthirsty subject from the Apocrypha brings out many facets of Schuman's resourceful and dynamic personality at its most serious. There are dramatic moments but also areas of melodic power (after 18'20") which are particularly characteristic of Schuman and sound like nobody else. His Fifth Symphony (1943) must be one of the most successful American works for string orchestra this century. Schwarz's performance is effective enough and it fills a gap in the catalogue for Schuman on both sides of the Atlantic. The Americana side of Schuman comes in the popular *New England Triptych* based on three choral pieces by the eccentric pioneer William Billings (1746–1800). When Schuman wrote *New England Triptych* in 1956, Billings was less recognized, and Schuman was linking up with part of his own New England heritage. But in 1963, when he orchestrated Ives's *Variations on America* (the tune is the same as *God save the Queen*) Ives was beginning to reach his special position in American music. This is a brilliantly witty transformation of the organ work Ives wrote in his teens and performed himself. Perhaps as a result the Ives is more often played by organists now. Its zest matches the exuberance of Schuman throughout his busy career and it makes a fun start to this recorded tribute.
Additional recommendations...
...New England Triptych. **Menin** Symphony No. 5. **Ives** Orchestral Set No. 1, "A New England Symphony". **Eastman-Rochester Orchestra / Howard Hanson.** Mercury Ⓜ 432 755-2MM (77 minutes: ADD).
...American Festival Overture. New England Triptych. Symphony No. 10, "American Muse". **Ives** (orch. Schuman) Variations on "America". **St Louis Symphony Orchestra / Leonard Slatkin.** RCA Victor Red Seal Ⓔ 09026 61282-2 (67 minutes: DDD: 5/93). *Gramophone Editor's choice.*
Further listening ...
...String Quartets Nos. 2, 3 and 5. **Lydian Quartet.** Harmonia Mundi HMU90 7114 (8/94).

Clara Schumann

German 1819-1896

Suggested listening ...
...Piano Trio in G minor, Op. 17[a]. *Coupled with works by* **Beach, Carreño, Mendelssohn-Hensel, Tailleferre, Boulanger** and **Chaminade** **Macalester Trio.** Vox Box 115845-2 (10/84). *See review in the Collections section; refer to the Index to Reviews.*
...Piano Trio in G minor, Op. 17. *Coupled with* **Mendelssohn-Hensel** Piano Trio in G minor, Op. 11. **Dartington Trio.** Hyperion CDA66331 (3/90).

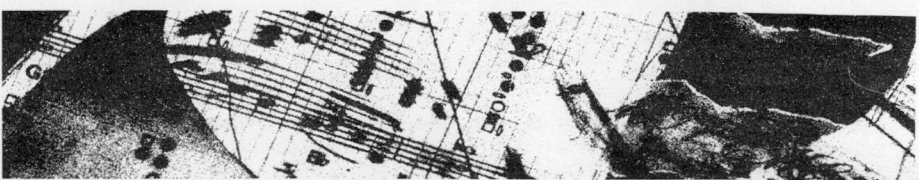

Robert Schumann   German 1810-1856

Schumann Cello Concerto in A minor, Op. 129[a]. Adagio and Allegro in A flat major, Op. 70[b].
Fantasiestücke, Op. 73[b]. Funf Stücke im Volkston, Op. 102[b]. **Heinrich Schiff** (vc); [b]**Gerhard
Oppitz** (pf); [a]**Berlin Philharmonic Orchestra / Bernard Haitink.** Philips Ⓟ 422 414-2PH
(60 minutes: DDD: 6/93). Item marked [a] recorded 1988, [b]arr. Grützmacher, recorded 1991.
Gramophone Editor's choice.   ⒼⒼ
New review
Schumann Cello Concerto in A minor, Op. 129.
Hindemith Cello Concerto. **János Starker** (vc); **Bamberg Symphony Orchestra / Dennis Russell
Davies.** RCA Victor Red Seal Ⓟ 09026 68027-2 (52 minutes: DDD: 10/95). Recorded 1994.
Schumann's Cello Concerto is a fairly dark, troubled work, and sometimes cellists are tempted to adopt
a somewhat overwrought approach when playing it. In fact, it responds best to a more balanced
approach, as exemplified in this performance by Heinrich Schiff. His playing is very eloquent, and quite
strong, but there is also a feeling of dignity and refinement in his response to the music. Everything is
perfectly in scale, and the work's essential nobility is allowed to emerge in a most moving fashion.
Schiff's technique is faultless, and his tonal quality is very beautiful. Haitink and the BPO seem totally
in sympathy with the soloist, and the recording is warm and well-detailed. The three items with piano
accompaniment comprise a series of short pieces which are for the most part sunnier in outlook than
the Concerto, and they make an effective contrast to the larger-scale work. Again Schiff's playing is
expressive, but his phrasing is full of subtlety and poetry, and Oppitz is a highly responsive partner.
   You'd never guess that Starker's disc is the work of a 70-year-old. The performance of the
Schumann is lean and wiry, although Starker's peculiarly 'inward' expressiveness (which is greatly
helped here by Dennis Russell Davies's subtle conducting) counters his more assertive side. It is a
fairly intimate rendition, very different in temper from, say, the more overtly intense Heinrich Schiff
or the lavishly demonstrative Casals. The performance incorporates Starker's own third-movement
cadenza. Hindemith's Cello Concerto is a joyous bag of tricks and strongly suggestive of 'games to
come' in the *Symphonic Metamorphoses on Themes of Weber*, composed some three years later (1943).
Starker is again a master of elegance; his tone is finely tensed, his sense of rhythm impeccable and
Davies's Bamberg players provide a suitably enthusiastic orchestral backdrop – though not one to
replace Karel Ančerl's dazzling 1955 Czech Philharmonic accompaniment for Paul Tortelier. Still,
that's another story (and another era), but Starker's reading will certainly make you sit up and listen.
A superb release for a man who could rightly assume the title 'Peter Pan of the Cello'!

Additional recommendations ...
...Cello Concerto[a]. **Lalo** Cello Concerto in D minor[a]. **Saint-Saëns** Cello Concerto in A minor,
Op. 33[b]. **János Starker** (vc); **London Symphony Orchestra /** [a]**Stanislaw Skrowaczewski,** [b]**Antál
Dorati.** Mercury Ⓜ 432 010-2MM (65 minutes: ADD: 4/92). *See review under Saint-Saëns; refer
to the Index to Reviews.*   ⒼⒼ
...Cello Concerto[a]. Piano Concerto in A minor, Op. 54[b]. Introduction and Allegro appassionato,
Op. 92[c]. [a]**Jacqueline du Pré** (vc); [a]**New Philharmonia Orchestra / Daniel Barenboim** ([b]pf); [bc]**London
Philharmonic Orchestra / Dietrich Fischer-Dieskau.** EMI Ⓜ CDM7 64626-2 (74 minutes:
ADD: 3/93).
...Cello Concerto[a]. Piano Trio No. 1 in D minor, Op. 63[b]. Funf Stücke im Volkston[c]. [b]**Alexander
Schneider** (vn); **Pablo Casals** (vc); [b]**Mieczyslaw Horszowski,** [c]**Leonard Mannes** (pfs); [a]**Prades
Festival Orchestra / Eugene Ormandy.** Sony Classical Casals Edition Ⓜ SMK58993 (74 minutes:
ADD: 5/94).   ⒼⒼ
...Cello Concerto. *Coupled with works by* **Dvořák, Saint-Saëns, Delius, Elgar, Haydn, Monn,
Chopin, Franck, Fauré, Bruch, Bach, Handel** *and* **Beethoven** Jacqueline du Pré (vc) with
various artists and orchestras. EMI Ⓑ CZS5 68132-2 (six discs: 437 minutes: ADD: 8/94). *See
review in the Collections section; refer to the Index to Reviews.*   ⒼⒼ
...Cello Concerto. **Brahms** Double Concerto in A minor, Op. 102[a]. [a]**Ilya Kaler** (vn); **Maria Kliegel**
(vc); **National Symphony Orchestra of Ireland / Andrew Constantine.** Naxos Ⓢ 8 550938 (59 minutes:
DDD: 10/95). *Gramophone Editor's choice. See review under Brahms; refer to the Index to Reviews.*
...Cello Concerto. **Dvořák** Cello Concerto in B minor, B191. **Arto Noras** (vc); **Finnish Radio
Symphony Orchestra / Sakari Oramo.** Finlandia Ⓟ 4509-98886-2 (64 minutes: DDD: 10/95).
...Cello Concerto. *Coupled with works by* **Bach, Kodály, Dohnányi, Boccherini, Haydn,
Saint-Saëns, Dvořák, Fauré, Milhaud** and **Prokofiev.** János Starker (vc); **Gerald Moore**
(pf); **Philharmonia Orchestra / Carlo Maria Giulini, Walter Susskind.** EMI mono/stereo Ⓜ CZS5
68485-2 (six discs: 398 minutes: ADD: 12/95) *See review in the Collections section; refer to the
Index to Reviews.*
...Romanze in A minor, Op. 94 No. 1. Adagio and Allegro. *Coupled with works by* **Bach, Handel,
Boccherini, Schubert, Chopin, Saint-Saëns, Debussy** and **Bloch** Mischa Maisky (vc);
Daria Hovora (pf). DG Ⓟ 439 863-2GH (67 minutes: DDD: 9/94). *See review in the Collections
section; refer to the Index to Reviews.*   Ⓖ

Schumann Piano Concerto in A minor, Op. 54[a]. Introduction and Allegro appassionato in
D minor (Concertstück), Op. 92[a]. Violin Concerto in D minor, Op. posth[b]. Cello Concerto in
A minor, Op. 129[c]. Konzertstücke in F major, Op. 86[d]. [d]**Gerd Seifert,** [d]**Norbert Hauptmann,**

[d]Christopher Kohler, [d]Manfred Klier (hns); [b]Gidon Kremer (vn); [c]Paul Tortelier (vc); [a]Daniel Barenboim (pf); [a]London Philharmonic Orchestra / Dietrich Fischer-Dieskau; [b]Philharmonia Orchestra / Riccardo Muti; [c]Royal Philharmonic Orchestra / Yan Pascal Tortelier; [d]Berlin Philharmonic Orchestra / Klaus Tennstedt. EMI Rouge et Noir Ⓜ CZS7 67521-2 (two discs: 121 minutes: ADD: 8/93). Items marked [a] from HMV ASD3053 (3/75), [b]ASD143519-1 (10/83), [c]ASD3728 (10/79), [d]ASD3724 (12/79).   Ⓖ

If ever a performance of Schumann's Piano Concerto stressed the principle of dialogue between soloist and conductor, then this is it. True, the Philharmonia's string ensemble isn't as water-tight under Fischer-Dieskau as it might have been under some other conductors; and poetry is invested at the premium of relatively low-level drama. Orchestral textures are absolutely right for Schumann – warm yet transparent, full-bodied yet never stodgy – and poetry is a major priority. Add Barenboim's compatible vision and keyboard finesse, and you indeed have a memorable reading. The more discursive *Introduction and Allegro appassionato* has plenty of interest, but remembering that this isn't exactly top-drawer Schumann, the performance could be more arresting. Conversely, the *Konzertstücke* has as much forthrightness as it could possibly take, certainly in terms of engineering: the four magnificent horns ring out with Olympian force, keenly supported by an animated BPO. The Cello Concerto is more smoothly recorded, but although Tortelier *père* had the measure of this fragile masterpiece's troubled spirit, his son was, at least at this stage in his career, less comprehensively perceptive. As for the Violin Concerto, one finds oneself frequently moved by Kremer's solo playing – his handling of the slow movement has a tonal richness – but less than happy with Muti's indulgent accompaniment. The repetitions in this work are frequently misunderstood as symptoms of creative decline rather than as the trenchant rhetorical devices that they in fact are, and Muti gives the impression of being unconvinced by them. Nevertheless, Kremer and Muti are, within the useful context of this competitively-priced set, certainly up to the task of communicating what is still a scandalously underrated work. They also have the benefit of good engineering.

Additional recommendations ...

...Violin Concerto. **Dvořák** Violin Concerto in A minor, B108. Romance in F minor, B39. **Thomas Zehetmair** (vn); **Philharmonia Orchestra / Eliahu Inbal.** Teldec Ⓜ 4509-91444-2 (72 minutes: DDD: 7/93).

...Violin Concerto. **Mendelssohn** Violin Concerto in E minor, Op. 64. **Georg Kulenkampff** (vn); **Berlin Philharmonic Orchestra / Hans Schmidt-Isserstedt.** Teldec Historic Series mono Ⓜ 4509-93672-2* (55 minutes: ADD: 9/94).

...Konzertstück. Symphonies Nos. 1-4. Overture, Scherzo and Finale, Op. 52. Etudes symphoniques, Op. 13 – Variation No. 11; Finale (arr. Tchaikovsky). . Piano Concerto in A minor, Op. 54. Manfred – Overture. **Bella Davidovich** (pf); **Seattle Symphony Orchestra / Gerard Schwarz.** Delos Ⓜ DE3146 (four discs: 231 minutes: DDD: 7/95).

...Violin Concerto. **Brahms** Violin Concerto in D, Op. 77. **Joshua Bell** (vn); **Cleveland Orchestra / Christoph von Dohnányi.** Decca Ⓕ 444 811-2DH (68 minutes: DDD: 5/96). *See review under Brahms; refer to the Index to Reviews.*

New review
Schumann Piano Concerto in A minor, Op. 54.
R. Strauss Burleske in D minor, AV85. **Hélène Grimaud** (pf); **Deutsches Symphony Orchestra, Berlin / David Zinman.** Erato Ⓕ 0630-11727-2 (52 minutes: DDD: 2/96). Recorded 1995.

Such is Grimaud's immediacy of response to every change of mood in the opening *Allegro affettuoso* of Schumann's concerto that some listeners may think it a little too excitable – at the expense of maturer composure and poise. But never in this movement, nor in a finale of unflagging vitality and *joie de vivre*, is there any hint of mere keyboard display. You could certainly never hope to hear the first movement's nostalgic main theme played with a more eloquent simplicity. Piano and orchestra are in exceptionally close accord throughout, and not least in the intimate conversational exchanges of the *Andantino grazioso*. Written when Strauss was a mere 22, the *Burleske* cries out for youthful virtuosity, volatility, caprice and charm – which we're given here with effortless fluency by all concerned. In what could vaguely be described as lyrical 'second subject' territory (from the start of track 5, *tranquillo*) who could fail to enjoy those amazing pre-echoes of irresistibly seductive, smiling (*con amore*) things-to-come a quarter of a century later in *Der Rosenkavalier*? The Erato sound is clear-cut rather than lusciously cushioned, but never hard-edged: it falls agreeably on the ear.

Additional recommendations ...

...Piano Concerto. **Prokofiev** Piano Concerto No. 3 in C major, Op. 26. **Van Cliburn** (pf); **Chicago Symphony Orchestra / Walter Hendl, Fritz Reiner.** RCA Victor Living Stereo 09026 62691-2 (61 minutes: ADD).

...Piano Concerto. **Grieg** Piano Concerto. **Radu Lupu** (pf); **London Symphony Orchestra / André Previn.** Decca Ovation Ⓜ 417 728-2DM (61 minutes: ADD: 12/87).   Ⓖ

...Piano Concerto[a]. Davidsbündlertänze, Op. 6. Kinderszenen, Op. 15. **Fanny Davies** (pf); [a]**Royal Philharmonic Society Orchestra / Ernest Ansermet.** Pearl mono Ⓕ GEMMCD9291* (65 minutes: ADD: 5/88).

...Piano Concerto. **Schoenberg** Piano Concerto, Op. 42. **Maurizio Pollini** (pf); **Berlin Philharmonic Orchestra / Claudio Abbado.** DG Ⓕ 427 771-2GH (51 minutes: DDD: 7/90).

...Piano Concerto. **Grieg** Piano Concerto. **Pascal Devoyon** (pf); **London Philharmonic Orchestra / Jerzy Maksymiuk.** Classics for Pleasure ℗ CD-CFP4574 (63 minutes: DDD: 2/91).

...Piano Concerto[a]. **Franck** Symphonic Variations, Op. 46[b]. **Grieg** Piano Concerto in A minor, Op. 16[c]. [a]**Friedrich Gulda,** [bc]**Clifford Curzon** (pfs); [a]**Vienna Philharmonic Orchestra / Volkmar Andreae;** [b]**London Philharmonic Orchestra / Sir Adrian Boult;** [c]**London Symphony Orchestra / Øivin Fjeldstad.** Decca Headline Classics ℗ 433 628-2DSP* (76 minutes: ADD: 1/92). *See review under Franck; refer to the Index to Reviews.* ⓖⓖⓖ

...Piano Concerto. **Grieg** Piano Concerto. **Lars Vogt** (pf); **City of Birmingham Symphony Orchestra / Sir Simon Rattle.** EMI ⓕ CDC7 54746-2 (62 minutes: DDD: 1/93).

...Piano Concerto[b]. Piano Quintet in E flat major, Op. 44[a]. **Alicia de Larrocha** (pf); [a]**Tokyo Quartet;** [b]**London Symphony Orchestra / Sir Colin Davis.** RCA Victor Red Seal ⓕ 09026 61279-2 (64 minutes: DDD: 5/93).

...Piano Concerto. Introduction and Allegro appassionato in G major (Concertstück), Op. 92. Introduction and Allegro in D minor, Op. 134. **Michel Dalberto** (pf); **Vienna Symphony Orchestra / Eliahu Inbal.** Denon ⓕ CO-75859 (62 minutes: DDD: 6/94).

...Piano Concerto. **Grieg** Piano Concerto in A minor, Op. 16. **Jean-Marc Luisada** (pf); **London Symphony Orchestra / Michael Tilson Thomas.** DG ⓕ 439 913-2GH (65 minutes: DDD: 12/94).

...Piano Concerto[b]. Kreisleriana, Op. 16. Kinderszenen, Op. 15. Fantasiestücke, Op. 12. Fantasie in C major, Op. 17. Etudes symphoniques, Op. 13. Drei Romanzen, Op. 94[c]. Abendlied, Op. 85 No. 12[c]. Adagio und Allegro in A flat major, Op. 70[c]. Fantasiestücke, Op. 73[c]. Funf Stücke in Volkston, Op. 102[c]. **Brahms** Piano Concertos – No. 1 in D minor, Op. 15; No. 2 in B flat major, Op. 83. Theme and Variations (from String Sextet No. 1, Op. 18). Four Ballades, Op. 10. **Alfred Brendel** (pf); [c]**Heinz Holliger** (ob); [a]**Berlin Philharmonic Orchestra,** [b]**London Symphony Orchestra / Claudio Abbado.** Philips Ⓜ 446 925-2PM5 (five discs: 334 minutes: ADD/DDD: 2/96).

...Piano Concerto[a]. **Grieg** Piano Concerto in A minor, Op. 16[a]. Piano Sonata in E minor, Op. 7[b]. [a]**Stephen Kovacevich,** [b]**Zoltán Kocsis** (pfs); [a]**BBC Symphony Orchestra / Sir Colin Davis.** Philips Solo Ⓜ 446 192-2PM (78 minutes: [a]ADD/[b]DDD: 6/96). *See review under Grieg; refer to the Index to Reviews.* ⓖⓖⓖ

New review

Schumann Piano Concerto in A minor, Op. 54[a].
Prokofiev Piano Concerto No. 3 in C major, Op. 26[b]. **Van Cliburn** (pf); **Chicago Symphony Orchestra /** [a]**Fritz Reiner,** [b]**Walter Hendl.** RCA Victor Living Stereo Ⓜ 09026 62691-2 (61 minutes: ADD. 8/96). Item marked [a] from SB2113 (8/61), [b]RA13002 (12/60). ⓠ

It is 37 years since Van Cliburn took Moscow by storm. The outright winner of the first Tchaikovsky Competition, his playing left an indelible mark and an enduring legend. Returning to these two wholly characteristic performances is to be forcibly reminded of his cardinal and unique qualities. Here, captured in RCA's magnificent remastering, is that sumptuously rich and burnished tone, that generous elasticity of phrase and rhythm, that open-hearted rhetorical splendour. Tempos, as so often with Cliburn, are expansive, allowing him an imperial breadth and majesty. Listen to the fullness and clarity he finds in Schumann's first movement *passionato* elaboration, or the way he sweeps all before him in the finale's exultant conclusion. On the other hand Cliburn's romantic generosity would probably have angered Prokofiev, whose austere performance of his own Third Concerto was bleak and angular. Yet even he would surely have marvelled at the way every note is made audible in his scintillating score. Given such superb assurance the final variation in the second movement sounds more than ever like two different forms of motion proceeding simultaneously and, all in all, both performances provide awe-inspiring evidence of Cliburn's once towering genius. In these too often lean times, when emotional aridity is often applauded to the skies, such magnificence is doubly rewarding.

Schumann Symphonies – No. 1 in B flat major, Op. 38, "Spring"; No. 2 in C major, Op. 61; No. 3 in E flat major, Op. 97, "Rhenish"; No. 4 in D minor, Op. 120. Overture, Scherzo and Finale, Op. 52. **Dresden Staatskapelle / Wolfgang Sawallisch.** EMI Sawallisch Edition Ⓜ CMS7 64815-2 (two discs: 148 minutes: ADD: 11/93). From HMV SLS867 (2/74). Recorded 1972. ⓖⓖⓖ

Schumann Symphonies. **Bavarian Radio Symphony Orchestra / Rafael Kubelík.** Sony Classical Essential Classics ℗ SBK48269/70 (two discs, oas: 74 and 76 minutes: ADD: 7/93). From CBS 79324 (10/79). Recorded 1978-79.

SBK48269 – No. 1 in B flat major, Op. 38, "Spring"; No. 2 in C major, Op. 61. *SBK48270* – No. 3 in E flat major, Op. 97, "Rhenish"; No. 4 in D minor, Op. 120. Manfred, Op. 115 – Overture. ⓖⓖⓖ

Schumann's symphonies come in for a lot of criticism because of his supposed cloudy textures and unsubtle scoring, but in the hands of a conductor who is both skilful and sympathetic they are most engaging works. Sawallisch's recordings, brightly transferred, provide us with a much admired set. His style, fresh and unforced, is not as high powered as some other conductors but it is sensible, alert and very pleasing. He achieves great lightness in the First and Fourth Symphonies – there's always a sense of classical poise and control but never at the expense of the overall architecture of the pieces. The Second and Third Symphonies, larger and more far-reaching in their scope, again benefit from Sawallisch's approach. The playing of the Staatskapelle Dresden is superlative in every department, with a lovely veiled string sound and a real sense of ensemble. These are real bargains and with the *Overture, Scherzo and Finale* thrown in for good measure, definitely not to be missed.

It is difficult to understand why Kubelík's wonderful cycle failed to make an impact when it was first issued. His sensitivity to detail, his refusal to bully Schumann's vulnerable structures and his ability to penetrate occasional thickets of orchestration, make these especially memorable. Just listen to the cheeky bassoon backing clarinet, 1'44" into the *Spring* Symphony's fourth movement, the limpid phrasing of the *Rhenish* Symphony's *Nicht schnell* third movement, or the to-ing and fro-ing between first and second violins (usefully separated, as virtually always with Kubelík) in the last movement of the Second. Only the first movement of the Fourth seems a little heavy-handed, but then the poetry of the *Romanze* and the exuberance of the finale more than make amends. First movement repeats are observed and the playing throughout is rich in felicitous turns of phrase. The sound, though, is a minor stumbling block: violins are thin (one of the few disadvantages of having them separated is that their massed tone becomes mildly diluted), brass a little fuzzy and the whole production less focused than Sawallisch's set. But Kubelík's insights are too varied and meaningful to miss, and there is much pleasure to be derived from them. What with a stirring *Manfred* Overture added for good measure, they also constitute exceptional value for money.

Additional recommendations ...

...Nos. 1-4. Overtures – Genoveva; Manfred. **Berlin Philharmonic Orchestra / Rafael Kubelík.** DG Double Ⓜ 437 395-2GX2 (two discs: 153 minutes: ADD).

...Nos. 1-4. **Suisse Romande Orchestra / Armin Jordan.** Erato Duo Bonsai Ⓑ 4509-95357-2 (two discs: 131 minutes: DDD).

...Nos. 1-4. **London Philharmonic Orchestra / Kurt Masur.** Teldec Ⓑ 4509-95501-2 (two discs: 122 minutes: DDD).

...Nos. 1-4. **Berlin Philharmonic Orchestra / Herbert von Karajan.** DG Symphony Edition Ⓜ 429 672-2GSE2 (two discs: 132 minutes: ADD: 7/90).

...Nos. 2 and 3. **Dresden Staatskapelle / Wolfgang Sawallisch.** EMI Studio Ⓜ CDM7 69472-2 (71 minutes: ADD: 11/88).   ⓖⓔⓖ

...Nos. 1 and 4. **Vienna Philharmonic Orchestra / Riccardo Muti.** Philips Ⓕ 442 121-2PH (65 minutes: DDD: 1/95).

...Nos. 1-4. **Staatskapelle Dresden / Giuseppe Sinopoli.** DG Ⓕ 439 923-2GH2 (two discs: 135 minutes: DDD: 9/95).

Schumann Symphonies – No. 1 in B flat major, Op. 38, "Spring"; No. 2 in C major, Op. 61; No. 3 in E flat major, Op. 97, "Rhenish"; No. 4 in D minor, Op. 120. Overture, Scherzo and Finale, Op. 52. **Hanover Band / Roy Goodman.** RCA Victor Red Seal Ⓕ 09026 61931-2 (two discs: 134 minutes: DDD: 3/95). 🎞 Recorded 1993.   ⓖ

This is one of those sets where so much sounds different, novel or challenging, that it will take quite a few playings before the full import of Roy Goodman's provocative performances, hits home. The main revelation is in textures that appear to have been turned inside out, something that will occur most to listeners weaned on the warmer-toned Schumann of, say, Sawallisch, Kubelík or Karajan. Here the brass are alarmingly prominent, while the strings are lightweight, neat and stylishly inflected. In the slow movements, shapeliness, mobility and a relatively chaste spirit will surprise those used to expressive intensity, breadth and lovingly nudged phrasing. Goodman dances hot-foot where *lebhaft* or *allegro* take the lead; his accents are punchy, his full tuttis impressively immediate. Goodman presents a less stylized reading of the original 1841 version of the Fourth Symphony than Harnoncourt did for Teldec (listed below) – one that really does convince one of the first alternative's musical superiority, the clarity of its middle voices and the sheer energy of it all. Divided violins are helpful throughout, most particularly in the first movement of the *Rhenish*: here the timpani also have a field day. Elsewhere, it is a case of logical transitions (nothing sounds awkward), lithe textures and thrillingly conclusive codas. Only the 'original' Fourth dispenses with familiar outer movement repeats. That's the good news. The 'bad' – or 'qualifying' – news will apply mainly to those readers for whom Schumann is first and foremost a musical poet. Although Goodman's readings are consistently intelligent and fairly sensitive to shifting nuances, it is the mellower, more introspective aspects of the music that occasionally seem rather under-projected. Throughout all four symphonies there are instances where Schumann's characteristic emotional equivocation suggests a more subtle, personal and recreative realization than it receives here. Still, this is a very significant set, and with a bracing account of the masterly *Overture, Scherzo and Finale* added as an enticing bonus, serves to teach us much about this great music. Use it to supplement existing recommendations, and you can't go wrong; but if you're thinking of making it a basic library choice, do try to listen before purchasing.

Additional recommendations ...

...Nos. 3 and 4. **London Classical Players / Roger Norrington.** EMI Ⓕ CDC7 54025-2 (57 minutes: DDD: 3/91). 🎞

...No. 3. **Schubert** Symphony No. 3 in D major, D200. **North German Radio Symphony Orchestra / Günter Wand.** RCA Victor Red Seal Ⓕ 09026 61876-2 (56 minutes: DDD: 2/94).

...No. 3; No. 4 (1841 version). **Chamber Orchestra of Europe / Nikolaus Harnoncourt.** Teldec Ⓕ 4509-90867-2 (57 minutes: DDD: 2/95).

...Nos. 2 and 4. **Polish National Radio Symphony Orchestra / Antoni Wit.** Naxos Ⓢ 8 550923 (68 minutes: DDD: 3/95).

...No. 4. **Bartók** Piano Concerto No. 3, Sz119[a].[a]**Géza Anda** (pf); **Staatskapelle Dresden / Herbert von Karajan.** DG Ⓜ 447 666-2GX (55 minutes: ADD: 10/95). *Gramophone Editor's choice. See review under Bartók; refer to the Index to Reviews.*

New review

Schumann Symphony No. 4 in D minor, Op. 120.
Schubert Symphony No. 4 in C minor, D417, "Tragic".
Mendelssohn Die schöne Melusine, Op. 32. **Berlin Philharmonic Orchestra / Nikolaus Harnoncourt.** Teldec Ⓕ 4509-94543-2 (77 minutes: DDD: 5/96). Recorded live in 1995.

"I think of it as one of the greatest symphonic poems" Harnoncourt has said of *Die schöne Melusine*. A bold claim, but here indeed is a bold and beauteous performance. Beauty first, "the beauty of calm waters" as Tovey described the opening: upwardly curling mother-of-pearl Berlin winds and strings. Then boldness: and here the strongly rhythmic second theme is subjected to such a dramatic *animato* that its definition may strike you as initially blurred (a momentary impression though, and the Overture as a whole benefits from Harnoncourt's tempo contrasts). The Berliners' musical collective would appear to have had a profound (and positive) effect on Harnoncourt in the Schubert. Compare the slow movement with his Concertgebouw recording (part of a cycle: see the review under Schubert; refer to the Index to Reviews): there, the *Andante*'s relatively detached period manners are here (at a slower tempo, though still an *Andante*) transformed into a very real beauty and eloquence of phrase and expression. Very startling, if you don't know the Abbado (listed under the Schubert/Harnoncourt review) or Harnoncourt's Amsterdam recording, is the removal of eight bars (from the printed editions) in the first movement's exposition, and Harnoncourt's fateful ('Tragic'?) half-tempo delivery of the finale's closing unison C chords. Dramatic delaying tactics – whether tiny hesitations, or huge fermatas – have always been a feature of Harnoncourt's conducting. Together with his insistent accentuation, sudden contrasts of dynamics, texture and tempo (for example, *Scherzo*/Trio tempos), you may feel that this Schumann Fourth (the familiar revision) sets out to contradict the symphony's apparent continuity, certainly compared to a performance like Wand's (reviewed below). But then, this is a performance that can catch fire spectacularly in a way that few others do, especially in the symphony's closing stages. The Berliners' playing is magnificent, and the sound is both satisfyingly present and spacious.

Schumann Symphony No. 4 in D minor, Op. 120.
Schubert Symphony No. 8 in B minor, D759, "Unfinished". **North German Radio Symphony Orchestra / Günter Wand.** RCA Victor Red Seal Ⓕ RD60826 (57 minutes: DDD: 5/92). Recorded live in 1991. ⒼⒼ

Wand's Schumann Fourth has impressive cumulative power; something the composer obviously intended with all four movements linked and sharing common themes. Wand's purposeful manner does not preclude many individual touches early in the work (the *Romanze* is darkly coloured and beautifully phrased), but as Schumann's thematic unity in continuity becomes more established, so Wand tightens his grip: the finale's introductory "darkness to dawn", for example, is here no interpolated episode, but an amassing of energies already in the air. The sound is full, deep and natural. Wand's is a traditionally unhurried unfolding of Schubert's *Unfinished*, and one which does not exploit its troubled lyrical expanses, bar by bar, for the utmost drama. Perceptible deviations from his well maintained pulse give heightened expressiveness to crucial moments in the 'symphonic' drama, such as the fearful start of the first movement's development section, and the second movement's haunting central transition. But the quality here that is most easy to recognize, and just as impossible to analyse, is its spirituality. The live origins may help to explain this, as they do a few trifling imprecisions in the playing.

New review

Schumann Piano Quintet in E flat major, Op. 44[a]. Andante and Variations, Op. 46[b]. Piano Quartet in E flat major, Op. 47[c]. Fantasiestücke, Op. 73[d]. Adagio and Allegro in A flat major, Op. 70[e]. Märchenbilder, Op. 113[f]. Violin Sonata No. 2 in D minor, Op. 121[g]. [be]**Marie-Luise Neunecker** (hn); [acg]**Dora Schwarzberg,** [a]**Lucy Hall** (vns); [acf]**Nobuko Imai** (va); [bcd]**Natalia Gutman,** [ab]**Mischa Maisky** (vcs); [abdfg]**Martha Argerich,** [bce]**Alexandre Rabinovitch** (pfs). EMI Ⓕ CDS5 55484-2 (two discs: 146 minutes: DDD: 1/96). Recorded live in 1994. Ⓖ

After "one memorable day of rehearsal", as the introductory note puts it, Martha Argerich and a group of friends recorded this generously long programme at a public concert in Holland "with the enthusiasm and intimate inspiration of a house-party". The rarity is the *Andante and Variations*, Op. 46, here brought up with all the spontaneous freshness of new discovery in a performance as enjoyable for its self-generating continuity as its diversity. Argerich and her fellow pianist, Rabinovitch, divide keyboard responsibilities in the remainder of the programme. Her own major triumph comes in the Quintet (with truly inspirational help from Maisky's cello). Every note tingles with life and colour in an arrestingly imaginative reading of exemplary textural transparency. In none of the more familiar works in the concert is that little extra stimulus of live as opposed to studio recording combined with more finesse and finish than here. In the Quartet Rabinovitch is a little less successful in concealing Schumann's inclination to entrust too much to his own instrument, with some aggressive accentuation *en route*. The finale is breathlessly, albeit excitably, fast. Rabinovitch is joined by Marie-Luise Neunecker in a hearty performance on the second disc of the *Adagio and Allegro* for horn and piano. In the smaller pieces Argerich reaffirms herself as an artist of 'temperament', much given to the impulse of the moment. In place of clarinet, the Op. 73 *Fantasiestücke* are played here with cello (Natalia Gutman), one of Schumann's two sanctioned alternatives despite its low-lying voice. However, in the *Märchenbilder* she partners the prescribed viola (Nobuko Imai). The recording itself is pleasingly natural, notwithstanding the odd moment of less than studio-perfected balance. And there is heartening audience applause, judiciously unprotracted, as a further reminder that we are in fact in the Concertgebouw at Nijmegen.

Additional recommendations ...

...Piano Quintet. **Brahms** Piano Quintet in F minor, Op. 34. **Kodály Quartet; Jenö Jandó** (pf). Naxos Ⓢ 8 550406 (67 minutes: DDD: 2/91).

...Piano Quintet. **Brahms** Piano Quartets Nos. 1-3. String Quartet No. 2 in A minor, Op. 51 No. 2. Piano Quintet in F minor, Op. 34. **Victor Aller** (pf); **Hollywood Quartet.** Testament mono Ⓕ SBT3063* (three discs: 220 minutes: ADD: 1/95).

...Piano Quintet[a]. Piano Quartet in E flat major, Op. 47. **Menahem Pressler** (pf); **Emerson Quartet** ([a]Eugene Drucker, Philip Setzer, vns; Lawrence Dutton, va; David Finckel, vc). DG Ⓕ 445 848-2GH (58 minutes: DDD: 1/96).

Schumann Piano Quartets – E flat major, Op. 47; C minor. **Young Uck Kim** (vn); **Heiichiro Ohyama** (va); **Gary Hoffman** (vc); **André Previn** (pf). RCA Victor Red Seal Ⓕ 09026 61384-2 (47 minutes: DDD: 5/93). Recorded 1991.

Schumann lovers the world over owe a great debt of gratitude to André Previn and his colleagues for giving us the "world première recording" of Schumann's C minor Piano Quartet, written when he was still a law student of only 18. Though favourably impressing several Leipzig musical friends at an informal try-out in 1829, the work remained unpublished for 150 years until a performing edition was prepared by that dedicated Schumann scholar, Wolfgang Boetticher. The nimble *Minuetto* and tenderly spun *Andante* are its gems: Schumann himself subsequently described the trio of the *Minuetto* (containing a phrase destined to reappear in the fourth of his Op. 4 *Intermezzos* for solo piano) as the moment he knew he belonged to a new world of romance. Though the more classically inspired flanking movements need (and in this splendidly vivid performance receive) a few discreet cuts, both have irrepressible buoyancy of spirit. His familiar second and last Quartet in E flat followed towards the end of 1842, a year almost exclusively devoted to chamber music, by which time he had an eminently distinguished pianist wife to help promote it. With his clear texture and rhythmic crispness, Previn ensures that the important keyboard part never dominates. And even though just now and again (notably in the meltingly heartfelt *Andante cantabile*) the sensitive cellist lacks the warmest and richest tonal glow, the playing, no less than the recording, holds its own with all the catalogue's rivals.

Additional recommendations ...

...Quartet, Op. 47[a]. Piano Quintet in E flat major, Op. 44[b]. **Beaux Arts Trio;** [b]**Dorf Bettelheim** (vn); [ab]**Samuel Rhodes** (va). Philips Ⓕ 420 791-2PH (58 minutes: ADD: 2/88).

...Quartet, Op. 47[a]. Piano Quintet, Op. 44[b]. [a]**Jiŕ Panocha** (vn); [a]**Miroslav Sehnoutka** (va); [a]**Jaroslav Kulhan** (vc); **Jan Panenka** (pf); [b]**Smetana Quartet.** Supraphon Ⓕ 11 0367-2 (57 minutes: DDD: 10/91).

...Quartet, Op. 47. Piano Quintet, Op. 44. **Schubert Ensemble of London.** Hyperion Ⓕ CDA66657 (58 minutes: DDD: 2/94).

...Quartet, Op. 47. **Beethoven** Piano Quartet in E flat major, Op. 16. **Isaac Stern** (vn); **Jaime Laredo** (va); **Yo-Yo Ma** (vc); **Emanuel Ax** (pf). Sony Classical Ⓕ SK53339 (65 minutes: DDD: 10/94). *See review under Beethoven; refer to the Index to Reviews.* ⊕⊕

New review

Schumann Piano Trios – No. 2 in F major, Op. 80; No. 3 in G minor, Op. 110. **Fontenay Trio** (Michael Mücke, vn; Niklas Schmidt, vc; Wolf Harden, pf). Teldec Ⓕ 4509-90864-2 (54 minutes: DDD: 12/95). Recorded 1993.

For anyone seeking the complete Schumann in this genre, there is obviously strong competition from the Borodins and Beaux Arts, whose mellow two-disc sets both include Schumann's Op. 88 *Fantasiestücke*. But taken on its own merits, this new Fontenay coupling of the Second and Third Trios has plenty to commend it in youthful verve and vividness of characterization, particularly welcome in No. 3 in G minor, where excessive repetition of initially arresting ideas can so easily sound merely patterned. Bigger tests come in the more personally motivated F major work, composed exactly ten years after Schumann's clandestine engagement to his beloved Clara, with the opening phrase of his 1840 love-song *Intermezzo* ("In the depths of my heart I keep a radiant image of you") as the secret underlying clue. Its introduction by the violin in the course of the first movement's development, though heartfelt, is surely just a little too backward. Also worrying is the almost aggressive accentuation of the pianist (a player certainly never backward in coming forward) in this movement's launching theme. All three artists respond warmly to the slow movement's *Mit innigem Ausdruck*, and they honour the third movement's slowish metronome marking rather than transforming it into a scherzo. Their relish of its quaint coda is particularly arresting. The recording is forward and bright albeit a bit hard.

Additional recommendations ...

...Nos. 1-3. Fantasiestücke, Op. 88. **Borodin Trio.** Chandos Ⓕ CHAN8832/3 (two discs:
110 minutes: DDD: 11/90).

...Nos. 1-3. Fantasiestücke, Op. 88. **Beaux Arts Trio.** Philips Ⓕ 432 165-2PH2 (two discs:
110 minutes: DDD: 8/93).

Schumann Fantasiestücke, Op. 73. Märchenbilder, Op. 113 – Nicht schnell; Langsam, mit
melancholischem Ausdruck. Funf Stücke im Volkston, Op. 102 – Langsam; Nicht schnell; Nicht
zu rasch. Drei Romanzen, Op. 94. Adagio and Allegro in A flat, Op. 70. **Paul Meyer** (cl); **Eric Le
Sage** (pf). Denon Ⓕ CO-75960 (51 minutes: DDD). Recorded 1993.

Of the engaging assortment of instrumental miniatures produced by Schumann (by way of temporary
respite from larger projects), only the three of Op. 73 were in fact originally conceived for clarinet. But
in every instance he sanctioned some or other alternative partner for the piano. Why worry, anyway,
when the young French artist, Paul Meyer, plays them all beautifully enough to make you
imagine that no other instrument could do them justice? Listening to the lullaby that closes the
Op. 113 *Märchenbilder* (originally composed for viola) one feels that no music could be more heart-
easing at the moment of one's passage from this world into the (hoped-for) next. Meyer's subtlety of
nuance within the *pianissimo* range, so often melting imperceptibly from sound into silence, is
spellbinding. Nor, of course, does he lack piercing incisiveness of articulation and agility when these
qualities are required – as in the spirited *Allegro* of Schumann's Op. 70 (originally for horn).
Throughout the disc he enjoys super-sensitive fluency and elegance from his French partner, Eric Le
Sage, whose biography inexplicably omits to mention that in 1989 he was the warmly acclaimed first
prize-winner at the Schumann International Piano Competition in Zwickau, the composer's
birthplace. The truthful recording justifies its full price but its playing-time of 51 minutes is not
over-generous.

Additional recommendation ...

...Fantasiestücke[ab]. Märchenbilder[bc]. Märchenerzählungen, Op. 132[abc]. **Kurtág** Neun Stücke[a].
Jelek, Op. 5[a]. Hommage à R. Sch, Op. 15d[abc]. [c]**Eduard Brunner** (cl); [a]**Kim Kashkashian** (va);
[b]**Robert Levin** (pf). ECM New Series Ⓕ 437 957-2 (76 minutes: DDD: 1/96).

Schumann Violin Sonatas – No. 1 in A minor, Op. 105; No. 2 in D minor, Op. 121. **Gidon Kremer**
(vn); **Martha Argerich** (pf). DG Ⓕ 419 235-2GH (49 minutes: DDD: 1/87).   ⓆⓆ

Schumann Violin Sonatas – No. 1 in A minor, Op. 105; No. 2 in D minor, Op. 121; No. 3 in
A minor – Intermezzo. **Ilya Kaler** (vn); **Boris Slutsky** (pf). Naxos Ⓢ 8 550870 (51 minutes: DDD:
9/94). Recorded 1993.

Schumann's two violin sonatas are late works, dating from 1851, and both were written quickly,
apparently in four and six days respectively. This rapidity of composition is nowhere evident except
perhaps in the vigour and enthusiasm of the music. Argerich and Kremer, both mercurial and
emotionally charged performers, subtly balance the ardent Florestan and dreamily melancholic
Eusebius elements of Schumann's creativity. This is even more striking in the Second Sonata, a greater
work than its twin, thematically vigorous with a richness and scope that make it at once a striking as
well as ideally structured work. Kremer and Argerich have established a close and exciting duo
partnership and this fine recording shows what like minds can achieve in music so profoundly
expressive as this.

The Naxos performances, powerfully recorded in Indiana by young Russian artists, are most
enjoyable. The passion of their playing is perhaps not wholly Germanic, but every artist legitimately
brings something of himself to the music he performs, and nothing here takes us out of touch with
Schumann's world. Indeed, there is an impressive intensity to this playing, although refinement and
tenderness are rightly also present. The single movement from the composite "FAE Sonata" dedicated
to Joseph Joachim, in which Schumann collaborated with the young Brahms and Albert Dietrich,
makes a useful bonus in a disc which would otherwise last under 50 minutes. The Naxos disc at super-
bargain price represents fine value.

Additional recommendation ...

...Nos. 1-3. **Mark Kaplan** (vn); **Anton Kuerti** (pf). Arabesque Ⓕ Z6662 (69 minutes: DDD: 2/96).

New review

Schumann Arabeske in C major, Op. 18. Davidsbünd-lertänze, Op. 6. Blumenstück in D flat
major, Op. 19. Etudes symphoniques, Op. 13 (1852 version). **András Schiff** (pf). Teldec Ⓕ 4509-
99176-2 (76 minutes: DDD: 11/95). Recorded 1995.

Schumann was a great re-thinker, in Schiff's opinion not always for the better in later life – hence his
choice of Schumann's original (1837) conception of the *Davidsbündlertänze* rather than its more
usually heard 1851 revision. Except for a touch of mischief (subsequently removed) at the end of
No. 9, textual differences are slight. But Schiff prefers the fewer repeat markings in the first edition,
so that ideas never lose their freshness. More importantly, the exceptional immediacy and vividness
of his characterization reminds us that initially Schumann signed nearly all of these 18 'bridal
thoughts' with an F (the impetuous Florestan) or an E (the introspective, visionary Eusebius) – or
sometimes both – as well as including literary inscriptions (and one or two more colourful expression
marks) as a clue to the mood of the moment. Schiff laughs and teases, storms and yearns, as if the

hopes and dreams of the youthful Robert, forbidden all contact with his distant beloved, were wholly his own – there and then. The impatient Florestan fares particularly well. For the much metamorphosed *Etudes symphoniques* Schiff chooses the generally used late version of 1852 (posthumously revised to restore two rejected earlier numbers) with its admirably tautened finale. Here, his bold, firmly contoured approach reaffirms it as the most magisterially 'classical' work the young Schumann ever wrote. Whereas Thibaudet, in his more fancifully brilliant recent recording, seeks its variety, Schiff emphasizes its continuity (partly by smoother tempo change *en route*) and unity as a whole. Even the five so-called supplementary variations emerge as more purposeful, less ruminative, than often heard. These Schiff wisely offers as a completely independent group at the end. The recital is completed by the *Arabeske* and *Blumenstück*, again played with a very strong sense of direction, even if Schiff is not yet Richter's equal in disguising the repetitiveness of the latter. Nothing but praise for the naturalness of the reproduction.

Schumann Fantasie in C major, Op. 17. March in G minor, Op. 76 No. 2. Concert Studies on Caprices by Paganini, Op. 10 – No. 4 in C minor; No. 5 in B minor; No. 6 in E minor. Novellette in F major, Op. 21 No. 1. Blumenstück in D flat major, Op. 19. Vier Nachtstücke, Op. 23.
Brahms Piano Sonatas – No. 1 in C major, Op. 1; No. 2 in F sharp minor, Op. 2. Variations on a Theme by Paganini, Op. 35. Capriccio in C major, Op. 76 No. 8. Intermezzo in E minor, Op. 116 No. 5. Ballade in G minor, Op. 118 No. 3. Rhapsody in E flat major, Op. 119 No. 4. **Sviatoslav Richter** (pf). Philips Ⓕ 438 477-2PH3 (three discs: 184 minutes: DDD: 8/94). ⒼⒼ

Variable reproduction, coupled with this highly-strung artist's own unpredictability, inevitably results in ups and downs. But for the one-and-a-half discs of Schumann alone, this album can be cherished as a collector's piece. There is surely no one on the concert platform today more finely attuned to Schumann's secret inner world. The miniatures give particular pleasure and how keenly he responds to that element of "strangeness blended with the beautiful" (as romanticism was once defined) in the four *Nachtstücke* written with a supernatural premonition of his brother's death. All technical challenges are dissolved into the purest poetry in the three all-too-rarely heard *Concert Studies on Caprices by Paganini* and in the major work, the great Op. 17 *Fantasie*, his own emotional warmth is fortunately matched by some of the ripest sonority that we're given in this album. It's a performance which obviously comes from the deepest places of his heart. There are memorable things too in the two early Brahms sonatas, not least the strain of nostalgic lyricism so beautifully drawn from the first movement of No. 1 in C major. The two sets of *Paganini* Variations in their turn bring bewitchingly light and delicate prestidigitation and seductively sung melody. But in burlier bravura, and notably in both excitable homecomings, there are some gaucheries and inaccuracies that would certainly not have got through in a studio recording. Of the miniatures, the intimate, elusive E minor *Intermezzo* is exquisitely phrased and shaded.

Additional recommendations ...

...Fantasie. Fantasiestücke, Op. 12. **Alfred Brendel** (pf). Philips Ⓕ 411 049-2PH (ADD: 4/84).

...Kreisleriana. Piano Sonata No. 2. Novellette in F sharp minor, Op. 21 No. 8. **Vladimir Ashkenazy** (pf). Decca Ⓕ 425 940-2DH (59 minutes: DDD: 4/92).

...Arabeske, Op. 18. Piano Sonata No. 2 in G minor, Op. 22. Vier Nachtstücke, Op. 23. Vier Klavierstücke, Op. 32. Toccata in C major, Op. 7. Presto passionato in G minor. **Bernd Glemser** (pf). Naxos Ⓢ 8 550715 (68 minutes: DDD: 10/94).

...Fantasie. **Schubert** Piano Sonata No. 21 in B flat major, D960. **Sir Clifford Curzon** (pf). Orfeo D'Or Ⓜ C401951B (66 minutes: ADD: 4/96).

...Fantasie. **Schubert** Fantasy in C major, D760, "Wanderer". **Maurizio Pollini** (pf). DG The Originals Ⓜ 447 451-2GOR (52 minutes: ADD: 6/96). *See review under Schubert; refer to the Index to Reviews.*

New review

Schumann Fantasiestücke, Op. 12[a] – No. 1, Des Abends; No. 2, Aufschwung; No. 3, Warum?; No. 5, In der Nacht; No. 7, Traumes Wirren; No. 8, Ende von Lied. Humoreske in B flat major, Op. 20[a]. Novelletten, Op. 21[b] – No. 1 in F major; No. 2 in D major; No. 8 in F sharp minor. **Sviatoslav Richter** (pf). Melodiya mono Ⓜ 74321 29464-2* (71 minutes: ADD: 6/96). Items marked [a] recorded 1956, [b]1960.

The booklet contains an anecdote about Arthur Rubinstein hearing Richter for the first time, "It really wasn't anything out of the ordinary. Then at some point I noticed my eyes growing moist: tears began rolling down my cheeks ...". What produces such a reaction cannot be put into words, but it probably has to do with Richter's uncanny ability to convey a sense of inevitability. In Schumann, for instance, Richter takes characterization and virtuosity in his stride and aims at the emotional truth beyond. Impetuosity and fantasy are there, but at the structural level rather than in the detail. The simplicity of his *Humoreske* gets to the heart of the matter as unerringly as the élan of his *Fantasiestücke* and the tensed steel of his *Novelettes*. Decent mono sound.

Schumann Humoreske in B flat major, Op. 20. Kinderszenen, Op. 15. Kreisleriana, Op. 16. **Radu Lupu** (pf). Decca Ⓕ 440 496-2DH (75 minutes: DDD: 4/95). Recorded 1993. *Gramophone Editor's record of the month.* ⒼⒼ

As piano playing this disc has an aristocratic distinction reminiscent of Lipatti. As music-making it is underpinned by a totally unselfconscious kind of intuition, making you feel you are discovering the truth of the matter for the first time. It is difficult to recall a more revealing performance of Schumann's *Humoreske*. Lupu captures all the unpredictability of its swift-changing moods while at the same time imparting a sense of inevitability to the sequence as a whole. Florestan's caprice is as piquant as Eusebius's tenderness is melting. Yet there is an underlying unity in the diversity from Lupu, enhanced by most beautifully timed and shaded 'links'. Goodness knows how long this work has been in his repertory. But here it emerges with the keen edge of new love. Next, *Kinderszenen*: simplicity is its keynote. To begin with (as notably in the opening "Von fremden Ländern und Menschen") you wonder if, in rejection of sentimentality, he might not be allowing himself enough time for wide-eyed wonderment. But you are soon won over by his limpid tonal palette and the sheer purity of his phrasing. Each piece tells its own magical little tale without the slightest trace of special pleading. Such pristine grace will never pall, however often heard. *Kreisleriana* in its turn offers rich contrasts of desperation, dedication and Hoffmannesque drollery. And except, perhaps, in the impetuous No. 7 (taken dangerously fast), it brings further reminders that we are in the presence of a master pianist – amongst so much else able to rejoice in this work's endless dialogues between left hand and right with his opulent bass and gleaming treble. Reproduction is totally faithful throughout.

Additional recommendations ...

...Kinderszenen. Kreisleriana, Op. 16. **Martha Argerich** (pf). DG Ⓕ 410 653-2GH (52 minutes: DDD: 5/84). Ⓖ

...Kinderszenen[a]. Faschingsschwank aus Wien, Op. 26[b]. Carnaval, Op. 9[b]. **Daniel Barenboim** (pf) DG Privilege Ⓑ 431 167-2GR (73 minutes: ADD: 8/91).

...Kreisleriana, Op. 16. Also includes other works by Schumann and Chopin. **Vladimir Horowitz** (pf). Sony Classical Ⓜ S2K53468 (two discs: 113 minutes: ADD: 7/94). *Gramophone classical 100*. ⒼⒼⒼ

...Kreisleriana, Op. 16. Faschingsschwank aus Wien, Op. 26. **Pamela Ross** (pf). Connoisseur Society Ⓕ CD4185 (52 minutes: DDD: 9/94).

...Kinderszenen. **Debussy** Children's Corner. **Tchaikovsky** Album for the young, Op. 39. **Idil Biret** (pf). Naxos Ⓢ 8 550885 (66 minutes: DDD: 10/94).

...Kreisleriana. Etudes symphoniques, Op. 13. **Franck** Prélude, Choral et Fugue. **Shura Cherkassky** (pf). Nimbus Ⓕ NI7705 (77 minutes: DDD: 3/95). *See review under Franck; refer to the Index to Reviews*. ⒼⒼ

...Kreisleriana. Carnaval, Op. 9. **Mitsuko Uchida** (pf). Philips Ⓕ 442 777-2PH (67 minutes: DDD: 5/95).

...Kinderszenen. Kreisleriana, Op. 16. Etudes symphoniques, Op. 13. Carnaval, Op. 9. Papillons, Op. 2. Davidsbündlertänze, Op. 6. Fantasiestücke, Op. 12 No. 1, Des Abends. Waldszenen, Op. 82 No. 7, Vogel als Prophet. **Alfred Cortot** (pf). Music & Arts mono Ⓕ CD858* (two discs: 131 minutes: ADD: 1/96).

Schumann Piano Sonata No. 1 in F sharp minor, Op. 11. Fantasie in C major, Op. 17. **Maurizio Pollini** (pf). DG Ⓕ 423 134-2GH (63 minutes: ADD: 5/88). From 2530 379 (5/74). ⒼⒼ
These works grew from Schumann's love and longing for his future wife Clara. Both performances are superb, not least because they are so truthful to the letter of the score. By eschewing all unspecified rubato in the *Fantasie*, Pollini reminds us that the young Schumann never wrote a more finely proportioned large-scale work; this feeling for structure, coupled with exceptional emotional intensity, confirms it as one of the greatest love-poems ever written for the piano. His richly characterized account of the Sonata is refreshingly unmannered. Certainly the familiar charges of protracted patterning in the faster flanking movements are at once dispelled by his rhythmic *élan*, his crystalline texture and his ear for colour. The sound re-emerges with all its original clarity on CD.

Additional recommendations ...

...Piano Sonata No. 1. Waldszenen, Op. 82. Kinderszenen, Op. 15. **Vladimir Ashkenazy** (pf). Decca Ⓕ 421 290-2DH (74 minutes: DDD: 2/89).

...Fantasie. Fantasiestücke, Op. 12. **Brahms** Variations and Fugue on a Theme by Handel, Op. 24. **Benno Moiseiwitsch** (pf). Testament mono Ⓕ SBT1023* (78 minutes: ADD: 1/94).

New review
Schumann Piano Works. **Alfred Cortot** (pf). Music & Arts mono Ⓕ CD-858* (two discs: 131 minutes: ADD: 1/96).
Etudes symphoniques, Op. 13 (from HMV DB1325/7, 8/30). Carnaval, Op. 9 (DB1252/4, 7/29). Kreisleriana, Op. 16 (DB2608/11, 5/38). Papillons, Op. 2 (HMV DA1442/3, 5/37). Kinderszenen, Op. 15 (DB2581/2, 1/36). Davidsbündlertänze, Op. 6 (DB3263/5, 8/38). Fantasiestücke, Op. 12 No. 1, Des Abends (DB3338, 1/38). Waldszenen, Op. 82 No. 7, Vogel als Prophet (DA1901, 1/49).
It is good to have this Music & Arts sharply focused issue of Cortot's evergreen, ever-fresh performances on a well-presented two-CD set. These recordings have been reissued many times before. How many artists, today, one wonders, could hope to garner such tribute? So here, again, is that magically floated *cantabile* tugging at the heart-strings in "Des Abends" (how one longs for the rest of the cycle) yet maintained with the flawless line and impetus of a great singer. In the *Davidsbündlertänze*, one of Cortot's most poetically potent if battle-scarred recordings, his confusion in Florestan's *schneller* in No. 3 or in the vaulting leaps of No. 12 is, perhaps, not quite what the composer had in mind in his instruction, *Mit Humor*. Yet who can resist his *dolce cantando* in No. 14,

the gem of his Schumann, alive with a rich polyphonic pianistic tradition that Alfred Brendel so sadly claims has virtually vanished from the music scene. In *Kinderszenen* the 'poet' of the epilogue is at once Schumann and Cortot, creator and re-creator, and in the *Etudes symphoniques* the gold-dust scattering of the posthumous studies throughout the main work is done with such passion and inwardness that only a Beckmesser could possibly object. Playing like this seems light years away from today's style or standard. But *pace* Cortot, his idiosyncrasy, his pell-mell virtuosity and poetic ecstasy may strike a foreign and even alien note in our more puritan times yet, as Yvonne Lefebure so eloquently put it, "even his wrong notes were those of a God".

Additional recommendation ...

...Etudes symphoniques. Arabeske in C major, Op. 18. **Brahms** Variations on a Theme by Paganini, Op. 35. **Jean-Yves Thibaudet** (pf). Decca Ⓕ 444 338-2DH (65 minutes: DDD: 10/95). *See review under Brahms; refer to the Index to Reviews.*

Schumann Theme and Variations on the name "Abegg", Op. 1. Fantasie in C major, Op. 17. Faschingsschwank aus Wien, Op. 26. **Vladimir Ashkenazy** (pf). Decca Ⓕ 443 322-2DH (58 minutes: DDD: 2/95). Recorded 1991.
The *Fantasie* in C is the centrepiece of this issue. Ashkenazy plays with a strong and consistently sustained sense of direction, as if trying to emphasize the continuity and coherence of the argument no less than the music's passion. It is an urgently committed, full-bodied performance and needless to say his command of the keyboard is superb, not least in the central march with its recklessly fast coda. It could well have been in response to Clara's plea for something less searching, something more brilliant and easily understood by the general public, that Schumann came up with the *Faschingsschwank aus Wien*. Ashkenazy gives a spirited enough performance to justify his resort to a considerably swifter tempo than prescribed for the three fast movements. The Decca recording is pleasingly warm and true.

Additional recommendation ...

...Theme and Variations on the name "Abegg". *Coupled with works by* **Schubert, Bach, Haydn, Chopin, Debussy, Scriabin, Rachmaninov** and **Prokofiev** Sviatoslav Richter (pf). DG Double Ⓜ 447 355-2GDB2 (two discs: 150 minutes: ADD: 12/95).

Schumann Allegro in B minor, Op. 8. Novelletten, Op. 21. Drei Fantasiestücke, Op. 111. Gesänge der Frühe, Op. 133. **Ronald Brautigam** (pf). Olympia Ⓕ OCD436 (79 minutes: DDD: 6/94). Recorded 1993.   Ⓖ
The note reminds us that even the eight *Novelletten* chosen as the centrepiece here are not often heard in sequence as a set. Brautigam prefaces them with the early (1931-32) B minor *Allegro* originally intended as the first movement of a sonata. They are followed by the last two suites Schumann ever wrote for the piano – the *Gesänge der Frühe* only a year before his final breakdown. Most enjoyable is Brautigam's vitality – vitality of imagination no less than of fingers. You are immediately gripped by his plunge into the Op. 8 *Allegro*, with its arresting octave 'motto'. His mercurial fancy and ear for hidden melodic strands in the ensuing stream certainly makes nonsense of hasty dismissal of this work as mere old-style virtuoso note-spinning. Moreover, such is his unflagging impulse in the eight *Novelletten* that never for a moment are you tempted to accuse Schumann of over-repetitively patterned figuration. Potently characterized and contrasted as are the three *Fantasiestücke*, Op. 111 of 1851, Brautigam leaves you in no doubt as to their unity as a set – as he does again, still more subtly and movingly, in the more elusive spiritual world of the five *Gesänge der Frühe*. The bright, clear tonal reproduction is acceptable enough.

Additional recommendation ...

...Carnaval, Op. 9. Drei Fantasiestücke, Op. 111. Etudes symphoniques, Op. 13. **Shura Cherkassky** (pf). Decca Ⓕ 433 652-2DH (66 minutes: ADD: 1/95).   ⒼⒼ

Schumann Davidsbündlertänze, Op. 6. Waldszenen, Op. 82. Fantasiestücke, Op. 111. **Andreas Haefliger** (pf). Sony Classical Ⓕ SK48036 (65 minutes: DDD: 10/92). Recorded 1991.   Ⓖ
Schumann Davidsbündlertänze, Op. 6. Fantasiestücke, Op. 12. **Benjamin Frith** (pf). Naxos Ⓢ 8 550493 (63 minutes: DDD: 3/93). Recorded 1991.
Although by 1851 Schumann had dropped overt references to that Laurel and Hardy of his creative imagination, Florestan and Eusebius (referring, more or less, to the *yin,* and *yang* – masculine and feminine, assertive and reflective – characters of individual pieces), frequent and telling changes of mood remained an essential ingredient of his mature style. *Davidsbündlertänze,* or "Dances of the League of David" exemplify this trend most vividly: two books, each containing nine separate pieces, alternating fast with slow, humorous with serious and invariably maintaining an element of surprise. There are two 'versions' of the *Davidsbündlertänze,* one from 1837, the other from 1851 and Andreas Haefliger achieves a felicitous musical balance by combining elements of both. His is an intelligent and thoughtful brand of pianism, sensitive to modulation and wonderfully warm in tone; one was was often reminded of the similarly perceptive art of our own much-loved (and much missed) master pianist, Solomon. What is most striking about the *Davidsbündlertänze* is the way Schumann plots key changes from one miniature to the next, effecting many magical contrasts, especially in the second book. Furthermore, the actual level of invention is always high, and the closing sequence utilizes some of Schumann's most bewitching invention: try, by way of example, the final pair – "Wie aus der

Ferne" and "Nicht schnell" (tracks 17 and 18). *Waldszenen* is less a sweeping inspiration than a series of lonely vignettes; "The Prophet Bird" (track 25), a frequently performed 'encore' in its own right, is possibly the most atmospheric evocation of tree-top bird song pre-Messiaen, an eerie, questioning *morceau* that twists and turns with the unpredictability of its natural model. If *Waldszenen* takes us deep into the woods, the late *Fantasiestücke* take us further still; here loneliness transforms to disorientation (second movement), and youthful passion becomes defiant grandeur (third). Haefliger charts both this and the disc's companion pieces with sure intuition, and he is most beautifully recorded.

The young prize-winning British pianist Benjamin Frith indulges the *Davidsbündlertänze*'s caprice, highlighting the contrasts between fast and slower pieces, and summoning his excellent technique for some exciting pianism. But then contrast lies at the very heart of Schumann's inspiration. Frith is quite unlike Haefliger in that he favours impulse over refinement, and isn't afraid to throw caution to the winds, if the mood dictates. His *Fantasiestücke*, too, are forthright and outspoken, although "Des Abends", "Warum" and "Ende vom Lied" each contain plenty of poetry. Naxos's recording is excellent. Certainly recommended, not only for the budget-conscious collector, but for those who enjoy youthful pianistic exuberance.

Additional recommendations ...

...Papillons, Op. 2. Davidsbündlertänze. Carnaval, Op. 9. Fantasie in C major, Op. 17. Etudes symphoniques, Op. 13. Kreisleriana, Op. 16. Kinderszenen, Op. 15. Piano Sonata No. 2 in G minor, Op. 22. Arabeske, Op. 18. Bunte Blätter, Op. 99 – Novellette. Drei Romanzen, Op. 28. Humoreske, Op. 20. Waldszenen. Nachtstücke, Op. 23. **Wilhelm Kempff** (pf). DG Ⓑ 435 045-2GX4 (four discs: 297 minutes: ADD: 5/92). 🅶🅶

...Waldszenen. Arabeske in C major, Op. 18. Drei Romanzen, Op. 28. Faschingsschwank aus Wien, Op. 26. **Maria-João Pires** (pf). DG Ⓕ 437 538-2GH (66 minutes: DDD: 6/95).

Schumann Six Studies, Op. 56. Four Sketches, Op. 58. Six Fugues on B-A-C-H, Op. 60. **Olivier Latry** (org). Sony Classical Ⓕ SK57490 (69 minutes: DDD: 10/94). Played on the Cavaillé-Coll organ of L'Eglise Notre-Dame de Saint-Omer, France. Recorded 1991. 🅶

Latry shows himself to be as sensitive and alert to the style of Schumann's miniatures as to Vierne's great symphonic structures. In the *Studies* and the *Sketches*, both written for pedal-piano, he manages to create a quasi-pianistic style while making it seem convincing organ music – and in the first *Sketch* he contrives to imitate by clever use of the swell pedal the kind of dynamic subtlety attainable on the piano by slight adjustment of finger pressure. His agile fingerwork and logical sense of phrasing belie the lack of intimacy between an organist and his instrument compared with that between pianist and piano, and his astute ear finds, usually, exactly the right registration. The *B-A-C-H* Fugues were written with the organ in mind (albeit very much as a second choice to the pedal-piano). Here Latry sheds any hint of pianism, something immediately apparent in the first fugue. He uses the unique sustaining power of the organ to trace unerringly the contrapuntal lines and the hierarchy of the inner detail, while increasing overall intensity by unobtrusively adding stops along the way to reach a truly thrilling climax.

New review

Schumann Frauenliebe und -leben, Op. 42. Gesänge, Op. 31 – No. 1, Die Löwenbraut; No. 2, Die Kartenlegerin. Gedichte, Op. 35 – No. 1, Lust der Sturmnacht; No. 8, Stille Liebe. Rose, Meer und Sonne, Op. 37 No. 9. Fünf Lieder, Op. 40. Der Schatzgräber, Op. 45 No. 1. Volksliedchen, Op. 51 No. 2. Die Soldatenbraut, Op. 64 No. 1. Lieder-Album für die Jugend, Op. 79 – No. 5, Vom Schlaraffenland; No. 22, Des Sennen Abscheid; No. 26, Schneeglöcken. Mein schöner Stern!, Op. 101 No. 4. Abendlied, Op. 107 No. 6. Die Meerfee, Op. 125 No. 1. Dein Angesicht, Op. 127 No. 2. **Anne Sofie von Otter** (mez); **Bengt Forsberg** (pf). DG Ⓕ 445 881-2GH (79 minutes: DDD: 11/95). Texts and translations included. *Gramophone Editor's choice.* Recorded 1993. 🅶

This is one of those records where the promise of something exceptional in the first phrases is fully borne out by all that follows. The *Frauenliebe* cycle is sung by a character, as vividly defined as any Fiordiligi, Senta or Mimì in opera. Von Otter is one of those rare artists who can adapt the voice and yet be true to its natural identity. In these songs of Schumann (not only in the *Frauenliebe*) she seems, unselfconsciously, to find a new voice-personality for each and still to confine herself to what lies naturally within her scope, forcing nothing and falsifying nothing. The woman of the 'life and love' starts out as a girl. "Seit ich ihn gesehen" has a shy, private rapture which then grows bold for "Er, der Herrlichste von allen", frank in its enthusiasm, buoyant in the spirit of its rhythm, radiant as the voice rises to its highest notes. "Ich kann's nicht fassen, nicht glauben" is fully outgoing, an expression of utter commitment, and the smile is always in the voice. The engagement-ring induces maturity, the girl now a woman. The wedding-day preparations, confiding of motherhood, dandling the baby, and then the emptiness of life at the husband's death: all are caught as in reality and in character. It is a completely absorbed and absorbing performance. The generous selection of songs which follows works its spell partly by contrasts. The pastoral sweetness of "Des Sennen Abschied" gives way to a grim, predatory ferocity of utterance in "Der Schatzgräber", and the big Brahmsy sweep of "Lust der Sturmnacht" throws into relief the wistfully tender mood of "Dein Angesicht". In these and in all else von Otter lights upon the right tone, and the right shades of that tone. The programme is well planned, too, rounded off with "Rose, Meer und Sonne", sketching the melodies of *Frauenliebe und -leben* with which the recital began. Occasionally the piano is recorded too heavily or too prominently for the voice. But generally the sympathy and unanimity of singer and pianist are all that could be desired – as is the recital *in toto*. No comparisons: it doesn't matter how much of Schumann you already have on the shelves, this will still be a prized addition.

Schumann Dichterliebe, Op. 48.
Mendelssohn Lieder, Op. 19*a* – No. 4, Neue Liebe; No. 5, Gruss. Lieder, Op. 34 – No. 2, Auf Flügeln des Gesanges; No. 6, Reiselied. Morgengruss, Op. 47 No. 2. Allnächtlich im Träume, Op. 86 No. 4.
Schubert Schwanengesang, D957 – Der Atlas; Ihr Bild; Das Fischermädchen; Die Stadt; Am Meer; Der Doppelgänger. **Christoph Prégardien** (ten); **Andreas Staier** (fp). Deutsche Harmonia Mundi Ⓕ 05472 77319-2 (57 minutes: DDD: 12/94). Texts and translations included. Recorded 1993.   Ⓖ

In their deeply poignant reading of *Dichterliebe,* these artists expose, even more than do the exemplary Schreier and Eschenbach, the wounded pain of the protagonist, and the participation of a fortepiano gives the performance an intimacy that a grand piano cannot match. The simple beauty of the singing in the early songs is rightly countermanded by the darker, more dramatic tone and manner in "Im Rhein" and "Ich grolle nicht", with the top A on "Herzen" piercing to the heart. These in turn give way to the plaintive sorrow of "Und wüssten's die Blumen", the *Innigkeit* of "Hör ich das Liedchen", the delicately etched line and feeling of "Am leuchtenden Sommermorgen", and the numbed emptiness, so Schreier-like, of "Ich hab im Traum geweinet". The draining of all passion is summed up in the repeated final line of the penultimate song, "Zerfliesst wie alte Schaum", with the fortepiano's afterthought so translucently played by Staier, whose postlude to the whole cycle, restrained and understated though it is, speaks volumes of the sadness experienced throughout. The truthfulness of the interpretation is seconded by the tenor's command of line and phrase, the player's close rapport with his partner. This intelligently planned programme then offers more Heine in the shape of settings by Mendelssohn and Schubert. The less demanding (for performers and listeners) Mendelssohn group allows an emotional respite between the soulful Schumann and the searing Schubert. From *Schwanengesang,* that extraordinary pair of anguished songs, "Ihr Bild" and "Die Stadt", are given their full measure of grief (and note the light, diaphanous evocation of the water on the fortepiano in "Die Stadt") with a gentle, rather fast "Das Fischermädchen" in between. Prégardien's silver-voiced sorrowing and communing in "Am Meer" is just right, the verbal accents present but, as throughout, never overdone. And so on to that Everest of a song, "Der Doppelgänger", a stark, nerve-tingling interpretation that proves a fitting climax to a superb recital, faultlessly recorded.

Additional recommendations ...
...Liederkreis, Op. 24. Frauenliebe und -leben, Op. 42. Tragödie, Op. 64 No. 3. Abends am Strand, Op. 45 No. 3. Lehn' deine Wang, Op. 142 No. 2. Mein Wagen rollet langsam, Op. 142 No. 2. **Brigitte Fassbaender** (mez); **Irwin Gage** (pf). DG Ⓕ 415 519-2GH (57 minutes: DDD: 2/86).
...Dichterliebe, Op. 48. Liederkreis, Op. 39. **Olaf Bär** (bar); **Geoffrey Parsons** (pf). EMI Ⓕ CDC7 47397-2 (54 minutes: DDD: 9/86).
...Dichterliebe. Liederkreis, Op. 39. **Josef Protschka** (ten); **Helmut Deutsch** (pf). Capriccio Ⓕ 10 215 (62 minutes: DDD: 12/88).
...Liederkreis, Opp. 24 and 39. Dichterliebe, Op. 48. Myrthen, Op. 25 – No. 1, Widmung; No. 2, Freisinn; No. 3, Der Nussbaum; No. 7, Die Lotosblume; No. 15, Aus den hebräischen Gesängen; No. 21, Was will die einsame Träne?; No. 24, Du bist wie eine Blume; No. 25, Aus den östlichen Rosen; No. 26, Zum Schluss. Lieder-Album für die Jugend, Op. 79 – No. 4, Frühlingsgruss; No. 7, Zigeunerliedchen; No. 13, Marienwürmchen; No. 26, Schneeglöckchen. Zwölf Gedichte, Op. 35 – No. 3, Wanderlied; No. 4, Erstes Grün; No. 8, Stille Liebe; No. 11, Wer machte dich so krank?; No. 12, Alte Laute. Liebesfrühling, Op. 37 – No. 1, Der Himmel hat eine Träne geweint; No. 5, Ich hab in mich gesogen; No. 9, Rose, Meer und Sonne. Fünf Lieder, Op. 40. Mein schöner Stern!, Op. 101 No. 4. Nur ein lächelnder Blick, Op. 27 No. 5. Geständnis, Op. 74 No. 7. Aufträge, Op. 77 No. 5. Meine Rose, Op. 90 No. 2. Kommen und Scheiden, Op. 90 No. 3. Lieder und Gesange, Op. 51 – No. 1, Sehnsucht; No. 3, Ich wandre nicht. An den Mond, Op. 95 No. 2. Dein Angesicht, Op. 127 No. 2. Lehn deine Wang, Op. 142 No. 2. Der arme Peter, Op. 53 No. 3. **Peter Schreier** (ten); **Christoph Eschenbach** (pf). Teldec Ⓕ 2292-46154-2 (three discs: 165 minutes: DDD: 6/91).   ⒼⒼ
...Myrthen, Op. 25 – No.1, Widmung; No. 3, Der Nussbaum; No. 7, Die Lotosblume; No. 9, Lied der Suleika; No. 11, Lied der Brait aus dem Liebesfrühling I; No. 12, Lied der Braut aus dem Liebesfrühling II; No. 15, Aus den hebräischen Gesängen; No. 21, Was will die einsame Träne?; No. 23, Im Westen. Sieben Gedichte, Op. 90. An den Sonnenschein, Op. 36 No. 4. Der Himmel hat ein Träne geweint, Op. 37 No. 1. Muttertraum, Op. 40 No. 2. Romanzen und Balladen, Op. 64 – No. 2, Das berlassne Mägdelein; No. 3, Tragödie. Melancholie, Op. 74 No. 6. Geisternähe, Op. 77 No. 3. Der Einsiedler, Op. 83 No. 3. **Mitsuko Shirai** (mez); **Hartmut Höll** (pf). Capriccio Ⓕ 10 445 (63 minutes: DDD: 11/93). *Gramophone Editor's choice.*
...Dichterliebe[d]. **Schubert** Der Jüngling und der Tod, D545[a]. Der Wanderer an den Mond, D870[a]. Schwanengesang, D957[a] – Liebesbotschaft; Ihr Bild. Der Schiffer, D536[a]. Ganymed, D544[a].

Erster Verlust, D226[a]. Die Forelle, D550[a]. Nacht und Träume, D827[a]. Seligkeit, D433[b].
Harfenspieler I, D478[c]. Fischerweise, D881[c]. Erlkönig, D328[c]. **Gérard Souzay** (bar); [acd]**Jacqueline Bonneau**, [b]**Dalton Baldwin** (pfs). Decca Historic Series mono Ⓜ 440 065-2DM* (71 minutes: ADD: 1/95).

...Dichterliebe. Liederkreis, Op. 24. Mein Wagen rollet langsam, Op. 142 No. 4. Es leuchtet meine Liebe, Op. 127 No. 3. Abends am Strand, Op. 45 No. 3. Myrthen, Op. 25 – No. 5, Lied aus dem Schenkenbuch im Divan I; No. 24, Du bist wie eine Blume. Der Kontrabandiste, Op. 74 No. 10. Erstes Grün, Op. 35 No. 4. Schöne Fremde, Op. 39 No. 6. **Dietrich Fischer-Dieskau** (bar); **Hartmut Höll** (pf). Erato Ⓕ 4509-98492-2 (69 minutes: DDD: 9/95).

...Myrthen, Op. 25 – No. 1, Widmung; No. 3, Der Nussbaum; No. 7, Die Lotosblume; No. 9, Lied der Suleika. Lieder-Album für die Jugend, Op. 79 – No. 10, Das Käuzlein; No. 12, Der Sandmann; No. 13, Marienwürmchen; No. 23, Er ist's; No. 26, Schneeglöckchen. Jasminenstrauch, Op. 27 No. 4. Die Blume der Ergebung, Op. 83 No. 2. Röselein, Op. 89 No. 6. Lieder und Gesänge, Op. 77 – No. 2, Mein Garten; No. 5, Aufträge. Gedichte, Op. 90 – No. 2, Meine Rose; No. 4, Die Sennin. Schmetterling, Op. 79 No. 2. Gedichte, Op. 35 – No. 4, Erstes Grün; No. 5, Sehnsucht nach der Waldgegend; No. 9, Frage. Die letzten Blumen starben, Op. 104 No. 6. Die Meerfee, Op. 125 No. 1. Waldesgespräch, Op. 39 No. 3. Loreley, Op. 53 No. 2. Die Kartenlegerin, Op. 31 No. 2. Sehnsucht, Op. 51 No. 1. Mein schöner Stern!, Op. 101 No. 4. *Coupled with works by* **Brahms, Telemann, C.P.E. Bach, J.S. Bach, Handel** and **Schubert Elly Ameling** (sop); **Various soloists.** Deutsche Harmonia Mundi Ⓕ 74321 26617-2 (four discs: 239 minutes: ADD: 12/95). *See review in the Collections section; refer to the Index to Reviews.*

New review

Schumann Liederkreis, Op. 24. Dichterliebe, Op. 48. Gesänge, Op. 142 – Lehn deine Wang; Mein Wagen rollet langsam. Myrthen, Op. 25 – Die Lotosblume; Was will die einsame Tränen?; Du bist wie eine Blume. Der arme Peter, Op. 53 No. 3. Tragödie, Op. 64 No. 3. **Wolfgang Holzmair** (bar); **Imogen Cooper** (pf). Philips Ⓕ 446 086-2PH (67 minutes: DDD: 9/95). Texts and translations included. Recorded 1994. *Gramophone Editor's choice.* Ⓖ

This is a hugely enjoyable disc: here we have an ideal partnership in a thoughtfully conceived programme perfectly suited to its extraordinary talents. Holzmair's plangent, tenorish, gently vibrating voice, just right for Schumann, is beautifully supported and encouraged by Cooper's discerning, subtly arched playing, both wholly responsive to the love and longing expressed in Heine's wonderful poetry. The interpretations themselves abound in verbal and musical perceptions yet nothing is ever in the least exaggerated. From the very first notes of the very first song, "Mein Wagen rollet langsam", you know you are in for a special experience as you sense the rapport between the two artists, notice the flow and freedom of Cooper's playing, the feeling for the text in Holzmair's singing. In Op. 24, revelations come apace, particularly the lovely playing in the postlude to the third song, the unanimity of thought in the fourth, the dramatic impetus of the sixth, the sense of finality in the last. *Dichterliebe* is if anything even more satisfying, tempos, phrasing, inner feeling all confidently welded into a convincing whole, so much so that to single out any song, any detail would be out of place. Just listen – and be moved and delighted by a superb interpretation. To contemplate one's pleasure, the recording, made in the Esterházá Palace at Eisenstadt, is faultlessly balanced, voice and instrument for ward yet never obtrusively so. This is a 'must' for all Lieder enthusiasts. Those who aren't in that category ought to be converted if they try this disc.

Schumann Liederkreis, Op. 39. Sieben Gedichte, Op. 90. Lieder, Op. 40 – No. 1, Märzveilchen; No. 2, Muttertraum; No. 3, Der Soldat; No. 4, Der Spielmann. Lieder und Gesänge aus Wilhelm Meister, Op. 98a – No. 4, Wer nie sein Brot mit Tränen ass; No. 6, Wer sich der Einsamkeit ergibt; No. 8, An die Türen will ich schleichen. Nachtlied, Op. 96 No. 1. **Robert Holl** (bass); **András Schiff** (pf). Decca Ⓕ 436 123-2DH (68 minutes: DDD: 7/94). Texts and translations included. Recorded 1990. *Gramophone Editor's choice.* Ⓖ

The structure of this recital, and the way in which it works on the ear and the spirit from first to last, is an inextricable part of the power of its performances: each one is typical of Robert Holl's deeply absorbed imaginative examination of everything he sings, and of András Schiff's minutely sentient accompanying. The Op. 39 *Liederkreis* is the central point of reference. Before this come the seven little Lenau settings of Op. 90, approached by Holl very much as private intimations and reflections, to be overheard by the listener. "Meine Rose" is a mere sigh in half-voice; a dark "Der schwere Abend" presages the state of mind of *Dichterliebe's* "Ich hab' im Traum". As a group, these songs breathe out the very essence of the *Waldeinsamkeit* which appears overtly in the Op. 39 *Liederkreis*. For Holl, these are songs of far distant exile, the first poem whispering its intimations of mortality in a mere fraction of his mighty bass. He also adds the dark fairytale miniatures of the Hans Andersen Songs (Op. 40) and the tortured, forward-looking *Wilhelm Meister* Harper-Songs, ending, wonderfully, with one of Schumann's and Goethe's very greatest, "Uber allen Gipfeln ist Ruh". An outstanding recital.

Additional recommendations ...

...Liederkreis, Op. 39. 12 Gedichte, Op. 35. **Dame Margaret Price** (sop); **Graham Johnson** (pf). Hyperion Ⓒ CDA66596 (59 minutes: DDD).

...Liebeslied, Op. 51 No. 5. Nachtlied, Op. 96 No. 1. Lieder und Gesänge aus Wilhelm Meister, Op. 98a – No. 1, Mignon; No. 5, Heiss mich nicht reden; No. 7, Singet nicht in Trauertönen. *Coupled with works by* **Schubert, Wolf** and **Mozart** Das Veilchen, K476. **Dawn Upshaw** (sop); **Richard Goode** (pf). Elektra-Nonesuch Ⓕ 7559-79317-2 (53 minutes: DDD: 8/94). *See review in the Collections section; refer to the Index to Reviews.* Ⓖ

...Liederkreis, Op. 39. *Coupled with works by* **Brahms Brigitte Fassbaender** (mez); **Elisabeth Leonskaja** (pf). Teldec Ⓕ 9031-74872-2 (69 minutes: DDD: 10/94). *See review under Brahms; refer to the Index to Reviews.* Ⓖ

New review

Schumann Liederkreis, Op. 39. Frauenliebe und -leben, Op. 42. Myrthen, Op. 25 – No. 3, Der Nussbaum; No. 7, Die Lotosblume; No. 15, Aus den Hebraïschen Gesängen. Der Soldat, Op. 40 No. 3. Lieder-Album für die Jugend, Op. 79 – No. 23, Er ist's; No. 28, Mignon. **Marjana Lipovšek** (mez); **Graham Johnson** (pf). Sony Classical Ⓕ SK57972 (65 minutes: DDD: 8/95). Texts and translations included. Recorded 1993.

It will be for the two cycles that most will be drawn to this disc. As each of these performances is so satisfying, striking a *via media*, perhaps under Johnson's influence, between reading too little or too much into the songs, and finding in every case the just tempo, they can be recommended wholeheartedly to anyone wanting the pair sung by a mezzo. The combination of romance and gothic mystery in the Op. 39 *Liederkreis* is captured unerringly by both artists, in technical and interpretive terms, though one might like a firmer line and a more hushed *piano* from the singer in "Mondnacht". Detailed analysis is hardly warranted as the cycle progresses in a wholly natural and acceptable way, line, tone, and particularly vibrato nicely judged, and certain phrases, such as the final one in "Auf einer Berg", given an added frisson of verbal emphasis. In *Frauenliebe*, the pair catch the sense of the girl's wonder, growing maturity, inner warmth, but any hint of sentimentality is firmly kept at bay. A sudden underlining of the word "mein" in "Helft mir, ihr Schwestern" evinces the woman's anti-feminist attitude of being at her master's command. "Weisst du nun die Tränen" in the sixth song is rightly the emotional core of the reading. The postlude is softly, hauntingly played by Johnson. The recording has presence and immediacy.

New review

Schumann Liederkreis, Op. 39. Frauenliebe und -leben, Op. 42. **Soile Isokoski** (sop); **Marita Viitasalo** (pf). Finlandia Ⓕ 0630-10924-2 (49 minutes: DDD: 3/96). Texts and translations included. Recorded 1993-5.

Hot on the heels of Sofie von Otter's *Frauenliebe* (reviewed above) comes an interpretation from this young Finnish soprano that can well stand comparison with the Swedish mezzo's reading. Indeed, they are complementary: von Otter, whose tone hasn't anything like the refulgence of Isokoski's, is just now the more measured and detailed interpreter, but Isokoski has other and contrasted virtues. In her wonderfully straightforward and musical performance, she marries a sincere spontaneity with a warming sense of line and phrase, a style well learnt yet put to her own, positive purpose. Before you is the rapturous bride-to-be in all her moods, then the young woman struck almost dumb by unexpected grief. Nothing in her portrayal is forced or in the least contrived yet everything, felt from the heart, goes to it. And the voice itself? Well, reminders of Flagstad's richness, Ameling's naturalness and Price's precision are here to be heard and enjoyed. She is just as imaginative in Op. 39 as in Op. 42 so here is yet another excellent choice for anyone wanting the two works on one disc. If you choose it you will have a very central, unaffected account of the *Liederkreis* encompassing all its varied moods and one that makes its points unobtrusively and, as with Op. 42, with the emphasis on long-breathed phrasing and rock-steady tone. The partnership with Viitasalo is obviously a fruitful one. The two artists think and 'breathe' alike and, though in Op. 42 the pianist isn't as positive as Forsberg for von Otter, he is just occasionally too prominent, at least as recorded. Since DG (and Sony Classical for Lipovšek) offer considerably more minutes of music, anyone wanting Op. 42 will probably still opt for one of the others, but quantity isn't everything and the quality found on Finlandia is of a high order and not on any account to be overlooked.

Additional recommendations ...

...Liederkreis, Op. 39. Lieder und Gesänge – Op. 27; Op. 51; Op. 77; Op. 96. **Nathalie Stutzmann** (contr); **Catherine Collard** (pf). RCA Victor Red Seal Ⓕ 09026 61728-2 (67 minutes: DDD: 8/94).

...Myrthen, Op. 25ª. Lieder und Gesänge, Op. 27. Die Löwenbraut, Op. 31 No. 1. ªLynne Dawson (sop); Ian Partridge (ten); Julius Drake (pf). Chandos Ⓕ CHAN9307 (72 minutes: DDD: 12/94).

New review

Schumannª Liederkreis, Op. 39 – No. 1, In der Fremde; No. 3, Waldesgespräch; No. 4, Die Stille; No. 10, Zwielicht; No. 12, Frühlingsnacht. Frauenliebe und -leben, Op. 42. Myrthen, Op. 25 – No. 1, Widmung; No. 3, Der Nussbaum; No. 7, Die Lotosblume; No. 9, Lied der Suleika. Fünf Gedichte der Königen Maria Stuart, Op. 135. Dein Angesicht, Op. 127 No. 2. Meine Rose, Op. 90 No. 2. Aufträge, Op. 77 No. 5. Stille Tränen, Op. 35 No. 10.

Brahmsᵇ Deutsche Volkslieder, WoO33 – Da unten im Tale; Feinsliebchen; In stiller Nacht. Die Trauernde, Op. 7 No. 5. **Irmgard Seefried** (sop); **Erik Werba** (pf). Orfeo D'Or Salzburg Festspieldokumente mono Ⓕ C398951B* (77 minutes: ADD: 3/96). Recorded live in ª1960, ᵇ1959.

Whatever performance may in the meantime have intervened, listening to Seefried's *Frauenliebe* again is like returning to base, to the *Ur* performance before which every other, however many merits it may have, must give place. It is simply that she brings before us with every fibre of her being, every tone at her command, every subtly emphasized word the eager, loving girl portrayed within. You instinctively know this must be the kind of voice, the kind of utterance Schumann had in mind to convey the varied emotions he explores. And here, at a live Salzburg performance, the effect is very immediate. Each of her choices from the *Liederkreis*, Op. 39 is presented as a picture palpitating with immediacy and life, something impossible to achieve to this extent in the studio, even if – at the start of a recital – the tone isn't yet well-oiled and there's a suspicion of flatness once in a while. Then comes *Frauenliebe* followed by four unforgettable performances from *Myrthen*. In "Lied der Suleika" listen to how Seefried whispers sensuously "Kuss auf Kuss", mark how unerring is her rubato in "Der Nussbaum" (as it is throughout) and how she underlines longingly, in the same song, "von nächsten Jahr". Those who were present were apparently most moved by the Mary Stuart settings. One hears why as the eloquent emotions of Schumann's settings are so keenly projected. Here the urgency and desperation of a lonely woman are perfectly encompassed. Then in the final group, the expectations of *Aufträge* taken very quickly – Werba has a job keeping up with his impulsive partner – and the wonderful generosity in that heartfelt outpouring, *Stille Tränen* stand out, but every interpretation stays in the mind. Don't miss them or the delightful Brahms encores taken from a recital the previous year at Salzburg. A few notes overload, the voice being recorded very near the microphone and Werba isn't always the most imaginative of pianists, but nothing, not even the regrettable absence, at full price, of texts and translations can mar one's enjoyment of a very special occasion caught on the wing.

New review

Schumann Complete Lieder, Volume 1. Das verlassene Mägdlein, Op. 64 No. 2. Melancholie, Op. 74 No. 6. Aufträge, Op. 77 No. 5. Op. 79 – No. 7a, Zigeunerliedchen I; No. 7b, Zigeunerliedchen II; No. 23, Er ist's!. Die Blume der Ergebung, Op. 83 No. 2. Röslein, Röslein!, Op. 89 No. 6. Sechs Gedichte und Requiem, Op. 90. Op. 96 – No. 1, Nachtlied; No. 3 Ihre Stimme. Lieder und Gesänge aus Wilhelm Meister, Op. 98a – No. 1, Kennst du das Land?; No. 3, Nur wer die Sehnsucht kennt; No. 5, Heiss' mich nicht reden; No. 7, Singet nicht in Trauertönen; No. 9, So lasst mich scheinen. Sechs Gesänge, Op. 107. Warnung, Op. 119 No. 2. Die Meerfee, Op. 125 No. 1. Sängers Trost, Op. 127 No. 1. Mädchen-Schwermut, Op. 142 No. 3. **Christine Schäfer** (sop); **Graham Johnson** (pf). Hyperion Ⓟ CDJ33101 (75 minutes; DDD; 8/96). Texts and translations included.

This disc launches Hyperion's Schumann Lieder project as auspiciously as Dame Janet Baker's recital opened their Complete Schubert Edition. As ever, Graham Johnson shows an unerring gift for matching singer and song. These are almost all late pieces, written between 1849 and 1852 under the shadow of depression and sickness; and their intense chromaticism can all too easily seem tortuous. However, imaginatively supported by Johnson, Christine Schäfer illuminates each of these songs with her pure, lucent timbre, her grace and breadth of phrase and her unselfconscious feeling for verbal meaning and nuance. The voice is an expressive, flexible lyric-coloratura; she can spin a scrupulously even legato, integrates the high notes of, say, "Er ist's" perfectly within the melodic line, and has the breath control to sustain the long phrases of "Requiem" with apparent ease. Aided by Johnson's lucid textures and uncommonly subtle feel for rubato and harmonic direction, Schäfer avoids any hint of mawkishness in songs like "Meine Rose", Op. 90 No. 2, "Mädchen-Schwermut" and "Abendlied. Several songs here have been overshadowed or totally eclipsed by the settings by Schubert, Wolf or Brahms, and Schäfer and Johnson do much to rehabilitate them: in "Der Gärtner" (from Op. 107), for instance, the gardener's hopeless adoration inspires a new glow and fullness in the tone, with Johnson cunningly clarifying the intricate cross-rhythms. Schäfer brings an exquisite wondering stillness to the Goethe "Nachtlied", more disturbed and earthbound than Schubert's sublime setting, but here, at least, scarcely less poignant. She also has the dramatic flair to bring off the difficult Mignon songs, especially the volatile, quasi-operatic "Heiss' mich nicht reden" and "Kennst du das Land", where the final verse, evoking Mignon's terrifying passage across the Alps, builds to a climax of desperate, almost demented yearning. At the other end of the emotional spectrum, Schäfer brings a guileful, knowing touch to the first of the *Zigeunerliedchen*; the Mendelssohnian "Die Meerfee" glistens and glances and "Aufträge" has a winning eagerness and charm, with a delicious sense of flirtation between voice and keyboard. In sum, a delectable, often revelatory recital. The recording is natural and well balanced, while Graham Johnson's typically searching commentaries complement the performances in presenting the most eloquent case possible for Schumann's much maligned and neglected late songs.

Schumann (arr. Beecham) Manfred – Incidental Music, Op. 115. **Gertrud Holt** (sop); **Claire Duchesneau** (mez); **Glyndwr Davies, Ian Billington** (tens); **Niven Miller** (bar); **Laidman Browne, Jill Balcon, Raf de la Torre, David Enders** (spkrs); **BBC Chorus; Royal Philharmonic Orchestra / Sir Thomas Beecham.** Sir Thomas Beecham Trust mono Ⓜ BEECHAM4* (78 minutes: ADD: 9/91). From Fontana CFL1026/7 (2/59). Recorded 1954-56.

Schumann was haunted by Byron's autobiographically-inspired dramatic poem, *Manfred*, from a very early age. When eventually writing his incidental music for it (15 numbers and an overture) in

1848-89 he confessed to never having devoted himself to any composition before "with such lavish love and power". No one in this country has ever done more for it than Sir Thomas Beecham, who even staged it at the Theatre Royal, Drury Lane, London, way back in 1918, some 36 years before reviving it for the BBC and at the Festival Hall in performances leading to this now legendary recording. Score-followers will at once note Beecham's appropriation and scoring of two of the composer's roughly contemporaneous keyboard miniatures as additional background music for the guilt-wracked, soliloquizing Manfred. But their choice and placing is so apt that even Schumann himself might have been grateful. By present-day standards Laidman Browne might be thought a shade too overtly emotional in the title-role. But speakers (including a splendidly awesome Witch of the Alps and rustic chamois-hunter), like singers, orchestra and the magnetic Sir Thomas himself, are all at one in vividness of atmospheric evocation. Splendid remastering also plays its part in making this medium-priced disc a collector's piece.

Additional recommendation ...
...Soloists; Basle Madrigalists; Swiss Workshop Philharmonic Orchestra / Mario Venzago. MGB Musiques Suisses Ⓕ CD6122 (62 minutes: DDD: 10/95).

Schumann Szenen aus Goethes Faust. **Karita Mattila, Barbara Bonney, Brigitte Poschner-Klebel, Susan Graham** (sops); **Iris Vermillion** (mez); **Endrik Wottrich, Hans-Peter Blochwitz;** **Bryn Terfel** (bass-bar); **Jan-Hendrik Rootering, Harry Peeters** (basses); **Tölz Boys' Choir; Swedish Radio Chorus; Berlin Philharmonic Orchestra / Claudio Abbado.** Sony Classical Ⓕ S2K66308 (two discs: 115 minutes: DDD: 5/95). Notes, text and translation included. Recorded live in 1994.   ⒼⒼⒼ

The *Szenen aus Goethes Faust* is now recognized as a masterpiece and you will find yourself bowled over by its imaginative vision and beauty. No one before Schumann had ever attempted to set Goethe's mystical closing scene, which he finished in time for the Goethe centenary in 1849. What eventually emerged as his own Parts 1 and 2 (in turn portraits of Gretchen and the by now repentant Faust) followed later, after his move from a Mendelssohn-dominated Leipzig to a Wagner-ruled Dresden, hence the striking difference in style. Nothing Schumann ever wrote is more dramatic than Faust's blinding and death in the course of Part 2. The Berlin Philharmonic is very fully and forwardly recorded – occasionally perhaps a little too much so for certain voices. But never in the case of Bryn Terfel in the title-role. Any advance fears that he might disappoint after the mature Fischer-Dieskau (for Klee) were immediately banished not only by the generosity and flow of his warm, round tone but also the total commitment and conviction of his characterization. Moreover as Dr Marianus in Part 3 he offers some wonderfully sustained *mezza* and *sotto voce*. Karita Mattila's Gretchen, less youthfully vulnerable than Elizabeth Harwood (for Britten) and certainly less excitably impressionable than Edith Mathis (Klee), is always sympathetically pure-toned, clean-lined and assured. As Ariel and Pater Ecstaticus Endrik Wottrich has more in common with the stylish, tighter-voiced Peter Pears (Britten) than the open-throated, uninhibited Nicolai Gedda (Klee). But like Jan-Hendrik Rootering's sinister Mephistopheles and Evil Spirit, and still more Harry Peeters's Pater Profundis, he at times, as platform positioned, seems outweighed by the orchestra. No praise can be too high for the Four Grey Sisters (so tellingly contrasted in vocal colour) led by Barbara Bonney: their midnight encounter with Faust and his eventual blinding, is brilliantly done. And there is splendidly characterful choral singing throughout from both adult and youthful choirs. Both Klee and Britten are fortunate in having Dietrich Fischer-Dieskau at the head of their casts, and in both performances he tellingly changes his style from the quasi-operatic demands of the title-role to the smoother, suaver lyricism of Doctor Marianus in the holier Part 3. With Walter Berry (Mephistopheles, the Evil Spirit and Pater Seraphicus), Nicolai Gedda (Ariel and Pater Ecstaticus) and Edith Mathis (Gretchen and Una Poenitentium) in support, Klee's Düsseldorf recording offers the stronger soloists, though the English team under Britten lack nothing in sensitivity. Alike in the more operatically conceived Parts 1 and 2 and the visionary Part 3, Abbado himself takes the music to heart just as closely and intensely as the spacious Britten and the more eagerly and urgently dramatic Klee, whose overall timing, incidentally is some five minutes shorter than Abbado's and almost eight minutes shorter than Britten's. And needless to say what Abbado draws from his orchestra (even if not matching the ECO and Britten's shattering outburst at the actual moment of Faust's death) makes nonesense of the charge that Schumann was an inept scorer. In sum, the Abbado is worth every penny of its full-price while at the same time not causing you any cause for regret if you have already purchased one or other of its two splendid mid-price rivals.

Additional recommendations ...
...Soloists; Wandsworth School Choir; Aldeburgh Festival Singers; English Chamber Orchestra / Benjamin Britten. Decca Ⓜ 425 705-2DM2 (two discs: 118 minutes: ADD: 7/90).   ⒼⒼⒼ
...Soloists; Tölz Boys' Choir; Düsseldorf Symphony Orchestra / Bernhard Klee. EMI Ⓜ CMS7 69450-2 (two discs: 110 minutes: DDD: 5/95).   Ⓖ

New review

Schumann Der Rose Pilgerfahrt, Op. 112. **Inga Nielsen, Helle Hinz** (sops); **Annemarie Møller, Elizabeth Halling** (mezzos); **Deon van der Walt** (ten); **Guido Päevatalu** (bar); **Christian Christiansen** (bass); **Danish National Radio Choir and Symphony Orchestra / Gustav Kuhn.** Chandos Ⓕ CHAN9350 (62 minutes: DDD: 7/95). Text included. Recorded 1993.

Amidst today's great upsurgence of interest in Schumann's later choral undertakings, the work's long neglect is no doubt due to its all-too-naïve tale of a rose who, after an eagerly sought transformation into a maiden to experience human love, chooses to sacrifice herself for her baby. Schumann's own ready response to Moritz Horn's poem can best be explained by its underlying moral message together with a strain of German rusticity then equally close to the composer's heart. Having said that, how grateful Schumann lovers should be to Chandos for at last introducing the work to the English catalogue in so sympathetic yet discreet a performance from this predominantly Danish cast. All credit to the conductor, Gustav Kuhn, for revealing so much fancy in fairyland, so much brio in peasant merriment, and so much charm in more tender lyricism without ever making heavy weather of this essentially *gemütlich* little score. No praise can be too high for the Danish National Radio Choir: such immediacy of response leaves you in no doubt as to their professional status. Nor do the soloists or orchestra disappoint. Tonal reproduction is agreeably natural.

Schumann Genoveva. **Julia Faulkner** (sop) Genoveva; **Keith Lewis** (ten) Golo; **Harald Stamm** (bass) Hidulfus, Caspar; **Alan Titus** (bar) Siegfried; **Renate Behle** (sop) Margaretha; **Carl Schultz** (bass) Drago; **Johann Tilli** (bass) Balthasar; **Hamburg State Opera Chorus; Hamburg Philharmonic Orchestra / Gerd Albrecht.** Orfeo Ⓕ C289932H (two discs: 178 minutes: DDD: 1/94). Notes, text and translation included. Recorded live in the Musikhalle, Hamburg in 1992. **Ⓖ**
Because of certain dramatic shortcomings, including a contrived, last-minute happy ending and an infusion of black magic once dismissed by George Bernard Shaw as "pure bosh", Schumann's one and only opera, *Genoveva*, never held the stage. After the unpardonably long omission of *Genoveva* from the British catalogue, we can now at last enjoy much lovely music in our armchairs through this Hamburg live recording under the directorship of that tireless champion of the unjustly neglected, Gerd Albrecht. Prime responsibility for the care of Genoveva, the luckless lady, wrongly accused of adultery while her husband is away at the war, rests with Golo, who is wracked by conscience about his secret passion for her until he is stung into vengeance by Genoveva's "Away, away, infamous bastard". The role is feelingly and lyrically sung by Keith Lewis. Genoveva herself, only fully portrayed in distress (Acts 2 and 4), is sung by the American, Julia Faulkner, with a pure-toned, girlish vulnerability. Albrecht sweeps the opera along with an effortlessly flowing, seam-concealing continuity that would have surely pleased the composer himself, who was anxious to emulate Wagner's ever-growing rejection of the self-contained operatic set-number. The sound quality offered by the Hamburg engineers is unfailingly mellifluous.

Further listening ...
...String Quartets, Op. 41 – No. 1 in A minor; No. 2 in F major. CRD CRD3333 (10/88).
...Carnaval, Op. 9. *Coupled with works by* **Matthay, Bach, D. Scarlatti, Brahms** and **Ferguson** Dame Myra Hess (pf). Biddulph mono Ⓜ LHW025* (76 minutes: ADD: 3/96). *See review in the Collections section; refer to the Index to Reviews.*
...Papillons, Op. 2. *Coupled with* **Bach** Overture in the French style in B minor, BWV831. **Scriabin** Mazurkas, Op. 3 – C sharp minor; E minor; G sharp minor. **Medtner** Fairy Tales – F sharp minor, Op. 26 No. 4; G sharp minor, Op. 31 No. 3; A minor, Op. 34 No. 3, "Wood-Goblin". **Konstantin Lifschitz** (pf) Denon CO-78907 (12/94).   **ⒼⒼ**
...Etudes symphoniques, Op. 13. Papillons, Op. 2. Arabeske in C major, Op. 18. **Vladimir Ashkenazy** (pf). Decca 414 474-2DH (6/87).
...Etudes symphoniques, Opp. 13 and posth. Bunte Blätter, Op. 99. *Coupled with works by* **Chopin** and **Beethoven** Sviatoslav Richter (pf). Olympia OCD339 and OCD338 (4/94). *See review under Beethoven; refer to the Index to Reviews.*   **ⒼⒼ**
...Spanische Liebeslieder, Op. 138. *Coupled with* **Brahms** Liebeslieder, Op. 52. Neue Liebeslieder, Op. 65. **Barbara Bonney** (sop); **Anne Sofie von Otter** (mez); **Kurt Streit** (ten); **Olaf Bär** (bar); **Bengt Forsberg, Helmut Deutsch** (pf duet). EMI CDC5 55430-2 (10/95).
...Das Paradies und die Peri, Op. 50[a]. Overture, Scherzo and Finale, Op. 52. [a]Soloists; [a]**Dresden State Opera Chorus; Staatskapelle Dresden / Giuseppe Sinopoli.** DG 445 875-2GH2 (12/95).
...Szenen aus Goethes Faust. **Soloists; Wandsworth School Choir; Aldeburgh Festival Singers; English Chamber Orchestra / Benjamin Britten.** Decca 425 705-2DM2 (7/90).   **ⒼⒼⒼ**

Gerard Schurmann   Dutch/British 1929-

Suggested listening ...
...Six Studies of Francis Bacon. Variants for Small Orchestra. **BBC Symphony Orchestra / Gerard Schurmann.** Chandos CHAN9167.
...Film scores (excerpts) – Horrors of the Black Museum. Attack on the Iron Coast. The Bedford Incident. The Ceremony. Claretta. Cone of Silence. Konga. The Long Arm. The Lost Continent. Doctor Syn – Smuggler's Rhapsody. **Original soundtrack.** Cloud Nine CNS5005* (10/93).

Heinrich Schütz   German 1585-1672

Schütz Symphoniae sacrae, SWV341-67. **Emma Kirkby, Suzie Le Blanc** (sops); **James Bowman** (alto); **Nigel Rogers, Charles Daniels** (tens); **Stephen Varcoe** (bass); **Richard Wistreich** (bass); **Jeremy West, Nicholas Perry** (cornets); **Purcell Quartet** (Catherine Mackintosh, Catherine Weiss, vns; Richard Boothby, va da gamba; Robert Woolley, hpd). Chandos Chaconne Ⓕ CHAN0566/7 (two discs: 139 minutes: DDD: 4/95). Text and translation included. ☞ Recorded 1993-4. *Gramophone Editor's choice.*   Ⓖ

These discs are in various ways revelatory. Schütz's collection is difficult to get through in one sitting, but each item in the collection is a jewel, albeit not ostentatiously displayed. This is church music on a small scale in terms of physical resources, but of enormous invention and beauty. Sometimes the Purcell Quartet do not push the music along quite enough. In general, however, the instrumentalists respond with enthusiasm and great understanding of the style of these rather recondite works. It takes considerable sensitivity to bring out the rich textures of *Meine Seele erhebt den Herren* or *Der Herr ist meine Stärke* without enjoying such moments at the expense of the vocal soloist. The relatively well-known bass solo *Herr, nun lässest du deinen Diener* is another example of a perfect match between voice and instruments. Emma Kirkby brings all her customary charm and precision to her two solo arias. Both tenors are in their element, if sometimes a little understated, and Stephen Varcoe and Richard Wistreich really understand and communicate the glowing black and gold colours of Schütz's writing for the bass voice. Schütz's debt to Monteverdi is very much evident in *Der Herr ist mein Licht* for two tenors and even more so in *Es steh Gott auf*, for the same scoring, but Schütz's natural reluctance to "deck out my work with foreign plumage" means that his own voice as a composer is always in evidence. It is difficult to be precise about this, especially when the second volume of *Symphoniae sacrae* does undeniably show such a strong Italian influence as compared with its predecessor. Yet this reconciliation of Italian *stile concertato* with Schütz's northern reticence is one of the challenges in performing his music, and one to which this recording rises magnificently.

New review

Schütz Die Auferstehung unsres Herren Jesu Christi, SWV50. **Jan Caals** (ten); **Kurt Widmer** (bass) Evangelist; **Bernadette Degelin** (sop); **Musica Polyphonica / Louis Devos.** Erato Ⓜ 0630-11230-2 (49 minutes: ADD: 5/96). Text and translation included. Recorded 1980.

The Resurrection of Jesus Christ was composed relatively early in Schütz's long and prolific career. Still fresh in 1623 from his Italian sojourns, Schütz had already set out his stall: the new histrionic world of Monteverdi radiating the intense and measured austerity of German strophes and antique polyphony. What might appear to a clinical twentieth-century mind as a brilliantly conceived synthesis of aesthetics – leading to a rebirth of German music – is more likely to have been a pragmatic means of representing the narrative with the best materials available at the time. Schütz allows himself a rich palette of viols to accompany a fluid recitation. Kurt Widmer is not always a secure Evangelist but he is deeply involving, mellow-toned, if slightly po-faced. Let down occasionally by insecure viol playing, he is nevertheless able to maintain a memorable and noble incantation. Schütz is inimitable in his characterization of Jesus and those whom the Saviour meets. Christ's words are set specially for a madrigalian tenor and bass and others, like the High Priests, are treated to splendidly figurative counterpoint, here depicting worried quasi-prison governors who have let another one through the net and need to think of their own *historia* fast. In addition there is Cleophas and his companion whose close imitative points almost trip over themselves as we imagine their excitement at seeing the Lord. All these dramatic interpolations are well served under Louis Devos, though Schütz's more theatrical moments rarely jump out of the page. Devos's priority is to achieve a constant and mellifluously unfolding story which retains its solemnity at every turn. René Jacobs's account is more restrained still in dramatic effect, though he can boast a rather more colourful instrumental backdrop. Widmer, however, has more to say than Martin Hummell as the Evangelist; he is better equipped to draw the listener into the spiritual and contemplative power of Schütz's setting, making this reissue first choice amongst the available versions.

New review

Schütz Geistliche Chormusik, SWV369-97 – Herr, auf dich traue ich, SWV377[a]; Die mit Tränen säen, SWV378[b]; So fahr ich hin zu Jesu Christ, SWV379[c]; O lieber Herre Gott, SWV381; Ich bin eine refende Stimme, SWV383; Die Himmel erzählen dei Ehre Gottes, SWV386; Herzlich lieb hab ich dich, o Herr, SWV387; Das ist je gewisslich wahr, SWV388; Unser Wandel ist im Himmel, SWV390; Selig sind die Toten, SWV391; Was mein Gott will, das gescheh allzeit, SWV392[bc]. Kleiner geistlichen Concerten, Erster Theil, SWV282-305 – Eile mich, Gott, zu erretten, SWV282[a]; O süsser, o freundlicher, SWV285[b]; Schaffe in mir, Gott, ein reines Herz, SWV291[ab]. Kleiner geistlichen Concerten, Anderer Theil, SWV306-37 – Ich liege und schlafe, SWV310[c]; Wann unsre Augen schlafen ein, SWV316[bc]. [a]**Agnes Mellon** (sop); [b]**Mark Padmore** (ten); [c]**Peter Kooy** (bass); **Collegium Vocale / Philippe Herreweghe.** Harmonia Mundi Ⓕ HMC90 1534 (61 minutes: DDD: 5/96). ☞ Texts and translations included.

This anthology shows both sides of Schütz's output: the solid *prima prattica* training which is evident in his fine handling of counterpoint, and the Monteverdian lessons learned and shown off in the *Kleiner geistlichen Concerten.* Common to both styles is an impressive economy of means, so that with very small resources Schütz obtains an extraordinary variety of colour and responds with immediacy to each text. To all this Collegium Vocale bring a brilliance of colour and a splendid choral blend (particularly evident in *Herr, auf dich* and *Die mit Tränen*, to pick two random examples), and a vivid response to Schütz's often difficult tempo changes. The speech-propelled writing in such motets as *O lieber Herre Gott* or *Die Himmel erzählen* is far from easy to bring across convincingly, but both are rendered here with impressive conviction and power. The *Concerte* are rather disappointing after such magnificent concerted choral singing, their highly baroque word-setting seeming superficial, but they are superbly sung, and it is especially good to hear Peter Kooy shown to such advantage.

Additional recommendation ...

...Geistliche Chormusik, SWV381-93. Ich weiss das mein Erlöser lebet, SWV457. **Emmanuel Music Chorus / Craig Smith.** Koch International Classics Ⓕ 37174-2 (67 minutes: DDD: 11/93).

Schütz Ich hab mein Sach Gott heimgestellt, SWV305. Ich will dem Herren loben allezeit, SWV306. Was hast du verwirket, SWV307. O Jesu, nomen dulce, SWV308. O misericordissime Jesu, SWV309. Ich leige und schlafe, SWV310. Habe deine Lust an dem Herren, SWV311. Herr, ich hoffe darauf, SWV312. Bone Jesu, verbum Patris, SWV313. Verbum caro factum est, SWV314. Hodie Christus natus est, SWV315. Wann unsre Augen schlafen ein, SWV316. Meister, wir haben die ganze Nacht gearbeitet, SWV317. Die Furcht des Herren, SWV318. Ich beuge meine Knie, SWV319. Ich bin jung gewesen, SWV320. Herr, wann ich nur dich habe, SWV321. Rorate coeli desuper, SWV322. Joseph, du Sohn David, SWV323. Ich bin die Auferstehung, SWV324. **Tölz Boys' Choir / Gerhard Schmidt-Gaden** with **Roman Summereder** (org). Capriccio Ⓕ 10 388 (77 minutes: DDD: 4/93). ✒ Texts and translations included. Recorded 1989-90.

Getting music published evidently encountered economic difficulties during the Thirty Years' War, for Heinrich Schütz had to issue his *Kleine Geistliche Konzerte* ("Little Sacred Concertos") – short motets for vocal soloists and continuo – in two parts in, respectively, 1636 and 1639. No. 24 from Part 1 and Nos. 1-19 from Part 2 comprise the programme for this second volume from soloists of the Tölz Boys' Choir and although, at first sight, this may seem too regimented an approach to produce satisfying listening for the whole disc, Schütz himself structured the items so that there is a progression throughout the set, not only in increased numbers of soloists but also in intensity and intellectual scope. The voices of the soloists here are typically very individual and characterful, and all are remarkably adroit and stylish, so the personal witness that is so pronounced in the text is particularly well portrayed. These are performers well used to the subtleties of baroque word setting and they highlight all the ingenuity that Schütz lavished on these seemingly simple texts. There is an evident delight in the way the composer deployed his limited resources, constantly ringing the changes on traditional formulas to produce a richness of ideas that it took a Bach or Handel to emulate. The rather close recording allows all these intricacies to emerge undiminished and although the resonance of the acoustic seems restrained, this is no bad thing for music that, despite its title, has the feel of chamber music.

Further listening ...

...Freue dich des Weibes deiner Jugend, SWV453 (with Frieder Lang, ten). Ist nicht Ephraim mein teuer Sohn, SWV40. Saul, Saul, was verfolgst du mich, SWV415. Auf dem Gebirge, SWV396 (Ashley Stafford, Michael Chance, altos). Musicalische Exequien, SWV279-81 (Lang). **Monteverdi Choir; English Baroque Soloists; His Majesties Sagbutts and Cornetts / John Eliot Gardiner.** Archiv Produktion 423 405-2AH (11/88). ✒

...Saul, Saul, was verfolgst du mich, SWV415. Ich danke dem Herrn, SWV34. Magnificat anima mia, SWV468. Stehe auf, meine Freundin, SWV499. *Coupled with* **G. Gabrieli** Magnificat, Lieto godea. **M. Praetorius** Meine Seele erhebt den Herren. **Monteverdi** Gloria in excelsis Deo. **Schütz Academy / Howard Arman.** Capriccio 10 409 (5/93).

...Psalmen Davids sampt etlichen Moteten und Concerten, SWV22-47. **Soloists; Stuttgart Chamber Choir; Cologne Musica Fiata / Frieder Bernius.** Sony S2K48042.   Ⓖ

...St Matthew Passion, SWV479. **Soloists; Heinrich Schütz Choir / Roger Norrington.** Decca 436 221-2DM. ✒

...Die Auferstehung unsres Herren Jesu Christi, SWV50. **Jan Caals** (ten); **Kurt Widmer** (bass); **Bernadette Degelin** (sop); **Musica Polyphonica / Louis Devos.** Erato 0630-11230-2 (5/96). ✒

Joseph Schwantner   American 1943-

Suggested listening ...

...From Afar ... . *Coupled with works by* **Corigliano** and **Foss** Sharon Isbin (gtr); **Saint Paul Chamber Orchestra / Hugh Wolff.** Virgin Classics CDC5 55083-2 (8/96). *See review under Corigliano; refer to the Index to Reviews.*   Ⓖ

Cornelius Schwehr   German 20th Century

Suggested listening ...

...Deutsche Tänze. *Coupled with* **Eisler** Woodburry-Liederbüchlein. **Rühm** Schöpfung. Foetus. Sprechquartette. **Van de Vate** Cocaine Lil. **Bel Canto Ensemble / Dietburg Spohr.** Koch Schwann 314322 (3/95).

Kurt Schwertsik

Austrian 1935-

Suggested listening ...
...da uhu schaud me so draurech au[a]. Gedichte an Ljuba. Op. 53[a]. Ich sein blumenbein, Op. 38[a].
Drei späte Liebeslieder ... für Christa[bc]. Fünf Nocturnes, Op. 10[bc]. [a]**Christa Schwertsik** (sngr);
[b]**Christopher van Kampen** (vc); [a]**Kurt Schwertsik**; [c]**Nicola Meecham** (pfs). Largo 5125 (9/94).

Cyril Scott

British 1879-1970

Suggested listening ...
...Aubade, Op. 77. Neapolitan Rhapsody. Three Dances, Op. 22. Suite Fantastique. Two
Passacaglias on Irish Themes. **South African Broadcasting Corporation Orchestra / Peter
Marchbank.** Marco Polo 8 223485 (7/94).

Alexander Scriabin

USSR 1872-1915

Scriabin Piano Concerto in F sharp minor, Op. 20.
Tchaikovsky Piano Concerto No. 1 in B flat minor, Op. 23. **Nikolai Demidenko** (pf); **BBC
Symphony Orchestra / Alexander Lazarev.** Hyperion Ⓕ CDA66680 (65 minutes: DDD: 10/94).
Recorded 1993.   ⓖ
The chief attraction here is the unusual coupling which pairs two sharply opposed examples of
Russian romanticism, and although the reasons for the neglect of Scriabin's Piano Concerto are not
hard to fathom (its lyrical and decorative flights are essentially inward-looking), its haunting,
bittersweet beauty, particularly in the central *Andante* is hard to resist. Demidenko's own comments,
quoted in the accompanying booklet, are scarcely less intense and individual than his performance:
"in the ambience, phrasing and cadence of his music we meet with a world almost without skin, a
world of nerve-ends where the slightest contact can bring pain". His playing soars quickly to meet the
music's early passion head on, and in the first *più mosso scherzando* he accelerates to produce a
brilliant lightening of mood. His flashing *fortes* in the *Andante*'s second variation are as volatile as his
pianissimos are starry and refined in the finale's period reminiscence, and although he might seem
more tight-lipped, less expansive than Ashkenazy (reviewed below), he is arguably more dramatic and
characterful. Demidenko's Tchaikovsky, too, finds him ferreting out and sifting through every texture,
forever aiming at optimum clarity. While this is hardly among the greatest Tchaikovsky Firsts on
record (see reviews under Tchaikovsky; refer to the Index to Reviews), it is often gripping and
mesmeric. The orchestra respond admirably to their mercurial soloist and certainly come alight at key
moments in both concertos. The recorded balance is not always ideal and the piano sound is
sometimes uncomfortably taut.

Scriabin Piano Concerto in F sharp minor, Op. 20[a]. Prometheus, Op. 60, "Le poème du feu"[b].
Le poème de l'extase, Op. 54[c]. [ab]**Vladimir Ashkenazy** (pf); [b]**Ambrosian Singers**; [ab]**London
Philharmonic Orchestra**; [c]**Cleveland Orchestra / Lorin Maazel.** Decca Ⓕ 417 252-2DH
(66 minutes: ADD: 4/89). Items marked [a] and [b] from SXL6527 (1/72), recorded 1971,
[c]SXL6905 (9/79), recorded 1978.   ⓖⓖ
This CD gives us the essential Scriabin. The Piano Concerto has great pianistic refinement and
melodic grace as well as a restraint not encountered in his later music. With *Le poème de l'extase* and
Prometheus we are in the world of *art nouveau* and Scriabin in the grip of the mysticism (and
megalomania) that consumed his later years. They are both single-movement symphonies for a huge
orchestra: *Prometheus* ("The Poem of Fire") calls for quadruple wind, eight horns, five trumpets,
strings, organ and chorus as well as an important part for solo piano in which Ashkenazy shines. The
sensuous, luminous textures are beautifully conveyed in these performances by the LPO and the
Decca engineers produce a most natural perspective and transparency of detail, as well as an
appropriately overheated sound in the sensuous world of *Le poème de l'extase*.
Additional recommendations ...
...Piano Concerto[a]. Le poème de l'extase. [a]**Garrick Ohlsson** (pf); **Czech Philharmonic Orchestra /
Libor Pešek.** Supraphon Ⓕ CO2047 (53 minutes: DDD: 11/89).   ⓖ
...Piano Concerto[a]. Symphony No. 3. [a]**Roland Pöntinen** (pf); **Stockholm Philharmonic Orchestra /
Leif Segerstam.** BIS Ⓕ CD475 (77 minutes: DDD: 1/91).   ⓖ
...Le poème de l'extase. Symphony No. 3. **Berlin Radio Symphony Orchestra / Vladimir Ashkenazy.**
Decca Ⓕ 430 843-2DH (70 minutes: DDD: 11/91).
...Prometheus. *Coupled with works by* **Liszt, Beethoven** and **Nono** Martha Argerich (pf); **Berlin
Singakademie.** Sony Classical Ⓕ SK53978 (75 minutes: DDD: 1/95). *See review in the Collections
section; refer to the Index to Reviews.*   ⓖⓖⓖ
...Le poème de l'extase[a]. **Bartók** Music for Strings, Percussion and Celesta,[b]. Dance Suite, Sz77[a].
The wooden prince, Sz60[a]. [a]**New York Philharmonic Orchestra**, [b]**BBC Symphony Orchestra /
Pierre Boulez.** Sony Classical Boulez Edition Ⓜ SM2K64100 (two discs: 123 minutes:
ADD: 9/95).

Scriabin Symphonies – No. 1 in E major, Op. 26[a]; No. 2 in C minor, Op. 29; No. 3, Op. 43, "Divine Poem"[b]. Le poème de l'extase, Op. 54. Piano Concerto in F sharp minor, Op. 20[c]. Prometheus, Op. 60. Rêverie, Op. 24. [a]**Tamara Siniawskaia** (sop); [a]**Alexander Fedin** (ten); [b]**Vladimir Krainev**, [c]**Gerhard Oppitz** (pfs); [a]**Figuralchor; Frankfurt Radio Symphony Orchestra / Dmitri Kitaienko.** RCA Victor Symphony Edition ℗ 74321 20297-2 (three discs: 225 minutes: DDD: 12/95). Recorded 1991-4.

These recordings are half the price of Muti's acclaimed Philadelphia set (listed below). What is more, Kitaienko's survey, unlike Muti's, includes the Piano Concerto and the short *Rêverie*. It also includes a chorus for the final bars of *Le Poème de l'extase* (a bizarre idea that has a dubious precedent in Scriabin's use of it at the same point in *Prometheus*), and there are copious unmarked parts for cymbals in the numbered symphonies, from a light dusting of metal to the occasional clash (there is a dubious precedent here too, in that generations of conductors, particularly Russian ones, have felt their use to be necessary). Kitaienko's textual deviations also include a fondness for silent pauses: they may be useful signposts, breathing spaces or dramatic interpolations; they may also be felt to be disruptive. So much for the extras. Is there anything missing? Most obviously, ample Philadelphia string tone, and some of the most voluptuous string playing (with portamento) to have come from that orchestra since Stokowski's days. Arguably Scriabin's music thrives on such things. Even the BBC Symphony Orchestra strings manage greater warmth and variety of tone colour (and portamento) in the opening minute of the central *Andante* from the Piano Concerto (the Oppitz/Kitaienko account could happily join a collection, but the Demidenko/BBCSO/Lazarev would grace one), and, staying with Scriabin's most hauntingly beautiful tune, is there not an imbalance when the clarinet (which must have been Scriabin's favourite orchestral instrument) takes over the tune? In Frankfurt, it is the piano decorations of the tune which dominate. The piano moves back a few metres for *Prometheus*, as it probably should, which is a way of saying that if you are used to the famous Ashkenazy/Maazel, you might feel that the piano part lacks projection and character (Alexeev is similarly distant for Muti), but then *everything* is much clearer and closer on that 25-year-old Decca recording. More generally, you may wish to know whether Scriabin's climaxes cause the earth to move as often (and by as much) as it does in the Muti set. Not quite. Kitaienko risks greater extremes of tempo than most. The ups and downs in *Le poème de l'extase* perhaps add to its allure. Elsewhere, one or two tempo transitions and manoeuverings are a little awkward, for example, from the slowest of all *Andantes* at the outset of the Second Symphony's slow movement to its necessarily much faster *più vivo* sections (Kitaienko takes 15'44" in this movement; Muti 13'40" and Järvi 11'30"). The exception is the vast first movement of the Third Symphony, where Kitaienko keeps a cool head and a long view, and where, untypically, Muti is all at sea. Swings and roundabouts then. If the idea appeals of a bargain acquisition of all Scriabin's work for orchestra – this is it, apart from an early symphonic poem.

Additional recommendation ...

...No. 1[a]; Nos. 2 and 3. Le poème de l'extase[b]. Prometheus[c]. [a]**Stefania Toczyska** (mez); [a]**Michael Myers** (ten); [b]**Frank Kaderabek** (tpt); [c]**Dmitri Alexeev** (pf); [a]**Westminster Choir**; [c]**Philadelphia Choral Arts Society; Philadelphia Orchestra / Riccardo Muti.** EMI ℗ CDS7 54251-2 (three discs: 188 minutes: DDD). ⓖ

Scriabin Complete Piano Sonatas – No. 1 in F minor, Op. 6; No. 2 in G sharp minor, Op. 19, "Sonata-fantasy"; No. 3 in F sharp minor, Op. 23; No. 4 in F sharp, Op. 30; No. 5 in F sharp major, Op. 53; No. 6 in G major, Op. 62; No. 7 in F sharp major, Op. 64, "White Mass"; No. 8 in A major, Op. 66; No. 9 in F major, Op. 68, "Black Mass"; No. 10 in C major, Op. 70. Fantasie in B minor, Op. 28. Sonata-fantaisie in G sharp minor. **Marc-André Hamelin** (pf). Hyperion ℗ CDA67131/2 (two discs: 146 minutes: DDD: 6/96).

Scriabin was an ambitious composer. A romantic alchemist, he saw his music as a transmuting agent. Through its influence pain would become happiness and hate become love, culminating in a phoenix-like rebirth of the universe. With Shakespearian agility he would change the world's dross into "something rich and strange". Not surprisingly, given Scriabin's early prowess as a pianist, the ten sonatas resonate with every exoticism, ranging through the First Sonata's cries of despair (complete with magnificent Russian funeral march), to the Second Sonata's Baltic Sea inspiration, the Third Sonata's "states of being", the "flight to a distant star" (No. 4) and "the emergence of mysterious forces" (No. 5). Nos. 7 and 9 are *White* and *Black Mass* Sonatas respectively, and the final sonatas blaze with trills symbolizing an extra-terrestrial joy and incandescence. Even less surprisingly such music makes ferocious demands on the pianist's physical stamina and imaginative resource. However, Marc-André Hamelin, a cool customer, takes everything in his stride. Blessed with rapier reflexes he nonchalantly resolves even the most outlandish difficulties. He launches the First Sonata's opening outcry like some gleaming trajectory and, throughout, his whistle-stop virtuosity is seemingly infallible. You might, however, miss a greater sense of the music's Slavonic intensity, its colour and character; a finer awareness, for example, of the delirious poetry at the heart of the Second Sonata's whirling finale. Hamelin's sonority is most elegantly and precisely gauged but time and again his fluency (admittedly breathtaking) erases too much of the work's originality and regenerative force. However, he shows a greater sense of freedom in the Fifth Sonata, and in the opalescent fantasy of the later sonatas, he responds with more evocative skill to subjective terms, as well as to moments where Scriabin's brooding introspection is lit by sudden flashes of summer lightning. Yet even here some collectors may miss Ashkenazy's romantic volatility in his set of the sonatas, or Horowitz's cunning and diablerie (in Sonatas Nos. 3, 5 and 9). Hyperion's recordings are a little tight and airless in the bass and middle register, but their two-disc set is beautifully presented and includes a superb essay on Scriabin.

Additional recommendations ...

...Piano Sonatas Nos. 1-10. **Vladimir Ashkenazy** (pf). Decca Ⓜ 425 579-2DM2 (two discs: 131 minutes: ADD/DDD: 1/90).

...Piano Sonatas Nos. 3 and 5. Preludes – Op. 11: Nos. 1, 3, 9, 13, 14 and 16; Op. 13 No. 6; Op. 15 No. 2; Op. 16 – Nos. 1 and 4; Op. 27 No. 1; A minor, Op. 51 No. 2; Op. 48 No. 3; Op. 67 No. 1; Op. 59 No. 2. Etudes – Op. 8 No. 7; Op. 42: Nos. 5 and 12. **Vladimir Horowitz** (pf). RCA Victor Gold Seal Ⓔ mono/stereo GD86215* (66 minutes: ADD: 1/90). Ⓖ

...Piano Sonatas Nos. 2 and 9. Etudes – Op. 8: Nos. 2, 4 and 5. Op. 42: Nos. 3, 4 and 7. Four Pieces, Op. 51. Vers la flamme, Op. 72. **Prokofiev** Visions fugitives, Op. 22. **Nikolai Demidenko** (pf). Conifer Ⓕ CDCF204 (73 minutes: DDD: 8/91). ⓖⓖ

...Poème-nocturne. Two Danses. Vers la flamme. Fantasie in B minor, Op. 28. **Shostakovich** 24 Preludes and Fugues, Op. 87 – No. 4 in E minor; No. 12 in G sharp minor; No. 14 in E flat major; No. 15 in D flat major; No. 17 in A flat major; No. 23 in F major. **Prokofiev** Piano Sonatas – No. 4 in C minor, Op. 29; No. 6 in A major, Op. 82. Legend, Op. 12 No. 6. Visions fugitives, Op. 22 Nos. 3-6, 8, 9, 11, 14, 15 and 18. Pieces, Op. 32 – No. 1, Danse; No. 4, Waltz. Pieces from "Cinderella" – Op. 95: No. 2, Gavotte; Op. 97: No. 3, Autumn fairy, No. 6, Oriental dance; Op. 102: No. 1, Grand waltz, No. 3, Quarrel. **Sviatoslav Richter** (pf). Philips Ⓕ 438 627-2PH2 (two discs: 152 minutes: DDD: 8/94). . ⓖⓖ

...Piano Sonata No. 3. Preludes – Op. 11 No. 1; Op. 39 No. 2; Op. 39 No. 3; Impromptu in B minor, Op. 12 No. 2. Etudes – Op. 8 No. 7; Op. 42 No. 4; Op. 42 No. 6. **Rachmaninov** Preludes – Op. 3 No. 2; Op. 23 No. 4; Op. 23 No. 6. Etudes-tableaux, Op. 39 Nos. 4-6. **Vladimir Sofronitzki** (pf). Multisonic Russian Treasure Ⓜ 310181-2* (58 minutes: ADD: 5/94). Ⓖ

...Piano Sonata No. 4. *Coupled with works by* **Stravinsky, Ravel, Berg, Messiaen, Britten** and **Copland** Shura Cherkassky (pf). Decca Ⓕ 433 657-2DH (79 minutes: ADD: 2/96). *See review in the Collections section; refer to the Index to Reviews.* Ⓖ

...Piano Sonatas Nos. 2 and 5. **Chopin** Etudes: Op. 10 – No. 4 in C sharp minor; No. 10 in A flat major; No. 11 in E flat major; Op. 25 – No. 5 in E minor; No. 8 in D flat major; No. 11 in A minor; No. 12 in C minor. Nocturnes – E major, Op. 62 No. 2; E minor, Op. 72 No. 1. Polonaise in A flat major, Op. 61. **Sviatoslav Richter** (pf). Praga mono/stereo Ⓑ CMX354007* (61 minutes: ADD: 6/96).

...Piano Sonata No. 6. Etudes – C sharp minor, Op. 2 No. 1; Op. 8: No. 5 in E major; No. 11 in B flat minor; Op. 42: No. 2 in F sharp minor; No. 3 in F sharp major; No. 4 in F sharp major; No. 5 in C sharp minor; No. 6 in D flat major; No. 8 in E flat major; Trois Etudes, Op. 65. **Miaskovsky** Piano Sonata No. 3 in C minor, Op. 19. **Prokofiev** Piano Sonata No. 7 in B flat major, Op. 83. **Sviatoslav Richter** (pf). Melodiya mono Ⓜ 74321 29470-2* (68 minutes: ADD: 6/96).

Scriabin Piano Sonatas – No. 3 in F sharp minor, Op. 23; No. 4 in F sharp, Op. 30; No. 5, Op. 53. 12 Etudes, Op. 8. **Yuki Matsuzawa** (pf). Pianissimo Ⓕ PP10394 (72 minutes: DDD: 6/94). *Gramophone* Editor's choice. ⓖⓖ

From the very first notes, this disc immediately makes it clear that Yuki Matsuzawa is indeed something special: in fact, she was, arguably, the most exciting newcomer to the record catalogue in 1994. It is not just that she has an unassailably secure technical mastery, dealing with apparent ease and panache with the formidable virtuosity required by, for example, the Ninth, Tenth and Twelfth Studies of Op. 8, nor that she commands a great range of dynamics, from Scriabin's *quietissimo* to his most thunderously passionate climaxes – and it is rare to find a pianist observing indications so absolutely exactly yet so seemingly naturally, without a trace of being applied mechanically. As the first *Etude* reveals, she possesses that almost teasing lightness that Pasternak (who knew Scriabin) tells us was typical of his playing; and in lyrical passages such as the dreamy poetic *Andante* of the Third Sonata her tone is ravishingly beautiful. She is meticulous about detail (note her distinction between detached quavers and legato crotchets in the right hand of Op. 8 No. 7), and she has a sensitive feeling for phrase and structure and a proper appreciation of the expressive implications of key shifts (e.g. in Op. 8 No. 8). She brings off the self-questioning of the Third Sonata, lingering over its initial subject, and the neurosis of the Fourth, with its passing echoes of *Tristan*, the chromatic appoggiaturas which give the first movement's harmonies a special character, and a truly fleeting *volando* in its second movement (which contains that direction in an Italian that never was, *giobilosco*). In the Fifth Sonata, written when Scriabin had fallen under the influence of theosophy, and making so great a change in his idiom (teetering as it does on the edge of atonality), she is convincingly deft, if taking the *languido* sections very freely. This is a brilliant recording début.

Scriabin Etude in C sharp minor, Op. 2 No. 1. 12 Etudes, Op. 8. Etudes, Op. 42. Etude in E flat major, Op. 49 No. 1. Etude, Op. 56 No. 4. Three Etudes, Op. 65. **Piers Lane** (pf). Hyperion Ⓕ CDA66607 (56 minutes: DDD: 12/92). Recorded 1992. *Selected by Sounds in Retrospect.* ⓖⓖ

Although Scriabin's *études* do not fall into two neatly packaged sets in the same way as Chopin's celebrated contributions, there is nevertheless a strong feeling of continuity and development running throughout the 26 examples produced between the years 1887 and 1912. This is admirably demonstrated in this excellent issue from Hyperion, which, far from being an indigestible anthology proves to be an intriguing and pleasurable hour's worth of listening charting Scriabin's progression from late-romantic adolescence, to harmonically advanced mystical poet. Indeed, although these studies can be counted as amongst the most digitally taxing and hazardous of their kind, Scriabin also saw them as important sketches and studies for his larger works, and as experiments in his gradually evolving harmonic language and mystical vision. Piers Lane attains the perfect balance between virtuoso display and poetic interpretation. Expressive detail and subtle nuance are finely brought out, and he is more than receptive to Scriabin's sometimes highly idiosyncratic sound-world; rarely, for instance, has the famous "Mosquito" *Etude* (Op. 42 No. 3) been captured with such delicate fragility as here, and in No. 1 of the three fiendishly difficult *Etudes,* Op. 65 (fifths, sevenths and ninths!) the tremulous, ghostly flutterings are tellingly delivered with a gossamer-light touch and an appropriate sense of eerie mystery. The clear, spacious recording is exemplary.

Additional recommendation ...

...Op. 2 No. 1; D sharp minor, Op. 8 No. 12 (two versions). *Coupled with works by* **Liszt, Chopin, Balakirev, Blumenfeld, Glazunov, Lully, Rameau** and **Schumann** Simon Barere (pf). APR mono Ⓔ APR7001* (two discs: 126 minutes: ADD: 5/91). *See review in the Collections section; refer to the Index to Reviews.* ⒼⒼⒼ

New review

Scriabin Etudes[a] – C sharp minor, Op. 2 No. 1; Op. 8: No. 5 in E major; No. 11 in B flat minor; Op. 42: No. 2 in F sharp minor; No. 3 in F sharp major; No. 4 in F sharp major; No. 5 in C sharp minor; No. 6 in D flat major; No. 8 in E flat major; Trois Etudes, Op. 65. Piano Sonata No. 6 in G major, Op. 62[b].
Miaskovsky Piano Sonata No. 3 in C minor, Op. 19[c].
Prokofiev Piano Sonata No. 7 in B flat major, Op. 83[d]. **Sviatoslav Richter** (pf). Melodiya mono Ⓜ 74321 29470-2* (68 minutes: ADD: 6/96). Items marked [a] recorded 1952, [b]1955, [c]1953, [d]1958.

Richter's interpretations in the 1950s had an elemental power and unselfconscious abandon that was refined and tempered in later life; the problem is the unreliable 1950s Soviet recording quality, compounded, presumably, by some decay in the master-tapes over the years, and not entirely redeemed by the NoNoise remastering technique. Nevertheless, here is an other-worldly Scriabin, cataclysmic and elevated, culminating in a vaporous, explosive, ultimately clamorous account of the Sixth Sonata. The Miaskovsky – formulaic Scriabin with an academic safety net – is probably better heard on elsewhere; from the amount of background noise on Melodiya you might think a *babushka* with her vacuum cleaner was competing for attention. Finally comes a muscular and emotionally searing Prokofiev Seventh which presents the only serious alternative to Pollini.

Further listening ...

...Fantasy in A minor. *Coupled with* **Tchaikovsky** Capriccio italien, Op. 45. Swan Lake, Op. 20 (arr. Debussy). The Sleeping Beauty, Op. 66 (arr. Rachmaninov). Marche slave, Op. 31 (arr. Batalini). **Katia Labèque, Marielle Labèque** (pfs). Philips 442 778-2PH (12/95).

...Mazurkas, Opp. 3, 25 and 40. **Artur Pizarro** (pf). Collins Classics 1394-2 (6/94). Ⓖ

...Preludes, Op. 11 – No. 2 in A minor; No. 4 in E minor; No. 5 in D major; No. 6 in B minor; No. 8 in F sharp minor; No. 9 in E major; No. 10 in C sharp minor; No. 11 in B major; No. 12 in G flat major; No. 13 in G flat major; No. 14 in E flat minor; No. 16 in B flat minor; No. 18 in F minor; No. 20 in C minor; No. 22 in G minor; No. 24 in D minor. *Coupled with* **Rachmaninov** Preludes – Op. 23: No. 1 in F sharp minor; No. 2 in B flat; No. 5 in G minor; No. 6 in E flat major; Op. 32: No. 12 in G sharp minor. Etudes-tableaux, Op. 39 – No. 3 in F sharp minor; No. 5 in E flat minor. Moments musicaux, Op. 16 – No. 3 in B minor; No. 4 in E minor; No. 5 in D flat major; No. 6 in C major. Elégie in E flat minor, Op. 3 No. 1. **Andrei Gavrilov** (pf). EMI Eminence CD-EMX2237 (12/95). Ⓖ

...Deux poèmes, Op. 32. Prélude et Nocturne, Op. 9. *Coupled with works by* **Liszt, Busoni, Liszt, Chopin, Debussy, Mendelssohn, Schumann, Rachmaninov** and **Weber** Anatol Ugorski (pf). DG 447 105-2GH 3/96). *See review in the Collections section; refer to the Index to Reviews.*

Peter Sculthorpe

New review

Sculthorpe Earth Cry. Irkanda IV[a]. Small Town[b]. Kakadu. Mangrove. [a]**Donald Hazelwood** (vn); [b]**Guy Henderson** (ob), Sydney Symphony Orchestra / Stuart Challender. ABC Classics Ⓓ 8 77000-2 (56 minutes: DDD: 11/95). *Gramophone Editor's choice.* Recorded 1989. Ⓖ

Peter Sculthorpe writes in an approachable, strongly characterful idiom, yet his music always retains its power to challenge and intrigue. Part of the fascination stems from his fruitful, indeed almost spiritual, identification with the Australian landscape. Not only does his inspiration evince a compelling sense of local colour, there is also a refusal to compromise – on this evidence Sculthorpe is a composer of undoubted integrity and strong personality. The earliest of the five works gathered here, *Irkanda IV* from 1961 (the Aboriginal title means "a remote and lonely place"), incorporates a strikingly imaginative threnody for solo violin to memorably eloquent effect (Sculthorpe, in fact, conceived the piece as a memorial to his father who had died the previous year). *Small Town* (1962) also combines a tender solo line (this time a sweetly lyrical, Coplandesque tune for principal oboe) with more obviously elegiac elements, most notably a moving double appearance of *The Last Post*. The 1979 piece, *Mangrove*, is a more ambitious essay, its characteristic block-like structure satisfyingly varied in mood, rhythm and texture. The impassioned, resonant *Earth Cry* comprises perhaps the most immediately arresting offering in the collection. Dating from 1986, its brooding stately outer sections effectively foil a more rhythmic central portion (which itself attains considerable power and momentum). By contrast, *Kakadu* (completed in 1988 and named after the vast Kakadu National Park in Northern Australia) boasts a reflective, exotic episode at its heart (with unmistakable echoes of the bird-song effects heard earlier in *Mangrove*), framed by much exhilarating, colourful faster material. Both *Earth Cry* and *Kakadu* are first-rate achievements, vibrantly scored and instantly communicative. The ripe recordings match the committed, disciplined performances.

Further listening ...

...Nourlangie[a]. From Kakadu. Into the Dreaming. *Coupled with* **Westlake** Antarctica[b]. **John Williams** (gtr); [a]**Australian Chamber Orchestra / Richard Hickox;** [b]**London Symphony Orchestra / Paul Daniel.** Sony Classical SK53361 (5/95).

Ruth Crawford Seeger
American 1901-1953

Suggested listening ...

...Andante for Strings. *Coupled with works by* **Ives** and **Ruggles** Cleveland Chorus and Orchestra / **Christoph von Dohnányi.** Decca 443 776-2DH (12/95). *See review under Ruggles; refer to the Index to Reviews.*

Mátyás Seiber
Hungarian 1905-1960

Suggested listening ...

...Clarinet Concertino. *Coupled with* **Blake** Clarinet Concerto. **Lutosławski** Dance Preludes. **Thea King** (cl); **English Chamber Orchestra / Andrew Litton.** Hyperion CDA66215 (1/88).

Carlos de Seixas
Portuguese 1704-1742

New review

Seixas Harpsichord Concerto in A major[a]. Sinfonia in B flat major[a]. Keyboard Sonatas – No. 1 in C major; No. 16 in C minor; No. 32 in E flat major; No. 33 in E flat major; No. 42 in F minor; No. 46 in G major; No. 47 in G major; No. 57 in A major; No. 71 in A minor; No. 79 in B flat major. [a]**Norwegian Baroque Orchestra / Ketil Haugsand** (hpd). Virgin Classics Veritas Ⓟ VC5 45114-2 (68 minutes: DDD: 3/96). 🖉 Recorded 1994.

Inevitably, Seixas's music for the harpsichord has always been overshadowed by Domenico Scarlatti's, which in several ways it resembles. Seixas was nearly two decades younger than Scarlatti and his style, although having much of the same waywardness and brilliance, is more given to the conventional expressive phraseology of the mid-eighteenth century. But it is still music of remarkable imagination, drama and intensity. The concerto that opens this CD is fairly ordinary, in a straight Vivaldian pattern, and the outer movements sound rather like sonatas with ritornellos pasted on (the finale a splendid gigue-like one). The Norwegian Baroque Orchestra are perfectly adequate but not a high precision group and the resonance of the recording, made in a Coimbra church, is no great help. However, the sonatas, played by Ketil Haugsand with great aplomb and a fine feeling for rhythm and how to flex it, to make rhetorical points without damaging momentum, are another matter. The fusion of the Scarlattian manner (or perhaps it is partly a more general Iberian-Lusitanian one) with the early *galant* flavour very attractive. Listen, for example, to the vivid series of flourishes that animate the C minor Sonata (No. 16), the elaborately worked and often chromatic lines of the E flat (No. 32), the deeply introspective music of the F minor (No. 42), with near-voluptuous textures in the minuet, and the brilliant *galanteries* of the final piece, the B flat (No. 79). There is plenty of variety here, and skilful and lively playing, on a very fine Antunes instrument of 1758.

Ludwig Senfl
Swiss/German c1486-1542/3

Suggested listening ...

...Will niemand singen. Ein Maidlein zue dem Brunnen ging. Dort oben auf dem Berge. Nun wöllt ihr hören neue Mär. Ich soll und müess ein'n Büehlen haben. Oho, so geb' der Mann. Es wollt' ein Maidlein Wasser hol'n. Es wollt' ein Frau zuem Weine gahn. Lamentatio. Ich stuend an einem Morgen. Albrecht mirs schwer. Ich weiss nit was er ihr verheiss (two versions). *Coupled with works by* **Isaac, Obrecht, Hofhaimer, Heinrich Finck, Ammerbach, A. Bruck, Küffer, G. Meyer** and **Rhau** Convivium Musicum; Villanella Ensemble / Sven Berger. Naxos 8 553352 (1/96). *See review in the Collections section; refer to the Index to Reviews.*

José Serebrier
Uruguayan 1938-

Suggested listening ...
...Poema elegíaco. Momento psicológico. *Coupled with* **Bloch** Violin Concerto. Baal Shem.
Michael Gutman (vn); **Royal Philharmonic Orchestra / José Serebrier.** ASV CDDCA785 (5/92).

Claudin de Sermisy
French c1490-1562

Suggested listening ...
...Chansons. *Coupled with* **Janequin** Chansons. **Ensemble Clément Janequin.** Harmonia Mundi HMC90 1271.
...Je ne menge point de porc. Las, je m'y plains, mauldicte soit fortune. Vien tost. *Coupled with works by* **Gombert, Clemens non Papa, Certon, G. Coste, Compère, De Bussy, Fresneau, Guiard, Hesdin, Josquin Desprez, La Rue, Ninot le Petit, Pipelare, Vermont le Jeune** *and* **Willaert.** Clément Janequin Ensemble / Dominique Visse.
Harmonia Mundi HMC90 1453 (5/95). *See review in the Collections section; refer to the Index to Reviews*

Roger Sessions
American 1896-1985

Sessions String Quintet[a]. Canon to the memory of Stravinsky[b]. String Quartet in E minor[b]. Six Pieces. **The Group for Contemporary Music** ([ab]Benjamin Hudson, [ab]Carol Zeavin, vns; [ab]Lois Martin, [a]Jenny Douglass, vas; Joshua Gordon, vc). Koch International Classics Ⓕ 37113-2 (66 minutes: DDD: 2/95). Recorded 1992.
The String Quartet in F minor (1938) is the essence of chamber music with its long lines in the extended *Adagio*, and impressive example of Sessions's visionary imagination. The final *Vivace* has some common ground with Tippett. The language of the Quintet (1958) is developed from the Schoenberg of the Third and Fourth Quartets, with a similar cantilena to the Quartet in a more advanced harmonic idiom. The energy of Sessions's faster movements, such as the finales of both works, is comparable and – in performances like these from New York's admirable Group for Contemporary Music – frequently electrifying. The short, elegiac *Canon to the memory of Stravinsky* shows that Sessions felt deeply about both the great innovators of early twentieth-century music. The solo cello pieces use all the scope available and make the most of Joshua Gordon's virtuosity, even if the rather close recording is inclined to catch breathing sounds.
Further listening ...
...Concerto for Orchestra. *Coupled with* **Panufnik** Symphony No. 8, "Sinfonia Votiva". **Boston Symphony Orchestra / Seiji Ozawa.** Hyperion CDA66050 (7/89).
...Symphonies Nos. 4 and 5. Rhapsody for Orchestra. **Columbus Symphony Orchestra / Christian Badea.** New World NW345-2 (10/87).
...Symphonies Nos. 6, 7 and 9. **American Composers Orchestra / Dennis Russell Davies.** Argo 444 519-2ZH (4/96).
...Piano Sonata No. 2. *Coupled with* **Griffes** Piano Sonata in F sharp minor. **Ives** Piano Sonata No. 1. **Peter Lawson** (pf). Virgin Classics VC7 59316-2 (2/94). *Gramophone Editor's choice. See review under Griffes; refer to the Index to Reviews.*

Déodat de Séverac
French 1873-1921

Suggested listening ...
...Tantum ergo[d]. *Coupled with* **Fauré** Requiem, Op. 48[a]. Messe basse[b]. Cantique de Jean Racine, Op. 11[b]. **Vierne** Pièces de fantaisie. Suite No. 1, Op. 51 – Andantino[c]. [a]**Lisa Beckley** (sop); [a]**Nicholas Gedge** (bass-bar); [abd]**Oxford Schola Cantorum;** [a]**Oxford Camerata / Jeremy Summerly** with [abc]**Colm Carey** (org). Naxos 8 550765 (9/94). *See review under Fauré; refer to the Index to Reviews.*

Vissarion Shebalin
USSR 1902-1963

Suggested listening ...
...Symphonies – No. 1 in F minor, Op. 6[a]; No. 3 in C major, Op. 17[b]. **USSR Radio Symphony Orchestra /** [a]**Mark Ermler,** [b]**Valery Gergiev** Olympia OCD577 (4/96).

Rodion Shchedrin

USSR 1932-

New review

Shchedrin Sotto voce.
Gagneux Triptyque. **Mstislav Rostropovich** (vc); **London Symphony Orchestra / Seiji Ozawa.** Teldec
Ⓟ 4509-94570-2 (56 minutes: DDD: 6/96). Recorded 1994.

Gagneux's *Triptyque* serves as a kind of atmospheric in-the-beginning prelude, complete with cells
and clusters, to Shchedrin's latest feat of the imagination. *Triptyque* comes across as a refined cocktail
of Dutilleux and Messiaen – two of Gagneux's teachers – whereas Shchedrin's concerto is a muted cry
from the heart, more personal than any other work of his (the article in the excellently produced
booklet invokes the Pushkin line, "My sorrow is bright"). The essence of the solo part – singing
legato, the frequent use of *pianissimo* and radiant harmonics – is a tribute to Rostropovich; but it
serves Shchedrin's belief in melody's closeness to speech intonations (in this case half-overheard) and,
in the final movement, a childhood memory of shepherds calling across fields by the river Oka. The
composer's re-creation, once the work's belligerent episodes have been laid to rest, is extraordinary:
the cello duets with one or two recorders, first imitating their sound and later weaving flageolet-note
patterns *quasi balalaika* around the descant and an echoing clarinet as the surrounding textures
become ever more rarefied. The ethereal pay-off is by no means the only remarkable thing about the
concerto. *Sotto voce* may be the title, but it is not the exclusive realm of the piece; the two brief
climaxes of the second movement – selectively scored, vividly played and recorded here – show a
master hand. Here, too, Shchedrin's keen balance between powering rhythmic patterns and careful
melodic lines helps to sustain a powerful argument, long-term shaping as sure as that of Schnittke or
Gubaidulina. Shchedrin's work joins the greatest of the many concertos dedicated to Rostropovich –
those of Prokofiev, Shostakovich, Britten and Schnittke.

Further listening ...
...Preludes and Fugues (1963-70). Preludes and Fugues, "Polyphonic notebook" (1972). **Murray
McLachlan** (pf). Olympia OCD438 (3/95).

Rich Shemaria

American 1955-

Suggested listening ...
...Pandora's Magic Castle. *Coupled with works by* **J. Nelson, Babbitt, Van Vliet, Wheeler, Zappa,
Stravinsky, H. Hancock** and **London** Meridian Arts Ensemble. Channel Classics Channel
Crossings CCS8195 (4/96). *See review in the Collections section; refer to the Index to Reviews.* Ⓖ

Bright Sheng

Chinese-American 1955-

Suggested listening ...
...H'un (Lacerations): In memoriam 1966-76[a]. The stream flows[b]. Three Chinese Love Songs[c]. My
song[d]. [c]**Lisa Saffer** (sop); [b]**Lucia Lin** (vn); [c]**Paul Neubauer** (va); [c]**Bright Sheng**, [d]**Peter Serkin** (pfs);
[a]**New York Chamber Symphony Orchestra / Gerard Schwarz.** New World 80407-2 (9/92).
...Two folksongs from Chinhai. *Coupled with* **McKinley** Four Text Settings. **Amlin** Time's
Caravan. **Carter** Emblems. The harmony of morning. Heart not so heavy as mine. Musicians
wrestle everywhere. **John Oliver Chorale / John Oliver.** Koch International Classics 37178-2 (5/95).

John Sheppard

British c1515-1559/60

Suggested listening ...
...Mass – "Be not afraide" (with plainsong Propers). Sacred Choral Works – Steven firste after
Christ. Sancte Dei pretiose. Impetum fecerunt unanimes. Gaudete caelicole omnes. *Coupled with*
Sampson Psallite felices. **The Cardinall's Musick / Andrew Carwood.** Meridian CDE84220
(12/92).
...In manus tuas Domine II. Gaude virgo Christiphera. Reges Tharsis et insulae. Libera nos, salva
nos I. Libera nos, salva nos II. *Coupled with* **Tye** Missa Euge Bone. Peccavimus Patribus nostris.
Clerkes of Oxenford / David Wulstan. Proud Sound PROUCD126 (5/90).
...Jesu salvator seculi, verbum. Deus tuorum militum II. Ave maris stella. Jesu salvator seculi,
redemptis Missa "Cantate". Salvator mundi Domine. **The Sixteen / Harry Christophers.** Hyperion
CDA66418 (12/92).
...Gaude, gaude, gaude Maria virgo. Dum transisset Sabbatum I. Spiritus Sanctus procedens II. In
manus tuas Domine II. Audivi vocem de caelo. Libera nos, salva nos II. Beata nobis gaudia.
Impetum fecerunt unanimes. Sancte Dei pretiose. Sacris solemniis iuncta sint gaudia.
The Sixteen / Harry Christophers. Hyperion CDA66570 (12/92).
...Verbum caro factum est. Laudem dicite Deo. Reges Tharsis et insulae. In manus tuas I. Filiae
Jerusalem. In pace in idipsum. Paschal Kyrie. Haec dies. Spiritus sanctus. Justi in perpetuum
vivent. Libera nos, salva nos I. **The Sixteen / Harry Christophers.** Hyperion CDA66259 (2/89).

...Aeterne Rex altissime. Dum transisset Sabbatum II. Hostis Hérodes impie. In manus tuas III. Te Deum laudamus. Mass, "The Western Wynde". The Second Service: Magnificat; Nunc dimittis. **The Sixteen / Harry Christophers.** Hyperion CDA66603 (8/93).

Richard M. Sherman/Robert B. Sherman   American 1928-; 1925-

Suggested listening ...
...Mary Poppins. Original film soundtrack. IMP/Disney DSMCD459.
...The Jungle Book. Original film soundtrack. IMP/Disney DSMCD457.

William Shield   British 1748-1829

Suggested listening ...
...String Quartet in C minor, Op. 3 No. 6. *Coupled with works by* **Abel, Marsh, Webbe** and **S. Wesley Salomon Quartet.** Hyperion CDA66780 (3/96). *See review in the Collections section; refer to the Index to Reviews.*

Dmitry Shostakovich   USSR 1906-1975

Shostakovich Cello Concertos – No. 1 in E flat major, Op. 107; No. 2 in G major, Op. 126. **Mischa Maisky** (vc); **London Symphony Orchestra / Michael Tilson Thomas.** DG Ⓕ 445 821-2GH (65 minutes: DDD: 4/95). Recorded 1993. *Gramophone Editor's choice.*   ⒼⒼ

New review
Shostakovich Cello Concertos – No. 1 in E flat major, Op. 107; No. 2 in G major, Op. 126. **Truls Mørk** (vc); **London Philharmonic Orchestra / Mariss Jansons.** Virgin Classics Ⓕ VC5 45145-2 (66 minutes: DDD: 2/96). Recorded 1995. *Selected by Soundings.*   Ⓖ
The Second Cello Concerto is one of the major concertos of the post-war period – as potent a representative of the composer's later style as the last three symphonies, be it through irony (second movement), poetry (first and third) or anger (beginning of the third). Few cellists have tended the *p espressivo* of the *Largo*'s opening bars as lovingly as Mischa Maisky does, while the rapt quality of his soft playing and the expressive eloquence of his double stopping wring the most from Shostakovich's extended soliloquy. Michael Tilson Thomas points and articulates with his usual skill. Only the opening of that movement (with its furious whoop horns) seems marginally underprojected, although the main climax later on is both immensely powerful and extraordinarily clear. The First Concerto harbours fewer mysteries than the Second and yet remains a pivotal work. Maisky phrases beautifully, while Tilson Thomas and the LSO again come up trumps, even though 1'33" into the finale the dramatic switch to 6/8 sounds less spontaneous than it does under, say, Maxim Shostakovich. In other respects, however, this is a forceful and fairly outgoing interpretation, beautifully recorded and a suitable coupling for the disc's star act – the finest available studio recording of the Second Concerto. In fact, this CD is now the prime recommendation for the two concertos coupled together.
  Although Truls Mørk and Mariss Jansons offer admirably strong, well-considered interpretations of both works, that recommendation stands. The Virgin release has the virtue of exceptional engineering; in fact, it's one of the best recordings to emerge from Abbey Road in recent years – a spacious, highly attentive production with a pin-sharp solo image and a consistently vivid orchestral backdrop. In that respect alone, Virgin score a definite point over their excellent DG rival. As to interpretation, Mørk is a less outwardly demonstrative player than Maisky and Jansons a rather less imaginative Shostakovich conductor than Michael Tilson Thomas.
Additional recommendations ...
...No. 1. **Barber** Cello Concerto, Op. 22. **Raphael Wallfisch** (vc); **English Chamber Orchestra / Geoffrey Simon.** Chandos Ⓕ CHAN8322 (59 minutes: DDD: 2/85).
...Nos. 1 and 2. **Heinrich Schiff** (vc); **Bavarian Radio Symphony Orchestra / Maxim Shostakovich.** Philips Ⓕ 412 526-2PH (61 minutes: DDD: 10/85).   ⒼⒼ
...Nos. 1 and 2. **Natalia Gutman** (vc); **Royal Philharmonic Orchestra / Yuri Temirkanov.** RCA Victor Red Seal Ⓕ RD87918 (66 minutes: DDD: 1/91).
...No. 1[a]. Symphony No. 5 in D minor, Op. 47. [a]**Miloš Sadló** (vc); **Czech Philharmonic Orchestra / Karel Ančerl.** Supraphon Crystal Collection Ⓜ 11 0676-2 (72 minutes: ADD: 8/93).   ⒼⒼ
...Nos. 1 and 2. **Torleif Thedéen** (vc); **Malmö Symphony Orchestra / James DePreist.** BIS Ⓕ CD626 (65 minutes: DDD: 7/94).
...No. 2[a]. Symphony No. 5 in D minor, Op. 47[b]. [a]**Boston Symphony Orchestra / Seiji Ozawa;** [b]**Washington National Symphony Orchestra / Mstislav Rostropovich** ([a]vc). DG Classikon ⓑ 439 481-2GCL (79 minutes: ADD/DDD: 9/95).

Shostakovich Piano Concertos – C minor for Piano, Trumpet and Strings, Op 35[ab]; No. 2 in F major, Op. 102[b]. Three Fantastic Dances, Op. 5 (all from French Columbia FCX769, 10/61).

24 Preludes and Fugues, Op. 87 – No. 1 in C major; No. 4 in E minor; No. 5 in D major; No. 23 in F major (FCX771); No. 24 in D minor (Parlophone PMC1056, 7/58). **Dmitri Shostakovich** (pf); [a]**Ludovic Vaillant** (tpt); [b]**French Radio National Orchestra / André Cluytens.** EMI Composers in Person mono Ⓕ CDC7 54606-2* (76 minutes: ADD: 4/93). Recorded 1958-59. ☉☉

Before devoting himself entirely to composition Shostakovich pursued a successful parallel career as a concert pianist, playing mostly romantic repertoire. These recordings were made at a time when he still played his own works in public, and they show him to have been a highly skilled player. His performances of both concertos are quite brilliant, and have a particularly vivacious, outgoing quality. In the First Concerto Ludovic Vaillant plays the trumpet part with character and great virtuosity, and the orchestral playing under Cluytens matches that of the composer in its joyous high spirits. The three little *Fantastic Dances* are wittily brought to life. A different, far more serious and academic world is evoked by Shostakovich in his Preludes and Fugues. Here the composer shapes his own long contrapuntal lines with great skill, and these are very compelling, highly concentrated performances. The mono recordings are all very acceptable, save that of the last Prelude and Fugue, where a certain rustiness creeps into the sound. All these items have obvious historical importance, but they also offer many rewards to the listener who is primarily interested in the music.

Additional recommendations ...

...Cello Sonata[a]. Concerto for Piano, Trumpet and Strings[b]. Piano Concerto No. 2[c]. [a]**Mstislav Rostropovich** (vc); **Dmitri Shostakovich** (pf); [b]**Moscow Radio Symphony Orchestra / Alexander Gauk;** [c]**Moscow Philharmonic Orchestra / Samuil Samosud.** Russian Disc Ⓕ RDCD15005 (64 minutes: ADD: 2/95).

...Concerto for Piano, Trumpet and Strings. **Borodin** Op. 35[d]. Prince Igor – Overture[a]. Symphony No. 2 in B minor[b]. **Liadov** Kikimora, Op. 63[c]. **Tchaikovsky** The Sleeping Beauty – Valse[e]. [d]**Eileen Joyce** (pf); [d]**Arthur Lockwood** (tpt); **Hallé Orchestra /** [b]**Constant Lambert,** [ad]**Leslie Heward,** [c]**Sir Adrian Boult,** [e]**Sir Malcolm Sargent.** Dutton Laboratories mono Ⓜ CDAX8010* (67 minutes: ADD: 2/95).

Shostakovich Piano Concertos – C minor for Piano, Trumpet and Strings, Op. 35[a]; No. 2 in F major, Op. 102. The Unforgettable Year 1919, Op. 89 – The assault on beautiful Gorky. **Dmitri Alexeev** (pf); [a]**Philip Jones** (tpt); **English Chamber Orchestra / Jerzy Maksymiuk.** Classics for Pleasure Ⓑ CD-CFP4547 (48 minutes: DDD: 1/89). From CFP414416-1 (11/83).

Shostakovich's Piano Concertos were written under very different circumstances, yet together they contain some of the composer's most cheerful and enlivening music. The First, with its wealth of perky, memorable tunes, has the addition of a brilliantly-conceived solo trumpet part (delightfully done here by Philip Jones) that also contributes to the work's characteristic stamp. The Second Concerto was written not long after Shostakovich had released a number of the intense works he had concealed during the depths of the Stalin era. It came as a sharp contrast, reflecting as it did the optimism and sense of freedom that followed the death of the Russian dictator. The beauty of the slow movement is ideally balanced by the vigour of the first, and the madcap high spirits of the last. The poignant movement for piano and orchestra from the Suite from the 1951 film *The Unforgettable Year 1919*, "The assault on beautiful Gorky", provides an excellent addition to this disc of perceptive and zestful performances by Alexeev. He is most capably supported by the ECO under Maksymiuk, and the engineers have done them proud with a recording of great clarity and finesse. A joyous issue.

Additional recommendations ...

...Concerto for Piano, Trumpet and Strings[a]. Chamber Symphony in C minor, Op. 110a. Preludes, Op. 34[b] – Nos. 5, 6, 10, 13, 14, 17 and 24. [ab]**Evgeni Kissin** (pf); [a]**Vassili Kan** (tpt); **Moscow Virtuosi / Vladimir Spivakov.** RCA Victor Red Seal Ⓕ RD87947 (58 minutes: DDD: 12/89).

...Concerto for Piano, Trumpet and Strings[c]. Piano Concerto No. 2 **Poulenc** Double Piano Concerto in D minor[c]. [a]**André Previn,** [c]**Arthur Gold,** [c]**Robert Fizdale** (pfs); [a]**William Vacchiano** (tpt); **New York Philharmonic Orchestra / Leonard Bernstein.** Sony Classical Bernstein Royal Edition Ⓜ SMK47618 (61 minutes: ADD: 6/94).

...Concerto for Piano, Trumpet and Strings[a]. **Haydn** Piano Concerto in D major, HobXVIII/11. **Martha Argerich** (pf); [a]**Guy Touvron** (trpt); **Württemberg Chamber Orchestra / Jörg Faerber.** DG Ⓕ 439 864-2GH (42 minutes: DDD: 1/95).

Shostakovich Violin Concerto No. 1 in A minor, Op. 99.
Prokofiev Violin Concerto No. 1 in D major, Op. 19. **Maxim Vengerov** (vn); **London Symphony Orchestra / Mstislav Rostropovich.** Teldec Ⓕ 4509-92256-2 (62 minutes: DDD: 2/95). Recorded 1994. Includes bonus sampler disc. *Gramophone Award Winner 1995. Gramophone Editor's choice.* ☉☉☉

New review
Shostakovich Violin Concerto No. 1 in A minor, Op. 99.
Prokofiev Violin Concerto No. 2 in G minor, Op. 63. **Vadim Repin** (vn); **Hallé Orchestra / Kent Nagano.** Erato Ⓕ 0630-10696-2 (59 minutes: DDD: 1/96).

There is an astonishing emotional maturity in Vengerov's Shostakovich. He uses Heifetz's bow but it is to David Oistrakh that he is often compared. His vibrato is wider, his manners less consistently refined, and yet the comparison is well-founded. Only one of Oistrakh's three commercial recordings of the Shostakovich is at present in the catalogue (listed below) and one can guess that Vengerov has been listening to those earlier Oistrakh renditions as there is nothing radically novel about his interpretation. It is possible that some will find Vengerov's impassioned climaxes a shade forced by comparison. Yet he achieves a nobility and poise worlds away from the superficial accomplishment of most modern rivals. He can fine down his tone to the barest whisper; nor is he afraid to make a scorching, ugly sound. While his sometimes slashing quality of articulation is particularly appropriate to the faster movements, the brooding, silver-grey *Nocturne* comes off superbly too, though it seems perverse that the engineers mute the low tam-tam strokes. Rostropovich has the lower strings dig into the third movement's passacaglia theme with his usual enthusiasm. Indeed the orchestral playing is very nearly beyond reproach. Vengerov and Rostropovich take an unashamedly epic, wide-open-steppes view of the Prokofiev concerto and it works well. Closely observed digital recording uncovers a wealth of detail, most of it welcome, with the conductor's erstwhile clumsy tendency barely noticeable. Towards the end of the first movement, the approach to the reprise of the opening melody on solo flute with harp, muted strings and lightly running tracery from the soloist is very deliberately taken, and the long-breathed finale builds to a passionate, proto-Soviet climax. The central scherzo is predictably breathtaking in its virtuosity. Need one go on? If you're looking for a recording of the Shostakovich, Vengerov's coupling may be less logical than Lydia Mordkovitch's (see below) but do not be deterred from investigating this extraordinary disc. However committed you are to alternative interpretations, these demand to be heard.

Vadim Repin's interpretation of the Shostakovich comes across as less quintessentially Russian in its avoidance of rhetorical overkill. Without in any way underplaying the bravura passages (the *Scherzo* is taken at an incredible speed), he stresses rather the chamber-like intimacy of Shostakovich's score. Rather surprising, perhaps, is the flowing tempo for the slow third movement, but, thanks also to Nagano and the Hallé, we do actually hear the music as a passacaglia. With Vengerov and Rostropovich intent on heightening strong emotions rather than clarifying textures, the LSO's contribution is comparatively impenetrable on Teldec. In the "Nocturne" the tam-tam, inaudible in Abbey Road, is perfectly caught in Manchester. Given Repin's dazzling achievement in the Shostakovich concerto, his Prokofiev is a shade disappointing. The violin is less sweetly caught and Repin sometimes makes the kind of uningratiating noises which imply some impatience with the straightforward *Romeo and Juliet*-style lyricism of the work. The finale sounds spontaneous but the lovely slow movement could do with more space to indulge its sweetly singing lines. However, if the coupling appeals, Repin represents a clear first choice – and anyone who cares about the Shostakovich will want to hear Repin's disc.

Additional recommendations ...

...No. 1; No. 2 in C sharp minor, Op. 129. **David Oistrakh** (vn); **Czech Philharmonic Orchestra / Evgeny Mravinsky.** Praga PR250 052*.

...No. 1. **Glazunov** Violin Concerto in A minor, Op. 82. **Itzhak Perlman** (vn); **Israel Philharmonic Orchestra / Zubin Mehta.** EMI Ⓕ CDC7 49814-2 (55 minutes: DDD: 1/90).

...Nos. 1 and 2. **Lydia Mordkovitch** (vn); **Scottish National Orchestra / Neeme Järvi.** Chandos Ⓕ CHAN8820 (69 minutes: DDD: 4/90). *Gramophone* Award Winner 1990. Ⓖ

...No. 1[a]. Piano Concerto No. 2 in F major, Op. 102[b]. [a]**Boris Belkin** (vn); [b]**Cristina Ortiz** (pf); **Royal Philharmonic Orchestra / Vladimir Ashkenazy.** Decca Ⓕ 425 793-2DH (60 minutes: DDD: 8/90).

...Nos. 1 and 2. **Dmitry Sitkovetsky** (vn); **BBC Symphony Orchestra / Andrew Davis.** Virgin Classics Ⓕ VC7 59601-2 (67 minutes: DDD: 9/90). Ⓖ

Shostakovich The Bolt. **Royal Stockholm Philharmonic Orchestra / Gennadi Rozhdestvensky.** Chandos Ⓕ CHAN9343/4 (two discs: 147 minutes: DDD: 6/95). Recorded 1994. Ⓖ

The Bolt (1931) can be neither laughed nor shrugged off. It is a disturbing symptom of a very sick society, and it is surely no wonder that Shostakovich was noticeably less keen to see it restaged than *Lady Macbeth* or *The Nose*. It has long been recognized that *The Bolt* contains some fine music. From the spoof-Tchaikovsky opening, through the Bureaucrat's music cunningly poised between ridicule and threat, through the naughty habanera and the coy Soviet ragtime of Kozelkov's Dance, to the nudge-and-wink of The Conciliator, the score is as stunningly talented as it is recklessly tossed off. Admittedly a lot of the unfamiliar music consists of off-the-top-of-the-head, Stravinsky-cum-Hindemithian scraps, and without the visual input of the choreography the not-quite-spontaneous radical cheek does get a bit tiring. But what a wonderful tease his music could be, and how deftly he orchestrated it, even when working at absurd speed. How he must have enjoyed composing a movement like the radio gymnastic exercises, and how Gennadi Rozhdestvensky must have enjoyed playing and declaiming them. The character of *The Bolt* fits Rozhdestvensky like a body-stocking. There are innumerable coquettish nuances of timing and balance, and despite some moments of tonal thinness (especially in the strings) the orchestra sound more at home in the idiom than they did with *The Golden Age* (see below). Recording quality is fine; entertainment value is intermittent but at its best very high; food for thought is abundant.

Shostakovich The Golden Age. **Royal Stockholm Philharmonic Orchestra / Gennadi Rozhdestvensky.** Chandos Ⓕ CHAN9251/2 (two discs: 134 minutes: DDD: 5/94). Recorded 1993.

The Golden Age (1930) is an industrial exhibition organized in a capitalist country, at which a group of Soviet sportsmen have been invited to compete. The general idea of Shostakovich's characterization is clearly to differentiate between goodies and baddies by assigning them respectively healthy-folk and decadent-bourgeois idioms. But then the trouble was, he couldn't stop himself enjoying being decadent. Not all of the 37 movements stand up independently of the stage-action. But the finales and the whole of Act 3 are top-notch stuff, at times surprisingly threatening in tone and symphonic in continuity; and there are several movements which could undoubtedly be promoted alongside the four in the familiar concert suite (the Tap Dance of Act 2 is especially appealing, for instance). Those who know their Shostakovich will be constantly intrigued by foretastes of *Lady Macbeth*, the Fourth Symphony and the *Hamlet* music, and by the appearance of Shostakovich's "Tea for Two" arrangement as an Interlude in Act 2. This first complete recording is a major coup for Chandos. Admittedly not even their flattering engineering can disguise a certain lack of confidence and idiomatic flair on the part of the Royal Stockholm Philharmonic Orchestra. But let that not deter anyone with the least interest in Shostakovich, or ballet music, or Soviet music, or indeed Soviet culture as a whole, from investigating this weird and intermittently wonderful score.

Shostakovich Symphonies. [a]**London Philharmonic Orchestra;** [b]**Concertgebouw Orchestra / Bernard Haitink.** Decca Ovation Ⓜ 444 430-2LC11 (11 discs, oas: ADD/DDD: 11/93). Texts and translations included.
425 063-2DM[a] (65 minutes) – No. 1 in F minor, Op. 10 (from SXDL7515, 5/81); No. 3 in E flat major, Op. 20, "The first of May" (with the London Philharmonic Choir. SXDL7535, 7/82). *425 064-2DM*[a] (76 minutes) – No. 2 in B major, Op. 14 (London Phil Ch. SXDL7535, 7/82); No. 10 in E minor, Op. 93 (SXL6838, 10/77). *425 065-2DM* (68 minutes) – No. 4 in C minor, Op. 43 (SXL6927, 11/79)[a]. *425 066-2DM* (76 minutes) – No. 5 in D minor, Op. 47 (SXDL7551, 12/82. *Gramophone Award Winner 1982-83*)[b]; No. 9 in E flat major, Op. 70 (SXDL7515, 5/81)[a]. *425 067-2DM*[b] (74 minutes) – No. 6 in B minor, Op. 54 (411 939-2DH2, 8/85. *Selected by Sounds in Retrospect*); No. 12 in D minor, Op. 112, "The year 1917" (SXDL7577, 6/83). *425 068-2DM* (79 minutes) – No. 7 in C major, Op. 60, "Leningrad" (D213D2, 11/80)[a]. *425 069-2DM* (73 minutes) – No. 15 in A major, Op. 141 (SXL6906, 3/79)[a]; From Jewish Folk Poetry, Op. 79 (Elisabeth Söderström, sop; Ortrun Wenkel, contr; Ryszard Karczykowski, ten. 417 261-2DH, 3/87)[b]. *425 071-2DM* (62 minutes) – No. 8 in C minor, Op. 65 (SXDL7621, 11/83)[b]. *425 072-2DM* (61 minutes) – No. 11 in G minor, Op. 103, "The year 1905" (411 939-2DH2, 8/85. *Selected by Sounds in Retrospect*)[b]. *425 073-2DM* (64 minutes) – No. 13 in B flat minor, Op. 113, "Babiy Yar". (Marius Rintzler, bass; Concertge-bouw Choir. 417 261-2DH, 3/87)[b]. *425 074-2DM*[b] (72 minutes) – No. 14, Op. 135 (Julia Varady, sop; Dietrich Fischer-Dieskau, bar. SXDL7532, 1/82). Six Marina Tsvetaeva Poems, Op. 143 (Ortrun Wenkel. 417 261-2DH, 3/87). 🔊🔊

We used to see Shostakovich's output discussed in terms of public and private utterance. Rigorously 'public' symphonies – giving new life to a monumental form that, in the opinion of Soviet ideologists, had become impossible to cultivate in the capitalist West – were ranged against ineluctably 'private' chamber works, intimate confessionals in which the composer was apt to reveal his secret heart. Paradoxically, despite today's much greater understanding of the symphonies' own allusive dimension, there have been few wholly successful recordings in recent years. As Western LPs of the 1960s and 1970s from conductors like Ormandy, Previn and Berglund have disappeared from the catalogue, so the more demonstrative Soviet tradition has splintered. The first complete Western cycle, that of Bernard Haitink, returns to the catalogue at midprice, Decca having jettisoned a few minor works and decoupled several major ones. It is hard to argue with the new presentation when it includes modern annotations and full recording data. Concerned for tradition, and with the need to challenge it, the young Shostakovich could be classical and modern, polemical and prankish by turns.

Haitink, not entirely po-faced, turns in a thoroughly decent account of the First Symphony, missing just a little of the element of pastiche. The recoupling with the Third does strike sparks, the language of the later music variously foreshadowed in divergent contexts. In the Fourth Symphony, Haitink offers no stupendous revelations, content to bring out the dignity of the writing in a piece where we have come to expect something more sensational, less perfectly controlled. Even the hurtling *moto perpetuo* fugato passage for strings which triggers the main climax of the first movement seems just a little studied. His outer movements are helpfully split, by additional cues – but his literalness and sobriety fall short of the ideal, as, marginally, does the playing. It is worth paying extra for Järvi's emotional candour (reviewed further on). Haitink's Fifth, deeply considered and almost indecently well-upholstered, is not easy to assess. Originally greeted with extreme reverence in these pages – its release followed hard on the heels of the publication of *Testimony* which surely influenced the critical response – it is an earnest attempt to make structural sense of the music's grand symphonic aspirations. It is only because the orchestral playing is generally so immaculate that one registers the curious glitch 2'13" into the *Largo*. That movement is generally less affecting than it can be, yet the preceding *Allegretto* is triumphantly brought off as a heavy-footed Mahlerian *Ländler*. Then again, the first movement's long-limbed second subject chugs along reluctantly, dourly unphrased, with none of the easeful balm to be found in other interpretations.

Haitink's Fifth is now generously paired with his solid, untrivial but scarcely earth-shattering Ninth. His Sixth and Twelfth is characterized by playing of predictable *gravitas* and tonal splendour. Indeed, this Twelfth could be seen as the 'best' modern version. The *Leningrad* is another matter. Rightly praised for its symphonic integrity and splendid sound, Haitink's *nobilmente* reappraisal is now a much cheaper option than Bernstein's two-disc epic on DG (reviewed further on), though some will respond more favourably to the raw authenticity of Rozhdestvensky. Haitink's stoical view of the Eighth is highly impressive, though not very varied in mood. Curiously, the finale is mis-cued. Kurt Sanderling's reading (listed under the review of No. 8) is also highly impressive. The Tenth has always seemed less dependent on a conductor steeped in the Russian tradition, and the only drawback of Haitink's well-played well-recorded account is his unsubtle, over-confident tone in the enigmatic third movement *Allegretto*. There is real demonic abandon in the scherzo. Karajan's Tenth is very desirable (reviewed further on) but he offers no makeweight. Haitink offers a carefully prepared account of No. 2, where the choral contribution has the odd awkward moment but the overall effect is very arresting. His Eleventh too has such weight and precision that his customary detachment is mostly less noticeable than his phenomenal control.

Haitink's Thirteenth boasts another of Decca's huge, reverberant recordings, of such 'cinematic' brilliance and range that it threatens to dwarf the music-making. While chorus and orchestra are on terrific form, even this monolithic work ideally requires greater flexibility and plasticity than the conductor seems willing to provide. The soloist, Marius Rintzler, would seem to be at one with Haitink's brooding approach. Kondrashin's account (listed further on) makes a very recommendable alternative. As one of the first of Shostakovich's late scores to be taken seriously in the West, it is odd that the Fourteenth should have been so poorly represented in the CD catalogue. Haitink's polyglot reading (not quite that authorized by the composer, incidentally) does not really represent a viable solution – too much vital and specific tone colour is lost along with the original note-values. To make matters worse, Fischer-Dieskau is in hectoring mode and both soloists' proximity to the microphones makes for uncomfortable listening, though the orchestral contribution is excellent. Barshai (listed below) can lay claim to *absolute* authenticity. It is a fascinating document, as he and Vishnevskaya rage against the dying of the light in every song, slicing seconds (sometimes minutes) off the timings of the Western account. Reshetin is superb too, less inclined to histrionics. Generally speaking the sound is close and crude, by no means intolerable but sufficiently prone to distortion to inhibit a general recommendation. In its way, however, this disc is indispensable. Haitink's Fifteenth has always been highly regarded, despite some less than needle-sharp contributions from the percussion where it matters most. At medium price, and with a rather high-level transfer of its coupling (whose historical significance is ably outlined in the insert-note), this merits a place at or near the top of anyone's list. To sum up: Haitink's set, superbly engineered, is nothing if not reliable. For those who prize technical finesse over raw passion, Haitink remains a plausible first choice. These are endlessly fascinating, endlessly equivocal works.

Additional recommendations ...

...Nos. 9[a] and 14[b]. [b]**Galina Vishnevskaya** (sop); [b]**Mark Reshetin** (bass); [b]**Moscow Chamber Orchestra / Rudolf Barshai**; [a]**USSR Symphony Orchestra / David Oistrakh**. Russian Disc ⒻRDCD11192 (73 minutes: ADD: 1/94). *Gramophone Editor's choice.*　🟢🟢

...No. 12. **Leningrad Philharmonic Orchestra / Evgeny Mravinsky**. Erato Ⓜ 2292-45754-2 (39 minutes: DDD: 6/92).　🟢🟢🟢

...No. 14[a]. King Lear, Op. 58[ab]. [a]**Makuara Kasrashubili** (sop); [b]**Nina Romanova** (mez); [a]**Anatoly Safiulin** (bass); [a]**USSR Ministry of Culture Symphony Orchestra / Gennadi Rozhdestvensky**; [b]**Leningrad Chamber Orchestra / Eduard Serov**. Olympia Ⓜ OCD182 (62 minutes: DDD: 12/88).

Shostakovich Symphonies – No. 1 in F minor, Op. 10; No. 6 in B minor, Op. 54. **Scottish National Orchestra / Neeme Järvi**. Chandos Ⓕ CHAN8411 (64 minutes: DDD: 6/86). Recorded 1984-85.　🟢

The First Symphony, the 19-year-old composer's graduation piece from the then Leningrad Conservatory in 1925, may be indebted to Stravinsky, Prokofiev, Tchaikovsky and even Scriabin. But it rarely sounds like anything other than pure Shostakovich. The sophisticated mask of its first movement is drawn aside for a slow movement of Slav melancholy and foreboding, and the finale brilliantly stage-manages a way out. The Sixth (1939) takes the familiar Shostakovichian extremes of explosive activity and uneasy contemplation (that the composer reconciles in the finale of the First) and separates them into individual movements. Two swift movements (a mercurial but menacing *Scherzo*, and a real knees-up of a finale) follow on from an opening *Largo* whose slow lyrical declamations eventually all but freeze into immobility. Järvi has a will (and Chandos, the engineering) to explore the extremes of pace, mood and dynamics of both symphonies; his account of the First Symphony convinces precisely because those extremes intensify as the work progresses. Some may crave a fuller, firmer string sound, but the passionate intensity of the playing (in all departments) is never in doubt.

Additional recommendations ...

...No. 6. **Rachmaninov** Symphony No. 3 in A minor, Op. 44. **London Symphony Orchestra / André Previn**. EMI Studio Ⓜ CDM7 69564-2 (75 minutes: ADD: 12/88).

...Nos. 1[a], 5[b] and 7[c]. Prelude in E flat minor, Op. 34[d] (orch. Stokowski). [abd]**Philadelphia Orchestra**; [c]**NBC Symphony Orchestra / Leopold Stokowski**. Pearl mono Ⓜ GEMMCD9044* (two discs: 156 minutes: ADD: 1/94).　🟢🟢

...No. 6; No. 12 in D minor, Op. 112, "The year 1917". **Leningrad Philharmonic Orchestra / Evgeny Mravinsky**. Praga Ⓕ PR254 017 (61 minutes: ADD: 8/94).

...Nos. 1 and 15. **Montreal Symphony Orchestra / Charles Dutoit**. Decca Ⓕ 436 838-2DH (75 minutes: DDD: 10/94).

...No. 1. Concerto for Piano, Trumpet and Strings in C minor, Op. 35[a]. [a]**Mikhail Rudy** (pf); [a]**Ole Edward Antonsen** (tpt); **Berlin Philharmonic Orchestra / Mariss Jansons.** EMI Ⓔ CDC5 55361-2 (55 minutes: DDD: 12/95).

Shostakovich Symphony No. 2 in B major, Op. 14, "To October"[a]. October, Op. 131. Festival Overture in A major, Op. 96. The Song of the Forests, Op. 81[b]. [b]**Mikhail Kotliarov** (ten); [b]**Nikita Storojev** (bass); [b]**New London Children's Choir**; [ab]**Brighton Festival Chorus; Royal Philharmonic Orchestra / Vladimir Ashkenazy**. Decca Ⓔ 436 762-2DH (72 minutes: DDD: 8/94). Texts and translations included. Recorded 1989-91.

Shostakovich Symphonies – No. 2 in B major, Op. 14, "To October"; No. 3 in E flat major, "The first of May", Op. 20. **London Voices; London Symphony Orchestra / Mstislav Rostropovich.** Teldec Ⓔ 4509-90853-2 (48 minutes: DDD: 10/94). Recorded 1993.   Ⓖ

Ashkenazy's offers a programme designed to show how Shostakovich negotiated the shifting sands of Soviet cultural politics, as an unwilling but adaptable composer laureate. At well over 30 minutes, *The Song of the Forests* is hardly an insignificant makeweight, whatever its musical shortcomings. Shostakovich completed the Second Symphony when barely into his twenties, prompted by an official commission to mark the tenth anniversary of the October Revolution. Despite material discomfort, he was living through a period of unprecedented freedom for Russian artists though the exploratory, futurist style of the first section was enough to keep it under wraps in the era of Stalin and Khrushchev. As often happens in Western recordings of this repertoire, the singing falls short of the ideal – a pity when the orchestral response is appropriately full-blooded, the dynamic range impressively wide. The more familiar *Festival Overture* receives a bright and breezy rendition with details superbly pointed. The symphonic poem *October* (1967) has its moments, not least because its material is so closely related to that of the Tenth Symphony. However, the piece, in Shostakovich's epic, brooding vein, is surely too long for its own good.

If in No. 2, Ashkenazy's version has the edge in terms of textural clarity it is Rostropovich who makes better sense of the notes. The disc is cut at a low level, which will make the dark opening pages implausibly opaque unless you reset the controls. The string playing then emerges as impressively polished, the wind aptly angular and spiky, more characterful than their rivals as the music gains pace. Only the LSO's leader seems a trifle thin of tone (as recorded). Under Rostropovich, uniquely among recent exponents of the score, the factory whistle is not doubled by brass. Thereafter the churchy acoustic ensures that his London Voices sound at least as numerous as Ashkenazy's Brighton chorus; and the men at least are more comfortable with the idiom. The climax is both fervent and unusually secure of pitch. Rostropovich's account of the Third is an outstanding achievement. Relishing the opportunities for display, the LSO find their best form – crisper of ensemble than in previous outings with this inspirational, if not always ideally lucid, conductor – and the recorded sound is surely the best in Teldec's cycle. The opening clarinet theme is exquisitely done and, amid the corybantic tumult of Revolution, the lyrical moments are empowered here with rare emotional clout. Already we hear the authentic voice of the composer Rostropovich knew as friend and mentor, the disillusioned chronicler of Soviet reality.

Additional recommendation ...

...Festival Overture. Ballet Suites – No. 1; No. 2; No. 3; No. 4; No. 5, Op. 27*a*. Katerina Izmaylova – Suite. **Royal Scottish Orchestra / Neeme Järvi.** Chandos Ⓜ CHAN7000/1 (two discs: 114 minutes: DDD: 5/95).

New review

Shostakovich Symphony No. 4 in C minor, Op. 43.
Britten Russian Funeral. **City of Birmingham Symphony Orchestra / Sir Simon Rattle.** EMI Ⓔ CDC5 55476-2 (68 minutes: DDD: 11/95). Recorded 1994.

This could just be the most important Western recording of the Fourth since the long-deleted Ormandy and Previn versions. Naturally, it complements rather than replaces Kondrashin's reading, taped shortly after the work's belated unveiling in December 1961: papery strings and lurid brass cannot disguise that conductor's unique authority even when Shostakovich's colouristic effects are muted by rudimentary Soviet sound engineering. In his new recording, Rattle's approach is more obviously calculated, supremely brilliant but just a little cold. A certain firmness and self-confidence is obvious from the first. The restrained Hindemithian episode is relatively square, the first climax superbly built. The second group unfolds seamlessly with the glorious *espressivo* of the strings not much threatened by the not very mysterious intrusions of harp and bass clarinet. Tension builds again, some way into the development, with the lacerating (Kondrashin-like) intensity of the strings' *moto perpetuo* fugato passage. Six miraculously terraced discords herald the two-faced recapitulation. Kondrashin and Järvi find more emotional inevitability in Shostakovich's destabilizing tactics hereabouts. Rattle doesn't quite locate a compensating irony, although his closing bars are convincingly icy, with nicely audible gong. Even in Rattle's experienced hands, the finale is not all plain sailing. The initial quasi-Mahlerian march is underpinned by disappointingly fuzzy timpani strokes which lose the point of their own lopsidedness. But then the section's mock-solemn climax is simply tremendous (and tremendously loud). The incisive *Allegro* is launched with (deliberate?) abruptness at an unbelievably fast tempo and, even if the music doesn't always make sense at this pace, the results are breathtaking. The denouement is approached with real flair. A superbly characterized trombone solo, hushed expectant strings and the most ambiguous of all Shostakovich perorations is unleashed with devastating force. The coda is mightily impressive too, not as slow as it might be, but with just the right dragging quality in the articulate and unanimous basses. After this, the Britten encore risks seeming beside the point; this really is emotional play-acting. In sum, neither Kondrashin or Järvi's more direct emotional involvement are easily passed over. On the other hand, Rattle does give us a thrilling example of what a relatively objective, thoroughly 'modern' approach has to offer in the 1990s. Among recent rivals only Inbal is granted sound of similar quality and his interpretation is comparatively soft-grained. With its huge dynamic range and uncompromising, analytical style, EMI's recording pulls no punches, and the awesome precision of the CBSO's playing makes for an unforgettable experience.

Additional recommendations ...
...**Scottish National Orchestra / Neeme Järvi.** Chandos Ⓕ CHAN8640 (61 minutes: DDD: 12/89). Ⓖ
...**National Symphony Orchestra / Mstislav Rostropovich.** Teldec Ⓕ 9031 76261-2 (65 minutes: DDD: 11/92).
...**Vienna Symphony Orchestra / Eliahu Inbal.** Denon Ⓕ CO-75330 (63 minutes: DDD: 7/93).

Shostakovich Symphony No. 5 in D minor, Op. 47. Ballet Suite No. 5, Op. 27a. **Scottish National Orchestra / Neeme Järvi.** Chandos Ⓕ CHAN8650 (76 minutes: DDD: 4/90). Recorded 1988.
There are more Shostakovich Fifths than you can shake a stick at in the CD catalogue at present, and several of them are very good. Järvi's makes perhaps the safest recommendation of them all: it has a generous coupling (which cannot be said of many of its rivals), it has no drawbacks (save, for some tastes, a slight touch of heart-on-sleeve in the slow movement) and a number of distinct advantages. A profound seriousness, for one thing, and an absolute sureness about the nature of the finale, which many conductors feel the need to exaggerate, either as brassy optimism or as bitter irony. Järvi takes it perfectly straight, denying neither option, and the progression from slow movement (the overtness of its emotion finely justified) to finale seems more natural, less of a jolt than usual. The SNO cannot rival the sheer massiveness of sound of some of the continental orchestras who have recorded this work, but while listening one hardly notices the lack, so urgent and polished is their playing. A very natural and wide-ranging recording, too, and the lengthy Suite (eight movements from Shostakovich's early ballet *The Bolt*, forming an exuberantly entertaining essay on the various modes that his sense of humour could take) makes much more than a mere fill-up.

Additional recommendations ...
...No. 5. Five Fragments, Op. 42. **Royal Philharmonic Orchestra / Vladimir Ashkenazy.** Decca Ⓒ 421 120-2DH (56 minutes: DDD: 6/88).
...Nos. 5 and 9. **Atlanta Symphony Orchestra / Yoel Levi.** Telarc Ⓕ CD80215 (78 minutes: DDD: 6/90).
...No. 5. Festival Overture, Op. 96. **London Symphony Orchestra / Maxim Shostakovich.** Collins Classics Ⓕ 1108-2 (59 minutes: DDD: 9/90).
...No. 5. **Hallé Orchestra / Stanislav Skrowaczewski.** IMP Classics Ⓜ PCD940 (48 minutes: DDD: 8/91).
...No. 5. **Leningrad Philharmonic Orchestra / Evgeny Mravinsky.** Erato Ⓜ 2292-45752-2 (44 minutes: ADD: 6/92). ⒼⒼ
...No. 5. **New York Philharmonic Orchestra / Leonard Bernstein.** Sony Classical Bernstein Royal Edition Ⓜ SMK47615 (71 minutes: ADD: 6/94).
...No. 5. Cello Concerto No. 1 in E flat major, Op. 107[a]. [a]**Miloš Sadló** (vc); **Czech Philharmonic Orchestra / Karel Ančerl.** Supraphon Crystal Collection Ⓜ 11 0676-2 (72 minutes: ADD: 8/93).
...No. 5. **Stravinsky** The Rite of Spring. **Cleveland Orchestra / Lorin Maazel.** Teldec Ⓜ CD82001 (81 minutes: DDD: 7/94).
...No. 5[a]. Festival Overture in A major, Op. 96[ab]. [a]**Russian Federation State Symphony Orchestra,** [b]**Bolshoi Theatre Brass Ensemble / Evgeni Svetlanov.** Canyon Classics Ⓕ EC3672-2 (53 minutes: DDD: 10/94).
...No. 5. Novorossisk Chimes, "The Fire of Eternal Glory". October, Op. 131. Overture on Russian and Kirghiz Folk Themes, Op. 115. **Royal Philharmonic Orchestra / Enrique Bátiz.** IMG Records Ⓕ IMGCD1609 (76 minutes: DDD: 2/95).
...No. 5. Festival Overture. **Royal Philharmonic Orchestra / Sir Charles Mackerras.** Tring International Royal Philharmonic Collection Ⓢ TRPO32 (53 minutes: DDD: 9/95).

Shostakovich Symphonies – No. 7 in C major, Op. 60, "Leningrad". No. 1 in F minor, Op. 10. **Chicago Symphony Orchestra / Leonard Bernstein.** DG Ⓕ 427 632-2GH2 (two discs: 120 minutes: DDD: 1/90). Recorded live in 1988. ⒼⒼ
The *Leningrad* Symphony was composed in haste as the Nazis sieged and bombarded the city (in 1941). It caused an immediate sensation, but posterity has been less enthusiastic. What business has the first movement's unrelated long central 'invasion' episode doing in a symphonic movement? Is the material of the finale really distinctive enough for its protracted treatment? Michael Oliver, in his original *Gramophone* review wrote that in this performance "the Symphony sounds most convincingly like a symphony, and one needing no programme to justify it". Added to which, and no disrespect is intended by this observation, the work's epic and cinematic manner has surely never been more powerfully realized. These are live recordings, with occasional noise from the audience (and the

conductor), but the Chicago Orchestra has rarely sounded more polished or committed under any conditions. The strings are superb in the First Symphony, full and weightily present, and Bernstein's manner in this Symphony is comparably bold and theatrical of gesture. A word of caution: set your volume control carefully for the *Leningrad* Symphony's start; it is scored for six of both trumpets and trombones, and in the above mentioned 'invasion' episode, no other recording has reproduced them so clearly, and to such devastating effect.

Additional recommendation ...
...No. 7. **Royal Scottish Orchestra / Neeme Järvi.** Chandos Ⓕ CHAN8623 (69 minutes: DDD: 8/88).

New review
Shostakovich Symphony No. 8 in C minor, Op. 65. **London Symphony Orchestra / André Previn.**
EMI Matrix Ⓜ CDM5 65521-2 (61 minutes: ADD: 10/95). From HMV ASD2917 (10/73).

The Eighth Symphony, written in 1943, two years after the *Leningrad*, offers a wiser, more bitterly disillusioned Shostakovich. The heroic peroration of the Seventh's finale is here replaced by numbed whimsy and eventual uneasy calm. André Previn has since re-recorded the symphony but this youthful account serves to remind us that the music is the product of a young man's imagination. The remake has greater breadth in every sense and, note for note, the orchestral playing is often finer. However, many will prefer the urgency of this earlier version. At that time, Previn seemed content to add a patina of mid-Atlantic gloss, and a good deal of subtlety, to the raw expressivity of the earlier Soviet recordings; he had not yet adopted the self-consciously epic manner thought appropriate today. There are few who know how to bring off the symphony as a gloomy and spiritless *in memoriam*, but the lithe freshness of the Previn remains a compelling alternative. EMI's transfer is punchy and focused.

Additional recommendations ...
...No. 8. **Washington National Symphony Orchestra / Mstislav Rostropovich.** Teldec Ⓕ 9031-74719-2 (61 minutes: DDD: 10/92).
...No. 8. Funeral-Triumphal Prelude, Op. 130. Novorossisk Chimes, "The Fire of Eternal Glory".
Royal Philharmonic Orchestra / Vladimir Ashkenazy. Decca Ⓕ 436 763-2DH (67 minutes: DDD: 4/94).
...No. 8. **London Symphony Orchestra / André Previn.** DG Ⓕ 437 819-2GH (68 minutes: DDD: 3/95).

New review
Shostakovich Symphonies – No. 9 in E flat major, Op. 70[a] ; No. 15 in A major, Op. 141[b].
Moscow Philharmonic Orchestra / Kyrill Kondrashin. Melodiya Ⓜ 74321 19846-2 (54 minutes: ADD: 11/94). Item marked [a] from HMV ASD2409 (1/69), [b]EX290387-3 (1974). ⒼⒼ

After Mravinsky's politically motivated refusal to undertake the première of the Thirteenth in 1962, Shostakovich found a stalwart interpreter in Kyrill Kondrashin. Shostakovich recordings don't come any more authentic than this. Objectively speaking, the playing of the Moscow Philharmonic is not uniformly distinguished. Kondrashin can be startlingly brisk, the panache and brilliance hardening into mannerism. The transfers are no more than serviceable and the badly translated accompanying notes are untrustworthy at best. That said, here is unbeatable music-making, and these are arguably among Kondrashin's greatest recordings. The classic Ninth (from 1965) is conveniently paired with a superbly vivid Fifteenth (from 1974), generally hard-driven *à la* Mravinsky but far more convincingly poised. The first movement goes at a frightening lick, deserting the toy shop for the asylum, the slow movement lacks only the very last ounce of desolation and the finale, always intelligently conceived, is suitably emotive at the close. The sound has immediacy and just enough depth. Though of earlier vintage, the Ninth enjoys a more generous acoustic, the tape a little prone to distortion at moments of stress (which for Kondrashin come more often than usual). Both interpretations have a tonal weight and sarcastic intent which cannot fail to shock the uninitiated . To sum up: he finds in these scores an unrivalled degree of dramatic tension, bringing to the surface raw emotions that more smoothly executed Western accounts play down. We may be impressed by the diligent literalness and sobriety of Haitink, but to what extent should we worry if he illuminates aspects of the music the composer himself thought unimportant? It isn't simply a matter of 'authentic' orchestral timbre. Kondrashin's versions document a very special kind of insight.

Additional recommendations ...
...Nos. 9 and 15. **Royal Philharmonic Orchestra / Vladimir Ashkenazy.** Decca Ⓕ 430 227-2DH (65 minutes: DDD: 10/92).
...No. 9. *Coupled with works by* **Wagner, Brahms, R. Strauss** and **Smetana** The Solti Orchestral Project, Carnegie Hall / Sir Georg Solti. Decca Ⓕ 444 458-2DH (77 minutes: DDD: 12/94). *See review in the Collections section; refer to the Index to Reviews.* Ⓖ

Shostakovich Symphony No. 10 in E minor, Op. 93. **Berlin Philharmonic Orchestra / Herbert von Karajan.** DG Galleria Ⓜ 429 716-2GGA (51 minutes: ADD: 8/90). From SLPM139020 (1/69). Recorded 1966.
Shostakovich Symphony No. 10 in E minor, Op. 93.
Mussorgsky (orch. Shostakovich) Songs and Dances of Death[a]. [a]**Robert Lloyd** (bass);
Philadelphia Orchestra / Mariss Jansons. EMI Ⓕ CDC5 55232-2 (72 minutes: DDD: 6/95). Recorded 1994.

Stalin died on 5th March 1953, the same day as Prokofiev. In the summer of that year Shostakovich produced a symphony which can be taken as his own return to life after the dark night of dictatorship – the last two movements included, for the first time in his output, his personal DSCH signature (the notes D, E flat, C, B natural, in the German spelling). In the West the Tenth Symphony is now widely regarded as the finest of the cycle of 15, not just for its sheer depth of personal feeling, but because it finds the purest and subtlest musical representation of that feeling. Perhaps this is why it is less dependent than some of Shostakovich's major works on a conductor steeped in the Russian idiom. Karajan's profound grasp of the overall drama unites with a superb instinct for atmosphere and mood to put the earlier of his two recordings into a class of its own. It is a performance of compelling integrity and sweep, with an almost palpable sense of what is at stake emotionally. The recording sounds a little bass-heavy in this digital remastering but is still far more realistic than Karajan's 1982 remake.

Anyone expecting a welter of hairpin *diminuendos* and expressive nudges will be disappointed by Jansons's Shostakovich – solid, sturdy and rhythmically taut rather than overly individualistic for the most part. Jansons's first movement is basically brisk with thrustful strings and conscientiously Soviet-style woodwind. It is a cogent enough view and yet the sense of underlying desolation is lacking, despite the conductor's vocal exhortations. The *Scherzo* is brilliantly articulated – even if the relatively leisurely pace robs the music of its potential to intimidate. The 'difficult' third movement is more convincing, though again unusually confident in tone. It would be churlish not to single out the superb horn playing. The main body of the finale (the introduction is separately tracked by the way) is launched with precise rhythmic clarity rather than irrepressible enthusiasm. In short, this is an excellent, sometimes dazzling choice among modern versions but it may strike seasoned listeners as slightly sterile, at once tightly controlled and spiritually disengaged. There is more passion in the coupling. Robert Lloyd is curiously under-represented on CD in the Russian repertoire that suits him so well. His admirers are bound to want this performance, which is very impressive as sheer singing. There is a gorgeously long-breathed "Serenade" and the more demonstrative songs are highly characterized without stooping to the coarse theatricality of some native singers. Throughout the disc, the close focus of the recording exposes a few instances of less than perfect synchronization but with playing so spectacularly accomplished, if not recognizably Philadelphian, this must be counted an outstanding achievement in its way.

Additional recommendations ...

...No. 10[a]. The Bolt – Suite, Op. 27*a*: Overture; The Bureaucrat; The Drayman's Dance; Intermezzo[b]. [a]**Leningrad Philharmonic Orchestra / Evgeny Mravinsky;** [b]**Czech Philharmonic Orchestra / Gennadi Rozhdestvensky.** Praga [a]mono/stereo Ⓔ PR250 053* (64 minutes: ADD: 9/95).

...No. 10. **Hallé Orchestra / Stanislaw Skrowaczewski.** IMP Classics Ⓜ PCD955 (52 minutes: DDD: 10/91).

Shostakovich Symphony No. 11 in G minor, Op. 103, "The year 1905". **Leningrad Philharmonic Orchestra / Evgeny Mravinsky.** Praga Ⓓ PR254 018* (61 minutes: ADD: 8/94). Recorded live in 1967. ⒼⒼ

Despite the rawness and occasional congestion of the sound this is a performance of extraordinary vehemence. There is an element in the work, of course, that is very close to agitprop; there are pages in the terrifying scherzo and in the finale that are not so much composed in primary colours as splashed on to a wall in broad strokes of dripping red and black. Many recent performances have refined this element with sheer orchestral virtuosity, but that is not Mravinsky's way: his brass players yell at the tops of their voices, his percussion threatens to overwhelm the rest of the orchestra, his violins come within an ace of breaking their strings with the sheer scorch of their bows' impact. It is valuable too for the unique sound of a Soviet orchestra during the Soviet period playing a profoundly Soviet work: you really do get the impression that every member of the orchestra knows and has complex reactions to all those quoted revolutionary or pre-revolutionary songs. The work is about a revolt against intolerable oppression. Such a revolt, suppressed like that in Leningrad in 1905, took place in Prague not long after this performance. It has such eloquence that you can almost persuade yourself that it played a part in that.

Additional recommendations ...

...No. 11. **Leningrad Philharmonic Orchestra / Evgeny Mravinsky.** Russian Disc Ⓕ RDCD11157 (56 minutes: ADD: 1/94).

...No. 11. **Vienna Symphony Orchestra / Eliahu Inbal.** Denon Ⓓ CO-78920 (62 minutes: DDD: 4/95).

New review

Shostakovich Symphony No. 11 in G minor, Op. 103, "The year 1905". **St Petersburg Philharmonic Orchestra / Vladimir Ashkenazy.** Decca Ⓔ 448 179-2DH (55 minutes: DDD: 5/96).

For his first all-Russian Shostakovich recording, Vladimir Ashkenazy has chosen one of the more problematic symphonies. There are many felicitous touches, rather less in the way of *gravitas*. For once, the motto theme is clearly audible from the start, just as, at the very end of the piece, the alternating major and minor thirds ring out cleanly against the orchestral clamour. Detail emerges vividly throughout, with the recording team favouring relatively close balances to convey the orchestra's distinctive sonority. The trumpets blaze through with the old fervour at key points in the second movement; the strings retain their characteristic huskiness even if they sound thinner than they used to. And yet to adopt generally brisk tempos without Mravinsky's insistent ferocity of address is to risk taming the beast. If the work is to be associated with big, universalized ideas of requiem and redemption – a (Brittenish?) search for eternal rest in the face of violence and death – it will require careful handling. Inbal has refashioned the Eleventh as a sequence of glowing icons. Ashkenazy is a discreet interpreter in the best sense but, given his avoidance of the *self-consciously* profound, you may feel that Shostakovich's rhetoric is not always empowered with sufficient clout to banish the doubts. To sum up: this is a fresh, unaffected reading. The disc comes attractively packaged with the orchestral layout helpfully reproduced in a session photo. Small wonder the percussion seem so prominent.

Shostakovich Symphony No. 13 in B flat minor, Op. 113, "Babiy Yar". **Robert Holl** (bass);
  Viennensis Chorus; Vienna Symphony Orchestra / Eliahu Inbal. Denon Ⓕ CO-75887 (60 minutes:
  DDD: 9/94). Text and translation included. Recorded live in 1993.   ⒼⒼ
Shostakovich confounds expectations not merely by selecting these vivid, dissenting verses (imagine Copland setting Bob Dylan *c*1963) but by presenting them in an idiom of Mussorgskian simplicity, unimpeachably 'correct' from the official Soviet point of view. It is no accident that the composer follows the Twelfth's revolutionary *Dawn of Humanity* with a consecutive opus focusing on the enduring legacy of Stalinism. Much more than Haitink, Eliahu Inbal takes us away from the dissident emotions which helped inspire the piece to give us a choral symphony, soft-grained and often very beautiful, scarcely focused on the drama of the texts. We are made aware of numerous instrumental details we perhaps haven't heard before, and an unrivalled lucidity of texture is faithfully conveyed by the engineers. The soloist Robert Holl sounds more committed than Haitink's but his tone is obviously non-Slav and he is occasionally unsteady or inaccurate. The third movement seems to set out to convey the nobility and restraint rather than the distress of the women queueing at the store. And yet the central climax is genuinely shattering with the stabbing chords deliberately articulated as anger ebbs away and submissiveness returns. The choir are practically inaudible at the start of the fourth movement – whether the consequence of the wide dynamic range or a deliberate effect (the poet's fears aren't really dying after all and it may be safer to mutter) – while the Mahlerian aspect of the orchestral writing has never been more obvious. Inbal is unidiomatic but fascinating.
Additional recommendations ...
...No. 13. **Vitaly Gromadsky** (bass); **USSR State Academic Choir; Moscow Philharmonic Orchestra /**
  Kyrill Kondrashin. Russian Disc Ⓕ RDCD11191* (57 minutes: ADD: 3/94).
...No. 13. **Sergei Leiferkus** (bar); **New York Male Choral Artists; New York Philharmonic Orchestra**
  / Kurt Masur. Teldec Ⓕ 4509-90848-2 (67 minutes: DDD: 10/94).

New review
Shostakovich Symphony No. 14, Op. 135[a]. Two Pieces for String Quartet (arr. Sikorski).
  [a]**Margareta Haverinen** (sop); [a]**Petteri Salomaa** (bass); **Tapiola Sinfonietta / Joseph Swensen.**
  Ondine Ⓕ ODE845-2 (59 minutes: DDD: 4/96). Text and translation included. Recorded 1994-5.
The multilingual version of the Fourteenth Symphony was sanctioned by the composer but it remains something of a rarity on disc; some vital and specific tone colour is lost along with the original note values, and the 'three lilies' adorn the grave of "The Suicide" more elegantly in the Russian. Bernard Haitink may not agree. He elected to use the multilingual text in his 1980 recording and now Joseph Swensen presents this compelling alternative. We tend to take sonic excellence for granted these days but this is a true state-of-the-art recording with the soloists more naturally placed than in the rival Decca issue and an orchestral sound combining great clarity with just enough hall resonance. The performance has character too, if lacking the pervasive chill of the earliest Soviet accounts. The conductor secures excellent results from the Tapiola Sinfonietta. They are a lean and super-efficient group, yet without the loss of character this can sometimes imply. Of the soloists, the young bass-baritone Petteri Salomaa is particularly impressive: his is a voice of rare tonal beauty, a Billy Budd rather than a Boris. His pronunciation is a little odd at times – something more noticeable in a version which has the singers feigning familiarity with four languages – but you may not see this as a problem. Tempos are perceptibly more 'extreme' than Haitink's, with the opening "De profundis" dangerously slow in the modern manner and a strikingly well-characterized instrumental contribution to "A la Santé" ("In the Santé Prison"). The fillers, larger than life, brilliantly dispatched and curiously inappropriate, are based on original quartet pieces which only came to light in the mid 1980s. The first shares material with *Lady Macbeth of Mtsensk*; the second appears as the polka from *The Age of Gold*! This is nevertheless a more rewarding, more probingly conducted disc than most of the current Shostakovich crop.

Shostakovich String Quartets. **Shostakovich Quartet** (Andrei Shishlov, Sergei Pishchugin, vns;
  Alexander Galkovsky, va; Alexander Korchagin, vc). Olympia Ⓕ OCD531/5 (five discs, oas:
  77, 78, 74, 78 and 73 minutes: ADD: 9/94). Recorded 1978-85.
  OCD531 – No. 1 in C major, Op. 49; No. 3 in F major, Op. 73; No. 4 in D major, Op. 83. Two
  Pieces for String Quartet (1931). *OCD532* – No. 2 in A major, Op. 68; No. 5 in B flat major,
  Op. 92; No. 7 in F sharp minor, Op. 108. *OCD533* – No. 6 in G major, Op. 101; No. 8 in C minor,

Op. 110; No. 9 in E flat major, Op. 117. *OCD534* – No. 10 in A flat major, Op. 118; No. 11 in F minor; No. 15 in E flat minor. *OCD535* – No. 12 in D flat major; No. 13 in B flat minor; No. 14 in F sharp major. ⒢

Any attempt to rank these players in relation to their more widely acclaimed opposite numbers in the Borodin Quartet seems pointless at this level of dedication; both teams have lived through this most extraordinary of twentieth-century quartet-cycles many times. If any general observation about the two can be made, it is that the Borodins find more corporate subtleties and passing shades in some of the earlier quartets, while the individual members of the Shostakovich Quartet make even stronger, more vibrant soloists. In the context of Shostakovich's many, very vocal solos and recitatives, it hardly seems invidious to single out the first violinist, Andrei Shishlov – dark, powerful and flawless of intonation throughout. Listen to his sleight-of-hand freedom in the unaccompanied melody of No. 6's finale: the Borodins' Mikhail Kopelman doesn't begin to touch imagination like that. These players also teach us to hold in equal awe the more classically contained quartets – No. 6 and the outer movements of No. 10 have a special grace – and all the slow movements are impressively unfolded with a steady fluency (notable in the passacaglias). As for the last rites of No. 15, not even the Borodins find such implicit human warmth in the still fugato of the Elegy. In tandem with the impassioned solos of the later movements, it's an impressive summing-up of this team's best intentions. Balances in the earlier recordings are less than kind to second fiddle and cellist and are uncomfortably boxy. You'll also have to adjust the volume-level for consecutive listening. If you seek only a single-disc token of the achievement, Vol. 4 (featuring Quartets Nos. 10, 11 and 15) is the one to have.

Additional recommendations ...

...Nos. 1-15. **Borodin Quartet.** EMI Ⓜ CMS5 65032-2 (six discs: DDD).

...Nos. 4, 8 and 11. **Coull Quartet.** ASV Ⓔ CDDCA631 (64 minutes: DDD: 4/89).

...No. 8. *Coupled with works by* **Crumb, Tallis, Marta** *and* **Ives Kronos Quartet.** Elektra Nonesuch Ⓔ 7559-79242-2 (62 minutes: DDD: 4/91). *See review in the Collections section; refer to the Index to Reviews.* ⒢⒢

...Nos. 1-15. **Fitzwilliam Quartet.** Decca Enterprise Ⓜ 433 078-2DM6 (six discs: 377 minutes: ADD: 6/92). *Gramophone classical 100.* ⒢⒢⒢

...No. 15 (arr. Rachlevsky). Chamber Symphony, Op. 110*a*. Symphony for Strings in A flat major, Op. 118*a*. **Kremlin Chamber Orchestra / Misha Rachlevsky.** Claves Ⓔ CD50-9115 (80 minutes: DDD: 3/93).

New review

Shostakovich String Quartets – No. 4 in D major, Op. 83; No. 11 in F minor, Op. 122; No. 14 in F sharp major, Op. 142. **Hagen Quartet** (Lukas Hagen, Rainer Schmidt, vns; Veronika Hagen, va; Clemens Hagen, vc). DG Ⓔ 445 864-2GH (71 minutes: DDD: 9/95). Recorded 1993-4.

The Hagens have chosen a fascinating journey to the unusual at-one-with-the-world radiance that ends the Fourteenth. Already in this interpretation of the Fourth we hear those voices from beyond the grave that trouble the later quartets. The introspective shading of the *Andantino*'s earlier stages, climax included, sounds as if the mutes are already on. And when in fact the players do take them up – for the rest of the movement and the whole of the ensuing *Allegretto* – the sound becomes even more refined; note how first violin Lukas Hagen sings out his solo at fig. 29 (track 2, 3'31") with a frail, unearthly beauty which sounds as if it emanates from a viola d'amore. Corporate work is faultlessly and subtly in sympathy with the essence of the piece; the only individual weakness occurs when Shostakovich asks the cellist to come to the fore in the finale's build-up of tension – Clemens Hagen's tone doesn't really make itself felt here – though the collective *fortissimo* cry from the heart shortly afterwards makes amends with even more intensity than some of the Hagen's senior counterparts (including the Shostakovich Quartet on Olympia) have previously found there. Clemens does rather lack the presence to take the lead in Quartet No. 14, dedicated to the cellist of the Beethoven Quartet, and emphasizing his role accordingly; the sound can be lovely, but right at the start he has the misfortune to be echoed by his more characterful brother. Still, the F sharp major ending is as implicitly moving as it can be, and joint string power in crises comes very close to the genuine Russian article. Indeed, in the fifth-movement *Humoresque* of the Eleventh the limelighted second violin – Rainer Schmidt, the quartet's febrile and ever-impressive outside influence – brings so much forceful tone to the swelling of his two repeated notes that it sounds for all the world as if two violins are playing in unison, not just the one. Again, the joint approach to chants and combats, not to mention Lukas's extraordinary handling of the *glissandos* in the second movement, bring an urgently vocal quality to the work.

New review

Shostakovich String Quartet No. 8 in C minor, Op. 110.

Schnittke String Quartet No. 2.

Tchaikovsky String Quartet No. 1 in D major, Op. 11. **Duke Quartet** (Louisa Fuller, Rick Koster, vns; John Metcalfe, va; Ivan McCready, vc). Collins Classics Ⓔ 1450-2 (70 minutes: DDD: 2/96). Recorded 1995.

Shostakovich has 15 String Quartet masterpieces to choose from, none of which is either 'early' or musically insubstantial; but because the Eighth has historical-political connotations – it does tell a story – it tends to be the most often recorded; the others tend to get ignored, at least outside of recorded or live cycles. The Duke Quartet 'go for the jugular', especially in the three *Largos*: the second in particular yields a handsome body of tone while the sudden ray of light at 3'44" has real pathos. The only minor reservation concerns the *Allegretto*, which sounds just a mite too cheerful for the ghostly, cynical statement that it is. Placing Schnittke's Second Quartet directly after Shostakovich's Eighth was a stroke of genius, especially as its opening harmonies seem to echo the D-S-C-H motif that closes the earlier work. Schnittke's piece incorporates a frenzied *Agitato* (with wild arpeggios to the fore), a prayer-like *Mesto* and an intense *Moderato* finale that retreats among ethereal harmonics. It is a very powerful piece; the programme ends with Tchaikovsky's classically proportioned First Quartet. Here the Duke Quartet's phrasing is somewhat fussy, especially in the first movement, and there are also some uncomfortable tempo relations. Still, the last two movements are sprightly enough, the recordings are good and the whole adds up to a programme that is certainly worth hearing – especially for the sake of the Shostakovich and the Schnittke.

Shostakovich Piano Quintet in G minor, Op. 57[a]. String Quartets – No. 7 in F sharp minor, Op. 108; No. 8 in C minor, Op. 110. [a]**Sviatoslav Richter** (pf); **Borodin Quartet** (Mikhail Kopelman, Andrei Abramenkov, vns; Dmitri Shebalin, va; Valentin Berlinsky, vc). EMI Ⓔ CDC7 47507-2 (70 minutes: ADD: 10/87). From EL270338-1 (11/85).   ⒼⒼⒼ

The Seventh and Eighth Quartets are separated by only one opus number and both works inhabit a dark and sombre sound world. The Seventh is dedicated to the memory of his first wife, Nina, who died in 1954 and is one of his shortest and most concentrated quartets. The Eighth Quartet provides a perfect introduction to Shostakovich's music. It is very much an autobiographical work. The Piano Quintet is almost symphonic in its proportions, lasting some 35 minutes and has been popular with audiences ever since its first performance in 1940. Much of its popularity stems from Shostakovich's highly memorable material, particularly in the boisterous and genial *Scherzo* and finale movements. The Borodin Quartet play with great authority and conviction and in the Seventh Quartet there is a fine sense of poetry and intimacy. Richter's performance of the Piano Quintet matches the grandeur of the work, with playing that has tremendous power and strength. The recording, taken from a live performance, is rather dry with a slightly hard piano sound, but this does little to distract from so commanding a performance as this. The earlier studio recordings of the string quartets are well recorded. This disc would be an excellent introduction to the chamber music of Shostakovich.

Additional recommendations ...

...Piano Quintet. **Britten** String Quartet No. 1 in D major, Op. 25. [a]**Clifford Benson** (pf); **Alberni Quartet**. CRD Ⓕ CRD3351 (57 minutes: DDD: 3/89).

...Piano Quintet[a]. Piano Trio No. 2 in E minor, Op. 67. [a]**Eugene Drucker** (vn); [a]**Lawrence Dutton** (va); **Beaux Arts Trio** (Isidore Cohen, vn; Peter Wiley, vc; Menahem Pressler, pf). Philips Ⓕ 432 079-2PH (57 minutes: DDD: 8/91).

...Piano Quintet. **Franck** Piano Quintet in F minor. **Victor Aller** (pf); **Hollywood Quartet**. Testament mono Ⓕ SBT1077* (67 minutes: ADD: 5/96).

New review

Shostakovich Piano Sonatas – No. 1, Op. 12; No. 2 in B minor, Op. 61. Five Preludes. 24 Preludes, Op. 34. **Colin Stone** (pf). Olympia Ⓜ OCD574 (79 minutes: DDD: 6/96). Recorded 1995.

Shostakovich's Five Preludes from student days are not otherwise currently available, and Colin Stone is to be congratulated for including these gauche but attractive pieces rather than the ubiquitous *Fantastic Dances*. Indeed his playing is well prepared throughout and the recording quality is as clean as his playing; the piano itself sounds pretty well ideally regulated. What you won't find is the wildness of the First Sonata, where Stone has gone for clarity rather than the impossibly frenetic metronome marks. Nor do the Op. 34 Preludes rival Mustonen (listed below) for point and characterization; some listeners may actually prefer the steadier approach to the impulsive Finn's shock tactics. Colin Stone offers an admirably sane view, then, and the expense of buying anything better is considerable. There is certainly a lot more to this music than sanity, but this survey can still be confidently recommended to anyone looking for a single-disc supplement to the Preludes and Fugues.

Additional recommendation ...

...24 Preludes, Op. 34. **Alkan** 25 Préludes dans les tons majeurs et mineur, Op. 31. **Olli Mustonen** (pf). Decca Ⓕ 433 055-2DH (76 minutes: DDD: 10/91). *Gramophone* Award Winner 1992. *See review under Alkan; refer to the Index to Reviews.*   ⒼⒼ

Shostakovich 24 Preludes and Fugues, Op. 87. **Tatyana Nikolaieva** (pf). Melodiya Ⓕ 74321 19849-2 (three discs: 168 minutes: DDD: 2/95). Recorded 1987.   ⒼⒼ

Tatyana Nikolaieva was in at the birth of Shostakovich's Preludes and Fugues, and she made them one of the cornerstones of her repertoire. But you don't need to know those facts in order to sense the authority and insight of her interpretations. She gives the three-hour cycle a wonderful over-arching sense of unity, of an unbroken voyage of exploration. That may not have been the composer's intention (he actually spoke out specifically against such a view of the work), but there are plenty of indications in the structure and character of his music to justify Nikolaieva's approach. Her recordings of the complete Preludes and Fugues are undoubtedly the finest monuments to a much lamented artist. It is truly sad that her playing was not fully appreciated in the West until so late in her career. Not that her performances on the Hyperion set are seriously flawed, but Hyperion's recorded sound is seriously over-resonant and distantly balanced and this is music which lives or dies by its clarity. By contrast the Melodiya acoustic is a fraction too close and dry, but still greatly preferable. It gives space for the music to breathe rather than suffocating it with unwanted stage-mist; and it enables many more of Nikolaieva's nuances to register. So the first choice is the Melodiya version. Owners of the Hyperion set without unlimited budgets may nevertheless feel that the more essential supplement is Richter's peerless accounts of six of them.

Additional recommendations ...

...**Tatyana Nikolaieva** (pf). Hyperion Ⓔ CDA66441/3 (three discs: 166 minutes: DDD: 3/91). *Gramophone Award Winner 1991.* Ⓖ

...24 Preludes and Fugues – No. 4 in E minor; No. 12 in G sharp minor; No. 14 in E flat major; No. 15 in D flat major; No. 17 in A flat major; No. 23 in F major. **Prokofiev** Piano Sonatas – No. 4 in C minor, Op. 29; No. 6 in A major, Op. 82. Legend, Op. 12 No. 6. Visions fugitives, Op. 22 – No. 3, Allegretto; No. 4, Animato; No. 5, Molto giocoso; No. 6, Con eleganza; No. 8, Commodo; No. 9, Allegretto tranquillo; No. 11, Con vivacita; No. 14, Feroce; No. 15, Inquieto; No. 18, Con una dolce lentezza. Pieces, Op. 32 – No. 1, Danse; No. 4, Waltz. Pieces from "Cinderella" – Op. 95: No. 2, Gavotte; Op. 97: No. 3, Autumn fairy, No. 6, Oriental dance; Op. 102: No. 1, Grand waltz, No. 3, Quarrel. **Scriabin** Poème-nocturne, Op. 61. Two Danses, Op. 73. Vers la flamme, Op. 72. Fantasie in B minor, Op. 28. **Sviatoslav Richter** (pf). Philips Ⓔ 438 627-2PH2 (two discs: 152 minutes: DDD: 8/94). ⒼⒼ

New review

Shostakovich Six Romances on Japanese Poems, Op. 21[a]. Six Poems of Marina Tsvetayeva, Op. 143[b]. Suite on Verses of Michelangelo, Op. 145[c]. [b]**Elena Zaremba** (contr); [a]**Ilya Levinsky** (ten); [c]**Sergei Leiferkus** (bar); **Gothenburg Symphony Orchestra / Neeme Järvi.** DG Ⓔ 447 085-2GH (71 minutes: DDD: 1/96). Texts and translations included. Recorded 1994.

Leiferkus has recorded nothing finer than this rightly daunting interpretation of the *Suite on Verses of Michelangelo*, Shostakovich's greatest, most monolithic song-cycle – equal first if you include the Fourteenth Symphony. Choice for the cycle depends on where your preferences lie. Fischer-Dieskau's is perhaps the more searching version, but one should never underestimate Leiferkus's sheer vocal beauty of line and sheen in the superb declamatory settings of "Dante" and its companion-piece hymn to the exiled poet (parallels with Solzhenitsyn were inescapable in 1974); nor is there that lack of a deeper understanding elsewhere in the cycle sometimes sensed in previous recordings by Leiferkus. It is simply that his tone is defiant where Fischer-Dieskau's inclines to heart-breaking introspection – the respective interpretations of the last line of the final song, "Immortality", says it all. Matters are further complicated by the greater introspection of Leiferkus's orchestra and conductor: the shadowy chords underpinning the earlier songs and punctuating the wonderful exchange of verses between Strozzi and Michelangelo on the sculptor's sleep in "Night" are carefully projected with all the infinite atmosphere one has come to expect from Järvi's rapport with his supremely resonant Gothenburg strings. The similar mood of the near-contemporary Tsvetayeva settings, no less profound in their reflection on creativity and the State, make a perfect coupling for the *Michelangelo* Suite. Zaremba, a true contralto, is another great Russian voice – very impressive indeed, like Leiferkus, in majestic declamation, but more distractingly loud (and her up-front role in the recording doesn't help) when she should be withdrawn. That is also true of the tenor Ilya Levinsky in the *Romances on Japanese Poems*. A dark sidelight on *Lady Macbeth of the Mtsensk District*, the plangent aspect of the sequence is best served when Levinsky plays respectively the rejected and the unrequited lovers of the fourth and the fifth songs. Investigate the first two cycles to check the vocal progress of two fine young Russian singers; but don't miss Leiferkus's *Michelangelo* Suite, even if Fischer-Dieskau already has an affectionate place on your shelves.

Further listening ...

...Chamber Symphony, Op. 110a. Two Pieces, Op. 11 – Scherzo. **Bartók** Romanian Folkdances, Sz68. Divertimento, Sz113. **Zagreb Soloists / Tonko Ninic.** IMP Classics PCD1000 11/92).

...The gadfly – Suite, Op. 97a. **USSR Cinema Symphony Orchestra / Emin Khachaturian.** Classics for Pleasure CD-CFP4463 (4/89).

...The Gadfly, Op. 97a – film music. King Lear, Op. 58a. Hamlet, Op. 116a – Introduction; The ghost; In the Garden. **KBS Symphony Orchestra / Vakhtang Jordania.** Koch International Classics 37274-2 (12/94).

...Hamlet, Op. 116a[b] – Introduction; Ball at the palace; The ghost; The poisoning; The players; Duel and death of Hamlet. *Coupled with* **Kabalevsky** Symphony No. 2 in C minor, Op. 19a. **Miaskovsky** Symphony No. 21, Op. 51, "Fantasy in F sharp minor"[a]. [a]**New Philharmonia Orchestra / David Measham;** [b]**National Philharmonic Orchestra / Bernard Herrmann.** Unicorn-Kanchana Souvenir UKCD2066 (2/95). *See review under Kabalevsky; refer to the Index to Reviews.*

...Incidental Music – Hamlet, Op. 32; King Lear, Op. 58a. **Louise Winter** (mez); **David Wilson-Johnson** (bar); **City of Birmingham Symphony Orchestra / Mark Elder.** Cala CACD1021 (1/96).

...Suites – New Babylon[a]; The Golden Hills[b]. [a]**Moscow Philharmonic Orchestra;** [b]**USSR Ministry of Culture Symphony Orchestra / Gennadi Rozhdestvensky.** Russian Disc RDCD11064 (5/95).

...Concertino, Op. 94. *Coupled with* **Stravinsky** Petrushka. **Scriabin** Romance in A minor.
  Rachmaninov Six Morceaux, Op. 11. **Duo Reine Elisabeth** (Wolfgang Manz, Rolf Plagge, pfs).
  Koch International Classics DICD920150 (11/94).
...Viola Sonata, Op. 147[a]. *Coupled with* **Bartók** Sonata for Solo Violin, Sz117 (arr. viola).
  Stravinsky Elegy. **Raphael Hillyer** (va); [a]**Reinbert de Leeuw** (pf). Koch Schwann 311612 (5/95).
...Hypothetically Murdered, Op. 31*a* (reconstructed McBurney). Five Fragments, Op. 42. Suite
  No. 1 for Jazz Band. Four Songs, Op. 46[a] (No. 4 orch. McBurney). [a]**Dmitri Kharitonov** (bass);
  City of Birmingham Symphony Orchestra / Mark Elder. Cala United 88001-2 (1/94).
...Two Fables (Krylov), Op. 4[a]. Four Songs, Op. 46[b]. Songs on Verses by British Poets, Op. 140[c].
  From Jewish folk poetry, Op. 79[d]. [d]**Luba Orgonasova** (sop); [a]**Larissa Dyadkova** (mez); [d]**Nathalie
  Stutzmann** (contr); [d]**Philip Langridge** (ten); [bc]**Sergei Leiferkus** (bar); [a]**Gothenburg Opera Chorus;
  Gothenburg Symphony Orchestra / Neeme Järvi.** DG 439 860-2GH (9/94).
...Lady Macbeth of the Mtsensk District. **Soloists; Ambrosian Opera Chorus; London Philharmonic
  Orchestra / Mstislav Rostropovich.** EMI CDS7 49955-2 (5/90).   ⊙⊙
...(cptd. K. Meyer) The Gamblers. **Soloists; North-West German Philharmonic Orchestra / Mikhail
  Yurovsky.** Capriccio 60 062-2 (6/95).

Konstantin Shvedov   USSR 1886-1954

Sugested listening ...
...Liturgy of St John Chrysostom, Op. 40. **Slavyanka / Aleksei Shipovalnikov.** Harmonia Mundi
  HMU90 7105 (1/95).

Jean Sibelius   Finnish 1865-1957

Sibelius Violin Concerto in D minor, Op. 47[a]. Serenade in G minor, Op. 69 No. 2[a]. En saga, Op. 9.
  [a]**Julian Rachlin** (vn); **Pittsburgh Symphony Orchestra / Lorin Maazel.** Sony Classical Ⓕ SK53272
  (60 minutes: DDD: 6/94). Recorded 1992. *Gramophone Editor's choice.*   ⊙
Sibelius Violin Concerto in D minor, Op. 47.
Tchaikovsky Violin Concerto in D major, Op. 35. **Kyung-Wha Chung** (vn); **London Symphony
  Orchestra / André Previn.** Decca The Classic Sound Ⓜ 425 080-2DCS (66 minutes: ADD: 5/95).
  From SXL6493 (11/70). Recorded 1970.   ⊙
Julian Rachlin was only 18 when he made his recording and here he is in one of the most challenging
of concertos, whose difficulties he takes easily in his stride. He has consistent beauty of tonal colour,
a pure silvery tone with intonation to match, and possesses the aristocratic quality this music calls for.
He is technically flawless – stunning in fact – and his eloquence is unfailingly persuasive: for example,
the beautifully articulate way in which he echoes the questioning phrase in the slow movement
(track 2, 2'34"). The tiny mannerisms in which he indulges would not inhibit a placing alongside such
classics as Oistrakh and Perlman. Certainly his artistry and sensitivity place him securely among the
finest players of the day. The G minor *Serenade* is quintessential Sibelius. It has a poignant, wistful
melancholy all its own, and there are few pieces which more keenly evoke the magic of the white
nights of the Scandinavian summer. Rachlin, coming as he does from the Baltic, though he left
Lithuania when he was six, would understand all that. Lorin Maazel's *En saga* is a straight, often very
fast, but thoroughly atmospheric account of the score. The recording is splendidly balanced.
Outstanding.
  If the vital test for a recording is that a performance should establish itself as a genuine one, not a
mere studio run-through, Chung's remains a disc where both works are made to leap out at you in
concentration and vitality, not just through the soloist's weight and gravity, expressed as though
spontaneously, but through the playing of the LSO under Previn at a vintage period. The great
melodies of the first two movements of the Sibelius are given an inner heartfelt intensity rarely
matched, and with the finale skirting danger with thrilling abandon. Chung's later Montreal version
of the Tchaikovsky is rather fuller-toned with the tiny statutory cuts restored in the finale. Yet the very
hint of vulnerability amid daring, a key element in Chung's magnetic, volatile personality, here adds
an extra sense of spontaneity. This remains breathtaking playing, and the central slow movement,
made to flow without a hint of sentimentality, has an extra poignancy. The Kingsway Hall sound, full
and sharply focused, gives a sense of presence to match or outshine today's digital recordings.

New review
Sibelius Violin Concerto in D minor, Op. 47. Two Serenades, Op. 69. Humoresque in D minor,
  Op. 87 No. 1. **Anne-Sophie Mutter** (vn); **Staatskapelle Dresden / André Previn.** DG Ⓕ 447
  895-2GH (49 minutes: DDD: 3/96). Recorded 1995. *Gramophone Editor's choice.*   ⊙
The power and intensity of Mutter's performance of the concerto emerges immediately in the opening
phrases. Where most violinists treat them as a deep meditation, Mutter with comparable intensity
makes them tougher than usual, using momentarily a vibratoless tone, slightly steely, establishing this
more clearly as an *Allegro moderato* first movement rather than a lyrical slow one. Even if one misses
some of the raptness of Mullova or Chung, it is a very valid view, and the power of the reading is

reinforced by the relatively close balance of the solo instrument. Not that her reading lacks inner qualities, for despite the close balance the opening of the slow movement finds Mutter playing in rapt meditation on a half-tone. In the middle of the movement she expands in romantic warmth before returning finally to the most intense *pianissimo*. Her timing for the finale is even faster than Perlman's, with power again the keynote, and as in the earlier movements Previn proves a most sympathetic, bitingly effective partner. The all-Sibelius coupling is apt if (at 49 minutes) hardly generous. On any count Mutter clearly establishes all three pieces as far more than just salon Sibelius, with Previn and the orchestra, beautifully recorded, relishing the atmospheric and original colourings.

Additional recommendations ...

...Violin Concerto. **Sinding** Suite for Violin and Orchestra, Op. 10, "In alten Stil". **Itzhak Perlman** (vn); **Pittsburgh Symphony Orchestra / André Previn.** EMI Ⓕ CDC7 47167-2 (ADD: 9/85).

...Violin Concerto. **Tchaikovsky** Violin Concerto in D major, Op. 35. **Viktoria Mullova** (vn); **Boston Symphony Orchestra / Seiji Ozawa.** Philips 416 821-2PH (67 minutes: DDD: 5/87).

...Violin Concerto[a]. **Brahms** Violin Concerto in D major, Op. 77[b]. **Ginette Neveu** (vn); **Philharmonia Orchestra /** [a]**Walter Susskind,** [b]**Issay Dobrowen.** EMI Références mono Ⓜ CDH7 61011-2* (70 minutes: ADD: 3/88).　　　　　　　　　　　　　　　　　　　　　　　　　Ⓖ

...Violin Concerto (original 1903-04 version and final 1905 version). **Leonidas Kavakos** (vn); **Lahti Symphony Orchestra / Osmo Vänskä.** BIS Ⓕ CD500 (75 minutes: DDD: 4/91). *Gramophone Award Winner 1991. Selected by Sounds in Retrospect.*

...Violin Concerto. **Brahms** Violin Concerto. **Tasmin Little** (vn); **Royal Liverpool Philharmonic Orchestra / Vernon Handley.** EMI Eminence Ⓜ CD-EMX2203 (72 minutes: DDD: 2/93). *See review under Brahms; refer to the Index to Reviews.*　　　　　　　　　　　　　Ⓖ

...Violin Concerto. **Beethoven** Violin Concerto in D major, Op. 61. **David Oistrakh** (vn); **Stockholm Festival Orchestra / Sixten Ehrling.** Testament mono Ⓕ SBT1032* (75 minutes: ADD: 7/94).　　　　　　　　　　　　　　　　　　　　　　　　　　　　　　　Ⓠ

...Violin Concerto. **Tchaikovsky** Violin Concerto in D major, Op. 35. **Vadim Repin** (vn); **London Symphony Orchestra / Emmanuel Krivine.** Erato Ⓕ 4509-98537-2 (67 minutes: DDD: 5/96).

...Violin Concerto[a]. Karelia Suite, Op. 11. Belshazzar's Feast – suite, Op. 51. [a]**Pekka Kuusisto** (vn); **Helsinki Philharmonic Orchestra / Leif Segerstam.** Ondine Ⓕ ODE878-2 (65 minutes: DDD: 5/96).

Sibelius Kullervo, Op. 7. **Marianne Rørholm** (contr); **Jorma Hynninen** (bar); **Helsinki University Chorus; Los Angeles Philharmonic Orchestra / Esa-Pekka Salonen.** Sony Classical Ⓕ SK52563 (70 minutes: DDD: 7/93). Text and translation included. Recorded 1992.　　　　　　　Ⓖ

Sibelius's *Kullervo* was the symphonic poem-cum-symphony with which he made his breakthrough in Finland in 1892. Common to all recordings, including this newcomer, is the magisterial presence of Jorma Hynninen. Salonen keeps a firm grip on the proceedings and maintains a real sense of momentum throughout. Moreover, temptations to dwell on beauty of incident or to indulge in expressive emphasis are resisted, and this extraordinary piece is all the more telling as a result. The dramatic force of the central scena is vividly realized and both Marianne Rørholm and Jorma Hynninen are impressive – as indeed are the male voices of the Finnish chorus. An impressive performance, and the orchestral playing and recording are absolutely first class. This is arguably the best *Kullervo* we have yet had.

Additional recommendations ...

...**Eeva-Liisa Saarinen** (mez); **Jorma Hynninen** (bar); **Estonian State Academic Male Choir; Helsinki University Male Choir; Helsinki Philharmonic Orchestra / Paavo Berglund.** EMI Matrix Ⓜ CDM5 65080-2 (72 minutes: DDD: 7/94).

...**Soile Isokoski** (sop); **Raimo Laukka** (bar); **Danish National Radio Choir and Symphony Orchestra / Leif Segerstam.** Chandos Ⓕ CHAN9393 (76 minutes: DDD: 3/96).

New review

Sibelius The Wood-Nymph, Op. 15 The Wood-Nymph (melodrama)[a]. A lonely ski-trail[a]. Swanwhite, Op. 54 – incidental music (original version). [a]**Lasse Pöysti** (narr); **Lahti Symphony Orchestra / Osmo Vänskä.** BIS Ⓕ CD815 (62 minutes: DDD: 6/96). Recorded 1996.

Although most Sibelians will know of the tone-poem, *The Wood-Nymph*, they will not have heard it, as the score has remained in Helsinki University Library. It opens very much in *Karelia* mode, and as one might expect, inhabits much the same world as the *Lemminkäinen Legends*. Though it is less developed than the 1892 *En Saga*, let alone the *Legends* in their definitive form, it still bears the characteristic Sibelian hallmarks. The present disc gives us an opportunity to put it alongside the melodrama of the same name, scored for speaker, horn, strings and piano. This is a setting of the mainland-Swedish poet, Viktor Rydberg, best known in the Sibelius context for *Autumn Evening* ("Höstkväll"). The tone-poem which was given a month after the première of the melodrama follows much the same basic layout, though the chamber music-like texture offers numerous felicities. Not content with these interesting novelties, the CD also gives us two other works new to the catalogue, another short melodrama, *A lonely ski-trail* to words by Bertel Gripenberg, which in its piano form comes from 1925 and which Sibelius scored for harp and strings as late as 1948, a short, slight and atmospheric piece; and above all, the complete incidental music to Strindberg's *Swanwhite*. The score runs to some 30 minutes and is full of that special light and sense of space characteristic of *Pelléas et*

Mélisande. The playing of the Lahti orchestra under Osmo Vänskä is excellent and the recording, too, is very fine: spacious, well-detailed and refined. Obviously a self-recommending issue which no Sibelian should miss.

Sibelius Finlandia, Op. 26. Karelia Suite, Op. 11. Tapiola, Op. 112. En Saga, Op. 9. **Philharmonia Orchestra / Vladimir Ashkenazy.** Decca Ovation Ⓜ 417 762-2DM (63 minutes: DDD: 12/88). From 417 378-1DM5. Recorded 1980-85.

More than 30 years separate *En Saga* and *Tapiola*, yet both works are quintessential Sibelius. The latter is often praised for the way Sibelius avoided 'exotic' instruments, preferring instead to draw new and inhuman sounds from the more standard ones; and the former is, in many ways, just as striking in the way Sibelius's orchestration evokes wind, strange lights, vast expanses and solitude. Both works suggest some dream-like journey: *En Saga* non-specific though derived from Nordic legend; *Tapiola* more of an airborne nightmare in, above and around the mighty giants of the Northern forests inhabited by the Green Man of the Kalevala, the forest god Tapio (the final amen of slow, bright major chords brings a blessed release!). Ashkenazy's judgement of long term pacing is very acute; the silences and shadows are as potent here as the wildest hurricane. And Decca's sound allows you to visualize both the wood and the trees: every detail of Sibelius's sound world is caught with uncanny presence, yet the overall orchestral image is coherent and natural. In addition, his *Finlandia* boasts some of the most vibrant and powerful brass sounds on disc.

Additional recommendations ...

...Tapiola. Pohjola's daughter, Op. 49. Rakastava, Op. 14. Andante lirico. **Gothenburg Symphony Orchestra / Neeme Järvi.** BIS Ⓕ CD312 (56 minutes: DDD: 6/87).

...Finlandia. Karelia Suite. En Saga. The Swan of Tuonela. Tapiola. Luonnotar, Op. 70[a]. [a]**Elisabeth Söderström** (sop); **Philharmonia Orchestra / Vladimir Ashkenazy.** Decca Ovation Ⓜ 430 757-2DM (73 minutes: DDD: 7/93).

...Finlandia (arr. H. Fricker). *Coupled with works by* **Nielsen, Alain, Mulet, Sløgedal, Lindberg, Mozart, Lefébure-Wély** and **Elgar** Christopher Herrick (org). Hyperion Ⓕ CDA66676 (75 minutes: DDD). *See review in the Collections section; refer to the Index to Reviews.*

Sibelius Six Humoresques, Opp. 87 and 89[a]. Two Serenades, Op. 69[a]. Two Pieces, Op. 77[a]. Overture in E major. Ballet scene. [a]**Dong-Suk Kang** (vn); **Gothenburg Symphony Orchestra / Neeme Järvi.** BIS Ⓕ CD472 (62 minutes: DDD: 2/91). Recorded 1989.

The music for violin and orchestra here is marvellously rewarding and gloriously played. The six *Humoresques*, Opp. 87 and 89 come from the same period as the Fifth Symphony, at a time when Sibelius was toying with the idea of a second violin concerto, and some of the material of the *Humoresques* was possibly conceived with a concerto in mind. Sibelius wrote that these radiant pieces convey something of "the anguish of existence, fitfully lit up by the sun", and behind their outward elegance and charm, there is an all-pervasive sadness. This is even more intense in the *Serenades*, which are glorious pieces and quintessential Sibelius. Dong-Suk Kang is an outstanding player. His impeccable technique and natural musical instinct serve this repertoire well and he seems to have established an excellent rapport with Järvi and the Gothenburg orchestra. The two fill-ups are juvenilia and are only intermittently characteristic. The Overture is very much in his *Karelia* idiom, though they are of undoubted interest to all Sibelians. The recording is of the usual high quality one has come to expect from BIS.

New review

Sibelius Karelia Suite, Op. 11. Luonnotar, Op. 70[a]. Andante festivo. The Oceanides, Op. 73. King Christian II, Op. 27 – Suite. Finlandia, Op. 26. [a]**Soile Isokoski** (sop); **Gothenburg Symphony Orchestra / Neeme Järvi.** DG Ⓕ 447 760-2GH (72 minutes: DDD: 6/96). Text and translation included. Recorded 1992-5.

This CD offers the *Karelia* and *King Christian II* suites, both from the 1890s, together with outstanding accounts of two of the strangest and most haunting masterpieces of Sibelius's maturity, *Luonnotar* and *The Oceanides*. Of special interest is *Luonnotar*, which tells of the creation of the world as related in Finnish mythology and was written for the legendary Aino Ackté. Not surprisingly, perhaps, it places cruel demands on the soloist both in terms of tessitura and dynamics. Soile Isokoski is magnificent and possesses an impressive accuracy both in intonation and dynamics above the stave. Järvi gets an excellent response from his fine Gothenburg players and tellingly conveys the atmosphere and mystery of this extraordinary score. James Hepokoski's excellent note speaks of it as "unlike anything else in the entire repertoire" – which indeed it is! What a wonderfully evocative score *The Oceanides* is, and what an atmospheric, and indeed magical account, we have here. The performances of the *Karelia* and *King Christian II* suites are not quite in this class but they are enjoyable, and the recording is quite exemplary.

Sibelius Pelleas and Melisande – Incidental Music, Op. 46. Swanwhite, Op. 54 – The Harp; The Maiden with the Roses; The Prince Alone; Swanwhite and the Prince; Song of Praise. King Christian II – Incidental Music, Op. 27[a]. [a]**Sauli Tiilikainen** (bar); **Iceland Symphony Orchestra / Petri Sakari.** Chandos Ⓕ CHAN9158 (79 minutes: DDD: 7/93). Text and translation included. Recorded 1992. *Gramophone Editor's choice.*

These performances are natural and unaffected and radiate immense care and pleasure in music-making. The *King Christian II* music includes "The Fool's Song", complete with soloist, and very good he is too, and a short "Minuet". Petri Sakari's performance is totally unaffected, plain and full of enthusiasm; the players sound as if they are enjoying this score and communicate their pleasure. Phrasing is attentive, musical through and through but never fussy. The *Pelleas and Melisande* is a version many collectors would want to have. It is imaginative, totally musical, strong on atmosphere and observant of dynamic subtleties. There may be readers who might find some of the tempos on the slow side; they are unhurried, but in context they feel right. Unfortunately there is only room for five movements from the *Swanwhite* music. All are beautifully played; every detail is allowed to take its time and the phrasing, though attentive, is free of the slightest taint of narcissism. Let "Swanwhite and the Prince" serve as an example of how well thought out and natural in feeling the phrasing is! Added to this, the Chandos recording is beautifully transparent, warm and well-detailed. Recommended with enthusiasm.

Sibelius The Tempest – Incidental Music, Op. 109 (from Philips ABR4045, 12/55)[a]. Scènes historiques: Op. 25 – No. 3, Festivo; Op. 66 (both from Columbia 33C1018, 11/53)[a]. Karelia Suite, Op. 11 – No. 1, Intermezzo; No. 3, Alla marcia (HMV DB6248. Recorded 1945)[b]. Finlandia, Op. 26 (Columbia LX704, 4/38)[c]. [a]**Royal Philharmonic Orchestra;** [b]**BBC Symphony Orchestra;** [c]**London Philharmonic Orchestra / Sir Thomas Beecham.** EMI Beecham Edition mono Ⓜ CDM7 63397-2* (73 minutes: ADD: 7/90). Recorded 1938-55.   ⒼⒼⒼ

Sibelius Symphonies – No. 4 in A minor, Op. 63[a] (from HMV DB3351/5, 3/38); No. 6 in D minor, Op. 104[b] (DB6640/42, 6/50). The Tempest – Incidental Music, Op. 109: Prelude[a] (DB3894, 12/39). Legends, Op. 22 – Lemminkäinen's return[a] (DB3355/6, 3/38). The bard, Op. 64[a] (DB3891, 12/39). [a]**London Philharmonic Orchestra;** [b]**Royal Philharmonic Orchestra / Sir Thomas Beecham.** EMI Beecham Edition mono Ⓜ CDM7 64027-2* (79 minutes: ADD: 3/92). Recorded 1937-47.   ⒼⒼⒼ

One of the special things about Beecham's Sibelius was its sheer sonority: there was a fresh, vernal sheen on the strings quite different from the opulence of Koussevitzky or Karajan but with all their flexibility and plasticity of phrasing, and a magic that is easier to discern than define. Suffice it to say that his feeling for atmosphere in Sibelius was always matched by a strong grip on the architecture. His 1956 recording of the two suites from *The Tempest* enjoys legendary status and is pure magic. The 1952 performances of four of the *Scènes historiques* have that similar ring of authenticity that transcend any sonic limitations. Beecham's stark account of the Fourth Symphony carries special authority since it was done after a long correspondence with the composer; and the 1947 RPO performance of the Sixth enjoyed Sibelius's imprimatur. The Prelude to *The Tempest* is as chillingly realistic as *Lemminkainen's return* is exciting.

Additional recommendations ...

...Legends. **Gothenburg Symphony Orchestra / Neeme Järvi.** BIS Ⓕ CD294 (49 minutes: DDD: 6/86).

...Scènes historiques – Suite No. 1, Op. 25; Suite No. 2, Op. 66. **Gothenburg Symphony Orchestra / Neeme Järvi.** BIS Ⓒ CD295 (56 minutes: DDD: 1/87).

...Legends. Luonnotar, Op. 70[a]. The bard. [a]**Phyllis Bryn-Julson** (sop); **Scottish National Orchestra / Sir Alexander Gibson.** Chandos Collect Ⓜ CHAN6586 (62 minutes: ADD: 11/92).

...Rakastava. Scènes historiques, Opp. 25 and 66. Valse lyrique. **Scottish National Orchestra / Sir Alexander Gibson.** Chandos Collect Ⓜ CHAN6591 (54 minutes: ADD: 11/93).

Sibelius Symphonies – No. 1 in E minor, Op. 39[a]; No. 7 in C major, Op. 105[b]. Karelia Overture, Op. 10[c]. **London Symphony Orchestra / Anthony Collins.** Beulah mono Ⓕ 1PD8* (62 minutes: ADD: 6/94). Item marked [a] from Decca LXT2694 (8/52), [b]LXT2940 (12/54), [c]LW5209 (3/56). Recorded 1952-55.   Ⓖ

Sibelius Symphonies – No. 2 in D major, Op. 43[a]; No. 6 in D minor, Op. 104[b]. **London Symphony Orchestra / Anthony Collins.** Beulah mono Ⓕ 2PD8* (69 minutes: ADD: 6/94). Item marked [a] from Decca LXT2815 (10/53), [b]LXT5084 (11/55). Recorded 1953-55.   Ⓖ

Sibelius Symphony No. 3 in C major, Op. 52[a]. Pohjola's Daughter, Op. 49[b]. Pelleas and Melisande[c] – No. 2, Melisande; No. 6, Pastorale; No. 7, At the spinning wheel; No. 8, Intermezzo; No. 9, Death of Melisande. Nightride and Sunrise, Op. 55[d]. **London Symphony Orchestra / Anthony Collins.** Beulah mono Ⓕ 3PD8* (68 minutes: ADD: 6/94). Item marked [a] from Decca LXT2960 (12/54), [b]LXT2962 (12/54), [c]LXT5084 (11/55), [d] LXT5083 (10/55). Recorded 1954-55.   Ⓖ

The name Anthony Collins (1893-1963) probably doesn't mean a great deal to the majority of younger readers, but for quite a few serious Sibelius *aficionados* his 1950s Decca recordings hold cult status. In these transfers the original recordings are revealed for the fine achievements they were: beautifully balanced, clear and vivid, allowing us to hear these performances in intimate detail – which is how they deserve to be heard. Collins is a first-rate musical landscape-painter. He doesn't just give us the bold sweeping brush-strokes, important as they are; he shows how the landscapes team with minute life. Rustling string textures aren't blandly homogenized – tiny details catch the ear, and then vanish again. Woodwind bird calls or horn calls can be acutely expressive – some passages remind one of Sibelius's comments about quasi-human voices in the nature sounds around his forest-home. But exaggeration is alien to the Collins approach. Nothing is forced, almost everything is fresh and vital, and it isn't only in the symphonies that the Collins touch is refreshing. *Pohjola's Daughter* comes to life as effectively as the symphonies, and Vol. 3 contains a real rarity, an entirely satisfactory *Nightride and Sunrise*.

Sibelius Symphonies – No. 1 in E minor, Op. 39 (from 414 534-1DH, 5/86); No. 2 in D major, Op. 43 (SXDL7513, 11/80); No. 3 in C major, Op. 52 (414 267-1DH, 8/85); No. 4 in A minor, Op. 63 (SXDL7517, 5/81); No. 5 in E flat major, Op. 82 (SXDL7541, 1/82); No. 6 in D minor, Op. 104 (414 267-1DH, 2/85); No. 7 in C major, Op. 105 (SXDL7580, 8/83). **Philharmonia Orchestra / Vladimir Ashkenazy.** Decca Ⓜ 421 069-2DM4 (four discs: 232 minutes: ADD/DDD: 12/87).

Of all the cycles of Sibelius's symphonies recorded during recent years this is one of the most consistently successful. Ashkenazy so well understands the thought processes that lie behind Sibelius's symphonic composition just as he is aware, and makes us aware, of the development between the Second and Third Symphonies. His attention to tempo is particularly acute and invariably he strikes just the right balance between romantic languor and urgency. The Philharmonia play for all they are worth and possess a fine body of sound. The recordings are remarkably consistent in quality and effectively complement the composer's original sound-world.

Additional recommendations ...

...Nos. 1-3. Luonnotar, Op. 70[a]. Pohjola's Daughter, Op. 49. [a]**Phyllis Curtin** (sop); **New York Philharmonic Orchestra / Leonard Bernstein.** Sony Classical Bernstein Royal Edition Ⓜ SM2K47619 (two discs: 129 minutes: ADD).

...Nos. 4-7. **New York Philharmonic Orchestra / Leonard Bernstein.** Sony Classical Bernstein Royal Edition Ⓜ SM2K47622 (two discs: 122 minutes: ADD).

...Nos. 1-7. Finlandia. Tapiola. The Swan of Tuonela. **Boston Symphony Orchestra / Sir Colin Davis.** Philips Ⓜ 416 600-2PH4 (four discs: 266 minutes: DDD: 11/86). ⒼⒼ

...Nos. 1-7. The Oceanides. Kuolema – Scene with cranes. Nightride and Sunrise, Op. 55. **City of Birmingham Symphony Orchestra; Philharmonia Orchestra / Sir Simon Rattle.** EMI Ⓜ CMS7 64118-2 (four discs: 267 minutes: DDD: 2/92). Ⓖ

...Nos. 1-7. **Vienna Philharmonic Orchestra / Lorin Maazel.** Decca Ⓑ 430 778-2DC3 (three discs: 212 minutes: ADD: 2/92). Ⓖ

...Nos. 4 and 5. **San Francisco Symphony Orchestra / Herbert Blomstedt.** Decca Ⓕ 425 858-2DH (68 minutes: DDD: 7/91). Ⓖ

...Nos. 4 and 6. **City of Birmingham Symphony Orchestra / Sir Simon Rattle.** EMI Ⓜ CDM7 64121-2 (67 minutes: DDD: 2/92). ⒼⒼ

...Nos. 4 and 6[a]. The Tempest: Prelude. Legends – Lemminkaïnen's return. The bard. **London Philharmonic Orchestra; [a]Royal Philharmonic Orchestra / Sir Thomas Beecham.** EMI mono Ⓜ CDM7 64027-2* (79 minutes: ADD: 3/92). ⒼⒼ

...Nos. 1 and 7. **Philharmonia Orchestra / Vladimir Ashkenazy.** Decca Ⓜ 436 473-2DM (62 minutes: DDD: 7/93). *These are the same recordings as those reviewed above.*

...Nos. 1 and 3. **Philharmonia Orchestra / Paul Kletzki.** Testament mono Ⓕ SBT1049* (63 minutes: ADD: 4/95).

...No. 7[a]. Pelleas and Melisande – No. 2, Melisande[a]; No. 4, Spring in the park[b]; No. 8, Intermezzo[b]; No. 9, Death of Melisande[b]. The Tempest – incidental music, Op. 109[b]: Prelude; The oak-tree; Humoresque; Caliban's Song; Berceuse; Prospero; Miranda. Scènes historiques, Op. 25 – Festivo[b]. In memoriam, Op. 59[b]. Legends, Op. 22 – Lemminkäinen's return[b]. [a]**New York Philharmonic Orchestra, [b]London Philharmonic Orchestra / Sir Thomas Beecham.** Dutton Laboratories mono Ⓜ CDAX8013* (76 minutes: ADD: 7/95).

New review

Sibelius Symphonies – No. 1 in E minor, Op. 39; No. 7 in C major, Op. 105. **San Francisco Symphony Orchestra / Herbert Blomstedt.** Decca Ⓕ 444 541-2DH (62 minutes: DDD: 5/96). Recorded 1993-4.

This performance of the Seventh is magisterial and majestic Sibelius without a trace of interpretative egotism. It is built up with real feeling for balance and proportion and as a whole, the reading is powerful and marvellously controlled, with no want of dignity or nobility. The First Symphony is among the best to have appeared lately. We have not been short of good versions in recent years – Ashkenazy and the Philharmonia, Jansons and the Oslo Philharmonic and Bernstein and the Vienna Philharmonic to name only three. Blomstedt admits no concessions to the gallery; we are given this symphony with plenty of fire and no lack of virtuosity on the part of the San Francisco players. Here we get Sibelius straight and unadorned. The sound is faithful and well balanced.

Sibelius Symphony No. 1 in E minor, Op. 39. Karelia Suite, Op. 11. Finlandia, Op. 26. **Oslo Philharmonic Orchestra / Mariss Jansons.** EMI Ⓕ CDC7 54273-2 (62 minutes: DDD: 1/92). Recorded 1990. Ⓖ

Jansons's account of the First Symphony was quite the most thrilling version to have appeared for some years. It has excitement and brilliance without exaggerations. Tempos throughout are just right, the phrasing breathes naturally and the sonority is excellently focused. Jansons never presses on too quickly but allows each phrase, each musical sentence to register so that the listener feels borne along on a natural currrent. Moreover, excitement is not whipped up but arises naturally from the music's forward momentum. The Oslo Philharmonic are a highly responsive orchestra of no mean virtuosity and they play with a splendid intensity and fire not only in the symphony but also the *Karelia Suite* and *Finlandia* which sound very fresh. All the artistic decisions in this reading seem to be right and the orchestral playing further enhances the high renown this ensemble now enjoys. Very good recording too.

Additional recommendation ...

...No. 1. **Vienna Philharmonic Orchestra / Leonard Bernstein.** DG 435 512-2GH (41 minutes: DDD: 4/92).

New review

Sibelius Symphonies – No. 2 in D major, Op. 43; No. 6 in D minor, Op. 104. **London Symphony Orchestra / Sir Colin Davis.** RCA Victor Red Seal Ⓕ 09026 68218-2 (73 minutes: DDD: 12/95). Recorded 1994.

Sir Colin is totally attuned to the Sixth Symphony, whose eloquent polyphony, purity of utterance and harmony of spirit give it a special place in the canon. As I have said elsewhere, in this symphony "Sibelius's mastery enables him to move with a freedom so complete that the musical events are dictated by their own inner necessity". And in Davis's hands this music unfolds with a freedom and naturalness that are totally convincing. As Sibelius said of the Fourth Symphony, this is music "with nothing of the circus about it", and in this reading there is no playing to the gallery. There is no playing to the gallery either in Sir Colin's account of the Second Symphony. He views the work as a whole and does not invest detail with undue expressive vehemence at its expense, but strikes just the right balance between the nationalist-romantic inheritance on the one side and the classical power of Sibelius's thinking on the other. The first movement has dignity and breadth, and as with Karajan, the pacing of climaxes is magisterial. The recording has splendid presence and space.

Additional recommendations ...

...No. 2. Romance in C major, Op. 42. **Gothenburg Symphony Orchestra / Neeme Järvi.** BIS Ⓕ CD252 (48 minutes: DDD: 10/84).

...No. 2. **Berlin Philharmonic Orchestra / Herbert von Karajan.** EMI Studio Ⓜ CDM7 69243-2 (48 minutes: ADD: 4/88).

...Nos. 2, 5 and 7. Swanwhite   The Maidens with roses. Tapiola. Pohjola's daughter. **Boston Symphony Orchestra; BBC Symphony Orchestra / Serge Koussevitzky.** Pearl mono Ⓕ GEMMCDS9408* (two discs: 125 minutes: AAD: 7/90).   Ⓖ

...No. 4. The Tempest – Suite No. 1. **Danish National Radio Symphony Orchestra / Leif Segerstam.** Chandos Ⓕ CHAN8943 (65 minutes: DDD: 8/91).

...Nos. 2 and 3. **City of Birmingham Symphony Orchestra / Sir Simon Rattle.** EMI Ⓜ CDM7 64120-2 (51 minutes: DDD: 2/92).

...No. 2. Finlandia. Karelia Suite. **Philharmonia Orchestra / Vladimir Ashkenazy.** Decca Headline Ⓑ 430 737 2DM (72 minutes: DDD: 8/92).

...No. 2. Tapiola. Kuolema – Valse triste. **San Francisco Symphony Orchestra / Herbert Blomstedt.** Decca Ⓕ 433 810-2DH (69 minutes: DDD: 3/93).   Ⓖ

...No. 2. The Swan of Tuonela, Kuolema – Valse triste. Andante festivo for Strings. **Oslo Philharmonic Orchestra / Mariss Jansons.** EMI Ⓕ CDC7 54804-2 (61 minutes: DDD: 7/93).

...No. 2. Romance in C major, Op. 42. Kuolema – Valse triste. Finlandia. **Boston Symphony Orchestra / Vladimir Ashkenazy.** Decca Ⓕ 436 566-2DH(65 minutes: DDD: 10/93).

...No. 2. Finlandia, Op. 26. Valse triste, Op. 44 No. 1. The Swan of Tuonela. **Boston Symphony Orchestra / Sir Colin Davis.** Philips Solo Ⓜ 442 389-2PM (69 minutes: ADD: 9/94).

...Nos. 2 and 7. **Philadelphia Orchestra / Eugene Ormandy.** Sony Classical Ⓑ SBK53509* (66 minutes: ADD: 9/94).

Sibelius Symphonies – No. 3 in C major, Op. 52; No. 5 in E flat major, Op. 82. **London Symphony Orchestra / Sir Colin Davis.** RCA Victor Red Seal Ⓕ 09026 61963-2 (61 minutes: DDD: 3/95). Recorded 1992.   Ⓖ

Some 20 years have passed since Davis's last Sibelius cycle, with the Boston Symphony Orchestra for Philips. Generally speaking Sir Colin's new version of the Third has greater breadth and sense of scale than his previous account or any other. His first movement has a majestic stride and great power; and he has the measure of the slow movement's pantheistic musings. The Fifth is more tautly held together than before; the first movement moves forward and onwards with a powerful feeling of inevitability and purpose. The transition in the first movement to the scherzo section is masterly. Listening to this disc, one wonders anew at the sheer originality of this piece, and that is, of course, the touchstone of a great performance. Sir Colin Davis understands Sibelius as do few others and senses the vital currents that flow through these symphonies, and the LSO know this and respond with playing of distinction. The recording is in every way first-class, vivid in detail and truthful in perspective.

Additional recommendations ...

...Nos. 4 and 5. **Philharmonia Orchestra / Vladimir Ashkenazy.** Decca 430 749-2DM (65 minutes: DDD).

…No. 3. King Christian II, Op. 27 – excerpts. **Gothenburg Symphony Orchestra / Neeme Järvi.** BIS
Ⓕ CD228 (DDD: 10/84).

…Nos. 3 and 6. **Philharmonia Orchestra / Vladimir Ashkenazy.** Decca Ⓜ 436 478-2DM (58 minutes:
DDD: 2/94).

…Nos. 3[a] and 5[a]. March of the Finnish Jaeger Battalion, Op. 91 No. 1[b]. [a]**London Symphony
Orchestra;** [b]**Helsinki Philharmonic Orchestra / Robert Kajanus.** Koch Historic mono Ⓜ 37133-2*
(62 minutes: ADD: 2/94). *Gramophone classical 100.*   ⒼⒼⒼ

…Nos. 5 and 6. **Berlin Philharmonic Orchestra / Herbert von Karajan.** DG Galleria Ⓜ 439
982-2GGA (69 minutes: ADD: 1/95).

…Nos. 3 and 5. **Oslo Philharmonic Orchestra / Mariss Jansons.** EMI Ⓕ CDC5 55533-2 (58 minutes:
DDD: 5/96).

New review

Sibelius Symphonies – No. 4 in A minor, Op. 63[a]; No. 7 in C major, Op. 105[b]. Kuolema, Op. 44
No. 1 – Valse triste[c]. **Berlin Philharmonic Orchestra / Herbert von Karajan.** DG Galleria Ⓜ 439
527-2GGA (66 minutes: ADD: 5/94). Item marked [a] from SLPM138974 (6/66), [b]SLPM139032
(10/68), [c]SLPM139016 (3/68).   Ⓖ

Karajan recorded the Fourth Symphony three times, once in the 1950s with the Philharmonia and
twice with the Berlin Philharmonic. The work obviously meant a great deal to him. He insisted on its
inclusion in his very first concert on his appointment at the Berlin Philharmonic in the early 1960s at
a time when Sibelius's cause had few champions in Germany, so keen was he to stake its claim as one
of the great symphonies of the day. Karajan's account has withstood the test of time as one of the
most searching, profound and concentrated performances of this masterpiece, and its reappearance
at mid price was very welcome. The Seventh is finer than his earlier Philharmonia version but does
not enjoy quite the same classic status. Karajan's *Valse triste* is wonderfully seductive. An
indispensable issue.

New review

Sibelius Symphony No. 5 in E flat major (original 1915 version). En Saga, Op. 9 (original 1892
version). **Lahti Symphony Orchestra / Osmo Vänskä.** BIS Ⓕ CD800 (58 minutes: DDD: 4/96).
Recorded 1995. *Gramophone Editor's choice. Selected by Soundings.*   ⒼⒼ

Every so often a CD appears which, by means of some interpretative insight, changes our view of a
piece of music. This disc changes our whole perspective in a wholly different sense, for it gives us a
glimpse of two familiar masterpieces in the making. Sibelius struggled with the Fifth Symphony for
almost seven years from about 1912 until it reached its definitive form in 1919. Although the finished
score of the first version does not survive, the orchestral material does, and thus it was not difficult
to reconstruct the score. The 1915 score is now available to the public at large in dedicated
performance. To study how the two scores differ is to learn something important about the creative
process and it is this mystery that makes the disc imperative listening – and not just for Sibelians. The
four-movement 1915 score has a more complex harmonic language than the final score and so it
provides a missing link, as it were, between the Fourth Symphony and the definitive Fifth. The
opening horn motive has yet to emerge, and the finale's coda has yet to acquire its original hammer-
blow chords. And in between you will find that the various themes, some distinctly recognizable,
others taking off in totally unexpected directions and charting unknown regions. Something of the
cosmic feel of this music emerges in a letter Sibelius wrote in 1914, "God opens the door for a moment
and his orchestra was playing the Fifth Symphony". Of course, Sibelius knew what he was doing, and
in the 1919 version, he managed to keep the door open for rather longer! The version of *En Saga* with
which we are familiar does not come between the *Kullervo* Symphony and the *Karelia* music but from
1901 between the First and Second Symphonies and was made for Busoni. The original offers
fascinating material for comparison: there is a brief glimpse of Bruckner, whose work he had
encountered in Vienna a year or two earlier, and the orchestral writing, though not always as polished
as in the later version, still has flair. There is so much more to say about this music but room must be
found to sing the praises of the Lahti orchestra and their fine conductor, and the excellent and natural
balance.

Additional recommendation …

…No. 5[a]. **Nielsen** Symphony No. 4, FS76, "The inextinguishable"[b]. Pan and Syrinx, FS87[b].
[a]**Philharmonia Orchestra;** [b]**City of Birmingham Symphony Orchestra / Sir Simon Rattle.** EMI
Ⓜ CDM7 64737-2 (78 minutes: DDD: 11/93).   ⒼⒼ

Sibelius Five Pieces, Op. 81. Novelette, Op. 102. Five Danses champêtres, Op. 106. Four Pieces,
Op. 115. Three Pieces, Op. 116. **Nils-Erik Sparf** (vn); **Bengt Forsberg** (pf). BIS Ⓕ CD625
(57 minutes: DDD: 5/95). Recorded 1993.

No one listening to this music would doubt that Sibelius had a special feeling for the violin. Whether
he is composing lighter music such as the captivating "Rondino" from the Op. 81 set or the more
substantial later pieces, such as the first of the *Danses champêtres*, which comes close to the world of
The Tempest. Neither the Op. 115 nor the Op. 116 set contains great music but they are much finer
than they have been given credit for. Both "On the heath" and the "Ballade", Nos. 1 and 2 of Op. 115
have an innocence that calls to mind the wonderful *Humoresques* for violin and orchestra. In

particular "The Bells", Op. 115 No. 4 is a rather cryptic miniature and the "Scène de danse" of Op. 116, with its striking tonal juxtapositions, is a kind of Finnish equivalent of the Bartók *Romanian Dances*. Nils-Erik Sparf and Bengt Forsberg are dedicated and sensitive exponents who make the most of the opportunities this repertoire provides. The piano tone sounds a little thick at the bottom end of the spectrum, and the violin is by no means the dominant partner in the aural picture. This reservation is a small one and the performances are to be recommended with enthusiasm.

Sibelius King Christian II, Op. 27 – Fool's Song of the Spider. Five Christmas Songs, Op. 1. Eight Songs, Op. 57. Hymn to Thaïs. Six Songs, Op. 72 – No. 3, The kiss; No. 4, The echo nymph; No. 5, Der Wanderer und der Bach; No. 6, A hundred ways. Six Songs, Op. 86. The small girls. **Monica Groop** (mez); **Love Derwinger** (pf). BIS Ⓔ CD657 (66 minutes: DDD: 9/94). Texts and translations included. Recorded 1994.

Monica Groop, following her success in the Cardiff Singer of the World Competition, has had a busy career. Communication is her strength, and unevenness of line a relative weakness. Sibelius's songs are a rich and still undervalued part of the song repertoire. Still only four or five are really well-known, and none of those is included here. Not all are of very special quality: the title is probably the best thing about the "Fool's Song of the Spider" (from *King Christian II*), and the *Hymn to Thaïs* gains interest through being Sibelius's only song in English rather than through intrinsic merit. Yet there are many delights here, including the closing waltz-song, *The small girls*. The acoustic is perhaps somewhat too reverberant but has plenty of presence.

New review

Sibelius Songs, Volume 3. Seven Songs, Op. 13. Six Songs, Op. 50. Six Songs, Op. 90. The Wood Nymph. Belshazzar's Feast – The Jewish Girl's Song. Resemblance. A Song. Serenade. The Thought[a]. **Anne Sofie von Otter**, [a]**Monica Groop** (mezzos); **Bengt Forsberg** (pf). BIS Ⓔ CD757 (67 minutes: DDD: 4/96). Texts and translations included. *Gramophone Editor's choice.*　　Ⓖ

The vast majority of Sibelius's songs are in Swedish, the language with which he grew up as a child, and here they are given by a distinguished native Swedish partnership. The *Seven Songs*, Op. 13, are all Runeberg settings and come from the composer's early years (1891-2). Best known, perhaps, are "Spring is flying" ("Våren flyktar hastigt") and "The dream" ("Drömmen"), but there are others, such as "The young hunter" ("Jägargossen"), that are no less delightful and characterful. The other Runeberg settings here, the *Six Songs*, Op. 90, come towards the end of Sibelius's career as a song composer (1917-18). "The month" ("Norden"), as in all the nature poetry of Runeberg, touches a very special vein of inspiration. Along with "Die stille Nacht" ("The silent city"), Op. 50 No. 5, which is equally affectingly given by these two artists – it is among his finest songs. Interest naturally focuses on the rarities. *The Wood Nymph* ("Skogsrået"), not to be confused with the melodrama or the tone-poem, is recorded here for the first time. As well as *A Song* ("En visa"), there are two other early Runeberg settings, the 1888 *Serenade*, and *Resemblance* ("Likhet"), both of them new to the catalogue. "The Jewish Girl's Song" ("Den judiska flickans sång") will be familiar from the incidental music to *Belshazzar's Feast*, and is affecting in this form – particularly sung as it is here. Given the artistry and insight of this splendid partnership, and the interest and beauty of the repertoire, this is a self-recommending issue.

Sibelius Arioso, Op. 3. Seven Songs, Op. 17. Row, row duck. Six Songs, Op. 36. Five Songs, Op. 37. Pelleas and Melisande, Op. 46 – The three blind sisters. Six Songs, Op. 88. Narcissus. **Anne Sofie von Otter** (mez); **Bengt Forsberg** (pf). BIS Ⓔ CD457 (57 minutes: DDD: 6/90). Texts and translations included.

In all, Sibelius composed about 100 songs, mostly to Swedish texts but his achievement in this field has, naturally enough, been overshadowed by the symphonies. Most music lovers know only a handful like "Black roses", Op. 36 No. 1, and "The Tryst" and the most popular are not always the best. Sibelius's output for the voice has much greater range, diversity and depth than many people suppose. For collectors used to hearing them sung by a baritone, the idea of a soprano will seem strange but a lot of them were written for the soprano Ida Ekman. Anne Sofie von Otter not only makes a beautiful sound and has a feeling for line, but also brings many interpretative insights to this repertoire. The very first song from the Op. 17 set is a marvellous Runeberg setting, "Since then I have questioned no further" and it was this that Ida Ekman sang for Brahms. Von Otter captures its mood perfectly and has the measure of its companions too. Her account of "Black roses" is particularly thrilling and she is very persuasive in the weaker Op. 88 set. She sings throughout with great feeling for character and her account of "Astray", Op. 17 No. 6, has great lightness of touch and charm. The Opp. 36 and 37 sets are among the finest lyrical collections in the whole of Sibelius's song output, and they completely engage this artist's sensibilities. These are performances of elegance and finesse; Bengt Forsberg proves an expert and stylish partner and both artists are well recorded.

New review

Sibelius Incidental Music – Everyman, Op. 83[a]; Belshazzar's Feast, Op. 51[b]. The Countess's Portrait, Op. posth. [ab]**Lilli Paasikivi** (mez); [a]**Petri Lehto** (ten); [a]**Sauli Tiilikainen** (bar); [a]**Pauli Pietiläinen** (org); [a]**Leena Saarenpää** (pf); [a]**Lahti Chamber Choir; Lahti Symphony Orchestra /** **Osmo Vänskä**. BIS Ⓔ CD735 (65 minutes: DDD: 5/96). Texts and translations included. Recorded 1995.

These are all first recordings and interest centres on the score Sibelius wrote for Hofmannsthal's morality play, *Jedermann* ("Everyman") in 1916. The final score comprises 16 numbers and runs to some 40 minutes. Some of the music is fragmentary and hardly makes sense out of context, though most of it is atmospheric and all of it is characteristic. The sustained *Largo* section for muted, divided strings (track 11), is among the most searching music Sibelius ever wrote for theatre and, artistically, is fit to keep company with *The Tempest* music. Overall the material does not lend itself to being turned into a suite in the same way as *Belshazzar's Feast* but this recording rescues from obscurity some strangely haunting and at times really inspired music – the last 25 minutes are very powerful. By all accounts Hjalmar Procopé's *Belshazzar's Feast* was a feeble play and when it first appeared, one newspaper cartoon showed the playwright being borne aloft in the composer's arms. There seems little doubt that his name would not be alive were it not for Sibelius's music. The latter certainly makes an expert job of creating an effective and (in the case of the "Notturno") a moving concert suite. The present issue gives us an additional six minutes or so of unfamiliar music; there are 11 numbers in all, though familiar passages from the suite are broken up. *The Countess's Portrait* (1906) is a wistful, pensive and charming piece for strings, which was only published two years ago. Obviously this is a self-recommending issue of exceptional interest.

Sibelius The Tempest – Incidental Music, Op. 109. **Kirsi Tiihonen** (sop); **Lilli Paasikivi** (mez);
  Anssi Hirvonen, Paavo Kerola (tens); **Heikki Keinonen** (bar); **Lahti Opera Chorus and Symphony
  Orchestra / Osmo Vänskä.** BIS Ⓟ CD581 (68 minutes: DDD: 2/93). Text and translation
  included. Recorded 1992. *Selected by Sounds in Retrospect.*   Ⓖ
A first recording of the full score! Sibelius's music for *The Tempest,* his last and greatest work in its genre, was the result of a commission for a particularly lavish production at the Royal Theatre, Copenhagen in 1926. The score is far more extensive than the two suites and consists of 34 musical numbers for soloists, mixed choir, harmonium and large orchestra. Readers will be brought up with a start by the music for the "Berceuse", the second item, which uses a harmonium rather than the strings with which we are familiar from the two suites and although it is still more magical in the familiar orchestral suite, the original has an other-worldly quality all its own. The music is played in the order in which it was used in the 1927 production of the play and there are ample and excellent explanatory notes. The "Chorus of the Winds" is also different but no less magical in effect. Of course, taken out of the theatrical context, not everything comes off – but even if the invention is not consistent in quality, at its best it is quite wonderful. The singers and chorus all rise to the occasion and Osmo Vänskä succeeds in casting a powerful spell in the "Intermezzo", which opens Act 4. The recording is marvellously atmospheric though it needs to be played at a higher than usual level setting as it is a little recessed. For Sibelians this is a self-recommending issue.

Further listening ...

…Suite champêtre, Op. 98*b*. Canzonetta, Op. 62*a*. *Coupled with* **Tchaikovsky** Elegy in G major (in
  honour of Ivan Samarin). **Dvořák** Two Waltzes, B105. Nocturne in B major, B47. Humoresque
  in G flat major, B187. **Elgar** Salut d'amour, Op. 12. Sospiri, Op. 70. **Grieg** Two Melodies,
  Op. 53. Two Nordic Melodies, Op. 63. Two Elegiac Melodies, Op. 34. **Serenata of London / Barry
  Wilde.** IMP Classics PCD1108 (2/95). .
…Scaramouche – Incidental Music, Op. 71. The Language of the Birds – Wedding March.
  Gothenburg Symphony Orchestra / Neeme Järvi. BIS CD502 (4/92).
…Piano Quintet in G minor (1890)[a]. String Quartet in D minor, Op. 56, "Voces intimae". **Gabrieli
  Quartet;** [a]**Anthony Goldstone** (pf). Chandos CHAN8742 (2/90).
…Piano Quartet in C minor[a]. Violin Sonata in F major[b]. String Trio in G minor[c]. Suite for String
  Trio in A major[c]. [b]**Ernst Kovacic,** [c]**Jan Söderblom,** [a]**Massimo Quarta,** [a]**Ilaria Miori** (vns); [c]**Ilari
  Angervo** (va); [c]**Jan-Erik Gustafsson,** [a]**Martti Rousi** (vcs); [b]**Juhani Lagerspetz,** [a]**Viatcheslav Novikov**
  (pfs). Ondine ODE826-2 (6/95).
…String Quartets – E flat major; A minor; B flat major, Op. 4; D minor, Op. 56, "Voces intimae".
  Sibelius Academy Quartet. Finlandia 4509-95851-2 (8/92).
…String Quartet in D minor, Op. 56, "Voces intimae". *Coupled with* **Grieg** String Quartet No. 1 in
  G minor, Op. 27. **Wolf** Italian Serenade. **Budapest Quartet.** Biddulph mono LAB098* (4/95).
…Piano Works, Volume 4. – Melody for the Bells of Berghäll Church, Op. 65. Five Pieces, Op. 75.
  13 Pieces, Op. 76. Five Pieces, Op. 85. Six Pieces, Op. 94. Six Bagatelles, Op. 97. **Annette Servadei**
  (pf). Continuum CCD1070 (12/95).
…Piano Works, Volume 5. – Valse lyrique, Op. 96*a*. Autrefois, Op. 96*b*. Valse chevaleresque, Op.
  96*c*. Eight Pieces, Op. 99. Five Pieces, Op. 101. Five Pieces, Op. 103. Five Esquisses, Op. 114.
  Finlandia, Op. 26. **Annette Servadei** (pf). Continuum CCD1071 (12/95).
…The maiden in the tower. Karelia Suite, Op. 11. **Soloists; Gothenburg Concert Hall Chorus and
  Symphony Orchestra / Neeme Järvi.** BIS CD250 (3/85).
…The Kiss. **Soloists; Brno Janáček Opera Chorus and Orchestra / František Vajnar.** Supraphon
  11 2180-2.

Thorkell Sigurbjörnsson
Icelandic 1938-

New review
Sigurbjörnsson Liongate[a]. Calaïs. Columbine[a]. Euridice[a]. **Manuela Wiesler** (fl); [a]**Southern Jutland Symphony Orchestra / Tamás Vetö**. BIS Ⓕ CD709 (67 minutes: DDD: 6/96).
Here is a welcome representative programme of works by one of Iceland's leading composers. Sigurbjörnsson is very much an assimilator, glad to write accessible music for specific players and occasions and, like Britten, eager to be "useful, and to the living". *Liongate* is a 20-minute concerto for flute, strings and percussion, inspired by a visit to the great gate of Lions at Mycenae and by Sigurbjörnsson's own incidental music for a production of the *Oresteia* at the National Theatre, Reykjavík. An irregular, ostinato-like pulse introduces the flute as a haunted, hovering Ariel of an instrument, thermalling in cadenzas above numb, pulsating orchestral chords and sparely employed, coppery percussion. *Euridice*, written five years earlier, has a stronger foreground: here the flute is a bewildered and tormented protagonist, moving in coiled, choreographic figures (the performer, ideally, should play with costume and lighting) above the deep brass and woodwind furies of Hades. These two substantial works frame a light-hearted Gluckian divertimento called *Columbine*, and the solo *Calaïs*, a highly imaginative virtuoso celebration of the eponymous son of Boreas, the North Wind.

Valentin Silvestrov
USSR 1937-

New review
Silvestrov Symphony No. 2[a]. Meditatsiya[b]. Serenade[c]. [a]**Oleg Hudiyakov** (fl); [a]**Ivan Sokolov** (pf); [a]**Mikhail Dunayev**, [a]**Konstantin Smirnov** (perc); **Musica Viva Chamber Orchestra / [ac]Alexander Rudin** ([b]vc), [b]**Nicolay Alexeiev**. Olympia Ⓜ OCD477 (58 minutes: DDD: 7/96). *Gramophone Editor's choice*. Recorded 1995.
Valentin Silvestrov is not exactly an unknown quantity. He has frequently been mentioned in the same breath as Schnittke, Denisov and Gubaidulina as one of the most talented of the generation of avant-garde-minded former-Soviet composers who came to maturity in the 1960s. His uniqueness lies in a curious temperamental mixture of the ascetic and the ecstatic, allied to the extraordinary acuteness of his ear. His style has followed a not unfamiliar route from avant-garde Polish 'sonoristics' (as in the 12-minute, single movement Second Symphony for flute, percussion, piano and strings of 1965) through mild polystylism (as in *Meditatsiya* for cello and chamber orchestra of 1972) to out-and-out sensuous atavism (as in his masterpiece, the Fifth Symphony of 1982, soon to be released on Sony Classical). The Second Symphony is the least interesting musical experience on this disc, though the presence of a burgeoning talent is unmistakable. *Meditatsiya* starts in an all-purpose-Darmstadt vein, but soon sets out on more intriguing zigzag pathways towards and away from triadic sonorities and romantically consoling textures. The manner is predominantly quietist, even in passages of apparent expressionist gesturing, and the sense of vistas opening up in the mind is almost tangible. In the second half Silvestrov pushes the stylistic polarities to wider extremes, risking charges of opportunism, of effects without cause. But helped by a wonderfully sensitive performance from Musica Viva, the piece retains its hypnotic grip, notably in a massively extended, shimmering coda, haunted by all sorts of dimly perceived ghosts. The *Serenade* for strings of 1978 shows Silvestrov apparently not quite ready to abandon himself to the sensuous other-worldliness that was to come in the Fifth Symphony. Yet just when the hypersensitive brush-strokes seem to be degenerating into mere doodles, he startles by introducing a visitor from that world-to-come, in the shape of profoundly disconsolate melodic fragments in an unequivocal E flat minor. Eccentric, maybe, but in a compelling world of its own. All these performances are superb, excellently recorded, and they document one composer's path towards one of the most treasurable and original voices in the music of our time.

Robert Simpson
British 1921-

Simpson Symphonies Nos. 3 and 5. **Royal Philharmonic Orchestra / Vernon Handley**. Hyperion Ⓕ CDA66728 (71 minutes: DDD: 2/95). Recorded 1994.
The RPO and Vernon Handley play the Third Symphony like the repertoire piece it deserves to be, and Hyperion's recording reveals a wealth of unsuspected detail and beauty. The Beethovenian impulse still comes across, and the abrasive edge is only slightly softened. But what has been gained is clarity, blend and perspective, plus a sense of dialogue (Simpson's polyphony never ceases to amaze) and an altogether subtler realization of the luminosity of Simpson's scoring. The Fifth Symphony is surely one of Simpson's most vivid pieces. Moods of terror, anger, anxious probing and fierce determination are right on the surface, and there is a feeling of terrific will-power being exerted to transmute those moods into a symphonic experience. This is one of the great symphonies of the post-war era, magnificently realized by all concerned.

Simpson Horn Trio. Horn Quartet[a]. **Richard Watkins** (hn); **Pauline Lowbury** (vn); [a]**Caroline Dearnley** (vc); **Christopher Green-Armytage** (pf). Hyperion Ⓕ CDA66695 (50 minutes: DDD: 12/94). Recorded 1993.

Nirvana for composers and performers alike is a state where music unfolds of its own accord, without apparent conscious effort; and not many composers could claim to have reached that enviable condition more consistently than Robert Simpson. Not that will-power and effort are absent from his music – when the situation demands, no one directs the flow more determinedly than he does. But often the entire course of the work seems to be latent in its very first notes, only needing him to open a window and let it flood in. Both the Horn Quartet of 1976 and the Trio of 1984 make their mark on first hearing. That may be because the performances are exceptionally fine but is probably down to enthralling qualities in the pieces themselves. What it is *not* down to is any special idiomatic treatment of the horn – if anything that side of things is kept too rigorously in check. But the sense of power in reserve, of a satisfying fluidity of texture, of tiny ideas snowballing with irresistible inevitability, of frowns easing into poetry, all these things proclaim a true kinship with late Beethoven, long before the Quartet's final variation movement openly reveals its debt to Beethoven's last piano sonata. Top-flight recordings from Hyperion.

New review

Simpson Violin Sonata. Trio for Violin, Cello and Piano. **Lowbury Piano Trio** (Pauline Lowbury, vn; [b]Ursula Smith, vc; [b]Elizabeth Burley, pf); [a]Christopher Green-Armytage (pf). Hyperion
Ⓕ CDA66737 (66 minutes: DDD: 7/95). Recorded 1993.

One might write that Simpson is one of those fortunate composers who find their niche early on and occupy it happily for the rest of their careers. But that would be to understate the breadth of experience he encompasses. Better perhaps to say that what he found was his own orbit. Because the essential quality of his music is its sense of movement and trajectory; because it gives the feeling of moving somehow above traditional tonality and yet aware of its gravitational pull; because it seems to be somewhat aloof from terrestrial concerns and yet keenly observant of them. Simpson's favoured chamber medium is the string quartet, and he tends to write for the piano trio as though it were an expanded quartet, with each of the pianist's hands a kind of translated super-violin or super-cello. And why not? This is music where clean, simple lines reveal inner beauties through contrapuntal interaction, where scales occasionally ignite and implacable chords challenge the unfolding of the music (both the Sonata and the Trio are haunted by dominant sevenths in oblique Busonian harmonic layerings), where disciplined rhythmic interweavings link hands with late Beethoven (for example the Sonata, Op. 111) and Nielsen (such as the *Chaconne*), where conclusions come as thoughtful reconciliation or spidery dispersal. If you are responsive to Simpson's exhilarating command of musical movement and space you will find this disc as rewarding as any in Hyperion's wonderful recorded cycle. Both performances are sustained, patient and alert in a way which brings out a maximum of power and poetry. Recording quality is once again clean and truthful.

New review

Simpson Piano Sonata. Variations and Finale on a Theme of Haydn. Michael Tippett, His Mystery. Variations and Finale on a Theme by Beethoven. **Raymond Clarke** (pf). Hyperion
Ⓕ CDA66827 (65 minutes: DDD: 5/96). Recorded 1995.

It's convenient that all Simpson's piano music fits on to a single CD. But if you were hoping to find representative works from all periods of his career, it's not so convenient to find that four decades separate the two earlier works from the two later ones. Yet the Piano Sonata and the *Variations and Finale on a Theme of Haydn*, composed in 1946 and 1948 respectively, have much in common with the *Beethoven* Variations from as recently as 1990. In each case the piano writing is rugged, plain-speaking and disdainful of colour and effect, often recalling Schubert in chunkiest *Wanderer* Fantasy vein. In each case, too, Simpson's compositional resources feel as limitless, as they are, in point of fact, strictly focused. Whether weirdly hanging in the air or nearly exploding with fierce joy, this music is absolutely single-minded in its exploitation of the potential energy of its material. The big-boned opening bars of the Sonata could be a homage to Nielsen's *Symphonic Pieces*, Op. 3, were it not for the fact that Simpson had yet to encounter that composer. As in Brahms's Op. 1 Sonata, the general strenuousness of texture and eagerness to take possession of musical space suggest a composer "springing ready-armed from the head of Zeus" (to quote Schumann).

The *Haydn* Variations are on the same palindromic theme Simpson was to take 34 years later for his huge masterpiece, the Ninth String Quartet, and the piece shares some of the same ideas. But this is no mere interesting forerunner. It works its compelling way through statuesque stillness and Diabellian humour, to Hammerklavierian energy. The tiny Tippett tribute from 1984 is like a response to the slow movement of the older man's Third Piano Sonata, heard through a prism of Scriabinesque tritones. And the last movement of that same Tippett work comes to mind in the characteristically engrossing *Beethoven* Variations. But all this mention of other composers is only a question of affinities, not overshadowing influences. Simpson dances to no one's tune but his own. The *Beethoven* Variations were composed for Raymond Clarke, who brings to them, and to the other pieces, an unimpeachable mastery of technique and idiom. His dedication to the Simpson cause is on a par with the other discs in the remarkable Hyperion series, as is the clarity of the recording.

Further listening ...
...Symphonies Nos. 2 and 4. **Bournemouth Symphony Orchestra / Vernon Handley.** Hyperion
CDA66505 (12/92). *Selected by Sounds in Retrospect.*

...Symphony No. 9. **Bournemouth Symphony Orchestra / Vernon Handley.** Hyperion CDA66299 (12/88). *Gramophone Award Winner 1989.* Ⓖ

...Music for Brass Band: Energy. The Four Temperaments. Introduction and Allegro on a Bass by Max Reger. Volcano. Vortex. **Desford Colliery Caterpillar Band / James Watson.** Hyperion CDA66449 (1/91).

...String Quartets Nos. 3 and 6. String Trio (Prelude, Adagio and Fugue). **Delmé Quartet.** Hyperion CDA66376 (7/90).

...String Quartets Nos. 7 and 8. **Delmé Quartet.** Hyperion CDA66117 (2/90).

...String Quartet No. 9. **Delmé Quartet.** Hyperion CDA66127 (2/90).

...String Quartet No. 12. String Quintet[a]. **Coull Quartet;** [a]**Roger Bigley** (va). Hyperion CDA66503 (7/92).

Christian Sinding
Norwegian 1856-1941

Suggested listening ...

...Suite for Violin and Orchestra, Op. 10, "In alten Stil". *Coupled with* **Sibelius** Violin Concerto in D minor, Op. 47. **Itzhak Perlman** (vn); **Pittsburgh Symphony Orchestra / André Previn.** EMI CDC7 47167-2 (9/85).

Maddalena Sirmen
Italian 1745-1818

Suggested listening ...

...String Quartets – No. 1 in E flat major; No. 2 in B flat major; No. 3 in G minor; No. 4 in B flat major; No. 5 in F minor; No. 6 in E major. **Allegri Quartet.** Cala CACD1019 (5/95).

Emil Sjögren
Swedish 1853-1918

Suggested listening ...

...Lieder from Wolff's "Tannhäuser", Op. 12 – No. 4, Hab'ein Röslein dir gebrochen; No. 6, Ich möchte schweben. Du schaust mich an mit stummen Fragen. *Coupled with works by* **Rangström, Stenhammar, Peterson-Berger, Sigurd von Koch** and **Alfvén Anne Sofie von Otter** (mez); **Bengt Forsberg** (pf). DG 449 189-2GH (5/96). *See review in the Collections section; refer to the Index to Reviews.* Ⓖ

Nikolaos Skalkottas
Greek 1904-1949

New review

Skalkottas Quartets for Piano and Wind[abc] – No. 1; No. 2. Concertino for Oboe and Piano[a]. Sonata concertante for Bassoon and Piano[b]. Concertino for Trumpet and Piano[c]. [a]**Heinz Holliger** (ob); [b]**Klaus Thunemann** (bn); [c]**Håkan Hardenberger** (tpt); **Bruno Canino** (pf). Philips Ⓔ 442 795-2PH (49 minutes: DDD: 10/95).

One reason why composers of supposedly second rank are so supposed is that their cause has never been taken up by front-rank performers. Or so one often suspects. It's refreshing then to see the Greek Schoenberg-pupil Nikolaos Skalkottas gaining the advocacy of four undoubted virtuosos with proven commitment to unfashionable causes. And they need every ounce of that virtuosity and commitment. Not that Skalkottas asks feats of pyrotechnic agility of them. But his fiercely contrapuntal, acerbic style demands stamina and concentration above and beyond the call of duty. The five pieces recorded here arose from suggestions from colleagues in the Athens State Orchestra around 1940. But the results must have over-faced the players, because the works had to wait until long after Skalkottas's premature death for their first performances. Hindemith, Stravinsky and early-12-note Schoenberg are the obvious influences, to which Skalkottas adds a porcupinal spikiness all his own. There are some telling moments of manic head-spinning pseudo-jazz too, which call to mind the 'Bad Boy of Music', George Antheil. Hearing top-class players meeting these challenges head-on gives much enjoyment, and the close recording suits the brittleness of the music.

Howard Skempton
British 1947-

Suggested listening ...

...Colomen. *Coupled with works by* **N. Hayes, Hallgrimsson, Weir, Finnissy, G. Jackson, S. Harrison, Crane** and **A. Fisher Tapestry.** British Music Label BML012 (12/95). *See review in the Collections section; refer to the Index to Reviews.*

...Lento. **BBC Symphony Orchestra / Mark Wigglesworth.** NMC NMCD005 (6/93).

Julian Slade   British 1930-

Suggested listening ...
...Salad Days. Cast includes **Jamie Dee, Simon Green, Roy Hudd, Leslie Phillips, Tony Slattery, Prunella Scales, Timothy West** and **Willie Rushton.** EMI CDC5 55200-2 (11/94).   ⓖ

Henry Smart   British 1813-1879

Suggested listening ...
...Postlude in D major. Air and Variations and Finale Fugato. Three Andantes – G major; A major; E minor. Minuet in C major. Grand Solemn March in E flat major. **Anne Marsden-Thomas** (org). Priory PRCD368 (9/92).

Bedrich Smetana   Bohemian 1824-1884

Smetana Má vlast. **Czech Philharmonic Orchestra / Rafael Kubelík.** Supraphon ⓕ 11 1208-2 (78 minutes: DDD: 9/91). Recorded live in 1990.   ⓖⓖ
Smetana Má vlast. **Concertgebouw Orchestra / Antál Dorati.** Philips Solo ⓜ 442 641-2PM (79 minutes: DDD: 6/95). Recorded 1987.

Smetana's great cycle of six tone-poems, *Má vlast*, celebrates the countryside and legendary heroes and heroines of Bohemia. It is a work of immense national significance encapsulating many of the ideals and hopes of that country. What a triumphant occasion it was when Rafael Kubelík returned to his native Czechoslovakia and to his old orchestra after an absence of 42 years and conducted *Má vlast* at the 1990 Prague Spring Festival. Supraphon's disc captures that live performance – not perfectly, since the sound is efficient rather than opulent – but well enough to show off what is arguably the finest performance on record since Talich's early LP set. You would never imagine that Kubelík had emerged from five years of retirement and a recent serious illness, such is the power and eloquence of his conducting. Typically he takes a lyrical rather than a dramatic view of the cycle, and if there is strength enough in more heroic sections there is also a refreshing lack of bombast. Kubelík's intimate knowledge of the score (this is his fifth recording of it) shows time and time again in the most subtle touches. Even the weakest parts of the score are most artfully brought to life, and seem of much greater stature than is usually the case. "Vltava" flows beautifully, with the most imaginative flecks of detail, and in "From Bohemia's Woods and Fields" there are vivid visions of wide, open spaces. The orchestra, no doubt inspired by the occasion, reward their former director with superlative playing.

The Concertgebouw Orchestra, vividly directed by Antál Dorati, give a strongly characterized performance of this epic cycle. The romantic opening of "Vyšehrad" benefits from the glowing hall ambience, while "Vltava" builds impressively from the gentle trickling streams to the river's powerful course through the St John's rapids – and how beautifully the Concertgebouw strings sing the main theme. "Sárka", for all its bloodthirsty scenario, never descends into melodrama, "From Bohemia's woods and fields" is gloriously diverse, and the darkly sombre opening of "Tábor" contrasts with the hammered forcefulness of "Blaník", which never becomes bombastic because of the crisply pointed orchestral articulation, while the performance is enhanced by the lovely playing in its enchanting pastoral interlude. Dorati's imaginative grip on this last, wayward 15-minute piece holds the listener throughout all its episodes to the grandiloquent final peroration. The recording is out of Philips's top-drawer.

Additional recommendations ...
...Má vlast. **Vienna Philharmonic Orchestra / James Levine.** DG ⓕ 431 652-2GH (76 minutes: DDD).
...Má vlast – Vltava[a]. **Dvořák** Symphonies[b] – No. 7 in D minor, B141; No. 8 in G major, B163; No. 9 in E minor, B178, "From the New World". The wild dove, B198[c]. [a]**Boston Symphony Orchestra;** [b]**Berlin Philharmonic Orchestra,** [c]**Bavarian Radio Symphony Orchestra / Rafael Kubelík.** DG Double ⓜ 439 663-2GX2 (two discs: 146 minutes: ADD).
...Má vlast. **Royal Liverpool Philharmonic Orchestra / Libor Pešek.** Virgin Classics ⓕ VC7 59576-2 (76 minutes: DDD: 7/90).   ⓖ
...Má vlast. **Czech Philharmonic Orchestra / Václav Talich.** Koch International Legacy mono ⓕ 37032-2* (79 minutes: ADD: 2/91).   ⓖⓖⓖ
...Má vlast. **Israel Philharmonic Orchestra / Walter Weller.** Decca Headline Classics ⓑ 433 635-2DSP (74 minutes: DDD: 1/92).   ⓐ
...Má vlast. **Czech Philharmonic Orchestra / Václav Talich.** Supraphon mono ⓕ 11 1896-2* (74 minutes: ADD: 1/94). *Gramophone classical 100.*   ⓖⓖⓖ
...Má vlast – Vltava[a]. **R. Strauss** Don Juan, Op. 20[b]. Till Eulenspiegels lustige Streiche, Op. 28[b]. Tod und Verklärung, Op. 24[c]. **Vienna Philharmonic Orchestra / Wilhelm Furtwängler.** EMI Références mono ⓜ CDH5 65197-2* (73 minutes: ADD: 10/94).
...Má vlast – Vltava. The bartered bride – Overture; Polka; Furiant; Dance of the Comedians. **Dvořák** Hussite, B132. Romance in F minor, B39[a]. Silent woods, B182[b]. **Fučík** Die lustigen Dorfschmiede, Op. 218. Der alte Brummbär, Op. 210[c]. Einzug der Gladiatoren, Op. 68. **Nedbal**

Valse triste. [a]**Malcolm Stewart** (vn); [b]**Timothy Walden** (vc); [c]**Alan Pendlebury** (bn); **Royal Liverpool Philharmonic Orchestra / Libor Pešek**. Virgin Classics Ⓕ VC7 59285-2 (76 minutes: DDD: 11/94).
…Má vlast. **Polish National Radio Symphony Orchestra / Antoni Wit**. Naxos Ⓢ 8 550931 (80 minutes: DDD: 4/95). *Gramophone Editor's choice*.

New review

Smetana Piano Trio in G minor, B104.
Tchaikovsky Piano Trio in A minor, Op. 50. **Golub Kaplan Carr Trio** (Mark Kaplan, vn; Colin Carr, vc; David Golub, pf). Arabesque Ⓕ Z6661 (75 minutes: DDD: 3/96). Recorded 1994.
The Tchaikovsky trio is well represented on CD with some 17 listings as opposed to a mere half-dozen of the Smetana, but no other version offers them together. The Golub Kaplan Carr Trio give exemplary, well-shaped accounts of both works, which grip the listener with their musicality and unforced, natural eloquence. They perform the Tchaikovsky trio complete without any of the cuts that the composer sanctioned and play it without the slightest overstatement. All three are fine players but when one sees the discography of some cellists (no disrespect intended to any of them), it is puzzling that Colin Carr has not enjoyed greater exposure as a soloist. The recording has great presence and though it may be a bit too forward for some tastes it is still well balanced.

New review

Smetana Má vlast – Vltava. The bartered bride – Overture; Polka[a]; Furiant; Dance of the Comedians. The Kiss – Overture. Libuše – Prelude. The two widows – Overture. [a]**Cleveland Orchestra Chorus; Cleveland Orchestra / Christoph von Dohnányi**. Decca Ⓕ 444 867-2DH (57 minutes: DDD: 2/96). Text and translation included. Recorded 1993-4.
Pride of place must go to the magnificent Overture to *Libuše*, a work that was completed in 1872 but not actually premièred until 1881, two years before Dvořák composed his *Hussite* Overture along vaguely similar lines. The opening brass-and-timpani fanfare anticipates Janáček's *Sinfonietta*, although ensuing incident is more reminiscent of 'Smetana's own *Má vlast* and, especially, Wagner (note the beautiful, *Lohengrin*-style descending passage from 5'27"). Dohnányi effects ideal pacing and tapers a beautifully graded *diminuendo* away from the bold opening (from, say, 1'10"), but the strings are occasionally less than precise – especially at around 4'17". *The two widows* opens somewhat in the manner of late Verdi though the overall flavour is unmistakable, especially at 3'20" where Smetana launches a quietly mischievous fugue over a held bass pedal. Then there is the delightful "Polka" and the lively Overture to *The Kiss*, both prime-cut samplings of Smetana's mature style. *The bartered bride* suite is very nicely done, although synchronization falters momentarily just after 1'00" into the Overture, and don't expect Dohnányi's "Dance of the Comedians" to match Szell's Cleveland recording of 30 years earlier for precision, especially among the strings. In the "Polka", vivid stereophony lends considerable presence to the chorus, who make a very bold entrance: You may feel you have been gatecrashed by a crowd of unannounced guests! "Vltava" is equally effective, what with its stylishly phrased opening, sensitive transitions (especially into the "Peasant's Wedding" episode) and powerful current later on. The sound is resonant and full-bodied, except that important 'hunting' horns are virtually inaudible at 1'46" and some louder climaxes want for detail. Still, this remains an enjoyable programme

---

Smetana The bartered bride. **Gabriela Beňačková** (sop) Mařenka; **Peter Dvorský** (ten) Jeník; **Miroslav Kopp** (ten) Vašk; **Richard Novák** (bass) Kecal; **Jindřich Jindrák** (bar) Krušina; **Marie Mrázová** (contr) Háta; **Jaroslav Horáček** (bass) Mícha; **Marie Veselá** (sop) Ludmila; **Jana Jonášová** (sop) Esmeralda; **Alfréd Hampel** (ten) Circus master; **Karel Hanuš** (bass) Indian; **Czech Philharmonic Chorus and Orchestra / Zdeněk Košler**. Supraphon Ⓕ 10 3511-2 (three discs: 137 minutes: DDD: 10/91). Notes, text and translation included. From 1116 3511 (7/82).
There is something special about a Czech performance of *The bartered bride* and this one is no exception. The hint of melancholy which runs through the work is wonderfully evoked, as well as its marvellous gaiety. Zdeněk Košler has the rhythm and lilt of the music in his bones, like any Czech conductor worth his salt. The Czech Philharmonic has long had one of the finest of all woodwind sections, and especially in this music they play with a sense of their instruments' folk background, with phrasing that springs from deep in Czech folk-music. This sets the musical scene for some moving performances. The warm, lyrical quality of Gabriela Beňačková's voice can lighten easily to encompass her character's tenderness in the first duet, "Věrné milováni", or "Faithful love", the considerable show of spirit she makes when Jeník appears to have gone off the rails. Her Act 1 lament is most beautifully song. Peter Dvorský as Jeník plays lightly with the score, as he should, or the character's maintaining of the deception can come to seem merely cruel. Even old Kecal comes to new life, not as the conventional village bumbler, but as a human character in his own right as Richard Novák portrays him – quite put out, the old boy is, to find his plans gone astray. In fact, all of the soloists are excellent. The chorus enjoy themselves hugely, never more so than in the Beer chorus. Altogether a delightful, touching and warming performance.
Additional recommendation ...
…**Soloists; Prague Radio Chorus and Symphony Orchestra / Karel Ančerl**. Multisonic mono Ⓜ 310185-2* (two discs: 120 minutes: ADD: 9/94).

...The bartered bride – Overture; Dance of the villagers; Polka; Furiant; Fanfare; Dance of the comedians. String Quartet No. 1 in E minor, "From my life" (orch. G. Szell). **London Symphony Orchestra / Geoffrey Simon.** Chandos Ⓕ CHAN8412 (DDD: 8/86).

...Overture. *Coupled with works by* **Wagner, Brahms, Shostakovich** and **R. Strauss The Solti Orchestral Project, Carnegie Hall / Sir Georg Solti.** Decca Ⓕ 444 458-2DH (77 minutes: DDD: 12/95). *See review in the Collections section; refer to the Index to Reviews.*   Ⓖ

...The bartered bride – Overture. **Dvořák** Violin Concerto in A minor, B108[a]. Symphony No. 9 in E minor, B178, "From the New World". [a]**Josef Suk** (vn); **Czech Philharmonic Orchestra / Karel Ančerl.** Orfeo Festspiel Dokumente mono Ⓕ C395951B* (78 minutes: ADD: 4/96).

Smetana Libuše. **Gabriela Beňačková** (sop) Libuše; **Václav Zítek** (ten) Přemysl; **Antonín Svorc** (bass) Chrudoš; **Leo Marian Vodička** (ten) Stáhlav; **Karel Průša** (bass) Lutbor; **René Tuček** (bar) Radovan; **Eva Děpoltová** (sop) Krasava; **Věra Soukupová** (mez) Radmila; **Prague National Theatre Chorus and Orchestra / Zdeněk Košler.** Supraphon Ⓕ 11 1276-2 (three discs: 166 minutes: DDD: 4/94). Notes, text and translation included. Recorded live in 1983.

Libuše is a patriotic pageant, static and celebratory, with such plot as there is concerning the mythical founder of Prague, Libuše, and her marriage to the peasant Přemysl, founder of the first Czech dynasty. Václav Zítek makes a fine, heroic Přemysl; but the triumphant performance comes, as it must, from Gabriela Beňačková. The opera concludes with a series of tableaux in which Libuše prophesies the future kings and heroes who will assure the stability and greatness of the nation. At the end of a long performance her voice is undimmed in its ringing splendour; and earlier, as near the very start, the beauty of her tone and line seeks out all the warmth, character and humanity which she proves to be latent in Smetana's spacious but seemingly plain vocal writing. *Libuše* is scarcely Smetana's greatest opera, as he liked to claim, but especially in so splendid a performance from Beňačková, and under the grave but impassioned direction of Zdeněk Košler, it makes compelling gramophone listening. The live recording includes some applause, but little other audience intervention.

Further listening ...

...Piano Trio in G minor, B104. *Coupled with* **Dvořák** Piano Trio No. 4 in E minor, B166, "Dumky". **Rostislav Dubinsky** (vn); **Yuli Turovsky** (vc); **Luba Edlina** (pf). Chandos CHAN8445 (7/87).

...String Quartets – No. 1 in E minor, "From my life"; No. 2 in D minor. **Lindsay Quartet.** ASV CDDCA777.

...String Quartet No. 1 in E minor, "From my life". *Coupled with* **Dvořák** String Quartet No. 14 in A flat major, B193. **Artis Quartet.** Sony Classical SK53282.

...String Quartet No. 1 in E minor, "From my life". *Coupled with* **Dvořák** String Quartet No. 12 in F major, B179, "American". **Kodály** String Quartet No. 2, Op. 10. **Hollywood Quartet.** Testament mono/stereo SBT1072* (5/96).   Ⓖ

...14 Czech Dances, T112. Bagatelles and Impromptus, B40. **Radoslav Kvapil** (pf). Unicorn-Kanchana DKPCD9139 10/93).   ⒼⒼ

...Three Choruses, T119. *Coupled with works by* **Dvořák, Eben** and **Suk Prague Chamber Choir / Josef Pancik.** Chandos CHAN9257 (12/95). *See review under Eben; refer to the Index to Reviews.*

...The Two Widows. **Soloists; Prague Radio Chorus and Symphony Orchestra / Jaroslav Krombholc.** Praga PR250 022/3 (6/93).

...The Brandenburgers in Bohemia. **Soloists; Prague National Theatre Chorus and Orchestra / Jan Hus Tichý.** Supraphon 11 1804-2 (5/94).

...Macbeth and the Witches. Six Rêves, T112. Trois Polkas de Salon, B94 (Op. 7). Trois Polkas poétiques, B95 (Op. 8). Quatre Souvenirs de Bohème en forme de polka, B115-16 (Opp. 12 and 13). **Radoslav Kvapil** (pf). Unicorn-Kanchana DKPCD9152 (2/95).

...The Devil's Wall. **Soloists; Prague National Theatre Chorus and Orchestra / Zdeněk Chalabala.** Supraphon 11 2201-2 (11/95).

...Dalibor. **Soloists; Prague National Theatre Chorus and Orchestra / Zdeněk Košler.** Supraphon SU0077-2 (12/95).

...The Kiss. **Soloists; Brno Janáček Opera Chorus and Orchestra / František Vajnar.** Supraphon 11 2180-2 (9/95).

Geoff Smith   British 1966-

Suggested listening ...

...The Last of England[a]. Six Wings of Bliss[a]. Possess Me. Fifteen Wild Decembers[a]. The Rainpools Are Happy. Speak of the North[a]. To the Old Place. Summer's Last Will and Testament[a]. [a]**Nicola Walker Smith** (sngr); **Geoff Smith** (kybds). Sony Classical SK66605 (11/95). Includes a bonus CD-single version of Six Wings.

Dame Ethel Smyth

New review

Smyth Concerto for Violin, Horn and Orchestra[a]. Serenade in D major. [a]**Sophie Langdon** (vn);
[a]**Richard Watkins** (hn); **BBC Philharmonic Orchestra / Odaline de la Martinez.** Chandos
Ⓔ CHAN9449 (64 minutes: DDD: 6/96).

This is recommended to those who have yet to discover Dame Ethel Smyth's music. The two works
here come from opposite ends of her composing career and where both of them score over her
opera, *The Wreckers*, is in the extra memorability of the thematic material. The *Serenade* at 35
minutes might have qualified as a full-scale symphony, except that there is no slow movement, and
the middle two movements, more lightly scored than the outer ones, are both rather like interludes,
the first a jolly scherzo with a rumbustious Trio, and the second an *Allegretto grazioso* of the kind
that Brahms often wrote in place of a scherzo. There are other places where Smyth has clearly taken
Brahms as a model, though the writing is more than distinctive enough to establish its own identity.
Written after long years of study in Leipzig and elsewhere, the *Serenade* is a fully mature piece, but
the concerto with its rare solo combination is even more striking, above all more lyrical. After a
grand opening worthy of Elgar, the soloists enter in turn on a broad melody, far more expansively
argued, leading to a third contrasting theme in jolly hornpipe rhythm. The lovely slow movement,
"In Memoriam", again brings warm lyricism, with themes of Brahmsian cut sounding in context
very different from Brahms. The finale starts with jagged writing for the violin, as though Smyth is
finally acknowledging a debt to the twentieth century, while the horn then offers a hunting theme
on rapid triplets. The exuberant mood is disturbed only by a ruminative accompanied cadenza for
the soloists. One problem of the piece is balancing them, with the horn tending to merge in to the
orchestral background far more than the violin. But with opulent recording and superb playing
from both Sophie Langdon and Richard Watkins, not to mention the BBC Philharmonic under de
la Martinez in both works, this is a delightful disc to bring home the strong musical character of
Dame Ethel.

New review

Smyth Violin Sonata in A minor, Op. 7. Cello Sonata in A minor, Op. 5. Piano Trio in D minor.
Chagall Trio (Nicoline Kraamwinkel, vn; Tim Gill, vc; Julian Rolton, pf). Meridian
Ⓔ CDE84286 (74 minutes: DDD: 10/95). Recorded 1993.

These are very fine performances indeed, so fine that it is hard to imagine many people being left in
much doubt of Dame Ethel Smyth's stature, even in her early works. The discovery here, in fact, is one
of the very earliest of them, a piano trio written when she was 22 but which had to wait until 1985
for its first public performance and until 1993 for its British première, by the artists who have now
recorded it. It is Brahmsian, of course – at this stage Smyth worshipped Brahms – but in the charming
variations of the slow movement, the delightful touch of humour that sparks off the coda of the
finale, and a certain willingness throughout to halt or turn aside pensively, an individual voice is
already there. What makes it individual can be immediately recognized at the outset of the Violin
Sonata of only a few years later. Its splendid opening theme is not so much Brahmsian as Brahmsian-
plus: a memorable and touching melody from which an attractive hint of melancholy will later be
distilled. By the time you have heard the Cello Sonata as well you will have heard others like it, and
will be well on the way to recognizing Smyth's own voice. Her tendency to pause in her argument is
not always merely discursive, but an expression of her own fantasy. The Cello Sonata's slow
movement, for example, is based on another most beautiful melody, like a sort of chaconne. It grows
and she passes on to other ideas, but there is real purpose to the melody's eloquent return and its
distillation into the moving, spare coda. The way she fancifully relates the episodes of the rondo finale
of the same sonata is another thing that one begins to recognize as typical Smyth. The Chagall Trio
shrewdly seek out her real qualities: in the Violin Sonata in particular her delicate sensitivity is most
beautifully conveyed. But the other performances are scarcely inferior, and they are all finely
recorded.

Further listening ...

...Violin Sonata in A minor, Op. 7[a]. String Quintet in E major, Op. 1[b]. Cello Sonata in A minor,
Op. 5[c]. String Quartet in E minor[d]. [c]**Friedmann Kupsa** (vn); [bc]**Johanna Varner** (vc); [ac]**Céline
Dutilly** (pf); [bd]**Fanny Mendelssohn Quartet.** Troubadisc TRO-CD03 (6/94).

...Piano Sonatas – No. 1 in C major; No. 2 in F sharp minor; No. 3 in D major. Four Four-Part
Dances. Two Canons. Invention in D major. Suite in E major. To Youth!. Piece in E major.
Variations on an Original Theme in D flat major. Prelude and Fugues – F sharp major; C major.
Liana Serbescu (pf). CPO CPO999 327-2 (3/96).

...Four Songs (1907)[a]. Three Songs (1913)[b]. Horn Trio in A major[c]. **Various soloists.** Troubadisc
TRO-CD01405 (6/94).

Antonio Soler

Soler Quintets – No. 3 in G major; No. 4 in A minor; No. 5 in D major. **Concerto Rococo** (Nicolas
Mazzoleni, Roberto Crisafulli, vns; Nadine Davin, va; Elena Andreyev, vc; Jean-Patrice Brosse,

hpd). Pierre Verany Ⓔ PV792111 (71 minutes: DDD: 4/94). 🎞 Recorded 1992. *Gramophone*
Editor's choice.

Soler's delightful and melodious quintets were written in 1776 – that's to say at the same time as
Mozart's *Haffner* Serenade – for private music-making in the villa near the Escorial (where Soler was
a monk) of the music-loving Infante, Don Gabriel de Borbón. The Hispanicisms that fascinated
Scarlatti, and appear in some of the keyboard sonatas of his disciple Soler, are rarely to be found here:
the style is closer to that of Boccherini, and it is not without significance that the latter was in the
Spanish royal service at the time. What is at once apparent is the vitality of Soler's writing: sparkling
in the G major's first movement and boisterously bucolic in its third; full of agitation in the A minor's
third movement and of fresh invention in its variation finale (in which viola and cello are suddenly
allotted starring roles); fiercely energetic in the D major's second movement (in which there are echoes
of the 'hunting' figures of Scarlatti's Sonata, Kk159) and Haydnesque in its finale. The Concerto
Rococo is an extremely good ensemble with the harpsichord a sweet-toned copy of a Cresci. The
playing is notably neat and crisp throughout and the recording is excellent.

Soler Keyboard Sonatas – No. 36 in C minor; No. 72 in F minor; No. 88 in D flat major; No. 119
in B flat major. Fandango.
D. Scarlatti Keyboard Sonatas – Kk7; Kk84; Kk185; Kk187; Kk193; Kk208; Kk491; Kk492.
Virginia Black (hpd). Cala United Ⓔ 88005-2 (58 minutes: DDD: 8/94). 🎞

This highly recommendable disc is particularly exhilarating, even among a multitude of Scarlatti
recordings. Thought has been given to the order of the sonatas selected, so as to provide a smooth
key-sequence as well as contrasts of mood and pace. Black starts off in fine style with the sturdy
Kk491 Sonata, complete with trumpet tuckets: she shows that it is perfectly possible to maintain strict
time without any danger of sounding mechanical. On the other hand, her slight flexibility for
expressive purposes in Kk208 is judged to a nicety. There is joyousness in Kk492, with its quasi-guitar
thrummings and rushing scales, and noisy high spirits in Kk187; the exuberant vivacity of Kk7 really
needed to be seen – not to check that there was no cheating in the perversely lengthy cross-handed
sections (for who could not trust Virginia Black), but to enjoy the left-hand leaps, as we do the sixths
and thirds of Kk84. The chosen sonatas by Scarlatti's disciple Soler are equally pleasurable. The
chattering repeated notes of No. 88 and the right-hand leaps of tenths in No. 119 are entirely in the
tradition of his mentor: the modulations in the second half of No. 36 and No. 119 point to Soler's
special interest in that subject. (By an unfortunate mis-reading, this latter is billed as *Allegro arioso*
instead of *Allegro airoso*, which is a very different thing.) The only disappointment in the disc is the
amazing and spectacular *Fandango* (which may or may not be by Soler, but is remarkable whoever
wrote it): not only does Virginia Black make numerous cuts in this, but her small inflexions of pace
undermine the relentlessly cumulative drive of the dance rhythm. No details are given of the
harpsichord employed, but it is a fine instrument with a magnificently rich tone.

Additional recommendations ...

...No. 1 in A major; No. 3 in B flat major; No. 24 in D minor; No. 25 in D minor; No. 28 in
C major; No. 29 in C major; No. 30 in G major; No. 31 in G major; No. 96 in E flat major;
No. 118 in A minor. Prelude No. 1 in D minor. **Bob van Asperen** (hpd). Auvidis Astrée Ⓔ E8768
(71 minutes: DDD: 7/92). 🎞

...No. 7 in C major; No. 8 in C major; No. 9 in C major; No. 20 in C sharp minor; No. 21 in
C sharp minor; No. 34 in E major; No. 95 in A major. Prelude No. 3 in C major. **Bob van Asperen**
(hpd). Auvidis Astrée Ⓔ E8769 (68 minutes: DDD: 7/92). 🎞

...No. 10 in B minor; No. 11 in B major; No. 12 in G major, "de la Cordorniz"; No. 13 in G major;
No. 14 in D major; No. 52 in E minor; No. 73 in D major; No. 74 in D major; No. 92 in D major,
"Sonata de clarines"; No. 106 in E minor. Prelude No. 6 in G major. **Bob van Asperen** (hpd).
Auvidis Astrée Ⓔ E8780 (69 minutes: DDD: 7/92). 🎞

...No. 37 in D major; No. 46 in C major; No. 56 in F major; No. 98 in B flat major; No. 100 in
C minor; No. 103 in C minor; No. 108 in C major, "del Gallo"; No. 109 in F major; No. 112 in
C major. Fandango. Prelude No. 5 in D major. **Bob van Asperen** (hpd). Auvidis Astrée Ⓔ E8771
(77 minutes: DDD: 7/92). 🎞

...No. 15 in D minor; No. 22 in D flat major; No. 23 in D flat major; No. 54 in D minor; No. 61 in
C major; No. 75 in F major; No. 76 in F major; No. 80 in G minor; No. 81 in G minor; No. 84 in
D major; No. 86 in D major. **Bob van Asperen** (hpd). Auvidis Astrée Ⓔ E8772 (70 minutes:
DDD: 7/92). 🎞

...No. 18 in C minor; No. 19 in C minor; No. 26 in E minor; No. 27 in E minor; No. 36 in C minor;
No. 85 in F sharp minor; No. 90 in F sharp minor; No. 91 in C major. No. 94 in G major. **Bob
van Asperen** (hpd). Auvidis Astrée Ⓔ E8773 (75 minutes: DDD: 7/92). 🎞

...No. 18 in C minor; No. 19 in C minor; No. 41 in E flat major; No. 72 in F minor. No. 78 in
F sharp minor; No. 84 in D major; No. 85 in F sharp minor; No. 86 in
D major; No. 88 in D flat major; No. 90 in F sharp major. Fandango. **Maggie Cole** (hpd).
Virgin Classics Veritas Ⓜ VER5 61220-2 (71 minutes: DDD: 1/96). 🎞

Further listening ...

...Canzonettas – La semplice; La volubile; La costanza; La mercede. *Coupled with works by*
Carulli, Giuliani, Sor and **Mertz** Marta Almajano (sop); **José Miguel Moreno** (gtr). Glossa
GCD920202 (2/96). *See review in the Collections section; refer to the Index to Reviews.*

Stephen Sondheim

Sondheim Passion. **Original Broadway cast** (with Donna Murphy, Jere Shea, Marin Mazzie, sngrs) **/ Paul Gemignani.** EMI Broadway Classics Ⓟ CDQ5 55251-2 (57 minutes: DDD: 12/95). Notes and text included. Recorded 1994. Ⓖ

Passion is effectively a musical without songs. The notes describe it as a "rhapsody on the theme of love" – and that is what it is, a rhapsody on the power of love unconditional, that most potent of all life-forces. The piece, like the emotions it chronicles, is more complex, more intricate than it might at first seem. Sondheim has a way of deploying thematic ideas so that they subliminally play on our senses: sometimes he's blatant (the *Leitmotif* principle), sometimes he goes for the subtle derivation. But *Passion*'s musical imperative is in the dream-like current of its narrative. It is at once the most febrile and effulgently lyrical of Sondheim. At its heart is a powerful and recurrent juxtaposition. Sondheim plants it right there at the opening. The clatter of military drum and shriek of dissonant winds rapidly dissolve into gentle palpitations – post-coital rhythms. The two principal love themes emerge and bond, ravishing creations, both, the latter "God, you are so beautiful" graced with an exquisite ornateness in the phrase "I love to see you in the light". Clara and Giorgio (the excellent Marin Mazzie and Jere Shea) physically, vocally, musically entwine. The drums invade once more. Love and War – backdrop and metaphor: fierce emotions, passion running high. It is remarkable that the work manages to see-saw our emotions between irritation at the sickly, self-pitying Fosca (the third and most potent force in the love triangle) and overwhelming compassion for her. One of the show's most electrifying and unsettling scenes comes with a letter she dictates to Giorgio. But it's a letter to herself *from* Giorgio, a fantasy in which she presumes to read his heart and mind. It is, of course, deeply prophetic. Sondheim gives Fosca the most hauntingly elusive of themes, a consumptive Chopinesque plaint (minor key, of course), heard first on distant piano but soon impatient for the oboe. Donna Murphy's extraordinary voice (a husky alto colour which belongs among the cellos) plumbs the depths of her melancholy: on her very first entrance, a bass clarinet accompanies her into shadow. The scoring throughout is most seductive (the 15-piece pit band gets 26 extra strings for the recording). This composer must adore Ravel. It's the fastidiousness, the harmonic luminosity that gives him away. There is some beautiful music in *Passion* – vocal lines that really do take wing. But equally, much – too much? – that is greyly recitative-like in character. Add to this the Sondheim mannerisms, the familiar rhythmic and intervallic tics that now and then begin to get to you ... . Then again, Sondheim just wouldn't be Sondheim without them.

Further listening ...

...Follies. **Original Broadway cast.** EMI Angel ZDM7 64666-2

...Into the Woods. **Original London cast.** RCA Victor RD60752 (9/91). *Gramophone Award Winner 1991.*

...Sunday in the Park with George. **Original Broadway cast.** RCA Victor RD85042 (7/90).

...Pacific Overtures. **English National Opera.** That's Entertainment CDTER2 1152 (8/88).

...Anyone Can Whistle – There won't be trumpets. Saturday Night – What more do I need? The Girls of Summer – The Girls of Summer. Merrily We Roll Along – Like it was. Evening Primrose – Take me to the world. *Coupled with works by* **Blitzstein, Weill** and **Bernstein** Dawn Upshaw (sop); **orchestra / Eric Stern.** Elektra Nonesuch 7559-79345-2 (12/94). *Gramophone Award Winner 1995. See review in the Collections section; refer to the Index to Reviews.* ⒼⒼ

...Company. **Original London cast.** Sony West End SMK53496.

Fernando Sor

New review

Sor Fantaisies – No. 12, Op. 58; No. 13, Op. 59, "Fantaisie elégiaque". Studies, Op. 60. **Nicholas Goluses** (gtr). Naxos Ⓢ 8 553342 (65 minutes: DDD: 8/96).

New review

Sor Grand Sonatas – C major, Op. 22; C major, Op. 25. Divertissement, Op. 23. Eight Short Pieces, Op. 24. **Adam Holzman** (gtr). Naxos Ⓢ 8 553340 (75 minutes: DDD: 8/96).

Sor's guitar works is an *oeuvre* the most consistent in quality, and most manageable in quantity of any major guitar composer of the period. At that time the styles of guitar composers lagged behind the leading edge, so that whilst Sor was born and died later than Beethoven his language was closer to that of Mozart, barely on the edge of romanticism. He was a polished and elegant composer, whose works have more quiet emotional content and expressiveness than those of any of his contemporaries, and though he often calls for technical virtuosity he doesn't lean too heavily on it. The *Fantaisie* Op. 58 is not one of Sor's more riveting works. Goluses plays it in a somewhat matter-of-fact way. The *Fantaisie elégiaque*, arguably Sor's finest single work, elicits a very different response from Goluses, a deeply sensitive and dignified reading in which the moments of silent grief are given the breathing-space and time they call for. Sor devoted five opus numbers to his 97 studies, of which Op. 60 was the last. Each has a clear technical and/or musical purpose and even the simplest is lovingly crafted music – which is how Goluses treats it, with lots of care lavished on it. It should be remembered that the guitar of Sor's time differed from today's in construction, stringing and sound, and that Sor played without using the right-hand nails. Goluses uses a modern instrument and plays with nails, which inevitably leads to differences in sound and, to some extent, interpretation. Given and accepting the differences, Goluses sets a bench-mark for present-day guitarists.

The major works in Holzman's programme are the two sonatas, each with four movements. Of these Op. 25 is by far the finer – and the best work of its kind from the period; the last movement is a Minuet, a final lightening of the atmosphere that was not then uncommon. The *Divertissement*, Op. 23 contains ten pieces – *Valses*, *Allegrettos*, *Andantes*, a *Minuetto* and an *Allemande*. With a few exceptions they are, like the studies, more likely to be of interest to guitarists than to the general listener. Holzman plays very well, with a softer sound than Goluses, and in a tighter acoustic. At slower tempos he exercises a pleasing degree of rubato and commendable dynamic shading; one wishes he had done likewise in the quicker ones, which incline to the metronomic. These are two discs that should, both in their own right and at super-budget price, be irresistible to guitarists.

Additional recommendation ...
...Fantasia élégiaque, Op. 59. Introduction and Variations on a Theme by Mozart, Op. 9. Etudes – Op. 6 No. 11; Op. 31 No. 12; Op. 35 No. 22. **Coste** Pièces originales, Op. 53 – No. 1, Rêverie. Morceaux episodiques, Op. 23 – No. 7, Les soirées d'Auteuil. Grande sérénade, Op. 30. **Raphaëlla Smits** (gtr). Accent Ⓕ ACC29182D (61 minutes: DDD: 8/93).

Further listening ...
...Minuet, Op. 11 No. 6. Studies, Op. 6 – No. 6 in A major; No. 9 in D minor; No. 11 in E major; No. 12 in A major. Etude in A major, Op. 31 No. 19. Etudes, Op. 35 – No. 13 in C major; No. 17 in D major; No. 22 in E minor. Minuetto, Op. 22. *Coupled with works by* **Aguado** *and* **Tárrega Norbert Kraft** (gtr). Naxos 8 553007 (1/95).
...(ed. P. Romero) Fantasía in D minor. *Coupled with* **Tárrega** (arr. P. Romero) Gran Jota. **Albéniz** (arr. C. Romero) Torre Bermeja, Op. 92 No. 12. **Granados** Tonadillas al estilo antiguo – No. 7, La maja de Goya[a]. **Mudarra** Tres libros – Fantasía que contrahaze la harpa en la manera de Ludovico[a]. **Guerau** Canarios[a]. **Milán** El Maestro – Fantasia XVI[a]. **Turina** Guitar Sonata, Op. 61. **Falla** Homenaje, "Le tombeau de Claude Debussy". **Rodrigo** Por tierras de Jerez. **Moreno Torroba** Aires de la Mancha. **C. Romero** Los Maestros. **Pepe Romero** (gtr). Philips 442 150-2PH (4/95). Items marked [a] trans. P. Romero.
...Thèmes variés et Douze Minuets, Op. 11 – Andante maestoso; Andante expressivo[b]. Introduction and Variations on a theme by Mozart, Op. 9[b]. *Coupled with* **Sanz** Instruccion de musica sobre la guitarra española – Canarios; Folías; Lantururú; Pavanas al ayre español[b]. **Guerau** Poema harmonico – Canario; Marionas[b]. **Murcia** Cumbés[b]. Giga[b]. **Mudarra** Tres libros de música en cifras para vihuela – Pavana de Alexandre; Fantasia que contrahaze la harpa en la manera de Ludovico[a]. **Milán** El Maestro – Pavana II[a]. **López** Fantasia[a]. **Narváez** Los seys libros del delphin – La canción del Emperador; Diferencias on "Guárdame las vacas"[a]. Paseavase el rey moro[a]. **José Miguel Moreno** ([a]vihuela/[b]gtr). Glossa GCD920103 (8/95). ✍
...Studies, Op. 31 – Mouvement de prière religieuse. Ariettas – Povero cor t'inganni; Lagrime; Io mentitor!; Perduta l'anima. Nel cor più non mi sento. Seguidillas – Muchacha, y los vergüenza; Si dices que mis ojos; Los canonigos, madre; Las mujeres y cuerdas; Mis descuidados ojos. *Coupled with works by* **Giuliani, Carulli, Soler** *and* **Mertz Marta Almajano** (sop); **José Miguel Moreno** (gtr). Glossa GCD920202 (2/96). *See review in the Collections section; refer to the Index to Reviews.*

Kaikhosru Shapurji Sorabji   British 1892-1988

New review
Sorabji Gulistān. **Charles Hopkins** (pf). Altarus (special price) AIR-CD-9036 (35 minutes: DDD: 4/96). Recorded 1994.
Gulistān ("The Rose Garden") dates from 1940 and is cast in a single movement lasting some 35 minutes, deriving inspiration from a Sufi text of the same name by the poet Sa'dī of Shīrāz. Not a programmatic representation of the text it is rather, as Charles Hopkins states in his own illuminating and extremely detailed booklet-notes, "a richly evocative response to the many layers on which the text operates, [and] through its meditative serenity we are brought closer to a higher level of consciousness". The sound-world, like *Le jardin parfumé* of 1923, is a heady, intoxicating brew that has much in common with the late piano music of Scriabin and is saturated in sensuality, yet at the same time somnambulistically sure-footed. Despite its florid, improvisatory, drifting quality the piece is exceptionally difficult to perform, though Charles Hopkins makes it sound deceptively easy as he delivers a most ravishing account of this extraordinary work. The recorded sound is generally very fine, though at times there is an audible knocking noise from the sustaining pedal that really should have been spotted and dealt with before recording. Nevertheless, a thoroughly rewarding and recommendable disc.

Sorabji Quaere reliqua hujus materiei inter secretiora. St Bertrand de Comminges, "He was laughing in the tower". Toccatinetta sopra C.G.F. Sutra sul nome dell'amico Alexis. Sutra "per il caro amico quasi Nipote – Alexis". Passeggiata arlecchinesca sopra un frammento di Busoni. **Donna Amato** (pf). Altarus Ⓕ AIR-CD-9025 (68 minutes: DDD: 4/95). Recorded 1994.
This is a very impressive achievement, distinguished by perceptive performances. The name of Kaikhosru Sorabji is far more widely known than his music, the celebrated *Opus clavicembalisticum*

(magnificently recorded by the late John Ogdon on the same label, listed below) notwithstanding. None of the works on this issue is on anything remotely approaching the same scale or complexity; indeed, the *Toccatinetta* aside, they are untypical of compositions recorded hitherto, such as the *Fantaisie espagnole* or *Le jardin parfumé. Quaere reliqua hujus materiei inter secretiora* ("Seek the rest of this Matter among the More Private Things", 1940) is the third of a group of four short piano works ('short' here meaning around 20 minutes' duration). It and *St Bertrand de Comminges*, completed in 1941, derived their inspiration from the ghost stories of M.R. James (1862-1936), though neither is programmatic as such. While the two *Sutras* (1981-84) are tiny, aphoristic miniatures lasting less than a minute each, *Passeggiata arlecchinesca* (1981-82) is on a similar scale to *Quaere reliqua*. Here, though, the source work is a musical one – Busoni's *Rondo arlecchinesca*. Sorabji retained a deep respect for the German-Italian all his life and it shows in this piece written nearly six decades after Busoni's death. Donna Amato's interpretations are formed through considerable knowledge. There is an excellent illustrated booklet.

Further listening ...

...Piano Sonata No. 1. **Marc-André Hamelin** (pf). Altarus AIR-CD-9050 (5/91). ⓖ

...Opus clavicembalisticum. **John Ogdon** (pf). Altarus AIR-CD-9075 (9/89). ⓖⓖ

...Fantaisie espagnole. **Donna Amato** (pf). Altarus AIR-CD-9022 (7/93). ⓖ

...Le jardin parfumé. **Yonty Solomon** (pf). Altarus AIR-CD-9037 (7/93). ⓖ

John Sousa
American 1854-1932

Suggested listening ...

...Fennell conducts Sousa. Sound Off. Nobles of the Mystic Shrine. Sabre and Spurs. The Picadore. Our Flirtation. The High School Cadets. The Invincible Eagle. Bullets and Bayonets. The Liberty Bell. Riders for the Flag. Solid Men to the Front. The Gallant Seventh. The Rifle Regiment. The Pride of the Wolverines. Golden Jubilee. The Gridiron Club. New Mexico. Sesqui-Centennial Exposition. The Black Horse Troop. The Kansas Wildcats. Manhattan beach. Ancient and Honorable Artillery Company (of Boston). The National Game. The Glory of the Yankee Navy. **Eastman Wind Ensemble / Frederick Fennell.** Mercury Living Presence 434 300-2MM.

Michael Spivakovsky
British 1919-1983

Suggested listening ...

...Harmonica Concerto. *Coupled with works by* **Arnold, Farnon, Moody** and **Villa-Lobos** Tommy Reilly (harmonica); **Munich Radio Orchestra / Charles Gerhardt.** Chandos CHAN9248 (5/94).

Louis Spohr
German 1784-1859

New review

Spohr Nonet in F major, Op. 31. Octet in E major, Op. 32. Waltz in A major, Op. 89, "Erinnerung an Marienbad". **Academy of St Martin in the Fields Chamber Ensemble.** Philips ⓕ 438 017-2PH (74 minutes: DDD: 11/95). Recorded 1992.

Spohr's two most popular chamber works go well together, here in performances that come closer to a lyrical, reflective, even sometimes wistful manner than the more extrovert style of the Nash Ensemble. Theirs was friendly chamber music playing in a comparatively light context; the Academy suggest greater depths, sometimes at the expense of the music's gaiety in the faster movements. The finale of the Octet can sound livelier than on this disc, and perhaps should, though there is at least consistency with all that has gone before; and the 'Harmonious Blacksmith' depicted in the variation movement is a more melancholy fellow than Handel surely intended. But the playing is thoughtful and well-judged, not only in matters of living ensemble (something more than merely timing) but in exploring and bringing to life the music through a flexible and sensitive application of its form. So the first movements of both works come off well as sonata structures as powerful and supple as Spohr must have intended, which will doubtless give these performances lasting satisfaction. The sound is well-balanced, with a proper attention to the rich middle registers. As a *bonne bouche*, there is the waltz which he wrote in salon manner for the typical spa ensemble of the day. It is amiable recreation music, just the thing to accompany the sipping of the waters on a sunlit terrace. Spohr was unnecessarily apologetic about it when he first heard it in 1834, having composed it, one can hardly avoid saying, last year in Marienbad.

Additional recommendations ...

...Nonet. Octet. **Gaudier Ensemble.** Hyperion ⓕ CDA66699 (61 minutes: DDD: 8/94).

...Nonet. Octet. **Nash Ensemble.** CRD ⓕ CRD3354 (56 minutes: ADD: 3/89).

New review

Spohr Piano Trios – No. 3 in A minor, Op. 124; No. 4 in B flat major, Op. 133. **Borodin Trio**
(Rostislav Dubinsky, vn; Laszlo Varga, vc; Luba Edlina, pf). Chandos Ⓕ CHAN9372
(66 minutes: DDD: 10/95). Recorded 1994.

Spohr's late piano trios are virtuoso works, in every sense. They are ingeniously composed and are
difficult to balance with true effect; above all they demand great technical dexterity, and the dexterity
to allow many extremely difficult passages to play a secondary or supporting role. In particular
No. 3 in A minor places demands on the players which need virtuosity of the kind which the Borodin
Trio are well able to provide. Their skills need no recommendation by now; here, they also have a
subtlety and quickness of response that come from a proper sympathy with Spohr's idiom. They rise
to the occasion with, for instance, the racing piano fingerwork in the Variations of No. 3; they also
respond with the flexibility of tempo the music needs for its full expressive effect. Moreover, in places
where Spohr seems to have lost concentration for a moment or two – his capacity to meander down
beguiling but distracting chromatic paths, his habit of striking a cliché chord like a dramatic attitude,
his gear-changing modulations – the Borodin hold faith and make the music come off effectively. The
A minor Trio is the more worthwhile piece, and deserves all this interpretative concentration; but the
rather less well-invented work in B flat, apparently here receiving a first recording, is worth having for
some pleasant and recreational music. The recording team cannot always have had an easy task with
balance; it all works excellently.

Additional recommendation ...

...Piano Trios – No. 3 in A minor, Op. 124; No. 5 in G minor, Op. 142. **Hartley Piano Trio.** Naxos
Ⓢ 8 553164 (62 minutes: DDD: 1/96).

New review

Spohr Duos concertants, Op. 67 – No. 1 in A minor; No. 2 in D major; No. 3 in A minor. **Heinz
Schunk, Ulrike Petersen** (vns). CPO Ⓕ CPO999 343-2 (51 minutes: DDD: 3/96). Recorded 1994.

Renewed teaching activities, and the exceptional abilities of his students Ferdinand David and Fredrik
Pacius, inspired Spohr to return to the violin duet in 1824, after a gap of eight years. However, as this
issue proves, the three *Duos concertants*, Op. 67 are more than mere teaching pieces. Schunk's and
Petersen's mix of deliciously clear counterpoint and dramatically potent lyricism in the opening
Allegro, rich tone in the *Andante* and carefree exuberance in the finale, confirm that this is first-rate
chamber music. The second piece displays what Rochlitz described as Spohr's "inclination to the
grand". Here, Schunk and Petersen give an enthralling account of the first movement, winningly
conveying the 'symphonic' breadth of Spohr's conception. They luxuriate in the *Larghetto*'s
emotionally rich, romantic language (often simulating larger forces), and conclude with tautly sprung
rhythms in the lively finale. The last piece offers a further opportunity to enjoy Schunk's and
Petersen's expert blend of warm sensitivity and engagingly athletic virtuosity. Excellently recorded,
this fascinating disc will have wide appeal.

Further listening ...

...Symphonies – No. 1 in E flat major, Op. 20; No. 5 in C minor, Op. 102. **Košice State Philharmonic
Orchestra / Alfred Walter.** Marco Polo 8 223363.

...Clarinet Concerto No. 1 in C minor, Op. 26[a]. *Coupled with works by* **Mozart** and **Weber** Ernst
Ottensamer (cl/[a]basset cl); **Vienna Philharmonic Orchestra / Sir Colin Davis.** Philips 438 868-2PH
(6/94). *See review under Mozart; refer to the Index to Reviews.*

...Septet in A minor, Op. 147[b]. *Coupled with* **Beethoven** Quintet for Piano and Wind in
E flat major, Op. 16[a]. [b]Chantal Juillet (vn); [b]Christopher van Kampen (vc); Pascal Rogé (pf);
London Winds. Decca 443 892-2DH (4/96). *See review under Beethoven; refer to the Index
to Reviews.*

...String Quintet in A minor, Op. 91. String Sextet in C major, Op. 140. Potpourri on themes of
Mozart in B flat major, Op. 22. **Academy of St Martin in the Fields Chamber Ensemble.** Chandos
CHAN9424 (4/96).

...Double Quartet in D minor, Op. 65. String Sextet, Op. 140. String Quintet in G major, Op. 33
No. 2. **L'Archibudelli** and **Smithsonian Chamber Players.** Sony Classical Vivarte SK53370
(4/94). ✍

...Fantasia in C minor, Op. 35. *Coupled with works by* **Rosetti, Debussy, Casella, Damase,
Tournier, Prokofiev, Renié** and **Fauré** Naoko Yoshino (hp). Philips 446 064-2PH (2/96).
See review in the Collections section; refer to the Index to Reviews.

...Sechs Lieder, Op. 103. Faust – Ich bin allein. Variations in B flat major on a Theme from
"Alruna". *Coupled with works by* **Mozart, Müller** and **Paer** Elizabeth Ritchie (sop); Victoria
Soames (cl); **Anna Coleman** (vn); **Matthew Souter** (va); **Alastair Blayden** (vc); **Jennifer Purvis** (pf).
Clarinet Classics CC0006 (3/94).

...Jessonda. **Soloists; Hamburg State Opera Chorus; Hamburg Philharmonic Orchestra / Gerd
Albrecht.** Orfeo C240912H (11/91).

...Faust. **Soloists; Bielefeld Opera Chorus; Bielefeld Philharmonic Orchestra / Geoffrey Moull.** CPO
CPO999 247-2 (8/94).

...Faust. **Soloists; Stuttgart Radio Chorus; Kaiserslautern Radio Orchestra / Klaus Arp.** Capriccio
60 049-2 (12/94).

Sir John Stainer
British 1840-1901

...The Crucifixion. Come, Thou long-expected Jesus. I saw the Lord. **Richard Lewis** (ten); **Owen Brannigan** (bass); **St John's College Choir, Cambridge / George Guest.** Decca Headline 436 146-2DSP.

Jan Stamitz
Bohemian 1717-1757

C. Stamitz Symphonies – F major, Op. 24 No. 3; Op. 13 – No. 4 in G major; No. 5 in C major; D major, "La chasse". **London Mozart Players / Matthias Bamert.** Chandos Ⓕ CHAN9358 (62 minutes: DDD: 5/95). Recorded 1994.

Besides showing Stamitz's flair for melody and effective use of contrast, the London Mozart Players are responsive to the touches of genuine originality in these pieces. Try the first movement of the C major Symphony, Op. 13 No. 5, where the slow introduction ingeniously returns as a coda, or the textural variety in the G major Symphony, Op. 13 No. 4, where flutes replace oboes in the outer movements, while the second movement, in which the LMP elegantly convey the music's spaciousness, is scored for strings and continuo alone. Bamert's firm, sympathetic direction is also evident in the F major Symphony, Op. 24 No. 3, where the second and third movements are particularly effective for the subtlety with which the LMP defuse the slow movement's dramatic intensity, with delightfully buoyant playing in the work's radiantly cheerful finale. The programmatic symphony, *La chasse* is the highlight of the disc. In this remarkable work, the declamatory character of the slow introduction gives way to operatic brilliance in the subsequent *Allegro*, and the slow movement's graceful stateliness culminates in a vividly descriptive portrayal of the hunt in the finale. These stylish performances make a strong case for a comprehensive recorded survey of this repertoire.

Further listening ...
...Sinfonia concertante in D major, Kaiser 19[c]. *Coupled with* **Dittersdorf** Sinfonia concertante in D major[a]. **Haydn** Sinfonia concertante in B flat major, HobI/105[b]. [b]**Jan Kolar** (ob); [b]**František Herman** (bn); [bc]**Oldřich Vlček** (vn); [ac]**Josef Suk** (va); [b]**František Host** (vc); [a]**Jiři Hudeč** (db); **Virtuosi di Praga / Rudolf Krecmer.** Koch International Classics DICD920274 (12/95).
...Trumpet Concerto in D major (realized Boustead). *Coupled with works by* **Hummel, Hertel** and **Haydn Håkan Hardenberger** (tpt); **Academy of St Martin in the Fields / Sir Neville Marriner.** Philips 420 203-2PH (12/87). *See review in the Collections section; refer to the Index to Reviews.*
...Viola Sonata in B flat major. *Coupled with* **Hummel** Viola Sonata in E flat major, Op. 5 No. 3. **Dittersdorf** Viola Sonata in E flat major. **Vanhal** Viola Sonata in E flat major. **Anna Barbara Duetschler** (va); **Ursula Duetschler** (fp). Claves CD50-9502 (11/95). ✍

Alexey Stanchinsky
USSR 1888-1914

...Piano Sonatas – E flat minor; No. 1 in F major; No. 2 in G major. Three Sketches. 12 Sketches. **Daniel Blumenthal** (pf). Marco Polo 8 223424 (11/94).

Charles Villiers Stanford
Irish/British 1852-1924

Stanford Symphony No. 3 in F minor, "Irish", Op. 28[a].
Elgar Scenes from the Bavarian Highlands, Op. 27[b]. [b]**Bournemouth Symphony Chorus; Bournemouth Sinfonietta / Norman Del Mar.** EMI British Composers Ⓜ CDM5 65129-2 (70 minutes: ADD: 7/95). Text included. Item marked [a] from HMV ASD4221 (8/82), [b]ASD4061 (9/81). Recorded 1981-82.

A valuable addition to the catalogue on its initial appearance, Norman Del Mar's characteristically enterprising 1982 recording of Stanford's *Irish* Symphony re-emerges in splendidly vital fashion on this beautifully presented release. Compared with Vernon Handley and the excellent Ulster Orchestra, Del Mar is perhaps just a touch lacking in charm and it is undoubtedly the former who more effectively minimizes the element of dutiful convention which occasionally afflicts both outer movements (Handley is nearly three minutes quicker in the opening *Allegro moderato*, yet there is no feeling of undue haste). However, Del Mar draws the threads together most satisfyingly for the symphony's ample peroration, and his Bournemouth band respond with commendable vigour throughout. Preceding the Stanford here is a rare outing for the orchestral version of Elgar's *Scenes from the Bavarian Highlands*. This six-movement choral suite shows Elgar at his most carefree and joyous, qualities savoured to the full in Del Mar's exuberant, nicely disciplined performance. A thoroughly enjoyable reissue.

Additional recommendation ...
...No. 3. Irish Rhapsody No. 5 in G minor, Op. 147. **Ulster Orchestra / Vernon Handley.** Chandos Ⓕ CHAN8545 (56 minutes: DDD: 1/88).

Stanford Morning and Evening Services – B flat major, Op. 10; C major, Op. 115. Benedictus and Agnus Dei in F major. **Durham Cathedral Choir / James Lancelot** with **Keith Wright** (org). Priory Ⓕ PRCD437 (80 minutes: DDD: 4/94). Recorded 1992.   Ⓖ

The mastery of composition is there for all to see. Moreover, it is seen with all the greater clarity when the opus is performed complete, as here. Excellent notes tell in outline of the evidence which could be amassed in a much longer study of the unity of these works, the thematic material and detailed cross-reference which bind the individual numbers into a work of art; and that is the special function of the record. The Choir of Durham Cathedral are fresh-toned and homogeneous in sound, stylish in phrasing and nuance, precise in attack and articulation. Exemplary, too, is the work of the organist, especially in Op. 115 where Stanford appears to be thinking so much more in terms of orchestration. The balance between organ and choir is effective.

Further listening ...

...Piano Concerto No. 1 in G major, Op. 59. *Coupled with* **Parry** Piano Concerto in F sharp major. **Piers Lane** (pf); **BBC Scottish Symphony Orchestra / Martyn Brabbins.** Hyperion CDA66820 (2/96). *See review under Parry; refer to the Index to Reviews.*

...Clarinet Concerto in A minor, Op. 80. *Coupled with* **Finzi** Clarinet Concerto in C minor, Op. 31. **Thea King** (cl); **Philharmonia Orchestra / Alun Francis.** Hyperion CDA66001 (6/87).

...Symphony No. 1 in B flat major. Irish Rhapsody No. 2 in F minor, Op. 84, "Lament for the son of Ossian". **Ulster Orchestra / Vernon Handley.** Chandos CHAN9049 (10/92).

...Symphony No. 2 in D minor, "Elegiac". Clarinet Concerto in A minor, Op. 80[a]. [a]**Janet Hilton** (cl); **Ulster Orchestra / Vernon Handley.** Chandos CHAN8991 (1/92).

...Symphony No. 4 in F major, Op. 31. Irish Rhapsody No. 6, Op. 191[a]. Oedipus tyrannus, Op. 29 – Prelude. [a]**Lydia Mordkovitch** (vn); **Ulster Orchestra / Vernon Handley.** Chandos CHAN8884 (3/91).

...Serenade (Nonet) in F major, Op. 95. *Coupled with* **Parry** Nonet in B flat major. **Capricorn.** Hyperion CDA66291 (9/89).

...Piano Trio No. 2 in G minor, Op. 73. *Coupled with works by* **Holst** *and* **Bax Pirasti Trio.** ASV CDDCA925 (9/95). *See review under Bax; refer to the Index to Reviews.*

...Fantasia and Toccata in D minor, Op. 57. *Coupled with works by* **Reger, Shostakovich, Schmidt** *and* **Ravanello** Keith John (org). Priory PRCD370 (11/92). *See review in the Collections Section; refer to the Index to Reviews.*   ⒼⒼⒼ

...Complete Organ Sonatas – No. 1 in F major, Op. 149; No. 2 in G minor, Op. 151, "Sonata Eroica"; No. 3 in D minor, Op. 152, "Britannia"; No. 4 in C minor, Op. 153, "Celtica"; No. 5 in A major, Op. 159, "Quasi una fantasia". Six Short Preludes and Postludes – Set 2, Op. 105. **Desmond Hunter** (org). Priory PRCD445 (9/94).

...Evening Service in A major, Op. 12[a]. *Coupled with works by* **S. Watson, G. Ives, Gibbons, Leighton, Howells** *and* **Dyson** Lichfield Cathedral Choir / Andrew Lumsden with **Mark Shepherd.** Priory PRCD505 (10/95). *See review in the Collections section; refer to the Index to Reviews.*

...Services in A major, Op. 12. Services in G major, Op. 81. **Durham Cathedral Choir / James Lancelot** with **Keith Wright** (org). Priory PRCD514 (6/95).

...Three Motets, Op. 38 – Justorum animae; Coelos ascendit hodie; Beati quorum via. *Coupled with* **Martin** Mass for Double Chorus. **Duruflé** Four Motets sur des thèmes grégoriens, Op. 10. **Górecki** Totus tuus, Op. 60. **Byron** Verba. [a]**Rebecca Outram** (sop); **Schola Cantorum, Oxford / Jeremy Summerly.** Proud Sound PROUCD129 (4/92).

John Stanley   British 1712-1786

Suggested listening ...

...Organ Concertos, Op. 10 – No. 1 in E major; No. 2 in D major; No. 3 in B flat major; No. 4 in C minor; No. 5 in A major; No. 6 in C major. **Northern Sinfonia / Gerald Gifford** (org). CRD CRD3365 (10/92).

...Voluntaries – A minor, Op. 6 No. 2; D minor, Op. 7 No. 4; G major, Op. 7 No. 9. *Coupled with works by* **Boyce, Handel, Heron, Hook, Russell, Stubley** *and* **S. Wesley** Jennifer Bate (org). Unicorn-Kanchana DKPCD9106 (11/91). *Selected by Sounds in Retrospect. See review in the Collections section; refer to the Index to Reviews.*   Ⓖ

Agostino Steffani   Italian 1654-1728

New review

Steffani Stabat mater.
Biber Requiem a 15 in A major[a]. **Marta Almajano, Mieke van der Sluis** (sops); **John Elwes, Mark Padmore** (tens); [a]**Frans Huijts** (bar); **Harry van der Kamp** (bass); **Chorus and Baroque Orchestra of the Dutch Bach Association / Gustav Leonhardt.** Deutsche Harmonia Mundi Ⓕ 05472 77344-2 (64 minutes: DDD: 8/96). Texts and translations included.

In his intimate and contemplative setting of the *Stabat mater*, Agostino Steffani matches the text with grief-stricken vocal declamation and agonized string suspensions. The scoring, as we should expect, is much more modest and subdued than that required for Biber's Requiem; Steffani calls for six vocal strands, six string parts and an organ. Comparatively small in scale it may be, but its emotional content is at least as affecting as Biber's more public demonstration of the Catholic faith. Leonhardt has picked a fine ensemble of vocalists from among whom the contribution of Marta Almajano (track 8) and Mieke van der Sluis (track 13) are particularly enjoyable. Biber's Requiem may well have been performed at the funeral in 1687 of his employer, Max Gandolph von Khuenberg, Archbishop of Salzburg. The two pieces on this disc are strikingly different in character – that much at least is suggested by Biber's choice of key – the F minor, melancholy and contemplative, the A major sonorous, stirring and noble. These qualities are at once encountered in the work's richly colourful opening, "Requiem aeternam dona eis" and to an even greater extent in the wrathful "Dies irae". This is a splendid section which inspires Leonhardt and his musicians to deliver it with fearful fervour. The occasions which prompted grand, ceremonial gestures of the kind which we encounter here must have been quite awe-inspiring since much of the music is redolent of processional solemnity highlighted by dashes of brilliant colour – the scoring includes trumpets and three trombones as well as the standard woodwind and strings. In summary, this is a strong release. The Chorus and Baroque Orchestra of the Dutch Bach Association perform well throughout and the programme, offering two starkly different baroque visions of heaven, is a richly rewarding one.

Further listening ...

...Scherzo, Guardati. *Coupled with works by* **Bononcini, Torelli, Ariosti** and **Corelli** Ann Monoyios (sop); **Berlin Barock Compagney.** Capriccio 10 459 (10/95). *See review in the Collections section; refer to the Index to Reviews.* Ⓖ

Max Steiner

Austrian/American 1888-1971

Suggested listening ...

...Film Scores – Now, Voyager – excerpts; King Kong – Suite; Saratoga Trunk – As long as I live; The Charge of the Light Brigade – Forward the Light Brigade; Four Wives – Symphonie moderne[a]; The Big Sleep – Suite; Johnny Belinda – Suite; Since You Went Away – Main Title; The Informer – excerpts[b]; The Fountainhead – Suite. [a]**Earl Wild** (pf); [b]**Ambrosian Singers; National Philharmonic Orchestra / Charles Gerhardt.** RCA Victor GD80136 (10/90).

...King Kong – Overture. *Coupled with* **Savino/Perry** The Phantom of the Opera – Through the Looking Glass. **Stravinsky** The Rite of Spring – Sacrificial Dance. **J.T. Williams** Jurassic Park – Theme[b]. Dracula – Night Journeys. **Herrmann** Vertigo – Prelude; Scène d'Amour. **Rósza** Spellbound Concerto[a]. **Barry** Body Heat – Main Theme. **Waxman** Sunset Boulevard – Sonata for Orchestra (arr. Mauceri). Dr Jekyll and Mr Hyde – Suite (arr. Palmer)[b]. **Goldsmith** The Omen – Main Title[b]. [a]**Stephen Hough** (pf); [b]**Los Angeles Master Chorale; Hollywood Bowl Orchestra / John Mauceri.** Philips 442 425-2PH (1/95).

...Gone with the Wind. **National Philharmonic Orchestra / Neeme Järvi.** RCA Victor Gold Seal GD80452 (6/90). Ⓖ

...Gone With The Wind: The Classic Max Steiner – Film Scores: The Adventures of Mark Twain – Overture. A Distant Trumpet. Casablanca – Suite. A Summer Place – Main Title; Young love. The Treasure of the Sierra Madre – Overture. Helen of Troy – Suite. The Caine Mutiny – march. Gone with the Wind – Suite. **Westminster Philharmonic Orchestra / Kenneth Alwyn.** Silva Screen FILMCD144 (8/94).

Wilhelm Stenhammar

Swedish 1871-1927

Stenhammar Piano Concerto No. 1 in B flat minor, Op. 1[a]. Symphony No. 3 in C major – fragment. [a]**Mats Widlund** (pf); **Stockholm Philharmonic Orchestra / Gennadi Rozhdestvensky.** Chandos Ⓕ CHAN9074 (51 minutes: DDD: 10/92). Recorded 1992.

Stenhammar Piano Concerto No. 2 in D minor, Op. 23[a]. Serenade in F major, Op. 31[b]. Florez och Blanzeflor, Op. 3[c]. [c]**Ingvár Wixell** (bar); [a]**Janos Solyom** (pf); [a]**Munich Philharmonic Orchestra;** [bc]**Swedish Radio Symphony Orchestra / Stig Westerberg.** EMI Matrix Ⓜ CDM5 65081-2 (73 minutes: ADD: 5/94). Text and translation included. Items marked [a] from Swedish HMV 4E 063 34284 (8/81), [bc] Swedish HMV 4E 061 35148 (8/80). Recorded 1970-74.

The First Piano Concerto comes from 1893, when Stenhammar was 22, and such was its success during the 1890s that he was invited to play it with the Berlin Philharmonic under Richard Strauss. In time, however, he grew tired of it and became careless as to its fate. Both the autograph and the orchestral parts were destroyed when Breslau was bombed during the Second World War. But recently a copy probably made for the American première came to light in the Library of Congress. Chandos also offer a short fragment from the Symphony No. 3 in C major, on which Stenhammar embarked in 1918-19. At not much under 50 minutes it is perhaps overlong, but still has much charm, and Widlund and Rozhdestvensky make a most persuasive case for it. The recording has great depth and warmth and the strings of the Stockholm Orchestra have great richness of sonority.

The *Serenade* is arguably Stenhammar's masterpiece. In its Overture the writing is vibrant and luminous, full of subtly changing textures and colours, and like the finale is of symphonic proportions. Apparently Stenhammar toyed at one stage with the idea of adding the word *selvaggio* or "wild" to the title of the *Scherzo*, the mercurial centrepiece of the whole work, which is played with captivating spirit here. Stig Westerberg's 20-year-old recording comes up very fresh indeed. The playing throughout is ardent, sensitive and vital. This issue offers two additional pieces, most notably János Solyom's brilliant account of the Second Piano Concerto with the Munich Philharmonic, sounding as if it were recorded yesterday. It is strongly indebted to Saint-Saëns, and the *Scherzo* has a Mendelssohnian effervescence and delicacy. The early and endearing if Wagnerian *Florez och Blanzeflor,* finely sung by Ingvár Wixell, is the admirable makeweight.

Additional recommendations ...

...Piano Concerto No. 1[a]. Two Sentimental Romances, Op. 28[b]. Florez och Blanzeflor, Op. 3[c]. [a]**Love Derwinger** (pf); [b]**Ulf Wallin** (vn); [c]**Peter Mattei** (bar); **Malmö Symphony Orchestra / Paavo Järvi.** BIS Ⓟ CD550 (68 minutes: DDD: 10/92). *Selected by Sounds in Retrospect.*

New review

Stenhammar Symphonies – No. 1 in F major; No. 2 in G minor, Op. 34. Excelsior!, Op 13. Serenade in F major, Op 31. **Gothenburg Symphony Orchestra / Neeme Järvi.** DG Ⓟ 445 857-2GH2 (two discs: 139 minutes: DDD: 8/95). Recorded 1992-3. *Gramophone Editor's choice.*

A year or so ago BIS issued a four-disc set (retailing at the price of three), repackaging all their Stenhammar orchestral music including the *Serenade* in F with the *Reverenza* movement inserted, the two piano concertos, the two *Sentimental Romances,* Op. 28 and a handful of other works. The earliest of these recordings was the First Symphony, recorded at a concert performance in 1982 in good analogue sound, and the most recent the First Piano Concerto recorded in 1992, in its newly discovered original form. This DG set, recorded in 1993, offers the two symphonies, the *Serenade* in its finished form without the *Reverenza* movement, which Stenhammar eventually rejected and the early overture, *Excelsior!* in a somewhat smaller box of two CDs. The first DG disc offers an exemplary performance of the brilliant overture, *Excelsior!* – full of youthful confidence and Wagnerian exuberance – as well as only the seond recording of the First Symphony. The Swedish daily press, reviewing the première of the overture in 1897, commented that Stenhammar "speaks more German than Swedish". They might well have said the same of the First Symphony, which Stenhammar himself called "idyllic Bruckner", but there are Brahmsian touches too. It is a marvellous score, fertile in invention and generous in spirit. Järvi brings to the glorious *Serenade* an appropriate lightness of touch though in the *Notturno* he takes more time over the piece in the earlier version; feelings are perhaps more delicately touched upon and there is a greater sense of wonder. Still, the performance as a whole is very sympathetic and, as one would expect, idiomatic. Järvi's version of the Second Symphony is a considerable improvement on his first. In sum, those who want only the orchestral music should not hesitate but those who have the BIS recordings need not change. There is splendid definition in the DG set but the earlier BIS has excellent presence and ambience.

New review

Stenhammar Seven Poems from Thoughts of Solitude, Op. 7. Five Songs to texts by Johann Ludvig Runeberg, Op. 8. Four Swedish Songs, Op. 16. Five Songs of Bo Bergman, Op. 20. Songs and Moods, Op. 26. Late Harvest. **Peter Mattei** (bar); **Bengt-Ake Lundin** (pf). BIS Ⓟ CD654 (79 minutes: DDD: 9/95). Texts and translations included. Recorded 1994.

Stenhammar's songs are at last coming into their own. Looking through his list of songs, Sibelians will have noted some familiar titles, settings of Fröding's *Ingalill* and Runeberg's *The maiden's tryst* ("Flickan kom ifrån sin älsklings möte"), the former to be found here among the *Four Swedish Songs,* Op. 16. And though Stenhammar may not always distil the same powerful atmosphere, his songs have an eloquence all their own. They are invariably short but are always perfectly fashioned: only two, "Miss Blond and Miss Brunette: ("Jungfru Blond och Jungfru Brunett") and "Prince Aladdin of the Lamp" ("Prins Aladin av Lampan"), both from *Songs and Moods* ("Visor och stämningar") Op. 26 exceed four minutes. The present disc is generously filled: there are 36 songs in all, some are outstandingly fine. In addition to the complete sets, it also gives us the posthumously published (1933) *Late Harvest* ("Efterskörd"). Many of these songs will be new to collectors, including "The Bell" ("Klockan") to words of Bo Bergman (1923) and the Fröding setting from *Late Harvest* (1904), "Comfort" ("Tröst"), two examples of Stenhammar's fastidious craftsmanship and impeccable taste. Peter Mattei possesses a voice of great beauty. He is a responsive, sensitive artist who understands and identifies with this repertoire and can characterize the songs with real feeling. The only problem is that he all too often colours the voice on the flat side of the note and at times, as in "Prince Aladdin of the Lamp", is flat. But there is so much that gives unalloyed pleasure that it would be wrong to dwell on reservations. One of the joys of this CD is the artistry of Bengt-Ake Lundin, whose accompanying is a model of its kind. He produces unfailing beauty of sound and responsiveness to the mood of the songs. The documentation is, as usual from this source, excellent and so, too, is the recorded sound.

Additional recommendation ...

...Songs and Moods – No. 1, The Wanderer; No. 4, Miss Blonde and Miss Brunette; No. 5, A ship sails; No. 9, Coastal song. Songs, Op. 37 – No. 1, Jutta comes to the Volkungs; No. 2, In the maple's shade. *Coupled with works by* **Peterson-Berger, Sigurd von Koch, Rangström, Alfvén** and **Sjögren** Anne Sofie von Otter (mez); **Bengt Forsberg** (pf). DG Ⓕ 449 189-2GH (74 minutes: DDD: 5/96). *See review in the Collections section; refer to the Index to Reviews.* Ⓖ

Further listening ...

...String Quartets – No. 1 in C major, Op. 2[a]; No. 2 in C minor, Op. 14[b]. [a]**Fresk Quartet;** [b]**Copenhagen Quartet.** Caprice CAP21337.

...String Quartets – No. 3 in F major, Op. 18; No. 4 in A minor, Op. 25. **Gotland Quartet.** Caprice CAP21338.

...String Quartets – No. 5 in C major, Op. 29, "Serenade"[a]; No. 6 in D minor, Op. 35[b]. [a]**Fresk Quartet;** [b]**Copenhagen Quartet.** Caprice CAP21339.

...Piano Sonatas – No. 1 in C major; No. 2 in C minor; No. 3 in A flat major; No. 4 in G minor. Fantasie in A minor. **Lucia Negro** (pf). BIS CD634 (3/96).

Rudi Stephan

New review

Stephan Music for Orchestra.
Zemlinsky Die Seejungfrau. **North Netherlands Orchestra / Jacek Kaspszyk.** Vanguard Classics Ⓜ 99065 (61 minutes: DDD: 4/96). Recorded 1994-5.

The North Netherlands Orchestra may not have quite the sheer luxuriant density of string tone of their southern neighbours, the Royal Concertgebouw, but they seem to have pretty well everything else that this music requires. And how very shrewd to couple the Zemlinsky with Rudi Stephan's striking piece, which, although it shares with Zemlinsky a good many influences (Strauss and Wagner, among others), uses the orchestra quite differently. Stephan was killed during the First World War at the age of only 28. His *Music for Orchestra* was written two years before his death, and shows him already moving away from his obvious models towards an orchestral sound that can be rhapsodically luscious but can equally well be lean and sinewy. Formally, the piece is both clever and satisfying: a sort of one-movement symphony, with two basic themes that are both obviously related and capable of fruitful development and of giving birth to further ideas. Thus a lyrical slow movement, with some especially beautiful string writing, and a vigorous fugal scherzo are both generated from variants of the opening themes, as is the jubilant major-key coda. In the Zemlinsky Kaspszyk is very good at demonstrating how many qualities it has, as well as opulence. Real urgency in the more dramatic sections, for example, which are fierily done. And an extreme delicacy of fine detail, no less difficult to achieve than warm richness. This is an orchestra that can already produce that most arresting of sonorities, a genuine *pianissimo*. The sound is very clear but pleasingly spacious, spacious enough for the strings to achieve a satisfying warmth.

Sir William Sterndale Bennett

Suggested listening ...

...Piano Concertos – No. 1 in D minor, Op. 1; No. 3 in C minor, Op. 9. Caprice in E major, Op. 22. **Malcolm Binns** (pf); **London Philharmonic Orchestra / Nicholas Braithwaite.** Lyrita SRCD204 (11/90).

...Piano Concertos – No. 2 in E flat major, Op. 4; No. 5 in F minor. Adagio. **Malcolm Binns** (pf); **Philharmonia Orchestra / Nicholas Braithwaite.** Lyrita SRCD205 (11/90).

...Piano Sextet in F sharp minor, Op. 8[a]. Sonata Duo in A major, Op. 32[b]. [a]**András Kiss,** [a]**Ferenc Balogh** (vns); [a]**László Bársony** (va); [a]**Károly Botvay,** [b]**György Kertész** (vcs); [a]**Péter Kubina** (db); [a]**Ilona Prunyi,** [b]**Kálmán Dráfi** (pfs). Marco Polo 8 223304 (11/94).

Bernard Stevens

Suggested listening ...

...Cello Concerto, Op. 18[a]. A Symphony of Liberation. [a]**Alexander Baillie** (vc); **BBC Philharmonic Orchestra / Sir Edward Downes.** Meridian CDE84124 (3/87).

...Violin Concerto, Op. 4[a]. Symphony No. 2, Op. 35. [a]**Ernst Kovacic** (vn); **BBC Philharmonic Orchestra / Sir Edward Downes.** Meridian CDE84174 (4/90).

...Dance Suite, Op. 28. Piano Concerto, Op. 26[a]. Variations, Op. 36. [a]**Martin Roscoe** (pf); **National Symphony Orchestra of Ireland / Adrian Leaper.** Marco Polo 8 223480 (11/94). Ⓖ

Ronald Stevenson

Suggested listening ...

...Passacaglia on DSCH. **Raymond Clarke** (pf). Marco Polo 8 223545 (9/95).

William Grant Still
American 1895-1978

W.G. Still Symphony No. 2 in G minor, "Song of a New Race".
Dawson Negro Folk Symphony.
Ellington (orch. Henderson) Harlem. **Detroit Symphony Orchestra / Neeme Järvi.** Chandos
Ⓕ CHAN9226 (74 minutes: DDD: 3/94).

It would be foolhardy to hail William Grant Still's First Symphony as a major find, but it is an affectingly lyrical, unpretentious offering. Not surprisingly, given Still's reputation as an expert arranger, the scoring is assured and effective; indeed, the richly textured string writing in particular seems tailor-made for the legendary skills of the work's première performers, namely Leopold Stokowski and the Philadelphia Orchestra. The latter also first performed William Levi Dawson's *Negro Folk Symphony*. That was in 1934, but the composer later revised the piece after a visit to Africa in 1952. Again, it is thoroughly diverting stuff, stylishly orchestrated. It was John Mauceri who most recently drew our attention to the provocative charms of Duke Ellington's steamy 1950 portrait-in-sound, *Harlem*, yet the relaxed virtuosity displayed by Järvi's Detroit players makes for an experience just as swaggeringly enjoyable. Given such consistently idiomatic, polished advocacy and agreeably velvety Chandos sound, this release must be deemed a great success.

Further listening ...

...Afro-American Symphony. *Coupled with* **Ellington** The River – Suite. **Detroit Symphony Orchestra / Neeme Järvi.** Chandos CHAN9154 (4/93).
...Songs – Pastorela. Here's one. Songs of Separation – If you should go. Song for the Lonely. Bayou Home (all arr. A. Still). Summerland. Quit dat fool'nish. Folk Suite No. 1[a]. Suite for Violin and Piano – Movements II and III (ed. A. Still). Prelude[ab]. **Alexa Still** (fl); **Susan DeWitt Smith** (pf); [a]**New Zealand String Quartet;** [b]**Michael Steer** (db). Koch International Classics 37192-2 (11/94).

Karlheinz Stockhausen
German 1928-

Suggested listening ...

...Michaels Reise um die Erde. **Markus Stockhausen** (tpt); **Suzanne Stephens** (basset-hn); **Kathinka Pasveer** (alto fl); **Ian Stuart** (cl); **Lesley Schatzberger** (cl/basset-hn); **Michael Svoboda** (tbn/bar hn); **Andreas Boettger, Isao Nakamura** (perc); **Michael Obst, Simon Stockhausen** (synths); **Karlheinz Stockhausen** (sound projection). ECM New Series 437 188-2 (3/93).
...Mantra. **Yvar Mikashoff, Rosalind Bevan** (pfs); **Ole Orsted** (electronics). New Albion NA025CD (1/91).
...Klavierstück XII-XIV. **Bernhard Wambach** (pf). Koch Schwann 310015 (5/90).
...Aus den sieben Tagen – Setz die Segel sur Sonne verbindung. **Ensemble Musique Vivante / Diego Masson** with **Karlheinz Stockhausen** (filters/potentionmeters). Harmonia Mundi HMA190 795 (9/89).
...Stimmung. **Singcircle / Gregory Rose.** Hyperion CDA66115 (2/87).

Thomas Stoltzer
German c1480/85-1526

Suggested listening ...

...Missa duplex per annum – Kyrie; Gloria; Sanctus (with plainchant Credo). Missa "Kyrie summum" – Agnus Dei. Levavi oculos meos. Benedicamus Dominum in omni tempore. Omnes gentes plaudite. Octo tonorum melodiae – Melodia quarti toni; Melodia quinti toni. **Weser-Renaissance / Manfred Cordes.** CPO CPO999 295-2 (2/96).

Alessandro Stradella
Italian 1644-1682

New review

Stradella Crocifissione e morte di N. S. Giesù Christo: Da cuspide ferrate. Benedictus dominus Deus[a]. O vos omnes qui transitis. Chare Jesu suavissime[a]. Lamentatione per il Mercoledì Santo: Et egressus est. [a]**Sandrine Piau** (sop); **Il Seminario Musicale / Gérard Lesne** (alto). Virgin Classics Veritas Ⓕ VC5 45175-2 (62 minutes: DDD: 4/96). 🖉 Texts and translations included. Recorded 1995.   Ⓖ

The sadly small portion of the current catalogue devoted to Stradella receives a helpful boost with this recording, which offers five motets for one or two voices with small, single-string ensemble. From these we can see that one thing Stradella certainly was not was formulaic, for each work is constructed very much on its own terms, from the sustained nobility of *Crocifissione e morte di N. S. Giesù Christo* (ending, intriguingly, on the dominant) to the alternating lively recitatives and sinuous two-part writing of *Benedictus dominus Deus*, and from the virtuoso vocal delights of *O vos omnes qui transitis* to the dignified syllabic setting of the *Lamentatione per il Mercoledì Santo* (so like Charpentier or Couperin in its austere expressiveness). Il Seminario Musicale are persuasive interpreters as usual. Led by Gérard

Lesne's smoothly controlled, rich countertenor voice, they relish Stradella's more anguished harmonies and summon up plenty of energy when the going gets more lively. Sandrine Piau's dark soprano is a good complement to Lesne and, as in their earlier recordings, the instrumental ensemble (bolstered by the unusual inclusion of a double-bass) produces a satisfyingly weighty sound.

Further listening ...

...San Giovanni Battista. **Catherine Bott, Christine Batty** (sops); **Gérard Lesne** (alto); **Richard Edgar-Wilson** (ten); **Philippe Huttenlocher** (bar); **Les Musiciens du Louvre / Marc Minkowski.** Erato 2292-45739-2 (10/92). ✍ *Gramophone Award Winner 1993.*

...(ed. Steele-Perkins) Sonata a 8 con una Tromba in D. *Coupled with* **Albinoni** (attrib.) Concerto for Trumpet, Oboes, Bassoon and Strings in C major. **Telemann** Concerto for Trumpet, Two Oboes and Strings in D major. **Biber** Fidicunium sacro-profanum – Sonata IV a 5 in C major. Sonatae tam aris quam aulis servientes – I a 8 in C major; X a 5 in G minor[a]. Duets for Two Trumpets[a] – No. 1 in C major; No. 5 in C major; No. 11 in G minor; No. 13 in A minor. **Vivaldi** Concerto for Two Trumpets and Strings in C major, RV537[a]. **Handel** (ed. Steele-Perkins) Airs from Vauxhall Gardens. **Crispian Steele-Perkins,** [a]**John Thiessen** (tpts); **Tafelmusik / Jeanne Lamon** (vn). Sony Classical Vivarte SK53365 (4/95). ✍

Eduard Strauss
Austrian 1835-1916

Johann Strauss I
Austrian 1804-1849

Johann Strauss III
Austrian 1866-1939

Josef Strauss
Austrian 1827-1870

Johann Strauss II
Austrian 1825-1899

Ein Straussfest II [a]**Cincinnati Pops Chorale and Orchestra / Erich Kunzel.** Telarc Ⓕ CD80314 (68 minutes: DDD: 7/93). Recorded 1991-92.
E. Strauss Ohne Aufenthalt, Op. 112. **Josef Strauss** Plappermäulchen, Op. 245. Sphärenklange, Op. 235. Jockey, Op. 278. **J. Strauss I** Chinese Galop, Op. 20. **J. Strauss II** Egyptischer Marsch, Op. 335[a]. Künstler-Quadrille, Op. 71. Kaiser-Walzer, Op. 437. Freikugeln, Op. 326. Jubelfest-Marsch, Op. 396. Tritsch-Tratsch-Polka, Op. 214. Geisselhiebe, Op. 60[a]. Klipp Klapp, Op. 466. Wein, Weib und Gesang, Op. 333. Perpetuum mobile, Op. 257.

This collection deliberately sets out to adorn popular Strauss pieces with sound effects to outdo anything one hears at a Vienna New Year Concert. It starts with a performance of Eduard Strauss's *Ohne Aufenthalt* that is accompanied throughout by steam railway effects, has bullets flying mercilessly in the *Freikugeln* Polka, and includes neighing nags and swishing whips in the *Jockey* Polka. The fun is increased by the inclusion of the *Künstler-Quadrille*, a sort of 1850s "Hooked on Classics" number that begins with Mendelssohn's "Wedding March" and continues through the likes of Mozart's Symphony No. 40 and Chopin's 'Funeral March' Sonata to Beethoven's *Ruins of Athens* and *Kreutzer* Sonata. If the Viennese lilt is just a shade lacking in the waltzes, the playing is nevertheless excellent and lively throughout. The Strausses themselves would have approved.

New Year's Day Concert, 1995 Vienna Philharmonic Orchestra / Zubin Mehta. Sony Classical Ⓕ SK66860 (78 minutes: DDD: 5/95). Recorded live in 1995.
Lanner Favorit-Polka, Op. 201. **E. Strauss** Electrisch. **J. Strauss I** Radetzky March, Op. 228. Alice, Op. 238. **J. Strauss II** Reitermarsch, Op. 428. Morgenblätter, Op. 279. Process, Op. 294. Mephistos Höllenrufe, Op. 101. Perpetuum mobile, Op. 257. Russische Marsch – Phantasie, Op. 353. An der schönen, blauen Donau, Op. 314. Schützen. **Josef Strauss** Arm in Arm, Op. 215. Thalia, Op. 195. Mein Lebenslauf ist Lieb und Lust, Op. 263. Auf Ferienreisen, Op. 133. Ⓖ

There was a high proportion of rarities in the 1995 New Year's Day Concert, and they included two total novelties, apparently buried for a century in some princely archive in Coburg. The slinky and lyrical Mazurka Polka, *Thalia*, by Josef Strauss is particularly delightful, and Eduard Strauss's *Electrisch* Polka is as breezily energetic as one would expect. Other rare charmers include the *Alice* Polka with Czech overtones by Johann Strauss the elder, dedicated to Princess Alice, daughter of Queen Victoria, and the *Russian March Fantasy* by Johann Strauss the younger, even more Slavonic in flavour. Lanner's *Favorit-Polka* includes an authentic Rossini crescendo, and even in this context the swinging waltz, *Mephistos Höllenrufe* ("Mephisto's Calls from Hell"), might win a prize for oddity of title. If Mehta's traditional rounding off for the *Perpetuum mobile* polka ("Und so weiter", and so on) comes in a little too quickly, and the audience start clapping in the *Radetzky March* much too soon (remember the way Karajan controlled them!), that plainly reflects the exuberance of the occasion, well caught on this well-filled disc.

Additional recommendation ...

...Radetzky March *Coupled with works by* **Nicolai, Smetana, J. Strauss I, Weber, Meyerbeer, Brahms, Thomas, Tchaikovsky, Suppe, Offenbach** and **Glinka** London

Symphony Orchestra / Sir Charles Mackerras. Mercury Living Presence Ⓜ 434 352-2MM
(75 minutes: ADD: 12/95).

New review

New Year's Day Concert 1996 Vienna Philharmonic Orchestra / Lorin Maazel ([a]vn). RCA
Victor Red Seal Ⓕ 09026 68421-2 (two discs: 94 minutes: DDD: 5/96). Recorded live in 1996.
J. Strauss II Fest-Marsch, Op. 452. Blumenfest, Op. 111. Lagunen-Walzer, Op. 411.
Waldmeister – Overture. Phönix-Schwingen, Op. 125. Die Göttin der Vernunft – Overture[a].
Sekunden-Polka, Op. 258. Kaiser-Walzer, Op. 437. Furioso-Polka, Op. 260. An der schönen,
blauen Donau, Op. 314. **Ziehrer** Wiener Bürger, Op. 419. **Josef Strauss** Die Nasswalderin,
Op. 267 (arr. Rot). Die Tanzende Muse, Op. 266. Jokey-Polka, Op. 278. **E. Strauss** Mit
Vergnügen!, Op. 228. **J. Strauss I** Radetzky-Marsch, Op. 228.
Not only are Maazel and the VPO on peak form, relaxed and glowing throughout, but the
programme includes an exceptionally strong crop of novelties, never heard at these concerts before,
and the recorded sound is among the finest from the Musikvereinsaal, giving cleaner focus than usual
and a firmer sense of presence. Maazel is pictured on the cover, violin in hand, grinning with delight,
and the performances consistently reflect that ease, his deep affection and understanding for the
idiom. Where last year his big violin solo came in a favourite number, *Tales from the Vienna Woods*,
this time it is in a rarity, the overture *Die Göttin der Vernunft* ("The Goddess of Reason"), Johann
Strauss II's last operetta, characteristically with waltz and polka themes alternating. Among the other
half-dozen or so works never heard before at a New Year concert, the waltz, *Phönix-Schwingen*
("Wings of the Phoenix"), exhilaratingly done, with one idea like "Chopsticks" in waltz-time, is
particularly enjoyable. There are many other items to cherish, new and old, such as the jaunty
Blumenfest polka and the aptly named *Furioso-Polka*. The whole concert is so long that the encores
have spilt over on to a second, much briefer CD, included free in the same jewel-case.

Viennese Dance Music [a]**Wolfgang Schulz** (fl); [b]**Ernst Ottensamer** (cl); [c]**Alois Posch** (db); [d]**Heinz
Medjimoreč** (pf); [e]**Alfred Mitterhofer** (harm); **Alban Berg Quartet** (Günter Pichler, Gerhard
Schulz, vns; Thomas Kakuska, va; Valentin Erben, vc). EMI Ⓕ CDC7 54881-2 (62 minutes:
DDD: 6/94). Recorded 1992.
J. Strauss I (arr. Weinmann) Wiener Gemüths, Op. 116[c]. Beliebte Annen, Op. 137[c]. Eisele und
Beisele Sprünge, Op. 202[c]. **J. Strauss II** Schatz, Op. 418 (arr. Webern)[de]. Wein, Weib und
Gesang, Op. 333 (arr. Berg)[de]. Kaiser-Walzer, Op. 437 (arr. Schoenberg)[abd]. **Lanner** (arr.
Weinmann) Marien-Walzer, Op. 143[c]. Steyrische-Tänze, Op. 165[c]. Die Werber, Op. 103[c].
In the Alexander Weinmann arrangements of Lanner and the elder Johann Strauss, one is able to
appreciate to the full the clear lyrical lines of works whose full orchestration is very much built upon
the foundation of the string quartet. Likewise, in the large-scale waltzes of the younger Strauss one
cannot but admire the skill and affection with which Webern, Berg and Schoenberg used the limited
resources available to their Society for Private Musical Performances. Indeed, if string quartet, piano,
flute and clarinet inevitably struggle to capture the full splendour of the march introduction to the
Kaiser–Walzer, the imaginative way in which Schoenberg finds a chamber ensemble substitute for
Strauss's full orchestral sound is perhaps the most impressive aspect of the various arrangements here.
On its own terms, the collection is extremely impressive. The Alban Berg Quartet have made a fine
selection of some of the most melodic works from over half a century of prodigious invention, and
they play them with affection and relish. From Lanner's tender *Marien–Walzer*, through to Strauss
junior's most magisterial waltz, the clarity and refinement of the playing is tempered with a sense of
lightheartedness and fun. If you fancy a Viennese dance collection with a different slant, don't
hesitate to go for this admirable release.

J. Strauss II Complete Edition, Volumes 34-36. [a]**Bratislava Radio Symphony Orchestra / Michael
Dittrich; Košice State Philharmonic Orchestra** / [b]**Johannes Wildner**, [c]**Alfred Walter.** Marco Polo
Ⓕ 8 223234/6 (three discs, oas: 69, 74 and 68 minutes: DDD: 7/94). Volumes marked [ab] recorded
1991, [c] 1989-91.
8 223234[a] – Russischer Marsch, Op. 426. Slaven-Potpourri, Op. 39. Fünf Paragraphe, Op. 105. La
favorite, Op. 217. Nikolai-Quadrille, Op. 65. Abschied von St Petersburg, Op. 210. Der Kobold,
Op. 226. Im russischen Dorfe, Op. 355 (orch. Schönherr). Dolci pianti (with Jozef Sikora, vc).
Niko-Polka, Op. 228. *8 223235*[b] – Zivio!, Op. 456 (orch. Fischer). Architecten-Ball-Tänze,
Op. 36. Jäger, Op. 229. Accelerationen, Op. 234. Der Liebesbrunnen, Op. 10 (orch. Kulling).
Die Zeitlose, Op. 302. Königslieder, Op. 334. Im Sturmschritt, Op. 348. Der Blitz, Op. 59
(orch. Babinski). Heut' ist heut', Op. 471 (orch. Babinski). Die Wahrsagerin, Op. 420. *8 223236*[c] –
Matador-Marsch, Op. 406 (orch. Fischer). Kreuzfidel, Op. 301. D'Woaldbuama (Die
Waldbuben), Op. 66 (orch. Babinski). Process, Op. 294. Elfen-Quadrille, Op. 16 (orch.
Kulling). Mephistos Höllenrufe, Op. 101. Bitte schön!, Op. 372. Die Extraganten, Op. 205.
Fledermaus-Quadrille, Op. 363. Der Klügere gibt nach, Op. 401. Neu-Wien, Op. 342.
Diplomaten-Polka, Op. 448.
Volume 34 offers a distinct Russian flavour. The most obviously familiar item is the opening
Russischer Marsch while the waltz *Abschied von St Petersburg* will also be familiar to some. It's a fine
swinging waltz, with an attractive cello solo in the introduction. *Dolci pianti*, one of three romances

surviving from Strauss's Russian visits, provides further material for a cello soloist, while the piquant *Niko–Polka* offers as good an example as any of the delights to be found among the unfamiliar works of the Waltz King. Not the least attraction of Vol. 34 is the conductor Michael Dittrich and his alert, *echt-Wienerisch* performances here. On Vol. 35 Johannes Wildner's conducting shows up to much better effect than has often been the case. Marches have always been his strong point, and the collection thus gets off to a good start with *Zivio!* from the operetta *Jabuka*. There are other attractive pieces on offer, too, from the perpetual favourite *Accelerationen,* through the delicate polka–mazurka *Die Zeitlose* to the magisterial *Königslieder* (a waltz from Strauss's most successful period) and the polka–mazurka *Die Wahrsagerin* on melodies from *The Gipsy Baron*. Volume 36 offers perhaps the most attractive music of the three volumes. Again the performance of the haunting waltz *Mephistos Höllenrufe* may not erase memories of some previous versions, but such pieces as the *Neu-Wien* waltz and the excellently played *Fledermaus–Quadrille* are among the composer's most agreeable creations. Perhaps the most pleasant surprise of all comes from the waltz *Die Extravaganten* which, with its endearing themes and richly inventive harmonic and orchestral touches, shows above all the merits of Marco Polo's voyage of Straussian rediscovery.

New review

J. Strauss II Complete Edition, Volumes 43, 44 and 45. **Slovak State Philharmonic Orchestra, Košice / [a]Christian Pollack, [b]Alfred Walter.** Marco Polo Ⓔ 8 223243/5 (three discs, oas: 58, 56 and 59 minutes: DDD: 3/96).

8 223243[a] – Reitermarsch, Op. 428. Walzer-Bouquet No. 1. Postillon d'amour, Op. 317. Simplicius-Quadrille, Op. 429. Wilde Rosen, Op. 42 (arr. Babinski/Kulling). Die Tauben von San Marco, Op. 414. Auf dem Tanzboden, Op. 454 (arr. Pollack). Des Teufels Antheil (arr. Pollack). Trifolien (with Josef and Eduard Strauss). Herrjemineh, Op. 464. *8 223244*[a] – Maskenfest-Quadrille, Op. 92. Aschenbrödel-Walzer. Von der Börse, Op. 337. Monstre-Quadrille (with Josef Strauss). Autograph Waltzes (arr. Cohen). Auf freiem Fusse, Op. 345. Schützen-Quadrille (with Josef and Eduard Strauss). Altdeutscher Walzer (arr. Pollack). Nur nicht mucken, Op. 472 (arr. Peak). Hinter den Coulissen (with Josef Strauss). *8 223245*[b] – Fest-Marsch, Op. 452. Zigeunerbaron-Quadrille, Op. 422. Ischler Walzer. Ritter Pasman – ballet music. Pasman-Quadrille (arr. Pollack). Eva-Walzer. Potpourri-Quadrille. Der Carneval in Rom – ballet music (arr. Schönherr).

As this Marco Polo series reaches its final stretches, it delves increasingly into the more remote corners of the Waltz King's output. Vols. 43 and 44 include as many as four collaborations between Johann and his two brothers, of which the *Trifolien* waltz and *Schützen-Quadrille* most engagingly permit a comparison of all three brothers' strengths. Both volumes also include a waltz from the composer's 1876 visit to the USA. The *Walzer-Bouquet* No. 1 (originally the *Manhattan Waltzes*) is a convincingly authentic Strauss arrangement of themes from his earlier waltzes, but it is difficult to feel as sure of the worth or authenticity of the *Autograph Waltzes*, which may merely comprise themes thrown off by Strauss and worked up by an eager US publisher.

The other particular curiosities of these two volumes are *Auf dem Tanzboden*, a musical evocation of a painting, and the *Altdeutscher Walzer*, which is really no more than an *entr'acte* from the operetta, *Simplicius*. Of the more conventional items, the attractive early waltz *Wilde Rosen* is already known from a previous recording by the same orchestra on this label (Marco Polo, 2/94). It receives a compelling performance here from Christian Pollack, without the somewhat heavy beat he imparts to the *Walzer-Bouquet*. Generally Pollack seems better in the polkas and quadrilles, which he gives genuine 'lift' and sparkle, as here in several delightful polkas and the *Maskenfest-Quadrille*, which contains themes familiar to anyone who knows *Graduation Ball*.

By contrast, Vol. 45 is relatively free of the polkas and polka-mazurkas that tend to sound somewhat leaden in the hands of Alfred Walter. Over half this CD is devoted to items from Strauss's only opera *Ritter Pasman* – not just the ballet music (played in a fuller version than on some occasions), but also the *Pasman-Quadrille* and *Eva-Walzer* arranged by other hands from the score. The posthumous *Ischler Walzer* proves a piece of genuine charm, and the *Potpourri-Quadrille* compiled by Strauss for his visit to London in 1867 provides fun value with its quotations from earlier Strauss quadrilles interspersed with a selection of Scottish airs. The inclusion of the *Carneval in Rom* ballet music in a modern arrangement seems unfortunate in a collection such as this with an accent on authenticity. As a whole, though, this proves one of the best of Walter's volumes, and all three CDs rank among the more interesting and enjoyable in this adventurous series.

J. Strauss I Radetzky March, Op. 228.
J. Strauss II Die Fledermaus – Overture. Perpetuum mobile, Op. 257. Accelerationen-Waltz, Op. 234. Unter Donner und Blitz-Polka, Op. 324. Morgenblätter-Waltz, Op. 279. Persischer Marsch, Op. 289. Explosionen-Polka, Op. 43. Wiener Blut-Waltz, Op. 354. Egyptischer Marsch, Op. 335. Künstlerleben-Waltz, Op. 316. Tritsch-Tratsch-Polka, Op. 214.
J. Strauss II/Josef Strauss Pizzicato Polka. **Vienna Philharmonic Orchestra / Willi Boskovsky** (vn). Decca Ovation Ⓜ 417 747-2DM* (65 minutes: ADD). Recorded 1958-73.

There have been no finer recordings of Johann Strauss than those by Boskovsky and the Vienna Philharmonic. The velvety sheen and elegance of the orchestra's sound, combined with the unique lilt that comes so naturally to Viennese players, produced magical results. For this compilation Decca have sensibly mixed seven of the most famous waltzes and polkas from those sessions with other popular Strauss compositions in various rhythms, from the celebrated *Die Fledermaus* Overture, through popular polkas and novelty pieces (for *Perpetuum mobile* Boskovsky himself can be heard explaining that it has no ending) to the ever-popular *Radetzky March*. The recorded sound is not up to the most modern digital standards, but reprocessing has produced a remarkably homogeneous sound for recordings originating over a 15-year period.

Additional recommendation ...

...Künstlerleben. Rosen aus dem Süden-Waltz, Op. 388. Der Zigeunerbaron – Overture. G'schichten aus dem Wienerwald-Waltz, Op. 325. Kaiser-Walzer, Op. 437. Die Fledermaus – Overture. An die schönen blauen Donau. **London Philharmonic Orchestra / Franz Welser-Möst.** EMI Ⓕ CDC7 54089-2 (66 minutes: DDD: 12/91).

J. Strauss II Die Fledermaus. **Dame Elisabeth Schwarzkopf** (sop) Rosalinde; **Rita Streich** (sop) Adele; **Nicolai Gedda** (ten) Eisenstein; **Helmut Krebs** (ten) Alfred; **Erich Kunz** (bar) Doctor Falke; **Rudolf Christ** (ten) Orlovsky; **Karl Dönch** (bar) Frank; **Erich Majkut** (ten) Blind; **Luise Martini** (sop) Ida; **Franz Böheim** (bar) Frosch; **Philharmonia Chorus and Orchestra / Herbert von Karajan.** EMI Ⓜ CHS7 69531-2* (two discs: 110 minutes: ADD: 11/88). From Columbia 33CX1309-10 (11/55). Recorded 1955.   ⒼⒼ

This 1955 recording can readily be recommended to anyone less concerned with modernity of sound than with enjoying a well-proven, classic interpretation of Strauss's operetta masterpiece. Herbert von Karajan, whose preference for slow tempos and beauty of sound above all else was then still in the future, here directs with affection and *élan*. Amongst the principals Elisabeth Schwarzkopf leads the cast majestically and ravishingly. Notably in the *Csárdás*, her firm lower notes swell gloriously into a marvellously rich and individual register. As her maid, Adele, Rita Streich is an agile-voiced, utterly charming foil, launching her "Laughing Song" with deliciously credible indignation. Nicolai Gedda also enters into the fun with supreme effect. Throughout he sings with youthful ardour and freshness, but he also has a high old time impersonating the stammering Blind in the Act 3 trio. Erich Kunz's rich, characterful baritone is also heard here to good effect as Doctor Falke, the character who arranges the 'bat's revenge' which forms the story of *Die Fledermaus*. Unconventionally, the young Prince is played by a tenor rather than the mezzo-soprano for whom the role was written. Purists may object, but the result is dramatically convincing, and musically could hardly be bettered when the singer is the sweet-toned Rudolf Christ. Altogether this set can still rival any later one in theatrical effectiveness and EMI have done a good job in refurbishing it, with the disc-break sensibly placed between Acts 1 and 2.

Additional recommendations ...

...(with Gala Sequence). **Soloists; Vienna State Opera Chorus and Orchestra / Herbert von Karajan.** Decca Ⓕ 421 046-2DH2* (two discs: 143 minutes: ADD: 12/87).

...**Vienna State Opera Chorus; Vienna Philharmonic Orchestra / André Previn.** Philips Ⓕ 432 157-2PH2 (two discs: 112 minutes: DDD: 9/91).

...**Soloists; Netherlands Opera Chorus; Concertgebouw Orchestra / Nikolaus Harnoncourt.** Teldec Ⓜ 4509-91974-2 (72 minutes: DDD: 7/93).

...**Soloists; Philharmonia Chorus; Philharmonia Orchestra / Otto Ackermann.** Classics for Pleasure Silver Doubles Ⓢ CD-CFPSD4793 (two discs: 113 minutes: ADD: 4/96).

New review

J. Strauss II Die Fledermaus (sung in English). **Rosemarie Arthars** (sop) Rosalinde; **Adey Grummet** (sop) Adele; **David Fieldsend** (ten) Eisenstein; **Khosrow Mahsoori** (ten) Alfred; **Gordon Sandison** (bar) Falke; **Deborah Hawksley** (mez) Orlovsky; **Lynton Black** (bar) Frank; **Howard Ludlow** (ten) Blind; **Wendy Schoemann** (sop) Ida; **Paul Barnhill** (spkr) Frosch; **D'Oyly Carte Opera Chorus and Orchestra / John Owen Edwards.** Sony Classical Ⓕ S2K64573 (two discs: 111 minutes: DDD: 1/96). Notes and texts included.

Recordings of *Die Fledermaus* in English were common enough during the early days of LP. Since then the work has tended to be regarded as the province of international star opera casts, which makes the D'Oyle Carte release all the more welcome. Comparisons with those international, German-language versions are scarcely appropriate, though on any terms this newcomer is a resounding success. It presents the score, extremely well played and sung (in Alistair Beaton's new translation), in a form that enables English-speaking listeners to keep unusually well apace of a notoriously complex plot. The tone of the performance is admirably set by the overture, in which symphonic pretensions are set aside in favour of a light and leisurely journey through the engaging material. John Owen Edwards never forces the tempo but allows the melodies to unfold naturally, and eases gently into the big waltz tunes. Musical standards remain uniformly high throughout the performance, which omits any ballet music but restores the two brief passages in Act 2 (in the opening chorus and the *csárdás*) that are usually cut. Without ever being sent up, the work once more becomes part of the international popular musical theatre tradition rather than part of an overblown operatic form. The cast is almost universally strong, with David Fieldsend (Eisenstein), Adey Grummet (Adele) and Gordon Sandison (Falke) each admirable in his or her way and Rosemarie Arthars a particular joy as she switches effortlessly between a testing singing part and dialogue that contributes so much to making this *Fledermaus* an integral experience.

J. Strauss II Der Zigeunerbaron. **Pamela Coburn** (sop) Saffi; **Herbert Lippert** (ten) Barinkay; **Wolfgang Holzmair** (bar) Homonay; **Rudolf Schasching** (ten) Zsupán; **Christiane Oelze** (sop) Arsena; **Júlia Hamari** (mez) Czipra; **Elisabeth von Magnus** (contr) Mirabella; **Jürgen Flimm** (bar) Carnero; **Robert Florianschutz** (bass) Pali; **Hans-Jürgen Lazar** (ten) Ottokar; **Arnold Schoenberg Choir; Vienna Symphony Orchestra / Nikolaus Harnoncourt.** Teldec Ⓔ 4509-94555-2 (two discs: 150 minutes: DDD: 6/95). Notes, text and translation included. Recorded live in1994.

This set comes with a sticker proclaiming the inclusion of 40 minutes of unpublished music. Well, 14 perhaps – certainly no more than 15. False claims aside, though, this proves an uncommonly interesting and enjoyable release. The extra music comes because Nikolaus Harnoncourt and Johann Strauss specialist Norbert Linke have sought to restore *Der Zigeunerbaron* to the form it had before Strauss made various cuts. The real merits of the set lie elsewhere. Not least, Harnoncourt has stripped away generations of Viennese schmaltz and performing tradition. This is the very first recording to include every number of the published score, and for once the music is sung at its original pitch, without the usual downward transpositions for Zsupán and Homonay. Most particularly Harnoncourt has completely rethought the style of the performance. *Der Zigeunerbaron* is a long work, described as "Komische Oper" rather than "Operette", and much of its music is unusually solid for Strauss. Harnoncourt gives the major numbers full weight, phrasing them beautifully, drawing refined singing from the soloists, among whom Herbert Lippert and Pamela Coburn combine beautifully in the duet "Wer uns getraut?", and Christiane Oelze is a delectably sweet Arsena. The necessary light relief comes not only from Zsupán (Rudolf Schasching in fine voice) but from usually omitted subsidiary numbers. Elisabeth von Magnus sings Mirabella's "Just sind es vierundzwanzig Jahren" with exhilarating comic zest, and joins with Jürgen Flimm (more actor than singer) to make the trio "Nur keusch und rein" an irresistible delight. The recording comes from a live concert performance, with some audience laughter and coughs but with applause suppressed. It is surely the best thing that Harnoncourt has done in the operetta field, and it deserves to win new admirers both for him and for Strauss's masterly score.

Further listening ...

...New Year's Day Concert, 1987 – Die Fledermaus – Overture. Annen-Polka, Op. 117. Vergnügungszug-Polka, Op. 281. Unter Donner und Blitz-Polka, Op. 324. Frühlingsstimmen-Waltz, Op. 410ª. An die schönen blauen Donau-Waltz, Op. 314. *Coupled with* **J. Strauss I** Beliebte Annen-Polka, Op. 137. Radetzky March, Op. 228. **J. Strauss II/Josef Strauss** Pizzicato Polka. **Josef Strauss** Sphärenklänge-Waltz, Op. 235. Delirien-Waltz, Op. 212. Ohne Sorgen-Polka, Op. 271. **Kathleen Battle** (sop); **Vienna Philharmonic Orchestra / Herbert von Karajan.** DG 419 616-2GH (11/87).

...New Year's Day Concert, 1989 – Accelerationen-Waltz, Op. 234. Bauern-Polka, Op. 276. Die Fledermaus – Overture. Künstlerleben-Waltz, Op. 316. Eljen a Magyar!-Polka, Op. 322. Im Krapfenwald'l-Polka française, Op. 336. Frühlingsstimmen-Waltz, Op. 410. Ritter Pasman – Csárdás. An die schönen blauen Donau-Waltz, Op. 314. *Coupled with* **J. Strauss I** Radetzky March, Op. 228. **J. Strauss II/Josef Strauss** Pizzicato Polka. **Josef Strauss** Die Libelle-Polka Mazur, Op. 204. Moulinet-Polka française, Op. 57. Plappermäulchen-Polka schnell, Op. 245. Jockey-Polka schnell, Op. 278. **Vienna Philharmonic Orchestra / Carlos Kleiber.** Sony Classical SK45938 (2/91).

...Complete Edition, Volume 37. Triumph-Marsch, Op. 69 (orch. Fischer). Jugend-Träume, Op. 12 (orch. Pollack). Das Komitat geht in die Höh!, Op. 457 (orch. Pollack). Die Königin von Leon-Quadrille, Op. 40 (orch. Pollack). Neue steirische Tänze, Op. 61 (orch. Pollack). Tanze mit dem Besenstiel!, Op. 458 (orch. Pollack). Spitzentuch-Quadrille, Op. 392. Schwungräder, Op. 223. Sonnenblume, Op. 459 (orch. Pollack). Romance No. 2 in G minor, Op. 255 (orch. Schönherr. With Regina Jauslin, vc). Traumbilder II, Op. posth. **Košice State Philharmonic Orchestra / ᵃChristian Pollack, ᵇAlfred Walter.** Marco Polo 8 223237 (9/95).

...(arr. Benatzky) Casanova – Nuns' Chorus and Laura's Song. *Coupled with works by* **Romberg, Offenbach, Novello, Lehár, Coward, Chabrier, Heuberger** and **Sullivan** Lesley Garrett (sop); **Crouch End Festival Chorus; Royal Philharmonic Concert Orchestra / James Holmes.** Silva Screen Classics SILKTVCD1 (2/96). *See review in the Collections section; refer to the Index to Reviews.*

Richard Strauss   German 1864-1949

R. Strauss Orchestral works, Volume 1 – Horn Concertos – No. 1 in E flat major, Op. 11ª; No. 2 in E flat major, AV132ᵇ. Oboe Concerto, AV144ᶜ. Duet Concertino, AV147ᵈ. Burleske in D minor, AV85ᶜ. Parergon, Op. 73ᶠ. Panathenäenzug Symphonic Study in the form of a Passacaglia, Op. 74ᵍ. Till Eulenspiegels lustige Streiche, Op. 28ʰ. Don Juan, Op. 20ⁱ. Ein Heldenleben, Op. 40ʲ. ᵃᵇ**Peter Damm** (hn); ᶜ**Manfred Clement** (ob); ᵈ**Manfred Weise** (cl); ᵈ**Wolfgang Liebscher** (bn); ᵉ**Malcolm Frager** (pf); ᶠᵍ**Peter Rösel** (pf); **Dresden Staatskapelle / Rudolf Kempe.** EMI Ⓜ CMS7 64342-2 (three discs: 224 minutes: ADD: 12/92). Items marked ᵃᵇᶜᵈᵉᶠᵍ from HMV SLS5067 (10/76), ʰSLS894 (3/75), ⁱSLS861 (10/73), ʲSLS880 (6/74). ⒼⒼ

R. Strauss Orchestral works, Volume 2 – Violin Concerto in D minor, Op. 8ª. Symphonia domestica, Op. 53ʰ. Also sprach Zarathustra, Op. 30ᶜ. Tod und Verklärung, Op. 24ᵈ. Der

Rosenkavalier – Waltzes[e]. Salome – Dance of the Seven Veils[f]. Le bourgeois gentilhomme – Suite,
Op. 60[g]. Schlagobers – Waltz[h]. Josephslegende – Suite[i]. [a]**Ulf Hoelscher** (vn); **Dresden Staatskapelle
/ Rudolf Kempe.** EMI Ⓜ CMS7 64346-2 (three discs: 222 minutes: ADD: 12/92). Items marked [a]
from HMV SLS5067 (10/76), [bfi]SLS894 (3/75), [cgh]SLS861 (10/73), [de]SLS880 (6/74).   ⒼⒼ
R. Strauss Orchestral works, Volume 3 – Metamorphosen for 23 Solo Strings, AV142[a]. Eine
Alpensinfonie, Op. 64[b]. Aus Italien, Op. 16[c]. Macbeth, Op. 23[d]. Don Quixote, Op. 35[e]. Dance
Suite on Keyboard Pieces by François Couperin, AV107[f]. [e]**Paul Tortelier** (vc); [e]**Max Rostal** (va);
Dresden Staatskapelle / Rudolf Kempe. EMI Ⓜ CMS7 64350-2 (three discs: 208 minutes: ADD:
12/92). Items marked [abd] from HMV SLS861 (10/73), [c]SLS894 (3/75), [ef]SLS880 (6/74).
Gramophone classical 100.   ⒼⒼⒼ
"From the store of glorious memories of my artistic career, the tones of this master orchestra ever
evoke feelings of deepest gratitude and admiration" (thus spoke Richard Strauss when greeting the
Dresden orchestra in 1948 on its 400th Anniversary). You get the feeling that this orchestra is
justifiably proud of its tones, and its Straussian associations; it takes only a few minutes of the wind
concertos disc (the first CD in Volume 1), with the principals as soloists, to be aware of those tones,
and to detect a special radiance that probably derives from that pride. Kempe, it seems, was the man
to draw it out, and give it purpose; after his *Till Eulenspiegel*, for example, virtually all others either
affect character, or are characterless. Some may find Kempe an occasionally circumspect Straussian,
one who preferred decorum to decibels in the protracted cacophony that concludes the *Symphonia
domestica*, and who ensures that the famous "2001" opening to *Also sprach Zarathustra* isn't so
awesome that the rest of the piece is an anti-climax. Neither did he have at his disposal the saturated
sonorities of the Berlin Philharmonic that supported Karajan's breadth and power. It is difficult,
though, to think of many other Straussians with the imagination and understanding to bring these
scores to life from within. To catalogue Kempe's Straussian credentials would take up more space
than is available; suffice it to say that, like Fritz Reiner, clarity of texture and a natural flexibility of
pacing were prerequisites for the characterful animation and interaction of orchestral soloists or
instrumental groups, but never at the expense of the long-term direction of the music. His technique,
too, ensured the kind of feats of ensemble and precision that you might have expected from the
Chicago Symphony Orchestra under Reiner, but Kempe's orchestra, of course, retains its warmer and
cherishably Old World tones.
   There are many self-evidently great Strauss performances here. A lithe, demon-driven *Don Juan*;
perhaps the most vital and communicative *Don Quixote* ever recorded (greatly ennobled by Tortelier's
presence); and *Ein Heldenleben* whose hero is drawn with humanity, even vulnerability and self-doubt
(the reaction to the critics is unbearably sad; the scene with the hero's wife, properly reactive) and the
ideal choice for those who find the work's egotism unpalatable. EMI have mixed the familiar with the
unfamiliar in each box, and dedicated Straussians will find the by-ways explored with comparable
commitment and skill. The recordings, made between 1970 and 1975 (the year before Kempe's
premature death), vary in perspective from an ideally distanced, natural layout (*Till* and *Aus Italien*),
to the closer and slightly 'contained' (*Eine Alpensinfonie* and *Ein Heldenleben*), and the vividly present
(*Le bourgeois gentilhomme* and *Metamorphosen*). Clear, light-toned timpani with very little bass
resonance further enhance Kempe's precise rhythmic control (even though they sound like tom-toms
at the start of *Also sprach Zarathustra*), and soloists are invariably up-front, but rarely at the expense
of orchestral detail. The whole invaluable enterprise benefits from the warm acoustics of the
Lukaskirche in Dresden.

Additional recommendations ...
...Don Juan. Till Eulenspiegels lustige Streiche. Also sprach Zarathustra. Ein Heldenleben. Le
   bourgeois gentilhomme – Suite. Tod und Verklärung. Symphonia domestica. **Vienna
   Philharmonic Orchestra / Richard Strauss.** Preiser mono Ⓕ 90216* (three discs: 206 minutes:
   AAD).
...Tod und Verklärung. Symphonia domestica, Op. 53. Salome, Op. 54 – Dance of the Seven Veils.
   Philadelphia Orchestra / Eugene Ormandy. Sony Classical Ⓑ SBK53511* (75 minutes: ADD). ⒼⒼ
...Metamorphosen. Tod und Verklärung. **Berlin Philharmonic Orchestra / Herbert von Karajan.**
   DG Ⓕ 410 892-2GH (52 minutes: DDD: 2/84).   ⒼⒼ
...Horn Concertos. **Weber** Horn Concertino in E minor, J188. **Hermann Bauman** (hn); **Leipzig
   Gewandhaus Orchestra / Kurt Masur.** Philips Ⓕ 412 237-2PH (DDD: 6/85).
...Horn Concertos[a]. **Hindemith** Horn Concerto[b]. **Dennis Brain** (hn); **Philharmonia Orchestra /
   [a]Wolfgang Sawallisch,** [b]**Paul Hindemith.** EMI Ⓕ CDC7 47834-2* (49 minutes: ADD: 10/87).
...Don Juan. Tod und Verklärung. Also sprach Zarathustra. **Vienna Philharmonic Orchestra /
   Herbert von Karajan.** Decca Ovation Ⓜ 417 720-2DM* (75 minutes: ADD: 12/87).
...Also sprach Zarathustra[b]. Don Juan. **Dresden Staatskapelle / Herbert Blomstedt.** Denon
   Ⓕ CO-2259 (51 minutes: DDD: 9/88).
...Le bourgeois gentilhomme – Suite. Divertimento, Op. 86. **Chamber Orchestra of Europe / Erich
   Leinsdorf.** ASV Ⓜ CDCOE809 (63 minutes: DDD: 11/88).
...Eine Alpensinfonie. **Vienna Philharmonic Orchestra / André Previn.** Telarc Ⓕ CD80211
   (48 minutes: DDD: 9/90).
...Aus Italien. Die Liebe der Danae, Op. 83 – Symphonic Fragment. Der Rosenkavalier,
   Op. 59 – Waltz Sequences, Acts 2 and 3. **Slovak Philharmonic Orchestra / Zdeněk Košler.** Naxos
   Ⓢ 8 550342 (59 minutes: DDD: 2/91).

...Don Juan. Don Quixote[a]. [a]**Franz Bartolomey** (vc); [a]**Heinrich Koll** (va); **Vienna Philharmonic Orchestra / André Previn.** Telarc Ⓕ CD80262 (60 minutes: DDD: 10/91).

...Ein Heldenleben[a]. Also sprach Zarathustra[b]. Don Quixote[cfg]. Tod und Verklärung[d]. Aus Italien – Am Strande von Sorrent[e]. [f]**Michel Piastro** (vn); [g]**René Pollain** (va); [e]**Alfred Wallenstein** (vc); **New York Philharmonic Symphony Orchestra /** [c]**Sir Thomas Beecham,** [a]**Willem Mengelberg;** [b]**Boston Symphony Orchestra / Serge Koussevitzky;** [d]**Philadelphia Orchestra / Leopold Stokowski;** [e]**Chicago Symphony Orchestra / Frederick Stock.** RCA Victor Gold Seal mono Ⓜ 09026-60929-2* (two discs: 146 minutes: ADD: 11/92).

...Metamorphosen. **Schoenberg** Verklärte Nacht. **Wagner** Siegfried Idyll. **Sinfonia Varsovia / Emmanuel Krivine.** Denon Ⓕ CO-79442 (64 minutes: DDD: 12/92). Ⓖ

...Also sprach Zarathustra. Ein Heldenleben, Op. 40. **Chicago Symphony Orchestra / Fritz Reiner.** RCA Ⓜ 09026 61494-2* (76 minutes: ADD: 4/93). *Gramophone classical 100.* ⒼⒼⒼ

...Le bourgeois gentilhomme – Suite. Salome, Op. 54 – Dance of the Seven Veils. **Brahms** Symphony No. 3 in F major, Op. 90. **Vienna Philharmonic Orchestra / Clemens Krauss.** Koch Legacy mono 37129-2* (75 minutes: ADD: 5/93).

...Eine Alpensinfonie. Sinfonische Fantasie aus "Die Frau ohne Schatten". **Chicago Symphony Orchestra / Daniel Barenboim.** Erato Ⓕ 2292-45997-2 (71 minutes: DDD: 6/93).

...Metamorphosen. **Honegger** Symphony No. 2. **Webern** Langsamer Satz (trans. Schwarz). **Seattle Symphony Orchestra / Gerard Schwarz.** Delos Ⓕ DE3121 (71 minutes: DDD: 4/94).

...Ein Heldenleben[a]. Also sprach Zarathustra[b]. Don Juan[b]. Till Eulensiegels lustige Streiche[b]. Eine Alpensinfonie[c]. [a]**Vienna Philharmonic Orchestra;** [b]**Chicago Symphony Orchestra;** [c]**Bavarian Radio Symphony Orchestra / Sir Georg Solti.** Double Decca Ⓜ 440 618-2DF2 (two discs: 152 minutes: ADD: 5/94).

...Don Quixote[a]. Burleske[b]. [a]**Milton Preves** (va); [a]**Antonio Janigro** (vc); [b]**Byron Janis** (pf); **Chicago Symphony Orchestra / Fritz Reiner.** RCA Victor Ⓜ 09026 61796-2 (63 minutes: ADD: 9/94).

...Capriccio – Prelude. Metamorphosen (arr. Leopold)[a]. **Mozart** String Quintet in C minor, K406/K516*b*. **Vienna String Sextet; Alois Posch** (db). EMI Ⓕ CDC5 55108-2 (61 minutes: DDD: 2/95).

...Don Quixote[a]. Ein Heldenleben. Eine Alpensinfonie. Festmusik zur Feier des 2600 jährigen Bestehens des Kaiserreichs Japan, Op. 84. Der Rosenkavalier – Waltz Sequence, Act 3. [a]**Philipp Haass** (va); [a]**Oswald Uhl** (vc); **Bavarian State Orchestra / Richard Strauss.** Preiser mono Ⓕ 90205* (two discs: 145 minutes: AAD: 8/95).

Metamorphosen. **Mahler** Symphony No. 6 in A minor. **New Philharmonia Orchestra / Sir John Barbirolli.** EMI Rouge et Noir Ⓜ CZS7 67816-2 (two discs: 111 minutes: ADD: 9/95).

...Also sprach Zarathustra. Der Rosenkavalier – suite. Don Juan. **Bavarian Radio Symphony Orchestra / Lorin Maazel.** RCA Victor Red Seal Ⓕ 09026 68225-2 (77 minutes: DDD: 10/95).

...Don Quixote[b]. **Lalo** Cello Concerto in D minor[a]. **Jacqueline du Pré** (vc); [b]**Herbert Downes** (va); [a]**Cleveland Orchestra / Daniel Barenboim;** [b]**New Philharmonia Orchestra / Sir Adrian Boult.** EMI Ⓕ CDC5 55528-2 (73 minutes: ADD: 11/95).

...Don Quixote[a]. **Tchaikovsky** Variations on a Rococo Theme in A major, Op. 33[b]. **Fauré** Elégie, Op. 24[c]. **Debussy** Cello Sonata[d]. **Tortelier** Le pitre[d]. Paul Tortelier (vc); [a]**Leonard Rubens** (va); [d]**Gerald Moore** (pf); **Royal Philharmonic Orchestra /** [a]**Sir Thomas Beecham,** [bc]**Norman Del Mar.** EMI Références mono Ⓜ CDH5 65502-2* (78 minutes: ADD: 12/95).

...Don Juan. *Coupled with works by* **Brahms, Wagner, Shostakovich** and **Smetana** The Solti Orchestral Project, Carnegie Hall / Sir Georg Solti. Decca Ⓕ 444 458-2DH (77 minutes: DDD: 12/95). *See review in the Collections section; refer to the Index to Reviews.* Ⓖ

...Burleske[a]. Der Rosenkavalier – suite. Salome – Dance of the seven veils. Festliches Präludium, Op. 61[b]. [a]**Jeffrey Kahane** (pf); [b]**Michael Chertok** (org); **Cincinnati Symphony Orchestra / Jésus López-Cobos.** Telarc Ⓕ CD80371 (65 minutes: DDD: 12/95).

...Burleske. **Schumann** Piano Concerto in A minor, Op. 54. **Hélène Grimaud** (pf); **Deutsches Symphony Orchestra, Berlin / David Zinman.** Erato Ⓕ 0630-11727-2 (52 minutes: DDD: 2/96).

New review

R. Strauss Horn Concertos[a] – No. 1 in E flat major, Op. 11, No. 2 in E flat major, AV132. Duett-Concertino, AV147[b]. Serenade, Op. 7. [a]**David Pyatt** (hn); [b]**Joy Farrall** (cl); [b]**Julie Andrews** (bn); **Britten Sinfonia / Nicholas Cleobury.** EMI Eminence Ⓜ CD-EMX2238 (66 minutes: DDD: 8/95). Recorded 1994. ⒼⒼⒼ

David Pyatt won the BBC's "Young Musician of the Year" Competition back in 1988. Since then the fledgling has well and truly flown. This is sensationally good horn playing. Primarily, there's his noble legato: the heart of the matter, a beautiful sound, full, even and unclouded. He is sparing with the brassy timbres, holding them in reserve for dramatic effect, for such times as the instrument's well-rounded jocularity must take on a brazen, huntsmen-like air, or rise to shining heroics – like the challenging motto theme of the First Concerto. His shaping of the big phrases rolls off the page with ease and authority, but equally, so much of his personality is conveyed in the rhythmic articulation: a dashing, Jack-be-nimble mischievousness (even a touch of impudence?) in Strauss's athletic *allegros*. Most of all, though – and this is rare – he loves to play quietly, really quietly. He is a master of those dreamy, far-away departures – twilit forest-murmurings: mysterious, unreal. The recording helps in this, too, with a beautifully integrated balance. The sound of the early *Serenade*, Op. 7 is particularly fine with ripe, euphonious tuttis and room enough for individual personalities (and the Britten Sinfonia boasts several) to open up. And that is the most remarkable aspect of the piece, the utterly natural way it blends and contrasts across the whole spectrum of wind voices. Two of them take centre-stage in the delightful *Duett-Concertino*. Joy Farrall's clarinet and Julie Andrews's bassoon are like Octavian and the Baron Ochs in this gentle but spirited opus. A spendid disc, then, sympathetically directed by Nicholas Cleobury.

R. Strauss Divertimento, Op. 86. Le bourgeois gentilhomme – Suite, Op. 60. **Orpheus Chamber Orchestra.** DG Ⓕ 435 871-2GH (68 minutes: DDD: 3/93). Recorded 1991. Ⓖ
This coupling should give much pleasure to those prepared to take a little New World zest and stringency with their Strauss; despite the absence of a conductor, there is nothing remotely bland or mechanical about the playing. The little-known *Divertimento* is often confused with the similar-sounding *Dance Suite* of 1923, also based on Couperin originals. The *Divertimento* came together as late as 1943 and has never established a firm place in the repertoire. Until now: the Orpheus Chamber Orchestra are mightily impressive here, eclipsing previous exponents by restoring something of the freshness of Couperin's *Pièces de clavecin* to Strauss's outrageous realizations. Behind the inauthentic, chocolate-box sonorities lurks an affecting undercurrent of nostalgia and there are obvious links with *Capriccio*'s pastiche of Passepied, Gigue and Gavotte. *Le bourgeois gentilhomme* is of course the stronger score and this stylish account of the suite is absolutely complete, unlike some famous versions of the past. Again, the players are on world-beating form, lacking perhaps the very last ounce of charm and flexibility but compensating with a dazzling display of technique. Sensitive microphone placement minimizes the problems of an over-resonant venue. This is modern music-making at its best.

R. Strauss Eine Alpensinfonie, Op. 64. Don Juan, Op. 20. **San Francisco Symphony Orchestra / Herbert Blomstedt.** Decca Ⓕ 421 815-2DH (70 minutes: DDD: 6/90). Recorded 1988. ⒼⒼ
The *Alpine* Symphony is the last of Richard Strauss's great tone-poems and is in many ways the most spectacular. The score is an evocation of the changing moods of an alpine landscape and the huge orchestral apparatus of over 150 players encompasses quadruple wind, 20 horns, organ, wind machine, cowbells, thunder machine, two harps and enhanced string forces. Its pictorialism may be all too graphic but what virtuosity and inspiration Strauss commands. Herbert Blomstedt's reading penetrates beyond the pictorialism into the work's deeper elements. It emerges as a gigantic hymn to nature on a Mahlerian scale. Tempos are slower, but these are justified by the noble expansiveness of the final pages, towards which the whole performance moves with impressive inevitability. The San Francisco Symphony's playing is magnificent, with subtle use of vibrato by the strings and superb performances, individual and corporate, by the wind sections. The recording is on a spacious scale to match the performance, the big climaxes really thrilling and the whole well balanced. The *Don Juan* performance is fine too.
Additional recommendations ...
...Eine Alpensinfonie. **Concertgebouw Orchestra / Bernard Haitink.** Philips Ⓕ 416 156-2PH
(50 minutes: DDD: 7/86). *Selected by Sounds in Retrospect.* Ⓖ
...Eine Alpensinfonie. Der Rosenkavalier – suite[a]. [a]**Tivoli Augmented Orchestra; Bavarian State Orchestra / Richard Strauss.** Koch Legacy mono Ⓜ 37132-2* (72 minutes: ADD: 1/93).

New review
R. Strauss Serenade, Op. 7. Suite in B flat major, Op. 4. Sonatina No. 2 in E flat major, AV143, "Fröhliche Werkstatt". Wind soloists of the **Chamber Orchestra of Europe / Heinz Holliger.** Philips Ⓕ 438 933-2PH (74 minutes: DDD: 9/95). Recorded 1993.
What the Orpheus Chamber Orchestra did for Strauss's *Bourgeois gentilhomme* Suite (reviewed above) the COE wind players have achieved with the second of the composer's late *Sonatinas* (also known as the Symphony for Wind Instruments) – in this case, making sure that outer-movement lines have plenty of muscle, that the bigger harmonies bloom without ever sounding overblown and that the whole adds up to a rainbow of generous invention, effects and colours such as one would hardly have thought possible even given Strauss's extraordinary knowledge of the medium. With a sophisticated, easy-going team like the Netherlands Wind Ensemble, the Indian summer burble has an instant charm that palls rather quickly; but while not even this team can quite stop the mind from wandering in the very prolix finale, there is a dynamic and tonal rigour about the first movement which rivets attention. The line of easy invention between the teenage Strauss's first characteristically happy inspirations in the *Serenade* and the octogenarian's refuge in his 'happy workshop' is broken by the more uneven qualities of the Op. 4 *Suite*. The COE players do it the credit of taking it seriously, making the most of the characteristic swing from an assumed pale cast of thought into the character of a prototype *Till Eulenspiegel*. Again, the full chordings – closely but deliciously captured by the excellent recording – are a constant delight, and one assumes Holliger's shaping hand in the flexible vocalizing of the many *bel canto* lines (starting with the *Serenade*'s ineffable counter-melody). A winner.
Additional recommendations ...
...Suite, Op. 4. Sonatinas Nos. 1 and 2. Serenade. **London Winds / Michael Collins** (cl). Hyperion
Ⓕ CDA66731/2 (two discs: 105 minutes: DDD: 8/93).

...Oboe Concerto. **Françaix** L' Horloge de flore. **Ibert** Symphonie concertante. **Satie** Three Gymnopédies – No. 1. **John de Lancie** (ob); **London Symphony Orchestra / André Previn.** RCA Victor Gold Seal Ⓜ GD87989 (72 minutes: ADD: 12/91).

...Serenade,[a]. Suite, Op. 4[b]. Sonatinas – No. 1 in F major, "Aus der Werkstatt eines Invaliden", AV135[b]; No. 2[a]. Oboe Concerto, AV144[c]. [c]**Heinz Holliger** (ob); [ab]**Netherlands Wind Ensemble;** [c]**New Philharmonia Orchestra / Edo de Waart.** Philips Ⓜ 438 733-2PM2 (two discs: 132 minutes: ADD: 7/94). Ⓖ

R. Strauss Till Eulenspiegels lustige Streiche, Op. 28. Ein Heldenleben, Op. 40. **Chicago Symphony Orchestra / Daniel Barenboim.** Erato Ⓕ 2292-45621-2 (63 minutes: DDD: 8/91).

This disc kicks off with Barenboim's suave reading of *Till Eulenspiegel*. The performance is brilliant, combining tenderness (as in the introduction) with exuberance. His pacing and judging of the tricky corners is exemplary and his approach shows an awareness that this above all is a young man's music. For sheer splendour and opulence it is quite staggering. Barenboim's hero in *Ein Heldenleben* is impetuous and romantic and he gives the Chicago Symphony Orchestra a free rein to bring their customary flair and virtuosity to the work. The battle sequence is properly exciting while Samuel Magad's violin solo is sweet and seductive. This reading is a major claimant for supremacy. Erato have given Barenboim a big full sound, eminently suited to the music. The entire recording is very fine, with plenty of inner detail and for sheer opulence and splendour it surpasses other versions.

Additional recommendations ...

...Ein Heldenleben. Don Juan. **Berlin Philharmonic Orchestra / Herbert von Karajan.** DG Galleria Ⓜ 429 717-2GGA* (ADD). Ⓖ

...Also sprach Zarathustra. Ein Heldenleben. **Chicago Symphony Orchestra / Fritz Reiner.** RCA Living Stereo Ⓜ 09026 61494-2 (76 minutes: ADD: 4/93). ⓖⒼ

...Ein Heldenleben[a]. Don Juan, Op. 20[b]. Till Eulenspiegels lustige Streiche[b]. [a]**Philadelphia Orchestra / Eugene Ormandy;** [bc]**Cleveland Orchestra / George Szell.** Sony Classical Essential Classics Ⓑ SBT48272 (75 minutes: ADD: 5/93). Ⓖ

...Ein Heldenleben. Till Eulenspiegels lustige Streiche. **Cleveland Orchestra / Christoph von Dohnányi.** Decca Ⓕ 436 444-2DH (61 minutes: DDD: 10/93).

...Don Juan, Op. 20[a]. Duett-Concertino, AV147[b]. Burleske in D minor, AV85[c]. Till Eulenspiegels lustige Streiche[d]. [b]**Heinrich Geuser** (cl); [b]**Willi Fugmann** (bn); [c]**Margrit Weber** (pf); [abc]**Berlin RIAS Orchestra;** [d]**Berlin Philharmonic Orchestra / Ferenc Fricsay.** DG Dokumente mono Ⓜ 445 403-2GDO* (67 minutes: ADD: 11/94).

R. Strauss Gesänge, Op. 33 – No. 3, Hymnus; No. 4, Pilgers Morgenlied. Gesänge, Op. 51. Grössere Gesänge, Op. 44 – No. 1, Notturno.

Mahler (orch. Berio) Lieder und Gesänge – No. 1, Frühlingsmorgen; No. 3, Hans und Grethe; No. 6, Um schlimme Kinder artig zu machen; No. 7, Ich ging mit Lust durch einen grünen Wald; No. 10, Zu Strassburg auf der Schanz; No. 13, Nicht wiedersehen! **Andreas Schmidt** (bar); **Berlin Radio Symphony Orchestra / Cord Garben.** RCA Victor Red Seal Ⓕ 09026 61184-2 (62 minutes: DDD: 8/94). Texts and translations included. Recorded 1992.

The real discovery here is Strauss's 15-minute-long, wholly neglected "Notturno", a narrative with orchestra to a poem by Richard Dehmel. It tells of the vision of a dream of Death in the shape of a much-loved friend who appears in bright moonshine, in the depths of the night, playing a beseeching air on his violin. As Norman Del Mar says in Vol. 3 of his biography of the composer (London. 1972). "The title *Notturno* is Dehmel's own and the long poem is one of great emotional intensity". So is Strauss's extraordinarily hypnotic and original setting. The mood of the piece is hallucinatory and tormented, uncannily recalling that of Tristan's desperate outbursts in Act 3. Schmidt interprets it with a notable feeling for its haunting, eerie quality, in a recording of presence. Almost as neglected are the two songs that comprise Strauss's Op. 51. The Uhland setting, "Das Thal" is the most ambitious, describing someone who wants to get away from it all. Its sustained lyricism and atmospheric scoring are Strauss at his most compelling. Berio's orchestrations of some of Mahler's early settings don't sound entirely Mahlerian, but Schmidt sings them all so beautifully that criticism is silenced.

R. Strauss Deutsche Motette, Op. 62[a]. Gesänge, Op. 34. An den Baum Daphne (epilogue to "Daphne"), AV137[b]. Die Göttin im Putzzimmer, AV120. [a]**Tina Kiberg,** [b]**Marianne Lund** (sops); [b]**Christian Lisdorf** (treb); [a]**Randi Stene** (contr); [a]**Gert Henning-Jensen** (ten); [a]**Ulrik Cold** (bass); [b]**Copenhagen Boys' Choir; Danish National Radio Choir / Stefan Parkman.** Chandos Ⓕ CHAN9223 (57 minutes: DDD: 5/94). Texts and translations included. Recorded 1993.

Under Stefan Parkman the Danish National Radio Choir have established a reputation second to none. Parkman handles his singers as if they were a fully fledged symphony orchestra; which is not at all inappropriate in this programme by the supreme master of orchestral colour. From the heart of the 16 chorus parts of the *Deutsche Motette* a further seven are projected by solo voices emerging imperceptibly from the midst of a dense, luxuriant texture. The depth of colour and range of emotions are every bit as extensive in these works as in the great orchestral tone-poems; indeed few orchestral tone-poems evoke dusk and sunset so vividly as "Der Abend", the first of the 1897 *Zwei Gesänge*. There is a wonderfully luminous soundscape here; a combination of superb compositional skill, sensitive musical direction, superlative choral singing and a warm, full-bodied recording.

New review

R. Strauss Lieder – Op. 10: No. 2, Nichts; No. 9, Allerseelen; Winternacht, Op. 15 No. 2;
Ständchen, Op. 17 No. 2; A11' mein Gedanken, Op. 21 No. 1; Op. 22: No. 3, Efeu; No. 4,
Wasserrose; Op. 27: No. 2, Cäcilie; No. 3, Heimliche Aufforderung; Op. 29: No. 1, Traum durch
die Dämmerung; No. 3, Nachtgang; Op. 32: No. 2, Sehnsucht; No. 3, Liebeshymnus; Der
Rosenband, Op. 36 No. 1; Op. 37: No. 3, Meinem Kinde; No. 4, Mein Auge; No. 5, Herr Lenz;
No. 6, Hochzeitlich Lied; Befreit, Op. 39 No. 4; Op. 49: No. 1, Waldseligkeit; No. 6,
Junggesellenschwur; Weihnachtsgefühl, AV94. **Simon Keenlyside** (bar); **Malcolm Martineau** (pf).
EMI Eminence Ⓜ CD-EMX2250 (64 minutes: DDD: 6/96). Texts and translations included.
Recorded 1995.

Simon Keenlyside understands and respects both Strauss's sentiment and his sentimentality for what
it is. With steady, thoughtfully considered word-placing, he relieves *Allerseelen* of its sicklier scents
and keeps its movement light and fresh, bringing the song to a strong, firmly syllabic climax. This skill
in estimating the expressive potential of verbal weight and measure also strengthens the contours of
his *Sehnsucht*; and in *Ständchen* keeps the vocal focus clear and bright in the more fleet, high notes.
Keenlyside exploits the heroic character of his baritone in the bold rhetorical questions of *Nichts*, and
in *Liebeshymnus* where the voice rings out with fearless resilience in its top register. This sense of
heroic address and acclamation tends to replace, for Keenlyside, the more tremulous, passionate
response some singers find in songs such as the *Hochzeitlich Lied* and *Heimliche Aufforderung*: the lip
seldom trembles here, the voice yields little to Strauss's harmonic sidesteps and melodic melismas.
Whether you miss that, or find it a relief, will be purely a matter of taste. With Malcolm Martineau
delighting equally in the complexity and the simplicity of the piano writing displayed in this 20 years'
worth of love songs, the recital should certainly take a significant place in any Strauss collection.

Additional recommendations ...

...Op. 10 – No. 1, Zueignung; No. 2, Nichts; No. 4, Die Georgine; No. 6, Die Verschwiegenen; No.
7, Die Zeitlose; No. 8, Allerseelen. Heimkehr, Op. 15 No. 5. Op. 21 – No. 2, Du meines Herzens
Krönelein; No. 3, Ach Lieb, ich muss nun scheiden. Vier Mädchenblumen, Op. 22. O wärst du
mein, Op. 26 No. 2. Morgen, Op. 27 No. 4. Traum durch die Dämmerung, Op. 29 No. 1. Ich
trage meine Minne, Op. 32 No. 1. Befreit, Op. 39 No. 4. Gefunden, Op. 56
No. 1. Op. 66 – No. 2, Einst kam der Bock als Bote; No. 6, O lieber Künstler sei ermahnt; No. 9,
Es war mal eine Wanze; No. 11, Die Händel und die Macher. Op. 67 – Wie erkenn' ich mein
Treulieb; No. 2, Guten Morgen, 's ist Sankt Valentinstag; No. 3, Sie trugen ihn auf der Bahre
bloss; No. 6, Wanderers Gemütsruhe. **Mitsuko Shirai** (mez); **Hartmut Höll** (pf). Capriccio
Ⓟ 10 497 (72 minutes: DDD: 2/95). Texts included.

...Die Drossel, AV34. Der müde Wanderer, AV13. Lass ruh'n die Toten, AV35. Abend- und
Morgenrot, AV42, Wiegenlied, AV41. Nebel, AV47. Weihnachtsgefühl, AV94. Weihnachtslied,
AV2. Ein Röslein zog ich mir im Garten, AV49. Lieder aus Letzte Blätter, Op. 10 – No. 1,
Zueignung; No. 3, Die Nacht; No. 8, Allerseelen. Wie sollten wir geheim sie halten, Op. 19 No. 4.
Schlichte Weisen, Op. 21 – No. 1, All' mein Gedanken, mein Herz und mein Sinn; No. 2, Du
meines Herzens Krönelein; No. 3, Ach Lieb, ich muss nun scheiden. Lieder, Op. 27 – No. 1, Ruhe,
meine Seele; No. 4, Morgen!. Schlagende Herzen, Op. 29 No. 2. Leises Lied, Op. 39 No. 1. Lieder,
Op. 49 – No. 2, In goldener Fülle; No. 3, Wiegenliedchen; No. 7, Wer lieben will, muss leiden;
No. 8, Ach, was Kummer, Qual und Schmerzen. Gefunden, Op. 56 No. 1. Das Bächlein, Op. 88
No. 1. **Marie McLaughlin** (sop); **Graham Johnson** (pf). Hyperion Ⓟ CDA66659 (63 minutes:
DDD: 8/95).

R. Strauss Four Last Songs, AV150. Zueignung, Op. 10 No. 1. Morgen, Op. 27 No. 4.
Wagner Wesendonk Lieder. **Elisabeth Meyer-Topsøe** (sop); **Copenhagen Philharmonic Orchestra /
Hans Norbert Bihlmaier.** Kontrapunkt Ⓟ 32156 (50 minutes: DDD: 1/94). Notes, texts and
translations included. Recorded 1993.   Ⓖ

R. Strauss Four Last Songs, AV150.
Wagner Wesendonk Lieder. Tristan und Isolde – Prelude and Liebestod. **Cheryl Studer** (sop);
Dresden Staatskapelle / Giuseppe Sinopoli. DG Ⓟ 439 865-2GH (61 minutes: DDD: 7/94). Notes,
texts and translations included. *Gramophone Editor's choice.*   Ⓖ

Here is a discovery, perhaps the most promising *Jugendlich-Dramatische* soprano to burst on the scene
since Cheryl Studer. With a full, glowing tone that soars easily above the stave without let or
hindrance, an even line, and an innate feeling for a long phrase, Elisabeth Meyer-Topsøe has chosen
repertory that shows off her gifts ideally. She sings the *Wesendonk Lieder* with a truly Wagnerian
amplitude of phrase and a fair feeling for the text. You only have to hear the generosity of "Stehe
still!", with vibrato used to enhance the expression (a lovely "Wesen in wesen", a refulgent close), or
the passage starting "Wohl ich weiss es" in "Im Treibhaus" to hear these matters made manifest.
Others have, of course, found deeper shades in the songs, but these will surely come to this young artist
in time. Similarly the sense of valediction in the *Four Last Songs* can be more easily encompassed by
maturer singing, but few have managed the long, tricky phrases of "Beim Schlafengehen" with such a
long breath or such daring, exciting fullness. The Wagner is faithfully recorded. In the Strauss items,
the voice sometimes seems to go out of focus and the orchestra is lacking real definition. The
conducting and playing are always adequate but not quite of the calibre this aspiring artist deserves.

In the Strauss Cheryl Studer need hardly fear comparison with the best of her predecessors (listed below), largely because her voice, lyrical yet with dramatic overtones, seems near-ideal for Strauss and for this work in particular, quite apart from the sheer beauty and technical accomplishment of her singing. In the first two songs there is the necessary ecstasy and longing in her singing as Strauss reviews, elegiacally, his musical credo. As an exemplar of the rest one could cite the loving treatment in "September" of the phrases beginning "Langsam tut er", the singer's tone poised, the shading of the line perfectly natural. It is the seamless legato and lovely voice that again make "Beim Schlafengehen" so rewarding while, in the final song, Studer is suitably hushed and reflective. Sinopoli and the Staatskapelle Dresden provide ideal support for their singer with the playing in all these works as lyrically expressive as the singing above it, all tempos ideally judged. Similar praise can be given to the reading of the *Wesendonk Lieder*. Here, once again, one notes Studer's amazing combination of vocal mastery and interpretative insight. Every dynamic and expressive mark is scrupulously followed (listen to the *piano* at "Luft" and "Duft" in the second song) in the pursuit of seamless phrasing and a due attention to the text. Her Liebestod makes one eager for her to sing the role on stage, or at least on CD. The richness of her singing, the thorough mastery of German diction and phraseology, make this another special performance. Sinopoli's reading of the Prelude to *Tristan* is flowing, intense and spontaneous and the playing is predictably superb, all adding to the disc's worth. The recordings are for the most part happily spacious and well focused.

R. Strauss Four Last Songs, AV150 (from LW5056, 12/53)[a]. Arabella – Er ist der Richtige nicht (with Hilde Gueden, sop. LW5029, 10/53)[b]; Der Richtige so hab ich stets zu mir gesagt (Paul Schoeffler, bass-bar. LXT5017, 4/55)[c]; Das war sehr gut, Mandryka (Alfred Poell, bar. LW5029)[b]. Ariadne auf Naxos – Es gibt ein Reich[c]. Capriccio – Closing scene (Franz Bierbach, bass. Both LXT5017)[c]. **Lisa della Casa** (sop); **Vienna Philharmonic Orchestra / [a]Karl Böhm, [b]Rudolf Moralt, [c]Heinrich Hollreiser.** Decca Historic mono Ⓜ 425 959-2DM* (67 minutes: ADD: 4/90). Texts and translations included. Recorded 1953-54.

Strauss's *Four Last Songs* are a perfect summation of the composer's lifelong love-affair with the soprano voice deriving from the fact that he married a soprano, Pauline Ahna. They are also an appropriate and deeply moving farewell to his career as a composer and to the whole romantic tradition and they have inspired many glorious performances. In recent times there has been a tendency to linger unnecessarily over what are already eloquent enough pieces. Lisa della Casa, in her naturally and lovingly sung performance under Karl Böhm (the first-ever studio recording of the pieces back in 1953) makes no such mistake. In this new incarnation this is a wonderful offering at medium price backed by other invaluable Strauss interpretations from the Swiss diva. Her particular gift is to sing the pieces in a natural, unforced manner with gloriously unfettered tone. Her and Böhm's tempos tend to be faster than those employed by most of her successors.

Additional recommendations ...

...Four Last Songs. Cäcilie, Op. 27 No. 2. Morgen, Op. 27 No. 4. Wiegenlied, Op. 41 No. 1. Ruhe meine Seele, Op. 27 No. 1. Meinem Kinde, Op. 37 No. 3. Zueignung, Op. 10 No. 1 (orch. Heger). **Jessye Norman** (sop); **Leipzig Gewandhaus Orchestra / Kurt Masur.** Philips Ⓕ 411 052-2PH (DDD: 2/84). **Ⓖ**

...Four Last Songs [a]. Muttertändelei, Op. 43 No. 2[a]. Waldseligkeit, Op. 49 No. 1[a]; Zueignung, Op. 10 No. 1[a]. Freundliche Vision, Op. 48 No. 1[a]. Die heiligen drei Könige, Op. 56 No. 6[b]. Ruhe, meine Seele, Op. 27 No. 1[b]. Meinem Kinde, Op. 37 No. 3[b], Wiegenlied, Op. 41 No. 1[b]. Morgen, Op. 27 No. 4 (with Edith Peinemann, vn)[b]. Das Bächlein, Op. 88 No. 1[b]. Das Rosenband, Op. 36 No. 1[b]. Winterweihe, Op. 48 No. 4. **Elisabeth Schwarzkopf** (sop); [a]**Berlin Radio Symphony Orchestra;** [b]**London Symphony Orchestra / George Szell.** EMI Ⓕ CDC7 47276-2 (64 minutes: ADD: 12/85). **ⒼⒼⒼ**

...Four Last Songs[a]. Capriccio – Morgen mittag um Elf[a]. Arabella[b] – Ich danke, Fräulein ... Aber der Richtige; Mein Elemer; Sie wollen mich heiraten; Das war sehr gut (all with Anny Felbermayer, sop; Josef Metternich, bar). **Dame Elisabeth Schwarzkopf** (sop); **Philharmonia Orchestra / [a]Otto Ackermann, [b]Lovro von Matačic.** EMI Références mono Ⓜ CDH7 61001-2* (68 minutes: ADD: 4/88). *Gramophone classical 100.* **ⒼⒼⒼ**

...Four Last Songs[a]. Metamorphosen for 23 Solo Strings. Oboe Concerto[b]. [a]**Gundula Janowitz** (sop); [b]**Lothar Koch** (ob); **Berlin Philharmonic Orchestra / Herbert von Karajan.** DG Galleria Ⓜ 423 888-2GGA (75 minutes: ADD: 12/88). **ⒼⒼ**

...Four Last Songs[a]. All' mein Gedanken, Op. 21 No. 1[b]. Allerseelen, Op. 10 No. 8[b]. Begegnung, AV72[b]. Cäcilie, Op. 27 No. 2[b]. Hat gesagt, Op. 36 No. 3[b]. Madrigal, Op. 15 No. 1[b]. Malven, Op. posth[b]. Morgen, Op. 27 No. 4[b]. Muttertändelei, Op. 43 No. 2[b]. Die Nacht, Op. 10 No. 3[b]. Schlechtes Wetter, Op. 69 No. 5[b]. Ständchen, Op. 17 No. 2[b]. Zueignung, Op. 10 No. 1[b]. **Dame Kiri Te Kanawa** (sop); [a]**Vienna Philharmonic Orchestra / Sir Georg Solti** ([b]pf). Decca Ⓕ 430 511-2DH (50 minutes: DDD: 9/91).

...Four Last Songs.[a]. Capriccio – Morgen mittag um elf! ... Kein andres[b]. Tod und Verklärung, Op. 24[c]. [ab]**Gundula Janowitz** (sop); [a]**Berlin Philharmonic Orchestra / Herbert von Karajan;** [b]**Bavarian Radio Symphony Orchestra;** [c]**Dresden Staatskapelle / Karl Böhm.** DG Classikon Ⓑ 439 467-2GCL (65 minutes: ADD: 4/95).

...Four Last Songs[a]. Oboe Concerto, AV144[b]. Lieder[c] – Cäcilie, Op. 27 No. 2; Befreit, Op. 39 No. 4; Muttertändelei, Op. 43 No. 2; Frühlingsfeier, Op. 56 No. 5; Die heiligen drei Könige, Op. 56

No. 6. [a]**Heather Harper**, [c]**Elizabeth Harwood** (sops); [b]**John Anderson** (ob); [a]**Royal Philharmonic Orchestra**, [b]**BBC Symphony Orchestra**, [c]**New Philharmonia Orchestra / Norman Del Mar.** BBC Radio Classics Ⓑ 15656 9138-2 (65 minutes: ADD: 5/96).

R. Strauss Lieder – Ruhe, meine Seele, Op. 27 No. 1; Waldseligkeit, Op. 49 No. 1; Freundliche Vision, Op. 48 No. 1; Morgen!, Op. 27 No. 4; Befreit, Op. 39 No. 4; Meinem Kinde, Op. 37 No. 3; Winterweihe, Op. 48 No. 4; Wiegenlied, Op. 41 No. 1; Die heiligen drei Könige aus Morgenland, Op. 56 No. 6[a]. Metamorphosen for 23 Solo Strings. [a]**Gundula Janowitz** (sop); **Academy of London / Richard Stamp.** Virgin Classics Ⓕ VC7 59538-2 (60 minutes: DDD: 2/91). Texts and translations included.   Ⓖ

Gundula Janowitz has given some of the most beautiful performances of the music of Richard Strauss in the last three decades. Why no one asked her to record more songs during her heyday is a great mystery, but here is a quite lovely collection that shows her musicality and fine feeling for the Strauss idiom at its best. Obviously, given the passing of the years, she is happiest in the gentler, more legato numbers where her quite exquisite breath control and beauty of tone reap rich rewards – the floated line in *Wiegenlied* is absolutely ravishing and her feeling for words has, if anything, deepened over the years. She instils appropriate drama into the ecstatic *Die heiligen drei Könige aus Morgenland*, a lovely song. Throughout the disc the Academy of London play with great feeling and a good regard for the sound-world that Richard Strauss's music demands. As a very substantial fill-up. Richard Stamp and his orchestra offer a sensitive reading of Strauss's heartrending *Metamorphosen*, that threnody for the great opera-houses of Germany destroyed by Allied bombing during the Second World War. The complex lines are interwoven with care and sensitivity, and the work's true character emerges powerfully in this passionate performance. The recording is rich and clear. A delightful disc.

New review

R. Strauss Friedenstag[a]. **Hans Hotter** (bass-bar) Commandant; **Viorica Ursuleac** (sop) Maria; **Herbert Alsen** (bass) Sergeant; **Josef Witt** (ten) Rifleman; **Hermann Wiedemann** (bass) Corporal; **Carl Bissuti** (bass) Musketeer; **Nikolaus Zec** (bass) Bugler; **Anton Dermota** (ten) A Piedmontese; **Hermann Gallos** (ten) Officer; **Georg Monthy** (bass) Front-line Officer; **Karl Kamann** (bass) Holsteiner; **Willy Franter** (ten) Burgomaster; **Viktor Madin** (bar) Prelate; **Mela Bugarinovic** (mez) Woman of the People.
Arabella – excerpts[b]. Ariadne auf Naxos – excerpts[c]. [b]**Margit Bokor**, [bc]**Adele Kern**, [c]**Dora Komarek**, [c]**Anny Konetzni**, [c]**Elisabeth Rutgers**, [c]**Else Schulz**, [b]**Viorica Ursuleac** (sops); [c]**Elena Nikolaidi**, [b]**Gertrud Rünger** (mezzos); [c]**Friedrich Jelinek**, [c]**Alexander Pichler**, [c]**Richard Sallaba**, [c]**Set Svanholm**, [c]**William Wernigk** (tens); [c]**Hermann Baier**, [c]**Alfred Poell** (bars); [bc]**Alfred Jerger** (bass-bar); [b]**Richard Mayr**, [c]**Alfred Vogel** (basses); [c]**Alfred Muzzarelli** (spkr); **Vienna State Opera** [ab]**Chorus and Orchestra /** [ab]**Clemens Krauss**, [c]**Rudolf Moralt.** Koch Schwann mono Ⓜ 314652* (two discs: 143 minutes: ADD: 10/95). Item marked [a] recorded live in 1939, [b]live in 1933, [c]1941.

This issue offers us a complete performance of Strauss's underrated and under-recorded *Friedenstag* given by its creators in 1939, shortly after its première in Munich. Here Krauss, Ursuleac and Hotter prove incontrovertibly that the work has a strength and validity not often accorded it by even the most dedicated of Straussians. You marvel at the immense conviction and energy Krauss brings to it. Then, his wife Ursuleac gives the performance of her life as Maria. She is fearless and tireless in tackling the high As, B flats and Bs in which the role abounds, singing with vibrant tone and in a possessed manner fitting an overwrought woman starved of the love of her husband (the Commandant) who has poured all his energies into war. Finally, she provides the necessary ecstasy when she wins him back and sees the war come to an end. As ever, Strauss glories in his writing for a *lirico-spinto*, and Ursuleac glories with him. The 30-year-old Hotter, in towering voice, gives to the Commandant's part the right sense of a man dedicated to his role of defending his Kaiser's cause and honour at whatever cost to his men or to his personal life. A team of Viennese stalwarts of the day fills the smaller roles satisfactorily, with the young Dermota notable as the Piedmontese youth musing on his beloved Italy and its girls: it's another role nicely etched in by the composer. The music is so different from most of what Strauss was writing at the time. Instead of harking back to romanticism, as in *Arabella* and *Daphne*, he composes here in a tougher style more in keeping with his own time, bringing into play Hindemithian, even Bergian ideas. The final paean to peace recalls the Mahler of the symphonies' choral sections. Mind you, the piece – as many have commented – is more dramatic oratorio than opera. The recorded sound, taken in this case off a broadcast, is good by the standard of these sets, but by no means anything special. However, the voices don't distort and much of the orchestral detail can be gleaned. *Friedenstag* is flanked by excerpts from two other works by Strauss. Those from a 1933 *Arabella*, also a Viennese 'first', featuring the original singers of the two main roles, are not so desirable since Ursuleac and Jerger recorded the most important passages commercially (Decca-Polydor, 12/33). Nevertheless, it is good to hear Krauss conducting with such *élan*.

R. Strauss Salome. **Cheryl Studer** (sop) Salome; **Bryn Terfel** (bar) Jokanaan; **Horst Hiestermann**
(ten) Herod; **Leonie Rysanek** (sop) Herodias; **Clemens Bieber** (ten) Narraboth; **Marianne Rørholm**
(contr) Page; **Friedrich Molsberger** (bass) First Nazarene; **Ralf Lukas** (bass) Second Nazarene;
William Murray (bass) First Soldier; **Bengt Rundgren** (bass) Second Soldier; **Klaus Lang** (bar)
Cappadocian; **Orchestra of the Deutsche Oper, Berlin / Giuseppe Sinopoli.** DG Ⓕ 431 810-2GH2
(two discs: 102 minutes: DDD: 9/91). Notes, text and translation included. Recorded 1990. ⒼⒼ

R. Strauss Salome. **Catherine Malfitano** (sop) Salome; **Bryn Terfel** (bass-bar) Jokanaan; **Kenneth**
Riegel (ten) Herod; **Hanna Schwarz** (mez) Herodias; **Kim Begley** (ten) Narraboth; **Randi Stene**
(contr) Page; **Peter Rose** (bass) First Nazarene; **Martin Gantner** (ten) Second Nazarene; **Frode**
Olsen (bass) First Soldier; **Georg Paucker** (bass) Second Soldier; **Walter Zeh** (bar) Cappadocian;
Rannveig Braga (mez) Slave; **Vienna Philharmonic Orchestra / Christoph von Dohnányi.** Decca
Ⓕ 444 178-2DHO2 (two discs: 100 minutes: DDD: 4/95). Notes, text and translation included.
Recorded 1994.   Ⓖ

Strauss's setting of a German translation of Oscar Wilde's play is original and erotically explicit. It
caused a sensation in its day and even now stimulates controversy. Sinopoli's recording is a
magnificent achievement, mainly because of Cheryl Studer's representation of the spoilt Princess who
demands and eventually gets the head of Jokanaan (John the Baptist) on a platter as a reward for her
striptease ("Dance of the Seven Veils"). Studer, her voice fresh, vibrant and sensuous, conveys exactly
Salome's growing fascination, infatuation and eventual obsession with Jokanaan, ending in the
arresting necrophilia of the final scene. She expresses Salome's wheedling, spoilt nature, strong will
and ecstasy in tones apt for every aspect of the strenuous role. She is supported to the hilt by
Sinopoli's incandescent conducting and by Bryn Terfel's convincing Jokanaan, unflaggingly delivered,
by Hiestermann's neurotic Herod, who makes a suitably fevered, unhinged sound as the near-crazed
Herod, and Rysanek's wilful Herodias. The playing is excellent and the recording has breadth and
warmth. This is eminently recommendable. For a newcomer to the work, Studer's superb portrayal
just tips the balance in favour of Sinopoli, though Sir Georg Solti's famous version (listed below)
comes a close second, with a gloriously sung Salome and the ravishingly beautiful playing of the
Vienna Philharmonia.

Concluding his excellent booklet-note for the Ozawa set, Michael Kennedy reminds us of Strauss's
description of *Salome* as "a scherzo with a fatal conclusion" and quotes Dallapiccola's verdict on a
1930 performance conducted by Zemlinsky which "made the score as transparent as that of *Così fan*
tutte". All three composers would undoubtedly be enthralled by Dohnányi's interpretation. The
conclusion may be less than overwhelmingly fatal, but the rest strokes and teases with a lighter touch
than the equally texture-conscious Sinopoli. Every new recording of the opera reveals details never
heard before, but this is richer than most in that respect: to single out a few from the long list would
be the constant refinement of the violin divisions, the trumpets' astonishing realization of Herodias's
peacock screams as Herod stalls for time and the string flailings, prophetic of the *Miraculous*
mandarin's urban panic, just before Salome's *Liebesverklärung*. The pace is swift and light and lends
all the smaller roles an extra degree of vividness in characterization, disappointing only in the lack of
a certain largesse for the final scene. Dohnányi certainly seems anxious to keep the oracular utterances
of Jokanaan on the move, which makes it the more interesting to have Terfel's characterization in
quite a different context from that of the Sinopoli recording. There, he made the prophet nobler and
broader of phrase than Strauss could ever have imagined; here, the big 'sea of Galilee' solo and the
later warning from the cistern begin with a tenderness and an intimacy which shed a new light on the
role. Terfel also brings out the terrifying side to Jokanaan right at the start of the confrontation with
Salome. Malfitano is exactly right here: girlish and fresh of tone, if less concerned with the colouring
of certain phrases than Cheryl Studer or Jessye Norman (for Ozawa). On the Philips set, Jessye
Norman's heroine provided the detailed case for another *Salome* single-handedly; here it is
Dohnányi's intelligent thoughts which command a special hearing.

Additional recommendations ...

...**Soloists; Vienna Philharmonic Orchestra / Sir Georg Solti.** Decca Ⓕ 414 414-2DH2 (two discs:
99 minutes: ADD: 7/85). *Gramophone classical 100.*   ⒼⒼⒼ

...**Soloists; Dresden Staatskapelle / Seiji Ozawa.** Philips Ⓕ 432 153-2PH2 (two discs: 103 minutes:
DDD: 10/94).

...**Soloists; Staatskapelle Dresden / Otmar Suitner.** Berlin Classics Ⓜ 0091 012BC (two discs:
94 minutes: ADD: 4/96).

R. Strauss Elektra. **Birgit Nilsson** (sop) Elektra; **Regina Resnik** (mez) Klytemnestra; **Marie Collier**
(sop) Chrysothemis; **Tom Krause** (bar) Orestes; **Gerhard Stolze** (ten) Aegisthus; **Pauline Tinsley**
(sop) Overseer; **Helen Watts** (contr), **Maureen Lehane, Yvonne Minton** (mezzos), **Jane Cook,**
Felicia Weathers (sops) First, Second, Third, Fourth and Fifth Maids; **Tugomir Franc** (Tutor);
Vienna Philharmonic Orchestra / Sir Georg Solti. Decca Ⓕ 417 345-2DH2 (two discs:
108 minutes: ADD: 12/86). Notes, text and translation included. From SET354/5 (11/67).   ⒼⒼ

Elektra is the most consistently inspired of all Strauss's operas and derives from Greek mythology,
with the ghost of Agamamenon, so unerringly delineated in the opening bars, hovering over the whole
work. The invention and the intensity of mood are sustained throughout the opera's one-act length,
and the characterization is both subtle and pointed. It is a work peculiarly well-suited to Solti's gifts

and he has done nothing better in his long career in the studios. He successfully maintains the nervous tension throughout the unbroken drama and conveys all the power and tension in Strauss's enormously complex score which is, for once, given complete. The recording captures the excellent singers and the Vienna Philharmonic in a warm, spacious acoustic marred only by some questionable electronic effects.

Additional recommendations ...

...**Soloists; Bavarian Radio Chorus and Symphony Orchestra / Wolfgang Sawallisch.** EMI Ⓕ CDS7 54067-2 (two discs: 102 minutes: DDD: 12/90).

...**Excerpts**[a] – Allein! Weh, ganz allein; Was willst du, fremder Mensch?; Elektra; Schwester! Salome – Dance of the seven veils[b]; Ach, du wolltest mich nicht deinen Mund küssen lassen[c]. [ac]**Inge Borkh** (sop) Elektra, Salome; [a]**Paul Schoeffler** (bass-bar) Orestes; [a]**Frances Yeend** (sop) Chrysothemis; [a]**Chicago Lyric Opera Chorus; Chicago Symphony Orchestra / Fritz Reiner.** RCA Victor Gold Seal Ⓜ GD60874* (67 minutes: ADD: 5/93). ⒼⒼ

...**Soloists; Berlin State Opera Chorus; Staatskapelle Berlin / Daniel Barenboim.** Teldec Ⓕ 4509-99175-2 (two discs: 101 minutes: DDD: 7/96).

R. Strauss Der Rosenkavalier. **Dame Elisabeth Schwarzkopf** (sop) Die Feldmarschallin; **Christa Ludwig** (mez) Octavian; **Otto Edelmann** (bass) Baron Ochs; **Teresa Stich-Randall** (sop) Sophie; **Eberhard Waechter** (bar) Faninal; **Nicolai Gedda** (ten) Italian Tenor; **Kerstin Meyer** (contr) Annina; **Paul Kuen** (ten) Valzacchi; **Ljuba Welitsch** (sop) Duenna; **Anny Felbermayer** (sop) Milliner; **Harald Pröghlöf** (bar) Notary; **Franz Bierbach** (bass) Police Commissioner; **Erich Majkut** (ten) Marschallin's Majordomo; **Gerhard Unger** (ten) Faninal's Majordomo, Animal Seller; **Karl Friedrich** (ten) Landlord; **Loughton High School for Girls and Bancroft's School Choirs; Philharmonia Chorus and Orchestra / Herbert von Karajan.** EMI Ⓕ CDS7 49354-2* (three discs: 191 minutes: ADD: 1/88). Notes, text and translation included. From Columbia SAX2269/72 (11/59). Recorded 1956. *Gramophone* classical 100. *Gramophone* Award Winner 1988. ⒼⒼⒼ

Der Rosenkavalier concerns the transferring of love of the young headstrong aristocrat Octavian from the older Marschallin (with whom he is having an affair) to the young Sophie, a girl of *nouveau riche* origins who is of his generation. The portrayal of the different levels of passion is masterly and the Marschallin's resigned surrender of her ardent young lover gives opera one of its most cherishable scenes. The comic side of the plot concerns the vulgar machinations of the rustic Baron Ochs and his attempts to seduce the disguised Octavian (girl playing boy playing girl!). The musical richness of the score is almost indescribable with stream after stream of endless melody, and the final trio which brings the three soprano roles together is the crowning glory of a masterpiece of our century. This magnificent 1956 recording, conducted with genius by Karajan and with a cast such as dreams are made of, has a status unparalleled and is unlikely to be challenged for many a year. The Philharmonia play like angels and Elisabeth Schwarzkopf as the Marschallin gives one of her greatest performances. The recording, lovingly remastered, is outstanding.

Additional recommendations ...

...**Soloists; Vienna State Opera Chorus; Vienna Philharmonic Orchestra / Sir Georg Solti.** Decca Ⓕ 417 493-2DH3 (three discs: 200 minutes: ADD: 3/87).

...**Soloists; Dresden Kreuzchor; Dresden State Opera Chorus; Dresden Staatskapelle / Bernard Haitink.** EMI Ⓕ CDS7 54259-2 (three discs: 223 minutes: DDD: 9/91).

...**(Abridged). Soloists; Vienna State Opera Chorus; Vienna Philharmonic Orchestra / Robert Heger.** Die Aegyptische Helena – Helen's awakening; Funeral march; Bei jener Nacht; Zweite Brautnacht, Zaubernacht!; **Rose Pauly** (sop); **Berlin State Opera Orchestra / Fritz Busch.** Breit über mein Haupt, Op. 19 No. 2. Morgen, Op. 27 No. 4. **Robert Hutt** (ten); **Richard Strauss** (pf). Pearl mono Ⓕ GEMMCDS9365* (two discs: 115 minutes: ADD: 3/90).

R. Strauss Ariadne auf Naxos. **Gundula Janowitz** (sop) Ariadne; **Teresa Zylis-Gara** (sop) Composer; **Sylvia Geszty** (sop) Zerbinetta; **James King** (ten) Bacchus; **Theo Adam** (bass-bar) Music Master; **Hermann Prey** (bar) Harlequin; **Siegfried Vogel** (bass) Truffaldino; **Hans Joachim Rotzsch** (ten) Brighella; **Peter Schreier** (ten) Scaramuchio, Dancing Master; **Erika Wustmann** (sop) Naiad; **Annelies Burmeister** (mez) Dryad; **Adele Stolte** (sop) Echo; **Erich-Alexander Winds** (spkr) Major-Domo; **Dresden Staatskapelle / Rudolf Kempe.** EMI Opera Ⓜ CMS7 64159-2 (two discs: 118 minutes: ADD: 11/92). Notes, text and translation included. From HMV SAN215/7 (11/68). Ⓖ

At mid price this classic set cannot be recommended too highly. Nobody knew more about how to pace Strauss's operas than Kempe and he was at his best when working with the Dresden Staatskapelle, a group of players who have Strauss in their veins. This reading brings out all the sentiment and high spirits of this delightful work, and the results are beautifully recorded. Janowitz's golden tones were ideal for the title role, which she sings with poise and inner feeling, though she makes little of the text. Zylis-Gara is a suitably impetuous Composer in the engaging Prologue where 'he' meets and has a gently erotic encounter with the charming but flighty Zerbinetta, a role here taken with brilliant accomplishment by Sylvia Geszty, who made it her own in the 1960s. James King is a forthright though none too flexible Bacchus. The smaller parts are also well taken. The more recent Masur version, with the admirable Leipzig Gewandhaus, has Jessye Norman as a stately

Ariadne, Julia Varady as a fiery Composer, Edita Gruberová as a bright-eyed, dexterous Zerbinetta, Paul Frey as an anonymous Bacchus. Masur, like Kempe, is steeped in the work's performing tradition and is the best of modern sets.

Additional recommendations ...

...Soloists; **Leipzig Gewandhaus Orchestra / Kurt Masur.** Philips Ⓕ 422 084-2PH2 (two discs: 118 minutes: DDD: 11/88).

...Soloists; **London Philharmonic Orchestra / Sir Georg Solti.** Decca Grand Opera Ⓜ 430 384-2DM2 (two discs: 121 minutes: ADD: 5/92).

...Ariadne auf Naxos[a]. **Wagner** Die Meistersinger von Nürnberg – excerpts[b]. **Soloists; Vienna State Opera** [b]**Chorus and Orchestra / Karl Böhm.** Koch Schwann mono Ⓜ 314732* (two discs: 156 minutes: ADD: 5/96).

New review

R. Strauss Ariadne auf Naxos[a]. **Maria Reining** (sop) Ariadne; **Irmgard Seefried** (sop) Composer; **Alda Noni** (sop) Zerbinetta; **Max Lorenz** (ten) Bacchus; **Paul Schoeffler** (bass-bar) Music Master; **Erich Kunz** (bar) Harlequin; **Marjan Rus** (bass) Truffaldino; **Peter Klein** (ten) Brighella; **Richard Sallaba** (ten) Scaramuchio; **Emmy Loose** (sop) Naiad; **Melanie Frutschnigg** (contr) Dryad; **Elisabeth Rutgers** (sop) Echo; **Josef Witt** (ten) Dancing Master; **Alfred Muzzarelli** (spkr) Majordomo; **Hans Schweiger** (bar) Footman; **Friedrich Jelinek** (ten) Officer; **Hermann Baier** (bar) Wigmaker.

Wagner Die Meistersinger von Nürnberg – excerpts[b]. **Maria Reining** (sop); **Martha Rohs** (mez); **Max Lorenz, Peter Klein** (tens); **Josef Herrmann, Erich Kunz** (bars); **Vienna State Opera** [b]**Chorus and Orchestra / Karl Böhm.** Koch Schwann mono Ⓜ 314732 (two discs: 156 minutes: ADD: 5/96). Item marked [a] recorded live in 1944, [b]1943.

This opens with some desirable extracts from a 1943 *Die Meistersinger*, conducted by the sterling Böhm. It is adorned by Herrmann's lyrical, poetic Sachs, a reading based on firm tone, incisive diction and finely etched legato singing, the best example of this underrated baritone's art on record. The *Flieder* receives an inward, thoughtful interpretation, followed by an account of the duet with Maria Reining's radiant Eva that approaches an ideal. Then he leads into the Act 3 Quintet as poetically as any Sachs on disc, the ensemble itself led off by Reining's poised singing. Lorenz is his usual over-effusive self in the Prize song, and the final track has Herrmann somewhat tiring in Sachs's final solo. The sound is mostly excellent. So, these are further important mementoes of the unrivalled ensemble then resident in Vienna. The same can be said of the complete *Ariadne*, conducted by Böhm at the Opera for Strauss's eightieth birthday. This is also available on Preiser (listed below), where the transfer yields marginally superior results. But, of course, you have here a bonus in the Wagner, and so better value for money in terms of quantity of music. Either way the *Ariadne* is a 'must', arguably the most idiomatic recording the Strauss masterpiece has ever received.

Additional recommendation ...

...Soloists; **Vienna State Opera Orchestra / Karl Böhm.** Preiser mono Ⓕ 90217* (two discs: 117 minutes: AAD: 11/94).

R. Strauss Die Frau ohne Schatten. **Julia Varady** (sop) Empress; **Plácido Domingo** (ten) Emperor; **Hildegard Behrens** (sop) Dyer's Wife; **José van Dam** (bar) Barak the Dyer; **Reinhild Runkel** (contr) Nurse; **Albert Dohmen** (bar) Spirit-Messenger; **Sumi Jo** (sop) Voice of the Falcon; **Robert Gambill** (ten) Apparition of a Young Man; **Elzbieta Ardam** (mez) Voice from above; **Eva Lind** (sop) Guardian of the Threshold; **Gottfried Hornik** (bar) One-eyed Brother; **Hans Franzen** (bass) One-armed Brother; **Wilfried Gahmlich** (ten) Hunchback Brother; **Vienna Boys' Choir; Vienna State Opera Chorus; Vienna Philharmonic Orchestra / Sir Georg Solti.** Decca Ⓕ 436 243-2DH3 (three discs: 195 minutes: DDD: 5/92). Notes, text and translation included. Recorded 1989-91.

Gramophone Award Winner 1992. ⒼⒼⒼ

This was the most ambitious project on which Strauss and his librettist Hugo von Hofmannthal collaborated. It is both fairy tale and allegory with a score that is Wagnerian in its scale and breadth. This Solti version presents the score absolutely complete in an opulent recording that encompasses every detail of the work's multi-faceted orchestration. Nothing escapes his keen eye and ear or that of the Decca engineers. The cast boasts splendid exponents of the two soprano roles. Behrens's vocal acting suggests complete identification with the unsatisfied plight of the Dyer's Wife and her singing has a depth of character to compensate for some tonal wear. Varady gives an intense, poignant account of the Empress's taxing music. The others, though never less than adequate, leave something to be desired. Domingo sings the Emperor with customary vigour and strength but evinces little sense of the music's idiom. José van Dam is likewise a vocally impeccable Barak but never penetrates the Dyer's soul. Runkel is a mean, malign Nurse as she should be though she could be a little more interesting in this part. It benefits from glorious, dedicated playing by the Vienna Philharmonic Orchestra.

Additional recommendations ...

...Soloists; **Tölz Boys' Choir; Bavarian Radio Chorus and Symphony Orchestra / Wolfgang Sawallisch.** EMI Ⓕ CDS7 49074-2 (three discs: 191 minutes: DDD: 9/88).

...Soloists; **Vienna State Opera Chorus; Vienna Philharmonic Orchestra / Sir Georg Solti.** Decca Grand Opera Ⓜ 430 387-2DM2 (two discs: 144 minutes: ADD: 5/92).

R. Strauss Die aegyptische Helena – excerpts[a]. Die Frau ohne Schatten – excerpts[b]. Daphne – excerpts[c]. [a]**Viorica Ursuleac**, [a]**Margit Bokor**, [b]**Hilde Konetzni**, [b]**Emmy Loose**, [b]**Else Schulz**, [c]**Maria Reining** (sops); [b]**Else Boettcher** (mez); [b]**Melanie Frutschnigg**, [b]**Elisabeth Höngen** (contrs); [a]**Franz Völker**, [a]**Helge Roswaenge**, [b]**Torsten Ralf**, [b]**Wenko Wenkoff**, [b]**William Wernigk**, [c]**Anton Dermota**, [c]**Alf Rauch** (tens); [a]**Alfred Jerger**, [b]**Josef Herrmann**, [b]**Alfred Poell**, [b]**Tomislav Neralic** (bars); [b]**Herbert Alsen**, [b]**Georg Monthy**, [b]**Marjan Rus**, [b]**Roland Neumann** (basses); **Vienna State Opera Chorus and Orchestra** / [a]**Clemens Krauss**, [b]**Karl Böhm**, [c]**Rudolf Moralt**. Koch Schwann mono Ⓜ 314552* (two discs: 145 minutes: ADD: 11/94). Item marked [a] recorded live in 1933, [b]1943, [c]1942.

Here is another significant document in Koch Schwann's historic series, because it enshrines valuable extracts from the original Viennese performances of *Helena* and *Daphne*, and some 90 minutes from what proves to be one of the most convincing readings ever of *Die Frau ohne Schatten*. The *Helena* provides the final proof that the somewhat maligned Ursuleac was, in the 1930s, a Strauss soprano *par excellence* and, supported by her husband Krauss's inspiriting direction, she fills the famous solo "Zweite Brautnacht" and other equally taxing passages with refulgent tone and soaring phraseology. For 1933 the sound is remarkable, and has the minimum amount of distortion. When *Die Frau* is sung and conducted as here at a 1943 revival, it does indeed sound like Strauss's outright masterpiece as many experts on the composer declare it to be. Böhm recognizes the virtues of sheerly beautiful sound (amply provided by his cast and the Vienna Philharmonic), textural clarity of a chamber-music kind and keeping the score on the move. Excellent as have been her successors as the Empress, Konetzni just about surpasses them all for the steadiness of her tone, her firm legato and her involvement. The first Daphne at the State Opera was Maria Reining. In her long opening solo, she is inclined to spoil her lovely singing by sliding into notes from below, but she reaches her glorious best in her duet with Apollo and from then on goes from strength to strength, making light of the extraordinary demands Strauss places on his soprano. Both Moralt and Böhm are ardent advocates of this vital but flawed score. Any Straussian must have this issue. Others who wish to find out just how to sing and conduct the composer's operas authentically may well like to sample it too.

R. Strauss Arabella. **Julia Varady** (sop) Arabella; **Helen Donath** (sop) Zdenka; **Dietrich Fischer-Dieskau** (bar) Mandryka; **Walter Berry** (bass) Waldner; **Helga Schmidt** (mez) Adelaide; **Elfriede Höbarth** (sop) Fiakermilli; **Adolf Dallapozza** (ten) Matteo; **Hermann Winkler** (ten) Elemer; **Klaus-Jürgen Küper** (bar) Dominik; **Hermann Becht** (bar) Lamoral; **Doris Soffel** (mez) Fortune Teller; **Arno Lemberg** (spkr) Welko; **Bavarian State Opera Chorus; Bavarian State Orchestra** / **Wolfgang Sawallisch**. Orfeo Ⓔ C169882H (two discs: 144 minutes: DDD: 1/89). Notes, text and translation included. From EMI SLS5224 (10/81).

Complete except for a brief cut in Matteo's part in Act 3, Sawallisch's 1981 Orfeo recording of *Arabella* has been easily fitted on to two CDs. Sawallisch is the most experienced conductor of Strauss's operas alive today and at his best in this one, his tempos just right, his appreciation of its flavour (sometimes sentimental, at others gently ironic and detached) unequalled. Helen Donath's delightful Zdenka is a perfect foil for Varady's Arabella. Varady's singing of the title-role is characterful and intelligent. One should be left with ambivalent feelings about this heroine; is she lovable or a chilling opportunist? Or both? And while Fischer-Dieskau's singing of Mandryka has not the total security of his earlier DG recording of the role with Keilberth (listed below), he remains the best Mandryka heard since the war.

Additional recommendation ...

...**Soloists; Bavarian State Opera Chorus and Orchestra** / **Joseph Keilberth**. DG Ⓜ 437 700-2GX3 (three discs: 159 minutes: ADD: 8/93).

Further listening ...

...*Intermezzo – symphonic interludes. Coupled with* **Schmidt** Symphony No. 1 in E major. **Detroit Symphony Orchestra** / **Neeme Järvi**. Chandos CHAN9357 (4/96). *See review under Schmidt; refer to the Index to Reviews.*

...*Symphonia domestica, Op. 53 (arr. Singer). Coupled with works by* **Dukas** *and* **Ravel** Martha **Argerich, Alexandre Rabinovitch** (pfs). Teldec 4509-96435-2 (7/96). *Gramophone Editor's choice. See review under Dukas; refer to the Index to Reviews.* ⒼⒼ

...*Cello Sonata in F major, Op. 6. Coupled with* **Thuillé** Cello Sonata, Op. 22. **Sophie Rolland** (vc); **Marc-André Hamelin** (pf). ASV CDDCA913 (3/95). Ⓖ

...*Violin Sonata in E flat major, Op. 18. Coupled with* **Respighi** Violin Sonata in B minor. **Kyung-Wha Chung** (vn); **Krystian Zimerman** (pf). DG 427 617-2GH (2/90). *See review under Respighi; refer to the Index to Reviews.* Ⓖ

...*Stiller Gang, Op. 31 No. 4. Coupled with works by* **Brahms, A. Busch, Loeffler, Dargomïzhsky, Marx, Reutter** *and* **Gounod.** **Mitsuko Shirai** (mez); **Tabea Zimmermann** (va); **Hartmut Höll** (pf). Capriccio 10 462 (9/95). *See review in the Collections section; refer to the Index to Reviews.* Ⓖ

...*Drei Hymnen, Op. 71[b]. Coupled with* **Rihm** Hölderlin-Fragmente[c] **Reger** An die Hoffnung, Op. 124[b]. **Brahms** Schicksalslied, Op. 54[a]. [b]**Karita Mattila** (sop); [c]**Johannes M. Kösters** (bar); [a]**Leipzig Radio Chorus; Berlin Philharmonic Orchestra** / **Claudio Abbado**. Sony Classical SK53975 (3/95).

...Arabella – Das war sehr gut, Mandryka. Der Rosenkavalier – Da geht er hin; Die Zeit, die ist ein
sonderbar Ding; Mein schöner Schatz ... Ich werd' jetzt in die Kirchen geh'n; Marie Theres'! ...
Hab' mir's gelobt. *Coupled with works by* **Wagner, Albert** and **Verdi Leonie Rysanek** (sop);
Various soloists and orchestras. EMI Références mono CDH5 65201-2* (2/95).
...Salome – Ach, du wolltest mich nicht deinen Mund küssen lassen[a]. Feuersnot – Feuersnot!
Minnegebot![b]. Der Rosenkavalier – Marie Theres'[c]. Daphne – Ich komme grünende Brüder[a].
Taillefer, Op. 52[d]. **Maria Cebotari,** [c]**Paula Buchner,** [c]**Tiana Lemnitz** (sops); [d]**Walther Ludwig** (ten);
[b]**Karl Schmitt-Walter** (bar); [d]**Hans Hotter** (bass-bar); [d]**Rudolf Lamy Singers; Berlin Radio
Symphony Orchestra / Artur Rother.** Preiser mono 90222* (8/95).
...Daphne[a]. Daphne – excerpts[b]. An den Baum Daphne, AV137[c]. **Soloists;** [ac]**Vienna State Opera
Chorus;** [a]**Vienna Philharmonic Orchestra;** [b]**Dresden State Opera Orchestra** / [ab]**Karl Böhm,** [c]**Walter
Hagen-Groll.** Preiser mono 90237* (11/95).
...Capriccio. **Soloists; Philharmonia Orchestra / Wolfgang Sawallisch.** EMI mono CDS7 49014-8*
(9/87).   ⊕⊕

Igor Stravinsky   USSR/French/American 1882-1971

Stravinsky Violin Concerto in D major[a].
Lutosławski Partita for Violin, Orchestra and Obbligato Solo Piano (1985)[b]. Chain 2 (1984)[c].
Anne-Sophie Mutter (vn); [b]**Phillip Moll** (pf); [a]**Philharmonia Orchestra / Paul Sacher;** [bc]**BBC
Symphony Orchestra / Witold Lutosławski.** DG Ⓕ 423 696-2GH (56 minutes: DDD: 2/89).   ⓖ
This disc contains some spellbinding violin playing in a splendidly lifelike recording, and it's a bonus
that the music, while unquestionably 'modern', needs no special pleading: its appeal is instantaneous
and long-lasting. Anne-Sophie Mutter demonstrates that she can equal the best in a modern classic –
the Stravinsky Concerto – and also act as an ideal, committed advocate for newer works not previously
recorded. The Stravinsky is one of his liveliest neo-classical pieces, though to employ that label is, as
usual, to underline its rough-and-ready relevance to a style that uses Bach as a springboard for an
entirely individual and unambiguously modern idiom. Nor is it all 'sewing-machine' rhythms and
pungently orchestrated dissonances. There is lyricism, charm, and above all humour: and no change of
mood is too fleeting to escape the razor-sharp responses of this soloist and her alert accompanists,
authoritatively guided by the veteran Paul Sacher. Lutosławski's music has strongly individual qualities
that have made him perhaps one of the most approachable of all contemporary composers. This
enthralling collaboration between senior composer and youthful virtuoso is not to be missed.
Additional recommendations ...
...Violin Concerto[a]. **Ravel** Tzigane[b]. **Berg** Violin Concerto[a]. **Itzhak Perlman** (vn); [a]**Boston
Symphony Orchestra / Seiji Ozawa;** [b]**New York Philharmonic Orchestra / Zubin Mehta.**
DG The Originals Ⓜ 447 445-2GOR (57 minutes: [a]ADD/[b]DDD).
...Violin Concerto. **Prokofiev** Violin Concertos – No. 1 in D major, Op. 19; No. 2 in G minor,
Op. 63. **Kyung-Wha Chung** (vn); **London Symphony Orchestra / André Previn.** Decca Ⓜ 425 003-
2DM (72 minutes: ADD: 7/90).   ⓖ
...Violin Concerto. **Prokofiev** Violin Concertos – No. 1 in D major, Op. 19; No. 2 in G minor,
Op. 63. **Cho-Liang Lin** (vn); **Los Angeles Philharmonic Orchestra / Esa-Pekka Salonen.** Sony
Classical Ⓕ SK53969 (70 minutes: DDD: 3/95).   ⓖ

Stravinsky The Rite of Spring. Apollon musagète. **City of Birmingham Symphony Orchestra / Sir
Simon Rattle.** EMI Ⓕ CDC7 49636-2 (65 minutes: DDD: 11/89).   ⓖ
Recordings of *The Rite of Spring* are legion, but it is rare to find Stravinsky's most explosive ballet
score coupled with *Apollon musagète*, his most serene. The result is a lesson in creative versatility,
confirming that Stravinsky could be equally convincing as expressionist and neoclassicist. Yet talk of
lessons might suggest that sheer enjoyment is of lesser importance, and it is perfectly possible to relish
this disc simply for that personal blend of the authoritative and the enlivening that Simon Rattle's
CBSO recordings for EMI so consistently achieve. Rattle never rushes things, and the apparent
deliberation of *The Rite*'s concluding "Sacrificial Dance" may initially surprise, but in this context it
proves an entirely appropriate, absolutely convincing conclusion. Rattle sees the work as a whole,
without striving for a spurious symphonic integration, and there is never for a moment any hint of a
routine reading of what is by now a classic of the modern orchestral repertoire. The account of *Apollo*
has comparable depth, with elegance transformed into eloquence and the CBSO strings confirming
that they have nothing to fear from comparison with the best in Europe or America. The recordings
are faithful to the intensity and expressiveness of Rattle's Stravinsky, interpretations fit to set beside
those of the composer himself.
Additional recommendations ...
...The Rite of Spring[a]. The Rite of Spring (trans. pianola)[b]. [b]**Rex Lawson** (pianola); [a]**Boston
Philharmonic Orchestra / Benjamin Zander.** IMP Classics Ⓕ MCD25 (69 minutes: DDD).
...The Rite of Spring. Apollon musagète. **Berlin Philharmonic Orchestra / Herbert von Karajan.**
DG Ⓕ 415 979-2GH (66 minutes: ADD: 9/86).
...The Rite of Spring. Symphony in E flat major. Symphony in Three Movements. Symphony in C.
Symphony of Psalms[a]. [a]**Festival Singers, Toronto; Columbia Symphony Orchestra;** [a]**CBC**

Symphony Orchestra / Igor Stravinsky. Sony Classical Ⓜ SM2K46294 (two discs: 142 minutes: ADD: 8/92). ⒼⒼⒼ

...The Rite of Spring. **Mussorgsky** Pictures at an Exhibition. **Philadelphia Orchestra / Riccardo Muti.** EMI Ⓜ CDM7 64516-2 (64 minutes: DDD: 11/92).

...The Rite of Spring. Four Etudes. Scherzo à la russe. **Philharmonia Orchestra / Eliahu Inbal.** Teldec Digital Experience Ⓜ 4509-91449-2 (50 minutes: DDD; 7/93).

...The Rite of Spring. Petrushka. **Oslo Philharmonic Orchestra / Mariss Jansons.** EMI Ⓕ CDC7 54899-2 (67 minutes: DDD: 1/94). Ⓖ

...Apollon musagète[a]. Petrushka[b]. The Firebird[b]. The Rite of Spring[b]. [a]**London Symphony Orchestra / Igor Markevitch;** [b]**London Philharmonic Orchestra / Bernard Haitink.** Philips Duo Ⓜ 438 350-2PM2 (two discs: 151 minutes: ADD: 1/94). Ⓖ

...The Rite of Spring[a]. Petrushka[b]. Movements[c]. [c]**Margrit Weber** (pf); [ab]**Berlin RIAS Orchestra;** [c]**Berlin Radio Symphony Orchestra / Ferenc Fricsay.** DG Dokumente mono/stereo Ⓜ 445 405-2GDO* (73 minutes: ADD: 11/94).

...Apollon musagète[a]. Two Suites for Small Orchestra[a]. Four Norwegian Moods[a]. Circus Polka[a]. L'histoire du soldat[b]. Symphony of Psalms[c]. **Soloists;** [c]**Russian State Academic Choir and Orchestra;** [a]**London Symphony Orchestra;** [b]**instrumental ensemble / Igor Markevitch.** Philips The Early Years Ⓜ 438 973-2PM2 (two discs: 128 minutes: 2/95).

New review

Stravinsky The Rite of Spring. Canticum sacrum[a]. Requiem canticles[b]. Choral Variations on "Vom Himmel hoch"[c]. [b]**Irène Friedli** (mez); [a]**Frieder Lang** (ten); [ab]**Michel Brodard** (bar); [a]**Lausanne Pro Arte Choir; Suisse Romande Chamber Choir and Orchestra / Neeme Järvi.** Chandos Ⓕ CHAN9408 (75 minutes: DDD: 3/96). Texts and translations included. Recorded 1994.

Järvi's is a weighty account of *The Rite* (it is scored, after all, for a very large orchestra; some analytical readings almost disguise this) and it packs a massive punch. He does not opt for showily fast tempos (save towards the end of the "Sacrificial Dance", where a combination of high speed and rather heavy sonority garbles a little of the detail) and at times – in the "Mystical Circle", for instance – he leans on the accents, diminishing the springiness of the rhythm. Elsewhere, though, the articulation tingles appropriately, and the orchestral sound is often beautiful, often cleanly detailed. One would not, even so, put it among the top half-dozen current recordings of *The Rite of Spring* were it not for the quite splendid couplings, where the very qualities that are a slight disadvantage in *The Rite* give urgency and eloquence to a couple of scores that are still regarded as among Stravinsky's most difficult. "Both soloists are good, especially the elegantly lyrical tenor, and the chorus sing with wonderfully jubilant confidence. A slight tendency to overmark dynamics, noticeable in *The Rite*, is evident at the beginning of the *Requiem canticles*, where Stravinsky firmly instructs that the strings are not to play loudly and Järvi just as firmly begs to differ. But he has obviously been moved by the fervour of the piece, and he demonstrates that a sonorous, full-voiced account can be just as effective as the more usual reading of the score as a quiet chamber ritual. After that there is no doubting how much fun Stravinsky had in so industriously outdoing Bach's contrapuntal ingenuity in the *Choral Variations*. Järvi obviously loves all those extra twiddly bits too, and is more successful than any other conductor at demonstrating what a Christmassy work it is. Decent recordings throughout, little lacking in resonance in the *Canticum sacrum* (its pauses very precisely tailored to the reverberation time of St Mark's in Venice, after all) and the organ-blower motor of the Victoria Hall in Geneva sounds as though it needs servicing. Otherwise a highly recommendable coupling, especially to those who love *The Rite* but have hitherto found late Stravinsky off-puttingly austere.

Stravinsky The Rite of Spring. Perséphone[a]. [a]**Anthony Rolfe Johnson** (ten); [a]**Anne Fournet** (narr); [a]**Tiffin Boys' Choir; London Philharmonic** [a]**Choir and Orchestra / Kent Nagano.** Virgin Classics Duo Ⓜ VCK7 59077 (two discs: 83 minutes: DDD: 6/92). Notes, text and translation included. ⒼⒼ

The American composer Elliott Carter described *Perséphone* as "a humanist *Rite of Spring*", so this makes a logical and thought-provoking coupling (timings are not generous on the two CDs but they do come at mid price). Twenty years separate both works, and they could not be more different. The primal energy of the earlier *Rite of Spring*'s very naturalistic setting of scenes from pagan Russia is almost wholly absent from the cool, hieratic beauty of *Perséphone*'s ritual, and predominantly lyrical mode of address. The latter fuses elements of melodrama (literally, speech with music), oratorio and ballet, is set in classical Greece and has a text that is spoken and sung in French. Nagano's recording is the first to have appeared since Stravinsky's own 1966 account (part of the Stravinsky Edition but not one of the items to be made available separately) and is, in many ways, finer. A modern dynamic range predictably benefits the thrilling theatre of the choral invocation for Perséphone's return from the underworld in the third part of the work (culminating in a triple *forte* cry of "Printemps" as powerful as anything in the *Rite*); and both Anne Fournet in the spoken role of Perséphone, and Anthony Rolfe Johnson as the priest of the Eleusinian mysteries are preferable to their predecessors. Nagano's tempos are swifter than Stravinsky's which, in music that is predominantly slow moving, will be welcomed by many. Nagano's *Rite* is balletic and sharply emphatic; closely miked in a way often reminiscent of Stravinsky's own, with strongly projected woodwind and a crisp, forceful, though never heavy presence for the percussion. Other versions may remind us more powerfully of the work's extremism, but Nagano is often strikingly individual – one thinks of the almost reptilian coiling of clarinets at the end of the "Ritual of the Ancestors" – with more expressive phrasing and pacing than usual in the work's mysterious moments.

Stravinsky Apollon musagète[a]. Pulcinella – suite[a]. Capriccio[b]. [b]**John Ogdon** (pf); **Academy of St Martin in the Fields / Sir Neville Marriner.** Decca The Classic Sound Ⓜ 443 577-2DCS (70 minutes: ADD: 4/95). Items marked [a] from Argo ZRG575 (10/68), [b]ZRG674 (2/72). Recorded 1967-70. Recorded 1993. ⒼⒼ

The Academy's 1968 coupling of the *Pulcinella* suite and *Apollo* was their first foray into twentieth-century repertoire on disc and it now returns with *Capriccio* a substantial bonus. The transfers are excellent. In *Pulcinella*, the unprecedented crispness of the Academy's ensemble may no longer inspire particular awe – we are accustomed to squeaky-clean Stravinsky nowadays – so it is the elegant, characterful solos and clear, warm (not quite plummy) Kingsway Hall ambience that places this account in a special category. *Apollo* sounds superb too, that final "Apotheosis" as blissful as ever, although, as its final chord dies, the improved clarity in the bass alerts us to the presence of an intruder – the London Underground. *Capriccio*, not perhaps one of Stravinsky's more inspiring works, is well served by John Ogdon, less so by the over-resonant acoustic of The Maltings, Snape, which sometimes obscures instrumental detail. This is nevertheless an outstanding collection.

Additional recommendation ...

...Symphony of Psalms[a]. Concerto for Piano and Wind Instruments[b]. Pulcinella – suite[c]. [b]**Seymour Lipkin** (pf); [a]**English Bach Festival Chorus;** [a]**London Symphony Orchestra;** [bc]**New York Philharmonic Orchestra / Leonard Bernstein.** Sony Classical Bernstein Royal Edition Ⓜ SMK47628 (68 minutes: ADD: 11/94).

Stravinsky The Firebird (1910 version). Symphonies of Wind Instruments (1920 version). **London Symphony Orchestra / Kent Nagano.** Virgin Classics Ⓕ VC5 45032-2 (59 minutes: DDD: 8/94). Recorded 1991. Ⓖ

This is the kind of vividly narrative performance that stimulates the imagination; one where every instrument and every turn of phrase has had its dramatic relevance considered and realized (but always in completely musical ways): for example, the last longing look from the departing princess (lamenting solo clarinet, track 12 at 1'13") memorably highlighted by a well controlled slowing and shading down, and the kind of look that would make any prince worth his salt risk life and limb. You sense that this is going to be a rather special performance right from the opening bars where Nagano has his trombones steal onto the scene (this 'Introduction' is full of subtle shadings and slowings); a rather special recording too that preserves a clean focus for both the physical impact and all the atmospheric workings of the score, and ensures a stereophonic spectacle for Stravinsky's 'in the wings' brass for "Daybreak" and the "Magic Carillon". All of which, and a great deal more than space will allow, adds up to an experience of *The Firebird* that, in terms of preparation, imagination, concentration and quality of playing and recording, rivals that of the competition.

Additional recommendations ...

...The Firebird – Concert Suite. **Rimsky-Korsakov** Scheherazade, Op. 35. **Paris Opera-Bastille Orchestra / Myung-Whun Chung.** DG Ⓕ 437 818-2GH (DDD).

...The Firebird. Scherzo à la russe (versions for jazz ensemble and orchestra). Quatre études (1952 version). **City of Birmingham Symphony Orchestra / Sir Simon Rattle.** EMI Ⓕ CDC7 491'/8-2 (65 minutes: DDD: 4/89). ⒼⒼ

...Symphonies of Wind Instruments. Concerto for Piano and Wind Instruments. Capriccio. Movements for Piano and Orchestra. **Paul Crossley** (pf); **London Sinfonietta / Esa-Pekka Salonen.** Sony Classical Ⓕ SK45797 (54 minutes: DDD: 10/90).

...The Firebird. Le chant de rossignol. Fireworks, Op. 4. Scherzo à la russe. Tango. **London Symphony Orchestra / Antál Dorati.** Mercury Ⓜ 432 012-2MM (74 minutes: ADD: 11/91). ⒼⒼⒼ

...The Firebird. Le Chant de Rossignol. **Danish National Radio Symphony Orchestra / Dmitri Kitaienko.** Chandos Ⓕ CHAN8967 (77 minutes: DDD: 9/92).

...The Firebird. Fireworks, Op. 4. Four Etudes. **Chicago Symphony Orchestra / Pierre Boulez.** DG Ⓕ 437 850-2GH (60 minutes: DDD: 11/93). *Selected by Sounds in Retrospect.*

...The Firebird. Symphonies of Wind Instruments. **London Philharmonic Orchestra / Franz Welser-Möst.** EMI Ⓕ CDC5 55030-2 (56 minutes: DDD: 6/94).

...The Firebird – Concert Suite (1919). **Falla** El amor brujo[a]. El sombrero de tres picos – Dance of the Miller's Wife; Neighbours' Dance; Miller's Dance; Final Dance. [a]**Grace Bumbry** (mez); **Berlin Radio Symphony Orchestra / Lorin Maazel.** DG The Originals Ⓜ 447 414-2GOR (65 minutes: ADD: 10/95). *See review under Falla; refer to the Index to Reviews.*

Stravinsky Symphony in C[a]. Symphonies of Wind Instruments[b]. Scherzo fantastique, Op. 3[c]. Symphony in Three Movements[a]. [a]**Suisse Romande Orchestra;** [bc]**Montreal Symphony Orchestra / Charles Dutoit.** Decca Ovation Ⓜ 436 474-2DM (71 minutes: DDD: 5/94). Items marked [a] from SXDL7543 (6/82), [b]414 202-2DII (4/85), [c]414 409-1DH (10/86). Recorded 1981 84. ⒼⒼ

In Geneva, Dutoit was conducting an orchestra with plenty of experience of these scores behind it; was recording with a company whose long-standing proven ability to reproduce this orchestra with needle-sharp definition reached a new high with these recordings (Ansermet's timps rarely sounded as good as this; Stravinsky's never); and in a hall (Victoria Hall) whose acoustics breathed just enough fresh, natural air into and around the proceedings. The inclusion of Dutoit's Montreal recordings of the *Scherzo fantastique* (like the composer's, daringly fast but more securely articulated) and the *Symphonies of Wind Instruments* (Montreal winds on peak form) generously extends what was in the 1980s *Gramophone*'s prime recommendation for the orchestral symphonies. It remains so now for the 1990s.

Additional recommendations ...

...Symphony in C. Symphony in Three Movements. **Royal Scottish Orchestra / Sir Alexander Gibson.** Chandos Collect Ⓜ CHAN6577 (51 minutes: DDD: 6/92).

...Scherzo fantastique. **Rimsky-Korsakov** Scheherazade, Op. 35. **Royal Concertgebouw Orchestra / Riccardo Chailly.** Decca Ⓕ 443 703-2DH (59 minutes: DDD: 10/94).

Stravinsky Petrushka (1947 version)[a]. Symphony in Three Movements. [a]**Peter Donohoe** (pf); **City of Birmingham Symphony Orchestra / Sir Simon Rattle.** EMI Ⓕ CDC7 49053-2 (57 minutes: DDD: 5/88). Ⓖ

Stravinsky's second great ballet score has been well served on disc from the earliest days of LP. He recorded it himself (rather indifferently) but there is in any event a good case for preferring the brilliance and clarity of digital sound in this of all works. Simon Rattle's performance is most notable for its fresh look at details of scoring and balance, with pianist Peter Donohoe making a strong impression. The results are robust and persuasive, though one sometimes has the impression that the characters are being left to fend for themselves. The atmospheric sound with its generous middle and bass is certainly very natural. The symphony too is eminently recommendable, sounding more grateful and high spirited than it sometimes has, with Rattle particularly relishing the jazzy bits.

Additional recommendations ...

...Petrushka. Firebird – Suite. Pastorale (arr. Stokowski). **Shostakovich** (arr. Stokowski). Prelude in E minor, Op. 34 No. 14. **Philadelphia Orchestra / Leopold Stokowski.** Dutton Laboratories mono Ⓜ CDAX8002* (60 minutes: ADD: 5/93).

...Orpheus. Petrushka. **Philharmonia Orchestra / Esa-Pekka Salonen.** Sony Classical Ⓕ SK53274 (64 minutes: DDD: 2/94).

...Symphony in C. Symphony in Three Movements. Symphony of Psalms[a]. **London Symphony** [a]**Chorus and Orchestra / Michael Tilson Thomas.** Sony Classical Ⓕ SK53275 (71 minutes: DDD: 7/94).

...Petrushka. *Coupled with works by* **Scriabin, Ravel, Berg, Messiaen, Britten** and **Copland Shura Cherkassky** (pf). Decca Ⓕ 433 657-2DH (79 minutes: ADD: 2/96). *See review in the Collections section; refer to the Index to Reviews.* Ⓖ

Stravinsky Petrushka (1947 version). Pulcinella[a]. [a]**Anna Caterina Antonacci** (sop); [a]**Pietro Ballo** (ten); [a]**William Shimell** (bar); **Royal Concertgebouw Orchestra / Riccardo Chailly.** Decca Ⓕ 443 774-2DH (73 minutes: DDD: 6/95). Text and translation included. Recorded 1993. *Gramophone Editor's choice.* ⒼⒼ

New review

Stravinsky Pulcinella[a]. Renard[b]. Two Suites. Rag-Time. [a]**Jennifer Larmore** (mez); [b]**John Aler,** [ab]**Frank Kelly** (tens); [ab]**Jan Opalach,** [b]**John Cheek** (basses); **Saint Paul Chamber Orchestra / Hugh Wolff.** Teldec Ⓕ 4509-94548-2 (73 minutes: DDD: 5/96). Texts and translations included. Recorded 1994.

In *Petrushka* Chailly has his players characterize even the smallest detail. Note the tongue-in-cheek lead-in to the "Russian Dance" and the carefree 'squeeze-box' character of the dance itself (with dynamic crossfire between wind and brass and some excellent piano playing). "Petrushka" (second tableau) is played *con amore*, with much humanity and not entirely without malice: perhaps the anger and frustration aren't as blatant as Bernstein's (listed below); but the pain and humiliation certainly are. It's a performance that breathes, that sings and neither rushes its fences nor loses sight of the score's very specific rhythmic profile. As for the recording, given top-ranking engineers – who could rightly expect anything less than exceptional? The coupling, too, is equally colourful: a pert, sweet-centred *Pulcinella*, with an expressive *concertino* in the "Ouverture", winsome phrasing elsewhere and extremely brilliant accounts of the two *Allegro assais* (tracks 23 and 35). Here there is an incisiveness, attack and buoyancy to the rhythms. The singing is vividly characterized and, again, the recording is spectacular, with a trombone "Vivo" that should serve the same 'demonstration' function as Ansermet's and Marriner's did in the days of LP. Now, as then, Decca take a definite sonic lead in this delightful music.

Hugh Wolff's *Pulcinella* is a witty, incisive alternative. Just try the *Vivo* with its frolicking trombone and wilting double-bass solo and note how stylishly they phrase their closing duet. His singers are generally above par, Jennifer Larmore especially. Wolff offers for couplings the best *Rag-Time* for 11 instruments on disc – gently swinging and without a hint of self-consciousness – plus keenly focused accounts of the two Suites for small orchestra and an exceedingly enjoyable *Renard*. Here the singing is again excellent and there's a novelty in that Wolff has tweaked the published translation and in so doing has effected a more natural flow to the comedy. Again, there is a plethora of detail – subtle underlinings, useful clarifications and felicitous turns of phrase, all to the benefit of the music – and the recording is excellent.

Additional recommendations ...

...Petrushka. The Rite of Spring. Firebird Suite (1919). Scènes de Ballet. Symphony in Three Movements. **Israel Philharmonic Orchestra / Leonard Bernstein.** DG Masters Series Ⓜ 445 538-2GMA2 (DDD).

...Pulcinella[a]. Le Chant du Rossignol. [a]**Ann Murray** (mez); [a]**Anthony Rolfe Johnson** (ten); [a]**Simon Estes** (bass); **French National Orchestra / Pierre Boulez.** Erato Ⓕ 2292-45382-2 (ADD: 5/86).

...Pulcinella[a]. Jeu de cartes. [a]**Teresa Berganza** (mez); [a]**Ryland Davies** (ten); [a]**John Shirley-Quirk** (bar); **London Symphony Orchestra / Claudio Abbado.** DG Galleria Ⓜ 423 889-2GGA (62 minutes: ADD: 1/89).

New review

Stravinsky Le baiser de la fée. Bluebird Pas-de-deux.
Tchaikovsky (orch. Stravinsky) The Sleeping Beauty – Variation d'Aurore; Entr'acte. **Hong Kong Philharmonic Orchestra / David Atherton.** Virgin Classics Ⓜ VM5 61281-2 (57 minutes: DDD: 4/96). Recorded 1995. *Selected by Soundings.*

A remarkably satisfying trio of performances, delicately executed and finely observed but by no means short on drama. In fact, it is difficult to think of any other conductor on disc who has so precisely gauged the colour, texture and overall 'fit' of Stravinsky's supple orchestrations. David Atherton's keen-eared direction inspires some extremely fine playing – from the first clarinet, for example, so beautifully accompanied at 6'25" into the Prologue; or from the eloquent lead cello at 2'18" into the *Pas-de-deux*'s *Adagio*. True, full string tuttis aren't as lustrous as they might have been from one of the older European or American orchestras and the otherwise excellent recording tends to harden at climaxes, but these are trifling inadequacies in a work that calls mainly on the qualities that Atherton and his players supply in abundance – namely precision, transparency and a genuinely balletic mobility. Atmosphere too, especially the sensitive manner in which Atherton dovetails the end of the second scene with the beginning of the third. Stravinsky's other Tchaikovsky orchestrations make for obvious couplings and again, Atherton and his players (their professional partnership dates back to 1989) maximize the music's wit and elegance. How nice to hear a clearly balanced piano in the *Bluebird Pas-de-deux*, while Mayumi Seiler's excellent solo violin playing enhances Stravinsky's rarely performed version of the *Entr'acte*. Here the recorded balance is first-rate and the effectiveness of Stravinsky's tasteful – and highly characteristic – chamber reductions tellingly underlined. The only other performances of the main work that one might turn to as alternatives to Atherton are Reiner's of the *Divertimento* (an orchestral arrangement of movements from the *Le baiser de la fée* on RCA), Mravinsky's passionate but indifferently engineered live 1983 performance and the composer's own stereo version (less alert than Atherton's, but instrumentally more distinctive). However, collectors in search of Stravinsky's Tchaikovsky 'complete' (as it were) could hardly do better than this Virgin Classics release.

Additional recommendations ...

...Le baiser de la fée. **Tchaikovsky** (arr. Stravinsky) The Sleeping Beauty – Bluebird pas de deux. **Scottish National Orchestra / Neeme Järvi.** Chandos Ⓕ CHAN8360 (51 minutes: DDD: 7/85).

...Divertimento from "Le baiser de la fée". Suites Nos. 1 and 2. Octet. "L'histoire du soldat" – Concert Suite. **London Sinfonietta / Riccardo Chailly.** Decca Enterprise Ⓜ 433 079-2DM (76 minutes: DDD: 5/92). Ⓖ

...Divertimento from "Le baiser de la fée". *Coupled with works by* **Prokofiev** *and* **Hovhaness** **Chicago Symphony Orchestra / Fritz Reiner.** RCA Victor Living Stereo Ⓜ 09026 61957-2 (64 minutes: ADD: 9/95). *See review under Hovhaness; refer to the Index to Reviews.*

...Le baiser de la fée. **Bartók** Two Pictures, Sz46. **La Scala Philharmonic Orchestra, Milan / Riccardo Muti.** Sony Classical Ⓕ SK58949 (61 minutes: DDD: 9/95).

Stravinsky the Composer Two Suites[d]. Four Etudes, Op. 7[b]. Four Norwegian Moods[d]. Concerto for Two Solo Pianos[bc]. Ode[d]. Rag-time[d]. Piano-rag-music[b]. Renard[ad]. [a]**Thom Baker,** [a]**Drew Martin** (tens); [a]**David Evitts, [a]Wilbur Pauley** (basses); [b]**Mark Wait,** [c]**Tom Schultz** (pfs); [d]**St Luke's Orchestra / Robert Craft.** MusicMasters Ⓕ 67110-2 (76 minutes: DDD: 9/94). Text and translation included. ⒼⒼ

This is Stravinsky on a relatively small scale – slick, light-textured and free-flowing, purged of expressive exaggeration but by no means slavishly literal. Indeed, the opening number of the Suite No. 1 is surprisingly romantic in feeling. More predictably, subsequent items find the musicians trying to achieve the appropriate spikiness in what can seem a rather resonant performance space. The short orchestral pieces are interleaved with an unpredictable assortment of keyboard works, the piano tone generally a little shallow though perfectly acceptable. Craft's restraint points up the unchanging aspects of Stravinsky's musical language. The effective English-text version of *Renard* uses a variant of Stravinsky's own translation but on its own, more intimate, fairy-tale terms Craft's performance is an undoubted success. The *Ode* will come as a delightful discovery to many. Its second movement (very convincingly done here) is drawn from music originally composed for the hunting scene in the Hollywood film of *Jane Eyre* (starring Orson Welles); its third achieves real profundity in a three-minute span.

Stravinsky Rag-time[bce]. Octet[be]. Three Pieces[b]. L'histoire du soldat – suite[bcf]. Pastorale[be]. Concertino[bce]. Septet[be]. Epitaphium[abd]. [a]**Lorna McGhee** (fl); [b]**Dmitri Ashkenazy** (cl); [c]**Alan Brind** (vn); [d]**Cristina Bianchi** (hp); [e]**European Soloists Ensemble / Vladimir Ashkenazy** ([f]pf). Decca Ⓕ 448 177-2DH (59 minutes: DDD: 8/96).

This is probably Ashkenazy's finest Stravinsky CD. The catchy but immensely clever Septet scores a double bulls-eye by employing formal ingenuity (the closing Gigue features four separate fugues on four versions of an eight-note row) without 'losing' the untutored listener. Written for violin, viola, cello, clarinet, horn, bassoon and piano, it is followed by the disc's closing selection, a 1'29" *Epitaphium* that offers brief confirmation of the older Stravinsky's serial leanings. The journey started with *Rag-time*, composed in 1918 and peppered with the metallic twang of a cimbalon. Ashkenazy's performance of this is very well played, as is the Octet, with its scampering variations and gentle, bossa-nova style final bars (did Stravinsky ever write anything more charming than this?). Again, the performance is confident and unfussy, while Dmitri Ashkenazy blows plenty of spirit into the *Three Pieces* for solo clarinet (the third especially) and Ashkenazy *père* joins him – together with violinist Alan Brind – for a no-nonsense account of a trio arrangement of *The Soldier's Tale* Suite. Here Brind favours light bowing and bland characterization, whereas the elegant *Pastorale* and lively *Concertino* are, by turns, colourful and punchy. Decca's recordings are uniformly good throughout; so is the standard of playing, and although one might maintain other preferences in this or that individual piece (with Stravinsky himself invariably leading the field), the programme is both stimulating and entertaining.

Stravinsky L'histoire du soldat – four movements. Petrushka – three movements. Apollon musagète. **Christopher O'Riley** (pf). Elektra Nonesuch Ⓕ 7559-79343-2 (58 minutes: DDD: 5/95).

Ⓖ

These performances are not quite what they seem. With the exception of the three movements from *Petrushka*, they are not concert arrangements but piano reductions of the kind that most composers make for rehearsal purposes. Like the *Petrushka* transcription, however, they show Stravinsky re-thinking his ideas in terms of another medium; and besides, like *Petrushka*, they were conceived at the piano. Christopher O'Riley, justifiably has edited the piano reductions of *The soldier's tale* and *Apollon musagète* to put back in some of those elements of the scores that Stravinsky felt obliged to leave out. The effect is curious but alluring. Pretty well all the notes are there (including the percussion part in the tango from *The soldier's tale*, achieved by a discreet 'prepared piano' effect), but their recasting for piano means that their perspectives have changed. Often enough the difficulty of this enterprise lies in tailoring a crisp, an elegant or a staccato figure conceived for cornet or for solo violin to the very different sound of the piano. O'Riley almost invariably succeeds in this admirably. He is also capable of using the amplitude of piano sound to make a pretty satisfactory substitute for the resonance of a full string orchestra in his uncommonly big-scaled and grand account of the "Apothéose" from *Apollo*. On the strength of the *Petrushka* transcriptions played, with delicacy of colour and rhythmic precision, O'Riley has at least three hands. All that and a real sense that he is having a whale of a time.

Additional recommendations ...

...Petrushka. *Coupled with works by* **Scriabin, Shostakovich** and **Rachmaninov Duo Reine Elisabeth.** Koch International Classics Ⓢ DICD920150 (66 minutes: DDD: 11/94). *See review in the Collections Section; refer to the Index to Reviews.*

...Petrushka – three movements. Valse pour les enfants. Ragtime. Piano-rag music. Les cinq doigts. Sonata. Serenade in A major. Tango. Circus Polka. Three Easy Pieces[a]. **Aleck Karis,** [a]**Robert Lubin** (pfs). Bridge Ⓕ BCD9051 (73 minutes: DDD: 3/95).

...Petrushka – three movements. *Coupled with workd by* **Webern, Prokofiev** and **Boulez Maurizio Pollini** (pf). DG The Originals Ⓜ 447 431-2GOR (68 minutes: ADD: 6/95). *See review in the Collections section; refer to the Index to Reviews.*

ⒼⒼ

Stravinsky Piano-rag music. Circus Polka. Sonata. Serenade in A major. Tango. Four Studies, Op. 7. Scherzo. Sonata in F sharp minor. **Victor Sangiorgio** (pf). Collins Classics Ⓕ 1374-2 (71 minutes: DDD: 9/93). Recorded 1991.

Victor Sangiorgio launches his Stravinsky programme with a superbly colourful account of the *Piano-rag music*. He commands an excellent variety of attack and resonance, and this combines with his natural rhythmic *élan* and his fine ear for textural voicing to make the *Circus Polka* and the *Tango* especially effective. The *Studies* go well too, especially the Chaplinified Scriabin of No. 4. The short 1902 *Scherzo* is the only seriously flawed performance, marred as it is by a tendency towards spasmodic over-punctuation. But at least Sangiorgio pays this slight piece, and the anything-but-slight F sharp minor Sonata, the compliment of meticulous preparation. Third-hand Tchaikovsky the Sonata may be, but there is still something irresistible about the Russian gung-ho of its finale as relished here by Sangiorgio. The recording is very immediate in its impact, possessing both warmth and clarity.

Stravinsky Pastorale[a]. Deux poèmes de Paul Verlaine[d]. Two poems of Konstantin Bal'mont[a]. Three Japanese lyrics[a]. Three little songs, "Recollections of my childhood"[a]. Pribaoutki[d]. Cat's

Cradle Songs[b]. Four Songs[a]. Mavra – Chanson de Paracha[a]. Three Songs from William Shakespeare[b]. In memoriam Dylan Thomas[c]. Elegy for J.F.K.[d]. Two Sacred Songs (after Wolf)[c]. [a]**Phyllis Bryn-Julson** (sop); [b]**Ann Murray** (mez); [c]**Robert Tear** (ten); [d]**John Shirley-Quirk** (bar); **Ensemble InterContemporain / Pierre Boulez.** DG 20th Century Classics Ⓜ 431 751-2GC (58 minutes: ADD: 2/92). Texts and translations included. From 2531 377 (7/82). Recorded 1980.

Ⓖ

It may be true that this disc lacks the focus of a single major work, but it is also much more than a random compilation of unrelated miniatures. Principally, it offers an aurally fascinating contrast between two groups of pieces: Stravinsky's relatively early Russian settings, as he worked through his own brand of nationalism, reaching from the salon style of *Pastorale* to the folk-like vigour of a work like *Pribaoutki*; then the late serial compositions, written in America, which prove that the rhythmic vitality and melodic distinctiveness of the early works survived undimmed into his final years. Stravinsky may have regarded texts as collections of sounds whose natural rhythms had no role to play in their musical setting, but the essential meaning still comes through unerringly, whether it is that of the plaintive Paracha's song from the opera *Mavra* or the sombre *Elegy for J.F.K.* (to an Auden text). The disc is rounded off by the very late Wolf arrangements, and whilst one might quibble here and there about Boulez's choice of tempo, or the balance of voice and instruments, the disc as a whole is immensely satisfying as a comprehensive survey of an important repertory.

The reviews which follow comprise part of "The Complete Edition" (Sony Classical Ⓜ *S22K46290 22 CDs: ADD: 7/91). The items reviewed here were subsequently issued as separate sets.* **Gramophone** *classical 100.*

Stravinsky The Complete Edition, Volume 1. **Various artists / Igor Stravinsky.** Sony Classical Ⓜ SM3K46291* (three discs: 194 minutes: ADD: 8/92). Recorded 1959-62. *Gramophone classical 100.*
The Firebird (Columbia Symphony Orchestra. From CBS 72046, 9/62). Scherzo à la russe (Columbia Symphony Orchestra). Scherzo fantastique (CBC Symphony Orchestra). Fireworks (Columbia Symphony Orchestra. All from CBS GM31, 2/82). Petrushka (Columbia Symphony Orchestra. Philips SABL175, 4/61). The Rite of Spring (Columbia Symphony Orchestra. SABL174, 4/61). Les noces (Mildred Allen, sop; Regina Sarfaty, mez; Loren Driscoll, ten; Richard Oliver, bass; Samuel Barber, Aaron Copland, Lukas Foss, Roger Sessions, pfs; American Concert Choir; Columbia Percussion Ensemble). Renard (George Shirley, Loren Driscoll, tens; William Murphy, bar; Donald Gramm, bass; Toni Koves, cimbalom; Columbia Chamber Ensemble. Both from CBS SBRG72071, 12/62). L'histoire du soldat – Suite (Columbia Chamber Ensemble. SBRG72007, 6/62).

ⒼⒼⒼ

Inspiration for this collection of mainly stage music came from Stravinsky's native folk-song, folk-dance, folk-tale and folk ritual; and the set contains virtually all the music from Stravinsky's 'Russian' period, including the three great ballets. It is fascinating to chart his development from the 1908 *Scherzo fantastique* with its orchestral colours scintillating in the best Rimsky-Korsakovian manner, to the wholly original language of *Les noces* with its almost exclusively metrical patterns and monochrome scoring (soloists, chorus, pianos and percussion) begun only six years later. The links are there: witness the Rimskian bumble-bee that flies through the *Scherzo* to find its winged counterpart two years on in *The Firebird*; and the primitive rhythmic force of Kastchei's "Infernal dance" in *The Firebird* finding its fullest expression, another three years later, in *The Rite of Spring*; and so on. Each work is a logical, if time-lapse progression from the previous one. The set concludes with the 15-minute long animal rites of the farmyard opera-cum-burlesque *Renard* (1916); and *L'histoire du soldat* (1918), a morality play designed for a small touring theatre company (the Suite included here omits the speaking roles); both, like *Les noces*, leaving behind the lavish orchestra of *The Rite* for small and unusual instrumental and vocal combinations.

To have the composer at the helm, and a consistent approach to the way the music is recorded, ensures that those links are clearly established. And the orchestra that takes the lion's share of the task, the Columbia Symphony, was assembled by CBS to include many of the finest players in America. It is possible to criticize the recordings (made between 1959 and 1963) for close balances and spotlighting, but many modern contenders, more distantly recorded, will more often than not deprive you of adequate articulation of the music's linear and rhythmic ingenuity. The dynamic range and contours of *The Rite of Spring* do seem momentarily reduced and disturbed by the techniques, otherwise all these recordings reproduce with good tone, range, openness and presence. As to Stravinsky the conductor, only *Les noces* finds him at less than his usual rhythmically incisive self. This *Petrushka* is more representative: it pulsates with inner life and vitality – incidentally, Stravinsky uses his leaner, clearer 1947 revision, not the original 1911 score as the booklet claims.

Stravinsky The Complete Edition, Volume 2. **Various artists / Igor Stravinsky.** Sony Classical Ⓜ SM3K46292 (three discs: 210 minutes: ADD: 8/92). *Gramophone classical 100.*
Apollo (Columbia Symphony Orchestra). From SBRG72355, (11/65). Agon (Los Angeles Festival Symphony Orchestra. SBRG72438, 8/66). Jeu de cartes (Cleveland Orchestra). Scènes de ballet (CBC Symphony Orchestra). Bluebird – Pas de deux (Columbia Symphony Orchestra. All from SBRG72270, 5/65). Le baiser de la fée (Columbia Symphony Orchestra. SBRG72407, 5/66).

Pulcinella (Irene Jordan, sop; George Shirley, ten; Donald Gramm, bass; Columbia Symphony Orchestra. SBRG72452, 7/66). Orpheus (Chicago Symphony Orchestra. SBRG72355).　　🅖🅖🅖
Volume 2 of Sony's Stravinsky Edition comprises ballets written between 1919 and 1957. *Pulcinella* was based on music originally thought to have been written by Pergolesi, but now known to be the work of various eighteenth-century composers. In 1919 Stravinsky had not long embraced neo-classical style, but here was a brilliant example of old wine in new bottles, with the melodies sounding as if they come from the pen of Stravinsky himself. The composer conducts a lively, sharply-accented account of the score. 1928 saw the production of two Stravinsky ballets. *Apollo*, a mainly quiet, contemplative score, written for string orchestra, has many passages of great beauty. Stravinsky the conductor does not linger over these, but allows the work's cool classical elegance to speak for itself. In *Le baiser de la fée* Stravinsky used themes by Tchaikovsky as the basis for his score. Once again, the music seems quite transformed, and the result is a most captivating work. Stravinsky's watchful, affectionate performance is perfectly proportioned. His arrangement of the "Pas de deux" from Tchaikovsky's *Sleeping Beauty* is no more than a reduction for small pit orchestra, however, and a mere curiosity.

In *Jeu de cartes*, which dates from 1936, Stravinsky used music by Rossini and others, but here the references are only fleeting, and merely enhance the humour of this robust, outgoing score. His performance brings out all the work's vigour and personality very effectively, but here and there rhythms become slightly unstuck, and a slightly hectic quality manifests itself. *Scènes de ballet* was written in 1944, and possesses a slightly terse quality in the main, though there are some more lyrical passages. Stravinsky does nothing to soften the work's edges in his performance, and it emerges as a strong, highly impressive piece. *Orpheus* was completed in 1947, and shows Stravinsky's neo-classical style at its most highly developed. Much of the music is quiet, after the manner of *Apollo*, but then the orchestra suddenly erupts into a passage of quite savage violence. Stravinsky conducts this passage with amazing energy for a man in his eighties, and elsewhere his performance has characteristic clarity and a very direct means of expression typical of a composer performance. Finally *Agon*, written in 1957, attracts the listener with its colourful opening fanfares, and then pursues an increasingly complex serial path in such a brilliant and highly rhythmical fashion that one is hardly aware that the technique is being used. This work, brilliantly conducted by Stravinsky, is an ideal introduction to his late style, and to the serial technique itself. Remastering has been carried out with the greatest skill, and all the recordings in this set sound very well indeed for their age.

Additional recommendations ...
...Orpheus. Jeu de cartes. **Royal Concertgebouw Orchestra / Neeme Järvi.** Chandos Ⓕ CHAN9014 (53 minutes: DDD: 3/92).

Stravinsky The Complete Edition, Volume 4. **Various artists / Igor Stravinsky.** Sony Classical Ⓜ SM2K46294 (two discs: 143 minutes: ADD: 8/92). *Gramophone* classical 100.
Symphonies – No. 1 in E flat major (Columbia Symphony Orchestra SBRG72569, 11/67). Stravinsky in rehearsal. Stravinsky in his own words (GM31). Symphony in Three Movements (Columbia Symphony Orchestra. SBRG72038, 9/62). Symphony in C (CBC Symphony Orchestra). Symphony of Psalms (Toronto Festival Singers, CBC Symphony Orchestra. SBRG72181, 8/64).　　　　　　　　　　　　　　　　　　🅖🅖🅖
The word 'symphony' appears in the title of each work on these two discs, but this term covers some very diverse material. Stravinsky was in his mid-twenties when he wrote his Symphony in E flat, and the score is very much in the style of his teacher Rimsky-Korsakov. It has genuine colour and flair, however, and the octogenarian conductor brings paternalistic affection and a good deal of vigour to his performance. The *Symphony in C* dates from 1940, when Stravinsky was in his neo-classical phase. The work has many beautiful pages, as well as much pungent wit. In this performance Stravinsky drives the music much harder than he did in his 1952 mono recording with the Cleveland Orchestra, and although there are some exciting moments the music does tend to lose its elements of grace and charm. The performance of the *Symphony in Three Movements* is also characterized by the use of fastish tempos. But this violent work, written in 1945, and inspired by events in the Second World War, responds more readily to a strongly driven interpretation. Stravinsky wrote his *Symphony of Psalms* in 1930, and this composition reflects his deep religious convictions in varied settings from the Book of Psalms. His use of a chorus is interestingly combined with an orchestra which lacks upper strings. Stravinsky conducts a fervent, serious, beautifully balanced performance. All the 1960s recordings in this set sound very well in their new CD transfers. In some quarters the elderly Stravinsky has been wrongly portrayed as a frail, inadequate figure who only took over performances when works had been thoroughly rehearsed for him. Nothing could prove more clearly that this was not true than the rehearsal excerpts in this set, which show a vigorous, alert octogenarian very much in control of proceedings, and rehearsing passages in some detail.

Additional recommendation ...
...Symphony of Psalms[c]. Pater noster. Credo. Ave Maria. Mass[c]. Canticum sacrum. [a]**John Mark Ainsley** (ten); [b]**Stephen Roberts** (bar); **Westminster Cathedral Choir;** [c]**City of London Sinfonia / James O'Donnell.** Hyperion Ⓕ CDA66437 (68 minutes: DDD: 9/91).

New review
Stravinsky L'histoire du soldat – Suite[a]. La Marseillaise[d]. Valse pour les enfants[e]. Sketches for a Sonata[e]. Pribaoutki[af]. Cats' Cradle Songs[af]. Monumentum pro Gesualdo di Venosa ad CD

annum[abcef]. Mass[abcefg]. The dove descending breaks[abcefg]. Canticum sacrum ad honorem Sancti Marci nominis[abcefg]. [a]**Catherine Ciesinski** (mez); [b]**Jon Humphries** (ten); [c]**David Evitts** (bar); [d]**Rolf Schulte** (vn); [e]**Mark Wait** (pf); [g]**The Gregg Smith Singers**; [f]**Orchestra of St Luke's / Robert Craft.** MusicMasters Ⓕ 67152-2 (78 minutes: DDD: 10/95). Recorded 1992-4.

Craft's 'hands-on' relationship with this music tells at virtually every juncture. *Canticum sacrum*, for example, sounds so much more confident than it does under the composer's own direction. Compare the two versions of the second movement ("Euntes in mundum") and Craft's extra urgency and superior blending immediately hold one's attention. Taken overall, the newer recording is notably faster than its predecessor, whereas the performance of the *Mass* seems to acknowledge Stravinsky's early music influences, especially in terms of a singing style which, in Stravinsky's own recording sounds – at least next to Craft – strangely unidiomatic. Craft was responsible for introducing Stravinsky to the work of Carlo Gesualdo, and the *Momentum pro Gesualdo di Venosa ad CD annum* – a wonderfully supple recomposition of three five-part madrigals for woodwinds, brass and strings – is in fact dedicated to him. Again, the playing is cleanly accomplished, while the *L'histoire du soldat* Suite is the only performance that rivals Stravinsky's third recording (included in Sony's 22-CD retrospective). Craft has taken great pains over the percussion parts, which are placed here as per the original score. The remaining items on this generously filled collection include a sensitive account of the *a cappella* anthem, *The dove descending*, the lively *Pribaoutki* (the first of which was particularly admired by Prokofiev), the *Cats' Cradle Songs* (admired by Webern) and three comparative rarities: the première on record of two gnomic piano pieces based on orchestral sketches (total timing: 44 seconds), a 50-second *Valse pour les enfants* and a highly palatable solo violin arrangement of *La Marseillaise* (composed on New Year's Day 1919, seven weeks after the Armistice), again presented for the first time on disc and extremely well played by Rolf Schulte. It would make a splendid recital 'encore'. An excellent disc, then. Craft balances scholarship and enthusiasm with perceptive musicianship, and his comprehensive annotations provide an invaluable listening aid.

Stravinsky Les noces[a]. Mass[b]. [a]**Anny Mory** (sop); [a]**Patricia Parker** (mez); [a]**John Mitchinson** (ten); [a]**Paul Hudson** (bass); **English Bach Festival Chorus;** [b]**Trinity Boys' Choir;** [a]**Martha Argerich,** [a]**Krystian Zimerman,** [a]**Cyprien Katsaris,** [a]**Homero Francesch** (pfs); [a]**English Bach Festival Percussion Ensemble;** [b]members of the **English Bach Festival Orchestra / Leonard Bernstein.** DG 20th Century Classics Ⓜ 423 251-2GC (44 minutes: ADD: 6/88). Texts and translations included. From 2530 880 (2/78). ⒼⒼ

Stravinsky Les noces.
Traditional Russian Village Wedding Songs Play, Skomoroshek. River. Trumpet. Cosmas and Demian. The drinker. Green forest. God bless, Jesus. My white peas. Steambath. Berry. Black beaver. In the house. Bunny with short legs. The bed. Birch tree. **Pokrovsky Ensemble / Dmitri Pokrovsky.** Elektra Nonesuch Ⓕ 7559-79335-2 (54 minutes: DDD: 9/94). English texts included. *Gramophone Editor's choice.* ⒼⒼ

Many readers will probably look askance at the timing here – could DG really not have done anything with the spare 30 minutes' capacity? However, never mind the width, feel the quality – these are top-drawer Bernstein performances, excellently recorded. *Les noces* sports an impressive array of pianists; but that need not be a decisive factor, since rhythmic precision and good balance are far more at a premium than individual flair or power – fortunately these individuals are equally fine ensemble players. It is even more important that the choir should be meticulously prepared (which they are), that the vocal soloists should be precise and full-blooded (which they are) and that the conductor should impart a sense of the profundity of the whole conception (which Bernstein emphatically does). The Mass is an ideal coupling for *Les noces*, not just because of the shared importance of the chorus, but because it too displays a fundamental ritual experience, in this case the sacrament of worship rather than marriage, with archetypal clarity. Bernstein's reading has all the calm devotion of the composer's own, even if the soloists are rather variable. A highly recommendable reissue.

For the Elektra Nonesuch recording Dmitri Pokrovsky and the singers in his ensemble travelled to southern and western Russia in search of melodies and texts related to *Les noces*; and they found rich pickings. True, the melodic similarities are not as tangible as the folk sources for *Petrushka* but the 15 songs, here recorded with immense flair and enjoyment to a variety of instrumental accompaniments, will be a revelation to non-specialists and specialists alike. Be prepared for some fairly acerbic sounds. Authentic Russian folk polyphony is an extraordinarily modern-sounding experience, as is authentic open-throated singing. The value of the disc is multiplied by the fact that the singers have carried over the style and expressive content of the folk-songs into their performance of *Les noces* itself, bringing it to life in a way that must surely be unprecedented and uniquely illuminating. Not only that, but Pokrovsky had the inspired idea of recreating the instrumental parts on an Apple Macintosh computer, thus continuing Stravinsky's search for the ideal mechanical realization.

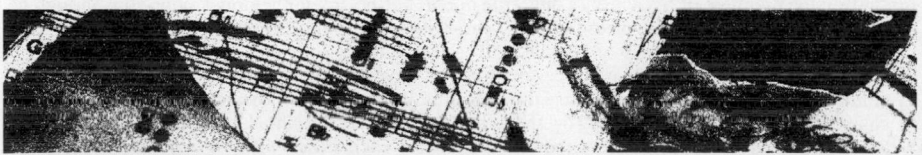

Stravinsky The Flood[a]. Abraham and Isaac[b]. Variations "Aldous Huxley in memoriam"[c]. Requiem canticles[d].
Wuorinen A Reliquary for Igor Stravinsky[e]. [d]**Susan Bickley** (sop); [a]**Peter Hall** (ten/spkr); [abd]**David Wilson-Johnson** (bar); [a]**Stephen Richardson** (bass); [a]**Michael Berkeley**, [a]**Bernard Jacobson**, [a]**Lucy Shelton** (spkrs); [d]**New London Chamber Choir; London Sinfonietta / Oliver Knussen.** DG Ⓕ 447 068-2GH (70 minutes: DDD: 10/95). Texts and translations included.   Ⓖ

There is a confidence and spontaneity about the music-making on this disc that signal something special. Under Oliver Knussen's authoritative direction the performances leap from the speakers with a vividness that is the ideal complement to the music's rhythmic litheness and intensity of colour. Not all the Stravinsky works represent the composer at his best. *The Flood* (a 'musical play' for television) has marvellous episodes, not least the 'flood' music itself, but other passages, like the melodrama in which God gives Noah his instructions, are less inspired. All four works make strong impressions in these recordings, however, and the *Huxley* Variations and *Requiem canticles* are the crowning glory, with an excellent balance between sharpness of detail and shapely, expressive phrasing. In *The Flood* Michael Berkeley's narration is rather too matter of fact alongside Bernard Jacobson's more actorish Noah, and in the *Requiem canticles'* 'Tuba mirum' David Wilson-Johnson is not ideally focused in tone, but these are very minor cavils. In *Abraham and Isaac* Wilson-Johnson is exemplary in projecting the lyricism as well as the drama of one of Stravinsky's most complex pieces of vocal writing. Charles Wuorinen's *Reliquary* refers to material which Stravinsky was working on at the time of his death, but the last thing Wuorinen was aiming at was pious imitation of the master. There's an exuberant elaboration here that is almost Schoenbergian, at least until the understated coda, and this strong piece fully earns its place on the disc. All the recordings are crisply focused, the sound very immediate in impact.

Stravinsky Oedipus Rex[a]. Symphony of Psalms[b]. **Ivo Zídek** (ten); Oedipus; **Věra Soukupová** (mez) Jocasta; **Karel Berman** (bass) Créon; **Eduard Haken** (bass); Tiresias; **Antonin Zlesák** (ten) Shepherd; **Zdeněk Kroupa** (bar) Messenger; **Jean Desailly** (narr); **Czech Philharmonic Chorus and Orchestra / Karel Ančerl.** Supraphon Historical Ⓕ 11 1947-2 (73 minutes: AAD: 3/93). Item marked [a] from SUAST50678 (1/68), [b]SUAST50778 (8/68). Recorded 1964-66.   Ⓖ

Oedipus Rex is one of Stravinsky's most compelling theatre pieces, a powerful drama that re-enacts the full force of a glorious highspot in ancient culture. The text is by Jean Cocteau, who once said, pertaining to his work on *Oedipus,* that "any serious work, be it of poetry or music, of theatre or of film, demands a ceremonial, lengthy calculation, an architecture in which the slightest mistake would unbalance the pyramid" (quoted from *Diary of an Unknown*, pub. Paragon House). The fusion of words and music in *Oedipus,* indeed its very 'architecture' is masterly and arrests the attention consistently, from the animated severity of the opening narration, through the cunningly calculated tension of its musical argument, to the tragic restraint of its closing pages. Stravinsky has nearly always been well served by Czech musicians, and the late Karel Ančerl was one of his most committed exponents. This particular recording of *Oedipus Rex* was taped in the Dvořák Hall of the House of Artists, Prague, and earned itself at least three major gramophone awards. Ančerl traces and intensifies salient points in the tragedy yet maintains a precise, sensitive touch; his vocal collaborators include the noble Karel Berman (Créon) who, like Anerl himself, suffered considerably during the Nazi occupation of Czechoslovakia; then there's a fine Jocasta in Věra Soukupová and the convincing but occasionally unsteady Ivo Zídek singing the part of Oedipus. Both here and in the *Symphony of Psalms* – one of the most serenely perceptive performances of the work ever recorded – the Czech Philharmonic Chorus excel, while Supraphon's 1960s engineering (not, alas, the DDD suggested on the box) has an appealing brightness .

Additional recommendations ...
...**Soloists; Swedish Radio Chorus; Eric Ericson Chamber Choir; Orphei Dranger; Swedish Radio Symphony Orchestra / Esa-Pekka Salonen.** Sony Classical Ⓕ SK48057 (50 minutes: DDD: 7/92).
...**Soloists; Shin-yu Kai Choir; Saito Kinen Orchestra / Seiji Ozawa.** Philips Ⓕ 438 865-2PH (53 minutes: DDD: 3/94).

Stravinsky The Rake's Progress. **Jerry Hadley** (ten) Tom Rakewell; **Dawn Upshaw** (sop) Anne; **Samuel Ramey** (bass) Nick Shadow; **Grace Bumbry** (mez) Baba the Turk; **Steven Cole** (ten) Sellem; **Anne Collins** (contr) Mother Goose; **Robert Lloyd** (bass) Trulove; **Roderick Earle** (bass) Keeper; **Chorus and Orchestra of Opéra de Lyon / Kent Nagano.** Erato Ⓕ 0630-12715-2 (two discs: 138 minutes: DDD: 8/96).

Any number of the world's opera houses would have given their eye teeth for the privilege of presenting the première of Stravinsky's only true opera, but he, intensely money-conscious though he was (and he had worked on the piece for three years without a commission fee), insisted on La Fenice in Venice. Because he was fond of the city, of course, but also because *The Rake's Progress* is a chamber opera. And this is a chamber performance of it, with a fairly small orchestra, much singing of almost *parlando* quality and crystal-clear words. It is also intimate, with a strong sense of the stage, of characters reacting to each other. Together with Nagano's on the whole brisk tempos, and no time wasted on pauses between numbers that should follow each other without a break, it gives the impression of a real performance, and a gripping one. Upshaw's is not the purest soprano voice to have attempted the role of Anne, and there have been more spectacular high Cs than hers, but she is movingly vulnerable, totally believable. So is Hadley, acting at times almost too vividly for the music's line: as he occasionally demonstrates he has a wonderfully beautiful head voice. He is not, therefore, quite the touchingly likeable "shuttle-headed lad" that Alexander Young portrayed so unforgettably in the composer's own recording, but no other Tom Rakewell surpasses him. Ramey's is a bigger voice than most of the others here – firm and superbly produced. He has recorded the role twice before, but never with such a light touch, and all the more dangerous for it. Collins and Lloyd are both first-class as Mother Goose and Trulove, Cole an unusually light-voiced, confidingly conspiratorial Sellem. Bumbry is the disappointment of the cast, over-loud and baritonal almost throughout, but the French chorus sing nimbly and in admirable English. Stravinsky's own recording is still to be cherished, particularly on account of Young, also for the composer's infectious enthusiasm and sheer rhythmic zest, but of modern recordings of *The Rake's Progress* this is by some way the most enjoyable.

Additional recommendations ...

...**Soloists; Sadler's Wells Opera Chorus; Royal Philharmonic Orchestra / Igor Stravinsky.** Sony Classical Ⓜ SM2K46299 (three discs: ADD: 8/92).

...**Soloists; Gregg Smith Singers; Orchestra of St Luke's / Robert Craft.** MusicMasters Ⓕ 67131-2 (two discs: 128 minutes: DDD: 3/95).

Further listening ...

...Concerto in D major. *Coupled with* **Honegger** Symphonies – No. 2; No. 3, "Liturgique", H186. **Berlin Philharmonic Orchestra / Herbert von Karajan.** DG The Originals 447 435-2GOR (12/95). *See review under Honegger; refer to the Index to Reviews.* ⒼⒼⒼ

...Fanfare for a New Theatre. *Coupled with works by* **Zappa, Wheeler, Van Vliet, Babbitt, J. Nelson, Shemaria, H. Hancock** and **London** Meridian Arts Ensemble. Channel Classics Channel Crossings CCS8195 (4/96). *See review in the Collections section; refer to the Index to Reviews.* Ⓖ

...Three Pieces. **Ravel** String Quartet in F major. **Debussy** String Quartet in G minor, Op. 10. **Lindsay Quartet.** ASV CDDCA930 (12/95).

...Les noces (sung in English. Kate Winter, sop; Linda Seymour, contr; Parry Jones, ten; Roy Henderson, bar; Berkeley Mason, Leslie Heward, Ernest Lush, Edwin Benbow, pfs; BBC Chorus; percussion ensemble / Igor Stravinsky). Octet (Marcel Moyse, fl; Emile Godeau, cl; Gustave Dhérin, Marius Piard, bns; Eugène Foveau, Pierre Vignal, tpts; André Lafosse, Raphaël Delbos, tbns / Stravinsky). Capriccio (Stravinsky, pf; Walther Straram Concerts Orchestra / Ernest Ansermet). Symphony of Psalms (Alexis Vlassov Choir; Straram Orchestra / Stravinsky). Pastorale (Louis Gromer, ob; Georges Durand, cor ang; André Vacellier, cl; Gabriel Grandmaison, bn; Samuel Dushkin, vn / Stravinsky). Petrushka – Danse russe. The Firebird – Scherzo; Berceuse. Le chant du rossignol – Airs du rossignol; Marche chinoise (all with Dushkin, vn; Stravinsky, pf). Rag-time (Lucien Lavaillotte, fl; Godeau, cl; Jean Devemy, hn; Foveau, tpt; Roger Tudesq, tbn; Roland Charmy, Henri Volant, vns; Etienne Ginot, va; Louis Juste, db; Aladar Racz, cimbalom; Jean Morel, perc / Stravinsky). Piano-rag-music (Stravinsky). Suite italienne – Serenata; Scherzino. Duo concertant (Dushkin; Stravinsky). Serenade in A major (Stravinsky). Concerto for Two Pianos (Soulima and Igor Stravinsky, pfs). **Various artists.** EMI Composers in Person mono CDS7 54607-2* (5/93). Recorded 1928-34.

Soulima Stravinsky
American 1910-1994

Suggested listening ...

...Piano Trio[ab]. Encounters. Three Pieces for Violin and Piano[a]. Three Etudes for Violin and Piano[a]. [a]**Thomas Moore** (vn); [b]**Christopher Pegis** (vc); **Elisha Gilgore** (pf). Centaur CRC2176 (2/95).

Alessandro Striggio
Italian c1540-1592

Suggested listening ...

...Ecce beatam lucem. *Coupled with works by* **Ockeghem, Josquin Desprez, Porta, Tallis, G. Gabrieli** and **Manchicourt** Huelgas Ensemble / **Paul van Nevel.** Sony Classical Vivarte SK66261 (4/96). *See review in the Collections section; refer to the Index to Reviews.*

Barbara Strozzi
Italian 1619-1664 or later

Suggested listening ...

...Merce di voi. Dimmi, ah dimmi dove sei. Bella madre d'amore. Gl'occhi superbi. Amor, non dormir più. Mi ferite oh begli occhi. Anima del mio core. Sete pur fastidioso. Oh dolci, oh cari, oh desiati baci! Sino alla morte. Mordeva un bianco lino. Godere e tacere. Che dolce udire. Non ci lusinghi più. **Musica Secreta.** Amon Ra CD-SAR61 (1/95). ✐

...Corrente terza. *Coupled with works by* **Salvatore, Frescobaldi, Lambardo, Buono, Picchi, Trabaci, A. Mayone, Giovanni de Macque, Facoli, A. Valente, Merula, M. Rossi, B. Storace, Stradella** and **A. Scarlatti** Rinaldo Alessandrini (hpd). Opus 111 OPS30-118 (4/95). ☞ *See review in the Collections section; refer to the Index to Reviews.* ⓖⓖ

Simon Stubley
British died 1754

Suggested listening ...
...Voluntary in C major. *Coupled with works by* **Boyce, Handel, Heron, Hook, Russell, Stanley** and **S. Wesley** Jennifer Bate (org). Unicorn-Kanchana DKPCD9106 (11/91). *Selected by Sounds in Retrospect. See review in the Collections section; refer to the Index to Reviews.* ⓖ

Jule Styne
American 1905-

Suggested listening ...
...Funny Girl. **Original Broadway cast.** EMI Angel ZDM7 64661-2.
...Gipsy. **Original 1990 Broadway revival cast.** Elektra Nonesuch 7559 79239-2.

Josef Suk
Bohemian 1874-1935

Suk Asrael, Op. 27. **Bavarian Radio Symphony Orchestra / Rafael Kubelík.** Panton Ⓕ 81 1101-2 (64 minutes: ADD: 1/94). Recorded 1981. ⓖⓖⓖ
To use large scale symphonic form for the purging of deep personal grief carries the danger that the result will seriously lack discipline. In 1904-05 Suk's world was shattered by two visits from *Asrael* (the Angel of Death in Muslim mythology): he lost his father-in-law (and revered teacher) Dvořák, and his beloved wife, Otylka. Forgivably, Suk does perhaps linger a little too long in the fourth movement's gentle, mainly lyrical portrait of Otylka, but elsewhere the progress is as satisfying psychologically as it is symphonically. Much of the music has a concentrated dream-like quality; at the extremes, spectral nightmare visions merge with compensatory surges of lyrical ardour. It seems that *Asrael's* time has well and truly come; there are now seven versions currently available. Set Kubelík's reading alongside any of the modern versions and one is immediately aware of a wholly compelling imaginative intensity and interpretative flair that betoken a true poet of the rostrum. Kubelík's control throughout is awesome and he conjures up playing of enormous expressive subtlety from his fine Munich orchestra. No other recorded performance – not even Václav Talich's legendary 1952 Supraphon account – succeeds in conveying the intensely personal nature of this music with such devastating emotional candour. Technically, too, one need have no qualms about this Panton disc – the Bavarian Radio engineers secure most truthful results.
Additional recommendations ...
...Asrael. **Royal Liverpool Philharmonic Orchestra / Libor Pešek.** Virgin Classics Ⓕ VC7 59638-2 (62 minutes: DDD: 9/91). ⓖⓖ
...Asrael. **Czech Philharmonic Orchestra / Jiří Bělohlávek.** Chandos Ⓕ CHAN9042 (59 minutes: DDD: 5/92).
...Asrael. **Dvořák** Stabat mater, B171. **Soloists; Czech Philharmonic Chorus and Orchestra / Václav Talich.** Supraphon Historical mono Ⓜ 11 1902-2* (two discs: 147 minutes: ADD: 12/93). ⓖⓖ
...Asrael. **Russian State Symphony Orchestra / Evgeni Svetlanov.** Russian Disc Ⓕ RDCD11011 (64 minutes: DDD: 1/94). ⓖ

Suk Ripening, Op. 34[a]. Praga, Op. 26. **Royal Liverpool Philharmonic [a]Choir and Orchestra / Libor Pešek.** Virgin Classics Ⓕ VC7 59318-2 (67 minutes: DDD: 1/94). Recorded 1992. *Gramophone Editor's choice.* ⓖ
Completed in 1917, *Ripening* shows Suk at the height of his powers. This vast yet tightly organized tone-poem shares many of the autobiographical concerns of both its large-scale orchestral predecessors (namely *Asrael* and *A Summer Tale*). Throughout, Suk handles his outsize forces with a truly Straussian confidence and virtuosity, nowhere more strikingly than in the extended Fugue which attains a climax of truly devastating proportions; the profound serenity of the ensuing coda (where a wordless female chorus is used to magical effect) could not have been harder won. The coupling, *Praga*, is an affectionate, enjoyably grandiloquent portrait-in-sound of that fair city dating from 1904. Pešek's direction is imaginative, the RLPO's playing accomplished and communicative. The engineering, too, is first-class.
Additional recommendation ...
...Praga. A Summer's Tale, Op. 29. **Czech Philharmonic Orchestra / Libor Pešek.** Supraphon Ⓕ 11 1984-2 (76 minutes: DDD: 8/95).

Suk Chamber works, Volumes 1-3. [l]Jiří Válek (fl); [eghijlno]Josef Suk, [g]Jitka Nováková, [o]Ludmila Vybíralová, [o]Miroslav Kosina, [o]Jaroslav Krištůfek, [o]Zdeněk Mann (vns); [e]Jan Talich (va);

[e]Michaela Fukačová, [k]Marek Jerie, [n]František Host, [o]Ivo Laniar (vcs); [o]Tomáš Josífko (db); [n]Renata Kodadová (hp); Josef Hála ([hl]pf/[m]harm); [eij]Jan Panenka, [f]Pavel Stěpán, [k]Iván Klánský (pfs); [o]Josef Fousek, [o]Libor Kubánek (perc); [cd]Suk Trio (Josef Suk, vn; Josef Chuchro, vc; [c]Josef Hála, [d]Jan Panenka, pfs); [abfmn]Suk Quartet ([afm]Antonín Novák, [bn]Ivan Straus, Vojtěch Jouza, vns; Karel Rehák, va; Jan Stros, vc). Supraphon Ⓜ 11 1874-2 (three discs, aas: 71, 74 and 63 minutes: ADD/DDD? 2/94). Recorded 1966-92.

11 1531-2: String Quartets – No. 1 in B flat major, Op. 11[a] (from 1111 2974, 10/82); No. 2, Op. 31[b]. Tempo di menuetto[b]. Meditation on an old Czech hymn, Op. 35*a*[b] (all from 1111 3370, recorded 1984). Quartet movement in B flat major[a] (recorded 1978, new to UK).
11 1532-2: Piano Trio in C minor, Op. 2[c]. Elégie, Op. 23[d] (SUAST50863, 12/69). Piano Quartet in A minor, Op. 1[e]. Piano Quintet in G minor, Op. 8[f] (recorded 1978, new to UK). *11 1533-2:* Mélodie[g]. Minuet[h]. Balada in D minor[i] (SUAST5077, 8/68). Four Pieces, Op. 17[j] (SUAST5077). Ballade in D minor, Op. 3 No. 1[k]. Serenade in A major, Op. 3 No. 2[k] (both recorded 1983, new to UK). Bagatelle, "Carrying a bouquet"[l]. Barcarolle in B flat major[m]. Balada in D minor[m] (both recorded 1978, new to UK). Elégie, Op. 23[n]. Sousedská[o].   ⓖⓖⓖ

A treasure-trove of heartfelt music performed with refinement and flair. Volume 1 concentrates on Suk's string quartet output (Suk himself was the second violinist in the great Czech Quartet for 40 years). If the First Quartet (1896) doesn't quite show the same freshness or entrancing melodic vein of the String Serenade of four years earlier, it remains a delightfully unassuming creation with the genial presence of Suk's teacher Dvořák looming large over the proceedings. It is followed by a rare hearing for the alternative finale Suk composed some 19 years later in 1915. By this time, of course, the composer had already found his own strongly personal voice. Both the resourceful Second Quartet of 1911 (an ambitious one-movement essay of nearly 28 minutes' duration and considerable emotional variety) and the deeply-felt *Meditation on an old Czech Hymn* (1914) are works of some substance well worth exploring, and these passionate accounts enjoy excellent sound. The remaining two volumes perhaps contain more to interest Suk *aficionados* than newcomers, though the adorable *Four Pieces* for violin and piano, Op. 17, have always remained great favourites.

Volume 2 features youthful offerings: the Piano Trio, the Piano Quartet, the likeable, if rather garrulous, Piano Quintet of 1893 and the touching *Elégie* for piano, violin and cello from 1902, written to celebrate the anniversary of the death of the poet and dramatist, Julius Zeyer. Apart from the *Four Pieces* already mentioned, the third and final volume also contains, amongst much else, the *Elégie* in its original guise for violin, cello, string quartet, harmonium and harp, no fewer than three different *Ballades* in D minor conceived for various instrumental combinations during Suk's days at the Conservatory, the "Barcarolle" slow movement of a very early String Quartet from 1888, as well as the composer's last completed piece from 1935, the engaging *Sousedská* for five violins, double bass, cymbals and triangle. Recording dates range from 1966 to 1992 (most of the material is designated as AAD), but the quality is consistently praiseworthy and the volumes are available either separately or gathered together within an attractive slipcase.

New review

Suk Six Pieces, Op. 7. Spring, Op. 22*a*. Summer moods, Op. 22*b*. About Mother, Op. 28. **Radoslav Kvapil** (pf). Unicorn-Kanchana Ⓔ DKPCD9159 (74 minutes: DDD: 2/96). Recorded 1994.

Suk wrote some 60-odd short piano pieces, many of them collected into groups sharing an experience; about a third of them are here, in four collections. Three of these, the Six Pieces (Op. 7), and the connected *Spring* and *Summer moods* (Op. 22), antedate the dreadful double blow that befell him in 1904 and 1905; the sequence *About Mother* belongs to 1907, and is more backward-looking and reflective, marked by sorrow but not with the darkness that was shadowing his large-scale orchestral works in these years. The latter are pieces written for his son, touching domestic vignettes that avoid sentimentality, and are marked by foreboding in the last of them, when the irregularity of the rhythms reflects the frail beat of his wife's heart. The pieces make an excellent anthology of Suk's music, and Kvapil has their manner ideally. He can touch off a mood of gentleness or wit or, more rarely, something almost wry in its oblique, private feeling. Some of the pieces are very simple, and would buckle under playing of greater intensity; some need a little intelligent help in holding them together, or in making the most of Suk's handling of a single idea permeating the invention. Kvapil is unerringly sensitive to their mood, and makes this a most affecting recital.

Further listening ...

...A Summer's Tale, Op. 29. **Royal Liverpool Philharmonic Orchestra / Libor Pešek.** Virgin Classics VC5 45057-2 (8/95).

...Fairy Tale, Op. 16. Serenade in E flat major, Op. 6. **Czech Philharmonic Orchestra / Jiří Bělohlávek.** Chandos CHAN9063 (3/93).

...Serenade in E flat major, Op. 6. *Coupled with* **Grieg** Holberg Suite, Op. 40[a]. **Tchaikovsky** Serenade in C major for Strings, Op. 48. [a]**Swiss Chamber Orchestra; Polish Radio Chamber Orchestra / Agnieszka Duczmal.** ASV CDQS6094 (3/94).

...Serenade in E flat major, Op. 6. Meditation on an old Czech hymn, Op. 35*a*. *Coupled with* **Janáček** Suite. **Virtuosi di Praga / Oldrich Vlcek.** Koch International Classics DICD920234 (9/95).

...Serenade in E flat major, Op. 6. *Coupled with* **Dvořák** Symphony No. 6 in D major, B112.**Czech Philharmonic Orchestra / Václav Talich.** Koch Legacy mono 37060-2* (1/92).   ⓖ

...Spring, Op. 22*a*. About Friendship, Op. 36. Things lived and dreamt, Op. 30. Pieces, Op. 7 – No. 1, Love song; No. 2, Humoreske; No. 4, Two Idylls. **Niel Immelman** (pf). Meridian CDE84269 (1/94).

...10 Songs, Op. 15[a]. *Coupled with works by* **Smetana, Dvořák** and **Eben Prague Chamber Choir / Josef Pancik** with [a]**Marian Lapsansky,** [a]**Daniel Buranovsky** (pf duet). Chandos CHAN9257 (12/95). *See review under Eben; refer to the Index to Reviews.*

Arthur Sullivan

British 1842-1900

Sullivan Cello Concerto in D major (reconstr. Mackerras and Mackie)[a]. Symphony in E major, "Irish"[b]. Overture di ballo[b].
Elgar Romance, Op. 62 (arr. vc)[a]. [a]**Julian Lloyd Webber** (vc); [a]**London Symphony Orchestra / Sir Charles Mackerras;** [b]**Royal Liverpool Philharmonic Orchestra / Sir Charles Groves.** EMI British Composers Ⓜ CDM7 64726-2 (71 minutes: ADD/DDD: 4/94). Items marked [a] from CDC7 47622-2 (2/87), recorded 1986; [b]HMV ASD2435 (2/69), recorded 1968.

Sir Charles Groves's sturdy yet affectionate reading of Arthur Sullivan's wholly charming *Irish* Symphony was always one of the best of his EMI offerings with the RLPO and the 1968 recording remains vivid. In the sparkling *Overture di ballo*, again, Groves conducts with plenty of character. There are also first-rate performances of Sullivan's undemanding Cello Concerto from 1866 (in a fine reconstruction by Sir Charles Mackerras – the manuscript was destroyed in Chappell's fire of 1964) as well as Elgar's wistful little *Romance* (originally for bassoon). This is a thoroughly attractive mid-price reissue.

Additional recommendation ...

...Symphony. Imperial March. Victoria and Merrie England – Suite No. 1. Overture in C major, "In memoriam". **BBC Concert Orchestra / Owain Arwel Hughes.** CPO Ⓕ CPO999 171-2 (72 minutes: DDD: 4/95).

New review
Sullivan Victoria and Merrie England. **RTE Sinfonietta / Andrew Penny.** Marco Polo Ⓕ 8 223677 (78 minutes: DDD: 6/96).

Five years before Edward German's comic opera *Merrie England*, this Sullivan ballet score was staged at the Alhambra Theatre as part of the celebrations of Queen Victoria's Diamond Jubilee. The original full score appears not to have survived. However, a complete piano reduction was published, along with an orchestral suite, and in addition Sullivan reused earlier material such as his *Imperial March* and music from his early ballet *L'île enchantée*. From all these sources Roderick Spencer has made this very convincing re-creation of the full score. And very worthwhile it proves too. As the notes explain, British ballet in those days was not classical ballet as we know it today but mime-drama. Spectacle was what it was all about, and Sullivan rose to the occasion admirably. There are some most attractive passages – not only in the recycled material but also, for instance, the Solo Variation for the May Queen and perhaps above all the Waltz of Wood Nymphs, which would well repay taking over into the light music repertory. In addition Sullivan skilfully weaves in various patriotic British melodies as well as traditional dances such as a morris dance and a sailors' hornpipe. Such pastiche is the sort of thing that Sullivan did particularly well, and Andrew Penny and the RTE Sinfonietta do the whole score proud. This is as rewarding as any of the CDs of Sullivan without Gilbert that Marco Polo have issued.

Sullivan HMS Pinafore. **Richard Suart** (bass) Sir Joseph Porter; **Felicity Palmer** (mez) Little Buttercup; **Rebecca Evans** (sop) Josephine; **Thomas Allen** (bar) Captain Corcoran; **Michael Schade** (ten) Ralph Rackstraw; **Donald Adams** (bass) Dick Deadeye; **Valerie Seymour** (sop) Hebe; **Richard Van Allan** (bass) Bill Bobstay; **John King, Philip Lloyd-Evans** (bars) Bob Becket; **Welsh National Opera Chorus and Orchestra / Sir Charles Mackerras.** Telarc Ⓕ CD80374 (74 minutes: DDD: 1/95). Notes and text included. Recorded 1994. *Gramophone Editor's choice.*   Ⓖ

As always, Mackerras keeps the livelier numbers moving along comfortably without ever a hint of rushing, whilst giving full weight to the tender moments and, above all, caressing all the details of Sullivan's delicious orchestration. Right from the overture, with its beautifully shaped *Andante* section, this is music-making to perfection. Of the singers, Felicity Palmer's Buttercup truly oozes plumpness and pleasure, while Thomas Allen's Captain does not just the crew of the *Pinafore*, but all of us, proud. If Rebecca Evans's Josephine is a shade lacking in colour, Mackerras has found in Michael Schade's Ralph Rackstraw a most elegant addition to his G&S team. As for Richard Suart's Sir Joseph Porter, this is surely as stylish a demonstration of patter singing as one can find anywhere on disc, while Donald Adams's Dick Deadeye is no worse for his 40-odd years singing the role. Add orchestral playing of refinement, choral work whose perfection extends from the formal numbers to the varied inflexions of "What nevers?", plus a recording that brings out the instrumental detail to perfection, and one has a *Pinafore* that is unadulterated delight from first note to last.

Additional recommendation ...

...Soloists; **D'Oyly Carte Opera Chorus; New Symphony Orchestra / Isidore Godfrey.** Decca London Ⓜ 414 283-2LM2 (98 minutes: ADD: 1/90).

Sullivan The Pirates of Penzance. **Eric Roberts** (bar) Major-General Stanley; **Malcolm Rivers** (bar) Pirate King; **Gareth Jones** (bar) Samuel; **Philip Creasy** (ten) Frederic; **Simon Masterton-Smith** (bass) Sargeant of Police; **Marilyn Hill Smith** (sop) Mabel; **Patricia Cameron** (sop) Edith; **Pauline Birchall** (mez) Kate; **Susan Gorton** (contr) Ruth; **D'Oyly Carte Opera Chorus and Orchestra / John Pryce-Jones.** TER Ⓕ CDTER2 1177 (two discs: 85 minutes: DDD: 9/90). Recorded 1990.

The revival of the D'Oyly Carte Opera Company produced the first digital recordings of complete Gilbert and Sullivan scores, and this TER set is a very happy example. Philip Creasy is an engaging and vocally secure Frederic, and Marilyn Hill Smith trips through "Poor wandering one" with a delectable display of vocal ability and agility. The couple's interplay with the chorus in "How beautifully blue the sky" is quite enchanting, and their exchanges in "Stay, Frederic, stay" splendidly convincing. Eric Roberts makes the Major-General a thoroughly engaging personality, and the dotty exchanges between Simon Masterson-Smith's Sargeant of Police and his police force are sheer joy. Even such details as the girls' screams at the appearance of the pirates in Act 1 have a rare effectiveness. John Pryce-Jones keeps the score dancing along. Those who want the dialogue as well as the music must look elsewhere, but this version is certainly to be recommended for its musical and acting values as well as its fine modern sound.

Additional recommendations ...

...**Soloists; D'Oyly Carte Opera Chorus; Royal Philharmonic Orchestra / Isidore Godfrey.** Decca Ⓜ 425 196-2LM2 (1/90).

...**Soloists; Welsh National Opera Chorus and Orchestra / Sir Charles Mackerras.** Telarc Ⓕ CD80353 (79 minutes: DDD: 11/93).

Sullivan The Mikado[a]. **John Holmes** (bass) The Mikado; **John Wakefield** (ten) Nanki-Poo; **Clive Revill** (bar) Ko-Ko; **Denis Dowling** (bar) Pooh-Bah; **John Heddle Nash** (bar) Pish-Tush; **Marion Studholme** (sop) Yum-Yum; **Patricia Kern** (mez) Pitti-Sing; **Dorothy Nash** (sop) Peep-Bo; **Jean Allister** (mez) Katisha.
Iolanthe[b] – excerpts. **Elizabeth Harwood, Elizabeth Robson, Cynthia Morey** (sops); **Heather Begg, Patricia Kern** (mezzos); **Stanley Bevan** (ten); **Eric Shilling, Denis Dowling, Julian Moyle** (bars); **Leon Greene** (bass); **Sadler's Wells Opera Chorus and Orchestra / Alexander Faris.** Classics for Pleasure Ⓑ CD-CFPD4730 (two discs: 135 minutes: ADD: 4/94). Item marked [a] from HMV CSD1458/9 (10/62), [b] CSD1434 (7/62). Recorded 1962.

At the core of these performances are some of the finest British singers of 30 years ago, all of whom were chosen not just for their singing but for their sense of the theatricality and humour of Gilbert and Sullivan. Just listen, for instance, to how John Heddle Nash gives full expression to every word of Pish-Tush's "Our great Mikado". Here, too, is Marion Studholme's delicious Yum-Yum and Elizabeth Harwood's joyous Phyllis. If one singles out Clive Revill for special mention, it is because his Ko-Ko is uniquely well-judged and imaginative, combining superb comic timing, verbal clarity and vocal dexterity. His "little list" is hilarious, and one can almost feel one's hand gripped at the words "shake hands with you *like that*". At the helm in both works is Alexander Faris who knew supremely well how to capture the lightness and sparkle of operetta. The new Overture put together for *The Mikado* by Stephen Dodgson may come as a surprise, but it is apt and cleverly done. The sound is inevitably dated when compared to more recent recordings, but it scarcely mars the enjoyment.

Additional recommendations ...

...**Soloists; D'Oyly Carte Chorus; Royal Philharmonic Orchestra / Royston Nash.** Decca Ⓜ 425 190-2LM2 (two discs: 90 minutes: ADD: 1/90).

...**Soloists; Welsh National Opera Chorus and Orchestra / Sir Charles Mackerras.** Telarc Ⓕ CD80284 (79 minutes: DDD: 5/92).

New review

Sullivan The Yeomen of the Guard. **Peter Savidge** (bar) Sir Richard Cholmondeley; **Neill Archer** (ten) Colonel Fairfax; **Donald Adams** (bass) Sergeant Meryll; **Peter Hoare** (ten) Leonard; **Richard Suart** (bar) Jack Point; **Donald Maxwell** (bar) Shadbolt; **Alwyn Mellor** (sop) Elsie; **Pamela Helen Stephen** (mez) Phoebe; **Felicity Palmer** (mez) Dame Carruthers; **Clare O'Neill** (sop) Kate; **Ralph Mason** (ten) First Yeoman; **Peter Lloyd Evans** (bar) Second Yeoman.
Sullivan Trial by Jury. **Rebecca Evans** (sop) Plaintiff; **Barry Banks** (ten) Defendant; **Richard Suart** (bar) Judge; **Peter Savidge** (bar) Counsel; **Donald Adams** (bass) Usher; **Gareth Rhys-Davies** (bar) Foreman; **Welsh National Opera Chorus and Orchestra / Sir Charles Mackerras.** Telarc Ⓕ CD80404 (two discs: 121 minutes: DDD: 2/96). Recorded 1995. Notes and texts included.

Between them, *The Yeomen of the Guard* and *Trial by Jury* contain all that is best in Sullivan's music for the theatre. In the former there is some of his more serious and ambitious writing, in the latter some of his most consistently light-hearted and engaging. All of this is brought out in the latest of Telarc's series of recordings with Welsh National Opera. As always, Sir Charles Mackerras paces the music impeccably, and he has assured contributions from such stalwarts as Donald Adams, Felicity Palmer and Richard Suart. The last-named may be a shade light-voiced compared with some of the more comic performers of Jack Point and the Learned Judge; but in *The Yeomen* it is surely his performance that stands out. His handling of the dialogue after "Here's a man of jollity" is masterly, and his "Oh, a private buffoon" is as winning as any, with impeccable clarity of diction and a perfectly judged French accent for "jests ... imported from France". Neill Archer and Alwyn Mellor are admirable as Fairfax and Elsie; but Pamela Helen Stephen could have displayed more of the minx in Phoebe Meryll's personality, while in *Trial by Jury* Barry Banks seems to have too small a voice to convince as the Defendant. If this set doesn't quite stand out in the same way as Mackerras's *Mikado* and *Pinafore* it would still be a clear recommendation from the versions of *The Yeomen of the Guard* listed below. Anyone who wants any of Gilbert's dialogue, though, must go for the Marriner version, while the D'Oyly Carte disc (TER) has a good sense of theatre. Yet perhaps the major competition still comes from the 1964 D'Oyly Carte coupling of the same works, with Sargent conducting *Yeomen* in relaxed but winning fashion and Elizabeth Harwood still unmatched as Elsie Maynard.

Additional recommendations ...

...The Yeoman of the Guard. **Soloists; Glyndebourne Festival Chorus; Pro Arte Orchestra / Sir Malcolm Sargent.** EMI Ⓜ CMS7 64415-2 (two discs: 93 minutes: ADD).

...The Yeoman of the Guard[a]. Trial by Jury[b]. **Soloists; D'Oyly Carte Opera Chorus,** [a]**Royal Philharmonic Orchestra / Sir Malcolm Sargent;** [b]**Orchestra of the Royal Opera House, Covent Garden / Isidore Godfrey.** Decca Ⓜ 417 358-2LM2 (two discs: 125 minutes: ADD: 1/90).

...The Yeoman of the Guard. **Soloists; D'Oyly Carte Opera Chorus and Orchestra / John Owen Edwards.** TER Ⓕ CDTER2 1195 (two discs: 115 minutes: DDD: 4/93). *Gramophone Editor's choice.*

...The Yeoman of the Guard. **Soloists; Academy and Chorus of St Martin in the Fields / Sir Neville Marriner.** Philips Ⓕ 438 138-2PH2 (two discs: 115 minutes: DDD: 11/93).

Sullivan The Gondoliers. Overture di Ballo (1870 version). **Richard Suart** (bar) Duke of Plaza-Toro; **Philip Creasey** (ten) Luiz; **John Rath** (bass) Don Alhambra; **David Fieldsend** (ten) Marco; **Alan Oke** (bar) Giuseppe; **Tim Morgan** (bar) Antonio; **David Cavendish** (ten) Francesco; **Toby Barrett** (bass) Giorgio; **Jill Pert** (contr) Duchess of Plaza-Toro; **Elizabeth Woollett** (sop) Casilda; **Lesley Echo Ross** (sop) Gianetta; **Regina Hanley** (mez) Tessa; **Yvonne Patrick** (sop) Fiametta; **Pamela Baxter** (mez) Vittoria; **Elizabeth Elliott** (sop) Giulia; **Claire Kelly** (contr) Inez; **D'Oyly Carte Opera Chorus and Orchestra / John Pryce-Jones.** TER Ⓕ CDTER2 1187 (two discs: 109 minutes: DDD: 5/92). Recorded 1991.

This is one of a series of recordings by the new D'Oyly Carte Opera Company that offers a vastly better quality of sound than any of its ageing competitors. Orchestral detail is the most immediate beneficiary, and the overture serves to demonstrate John Pryce-Jones's lively tempos and lightness of touch. Outstanding among the singers are perhaps John Rath, who gives Don Alhambra's "I stole the prince" and "There lived a king" real presence, and Jill Pert, a formidable Duchess of Plaza-Toro. Richard Suart not only provides the leading comedy roles with exceptionally clear articulation and musicality, but also adds considerable character to his portrayals; his "I am a courtier grave and serious" is a sure winner. David Fieldsend and Alan Oke provide attractive portrayals of the two gondoliers, and Lesley Echo Ross and Regina Hanley are also most agreeable. Seasoned listeners may note numerous changes of detail as a result of the purging of the performance material of changes made to the parts around the time of the 1920s Savoy Theatre revivals. There is no dialogue, but added value is provided by Sullivan's sunniest comic opera score being accompanied by the sparkling *Overture di Ballo*, played in its original version with some traditional cuts opened up.

Additional recommendation ...

...**Soloists; D'Oyly Carte Opera Chorus; New Symphony Orchestra / Isidore Godfrey.** Decca Ⓜ 425 177-2LM2 (two discs: 129 minutes: ADD: 1/90).

Further listening ...

...The Contrabandista – Only the night wind sighs alone. *Coupled with works by* **Lehár, Offenbach, J. Strauss II, Romberg, Novello, Coward, Chabrier** and **Heuberger Lesley Garrett** (sop); **Crouch End Festival Chorus; Royal Philharmonic Concert Orchestra / James Holmes.** Silva Screen Classics SILKTVCD1 (2/96). *See review in the Collections section; refer to the Index to Reviews.*

...Guinevere and other Ballads – O mistress mine. She is not fair to outward view. Golden days. A life that lives for you. Guinevere!. Thou art lost to me. Once again. County guy. Mary Morison. If doughty deeds. Orpheus with his lute. Sigh no more, ladies. Sweet day, so cool. Ich möchte hinaus es jauchzen. Arabian love song. Tears, idle tears. Oh! ma charmante. I would I were a King. **Richard Conrad** (bar); **William Merrill** (pf). Pearl SHECD9636 (2/95).

...Overtures – HMS Pinafore; The Pirates of Penzance; Patience; Iolanthe; Princess Ida; The Mikado; The Gondoliers; The Yeoman of the Guard; Di ballo; Ruddigore. **New Sadler's Wells Opera Orchestra; D'Oyly Carte Opera Orchestra / John Pryce-Jones, Simon Phipps, John Owen Edwards.** TER CDVIR8316 (5/93).

...Iolanthe. **Glyndebourne Festival Chorus; Pro Arte Orchestra / Sir Malcolm Sargent.** EMI CMS7 64400-2.

...Ruddigore. The Pirates of Penzance. **Soloists; Glyndebourne Festival Chorus; Pro Arte Orchestra / Sir Malcolm Sargent.** EMI CMS7 64412-2.

...Pineapple Poll – excerpts. *Coupled with* **Verdi** The Lady and the Fool. **London Philharmonic Orchestra / Sir Charles Mackerras.** Classics for Pleasure CD-CFP4618.

...Patience. **Soloists; D'Oyly Carte Opera Chorus; New Symphony Orchestra / Isidore Godfrey.** Decca 425 193-2LM2 (1/90).

Lepo Sumera

Suggested listening ...
...Musica tenera. Piano Concerto[a]. Symphony No. 4, "Serena borealis". [a]**Kalle Randalu** (pf);
Malmö Symphony Orchestra / Paavo Järvi. BIS CD690 (9/95).
...Symphonies Nos. 1-3. **Malmö Symphony Orchestra / Paavo Järvi.** BIS CD660 (12/94).
...For B.B.B. and his Friend. *Coupled with works by* **Kangro, Mägi, Põldmäe, Eespere** and
Vähi Tallinn Camerata. Finlandia 4509-95705-2 (5/95).
...Piece from the Year 1981. *Coupled with* **Rääts** Toccata. **Kangro** Suite, Op. 1. **Mägi** The Ancient
Kannel. **Tüür** Sonata. **Vähi** Fata Morgana. **Pärt** Partita. **Lauri Väinmaa** (pf). Finlandia
4509-95704-2 (7/95).

Herbert Sumsion

Suggested listening ...
...Introduction and Theme. *Coupled with works by* **Elgar, Hollins, Cocker, Spicer, C.S. Lang,
Lemare** and **Wagner Christopher Herrick** (org). Hyperion CDA66778 (3/96). *See review in the
Collections section; refer to the Index to Reviews.*

Franz von Suppé

New review
Suppé Overtures – Leichte Kavallerie; Tricoche und Cacolet; Boccaccio. Afrikareise – Titania
Waltz. Fatinitza. Humorous variations on the popular song, "What comes there from on high?"
Die Heimkehr von der Hochzeit. Herzenseintracht – polka. Franz Schubert. Triumph Overture.
Slovak State Philharmonic Orchestra, Košice / Alfred Walter. Marco Polo Ⓟ 8 223683
(62 minutes: DDD: 12/95). Recorded 1994.
This volume of Marco Polo's Suppé series offers another fascinating insight into the wider output of
a composer unjustly typecast through the brilliance of his rousing overtures. Here the familiar *Leichte
Kavallerie* and *Fatinitza* overtures serve to demonstrate the thoroughly reliable conducting and
playing of Alfred Walter and the Košice orchestra, without quite offering a challenge to the most
rousing interpretations available elsewhere. What are of interest are the rarities. Of the unfamiliar
overtures, that to *Tricoche und Cacolet*, a Viennese adaptation of a Meilhac and Halévy play, is
perceptibly in the French style of Offenbach, with some attractive themes and a marvellous passage
for bassoon, while the *Triumph Overture* has a typically exciting ending. The overture to *Die Heimkehr
von der Hochzeit* is perhaps less striking, while that to *Franz Schubert* (a one-act operetta portraying
the composer on stage) is mainly notable for its use of Schubertian themes – *Der Erlkönig, Der
Wanderer*, the German Dance No. 7 (also used later in *Lilac Time*), *Der Schäfer und der Reiter* and
Die Taubenpost. Among the other pieces, the *Afrikareise* waltz finds Suppé very much in Straussian
territory, while *Herzenseintracht* proves that he could also produce a polka with the best. Perhaps the
most intriguing item is Suppé's set of humorous variations on the *Fuchslied*, a popular Viennese
student song which we would recognize as *A-hunting we will go*. It all provides further enjoyable proof
that Suppé's entertaining writing extended way beyond his overtures.
Additional recommendations ...
...Overtures – Die schöne Galathee; Boccaccio; Dichter und Bauer; Leichte Kavallerie; Ein Morgen,
ein Mittag, ein Abend in Wien; Pique Dame. **Auber** Overtures – Le Cheval de bronze; Fra
Diavolo; La Muette de Portici. **Detroit Symphony Orchestra / Paul Paray.** Mercury Living
Presence Ⓜ 434 309-2MM (66 minutes: ADD).   Ⓖ
...Overtures – Leichte Kavallerie; Tantalusqualen; Die Irrfahrt um's Glück; Die Frau Meisterin, Ein
Morgen, ein Mittag, ein Abend in Wien; Pique-Dame; Wiener Jubel; Dichter und Bauer.
Academy of St Martin in the Fields / Sir Neville Marriner. EMI Ⓔ CDC7 54056-2 (61 minutes:
DDD: 10/90).
...Overtures – Die schöne Galathee; Isabella; Das Modell; Tantalusqualen; Der Krämer und sein
Kommis; Paragraph drei; Boccaccio. Fatinitza – March. Donna Juanita. **Slovak Philharmonic
Orchestra, Košice / Alfred Walter.** Marco Polo Ⓟ 8 223648 (71 minutes: DDD: 6/95).

Tylman Susato

Suggested listening ...
...Dansereye – excerpts. **New London Consort / Philip Pickett.** L'Oiseau-Lyre 436 131-2OH (1/94).

Johann Svendsen

Svendsen Symphony No. 2 in B flat major, Op. 15. Romance in G major, Op. 26[a]. Carnival in Paris, Op. 9. Norwegian Artists' Carnival, Op. 14. Norwegian Rhapsody No. 2, Op. 19.
[a]**Marianne Thorsen** (vn); **Stavanger Symphony Orchestra / Grant Llewellyn.** Chatsworth Ⓕ FCM1002 (70 minutes: DDD: 9/94). Recorded 1993.

Even though he and Grieg were good friends, Svendsen did not involve himself in the folk-song movement to anywhere near the same extent as his great countryman. His basic sympathies remained predominantly classical and he continued to work within the sonata-form discipline; yet there is a distinctive Norwegian feel to his melodic ideas. The Second Symphony was Svendsen's last large-scale work for, alas, the creative fires burnt themselves out prematurely, and after the popular *Romance* in G major, he virtually gave up composing. The Stavanger orchestra under the Welsh conductor Grant Llewellyn give a straightforward, enthusiastic account of the piece, not preferable to Järvi on BIS (listed below): the Stavanger orchestra is not the equal of Gothenburg. All the same, they acquit themselves well in the *Norwegian Rhapsody* No. 2 and the other orchestral pieces, as for that matter does the 21-year-old Marianne Thorsen, who plays with an unaffected simplicity and purity that is touching. Very clean, well-balanced sound with plenty of presence and body throughout.

Additional recommendations ...

...Symphonies – No. 1 in D major, Op. 4; No. 2. Two Swedish folk-melodies, Op. 27. **Gothenburg Symphony Orchestra / Neeme Järvi.** BIS Ⓕ CD347 (71 minutes: DDD: 11/87).

...Romance[a]. Octet in A major, Op. 3. **Nielsen** String Quintet in G major, FS5. [a]**Kenneth Sillito** (vn); **Academy of St Martin in the Fields Chamber Ensemble.** Chandos CHAN9258 (5/94).   Ⓖ

Gyorgy Sviridov

Sviridov Three Choruses from the music to Alexei Tolstoy's "Tsar Feodor Ioannovich". Pushkin's Garland. Four Choruses, "Songs of Troubled Times". Night Clouds. **Moscow New Choir / Elena Rastvorova.** Olympia Ⓜ OCD541 (68 minutes: DDD: 9/95). Translations included. Recorded 1994.

Fans of the 'new spirituality' – be they seekers after the 'what next?' line following up Górecki's Third Symphony or hungry for *a cappella* choral music in the Russian Orthodox tradition – will be well pleased by the way this disc begins; and so might the rest of us, for Sviridov balances simplicity and originality to perfection in his three choruses for Alexei Tolstoy's *Tsar Feodor Ioannovich*. The melodic lines are cleanly projected by members of the Moscow New Choir, with scrupulous concern for the text, the harmonies (Orthodox with a Sviridov twist in the second setting) atmospherically supportive. And that's only the first ten minutes. More quasi-religious settings crop up at key points in the Pushkin and Blok settings, but Sviridov's emotional range is much wider, and it is incredible just how many effects and subtleties he achieves between the lines in music that is rooted – but not fixed – in major and minor triads. This marvellous choir's bright, intelligent and dynamically varied approach, their attention perfectly focused on both the words and the music, should help to establish the reputation of *Pushkin's Garland* as one of the richest Russian choral works of the twentieth century as well as a first-rate tribute to Russia's greatest poet. Pushkin's full emotional range is here, including alternately crystal-clear and solemn nature-poetry, tenderly intimate tributes to dear friends, beautifully light-of-touch in the setting (tracks 6 and 11), and poetical introspections verging on the mystical (tracks 10 and 12). Sviridov even brings in an Orff-ian percussion and keyboard ensemble to heighten the antique brilliance of "The Greek Feast", and the tributes to Russian folk-tradition in the second and last settings are splendidly vibrant here. The Blok choruses are more concentrated in mood, no less perfect in the matching of musical means to poetic ends; the rich blend of Orthodox ritual and passionate response in the 'child's burial' poem of the *Night Clouds* cantata seems to touch a special emotional chord in the singers as well as the listener. Pitching may not always be absolutely perfect, but it's a small price to pay for such a sympathetic presentation of Sviridov's late-flowering choral garlands and wreaths; they should enter the repertoire of our own chamber choirs sooner rather than later.

Sviridov Russia cast adrift.
Rachmaninov Oh thou, my field, Op. 4 No. 5. Op. 14 – No. 1, I wait for thee; No. 7, Believe me not, friend. Op. 21 – No. 4, They answered; No. 7, How fair this spot. Op. 26 – No. 9, Again I am alone; No. 12, Night is mournful; No. 15, All things pass by. Night. **Dmitri Hvorostovsky** (bar); **Mikhail Arkadiev** (pf). Philips Ⓕ 446 666-2PH (55 minutes: DDD: 8/96). Texts and translations included.

Quite a few of Sviridov's works have been entering the catalogue lately, and the addition of this haunting cycle is welcome. The simplicity is as deceptive as is that of the poet in whom he found a kindred spirit, Sergey Yesenin. Plain metres and rhymes, direct imagery and metaphor carry an unexpected charge of meaning, just as simple chords, uncomplicated melodies and diatonic harmony are reinvented with an oblique twist or an allusiveness that catches in the memory. There is an analogy here with Britten. Behind the poetry's reticence lies a passionate devotion, leaping out of some of the verses, for the land and feel and smell of Russia, for her eternal plight, for the candle of Orthodox belief burning in the darkness and tugged at by winds from every quarter. In the music this fervour can break free from plain statements, or may seem to be at odds with the words until an expressive resonance is gradually discerned. With Arkadiev in ideally sympathetic support, Hvorostovsky has the range of the music within his voice, cradling it lyrically in the more pastoral songs, discharging a Mussorgskian gruffness for the song of death about the fateful trumpet, blanching his tone for the strange song of Christ calling for Peter to follow him and being answered by Judas. The nine Rachmaninov songs, from most periods of his song-writing life, are sensitively sung, with only occasionally an emphasis on the tone that brings in a strong vibrato, but it is really for Sviridov's cycle that interest attaches to this disc. Philips have thankfully supplied the original Russian texts with English, German and French translations.

Further listening ...
...Piano Trio[a]. St Petersburg Songs[b]. Music for Chamber Orchestra[c]. [b]**Natalia Gerasimova** (sop); [b]**Tatiana Vinogradova** (mez); [b]**Alexander Vasiliev** (bar); [b]**Alexander Vedernikov** (bass); [a]**Olga Kolgatina**, [b]**Alexander Mayorov** (vns); [b]**Alexei Makarov** (vc); [ab]**Marina Butir** (pf); [c]**Musica Viva Chamber Orchestra / Alexander Rudin** ([a]vc). Olympia OCD540 (1/96).

Giles Swayne
British 1946-

Suggested listening ...
...Cry. **BBC Singers / John Poole.** NMC NMCD016 (10/94). Ⓖ

Jan Pieterszoon Sweelinck
Dutch 1562-1621

Sweelinck Toccata in C major. Ballo del granduca. Ricercar. Malle Sijmen. Mein junges Leben hat ein End'. Aeolian Echo Fantasia. Onder een linde groen. Toccata in A minor I. Erbarm dich mein, o Herre Gott. Poolsche dans. **James David Christie** (org). Naxos Ⓢ 8 550904 (64 minutes: DDD: 2/95). Played on the C.B. Fisk Organ, Houghton Chapel, Wellesley College, USA. Recorded 1993.

James David Christie presents what is, in effect, a most satisfactory re-creation of one of Sweelinck's organ recitals, given daily between 1580 and 1621, for the burghers of Amsterdam. One hopes they were properly appreciative of the most consistently witty and generous-spirited keyboard music before the era of Buxtehude, Couperin and Bach. While Christie may not possess the lyricism of a Leonhardt, the humane warmth of a Piet Kee, or the mercurial whimsy of a Koopman, he is, in his own right, a bold, stylish, unhasty player, clearly thoroughly versed in early performance practice, with an incisive technique disclosing musical intelligence and common sense. He is particularly successful in the five major variation sets here, relishing the variety of decorative motifs but still conveying an impression of structural coherence and unity. Just occasionally his articulation might have worked better in a somewhat larger acoustic: at times a more obviously singing touch might have suggested greater tenderness in quieter moments and more ample majesty in louder ones. Nevertheless, with appealing registrations, an almost ideal choice of programme, good notes and undistractingly natural recording, Naxos have produced a single-disc anthology of this most companionable of organ composers that merits general recommendation, particularly at super-bargain price.

Further listening ...
...Fantasia. *Coupled with* **Mozart** Piano Sonata in C major, K330/K300h. **Bach** Goldberg Variations, BWV988. **Schoenberg** Suite, Op. 25. **Glenn Gould** (pf). Sony Classical mono SMK53474* (9/95)

...Or soit loué l'Etérnal. Mon Dieu, j'ay en toy esperance. Qui au conseil des malins. Vous tous qui la terr' habitez. Revenge moy, pren la querelle. Mon am'en Dieu taut seulement. Les cieux en chacun lieu. Du Seigneur les bontez. Ne sois fasché. Or sus serviteurs de Seigneur. Jamais ne cesseray. Vouloir m'est pris. Le Toutpuissant à mon Seigneur. D'ou vient, Seigneur. Vous tous les habitans. **Trinity College Choir, Cambridge / Richard Marlow.** Conifer CDCF205 (8/92).

András Szöllösy
Hungarian 1921-

Suggested listening ...
...Paesaggio con morti. *Coupled with works by* **Liszt, Dohnányi, Kodály, Bartók, Weiner** and **Kurtág** Peter Frankl (pf). ASV CDDCA860 (6/93). *See review in the Collections section; refer to the Index to Reviews.* ⒼⒼⒼ

Karol Szymanowski   Polish 1882-1937

New review
Szymanowski Violin Concertos[a] – No. 1, Op. 35; No. 2, Op. 61. Three Paganini Caprices, Op. 40[b]. Romance in D, Op. 23[b]. **Thomas Zehetmair** (vn); [b]**Silke Avenhaus** (pf); [a]**City of Birmingham Symphony Orchestra / Sir Simon Rattle.** EMI Ⓕ CDC5 55607-2 (65 minutes: DDD: 8/96).   Ⓖ

They make an admirable coupling, the two Szymanowski violin concertos, but a demanding one for the soloist. They are both so beautiful that it must be tempting to embellish both with a similarly glowing tone. They inhabit quite different worlds (they were written 16 years apart) and Zehetmair shows how well they respond to quite different approaches. In the First, after a rapt solo entry, he uses for the most part a lovely but delicate tone, expanding to athletic incisiveness but not often to lushness. It fits very well with Rattle's handling of the orchestra: occasionally full and rich but mostly a sequence of exquisitely balanced chamber ensembles. Generous but finely controlled rubato from both soloist and conductor allows the concerto's improvisatory fantasy to flower; and the quiet close even has a touch of wit to it. Zehetmair's sound is immediately less ethereal, more robust, for the opening melody of the Second Concerto. This is the sort of tone, you suspect, that he would use in Bartók's Second Concerto, and it points up a vein of indeed Bartókian strength to this work's longer and firmer lines. Rattle, too, seeks out bolder and more dense colours. It is characteristic that even the more musing lyrical pages here are given a warmer colour than superficially similar moments in the First Concerto. The *Paganini Caprices* were equipped by Szymanowski not with deferential accompaniments but with independent and quite freely composed piano parts. They change Paganini, even where the violin part is unmodified (most of the time but not quite all), into a late romantic virtuoso, with a hint of Lisztian poetry alongside the expertly pointed-up fireworks of the Twenty-Fourth *Caprice*; even here Zehetmair is a listening violinist, not one to upstage his excellent pianist. The *Romance*, the warmest and most luscious piece here, is beautifully done but with a touch of restraint to prevent it cloying. A first-class coupling, and a recording that makes the most of the superb acoustic of Symphony Hall in Birmingham.

Additional recommendation ...
...Violin Concertos Nos. 1[a] and 2[a]. **Górecki** Three Pieces in Old Style[b]. **Baird** Colas Breugnon – suite[b]. [a]**Konstanty Kulka** (vn); [a]**Polish National Radio Symphony Orchestra,** [b]**Polish Chamber Orchestra / Jerzy Maksymiuk.** EMI Matrix Ⓜ CDM5 65418-2 (73 minutes: ADD: 3/96).

Szymanowski Harnasie, Op. 46[a]. Symphony No. 4, Op. 60, "Symphonie concertante"[b]. Mazurkas, Op. 50[c] – No. 1 in C major; No. 2 in A major. Theme and Variations in B flat minor, Op. 3[c]. [a]**Andrzej Bachleda** (ten); [a]**Wiestaw Kwasny** (vn); [bc]**Felicja Blumental** (pf); [a]**Cracow Radio Chorus and Symphony Orchestra / Antoni Wit;** [b]**Polish National Radio Symphony Orchestra / Jerzy Semkow.** EMI Matrix Ⓜ CDM5 65307-2 (75 minutes: ADD: 4/95). Items marked [ab] from HMV SLS5242 (9/82), [c]Unicorn RHS347 (6/78). Recorded 1974-79.   Ⓖ

With the exception of the early and accomplishedly Brahmsian *Theme and Variations*, this is all late Szymanowski, Szymanowski giving up just a little of the colour and opulence of his middle period to respond with delight to the fresh and invigorating rawness of the folk music of the Tatra region. He responds most obviously, of course, in the folk ballet *Harnasie*, with its frequent imitations of raucous folk fiddling and the fervour of choral folk-song and its heartfelt evocations of Poland's mountain country. But surely the wonderfully poised opening theme of the *Symphonie concertante* owes something to this influence too (a theme so beautiful that Szymanowski cannot resist returning to it as the true destination of all the previous beauties of his slow movement)? The last movement might almost be a supplement to *Harnasie*, but the use throughout of wind and string solos sounds very much like a 'refinement' of the peasant fiddle and trumpet in the ballet. Since the performances are very good indeed, and the recordings clean and decent, the coupling is a very recommendable one. All the more so since Western pianists still seem reluctant to programme the *Symphonie concertante* (perhaps they would if it were called a concerto), and *Harnasie*, which calls for tenor and violin soloists and a chorus as well as orchestra, is unlikely ever to prove popular in the concert-hall. Both are full of delights. The *Theme and Variations* and the two *Mazurkas* are well-played; the latter will undoubtedly whet your appetite for the more intimate and subtle aspects of 'late Szymanowski', and will send you off hunting for the other 18 *Mazurkas*.

Additional recommendations ...
...Harnasie[a]. Mandragora, Op. 43[b]. [a]**Jozef Stepién,** [b]**Paulos Raptis** (tens); **Polish National Opera Chorus; Polish National Opera Orchestra / Robert Satanowski.** Koch Schwann 311064 (12/91).
...Symphonies – No. 3, Op. 27[b], "The Song of the Night"; No. 4. **Panufnik** Symphony No. 8, "Sinfonia Votiva"[a]. [b]**Philip Langridge** (ten); [c]**Piotr Paleczny** (pf); [b]**BBC Singers; BBC Symphony** [b]**Chorus and Orchestra /** [a]**Andrzej Panufnik,** [b]**Norman Del Mar,** [c]**Mark Elder.** BBC Radio Classics Ⓑ BBCRD9124 (77 minutes: ADD: 12/95).

Szymanowski String Quartets – No. 1 in C major, Op. 37; No. 2, Op. 56.
Webern Langsamer satz (1905). **Carmina Quartet** (Matthias Enderle, Susanne Frank, vns; Wendy Champney, va; Stephan Goerner, vc). Denon Ⓕ CO-79462-2 (45 minutes: DDD: 3/92).
Gramophone Award Winner 1992. Selected by Sounds in Retrospect.   ⒼⒼ

Szymanowski's sound world is totally distinctive: there is an exotic luxuriance, a sense of ecstasy and longing, a heightened awareness of colour and glowing, almost luminous textures. The two quartets are separated by a decade: the First, whose sense of ecstasy and longing permeates its opening, is a subtle and deeply-felt performance and much the same can be said of No. 2. Again heady perfumes and exotic landscapes are in evidence, though with his increasing interest in folk-music, the finale has slight overtones of Bartók. The Swiss-based Carmina Quartet play both Szymanowski works with great understanding and emotional involvement, and technically they are quite brilliant. If we associate Webern with brief, highly compressed atonal and serial works, the *Langsamer satz* for String Quartet shows the composer in his early twenties still writing in a late-romantic style, appropriately enough for a piece which reflects for Webern the pleasures of a walk through Austrian woods with his future wife. The movement sprawls a little, but is very pleasingly written. The Carmina Quartet give a sympathetic, warm-hearted performance of this piece, and the sound obtained by Denon's largely Japanese team throughout the disc is very detailed, but also has a very attractive bloom.

Additional recommendations ...

...String Quartets. **Lutosławski** String Quartet. **Penderecki** String Quartet No. 2. **Varsovia Quartet.** Olympia Ⓜ OCD328 (68 minutes: AAD: 6/89).

...String Quartets. **Bacewicz** String Quartet No. 4. **Maggini Quartet.** ASV Ⓕ CDDCA908 (59 minutes: DDD: 2/95).

New review

Szymanowski Mazurkas, Op. 50 Nos. 1-4. Metopes, Op. 29. Four Etudes, Op. 4. Piano Sonata No. 2 in A major, Op. 21. **Martin Roscoe** (pf). Naxos Ⓢ 8 553016 (67 minutes: DDD: 9/95). Recorded 1994. *Gramophone Editor's choice.*   Ⓖ

This collection appears as "Szymanowski: Piano Works Vol. 1", which rightly suggests that Martin Roscoe is recording a complete Szymanowski cycle for Naxos. So is Martin Jones for Nimbus, of course. Jones's looks like being a distinguished series. So does Roscoe's, and the differences between their approaches are interesting. Very broadly speaking Jones is a bit more open to fantasy, to the mercurial element in Szymanowski, while Roscoe is more concerned with bolder gestures and marked contrasts. Both bring off the extremely difficult Second Sonata very well, for example, but at the beginning of the second movement Jones etches the lines of the theme with delicate staccato while Roscoe, perhaps reflecting that it is after all a theme, not yet a variation, plays it more simply, more slowly, and thus effectively marks it off from the ensuing first variation in tempo as well as in manner. Jones's filigree effects are often beautiful, Roscoe's clearer outlines often no less so. If Roscoe is on the whole preferable, it is because Naxos's ample and natural piano sound is preferable to Nimbus's which is rather disembodied and brittle at the top of the instrument in staccato, resulting in a slight miniaturization of Jones's excellent performances. The very low price of the newer version, and the fact that Naxos are issuing their Szymanowski series as single CDs, are strong arguments in Roscoe's favour as well. A bargain, and strongly recommended.

Additional recommendations ...

...Four Etudes. Metopes, Op. 29. Fantasy. Masques, Op. 34. **Dennis Lee** (pf). Hyperion Ⓕ CDA66409 (64 minutes: DDD: 7/91).

...Mazurkas, Op. 50 Nos. 1-4[a]. *Coupled with works by* **Debussy, Prokofiev, Villa-Lobos, Schumann** *and* **Albéniz** Navarra[a]. **Artur Rubinstein** (pf). RCA Victor Gold Seal Ⓜ 09026 61445-2 (64 minutes: ADD: 10/93). *See review in the Collections section; refer to the Index to Reviews.*   ⒼⒼ

...Nine Preludes, Op. 1. Variations in B flat minor, Op. 3. Variations on a Polish folk theme, Op. 10. Four Etudes, Op. 4. Piano Sonatas – No. 1 in C minor; No. 2 in A major, Op. 21. Fantasy, Op. 14. Prelude and Fugue in C sharp minor. **Martin Jones** (pf). Nimbus Ⓕ NI5405/06 (two discs: 135 minutes: DDD: 9/94).

Szymanowski Stabat mater, Op. 53[a]. Litany to the Virgin Mary, Op. 59[b]. Symphony No. 3, Op. 27, "The song of the night"[c]. [ab]**Elzbieta Szmytka** (sop); [a]**Florence Quivar** (contr); [c]**Jon Garrison** (ten); [a]**John Connell** (bass); **City of Birmingham Symphony Orchestra and Chorus / Sir Simon Rattle.** EMI Ⓕ CDC5 55121-2 (56 minutes: DDD: 8/94). Texts and translations included. *Gramophone Award Winner 1995. Gramophone Editor's choice.*   ⒼⒼⒼ

The first impression here is that Rattle is relatively new to Szymanowski. There's a huge enthusiasm here, a missionary quality that bespeaks the recent convert. On the other hand the care over matters of balance, the knowledge of just those points where Szymanowski's complexity needs very careful handling if it's not simply to blur into opacity, suggest a conductor who has been there before and knows the dangers. You get the feeling that a conscious decision was made to delay recording this music until the circumstances were right. The CBSO Chorus not only sound thoroughly at home in the music but in the language too. The clincher on the decision to go ahead with this recording might well have been Rattle's realization that in Elzbieta Szmytka he had a soprano who might have been born to sing Szymanowski's pure, floated and very high-lying soprano lines (in the *Stabat mater* and the *Litany*; in the symphony he uses a tenor, which was Szymanowski's own first choice). The result is very fine indeed: one of the most beautiful Szymanowski recordings ever made. And yet 'beautiful Szymanowski' isn't all that hard if the orchestra's good enough and the conductor capable. Rattle's insistence that all of the music be heard, its bones and sinews as well as its flesh, its urgency and passion as well as its deliquescent loveliness, makes for uncommonly gripping Szymanowski as well. He reminds one of how much more there is to the Third Symphony than voluptuous yearning: solemnity, for one thing, and a fierce ardour that can indeed knock you sideways. The choice of soloists for the *Stabat mater* is interesting: alongside Szmytka's radiant purity are Quivar's throaty vibrancy and Connell's weighty darkness. Not a matching trio, but the contrast is appealing; it adds to the rich differentiation of sonority that Rattle draws from his chorus and orchestra. Garrison in the symphony is a touch hard and strenuous, less enraptured than one or two of the Polish tenors (and sopranos) who've recorded it, but he's a musicianly and likeable singer. The recording is outstanding: lucid, rich and spacious, with tremendous and perfectly focused climaxes.

Additional recommendation ...

...Stabat mater[a]. Symphony No. 3[b]. Three Fragments from poems by Jan Kasprowicz, Op. 5[c]. [ab]**Stefania Woytowicz** (sop); [ac]**Krystyna Szostek-Radkowa** (mez); [a]**Andrzej Hiolski** (bar); **Polish Radio and Television** [ab]**Choir and** [b]**Symphony Orchestra, Cracow;** [ac]**Polish Radio and Television Great Symphony Orchestra, Katowice /** [a]**Stanislaw Wislocki,** [b]**Tadeusz Strugala,** [c]**Jerzy Maksymiuk.** Koch Schwann Ⓕ 312652 (70 minutes: ADD: 4/94).

Further listening ...

...Symphonies – No. 2 in B flat major, Op. 19[b]; No. 3, Op. 27, "The song of the night"[a]. Concert Overture in E major, Op. 12[b]. [a]**Wieslaw Ochman** (ten); [a]**Cracow Polish Radio Chorus; Polish National Radio Symphony Orchestra /** [a]**Jerzy Semkow,** [b]**Jacek Kaspszyk.** EMI Matrix CDM5 65082-2 (7/94).

...Violin Sonata in D minor, Op. 9. Mythes, Op. 30. Nocturne and Tarantella, Op. 28. **Lydia Mordkovitch** (vn); **Marina Gusak-Grin** (pf). Chandos CHAN8747 (6/91).

...Violin Sonata in D minor, Op. 9. *Coupled with* **Franck** Violin Sonata in A major. **Chee-Yun** (vn); **Akira Eguchi** (pf). Denon CO-78954 (1/96).

Toru Takemitsu
Japanese 1930-1996

New review

Takemitsu Gémeaux[a]. Dream/Window. Spirit Garden. [a]**Masashi Honma** (ob); [a]**Christian Lindberg** (tbn); **Metropolitan Symphony Orchestra / Hiroshi Wakasugi,** [a]**Ryusuke Numajiri.** Denon Ⓕ CO-78944 (59 minutes: DDD: 10/95). Recorded 1994.

Takemitsu views the orchestra as an elaborate Japanese garden, soundscaped to the finest detail and abundantly rich in colour. The parallel works well, except that the scenic scope of Takemitsu's scores (or at least those of them programmed on this superbly recorded CD) seems to incorporate – even to embrace – some vast, unpeopled horizon. Of the three works included, *Spirit Garden* is both the most recent (1994) and the most rigorously designed, having been constructed on the basis of a specific 12-tone series. And yet there's absolutely no hint of dryness to the score. Rather, *Spirit Garden* is awash in sensuously harmonized textures, backed – towards the end of the piece – by the "wistful and nostalgic" sound of ritual drums. The structure of *Dream/Window* (1985) sets an 'inner sphere' of flute, clarinet and string quartet against the orchestra, with a 'mediatory' group that consists of two harps, celesta and guitar. The 'outer sphere' is represented by strings and the main body of musical activity is marked by luminous sphereal interplay. However, the disc's most ambitious item is *Gémeaux* ("Gemini", 1972-86), where two orchestras and two soloists suggest, via four separate movements, androgyny, differentiation, role reversal and unity. Musically, there are echoes of Messiaen, Ravel and the Scriabin of *Prometheus*; but the overall design bears Takemitsu's usual fingerprints: delicacy of timbre, textural warmth, sharp focusing and a powerful sense of atmosphere. The performers seem wholly committed to each score, and the recordings capture the music's every tapered strand. The documentation, too, is excellent. Those readers who normally fight shy of modern music but who have a taste for the more exotic romantics, impressionists and post-impressionists, might like to give it a try.

Takemitsu To the Edge of Dream[c]. Folios – I, II and III. Toward the Sea III[a]. Here, There and Everywhere. What a Friend. Amours Perdues. Summertime. Vers, l'Arc-en-ciel, Palma[bc]. **John Williams** (gtr); [a]**Sebastian Bell** (alto fl); [b]**Gareth Hulse** (ob d'amore); [c]**London Sinfonietta / Esa-Pekka Salonen.** Sony Classical Ⓕ SK46720 (60 minutes: DDD: 1/92). Ⓖ

Toru Takemitsu is an original, refined composer and something of a latter-day impressionist, as titles like *To the Edge of Dream* suggest. It may therefore come as a surprise to find him arranging songs by Lennon and McCartney, Gershwin and others, for solo guitar. Yet these prove to have attractive touches of the subtlety found in Takemitsu's own compositions, and they also provide useful contrast to the more substantial works on this beguiling disc. *Folios*, the earliest composition included, already reveal Takemitsu's musical catholicity in its reference to a Bach chorale. *Toward the Sea* and *Vers, l'Arc-en-ciel, Palma* are both more expansive mood pieces, the former (for guitar and alto flute) almost too reticent and hesitant beside the richer textures of the latter, which is enhanced by the additional solo role given to the oboe d'amore as well as its beautifully laid out orchestral accompaniment. *To the Edge of Dream* is in effect a guitar concerto, with a wider range of mood and an even more developed role for the orchestra than *Vers, l'Arc-en-ciel, Palma*. It provides a particularly satisfying focus for a sensitively performed and well recorded disc. Even if we hear rather more of the guitar relative to the orchestra than we would in the concert-hall, there is nothing unreasonably artificial about the result.

Additional recommendation ...

...To the Edge of Dream. **Arnold** Guitar Concerto, Op. 67. **Rodrigo** Concierto de Aranjuez. **Julian Bream** (gtr); **City of Birmingham Symphony Orchestra / Sir Simon Rattle.** EMI Ⓕ CDC7 54661-2 (58 minutes: DDD: 7/93). Ⓖ

Further listening ...

...Fantasma/Cantos. Water-Ways. Waves. Quatrain II. **Soloists;** [a]**BBC Welsh Symphony Orchestra / Tadaaki Otaka.** RCA Victor Red Seal 09026 62537-2 (1/95).

...November Steps[a]. Eclipse[b]. Viola Concerto, "A String around Autumn"[c]. [ab]**Katsuya Yokoyama** (shakuhachi); [ab]**Kinshi Tsuruta** (biwa); [c]**Nobuko Imai** (va); [ac]**Saito Kinen Orchestra / Seiji Ozawa.** Philips 432 176-2PH (8/92). Ⓖ

...Visions[b]. *Coupled with works by* **Carter** and **Berio** Chicago Symphony Orchestra / Daniel Barenboim. Teldec 4509-99596-2 (8/95). *See review under Berio; refer to the Index to Reviews.*

...A Way A Lone. *Coupled with* **Barber** String Quartet, Op. 11. **Britten** String Quartet No. 2 in C major, Op. 36. **Tokyo Quartet.** RCA Victor Red Seal 09026 61387-2 (2/94). *See review under Barber; refer to the Index to Reviews.* Ⓖ Ⓖ

...Cherry Blossoms. Songs I – Small Sky; I Just Sing; In a Small Room; The Game of Love; Unseen Child; Will Tomorrow, I Wonder, Be Cloudy or Clear? To the Island. All that the Man Left Behind When He Died. A Song of Circles and Triangles. Sayonara. Wings. **Shin-yu Kai Choir / Shin Sekiya.** Philips 438 135-2PH (8/94).

Otar Taktakishvili USSR 1924-1989

Suggested listening ...

...Flute Sonata. *Coupled with works by* **Feld, Gubaidulina, Amirov** and **Martinů** Leslie Newman (fl); **Amanda Hurton** (pf). Cala CACD88026 (6/96). *See review in the Collections section; refer to the Index to Reviews.*

Thomas Tallis British c1505-1585

Tallis Lamentations of Jeremiah. Motets – Absterge Domine; Derelinquat impius; Mihi autem nimis; O sacrum convivium; In jejunio et fletu; O salutaris hostia; In manus tuas; O nata lux de lumine. Salve intemerata virgo. **The Tallis Scholars / Peter Phillips.** Gimell Ⓕ CDGIM025 (68 minutes: DDD: 5/92). Texts and translations included.

This, the third volume of the survey by The Tallis Scholars of the music of the Tudor composer, Thomas Tallis, contains the well-known *Lamentations*, eight motets, and the extended motet *Salve intemerata virgo*. The *Lamentations* and motets are typical of the style of late Renaissance English composers. The overall mood is one of considerable austerity and their simplicity is indicative of the probability of their having been written for the private use of loyal Catholics rather than for formal ritual. *Salve intemerata virgo*, on the other hand, looks back to the glories of the late fifteenth century. In particular Tallis's use of the phrygian mode gives the work as a whole a strong sense of the medieval. Despite this disparity of styles the Tallis Scholars acquit themselves, as always, with great distinction. In the *Lamentations* and motets they achieve an appropriate sense of intimacy, while in *Salve intemerata virgo* they rise fully to the challenges of one of the more extended and demanding examples of Tudor choral composition. In addition the formidable challenges which this latter work sets for the conductor, such as the sense of pace, variation of dynamics, and overall architecture of the work, are all extremely well handled by Peter Phillips. Like much music of this era, the compositions of Thomas Tallis repay repeated listening, and in these distinguished readings, aided by Gimell's fine recording, Tallis's genius is fully revealed.

Additional recommendation ...

...Lamentations of Jeremiah. Salvator mundi II. O sacrum convivium. Mass a 4. Absterge Domine. **The Hilliard Ensemble / Paul Hillier.** ECM New Series Ⓕ 833 308-2 (DDD: 4/88).

New review

Tallis Lamentations of Jeremiah[a]. Absterge Domine[b]. In jejunio et fletu[a]. If ye love me[a]. O sacrum convivium[b]. Audivi vocem de caelo[a]. Derelinquat impius[a]. Salvator mundi, salva nos I[a]. Solfa-ing Song a 5[b]. In Nomine a 4 No. 1[b]. Benedictus[a]. Fond youth is a bubble[b]. Psalm Tunes for Archbishop Parker's Psalter[a] – No. 3, Why fum'th in sight; No. 8, Tallis's Canon. Like as the doleful dove[b]. When shall my sorrowful sighing slake[b]. Te lucis ante terminum I[a]. [a]**Theatre of Voices / Paul Hillier;** [b]**The King's Noyse / David Douglass.** Harmonia Mundi Ⓕ HMU90 7154 (71 minutes: DDD: 7/96).

This is imaginative programme planning – atmospheric renaissance music performed by choral and instrumental forces in amiable juxtaposition rather than combination. The 16-strong Theatre of Voices, who are based at the University of California at Davis, sing throughout with a dark-browed *gravitas* and warmth of feeling that are thoroughly appropriate and give considerable pleasure. The secular music plus (surprisingly perhaps, but interestingly) *Absterge Domine* and *O sacrum convivium* are done by The King's Noyse, an expert renaissance violin consort, though they realize the sombre harmonic undertow so characteristic of Tallis less successfully than the singers. It ends with the tranquil evening office hymn, *Te lucis ante terminum* (complete with its alternating plainchant). Unlike most English groups in this repertoire, the Theatre of Voices do not use falsettists (authenticity may be on their side). Compared with The Tallis Scholars, the high-lying tenor parts here – often assigned by other groups to male altos – are perhaps not always impeccably blended, and the female voices sometimes have a slight flatward colouring. But, in compensation, this American group certainly taps a rich vein of pathos in this affecting music while remaining stylistically convincing, and Tallis's two most famous psalm-tunes are done with much relish. A distinctive, and on the whole, commendable issue, warmly recorded, if in a rather neutral acoustic, and with a sumptuously produced CD booklet.

Tallis Videte miraculum[b]. Homo quidam[b]. Audivi vocem[a]. Candidi facti sunt Nazarei[b]. Dum transisset Sabbatum[b]. Honor, virtus et potestas[b]. Hodie nobis[a]. Loquebantur variis linguis[b]. In pace, in idipsum[a]. Spem in alium (with Wim Becu, bass sackbut; Paul Nicholson, Alan Wilson, orgs)[ab]. [a]**Taverner Consort;** [b]**Taverner Choir / Andrew Parrott.** EMI Reflexe Ⓕ CDC7 49555-2 (two discs, oas: 62 and 68 minutes: DDD: 5/89). ✍ Texts and translations included.   ⒼⒼ

Tallis, one of the greatest composers of sacred music, has been sympathetically and generously acknowledged by Andrew Parrott and the Taverner Choir with this disc of Latin church music. It includes the masterly 40-part responsary *Spem in alium* written, it would seem, in reply to a similarly ambitious one by Tallis's Italian contemporary, Alessandro Striggio. The performances are characterized by translucent textures, a wonderful feeling for structure and a fluent understanding of the composer's contrapuntal ingenuity. Certainly there are occasional hints of vocal strain in the uppermost reaches of the part writing but they do little to spoil an affectionate, technically assured account of thrilling music. Parrott illuminates the music with his own deep understanding of it, but above all with the skilful deployment of vocal talent that he has at his command.

Additional recommendations ...

...Spem in alium. Salvator mundi I and II. Sancte Deus, sancte fortis. Gaude gloriosa Dei mater. Miserere nostri. Loquebantur variis linguis. **The Tallis Scholars / Peter Phillips.** Gimell Ⓕ CDGIM006 (43 minutes: DDD: 3/86).

...Dum transisset Sabbatum. Gaude gloriosa Dei mater. Magnificat and Nunc dimittis. In jejunio et fletu. Derelinquat impius. Candidi facti sunt Nazarei. Salvator mundi II. Absterge Domine. **New College Choir, Oxford / Edward Higginbottom.** CRD Ⓕ CRD3429 (57 minutes: DDD: 4/87).

...O salutaris hostia. In jejunio et fletu. Salvator mundi I and II. In manuas tuas, Domine. Lamentations of Jeremiah. O sacrum convivium. O nata lux de lumine. Te lucis ante terminum. Spem in alium (with Winchester College Quiristers; Vocal Arts; Timothy Byram-Wigfield, org). **Winchester Cathedral Choir / David Hill.** Hyperion Ⓕ CDA66400 (59 minutes: DDD: 5/90).   Ⓖ

...Spem in alium. *Coupled with works by* **Porta, Josquin, Desprez, Ockeghem, Manchicourt, G. Gabrieli** and **Striggio** ✍ **Huelgas Ensemble / Paul van Nevel.** Sony Classical Vivarte Ⓕ SK66261 (53 minutes: DDD: 4/96). *See review in the Collections section; refer to the Index to Reviews.*

...Salvator mundi, salva nos I. O nata lux de lumine. In manus tuas. *Coupled with works by* **Allegri, Palestrina, Byrd, Parsons, Viadana, Tallis, Philips, G. Gabrieli, Lotti, Tye, Victoria** and **Monteverdi** Soloists; Westminster Cathedral Choir / James O'Donnell. Hyperion Ⓕ CDA66850 (72 minutes: DDD: 5/96). *See review in the Collections section; refer to the Index to Reviews.*

Further listening ...

...Anthems – If ye love me; Hear the voice and prayer; A New commandment; O Lord, give thy Holy Spirit; Purge me, O Lord; Verily, verily say I unto you; Remember not, O Lord God; Out from the deep; O Lord, in Thee is all my trust; Christ rising again; Blessed are those that be undefiled. Psalm Tunes for Archbishop Parker's Psalter. **The Tallis Scholars / Peter Phillips.** Gimell CDGIM007 (12/86).

...Mass Puer natus est nobis. Suscipe quaeso Dominus. Salvator mundi Domine ... Adesto nunc proprius. *Coupled with* **White** Regina coeli. Portio mea Domine. Domine quis habitavit. Christe, qui lux es et dies. **The Clerkes of Oxenford / David Wulstan.** Calliope Approche CAL6623 (11/95).

Sergey Ivanovich Taneyev   USSR 1856-1915

New review

A. Taneyev String Quartets – No. 1 in G major, Op. 25; No. 2 in C major, Op. 28; No. 3 in A major, Op. 30. **Talan Quartet** (Vladimir Talanov, Alexander Talanov, vns; Olga Bulakova, va; Alexei Steblov, vc). Olympia Ⓜ OCD543 (68 minutes: DDD: 10/95). Recorded 1994.

Alexander Taneyev is said by most Western musical dictionaries to be the uncle of the better-known Sergey Taneyev, but the standard Russian encyclopaedia, which gives him only a few rather laconic comments, insists that he was really a second cousin. He was yet another of the amateurs who contributed so much to Russian music, scribbling away secretly under his desk at the Imperial

Chancellery, and even managing to write a couple of operas as well as orchestral and chamber music. In his three string quartets, at any rate, he reveals a fluent charm that owes most to the Russian lyrical tradition upheld by his namesake, among many others, and glorified by Tchaikovsky, but also taking account of the long Viennese inheritance. His qualities show best in a melodic charm and an ability to produce music in various manners well suited to the medium; he was also professional enough to write a decent fugue. If he does not really sustain the forms of the movements well, and can occasionally seem to get a bit caught up in processes that do not have sufficient musical motivation, there are some lively *Scherzo*s and some lyrical meditations in the *Larghetto* movements of, in particular, Nos. 2 and 3. Collectors of Russian music will no doubt want to add these rarities to their shelves, and may find themselves taking them down to play for relaxation quite often; they will also find sympathetic and well-turned performances from the Talan Quartet.

Further listening ...

...Symphony No. 4 in C minor, Op. 12. The Oresteia – Overture. **Philharmonia Orchestra / Neeme Järvi.** Chandos CHAN8953 (4/92).

...Piano Quintet in G minor, Op. 30. **Jerome Lowenthal** (pf); **Paul Rosenthal**, **Yukiko Kamei** (vns); **Marcus Thompson** (va); **Stephen Kates** (vc). Arabesque Z6539.

...Piano Trio in D major, Op. 22. **Borodin Trio.** Chandos CHAN8592 (2/89).

Alexandre Tansman
Polish/French 1897-1986

Suggested listening ...

...Le Jardin du Paradis – Danse de la sorcière[abcde]. *Coupled with works by* **Saint-Saëns, d'Indy, Roussel, Françaix, Poulenc and Milhaud** [a]**Catherine Cantin** (fl); [b]**Maurice Bourgue** (ob); [c]**Michel Portal** (cl); [d]**Amaury Wallez** (bn); [e]**André Cazalet** (hn); **Pascal Rogé** (pf). Decca 425 861-2DH (5/91). *See review in the Collections Section; refer to the Index to Reviews.*

Johannes Tapissier
French c1370-1410

Suggested listening ...

...Eya dulcis adque vernans rosa/Vale placens peroratrix. *Coupled with works by* **Velut, Ciconia, Philipoctus de Caserta, Johanne Eyidius, Matheus de Sancto Johanne, Bartolomeus da Bologna, Antonius de Civitate Austrie, Anonymous, Zacharias, Brassart** and **Dufay Orlando Consort.** Metronome METCD1008 (11/95). *See review in the Collections section; refer to the Index to Reviews.* Ⓖ

Francisco Tárrega
Spanish 1852-1909

Suggested listening ...

...Rosita. Four Mazurkas. Estudio brillante de Alard. Gran vals. Preludios – No. 1 in E major; No. 8 in E major (Lágrima); No. 9 in D minor (Endecha); No. 11 in D major. Alborada. Recuerdos de la Alhambra. Maria. *Coupled with* **Sor** Minuet, Op. 11 No 6, Studies, Op. 6 – No. 6 in A major; No. 9 in D minor; No. 11 in E major; No. 12 in A major. Study in A major, Op. 31 No. 19. Studies, Op. 35 – No. 13 in C major; No. 17 in D major; No. 22 in E minor. Minuetto, Op. 22. **Aguado** Menuett. Andante. Guitar Method Lessons – Nos. 15, 19, 24, 26 and 29. Guitar Method Studies – No. 17. **Norbert Kraft** (gtr). Naxos 8 553007 (1/95).

...Preludios – Endecha; Oremus; Allegro; Andante sostenuto; Lágrima. Capricho árabe. Mazurkas – Adelita; Marieta; Sueño. Pavana. Alborada. *Coupled with* **Mertz** Six Schubertian Songs. **Paganini** Grand Sonata in A major – second and third movements. Ghiribizzi, MS43 – No. 20, Andante in C major on Mozart's "Là ci darem la mano"; No. 37, Adagietto con espressione in A major. Sonatina No. 1 in C major. **Regondi** Introduction and Caprice, Op. 23. **Schubert** (arr. Tárrega) Piano Sonata in G major, D894 – Menuetto. Moment musical in F minor, Op. 94 No. 3. **Chopin** (arr. Tárrega) Preludes – No. 7 in A major; No 15 in D flat major; No. 20 in C minor. **Tom Kerstens** (gtr). Conifer CDCF518 (9/94).

Giuseppe Tartini
Italian 1692-1770

Tartini Sonate e una pastorale – No. 2 in F major; No. 8 in C minor; No. 10 in G minor, "Didone abbandonata"; No. 12 in F major; Pastorale in A major. Sonata in G minor, "Le trille du diable". **Locatelli Trio** (Elizabeth Wallfisch, vn; Richard Tunnicliffe, vc; Paul Nicholson, hpd). Hyperion Ⓔ CDA66430 (73 minutes: DDD: 4/92). 🎵 Recorded 1990.

The members of the Locatelli Trio have an impressive pedigree as performers of baroque music. Here they bring their wealth of experience most fruitfully to bear upon six of about 42 authenticated violin sonatas by Giuseppe Tartini, the violin virtuoso and pedagogue who established such an influential school of playing in Padua in the second quarter of the eighteenth century. These sonatas have been well selected to illustrate the range of Tartini's style and to produce a balanced, developing programme. Two important and better known works – nicknamed *Didone abbandonata* and *Le trille du diable* – frame others that are equally rich in graceful melody, dazzling passagework and innovative scoring but which perhaps lack a distinctive selling point. The three-movement *Pastorale* in A major is a particularly effective work, worthy of much wider dissemination in recital programmes. The multi-sectioned final movement is a triumph of novel ideas and balanced structure. This performance is especially affecting, with the lightness of approach nevertheless conveying a depth of feeling not always to the fore elsewhere on this disc. In general, warmth and invention abound in this playing, yet the galant style is never transgressed, the emotions never pushed to romantic proportions. Elizabeth Wallfisch's baroque violin has a full, rounded tone and she plays with admirable security of technique, even in the most demanding sections. The resonance of the ensemble is delightfully reflected in the spacious acoustic of the recording, further helping the cause of such fine music that has for too long been neglected.

Tartini Violin Sonatas – D major, BD19; B flat major, BB1; A major, BA4, "sopra lo stile che suona il Prette dalla Chitarra Portoghese"; B flat major, BB5 (Op. 5 No. 6). **Locatelli Trio** (Elizabeth Wallfisch, vn; Richard Tunnicliffe, vc; Paul Nicholson, hpd). Hyperion Ⓕ CDA66485 (67 minutes: DDD: 11/92). ✒ Recorded 1991.

The four works here are unfailingly inventive, ranging in style from the militaristic first *Allegro* of the D major Sonata to the delicate *Largo* of the B flat work. Each sonata here receives performances of the highest calibre from the Locatelli Trio, richly detailed and compelling in tone. Listen to the extraordinary Sonata, BA4 "In the style of the priest who plays the Portuguese guitar". The second movement *Andante* sets biting double-stopped dissonances of the violin against limpid pizzicato cello in such a manner as to sound almost improvised. Tempos are unfailingly apt – in the B flat Sonata, Op. 5 No. 6, the opening *Affetuoso* is given ample space before launching into the breezy *Allegro*, with Elizabeth Wallfisch throwing off the intricate figurations with effortless grace and impeccable tuning, even in the top-most registers, of which Tartini was inordinately fond. Unless the very thought of original instruments brings you out in a rash, there is much to delight here, both in the pieces and the performances. The immediate recording brings the players right into the room with the listener and the scholarly yet readable notes from Peter Holman set the works in their proper context.

Further listening ...

...Concerto in D major. *Coupled with works by* **Arban, Eben, Enescu, Fantini, Françaix** and **Goedicke** John Wallace (tpt/cornet); **Meyrick Alexander** (bn); **Simon Wright** (pf/org/hpd). EMI Virtuosi CDC5 55086-2 (11/94).

Phyllis Tate
British 1911-1987

Suggested listening ...

...String Quartet in F major. *Coupled with* **Rubbra** String Quartet No. 2 in E flat major. **P. Wishart** String Quartet No. 3 in A major. **English Quartet**. Tremula TREM102-2 (12/93).

Carl Tausig
Polish 1841-1871

Suggested listening ...

...Nouvelles soirées de Vienne – Nachtfalter, Op. 157; Man lebt nur einmal, Op. 167; Wahlstimmen, Op. 250. *Coupled with works by* **Schulz-Evler, Friedman, M. Rosenthal** and **Godowsky** Piers Lane (pf). Hyperion CDA66785 (2/96).

John Tavener
British 1944-

Tavener The Protecting Veil[a]. Thrinos.
Britten Solo Cello Suite No. 3, Op. 87. **Steven Isserlis** (vc); [a]**London Symphony Orchestra / Gennadi Rozhdestvensky**. Virgin Classics Ⓕ VC7 59052-2 (74 minutes: DDD: 3/92). *Gramophone Award Winner 1992.*   ⊖⊖

New review

Tavener The Protecting Veil[a]. Thrinos. Eternal Memory[a]. **Raphael Wallfisch** (vc); [a]**Royal Philharmonic Orchestra / Justin Brown**. Tring International Royal Philharmonic Collection Ⓢ TRP048 (58 minutes: DDD: 1/96). Recorded 1994.

The Protecting Veil is one of the feasts of the Mother of God, according to the ritual of the Orthodox Church. John Tavener's ability to transfer such a concept into a concert work of wide appeal and proven impact is indeed remarkable, even if its success has more to do with the simple, direct emotionalism of the music than with its specific religious connotations. Direct emotionalism, certainly – but the music's predominantly slow pace and sustained lyricism, offset by occasional, striking dramatic gestures of sorrow and lamentation, make huge demands on the stamina and technique of the performers. Both Steven Isserlis and Gennadi Rozhdestvensky, not normally one of the more self-effacing of conductors, deserve high praise for the way they sink themselves into the music's contemplative but constantly illuminating ethos, and refugees from the battering of more complex contemporary music need look no further for solace and consolation. The brief lament of the unaccompanied cello piece *Thrinos* is no less affecting, while the Britten suite provides valuable contrast through music from which the intense and unshakeable religious faith of Tavener's work is conspicuous by its absence. Even by modern standards, the recording quality is outstandingly good.

In *The Protecting Veil* the differences between Raphael Wallfisch and Steven Isserlis are primarily a matter of rhapsodic and lyrical intensity versus spiritual and lyrical intensity. Wallfisch is pretty direct in his approach, that is he projects the work's rhapsodic and dramatic qualities extremely well and overall he gives a more extrovert reading. Isserlis, on the other hand, focuses much more on the spiritual dimensions of the piece, creating an altogether greater sense of internal stillness and intensity. Wallfisch does not quite match the intensity of Isserlis's RCA recording of *Eternal Memory* either; again Wallfisch gives a reading more dramatic than spiritually intense, though it is a thoroughly valid account, none the less. Justin Brown coaxes some extremely sensitive performances from the Royal Philharmonic Orchestra strings in both items. All in all the Tring disc is an excellent bargain

Additional recommendation ...

...Eternal Memory. *Coupled with* **Bloch** From Jewish Life. **Steven Isserlis** (vc); **Moscow Virtuosi / Vladimir Spivakov.** RCA Victor Red Seal (special price) 09026 61966-2 (21 minutes: DDD: 4/94). **Ⓖ**

Tavener String Quartets – The Last Sleep of the Virgin; The Hidden Treasure.
Pärt String Quartets – Summa; Fratres. **Chilingirian Quartet** (Levon Chilingirian, Mark Butler, vns; Louise Williams, va; Philip De Groote, vc). Virgin Classics Ⓔ VC5 45023-2 (74 minutes: DDD: 5/94). Recorded 1993. **Ⓖ**

Tintinnabulation (a tinkling ringing of bells), a word that Arvo Pärt uses for describing his style, might equally apply to John Tavener's meditative *The Last Sleep of the Virgin* (1992). "Still, quiet and intensely fragile" writes Tavener at the head of his score. Music such as this aims at suggestion rather than argument, and with production and performance standards that are uniformly high, it's best to take this work on its own terms and leave it at that. *The Hidden Treasure* (1989) is another continuous piece, one that centres on the idea of longing for Paradise. Contrast is the key word here – forceful and static passages alternate, but words mean nothing, you *must* hear it for yourself! In fact, virtually the whole of Tavener's recent output is single-mindedly intent on defining and exploring areas beyond the busy prisons of language, a trend that Arvo Pärt has been exploring since the mid-1970s. *Fratres* and *Summa* are wordless prayers that take specific liturgy as their starting point and ultimately convey a universal message. Approach them as you might a lonely walk among hills or mountains at dusk, where (to paraphrase Pärt) the many-faceted is abandoned and "everything that is unimportant falls away". Anything more or less, and the point is lost entirely.

New review

Tavener Innocence[a]. The Lamb. The Tiger. The Annunciation. Hymn to the Mother of God. Hymn for the Dormition of the Mother of God. Little Requiem for Father Malachy Lynch[b]. Song for Athene. [a]**Patricia Rozario** (sop); [a]**Leigh Nixon** (ten); [a]**Graham Titus** (bass); [a]**Alice Neary** (vc); [a]**Charles Fullbrook** (bells); [a]**Martin Baker** (org); **Westminster Abbey Choir**; [b]**English Chamber Orchestra / Martin Neary.** Sony Classical Ⓔ SK66613 (64 minutes: DDD: 12/95). Texts included. Recorded 1994-5.

This is recommended as a single disc to convince anyone of the mastery of John Tavener. As well as the superb new work, *Innocence*, specially written for Westminster Abbey – encapsulating in 25 minutes what many of his more expansive pieces have told us – we have a rich and rewarding selection of other shorter choral pieces. They include not just the established favourites like the two intense Blake settings, *The Lamb* and *The Tiger*, and the two hymns for the Mother of God – here more openly passionate than in previous recordings – but the bald and direct *Little Requiem for Father Malachy Lynch*, the sharply terraced *Annunciation* and the *Song for Athene* of two years ago, all among Tavener's most beautiful and touching inspirations. The theme of *Innocents* is Innocent Victims, which prompted Tavener to compose a ritual built on texts from varied sources, Christian, Jewish, Islamic and Hindu. This involves a range of elements, set physically apart from each other. So the main choir, soprano (representing Holy Wisdom) and cello are at the centre, with the baritone soloist on one side intoning prayers for mercy in the language of the Orthodox church, and with the tenor soloist entering behind with Islamic prayers, and far away the pure sounds of a boys' choir. The result is both moving and atmospheric, with the climax introducing one element after another in rich crescendo, to provide a resolution very comparable to Britten's in the *War Requiem*. Neary draws intensely committed singing from his choir, with the principal soloists, Patricia Rozario and Graham Titus, both excellent, as well as the tenor, Leigh Nixon, with Alice Neary an expressive cellist. All the performances have a warmth of expressiveness which defies any idea of ecclesiastical detachment. The discs of shorter Tavener works from both The Sixteen (Collins, 6/94) and St George's Chapel Choir (Hyperion) offer excellent performances of the four shortest and best-known works, but they seem relatively cool next to Neary's, whose reading of the *Hymn to the Mother of God* is overwhelmingly powerful within its three-minute span. The recording vividly captures Westminster Abbey's acoustic with extreme dynamics used impressively to convey space and distance.

Tavener Hymn for the Dormition of the Mother of God. Hymn to the Mother of God. Little Lamb, who made thee? (The Lamb)[b]. The Tiger. Ikon of Light[a]. Today the Virgin. Eonia. [a]**Duke Quartet** (Louisa Fuller, Rick Koster, vns; John Metcalfe, va; Ivan McCready, vc); **The Sixteen / Harry Christophers.** Collins Classics Ⓕ 1405-2 (67 minutes: DDD: 6/94). Item marked [b] from 1270-2 (12/90), recorded 1990; remainder new to UK, recorded 1993.

Lavish soundscapes, like *The Protecting Veil*, may have caught the public imagination, but perhaps Tavener's real genius is encapsulated in his two Blake settings. Just as the true believer can find more profound beauty in a tiny icon than a church full of frescoes, so in these short works Tavener's spiritual and musical vision seems more intense than in his more expansive works. What's more, he reaches into the very soul of Blake's famous but none the less obscure poetry. It is not just the Blake settings that show Tavener focusing his writing without losing that intangible sense of depth and mystery which so informs the larger scores, and whether it is the gloriously full-bodied crescendo in the *Hymn to the Mother of God*, or the deliberate absence of colour and expression in *Eonia*, The Sixteen seem to have an instinctive feel for the inner spirit of the music, creating compelling performances of all six of these miniature *a cappella* masterpieces. With the *Ikon of Light*, though, maybe the more prayerful and distant style adopted by The Tallis Scholars (listed below) is preferable. The Sixteen bring a satisfying warmth and richness, but is this entirely appropriate in a work of such mystery and spiritual intensity? It can be powerful – not least with the initial five gradually expanding choral statements of the word "Fos" ("light") set against the sparse back-drop of a string trio which here have all the blinding awesomeness of nuclear explosions.

Additional recommendation ...

...Ikon of Light[a]. Funeral Ikos[b]. The Lamb[c]. Members of the **Chilingirian Quartet; The Tallis Scholars / **[ab]**Peter Phillips,** [c]**John Tavener.** Gimell Ⓕ CDGIM005 (55 minutes: DDD: 6/91).

Tavener The Annunciation. Ikon of the Nativity. The Lamb. A Nativity. Today the Virgin. The Lord's Prayer. Many Years. Wedding Prayer. He Hath Entered the Heven. The Acclamation. **Górecki** Euntes Ibant et Flebant, Op. 32. Totus tuus, Op. 60. Amen, Op. 35. **Pärt** Magnificat. Summa. **Oxford Pro Musica Singers / Michael Smedley.** Proud Sound Ⓕ PROUCD136 (77 minutes: DDD: 12/94). Recorded 1993.

It is good to have on one disc music by these three composers, whose names are so often bracketed together, in order to appreciate just how different from each other they really are. Each has a distinctive style and it would be difficult to confuse their pieces. It is also startling to realize how brave Górecki was to write such a piece as *Euntes Ibant et Flebant* in 1972. Both this and the slightly later *Amen* are economical in their means and powerful in their effect in a way that most would associate much more with pieces written in the last ten years, and they more than stand the test of time. Almost all the Tavener works here are first recordings, and it is particularly valuable to have the beautiful *Annunciation*, *The Acclamation* and especially *He Hath Entered the Heven* in such excellent performances. The last of these, including handbells, has hardly ever been performed and yet is one of Tavener's most powerful and haunting works, seeming to last at least twice its actual length of just over six minutes. Pärt's splendid *Magnificat* and *Summa*, an arch-representative of his *tintinnabuli* style, are also sung superbly, and their clarity and austerity sit well between the Eastern grandeur of much of the Tavener and the far more western approach of Górecki. All of the music is wonderfully well sung, with precise intonation and a full-bodied sound.

Additional recommendation ...

...Angels[a]. The Annunciation. The Lament of the Mother of God[b]. Thunder entered Her[c]. Hymns of Paradise[d]. God is with us. [b]**Solveig Kringelborn** (sop); [c]**William Kendall** (ten); [d]**Donald Sweeney** (bass); [d]**violin ensemble;** [c]**Iain Simcock** (handbells); [ace]**David Dunnett** (org); **Winchester Cathedral Choir / David Hill.** Virgin Classics Ⓕ VC5 45035-2 (63 minutes: DDD: 8/94).

Tavener We shall see Him as He is. **Patricia Rozario** (sop); **John Mark Ainsley, Andrew Murgatroyd** (tens); **Britten Singers; Chester Festival Chorus; BBC Welsh Symphony Chorus and Orchestra / Richard Hickox.** Chandos Ⓕ CHAN9128 (61 minutes: DDD: 1/93). Text included. Recorded live in 1992.

We shall see Him as He is was given its first performance in the Chester Summer Music Festival in 1992. This recording is a remarkable achievement in every respect – balance and sound are superb and the spellbound audience are as quiet as mice. The text depicts, in simple but powerful words, various events in the life of Christ – His baptism, the miracle at Cana, the cleansing of the temple, His healing of the cripple, the Last Supper and the Crucifixion, to name a few. These are presented as a series of 12 musical episodes (ikons) headed by an introduction entitled "The Unfolding of the Great Mystery"; perhaps the best way for the listener to think of the work is as one large iconostasis comprising of 12 smaller ikons which gradually unfold as the work progresses. Although the piece could scarcely be described as modest in its scoring, Tavener's handling of the forces could hardly be more economical. Most of the musical focus is in the sumptuous and melismatic vocal writing, with the instrumental material providing iconographical colour and, at key points in the narrative, declamatory and monumental "blazes of light", as for example in the turning of water into wine and the healing of the cripple. The performances are astonishingly persuasive and committed in this compelling and intensely moving work. Those who have come to Tavener's music via *The Protecting Veil* will not be disappointed.

...To a child dancing in the wind[a]. Lamentation, Last Prayer and Exultation[b]. A Mini Song Cycle
for Gina[c]. Melina. **Patricia Rozario** (sop); [a]**Kathryn Lukas** (fl); [a]**Stephen Tees** (va); [a]**Helen Tunstall**
(hp); [b]**Iain Simcock** (handbells); [ac]**John Tavener** (pf). Collins Classics 1428-2 (2/95).
...Akathist of Thanksgiving. **James Bowman, Timothy Wilson** (altos); **Westminster Abbey Choir;**
BBC Singers; BBC Symphony Orchestra / Martin Neary (org). Arc of Light SK64446 (9/94).
...The Whale. **Soloists; London Sinfonietta Chorus; London Sinfonietta / David Atherton.** EMI Apple
CDSAPCOR15 (6/93).
...Mary of Egypt. **Soloists; Ely Cathedral Choristers; Britten-Pears Chamber Choir; Aldeburgh**
Festival Ensemble / Lionel Friend. Collins Classics 7023-2 (5/93).

John Taverner   British c1490-1545

Taverner Hodie nobis caelorum Rex. Mater Christi sanctissima. Magnificat sexti toni. Nesciens
mater. Quemadmodum a 6[a]. Missa Mater Christi sanctissima. In nomine a 4[a]. [a]**Fretwork** (Wendy
Gillespie, Richard Campbell, treble viols; Susanna Pell, Julia Hodgson, Richard Boothby, bass
viols; William Hunt, great bass viol); **The Sixteen / Harry Christophers.** Hyperion Ⓕ CDA66639
(65 minutes: DDD: 3/94). 🗡 Texts and translations included. Recorded 1992.
The Sixteen offer an impressive account of the composer's five-part *Missa Mater Christi sanctissima*,
based on his votive anthem of the same name. It is a lively and vigorous work, beautifully crafted, and
this performance amply matches that craftsmanship. Harry Christophers attempts no liturgical
reconstruction, concentrating instead upon sheer musical quality. Three female sopranos replace the
boy trebles. The music is all pitched up a tone, which has the effect of adding brilliance to every
climax. He demonstrates the surprisingly good acoustic of St Jude's in Hampstead – an acoustic of
space and definition, ideal for the interweaving of the strands of early Tudor polyphony; indeed,
clarity and a sense of space are hallmarks of the recording. The supporting programme of the
Christmas responsory, *Hodie*, the votive anthem *Mater Christi* and a four-part *Magnificat* is
completed – unexpectedly, but most delightfully – by two pieces for viols.

New review
Taverner Missa Gloria tibi Trinitas[a]. Kyrie, "Leroy"[a]. Dum transisset Sabbatum I[a]. Mass a 4,
"Western Wynde"[b]. **The Tallis Scholars / Peter Phillips.** Gimell Ⓕ CDGIM995 (79 minutes:
DDD: 12/95). Texts and translations included. Items marked [a] from CDGIM004 (7/86),
[b]CDGIM027 (9/93). Recorded 1984-93.
This disc shows a striking panorama of The Tallis Scholars over the past ten years. Most of this
comes from a CD of 1986. But by adding their more recent recording of the *Western Wynde* Mass
they have created an anthology containing some of Taverner's most remarkable music: the two most
famous Masses alongside two of his loveliest smaller works. For the *Western Wynde* Mass The Tallis
Scholars present themselves at their most mandarin: everything beautifully in place, gentle, soothing,
immaculate. The marvellous range of inventive lines that Taverner weaves around this trite little
melody is given full scope to blossom and grow. Nothing is hurried or allowed to stand out too much.
This is in striking contrast to their much earlier approach to the Mass *Gloria tibi Trinitas*: here Peter
Phillips takes the music very much by the scruff of the neck, changing pace and textures to articulate
the massively complex six-voice textures. This is a tremendously exciting performance because it so
often throws caution to the winds. In other words, some listeners may find the *Western Wynde* a touch
bland and *Gloria tibi Trinitas* a touch rough, but it makes for an exciting and varied record. And
nobody could possibly resist the still beauty they give to the *Leroy Kyrie*.
Additional recommendation ...
...Mass a 4, "Western Wynde". Mater Christi. **Tallis** Motets – Sancte Deus; Audivi vocem de caelo;
Honor, virtus et potestas; O sacrum convivium; Salvator mundi I a 5. **New College Choir, Oxford**
/ Edward Higginbottom. CRD Ⓕ CRD3372 (60 minutes: ADD: 4/89).

Taverner Missa Sancti Wilhelmi. Motets – O Wilhelme, pastor bone; Dum transisset Sabbatum;
Ex eius tumba. **The Sixteen / Harry Christophers.** Hyperion Ⓕ CDA66427 (52 minutes: DDD:
4/92). Texts and translations included.
The *Missa Sancti Wilhelmi* is not one of Taverner's best known works, but there is no reason why this
should be the case. Though it does not have the sometimes rather wild melodic beauty of the six-voice
Masses, it is nevertheless an impressive work in a more modern imitative style, in keeping with its
model *O Wilhelme, pastor bone*. The Sixteen perform with their customary clarity and precision, and
convey enthusiasm even in the somewhat syllabic *Gloria* and *Credo* movements of the Mass,
something which is not always easy to do. While both the 'Wilhelm' works and *Dum transisset*
Sabbatum are among Taverner's later works, there is no doubt at all that *Ex eius tumba* is one of the
earliest. It is firmly late medieval in style, and the intricate tracery of its construction, so well captured
here by The Sixteen, makes a thought-provoking contrast to the pieces in a more 'continental'
imitative style. At 15 minutes this is a substantial composition, and one can only be surprised that it
is so little known: perhaps the large amount of chant which forms an integral part of the work has
discouraged performers. *Dum transisset Sabbatum* is, however, the high point of the disc, and if The

Sixteen do not quite attain the ecstatic heights achieved in the recording by The Tallis Scholars (reviewed above), neither do they fail to rise to Taverner's inspiration.

Additional recommendation ...

...Dum transisset Sabbatum. Missa Gloria tibi Trinitas. Kyrie a 4, "Leroy". **The Tallis Scholars / Peter Phillips.** Gimell Ⓕ CDGIM004 (47 minutes: DDD: 7/86).

Further listening ...

...Missa Corona spinea. Motets – Gaude plurimum; In pace in idipsum. **The Sixteen / Harry Christophers.** Hyperion CDA66360 (1/90).

...Missa Mater Christi. O Wilhelme, pastor bone. Mater Christi sanctissima. **Christ Church Cathedral Choir, Oxford / Stephen Darlington.** Nimbus NI5218 (4/90).

André Tchaikovsky
Polish/British 1935-1982

Suggested listening ...

...String Quartet No. 2 in C major, Op. 5. *Coupled with works by* **Wirén, Hugh Wood** and **Barber** Lindsay Quartet. ASV CDDCA825 (1/93). *See review in the Collections section; refer to the Index to Reviews.*

Pyotr Ill'yich Tchaikovsky
USSR 1840-1893

Tchaikovsky Piano Concerto No. 1 in B flat major, Op. 23[b].

Prokofiev Piano Concerto No. 3 in C major, Op. 26[a]. **Martha Argerich** (pf); [a]**Berlin Philharmonic Orchestra / Claudio Abbado;** [b]**Royal Philharmonic Orchestra / Charles Dutoit.** DG Ⓕ 415 062-2GH (63 minutes: ADD: 5/85). Item marked [a] from 138349 (2/68), [b]2530 112 (10/71). Ⓖ Ⓖ Ⓖ

New review

Tchaikovsky Piano Concerto No. 1 in B flat minor, Op. 23[a]. The Seasons, Op. 37[b] – January; February; April; May; August; October; November; December. **Ronan O'Hora** (pf); [a]**Royal Philharmonic Orchestra / James Judd.** Tring International Royal Philharmonic Collection Ⓢ TRP023 (65 minutes: DDD: 10/95). Recorded 1994.

By general consensus Martha Argerich's 1971 recording of Tchaikovsky's B flat minor Piano Concerto is still among the best of the currently available recordings. The opening of the first movement sets the mood of spaciousness and weight, with the lovely secondary material bringing poetic contrast. The *Andantino* has an appealing delicacy, with the centrepiece dazzling in its light-fingered virtuosity to match the exhilaration of the last movement. The admirably balanced recording has plenty of spectacle, the strings are full and firm and the piano image is strikingly real and tangible. The unexpected but inspirational coupling was one of Argerich's début recordings, and for those less familiar with Tchaikovsky's twentieth-century compatriot, the music itself will come as a refreshing surprise. The apparent initial spikiness soon dissolves with familiarity and Prokofiev's concerto reveals itself as very much in the romantic tradition. Its harmonies are more pungent than those of Tchaikovsky, but the melodic appeal is striking and the sheer vitality of the outer movements is irresistible as projected by Martha Argerich's nimble fingers.

After Richter, Gilels, Argerich and others, hopes of making an impact in the Tchaikovsky First Piano Concerto can seem depressingly remote. Yet Ronan O'Hora provides his own direct answer to such a conundrum when he both acknowledges and ignores such illustrious predecessors. Few young pianists remain so scrupulously true to their own musical and poetic lights. Superbly partnered by James Judd and the Royal Philharmonic (the opening a magnificent clarion call to attention, the tempo at once *andante* and *maestoso* as instructed), his playing is subtle, lucid and powerful throughout. Try the start of the Concerto proper at 4'21" and you will hear an impish vitality. The second subject sounds as natural as it is deeply felt (*dolce e molto espressivo*), the champing split-chord ascent at 8'06" pulses with virtuoso excitement and the following octave roulades are inflected with thrilling romantic rhetoric. The *Andantino* is a true oasis of calm amid so many storms, the central *prestissimo* for once *pp* and *leggiero* and the resistance to all obvious display is exceptionally poised and aristocratic. The finale, too, taken at a brisk tempo, dances with an acute rhythmic impetus rather than the more familiar flat-footed emphasis. Just occasionally eyebrows – and particularly Russian eyebrows – may be raised at what might arguably be seen as English understatement, yet the absence of all bombast and the presence of such clarity and finesse are rare attributes in this often heavily tarnished masterpiece. O'Hora's encores, a selection from *The Seasons*, are less successfully, and even claustrophobically recorded, but nothing can cloud his clear instinct for poetry or his undemonstrative yet unmistakable command. "December", a gently dipping and gyrating waltz, glows with warmth and affection and so, too, does "October", ultra-Russian poem for autumn. All in all, that rare thing, a bargain release of the highest quality.

Additional recommendations ...

...No. 1. **Grieg** Piano Concerto in A minor, Op. 16[a]. **Artur Rubinstein** (pf); **Boston Symphony Orchestra / Erich Leinsdorf;** [a]**orchestra / Alfred Wallenstein.** RCA Victor Gold Seal Ⓜ 09026 61262-2 (63 minutes: ADD). Ⓖ

...No. 2 in G major, Op. 44; No. 3 in E flat major, Op. 75. **Peter Donohoe** (pf); **Bournemouth Symphony Orchestra / Rudolf Barshai.** EMI Ⓕ CDC7 49940-2 (63 minutes: DDD). Ⓖ

...No 2. **Rachmaninov** Piano Concerto No. 2 in C minor, Op. 18. **Alexei Sultanov** (pf); **London Symphony Orchestra / Maxim Shostakovich.** Teldec Digital Experience Ⓜ 9031-77601-2 (70 minutes: DDD: 9/92).

...No 1. Concert Fantasia, Op. 56. **Mikhail Pletnev** (pf); **Philharmonia Orchestra / Vladimir Fedoseyev.** Virgin Classics Ⓕ VC7 59612-2 (64 minutes: DDD: 4/91).

...No. 1ᵃ. Morceau, Op. 19 No. 6. **Balakirev** Islamey. **Prokofiev** Piano Concerto No. 1 in D flat major, Op. 10ᵇ. Piano Piece, Op. 4 No. 4. **Andrei Gavrilov** (pf); ᵃ**Philharmonia Orchestra / Riccardo Muti.** ᵇ**London Symphony Orchestra / Sir Simon Rattle.** EMI Studio Plus Ⓜ CDM7 64329-2 (74 minutes: DDD: 11/92). Ⓖ

...No. 2. **Mozart** Piano Concerto No. 21 in C major, K467. **Emil Gilels** (pf); **USSR Symphony Orchestra / Kyrill Kondrashin.** Mezhdunarodnaya Kniga Ⓕ MK417106 (63 minutes: AAD: 5/93).

...No. 1ᵃ. **Mussorgsky** Pictures at an Exhibition. **Vladimir Horowitz** (pf); ᵃ**NBC Symphony Orchestra / Arturo Toscanini.** RCA Victor Gold Seal Ⓜ GD60321 (61 minutes: ADD: 9/93). ⒼⒼ

...Nos. 1-3. Concert Fantasia in G major, Op. 56. **Barry Douglas** (pf); **Philharmonia Orchestra / Leonard Slatkin.** RCA Victor Ⓜ 09026 61631-2 (two discs: 124 minutes: DDD: 6/94).

...Nos. 2 and 3. **Victoria Postnikova** (pf); **Vienna Symphony Orchestra / Gennadi Rozhdestvensky.** Decca Ovation Ⓜ 436 485-2DM (68 minutes: DDD: 6/94).

...No. 1ᵃ; No. 2ᵇ. ᵃ**Sviatoslav Richter,** ᵇ**Emil Gilels** (pfs); ᵃ**Leningrad Philharmonic Orchestra / Evgeny Mravinsky;** ᵇ**USSR Symphony Orchestra / Evgeny Svetlanov.** Melodiya mono Ⓜ 74321 17083-2* (73 minutes: ADD: 9/94).

...No. 1. **Scriabin** Piano Concerto in F sharp minor, Op. 20. **Nikolai Demidenko** (pf); **BBC Symphony Orchestra / Alexander Lazarev.** Hyperion Ⓕ CDA66680 (65 minutes: DDD: 10/94). *See review under Scriabin; refer to the Index to Reviews.* Ⓖ

...No. 1ᵇ. **Rachmaninov** Piano Concerto No. 3 in D minor, Op. 30ᵃ. **Martha Argerich** (pf); ᵃ**Berlin Radio Symphony Orchestra / Riccardo Chailly;** ᵇ**Bavarian Radio Symphony Orchestra / Kyrill Kondrashin.** Philips Ⓕ 446 673-2PH (73 minutes: DDD: 8/95). *See review under Rachmaninov; refer to the Index to Reviews.* ⒼⒼⒼ

...No. 1ᵃ. **Rachmaninov** Piano Concerto No. 2 in C minor, Op. 18ᵃ. Preludes – G minor, Op. 23 No. 5; G major, Op. 32 No. 5. **Géza Anda** (pf); ᵃ**Philharmonia Orchestra / Alceo Galliera.** Testament mono Ⓕ SBT1064* (76 minutes: ADD: 10/95).

Tchaikovsky Violin Concerto in D major, Op. 35ᵃ.
Brahms (arr. Joachim) Hungarian Dancesᵇ – No. 1 in G minor; No. 2 in D minor; No. 4 in B minor; No. 7 in A major. **Sarah Chang** (vn); ᵇ**Jonathan Feldman** (pf); ᵃ**London Symphony Orchestra / Sir Colin Davis.** EMI Ⓕ CDC7 54753-2 (49 minutes: DDD: 12/93). Recorded 1992-93.

New review

Tchaikovsky Violin Concerto in D major, Op. 35.
Prokofiev Violin Concerto No. 1 in D major, Op. 19. **Julian Rachlin** (vn); **Moscow Radio Symphony Orchestra / Vladimir Fedoseyev.** Sony Classical Ⓕ SK66567 (58 minutes: DDD: 8/95). Recorded live in 1994.

The range of dynamic truthfulness conveyed in Sarah Chang's performance, helped by a clear, full, naturally-balanced recording, brings not just momentary delight in individual phrases but cumulative gain, in this reading which so strongly hangs together. Not only does Chang play with exceptionally pure tone, avoiding heavy coloration, but her individual artistry does not demand the wayward pulling-about often found in this work. In that she is enormously helped by the fresh, bright and dramatic accompaniment provided by the LSO under Sir Colin Davis. In the outer movements Chang conveys wit along with the power and poetry, and the intonation is immaculate. Brahms's *Hungarian Dances* are delectable, marked by the sort of naughty pointing of phrase and rhythm that tickles one's musical funny-bone just as the playing of Kreisler always did. Here is a young artist who really does live up to the claims of the publicists.

Julian Rachlin gives exceptionally characterful and distinctive readings of both these concertos, not because they are conventionally high-powered, but because of their thoughtfulness and hushed intensity. He is helped by a natural balance for the solo instrument in these live recordings made in the Moscow Conservatoire. Some may feel that the relatively backward balance and Rachlin's determination to observe every *pianissimo* marking detracts from the power of these readings; however, in the Tchaikovsky, by establishing at the start a rapt, meditative manner, instantly magnetic, he has you accepting and welcoming his own scale of dynamic values. In the big cadenza of the first movement, for example, he may not provide such dazzling fireworks as others do but with his intense concentration he makes it sound like spontaneous expression, volatile and mercurial, not just a display vehicle. The central "Canzonetta", taken at a flowing *Andante*, is a hushed meditation, with Rachlin adopting an extra degree of *pianissimo* for the second half of the main reprise. He uses such echo effects – not always marked in the score – in the lyrical episodes of the finale, notably the *Molto meno mosso* section, which he takes so slowly than no further *rallentando* is possible. In that movement too Rachlin, rather than thrusting on with sheer power, makes the music sparkle. The volatile quality of this live recording sets problems for the orchestra, which could be crisper. In the Prokofiev they have fewer problems, and here even more the yearning, hushed beauty of Rachlin's treatment of the great melodies is very moving. This is not only a poetic performance, with the outer movements both lighter and faster-flowing than usual, but one which consistently brings out the wit and fun in the writing.

Additional recommendations ...

...Violin Concerto. **Mendelssohn** Violin Concerto in E minor, Op. 64. **Takako Nishizaki** (vn); **Slovak Philharmonic Orchestra / Kenneth Jean.** Naxos Ⓢ 8 550153 (67 minutes: DDD).

...Violin Concerto. **Mendelssohn** Violin Concerto in E minor, Op. 64. **Nathan Milstein** (vn); **Vienna Philharmonic Orchestra / Claudio Abbado.** DG Galleria Ⓜ 419 067-2GGA (58 minutes: DDD: 8/87).

...Violin Concerto. Sérénade mélancolique in B minor, Op. 26. Souvenir d'un lieu cher, Op. 42 – No. 3, Mélodie (orch. Glazunov). Valse-scherzo in C major, Op. 34. **Xue-Wei** (vn); **Philharmonia Orchestra / Salvatore Accardo.** ASV Ⓕ CDDCA713 (54 minutes: DDD: 9/90).

...Violin Concerto[a]. **Bazzini** La ronde des lutins, Op. 25[b]. **Bloch** Baal shem – Nigun[b]. **Kreisler** Liebesleid[b]. **Prokofiev** (arr. Heifetz) The Love for Three Oranges – March[b]. **Tartini** Violin Sonata in G minor, "The devil's trill"[b]. **Tchaikovsky** (arr. Kreisler) String Quartet No. 1 in D major, Op. 11 – Andante[b]. **Wieniawski** (arr. Kreisler) Caprice in A minor[b]. **Itzhak Perlman** (vn); [b]**Janet Goodman Guggenheim** (pf); [a]**Israel Philharmonic Orchestra / Zubin Mehta.** EMI Ⓕ CDC7 54108-2 (72 minutes: DDD: 2/91).

...Violin Concerto. **Prokofiev** Violin Concerto No. 2 in G minor, Op. 63. **Kyoko Takezawa** (vn); **Moscow Radio Symphony Orchestra / Vladimir Fedoseyev.** RCA Victor Red Seal Ⓕ 09026 60759-2 (63 minutes: DDD: 12/93).

...Violin Concerto. **Brahms** Violin Concerto in D major, Op. 77. **Jascha Heifetz** (vn); **Chicago Symphony Orchestra / Fritz Reiner.** RCA Living Stereo Ⓜ 09026 61495-2* (64 minutes: ADD: 4/93).   ⒺⒺⒺ

...Violin Concerto. Sérénade mélancolique in B minor, Op. 26. Valse-scherzo in C major, Op. 34. **Pierre Amoyal** (vn); **Philharmonia Orchestra / Charles Dutoit.** Erato Libretto Ⓜ 2292-45971-2 (51 minutes: ADD: 5/93).

...Violin Concerto. **Sibelius** Violin Concerto in D minor, Op. 47. **Gil Shaham** (vn); **Philharmonia Orchestra / Giuseppe Sinopoli.** DG Ⓕ 437 540-2GH (67 minutes: DDD: 9/93).

...Violin Concerto[a]. **Brahms** Violin Concerto in D major, Op. 77[b]. **Ida Haendel** (vn); [b]**London Symphony Orchestra / Sergiu Celibidache;** [a]**Royal Philharmonic Orchestra / Sir Eugene Goossens.** Testament mono Ⓕ SBT1038* (76 minutes: ADD: 10/94).

...Violin Concerto. **Sibelius** Violin Concerto in D minor, Op. 47. **Kyung-Wha Chung** (vn); **London Symphony Orchestra / André Previn.** Decca The Classic Sound Ⓜ 425 080-2DCS (66 minutes: ADD: 5/95). *See review under Sibelius; refer to the Index to Reviews.*   Ⓔ

...Violin Concerto[c]. **Brahms** Violin Concerto in D major, Op. 77[c]. **Beethoven** Romances[b] – No. 1 in G major, Op. 40; No. 2 in F major, Op. 50. **Bach** Violin Concertos[a] – A minor, BWV1041; E major, BWV1042. Concerto for Two Violins and Strings in D minor, BWV1043[b] (with Igor Oistrakh, vn). **David Oistrakh** (vn); [a]**Vienna Symphony Orchestra;** [b]**Royal Philharmonic Orchestra / Sir Eugene Goossens;** [c]**Dresden Staatskapelle / Franz Konwitschny.** DG The Originals [ab]stereo/[c]mono Ⓜ 447 427-2GOR2 (two discs: 142 minutes: ADD: 6/95).

...Violin Concerto. **Glazunov** Violin Concerto in A minor, Op. 82. **Maxim Vengerov** (vn); **Berlin Philharmonic Orchestra / Claudio Abbado.** Teldec Ⓕ 4509-90881-2 (55 minutes: DDD: 11/95). *Gramophone Editor's choice. See review under Glazunov; refer to the Index to Reviews.*

Tchaikovsky 1812 – Overture, Op. 49. Capriccio italien, Op. 45. Mazeppa – Cossack Dance. **Cincinnati Symphony Orchestra / Erich Kunzel.** Telarc Ⓕ CD80041 (35 minutes: DDD: 12/83). From DG10041 (4/80).

Kunzel's recording of the *1812* is an unashamed hi-fi spectacular, so much so that purchasers are warned that the cannon at the end can damage loudspeakers with their extreme volume. At the time of the recording it is claimed that windows nearby were shattered. In the *Capriccio italien* too, another colourful popular favourite, this version uses the full range of high-fidelity digital sound with the bass drum very prominent and astonishingly vivid in its exploitation of the lowest register. The forwardness of such effects may detract from the purely musical qualities of the performances, which are strong and energetic without being so perceptive or so exciting as some, though very well played. Particularly enjoyable is the third item, the vigorous and colourful "Cossack Dance".

Additional recommendation ...

...Capriccio italien. Marche slave. Eugene Onegin – Waltz; Polonaise. *Coupled with works by* **Liadov** *and* **Mussorgsky Kirov Theatre Chorus and Orchestra / Valery Gergiev.** Philips Ⓕ 442 775-2PH (54 minutes: DDD: 7/95). *See review under Liadov; refer to the Index to Reviews.*

Tchaikovsky Serenade in C major, Op. 48. Souvenir de Florence, Op. 70. **Vienna Chamber Orchestra / Philippe Entremont.** Naxos Ⓢ 8 550404 (65 minutes: DDD: 10/91). Recorded 1990.

This is one of the many CDs now on the market that dispel the myth once and for all that only full-price recordings contain really outstanding performances. The Naxos label is just about as 'bargain' as you can get, and here they have given us superlative performances of two of Tchaikovsky's most endearing works. The Serenade in C contains a wealth of memorable and haunting music, beautifully and inventively scored and guaranteed to bring immense pleasure and delight to those dipping their toes in to the world of classical music for the first time. Philippe Entremont and the Vienna Chamber

Orchestra give a marvellously polished and finely poised performance full of warmth, affection and high spirits, and the famous second movement Waltz in particular is played with much elegance and grace. The *Souvenir de Florence*, originally written for string sextet, makes a welcome appearance here in Tchaikovsky's own arrangement for string orchestra. This is a delightfully sunny performance, full of suavity, exuberance and romantic dash, but always alert to the many subtleties of Tchaikovsky's skilful and intricate part-writing. The *Adagio cantabile* is particularly notable for some extremely fine and poetic solo playing from the violin and cello principals of the VPO. The beautifully spacious recording does ample justice to the performances.

Additional recommendations ...

...Serenade. Suite No. 4 in G major, Op. 61, "Mozartiana". Elegy in G major in honour of Ivan Samarin. String Quartet No. 1 in D major, Op. 11 – Andante cantabile (orch. Serebrier). The Sleeping Beauty (orch. Stravinsky) – Variations de la Fée de lilas; Entr'acte. **Scottish Chamber Orchestra / José Serebrier.** ASV Ⓕ CDDCA719 (77 minutes: DDD: 3/91).

...Serenade. **Grieg** Holberg Suite, Op. 40. Two Norwegian Melodies, Op. 63. **Moscow Soloists / Yuri Bashmet.** RCA Victor Red Seal Ⓕ RD60368 (61 minutes: DDD: 3/91).

...Serenade. Souvenir de Florence. **Auvergne Orchestra / Jean-Jacques Kantorow.** Denon Ⓕ CO-75026 (62 minutes: DDD: 3/93).

...Serenade in C major. **Mozart** Serenade No. 13 in G major, K525, "Eine kleine Nachtmusik". Divertimento for Strings in D major, K136. **Saito Kinen Orchestra / Seiji Ozawa.** Philips Ⓕ 438 137-2PH (60 minutes: DDD: 9/94).

Tchaikovsky 1812 – Overture, Op. 49. Romeo and Juliet – Fantasy Overture. Marche slave, Op. 31. Francesca da Rimini, Op. 32. **Royal Liverpool Philharmonic Orchestra / Sian Edwards.** EMI Eminence Ⓜ CD-EMX2152 (66 minutes: DDD. 12/89).

It is an extraordinary achievement that the young British conductor, Sian Edwards, should have made her recording début with a Tchaikovsky programme of such distinction. She immediately achieves a splendid artistic partnership with the Royal Liverpool Philharmonic Orchestra, whose playing is so full of vitality, and whether in *1812* with its vigour and flair, its cluster of lyrical folk melodies, and a spectacular finale with thundering canon, or in *Marche slave*, resplendently patriotic, in a uniquely Russian way, together they bring the music tingling to life in every bar. *Romeo and Juliet*, on the other hand, needs a finely judged balance between the ardour and moonlight of the love music, the vibrant conflict of the battle, and the tragedy of the final denouement, which is uncannily well managed. Most intractable interpretatively is *Francesca da Rimini*, with its spectacularly horrifying picture of Dante's inferno which the composer uses to frame the central sequence depicting the lovers, Francesca and Paolo, and the doom-laden atmosphere which surrounds their intense mutual passion. Edwards's grip on this powerfully evocative sequence of events is unerringly sure, and she takes the orchestra through the narrative as only an instinctive Tchaikovskian could. The work opens with an unforgettable sense of nemesis and ends with a truly thrilling picture of the whirlwinds of Hell, into which the lovers are cast, still in their final passionate embrace. All in all this is one of the best Tchaikovsky discs in the mid-price catalogue and the fine EMI Eminence recording combines weight and sonority with brilliance, and brings a most attractive ambient effect.

Additional recommendations ...

...Romeo and Juliet (1869 version). Hamlet – Incidental Music, Op. 67a[a]. Festival Overture on the Danish national hymn, Op. 15. Serenade for Nikolai Rubinstein's name day. Mazeppa – Battle of Poltava; Cossack Dance. [a]**Janis Kelly** (sop); [a]**Derek Hammond-Stroud** (bar); **London Symphony Orchestra / Geoffrey Simon.** Chandos Ⓕ CHAN8310/11 (two discs: 94 minutes: DDD: 7/84). Ⓖ

...Francesca da Rimini. Hamlet – Fantasy Overture, Op. 67. **New York Stadium Orchestra / Leopold Stokowski.** dell'Arte Ⓕ CDDA9006* (ADD: 4/88). *Gramophone classical 100.* ⒼⒼⒼ

...Romeo and Juliet. Francesca da Rimini. Mazeppa – Cossack Dance. Festival Coronation March in D major. **Leipzig Gewandhaus Orchestra / Kurt Masur.** Teldec Ⓕ 9031-76456-2 (53 minutes: DDD: 5/93).

...Romeo and Juliet[a]. 1812[a]. Capriccio italien, Op. 45[b]. None but the lonely heart, Op. 6 No. 6 (arr. Riley)[c]. Eugene Onegin – Faint echo of my youth[c]. [b]**Ofra Harnoy** (vc); **Philharmonia Orchestra / [ab]Plácido Domingo** ([c]ten); [c]**Randall Behr.** EMI Ⓕ CDC5 55018-2 (68 minutes: DDD: 4/94).

...Marche slave. Suite No. 1, Op. 43 – Marche miniature. *Coupled with works by* **Mussorgsky, Borodin, Kabalevsky** and **Glinka Chicago Symphony Orchestra / Fritz Reiner.** RCA Victor Living Stereo Ⓜ 09026 61958-2 (71 minutes: ADD: 8/94). *See review in the Collections section; refer to the Index to Reviews.* ⒼⒼⒼ

...Francesca da Rimini. Symphony No. 1 in G minor, Op. 13, "Winter Daydreams". **USSR Symphony Orchestra / Evgeni Svetlanov.** Melodiya Ⓜ 74321 17092-2 (65 minutes: ADD/DDD: 12/94).

...Francesca da Rimini. **Schubert** Symphony No. 4 in C minor, D417, "Tragic". **Debussy** Images – Ibéria. **New York Philharmonic Symphony Orchestra / Sir John Barbirolli.** Dutton Laboratories Essential Archive mono Ⓑ CDEA5000* (69 minutes: ADD: 1/96).

...Francesca da Rimini. Suite No. 3 in G major, Op. 55. **Detroit Symphony Orchestra / Neeme Järvi.** Chandos Ⓕ CHAN9419 (69 minutes: DDD: 4/96).

Tchaikovsky Swan Lake, Op. 20. **Montreal Symphony Orchestra / Charles Dutoit.** Decca Ⓕ 436 212-2DH2 (two discs: 154 minutes: DDD: 2/93). Recorded 1991.   ⒼⒼ

New review

Tchaikovsky Swan Lake. Op. 20. **Philadelphia Orchestra / Wolfgang Sawallisch.** EMI Ⓕ CDS5 55277-2 (two discs: 159 minutes: DDD: 1/95).   Ⓖ

No one wrote more beautiful and danceable ballet music than Tchaikovsky, and this account of *Swan Lake* is a delight throughout. This is not only because of the quality of the music, which is here played including additions the composer made after the première, but also thanks to the richly idiomatic playing of Charles Dutoit and his Montreal orchestra in the superb and celebrated location of St Eustache's Church in that city. Maybe some conductors have made the music even more earthily Russian, but it is worth remembering that the Russian ballet tradition in Tchaikovsky's time was chiefly French and that the most influential early production of this ballet, in 1895, was choreographed by the Frenchman Marius Petipa. Indeed, the symbiosis of French and Russian elements in this music (and story) is one of its great strengths, the refinement of the one being superbly allied to the vigour of the other, notably in such music as the "Russian Dance" with its expressive violin solo. This is a profoundly romantic reading of the score, and the great set pieces such as the Waltz in Act 1 and the marvellous scene of the swans on a moonlit lake that opens Act 2 are wonderfully evocative; yet they do not for that reason overshadow the other music, which supports and strengthens them as gentler hills and valleys might surround and enhance magnificent, awe-inspiring peaks, the one being indispensable to the other. You do not have to be a ballet *aficionado* to fall under the spell of this wonderful music, which here receives a performance that combines romantic passion with an aristocratic refinement and is glowingly recorded.

Full marks to EMI for capacity-filled discs with the minimum necessary missing (two short double bar line repeats in Act 3's early stages). Forest, lake, moonlight and melancholy; these are the scenes that find Sawallisch in his element. The superb solo oboe is free to float his sad song in the swan scene (end of Act 1 and beginning and end of Act 2; how marvellous to hear the slurred staccato so well taken); the tempo is broad, the perspective deep, and Sawallisch's control of dynamics and his fluid pace (different in all three scenes) is masterly. Also impressive is the ballet's storm-tossed finale, less elemental at the start than Dutoit, but the moment these strings ride that storm, you know you are in Philadelphia. At this point, Sawallisch loosens the reins on his elsewhere tightly controlled brass (Dutoit's use of the brass is more judiciously opportunist). In general, Sawallisch uses a narrow range of tempos: Tchaikovsky's slower dances, such as the "Intrada" to the Act 1 "Pas de trois", can initially seem surprisingly brisk, and the difference between the *Andante* and the *Allegro* in the second part of the succeeding "Pas de deux" is small. Arguably, this moderation of speed brings an appreciable continuity to the musical scheme of things, and is a welcome corrective to the short-term, maximum contrast approach. The symphonic aspirations of the ballet can be overstressed, and it is significant that Sawallisch is at his most convincing in the most obviously 'symphonic' section of the score—the whole of Act 4. Significant, too, is Sawallisch's complete avoidance of the familiar theatrical tricks of the trade, such as rhetorical slowings at the ends of numbers. EMI's sound, apart from an occasional hollow 'ring' to tuttis, is full, spacious and well balanced. Woodwind are more consistently featured than on the Dutoit set, and percussion is well controlled. The tracking is generous; the documentation, wide ranging; and the presentation, classy. All in all, a deeply considered, seriously intentioned *Swan Lake*; one to stir the mind, if not the limbs.

Additional recommendations ...

...Swan Lake. **Russian State Symphony Orchestra / Evgeni Svetlanov.** Melodiya Ⓜ 74321 17082-2 (three discs: 153 minutes: DDD).

...Swan Lake. **Royal Opera House Orchestra, Covent Garden / Mark Ermler.** Royal Opera House Records Ⓕ ROH301/03 (three discs: 153 minutes: DDD: 12/89).

...Swan Lake. **Philharmonia Orchestra / John Lanchbery.** Classics for Pleasure Ⓑ CD-CFPD4727 (two discs: 154 minutes: DDD: 9/89).   Ⓖ

...Swan Lake – excerpts. The Nutcracker – Ballet Suite. Romeo and Juliet. **Chicago Symphony Orchestra / Sir Georg Solti.** Decca Ovation Ⓜ 430 707-2DM (70 minutes: DDD: 8/91).

...Swan Lake. **Slovak Radio Symphony Orchestra, Bratislava / Ondrej Lenárd.** Naxos Ⓢ 8 550246/7 (two discs: 140 minutes: DDD: 12/91).

...Swan Lake – excerpts. *Coupled with works by* **Beethoven, Brahms, Debussy, Ravel** *and* **Schubert** London Symphony Orchestra / Pierre Monteux. Philips The Early Years Ⓜ 442 544-2PM5 (five discs: 311 minutes: ADD: 12/94). *See review in the Collections section; refer to the Index to Reviews.*   ⒼⒼⒼ

Tchaikovsky The Sleeping Beauty, Op. 66. **Kirov Theatre Orchestra / Valery Gergiev.** Philips Ⓕ 434 922-2PH3 (three discs: 164 minutes: DDD: 7/93). Recorded 1992.

Many authorities regard this as Tchaikovsky's finest ballet score and, indeed, one of the greatest ballet scores of all time. It contains many wonderful things: the Waltz from Act One includes some wonderfully arching phrasing that soars with tremendous passion, while the "Panorama" of Act 2 is one of the composer's finest melodic ideas. The "Pas de six" of Act 1 and the contrasted Fairy dances of Act 3 bring the same almost Mozartian grace (combined with Tchaikovsky's own very special feeling for orchestral colour) that he displays in the *Nutcracker* characteristic dances, which turn simple ballet vignettes into great art. Valery Gergiev, the conductor of the Kirov Theatre Orchestra of St Petersburg is at home in this score. He secures splendidly alive and sympathetic playing from his orchestra and the Philips recording is full and sumptuous, with a rich theatrical atmosphere. Tchaikovsky's big climaxes expand properly, the strings are full and natural and the woodwind colours glow.

Additional recommendations ...

...The Sleeping Beauty (incomplete). **Philharmonia Orchestra / George Weldon.** Classics for Pleasure Ⓑ CD-CFPD4458* (two discs: 117 minutes: ADD: 1/89). Ⓖ

...The Sleeping Beauty. **Royal Opera House Orchestra, Covent Garden / Mark Ermler.** Royal Opera House Records Ⓕ ROH306/8 (three discs: 173 minutes: DDD: 5/90).

...The Sleeping Beauty – excerpts. **Royal Opera House Orchestra, Covent Garden / Mark Ermler.** Royal Opera House Records Ⓕ ROH003 (72 minutes: DDD: 5/90).

...The Sleeping Beauty – excerpts (arr. Pletnev). **Mussorgsky** Pictures at an Exhibition. **Mikhail Pletnev** (pf). Virgin Classics Ⓕ VC7 59611-2 (64 minutes: DDD: 4/91).

...The Sleeping Beauty. **Czecho-Slovak State Philharmonic Orchestra / Andrew Mogrelia.** Naxos Ⓢ 8 550490/2 (three discs: 173 minutes: DDD: 4/93).

Tchaikovsky The Nutcracker. The Sleeping Beauty – Aurora's Wedding. **Montreal Symphony Orchestra / Charles Dutoit.** Decca Ⓕ 440 477-2DH2 (two discs: 135 minutes: DDD: 3/94). Recorded 1992.

Many of the favourite characteristic dances seem freshly minted, notably the "Dance of the Sugar-plum Fairy", with its deliciously liquid celesta, and the perky "Chinese Dance". The "Waltz of the Snowflakes" (Act 1) with the children's chorus also has great charm. The transparency of the recorded sound, which helps to make all this possible, is immediately noticeable in the delightful gossamer string textures of the "Miniature Overture". But the big Act 2 *Adagio*, too, is exceptionally satisfying, its histrionics conveyed with passionate flair, yet without hysterical rhetoric at the excitingly grand climax. The recording is extremely vivid: bright but without glare, and the balance between detail, weight and hall resonance seems exactly right. "Aurora's Wedding" is the very much truncated version of *The Sleeping Beauty* which Diaghilev adopted in repertory after his extravagant London production of the complete ballet in 1921 nearly bankrupted him. The music, after introducing both Carabosse and the Lilac Fairy, passes on to the christening, includes the hunting scene in Act 2, where the Prince has a vision of his sleeping princess, then moves on to the happy ending and the dances which form the highlight of the last act. Top choice for *The Nutcracker* can safely rest between Dutoit and Ashkenazy (listed below). Previn's mid-price 1972 LSO version also emerges very favourably against the competition.

Additional recommendations ...

...The Nutcracker[a]. Queen of Spades – Duet of Daphnis and Chloë[b]. [b]**Cathryn Pope** (sop); [b]**Sarah Walker** (mez); [a]**Tiffin Boys' School Choir; London Symphony Orchestra / Sir Charles Mackerras.** Telarc Ⓕ CD80137 (two discs: 88 minutes: DDD: 5/87).

...The Nutcracker[a]. **Glazunov** The Seasons, Op. 67. [a]**Finchley Children's Music Group; Royal Philharmonic Orchestra / Vladimir Ashkenazy.** Decca Ⓕ 433 000-2DH2 (two discs: 131 minutes: DDD: 4/92). *Selected by Sounds in Retrospect. See review under Glazunov; refer to the Index to Reviews.*

...The Nutcracker. Serenade in C major, Op. 48[a]. **London Symphony Orchestra;** [a]**Philharmonia Hungarica / Antál Dorati.** Mercury Ⓜ 432 750-2MM2* (two discs: 109 minutes: ADD: 9/92). ⒼⒼ

...The Nutcracker. **Ambrosian Singers; London Symphony Orchestra / André Previn.** Classics for Pleasure Ⓜ CD-CFPD4706 (two discs: 86 minutes: ADD: 3/93).

Tchaikovsky Manfred Symphony, Op. 58. The Tempest, Op. 18. **Russian National Orchestra / Mikhail Pletnev.** DG Ⓕ 439 891-2GH (76 minutes: DDD: 12/94). *Gramophone Editor's choice.* ⒼⒼ

There are no cheap thrills in Pletnev's *Manfred*. Percussion and brass are very carefully modulated, their brilliance and power reserved quite noticeably for what Pletnev sees as the few crucial climactic passages in the outer movements. Timpani in particular provide support rather than make a show – it is the lower strings that course through Manfred's outburst in the second movement (from 5'50"), not the almost standard spurious timpani swells. It is the strong, dark woodwind, not the more usual stuttering horns, that you initially hear in the first movement's concluding *Andante con duolo* (from 13'09"). The deep satisfaction to be had from this account comes from the superlative strings, and from Pletnev's pacing which, more often than any of the listed additional recommendations takes notice of Tchaikovsky's tempo indications, most obviously in the properly flowing third movement's pastoral, and in the successful bonding of the finale's episodic structure (the magniloquent Muti's Achilles' heel). More eccentric is Pletnev's drop in tempo for those rising unison scales on strings at the start of the bacchanale (from 0'18"), but it is less troubling than Toscanini's and particularly Jansons's speeding up for those hammering chords before Astarte returns; and, mercifully, there are none of the cuts made by Toscanini. *The Tempest*, a generous coupling (Muti and Jansons, listed below, have none), brings much the same priorities and equal rewards – no more need be said, except to observe that the horns receive a better deal from the balance than in the symphony. As to the recording generally, timpani are probably less focused than Pletnev would have wanted; in all other respects, the sound does full justice to the riches of his orchestra and the seriousness of his intent.

Additional recommendations ...

...Manfred Symphony. **Oslo Philharmonic Orchestra / Mariss Jansons.** Chandos Ⓕ CHAN8535 (53 minutes: DDD: 5/88).

...Manfred Symphony. Romeo and Juliet – Fantasy Overture. **NBC Symphony Orchestra / Arturo Toscanini.** RCA Victor Gold Seal mono Ⓜ GD60298* (67 minutes: ADD: 6/92).

...Manfred Symphony. **Philharmonia Orchestra / Riccardo Muti.** EMI Studio Plus Ⓜ CDM7 64872-2 (59 minutes: DDD: 3/94).

...Manfred Symphony. Festival Overture on the Danish national hymn in D major, Op. 15ᵇ. **USSR Symphony Orchestra / Evgeni Svetlanov.** Melodiya Ⓜ 74321 17098-2 (70 minutes: ADD: 12/94).

...Manfred Symphony. **Borodin** Symphony No. 2 in B minor. **Philharmonia Orchestra / Paul Kletzki.** Testament mono Ⓕ SBT1048* (78 minutes: ADD: 3/95).

New review

Tchaikovsky Suite No. 2, Op. 53. The Tempest, Op. 18. **Detroit Symphony Orchestra / Neeme Järvi.** Chandos Ⓕ CHAN9454 (64 minutes: DDD: 8/96).

Tchaikovsky's elusive blend of instrumental precision and free-flowing thematic fantasy in the Second Suite meets its match in the Detroit/Järvi partnership: the conductor's imagination works alongside the lean, clean Detroit sound with interesting results. The strings are not always the ideal: the lush chordings and central fugal energy of the opening movement, "Jeu de sons", cry out for a richer, Russian tone. But the semiquaver patter is beautifully done, the lower lines clear and personable. Keen articulation and driving force go hand-in-glove as Järvi prepares for the entry of the four accordions in the virile "Rondo-Burlesque", sweeping on to the folk-song of the central section with characteristic aplomb. And yes, the accordions are here: "the engagement of these instruments is not indispensible ... but the composer believes that their sonority is apt to increase the effectiveness", it says in the score. It is in the Schumannesque phrases and the subtly shifting moods of the most poetic movement, "Rêves d'enfant", that Järvi really comes into his own; the short-lived, other-worldly radiance at the heart of the movement seems more than ever like a preliminary study for the transformation scenes of *The Nutcracker*, just as the woodwind choruses throughout the work look forward to that and *Sleeping Beauty.* The magical haze surrounding Prospero's island in *The Tempest* doesn't quite come off; here it's Pletnev (reviewed above) who surprises us with the true magician's touch, but then his Russian horns, and later his trumpeter, cast their incantations more impressively. Järvi is no more successful than any other conductor in stitching together Tchaikovsky's strong impressions of the play, though a little more forward movement in the love-music might not have gone amiss.

Tchaikovsky Symphonies – No. 1 in G minor, Op. 13, "Winter Daydreams"ᵃ; No. 2 in C minor, Op. 17, "Little Russian"ᵇ; No. 3 in D major, Op. 29, "Polish"ᶜ; No. 4 in F minor, Op. 36ᵈ; No. 5 in E minor, Op. 64ᵉ; No. 6 in B minor, Op. 74, "Pathétique"ᶠ. **London Symphony Orchestra / Igor Markevitch.** Philips Ⓑ 426 848-2PB4 (four discs: 256 minutes: ADD: 3/91). Recorded 1962-66. Item marked ᵃ from SAL3578 (10/66), ᵇSAL3601 (3/67), ᶜSAL3549 (2/66), ᵈSAL3481 (2/65), ᵉSAL3579 (12/66), ᶠ835126AY (10/62). ⒼⒼⒼ

If you want to avoid routine in standard repertoire, then entrust its interpretation to a composer-performer. It's a formula that doesn't always work, but when it does the results are usually illuminating beyond belief. Igor Markevitch started life as a composer; in fact, before the Second World War he was considered one of Nadia Boulanger's most promising protégées, and his compositions were held in high esteem. Markevitch's approach to Tchaikovsky is refreshing, spontaneous and perceptive; no wonder Stravinsky (another Markevitch speciality) felt such a deep love for this music, with its piquant scoring, acute sense of harmonic development and dramatic impact. Markevitch avoids a blanket approach to the six symphonies. He doesn't merely select and indulge those aspects of the music that appeal to him; rather, he treats each separate work as a unique phase in an ongoing symphonic journey. His are more recreations than interpretations; and although attentive to structure, he's quite willing to underline small details, varying the pulse to expressive ends – as he does in the first movements of the Fourth and Sixth Symphonies – and guiding us through musical events that we might otherwise have missed. But where a lesser conductor might turn selective observation into tiresome point-making, Markevitch always retains a sense of structural proportion. His handling of the Third Symphony's introduction is masterly, with the transition into the main *Allegro* as effective as it is cunning. He brings both expressive weight and balletic sensibility to the early symphonies, and although Bernard Haitink's versions (now reissued on a six-disc, bargain-price set) are not displaced, Markevitch's are especially supple, with the LSO strings and woodwinds excelling themselves in keenness of attack and clarity of articulation. The Fifth, too, is supremely alive and eager to yield its secrets, with a first movement that forges forwards and resists the temptation to linger over the big tunes. Musical punctuation can be a problem in Tchaikovsky, but Markevitch understands how to make this music breathe; and with clean, open recordings (just a little short on lustre), his work is borne to us much as it sounded on the day.

Additional recommendations ...

...Nos. 1-6. Capriccio italien, Op. 45. Manfred Symphony, Op. 58. **Oslo Philharmonic Orchestra / Mariss Jansons.** Chandos Ⓜ CHAN8672/8 (seven discs: 319 minutes: DDD: 1/89). Ⓖ

...No. 1[a]; Nos. 2-6[b]. Romeo and Juliet – Fantasy Overture[b]. [a]**New Philharmonia Orchestra;** [b]**Philharmonia Orchestra / Riccardo Muti.** EMI Ⓜ CZS7 67314-2 (four discs: 272 minutes: ADD: 9/91). Ⓖ

...Nos. 1-6. Romeo and Juliet. **Vienna Philharmonic Orchestra / Lorin Maazel.** Decca Ⓑ 430 787-2DC4 (four discs: 267 minutes: ADD: 4/92).

...Nos. 1-6. Francesca da Rimini, Op. 32. Marche slave, Op. 31. Fate, Op. 77. Romeo and Juliet. Capriccio italien, Op. 45. Swan Lake – Suite. **Royal Philharmonic Orchestra / Yuri Temirkanov.** RCA Victor Red Seal Ⓜ 09026 61821-2 (six discs: 391 minutes: DDD: 5/94).

...Nos. 1-6. Romeo and Juliet. Manfred Symphony. Capriccio italien. 1812 – Overture, Op. 49. Marche slave, Op. 31. Francesca da Rimini. The storm, Op. 76. **Concertgebouw Orchestra / Bernard Haitink.** Philips Bernard Haitink Symphony Edition Ⓜ 442 061-2PB6 (six discs: 423 minutes: ADD: 10/94).

...Nos. 1-6. Francesca da Rimini. Serenade in C major, Op. 48. Romeo and Juliet. Fate, Op. 77. Capriccio italien. The Tempest, Op. 18. Voyevoda, Op. 78. Andante cantabile for Cello and Strings, Op. 11. **USSR Symphony Orchestra / Evgeni Svetlanov.** Melodiya Ⓑ 74321 17101-2 (six discs: 403 minutes: ADD/DDD: 12/94).

...No. 2, Op. 17. Romeo and Juliet. 1812 – Overture, Op. 49[a]. **Culver Girls Academy Choir; St Louis Symphony Orchestra / Leonard Slatkin.** RCA Victor Red Seal Ⓕ 09026 68045-2 (68 minutes: DDD: 11/95).

...No. 3. **Oslo Philharmonic Orchestra / Mariss Jansons.** Chandos Ⓕ CHAN8463 (45 minutes: DDD: 7/86).

...No. 3. Capriccio italien. **Berlin Philharmonic Orchestra / Herbert von Karajan.** DG Ⓕ 419 178-2GH (64 minutes: DDD: 12/86).

...Nos. 4-6. **London Symphony Orchestra / Igor Markevitch.** Philips Duo Ⓜ 438 335-2PM2 (two discs: 132 minutes: ADD). ⒼⒼⒼ

...No. 6. **Leningrad Philharmonic Orchestra / Evgeny Mravinsky.** Erato Ⓜ 2292-45756-2 (45 minutes: DDD: 6/92). ⒼⒼⒼ

...No. 6. Romeo and Juliet[b]. **National Symphony Orchestra / Albert Coates.** Beulah mono Ⓕ 1PD6* (66 minutes: ADD: 7/94).

...No. 6. Voyevoda, Op. 78. Andante cantabile for Cello and Strings, Op. 11. **USSR Symphony Orchestra / Evgeni Svetlanov.** Melodiya Ⓜ 74321 17097-2 (65 minutes: ADD/DDD: 12/94).

Tchaikovsky Symphony No. 1 in G minor, Op. 13, "Winter Daydreams". **Oslo Philharmonic Orchestra / Mariss Jansons.** Chandos Ⓕ CHAN8402 (44 minutes: DDD: 2/86). Ⓖ

Tchaikovsky Symphony No. 2 in C minor, Op. 17, "Little Russian". Capriccio italien, Op. 45. **Oslo Philharmonic Orchestra / Mariss Jansons.** Chandos Ⓕ CHAN8460 (48 minutes: DDD: 11/87).

The composer himself gave the work the title *Winter Daydreams*, and also gave descriptive titles to the first two movements. The opening *Allegro tranquillo* he subtitled "Dreams of a winter journey", while the *Adagio* bears the inscription "Land of desolation, land of mists". A *Scherzo* and finale round off a conventional four-movement symphonic structure. In the slow movement Jansons inspires a performance of expressive warmth and tenderness, while the *Scherzo* is managed with great delicacy and sensitivity. Both the opening movement and the finale are invested with vigour and passion, and everywhere the orchestral playing is marvellously confident and disciplined. The recording has not only impact and immediacy but also warmth and refinement. Jansons also has the full measure of Tchaikovsky's Second Symphony. It is a direct performance – the first movement allegro is relatively steady, but never sounds too slow, because of crisp rhythmic pointing – and the second movement goes for charm and felicity of colour. The finale is properly exuberant, with the secondary theme full of character, and there is a fine surge of adrenalin at the end. The *Capriccio italien*, a holiday piece in which the composer set out to be entertaining, is also played with great flair and the hint of vulgarity in the Neapolitan tune is not shirked. Again the closing pages produce a sudden spurt of excitement which is particularly satisfying. The recording here is just short of Chandos's finest – the massed violins could be sweeter on top, but the hall resonance is right for this music and there is a proper feeling of spectacle.

Tchaikovsky Symphony No. 4 in F minor, Op. 36. **Oslo Philharmonic Orchestra / Mariss Jansons.** Chandos Ⓕ CHAN8361 (42 minutes: DDD: 9/86). From ABRD1124 (7/85). *Selected by Sounds in Retrospect.*

A high emotional charge runs through Jansons's performance of the Fourth, yet this rarely seems to be an end in itself. There is always a balancing concern for the superb craftsmanship of Tchaikovsky's writing: the shapeliness of the phrasing; the superb orchestration, scintillating and subtle by turns; and most of all Tchaikovsky's marvellous sense of dramatic pace. Rarely has the first movement possessed such a strong sense of tragic inevitability, or the return of the 'fate' theme in the finale sounded so logical, so necessary. The playing of the Oslo Philharmonic Orchestra is first rate: there are some gorgeous woodwind solos and the brass manage to achieve a truly Tchaikovskian intensity. Recordings are excellent: at once spacious and clearly focused, with a wide though by no means implausible dynamic range.

Additional recommendations ...

...No. 4. Capriccio italien, Op. 45. **Berlin Philharmonic Orchestra / Herbert von Karajan.** DG Galleria Ⓜ 419 872-2GGA (59 minutes: DDD).

...Nos. 4-6. **Leningrad Philharmonic Orchestra / Evgeny Mravinsky.** DG Ⓕ 419 745-2GH2
(two discs: 129 minutes: ADD: 8/87). *Gramophone classical 100.*   ⒼⒼⒼ
...No. 4. Marche slave, Op. 31. **London Symphony Orchestra / Gennadi Rozhdestvensky.** IMP
Classics Ⓜ PCD867 (53 minutes: DDD: 12/87).
...No. 4. Francesca da Rimini, Op. 32. **New York Philharmonic Orchestra / Leonard Bernstein.**
DG Ⓕ 429 778-2GH (76 minutes: DDD: 4/91).
...Nos. 2[a] and 4[b]. [a]**New Philharmonia Orchestra,** [b]**Vienna Philharmonic Orchestra / Claudio Abbado.**
DG Galleria Ⓑ 429 527-2GR (75 minutes: ADD: 8/91).
...Nos. 2 and 4. **Polish National Radio Symphony Orchestra / Adrian Leaper.** Naxos Ⓢ 8 550488
(79 minutes: DDD: 5/93).
...Nos. 4-6. **London Symphony Orchestra / Igor Markevitch.** Philips Duo Ⓜ 438 335-2PM2
(two discs: 132 minutes: ADD: 2/94). *These are the same recordings as those reviewed
above.*   ⒼⒼⒼ

Tchaikovsky Symphonies – No. 4 in F minor, Op. 36[a]; No. 5 in E minor, Op. 64[b]; No. 6 in
B minor, Op. 74, "Pathétique"[c]. Romeo and Juliet – Fantasy overture[d]. Serenade in C major,
Op. 48 – Waltz[e]. **Concertgebouw Orchestra / Willem Mengelberg.** Music and Arts mono
Ⓕ CD809* (two discs: 149 minutes: AAD: 10/94). Item marked [a] from Columbia L2366/70
(2/30), [b]L2176/82 (1/29), [c]Telefunken SK2214/18 (recorded 1937), [d]Columbia LX55/6 (10/30),
[e]L2182.   ⒼⒼ

Those readers who treat Tchaikovsky's written scores as sacrosanct will likely baulk at these provocative
re-creations; but, be warned, those who risk sampling Mengelberg's realization of the music's emotional
core could quite easily be mesmerized into forgetting the very existence of a printed source. So forget his
dynamic adjustments, his re-harmonizing a crucial chord at the end of the Fifth Symphony, or the
dazzling array of tempos that he inflicts on the Fourth's finale. That was his way, his manner of
communication; yet the end products are nothing short of spellbinding, even on those occasions when
we are prompted to shake our heads at the sheer nerve of it all. Mengelberg's charting of the Fourth
Symphony's first movement is a masterpiece of interpretative rhetoric: the central development is
angrily impatient, the final build-up a terrifying tread towards some unimaginable catastrophe. The
Andantino is played with a degree of rubato that would tax even an accomplished soloist, while the
Romeo and Juliet Fantasy Overture, the *1812* Overture and the first two movements of the Fifth
Symphony rage, riot or relax as the spirit dictates. Under Mengelberg's inspired baton, the Fifth's first
movement in particular is like a tightly-coiled spring that snaps loose whenever the temperature rises, and
the equally charismatic *Pathétique* climaxes with a desperately weeping *Adagio lamentoso*. The Music and
Arts transfers are remarkably quiet and detailed but the Fifth Symphony is split between two CDs.

Tchaikovsky Symphony No. 5 in E minor, Op. 64.
Mussorgsky Songs and Dances of Death[a]. [a]**Anatoly Kotscherga** (bass); **Berlin Philharmonic
Orchestra / Claudio Abbado.** Sony Classical Ⓕ SK66276 (65 minutes: DDD: 3/95). Text and
translation included. Recorded live in 1994.

Sony's booklet tells us that Shostakovich's orchestration was used for the Mussorgsky songs;
"Shostakovich ed. Abbado" would be more accurate, though you will need a score to pick up most of
Abbado's changes, mainly small additions and alterations to the string parts. These alterations tie in
with an approach to all four songs that finds soloist and conductor generally avoiding the Grand
Guignol tactics and timing that Hvorostovsky and Gergiev so obviously relish. Kotscherga has the
richer, darker bass voice that seems ideal for these songs, and which he varies to great effect: ashen-
voiced and gravelly for the opening of "Lullaby", turning to a silken whisper for its haunting refrain;
and he judiciously coarsens tone and manner to mimic and menace the doomed drunkard in
"Trepak". When Kotscherga 'opens up', the power and pitching are thrilling, not least in the "Ty
maja!" ("You are mine!") at the end of "Serenade". With Abbado's alterations giving the strings a
little more to do, and the Berlin strings at their expressive finest, their contribution to the success of
the Mussorgsky songs is considerable. And so it is in the Tchaikovsky. Though they never appear to
dominate the scene, as has often been the case in DG's Berlin recordings, such moments as their full-
toned, impassioned song at the climax of the symphony's slow movement, and *feroce* and
marcatissimo playing in the finale's main *Allegro*, duly astonish. This is Abbado's third recording of
Tchaikovsky's Fifth and, as before, he allows himself a fair measure of freedom in pacing
(considerably more than Jansons). On balance, Abbado finds more shadow in the score than the
breezy Jansons, especially in the symphony's opening minutes and the finale is one of the most
exciting on disc, with superb brass. The orchestra are present, but the Philharmonie's ambience adds
just enough warmth and space to the proceedings. Those who prefer the more obviously spacious
setting that Chandos gave to Jansons may find it a little dry.

Additional recommendations ...

...No. 5. Sérénade mélancolique[a]. [a]**Shizuka Ishikawa** (vn); **Czech Philharmonic Orchestra / Lovro
von Matačic,** [a]**Zdenek Kosler.** Supraphon Crystal Collection Ⓜ 11 0656-2 (52 minutes: ADD).
...No. 5. **Oslo Philharmonic Orchestra / Mariss Jansons.** Chandos Ⓕ CHAN8351 (43 minutes:
DDD: 3/85). *Gramophone classical 100.*   ⒼⒼⒼ
...No. 5. Eugene Onegin – Tatyana's letter scene[a]. [a]**Eilene Hannan** (sop); **London Philharmonic
Orchestra / Sian Edwards.** EMI Eminence Ⓜ CD-EMX2187 (59 minutes: DDD: 1/92).

...No. 5. Romeo and Juliet – Fantasy Overture. Piano Concerto No. 1 in B flat minor, Op. 23[a].
[a]John Ogdon (pf); **London Symphony Orchestra / Pierre Monteux.** Vanguard Classics
Ⓜ 08.8032.72 (two discs: 97 minutes: ADD: 3/95).
...No. 5. **Mozart** Symphony No. 40 in G minor, K550. **North German Radio Symphony Orchestra /
Günter Wand.** RCA Victor Red Seal Ⓕ 09026 68032-2 (73 minutes: DDD: 6/95).   Ⓖ
...No. 5. 1812 – Overture. Again, as before, alone, Op. 73 No. 6 (orch. Stokowski). Chant sans
paroles in A minor, Op. 40 No. 6 (orch. Stokowski). **Philadelphia Orchestra / Leopold Stokowski.**
Biddulph mono Ⓜ WHL015* (69 minutes: ADD: 11/95).

New review

Tchaikovsky Symphony No. 5 in E minor, Op. 64[a]. 1812 – Overture, Op. 49. **Chicago Symphony
Orchestra / Daniel Barenboim.** Teldec Ⓕ 0630-10904-2 (60 minutes: DDD: 8/96). Item marked [a]
recorded live in 1995.
Recorded live, Barenboim and the Chicago orchestra give a warm, powerful and beautifully paced
reading of the Fifth, freely expressive without self-indulgence in a winningly spontaneous way.
Barenboim is a degree more impulsive and volatile than other conductors in a way that might be
counted more idiomatic. It almost goes without saying too that the Chicago orchestra play with a
refinement second to none, with much outstanding solo work, not least from the horn in the slow
movement. Where the new recording falls down is in the sound. Orchestra Hall, Chicago, is not an
easy venue, particularly when there is an audience present, damping down the acoustic, and though
many will be perfectly satisfied, the Teldec recording is certainly drier than most others, becoming
constricted in loud tuttis. Not only do the brass suffer, the Chicago violins also lack the bloom we
know they genuinely have, and the proof comes in the fill-up, *1812*, recorded in the same hall but
without an audience. The difference may be marginal but it is a crucial one, with the violins opening
up far more sweetly, and with brass antiphonies given their full bloom and proper focus thanks to the
more spacious acoustic. Barenboim directs a strong, urgent and very exciting reading without
bombast, minimizing the vulgarity with crisply pointed, purposeful playing. Anyone wanting this
coupling may well find that the limitations of sound in the symphony are easily borne.

Tchaikovsky Symphony No. 6 in B minor, Op. 74, "Pathétique". Marche slave, Op. 31.
Russian National Orchestra / Mikhail Pletnev. Virgin Classics Ⓕ VC7 59661-2 (53 minutes:
DDD: 1/92). *Gramophone classical 100.*   ⒼⒼⒼ
There's no denying that Russian orchestras bring a special intensity to Tchaikovsky, and this
Symphony in particular. But, in the past, we have had to contend with lethal, vibrato-laden brass, and
variable Soviet engineering. Not any more. Pianist Mikhail Pletnev formed this orchestra in 1990 from
the front ranks of the major Soviet orchestras, and the result here has all the makings of a classic. The
brass still retain their penetrating power, and an extraordinary richness and solemnity before the
Symphony's coda; the woodwind (soft, veiled flute tone, dark-hued bassoons) make a very
melancholy choir; and the strings possess not only the agility to cope with Pletnev's aptly death-
defying speed for the third movement march, but beauty of tone for Tchaikovsky's yearning
cantabiles, and their lower voices add thunderous black density to the first movement's development's
shattering intrusion. Pletnev exerts the same control over his players as he does over his fingers, to
superb effect. The dynamic range is huge and is comfortably reproduced here with clarity, natural
perspectives, a sense of instruments playing in a believable acoustic space, and a necessarily higher
volume setting than usual. *Marche slave's* final blaze of triumph, under the circumstances, seems apt
Additional recommendations ...
...No. 6. **Oslo Philharmonic Orchestra / Mariss Jansons.** Chandos Ⓕ CHAN8446 (44 minutes:
DDD: 5/87).
...No. 6[a]. Romeo and Juliet[a]. Swan Lake – excerpts[b]. The Nutcracker – excerpts[b]. Sleeping Beauty
– excerpts[b]. **Philadelphia Orchestra / [a]Carlo Maria Giulini, [b]Efrem Kurtz.** EMI Seraphim
Ⓢ CES5 68537-2 (two discs: 145 minutes: ADD: 1/96).

Tchaikovsky String Quartets – No. 1 in D major, Op. 11; No. 2 in F major, Op. 22; No. 3 in E flat
minor, Op. 30. Quartet Movement in B flat major. Souvenir de Florence, Op. 70[a]. [a]**Yuri Yurov**
(va); [a]**Mikhail Milman** (vc); **Borodin Quartet** (Mikhail Kopelman, Andrei Abramenkov, vns;
Dmitri Shebalin, va; Valentin Berlinsky, vc). Teldec Ⓕ 4509-90422-2 (two discs: 151 minutes:
DDD: 1/94). Recorded 1993. *Gramophone Award Winner 1994.*   ⒼⒼⒼ
Who could fail to recognize the highly characteristic urgency and thematic strength of the F major
Quartet's first movement development section, or miss premonitions of later masterpieces in the
Third Quartet's *Andante funèbre*. None of these works is 'late' (the last of them predates the Fourth
Symphony by a couple of years), yet their rigorous arguments and sweeping melodies anticipate the
orchestral masterpieces of Tchaikovsky's full maturity. So why the neglect – that is, of all but the First
Quartet? The most likely reason is our habitual expectation of orchestral colour in Tchaikovsky, a
situation that doesn't really affect our appreciation of the early, almost Schubertian D major Quartet
(the one with the *Andante cantabile* that moved Tolstoy to tears). The Second and Third Quartets are
noticeably more symphonic and particularly rich in the kinds of harmonic clashes and sequences that
Tchaikovsky normally dressed for the orchestral arena. Even minor details, like the quick-fire
exchanges near the beginning of No. 3's *Allegretto*, instantly suggest 'woodwinds' (you can almost

hear oboes, flutes and clarinets jostle in play), while both finales could quite easily have been transposed among the pages of the early symphonies. But if these and other parallels are to register with any conviction, then performers need to locate them, and that's a challenge the Borodins meet with the ease of seasoned Tchaikovskians. Generally speaking, the earlier performances (listed below) have the more incisive attack (especially in the First Quartet); but the newer ones are marginally more 'natural' and spontaneous, most noticeably in the first movement of the exuberant *Souvenir de Florence* sextet, and in that wonderful passage from the Second Quartet's first movement where the lead violin calms from agitated virtuosity to a magical recapitulation of the principal theme – an unforgettable moment, superbly paced in the Teldec reading. We also get a bonus in the shape of a 15-minute B flat Quartet movement – an appealing torso imbued with the spirit of Russian folk-song – which is accommodated partially at the expense of the First Quartet's last movement repeat (included in the 1979 recording).

Additional recommendations ...

...Nos. 1-3. Souvenir de Florence[a]. [a]**Natalia Gutman** (vc); [a]**Yuri Bashmet** (va); **Borodin Quartet.** EMI Ⓕ CDS7 49775-2 (two discs: 140 minutes: ADD: 8/88).   ⒼⒼ

...Nos. 1-4. Quartet Movement in B flat major. Souvenir de Florence, Op. 70[a]. [a]**Genrikh Talalyan** (va); [a]**Mstislav Rostropovich** (vc); **Borodin Quartet.** Melodiya Ⓕ 74321 18290-2 (two discs: 154 minutes: ADD: 10/94).

...No. 1. **Borodin** String Quartet No. 2 in D major. **Glazunov** Five Novelettes, Op. 15. **Hollywood Quartet.** Testament mono Ⓕ SBT1061* (80 minutes: ADD: 8/95).

...No. 1. **Schnittke** String Quartet No. 2. **Shostakovich** String Quartet No. 8 in C minor, Op. 110. **Duke Quartet.** Collins Classics Ⓕ 1450-2 (70 minutes: DDD: 2/96). *See review under Shostakovich; refer to the Index to Reviews.*

Tchaikovsky Piano Trio in A minor, Op. 50.
Arensky Piano Trio No. 1 in D minor, Op. 32. **Cho-Liang Lin** (vn); **Gary Hoffman** (vc); **Yefim Bronfman** (pf). Sony Classical Ⓕ SK53269 (76 minutes: DDD: 9/94). Recorded 1992.
Gramophone Editor's choice.   Ⓖ

This is a recording of Tchaikovsky's Trio to take its place in some very august company, and that in particular offers new insight into the nature and structure of the long, difficult opening movement. The work is dedicated "To the memory of a great artist" (Tchaikovsky's mentor Nikolay Rubinstein), and the movement is entitled *Pezzo elegiaco*. The players treat it with considerable flexibility of tempo, which works extremely well when their understanding of its unusual structure is so acute. This is the finest kind of chamber music-making. It is fresh, and it takes risks, as all performances do that deal in the making of music and not the execution of a plan of campaign. The ensuing variations are delightfully done, with a nimble scherzo, a tinkling musical clock, a waltz that has a charming, even witty lilt, and a fugue that proves the point of including it (Tchaikovsky nervously said it could be cut). They even bring off the rather noisy finale before the touching return of the opening elegy. Arensky's Trio, now a regular partner to Tchaikovsky's on record, is also given a fine performance, with a brilliant scherzo and grave, intense playing of the beautiful *Elegia*. The recording is particularly sensitive to the demands put upon everyone by Tchaikovsky, who wrote some notoriously thick chords for the piano. They need careful handling by the pianist, but much can be contributed by engineers sensitive to the problems. This is as fine a performance as any on record, and in many ways the most interesting.

Additional recommendations ...

...Piano Trio. **Pierre Amoyal** (vn); **Frédéric Lodéon** (vc); **Pascal Rogé** (pf). Erato Ⓜ Libretto 2292-45972-2 (47 minutes: DDD: 5/83).

...Piano Trio. **Smetana** Piano Trio in G minor, B104. **Golub Kaplan Carr Trio.** Arabesque Ⓕ Z6661 (75 minutes: DDD: 3/96). *See review under Smetana; refer to the Index to Reviews.*

New review

Tchaikovsky Capriccio italien, Op. 45. Swan Lake, Op. 20 (arr. Debussy). The Sleeping Beauty, Op. 66 (arr. Rachmaninov). Marche slave, Op. 31 (arr. Batalini).
Scriabin Fantasy in A minor. **Katia Labèque, Marielle Labèque** (pfs). Philips Ⓕ 442 778-2PH (56 minutes: DDD: 12/95).

This is a fascinating and, for the most part, brilliantly played collection. The 20-year-old Debussy's arrangement of three dances from *Swan Lake* opens with a glittering flourish, and then presents the music in totally pianistic terms: the "Danse russe" is most engaging and the "Danse napolitaine" invites and receives scintillating brilliance at its close. Rachmaninov was just 18 when he arranged the suite from *Sleeping Beauty* and Tchaikovsky was greatly displeased with the result. "It was a mistake to entrust this work to a *boy*", said he angrily to Ziloti, who had arranged the commission. The latter hastily re-edited Rachmaninov's work. But Rachmaninov deplored his failure and probably had a hand in revising the final version, which is certainly pianistically effective. The Labèques obviously enjoy the drama of the "Introduction", attacking it with relish and then putting in a splendid pianistic 'bang' at the climax of "La fée des lilas". The surprise here is that they entirely miss the rhythmic point (and all the magic) of the famous "Panorama", playing it too fast, and failing to notice that it should float gently above the (almost syncopated) bass, which here rocks prosaically. They are at home in the "Waltz", however, which is played with fine sparkle, and they make the most of

Rachmaninov's extra decorations, though they are inclined to rush their fences a little here and there. Alexandra Batalini's transcription of the *Marche slave* ends the recital grandiloquently – the orchestral detail is all there, particularly the effulgent twiddly bits in the treble, and it is made to sound so commandingly pianistic that one does not miss the orchestra (and that's saying a good deal with a composer like Tchaikovsky). The coda is quite splendid and this performance, with its thrilling fireworks at the end, would deservedly bring the house down at a live recital, which is just what it sounds like, with a very real and immediate piano recording. It is a pity the recital was programmed to open with Tchaikovsky's own four-handed piano transcription of the *Capriccio italien*, for the composer (although he admired his own efforts) showed no real skill at re-thinking a spectacular orchestral show-piece for the piano. It opens with the famous bugle call played by one hand(!), and as "the rest of the brass joins in", the extended fanfare is little short of tedious. Fortunately when the Labèque sisters get to the echo theme they are able to invest it with their own effervescence, even if they are a bit impetuous, and the "Tarantella" finale certainly tests their virtuosity, just as the composer intended. The Scriabin *Fantasy* follows, opening nocturnally and later becoming harmonically more complex.

Tchaikovsky Two Pieces, Op. 1. Three Souvenirs de Hapsal, Op. 2. Valse caprice in D major, Op. 4. Romance in F minor, Op. 5. Valse-scherzo in A major, Op. 7. Capriccio in G flat major, Op. 8. Three Morceaux, Op. 9. Two Morceaux, Op. 10. Six Morceaux, Op. 19. Six Morceaux composés sur un seul theme, Op. 21. Impromptu in A flat major. Valse-scherzo in A major. Impromptu-caprice in G major. Aveu passione in E minor. Military March in B flat major. Piano Sonata in G major, Op. 37. Album for the young, Op. 39. Dumka, Op. 59. The Seasons, Op. 37b[a]. Piano Sonata in C sharp minor, Op. 80[d]. 50 Russian Folk Songs (with Gennadi Rozhdestvensky, pf, four hands). Potpourri on Themes from the opera "Voyevoda". Three Romances. Theme and Variations in A minor. 12 Morceaux, Op. 40. Six Morceaux, Op. 51. 18 Morceaux, Op. 72. Momento lirico in A flat major. **Victoria Postnikova** (pf). Erato Ⓔ 2292-45969-2 (seven discs: 533 minutes: DDD: 7/93). Items marked [a] from 2292-45512-2 (6/92). Recorded 1990-92. ⒼⒼⒼ

Why, given the indestructible popularity of the B flat Piano Concerto, should Tchaikovsky's solo piano music be so little heard? The solo works are no less gratefully written than the concertos – if anything they tend to suit the instrument rather better – and it is only at times in the later pieces, when Tchaikovsky looks self-consciously towards Lisztian layouts, that embarrassment ensues. Nor can the blame be laid at the door of Robert Schumann, the model for an overwhelming proportion of the writing. In fact the problem seems to be more that, without the colouristic resources of contrasting instruments to fall back on, as soon as Tchaikovsky wants to extend a miniature time-span into something dramatic he has a tendency to rant. Of course, not all these works had elevated artistic intentions. Some, like the *Potpourri*, were obviously pot-boilers. It would be absurd to expect consistency of inspiration here. And yet there are surprisingly few instances of zero musical interest, and in every cycle of shorter pieces there are items to be treasured. Postnikova brings to every single piece a virtually ideal blend of affection, respect and intelligence, not to speak of virtuoso command. Not only does this give the textures the best possible chance to 'come off the page', she also has the instinct for inflexions which get us to the heart of Tchaikovsky's individual moods. The piano tone is generally fine, though occasionally dry. A highly desirable library acquisition for all Tchaikovskians and serious lovers of the piano repertoire.

Additional recommendations ...

...Album for the young (orig. piano version)[a]. Album for the young (for string quartet, arr. Dubinsky)[b]. [a]**Luba Edlina** (pf); [b]**Rostislav Dubinsky** (vn); [b]**Mimi Zweig** (vn); [b]**Jerry Horner** (va); [b]**Yuli Turovsky** (vc). Chandos Ⓕ CHAN8365 (59 minutes: DDD: 11/85).

...Album for the young, Op. 39. **Debussy** Children's Corner. **Schumann** Kinderszenen, Op. 15. **Idil Biret** (pf). Naxos Ⓢ 8 550885 (66 minutes: DDD: 10/94).

...Piano Sonata in G major, Op. 37. **Mussorgsky** Pictures at an Exhibition. **Sviatoslav Richter** (pf). Melodiya mono Ⓜ 74321 29469-2* (61 minutes: ADD: 6/96).

Tchaikovsky The Seasons, Op. 37b. Six Morceaux composés sur un seul thème, Op. 21. **Mikhail Pletnev** (pf). Virgin Classics Ⓕ VC5 45042-2 (66 minutes: DDD: 12/94). Recorded 1994. ⒼⒼ

Pletnev finds colours and depths in *The Seasons* that few others have found even intermittently. Schumann is revealed as a major influence, not only on the outward features of the style, but on the whole expressive mood and manner. The opening of "May" is straight from the contemplative Schumann – his Eusebius persona – while the mercurial staccato-legato exchanges near the start of "January" are intrusions from the lighter Florestan. That alternation of civilized soulfulness and delicious, faintly wicked humour recurs again and again in this performance. Even the melancholy song of "October" has its tiny touches of Pletnevian naughtiness, but how beautifully the tune itself sings. And as a display of pianism the whole record is outstanding, all the more so because Pletnev's brilliance isn't purely egoistic. Even when he does something unmarked – like attaching the hunting fanfares of "September" to the final unison of "August" – he's so persuasive that you could believe that this is somehow inherent, if not actually explicit, in the material. There's plenty of poetry, colour and panache in Postnikova's interpretation (see above), but Pletnev has the edge – a touch more brilliance here, more singing eloquence there, a slightly broader palette, and above all a unique ability to surprise. Pletnev's coupling, the six *Morceaux*, Op. 21, emerge here as fascinating, richly enjoyable works. This is all exceptional playing, and the recording – bright in the treble, but also warm in tone – is ideally attuned to all its moods and colours.

Tchaikovsky Morceaux – Op. 10 (Nos. 1 and 2 from Eurodisc 205 455, 9/84; remainder new to UK, recorded 1983); Op. 19 – No. 1, Rêverie du soir, No. 5, Capriccioso; Op. 40 – No. 2, Chanson triste, No. 8, Valse; Op. 51 – No. 1, Valse de salon, No. 3, Menuetto scherzoso, No. 5, Romance; Op. 72 – No. 5, Méditation, No. 12, L'espiègle, No. 15, Un poco di Chopin. Romance in F minor, Op. 5. Valse-scherzo in A major, Op. 7 (all from 205 455). The Seasons, Op. 37*b* – No. 1, January; No. 5, May; No. 6, June; No. 11, November (Eurodisc 610 075, 10/84). **Sviatoslav Richter** (pf). Olympia Ⓟ OCD334 (80 minutes: DDD/ADD: 1/94). Recorded 1983.   ⓖⓖⓖ
Richter elevates Tchaikovsky's miniatures far beyond the salon. No interpretative frills, just trenchant fingerwork and perfectly sculpted sound, so that slight unbendings become immensely touching. The effect is to convey not so much the surface melancholy of these pieces as their underlying strength of character. A curious sense of permanence comes through, as though the music is being contemplated rather than felt. Not for imitation, perhaps (and who could imitate such perfect harmonic and structural weighting?), but this is breathtaking, inspiring artistry, and it sets its own terms. Sound-quality is on the dry side. But Richter's is the sort of playing which positively benefits from close analytical scrutiny, and serious collectors of piano recordings should need no further encouragement.

New review

Tchaikovsky Eugene Onegin – Let me perish, but first let me summon. The Queen of Spades – What am I crying for, what is it?. The Enchantress – Where are you, beloved? ... Hurry to my side. Oprichnik – I heard voices and footsteps.
Verdi La forza del destino – Son giunta! ... Madre, pietosa Vergine[a]; Pace, pace, mio Dio. Otello – Mia madre aveva ... Piangea cantando ... Ave Maria. Aida – Qui Radames verra? ... O patria mia. Il trovatore – Tacea la notte placida ... Di tale amor. **Galina Gorchakova** (sop); [a]**Chorus and Orchestra of the Kirov Opera / Valery Gergiev.** Philips Ⓟ 446 405-2PH (60 minutes: DDD: 3/96). Texts and translations included. Recorded 1995. *Gramophone Editor's choice.*   ⓖ
Gorchakova promises to be one of the vocal giants of her generation. This recital programme marks her first steps into the Italian repertoire on disc. For a star of the Kirov, Verdi's St Petersburg opera – *La forza del destino* – makes an apt choice. Arriving at the monastery gate, her Leonora immediately announces herself as a Verdi soprano of tragic stature, shaping "Madre, pietosa Vergine" with the dark colouring of a troubled soul. The Willow Song from *Otello* is predictably doom-laden, for Gorchakova is no simple, creamy, lyrical Desdemona. The Aida is less successful and sounds as if it is not yet fully in her voice. It might have been better to offer "Ritorna vincitor", as she seems uncomfortable with long, slow phrases around the top of the stave. The top C is very loud and the conclusion, broken off sharply in full voice, is not what Verdi asks for. After that, the *Trovatore* goes much better: the aria has splendid vocal depth and the cabaletta (one verse only) is surprisingly nimble, especially at Gergiev's brilliant pace. Elsewhere his conducting of the Verdi could do with more pace.
As an interpreter of Tchaikovsky, Gorchakova has already won her laurels on the stage. Despite the size and dark colour of the voice, her soprano is still youthful enough for her to play a plausible Tatyana and the Letter Scene will be one of the major reasons for acquiring this disc. The heart of the scene is sung with the kind of *pianissimo* that one would use to carry to the back of the theatre, rather than an inward *pianissimo* intended for the microphone. The *Queen of Spades* aria (Lisa's short solo from Act 1, not her main aria) is so full of beautiful, soaring tone that one resents being cut off just at the point where Herman enters for their duet. The brief aria from *The Enchantress* includes an exciting high B. Elsewhere there is one worrying sign to be mentioned. That is a tendency to go flat when the music is soft and slow (both the *Otello* and the *Aida* suffer from passages of sinking pitch) and one has to hope that difficulties like this are not allowed to defeat her. Gorchakova is no highly polished automaton as a singer, as we know from a couple of problematical live appearances. Her artistry is about letting this voice out of its cage and harnessing its formidable energy. The Philips recording team have done well to capture it so truthfully in the studio. A vocal beast like this is not easily tamed.

Tchaikovsky My genius, my angel, my friend. Take my heart away. Songs, Op. 6 – No. 1, Do not believe, my friend; No. 2, Not a word, o my friend; No. 5, Why?; No. 6, None but the lonely heart. Cradle song, Op. 16 No. 1. Reconciliation, Op. 25 No. 1. The fearful minute, Op. 28 No. 6. It was in the early spring, Op. 38 No. 2. Songs, Op. 60 – No. 6, Frenzied nights; No. 7, Gipsy's song; No. 12, The mild stars shone for us. Songs, Op. 63 – No. 4, The first meeting; No. 5, The fires in the rooms were already out. Serenade, Op. 65 No. 1. Songs, Op. 73 – No. 2, Night; No. 4, The sun has set; No. 6, Again, as before, alone. **Olga Borodina** (mez); **Larissa Gergieva** (pf). Philips Ⓟ 442 013-2PH (60 minutes: DDD: 6/94). Translations included. Recorded 1993. *Gramophone Editor's choice.*   ⓖⓖ
Olga Borodina is among the most considered of Tchaikovsky interpreters on disc. In the "Cradle song", one of Tchaikovsky's most haunting pieces, Joan Rodgers sounds carefree as she rocks her baby to sleep, where Borodina is heavier, sensing dark threats all around. Larissa Gergieva adds to the unsettling atmosphere of that song by stressing the chromatic tensions in the accompaniment. In general, it might have been better to have had a pianist less amenable to slow speeds than Gergieva, but Borodina has such a range of colour and expression in her voice that she can fill the time

profitably. One marvels at the beauty of the singing and admires its sustained intensity. In "Night" a darkness descends over the voice from the opening lines, but in "Again, as before, alone" she tries something even more daring, draining all the life and vibrancy from her tone in a way that is quite unforgettable. One would hardly dare play the final track often (Hvorostovsky is matter-of-fact by comparison). The booklet does not include Russian texts either in Cyrillic or transliteration, but there is a free CD, "Presenting Olga Borodina" in three excerpts from existing Philips opera sets. In fact, there is no need to persuade us that the young Russian mezzo is a star: Borodina is one of the major singers of her generation and this recital demands that she be accepted on her own terms.

Additional recommendations ...

...Songs – Op. 6: No. 4, A tear trembles; No. 6, None but the lonely heart. Op. 25: No. 1, Reconciliation. Op. 28: No. 6, The fearful minute. Op. 38: No. 1, Don Juan's Serenade. Op. 60: No. 4, The nightingale; No. 11, Exploit. Op. 63: No. 2, I opened the window. Op. 73: No. 6, Again, as before, alone. **Rachmaninov** Op. 4: No. 1, Oh no, I beg you, forsake me not; No. 3, In the silence of the secret night; No. 4, Sing not to me, beautiful maiden. Op. 8: No. 5, The dream. Op. 14: No. 9, She is as lovely as the noon. Op. 21: No. 6, Fragment from Musset. Op. 26: – No. 2, He took all from me; No. 6, Christ is risen; No. 13, When yesterday we met. **Dmitri Hvorostovsky** (bar); **Oleg Boshniakovich** (pf). Philips Ⓟ 432 119-2PH (52 minutes: DDD: 10/91).

...Songs – Op. 6: No. 1, Do not believe, my friend; No. 2, Not a word, o my friend; No. 5, Why?; No. 6, None but the lonely heart. Cradle song, Op. 16 No. 1. The canary, Op. 25 No. 4. Op. 28: No. 3, Why did I dream of you?; No. 6, The fearful minute. Op. 38: No. 2, It was in the early spring; No. 3, At the ball. Op. 47: No. 1, If only I had known; No. 6, Does the day reign?; No. 7, Was I not a little blade of grass?. Op. 54: No. 8, The cuckoo; No. 9, Spring song; No. 10, Lullaby in a storm. Op. 60: No. 1, Last night; No. 4, The nightingale; No. 10, Behind the window in the shadow. Op. 63 – Serenade: O child beneath thy window. To forget so soon. **Joan Rodgers** (sop); **Roger Vignoles** (pf). Hyperion Ⓟ CDA66617 (65 minutes: DDD: 2/93).

...Songs, Op. 47 – No. 1, If only I had known; No. 6, Does the day reign?; No. 7, Was I not a little blade of grass? Zemfira's song. *Coupled with works by* **Mussorgsky** and **Rachmaninov** Ewa **Podles** (contr); **Graham Johnson** (pf). Forlane Ⓟ UCD16683 (70 minutes: DDD: 5/95). *See review in the Collections section; refer to the Index to Reviews.*

New review

Tchaikovsky Songs, Op. 6 – No. 1, Do not believe, my friend; No. 2, Not a word, o my friend; No. 4, A tear trembles; No. 5, Why?; No. 6, None but the lonely heart. Reconciliation, Op. 25 No. 1. No response, or word, or greeting, Op. 28 No. 5. Songs, Op. 38 – No. 1, Don Juan's Serenade; No. 2, It was in the early spring; No. 3, At the ball; No. 5, The love of a dead man. Songs, Op. 47 – No. 3, Dusk fell on the earth; No. 4, Sleep, poor friend; No. 5, I bless you, forests. Songs, Op. 57 – No. 2, On the golden cornfields; No. 5, Death. Frenzied nights, Op. 60 No. 6. I should like in a single word. My genius, my angel, my friend. **Sergei Leiferkus** (bar); **Semion Skigin** (pf). BMG Conifer Ⓟ 75605-51266-2 (62 minutes: DDD: 8/96). Texts and translations included.

This first volume in Leiferkus's collection of Tchaikovsky's songs with Semion Skigin contains a good number of favourites. He has the innate sympathy for the melodic lines to refresh even so well-known, and often abused, a song as the one usually called in this country *None but the lonely heart*. This is beautifully sung, with a tinge of mournfulness in the tone and a long, carefully crafted shading of the melody. He can also turn to a hearty, even ruthless tone for the vehemence of *Don Juan's Serenade*, a fine partnership with Skigin as the piano hurtles forward mercilessly under the rollicking of the tune. Two songs of oblique love are among the best in the whole recital. *My genius, my angel, my friend* is tenderly phrased, as if all leading towards the long, held note that closes the song, on the cherished words "moy drug" – "my friend". There is also gentleness, and that sense of love never wholly grasped which haunted Tchaikovsky so bitterly, in *At the ball* – one of his most moving songs – as the singer cannot bear to let the vision glimpsed across the crowded dance floor vanish altogether. Leiferkus seems in a few of the songs to be placed a little far back for the best effect, but in general the balance is carefully arranged so as to keep voice and piano in proper focus with each other. Certainly this is necessary in songs where melodic lines can blend so skilfully. Here is a recital of the quality one would expect from so fine an artist.

Tchaikovsky The Snow Maiden. **Irina Mishura-Lekhtman** (mez); **Vladimir Grishko** (ten); **Michigan University Musical Society Choral Union; Detroit Symphony Orchestra / Neeme Järvi**. Chandos Ⓟ CHAN9324 (79 minutes: ADD: 3/95). Text and translation included. Recorded 1994.

Tchaikovsky wrote his incidental music for Ostrovsky's *Snow Maiden* in 1873, and though he accepted it was not the best of which he was capable, he retained an affection for it and was upset when Rimsky-Korsakov came along with his full-length opera on the subject. The tale of love frustrated had its appeal for Tchaikovsky, even though he was not to make as much as Rimsky was of the failed marriage between Man and Nature. But though he did not normally interest himself much in descriptions of the natural world, there are charming numbers that any lover of Tchaikovsky's music will surely be delighted to encounter. A strong sense of a Russian folk celebration, and of the interaction of the natural and supernatural worlds, also comes through, especially in the earlier part of the work. There is a delightful dance and chorus for the birds, and a powerful monologue for Winter; this is vigorously but somewhat hectoringly sung by Alexander Arkhipov for Chistiakov (listed below), where Vladimir Grishko, placed further back, sounds more magical. Natalia Erassova (also for Chistiakov) gets round the rapid enunciation of Lel's second song without much difficulty, but does not quite bring the character to life; Irina Mishura-Lekhtman has a brighter sparkle. Chistiakov's Shrove Tuesday procession goes at a much steadier pace than Järvi's, and is thus the more celebratory and ritual where the other is a straightforward piece of merriment. Both performances have much to recommend them, and it is not by a great deal that Järvi's is preferable. The balance is further tilted by CdM providing only an English (and French) translation of the text unmatched to a Russian text or transliteration, making it hard to gather what is going on at any given moment; Chandos provide transliteration and English translation.

Additional recommendation ...

…**Natalia Erassova** (sop); **Alexander Arkhipov** (ten); **Nikolai Vassiliev** (bar); **Russian State Choir; orchestra / Andrey Chistiakov.** CdM Russian Season Ⓔ LDC288 090 (73 minutes: DDD: 3/95).

Tchaikovsky Eugene Onegin. **Dmitri Hvorostovsky** (bar) Eugene Onegin; **Nuccia Focile** (sop) Tatyana; **Neil Shicoff** (ten) Lensky; **Olga Borodina** (mez) Olga; **Alexander Anisimov** (bass) Prince Gremin; **Sarah Walker** (mez) Larina; **Irina Arkhipova** (mez) Filipievna; **Francis Egerton** (ten) Triquet; **Hervé Hennequin** (bass-bar) Captain; **Sergei Zadvorny** (bass) Zaretsky; **St Petersburg Chamber Choir; Orchestre de Paris / Semyon Bychkov.** Philips Ⓔ 438 235-2PH2 (two discs: 141 minutes: DDD: 12/93). Notes, text and translation included. Recorded 1992. *Gramophone Editor's choice.*   Ⓖ

Tchaikovsky Eugene Onegin. **Evgeny Belov** (bar) Eugene Onegin; **Galina Vishnevskaya** (sop) Tatyana; **Sergei Lemeshev** (ten) Lensky; **Larissa Adyeva** (mez) Olga; **Ivan Petrov** (bass) Prince Gremin; **Valentina Petrova** (sop) Larina; **Evgenya Verbitskaya** (mez) Filipyevna; **Andrei Sokolov** (ten) Triquet; **Igor Mikhailov** (bass) Zaretsky; **Georgi Pankov** (bass) Captain; **Bolshoi Theatre Chorus and Orchestra / Boris Khaikin.** Melodiya mono Ⓜ 74321 17090-2* (two discs: 140 minutes: ADD: 12/94). From Parlophone PMA1050/52 (7/59). Recorded 1955.   Ⓖ

Entirely at the service of Tchaikovsky's marvellous invention, Semyon Bychkov illuminates every detail of the composer's wondrous scoring with pointed delicacy and draws playing of the utmost acuity and beauty from his own Paris orchestra – enhanced by the clear, open recording – and the St Petersburg Choir are superbly disciplined and alert with their words. Focile offers keen-edged yet warm tone and total immersion in Tatyana's character. Aware throughout of the part's dynamic demands, she phrases with complete confidence, eagerly catching the girl's dreamy vulnerability and heightened imagination in the Letter scene, which has that sense of awakened love so essential to it. Hvorostovsky is in his element. His singing has at once the warmth, elegance and refinement Tchaikovsky demands from his anti-hero. Together he, Focile and Bychkov make the finale the tragic climax it should be; indeed the reading of this passage is almost unbearably moving. Shicoff has refined and expanded his Lensky since he recorded it for Levine and Anisimov is a model Gremin, singing his aria with generous tone and phrasing while not making a meal of it. Olga Borodina is a perfect Olga, spirited, a touch sensual, wholly idiomatic with the text – as, of course, is the revered veteran Russian mezzo Arkhipova as Filipievna, an inspired piece of casting. An outright recommendation for a magnificent achievement.

The classic Khaikin version, generally accepted as the most convincing and knowledgeable performance the work has yet received, wears its 40 years lightly: indeed, the recording of the voices and even the orchestra, albeit in mono, has a great deal to teach producers today in terms of a natural sound. The reading's virtues are, above all, Khaikin's unforced, unexaggerated, wholly integrated direction, with players and singers who know the score from the inside giving an entirely idiomatic reading (if you can forgive the watery horns). From the very first scene you feel the impetus of the performance and are drawn into its truly Russian ambience. Khaikin brings into perfect balance the dramatic and yearning aspects of the score in a lyrical, delicate reading. With his incisive but sympathetic beat, he clearly characterizes those many passages of intimate feeling without which any account of the piece crucially fails. The young Vishnevskaya is a near-ideal Tatyana, having exactly the right voice for the part and totally convincing us that she *is* Tatyana. She is incomparable. What a genuine, unsophisticated outpouring of passion the Letter scene becomes as she interprets it, and how superbly she sings it! Few tenors before or since Lemeshev have offered precisely the right tone and character for Lensky. From his first entry we hear a plaintive timbre and easy way with the language that proclaim a true poet. Belov's Onegin, though not quite in that class, is a resolute member of a real ensemble and rises to the challenge of the final scenes. All that disappoints is the presentation: numerous spelling mistakes and no libretto.

Additional recommendations ...

…**Soloists; John Alldis Choir; Orchestra of the Royal Opera House, Covent Garden / Sir Georg Solti.** Decca Ⓔ 417 413-2DH2 (two discs: 143 minutes: ADD: 8/87).

…**Soloists; Leipzig Radio Chorus; Dresden Staatskapelle / James Levine.** DG Ⓔ 423 959-2GH2 (two discs: 149 minutes: DDD: 3/89).

…**Soloists; Sofia National Opera Chorus; Sofia Festival Orchestra / Emil Tchakarov.** Sony Classical Ⓔ S2K45539 (two discs: 143 minutes: DDD: 3/91).

Tchaikovsky Iolanta. **Galina Gorchakova** (sop) Iolanta; **Gegam Grigorian** (ten) Vaudémont; **Dmitri Hvorostovsky** (bar) Robert; **Sergei Alexashkin** (bass) King René; **Nikolai Putilin** (bar) Ibn-Hakia; **Larissa Diadkova** (mez) Martha; **Nikolai Gassiev** (ten) Alméric; **Tatiana Kravtsova** (sop) Brigitta; **Olga Korzhenskaya** (mez) Laura; **Gennadi Bezzubenkov** (bar) Bertrand; **Chorus and Orchestra of the Kirov Opera, St Petersburg / Valery Gergiev.** Philips Ⓕ 442 796-2PH2 (two discs: 96 minutes: DDD: 7/96). Notes, text and translation included.

Iolanta, the touching little princess, blind and virginal, into whose darkness and isolation there eventually shines the 'bright angel' of Duke Robert, is delightfully sung by Galina Gorchakova. There is a freshness and sense of vulnerability here, especially in the opening scenes with Martha in the garden as she sings wistfully of something that appears to be lacking in her life: the Arioso is done charmingly and without sentimentality. Gegam Grigorian sometimes sounds pinched and under strain, even in the Romance. He is also overshadowed by Dmitri Hvorostovsky who is here at his best: warm and with a somewhat dusky tone, responding with great sensitivity to the often elusive melodic lines which Tchaikovsky writes in this, his last opera. The King, Provence's 'bon roi René', is benignly if a little throatily sung by Sergei Alexashkin, and he has at hand a sturdy-voiced Ibn-Hakia in Nikolai Putilin. Valery Gergiev conducts a sensitive performance, responding constructively to the unusual scoring (much disliked by the possibly jealous Rimsky-Korsakov), and not overplaying the more demonstrative elements in a score that gains most through some understatement. The booklet very sensibly prints in parallel columns a transliteration of the Russian, then English, German and French; the text in the original Cyrillic is printed separately at the end.

Tchaikovsky Mazeppa. **Sergei Leiferkus** (bar) Mazeppa; **Galina Gorchakova** (sop) Mariya; **Anatoly Kotscherga** (bass) Kochubey; **Larissa Dyadkova** (mez) Liubov; **Sergei Larin** (ten) Andrei; **Monte Pederson** (bar) Orlik; **Richard Margison** (ten) Iskra; **Heinz Zednik** (ten) Drunken Cossack; **Stockholm Royal Opera Chorus; Gothenburg Symphony Orchestra / Neeme Järvi.** DG Ⓕ 439 906-2GH3 (three discs: 166 minutes: DDD: 11/94). Notes, text and translation included. Recorded 1993. Ⓖ

It was *Eugene Onegin* that turned Tchaikovsky into Russia's best-loved composer, not the more calculated recipes for success of *The Maid of Orleans*, *Mazeppa* or *Charodeyka* ("The Enchantress"). *Onegin* works for us today because it is sincerely felt from start to finish; but the fascination of those lesser-known operas lies in the way they move in and out of scenes and predicaments which clearly touched the composer. Of the three, *Mazeppa* has the greatest share of first-rate music, extending our appreciation of Tchaikovsky's blacker side as he attempts to reflect the cruelty inflicted by the anti-hero. Gorchakova's response to Mazeppa's patriotic scheme in Act 2 gives us a fairer picture of the Gorchakova phenomenon than ill-focused earlier stages of this semi-interpretation: shining strength above the stave goes some way towards redeeming the placidity of the whole. It takes Larissa Dyadkova's far more committed cut and thrust in the electrifying scene between Mariya and her mother to spur Gorchakova to a more consistent sense of occasion. Anatoly Kotscherga would clearly like to deliver more than his limited vocal resources permit him as the outraged father seethes in Act 1 but he rises to his supreme challenge as Tchaikovsky plumbs the depths for Kochubey's prison monologue: here, indeed, are the range of tone-colour and introspection missing from Gorchakova's mad scenes. Leiferkus has less to deal with as the headstrong tyrant; even so, he strikes firmly at the heart of darkness, and there could be no more free- and easy-sounding delivery of the wonderful aria that Tchaikovsky gave his baritone at a late stage in the compositional process. In the cases of both the victim's darkest hour and this, the conqueror's most sensitive one, Järvi reinforces the orchestra's role as an equal partner in characterization – driving home the lower-instrument gloom and terror of Kochubey's circumstances, underlining the light and lovely, woodwind-dominated scoring of "O, Mariya!" as Mazeppa muses Gremin-like on the sincerity of his late-flowering love. As a whole the set is a faithful testament to *Mazeppa*'s intermittent power to move and appal.

Tchaikovsky The Queen of Spades. **Gegam Grigorian** (ten) Herman; **Maria Gulegina** (sop) Lisa; **Irina Arkhipova** (mez) Countess; **Nikolai Putilin** (bar) Count Tomsky; **Vladimir Chernov** (bar) Prince Yeletsky; **Olga Borodina** (mez) Pauline; **Vladimir Solodovnikov** (ten) Chekalinsky; **Sergei Alexashkin** (bass) Surin; **Evgeni Boitsov** (ten) Chaplitsky; **Nikolai Gassiev** (ten) Major-domo; **Gennadi Bezzubenkov** (bass) Narumov; **Ludmila Filatova** (mez) Governess; **Tatiana Filimonova** (sop) Masha; **Kirov Theatre Chorus and Orchestra / Valery Gergiev.** Philips Ⓕ 438 141-2PH3 (three discs: 166 minutes: DDD: 10/93). Notes, text and translation included. Recorded 1992.

There are major problems with all the current sets of *The Queen of Spades*, but Valery Gergiev, one of the outstanding Tchaikovskians of the day, here coaxes from a thoroughly Western-sounding Kirov Theatre Orchestra what is surely the most refined account of the score yet recorded, and one that is never lacking energy or full-blooded attack. His is not so much a compromise approach as one which stresses fatalism and underlying sadness. The recording was made in the Kirov Theatre itself, and there is admittedly some constriction to the orchestral sound-picture; but for many the atmosphere of a real stage-venue will be a plus, and the all-important balance between voices and orchestra is just right. If the spine still fails to tingle as often as it should, that is mainly a reflection of the respectable but unexciting singing, though it would be folly to expect greater thrills from any of the three rival sets, and in many ways Gergiev's conducting elevates his above them all.

Additional recommendations ...

...**Soloists; Gouslarche Boys' Choir; Svetoslav Obretenov National Chorus; Sofia Festival Orchestra / Emil Tchakarov.** Sony Classical Ⓕ S3K45720 (three discs: 159 minutes: DDD· 12/90).

...**Soloists; American Boychoir; Tanglewood Festival Chorus; Boston Symphony Orchestra / Seiji Ozawa.** RCA Victor Red Seal Ⓕ 09026-60992-2 (three discs: 156 minutes: DDD: 11/92).

Further listening ...

...Variations on a Rococo Theme in A major, Op. 33. Nocturne in D minor, Op. 19, No. 4. Pezzo capriccioso in B minor, Op. 62. Legend: Christ had a garden, Op. 54 No. 5. Was I not a little blade of grass. Andante cantabile for Cello and Strings, Op. 11. **Raphael Wallfisch** (vc); **English Chamber Orchestra / Geoffrey Simon.** Chandos CHAN8347 (2/85).

...Variations on a Rococo Theme in A minor, Op. 33. Nocturne in C sharp minor, Op. 19 No. 4. *Coupled with* **Miaskovsky** Cello Concerto in C minor, Op. 66. **Shostakovich** The Limpid Stream, Op. 39 – Adagio. **Julian Lloyd Webber** (vc); **London Symphony Orchestra / Maxim Shostakovich.** Philips 434 106-2PH (5/92).

...Variations on a Rococo Theme, Op. 33. *Coupled with* **Dvořák** Cello Concerto in B minor, B191. **Mstislav Rostropovich** (vc); **Berlin Philharmonic Orchestra / Herbert von Karajan.** DG The Originals 447 413-2GOR (5/95). *See review under Dvořák; refer to the Index to Reviews.* *Gramophone classical 100.*   ⒼⒼⒼ

...Méditation, Op. 42 No. 1 (arr. Glazunov). **Khachaturian** Violin Concerto in D minor. **Itzhak Perlman** (vn); **Israel Philharmonic Orchestra / Zubin Mehta.** EMI CDC7 47087-2 (7/85). *See review under Khachaturian; refer to the Index to Reviews.*

...Andante cantabile, Op. 11ᶜ. *Coupled with* **Dvořák** Cello Concerto in B minor, B191ª. Silent woods, B173ᶜ. Rondo in G minor, B171ᵇ. **Arensky** Chant triste, Op. 56 No. 3ᶜ. **Davïdov** At the fountain, Op. 20 No. 2ᵇ. **Pieter Wispelwey** (vc); **Paul Giacometti** (ᵇpf/ᶜharm); ªNetherlands Philharmonic Orchestra / Lawrence Renes. Channel Classics CCS8695 (6/96).

...Suites – No. 3 in G major, Op. 55. No. 4. **USSR Symphony Orchestra / Evgeni Svetlanov.** Melodiya 74321 17100-2.

...Symphony No. 7 in E flat major (cptd. Bogatryryev). Piano Concerto No. 3 in E flat major, Op. 73ª. ªGeoffrey Tozer (pf); London Philharmonic Orchestra / Neeme Järvi. Chandos CHAN9130 (4/93).

...Elegy in G major (in honour of Ivan Samarin). *Coupled with* **Sibelius** Suite champêtre, Op. 98ᵇ. Canzonetta, Op. 62ª. **Dvořák** Two Waltzes, B105. Nocturne in B major, B47. Humoresque in G flat major, B187. **Elgar** Salut d'amour, Op. 12. Sospiri, Op. 70. **Grieg** Two Melodies, Op. 53. Two Nordic Melodies, Op. 63. Two Elegiac Melodies, Op. 34. **Serenata of London / Barry Wilde.** IMP Classics PCD1108 (2/95).

...Souvenir d'un lieu cher, Op. 42 – No. 1, Méditation in D minor. Valse-scherzo, Op. 34. *Coupled with works by* **Bartók, Brahms, Chaminade** and **Falla** Kyoko Takezawa (vn); **Philip Moll** (pf). RCA Victor Red Seal 09026 60704-2 (2/93). *See review in the Collections section; refer to the Index to Reviews.*

Alexander Tcherepnin   USSR/French/American 1899-1977

New review

A. Tcherepnin Piano Concertos – No. 1, Op. 12; No. 4, Op. 78, "Fantaisie"; No. 5, Op. 96. **Murray McLachlan** (pf); **Chetham's Symphony Orchestra / Julian Clayton.** Olympia Ⓕ OCD440 (71 minutes: DDD: 12/95). Recorded 1995.

The Tcherepnin piano concertos are in their various ways cast in the same exuberant, heartfelt romantic manner. However, there is considerable variety within this general approach. The First, written in Paris in 1920, takes not the slightest interest in what was beginning to occupy French musicians and most other Parisian expatriates at the beginning of that exciting decade: it looks east, to a Georgia which Tcherepnin had known before exile, and north to an influence from, of all composers, Sibelius. The result is inventive but, predictably, less original than the later concertos. The Fourth, written in 1947, looks further east to China, a country which Tcherepnin had toured in the 1930s and where he met his future wife. It is more a set of three tone-poems, lightly accommodating Chinese musical gestures into the familiar romantic language, than a symphonic concerto. The Fifth belongs to 1963, and is a much more enigmatic work, and also by some way the most original of the entire set of six. Murray McLachlan is a fine advocate of this music, which is technically demanding and, in the Fifth Concerto, also demanding of a subtle understanding if the most is to be made of its laconic gestures and rather greyer lyricism. The Chetham's Symphony Orchestra reaffirm their ability to cope with technically testing scores and, guided by Julian Clayton, to make musical sense of them with the command of more experienced musicians.

Further listening ...

...Piano Concertos – No. 2, Op. 26; No. 3, Op. 48; No. 6, Op. 99. **Murray McLachlan** (pf); **Chetham's Symphony Orchestra / Julian Clayton.** Olympia OCD439 (11/94).

...Symphony No. 4, Op. 91. Suite, Op. 87. Russian Dances. Romantic Overture, Op. 67. **Košice State Philharmonic Orchestra / Win-Sie Yip.** Marco Polo 8 223380 (10/92).

Georg Philipp Telemann
German 1681-1767

Telemann Concerto for Three Horns, Violin and Orchestra in D major[a]. Overture-Suites – C major, TWV55: C5, "La Bouffonne"; F major, TWV55: F11, "Alster Echo". Concerto in G major, "Grillen-Symphonie". [a]**Anthony Halstead**, [a]**Christian Rutherford**, [a]**Raul Diaz** (hns); **Collegium Musicum 90 / Simon Standage** (vn). Chandos Chaconne Ⓕ CHAN0547 (70 minutes: DDD: 7/94). ✐   Ⓖ

This release provides some very varied and exotic fare, in the form of an assorted programme of orchestral music showing Telemann at his most irrepressibly good-humoured and imaginative. There's a concerto for three rattling horns and a solo violin (a splendid sound, with the horns recorded at what seems like the ideal distance), and an elegant suite for strings which sounds like Handel, Bach and a few French composers all thrown in together. More striking, though, is the most substantial piece on the disc, the *Alster Echo* Overture-Suite, a nine-movement work for strings, oboes and horns full of tricks and surprises occasioned by a whole host of representative titles. Thus "Hamburg Carillons" brings us horns imitating bells, "Concerto of Frogs and Crows" has some mischievously scrunchy wrong notes, and in "Alster Echo" there's a complex network of echoes between oboes and horns. But the show-stealer by a long way on this disc is the *Grillen-Symphonie* ("Cricket Symphony"), which Telemann jokingly noted on the manuscript as being "in the Italian, English, Scottish and Polish styles". What he meant by that is hardly the point; this is a work for the gloriously silly scoring of piccolo, alto chalumeau, oboe, violins, viola, and two double-basses, a somewhat Stravinskian combination that you're unlikely to encounter every day. But it's not just the instrumentation that's irresistibly odd. There is a slow movement with curious, melancholy woodwind interventions a little reminiscent of *Harold in Italy*, and a finale which, with its boisterously galumphing double-basses, is quite a hoot. You'll be hard put not to enjoy this release.

New review

Telemann Oboe Concertos – No. 2 in C minor[a]; No. 3 in D major[a]; No. 4 in D minor[a]; No. 6 in E minor[a]. Concertos for Oboe d'amore and Strings – No. 1 in G major[b]; No. 2 in A major[b]. **Il Fondamento / Paul Dombrecht.** Vanguard Classics Pasacaille Collection Ⓜ 99701 (72 minutes: DDD: 2/96). ✐ Recorded 1994.

The oboe was an instrument for which Telemann wrote unfailingly well. One of the finest achievements here is a Concerto in C minor whose sustained, uncompromising dissonant first utterance commands an attention which is never allowed to wander throughout its four tautly constructed movements. The Flemish baroque oboist Paul Dombrecht, who also directs his group Il Fondamento, gives an emotionally charged performance which benefits from effectively shaded dynamics. Of the three remaining oboe concertos on the disc only that in E minor, one of the best known, is comparably well sustained musically. The most arresting of its four movements, a layout shared with all the concertos here, is the melancholy opening *Andante*, which is among the high points of affective oboe writing in the late baroque period. There are some poignant moments in this eloquent movement and Dombrecht explores them to the full. In the vigorous *Allegro* that follows there is some wonderfully conversational writing between oboe and strings, arrested momentarily by an expressive passage of wistful *andante* before the main thread of the piece is drawn together again. The two remaining concertos of the programme are for oboe d'amore and strings. Both contain music in Telemann's headiest vein. There are sonorities here that no lover of Telemann's music should miss and by and large the performances are first-rate.

Additional recommendation ...

...Oboe Concertos – No. 4[a]; No. 8 in F minor[a]; Oboe d'amore and Strings No. 2 in A major[b]; Oboe and Strings No. 2 in C minor[a]; Oboe d'amore Concerto in E minor[b]; Flute, Oboe d'amore and Viola Concerto in E major[c]. [c]**Graham Mayger** (fl); [c]**Elizabeth Watson** (va d'amore); **London Harpsichord Ensemble / Sarah Francis** ([a]ob/[b]ob d'amore). Unicorn-Kanchana Ⓕ DKPCD9131 (67 minutes: DDD: 8/94).

Telemann Concerto for Two Oboes, Three Trumpets, Timpani and Strings[d]. Overture-Suite in G minor, TWV55: g 4. Musique de table – Overture-Suite in D major, TWV55: D 1. **Paul Goodwin**, [a]**Lorraine Wood** (obs); [a]**Mark Bennett**, [a]**Michael Harrison**, [a]**Nicholas Thompson** (tpts); **The English Concert / Trevor Pinnock.** Archiv Produktion Ⓕ 439 893-2AH (59 minutes: DDD: 8/94). ✐   ⒼⒼ

This extensive D major work is well represented in the catalogue. In the circumstances, this piece for solo oboe and trumpet with strings is a less desirable proposition than the richly endowed and little-known gems which we have been introduced to by Pinnock so far. This disc contains only one such work but it is a flawless G minor Suite displaying Telemann's brilliant and variegated ideas of blending and offsetting three *concertante* oboes with strings. After the exquisitely balanced overture the picturesque dances are executed with refined characterization, most notably in the robustly Ramellian, "Les Irresoluts". If the inclusion of the Produktion II suite (from Musique de table) is perhaps a missed opportunity for more *objets inconnus*, it is certainly not a waste of air time since it rivals, if not improves upon Goebel's account with the trumpeter, Friedemann Immer (see below). Pinnock's approach is about right in its bold gestures, with the forward placing of the trumpet and oboe making for a persuasive dialogue, even if Mark Bennett's gleaming tone tends to predominate.

Bennett's virtuoso 'natural' trumpet playing is demanded again in a performance of one or two extant concertos Telemann wrote for three trumpets. He and his colleagues are meticulously matched here in a thrilling performance which simply has to be heard by those who relish baroque music at its grandest and most rhetorical. Overall then, another fine achievement.

Additional recommendation ...
...Musique de table – Produktions I-III. **Cologne Musica Antiqua / Reinhard Goebel.** Archiv Produktion Ⓕ 427 619-2AH4 (four discs: 254 minutes: DDD: 10/89). ✐

Telemann Concertos, Volumes 1 and 2. **Collegium Musicum 90 / Simon Standage** (vn). Chandos Ⓕ CHAN0519 and CHAN0512 (two discs, oas: 63 and 64 minutes: DDD: 4/92). ✐ Recorded 1990-91.
   CHAN0519: Concertos – A minor for Violin; E minor for Flute and Violin (Rachel Brown, fl); G major for Four Unaccompanied Violins; A major for Four Violins (Micaela Comberti, Miles Golding, Andrew Manze, vns); E major for Violin. Orchestral Suite in G minor, "La Changeante". *CHAN0512:* Concertos – G major for Violin; D major for Two Flutes, Violin and Cello (Brown, Siu Peasgood, fls; Jane Coe, vc); F sharp minor for Violin; G major for Two Violins (Comberti). Orchestral Suite in B flat major, "Ouverture burlesque".   Ⓖ
It is difficult to mention Telemann without referring to the prolific and eclectic nature of his output, both of which are reflected in his very numerous concertos, and in these recordings the two works that are *not* concertos – *La Changeante* and *Ouverture burlesque*, both of which evoke the spirit of the *commedia dell'arte*. What changes in *La Changeante* is not only the moods of the movements but also their keys; only the first and last of the eight are in the home key of G minor, the others are in a variety of different ones, a most unusual feature at that time. The ouverture-suites are predominantly French in style but the concertos represent Telemann's highly individual variant of Venetian models. Whilst Vivaldi's concertos are predominantly in three movements (quick-slow-quick), Telemann's are usually in four or five, with no set pattern of pace, and they take both *da chiesa* and *da camera* forms. Telemann's muse seems rarely to have slept, likewise his acute sense of instrumental colour. When Playford wrote of "Sprightly and cheerful musick" he was referring to that of the cittern; had he lived a little longer he might have felt the same about that of Telemann, not least if he had heard it played so expertly by Collegium Musicum 90, who are brought into your home by most faithful recorded sound.

Additional recommendation ...
...Concertos – E major for Flute, Oboe d'amore, Viola d'amore and Strings; E minor for Flute, Violin and Strings; D major for Flute, Strings and Continuo; E flat major for Strings and Continuo; G major for Flute, Chalumeau, Oboe, Two Double-Basses, Strings and Continuo. **La Stravaganza, Cologne / Andrew Manze** (vn). Denon Aliare Ⓕ CO-78933 (60 minutes: DDD: 11/95). ✐

Telemann Overture-Suite in A minor[a]. Concerto in E minor for Recorder and Flute[b]. Viola Concerto No. 1 in G major[c]. Overture des Nations: anciens et modernes for Strings and Continuo, TWV55[d]. [b]**Franz Verster** (fl); [c]**Paul Doctor** (va); [a]**South-West German Chamber Orchestra / Friedrich Tilegant**; [bd]**Amsterdam Chamber Orchestra / André Rieu**; [c]**Concerto Amsterdam / Frans Brüggen** ([ab]rec). Teldec Das Alte Werk Ⓜ 9031-77620-2 (69 minutes: ADD: 7/93). ✐ Items marked [abd] recorded 1967, [c]1968.   ⒼⒼ
Four performances of the highest calibre, marvellously recorded in the 1960s and now sounding as fresh as the day they were made. Two of them feature the distinguished recorder player Frans Brüggen (who is now more often heard on disc as a conductor). He is at his inimitable finest, and this is very fine indeed, in the masterly Suite in A minor for recorder and strings (every bit as fine a work as the Bach B minor Suite for the same instrumentation) and the E minor Concerto for recorder, transverse flute and strings with its attractive interplay of solo texture. Here he is joined by Franz Verster. Brüggen then moves to the conductor's podium to direct the Concerto Amsterdam, joined by a superb viola player, Paul Doctor, in the justly famous G major Viola Concerto. The *Ouverture des Nations: anciens et modernes* is another suite (comprising nine movements), full of the composer's most felicitous invention. The music is played with great verve and character and the CD transfer is exemplary. This is possibly one of the finest Telemann collections ever issued on CD.

New review
Telemann Overture-Suite in C major, "Hamburger Ebb und Fluth". Overture-Suite in D major[a]. Concerto in A minor for Two Recorders, Two Oboes and Strings[b]. Concerto in E minor for Recorder, Flute and Strings[c]. [b]**Dominique Gauthier** (fl); [a]**Philippe Foulon** (va da gamba); **Orchestre Musica Antiqua / Christian Mendoze** ([bc]rec). Pierre Verany Ⓕ PV796022 (68 minutes: DDD: 7/96). ✐
An attractive programme of suites and concertos – two of each – comes from the Orchestre Musica Antiqua under their director, Christian Mendoze. Musica Antiqua were founded some 15 years ago but their representation on disc, at least in the UK, has been infrequent. As we might expect, these musicians bring a markedly French atmosphere to Telemann's Suites. And why not? Telemann was drawn to French ouvertures and their appended suites of dances at an early age and his love of them never deserted him. In the Suite in C major, variously subtitled *Wassermusik* and *Hamburger Ebb und*

Fluth, indigenous French gestures especially can be felt in rhythmic *inégalités* and in the ornamented resolution of several final cadences. This Suite is colourfully scored for pairs of recorders and oboes with bassoon and strings and it is the woodwind department of the Ensemble which gives the performance its lustre. That is not to imply any serious shortcoming in the string playing but rather that the recording balance favours the wind instruments. None of the four works, in fact, is well served by the acoustic, which is hollow in sound and reverberant in a way that only intermittently captures the character of the instruments; and the solo and *concertino* players are placed too close to the microphone. Whatever the shortcomings of the recording itself, however – and anyway this is purely a matter of personal preference – the spirited and mainly stylish playing of these musicians is hardly open to question. In the D major Suite the solo viola da gamba, to which Telemann gives pride of place throughout, is expressively played by Philippe Foulon. He is a gambist who proves his eloquence above all in the fine Sarabande of the work. The two concertos are for solo woodwind and strings. The A minor work is scored for pairs of recorders, oboes and violins with basso continuo, while that in E minor, the best-known piece in the programme, features an unusual partnership of recorder and flute, the old and the new, so to speak. The A minor Concerto is the slighter of the two and is the one work here which Telemann enthusiasts may not have in their library. It is an engaging piece with lively dialogue among the three instrumental groups; but it lacks the colourful invention of the E minor Concerto, with its tender slow movements and wild, swirling Polish dance finale. What the performances lack in finesse is generously compensated for in sheer interpretative *esprit*.

Telemann Overture-Suites – G minor, TWV55: g4; A minor, TWV55: a2[a]; C major, TWV55: C6; D major, TWV55: D15; D minor, TWV55: d3; F minor, TWV55: f1[a]. **Vienna Concentus Musicus / Nikolaus Harnoncourt.** Teldec Das Alte Werk Ⓜ 4509-93772-2 (two discs: 148 minutes: ADD: 12/94). ✎ Items marked [a] from SAW19507 (3/68), others recorded 1978. 🄴🄴

Harnoncourt is nowhere more at home than in the aesthetic world of this music. The Overtures of the ravishing G minor Suite and the bolder C major work show him to be a master of noble gesture and purposeful articulation. Compared with Trevor Pinnock's accounts of these two works (see reviews elsewhere), the current performances are less even in terms of orchestral exactitude and pure luxuriance of texture but there is a robust, biting energy about Harnoncourt which is infectious; often, as in the Bourée *en trompette* of the C major work, one imagines that the exaggerated contrasts and deliberate accentuations would appear mannered if executed by anyone other than Harnoncourt. Throughout, he conjures up subtle rhythmic deviations, each paragraph flexibly shaped but still controlled and naturally breathed. If pliancy of this kind is an answer to making sense of baroque phrasing, then texture speaks volumes too: Telemann's oboe writing in particular, and its place within a string body is exceptionally skilled; his scoring of three oboes is especially effective and the oboists play with irresistible *esprit*. The D major Suite is full of instances where their performances brim with personality, contributing greatly to that fruity and ever so musty nose which characterizes Concentus Musicus on vintage form. The recorded sound is full of presence. To sum up: with Harnoncourt one can imagine few exponents better suited to this colourful repertoire. Pinnock's two recent recordings of suites are obligatory for baroque collectors generally but this release is full of many unique delights and it contains three works not otherwise available in the catalogue.

Additional recommendations ...

...A minor, TWV55: a2[a]. Concertos – F major; C major. Sinfonia in F major[a]. **Peter Holtslag** (rec); **The Parley of Instruments / Peter Holman,** [a]**Roy Goodman.** Hyperion Ⓕ CDA66413 (66 minutes: DDD: 10/91). ✎

...A minor. Concerto in C major. Concerto for Recorder, Viola da gamba and Strings in A minor[a]. [a]**Mark Levy** (va da gamba); **New London Consort / Philip Pickett** (rec). L'Oiseau-Lyre Ⓕ 433 043-2OH (68 minutes: DDD: 11/92). ✎

...C major, TWV55: C6; D major, TWV55: D19; B flat major, TTWV55: B10. **The English Concert / Trevor Pinnock.** Archiv Produktion Ⓕ 437 558-2AH (77 minutes: DDD: 6/93). ✎ 🄴🄴

...D major, TWV55: D6[b]; A minor, TWV55: A2[a]. Sinfonia in F major, TWV50: 3[ab]. Concerto for Recorder, Viola da gamba and Strings in A minor[ab]. [a]**Marion Verbruggen** (rec); [b]**Sarah Cunningham** (va da gamba); **Orchestra of the Age of Enlightenment / Monica Huggett.** Harmonia Mundi Ⓕ HMU90 7093 (74 minutes: DDD: 1/94). ✎ 🄴

Telemann Overture-Suites – G major, TWV55: G10, "Burlesque de Quichotte"; F minor, TWV55: f1; D major, TWV55: D15. Concerto for Two Violins and Strings in E minor. **Freiburg Baroque Orchestra / Gottfried von der Goltz.** Deutsche Harmonia Mundi Ⓕ 05472 77321-2 (74 minutes: DDD: 1/95). ✎ Recorded 1993. 🄴

The spontaneous musical gestures and lively imagination of the Freiburg Baroque Orchestra are particularly well suited to the Overture-Suites of Telemann with their colourfully depictive, sometimes programmatic slant. The pieces they have chosen for this new release might almost have been tailor-made for them, so well does their idiom suit the theatrically inclined style of the players. Best known, by far, is the Suite in G major for strings in which Telemann deftly and with humour paints vignettes of the adventures and misadventures of Don Quixote, his horse Rosinante, and his knight Sancho Panza. The suite is one of the most engaging from Telemann's pen and also one of the most imaginatively written of them. Entirely different is the Suite in F minor, its darkly coloured but highly motivated overture establishing an atmosphere of melancholy. The remaining dances are attractive, with the surprising entry of two recorders, otherwise absent from the suite, in the penultimate movement, a Chaconne. This rarely performed work also exists in a two-disc album of suites by Telemann directed by Nikolaus Harnoncourt (reviewed above). The Freiburg account is, in some respects, more polished, but Harnoncourt achieves more interesting sonorities and the elegiac mood is better sustained. The remaining Suite in D major is more richly scored than the other two, with three oboes and a continuo bassoon added to the strings. This piece, too, is included in Harnoncourt's mid-price set and there is little to choose between the two performances other than that Harnoncourt affords greater prominence to the woodwind. In summary, a delightful programme, played with panache and very well recorded.

Telemann Overture-Suites – D major, TWV55: D23; A minor, TWV55: a2; D major, TWV55: D6.
  Cologne Camerata / Michael Schneider (rec). Deutsche Harmonia Mundi Ⓟ 05472 77324-2
  (77 minutes: DDD: 6/95). ✒   ⒼⒼ
In this new release Schneider, both as director and treble recorder player, gives us three of Telemann's overture-suites. Telemann's fecundity in this type of composition seems virtually inexhaustible and, if there is one sphere of activity in which he seldom if ever disappoints, it is this one. The most well-known work here is the Suite in A minor for treble recorder and strings (TWV55: a2) which has enjoyed wide currency over the past 30 years or so. Schneider's playing is agile and he is supported by animated string playing of great character. He is also imaginative if not always entirely apposite in his ornamentation. The "Air à l'Italien" and the Menuets fare especially well in this respect. Where the third suite is concerned (TWV55: D23), this is the first time it has been commercially recorded. It is a late work (1763) dating from near the end of Telemann's life when the composer, though in his eighties, was revealing a fluency in the classical style of composers two generations younger than himself. This spirited piece, which begins with a French ouverture full of interest and fantasy, contains an appealing blend of the old and the new with two captivating Menuets full of *galanteries*, a poignant lament (Plainte), a trio for two flutes and bassoon, and a rousing Fanfare for flutes, bassoon, horn and strings, which stand out from a notably colourful assembly of movements.

Telemann Essercizii Musici – Trio No. 2 in G major, TWV42: G6[a]; Trio No. 4 in A major,
  TWV42: A6[b]; Solo No. 6 in C major, TWV41: 3 (arr. Christensen)[e]; Trio No. 8 in B flat
  major, TWV42: B 4[d]; Solo No. 12 in F major, TWV32: 4 (arr. Christensen)[e]; Trio No. 12 in
  E flat major, TWV42: Es 3[f]. [d]**Conrad Steinmann** (rec); [b]**Oskar Peter** (fl); [f]**Miguel Piguet** (ob);
  [a]**Paolo Pandolfo** (va da gamba); [abdf]**Imke David** (vc); [abdf]**Andreas Staier**, [ce]**Jesper Bøje Christensen**
  (hpds). Deutsche Harmonia Mundi Ⓟ 05472 77169-2 (74 minutes: DDD: 8/93). ✒
  Recorded 1990.   Ⓖ
Telemann's *Essercizii Musici* (1739) is a collection of alternating "Solos" and "Trios" a summary of the composer's best work in these forms; but while the Trios have been frequently performed both in concert and on disc some of the Solos remain less well-known. This delightful programme devised and performed by members of the Schola Cantorum Basiliensis offers all the pieces in *Essercizii Musici* calling for obbligato harpsichord. The four Trios with obbligato harpsichord each has a different instrument to partner it and are captivating works, skilfully and appealingly written. They are among the most impressive testaments to his ability in writing in a form for which he was greatly admired by his own colleagues both at home and abroad. The performances are full of insight and sparkle with lively humour.

New review
Telemann Essercizii Musici[a] – Trios: No. 4 in A major, TWV42: A6; No. 7 in F major, TWV42:
  F3; No. 8 in B flat major, TWV42: B4. Trio Sonatas[a] – F major, TWV42: F14; A minor, TWV42:
  a1; A minor,TWV42: a6. Fantaisies for Flute without Continuo, TWV40: 2-13 – No. 1 in
  A major; No. 5 in C major (played in F major). Der getreue Music-Meister – Sonata in C major,
  TWV41: C2[a]. **Sébastien Marq** (rec); [a]**Le Concert Français.** Auvidis Astrée Ⓟ E8554 (70 minutes:
  DDD: 2/96). ✒ Recorded 1994.
The title of this entertaining disc is misleading, since only three of its nine items belong to Telemann's chamber music anthology, *Essercizii Musici* (c1739). What all of the pieces have in common is the presence of a recorder and Sébastien Marq is a dextrous, refreshingly ungimmicky player, his playing warmly sympathetic to the music and his phrasing eloquent and communicative. He is exceptionally well supported by his fellow instrumentalists and it is this, above all, which makes the programme such rewarding listening. The oboist, Alfred Bernardini, violinist François Fernandez, viola da gambist and harpsichordist Jérôme and Pierre Hantaï, respectively, are among those who make excellent contributions. The continuo line-up, too, is responsive though the recording acoustic does not serve the double-bass as faithfully as it should. The choice of pieces is discerning. There are no disappointments to be found among the solos and trios which Telemann included in his *Essercizii Musici*. The three pieces included here perhaps take pride of place in the programme, though the two somewhat melancholic Trio Sonatas in A minor are hardly their inferior. Most unusual is a chamber concerto in F major (TWV42:F14) for the unlikely partnership of recorder and horn. It is pieces such as this which reveal Telemann's fascination with instrumental colour, his penchant for experimentation but, above all, his deeply informed knowledge of the strengths and weaknesses of the instruments themselves. The interpretative know-how of these players is reason enough to become

acquainted with the disc but the sheer variety and sustained invention of the composer is what will lead you to it over and over again.

Telemann Paris Quartets (Quadri), Volume 2 – Concerto secondo in D major, TWV43: D 1; Première Suite in E minor, TWV43: e 1. Paris Quartets (Nouveaux quatuors en six suites) – G major, TWV43: G 4; B minor, TWV43: h 2. **Wilbert Hazelzet** (fl); **Trio Sonnerie** (Monica Huggett, vn; Sarah Cunningham, va da gamba; Mitzi Meyerson, hpd/org). Virgin Classics Veritas Ⓟ VC5 45020-2 (73 minutes: DDD: 11/94). ✍ Recorded 1993. Ⓖ

Here we have superbly refined performances of some of the most alluring chamber music of the entire baroque era. Telemann's musical personality is seldom less than charming, but these quartets surely take the prize with their tasteful and elegant discourse, helped out by effective (and of course greatly attractive) scoring. All this is brought out unerringly by our four musicians: the polished playing of Trio Sonnerie will already be familiar to many readers, while Hazelzet is an uncommonly accomplished and tasteful performer. Occasionally there is the odd tempo which seems a little on the slow side but in general the touch is light and graceful, without being in any way insubstantial. And it's all helped by a well-judged and clean recording.

Additional recommendations ...

...Six Paris Quartets[a]. Suite in F major[b]. Overture-Suite in E flat major, TWV55: Es3[c].
[a]**Amsterdam Quartet;** [b]**Jaap Schroder** (vn); [bc]**Concerto Amsterdam / Frans Brüggen.** Teldec 4509-92177-2. ✍ Ⓖ

...Musique de table – Quartet in E minor. Paris Quartets – No. 1 in D major, TWV43: D3; No. 2 in A minor, TWV43: a2. Six Concerts et Six Suites – Concert No. 3 in A major, TWV42: A3. **Hortus Musicus / Andres Mustonen** (vn). Finlandia Ⓟ 4509-95578-2 (52 minutes: DDD: 9/95). ✍

Telemann Sonates Corellisantes – No. 1 in F major, TWV42: F2. Paris Quartets, "Nouveaux quatuors en Six Suites" – No. 6 in E minor, TWV43: e4. Essercizii Musici – Trio No. 8 in B flat major, TWV42: B4. Quartets – A minor, TWV43: a3; G minor, TWV43: g4. **Florilegium Ensemble.** Channel Classics Ⓟ CCS5093 (53 minutes: DDD: 10/93). ✍ Recorded 1992. Ⓖ

The rarity here is the *Sonata Corellisante* for two violins and continuo in which Telemann pays tribute to Corelli. The remaining works are the sixth and perhaps finest of the 1738 *Nouveaux Quatuors* or *Paris Quartets* as they have become known, a little *Quartet* (or *Quadro*) in G minor, a B flat Trio from the *Essercizii Musici* collection (*c.*1739) and a fine Concerto da camera (Quartet) in A minor, very much along the lines of Vivaldi's pieces of the same kind in which each instrument other than the continuo has an obbligato role. The finest work here is the *Paris Quartet* which consists of a Prelude, a sequence of dance-orientated movements and an elegiac Chaconne that lingers long in the memory. The performance is full of vitality and probes beneath the music's superficialities. There is, throughout the programme, an intensity and a youthful spontaneity about this playing which has considerable appeal; and the continuo line, furthermore, is handled with boldness and imagination.

New review

Telemann 12 Fantaisies for Violin without Continuo, TWV40: 14-25. Der Getreue Music-Meister – "Gulliver" Suite in D, TWV40:108[a]. **Andrew Manze,** [a]**Caroline Balding** (vns). ✍ Harmonia Mundi Ⓟ HMU90 7137 (78 minutes: DDD: 6/96). Recorded 1994.

Andrew Manze's recording of the 12 *Fantaisies* marks the fourth version in as many years (Peter Sheppard's and Maya Homburger's are the two comparable versions on period instruments, the other, on a modern violin, is by Betina Maag Santos on Gallo (all listed below) and not surprisingly he brings a very definite and distinctive angle to them, one which we can hear from the outset delicately balances clarity of thought with the sense of restoring the lost art of extemporization. We have learnt to take virtuosity for granted with Manze – his remarkable feats allow the most prejudiced to forget that he is playing a baroque fiddle. But without such an instrument he could barely create such a biting astringency in the more self-effacing and tortured moments (*Fantaisie* No. 6) or a cultivated assurance and definition in articulation to the recognizably regular sections, such as *Fantaisie* No. 10, where Telemann is working in established forms – particularly in the latter works in the set where dance forms predominate. If characterization is the key, Manze is arguably the most persuasive of all his rivals. He grows through phrases in the Gigue of the Fourth *Fantaisie* in a fashion which gives the work a peculiarly stoical strength, purrs through the contrapuntally conceived *Fantaisies* (Nos. 1-6 in particular) with nonchalant disdain for their often extreme technical demands and leaves sighs and pauses hanging with supreme eloquence. If Homburger brings some moments of keener grace and repose, then one must also recognize the robust integrity and humour of Sheppard's accounts. But for sheer lucidity, breadth of imagination and colour, One is drawn again and again to Manze's version; he most acutely captures the sense of a famous public figure ensconced in a private world against the backdrop of a musical world in a state of flux. To add spice to an already outstanding release, we have the short and delightful *Gulliver* Suite for two violins where Manze is joined by Caroline Balding trust Telemann to be up-to-the-mark only a year or two after *Gulliver's Travels* was published!

Additional recommendations ...

...12 Fantaisies. **Betina Maag Santos** (vn). Gallo Ⓕ CD-718 (75 minutes: ADD: 8/94).   Ⓖ

...12 Fantaisies. **Maya Homburger** (vn). Maya Recordings Ⓕ MCD9302 (72 minutes: DDD: 8/94). ✍

...12 Fantaisies. **Peter Sheppard** (vn). Meridian Ⓕ CDE84266 (67 minutes: DDD: 8/94).   Ⓖ

| New review |

Telemann 12 Sonate metodiche. **Barthold Kuijken** (fl); **Wieland Kuijken** (va da gamba); **Robert Kohnen** (hpd). Accent Ⓕ ACC94104/5D (two discs: 140 minutes: DDD: 5/96). ✍ Recorded 1994.

No, the title is hardly an incentive to part with one's pocket-money. But with Telemann we should know better than to be taken in by such packaging details. These are, in fact, 12 skilfully written and entertaining sonatas, published in two sets of six and issued in 1728 and 1732. Telemann seems, right from the start, to have had two instruments in mind: flute or violin, and though Barthold Kuijken has elected to play all of them on a baroque flute, he does so with such technical mastery that there is little cause for regret. He savours the many playful ideas contained in the faster movements and realizes a touching sense of melancholy in several of the slow ones. Among the most impressive of the sonatas is that in B minor which Kuijken plays with sensitivity and technical panache. Overall, the interpretation is on a sufficiently elevated level to warrant unqualified praise. The recorded sound is first-rate.

Telemann Der Tag des Gerichts[a]. Ino[b]. [a]**Gertraud Landwehr-Herrmann**, [b]**Roberta Alexander** (sops); [a]**Cora Canne-Meijer** (contr); [a]**Kurt Equiluz** (ten); [a]**Max van Egmond** (bass); [a]**Vienna Boys' Choir**; [a]**Hamburg Monteverdi Choir; Vienna Concentus Musicus / Nikolaus Harnoncourt**. Teldec Das Alte Werk Ⓜ 9031-77621-2 (two discs: 121 minutes: ADD/DDD: 7/93). ✍ Texts and translations included. Item marked [a]2292-42722-2 (12/89, recorded 1966), [b]2292-44633-2 (4/91, recorded 1988). Recorded 1996-7.   ⒼⒼ

Der Tag des Gerichts ("The Day of Judgement") is another one of Telemann's greatest achievements from that miraculous decade of his creative rejuvenation. The work was first performed in Hamburg in 1762 when Telemann was 81 years old. From start to finish this beautiful score has all the freshness of invention and vitality that we might have expected from a man half his age. The text is by Wilhelm Alers who described it as a "Poem for Singing in Four Contemplations". It must have appealed to the octogenarian composer who brings it to life with a wealth of instrumental colour, affective word-painting and striking contrasts. The disc further includes Telemann's masterly dramatic cantata, *Ino*, belonging to the same period. The performances are equal to almost everything in these vital and rapturous scores. Twenty-two years separate the recordings of the two works, revealing the remarkable consistency with which Harnoncourt's limpid sense of enactment has been pursued.

| New review |

Telemann Die Auferstehung und Himmelfahrt Jesu, TWV6:6. **Monika Frimmer, Veronika Winter** (sops); **Matthias Koch** (alto); **Nico van der Meel** (ten); **Klaus Mertens** (bass); **Rheinische Kantorei; Das Kleine Konzert / Hermann Max**. Capriccio Ⓕ 10 596 (59 minutes: DDD: 7/96). Notes and text included.

What motivated Telemann to produce a succession of oratorios in old age is unclear. Perhaps, as is sometimes suggested, it was contact with Handel in London, though the two composers' approaches to oratorio are vastly different. *Die Auferstehung und Himmelfahrt Jesu* ("The Resurrection and Ascension of Jesus") was completed by Telemann in 1760. The text was commissioned from the Berlin enlightenment poet, Carl Wilhelm Ramler, with whom Telemann had previously collaborated and who was to provide him, five years later, with a fine text for *Ino*. In a letter to a fellow poet, Ramler wrote, "I gave a solemn promise to prepare something for Easter at which an old musician will sing his last. Herr Telemann, an elderly man of 78, wants to sing his swansong." In fact it was anything but a swansong since two further oratorios were to come, one of them *Der Tag des Gerichts*. Telemann's late oratorios follow no set pattern; indeed, certain of them reveal a pioneering quality in which we sense the composer exploring new ground, not without trepidation. A distinctive feature in all of them, however, is one of lyricism achieved in some measure by the breaking down of older, rigid structures in favour of new and different means of textual elucidation. Having said that, the present work does adhere mainly to an alternating pattern of recitative and aria with choruses and two duets interspersed. But there is great formal and expressive variety within this scheme in which Telemann's acute sensibility to affective textual setting is almost constantly on display. By no means least of the oratorio's attractions is its Janus-like stance created by baroque forms and means of expression jostling with newer concepts. The performance under Hermann Max is stylish and affectionate. The solo cast is mostly excellent, with Monika Frimmer and Veronika Winter proving evenly matched and youthful in sound in their duets. Nico van der Meel and Klaus Mertens are admirably clear in their declamation, Mertens above all understanding and thus able to convey Telemann's wonderful feeling for recitative and arioso. Only Matthias Koch failed to please in every instance. His voice can lack warmth and his tone sounds brittle in the present company. The Rheinische Kantorei and Das Kleine Konzert acquit themselves well. Telemann's innate sense of orchestral colour had lost none of its charm by 1760 and there are splendid numbers for pairs of flutes (track 4), oboes (track 9), horns (track 14), trumpets (track 17) and trumpets with drums (track 7). In conclusion, this is an issue which not only adds to our picture of an extraordinarily inventive composer, but also provides musical enrichment which grows perceptibly on acquaintance. One black mark, : the text is printed in German only, a questionable economy. Otherwise, a stimulating and rewarding release, well recorded.

New review

Telemann Der Herr ist König, TWV8:6[a]. Die Donner-Ode, TWV6:3[b]. [a]**Ann Monoyios**, [b]**Barbara Schlick** (sops); [b]**Axel Köhler** (alto); **Wilfried Jochens** (ten); [a]**Harry van der Kamp**, [b]**Hans-Georg Wimmer, Stephan Schreckenberger** (basses); **Rheinische Kantorei; Das Kleine Konzert / Hermann Max.** Capriccio Ⓕ 10 556 (65 minutes: DDD: 11/95). Texts and translations included. Recorded 1990-92.

The *Donner-Ode* was one of Telemann's biggest public successes during his lifetime and is a striking piece in its own right, a vivid reaction to the Lisbon earthquake of 1755. The shock caused to the international community by this dreadful event (in which some 60,000 people were killed) was enormous, and in Hamburg a special day of penitence was the occasion for this "Thunder Ode", though it does perhaps suggest a rather smug satisfaction that such a disaster didn't befall northern Germany. "The voice of God makes the proud mountains collapse", the text proclaims, "Give thanks to Him in His temple!". The music, too, both in its mood and in that extraordinarily up-to-date style of Telemann's later years, frequently conjures the benign, entertainingly song-like pictorial mood of a Haydn Mass or oratorio. Entertaining is the word, though, especially in this energetic performance under Hermann Max. He is more fleet-footed and buoyantly athletic than Richard Hickox, benefiting from what is becoming his customary excellent team of German soloists. Hickox's *Donner-Ode* is coupled with Telemann's charmingly Frenchified motet, *Deus judicium tuum*, but Max chooses another German work, the cheerful cantata *Der Herr ist König*, written much earlier in the composer's life and rather more Bach-like in character and form (though it is worth pointing out that since it survives partly in Bach's hand, we ought perhaps to conclude that Telemann was the one wielding the influence here). As in the *Ode*, choir, soloists and orchestra are bright, tight-knit and well recorded, making this release as a whole an enjoyable one.

Additional recommendation ...

...Die Donner-Ode[a]. Deus judicium tuum. **Patrizia Kwella** (sop); **Catherine Denley** (mez); **Mark Tucker** (ten); **Stephen Roberts** (bar); [a]**Michael George** (bass); **Collegium Musicum 90 Chorus; Collegium Musicum 90 / Richard Hickox.** Chandos Chaconne Ⓕ CHAN0548 (61 minutes: DDD: 8/94). ✎   Ⓖ

Telemann Don Quichotte auf der Hochzeit des Comacho. **Raimund Nolte** (bass) Don Quichotte; **Michael Schopper** (bass) Sancho Panza; **Silke Stapf** (sop) Pedrillo; **Mechthild Bach** (sop) Grisostomo; **Heike Hallaschka** (sop) Quiteria; **Annette Kohler** (mez) Comacho; **Karl-Heinz Brandt** (ten) Basilio; **Bremen Vocal Ensemble for Ancient Music; La Stagione / Michael Schneider.** CPO Ⓕ CPO999 210-2 (59 minutes: DDD: 9/94). ✎ Notes, text and translation included. Recorded live in 1993.   Ⓖ

Telemann's delightful comic-opera/serenata, *Don Quichotte auf der Hochzeit des Comacho* ("Don Quixote at Camacho's Wedding"), dates from 1761; he selected for a libretto a text by a young Hamburg poet, Daniel Schiebeler. Schiebeler took an episode from Part 2 of Cervantes's celebrated burlesque novel, in which the Knight of the Lions and his squire Sancho Panza encounter some rather strange wedding celebrations as they roam the world in search of adventure. The bride, Quiteria is to marry Camacho, a rich sheep farmer. But *she* loves Basilio who is, however, poor and therefore disqualified from marrying his childhood sweetheart. Just as the marriage is about to take place Basilio is led in with a dagger in his breast. He implores Quiteria to grant him one last wish – to give a dying man her hand in marriage, since that would strengthen his heart and give him breath for confession. Quiteria agrees to this, gives Basilio her hand and the priest blesses them, whereupon Basilio leaps to his feet pulling the dagger deftly from his breast. It was all a trick, he exclaims, jubilantly. Camacho is furious and demands instant justice but Don Quixote intervenes: "Quiteria was Basilio's, and Basilio Quiteria's, by Heaven's just and favourable decree". Drinking, dancing and merrymaking follow as Quixote and a reluctant Sancho leave the feast for the open road once more. Most sharply and wittily characterized is the role of Sancho, a character in whom Telemann, like us, clearly delighted. Athletic leaps accompany his recollection of an earlier unpleasant escapade when playful rogues tossed him in a blanket. Michael Schopper revels in the part, giving a larger-than-life picture of this lovable squire. Quixote is another bass role, here sung by Raimund Nolte. His, too, is a splendidly robust performance, as we can hear, for instance, in his vigorous chiding of the timorous tendencies in Sancho's nature (tracks 5 and 6). The remaining roles are smaller, but uniformly well sung and the choruses, often adorned with rhythmic and instrumental ideas which evoke splashes of local colour, are first-rate. In summary, here is a work which should have a wide appeal for its musical diversity, skilful characterization and captivating melodies. The sound is excellent.

New review

Telemann Der getreue Music-Meister. **Edith Mathis** (sop); **Hertha Töpper** (mez); **Rosemarie Sommer** (contr); **Ernst Haefliger, Gerhard Unger** (tens); **Barry McDaniel** (bar); **Hartmut Hein** (bar); **Würzburg Bach Choir; Instrumental ensemble / Josef Ulsamer,** Archiv Produktion Ⓑ 447

722-2AX4 (four discs: 271 minutes: ADD: 4/96). Texts and translations included. From
SKL943/7 (12/67). Ⓖ

"The cow, but stay! no, no, the she-goat bowed down her horns to the earth and begged the lion to be
her lifetime's mate; the lion well knew how false the she-goat was, pretended to be dumb, took a pinch
of snuff and paid no heed to her; until the she-goat piteously cried out: O merciful Lord lion! I'll be
forever true. The lion said: No! The she-goat cried: Ye Gods! is there then no saviour? The lion said:
I trust thee not; and then his lordship took his watch which he looked at and said: Take thyself off!
the hour has struck and I must post my mail." Such is the stuff Telemann's unique anthology *Der
getreue Music-Meister* is made of: fable by Aesop, text by Mattheson, music by Telemann. Ironically,
this entertaining setting contains in its depictive, onomatopoeic passages an aspect of Telemann's art
which the testy, irascible Mattheson deplored. But it little matters what he thought since the piece
from Telemann's opera *Aesopus* is a gem of absolute enchantment, as is much else in the collection.
Telemann launched what is generally accepted as the first musical periodical in Hamburg in 1728. It
ran to 25 instalments, or 'lessons' as he called them. This was pioneering stuff in the 1720s, as indeed
it was in 1967 when Archiv bravely issued a box of five LPs to mark the two-hundredth anniversary
of Telemann's death. He probably intended his *Getreue Music-Meister* as an amateur musician's vade-
mecum and, with characteristic flair, included idiomatically written pieces in a wide variety of forms
for voice and virtually every instrument then in use. The result is a rich and extraordinarily colourful
compendium in which Telemann's own encyclopaedic learning in many different areas is reflected.

This musical bran-tub probably has at least one item of interest for every single reader of the guide.
For some, it contains a great deal more than that. The set is not quite as complete as its rival, more
recent account by Cologne Camerata (Deutsche Harmonia Mundi RD77239, 4/93); but it is in about
every respect far more entertaining, even if its period-instrument credentials are not quite so squeaky
clean as those of the Cologne group. This was 1967, after all, when the 'early music' revival was in its
infancy. In fact little or nothing of real significance is missing but the real gain in the Archiv set is the
spirited and characterful contribution of the singers. The aforementioned Fable is sung with
consummate artistry by Gerhard Unger, while Edith Mathis, athletically accompanied by Sebastian
Kelber's dazzling descant recorder obbligato, gives a scintillating performance of "Più del fiume",
another *da capo* aria from the opera *Aesopus*, this one with a particularly well-contrasted middle
section. Other delights include a "Carillon" for two chalumeaux – for which, unforgivably, two
recorders have been substituted in the Cologne version – a fine Oboe Sonata in A minor, several free-
standing secular songs of a kind which had become popular with the new, leisured, culture-loving
Hamburg middle-class, and a wealth of pieces for solo instruments and small ensembles. Among the
most impressive of the latter is the trio sonata or "Introduzione" with which Telemann launched the
project, here played in its proper key of C major rather than in the inexplicably transposed key of
A major which is preferred in the newer recording.In short, this is a winner. Not everything, of course,
is done as we should set about it today, but the consistently elevated level of artistry and the spirit in
which Telemann's anthology has been brought to life make it an irresistible choice.

Further listening ...

...Concerto for Trumpet, Two Oboes and Strings in D major. *Coupled with* **Biber** Fidicunium
sacro-profanum – Sonata IV a 5 in C major. Sonatae tam aris quam aulis servientes – I a 8 in
C major; X a 5 in G minor[a]. Duets for Two Trumpets[a] – No. 1 in C major; No. 5 in C major;
No. 11 in G minor; No. 13 in A minor. **Vivaldi** Concerto for Two Trumpets and Strings in
C major, RV537[a]. **Stradella** (ed. Steele-Perkins) Sonata a 8 con una Tromba in D major.
Albinoni (attrib.) Concerto for Trumpet, Oboes, Bassoon and Strings in C major. **Handel** (ed.
Steele-Perkins) Airs from Vauxhall Gardens. **Crispian Steele-Perkins,** [a]**John Thiessen** (tpts);
Tafelmusik / Jeanne Lamon (vn). Sony Classical Vivarte SK53365 (4/95). ✍

...Sonata (Septett) in E minor. *Coupled with works by* **Gluck** and **Rebel** Cologne Musica Antiqua /
Reinhard Goebel. Archiv Produktion 445 824-2AH (12/95). ✍ *See review under Gluck; refer to
the Index to Reviews.*

...Paris Quartets (Nouveaux quatuors en six suites), Volume 1 – No. 1 in D major, TWV43: D 3;
No. 5 in A major, TWV43: A 3. Paris Quartets (Quadri) – No. 4, Sonata seconda in G minor,
TWV43: g 1; No. 6, Deuxième Suite in B minor, TWV43: h 1. **Wilbert Hazelzet** (fl); **Trio
Sonnerie.** Virgin Classics Veritas VC5 45045-2 (3/92). ✍

...Six Sonates sans Basse, TWV40: 101-106. **Michala Petri, Elisabeth Smith** (recs). RCA Victor Red
Seal RD87903 (4/91).

...12 Fantaisies for Flute without Continuo, TWV40: 2-13. **Peter Holtslag** (rec). Globe GLO5117
(12/94). ✍ Ⓖ

...Cantatas – Tirsis am Scheidewege; Nach Finsternis und Todesschatten; Meines Bleibens ist nicht
hier. Das Frauenzimmer verstimmt sich immer. Vergiss dich selbst, mein schönster Engel. An der
Schlaf. Die Einsamkeit. Concerto grosso in E minor – Adagio. **René Jacobs** (alto); **Berlin
Academy for Ancient Music.** Capriccio 10 338 (11/92). ✍

...Du aber Daniel, gehe hin – Mit sehnenden verlangen; Richt ihr müde Augen nieder. *Coupled with
works by* **C.P.E. Bach, J.S. Bach, Handel, Brahms, Schumann** and **Schubert** Elly
Ameling (sop); **Various soloists.** Deutsche Harmonia Mundi 74321 26617-2 (12/95). *See review in
the Collections section; refer to the Index to Reviews.*

...Schwanengesang, TWV4: 6 Herr, strafe mich nicht in Deinem Trinitatis, TWV1: 771. **Soloists; La
Stagione / Michael Schneider.** CPO CPO999 212-2 (7/94). ✍

...Missa brevis. Deus judicium tuum. Alles redet jetzt und singet. **Soloists; Rheinische Kantorei; Das Kleine Konzert / Hermann Max.** Capriccio 10 315 (11/91). 🖋

...St Matthew Passion. **Soloists; Darmstadt Chorus and Chamber Orchestra / Wolfgang Seeliger.** Christophorus CHR77149 (5/95).

...Pimpinone. **John Ostendorf** (bass); **Julianne Baird** (sop); **St Luke's Baroque Orchestra / Rudolph Palmer.** Newport Classic NCD60117 (1/92). 🖋

Alec Templeton

Suggested listening ...

...Bach goes to Town. *Coupled with works by* **F. Couperin, Rameau, Rimsky-Korsakov, Daquin, Paradis, Bach** and **Malcolm** George Malcolm (hpd). 🖋 Decca 444 390-2DWO (11/95).

Sigismond Thalberg

German/Austrian 1812-1871

Suggested listening ...

...Fantasies on operas by Donizetti. **Francesco Nicolosi** (pf). Marco Polo 8 223365 (7/94).

...Fantasias on themes from Rossini's operas – Semiramide, Op. 51; La donna del lago, Op. 40*a*; Il barbiere di Siviglia, Op. 63; Moïse, Op. 33. **Francesco Nicolosi** (pf). Marco Polo 8 223366 (1/96).

Ambroise Thomas

French 1811-1896

Thomas Hamlet. **Thomas Hampson** (bass) Hamlet; **June Anderson** (sop) Ophélie; **Gregory Kunde** (ten) Laërte; **Denyce Graves** (mez) Gertrude; **Samuel Ramey** (bass) Claudius; **Jean-Philippe Courtis** (bass) Ghost; **Gérard Garino** (ten) Marcellus; **Michel Trempont** (ten) Polonius; **François Le Roux** (bar) Horatio; **Thierry Félix** (bar) First Gravedigger; **Jean-Pierre Furlan** (ten) Second Gravedigger; **Ambrosian Opera Chorus; London Philharmonic Orchestra / Antonio de Almeida.** EMI ℗ CDS7 54820-2 (three discs: 198 minutes: DDD: 1/94). Notes, text and translation included. Recorded 1993.
Variously described as a "powerful, dark-hued masterpiece" and as, dramatically, a travesty with some musical high spots amid a sea of commonplace sentimentalities, Thomas's *Hamlet* seems to demand being looked at afresh. Forget Shakespeare if you can, and though the contrived happy ending, with Hamlet being proclaimed king, takes some swallowing, responsibility for this lies not with Thomas but with the French audiences of the 1860s. For the Covent Garden production of *Hamlet* a year after the Paris première, the ending was changed as a sop to British sensibilities, and Hamlet kills himself. The present recording goes back to Thomas's original but also includes the Covent Garden ending in an appendix, to which is also banished the ballet (dramatically irrelevant) on which Parisian audiences insisted. Also as an appendix is the inclusion of a duet between Claudius and Gertrude only recently discovered. So, what impression does it make? There are indeed undistinguished sections, where Thomas lapses into the conventional, and lead-ins to arias are too often like ballet-dancers' "take up position" (though the introduction to "To be or not to be" is almost Verdian) – but against this must be set the tense scene of the ghost's appearance, Hamlet's highly dramatic confrontation of Gertrude, such arias as Claudius's prayer for forgiveness and Hamlet's "Comme une pâle fleur", and Thomas's orchestration – colourful and full of felicities. Almeida secures the utmost commitment from the LPO – the initial coronation march has tremendous impact and the Ambrosian Singers are splendidly firm-voiced and tonally sensitive. The casting is admirable: Anderson, with her seductive voice and sparkling technique, presents a touching and vulnerable Ophelia, and manages even to make the protracted mad scene that occupies all of Act 3 something more than the mere display-piece for prima donnas and canary-fanciers. Hampson's Hamlet is full of subtle shadings of tone and colour, and the recitatives (his as well as the others') are invested with life and character. Ramey brings weight to his portrayal of Claudius, Denyce Graves has a secure facility as Gertrude, and all the minor parts are well taken. In sum, listeners should give Thomas another chance.

Further listening ...

...Raymond – Overture. *Coupled with* **Chabrier** Joyeuse marche. España. **Dukas** L'apprenti sorcier. **Satie** (orch. Debussy) Gymnopédies – Nos. 1 and 3. **Saint-Saëns** Samson et Dalila – Bacchanale. **Bizet** Jeux d'enfants. **Ibert** Divertissement. **Montreal Symphony Orchestra / Charles Dutoit.** Decca 421 527-2DH (6/89). 🄶

...String Quartet in E minor. *Coupled with* **Gounod** String Quartet No. 3 in A minor. **Lalo** String Quartet in E flat major, Op. 45. **Daniel Quartet.** Koch Discover International DICD920159 (12/94). 🄶

Randall Thompson
American 1899-1984

Suggested listening ...

...Symphony No. 2. *Coupled with* **Chadwick** Rip Van Winkle. Melpomene – overture. Tam O'Shanter. **Detroit Symphony Orchestra / Neeme Järvi.** Chandos CHAN9439 (6/96).

Virgil Thomson
American 1896-1989

Suggested listening ...

...Symphony on a Hymn Tune[b]. Symphony No. 2[b]. Lord Byron[ac] – Alas! the love of woman!; A wanderer from the British world of fashion; Sweet Lady; I'd sooner burn in hell; Fare thee well thus disunited. Shipwreck and Love Scene from Byron's Don Juan[ac]. A Solemn Music[c]. A Joyful Fugue[c]. [a]**Martyn Hill** (ten); [b]**Monadnock Festival Orchestra;** [c]**Budapest Symphony Orchestra / James Bolle.** Albany TROY017-2 (4/90).

...Susie Asado[a]. Pigeons on the Grass Alas[b]. Praises and Prayers[c]. Five Phrases from the Song of Solomon[d]. Mostly about Love[e]. Commentaire sur St Jérome[f]. From Sneden's Landing Variations[g]. Five Shakespeare Songs[h]. Oraison funèbre de Henriette-Marie de France, Reine de la Grande-Bretagne[i]. Capital Capitals[j]. [adegi]**Nancy Armstrong** (sop); [ch]**D'Anna Fortunato** (contr); [j]**Frank Kelley,** [fj]**Paul Kirby** (tens); [bj]**Sanford Sylvan** (bar); [j]**David Ripley** (bass); [d]**James Russell Smith** (perc); [abcefghij]**Anthony Tommasini** (pf). Northeastern NR250-CD.

...The River – Suite. The Plow that Broke the Plains – Suite. *Coupled with* **Stravinsky** L'histoire du soldat – Suite[a]. [a]**instrumental ensemble; Symphony of the Air (New York) / Leopold Stokowski.** Vanguard Classics 08.8013.71.

Ludwig Thuillé
Austrian 1861-1907

Suggested listening ...

...Cello Sonata, Op. 22. *Coupled with* **R. Strauss** Cello Sonata in F major, Op. 6. **Sophie Rolland** (vc); **Marc-André Hamelin** (pf). ASV CDDCA913 (3/95).   Ⓖ

Michael Tippett
British 1905-

New review

Tippett Concerto for Double String Orchestra[b]. Divertimento on Sellinger's Round[b]. Little Music for Strings[b]. Sonata[a]. [a]**Michael Thompson Horn Quartet** (Michael Thompson, Jeffrey Bryant, Richard Watkins, Hugh Seenan, hns); [b]**Academy of St Martin in the Fields / Sir Neville Marriner.** EMI British Composers Ⓕ CDC5 55452-2 (66 minutes: DDD: 1/96). Recorded 1995.

New review

Tippett Divertimento on Sellinger's Round. Little Music for Strings. The Heart's Assurance (orch. Bowen)[a]. Concerto for Double String Orchestra. [a]**John Mark Ainsley** (ten); **City of London Sinfonia / Richard Hickox.** Chandos Ⓕ CHAN9409 (71 minutes: DDD: 3/96). Text included. Recorded 1995.

The EMI disc provides firm enjoyment from start to finish. Marriner and the Academy recorded two of these pieces (namely the *Concerto for Double String Orchestra* and *Little Music*) in the early 1970s for Argo – a much-loved collection, currently unavailable. So how do these new accounts measure up to those distinguished predecessors? Very well indeed, is the answer. There is the same combination of stunning discipline and joyous swagger on show, whilst Marriner's purposeful, clear-headed direction once again betokens considerable affection as well as commitment to the cause. If the central *Adagio cantabile* of the concerto now emerges in marginally less rapt fashion than before, it still sounds surpassingly beautiful, and surely no one could resist the stirring passion behind the big-hearted C major home-coming in the finale. A similar sense of dedication informs Marriner's crisply poised performance of the *Divertimento on Sellinger's Round.* This is a sparkling, richly inventive creation, its beguiling grace and bubbling, at times anarchic wit extremely well conveyed here. That just leaves the Sonata for four horns of 1955, a pithy, concentrated offering which well repays repeated hearings (the slow movement is particularly haunting), and whose technical demands hold no terrors for the four superbly assured principals who comprise the Michael Thompson Horn Quartet. The engineering throughout is ideally ripe and realistic.

    The advantage Chandos have is in securing the first recording of the orchestral version of Tippett's major song-cycle, *The Heart's Assurance.* EMI's Sonata for four horns may seem relatively slight beside this, although it is a fine piece, and 100 per cent genuine Tippett. The *Concerto for Double String Orchestra* is Tippett's first masterwork, and it's marvellous to have a recording that does justice to all those antiphonal textural subtleties. One might wish for a touch more brio in the first movement, and a richer, stronger tone in places: for example, the slow movement's sublime outer sections. But this is still a very satisfying performance, not least because the finale comes across with such a winning blend of vitality and eloquence. Meirion Bowen's orchestration of *The Heart's*

Assurance has Tippett's approval, and it is undoubtedly a resourceful piece of work. What makes the effect so different from the voice and piano original is that the all-important doublings of voice and instrument seem so much more prominent when the instrument in question can sustain the sound for as long as the voice itself. For this reason the original may be preferable, and in addition, despite John Mark Ainsley's excellent contribution to this recording, the final song doesn't build to its overwhelming climax as inexorably as it should. However, this is another valuable Tippett issue from Chandos, and the recording is satisfyingly rich in detail and atmosphere.

Additional recommendation ...

...Little Music for Strings[c]. **Rubbra** Symphony No. 5 in B flat major, Op. 63[a]. **Bliss** Checkmate – excerpts[b]. [a]**Melbourne Symphony Orchestra;** [b]**West Australian Symphony Orchestra;** [c]**Soloists of Australia /** [c]**Ronald Thomas;** [ab]**Hans-Hubert Schönzeler.** Chandos Collect Ⓜ CHAN6576 (60 minutes: ADD/DDD: 6/92).

Tippett Symphony No. 1. Piano Concerto[a]. [a]**Howard Shelley (pf); Bournemouth Symphony Orchestra / Richard Hickox.** Chandos Ⓕ CHAN9333 (72 minutes: DDD: 4/95). Recorded 1994. *Selected by Sounds in Retrospect.* Ⓖ

The riot of proliferating counterpoint that is Tippett's Symphony No. 1 presents enough problems of orchestral balance to give recording teams (not to mention conductors) nightmares. Chandos have managed highly creditable degrees of containment and clarity, without loss of realism, and the impact, when the last movement finally settles on to its long-prepared harmonic goal, is powerful and convincing. As with other Hickox performances in this Tippett series, doubts as to whether initial impetus is sufficient to keep the complex structures on course prove groundless – even in the extraordinary slow movement, with its endlessly rotating ground bass. This is a fine account, well-balanced between lively rhythmic articulation and broad melodic sweep. The performance of the Piano Concerto is no less notable for the inexorable way in which its mighty design unfolds. There may be too much decorum, too little passion, in certain episodes, yet Howard Shelley makes persuasive sense of the *con bravura* marking in the finale, and his shaping of the first movement's long, dreamingly decorative lines is as alert and sensitive as his control of the second movement's more dynamic discourse. This is a truly symphonic concerto, with a wealth of invention, remarkable textural ingenuity and a particularly imaginative use of the orchestra (especially the celesta) to complement the bright colours of the solo instrument. In this excellent recording, all doubts about the musical merits of the work should finally be stilled.

Tippett Symphony No. 2. New Year – Suite. **Bournemouth Symphony Orchestra / Richard Hickox.** Chandos Ⓕ CHAN9299 (65 minutes: DDD: 10/94). Recorded 1994. *Gramophone Editor's choice.* Ⓖ

The balance Hickox achieves between attention to detail and large-scale symphonic sweep is exemplary, and especially impressive in the tricky finale, where he conveys the essential ambiguity of an ending which strives to recapture the optimistic *élan* of the work's opening without ever quite managing it. The Chandos recording, too, gives us much more of the symphony's contrapuntal detail. The first recording of music from Tippett's latest opera *New Year*, premièred in 1989, is thoroughly welcome. The music of this suite may seem over-emphatic to anyone who hasn't experienced the opera in the theatre, and the recording relishes the booming electric guitars and wailing saxophones, as well as the taped spaceship effects. Yet there are many imaginative moments, like the use of the 'paradise garden' sarabande borrowed from *The Mask of Time*, and the exotic arrangement of *Auld Lang Syne* near the end. This is Tippett firing on all cylinders, with a performance and recording to match.

Tippett Praeludium. Symphony No. 3[a]. [a]**Faye Robinson (sop); Bournemouth Symphony Orchestra / Richard Hickox.** Chandos Ⓕ CHAN9276 (64 minutes: DDD: 6/94). Text included. Recorded 1993.

The Third Symphony, first heard in 1972, is one of Tippett's most complex and highly charged attempts to create a convincing structure from the collision between strongly contrasted musical characteristics. The work evolves from a purely orchestral drama – fast first movement, slow second movement, both large-scale, followed by a shorter scherzo – to a less extended but also tripartite sequence of blues settings, the whole capped by a huge, climactic coda in which the soprano voice finally yields the last word to the orchestra. The first two movements (Part 1, as Tippett calls it) remain a considerable technical challenge, especially to the strings, but this performance manages to sustain an appropriate level of tension without sounding merely effortful, and without skimping on the opportunities for eloquence of phrasing. It could well be that Tippett has over-indulged the percussion in the slow movement, but this vivid and well-balanced Chandos recording lets us hear ample detail without exaggerating the bright colours and hyper-resonant textures. The later stages have the advantage of a superbly characterful singer in Faye Robinson. She has the power, the edge, and also the radiance, to make Tippett's progression from idiosyncratic blues to Beethoven-quoting peroration utterly convincing. The work ends, famously, on a question-mark, dismissing the unrestrained affirmation of Beethoven's *Choral* finale in favour of the unresolved opposition of loud brass and soft strings. Will that "new compassionate power/To heal, to love" which the text "senses" actually be achieved? Twenty years on, the jury is still out on Tippett's great humanist challenge.

Meanwhile, there can be no questioning the achievement of this performance and recording, coupled strikingly with the highly characteristic *Praeludium* for brass, bells and percussion of 1962. Sir Colin Davis's account of the symphony (currently unavailable), will always be admired as a magnificent pioneering effort, but Chandos have given us the version for our time.

New review

Tippett String Quartets – No. 1[a]; No. 2 in F major[a]; No. 3[a]; No. 4[b]; No. 5[c]. **Lindsay Quartet** (Peter Cropper, Ronald Birks, vns; [a]Roger Bigley, [bc]Robin Ireland, vas; Bernard Gregor-Smith, vc). ASV Ⓕ CDDCS231 (two discs: 123 minutes: ADD/DDD: 5/96). Items marked [a] from L'Oiseau-Lyre DSLO10 (12/75), [b]DCA608 (5/88), [c]CDDCA879 (1/94). Recorded 1975-92.

Tippett coached the Lindsay Quartet for these recordings of his first three quartets, and the other two were written for them. In a note written for their twenty-fifth anniversary in 1992 he said that in these recordings they were "concerned to establish good precedents in matters of style, so that succeeding generations of interpreters start at an advantage". In fact one of the most enjoyable things about these readings is that they are so very characteristic of the Lindsay Quartet. Of course a number of the qualities that one might call 'characteristic' are uncommonly well-suited to Tippett's earlier quartets: big tone, sheer vigour of attack and an infectious enjoyment of his lithe sprung rhythms. These performances are indeed excellent precedents for later interpreters. They do establish a style – big-scaled, urgently communicative – that is presumably 'authentic' and yet they challenge listeners as well as other performers to imagine how else they might be done. They also affirm the aching absence of a quartet between the Third and the Fourth (Tippett intended to write one in the late 1940s or early 1950s but got side-tracked by *The Midsummer Marriage* and did not write another for over 20 years) and make one wonder what the rejected two movements of the First Quartet might be like. It is wonderful, though, to hear the five as a sequence in such authoritative readings. The recordings sound very well, but have been transferred at an exceptionally high level.

Additional recommendations ...

...Nos. 1-4. **Britten Quartet.** Collins Classics Ⓕ 7006-2 (two discs: 97 minutes: DDD: 12/91).

...No. 4. **Britten** String Quartet No. 3, Op. 94. **Lindsay Quartet.** ASV Ⓕ CDDCA608 (53 minutes: DDD: 5/88).

Tippett String Quartet No. 5. **Lindsay Quartet** (Peter Cropper, Ronald Birks, vns; Robin Ireland, va; Bernard Gregor-Smith, vc). ASV Ⓕ CDDCA879 (76 minutes: DDD: 1/94).
Brown Fanfare to welcome Sir Michael Tippett. **Purcell** Fantasias – F major, Z737; E minor, Z741; G major, Z742. **Morris** Canzoni Ricertati – No. 1, Risoluto; No. 6, Lento sostenuto.
C. Wood: String Quartet in A minor.

This curious mixture of a programme is a precise re-creation of the concert at which Tippett's Fifth String Quartet had its first performance. Music by two of his teachers and one of his great inspirers is preceded by a greeting prelude that quotes both Purcell and Tippett himself. Tippett's Quartet is quite typical of him, both in its exquisitely singing lyricism and in the fact that it is by no means a mere looking back towards his earlier lyrical phases. Here intensification of expression is often achieved by distillation, towards such a simplicity of utterance that at crucial moments the music thins sometimes to one, often to no more than two, of the quartet's voices. R.O. Morris's *Canzoni Ricertati* subject faintly folk-like melodies to ingenious fugal and canonic treatment. In Charles Wood's quartet, the ingenious interplay of short motives in his scherzo is something that might have caught the young Tippett's ear, and his finale dresses up the Irish folk-song *The lark in the clear air* in its best Sunday clothes. The Purcell *Fantasias* point up Tippett's Purcell-ancestry rather touchingly as does Christopher Brown's miniature *Fanfare*. The Lindsay's beautiful performances are cleanly but not clinically recorded.

New review

Tippett The Windhover. The Source. Magnificat and Nunc dimittis, "Collegium Sancti Johannis Cantabrigiense"[a]. Lullaby. Four Songs from the British Isles. Dance, Clarion Air. A Child of Our Time – Five Negro Spirituals. Plebs angelica. The Weeping Babe. **Finzi Singers / Paul Spicer** with [a]**Andrew Lumsden** (org). Chandos Ⓕ CHAN9265 (55 minutes: DDD: 7/95). Texts included. Recorded 1994.

The Finzi Singers are eloquent in the Spirituals, and polished in the *British Songs* (especially the beguiling "Early One Morning"). However, it is especially good to have the works which represent early sightings of Tippett's later, less lusciously lyrical style – the *Lullaby* (with countertenor, reminding us that it was written for the Deller Consort) and the *Magnificat* and *Nunc dimittis*: here not only are the intonation and phrasing of the tricky lines supremely confident, but the accompanying organ is recorded with exemplary naturalness. The vocal sound throughout is generally no less successful. There may be almost too full and rich a texture for the linear intricacies of *Plebs angelica* and *The Weeping Babe* to make their maximum effect, but there is no lack of exuberance in *Dance, Clarion Air* and the other secular pieces.

Additional recommendation ...

...Dance, Clarion Air. The Weeping Babe. Plebs angelica. Bonny at Morn. Crown of the Year. Music. A Child of Our Time – Five Negro Spirituals. **Soloists; Christ Church Cathedral Choir / Stephen Darlington.** Nimbus Ⓕ NI5266 (51 minutes: DDD: 1/91).

Tippett Songs and Purcell Realizations. **Martyn Hill** (ten); [a]**Craig Ogden** (gtr); [b]**Andrew Ball** (pf). Hyperion Ⓕ CDA66749 (70 minutes: DDD: 4/95). Texts included. Recorded 1994. *Gramophone Editor's choice.*
Music[b]. Songs for Ariel[b]. Songs for Achilles[a]. Boyhood's End[b]. The Heart's Assurance[b]. **Purcell** If music be the food of love, Z379/2[b]. The Fairy Queen – Thrice happy lovers[b]. The Fatal hour comes on apace, Z421[a]. Bess of Bedlam, Z370[b]. Pausanias – Sweeter than roses[b].

The two longest works – the cantata *Boyhood's End* and song-cycle *The Heart's Assurance* – challenge the musicianship and sensitivity of singer and pianist alike. *Boyhood's End* (1943), a setting of prose that is never prosaic, shows the ecstasy of *Midsummer Marriage* to be already within the system, and the profusion of notes has to be mastered so that the dance shall seem as delicate and natural as graceful improvisation. In *The Heart's Assurance* (1951) the spirit is similar though the technical accomplishment of all concerned, composer and performers, is heightened. For the singer, in addition to fearsome difficulties of pitch and rhythm, there is likely to be some problem of tessitura, particularly in the third of the songs, "Compassion". For the pianist, concentration has to be divided between the virtuosic writing of his own part and responsiveness to the singer, his notes, words and expression. Martyn Hill and Andrew Ball are wonderfully at one in all this, and the balancing of voice and piano has been finely achieved. The *Songs for Achilles*, with guitar, also convey a sense of ardent improvisation, and the voice rings out freely. The *Songs for Ariel* here work their natural magic. Tippett's affinities with Purcell are felt at one time or another in most of these compositions, starting indeed with the opening of the programme, the setting of Shelley's *Sleep*. It is good also to have the Purcell 'realizations' included. The recording was issued to mark the composer's ninetieth birthday, a most touching and eloquent tribute.

New review
Tippett The Knot Garden[a]. A Child of Our Time[b]. [a]**Raimund Herincx** (bass) Faber; [a]**Yvonne Minton** (mez) Thea; [a]**Jill Gomez** (sop) Flora; [a]**Dame Josephine Barstow** (sop) Denise; [a]**Thomas Carey** (bar) Mel; [a]**Robert Tear** (ten) Dov; [a]**Thomas Hemsley** (bar) Mangus; [b]**Jessye Norman** (sop); [b]**Dame Janet Baker** (mez); [b]**Richard Cassilly** (ten); [b]**John Shirley-Quirk** (bar); [b]**BBC Singers**; [b]**BBC Choral Society**; [a]**Orchestra of the Royal Opera House, Covent Garden**, [b]**BBC Symphony Orchestra / Sir Colin Davis.** Philips Ⓕ 446 331-2PH2 (two discs: 145 minutes: ADD: 9/95). Notes and texts included. Item marked [a] from 6700 063 (4/74, recorded 1993), [b]6500 985 (11/75, recorded 1975).

The Knot Garden is a classic of its period and a central work in its composer's output. Some of the more enthusiastic reviews after the first performance of *The Knot Garden* were rather perplexed by its structure: it is a short opera, but its three acts are divided into 23 scenes, often brief and abruptly juxtaposed. However, the form of the piece now seems to be admirably clear, musically strong and ideally appropriate to the subject. It is not so much a narrative as an examination of a set of relationships. The First Act introduces six of the seven characters, briefly demonstrates their problems and then introduces a catalyst in the person of Denise, the freedom-fighter disfigured by torture. She sings an updated version of an ancient operatic form – the virtuoso display aria, here brilliantly put to new purposes – which in turn prompts an ensemble-finale in the again updated form of a blues with a fast boogie-woogie middle section. As an opera about relationships it needs particularly sensitive handling by the singers, and the cast (that of the first performance) is outstanding. Tear gives his character ("a homosexual in pink socks!", sneered one reviewer) real charm and pathos as well as singing his uncommonly difficult lines with great flair. Barstow is even finer: an electric presence with a visionary intensity to her aria of remembered anguish. Minton and Herincx are both excellent, Gomez touchingly vulnerable, while Hemsley's immaculate diction and gentlemanly tones are perfect for Mangus, the psychiatrist Prospero who "puts them all to rights". Davis is as eloquently urgent in the opera as in the oratorio, *A Child of Our Time*, which, in a generally fine, rather opera-scaled reading, makes an ideal coupling: two complementary aspects of Tippett the maker of healing images. In the opera the voices sound a little further forward than on the original LPs, the sound a bit harder-edged; the oratorio, appropriately, is placed in a warmer acoustic.

Additional recommendations ...
...Soloists; **City of Birmingham Symphony Chorus and Orchestra / Sir Michael Tippett.** Collins Classics Ⓕ 1339-2 (69 minutes: DDD: 9/92).
...Soloists; **London Symphony Chorus and Orchestra / Richard Hickox.** Chandos Ⓕ CHAN9123 (73 minutes: DDD: 2/93).

New review
Tippett The Midsummer Marriage. **Alberto Remedios** (ten) Mark; **Joan Carlyle** (sop) Jenifer; **Raimund Herincx** (bass) King Fisher; **Elizabeth Harwood** (sop) Bella; **Stuart Burrows** (ten) Jack; **Helen Watts** (contr) Sosostris; **Stafford Dean** (bass) He-Ancient; **Elizabeth Bainbridge** (mez) She-Ancient; **David Whelan** (bar) Half-Tipsy Man; **Andrew Daniels** (ten) Dancing Man; **Chorus and Orchestra of the Royal Opera House, Covent Garden / Sir Colin Davis.** Lyrita Ⓕ SRCD2217 (two discs: 154 minutes: ADD: 1/96). Notes and text included. From Philips 6703 027 (5/71). Recorded 1970.

Here was Tippett in 1955 expressing joy, boundless optimism and faith in beauty and humanity; doing so, moreover, with such richness of imagery that even those who loved it at first hearing were a bit taken aback by its overwhelming abundance. As so often with his pieces, it took a while to sink in, and for players and singers to get their fingers and their vocal chords around those springing rhythms and sinewy lines. The moment at which that happened was the moment of this recording and the performances that preceded it. Remedios and Carlyle are not simply managing those exuberant hocketings above the stave in their final duet; you would swear that they were enjoying them, and as they do so the image of love as a consuming flame is vividly projected. Burrows and the adorable Harwood are audibly moved by how much tenderness and innocence there is in their music, and they make a real and most touching couple. Herincx is wonderfully suave and bossy as King Fisher; Watts not only survives her forays into the bass-baritone register but makes an awesomely Sibylline figure of Sosostris. And Davis, raptly in love with this score and communicating that to his singers and players so effectively that one is never aware of them gritting their teeth and counting beats as though their lives depended on it, reveals again and again the opera's magical sonorities. It is a superb performance: after it one can hardly read those early reviews ("incomprehensible libretto", "too much counterpoint", "half an hour too long") without laughing. The recording, too, communicates a real sense of live performance. A masterpiece, in short, and one that can be listened to again and again without exhausting its exuberant generosity.

New review

Tippett King Priam. **Norman Bailey** (bar) Priam; **Heather Harper** (sop) Hecuba; **Thomas Allen** (bar) Hector; **Felicity Palmer** (sop) Andromache; **Philip Langridge** (ten) Paris; **Yvonne Minton** (mez) Helen; **Robert Tear** (ten) Achilles; **Stephen Roberts** (bar) Patroclus; **Ann Murray** (mez) Nurse; **David Wilson-Johnson** (bar) Old Man; **Peter Hall** (ten) Young Guard; **Kenneth Bowen** (ten) Hermes; **Julian Saipe** (treb) Young Paris; **Linda Hirst** (sop) Servant; **London Sinfonietta Chorus; London Sinfonietta / David Atherton.** Chandos Ⓟ CHAN9406/7 (two discs: 127 minutes: DDD: 2/96). Notes and text included. From Decca D246D3 (11/81). Recorded 1980.

King Priam was a great shock when it was first performed in 1962. In place of the ecstatic lyrical warmth of Tippett's previous opera, The Midsummer Marriage, a plot drawn from the Trojan War drew from him a new and bracing style, hard-edged, disjunct and often barbaric in colour. His vocal writing also became very much more taxing. All the principal roles demand unsparing vocal intensity, precision in pitching the often very awkward intervals and, often enough, athletic flexibility. In its own way it is as difficult to cast as Il trovatore, and the fearlessness of, in particular, Harper, Minton, Palmer, Langridge and Tear is quite remarkable. But a lot more is required of the singers than merely standing up with fortitude to the demands made of them. In that way, too, this is an exceptionally fine performance. One only has to compare the ardour of Langridge's Paris with the range from languor to ferocity of Tear's Achilles to realize that Tippett is very far from writing all-purpose angular modernisms for both his principal tenors. Hecuba, Andromache and Helen are equally sharply characterized by the composer, and as vividly realized by these singers.

Alongside the shock at this opera's new sound-world went a deeper shock at how poignantly moving it could be. The title-role is less spectacularly difficult than some of the others, but Priam is given many of the opera's most telling pages, from 'his' motif of sonorous chordal strings (an archetypal Tippett sound) to the bare but profoundly affecting scene in which he begs Achilles for the body of his son. Bailey has just the right blend of proud dignity and vulnerability for the role, and his projection of the text is immaculate. Atherton is at his best, not just steering the cast and the orchestra past the score's many pitfalls but searching out all the wonderfully sensuous sounds that it contains. He knows just what Tippett means by marking Paris's love music 'winged', and that is exactly how it sounds. The performance and the clean, transparent recording are in short fully worthy of this wonderful opera.

Further listening ...

...Symphony No. 4[a]. Byzantium[b]. [b]**Faye Robinson** (sop); **Chicago Symphony Orchestra / Sir Georg Solti.** Decca 433 668-2DH (4/93).   Ⓖ

...Symphony No. 4. Fantasia on a Theme of Handel[a]. Fantasia concertante on a Theme of Corelli. [a]**Howard Shelley** (pf); **Bournemouth Symphony Orchestra / Richard Hickox.** Chandos CHAN9233 (11/93).

...Piano Sonatas Nos. 1-4. **Paul Crossley** (pf). CRD CRD3430/1 (6/92).

...Piano Sonata No. 2. Coupled with works by **Sackman, Saxton** and **Connolly** Steven Neugarten (pf). Metier MSVCD92008 (1/96). See review in the Collections section; refer to the Index to Reviews.

...Piano Sonata No. 4. Coupled with works by **Saxton, C. Matthews** and **C. Lambert** Nicholas Unwin (pf). Metier MSVCD92009 (1/96). See review in the Collections section; refer to the Index to Reviews.

...The Mask of Time. **Soloists; BBC Singers; BBC Symphony Chorus and Orchestra / Andrew Davis.** EMI British Composers CMS7 64711-2 (10/93).

Boris Tishchenko

New review

Tishchenko String Quartets – No. 1, Op. 8[a]; No. 4, Op. 77[b]. **Glazunov Quartet** (Olga Kolgatina, [a]Elena Kharitonova, [b]Natalia Kolgatina, vns; Inna Peskova, va; Elena Erofeyeva, vc). Olympia Ⓜ OCD547 (60 minutes: DDD: 7/96).

These two string quartets by Boris Tischenko, Shostakovich's 'favourite pupil', contain music of a quality not wholly eclipsed by his teacher. Tishchenko can emulate the obsessiveness of Shostakovich without sounding second-hand. His music has rhythmic backbone, not being afraid of crotchets and quavers, but not making a fetish out of them either. It is remarkable to discover that the First Quartet is the work of an 18-year-old, written long before he began his studies with Shostakovich. True it is somewhat short (it lasts a mere 13 minutes) and underdeveloped, as though he was still testing the water, and the aggressive dance of the second movement is eclipsed by its counterpart in the Fourth Quartet, while the last movement ducks the issues somewhat. But the opening slow movement is successful in elevating introversion to the main topic for discussion, and its harmonic control and calculated open-endedness are admirable. Plenty of student quartets get written, but few could survive the critical scrutiny of maturity as well as this one can. The Fourth Quartet goes to the other extreme of length, its five *attacca* movements lasting a full 47 minutes. The barbaric central movement, exhausting in its remorseless intensity, makes the strongest initial impression, but the rest of the piece doesn't entirely sustain its exceptional length. However, the intriguing, spectral silences and long arcs of dramatic tension of the first two movements are deeply impressive, as are the catatonic cello of the fourth movement and the shell-shocked ostinato, jazzy overlay and deliberate non-tying of loose ends in the finale. The performances by the Glazunov Quartet are as gritty and forthright as the music demands. There are some audible edits, but otherwise the recording is close and clear, maximizing the impact of the playing. These are welcome additions to the catalogue

Further listening ...
...Symphony No. 5. **USSR Ministry of Culture Symphony Orchestra / Gennadi Rozhdestvensky.** Olympia OCD213 (12/88).

Loris Tjeknavorian

Suggested listening ...
...Danses fantastiques. *Coupled with* **Khachaturian** The Widow of Valencia – Suite. Gayaneh – Suite No. 2. **Armenian Philharmonic Orchestra / Loris Tjeknavorian.** ASV CDDCA884 (3/94). *See review under Khachaturian; refer to the Index to Reviews.* Ⓖ

Rudolf Tobias

New review

Tobias String Quartets – No. 1 in D minor; No. 2 in C minor. **Tallinn Quartet** (Urmas Vulp, Toomas Nestor, vns; Viljar Kuusk, va; Teet Järvi, vc). BIS Ⓕ CD704 (64 minutes: DDD: 6/96). Recorded 1994.

The Estonian composer Rudolf Tobias gets scant mention in Western musical dictionaries, and hardly more than this in ones for Eastern European countries. Yet he has a strong claim to be considered the father of modern Estonian composition. He made a career teaching in Leipzig and Berlin, and took German nationality just before the outbreak of the First World War. The privations he suffered on active service in that conflict led to his early death at the age of 45. The two quartets, written in 1899 and 1902, show evidence of abundant, if not yet fulfilled, talent (he was at work on a third when he died, but only fragments exist). The First has the appealing freshness and Nordic – or should one say Baltic – clarity of air that one finds in the early Sibelius quartets. The Second is more mature and ambitious, but its sacrifice of spontaneity is not unreservedly to be welcomed. The slow third movement, *Nachtstück*, is particularly fine. The Tallinn Quartet are exemplary advocates, giving incisive, invigorating performances (occasionally rough around the edges) and total commitment. BIS's sound is warm and beautifully natural.

New review

Tobias Jonah's Mission. **Pille Lill** (sop); **Urve Tauts** (mez); **Peter Svensson** (ten); **Raimo Laukka** (bar); **Mati Palm** (bass); **Tallinn Boys' Choir; Estonian Philharmonic Chamber Choir; Oratorio Choir; Estonian State Symphony Orchestra / Neeme Järvi.** BIS Ⓕ CD731/2 (two discs: 114 minutes: DDD: 8/96). Notes, text and translation included.

The informative insert-note to this disc claims Tobias as a major figure and *Jonah's Mission* as "one of the most magnificent and monumental compositions an Estonian composer has ever written". It is an oratorio much influenced by Mendelssohn, both in the free construction, a good deal of the idiom, and in some of the subtle use of motive. However, the work is on a scale never envisaged by Mendelssohn, calling for two mixed choirs, a children's choir, five soloists and a very large orchestra with organ. Only occasionally are there suggestions (as with a harmonized descending chromatic scale) that Tobias is aware of Wagner, and perhaps of Mahler. It is certainly constructed with an expert hand, well written especially for the chorus, and laying out the story of Jonah with a skilful sense of drama that Tobias may have developed during his years working in the St Petersburg opera. The plot is the one familiar from the Old Testament of Jonah fleeing Nineveh, being cast overboard so as to calm a storm and then swallowed by a whale, eventually being restored to God's mercy. However, the narrative elements are less important than meditative ones (the whale is, so to speak, only small fry). Tobias's intention is clearly to marry religious reflection on the matter of divine mercy with the conflict between the oppressive and worldly Nineveh and the sufferings of a small nation, drawing a parallel between the fate of the Israelites and that of the Estonians. The vigour of the enterprise, and its boldness, command respect, and there is some truly splendid music, especially at the moments of high drama – the storm, over which Tobias does not linger – and at some of the more introspective, prayerful meditations. Tobias himself seems to have been largely responsible for the failure of the first performance, at Leipzig in 1909, being obliged to cut down on the forces and overestimating his abilities as a conductor. With the escape of Estonia from Soviet rule, the work has apparently embarked on a new lease of life, in particular since the first performance of the fully restored version in 1989. It is a pity that the recording and some aspects of the solo singing leave much to be desired; but the choir and orchestra rise wholeheartedly to an event of obvious significance for them, and they could hardly expect a more inspiring and committed conductor than Neeme Järvi.

Further listening ...

...Julius Caesar. *Coupled with* **Lemba** Symphony in C sharp minor. **Eller** Twilight. **Tormis** Overture No. 2. **Pärt** Cantus in memory of Benjamin Britten. **Royal Scottish Orchestra / Neeme Järvi.** Chandos CHAN8656 (11/89).

Ernst Toch

American 1887-1964

Suggested listening ...

...Five Pieces for Wind and Percussion, Op. 83. *Coupled with* **Hindemith** Wind Septet. **Weill** Violin Concerto, Op. 12[a]. [a]**Christian Tetzlaff** (vn); **Deutsche Kammerphilharmonie.** Virgin Classics VC5 45056-2 (7/95).

Henri Tomasi

French 1901-1971

Suggested listening ...

...Trumpet Concerto. *Coupled with works by* **Jolivet, Hummel** and **Haydn** Sergei Nakariakov (tpt); [a]**Alexander Markovich** (pf); **Lausanne Chamber Orchestra / Jésus López-Cobos.** Teldec 4509-90846-2 (10/93). *See review in the Collections section; refer to the Index to Reviews.*

Thomas Tomkins

British 1572-1656

Tomkins Third Service[a]. O Lord, let me know mine end[a]. O that the salvation were given[a]. Know you not[a]. In Nomine (1648). In Nomine (1652). Voluntaries – G major; C major; A minor. [a]**New College Choir, Oxford / Edward Higginbottom** with **David Burchell** (org). CRD Ⓕ CRD3467 (62 minutes: DDD: 9/94). Texts included. Recorded 1990. *Gramophone Editor's choice.*

This is a well-balanced programme of sacred music by Thomas Tomkins. The four movements of the Third, or Great Service, together with the three anthems are spaced out with five organ pieces – two *In Nomines* and three voluntaries – chosen and arranged in such a way that the resulting key sequence has a satisfying natural flow. After an unassuming intonation, the truly royal *Te Deum* of the Great Service takes off with great verve and vigour, the rich ten-part texture of the full sections contrasting well with the lighter scoring of the verses. This energy and these contrasts are characteristic of the performances as a whole. There is some delightful solo singing in the verse anthems, in particular the alto solo in *O Lord, let me know mine end.* The two solo trebles are kept busy: they have a rather distinctive but complementary tone-quality, which makes up for a slight imbalance in volume. In general, however, the balance is good and the ensemble and dovetailing excellent. The trebles are a confident group with good articulation; they soar up to their top B flats with the utmost ease.

Additional recommendations ...

...Third Service – Magnificat and Nunc dimittis. Cathedral Music – O sing unto the Lord a new song. Then David mourned. My beloved spake unto me. Above the stars my saviour dwells. Glory be to God on high. Almighty God, the fountain of all wisdom. When David heard. My shepherd is the living Lord. Sing unto God. Behold, the hour cometh. O God, the proud are risen against me. **St George's Chapel Choir, Windsor / Christopher Robinson** with **Roger Judd** (org). Hyperion Ⓕ CDA66345 (63 minutes: DDD: 3/90).

...Third Service. Anthems – Almighty God, the fountain of all wisdom; Be strong and of good courage; O God, the proud are risen against me; O sing unto the Lord; Then David mourned; When David heard; Woe is me. **The Tallis Scholars / Peter Phillips.** Gimell Ⓕ CDGIM024 (58 minutes: DDD: 3/92).

Further listening ...
...Barafostus' Dream. *Coupled with works by* **Gibbons, Byrd, Anonymous, Aston** and **J. Bull** In Nomine. **Sophie Yates** (virg). ✍ Chandos Chaconne CHAN0574 (12/95). *See review under Byrd; refer to the Index to Reviews.*

Ernest Tomlinson   British 1927-

Suggested listening ...
...Little Serenade. An English Overture. The Story of Cinderella – Fairy Coach; Cinderella Waltz. Kielder Water. Silverthorne Suite. Second Suite of English Folk-Dances. Lyrical Suite – Nocturne. Pastoral Dances – Hornpipe. Gaelic Sketches – Gaelic Lullaby. Nautical Interlude. Sweet and Dainty. **Bratislava Radio Symphony Orchestra / Ernest Tomlinson.** Marco Polo 8 223413 (12/92).
...Comedy Overture. First Suite of English Folk-Dances. Light Music Suite. Shenandoah. Cumberland Square. Rhapsody and Rondo[a]. Passepied. Miniature Dances. Aladdin – Birdcage Dance; Cushion Dance; Belly Dance. A Georgian Miniature. [a]**Richard Watkins** (hn); **Slovak Radio Symphony Orchestra / Ernest Tomlinson.** Marco Polo 8 223513 (3/95).

Giuseppe Torelli   Italian 1658-1709

Suggested listening ...
...12 Concerti grossi, Op. 8 No. 2 in A minor; No. 3 in E major; No. 6 in G minor; No. 8 in C minor; No. 9 in E minor; No. 12 in D major. **Mariana Sirbu, Antonio Perez** (vns); **I Musici.** Philips 432 118-2PH (1/94).
...Complete Works for One, Two and Four Trumpets and Orchestra. **San Petronio Cappella Musicale Orchestra** (Per-Olov Lindeke, David Staff, Edward Tarr, Gabriele Cassone, tpts) **/ Sergio Vartolo.** Bongiovanni GB5523/5-2 (5/95).
...Concerto in E minor for Four Violins and Strings. *Coupled with works by* **Locatelli, Leo, Mossi** and **Valentini** Cologne Musica Antiqua / Reinhard Goebel. Archiv Produktion 435 393-2AH (9/92). ✍ *See review in the Collections section; refer to the Index to Reviews.*
...Sonata in G major, Op. 1 No. 1. Concerto a quattro in D minor, Op. 6 No. 10. *Coupled with works by* **Bononcini, Ariosti, Corelli** and **Stoffani** Berlin Barock Compagney. Capriccio 10 459 (10/95). ✍ *See review in the Collections section; refer to the Index to Reviews.*   ⓗ
...Sonata a 5 con tromba, G7. *Coupled with works by* **Albinoni, Corelli, Vivaldi, A. Marcello, Viviani, Franceschini** and **Baldassare** Håkan Hardenberger (tpt); **I Musici.** Philips 442 131-2PH (5/95). *See review in the Collections section; refer to the Index to Reviews.*   ⓖ

Michael Torke   American 1961-

New review
Torke Javelin[a]. December[h]. Run[a]. Adjustable Wrench[cd]. Green[f]. Music on the Floor – second movement[ce]. Bright Blue Music[f]. [a]**Atlanta Symphony Orchestra / Yoel Levi;** [b]**Philharmonia Orchestra / Michael Torke;** [cde]**London Sinfonietta /** [d]**Kent Nagano,** [e]**Lothar Zagrosek;** [f]**Baltimore Symphony Orchestra / David Zinman.** Argo Ⓟ 452 101-2ZH (63 minutes: DDD: 8/96). Items marked [a] and [b] new to UK, [cd] from 430 209-2ZH (12/90), [ce]443 528-2ZH (1/95). *Gramophone Editor's choice.*   ⓖⓖ

Under the collective title, "Javelin. The Music of Michael Torke", this excellent anthology contains both new and previously unrecorded material. It also brings together on one disc some of the most optimistic, joyful and thoroughly uplifting music to appear in recent years. Admittedly, Torke's music may not be heavily laden with the socio-political messages of our time or deal with the darker corners of man's psyche, but that certainly doesn't make it any less relevant. Of the new pieces presented here the main attraction is *Javelin*, which was composed in 1994 and is the official commission of the 1996 Olympic Games. *Javelin* is lithe and sleek and very athletic and heroic in tone – its bright and breezy countenance more than fulfilling its sporting brief. The work's classical reverberations place it alongside pieces such as *Green* and *Bright Blue Music*. *December*, too, is very classical in tone. Scored for strings the writing has a certain English quality about it, recalling at times Tippett. *Run*, which dates from 1992, can be counted amongst Torke's process pieces, though the word 'process' should be used with caution, as the result tends away from minimalism rather than towards it. Torke's own description of the piece as "someone setting out on their morning run, taking in the ever-changing panorama of the rising sun over a still-sleeping city" is very evocative; it's a high-energy, invigorating work. The remaining pieces are taken from earlier Torke/Argo releases, and consist of the beautiful central movement from *Music on the Floor*, the 'pop'-inspired chamber work *Adjustable Wrench* (Torke's most frequently performed composition) and the two exhilarating roller-coaster-ride orchestral pieces *Bright Blue Music* and *Green*. Performances and recordings of all the pieces on this disc are superb, and if you are coming to Torke's music for the first time it cannot be recommended too highly. Even if you already have the original recordings of some of these pieces the disc is worth considering for the new items alone.

Additional recommendations ...

...Colour Music – Green; Purple; Ecstatic Orange; Ash; Bright Blue Music. **Baltimore Symphony Orchestra / David Zinman.** Argo Ⓔ 433 071-2ZH (54 minutes: DDD: 2/92). ⒼⒼⒼ

...The Yellow Pages[e]. Slate[abcd]. Adjustable Wrench[d]. Vanada[d]. Rust[e]. **Michael Torke** (pf); [a]**Edmund Niemann, Nurit Tilles** (pf, four hands); [b]**James Pugliese** (xylophone); [c]**Gary Schall** (marimba); **London Sinfonietta /** [d]**Kent Nagano,** [c]**David Miller.** Argo Ⓔ 430 209-2ZH (55 minutes: DDD: 12/90). Ⓖ

Torke Four Proverbs[a]. Monday[b]. Music on the floor[b]. Tuesday[b]. [a]**Catherine Bott** (sop); [a]**Argo Band / Michael Torke;** [b]**London Sinfonietta / Lothar Zagrosek.** Argo Ⓔ 443 528-2ZH (60 minutes: DDD: 1/95). Texts included. Recorded 1993. Ⓖ

Those familiar with Torke's music will not be surprised to learn that his vocal writing has a strong lyrical impulse; they may not know, however, that he also appears to have a natural flair for the medium. The *Four Proverbs* (settings of proverbs from the New Testament) are attractive examples of Torke's approachable style – lyrical melodies and a disciplined, economical working of his chosen material. In each of the settings Torke ingeniously constructs, deconstructs and finally reconstructs the vocal line in such a way that the technical process actually becomes an integral part of the music's attractiveness. Catherine Bott certainly makes an ideal and persuasive exponent, and clearly relishes the curvaceousness of Torke's melodic writing. The remaining pieces, *Monday*, *Tuesday* and *Music on the floor*, are for chamber ensemble and are more abstract in style. The pieces *Monday* and *Tuesday* may be a musical response to those days of the week, or they may not. In fact, the music needs no hidden agenda to justify itself; its beautiful sense of organic flow and development and its pulsing kinetic energy are enough in themselves. The same goes for *Music on the floor*, a three-movement work colourfully scored for two vibraphones (spatially separated left and right), piano, string quartet and two woodwind; the slow movement is particularly haunting and attractive. The one thing that really stands out about this composer is his highly individual voice, because, for all of its echoes of Copland and Stravinsky, there is an overall sound that is uniquely Torkean. Splendid performances and recorded sound.

Further listening ...

...Soprano Saxophone Concerto. *Coupled with works by* **R.R. Bennett** and **Myers** John Harle (sax); **Albany Symphony Orchestra / David Alan Miller.** Argo 443 529-2ZH (7/95).

...Soprano Saxophone Concerto. *Coupled with works by* **I. Wilson, D. Heath, McGlynn** and **Nyman** Gerard McChrystal (sax); **London Musici / Mark Stephenson.** Silva Classics SILKD6010 (6/96). *See review in the Collections section; refer to the Index to Reviews.*

...Black and White – Charcoal. *Coupled with* **Harbison** Remembering Gatsby. **Larsen** Collage: Boogie. **Schiff** Stomp. **Kernis** New Era Dance. **J. Adams** The Chairman Dances. **Bernstein** West Side Story – Mambo. **Moran** Points of Departure. **Agento** The Dream of Valentino – Tango. **Daugherty** Desi. **Rouse** Bonham. **Baltimore Symphony Orchestra / David Zinman.** Argo 444 454-2ZH (7/95).

José de Torres
Spanish

Suggested listening ...

...Más no puedo ser. Al clamor. *Coupled with works by* **C. Galán, Literes, Anonymous, F. Valls** and **F. de Iribarren** Al Ayre Español / Eduardo López Banzo. Deutsche Harmonia Mundi 05472 77325-2 (8/95). ✐ *See review in the Collections section; refer to the Index to Reviews.* **Gramophone** *Editor's choice.* Ⓖ

Veljo Tormis
Estonian 1930-

Suggested listening ...

...Livonian Heritage. Votic Wedding Songs. Izhorian Epic. Ingrian Evenings. Vespian Paths. Karelian Destiny. **Estonian Philharmonic Chamber Choir / Tonu Kaljuste.** ECM New Series 434 275-2 (10/92).

...The Curse of Iron. *Coupled with* **Nørgård** And time shall be no more. **Rautavaara** Suite de Lorca, Op. 72. **Sandström** A Cradle Song/The Tyger. **Jersild** Three Romantic Songs. **Danish National Radio Choir / Stefan Parkman.** Chandos CHAN9264 (4/95).

...Overture No. 2. *Coupled with* **Tobias** Julius Caesar. **Lemba** Symphony in C sharp minor. **Eller** Twilight. **Pärt** Cantus in memory of Benjamin Britten. **Royal Scottish Orchestra / Neeme Järvi.** Chandos CHAN8656 (8/89).

Charles Tournemire   French 1870-1939

Tournemire Suite Evocatrice, Op. 74.
Vierne Symphony No. 3, Op. 28.
Widor Symphonie Gothique, Op. 70. **Jeremy Filsell** (org). Herald Ⓕ HAVPCD145 (71 minutes:
   DDD: 3/92). Played on the Harrison and Harrison organ of Ely Cathedral. Recorded 1991. ⒼⒼ
Compared with, say, the symphonies of Tchaikovsky or Sibelius the organ symphonies of Widor and
his pupil Vierne are not particularly long. But in terms of organ music they are among the longest
single works in the repertory. Within their five-movement form the composers set out to exploit the
full expressive range of the organ and it was no coincidence that the organ symphony developed in
turn of the century France. The great French organ builder Aristide Cavaillé-Coll was then producing
instruments capable of hitherto undreamt-of colour and expression. Both Widor (at St Sulpice) and
Vierne (at Notre Dame) had at their disposal the finest instruments in Paris and they indulged
themselves fully in their symphonies. The subtitle of Widor's Ninth (*Gothic*) says it all. The structure
is vast, intricately detailed, and almost forbidding in its grandness. Vierne's Third also presents an
awesome spectacle, full of complex music and technically demanding writing, while Tournemire's neo-
classical Suite provides a moment almost of light relief in such heavyweight company. Jeremy Filsell
is an outstanding virtuoso player with a gift for musical communication and, in the Ely Cathedral
organ, an instrument which produces the range of the great French instruments, but within an
altogether clearer acoustic. These are performances of exceptional quality captured in a recording of
rare excellence from the small independent company, Herald.

Marcel-Lucien Tournier   French 1879-1951

Suggested listening ...
...Jazz Band. *Coupled with works by* **Renié, Casella, Rosetti, Spohr, Debussy, Damase,
   Prokofiev** and **Fauré** Naoko Yoshino (hp). Philips 446 064-2PH (2/96). *See review in the
   Collections section; refer to the Index to Reviews.*

Colin Towns   British 20th Century

Suggested listening ...
...Trumpet Concerto. Cityscape. Full Circle: The Haunting of Julie – film score. Koch 38703-2 (9/95).
...The Buccaneers – original TV soundtrack. Mercury 526 866-2 (9/95).

Geoffrey Toye   British 1889-1942

Suggested listening ...
...The Haunted Ballroom. *Coupled with works by* **Binge, Williams, Coates, Collins, Farnon,
   Baynes, Curzon, Lutz, Gibbs, White, Ketèlbey, Joyce, Ellis** and **Ancliffe** New London
   Orchestra / Ronald Corp. Hyperion CDA66868 (7/96). *See review in the Collections section; refer
   to the Index to Reviews.* **Gramophone** *Editor's record of the month.*

Giovanni Trabaci   Italian c1575-1647

Suggested listening ...
...Partite sopra "Rugiero". *Coupled with works by* **A. Mayone, Giovanni de Macque, Facoli,
   A. Valente, Picchi, Buono, Frescobaldi, Lambardo, Merula, M. Rossi, Salvatore,
   B. Storace, G. Strozzi, Stradella** and **A. Scarlatti** Rinaldo Alessandrini (hpd). Opus 111
   OPS30-118 (4/95). ☞ *See review in the Collections section; refer to the Index to Reviews.*   ⒼⒼ

Harold Truscott   British 1914-1992

Truscott Symphony in E major. Suite in G major. Elegy. **Ireland National Symphony Orchestra /
   Gary Brain.** Marco Polo Ⓕ 8 223674 (61 minutes: DDD: 2/95). Recorded 1993.   Ⓖ
During his lifetime Harold Truscott was known to a good many as a teacher and as a perceptive and
truculent critic, as a composer to very few. The Symphony seems to date from the late 1940s, and it
sounds neither English nor 'modern', with references to Nielsen, Bruckner and Mahler (roughly in
that order, with perhaps a hint or two of Franz Schmidt, on whose music Truscott was an authority).
It is a work of considerable power and eloquence, with a personal voice clearly audible above those
'quotations' (they sound more like that than influences). Guy Rickards's note on the work and a pair
of superscriptions in Truscott's piano reduction of the Symphony suggest that it has a religious
'programme'. The doomed processional of the first movement, the combination of Shostakovich-like

humour and malign grimness in the central scherzo and the progress of the finale from a cold funeral march to a bleakly tragic coda make this seem likely: a 'Good Friday Symphony', perhaps. As Truscott's only completed symphony it has remarkable assurance in its handling of the orchestra and its ability to build structures of real scale and grandeur. The *Elegy* is earlier, but also symphonic in the size of its gestures. The diminutive Suite is slighter than these other works, but an echo of them is heard in the slow movement (nearly as long as the other three movements put together), suggesting that Truscott was happiest writing in symphonic dimensions. The performances are decent enough, the recording a shade reverberant. What matters is the music, the Symphony above all: it is a remarkable work.

Further listening ...

...Trio in A minor[a]. Clarinet Sonata No. 2 in C major[b]. Solo Violin Sonata in C major[c]. Meditation on themes from Emmanuel Moór's Suite for Four Cellos[d]. Cello Sonata in A minor[e]. [a]**Imre Kovács** (fl); [b]**István Varga** (cl); [a]**Béla Nagy,** [c]**Violetta Eckhardt** (vns); [a]**László Bársony** (va); [de]**Judit Kis Domonkos** (vc); [be]**Melinda Lugossy** (pf). Marco Polo 8 223727 (6/95).

Eduard Tubin
Estonian/Swedish 1905-1982

Suggested listening ...

...Symphonies – No. 2, "The Legendary"; No. 6. **Swedish Radio Symphony Orchestra / Neeme Järvi.** BIS CD304 (4/86).

...Symphonies Nos. 3 and 8. **Swedish Radio Symphony Orchestra / Neeme Järvi.** BIS CD342 (9/88). *Gramophone Award Winner 1989.*

...Symphonies – No. 4, "Sinfonia lirica"[a]; No. 9[b]. Toccata[b]. [a]**Bergen Symphony Orchestra;** [b]**Gothenburg Symphony Orchestra / Neeme Järvi.** BIS CD227 (10/86).

...Symphony No. 5. Kratt. **Bamberg Symphony Orchestra / Neeme Järvi.** BIS CD306 (9/86).

...Symphony No. 7. Piano Concerto[a]. Sinfonietta on Estonian motifs. [a]**Roland Pöntinen** (pf); **Gothenberg Symphony Orchestra / Neeme Järvi.** BIS CD401 (1/89).

...Elegy for Strings (arr. Raid). Symphony No. 11 (orch. Raid). *Coupled with* **Raid** Symphony No. 2, "Stockholm". **Estonian State Symphony Orchestra / Arvo Volmer.** Koch International Classics Ⓟ 37291-2 (48 minutes: DDD: 1/96). *See review under Raid; refer to the Index to Reviews.*

...String Quartet. Piano Quartet in C sharp minor[a]. Elegy. *Coupled with* **Pärt** Fratres. **Tüür** String Quartet. **Tallinn Quartet;** [a]**Love Derwinger** (pf). BIS CD574 (1/94).

...Six Preludes. Piano Sonatas Nos. 1 and 2. Lullaby. Album Leaf. Three Pieces for Children. A little March, for Rana. Three Estonian Folk-dances. Prelude No. 1. Variations on an Estonian Folk Tune. Ballad on a Theme by Mart Saar. Four Folk-songs from my country. Sonatina in D minor. Seven Preludes. Suite on Estonian Shepherd Melodies. **Vardo Rumessen** (pf). BIS CD414/16 (three discs: 3/89).

...Barbara von Tisenhusen. **Soloists; Estonia Opera Chorus; Estonia Opera Orchestra / Peeter Lilje.** Ondine ODE776-2 (4/93).

Antonín Tučapsky
Czechoslovakian/British 1928-

New review

Tučapský The Sacrifice[a]. Five Lenten Motets. Lauds. The Seven Sorrows[b]. [a]**Stephen Foulkes** (bar); [b]**Tomáš Tuláček** (vn); [a]**Colin Hunt** (org); **Bath Camerata / Nigel Perrin.** Somm Ⓟ SOMMCD205 (65 minutes: DDD: 7/96). Texts included. Recorded 1995.

Antonin Tučapský is known as the conductor of some fine performances of Janáček with the Moravian Teachers choir; he is less well known as a composer, even though he has written much and has been living in England since life was made impossible for him in his own country after the 'Prague Spring' of 1968. It comes as no surprise that he writes well for a small chorus; though quite how well and inventively may come as a highly agreeable surprise. He has the enterprise to experiment, as with the spoken passages and the eerie *glissandos* of his setting of two Auden poems in *Lauds*, but this is less impressive than the range of textures – sometimes dense and luminous, sometimes translucent, sometimes packed and brooding – which marks the major work on this record, *The Sacrifice*. This is a setting of George Herbert's marvellous devotional poem of Christ before his Passion, with its repeated cry, "Was ever grief like mine?" Tučapský selects and slightly rearranges the verses but effectively divides them up into seven sections, bringing in a solo baritone for some of them. There is something of the Britten of *Rejoice in the Lamb* here, and not only in the mastery of the choral writing, but essentially the voice is a strong and individual one, with a subtle harmonic idiom and a vivid sense of drama. The work lasts a little over half an hour, and sustains its atmosphere unfalteringly. This is a real discovery; it should be more widely heard, and perhaps this disc will encourage that. It somewhat overshadows the *Five Lenten Motets*, and even the ambitious and ingenious setting of Ted Hughes's *The Seven Sorrows*, though the mastery of choral writing is very much in evidence in both works. Nigel Perrin directs very carefully prepared and effective performances.

Joaquín Turina
Spanish 1882-1949

Turina Danzas fantásticas, Op. 22. La procesión del Rocio, Op. 9. Sinfonía sevillana, Op. 23. Ritmos, Op. 43. **Bamberg Symphony Orchestra / Antonio de Almeida.** RCA Victor Red Seal Ⓔ RD60895 (63 minutes: DDD: 7/92).

An hour's worth of musical sunshine, with the occasional cloud drifting by just for tonal contrast. Turina was a magnificent orchestrator and although he was – as Antonio de Almeida points out in his useful booklet annotations – a "quintessential Sevillian", he was also acutely aware of musical trends beyond his own locality. His style approximates the youthful opulence of early Debussy (whose sensuous *Printemps* frequently comes to mind), yet the piquant instrumentation that graces, say, "Exaltación" from the *Danzas fantásticas*, or the whole of *La procesión del Rocio* is refreshingly individual – beautifully aired and crafted, with the sum of its gleaming parts amounting to an appealing tonal blend. Were it not for the give-away nature of specifically Spanish melodies, Dvořák (of the *Slavonic Dances*) would as likely come to mind as Falla – particularly in the *Danzas*. *La procesión* (1912) predates the other pieces on the disc, while *Ritmos* was composed as late as 1928. It was premièred by Casals, but here more than anywhere else on the disc, one is reminded of Almeida's great mentor, Sir Thomas Beecham. Just listen to the way he points *Ritmos*'s atmospheric "Danza lenta", or sample the excitement he generates in the "Danza exótica" from the same work; then turn back to "Fiesta en San Juan de Aznalfarache" from *Sinfonía sevillana* – awash with colour from the first bar to the last – and witness how the Bamberg players exploit Turína's varied tonal palette. As for the recording (a co-production between BMG Classics and Bavarian Radio), it's truly demonstration-worthy; a fair sampling point is the "Valse trágico" from *Ritmos*, which features a spectacular mushrooming tam-tam. But then Turina is the answer to a recording engineer's dream: his use of winds, brass and percussion, in particular, is as judicious as it is impressive, and he never overcrowds his orchestral climaxes. Quite simply, this disc is unalloyed delight from start to finish – *Fantásticas* in name and nature!

Further listening ...

...Rapsodia sinfónica, Op. 66. *Coupled with* **Albéniz** (orch. Halffter). Rapsodia española, Op. 70. **Falla** Noches en los jardines de España. **Alicia de Larrocha** (pf); **London Philharmonic Orchestra / Rafael Frühbeck de Burgos.** Decca 410 289-2DH (10/84). *See review under Albéniz; refer to the Index to Reviews.* Ⓖ

...La oración del torero, Op. 34. *Coupled with works by* **Debussy, Ravel, Villa-Lobos** and **Creston** Arthur Gleghorn (fl); Mitchell Lurie (cl); Ann Mason Stockton (hp); Hollywood Quartet; Concert Arts Strings / Felix Slatkin. Testament mono SBT1053* (3/95). *See review in the Collections section; refer to the Index to Reviews.* ⒼⒼ

...Piano Trios – No. 1, Op. 35; No. 2, Op. 76. Círculo, Op. 91. **Munich Piano Trio.** Calig CAL50 902.

...Guitar Sonata, Op. 61. *Coupled with* **Sor** (ed. P. Romero) Fantasía in D minor. **Tárrega** (arr. P. Romero) Gran Jota. **Albéniz** (arr. C. Romero) Torre Bermeja, Op. 92 No. 12. **Granados** Tonadillas al estilo antiguo No. 7, La maja de Goya[a]. **Mudarra** Tres libros – Fantasía que contrahaze la harpa en la manera de Ludovico[a]. **Guerau** Canarios[a]. **Milán** El Maestro – Fantasia XVI[a]. **Falla** Homenaje, "Le tombeau de Claude Debussy". **Rodrigo** Por tierras de Jerez. **Moreno Torroba** Aires de la Mancha. **C. Romero** Los Maestros. **Pepe Romero** (gtr). Philips 442 150-2PH (4/95). Items marked [a] trans. P. Romero.

...Mujeres de Sevilla, Op. 89. Mujeres Españolas, Op. 17. Mujeres Españolas, Op. 73. Danzas Andaluzas, Op. 8. Bailete, Op. 79. **David Buechner** (pf). Connoisseur Society CD4186 (10/94). Ⓖ

Mark-Anthony Turnage
British 1960-

Turnage Drowned Out[a]. Kai[b]. Three Screaming Popes[c]. Momentum[a]. [b]**Ulrich Heinen** (vc); [b]**Birmingham Contemporary Music Group;** [ac]**City of Birmingham Symphony Orchestra / Sir Simon Rattle.** EMI Ⓔ CDC5 55091-2 (72 minutes: DDD: 9/94). Item marked [c] from TSP204681-2 (9/92), remainder new to UK. Recorded 1994. *Gramophone Editor's choice.* ⒼⒼ

This is a stunning collection, even more convincing proof than the recording of his opera *Greek* (listed below) that Mark-Anthony Turnage is a talent of major importance. The influences on his musical language are obvious, but even to name Stravinsky and Copland, jazz and certain areas of popular music, is misleading, since the most attractive feature of his style is its unified individuality, its personal voice. In *Drowned Out*, for example, one could waste a good deal of time ascribing the regular pulse of its lyrical but tense opening section to the influence of jazz, or examining its gradually intensifying melodic line for traces of an affinity with blues or 'soul' music. They may be there, but the sustained eloquence of this music is what matters; it is Turnage's own, and an impressive achievement. The 'influences' are more overt in *Kai*, a one-movement concerto for cello and chamber orchestra in which saxophones and brass are prominent. The cello line, and that of its lyrical 'companions' (other solo strings, flute, bassoon), are often blues-inflected, sometimes Gershwin-tinged; the 'attacking' forces here are an aggressive double-bass pizzicato and a sort of big-band toccata. *Three Screaming Popes* offers further evidence of the range that Turnage's style can command: the impetus and sometimes troubled lyricism of the two longer works, but also a grave, mysterious solemnity, and it shares with *Kai* and *Drowned Out* a pungent sense of orchestral colour. So does *Momentum*, a sort of extended fanfare written for the opening of Symphony Hall in Birmingham. This has the feeling, by analogy with Janáček, of Turnage's *Sinfonietta*, a bold opposition of brass-led and saxophone-dominated sonorities from which a striding string theme emerges. Most welcome of all, this music is insistently approachable without being simplistic. Turnage's 'recipe' is not 'Stravinsky plus palatable pop'. The 'influences' are used as we use imagery in speech, to aid urgent communication, not to reduce communication to the lowest common denominator. The performances have a strong sense that the players realize this: they are urgently eloquent and gratefully virtuoso. The recordings are appropriately direct and vivid.

Further listening ...

...On All Fours[a]. Lament for a Hanging Man[b]. Sarabande[c]. Release[d]. [bc]**Fiona Kimm** (mez); [abd]**Martin Robertson** (sax); [a]**Christopher Van Kampen** (vc); [cd]**Ian Brown** (pf); [abd]**Nash Ensemble / Oliver Knussen.** NMC NMCD024M (9/95).

...Greek. **Soloists; Greek Ensemble / Richard Bernas.** Argo 440 368-2ZHO (7/94).

Erkki-Sven Tüür

Estonia 1959-

New review

Tüür Architectonics VI. Passion. Illusion. Crystallisatio. Requiem[a]. [a]**Estonian Philharmonic Chamber Choir; Tallinn Chamber Orchestra / Tönu Kaljuste.** ECM New Series Ⓕ 449 459-2 (64 minutes: DDD: 7/96). Text and translation included.

Architectonics VI sounds like one of those titles that are too good to resist, and it is to the credit of Erkki-Sven Tüür that he admits as much in the brief interview in the booklet to this beguiling disc (the sumptuous annotation in English is translated in reduced form in German and French). Tüür's piece – written in 1992 – isn't architectonic in construction (well, any more than the music of a hundred other composers), but it is well put together and effective on its own terms. *Passion* and *Illusion*, both for string orchestra and composed in 1993, are closer in spirit to the prevailing 'New Simplicity' of current East Baltic composition. *Passion*, indeed, is occasionally reminiscent of Tüür's better-known compatriot, Arvo Pärt, although the brief *Illusion* has a curiously English feel to it. The title track, *Crystallisatio* (1995), is scored for three flutes, bells, string orchestra and live electronics and is somewhat more demanding in scope. It is here that Tüür's synthesis of minimalism with serial techniques is heard most eloquently; not wholly achieved, perhaps, but fascinating in application. By far the biggest piece is the Requiem (1992-3; in memory of the conductor Peeter Lilje). It is a deeply felt, half-hour-long setting of the mass for the dead, and is of markedly different character to the other pieces on this release. This is a handsomely produced, thought-provoking release. ECM may be looking for a new Pärt, but Tüür is his own man. Anyone wanting to hear up-to-the-minute new music that will not sear the ears off his (or her) head could do little better than try this new disc.

Further listening ...

...Insular Deserta. *Coupled with* **Urbaitis** Lithuanian Folk Music. **Juozapaitis** Perpetuum mobile. **Vasks** Cantabile. **Kutavičius** Northern Gates. **Rekašius** Music for Strings. **Ostrobothnian Chamber Orchestra / Juha Kangas.** Finlandia 4509-97893-2 (11/95).

...String Quartet. *Coupled with* **Pärt** Fratres. **Tubin** String Quartet. Piano Quartet in C sharp minor[a]. Elegy. **Tallinn Quartet;** [a]**Love Derwinger** (pf). BIS CD574 (1/94).

...Sonata. *Coupled with* **Sumera** Piece from the Year 1981. **Rääts** Toccata. **Kangro** Suite, Op. 1. **Mägi** The Ancient Kannel. **Vähi** Fata Morgana. **Pärt** Partita. **Lauri Väinmaa** (pf). Finlandia 4509-95704-2 (7/95).

Christopher Tye

British *c*1505-1572

Suggested listening ...

...Consort Music – Complete Instrumental Works. **Hespèrion XX / Jordi Savall.** Auvidis Astrée E8708 (11/89). ✐

...Mass, "Euge Bone". Peccavimus cum patribus. *Coupled with* **Sheppard** In manus tuas II. Gaude virgo Christiphera. Reges Tharsis et insulae. Libra nos, salva nos I and II. **The Clerkes of Oxenford / David Wulstan.** Proud Sound PROUCD126 (5/90).

...Kyrie, "Orbis factor". Mass, "Euge bone". Quaesumus omnipotens. Miserere mei, Deus. Omnes gentes, plaudite. Peccavimus cum patribus. **Winchester Cathedral Choir / David Hill.** Hyperion CDA66424 (1/91).

...Mass, "Euge Bone". Omnes gentes, plaudite. Peccavimus cum patribus. *Coupled with* **W. Mundy** Kyrie. Magnificat. **Oxford Camerata / Jeremy Summerly.** Naxos 8 550937 (2/95).

Marco Uccellini
Italian c1603-1680

Suggested listening ...
...Sonatas – Op. 2: Sonata ottava a due violini. Op. 3: Sonata quarta detta "La Trasformata"; Aria quinta sopra "La Bergamasca"; Aria sesta sopra un balletto; Sonata nona a doi violini detta "La Reggiana". Op. 4: Sonata seconda detta "La Luciminia contenta"; Sonata quarta a violino solo detta "La Hortensa virtuosa"; Aria undecima a doi violini sopra "Il Caporal Simon"; Aria decima quarta a doi violini "La mia Pedrina"; Aria decima quinta sopra "La Scatola dagli agghi"; Sonata decima ottava a doi violini; Sonata vigesima a doi violini; Sonata vigesima prima a doi violini; Sonata vigesima quinta; Sonata vigesima sesta sopra "La Prosperina"; Sonata vigesima settima. Op. 7: Sonata nona. **Arcadian Academy / Nicholas McGegan** (hpd, org). Harmonia Mundi HMU90 7066 (7/94). ✍

Viktor Ullmann
Austrian/Hungarian 1898-1944

New review
Ullmann Liebeslieder, Op. 18[a]. Lieder, Op. 17[a]. Three Sonnets from the Portuguese, Op. 29[a]. Six Sonnets, Op. 34[a]. Geistliche Lieder, Op. 20[a]. Liederbuch des Hafis, Op. 30[b]. Der Mensch und sein Tag, Op. 47[b]. Immer inmitten[c]. Chinese Songs – Wanderer erwacht in der Herberge; Der mude Soldat[b]. Drei Lieder (1942)[b]. Sonnen-untergang[a]. Der Frühling[a]. Abendphantasie[a]. [a]**Christine Schäfer** (sop); [c]**Liat Himmelheber** (mcz); [b]**Yaron Windmüller** (bar); **Axel Bauni** (pf). Orfeo ℗ C380952 (two discs: 112 minutes: DDD: 5/96). Texts and translations included. Recorded 1994-5.
This collection (all Ullmann's surviving songs are here, sung in roughly chronological order) demonstrates that he was a very gifted song-writer by the late 1930s, and a masterly one by the time he arrived at Terezin concentration camp in 1942 where he was to die two years later. The Opp. 17 and 18 sets already show a resourceful way of developing short, arresting and pregnant melodic ideas. They suggest a composer moving from the region of Wolf and late Brahms to that of the young Alban Berg (Ullmann had been a pupil of Schoenberg) but in the subsequent groups he is tonally adventurous, never atonal. In fact with the three Elizabeth Barrett Browning sonnets of Op. 29 (set in Rilke's German translation), he is writing bolder, longer lines than before, and expanding emotionally, too, expressing moods from passion to quiet ecstasy. Of the songs written in Terezin, *Der Mensch und sein Tag* ("Man and his Day"), Op. 47, is a striking sequence of 12 lyrical epigrams, all very short but none seeming hurried or truncated, most having a reflective or culminatory epilogue for the piano alone: Axel Bauni, the excellent pianist in this set, is particularly impressive in these. Like the other 'late' songs they exemplify Ullmann's determination to demonstrate that "by the waters of Babylon we did not merely bewail our fate; our will to create was as strong as our will to live". In the incomplete solo cantata *Immer inmitten* ("Always amidst") he earnestly protests; in the three songs of 1942 a grotesque, sharp-edged wit is his response; but in what may have been his last song, a setting of Hölderlin's *Abendphantasie*, his plea for sleep and the peace and contentment that old age will bring is without irony, and quite haunting. Above all, in these final songs he continues to develop, to refine his language and his response to words. The performances are good enough to leave one in no doubt of Ullmann's stature as a song-writer of outstanding gifts. The recordings are excellent.

New review
Ullmann Die Weise von Liebe und Tod des Cornets Christoph Rilke[a]. Variationen und Doppelfuge über ein Theme von Arnold Schoenberg, Op. 3a[b].
Schoenberg Sechs Klavierstücke, Op. 19[c]. Ode to Napoleon, Op. 41[d]. [a]**Gert Westphal**, [d]**Roland Hermann** (spkrs); [d]**Tim Vogler**, [d]**Frank Reinecke** (vns), [d]**Stefan Fehlandt** (va); [d]**Michael Sanderling** (vc); [a]**Michael Allan**, [bc]**Günther Herzfeld**, [d]**Frank-Immo Zichner** (pfs). Edition Abseits ℗ EDA008-2 (65 minutes: DDD: 11/95). Texts and translations included. Recorded 1994.
Coupling Ullmann and Schoenberg makes sense. Even in the desperate conditions of the concentration camp Theresienstadt, where his Rilke setting was composed, Ullmann followed a more recognizably German compositional path than his fellow internees. His teacher's work was the yardstick against which he would have gauged his own development. Listening to the *Variations* in conjunction with *Die Weise von Liebe und Tod des Cornets Christoph Rilke* (also set by Frank Martin – see new review under Martin; refer to the Index to Reviews) one is aware of a simplification of technique and expression not solely attributable to the practical constraints of Ullmann's last years. But then he was never a slavish Schoenbergian: the *Variations* begin with an artfully academic inversion of the theme, extend its possibilities in a language that owes more to Berg and take a quasi-Hindemithian line in the rhetorical counterpoint of the fugue. Herzfeld gives what seems to be an accurate, often bravura performance, whereas his Schoenberg Op. 19 pieces (the source of Ullmann's theme) lack a certain tension, the sound itself rather too soft-grained. Competition in this repertoire is fierce. Ullmann's setting of 12 extracts from Rilke's novella is a quirky but compelling assertion of self against insurmountable odds. The problem of integrating speech and music into a unified whole is not so much solved as avoided, in favour of a series of vignettes depicting stages in the protagonist's journey towards a mythical future. Simple leitmotivic fragments provide overall coherence, although

the text's evocative qualities are inevitably cramped by the two-dimensional effect of the medium: Ullmann did not live to complete an orchestral version. When performed with this degree of conviction, *Die Weise von Liebe und Tod des Cornets Christoph Rilke* is more than a historical curiosity, even if Ullmann cannot match the ironic force that Schoenberg draws from Lord Byron's withering 'tribute'. The present performance of the *Ode to Napoleon* lacks the flexibility and élan one expects to hear in the English language original but Hermann makes a solid case for Schoenberg's own (unpublished) German translation. The players capture the intricacy, if not always the immediacy, of the instrumental commentary – the recording is spacious but could be better focused. An uneven disc then, but definitely one of the more interesting Ullmann offerings to date.

Further listening ...

...Piano Concerto, Op. 25[a]. Five Variations and Double Fugue on a Piano Piece of Arnold Schoenberg. Symphony No. 2 in D. [a]**Konrad Richter** (pf); **Brno State Philharmonic Orchestra / Israel Yinon.** Bayer BR100228 (10/94).

...String Quartet No. 3, Op. 43. *Coupled with* **Klein** String Trio. Fantasie a Fuga. Piano Sonata[a]. String Quartet, Op. 2. **Hawthorne Quartet;** [a]**Virginia Eskin** (pf). Channel Classics CCS1691 (12/91). *See review under Klein; refer to the Index to Reviews.* ⓖⓖ

...Der Kaiser von Atlantis, oder Die Tod-Verweigerung. Hölderlin-Lieder – Abend-phantasie; Der Frühling; Wo bist du?. **Soloists; Leipzig Gewandhaus Orchestra / Lothar Zagrosek.** Decca Entartete Musik 440 854-2DH (12/94). *Gramophone Award Winner 1995.* ⓖ

Chinary Ung
Cambodian/American 1942-

Suggested listening ...

...Inner Voices. *Coupled with works by* **L. Harrison** and **McPhee** **American Composers Orchestra / Dennis Russell Davies.** Argo 444 560-2ZH (4/96). *See review under McPhee; refer to the Index to Reviews.*

Mindaugas Urbaitis
USSR/Lithuanian 1952-

Suggested listening ...

...Lithuanian Folk Music. *Coupled with* **Juozapaitis** Perpetuum mobile. **Vasks** Cantabile. **Kutavičius** Northern Gates. **Tüür** Insular Deserta. **Rekašius** Music for Strings. **Ostrobothnian Chamber Orchestra / Juha Kangas.** Finlandia 4509-97893-2 (11/95).

Galina Ustvol'skaya
USSR 1919-

Suggested listening ...

...Grand (Bolshoi) Duet[b]. *Coupled with* **Gubaidulina** In croce[a]. Ten Preludes (Etudes). **Maya Beiser** (vc); [a]**Dorothy Papadakos** (org); [b]**Christopher Oldfather** (pf). Koch International Classics 37258-2 (11/95). *See review under Gubaidulina; refer to the Index to Reviews.*

Peeter Vähi
Estonian 1955-

Suggested listening ...

...To His Highness Salvador D. *Coupled with* **Sumera** For B.B.B. and his Friend. **Kangro** Idioms, Op. 43a. **Mägi** Cantus and Processus. **Põldmäe** Sonatina, Op. 9. **Eespere** Trivium. **Tallinn Camerata.** Finlandia 4509-95705-2 (5/95).

...Fata Morgana. *Coupled with* **Tüür** Sonata. **Sumera** Piece from the Year 1981. **Rääts** Toccata. **Kangro** Suite, Op. 1. **Mägi** The Ancient Kannel. **Pärt** Partita. **Lauri Väinmaa** (pf). Finlandia 4509-95704-2 (7/95).

Moysey Vainberg
Polish 1919-

Vainberg The Golden Key, Op. 55: Suites Nos. 1-3; No. 4 – excerpts. **Bolshoi Theatre Orchestra / Mark Ermler.** Olympia Ⓜ OCD473 (78 minutes: ADD: 5/95). Recorded 1966.

Interest in Moishei Vainberg has been growing, with several of his symphonies and other pieces now available on record. Now here comes this set of suites from a full-length ballet of 1955. The story, by Alexey Tolstoy, is rather a jumbled one concerning a troupe of puppets, with at their centre the Pinocchio/Petrushka figure of Buratino (the note claims this name as a nonsense jumble of the Russian words for borax and slime, but *burattino* is simply Italian for puppet). It gives Vainberg the chance for plenty of short pieces, 26 of them here, many lasting as little as a minute or two, and hence the need to characterize or depict quickly and wittily. This he does, if not with the sardonic swiftness of his revered Shostakovich, at any rate deftly and often quite amusingly. There is a dance for Pierrot with a sleazy saxophone, a noble-minded but somewhat eccentric tortoise, a march for a manic firefly, a solo for an unappealing rat, and a beautiful *Adagio*, the longest number in the score, in which Vainberg touches on a deeper lyrical vein. It is all quite lightly and engagingly done, and neatly played here by Ermler and the Bolshoi orchestra.

Vainberg Piano Quintet, Op. 18[a]. String Quartet No. 12, Op. 103[b]. [a]**Moishei Vainberg** (pf);
[a]**Borodin Quartet** (Rostislav Dubinsky, Jaroslav Alexandrov, vns; Dmitri Shebalin, va; Valentin
Berlinsky, vc); [b]**Yevgeni Smirnov**, [b]**Arnold Kobyhyansky** (vns); [b]**Vyatcheslav Trushin** (va); [b]**Alla**
Vasilieva (vc). Olympia Ⓜ OCD474 (70 minutes: ADD: 4/95). Recorded in 1963 and 1970. Ⓖ
The recording of the Piano Quintet does full justice to the often demanding range of textures, which includes densely packed chords and the aloof, widely spaced spread of sound which Vainberg avowedly learnt from Shostakovich. It is in many ways an engaging work, expertly written and played with great address by the composer himself. He is a sympathetic artist, even when one has set aside the appalling sufferings to which he and his family were subjected by both Nazis and Communists. To survive so much and to retain such creative energy compels admiration. It does not consistently compel more, for not always does he seem to control his material with the magisterial command of Shostakovich, nor is the material itself always as beguiling. If the Piano Quintet may seem to be more rewarding for the surprising range of invention (which includes a wild Irish fiddle), the String Quartet gains for its greater compactness. It draws close to dodecaphonic techniques, which had become more possible by 1976, and perhaps the demands of the method helped concentration. It is worth several hearings, and though less immediately intriguing and less eccentric than the Quintet, it has rather more substance. The performance is admirable. Vainberg is a remarkable figure; he deserves this attention from a record company, and deserves the curiosity of Western listeners who have little other chance of getting to know his music.
Further listening ...
...Symphonies – No. 7, Op. 81[a]; No. 12, Op. 114, "In memory of Shostakovich"[b]. [a]**Moscow**
Chamber Orchestra / Rudolf Barshai; [b]**USSR TV and Radio Symphony Orchestra / Maxim**
Shostakovich. Olympia OCD472 (11/94).

Antonio Valente
Italian c1529-c1580

Suggested listening ...
...Tenore del passo e mezzo. *Coupled with works by* **Facoli, Giovanni de Macque, A. Mayone,**
Trabaci, Picchi, Buono, Frescobaldi, Lambardo, Merula, M. Rossi, Salvatore,
B. Storace, G. Strozzi, Stradella and **A. Scarlatti** Rinaldo Alessandrini (hpd).
Opus 111 OPS30-118 (4/95). ☞ *See review in the Collections section; refer to the Index to*
Reviews. ⒼⓈ

Francisco Valls
Spanish 1665-1747

New review
Valls Mass, "Scala Aretina". **Mavis Beattie, Valerie Hill, Nancy Long** (sops); **Christopher Robson,**
Ashley Stafford (altos); **Edgar Fleet** (ten); **Antony Shelley** (bar); **London Oratory Choir; Thames**
Chamber Orchestra / John Hoban. CRD Ⓔ CRD3371 (43 minutes: ADD: 9/95). Text and
translation included. From CRD1071 (11/80).
It was indeed enterprising of John Hoban in 1978 to perform in Barcelona this 1702 Mass by the rarely heard Catalan musician Francisco Valls (then *maestro de capilla* in the cathedral there) based on Guido d'Arezzo's hexachord, and then to record it. The fervour, vitality and shading of this performance more than compensate for a few small flaws of ensemble. The work's use of expressive unprepared dissonances and bold modulations (still surprising today) caused long-running controversy among the composer's contemporaries, which he countered with a theoretical treatise entitled *Mapa armónico*. What is disappointing is the failure of other conductors to follow Hoban's lead and explore the very considerable range of Valls's other works (including nine more Masses, 17 psalms, 30 motets and much else) preserved in the Biblioteca Central in Barcelona. A feature of this particular work is its scoring for three choirs (each with their own continuo) plus a separate instrumental group of violins, oboes, trumpets and violone, the spatial layout lending the elaborate polyphony a special richness. Valls knew how to create striking effects, such as – in the *Credo* alone – the overlapping solo sopranos at "Deum de Deo", the running scales behind "Et in unum Dominum", the remarkable harmonic progression at "passus et sepultus est", the sheer jubilation of "et resurrexit", and a magnificent Amen (the trumpets, splendid throughout, much in evidence). However, the gem of the work is the deeply moving *Agnus Dei*.
Further listening ...
...En un noble, sagrado firmamento. *Coupled with works by* **J. de Torres, C. Galán, Literes,**
Anonymous and **F. de Iribarren** Al Ayre Español / Eduardo López Banzo. Deutsche
Harmonia Mundi 05472 77325-2 (8/95). ☞ *See review in the Collections section; refer to the*
Index to Reviews. Ⓖ

Nancy Van de Vate   American 1930-

Suggested listening ...
...Cocaine Lil. *Coupled with* **Eisler** Woodbury-Liederbüchlein. **Rühm** Schöpfung. Foetus.
Sprechquartette. **Schwehr** Deutsche Tänze. **Bel Canto Ensemble / Dietburg Spohr.** Koch
Schwann 314322 (3/95).

Edgard Varèse   French/American 1883-1965

Varèse Ionisation[ce]. Amériques[ce]. Arcana (All from CBS 76520, 6/78)[ce]. Density 21.5[b].
Offrandes[ade]. Octandre[de]. Intégrales (All from IM39053, 3/85)[de]. [a]**Rachel Yakar** (sop); [b]**Lawrence**
Beauregard (fl); [c]**New York Philharmonic Orchestra**; [d]**Ensemble InterContemporain /** [e]**Pierre**
Boulez. Sony Classical Ⓜ SMK45844 (77 minutes: ADD/DDD: 10/90). Texts and translations
included.   Ⓖ
The music of Varèse has been poorly represented on disc and in the concert-hall in recent years. Quite
why so important a figure in twentieth-century music should be neglected like this is hard to say, and
even more difficult to comprehend when one samples the quality of the music presented here. Varèse
was a pioneer, a quester and above all a liberator. Music for him was a form of twentieth-century
alchemy – the transmutation of the ordinary into the extraordinary, an alchemical wedding of
intellectual thought with intuitive imagination. It was the writings of the fourteenth-century
cosmologist and alchemist Paracelsus that formed the inspiration behind his orchestral work *Arcana*,
a vast canvas of sound built entirely out of one melodic motive. Echoes of Stravinsky and others are
discernible, but the totality of *Arcana* is pure Varèse. The same is true of *Amériques*, a title that Varèse
emphasized was not to be taken as "purely geographical but as symbolic of discoveries – new worlds
on earth, in the sky or in the minds of men". Here romanticism and modernism seem to coexist side
by side, where allusions from works such as *La mer* and *The Firebird* seem like memories carried into
his brave new world. The remaining items consist of smaller chamber works which display Varèse's
most radical, though equally rewarding, styles. Boulez and his players give committed, virtuosic
performances of these challenging and intriguing works. Well worth exploring.

Peteris Vasks   Latvian 1946-

Suggested listening ...
...Symphony for Strings, "Stimmen". *Coupled with works by* **Narbutaite** and **Balakauskas**
Ostrobothnian Chamber Orchestra / Juha Kangas. Finlandia 4509-97892-2 (11/95). *See review*
under Narbutaite; refer to the Index to Reviews.
...Cantabile. Cor Anglais Concerto[a]. Message. Musica Dolorosa. Lauda. [a]**Normunds Schnee**
(cor ang); **Riga Philharmonic Orchestra / Kriss Rusmanis.** Conifer CDCF236 (1/95).

Juan Vásquez   Spanish *c*1510-*c*1560

Suggested listening ...
...Orphenica lyra – De los álamos vengo; Con qué la lavaré; Glosa sobre Tan que vivray; De
Antequera sale el moro. *Coupled with works by* **Pisador, D. Ortiz, Encina, Anonymous,**
Narvaez and **Mudarra La Romanesca / José Miguel Moreno** (vihuela). Glossa GCD920203
(5/96). ☞ *See review in the Collections section; refer to the Index to Reviews.*   Ⓖ

Ralph Vaughan Williams   British 1872-1958

Vaughan Williams Double Piano Concerto. Symphony No. 5 in D major. **Ralph Markham,**
Kenneth Broadway (pfs); **Royal Philharmonic Orchestra / Sir Yehudi Menuhin.** Virgin Classics
Virgo Ⓑ VJ5 61105-2 (69 minutes: DDD: 1/94). Recorded 1987.
The fine duo, Ralph Markham and Kenneth Broadway join Sir Yehudi Menuhin and the RPO for this
performance of the Double Piano Concerto. This was arranged by the composer in 1946 from the
(solo) Piano Concerto, the ending being altered to advantage. It remains a somewhat uneven work,
but when presented so vigorously and persuasively, well worth exploring. Here is a case where a
bargain price should tempt any Vaughan Williams *aficionado* to explore less well-known territory.
More particularly so since Menuhin's strongly paced, yet passionately lyrical account of the glorious
Fifth Symphony is quite different from the Vernon Handley version (a front-runner in this work) and
would grace any collection. The recording of both pieces is first-class.

Vaughan Williams Symphonies – No. 1, "A Sea Symphony"[a]; No. 2, "A London Symphony"[b];
No. 3, "A Pastoral Symphony"[c]; No. 4 in F minor[d]; No. 5 in D major[e]; No. 6 in E minor[g];
No. 7, "Sinfonia antartica"[h]; No. 8 in D minor[b]; No. 9 in E minor[g]. Flos campi[f]. Serenade to

Music[i]. [c]**Alison Barlow,** [h]**Alison Hargan,** [a]**Joan Rodgers** (sops); [a]**William Shimell** (bar);
[f]**Christopher Balmer** (va); [afh]**Liverpool Philharmonic Choir; Royal Liverpool Philharmonic
Orchestra / Vernon Handley.** EMI Eminence Ⓜ CDBOX-VW1 (six discs: 396 minutes: DDD:
1/95). Items marked [a] from CD-EMX2142 (2/89), [b]CD-EMX2209 (8/93), [cd]CD-EMX2192
(11/92), [ef]CD-EMX9512 (3/88), [g]reviewed below, [hi]CD-EMX2173 (9/91). No. 2 *Gramophone
Editor's choice.* Nos. 2 and 8 *selected by Sounds in Retrospect.* ⒼⒼ

Vaughan Williams Symphonies – No. 6 in E minor; No. 9 in E minor. **Royal Liverpool
Philharmonic Orchestra / Vernon Handley.** EMI Eminence Ⓜ CD-EMX2230 (67 minutes: DDD:
1/95). Recorded 1994. *Gramophone Editor's choice.* ⒼⒼ

Handley's performances can withstand comparison with the very best. The first to appear was the Fifth
Symphony. Rightly acclaimed on its initial release, this remains a gloriously rapt, yet formidably lucid
realization. The coupling, a supremely dedicated rendering of the exquisite *Flos campi*, is just as
distinguished. Handley's masterly pacing is a compelling feature of both the *Sea Symphony* and
Sinfonia antartica, but, whilst it is difficult to fault either performance on artistic grounds, here more
than elsewhere one notes the limitations of the slightly cramped acoustic of Liverpool's Philharmonic
Hall. There are no technical shortcomings about the Third or Fourth. Handley's illuminatingly intense
Pastoral yields only to André Previn's sublime LSO account and his Fourth only (amongst modern
counterparts) to Slatkin's in terms of unbridled ferocity and orchestral virtuosity. The second and
Eighth bring outstandingly perceptive, marvellously communicative music-making, with both scores
emerging as fresh as the day they were conceived. Handley's interpretation of the Sixth Symphony is a
model of cogency and long-term control. Don't be deceived by the element of slight reserve in the
opening movement. It soon transpires that Handley already has his eyes firmly set on the work's
terrifying apex, namely the baleful climax of the succeeding *Moderato*. Handley's scherzo teems with
busy detail, its feverish contrapuntal workings laid out before us with maximum clarity and force. So
many performances have come to grief in the extraordinary finale; Handley's is a triumphant
exception. In this desolate, inconsolable landscape (with not an *espressivo* marking in sight), Handley,
even more than the admirable Andrew Davis, achieves a truly awesome hush and concentration. And
what of the Ninth, VW's other 'E minor'? Few interpreters on disc have probed much beneath the
surface of this elusive, craggy masterpiece. Though Handley's memorably responsive Liverpool
orchestra can't quite boast a string section as lustrous or refined as Slatkin's Philharmonia, he captures
more of the music's mordant wit, whilst allowing the listener to revel afresh in the astonishing vitality
and startlingly original sonorities of VW's ever-imaginative inspiration. The overriding impression left
by both performances is one of supreme sensitivity and utter dedication to the cause. In the visionary
finale, whose monumental, block-like structure gradually takes shape before our eyes like Stonehenge
itself, Handley's conception just has the edge in terms of elemental power and effortless inevitability.
A final word of praise for the admirably natural results obtained by the recording engineers.

Additional recommendations ...

...Nos. 1-9. **Soloists; London Symphony Chorus and Orchestra / Bryden Thomson.** Chandos
Ⓕ CHAN9087/91 (five discs: 352 minutes: DDD).

...Nos. 1-9. Norfolk Rhapsody No. 1. Fantasia on a Theme by Thomas Tallis. Fantasia on
"Greensleeves". Five Variants of "Dives and Lazarus". **Soloists; Philharmonia Chorus and
Orchestra / Leonard Slatkin.** RCA Victor Ⓜ 09026 61460-2 (six discs: DDD).

...Nos. 3 and 5. **London Philharmonic Orchestra / Sir Adrian Boult.** Belart Ⓢ 461 118-2 (72 minutes:
ADD).

...No. 5. Flos campi[a]. [a]**Christopher Balmer** (va); [a]**Liverpool Philharmonic Choir; Royal Liverpool
Philharmonic Orchestra / Vernon Handley.** EMI Eminence Ⓜ CD-EMX9512 (62 minutes: DDD:
3/88).

...No. 2. Fantasia on a Theme by Thomas Tallis. **London Philharmonic Orchestra / Bernard Haitink.**
EMI Ⓕ CDC7 49394-2 (66 minutes: DDD: 7/88). Ⓖ

...No. 3. Oboe Concerto in A minor[a]. **Yvonne Kenny** (sop); [a]**David Theodore** (ob); **London
Symphony Orchestra / Bryden Thomson.** Chandos Ⓕ CHAN8594 (56 minutes: DDD: 8/88).

...No. 2. Concerto grosso. **London Symphony Orchestra / Bryden Thomson.** Chandos Ⓕ CHAN8629
(65 minutes: DDD: 10/89).

...No. 2. Concerto Accademico[a]. The Wasps – Overture. [a]**James Oliver Buswell IV** (vn); **London
Symphony Orchestra / André Previn.** RCA Gold Seal Ⓜ GD90501 (71 minutes: ADD: 3/91). Ⓖ

...Nos. 3 and 4. **Heather Harper** (sop); **London Symphony Orchestra / André Previn.** RCA Victor
Gold Seal Ⓜ GD90503 (73 minutes: ADD: 3/91).

...Nos. 7[a] and 8. [a]**Heather Harper** (sop); [a]**Ambrosian Singers; London Symphony Orchestra / André
Previn.** RCA Victor Gold Seal Ⓜ GD90510 (72 minutes: ADD: 3/91).

...No. 2. Fantasia on a Theme by Thomas Tallis. **London Philharmonic Orchestra / Sir Adrian Boult.**
EMI Ⓜ CDM7 64017-2 (60 minutes: ADD: 5/92)

...Nos. 3 and 4. [a]**Alison Barlow** (sop); **Royal Liverpool Philharmonic Orchestra / Vernon Handley.**
EMI Eminence Ⓜ CD-EMX2192 (67 minutes: DDD: 11/92).

...Nos. 2 and 8. **Royal Liverpool Philharmonic Orchestra / Vernon Handley.** EMI Eminence
Ⓜ CD-EMX2209 (72 minutes: DDD: 8/93). *Gramophone Editor's choice.* ⒼⒼ

...No. 2. Fantasia on "Greensleeves". Serenade to Music. The Wasps – Overture. **Soloists; Queen's
Hall Orchestra / Sir Henry Wood.** Dutton Laboratories mono Ⓜ CDAX8004* (63 minutes: ADD:
10/93). Ⓖ

...Nos. 3[a] and 4. Fantasia on "Greensleeves". [a]**Linda Hohenfeld** (sop); **Philharmonia Orchestra / Leonard Slatkin.** RCA Victor Red Seal Ⓕ 09026 61194-2 (73 minutes: DDD: 11/93). *Gramophone Editor's choice.*

...No. 2[a]. Partita for Double String Orchestra[b]. **London Philharmonic Orchestra / Sir Adrian Boult.** Belart [a]mono/[b]stereo Ⓢ 461 008-2* (65 minutes: ADD: 12/94).

Vaughan Williams Symphony No. 1, "A Sea Symphony". **Felicity Lott** (sop); **Jonathan Summers** (bar); **Cantilena; London Philharmonic Choir and Orchestra / Bernard Haitink.** EMI Ⓕ CDC7 49911-2 (71 minutes: DDD: 1/90). Text included. Recorded 1989. ⓋⓋ

A firm hand on the tiller is needed to steer a safe course through this, Vaughan Williams's first and most formally diffuse symphony, completed in 1909. Haitink is clearly an ideal choice of helmsman and he is helped by a remarkably lucid recording that resolves details that would rarely be revealed in live performance. What might be more unexpected here is the obvious affinity he shows for this music: whilst never transgressing the bounds of Vaughan Williams's characteristically English idiom, he manages to place the work in the European mainstream, revealing a whole range of resonances, from Bruckner and Mahler to the Impressionists. Not all the glory should go to the conductor, of course. Both soloists are particularly fine, the vulnerability behind the spine-tingling power of Felicity Lott's voice providing excellent contrast to the staunch solidity of Jonathan Summers. The LPO Chorus, aided by Cantilena, are on top form and the whole enterprise is underpinned by the London Philharmonic's total commitment and expertise. Here is the recording of this glorious work for which the catalogue was waiting.

Additional recommendations ...

...**Margaret Marshall** (sop); **Stephen Roberts** (bar); **London Symphony Chorus; Philharmonia Orchestra / Richard Hickox.** Virgin Classics Virgo Ⓑ VJ7 59687-2 (64 minutes: DDD).

...**Joan Rodgers** (sop); **William Shimell** (bar); **Royal Liverpool Philharmonic Choir and Orchestra / Vernon Handley.** EMI Eminence Ⓜ CD-EMX2142 (70 minutes: DDD: 2/89).

...**Yvonne Kenny** (sop); **Brian Rayner Cook** (bar); **London Symphony Chorus and Orchestra / Bryden Thomson.** Chandos Ⓕ CHAN8764 (66 minutes: DDD: 2/90).

...**Heather Harper** (sop); **John Shirley-Quirk** (bar); **London Symphony Chorus and Orchestra / André Previn.** RCA Victor Gold Seal Ⓜ GD90500 (66 minutes: ADD: 3/91).

...**Dame Isobel Baillie** (sop); **John Cameron** (bar); **London Philharmonic Choir and Orchestra / Sir Adrian Boult.** Belart mono Ⓢ 450 144-2* (68 minutes: ADD: 7/94). Ⓖ

New review

Vaughan Williams Symphony No. 1, "A Sea Symphony". **Elaine Blighton** (sop); **John Cameron** (bar); **Christchurch Harmonic Choir, New Zealand; BBC Choral Society; BBC Chorus and Symphony Orchestra / Sir Malcolm Sargent.** BBC Radio Classics Ⓑ 15656 9150-2 (60 minutes: ADD: 4/96). Recorded live in 1965.

In large-scale choral repertory Sir Malcolm Sargent had few peers and this performance of *A Sea Symphony* possesses a vibrancy and easy authority which communicate strongly. He certainly draws an enthusiastic, full-blooded response from his assembled choral and orchestral forces and his mobile, fluent reading as a whole has its exciting moments. However, eyebrows may well be raised at Sargent's controversial (and dramatically unconvincing) lengthening of the chorus's final chord in the scherzo (and whence, for that matter, the extra cymbal clash at 2'02" in the opening movement?). Both soloists are excellent, though: the Australian soprano Elaine Blighton makes a pleasing impression with her silvery, light-toned timbre, whilst her fellow countryman John Cameron gives a commanding and intelligent performance. Sir Malcolm's many admirers will rightly want this budget-price BBC Radio Classics offering.

Vaughan Williams Symphonies – No. 4 in F minor[a]; No. 5 in D major[b]. [a]**BBC Symphony Orchestra / Ralph Vaughan Williams;** [b]**Hallé Orchestra / Sir John Barbirolli.** Dutton Laboratories mono Ⓜ CDAX8011* (66 minutes: ADD: 6/95). Item marked [a] from HMV DB3367/70 (1/38), recorded 1937; [b]HMV C3388/92 (5/44), recorded 1944. ⓋⓋ

No performance on record of Vaughan Williams's Fourth Symphony has ever quite matched this very first one, recorded under the composer's baton in October 1937. As Michael Kennedy says in his highly illuminating note for the Dutton Laboratories reissue, it is "taken at a daredevil pace", and more importantly has a bite and energy beyond any rival. If early listeners to this violent work were shocked by the composer's new boldness, here his conducting demonstrates the passionate emotion behind the piece – paradoxically the most conventional of his symphonies in structure, as it is the most radical in idiom. The remastered sound is so vivid and immediate, so full of presence, that in places one almost has the illusion of stereo before its time. Sir John Barbirolli's première recording of the Fifth Symphony, made in February 1944 eight months after the first performance, is hardly less remarkable. This, too, has never quite been matched since for the stirring passion of the great climaxes in the first and third movements, with Barbirolli in each carefully grading the intensity between exposition and recapitulation. It is also a revelation to find him taking the triple-time of the Passacaglia finale much faster than latter-day rivals, relating it far more closely than usual to the great example of the finale of Brahms's Fourth Symphony, making it no pastoral amble but a searing argument. Here again hiss – very high on the original wartime 78s, has been virtually eliminated, but that has left the high violins sounding rather papery. Even so, there is no lack of weight or bite in the big climaxes, with brass and wind atmospherically caught. An outstanding issue for all lovers of this composer's music, not just those who specialize in historic recordings.

Additional recommendations ...

...No. 4. Violin Concerto in D minor, "Concerto Accademico"[a]. [a]**Kenneth Sillito** (vn); **London Symphony Orchestra / Bryden Thomson.** Chandos Ⓕ CHAN8633 (50 minutes: DDD: 1/89).

...No. 5. The England of Elizabeth – excerpts. **London Symphony Orchestra / André Previn.** RCA Victor Gold Seal Ⓜ GD90506 (59 minutes: ADD: 3/91).

...No. 4[a]. **Holst** The Planets, H125[b]. [a]**BBC Symphony Orchestra / Ralph Vaughan Williams;** [b]**London Symphony Orchestra / Gustav Holst.** Koch International Classics mono Ⓕ 37018-2* (69 minutes: ADD: 4/91).   Ⓖ

...Nos. 4 and 6. **New Philharmonia Orchestra / Sir Adrian Boult.** EMI Ⓜ CDM7 64019-2 (69 minutes: ADD: 5/92).

...No. 5[a]. **Bax** Tintagel[b]. [a]**Philharmonia Orchestra;** [b]**London Symphony Orchestra / Sir John Barbirolli.** EMI British Composers Ⓜ CDM5 65110-2 (54 minutes: ADD: 3/95).

New review

Vaughan Williams Symphonies – No. 4 in F minor[a]; No. 8 in D minor[b]. **BBC Symphony Orchestra / [a]Sir Malcolm Sargent, [b]Leopold Stokowski.** BBC Radio Classics Ⓑ 15656 9131-2 (62 minutes: ADD: 4/96). Recorded live in [a]1963, [b]1964.

Sargent presides over a strong performance of the Fourth Symphony, emanating from a 1963 Promenade Concert at the Royal Albert Hall. True, the main portion of the first movement can at times verge on the hectic, but there's some truly eloquent string playing in the bleached coda, and the succeeding *Andante moderato* again plumbs genuine depths (the concluding, inconsolably bleak flute solo really captures the imagination here). Sargent brings a distinctively dapper, well-sprung elegance to both the scherzo and finale. The cumulative effect is less intimidatingly relentless than usual, but no less compulsive and powerful for all that. The coupling (captured at the following year's Proms) is an extraordinarily characterful, heart-warming account of the Eighth Symphony from Stokowski. This is a reading of daring individuality, riskily spacious and hyper-expressive one moment, impishly mischievous the next, yet such is the sheer magnetism of Stokowski's personality that it somehow all holds together. Both the first and third movements glow with affectionate warmth, with Stokowski drawing the most tenderly pliant response from the BBC Symphony strings in the lovely *Cavatina*. By contrast, the *Scherzo alla marcia* fairly rattles along, the BBC SO winds and brass pushed to their very limits, whilst the finale combines gleeful clangour with plenty of twinkling good humour. BBC Sound Archive (stereo) tapes yield a more than acceptable sound quality.

New review

Vaughan Williams Symphony No. 5 in D major[a]. Sancta civitas[b]. [b]**Gareth Roberts** (ten); [b]**Brian Rayner Cook** (bar); [b]**BBC Singers;** [b]**BBC Symphony Chorus and Orchestra / Gennadi Rozhdestvensky.** BBC Radio Classics Ⓑ BBCRD9125 (74 minutes: ADD: 10/95). Item marked [a] recorded live in 1980, [b]1979.

Gennadi Rozhdestvensky can be an invigorating interpreter of British fare, as this generous Vaughan Williams pairing testifies. The former BBC SO chief directs the Fifth Symphony as if to the manner born. His reading is lucid, admirably paced and consistently warm-hearted. Moreover, the commitment and dedication of the orchestral response is most striking. Then again, this was in fact a rather special occasion: the present Royal Festival Hall performance dates from October 1980, the fiftieth anniversary to the day of the first-ever concert given by the BBC SO under their founder, Sir Adrian Boult. Newcomers to this glorious symphony should perhaps stick with Vernon Handley's account (nor should one overlook those essential mono recordings from Barbirolli and Boult – see above), yet Rozhdestvensky's deeply sympathetic, often very moving interpretation is a worthy addition to the catalogue. The 1926 oratorio *Sancta civitas* remains one of Vaughan Williams's least familiar masterworks and performances of it are decidedly rare. No VW enthusiast, therefore, should pass up the opportunity of hearing Rozhdestvensky's admirably prepared, excitingly vibrant live rendering from 1979. Though Richard Hickox's magnificent studio recording for EMI is not seriously challenged by this BBC newcomer (reviewed further on), there is a refreshing ardour about Rozhdestvensky's conception that communicates strongly. Sound and balance throughout are eminently natural. An enticing coupling, this, and a genuine bargain too.

Vaughan Williams Symphony No. 6 in E minor. Fantasia on a Theme by Thomas Tallis. The Lark Ascending[a]. [a]**Tasmin Little** (vn); **BBC Symphony Orchestra / Andrew Davis.** Teldec British Line Ⓕ 9031-73127-2 (62 minutes: DDD: 8/91). Recorded 1990. *Selected by Sounds in Retrospect.*
Ⓖ

Andrew Davis has clearly thought long and hard before committing this enigmatic and tragic symphony to disc, and the result is one of the most spontaneous and electrifying accounts of the Sixth Symphony available. The urgency and vigour of the first and third movements is astonishing, leaving one with the impression that the work might have been recorded in one take. His treatment of the second subject's reprise in the closing pages of the first movement is more underplayed and remote than the beautifully sheened approach of some recordings, but is arguably more nostalgic for being so. The feverish, nightmare world of the *Scherzo* is a real *tour de force* in the hands of an inspired BBC Symphony Orchestra, and the desolate wasteland of the eerie final movement has rarely achieved such quiescence and nadir as here. Davis's searchingly intense *Tallis Fantasia* is finely poised with a beautifully spacious acoustic. The disc concludes on a quietly elevated note with Tasmin Little's serene and gently introspective reading of *The Lark Ascending*. The recording is excellent.

Additional recommendations ...

...Fantasia on a Theme by Thomas Tallis[a]. Fantasia on Greensleeves[a]. **Elgar** Introduction and Allegro for String Quartet and Strings[a]. Serenade in E minor[a]. Elegy for Strings[b]. Sospiri[b]. [a]**Sinfonia of London; [b]New Philharmonia Orchestra / Sir John Barbirolli.** EMI Ⓕ CDC7 47537-2* (58 minutes: ADD: 2/87).   ⓆⓆⓆ

...Fantasia on a Theme by Thomas Tallis. Norfolk Rhapsody No. 1. In the Fen Country. Five Variants of "Dives and Lazarus". **London Philharmonic Orchestra / Bryden Thomson.** Chandos Ⓕ CHAN8502 (59 minutes: DDD: 5/87).

...Nos. 6 and 9. **London Symphony Orchestra / André Previn.** RCA Victor Gold Seal Ⓜ GD90508 (73 minutes: ADD: 3/91).

...Fantasia on a Theme by Thomas Tallis. Partita for Double String Orchestra. Oboe Concerto[a]. English Folk-Song Suite (orch. Jacob). Fantasia on "Greensleeves" (arr. Greaves). [a]**Jonathan Small** (ob); **Royal Liverpool Philharmonic Orchestra / Vernon Handley.** EMI Eminence Ⓜ CD-EMX2179 (68 minutes: DDD: 12/91).

...Fantasia on a Theme by Thomas Tallis. *Coupled with works by* **Brahms, Klemperer** and **Ravel** **New Philharmonia Orchestra / Leopold Stokowski.** BBC Radio Classics Ⓑ BBCRD9107 (74 minutes: ADD: 3/95). *See review in the Collections section; refer to the Index to Reviews.*   Ⓠ

...The Lark Ascending[b]. **Gardiner** Shepherd Fennell's Dance. **Coleridge Taylor** Scenes from "The Song of Hiawatha", Op. 30 – Onaway, awake, beloved[a]. **Harty** A John Field Suite. **Ireland** A London Overture. **Holst** The Hymn of Jesus, H140[c]. [a]**Webster Booth** (ten); [b]**David Wise** (vn); [c]**Huddersfield Choral Society; Liverpool Philharmonic Orchestra / Sir Malcolm Sargent.** Dutton Laboratories mono Ⓜ CDAX8012* (75 minutes: ADD: 5/95).

Vaughan Williams Symphony No. 7, "Sinfonia antartica". **Sheila Armstrong** (sop); **London Philharmonic Choir and Orchestra / Bernard Haitink.** EMI Ⓕ CDC7 47516-2 (42 minutes: DDD: 1/87). From EL270318-1 (10/85). Recorded 1984.   Ⓠ

Scored for wordless soprano solo and chorus plus a large orchestra, this Seventh Symphony was based on the composer's music for the film *Scott of the Antarctic*. It comprises five movements; the Prelude, which conveys mankind's struggle in overcoming hostile natural forces; a *Scherzo*, which depicts the whales and penguins in their natural habitat; "Landscape", which portrays vast frozen wastes; Intermezzo, a reflection of the actions and thoughts of two members of the party; and "Epilogue", describing the final tragic assault on the South Pole. Bernard Haitink's conducting is highly imaginative, very concentrated and very committed and the LPO respond to him with some wonderfully atmospheric playing, full of personality and colour. Sheila Armstrong's eerie disembodied soprano voice and the remote chorus heighten the atmosphere, so that the score emerges as a powerful, coherent essay in symphonic form. Every detail has been captured by a magnificently sonorous and spacious recording.

Additional recommendations ...

...No. 7[a]. Toward the Unknown Region. [a]**Catherine Bott** (sop); **London Symphony Chorus and Orchestra / Bryden Thomson.** Chandos Ⓕ CHAN8796 (55 minutes: DDD: 4/90).

...No. 7[a]. Serenade to Music. [a]**Alison Hargan** (sop); **Royal Liverpool Choir and Orchestra / Vernon Handley.** EMI Eminence Ⓜ CD-EMX2173 (57 minutes: DDD: 9/91).

Vaughan Williams Symphony No. 9 in E minor. Piano Concerto in C major[a]. [a]**Howard Shelley** (pf); **London Symphony Orchestra / Bryden Thomson.** Chandos Ⓕ CHAN8941 (57 minutes: DDD: 7/91). Recorded 1990. *Selected by Sounds in Retrospect.*   Ⓠ

Alongside the scorching account of the apocalyptic Fourth Symphony, this clear-headed, perceptive traversal of the enigmatic Ninth has fair claims to be regarded as the best thing in Bryden Thomson's underrated VW cycle for Chandos. Thomson's urgent conception of the opening *Moderato maestoso* in particular has a sweep and momentum one might not have previously associated with this movement, yet the gain in terms of sheer concentration and symphonic stature is irrefutable. Granted, some may find the outer sections of the succeeding *Andante sostenuto* just a little too lacking in evocative magic, but there's no gainsaying the effectiveness of gallumphing woodwind in the oafish scherzo; certainly, the LSO's saxophone trio seem to be enjoying their day out hugely. In the finale, too, Thomson's approach is more boldly assertive than usual – not the way one would always want to hear this music, perhaps, but a thoroughly valid and convincing performance all the same. The coupling, Howard Shelley's distinguished remake of the same composer's craggily elusive Piano Concerto, is both imaginative and desirable. All in all, a highly recommendable disc: the LSO are in fine fettle throughout, whilst Chandos's glowing sound come close to the ideal.

Additional recommendations ...

...Nos. 8 and 9. **London Philharmonic Orchestra / Sir Adrian Boult.** EMI Ⓜ CDM7 64021-2 (64 minutes: ADD: 5/92).

...Piano Concerto. **Foulds** Dynamic Triptych, Op. 88. **Howard Shelley** (pf); **Royal Philharmonic Orchestra / Vernon Handley.** Lyrita Ⓕ SRCD211 (57 minutes: DDD: 3/93).   Ⓠ

... Nos. 8 and 9. Flourish for Glorious John (Barbirolli). **Philharmonia Orchestra / Leonard Slatkin.** RCA Victor Red Seal Ⓔ 09026 61196-2 (63 minutes: DDD: 8/93). Ⓖ

...No. 9[a]. **Arnold** Symphony No. 3, Op. 63[b]. **London Philharmonic Orchestra / [a]Sir Adrian Boult, [b]Sir Malcolm Arnold.** Everest Ⓔ EVC9001* (70 minutes: ADD: 4/95).

...Piano Concerto. **Finzi** Eclogue, Op. 10. **Delius** Piano Concerto in C minor. **Piers Lane** (pf); **Royal Liverpool Philharmonic Orchestra / Vernon Handley.** EMI Eminence Ⓜ CD-EMX2239 (61 minutes: DDD: 11/95).

New review

Vaughan Williams Job[a]. The Wasps – Overture[b].

Arnold Four Scottish Dances, Op. 59[c]. **London Philharmonic Orchestra / [ab]Sir Adrian Boult, [c]Sir Malcolm Arnold.** Everest Ⓔ EVC9006 (57 minutes: ADD: 5/95). Item marked [a] from SDBR3019 (2/68, recorded 1958), [b]new to UK, [c]World Record Club ST99 (1/62). ⒼⒼⒼ

This is the third of Sir Adrian Boult's four recordings of *Job*, a work he conducted with peerless authority for over 40 years (he was, of course, the score's dedicatee). The performance is one of enormous dedication and considerable insight, achieving a rare serenity in Scene 3 ("Minuet of the Sons of Job and their Wives"), Scene 5 ("Dance of the Three Messengers") and, above all, in the Epilogue, which is more movingly realized than ever before or since. However, the chosen venue of London's Royal Albert Hall evidently brought problems for the Everest recording team: it's an odd sound, tightly miked and rather lacking in body, with brass balance closer than is ideal. Nor was the London Philharmonic in the healthiest of shape at the time: string tone can be unreliable and intonation occasionally suspect. Boult also directs a cherishable, delectably pointed rendering of *The Wasps* Overture, whose glorious central melody really does seem to unfold with all the time in the world here. Finally, Sir Malcolm Arnold conducts his own, irresistibly tuneful *Scottish Dances*. The sound in both these items is impressively vivid for its late-1950s vintage. All in all, then, a very useful and welcome reissue.

Vaughan Williams Mass in G minor (1922)[b]. Te Deum in G major (1928)[c].

Howells Requiem (1936)[a]. Take him, earth, for cherishing (1963). [a]**Mary Seers** (sop); [ab]**Michael Chance** (alto); [ab]**Philip Salmon** (ten); [ab]**Jonathan Best** (bass); **Corydon Singers / Matthew Best** with [c]**Thomas Trotter** (org). Hyperion Ⓔ CDA66076 (60 minutes: ADD: 10/87). Texts included. From A66076 (8/83). ⒼⒼ

Vaughan Williams's unaccompanied Mass in G minor manages to combine the common manner of Elizabethan liturgical music with those elements of his own folk-music heritage that make his music so distinctive, and in so doing arrives at something quite individual and new. The work falls into five movements and its mood is one of heartfelt, if restrained, rejoicing. Herbert Howells wrote his unaccompanied Requiem in 1936, a year after the death of his only son. The work was not released in his lifetime but was reconstructed and published in 1980 from his manuscripts. It is a most hauntingly beautiful work of an obviously intensely personal nature. *Take him, earth, for cherishing* was composed to commemorate the assassination of President John F. Kennedy. The text is an English translation by Helen Waddell of Prudentius's fourth-century poem, *Hymnus circa Exsequias Defuncti*. Again it demonstrates the great strength of Howells's choral writing, with a clear outline and aptly affecting yet unimposing harmonic twists. The Corydon Singers give marvellous performances of these works and the sound is very fine indeed. An hour of the finest English choral music and not to be missed.

Vaughan Williams Dona nobis pacem[a]. Sancta civitas[b]. [a]**Yvonne Kenny** (sop); [b]**Philip Langridge** (ten); **Bryn Terfel** (bass-bar); [b]**St Paul's Cathedral Choir; London Symphony Chorus and Orchestra / Richard Hickox.** EMI British Composers Ⓔ CDC7 54788-2 (63 minutes: DDD: 12/93). Texts included. Recorded 1992. *Selected by Sounds in Retrospect.*

This is a generous and inspiring coupling of two of Vaughan Williams's most important choral utterances. Hickox coaxes magnificent sounds from the LSO throughout: in *Dona nobis pacem*, for example, the sense of orchestral spectacle during "Beat! Beat! drums!" is riveting in its physical impact. As ever, the contribution of the London Symphony Chorus combines full-throated discipline and sensitivity to nuance, and Hickox's trio of soloists are all excellent, with Bryn Terfel outstandingly eloquent. *Sancta civitas* is a work whose multi-layered scoring places great demands on both conductor and production team alike: suffice it to report, it is difficult to see Hickox's inspirational account of this still-underrated score (with its striking pre-echoes of *Job* and the Fourth Symphony) being surpassed for years to come. EMI's clean, wide-ranging sound sets the seal on a memorable pair of performances.

Additional recommendation ...

...Dona nobis pacem[a]. Five Mystical Songs. [a]**Edith Wiens** (sop); **Brian Rayner Cook** (bar); **London Philharmonic Choir and Orchestra / Bryden Thomson.** Chandos Ⓔ CHAN8590 (57 minutes: DDD: 3/89).

Vaughan Williams Serenade to Music[a]. Flos campi[b]. Five mystical songs[c]. Fantasia on Christmas carols[d]. [a]**Elizabeth Connell, [a]Linda Kitchen, [a]Anne Dawson, [a]Amanda Roocroft** (sops); [a]**Sarah Walker, [a]Jean Rigby, [a]Diana Montague** (mezzos), [a]**Catherine Wyn-Rogers** (contr); [a]**John Mark**

Ainsley, [a]Martyn Hill, [a]Arthur Davies, [a]Maldwyn Davies (tens); [acd]Thomas Allen, [a]Alan Opie (bars); [a]Gwynne Howell, [a]John Connell (basses); [b]Nobuko Imai (va); [bcd]Corydon Singers; English Chamber Orchestra / Matthew Best. Hyperion Ⓕ CDA66420 (68 minutes: DDD: 8/90). Texts included. Recorded 1990.

In 1938 Sir Henry Wood celebrated his 50 years as a professional conductor with a concert. Vaughan Williams composed a work for the occasion, the *Serenade to Music*, in which he set words by Shakespeare from Act 5 of *The Merchant of Venice*. Sixteen star vocalists of the age were gathered together for the performance and Vaughan Williams customized the vocal parts to show off the best qualities of the singers. The work turned out to be one of the composer's most sybaritic creations, turning each of its subsequent performances into a special event. Hyperion have gathered stars of our own age for this outstanding issue and Matthew Best has perceptively managed to give each their head whilst melding them into a cohesive ensemble. A mellow, spacious recording has allowed the work to emerge on disc with a veracity never achieved before. The coupled vocal pieces are given to equal effect and the disc is substantially completed by Nobuko Imai's tautly poignant account of *Flos campi*, in which the disturbing tension between solo viola and wordless chorus heighten the work's crypticism. Altogether, an imaginative issue that is a must for any collection.

Additional recommendation ...

...Flos campi[a]. Viola Suite[b]. Two Hymn-Tune Preludes[c]. The Poisoned Kiss – Overture[c]. The Running Set[c]. [ab]Frederick Riddle (va); [a]Bournemouth Sinfonietta Chorus; Bournemouth Sinfonietta / [ab]Norman Del Mar, [c]George Hurst. Chandos Collect Ⓜ CHAN6545 (66 minutes: ADD: 11/92).

Vaughan Williams On Wenlock Edge[a]. Songs of Travel[b].
Butterworth Love blows as the wind blows[c].
Elgar Pleading, Op. 48 No. 1[c]. Song Cycle, Op. 59[c]. Two Songs, Op. 60[c]. [ac]Robert Tear (ten); [b]Thomas Allen (bar); City of Birmingham Symphony Orchestra / [ab]Sir Simon Rattle, [c]Vernon Handley. EMI British Composers Ⓕ CDM7 64731-2 (69 minutes: DDD/ADD: 3/94). Items marked [ab] from EL270059-2 (9/84), [c]HMV ASD3896 (9/80). Texts included. Recorded 1979-83.

Neither of Vaughan Williams's song cycles was originally written with orchestral accompaniment. *On Wenlock Edge* was scored for accompaniment of piano and string quartet, while the *Songs of Travel* were written with piano. Both lose a little when sung with orchestra but the gain seems to considerably outweigh any loss, especially when three such superb artists are involved. Tear's singing is notable for some wonderfully long phrases (as also is Allen's in the other cycle) together with the other Tear qualities, of clarity of words and such matters. The CBSO play especially well for Rattle, as they always do. All in all, superb performances that do real justice to Vaughan Williams's imagination, his care for words and his orchestration. The Tear/Handley Elgar and Butterworth items are rarities and were all première recordings. Throughout, Tear sings with his customary sensitivity and intelligent word-pointing. Equally, the CBSO under Handley tender irreproachably alert and imaginative support. EMI's warm-toned engineering is vivid and beautifully balanced. This is a most desirable reissue.

Additional recommendation ...

...Songs of Travel. **Butterworth** Bredon Hill and other songs. A Shropshire Lad. **Finzi** Let us garlands bring, Op. 18. **Ireland** Sea Fever. The Vagabond. The Bells of San Marie. **Bryn Terfel** (bass-bar); **Malcolm Martineau** (pf). DG Ⓕ 445 946-2GH (77 minutes: DDD: 8/95). *Gramophone Editor's record of the month. See review under Butterworth; refer to the Index to Reviews.* ⒼⒼⒼ

Vaughan Williams Riders to the Sea[a]. Merciless Beauty[b]. Epithalamion[c]. [a]Norma Burrowes (sop) Nora; [a]Dame Margaret Price (sop) Cathleen; [a]Helen Watts (contr) Maurya; [a]Benjamin Luxon (bar) Bartley; [a]Pauline Stevens (mez) Woman; [a]Ambrosian Singers; [a]Orchestra Nova of London / Meredith Davies. [b]Philip Langridge (ten); [c]Stephen Roberts (bar); [c]Jonathan Snowden (fl); [c]Howard Shelley (pf); [b]members of the Endellion Quartet (Andrew Watkinson, James Clark, vns; David Waterman, vc); [c]Bach Choir; [c]London Philharmonic Orchestra / Sir David Willcocks. EMI British Composers Ⓜ CDM7 64730-2 (75 minutes: ADD/DDD: 4/94). Item marked [a] from HMV ASD2699 (9/71), recorded 1970; [bc]CDC7 47769-2 (3/88), recorded 1986. Texts included. Ⓖ

Vaughan Williams completed his masterly setting of J.M. Synge's one-act drama, *Riders to the Sea*, in 1932. Although it has enjoyed the occasional revival, it remains one of the least-known and most under-appreciated of Vaughan Williams's major works. Indeed, with scoring that is both economical and intensely evocative, it can be a gripping experience, especially when presented as sympathetically as here. The cast is a uniformly strong one, and Meredith Davies inspires everyone to give of their very best. The 1970 sound has come up superbly, creating a rather more vivid impression, in fact, than its two digitally recorded partners here from 1986. These are also both considerable rarities. *Epithalamion* is a large-scale cantata from 1957 based on Edmund Spenser's love-poem of the same name: musically, it draws extensively on material used in Vaughan Williams's 1938 masque, *The Bridal Day*, and its emotional centrepiece, "The Lover's Song", boasts a viola solo of exquisite beauty. Finally, there is *Merciless Beauty*, three pithy Chaucer settings for tenor and string trio dating from 1921. Performances are once again all one could wish.

Additional recommendation ...

...Riders to the Sea[a]. Household Music. Flos campi[b]. [a]Soloists; [b]Philip Dukes (va); [b]Northern Sinfonia Chorus; Northern Sinfonia / Richard Hickox. Chandos Ⓕ CHAN9392 (79 minutes: DDD: 11/95).

Further listening ...

...Job. Variations for Brass Band (orch. G. Jacob). **Bournemouth Symphony Orchestra / Richard Hickox.** EMI CDC7 54421-2 (7/92).

...Phantasy Quintet. Violin Sonata in A minor. String Quartet No. 2 in A minor. Six Studies in English folk song. **Music Group of London.** EMI British Composers CDM5 65100-2 (9/94).

...Job. **David Nolan** (vn); **London Philharmonic Orchestra / Vernon Handley.** Classics for Pleasure CD-CFP4603 (3/93).

...49th Parallel – Prelude. The Story of a Flemish Farm – Suite. Coastal Command – Suite. The England of Elizabeth – Explorer; Poet; Queen. **Radio Telefis Eire Concert Orchestra / Andrew Penny.** Marco Polo 8 223665 (10/95).

...Scott of the Antarctic – Prologue; Pony March; Penguins; Climbing the Glacier; Final Music. *Coupled with works by* **Frankel, Alwyn, Arnold, Addinsell, C. Williams, Brodszky, C. Parker, J. Addison II, Allan Gray, Greenwood, Spoliansky** and **P. Green** Various orchestras and conductors. EMI mono CDGO2059* (9/94). *See review in the Collections section; refer to the Index to Reviews.*

...Six Studies in English folk song. *Coupled with* **Bozza** Pulcinella. **Milhaud** Duo concertante, Op. 351. Caprice, Op. 335a. **Françaix** Tema con variazioni. **Honegger** Clarinet Sonatina, H42. **Hindemith** Clarinet Sonata in B flat major. **Kupferman** Moonflowers, Baby!. **Jonathan Cohler** (cl); **Judith Gordon** (pf). Crystal CD733 (5/95).

...Bushes and briars. Loch Lomond. John Dory. Greensleeves. Ward the Pirate. Ca' the Yowes. The unquiet grave. The Seeds of Love. Early in the spring. The Turtle Dove. An Acre of Land. Five English Folksongs. Bushes and briars. Wassail song. *Coupled with works by* **Elgar, Howells, Bax, Delius, Warlock, Britten** and **Holst** London Madrigal Singers / Christopher Bishop; Baccholian Singers of London; Philip Jones Brass Ensemble; English Chamber Orchestra / Ian Humphris. EMI British Composers CMS5 65123-2 (2/96). *See review in the Collections section; refer to the Index to Reviews.*

...A Bunyan Sequence. **Sir John Gielgud, Richard Pasco, Ursula Howells** (narrs); **Aiden Oliver** (treb); **Corydon Singers; City of London Sinfonia / Matthew Best.** Hyperion CDA66511 (8/91).

...A Song of Thanksgiving[a]. Three Choral Hymns[b]. Magnificat[c]. The Shepherds of the Delectable Mountains[d]. The Old Hundredth Psalm Tune[e]. [a]**Sir John Gielgud** (narr); [a]**Lynne Dawson,** [d]**Linda Kitchen** (sops); [c]**Catherine Wyn-Rogers** (contr); [d]**John Mark Ainsley,** [b]**John Bowen,** [d]**Adrian Thompson** (tens); [d]**Alan Opie** (bar); [d]**Bryn Terfel** (bass-bar); [d]**Jonathan Best** (bass); [a]**John Scott,** [bce]**Roger Judd** (orgs); [a]**London Oratory Junior Choir; Corydon Singers; City of London Sinfonia / Matthew Best.** Hyperion CDA66569 (8/92).

...The Old Hundreth Psalm Tune. Toward the Unknown Region. O taste and see. O clap your hands. Let us now praise famous men. Benedicite. *Coupled with* **Walton** Orb and Sceptre. Set me as a seal upon thine heart. Jubilate Deo. A Litany. Coronation Te Deum. **Soloists; Waynfelte Singers; Winchester Cathedral Choir; Bournemouth Symphony Orchestra / David Hill.** Argo 436 120-2ZH (5/93).

...Hugh the Drover. **Soloists; New London Children's Choir; Corydon Singers; Corydon Orchestra / Matthew Best.** Hyperion CDA66901/2 (10/94).

...Hugh the Drover. **Soloists; St Paul's Cathedral Choir; Ambrosian Opera Chorus; Royal Philharmonic Orchestra / Sir Charles Groves.** EMI British Composers CMS5 65224-2 (10/94).

Orazio Vecchi
Italian 1550-1605

Suggested listening ...

...L'Amfiparnaso. Il convito musicale – o giardiniero; Lunghi danni; Bando del asino. **Clément Janequin Ensemble / Dominique Visse** (alto). Harmonia Mundi HMC90 1461 (12/93). ✒

Glauco Velasquez
Brazilian 1884-1914

Suggested listening ...

...Valsa romântica. Brutto sogno. Rêverie. Valsa lenta. Prelúdio e Scherzo. Prelúdios Nos. 1 and 2. Divertimento No. 2. Petite Suite. Two Folha d'album. Minuetto e Gavotte Moderni. Danse de silphes. Canzone Strana. Impromptu. Melancolia. Devaneio. **Clara Sverner** (pf). Marco Polo 8 223556 (7/95).

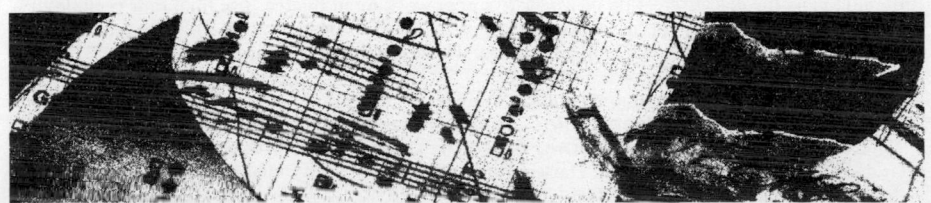

Gilet Velut

French fl early 15th century

Suggested listening ...

...Benedicta viscera/Ave mater gratie/Ora pro nobis Deum alleluya. *Coupled with works by* **Ciconia, Philipoctus de Caserta, Johanne Egidius, Matheus de Sancto Johanne, Bartolomeus da Bologna, Anonymous, Tapissier, Antonius de Civitate Austrie, Brassart, Zacharias** and **Dufay. Orlando Consort.** Metronome METCD1008 (11/95). *See review in the Collections section; refer to the Index to Reviews.* Ⓖ

...Lassies ester vostres chans de liesse. Un petit oyselet chantant. *Coupled with works by* **Legrant Johannes de Lymburga, Fontaine, Dunstable, Cardot, Anonymous, Bittering, Binchois, Machaut** and **Power Gothic Voices / Christopher Page.** Hyperion CDA66783 (1/96). *See review in the Collections section; refer to the Index to Reviews.*

Francesco Veracini

Italian 1690-1768

New review

Veracini Sonate accademiche, Op. 2 – No. 7 in D minor; No. 8 in E minor; No. 9 in A major; No. 12 in D minor. Capriccio sesto con due soggetti in G minor. **Fabio Biondi** (vn); **Maurizio Naddeo** (vc); **Rinaldo Alessandrini** (hpd); **Pascal Monteilhet** (theorbo). Opus 111 Ⓕ OPS30-138 (61 minutes: DDD: 9/95). Recorded 1995.

Despite the continuing re-discovery of so much of the Italian baroque, Veracini's music remains comparatively unknown both in the concert-hall and on record. This neglect is as unjustified as the traditional unfavourable comparison of his music with that of Vivaldi. He was a performer whose curious style was already noticed during his lifetime by the English writer Charles Burney, who once said that by travelling and playing all over Europe Veracini had formed a "style of playing peculiar to himself". The same might be said of his composing, which far from being simply an assimilation of contemporary modes, speaks with a sharply individual voice that constantly surprises with its freshness and originality. This almost kaleidoscopic shifting of moods and manners is fully evident in the *Sonate accademiche*, a collection of pieces published in 1744, but the fruits of a lifetime's experience playing in Dresden, London and Venice. As such they are shot through with virtuoso passagework, double-stopping and other technical features characteristic of Veracini's performances. These are here negotiated by Fabio Biondi with an easy brilliance that nevertheless does not sacrifice poetry for mere outward display. His approach is vigorous, with plenty of tone when required, and attractively alive. The overall sound is sharp and clean. Both he and the other performers use either period instruments or modern copies, and Rinaldo Alessandrini's informed and committed direction, and support, brings out all the delicacy of Veracini's rich and varied textures. There is much to savour on this record – no connoisseur of the period can afford to be without it.

Further listening ...

...Overtures – No. 1 in B flat major; No. 2 in F major; No. 3 in B flat major; No. 4 in F major; No. 6 in B flat major. **Cologne Musica Antiqua / Reinhard Goebel.** Archiv Produktion 439 937-2AH (12/94). ✒ Ⓖ

...Overture No. 5 in B flat major. *Coupled with works by* **Heinichen, Dieupart, Fasch, Pisendel** and **Quantz Cologne Musica Antiqua / Reinhard Goebel.** Archiv Produktion 447 644-2AH (1/96). ✒ Ⓖ

Giuseppe Verdi

Italian 1813-1901

Verdi Overtures and Preludes – Nabucco; Ernani; I Masnadieri; Macbeth; Il Corsaro; La Battaglia di Legnano; Luisa Miller; Rigoletto; La traviata; I Vespri Siciliani; Un ballo in maschera; La forza del destino; Aida. **Berlin Philharmonic Orchestra / Herbert von Karajan.** DG Ⓕ 419 622-2GH (73 minutes: ADD: 10/87). From 413 544-1GX2 (2/86). Recorded 1975.

Karajan was one of the most adaptable and sensitive of dramatic conductors. His repertoire in the theatre is extraordinarily wide being at home equally in Verdi, Wagner, Richard Strauss and Puccini. In this selection from his celebrated 1976 collection of all of Verdi's overtures, he gives us some fine insights into the composer's skill as an orchestrator, dramatist and poet. Though Karajan had only recorded *Aida* complete his dramatic instincts bring some fine performances of the lesser known preludes. The earliest, *Nabucco* from 1842 (the collection is arranged chronologically), already shows a mastercraftsman at work, with a slow introduction promising much. *La traviata* shows a quite different skill – the delcate creation of a sensitive poet working in filigree. The final four preludes are great works fully worthy of this individual presentation. Even the lesser known Preludes are enhanced by Karajan's dramatic instincts. Good recordings, though less than outstanding.

Additional recommendation ...

...I vespri siciliani – Overture. Luisa Miller – Oh! fede negar potessi ... Quando le sere al placido. *Coupled with works by* **Donizetti, Cilea, Leoncavallo, Mascagni, Bixio, Ellington, Di Lazzaro, Sibella, Denza, Borne, Crescenzo, De Curtis, Massenet, Puccini** and **Di Capua** Luciano Pavarotti; Harlem Boys' Choir; New York Philharmonic Orchestra / Leone Magiera. Decca 444 450-2DH (2/95).

Verdi Messa da Requiem[a]. Quattro pezzi sacri[b]. [a]**Luba Orgonasova**, [b]**Donna Brown** (sops); [a]**Anne Sofie von Otter** (mez); [a]**Luca Canonici** (ten); [a]**Alastair Miles** (bass); **Monteverdi Choir; Orchestre Révolutionnaire et Romantique / John Eliot Gardiner**. Philips Ⓕ 442 142-2PH2 (two discs: 120 minutes: DDD: 4/95). ✏ Notes, texts and translations included. Recorded 1992.
Gramophone Editor's choice. ⓖⓖ

In terms of instrumental and vocal detail, internal balance, textural clarity and dynamic grading Gardiner's Verdi Requiem is in a class of its own, an achievement made possible by discipline over forces who know him well and who are dedicated to his will. Listen to the perfectly graded crescendo in the *Kyrie* at "luceat eis" just before the soloists first enter, the really hushed *sotto voce* in the *Dies irae*, the double and triple dotting in "Rex tremenda", the discipline and detail throughout an exhilarating *Sanctus*, the exquisitely judged *senza misura* at the start of the "Libera me", then the attack in the same movement's fugue – and the dramatic intensity of the "Stabat mater" climaxes in the *Quattro pezzi sacri*. These are just a few of the many moments of revelation in readings that combine a positive view and interpretative integrity from start to finish, something possible only in the context of the superb professionalism of the (augmented) Monteverdi Choir, who sing with burnished, steady tone throughout and suggest, rightly, a corporate act of worship. Their contribution is beyond praise – and Verdi would surely have marvelled at that. He might also have been surprised and delighted to hear the soloists' contribution sung with such precision by such a finely integrated quartet, who perform the important unaccompanied passages with special grace and sensitivity. Instead of hearing the usual jostle of vibratos, here the four voices are firm and true. Individually they are also distinguished. Pride of place must go to Orgonasova who gives the performance of her life. The exactly placed high B in the "Quid sum miser" section of the *Dies irae*, the perfect blending with von Otter at "Dominum", the whole of the *Andante* section of the "Libera me", sung with ethereal tone and a long breath, make the heart stop in amazement. In "Oro supplex" Gardiner follows Verdi's tempo marking. More often he follows tradition, with slower speeds than those suggested, and he allows more licence than the score, or conductors like Toscanini (listed below). But as his liberties all seem so convincing in the context of the whole, who should complain? In the *Pezzi sacri*, Gardiner gives the most thrilling account yet to appear. The recording, made in Westminster Cathedral, has a huge range which may cause problems in confined spaces. If you have the volume high enough to catch the many *ppp* passages you are liable to be overwhelmed by, for instance, the *Dies irae*.

Additional recommendations ...

...Messa da Requiem. Quattro pezzi sacri. **Soloists; Philharmonia Chorus and Orchestra / Carlo Maria Giulini.** EMI Ⓕ CDS7 47257-8 (two discs: 129 minutes: ADD: 4/87). ⓖⓖ

...Messa da Requiem[a]. Opera choruses – Don Carlos – Spuntato ecco il di. Macbeth – Patria oppressa. Otello – Fuoco di gioia. Nabucco – Va, pensiero, sull'ali dorate. Aida – Gloria all'Egitto. [a]**Susan Dunn** (sop); [a]**Diane Curry** (mez); [a]**Jerry Hadley** (ten); [a]**Paul Plishka** (bass); **Atlanta Symphony Chorus and Orchestra / Robert Shaw.** Telarc Ⓕ CD80152 (two discs: 113 minutes: DDD: 3/88). *Gramophone* Award Winner 1988. *Selected by Sounds in Retrospect.*

...Messa da Requiem. Quattro pezzi sacri. **Soloists; Vienna State Opera Concert Chorus; Vienna Philharmonic Orchestra / Claudio Abbado.** DG Ⓕ 435 884-2GH2 (two discs: 127 minutes: DDD: 9/93).

...Messa da Requiem. **Soloists; Chicago Symphony Chorus and Orchestra / Sir Georg Solti.** RCA Victor Gold Seal Ⓜ 09026-61403-2 (two discs: 82 minutes: ADD: 9/93).

...Messa da Requiem. **Soloists; Chicago Symphony Chorus and Orchestra / Daniel Barenboim.** Erato Ⓕ 4509-96357-2 (two discs: 83 minutes: DDD: 11/94). *Selected by Sounds in Retrospect.*

...Messa da Requiem[a]. Quattro pezzi sacri – No. 4, Te Deum. [a]**Zinka Milanov** (sop); [a]**Bruna Castagna** (mez); [a]**Jussi Björling** (ten); [a]**Nicola Moscona** (bass); **Westminster Choir; NBC Symphony Orchestra / Arturo Toscanini.** Music and Arts mono Ⓜ CD240* (two discs: 99 minutes: AAD: 3/95).

...Messa da Requiem. **Soloists; Chorus and Orchestra of the Rome Opera / Tullio Serafin.** Dutton Laboratories mono Ⓜ CDLX7010* (73 minutes: ADD: 3/95).

...Messa da Requiem[a]. La traviata[b] – Preludes, Act 1 and 3. I vespri siciliani – Overture[b]. **Wolf-Ferrari** I quattro rusteghi – Intermezzo[b]. Il segreto di Susanna – Overture[b]. **Respighi** Fountains of Rome[b]. **Rossini** Guillaume Tell – Overture[b]. [a]**Dame Elisabeth Schwarzkopf** (sop); [a]**Oralia Dominguez** (mez); [a]**Giuseppe di Stefano** (ten); [a]**Cesare Siepi** (bass); [a]**Chorus and Orchestra of La Scala, Milan,** [b]**Santa Cecilia Academy Orchestra, Rome / Victor de Sabata.** EMI Références mono Ⓜ CHS5 65506-2* (two discs: 148 minutes: ADD: 9/95).

...Messa da Requiem[b]. **Cherubini** Requiem Mass No. 1 in C minor[a]. **Soloists;** [a]**Ambrosian Singers;** [b]**Ambrosian Chorus; Philharmonia Orchestra / Riccardo Muti.** EMI Forte Ⓜ CZS5 68613-2 (two discs: 135 minutes: [a]ADD/[b]DDD: 7/96).

Verdi Opera choruses – Nabucco – Gli arredi festivi giù cadano infranti; Va, pensiero, sull'ali dorate. I Lombardi – Gerusalem!; O Signore, dal tetto natio. Macbeth – Tre volte miagola; Patria oppressa. I Masnadieri – Le rube, gli stupri. Rigoletto – Zitti zitti. Il trovatore – Vedi! le fosche notturne spoglie; Squilli, echeggi la tromba guerriera. La traviata – Noi siamo zingarelle ... Di Madride noi siam mattadori (with Marsha Waxman, mez; David Huneryager, Richard Cohn, basses). Un ballo in maschera – Posa in pace. Don Carlos – Spuntato ecco il dí. Aida – Gloria all'Egitto. Otello – Fuoco di gioia. Requiem – Sanctus. **Chicago Symphony Chorus and Orchestra / Sir Georg Solti.** Decca Ⓕ 430 226-2DH (70 minutes: DDD: 4/91). Texts and translations included. Recorded 1989.

Verdi's choruses occupy a special place in his operas. They are invariably red-blooded and usually make a simple dramatic statement with great impact. The arresting "Chorus of the Hebrew Slaves" ("Va, pensiero") from *Nabucco* is probably the best-known and most popular chorus in the entire operatic repertoire, immediately tugging at the heart-strings with its gentle opening cantilena, soon swelling out to a great climax. Solti shows just how to shape the noble melodic line which soars with firm control, yet retaining the urgency and electricity in every bar. He is equally good in "Gli arredi festivi", from the same opera, not only in the bold opening statement, shared between singers and the resplendent sonority of the Chicago brass, but also later when the mood lightens, and women's voices are heard floating over seductive harp roulades. The dramatic contrasts at the opening of "Gerusalem!" from *I Lombardi* are equally powerfully projected, and the brass again makes a riveting effect in "Patria oppressa" from *Macbeth*. But, of course, not all Verdi choruses offer blood and thunder: the volatile "Fire chorus" from *Otello* flickers with an almost visual fantasy, while the wicked robbers in *I Masnadieri* celebrate their excesses (plunder, rape, arson and murder) gleefully, and with such rhythmic jauntiness that one cannot quite take them seriously. The "Gipsies chorus" from *La traviata* has a nice touch of elegance, and the scherzo-like "Sanctus", from the *Requiem*, which ends the concert, is full of joy. But it is the impact of the dramatic moments which is most memorable, not least the big triumphal scene from *Aida*, complete with the ballet music, to provide a diverse interlude in the middle. The recording is in the demonstration class.

Additional recommendations ...

...Nabucco – Gli arredi festivi giù cadano infranti; Va, pensiero, sull'ali dorate. Macbeth – Patria oppressa. Il trovatore – Vedi! le fosche notturne spoglie; Ora co'dadi, ma fra poco. La traviata – Noi siamo zingarelle; Si ridesta in ciel (with Alena Cokova, mez; Stanislav Vrabel, bass). Don Carlos – Spuntato ecco il dì d'esultanza. Aida – Gloria all'Egitto. Otello – Fuoco di gioia. La Battaglia di Legnano – Deus meus, pone illos ut rotam (Eva Jenisova, sop; Cokova); Giuramento (L'udovit Ludha, ten). Ernani – Si rideste il Leon di Castiglia. La forza del destino – Rataplan! rataplan! (Ida Kirilová, mez). **Slovak Philharmonic Choir; Slovak Radio Symphony Orchestra / Oliver Dohnányi.** Naxos Ⓢ 8 550241 (56 minutes: DDD: 4/91).

...Nabucco – Gli arredi festivi; Va, pensiero, sull'ali dorata. Macbeth – Tre volte miagola; Patria oppressa! La Battaglia di Legnano – Giuriam d'Italia. I Lombardi – Gerusalem!; O Signore, del tetto natio. Il trovatore – Vedi! le fosche. Don Carlo – Spuntato ecco il di d'esultanza. Otello – Fuoco di gioia! Aida – Gloria all' Egitto. **Santa Cecilia Academy Chorus and Orchestra, Rome / Carlo Rizzi.** Teldec Ⓕ 4509-90267-2 (61 minutes: DDD: 8/93). *Gramophone Editor's choice.*

...La forza del destino – Son giunta! ... Madre, pietosa Vergine[a]; Pace, pace, mio Dio. Otello – Mia madre aveva ... Piangea cantando ... Ave Maria. Aida – Qui Radames verra? ... O patria mia. Il trovatore – Tacea la notte placida ... Di tale amor. *Coupled with works by* **Tchaikovsky** Galina Gorchakova (sop); [a]**Chorus and Orchestra of the Kirov Opera / Valery Gergiev.** Philips Ⓕ 446 405-2PH (60 minutes: DDD: 3/96). *See review under Tchaikovsky; refer to the Index to Reviews.* *Gramophone Editor's choice.*

New review

Verdi Opera Arias: Nabucco – Ben io t'avenni ... Anch'io dischiuso un giorno. Il trovatore – Tacea la notte placida ... Di tale amor; Timor di me? ... D'amor sull'ali rosee. La traviata – E strano! ... Ah, fors'è lui ... Follie! Sempre libera[a]; Teneste la promessa ... Addio del passato. Un ballo in maschera – Ecco l'orrido campo ... Ma dall'arido stelo divulsa ... Morro, ma prima in grazia. La forza del destino – Pace, pace, mio Dio. **Julia Varady** (sop); [a]**Lothar Odinius** (ten); **Bavarian State Orchestra / Dietrich Fischer-Dieskau.** Orfeo Ⓕ C186951 (51 minutes: DDD: 1/96). Recorded 1995.

Varady endows these arias we have heard hundreds of times, and of which we all have our favourite memories and recordings, with renewed life through an art which is fully responsive, highly fastidious, lovely in the quality of its sound and individual in its timbre and inflexion. The beauty of tone is evident first of all in its well-preserved purity (and Varady, born in 1941, is of an age when normally allowances have to be made). Here is not a full-bodied, rich Ponselle-like voice, but she makes wonderfully effective use of her resources, which include a surprisingly strong lower register and an upward range that (as we hear) easily encompasses the high D flat and has an E flat available. She is dramatic in style yet also thoroughly accomplished in her scales, trills and other *fioriture*. Her first *Trovatore* aria, for instance, includes the cabaletta with its full complement of technical brilliances. The musical instinct seems almost infallible – a 'wrong' portamento or rubato always irritates and here everything seems right. A remarkable sensitivity is at work throughout. The orchestra is conducted by Fischer-Dieskau, Varady's husband, and here too is a fine example of a positive, non-routine collaboration, the pacing and shading of the orchestral parts so frequently having something specific to offer (for example, in the letter passage from *La traviata*). The recording is well-balanced.

Verdi Stiffelio. **José Carreras** (ten) Stiffelio; **Sylvia Sass** (sop) Lina; **Matteo Manuguerra** (bar) Stankar; **Wladimiro Ganzarolli** (bass) Jorg; **Ezio di Cesare** (ten) Raffaele; **Maria Venuti** (mez)

Dorotea; **Thomas Moser** (ten) Federico; **Austrian Radio Chorus and Symphony Orchestra / Lamberto Gardelli.** Philips Ⓜ 422 432-2PM2 (two discs: 109 minutes: ADD: 3/90). Notes, text and translation included. From 6769 039 (10/80). Recorded 1979.

This work is gradually gaining the reputation it deserves as companies and audiences realize its quality (it gains its first performance at Covent Garden in the 1992-23 season). It tells of Stiffelio, a Protestant clergyman, in a Catholic country, whose wife Linda has committed adultery and finds it in his heart, after her father has killed her lover, to forgive her. The work has elements that pre-echo *Otello* and is yet another example of Verdi finding the specific music for a specific predicament. This performance, firmly conducted by Gardelli, has an involved, involving assumption of the title-role by Carreras. This role is a gift for an accomplished tenor and he catches the moral fervour and uncertainties of the part with his open-hearted, spontaneous performance. Sylvia Sass also offers a rewarding, strongly emotional performance as Lina.

Verdi Macbeth. **Piero Cappuccilli** (bar) Macbeth; **Shirley Verrett** (mez) Lady Macbeth; **Nicolai Ghiaurov** (bass) Banquo; **Plácido Domingo** (ten) Macduff; **Antonio Savastano** (ten) Malcolm; **Carlo Zardo** (bass) Doctor; **Giovanni Foiani** (bass) Servant; **Sergio Fontana** (bass) Herald; **Alfredo Mariotti** (bass) Assassin; **Stefania Malagú** (mez) Lady-in-waiting; **Chorus and Orchestra of La Scala, Milan / Claudio Abbado.** DG Ⓕ 415 688-2GH3 (three discs: 154 minutes: ADD: 9/86). Notes, text and translation included. From 2709 062 (10/76). Recorded 1976.

Verdi's lifelong admiration for Shakespeare resulted in only two operas based on his plays. *Macbeth*, the first, originally written in 1847, was extensively revised in 1865. Without losing the direct force of the original, Verdi added greater depth to his first ideas. Once derided as being un-Shakespearian, it is now recognized as a masterpiece for its psychological penetration as much as for its subtle melodic inspiration. Abbado captures perfectly the atmosphere of dark deeds and personal ambition leading to tragedy, projected by Verdi, and his reading holds the opera's disparate elements in the score under firm control, catching its interior tensions. He is well supported by his Scala forces. Shirley Verrett may not be ideally incisive or Italianate in accent as Lady Macbeth, but she peers into the character's soul most convincingly. As ever, truly inspired by Abbado, Cappuccilli is a suitably haunted and introverted Macbeth who sings a secure and unwavering legato. Domingo's upright Macduff and Ghiaurov's doom-laden Banquo are both admirable in their respective roles.

Additional recommendations ...

...**Soloists; Berlin Deutsche Opera Chorus and Orchestra / Giuseppe Sinopoli.** Philips Ⓕ 412 133-2PH3 (three discs: 135 minutes: DDD: 2/85).

...**Soloists; Metropolitan Opera Chorus and Orchestra / Erich Leinsdorf.** RCA Victor Ⓜ GD84516 (two discs: 130 minutes: ADD: 9/88).

...**Soloists; Ambrosian Opera Chorus; New Philharmonia Orchestra / Riccardo Muti.** EMI Ⓜ CMS7 64339-2 (two discs: ADD: 2/93).

Verdi Luisa Miller. **Montserrat Caballé** (sop) Luisa; **Luciano Pavarotti** (ten) Rodolfo; **Sherrill Milnes** (bar) Miller; **Bonaldo Gaiotti** (bass) Count Walter; **Anna Reynolds** (mez) Federica; **Richard Van Allan** (bass) Wurm; **Annette Céline** (mez) Laura; **Fernando Pavarotti** (ten) Peasant; **London Opera Chorus; National Philharmonic Orchestra / Peter Maag.** Decca Ⓕ 417 420-2DH2 (two discs: 144 minutes: ADD: 10/88). Notes, text and translation included. From SET606/08 (5/76).

This transitional work shows Verdi enhancing his skills and refining his musical style. The plot, based on a Schiller drama, involves the tragedy and death of Luisa and her beloved Rodolfo brought about by the evil Wurm, apt predecessor of Verdi's Iago. The title-role could not find a more appealing interpreter than Caballé, who spins a fine line and is highly responsive to Luisa's sad situation. She is partnered by Pavarotti at the height of his powers as Rodolfo. He excels in "Quando le sere al polacido", the work's most famous aria. As Luisa's equivocal father, Miller, Milnes gives one of his best performances on disc and Van Allan is a properly snarling Wurm. Maag, an underrated conductor, directs a strong, well-proportioned performance. He gives the impression of being in love with this opera and he goes right to the heart of the score, finding its seriousness as well as its fire. The last act is specially fine, containing what are regarded as among the gramophone classics, the two duets of Luisa, first with her father, then with Rodolfo. The production is unobtrusively effective in creation of atmosphere and is spaciously recorded.

Additional recommendation ...

...**Soloists; Chorus and Orchestra of the Royal Opera House, Covent Garden / Lorin Maazel.** DG Ⓕ 423 144-2GH2 (two discs: 133 minutes: ADD: 5/88).

Verdi Rigoletto. **Tito Gobbi** (bar) Rigoletto; **Giuseppe di Stefano** (ten) Duke; **Maria Callas** (sop) Gilda; **Nicola Zaccaria** (bass) Sparafucile; **Adriana Lazzarini** (mez) Maddalena; **Giuse Gerbino** (mez) Giovanna; **Plinio Clabassi** (bass) Monterone; **William Dickie** (bar) Marullo; **Renato Ercolani** (ten) Borsa; **Carlo Forti** (bar) Count Ceprano; **Elvira Galassi** (sop) Countess Ceprano; **Chorus and Orchestra of La Scala, Milan / Tullio Serafin.** EMI mono Ⓕ CDS7 47469-8* (two discs: 118 minutes: ADD: 2/87). Notes, text and translation included. From Columbia 33CXS1324, 33CX1325/6 (2/56). Recorded 1955. Ⓖ

The story of the hunchbacked jester Rigoletto at the court of a licentious Duke who seduces the Fool's daughter Gilda by masquerading as a poor student, and the consequent attempts at revenge on the part of Rigoletto, produced from Verdi one of the most telling of his middle-period triumphs. His identification with each of the characters and the sheer energy and sensuous ardour of the score is quite remarkable. Nowhere else on record have these characterizations been delineated with such intelligence and commitment as by Gobbi, Callas and di Stefano on this 41-year-old set. Serafin presides over everything with an unerring grasp of Verdian timing.

Additional recommendations ...

...**Soloists; Vienna State Opera Chorus; Vienna Philharmonic Orchestra / Carlo Maria Giulini.** DG Ⓕ 415 288-2GH2 (two discs: DDD: 11/85).

...**Soloists; RCA Italiana Opera Chorus and Orchestra / Sir Georg Solti.** RCA Victor Gold Seal Ⓕ GD86506 (two discs: 113 minutes: ADD: 9/88).

...**Soloists; Chorus and Orchestra of La Scala, Milan / Riccardo Muti.** EMI Ⓕ CDS7 49605-2 (two discs: 116 minutes: DDD: 11/89).

...**Soloists; Chorus and Orchestra of the Teatro Communale, Bologna / Riccardo Chailly.** Decca Ⓕ 425 864-2DH2 (two discs: 107 minutes: DDD: 1/90).

...**Soloists; Slovak Philharmonic Chorus; Czecho-Slovak Radio Symphony Orchestra / Alexander Rahbari.** Naxos Ⓢ 8 660013/4 (two discs: 115 minutes: DDD: 3/92).

...**Soloists; Stockholm Royal Opera Chorus and Orchestra / Sixten Ehrling.** BIS mono Ⓜ CD296* (116 minutes: ADD: 8/94).

...**Rigoletto, with additional items by Benedict, Bizet, Donizetti, Evans, Kaper, Lehár, Martin y Guerrero, Payán and Serrano sung by Lina Pagliughi** (sop) and **Tino Folgar** (ten). **Soloists; Chorus and Orchestra of La Scala, Milan / Carlo Sabajno.** Pearl mono Ⓜ GEMMCDS9180* (two discs: 155 minutes: ADD: 6/96),

---

New review

Verdi Rigoletto. **Renato Bruson** (bar) Rigoletto; **Andrea Rost** (sop) Gilda; **Roberto Alagna** (ten) Duke; **Dimitri Kavrakos** (bass) Sparafucile; **Mariana Pentcheva** (contr) Maddalena; **Giorgio Giuseppini** (bass) Monterone; **Antonella Trevisan** (mez) Giovanna; **Ernesto Gavazzi** (ten) Borsa; **Silvestro Sammaritano** (bass) Marullo; **Nicoletta Zanini** (mez) Countess Ceprano; **Antonio de Gobbi** (bass) Count Ceprano; **Marilena Laurenza** (sop) Page; **Ernesto Panariello** (bass) Usher; **Chorus and Orchestra of La Scala, Milan / Riccardo Muti.** Sony Classical Ⓕ S2K66314 (two discs: 121 minutes: DDD: 12/95). Recorded live in 1994.

Muti's previous recording of this opera is only six-and-a-half years old. That was made with the forces of La Scala in La Scala for EMI but not at a live performance, unlike this one. You immediately feel that added *frisson* of a 'real' occasion and that continues throughout a well-prepared and well-integrated performance, applause restricted to ends of acts, virtually no audience noise. As for Muti's interpretation, it has changed very little during the intervening period. It remains rewardingly vital, rhythmically speaking. Every moment is acutely and alertly sprung with speeds tending to be on the brisk side. It is at the furthermost extreme from Giulini's grand, leisurely approach, more akin to Chailly's. It is a pleasure to hear how Muti, in both versions, observes the importance Verdi gives to oboe, clarinet and bassoon, how profitably he makes all his singers observe to the letter what Verdi wrote. Ah, Roberto Alagna! Many will want this set for the participation of the new star. Listen to the Duke's aria and cabaletta at the start of Act 3 and you will hear this young tenor's tone perfectly suited and his phrasing immaculately turned. Both in "La donna è mobile" and the opening of the Quartet one might like a shade more variation in dynamics and tonal colour, just the things provided by La Scola on the EMI version, but then Alagna has the more sappy, brilliant voice and, above all, the *slancio* the part demands, and his singing reflects the Duke's wilful, libidinous nature. His is a most attractive contribution to the set. At the end of the Duke-Gilda duet, Muti demands and gets the full cadenza written into the score. It is finely turned by Alagna, and by Rost, who offers an altogether lovely performance, ideal in almost every respect. With just the right weight of voice for the role, all her singing is full-toned and precisely articulated, and the tone itself is vibrant and tangy. She very much recalls Cotrubas on the Giulini set, but Rost has the firmer tone, and this Gilda dies heart-rendingly. Rost hasn't the specifically Italian sound of Muti's Dessì (EMI), who also makes a most affecting Gilda, but Rost is the more accomplished technician.

The years have been kind to Bruson's voice (he was 58 when this recording was made), but it has to be said that, especially in the first half of the opera, the vibrato is now disturbing when the tone comes under pressure. Perhaps because he is afraid he cannot sustain a line at a lower dynamic level, he seems unwilling to sing at less than *mezzo-forte*. His remains a considered, eloquent interpretation through which courses a father's concern and anguish. But turn to Muti's Zancanaro (EMI) and you hear the exact voice for the jester, more biting, stronger, more flexible and varied in tone than Bruson's, at least the equal of Cappuccilli's on the Giulini set. Only Gobbi for Serafin provides a range of colour and shades of meaning beyond all his rivals. Kavrakos is a suitably sturdy, dour Sparafucile. After a blowzy start Pentcheva proves a seductive-sounding Maddalena, but these and the smaller roles are as well if not better cast on EMI. So that set is by no means put out of court by this one; indeed the earlier Muti is probably the most overall recommendable one among modern versions, just about superior to the Decca/Chailly – unless that is you want Giulini's appealingly sung, deeply thought-through version. But this set does boast Alagna's superbly vital Duke and Rost's greatly appealing Gilda, which may well sway you in its favour. Had the recording more presence it would run the EMI close and in any case it certainly deserves to be up among the top versions. However, as engineered here – the action seems somewhat distanced, as though you are sitting in the balcony rather than the stalls. You need a very high volume setting to get a satisfactory level from the singers; then the orchestra sound too loud. Of course the Serafin will remain unrivalled for many, but its aged sound and the disfiguring cuts must be a serious drawback to anyone coming afresh to the work's discography.

Verdi La traviata. **Tiziana Fabriccini** (sop) Violetta; **Roberto Alagna** (ten) Alfredo; **Paolo Coni** (bar) Germont; **Nicoletta Curiel** (mez) Flora; **Antonella Trevisan** (mez) Annina; **Enrico Cossutta** (ten) Gastone; **Orazio Mori** (bass) Baron; **Enzo Capuano** (bass) Marquis; **Francesco Musinu** (bass) Doctor; **Ernesto Gavazzi** (ten) Giuseppe; **Ernesto Panariello** (bass) Servant; **Silvestro Sammaritano** (bass) Messenger; **Chorus and Orchestra of La Scala, Milan / Riccardo Muti.**
Sony Classical Ⓕ S2K52486 (two discs: 136 minutes: DDD: 10/93). Notes, text and translation included. Recorded live in 1992. *Gramophone Editor's choice.* ⒼⒼ

New review

Verdi La traviata. **Angela Gheorghiu** (sop) Violetta; **Frank Lopardo** (ten) Alfredo; **Leo Nucci** (bar) Germont; **Leah-Marian Jones** (mez) Flora; **Gillian Knight** (mez) Annina; **Robin Leggate** (ten) Gaston; **Richard Van Allan** (bass) Baron; **Roderick Earle** (bass) Marquis; **Mark Beesley** (bar) Doctor; **Neil Griffiths** (ten) Giuseppe; **Bryan Secombe** (bass) Messenger; **Rodney Gibson** (ten) Servant; **Chorus and Orchestra of the Royal Opera House, Covent Garden / Sir Georg Solti.**
Decca Ⓕ 448 119-2DHO2 (two discs: 127 minutes: DDD: 8/95). Notes, text and translation included. Recorded live in 1994. Ⓖ

An exciting and eloquent reading on all sides, this version must now be rated with the established frontrunners (listed below) – but, as with some of those, most notably any of Callas's versions, it is not for the fainthearted, or for those who like their Violettas to have full, equally, produced voices. Fabriccini is evidently not an Act 1 Violetta. But even without assured coloratura and with problems at the *passagio*, she is one who is going to hold our attention and move us. In the Second Act so much bespeaks not only complete identification with Violetta's predicament but also vocal acumen of an exceptional kind, often based on the seemingly lost art of portamento. Because this is a live performance we are conscious that the singer's acting is part of the secret of the reading's success, that and the obvious youth of a soprano who is not yet a preening prima donna. The final tragedy is still better, very much modelled on Callas. The voice, more settled now than anywhere in the performance manages her role with long-breathed phrasing and pathetic accents, the result of a true understanding of Verdian style yet never self-conscious in its effect – this is undoubtedly great singing *and* interpretation. The death is deeply moving. Alagna, in the role that brought him to attention, is just the Alfredo for this Violetta; youthfully ardent, with keen-edged tone, finely attuned to the legato essential in Verdi. The recording is taken from four performances, given at La Scala, and is a theatrical view full of electricity, vitally executed by the forces of La Scala, as vital as any in the recorded history of the work. Don't miss it.

Turning to the Decca set, for Angela Gheorghiu, a young Romanian of great promise, Violetta was the right role at the right time. The whole drama is there in her voice, every expression in the eyes and beat of the heart reflected in the way she shapes and colours Verdi's vocal lines. Her quiet singing is particularly lovely, affording subtle variations of tenderness and inner anxiety. When she does choose to make a point with force, as in her sudden warmth of feeling towards Giorgio Germont at "Qual figlia m'abbracciate" or her chilling cry of "Morro!", accompanied by a loud thump on the table, her ideas always hit home. A few moments of vocal weakness are accentuated by the microphone, mainly a tendency to go sharp and some hardness at the top of the voice that was not troublesome in the theatre. Otherwise, she is the most complete and moving Violetta we have had since her compatriot, Ileana Cotrubas. These live performances were remarkably the first time that Sir Georg Solti, at the age of 82, had conducted a staged *La traviata* and he wanted two young singers who were coming fresh to the opera, as he was himself. What was so spellbinding in the theatre was the touching intimacy they brought to their scenes together. Instead of the duets for Violetta and Alfredo turning into standard Italian operatic bawling, they became lovers' whispers, each phrase floating like a kiss from one set of lips to the other. The effect comes across here in the cadenzas, where Gheorghiu and Frank Lopardo really seem to be listening to each other. Elsewhere, one is more aware than in the theatre that Lopardo's light tenor is far from being an idiomatic Italian voice. His idiosyncratic tone quality and un-Italian vowels can be problematical, as is some ungainly lifting up into notes in the earlier scenes.

Leo Nucci, Decca's resident Verdi baritone at the moment, makes a standard Giorgio Germont, not more, and apart from Leah-Marian Jones's energetic Flora, the smaller roles do not say a great deal for the Royal Opera's depth of casting, with its selection of gruff bass voices and prim Anglo-Saxon accents. Solti insisted that the opera be performed complete (more unusual in the theatre than it is on disc). But there is nothing studied about his conducting: the performance is fresh and alive from the first note to the last, the result of a lifetime's experience of how to pace a drama in the opera-house. With the increasing number of live opera sets, a recommendation for *La traviata* is likely to be based on whether one is prepared to accept noises-off or not. (Decca's recording is well-balanced and vivid, dancing feet and banging doors included.) Levine on DG is a stronger contender, as he has an all-purpose theatricality and Pavarotti as his tenor, but Studer is a generalized and unmoving Violetta next to Gheorghiu. Among the live sets, Giulini and Callas at La Scala in 1955 must be *hors concours*, an unforgettable performance of the greatest inspiration, but in rather awful sound. Muti's more recent La Scala set, in which he has to wrestle with Tiziana Fabbricini's wayward talents as Violetta, is the nearest comparison.

Additional recommendations ...

...**Soloists; Rome Opera Chorus and Orchestra / Fernando Previtali.** RCA Victor Gold Seal Ⓜ GD84144 (two discs: 113 minutes: ADD).

...**Soloists; Bavarian State Opera Chorus and Orchestra / Carlos Kleiber.** DG Ⓕ 415 132-2GH2 (two discs: DDD: 3/86).

...**Soloists; Ambrosian Opera Chorus; Band of HM Royal Marines; Philharmonia Orchestra / Riccardo Muti.** EMI Ⓕ CDS7 47538-8 (two discs: 129 minutes: DDD: 11/87). ⒼⒼⒼ

...**Soloists; Chorus and Orchestra of the Teatro Nacional de San Carlos, Lisbon / Franco Ghione.** EMI mono Ⓕ CDS7 49187-8* (two discs: 123 minutes: ADD: 11/87).

...**Soloists; Chorus and Orchestra of La Scala, Milan / Carlo Maria Giulini.** EMI mono Ⓜ CMS7 63628-2* (two discs: 124 minutes: ADD: 2/91).

...**Soloists; Metropolitan Opera Chorus and Orchestra / James Levine.** DG Ⓕ 435 797-2GH2 (two discs: 122 minutes: DDD: 11/92).

New review

Verdi La traviata (sung in English). **Valerie Masterson** (sop) Violetta; **John Brecknock** (ten) Alfredo; **Christian du Plessis** (bar) Germont; **Della Jones** (mez) Flora; **Shelagh Squires** (mez) Annina; **Geoffrey Pogson** (ten) Gaston; **John Gibbs** (bar) Baron; **Denis Dowling** (bar) Marquis; **Roderick Earle** (bass) Doctor; **Edward Byles** (ten) Joseph; **Chorus and Orchestra of English National Opera / Sir Charles Mackerras.** Classics for Pleasure Silver Doubles Ⓢ CD-CFPSD4799 (two discs: 119 minutes: ADD: 4/96). From HMV SLS5216 (10/81). Recorded 1980.

This recording was made after the end of Sir Charles Mackerras's reign at the London Coliseum, but still in time to capture the traditional values over which he presided at English National Opera. Above all, the set is a perfect example of what recording opera in English should be about. The translation is remarkably close to the Italian, always using words with the same linguistic origin where possible, and the singers take the text to heart. There is no libretto in the booklet and none is needed. John Brecknock, in particular, used to be renowned for the clarity of his words in the theatre. His Alfredo sounds a young man of good bearing, singing with an attractive English ardour even if he was slightly past his best by this time. Christian du Plessis makes a Giorgio Germont with enough voice, but limited imagination. Both artists get a single verse of their cabalettas, Brecknock ending his with a dutiful top C. Among the supporting cast Della Jones's spitfire Flora briefly snatches the spotlight, as she makes her consonants crackle with energy. All of them worked regularly with Mackerras at ENO and sing with a care for the details of the score that must emanate from him. There is not, however, much passion about the performance. So far the set's virtues may be ephemeral, but Valerie Masterson's delectable Violetta deserves her chance with posterity. There is a moment towards the end of "Un di felice" where Mackerras gives her a little extra time and she floats the high A with an intuitive freedom that seems to cradle the very spirit of the opera in the palm of her hand. As much as any international singer, Masterson knows where to find Violetta's heart in the music. She is not in equally good voice throughout (the recording was made over a period of three months) but at its best her soprano has a delicate, bone-china fragility that very nearly embodies the role. It is difficult to imagine anyone who wants La traviata in English being disappointed.

Verdi Il trovatore. **Plácido Domingo** (ten) Manrico; **Aprile Millo** (sop) Leonora; **Vladimir Chernov** (bar) Conte di Luna; **Dolora Zajick** (mez) Azucena; **James Morris** (bass) Ferrando; **Sondra Kelly** (contr) Ines; **Anthony Laciura** (ten) Ruiz; **Glenn Bater** (bass) Old Gipsy; **Tim Willson** (ten) Messenger; **New York Metropolitan Opera Chorus and Orchestra / James Levine.** Sony Classical Ⓕ S2K48070 (two discs: 129 minutes: DDD: 6/94). Notes, text and translation included. Recorded 1991. Ⓖ

This is the most recommendable among modern versions of Trovatore, with a reading all-round that finely balances the lyrical and melodramatic elements in the score. Once Leonora appears, the reading takes on true Verdian style. Millo floats "Come d'aurato" effortlessly on a fine line and throughout her part is replete with the right kind of Verdian spinto sound, the correct phraseology. This is a reading to please the ear and move the heart. Immediately this Leonora is confronted with Conte di Luna, we hear the firm, vibrant, implacable tones of Chernov. His voice is surely now in its absolute prime and he sings everything with the confident panache that suggests as much. Our upright hero is Domingo, aged a little since his earlier recordings of Manrico for Mehta Giulini (listed below). The artistry and management of the voice are as rewarding as of old and Domingo reserves his best for the last and greatest scene when both his sovereign phrasing – "Riposa, o madre" sung in a single breath – and his involvement take on the aura of active participation. Manrico's feelings of love for his mother, momentary contempt for Leonora and eventual tragic pathos are firmly targeted: we hear once more the noble tenor we know and can listen to in sappier voice for Giulini. As Azucena, Zajick gives an effective and strong-willed performance, wanting only the last ounce of character: she is also at her best in the final act. The Met chorus is no more than adequate on this occasion, but as ever the house's orchestra plays with the virtuosity it reserves for its Musical Director. Levine's reading is well timed, properly earthy yet refined in the many delicate touches Verdi evinces in arias and duets. His is a more dramatically vital reading than Giulini's which is at times unconscionably slow (his version runs to three discs), and rivals Karajan's in projecting incisively the drama's essence. Luciano Pavarotti's predominantly lyrical tenor (for Mehta on Decca) is not ideal for Manrico but he sings it with such unfailing musicality and sense of line that Pavarotti enthusiasts need not hesitate to acquire this version, confident that their hero's portrayal is set in suitable surroundings. However, the whole reading is not as well integrated as the Levine, and by a hair's breadth that is probably the better sung. Mehta's earlier, much-lauded recording for RCA remains very much in the frame.

Additional recommendations ...

...**Soloists; Saint Cecilia Academy Chorus and Orchestra / Carlo Maria Giulini.** DG Ⓕ 423 858-2GH2 (two discs: 140 minutes: DDD: 2/85).

...**Soloists; Chorus and Orchestra of La Scala, Milan / Herbert von Karajan.** EMI mono Ⓕ CDS7 49347-2* (129 minutes: ADD: 12/87).

...**Soloists; Ambrosian Opera Chorus; New Philharmonia Orchestra / Zubin Mehta.** RCA Victor Red Seal Ⓕ RD86194 (two discs: 137 minutes: ADD: 8/88).

...**Soloists; Robert Shaw Chorale; RCA Victor Orchestra / Renato Cellini.** RCA Victor mono Ⓜ GD86643* (two discs: 117 minutes: ADD: 8/88).

...Il trovatore[a]. La forza del destino[b] – excerpts. [ab]Soloists; [a]**Chorus of the Royal Opera House, Covent Garden; [a]London Philharmonic Orchestra / Vittorio Gui; [b]Chorus and Orchestra of RAI, Rome / Oliviero de Fabritiis.** Legato Classics mono Ⓜ LCD-173* (two discs: 158 minutes: ADD: 2/94).

...**Soloists; Chorus and Orchestra of the Maggio Musicale Fiorentino / Zubin Mehta.** Decca Ⓕ 430 694-2DHO2 (two discs: 132 minutes: DDD: 7/95).

...**Soloists; Chorus and Orchestra of La Scala, Milan / Tullio Serafin.** DG Double Ⓜ 445 451-2GX2 (two discs: 126 minutes: ADD: 1/96).

Verdi Un ballo in maschera. **Giuseppe di Stefano** (ten) Riccardo; **Tito Gobbi** (bar) Renato; **Maria Callas** (sop) Amelia; **Fedora Barbieri** (mez) Ulrica; **Eugenia Ratti** (sop) Oscar; **Ezio Giordano** (bass) Silvano; **Silvio Maionica** (bass) Samuel; **Nicola Zaccaria** (bass) Tom; **Renato Ercolani** (bar) Judge; **Chorus and Orchestra of La Scala, Milan / Antonino Votto.** EMI mono Ⓕ CDS7 47498-8* (two discs: 130 minutes: ADD: 9/87). Notes, text and translation included. From Columbia 33CX1472/4 (10/57).

Ballo manages to encompass a vein of lighthearted frivolity (represented by the page, Oscar) within the confines of a serious drama of love, infidelity, noble and ignoble sentiments. None of the more recent recordings has quite caught the opera's true spirit so truly as this one under Votto's unerring direction. Callas has not been surpassed in delineating Amelia's conflict of feelings and loyalties, nor has di Stefano been equalled in the sheer ardour of his singing as Riccardo. Add to that no less a singer than Tito Gobbi as Renato, at first eloquent in his friendship to his ruler, then implacable in his revenge when he thinks Riccardo has stolen his wife. Fedora Barbieri is full of character as the soothsayer Ulrica, Eugenia Ratti a sparky Oscar. It is an unbeatable line-up.

Additional recommendations ...

...**Soloists; London Opera Chorus; Royal College of Music Junior Department Chorus; National Philharmonic Orchestra / Sir Georg Solti.** Decca Ⓕ 410 210-2DH2 (two discs: DDD: 9/85).

...**Soloists; Chorus and Orchestra of La Scala, Milan / Claudio Abbado.** DG Ⓕ 415 685-2GH2 (two discs: DDD: 9/86).

...**Soloists; Haberdashers' Aske's School Girls' Choir; Medici Quartet; Royal Opera House Chorus, Covent Garden; New Philharmonia Orchestra / Riccardo Muti.** EMI Ⓜ CMS7 69576-2 (two discs: 127 minutes: ADD: 11/88).

...**Soloists; RCA Italiana Opera Chorus and Orchestra / Erich Leinsdorf.** RCA VictorGold Seal Ⓜ GD86645 (two discs: 128 minutes: ADD: 11/88).

...**Soloists; Robert Shaw Chorale; NBC Symphony Orchestra / Arturo Toscanini.** RCA Victor Gold Seal mono Ⓜ GD60301* (two discs: 122 minutes: ADD: 7/91).

...**Soloists; Metropolitan Opera Chorus and Orchestra / Ettore Panizza.** Myto mono Ⓕ 2MCD90317* (two discs: 147 minutes: ADD: 2/94).

...Excerpts. Aida[b] – excerpts. Falstaff[c] – excerpts. **Soloists; Vienna State Opera Chorus and Orchestra / [a]Karl Böhm, [b]Vittorio Gui, [c]Clemens Krauss.** Koch Schwann mono Ⓜ 314582* (two discs: 149 minutes: ADD: 4/95).

Verdi La forza del destino. **Martina Arroyo** (sop) Leonora; **Carlo Bergonzi** (ten) Don Alvaro; **Piero Cappuccilli** (bar) Don Carlos; **Ruggero Raimondo** (bass) Padre Guardiano; **Biancamaria Casoni** (mez) Preziosilla; **Sir Geraint Evans** (bar) Melitone; **Antonio Zerbini** (bass) Marchese; **Florindo Andreolli** (ten) Trabuco; **Mila Cova** (mez) Curra; **Virgilio Carbonari** (ten) Mayor; **Derek Hammond-Stroud** (bar) Surgeon; **Ambrosian Opera Chorus; Royal Philharmonic Orchestra / Lamberto Gardelli.** EMI Opera Ⓜ CMS7 64646-2* (three discs: 168 minutes: ADD: 6/93). Notes, text and translation included. From HMV SLS948 (3/70). Recorded 1969. *Gramophone Editor's choice.*

This wonderfully multifarious opera demands an array of principal singers who need to be skilled in an unusually wide range of vocal and dramatic skills. It is a 'chase' opera in which Carlos pursues

Alvaro and Leonora through two countries, through cloister and convent, through scenes popular and martial, all treated on the most expansive scale. It is dominated by its series of magnificent duets that are composed so that the music marches with the development of situation and character. This reissue is an excellent and completely satisfying mid-price buy. It features Bergonzi, that prince among Verdi tenors, as an exemplary and appealing Alvaro, the best in any complete set, and Piero Cappuccilli – like Bergonzi at the peak of his powers when this set was made – as a full-blooded and Italianate Carlos. In the three all-important duets, their voices blend ideally. Leonora was the most successful of Arroyo's recorded roles, and she sings here with a feeling and urgency appropriate to Leonora's desperate situation. Casoni's vital Preziosilla, Raimondi's grave but over-lugubrious Padre Guardiano and Sir Geraint's keenly characterized Melitone complete a well-chosen cast. Over all presides Gardelli, a Verdi conductor with an instinctive feeling for the ebb and flow of his music, always attending to the needs of the music, never calling attention to himself. All of the versions listed here have much to commend them. The Levine is more opulently but not so stylishly sung and perhaps a little too hectically conducted. The *Gramophone* Award-winning Sinopoli is the stuff of which great music drama is made, especially in the opera's closing pages. It is wonderfully enacted by Paata Burchuladze (Padre Guardiano), Rosalind Plowright (Leonora) and José Carreras (Alvaro), with subtle changes of pace and perspective from Sinopoli and glorious string playing. The Serafin boasts the irreplaceable Callas and conducting on the Gardelli level but has some indifferent singing, significant excisions and a mono recording.

Additional recommendations ...

...**Soloists; Ambrosian Opera Chorus; Philharmonia Orchestra / Giuseppe Sinopoli.** DG Ⓕ 419 203-2GH3 (three discs: 178 minutes: DDD: 5/87). *Gramophone Award Winner 1987. Selected by Sounds in Retrospect.*

...**Soloists; Chorus and Orchestra of La Scala, Milan / Riccardo Muti.** EMI Ⓕ CDS7 47485-8 (three discs: 164 minutes: DDD: 5/87).

...**Soloists; Chorus and Orchestra of La Scala, Milan / Tullio Serafin.** EMI mono Ⓜ CDS7 47581-8* (three discs: 164 minutes: ADD: 10/87).

...**Soloists; John Alldis Choir; London Symphony Orchestra / James Levine.** RCA Ⓕ RD81864 (three discs: 171 minutes: ADD: 10/87).

Verdi Don Carlo. **Plácido Domingo** (ten) Don Carlos; **Montserrat Caballé** (sop) Elisabetta; **Shirley Verrett** (mez) Princess Eboli; **Sherrill Milnes** (bar) Rodrigo; **Ruggero Raimondi** (bass) Philip II; **Giovanni Foiani** (bass) Grand Inquisitor; **Delia Wallis** (mez) Thibault; **Ryland Davies** (ten) Count of Lerma; **Simon Estes** (bass) A Monk; **John Noble** (bar) Herald; **Ambrosian Opera Chorus; Royal Opera House Orchestra, Covent Garden / Carlo Maria Giulini.** EMI Ⓕ CDS7 47701-8 (three discs: 208 minutes: ADD: 7/87). Notes, text and translation included. From SLS956 (7/71).　　Ⓖ

In no other Verdi opera, except perhaps *Aida*, are public and private matters so closely intermingled, so searchingly described as in this large-scale, panoramic work, in which the political intrigues and troubles of Philip II's Spain are counterpointed with his personal agony and the lives and loves of those at his court. This vast canvas inspired Verdi to compose one of his most varied and glorious scores. Giulini, more than any other conductor, searches out the inner soul of the piece and his cast is admirable. The young Plácido Domingo makes a vivid and exciting Carlos, whilst Montserrat Caballé spins glorious tone and phrases in encompassing Elisabeth's difficult music. Shirley Verrett is a vital, suitably tense Eboli, Sherrill Milnes an upright, warm Rodrigo and Ruggero Raimondi a sombre Philip. Throughout, the Covent Garden forces sing and play with fervour and understanding for their distinguished conductor.

Additional recommendation ...

...**(Includes appendix). Soloists; Chorus and Orchestra of La Scala, Milan / Claudio Abbado.** DG Ⓕ 415 316-2GH4 (four discs: DDD: 12/85).

Verdi Aida. **Maria Callas** (sop) Aida; **Richard Tucker** (ten) Radames; **Fedora Barbieri** (mez) Amneris; **Tito Gobbi** (bar) Amonasro; **Giuseppe Modesti** (bass) Ramfis; **Nicola Zaccaria** (bass) King of Egypt; **Elvira Galassi** (sop) Priestess; **Franco Ricciardi** (ten) Messenger; **Chorus and Orchestra of La Scala, Milan / Tullio Serafin.** EMI mono Ⓕ CDS7 49030-8* (three discs: 144 minutes: ADD: 11/87). Notes, text and translation included. From Columbia 33CX1318/20 (1/56). Recorded 1955.　　ⒼⒼ

Aida, the daughter of the Ethiopian king, is a prisoner at the Egyptian court where she falls in love with Radames, an Egyptian captain of the guard; Amneris, the Egyptian princess, also loves him. The tensions between these characters are rivetingly portrayed and explored and the gradual build-up to Aida's and Radames's union in death is paced with the sureness of a master composer. Callas's Aida is an assumption of total understanding and conviction; the growth from a slave-girl torn between love for her homeland and Radames, to a woman whose feelings transcend life itself represents one of the greatest operatic undertakings ever committed to disc. Alongside her is Fedora Barbieri, an Amneris palpable in her agonized mixture of love and jealousy – proud yet human. Tucker's Radames is powerful and Gobbi's Amonasro quite superb – a portrayal of comparable understanding to stand alongside Callas's Aida. Tullio Serafin is quite simply ideal and though the recording may not be perfect by current standards, nowhere can it dim the brilliance of the creations conjured up by this classic cast.

...Soloists; Chorus of the Royal Opera House, Covent Garden; Trumpeters of the Royal Military School of Music, Kneller Hall; New Philharmonia Orchestra / Riccardo Muti. EMI Ⓕ CDS7 47271-8 (three discs: 148 minutes: DDD: 1/87). *Gramophone classical 100.* ⓖⓖⓖ

...Soloists; Rome Opera House Chorus and Orchestra / Sir Georg Solti. Decca Ⓕ 417 416-2DH3 (three discs: 152 minutes: ADD: 9/87).

...Soloists; Vienna State Opera Chorus; Vienna Philharmonic Orchestra / Herbert von Karajan. EMI Ⓜ CMS7 69300-2 (three discs: 155 minutes: ADD: 4/88).

...Soloists; Rome Opera House Chorus and Orchestra / Jonel Perlea. RCA Victor mono Ⓜ GD86652* (three discs: 149 minutes: ADD: 8/88).

...Soloists; Chorus of La Scala, Milan; Milan Symphony Orchestra / Lorenzo Molajoli. VAI Audio mono Ⓕ VAIA1083* (two discs: 136 minutes: ADD: 4/96).

Verdi Otello. **Plácido Domingo** (ten) Otello; **Cheryl Studer** (sop) Desdemona; **Sergei Leiferkus** (bar) Iago; **Ramon Vargas** (ten) Cassio; **Michael Schade** (ten) Roderigo; **Denyce Graves** (mez) Emilia; **Ildebrando d'Arcangelo** (bass) Lodovico; **Giacomo Prestia** (bass) Montano; **Philippe Duminy** (bass) Herald; **Hauts-de-Seine Maîtrise; Chorus and Orchestra of the Opéra-Bastille, Paris / Myung-Whun Chung.** DG Ⓕ 439 805-2GH2 (two discs: 132 minutes: DDD: 12/94). Notes, text and translation included. Recorded 1993. *Gramophone Editor's choice. Selected by Sounds in Retrospect.* ⓖⓖ

Just as *Othello* is a difficult play to bring off in the theatre, so *Otello* is a difficult opera to bring off out of it. For some years now, Domingo has been, on stage, the greatest Otello of our age. On record, though, he has had less success. Leiferkus and Domingo have worked closely together in the theatre; and it shows in scene after scene – nowhere more so than in the crucial sequence in Act 2 where Otello so rapidly ingests Iago's lethal poison. By bringing into the recording studio the feel and experience of a stage performance – meticulous study subtly modified by the improvised charge of the moment – both singers help defy the jinx that so often afflicts *Otello* on record. The skill of Leiferkus's performance is rooted in voice and technique: clear diction, a disciplined rhythmic sense and a mastery of all ornament down to the most mordant of mordents. Above all, he is always *there* (usually stage right in this recording), steely-voiced, rabbiting on obsessively. We even hear his crucial interventions in the great Act 3 *concertato*. Domingo is in superb voice; the sound seems golden as never before. Yet at the same time, it is a voice that is being more astutely deployed. To take that cruellest of all challenges to a studio-bound Otello, the great Act 3 soliloquy "Dio! mi potevi", Domingo's performance is now simpler, more inward, more intense. He has rethought the role for the microphone, much as a great actor might adapt his Othello for the radio, or a singer might shift from the broad brush-strokes of theatre performance to the keener disciplines of Lieder-singing. It helps, perhaps, that Domingo's voice has darkened, winning back some of its russet baritonal colourings. But in the end the genius of the performance lies in its ability to distil. Chung's conducting is almost disarmingly vital. Verdi's scoring is more Gallic than Germanic. The score sounds very brilliant in the hands of the excellent Opéra-Bastille orchestra, and, in Act 4, very beautiful. Maybe Chung is wary of the emotional depths and, occasionally, the rhythmic infrastructure is muddled and unclear. And yet, the freshness is all gain. He is already a master of the big ensemble, and the line of an act. Tension rarely slackens. Where it does the mixing and matching of takes is probably to blame. Studer's is a carefully drawn portrait of a chaste and sober-suited lady. Perhaps Verdi had a sweeter-voiced singer in mind for this paragon of "goodness, resignation, and self-sacrifice" (Verdi's words, not Shakespeare's). Studer's oboe tones keep us at a certain distance. There is little of Rysanek's warmth and vulnerability (Serafin) and yet you will look in vain for a better Desdemona. What's more, Studer is a singer who can single-mindedly focus the drama afresh, as she does more than once in Act 3. DG's recording is clear and unfussy and satisfyingly varied; Studer, in particular, is much helped by the beautifully open acoustic the engineers provide for the closing act. This is undoubtedly the best *Otello* on record since the early 1960s. It also happens to be the first time on disc that a great Otello at the height of his powers has been successfully caught in the context of a recording that can itself be generally considered worthy of the event, musically and technically.

...Soloists; Chorus and Orchestra of La Scala, Milan / Lorin Maazel. EMI Ⓕ CDS7 47450-8 (two discs: 142 minutes: DDD: 12/86).

...Soloists; Rome Opera Chorus and Orchestra / Tullio Serafin. RCA Victor Gold Seal Ⓜ GD81969* (two discs: 144 minutes: ADD: 11/88).

...Soloists; Metropolitan Opera Chorus and Orchestra / Ettore Panizza. Music and Arts mono Ⓕ CD645* (two discs: 139 minutes: AAD: 9/91).

...Soloists; Metropolitan Opera Children's Chorus; Chicago Symphony Chorus and Orchestra / Sir Georg Solti. Decca Ⓕ 433 669-2DH2 (two discs: 129 minutes: DDD: 11/91).

...Soloists; NBC Chorus and Symphony Orchestra / Arturo Toscanini. RCA Victor Gold Seal mono Ⓜ GD60302* (two discs: 125 minutes: ADD: 3/92). *Gramophone classical 100.* ⓖⓖⓖ

Verdi Falstaff. **Tito Gobbi** (bar) Falstaff; **Rolando Panerai** (bar) Ford; **Luigi Alva** (ten) Fenton; **Elisabeth Schwarzkopf** (sop) Alice; **Anna Moffo** (sop) Nannetta; **Fedora Barbieri** (mez) Quickly; **Renato Ercolani** (ten) Bardolfo; **Nicola Zaccaria** (bass) Pistola; **Tomaso Spataro** (ten) Dr Caius;

Nan Merriman (mez) Meg Page; **Philharmonia Chorus and Orchestra / Herbert von Karajan.** EMI
Ⓕ CDS7 49668-2* (two discs: 120 minutes: ADD: 9/88). Notes, text and translation included.
From SAX2254/6 (7/61). Recorded 1956.   ⒼⒼ

Verdi's *Falstaff* is one of those works that sum up a career with perfection, yet though it was his last
opera it was also his first comic opera. This classic EMI recording enshrines one of the finest Falstaffs
to have graced the stage in post-war years, Tito Gobbi. His assumption of the role is magnificent, and
the completeness with which he embraces the part tends to overshadow his many successors.
Assembled around this larger-than-life character is a near ideal cast, sprightly of gait, sparklingly
comic and above all, beautifully sung. Karajan's conducting is always deeply cherishable as he leads
the Philharmonia Orchestra surefootedly through the score and the recording has come up sounding
as fresh as the day it was set down.

Additional recommendations ...

...**Soloists; Los Angeles Master Chorale and Philharmonic Orchestra / Carlo Maria Giulini.** DG
Ⓕ 410 503-2GH2 (two discs: 123 minutes: ADD: 12/83).

...**Soloists; RCA Italiana Opera Chorus and Orchestra / Sir Georg Solti.** Decca Grand Opera Ⓜ 417
168-2DM2 (two discs: 115 minutes: ADD: 3/90).

...**Soloists; Chorus and Orchestra of La Scala, Milan / Riccardo Muti.** Sony Classical Ⓕ S2K58961
(two discs: 123 minutes: DDD: 11/94).

Further listening ...

...**String Quartet in E minor.** *Coupled with* **Puccini** Crisantemi. **Donizetti** String Quartet No. 13
in E minor. **Alberni Quartet.** CRD CRD3366 (5/89).

...**La forza del destino** – Pace, pace, mio Dio[i]. Aida[i] – Qui Radames verrà! ... O patria mia; La fatal
pietra[d]; O terra, addio[cd]. *Coupled with* **Wagner** Der Fliegende Holländer[g] – Joho hoe! Traft ihr
das Schiff[f]; Wie aus der Ferne[e]. **Albert** Tiefland – Ich weiss nicht, wer mein Vater war[g].
R. Strauss Arabella – Das war sehr gut, Mandryka[g] (both from LX1559, 10/52). Der
Rosenkavalier[h] – Da geht er hin; Die Zeit, die ist ein sonderbar Ding[a]; Mein schöner Schatz ...
Ich werd' jetzt in die Kirchen geh'n[a]; Marie Theres'! ... Hab' mir's gelobt[ab]. **Leonie Rysanek,**
[a]**Elisabeth Grümmer,** [b]**Erika Köth** (sops); [c]**Sieglinde Wagner** (mez); [d]**Rudolf Schock** (ten); [e]**Sigurd
Björling** (bar); [f]**Royal Opera House Chorus, Covent Garden;** [c]**Berlin Deutsche Oper Chorus;**
[g]**Philharmonia Orchestra;** [h]**Berlin Philharmonic Orchestra;** [i]**Berlin Symphony Orchestra / Wilhelm
Schüchter.** EMI Références mono CDH5 65201-2* (2/95).

...**I Due Foscari. Soloists; Austrian Radio Chorus and Symphony Orchestra / Lamberto Gardelli.**
Philips 422 426-2PM2 (12/89).

...**Attila. Soloists; Chorus and Orchestra of La Scala, Milan / Riccardo Muti.** EMI CDS7 49952-2
(5/90).

...**I vespri siciliani. Soloists; Chorus and Orchestra of La Scala, Milan / Riccardo Muti.** EMI
CDS7 54043-2 (1/91).

...**Simon Boccanegra. Soloists; Milan La Scala Chorus; Milan La Scala Orchestra / Claudio Abbado.**
DG 415 692-2GH2 (9/86).   Ⓖ

...**Simon Boccanegra. Soloists; RCA Victor Chorus and Orchestra / Gianandrea Gavazzeni.** RCA
Victor Red Seal RD70729 (9/87).

Sándor Veress   Hungarian 1907-1992

Suggested listening ...

...**Passacaglia concertante**[a]. **Musica concertante**[b]. **Songs of the Seasons**[c]. [c]**London Voices / Terry
Edwards;** [ab]**Berne Camerata / Heinz Holliger** ([a]ob). ECM New Series 447 390-2 (9/95).

...**Solo Violin Sonata**[a]. *Coupled with* **Kodály** Duo, Op. 7[ab]. Solo Cello Sonata, Op. 8[b]. [a]**Sergiu Luca**
(vn); [b]**Roel Dieltiens** (vc). Harmonia Mundi HMC90 1560 (3/96). *See review under Kodály; refer
to the Index to Reviews.*

Tomas Luis de Victoria   Spanish 1548-1611

New review

Victoria Officium defunctorum (1605). **Gabrieli Consort / Paul McCreesh.** Archiv Produktion
Ⓕ 447 095-2AH (60 minutes: DDD: 12/95). Text and translation included. Recorded 1994.
    Gramophone Editor's record of the month.   ⒼⒼⒼ

This is a remarkable recording. In some ways it is like a rediscovery, for here is an approach not too
far from Pro Cantione Antiqua at their best and yet that group never recorded the work. That sense
of rediscovery comes in fact as much from the difference between this and the versions by The Tallis
Scholars and Westminster Cathedral Choir (under David Hill): though the latter places the Matins
lesson *Taedet animam meam* in a semi-liturgical reconstruction of Lauds, this Gabrieli Consort
recording takes a different approach and adds chant to the Requiem Mass itself, thus creating even
more of a context for Victoria's magisterial work. We have therefore the Epistle and preceding prayer,
the Tract, Sequence, Gospel, Preface, Lord's Prayer and Postcommunion in addition to the
polyphony; this also means, for example, that the *Kyrie* is sung nine-fold with alternating chant

instead of simply three-fold only in polyphony. One may presume that the chant was taken from a suitable Spanish source by Luis Lozano Virumbrales, an expert in this field and author of the insert-notes together with Paul McCreesh. The performance itself is stately and imposing, with a tremendous homogeneity of sound: the use of an all-male choir, together with the added chant, lends it a tangibly monastic feel, though it would have been a fortunate monastery indeed that had falsettists of this quality. About the performance of the chant there are two points of interest: firstly, that it is doubled, like the polyphony, by a bajón, common Spanish practice at this period, and secondly, that McCreesh is not afraid to have the falsettists singing the chant too. The pace of the polyphony often seems to be unhurried, but it never feels slow. Indeed, in almost every case the polyphonic sections are taken slightly quicker than The Tallis Scholars, and Westminster Cathedral Choir are of course faced with the hugely reverberant acoustics of their home building. From the beginning the singing is involving and incarnate, but the real magic comes nearer the end: from the *Agnus Dei* onwards one feels that the Gabreli Consort have really got the measure of the music and are allowing it to speak through them. The final great responsory, the "Libera me" is performed with heart stopping power and conviction. The Tallis Scholars approach the music as though it were a concert suite, with no added chant, and in many respects this pays dividends, since they are able to build it up in an almost architectural way, whereas the Westminster choir, though they also add no chant except for the opening Matins lesson, somehow concentrate more on each separate section of the Mass. Of course this works: Victoria's sublime music is indeed conceived architecturally. And yet this is not all; McCreesh's approach shows something else, shows how it would have fitted into and complemented the liturgical framework without ever losing its own internal power and drama (for that of course is what it was intended for). A revelatory disc.

Additional recommendations ...

...Officium defunctorum. **Lôbo** Versa est in luctum. **The Tallis Scholars / Peter Phillips.** Gimell Ⓕ CDGIM012 (47 minutes: DDD: 9/87). Ⓖ

...Officium defunctorum. **Westminster Cathedral Choir / David Hill.** Hyperion Ⓕ CDA66250 (58 minutes: DDD: 9/87). Ⓐ

Victoria Missa Trahe me post te. Trahe me post te. Alma redemptoris mater. Ave regina coelorum. Regina coeli. Salve regina. Magnificat primi toni. **Westminster Cathedral Choir / James O'Donnell.** Hyperion Ⓕ CDA66738 (68 minutes: DDD: 3/95). Texts and translations included. Recorded 1994. *Gramophone Editor's choice.*

The Westminster Cathedral Choir are in excellent shape, and some of the pieces on this recording are quite simply stunning examples of Victoria's most expressive and dramatic writing. The *Missa Trahe me post te* is yet another witness to the melodious, spacious style that the Spanish composer cultivated in his Mass settings. The double canon on which the motet that forms the model for the Mass is based only reappears in the final *Agnus Dei*, but as a whole it is nevertheless a paragon of contrapuntal virtue. More striking, however, are the polychoral works included here, notably Victoria's setting of the Marian antiphon *Alma redemptoris mater* and, above all, the *Salve regina*. Scarcely less impressive is the double-choir *Magnificat*, with soaring lines in all voice parts. These dramatic pieces are given intense readings by O'Donnell and the choir, and the *Salve regina* in particular is definitely a desert island choice. Victoria in sustained, less contrapuntal vein demands the fullness of tone and forthright expressiveness that are the hallmarks of Westminster's interpretations; nothing mealy-mouthed or overly polite will do. The resonant acoustic of Westminster Cathedral is clearly an important ingredient in the success of the choir's recordings, which have an atmospheric quality that is sometimes lacking from other clearer but also more clinical contexts.

Further listening ...

...Missa O magnum mysterium. Missa Ascendens Christus in altum. Motets – O magnum mysterium. Ascendens Christus. **Westminster Cathedral Choir / David Hill.** Hyperion CDA66190 (9/87).

...Missa O quam gloriosum. Motet – O quam gloriosum. Missa Ave maris stella. **Westminster Cathedral Choir / David Hill.** Hyperion CDA66114 (6/86). ⒼⒼ

...Responsories for Tenebrae. **Westminster Cathedral Choir / David Hill.** Hyperion CDA66304 (7/89).

...Et egressus est. Ecce vidimus eum. Amicus meus. Unus ex discipulis. Eram quasi agnus. Seniores populi. Benedictus Deus Dominus Israel. Vere languores nostros. *Coupled with* **Morales** (attrib.) Vigilate et orate. **Brito** Lamentations of Jeremiah – Incipit lamentatio Jeremiae. **F. Vásquez** In te, Domine, speravi. **Lienas** Coenantibus autem. **Cardoso** Magnificat Primi Toni. **La Colombina.** Accent ACC9394D (8/94).

Gerard Victory
Irish 1921-

Suggested listening ...

...Ultima Rerum. **Virginia Kerr** (sop); **Bernadette Greevy** (mez); **Adrian Thompson** (ten); **Alan Opie** (bar); **Eire Radio Telefis Philharmonic Choir; Ireland National Chamber Choir; National Symphony Orchestra of Ireland / Colman Pearce.** Marco Polo 8 223532/3 (6/95).

Louis Vierne

French 1870-1937

Vierne Symphonies – No. 2, Op. 20; No. 3, Op. 28. **Colin Walsh** (org). Priory Ⓕ PRCD446
(72 minutes: DDD: 10/94). Played on the organ of Lincoln Cathedral. Recorded 1992.   ⒼⒼⒼ
Here is something out of the ordinary. It's not just that Colin Walsh is an impassioned advocate of
the French romantic school or that he possesses a technique which all but takes one's breath away.
Neither is it the ravishing Lincoln instrument, glorious though it sounds here in one of Priory's most
vivid recordings to date. It's the way Walsh brings the music itself into such sharp focus. Vierne's
creation takes centre stage, unobscured either by a player's virtuosity or an organ's enticing allure: the
latter something of a rare feat since organ buffs seem to prefer to listen to the instrument rather than
what's being played on it. Walsh manages the instrument deftly enough – after all, he knows it as
intimately as anyone (and certainly more intimately than Priory's typesetters who have missed out a
whole division from the printed specification) – so we never really notice his subtle and skilful
registrations, giving all the more impact to those great climactic moments. So often a Vierne
symphony can sound like a well-ordered sequence of individual pieces, but here the essential
interdependence of the movements is most powerfully demonstrated. The composer's marvellous
sense of structure and ingenious architectural designs are shown for the great musical gifts they are.
Additional recommendations ...
...No. 3. **Tournemire** Suite Evocatrice, Op. 74. **Widor** Symphonie Gothique, Op. 70. **Jeremy Filsell**
(org). Herald Ⓕ HAVPCD145 (71 minutes: DDD: 3/92). *See review under Tournemire; refer to the
Index to Reviews.*   ⒼⒼ
...No. 1, Op. 14; No. 3. **Michael Murray** (org). Telarc Ⓕ CD80329 (75 minutes: DDD: 5/94).
Further listening ...
...Triptyque, Op. 58. Pièces en style libre, Op. 31. **Colin Walsh** (org). Priory PRCD319 (3/92).
...Les cloches de Hinckley, Op. 55 No. 6. *Coupled with works by* **Langlais, Honegger, Dupré,
Roussel, d'Indy, R. Vierne** *and* **Barié** Marie-Bernadette Dufourcet (org). Priory PRCD422
(6/95). *See review in the Collections section; refer to the Index to Reviews.*
...Pièces de fantaisie. Suite No. 1, Op. 51 – Andantino[c]. *Coupled with* **Fauré** Requiem, Op. 48[a]. Messe
basse[b]. Cantique de Jean Racine, Op. 11[b]. **Séverac** Tantum ergo[d]. [a]**Lisa Beckley** (sop); [a]**Nicholas
Gedge** (bass-bar); [abd]**Oxford Schola Cantorum**; [a]**Oxford Camerata / Jeremy Summerly** with
[abc]**Colm Carey** (org). Naxos 8 550765 (9/94). *See review under Fauré; refer to the Index to Reviews.*

René Vierne

French 1878-1918

Suggested listening ...
...Six pièces de différents caractères. *Coupled with works by* **Barié, d'Indy, Roussel, Honegger,
Dupré, Langlais** *and* **L. Vierne** Marie-Bernadette Dufourcet (org). Priory PRCD422 (6/95).
See review in the Collections section; refer to the Index to Reviews.

Henry Vieuxtemps

Belgian 1820-1881

Vieuxtemps Violin Concerto No. 5 in A minor, Op. 37.
Mendelssohn Violin Concerto in E minor, Op. 64. **Chee-Yun** (vn); **London Philharmonic
Orchestra / Jésus Lopez-Cóbos.** Denon Ⓕ CO-78913 (50 minutes: DDD: 1/95). Recorded 1993.
Recorded 1994.
Chee-Yun's Mendelssohn is full of sparkle and imagination. Her tone is sweet and full, her playing
wonderfully polished, her feeling for Mendelssohn's line and phrase quite extraordinarily sure. Lopez-
Cóbos is a supportive and understanding accompanist, and in the finale the woodwind support the
vivacious solo line in a lively fashion, adding to the colour we expect from the LPO on top form. The
Vieuxtemps was the work with which the 13-year-old Chee-Yun made her début with the New York
Philharmonic. That was in the 1980s and now she essays it with an attractive mixture of affection and
maturity: her reflective approach to the rhapsodical first movement is very appealing in its shaping
and use of contrast. The simple *Adagio* brings an elegiac response to its serene yet plaintive arioso
which is most touching, with another exquisite *pianissimo* before the climax. The dashing finale of
this unusual concerto lasts for little more than a minute, but nevertheless caps the piece satisfactorily.
The recording balance is very well judged, the microphones ideally placed in relation to the solo
violin. The orchestra sounds full and spacious, with just a touch of studio boominess in the bass: not
enough, however, to prevent one from thoroughly enjoying this splendid music-making.
Additional recommendations ...
...No. 5[a]. **Mendelssohn** Violin Concerto in E minor, Op. 64[b]. **Mozart** Violin Concerto in A
major, K219[c]. **Jascha Heifetz** (vn); [a]**London Symphony Orchestra / Sir Malcolm Sargent;** [b]**Royal
Philharmonic Orchestra / Sir Thomas Beecham;** [c]**London Philharmonic Orchestra / Sir John
Barbirolli.** EMI Références mono Ⓜ CDH5 65191-2* (69 minutes: ADD: 10/94).
...No. 5[b]. **Lalo** Symphonie espagnole, Op. 21[a]. **Sarah Chang** (vn); [a]**Royal Concertgebouw Orchestra,**
[b]**Philharmonia Orchestra / Charles Dutoit.** EMI Ⓕ CDC5 55292-2 (52 minutes: DDD: 5/96). *See
review under Lalo; refer to the Index to Reviews.*   Ⓖ

Heitor Villa-Lobos

New review

Villa-Lobos Bachianas Brasileiras Nos. 2, 4 and 8. **Cincinnati Symphony Orchestra / Jesús López-Cobos.** Telarc Ⓕ CD80393 (70 minutes: DDD: 2/96). Recorded 1995. *Gramophone Editor's choice.*

Ⓖ

If any parallels existed between Bach and Brazilian idioms, they were largely in Villa-Lobos's mind – even the Fugue in No. 8 of these *Bachianas Brasileiras* is totally un-Bach-like; so anyone coming fresh to these exotically coloured, rather sprawling works should not be misled by false expectations. But fascinating, indeed haunting, in a highly individual way, they are; and the present performances are welcome, all the more since no other version of No. 8 is currently available. In view of the composer's sublime indifference to instrumental practicalities (as, for instance, the feasible length of a trombone *glissando*), his carelessness over detail in his scores, his Micawber-like trust that problems of balance he had created would be sorted out in performance, the chaotic state of the printed scores and orchestral parts of his music (littered as they are with wrong notes and questionable points), and numerous misreadings in past performances, the only half-way reliable yardstick for conductors or critics is the composer's own recordings, made in the 1950s and now preserved in a six-CD box on EMI. Compared to them, the present issue shows a number of differences. Chief of these is the warmer, more generalized sound, with less emphasis on clarity of detail. This works reasonably well in the Preludio of No. 8, where concentration on the melodic line and the adoption of a slower tempo aid the movement's lyricism (likewise the more sentimental approach to the Aria of No. 2); the Aria of No. 8 is unquestionably more poetic and the Dansa of No. 4 lighter; but in the most famous movement, the hilarious and ingenious "Little train of the Caipira" of No. 2, the rasps near the start and the clatter of wheels on the track (evoked by the fiendishly difficult piano part) are far too subdued in favour of the 'big tune'. López-Cobos deals persuasively with knotty questions of balance such as in the middle section of No. 3's Toccata, and brings to the fore the bell-like araponga bird's cry in No. 4's Coral, but makes less of that movement's jungle screeches. He makes clear the thematic link between the sections of No. 4's Aria, and seeks to overcome the repetitious pattern of its Preludio by taking a faster speed rather than by the wealth of tonal nuance the composer himself introduced. Perhaps such detailed comparisons are superfluous: enjoy, enjoy!

Villa-Lobos Dança frenética. Danças características africanas. Dança dos mosquitos. Rudepoema. **Bratislava Radio Symphony Orchestra / Roberto Duarte.** Marco Polo Ⓕ 8 223552 (55 minutes: DDD: 2/95). Recorded 1993.

How far we have come in 75 years is forcibly brought home by the *Dança frenética*, which an influential critic in Brazil, when it was first played in 1919, recommended as suitable only for epileptic musicians and paranoiac listeners. To today's ears it seems little more than an energetic, in places slightly sinister, romp (but with one delicate and charming interlude for woodwind, harp and celesta), far from disturbing in its idiom, and making its effect by its colour and rhythmic exuberance. Villa-Lobos's remarkable inventive ingenuity in orchestration is most striking of all in the *Dança dos mosquitos* of three years later. He was still only 35 at the time, and had yet to emerge from his native country and go to Paris, where much was made much of him. What fascinated the French avant-garde of the day was his exoticism – well illustrated here by the *Danças características africanas*, which despite their title draw on rhythmic and melodic traits obsessional in the third dance – of the Indians of the Matto Grosso (near the Bolivian border). These pieces were originally written for piano in 1914 and orchestrated two years later. The main work on this disc is also an orchestration of a piano piece, the composition of which was spread over five years in Paris. This is the discursive and wild *Rudepoema*, which if it really was intended as a musical portrait of Artur Rubinstein (a staunch champion of his music) rather than himself, depicts him not only as a sensational virtuoso (which we know he was) but a particularly violent and noisy character: it is definitely not a work for bedtime listening or for old ladies of nervous disposition. The orchestra strive manfully with its formidable demands, and except for some occasional and understandable dizzied insecurity by the violins, succeeds in conveying the composer's extraordinary vision, and thanks are due to the very skilful sound engineers.

Villa-Lobos The Discovery of Brazil – Suites Nos. 1-4. **Slovak Philharmonic Chorus; Slovak Radio Symphony Orchestra / Roberto Duarte.** Marco Polo Ⓕ 8 223551 (79 minutes: DDD: 8/94). Recorded 1993. *Gramophone Editor's choice.*

Ⓖ

It has taken a very long time for *The Discovery of Brazil*, one of Villa-Lobos's most significant works, to reach the record catalogue. The original score – which incorporated orchestrations of three earlier pieces – was intended for a 1937 nationalist film, which however used only a fraction of it: the composer then expanded his version into the present four suites (totalling ten items), of which he conducted the first performance in Paris in 1952. Predictably picturesque and colourful in nature, the work depicts the journey of the caravels, with the varied feelings of the aristocrats and seamen on board, the arrival in the strange new continent, and the celebration, amid friendly Indian spectators, of the first Mass in Brazil on May 1st, 1500. For this, Villa-Lobos had recourse to a very large orchestra and a great diversity of styles – Indian chants, popular Portuguese dances and *saudades*, Andalusian rhythms and Moorish melodic contours (since Spaniards and Moors may have been among the crew), plainchant, the *Ave verum* and *Tantum ergo*. Taken as a whole it achieves a certain epic quality, as the composer intended: what it lacks in homogeneity is counterbalanced by the sheer exuberance of invention. The Fourth Suite, in which the orchestra is joined by the chorus, is the most substantial, and the finale the most musically impressive, with some remarkable counterpoint; but the elaborate intertwining of Indian elements and the liturgical would have been more effective with more secure intonation from the chorus, especially the sopranos. Except for occasional anxieties in the very highest register of the violins, the orchestra rises splendidly to the whole score.

Villa-Lobos Gênesis. Erosño (Origem do rio Amazonas). Amazonas. Dawn in a tropical forest.
  Czecho-Slovak Radio Symphony Orchestra, Bratislava / Roberto Duarte. Marco Polo Ⓔ 8 223357 (62 minutes: DDD: 3/92). Recorded 1990.
Do not be deterred by the thought of an Eastern European orchestra playing unfamiliar Villa-Lobos. The Czecho-Slovak Radio Orchestra is clearly a very skilled and flexible body, and the conductor Roberto Duarte, a Brazilian authority on Villa-Lobos, has instilled South American colour and rhythmic vitality into his players quite brilliantly. The best of the four works is probably the earliest, *Amazonas*, which was written in 1917. Here, at the age of 30, Villa-Lobos's imagination was extraordinarily fertile, and this early evocation of Brazilian folklore, with its use of unusual instruments and strange orchestral timbres, is remarkably advanced for its date. The short tone poem *Dawn in a tropical forest* is a late work dating from 1953, and this has a more lyrical, more classical style. The remaining two works also come from the last phase in Villa-Lobos's career, and have similar themes. *Gênesis*, written in 1954, is a large-scale symphonic poem and ballet which depicts its enormous subject with all the extravagant colour and use of complex rhythms which were the composer's trademark. *Erosño*, or *The origin of the Amazon*, composed in 1950, is another ambitiously complex work. All four items are captured in faithful, wide-ranging sound.

Villa-Lobos Quinteto em forma de chôros[a]. Modinha[b]. Bachianas Brasileiras No. 6[c]. Distribuçiño de flôres[b]. Assobio a jato[d]. Chôros No. 2[e]. Cançño do amor[b]. Trio for Oboe, Clarinet and Bassoon[f]. **William Bennett** (fl); [ae]**Neil Black** (ob); [a]**Janice Knight** (cor ang); [aef]**Thea King** (cl); [acf]**Robin O'Neill** (bn); [d]**Charles Tunnell** (vc); [b]**Simon Weinberg** (gtr). Hyperion Ⓔ CDA66295 (61 minutes: DDD: 9/89).
If there is one consistent feature in Villa-Lobos's enormous and diverse output, it is his unpredictability. His restless, supercharged mind never tired of experimenting with new sonorities, and he never felt inhibited, in the course of a work, from following unrelated new impulses. This has the effect of making his music at the same time attractive and disconcerting. The multi-sectional Quintet, the most significant item here, is highly complex but extremely entertaining in its quirky way; and it is played with marvellous neatness, finely judged tonal nuances and high spirits. The rarely heard Trio, the earliest work here, is a particularly spiky atonal piece, typical of its period (1921), depending almost entirely on exuberantly thrusting and counter-thrusting rhythm: it calls for virtuosity, and gets it. The sixth of the *Bachianas Brasileiras* (easily the best available recorded performance) is most sensitively shaped, and the second *Chôros*, which makes great demands on the two players both individually and in mutual responsiveness, is outstandingly polished. A disc of outstanding artistry.

New review

Villa-Lobos Bachianas Brasileiras – No. 2: Toccata[a]; No. 4[b]; No. 5[c]. Miniaturas – No. 2, A Viola[d]. Modinhas e Canções, Series I – No. 3, Cantilena[d]. Momoprecoce[e]. Chôros No. 10, "Rasga o coração"[f]. [c]**Victoria de los Angeles** (sop); [d]**Frederick Fuller** (bar); [e]**Magda Tagliaferro** (pf); [f]**Chorale des Jeunesses Musicales de France;** [abcef]**French Radio National Orchestra / Heitor Villa-Lobos** ([d]pf). EMI Composers in Person mono Ⓔ CDC5 55224-2* (78 minutes: ADD: 6/95). Items marked [ac] from HMV ALP1603 (9/58, recorded 1956), [b]Columbia 33CX1648 (6/59, recorded 1957), [d]HMV B9700 (12/48), [e]French Columbia FCX346 (1954), [f]FCX603 (1/63. 1957). ⓖⓖ
No one disc could fully illustrate the extent of Villa-Lobos's bewilderingly vast and unruly output's stylistic diversity; but this one makes a very good attempt. For those encountering him for the first time the simplest approach is via his purely lyrical side – the two songs so sympathetically sung by Frederick Fuller, *A Viola* with its gently insistent rumba rhythm and *Cantilena* wending its way above an unchanging pedal-note before repeating the melody wordlessly. The same wordless treatment is adopted in the haunting first movement of the *Bachianas Brasileiras* No. 5 for soprano and eight cellos (which has become Villa-Lobos's best-known piece, thanks partly to commercial exploitation): the radiance of Victoria de los Angeles's voice more than compensates for the less than tidy ensemble in places that the composer achieves as conductor. Moving to the non-vocal works, nobody could fail to enjoy the Toccata from the Second *Bachianas Brasileiras*, a brilliantly vivid sound-picture of a little country train determinedly and happily chuffing along – as inventive as Honegger's earlier *Pacific 231* but more fun: the final exhausted long emission of steam cannot but make you laugh. The orchestral virtuosity which that piece demands reappears in the complex rhythms of the finale of *Bachianas Brasileiras* No. 4, whose much more straightforward first three movements, however, provide some clue to the composer's avowed preoccupation with Bach. Villa-Lobos's lifelong interest in children is illustrated by the noisily high-spirited fantasy *Momoprecoce* (derived from the piano suite *Children's carnival*): its dedicatee, Magda Tagliaferro, brings to it all the requisite energy and boisterousness. The

newcomer to Villa-Lobos, having weathered its strikingly individual scoring and sometimes strident dissonances, can now advance to the exotic atmosphere of the heartfelt cry for "Brazilian heart and Brazilian earth" of the *Chôros* No. 10, which brings into play a chorus chanting against a hail of staccato syllables: the overall effect is totally unique and immensely exciting. It should be added that the quality of transfer throughout the disc is bright and clear.

Additional recommendation ...

...Bachianas Brasileiras No. 5[a]. **Canteloube** Chants d'Auvergne. **Dame Kiri Te Kanawa** (sop); [a]**Lynn Harrell** (vc); **English Chamber Orchestra / Jeffrey Tate.** Double Decca Ⓜ 444 995-2DF2 (two discs: 111 minutes: DDD: 1/96). *See review under Canteloube; refer to the Index to Reviews.* Ⓖ

New review

Villa-Lobos Forest of the Amazon. **Renée Fleming** (sop); **Moscow Institute Male-Voice Choir; Moscow Radio Symphony Orchestra / Alfred Heller.** Consonance Ⓔ 810012 (73 minutes: DDD: 5/96). Text and translation included. Recorded 1905-11.

Forest of the Amazon had – even more than usual with Villa-Lobos – a confusing genesis. It started out as music for a film of W.H. Hudson's *Green Mansions* (with Anthony Perkins, and Audrey Hepburn as the bird-woman Rima), but the film producers had jettisoned most of the score in favour of another by Bronislau Kaper. Not surprisingly, Villa-Lobos was furious and decided to re-use and recast his music, transferring sections and adding a brief overture and four new songs to Portuguese texts – to become an extended symphonic poem, or rather, a multi-section rhapsody, which breathes a pantheistic doctrine of Nature, universal love and extinction. As might be expected from this composer and with this subject, this is a busily inventive score of great complexity for very large orchestral forces (including numerous metallophones and native percussion), making virtuoso demands on the participants (all of whom acquit themselves brilliantly under Alfred Heller's expert direction). Exotic colorations and intricate textures abound, with Amerindian chants, bird-song, energetic dance rhythms and occasional folk-like themes in this vast melting-pot. In it are found both frenzied violence and passionate lyricism, with, here and there, simpler interludes of sweetness (notably the start of "Rima's music", various vocalises and the songs, delightfully sung by Renée Fleming – the "Love song" and the "Sentimental melody", first cousin to the famous Aria in *Bachianas Brasileiras* No. 5, enticingly lyrical). One feels a bit steamrollered at the end of 73 minutes, but without question this is an important addition to the available Villa-Lobos repertoire, especially as the technical quality of the recording is deserving of the highest praise.

Villa-Lobos Missa São Sebastião. Bendita sabedoria. Praesepe (with Ansy Boothroyd, mez). Cor dulce, cor amabile. Panis angelicus. Sub tuum praesidium. Ave Maria (a 5). Ave Maria (a 6). Pater noster. Magnificat-alleluia (Elizabeth McCormack, mez)[a] **Corydon Singers and** [a]**Orchestra / Matthew Best.** Hyperion Ⓕ CDA66638 (77 minutes: DDD: 8/93). Texts and translations included.

Any listener not informed in advance and asked to identify the composer of all these religious works except the Mass (the earliest here) would be most unlikely to think of Villa-Lobos. That larger-than-life exotic, that extravagantly experimental and boisterous figure, the composer of such chastely restrained music, the sweetly gentle *Cor dulce*, the mellifluous imitative counterpoint of the first of the *Bendita sabedoria* (six brief choral pieces on biblical texts), the controlled fervour of the *Pater noster*? Even the impressive and grandiose *Magnificat-alleluia* (written in 1958 at the request of Pope Pius XII to celebrate Lourdes Year) gives no hint of its country of origin. The one clue here might be that, of the two *Ave Marias*, the (earlier) five-part setting is in Portuguese. It is only the Mass that reveals all. Amid its austere style and purely diatonic, contrapuntal idiom the *Sanctus* suddenly seems to come from a different background: then one remembers that Sebastian is the patron saint of Rio de Janeiro; and looking into the score one finds that the liturgical heading of each movement is followed by a local one, the final *Agnus Dei* bearing the subtitle "Sebastian, protector of Brazil". In an exceptionally informative note, Simon Wright, besides sketching in the politico-social background to Villa-Lobos's religious music, also points out that vestiges of old magical beliefs brought by African slaves still tinge Catholicism in Brazil. This programme, all of unaccompanied music except for the *Magnificat-alleluia*, should not be listened to as a continuity if some feeling of sameness is to be avoided: the Corydon Singers are most efficient in all they do, even if their tone is not the most seductive, but the outstanding performance is that of the Mass.

Further listening ...

...String Quartets. **Danubius Quartet.** Marco Polo 8 223389/91 (11/92): *8 223389* – Nos. 1, 8 and 13. *8 223390* – Nos. 11, 16 and 17. *8 223391* – Nod. 4, 6 and 14.

...String Quartet No. 6. *Coupled with works by* **Turina, Debussy, Ravel** and **Creston** Arthur Gleghorn (fl); Mitchell Lurie (cl); Ann Mason Stockton (hp); Hollywood Quartet; Concert Arts Strings / Felix Slatkin. Testament mono SBT1053* (3/95). *See review in the Collections section; refer to the Index to Reviews.* Ⓖ Ⓖ

...Suite for Strings. Bachianas Brasileiras No. 9. *Coupled with works by* **Ginastera** and **Evangelista** I Musici de Montréal / Yuli Turovsky. Chandos CHAN9434 (5/96). *See review under Evangelista; refer to the Index to Reviews.*

...String Quartets Nos. 2 and 7. **Danubius Quartet.** Marco Polo 8 223394 (2/95). Ⓖ Ⓖ

...Caixinha de música quebrada. Próle do bébé, Book 1. Cirandinhas. Carnaval das crianças.
   Marcelo Bratke (pf). Olympia OCD455 (2/95).
...Próle do bébé, Book 1. *Coupled with works by* **Debussy, Szymanowsksi, Prokofiev,
   Schumann** and **Albéniz Artur Rubinstein** (pf). RCA Victor Gold Seal 09026 61445-2 (10/93).
   See review in the Collections section; refer to the Index to Reviews.   ⓔⓔⓔ

Pierre Villette
French 1926-1969

Suggested listening ...
...Attende Domine. Hymne à la Vierge. O magnum mysterium. O sacrum convivium. Salve regina.
   Coupled with works by **Bax Rodolfus Choir / Ralph Allwood** with **Christopher Hughes** (org).
   Herald HAVPCD176 (9/95). *See review under Bax; refer to the Index to Reviews.*

Carl Vine
Australian 1954-

New review

Vine MicroSymphony. Symphonies – No. 2; No. 3. **Sydney Symphony Orchestra / Stuart
   Challender.** ABC Classics ⓔ 8 77000 5 (56 minutes: DDD: 10/95). Recorded 1990.
Carl Vine writes Big Tunes. More: he scores them with Technicolor richness, and he writes them not
only in (say) E major but with a precise knowledge of what effect can be gained in that key by a brazen
last-minute shift to A flat. His music is rhythmically cogent (you may be occasionally reminded of Roy
Harris or of Copland) and makes frequent use of ostinato. Aha! So he's a minimalist, then? Hardly:
some of his most striking effects are in fact quite complex, with richly embroidered polyphony and
multiple ostinatos that enable the music to move at two different speeds at once. There is abundant
floridly ornamental melody, but beneath the tendrils the melodic substance is often quite simple, even
innocent, derived from scale figures or from brief cells. The Third Symphony progresses from
darkness to brilliance by starting with a simple juxtaposition of restless chromatic meanderings and
diatonic melody of such simplicity that one doubts whether a single sharp or flat darkens the page.
Yet there is no real sense of light *triumphing* over dark, and those who like symphonies to be about
risks and dangers and triumphs will be disappointed. The moment you hear those almost naïve
woodwind solos over a harp ostinato, observe them growing in length and strength to a first climax
(with fanfares and bells!) you know perfectly well that the outcome will be positive: flags wave, the sun
blazes and Humphrey Bogart and Ingrid Bergman get to stay together after all. Some will find that it
all sounds too much like film music for comfort, others that Vine is dangerously retrogressive. But he
is not proposing a Solution to the Problem of the Symphony in the Late Twentieth Century. What he
wants to do is write big orchestral pieces at the ends of which people feel better. The Sydney
Symphony Orchestra presumably did, by the sound of it. The recordings are satisfyingly rich and
vociferous.

Giovanni Viotti
Italian 1755-1824

Suggested listening ...
...(arr. Nordmann) Adagio non troppo in C minor. *Coupled with works by* **Parish Alvars** and
   Boieldieu Marielle Nordmann (hp); **Franz Liszt Chamber Orchestra / Jean-Pierre Rampal.** Sony
   Classical SK58919 (10/95). *See review under Boieldieu; refer to the Index to Reviews.*

Robert de Visée
French c1660-1725

Suggested listening ...
...Suites – G major; C minor; A major; E minor. Ouverture de la Grotte de Versailles de
   M. Lully. Logistille de Roland de M. Lully. Les Baricades Mistérieuses de M. Couperin. La
   Ménetou de M. Couperin. **Yasunori Imamura** (theorbo). Capriccio 10 464 (8/94). ✐

Zacharie de Vitré
French 1659-?

Suggested listening ...
...Comme trois forgerons. *Coupled with works by* **Ceppede, Gilles, Carpentras, Bouzignac**
   and **Godolin Soloists; Boston Schola Cantorum; Boston Camerata / Joel Cohen.** Erato 4509-
   98480-2 (11/95). ✐

Philippe de Vitry

Suggested listening ...
...De Vitry and the Ars Nova. **The Orlando Consort.** Amon Ra CD-SAR49 (10/91).

Antonio Vivaldi

New review
Vivaldi Bassoon Concertos – C major, RV472; D minor, RV482; E minor, RV484; F major, RV491;
    G major, RV494; G minor, RV495; A minor, RV499. **Klaus Thunemann** (bn); **I Musici.** Philips
    Ⓕ 446 066-2PH (57 minutes: DDD: 2/96). Recorded 1994.
Vivaldi's distinctive individuality is in full flower in the rich invention which characterizes the tuttis of
the fast movements of his bassoon concertos; and in the slow movements, as so often elsewhere, he
proves himself a poet with the most delicate of sensibilities. In all of them, he seems to have been
inspired by the colour and range of the instrument itself, exploring almost every possibility available
to him in the bassoon of his day and, like Rameau in France, writing especially rewardingly for it in
the tenor register. Thunemann, of course, plays an instrument of present-day manufacture, in keeping
with the modern string instruments of I Musici; but he makes a very beautiful sound indeed,
capitalizing on the inherent virtues of up-to-date technology. To all but the most committed
Vivaldians only one of the seven concertos here may seem at all familiar. That is the atmospheric
Concerto in E minor (RV484) with its undulating first movement tuttis inspired, one might suspect,
by Venetian waters. Thunemann instils life into every bar of his interpretation, performing dazzling
feats of athleticism apparently with the utmost of ease, while at the same time giving thought to
ornamentation. Not a note is either out of tune or misplaced and, in slow movements, many of which
possess beguiling lyrical charm, Thunemann reveals himself as a musician of great sensitivity. The
Largo of the first concerto on the disc (RV491) is a striking example. Readers familiar with Vivaldi's
sacred vocal music will recognize its derivation in part from a passage to be found both in his
Magnificat(RV610) and his *Kyrie* (RV587). In the present context Vivaldi imbues an already arresting
harmonic pattern with a drowsy, almost dreamlike fantasy in which the bassoon writing, treated here
with an affecting improvisatory freedom, ranges widely with some striking intervals against sustained,
softly modulating strings It's a brief moment of magic.

Vivaldi Bassoon Concertos – C major, RV474; F major, RV489; A minor, RV498. Chamber
    Concertos – F major, RV571; G minor, RV576; G minor, RV577. **Danny Bond** (bn); **Academy
    of Ancient Music / Christopher Hogwood.** L'Oiseau-Lyre Ⓕ 436 867-2OH (58 minutes:
    DDD: 4/95). ✏ Recorded 1992.   Ⓖ
One of the mysteries surrounding Vivaldi's 37 complete bassoon concertos is that they are so difficult;
recordings tended to prove the point – they *are* tough nuts. But here Danny Bond surmounts every
obstacle with rounded tone, secure intonation, every note clearly played, with musicality to match that
of his colleagues – and on a period bassoon to boot. The other three works are *concerti grossi ("con
molti strumenti")* of which RV571, the most virtuosic, has no other listed recording. The Concertos,
RV576 and 577 were, as their large wind band proclaims, written for the ample resources of the
Dresden orchestra. All the soloists are on superb form, the ensemble is spirited and beautifully
balanced – as is the recording thereof. A wholly delightful disc.

Vivaldi Cello Concertos – C minor, RV402; D minor, RV406; G major, RV414. Sonatas – A minor,
    RV44; E flat major, RV39; G minor, RV42. **Christophe Coin** (vc); **Academy of Ancient Music /
    Christopher Hogwood** (hpd). L'Oiseau-Lyre Ⓕ 433 052-2OH (67 minutes: DDD: 1/92). ✏
    Recorded 1990.   ⒼⒼ
Vivaldi wrote rewardingly for the cello as the music on this issue demonstrates. Christophe Coin's
feeling for dance rhythms, his clear articulation and musical phrasing and his sharp ear for detail
bring the concertos and sonatas alive in an infectious way. He is both firmly and imaginatively
supported in the sonatas by a fine continuo group, and in the concertos by the strings of the Academy
of Ancient Music. In the sonatas Christopher Hogwood varies the colour of the accompaniments by
moving between harpsichord and organ while cello and baroque guitar add further variety and
support. In the concertos, fast movements are characterized by vigorous, idiomatic passagework for
the solo instrument punctuated by pulsating Vivaldian rhythms in the tuttis. In the slow movements,
richly endowed with lyricism, the expressive intensity of the music is, on occasion, almost startling,
revealing Vivaldi as a composer capable of far greater affective gestures than he is often given credit
for. This music was intended to move the spirit, to appeal to the senses, and it seldom, if ever, fails to
do so.
Additional recommendations ...
...Cello Concertos – C minor, RV402; D major, RV403; D minor, RV406; F major, RV412; G major,
    RV414; A minor, RV422; B minor, RV424. **Ofra Harnoy** (vc); **Toronto Chamber Orchestra / Paul
    Robinson.** RCA Victor Red Seal Ⓕ RD60155 (73 minutes: DDD: 4/90).
...Cello Concertos – D major, RV404; D minor, RV407; F major, RV411; G minor, RV417;
    A minor, RV420. Concerto for Violin, Cello and Strings in F major, "Il Proteo ò sia il mondo al

rovescio", RV544[a]. **Ofra Harnoy** (vc); [a]**Igor Oistrakh** (vn); **Toronto Chamber Orchestra / Paul Robinson.** RCA Victor Red Seal Ⓕ 09026 61578-2 (59 minutes: DDD: 1/94).

...Cello Concertos, Volume 1 – C major, RV398; C major, RV399; RV404; D minor, RV406; F major, RV410; F major, RV412; A minor, RV419. **Raphael Wallfisch** (vc); **City of London Sinfonia / Nicholas Kraemer** (hpd/org). Naxos Ⓢ 8 550907 (57 minutes: DDD: 1/96).

...Cello Concertos, Volume 3 – RV402; D major, RV403; D minor, RV407; E minor, RV409; A minor, RV418; B flat major, RV423; B minor, RV424. **Raphael Wallfisch** (vc); **City of London Sinfonia / Nicholas Kraemer** (hpd/org). Naxos Ⓢ 8 550909 (54 minutes: DDD: 1/96).

...Cello Concertos, Volume 4 – D minor, RV405; RV411; G major, RV414; G minor, RV416; G minor, RV417; RV420; A minor, RV421. **Raphael Wallfisch** (vc); **City of London Sinfonia / Nicholas Kraemer** (hpd/org). Naxos Ⓢ 8 550910 (61 minutes: DDD: 1/96).

Vivaldi Six Flute Concertos, Op. 10. **Patrick Gallois** (fl); **Orpheus Chamber Orchestra.** DG Ⓕ 437 839-2GH (49 minutes: DDD: 5/94). Recorded 1992. *Gramophone Editor's choice.* Ⓖ
Patrick Gallois is a player of agility and sensitivity, an intelligent artist who can make his metal flute speak with all the subtlety of varied articulation and tone colour that some of us had come to assume was only possible on the wooden baroque instrument. These are deliciously light performances, in the best sense of the word; plenty of air allowed in, sparing and thoughtful use of vibrato, and above all an infectious bounce to the music-making in general. Gallois's sunny approach is matched by the excellent string players of the Orpheus Chamber Orchestra, whose stunning unanimity of ensemble, crispness of attack and sheer concentration-level once again make it hard to believe that they operate without a conductor. And both soloist and orchestra are equally responsive, too, to the uniquely tranquil beauties of the Vivaldian slow movement.

New review
Vivaldi Double and Triple Concertos – Two Cellos and Strings in G minor, RV531; Violin, Cello and Strings in F major, RV544, "Il Proteo ò sia il mondo rovescio"; Three Violins and Strings in F major, RV551; Violin and Strings in A major, RV552, "violine per eco in lontano"; Violin, Two Cellos and Strings in C major, RV561; Two Violins, Two Cellos and Strings in D major, RV564. **Christophe Coin** (vc); **Il Giardino Armonico / Giovanni Antonini.** Teldec Das Alte Werk Ⓕ 4509-94552-2 (64 minutes: DDD: 8/95). Recorded 1994. *Gramophone Editor's choice.* Ⓖ
This is a strong programme which almost unfailingly presents the Venetian composer in his most colourful clothing. Though Vivaldi often wrote imaginatively for pairs of wind instruments his musical ideas were of necessity confined by their technical limitations. With violins and cellos, on the other hand, he was better able to extend his creative faculties, which resulted in music of more sustained interest. This is certainly true of the two concertos which he wrote for two violins, two cellos and strings, one of them (RV564) included here. Making an even rarer appearance on disc is a Concerto in F major for violin and cello (RV544), the least well-known of three such works from Vivaldi's pen. Two versions of this concerto exist, the other (RV572) containing additional parts for pairs of flutes and oboes. Both carry the engaging title *Il Proteo ò sia il mondo al rovescio*. Infrequently performed, too, is a C major piece for violin, two cellos and strings (RV561), though the characteristically Vivaldian ritornello of the opening movement may recall other contexts in the minds of listeners. The three remaining works are fairly mainstream Vivaldi: the G minor Concerto for two cellos (RV531), the F major Concerto for three violins (RV551) and the A major Concerto for two violins, one of them functioning as an echo, the *violine per eco in lontano* (RV552). From this, readers will infer a pleasing variety of texture and, within the limits of a purely string programme, colour. Il Giardino Armonico have thought carefully about the latter, ringing the changes in the keyboard continuo between organ and harpsichord, and introducing a theorbo, too. But what makes this disc a real winner is the exhilarating character of the playing, both solo and ripieno. Playing of vitality and lyricism brings Vivaldi's music to life in a thrilling manner. Indeed, the integrity and musicianly character of these performances is in no small measure heightened by the presence of Christophe Coin. Fine music, fine playing and a fine recording. An outstanding issue.

Vivaldi Oboe Concertos – C major, RV447[b]; F major, RV457[a]; A minor, RV461[a]; A minor, RV463[b]; D minor, RV535[ab]. Concerto for Two Clarinets, Two Oboes and Strings in C major, RV559[abc]. [a]**Stephen Hammer**, [b]**Frank de Bruine** (obs); [c]**Eric Hoeprich**, [c]**Antony Pay** (cls); **Academy of Ancient Music / Christopher Hogwood.** L'Oiseau-Lyre Ⓕ 433 674-2OH (60 minutes: DDD: 7/93). 🖉
Recorded 1991.
This delightful miscellany of concertos by Vivaldi for one and two oboes – in a single instance, here, they are joined by a pair of clarinets – confirms Stephen Hammer as one of the very finest baroque oboe players around. He and Christopher Hogwood have achieved a happy partnership which realizes on the one hand the exuberant vitality of Vivaldi's rhythms, and on the other the rich seam of fantasy running through so much of his music. Few if any of Vivaldi's 18 or so surviving solo concertos for the instrument are disappointing. Stephen Hammer and Frank de Bruine have picked four of the best constructed and most alluring of them, taking two concertos each. They join forces in the D minor Concerto for two oboes, and are further joined by Eric Hoeprich and Antony Pay for one of Vivaldi's two concertos for two oboes and two clarinets. The latter piece is effectively written with the focus on the contrasting sonorities of the single and double reed families. Hammer negotiates the solo writing

with consummate skill, athletic, precise in tuning and articulation and tasteful in his ornamentation and the remainder comes over with comparable panache. Both oboists unfailingly bring out the poetry in the music with sensibility and restraint. Fine recorded sound.

Vivaldi Oboe Concertos – C major, RV447; C major, RV450; D major, RV453; A minor, RV461; A minor, RV463. Concerto for Violin and Oboe in B flat major, RV548. **Douglas Boyd** (ob); [a]**Marieke Blankestijn** (vn); **Chamber Orchestra of Europe.** DG Ⓕ 435 873-2GH (59 minutes: DDD: 5/93). Recorded 1991.   ⊙⊙

As well as being an inspired composer for his own instrument – the violin – Vivaldi could equally turn his hand to concertos for a great many other instruments. One of the principal beneficiaries of his skill was the oboe, for which he wrote 17 solo concertos, three for two oboes and another for oboe and violin. In this virtuoso programme the oboist, Douglas Boyd, has chosen five of the solo oboe concertos together with the more modestly conceived but no less captivating Concerto in B flat for oboe and violin. The oboe concertos have been selected discerningly, not only for their musical interest but also, it would seem, with an eye to their rarity value on the concert platform. Boyd, playing a modern oboe, gives fluent, sensitively shaped performances and is supported in a lively manner by the strings of the Chamber Orchestra of Europe. Boyd is expressive in slow movements – they almost invariably possess considerable lyrical appeal – and athletic in faster ones; and he needs to be, for Vivaldi seldom showed mercy on his soloists. From among the many beautiful movements here the *Larghetto* of the Concerto in A minor (RV461) stands out and may be ranked among Vivaldi's happiest creations for the oboe. Fine recorded sound.

New review

Vivaldi Viola d'amore Concertos – D major, RV392; D minor, RV393; D minor, RV394; D minor, RV395; A major, RV396; A minor, RV397. **Orchestra of the Age of Enlightenment / Catherine Mackintosh** (va d'amore). Hyperion Ⓕ CDA66795 (67 minutes; DDD: 4/96). 🖉 Recorded 1995.   ⊙

John Evelyn (1620-1706) was beguiled and surprised by the sound of the viola d'amore, but he should hardly have been so by the fact that it was on that occasion "played ... by a *German*"; that was the nationality of most of the composers who wrote for it – Bach, Biber, Telemann and Mattheson. The instrument was distinguished by its wide compass, its use of sympathetic strings (not bowed but allowed to resonate), and the fact that it lent itself to playing "the lyra way" (as with the bass viola da gamba), facilitating the use of multiple stopping and contrapuntal textures. Vivaldi was obviously no less attracted by it; six concertos are a lot for such an unusual instrument, and it is fair to say that they represent some of the most beguiling music he wrote. Mackintosh, on top form, acts her role with the utmost virtuosity, lovely tone, unimpeachable intonation, and fine style – with some elegant embroidery. The OAE rise to the occasion, making this splendidly engineered recording one to treasure.

Vivaldi Concerto for Four Violins and Strings in D minor, RV549[abcf]. Cello Concertos[d] – G major, RV413; A minor, RV418. Concerto for Violin, Cello and Strings in B flat major, RV547[df]. Concerto for Two Violins, Two Cellos and Strings in G major, RV575[adef]. Concertos for Strings – C major, RV117; E minor, RV134; F minor, RV143; A major, RV159. [a]**Stephen Marvin,** [b]**Chantal Rémillard,** [c]**Cynthia Roberts** (vns); [d]**Anner Bylsma,** [e]**Christina Mahler** (vcs); **Tafelmusik / Jeanne Lamon** ([f]vn). Sony Classical Vivarte Ⓕ SK48044 (66 minutes: DDD: 9/92). 🖉 Recorded 1990.   ⊙⊙

The Canadian period-instrument group Tafelmusik has been building up an impressive discography of music ranging from Corelli to Mozart. Here the players address themselves to Vivaldi in a first-rate recording of concertos for various combinations of strings. Though Vivaldi himself was a violinist he wrote for almost every other instrument of his day with informed skill. One of those to benefit was the cello which features as a solo instrument to a greater or lesser extent in five of the concertos in this programme. The soloist is the Dutch virtuoso Anner Bylsma whose animated playing generates a feeling of excitement and spontaneity by no means easily captured on disc. If he has a fault then it is that he is too often attracted by breakneck tempos and it is that which detracts from the opening movement of the G major Concerto (RV413). Apart from that one minor criticism the disc is one to be treasured not only for the excellence of the playing but also for the judicious choice of repertory. The Concerto in G major for two violins, two cellos and strings (RV575) is a beautifully crafted work with notably expressive writing for the solo instruments. The four concertos for ripieno strings, in which Vivaldi foreshadows the early classical symphonists, provide a rewarding contrast with the remaining programme and are played here with accomplishment and affection.

Additional recommendations ...

...Concertos – RV575[f]; Strings in G minor, RV156; Oboe and Strings in C major, RV449[a]; Bassoon and Strings in F major, RV485[b]; Strings in B flat major, RV166; Violin, Two Recorders, Two Oboes and Strings in G minor, RV577[d], "per l'orchestra di Dresda"; Piccolo and Strings in C major, RV444[e] [de]**Peter Holtslag,** [d]**Catherine Latham** (recs); [ad]**Paul Goodwin,** [d]**Lorraine Wood** (obs); [b]**Alberto Grazzi** (bn); [df]**Peter Hanson,** [f]**Walter Reiter** (vns); [f]**Jane Coe,** [f]**David Watkin** (vcs); **The English Concert / Trevor Pinnock.** Archiv Production Ⓕ 445 839-2AH (59 minutes: DDD: 10/95). 🖉

...Cello Concertos, Volume 2 – C major, RV400; C minor, RV401; E flat major, RV408; RV413; A minor, RV422. Concerto for Two Cellos and Strings in G minor, RV531[a]. [a]**Keith Harvey, Raphael Wallfisch** (vcs); **City of London Sinfonia / Nicholas Kraemer** (hpd/org). Naxos Ⓢ 8 550908 (57 minutes: DDD: 1/96).

Vivaldi Violin Concertos – D major, RV223; A major, RV349; D minor, RV248; D major, RV229; A major, RV343; F major, RV267. **Israel Chamber Orchestra / Shlomo Mintz** (vn). MusicMasters Ⓕ 67120-2 (59 minutes: DDD: 10/94). ⓖⓖ

Shlomo Mintz has hit on the charming idea of assembling six concertos which Vivaldi intended expressly at one time or another for his gifted pupil, Anna Maria at the Pietà in Venice. If the music is anything to go by then Signora Anna Maria must have been prodigiously talented; much of the music here is of a markedly virtuoso character and of enormous appeal, melodic and rhythmic. Mintz himself does considerable justice to the works, effortlessly surmounting the technical difficulties posed by Vivaldi's writing. Equally admirable is his spirited approach and the wholehearted enthusiasm with which he throws himself into the playful invention, often strikingly varied, of the outer movements. The only reservation, a small one, lies in the recorded sound which has a slight hollowness, especially noticeable in slow movements and in passages where the solo violin is accompanied solely by cello and keyboard continuo. Otherwise a captivating issue containing music which even the most assiduous Vivaldi enthusiasts may not have heard.

Vivaldi Chamber Concertos – D major, RV93. D major, RV94. F major, RV98, "La tempesta di mare". G minor, RV104, "La notte". G minor, RV107, A minor, RV108. F major, RV442. Trio Sonata in D minor, RV63. **Il Giardino Armonico.** Teldec Ⓕ 4509-91852-2 (67 minutes: DDD: 7/94). ✍ Recorded 1990-92. ⓖ

There are baroque groups that are frankly dull and there are others on whom stylistic felicity sits naturally and gracefully. Il Giardino Armonico, an 11-strong group of young Italians, is one of the best. Italy, the birthplace of the baroque, has been curiously slow in coming forward with a specialized unit such as this, but the wait has been worthwhile; Il Giardino Armonico are as Italian as the music itself – brightly coloured, individualistic, confident, stylish, arrestingly decorated, bubbling with enthusiasm and ... add your own adjectives. The only un-Italian thing about them is their collective unanimity! Set these performances against any others in the catalogue and, with no detriment to the others, the differences are likely to deal you a blow to the solar plexus. Any sneaking fear that such unbridled *élan* leads to a uniformly vigorous approach is unfounded; equally 'Italian' is their wide dynamic range, dramatically exploited in RV104 and RV63, and all calls for serenity are answered. The recording is as bright and clear as the music.

Additional recommendation ...

...Chamber Concertos – A minor, RV86; C major, RV88; F major, RV99; G minor, RV103; G minor, RV105; G minor, RV107. Sonata for Recorder, Bassoon and Continuo in A minor, RV86. **Philidor Ensemble.** Philips Ⓕ 434 995-2PH (53 minutes: DDD: 9/93).

Vivaldi 12 Violin Concertos, Op. 4, "La stravaganza" – No. 3 in G major, RV301; No. 4 in A minor, RV357; No. 5 in A major, RV347; No. 8 in D minor, RV249; No. 10 in C minor, RV196; No. 12 in G major, RV298. **La Stravaganza, Cologne / Andrew Manze** (vn). Denon Aliare Ⓕ CO-75598 (51 minutes: DDD: 8/94). ✍ Recorded 1991. ⓖⓖ

In *La stravaganza* Vivaldi makes a further decisive step towards the virtuoso solo violin concerto and though the quality of the music is a little uneven, the set nevertheless contains several movements of outstanding beauty. Andrew Manze's feeling for detail, his lightly articulated bowing, in a word his sensibility, bring out the charm of the music; and in this set, with its many affecting slow movements – the *Grave* of No. 4 is exquisitely played – the charm is considerable. Both Manze and the ensemble savour the sonorities inherent in Vivaldi's textures but what is perhaps most welcome is their belief, well founded, that there is far more to this music than meets the eye; and the proof is in their playing of it. Manze's athletic technique and his disavowal of overstatement are in themselves noteworthy features of his playing but, more than that, he seems to revel in the composer's little *jeux d'esprit*, the caprices and the fantasy which suffuse so many of these movements. Six concertos from *La stravaganza* are no substitute for 12, but Vivaldi enthusiasts will certainly not need any further encouragement to add this disc to their complete sets.

Additional recommendations ...

...**I Solisti Italiani.** Denon Ⓕ CO-75889/90 (two discs: 105 minutes: DDD: 1/95).
...**Soloists; Academy of St. Martin in the Fields / Sir Neville Marriner.** Decca Ⓜ 444 821-2DF2 (two discs: 110 minutes: ADD: 1/96).

Vivaldi Violin Concertos, Op. 8 – Nos. 1-4, "The Four Seasons"[a]; No. 8 in G minor[a]; No. 9 in D minor[b]. [a]**Enrico Onofri** (vn); [b]**Paolo Grazzi** (ob); **Il Giardino Armonico Ensemble.** Teldec Ⓕ 4509-96158-2 (61 minutes: DDD: 1/95). ✍ Recorded 1993. ⓖ

New review

Vivaldi Violin Concertos, Op. 8, "Il cimento dell'armonia e dell'inventione" – No. 5 in E flat major, RV253, "La tempesta di mare"; No. 6 in C major, RV180, "Il piacere"; No. 7 in D minor, RV242; No. 9 in D minor, RV236; No. 10 in B flat major, RV362, "La caccia"; No. 11 in D major, RV210;

No. 12 in C major (two versions, RV178 and RV449[a]). **Enrico Onofri** (vn); [a]**Paolo Grazzi** (ob); **Il Giardino Armonico Ensemble / Giovanni Antonini.** Teldec Das Alte Werk Ⓔ 4509-94566-2 (74 minutes: DDD: 4/96). ✏ Recorded 1994-5.

Il Giardino Armonico don't do anything extraordinary; it is more a matter of their demonstration of what can be achieved with small forces – 5.1.2.1 plus soloist and continuo. Here, small is flexible and it highlights the differences in colour achieved by varying the continuo – bassoon, cello, organ, harpsichord and theorbo, unobscured by the *ripieno*, all have their moments. Numbers of 'chamber' dimensions also favour unanimity of attack and changes of dynamics and pace, all vividly accomplished by IGA. The dog barks harshly in "Spring" but without disturbing the shepherd's peaceful dreams, and the chill of "Autumn" in the *Adagio molto* is conveyed by the ethereal strings with the harpsichord firmly relegated to a supporting role. Onofri is as good a soloist as may be met in a long march, pitch-perfect, incisive but not 'edgy', and effortlessly alert to every nuance. All the foregoing good things are also to be found in the other two concertos from Op. 8, together with Grazzi's liquid-toned and agile oboe playing in that in D minor, attractively supported in the *Largo* by theorbo and bassoon. A tasty addition to even the most highly-seasoned collection.

In the completion disc of Il Giardino Armonico's Op. 8, as two of the concertos exist in alternative forms, with oboe *vice* violin (RV236 = 454, RV178 = 449), they are given in both versions – with negligible differences in tempo. The virtues of Il Giardino Armonico are, if anything, even more vividly apparent in this recording. Onofri is once again spellbinding in his imaginative use of a varied continuo, here highlighted in the *Adagio* of RV362 (*La caccia*) played only by violin and theorbo. One complaint: if there is logic behind the order in which the concertos are presented, it is not apparent. The first volume has six concertos (61 minutes), Vol. 2 has eight (74 minutes), whereas to place Nos. 1-6 and RV454 on one disc, and Nos. 7-12 and RV449 on the other would have created no apparent problem. One would, however, need a far more compelling reason not to make a beeline for the nearest record store in search of these magical and finely recorded discs.

Additional recommendations ...

...Op. 8 Nos. 1-12. Flute Concerto in D major, RV429. Cello Concerto in B minor, RV424. **Stephen Preston** (fl); **Simon Standage** (vn); **Anthony Pleeth** (vc); **The English Concert / Trevor Pinnock.** CRD Ⓔ CRD3348/9 (two discs: 154 minutes: ADD: 8/88). ✏

...Op. 8 Nos. 2 and 10. Violin Concertos, Op. 11 – C minor; RV199, "Il sospetto"; E major, RV271, "L'amoroso"; A major, RV335, "Il cucù". **Jaap van Zweden** (vn); **Combattimento Consort Amsterdam / Jan Willem de Vriend.** Sony Classical Ⓔ SK53265 (58 minutes: DDD: 8/93). ✏　　ⒼⒼ

...Op. 8 Nos. 1-6. **European Community Chamber Orchestra / Marieke Blankestijn** (vn); **Richard Lester** (vc); **Harold Lester** (hpd). Teldec Ⓔ 4509-91683-2 (59 minutes: DDD: 6/94).

...Op. 8 Nos. 1-4. **Kreisler** Violin Concerto in C major, "in the style of Vivaldi". **Gil Shaham** (vn); **Orpheus Chamber Orchestra.** DG Ⓔ 439 933-2GH (50 minutes: DDD: 3/95).

New review

Vivaldi Violin Concertos, Op. 8 – Nos. 1-4, "The Four Seasons"[a]. Oboe Concertos, Op. 7[b]　No. 1 in B flat major, RV465; No. 5 in F major, RV285a. [a]**Andrew Manze** (vn); [b]**Marcel Ponseele** (ob); **Amsterdam Baroque Orchestra / Ton Koopman.** Erato Ⓔ 4509-94811-2 (56 minutes: DDD: 8/96). ✏　　ⒼⒼⒼ

There are already enough versions of the *Four Seasons* to make the choice of a clear leader a headache that no reviewer would want. However, suffice it to say that this is one of the very best, valid for a lifetime of pleasure. Little differences in attention to detail soon begin to show, first at 0'17" of the first movement of "Spring", where the chords that are usually hit hard are here given a happy little squeeze. Amsterdam Baroque (consisting here of 13 instrumentalists) play with the unanimity of one mind and body, with extreme changes of volume that never sound theatrically contrived, as concerned with the fate of every note as with the shaping of each phrase. Manze's bow breathes vocal life into his strings; in the slow movements many notes whisper their way into being, and his *fortissimo* whiplashes have rasp-free edges. There are many delightful little personal touches – his slurred resolution of the sighing appoggiatura at 2'50" in the third movement of "Spring", and the way he nudges his way up the ladder of trills in the first movement of "Autumn" are just two. The remaining works come from Op. 7, in the first of which (RV465) the oboe is the designated soloist; its transcribed role in No. 5 (RV285a) accords with baroque practice. Both are charming works with a high level of inspiration, played with no less affection than the *Seasons*.

Vivaldi Violin Concertos – C minor, RV199, "Il sospetto"; D major, RV234, "L'inquietudine"; E major, RV270, "Il riposo"; E major, RV271, "L'amoroso"; E minor, RV277, "Il favorito"; C major, RV581. **Mariana Sirbu** (vn); **I Musici.** Philips Ⓔ 442 145-2PH (63 minutes: DDD: 7/95). Recorded 1993.　　ⒼⒼ

All but one piece (RV581) in this attractive programme from I Musici were included in a 1958 recording by the same ensemble (no longer available). This newer issue is by and large more enjoyable, with livelier, more sharply defined rhythms, clearer articulation and brisker tempos. The last-mentioned need not necessarily imply virtue but in this instance it is a decided plus, above all in *L'inquietudine* whose restless character was only partly realized in the earlier recording. While the solo work was spread among five players on the 1958 disc, it is allotted to just one on the new issue – Mariana Sirbu. She is manifestly a fine violinist with a warm, even tone, a sharp ear for tonal and interpretative detail and a feeling for the various states of mind suggested in some of the subtitles. The expressive *Andante* of *Il favorito* is beautifully controlled and, in the hands of a soloist of this calibre, explains how the concerto, quite austere on first acquaintance, acquired its title. *L'amoroso* comes over well, too, with tenderly spoken phrases and a playful lyricism in the outer movements. Sirbu ornaments both tastefully and with admirable discretion. Only in *Il riposo* does one feel some disappointment. This delicately crafted piece is scored for muted strings throughout and at some stage in Vivaldi's life acquired Christmas connotations with an additional subtitle "per il Santissimo Natale". Sirbu and I Musici set too brisk a pace in the opening movement and the result is a shade perfunctory. Even so, the playing itself maintains the high level of excellence achieved throughout the remainder of the programme, with impressive virtuosity from Sirbu in the C major Concerto, RV581, recorded here in its version for solo violin and double orchestra. In short, a delightful issue, recommended for music and performances alike.

Additional recommendation ...

...RV199; RV234; D major, RV208; RV270; RV271; B flat major, RV363; RV553. **Soloists; I Solisti Veneti / Claudio Scimone.** Erato 4509-97415-2.

Vivaldi L'estro armonico, Op. 3. **Academy of Ancient Music / Christopher Hogwood.** L'Oiseau-Lyre Florilegium Ⓜ 414 554-2OH2 (two discs: 96 minutes: DDD: 1/86). ✍ From D245D2 (12/81).

This set of Concertos is arranged as a display of variety, and ordered in a kaleidoscopic way that would maintain interest were it to be played in its entirety. These works are often played with an inflated body of *ripieno* (orchestral) strings, but in this recording they are played as Vivaldi intended them; only four violins are used. The contrast does not come from antiphony or weight of numbers but is provided through the *tutti* versus episodic passages. One could not assemble a more distinguished 'cast' than that of the AAM in this recording, showing clearly just why this music is best played on period instruments, by specialists in baroque style, who are not afraid to add a little embellishment here and there. Neither the enchanting performances nor the quality of their recording could be better; this is required listening.

Additional recommendations ...

...**I Solisti Italiani.** Denon Ⓕ CO-72719/20 (two discs: 109 minutes: DDD: 8/89). ✍

...**Roberto Michelucci** (vn); **I Musici.** Philips Ⓜ 426 932-2PM2 (two discs: ADD: 7/91). ✍

Vivaldi Concertos for Strings – C major, RV117; C minor, RV118; D major, RV123; D minor, RV128; F major, RV136; F minor, RV143; G major, RV146; A major, RV159; A major, RV160; B flat major, RV163, "Conca". **I Musici.** Philips Ⓕ 438 876-2PH (55 minutes: DDD: 5/94). Recorded 1992.

Here is a generous and varied selection from among the concertos which Vivaldi wrote for strings without soloist. He composed over 40 such pieces of which ten are included here. Anyone who still thinks that one Vivaldi concerto sounds much the same as another should address himself to these vital, often forward-looking pieces. They are full of striking contrasts and ideas which point strongly in the direction of the early symphony and the tautly constructed fugues at the conclusion of the Concerto in D major (RV123) and the beginning of the Concerto in F minor (RV143) are but two reminders of how effective a contrapuntist Vivaldi could be if he so wished. I Musici give a lively view of these engaging concertos with tidy ensemble and good intonation and should disappoint only those who no longer find enjoyment in listening to baroque repertory played on modern instruments. Good recorded sound.

Additional recommendation ...

...C major, RV114; RV118; C minor, RV120; RV128; E minor, RV133; E minor, RV134; RV143; G major, RV151, "Alla rustica"; G minor, RV152; G minor, RV157; A major, RV158; "Conca"; B flat major, RV167. Sinfonias for Strings – C major, RV116; E major, RV132; F major, RV137; F major, RV140; G major, RV146; B minor, RV168. **I Solisti Veneti / Claudio Scimone.** Erato Ⓕ 4509-96382-2 (two discs: 127 minutes: ADD/DDD). ⊙⊙

Vivaldi Concertos for Two Violins and Strings – C major, RV505; D major, RV511; A minor, RV523 (Micaela Comberti, vn). Concerto for Two Cellos and Strings in G minor, RV531 (Jane Coe, David Watkin, vcs). Concerto for Two Oboes and Strings in D minor, RV535 (Anthony Robson, Catherine Latham, obs). Concerto for Two Violins, Oboe and Strings in C major, RV554. **Collegium Musicum 90 / Simon Standage** (vn). Chandos Chaconne Ⓕ CHAN0528 (65 minutes: DDD: 3/93). ✍ Recorded 1991.

It was natural, with so many talented young ladies available at the Pietà, that Vivaldi should have written a large number of concertos with two or more soloists. More than two dozen are for two violins and most remain unrecorded; RV505 and 511 are both mature works, the former leaning toward *galant* style and the latter 'unified' by elements that are common to its outer movements. RV554, originally a triple concerto for violin, oboe and organ, was rewritten by Vivaldi for oboe and two violins, in which latter form it is given in this recording. The Concerto for two oboes, RV535, is 'Corellian' in its four-movement *da chiesa* form and in its 'conversations' between the soloists and the *ripieno* strings – a Vivaldian rarity. If Vivaldi wrote a more eloquently pathetic melody than that of the *Largo* of the Double Cello Concerto, RV531, it is hard to bring it to mind; it is an early work – why did he never return to that most rewarding of media? Collegium Musicum 90 field a modest string band, which adds leanness of sound to their other virtues of stylishness and crispness of ensemble. Excellent oboe soloists contribute to the allure of this recording.

Vivaldi Concertos – G major, RV151, "Alla rustica"; B flat major for Violin and Oboe, RV548; G major for Two Violins, RV516; A minor for Oboe, RV461; G major for Two Mandolins, RV532; C major, RV558. **The English Concert / Trevor Pinnock.** Archiv Produktion Ⓕ 415 674-2AH (53 minutes: DDD: 9/86). ✔   Ⓖ

The *Concerto con molti stromenti*, RV558, calls for a plethora of exotic instruments and Vivaldi's inventiveness, everywhere apparent, seems to know no bounds. The vigorous melodies have splendid verve whilst the slow movements are no less exciting. The concertos which employ plucked instruments, are particularly entrancing to the ear – here is virtuosity indeed, with Pinnock sensibly opting for an organ continuo to emphasize the difference between the plucked strings and the bowed. The Double Mandolin Concerto, RV532, is beautifully played with a real build-up of tension in the tuttis. The playing of The English Concert is affectionate and rhythmically precise and the recording is good, with the gentler sounding instruments well brought out of the fuller textures.

Vivaldi String Concertos – C minor, RV761; D minor, RV129, "Concerto madrigalesco"; G minor, RV517[a]; B flat major, RV547[b]; C minor, RV202; E flat major, RV130, "Sonata al santo sepolcro". Sinfonia in B minor, RV169, "Sinfonia al santo sepolcro". [a]**Adrian Chamorro** (vn); [b]**Maurizio Naddeo** (vc); **L'Europa Galante / Fabio Biondi** (vn). Opus 111 Ⓕ OPS309004 (52 minutes: DDD: 9/91). ✔ Recorded 1990.   ⒼⒼ

This invigorating programme contains well-known and less well-known concertos by Vivaldi. The performances sparkle with life and possess an irresistible spontaneity. The Concertos for one and two violins (RV761 and RV202) are comparative rarities and are played with agility and insight by the soloist director Fabio Biondi and his alert and responsive ensemble. Biondi himself is capable of light and articulate bowing and has a natural feeling for graceful turns of phrase. Vivaldi's virtuoso writing occasionally finds chinks in his armour but with enlightened music-making of this order it matters little. Everywhere Vivaldi's infectious rhythms are tautly controlled and the music interpreted with character and conviction. Perhaps the highlight of the disc is the Concerto in B flat for violin and cello. Outer movements are crisply articulated and played with almost startling energy while the poignant lyricism of the *Andante* is touchingly captured. A refreshing and illuminating disc whose imaginative and passionate interpretations have few rivals in the catalogue. The recorded sound is clear and ideally resonant.

Vivaldi Cello Sonatas – E flat major, RV39; E minor, RV40; G minor, RV42; A minor, RV44; B flat major, RV45; B flat major, RV46. **Pieter Wispelwey** (vc); **Florilegium Ensemble** (Elizabeth Kenny, William Carter, ltes/theorboes/gtrs; Daniel Yeadon, vc; Neal Peres da Costa, hpd/org). Channel Classics Ⓕ CCS6294 (66 minutes: DDD: 11/94). ✔ Recorded 1994.

Vivaldi wrote with great imagination for the cello, and the sonatas like the concertos, of which three times as many exist, are plentifully endowed with affecting melodies – the third movement of the E minor Sonata is a superb example – and virtuoso gestures. It would seem, on the strength of these pieces, that Vivaldi possessed a rare sensibility to the expressive *cantabile* possibilities in writing for the cello. Certainly, few baroque composers other than Bach and perhaps Geminiani realized the instrument's solo potential better than he. Wispelwey is a sensitive player who draws a warm if at times under-assertive sound from his instrument. Fast movements are clearly articulated, slow ones lyrically played with some feeling for the poetry of the music. The performances are thoughtful and enlightened, with a continuo group that includes organ, harpsichord, cello, archlutes, theorboes and guitars in a variety of combinations. The recorded sound is fine. Well worth exploring though Anthony Pleeth's ASV recording of all nine sonatas (listed below) may ultimately prove the more satisfying of the two.

Additional recommendation ...

...RV40; F major, RV41; A minor, RV43; RV45; RV46; B flat major, RV47. **Christophe Coin** (vc); **Christopher Hogwood** (hpd). L'Oiseau-Lyre Florilegium Ⓕ 421 060-2OH (72 minutes: DDD: 4/89). ✔

...RV39; RV40; RV41; RV42; RV43; RV44; RV45, RV46, RV47. **Anthony Pleeth, Suki Towb** (vcs); **Robert Woolley** (hpd/org). ASV Gaudeamus Ⓕ CDGAD201 (two discs: 123 minutes: DDD: 11/91). ✔

...RV39, RV40; RV41; RV42, RV43; RV44, RV45; RV46; RV47. **David Watkin** (vc); **Helen Gough** (vc continuo), **David Miller** (lte/theorbo/gtr); **Robert King** (org/hpd). Hyperion Ⓕ CDA66881/2 (two discs: 116 minutes: DDD: 8/95). ✔

Vivaldi 12 Violin Sonatas, "Manchester Sonatas" – No. 1 in C major, RV3. No. 2 in D minor, RV12. No. 3 in G minor, RV757. No. 4 in D major, RV755. No. 5 in B flat major, RV759. No. 6 in A major, RV758. No. 7 in C minor, RV6. No. 8 in G major, RV22. No. 9 in F minor, RV17a. No. 10 in B minor, RV760. No. 11 in E flat major, RV756. No. 12 in C major, RV754. **La Romanesca** (Andrew Manze, vn; Nigel North, lte/theorbo/gtr; John Toll, hpd). Harmonia Mundi

Ⓕ HMU90 7089/90 (two discs: 145 minutes: DDD: 1/94). ⏺ Recorded 1992. *Gramophone*
Editor's choice.

Vivaldi is so well-known for his concertos that we are apt to overlook his admittedly much smaller
output of sonatas. This set of 12 for violin and continuo was discovered in Manchester's Central
Music Library during the 1970s though five of them exist in versions which have been known for
much longer. It is probable that all of them date from the early- to mid-1720s when Vivaldi assembled
them to present to Cardinal Ottoboni on the occasion of his visit to Venice, the city of his birth, in
1726. The violinist Andrew Manze has an appealing rapport with this music and is expressive in his
shaping of phrases. He reveals sensibility towards Vivaldi's pleasing melodic contours. Indeed, this is
a quality in which these sonatas abound, not only in the varied Preludes with which each Sonata
begins but also in the brisker, sometimes very brisk allemandes and correntes. He ornaments the
music with an effective blend of fantasy and good taste and he dispenses with bowed continuo
instruments, preferring the lighter textures provided by harpsichord, archlute, theorbo or guitar. This
is music of great beauty and vitality which will delight most if not all lovers of the late baroque; and
it is sympathetically interpreted and warmly and intimately recorded.

Vivaldi Opera Arias and Sinfonias: Griselda – Sinfonia; Ombre vane, ingiusti orrori; Agitata da
due venti. Tito Manlio – Non ti lusinghi la crudeltade. Ottone in Villa – Sinfonia; Gelosia, tu già
rendi l'alma mia; L'ombre, l'aure, e ancora il rio[a]. L'Atenaide – Ferma, Teodosio. Bajazet –
Sinfonia. L'Incoronazione di Dario – Non mi lusinga vana speranza. Catone in Utica – Se mai
senti spirarti sul volto; Se in campo armato. **Emma Kirkby, [a]Liliana Mazzarri** (sops); **The
Brandenburg Consort / Roy Goodman.** Hyperion Ⓕ CDA66745 (75 minutes: DDD: 5/95). ⏺
Texts and translations included. Recorded 1994.   ⊕⊕

This release of arias and sinfonias from Vivaldi's operas gives us a *bonne bouche* of what lies in store
for artists and record companies inclined to explore this still somewhat overlooked aspect of Vivaldi's
output. The programme is also an entertaining one in its own right and it is far from being a mere
highlights disc. The arias have been chosen with discernment, thoughtfully grouped and effectively
interspersed with three of Vivaldi's opera *sinfonias*. The formula proves so successful that it even
occurs to you that this was maybe the happiest solution to reviving at least the more problematic of
Vivaldi's operas. Emma Kirkby's voice is still maturing, filling out, and she is able to achieve an ever
increasing variety of colour. Her "Ombre vane, ingiusti orrori", a ravishing piece from *Griselda*
(1735), is beautifully and effortlessly controlled, delicately shaded and rhythmically vital; and her
feeling for apposite embellishment comes across with pleasing spontaneity and stylistic assurance.
The voice is supported and highlighted by the sympathetic partnership of The Brandenburg Consort
conducted by Roy Goodman. In summary, this is a disc which will delight both Vivaldi enthusiasts
and lovers of baroque music generally. Excellent recorded sound.

New review

Vivaldi Stabat mater in F minor, RV621[a]. Cessate, omai cessate, RV684[a]. Filiae mestae Jerusalem in
C minor, RV638[a]. Concertos for Strings – C major, RV114; E flat major, RV130, "Sonata al
Santo Sepolcro". [a]**Andreas Scholl** (alto); **Ensemble 415 / Chiara Banchini** (vn). Harmonia Mundi
Ⓕ HMC90 1571 (52 minutes: DDD: 4/96). Texts and translations included. Recorded 1995.
Gramophone Editor's choice. Selected by Soundings.   ⊕⊕⊕

Here is a very attractively prepared menu whose main course is the *Stabat mater* for countertenor and
strings. Hors-d'oeuvres and side-dishes consist of a ripieno concerto (RV114), a chamber cantata for
countertenor and strings (RV684), a string sonata in E flat (RV130) and an introductory motet to a
lost *Miserere* (RV638). Taken together, the pieces demonstrate something of Vivaldi's diverse style as
a composer. The two instrumental works offer the strongest contrasts, the Concerto suggestive, above
all in its opening movement, of an opera sinfonia, the Sonata redolent with poignant suspensions and
darkly sonorous in its first movement, but yielding to a tautly constructed fugue in the second. The
chamber cantata, if closely related to the two sacred vocal items on the disc in respect of tonal colour,
differs from them in character. Conforming with the standard Italian cantata pattern at the time of
two pairs of alternating recitative and *da capo* aria Vivaldi enlivens his pastoral idyll with two
particularly affecting arias, the first with a palpitating pizzicato violin, the second a virtuoso vocal
tour de force illustrating the plight of the forsaken lover. Andreas Scholl brings the whole thing off
superbly with only a moment's faulty intonation at the close of the first aria. Unlike settings of the
Stabat mater by Pergolesi and others, Vivaldi used only the first ten of the 20 stanzas of the poem.
His deeply expressive setting of the poem will be familiar to many readers but few will have heard such
an affecting performance as Scholl achieves here. The lyrical prayer of human yearning for faith
contained in the "Fac ut ardeat" movement is tenderly sung and here, as throughout the programme,
sympathetically supported by Ensemble 415 under Chiara Banchini's experienced direction.

Vivaldi Domine ad adiuvandum me festiana, RV593. Beatus vir, RV597. Stabat mater, RV621.
Magnificat, RV610*a*. **Ex Cathedra Chamber Choir and Baroque Orchestra / Jeffrey Skidmore.**
ASV Gaudeamus Ⓕ CDGAU137 (70 minutes: DDD: 12/92). ⏺ Texts and translations
included. Recorded 1991.   ⊕⊕

This is an interesting and mainly successful attempt to place a handful of Vivaldi's sacred pieces in a
liturgical context. The most well-known work here is the *Stabat mater* for alto voice and strings, but

the others deserve to be heard more often than they are. Ex Cathedra Chamber Choir is a well-disciplined, youthful sounding ensemble whose contribution to the recording is first-rate. And it is from the choir that solo voices emerge as required, giving the performances a homogeneity of sound and intent. The instrumentalists, too, make a strong contribution and together with the voices project interpretations which are full of vitality. There are, of course, rival versions on disc of all the music sung here but, on the strength of the thoughtful way it has been presented by the director of Ex Cathedra, Geoffrey Skidmore, this is perhaps the most affecting of them. Few will be disappointed, for example, by the gently inflected, poignant account of the *Stabat mater* by the countertenor Nigel Short. Hardly a detail has been overlooked, even to the extent of allowing the listener to hear a distant bell during the opening Versicle. In short, only the painfully and unnecessarily small typeface of the accompanying texts fails to please.

Additional recommendations ...

...Magnificat. In turbato mare irato, RV627. Concertos – D minor, RV129, "Concerto madrigalesco"; G minor, RV157; G major, RV151, "Concerto alla rustica". Lungi dal vago volto, RV680. **Soloists; Tafelmusik Chamber Choir and Orchestra / Jean Lamon** (vn). Hyperion Ⓕ CDA66247 (57 minutes: DDD: 12/87). ✒   Ⓖ

...Vestro Principi divino, RV633. Stabat mater. Filiae mestae, RV638. Nisi Dominus, RV608. **Gérard Lesne** (alto); **Il Seminario Musicale Ensemble.** Harmonic Ⓕ H/CD8720 (58 minutes: DDD: 3/91). ✒

...Laudate pueri Dominum, RV600[a]. Stabat mater[b]. Deus tuorum militum, RV612[c]. Sanctorum meritis, RV620[d]. [ad]**Margaret Marshall** (sop); [bc]**Jochen Kowalski** (alto); [ad]**Jacques Ogg** (org); **Concertgebouw Chamber Orchestra / Vittorio Negri.** Philips Ⓕ 432 091-2PH (49 minutes: DDD: 2/92).

...Gloria in D major, RV589[a]. Magnificat[b]. Laetatus sum, RV607[c]. Laudate Dominum in D minor, RV606[e]. In exitu Israel in C major, RV064[c]. Sinfonia al Santo Sepolcro in B minor, RV169. Sonata al Santo Sepolcro in E flat major, RV130. (All using womens' voices only) [ab]**Emily Van Evera,** [b]**Nancy Argenta** (sops); [ab]**Alison Place,** [b]**Catherine King** (mezzos); [ab]**Margaret Cable** (contr); [abc]**Taverner Choir; Taverner Players / Andrew Parrott.** Virgin Classics Veritas Ⓕ VC7 59326-2 (68 minutes: DDD: 1/95). ✒

Vivaldi Magnificat in G minor, RV610[a]. Lauda Jerusalem in E minor, RV609[b]. Kyrie in G minor, RV587[c]. Credo in E minor, RV591[d]. Dixit Dominus in D major, RV594[e]. [abe]**Susan Gritton,** [abe]**Lisa Milne** (sops); [ae]**Catherine Denley** (mez); [ae]**Lynton Atkinson** (ten); [e]**David Wilson-Johnson** (bar); **King's Consort Choristers and Choir; King's Consort / Robert King.** Hyperion Ⓕ CDA66769 (63 minutes: DDD: 6/95). ✒ Texts and translations included. Recorded 1994. *Gramophone Editor's choice.*   Ⓖ

King's 'super-group' featuring choristers drawn from seven English cathedral and collegiate choirs sound better than ever – technically reliable, with a good, full sound – and are a credit to King's vision in bringing them together. This volume has five typically uplifting works, three of which – *Lauda Jerusalem*, *Dixit Dominus* and the G minor *Kyrie* – offer the opulent sound of double choir and orchestra. *Dixit Dominus* is the most substantial, a colourful 23-minute sequence of varied solos and choruses, with trumpets, oboes and two organs all chipping in, most notably in an awe-inspiring depiction of the Day of Judgement. The other two are perhaps less striking, though *Lauda Jerusalem* is certainly charming in its two-soprano interchanges. Highlights of the single-chorus works include another exquisite soprano duet and a fiery "Fecit potentiam" in the *Magnificat*, and an extraordinary "Crucifixus" in the *Credo* which departs from the pain-wracked norm by seemingly depicting with lugubrious slow tread Christ's walk to Calvary. King manages very well in capturing the essence of Vivaldi's bold, sometimes disarmingly straightforward style. These tidy performances are driven with just the right amount of springy energy – neither too much nor too little – and are well recorded in the warm resonance of St Jude's Church, Hampstead in London.

New review

Vivaldi In furore gustissimae irae, RV626[a]. Longe mala, umbrae, terrores, RV629[b]. Clarae stellae, scintillate, RV625[c]. Canta in prato, ride in monte, RV623[a]. Filiae mestae Jerusalem in C minor, RV638[c]. Nulla in mundo pax sincera, RV630[a]. [a]**Deborah York** (sop); [b]**Catherine Denley** (mez); [c]**James Bowman** (alto); **King's Consort / Robert King.** Hyperion Ⓕ CDA66779 (69 minutes: DDD: 7/96). ✒ Texts and translations included.   Ⓖ

The promising first volume of Robert King's exploration of Vivaldi's sacred music (reviewed above) gave us a selection of large-scale choral works; Vol. 2 offers five of his motets for solo voice and strings, together with RV623, one of the *Introduzioni* he composed to precede his liturgical choral pieces. As ever with Vivaldi, they are utterly beguiling pieces of music, impossible to dislike and easy to be beguiled by. Their Latin texts – which usually allow for two arias separated by a recitative and followed by an "Alleluia" – are about as profound as the sonnets which accompany *The Four Seasons*, but they inspire in Vivaldi just the same kind of charmingly uncomplicated reaction. Nightingales, scenes of general Arcadian bliss, the storms of God's wrath and the touching sorrow of the mournful daughters of Jerusalem before the Cross – all bring forth what you might be tempted to call stock responses were it not for the fact that the music is always so instantly recognizable as being by Vivaldi. Vivaldi's singers must have been good to judge from these pieces, which show a brand of virtuosity more at home in the instrumental concerto than the aria. James Bowman and Catherine Denley are both on good form (the latter having a particularly taxing number to sing), but the star of the disc is Deborah York, yet another of the many outstanding young sopranos to have arrived on the scene in recent years. Her *In furore iustissimae irae* is a *tour de force* of vocal power and agility with a teasing little top C at the end of the first aria; while the deceptive beauties of *Nulla in mundo pax sincera* are artfully conjured by sly little portamentos. The string accompaniments throughout are buoyant but beefy, aided by an excellent recorded sound, and the tempos seem well judged. With such things as these on its side, this looks like a Vivaldi series that cannot go wrong.

Vivaldi Salve regina in C minor, RV616[a]. Introduzione al Miserere, RV641[a]. Introduzione al Gloria, RV637[a]. Salve regina in G minor, RV618[a]. Concerto for Violin and Strings in C major, RV581[b] ("per la Santissima Assenzione di Maria Vergine"). [a]**Gérard Lesne** (alto); [b]**Fabio Biondi** (vn); **Il Seminario Musicale**. Virgin Classics Veritas Ⓕ VC7 59232-2 (77 minutes: DDD: 6/93). ✍ Texts and translations included. Recorded 1991.

The principal works here are two settings of the Marian antiphon *Salve regina*, but the French countertenor Gérard Lesne follows this with an extended *Introduzione* to a *Miserere*, one of two by Vivaldi, and an *Introduzione* to a *Gloria*; and by way of making up a programme, he divides the four vocal pieces into two groups inserting a Violin Concerto between them. The main bias of this music is contemplative, often deeply so, as is the case with the darkly expressive, sorrowful introduction to the *Miserere non in pratis*. Lesne approaches the music with style. Indeed, a stronger advocate for these affecting compositions is hard to imagine since he is technically almost faultless. Then there is the Concerto in C major (*in due cori*), a splendid example of Vivaldi's skill in this medium, admirably played by the violinist Fabio Biondi with Lesne's own group Il Seminario Musicale. Vivaldi enthusiasts will require no further proof of this disc's merit, but readers in general should also find much to enjoy here, both in the singing and playing. The recorded sound is pleasantly resonant, serving the best interests of Lesne's voice and of the instruments too. A fine release.

New review

Vivaldi Tito Manlio. **Giancarlo Luccardi** (bass) Tito Manlio; **Norma Lerer** (mez) Decio; **Margaret Marshall** (sop) Lucio; **Júlia Hamari** (mez) Servilia; **Rose Wagemann** (mez) Manlio; **Birgit Finnilä** (mez) Vitellia; **Domenico Trimarchi** (bar) Lindo; **Claes Hakon Ahnsjö** (ten) Geminio; **Berlin Radio Chorus; Berlin Chamber Orchestra / Vittorio Negri**. Philips Ⓜ 446 332-2PM4 (four discs: 238 minutes: ADD: 7/96). Notes, text and translation included. From 6769 004 (9/78).

Tito Manlio was produced for the Mantuan Carnival season in 1719 and, if we are to believe a note by Vivaldi himself at the head of the score, was written in the space of five days. This recording of the work was first issued on LP in 1978 but only now makes its début on CD. *Tito Manlio* certainly ranks among the most successful of all the ten Vivaldi operas so far commercially recorded. The libretto, by Matteo Noris, whom Vivaldi set on more than one occasion, centres round a dispute between the Romans and the Latins which has arisen because the Roman Senate, headed by Titus Manlius, has denied the Latins a consul of Latin birth. The Latins declare war on Rome but, since until now the opposing camps have been on friendly terms, Titus forbids his son Manlius to engage the enemy in single combat. Manlius disobeys him and is sentenced to death by his father. These events, together with drama provided by lovers separated by war, sustain the opera successfully and by large, through three substantial acts. All this takes place in about 340 BC, by the way. Vivaldi's melodic invention is alluring and, if the libretto is no masterpiece, at least it provides a wealth of opportunities for evocative image painting. The role of Lucio is stylishly sung by Margaret Marshall. Titus's daughter Vitellia, sung by Birgit Finnilä, is also allotted some engaging music. Then there is Titus's music, sung by Giancarlo Luccardi; he had a reputation as a stern consul and Vivaldi underlines this side of his character with some robust arias. Manlius, Titus's son, sung by Rose Wagemann, also has some strong arias – not surprisingly since his predicament seems hopeless on all fronts. In short, this is an opera which both in content and performance, albeit dated in some respects, goes some way towards rehabilitating Vivaldi in the minds of readers who, over the years, have encountered more than their fair share of indifferent recordings. The cast is mainly a strong one with the Berlin Chamber Orchestra (using modern instruments) providing solid support. If the overture to the work has survived it can no longer be identified. Negri, instead, has chosen three movements from three different concertos (RV562, 579 and 141). The solution is both apt in context and extremely effective. A welcome and stimulating reissue.

Further listening ...

...Concertos – Two Horns and Strings: F major, RV539[a]; F major, RV538[b]; Two Trumpets and Strings in C major, RV537[c]; Two Oboes and Two Clarinets in C major, RV560[d]; Oboe, Bassoon and Strings in G major, RV545[e]; Two Flutes and Strings in C major, RV533[f]. Sinfonia for Strings in D major, RV122[g]. [f]**Duke Dobing**, [f]**Deborah Davis** (fls); [deg]**Christopher Hooker**, [deg]**Helen McQueen** (obs); [d]**Ruth McDowall**, [d]**David Rix** (cls); [eg]**Joanna Graham** (bn); [c]**Crispian Steele-Perkins**, [c]**Michael Meeks** (tpts); [ab]**Stephen Stirling**, [ab]**Tim Caister** (hns); **City of London Sinfonia / Nicholas Kraemer** (hpd). Naxos Ⓢ 8 553204 (54 minutes: DDD: 1/96).

...Concerto for Two Trumpets and Strings in C major, RV537[a]. *Coupled with* **Stradella** (ed. Steele-Perkins) Sonata a 8 con una Tromba in D major. **Biber** Fidicunium sacro-profanum – Sonata IV a 5 in C major. Sonatae tam aris quam aulis servientes – I a 8 in C major; X a 5 in G minor[a].

Ducts for Two Trumpets[a] – No. 1 in C major; No. 5 in C major; No. 11 in G minor; No. 13 in A minor. **Albinoni** (atrib.) Concerto for Trumpet, Oboes, Bassoon and Strings in C major. **Telemann** Concerto for Trumpet, Two Oboes and Strings in D major. **Handel** (ed. Steele-Perkins) Airs from Vauxhall Gardens. **Crispian Steele-Perkins,** [a]**John Thiessen** (tpts); **Tafelmusik / Jeanne Lamon** (vn). Sony Classical Vivarte SK53365 (4/95). ✍

…Concerto for Two Trumpets and Strings in C major, RV537 (rev. Malipiero). *Coupled with works by* **Corelli, Albinoni, Torelli, A. Marcello, Viviani, Franceschini** and **Baldassare** Håkan **Hardenberger, Reinhold Friedrich** (tpts); **I Musici.** Philips 442 131-2PH (5/95). *See review in the Collections section; refer to the Index to Reviews.*   Ⓖ

…Dorilla in Tempe. **Soloists; Nice Opera Chorus; Nice Baroque Ensemble / Gilbert Bezzina.** Pierre Verany PV794092 (2/95).   Ⓖ

…Gloria in D major, RV588. *Coupled with* **A. Scarlatti** Dixit Dominus II. **Soloists; The English Concert Choir; The English Concert / Trevor Pinnock.** Archiv Produktion 423 386-2AH (5/88). ✍

…Glorias – D major, RV588; D major RV589. **Soloists; St John's College Choir, Cambridge. Wren Orchestra. George Guest.** Decca Eclipse 448 223-2DEC (2/96).

Amadeo Vives   Spanish 1871-1932

Suggested listening …
…Bohemios. **Soloists; La Laguna University Polyphonic Chorus and Choir; "Reyes Bartlet" Choir, Puerto de la Cruz; Tenerife Symphony Orchestra / Antoni Ros Marbà.** Auvidis Valois V4711 (43 minutes: DDD: 3/95).

Giovanni Viviani   Italian 1638-1692 or later

Suggested listening …
…Capricci armonici – Sonata prima. *Coupled with works by* **A. Marcello, Torelli, Albinoni, Corelli, Vivaldi, Franceschini** and **Baldassare** Håkan Hardenberger (tpt); **I Musici.** Philips 442 131-2PH (5/95) *See review in the Collections section; refer to the Index to Reviews.*   Ⓖ

Kevin Volans   South African 1949-

Volans String Quartets – No. 2, "Hunting: Gathering"; No. 3, "The Songlines". **Balanescu Quartet** (Alexander Balanescu, Clare Connors, vns; Bill Hawkins, va; Nick Cooper, vc). Argo Ⓔ 440 687-2ZH (57 minutes: DDD· 8/94). Recorded 1993.
Both works here call on ideas from native African peoples, including the Hamar of Ethiopia and the Zulus, but Volans's style is also reminiscent of Western models, Stravinsky, Bartók and Messiaen most especially. In fact, the mesmeric, 19-minute second movement of *The Songlines* features one passage (roughly 12'00" to 15'00") that suggests the joint influence of Messiaenic bird song and Bartókian nocturnal atmosphere. Volans favours speech-like phrase constructions and punctuation, although his work appears not to have mirrored specific words. *Hunting: Gathering* is certainly the place to start: its language is less discursive than *The Songlines*, its melodic material easier to assimilate. There's even what sounds like a passing reference to the theme for the TV 'cop' show "Cagney and Lacey" (near the beginning of the second movement)! *The Songlines* was intended as "an extension in another medium" on Bruce Chatwin's novel of the same name and is altogether darker, more austere and more obviously outspoken than its predecessor. However, both works are beautifully realized, and the recordings have a clarity and refinement that reflects similar priorities on the part of the performers. Recommended.
Further listening …
…White man sleeps (1982[d] and 1986[a] versions). Mbira[b]. She who sleeps with a small blanket[c]. [bd]**Kevin Volans,** [b]**Deborah James,** [d]**Robert Hill** (hpds); [d]**Margriet Tindemans** (va da gamba); [bcd]**Robyn Schulkowsky** (perc); [a]**Smith Quartet.** Cala United 88034 (10/91).
…String Quartets – No. 4, "Ramanujan Notebooks"; No. 5, "Dancers on a Plane". Movement for String Quartet. **Duke Quartet.** Collins Classics 1417-2 (7/95).

Jan Voříšek   Bohemian 1791-1825

Voříšek Symphony in D major, Op. 24.
Schubert Symphony No. 2 in B flat major, D125. **West German Sinfonia / Dirk Joeres.** IMP Classics Ⓜ PCD1052 (57 minutes: DDD: 8/94). Recorded 1989-90.   ⒼⒼ
Voříšek was a lively and intelligent composer, admired by Beethoven and Schubert among many others in his circle of Viennese friends. These are fresh and vigorous performances, sometimes rather too much so for their own good. The opening *Allegros* of both symphonies are taken at high speed.

An immediate consequence is that not only do the main themes lose a little of their lyrical charm, but some of the accompanying figuration, whose role is to add their own tension, becomes hardly more than gabbled. Matters improve: Schubert's *Andante* variations are charmingly played, with tempo now easy and affable; the minuet has a good thrust to it; and the finale whirls along with genuine liveliness and not merely speed. Similarly, Vořišek's Symphony has a delightfully played *Andante*, a *Scherzo* (unusually, in 9/8) that drives forward with positively Schubertian energy, and a vigorously handled finale. The recording is pleasantly sharp and clear, with a good ear for the clarity and invention of texture that mark both works: the beautiful viola and cello melody at the start of Vořišek's *Andante* is exactly judged, as is the often quite elaborate string figuration contrasting with more drawn out wind phrases later on.

Additional recommendation ...
...Symphony in D major. **Arriaga** Symphony in D major Los esclavos felices – Overture. **Scottish Chamber Orchestra / Sir Charles Mackerras.** Hyperion Ⓕ CDA66800 (58 minutes: DDD: 11/95). *Gramophone Editor's choice. See review under Arriaga; refer to the Index to Reviews.* ⒼⒼ

New review
Vořišek Fantasia in C major, Op. 12. Piano Sonata in B flat major, Op. 20. Variations in B flat major, Op. 19. Six Impromptus, Op. 7. **Artur Pizarro** (pf). Collins Classics Ⓕ 1458-2 (74 minutes: DDD: 10/95). Recorded 1994.
This disc covers the same ground as Radoslav Kvapil's Unicorn-Kanchana recording, with four rewarding and enjoyable works by one of the most talented of the Bohemians who migrated to Vienna and came under the spell of both Beethoven and Schubert. On the whole, Pizarro is more reflective, less classically inclined than Kvapil, and he emphasizes the romantic adumbrations in the very striking *Fantasia*. However, he sensibly does not overplay the sonata, which owes a good deal to the manner of middle-period Beethoven but, not surprisingly, lacks the charge of energy. With the *Impromptus*, there are suggestions of Schubert, but (though the captivating A major piece meets Schubert on his own ground) comparisons between talent and genius are hardly fair. Rather than emphasize them, one may hope to do Vořišek better justice by suggesting that the harmonic simplicity is part of these pieces' charm. The *Variations* are less interesting, though occasionally – in the sombre minor-key variation, even in the graceful *Siciliano* – there are signs that Vořišek was ready to move beyond this fairly conventional but well-turned manner in favour of something more enterprising. His death from tuberculosis at the age of 34 in 1825 was tragic: he might well have found a more distinctive voice in the coming decade.

Additional recommendation ...
...Fantasia. Piano Sonata. Variations. Six Impromptus. **Radoslav Kvapil** (pf). Unicorn-Kanchana Ⓕ DKPCD9145 (72 minutes: DDD: 6/94).

Ladislav Vycpálek   Czechoslovakian 1882-1969

Suggested listening ...
...Cantata of the Last Things of Man, Op. 16[a]. Czech Requiem, Op. 24[b]. [a]**Drahomíra Tikalová,** [b]**Mariana Reháková** (sops); [b]**Marie Mrázová** (contr); [a]**Ladislav Mráz,** [b]**Theodor Srubař** (bars); **Czech Philharmonic Chorus and Orchestra / Karel Ančerl.** Supraphon Historical 11 1933-2* (7/93). Ⓖ

Richard Wagner   German 1813-1883

New review
Wagner Rienzi – Overture. Tristan und Isolde – Prelude; Liebestod[a]. Die Meistersinger von Nürnberg – Prelude. Siegfried Idyll. Parsifal – Prelude. Lohengrin – Prelude. [a]**Jane Eaglen** (sop); **London Classical Players / Roger Norrington.** EMI Ⓕ CDC5 55479-2 (64 minutes: DDD: 11/95). Recorded 1994.
The born-again New Queen's Hall Orchestra and Barry Wordsworth were first in the field with a whole disc of period instrument Wagner. The London Classical Players and Norrington have, of course, been playing together rather longer, and it shows nearly everywhere. How much of the extra polish and precision of the LCP's finished product is due to editing is not the issue. That Norrington is much more a man of the theatre is immediately apparent from the anticipatory hush of the first bars of *Rienzi*, and generally from the greater contrasts of tempo and dynamics (and the extra brass bite and brilliance). From Norrington's group, there are also more revelations of texture (apart from the tuba) and timbre. In matters of tempo, Norrington's disc, true to form, sets the cat among the pigeons. There's a *Meistersinger* Prelude almost two minutes shorter than the average. Perhaps its most startling feature (once you have adjusted to the slimline Masters) is a sudden increase in speed at 5'55" where, as Ernest Newman put it, "the Masters sweep the apprentices aside, [the Masters' theme] thundering out in trumpets and trombones". Norrington's way here would seem to propose that the Masters are simply joining in with the fun. Even more controversial will be the *Tristan* Prelude. For this 6/8, Norrington has two slow beats in the bar (all others, six moderate ones) and he

ignores Felix Mottl's injunction to remain in tempo up to the climax. The *Parsifal* Prelude is a human, immediate and musical experience (look elsewhere for mystical refulgence and long-drawn reverence). And the *Siegfried Idyll* is a real charmer; less of the traditional fireside warmth (the cradle song almost dances), but considerably more than usual woodland magic (period woodwind coming into their own). In short, vintage Norrington.

Additional recommendations ...

...Götterdämmerung – Siegfried's Rhine Journey; Siegfried's Funeral March. Parsifal – Prelude, Act 1. Siegfried – Forest Murmurs. Tristan und Isolde – Prelude and Liebestod. Die Walküre – Ride of the Valkyries. **Philharmonia Orchestra / Yuri Simonov.** Collins Classics Ⓕ 1207-2 (68 minutes: DDD: 10/91).

...Götterdämmerung – Dawn and Siegfried's Rhine Journey. Siegfried Idyll. **NBC Symphony Orchestra / Arturo Toscanini.** RCA Victor Gold Seal Ⓜ GD60296* (69 minutes: ADD: 11/92).

...Overtures – Rienzi; Tannhäuser. Preludes – Lohengrin, Act 1; Tristan und Isolde, Act 3; Die Meistersinger von Nürnberg, Act 1; Parsifal, Act 1 and close of Act 3. **New Queen's Hall Orchestra / Barry Wordsworth.** Eye of the Storm (special price) EOS5001 (two discs: 144 minutes: DDD: 6/95). Set includes two performances of each work together with an illustrated talk on "The Instruments". ✍

...Der Fliegende Holländer – Overture. Tannhäuser – Overture. Lohengrin – Prelude, Act 1; Prelude, Act 3. Die Meistersinger von Nürnberg – Prelude, Act 1. Tristan und Isolde – Prelude and Liebestod. **Chicago Symphony Orchestra / Daniel Barenboim.** Teldec Ⓕ 4509-99595-2 (63 minutes: DDD. 4/96). *Selected by Soundings.*

Wagner Die Meistersinger von Nürnberg – Prelude, Act 1[a]; Da zu dir der Heiland kam[b]; Wach auf![b]; Morgenlich leuchtend[b]. Der Fliegende Holländer – Overture[c]. Tannhäuser – Overture[d]; Entry of the Guests[e]. Lohengrin – Prelude, Act 3[f]. Götterdämmerung[g] – Hier sitz' ich zur Wacht; Hoiho! Ihr Gibichsmannen. [b]**Tiana Lemnitz** (sop); [b]**Torsten Ralf** (ten); [g]**Herbert Janssen** (bar); [g]**Ludwig Weber** (bass); [bg]**Royal Opera House Chorus, Covent Garden; London Philharmonic Orchestra / Sir Thomas Beecham.** Dutton Laboratories mono Ⓜ CDLX7007* (69 minutes: ADD: 6/94). Item marked [a] from Columbia LX557 (12/36), [b]LX645/6 (10/37, recorded live in the Royal Opera House, Covent Garden in 1936), [c]LX732/3 (9/38), [d]LX768/9 (2/39), [e]LX733 (9/38), [f]LX482 (5/36), [g]LX636/7 (9/37. Royal Opera House, 1936).　　ⒼⒼ

Beecham was a lifelong Wagnerian and these superlative performances make one regret all the more that he never recorded a Wagner opera complete in the studio. The greatest 'might have been' would be a complete Covent Garden *Die Meistersinger* of 1936, when a superb cast had been assembled: given that the recording facilities were there to make the sides included here, one wonders why the rest of the opera wasn't also committed to disc. A month after those excerpts were taken live Beecham went into the studio to record his masterly account of the Prelude to Act 1. Here the whole panoply of the score is set expectantly before us. The Royal Opera House Chorus sing well, though not exceptionally so. Ralf, a compact, musical tenor sings a pleasing, poetic Prize song, for which he duly receives the crown from Lemnitz's nonpareil of an Eva, perfect trill and all. Nine days after the *Meistersinger* extracts were made, EMI were back at Covent Garden for *Götterdämmerung*. All that officially resulted were two solos, in which we hear Weber as an implacable then fiendishly celebratory Hagen. The rest of the items demonstrate Beecham's ability to inject zestful conviction into pre-*Ring* Wagner without ever overblowing the sound, as so often happens today. These readings also confirm the virtuoso calibre of his pre-war LPO, who play with a precision and character that leap from the loudspeakers with amazing freshness and vitality in these faultless transfers, not a 78rpm surface to be heard, a tribute to Dutton Laboratories' skills in using the CEDAR system to best advantage.

Additional recommendations ...

...Die Meistersinger von Nürnberg – Prelude, Act 1. *Coupled with works by* **Brahms, Shostakovich, R. Strauss** and **Smetana** The Solti Orchestral Project, Carnegie Hall / **Sir Georg Solti.** Decca Ⓕ 444 458-2DH (77 minutes: DDD: 12/94). *See review in the Collections section; refer to the Index to Reviews.*　　Ⓖ

...Die Meistersinger von Nürnberg – Prelude, Act 1. Die Walküre – Ride of the Valkyries. Götterdämmerung – Siegfried's Funeral March; Dawn and Siegfried's Rhine Journey. Tannhäuser – Overture; Venusberg Music. Lohengrin – Prelude, Act 3. **Royal Concertgebouw Orchestra / Riccardo Chailly.** Decca Ⓕ 448 155-2DH (64 minutes: DDD: 3/96).

Wagner Tannhäuser – Overture. Siegfried Idyll. Tristan und Isolde – Prelude and Liebestod[a]. [a]**Jessye Norman** (sop); **Vienna Philharmonic Orchestra / Herbert von Karajan.** DG Ⓕ 423 613-2GH (54 minutes: DDD: 8/88). Text and translation included. Recorded live in 1987.　　ⒼⒼ

For the Wagner specialist who has a complete *Tannhäuser* and *Tristan* on the shelves, this disc involves some duplication. Even so, it is not hard to make room for such performances as are heard here. For the non-specialist, the programme provides a good opportunity for a meeting halfway, the common ground between Master and general music-lover being the *Siegfried Idyll*. This offers 20 minutes of delight in the play of musical ideas, structured and yet impulsive, within a sustained mood of gentle affection. The orchestration is something of a miracle, and it can rarely have been heard to better advantage than in this recording, where the ever-changing textures are so clearly displayed and where from every section of the orchestra the sound is of such great loveliness. It comes as a welcome contrast to the *Tannhäuser* Overture, with its big tunes and *fortissimos*, the whole orchestra surging in a frank simulation of physical passion. A further contrast is to follow in the *Tristan* Prelude, where again Karajan and his players are at their best in their feeling for texture and their control of pulse. Jessye Norman, singing the *Liebestod* with tenderness and vibrant opulence of tone, brings the recital to an end. There is scarcely a single reminder that it was recorded live.

Additional recommendations ...

...Siegfried Idyll. Lohengrin – Preludes, Acts 1 and 3. Die Meistersinger von Nürnberg – Prelude, Act 1. Die Walküre – Ride of the Valkyries; Wotan's Farewell and Magic Fire Music[a]. [a]**John Tomlinson** (bass); **Philharmonia Orchestra / Francesco d'Avalos.** ASV Ⓕ CDDCA666 (64 minutes: DDD: 3/90).

...Opera Choruses – Der Fliegende Holländer; Tannhauser; Lohengrin; Die Meistersinger von Nürnberg; Götterdämmerung; Parsifal. **Bayreuth Festival Chorus and Orchestra / Wilhelm Pitz.** DG Privilege Ⓑ 429 169-2GR* (53 minutes: ADD: 4/90).

...Rienzi – Overture. Tannhäuser – Overture; Venusberg Music. Die Meistersinger von Nürnberg – Prelude, Act 1. Lohengrin – Prelude Act 3. Der Fliegende Holländer – Overture. **Orchestra of the Metropolitan Opera, New York / James Levine.** DG Ⓕ 435 874-2GH (60 minutes: DDD: 10/93).

...Tannhäuser – Overture[a]. Lohengrin – Prelude, Act 1. Die Walküre – Ride of the Valkyries[a]. Götterdämmerung – Prelude and Siegfried's Rhine Journey[a]; Siegfried's Funeral March; Immolation Scene[b]. Der Fliegende Holländer – Overture[a]. Tristan und Isolde – Prelude and Liebestod[c]. Die Meistersinger von Nürnberg[a] – Preludes – Acts 1 and 3; Dance of the Apprentices. Parsifal – Prelude and Good Friday Music[c]. [b]**Kirsten Flagstad** (sop); [a]**Vienna Philharmonic Orchestra;** [b]**Philharmonia Orchestra;** [c]**Berlin Philharmonic Orchestra / Wilhelm Furtwängler.** EMI Références mono Ⓜ CHS7 64935-2* (two discs: 144 minutes: ADD: 4/94).

...Rienzi – Overture. Tannhäuser – Venusberg Music. Tristan und Isolde – Prelude and Liebestod. Die Meistersinger von Nürnberg – Prelude, Act 3; Dance of the Apprentices; Entry of the Masters. Siegfried Idyll. **New York Philharmonic Orchestra / Sir John Barbirolli.** Dutton Laboratories mono Ⓕ CDSJB1001* (76 minutes: ADD: 3/95). ⒼⒼ

...Tristan und Isolde – Doch nun von Tristan![a]; Isolde! Tristan! geliebter[b]; Mild und leise. **Martha Mödl** (sop); [ab]**Johanna Blatter** (mez); [b]**Wolfgang Windgassen** (ten); **Berlin City Opera Orchestra / Artur Rother.** Teldec mono Ⓜ 4509-95516-2* (64 minutes: ADD: 5/95).

Wagner Rienzi. **René Kollo** (ten) Cola Rienzi; **Siv Wennberg** (sop) Irene; **Janis Martin** (sop) Adriano; **Theo Adam** (bass) Paolo Orsini; **Nikolaus Hillebrand** (bass) Steffano Colonna; **Siegfried Vogel** (bass) Raimondo; **Peter Schreier** (ten) Baroncelli; **Günther Leib** (bass) Cecco del Vecchio; **Ingeborg Springer** (sop) Messenger of Peace; **Leipzig Radio Chorus; Dresden State Opera Chorus; Dresden Staatskapelle / Heinrich Hollreiser.** EMI Ⓜ CMS7 63980-2 (three discs: 225 minutes: ADD: 2/92). Notes, text and translation included. From SLS990 (11/76). Recorded 1974-6.

Rienzi is grand opera with a vengeance. Political imperatives count for more than mere human feelings, and politics means ceremony as well as warfare: marches, ballet music and extended choruses are much in evidence, while even the solo arias often have the rhetorical punch of political harangues. It could all be an enormous bore. Yet the young Wagner, basing his work on Bulwer Lytton's story of the tragic Roman tribune, did manage to move beyond mere tub-thumping into a degree of intensity that – for those with ears to hear – prefigures the mature genius to come. In the end, Rienzi himself is more than just a political animal, and the existential anguish of Tannhäuser, Tristan and even Amfortas glimmers in the distance. It would be idle to pretend that this performance is ideal in every respect, either musically, or as a recording. But its virtues outweigh its weaknesses by a considerable margin. Siv Wennberg was not in best voice at the time, but the other principals, notably René Kollo and Janis Martin, bring commendable stamina and conviction to their demanding roles. Above all the conductor Heinrich Hollreiser prevents the more routine material from sounding merely mechanical, and ensures that the whole work has a truly Wagnerian sweep and fervour. Moreover, it is the only complete recording in the current edition of *The **Gramophone** Classical Catalogue*.

Wagner Der fliegende Holländer. **Robert Hale** (bass-bar) Holländer; **Hildegard Behrens** (sop) Senta; **Kurt Rydl** (bass) Daland; **Josef Protschka** (ten) Erik; **Iris Vermillion** (mez) Mary; **Uwe Heilmann** (ten) Steuermann; **Vienna State Opera Concert Choir; Vienna Philharmonic Orchestra / Christoph von Dohnányi.** Decca Ⓕ 436 418-2DHO2 (two discs: 145 minutes: DDD: 4/94). Notes, text and translation included. Recorded 1991. *Gramophone Editor's choice.* Ⓖ

Singers, conductor, chorus, orchestra and engineers combine to make this the most successful recording of the work to date. In consequence its revolutionary character is fully realized. With the Vienna Philharmonic responding to Dohnányi's precise and energizing beat from start to finish the sea does really seem to course through the score as Wagner intended. Dohnányi emphasizes the raw, even untutored sound of much of the orchestration, giving the wind and brass the prominence they deserve. Taut, springy rhythms abound from the Overture onwards. He opts for the three-act version and the full ending. Hale is an exemplary Dutchman and sings with great depth and understanding. This is evident throughout a masterly traversal of his long monologue, where the required torment in the tone is revealed to the full. Behrens captures Senta's single-minded passion and infatuation, singing the quieter passages with refined sensitivity, the forceful ones with fearless attack; and satisfaction extends to the lesser roles. The chorus are superb as sailors, ghost crew and townspeople, singing with firm tone and exact attack. Nothing here is left unconsidered yet, amazingly, for the most part a real sense of the theatre is achieved throughout. For that we have to thank the Decca team. Balance, depth, perspectives all seem blessedly natural; undoctored and inevitable, so that one is able to take the sound-picture for granted.

Additional recommendations ...

...**Soloists; Bayreuth Festival Chorus and Orchestra / Woldemar Nelsson.** Philips Ⓜ 434 599-2PH2 (two discs: 134 minutes: DDD: 10/92).

...**Soloists; Bayreuth Festival Chorus and Orchestra / Karl Böhm.** DG Ⓜ 437 710-2GX2 (two discs: 134 minutes: ADD: 8/93).

...**Soloists; Austrian Radio Chorus and Symphony Orchestra / Pinchas Steinberg.** Naxos Ⓢ 8 660025/6 (two discs: 139 minutes: DDD: 9/93). *Gramophone Editor's choice.*

...**Soloists; Bayreuth Festival Chorus and Orchestra / Wolfgang Sawallisch.** Philips Ⓜ 442 103-2PM2 (two discs: 124 minutes: ADD: 9/94).

...**Soloists; Berlin Deutsche Oper Chorus and Orchestra / Franz Konwitschny.** Berlin Classics Ⓕ BC2097-2 (two discs: 141 minutes: ADD: 9/94).

...**Soloists; Bavarian State Opera Chorus and Orchestra / Clemens Krauss.** Preiser mono Ⓕ 90250* (two discs: 143 minutes: ADD: 6/96).

...**Der fliegende Holländer**[a]. **Die Meistersinger von Nürnberg – Was duftet.Wahn! Wahn!**[b] **Uberall Wahn!**[c]. **Soloists;** [a]**Bayreuth Festival Chorus and Orchestra / Richard Kraus;** [c]**Joel Berlund** (bar); [b]**Ludwig Hofmann** (bass); [b]**Berlin State Opera Orchestra / Franz Alfred Schmidt;** [c]**Royal Stockholm Orchestra / Nils Grevillius.** Preiser mono Ⓕ 90232* (two discs: 153 minutes: ADD: 6/96).

Wagner Tannhäuser (Paris version). **Plácido Domingo** (ten) Tannhäuser; **Cheryl Studer** (sop) Elisabeth; **Andreas Schmidt** (bar) Wolfram; **Agnes Baltsa** (mez) Venus; **Matti Salminen** (bass) Hermann; **William Pell** (ten) Walther; **Kurt Rydl** (bass) Biterolf; **Clemens Biber** (ten) Heinrich; **Oskar Hillebrandt** (bass) Reinmar; **Barbara Bonney** (sop) Shepherd Boy; **Chorus of the Royal Opera House, Covent Garden; Philharmonia Orchestra / Giuseppe Sinopoli.** DG Ⓕ 427 625-2GH3 (three discs: 176 minutes: DDD: 9/89). Notes, text and translation included. Ⓖ

Plácido Domingo's Tannhäuser is a success in almost every respect. He evokes the erotic passion of the Venusberg scene and brings to it just the right touch of nervous energy. This is boldly contrasted with the desperation and bitterness of the Rome Narration after the hero's fruitless visit to the Pope seeking forgiveness: Domingo's description of how Tannhäuser avoided every earthly delight on his pilgrimage is delivered with total conviction. In between he berates the slightly prissy attitude of his fellow knights on the Wartburg with the dangerous conceit of someone who knows a secret delight that they will never enjoy in their measured complacency. His tenor must be the steadiest and most resplendent ever to have tackled the part, although his German is far from idiomatic with several vowel sounds distorted. Baltsa also has some problems with her German, but she has the range and attack, particularly in the upper register, for an awkwardly lying part. Here comparisons have to be made with Christa Ludwig for Solti (listed below), in one of her most successful assumptions. She is not only more familiar with the role but also has the more voluptuous voice and is superbly seconded by Solti; which brings us to Sinopoli. It is obviously his concern throughout to bring out every last ounce of the drama in the piece, both in terms of orchestral detail, which receives very special attention from the Overture, given a big, full-blooded reading, onwards, but also in his awareness in this opera of the longer line, often sustained by the upper strings. The Philharmonia's violins respond with their most eloquent playing. The kind of frisson Sinopoli offers is evident in the anticipatory excitement at the start of Act 2 and the iron control he maintains in the big ensemble later in the same act. Cheryl Studer's secure, beautiful voice has no difficulty coping with Sinopoli's deliberate tempos. She takes her part with total conviction, both vocal and interpretative, phrasing with constant intelligence. Andreas Schmidt is a mellifluous, concerned Wolfram, Salminen a rugged, characterful Landgrave and Barbara Bonney an ideally fresh Shepherd Boy. As knights, ladies and pilgrims the Covent Garden Chorus sing with consistent beauty of sound, and have been sensibly balanced with the orchestra. As Sinopoli has chosen to conduct the Paris version, the Solti set is its main rival. It has always been one of Solti's most recommendable opera recordings, and in its CD format it remains a formidable achievement. Domingo and Studer, however, incline one towards this version, as does the wide range of the finely engineered recording, which makes the excellent Decca seem just a shade dated.

Additional recommendation ...

...**Soloists; Vienna Boys' Choir; Vienna State Opera Chorus; Vienna Philharmonic Orchestra / Sir Georg Solti.** Decca Ⓕ 414 581-2DH3 (three discs: DDD: 2/86).

Wagner Lohengrin. **Paul Frey** (ten) Lohengrin; **Cheryl Studer** (sop) Elsa of Brabant; **Gabriele Schnaut** (sop) Ortrud; **Ekkehard Wlaschiha** (bar) Telramund; **Manfred Schenk** (bass) King Henry; **Eike Wilm Schulte** (bar) Herald; **Bayreuth Festival Chorus and Orchestra / Peter Schneider.** Philips Ⓜ 434 602-2PH4 (four discs: 212 minutes: DDD: 10/92). Recorded 1990.

New review

Wagner Lohengrin. **James King** (ten) Lohengrin; **Gundula Janowitz** (sop) Elsa; **Dame Gwyneth Jones** (sop) Ortrud; **Thomas Stewart** (bar) Telramund; **Karl Ridderbusch** (bass) King Henry; **Gerd**

Nienstedt (bass) Herald; **Bavarian Radio Chorus and Symphony Orchestra / Rafael Kubelík.** DG
Ⓜ 449 591-2GX3 (three discs: 222 minutes: ADD: 8/96). Notes, text and translation included.
From 2720 036 (12/71).

Schneider's is a splendidly absorbing performance of *Lohengrin*. This underrated conductor provides
a straightforward, no-nonsense reading in the best Kapellmeister tradition, avoiding the extremes of
tempo interpretation of some more highly-powered conductors. He obtains playing and singing of the
highest calibre from the Bayreuth orchestra and chorus, sustains the long and sometimes tedious-
seeming paragraphs of Acts 1 and 2 without ever allowing boredom to intervene, and brings
extraordinary tension to such forward-looking scenes as Lohengrin's arrival, the Ortrud-Telramund
dialogue and the psychologically intense duet for Elsa and Lohengrin in Act 3. Elsa was one of the
roles with which Studer made her name on the international scene; she sings it here once more with
refulgent tone, understanding of the text and comprehension of Elsa's dreamy then troubled
personality. Particularly affecting is her desperate appeal to Lohengrin at the end of Act 2. Paul Frey
is a sensitive, chivalrous Lohengrin, even if his voice hasn't quite the Heldentenor strength of some of
his predecessors. Evil is reasonably well represented. Wlaschiha is a vital and nasty Telramund, keenly
projecting the character's chip-on-the-shoulder malevolence of the words. Schnaut has an imposing,
powerful soprano although more could have been made of the words than she achieves. Schenk is a
well-routined King, Schulte a superb Herald. Incidentally, Schneider observes the traditional
(Wagner's) cut just before Lohengrin's Farewell, although the passage is printed in full in the booklet.
This set is well worth considering in a sparse recommendable field of available versions.

The attributes of Kubelík's *Lohengrin*, which appears for the first time on CD, have been
underestimated. It will hold your interest from first to last, not least thanks to Kubelík's masterly
overview. Not only does he successfully hold together all the disparate strands of the sprawling work,
he also imparts to them a sense of inner excitement through his close attention to the small notes and
phrases that so often delineate character in this score and through his vital control of the large
ensembles. He is helped inestimably by the Bavarian Radio forces – gloriously singing strings,
characterful winds, trenchant, involving chorus – of which he was, in 1971, a beloved chief. There's
never a dull moment in his vivid, theatrical *Lohengrin*. The recording imparts a suitably spacious
atmosphere to the piece but also places the principals up front where they should be except when
distancing is required – as at Lohengrin's first appearance and at the moment when Elsa appears on
the balcony to address the night breezes. Janowitz's Elsa is one of the set's major assets. Pure in tone,
imaginative in phrasing, she catches the ear from her first entry, very much suggesting Elsa's
vulnerability. Later she eloquently conveys her deep feelings in the love duet, followed by her voicing
of all the doubts that beset her character. King's Lohengrin is more ordinary; today we would be
grateful for such solid, musical and well-judged singing. Few if any Lohengrins can sing the passage
starting "Höchstes Vertraun" (third disc, track 5) with anything like King's true tone and powerful
conviction. Though not as detailed or subtle in his colouring of the text as some, Thomas Stewart
sings a sturdy Telramund, managing the high tessitura with consummate ease. He is horribly plausible
in his complaints against Elsa. This portrayal discloses him as a grossly undervalued singer. Dame
Gwyneth Jones's portrayal, taken all-round, is reasonably convincing despite turning a vibrato that
might flatteringly be called opulent into something more objectionable. Her Ortrud registers high on
the scale of vicious malevolence in the part. The difficulty, as it always has been with this intelligent
artist, is that the subtlety evinced in quiet passages is vitiated when the tone comes under pressure –
but some Ortruds today are far more guilty in that respect than Jones. As King Henry, Ridderbusch
offers a judicious blend of sympathy and authority dispensed in fluent, warm tone. Nienstedt makes
the Herald's pronouncements moments to savour. The chorus are nothing short of superb. So, this
makes an irresistible bid for recommendation. It is well recorded, sounding wholly resplendent and as
cogently conducted as any of its rivals.

Additional recommendations ...

...**Soloists; Vienna State Opera Chorus; Vienna Philharmonic Orchestra / Sir Georg Solti.** Decca
Ⓕ 421 053-2DH4 (four discs: 223 minutes: DDD: 10/87).

...**Soloists; Vienna State Opera Chorus; Vienna Philharmonic Orchestra / Rudolf Kempe.** EMI
Ⓔ CDS7 49017-2 (three discs: 219 minutes: ADD: 2/88).

...**Soloists; Bayreuth Festival Chorus and Orchestra / Joseph Keilberth.** Teldec Historic Series mono
Ⓜ 4509-93674-2* (four discs: 220 minutes: ADD: 10/94).

...**Soloists; Cologne Radio Chorus; North German Radio Chorus and Symphony Orchestra / Wilhelm
Schüchter.** EMI Références mono Ⓜ CHS5 65517-2* (three discs: 197 minutes: ADD: 12/95).

Wagner Tristan und Isolde. **Wolfgang Windgassen** (ten) Tristan; **Birgit Nilsson** (sop) Isolde; **Christa
Ludwig** (mez) Brangäne; **Eberhard Waechter** (bar) Kurwenal; **Martti Talvela** (bass) King Marke;
Claude Heater (ten) Melot; **Peter Schreier** (ten) Sailor; **Erwin Wohlfahrt** (ten) Shepherd; **Gerd
Nienstedt** (bass) Helmsman; **Bayreuth Festival Chorus and Orchestra / Karl Böhm.** Philips Ⓜ 434
425-2PH3 (three discs: 219 minutes: ADD: 10/92). From DG 419 889-2GH3 (7/88). Notes, text
and translation included. Recorded live in 1966. ⓖⓖⓖ

New review

Wagner Tristan und Isolde. **Siegfried Jerusalem** (ten) Tristan; **Waltraud Meier** (mez) Isolde;
Marjana Lipovšek (mez) Brangäne; **Matti Salminen** (bass) King Marke; **Falk Struckmann** (bar)
Kurwenal; **Johan Botha** (ten) Melot; **Peter Maus** (ten) Shepherd; **Roman Trekel** (bar) Helmsman;

Uwe Heilmann (ten) Sailor; **Berlin State Opera Chorus; Berlin Philharmonic Orchestra / Daniel Barenboim.** Teldec Ⓕ 4509-94568-2 (four discs: 235 minutes: DDD: 9/95). Notes, text and translation included.

Böhm's recording is a live Bayreuth performance of distinction, for on stage are the most admired Tristan and Isolde of their time, and in the pit the 72-year-old conductor directs a performance which is unflagging in its passion and energy. Böhm has a striking way in the Prelude and *Liebestod* of making the swell of passion seem like the movement of a great sea, sometimes with gentle motion, sometimes with the breaking of the mightiest of waves. Nilsson characterizes strongly and her voice with its marvellous cleaving-power can also soften quite beautifully. Windgassen's heroic performance in the Third Act is in some ways the crown of his achievements on record, even though the voice has dried and aged a little. Christa Ludwig is the ideal Brangäene, Waechter a suitably-forthright Kurwenal, and Talvela an expressive, noble-voiced Marke. Orchestra and chorus are at their finest.

Over several seasons of conducting the work at Bayreuth, Barenboim has by now thoroughly mastered the pacing and shaping of the score as a unified entity. Even more important he has peered into the depths of both its construction and meaning, emerging with answers that satisfy on almost all counts, most tellingly so in the melancholic adumbration of Isolde's thoughts during her narration, in the sadly eloquent counterpoint of bass clarinet, lower strings and cor anglais underpinning King Marke's lament, and in the searingly tense support to Tristan's second hallucination. These are but the most salient moments in a reading that thoughtfully and unerringly reveals the inner parts of this astounding score. The obverse of this caring manner is a certain want of spontaneity, and a tendency to become a shade self-regarding. You occasionally miss the overwhelming force of Furtwängler's metaphysical account or the immediacy and excitement of Böhm's famous live Bayreuth reading but the very mention of those conductors suggests that Barenboim can live in their world and survive the comparions with his own perfectly valid interpretation. Besides, he has the most gloriously spacious yet well-focused recording so far of this opera and an orchestra not only familiar with his ways but ready to execute them in a disciplined and sensitive manner. The recording also takes account of spatial questions, in particular the placing of the horns offstage at the start of Act 2 and the approach of the subsidiary characters after Tristan's death in Act 3.

Salminen delivers a classic account of Marke's anguished reproaches to Tristan, his singing at once sonorous, dignified and reaching to the heart, a reading on a par with that of his fellow-countryman Talvela for Böhm. Meier's Isolde is a vitally wrought, verbally alert reading, which catches much of the venom of Act 1, the visceral excitement of Act 2, the lambent utterance of the Liebestod. Nothing she does is unmusical, everything is keenly intelligent, yet possibly her tone is too narrow for the role. Lipovšek's Brangäne tends to slide and swim in an ungainly fashion, sounding at times definitely overparted. Listening to Ludwig (Böhm) only serves to emphasize Lipovšek's deficiencies. Then it is often hard on the new set to tell Isolde and Brangäne apart, so alike can be their timbre. As with his partner, Jerusalem sings his role with immaculate musicality; indeed he may be the most accurate Tristan on disc where note values are concerned, one also consistently attentive to dynamics and long-breathed phrasing. On the other hand, although he puts a deal of feeling into his interpretation, he hasn't quite the intensity of utterance of either Windgassen (Böhm), or, even more, Suthaus (Furtwängler). His actual timbre is dry and occasionally rasping: in vocal terms alone Suthaus is in a class of his own. Yet, even with reservations about the Isolde and Tristan, this is a version that will undoubtedly hold a high place in my, or indeed any, survey of this work, for which one performance can never hope to tell the whole story. As for more mundane matters, Böhm is available at mid price on three discs as compared with Barenboim at full price on four.

Additional recommendations ...

...Soloists; **Bavarian Radio Chorus and Symphony Orchestra / Leonard Bernstein.** Philips Ⓕ 438 241-2PH4 (four discs: 266 minutes: DDD).

...Soloists; **Chorus of the Royal Opera House, Covent Garden; Philharmonia Orchestra / Wilhelm Furtwängler.** EMI mono Ⓕ CDS7 47322-8* (four discs: 236 minutes: ADD: 5/86).　　　ⒼⒼⒼ

...Soloists; **Leipzig Radio Chorus; Dresden Staatskapelle / Carlos Kleiber.** DG Ⓕ 413 315-2GH4 (four discs: 235 minutes: DDD: 11/86).

...Soloists; **Chorus of the Royal Opera House, Covent Garden; London Philharmonic Orchestra / Fritz Reiner, Sir Thomas Beecham.** EMI Références mono Ⓜ CHS7 64037-2* (three discs: 212 minutes: ADD: 1/92).

...Soloists; **Welsh National Opera Chorus and Orchestra / Sir Reginald Goodall.** Decca Grand Opera Ⓜ 443 682-2DMO4 (four discs: 259 minutes: DDD: 5/95).

...excerpts. Soloists; **Vienna State Opera Chorus and Orchestra / Wilhelm Furtwängler.** Koch Schwann mono Ⓜ 314612* (two discs: 140 minutes: ADD: 5/95).

...Soloists; **Bavarian State Opera Chorus; Bavarian State Orchestra / Hans Knappertsbusch.** Orfeo mono Ⓕ C355943D (three discs: 232 minutes: ADD: 5/95).　　　ⒼⒼ

...Soloists; **Berlin State Opera Chorus; Berlin Philharmonic Orchestra / Daniel Barenboim.** Teldec Ⓕ 4509-94568-2 (four discs: 235 minutes: DDD: 9/95).

Wagner Die Meistersinger von Nürnberg. **Bernd Weikl** (bar) Hans Sachs; **Ben Heppner** (ten) Walther; **Cheryl Studer** (sop) Eva; **Kurt Moll** (bass) Pogner; **Siegfried Lorenz** (bar) Beckmesser; **Deon van der Walt** (ten) David; **Cornelia Kallisch** (contr) Magdalene; **Hans-Joachim Ketelsen** (bar) Kothner; **Michael Schade** (ten) Vogelgesang; **Hans Wilbrink** (bar) Nachtigall; **Ulrich Ress**

(ten) Zorn; **Hermann Sapell** (bar) Eisslinger; **Roland Wagenführer** (ten) Moser; **Rainer Büse** (bass)
Ortel; **Guido Götzen** (bass) Schwarz; **Friedmann Kunder** (bass) Foltz; **René Pape** (bass)
Nightwatchman; **Bavarian State Opera Chorus; Bavarian State Orchestra / Wolfgang Sawallisch.**
EMI Ⓕ CDS5 55142-2 (four discs: 257 minutes: DDD: 8/94). Notes, text and translation
included. Recorded 1993.

It is, surprisingly, 19 years since we had a new recording of Wagner's great comedy, although in the
meantime several old and/or historic sets have been reissued or have appeared for the first time. We
needed a new, carefully prepared performance employing modern technology, and here we have it. It
is very much a version for today – profoundly musical, as it was bound to be under Sawallisch, sung
with a consistent beauty of sound perhaps encountered in no other version, and recorded truthfully
and spaciously. Anybody coming to the work for the first time, and wanting a version backed by
modern sound, will find it a sensible choice, a performance for the most part measuring up to the
score's many demands on its interpreters. Working with what were then his own Bavarian State Opera
forces, Sawallisch obtains singing and playing on the highest level of achievement, observant of detail,
rich in texture, sure in pacing and – very important in this score – anxious to move forward where
there is any danger of the music seeming over-extended, as in the recital of the tones and the Act 2
episode of Beckmesser's courting. Sawallisch's reading also catches the warmth that pervades the
whole opera, yet is also successful in deftly projecting its comedy. It must be said, however, that with
Sawallisch the earth doesn't move, the spirit is seldom lifted as it should be – and can be, witness
Karajan (until recently, the *Guide*'s top recommendation, now sadly deleted) and Abendroth. On the
other hand, nobody is better than Sawallisch at characterizing the disputes between the Masters in
Act 1, or the pointed humour of the Act 2 Sachs/Beckmesser scene, and much else of that nature is
unobtrusively right. Where the recording itself is concerned, great care has been taken over the
placing of the singers in relation to one another and the correct distancing of the voices where called
for. The balance in relation to the orchestra seems just about ideal. In the modern manner the chorus
is placed a little too far back. Karajan's Dresden account would present a strong challenge to the
newcomer were it available, and the inspiriting, marvellously sincere Hermann Abendroth (what feeling
in every bar here!). None of these is so note perfect, so exact or well considered as the Sawallisch, but
thay all suggest that frisson of a live performance occasionally missing in the new set. Even so,
Sawallisch takes an honoured place in this company and context. His reading is full of thoughtful
apercus and natural flow, and displays a sensible overview of the score. Vocally it will satisfy all but
those with the most demanding tastes in, and/or, long experience in Wagnerian interpretation.

Additional recommendations ...

...**Soloists; Bayreuth Festival Chorus and Orchestra / Herbert von Karajan.** EMI Références mono
Ⓜ CHS7 63500-2* (four discs: 267 minutes: ADD: 9/90). *Gramophone classical 100.*　　ⒼⒼⒼ

...**Soloists; St Hedwig's Cathedral Choir, Berlin; Chorus of the Deutsche Oper, Berlin; Berlin State
Opera Chorus; Berlin Philharmonic Orchestra / Rudolf Kempe.** EMI mono Ⓜ CMS7 64154-2*
(four discs: 260 minutes: ADD: 2/93).　　ⒼⒼ

...**Soloists; Bayreuth Festival Chorus and Orchestra / Hermann Abendroth.** Preiser mono Ⓕ 90174*
(four discs: 262 minutes: ADD: 2/94).

...**Soloists; Vienna State Opera Chorus; Vienna Philharmonic Orchestra / Hans Knappertsbusch.**
Decca Historic Series mono Ⓜ 440 057-2DMO4* (four discs: 266 minutes: ADD: 10/94).

...**Soloists; Vienna State Opera Chorus; Vienna Philharmonic Orchestra / Karl Böhm.** Preiser mono
Ⓕ 90234* (four discs: 266 minutes: AAD: 6/95).

Wagner Der Ring des Nibelungen – spoken introduction with 193 musical examples. **Deryck
Cooke** (narr); **various singers; Vienna Philharmonic Orchestra / Sir Georg Solti.** Decca The Classic
Sound Ⓜ 443 581-2DCS2 (two discs: 141 minutes: ADD: 5/95). Booklet of musical illustrations
included. From RING1/22 (12/68). Recorded 1967.　　ⒼⒼⒼ

Deryck Cooke died, prematurely, in 1976 before he completed his comprehensive study on *The Ring*.
Fortunately, in 1967, Decca had had the foresight to invite him to record this introduction to the cycle.
In this he developed at length his ideas on its leitmotifs using 193 examples, most of them taken from
the Solti recording, and a few made specifically to illustrate a point Cooke was making. Wagner, as
he avers, described the motifs as "melodic moments of feeling", not signposts or tags. He also adds
that their psychological significance and development are of the essence in comprehending *The Ring*,
and divides them into four groups – character, objects, events and emotions – which he then proceeds
to describe, in simple, pungent language, how they are deployed throughout the work. His
straightforward, unfussy method and delivery, so typical of a man quite without egotistical
pretension, enhances one's understanding and, more important, enjoyment of this mighty work. It is
an absorbing and essential adjunct to anybody's recording of the cycle.

Wagner Das Rheingold. **John Tomlinson** (bass) Wotan; **Linda Finnie** (mez) Fricka; **Graham Clark**
(ten) Loge; **Helmut Pampuch** (ten) Mime; **Günter von Kannen** (bar) Alberich; **Eva Johansson** (sop)
Freia; **Kurt Schreibmayer** (ten) Froh; **Bodo Brinkmann** (bar) Donner; **Birgitta Svendén** (mez) Erda;
Matthias Hölle (bass) Fasolt; **Philip Kang** (bass) Fafner; **Hilde Leidland** (sop) Woglinde; **Annette
Küttenbaum** (mez) Wellgunde; **Jane Turner** (mez) Flosshilde; **Bayreuth Festival Orchestra / Daniel
Barenboim.** Teldec Ⓕ 4509-91185-2 (two discs: 149 minutes: DDD: 10/93). Notes, text and
translation included. Recorded live in 1991.

Wagner Die Walküre. **Poul Elming** (ten) Siegmund; **Nadine Secunde** (sop) Sieglinde; **Anne Evans** (sop) Brünnhilde; **John Tomlinson** (bass) Wotan; **Linda Finnie** (mez) Fricka, Siegrune; **Matthias Hölle** (bass) Hunding; **Eva Johansson** (sop) Gerhilde; **Eva-Maria Bundschuh** (sop) Helmwige; **Ruth Floeren** (sop) Ortlinde; **Shirley Close** (mez) Waltraute; **Hebe Dijkstra** (mez) Rossweisse; **Birgitta Svendén** (mez) Grimgerde; **Hitomi Katagiri** (mez) Schwertleite; **Bayreuth Festival Orchestra / Daniel Barenboim.** Teldec Ⓕ 4509 91186-2 (four discs: 233 minutes: DDD: 10/93). Recorded live in 1992.

These are enthralling performances. Tomlinson's volatile Wotan is the most potent reading here. He manages to sing every word with insistent meaning and forceful declamation while maintaining a firm legato. His German is so idiomatic that he might have been speaking the language his whole life and he brings breadth and distinction of phrase to his solos at the close of both operas. Anne Evans has a single, important advantage over other recent Brunnhildes in that her voice is wholly free from wobble and she never makes an ugly sound. Hers is a light, girlish, honest portrayal, sung with unfailing musicality if not with the ultimate insights. Linda Finnie is an articulate, sharp-edged Fricka, and Graham Clark a sparky, incisive Loge. Nadine Secunde's impassioned Sieglinde is matched by the vital, exciting Siegmund of Poul Elming and Matthias Hölle as both Hunding and Fasolt is another of those black basses of which Germany seems to have an inexhaustible supply. The whole of *Das Rheingold* is magnificently conducted by Barenboim, a more expansive Wagnerian than Böhm. By 1991 he had the full measure of its many facets, brought immense authority and power to building its huge climaxes, yet finds all the lightness of touch for the mercurial and/or diaphanous aspects of this amazing score. He has the inestimable advantage of a Bayreuth orchestra at the peak of their form, surpassing – and this says much – even the Metropolitan orchestra for Levine, and Barenboim's reading is more convincing as a whole than Levine's. Similar qualities inform his interpretation of *Die Walküre*. Barenboim has now learnt how to match the epic stature of Wagner's mature works, how to pace them with an overview of the whole and there is an incandescent, metaphysical feeling of a Furwänglerian kind in his treatment of such passages as Wotan's anger and the Valkyrie ride. Again, the orchestra are superb. They are backed by a recording of startling presence and depth, amply capturing the Bayreuth acoustic.

Additional recommendations ...

...Das Rheingold. **Soloists; Vienna Philharmonic Orchestra / Sir Georg Solti.** Decca Ⓕ 414 101-2DH3 (three discs: ADD: 10/84).

...Das Rheingold. **Soloists; Bavarian Radio Symphony Orchestra / Bernard Haitink.** EMI Ⓕ CDS7 49853-2 (two discs: 149 minutes: DDD: 12/89).

...Die Walküre. **Soloists; Bayreuth Festival Orchestra / Clemens Krauss.** Foyer mono Ⓕ 4-CF2008* (four discs: 212 minutes: ADD: 6/88).

...Die Walküre – Act 1. **Soloists; Bayreuth Festival Orchestra / Karl Böhm.** Philips Solo Ⓜ 442 640-2PM (62 minutes: ADD: 7/95).

Wagner Der Ring des Nibelungen.

Das Rheingold. **Theo Adam** (bass-bar) Wotan; **Annelies Burmeister** (mez) Fricka; **Wolfgang Windgassen** (ten) Loge; **Erwin Wohlfahrt** (ten) Mime; **Gustav Neidlinger** (bass) Alberich; **Anja Silja** (sop) Freia; **Hermin Esser** (ten) Froh; **Gerd Nienstedt** (bass) Donner; **Vera Soukupova** (mez) Erda; **Martti Talvela** (bass) Fasolt; **Kurt Boehme** (bass) Fafner; **Dorothea Siebert** (sop) Woglinde; **Helga Dernesch** (sop) Wellgunde; **Ruth Hesse** (mez) Flosshilde; **Bayreuth Festival Chorus and Orchestra / Karl Böhm.** Philips Ⓕ 412 475-2PH2 (two discs: 137 minutes: ADD: 7/85). Notes, text and translation included. Recorded at a performance in the Festspielhaus, Bayreuth in 1967. From 6747 037 (9/73). ⒺⒺⒺ

Die Walküre. **James King** (ten) Siegmund; **Leonie Rysanek** (sop) Sieglinde; **Birgit Nilsson** (sop) Brünnhilde; **Theo Adam** (bass) Wotan; **Annelies Burmeister** (mez) Fricka, Siegrune; **Gerd Nienstedt** (bass) Hunding; **Danica Mastilovic** (sop) Gerhilde; **Liane Synek** (sop) Helmwige; **Helga Dernesch** (sop) Ortlinde; **Gertraud Hopf** (mez) Waltraute; **Sona Cervená** (mez) Rossweisse; **Elisabeth Schärtel** (contr) Grimgerde; **Sieglinde Wagner** (contr) Schwertleite; **Bayreuth Festival Chorus and Orchestra / Karl Böhm.** Philips Ⓕ 412 478-2PH4 (four discs: 210 minutes: ADD: 2/85). Notes, text and translation included. Recorded live in 1967. From 6747 037 (9/73). ⒺⒺⒺ

Siegfried. **Wolfgang Windgassen** (ten) Siegfried; **Theo Adam** (bass) Wanderer; **Birgit Nilsson** (sop) Brünnhilde; **Erwin Wohlfahrt** (ten) Mime; **Gustav Neidlinger** (bass) Alberich; **Vera Soukupova** (mez) Erda; **Kurt Boehme** (bass) Fafner; **Erika Köth** (sop) Woodbird; **Bayreuth Festival Orchestra / Karl Böhm.** Philips Ⓕ 412 483-2PH4 (four discs: 223 minutes: ADD: 8/85). Notes, text and translation included. Recorded live in 1967. From 6747 037 (9/73). ⒺⒺⒺ

Götterdämmerung. **Birgit Nilsson** (sop) Brünnhilde; **Wolfgang Windgassen** (ten) Siegfried; **Josef Greindl** (bass) Hagen; **Gustav Neidlinger** (bass-bar) Alberich; **Thomas Stewart** (bar) Gunther; **Ludmila Dvořáková** (sop) Gutrune; **Martha Mödl** (mez) Waltraute; **Dorothea Siebert** (sop) Woglinde; **Helga Dernesch** (sop) Wellgunde; **Sieglinde Wagner** (contr) Flosshilde; **Marga Höffgen** (contr) First Norn; **Annelies Burmeister** (mez) Second Norn; **Anja Silja** (sop) Third Norn; **Bayreuth Festival Chorus and Orchestra / Karl Böhm.** Philips Ⓕ 412 488-2PH4 (four discs: 249 minutes: ADD: 5/85). Notes, text and translation included. Recorded live in 1967. From 6747 037 (9/73). ⒺⒺⒺ

Wagner's *Der Ring des Nibelungen* is the greatest music-drama ever penned. It deals with the eternal questions of power, love, personal responsibility and moral behaviour, and has always been open to numerous interpretations, both dramatic and musical. For every generation, it presents a new challenge, yet certain musical performances have undoubtedly stood the test of time. One would recommend the recording made at Bayreuth in 1967 because, above all others, it represents a true and living account of a huge work as it was performed in the opera house for which it was largely conceived. Every artist who appears at Bayreuth seems to find an extra dedication in their comportment there, and on this occasion many of the singers and the conductor surpassed what they achieved elsewhere. Böhm's reading is notable for its dramatic drive and inner tension. For the most part he also encompasses the metaphysical aspects of the score as well, and he procures playing of warmth and depth from the Bayreuth orchestra. Birgit Nilsson heads the cast as an unsurpassed Brünnhilde, wonderfully vivid in her characterization and enunciation, tireless and gleaming in voice. Wolfgang Windgassen is equally committed and alert as her Siegfried and Theo Adam is an experienced, worldly-wise Wotan. No *Ring* recording is perfect or could possibly tell the whole story but this faithfully recorded, straightforward version conveys the strength and force of the epic's meaning.

Additional recommendations ...

...Der Ring des Nibelungen. **Vienna State Opera Chorus; Vienna Philharmonic Orchestra / Sir Georg Solti.** Decca Ⓜ 414 100-2DM15* (15 discs: 877 minutes: ADD: 3/89). *Gramophone classical 100.*   ⓖⓖⓖ

...Der Ring des Nibelungen. **Soloists; Chorus and Orchestra of RAI, Rome / Wilhelm Furtwängler.** EMI mono Ⓜ CZS7 67123-2* (13 discs: 902 minutes: ADD: 2/91).   ⓖⓖⓖ

...Der Ring des Nibelungen. **Soloists; Metropolitan Opera Chorus and Orchestra / James Levine.** DG Ⓜ 445 354-2GX14 (14 discs: 920 minutes: DDD: 10/94).

...Der Ring des Nibelungen. **Soloists; Bayreuth Festival Chorus and Orchestra / Karl Böhm.** Philips Ⓑ 446 057-2PB14 (14 discs: 819 minutes: ADD: 10/94). *This is the same recording as the one reviewed above.*

...Das Rheingold. **Soloists; Bayreuth Festival Orchestra / Clemens Krauss.** Foyer mono Ⓕ 3-CF2007* (three discs: 145 minutes: ADD: 6/88).   ⓖⓖⓖ

...Die Walküre. **Soloists; Bayreuth Festival Orchestra / Clemens Krauss.** Foyer mono Ⓕ 4-CF2008* (four discs: 212 minutes: ADD: 6/88).   ⓖⓖⓖ

...Siegfried. **Soloists; Bayreuth Festival Orchestra / Clemens Krauss.** Foyer mono Ⓕ 4-CF2009* (four discs: 237 minutes: ADD: 6/88).

...Siegfried (sung in English). **Soloists; Sadler's Wells Opera Orchestra / Sir Reginald Goodall.** EMI Ⓜ CMS7 63595-2 (four discs: 278 minutes: ADD: 3/91).

...Götterdämmerung. **Soloists; Bayreuth Festival Orchestra / Clemens Krauss.** Foyer mono Ⓕ 4-CF2010* (four discs: 260 minutes: ADD: 6/88).   ⓖⓖⓖ

...Götterdämmerung. **Soloists; Metropolitan Opera Chorus and Orchestra / James Levine.** DG Ⓕ 429 385-2GH4 (four discs: 270 minutes: DDD: 8/91).

...Götterdämmerung (sung in English). **Soloists; English National Opera Chorus and Orchestra / Sir Reginald Goodall.** EMI Ⓜ CMS7 64244-2 (five discs: ADD: 11/92).

...Götterdämmerung – excerpts. **Soloists; English National Opera Chorus and Orchestra / Sir Reginald Goodall.** EMI Ⓜ CMS7 64244-2 (66 minutes: ADD: 11/93).

Wagner Der Ring des Nibelungen – abridged. Pearl mono Ⓜ GEMMCDS9137* (seven discs: 500 minutes: AAD: 4/95). From HMV D1080 (5/26), D1088 (6/26), D1092 (6/26), D1319 (3/29), D1320/33 (12/27), D1530/35 (3/29), D1546 (3/29), D1572/87 (4/29), D1690/94 (4/30), D1836/7 (4/31), HMV C2237/8 (11/32), HMV DB963 (11/26), DB1578/83 (2/32), DB1710/13 (12/32), DB1720/21 (6/33).

Sopranos – Florence Austral, Noel Eadie, Florence Easton, Tilly de Garmo, Nora Gruhn, Genia Guszalewicz, Frida Leider, Göta Ljüngberg, Elsie Suddaby, Louise Trenton. *Mezzos* – Evelyn Arden, Lydia Kindermann, Elfriede Marherr-Wagner, Maartje Offers, Maria Olczewska. *Contraltos* – Emmi Leisner, Gladys Palmer, Nellie Walker. *Tenors* – Waldemar Henke, Rudolf Laubenthal, Kennedy McKenna, Lauritz Melchior, Albert Reiss, Heinrich Tessmer, Walter Widdop. *Baritones* – Howard Fry, Emil Schipper, Deszö Zádor. *Bass-baritones* – Rudolf Bockelmann, Friedrich Schorr. *Basses* – Ivar Andrésen, Frederick Collier, Arthur Fear, Eduard Habich, Emanuel List. *Orchestras* – Berlin State Opera, London Symphony, Vienna State Opera. *Conductors* – Karl Alwin, Sir John Barbirolli, Leo Blech, Albert Coates, Lawrance Collingwood, Robert Heger, Karl Muck.   ⓖⓖⓖ

Here we have, in its entirety, what one might term the Old Testament of *The Ring* recordings, the discs made in the late 1920s and early 1930s in London and Berlin. The operas given the major share are *Die Walküre* and *Siegfried*. The four extracts from *Das Rheingold* are notable only for Friedrich Schorr's magisterial "Abendlich strahlt". *Götterdämmerung* suffers most from being reduced to brief extracts, although the passages have been well chosen to give a substantial flavour of the vast work. Coates and the slightly less admirable Blech share the conducting with a few incursions from Heger, the young Barbirolli and others. The playing, mostly by the LSO of the day and the Berlin State Opera Orchestra, is remarkable for its sweep, also for its care over detail, much of which has astonishing clarity considering the dates of the recordings. Coates is particularly successful in projecting the ardour of the *Walküre* love duet and the forging of the sword in *Siegfried*. His speeds are always on the swift side. Of course, the singing is the most treasurable aspect of the whole enterprise.

Encountering Leider again one realizes anew that few, if any, have equalled her combination of vocal security, close-knit line and phrasing, and that matching of feeling with a goddess's natural dignity. Her Brünnhilde is an assumption all aspiring heroic sopranos should closely study (but they don't!). Fledgling Heldentenors would be unwise to listen to Melchior for they might be inclined to suicide. The sheer *élan*, strength and verbal acuity of his singing are, and will surely remain, unique. For these reasons alone he is unsurpassable as Siegfried, a role that ideally suited his remarkable attributes. Schorr's Wotan is just as remarkable. Once again tone, technique and text are in perfect accord as his noble bass-baritone fills every passage grandly, movingly. The sound is vivid throughout these seven (for the price of five), generously filled CDs. The voices are recorded more successfully than in most modern versions of these works, and their relationship with the orchestra is more natural than that favoured in studios today. This is a set no enquiring Wagnerian, whatever complete version of *The Ring* he or she owns, should be without.

Wagner Parsifal. **Jess Thomas** (ten) Parsifal; **George London** (bass-bar) Amfortas; **Hans Hotter** (bass) Gurnemanz; **Irene Dalis** (mez) Kundry; **Gustav Neidlinger** (bass) Klingsor; **Martti Talvela** (bass) Titurel; **Niels Möller** (ten) First Knight; **Gerd Neinstedt** (bass) Second Knight; **Sona Cervená** (mez), **Ursula Boese** (contr), **Gerhard Stolze, Georg Paskuda** (tens) Squires; **Gundula Janowitz, Anja Silja, Else-Margrete Gardelli, Dorothea Siebert, Rita Bartos** (sops), **Sona Cervená** (mez) Flower Maidens; **Bayreuth Festival Chorus and Orchestra / Hans Knappertsbusch.** Philips Ⓕ 416 390-2PH4 (four discs: 250 minutes: ADD: 6/86). Notes, text and translation included. Recorded live in 1962. From SAL3475 (11/64). ⒼⒼⒼ

There have been many fine recordings of this great Eastertide opera, but none have so magnificently captured the power, the spiritual grandeur, the human frailty and the almost unbearable beauty of the work as Hans Knappertsbusch. This live recording has a cast that has few equals. Hotter is superb, fleshing out Gurnemanz with a depth of insight that has never been surpassed. London's Amfortas captures the frightening sense of impotence and anguish with painful directness whilst Thomas's Parsifal grows as the performance progresses and is no mean achievement. Dalis may lack that final degree of sensuousness but gives a fine interpretation. Throughout Knappertsbusch exercises a quite unequalled control over the proceedings; it is a fine testament to a great conductor. The Bayreuth acoustic is well reproduced and all in all it is a profound and moving experience.

Additional recommendations ...
...Soloists; **Berlin Deutsche Oper Chorus; Berlin Philharmonic Orchestra / Herbert von Karajan.** DG Ⓕ 413 347 2GH4 (four discs: 256 minutes: DDD: 10/84). ⒼⒼ
...Soloists; **Berlin State Opera Chorus; Berlin Philharmonic Orchestra / Daniel Barenboim.** Teldec Ⓕ 9031-74448-2 (four discs: 256 minutes: DDD: 10/91).
...Soloists; **Bayreuth Festival Chorus and Orchestra / Hans Knappertsbusch.** Teldec Historic Series mono Ⓜ 9031-76047-2* (four discs: 272 minutes: ADD: 8/93). *Gramophone Editor's choice.*

Further listening ...
...Overtures – A Faust Overture. *Coupled with works by* **Rossini, Berlioz, Weber, Brahms** and **Mozart** London Philharmonic Orchestra; Berlin Philharmonic Orchestra / Sir Thomas Beecham. Dutton Laboratories mono CDLX7009* (10/94). *See review in the Collections section; refer to the Index to Reviews.*
...Wesendonk Lieder. *Coupled with works by* **Liszt, Wolf** and **Cornelius** Dame Margaret Price (sop); **Graham Johnson** (pf). Forlane UCD16728 (2/95). *See review in the Collections section; refer to the Index to Reviews.*
...Tannhäuser – Dich teure Halle; Allmächt'ge Jungfrau. Lohengrin – Einsam in trüben Tagen; Euch Lüften, die mein Klagen. Rienzi – Gerechter Gott. *Coupled with works by* **Mozart, Weber** and **Schubert.** Gundula Janowitz (sop); Irwin Gage (pf); **Vienna Symphony Orchestra / Wilfried Boettcher; Orchestra of the Deutsche Staatsoper, Berlin / Ferdinand Leitner.** DG Double 447 352-2GDB2 (12/95).
...Der fliegende Holländer[g] – Joho hoe! Traft ihr das Schiff[f]; Wie aus der Ferne[e]. *Coupled with* **Albert** Tiefland – Ich weiss nicht, wer mein Vater war[g]. **R. Strauss** Arabella – Das war sehr gut, Mandryka[g]. Der Rosenkavalier[h] – Da geht er hin; Die Zeit, die ist ein sonderbar Ding[a]; Mein schöner Schatz ... Ich werd' jetzt in die Kirchen geh'n[a]; Marie Theres'! ... Hab' mir's gelobt[ab]. **Verdi** La forza del destino – Pace, pace, mio Dio[i]. Aida[i] – Qui Radames verrà! ... O patria mia; La fatal pietra[d]; O terra, addio[cd]. **Leonie Rysanek,** [a]**Elisabeth Grümmer,** [b]**Erika Köth** (sops); [c]**Sieglinde Wagner** (mez); [d]**Rudolf Schock** (ten); [c]**Sigurd Björling** (bar); [f]**Royal Opera House Chorus, Covent Garden;** [c]**Berlin Deutsche Oper Chorus;** [g]**Philharmonia Orchestra;** [h]**Berlin Philharmonic Orchestra;** [i]**Berlin Symphony Orchestra / Wilhelm Schüchter.** EMI Références mono CDH5 65201-2* (4/95).
...Das Liebesmahl der Apostel. *Coupled with* **Bruckner** Helgoland. **Ambrosian Chorus; Symphonica of London / Wyn Morris.** IMP Classics PCD1042.

...Die Feen. **Soloists; Bavarian Radio Chorus; Bavarian Radio Symphony Orchestra / Wolfgang Sawallisch.** Orfeo C062833F.

...Paraphrase on Isolden's Liebestod from "Tristan und Isolde", S447 (trans. Liszt). *Coupled with works by* **Haydn, Chopin** and **Liszt Vladimir Horowitz** (pf). Sony Classical SK45818 (8/90). *See review in the Collections section; refer to the Index to Reviews.* ⓖⓖⓖ

...Das Rheingold – Prelude ... Bangt euch noch nicht?[a]; Bin ich nun frei? ... Abendlich strahlt[b] (both from HMV ASD535, 7/63). Die Walküre – Act 1, complete[c] (HMV SLS968, 5/73); Siegmund! Sieh auf mich![d] (HMV DB6962/3, 11/49); War es so schmählich[e] ... Leb' wohl[ef] ... Der Augen leuchtendes Paar[ef] ... Loge, hör[ef] ... Magic Fire Music[ef] ([e]Columbia SAX2296, 12/59; [f]ASD3499, 7/78). Siegfried – Heil dir, Sonne! ... Ewig war ich, ewig bin ich[g] (HMV BLP1035, 11/53). Götterdämmerung – Zu neuen Taten ... O heilige Götter![g] (HMV EX291227-3, 7/87. Recorded 1951); Siegfried's Rhine Journey[h] (Columbia 33CX1655, 11/59); Hier sitz' ich zur Wacht[i]; Hoiho! ihr Gibichsmannen[j] (ASD363, 9/60); Helle Wehr! Heilige Waffe![k] (EX291227-3). Siegfried's Funeral March[h] (33CX1655); Starke Scheite[l] (DB6792/4, 12/48). [ab]**Lisa Otto,** [ab]**Melitta Muszely,** [dgkl]**Kirsten Flagstad,** [c]**Helga Dernesch,** [e]**Birgit Nilsson** (sops); [ab]**Sieglinde Wagner,** [b]**Johanna Blatter** (mezzos); [b]**Ruth Siewert** (contr); [b]**Helmut Melchert,** [b]**Rudolf Schock,** [dgk]**Set Svanholm,** [c]**William Cochran** (tens); [ab]**Benno Kusche,** [b]**Josef Metternich,** [f]**Dietrich Fischer-Dieskau** (bars); [b]**Ferdinand Frantz,** [e]**Hans Hotter** (bass-bars); [c]**Hans Sotin,** [ij]**Gottlob Frick** (basses); [j]**Chorus and** [ij]**Orchestra of the Deutsche Oper, Berlin / Franz Konwitschny;** [ab]**Berlin Staatskapelle / Rudolf Kempe; Philharmonia Orchestra /** [d]**Karl Böhm,** [e]**Leopold Ludwig,** [g]**Georges Sébastian,** [h]**Wolfgang Sawallisch,** [l]**Wilhelm Furtwängler,** [k]**Hermann Weigert;** [c]**New Philharmonia Orchestra / Otto Klemperer;** [f]**Bavarian Radio Symphony Orchestra / Rafael Kubelík.** EMI [abcefhij]stereo/[dgkl]mono CMS5 65212-2* (four discs: 10/94). ⓖⓖ

Siegfried Wagner   German 1869-1930

Suggested listening ...

...Der Bärenhäuter. **Soloists; Thüringian Landestheater Chorus; Thüringian Symphony Orchestra / Konrad Bach.** Marco Polo 8 223713/4 (6/95).

...Schwarzschwanenreich. **Soloists; Thüringian Landestheater Chorus; Thüringian Symphony Orchestra / Konrad Bach.** Marco Polo 8 223777/8 (11/95).

Emile Waldteufel   French 1837-1915

New review

Waldteufel, Flots de joie, Op. 145. Château en Espagne, Op. 225. Gaîté, Op. 164. Tout à vous, Op. 142. Bella, Op. 113. Brune ou blonde, Op. 162. Acclamations, Op. 223. La Barcarolle, Op. 178. Béobile. **Slovak State Philharmonic Orchestra, Košice / Alfred Walter.** Marco Polo Ⓟ 223684 (66 minutes: DDD: 6/96). Recorded 1992-5.

Alfred Walter's Waldteufel series is distinguished by his characteristic professionalism and the Slovak orchestra at Košice play with warmth and considerable polish. This volume contains entirely unfamiliar repertoire, and much of it deserves to be better known: *Gaîté*, *Brune ou blonde* and *La Barcarolle* all have attractive ideas, the last-named nothing like Offenbach, but with a gently bouncing lilt. Vol. 7 again brings several striking numbers: *Rêverie* and the nostalgic *Au revoir* are aptly named, while *Trésor d'amour* uses flutes to usher in a tune of graceful delicacy. *Coquetterie*, too, has a capricious, winningly scored introduction entirely in keeping with its title. The highlight of the disc is *Béobile*, a pizzicato novelty of such verve that if better known it could be a great favourite. The recording is excellent, with a nice ballroom resonance.

Johann Gottfried Walther   German 1684-1748

Suggested listening ...

...Concertos – del Signor Torelli; del Signor Taglietti; del Signor Telemann in G major and C minor; del Signor Meck. Chorale Preludes – Herr Jesu Christ, ich weiss gar wohl; Es ist das Heil uns kommen her; Hilf mir Gott, dass mir's gelinge; Herr Gott, nun schleuss der Himmel auf; Schmücke dich, o liebe Seele. Partita – Jesu meine Freude. **Stephen Farr** (org). Meridian CDE84213 (8/92).

William Walton   British 1902-1983

New review

Walton Cello Concerto[a]. Symphony No. 1 in B flat minor. [a]**Robert Cohen** (vc); **Bournemouth Symphony Orchestra / Andrew Litton.** Decca London Ⓟ 443 450-2LH (74 minutes: DDD: 10/95). Recorded 1993.

Walton Scapino. Violin Concerto in B minor[a]. Symphony No. 2. [a]**Tasmin Little** (vn); **Bournemouth Symphony Orchestra / Andrew Litton.** Decca London Ⓕ 444 114-2LH (68 minutes: DDD: 10/95). Recorded 1994.

Walton Belshazzar's Feast[a]. Henry V. Crown Imperial. [a]**Bryn Terfel** (bass-bar); [a]**Waynflete Singers;** [a]**L'Inviti;** [a]**Bournemouth Symphony Chorus and Orchestra / Andrew Litton.** Decca London Ⓕ 448 134-2LH (60 minutes: DDD: 10/95). Text included. Recorded 1995.

More than anyone since Previn, Litton thrillingly conveys the element of wildness in Walton's finest inspirations, notably in the works of the pre-war period. It is partly a question of his treatment of the jazzy syncopations which are such a vital element in Walton. Litton is not alone in treating them with a degree of idiomatic freedom – the composer himself as interpreter set the pattern – but as with Previn Litton's affinity with the jazz element comes from inside, clearly reflecting his American background. Consistently he makes the music crackle with high voltage electricity, and again he echoes Previn in the way he can screw tension up to the limit and beyond, resolving grinding dissonances on heart-warming concords. That is particularly important in the First Symphony. The Rattle version is superb, but next to Litton's it seems almost too safe, too closely controlled, lacking the extremes of tension, the wildness. Litton even surpasses Previn in the climactic resolution of the finale. With him this movement in no way seems a let-down after the rest, as it easily can – reflecting the composer's problems over completing it. The climactic resolution on an outburst from multiple timpani and percussion is more shattering than ever before on disc, with the Decca recording team achieving wonders in the weight and brilliance of the sound. In general the transfer level is a degree lower than in most rival versions. In the Cello Concerto too the sound is a degree less immediate than in Rattle's version with Lynn Harrell, and that matches a broad contrast of interpretation. Where Harrell remains unrivalled in power and tonal resonance, Robert Cohen for Litton follows a deeper, more hushed, more meditative approach, even when as in the first movement he has a more flowing speed. Harrell is the more powerful, Cohen the more mercurial as well as the more tender. The way that Cohen makes the opening notes of the slow finale seem to emerge from afar is magical.

In all three discs the exceptionally full and vivid recording brings out the opulence as well as the sensuousness of Walton's orchestration, regularly enhancing Litton's expressive warmth as a Waltonian in the great romantic melodies. Not only that, the bitingly dramatic contrasts of brass and percussion have never been more vivid, with the Bournemouth orchestra playing magnificently, not just with brilliance but with passionate commitment. On the second disc the Symphony No. 2 is given an even sharper focus than in Ashkenazy's Decca version with the RPO. On the disc it follows – as in a concert – the *Scapino* overture and the Violin Concerto. Tasmin Little as soloist gives the most tenderly beautiful performance, matching Litton in her control of Waltonian contrasts between tender lyricism and sparkling wit. Like Litton, too, Little is able to hold full tension through pauses, often daringly extending them as in a live performance, so that the cadenzas in the first and last movements have a rare intensity. This is a work which has inspired many outstanding performances, not least from women violinists, and Little in spontaneity and tenderness is unsurpassed.

Where the first two discs were recorded in the helpful acoustic of the Southampton Guildhall, *Belshazzar's Feast* was put into the grander setting of Winchester Cathedral. The problems for the engineers must have been daunting, for the reverberation time is formidably long, yet thanks to brilliant balancing there is ample detail and fine focus in exceptionally incisive choral and orchestral sound. The great benefit is that this emerges as a performance on a bigger scale than its rivals, with the contrasts between full chorus and semi-chorus the more sharply established. The vividly dramatic soloist is Bryn Terfel, spine-chilling in his narration describing the writing on the wall. In *Crown Imperial* a cathedral acoustic does bring some lack of clarity, but it is a stirring performance. Andrew Litton's years as Principal Conductor of the Bournemouth Symphony Orchestra could hardly have had a richer culmination on disc.

Walton Violin Concerto. Viola Concerto. **Nigel Kennedy** (vn/va); **Royal Philharmonic Orchestra / André Previn.** EMI Ⓕ CDC7 49628-2 (57 minutes: DDD: 4/88). From EL749628-1 (1/88).
Selected by Sounds in Retrospect. Ⓖ

These concertos are among the most beautiful written this century. Walton was in his late twenties when he composed the viola work and in it he achieved a depth of emotion, a range of ideas and a technical assurance beyond anything he had so far written. Lacking in the brilliance of the violin, the viola has an inherently contemplative tonal quality and Walton matches this to perfection in his score, complementing it rather than trying to compensate as other composers have done. There is a larger element of virtuosity in the Violin Concerto, but it is never allowed to dominate the musical argument. Nigel Kennedy gives wonderfully warm and characterful performances which are likely to stand unchallenged as a coupling for a long time. He produces a beautiful tone quality on both of his instruments, which penetrates to the heart of the aching melancholy of Walton's slow music, and he combines it with an innate, highly developed and spontaneous-sounding sense of rhythmic drive and bounce which propels the quick movements forward with great panache. Previn has long been a persuasive Waltonian and the RPO respond marvellously, with crisp and alert playing throughout. The recordings are very clear and naturally balanced with the solo instrument set in a believable perspective.

Additional recommendation ...

...Violin Concerto. Violin Sonata. Two Pieces. **Lydia Mordkovitch** (vn); **London Philharmonic Orchestra / Jan Latham-Koenig.** Chandos Ⓕ CHAN9073 (69 minutes: DDD: 10/92).

New review

Walton Viola Concerto in A minor[a]. Symphony No. 2. Johannesburg Festival Overture. [a]**Lars Anders Tomter** (va); **English Northern Philharmonia / Paul Daniel.** Naxos ⑨ 8 553402 (61 minutes: DDD: 5/96). Recorded 1995.

This disc opens with one of the wittiest, most exuberant performances of the *Johannesburg Festival Overture*: characteristically Daniel encourages the orchestra's virtuoso wind and brass soloists to point the jazz rhythms idiomatically, making the music sparkle. The Viola Concerto is just as delectably pointed, the whole performance instantly magnetic. Tomter's tone, with its rapid flicker-vibrato, lacks the warmth of Kennedy's (reviewed above), but the vibrato is only obtrusive in that upper-middle register and his intonation is immaculate, his attack consistently clean, to match the crisp ensemble of the orchestra. Although he adopts relatively measured speeds both for the scherzo and the jaunty opening theme of the finale, the rhythmic lift brings out the *scherzando* jollity of the latter all the more. Daniel's keen observance of dynamic markings is again brought out in the stuttering fanfare theme of the scherzo, with muted trumpets and trombones for once played *pianissimo* as marked. The close of the slow epilogue has never been recorded with such a profound hush as here, subsiding in darkness, and the recording team are to be complimented on getting such beautiful sound, clean with plenty of bloom. Paul Daniel adopts a relatively broad tempo in the Symphony's first movement, which makes less impact than in Andrew Litton's powerful Decca version (reviewed above), and the flowing tempo for the central slow movement makes for a lighter, less passionate result too. The finale, with its brassy first statement of the Passacaglia theme, brings fine dynamic contrasts, but again Litton and others produce a fatter, weightier sound, which on balance is preferable. Yet Daniel's view is a very valid one, to round off most convincingly an invaluable addition to the Walton discography.

Walton Façade – Suites Nos. 1-3[a]. Siesta[b]. Sinfonia concertante[ca]. Portsmouth Point[a].
Arnold Popular Birthday[a]. [c]**Eric Parkin** (pf); **London Philharmonic Orchestra /** [a]**Jan Latham-König,** [b]**Bryden Thomson.** Chandos Ⓕ CHAN9148 (59 minutes: DDD: 1/94). Recorded 1990-92.

The *Sinfonia concertante* (1926-27) with its sharply memorable ideas in each movement and characteristically high voltage, has never had the attention it deserves, and that is all the more regrettable when there is such a dearth of attractive British piano concertos. The soloist, Eric Parkin, is perfectly attuned to the idiom, warmly melodic as well as jazzily syncopated. He points rhythms infectiously and shapes melodies persuasively, though the recording sets the piano a little backwardly, no doubt to reflect the idea that this is not a full concerto. Jan Latham-König proves most understanding of the composer's 1920s idiom, giving the witty *Façade* movements just the degree of jazzy freedom they need. The Third Suite, devised and arranged by Christopher Palmer, draws on three apt movements from the *Façade* entertainment, ending riotously with the rag-music of "Something lies beyond the scene". That is a first recording, as is Constant Lambert's arrangement of the Overture, *Portsmouth Point*. *Siesta* is given an aptly cool performance under Thomson, and the *Popular Birthday* is Malcolm Arnold's fragmentary linking of *Happy Birthday to You* with the "Popular Song" from *Façade*, originally written for Walton's seventieth birthday. The impact of some of the pieces, notably in *Façade*, would have been even sharper, had the warmly atmospheric Chandos recording placed the orchestra a fraction closer.

Walton Overtures – Johannesburg Festival; Portsmouth Point; Scapino. Capriccio burlesco. The First Shoot (orch. Palmer). Granada Prelude. Prologo e Fantasia. Music for Children. Galop final (orch. Palmer). **London Philharmonic Orchestra / Bryden Thomson.** Chandos Ⓕ CHAN8968 (70 minutes: DDD: 11/91).

While enthusiasts for Walton's music may justifiably complain that there is not enough of it, they usually concede that what there is is readily available in good recorded performances. However, thanks to the dedicated and skilful work of Christopher Palmer, still more of it is now coming to light. How many people, one wonders, have ever heard *The First Shoot*, a miniature ballet written for a C.B. Cochran show in 1935, the *Granada Prelude* devised for that television company in the 1960s, or the *Prologo e Fantasia* which was the composer's last work, written for Rostropovich and his National Symphony Orchestra of Washington. Such fresh and welcome goodies as these appear along with familiar material such as the splendidly open-air, nautical overture *Portsmouth Point* that Walton wrote nearly 40 years earlier, at the very start of his career. The Cochran piece, as orchestrated by Palmer, has five little sections that are delightfully jazzy in a way that recalls *Façade* and one's only regret is that there's not more of it. All this music is in the excellent hands of Bryden Thomson and the LPO, and Palmer's booklet essay is a model of stylish, informative writing. The recording is richly toned in the successful Chandos style, which takes some edge off the composer's characteristically sharp scoring but is still most enjoyable.

Walton Symphony No. 1 in B flat minor. Cello Concerto[a]. [a]**Lynn Harrell** (vc); **City of Birmingham Symphony Orchestra / Sir Simon Rattle.** EMI British Composers Ⓕ CDC7 54572-2 (74 minutes: DDD: 12/92). Recorded 1990-91.

Simon Rattle's version of Walton's First Symphony is as intelligent and dynamic a traversal as one would expect from this talented figure. Texturally speaking, the inner workings of Walton's score are laid bare as never before, aided by what sounds like a meticulously prepared CBSO. Some may find a touch of contrivance about Rattle's control of dynamics in the scorching first movement, but there's absolutely no gainsaying the underlying tension or cumulative power of the whole. Under Rattle the *Scherzo* darts menacingly (the most convincing account of this music since the classic 1966 Previn account), whilst the slow movement is an unusually nervy, anxious affair. Certainly, the finale is superbly athletic and lithe, though by now one is beginning to register that EMI's sound is, for all its transparency and natural perspective, perhaps a little lightweight for such enormously red-blooded inspiration. Overall, though, Rattle's is a very strong account – indisputably one of the finest we've had in recent years – and his disc's claims are enhanced by the coupling, a wholly admirable performance of the same composer's luxuriant Cello Concerto. Here Rattle and Lynn Harrell form an inspired partnership, totally dedicated and achieving utter concentration throughout – no mean feat in this of all works, whose predominantly slow-moving progress demands so much from both performers and listeners.

Additional recommendations ...

...Nos. 1[a] and 2[b]. [a]**London Philharmonic Orchestra;** [b]**London Symphony Orchestra / Sir Charles Mackerras.** EMI Eminence Ⓜ CD-EMX2206 (74 minutes: DDD: 12/89). Ⓖ

...No. 1. **Vaughan Williams** The Wasps – Overture. **London Symphony Orchestra / André Previn.** RCA Victor Gold Seal Ⓜ GD87830 (52 minutes: ADD: 2/89). *Gramophone classical 100.* ⓄⓄⓄ

...No. 1[a]. Viola Concerto[b]. Façade – excerpts[c]. [b]**Frederick Riddle** (va); [c]**Dora Stevens** (sop); [c]**Hubert Foss** (pf); **London Symphony Orchestra /** [a]**Hamilton Harty,** [b]**Sir William Walton.** Dutton Laboratories mono Ⓜ CDAX8003* (72 minutes: ADD: 12/93).

Walton Symphonies – No. 1 in B flat minor; No. 2. **Royal Philharmonic Orchestra / Vladimir Ashkenazy.** Decca Ⓕ 433 703-2DH (72 minutes: DDD: 4/93). Recorded 1991. Ⓖ

Even in the face of intense competition from the similarly coupled EMI Eminence issue with Sir Charles Mackerras, Ashkenazy's pairing has a lot going for it. Although not quite as glowingly rich as some of this company's previous efforts from Walthamstow Assembly Hall, Decca's production is a splendidly analytical affair, and the ear revels in the thrilling amount of detail captured by the engineers in these superbly orchestrated scores. The RPO, too, respond with no little dash or commitment; certainly, the *Scherzo* of the First Symphony is delivered with impressive poise and rhythmic (indeed almost balletic) flair, and if one might crave a rather larger, more refulgent body of string tone on occasion (as in the gorgeous Mediterranean seascape which comprises the Second Symphony's slow movement), the brass playing has exemplary thrust and flashing brilliance throughout. Ashkenazy's conception of the First is laudably clear-sighted and undisruptive. What's missing, however, is simply that last ounce of crackling tension one finds on rival readings from the likes of Rattle, Mackerras and, above all, Previn. Indeed, the latter's blistering 1966 LSO account remains pre-eminent, and in the Second, too, many will understandably prefer the greater emotional pungency of Mackerras and sheer orchestral spectacle of George Szell's famous Cleveland recording from 1961 (listed below). Still, the present coupling is a generous one, and no one will be disappointed with either Ashkenazy's achievement here or the impact of the Decca engineering.

Additional recommendation ...

...No. 2. Partita. Variations on a Theme by Hindemith. **Cleveland Orchestra / George Szell.** CBS Masterworks Ⓜ CD46732 (65 minutes: ADD: 12/91). ⓄⓄ

New review

Walton Piano Quartet[a]. Violin Sonata[b]. Five Bagatelles[c]. [ab]**Janice Graham** (vn); [a]**Paul Silverthorne** (va); [a]**Moray Welsh** (vc); [c]**Tom Kerstens** (gtr); [a]**Israela Margalit,** [b]**John Alley** (pfs). EMI Anglo-American Chamber Music Ⓕ CDC5 55404-2 (69 minutes: DDD: 8/96).

This is a splendid addition to EMI's Anglo-American Chamber Music series, with superb string players from the LSO, and with Israela Margalit making a distinguished contribution. The two major works are also coupled on the Chandos disc, but here you get a bonus in an outstanding performance of the *Five Bagatelles* for guitar, originally written for Julian Bream. With Israela Margalit injecting fire, the performance of the Piano Quartet is also lighter and more volatile than that in the Chandos set with Hamish Milne as pianist. That impression is enhanced by the EMI recording balance, with textures rather more open, letting the solo work stand out more. But where the first two movements in the new performance have more sparkle and fantasy, the Chandos team gain increasingly in the slow movement and finale, which have extra weight and intensity. You could argue that the EMI team's treatment of the slow movement – lighter, more flowing yet still warm – is more apt for the work of a precocious 16-year-old composer, and though the finale is not quite as biting as in the Chandos performance, the vigour is hardly less, and the players more readily respond to the moments of repose, as in the pause before the final coda. Janice Graham is the brilliant, winningly expressive violinist in both works, again more fanciful, more volatile in the Violin Sonata than her opposite number, Kenneth Sillito, notably in the first movement. In the slow variations which form the second of the two movements Sillito grows ever warmer, conveying an extra weight and intensity, but both performances are outstanding, bringing warmth and purposefulness to what can easily seem one of the more wayward of Walton's major works. Though the three pieces were recorded in three different venues, the sound is remarkably consistent, excellent in each.

Additional recommendation ...

...Piano Quartet[a]. Violin Sonata. **Kenneth Sillito** (vn); [a]**Robert Smissen** (va); [a]**Stephen Orton** (vc); **Hamish Milne** (pf). Chandos CHAN8999 (3/92).

Walton Belshazzar's Feast[a]. Coronation Te Deum. Gloria[b]. [b]**Ameral Gunson** (contr); [b]**Neil Mackie** (ten); [a]**Gwynne Howell**, [b]**Stephen Roberts** (bars); **Bach Choir; Philharmonia Orchestra / Sir David Willcocks.** Chandos Ⓕ CHAN8760 (62 minutes: DDD: 1/90). Texts included. Recorded 1989.

With Sir David Willcocks in charge of the choir which he has directed since 1960, one need have no fears that the composer's many near-impossible demands of the chorus in all three of these masterpieces will not be met with elegance and poise. There is as well, in *Belshazzar*, a predictably fine balance of the forces to ensure that as much detail as possible is heard from both chorus and orchestra, even when Walton is bombarding us from all corners of the universe with extra brass bands and all manner of clamorous percussion in praise of pagan gods. Such supremely musical concerns bring their own rewards in a work that can often seem vulgar. The revelation here is the sustained degree of dramatic thrust, exhilaration and what Herbert Howells called "animal joy" in the proceedings. How marvellous, too, to hear the work paced and scaled to avoid the impression of reduced voltage after the big moments. Gwynne Howell is the magnificently steady, firm and dark toned baritone. The *Gloria* and *Coronation Te Deum* are informed with the same concerns: accuracy and professional polish are rarely allowed to hinder these vital contributions to the British choral tradition. The recording's cathedral-like acoustic is as ideal for the *Te Deum*'s ethereal antiphonal effects, as it is for *Belshazzar's* glorious spectacle; and Chandos match Willcocks's care for balance, bar by bar.

Walton Façade[a]. Overtures – Portsmouth Point; Scapino[b]. Siesta[b].
Arnold English Dances, Op. 33[c]. [a]**Dame Edith Sitwell**, [a]**Sir Peter Pears** (spkrs); [a]**English Opera Group Ensemble / Anthony Collins**; [bc]**London Philharmonic Orchestra / Sir Adrian Boult.** Decca London mono Ⓜ 425 661-2LM* (74 minutes: DDD). Items marked [a] from LXT2977 (11/54), [b]LXT5028 (6/55), [c]LW5166 (6/55).   Ⓖ

This is the classic and authoritative reading of the fully approved selection of *Façade* settings. Dame Edith herself reads two-thirds of the numbers, Sir Peter the remaining third. The poetess herself reads them with such *joie de vivre*, such a natural feeling for her own verses and inflexions that nobody could be expected to rival her. Her timing is perfect, her delivery deliciously idiosyncratic, the intonations obviously what she and presumably Walton wanted. Sir Peter isn't far behind her in ability to relish the writing and the instrumental ensemble plays with refinement allied to virtuosity. The 1950s mono recording stands the test of time remarkably well.

Additional recommendations ...

...Façade[a]. **Sitwell** Poems: Two Kitchen Songs. Five Songs – Daphne; The Peach Tree; The Strawberry; The Greengage Tree; The Nectarine Tree. On the Vanity of Human Aspirations. Two Poems from "Façade" – The Drum; Clowns' Houses. The Wind's Bastinado. The Dark Song. Colonel Fantock. Most Lovely Shade. Heart and Mind. **Prunella Scales, Timothy West** (spkrs); [a]members of **London Mozart Players / Jane Glover.** ASV Ⓕ CDDCA679 (64 minutes: DDD/ADD: 4/90).

...Façade – Suites Nos. 1 and 2. **Bliss** Checkmate – Suite. **Lambert** Horoscope – Suite. **English Northern Philharmonia / David Lloyd-Jones.** Hyperion Ⓕ CDA66436 (74 minutes: DDD: 3/91). *Selected by Sounds in Retrospect.*   Ⓖ

Walton Troilus and Cressida. **Judith Howarth** (sop) Cressida; **Arthur Davies** (ten) Troilus; **Clive Bayley** (bass) Calkas; **Nigel Robson** (ten) Pandarus; **Alan Opie** (bar) Diomede; **James Thornton** (bar) Antenor; **David Owen-Lewis** (bass) Horaste; **Yvonne Howard** (mez) Evadne; **Peter Bodenham** (ten) Priest; **Keith Mills** (ten) Soldier; **Bruce Budd** (bass) First Watchman; **Stephen Dowson** (bass) Second Watchman; **Brian Cookson** (ten) Third Watchman; **Chorus of Opera North; English Northern Philharmonia / Richard Hickox.** Chandos ⒻCHAN9370/1 (two discs: 133 minutes: DDD: 5/95). Notes and text included. Recorded 1995. *Gramophone Award Winner 1995.* ⒼⒼⒼ

Troilus and Cressida is here powerfully presented as an opera for the central repertory, traditional in its red-blooded treatment of a big classical subject. Few if any operas since Puccini's have such a rich store of instantly memorable tunes as *Troilus and Cressida*. Walton wrote the piece in the wake of the first great operatic success of his rival, Benjamin Britten. What more natural than for Walton, by this time no longer an *enfant terrible* of British music but an Establishment figure, to turn his back on operas devoted like Britten's to offbeat subjects, and to go back to an older operatic tradition using a classical love story, based on Chaucer (not Shakespeare). Though he was much praised for this by early critics in 1954, he was quickly attacked for being old-fashioned. Even when in the tautened version of the score he offered for the 1976 Covent Garden revival – with the role of the heroine adapted for the mezzo voice of Dame Janet Baker – the piece was described by one critic as a dodo. Yet as Richard Hickox suggests, fashion after 40 years matters little, and the success of the Opera North production in January 1995 indicated that at last the time had come for a big, warmly romantic, sharply dramatic work to be appreciated on its own terms. This recording was made under studio conditions during the run of the opera in Leeds in the UK. The discs amply confirm what the live performances suggested, that Walton's tautening of the score, coupled with a restoration of the original soprano register for Cressida, has proved entirely successful.

Hickox conducts a performance that is magnetic from beginning to end. The scene is atmospherically set in Act 1 by the chorus, initially off-stage, but then with the incisive Opera North chorus snapping out thrilling cries of "We are accurs'd!". The libretto is unashamedly archaic in its use of 'opera-speak' like that, with "thee"s and "thou"s and the occasional "perchance". Though the text may put some off, it is plainly apt for a traditional 'well-made opera' on a classical subject. The first soloist one hears in the High Priest, Calkas, Cressida's father, about to defect to the Greeks, and the role is superbly taken by the firm, dark-toned Clive Bayley. Troilus's entry and his declaration of love for Cressida bring Waltonian sensuousness and the first statements of the soaring Cressida theme. Arthur Davies is not afraid of using his head voice for *pianissimos*, so contrasting the more dramatically with the big outbursts and his ringing top notes. This is a younger-sounding hero, more Italianate of tone than the very English-sounding Lewis on the Walton set. Similarly, Judith Howarth's Cressida is much more girlish than either Dame Janet Baker in the Covent Garden set conducted by Lawrence Foster or Dame Elisabeth Schwarzkopf on the Walton excerpts disc. More than those great predecessors Judith Howarth brings out the vulnerability of the character along with sweetness and warmth. After Calkas has defected to the Greeks, her cry of "He has deserted us and Troy!" conveys genuine fear, with her will undermined. All told, although some fine music has been cut, the tautened version is far more effective both musically and dramatically, with no *longueurs* at all. The role of Diomede, Cressida's Greek suitor, can seem one-dimensional, but Alan Opie in one of his finest performances on record sharpens the focus, making him a genuine threat, with the element of nobility fully allowed. As Antenor, James Thornton sings strongly, but is less steady than the others, while Yvonne Howard is superb in the mezzo role of Evadne, Cressida's treacherous servant and confidante.

Not just the chorus but the orchestra of Opera North, the English Northern Philharmonia, respond with fervour. Naturally and idiomatically they observe the Waltonian rubato and the lifting of jazzily syncopated rhythms which Hickox as a dedicated Waltonian instils, echoing the composer's own example. As for the recorded sound, it brings a complete contrast with the dry Covent Garden acoustic on the old EMI complete set or even the close-up mono sound of the Walton extracts. The bloom of the acoustic allows the fullest detail from the orchestra, enhancing the Mediterranean warmth of the score, helped by the wide dynamic range.

Additional recommendations ...

...**Soloists; Chorus and Orchestra of the Royal Opera House, Covent Garden / Lawrence Foster.** EMI British Composers Ⓜ CMS5 65550-2 (two discs: 126 minutes: ADD: 7/95).

...Excerpts **Soloists; Philharmonia Orchestra; Orchestra of the Royal Opera House, Covent Garden / Sir William Walton.** EMI British Composers mono Ⓜ CDM7 64199-2* (55 minutes: ADD: 1/94).

Walton The Bear. **Della Jones** (mez) Madame Popova; **Alan Opie** (bar) Smirnov; **John Shirley-Quirk** (bar) Luka; **Northern Sinfonia / Richard Hickox.** Chandos Ⓕ CHAN9245 (53 minutes: DDD: 1/94). Text included. Recorded 1993.

If Walton's sense of humour was firmly established from the start in *Façade*, his one-acter, *The Bear*, among his later works brings out very clearly how strong that quality remained throughout his life. In this Chekhov tale, Walton times the melodramatic moments marvellously - notably the climactic duel between the mourning widow and her husband's creditor (the bear of the title) and Hickox brings that out most effectively. Walton also deftly heightens the farcical element by introducing dozens of parodies and tongue-in-cheek musical references, starting cheekily with echoes of Britten's *Midsummer Night's Dream*. Hickox brings out the richness of the piece as well as its wit, helped by the opulent Chandos recording which still allows words to be heard clearly. The casting of the three characters is as near ideal as could be. Della Jones is commanding as the affronted widow, consistently relishing the melodrama like a young Edith Evans. Alan Opie as Smirnov, 'the bear' is clean-cut and incisive, powerfully bringing out the irate creditor's changing emotions, while John Shirley-Quirk, still rich and resonant, is very well cast as the old retainer, Luka. With the duel scene leading delectably to an amorous *coup de foudre* – *The Bear* in many ways comes off even better on disc than on stage.

Further listening ...

...Film Music, Volume 2 – Spitfire Prelude and Fugue. A Wartime Sketchbook (arr. Palmer). Escape Me Never – Suite (arr. Palmer). The Three Sisters (ed. Palmer). The Battle of Britain – Suite. **Academy of St Martin in the Fields / Sir Neville Marriner.** Chandos CHAN8870 (12/90).

...The Quest (ed. Palmer). The Wise Virgins – Ballet Suite. **London Philharmonic Orchestra / Bryden Thomson.** Chandos CHAN8871 (4/91).

...String Quartets – No. 1; A minor. **Gabrieli Quartet.** Chandos CHAN8944 (10/91).

...String Quartet in A minor. *Coupled with* **Bridge** Three Idylls, H67. **Elgar** String Quartet in E minor, Op. 83. **Coull Quartet.** Hyperion CDA66718 (10/94). *See review under Bridge; refer to the Index to Reviews.*

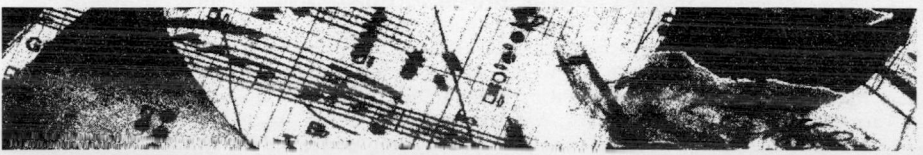

...String Quartet in A minor. *Coupled with* **Hindemith** String Quartet No. 3, Op. 22. **Prokofiev** String Quartet No. 2 in F major, Op. 92. **Hollywood Quartet.** Testament mono SBT1052* (3/95). *See review under Hindemith; refer to the Index to Reviews.* ⒼⒼ

...Toccata in A minor[bd]. Ten duets for children[de]. Façade – Valse[d]. Two Pieces[bd]. Five Bagatelles[c]. Anon in Love[ac]. The Winds[ad]. Tritons[ad]. [a]**John Mark Ainsley** (ten); [b]**Kenneth Sillito** (vn); [c]**Carlos Bonell** (gtr); [d]**Hamish Milne**, [e]**Gretel Dowdeswell** (pfs). Chandos CHAN9292 (10/94).

...Henry V – a Shakespeare scenario (arr. Palmer). **Christopher Plummer** (narr); **Westminster Abbey Choristers; Chorus and Academy of St Martin in the Fields / Sir Neville Marriner.** Chandos CHAN8892 (4/91).

...Magnificat and Nunc dimittis. Cantico del sole. Antiphon. Set me as a seal upon thine heart. Missa brevis. Where does the uttered music go?. Jubilate Deo. A Litany. The Twelve. Carols – All this time; What cheer?; King Herod and the Cock. Make we joy now in this fest. **Trinity College Choir, Cambridge / Richard Marlow.** Conifer CDCF164 (5/89).

John Ward
British 1571-1638

Suggested listening ...

...Vocal and Instrumental Works – No object dearer. If Heaven's just wrath. Down in a dale. Cruel unkind. My breast I'll set upon a silver stream. Cor mio, deh non languire. Well-sounding pipes. Fantasias a 6 – No. 1 in A minor; No. 2 in F major; No. 3 in A minor; No. 4 in G minor; No. 7 in C minor. In Nomine a 6 No. 1 in G minor. Fantasia on In Nomine a 6 No. 2 in C minor. **The Consort of Musicke / Anthony Rooley.** Musica Oscura 070981 (7/95). ✍

...Vocal and Instrumental Works – Praise the Lord, O my soul (3vv). How long wilt thou forget me. O Lord consider my great moans. I will praise the Lord. Praise the Lord, O my soul (6vv). Let God arise. O let me tread in the right path. Have mercy upon me. Down caitive wretch/Prayer is an endless chain. This is a Joyful, Happy, Holy Day. **The Consort of Musicke / Anthony Rooley.** Musica Oscura 070982 (7/95). ✍

Peter Warlock
British 1894-1930

Warlock The Wind from the West. To the Memory of a Great Singer. Take, o take those lips away. As ever I saw. The Bayly berith the bell away. There is a lady sweet and kind. Lullaby. Sweet content. Late summer. The Singer. Rest, sweet nymphs. Sleep. A Sad Song. In an arbour green. Autumn Twilight. I held love's head. Thou gav'st me leave to kiss. Yarmouth Fair. Pretty Ring Time. A Prayer to St Anthony of Padua. The Sick Heart. Robin Goodfellow. Jillian of Berry. Fair and True. Ha'nacker Mill. The Night. My Own Country. The First Mercy. The Lover's Maze. Cradle Song. Sigh no more, ladies. Passing by. The Contented Lover. The Fox. **John Mark Ainsley** (ten); **Roger Vignoles** (pf). Hyperion Ⓕ CDA66736 (69 minutes: DDD: 1/95). Texts included. Recorded 1994. **Gramophone** *Editor's choice.* Ⓖ

Singer and song are ideally matched, pianist and piano-part likewise, and the shade of Philip Heseltine, so strangely renamed, should gain contentment. He – the composer – did not facilitate either the singing or the playing of his songs. For the voice they have a way of passing awkwardly between registers, and though the high notes are not very high they tend to be uncomfortably placed. The pianist, caught for long in a pool of chromatics, suddenly finds his hands flying in both directions. Yet for the singer with the control of breath and command of voice that John Mark Ainsley so splendidly employs here, and for a pianist with Roger Vignoles's sureness of touch and insight, they must be wonderfully satisfying to perform, for there is such a love of song implicit in them and such a personal voice speaks through them. The programme here is arranged chronologically, from 1911 to 1930. Early and Elizabethan poems are the favourite source, and then the poems of contemporaries such as Belloc, Symons and Bruce Blunt. Even the earliest of the songs, *The Wind from the West*, has the characteristic touch of a lyrical impulse, directly responsive to words, and a fastidious avoidance of strophic or harmonic banality. Often a private unease works within the chromaticism as in the *Cradle Song* ("Be still, my sweet sweeting"), yet nothing could be more wholehearted in gaiety when he is in the mood for it (viz. *In an arbour green*, *Robin Goodfellow*, *Jillian of Berry*). Ainsley sings with fine reserves of power as well as softness; he phrases beautifully, and all the nuance that is so essential for these songs (in *Sleep*, for instance) is most sensitively judged. Vignoles is entirely at one with singer and composer. There are also excellent notes by Fred Tomlinson, and a strikingly fine watercolour by Peter de Wint graces the booklet.

Additional recommendation ...

...I held love's head. Thou gav'st me leave to kiss. The Singer. Consider. A Sad Song. Rutterkin. *Coupled with songs by* **Ireland, Howells, Bridge** *and* **Holst** Sarah Leonard (sop); **Malcolm Martineau** (pf). Cala United Ⓕ 88016-2 (61 minutes: DDD: 3/95).

Further listening ...

...Capriol Suite. Serenade. The Curlew. Where riches is everlasting. The Shrouding of the Duchess of Malfi. The lady's birthday. Pretty Ring Time. Autumn Twilight. Captain Stratton's Fancy. Yarmouth Fair. **Traditional** (arr./ed. Warlock) Bethlehem Down. Adam lay y-bounden. I saw a fair maiden. Balulalow. **Various artists.** EMI British Composers CDM5 65101-2 (9/94).

...Capriol Suite. **Britten** Variations on a theme of Frank Bridge, Op. 10. **Butterworth** Two English Idylls. A Shropshire Lad. The banks of green willow. **Academy of St Martin in the Fields / Sir Neville Marriner.** Decca Ⓜ 421 391-2LM (62 minutes: ADD: 8/89).

...A Cornish Carol. I saw a fair maiden. Benedicamus Domino. The full heart. The rich cavalcade. Corpus Christi. All the flowers of the Spring. As dew in Aprylle. Bethlehem Down. A Cornish Christmas Carol. *Coupled with* **Moeran** Songs of Springtime. Phyllida and Corydon. **Finzi Singers / Paul Spicer.** Chandos CHAN9182 (10/93). *Gramophone Editor's choice. See review under Moeran; refer to the Index to Reviews.*   Ⓖ

...The Shrouding of the Duchess of Malfi. The lady's birthday. *Coupled with works by* **Bax, Elgar, Vaughan Williams, Howells, Delius, Britten** and **Holst.** London Madrigal Singers / Christopher Bishop; Baccholian Singers of London; Philip Jones Brass Ensemble; English Chamber Orchestra / Ian Humphris.** EMI British Composers CMS5 65123-2 (2/96). *See review in the Collections section; refer to the Index to Reviews.*

Harry Warren
American 1893-1981

The Busby Berkeley Album [ac]Judith Blazer, Debbie Shapiro Gravitte, [abc]Ann Morrison, [d]Jayne Sylvester, [b]Nancy Long, Brent Barrett, [acd]Guy Stroman, [abd]Stan Chandler, [abd]Larry Raben, [bd]David Engel (sngrs); **London Sinfonietta Chorus and Orchestra / John McGlinn** ([d]sngr). EMI Angel Ⓟ CDC5 55189-2 (70 minutes: DDD: 12/94). Texts included. Recorded 1993.
Warren (orch. Heindorf) Gold Diggers of 1933 – We're in the money; Remember my forgotten man; Pettin' in the park[a]. Gold Diggers of 1935 – Lullaby of Broadway; I'm going shopping with you[b]. 42nd Street – 42nd Street; Shuffle off to Buffalo; You're getting to be a habit with me; Young and healthy[c]. Dames – Dames[d].   Ⓖ

In his introduction to the admirable booklet that accompanies this sizzling disc, Miles Kreuger writes that if "by some miracle" anyone has reached the record-purchasing age without seeing the great Busby Berkeley movies, then they can "make up their own images" to go with the exhilarating routines. You might think that without the sight of Ginger Rogers, Ruby Keeler, Dick Powell and supporting cast, the songs would fall a bit flat. The opposite is true of this CD. The sound is terrific and the original orchestrations by Ray Heindorf for Warner Brothers studio come up fresh and inventive. On the whole the modern singers have managed to hit off the required style without resorting to camp impersonations. Brent Barrett is especially successful in the Dick Powell numbers, "Young and healthy", "Pettin' in the park" and "I'm going shopping with you" from the less well-known *Gold Diggers of 1935*. On screen, the finale "Lullaby of Broadway" can seem interminable at the end of a long evening, but here it is the fitting climax to John McGlinn and the London Sinfonietta's enterprising foray into the field of the musical film. If you're feeling blue, just put on this CD and, in no time at all, the "hi-dee-hi and boop-a-do" will get you feeling "naughty, bawdy, gaudy and sporty".

Anthony Watson
New Zealand 1933-1973

Suggested listening ...
...Prelude and Allegro for Strings. *Coupled with* **Pruden** Soliloquy. **Lilburn** Diversions. Landfall in unknown seas[a]. Allegro. [a]Sir Edmund Hillary (narr); **New Zealand Chamber Orchestra.** Koch International Classics 37260-2 (12/95).

...Prelude and Allegro for Strings. *Coupled with works by* **Lilburn, A. Ritchie, C. Blake, Whitehead, Jenny McLeod, Farquhar, Pruden** and **Carr** New Zealand Symphony Orchestra / Kenneth Young.** Continuum CCD1073 (5/96). *See review in the Collections section; refer to the Index to Reviews.*

Unico Wilhelm, Graf van Wassenaer
Dutch 1692-1766

Suggested listening ...
...Concerti armonici – No. 1 in G major; No. 2 in B flat major; No. 3 in A major; No. 4 in G major; No. 5 in F minor; No. 6 in E flat major. **The Brandenburg Consort / Roy Goodman.** Hyperion CDA66670 (4/94). ✍

Sydney Watson
British 1903-

Suggested listening ...
...Evening Service in E major. *Coupled with works by* **Stanford, G. Ives, Gibbons, Leighton, Howells** and **Dyson** Lichfield Cathedral Choir / Andrew Lumsden with Nigel Potts (orgs). Priory PRCD505 (10/95). *See review in the Collections section; refer to the Index to Reviews*

Franz Waxman
German/American 1906-1967

Suggested listening ...

...Fantasy on Bizet's "Carmen". *Coupled with works by* **Korngold** and **Rózsa** Jascha Heifetz (vn); **RCA Victor Symphony Orchestra / Donald Voorhees.** RCA Victor Gold Seal mono/stereo GD87963* (4/89). *See review under Korngold; refer to the Index to Reviews.* ⒼⒼⒼ

...Film Scores: Prince Valiant – Suite. A Place in the Sun – Suite. The Bride of Frankenstein – Creation of the female monster. Sunset Boulevard – Suite. Rebecca – Suite. The Philadelphia Story. Old Acquaintance – Elegy for Strings. Taras Bulba – Ride to Dubno. **National Philharmonic Orchestra / Charles Gerhardt.** RCA Victor Gold Seal GD80708 (11/91).

...Rebecca. **Bratislava Radio Symphony Orchestra / Adriano.** Marco Polo 8 223399 (10/92).

...The Bride of Frankenstein. **Westminster Philharmonic Orchestra / Kenneth Alwyn.** Silva Screen FILMCD135 (3/94).

...Carmen Fantasia. *Coupled with works by* **Arban, Falla, Saint-Saëns, Paganini, Tchaikovsky, Sarasate, Fauré** and **W. Brandt** Sergei Nakariakov (tpt); **Alexander Markovich** (pf). Teldec 4509-94554-2 (6/95). *See review in the Collections section; refer to the Index to Reviews.* ⒼⒼ

...Sunset Boulevard – Sonata for Orchestra (arr. Mauceri). Dr Jekyll and Mr Hyde – Suite (arr. Palmer)[a]. *Coupled with works by* **Savino/Perry, Steiner, Stravinsky, J.T. Williams, Herrmann, Rósza, Barry** and **Goldsmith** [a]**Los Angeles Master Chorale; Hollywood Bowl Orchestra / John Mauceri.** Philips 442 425-2PH (1/95). *See review in the Collections section; refer to the Index to Reviews.*

Samuel Webbe II
British c1770-1843

Suggested listening ...

...Variations in A major on "Adeste Fideles". *Coupled with works by* **Marsh, Shield, Abel** and **S. Wesley** Salomon Quartet. Hyperion CDA66780 (3/96). *See review in the Collections section; refer to the Index to Reviews.*

Carl Maria von Weber
German 1786-1826

New review

Weber Symphonies – No. 1 in C major, J50; No. 2 in F minor, J51. Konzertstück in F minor, J282[a]. [a]**Melvyn Tan** (fp); **London Classical Players / Roger Norrington.** EMI Ⓕ CDC5 55348-2 (60 minutes: DDD: 9/95). 🎙 Recorded 1994. Ⓖ

Weber's symphonies may not be conventional symphonies nor his *Konzertstück* a conventional piano concerto, but they are highly original pieces and the performer who does not start from that premise will get nowhere with them. Norrington plays both symphonies more as sequences of remarkable orchestral inventions, and does so with great wit and style. He has flexibility, a gift for a neat rhythmic swerve or a sly rubato, a sense of timing as he makes the most of the unexpected pauses or abrupt explosions of sound; not least, he has a quick ear for the textures, and appreciates how the use of viola tone, or of hand-horns and their variously coloured notes, or of the contrast of solo woodwind instruments, is of the essence of the invention and not simply a colouring of it. These are delightfully fresh, enjoyable performances. Melvyn Tan's of the *Konzertstück* is in similar vein. The instrument he uses, a copy of an 1815 Streicher, is ideally suited to the light textures but can also produce enough weight to balance with the full orchestra; and he spares himself nothing with his hurtling tempos. A substantial element in this pioneering work is about virtuosity as a stimulus for invention, rather than difficulties for their own sake, and about how that can express itself in originality of form. Tan has the sense of relishing difficulties and fearlessly overcoming them, together with a vein of poetry in it all, which reminds one of accounts of Weber's own playng. The recording does full justice to all this artistry.

Additional recommendations ...

...Konzertstück, J282. Piano Concertos Nos. 1 and 2. **Nikolai Demidenko** (pf); **Scottish Chamber Orchestra / Sir Charles Mackerras.** Hyperion Ⓕ CDA66729 (57 minutes: DDD: 6/95).

...Symphonies Nos. 1 and 2. Turandot – Overture; Act 2 March; Act 5 Funeral March. Silvana – Tanz der Edelknaben; Fackel Tanz. Die drei Pintos – Entr'acte. **Queensland Philharmonic Orchestra / John Georgiadis.** Naxos Ⓢ 8 550928 (65 minutes: DDD: 2/95).

Weber Piano Sonatas – No. 1 in C major, J138; No. 2 in A flat major, J199. Rondo brillante in E flat major, J252, "La gaité". Invitation to the dance, J260. **Hamish Milne** (pf). CRD Ⓕ CRD3485 (76 minutes: DDD: 9/92). Recorded 1991.

Weber's piano music, once played by most pianists, has since suffered neglect and even the famous *Invitation to the dance* is now more often heard in its orchestral form. Since he was a renowned pianist as well as a major composer, the neglect seems odd, particularly when other pianist composers such as Chopin and Liszt are at the centre of the concert repertory; but part of the trouble may lie in the difficulty of the music, reflecting his own huge hands and his tendency to write what the booklet-essay calls "chords unplayable by others". Hamish Milnes makes out a real case for this music, and his playing of the two sonatas is idiomatic and resourceful, even if one cannot banish the feeling that Weber all too readily used the melodic and harmonic formulae of eighteenth-century *galanterie* and simply dressed them up in nineteenth-century salon virtuosity. From this point of view, a comparison with Chopin's mature sonatas or Liszt's magnificent single essay in the form reveals Weber as a lightweight. A hearing of the first movement in the First Sonata will quickly tell you if this is how you may react, while in its *Presto* finale you may praise a Mendelssohnian lightness but also note a pomposity foreign to that composer. Leaving aside the musical quality of these sonatas, this is stylish playing which should win them friends. The *Rondo brillante* and *Invitation to the dance* make no claim to be other than scintillating salon music, and are captivating in Milne's shapely and skilful performances. The recording is truthful and satisfying.

Additional recommendations ...

...No. 2. **Brahms** Four Ballades, Op. 10. **Alfred Brendel** (pf). Philips Ⓕ 426 439-2PH (53 minutes: DDD: 6/91).

...Nos. 1 and 2. **Martin Jones** (pf). Pianissimo Ⓕ PP20792 (58 minutes: DDD: 9/92).

...No. 1. Nine Variations on a Russian theme, "Schöne Minka", J179. Six Variations on an original theme, J7. Invitation to the dance, J260. **Alexander Paley** (pf). Naxos Ⓢ 8 550988 (66 minutes: DDD: 2/95).

...No. 2. Six Variations on Naga's air (from Vogler's opera "Samori"), J43. Seven Variations on a Gipsy song, J219. Grande polonaise, J59. **Alexander Paley** (pf). Naxos Ⓢ 8 550989 (61 minutes: DDD: 2/95).

Weber Meine Lieder, meine Sänge, J73. Klage, J63. Der Kleine Fritz an seine jungen Freunde, J74. Was zieht zu deinem Zauberkreise, J86. Ich sah ein Röschen am Wege stehn, J67. Er an Sie, J57. Meine Farben, J62. Liebe-Glühen, J140. Uber die Berge mit ungestüm, Op. 25 No. 2. Es stürmt auf der Flur, J161. Minnelied, J160. Reigen, J159. Sind es Schmerzen, J156. Mein Verlangen, J196. Wenn ich ein Vöglein war', J233. Mein Schatzerl ist hübsch, J234. Liebesgruss aus der Ferne, J257. Herzchen, mein Schätzchen, J258. Das Veilchen im Thale, J217. Ich denke dein, J48. Horch'!, Leise horch', Geliebte, J56. Elle était simple et gentilette, J292. **Dietrich Fischer-Dieskau** (bar); **Hartmut Höll** (pf). Claves Ⓕ CD50-9118 (52 minutes: DDD: 11/93). Texts and translations included. Recorded 1991.
Ⓖ

"In my opinion the first and most sacred duty of a song-writer is to observe the maximum of fidelity to the prosody of the text that he is setting." Weber was writing in defence of a number he composed for an obscure play, but his words can stand as an apologia for his 90-odd songs. His contribution to German song has been underrated, for his ideas were different from those of his contemporaries. Fischer-Dieskau used to resist suggestions that he might take up Weber's songs, and it is good that he has now done so, even late in his career. Always sensitive to words, he now responds with the subtlety of understanding that comes from many years of closeness to German poetry. Only very occasionally is there the powerful emphasis on the single expressive word that sometimes used mar his interpretations, keeping them too near the surface of the poetry. He can still use individual colour marvellously: the tonal painting of 'blue', 'white' and 'brown' in *Meine Farben* is exquisitely done. But more remarkable, here and in other songs, is the manner in which he follows the novel melodic lines which Weber has contrived out of the poetry. *Ein steter Kampf* is a masterly example; so is *Was zieht zu deinem Zauberkreise*, one of the few songs in which Weber enters Schubertian territory; so are *Es stürmt auf der Flur* and *Liebesgruss aus der Ferne*. Not even Fischer-Dieskau can quite bring off the coy *Der Kleine Fritz* by slightly sending it up (the only hope), and there is something a bit hefty about *Reigen*, a very funny wedding song full of "Heissa, lustig!" and "Dudel, didel!", though Hartmut Höll does wonders with the clanking accompaniment. Höll varies his tone so much here from the warmth and depth of his touch elsewhere that one wonders if the engineers did not take a small hand: why not? These are charming, touching, witty, colourful verses, often by minor figures of Weber's circle, and they drew from him music that heightens their point. Fischer-Dieskau's intelligent artistry could not more eloquently support the praise for Weber from Wilhelm Müller, poet of *Die schöne Müllerin* and *Winterreise*, as "master of German song".

Weber Der Freischütz. **Peter Schreier** (ten) Max (Hans Jörn Weber); **Gundula Janowitz** (sop) Agathe (Regina Jeske); **Edith Mathis** (sop) Aennchen (Ingrid Hille); **Theo Adam** (bass) Caspar (Gerhard Paul); **Bernd Weikl** (bar) Ottokar (Otto Mellies); **Siegfried Vogel** (bass) Cuno (Gerd Biewer); **Franz Crass** (bass) Hermit; **Gerhard Paul** (spkr) Samiel; **Günther Leib** (bar) Kilian (Peter Hölzel); **Leipzig Radio Chorus; Dresden Staatskapelle / Carlos Kleiber.** DG Ⓕ 415 432-2GH2 (two discs: 130 minutes: ADD: 11/86). Notes, text and translation included. From 2720 071 (11/73).

This opera tells of a forester Max and his pact with the forces of darkness to give him the ability to shoot without missing. Carlos Kleiber's recordings are always fascinating and for this one he went back to the manuscript, seeking out details rarely heard in the standard opera house text. His direction is imaginative and where controversial (his tempos do tend to extremes) one feels he presents a strong case. His cast is very fine too: Schreier's Max is more thoughtful than some, though always ready to spring back after his hellish encounters. Janowitz is a lovely Agathe and Mathis a perky

Aennchen, whilst Adam's Caspar is suitably diabolic. The use of actors to speak the dialogue does take a little getting used to, but the recording is good and the Dresden orchestra play magnificently.

Additional recommendations ...

...**Soloists; Chorus of the Deutsche Oper, Berlin; Berlin Philharmonic Orchestra / Joseph Keilberth.** EMI Ⓜ CMS7 69342-2 (two discs: 134 minutes: ADD: 9/89).

...**Soloists; Bavarian Radio Chorus and Symphony Orchestra / Eugen Jochum.** DG Double Ⓜ 439 717-2GX2* (two discs: 120 minutes: ADD: 12/94).

...**Soloists; Berlin Radio Chorus and Symphony Orchestra / Marek Janowski.** RCA Victor Red Seal Ⓕ 09026 62538-2 (two discs: 131 minutes: DDD: 1/95).

...**Soloists; Berlin Deutsche Oper Chorus and Orchestra / Lovro von Matačić.** RCA Victor Ⓜ 74321 25287-2 (two discs: 139 minutes: ADD: 6/95).

...**Overtures** – Der Freischütz; Oberon. *Coupled with works by* **Brahms, Mozart, Wagner, Berlioz** and **Rossini** London Philharmonic Orchestra; [b]Berlin Philharmonic Orchestra / Sir Thomas Beecham. Dutton Laboratories mono Ⓜ CDLX7009* (75 minutes: ADD: 10/94). *See review in the Collections section; refer to the Index to Reviews.*

...**Soloists; Bavarian Radio Chorus and Symphony Orchestra / Rafael Kubelík.** Decca Ⓜ 443 672-2DMO2 (two discs: 134 minutes: ADD: 8/95).

...**Der Freischütz** – Wie nahte mir der Schlummer ... Leise, leise, fromme Weise; Und ob die Wolke. Oberon – Ozean du Ungeheuer! ... Wolkenlos strahlt denn die Sonne; Traure, mein Herz. *Coupled with works by* **Mozart, Wagner** and **Schubert** Gundula Janowitz (sop); Irwin Gage (pf); Vienna Symphony Orchestra / Wilfried Boettcher; Orchestra of the Deutsche Staatsoper, Berlin / Ferdinand Leitner. DG Double Ⓜ 447 352-2GDB2 (two discs: 152 minutes: ADD: 12/95).

Further listening ...

...**Clarinet Concertos** – No. 1 in F minor, J114; No. 2 in E flat major, J118. Clarinet Concertino in E flat major, J109. **Paul Meyer** (cl); **Royal Philharmonic Orchestra / Günther Herbig.** Denon CO-79551 (10/92).

...**Clarinet Concertino.** *Coupled with* **Rossini** Introduction, Theme and Variations in B flat major. **Crusell** Clarinet Concerto No. 2 in F minor, Op. 5. **Baermann** Quintet (Septet) in E flat major, Op. 23 – Adagio. **Emma Johnson** (cl); **English Chamber Orchestra / Sir Charles Groves.** ASV CDDCA559 (11/86). ⒼⒼ

...**Invitation to the dance.** Overtures – Der Beherrscher der Geister; Euryanthe; Oberon; Abu Hassan; Der Freischütz; Peter Schmoll. **Berlin Philharmonic Orchestra / Herbert von Karajan.** DG Galleria 419 070-2GGA (6/88).

...**Grand duo concertant, J204.** *Coupled with* **Danzi** Clarinet Sonata in B flat major. **Mendelssohn** Clarinet Sonata in E flat major. **Charles Neidich** (cl); **Robert Levin** (fp). Sony Classical SK64302 (9/95). ✐

...**Clarinet Quintet in B flat major, J182.** *Coupled with* **Hummel** Clarinet Quintet in E flat major. **Reicha** Clarinet Quintet in B flat major, Op. 89. **Charles Neidich** (cl); **L'Archibudelli.** Sony Classical SK57968 (9/95). ✐

...**Piano Sonata No. 3 in D minor, J206.** Eight Variations on an air from Vogler's ballet "Castore e Polluce", J40. Seven Variations on Bianchi's air "Vien quà, Dorina bella", J53. Seven Variations on an original theme, J55. Momento capriccioso in B flat major, J56. **Alexander Paley** (pf). Naxos 8 550989 (2/95).

...**Piano Sonata No. 4 in E minor, J287.** Seven Variations on a theme from Méhul's opera "Joseph", J141. Les adieux, 'Op. 81'. Rondo brillante in E flat major, "La gaité", J252. Polacca brillante, "L'hilarité", J268. **Alexander Paley** (pf). Naxos 8 553006 (2/95).

...**Peter Schmoll und seine Nachburn.** **Soloists; Hagen Philharmonic Orchestra / Gerhard Markson.** Marco Polo 8 223592/3 (4/94).

...**Oberon.** **Soloists; Bavarian Radio Chorus and Symphony Orchestra / Rafael Kubelík.** DG 419 038-2GX2 (12/91).

...**Abu Hassan**[b]. **Humperdinck** Hänsel und Gretel[a]. **Soloists;** [a]**Mozart Chorus;** [a]women's voices of the **Deutsche Oper Chorus, Berlin;** [b]**chorus; Berlin Radio Symphony Orchestra /** [a]**Artur Rother,** [b]**Leopold Ludwig.** Preiser mono Ⓕ 90209* (two discs: 145 minutes: ADD: 3/96).

Frederick Weber
German 1766-1842

Suggested listening ...

...**Variations in F major.** *Coupled with works by* **Haydn, Neruda, Hummel** and **C.F.C. Fasch** **John Wallace** (tpt); **John Anderson** (ob d'amore); **Peter Thomas** (vn); **Philharmonia Orchestra / Christopher Warren-Green, Simon Wright.** Nimbus NI7016 (2/95). *See review in the Collections section; refer to the Index to Reviews.*

Anton Webern
Austrian 1883-1945

Webern Passacaglia, Op. 1. Six Pieces, Op. 6. Five Pieces, Op. 10. Variations, Op. 30.
Bach (arr. Webern) Musikalisches Opfer, BWV1079 – Ricercar a 6.

Schoenberg A Survivor from Warsaw, Op. 46[a]. [a]**Gottfried Hornik** (narr); [a]**Vienna State Opera Chorus; Vienna Philharmonic Orchestra / Claudio Abbado.** DG Ⓕ 431 774-2GH (50 minutes: DDD: 5/93). Text and translation included. Recorded 1989-92.　　　　　　　Ⓖ

Claudio Abbado has recorded rather more in the way of progressive twentieth-century music over the years than many other star conductors. It would be good to have much more. Meanwhile, we must be grateful for these recordings of Webern, including a fine reading of the rarely-heard and forcefully dramatic Variations, Op. 30. Abbado and the VPO are predictably responsive to the romantic intensity of the early *Passacaglia*, with nothing routine in their performance, and the sets of expressionist miniatures are even more convincing in their blend of delicacy and power. The fourth piece from Op. 6, the closest Webern ever came to concentrating the essence of a Mahlerian funeral march, and ending with an ear-splitting percussion crescendo, is all the more effective for Abbado's refusal to set a self-indulgently slow tempo. Technically, these recordings outshine the competition, though both Boulez and Karajan remain memorable as interpreters – Boulez especially in Op. 30, Karajan most notably in Op. 6. Given the evident rapport between Webern and Abbado it seems odd that the disc doesn't include more of Webern's music – for example, the Symphony, Op. 21. The Bach arrangement is nevertheless an ear-opening exercise in passing baroque counterpoint through a kaleidoscope of expressionist tone-colours, and Schoenberg's *A Survivor from Warsaw* retains its special power to move and disturb.

Additional recommendations ...

...Passacaglia. Five Movements, Op. 5. Six Pieces. Symphony, Op. 21. **Berlin Philharmonic Orchestra / Herbert von Karajan.** DG 20th Century Classics Ⓜ 423 254-2GC (46 minutes: ADD: 7/88).　Ⓖ Ⓖ

New review

Webern Passacaglia, Op. 1. Five Pieces, Op. 5. Six Pieces, Op. 6. Im Sommerwind.
Bach (orch. Webern) Musikalisches Opfer, BWV1079 – Ricercar a 6.
Schubert (orch. Webern) Deutsche Tänze, D820. **Berlin Philharmonic Orchestra / Pierre Boulez.**
DG Ⓕ 447 099-2GH (67 minutes: DDD: 3/96). Recorded 1993-4. *Selected by Soundings.*

With the exception of the Bach and Schubert arrangements this is all relatively early, pre-serial Webern, yet Boulez devotes as much care and as much affection to the D minor *Passacaglia* and to the undeniably immature but irresistibly luscious *Im Sommerwind* as to the far more characteristic Op. 5 and Op. 6 pieces. Indeed, if the *Passacaglia* is anything to go by, a Brahms symphony cycle from Boulez would be a fascinating prospect, while his reading of the 'idyll for large orchestra' suggests that his Delius might be no less interesting. Boulez does not imply that the mature Webern is present here in embryo; but he does perhaps make us ask how much of that later music is, like this, inspired by nature. To be reminded of Brahms by the *Passacaglia* is no less appropriate. This is a Janus of a piece, looking back not only to Brahms's Fourth Symphony but beyond (the presence of the Bach/Webern *Ricercar* points that up), and at the same time moving onwards from the delicate chamber passages in *Im Sommerwind* towards the 'orchestral chamber music' of Op. 5 and Op. 6. Boulez looks both ways too, with rich orchestral amplitude and expressive phrasing (very broad rubato) but he also notices Webern's already marked liking for transparent textures, quiet subtleties of string colour and the sound of the muted trumpet. And yes: heard in this context the shorter pieces are a logical progression. They are intensely expressive, with a wide range of emotion often within a very few bars; no wonder Boulez prefers the earlier, richer scoring of Op. 6. He obviously loves their Mahler-derived dissolution of the boundary between orchestral and chamber music, and encourages the Berlin Philharmonic to play with great tonal beauty, aware that a recurrent marking in mature Webern is "tenderly". Those qualities recur in the Bach and Schubert arrangements; the rubato in the Fourth Schubert Dance and the Viennese charm of the Fifth suggest that a Boulez *Fledermaus*, even, might be a gleam at the back of his mind. The recordings, very properly, are warm as well as clean.

Webern Complete works, Opp. 1-31. **Various artists.** Sony Classical Ⓜ SM3K45845 (three discs: 223 minutes: ADD: 6/91). Notes, texts and translations included. From 79204 (12/78). Recorded 1967-72. *Gramophone* classical 100. *Gramophone* Award Winner 1978.　　Ⓖ Ⓖ Ⓖ

Passacaglia, Op. 1 (London Symphony Orchestra / Pierre Boulez). Entflieht auf leichten Kähnen, Op. 2 (John Alldis Choir / Boulez). Five Songs from "Der siebente Ring", Op. 3. Five Songs, Op. 4 (Heather Harper, sop; Charles Rosen, pf). Five Movements, Op. 5 (Juilliard Quartet). Six Pieces, Op. 6 (LSO / Boulez). Four Pieces, Op. 7 (Isaac Stern, vn; Rosen, pf). Two Songs, Op. 8 (Harper, sop; chamber ensemble / Boulez). Six Bagatelles, Op. 9 (Juilliard Qt). Five Pieces, Op. 10 (LSO / Boulez). Three Little Pieces, Op. 11 (Gregor Piatigorsky, vc; Rosen, pf). Four Songs, Op. 12 (Harper, sop; Rosen, pf). Four Songs, Op. 13. Six Songs, Op. 14 (Harper, sop; chbr ens / Boulez). Five Sacred Songs, Op. 15. Five Canons on Latin Texts, Op. 16 (Halina Lukomska, sop; chbr ens / Boulez). Three Songs, Op. 18 (Lukomska, sop; John Williams, gtr; Colin Bradbury, cl / Boulez). Two Songs, Op. 19 (John Alldis Ch, mbrs LSO / Boulez). String Trio, Op. 20 (mbrs Juilliard Qt). Symphony, Op. 21 (LSO / Boulez). Quartet, Op. 22 (Robert Marcellus, cl; Abraham Weinstein, sax; Daniel Majeske, vn; Rosen, pf / Boulez). Three Songs from "Viae inviae", Op. 23 (Lukomska, sop; Rosen, pf). Concerto, Op. 24 (mbrs LSO / Boulez). Three Songs, Op. 25 (Lukomska, sop; Rosen, pf). Das Augenlicht, Op. 26 (John Alldis Ch, LSO / Boulez). Piano Variations, Op. 27 (Rosen, pf). String Quartet, Op. 28 (Juilliard Qt). Cantata No. 1, Op. 29 (Lukomska, sop; John Alldis Ch; LSO / Boulez). Variations, Op. 30 (LSO / Boulez). Cantata

No. 2, Op. 31 (Lukomska, sop; Barry McDaniel, bar; John Alldis Ch; LSO / Boulez). Five Movements, Op. 5 – orchestral version (LSO / Boulez). **Bach** (orch. Webern) Musikalischen Opfer, BWV1079 – Fuga (Ricercata) No. 2 (LSO / Boulez). **Schubert** (orch. Webern) Deutsche Tänze, D820 (Frankfurt Radio Orchestra / Anton Webern. Recorded live in 1932). 🅖🅖🅖

Webern is as 'classic' to Pierre Boulez as Mozart or Brahms are to most other conductors, and when he is able to persuade performers to share his view the results can be remarkable – lucid in texture, responsive in expression. Despite his well-nigh exclusive concern with miniature forms, there are many sides to Webern, and although this set is not equally successful in realizing all of them, it leaves the listener in no doubt about the music's sheer variety, as well as its emotional power, whether the piece in question is an ingenious canon-by-inversion or a simple, folk-like *Lied*. From a long list of performers one could single out Heather Harper and the Juilliard Quartet for special commendation; and the smooth confidence of the John Alldis Choir is also notable. The recordings were made over a five-year period and have the typical CBS dryness of that time. Even so, in the finest performances which Boulez himself directs – as indicated in the review above, the *Orchestral Variations*, Op. 30 is perhaps the high point – that remarkable radiance of spirit so special to Webern is vividly conveyed. It is a fascinating bonus to hear Webern himself conducting his Schubert arrangements – music from another world, yet with an economy and emotional poise that Webern in his own way sought to emulate.

Additional recommendations ...

...Movement. String Quartet (1905). Five Movements. Six Bagatelles. String Quartet, Op. 28. **Quartetto Italiano.** Philips Ⓔ 420 796-2PH (53 minutes: ADD: 4/88). 🅖🅖

...Five Movements. Six Bagatelle. String Quartet, Op. 28. Trio. Movement (1925). String Quartet (1905). Slow Movement (1905). Rondo (c. 1906). **Arditti Quartet.** Auvidis Montaigne Ⓔ MO789008 (66 minutes: DDD; 12/91). 🅖🅖

... Five Movements. Langsamer Satz. **Schoenberg** String Quartet No. 2 in F sharp minor, Op. 10[a]. **Berg** String Quartet, Op. 3. [a]**Christiane Oelze** (sop); **Brindisi Quartet.** Metronome Ⓔ METCD1007 (70 minutes: DDD: 6/95). 🅖🅖

...Piano Variations, Op. 27[b]. *Coupled with works by* **Stravinsky, Prokofiev** and **Boulez** Maurizio **Pollini** (pf). DG The Originals Ⓜ 447 431-2GOR (68 minutes: ADD: 6/95). *See review in the Collections section; refer to the Index to Reviews.* 🅖🅖

...Piano Variations, Op. 27. *Coupled with* **Schoenberg** Piano Concerto, Op. 42[a]. Drei Klavierstücke, Op. 11. Suite, Op. 25. **Berg** Piano Sonata, Op. 1. **Glenn Gould** (pf); [a]**CBC Symphony Orchestra / Jean-Marie Beaudet.** CBC Records Perspective Series mono Ⓔ PSCD2008* (65 minutes: ADD: 1/96).

...Two Pieces for Cello and Piano. Four Pieces, Op. 7. Three Little Pieces, Op. 11. Cello Sonata. *Coupled with works by* **Mahler, Schoenberg** and **Berg** Sabine Meyer (cl); **Gidon Kremer** (vn); **Veronika Hagen** (va); **Clemens Hagen** (vc); **Oleg Maisenberg** (pf). DG Ⓔ 447 112-2GH (76 minutes: DDD: 4/96). *See review in the Collections section; refer to the Index to Reviews.*

Webern Slow movement (Langsamer Satz). Five Movements, Op. 5. String Quartet (1905). Six Bagatelles, Op. 9. Rondo. Movement (Sehr lebhaft), Op. posth. Three Little Movements[a]. String Trio, Op. 20. String Quartet, Op. 28. [a]**Mary Ann McCormick** (mez); **Emerson Quartet** (Eugene Drucker, Philip Setzer, vns; Lawrence Dutton, va; David Finckel, vc). DG Ⓔ 445 828-2GH (68 minutes: DDD: 5/95). Recorded 1992. 🅖🅖

Webern being Webern, almost half the playing time is occupied by late-romantic juvenilia not published until after the composer's death, and which he might have been horrified to think of as being interlaced, as here, with his mature, radical and aphoristic works. Yet even the neo-Schoenbergian exercises of the 1905 Quartet are not without interest, the main motive signalling its serial potential until it gives way to a warm, well-upholstered tonality. Nor is there anything in the least perfunctory in the Emerson's performances of these early efforts. Their command of the multifarious techniques Webern calls for from Op. 5 onwards is complete, and they play with wholehearted freedom of expression in a well-balanced, rather closely focused recording. An attractive flexibility in the already intense compression of Op. 5 is complemented by a special refinement, which ensures that every note counts in the miniscule *Bagatelles*. It also pays dividends in the fiercely coherent lines of the Trio and its gossamer-like satellite *Movement*. To end with, the Quartet, Op. 28 inhabits a different, more sober world, at least until the finale brings back some of the old expressionistic turbulence to counter the rhythmic smoothness and motivic balance which dominate the earlier movements. This admirable performance sets the seal on a most distinguished enterprise.

New review

Webern Drei Gedichte (1899-1903). Acht frühe Lieder (1901-04). Fünf Lieder (1906-08). Fünf Lieder aus "Der siebente Ring", Op. 3. Fünf Lieder, Op. 4. Vier Lieder nach Gedichten von Stefan George (1908-09). Vier Lieder, Op. 12. Drei Lieder aus, Op. 23, "Viae inviae". Drei Lieder, Op. 25. **Christiane Oelze** (sop); **Eric Schneider** (pf). DG Ⓔ 447 103-2GH (76 minutes: DDD: 4/96). Texts and translations included. Recorded 1994.

Webern's songs are quiet and mostly brief (there are 40 of them here in the space of 76 minutes). They are intimate, ethereal, more concerned with distilling subtle emotional states than with telling stories or painting pictures. Christiane Oelze's voice and musicianship are well suited to them. Her voice is not large, but by careful control of dynamics she can easily encompass those infrequent moments where a big phrase or an ample gesture is required. The sound is pure and bright, her sense of line as admirable as her intonation and her pianist is an artist of great intelligence, refinement and command of colour. The recording balances them very well, not tempted by Oelze's confiding manner to come too close. The first mature songs here are those with opus numbers, the three earlier sets an account of how that maturity was achieved. In the two outer songs of the *Drei Gedichte* (charming, lyrical epigrams both, like thinned-down Wolf) we already hear a prediction of Webern's later manner, but the central setting of Richard Dehmel's "Nachtgebet der Braut" might be by another composer, with its four verses of overheated Wagnerian passion. Real urgency arrives with serialism and the last three sets of songs on this disc. With it arrives also fantasy, wit and a feeling of being at ease with the past; now Webern can make subtle but unmistakable allusions to (among others) Bachian aria and Viennese *Ländler* (this latter hint beautifully picked up by Oelze and Schneider). And by now he is also choosing poems, either very simple or exaltedly religious, that are ideally suited to his distilled, immaculate precision. Webern became a great songwriter with Op. 12, but the path to that achievement is absorbingly charted in these carefully studied performances.

Thomas Weelkes

British 1576-1623

Suggested listening ...
...Alleluia, I heard a voice. All laud and praise. Laboravi in gemitu meo. Give the king thy judgements. O Lord, arise. If King Manasses. When David heard. O how amiable are they dwellings. Gloria in excelsis Deo (Sing my soul to God). O Jonathan, woe is me. Hosanna to the Son of David. Pavane[a]. Evening Service for Trebles – Magnificat; Nunc dimittis. Voluntaries I and II[a]. **Winchester Cathedral Choir / David Hill** with [a]**Timothy Byram-Wigfield** (org). Hyperion CDA66477 (10/92).
...Alleluia, I heard a voice. Give ear, O Lord. Hosanna to the Son of David. When David heard. O Lord, grant the King a long life. Give the King thy judgements. Gloria in excelsis Deo (Sing my soul to God). Evening Service a 5. Ninth Service. **Christ Church Cathedral Choir, Oxford / Stephen Darlington.** Nimbus NI5125 (3/89).

Karl Weigl

Austrian 1881-1940

Suggested listening ...
...Sieben Gesänge, Op. 1. Liebeslied. *Coupled with* **Korngold** Unvergänglichkeit, Op. 27. Lieder, Op. 38 – No. 1, Glückwunsch; No. 2, Der Kranke. **Schreker** Entführung. Und wie mag die Liebe dir kommen sein?. Lieder, Op. 4 – No. 1, Unendliche Liebe; No. 2, Frühling; No. 3, Wohl fühl' ich wie das Leben rinnt; No. 4, Die Liebe als Rezensenten. Wiegenliedchen, Op. 7 No. 1. Ein Rosenblatt. **Schoenberg** In hellen Träumen. Warum bist du aufgewacht. Mannesbangen. Mailied. Gruss in die Ferne. **Steven Kimbrough** (bar); **Dalton Baldwin** (pf). Koch Schwann 310942 (2/95).

Kurt Weill

German/American 1900-1950

Weill Concerto for Violin and Wind Orchestra, Op. 12[a]. Kleine Dreigroschenmusik. [a]**Naoko Tanaka** (vn); **St Luke's Orchestra / Julius Rudel.** MusicMasters Ⓟ 67007-2 (48 minutes: DDD: 2/94).
Weill's Violin Concerto, although composed four years before *Die Dreigroschenoper,* is a definite precursor of the sound we associate with the more obviously popular music he wrote for his theatre pieces with Brecht. The parallel is especially striking in the scoring for wind orchestra and the flirtatious second movement, which Naoko Tanaka plays with a seemingly relaxed manner, in fine contrast to the 'duel' of the first, more skeletal movement. The Concerto has a handful of recordings, but Rudel's sympathetic conducting makes this the natural contender for first choice. The suite from *Dreigroschenoper,* first performed by an ensemble from the Berlin Opera under Klemperer, is one of Weill's most frequently performed works. Rudel's direction of the suite is beautifully light and elegant, with a splendid feel for the wit and balletic subtlety of Weill's orchestration.
Additional recommendations ...
...Kleine Dreigroschenmusik. Symphonies – No. 1; No. 2. **Lisbon Gulbenkian Foundation Orchestra / Michel Swierczewski.** Nimbus Ⓟ NI5283 (74 minutes: DDD).
...Violin Concerto[a]. Kiddush[b]. Kleine Dreigroschenmusik. [a]**Yuval Waldman** (vn); [b]**Grayson Hirst** (ten); [b]**Ray Pellerin** (org); [b]**Amor Artis Chamber Choir and Orchestra / Johannes Somary.** Newport Classic Ⓟ NCD60098 (55 minutes: DDD: 12/91).
...Violin Concerto[a]. **Hindemith** Wind Septet. **Toch** Five Pieces for Wind and Percussion, Op. 83. [a]**Christian Tetzlaff** (vn); **Deutsche Kammerphilharmonie.** Virgin Classics Ⓟ VC5 45056-2 (58 minutes: DDD: 7/95).

Weill Der Silbersee – Ich bin eine arme Verwandte (Fennimores-Lied); Rom war eine Stadt (Cäsars Tod); Lied des Lotterieagenten. Die Dreigroschenoper – Die Moritat von Mackie Messer; Salomon-Song; Die Ballade von der sexuellen Hörigkeit. Das Berliner Requiem – Zu Potsdam unter den Eichen (arr. Hazell). Nannas-Lied. Aufstieg und Fall der Stadt Mahagonny – Alabama Song; Wie man sich bettet. Je ne t'aime pas. One Touch of Venus – I'm a stranger here myself; Westwind; Speak low. **Ute Lemper** (sop); **Berlin Radio Ensemble / John Mauceri.** Decca New Line Ⓕ 425 204-2DNL (50 minutes: DDD: 3/89). Texts and translations included.

The songs in this collection are mostly from the major works Weill composed between 1928 and 1933, but also included are one from his years in France and three others from the 1943 Broadway musical *One Touch of Venus*. The collection introduces a most exciting talent in the person of Ute Lemper. By comparison with the husky, growling delivery often accorded Weill's songs in the manner of his widow Lotte Lenya, we here have a voice of appealing clarity and warmth. What distinguishes her singing, though, is the way in which these attributes of vocal purity are allied to a quite irresistible dramatic intensity. Her "Song of the Lottery Agent" is an absolute *tour de force*, apt to leave the listener emotionally drained, and her *Je ne t'aime pas* is almost equally overwhelming. Not least in the three numbers from *One Touch of Venus*, sung in perfect English, she displays a commanding musical theatre presence. With John Mauceri on hand to provide authentic musical accompaniments, this is, one feels, how Weill's songs were meant to be heard.

Additional recommendations ...

...(arr. Berio. Sung in English) Der Dreigroschenoper – Die Ballade von der sexuellen Hörigkeit. Marie Galante – Le grand Lustucru. Happy End – Surabaya-Johnny. **Berio** Recital I for Cathy[a]. 11 Folk Songs[b]. **Cathy Berberian** (mez); [a]**London Sinfonietta;** [b]**Juilliard Ensemble / Luciano Berio.** RCA Victor Gold Seal Ⓜ 09026 62540-2 (65 minutes: ADD: 7/95). *See review under Berio; refer to the Index to Reviews.* ⒼⒼ

...Zu Potsdam unter den Eichen. Divertimento, Op. 5 – Chorale-Fantasy: Herr Gott dein Zorn tu von uns wenden. *Coupled with works by* **Blacher, Shortall, B. Goldschmidt, Milhaud** and **Vaughan Williams** BBC Symphony Chorus / Stephen Jackson; Poznan Opera Chorus; Poznan Philharmonic Orchestra / Andrzej Borejko. Largo Ⓕ Largo5130 (two discs; 117 minutes: DDD: 7/95). *See review in the Collections section; refer to the Index to Reviews.*

Weill Die Sieben Todsünden[a]. Songs[b] – Complainte de la Seine; Youkali; Nannas Lied, "Meine Herren, mit Siebzehn Jahren"; Wie lange noch?; Es regnet; Berlin im Licht. **Brigitte Fassbaender** (mez); [a]**Karl-Heinz Brandt,** [a]**Hans Sojer** (tens); [a]**Hidenori Komatsu** (bar); [a]**Ivan Urbas** (bass); [a]**Hanover Radio Philharmonic Orchestra / Cord Garben** ([b]pf). Harmonia Mundi Ⓕ HMC90 1420 (55 minutes: DDD: 12/93). Texts and translations included. Recorded 1992-3. *Gramophone Editor's choice.*

Ⓖ

Weill Die Sieben Todsünden[a].

Berg Lulu – Symphonie. **Angelina Réaux** (sop); [a]**Hudson Shad** (Hugo Munday, Mark Bleeke, tens; Peter Becker, bar; Wilbur Pauley, bass); **New York Philharmonic Orchestra / Kurt Masur.** Teldec Ⓕ 4509-95029-2 (68 minutes: DDD: 12/94). Recorded live in 1993.

Weill Die Sieben Todsünden[a]. Songs – Lady in the Dark – One life to live; My ship[c]. Propaganda Songs – Schickelgruber; Buddy on the nightshift[b]. Nannas Lied[b]. Happy End – Bilbao Song; Surabaya-Johnny; Das Lied von der harten Nuss[c]. Je ne t'aime pas[b]. Der Abschiedsbrief[b]. One Touch of Venus – I'm a stranger here myself; Foolish heart; Speak low[c]. **Anne Sofie von Otter** (mez); [a]**James Sims,** [a]**Karl-Heinz Lampe** (tens); [a]**Christoph Bierbrach** (bar); [a]**Frederick Martin** (bass); [b]**Bengt Forsberg** (pf); [ac]**North German Radio Symphony Orchestra / John Eliot Gardiner.** DG Ⓕ 439 894-2GH (78 minutes: DDD: 12/94).

Weill and Brecht's *Seven Deadly Sins*, written in haste just after their flight from Hitler's Germany, was their last major collaboration. The question of its interpretation will always be bound up with the memory of Lotte Lenya, who created the role of Anna I. Brigitte Fassbaender is the first great Lieder singer to record it, the others have all been singing actresses or opera stars; her performance is stupendous – one of the best things she has ever done on disc. Of course she sounds rather aristocratic compared with the knowing street-singer style adapted by Ute Lemper (for Mauceri on Decca), but listen to "Lust", the very heart of the work, and marvel at the detail she extracts from both text and music. The rest of Fassbaender's disc is a judiciously chosen selection of Weill songs, all of which have some bearing on *The Seven Deadly Sins*. Cord Garben's conducting and the soloists in the male quartet are fine but compared with Rattle's interpretation, the pacing sounds a bit pedestrian. One cannot, however, imagine a dancer being able to keep up with Rattle's frantic speed in the Schneller Walzer section of "Pride". Elise Ross's performance (for Rattle, listed below) has been generally underrated, her singing is full of interesting detail, but inevitably she sounds pale compared with Fassbaender.

Angelina Réaux for Masur is the most operatic sounding of all the singers who have recorded it. Her interpretation is on the cool side, and although her diction is very clear it does not always sound idiomatic when compared with the authentic Berlin sound provided by Fassbaender, who is much more passionate. But Réaux is especially good at differentiating between the two sisters at the moments when she has to provide a voice for Anna II, the dancer. The key moment comes in "Lust" – when both girls, the practical Anna I and the beautiful Anna II have fallen in love with the same man in Boston but are forced to reject him in favour of a richer client. When she sings "Es war gar nichts zwischen uns, Lächerlich!" ("There was really nothing between us, ridiculous!") it is almost a cry of disgust. Fassbaender sounds angry, Réaux just apprehensive at this point. As for the *Lulu* suite, it is a very apt companion. Réaux has not sung Lulu on the stage – but it would be interesting to see her try it; she is one of the most touching actresses in American opera today. In his essay in the booklet, Kim Kowalke points out that "most of the memorable Lulus of our time have also performed *Sins*". (It's true – Lear, Migenes, Stratas, Silja.)

Von Otter's performance with John Eliot Gardiner is without question the most beautifully sung version of *Die sieben Todsünden* that has yet appeared. This is not altogether an advantage: the work is a grim parable about the triumph of materialism over human emotions and it needs that note of harshness and cynicism which Réaux certainly manages. On stage perhaps some of the subtle effects that von Otter and Gardiner try for might work but often the beauty of tone and line sacrifices the dramatic impact of the text. Gardiner's conducting seems rather erratic, in places as slow as Mauceri's for Lemper (the longest drawn-out on disc) but with good danceable rhythms elsewhere. It almost goes without saying that von Otter's diction is excellent, but at key moments she just misses the anguish that is so clearly needed. There are now so many recordings of *Die sieben Todsünden* that it isn't possible to make an out-and-out recommendation – it depends on the voice you respond to most. Fassbaender remains the present writer's own favourite, but Masur's pacing of the score is preferable to that of Garben.

Additional recommendations ...

...Die Sieben Todsünden. Mahagonny-Gesänge[a]. **Soloists; Berlin RIAS Sinfonietta / John Mauceri.** Decca Ⓕ 430 168-2DH (66 minutes: DDD: 4/91).

...Die Sieben Todsünden[a]. **Stravinsky** Pulcinella[b]. **Soloists;** [b]**Northern Sinfonia;** [a]**City of Birmingham Symphony Orchestra / Sir Simon Rattle.** EMI Ⓜ CDM7 64739-2 (73 minutes: ADD/DDD: 12/93).

Weill Street Scene. **Kristine Ciesinski** (sop) Anna Maurrant; **Richard Van Allan** (bass) Frank Maurrant; **Janis Kelly** (sop) Rose Maurrant; **Bonaventura Bottone** (ten) Sam Kaplan; **Terry Jenkins** (ten) Abraham Kaplan; **Meriel Dickinson** (mez) Emma Jones; **Angela Hickey** (mez) Olga Olsen; **Claire Daniels** (sop) Jennie Hildebrand; **Fiametta Doria** (sop) First Nursemaid; **Judith Douglas** (mez) Second Nursemaid; **English National Opera Chorus and Orchestra / Carl Davis.** TER Classics Ⓕ CDTER21185 (two discs: 146 minutes: DDD: 11/91). Recorded 1989.

Street Scene is the most ambitious product of Weill's American years. It's something of a *Porgy and Bess* transferred from Catfish Row to the slum tenements of New York. Where *Porgy and Bess* is through-composed with recitatives, though, *Street Scene* offers a mixture of set musical numbers, straight dialogue, and dialogue over musical underscoring. The musical numbers themselves range from operatic arias and ensembles to rousing 1940s dance numbers. It is consistently well sung, particularly where style is concerned. Weill described the work as a "Broadway opera", and it demands a vernacular rather than a classical operatic singing style. This it duly gets from Kristine Ciesinski as Anna Maurrant, while Janis Kelly's beautifully clear but natural enunciation and her sense of emotional involvement make daughter Rose's "What good would the moon be?" a performance of real beauty. Praiseworthy too is Richard Van Allan as the murderous husband, his "Let things be like they always was" creating a suitably sinister effect. Among the subsidiary attractions is the appearance of Catherine Zeta Jones, performing the swinging dance number "Moon-faced, starry-eyed".

Weill Lost in the Stars. **Gregory Hopkins** (ten) Leader; **Arthur Woodley** (bass-bar) Stephen Kumolo; **Reginald Pindell** (bar) Absalom, John, Man, Villager; **Cynthia Clarey** (sop) Irina; **Carol Woods** (sngr) Linda; **Jamal Howard** (treb) Alex; **Richard Vogt** (spkr) Stationmaster, Judge; **New York Concert Chorale; St Luke's Orchestra / Julius Rudel.** MusicMasters Ⓕ 67100-2 (72 minutes: DDD: 11/93). Recorded 1992.

Lost in the Stars is subtitled "A Musical Tragedy" and was adapted by Maxwell Anderson from Alan Paton's novel *Cry the Beloved Country*. Weill and Anderson's use of a chorus to comment on the action and advance the story makes the play difficult to stage, and Anderson's sentimentalization of the Paton original has made it one of the most dated of Weill's works. Julius Rudel conducted a production of *Lost in the Stars* for the New York City Opera in 1959, and observes in the booklet that he found these recording sessions "somewhat akin to a religious experience". This certainly communicates itself, especially in the choral sequence "Cry the Beloved Country" which frames the death-cell confrontation between father and son. Without much recorded dialogue, the condescending sugariness of the Anderson contribution is reduced and Weill's experimentation with the choruses as well as his usual high quota of great melodies make this one of the finest modern recordings of his work. In the main role of the black preacher, Kumolo, Arthur Woodley sings with fervour and fine diction and the Orchestra of St Luke's manage an accurate 1940s sound; a real achievement. This is a major addition to the catalogue and essential to any collection of Weill's work – or of twentieth-century opera.

Further listening ...

...Symphonies Nos. 1 and 2. *Coupled with* **Busoni** Berceuse élégiaque, Op. 42. **Schoenberg** Chamber Symphony No. 2, Op. 38. **New Philharmonia Orchestra / Frederik Prausnitz; BBC Symphony Orchestra / Gary Bertini.** EMI Matrix CDM5 65869-2 (4/96).

...String Quartet. *Coupled with works by* **Schulhoff** *and* **Hindemith** Brandis Quartet. Nimbus NI5410 (3/95). *See review under Schulhoff; refer to the Index to Reviews.* Ⓖ

...One Touch of Venus – That's him. Lady in the Dark – The saga of Jenny; My ship. Lost in the Stars – Stay well. *Coupled with works by* **Sondheim, Blitzstein** *and* **Bernstein** Dawn Upshaw (sop); orchestra / Eric Stern. Elektra Nonesuch 7559-79345-2 (12/94). *See review in the Collections section; refer to the Index to Reviews.* **Gramophone** *Award Winner 1995.* ⒼⒼ

...Der Silbersee. Soloists; Cologne Pro Musica; Cologne Radio Symphony Orchestra / Jan Latham-König. Capriccio 60 011-2 (8/90).

...Die Dreigroschenoper. Soloists; Berlin RIAS Chamber Choir and Sinfonietta / John Mauceri. Decca 430 075-2DH (3/90).

Leó Weiner
British 1885-1960   *(Hungarian 1885-1960)*

Suggested listening ...

...Suite on Hungarian Folk-tunes, Op. 18. *Coupled with* **Bartók** The miraculous mandarin, Sz73[a]. [a]**London Voices; Philharmonia Orchestra / Neeme Järvi.** Chandos CHAN9029 (3/92). Ⓖ

...Three Hungarian Rural Dances. *Coupled with works by* **Kodály, Liszt, Dohnány, Bartók, Kurtág** *and* **Szöllösy** Peter Frankl (pf). ASV CDDCA860 (6/93). *See review in the Collections section; refer to the Index to Reviews.* ⒼⒼⒼ

Judith Weir
British 1954-

New review

Weir The Art of Touching the Keyboard[d]. I Broke off a Golden Branch[d]. El Rey de Francia[d]. The King of France[a]. Distance and Enchantment[ae]. The Bagpiper's String Trio[e]. Ardnamurchan Point[bc]. [a]**Susan Tomes,** [b]**William Howard,** [c]**Petra Casén** (pfs); [d]**Schubert Ensemble of London;** [e]**Domus** (Krysia Osostowicz, vn; Timothy Boulton, va; Richard Lester, vc). Collins Classics Ⓟ 1453-2 (58 minutes: DDD: 12/95). Recorded 1995.

Judith Weir's music is not simplistic, nor does it ape any style from the past, and it is not in the least minimalist, but it has qualities that could appeal to a vastly wider audience than the 'contemporary music public'. Her music is bold, clean and uncluttered, with a strong melodic line and purposeful forward movement. Those qualities are present even when she is paying an overt homage to Schubert, as in the exquisitely lyrical opening of *I Broke off a Golden Branch* (written for the Schubert Ensemble of London, and for the forces of the *Trout* Quintet), all the more so since the other preoccupation of this fine work is to avow a debt: to the beautiful, ancient folk music of the region we used to call Yugoslavia. Anyone who can carry out both of these objectives – and the gesture to Schubert is as delightfully affectionate as the tribute to Croatia is eloquent – and still remain unmistakably herself is evidently a very considerable composer. Strong melody is a feature of all these pieces: long, eventful, often florid melody. Indeed, despite changes of mood, direction, tempo and texture you can hear each piece as a single long melody. Even *The Art of Touching the Keyboard*, an avowed study of types of keyboard attack, has a surprising unity, a feeling that the whole piece is in a single span. *Ardnamurchan Point*, despite being for two keyboards, is mostly a single line throughout, a sort of journey; as with the tortuous road that suggested the title, you know that there will be a grand view at the end of it. That this sort of line has its roots in folk music is acknowledged in *Distance and Enchantment*, a piano quartet based on two folk melodies about mysterious vanishings (an appendix, in fact, to Weir's opera *The Vanishing Bridegroom*) and in *The Bagpiper's String Trio*. Nearly all these pieces were written for close friends, in most cases the artists on this disc; Weir says that of all her works these (for that very reason?) are the ones she most enjoys listening to. That quality too, of the anticipation of shared pleasure, is clearly audible in the performances, and adds to the enjoyment of the collection as a whole.

Further listening ...

...The Consolations of Scholarship – Chinese Yuan drama[a]. King Harald's Saga[b]. [a]**Linda Hirst** (sop); [b]**Jane Manning** (sop); [a]**Lontano / Odaline de la Martinez.** Cala United 88040 (3/90).

...Don't let that horse. *Coupled with works by* **P.P. Nash, Connolly, Bauld, Elias, Payne** *and* **A. Gilbert** Jane Manning (sop); Jane's Minstrels. NMC Artists' Series NMCD025 (10/95). *See review in the Collections section; refer to the Index to Reviews.* Ⓖ

...(arr. Finnissy) Songs from the Exotic (on the rocks). *Coupled with works by* **N. Hayes, Hallgrimsson, Finnissy, G. Jackson, S. Harrison, Crane, A. Fisher** *and* **Skempton** Tapestry. British Music Label BML012 (12/95). *See review in the Collections section; refer to the Index to Reviews.*

...Blond Eckbert. **Soloists; English National Opera Chorus and Orchestra / Sîan Edwards.** Collins Classics 1461-2 (7/95).

Hugo Weisgall
American 1912-

Suggested listening ...
...Six Characters in Search of an Author. **Soloists; Chorus and Orchestra of the Lyric Opera, Chicago / Lee Schaenen.** New World 80454-2 (3/96).

Silvius Weiss
German 1686-1750

Suggested listening ...
...Sonata in A minor, "L'infidèle". Prelude, Fantasia and Fugue in C major. Tombeau sur la mort de M. Comte de Logy. *Coupled with* **Bach** (trans. North) Partita in D minor, BWV1004 – Chaconne. **Vivaldi** (trans. North, after Bach) Concerto in D major, RV230. **Nigel North** (lte). Linn Records CKD006 (12/92). 🎵
...L'Amant malheureux in A minor. Capriccio in D major. Plainte in B flat major. Prelude in D major. Prelude in E flat major. Suite I – B flat major; D minor; F major. Suite II in G minor. Suite in A major "L'esprit italien". **Lutz Kirchhof** (lte). Sony Classical S2K48391.

Samuel Wesley
British 1766-1837

New review

S. Wesley In exitu Israel[a]. Ave regina caelorum[a]. Magnificat anima mea[a]. 12 Short Pieces with a Voluntary added[b] – A minor; Gavotte in F. Services in F[a] – Te Deum laudamus; Jubilate Deo. Ostende nobis Domine[a]. Ecce panis angelorum[a]. Domine salvam fac regem nostrum[a]. Omnia vanitas (Carmen funebre)[i]. Voluntary in D[b]. Tu es sacerdos[a]. Might I in Thy sight appear[a]. O Lord God most Holy[a]. Dixit Dominus[a]. [a]**Gonville and Caius College Choir, Cambridge / Geoffrey Webber** ([b]org). ASV Gaudeamus Ⓟ CDGAU157 (65 minutes: DDD: 6/96). Recorded 1995.

Samuel, the father, has been rather neglected in favour of Samuel Sebastian, the son; and this excellent recital is the first to be devoted to him on CD. It opens with the eight-part motet *In exitu Israel* which is probably his masterpiece. Notoriously difficult to sing without some smudging of the quavers, it also requires firm direction to stop it from 'running away'. Here the cleanness of line is impeccable as is the steadiness of tempo, and the clarity of the performance is both aided and tested by the unreverberant acoustic of Selwyn Chapel in which it was recorded. The Gonville and Caius College Choir have a deservedly growing reputation, with voices of good, fresh quality, ears well-attuned to each other, and admirable alertness in matters of phrasing and rhythm. The inner parts perhaps need strengthening, especially in relation to the robust bass-line, which one would not wish to hear 'tamed' at the expense of colour and character. The sopranos are as good treble-substitutes as any, and provide some very adequate soloists. Wesley's genius worked largely within the restraints of his period: essentially he was an eighteenth-century composer, ten years younger than Mozart but apparently having nothing of Beethoven about him. It is an unostentatious style, graceful and economical. An extension comes with his unfashionable enthusiasm for Bach, which brings a contrapuntal vigour into many of his best pieces. The bravura accompaniment to *Domine salvam fac* reminds us that he was also the leading British organist of his time, and an attractive feature of this recital is its inclusion of organ works that are not always so easy to play as they may look. Geoffrey Webber gives a tasteful account, playing (for instance) the Gavotte as a dance-movement, and not in the grandiose disguise of its frequent appearances at the end of Cathedral Evensong.

Further listening ...
...Symphonies – No. 3 in A major; No. 4 in D major; No. 5 in E flat major; No. 6 in B flat major. **Milton Keynes Chamber Orchestra / Hilary Davan Wetton.** Unicorn-Kanchana DKPCD9098 (10/91).
...Voluntaries – E flat major, Op. 6 No. 7; B flat major. *Coupled with works by* **Boyce, Handel, Heron, Hook, Russell, Stanley** and **Stubley** **Jennifer Bate** (org). Unicorn-Kanchana DKPCD9106 (11/91). *Selected by Sounds in Retrospect. See review in the Collections section; refer to the Index to Reviews.*

Samuel Sebastian Wesley
British 1810-1876

Suggested listening ...
...String Quartet in E flat major. *Coupled with works by* **Webbe, Marsh, Shield** and **Abel Salomon Quartet.** Hyperion CDA66780 (3/96). *See review in the Collections section; refer to the Index to Reviews.*

…Anthems – Ascribe unto the Lord. Blessed be the God and Father. Cast me not away. Thou wilt keep him in perfect peace. Wash me throughly. The wilderness and the solitary place. Organ works – Andante in E minor. Choral Song and Fugue. Larghetto in F minor. **New College Choir, Oxford / Edward Higginbottom** (org). CRD CRD3463 (10/91).

…Morning and Evening Service in E major – Te Deum; Jubilate Deo. *Coupled with* **Britten** Te Deum in C major. **Howells** Collegium Regale – Te Deum; Jubilate. **Moeran** Te Deum and Jubilate in E flat major. **Elgar** Te Deum and Benedictus, Op. 34 – Te Deum. **Statham** Te Deum in D minor. Te Deum in C major. **Gladstone** Te Deum in F major. **Norwich Cathedral Choir / Michael Nicholas** with **Neil Taylor** (org). Priory PRCD470 (10/94).

Nigel Westlake

Australian 1958-

Suggested listening …

…Antarctica[a]. *Coupled with* **Sculthorpe** Nourlangie[b]. From Kakadu. Into the Dreaming. **John Williams** (gtr); [a]**London Symphony Orchestra**[b], **Australian Chamber Orchestra / Richard Hickox / Paul Daniel.** Sony Classical SK53361 (5/95).

William Wheeler

American 1952-

Suggested listening …

…Song for Someone. *Coupled with works by* **Zappa, Stravinsky, Van Vliet, Babbitt, J. Nelson, Shemaria, H. Hancock** and **London** Meridian Arts Ensemble. Channel Classics Channel Crossings CCS8195 (4/96). *See review in the Collections section; refer to the Index to Reviews.* ⓖ

Edward White

British 1910-1994

Suggested listening …

…Puffin' Billy. *Coupled with works by* **Binge, Williams, Coates, Toye, Collins, Farnon, Baynes, Curzon, Lutz, Gibbs, Ketèlbey, Joyce, Ellis** and **Ancliffe** New London Orchestra **/ Ronald Corp.** Hyperion CDA66868 (7/96). *See review in the Collections section; refer to the Index to Reviews.* **Gramophone** *Editor's record of the month.* ⓖ

Robert White

British c1538-1574

New review

R. White Domine, quis habitabit I. Domine, quis habitabit III. Ad te levavi oculos meos. Deus misereatur nostri. Miserere mei, Deus. Appro-pinquet deprecatio mea. Exaudiat te Dominus. Libera me, Domine, de morte aeterna. Regina caeli. **Henry's Eight.** Meridian Ⓔ CDE84313 (69 minutes: DDD: 5/96). Texts and translations included.

Robert White is one of those hugely gifted composers whose posthumous reputation has suffered from the proximity of an even greater figure; yet his finest pieces may stand comparison with anything written in his lifetime, by Byrd or anyone else. What strikes one at first hearing is the variety of techniques the composer employs. Most of the pieces heard here are psalm-motets, but White follows many different approaches ranging from imitation of a quasi-continental strictness to a free alternation of homophonic and polyphonic textures in the *Miserere* (reminiscent, though perhaps in that respect only, of Tallis's *Lamentations*). His melodic style is at times rather more florid than that of Tallis or Byrd. Another immediate impression is that of the commitment of the singers to this undervalued figure. The all-male Henry's Eight belong audibly to the Oxbridge tradition of choral scholars: that is to say that ensemble, intonation and textural clarity are pretty well faultless throughout. On the other hand, their capacity to shape individual pieces, to produce an incredibly vibrant and full sound when required (in short, to 'let rip'), is not so often met with in that tradition. This allows them to make the most of the textural contrasts of the *Miserere*, for example; equally, the long paragraphs of through-composed imitation are carefully paced, sometimes starting quietly, then building up, subsiding and building up again (listen to the very first track, *Domine, quis habitabit*). Supported by a fine recording on their home turf, the chapel of Trinity College, Cambridge, they sound very impressive indeed.

Additional recommendations …

…Christe, qui lux es et dies III and IV. Exaudiat te Dominus. Lamentations of Jeremiah. Magnificat. Portio mea Domine. Regina caeli. **The Tallis Scholars / Peter Phillips.** Gimell Ⓔ CDGIM030 (68 minutes: DDD: 6/95).

…Portio mea Domine. Regina caeli. Domine quis habitavit. Christe, qui lux es et dies. **Tallis** Mass Puer natus est nobis. Suscipe quaeso Dominus. Salvatore mundi Domine … Adesto nunc proprius. **The Clerkes of Oxenford / David Wulstan.** Calliope Approche Ⓜ CAL6623 (70 minutes: 11/95).

Gillian Whitehead
New Zealand 1941-

Suggested listening
…Resurgences. *Coupled with works by* **C. Blake, A. Ritchie, A. Watson, Lilburn, Whitehead, Jenny McLeod, Farquhar, Pruden** and **Carr** New Zealand Symphony Orchestra / Kenneth Young. Continuum CCD1073 (5/96). *See review in the Collections section; refer to the Index to Reviews.*

Percy Whitlock
British 1903-1946

New review
Whitlock Organ Sonata in C minor. Five Short Pieces. Three Reflections. Wessex Suite – March: Rustic Cavalry. **Robert Gower** (org). ASV Ⓕ CDDCA957 (75 minutes: DDD: 7/96). Played on the organ of Selby Abbey. From Abacus ABA505-2 (4/89).
The more you hear Whitlock's Organ Sonata the more convinced you will be that this is one of the unsung masterpieces of British organ music, so it's good that Robert Gower's première recording of the work should be reissued in time to mark the fiftieth anniversary of the composer's death in 1946. The sonata's none too subtle allusions to Rachmaninov and Delius, not to mention a plethora of other references and influences, enrich Whitlock's already luscious harmonic vocabulary, and it all gels together splendidly in an organ work with orchestral aspirations perfectly suited to the big English symphonic organ – of which Selby Abbey's 1909 Hill is a classic example. You would expect Robert Gower, as a leading light in the Percy Whitlock Society, to be an enthusiastic advocate and with his undoubted virtuosic skills he produces an immensely rewarding performance. His own reconstruction of the March from one of Whitlock's lost orchestral scores rounds this rewarding disc off in a surprisingly rousing fashion.
Further listening ...
…Hymn Preludes – Darwall's 148th; Song 13. *Coupled with works by* **C.S. Lang, Howells, Elgar, Vaughan Williams** and **Cocker** Gareth Green (org). Naxos 8 550582 (3/93). *See review in the Collections section; refer to the Index to Reviews.*

Charles Marie Widor
French 1844-1937

Widor Organ Symphonies, Op. 42: No. 5 in F minor – Adagio; Toccata. No. 6 in C minor – Allegro. No. 7 – Moderato cantabile; Allegro. Symphonie gothique, Op. 70. Trois Nouvelles Pièces, Op. 87. **Thomas Trotter** (org). Argo Ⓕ 433 152-2ZH (74 minutes: DDD: 10/92). Played on the Cavaillé-Coll organ of Saint François-de-Sales, Lyon, France. Recorded 1990.
Two pieces of organ music stand head and shoulders above anything else in sheer popularity. After Bach's Toccata and Fugue in D minor, Widor's Toccata has justifiably attracted admiration from generations of music-lovers. Any church organist will tell you that it's requested as frequently for weddings as any music, and in performance it displays not only the player's virtuosity but also the power and glory of the instrument itself. But to assess Widor's qualities as a composer on the strength of this one piece is to do him a major disservice. Let's say straight away that Thomas Trotter's sturdy performance is the equal of any, and this full-throated French organ makes a simply wondrous noise. The Toccata comes from one of ten full-scale symphonies Widor wrote for the organ, attempting to recreate in scope and range on one instrument what other symphonists achieve through the medium of a large orchestra. These organ symphonies exploit a vast array of colours and effects and in addition to a complete symphony (the aptly named *Gothic*) Trotter has selected a number of individual movements – the majestic opening of the Sixth, the lyrical *moderato cantabile* from the Eighth and not only the Toccata but the reflective *Adagio* which precedes it in the Fifth (and without which no performance of the Toccata should be considered complete). Argo have captured these splendid performances in a most atmospheric recording which will hopefully inspire the inquisitive listener to delve beyond the flamboyant Toccata.
Additional recommendations ...
…No. 5. **Poulenc** Concerto for Organ, Strings and Percussion in G minor[a]. **Guilmant** Organ Symphony No. 1 in D minor, Op. 42[a]. **Ian Tracey** (org); [a]BBC Philharmonic Orchestra / Yan Pascal Tortelier. Chandos Ⓕ CHAN9271 (80 minutes: DDD: 11/94). *See review under Guilmant; Refer to the Index to Reviews.* ⓆⒶ
…Symphonie Gothique. **Vierne** Symphony No. 3, Op. 28. **Tournemire** Suite Evocatrice, Op. 74. **Jeremy Filsell** (org). Herald Ⓕ HAVPCD145 (71 minutes: DDD: 3/92). *See review under Tournemire; refer to the Index to Reviews.* ⓆⒶ
Further listening ...
…Sinfonia sacra, Op. 81[a]. Symphony No. 3, Op. 69[b]. **Paul Wisskirchen** (org); [a]Cologne Gurzenich Orchestra; [b]Philharmonia Hungarica / Volker Hempfling. Motette CD40071.
…Scherzo in E major, "La Chasse". *Coupled with* **Malengreau** Symphonie de la Passion, Op. 20. **Peeters** Suite, Op. 71. **P. Pierné** Pastorale. **Guillou** Toccata. **John Scott Whiteley** (org). Priory PRCD487 (2/96).

Henryk Wieniawski
Polish 1835-1880

Suggested listening ...
...Violin Concerto No. 2 in D minor, Op. 22[a]. *Coupled with* **Vieuxtemps** Violin Concerto No. 4 in
D minor, Op. 31[a]. **Saint-Saëns** Introduction and Rondo capriccioso, Op. 28[a]. **Sarasate**
Zigeunerweisen, Op. 20 No. 1[b]. **Jascha Heifetz** (vn); [a]**London Philharmonic Orchestra;** [b]**London
Symphony Orchestra / Sir John Barbirolli.** EMI Références mono Ⓜ CDH7 64251-2* (69 minutes:
ADD: 5/92).
...Violin Concerto No. 2 in D minor, Op. 22. *Coupled with* **Saint-Saëns** Violin Concerto No. 3 in
B minor, Op. 61. **Julian Rachlin** (vn); **Israel Philharmonic Orchestra / Zubin Mehta.** Sony Classical
SK48373 (12/92). *See review under Saint-Saëns; refer to the Index to Reviews.*
...Polonaise No. 1 in D major, Op. 4. Légende, Op. 17. *Coupled with works by* **Paganini, Kreisler,
Bloch, Tchaikovsky, Messiaen, Sarasate** and **Bazzini** Maxim Vengerov (vn); Itamar Golan
(pf). Teldec 9031-77351-2 (4/94). *See review in the Collections section; refer to the Index to Reviews.*
...Légende, Op. 17. Zigeunerweisen.*Coupled with works by* **Massenet, Glazunov,
Rachmaninov, Sarasate, Rimsky-Korsakov, Tchaikovsky** and **Kreisler** Itzhak Perlman
(vn); **Abbey Road Ensemble / Lawrence Foster.** EMI CDC5 55475-2 (1/96).

Adolf Wiklund
Swedish 1879-1950

Suggested listening ...
...Piano Concertos – No. 1 in E minor, Op. 10[a]. No. 2 in B minor, Op. 17[b]. Summer night and
sunrise, Op. 18. [a]**Ingemar Edgren,** [b]**Greta Erikson** (pfs); **Swedish Radio Symphony Orchestra / Stig
Westerberg; Gothenburg Symphony Orchestra / Jorma Panula.** Caprice CAP21363.
...Souvenir de Moscou, Op. 6. Capriccio-Valse, Op. 7. Variations on an Original Theme, Op. 15.
Polonaise No. 1 in D major, Op. 4. Russian Carnival, Op. 11. Gigue in E minor, Op. 23. Saltarello
(arr. Lenehan). Mazurka in G minor, Op. 12 No. 2. Two Mazurkas, Op. 19. Kujawiak in
A minor. Légende, Op. 17. Scherzo-tarantelle in G minor, Op. 16. **Marat Bisengaliev** (vn); **John
Lenehan** (pf). Naxos 8 550744 (10/94).

Johan Wikmanson
Swedish 1753-1800

Suggested listening ...
...String Quartet No. 2 in E minor, Op. 1 No. 2. *Coupled with* **Berwald** String Quartet No. 1 in
G minor. **Chilingirian Quartet.** CRD CRD3361 (3/95).

Alec Wilder
American 1907-1978

Wilder Concerto for Oboe, String Orchestra and Percussion. Piece for Oboe and Improvisatory
    Percussion[a].
Barlow The Winter's Past.
Bloom Requiem. Narrative.
Corigliano Aria. **Humbert Lucarelli** (ob); [a]**Mark Wood** (perc); **Brooklyn Philharmonic Orchestra /
    Michael Barrett.** Koch International Classics Ⓕ 37187-2 (51 minutes: DDD: 7/94).
    Recorded 1993.
Although John Corigliano receives top billing for his intensely moving *Aria* (an effective arrangement
for strings and oboe from the slow movement of his Concerto for oboe and orchestra), it is Alec
Wilder's catchy, easygoing Concerto for Oboe, String Orchestra and Percussion which occupies the
lion's share of this CD (roughly half its playing time, in fact). Wilder's work ranges in tone from
'classical' music to popular ballads; Sinatra is one of his great fans (he made a famous record of
Wilder's beautiful song, *I'll be Around*) and many other prestigious artists have espoused his cause. Yet
mindless categorizing has sometimes inhibited a fuller appreciation of his skills as a 'serious' composer.
The concerto's gentle demeanour and subtle echoes of various contemporary masters (Lucarelli
himself suggests Gershwin, Poulenc and Villa-Lobos) make for an utterly bewitching 25 minutes. Then
there's Wayne Barlow's vernal *The Winter's Past*. His style reflects lazy, sun-soaked afternoons, rather
in the manner of Copland or Vaughan Williams. Here, as elsewhere in this warming miscellany,
Lucarelli weaves a warm, sinewy tone and receives responsive support from the Brooklyn Philharmonic
under Michael Barrett. Robert Bloom's nicely crafted, neo-romantic Requiem (with its Hebraic
undertones) and his rather more 'personal' *Narrative* are both prime contenders for any oboist's

repertoire. Lucarelli ends his programme with Wilder's wistful, upbeat *Piece for Oboe and Improvisatory Percussion* – a pleasant encore to an altogether charming, well-recorded disc.

William, Monk of Stratford
British fl. 15th-16th centuries

Suggested listening ...
...Magnificat. *Coupled with works by* **Plummer, Lambe** and **Davy** The Sixteen / Harry Christophers. Collins Classics 1462-2 (3/96). *See review in the Collections section; refer to the Index to Reviews.*

Charles Williams
British 1893-1985

Suggested listening ...
...The Dream Of Olwen (from the film "While I live"). *Coupled with* **Addinsell** Warsaw Concerto (from the film "Dangerous Moonlight"). **Rózsa.** Spellbound Concerto (from the film "Spellbound"). **Bath** Cornish Rhapsody (from the film "Love Story"). **Gershwin** Rhapsody in Blue. **Daniel Adni** (pf); **Bournemouth Symphony Orchestra / Kenneth Alwyn.** Classics for Pleasure CD-CFP9020.
...The Night Has Eyes – Theme. *Coupled with works by* **Brodszky, Addinsell, C. Parker, J. Addison II, Arnold, Allan Gray, Frankel, Greenwood, Alwyn, Spoliansky, P. Green** and **Vaughan Williams** Various orchestras and conductors. EMI mono CDGO2059* (9/94). *See review in the Collections section, refer to the Index to Reviews.*

Grace Williams
British 1906-1977

Suggested listening ...
...Fantasia on Welsh Nursery Tunes[a]. Carillons[b]. Penillion[c]. Trumpet Concerto[d]. Sea Sketches[e]. [b]**Anthony Camden** (ob); [d]**Howard Snell,** [c]**Raymond Allan** (tpts); [abd]**London Symphony Orchestra;** [c]**Royal Philharmonic Orchestra / Sir Charles Groves;** [e]**English Chamber Orchestra / David Atherton.** Lyrita SRCD323 (6/95).

Graham Williams
British 1940-

Suggested listening ...
...The song within. *Coupled with works by* **Powers, Lutyens, LeFanu** and **R. Marsh** Mühlfeld Ensemble. Clarinet Classics CC0007 (10/94). *See review in the Collections section, refer to the Index to Reviews.*

John Williams
American 1932-

Suggested listening ...
...Flute Concerto[a]. Violin Concerto[b]. [a]**Peter Lloyd** (fl); [b]**Mark Peskanov** (vn); **London Symphony Orchestra / Leonard Slatkin.** Varèse Sarabande VSD5345.
...Jurassic Park – Theme. Dracula – Night Journeys. *Coupled with works by* **Savino/Perry, Steiner, Stravinsky, Herrmann, Rósza, Waxman, Barry** and **Goldsmith** Stephen Hough (pf); **Los Angeles Master Chorale; Hollywood Bowl Orchestra / John Mauceri.** Philips 442 425-2PH (1/95). *See review in the Collections section; refer to the Index to Reviews.*
...E.T.: The Extra-Terrestrial – original film soundtrack. MCA MCLD19021.
...Jaws – original film soundtrack. MCA MCLD19021.
...Jurassic Park – original film soundtrack. MCA MCD10859.
...Schindler's List – original film soundtrack. MCA MCD10969 (8/94).
...Star Wars Trilogy – original film soundtracks. Fox 07822 11012-2 (11/94).
...The Reivers – original film soundtrack. Columbia Legacy CK66130.

Meiron Williams
Welsh 1901-1976

Suggested listening ...
...Aros Mae'r Mynyddau Mawr (The mountains remain). Gwynfyd (Paradise). Awelon y Mynydd (Mountian breezes). O Fab y Dyn (O! son of man). Y lyn (The lake). Cloch y Llan (The Church bell). Rhosyun yr Haf (Summer rose). Ora Pro Nobis (Pray for us). Ffarwel iti, Cymru (Farewell, fair Wales). Pan Ddaw'r Nos (When night comes). Adlewych (Reflection). **Bryn Terfel** (bass-bar); **Annette Bryn Parri** (pf). Sain SCDC2013 (8/93). Ⓖ

Meredith Willson

American 1902-1984

Suggested listening ...
...The Music Man. **Original Broadway cast.** EMI Angel ZDM7 64663-2.

Ian Wilson

Irish 1964

Suggested listening ...
...Winter's Edge. *Coupled with works by* **Kinsella, Beckett** and **Boydell** Vanbrugh Quartet
Chandos CHAN9295 (10/94).
...I Sleep at Waking. *Coupled with works by* **D. Heath, Torke, McGlynn** and **Nyman** Gerard
McChrystal (sax); **London Musici / Mark Stephenson.** Silva Classics SILKD6010 (6/96). *See
review in the Collections section; refer to the Index to Reviews.*

Sandy Wilson

British 1924-

Suggested listening ...
...The Boy Friend. **Original 1984 London revival cast.** That's Entertainment CDTER1095 (3/87).

Dag Wirén

Swedish 1905-1986

Suggested listening ...
...String Quartet No. 3 in D minor, Op. 18. *Coupled with works by* **A. Tchaikovsky, Hugh Wood**
and **Barber Lindsay Quartet.** ASV CDDCA825 (1/93). *See review in the Collections section; refer
to the Index to Reviews.*

Peter Wishart

British 1921-1984

Suggested listening ...
...String Quartet No. 3 in A major. *Coupled with* **Rubbra** String Quartet No. 2 in E flat major.
Tate String Quartet in F major. **English Quartet.** Tremula TREM102-2 (12/93).

Hugo Wolf

Austrian 1860-1903

Wolf Italienisches Liederbuch. **Barbara Bonney** (sop); **Håkan Hagegård** (bar); **Geoffrey Parsons**
(pf). Teldec Ⓟ 9031-72301-2 (76 minutes: DDD: 7/94). Texts and translations included.
Recorded 1992. *Gramophone Editor's choice.*   Ⓖ
Wolf Italienisches Liederbuch. **Felicity Lott** (sop); **Peter Schreier** (ten); **Graham Johnson** (pf).
Hyperion Ⓟ CDA66760 (80 minutes: DDD: 9/94). Texts and translations included. Recorded
1993-4.   Ⓖ

The three vital and well-equipped interpreters on the Teldec disc give a reading of *Italienisches
Liederbuch* that can be spoken of in the same breath as the superb generation of Wolf interpreters
(listed below). Bonney and Hagegård are both highly versed in Lieder interpretation, both possess
attractive and individual voices allied to sound techniques, so we can take the vocal and verbal
accomplishments as such for granted. Both enter fully into the spirit of these charmed miniatures;
both have the art of immediately setting the mood of each song and shaping it swiftly into a
convincing whole, keenly supported by Parsons. Bonney catches the petulant anger of "Wer rief dich
denn?", then she relaxes into the wheedling urgency, two songs later, of "Nun lass uns Frieden
schliessen". In "Ihr jungen Leute" she is to the life the worried girlfriend taking leave of her soldier.
The dramatic power and range of emotional colour she can release in her voice come into play in
"Lass sie nur gehen" and the succeeding song "Wie soll ich fröhlich sein" and she ends the CD with
an exuberant "Ich hab' in Penna". Hagegård can also encompass every mood in his far-ranging
interpretations. The ninth song, "Dass doch gemalt" can stand as an exemplar for the rest – a hushed
and wondrous start, then a fine line and shaping to a heroic climax. He manages the ecstatic love
songs that lie at the Book's centre with a beauty and strength that would be hard to beat. "Und willst
du deinen Liebsten" and "Wir haben beide lange Zeit" have the touch of greatness on them; so, later
on, does "Benedeit die sel'ge Mutter". Parsons is a model of discernment and unexaggerated
musicianship throughout, never missing an interpretative point yet never underlining any to excess.
He is ideally balanced with the voices and the recording is truthful.

On the Hyperion disc it is gratifying to hear again a tenor rather than a baritone in all the lyrical
masterpieces so liberally distributed over the *Italian Songbook* and to hear each sung with such
understanding and feeling. You will surely be uplifted at Schreier's perceptive, natural way of
encompassing the awe of "Der Mond hat eine schwere Klag", the ecstatic adoration of "Und willst

du deinen Liebsten", the swagger of "Ein Ständchen euch zu bringen", the tenderness of "Und steh Ihr früh am Morgen auf", the simple beauty of "Benedeit die sel'ge Mutter", or any other of the man's songs calling for the pure, spontaneous art of this great tenor, with its refined line and ideal placing of words on tone. Where the woman's pieces are concerned, Felicity Lott seems perfectly attuned to the serious songs of love, but she is somewhat affected and exaggerated in the comic and ironic ones. The contrast can be felt in successive songs. In "Du sagst mir" she seems to be straining to convey its mocking mood; in "Wohl kenn ich Euren Stand" she perfectly conveys hopeless, true love through her sincere, lovely singing. She is also excellent in the scorn of "Was soll der Zorn?" and earlier "Wer rief ich denn?", sung in an all-in, Schwarzkopf-like vein, but as soon as Wolf adopts his humorous mode she sounds unnatural. Bonney, with a smaller range of vocal and emotional colour, is by and large more satisfying. Partnering both singers, Johnson is at his most positive; the playing is at once luminous and exact (similar qualities inform the excellent recording) and, as ever, his notes are masterly in their insights. If you want a version with a tenor soloist, this one will be a definite choice.

Additional recommendations ...

...**Elisabeth Schwarzkopf** (sop); **Dietrich Fischer-Dieskau** (bar); **Gerald Moore** (pf). EMI Ⓜ CDM7 63732-2 (79 minutes: ADD: 12/90).

...Italienisches Liederbuch[a]. Eichendorff Lieder. Nachruf. In der Fremde – I, II and VI. Rückkehr. Drei Gedichte von Michelangelo. [a]**Christa Ludwig** (mez); **Dietrich Fischer-Dieskau** (bar); **Daniel Barenboim** (pf). DG Galleria Ⓜ 439 975-2GGA2 (two discs: 142 minutes: ADD: 4/95).

Wolf Goethe Lieder – Harfenspieler I-III; Der Rattenfänger; Coptisches Lied I; Frech und froh I and II: Epiphanias; Genialisch Treiben; Der Schäfer; Blumengruss; Frühling übers Jahr; Anakreons Grab; Phänomen; Ob der Koran von Ewigkeit sei?; Trunken müssen wir alle sein!; So lang man nüchtern ist; Sie haben wegen der Trunkenheit; Hätt' ich irgend wohl Bedenken; Komm, Liebchen, komm!; Wie sollt ich heiter bleiben; Wenn ich dein gedenke; Ganymed. **Wolfgang Holzmair** (bar); **Thomas Palm** (pf). Collins Classics Ⓕ 1402-2 (55 minutes: DDD: 9/93). Texts and translations included. Recorded live in 1988. *Gramophone Editor's choice.*

Holzmair is a refreshing and challenging singer. He follows no known school and quite avoids the influence of Fischer-Dieskau. His voice is individual and tangy; his interpretations here, as elsewhere, are apparently spontaneous (the live recording helps) and unmarked by convention. His tone doesn't please everyone; it has a quick vibrato of a kind more frequently encountered in the earlier decades of the century than in the later, and it can harden under pressure. That's part of the price of taking risks: like Wolf he isn't always well behaved – and he's all the more stimulating for his immediacy of manner. Nowhere is that more apparent than in *Ganymed* where the wonder of the poem and its setting is wholly conveyed in this soaring interpretation. At the other end of the emotional scale in the inexhaustible variety of the Goethe settings is the desolation of the *Harfenspieler* ones, in the first of which the line "Dann bin ich nicht allein" carries all the inner torment of the mysterious old man. Nor at the end of the next verse is Holzmair averse to bursting out in operatic-like pain at "Mich Einsamen die Pein". The all-important piano parts are in the safe hands of Thomas Palm, a most sensitive player. He is placed a shade too far backward in relation to the voice but this probably reflects what you would have heard in the concert-hall. Too much applause is included and the length is short by today's standards on CD. But, as they say, the quality is what matters and here it is high.

Additional recommendations ...

...Mignon I; Mignon II; Mignon III; Mignon ("Kennst du das Land?"), Blumengruss; Die Bekehrte; Frühling übers Jahr; Anakreons Grab. *Coupled with works by* **Mozart, Beethoven, Schubert** and **Schumann** Irmgard Seefried (sop); Erik Werba (pf). Orfeo D'Or mono Ⓕ C297921B* (71 minutes: ADD: 9/93). *See review in the Collections section; refer to the Index to Reviews.* ⒼⒼ

...Wanderers Nachtlied. Der Rattenfänger. Coptisches Lied II. Genialisch Treiben. Frühling übers Jahr. Anakreons Grab. Phänomen. Ob der Koran von Ewigkeit sei?. *Coupled with works by* **Amalia, Reichardt, Zelter, Schumann, Schubert, Brahms, R. Strauss, Schoeck, Reger, Busoni** and **Beethoven** Dietrich Fischer-Dieskau (bar); Karl Engel (pf). Orfeo D'Or mono Ⓕ C389951B* (72 minutes: ADD: 2/96).

New review

Wolf Spanisches Liederbuch. **Anne Sofie von Otter** (mez); **Olaf Bär** (bar); **Geoffrey Parsons** (pf). EMI Ⓕ CDS5 55325-2 (two discs: 109 minutes: DDD: 8/95). Texts and translations included. Recorded 1992-4.

The songs are performed not in the published order but in one devised by Bär for several recitals of the set given by this trio, and now carried over into the recording studio. For the ten religious songs the reordering works well. In any case here the two singers show a deep and rewarding comprehension of the agony and ecstasy of poems and music. Listen, too, to von Otter's sense of smiling wonder in "Ach, des Knaben Augen" as the holy mother looks into her son's eyes. By contrast in "Mühvoll komm' ich und beladen" she changes to a scaring, soul-searching manner that captures completely the woman's remorse, magnificently so at the climactic "Nimm mich an". Bär is as tense and inward in the great "Herr, was trägt der Boden hier", capturing the voices of penitent and Christ to perfection. Note, too, Parsons's deliberately heavy gait in "Die du Gott gebarst". There are problems, however, in the more numerous secular songs. With von Otter, apart from downward transpositions that make the piano parts sound unduly dark and Parsons consequently a shade heavy-handed, there is little to quarrel with. She teases, flirts, falls in love with the best of them, alert with her words, but never overdoing the archness as Schwarzkopf sometimes does. Bär, though, is not only up against the perhaps more formidable challenge of Fischer-Dieskau but also against his own reordering. He does not have – how could he? – the immense tonal range and emotional charge of the older baritone. "Herz, verzage nicht geschwind" is broader, more biting in Fischer-Dieskau's reading, for instance, "Ach im Maien" that much more mellifluous, but you could say that Bär's more contained, but by no means reticent approach has its own, Wolfian justification. But it is entirely Bär's fault that songs Nos. 21 and 24, which should be sung as a group, lose some of their force when separated as here, thoughtfully as Bär sings each in its turn. However, the readings as a whole are worthy of the collection. In the modern manner there is more space around the voices than on the closer-miked DG set, where Fischer-Dieskau is very much a presence in the room with you: you listen to the new pair in more of a recital ambience. This new version doesn't replace the old, which also has the advantage of price over the newcomer, but those who want another, fresh, valid view of the *Spanisches Liederbuch* or just want to hear von Otter in her element will wish to acquire these two absorbing discs.

New review

Wolf Spanisches Liederbuch – Die ihr schwebet um diese Palmen; Ach, des Knaben Augen; Mühvoll komm' ich und beladen; In dem Schatten meiner Locken; Sagt, seid Ihr es, feiner Herr; Mögen alle bösen Zungen; Alle gingen, Herz, zur Ruh; Tief im Herzen trag' ich Pein; Komm, o Tod, von Nacht umgeben; Ob auch finstre Blicke glitten; Bedeckt mich mit Blumen; Sie blasen zum Abmarsch; Wer tat deinem Füsslein weh; Geh' Geliebter, geh' jetz. Mörike Lieder – Das verlassene Mägdlein; Nimmersatte Liebe; Verborgenheit; Im Frühling; Elfenlied; Auf ein altes Bild; Lied vom Winde. **Elly Ameling** (sop); **Rudolf Jansen** (pf). Hyperion Ⓕ CDA66788 (59 minutes: DDD: 10/95). Texts and translations included. Recorded 1991.

This is a gratifying distillation of Ameling as a Wolf interpreter, a late flowering of her art in which we are consoled for some loss in the quality and quantity of tone by the insights offered. Indeed, in so many of these readings, her performance represents Wolf singing of the most telling kind. The four central songs tell us all. To "Ob auch finstre Blicke glitten" she brings a depth of verbal accent and inner expression that places it among Wolf's highest achievements. There follow a properly weary, care-ridden account of "Alle gingen, Herz, zur Ruh", a languorous evocation of "Bedeckt mich mit Blumen" and a tragic entry into the abasing world of "Mühvoll komm' ich und beladen". The two sacred songs are hardly less impressive. Her choice ends with a reading of "Geh' Geliebter", in which Ameling sheds the years to give us all the ardent thoughts of the girl reluctant at dawn to leave her lover. If you have hesitated before buying the complete EMI set, you might prefer to try this rewarding and distinguished selection. Ameling shows equal discernment in her choice from the Mörike settings, catching – as the best Wolf interpreters can do – the specific mood of each. If there is a favourite here it has to be "Das verlassene Mägdlein", where the dreadful anguish of the abandoned girl, so unerringly caught by Wolf, is expressed in a mood of almost toneless lassitude – just right. As ever, Jansen is an ideal partner for this singer, nowhere more so than when he rightly underplays the rhythm of "Sie blasen zum Abmarsch". Altogether as an introduction into the wonderfully satisfying world of Wolf song, this is a winner.

Wolf Mörike Lieder – Im Frühling; Auf eine Christblume I; Lied vom Winde. Goethe Lieder – Philine; Mignon; Der Schäfer; Blumengruss; Frühling übers Jahr; Anakreons Grab; Phänomen; Ganymed. Spanisches Liederbuch – Mühvoll komm' ich und beladen; In dem Schatten meiner Locken; Bedeckt mich mit Blumen; Wer tat deinem Füsslein weh; Wehe der, die mir verstrickte. Italieniches Liederbuch – Nun lass uns Frieden schliessen. Sechs Lieder für eine Frauenstimme – Mausfallen-Sprüchlein. Sechs alte Weisen. **Dame Elisabeth Schwarzkopf** (sop); **Gerald Moore** (pf). EMI Festspieldokumente mono Ⓕ CDH7 64905-2* (71 minutes: ADD: 10/93). Texts included. Recorded live in 1958. *Gramophone Editor's choice.* ⓖⓖⓖ

"A blissful experience of the purest lied art" reported the *Salzburger Nachrichten* on Schwarzkopf's recital. The recording derives from the Austrian Broadcasting Corporation's archive. It gives a marvellous sense of presence, recalling most vividly what it was that made the memory of Schwarzkopf's song recitals precious. First, the quality of voice, caught here at its purest and most radiant; then the full concentration of a total sensibility, emotion and intellect fused, upon the songs: every one of them lived a special life on each separate occasion. The riches of this recital are beyond the scope of a short review. Every song here deserves a paragraph to itself, and the appreciation of Gerald Moore's work would have a large share in each. The disc, for one who cares for Wolf's songs and the art of their performance, is beyond price.

Additional recommendation ...

...Spanisches Liederbuch. **Elisabeth Schwarzkopf** (sop); **Dietrich Fischer-Dieskau** (bar); **Gerald Moore** (pf). DG Galleria Ⓜ 423 934-2GGA2 (two discs: 102 minutes: ADD: 3/89).

Wolf Eichendorff Lieder – Der Freund; Der Musikant; Verschwiegene Liebe; Das Ständchen; Der Soldat I; Der Soldat II; Nachtzauber; Der Schreckenberger; Der Glücksritter; Lieber Alles;

Heimweh; Der Scholar; Der verzweifelte Liebhaber; Unfall; Liebesglück; Seemanns Abschied; Erwartung; Die Nacht. In der Fremde – I, UP87; II, UP88; VI, UP93. Rückkehr, UP90. Nachruf, UP81.

Korngold Einfache Lieder, Op. 9 – No. 1, Schneeglöckchen; No. 2, Nachtwander; No. 3, Ständchen. Der Kranke, Op. 38 No. 2. **Boje Skovhus** (bar); **Helmut Deutsch** (pf). Sony Classical Ⓕ SK57969 (62 minutes: DDD: 1/95). Texts and translations included. Recorded 1993.

Lovers of good Lieder singing will surely respond eagerly to Skovhus's bold and velvet-toned singing and welcome a disc of songs which are currently under-represented in the catalogue. Eichendorff and Wolf are here predominantly outside, walking or riding along, and Wolf is free of the cares marking the Mörike settings that went before in his opus. Skovhus is the Musician, Soldier, Sailor, Swashbuckler, Fortune-hunter and Scholar to the life. But he can also encompass a more thoughtful mood, as expressed in pieces such as *Die Nacht*, where his quiet singing is perfection. Deutsch's mastery of Wolf's intricate rhythms and harmonies is never less than masterly, and he is recorded as an equal partner with the singer. Four of Korngold's Eichendorff settings form a neat pendant to the Wolf. Although his version of *Ständchen* is more obviously sentimental than Wolf's, it has its own character. *Schneeglöckchen* is suffused in Debussian harmony (Op. 9 was composed in 1917), and the final song, written 30 years later, is peculiarly Korngoldian in its passing-note harmony and deliberately post-romantic idiom. The interpreters are just as subtle yet unexaggerated in their performing here as in the Wolf.

Further listening ...
...Italian Serenade. *Coupled with* **Grieg** String Quartet No. 1 in G minor, Op. 27. **Sibelius** String Quartet in D minor, Op. 56, "Voces intimae". **Budapest Quartet** Biddulph mono LAB098* (4/95).

Julia Wolfe
American 1958-

Suggested listening ...
...Lick. *Coupled with works by* **L. Andriessen, D. Lang** and **Gordon** Bang on a Can All-Stars. Sony Classical SK66483 (2/96). *See review in the Collections section; refer to the Index to Reviews.*

Ermanno Wolf-Ferrari
Italian 1876-1948

Suggested listening ...
...Piano Trios – D major, Op. 5; F sharp major, Op. 7. **Raphael Trio.** ASV CDDCA935 (11/95).
...I quattro rusteghi – Intermezzo[b]. Il segreto di Susanna – Overture[b]. *Coupled with* **Rossini** Guillaume Tell – Overture[b]. **Respighi** Fontane di Roma[b]. **Verdi** Messa da Requiem[a]. La traviata[b] – Preludes, Act 1 and 3. I vespri siciliani – Overture[b]. [a]**Dame Elisabeth Schwarzkopf** (sop); [a]**Oralia Dominguez** (mez); [a]**Giuseppe di Stefano** (ten); [a]**Cesare Siepi** (bass); [a]**Chorus and Orchestra of La Scala, Milan,** [b]**Santa Cecilia Academy Orchestra, Rome / Victor de Sabata.** EMI Références mono CHS5 65506-2* (9/95).

Stefan Wolpe
German/American 1902-1972

Suggested listening ...
...Quartet for Oboe, Cello, Percussion and Piano[a]. Violin Sonata[b]. Trio in Two Parts[c]. [c]**Harvey Sollberger** (fl); [a]**Stephen Taylor** (ob); [b]**Jorja Fleezanis** (vn); [ac]**Fred Sherry** (vc); [a]**Daniel Kennedy** (perc); [a]**Aleck Karis,** [b]**Garrick Ohlsson,** [c]**Charles Wuorinen** (pfs). Koch International Classics 37112-2 (2/94).
...In Two Parts[c]. Three Lieder[ac]. Quartet[c]. Hamlet[c]. Piece for Two Instrumental Units[c]. To the Dancemaster[ac]. Solo Piece for Trumpet[b]. Piece for Trumpet and Seven Instruments[bc]. [a]**Joyce Castle** (mez); [b]**Raymond Mase** (tpt); [c]**Parnassus / Anthony Korf.** Koch International Classics 37141-2 (12/92).

Charles Wood
Irish 1866-1926

Suggested listening ...
...St Mark Passion[a]. *Coupled with* **Holloway** Since I believe in God the Father Almighty. [a]**William Kendall** (ten); [a]**Paul Robinson,** [a]**Kwame Ryan** (bars); [a]**Peter Harvey** (bass); **Gonville and Caius College Choir, Cambridge / Geoffrey Webber** with **Richard Hill** (org). ASV CDDCA854 (5/93).

Haydn Wood

British 1882-1959

Suggested listening ...
...Sketch of a Dandy. Serenade to Youth. Mannin Veen. Three London Cameos – Suite.
Mylecharane. Moods Suite No. 6, "Joyousness". A Brown Bird Singing. Apollo. The Seafarer.
Bratislava Radio Symphony Orchestra / Adrian Leaper. Marco Polo 8 223402 (8/92).

Hugh Wood

British 1932-

Hugh Wood String Quartets – No. 1 (1962); No. 2, Op. 13; No. 3, Op. 20; No. 4 (1992-93).
   Chilingirian Quartet (Levon Chilingirian, Charles Stewart, vns; Simon Rowland, va; Philip de
   Groote, vc). Conifer Ⓕ 75605-51239-2 (78 minutes: DDD: 6/95). Recorded 1994.
What Wood is about is already evident in the First Quartet, where the angular gestures of the
introduction propose ideas for future discussion, thus prompting references back to the opening
movement, while another strategy gradually reveals ideas that become dominant in the finale. The
result is a sketch, as yet somewhat tentative, of a quartet whose four movements are unified, finale-
directed rather than first-movement dominated. The Second and Third Quartets, seemingly stepping
aside from this path, in fact investigate it further. The Second, in 39 very brief linked sections, some
of them mildly aleatoric, gradually builds a powerful sense of forward impetus from an opening in
which each brief and violently juxtaposed musical event seems to propose a different direction. The
Third has fewer sections and a longer span, but a still greater emotional range, from its chilly opening
to the big, confident gestures with which it ends. Here there is no hint of the aleatory nor of disjunct
juxtaposition, but a gradual growth of eloquence, of a hard-won long line. It was written after an
unproductive period, and towards the end there is a distinctly Beethovenian sense of 'feeling new
strength'. The recent Fourth Quartet is a superb demonstration of that strength at full stretch: an
expository prelude, a tense *Scherzo* (itself expository also), a noble *Adagio* whose long lines can easily
bridge silences and quite sharp angles, and a finale that is most satisfyingly the audible (but not
predictable) destination of all that preceded it. It is a masterly piece, and it gains greatly from being
heard as the culmination of its predecessors. Finely and cleanly recorded, the Chilingirian Quartet
sound passionately involved with this music, but they know better than to overstate it: for all its
urgency it is true chamber music, of great distinction.
Additional recommendation ...
...No. 3. *Coupled with works by* **Wirén, A. Tchaikovsky** and **Barber** Lindsay Quartet. ASV
   Ⓕ CDDCA825 (77 minutes: ADD: 1/93). *See review in the Collections section; refer to the Index
   to Reviews.*
Further listening ...
...Piano Concerto, Op. 31. **Joanna MacGregor** (pf); **BBC Symphony Orchestra / Andrew Davis.**
   Collins 20th Century Plus 2007-2 (6/93).

William Wordsworth

British 1908-1988

Suggested listening ...
...Symphonies – No. 2 in D major, Op. 34; No. 3 in D major, Op. 48. **London Philharmonic
   Orchestra / Nicholas Braithwaite.** Lyrita SRCD207 (11/90). *Gramophone Award Winner 1991.*

Robert Wright

American 1914-

Suggested listening ...
...Kismet (Wright/Forrest, after Borodin). Cast includes **Valerie Masterson, Donald Maxwell, David
   Rendall, Richard Van Allan, Judy Kaye; Ambrosian Chorus; Philharmonia Orchestra / John Owen
   Edwards.** TER Classics CDTER2 1170 (7/90).

Charles Wuorinen

American 1938-

Wuorinen A Winter's Tale[a]. Album Leaf (piano). String Sextet. Twang[a]. New York Notes. [a]**Phyllis
   Bryn-Julson** (sop); **Lincoln Center Chamber Music Society / Charles Wuorinen.** Koch
   International Classics Ⓕ 37272-2 (75 minutes: DDD: 2/95). Recorded 1991-3.
The earliest work, *New York Notes* (1981-82) intrigues in the way in which computer-generated
sounds are grafted on to the live instrumental texture. It's not that Wuorinen is economical with the
notes, but busyness never becomes over-insistent, and purposeful activity is well diversified over the
piece's 25-minute time-span. The String Sextet (1988-89) is more lyrical, and also more intense,
revelling as much in the expansive homogeneity of the medium as in its potential for richness of
expression. The clinging to continuity here – a kind of anti-minimalist hyper-consistency – risks
suggesting self-conscious eccentricity. But Wuorinen's imagination, in a first-class performance, wins

out, and the Sextet's purely formal conviction keeps the ears absorbed to the very end. *A Winter's Tale* (1990-91) is more challenging, less persuasive, in its setting of Dylan Thomas's long, intricate poem of that title. There are occasional, arresting moments of characterization in the interaction of voice and ensemble, but with so many words it is hard for any composer to shape a memorable line, to let the music take over. When at last it does, in the exuberant cadenza of the last few minutes, the result – in this wholly admirable performance – is appropriately liberating.

Further listening ...

...Album Leaf (violin and cello). Fortune. Cello Variations II. Violin Variations. Tashi. **The Group for Contemporary Music.** Koch International Classics 37242-2 (9/94).

...A Reliquary for Igor Stravinsky. *Coupled with works by* **Stravinsky** Soloists; New London Chamber Choir; London Sinfonietta / Oliver Knussen. DG 447 068-2GH (10/95). *See review under Stravinsky; refer to the Index to Reviews.* Ⓖ

Iannis Xenakis
Greek/French 1922-

Suggested listening ...

...Palimpsest. Dikhthas[a]. Epeï. Akanthos[b]. [a]**Irvine Arditti** (vn); [a]**Claude Helffer** (pf); [b]**Penelope Walmsley-Clark** (sop); **Spectrum / Guy Protheroe.** Wcrgo WER6178-2. Ⓖ

...Jalons[a]. Phlegra[b]. Thalleïn[b]. Keren[c]. Nomos Alpha[d]. [c]**Benny Sluchin** (tbn); [d]**Pierre Strauch** (vc); **Ensemble InterContemporain /** [a]**Pierre Boulez,** [b]**Michel Tabachnik.** Erato 2292-45770-2. Ⓖ

...Naama[b]. A l'ile de Gorée[bc]. Khoaï[b]. Komboï[ab]. [a]**Sylvio Gualda** (perc); [b]**Elisabeth Chojnacka** (hpd); [c]**Xenakis Ensemble / Huub Kerstens.** Erato MusiFrance 2292-45030-2 (10/90).

...Metastasis. Pithoprakta. Eonta[a]. **French Radio National Orchestra / François Le Roux;** [a]**Paris Contemporary Music Instrumental Ensemble / Konstantin Simonovic.** Le Chant du Monde LDC278 368.

...Orestia. **Strasbourg University Music Department; Colmar Women's Voices; Anjou Vocal Ensemble; Basse-Normandie Ensemble / Dominique Debart.** Salabert Actuels SCD8906 (9/90).

José Ximénez
Spanish 1601-1672

Suggested listening ...

...Obra del primer tono de lleno. *Coupled with works by* **A. de Cabezón, Coelho, Anonymous, Carreira, H. de Cabezón** and **Cabanilles** Sophie Yates (hpd). Chandos Chaconne CHAN0560 (11/94). *See review in the Collections section; refer to the Index to Reviews.* Ⓖ

Yuquijiro Yochoh
Japanese 1929-

Suggested listening ...

...Sakura. *Coupled with* **Berio** Sequenza XI. **Britten** Nocturnal after John Dowland, Op. 70. **Brouwer** La Espiral Eterna. **Takemitsu** All in Twilight. **Torres** Mil y una caras. **Eduardo Fernández** (gtr). Decca 433 076-2DH (7/93).

Takashi Yoshimatsu
Japanese 1953-

New review

Yoshimatsu Symphony No. 2, "At terra". Guitar Concerto, "Pegasus Effect", Op. 21[a]. Threnody to Toki, Op. 12. [a]**Craig Ogden** (gtr); **BBC Philharmonic Orchestra / Sachio Fujioka.** Chandos Ⓟ CHAN9438 (69 minutes: DDD: 6/96).

Takashi Yoshimatsu, who until this recording was not represented in *The Gramophone Classical Catalogue* is a sort of oriental Hovhaness, who looks to North (and Latin) America for exotic inspiration. His accomplished, brightly coloured music is never less than engaging, if occasionally prolix, though it is doubtful that the innocent ear would identify it as Japanese. *At terra* (1991-2) is a very effective and exciting suite, and might have made a fine concerto for the cello, which has several important solos (exquisitely delivered by Peter Dixon), but by no stretch of the imagination is it a symphony. The Guitar Concerto (1981) is a welcome addition to a still meagre repertoire, the ecologically minded *Threnody to Toki* (mourning the extinction in the wild of a rare bird) rather less compelling. Sound and performance quality are uniformly excellent; a very enjoyable disc.

Eugène Ysaÿe
Belgian 1858-1931

Suggested listening ...

...Caprice d'après l'etude en forme de valse de Saint-Saëns. *Coupled with works by* **Saint-Saëns, Massenet, Sarasate, Chausson** and **Ravel** Joshua Bell (vn); **Royal Philharmonic Orchestra /**

Andrew Litton. Decca 433 519-2DH (1/92). *See review in the Collections section; refer to the Index to Reviews.*

…Solo Violin Sonatas, Op. 27 – No. 1 in G minor; No. 2 in A minor; No. 3 in D minor, "Ballade"; No. 4 in E minor; No. 5 in G major; No. 6 in E major. **Lydia Mordkovitch** (vn). Chandos CHAN8599 (5/88).

Isang Yun
Korean 1917-

Suggested listening …

…Gagok. Contrasts. Duo. Sori. Novellette. **L'Art Pour l'Art.** CPO CPO999 118-2.

Nicola Zacharias
Italian fourteenth-fifteenth centuries

Suggested listening …

…Gia per gran nobelta. *Coupled with works by* **Antonius de Civitate Austrie, Tapissier, Anonymous, Velut, Ciconia, Philipoctus de Caserta, Johanne Egidius, Matheus de Sancto Johanne, Bartolomeus da Bologna, Brassart** and **Dufay** Orlando Consort. Metronome METCD1008 (11/95). *See review in the Collections section; refer to the Index to Reviews.*   Ⓖ

Friedrich Zachow
German 1663-1712

Suggested listening …

…Ruhe, Friede, Freud und Wonne. *Coupled with works by* **Scheidt** and **Handel** Axel Köhler (alto); **Andreas Conrad** (ten); **Thomas Riehl** (bass); Stadtsingechor, Halle; Berolina Quartet; Camerata Musica / Dorothea Köhler. Berlin Classics 0011 312BC (6/96).

Roger Zahab
American 1957-

Suggested listening …

…Verging Lightfall. *Coupled with* **Cage** 13 Harmonies. **Roger Zahab** (vn); **Eric Moe** (pf/hpd/org). Koch International Classics 37130-2 (11/95).

Riccardo Zandonai
Italian 1883-1944

Suggested listening …

…Francesca da Rimini[a] – Act 2: E ancora sgombro il campo del comune? … Date il segno, Paolo, date … Un'erba io m'avea, per sanare … Onta et orrore sopra. Act 3: No, Smadragedi, no! … Paolo, datemi pace! … Ah la parola chi i miei occhi incontrano. Act 4: Ora andate … E così, vada s'è pur mio destino. *Coupled with* **Giordano** Fedora[b]. **Soloists;** [b]**Monte-Carlo Opera Chorus and** [ab]**Orchestra /** [a]**Nicola Rescigno,** [b]**Lamberto Gardelli.** Decca Grand Opera 433 033-2DM2 (3/92). *See review under Giordano; refer to the Index to Reviews.*

Frank Zappa
American 1940-1993

Suggested listening …

… (arr. Nelson) Peaches en Regalia. Let's make the water turn black. Oh No. Igor's boogie. Eat that question. Echidna's arf. *Coupled with works by* **Stravinsky, Wheeler, Van Vliet, Babbitt, J. Nelson, Shemaria, H. Hancock** and **London** Meridian Arts Ensemble. Channel Classics Channel Crossings CCS8195 (4/96). *See review in the Collections section; refer to the Index to Reviews.*   Ⓖ

Lorenzo Zavateri
Italian 1690-1764

New review

Zavateri 12 Concerti da chiesa e da camera, Op. 1. **Freiburg Baroque Orchestra / Gottfried von der Goltz** (vn). Deutsche Harmonia Mundi Ⓟ 05472 77352-2 (two discs: 103 minutes: DDD: 8/96). ✐   Ⓖ

Now here is a name that will almost certainly be new to every collector of baroque music on CD. Lorenzo Zavateri was a one-time pupil of Giuseppe Torelli. Zavateri joined the esteemed orchestra of San Petronio in Bologna during the mid 1720s. Little of his music was published, but among that which was is his set of 12 *Concerti da chiesa e da camera,* Op. 1. There is less differentiation here between 'church' and 'chamber' styles. Concertos Nos. 7 and 9, for example, are termed "Teatrale" his almost exact contemporary, Locatelli, published six *Introduttioni Teatrali* in the same year, which are, like Zavateri's pieces, *concerti grossi* in the three-movement form of the Italian opera *sinfonia* – while the tenth Concerto is "a Pastorale" and the twelfth "a Tempesta di mare"; the first work is perhaps rather unnecessarily subtitled "Introducione". The 12 concertos contain enough individual gestures and a sufficient diversity of ideas to hold our attention without difficulty. But perhaps it is those readers whose ears savour that Janus-like stance characteristic of vocabulary which draws upon the obsolescent and the new, who will derive the most constant pleasure from the music. Four of the works are ripieno concertos while two others are opera *sinfonias* in character and layout. The remaining six occupy a middle ground between *concerto grosso* and solo violin concerto – one of them, No. 10, is for two violins – and it is these which make a deeper impression. There is sometimes an element of dazzling, if short-winded virtuosity, and at other times an affecting expressive intimacy in Zavateri's concertos. Like so many Italian composers of his generation and earlier, he embraces a tradition of including a "Pastorale" movement within the set. Yet though not at that time published, it may have been Corelli's well-known *Christmas Concerto* (Op. 6 No. 8) which set the trend. Zavateri's "Pastorale" is an altogether more *galant* affair than those of his fellow Italians, airier in character, with trio episodes for two solo violins and continuo, and containing some striking key shifts. Of a completely different character is the splendidly vibrant *Tempesta di mare* which concludes the set. There are some telling contrasts here with rhythmically undulating passages juxtaposed with thrashing waves depicted chordally. Almost all is played with imagination and finesse – the Concerto No. 11 in G minor has a few rough moments – by the Freiburg Baroque Orchestra under their leader and solo violinistGottfried von der Goltz. A fascinating release.

Jan Dismas Zelenka Bohemian 1679-1745

New review

Zelenka Trio Sonatas, Volume 2 – No. 1 in F major; No. 3 in B flat major; No. 4 in G minor.
  Ensemble Zefiro (Paolo Grazzi, Alfredo Bernardini, obs; Alberto Grazzi, bn; Manfred Kraemer, vn; Lorenz Duftschmid, violone; Gian Carlo Rado, theorbo; Rinaldo Alessandrini, hpd/org). Auvidis Astrée Ⓟ E8563 (52 minutes: DDD: 2/96). Recorded 1995.

Zelenka was one of a gifted group of composers associated with the Dresden court during the first half of the eighteenth century. The court orchestra, one of the best around at that time, boasted a particularly accomplished wind section, and it may have been for some of these players that Zelenka wrote his six trios. The sources have not survived complete in all cases and the realization, for example, of the bass parts in the First and Third Sonatas, both of them included here, must always be conjectural. Ensemble Zefiro have thought carefully about this and have arrived at a solution which is both idiomatic and, it seems, in keeping with the surviving material. The playing is spirited and plentifully endowed with virtuosity. The oboists Paolo Grazzi and Alfredo Bernardini are technically secure and tastefully imaginative in their ornamentation. Bassoonist Alberto Grazzi is also fluent and furthermore a sensitive ensemble player. Keyboard continuo is stylishly provided by Rinaldo Alessandrini, sometimes playing harpsichord, at other times organ; and additional continuo support includes violone and theorbo. Readers so far unacquainted with these sonatas are in for a treat for this is music rich in fantasy, exciting for its virtuosic content, unusually extended in the working out of its ideas, and effectively constructed.

Additional recommendation ...
...Nos. 1-6. **Paul Dombrecht, Marcel Ponseele, Ku Ebbinge** (obs); **Danny Bond** (bn); **Chiara Banchini** (vn); **Richte van der Meer** (vc); **Robert Kohnen** (hpd). Accent Ⓟ ACC8848D (two discs: 109 minutes: DDD: 3/89). 🖙 Ⓖ

Zelenka Trio Sonatas – No. 2 in G minor, No. 5 in F major; No. 6 in C minor. **Ensemble Zefiro** (Paolo Grazzi, Alfredo Bernardini, obs; Alberto Grazzi, bn; Roberto Sensi, db; Rolf Lislevand, theorbo; Rinaldo Alessandrini, hpd/org). Auvidis Astrée Ⓟ E8511 (52 minutes: DDD: 6/94). 🖙 Recorded 1993. Ⓖ

For sheer *élan* and spirit the baroque instrumental players on this disc take some beating. Zelenka's six sonatas for two oboes, bassoon and continuo are among the most rewarding and at times most difficult pieces of baroque chamber music in the oboe repertory. Indeed, pieces demanding such virtuosity from these instruments were probably without precedent at the time (1715). We can only speculate as to the circumstances which led to their composition but the writing is often such as to make us wonder if they were destined for friends or enemies of the composer. Here, then, is splendidly invigorating playing of music which offers a great deal beyond face value. The sounds of the solo instruments themselves, together with an effective continuo group of double-bass, harpsichord/organ and theorbo are admirably captured in the recording.

Zelenka The Lamentations of Jeremiah. **Michael Chance** (alto); **John Mark Ainsley** (ten); **Michael George** (bass); **Chandos Baroque Players.** Hyperion Ⓟ CDA66426 (73 minutes: DDD: 7/91). 🖙 Texts and translations included. Recorded 1990.

Between the incomparable settings by Thomas Tallis and the extremely austere one by Stravinsky (which he called *Threni*) the "Lamentations of Jeremiah" have attracted surprisingly few composers. Perhaps the predominantly sombre tone, without even the dramatic opportunities presented by the *Dies irae* in a Requiem, is off-putting. Be that as it may, Zelenka showed remarkable resourcefulness in his 1722 setting for the electoral chapel at Dresden, where he was Kapellmeister. His musical language is in many ways similar to that of J.S. Bach but there are also daring turns of phrase which are entirely personal. The six *Lamentations* feature each singer twice; this performance is intimate, even mystical, slightly spacious in tempo and with a resonant acoustic.

Further listening ...

...Hipocondrie a 7 in A major. Concerto a 8 in G major. Sinfonia a 8 in A minor. *Coupled with* **Pisendel** Violin Concerto in D major. Sonata in C minor. **Freiburg Baroque Orchestra / Gottfried von der Goltz.** Deutsche Harmonia Mundi 05472 77339-2 (10/95). ✒ *See review under Pisendel; refer to the Index to Reviews.*

...Capriccios – No. 1 in D major; No. 2 in G major; No. 3 in F major; No. 4 in A major; No. 5 in G major. Concerto a 8 in G major. Sinfonia a 8 in A minor. Hipocondrie a 7 in A major. Overture a 7 in F major. **Berne Camerata / Alexander van Wijnkoop.** Archiv Produktion 423 703-2AX3 (1/89).   Ⓖ

Alexander Zemlinsky   Austrian 1871-1942

New review

Zemlinsky Ländliche Tänze, Op. 1. Balladen. Fantasien über Gedichte von Richard Dehmel, Op. 9. Albumblatt. Skizze. Fugue in G minor. **Siegfried Mauser** (pf). Virgin Classics Ⓕ VC5 45125-2 (63 minutes: DDD: 9/95). Recorded 1993.

All of Zemlinsky's piano music is early; most of it is enjoyable, some of it is quite delightful, and throughout there are unexpected turns, abrupt changes which signal a really individual mind. The *Ländliche Tänze* ("Country Dances") are post-Schubertian *Ländler*, post-Brahmsian waltzes of real charm, with occasionally a Schumannesque singing line and often a quite unpredictably contrasting trio section (or no trio section at all, just when you were expecting one) to keep you entertained throughout 12 movements, all in triple time. The *Balladen* and *Fantasien* are all in a sense 'songs without words' in that they illustrate particular poems. Here the style is often much bolder, owing a good deal in the *Balladen* to Brahms, in the *Fantasien* to Wagner as well. In the first of the *Fantasien* the two influences are juxtaposed, together with a beautifully pure lyrical line that seems to be Zemlinsky's own, but in the second of them, "Waldseligkeit", the three elements fuse together. By this time Schoenberg, already Zemlinsky's pupil, was working on *Verklärte Nacht*, and as Siegfried Mauser says in his notes, it is fascinating to watch teacher and pupil attempting a similar task. Zemlinsky's formal solution is the more traditional (an ABA structure) but when his opening melody, a sort of bright moonlit nocturne, returns beautifully embellished after a passionate outburst, only the word 'transfigured' (*verklärt*) will do. The *Albumblatt* is a tiny mood piece, the *Skizze* a return (like the last of the *Fantasien*) to the 'country dance' mood of Zemlinsky's Op. 1. The darkly eloquent fugue is an indication of what Zemlinsky's 'mature' piano music might have been like. Mauser plays this music with real flair and enthusiasm. The recording is first-class.

Zemlinsky Ein lyrische Symphonie, Op. 18[a]. Symphonische Gesänge, Op. 20[b]. [a]**Alessandra Marc** (sop); [a]**Håkan Hagegård** (bar); [b]**Willard White** (bass); **Royal Concertgebouw Orchestra / Riccardo Chailly.** Decca Entartete Musik Ⓕ 443 569-2DH (65 minutes: DDD: 12/94). Texts and translations included. Recorded 1993. **Gramophone** *Award Winner 1995.* **Gramophone** *Editor's choice.*   ⒼⒼ

With the Concertgebouw one has no fear that the sheer beauty of Zemlinsky's orchestral textures will be understated, but the urgency and strength beneath the surfaces are evident too, and it's quite an achievement for such an orchestra of Mahler specialists to get Zemlinsky's sound, so like Mahler and yet so very unlike, unerringly right. The soloists are simply superb: Marc is voluptuously caressing, not least in her sensuous use of portamento, but very intelligent in her use of words, her understanding of the dramatic gist of her three songs, and her extended lower register gives her both security at the bottom of the range and a beautiful shading of mezzo-ish warmth; Hagegård has nobility and strength as well as tenderness, and the Lieder singer's subtlety that the third and last songs need. Throughout, the orchestral playing is immaculately balanced. Was Willard White chosen for the *Symphonische Gesänge* because they are settings of black American poets? If so, he has the intelligence to realize that there is nothing especially 'ethnic' about them; to realize also, as does Chailly, that although only one opus number separates them from *Ein lyrische Symphonie* they inhabit a different world, harsher and more bitter. They require great vocal splendour but also a certain reserve, the ability not to underline emotions that are already clear enough in words and music. White and Chailly succeed admirably, and thus give this coupling the added benefit of presenting a more rounded portrait of Zemlinsky than any other recording of either work.

Zemlinsky Posthumous Songs – Sechs Lieder[a]. Zwei Lieder[b]. Zwei Preislieder[c]. Wandl' ich im Wald des Abends[d]. Vier Lieder[e]. Zwei Brettl-Lieder[f]. Drei Lieder[g]. Zwei Balladen[h]. Lieder auf

Gedichte von Richard Dehmel – Ansturm; Vorspiel; Auf See[i]. Vier Lieder[j]. Und einmal gehst du[k]. [acej]**Ruth Ziesak** (sop); [abefg]**Iris Vermillion** (mez); [abegi]**Hans-Peter Blochwitz** (ten); [adhk]**Andreas Schmidt** (bar); **Cord Garben** (pf). Sony Classical Ⓕ SK 57960 (70 minutes: DDD: 6/95). Texts and translations included. Recorded 1993.

A few years ago Blochwitz, Schmidt and Garben, together with Barbara Bonney as soprano and Anne Sofie von Otter as mezzo, recorded all of Zemlinsky's published songs (DG 427 348-2GH2, 10/89). These are the ones he didn't publish; why not? When sung as they are here in chronological order the reason for a while seems obvious: they have little individuality until about a third of the way through the collection. From then on things get much more interesting. The three settings of Richard Dehmel have a concentrated, poignant intensity so impressive that one is tempted to speculate about hidden reasons for Zemlinsky's reticence. "Jane Grey" (from *Zwei Balladen*), for example, was entered for a competition to which Schoenberg submitted a setting of exactly the same text. Is that why it almost out-Schoenbergs Schoenberg in its tenuous hold on tonality, its curiously gripping bare angularity? But in "Der verlorene Haufen" (*Zwei Balladen*), also set by Schoenberg for the same competition, Zemlinsky seems to be out-Mahlering Mahler in the fearsome march-toccata that accompanies this grim tale of a front-line regiment contemplating death each morning. The manner of the Dehmel songs is recaptured in a haunting group of settings of Hofmannsthal (*Vier Lieder*); there are also two curious comic ballads (the *Brettl-Lieder*, one quite funny, the other – about a man who eats so much that he bursts – rather disgusting), a most beautiful cradle-song over a dead child ("Über eine Wiege", *Drei Lieder*) and a much later, nobly stoic contemplation of old age (*Und einmal gehst du*) that are in no way inferior to the best of Zemlinsky's published songs. Blochwitz, Schmidt and Garben are as reliable as they were in the earlier set, Vermillion matches them admirably and Ziesak, if a little hard and bright at times, can fine her voice down to an effective intimacy. The recordings are excellent.

Further listening ...
...Die Seejungfrau. *Coupled with* **Stephan** Music for Orchestra. **North Netherlands Orchestra / Jacek Kaspszyk.** Vanguard Classics 99065 (4/96). *See review under Stephan; refer to the Index to Reviews.*
...Humoreske. *Coupled with* **Holst** Wind Quintet in A flat major, H67. **Nielsen** Wind Quintet, FS100. **Jolivet** Sérénade for Oboe, Piano and Wind Quintet. **P. Pierné** Suite pittoresque. **Aulos Wind Quintet.** Koch Schwann 310100. Ⓔ
...Gesänge nach Maeterlinck, Op. 13[a]. *Coupled with* **Reger** Variations and Fugue on a Theme of J.A. Hiller. [a]**Hedwig Fassbender** (mez); **Czech Philharmonic Orchestra / Václav Neumann.** Supraphon 11 1811-2 (7/93).
...Eine Florentinische Tragödie, Op. 16. **Soloists; Berlin Radio Symphony Orchestra / Gerd Albrecht.** Koch Schwann 314012 (12/85).
...Der Kreiderkreis. **Soloists; Berlin Radio Symphony Orchestra / Stefan Soltesz.** Capriccio 60016-2 (1/92).

Hans Zender
German 1936-

Suggested listening ...
...Schubert's Winterreise – a composed interpretation. **Hans-Peter Blochwitz** (ten); **Ensemble Modern / Hans Zender.** RCA Victor Red Seal 09026 68067-2 (9/95).

Bernd Alois Zimmermann
German 1918-1970

Zimmermann Concertos – Oboe and Small Orchestra[a]; Trumpet and Orchestra, "Nobody knows the trouble I see"[b]; Canto di speranza[c]; Cello and Orchestra, "en forme de pas de trois"[c]. [a]**Heinz Holliger** (ob); [b]**Håkan Hardenberger** (tpt); [c]**Heinrich Schiff** (vc); **South-West German Radio Symphony Orchestra / Michael Gielen.** Philips Ⓕ 434 114-2PH (71 minutes: DDD: 11/93). Recorded 1989-92.

The Oboe Concerto (1952) vigorously confronts the central post-war challenge: if you want to embrace the new (serialism) alongside the old (neo-classicism), how do you keep your balance? The answer, for Zimmermann, was 'precariously'. In the Trumpet Concerto (1954) the absorption of a negro spiritual and elements of jazz serve to intensify the trauma of a search for stylistic equilibrium. Yet again the result is an impressive work of art strongly built and progressing inexorably to a bleak conclusion. *Canto di speranza* (1953-57) brings us still closer to the apocalyptic modernism of the opera *Die Soldaten* (begun in 1958) as models – notably Webern – become objects of mockery. The Cello Concerto *en forme de pas de trois*, written after the opera in 1965-66, completes the process of recreative rejection. It is a haunting fantasy, at once ballet score and concert work, a parody of nineteenth-century terpsichorean conventions which is as bitter in tone as it is beguiling in sound. Philips have assembled three star soloists for this well-recorded disc, and with sterling orchestral support they do the music proud.

Further listening ...
...Enchiridion[b]. Cello Sonata[a]. Four Short Studies[a]. Intercommunicazione[ab]. [a]**Michael Bach** (vc); [b]**Bernhard Wambach** (pf). CPO CPO999 198-2 (8/94).

Manuel de Zumaya

Suggested listening ...

...Sol-fa de Pedro. Hieremiae Prophetae Lamentationes. Celebren, publiquen. *Coupled with*
Jerúsalem Responsorio Segundo de S. S. José: "Esuriente terra Aegypti". Dixit Dominus.
Polychoral Mass in D major. **Chanticleer Chorus and Sinfonia / Joseph Jennings.** Teldec Das Alte
Werk 4509-93333-2 (12/94). *See review under Jerúsalem; refer to the Index to Reviews.*

Collections

Orchestral

A la carte Itzhak Perlman (vn); **Abbey Road Ensemble / Lawrence Foster.** EMI Ⓔ CDC5 55475-2
(63 minutes: DDD: 1/96). Recorded 1995.
Massenet Thaïs – Méditation. **Glazunov** Mazurka-Oberek in D major. Meditation, Op. 32.
   Rachmaninov Vocalise, Op. 34 No. 14. **Sarasate** Zigeunerweisen, Op. 20. Introduction and
   Tarantella, Op. 43. **Rimsky-Korsakov** (arr. Kreisler) Fantasia on Two Russian Themes, Op. 33.
   Tchaikovsky (orch. Glazunov) Scherzo in C minor, Op. 42 No. 2. **Wieniawski** Légende,
   Op. 17. Zigeunerweisen. **Kreisler** The Old Refrain. Schön Rosmarin.
A most enjoyable programme. Perlman approximates the 'old school' with something of an actor's
skill: he feels the period, not as a first-hand witness (even at 50, he is far too young for that), but as a
respectful recipient of a great tradition. His "Méditation" is an elevated 'easy listen', sensitively
accompanied. The Glazunov *Mazurka-Oberek* should be at least as popular as Saint-Saëns's concert
pieces for violin and orchestra, and Perlman does it proud. The initial pages of Rachmaninov's
Vocalise are a little over-sweet (too many well-oiled slides), but its latter half achieves genuine
expressive eloquence. Glazunov's *Meditation* is suitably honeyed and the Kreisler-Rimsky *Fantasia*
(where Goldmark's A minor Concerto hovers around the main theme) is given a truly splendid
performance. Of the rest, the two Kreisler pieces are exceptional, *Schön Rosmarin* especially, while
Lawrence Foster's expert Abbey Road Ensemble provide a discreet but flavoursome orchestral base.

American Music Boston Symphony Orchestra / Serge Koussevitzky. Pearl mono
   Ⓜ GEMMCD9492* (79 minutes: AAD: 12/91). Recorded 1934-40.   ⊖⊖⊖
   Foote Suite in E minor, Op. 63 (from RCA Victor 11-8571/2.). **McDonald** San Juan Capistrano
   (RCA Victor 17729. 1939). **Copland** El salón México (HMV DB3812/3, 10/40). **Harris**
   Symphonies – No. 1 (American Columbia 68183/6. 1934); No. 3 (DB6137/8, 12/42).
Music lovers with a romantic hankering for the American desert and the Great Outdoors may well know
Roy Harris's high, wide and handsome Third Symphony already, but the chances of having heard Serge
Koussevitzky's 1939 recording of it are somewhat more remote. If you can accept and enjoy the
soundtracks of classic Westerns, then you'll have no trouble with this CD: the playing of the Boston
Symphony burns through a veil of surface hiss with the ease and accuracy of a blow-torch, and
Koussevitzky's conducting tends to confirm the judgement of many, that this is indeed the greatest
American symphony. It's a tremendous experience, and although the work is barely 17 minutes long, it
none the less constitutes an epic journey. Koussevitzky was a great musical pioneer, and his recordings
of Copland's saucy *El salón México* and Arthur Foote's delightful Suite (easily as appealing as, say,
Grieg's *Holberg Suite*) are rightly regarded as classics. Add Harris's First Symphony – a poorer
recording, but a fascinating prophecy of greater work to come – and Harl McDonald's colourful essays,
and you have the basis of an absorbing concert, one that is likely to give you a great deal of enjoyment.

Géza Anda Columbia Recordings, 1953-6. Géza Anda (pf); ªPhilharmonia Orchestra / Alceo
   Galliera. Testament mono Ⓔ SBT1064/7* (four discs, oas: 76, 79, 80 and 63 minutes: ADD:
   10/95). Recorded 1953-6.   ⊖
   SBT1064 – **Rachmaninov** Piano Concerto No. 2 in C minor, Op. 18ª. Preludes – G minor,
   Op. 23 No. 5; G major, Op. 32 No. 5 (both from 33CX1143, 9/54). **Tchaikovsky** Piano
   Concerto No. 1 in B flat minor, Op. 23ª (from 33CX1156, 11/54). *SBT1065* – **Bartók** For
   Children, Sz42 (33CX1176, 11/54 and 33CX1316, 5/56). *SBT1066* – **Chopin** Piano Concerto
   No. 1 in E minor, Op. 11ª (33C1057, 2/59). 12 Etudes, Op. 25. Ballade No. 1 in G minor, Op. 23
   (33CX1459, 9/57). *SBT1067* – **Liszt** Piano Sonata in B minor, S178. Mephisto Waltz No. 1,
   S514. Concert Study, S144 No. 3, "Un sospiro". Etudes d'exécution transcendante d'après
   Paganini, S140 – No. 3, La campanella (all from 33CX1202, 6/55). **Bartók** Sonatina, Sz55
   (33CX1176). **Delibes/Dohnányi** Coppélia – Valse lente Paraphrase (33CX1156).
Géza Anda was a pianist of contradictions, a fastidious technician prone to impulsive gestures and a
master of natural rubato whose imagination occasionally ran riot. He was unquestionably among the
greatest players of his generation and these are among his finest recordings. The Tchaikovsky
concerto opens with a vintage Philharmonia in full cry, while the ensuing dialogue is poised on a
nerve's edge, inspired but excitable (Anda courts extremes, both in terms of tempo and inflexion) and
with some ravishing solo work. In the Rachmaninov Second Concerto, the pianist's control of
sonority facilitates lightning switches between a richly voiced *bel canto* and bustling passagework.
Anda certainly knew how to subdue his tone to a murmur then rise to the fray with a swingeing
fortissimo. He glides through the *Adagio sostenuto*, and although his finale seems more decorative
than demonic, there is little suggestion of the theatrical overkill that mars his reading of
Tchaikovsky's finale. Furthermore, the actual recording reveals – via judicious balancing – more
detail, more internal interplay than many of its DDD successors. Bartók's music was, of course,
something of an Anda speciality. *For Children* is not so much designed 'for children' as for 'beginners
of all ages' (many of the pieces are in any case technically demanding), but Anda's approach suggests

more the world of Schumann's *Kinderszenen* than the tangy flavour of Hungarian and Slovakian folk-music. He cajoles, distends, lingers, colours, teases – in fact, he does everything you would expect of a master colourist working within a sequence of 78 miniatures. Chopin, however, is a more frequent victim of phrasal distortion and it is here in particular that Anda's finesse pays high dividends. Furthermore, the First Concerto is granted a superb accompaniment under Galliera, whose keen response to the soloist is a constant source of pleasure. Anda approaches Chopin from a Mozartian axis, with clean fingerwork, agile phrasing and a singing line that frequently recalls the playing style of Alfred Cortot. The Liszt Sonata is a brave shot that just misses its target. Anda's view of the work was, as of 1954, reckless, frequently heart-rending and full of tender ideas; furthermore, he had the technical equipment to take risks and triumph. However, minute instances of imperfect timing rather spoil the effect. The other items are mostly notable and include mesmerizing accounts of the First *Mephisto Waltz* and Third *Consolation*, a glittering Liszt/Busoni *La campanella*, a rather glum Bartók *Sonatina* and a performance of Dohnányi's *Coppélia* "Valse lente" Paraphrase that, for sheer style and pianistic bravura, deserves a place beside Horowitz's *Carmen* Variations and Rosenthal's *Carnaval de Vienne*. A real feast then, and all the more absorbing for the odd spot of interpretative controversy. The transfers give a clean, rounded piano tone, only occasionally troubled by tape flutter.

Baroque Classics Taverner Players / Andrew Parrott. EMI Reflexe Ⓜ CDM7 69853-2
(60 minutes: DDD: 12/88). 🖙
    Handel Solomon – Arrival of the Queen of Sheba. Harp Concerto in B flat major, Op. 4 No. 6 (with Andrew Lawrence-King, hp). **Purcell** Three Parts upon a Ground. A Suite of Theatre Music: The Indian Queen – Trumpet Overture; Symphony; Dance. Abdelazer – Rondeau; The Gordion Knot Unty'd – Chaconne. **Pachelbel** Canon and Gigue. **Bach** Wir danken dir, Gott, wir danken dir, No. 29 – Sinfonia. Ich steh mit einem Fuss im Grabe, No. 156 – Sinfonia. Der Himmel lacht! die Erde jubiliert, No. 31 – Sonata. Ich liebe den Höchsten von ganzem Gemüte, No. 174 – Sinfonia. Gottes Zeit ist die allerbeste Zeit, No. 106 – Sonatina. Herz und Mund und Tat und Leben, No. 147 – Chorale, Jesus bleibet meine Freude ("Jesu, joy of man's desiring"; with Taverner Consort). Christmas Oratorio, BWV248 – Sinfonia.

If you have ever felt the desire to hear 'baroque classics' as the composer might have heard them, but have been deterred by the unfriendly sounds and deadpan renditions offered by some early-instrument groups, you may do the former without suffering the latter by adding this disc to your collection. Though the performances have every benefit of stylistic scholarship and early-instrumental mastery they are in no way 'dry', nor are there any chalk-on-blackboard sounds to set the teeth on edge; on the contrary, the late David Reichenberg's oboe playing is likely to be a delightful revelation. Like other baroque composers, Bach was wont to rework some of his music for other media: thus you may recognize the Sinfonias from Cantatas Nos. 29, 156 and 31 as being related to the *Preludium* of the Third Violin Partita (BWV1006), the *Largo* of the F minor Harpsichord Concerto (BWV1056) and the first movement of the Third *Brandenburg Concerto* (BWV1048). This represents a doorway to the appreciation of baroque music in authentic performance, through which you may enter with as much enthusiasm as do the Taverner Players.

Baroque Trumpet Concertos Håkan Hardenberger (tpt); I Musici. Philips Ⓔ 442 131-2PH
(54 minutes: DDD: 5/95). Items marked [a] transcribed for trumpet. Recorded 1993.   Ⓖ
    Vivaldi (rev. Malipiero) Concerto for Two Trumpets and Strings in C major, RV537 (with Reinhold Friedrich, tpt). **Corelli** Sonata for Trumpet and Strings in D major. **Albinoni** Concerto in B flat major, Op. 7 No. 3[a]. **Torelli** Sonata a 5 con tromba, G7. **A. Marcello** Concerto for Oboe and Strings in D minor[a]. **Viviani** Capricci armonici – Sonata prima. **Franceschini** Sonata for Two Trumpets, Strings and Continuo in D major (Friedrich). **Baldassare** Sonata for Cornett, Strings and Continuo in F major[a].

No trumpet player can make a career as a baroque player on a modern instrument without performing music originally written for other instruments; the domestic repertoire is simply not sustainable (it could be argued that the Torelli and Corelli works only sound truly colourful on a natural trumpet and tonally bland even with Hardenberger's modern playing). No complaints with transcriptions *per se*: a good one can leave the original looking to its laurels. Some disappointment must be registered, however, that Hardenberger has not investigated his own fare from the multifarious collections of fine eighteenth-century concertos. Most listeners will enjoy this highly exacting playing and his silky articulation and rhythmic discipline – the Vivaldi is as high-tech and effortless as you will ever hear. I Musici are a curious choice of accompanists. Still sporting their timelessly vigorous and yet unashamedly Mediterranean approach to baroque chamber playing, there is quite a temperamental polarity here, one would suspect, between their style and Hardenberger's Nordic and less overtly emotional playing. The result, however, is not as marked as you might expect, since Hardenberger vocalizes more in this recording than in the past (all slow movements are warmer and less 'worked out' than in previous discs of this nature) and he responds to I Musici's full-blooded playing in a similarly jaunty way. The Marcello D minor Concerto contains some especially sweet moments.

New review

Alexander Brailowsky The Berlin Recordings, Volumes 1 and 2. **Alexander Brailowsky** (pf); [a]**Berlin Philharmonic Orchestra / Julius Prüwer.** Danacord mono Ⓟ DACOCD336/7*, DACOCD338/9* (two two-disc sets, oas: 135 and 117 minutes: ADD: 11/95). From Polydor originals; recorded 1928-34.
DACOCD336/7 – **Chopin** Piano Concerto No. 1 in F minor, Op. 11[a]. Piano Sonata No. 2 in B flat minor, Op. 35. Also includes 23 short works by Chopin. *DACOCD338/9* – **Liszt** Piano Concerto No. 1 in E flat major, S124[a]. Also includes works by **Debussy, Falla, Liszt, Mendelssohn, D. Scarlatti, Schubert, Schumann, Scriabin** and **Weber**

It's difficult not to be bowled over by Brailowsky's charm, delicacy and vitality, quite apart from his technical brilliance. Fortunately the Polydor engineers produced recordings of remarkable fidelity which allow his finely graded nuances to be fully appreciated, and in the modern transfer process used here, noise from the old 78rpm surfaces is minimal: there is, however, considerable variation in recording levels and in pitch (the piano used in 1928 was tuned very flat, so that a juxtaposition here of two Chopin *Etudes* in F minor and major from 1928 and 1934 respectively is jarring) – and there is a horrid discrepancy of pitch between what were the two sides of Liszt's *Hungarian Rhapsody* No. 12. By and large, the Chopin set is the better of the two. What is striking in the concerto is Brailowsky's shaping of phrases, his sensitivity and his delicately sparkling passagework. In the sonata he employs quite a lot of *affettuoso* rubato but shows he can also be simple: its *Scherzo* is scintillating and the finale (taken *prestissimo*) breathtaking. There is much finesse and convincing moulding of phrases in the *Barcarolle* and poetically tender caressing tone in the E flat *Nocturne*; the G minor *Ballade* is dazzling; and five Op. 25 *Etudes* are especially treasurable. Just occasionally he is too free for modern tastes in his rhythm, as in the middle section of the *Fantaisie-impromptu* and the Op. 69 A flat *Waltz*; but only in a B flat *Mazurka* are his rhythmic distortions unacceptable. The Liszt Concerto starts rather less well, with the opening cadenza over-pedalled and the first movement excessively wayward in rhythm (as is *Liebestraum* later on); but the *Allegretto vivace* section is deliciously playful, and by the end of the work one is completely won over. Brailowsky declines to treat three *Hungarian Rhapsodies* merely as barnstorming razzle-dazzle but discovers in them veins of poetry that are too often ignored. He is impressive in Liszt's arrangement of the *Tannhäuser* Overture and coquettish in his *Valse impromptu*, wonderfully vivacious in Mendelssohn's E minor *Scherzo* and the Scarlatti/Tausig *Capriccio*, and displays his virtuosity in Weber's *Moto perpetuo* and the Debussy *Toccata*. Elsewhere one has to forgive some mannered readings of familiar pieces; but what stays in my mind is an exceptionally beautiful, tenderly hushed performance of Debussy's *Serenade for the doll*. Yes, undoubtedly one of the great pianists.

British Film Music from the 1940s and 1950s [ab]Two Cities Symphony Orchestra; [cfkl]London Symphony Orchestra; [eim]Queen's Hall Light Orchestra; [do]Philharmonia Orchestra; [gjn]orchestra; [h]Royal Philharmonic Orchestra / [abeim]Charles Williams, [bdfkl]Muir Mathieson, [g]Ron Goodwin, [h]Malcolm Arnold, [j]George Melachrino, [n]Philip Green, [o]Ernest Irving. EMI mono Ⓟ CDGO2059* (65 minutes: ADD: 9/94). Recorded 1945-57.
Brodszky The Way to the Stars – Suite (from Columbia DB2180, 7/45)[a]. Carnival – Intermezzo (DB2225, 12/46)[b]. **Addinsell** Blithe Spirit – Prelude and Waltz (DX1186, 4/45)[c]. Passionate Friends – Suite (DX1551, 3/49)[d]. **C. Williams** The Night Has Eyes – Theme (DB2272, 11/46)[e]. **C. Parker** Western Approaches – Seascape (Decca K1544, 11/46)[f]. **J. Addison II** The Man Between – Theme (Parlophone R3775, 12/53)[g]. **Arnold** The Sound Barrier, Op. 38 (Columbia SED5542, 12/57)[h]. **Allan Gray** A Matter of Life and Death – Prelude (DX1320, 1/47)[i]. **Frankel** A Kid for Two Farthings – Theme (HMV B10903, recorded 1955)[j]. **Greenwood** Hungry Hill – Waltz into Jig (Decca K1579, 5/47)[k]. **Alwyn** The Rake's Progress – Calypso Music (Decca K1544, 11/46)[l]. **Spoliansky** Wanted for Murder – A Voice In the Night (with Eric Harrison, pf. DX1264, 8/46)[m]. **P. Green** Ha'penny Breeze – Theme (DX1724, recorded 1950)[n]. **Vaughan Williams** Scott of the Antarctic – Prologue; Pony March; Penguins; Climbing the Glacier; Final Music (HMV C3834, 2/49)[o].

This generously filled disc of 15 tracks in digitally refurbished sound should be an essential item in the libraries of all serious cinema buffs. Except in two cases (one of them the Ministry of Information *Western Approaches*, for the fine score of which Clifton Parker received the princely sum of £100), the films represented here come from the immediately post-war period – the latest is the 1955 *A Kid for Two Farthings* (with delightful music by that master craftsman Benjamin Frankel). The composers range from respected musical figures to notoriously near-illiterates like "Slug" Brodszky, who, it is frankly admitted here, needed to have "collaborators", who were rarely credited. Some film directors wanted incidental music that would enhance the atmosphere without attracting too much attention to the soundtrack (sometimes resulting in scores so dependent on the visual sequence – like Malcolm Arnold's *Sound Barrier* – as to undermine their understandable independent existence); some films included a featured musical episode, like John Greenwood's exhilarating Irish jig in *Hungry Hill* and William Alwyn's subtly scored calypso in *The Rake's Progress*; fortunately we are given only one blatant example of the artistically often ruinous policy of basing a film's music on a theme song or tune specifically designed for commercial exploitation. There is one famous example, too, of a composer taking a film score of his as the basis for a concert work – Vaughan Williams's *Scott of the*

Antarctic, which was elaborated into a symphony – though it was generally thought to be more effective in its original form.

New review

British Light Music Classics New London Orchestra / Ronald Corp. Hyperion Ⓕ CDA66868 (78 minutes: DDD: 7/96). *Gramophone Editor's record of the month.* Ⓖ

Binge Elizabethan Serenade. The Watermill. **Williams** The Devil's Galop. The Old Clockmaker. **Coates** Calling All Workers. **Toye** The Haunted Ballroom. **Collins** Vanity Fair. **Farnon** Jumping Bean. **Baynes** Destiny. **Curzon** The Boulevardier. **Lutz** Pas de quatre. **Gibbs** Dusk. **White** Puffin' Billy. **Ketèlbey** Bells across the meadows. **Joyce** Dreaming. **Ellis** Coronation Scot. **Ancliffe** Nights of Gladness.

This splendid Hyperion collection emphatically proves that there is much to be said about British Light Music. Here are 17 numbers whose melodies may be familiar even if their titles and composers are not, ranging from theatre music of the 1890s to radio theme tunes of the 1950s. Although several of these items have been recorded many times before, this Hyperion disc adds an extra dimension. Corp's measured approach to numbers such as *Dreaming*, *Dusk*, *Destiny* and *Nights of Gladness* results in him taking significantly longer than other versions: this is due in part to slower tempos and in part to scrupulous observance of repeats; but in every case the stature of the music is enhanced thereby, thanks to the security of the playing, sympathetic phrasing and intelligent use of dynamics and rubato. In *The Boulevardier*, Corp captures the impression of a strutting man-about-Paris, adding the important saxophone colouring that helps to catch the Parisian ambience. The collection is also welcome for the inclusion of Meyer Lutz's *Pas de quatre* – crudely orchestrated, perhaps, but most engaging and not recorded for many a year. For light music specialist and general music lover alike, this collection should prove pure delight. The recorded sound throughout is exemplary.

New review

Carnegie Hall Project The Solti Orchestral Project, Carnegie Hall / Sir Georg Solti. Decca Ⓕ 444 458-2DH (77 minutes: DDD: 12/95). Recorded live in 1994. Ⓖ

Wagner Die Meistersinger von Nürnberg – Prelude. **Brahms** Variations on a Theme by Haydn, Op. 56*a*, "St Antoni Chorale". **Shostakovich** Symphony No. 9 in E flat major, Op. 70. **R. Strauss:** Don Juan, Op. 20. **Smetana** The bartered bride – Overture.

Over a 16 day period in June 1994 Sir Georg Solti supervised a series of rehearsals and study-sessions with an orchestra unique in America. Two years earlier he had been approached by Carnegie Hall to conduct an orchestra made up of young musicians. The idea developed to include 15 musicians from five top American orchestras – to act not only as leading players but to coach their respective sections. These live recordings, made at the two concerts, crowned the whole project. As a revelation not just of the orchestra's superb quality but of Solti as interpreter the most remarkable performance here is of the Shostakovich symphony. It would be hard to imagine a happier, more genial account of this equivocal work, witty and pointed, with humour unforced and buoyant. It is remarkable, too, what natural flexibility marks the playing in such a work as the *Meistersinger* Prelude, with free rubato in the big melodies coupled with perfect ensemble. The syncopations in the Smetana work have an infectious freedom too, seemingly spontaneous, again achieved with total precision. As for the Brahms Variations, it would be hard to find a performance so sharply characterized, with each section beautifully contrasted. The clarity of texture allows some magical solo playing to be fully appreciated in all the works, notably from the principal oboe and horn. Hard-headed orchestral musicians, noting the ideal conditions set up for the project, might well comment that it is no surprise that the results are so fine.

Classical Trumpet Concertos John Wallace (tpt); ᶜJohn Anderson (ob d'amore); ᶜPeter Thomas (vn); Philharmonia Orchestra / Christopher Warren-Green, ᶜSimon Wright. Nimbus Ⓕ NI7016 (75 minutes: DDD: 2/95). Items marked ᵃ from NIM2141 (7/84) ᵇNI5065, recorded 1986, ᶜNI5121 (4/89).

Haydn Concerto in E flat major, HobVIIe/1ᵃ. **Neruda** Concerto in E flat majorᵇ. **Hummel** Concerto in E flat majorᵇ. **F. Weber** Variations in F majorᵇ. **C.F.C. Fasch** Concerto for Trumpet, Oboe d'amore, Violin and Strings in E majorᶜ.

The famous Haydn Concerto sounds bright and forthright with trumpeter and orchestra freshly caught in the spacious Church of All Saints, Tooting. Wallace's technical strength and impish articulation are characterized by crisp tonguing and a strident (if at times fairly uncompromising) trumpet sound in the outer movements. Peace is restored in a beautifully judged slow movement in which Wallace floats rather than imposes. Less refined than some other recordings of this work (track 2 at 3'43" has an extraordinary blemish in the lower register of the strings), there is a natural freshness here which one rarely hears in this old war-horse. The Neruda Concerto, written originally for the corno da caccia, makes an attractive trumpet piece, flawed only by its unbalanced episodic structure. Hummel's Concerto is a persuasive work, by and large, and it is given a bold reading here by Wallace, full of incident, some examples of which trip out of the bell in a fairly conventional manner. Others are decidedly quirky, such as the mock antiquated tuning on the opening trill of the second movement. Rather more effective are the dazzling embellishments which look forward to the salon and the new virtuoso tradition of the nineteenth century which the trumpet inhabited once valves had been invented. Friedrich Dionysius Weber's Variations in F are typical of this musically slight but entertaining world in which the cornet/trumpet was beginning to thrive. Wallace is utterly at home in this idiom, bringing to the music the swagger and facility upon which its characterization depends. Finally we step back to the Indian summer of the trumpet, the early classical years and the stratospherically high trumpet range demanded by Carl Friedrich Christian Fasch. His Concerto for trumpet, oboe d'amore and violin is an exciting work, brilliantly played.

New review

Concerti per l'orchestra di Dresda Cologne Musica Antiqua / Reinhard Goebel. Archiv
Produktion Ⓕ 447 644-2AH (70 minutes: DDD: 1/96). ✍ Recorded 1993-5.   Ⓖ
Heinichen Concerto in F major. Pastorale in A major, "Per la notte della Nativitate Christi".
Dieupart Concerto for Sopranino Recorder and Orchestra in A minor. **Fasch** Lute Concerto
in D minor. **Pisendel** Sonata in C minor. **Quantz** Double Flute Concerto in G major.
Veracini Overture No. 5 in B flat major.

If readers judge some of the pieces on this recording to be a little lacking in musical substance they will be generously compensated in matters of instrumental colour. During the first half of the eighteenth century the Dresden court orchestra enjoyed international renown. Its excellence was largely thanks to Pisendel, who directed the court orchestra for over a quarter of a century and whose prowess as a violin virtuoso was probably unrivalled in Germany during his lifetime. To some extent this disc is a tribute to Pisendel for, although only one short work by him appears on Goebel's menu, much of the remaining music and above all the sumptuous scoring of the Heinichen 'concerto' – it is in fact a suite – reflects his imaginative and innovative flair as a Konzertmeister. All but one of the pieces here are representative of the kind of music performed by the Dresden orchestra in what Goebel has aptly described as its Augustan Age. Indeed, much of it may well have actually been played by the court band, with the exception of Veracini's Overture No. 5 in B flat. Cologne Musica Antiqua are on crisply incisive form throughout the programme. Horns are stretched to their limits in the Heinichen but such cliff-hanger writing only serves to remind us of the virtuosity of the Dresden wind section. French composer, Charles Dieupart is represented by a pretty though lightweight Concerto for sopranino recorder and strings with *colla parte* oboes. Fasch is more impressive with his Concerto in D minor for lute and strings. Indeed, we may reckon him as among the greatest talents on the disc, and not least for the work's imaginative middle movement *Andante*. Pisendel's two-movement orchestral Sonata in C minor is a splendid composition with a vigorous and effectively worked *Allegro*. Quantz the composer too often gets a bad press from critics. This virtuoso Concerto in G major for two flutes has qualities of sterling merit, with dazzling solo parts and tutti episodes whose interest extends well beyond the merely functional. A laurel wreath to Maestro Goebel for investigative, imaginative programming, and for the disciplined, vital direction of his band, a veritable Dresden court orchestra reborn.

Concertos for Four Violins Cologne Musica Antiqua / Reinhard Goebel. Archiv Produktion
Ⓕ 435 393-2AH (66 minutes: DDD: 9/92). ✍ Recorded 1991.
Torelli Concerto in E minor for Four Violins and Strings. **Mossi** Concertos, Op. 4 – No. 12 in
G minor. **Valentini** Concerti grossi, Op. 7 – No. 11 in A minor. **Locatelli** Introduttioni teatrali
and Concerti, Op. 4 – No. 12 in F major. **Leo** Concerto in D major for Four Violins and Strings.
Even the most assiduous collectors and discerning connoisseurs of baroque concertos are likely to find novelties in this 'off the beaten track' programme from Cologne Musica Antiqua. Mossi, Valentini and Locatelli belong to the Roman school, though the latter shows marked Venetian leanings, while the remaining two composers are products of Bologna (Torelli) and Naples (Leo). Whatever doubts there may be concerning the intrinsic merit of these works they nevertheless provide a fascinating and valuable glimpse of what composers other than Corelli (Rome) on the one hand or Vivaldi (Venice) on the other were up to. Reinhard Goebel who, alas, was unable to lead his group from the violin in his usual manner, following an injury to his arm, directs effectively. The textures in these concertos are rich and contrasting and the players draw subtle resonances from them. The opening *Largo* and ensuing fugue of the Valentini work affords striking examples of Musica Antiqua's skill in pointing up the variety of string sound inherent in this repertory. This is a fascinating programme performed with Musica Antiqua's customary *élan* and precision.

Favourite Overtures, Volume 2. London Philharmonic Orchestra; ᵃBerlin Philharmonic Orchestra
/ Sir Thomas Beecham. Dutton Laboratories mono Ⓜ CDLX7009* (75 minutes: ADD: 10/94).
Recorded 1933-40.
Mozart Le nozze di Figaro (from Columbia LX639, 10/37). Don Giovanni (LX893, 10/40). Die
Zauberflöteᵃ (HMV DB3465, 7/38). **Weber** Oberon (LX746, 11/38). Der Freischütz (LX481/2,
5/37). **Brahms** Tragic Overture, Op. 81 (LX638/9, 10/37). **Wagner** A Faust Overture (LX481/2,
5/36). **Berlioz** Le carnaval romain, Op. 9 (LX570, 2/37). **Rossini** La scala di seta (LX255, 7/33).
The *Zauberflöte* Overture is taken from Beecham's complete recording of the opera, and he shows a measured, profound response to Mozart's inspiration. All his characteristic elegance is still there, but the 43 players of the Berlin Philharmonic are made to play in a concentrated, highly characterful fashion. He provides a strong, arrestingly dramatic account of the *Don Giovanni* Overture, yet his *Nozze di Figaro* bubbles over with charm and wit. He finds plenty of drama in the Wagner, and the Brahms has an appropriate and highly impressive strength and profundity of feeling. A reading such

as this effectively gives the lie to Beecham's reputation in some quarters as a lightweight interpreter. Perhaps the best performance of all is the overture by his beloved Berlioz, for energy and excitement are matched by playing of the most affecting delicacy and poetry in the piece's more reflective passages. All the engineering is outstanding.

Flute Concertos Michael Faust (fl); **Cologne Radio Symphony Orchestra** / [a]Alun Francis, [b]Serge Baudo. Capriccio Ⓕ 10 495 (64 minutes: DDD: 12/94). Recorded 1991-2.
Martin (arr. Ansermet) Ballade[a]. **Nielsen** Flute Concerto, FS119[a]. **Bernstein** Halil[a]. **Ibert** Flute Concerto[b].

Here is a valuable juxtaposition of twentieth-century works written in four countries between 1926 and 1981, and Michael Faust, a splendid flautist and artist, has the range to illuminate them all. The Martin is a coolly elegant piece that begins quietly but then has a good deal of animation; although essentially non-tonal, it has a clear sense of direction and is distinctly harmonious. Indeed, after around 4'30", we are reintroduced to Debussy's *faune* in an irresistibly slinky and sexy mood. The Danish peasant quirkiness of Nielsen's Concerto also comes across well, goat-footed Pan's flute now serving a northern wit and wildness. The writing for the soloist's orchestral colleagues individuality in a way that was new in Nielsen's time but, thanks to him, is something of a feature in much of today's music. Indeed, this work has an oddly modern and faintly irresponsible feeling. Bernstein's threnody in memory of a young Israeli flautist killed in battle in 1973 is a fine piece and eloquently moving. Finally, Ibert's Concerto of 1934, along with Gallic wit, again evokes Arcadia, although it is here (according to the booklet-essay) "unreal as through a frosted-glass window". A well-planned and deftly performed programme.

Flute Concertos of the Sans-Souci Patrick Gallois (fl); **CPE Bach Chamber Orchestra** / Peter Schreier. DG Ⓕ 439 895-2GH (77 minutes: DDD: 2/95). Recorded 1993.
C.P.E. Bach Flute Concerto in G major, H445. **F. Benda** Flute Concerto in E minor.
Frederick the Great Flute Concerto in C major. **Quantz** Flute Concerto in G major.

It is a nice peg on which to hang a programme – that of music by an employer (Frederick the Great of Prussia) and three of his employees, every item of which was first played by the King himself. Quantz was employed as Frederick's flute teacher from 1741; in 1752 he published a treatise on flute playing in which he described how a good concerto should be: a first movement with a "majestic" ritornello and "pleasing and intelligible melodies", a second movement whose "melody must be just as moving and expressive as one with accompanying words", and a finale that is "short, gay and fiery". The King is said to have disapproved of "mournful or sad" slow movements – saying that they should be "peaceful, contented or seductive". With the exception of the *Aria, mesto* of Quantz's own Concerto, all the works in this recording meet these regal requirements. We cannot know whether Frederick was as good a flautist as he was (flatteringly?) reported to be, but we do know that Gallois is a remarkable one; he cannot obliterate the differences between the baroque and modern flutes but, so soft-edged is his tone and so subtle his nuances, he reduces them to relative unimportance. One cannot speak too highly of the CPE Bach Chamber Orchestra or of Schreier's direction of it, a model of stylish, on-the-toes alertness and sympathetic response. The concertos by Frederick and Benda have no other currently listed recording, which, together with the 'virtual reality' recording, help to make this a disc to delight and to brighten the dullest day.

French Baroque Harpsichord Works Sophie Yates (hpd). Chandos Chaconne Ⓕ CHAN0545 . (71 minutes: DDD: 11/93). 🎵 Recorded 1993.
D'Anglebert Pièces de Clavecin – Suite in G minor; Tombeau de M. de Chambonnières.
F. Couperin L'Art de toucher le clavecin – Prélude in D minor. Livre de clavecin, Deuxième ordre – Seconde Courante; Sarabande, "La Prude"; Les Idées heureuses; La Voluptueuse.
Forqueray La Rameau; La Boisson; La Sylva; Jupiter. **Rameau** L'enharmonique.
L'Egyptienne. La Dauphine.

Sophie Yates has a real understanding of the French style - so difficult to capture, with its special conventions and elaborate ornamentation. Her phrasing is subtle as well as musical; and she proves herself capable of the flexibility proper to this music without risk to the underlying pulse or to continuity. Her reading of *La Dauphine*, Rameau's last harpsichord piece, is justifiably free and improvisatory, since it is thought to be a transcription of Rameau's extemporization at the wedding of the Dauphin in 1747. She savours Rameau's bold enharmonics, too, shows drive and energy in his *L'Egyptienne*, impressive dignity in Forqueray's tribute to his great contemporary and in a d'Anglebert sarabande, expressiveness in Forqueray's *La Sylva* and a sense of enjoyment in the trenchant drama of the flashing thunderbolts of his *Jupiter*. Yates also has the advantage of admirable recording of a particularly beautiful and rich-sounding instrument (a copy of a Goujon).

French Orchestral Works [a]French Radio National Orchestra; [b]Royal Philharmonic Orchestra / Sir Thomas Beecham. EMI Beecham Edition Ⓜ CDM7 63379-2* (68 minutes: ADD: 7/90). ⒼⒼ
Bizet Carmen – Suite No. 1 (from HMV HQS1108, 12/67)[a]. **Fauré** Pavane, Op. 50 (HMV ASD518, 4/63)[a]. Dolly Suite, Op. 56 (orch. Rabaud. HQS1136, 5/68)[a]. **Debussy** Prélude à l'après-midi d'un faune (ASD259, 6/59)[b]. **Saint-Saëns** Le rouet d'Omphale, Op. 31 (ASD259)[b].
Delibes Le Roi s'amuse – Ballet Music (HQS1136)[b].

Even to those who never heard him in the flesh there is no mistaking Beecham's relish in, and flair for, the French repertoire. His combination of mischievous high spirits, almost dandyish elegance, cool outer classicism masking passionate emotion, swagger, refined nuance and delicate charm was perhaps unique – not matched even by such committed Francophiles as Constant Lambert. *Elan* is at once in evidence here in the *Carmen* prelude, and subtle dynamic gradations in the entr'actes to Acts 2 and 4; there is lightness, vivacity and tenderness in Fauré's *Dolly Suite* and a true Gallic reserve in his *Pavane*; and he enters with prim finesse into Delibes's pastiche dances. Debussy's erotic study, on repeated hearings of this performance, becomes the more Grecian and effective for its conscious understatement; and only the Saint-Saëns symphonic poem, for all the RPO's delicacy, seems to hang fire. But four or five bull's-eyes out of six is a pretty good score, and at medium price not to be missed.

New review

Clara Haskil: The Legacy Clara Haskil (pf); [a]Arthur Grumiaux (vn); **Vienna Symphony Orchestra / **[b]**Paul Sacher,** [c]**Bernhard Paumgartner;** [d]**Lamoureux Concerts Orchestra / Igor Markevitch;** [e]**The Hague Philharmonic Orchestra / Willem van Otterloo.** Philips mono/stereo Ⓜ 442 685-2PM12 (12 discs: 809 minutes: ADD: 11/95). Also available in three boxed sets, as detailed below.

442 625-2PM5 (five discs) – **Beethoven** Violin Sonatas[a] – No. 1 in D major, Op. 12 No. 1 (from ABL3204, 5/58); No. 2 in A major, Op. 12 No. 2; No. 3 in E flat major, Op. 12 No. 3 (both from ABL3199, 4/58); No. 4 in A minor, Op. 23; No. 5 in F major, Op. 24, "Spring" (ABL3204); No. 6 in A major, Op. 30 No. 1 (ABL3226, 12/58); No. 7 in C minor, Op. 30 No. 2 (ABL3207, 6/58); No. 8 in G, Op. 30 No. 3 (ABL3199); No. 9 in A major, Op. 47, "Kreutzer" (ABL3226); No. 10 in G major, Op. 96 (ABL3207). **Mozart** Piano and Violin Sonatas[a] – G major, K301/K293*a*; E minor, K304/K300*c*; F major, K376/K374*d*; B flat major, K378/K317*d* (all from A00432L, 10/60); B flat major, K454; A major, K526 (ABL3144, 10/57). *442 631-2PM4* (four discs) – **Beethoven** Piano Concerto No. 3 in C minor, Op. 37[d] (SABL172, 1/61). **Mozart** Piano Concertos – No. 9 in E flat major, K271[b] (ABL3143, 7/57); No. 20 in D minor, K466 (two versions: [c]ABL3129, 4/57 and [d]SABL212, 4/62); No. 23 in A major, K488[b] (ABL3129); No. 24 in C minor, K491[d] (SABL212). Rondo in A major, K386 (ABL3143). **Schumann** Piano Concerto in A minor, Op. 54[e] (ABR4080, 2/55). **Falla** Noches en los jardines de España[d]. **Chopin** Piano Concerto No. 2 in F minor, Op. 21[d] (SABL173, 8/61). *442 635-2PM3* (three discs) – **Beethoven** Piano Sonatas – No. 17 in D minor, Op. 31 No. 2, "Tempest" (two versions: new to UK, recorded 1955 and ABL3358, 3/61); No. 18 in E flat major, Op. 31 No. 3 (two versions: new to UK, recorded 1955 and ABL3358). **Mozart** Nine Variations in D major on a minuet by Duport, K573 (6768 366, 11/83. 1954). Piano Sonata in C major, K330/K300*h* (ABL3365, 9/61). **Schumann** Bunte Blätter, Op. 99 (ABL3029, 2/55). Theme and Variations on the name "Abegg", Op. 1 (A11213G. 1951). Kinderszenen, Op. 15 (1955). Waldszenen, Op. 82 (both A00775R. 1954). **D. Scarlatti** Keyboard Sonatas – B minor, Kk87; E flat major, Kk193; F minor, Kk386. **Ravel** Sonatine (all A00143L. 1951). **Schubert** Piano Sonata in B flat major, D960 (ABL3029).

What a legacy this is, brimming over with musical zest yet drawing on an exalted delicacy and inwardness from what was clearly a 'still centre', a well of endless resource and nourishment. Haskil may have enjoyed a low profile until the autumn of her tragically short career, but her friends and admirers included Lipatti, Enescu, Stokowski, Cortot, Giulini and Tatyana Nikolaieva among others. Her range was exceptional. Before ill-health intervened her specialities included Brahms's Second and Saint-Saëns's Fifth Concertos, while Brahms's *Paganini* Variations and Liszt's *Feux follets* featured in her solo recitals. Later, such exuberance was not so much cautioned or restrained as channelled into her superlative Beethoven, Schumann (has any one played the *Abegg* Variations with such dizzy aplomb or captured the Prophet Bird's quizzical stare with such uncanny directness?) and, most of all, her Mozart. Indeed, listening once again to Haskil's Mozart is like re-entering a musical Elysium. Everything sounds so exactly 'right', so gently but firmly unarguable. Her sense of difference between Mozart and Beethoven is finely but unmistakably drawn. For just as she locates the underlying storms of Beethoven's more outgoing spirit, she finds no less exactly an equilibrium beneath even the clouded surface of Mozart's E minor Sonata, K304. In the greater, more ambitious utterances of K454 and in the *moto perpetuo* finale of K526 she miraculously makes every bar subtle and ambiguous without recourse to anything approaching overt drama or idiosyncrasy. The concertos, too, find this heaven-sent artist at her greatest. Here is no impersonal sheen or expertise, but a deeply committed poetry resolved in playing of the most crystalline perfection. Listen to her in the second movement cadenza of K271 and you may wonder when you last heard playing of such speculative beauty. Haskil was famous for lifting her partner's performances on to the highest level. Instantly aware of her quality Grumiaux rarely played better than he does here in the Beethoven sonatas, and you will have to go a long way to hear two artists in more perfect accord than in the great final G major Sonata's other-worldly musings.

Clearly, one could go on for ever celebrating this or that aspect of such life-enhancing artistry. You may demur at Haskil's Schubert (perhaps predictably it has a classical rather than romantic bias), Chopin, Ravel and Falla (an exotic departure from her principally German repertoire) yet all these performances are alive with passing felicities. Is the Schumann Concerto disappointingly non-committal, without, say, Dame Myra Hess's warmth and affection? Did Haskil's energy start to fail at the time of the second recording of Beethoven's Op. 31 Sonatas (those tell-tale pauses for breath in the headlong equestrian finale of No. 3)? Such questions may well be asked. Yet her Mozart – that litmus test of musical quality – surely defies criticism, is profoundly musical rather than decorous; totally devoid of what Dr Leavis, in one of his most trenchant phrases, called "the extant social world". The recordings vary but have been for the most part beautifully refurbished and no praise could be high enough for Philips's presentation. There are three superb accompanying essays and a beautiful selection of photographs.

Hollywood Nightmares [a]Stephen Hough (pf); [b]Los Angeles Master Chorale; Hollywood Bowl Orchestra / John Mauceri. Philips Ⓕ 442 425-2PH (72 minutes: DDD: 1/95). Recorded 1993.
Savino/Perry The Phantom of the Opera – Through the Looking Glass. **Steiner** King Kong – Overture. **Stravinsky** The Rite of Spring – Sacrificial Dance. **J.T. Williams** Jurassic Park – Theme[b]. Dracula – Night Journeys. **Herrmann** Vertigo – Prelude; Scène d'Amour. **Rósza** Spellbound Concerto[a]. **Barry** Body Heat – Main Theme. **Waxman** Sunset Boulevard – Sonata for Orchestra (arr. Mauceri). Dr Jekyll and Mr Hyde – Suite (arr. Palmer)[b]. **Goldsmith** The Omen – Main Title[b].

John Mauceri explores Hollywood's musical past with this entertaining programme of music from movies that deal with various manifestations of horror, from giant monsters and diabolical intervention to far less visible psychological phenomena. The disc opens imaginatively with a brief dialogue excerpt from the soundtrack of *The Phantom of the Opera* (the 1925 Lon Chaney version that was reissued four years later with sound effects and music) synchronized to a new recording of the background score, but rather more familiar are the excerpts from *Jurassic Park*, *Vertigo* and *The Omen*, though Mauceri's readings are not particularly distinctive. He fares much better with Max Steiner's bold, dramatic Overture to *King Kong* written specifically for the film's 1933 première, Rózsa's richly romantic *Spellbound Concerto* (heard here in a lengthier, more restrained and beautifully shaded performance than is customary, led by a fluent contribution from Stephen Hough that fully merits the "Bravo!" expressed by the composer just as the music dies away) and, most notably, the two Waxman suites, both of which differ in several fascinating ways from the performances already recorded. *Sunset Boulevard*, for example, has been edited by Mauceri himself. The lush but appropriately *noir*-ish sourness of this Oscar-winning score (which clearly influenced David Cullen's superb orchestrations for Lloyd Webber's stage version of the film) is never less than compelling here, whilst the vivid suite from the 1941 adaptation of *Dr Jekyll and Mr Hyde* is most impressive in Mauceri's hands, particularly in the sequence where a distant chorus sing "You should see me dance the polka" in counterpoint with the unsettling phrases describing Jekyll's transformation into his evil alter-ego. The warmth of the old MGM sound-stage provides a reliably beefy and sympathetic acoustic.

Hungarian Connections [a]Laurence Kaptain (cimb); Chicago Symphony Orchestra / Sir Georg Solti. Decca Ⓕ 443 444-2DH (72 minutes: DDD: 1/95). Recorded live in 1993. *Gramophone Editor's choice.* 🄶🄶
Bartók Hungarian Sketches, Sz97. Romanian folkdances, Sz68. **Kodály** Háry János, Op. 15 Suite[a]. **Liszt** Two Episodes from Lenau's Faust, S110 – Der Tanz in der Dorfschenke. Hungarian Rhapsody No. 2 in D minor (orch. Döppler). **L. Weiner** Csongor és Tünde, Op. 10b – Introduction; Scherzo.

This is a terrific programme. The sequence is imaginative, the material extremely attractive, and the standard of performance high. The *Mephisto Waltz* swirls in heady abandon, with strings as delicate as thistledown, and some snappy work from the Chicago brass. The once-ubiquitous Second *Hungarian Rhapsody* is wittily turned, although Döppler's sundry added counterpoint and rather tame orchestration tend to mute the rustic edge of Liszt's original. The performance, though, has plenty of life and the recording conjures up a realistic sense of aural perspective. Sir Georg's empathy for this idiom is everywhere in evidence, and never more so than in Bartók's *Romanian folkdances*, where lightness of touch and sensitive rubato recreate a crucial feeling of improvisation. The *Hungarian Sketches* are tellingly pointed, with fluid lines in "Evening in the Village" and "Melody", a hilarious *ff* trombone/tuba belch in "A Little Tipsy" and cleanly differentiated percussion in the "Bear Dance". Solti's version is now perhaps the current front-runner, and makes for a most entertaining musical diversion. Nice, too, to hear music by the much underrated Leó Weiner, his *Csongor és Tünde* ballet with its subtle reminiscences of Nicolai's *Merry Wives of Windsor* Overture and Liszt's *Dante* Symphony. The busy scherzo is the sort of thing Bartók might have composed had he not outgrown the worlds of Strauss and Dohnányi, while the Introduction is reminiscent of Kodály in pastoral vein. Kodály himself is represented by a genial, often brilliantly played account of the *Háry János* Suite, superbly recorded and with some distinctive solo work. And what a blessed relief to hear the cimbalom properly integrated into the orchestral texture.

Les Introuvables de Jacqueline Du Pré Jacqueline du Pré (vc); [a]Gerald Moore, [b]Ernest Lush, [c]Stephen Kovacevich (pfs); [d]London Symphony Orchestra / Sir John Barbirolli; [e]Royal Philharmonic Orchestra / Sir Malcolm Sargent; [f]New Philharmonia Orchestra, [g]Chicago Symphony Orchestra, [h]English Chamber Orchestra / Daniel Barenboim ([i]pf). EMI Ⓑ CZS5 68132-2 (six discs. 857 minutes: ADD: 8/94). 🄶🄶

Elgar Cello Concerto in E minor, Op. 85[d] (from HMV ASD655, 12/65). **Delius** Cello Concerto[e] (ASD644, 8/65). **Saint-Saëns** Cello Concerto No. 1 in A minor, Op. 33[f]. **Schumann** Cello Concerto in A minor, Op. 129[f] (both from ASD2498, 11/69). **Dvořák** Cello Concerto in B minor, B191[g]. Silent woods, B182[g] (ASD2751, 1/72). **Haydn** Cello Concertos – No. 1 in C major[h] (ASD2331, 10/67); No. 2 in D major[d]. **Monn** (arr. Schoenberg) Cello Concerto in G minor[d] (ASD2466, 4/69). **Chopin** Cello Sonata, Op. 65[i]. **Franck** Violin Sonata in A major[i] (arr. vc/pf. ASD2851, 2/73). **Fauré** Flégie, Op. 24[a] (HMV SAN255, 7/69). **Bruch** Kol Nidrei, Op. 47[a] (HMV CSD1499, 8/63). **Bach** Cello Suites – No. 1 in G major, BWV1007; No. 2 in D minor, BWV1008 (from broadcast performances in 1962. CDM7 63165-2, 9/89). **Handel** Oboe Concerto in G minor, HWV287[b] (arr. vc/pf Slatter. Broadcast, 1961. CDM7 63166-2, 9/89). **Beethoven** 12 Variations on Handel's "See the conqu'ring hero comes", Wo045[i]. Seven Variations in E flat major on Mozart's "Bei Männern, welche Liebe fühlen", Wo046[i]. 12 Variations in F major on "Ein Mädchen oder Weibchen", Op. 66[i] (recorded live in 1970. All from HMV SLS5042, 5/76). Cello Sonatas[c] – No. 3 in A major, Op. 69; No. 5 in D major, Op. 105 No. 2 (HMV HQS1029, 10/66).

As the title suggests, this fine six-disc retrospective of Jacqueline du Pré's recording career – a mere ten years long – was masterminded by French EMI. Aptly the English commentary by Jeremy Siepmann quotes Sir John Barbirolli's memorable remark in Christopher Nupen's television film, *Jacqueline*: "If you have no excesses in the full bloom of youth, what will there be to pare away on the long road to maturity?" The wonder was that Jacqueline du Pré was mature in her artistry from the start, and it is good that from the period even before the first official EMI sessions the collection includes three BBC recordings: Bach's Cello Suites Nos. 1 and 2 and a Handel sonata arranged from the Oboe Concerto in G minor. Those early BBC recordings are inevitably flawed, but the sheer scale of the artistry is never for a moment in doubt. Of the handful of items recorded by EMI in July 1962 with Gerald Moore accompanying, only Bruch's *Kol Nidrei* is included. The Delius was du Pré's first concerto recording, and she was not nearly as much at ease as she came to be later. The CD transfers do not minimize any of the flaws in the original recordings, notably the disappointing sound given to her Chicago recording of the Dvořák Concerto. Not only is the orchestral sound both coarse and thin with a high degree of background hiss, the cello is balanced far too close. Even with that balance one registers clearly the wide dynamic range of du Pré's playing, down to a whispered *pianissimo*. It was right to include it and also the cello sonata recordings of Chopin and Franck, the last recordings ever made by du Pré on December 10th and 11th, 1971. The tone may not have been quite so even as earlier, but the fire and warmth are undiminished. All the concerto recordings are welcome with the tear-laden quality in the slow movement of the Schumann matching that in the Elgar. It is good that the supreme Beethoven sonata recordings she made with Stephen Bishop (later Kovacevich) are included here, both sparkling and darkly intense. From the Beethoven series recorded at the 1970 Edinburgh Festival by the BBC only the three sets of variations are included, artistically fascinating but with sound curiously distanced and uninvolving. This is a treasure-house for anyone who was ever magnetized by du Pré's playing, and at bargain price as well.

New review

Les introuvables de János Starker János Starker (vc); [a]Gerald Moore (pf); Philharmonia Orchestra / [b]Carlo Maria Giulini, [c]Walter Susskind. EMI mono/stereo Ⓜ CZS5 68485-2* (six discs: 398 minutes: ADD: 12/95). Recorded 1956-9.
Bach Solo Cello Suites, BWV1007-12 (from Columbia 33CX1515, 4/58; 33CX1656, 9/59 and 33CX1745, 6/61). **Kodály** Solo Cello Sonata, Op. 8. **Dohnányi** Konzertstück in D major, Op. 12[c] (both from 33CX1595, 11/58). **Boccherini** Cello Concerto in B flat major, G482[b]. **Haydn** Cello Concerto No. 2 in D major, HobVII*b*/2[b] (33CX1665, 10/59). **Schumann** Cello Concerto in A minor, Op. 129[b]. **Saint-Saëns** Cello Concerto No. 1 in A minor, Op. 33[b] (33CX1579, 2/59). **Dvořák** Cello Concerto in B minor, B191[c]. **Fauré** Elégie, Op. 24[c] (Columbia SAX2263, 1/59). **Milhaud** Cello Concerto No. 1, Op. 136[c]. **Prokofiev** Cello Concerto in E minor, Op. 58[c] (33CX1425, 7/57). Also contains short items [a] by Bach, Chopin, Debussy, Kreisler, Mussorgsky, Paganini, Popper, Saint-Saëns, Schubert, Schumann and Tcherepnin (all from 33CX1700, 6/60).

A few seconds' worth of sampling is all that is needed to establish the tonal identity of János Starker, a supremely accomplished player whose tough, dry, vibrant sound was fuller in youth than in older age but whose every stroke of the bow suggests profound musicality, at once forthright and ardently expressive. In the Bach Cello Suites the approach is 'classical-romantic' rather than 'authentic baroque', with propulsive Preludes, buoyant Bourrées, Gavottes and Gigues, and deeply introspective accounts of the slower movements. He has recorded the Kodály Sonata on other occasions, but it would be difficult to upstage the well-employed virtuosity of this 1957 performance, especially in the raging final *Allegro molto vivace*, a dazzling dance sequence and the nearest Kodály ever came to sounding like Bartók. Of the concerto's, the Dvořák, in particular, features a most touching account of the slow movement, but EMI slip up in their tracking of the individual movements of the Saint-Saëns Concerto (the *Allegretto con moto* actually starts during track 7, and not at the beginning of track 8). The Schumann Concerto is more full-bodied but less subtle than Starker's new RCA recording (see review under Schumann; refer to the Index to Reviews); Dohnányi's delightful *Konzertstück* receives smiling advocacy, Fauré's *Elégie* weeps inwardly, while both the Milhaud and

Prokofiev concertos – the former with its Mahlerian resonances (try the *Grave* second movement for side-glances towards *Das Lied*), the latter, a restless precursor of a musically superior *Symphony-Concerto* – are treated to typically lithe, finely honed playing. Boccherini (with cadenzas by Hutter) and Haydn (where the cellist provides his own cadenzas) both respond to Starkerian tonal tapering, and then there are the encores – wistful, lean and tastefully turned. A veritable feast, then. The majority of EMI's transfers are excellent.

New review

Dinu Lipatti Les Inédits. [a]**Dinu Lipatti,** [b]**Madeleine Lipatti,** [b]**Béla Siki** (pfs); [c]**Suisse Romande Orchestra / Ernest Ansermet;** [d]**South-West German Radio Orchestra / Paul Sacher;** [e]**orchestra.** Archiphon mono Ⓕ ARC112/13* (two discs: 139 minutes: ADD: 10/95). From private and test recordings and public performances; recorded 1936-51.
 Liszt Piano Concerto No. 1 in E flat major, S124[c] (recorded at a performance in Geneva on June 6th, 1947). **Lipatti** Concertino en style classique, Op. 3[ae] (venue unknown, *c*1948). Three Romanian Dances[ac] (Geneva, October 10th, 1945). Symphonie concertante[bc] (Geneva, September 14th, 1951). Tziganes[c] (Geneva, *c*1951). Also includes works (some with various artists) by **Bach, Bartók**[d]**, Brahms, Chopin, Enescu, Fauré, Liszt, Ravel, Rimsky-Korsakov, D. Scarlatti** and **Schumann.**

The originators of this full-price, two-disc anthology make no secret of their problems in transferring old, imperfect, predominately private recordings to CD, or of their awareness when the odds go against them. But never mind the 'surface noise' and all that. Surely no Lipatti lover will want to be without these previously commercially unobtainable precious memories. Solos on the first disc range from Lipatti's first Parisian recordings of 1936 to extracts from a Zurich concert given only ten months before he died. Even as a 19-year-old student, in the *Presto vivace* of an F sharp minor Sonata by his godfather, Enescu, you recognize the pinpoint clarity of articulation and the rhythmic alacrity and precision that were to remain hallmarks of his style for life. This disc's main discoveries are, nevertheless, the two concertos, notably Lipatti's only known recording of Liszt's in E flat (a lifelong favourite) with Ansermet and the Suisse Romande, embodying his maturer 'rethoughts' after hearing a recording by Liszt's pupil, Emil von Sauer. The expansive grandeur of his bolder gestures, the exquisitely intimate poetry of his lyricism, and the delicately tingling scintillation of his prestidigitation are unforgettable. So, too, are the intensity underpinning his purity and his fingertip atmospheric evocation in the central *Adagio religioso* of Bartók's Third Concerto (also a work very close to his heart) in a much cleaner and truer recording than the Liszt – superior enough, in fact, to make it hard to forgive the conductor, Paul Sacher, for forbidding the issue of this 1948 Baden-Baden performance in its entirety. The second disc, invaluable for its reminders of the lure of composition for the younger Lipatti, "reunites for the first time all his symphonic work", as the very generously informative and caring accompanying booklet puts it. The collector's piece (despite inferior reproduction) is surely the Geneva world première of his *Three Romanian Dances* with himself as customarily close knit soloist with Ansermet and the Suisse Romande. Here, irrepressible love of his own country's folk heritage emerges with near Bartók-like voltage. No one did more to canalize Lipatti's overflowing romantic imagination than his Parisian mentor, Nadia Boulanger, as is clearly revealed here in his Bach-cum-Haydn-inspired *Concertino en style classique*, Op. 3 of 1936, with himself as an even more lithe and light-hearted soloist. The fuller impact of the then eclectic Paris, not forgetting Stravinsky, is nevertheless more potently revealed in his *Symphonie concertante* for two pianos and string orchestra (1938), here with his widow and Béla Siki alongside Ansermet in 1951. Its central *Molto adagio* has the same haunting nocturnal mystery of many of Bartók's slow movements. Nothing brings home our loss in December 1950 more than this, not only of a pianist over-blessed and over-loved by the gods, but of a potentially spellbinding post-impressionist Romanian composer.

New review

The London Viola Sound Viola sections from **Academy of St Martin in the Fields, BBC Symphony Orchestra, London Philharmonic Orchestra, English National Opera Orchestra / Geoffrey Simon.** Cala (special price) CACD0106 (36 minutes: DDD: 9/95). Items marked [a] arranged Milone, [b]Runswick, [c]Balcombe. Recorded 1995.
 Gershwin Porgy and Bess – It ain't necessarily so[a]. **Weill** Kiddush[a] (with Rivka Golani, va). **Shostakovich** Moscow, Cherymushki – Galop[a]. **Dvořák** Slavonic Dance in E minor, B147 No. 2[a]. **Grainger** Arrival Platform Humlet, RMTB1[c]. **Ravel** Pavane pour une infante défunte[a]. **Prokofiev** War and Peace – Waltz[a]. **Bacharach** This guy's in love with you[b]. **Strayhorn** Take the "A" Train[a].

Every one of these pieces is given a new dimension by its arrangement. "It ain't necessarily so" creeps in seductively, at an enticing, lazy gait, on 48 violas; while in Weill's *Kiddush*, Rivka Golani/viola acts as a cantor in the bluesy solo line. Her warm timbre is ultimately nearly as succulent as the ripieno, yet she manages somehow to keep something of the music's underlying traditional Jewish religious feeling. It is a haunting piece. However, the highlight of the programme is the Shostakovich "Galop" (from his 1959 operetta, *Cherymushki*), which is a kind of civilized *moto perpetuo* sabre dance. It sounds wonderfully spirited on these massed violas, while in the more familiar, warm and elegant Dvořák *Slavonic Dance* the violins are not missed one bit. Grainger actually wrote on his score that he intended the jaunty, folksy, at times dark-throated *Arrival Platform Humlet*, for "massed-middle-fiddles". It was conceived on the platforms of London's Liverpool Street and Victoria stations and is, as its composer details, "the sort of thing one hums to oneself as an accompaniment to one's tramping feet as one happily, excitedly paces up and down the arrival platform ... awaiting the arrival of belated train bringing one's sweetheart from foreign parts; great fun!". Ravel's lovely *Pavane* and the bittersweet Prokofiev *Waltz* bring subtle differences of colour, the sound warmly orientated, yet never exaggeratedly so, thus allowing the music's character to remain. As for Burt Bacharach's *This guy's in love with you*, well, like the Gershwin it's a great tune of our time, here richly arranged by Daryl Runswick, but without ostentatious schmalz. It is given a light rhythmic touch by Geoffrey Simon, who throughout is a model of good taste. The recording is full-toned, spacious and very easy on the ear.

Marches and Overtures à la Française Detroit Symphony Orchestra / Paul Paray. Mercury Living Presence Ⓜ 434 332-2MM (66 minutes: ADD: 11/93). Items marked [a] from AMS16077 (3/61), [b]AMS16121 (11/62), [c]sex15050 (3/62), [d]sex15024. Recorded 1959-60. ⒼⒼⒼ
Meyerbeer Coronation March[a]. **Gounod** Marche funèbre d'une marionnette[a].
Saint-Saëns Suite algérienne in C major, Op. 60 – March militaire française[a]. Marche héroïque in E flat major, Op. 34[a]. **Rouget de Lisle** La marseillaise[a]. **Adam** Si j'étais roi – Overture[b].
Boieldieu La dame blanche – Overture[b]. **Offenbach** La belle Hélène – Overture[c]. Orphée aux enfers – Overture[c]. Les contes d'Hoffmann – Prelude[c]. **Rossini** Guillaume Tell – Overture[d].
They don't make collections like this any more! Or so it seems. Yet can musical tastes really have changed so radically from the days when people would patiently turn over a 78rpm record for the second half of Boieldieu's *La dame blanche* Overture? Unlikely, and there must surely be a welcome for such a collection of charmingly melodious, unpretentious and yet well-crafted pieces as on this CD. Paul Paray (1886–1979) was a genuine son of Normandy who in his seventies could still bring out the Gallic warmth, excitement and sparkle of these pieces. The recording sounds just a shade raw with the violins at the top of their range, but generally the warmth and richness of sound make it quite unbelievable that these recordings are now 35-odd years old.

New review
Meeting Point Gerard McChrystal (sax); [a]London Musici / Mark Stephenson. Silva Classics
Ⓕ SILKD6010 (55 minutes: DDD: 6/96). Recorded 1995.
D. Heath Soprano Saxophone Concerto, "The Celtic"[a]. **I. Wilson** I Sleep at Waking. **Torke** Soprano Saxophone Concerto[a]. **McGlynn** From Nowhere to Nowhere. **Nyman** Where the Bee Dances[a].
McChrystal has an enviably full and warm soprano saxophone tone, and his intonation is as secure as his gift for melodic phrasing is unfailing. This is of inestimable advantage in a work such as Heath's Concerto, where the solo instrument is entirely dominant. The solo piece by Ian Wilson finds McChrystal on alto saxophone, and here his tone is pellucid, while his control of alternating fingering is precise and affecting. The music itself is cryptic and melancholy. McGlynn's solo effort is a good deal more conventional, closer to its folk music source, and is accordingly somewhat less striking. The two major works here are the Nyman and Torke concertos. Nyman's typical rhythmic and melodic patterns are to be found in abundance in *Where the Bee Dances*, but there is also a more discernible willingness to allow the music sequential development and several chances to pause and reflect than one normally associates with this composer. The gem in this collection, however, is the Torke, a three-movement concerto revelling in constantly transmuting thematic shards, unravelling orchestral colours and timbres, and genuinely engaging rhythmic complexities, often hinting at Far-Eastern influences. The outer movements are full of brilliant light, generated by the predominantly percussive scoring, supported by woodwinds and strings. The slow second movement is that modern rarity – a warm and moving construction with a ravishing theme which avoids any hint of sentimentality. It is also brilliantly scored. Unfortunately, this is the least well executed piece on the entire disc, with the London Musici woodwinds falling short of the high standards set elsewhere.

Pierre Monteux Edition [a]San Francisco Symphony Orchestra; [b]Chicago Symphony Orchestra; [c]Boston Symphony Orchestra; [d]RCA Victor Symphony Orchestra / Pierre Monteux. RCA Victor Pierre Monteux Edition mono/stereo Ⓜ 09026 61893-2* (15 discs: 16 hours 55 minutes: ADD: 9/94). ⒼⒼ
Beethoven Die Ruinen von Athen – Overture[a] (Recorded 1949). Symphonies[a] – No. 4 in B flat major, Op. 60 (Victor LM1714. 1952); No. 8 in F major, Op. 93 (GL43357, 11/82. 1950). **Bach** (orch. Respighi) Passacaglia and Fugue in C minor, BWV582[a] (HMV DB21053/4, 5/50). **Berlioz** Symphonie fantastique, Op. 14[a] (DB6670/5. 1945). Benvenuto Cellini – Overture[a] (1952). Les troyens – Prélude, Act 3[a] (previously unpublished. 1945). La damnation de Faust, Op. 24 – Hungarian March[a] (Camden CDN1009, 5/59. 1951). **Brahms** Symphony No. 2 in D major, Op. 73[a] (Victor 11-9237/40. 1945). Schicksalslied, Op. 54[a] (Stanford University Chorus. Victor LM149. 1949). **Mahler** Kindertotenlieder[a] (Marian Anderson, contr. HMV ALP1138, 5/54). **Chausson** Symphony in B flat major, Op. 20 (LM1081. 1950). Poème de l'amour et de la mer, Op. 19[d] (with Gladys Swarthout, mez. 12-0978. 1947). **Chabrier** Le roi malgré lui – Fête polonaise[a] (12-0978. 1947). **Debussy** Images[a] (LM1197. 1951). Images oubliées – Sarabande[a] (orch. Ravel. 11-9684. 1946). Nocturnes[c] (Berkshire Festival Chorus. GL43366, 11/82. 1955). La

mer[c] (GL43366. 1954). **Liszt** Les Préludes, S97[c]. **Scriabin** Le poème de l'extase, Op. 54[c] (both LM1775. 1952). **Saint-Saëns** Havanaise in E major, Op. 83[c] (Leonid Kogan, vn. VICS1153, 2/66). **Delibes** Coppélia – Suite[c]. Sylvia – Suite[c] (both ALP1475, 10/57. 1953. **Gounod** Faust – Ballet Music[a] (prev. unpub. 1947). **Franck** Symphony in D minor[b] (SB6631, 10/65. 1961). Pièce héroique in B minor[a] (orch. O'Connell. DB6135, 10/42). **d'Indy** Istar, Op. 42[a] (CDN1009. 1945). Symphonie sur un chant montagnard français in G major, Op. 25[a] (Maxim Shapiro, pf. 11-8367/9. 1941). Fervaal, Op. 40 – Prélude[a] (CDN1009. 1945). Symphony No. 2 in B flat major, Op. 57[a] (11-8441/5. 1942). **Ravel** Daphnis et Chloé – Suite No. 1[a] (11-9683/4. 1946). Valses nobles et sentimentales[a] (DB6676/7. 1946). Alborada del gracioso[a] (12-1107. 1947). La valse[a] (DB5964/5, 4/42). **Lalo** Le roi d'Ys – Overture[a] (11-8489. 1942). **Ibert** Escales[a] (11-9907/8. 1946). **Rimsky-Korsakov** Scheherazade, Op. 35[a] (11-8384/8. 1942). Sadko, Op. 5[a] (12-0501/2. 1945). Symphony No. 2, Op. 9, "Antar"[a] (DB6918/20. 1946). **R. Strauss** Ein Heldenleben, Op. 40[a] (prev. unpub. 1947). Tod und Verklärung, Op. 24[a] (new to UK. 1960). **Stravinsky** Petrushka[a] (VICS1297, 6/68. 1959). The Rite of Spring[a] (GL85239, 8/85. 1951). **Tchaikovsky** Symphonies[c] – No. 4 in F minor, Op. 36 (SB2093, 12/60); No. 5 in E minor, Op. 64 (SB2045, 10/59); No. 6 in B minor, Op. 74, "Pathétique" (SB2029, 5/59).

"Under-heralded, under-sung, under-appreciated except by those who knew" runs Leon Fleischer's tribute, one of many, in the booklet of this important box-set. Inevitably, as the majority of these RCA Victor recordings were made during Monteux's 17-year tenure in San Francisco, you may wonder how to interpret the claims of colleagues at the time that Monteux had achieved marvels there. Be not anxious: the only San Francisco recording here that reveals the orchestra as seriously less than world-class is the *Tod und Verklärung* which Monteux recorded in 1960 as a guest, eight years after his directorship there had ceased. For the rest, what this playing lacks in ultimate refinement of tone, it more than makes up for with unfailing responsiveness to its conductor's priorities; and as the conductor is Monteux, that means a lot. There is not one single routinely played or badly balanced bar of music, though tolerance may be needed for unexpected gremlins in the machinery (moments of distortion and congestion) in the pre-tape San Francisco recordings (i.e. about a third of the set).

As Monteux was the conductor of the most (in)famous première this century, Stravinsky's *Rite*, and its subsequent champion, you might expect these two restored recordings of the work (he recorded it four times) to shine more brightly than they do. Ensemble is generally tighter in Boston but there are moments of untypical laxity and coarseness. The less heavyweight Paris Conservatoire reading (in stereo) shares much with the 1960 Stravinsky: not as incisive but quite as revealing of the score's no less revolutionary intimate secrets, in other words, for the connoisseur, more rewarding than the endless list of modern recordings that turn the work into a percussion concerto. Throughout the stereo account of *Petrushka*'s Fair scenes, the characterization is earthy without ever being clumsy, and Petrushka himself is pathos in person. Again, if you are looking for the general whipcrack impact of many a modern version, you will be disappointed, though there are numerous instances where Monteux knows and shows how to articulate a difficult figure or a whole passage (for example, the final chase and death of Petrushka) with greater precision than in the average showpiece account. Stravinsky also praised Monteux's 1950 San Francisco Beethoven Eighth. No wonder. Here is the jester in the Age of Elegance; and Monteux has the measure of both. His airborne 1952 Beethoven Fourth is strong without heaviness or overemphasis; and that, to oversimplify, is the secret of Monteux's success in the Austro-German repertoire; the repertoire he loved more than any other, but which the public, or to be more precise, those that chose what the public should receive, decided was not his forte. All credit to RCA for the courage to release this previously unissued 1947 San Francisco *Heldenleben*; as well as the wisdom to record it in the first place.

Monteux recorded Brahms's Second Symphony four times, and the first two were made in San Francisco. The box includes his first (1945) recording and it has all the *joie de vivre* and superb string detailing that you would expect from a Monteux performance, but the extent of which always takes you by surprise. Another surprise is the tensely blazing first movement development. Don't be put off by the constricted sound, or the lack of a proper *sotto voce* at the start of the finale; most Brahms Seconds sound hopelessly retentive after this. His 1945 Berlioz *Symphonie fantastique* is a properly volatile reading: one that lives close to the edge. The playing in an excitable and sharp-featured Waltz (with superbly managed *rits.*) may perhaps strike you as often too loud, but Monteux will then suddenly surprise you with a brilliantly placed hush. This was a real Monteux speciality – establishing a mean of quiet that was practical for projecting clarity (especially for gramophone listeners) and to allow players to phrase properly, and then to select the right moment to drop from it. Was there ever a more accomplished architect of the climactic paragraph? The accomplishment is that you are rarely aware of the mechanics of the operation. To analyse how he does it would probably take a week-long conductors' symposium, so let us settle for shorthand and call it an inspired mix of planning and spontaneity.

The set contains all Monteux's d'Indy recordings. A good decision; d'Indy needs his champion's recordings returned to circulation as a new generation of French conductors take up the cause. If the record moguls and opera impresarios of the time were unwilling to allow Monteux to indulge his passion for Wagner, he undoubtedly found a ready outlet in d'Indy, Franck and Chausson (and Lalo's *Le roi d'Ys* Overture). His celebrated 1961 Chicago Franck Symphony must be in the collection of anyone who loves the work. Monteux's Delibes and Gounod ballet suites are stylish, but also vital and strong. Typically, tempos here and in his Rimsky-Korsakov, are swift but fluid. There are references in the accompanying booklets to his knack of finding *Le tempo juste*, and time and again a phrase of Christoph von Dohnányi's came to mind: "when the music is on its feet, it does the right thing". Music on its feet was, of course, the making of Monteux, but well before the Diaghilev connection, the teenage Monteux had played second violin in the Folies Bergères. Years later Gershwin complimented him on his marvellous rhythmic sense, and Monteux cited his Folies experience as the training for it. This rhythmic sense ... the spirit of the dance (call it what you will) permeated everything Monteux conducted, especially his Ravel. The Boston Debussy *La mer* and *Nocturnes* – 1954 and 1955 respectively, the latter in stereo – are among the finest on disc. Suffice it to say that Monteux understood that Debussy knew exactly what he wanted. This *La mer* is an all too rare case of the conductor working *with* the composer, not imagining he knows better. The discs are also available separately.

Pierre Monteux The Early Years. [a]**Concertgebouw Orchestra;** [b]**London Symphony Orchestra /**
Pierre Monteux. Philips The Early Years Ⓜ 442 544-2PM5 (five discs: 311 minutes: ADD: 12/94).
Recorded 1961-4.   ⒼⒼⒼ
Beethoven Symphony No. 3 in E flat major, Op. 55, "Eroica"[a] (from 835132AY, 2/63).
Schubert Symphony No. 8 in B minor, D759, "Unfinished"[a] (GL5788, 1/65). **Tchaikovsky**
Swan Lake – excerpts[b] (835142AY, 3/63). **Brahms** Symphony No. 2 in D major, Op. 73[b].
Academic Festival Overture, Op. 80[b] (both from SAL3435, 11/63). Tragic Overture, Op. 81[b]
(previously unpublished. Recorded 1962). **Ravel** Boléro[b]. La valse[b]. Ma mère l'oye[b] (all from
SAL3500, 5/65). **Debussy** Images[b]. Le martyre de St Sébastien – symphonic fragments[b]
(SAL3459, 12/64).

"The Early Years – Pierre Monteux" it says on the box. The early years are, of course, those of Philips, not Monteux. This mid-price set offers his very last stereo recordings, made between 1962 and 1964, when Monteux was in his late eighties – vintage years to be sure, for the conductor, the LSO and Philips engineering – on five discs for the price of four. The new CDs have been "digitalized by Bitstream", a process which has fractionally opened out and brightened up the treble. Compared with today's average offerings from London or Amsterdam, hall ambience is minimal (especially in the Brahms symphony), but the balances are flawless, and the benefits of Monteux's separated first and second violin sections are everywhere to be heard. Of Monteux's two *Eroica* recordings, this 1962 Amsterdam account is the one to have: "textures have a Stravinskyan bite and clarity ... the Concertgebouw are producing that fierce, bright, glistening tone which has always been a sure sign that their collective psyche is aflame", wrote *Gramophone*'s Richard Osborne in 1988. The first movement of Monteux's Amsterdam *Unfinished* (with repeat) is unusually fast, relaxing beautifully for the second subject (good, focused tone and phrasing here, not the common *pianissimo* thread).The LSO *Swan Lake* selection (with some numbers pruned, and a couple of concert endings) is well chosen for contrast, and the opening number sets the scene with some rapid string playing of effortless precision and point. Rarely, if ever, do you hear the swan theme (solo oboe) sung with such dignity and melancholy, the syncopations in the Act 1 *Pas de Deux* Waltz handled with such elegance, or the ballet's closing minutes played with such tragic grandeur. On occasions Tchaikovsky sounds like Delibes, but Tchaikovsky would undoubtedly have approved of that. In the last of Monteux's four recordings of the Brahms Second Symphony, subtleties of nuance and timing, and modifications of pacing, reflect a lifetime's love and experience of the work. Typically, it is light-toned and gentle in cast, almost symphonic chamber music. You would expect a Monteux *Academic Festival Overture* to raise the spirits, and you won't be disappointed. The *Tragic Overture* is articulated more powerfully than the symphony, always on its feet, and with heaven-sent, *pianissimo* muted violins preparing the way for the noble brass transformation of the opening theme. Monteux's LSO strings come into their own for the Debussy and Ravel items. There is a very good case for suggesting that, in the range of expression he was capable of encouraging from his string desks, Monteux (himself originally an orchestral violinist, and then a violist in a string quartet) had no peers.You will hear a great range of vibrato, very prominent, for example, in the gorgeous husky tone for the viola and violin gipsy song solos in the first two movements of "Ibéria" (it is worth mentioning that Monteux's ancestors were Spanish), or the more exalted moments from *Le martyre*. And if you are unable to succumb totally to the maximum vibrato and extraordinary textures as Monteux leads us through the "Fairy Garden" at the end of *Ma mère l'oye*, then you are a lost cause.

New review
New Zealand Composers New Zealand Symphony Orchestra / Kenneth Young. Continuum
Ⓜ CCD1073 (two discs: 124 minutes: DDD: 5/96). Recorded 1995.
Lilburn Aotearoa Overture. **A. Watson** Prelude and Allegro for Strings. **A. Ritchie** The
Hanging Bulb. **C. Blake** Till human voices wake us (with Christopher Doig, ten). **Whitehead**
Resurgences. **Jenny McLeod** Little Symphony. **Farquhar** Ring around the Moon – Short
Suite. **Pruden** Harbour Nocturne. **Carr** The Snow Maiden.
Douglas Lilburn kicks off proceedings with his appealing *Aotearoa Overture* from 1940, whose bracing, open-air manner suggests a definite kinship with Sibelius and Tubin. The youngest figure represented here is Anthony Ritchie (b.1960), whose impressive 1989 orchestral essay, *The Hanging Bulb*, proves to be a beautifully crafted, resourceful and readily approachable creation. Its four interlinked sections contain much attractive invention; certainly, the wistfully melancholic opening

pages cast quite a spell. Gillian Whitehead (b.1941) studied with Sir Peter Maxwell Davies and her teemingly active *Resurgences* (1990) evinces a refined, colourful orchestral palette as well as a strong feeling for landscape – the overall effect is not dissimilar to certain offerings by her Australian colleague, Peter Sculthorpe. The second disc starts brightly with the lean and lucid *Little Symphony* by Jenny McLeod (b.1941), an antipodean cousin to Stravinsky's *Symphony in C*. *Harbour Nocturne* by Larry Pruden (1925-82) is an evocative essay dating from 1956, its cool beauty and fastidious manner reminiscent of Copland and Britten. Finally comes Edwin Carr (b.1926) and his attractive ballet score from 1963, *The Snow Maiden*. Based on the same Ostrovsky play which inspired both Rimsky-Korsakov and Tchaikovsky, it is an unashamedly tuneful, witty confection which will appeal strongly to anyone with a sweet tooth. This enterprising set offers over two hours of music in first-rate performances and recordings; moreover, it retails for the price of just one CD.

Orchestral works New Philharmonia Orchestra / Leopold Stokowski. BBC Radio Classics
Ⓟ BBCRD9107 (74 minutes: ADD: 3/95). Recorded live in 1974.　　　　　　　Ⓡ
Brahms Symphony No. 4 in E minor, Op. 98. **Klemperer** Das Ziel – Merry Waltz. **Ravel** Rapsodie espagnole. **Vaughan Williams** Fantasia on a Theme by Thomas Tallis.
Stokowski in his ninety-third year – fiery, impulsive, provocative and above all, youthful. Listen to the coda of Brahms's first movement and you could as well be hearing an outrageously gifted teenage firebrand. True, the movement's earlier episodes betray a few loose joints (the tempo is, after all, alarmingly swift). The *Andante moderato* is warm and sinuous, the *Scherzo*, a balletic *tour de force* and the finale, a box of rhetorical tricks calculated to raise the roof – which it certainly did. The rest of the programme is scarcely less compelling. Vaughan Williams's *Tallis* Fantasia is warmly wrapped, its string choirs pure bowed velvet, even though Stokowski's moulding of dynamics is less theatrical than it probably would have been 20 years earlier. In the Ravel the "Prélude à la nuit" is positively hypnotic and the "Féria" graced by some unmistakably Stokowskian swoops. The only thing missing is that clinching element of control, the sort that distinguished Stokowski's greatest pre-war recordings with the Philadelphia Orchestra. Still, with lively, ambient sound and a generous programme, this CD must serve as irrefutable evidence that for Stokowski – as indeed for Toscanini, Casals, Végh and Wand – the ravages of age do not preclude fire and passion. A unique bargain.

Orchestral works Cristina Ortiz (pf); Royal Philharmonic Orchestra / Moshe Atzmon. Decca
Ⓕ 414 348-2DH (58 minutes: DDD: 9/86). From 414 348-1DH (5/86). Recorded 1984.　　　Ⓡ
Rachmaninov Piano Concerto No. 2 in C minor, Op. 18. **Addinsell** Warsaw Concerto.
Litolff Concerto Symphonique No. 4 in D minor, Op. 102 – Scherzo. **Gottschalk** (orch. Hazell) Grande fantaisie triomphale sur l'hymne national brésilien, RO108.
The C minor Concerto of Rachmaninov symbolizes romanticism at its ripest. Its combination of poetry and sensuous warmth with languorously memorable melodic lines balanced by exhilarating pianistic brilliance happily avoids any suggestion of sentimentality. The simple chordal introduction from the soloist ushers in one of the composer's most luscious tunes, yet the slow movement develops even greater ardour in its melodic contour, and the composer holds back a further haunting expressive idea to bring lyrical contrast to the scintillating finale. The couplings here are most apt. The genuinely inspired pastiche *Warsaw Concerto* by Richard Addinsell has a principal theme worthy to stand alongside those of Rachmaninov and its layout shows satisfying craftsmanship. Ortiz plays this main theme with great affection and she is equally beguiling in the delicious Litolff *Scherzo*. The effect here is of elegance rather than extrovert brilliance: this is reserved for the Gottschalk *Grande fantaisie triomphale*, which is played with a splendid panache that almost covers its inherent vulgarity and certainly emphasizes its ingenuous charm. Throughout the recording balance is realistic and the reverberation adds the most attractive bloom.

The Itzhak Perlman Collection Itzhak Perlman (vn) with various artists. EMI Perlman Edition
Ⓢ CZS4 83177-2 (20 discs: 22 hours 36 minutes: ADD/DDD: 6/95).　　　　　　　　　　Ⓡ
Violin Concertos – Bach, Bartók, Beethoven, Brahms, Bruch, Castelnuovo-Tedesco, Conus, Dvořák, Glazunov, Khachaturian, Korngold, Mendelssohn, Prokofiev, Shostakovich, Sibelius, Tchaikovsky, Vieuxtemps, Vivaldi and Wieniawski. Other concertante works – Bruch, Ravel, Saint-Saëns, Sinding and Tchaikovsky. *Chamber works* – Beethoven, Brahms, Mozart, Paganini, Spohr, Stravinsky and Tchaikovsky. *Short works* – Albéniz, Bach, Ben Haim, Chaminade, Chopin, Debussy, Dvořák, Elgar, Foster, Gluck, Grainger, Granados, Joplin, Kreisler, Lehár, Massenet, Moszkowski, Nováček, Paradies, Pollack, Ponce, Poulenc, Previn, Rachmaninov, Raff, Saint-Saëns, Sarasate, Schumann, Tchaikovsky, Toselli, Tosti, Vieuxtemps and Wieniawski.
This collection, offered at lower mid price, provides a formidable survey of Perlman's work, bringing home the consistent richness of his playing both tonally and expressively, his total assurance along with his peerless virtuosity and the strength of his artistic personality. What other violinist today could offer such a range of music in such performances? One great merit of these discs, at least the majority of them, is that they provide generous and well-planned couplings. So Perlman's peerless versions of the two Wieniawski concertos with Ozawa and the LPO, dating from 1973, here have five Wieniawski lollipops as supplement, not just the well-known *Polonaise de concert* and *Scherzo tarantelle*, but the little *Obertass Mazurka*, made all the wittier thanks to Perlman's delicious rubato. It is surprising that Perlman's studio recording of the Brahms concerto with Giulini and the Chicago

orchestra have been chosen in preference to his later Berlin version with Barenboim, recorded live and more consistently magnetic, but by contrast the Beethoven is here offered not in the studio version with Giulini and the Philharmonia but in the live Berlin account with Barenboim, which is even more compelling. One classic Perlman recording with Previn and the LSO which now at last belatedly arrives on CD is of the Bartók No. 2. As a performance, it has rarely been matched, helped by analogue recording that has fine presence. The transfer here has a much higher tape hiss than one would expect, which perhaps explains the long delay over its issue on CD. The Bach concerto disc offers in addition to three of Perlman's recordings with Barenboim and the ECO from the 1970s – the E major, the Double Concerto (with Zukerman) and the G minor arranged from the F minor Harpsichord Concerto – his much more recent account of the Violin and Oboe Concerto with Mehta and the Israel Philharmonic, where he is joined by the bright oboist, Ray Still. These are weighty Bach performances with unashamedly romantic, expansive slow movements. It is good that room has been found for some of Perlman's collaborations with André Previn, both on jazz pieces and on Scott Joplin rags. There are some discrepancies between the recordings of different vintage; some of the earliest convey the most vivid sense of presence. Perlman's violin is consistently caught in all its fullness and warmth, even if some of the recordings give it an extra edge. And if the balance of the violin is regularly on the close side, that is no more than such masterly playing deserves in such a celebratory set.

New review

Karl Richter Edition Various artists; **Karl Richter.** Teldec Ⓑ 0630-12155-2 (19 discs, aas: 17 hours and 40 minutes: ADD: 5/96).

Bach Fantasia in G major, BWV572[a]. Trio Sonatas, BWV525-30 – No. 3 in D minor; No. 6 in G major[a]. Pastorale in F major, BWV590[a]. Prelude and Fugue in D minor, BWV538, "Dorian". Partita diverse sopra Sei gegrüsset, Jesu gütig, BWV768. **Karl Richter** (org). Ⓑ 4509-97901-2 (two discs: 87 minutes: ADD: 5/96). Items marked [a] from Telefunken SAWD9915B (7/73), [b]recorded 1958, from Telefunken DX6.35054. Recorded 1958-71.

Bach Christmas Oratorio, BWV248. **Chloe Owen** (sop); **Hertha Töpper** (mez); **Gert Lutze** (ten); **Horst Günter** (bar); **Kieth Engen** (bass); **Munich Bach Choir and Orchestra / Karl Richter.** Ⓑ 4509-97902-2 (three discs: 169 minutes: ADD: 5/96). Recorded 1955, new to UK. Recorded 1958-71.

Bach Brandenburg Concertos, BWV1046-51. **chamber orchestra / Karl Richter.** Ⓑ 4509-97903-2 (two discs: 106 minutes: ADD: 5/96). Recorded 1958, new to UK. Recorded 1958-71.

Bach Goldberg Variations, BWV988. Keyboard Partitas, BWV825-30. **Karl Richter** (hpd). Ⓑ 4509-97904-2 (two discs: 135 minutes: ADD: 5/96). Recorded 1958 and 1960, new to UK. Recorded 1958-71.

Bach Harpsichord Concerto in D minor, BWV1052[a]. Concerto for Two Harpsichords in C major, BWV1061[b]. Concerto for Three Harpsichords in C major, BWV1064[c]. Concerto for Four Harpsichords in A minor, BWV1065[d]. [b]**Eduard Müller,** [cd]**Gerhard Aeschbacher,** [d]**Heinrich Gurtner** (hpds); **Ansbach Bach Week Soloists / Karl Richter** (hpd). Ⓑ 4509-99873-2 (73 minutes: ADD: 5/96). Items marked [ab] from Decca LXT5203 (10/56), [cd]recorded 1964, new to UK. [ab]Recorded 1955.

Bach Cantatas – No. 67, Halt im Gedächtnis Jesum Christ[a]; No. 108, Es ist euch gut, dass ich hingehe[a]; No. 127, Herr Jesu Christ, wahr' Mensch und Gott[b]. [b]**Antonia Fahberg** (sop); [a]**Lilian Benningsen** (contr); **Sir Peter Pears** (ten); **Kieth Engen** (bass); **Munich Bach Choir; Munich State Opera Orchestra / Karl Richter.** Ⓑ 4509-99874-2 (61 minutes: ADD: 5/96). Recorded 1959-60, from 9031-77614-2 (5/93).

Bach Cantata No. 4, Christ lag in Todesbanden[a]. Sonatas for Flute and Harpsichord, BWV1030-35 – No. 1 in B minor; No. 2 in A major[b]. [a]**Kieth Engen** (bass); [b]**Aurèle Nicolet** (fl); [a]**Munich Bach Choir;** [a]**Munich State Opera Orchestra / Karl Richter** ([b]hpd). Ⓑ 0630-11427-2 (66 minutes: ADD: 5/96). Recorded 1959 and 1963, new to UK.

C.P.E. Bach Symphony in D major, H663.

J.C. Bach Symphony in B flat major, Op. 18 No. 2.

Mozart Symphony No. 29 in A major, K201/K186a. **Munich Bach Orchestra / Karl Richter.** Ⓑ 4509-99872-2 (49 minutes: ADD: 5/96). From Telefunken SAWT9420 (6/67).

Handel Organ Concertos – Op. 4; Op. 7. **chamber orchestra / Karl Richter** (org). Ⓑ ① 4509 97900-2 (two discs: 157 minutes: ADD: 5/96). From Decca SXL2115 (6/59), SXL2187 (4/60) and SXL2201 (6/60).

Mozart Mass in D minor, K626, "Requiem". **Maria Stader** (sop); **Hertha Töpper** (mez); **John van Kesteren** (ten); **Karl Christian Kohn** (bass); **Munich Bach Choir and Orchestra / Karl Richter.** Ⓑ 4509-97926-2 (51 minutes: ADD: 5/96). From Telefunken SMA56 (6/62).

Mozart Flute Concertos – No. 1 in G major, K313/K285c[a]; No. 2 in C major, K314/K285d[b]. Flute and Harp Concerto in C major, K299/K297c[c]. Andante for Flute and Orchestra in C major, K315/K285e[d].

Gluck Orfeo ed Euridice – Ballet in D minor[d].

Hoffmeister Flute Concerto in D major[a]. **Aurèle Nicolet** (fl); [c]**Rose Stein** (hp); **Munich Bach Orchestra / Karl Richter.** Ⓑ 0630-10329-2 (two discs: 108 minutes: ADD: 5/96). Items marked [a] from Telefunken GMA80 (2/64), [bcd]GMA63 (9/62).

The aura of Karl Richter, experienced by so many who witnessed his performances, is not something easily comprehended these days. To some he was a saviour, bringing baroque music out of the mainstream towards a culture of specialism, to others the revered last frontier before *terra authentica* became the promised land – a transformation which Karl Schumann cynically describes as elevating performance practice to an article of faith. The importance of Teldec's significant Karl Richter Edition, which covers the early years of the conductor, harpsichordist and organist, is that the debates of the 1970s and 1980s were still in the embryonic stages: Richter is simply Richter and this is where the aura begins and ends. This is also consistent with the splendid cantata reissues from Archiv (see reviews under Bach), where again the earlier recordings in particular reveal an artist whose passionate, vital and profoundly committed performances are often treasures of the catalogue.

If Bach was understandably to dominate Richter's career, this set demonstrates that his interests spanned the whole of the eighteenth century. Whilst the qualities we most readily associate with Richter's concentrated, muscular and intense approach seem wedded to Lutheran spirituality and Bach, his way with Mozart is not as unforgiving as one might expect. Certainly, the A major Symphony is one of the most lugubrious and Teutonic post-war readings, humourless and lacking the sparkle he brings to C.P.E. Bach's D major Symphony, but the Requiem is a real discovery. It may seem that for Richter life was an unremittingly serious business – though this is not quite true, as one discovers in his robust and sensitive accompaniments to Aurèle Nicolet's animated and lovingly radiant playing in the flute concertos – but the Requiem is, at gut level at least, Richter country. As so often with Richter, the phrasing is short on ebb and flow but the conviction of intent, within an intractable articulation (especially in the granite-like "Quam olim Abrahae") results in a remarkably distinctive and powerful perspective of the work.

Pulsating and genuine fervour of that type is really only found again in the disc containing three cantatas dating from 1959/60, including several notable contributions, not least Sir Peter Pears's invigorating singing in No. 67 and Kieth Engen's deeply moving 'vox Christi' in the same work. Teldec have risked including two other Bach recordings which stand short alongside Richter's later readings: the *Brandenburg Concertos* of 1958 sound demonstrably like a trial run for the formation of a group which within two or three years had become a chamber orchestra *par excellence*, the Munich Bach Orchestra; Richter's solid and technically accomplished accounts of 1967 are in a different league. The same can be said of the *Christmas Oratorio*, which for 1958 (mistakenly listed as three years earlier) is a disappointment.

If posterity remembers Richter more as a director than a formidable virtuoso of the organ and harpsichord, then that is perhaps because we tend to be less tolerant of old-fashioned performance practices on instruments, particularly the harpsichord, where research and developments in reconstruction have opened our eyes to new possibilities. Consequently, we are left with some pretty uncompromising and Gothic performances here: Richter's overbearing gravity and some perplexing registral changes are about all one remembers of the *Goldberg Variations*. The six *Partitas* are rather unmalleable but more fleet-of-foot, with a balletic spring which reaches into the soul of the music. As a soloist-director in harpsichord and organ concertos, Richter's performances have a more endearing and enduring quality. A disc of harpsichord concertos, the earliest performances, recorded at the Ansbach Bach Festival in 1955, is fresh and buoyant, conveying something of that unique vitality which characterizes the best of his early choral recordings. The complete set of Handel Organ Concertos, Opp. 4 and 7 is in scale and conception intermittently absurd but deeply impressive at the same time and well recorded. Richter was unquestionably one of the most notable post-war organists; not surprisingly he sits far more comfortably on record as an organist than as a clavier player. There is a more joyous bravura at the console, and an awesome authority too. A mixed bag, yes, but a crucial one in gaining a more refined perspective on a potent and much-misunderstood figure. As you will have gathered from the titles at the head of this review, the many delights of this set are also available separately.

Russian Showpieces Chicago Symphony Orchestra / Fritz Reiner. RCA Victor Living Stereo
Ⓜ 09026 61958-2* (71 minutes: ADD: 8/94). Items marked ᵃ from SB2001 (10/58), ᵇVIC1068 (2/65). Recorded 1957-59.   ⊖⊖⊖
Mussorgsky (orch. Ravel) Pictures at an Exhibitionᵃ. A Night on the Bare Mountainᵃ.
Tchaikovsky Suite No. 1, Op. 43 – Marche miniatureᵇ. Marche slave, Op. 31ᵇ. **Borodin** Prince Igor – Polovtsian Marchᵇ. **Kabalevsky** Colas Breugnon – Overtureᵇ. **Glinka** Ruslan and Ludmilla – Overtureᵇ.

Reiner's *Pictures at an Exhibition* was one of the glories of the early stereo LP catalogue offering orchestral playing of the highest calibre. The richness of the brass sounds is apparent in the very opening "Promenade" and "Bydlo" really does sound like a heavy ox wagon. Reiner pictures the "Tuileries" lightly but nostalgically and the "Unhatched chicks" daintily, while the image of "Samuel Goldenburg" is unctiously conveyed by the full-bodied lower strings, which makes Schmuyle's bleating the more telling in consequence, "Market Place at Limoges" becomes a lightly articulated orchestral scherzo. The finale is predictably and grandly spacious. After Mussorgsky's sonorous climax dies away, Tchaikovsky's piquant little march sounds like a gnat after an elephant, and makes a charming diversion before the menacing brass growls of *Night on the Bare Mountain* (in Rimsky's version) and the robustly accented Borodin "Polovtsian March", which takes us back to the world of Slavonic orchestral spectacle. *Marche slave* is slow and sombre, but certainly makes a powerful climax.

Then the mood lightens again for the last two items, the *Colas Breugnon*, with its exuberant cross sycopations, matched by the racy *Ruslan and Ludmilla* Overture. One can only marvel at the consistency of the recording, so resplendent in its opulent concert-hall ambience.

Saxophone Concertos John Harle (sax); Academy of St Martin in the Fields / Sir Neville Marriner. EMI Ⓕ CDC7 54301-2 (71 minutes: DDD: 1/92).
     Debussy (ed. Harle) Rapsodie. **Glazunov** Saxophone Concerto in E flat major, Op. 109. **Heath** Out of the Cool. **Ibert** Concertino da camera. **R.R. Bennett:** Saxophone Concerto. **Villa-Lobos** Fantasia.

As the issue of a mixed marriage the saxophone has had problems in gaining general acceptance in 'respectable' (musical) society. Sigurd Rascher did wonders for it in the pre-war years, but overall its image has remained what it has been throughout this century, that of an instrument which rose to fame in houses of ill repute and smoky dens in which jazz developed – and from which came the players with the most fluent techniques. At the same time the saxophone's potential as a solo instrument was recognized by a number of notable composers, among them Glazunov and Ibert in the 1930s, Villa-Lobos in 1958 and, some decades later, by Bennett and Heath – the last a composer with a jazz pedigree. Debussy preceded all these but, writing for a lady of his acquaintance who had breathing problems, didn't really have his heart in it; his *Rapsodie* is here presented with worthier orchestration by John Harle. Harle is the virtuoso for whom the saxophone may have long been waiting; the selected works show his splendid musicianship and spectacular technical command to good advantage. If you have any prejudice against the saxophone that is less than incurable, this outstanding disc could easily change your mind – as well as introducing you to some unfamiliar and attactive music.

New review

Stokowski Transcriptions Philadelphia Orchestra / Wolfgang Sawallisch. EMI Ⓕ CDC5 55592-2 (66 minutes: DDD: 5/96). Recorded 1995.   Ⓖ
     Bach Cantatas: No. 208 – Schafe können sicher weiden; No. 140 – Wachet auf!; No. 80 – Ein' feste Burg. Toccata and Fugue in D minor, BWV565. **Boccherini** String Quintet in E major, G275 – Minuet. **Beethoven** Piano Sonata No. 14 in C sharp minor, Op. 27 No. 2, "Moonlight" – Adagio sostenuto. **Chopin** Prelude in E minor, Op. 28 No. 4. **Franck** Panis angelicus. **Tchaikovsky** String Quartet No. 1 in D major, Op. 11 – Andante cantabile. At the ball, Op. 38 No. 3 (with Marjana Lipovšek, mez). **Debussy** Suite bergamasque – Clair de lune. Préludes, Book 1 – No. 10, La cathédrale engloutie. **Rachmaninov** Prelude in C sharp minor, Op. 3 No. 2.

Quite apart from reissues of the Stokowski's own recordings, there are several other discs of these highly coloured arrangements, notably that of Matthias Bamert and the BBC Philharmonic (reviewed below). Though Stokowski's own recordings, even those he made in extreme old age, generally have a degree more flair and dramatic bite than any others, the contrasts are not always what you would expect. So it is surprising to find that the BBC Philharmonic strings are more ripely resonant than those of the Philadelphia Orchestra in Franck's *Panis angelicus*, though that is an exception, and possibly Sawallisch simply wanted to minimize the piece's bold vulgarity. One of the items common to these discs is the *Adagio* from Beethoven's *Moonlight* Sonata, and there Sawallisch brings out far more of the mystery of what becomes an evocative, atmospheric piece, making the Bamert disc seem clinical. This collection also gains in glamour from having Marjana Lipovšek as an appropriately Slavonic-sounding soloist in the orchestration of the Tchaikovsky song, *At the ball*. This EMI disc provides a generous programme together with richly rounded recording, well defined in the bass. Yet Bamert's even more generous selection of 15 encore pieces overlaps on only three items, and includes more in which Stokowski has the greatest fun tweaking the ear provocatively, such as Mozart's *Turkish Rondo*: the advice to anyone with a sweet tooth is to get both discs for maximum indulgence.

Stokowski Encores BBC Philharmonic Orchestra / Matthias Bamert. Chandos Ⓕ CHAN9349 (73 minutes: DDD: 6/95). All items orch. Stokowski. Recorded 1994.
     Handel Chandos Anthem No. 2, HWV247, "In the Lord will I put my trust" – Overture. **Gabrieli** Sacrae symphoniae – Sonata pian e forte alla quarta bassa, a 8. **J. Clarke** Prince of Denmark's March (Trumpet Voluntary). **Mattheson** Suite No. 5 – Air. **Mozart** Keyboard Sonata No. 11 in A major, K331/K300*i* – Rondo alla turca. **Beethoven** Piano Sonata No. 14 in C sharp minor, Op. 27 No. 2, "Moonlight" – Adagio sostenuto. **Schubert** Schwanengesang, D957 – Ständchen. **Franck** Panis angelicus. **Chopin** Piano Sonata No. 2 in B flat minor, Op. 35 – Marche funèbre. **Debussy** Préludes – La fille aux cheveux de lin. **Ippolitov-Ivanov** In the Manger. **Shostakovich** Counterplan – United Nations Overture. **Tchaikovsky** String Quartet No. 1 in D major, Op. 11 – Andante cantabile. **Albéniz** Iberia – El corpus en Sevilla. **Sousa** The Stars and Stripes Forever.

Matthias Bamert and the BBC Philharmonic follow up their defiantly successful disc of Stokowski's opulent Bach arrangements with this mixed bag of 15 items, six of them new to disc, again showing what a master of sound quality the cunning old maestro was. In today's climate it may seem outrageous to take a tiny harpsichord piece by a contemporary of Bach and Handel, Johann Mattheson, and inflate it using full orchestral strings. Yet as in the Bach arrangements one readily revels in opulence, and the Chandos engineers come up with a recording to match. Mozart's *Rondo alla turca* becomes a sparkling *moto perpetuo*, Paganini-like, with Stokowski wittily using the same 'Turkish' percussion which Mozart himself has for the *Entführung* Overture. The opening *Adagio* of Beethoven's *Moonlight* Sonata then acquires through lush orchestration an astonishing likeness to Rachmaninov's *Isle of the dead*: one suddenly appreciates the menace in the music in a new way. It is fascinating to compare Stokowski's arrangement of the Handel Overture in D minor (taken from the *Chandos Anthem* No. 2) with Elgar's transcription of the same piece, made only a year or so earlier. They are both opulent but in different ways, with Elgar moulding the orchestra into a brilliant and complex web of sound, where Stokowski more often sets the different timbres in antiphonal contrasts: more than Elgar he clarifies the entries in the fugue. Antiphonal contrasts recur in many of the pieces, as for example the 'Purcell' (Jeremiah Clarke) *Trumpet Voluntary* and the little chant-based Christmas piece, *In the Manger*, by Ippolitov-Ivanov.

Testimonies of War [i]Endrik Wottrich, [e]Michael Kraus (tens); [d]Sylvie Lechevalier, [e]Walter Moore (pfs); [g]BBC Symphony Chorus / Stephen Jackson; [f]Wallace Collection; [a]Berlin Radio Symphony Orchestra; [b]London Philharmonic Orchestra / Noam Sheriff; [h]Poznan Opera Chorus; [ch]Poznan Philharmonic Orchestra / Andrzej Borejko; [i]Berlin RSO / Berthold Goldschmidt. Largo
Ⓟ Largo5130 (two discs: 117 minutes: DDD: 7/95).
Blacher Alla marcia[a]. Dance Scenes[b]. Chiarina[a]. Partita, Op. 24[c]. Piano Sonatina, Op. 14 No. 2[d]. Drei Psalmen[e]. **Shortall** Fanfare for those who will not return[f]. **Weill** Workers' Choruses Zu Potsdam unter den Eichen[g]. Divertimento, Op. 5 – Chorale-Fantasy: Herr Gott dein Zorn tu von uns wenden[h]. **B. Goldschmidt** Zwei Psalmen[i]. **Milhaud** Chorale[d]. **Vaughan Williams** Valiant for truth[g].

This collection has three objectives, only one of them referred to in its title – "Testimonies of War". One of the most direct 'testimonies' here, one with a chilling, shocking force, is Boris Blacher's *Three Psalms*. Blacher remained in Germany during the Nazi period, and although his music was disliked by the authorities it received occasional performances. Then, in 1943, the Nazis discovered that he had a Jewish grandmother and banned his music outright. The *Psalms* seem to be his reaction: a bleakly austere cry for God's justice, a vehemently angry denunciation, an intense and heartfelt prayer for deliverance (and, by their choice of text, a defiant acceptance of his Jewish ancestry). They gain greatly in impact from being so closely coupled with a genial, francophile, neo-classical *Sonatina* that Blacher had written before the blow fell (but which had already been denounced as 'counter to German musical susceptibilities') and with the two psalm settings that Berthold Goldschmidt wrote immediately before his flight from Germany and which movingly, by purely musical means, express a fugitive's hope: "Our soul is escaped, as a bird from the fowler's snare". That is the second of this collection's functions, the making of startling juxtapositions. Kurt Weill's grimly penitential *Chorale-Fantasy* ("Lord God, turn away thy wrath; thy bloody scourge justly tormenteth and flayeth us at every turn") is in the solemnly denunciatory language of the chorale in *Mahagonny*; it is a reflection on post-1918 Germany, and could easily be read as an apocalyptic warning. To follow it with Vaughan Williams's radiant vision of Mr Valiant-for-truth's passing ("and all the trumpets sounded for him on the other side") is deeply moving. But not a facile epilogue: this collection was compiled in the knowledge that it would be issued around the time of the fiftieth anniversary of VE Day, and most listeners will hear Vaughan Williams's serene motet with the sounds of Harrington Shortall's haunting *Fanfare for those who will not return* and Blacher's remarkable *Partita* still ringing in their ears.

Shortall is an otherwise completely unknown composer who – however rash it may be to make such a statement on the basis of a piece lasting less than three minutes – had an obvious and remarkable talent. By the use of intervals natural to brass instruments, a 'mode' achingly omitting the tonic, a simple metrical palindrome and the natural resonance of other instruments in the hall (on the presumption that the fanfare would precede an orchestral concert) it produces an effect out of all proportion to its duration. But although Shortall's rediscovery is a valuable side-effect of the programme-planning, the third and primary objective of this compilation is to promote a re-evaluation of Blacher. The *Partita* is a major work, haunted by memories of the war; it was written amid the ashes of Berlin and its copyright sold for a few packets of cigarettes. The echoes of war in the edgy first movement (there are six percussionists in uneasy concert with the string orchestra) give way to growing confidence and intense eloquence in the central *Andante*, but a composer who has been through so much cannot write a jubilant or a radiant finale. Instead its resolve gives way to a strange epilogue: a walking bass, slowly modulating string chords, an unchanging ostinato figure. A ghost that cannot and must not be exorcized? It is that sort of strangeness and unease that fills the music of Blacher's two ballet scores with shadow. Both contain a great many jovial, topical references to the popular dance music of their time (tangos, rumbas and ragtimes), but they are often undercut by disquiet, or when brashly scored their heaviness takes on something of the threat of Ravel's *La valse*. There is nostalgia, too, but a complex nostalgia: a suggestion of Stravinskian neo-classicism at the beginning of the big *pas de deux* in *Chiarina* (nothing to do with Clara Schumann: it's the name of an imaginary spa town) gives way to a Prokofiev-like string *cantabile*, but yes, like Prokofiev it is also deeply rooted in Tchaikovsky, and all of a sudden we realize that Mahler is also present; Weill has been there all along. The collection fulfils all its objectives handsomely; whichever appeals to you, the others will provoke you into absorbed re-hearings. The performances (some reedy string playing from the Poznan Philharmonic apart) and recordings are excellent. An ideal way of presenting unfamiliar repertory: each constituent both gains and receives illumination from its context.

The Toscanini Collection New York Philharmonic Orchestra / Arturo Toscanini. RCA Victor Gold Seal mono Ⓜ GD60318* (64 minutes: ADD: 11/92). Recorded 1929-36.
 Gluck Orfeo ed Euridice – Ballet in D minor (from HMV D1784, 7/30). **Rossini** Il barbiere di Siviglia – Overture (D1835, 10/30). L'italiana in Algeri – Overture (HMV DB2943, 10/36). Semiramide – Overture (DB3079/80, 3/37). **Verdi** La traviata – Preludes, Acts 1 and 3 (D1672, 6/30). **Wagner** Götterdämmerung – Dawn and Siegfried's Rhine Journey (DB2860/61, 7/36). Lohengrin – Preludes, Acts 1 (DB2904, 9/36) and 3 (DB2861).

RCA's Toscanini Collection contains many very desirable reissues, but this disc has a particular quality in that it shows very clearly several outstanding but differing aspects of the great conductor's genius. The recordings, made in 1929 and 1936, have been made to yield a quality of sound which most listeners will find perfectly acceptable, and they date from a period when, as chief conductor of the New York Philharmonic Orchestra, Toscanini was in his artistic prime. Those who still imagine him always to be a hard, relentless interpreter should hear the exquisitely poised Gluck ballet music, or the tender, extraordinarily eloquent *Traviata* preludes. The Rossini Overtures are certainly propelled with a good deal of energy, but there's plenty of air in the rhythms, and some elegant phrasing amid the virtuoso playing of the magnificent New York Philharmonic. Wagner was particularly near to Toscanini's heart: the *Lohengrin* Act 1 Prelude has a wonderfully luminous quality, and "Siegfried's Rhine Journey" is played with tremendous strength and majesty.

Trumpet Concertos Håkan Hardenberger (tpt); **Academy of St Martin in the Fields / Sir Neville Marriner.** Philips Ⓕ 420 203-2PH (59 minutes: DDD: 12/87). Recorded 1986.
 Hummel Trumpet Concerto in E flat major. **Hertel** Trumpet Concerto in D major.
 J. Stamitz (realized Boustead) Trumpet Concerto in D major. **Haydn** Trumpet Concerto in E flat major, HobVIIe/1.

This recording made such a remarkable impression when it first appeared in 1987 that it created overnight a new star in the firmament of trumpeters. The two finest concertos for the trumpet are undoubtedly those of Haydn and Hummel and Hardenberger plays them here with a combination of sparkling bravura and stylish elegance that are altogether irresistible. Marriner and his Academy accompany with characteristic finesse and warmth, with the lilting dotted rhythms of the first movement of the Hummel, seductively jaunty. The lovely *Andante* of the Haydn is no less beguiling and both finales display a high spirited exuberance and an easy bravura which make the listener smile with pleasure. He is no less distinctive in the lesser concerto of Johann Hertel and the other D major work attributed to Johann Stamitz but probably written by someone with the unlikely name of J.B. Holzbogen. This takes the soloist up into the stratosphere of his range and provides him also with some awkward leaps. The Hertel work also taxes the soloist's technique to the extremities but Hardenberger essays all these difficulties with an enviably easy aplomb and remains fluently entertaining throughout. The recording gives him the most vivid realism and presence but it is a pity that the orchestral backcloth is so reverberant; otherwise the sound is very natural.

Trumpet Concertos Sergei Nakariakov (tpt); [a]Alexander Markovich (pf); **Lausanne Chamber Orchestra / Jésus López-Cobos.** Teldec Ⓕ 4509-90846-2 (56 minutes: DDD: 10/93). Recorded 1993.
 Jolivet Concertino for Trumpet, Piano and Strings[a]. **Hummel** Trumpet Concerto in E flat major. **Tomasi** Trumpet Concerto. **Haydn** Trumpet Concerto in E flat major, HobVIIe/1.

The young Russian, Sergei Nakariakov is in his element in the opening Jolivet Double Concerto, standing well out in front of his partner, Alexander Markovich. The balance is less than ideal, with the piano set rather backwardly and the orchestra in a dryish acoustic. The piano emerges more strongly in the very florid finale, the bubbling animation of the playing reaching a frenzy of activity towards the end. The Tomasi (1901-71) is an even better piece and could hardly be better played. In the Haydn and Hummel, the Nakariakov/López-Cobos performances do not quite match the famous version (reviewed above) by Håkan Hardenberger, who has the inestimable advantage of wonderfully smiling accompaniments from Marriner and the ASMF. However, the lovely *Andante* of the Haydn is so gracefully phrased by Nakariakov, that the ear is ravished and the finale sparkles delectably, as does, for that matter, the finale of the Hummel. As a whole this new CD is a distinctive compilation, and confirms Nakariakov's position as one of the world's leading trumpeters. The Teldec recording is truthful.

Twentieth Century Plus [f]Andrew Marriner (cl); [ace]BBC Sympony Orchestra / [a]Peter Eötvös, [c]Matthias Bamert, [e]Lothar Zagrosek; [b]BBC Philharmonic Orchestra / Sir Peter Maxwell Davies; [f]London Symphony Orchestra / Michael Tilson Thomas; [d]English Chamber Orchestra / Steuart Bedford. Collins Classics Ⓜ 2001/5-2 (five discs, oas: 37, 25, 30, 16 and 20 minutes: DDD: 3/92). Items marked [a] and [b] recorded live in 1990. ⒼⒼ
 2001-2: **Birtwistle** Earth Dances[a]. *2002-2:* **Maxwell Davies** Caroline Mathilde – Concert Suite from Act 1[b]. *2003-2:* **Saxton** In the beginning[c]. Music to celebrate the resurrection of Christ[d]. *2004-2:* **Mason** Lighthouses of England and Wales[e]. *2005-2:* **Tavener** The Repentant Thief[f].

No, not a five-CD set, but five separately available CD singles, each featuring the music of a contemporary British composer. At first sight the overall title "Twentieth Century Plus" may seem a contradiction in terms (the longest CD has a duration of only 37 minutes) but when one considers that the price of each CD is considerably less than that of a full-price issue and that both performances and recordings are of exceptionally high quality then these are bargains indeed. The most important (and long awaited) issue here is perhaps Birtwistle's large and impressive orchestral work – *Earth Dances*. Though massively complex in its construction and organization of material, *Earth Dances* can be a richly rewarding experience for the listener. Its title relates both to the 'geological' strata-like layers of the music, and often violent surface energy that almost makes the earth dance. Tavener's *The Repentant Thief* for clarinet and orchestra is built around a rondo-like structure made up of 10 segments – five "Refrains", three "Dances" and two "Laments", and its title refers to the thief who was crucified with Jesus on Golgotha. It was composed shortly after Tavener had finished work on two large-scale works (*Resurrection* and the opera *Mary of Egypt*) and is described by the composer as "a shorter, simple and rather primitive piece". Its simplicity, clear-cut formal scheme and tunefulness make it an immediately accessible and absorbing experience, and this is all the more enhanced by a magical performance of the solo clarinet part by Andrew Marriner. Like the *Eight Songs for a Mad King* before it, the Concert Suite from Act 1 of the ballet *Caroline Mathilde* by Maxwell Davies explores the subject of madness – Caroline Mathilde was the wife of the unbalanced King Christian VII of Denmark. The ballet traces the King's gradual mental deterioration, and his wife's subsequent love affair with the King's physician (Dr Struensee) through a series of short tableaux that mix Maxwell Davies's musical parody style with his more acerbic and intricate methods of composing. The remaining discs feature music by the younger composers Benedict Mason and Robert Saxton. The highly original, if somewhat unusual *Lighthouses of England and Wales* reveals Mason to be a composer of a striking individuality, not to mention an extremely gifted orchestrator, and Saxton's richly colourful pieces – *In the beginning* and *Music to celebrate the resurrection of Christ* – continue the composer's interest in the religious theme of darkness into light.

New review
United Nations Fiftieth Anniversary Concert
Bartók Concerto for Orchestra, Sz116.
Beethoven Fidelio – Final Scene[a].
Rossini Guillaume Tell – Overture. [a]**Evelyn Herlitzius** (sop) Leonore; [a]**Ruth Ziesak** (sop) Marzelline; [a]**Stig Andersen** (ten) Florestan; [a]**Herbert Lippert** (ten) Jaquino; [a]**Albert Dohmen** (bar) Don Pizarro; [a]**Hans Tschammer** (bass-bar) Rocco; [a]**Andreas Kohn** (bass) Don Fernando; [a]**London Voices; World Orchestra for Peace / Sir Georg Solti.** Decca ℗ 448 901-2DH (62 minutes: DDD: 3/96). Text and translation included. Recorded live in 1995.

Anniversary concerts come and go, but to grace the occasion with a specially formed orchestra (and a pretty good one at that) – now that really *is* big news. "Today in one corner of Europe there is a desperate war", wrote Sir Georg Solti towards the end of 1995; "we watch it on television and do nothing. This concert is the one thing I can do." The World Orchestra for Peace employs the talents of top-ranking orchestral players from America, Europe, Russia and Israel, most of them – including the 15 section leaders – having been chosen by Solti himself. Musically, things get off to a spectacular start with a most compelling *William Tell* Overture – at once tender (Stephen Geber's lead cello is eloquent beyond words), rousing and positively Toscanini-like in the quick-fire excitement of its closing "Gallop". Bartók's *Concerto for Orchestra* is hardly less remarkable, not so much for its showmanship (the finale, although typically energetic, occasionally blurs around the edges) but more for its poetry. Solti's unaffected lyricism touches our hearts and impulsiveness only occasionally turns to impatience. *Fidelio* is of course *the* musical symbol for what Solti terms "the qualities of brotherhood, liberty and humanity" and this vigorous account of the finale finds all concerned entering the fray – with a particularly distinctive contribution from the Don Fernando of Andreas Kohn. "Never can we praise too much ..." sing the assembled: apposite words that might equally apply – both in musical and humanistic terms – to this admirable venture. Decca's sound is lively and full-bodied.

Works for Oboe and Orchestra John de Lancie (ob); [a]London Symphony Orchestra / André
Previn; [b]chamber orchestra / Max Wilcox. RCA Victor Gold Seal Ⓜ GD87989 (72 minutes: ADD/DDD: 12/91). Items marked [a] from SB6721, 11/67, [b]recorded 1987 and new to UK. Ⓖ
Françaix L'horloge de flore[a]. **Ibert** Symphonie concertante[a]. **Satie** (orch. Debussy) Gymnopédie No. 1[a]. **R. Strauss** Oboe Concerto[b].

This delightful collection focuses on the career and talent of the American oboist John de Lancie. De Lancie was the American soldier who in 1945 asked Strauss to write him a few bars of music for the oboe – the result, no less, was the delightfully sunny Oboe Concerto. De Lancie's return to the United States prevented him from attending the première, but a few years later Strauss granted him permission to give the work its American première. Bureaucracy and protocol intervened however, and in the event the solo part was entrusted to Mitchell Miller. This 1987 recording (and a very fine one it is too) therefore closes the circle that began over 45 years ago in the Bavarian Alps. It was de Lancie too, who commissioned Françaix's gorgeous suite for oboe and orchestra, *L'horloge de flore*

("The flower clock"). Each of its seven movements represent a flower (and the time of day that the bloom opens), in the Flower Clock developed by the Swedish botanist Carl von Linne. Quite why this charming and melodious work should not be more well known and indeed performed is a complete mystery – it would certainly be a winner with any audience. Inexplicable, too, is the apparent neglect in the catalogue at present of Ibert's *Symphonie concertante* for oboe and strings. This substantial work is a fine example of Ibert's natural gift for seamless melodic invention and exquisite string writing; if you know and love the Flute Concerto then this work should be next on your list of acquisitions. The Françaix and Ibert items were recorded in 1966 but are remarkably fresh and clear, with Previn and the LSO providing most sympathetic accompaniments.

Works for Violin and Orchestra Joshua Bell (vn); **Royal Philharmonic Orchestra / Andrew Litton.** Decca Ⓕ 433 519-2DH (60 minutes: DDD: 1/92). Recorded 1991.
     Saint-Saëns Introduction and Rondo capriccioso, Op. 28. **Massenet** Thaïs – Méditation. **Sarasate** Zigeunerweisen, Op. 20. **Chausson** Poème, Op. 25. **Ysaÿe** Caprice d'après l'étude en forme de valse de Saint-Saëns. **Ravel** Tzigane.
The Spaniard, Pablo de Sarasate, and the great Belgian virtuoso, Eugene Ysaÿe, both travelled to study in Paris during the second half of the last century, and although both were celebrated as distinguished exponents of violin technique, their collective influence upon the composers active in France at much the same time proved to be far more significant, as this brilliant selection of virtuoso showpieces will readily confirm. The young American violinist, Joshua Bell, himself a grand-pupil of Ysaÿe via his teacher, Joseph Gingold, is heard to superb advantage here in commanding performances of music which will captivate as much as it will astonish. Bell captures the heady bravura of Saint-Saëns *Introduction and Rondo capriccioso* with breathtaking ease, and his spiccato playing in the coda is little short of phenomenal. Sarasate's perennial favourite *Zigeunerweisen* will also astound, with Bell's mastery of the whole panoply of technical effects, including multiple-stopping and left hand pizzicato, contributing to an authentic gipsy-style performance. No recording of this kind would be complete without the celebrated "Méditation" from Massenet's *Thaïs*, made especially compelling here, in Bell's affectionately rich-toned account. The same tonal refinement and sensitivity characterize his elegiac reading of the *Poème* by Chausson, ably supported by the Royal Philharmonic Orchestra under Andrew Litton. Ysaÿe's *Caprice d'après l'etude* is another, although rather less familiar *tour de force*, affording every possibility for virtuosic display, although it does not challenge Ravel's devilish *Tzigane* in terms of pure technical difficulty. This truly hair-raising rendition of the *Tzigane* would bring any concert audience to its feet, and Bell is wholly at ease with its Bartókian gipsy style. This thrilling playing crowns a hugely enjoyable collection from this dazzling young virtuoso. The clear and incisive Decca sound ensures that the forces are balanced effectively, and the natural ambience of Watford Town Hall lends a realistic dramatic weight to full orchestral climaxes, without undue spotlighting of the soloist. An admirable and meticulous release, then, whose appeal will gain Joshua Bell many new admirers.

Chamber

A Gift of Nature Seventeenth-Century English Chamber Music. **Trio Sonnerie** (Monica Huggett, vn; Sarah Cunningham, va da gamba; Gary Cooper, virg/org); **Stephen Stubbs** ([a]theorbo/[b]gtr); **Andrew Lawrence-King** ([c]hp/[d]org). Teldec Das Alte Werk Ⓕ 4509-90841-2 (70 minutes: DDD: 5/94). 🎜 Recorded 1992.
     Baltzar A Prelude for the Violin by Senior Balshar, a Germaine. Divisions on "John Come Kiss me Now"[ac]. **Schop** Lachrime pavaen[b]. **N. Matteis** Ayres for the Violin, Book 4[bc] – Ground after the Scotch Humour; Passagio a solo; Allegro Prestissimo; Ground; Aria Amorosa; Ground in D, la sol re. **Brade** Coral. **W. Lawes** Fantasia-Suite No. 8 in D major. **C. Simpson** Prelude. Divisions on a Ground. **Jenkins** Fantasia in D minor. **Byrd** John Come Kiss me Now, BK81. **Farinel** Faronell's Ground[b]. **Anonymous** A Division for a trible viol to play with a virginall[ad]. Paul's Steeple[ac].
Henry Purcell and his Time Scaramouche (Andrew Manze, Caroline Balding, vns; Jaap ter Linden, bass viol; Ulrike Wild, hpd/org); [a]**Foskien Kooistra** (vn); [b]**Konrad Junghänel** (theorbo). Channel Classics Ⓕ CCS4792 (60 minutes: DDD: 5/94). 🎜 Recorded 1992.
     Locke The Broken Consort – Suites Nos. 3[b] and 4. **W. Lawes** Fantasia-Suite No. 7 in D minor. **Jenkins** Fantasia in three parts. **C. Simpson** Prelude. Divisions on a Ground[b]. **Baltzar** Divisions on "John Come Kiss me Now"[b]. **Purcell** Pavans – B flat major, Z750; G minor, Z752[a]. Fantasia upon a Ground, Z731[ab].
The contents of these two discs of English seventeenth-century chamber music may look alike, but no one finding themselves in possession of both should consider their money wasted. It's not just that, a little surprisingly, no piece appears twice; rather, it's that the respective approaches to programming and interpretation are happily complementary, so you can take your pick as your mood carries you. In the Teldec release the emphasis is on fleeting 'divisions' or variation sets by relatively minor figures, mostly on catchy popular tunes and mostly for violin. They are despatched with effortless ease by

Monica Huggett and happily enhanced by the gentle and spacious acoustic of The Maltings, Snape. There's a solo spot for each of Trio Sonnerie's other members, however, and a constantly changing array of guest continuo instruments (including, unusually for this repertoire, a harp).

For Channel Classics, Scaramouche offer a more homogeneous selection of music and instrumental combinations. (The disc advertises itself, by the way, as offering the music of "Henry Purcell and His Time", a claim whose level of accuracy – Lawes, for one, died over a decade before Purcell was born – is eloquently symbolized by a portrait of an unmistakably Elizabethan lady on the front of the box!) Here the innocent charm of the Trio Sonnerie selection is largely replaced by the weightier, more sober pronouncements of Lawes, Locke and Purcell, but also by a bold interpretative vigour which makes it just as lively a listen in its own way. Jaap ter Linden's rendition of his Simpson piece is a little more poetic than Sarah Cunningham's is of hers, while Andrew Manze's version of *John Come Kiss me Now* has a Turkey-in-the-Straw ending that will make you chuckle.

American Works for Wind Quintet Reykjavik Wind Quintet (Bernhardur Wilkinson, fl; Dadi Kolbeinsson, ob; Einar Jóhannesson, cl; Joseph Ognibene, hn; Hafsteinn Gudmundsson, bn). Chandos Ⓕ CHAN9174 (66 minutes: DDD: 11/93). Recorded 1991-2.　　Ⓖ
 Barber Summer Music, Op. 31. **Beach** Pastorale. **Fine** Partita. **Harbison** Wind Quintet.
 Villa-Lobos Quinteto em forma de chôros. **Schuller** Suite.

American music, Icelandic instrumentalists, British venue. Barber's *Summer Music* is delightfully relaxed and playful here, helped by the familiar glow of The Maltings' acoustic. Schuller's little Suite, his first published work, is a teenage *jeu d'esprit* which already shows him experimenting with aspects of jazz in the central Blues movement. Harbison's Wind Quintet is certainly serious in intent, its musical language not always as approachable as we expect from this composer though the outer movements are immediately striking. While eminently lean, lucid and fluent, Beach's brief *Pastorale* risks sounding old hat after this – its idiom would have been considered antiquated in 1942 – and the programme ends on a slightly disconnected note with one of Villa-Lobos's less shapely utterances. Even so, this is a thoroughly recommendable package.

New review

First and Foremost Apollo Saxophone Quartet (Tim Redpath, Rob Buckland, Andrew Scott, Jonathan Rebbeck, saxs); **John Harle** ([a]alto sax/[b]keybds); [c]**Roy Powell** (keybds); [d]**Will Gregory** (bar and bass saxes); [e]**Mike Hamnett** (perc), Argo Ⓕ 443 903-2ZH (52 minutes: DDD: 8/95).
 Corea (arr. Apollo Saxophone Quartet) Children's Songs Nos. 2-4, 6, 7, 11, 16 and 18[be].
 Nyman Four Songs for Tony. **D. Bedford** Fridiof Kennings[e]. **W. Gregory** Hoe down[ade].
 R. Powell Bow out[c].

If you chance to be a saxophobe but have a friend who isn't, buy him or her a copy of this disc as a present, though after hearing it you may possibly regret parting with it. All the music was written or arranged (by the composer) for saxophone quartet, and it spans a variety of idioms from that of classical music to those of jazz, the hoe down, film music and the Icelandic saga. A saxophone quartet is in effect a 'whole consort', to be listened to (unless you are certifiably allergic to its sound) like any other – a recorder consort, a brass ensemble, or a string quartet. In their first recording, the Apollo Quartet prove to be musically sensitive, tight in ensemble and painless in intonation. Dear old Adolphe, who even proposed the erection of a giant 'muzak machine' overlooking Paris, could never have visualized anything like this. Powell's comment on *Bow out* perhaps epitomizes the best approach to the programme as a whole: "neither 'jazz' nor 'classical' ... [it] occupies its own space". The recording is of high quality in all respects.

Balanescu Quartet Balanescu Quartet (Alexander Balanescu, Clare Connors, vns; Bill Hawkes, va; Caroline Dale, vc). Argo Ⓕ 436 565-2ZH (52 minutes: DDD: 3/93). Recorded 1992.　　Ⓖ
 Byrne High Life. **Moran** Music from the Towers of the Moon. **Lurie** Stranger than Paradise.
 Torke Chalk.

Heterodox these pieces might be, but together they make a recital that's surprisingly and delightfully integrated. All four of the American composers represented here write in easily approachable styles. Each work is excellently served by highly dedicated, expert performances from the Balanescu Quartet, and by a faithful, well-defined recording. David Byrne's extraordinary hybrid of a piece, *High Life*, is the shortest piece on the disc, and consists of syncopated, repeated patterns over which apparently random, free-floating ideas come into being and then dissolve away. Robert Moran's contribution uses material from his opera *From the Towers of the Moon* and is in four short sections. His style is readily enjoyable, with fresh and energetic ideas, and attractive melodic invention. John Lurie's *Stranger than Paradise* is based on music written for a film of the same name: six descriptive episodes form a pleasantly evocative work which is influenced by blues and minimalist styles. *Chalk* is Michael Torke's word for the resinous residue formed by the action of a bow drawn strongly across a stringed instrument. The basic pulse of his piece is constant, in the style of the minimalists, and indeed there is plenty of vigorous, even hectic writing for the four instruments. Torke's insert-notes indicate that he much admires the Balanescu players, and they certainly play their hearts out for him.

Beyond the Iron Curtain Leslie Newman (fl); Amanda Hurton (pf). Cala Ⓕ CACD88026
(76 minutes: DDD: 6/96). Recorded 1994.
    Taktakishvili Flute Sonata. **Feld** Flute Sonata. **Gubaidulina** Allegro rustico. Sounds of the
Forest. **Amirov** Six Pieces. **Martinů** Flute Sonata No. 1.

The familiar work here is the Martinů Sonata, an unobtrusive masterpiece which contains the
quintessence of his gentle, sympathetic personality. Admittedly it is hardly 'Beyond the Iron Curtain',
for it was composed in America in 1945, and the descent of the Iron Curtain a few years later was the
precise reason why Martinů was never again to return to his homeland. But never mind. It is a lovely,
warm performance, beautifully recorded. The same could be said of the recital as a whole. Well-
written flute music has a way of sounding French, no matter where it was written. So it should be no
surprise to find the Georgian Taktakishvili taking his cue from Fauré, or his Czech contemporary
Feld embracing a garrulous neo-classicism that could easily pass for Milhaud, or the Azerbaijani
Amirov, another near-contemporary, hitting on an attractive blend of Ravel and Khachaturian. But
you may be more than a bit surprised to find Gubaidulina sounding like Dutilleux in her charming,
tarantella-like *Allegro rustico*. Her *Sounds of the Forest* is closer to her familiar world of mystic
rustlings, but this too is far more instantly appealing than the music for which she is best known. A
delightful programme, warmly recorded.

Black Angels Kronos Quartet (David Harrington, John Sherba, vns; Hank Dutt, va; Joan
Jeanrenaud, vc). Elektra Nonesuch Ⓕ 7559-79242-2 (62 minutes: DDD: 4/91).   ⒼⒼ
    Crumb Black Angels. **Tallis** (arr. Kronos Qt) Spem in alium. **Marta** Doom. A sigh. **Ives**
(arr. Kronos Qt/Geist) They are there! **Shostakovich** String Quartet No. 8 in C minor,
Op. 110.

This is very much the sort of imaginative programming we've come to expect from this talented young
American quartet. With an overall theme of war and persecution the disc opens with George Crumb's
Black Angels, for electric string quartet. This work was inspired by the Vietnam War and bears two
inscriptions to that effect – *in tempore belli* (in time of war) and "Finished on Friday the Thirteenth
of March, 1970", and it's described by Crumb as "a kind of parable on our troubled contemporary
world". The work is divided into three sections which represent the three stages of the voyage of the
soul – fall from grace, spiritual annihilation and redemption. As with most of his works he calls on
his instrumentalists to perform on a variety of instruments other than their own – here that ranges
from gongs, maracas and crystal glasses to vocal sounds such as whistling, chanting and whispering.
Doom. A sigh is the young Hungarian composer István Marta's disturbing portrait of a Roumanian
village as they desperately fight to retain their sense of identity in the face of dictatorship and
persecution. Marta's atmospheric blend of electronic sound, string quartet and recorded folk-songs
leave one with a powerful and moving impression. At first sight Tallis's *Spem in alium* may seem oddly
out of place considering the overall theme of this disc, but as the insert-notes point out the text was
probably taken from the story of Judith, in which King Nebuchadnezzar's general Holofernes
besieged the Jewish fortress of Bethulia. Kronos's own arrangement of this 40-part motet (involving
some multi-tracking) certainly makes a fascinating alternative to the original. A particularly fine
account of Shostakovich's Eighth String Quartet (dedicated to the victims of fascism and war) brings
this thought-provoking and imaginative recital to a close. Performances throughout are outstanding,
and the recording first class.

Cello Song Julian Lloyd Webber (vc); John Lenehan (pf). Philips Ⓕ 434 917-2PH (53 minutes:
DDD: 10/93). Recorded 1992.
    Villa-Lobos O Canto do capadócio. **Bach** Cantata No. 156, Ich steh mit einem Fuss im Grabe
– Sinfonia. **Castelnuovo-Tedesco** Sea murmurs, Op. 24a. **Schumann** Funf Stücke im
Volkston, Op. 102 – No. 2, Langsam. **Scriabin** Etudes in B flat minor, Op. 8 No. 11.
Rachmaninov Romance in F minor. **Grieg** Lyric Pieces, Book 3, Op. 43 – To the Spring.
Delius Hassan – Serenade. **Elgar** Romance, Op. 62. **Chopin** Cello Sonata in G minor, Op. 65 –
Largo. **Brahms** Five Lieder, Op. 105 – Wie Melodien zieht es mir. **Dvořák** Seven Gipsy
Melodies, B104 (Op. 55) – Songs my mother taught me. **Debussy** Beau soir. **Messiaen**
Quatuor pour la fin du temps – Louange à l'Eternité de Jésus. **Traditional** The Star of the
County Down.

As the title of this disc implies, all the pieces contained therein are rather in the same slowish-paced,
lyrical vein, but their sequence has been cleverly chosen so that there is still plenty of variety to keep
the listener's attention. Some of the items are original cello and piano pieces, others are skilful
arrangements, and there is a good mixture of well-known and unusual offerings. Elgar's bassoon
Romance translates particularly well to the cello, as do the Brahms, Debussy and Dvořák songs and
only in the arrangement of Grieg's piano piece, *To the Spring* does one feel that a cello is a little out
of place. The Messiaen excerpt is the longest and the most profound item, and it exists quite happily
as an entity away from the rest of the *Quatuor*. Throughout the programme Julian Lloyd Webber
plays with exceptional sensitivity, sympathy and tonal beauty – in fact it would be difficult to find
better performances of this kind of repertoire anywhere on records of today or yesterday. John
Lenehan gives good support, and Philips have provided a mellow, roomy recording.

Chamber Works [a]Arthur Gleghorn (fl); [a]Mitchell Lurie (cl); [ab]Ann Mason Stockton (hp); [acd]Hollywood Quartet (Felix Slatkin, Paul Shure, vns; Paul Robyn, va; Eleanor Aller, vc); [b]Concert Arts Strings / Felix Slatkin. Testament mono Ⓕ SBT1053* (73 minutes: ADD: 3/95). Items marked [ab] from Capitol CCL7509 (7/52), [c]Capitol CTL7063 (9/54), [d]CTL7004 (6/51). Recorded 1949-53. ⒼⒼ

Ravel Introduction and Allegro[a]. **Debussy** Danse sacrée et danse profane[b]. **Turina** La oración del torero, Op. 34[c]. **Villa-Lobos** String Quartet No. 6[d]. **Creston** String Quartet, Op. 8[c].

What a wonderful feeling for line these players had, what an incredible, perfectly matched and blended ensemble they produced – and how well these transfers sound! The Sixth Quartet of Villa-Lobos (1940) is slight but attractive and receives here a performance of the utmost brilliance and clarity. Paul Creston's String Quartet is slightly Gallic in feeling, and sweeter and more euphonious than those of Piston or William Schuman. The sound, as elsewhere in these recordings, is slightly on the dry side, save in the Ravel *Introduction and Allegro*, which also offers the additional attraction of Arthur Gleghorn's flute playing (though given the excellence of Mitchell Lurie and Ann Mason Stockton, it seems invidious to single him out). The Debussy *Danse sacrée et danse profane* sounds every bit as magical as it did 40 years ago.

Chamber Works by Women Composers [a]Macalester Trio; [b]Joseph Roche, [c]Robert Zelnick (vns); [c]Tamas Strasser (va); [c]Camilla Heller (vc); [d]Paul Freed (pf). Vox Box Ⓑ 115845-2 (two discs: 141 minutes: ADD: 10/94).

C. Schumann Piano Trio in G minor, Op. 17[a]. **Beach** Piano Trio in A minor, Op. 150[a]. **Tailleferre** Violin Sonata No. 1[bd]. **Boulanger** Pièces – Nocturne; Cortège[bd]. **Mendelssohn-Hensel** Piano Trio in G minor, Op. 11[a]. **Carreño** String Quartet in B minor[bc]. **Chaminade** Piano Trio No. 1 in G minor, Op. 11[a].

Four of the seven works here are première recordings. For such chivalrous acts of rescue gratitude is primarily due to Joseph Roche, leader of the Macalester Trio. Hearing Fanny Mendelssohn-Hensel's Piano Trio alongside the by now familiar G minor Piano Trio by Fanny's renowned pianist acquaintance, Clara Schumann, it reveals Clara as the neater craftswoman but Fanny as the more urgent communicator – especially its surging first movement. Too bad that as wife of the Prussian court painter, Wilhelm Hensel, the professional concert platform for her was decidedly out of bounds. Not so for this disc's sole American representative, Amy Marcy Cheney, who after marriage at 18, in 1885, pursued an active career as a pianist and composer under the name of Mrs H.H.A. Beach for her remaining 59 years. Dating from 1938, her Op. 150 Piano Trio testifies to a generously romantic heart, albeit occasionally too openly worn on the sleeve in so far as melody is concerned. In the last of the four piano trios we meet the young Cécile Chaminade, already anticipating later conquests with the ear-catching charm of this work's fancifully scored *Scherzo*. The solitary string quartet (like the last two works new to the catalogue) comes from that legendary Venezuelan firebrand, Teresa Carreño, here in surprisingly assuaging, quasi classical trim – even to the inclusion of a fugal episode (as if in emulation of Clara Schumann) in the finale. Each work included merits its place, but none, surely, more than those for just violin and piano. Lili Boulanger's "Nocturne" and "Cortège" are sensitive and subtle. As for Tailleferre's finely crafted, emotionally sophisticated First Sonata in C sharp minor, its previous omission from the catalogue is inexplicable. Apart from a bland account of Clara Schumann's Trio, the playing throughout is as acceptable as the recording.

New review
A Choice Collection Palladian Ensemble (Pamela Thorby, rec; Rachel Podger, vn; Susanne Heinrich, va da gamba; William Carter, gtr/theorbo). Linn Records Ⓕ CKD041 (66 minutes: DDD: 5/96). Recorded 1995.

Locke Broken Consorts – D major; C major. **Matteis** Setts of Ayres – Book 2: No. 10, Preludio in ostinatione; No. 12, Andamento malincolico; Book 3: No. 7, Preludio-Prestissimo; No. 8, Sarabanda-Adagio; No. 9, Gavotta con divisioni; Book 4: No. 27, Bizzararrie sopra un basso malinconico; No. 28, Aria amorosa-Adagio. **Baltzar** John come kiss me now. **Weldon** Sett of Ayres in D major. **Blow** Ground in G minor. **Butler** Variations on Callino Casturame. **J. Banister** Divisions on a Ground. **Anonymous** Old Simon the King.

The "choice collection" of "music of Purcell's London" is of items such as might have been heard at the concerts of then contemporary music held on the premises of Thomas Britton, the "small coal man", surely one of the most unlikely patrons in the history of music. It is in effect complementary to the Palladian Ensemble's earlier disc ("An Excess of Pleasure", also on Linn Records, ① CKD010, 7/93), with another liberal helping of Matteis's various and sometimes agreeably bizarre *Ayres* and two more of Locke's *Broken Consorts*, which we find absorbing rather than confusing – as Charles II did. John Weldon and Henry Butler are newcomers to the catalogue, the former with what amounts to an irregularly ordered suite, the latter with splendid variations on *Callino Casturame* in which Susanne Heinrich plays most expressively – and proves that chords played on the viola da gamba do not have to sound like teeth being pulled. *Old Simon the King* could not have been heard in Purcell's own time in this anonymous setting from *The division flute* of 1706, though it might have featured in one of Britton's concerts, but the tune was printed as early as 1652. If you are not already aware of the high quality of the instrumental playing, stylish musicality, imaginative approach and oneness of the Palladian Ensemble this disc provides as good an opportunity as any to find what you have been missing. Youth is at the helm in what amounts to (and sounds like) a joyous voyage of discovery. Join them on board. Music for pleasure is not just another record label!

Classical Works for Horn and Strings Hermann Baumann, [a]Vladimir Dshambasov (hns); **Gewandhaus Quartet** (Karl and Conrad Suske, vns; Dieter Hallmann, va; Jürnjakob Timm, vc); [b]**Olaf Hallmann** (va); [c]**Christian Ockert** (db). Philips Ⓔ 426 440-2PH (73 minutes: DDD: 9/93). Recorded 1992.
   Mozart Horn Quintet in E flat major, K407/K386c[b]. **Haydn** Divertimento a tre in E flat major, HobIV/5. **M. Haydn** Romanze in A flat major. **Beethoven** Sextet in E flat major, Op. 81b[a]. **Reicha** Horn Quintet, Op. 106[c].

In the insert-notes, horn-player Hermann Baumann describes the pieces on this disc as "the essential chamber works for horn and strings of the Classical and Romantic periods". The core work of the recording is Mozart's Horn Quintet and, according to Baumann, the horn part is the most difficult that Mozart wrote for the instrument. Michael Haydn's *Romanze*, an arrangement of the slow movement from Mozart's Third Horn Concerto, K447, is affectionately played with satisfying warmth of tone and unity of ensemble, and Joseph Haydn's E flat *Divertimento* provides an entertaining contrast. Antoine Reicha (1770-1836) is best known as a theorist. However, his E major Quintet, Op. 106, recorded here for the first time, blends virtuosity and lyricism in music of rhythmic and contrapuntal ingenuity, and deserves to be better known. These are excellent performances, superbly recorded.

Composers in Person [a]Maria Barrientos, [b]Ninon Vallin (sops); [c]**Enrique Granados**, [d]**Federico Mompou**, [b]**Joaquin Nin** (pfs); **Manuel de Falla** ([a]pf/[e]hpd); [e]**instrumental ensemble.** EMI Composers in Person mono Ⓔ CDC7 54836-2* (78 minutes: ADD: 11/93). Texts and translations included. Recorded between 1912 and 1950.
   Granados Danzas españolas, Op. 37[c] – No. 7, Valenciana; No. 10, Danza triste (both from Odeon 68649/50). Goyescas – No. 7, El pelele[c] (68651. All recorded c1912). **Falla** Siete canciones populares españolas[a] (French Columbia D11701 and PFX1/2. 1928-30). El amor brujo[a] – Canción del fuego fátuo. Soneto a Córdoba (PFX2. 1930). Harpsichord Concerto[e] (French Columbia LFX92/3. 1930). **Mompou**[d] Scènes d'enfants – No. 5, Jeunes filles au jardin. Suburbis – No. 1, El carrer, el guitarrista i el vell cavall. Cançons i dansas – No. 5 (all from French Columbia FCX184); No. 6 (previously unpublished); No. 8. Paisajes – No. 1, La fuente y la campana (FCX184. All 1950). **Nin**[b] Cantos populares españolas – No. 3, Tonada de la niña perdida; No. 4, Montañesa; No. 6, Malagueña; No. 7, Granadina; No. 19, Canto Andaluz; No. 20, Polo (Odeon 188693/5. 1929).

With few exceptions all Spain's leading composers in the early part of this century were excellent pianists. Granados is represented by some discs dating from 1912. Despite their surface noise (very heavy in an improvised ramble on "El pelele"), his qualities are evident, particularly in a light, airy and crisply rhythmic "Valenciana". The major part of the present disc is given over, reasonably enough, to Falla, an indisputably greater composer than the others and a conspicuously first-class keyboard player. His playing of the Harpsichord Concerto is masterly, especially of the *Lento* which, exemplifying his plea that it should be taken as slowly as humanly possible, is enormously atmospheric and evocative of great bells during the Corpus Christi procession. Falla is equally outstanding in the seven folk-songs accompanying Maria Barrientos. Ninon Vallin's bright, clear voice is artlessly attractive in the folk-song settings of Nin, a virtuoso pianist who is evidently enjoying himself in the "Malagueña". In a totally different style, far more introspective and subtle, is the playing of Mompou. He takes the dance of the fifth *Canço i dansa* slower than usual, gives a fine lift to the sixth (dedicated to Rubinstein), and is utterly seductive in the sentimental tune of "Jeunes filles au jardin", played very slowly and freely.

New review
Cradle Song Julian Lloyd Webber (vc); [a]**John Lenehan**, [b]**Pam Chowhan**, [c]**Richard Rodney Bennett** (pfs). Philips Ⓔ 442 426-2PH (57 minutes: DDD: 1/96). Recorded 1993.
   J. Lloyd Webber Song for Baba[b]. **Schumann** Kinderszenen, Op. 15 – No. 7, Träumerei[a]. **Schubert** Wiegenlied, D498[a]. **Montsalvatge** Canciones negras – Cancion de cuna para dormir a un negrito[a]. **T.J. Hewitt** (arr. Chowhan) Shepherd's Lullaby[b]. **Dvořák** Sleep, my baby, B142 No. 1[a]. Songs my mother taught me, B104 No. 4[a]. **R.R. Bennett** (arr. Bennett) Dream Sequence[c]. **Quilter** Slumber Song[a]. Child Songs, Op. 5 – Where Go the Boats?[a]. **C. Scott** Lullaby, Op. 57 No. 2[a]. **W. Lloyd Webber** Slumber Song[a]. **Canteloube** Chants d'Auvergne – Brezairola[a]. **Khachaturian** Scenes from childhood – A little song[a]. **Lenehan** Alice[a]. **Poulenc** L'histoire de Babar – Lent et mélancolique[a]. **D. Heath** Gentle dreams[a]. **Rutter** (arr. Willcocks) Mary's lullaby[a]. **Fauré** Dolly Suite, Op. 56 – Berceuse[a]. **Brahms** Wiegenlied, Op. 49 No. 4[a]. **Traditional** (arr. Chowhan) Nursery Suite[b]. Recorded 1993.

This album provides a companion to Julian Lloyd Webber's much admired "Cello Song" (reviewed above), and once again he has skilfully managed to choose a sequence of pieces that retains the same overall mood without monotony – though that consideration may in any case not much worry someone seeking late-night 'easy listening'. This attractive disc actually begins with a piece by Lloyd Webber – his first ever and written in 1992 for his six-week-old son David. Indeed, the inspiration for this whole album of lullabies is, he tells us, "the innocence of childhood" and the cellist also describes it as his "most personal recording". There are 21 tracks here and all are attractive music from, and for, a child's world, though not everything is strictly speaking a cradle song. Lloyd Webber plays consistently with an ideal intimacy and care, and John Lenehan, who also composed the lullaby called *Alice*, is an excellent partner – though Richard Rodney Bennett and Pam Chowhan also participate in their own arrangements. The thoughtful and imaginative booklet-essay is on cradle songs generally and doesn't attempt to deal with the individual pieces, but few purchasers of this disc will mind that. They will also not mind that the recording, close but not distractingly so, favours the lovely sound of Lloyd Webber's cello.

Début **Sarah Chang** (vn); **Sandra Rivers** (pf). EMI Ⓔ CDC7 54352-2 (51 minutes: DDD: 1/93). Recorded 1991.

> **Sarasate** Concert Fantasy on "Carmen", Op. 25. **Elgar** Salut d'amour, Op. 12. La Capricieuse, Op. 17. **Khachaturian** Gayaneh – Sabre Dance. **Kreisler** Tempo di Menuetto in the style of Pugnani. **Paganini** Caprices, Op. 1 – No. 1 in E major; No. 15 in E minor. **Chopin** (arr. Milstein) Nocturne in C sharp minor, Op. posth. **Shostakovich** (arr. Zyganow) Preludes, Op. 34 – No. 10 in C sharp minor; No. 15 in D major. **Gershwin** (trans. Heifetz) Porgy and Bess – It ain't necessarily so. **Liszt** (arr. Milstein) Consolations, S172 – Lento placido. **Tchaikovsky** Souvenir d'un lieu cher, Op. 42 – Mélodie in E flat major. **Prokofiev** (arr. Heifetz) The Love for Three Oranges – March.

This astonishing disc heralds the recording début of another much-vaunted violinistic phenomenon, the 11-year-old Sarah Chang. A student of the acclaimed pedagogue Dorothy DeLay, Chang actually made this recording at the age of nine, playing a quarter-sized violin. With an impressive catalogue of major orchestral engagements to her credit, she is now continuing her studies at the Juilliard School in New York. Her taxing programme opens with an impeccable account of Sarasate's *Carmen* Fantasy, in an edition prepared by Zino Francescatti; dazzling playing, even if that last *frisson* of excitement is held in check. The two Elgar favourites are charming, even if slightly mannered, but Chang's bristling performances of Khachaturian's "Sabre Dance" and the famous Heifetz transcription of the March from Prokofiev's *The Love for Three Oranges* are both sensational. Her Paganini, too, is electrifying – she despatches the First and Fifteenth *Caprices* with the confident *élan* of a seasoned virtuoso. The same technical assurance is evident in two Preludes by Shostakovich, but undemonstrative offerings are marginally less convincing perhaps, at this very early stage, with some inflexibility in the Tchaikovsky and Kreisler works. She is a shade unyielding in her approach to Nathan Milstein's winning Chopin and Liszt arrangements, but her natural spontaneity works to greater advantage in "It ain't necessarily so", from *Porgy and Bess*, in the famous Heifetz version. "Sarah Chang is the most ideal violinist I have ever heard" was Sir Yehudi Menuhin's verdict on this monumentally gifted young virtuoso. Her recording début will enthral and captivate in equal measure – hear it as a matter of priority!

Jacqueline du Pré – Her Early BBC Recordings Jacqueline du Pré, [f]William Pleeth (vcs); [deg]Ernest Lush, [c]Stephen Kovacevich (pfs). EMI Studio mono Ⓜ CDM7 63165/6-2* (two discs: 112 minutes: ADD: 9/89). Recorded at broadcast performances on [a]January 7th, 1962, [b]January 26th, 1962, [c]February 25th, 1965, [dg]March 22nd, 1961, [e]September 3rd, 1962, [f]March 17th, 1963. ⒼⒼ

> *CDM7 63165-2*: **Bach** Solo Cello Suites – No. 1 in G major, BWV1007[a]; No. 2 in D minor, BWV1008[b]. **Britten** Cello Sonata in C major, Op. 65 – Scherzo and March[c]. **Falla** (arr. Maréchal) Suite populaire espagnole[d]. *CDM7 63166-2*: **Brahms** Cello Sonata No. 2 in F major, Op. 99[e]. **F. Couperin** Nouveaux Concerts – Treizième Concert[f]. **Handel** (arr. Slatter) Oboe Concerto in G minor, HWV287[g].

We owe the BBC and EMI a debt of gratitude for making these valuable recordings available on disc. The performances date from her mid- to late- teens, and reveal a maturity and passion that is rare in so young a performer. This, together with her wonderful gift of communication, make these performances very special indeed. The two Bach Cello Suites have a magical, intimate poetry that transfixes the attention from the very first note and her beautifully phrased and lyrical readings more than compensate for any slight imperfections of articulation. Sadly we have only the "Scherzo" and "March" movements from the Britten Cello Sonata, and judging by the quality of these, a complete performance would surely have been a recording to treasure. These are sparkling performances, full of wit and good humour, reflecting the obvious rapport between the two young artists. The recording of Falla's *Suite populaire espagnole* dates from 1961 when du Pré was only 16 but is no less assured or technically accomplished. The performance is full of life and rhythmic vitality, with some very tender and expressive playing, as in the cantabile melodies of the "Nana" and "Cancion" movements. The mono recordings are not of the highest quality (the Bach Suites are taken from transcription discs, so there are traces of surface noise and clicks) but this is of little relevance when we are presented with playing as beautiful and captivating as this.

Espana! Katia and Marielle Labèque (pfs). Philips Ⓕ 438 938-2PH (59 minutes: DDD: 9/94). Recorded 1993.

    Falla La vida breve – Danses espagnoles. El amor brujo – Ritual Fire Dance. **Lecuona** Malagueña. **Albéniz** Suite española, Op. 47 – Sevilla; Cádiz; Aragon; Castilla. Pavana capricho, Op. 12. Iberia – Triana. Navarra. **Infante** Danses Andalouses.

The Labèque sisters give us the right Iberian mixture of vigour, brilliance, shadows and languor, and seem to be thoroughly enjoying themselves in music that they know well. There is no more exciting keyboard performance of Falla's "Ritual Fire Dance". This is actually a transcription by Mario Bragiotti. Indeed, save for the *Danses Andalouses* by Manuel Infante, every piece here is a transcription and the Labèques themselves have had a hand in that of Lecuona's exquisitely sultry *Malagueña*, which includes quietly plucked strings at the two-minute mark. But no one would know that this music was not originally written for two pianos, for everything is idiomatic. Indeed, the transcription of Albéniz's *Suite española* and *Pavana capricho* is by the composer, while that of his "Triana" (music that beautifully blends vivacity and delicacy) is by his friend Granados. The recording is intimate yet atmospheric.

English Viola Music Paul Coletti (va); [a]**Leslie Howard** (pf). Hyperion Ⓕ CDA66687 (67 minutes: DDD: 10/94). Recorded 1993.   Ⓖ

    Britten Elegy. **Vaughan Williams** Romance[a]. **R. Clarke** Lullaby[a]. Morpheus[a]. Viola Sonata[a]. **Grainger** Sussex Mummers' Christmas Carol, BFMS17[a]. Arrival Platform Humlet, RMTB1. **Bax** Legend for Viola and Piano[a]. **Bridge** Pensiero, H53a[a]. Allegro appassionato, H82[a].

The centre-piece to Scottish violist Paul Coletti's enterprising recorded début is the very fine Sonata by Rebecca Clarke (1886-1979). Displaying a most beguiling harmonic resource (the sound-world is distinctly Gallic with distant echoes of such English contemporaries as Bax and Ireland), idiomatic mastery (the viola was Clarke's own chosen instrument) and exquisite finish. That other English violist-composer of note, Frank Bridge, is represented by his *Pensiero* and *Allegro appassionato* (both from 1908, and surprisingly the only two pieces he wrote for his own instrument). Vaughan Williams's *Romance* turned up amongst the composer's papers after his death: although only 5'40" in length, it squeezes a wealth of incident and emotion into its compact frame. Percy Grainger's heart-warming *Sussex Mummers' Christmas Carol* finds these performers at their most touchingly eloquent, whilst Coletti audibly relishes the bracing sonorities of the unaccompanied *Arrival Platform Humlet* (a 'little hum', in case you were wondering). Bax's *Legend* dates from July 1929, a peak period between his Third Symphony and *Winter Legends*. It's a ten-minute essay of slumbering power and richly-stocked invention; indeed, as so often with this composer's instrumental output, the writing is almost orchestral in its emotional scope and remarkable range of colour. The performances throughout are past praise in their sensitivity and dedication and the engineering is impeccable.

New review

Fascinatin' rhythm Alan Feinberg (pf); **Daniel Druckman** (marimba)[a]. Argo Ⓕ 444 457-2ZH (76 minutes: DDD: 11/95). Recorded 1994.

    Gershwin Lady, Be Good! – Fascinatin' rhythm (arr. Wild); The Man I love (arr. Grainger). Tip-Toes – That certain feeling (trans. Wodehouse). Oh, Kay! – Clap yo' hands (trans. Wodehouse). **Waller** Ain't misbehavin' (trans. Distler). Squeeze me (trans. Scivales). **Ellington** Solitude (trans. Tucker). **J.P. Johnson** The Mule Walk (trans. Scivales). **Gottschalk** Bamboula, RO20. **Columbia** Caprice americain, RO61. **Rube Bloom** Spring Fever. Silhouette. **Cowell** Two Woofs. **Nancarrow** Study for Player Piano No. 6[a] (trans. Druckman). **B. Powell** Dusk in Sandi (trans. Brody). **Beiderbecke** Candlelights. **Jelly Roll Morton** Mamanita (trans. Dapogny). **Joplin** Magnetic Rag. **Cervantes** Por que, eh? **Grainger** In Dahomey. **Confrey** Kitten on the Keys.

Feinberg has said that his collections are "personal views ... about putting pieces together in a way that makes each piece speak most eloquently" rather than conventional catalogues or sets of complete works. He starts with Earl Wild's own transcription of *Fascinatin' rhythm* which is on Wild's own all-Gershwin CD (Chesky ① CD32, 10/90). Wild himself made a strong impression in these sometimes Lisztian interpretations, but Feinberg plays this one more dazzlingly right through. Two of the Gershwin numbers are in Artis Wodehouse's transcriptions from Gershwin's own disc recordings rather than the short-winded workings in Gershwin's *Songbook*. Without exception Feinberg makes these sound spontaneous and vivid. An odd decision is the inclusion of an arrangement of Nancarrow's player piano Study No. 6 for marimba and piano, which simply doesn't balance. Jelly Roll Morton's *Mamanita*, played in James Dapogny's transcription, is convincing but the master himself was rather more delicate. Grainger's crazy *In Dahomey* is a rarity on record; the Fats Waller numbers are further transcriptions; but an unmitigated hit is kept for the end. This is a performance of *Kitten on the Keys* which for sheer speed and panache would have left the best novelty pianists of the 1920s and 1930s simply gasping. With so many treats in this CD recital the packaging hardly matters: strongly recommended and good value at 76 minutes.

New review

Industry Bang on a Can All-Stars ([ae]Maya Beiser, vc; [abd]Evan Ziporyn, saxcs; [abd]Mark Stewart, gtrs; [ad]Robert Black, db; [abd]Lisa Moore, kbds; [abcd]Steven Schick, perc); [d]**Cees van Zeeland,**

[d]Gerard Bouwhuis (pfs); [d]Amy Knowles (congas); [d]Icebreaker (Katherine Pendry, James Poke, panpipes; Richard Craig, sax; Damian le Gassick, fender rhodes). Sony Classical Ⓟ SK66483 (61 minutes: DDD: 2/96).

Wolfe Lick[a]. **L. Andriessen** Hout[b]. Hoketus[d]. **D. Lang** The Anvil Chorus[c]. **Gordon** Industry[e].

The All-Stars come across here as a fiercely aggressive group, combining the power and punch of a rock band with the precision and clarity of a chamber ensemble. The individual pieces cover a considerable idiomatic range but share the minimalist fascination with repetitive, gradually evolving structures. Rhythm is constant and vital, melody and harmony either stunted or non-existent. The programme kicks off with Julia Wolfe's *Lick* – sensibly enough as it's the most approachable work on the disc. In a surprisingly affectionate tribute to the rock music of her youth, Wolfe toys with the expectations of the genre with considerable formal cunning; and no one could deny the extraordinary panache of the playing. The Andriessen compositions lack any comparable lightness of touch. This is not to deny that they matter. They articulate in purest form the seminal impulse behind the other music here, remaking the static, consonant sounds of Terry Riley, Steve Reich and the rest into a vehicle of protest – edgy, jarring and *Angst*-ridden. *Hout* and *Hoketus* are as severe in their canonic processes as any of Reich's early phase pieces, and their halting angular ideas evoke the back streets of some dark and impenetrable urban jungle (possibly best left unexplored). Is there another composer who would think of obtaining a monolithic sonority from panpipes and saxophones over acoustic and electric pianos with bass guitars and a conga rhythm? Like it or not, this disc makes an impressively cogent, individualistic statement. The music certainly isn't subtle: it's a bruising assault on the soothing, pseudo-spiritual escapism of the Holy Minimalists on the one hand and the excessive, barely-heard complexities of the Modernist Old Guard on the other. The results are technically outstanding but definitely not for the faint-hearted.

Kiss On Wood Maria Bachmann (vn); Jon Klibonoff (pf); [a]James Saporito (perc). Catalyst Ⓟ 09026 62668-2 (67 minutes: DDD: 5/95). Recorded 1994. Ⓖ

MacMillan Kiss on Wood. **Bolcom** Violin Sonata No. 2. **Copland** Nocturne. **Schnittke** Violin Sonata No. 1. **Dresher** Double Ikat – Part Two[a].

Maria Bachmann's recital exhibits warm, expressive tone, easy virtuosity and winning musicianship. True, parts of James MacMillan's *Kiss on Wood* of 1994 – a strong, somewhat spartan dialogue that becomes progressively more serene – find Bachmann having occasional trouble sustaining the line (or so it sounds), but the music's tense character is very well captured and the players' timing seems immaculate. Total contrast is afforded by William Bolcom's Second Sonata (1938), a winsome scrapbook of a piece, alternating dreams and brutality and with a finale "In Memory of Joe Venuti" that wouldn't be out of place on BBC Radio 3's "Jazz Record Requests". Here Bachmann weaves a cool, Grappelli-style line, whereas her sensitive handling of Copland's smoky *Nocturne* (1928) makes a strong case for an atmospheric *morceau* other violinists might do well to investigate. Schnittke of course keeps both players on their toes: his largely playful First Sonata (1963) flirts with atonalism ("a tonal world with atonal highways", to quote the composer himself) and turns grandly solemn for a *Largo* that recalls the parallel movement in Shostakovich's Second Piano Trio. Then there is Paul Dresher, whose transcontinental eclecticism makes for an interesting marriage between Western and south-east Asian musical styles. *Double Ikat – Part Two* for violin, piano and percussion (1988-90) is fitfully animated and dies to a wailing, curvaceous solo line backed by simple piano chords, a gong and sighing cymbal. It is a restful finale to a pleasing sequence of musical explorations, stylishly played and expertly recorded.

▌New review

Kremerata Musica [a]Sabine Meyer (cl); [b]Gidon Kremer (vn); [c]Veronika Hagen (va); [d]Clemens Hagen (vc); [e]Oleg Maisenberg (pf). DG Ⓔ 447 112-2GH (76 minutes: DDD: 4/96).

Mahler Quartet in A minor[bcde]. **Schoenberg** Piece in D minor[be]. String Trio, Op. 45[bcd]. Phantasy, Op. 47[be]. **Webern** Two Pieces for Cello and Piano[de]. Four Pieces, Op. 7[bc]. Three Little Pieces, Op. 11[de]. Cello Sonata[de]. **Berg** Four Pieces, Op. 5[ae]. Chamber Concerto – Adagio (arr. cpsr)[abe]. Recorded 1994.

This is a Second Viennese School disc that revels in extremes: for example, there could hardly be a greater contrast than that between Schoenberg's very early, very anodyne piece for violin and piano (it could easily be mistaken for Schubert at his least poetic) and his last instrumental work, the forceful, economical *Phantasy*. Even so, the playing throughout is so refined and expressive that the later music's eroded but still potent links with the romantic tradition are unmistakable. The result is fascinating, and one of the best releases of its kind for some years. Mahler's honorary membership of the Schoenberg school – as early patron and model – is acknowledged in his own youthful movement for piano quartet, an evocative mixture of Brahmsian and Wagnerian elements that showed the way forward with exemplary clarity. As for Schoenberg's pupils, Webern's rapid progress from languid late romanticism (in the two cello pieces of 1899) to aphoristic expressionism is powerfully displayed, the close positioning of the cello in the Op. 11 Pieces adding to the larger-than-life impression of these performances. Sabine Meyer's clarinet is also closely recorded in the Berg pieces, but music so rich in striking incident can stand such immediacy, as can Berg's arrangement of the *Chamber Concerto*'s slow movement for clarinet, violin and piano. Nevertheless, the finest music-making of all is heard in Schoenberg's Trio, an account in which technical mastery and expressive fantasy combine to brilliant effect.

Kronos Quartet Released 1985-95. [a]**Dumisani Maraire** (ngoma/hosho); [b]**Astor Piazzolla**
(bandoneon); [c]**Patty Manning,** [c]**John Taylor,** [c]**Larry Caballero** (vocs); [d]**Djivan Gasparian** (duduk).
Kronos Quartet (David Harrington, John Sherba, vns; Hank Dutt, vn; Joan Jeanrenaud, vc).
Nonesuch Ⓟ 7559-79394-2 (two discs: 101 minutes: DDD: 2/96). Recorded 1987-95.
Maraire Mai Nozipo (from 7559-79275-2, 11/92)[a]. **Piazzolla** Asleep (7559-79254-2)[b].
B. Johnston Amazing Grace (7559-79163-2, 11/87). **Reich** Different trains – America: before
the war (7559-79176-2, 6/89). **Górecki** String Quartet No. 2 (Quasi una fantasia), Op. 64 –
Arioso: Andante cantabile (7559-79319-2, 4/93). **Riley** Salome Dances for Peace – The Ecstasy:
excerpt (7559-79217-2, 9/90). **Crumb** Black Angels: 13 Images from the Dark Lands (Images I) –
God-music (7559-79242-2, 4/91). **Glass** String Quartet No. 5 – third movement (7559-79356-2).
Tahmizyan A Cool Wind is Blowing (7559-79346-2)[d]. **Barber** String Quartet – Adagio, Op. 11.
Pärt (arr. Hofer) Fratres (both from 7559-79181-2). **R. Scott** (arr. S. Mackay) Dinner Music for
a Pack of Hungry Cannibals. **S. Johnson** How it Happens (The Voice of I.F. Stone) – It raged.
Daugherty Elvis everywhere[c]. **Hendrix** (arr. S. Rifkin and Kronos Qt) Purple Haze (all new to
UK).

Kronos is a quality act. No quartet currently performing has done more to bridge the divide between
popular and 'serious' music, and although others have served contemporary repertoire with equal
dedication (the Arditti Quartet being among the most notable), Kronos take top laurels for
imagination, presentation and an intuitive sense of what best 'connects' with a non-specialist music-
loving audience. This superb retrospective is both representative and symbolic of their best work –
representative in that the styles of voices are uncommonly wide; symbolic in that the planning of the
disc, its telling juxtaposition of chosen material, actually reflects the compositional methods of
certain composers programmed. "Released" opens with Dumisani Maraire's breezy *Mai Nozipo* and
goes on to include Ben Johnston's prolix but engrossing variations for quartet on *Amazing Grace*, an
appealing extract from Terry Riley's epic *Salome Dances for Peace*, Crumb's mysterious *God-music*,
Pärt's ubiquitous *Fratres* (one of the work's earlier recordings), an eerie piece for *duduk* (a sort of
Eastern-sounding saxophone) by Tigran Tahmizyan and then, to finish, a poignant return home to
the familiar strains of Barber's *Adagio*. All are superbly performed and very well recorded. However,
the real highlight of the set – at least for those of us who already own the albums from which
"Released" has been compiled – is the relatively brief second disc "Unreleased", starting with the
upbeat hilarity of Raymond Scott's *Dinner Music for a Pack of Hungry Cannibals*, then progressing
to Scott Johnson's humbling "It raged" from *How it Happens* (urgent dialogue centring on I.F.
Stone's reasoned arguments against the stupidity of 'Holy Wars'), Michael Daugherty's astonishing *Elvis
everywhere* (three brilliant mimics, fragments of song and a tragicomic coda) and a raw-and-rowdy
remake of Hendrix's *Purple Haze*. There are no proper insert-notes on the music but the chosen
selections are so vivid, so powerfully communicative, that written explanations would serve little
purpose.

Lament [a]**Wilhelmenia Fernandez** (sop); [b]**Elvis Costello** (sngr); **Brodsky Quartet** (Michael Thomas,
Ian Belton, vns; Paul Cassidy, va; Jacqueline Thomas, vc); [c]**Susan Monks** (vc); [c]**Mary Scully** (db).
Silva Classics Ⓟ SILKD6001 (71 minutes: DDD: 10/94). Recorded 1994.
Stravinsky Three Pieces for String Quartet. **J. Alvarez** Metro Chabacano. **Traditional** She
moved through the fair[b]. **D. Matthews** Adagio. **Szymanski** Five Pieces. **Massenet** Elégie[a].
M. Thomas Harold In Islington. Variations on a theme of Banjo Patterson, "Waltzing
Matilda". **Sculthorpe** Lament[c].

Whether you find this programme annoyingly bitty or profoundly stimulating will be very much a
matter of personal taste. The music-making has real integrity. The sound is excellent too, bright and
vivid without adopting a clinical 'pop' ambience. Only the Stravinsky pieces are at all familiar and
they receive a hyper-brilliant, realization which allows them to sit happily with the knowing
minimalism of Javier Alvarez. His *Metro Chabacano* is a real discovery – if a Latinized combination
of early Tippett, Steve Reich and sophisticated pop is your idea of fun. The plangent simplicity of the
original folk melody is not necessarily best served by the treatment accorded to *She moved through the
fair* which features rock musician Elvis Costello on vocals, palpably sincere but quavery. Should you
find the restrained English eloquence of David Matthews's *Adagio* a little too mainstream, the post-
modern polystylism of Pawel Szymanski's *Five Pieces* may be more to your taste. The Massenet
arrangement is sensitive and unobtrusive with *Diva* star Wilhelmenia Fernandez conveying an
appealing mixture of seductiveness and melancholy. The most significant new(ish) music on the disc
is Peter Sculthorpe's *Lament*, an arrangement of a piece originally scored for string orchestra in 1976.
Coherently structured, stylistically consistent and beautifully reworked for string sextet, the second
cello and double-bass lending a dark, oppressive sonority, its musical argument seems almost old-
fashioned in its convincing continuity. The climax is genuinely moving. Recommended to those with
a post-modernist sensibility.

The Lindsays: 25 Years Lindsay Quartet (Peter Cropper, Ronald Birks, vns; [a]Robin Ireland,
[b]Roger Bigley, vas; Bernard Gregor-Smith, vc). ASV Ⓟ CDDCA825 (77 minutes: ADD: 1/93).
Recorded 1978-88.

Wirén String Quartet No. 3 in D minor, Op. 18 (recorded 1987)[a]. **A. Tchaikovsky** String Quartet No. 2 in C major, Op. 5 (1978)[b]. **Hugh Wood** String Quartet No. 3, Op. 20 (1980)[b]. **Barber** String Quartet, Op. 11 (1988)[a].

As its title suggests, this issue celebrates the Lindsay String Quartet's twenty-fifth anniversary, with all but the present violist Robin Ireland chalking up over 20 years' membership. The quartet has played works ranging from the classics to the less familiar modern ones by André Tchaikovsky and Hugh Wood that feature here. Indeed, what we have here is in no way central twentieth-century repertory: no 'great' composer at all, some will say, and regret it. Furthermore, these are recordings of BBC concert performances from 1978-88, and inevitably there are a few rustles that would otherwise have been edited out and applause after all the works except the Tchaikovsky. However, such is the vitality of the playing that one can overlook these matters, and the overall quality of the sound is good. Dag Wirén is a Swedish composer known mainly for just one work, a *Serenade for Strings*, but his Third Quartet has plenty of personality although in a conservative idiom. André Tchaikovsky was Polish-born but spent much of his life in England before dying by his own hand at the age of 46; a fine pianist as well as a composer, he had a prickly personality that is strongly reflected in his Second Quartet, written for the Lindsays and first played by them in this BBC performance of January 1978. Hugh Wood's Third Quartet, which the Lindsays premièred, is also a tough piece, and relies heavily on Second Viennese School gesturings, but the Lindsays play it with commitment. Finally, Samuel Barber's Quartet is maybe the best music here. Its celebrated central *Adagio* sounds strikingly fresh played in context on four instruments instead of alone in the usual version for string orchestra. It is a pleasure to salute the Lindsays and to welcome this excellent tribute disc.

Made in America Yo-Yo Ma (vc); [c]Ronan Lefkowitz, [d]Lynn Chang (vns); [ab]Jeffrey Kahane, [c]Gilbert Kalish (pfs). Sony Classical Ⓟ SK53126 (65 minutes: DDD: 4/94). Recorded 1991-92. Ⓖ

Bernstein (trans. Ma) Clarinet Sonata[a]. **Gershwin** (arr. Heifetz, trans. Ma)[b] Three Preludes. **Ives** Trio for Violin, Clarinet and Piano[c]. **Kirchner** Triptych[d].

In Ives's Trio you have the feeling that hiss only way of coping with his love for the 'old tunes' was to send them up; yet he did so with such aplomb, daring and imagination that one can't help but respond gratefully. Ives's Trio is the final work in Yo-Yo Ma's absorbing programme. The first, Bernstein's wartime Clarinet Sonata, was arranged with the composer's authorization and is pure delight from start to finish: mild, melodious and ultimately high-spirited. Which leaves Gershwin and Kirchner, the former represented by a sensuous re-working of Heifetz's famous *Prelude* transcriptions, the latter by an astonishingly outspoken *Triptych*. Scored, respectively, for "Cello Solo" and "Violin and Cello Obbligato" (the movement subtitles), *Triptych* ends with a vigorous *Presto*. The entire programme is superbly performed, the Ives being particularly adroit, the Gershwin smoochy and playful. This is the sort of recital that will have you reaching for *The Gramophone Classical Catalogue* in search of more of the same.

Neapolitan Chamber Works Il Giardino Armonico / Giovanni Antonini (rec). Teldec Das Alte Werk Ⓟ 4509-93157-2 (54 minutes: DDD: 11/94). 🎵 Recorded 1993. ⒼⒼ

Sarri Concerto for Recorder, Two Violins, Viola and Continuo in A minor. **D. Scarlatti** Sonata for Mandolin and Continuo in D minor, Kk90. **Durante** Concerto for two Violins, Viola and Continuo in G minor. **A. Scarlatti** Sonata for Recorder, two Violins and Continuo in A minor. **Mancini** Sonata for Recorder, Two Violins and Continuo in D minor.

The idea of a selection of music that might have been heard in early eighteenth-century Naples is not a new one but, in the area of chamber music, it has not been more vividly brought to life than on this disc. Domenico Scarlatti's Sonata is one of several believed to have been intended for a solo instrument with continuo, and here the soloist is as clean and quick-fingered a mandolinist as you could find, even if you hired a private detective (he is also the violist!) — a beguiling performance indeed. The remaining items lack any other recording, and all are to be welcomed. Sarri was a prolific composer of vocal music and the Concerto was his only instrumental work, with the recorder singing 'arias' that would tax any diva. There is something in each of the others to surprise and delight, such as the subtly tear-shedding chromatics of the opening *Affetuoso* of Durante's Concerto and the *Piano* of Alessandro Scarlatti's Sonata, a recorder/violin duo. Every item is illuminated by sensitivity to expressive nuance and dynamics, and the recording is close to perfection. This disc can do more for your sense of well-being than any medication.

New English Clarinet Music Mühlfeld Ensemble (Victoria Soames, cls; Julia Vohralik, vc; Jonathan Higgins, pf). Clarinet Classics Ⓟ CC0007 (74 minutes: DDD: 10/94).

Powers Trio. **Lutyens** Trio, Op. 135. **LeFanu** Lullaby. Nocturne **G. Williams** The song within. **R. Marsh** Ferry Music.

All the pieces in this collection were commissioned by the Mühlfeld Ensemble (then known as the Mühlfeld Trio; they have since added a violinist to the group and will soon be commissioning works for clarinet quartet under their new name). Their seriousness of intention is indicated by the composers they have chosen: there is no easy-access minimalism or neo-romanticism here. What most of these composers have in common is something much more challenging for performers: an economy of utterance that makes every note and every interval count. Of this Elisabeth Lutyens's late Trio is a perfect example, a little masterpiece of refined and pared-down expressiveness, beautifully made and no less beautifully played, each member of the trio realizing the importance of every inflexion to the overall design. It has the spareness of Webern, but longer lines. Anthony Powers's piece (what an under-represented composer in the record catalogue he is!) is well described by his own phrase: "subdued drama". A gradual progress from a slow prelude through a continually arrested scherzo to an eventual flowering of melody and of unified trio writing in the finale, it needs very concentrated playing if its line is to be perceived and its discontinuities bridged. Played as well as this it's an absorbing piece. Nicola LeFanu's two linked duos require no less concentration, the first because of its constant changes of direction away from the 'islands' of very slow lyrical intensity that are eventually shown to be its centre, the latter because it is in effect an unbroken melody, or series of self-regenerating melodies, some seven minutes long. The secret of performing such pieces is that the end of each should sound like an end: they do, most satisfyingly. Graham Williams, as the title of his piece suggests, surrounds a darkly expressive slow 'song' (for bass clarinet) with spikier, faster music that is related to it by a readily audible unifying melodic cell. Roger Marsh's five epigrammatic miniatures use a similar device and obvious 'mirrorings' between movements to create a sort of bridge structure, peaking of course in the centre but leaving no doubt that the fifth movement is the destination. All five pieces are better than 'interesting' and one wants a better word than 'enterprising' (which so often means 'a good try, but ... ') for the Mühlfeld Ensemble's remarkable success-rate in their commissioning. The recording is first-class.

Pastoral **Emma Johnson** (cl); [b]**Judith Howarth** (sop); [a]**Malcolm Martineau** (pf). ASV
Ⓔ CDDCA891 (74 minutes: DDD: 7/94).
    Ireland Fantasy-Sonata in E flat major[a]. **Vaughan Williams** Six Studies in English folk song[a].
Three Vocalises for Soprano Voice and Clarinet[b]. **Bax** Clarinet Sonata[a]. **Bliss** Pastoral (posth.)[a].
Two Nursery Rhymes[b]. **Stanford** Clarinet Sonata, Op. 129.

A lovely programme, radiantly performed and most judiciously chosen. Things get under way in fine style with John Ireland's marvellous *Fantasy-Sonata*: beautifully written, passionately argued and encompassing (for Ireland) a wide range of moods; it's certainly a work that shows this underrated figure at the height of his powers. The Clarinet Sonata by Ireland's teacher, Stanford, is one of that composer's most successful works: formally elegant and most idiomatically laid out, it boasts a central *Adagio* (entitled "Caoine" – an Irish lament) of considerable eloquence. Johnson is a gloriously mellifluous exponent in both Vaughan Williams's *Six Studies* and the Bax Sonata, and in the first movement of the latter she manages to convey a slumbering mystery that is somehow almost orchestral in its imaginative scope. Judith Howarth joins Johnson for the haunting *Three Vocalises* (one of Vaughan Williams's very last utterances from his final year) and makes an equally agile showing in Bliss's delightful *Two Nursery Rhymes* and touching *Pastoral*. A real pleasure, then, from start to finish and Malcolm Martineau proffers superb accompaniments.

Percussion Works **Safri Duo** (Morten Friis, Uffe Savery, perc). Chandos New Direction
Ⓕ CHAN9330 (62 minutes: ADD: 4/95). Recorded 1994.
    A. Koppel Toccata. **Fuzzy** Fireplay. **Pape** CaDance 4 2. **Miki** Marimba Spiritual II. **Nørgård**
Echo Zone I-III.

This is a corker of a disc. It is hard to imagine anyone who responds to top-notch virtuosity not being caught up by these two young Danes, both of whom sound as if they could give Evelyn Glennie a good run for her money. Certainly their playing here is stunning, captured in a warm but not over-resonant recording. The Safri Duo are not just highly accomplished players technically; as the individual notes by Fuzzy (yes, that is his working name, b.1939), Per Nørgård (b.1932) and Minoru Miki (b.1930) confirm, Morten Friis and Uffe Savery are musicians who both inspire the best from composers and actively take part in the music's evolution. Only the high standard of their playing was able to realize the longstanding conception that lay behind Nørgård's *Echo Zone I-III*, while in *Fireplay*, originally written in 1991 for percussion and tape, the passages constructed for the Duo to improvise have taken on an almost separate development, culminating – for the moment – in the present version recorded in 1994. In the case of Miki's *Marimba Spiritual II*, it would seem the Duo are responsible for the piece in its present form, the 1983 original being for marimba accompanied by a larger ensemble. The disc opens in entertaining fashion with the brilliant, light *Toccata* (1990) of Anders Koppel (b.1947), a straightforward duet for vibraphone and marimba. The other works all use larger arrays, not least Andy Pape's (b.1955) invigorating *CaDance 4 2* – the title punning cadence and dance – which is written for various species of drums.

New review
Prime Meridian **Meridian Arts Ensemble.** Channel Classics Channel Crossings Ⓕ CCS8195
(70 minutes: DDD: 4/96). Texts included. Recorded 1995.   Ⓖ
    Stravinsky Fanfare for a New Theatre. **Zappa** (arr. Nelson) Peaches en Regalia. Let's make the water turn black. Oh No. Igor's boogie. Eat that question. Echidna's arf. **Wheeler** Song for Someone. **Van Vliet** (arr. Grabois/Nelson) Ice rose. A carrot. When I see mommy. Apes-ma. Dropout boogie. Suction prints. **Babbitt** Fanfare for all. **J. Nelson** Song for a dead king. Paterson 2:35. **Shemaria** Pandora's Magic Castle. **H. Hancock** Jessica. **London** (arr. Stewart) Shvitz Suite.

The phrase 'arranged for brass quintet' too often means 'emasculated and equipped with brass-band clichés and showy solos for the lead trumpet'. Meridian, however, is a *sextet* (brass plus drums), most of whose players can either double on a non-brass instrument (guitar, saxophone, more drums) or can sort of sing. So no worries: the mercurial Zappa and the anarchic Don Van Vliet (also known as Captain Beefheart) are not excessively neatened and tidied by these arrangements. Zappa's melodic distinction, in particular, could withstand even a less sympathetic and affectionate treatment than Don Nelson gives him here. *Let's make the water turn black* has had its hair smarmed down a little (something to do with Meridian's dapper staccato manner; the disco-ish one-*two* rhythm is also a bit of a strait-jacket), but the archetypally Zappa *Peaches en Regalia* sounds almost as though he'd arranged it himself. No one, since the Captain's lamented retirement, can match his raucously gravelly vocalism, but Daniel Grabois makes a good shot at it. Stravinsky and Babbitt aside, the best composer here after Zappa and Beefheart is Nelson himself: his *Song for a dead king* (the monarch being Elvis Presley) is in the spirit of Zappa both in its derision and its exuberant solo writing. *Paterson 2:35* is catchy, joyous and Latin; so, if overextended, is Rich Shemaria's piece. Closer to the standard brass quintet style are Kenny Wheeler's only faintly blues-y lyric and Herbie Hancock's attractive ballad (used as an excuse for at any rate one brass cliché: chords in which instruments enter one at a time, from the bottom up). Stravinsky's brilliant fanfare ("two golden cockerels crowing at each other", said George Balanchine) makes an ideal prelude, Milton Babbitt's an ingeniously varied, toccata-like centrepiece. Frank London's suite might be described as Klezmer with added gritty dissonance. The performances throughout are quite stunningly good: all the brilliance one has learned to expect from the best traditional brass groups, plus a whole range of jazz- and rock- and funk- and who-knows-what-else-derived virtuosities. A close, brilliant recording: play it *very* loud.

Romantic Music for Violin and Piano Vera Vaidman (vn); Emanuel Krasovsky (pf). CDI/IMP
Classics Ⓑ PWK1137 (71 minutes: DDD: 6/90).
Tchaikovsky Méditation, Op. 42 No. 1. Valse-Scherzo, Op. 34. Mélodie, Op. 42 No. 3. **Dvořák** Violin Sonatina in G major, B183. **Schubert** Violin Sonata in A minor, D385. **Kreisler** Schön Rosmarin. Liebesleid. Liebesfreud.

Here is a splendid collection of inspired music for violin and piano, marvellously played and given a digital recording of great realism and immediacy. The Dvořák *Sonatina* was written in New York at around the same time that the great Czech composer created his most popular work, the *New World Symphony*, and it deserves to be equally well known. All four movements are brimming over with the same kind of memorable melody that makes the symphony such a favourite with the public. The first movement makes an impression of great vigour and impulse, the *Larghetto* sings beguilingly, the *Scherzo* dances vivaciously and the finale sparkles and introduces another quite lovely lyrical folksy melody which is instantly memorable and stays in the mind long after the work has concluded. Vera Vaidman's performance has great sympathy and spontaneity and her partner, Emanuel Krasovsky gives all the support she could ask for, though it is she who dominates – for that is the way the music is written. The programme opens with an engaging Tchaikovsky triptych, each miniature strikingly characterful and the third, *Mélodie*, having that bittersweet Russian melancholy for which the composer is famous. The Schubert Sonata which follows the Dvořák has a disarming, simple lyricism. Like the Dvořák it is in four movements: the *Andante* is gently eloquent, and the finale flows with captivating innocence. The programme ends with three Kreisler lollipops, dashingly played, to end the recital exuberantly. This disc is in the bargain price range and the recording is in the demonstration class; seek it out for its rewards are very considerable.

Russian Music for Two Pianos Duo Reine Elisabeth (Wolfgang Manz, Rolf Plagge, pfs). Koch
Discover International Ⓢ DICD920150 (66 minutes: DDD: 11/94). Recorded 1992.
Stravinsky Petrushka. **Scriabin** Romance in A minor. **Shostakovich** Concertino, Op. 94. **Rachmaninov** Six Morceaux, Op. 11.

This is essentially a 'fun' disc. The opening of *Petrushka* is relatively easygoing, without hammered rhythms or self-conscious virtuosity the music's colour and charm immediately come over. Yet characterization is perceptive. The scene in Petrushka's cell is gentle and touching although it does not lack drama, and the Blackamoor is darkly introduced without overdoing the menace. The closing fairground sequence is richly hued, with an almost orchestral palette. The rest of the programme is well contrasted. The Scriabin *Romance*, an endearing early piece, is melodically rich and the Shostakovich *Concertino*, which opens with a dramatic echo of the slow movement of Beethoven's Fourth Piano Concerto, has audaciously witty, toccata-like writing which really makes one smile when the playing is so infectious. The six Rachmaninov *Morceaux* are played with much sympathy and a natural charm. Good recording, forward and not too reverberant. A worthwhile and very real bargain.

New review
Smetana Quartet [b]Pavel Štěpán (pf); Smetana Quartet (Jiří Novák, Lubomir Kostecký, vns; Milan Škampa, va; Antonín Kohout, vc). Testament Ⓕ SBT1074/5 (two discs, oas: 79 and 77 minutes: ADD: 3/96). Items marked [ab] from HMV ASD2350 (2/68), [c]ASD2402 (6/69), [d]new to UK (recorded 1965).Recorded 1965-6. ⓐⓐ
SBT1074 – **Dvořák** String Quartet No. 12 in F major, B179, "American"[a]. Piano Quintet in

A major, B155[b]. **Janáček** String Quartet No. 1, "The Kreutzer Sonata"[d]. *SBT1075* – **Dvořák**
Terzetto in C major, B148[c]. String Quartet No. 14 in A flat major, B193[c]. **Janáček** String
Quartet No. 2, "Intimate Letters"[d].

Listening to these discs tempts one to think that in the 1960s the Smetana were the Berlin
Philharmonic of quartets – just as in the 1950s the Hollywoods might have been fancifully called the
Philadelphia Orchestra of quartets. Much of the playing here is in a class of its own, only later
equalled by the Borodin and Alban Berg Quartets in terms of finesse and ensemble. The Dvořák
performances must be numbered among the very best now in the catalogue: their phrasing has none
of the artificiality that marks some professional quartets (that is to say that a phrasing once rehearsed
becomes, as it were, mechanically reproduced so that while the line rises and falls it doesn't genuinely
breathe) and it is an enormous relief to hear genuine *pianissimo* tone and so natural and unforced an
ensemble. The present catalogue boasts over a dozen recordings of each of the Janáček Quartets but
in terms of tonal finesse, perfection of ensemble and depth of feeling the present issues would be
difficult to beat. They have a controlled passion that is wonderfully impressive.

New review

The String Quartet in Eighteenth-Century England Salomon Quartet (Simon Standage,
Micaela Comberti, vns; Trevor Jones, va; Jennifer Ward-Clarke, vc). Hyperion Ⓕ CDA66780
(69 minutes: DDD: 3/96). ✍ Recorded 1995.
Abel String Quartet in A major, Op. 8 No. 5. **Shield** String Quartet in C minor, Op. 3 No. 6.
Marsh Quartetto in B flat major in imitation of the Stile of Haydn's Opera Prima. **Webbe**
Variations in A major on "Adeste Fideles". **S. Wesley** String Quartet in E flat major.

For various reasons connected with the patterns of its social life, the string quartet was slow to
become established in England. The work that opens this CD, by the German-born Abel, comes from
the first set of quartets to be published in London (in 1769); it is an amiable piece, graceful enough,
harmonically rather static and texturally unenterprising. The few Englishmen who ventured into the
string quartet genre did rather better. William Shield's work, the sixth of a set published in 1782,
begins with a passionate C minor gesture and has some echoes of Haydn both in the ingenuity of its
humour and in its seriousness, though not in his technique nor his sureness of taste; but the *Adagio*
is very remarkable, quite individual in the tone of its expression and reaching an extraordinarily
imaginative climax in each half with a sort of free-flying violin passage, in its way breathtaking. The
finale too is sombre in quite an original way. John Marsh (a lawyer and a landowner, though music
was his passion), wrote his quartet "in imitation of the Stile of Haydn's Opera Prima" in the 1780s: it
is a very fluent, polished piece, close in manner to Haydn's Op. 1 No. 1, with a spirited 6/8 opening
movement, two minuets (the second particularly delightful) with an appealing *Largo* of charm and
warmth, between them, and a witty finale with some lively invention. Samuel Webbe, too, used Haydn
as his model – the slow movement of the *Emperor* Quartet – for his variations on *Adeste Fideles*: it is
a beautiful, highly ingenious piece, harmonically rich, exquisitely crafted. But the most unexpected
work here is certainly the Samuel Wesley Quartet, usually supposed to date from the very beginning
of the nineteenth century but surely more likely, as Peter Holman says in his note, to be 20 years later
– the energetic, leaping lines, the complex figuration, the abrupt gestures, the free textures: all this
speaks of a later, post-classical era. It is a substantial and powerful piece, wholly individual in tone.
The Salomon bring a good deal of fire to this piece, and indeed, once past the Abel, they play this
music with splendid conviction, as it amply merits. This CD is something of a revelation.

Joseph Szigeti The Recordings with Béla Bartók and Andor Foldes. **Joseph Szigeti** (vn); [a]**Andor
Foldes**, [b]**Béla Bartók** (pfs). Biddulph mono Ⓜ LAB070/71* (two discs: 129 minutes: ADD: 7/94) .
From American Columbia and New Music Quarterly originals; recorded 1940-41. ⒼⒼ
Bartók Rhapsody No. 1, Sz86[b]. Contrasts, Sz111[b] (with Benny Goodman, cl). **Bloch** Baal
Shem[a]. **Debussy** Violin Sonata in G minor[a]. **Ives** Violin Sonata No. 4, "Children's Day at the
Camp Meeting"[a]. **Schubert** Violin Sonata in D major, D384[a]. Also includes works by **Bach,
Brahms, Corelli, Debussy, Dvořák, Falla, Hubay, Kodály, Lalo, Milhaud,
Mussorgsky** and **Schubert**

Ever the thinker among conjurors, Joseph Szigeti didn't so much transcend pyrotechnics as harness
them to expressive ends. Szigeti's technique was in good working order on this set and fully up to
realizing the sensuality implicit in works like Debussy's Sonata and "Clair de lune" from the *Suite
bergamasque* (heard here in Rölens's effective arrangement). *Baal Shem* is gripping in its confessional
ardour, enshrining profoundly perceptive interpretations. It was also fascinating to encounter the rare
Ives Fourth Sonata. It is difficult to imagine the tender, central *Largo cantabile* sounding with greater
melancholy than it does here. It is a strangely alluring piece, full of stylistic contradictions and ending
with an engagingly off-beam *Allegro*. The Milhaud and Falla items (the booklet prints them in reverse
order) are delightfully adroit, but Szigeti's own transcription of the *Háry János* Intermezzo is rather
discursive and heavy-handed. The Bartók *Rhapsody* is given with appropriate rustic gaiety, while
Contrasts – heard here in its best CD transfer yet – has just the right feeling of improvised burlesque.
The Bach, Corelli and Schubert items convey the very essence of Szigeti's violinistic personality, his
warmth, elegance and superior intelligence. The Corelli *La folia* will stop you in your tracks, especially
the closing cadenza with its felicitous chord-work, a remarkable piece of playing by any standards.
The Schubert D major *Sonatina*'s opening *Allegro molto* displays acute sensitivity to line, while in the

carefree *Rondo* (taken from the big D major Piano Sonata, D850) Szigeti's quick-wristed, capricious phrasing is reminiscent of Heifetz's. The Bach *Bourrée* is typically crisp, deliberate and rhythmically supple. Quite honestly, everything here is so rich in incident that no amount of listening will dull its appeal. Joseph Szigeti's art is truly inexhaustible!

Toward the Sea III [a]Aurèle Nicolet (fl); Nobuko Imai (va); [b]Naoko Yoshino (hp). Philips Ⓕ 442 012-2PH (64 minutes: DDD: 12/94). Recorded 1993.
   Honegger Petite Suite, H89[ab]. **Denisov** Duo for Flute and Viola[a]. **Takemitsu** Toward the Sea III[ab]. And then I knew 'twas wind[ab]. **Britten** Lachrymae, Op. 48[b]. **Debussy** Sonata for Flute, Viola and Harp[ab].

The combination of flute, viola and harp has not been exactly over-employed since Debussy composed his Sonata of 1916. However, here is an imaginative and attractive collection of pieces that use various duo combinations of the ensemble or, as is the case in the works by Takemitsu, pieces that have been composed with Debussy's instrumental texture specifically in mind. Honegger's tiny, three-movement *Petite Suite* lasts no longer than 2'31", yet despite its brevity is perfectly formed in every respect. The scoring is flexible; Honegger asks simply for two melody instruments with piano. Here, the piano part is successfully taken by the harp and the melodic lines by flute and viola. Edison Denisov is generally known for his use of aleatoric techniques and unconventional textures, but his *Duo* for flute and viola establishes a strange and haunting atmosphere using traditional musical means; the resulting sound-world is not unlike that of Villa-Lobos's *Bachianas brasileiras* No. 6 for flute and bassoon. The surprise item of the disc is Britten's *Lachrymae*, though the pairing of viola and harp seems utterly natural considering the Elizabethan roots of the thematic material. The two Takemitsu works find the composer in his most sensuous and impressionistic mood. The performances throughout are uniformly excellent – as one would expect with such fine artists as Aurèle Nicolet and Nobuko Imai – and the atmospheric, well-balanced recording complements the repertoire perfectly.

Violin Recital Kyoko Takezawa (vn); Philip Moll (pf). RCA Victor Red Seal Ⓕ 09026 60704-2 (65 minutes: DDD: 2/93). Recorded 1990.
   Bartók Solo Violin Sonata, Sz117. **Brahms** Hungarian Dance No. 1 in G minor. **Chaminade** (arr. Kreisler) Sérénade espagnole. **Falla** (trans. Kochanski) Suite populaire espagnole.
   Tchaikovsky Souvenir d'un lieu cher, Op. 42 – No. 1, Méditation in D minor. Valse-scherzo, Op. 34.

Brave indeed is the violinist who elects to open a début recital disc with the Bartók Solo Sonata! Kyoko Takezawa's fearless performance is outstandingly good; her playing has idiomatic refinement and formidable virtuosity, sufficient to guarantee success in this most taxing of works for unaccompanied violin. For the remainder of her programme, this Gold Medal winner at the 1986 Indianapolis Violin Competition, and former student of Dorothy DeLay at the Juilliard School is joined at the piano by Philip Moll. Their Tchaikovsky performances are particularly memorable; affecting and nostalgic in the "Méditation" in D minor, and appropriately zestful in the case of the "Valse-scherzo". Takezawa's dazzling account of Falla's *Suite populaire espagnole* (Paul Kochanski's arrangement) has an intuitive flair and individuality, also much in evidence in the other Spanish-flavoured offering here, Chaminade's *Sérénade espagnole*, once a regular Kreisler encore piece, but seldom heard these days. Takezawa shows her true mettle in a spirited rendition of the *Hungarian Dance* No. 1 by Brahms, which concludes the programme. This is an outstanding release, a brilliantly played and perceptively chosen programme crowned by her stunning version of the Bartók Sonata. A must for all lovers of the violin.

Virtuoso Music for Trumpet Sergei Nakariakov (tpt); Alexander Markovich (pf). Teldec Ⓕ 4509-94554-2 (59 minutes: DDD: 6/95). Items marked [a] arr. Markovich, [b]Nakariakov, [c]Dokshitzer. Recorded 1994. ⒼⒼ
   Waxman Carmen Fantasia[a]. **Arban** Variations on a theme from Bellini's "Norma"[a]. Variations on a Tyrolean Theme[a]. **Falla** La vida breve – Danse espagnole[b]. **Saint-Saëns** Le carnaval des animaux – The swan[b]. **Paganini** Caprice in E flat major, Op. 1 No. 17[b]. Moto perpetuo in C major, Op. 11[b]. **Tchaikovsky** Valse-scherzo in C major, Op. 34[b]. **Sarasate** Zigeunerweisen, Op. 20[c]. **Fauré** Le Réveil[b]. **W. Brandt** Concert Piece No. 2.

Sergei Nakariakov is an extraordinary talent. It is one thing to be able to play the violin at the age of 17 with the technical aplomb of one's elders but a brass instrument – on a purely physical level – requires a strength and maturity which can be accelerated only so fast. His prowess as a trumpeter lies not only in the sphere of technical wizardry, which he has in super-abundance, but in a security of tone and interpretational vision: the subtle tuning in this selection of mainly-transcribed violin pieces and the gipsyish portamentos are astute and accomplished. The Russian-ness of his playing is fascinating; he has that intensity of tone that Westerners find so hard to emulate without sounding corny or chastened. Nakariakov has a focused but fat, epic sound (though no doubt it will get even more wholesome with age) and a total security and command in all registers. His technique is particularly admirable in the lower reaches where he seems rarely to need the air at his disposal to progress through phrases. Nakariakov's slow playing is fluid, especially in his smoky rendering of Fauré's *Le Réveil*.

Virtuoso Works for Violin and Piano Maxim Vengerov (vn); **Itamar Golan** (pf). Teldec
Ⓕ 9031-77351-2 (67 minutes: DDD: 4/94). Recorded 1993.
Wieniawski Polonaise No. 1 in D major, Op. 4. Légende, Op. 17. **Paganini** I palpiti, Op. 13.
Kreisler Schön Rosmarin. Tambourin chinois. Caprice viennois. **Bloch** Baal shem – Nigun.
Tchaikovsky Souvenir d'un lieu cher, Op. 42 – No. 2, Scherzo in C minor; No. 3, Mélodie in
E flat major. **Messiaen** Theme et Variations. **Sarasate** Caprice basque, Op. 24. **Bazzini** La
Ronde des lutins, Op. 25.

Maxim Vengerov is such a masterful musician that everything he touches turns to gold. Firstly, his
intonation is impeccable. The purity and steadiness of Paganini's *I palpiti* is such that one never has
the impression of his being under any strain. The double-stopping episodes in Wieniawski's *Légende*
appear to come as naturally to him as single notes. He captures the mawkish Slavonic melancholy with
real intensity. In the Kreisler selection Vengerov is gentle and generous-spirited, charmingly pure in
Schön Rosmarin and idiomatic for the tongue-in-cheek *Tambourin chinois*. The Bazzini has terrific
attack, too, though it might have been more impish. The piece is undeniably inconsequential, but one
is left gawping at the phenomenal accuracy and confidence of the left-hand pizzicato section at the
end. In conclusion it must be said that rarely if ever does one hear the Tchaikovsky *Mélodie* played
with more eloquence or refined tone colour.

Works for Clarinet and Piano Michael Collins (cl); **Kathryn Stott** (pf). EMI Virtuosi
Ⓕ CDC7 54419-2 (67 minutes: DDD: 9/92). Recorded 1992.
Schumann Fantasiestücke, Op. 73. **Debussy** Première rapsodie. **Poulenc** Clarinet Sonata.
Lovreglio Fantasia on Verdi's "La traviata", Op. 45. **Weber** Grand duo concertant, J204.
Messager Solo de concours.
Works for Clarinet and Piano Victoria Soames (cl); **Julius Drake** (pf). Clarinet Classics
Ⓕ CC0001 (68 minutes: DDD: 9/92).
Copland Clarinet Sonata. **Tailleferre** Arabesque. Solo Clarinet Sonata. **Honegger** Sonatine.
Poulenc Clarinet Sonata. **Milhaud** Sonatine, Op. 100. Duo Concertant, Op. 351.

One wishes that more music existed for the clarinet as a solo instrument, and it seems unfair that an
instrument loved by Mozart, Weber and Brahms (to name but three composers) has such a small solo
repertory. But there it is, and besides music by the men just mentioned there are other works of
importance such as Schumann's *Fantasiestücke,* Debussy's *Rapsodie* and the Poulenc Sonata which
appears on both these British discs. Michael Collins is one of the finest clarinettists active today, and
certainly earns the title of virtuoso with the performances on the EMI disc. Messager's "competition
solo" demands and receives great agility and panache, and Debussy's later piece is no less well served
by this artist's refinement and subtlety. Weber's *Grand duo concertant* is a sonata in all but name, with
fine melodies in its central *Andante* and a theatrical finale, and here Kathryn Stott matches Collins in
her handling of the challenging piano part. The recording is excellent. On the Clarinet Classics disc,
Copland's Clarinet Sonata nominally dates from the very end of his life but proves to be an expert
reworking of the Violin Sonata which he composed four decades earlier in 1943. This was a vintage
period for him and he described the work as mainly lyrical, with little virtuosity. In fact there is an
American purity of flavour here that is uniquely his and which we also find in other works of this time
such as the ballet, *Appalachian Spring.* Victoria Soames and Julius Drake give this sonata due weight
as well as quiet poetry, and they are no less good in Poulenc's, which has the same blend of energy
and tenderness, although Collins and Stott bring even more brilliance to its finale. The music by four
members of Les Six is not all of the same stature, and although Milhaud's two pieces (separated by
some three decades) are good value in their quirky way, the Honegger is not so interesting until its
vivid finale. But it is good to have all these works together and the performances by Soames and
Drake are unfailingly stylish, while the recording is well balanced and faithful.

Instrumental

American Piano Sonatas, Volume 1. **Peter Lawson** (pf). Virgin Classics Ⓕ VC7 59008-2
(76 minutes: DDD: 5/91).   ⓖⓖ
Copland Piano Sonata in E flat major, Op. 26. **Ives** (ed. Cowell) Three-page Sonata. **Carter**
Piano Sonata. **Barber** Piano Sonata, Op. 26.

This disc offers four relatively unfamiliar but highly characterful American piano works in
authoritative performances by a British-born pianist who clearly has their idiom at his fingertips – as
well as their pretty challenging notes. As played here, the Copland Piano Sonata of 1941 has softness
as well as strength, and for all its powerful utterance there is a strangely compelling lyricism at work
too; one can see why the young Leonard Bernstein adored the work. The recording matches the music,
being on the close side but extremely lifelike as piano sound. Ives's *Three-page Sonata,* which at over
seven minutes is longer than the miniature that its title suggests, is a gnomic utterance, but as always
with this composer we feel that he has something to say that could be said in no other way. Carter's

Piano Sonata is an early work of 1946, which the composer revised much later in 1982; its debt to Copland is evident, but there is also a personal voice and the scope and sweep of the music is deeply impressive. Barber's Sonata (1949), which was written for Horowitz, is less radical in idiom than the other works played and thus more immediately approachable if by no means conventional, being a work of considerable power and eloquence, very well written for the piano.

Martha Argerich Début Recital. **Martha Argerich** (pf). DG The Originals Ⓜ 447 430-2GOR (71 minutes: ADD: 6/95). Items marked [a] from SLPM138672 (1/63), [b]2530 193 (6/72). Recorded 1960-71. *Gramophone classical 100.* 🅖🅖
Chopin Scherzo No. 3 in C sharp minor, Op. 39[a]. Barcarolle in F sharp major, Op. 60[a]. **Brahms** Two Rhapsodies, Op. 79[a]. **Prokofiev** Toccata in C major, Op. 11[a]. **Ravel** Jeux d'eau[a]. **Liszt** Hungarian Rhapsody No. 6 in D flat major[a]. Piano Sonata in B minor, S178[b].

Here, on this richly filled CD, is a positive cornucopia of musical genius. Martha Argerich's 1961 disc remains among the most spectacular of all recorded débuts, an impression reinforced by an outsize addition and encore: her 1972 Liszt Sonata. True, there are occasional reminders of her pianism at its most fraught and capricious (Chopin's *Barcarolle*) as well as tiny scatterings of inaccuracies, yet her playing always blazes with a unique incandescence and character. The Brahms *Rhapsodies* are as glowingly interior as they are fleet. No more mercurial Chopin *Scherzo* exists on record and if its savagery becomes flighty and skittish (with the chorale's decorations sounding like manic bursts of laughter), Argerich's fine-toned fluency will make other, lesser pianists weep with envy. Ravel's *Jeux d'eau* is gloriously indolent and scintillating and the Prokofiev *Toccata* (a supreme example of his early iconoclasm) is spun off in a manner that understandably provoked Horowitz's awe and enthusiasm. Liszt's Sixth *Hungarian Rhapsody* is a marvel of wit and daring and the B minor Sonata is among the most dazzling ever perpetuated on disc. The recordings have worn remarkably well and the transfers have been expertly done.

Simon Barere The Complete HMV Recordings, 1934-36. **Simon Barere** (pf). APR mono
Ⓕ APR7001* (two discs: 126 minutes: ADD: 5/91). 🅖🅖🅖
Liszt Etudes de Concert, S144 – La leggierezza (from HMV DB2166, 7/34). Années de pèlerinage, Deuxième année, S161, "Italie" – Sonetto 104 del Petrarca. Etudes de Concert, S145 – Gnomenreigen (both from DB2167, 9/34). Etudes de Concert, S418 (two versions. DB2749/50. Recorded 1934 and 1936). Valse oubliée, S215 No. 1. Rhapsodie espagnole, S254 (DB2375/6, 6/35). **Chopin** Scherzo No. 3 in C sharp minor, Op. 39 (APR7001, 12/85. 1935). Mazurka in F sharp minor, Op. 59 No. 3 (two versions. DB2674, 1/37; second previously unpublished. 1935-36). Waltz in A flat major, Op. 42 (DB2166). **Balakirev** Islamey (two versions. DB2675, 4/36). **Blumenfeld** Etude for the Left Hand. **Glazunov** Etude in C major, Op. 31 No. 1 (DB2645, 12/35). **Scriabin** Etudes – C sharp minor, Op. 2 No. 1 (1934); D sharp minor, Op. 8 No. 12 (two versions. 1934-35). **Lully** (arr. Godowsky) Gigue in E major. **Rameau** (arr. Godowsky) Tambourin in E minor (both 1934. All from APR7001). **Schumann** Toccata in C major, Op. 7 (three versions – two on DB2674, 1/37; third previously unpublished. 1935-36).

For many years following his death in 1951 Simon Barere was simply a legendary name to conjure with, whose phenomenal pianism appeared to have been lost to future generations of music lovers. Then in the late 1980s a small specialist company, Appian Recordings, began to reissue his recordings – all extremely rare – in a series of three volumes. This, the first, contains all of the recordings (including rejected takes) which Barere made for HMV between 1934 and 1936, following his emigration from Russia and then Germany to the USA where his reputation was firmly, if briefly, established. Barere was part of the generation of super-pianists, including Horowitz, who succeeded the first wave of Russian virtuosos such as Rachmaninov and Josef Lhévinne. For musicians such as these the normal peaks of the piano literature became mere starting points for complete and thorough investigations of the musical and technical capabilities of the instrument itself. The HMV sessions included such monumental tests of virtuosity as Balakirev's fantasy, *Islamey*, Liszt's *Réminiscences de Don Juan*, and "Gnomenreigen", together with a whole range of shorter but equally testing pieces by Schumann, Chopin, Scriabin, Godowsky and Barere's last teacher, Blumenfeld. To all of this music Barere brought a technique which knew no difficulties and a sense of musical taste which kept vulgar display firmly at bay. The results are frankly benchmarks of performance by which all aspiring virtuosos must be tested and which few will ever equal. Simon Barere's playing is simply breathtaking in its unrestrained vigour and superb technical control, both laid at the feet of a unique and powerful musical insight. This two-CD set is an essential memorial to one of the greatest, if unsung, heroes of the piano this century. The production by Bryan Crimp is faultless, with full and highly faithful transfers from the original 78s, and comprehensive accompanying documentation. No lover of truly great piano playing can afford to be without this issue.

Beau Génie Pieces from the Bauyn Manuscript, Volume 1. **Jane Chapman** (hpd). Collins Classics
Ⓕ 1420-2 (69 minutes: DDD: 3/95). 🎶 Recorded 1994.
Suites and pieces by **Chambonnières, L. Couperin, Pinel, D'Anglebert, Mezangeot, Rossi** and unidentified members of the **Monnard, Gautier, Richard** and **La Barre** families

This release presents an enterprising and well-balanced programme, and one, too, which reflects the sort of practical contact with music that your average wealthy seventeenth-century enthusiast might actually have enjoyed. It is the first of three devoted to a manuscript collection named after the family for which it was copied around 1670, and whose musical tastes it presumably reflects. Two of the greatest figures of the French harpsichord school are here: Louis Couperin (represented by his solemn G minor Suite) and his teacher Chambonnières (a C major Suite which includes ornamented repeats by Couperin). The bulk of the disc, though, is given over to lesser figures; true, there is a fine Sarabande by D'Anglebert, but the rest consists of a mixture of transcriptions of lute pieces by composers such as Mezangeot and Gautier, and dances by unidentified members of minor composer dynasties such as the La Barres and the Richards. Jane Chapman uses Dartington Hall Trust's much rebuilt 1614 Flemish harpsichord rather than a more sonorous and resonant French model. And why not? What really matters is her command of the French style, which is fluent and tidy and shows good judgement in the use of generally lively tempos.

Divers styles dans l'Eloquence Pieces from the Bauyn Manuscript, Volume 2. **Jane Chapman** (hpd). Collins Classics Ⓕ 1421-2 (71 minutes: DDD: 4/95). ☞ Recorded 1994.
L. Couperin Suites – A minor; D minor; Prélude in C major. Pavanne in F sharp minor.
Froberger Toccatas in A minor and G major. Suite in A minor. Ricercare in C major.
Frescobaldi Capriccio in G major. Fantasia in E minor. **Anonymous** Four Pavannes.

Here are pieces by three of the undisputed keyboard masters of the early baroque. Louis Couperin provides the main substance of the programme, in the shape of two large-scale suites, a lengthy *Pavanne* in the unusual key of F sharp minor to open the disc, and a solemn *Prélude* to end. One of the advantages, however, of this type of release over the single-composer (or, for that matter, single-country) species is that new cross-connections can be illustrated, and it is fortunate the Bauyn collection contains both a Couperin *Prélude* explicitly "a l'imitation de Mr Froberger" and the Froberger *Toccata* which was its model. Chapman includes both, and then takes the opportunity to give us more of the German composer's attractive and influential music, including a three-movement suite to go with the *Toccata*. Two pieces by Froberger's teacher Frescobaldi complete the disc, along with four short *Pavannes* which are anonymous but by no means worthy of disownment. Chapman's grasp of the French idiom is secure, her application of it once again eloquent and attractive. If she is a shade more convincing in the dance movements than in the grander *Préludes* and *Toccatas*, then that could well be partly down to her instrument, a 1614 Ruckers from Dartington Hall which has its own beauties, for sure, but which doesn't quite have the resonance and sheer weighty presence of a French model. If that's the only drawback, though, it's not much of one; this is a thoroughly worthwhile and enjoyable release.

Carnegie Hall Highlights Artur Rubinstein (pf). RCA Victor Gold Seal Ⓜ 09026 61445-2 (64 minutes: ADD: 10/93). Items marked [a] from SB6504 (9/62), [b]RL13850 (7/81). Recorded live in 1961.   ⒼⒼⒼ
Debussy Préludes – La cathédrale engloutie; Ondine[a]. Images – Hommage à Rameau; Poissons d'or[a]. **Szymanowski** Mazurkas, Op. 50 – Nos. 1-4[a]. **Prokofiev** Vision fugitives, Op. 22 – Nos. 1-3, 9-14 and 16[a]. **Villa-Lobos** Próle do bébé, Book 1[a]. **Schumann** Arabeske in C major, Op. 18[b]. **Albéniz** Navarra[a].

Artur Rubinstein had a unique flair for live musical communication and these concert performances have great spontaneity. In fact, the whole disc might have been billed as 'The Essential Rubinstein', thus providing one of the few occasions where the 'essential' epithet would have been fully justified. And it's certainly all here – the wistful reverie (*Arabeske*), the mastery of rhythm and exotic colours (Szymanowski *Mazurkas*, *Navarra*, *Próle do bébé*), acute sensitivity to miniature forms (*Visions fugitives*), unforced virtuosity employed to musical ends (*Próle*) and a natural inclination towards musical impressionism (Debussy). RCA are more active with their back catalogue than most of their rivals so we can only hope that more Rubinstein is waiting in the wings.

Cellissimo Mischa Maisky (vc); **Daria Hovora** (pf). DG Ⓕ 439 863-2GH (67 minutes: DDD: 9/94). Items marked [a] arr. M. Maisky. Recorded 1993.   Ⓖ
Bach Orchestral Suite No. 3, BWV1068 – Air[a]. Toccata, Adagio and Fugue in C major, BWV564 – Adagio[a]. Nun komm' der Heiden Heiland, BWV659 (arr. V. Maisky). **Handel** (arr. anon.) Aria in C minor. **Boccherini** String Quintet in E major, G275 – Minuet[a]. **Schubert** Moments musicaux No. 3 in F minor, D780[a]. **Schumann** Romanze in A minor, Op. 94 No. 1. Adagio and Allegro in A flat major, Op. 70. **Chopin** Etude in C sharp minor, Op. 25 No. 7 (trans. Glazunov)[a]. Nocturne in C sharp minor, Op. posth. (trans. Ginsburg)[a]. **Saint-Saëns** Allegro appassionato in B minor, Op. 43. **Debussy** Suite bergamasque – Clair de lune (trans. Roelens)[a]. Préludes, Book 1 – No. 12, Minstrels[a]. **Bloch** Baal shem – Nigun (arr. Schuster).

Bach's "Air", *Adagio* and *Nun komm' der Heiden Heiland* are loaned for the sake of a glorious 'top line' and lovingly turned by Mischa Maisky and his sensitive pianist, Daria Hovora. There is bravura, too – especially in Saint-Saëns's earnest *Allegro appassionato* (an original cello composition) and Maisky's own fun transcription of Debussy's "Minstrels", complete with vibrant, sliding pizzicatos. Joseph Schuster renders Bloch's "Nigun" suitably cantorial and while piano purists might object to the hijacking of Chopin just for the sake of melody, one hopes that the warmth and seamlessness of

Maisky's playing minimizes any suggestion of offence. One might also care to remember that the *Etude* Op. 25 No. 7 (programmed here) is sometimes known as the 'Cello' Study. Schubert and Boccherini are pleasingly graceful, Debussy's "Clair de lune" is tastefully restrained, and the Schumann items are played with genuine affection. It's an appetizing, well-balanced menu, one that recalls long-cherished memories of Pablo Casals, Emanuel Feuermann, Gregor Piatigorsky and others in similar fare, but without in any way attempting to replicate their very individual styles. A very pleasant diversion, beautifully recorded.

Alfred Cortot Piano works by Albéniz, Chopin, Debussy, Fauré, Liszt, Mendelssohn, Ravel,
   Saint-Saëns, Scriabin and Weber. **Alfred Cortot** (pf). Biddulph mono Ⓜ LHW014/15* (two discs:
   133 minutes: ADD: 10/94). From Victor originals; recorded 1919-25.   Ⓖ
Cortot was, arguably, the most vivacious of all keyboard sophisticates, one whose dazzling mind and fingers flashed with a happy disregard for mere accuracy or musical propriety. Like the heroine of Muriel Spark's novel, *The Prime of Miss Jean Brodie*, Cortot proclaimed that beauty and truth rather than safety always came first. With exemplary completeness Biddulph present in this invaluable two-disc set Cortot's complete acoustic recordings, admirably transferred by Ward Marston from records dating from 1919-25. Cortot's inimitable wit and seduction grace Albéniz's *Triana* as well as *Seguidilla* and *Malagueña*, and two Fauré items offer further enchantment. Elsewhere there is a reminder in Cortot's death-defying spin through Saint-Saëns's *Etude en forme de valse* of a brilliance and rapidity that aroused the awe and envy of Horowitz and, in Scriabin's D sharp minor *Etude*, of a blazing rhetoric and insinuation that suggest total sympathy for the Russian romantic idiom. Alas, there are savage cuts in several pieces (Chopin's Op. 22 *Grande Polonaise*, minus its introductory *Andante Spianato*, is butchered virtually beyond recognition, the price of early recording techniques. This would also explain a pell-mell rush in several other works (try the 1923 Chopin *Berceuse*). Yet Cortot was always happy to risk a speeding ticket rather than modify his mood of the moment in the interests of mere expediency.

Alfred Cortot Piano Works by Albéniz, Bach, Brahms, Chopin, Handel, Liszt, Purcell, Saint-
   Saëns and Schubert. **Alfred Cortot** (pf). Biddulph mono Ⓜ LHW020* (77 minutes: ADD: 5/95).
   From HMV and Victor originals; recorded 1925-39.   ⒼⒼ
Biddulph have unearthed some astonishing gems. Cortot's whirl through Albéniz's *Malagueña* and joyous charge through the *Seguidillas* (a kind of Spanish *Chopsticks*) may be familiar, but what of *Sous la Palmier*? Here Cortot spins a tale beneath the palms that would seduce a saint. As the insert-note so nicely puts it, all these performances have "an almost tangible Iberian heat", a lilt and insinuation that can make even the redoubtable Alicia de Larrocha sound sober and lacking in *joie de vivre*. Schubert's *12 Ländler*, D681, too, seem to dance off the page, and in the *Arioso* from Bach's F minor Concerto (the pianist's own arrangement) Cortot shows himself an incomparable 'singer' of the keyboard. Even his finest partners in artistry (and they include Dame Maggie Teyte and Gérard Souzay) must have marvelled at that exquisitely floating *pianissimo* and his alternately full and delicate *cantabile*. Then there is Cortot's Purcell selection, all within style but with that instantly recognizable rhythmic spring and vivacity, yet another recording of Saint-Saëns's *Etude en forme de valse* (which made Horowitz pale with envy) and Chopin performances as sprightly and elemental as any on record. The *Berceuse*'s figurations foam and race with a happy disregard for tranquillity yet the playing is as mesmeric as it is iridescent. And although the First *Ballade* and Second *Impromptu* are periodically invaded by inaccuracies like swarms of locusts, nothing can detract from Cortot's innate elegance, fire and poetry. Ward Marston's transfers are exemplary, beautifully transcending age and crackles to capture performances which make most contemporary piano playing seem as insignificant as chaff in the wind.

Piano Works Shura Cherkassky (pf); [a]**Philharmonia Orchestra / Anatole Fistoulari.** Testament
   mono Ⓔ SBT1033* (62 minutes: ADD: 9/94). Recorded 1952-8.   Ⓖ
   Liszt Piano Concerto No. 1 in E flat major, S124[a] (from HMV DB9763/4, 10/52). Liebestraum
   in A flat major, S541 No. 3 (HMV 7ER5113, 1/59). Réminiscences de Don Juan (Mozart), S418
   (HMV ALP1154, 10/54). Hungarian Rhapsody No. 13 in A minor, S244. Faust (Gounod) -
   Waltz, S407. **Saint-Saëns** Le carnaval des animaux - Le cygne. **Liadov** A musical snuffbox,
   Op. 32 (all from ALP1527, 11/57).
Here, in excellent transfers of HMV recordings dating from the 1950s, is a vintage Cherkassky recital. Mercurial and hypnotic, his way with Liszt's E flat Concerto reminds us in every nook and cranny that he has always been able to enliven and transform even the most over-familiar score. True, there are moments – such as the start of the *Allegro vivace* – where he is less than ideally poised or balletic (one of those instances where his elfin caprice can seem close to uncertainty and where he leads Fistoulari and the Philharmonia a Puckish dance: now you hear me, now you don't), yet his sparkle and charm are inimitable. Again, in Var. 1 of the *Don Juan* Fantasy he is perhaps more flustered than *elegantamente*, but even when his virtuosity is less than watertight, his playing is infinitely more fascinating and imaginatively varied. Cherkassky can be garrulous or somnolent, his phrasing languorous or choppy, yet in the ecstatic, long-breathed descent just before the coda of the *Liebestraum* No. 3 and in all of the *Hungarian Rhapsody* No. 13 and the *Faust* Waltz, his mastery has seldom sounded more effortless or unalloyed. Finally, two encores of *friandises*: Godowsky's fine-spun elaboration of Saint-Saëns's "Le cygne",

Shura Cherkassky Live, Volume 3. **Shura Cherkassky** (pf). Decca Ⓕ 433 650-2DH (63 minutes: ADD: 6/93). Recorded between 1973 and 1991. *Gramophone Editor's choice.*   Ⓖ Ⓖ
   Chopin Piano Sonatas – No. 2 in B flat minor, Op. 35; No. 3 in B minor, Op. 58. Fantasie in F minor, Op. 49.

There are few pianists around who have the innate intelligence and resourcefulness to explore the possibilities of a score as does Cherkassky. His mastery of tone-colour is unique, where there are so many musicians who fail to produce an individual piano sound. Always more at home in the recital hall, where he can be in complete control of the proceedings, he commands the attention not as a musician too frequently capable of distorting a score, but as a man wholly dedicated to communicating the beauty and drama of the music he plays. Of course, one accepts and embraces some of the weird and wonderful inner lines that surface in familiar pieces by Chopin, but these highlights serve to add to the polyphonic richness of the score, rather than detract from the overall effect. Taken from live recitals, the sound-quality varies but is nearly always true to Cherkassky's tone. Altogether, not be missed by anyone who loves really fine piano-playing.

New review

Shura Cherkassky Live, Volumes 7 and 8. **Shura Cherkassky** (pf). Decca Ⓕ 433 657-2DH and 433 655-2DH (two discs, oas: 79 and 68 minutes: ADD: 2/96). Recorded at BBC broadcasts between 1973 and 1989.   Ⓖ
   433 657-2DH – **Scriabin** Piano Sonata No. 4 in F sharp major, Op. 30. **Stravinsky** Petrushka – Three movements. **Ravel** Piano Sonatine. **Berg** Piano Sonata, Op. 1. **Messiaen** Etudes de rythme – Ile de feu I; Ile de feu II. **Britten** Holiday diary, Op. 5. **Copland** (arr. Bernstein) El salón México. *433 655-2PH* – **Mendelssohn** Prelude and Fugue in E minor, Op. 35 No. 1. **Bach** (arr. Busoni) Toccata, Adagio and Fugue in C major, BWV564. **Brahms** Variations on a Theme by Paganini, Op. 35 – Book 2. **Tchaikovsky** Theme and Variations, Op. 19 No. 6. **Rachmaninov** Variations on a theme of Corelli, Op. 42.

No other pianist has left his mark with such teasing idiosyncrasy or with such fluid and scintillating pianism. Nothing is fixed, everything is seemingly improvised on the spot, new colours, angles and perspectives coming to him willy-nilly, on the spur of the moment. He can induce smiles and frowns, provoke pleasure and irritation, acceptance and rejection in equal proportions but he is always true to himself. As he himself puts it with delightful vagueness, "I just play the way I play". *Petrushka* is the star in this particular firmament of performances. Melodic patterns vanish and appear like rabbits from a conjuror's hat and it is difficult to recall a reading, save from Cherkassky himself, more mischievously or acutely characterized. In Scriabin's Fourth Sonata Cherkassky gives new meaning to terms such as *dolce* (from him invariably *dolcissimo*) and his flight through the concluding *prestissimo* flashes and sparkles with one piquant off-the-cuff surprise after another. In the *Paganini* Variations (Book 2 only, alas) Cherkassky resolves Brahms's daunting opacity with elfin and magisterial ease, his Mendelssohn is a marvel of colour, novelty and adventure and in romantically hyphenated Bach he relishes every opportunity for experiment and textural realignment. His Ravel is quirky but never less than affectionate and he even manages a sense of occasion for Britten's vapid *Holiday diary*. Finally, Cherkassky's Berg may be more garrulous than lucid, but it is always fascinating. The majority of these performances date from the 1980s; both discs are lavishly illustrated and documented and the recordings, given their provenance, are brilliantly faithful. And so although you may feel, like the protagonists in Robert Graves's *The Troll's Nosegay*, "awed, charmed, distracted, a trifle piqued ... who knows?" you will never remain indifferent, not for a minute, not for a second.

English Organ Music Gareth Green (org). Naxos Ⓢ 8 550582 (64 minutes: DDD: 3/93). Played on the organ of Chesterfield Parish Church. Recorded 1991.
   C.S. Lang Tuba tune. **Howells** Three Psalm-Preludes (Set 1), Op. 32. **Elgar** Organ Sonata No. 1 in G major, Op. 28. **Vaughan Williams** Three Preludes on Welsh Hymn Tunes – Rhosymedre. **Whitlock** Hymn Preludes – Darwall's 148th; Song 13. **Cocker** Tuba tune.

Most large English church and cathedral organs boast at least one tuba stop – making a huge, fat, trumpet-like noise so powerful it can overwhelm every other stop on the organ. The *Tuba tune*, of which there are two classic examples on this CD, is a uniquely English creation in which the tuba stop is pitted against the rest of the instruments in a light-hearted, tuneful battle. C.S. Lang's jovial romp with its instantly singable tune is certainly the most famous tuba tunes of all while Norman Cocker's slightly more demanding one runs it a close second. The Chesterfield organ possesses a fine tuba which brings these two pieces thrillingly to life in this thoroughly enjoyable CD. The remainder of the programme represents the very best of early twentieth-century English organ music with a handful of characteristic pieces; memorable for their fine melodies and stirring qualities. Gareth Green has an instinctive feel for this music and plays it all with great aplomb and this organ suits it to a tee – although Naxos's recording might have been a little clearer.

French Organ Works Simon Lindley (org). Naxos Ⓢ 8 550581 (74 minutes: DDD: 3/93). Played on the organ of Leeds Parish Church. Recorded 1991.
   Guilmant Grand Choeur in D major, "alla Handel". Cantilene pastorale, Op. 19.
   Vierne 24 Pièces en stile libre, Op. 31 – Epitaphe; Berceuse. Stele pour un enfant défunte.

M-A. Charpentier Te Deum, H146 – Prelude. **Langlais** Trois méditations (1962). **Bonnet**
Romance sans paroles. **de Maleingreau** Suite mariale. **Boëllmann** Suite gothique, Op. 25.
Widor Symphony No. 5 in F minor, Op. 42 No. 1 – Toccata.

Two of the most popular organ showpieces are here – Widor's Toccata and the Toccata which comes
as the last movement of Boëllmann's *Suite gothique*. In addition there is the majestic *Te Deum* Prelude
by Charpentier (familiar to a wide audience as the Eurovision signature tune) and the gentle *Berceuse*
which Vierne wrote for his baby daughter. Alongside these evergreens, mainstays of any organ-lover's
CD collection, are some more unusual but no less enjoyable pieces: Guilmant's glorious *Grand Choeur
"alla Handel"*, Bonnet's delightful *Romance sans paroles* and Paul de Maleingreau's *Suite mariale*. In
short, a real feast of some of the best French organ music. Simon Lindley, organist at the musically-
renowned Leeds Parish Church, gives fine, no-nonsense performances which should appeal especially
to those exploring this music for the first time. The organ makes a super noise, and the Naxos
recording is highly commendable. It may not be an instrument of which the *cognoscenti* of French
organ music would immediately approve, but there is enough sensitivity and interpretative insight in
Lindley's performances to make this a worthwhile buy for casual listener and specialist alike.

From Stanley to Wesley, Volume 6. **Jennifer Bate** (org). Unicorn-Kanchana Ⓔ DKPCD9106
(65 minutes: DDD; 11/91). Played on the organs of Adlington Hall, Cheshire; The Dolmetsch
Collection, Haslemere, Surrey; The Chapel of St Michael's Mount, Cornwall; The Iveagh Bequeast,
Kenwood, London; Killerton House, Broadclyst, Exeter, Devon and The Chapel of Our Lady and
St Everilda, Everingham, Yorkshire. Recorded 1989-91. *Selected by Sounds in Retrospect.* Ⓖ
Boyce Voluntary in D major. **Handel** Fugue in G major. Voluntary in C major.
Heron Voluntary in G major. **Hook** Voluntary in C minor. **Russell** Voluntary in F major.
Stanley Voluntaries – A minor, Op. 6 No. 2; D minor, Op. 7 No. 4; G major, Op. 7 No. 9.
Stubley Voluntary in C major. **S. Wesley** Voluntaries – E flat major, Op. 6 No. 7; B flat major.

Whilst most people would regard Bach and his North German contemporaries as synonymous with
all that is best in eighteenth-century organ music there was also a significant school of organist-
composers thriving in England. Chief amongst these was John Stanley whose music was greatly
admired at the time, in particular by a recent immigrant from Germany, one George Frederic Handel
(two fine examples of his own organ music are to be found on this CD). But while the German
composers were writing for their great, majestic organs, their English counterparts were faced with
something far humbler in scope and more delicate and intimate in character. To hear this music played
on such an instrument is to have its true beauty revealed: here it is played not just on one authentic
contemporaneous instrument, but the Unicorn-Kanchana team have scoured the length and breadth
of England, from Cornwall to Yorkshire, to unearth six classic, and virtually unaltered examples.
Jennifer Bate's immense musical and technical powers and her innate, native sense of style, imbues this
disc with compelling musical authority which, added to the captivating sound of these six delightful
organs, makes it an intriguing historical document – real 'living history', if you like. This CD is the
sixth in a series and while each is a valuable addition to the recorded legacy of English music, this one
in particular gives the less specialist collector a representative and varied selection of this wonderful,
yet woefully overlooked area of our musical heritage.

New review

Grand Piano

The Polish Virtuoso [a]Josef Hofmann, [b]Ignaz Friedman, [c]Ignaz Jan Paderewski (pfs). Nimbus
Ⓜ NI8802* (71 minutes: DDD: 12/95). From piano rolls released between 1919 and 1932.
Hofmann Impressions for Piano – No. 3, The Sanctuary[a]. Kaleidoscope, Op. 40 No. 4[a].
Moszkowski La jongleuse, Op. 52 No. 4[a]. Etincelles, Op. 36 No. 6[a]. Serenata, Op. 15 No. 1[b].
Guitarre, Op. 45 No. 2[a]. Caprice espagnol, Op. 37[a]. **Friedman** Viennese Waltzes on Themes
from Gärtner – Nos. 1-4[b]. Estampes, Op. 22 – Nos. 2 and 4[b]. Elle danse, Op. 10 No. 5[b].
Paderewski Humoresques de concert, Op. 14[c] – No. 1, Minuet; No. 3, Caprice; No. 6,
Cracovienne fantastique. Miscellanea, Op. 16[c] – No. 1, Légende in A flat major; No. 4, Nocturne
in B flat major. Mélodie, Op. 8 No. 3[c].
Chopin Piano Sonata No. 2 in B flat minor, Op. 35. Nocturnes – D flat major, Op. 27 No. 2;
F minor, Op. 55 No. 1. Polonaises – A major, Op. 40 No. 1; A flat major, Op. 53. Scherzos –
No. 1 in B minor, Op. 20; No. 3 in C sharp minor, Op. 39. Waltz in A flat major, Op. 42. Berceuse
in D flat major, Op. 57. **Josef Hofmann** (pf). Nimbus Ⓜ NI8803* (76 minutes: DDD: 12/95).
From piano rolls released between 1920 and 1927.

These performances taken from Duo-Art rolls made between 1915 and 1930 are played, via a 'robot'
created in 1973, on a modern concert Steinway under the supervision of Gerald Stonehill, a world
authority on the Duo-Art catalogue. As a result, they sound as vivid and sparkling as if they had been
given yesterday – indeed, so vivid is the piano tone that it emphasizes brightness at the expense of
warmth. To some extent this may be due to the difference in tone-quality between the instruments on
which the recordings were made and that used for the reproduction, but sneaking doubts remain
about the matching of the robot's responses, resulting in some lack of really soft passages.

Doubts about realism are lessened by a performance of Chopin's 'funeral march' Sonata by
Hofmann (Cherkassky's teacher), revered by contemporaries such as Rachmaninov. Though the
dynamic range in the piece is not large (the limitations being at the *ff* end), it sounds a convincingly

natural reading. But better still are the A flat *Polonaise*, which boasts a fine crisp *élan*, the B minor *Scherzo*, which employs a very full dynamic range and, like the C sharp minor *Scherzo*, illustrates the real meaning of *Presto con fuoco*, and a delicately pearly A flat *Waltz*. The *Berceuse*, coolly played, slightly suffers from a weakness also found elsewhere in the series – too obtrusive a middle register in relation to the melody above, whether due to the voicing of the piano or to a miscalculation in the adjustment of Duo-Art's two dynamic systems ('accompaniment' and 'theme').Hofmann is heard again, and at his stunning best, on the disc devoted to three Polish virtuosos. A group of five pieces by his teacher Moszkowski is notable for perfectly controlled staccato touch, vital rhythmicality, neat rapid repeated notes and some delectable lightness; and two works of his own show limpid arpeggios (*La jongleuse*) and breath-taking mercurial virtuosity (*Kaleidoscope*).

Ignaz Friedman is represented by Moszkowksi's once popular *Serenata* and by a handful of his own pieces in which he can display the superb technique for which he was famous. There is undeniably an air of exhibitionism about *Elle danse* and the elaborate fantasias on waltz themes by a singer friend (No. 3 particularly lavishly ornate); but with such coruscating playing who would want to complain? Paderewski did not have the natural facility of the others – he was a late starter – but attracted huge and adoring crowds everywhere and was the most highly paid. There is a sparkle about his lively "Caprice" in the style of Scarlatti and a quite attractive, if conventional, nationalist feeling in the "Cracovienne fantastique". The series is provided with first-class notes and Nimbus are to be applauded for their courageous enterprise.

Great European Organs, Volume 26. **Keith John** (org). Priory ℗ PRCD370 (73 minutes: DDD: 11/92). Played on the organ of Gloucester Cathedral, UK. Recorded 1991. *Selected by Sounds in Retrospect.* ⓖⓖⓖ

Stanford Fantasia and Toccata in D minor, Op. 57. **Reger** Five Easy Preludes and Fugues, Op. 56 – No. 1 in E major. **Shostakovich** Lady Macbeth of the Mtsensk district – Passacaglia. **Schmidt** Chaconne in C sharp minor. **Ravanello** Theme and Variations in B minor.

On the face of it this CD might look as if its appeal is purely for those with a specialist taste in large-scale post-romantic organ music. Certainly Schmidt's gargantuan *Chaconne* represents a daunting prospect both to player and listener, while Shostakovich's only organ solo begins with the kind of chilling dissonance which would certainly scare off those of a delicate disposition. Similarly neither Stanford nor Reger usually attract a crowd when their organ music played – and who has ever heard of Ravanello? But if ever a recording was made to shatter preconceptions, this is it. For a start the Gloucester organ makes a wondrous sound and Priory's recording is in a class of its own; in terms of sound alone this surely ranks as one of the best ever CDs of organ music. Then Keith John quite literally pulls out all the stops to produce an unparalleled display of virtuosity and musicianship. His technical prowess turns the Schmidt into a thrilling *tour de force* while few could question, after hearing his performances, that the Stanford is one of the best works ever written by a British composer or that Ravanello's music doesn't deserve the neglect it currently suffers. An essential disc in anyone's CD collection – what more is there to say?

Great European Organs, Volume 36. **Marie-Bernadette Dufourcet** (org). Priory ℗ PRCD422 (67 minutes: DDD: 6/95). Played on the Cavaillé-Coll organ of Notre-Dame-des-Champs, Paris. Recorded 1992.

Barié Trois Pièces, Op. 7. **R. Vierne** Six pièces de différents caractères. **d'Indy** Prélude in E flat minor, Op. 66. **Roussel** Prelude and Fughetta, Op. 41. **Honegger** Fugue and Chorale. **Dupré** Scherzo, Op. 16. **Langlais** Prelude and Fugue, Op. 1. **L. Vierne** Pièces de fantaisie, Op. 55 – Les cloches de Hinckley.

This is an immensely rewarding programme concentrating on works written between 1911 and 1929 and finding, not least in the six pieces by René Vierne (Louis's brother), true gems of great charm and individuality which really deserve to be better known. It is good, too, to have such authoritative performances of Honegger's two dark, almost tragic contributions to the instrument's repertoire as well as Vincent d'Indy's once popular *Prélude* in E flat minor (*not* B minor as the booklet suggests). The recording is first-rate, the performances infinitely satisfying but the booklet is inadequate.

New review

Great European Organs, Volume 41. **Roger Sayer** (org). Priory ℗ PRCD495 (76 minutes: DDD: 4/96). Played on the Klais organ of the Hallgrímskirkja, Reykjavík. Recorded 1994.

Bach Prelude and Fugue in D major, BWV532. Clavier-Ubung III, BWV669-89 – Christe, aller Welt Trost, BWV670. **Bonnal** Paysages Euskariens. **Langlais** Triptyque. **B. Ferguson** South and West Suite. **Dupré** Evocation, Op. 37 – Allegro deciso. Recorded 1994.

Here is an organ which makes a truly dazzling sound. Its 32-foot pedal reeds and three ranks of *chamade* Trumpets certainly add pizzazz to Bach's D major Prelude and Fugue. Roger Sayer gives first-rate performances which are both musically perceptive and technically assured – no sense here of allowing the thrill of the instrument to subvert musical integrity. The French works, particularly Langlais's divine *Triptyque*, sound absolutely spectacular, as does a remarkably French-sounding Suite, ostensibly reflecting aspects of the very English county of Devon, by Sayer's predecessor at Rochester Cathedral, Barry Ferguson. The hefty sound of this instrument reflects its bulk – apparently it weighs 25 tons. A pointless statistic, maybe, but without it we would learn precious little about the instrument from the accompanying booklet and the minimalist notes on the music are pitiful. When the music, the playing and the recording quality are as outstanding as this, it seems a shame to mar the result with shabby accompanying documentation.

New review

Myra Hess 1938-42 HMV Recordings. **Dame Myra Hess** (pf). Biddulph mono ① LHW025*
(76 minutes: ADD: 3/96). Recorded 1938-42.　　　　　　　　　　　　　　　　　Ⓖ
　　Schumann Carnaval, Op. 9 (from C3008/10, 6/38). **Matthay** Elves, Op. 17. Stray Fancies,
　　Op. 22 (both from B8758, 8/38). **Bach** (arr. Hess) Cantata No. 147, Herz und Mund und Tat und
　　Leben – Jesu, bleibet meine Freude ("Jesu, joy of man's desiring"). **D. Scarlatti** Keyboard
　　Sonata in G major, Kk14 (B9035, 4/40). **Brahms** Piano Pieces, Op. 76 – No. 2, Capriccio in
　　B minor; No. 3, Intermezzo in A flat major (B9189, 8/41). Capriccio in D minor, Op. 116 No. 7.
　　Intermezzo in E flat major, Op. 117 No. 1. Intermezzo in C major, Op. 119 No. 3 (all from
　　C3226, 6/41). **Ferguson** Piano Sonata in F minor, Op. 8 (C3335/7, 5/43).
Those who, sadly, retain an image of Dame Myra Hess as either a sober-suited pianist inclined towards severity or a 'graciousness' that excluded the toughest, most durable virtues, are in for a surprise. For here, on this truly glorious record, she ranges effortlessly from sheer wit and style (Schumann's *Carnaval*) to a dancing rhythmic magic (Scarlatti), from a glowing poetic inwardness (all the Brahms, with perhaps Op. 76 No. 3 as the distantly shining star of the set) to a matchless eloquence (Howard Ferguson's tragic masterpiece, his 1938-40 Piano Sonata). Yet all such qualities are seamlessly joined. Nothing is forced and whether you consider her regal tonal resource (tirelessly celebrated by Stephen Kovacevich, her finest pupil), or a naturalness and candour easy to underestimate, everything is achieved with supreme authority; an illusion achieved by only the truest artists. What an object-lesson, then, for today's harassed young pianists, jostling for attention in an increasingly commercial market-place, a reminder of a poetic and speculative artistry beyond price. Finally, David Lennick's transfers are masterly and Wayne Kiley's notes refer movingly to the legendary wartime National Gallery concerts held in London, where Hess's performances created an "indelible image of hope and vision in adversity".

Historic Organs, Volume 1. **Various artists.** Beulah mono Ⓔ 1PD5* (63 minutes: ADD: 9/94).
　　From HMV originals; recorded 1926-31 on the organs of [a]Alexandra Palace and [b]Queen's Hall,
　　London.
　　Reginald Goss-Custard – MacDowell[a], Saint-Saëns[a] and Watling[b] **Sir George Thalben-Ball**[a] –
　　Sibelius, Wagner and S. Wesley. **George D. Cunningham**[a] – Elgar and Widor. **J. Arthur Meale**[b] –
　　Batiste. **Albert Schweitzer**[b] – Bach. **Marcel Dupré**[b] – Clérambault, Daquin, Franck and
　　Saint-Saëns.
This disc allows us to hear the Alexandra Palace organ at the peak of its condition. Behind a thin veneer of hiss (which the ear quickly gets used to, anyway) the sound has remarkable depth and perspective and the innate character of both these magnificent organs, not to mention the contrasting acoustic of the two famous London halls, is vividly resurrected in Beulah's stunning remastering. How many brides wish the organist at their wedding had performed Wagner's Bridal chorus from *Lohengrin* with the virility of Thalben-Ball? His playing, particularly in Wesley's *Holsworthy Church Bells* complete with tubular bells, seems to have boundless energy and a wonderful sense of style, as does G.D. Cunningham's, who brings magisterial flair to a stirring Elgar Sonata. On the long-lost Queen's Hall organ, we have two famous players in repertoire with which they will always be closely associated: Dupré performing at great speed French music from Clérambault to Saint-Saëns and Schweitzer rather more sedately expounding his interpretative views on Bach. If most of us have had to rely on hearsay to justify our respect for these organists' reputations, then here we have convincing testament to their legendary status – in particular Schweitzer's performance of the Prelude and Fugue in E minor, BWV533, which surely overwhelms all advances in Bach scholarship and performance practice to stand as an interpretation of signal stature.

Vladimir Horowitz Piano works. **Vladimir Horowitz** (pf). RCA Victor Gold Seal mono/[a]stereo
Ⓜ GD60377* (65 minutes: ADD: 6/92).　　　　　　　　　　　　　　　　　　Ⓖ Ⓖ Ⓖ
　　Prokofiev Piano Sonata No. 7 in B flat major, Op. 83 (from RB6555, 12/63. Recorded 1945).
　　Toccata, Op. 11. **Poulenc** Presto in B flat major (both from HMV DB6971, 1947).
　　Barber Piano Sonata in E flat major, Op. 26 (RB6555, 1950). **Kabalevsky** Piano Sonata No. 3,
　　Op. 46 (new to UK. 1947). **Fauré** Nocturne No. 13 in B minor, Op. 119[a] (RL12548, 2/78. 1977).
Even today, when there is a six-deep queue of virtuosos who, laid end to end, would stretch halfway round the world, Vladimir Horowitz's playing is something to make the listener gasp and sit up. He has been called, with justification, "the greatest pianist alive or dead". Horowitz was associated with all three of the sonatas on this disc from their very beginnings. Prokofiev wrote his Seventh Sonata in 1942, and Horowitz gave the first American performance less than two years later. He sent a copy of this 1945 recording to the composer, and Prokofiev sent him an autographed copy of the score in return, inscribed "to the miraculous pianist from the composer". The performance is indeed superlative, with playing of extraordinary virtuosity, and Horowitz responds with equal flair to the sonata's 'barbaric' and lyrical elements. Kabalevsky's Third Sonata dates from 1946, and Horowitz gave the American première in February 1948, two months after he made this recording. The work is

of lesser stature than the Prokofiev, but its three well-contrasted movements make up an effective enough sonata. Again, Horowitz plays brilliantly and very sympathetically throughout the work. The world première of Barber's Piano Sonata was given by Horowitz in 1949. This piece is brilliantly written and technically extremely demanding to play – a perfect vehicle, in fact, for Horowitz the virtuoso. The great pianist brings great flair to the shorter Poulenc and Prokofiev items: the Fauré was recorded at a later stage of his career, and is played in a more deliberate, though perfectly idiomatic fashion. Four of the items have been transferred from 78s in good sound. The Barber and Fauré come from tape sources and sound well – the latter is even in stereo. This is a disc all pianists and piano enthusiasts should have – and it's mid price too!

Vladimir Horowitz The Last Recording. **Vladimir Horowitz** (pf). Sony Classical Ⓕ SK45818
(58 minutes: DDD: 8/90). Recorded 1989.   ⒼⒼⒼ
  Haydn Piano Sonata in E flat major, HobXVI/49. **Chopin** Mazurka in C minor, Op. 56
  No. 3. Nocturnes – E flat major, Op. 55 No. 2; B major, Op. 62 No. 1. Fantaisie-impromptu in
  C sharp minor, Op. 66. Etudes – A flat major, Op. 25 No. 1; E minor, Op. 25 No. 5. **Liszt**
  "Weinen, Klagen, Sorgen, Zagen", Präludium, S179. **Wagner/Liszt** Paraphrase on Isolde's
  Liebestod from "Tristan und Isolde", S447.
More than any other pianist of his generation, Vladimir Horowitz was a legend in his lifetime, not only for his staggering technique but also for the personality and authority of his playing. Other pianists such as Rubinstein and Arrau may have been finer all-rounders (there were gaps in his repertory even in the classical and romantic field), but none has left so many performances distinguished by a special individuality that is covered, though hardly explained, by the word magic. As Murray Perahia has written, from the point of view of a pianist over 40 years his junior, "he was a man who gave himself completely through his music and who confided his deepest emotions through his playing". The performances in this last of his recordings, made in New York in 1989 and with superlative piano sound, are wonderfully crystalline and beautifully articulated, yet there is warmth, too, in the Haydn sonata that begins his programme and nothing whatever to suggest that octogenarian fingers were feeling their age or that his fine ear had lost its judgement. The rest of the disc is devoted to Chopin and Liszt, two great romantic composers with whom he was always associated, the last piece being Liszt's mighty transcription of Wagner's *Liebestod*, in which the piano becomes a whole operatic orchestra topped by a soprano voice singing out her love for the last time. Apparently this was the last music Horowitz ever played, and no more suitable ending can be imagined for a great pianistic career informed by a consuming love of music that was expressed in playing of genius. A uniquely valuable record.

The Hungarian Anthology Peter Frankl (pf). ASV Ⓕ CDDCA860 (78 minutes: DDD: 6/93).
Recorded 1992.   ⒼⒼⒼ
  Liszt Csárdás macabre, S224. **Dohnányi** Gavotte and Musette. **Kodály** Seven Pieces, Op. 11.
  Bartók (trans. cpsr.) Dance Suite, Sz77. **Weiner** Three Hungarian Rural Dances. **Kurtág** Plays
  and Games for Piano, Book 3 – excerpts. **Szöllösy** Paesaggio con morti.
An important reminder, this, of how and where Hungarian piano music is progressing. The last piece of Peter Frankl's programme dates from 1988; the *Paesaggio con morti* by András Szöllösy, an impressive, 11-minute study in musical shades and textures. Working back from there, and tracing the general direction of Szöllösy's route, is a relatively simple task. Oddly, Kodály more than Bartók seems – in this case, at least – the overriding influence: his *Seven Pieces*, Op. 11 have never sounded more engaging than here, and the largest of them, "Epitaphe", is surely among the composer's most dramatic inspirations. With György Kurtág's *Plays and Games for Piano*, credits revert back to Bartók. Leó Weiner's spicy *Hungarian Rural Dances* include a "Ronde de Marosszek"; but here again, it's more Bartók than Kodály who springs to mind. Bartók's own *Dance Suite* is, of course, a pivotal creation in its use of Eastern European and Arabic modes, and the way they are so expertly welded on to the work's overall structure. And then to Dohnányi and Liszt, although the former's pleasant *Gavotte and Musette* seems more a side-long glance at Smetana than an extension of the bold, bald and audacious world of Liszt's menacing *Czárdás macabre*. Here we can locate the seeds of Bartók's mature style, sown not merely among the realms of local folklore (although this disturbing *Csárdás* is profoundly Hungarian in spirit), but deep within the furthest recesses of our collective musical unconscious. Performances and recording are sympathetic.

Les introuvables de Marcelle Meyer, Volume 2. **Marcelle Meyer** (pf). EMI mono Ⓜ CZS5
68092-2* (four discs: 275 minutes: ADD: 6/95). From Les Discophiles Françaises originals;
recorded 1946-55.   ⒼⒼⒼ
  Rameau Pièces de clavecin – Suites: A minor (1706); E minor (1724); D major (1724); A minor
  (c1729); G major (c1729). Quatre Pièces en concert. **F. Couperin** Livres de clavecin, Book 2 –
  Les Barricades Mistérieuses; Passacaille; Book 3 – Les Folies françoises, ou Les Dominos; Les
  Fauvétes Plaintives; Le Dodo, ou L'Amour en berceau; Le Tic-Toc-Choc, ou Les Maillotins; La
  Muse-Plantine; Book 4 – L'Arlequine; Les Ombres Errantes. **D. Scarlatti** 32 Keyboard Sonatas.
  Rossini Péchés de ma vieillesse, Book 5, "Album pour les enfants adolescents" – Ouf! les petits
  pois; Un sauté; Book 8, "Album de château" – Un regret, un espoir; Prélude prétentieux; Book 9
  – La savoie aimante.

Unlike her contemporary, Wanda Landowska, Marcelle Meyer had no mission to rehabilitate the harpsichord, but simply treasured its repertoire on its own merit and was indefatigable in her determination to bring it before as wide an audience as possible. Meyer's Rameau is full of poetic insight, illuminatingly expressive but devoid of any misplaced sentimentality. But inevitably, the more stylistically and technically advanced pieces of the 1724 and c1729 collections fare better on a modern piano than the miniatures of the 1706 anthology, which remains more firmly rooted in the harpsichordist's realm. The other chief beneficiary of this precious four-disc compilation is Domenico Scarlatti, 32 of whose sonatas Meyer recorded in the 1950s. Not a single disappointment awaits the listener here. Her athletic technique, her love of clearly defined articulation and her unfailingly lucid textures are but among the more obvious qualities in her playing; over and above that are her ability to capture and sustain a particular effect and her feeling for the underlying poetry of Scarlatti's music. There are delights, too, to be found among the Couperin pieces – Meyer carefully chose those which lend themselves to the piano – and a selection of five pieces from Rossini's *Péchés de ma vieillesse*. Meyer was an artist who was skilled in evoking a wide spectrum of moods but it was in the evocation of that quietly contemplative, melancholy spirit that she excelled. The discs have been carefully and effectively remastered and the warm, intimate sound of the piano is a constant pleasure.

Piet Kee at the Concertgebouw Piet Kee (org). Chandos Ⓕ CHAN9188 (72 minutes: DDD: 10/93). Recorded 1993.
Franck Fantaisie in A major. **Mendelssohn** Organ Sonata in C major/minor. **Schumann** Fugue on B-A-C-H, Op. 60 No. 3. **Andriessen** Sonata da chiesa. **Saint-Saëns** Fantaisie in C major, Op. 157. **Alain** Deuxième fantaisie. Le jardin suspendu. **Messiaen** Les corps glorieux Joie et clarté des corps glorieux.

Kee has made an ingenious choice of pieces which all treat the organ orchestrally, while at the same time finding some of these composers' finest, yet less familiar, creations. Alain's *Deuxième fantaisie* ranks considerably higher in musical worth than almost anything else he wrote – and if you doubt this, listen to the stimulating performance here. It is good, too, to see the name of Hendrik Andriessen appear on record again. A couple of decades or so ago he seemed to be all the rage; now representation of his music in the catalogues is minimal, to say the least, and to have his *Sonata da chiesa* back again alone makes this an invaluable release. For the most part these are outstanding performances. Kee is a master in the art of organ colour and, coupled with his meticulous and scholarly approach, one can't seriously question either the authority or sincerity of anything here – from a disarmingly delicate *Jardin suspendu* to a magisterial reading of the Mendelssohn sonata.

Evgeni Kissin in Tokyo Evgeni Kissin (pf). Sony Classical Ⓕ SK45931 (73 minutes: DDD: 11/90). Recorded live in 1987. ⓠⓠ
Rachmaninov Lilacs, Op. 21 No. 5. Etudes tableaux, Op. 39 – No. 1 in C minor; No. 5 in E flat minor. **Prokofiev** Piano Sonata No. 6 in A major, Op. 82. **Liszt** Concert Studies, S144 – La leggierezza; Waldestrauschen. **Chopin** Nocturne in A flat major, Op. 32 No. 2. Polonaise in F sharp minor, Op. 44. **Scriabin** Mazurka in E minor, Op. 25 No. 3. Etude in C sharp minor, Op. 42 No. 5. **Anonymous** (arr. Saegusa) Natu – Wa Kinu. Todai – Mori. Usagi.

One reason for buying this CD is that it contains dazzling piano playing by a 15-year-old Russian set fair for a career of the highest distinction. A better reason is that the recital contains as full a revelation of the genius of Prokofiev as any recording ever made in any medium. The Sixth Sonata is the first of a trilogy which sums up the appalling sufferings of Russia under Stalin in a way only otherwise found in Shostakovich's 'middle' symphonies. Kissin plays it with all the colour and force of a full orchestra and all the drama and structural integrity of a symphony, plus a kind of daredevilry that even he may find difficult to recapture. As for the rest of the recital only the Rachmaninov pieces are as memorable as the Prokofiev, though everything else is immensely impressive (the Japanese encore-pieces are trivial in the extreme, however). Microphone placing is very close, presumably in order to minimize audience noise; but the playing can take it, indeed it may even be said to benefit from it.

New review

Fritz Kreisler The Complete Victor Recordings. **Fritz Kreisler** (vn) with various artists. RCA Victor Gold Seal mono Ⓜ 09026 61649-2* (11 discs: 781 minutes: ADD). Recorded 1910-46. ⓠ
Works by Albéniz, Bach, Balogh, Bass, Beethoven, Berlin, Bizet, Boccherini, Braga, Brahms, Böhm, Cadman, Chaminade, Chopin, Cottenet, De Curtis, Dawes, Debussy, Dohnányi, Drdla, Dvořák, Earl, Falla, Foster, Friedberg, Friml, Gärtner, Gluck, Godard, Godowsky, Gounod, Grainger, Granados, Grieg, Handel, Haydn, Herbert, Heuberger, Hirsch, Hubbell, Jacobi, Johnson, Korngold, Koschat, Koželuch, Krakauer, Kramer, Kreisler, Lalo, Lehár, Lemare, Leroux, Liliuokalani, Logan, Mascagni, Massenet, Mendelssohn, Meyer-Helmund, Moszkowski, Nevin, Offenbach, Openshaw, Owen, Paderewski, Paganini, Poldini, Rachmaninov, Raff, Rameau, Ravel, Rimsky-Korsakov, Romberg, Schubert, Schütt, Scott, Seitz, Smetana, Spencer, Tchaikovsky, Thomas, Tosti, Townsend, Valdez, White and Winternitz.

If Jascha Heifetz was the firebrand among virtuosos, Bronislaw Huberman the passionate intellectual and Joseph Szigeti the articulate thinker, Fritz Kreisler was the ultimate gentleman – an easygoing, genial and comforting old-world master whose large discography centres mainly on the many sweetmeats associated with his name. This neatly packaged and beautifully transferred collection of "The Complete Victor Recordings" is in many respects the ultimate tribute: over 200 tracks covering the period 1910-46 and tracing a subtle stylistic curve from the vibrant and quick-wristed performances of the teens to the wistful, elegant and slightly off-colour 1946 recording of Kreisler's Straussian *Viennese Rhapsodic Fantasietta*. However, readers unable to stomach acoustic 78s are duly warned that primitive technology dominates the first six CDs, whereas the rest is made up of generally well-engineered electrical recordings. Still, such was Kreisler's sure projection and richness of tone that, like certain great singers of the period (McCormack being a fair case in point), he triumphed over inadequacies of sound. High points of his early discography include revealing 'one off' recordings of the "Canzonetta" from Tchaikovsky's Violin Concerto and the *Scherzando* from Lalo's *Symphonie espagnole* (both 'first commercial releases'), Kreisler's own arrangement of Chopin's A minor *Mazurka*, Op. 67 No. 4, a truncated Bach Double Concerto with Efrem Zimbalist and the various items with John McCormack.

Kreisler's electrical RCA recordings are dominated, at least in terms of repertoire, by the oft-reissued sonata performances with Rachmaninov, all of them combining violinistic poise with taut, muscular pianism. As to the rest, there are countless gems and a plethora of duplications: six of the *Thaïs* "Méditation", five each of *Caprice viennois*, *Liebesleid* and *Liebesfreud*, four of Dvořák's *Humoresque*, etc. – so many subtle varieties of a single basic conception, whether in terms of colour, rubato or phrasing. Some contrasts are fairly marked; one can think in particular of *Mighty Lak' a Rose*, where the electrical recording with pianist Carl Lamson is so much more stylish than Kreisler's acoustical duet with Geraldine Farrar. Then there are the previously unissued 1929 sessions with Lamson, recorded within weeks of the Wall Street crash (where Kreisler himself lost money): poignant, reflective performances, though technically somewhat stronger than the 1945 recordings with orchestra which coincided almost to the minute with the German surrender. Kreisler's RCA discography is, of course, deficient in one very significant respect: there are no full-length major concertos. Readers are therefore urged to supplement this invaluable set with one or other of Kreisler's Brahms, Beethoven or Mendelssohn concerto recordings (available on either Biddulph or Pearl). "The King of Violinists" (as he was sometimes known) was an undisputed master of musical aperitifs and desserts: taken in moderation, these recordings will give boundless pleasure. Enjoy, certainly – but watch the calories!

The Last Recital for Israel Artur Rubinstein (pf). RCA Victor Red Seal Ⓔ 09026 61160-2
(75 minutes: ADD: 3/93). Recorded 1975.   ⓠⓠ
   Beethoven Piano Sonata No. 23 in F minor, Op. 57, "Appassionata". **Debussy** La plus que lente. Pour le Piano – Prélude. **Schumann** Fantasiestücke, Op. 12. **Chopin** Etudes – C sharp minor, Op. 10 No. 4; E minor, Op. 25 No. 5. Nocturne in F sharp major, Op. 15 No. 2. Polonaise in A flat major, Op. 53.
Ever a supporter of youth in music, Artur Rubinstein gave a special concert in January 1975 at Ambassador College (California) for the benefit of the International Cultural Centre for Youth in Jerusalem; it was merely days before his eighty-eighth birthday. The event was sponsored entirely by contributions, and Rubinstein played to a packed house, which of course was no great surprise. However, what does truly amaze is the vitality and concentration of the performances. It might seem something of a cliché to say that Rubinstein plays the *Appassionata* like a man half his age, but it also happens to be the truth: the sheer energy and panache of the first movement so far exceeds expectations that one finds oneself checking the recording date to make sure that this isn't a reissue of an earlier Rubinstein recording. And in truth, the recording – taken from a video soundtrack – tends, unlike the playing, to sound older than it is. In addition to barnstorming Beethoven and endearingly warm-hearted Schumann, Rubinstein plays two Chopin *Etudes* that, believe it or not, he never recorded commercially: Op. 25 No. 5 and Op. 10 No. 4. Both are remarkable, as is a battle-scarred but riveting A flat major *Polonaise* (a Rubinstein speciality). But best of all is the famous E flat *Nocturne*, Op. 15 No. 2 – an intimate, beautifully phrased performance, so typical of the man and the best possible way to remember him. A simultaneously-released RCA video contains the entire programme, but the best items are on this CD. A life-affirming experience.

Dinu Lipatti The Last Recital. **Dinu Lipatti** (pf). EMI Références mono Ⓜ CDH5 65166-2*
(73 minutes: ADD: 12/94). Items marked [a] from Columbia 33CX1499 (2/58), [b]33CX1500 (2/58).
Recorded live in 1950.   ⓠⓠⓠ
   Bach Partita in B flat major, BWV825[a]. **Mozart** Piano Sonata No. 8 in A minor, K310/K300*d*[a].
Schubert Impromptus, D899[a] – No. 2 in E flat major; No. 3 in G flat major. **Chopin** Waltzes[b] – No. 1 and Nos. 3-14.
Apart from the two Schubert *Impromptus*, the programme of Lipatti's last recital consisted of works he had recorded only some ten weeks earlier for EMI, in a Geneva studio, while enjoying a miraculous cortisone-wrought new lease of life. However, when honouring this Besançon Festival engagement on September 16th, 1950, very much against the advice of his doctors, leukaemia had once more gained the upper hand. Less than three months later he was dead, aged only 33. As those of us who have long cherished the original LPs already know, the only evidence of weakness was the omission of the last of the concluding Chopin *Waltzes* (in his own favoured sequence, that in A flat major, Op. 34 No. 2). For the rest, the recital stands as "one of the great musical and human statements, a testimony to his

[Lipatti's] transcendental powers, an almost frightening assertion of mind over matter" as the sympathetic introductory note puts it in the insert-booklet. One has to marvel at the clarity of articulation and part-playing in the Bach Partita, at once so attentive to craftsmanly cunning yet so arrestingly unpedagogic and alive. For Mozart he finds a wonderfully translucent sound-world, rich in subtleties of colouring – not least in the slow movement's laden song. And as in the two Schubert *Impromptus*, the musical message is all the more affecting for its totally selfless simplicity and purity of expression. Even if just one or two of the *Waltzes* might be thought too fast, with over-swift internal tempo changes for contrasting episodes, his gossamer lightness of touch and mercurial imaginative fancy explain why his way with them has now acquired legendary status. The only small regret is that this most excellently remastered medium-price CD deprives us of the endearingly spontaneous extended arpeggio with which Lipatti prefaced the opening Partita, as if in greeting to his instrument, and likewise the improvisatory modulation with which he carried his Besançon listeners from Bach's B flat major to Mozart's A minor.

Nocturnal Julian Bream (gtr). EMI Ⓟ CDC7 54901-2 (73 minutes: DDD: 4/94). Recorded 1992.
    Martin Quatre Pièces Brèves. **Britten** Nocturnal after John Dowland, Op. 70. **Brouwer** Guitar Sonata. **Takemitsu** All in Twilight. **Lutosławski** (trans. cpsr): 12 Folk Melodies.
No one can truly reach into the depths of Britten's *Nocturnal* until Life has taught them some hard lessons, nor, perhaps, can they perceive the *Innigkeit* of Martin's work; Bream, now in his sixties and with his technical armoury totally at the service of his emotions, demonstrates the truth of this in performances of moving intensity. Age has not dimmed his enthusiasm for pastures new: Brouwer's strong, and in places wryly humorous, Sonata with its teasing references to the composers to whom its three movements pay tribute, and Takemitsu's introspective *All in Twilight*, were written at his behest and are communicated with wonderful clarity. What Gareth Walters, the annotator, aptly describes as the "simple charm" of Bream's arrangements of Polish folk-melody settings by Lutosławski brings the recital to a lighter conclusion. The old wine has matured beautifully and the new is of vintage status. The temptation to say that Bream has rarely played (or been recorded) better than here is too strong to resist!

Organ Fireworks, Volume 3. **Christopher Herrick** (org). Hyperion Ⓟ CDA66457 (71 minutes: DDD: 9/91). Played on the organ of St Eustache, Paris. Recorded 1990.   ⒶⒶⒶ
    Batiste Offertoire in D minor. **Bossi** Pièce héroïque in D minor, Op. 128. Scherzo in D minor, Op. 49 No. 2. **Dubois** Grand Choeur in B flat major. **Dupré** Cortège et Litanie, Op. 19 No. 2. **Jolivet** Hymne à l'Univers. **Lefebure-Wély** Marche in F major, Op. 122 No. 4. **Lemare** Concert Fantasy on "Hanover", Op. 4. Marche héroïque in D major, Op. 74. **Saint-Saëns** Allegro giocoso in A minor, Op. 150 No. 7.
Here is something truly spectacular. The brand new organ in St Eustache's Church, Paris was designed by the organist Jean Guillou who made sure it was an instrument fit for the finest of players and the greatest of music. In addition to a large array of stops, manuals and pipes it also boasts such extravagances as two consoles and a playback facility which enables the organ to play unattended. For this disc Christopher Herrick took advantage of this latter facility so that performances made during the day could be recorded in the small hours when extraneous noise was at a minimum. But the organ itself makes such a tremendously powerful, not to say, awesome noise, that one would have thought such a precaution unnecessary. Hyperion's vivid recording of this magnificent instrument stands out as one of the best recordings of an organ currently available on CD. Herrick's programme shows off both the instrument and his own amazing virtuosity to brilliant effect. There is great fun to be had from these pieces, none of which can really be said to be well-known. This is a disc of pure, unadulterated pleasure.

Organ Fireworks, Volume 5. **Christopher Herrick** (org). Hyperion Ⓟ CDA66676 (75 minutes: DDD: 8/94). Played on the Virtanen organ in Turku Cathedral, Finland. Recorded 1993.
    Alain Litanics, Op. 79. **Sibelius** (arr. H. Fricker) Finlandia, Op. 26. **Sløgedal** Variations on a Norwegian Folk Tune. **Mulet** Carillon-sortie in D major. **Lindberg** Organ Sonata in G minor, Op. 23 – Alla Sarabanda; Allegro con brio. **Mozart** Orgelstück (Fantasia) für eine Uhr, K608. **Lefébure-Wély** Marche. **Nielsen** Commotio, FS155. **Elgar** Pomp and Circumstance March in G major, Op. 39 No. 4.
This disc mines a rich seam of repertoire ranging from the sublime (Mozart's *Fantasia*) to the ridiculous (Lefébure-Wély's *Marche*), from the obscure (Sløgedal's Variations) to the familiar (Elgar's *Pomp and Circumstance* March). All have in common a virtuosity, be it simple showiness or something of greater musical substance, which, articulated by such an able player as Christopher Herrick and on an organ the mere sound of which can send shivers down the spine, means that we are treated to a thoroughly satisfying, carefully balanced display of aural pyrotechnics. Breathtaking clarity and an almost electrically charged brilliance of tone are the hallmarks of this magnificent Finnish organ. Never has *Finlandia* sounded quite as thrilling as it does with these flashing trumpets; never has Mulet's evergreen *Carillon-sortie* crackled as it does in this cold, clear Northern atmosphere. It gives a wonderful radiance to those less overtly flashy pieces and, combined with Herrick's intuitive musicianship, we have here performances of the Mozart *Orgelstück*, and Nielsen's mammoth *Commotio*, of great stature. This is a splendid disc, as thrilling and truly spectacular as anything Hyperion have so far produced.

New review

Organ Fireworks, Volume 6. **Christopher Herrick** (org). Hyperion Ⓕ CDA66778 (76 minutes: DDD: 3/96). Played on the Norman and Beard organ in the Town Hall, Wellington, New Zealand. Recorded 1995.

Hollins A Trumpet Minuet. **Elgar** Organ Sonata No. 1 in G major, Op. 28. **Cocker** Tuba tune. **Sumsion** Introduction and Theme. **Spicer** Kiwi Fireworks – Variations on "God defend New Zealand". **C.S. Lang** Tuba tune. **Lemare** Concertstück in the form of a Polonaise, Op. 80. **Wagner** (trans. Lemare, arr. Westbrook and Herrick) Die Meistersinger von Nürnberg – Prelude, Act 1.

This series is turning into something of a world tour for Christopher Herrick and the "Organ Fireworks" team, and they have now travelled about as far as it is possible to go from Hyperion's London headquarters. They have come up with one genuine piece of 'home-grown' music (although C.S. Lang left New Zealand for England almost before he could tell a nappy from a nazard) and a connection with Edwin Lemare; he played this organ three months after its completion in 1906. However, the starting-point for this programme is the tradition of civic organ concerts which was exported from the town halls of Edwardian England to such far-flung corners of the British Empire as Singapore, South Africa and, of course, New Zealand. The Wellington Town Hall organ is typical of a large turn-of-the-century English symphonic organ and while it might seem a little extravagant to go half-way round the world to find one, it is, following its 1985-6 restoration, rare in being substantially unaltered and in excellent working condition. Full organ is gloriously meaty, the flue tone beautifully blended and the solo reeds a joy to behold – a silvery Tromba perfect for Hollins's elegant Minuet; a gutsy Tuba ideal for both Cocker and Lang. As ever Herrick's performances have both musical integrity and great communicative flair: his is a matchless performance of the Elgar Sonata, in which the composer's strangely awkward use of the organ, in places treating it almost orchestrally, is immaculately managed.

Organ Showpieces from St Paul's Cathedral **Andrew Lucas** (org). Naxos Ⓢ 8 550955 (71 minutes: DDD: 11/94). Recorded 1994.

T. Dubois Toccata in G minor. **Franck** Chorale No. 3 in A minor. **Gigout** Scherzo. **Langlais** Poèmes évangéliques, Op. 2 – No. 2, La Nativité. Paraphrases grégoriennes, Op. 5 – Hymne d'actions de grâce. **Murrill** Carillon. **Peeters** Aria, Op. 51. **Reger** Pieces, Op. 59 – No. 5, Toccata in D minor; No. 6, Fugue in D major; No. 9, Benedictus. **Vierne** Pièces de fantaisie, Op. 54 – No. 6, Carillon de Westminster.

A populist programme: with the possible exception of Langlais's magical "La Nativité" these pieces will already be well represented in most organ buffs' collections. But the very absence of such stalwarts as Widor and Bach points to a programme designed to be, if not actually adventurous, at least different. We have relatively concise Reger unencumbered by a morass of seething chromaticisms, a selection of French toccatas and scherzos offering more than mere flamboyance, and it's good to have plenty of moments for peaceful reflection – most memorably a lovely account of Flor Peeters's *Aria*. Andrew Lucas isn't just interested in showing off his technical prowess, impressive though this is (although those tricky pedal solos in Murrill's *Carillon* would not bear close scrutiny in a less generous acoustic). He knows the organ, the building, the music and how to communicate to his invisible audience. Listen to the rare elegance he brings to the Dubois *Toccata*, the wonderfully seamless flow of the Franck *Chorale*. Naxos have done well to secure the services of Gary Cole, no stranger to the art of organ recording or to this venue. He has given them a superbly atmospheric, if slightly subdued recording that effectively balances instrument and building.

Piano works **Maurizio Pollini** (pf). DG The Originals Ⓜ 447 431-2GOR (68 minutes: ADD: 6/95). Items marked [a] from 2530 225 (6/72), [b]2530 803 (7/78). Recorded 1971-6. *Gramophone classical 100.*   ⒼⒼ

Prokofiev Piano Sonata No. 7 in B flat major, Op. 83[a]. **Boulez** Piano Sonata No. 2[b]. **Stravinsky** Petrushka – three movements[a]. **Webern** Piano Variations, Op. 27[b].

Perfection needs to be pursued so that you can forget about it. Pollini's *Petrushka* movements are almost inhumanly accurate and fast; but what comes across is an exhilarating sense of abandon, plus an extraordinary cumulative excitement. The Prokofiev Seventh Sonata remains a benchmark recording not only for the athleticism of its outer movements but for the epic remorselessness of the central *Andante*. The Webern Variations are a magical fusion of intellectual passion and poetry, and the Boulez Sonata vividly reminds us why the European avant-garde was such a powerful force in the 1950s. These recordings are a monument to what it is possible for two hands to achieve on one musical instrument. The 'original-image bit-processing' has given a notch more brilliance and presence, just as claimed, and another definite gain is the retention of atmosphere between movements.

Piano Recital Nicholas Unwin (pf). Metier Ⓔ MSVCD92009 (63 minutes: DDD: 1/96).
   Tippett Piano Sonata No. 4. **Saxton** Piano Sonata. **C. Matthews** 11 Studies in Velocity.
   C. Lambert Elegy.
Piano Recital Steven Neugarten (pf). Metier Ⓔ MSVCD92008 (53 minutes: DDD: 1/96).
   Tippett Piano Sonata No. 2. **Sackman** Piano Sonata. **Saxton** Chacony. **Connolly** Sonatina in
   Five Studies, Op. 1.

There are audible debts here, acknowledged by Robert Saxton in an affectionate tribute to Sir Michael printed among the other notes, but also clearly perceptible in Nicholas Sackman's fine Sonata. Placing the Tippett sonatas in these contexts, to which they stand up very well, also points up what a very distinguished cycle they are. Not least, each disc is an admirable visiting card for a young pianist of real interpretative gifts. Unwin is the more immediately striking of the two, perhaps because he has the challenge and the attendant rewards of Tippett's Fourth Sonata: the characteristic sonorities, the spare lyricism and the formal ingenuities are spot on. Saxton's one-movement Sonata, seemingly much freer than the Tippett but in fact controlled through all its splendid pianistic gestures by a firm and quite perceptible thematic discipline, is also very perceptively played, and Unwin enjoys himself hugely in Colin Matthews's boldly virtuoso Studies. The brief and ambiguous Constant Lambert *Elegy*, darkly vehement but bleak, is no less shrewdly characterized: a distinguished début recording.

However, one should not underestimate Steven Neugarten. Although in Tippett's Second Sonata there is a slight lack of that heady, ecstatic lyricism to which this grand and on the whole percussive sonata occasionally turns, you are impressed by the power and the attack of his playing, and he gives a sympathetic reading of Justin Connolly's misleadingly numbered Op. 1 (it was written in 1962 but revised and expanded in 1983). This is a gripping piece, vividly visual and dramatic within its spare, angular style. Saxton's *Chacony* is a curious but attractive "fantasy on a scale", giving Neugarten plenty of opportunity for agreeable pianistic rhetoric. Sackman's Sonata, with a long *cantabile* at its centre radiating stillness and lyricism into the more mechanistic and virtuoso outer movements, also amply deserves a recording, and a performance as compelling as this one. Like Unwin's recital it is excellently recorded, cleanly but not clinically.

Piano Recital Claudio Arrau (pf). Philips Insignia Ⓜ 438 305-2PM (79 minutes: ADD: 10/93).
   Liszt Liebesträume, S541 – No. 3, O lieb, so lang du lieben kannst (S298). Etudes d'exécution
   transcendante, S139 – Harmonies du soir. **Chopin** Nocturnes – B major, Op. 62 No. 1; E major,
   Op. 62 No. 2. **Brahms** Scherzo in E flat minor, Op. 4. **Beethoven** Rondo in G major, Op. 51
   No. 2. **Schubert** Impromptus in D flat major, D899 No. 3. **Schumann** Waldszenen, Op. 82 –
   No. 7, Vogel als Prophet. Three Romanzen, Op. 28 – No. 2 in F sharp major. Arabeske in C
   major, Op. 18. **Debussy** Estampes – Soirées dans Grenade. Images, Book 2 – Poissons d'or.

The late lamented Claudio Arrau took recording very seriously, although at times that robbed his playing in the studio of the last degree of spontaneity. Thus, in Liszt's *Liebesträume* No. 3, which opens his recital, and the two Chopin *Nocturnes* which follows, Arrau's gentle, poetic nudgings of the melodic line sound a little self-conscious. However, then he gives us his fine Brahms *Scherzo* in E flat minor, and the wonderful Schubert *Impromptu* in D flat from D899, which he plays magically. His Schumann is pretty impressive, too – "Vogels als Prophet" (from *Waldszenen*), the *Romance* in F sharp, Op. 28 No. 2 and the *Arabeske* in C major, Op. 18. These pieces are followed by another composer-pianist he understood so well: Debussy who is represented by his "Soirée dans Grenade" from *Estampes* and a superb "Poisson d'or" (*Images*, Book 2). The recital ends with a dazzling "Harmonies du soir" (from Liszt's *Etudes d'exécution transcendante*). All reveal extremely distinguished playing, backed by a recorded sound that is very real. One would certainly have had to pay far more for a good seat at an Arrau recital, and that is just what one has here with this disc.

Romantic Music for Harp Naoko Yoshino (hp). Philips Ⓔ 446 064-2PH (69 minutes: DDD: 2/96).
   Spohr Fantasia in C minor, Op. 35. **Rosetti** Piano Sonata No. 2 in E flat major. **Debussy**
   Suite bergamasque – Clair de lune. **Prokofiev** 10 Pieces, Op. 12 – Prelude. **Casella** Harp
   Sonata, Op. 68. **Damase** Sicilienne variée. **Reniè** Contemplation. **Tournier** Jazz Band. **Fauré**
   Impromptu, Op. 86. Recorded 1994.

Naoko Yoshino's status as a cultured musician and a harpist of superb technical control is asserted in the opening track of this, her first solo recording. Her phrasing is finely moulded, her articulation splendidly varied and clear, her use of tone colour enhancing but not obtrusive, her sound happily free from mechanical noises. In short, one may listen to the message without being overly conscious of the medium. Recordings of romantic harp music often lean heavily on pleasant pieces by harpists, spiced with tricks of the instrument's trade, and arrangements; here, only the Debussy is arranged (the Prokofiev is marked "for piano or harp"), and the only tricksy moments are in Tournier's piece, more ragtime than jazz; gestural sweeps across the strings, and sound 'cumuli' are in thankfully short supply. Casella offers the most substantial fare in what is in fact a more than usually interesting programme of this instrumental genre. Suppress any hesitation you may feel when faced with a disc of solo-harp music; this one is highly recommended.

Russian Piano Works Boris Berezovsky (pf). Teldec Ⓔ 4509-96516-2 (61 minutes: DDD: 7/96).
   Mussorgsky (arr. Tchernov) A Night on the Bare Mountain. **Rachmaninov** Etudes-tableaux,
   Op. 39 – No. 3 in F sharp minor; No. 4 in B minor; No. 7 in C minor; No. 9 in D major. **Liadov**
   Preludes – C major, Op. 39 No. 4; F sharp minor, Op. 40 No. 2; D flat major, Op. 57 No. 1.
   Medtner Four Fairy Tales, Op. 34 – No. 2 in E minor; No. 3 in A minor. Fairy Tale in B flat
   minor, Op. 20 No. 1. Fairy Tale in D minor, Op. 51 No. 1. Romantic Sketches for the Young,
   Op. 65 – Book 2: Tale. **Balakirev** Islamey.
In this most imaginative programme Boris Berezovsky displays a formidable technique and, for the
greater part, the sort of emotional commitment that is second nature to the greatest Russian pianists.
His selection from the Op. 39 *Etudes* confirms that he is among Rachmaninov's most powerful and
eloquent interpreters. In No. 3 in F sharp minor Berezovsky's romantic freedom and richness of
expression are several removes from other, more conventional, approaches. His rubato is pained and
ecstatic and the music seems to move across an immense emotional and dynamic spectrum within its
brief but intricate space. What drama he achieves too, in the great funeral elegy of No. 7,
complementing a hair-raising advance to the dissonant and audacious climax with a rare finesse in
the central triple *piano* and *legatissimo* reminder of the Russian liturgy. And it is this finesse which
makes every bar of the Liadov *Preludes* memorable, whether in the ultra-Russian memory of Chopin
in No. 1, or the octave storms of No. 3 (where the parallel with Scriabin's *Etude*, Op. 8 No. 9 is
remarkably close). Medtner's dark-hued *Fairy Tales*, too, find a potent and ideal interpreter both in
malignant antics (the "Wood goblin", Op. 34 No. 3) and subtle and elusive attributes (the *Romantic
Sketch*: the perfect encore to keep an audience guessing). The recital is framed by two towering feats
of virtuoso pianism. Mussorgsky's *Night on the Bare Mountain*, arranged by Konstantin Tchernov, is
a pulverizing experience – *allegro feroce*, indeed! And Balakirev's *Islamey* is tossed off at breakneck
speed, its sadistic, madcap difficulties resolved like so much child's play. In its stunningly imperious
way this performance is unrivalled. The recordings are close and airless, the accompanying notes
inadequate, but no piano buff should miss an awe-inspiring addition to this young artist's rapidly
expanding discography.

Short Stories Anatol Ugorski (pf). DG 447 105-2GH (62 minutes: DDD: 3/96). Recorded 1994.
   Busoni An die Jugend – Giga, bolero e variazione (study after Mozart). **Liszt** Liebestraum in
   A flat major, S541 No. 3. **Debussy** Suite bergamasque – Clair de lune. **Mendelssohn**
   Capriccio in E minor, Op. 16 No. 2. **Schumann** Kinderszenen, Op. 15 – Träumerei. **Chopin**
   Fantaisie-impromptu in C sharp minor, Op. 66. **Scriabin** Deux poèmes, Op. 32. Prélude et
   Nocturne, Op. 9. **Rachmaninov** Prelude in C sharp minor, Op. 3 No. 2. **Weber** Piano Sonata
   No. 1 in C major, J138 – Rondo (Perpetuum mobile). Invitation to the Dance, J260.
Anatol Ugorski, described in some quarters as a genius, in others as a charlatan (though frankly, you
would have to be as deaf as a post to make such a claim), is nothing if not versatile, and all these
performances are touched with a special individuality and commitment. He starts with a sophisticated
surprise, the Mozart/Busoni *Giga, bolero e variazione*. Here, Mozart's spare and near-Alkanesque
Gigue is viewed from a witty angle or prism and is played with great vitality. Old favourites such as
Liszt's Third *Liebestraum*, Debussy's *Clair de lune* and *the* Rachmaninov Prelude come up as fresh as
paint, fascinatingly and responsibly reconsidered so that, remarkably, one seems to be hearing them
for the first time. Chopin's *Fantaisie-impromptu*, too, is as inflammatory in its outer virtuosity as it is
lost in wonder in its central reveries, and the Scriabin items emerge with a hypnotic potency and
character. True, Ugorski's tempos for the *Prélude et Nocturne* for the left hand are dangerously slow
yet he holds one's attention throughout. Again, he can be heavy-footed on Weber's ballroom floor and
seems momentarily strenuous in the, ideally, nonchalant glitter of the composer's *Perpetuum mobile*.
One may have heard more fleet and tonally iridescent performances of all these pieces (Moiseiwitsch
comes to mind), yet Ugorski's mix of high seriousness and idiosyncrasy is unusual, intriguing and
rarely less than engaging. The recordings are excellent.

Solomon in Berlin Piano works. Solomon (pf). APR mono Ⓜ APR7030* (two discs: 92 minutes:
   ADD: 4/95). Recorded live in 1956.   ⊖⊕
   Bach Concerto in the Italian style, BWV971. **Beethoven** Piano Sonatas – No. 3 in C major,
   Op. 2 No. 3; No. 14 in C sharp minor, Op. 27 No. 2, "Moonlight". **Chopin** Fantasie in F minor,
   Op. 49. Nocturne in B flat minor, Op. 9 No. 1. Scherzo No. 2 in B flat minor, Op. 31. **Brahms**
   Intermezzos – E major, Op. 116 No. 4; E flat minor, Op. 118 No. 6. Rhapsody in B minor, Op. 79
   No. 1.
This invaluable issue brings together on two short CDs recitals given by Solomon in 1956 for Berlin
Radio. This was the time of Solomon's greatest success when, as Bryan Crimp puts it in his excellent
notes, he had acquired a Midas touch, at long last reaping the rewards his artistry deserved. The
recordings are clean but airless, yet they do little to dim one's sense of Solomon's quality, his masterly
but unobtrusive virtuosity, his unsullied honesty and musicianship. How typical is his robust, pacy
opening *Allegro* in the Bach, how impeccable his unfolding of the central *Andante*; a truly seamless
aria in such hands. His rhythmic zest in the finale, too, is hard to resist. In Beethoven Solomon is, not

surprisingly, no less remarkable. By 1956 he had modified his celebrated slow tempo for the first movement of Op. 27 No. 2, yet the playing remains sculpted and marmoreal, a statement mixing abstraction and elegy and wholly devoid of impressionism or 'moonlit' overtones. Solomon's Brahms is no less lucid and classic, though his B minor *Rhapsody* has a truly *agitato* sweep and propulsion. Here Solomon's poise and *sang-froid* are only just on the right side of detachment. The same might be said of his Chopin *Fantasie*. Solomon was hardly a pianist to wear his heart on his sleeve, and although there have been other, more richly idiosyncratic *Fantasies* on record, there are few more masterly or refined. Finally, criticism falls silent when you listen to Solomon in the B flat minor *Nocturne*, where his magically 'contained' eloquence re-creates a pearl beyond price. Here, heart and mind work in faultless harmony and alliance.

New review

Virtuoso Piano Transcriptions Earl Wild (pf). Sony Classical Ⓟ SK62036 (67 minutes: DDD: 12/95). Recorded 1995.　　　　　　　　　　　　　　　　　　　　　　　　Ⓖ
  Saint-Saëns (trans. Wild) Le rouet d'Omphale in A major, Op. 31. **Handel** Keyboard Suite No. 5 in E minor, HWV430 – Adagio and Variations, "The Harmonious Blacksmith". **Chopin** (trans. Wild) Concerto for Piano and Orchestra No. 2 in F minor, Op. 21 – Largo. **Rachmaninov** (trans. Wild) These summer nights, Op. 12 No. 5. **Pabst** Paraphrase on "Sleeping Beauty" (Tchaikovsky). **Wild** Improvisation on "Après un rêve" (Fauré). Hommage à Poulenc. Reminiscences of "Snow White and the Seven Dwarfs" (Churchill). **Mozart** (trans. Backhaus) Don Giovanni – Deh! vieni alla finestra. **Tchaikovsky** (trans. Wild) At the ball, Op. 38 No. 3. Swan Lake – Dance of the Swans. **Tausig** Man lebt nur einmal. **Kreisler** (trans. Rachmaninov) Liebeslied.

A pianist with a sweet tooth blessed with an autocratic and crystalline technique, Wild resurrects some of his old favourites (Rachmaninov's *These summer nights* and the Kreisler/Rachmaninov *Liebeslied*, for example) but for the most part provides new and delectable offerings. Take the Wild *Hommage à Poulenc* for example, where the Sarabande from Bach's First *Partita* is held in a relentlessly 'blue' spotlight, enveloped in luscious night-club harmony; a naughty but affectionate tilt at 'the old wig' and also at all purists and Beckmessers. His arrangement of Saint-Saëns's *Le rouet d'Omphale*, deriving in style from the Wagner-Liszt Spinning Chorus from *Der fliegende Holländer*, is dazzlingly resourceful and Handel's *Harmonious Blacksmith* takes on a new lease of life, decked out with mischievous but stylish additions. The decadent commentary on the Rachmaninov song ends with comic abruptness while Tchaikovsky's *At the ball* concludes with a flight nimble enough to show how lightly Wild has worn his years. Lovers of easy sentiment will enjoy the effusive *Reminiscences of "Snow White"* though admirers of Fauré's chaste voluptuousness will react to Wild's way with *Après un rêve* with more than a raised eyebrow. The *Dance of the Swans* from *Swan Lake* is as ear-tickling as ever and so, all in all, the instantly recognizable sheen and sparkle of this recital reflect a great pianist's tireless relish and delight in all things pianistic and seductive. The recordings are superb.

New review

Virtuoso Strauss Transcriptions Piers Lane (pf). Hyperion Ⓔ CDA66785 (74 minutes: DDD: 2/96). Recorded 1994.
  Schulz-Evler An der schönen, blauen Donau. **Friedman** Frühlingsstimmen. **M. Rosenthal** Carnaval de Vienne. Fantasia on themes by Johann Strauss II. **Tausig** Nouvelles soirées de Vienne – Nachtfalter, Op. 157; Man lebt nur einmal, Op. 167; Wahlstimmen, Op. 250. **Godowsky** Symphonic metamorphosis on "Die Fledermaus".

Here is a recital lovingly planned to tickle even the most jaded palette. Familiar and unfamiliar transcriptions jostle for attention and culminate in the grandest of grand finales, one where previously heard material resurfaces in a truly uproarious display. Schulz-Evler's introduction sends fabulous spangles of sound spinning through the air and Rosenthal's mock-canonic start to his *Carnaval de Vienne* evolves into a crazy course of events. All these works, including Friedman's much less well-known *Frühlingsstimmen* pose some near insuperable problems, even for those blessed with Piers Lane's enviable energy and facility. Somehow the pianist has to create an illusion of effortlessness, a nonchalant capacity to juggle four, five and six jewelled batons simultaneously. Then, and only then, is he free to explore with the most lavish variety of colour and nuance the evocative Viennese memories lingering beneath so much incessant surface activity. Fancifully speaking, Lane leaps rather than glides across the dance floor, revelling in the kaleidoscopic configurations of Friedman's *Frühlingsstimmen* and whirling Rosenthal's final fantasy into a virtuoso vortex; you can almost hear an audience's roar of approval at the end. One occasionally misses an elegance inseparable from such music, the sort of rhetoric or quality that came more easily to pianists of the past. But if Lane is sometimes happier in athleticism than lyricism his record will still grab virtuoso fanciers by the ears. The recordings are excellent.

Choral and song

Album de Musique, offert par G. Rossini à Mademoiselle Louise Carlier Suzanne
Danco (sop); **Ester Orel** (mez); **Francesco Molinari-Pradelli** (pf). Philips The Early Years mono
Ⓜ 438 952-2PM* (45 minutes: ADD: 9/94). Texts and translations included. From A00427L
(2/60). Recorded 1956.
> **Bazzini** Chi ami? **Bellini** Dolente immagine. **Bertin** Ah, dors en paix, mon bel enfant. **Berton**
> Air à trois notes. **Brugière** Le printemps arrive. **Cherubini** La pietosa bugia. **Costa** Trova un
> sol, mia bella Clori. **Gordigiani** Ognuno tira l'acqua al suo mulino. **Marliani** La gita in
> gondola. **Mercadante** Aure amiche, ah! non spirate. **Meyerbeer** Soave l'istante. **Morlacchi**
> La rosa appassita. **Onslow** La Dante dans le paradis. **Panseron** Il n'aurait pas dû venir. **Paer**
> Ange à la voix tendre. **Rossini** Mi lagnerò tacendo. **Spontini** L'adieu. **Tadolini** Com'e soave a
> l'anima.

This utterly charming recital, recorded in 1956, owes its origins to two men: the celebrated Milanese
collector of antiquarian curiosities Natale Gallini and the man who first put the collection together,
a certain Gioachino Rossini. It was in Paris in the early 1830s that Rossini had the idea of assembling
a decorative and handsomely inscribed Song Book for the daughter of a well-known Parisian
impresario. The result: an "Album de Musique, offert par G. Rossini à Mademoiselle Louise Carlier,
Mars 1835". Mme Benazet (as she was soon to become) later added to the volume; the Spontini song
bears the inscription "Paris, 1839". But most of it was Rossini's doing. Naturally, one looks to the
great names who contributed to Mlle Carlier's book: Bellini and Meyerbeer and the ageing Cherubini.
They don't disappoint; the Bellini song is especially lovely and even the Cherubini has its own quirky
interest. Some old lags turn up – Paer and the man who helped Rossini draft the original version of
his *Stabat mater*, Giovanni Tadolini. The real surprises, though, are elsewhere. Just when you think
the format is becoming a shade predictable – a chance perhaps to doze off whilst mademoiselle's
mother isn't looking – along comes some small gem of a piece by Signor Morlacchi or Signor Bazzini.
('My dear, isn't he the famous *violinist* – the man that scallywag Paganini thinks so highly of?')
Indeed, he is. In fact, I would say Bazzini's *Chi ami?* is one of the highlights of the collection. Suzanne
Danco is the impeccable interpreter for all this. She neither indulges the music, nor condescends to it.
Fine diction, elegant phrasing, vocal colour judiciously used. The same could be said of the
conductor-turned-pianist Francesco Molinari-Pradelli: impeccable. To complete one's pleasure, there
is the recital's equally impeccable presentation: a recording that sounds almost new-minted, full texts
and translations, and a set of beautifully written biographical vignettes of the various composers by
Gallini himself. Rossini, I feel, would be touched – and gratified. The whole production has what was
always for him an indispensable attribute: style.

New review

The Early Recordings Elly Ameling (sop); [a]**Hans-Martin Linde** (rec); [b]**Hans Deinzer** (cl);
[c]**Angelica May** (vc); [d]**Jörg Demus** (pf); [e]**Gustav Leonhardt** (hpd); [f]**Collegium Aureum /** [g]**Franzjosef
Maier** (vn), [h]**Gerhard Schmidt-Gaden**, [i]**Rudolf Pohl**. Deutsche Harmonia Mundi Ⓟ 74321 26617-2
(four discs: 239 minutes: ADD: 12/95). Texts and translations included. Recorded 1964-8.
> **Bach** Anna Magdalena Notenbuch – Bist du bei mir[e]. Cantata No. 82, Ich habe genug[e] – Ich
> habe genug!; Schlummert ein (from BASF BAC3054, 8/74). Cantata No. 202, Weichet nur,
> betrübte Schatten[fg]. Cantata No. 209, Non sa che sia dolore[fg]. Cantata No. 211, Schweigt stille,
> plaudert nicht (Coffee Cantata) – Nun folge; Heute noch[fg]. Cantata No. 212, Mer hahn en neue
> Oberkeet (Peasant Cantata) – Im Ernst ein Wort!; Kleinzschocher müsse[fg] (BASF BAC3052/3,
> 7/74). **C.P.E. Bach** Magnificat in D minor, H772 – Quia respexit[fh] (BASF BAS29368-9, 12/73).
> **Telemann** Du aber Daniel, gehe hin – Mit sehnenden verlangen; Richt ihr müde Augen nieder[fi]
> (1C 065 99751, 10/78). **Handel** Pensieri notturni di Filli, "Nel dolce dell'oblio", HWV134[af]. Ah,
> che troppo ineguali, HWV230[f] (BASF BAC3058/9, 1/75). **Brahms** Lieder, Op. 57 – No. 2, Wenn
> du nur zuweilen lächelst; No. 3, Es träumte mir; No. 4, Ach, wende diesen Blick; No. 8,
> Unbewegte laue Luft[d]. Deutsche Volkslieder, WoO33 – No. 12, Feinsliebchen, du sollst mir nicht
> barfuss geh'n; No. 15, Schwesterlein, Schwesterlein; No. 33, Och Moder, ich well en Ding han!;
> No. 41, Es steht ein' Lind'; No. 42, In stiller Nacht, zur ersten Wacht[d]. Lieder, Op. 107 – No. 3,
> Das Mädchen spricht; No. 5, Mädchenlied[d]. Vergebliches Ständchen, Op. 84 No. 4[d]. Ständchen,
> Op. 106 No. 1[d]. Am Sonntag Morgen, Op. 49 No. 1[d]. Trennung, Op. 97 No. 6[d]. Während des
> Regens, Op. 58 No. 2[d]. O kühler Wald, Op. 72 No. 3[d]. Von ewiger Liebe, Op. 43 No. 1[d] (BASF
> BAC3065, 1/75). **Schumann** Myrthen, Op. 25 – No. 1, Widmung; No. 3, Der Nussbaum; No. 7,
> Die Lotosblume; No. 9, Lied der Suleika[d]. Lieder-Album für die Jugend, Op. 79 – No. 10, Das
> Käuzlein; No. 12, Der Sandmann; No. 13, Marienwürmchen; No. 23, Er ist's; No. 26,
> Schneeglöckchen[d] (1C 065 99631, 11/78). Jasminenstrauch, Op. 27 No. 4[d]. Die Blume der
> Ergebung, Op. 83 No. 2[d]. Röselein, Op. 89 No. 6[d]. Lieder und Gesänge, Op. 77 – No. 2, Mein
> Garten; No. 5, Aufträge[d]. Gedichte, Op. 90 – No. 2, Meine Rose; No. 4, Die Sennin.
> Schmetterling, Op. 79 No. 2[d]. Gedichte, Op. 35 – No. 4, Erstes Grün; No. 5, Sehnsucht nach der
> Waldgegend; No. 9, Frage[d]. Die letzten Blumen starben, Op. 104 No. 6[d]. Die Meerfee, Op. 125
> No. 1[d]. Waldesgespräch, Op. 39 No. 3[d]. Loreley, Op. 53 No. 2[d]. Die Kartenlegerin, Op. 31 No. 2[d].

Sehnsucht, Op. 51 No. 1[d]. Mein schöner Stern!, Op. 101 No. 4[d] (1C 065 99631, 11/78). **Schubert** Der Hirt auf dem Felsen, D965[bd]. Seligkeit, D433[d]. Gretchen am Spinnrade, D118[d]. Du liebst mich nicht, D756[d]. Heimliches Lieben, D922[d]. Im Frühling, D882[d]. Die Vögel, D691[d]. Der Jüngling an der Quelle, D300[d]. Der Musensohn, D764[d] (BASF SAC3088, 2/75).

If, for instance, you have had a little too much of voices under stress, whether in the quest for volume to compete with orchestras and powerful colleagues or for expression in the emotional turmoils of big operatic business, then here is the singer to bring calm and comfort. The young Elly Ameling had a voice which was as clear as a bell, not a fleck of impurity in its consistency, not a scratch on the lovely surface of a tone-quality which served the happy spirit of its owner to perfection. When the earliest of these records was made, in 1964, she had been singing in public for some five or six years and was already an artist of note, but the outstanding feature (along with an admirable technique and scrupulous musicianship) is the freshness. She sings with a straightforward delight in the music of the masters, seemingly content to impose upon it nothing of herself save the beauty of her voice and the devotion of her study. For the most part, her repertoire is ideally chosen. Only one of the songs, Brahms's *Von ewiger Liebe*, exceeds her vocal means, wanting greater resources of power and a more opulent body of tone to match the grand swell of the melody and the generous amplitude of the accompaniment. Her ability at that time as an expressive singer is more severely tested, and one reflects that in later years she would discover more, both in the music and in her own inner store of emotion and understanding. *Gretchen am Spinnrade* is an obvious example. These are still exceptions, however. Mostly the songs are of happiness, youth and spring, with only the occasional overshadowing, as in the wistful mood of Brahms's *Es träumte mir* or the middle section of Schubert's *Der Hirt auf dem Felsen*. In the booklet which comes with the boxed set (and which needs careful handling or it will fall apart), Ameling recalls the Deutsche Harmonia Mundi sessions at Schloss Fugger in Kircheim unter Teck. "I was only 31," she says, "still wet behind the ears." She acknowledges the helpfulness of her producer, and of Jörg Demus. The performances certainly convey the feeling of a sympathetic collaboration, the playing being often of exquisite quality, with a refreshing tendency to bring out the Schubertian side of Brahms. Unfortunately, the acoustics of the castle were less amenable, and some of the sessions (Schubert and Schumann particularly) catch far too much echo. This is so with some of the orchestrally accompanied pieces as well, such as the otherwise captivating aria by Telemann. Still, the collection stands as a fine tribute to a greatly loved singer. Her art was to develop, so that the recordings here might be considered as the equivalent of an author's juvenilia. But we all know how unexpectedly moving that can be.

Arie Antiche Cecilia Bartoli (mez); György Fischer (pf). Decca Ⓟ 436 267-2DH (66 minutes; DDD: 12/92). Texts and translations included. Recorded 1990-91.
  A. Scarlatti Già il sole dal Gange. Son tutta duolo. Se Florindo è fedele. O cessate di piagarmi. Spesso vibra per suo gioco. **Giordani** Caro mio ben. **Lotti** Pur dicesti, o bocca bella. **Cesti** Intorno all'idol mio. **Paisiello** Nel cor più non mi sento. Il mio ben quando verrà. Chi vuol la zingarella. **Anonymous** O leggiadri occhi belli. **Marcello** Quella fiamma che m'accende. **Caldara** Selve amiche. Sebben, crudele. **Caccini** Tu ch'hai le penne, amore. Amarilli. **Parisotti** Se tu m'ami. **Cavalli** Delizie contente. **Vivaldi** Sposa son disprezzata. **Carissimi** Vittoria, vittoria!

With Scarlatti and Vivaldi among the composers, these *arie antiche* are not necessarily very old. Italian singers have long been accustomed to lumping together all songs earlier than Mozart (or perhaps Haydn) under this heading, piously including them at the start of a recital so as to establish a classical tone and give them time to try out their voices before entering on the more strenuous and popular part of their programme. Bartoli here devotes a whole disc to them, as things delightful in themselves, varied in mood and style, and calling in turn on almost all the essential arts of a good singer. No one can come away with a feeling of having been short-changed at the end of this. Her voice is ideal, both silken and chaste, finely controlled, cleanly produced. With a simple, direct song such as the famous *Caro mio ben* she will never fuss or show off; with Vivaldi's *Sposa son disprezzata* she exploits the most deliciously languishing tone and sometimes one more frankly passionate and 'operatic'. Most of the items are gems, and to all of them György Fischer brings the touch of the expert jeweller, knowing exactly how best to set off the beauties of voice and melody.

The Art of Arleen Auger Arleen Auger (sop); [a]members of the **Saint Paul Chamber Orchestra** and the **Minnesota Orchestra / Joel Revzen** ([bc]pf). Koch International Classics Ⓟ 37248-2 (55 minutes: DDD: 4/94). Texts and translations included. Recorded 1986-91.
  Larsen Six Sonnets from the Portuguese[a]. **Purcell** (ed. Britten) If music be the food of love, Z379 No. 3. The Libertine – Nymphs and shepherds[b]. Pausanias – Sweeter than roses.
  Schumann Myrthen, Op. 25 – No. 1, Widmung; No. 3, Der Nussbaum; No. 11, Lied der Braut I; No. 12, Lied der Braut II. Romanzen und Balladen, Op. 64 – No. 1, Die Soldatenbraut.
  Mozart Das Veilchen, K476. Dans un bois solitaire, K308/K295b. Das Lied der Trennung, K519. Als Luise die Briefe, K520[c]. Abendempfindung, K523.

Here is a record to cherish, and with it, of course, a memory. The late Arleen Auger was loved for her voice, her art and herself. All items here are taken from live performances, and the recorded balance favours the accompaniment, but a great and very special beauty remains. Libby Larsen's settings of six of Elizabeth Barrett-Browning's sonnets were written for the singer, and they suit her to perfection.

The idiom is lyrical, the writing for voice full of understanding about what should and should not be asked of a singer. Auger sings unerringly, with great beauty of tone and feeling for words. This, the Purcell songs, and the Mozart (Schumann on the whole suits her less well) are a lovely memorial: the fine legato (in Mozart), the even runs (in Purcell) and the gentle beauty of tone throughout. At the end of the programme comes Mozart's *Abendempfindung* with its quiet presentiment of death and its modest wish for remembrance, a wish that this record aptly helps to fulfil.

Janet Baker Song Recital. **Dame Janet Baker** (mez); **Gerald Moore** (pf). EMI Ⓜ CDM5 65009-2 (75 minutes: ADD: 11/94). Texts and translations included. Items marked [a] from HMV ASD2590 (9/70), [b]ASD2431 (1/69), [c]HMV HQS1091 (7/67). Recorded 1967-69.
    Fauré[a] Automne, Op. 18 No. 3. Prison, Op. 83 No. 1. Soir, Op. 83 No. 2. Fleur jetée, Op. 39 No. 2. En sourdine, Op. 58 No. 2. Notre amour, Op. 23 No. 2. Mai, Op. 1 No. 2. La chanson du pêcheur, Op. 4 No. 1. Clair de lune, Op. 46 No. 2. **Schubert**[b] Am Grabe Anselmos, D504. Abendstern, D806. Die Vögel, D691. Die Götter Griechenlands, D677. Gondelfahrer, D808. Auflösung, D807. **R. Strauss**[b] Morgen, Op. 27 No. 4. Befreit, Op. 39 No. 4. Stanford[c] La Belle Dame sans merci. **Parry**[c] Proud Maisie. O mistres mine. **Busch**[c] Rest. **Warlock**[c] Pretty ringtime. **Vaughan Williams**[c] Linden Lea. **Gurney**[c]: The fields are full. **Britten**[c] Corpus Christi carol. **Ireland**[c] The Salley Gardens. **Quilter**[c] Love's philosophy, Op. 3 No. 1.

This CD is a timely reminder, a generous one too, of Baker in her prime. At the peak of her career at the end of the 1960s, the tone is at its most beautiful, the singing as secure as it is intelligent. One realizes anew that here is one of the great singers of the century and one comfortable in so many idioms. It may be that some native singers of Fauré and Schubert capture the soul of these songs more unerringly, but few actually sing them so glowingly, so intensely. The typical Schubertian sadness brings out the very best in her. Nobody has sung *Am Grabe Anselmos* with so much sincere and deep feeling, nor have the lamenting echoes of *Die Götter Griechenlands* ever sounded more haunting. Technically the performances are also without fault. In her own language, Dame Janet is at home in every sense. The gems here are the Stanford ballad, the tensions of the tale sustained throughout by both artists, the tender sorrow of Britten's *Corpus Christi*, the fervent outpouring of Quilter's *Love's philosophy*. Everywhere Moore is at one with his partner, always supportive, perceptive, with that soft and inimitable touch of his. The recordings, for their dates, are exemplary in balance and presence.

New review

Bushes and Briars [a]London Madrigal Singers / Christopher Bishop; [b]Baccholian Singers of London; Philip Jones Brass Ensemble; English Chamber Orchestra / [c]Ian Humphris. EMI British Composers Ⓜ CMS5 65123-2 (two discs: 149 minutes: ADD: 2/96). Texts included. Recorded 1969-76.
    Vaughan Williams Bushes and briars. Loch Lomond. John Dory. Greensleeves. Ward the Pirate. Ca' the Yowes. The unquiet grave. The Seeds of Love. Early in the spring. The Turtle Dove. An Acre of Land. Five English Folksongs (all from HMV HQS1215, 7/70[a]). Bushes and briars. Wassail song. **Elgar** Five Partsongs from the Greek Anthology, Op. 45. The Wanderer. Reveille, Op. 54. **Howells** A Dirge. **Bax** The Boar's Head. **Delius** Wanderer's Song. **Warlock** The Shrouding of the Duchess of Malfi. The lady's birthday. **Britten** The Ballad of Little Musgrave and Lady Barnard (HMV CSD3783, 2/78[b]). **Holst** The Homecoming, H120. Choral Hymns from the Rig Veda (Group 4), H100 – No. 3, Hymn to Manas. Canons, H187 – No. 3, The fields of sorrow; No. 4, David's lament for Jonathan; No. 6, Truth of all truth. Choral Folk Songs, H136 – No. 1, I sowed the seeds of love; No. 3, Matthew, Mark, Luke and John; No. 4, The song of the blacksmith; No. 5, I love my love; No. 6, Swansea Town. Male Choruses, H186 – No. 1, Intercession; No. 2, Good Friday; No. 3, Drinking song; No. 4, A love song; No. 6, Before sleep. A Dirge for Two Veterans, H121 (CSD3764, 7/75[bc]).

From soulful first to sociable last, these part-songs are a delight for listeners as for singers. All who have warbled their way "through bushes and through briars" or taken tuneful farewell of their "little turtle dove" will know what pleasures they can bring, though no doubt many will reflect that the pleasure might have been heightened if their own group had numbered among them a few singers half as expert as those who perform so musically and intelligently on these recordings. The groups have in common a fine discipline that feels like instinct, a care for homogeneity of tone and style, and a keen appreciation of the civilized use of words, music and human society that such things betoken. Christopher Bishop's madrigal singers in the Vaughan Williams folk-song arrangements need more pace and more passion. For the rest, these performances deserve only praise. The Baccholians are particularly good in their rhythmic alertness, catching perfectly the subdued excitement of the *Wassail song* and the tricky syncopations of *The song of the blacksmith*. And what fine, fresh, considered and considerate compositions they are! The Six *Choral Folk Songs* of Holst are rich in variety, while the Six *Choruses* with strings have an equally satisfying unity. The *Dirge for Two Veterans* is a masterpiece, and indeed much could be said about them all which will have to go unsaid. Fortunately, it is hearing rather than 'saying' that really matters, and hearing is highly recommended.

Cabaret Classics Jill Gomez (sop); **John Constable** (pf). Unicorn-Kanchana Ⓔ DKPCD9055
(57 minutes: DDD: 6/88). Texts and translations included.
Weill Marie Galante – Les filles de Bordeaux; Le grand Lustucru; Le Roi d'Aquitaine; J'attends
un navire. Lady in the Dark – My ship. Street Scene – Lonely house. Knickerbocker Holiday – It
never was you. **Zemlinsky** Songs, Op. 27 – Harlem Tänzerin; Elend; Afrikanischer Tanz.
Schoenberg Arie aus dem Spiegel von Arcadien. Gigerlette. Der genügsame Liebhaber.
Mahnung. **Satie** La diva de l'Empire. Allons-y, Chochotte. Je te veux.
Schoenberg writing cabaret songs with a popular touch? Yes, and quite catchy ones too, as can be
heard particularly in *Gigerlette* – prompting the intriguing speculation of what might have been had
he not concentrated on *Gurrelieder*. On the other hand, his *Der genügsame Liebhaber* and Zemlinsky's
three songs would have been most unlikely to go down well with cabaret audiences, however
intellectual. At the other end of the spectrum are Satie's café-concert songs (the sentimental waltz *Je
te veux* is languidly attractive) and the Weill items, which were not written for cabaret but are drawn
from a 1934 Paris play and post-war Broadway musicals. That all these songs do not require a gin-
sodden voice or raucous delivery is demonstrated with the utmost artistry by Jill Gomez, in turn
seductive, pathetic, sly, sweet, swaggering, passionate, salacious – or simply singing beautifully. Her
performance of Weill's *Lonely house* (one of his best) remains hauntingly in the mind.

Carnaval! Sumi Jo (sop); **English Chamber Orchestra / Richard Bonynge.** Decca Ⓔ 440 679-2DH
(68 minutes: DDD: 9/94). Texts and translations included. Recorded 1993.
Adam Les Pantins de Violette – Le chanson du canari. Si j'étais roi – De vos nobles aïeux. **Balfe**
Les puits d'amour – Rêves d'amour, rêves de gloire. **Boïeldieu** La fête du village voisin –
Profitez de la view (Boléro). **F. David** La perle du Brésil – Couplets du Mysoli. **Delibes** Le roi
l'a dit – Portons toujours des robes sombres. **Grétry** Les fausses apparences ou L'amant jalous –
Je romps la chaîne qui m'engage. **Hérold** Le pré aux clercs – Jours de mon enfance. **Massenet**
Don César de Bazan – Sevillana. **Massé** La reine Topaze – Ninette est jeune et belle ("Carnaval
de Venise"). **Messager** Madame Chrysanthème – Le jour sous le soleil béni. **Offenbach** Un
mari à la porte – J'entends, ma belle ("Valse tyrolienne"). **A. Thomas** Le songe d'une nuit d'été
– Malgré l'éclat qui m'environne.
Sumi Jo is fortunate to have Bonynge as conductor and researcher to come up with a sequence of
really rare and fascinating music although the selection is a little like being confronted with a
patissier's window display. Sumi Jo's coloratura is accurate and apparently effortless. Although her
diction is not completely unintelligible, a lot of it is rather approximate. She is very affecting in the
Messager aria and in another bird-song, from Adam's *Les Pantins de Violette*. In general she seems to
be on firmer ground in the early nineteenth-century repertory – David, Adam and Hérold – than with
the *fin de siècle* style where once or twice the demands of the long lines seem to encourage her to stray
slightly off pitch. The Ambroise Thomas *Midsummer Night's Dream* is not an adaptation of the
Shakespeare play, but a fantasy set at the court of Queen Elizabeth I, whose aria is heard here; very
silly it all seems too. All in all, amongst these show-pieces there are valuable glimpses of the
extraordinary richness of the seldom-heard *opéra-comique* repertory.

New review

Contemporary Vocal Works Jane Manning (sop); [a]Jane's Minstrels / [b]Roger Montgomery. NMC
Artists' Series Ⓔ NMCD025 (64 minutes: DDD: 10/95). Texts included. Recorded 1993.　　　Ⓖ
Weir Don't let that horse[a]. **P.P. Nash** In a walled garden[ab]. **Connolly** Poems of Wallace
Stevens II, Op. 14[a]. **Bauld** Farewell Already[ab]. **Elias** Peroration. **Payne** Adlestrop[ab].
A. Gilbert Beastly Jingles[ab].
For the last 30 years Jane Manning has been an indispensable friend of and spur to British (and other)
composers, with her formidable blend of musical intelligence, precision, enterprise and readiness to
attempt the apparently impossible (Brian Elias's piece invites her to give the illusion of singing in two,
even three parts). Getting on for 350 works have so far been specially written for her, and this
collection is not only an absorbing cross-section of her repertory, but a sort of portrait as well. Her
sense of humour is briefly indicated in Judith Weir's deft setting of a poem by Lawrence Ferlinghetti
("Don't let that horse/eat that violin/cried Chagall's mother ..."), but comes fully into its own in
Anthony Gilbert's *Jingles*. Here the objects of humour include Manning's virtuosity itself (a
demented coloratura aria about the deplorable habits of rabbits) but the abiding impression is of vivid
inventiveness and richly bright sound. We select this track for a laugh, and we get it, but end up
wondering why such a gifted composer should not be at least as well known as ... but one does not
wish to be uncharitable. Another of Manning's gifts to present each of her composers in the most
compelling light. Much the same happens with Justin Connolly's Wallace Stevens songs. This is the
most 'modernist' music here: spare, angular and challenging. But it has a strange evocative power, too,
and an hour after hearing it you will still remember, even swear you can see, the fearsome "firecat" of
the first song, the prairie as solidified ocean of the second, the ritual dance of the third. Manning's
gifts as an actress are also at full stretch in Alison Bauld's moving setting (combining speech, song
and something precisely half-way between) of Lady Anne's lament over her murdered husband from
Richard III. Peter Paul Nash's Tennyson setting is another miniature concert opera, cleverly
constructed, finely cumulative, as well as an exquisitely written counterpoint of beautiful lines (Jane's

Minstrels, a carefully selected group of young virtuosos, enjoy them as much as she does). Jane Manning's voice will not take the pressure that once it did, and her lower register has retreated somewhat. She treats these facts not as restrictions but as useful additions to her armoury of vocal resource. A distinguished recital, and a most entertaining one.

Farewell to Salzburg Christa Ludwig (mez); **Charles Spencer** (pf). RCA Victor Red Seal
Ⓔ 09026 61547-2 (69 minutes: DDD: 10/93). Texts and translations included. Recorded 1993.
Gramophone Editor's choice.
Brahms Lieder, Op. 19 – No. 4, Der Schmied; No. 5, An eine Aolsharfe. Dein blaues Auge, Op. 59 No. 8. Vergebliches Ständchen, Op. 84 No. 4. Mädchenlied, Op. 95 No. 6. Immer leiser wird mein, Schlummer, Op. 105 No. 2. Ständchen, Op. 106 No. 1. **Mahler** Lieder aus "Des Knaben Wunderhorn" – Das irdische Leben; Rheinlegendchen. Rückert-Lieder – Ich bin der Welt abhanden gekommen; Um Mitternacht. **Schumann** Stille Tränen, Op. 35 No. 10. Myrthen, Op. 25 – No. 3, Der Nussbaum; No. 15, Aus dem hebräischen Gesängen. Marzveilchen, Op. 40 No. 1. Der Himmel hat ein Träne geweint, Op. 37 No. 1. Liederkreis, Op. 39 – No. 4, Die Stille; No. 5, Mondnacht. **R. Strauss** Gefunden, Op. 56 No. 1. Begegnung, Av72. Du meines Herzens Krönelein, Op. 21 No. 2. Die Nacht, Op. 10 No. 3. Lieder, Op. 27 – No. 1, Ruhe, meine Seele; No. 4, Morgen.
The inevitable loss of some of the voice's characteristic bloom and mobility, and the passing moments of instability at the bottom of the register do nothing to compromise the projection of character and spirit in everything Christa Ludwig sings here. Two songs from Mahler's *Des Knaben Wunderhorn* settings reveal that fusion of winsome, folk-art simplicity with the sense of a darker vision beyond which she, like Mahler, excels at conveying. Ludwig's voice warms to the tender containment of Richard Strauss's writing in songs like the little Goethe setting *Gefunden*, and finds a particular solemnity of concentration for *Ruhe, meine Seele* and a daringly slow *Morgen*. Schumann and Brahms celebrate the intimate confidence of Ludwig as Lieder singer, *Der Nussbaum* and *Die Stille* seem dream-like extensions of speech, even thought. By contrast, Byron's Hebrew melody and Brahms's Blacksmith light a bright flare, still burning effortlessly at the top of the voice. Most telling, though, are the more harmonically and methodically elusive songs: the secrets of sleep and of the Aeolian harp are now what Ludwig understands best and re-creates most affectingly.

New review

Lesley Garrett Soprano in Red. **Lesley Garrett** (sop); [a]**Crouch End Festival Chorus; Royal Philharmonic Concert Orchestra / James Holmes.** Silva Screen Classics Ⓔ SILKTVCD1
(60 minutes: DDD: 2/96). All items sung in English. Recorded 1995.
Romberg The New Moon – Softly, as in a morning sunrise; Lover, come back to me.
J. Strauss II (arr. Benatzky) Casanova – Nuns' Chorus and Laura's Song[a]. **Offenbach** La belle Hélène – On me nomme Hélène la Blonde. Orphée aux enfers – J'ai vu le Dieu Bacchus[a]; Ce bal est original[a]. **Novello** Perchance to dream – We'll gather lilacs. The Dancing Years – Waltz of my heart. **Lehár** Zigeunerliebe – Hör' ich Cymbalklänge. Friederike – Warum hast du mich wachgeküsst? Die lustige Witwe – Es lebt eine Vilja, ein Waldmägdelein[a]. **Coward** Bitter Sweet – If love were all. **Chabrier** L'étoile – O petite étoile; Je suis Lazuli!. **Heuberger** Der Opernball – Im chambre séparée. **Sullivan** The Contrabandista – Only the night wind sighs alone.
Lesley Garrett has won herself a huge following of those who respond to her straightforward, unaffected vocalizing, to the clarity and brightness of her voice and its ringing top notes. What also appeals about Garrett's recordings is the attention paid to less familiar material and the quest for authenticity of period style. Both facets are fully evident in this collection of operetta numbers from Paris, Vienna, Berlin, London and New York, ranging in time from classical Offenbach through to Coward, Novello and Romberg. The eager entreaties of Laura's Song from *Casanova*, the bright expressiveness of "If love were all" and the sheer joyfulness of "Waltz of my heart" (complete with piano contribution) are highlights. Especially gratifying, though, are the rarities. In the pedlar Lazuli's two numbers from Chabrier's *L'étoile*, Garrett's clarity of diction shows off Jeremy Sams's lyrics to fine effect and she should certainly win over the Sullivan faction with the first ever recording of an engaging little number from the pre-Gilbert operetta *The Contrabandista*. The aria from *La belle Hélène* is performed to Michael Frayn's text for the ENO adaptation of the work as *La belle Vivette*, while in Novello's "We'll gather lilacs" double tracking permits Garrett to duet with herself. Ensemble and momentum go curiously adrift at the choral entries in Offenbach's "Hymn to Bacchus", but this detracts only a little from another delightful Garrett collection.

Goethe Lieder Irmgard Seefried (sop); **Erik Werba** (pf). Orfeo D'Or mono Ⓔ C297921B*   ⓖⓖ
(71 minutes: ADD: 9/93). Recorded live in 1957. *Gramophone Editor's choice.*
Mozart Das Veilchen, K476. Das Kinderspiel, K598. **Beethoven** Egmont – Incidental Music, Op. 84: Die Trommel gerühret!; Freudvoll und leidvoll. Wonne der Wehmut, Op. 83 No. 1.
Schubert Suleika I, D720. Suleika II, D717. Heidenröslein, D257 (includes a false start). Der König in Thule, D367. Ganymed, D544. Gretchen am Spinnrade, D118. Im Frühling, D882. Ave Maria, D839. **Schumann** Myrthen, Op. 25 – No. 9, Lied der Suleika. **Wolf** Mignon I; Mignon II; Mignon III; Mignon ("Kennst du das Land?"); Blumengruss; Die Bekehrte; Frühling übers Jahr; Anakreons Grab.

All the performances on this disc are taken live from a single recital (devoted entirely to Goethe settings), a singer caught at the peak of her powers at a Salzburg recital of 1957. Listen to just four examples of her art and you will know all; the repeat of "Trocknet nicht" in Beethoven's *Wonne der Wehmut*, the first line of Schumann's ineffably beautiful and touching *Lied der Suleika* or the erotic close to Schubert's "Was bedeutet die Bewegung" (Suleika I) or the start of Wolf's "So lass mich scheinen" (Mignon III). Here caught on the wing is the kind of sincere, innig singing that can't be learnt: it is instinctive. But, of course, that is not the end of it. Seefried knew as well as anyone that essential in Lieder performance: how to shape a song from start to finish in speeds that never ever drag, evident throughout this arresting recital, but most particularly in Wolf's *Mignon*, "Kennst du das Land?" (the intensity evinced here not equalled even by Schwarzkopf herself – how searing are the repeated cries of "Kennst du es wohl?") and *Gretchen am Spinnrade*, which – probably because this is a real event and not a studio invention – has a cumulative, riveting effect seldom if ever heard matched; eternal longing expressed in simple yet overwhelmingly poignant diction and expression – slight signs of strain at the top here wholly appropriate. We are given the recital unedited except for the excision of some applause. Thus endearingly we hear a Heidenröslein where the singer 'dries', makes an amusing apology and starts again. Erik Werba was the perfect pianist for this singer. An unforgettable recital, worth every penny even at full price. Don't miss it.

Goethe Lieder Dawn Upshaw (sop); **Richard Goode** (pf). Elektra Nonesuch Ⓕ 7559-79317-2
(53 minutes: DDD: 8/94). Texts and translations included. Recorded 1993. *Gramophone Editor's record of the month.* Ⓖ
Schubert Rastlose Liebe, D138. Gretchen am Spinnrade, D118. Mignons Gesang, D877 No. 4.
Suleika I, D720. Versunken, D715. Wanderers Nachtlied II, D768. Ganymed, D544. An den
Mond, D296. **Schumann** Liebeslied, Op. 51 No. 5. Nachtlied, Op. 96 No. 1. Lieder und
Gesänge aus Wilhelm Meister, Op. 98a – No. 1, Mignon; No. 5, Heiss mich nicht reden; No. 7,
Singet nicht in Trauertönen. **Wolf** Blumengruss. Die Bekehrte. Die Spröde. Frühling übers Jahr.
Mozart Das Veilchen, K476.

Upshaw and Goode are a musical marriage made in heaven, each a highly individual, probing and sincere artist prepared to challenge received views on a song. Thus their *Gretchen am Spinnrade* in this programme of all-Goethe settings is an outburst of a desperate and infinitely perturbed woman breaking conventional bonds. To emphasize the point Upshaw leans into the first syllable of "nimmer" at each repetition with added feeling and times the climax of the great song at the word "Kuss" in an overwhelming way, only such a similarly involving (although very different) interpreter as Lotte Lehmann could. Goode's playing simply underlines and reinforces the singer's intense utterance. The Schumann settings are filled with just as much spontaneous emotion and direct imagination. The pair make as strong a case as is possible for Schumann's setting of Mignon's *Kennst du das Land* being superior even to Wolf's, the repeated "Kennst du das wohl?" carrying an extraordinary charge. The singer's voice is also ideally fitted for Wolf's teasingly sensual *Die Spröde* and *Die Bekehrte* and the pair bring the lightest touch to *Blumengruss*. Finally they give Mozart's *Das Veilchen* a deeper meaning than almost any interpreters from the past. An ideally balanced, forward yet spacious recording enhances the pleasure to be derived from this deeply satisfying disc.

Hail, Gladdening Light Cambridge Singers / **John Rutter**. Collegium Ⓕ COLCD113 (72 minutes:
DDD; 4/92). Texts and translations included.
Anonymous Rejoice in the Lord. **Purcell** Remember not, Lord, our offences, Z50. **J. Amner**
Come, let's rejoice. **Tomkins** When David heard. **Bairstow** I sat down under his shadow.
J. Goss These are they that follow the lamb. **Taverner** Christe Jesu, pastor bone. **Philips** O
beatum et sacrosanctum diem. **Howells** Nunc dimittis. **Vaughan Williams** O vos omnes.
Dering Factum est silentium. **Stanford** Justorum animae, Op. 38 No. 1. **C. Wood** Hail,
gladdening light. **Tavener** A hymn to the mother of God. Hymn for the dormition of the
mother of God. **Elgar** They are at rest. **Walton** A litany. **Morley** Nolo mortem peccatoris.
Tallis O nata lux. **Rutter** Loving shepherd of Thy sheep. **R. Stone** The Lord's Prayer.
J. Sheppard In manus tuas. **W.H. Harris** Bring us, O Lord God.

This has the subtitle "Music of the English Church" and it is arranged under four main headings: anthems and introits (these count as one), Latin motets, settings of hymns and other poetry, and prayer-settings. Each of them is well represented in a programme that varies delightfully in period and style, and in performances which are remarkably consistent in quality. Some of the items will come as discoveries to most listeners: for example, the anthem *Come, let's rejoice*, a splendid, madrigal-like piece written by John Amner, organist from 1610 to 1641 at Ely Cathedral where these recordings were made. Others are equally impressive in their present performance: a deep quietness attends the opening of Richard Dering's *Factum est silentium*, which ends with rhythmic Alleluias set dancing in subdued excitement. Among the hymn-settings is one by a 16-year-old called William Walton. Included in the prayers is the choirmaster's own setting, characteristically made for pleasure, of *Loving shepherd of Thy sheep*. All are unaccompanied, and thus very exactingly test the choir's blend of voices, its precision, articulation and feeling for rhythm. In all respects they do exceptionally well; the tone is fresh, the attack unanimous, the expression clear and sensitive, the rhythm on its toes. These are young and gifted singers, formed with disciplined enthusiasm into a choir with a distinctive style – and, incidentally, recorded with admirable results by a family firm which operates from a studio built at the bottom of the garden.

Hear my Prayer [a]Jeremy Budd (treb); **St Paul's Cathedral Choir / John Scott** with [b]**Andrew Lucas** (org). Hyperion Ⓕ CDA66439 (76 minutes: DDD: 10/91). Texts and translations included. Recorded 1990.

Allegri Miserere mei (with Nicholas Thompson, treb; Wilfred Swansborough, alto; Timothy Jones, bass)[a]. **B. Rose** Feast Song for St Cecilia (Simon Hill, alto; Alan Green, ten)[a]. **Brahms** Ein deutsches Requiem – Ich hab nun Traurigkeit (sung in English)[ab]. **Britten** Festival Te Deum, Op. 32[ab]. **Harvey** Come, Holy Ghost (Andrew Burden, ten; Nigel Beaven, bass)[a]. **Mendelssohn** Hear my prayer[ab]. **Stanford** Evening Canticles in G major (Jones)[ab]. **Tavener** I will lift up mine eyes. **Wise** The ways of Zion do mourn (Charles Gibbs, bass)[ab].

The special distinction of this disc is the work of the treble soloist, Jeremy Budd. He sings in a programme which is very much the choirboy's equivalent of an operatic soprano's "Casta diva" and more of that sort (come to think of it, Master Budd could probably have sung a splendid "Casta diva" into the bargain). As it is, he crowns the Allegri *Miserere* with its five top Cs, spot-on, each of them (rather like Melba singing "Amor" at the end of Act 1 in *La bohème* five times over). He commands the breath, the long line and the purity of tone necessary for the solo in Brahms's Requiem and copes with the difficult modern idiom of Jonathan Harvey's *Come, Holy Ghost* with an apparent ease that to an older generation may well seem uncanny. Other modern works are included. John Tavener's *I will lift up mine eyes*, written for St Paul's in 1990, has its characteristic compound of richness and austerity; and in this, the words penetrate the mist of echoes more successfully than do those of the *Feast Song for St Cecilia*, written by Gregory Rose and set to some very beautiful music by his father Bernard. It is good, as ever, to hear Stanford's Evening Service in G, with its almost Fauré-like accompaniment finely played by the excellent Andrew Lucas; and for a morning canticle there is Britten's *Te Deum* with its effective build-up to "Lord God of Sabaoth" and its faint pre-echo of *The Turn of the Screw* at "O Lord, save Thy people". There is also a melancholy anthem by Michael Wise, whose fate it was to be knocked on the head and killed by the watchman to whom he was cheeky one night in 1687.

Hölderlin Songs Mitsuko Shirai (mez); Hartmut Höll (pf). Capriccio Ⓕ 10 534 (69 minutes: DDD: 12/94). Texts and translations included. Recorded 1986-93.

Ullmann Abendphantasie. Der Frühling. **Eisler** Sechs Hölderlin-Fragmente. **Komma** Fünf Hölderlin Fragmente. **Reutter** Drei Hölderlin Lieder, Op. 67. **Fröhlich** Rückkehr in die Heimat. **Cornelius** Sonnenuntergang. **Jarnach** An eine Rose. **Hauer** Ehmals und jetzt. **Pfitzner** Abbitte, Op. 29 No. 1. **Fortner** Geh unter, schöne Sonne. **Britten** Hölderlin Fragments, Op. 61 – No. 5, Hälfte des Lebens.

Hölderlin evoked a unique world in those composers who have felt able to approach him, and this ingeniously compiled and finely performed recital amply and absorbingly bears that out. He was mad, of course, but in the midst of his mental whirlwind often achieved a lucid stillness that is profoundly sane. Viktor Ullmann, setting his verse in the Terezin concentration camp, matches this strange serenity very precisely with pure line and long curves that are tonally scarcely tethered. Hanns Eisler, setting him as an exile in California not long before Ullmann was killed, casts a quiet spell with sparely accompanied, atonal but graceful melodies, but is drawn into fierce vehemence and back to tonality by Hölderlin's and his own nostalgia for a Germany before chaos broke upon her. Karl Michael Komma, the only living composer here and in any case better known as a musicologist, is less interesting: his fragmentary but intense vocal lines reflect Hölderlin more precisely than his ungratefully clumpy keyboard writing. Fröhlich and Cornelius, contemporaries of Schubert and Brahms respectively, find the idiom more elusive, though Fröhlich at least hints at what a Hölderlin setting by Schubert might have been like. But in Hermann Reutter's three songs you can almost see him escaping from the almost salon style of No. 1 to find in No. 3 a vehemently bold vocal line that very aptly reflects Hölderlin's imagery of a hidden straight line underlying the crooked paths of fate. Pfitzner, too, gets very close both to the pain of *Abbitte* (a plea for forgiveness for troubling God with complaints) and to the wonderful serenity of the poem's end. Wolfgang Fortner's tolling ostinatos and beautiful melismatic lines suggest a song-writer of real distinction. Mitsuko Shirai's clear high mezzo and her subtle way with words make such a beautiful thing of a single song from Britten's Hölderlin cycle that one wishes she had recorded the whole set. The performances are consistently fine, though Hartmut Höll's piano is done no favours by a close, dry recording.

New review

Inessa Galante: Début Recital Inessa Galante (sop); **Latvian National Symphony Orchestra / Alexander Vilumanis.** Campion Ⓕ RRCD1335 (72 minutes: DDD: 11/95). Recorded 1994.

Bellini Norma – Casta diva. **Gounod** Roméo et Juliette – Je veux vivre. **Bach/Gounod** Ave Maria. **Puccini** La rondine – Chi il bel sogno di Doretta. La bohème – Sì, mi chiamano Mimì; Donde lieta uscì. Gianni Schicchi – O mio babbino caro. **Bizet** Carmen – Je dis que rien ne m'épouvante. **Leoncavallo** Pagliacci – Qual fiamma avea nel guardo!. **Verdi** La traviata – Addio del passato. I vespri siciliani – Mercè, dilette amiche. **Caccini/Brinums** Ave Maria. **Franck** Panis angelicus. **Mozart** Die Zauberflöte – Ach, ich fühl's. **Boito** Mefistofele – L'altra notte. **Villa-Lobos** Bachianas Brasileiras No. 5.

This must be one of the most exciting début recitals from any opera singer for a long time. Galante's voice is a lyrical, sappy one with prospects of entering the *spinto* repertory. It most resembles that of the young Carol Vaness. At the moment it is ideally suited to the lighter Puccini heroines, most particularly Mimì. Indeed Mimì's Farewell (wrongly labelled on the disc) is the most affecting performance here, finely shaded, warmly sung, tenderly felt, but the same character's narration and Lauretta's "O mio babbino caro" aren't far behind. Nedda's soaring Ballatella and Margarita's heartbroken solo (from *Mefistofele*) are other well-known solos that find Galante responding in a free-ranging, spontaneous manner. The downsides of this enormous talent are faults in stylistic approach that urgently call for attention by a good coach, who would teach her to phrase more idiomatically and to use words, particularly consonants, to enhance expression. In the meantime, enjoy the lovely sound and the secure, easy technique, particularly welcome in the soupy arrangements of Bach and Caccini, not incidentally for the fastidious. The support is undistinguished: Vilumanis's lethargic tempo contradicts the message of Juliette's "Je veux vivre". The recording catches the full bloom of Galante's tone. The documentation is inadequate.

Intermedios del Barroco Hispanico [a]**Montserrat Figueras** (sop); **Hespèrion XX / Jordi Savall** (va da gamba). Auvidis Astrée Ⓕ E8729 (71 minutes: DDD: 2/92). 🍏 Recorded 1987.
M. Romero Caiase de un espino[a]. **Aguilera de Héredia** Tiento de Batalla. Ensalada.
F. Guerrero Si tus penas[a]. **J. Cabanilles** Pasacalles V. Tiento lleno. Corrente italiana.
J.K. Keril Batalla Imperial. **M. Machado** Afuera, afuera que sale[a]. **Correa de Arauxo**
Batalla des Morales. **J. Blas de Castro** Desde las torres del alma[a]. Entre dos Alamos verdes[a].
J. Marin Ojos, que me desdenais[a]. **Lope de Vega/Anonymous** De pechos sobre una torre[a].
Como retumban los remos[a]. **Anonymous** No hay que decirle el primor[a].

A heady Hispanic baroque cocktail. All the vocal numbers here are settings of texts by the colourful and astonishingly prolific Spanish poet and dramatist Lope de Vega (1562-1635), described by Cervantes as "a monster of nature". They range from blithe, folkish pieces through the powerful *De pechos sobre una torre*, in which a woman laments for her lover who has sailed for England with the Armada, to Guerrero's haunting prayer to Jesus, declaimed over a bare string bass and culminating in an extraordinary spoken climax. The instrumental items interspersed with the vocal settings include several rousing battle pieces – a popular seventeenth-century genre – and, for contrast, three beautiful polyphonic numbers by one of the greatest figures of the Spanish Baroque, Joan Cabanilles. If Jordi Savall has touched up the scoring of some of the pieces, no matter: the performances are exciting, sensual, dramatic, with kaleidoscopically varied instrumental colouring, from the entertaining percussion effects of Machado's *Afuera, afuera que sale* to the grave viol consort of Cabanilles's *Pasacalles V* (strong Purcellian associations here). And Montserrat Figueras, with her distinctive, plangent tone, makes a subtle, stylish, richly imaginative soloist. An irresistible disc, and an ideal introduction to the largely unexplored treasures of the Spanish baroque.

Italian Songs **Cecilia Bartoli** (mez); **András Schiff** (pf). Decca Ⓕ 440 297-2DH (68 minutes: DDD: 11/93). Texts and translations included. Recorded 1992. *Gramophone Editor's choice.*
Beethoven La Partenza, WoO124. Four Ariettas, Op. 82. In questa tomba oscura, WoO133.
Mozart Ridente la calma, K152/K210a. **Schubert** Didone abbandonata, D510. Im Haine,
D738. An die Leier, D737. La Pastorella al Prato, D528. Vier Canzonen, D688. Pensa, che questo istante, D76. Willkommen und Abschied, D767. **Haydn** Arianna a Naxos, HobXXVI*b*/2.

It is good to be reminded of these composers' responses to the Italian muse in this particularly well-cast recital. Central Europe, in the person of András Schiff, meets Italy, in Cecilia Bartoli, to delightful, often revelatory effect. The simple form and undemanding vocal line of Beethoven's little *La Partenza* makes for a truthfulness of expression which Bartoli's clear, light-filled enunciation recreates to the full. With her warm breath gently supporting the voice's lively, supple inflexion, she reveals Beethoven's own skill in word-setting both here and in two fascinatingly contrasted settings of "L'amante impaziente" in the *Ariettas*, Op. 82. Schubert's ten *Canzone* selected here show a wide range of treatment, from the compressed lyric drama of Dido's lament "Vedi quanto adoro", in which Bartoli lives intensely from second to second, to the honeyed Goldoni *pastorella* and the thrumming, pulsating serenade of "Guarda, che bianca luna", D688 No. 2. A gently, fragrantly shaped Mozart *Ridente la calma*, and a Haydn *Arianna a Naxos* of movingly immediate and youthful response complete this unexpectedly and unusually satisfying recital.

I wish it so **Dawn Upshaw** (sop); **orchestra / Eric Stern.** Elektra Nonesuch Ⓕ 7559-79345-2 (45 minutes: DDD: 12/94). Texts included. Recorded 1993. *Gramophone Award winner 1995.* 🅖🅖
Blitzstein Juno – I wish it so. No for an Answer – In the clear. Reuben, Reuben – Never get lost. **Sondheim** Anyone Can Whistle – There won't be trumpets. Saturday Night – What more do I need? The Girls of Summer – The Girls of Summer. Merrily We Roll Along – Like it was. Evening Primrose – Take me to the world. **Weill** One Touch of Venus – That's him. Lady in the Dark – The saga of Jenny; My ship. Lost in the Stars – Stay well. **Bernstein** West Side Story – I feel pretty. Candide – Glitter and be gay. The Madwoman of Central Park West – My new friends.

Bernstein, Blitzstein, Sondheim and Weill are a good quartet to explore in a recital and Dawn Upshaw's clear soprano is well suited to nearly all these songs. The Blitzstein numbers will only be familiar to specialists. "I wish it so" from Blitzstein's adaptation of O'Casey's *Juno* seems to herald the mood of the whole disc, songs of longing, some optimistic, some resigned. "In the clear" is one of the songs from *No for an Answer*, Blitzstein's follow-up to *The Cradle Will Rock*; it was first given in 1940, the same week that saw the first night of Weill's *Lady in the Dark*. In the Blitzstein, Eric Stern's arrangement with a solo cello part played by Matthias Niegele turns the song into a melancholy lullaby. This and a brilliant performance of "Glitter and be gay" from *Candide* show off Dawn Upshaw's impressive range – from the coloratura of the Bernstein to the mezzo-ish moodiness for the Blitzstein. Of the Weill songs, "Stay well" from *Lost in the Stars* is especially successful, and "That's him" from *One Touch of Venus* is playful. The two numbers from *Lady in the Dark* are given the most extensive overhaul, the melody of "The saga of Jenny" such as it is disappears beneath Larry Wilcox's rearrangement and although Upshaw sings "My ship" quite beautifully, again Daniel Troob has made an arrangement that pulls it about rather. All in all, this is a very attractive foray into the Broadway territory.

New review

Lotte Lehmann Songs – Balogh, Beethoven, Brahms, Cimara, Franz, Gounod, Grechaninov,
   Hahn, Jensen, Marx, Mozart, Pfitzner, Sadero, Schubert, Schumann, Sjöberg, Wolf and Worth.
   Lotte Lehmann (sop) with various artists. Romophone mono Ⓟ 81013-2* (two discs: 157 minutes:
   ADD: 5/96). From Victor originals; recorded 1935-40.

Lotte Lehmann was at the height of her powers as a song interpreter in the late 1930s: the bloom of youth is still in the tone, now enhanced by the experience of many years of stage interpretation. Thus, her characters *in extremis* become something of a talisman of suffering women. Her impassioned Gretchen in Schubert's great song is sister to, and inhabits the same world as, Lehmann's Leonore and Sieglinde. The searing intensity of "Was hör ich alte Laute?" in Schumann's *Alte Laute* goes through you, becomes etched in the mind, just as do certain phrases in her operatic portrayals. Yet while the passions are felt on a large scale throughout these songs, the intimate mould of Lieder singing is never breached. The readings are generous and free, never dull, careful or limited, or by another token overladen with detailed word-painting in the Schwarzkopf manner. Unlike many of her contemporaries Lehmann ranged wide in her choice of repertory. She digs out Jensen's *Lehn' diene Wang' an meine Wange* and makes you believe that this little sentimental song is a masterpiece. However, it is for the Schubert (including 12 songs from *Winterreise*, so immediate in effect, no holds barred), Schumann, Brahms and Wolf, that the myriad admirers of this artist will want these two lavishly filled CDs. The transfers are clean and clear, but at times impart a slight glare to Lehmann's tone. This offering is an essential addition to the Lehmann discography.

New review

Lieder by German Opera Composers Olaf Bär (bar); Helmut Deutsch (pf). EMI
   Ⓟ CDC5 55393-2 (67 minutes: DDD: 1/96). Texts and translations included. Recorded 1994.
   Kreutzer Frühlingsglaube. Die Post. Die Kapelle, Op. 64 No. 1. Nachtreise. Entschluss,
   Op. 64 No. 2. Nähe des Geliebten. **Nicolai** Scarco d'affanni. Herbstlied, Op. 37. Il mistero,
   Op. 24 No. 2. **Goetz** Lieder, Op. 12 – No. 1, Geheimnis; No. 2, Schliesse mir die Augen beide;
   No. 3, Wandervöglein. Lieder, Op. 19 – No. 1, Ein Frühlingstraum; No. 2, Der Frühling kommt!;
   No. 3, Wandrers Nachtlied, "Der du von dem Himmel bist". **Humperdinck** Romanze.
   Blauveilchen. Entsagung. Oft sinn ich hin und wieder. Das Lied von Glück. Sonntagsruhe.
   Marschner Rheinromanzen, Op. 128 – No. 1, Die sieben Freier. Gesänge und Balladen,
   Op. 160 – No. 1, Der König von Thule; No. 2, Die Rache. Das Flämmchen auf der Heide,
   Op. 80 No. 12. Die Monduhr, Op. 102 No. 2. Das Lied von alten König, Op. 82 No. 2. Der
   betrogene Teufel, Op. 87 No. 1.

For all but the most knowledgeable in Lieder this will be a real and fascinating voyage of discovery. Each of the composers represented is known, if at all, by one or two operas, but all wrote liberally as song composers. Kreutzer's setting of *Die Post*, written before Schubert's, is worthy to stand beside it. *Die Kapelle* is even better, a funeral piece in the minor of much more than passing interest in its acute setting of an Uhland text, changes of key worthy of Schubert and intense repeats of the single word "Hirtenknabe". The three songs by Nicolai are pleasing but slight. Goetz, who died all too young, was admired by Brahms and one can hear why in the very Brahmsian *Schliesse mir die Augen beide*, a setting of an admirable poem by Ludwig Sturm. Goethe's other Lieder here are not so remarkable. Humperdinck also proves something of a disappointment except in the Wagnerian *Sonntagsruhe*. The remainder do not evince sufficiently individual personality. Marschner is quite another matter. Each song here is at least to be spoken of in the same breath as those by his contemporary, Loewe, whom he much resembles in style. *Die sieben Freier* is another of those Lorelei-inspired poems so beloved of the German romantics. This one deserves to stand alongside the best. Even better is the Gothic horror of both *Die Rache*, with its ostinato imitation of hoofbeats, and *Die Monduhr*, imbued throughout with a constantly varied motif in thirds. Perhaps these pieces aren't so unexpected from the composer of *Der Vampyr*. *Der betrogene Teufel* is a nice essay in the ribald, which is delivered by Bär in an appropriately biting timbre. But then throughout he is back on his most convincing form, relishing every word and note and singing with restored freedom. Deutsch, who also contributes the booklet-notes, proves a worthy partner. The recording is forward and well-balanced.

Lieder Recital Dame Janet Baker (mez); **Martin Isepp** (pf). Saga Classics Ⓜ EC33612
(47 minutes: AAD: 3/92). Texts and translation included. From STXID5277 (4/66). Recorded
1966.
> **Schumann** Frauenliebe und -leben, Op. 42. **Brahms** Die Mainacht, Op. 43 No. 2. Das
> Mädchen spricht, Op. 107 No. 3. Nachtigall, Op. 97 No. 1. Von ewiger Liebe, Op. 43 No. 1.
> **Schubert** Heimliches Lieben, D922. Minnelied, D429. Die abgeblühte Linde, D514. Der
> Musensohn, D764.

This recording was rapturously reviewed in *Gramophone* when it first appeared, and there was no
doubt that a singer of great achievement and still greater promise had arrived in our midst. Over the
next many years, the name of Janet Baker (Dame-to-be) graced the monthly lists of new recordings
and unfailingly brought distinction with it. Her interpretative powers were to mature, and she was
certainly to be better recorded, but it is quite likely that nothing brought greater pleasure in the sheer
sound of the voice than this early recital of Lieder. Her *Frauenliebe und -leben* here has the mark of
a great interpreter upon it particularly in the song of happy motherhood, "An meinem Herzen"; but
earlier, the conviction of her singing irradiates the performance, and in the last song the fine dark tone
and change of expression on the 'face' of the voice are both eloquent and moving. In the Schubert
group, her *Musensohn* has a joyous unselfconsciousness, and in the Brahms her *Von ewiger Liebe* still
ranks among the finest of all.

Lieder Recital Karl Erb (ten); **Bruno Seidler-Winkler** (pf). Preiser Lebendige Vergangenheit mono
Ⓕ 89208* (two discs: 149 minutes: AAD: 6/94). From HMV and Electrola originals; recorded
1934-9.   ⒼⒼⒼ
> Lieder by **Adam, Bach, Beethoven, Brahms, Liszt, Loewe, Schoeck, Schubert,**
> **Schumann, Wolf** and **Zilcher**

Erb's career, voice and style closely resemble those of Peter Schreier today; their voices are uncannily
similar in timbre, for they possess a tone of strange, plangent beauty that can on the other hand sound
a shade piercing and uncomfortable. Almost all of the first CD is devoted to Erb's Schubert, covering
a wide range of the better-known songs. Few, except perhaps for Schreier himself, have come closer
to conveying the inner desolation and/or loneliness of such pieces as *Wanderers Nachtlied II, Dass sie
hier gewesen* and "Der Wegweiser" and "Das Wirtshaus" from *Winterreise*. The piercing, sad quality
of tone, the acute accentuation of words are here wholly appropriate. Yet Erb can lighten his voice
and manner for such charmers as *An Sylvia* and *Liebesbotschaft*. The second disc in the main
comprises Erb's Beethoven, Schumann, Brahms and Wolf. Some of his Schumann is beyond praise.
His intimate, spontaneous readings of such favourites as *Meine Rose, Mondnacht* and *Der Nussbaum*
sound newly minted. The same can be said of Brahms's glorious *O wüsst' ich doch den Weg zurück*.
Again, his reading of Wolf's religious (Mörike and Ocana) settings are held on a thread of perfectly
sustained legato. The transfers are excellent.

Lieder Recital Nicolai Gedda (ten); **Erik Werba** (pf). EMI Salzburg Festival Edition mono
Ⓜ CDH5 65352-2* (69 minutes: ADD). Recorded live in 1961.
> **Handel** Atalanta – Di ad Irene, tiranna. **Schubert** Die Liebe hat gelogen, D751. Der Schiffer,
> D536. Nacht und Träume, D827. Rastlose Liebe, D138. **R. Strauss** Heimliche Aufforderung,
> Op. 27 No. 3. Die Nacht, Op. 10 No. 3. Heimkehr, Op. 15 No. 5. Liebeshymnus, Op. 32 No. 3.
> **Duparc** L'invitation au voyage. Le Manoir de Rosemonde. Phidylé. Chanson triste, Op. 2 No. 4.
> **Poulenc** Airs chantés – Air champêtre; Air grave. **Miaskovsky** The moon and the cloud.
> **Khachaturian** Nina's Song. **Rachmaninov** Christ is risen, Op. 26 No. 6. How fair this spot,
> Op. 21 No. 7. Aleko – Young Gipsy's song. **Napravnik** Dubrovsky – Romanze. **Massenet**
> Werther – Pourquoi me reveiller? **Malawski** Russian Song.

Gedda is in his marvellous prime here – a mature one, at the age of 36, singing like a young man who
might be a dozen years his junior, and with all the experience and assurance of an absolute master.
His voice is of the utmost beauty: sweetness and power combined. In this recital he goes through his
paces, classical aria first, with a long and testing run to make sure the lungs are in good working order,
and with plenty of opportunity for that lively play of varied moods which has always been such a
feature of his singing. Schubert brings a silvery yet passionate *Die Liebe hat gelogen*, a beautifully
sustained *Nacht und Träume* (with an extra beat to the bar at one point) and the two more vigorous
songs whose vitality is never rendered with over-emphasis. The Strauss group is superb throughout;
the Duparc has that right degree of greater intimacy, with *Phidylé* allowed a very French touch in
which for a while resonance is shut-off, the singing a melodious extension of the speaking-voice.
Poulenc's "Air grave" would surely have redeemed itself in the composer's judgement from his
condemnation as "indefensibly trite" if he could have heard this performance. The Rachmaninov
songs are perhaps best of all, *Christ is risen* having a fine agony of expression, *How fair this spot*
unforgettable in its sense of actuality (and glorious high B natural), and the song from *Aleko* sung
with thrilling resonance (as well as having, dare one suggest, just about the best tune Rachmaninov
ever wrote). Encores raise the temperature still further, the audience (who, incidentally, applaud
everything, mid-group or not) being by now high with very understandable enthusiasm, thoroughly
shared by the reviewer except when engaged in trying to extract something useful from the booklet,
which is less than adequate.

Lieder Recital Irmgard Seefried (sop) with various artists. Testament mono Ⓕ SBT1026*
(74 minutes: ADD: 9/93). From Columbia originals; recorded 1946-53.
    Lieder by **Brahms, Flies, Mozart, Schubert** and **Wolf**

Another 'must' for anyone who loves Seefried. In these wonderfully immediate and faithful transfers of performances made between 1946 and 1953 in Vienna and London, Seefried is heard at the peak of her powers, when her voice was at its freshest and easiest. In the Mozart whether the mood is happy, reflective or tragic, Seefried goes unerringly to the core of the matter. Here we have the archness of *Die kleine Spinnerin*, the naughty exuberance of *Warnung*, the deep emotion of *Abendempfindung* and *Unglückliche Liebe*. We are offered five Schubert songs, including an unsurpassed *Auf dem Wasser zu singen*, so airy and natural; a pure, elevated *Du bist die Ruh* and a poised, ravishing *Nacht und Träume*. The lullabies of Flies, Schubert and Brahms are all vintage Seefried. The Wolf items are a real treasure trove: a sorrowful, plangent account of *Das verlassene Mägdelein* (perhaps the most compelling interpretation of all here; unutterably moving), an enchanting, spontaneous *Elfenlied* (with Gerald Moore marvellously delicate here). For the most part, Moore is in attendance to complete one's pleasure in an irresistible and generously filled disc.

New review

Magnificat and Nunc Dimittis, Volume 3. Lichfield Cathedral Choir / Andrew Lumsden with [a]Mark Shepherd, [b]Nigel Potts (orgs). Priory Ⓕ PRCD505 (56 minutes: DDD: 10/95). Texts included. Recorded 1994.
    Stanford Evening Service in A major, Op. 12[a]. **S. Watson** Evening Service in E major[b].
    G. Ives Evening (Edington) Service[a]. **Gibbons** First (Short) Service[a]. **Leighton** Evening (Magdalen) Service[a]. **Howells** Evening Service in G major[a]. **Dyson** Evening Service in D major[a].

Why do keys have characters? Maybe it's the 'feel' of the keyboard and the 'look' of the key-signature – with A major those three spiky sharps suggest something quite different from the laid-back four flats of their neighbour. Anyway, Stanford has caught the very essence of A major at the start of his *Magnificat*; and this performance has caught the essence of Stanford. Crisp, clear-headed, purposeful and glad-to-be-alive that is the A majorish character of the opening bars, splendidly played by Mark Shepherd. The choir, too, are alert and responsive, a thorough credit to Andrew Lumsden, their Director. This is an excellent record. Each of the settings has its special character, and all in their different ways are skilful in craftsmanship, the joinery of the business. Sydney Watson, whose Service in E follows Stanford in A, has a fine economy of means, discreet in its more modern harmonic flavouring. Howells ("my son in music" as Stanford called him) wrote more adventurous and memorable settings than this one in G, yet its affectionate traditionalism impresses too, and as it opens out in the *Gloria* of the Magnificat it conveys that rush of ecstasy or apprehension of the sublime that is so characteristic. The Lichfield sound is refreshing, and the vitality of their performances remains a good, bracing pleasure throughout.

New review

Magnificat and Nunc Dimittis, Volume 4. Portsmouth Cathedral Choir / Adrian Lucas with David Thorne (org). Priory Ⓕ PRCD527 (79 minutes: DDD: 2/96). Texts included. Recorded 1995.
    Brewer Evening Service in E flat major. **Andrews** Evening Service in G major. **Howells** Evening Service in E major. Evening Service in B minor. **Lassus** Magnificat quarto toni.
    Victoria Nunc dimittis. **Stanford** Evening Service in C major, Op. 115. **Weelkes** Evening Service for Trebles – Magnificat; Nunc dimittis. **Darke** Evening Service in F major.
    R. Shephard Salisbury Service. **Bairstow** Evening Service in D major.

One good thing after another; it almost surprises that a succession of *Mags* and *Nuncs* can be so varied, satisfying and enjoyable. The programmes in this excellent series allow for a fair variety of styles and centuries, but in this instance a particularly generous share of the credit must go to the performances. Forthright and invigorating, they give rise to a distinct suspicion that the whole business may be a pleasure: that the choristers have some rhythm in their bones and at certain points might even have a smile on their faces. It is there right from the start, with Brewer in E flat (and how undeservedly stodgy that can sound in performance) bright with energy and encouraging a conviction that there genuinely is something in which to rejoice. This extends to Lassus, Victoria and Weelkes, where, instead of the more usual formal reading of notes, there is a common effort of understanding and imagination, lifting the notes off the page and sometimes, with a little judicious semi-staccato, setting them a-dance. Nor is there any lack of sensitive shading or of repose in the right places – a fine feeling for mood in the lovely and little-known B minor setting of Howells, for example. A splendid recital, with a fine choice of repertoire, and consistently admirable playing by the organist, David Thorne.

Miserere and other choral works Trinity College Choir, Cambridge / Richard Marlow. Conifer Ⓕ CDCF219 (79 minutes: DDD: 2/94). Recorded 1993.
    Parry I was glad. Jerusalem. **Schubert** Deutsche Messe, D872 – Sanctus. Ave Maria, D839.
    Barber Agnus Dei, Op. 11. **Burgon** Nunc dimittis. **Bach** Cantata No. 129, Gelobet sei der

Herr, mein Gott – Dem wir das Heilig itzt (sung in English). **Allegri** Miserere. **Mendelssohn**
Hear my prayer. **Gardiner** Evening Hymn. **Walford Davies** God be in my head. **Berlioz**
L'Enfance du Christ – Shepherds' Farewell. **Franck** Panis angelicus. **Purcell** Hear my prayer,
O Lord, Z15. **C. Wood** Hail, gladdening light. **Mozart** Ave verum corpus in D, K618. **Gounod**
Ave Maria. **Vaughan Williams** The Old Hundredth Psalm Tunes. O taste and see.

The choir is at its absolute best here in Barber's arrangement of his famous *Adagio* for strings as an
Agnus Dei for unaccompanied voices. In texture and balance, as in the precision of attack and
chording, they are really superb. *Jerusalem* is phrased with breadth and care for sense. Breadth, too,
distinguishes the performance of *I was glad*, the choir's fine sustaining power serving them well. They
are expert in making the most of their resources, so that the quiet "O pray for the peace of
Jerusalem", like the solo choir in the Allegri *Miserere*, makes doubly effective the rich sonority to
come. All the solo work is good, with a remarkably authentic treble tone supplied by Andrea
Cockerton in Mendelssohn's *Hear my prayer*. Purcell's *Hear my prayer* is probably the gem of the
whole programme, which is broadly popular in character, a generous mix of periods and styles, with
the choir's own style helping to impose a unity and always guaranteeing performances that will be
careful in preparation and scrupulous in beauty of tone.

The Mistress Settings of Abraham Cowley's Poems. **The Consort of Musicke** (Emma Kirkby,
Evelyn Tubb, sops; Joseph Cornwell, Andrew King, tens; Simon Grant, bass) / **Anthony Rooley**
(lte). Musica Oscura Ⓟ 070986 (77 minutes: DDD: 1/95). Recorded 1993.
Purcell I came, I saw, and was undone, Z375. They say you're angry, Z422. No, to what purpose,
Z468. She loves, and she confesses, Z413. **Blundeville** Beneath this gloomy shade. **Reggio** Now
by my Love. By Heav'n I'll tell her boldly. 'Tis well, 'tis well with them. Then like some wealthy
Island. I thought, I'll swear. Unhurt, untoucht. 'Tis a strange kind of Ignorance. Though all thy
gestures. **W. King** I wonder what those Lovers mean. What Mines of Sulphur. Go bid the
Needle. It gave a piteous groan. **R. King** False, foolish Heart. No, to what purpose. **Blow** I little
thought. **W. Hall** These full two hours now. **Turner** See where she sits. **Pigott** Ask me not.

Abraham Cowley's *The Mistress* was first published in London in 1647 and was the most successful
collection of love poems of its time. Cowley's strength was that he wrote in a style that was courtly
and clever yet comparatively easy to read, an assessment which calls to mind the customary
disparagement of Betjeman as a poet for people who don't normally read poetry. The result is verse
which is ideally suited to musical setting. Just over a third of the surviving Cowley settings are to be
heard here, offering the chance to hear songs by such rarely heard men as John Blundeville, Francis
Pigott and William Turner alongside their great contemporaries Purcell and Blow. Their music is
always charming and often touching – Pietro Reggio, the most highly represented composer here, is a
happy find for instance – but, predictably, the less strophe-bound Purcell knocks them well into a
cocked hat for sheer depth of emotion and resourceful word-setting; it is hard to imagine any of them
coming up, for instance, with a *tour de force* such as his unpredictable, chaconne-like setting of *She
loves, and she confesses*. Equally hard to imagine, however, are performances which could do them
better justice, interpretations which take each song seriously and look for whatever strengths it may
contain. Emma Kirkby is as intelligent and perceptive as ever, Evelyn Tubb a little more artful and
dramatic; while the two tenors complement each other nicely, Joseph Cornwell providing a richer and
warmer counterpart to Andrew King's light, incisive tones. A beautiful and refined achievement all
round.

New review

Las mujeres y cuerdas [a]Marta Almajano (sop); José Miguel Moreno (gtr). Glossa
Ⓟ GCD920202 (68 minutes: DDD: 2/96). Texts and translations included.Recorded 1994-5.
Soler Canzonettas – La semplice; La volubile; La costanza; La merced[a]. **Carulli** Andante
affetuoso, Op. 320. **Giuliani** Ariette, Op. 95 – Quando sarà quel di; Le dimore amore non ama;
Ad altro laccio[a]. Cavatine, Op. 39 – Confuso, smarrito[a]. Amor, perché m'accendi[a]. Di tanti
palpiti, Op. 79[a]. Andantino sostenuto, Op. 71 No. 3. **Sor** Studies, Op. 31 – Mouvement de prière
religieuse. Ariettas – Povero cor t'inganni; Lagrime; Io mentitor!; Perduta l'anima[a]. Nel cor più
non mi sento[a]. Seguidillas – Muchacha, y los vergüenza; Si dices que mis ojos; Los canonigos,
madre; Las mujeres y cuerdas; Mis descuidados ojos[a]. **Mertz** Bardenklänge, Op. 13 – Lied ohne
Worte.

The album title is that of the final song, Sor's *Las mujeres y cuerdas*, with its caveat that both women
and strings need 'tuning' – but carefully. The cover is adorned with Madrazo's painting (1853) of the
Countess of Vilches (seated in the luxurious surroundings appropriate to her rank), whose demeanour
suggests that she may be dreaming of romantic love, or perhaps listening to musical expressions of it.
The gentle guitar was at that time popular as an accompanying instrument in the home or salon,
incapable of supporting anything vulgar or excessive; the publishing of guitar-accompanied songs
was a flourishing trade. The song by Martin y Soler, a composer of *opera buffa*, was published with
the option of guitar or keyboard; all the others were composed or arranged by guitarists. Giuliani,
the darling of the Viennese salons, exercised his (Italian) gift of melody in responding generously to
the market, whilst Sor worked as a singing teacher during his sojourn in London, from which time the
songs in this recording (and many others) date. These graceful and sometimes coquettish songs of the
joys, frustrations and pains of love are punctuated by suitably day-dreaming guitar solos. Marta

Almajano sings them beguilingly though not without sacrificing consonants to beauty of tone, but the texts are printed in the substantial booklet, as are a number of charming reproductions of paintings. Moreno's contribution is excellent in all respects. This well-recorded and lavishly produced album should appeal to all who care to share the dreams of the Countess of Vilches, in whatever surroundings they may find themselves.

Music in the time of Velázquez La Romanesca (Marta Almajano, sop; Paolo Pandolfo, va da gamba; Juan Carlos de Mulder, theorbo; Nuria Llopis, hp; Tony Millan, hpd) / **José Miguel Moreno** (gtr/vihuela). Glossa Ⓟ GCD920201 (63 minutes: DDD: 11/94). 🖋 Texts and translations included.

Sanz Instrucción de música sobre la guitarra española – Folías; Lantururú; Canarios. **Martín y Coll** Folías. Canarios. **Hidalgo** El templo de Palas – Ay que si, ay que no. Los celos hacen estrellas – De los luces que en el mar; Peynándose estaba un olmo. Ay, que me río de Amor. La Estatua de Prometeo – Tonante Dios! Cuydado, pastor. **Marín** Ojos, que me desdeñais. Cambridge Song Book – Aquella sierra nevada; No piense menguilla ya. **Selma y Salaverde** Primo libro de canzoni – Fantasia sobre el "Canto del Cabellero". Susanna passeggiata. **Ruiz de Ribayaz** Luz y norte musical para caminar – Españoleta. **Guerau** Poema harmonico – Marionas. **Durón** Salir el Amor del Mundo – Sosieguen, descansen.

On this recording of Spanish instrumental and theatre music from the seventeenth century, both the instrumental playing and the solo singing are of a high order. Soprano Marta Almajano has a clear and well focused voice, that is both full and nuanced with a wide range of expression. She is at her most expressive, perhaps, in José Marín's *Ojos, que me desdeñais*, and is scintillatingly alive to the drama of some of the other pieces by Juan Hidalgo, the Spanish equivalent of Purcell. In some items (for example, Hidalgo's *Peynándose estaba un olmo*) the balance between voice and instruments is rather odd, with the latter too prominent or, at least, with the voice sounding curiously distant by comparison. At other times (in Hidalgo's *Cuydado, pastor*) the balance seems better. Both José Miguel Moreno on vihuela and baroque guitar and Paolo Pandolfo on gamba are technically assured and imaginative players, and lead the rest of the team in performances that are full of rhythmic zest and imagination. The music itself is charming and dramatic by turn, and certainly bears repeated listening. It is generally less harmonically adventurous than Purcell (despite some telling chromaticisms in Marín's *Aquella sierra nevada*), but has a cogent harmonic idiom of its own and is full of rhythmic interest.

New review

Music from Charlottenburg Castle [a]Ann Monoyios (sop); **Berlin Barock Compagney.** Capriccio Ⓟ 10 459 (61 minutes: DDD: 10/95). 🖋 Texts included. Recorded 1993.   Ⓖ

Corelli Sonata in G minor, WoO2. Trio Sonata in G major, Op. 2 No. 12. **Ariosti** La rosa[a]. **Torelli** Sonata in G major, Op. 1 No. 1. Concerto a quattro in D minor, Op. 6 No. 10. **Bononcini** Polifemo – Respira, alma, respira ... Dove sei, dove t'ascondi; Non soffrirà, mai Circe ... Pensiero di vendetta[a]. Cefalo e Procride – Cintia, il tuo nome invoco ... Sacro dardo, in te confido; Numi del ciel pietosi ... Bella auretta[a]. **Steffani** Scherzo, Guardati[a].

In the history of arts patronage Sophie Charlotte, wife of the Elector of Brandenburg and later Queen of Prussia, holds an honoured place. Besides building a fine summer palace on the river Spree, as a keen music-lover (with a reputation herself as a harpsichordist) she was at pains to engage leading composers, singers and instrumentalists for her court. Among them was the great violinist Torelli (one of the earliest to publish *Concerti grossi*) and, after him, the opera composer Ariosti, who in 1702 engaged the Bononcini brothers (of whom Giovanni was to become Handel's rival in London). Corelli was outside her immediate circle, but she took a lively interest in his work, and he dedicated his famous Op 5 set of sonatas to her. He is represented here by two works, a sonata containing a *Grave* of arresting chromaticisms, and a *Ciacona* that could easily become a popular hit like the now omnipresent Pachelbel Canon. Of the two Torelli works, the G major Sonata is a delight, with a charmingly springy initial *Allegro* and a dancingly light finale. The playing of this well-balanced group of (period) solo strings plus chamber organ is splendidly neat and crisply rhythmic, and the leader's embellishments – lots of *tirades* – are animated and stylish. The little Ariosti cantata (published in London and dedicated to Charlotte's brother, King George I) is preceded by a brilliant instrumental prelude and consists of two arias, one reflective and one fast. The scherzo – a warning against the wiles of Cupid – by one of Charlotte's favourite composers, Agostino Steffani, is more substantial, and displays a notable variety of mood. Bononcini's appeal as an opera composer is well illustrated by extracts from two works of 1702 outstanding are a deeply expressive *siciliana* for the hapless Galatea and a florid vengeance aria for Circe from *Polifemo*. Ann Monoyios, the possessor of a fresh, youthful-sounding voice with pure intonation, invests the former with pathos and reveals real virtuosity in the second; and her ornamentation of *da capos* in all the works she sings betokens an accomplished mastery of period practice. Most enjoyable. It is a pity that the texts are printed with only a German translation, and that the accompanying note is amateurishly rendered into English; but this is a delectable disc.

Officium Jan Garbarek (sax); **Hilliard Ensemble** (David James, alto; Rogers Covey-Crump, John Potter, tens; Gordon Jones, bar). ECM New Series Ⓟ 445 369-2 (78 minutes: DDD: 10/94). Latin texts included. Including Plainchant, Notre Dame polyphony and motets by Dufay, de la Rue and Morales – with saxophone. Recorded 1993. Ⓖ

The play between ancient chant and structured jazz-style improvisation creates a sort of spiritual time warp where past and present happily co-exist on the basis of shared musical goals. For no matter how one views so-called crossover (such a silly term), or the relative lack of wisdom in sticking to rigid musical boundaries, the evidence remains conclusive: "Officium" successfully transcends any limitations imposed by time and style. If you have any doubts, then play either the opening or closing tracks, both of which find Jan Garbarek (a master of apposite extemporization) easing around Christóbal de Morales's polyphonic "Pace mihi domine" (from the *Officium defunctorum*) as if it were his own creation. The effect is enchanting and when, eight tracks later (or earlier, according to whether you're in 'forward' or 'reverse' mode), the same piece is presented *sans* Garbarek's saxophone, we somehow miss the commentary. If the probable success of this album prompts certain jazz fans and early music specialists to commiserate over their invaded territories, or cynics to align Garbarek and the Hilliards with Górecki and the Monks, then take heart: we're still listening to Respighi's ancient masters, Stravinsky's 'Pergolesi', Tchaikovsky's Mozart and Loussier's Bach, not to mention Ellington's Tchaikovsky – none of which is in the current pop charts. Stylistic cross-pollination makes for a healthy creative environment, and this CD is one of its happiest symptoms. Recordings, documentation and presentation are exemplary.

On Wings of Song Songs and Duets. [a]**Felicity Lott** (sop); [b]**Ann Murray** (mez); **Graham Johnson** (pf). EMI Ⓔ CDC7 54411-2 (76 minutes: DDD: 7/92). Texts and translations included. Recorded 1991.

Purcell (arr. Britten) Come ye sons of art, away, Z323 – Sound the trumpet[ab]. The Indian Queen – I attempt from love's sickness[b]. Lost is my quiet for ever, Z502[ab]. King Arthur – Fairest isle[a]. What can we poor females do, Z518[ab]. **Mendelssohn** Wasserfahrt[ab]. Duets, Op. 63[ab] – No. 5, Volkslied; No. 6, Maiglöckchen und die Blümelein. Auf Flügeln des Gesanges, Op. 34 No. 2[b]. Neue Liebe, Op. 19a No. 4[ab]. Abendlied[ab]. **Rossini** Soirées musicales – No. 1, La promessa[a]; No. 10, La pesca[ab]. Péchés de vieillesse, Book 1 – Anzoletta co passa la regata[b]. Duetto buffo di due gatti[ab]. **Gounod** La siesta[ab]. **Delibes** Les trois oiseaux[ab]. **Massenet** Rêvons, c'est l'heure[ab]. Joie![ab]. **Paladilhe** Au bord de l'eau[ab]. **Aubert** Cache-cache[ab]. **Balfe** Trust her not[ab]. **Sullivan** Coming home[ab]. **Quilter** It was a lover and his lass, Op. 23 No. 3[ab]. **Britten** Mother comfort[ab]. Underneath the abject willow[ab].

These expert duettists (fellow contributors to the Songmakers's Almanac and Marschallin and Octavian in many a *Rosenkavalier*) have already one highly successfully disc ("Sweet Power of Song" – reviewed further on) to their joint credit, and now achieve what often proves the more difficult task of providing an equally good sequel. But of course this is not really a double-act but a trio, and Graham Johnson is, as ever, more than accompanist. When he arranges a programme, delight follows as sure as night follows day. Here the delight lies partly in discovery (for instance, there is a charmer of Gounod's, in Spanish style, the voices in dreamy thirds, the ending softly delicate). Then there is the range of mood, from Purcell's assured, outward-going "Sound the trumpet" at the start to the desolation that burrows within Britten's haunting *Mother comfort* near the end. Solos are deftly chosen to bring out the best in each singer, as in the clean style and unostentatious manner of Felicity Lott's "Fairest isle" and Ann Murray's finely phrased, evenly sustained *Auf Flügeln des Gesanges*. Then there are the charming oddities: Sullivan's "Coming home" turns out to be a duet from *Cox and Box* (but with different words), and 'Rossini's' cat-duet is now attributed to that singularly unpredictable minor genius, Robert Pearsall. The recording is exemplary.

A Program of Song Leontyne Price (sop); David Garvey (pf). RCA Victor Living Stereo Ⓜ 09026 61499-2 (40 minutes: ADD: 5/93). Texts and translations included. Recorded 1959. New to UK.

Fauré Clair de lune, Op. 46 No. 2. Notre amour, Op. 23 No. 2. Au cimetière, Op. 51 No. 2. Au bord de l'eau, Op. 8 No. 1. Mandoline, Op. 58 No. 1. **Poulenc** Main dominée par le coeur. Miroirs brûlants. Ce doux petit visage. **R. Strauss** Allerseelen, Op. 10 No. 8. Schlagende Herzen, Op. 29 No. 2. Freundliche Vision, Op. 48 No. 1. Wie sollten wir geheim, Op. 19 No. 4. **Wolf** Mörike Lieder – Der Gärtner; Lebe wohl. Lieder für eine Frauen-stimme – Morgentau. Spanisches Liederbuch – Geh' Geliebter, geh' jetz.

There can be few recordings which so vividly resemble the sound of singer and pianist performing live in one's own home. This forward, warts-and-all 1959 RCA recording has a disconcerting immediacy, but it's not just the recorded sound which creates this sense of close intimacy. Leontyne Price sings with a captivating directness which belongs more to a domestic setting than the concert-hall – or even the opera house, for it was here that her reputation was made, becoming revered as one of the foremost Verdi sopranos. Her recorded legacy encompasses major roles from Mozart through Berlioz and Puccini to Gershwin and Samuel Barber, but this CD is special. This was her recording début made in the Town Hall, New York City, and shows her in repertoire with which she has not generally been associated. Yet she sings it with an intuition and sensitivity which would be the envy of singers whose lifetimes' work has been in Lieder and *chanson*. The French and German accents have an unmistakable American twang, but it's not the words which matter so much as the sense of involvement she brings to each and every one of these beautiful and memorable songs. A CD of great historic and artistic value.

Prometheus [a]Ingrid Ade-Jesemann, [a]Monika Bair-Ivenz (sops); [a]Susanne Otto (contr); [a]Peter Hall (ten); [a]Ulrike Krumbiegel, [a]Mathias Schadock (spkrs); [a]Michael Hasel (bass fl); [a]Manfred Preis (bass cl); [a]Christhard Gössling (euph/tuba); [b]Martha Argerich (pf); [b]Berlin Singakademie; [a]Freiburg Soloists Choir; Berlin Philharmonic Orchestra / Claudio Abbado. Sony Classical Ⓟ SK53978 (75 minutes: DDD: 1/95). Texts and translations included. Recorded live in 1993 *Gramophone Editor's choice.*. ⊙⊙⊙
Beethoven Der Geschöpfe des Prometheus – excerpts. **Liszt** Prometheus, S99. **Scriabin** Prometheus, "Le poème du feu", Op. 60[b]. **Nono** Promoteo – suite[a].

Prometheus's theft of fire from Zeus and the cruelty of his punishment are all but absent from Beethoven's ballet. Even Melpomene's outburst of violence sounds disarmingly Schubertian, while the ensuing dances and finale are among the most diverting in the whole of Beethoven's orchestral output. It would be difficult to imagine a more beautifully shaped performance than Abbado's, where relative tensions are artfully judged, instrumental solos given with real style and the whole is captured in a warm, luminous recording. Liszt's glowering outburst – one of his most daring symphonic poems – is more an informed commentary than a genuine 'performance': lean, sinewy and consistent, yes, but too cool-headed by far. The disc's real *tour de force*, both sonically and musically, is Scriabin's Promethean effusion, his *Poem of fire*. Abbado serves as master of ceremonies, Argerich as a crazed high priestess, her delirious, delicate and unpredictable solo weaving through the orchestra like a bubbling stream of consciousness. That is how it *should* sound – overwrought, overpowering, utterly unhinged and yet calculated even to the smallest detail. The stylistic leap from Scriabin's tantalizing chromatics to Nono's non-gravitational soundscape – with its solo voices, synthesized sounds and woodwind-blown choruses – is tantamount to leaving the earth's orbit, and one's earthly body with it. Here we meet Prometheus head-on, lynched on an aural anxiety-loop where vague distortions are as many ripples on a sickly sea of sound. In short, this is a hugely stimulating, thoughtfully planned production.

New review

Requiem of Reconciliation Tobias Janzik (treb); Donna Brown, Julie Moffat (sops); Ingeborg Danz (mez); Thomas Randle (ten); Andreas Schmidt (bar); Stuttgart Gächinger Kantorei; Cracow Chamber Choir; Israel Philharmonic Orchestra / Helmuth Rilling. Hänssler Classic Ⓟ 98 931 (two discs: 107 minutes: DDD: 11/95). Notes, text and translations included. Recorded live in 1995.
Berio Prolog. **Cerha** Introitus and Kyrie. **Dittrich** Dies irae. **Kopelent** Judex ergo. **Harbison** Juste judex. **Nordheim** Confutatis. **Rands** Interludium. **Dalbavie** Domine Jesu Christe, Rex Gloriae. **Weir** Sanctus. **Penderecki** Agnus Dei. **Rihm** Communio I. **Schnittke/ Rozhdestvensky** Communio II. **Yuasa** Responsorium. **Kurtág** Epilog.

It was a great event in Stuttgart on August 16th, 1995 when 14 very different composers each contributed a section to a setting of the Requiem liturgy. It was the idea of Helmuth Rilling to celebrate the fiftieth anniversary of the end of the Second World War. The wonder is that the results are so consistent, the reflection – so the composers themselves felt – of concentrating on the theme of suffering, as well, of course, as Rilling's shrewd choice of contributors. Reflecting the text, the first half – up to Arne Nordheim's *Confutatis* – is the darker and more taxing. Only towards the end of that sequence does John Harbison's fine setting of *Juste judex* lighten the mood and textures, with Nordheim then the first identifiably to use the secondary idea presented to the composers of linking the Requiem with Gregorian chant. Nordheim uses the notes of the chant vertically as well as horizontally, while in the second half the Frenchman, Marc-André Dalbavie, in his *Domine Jesu Christe* goes much further in direct Gregorian echoes. Bernard Rands's thoughtful introduction to the second half gives just one word to the chorus, "Deus!". Then, after the Dalbavie, comes the most incandescent of the pieces, Judith Weir's brilliant setting of the *Sanctus* with its brass commentaries. The Japanese, Joji Yuasa, as a Buddhist was initially doubtful about taking part, but in the event his atmospheric, finely terraced setting of the *Responsorium* and *Libera me* makes a fine culmination before the rather perfunctory, if striking, *Epilog* of György Kurtág. Only one of the 14 contributions is a disappointment, but that is a serious one, the *Dies irae* of the German composer, Paul-Heinz Dittrich. As to the singing generally, the soloists make an outstanding team, with the Canadian soprano, Donna Brown, particularly impressive, while choruses and orchestra consistently respond to Rilling's direction with thrilling attack. With the vast forces superbly balanced, there is a bite and immediacy which allows one to appreciate every detail.

The Romantic Lied Dame Margaret Price (sop); Graham Johnson (pf). Forlane Ⓟ UCD16728 (71 minutes: DDD: 2/95). Texts and translations included. Recorded 1993.
Wolf Mörike Lieder – Er ist's; Begegnung; Der Gärtner; In der Frühe; Lebe wohl; Heimweh; Gesang Weylas; Bei einer Trauung. **Cornelius** Trauer und Trost, Op. 3. **Liszt** Freudvoll und leidvoll, S280. Uber allen Gipfeln ist Ruh, S306. Mignons Lied, S275. Der du von dem Himmel bist, S279. **Wagner** Wesendonk Lieder.

Price and Johnson have done it again. He has chosen a programme for her that exactly suits her talents and style, and she (with his inestimable help) has executed it with commitment and understanding. The programme in itself is fascinating, comparing and contrasting composers of roughly the same generation and period. The cross-fertilization of musical ideas is apparent, yet each emerges as an artist with something highly individual to say. Wolf isn't a composer with whom Price has been very much associated until now, but in a group of the Mörike settings, she proves herself at one with the poems and their music, catching in particular the restless ardour of *Begegnung*, the timeless mystery of *Gesang Weylas*, and the peculiarly Wolfian charm of the lighter pieces. Liszt is even more to her liking. She and Johnson choose the later, longer version of *Freudvoll und leidvoll* and make a grand romantic statement of it that is just right. The interpretation of the *Wesendonk Lieder* is the crowning glory of this wonderful recital. A virtually faultless reading, speeds (no unwanted lingering), phrasing, line and tone ideally adapted to the words and music. Johnson places the piano part in perfect relationship with the voice, helped by the exemplary recording of both.

Russian Songs Ewa Podles (contr); **Graham Johnson** (pf). Forlane Ⓕ UCD16683 (70 minutes: DDD: 5/95). Translations included.
Rachmaninov Op. 4 – No. 2, Morning; No. 3, In the silence of the secret night. Op. 14 – No. 1, I wait for thee; No. 8, Oh, do not grieve; No. 9, She is as lovely as the moon; No. 11, Spring waters. Op. 26 No. 6, Christ is risen. **Mussorgsky** The Nursery. Songs and Dances of Death.
Tchaikovsky Op. 47 – No. 1, If only I had known; No. 6, Does the day reign?; No. 7, Was I not a little blade of grass? Zemfira's song.
Podles is a welcome throwback to a more idiosyncratic style of singing. Taking risks in her interpretations, she earns her rewards. The voice itself is a vibrant, almost fruity contralto, far from the more refined, genteel kind we have become used to of late. In the two Mussorgsky cycles Podles comes into competition with Leiferkus, whose readings leave such a profound impression (see review under Mussorgsky; refer to the Index to Reviews). Without quite the vocal acuity of her Russian counterpart, the Polish-born Podles makes her own mark. Her inveigling, impulsive child in *The Nursery* cycle is a delight. She and Johnson capture all the charming innocence of the cycle without ever becoming whimsical or cute. They achieve even greater success in the more formidable demands of *Songs and Dances of Death* (usually a man's task). In the first song, a kind of Russian *Erlkönig*, Podles is insinuating; in the second, a sinister barcarolle, she is deliberately sensual; in the third, appropriately fantastic (Johnson is superb here); while in the finale, the mood of heroic pessimism is exactly caught. This reading is just as valid as Leiferkus's more incisive, extrovert approach. Podles takes a big-scale, romantic view of Rachmaninov and Tchaikovsky. In Rachmaninov's Op. 14 No. 8, she uses a huge range of dynamics from an almost crooning start to an operatic *forte* at the song's climax, while *Christ is risen* is properly visionary. The recording is excellent in balance and perspective.

A Salute to American Music [a]Leontyne Price, [b]Maureen O'Flynn, [c][i]Renée Fleming, [f]Karen Holvik, [l]Denise Woods, [o]Carol Vaness (sops); [b]Phyllis Pancella, [j]Tatiana Troyanos, [n]Frederica von Stade, [q]Marilyn Horne (mezzos); [b][h][i]Jerry Hadley, [b]Paul Groves (tens); [b]Daniel Smith, [b]Jeff Mattsey, [d][m]Sherrill Milnes, [c]Robert Merrill (bars); [p]Samuel Ramey (bass); [g][i][k][l]Collegiate Chorale; Metropolitan Opera Orchestra / James Conlon. RCA Victor Red Seal Ⓕ 09026 61509-2 (72 minutes: DDD: 6/93). Recorded live in 1991.
S. Ward America the Beautiful[a]. **Menotti** Amelia al ballo – Overture. **Weill** Street Scene – Ice-Cream Sextet[b]. Knickerbocker Holiday – September Song[c]. **V. Thomson** Five Songs from William Blake – Tiger! Tiger! burning bright[d]. **Griffes** Fiona Macleod Poems, Op. 11 – The Lament of Ian the Proud[e]. **Foster** Ah! May the red rose live alway[f]. **Bernstein** Chichester Psalm No. 1[g]. West Side Story – Maria[h]. Candide – Make our garden grow[i]. **Copland** Old American Songs, Set 2 – At the river[j]. **Bolcom** The Tyger[k]. **Gershwin** Porgy and Bess – Leavin' for the Promised Land[l]. **M.D. Levy** Mourning becomes Electra – Too weak to kill the man I hate[m]. **Barber** Vanessa – Must the winter come so soon?[n]. Antony and Cleopatra – Give me my robe[o]. **Floyd** Susannah – Hear me, O Lord[p]. **Berlin** God bless America[q].
This 'look at an era just gone by' starts with a great lift-off: America the Beautiful sung by Leontyne Price. At the age of 63 she can still summon enough patriotic fervour to make non-Americans want to apply for citizenship papers on the spot! And she isn't the oldest performer by any means. Robert Merrill is ten years her senior and delivers Weill's "September Song" touchingly. One of the most moving performances is Karen Holvik in Stephen Foster's immaculate Ah! May the red rose live alway, with piano (Steven Blier). More calculating, but equally polished nostalgia comes from Barber, especially "Must the winter come so soon?" from Vanessa, hauntingly sung by Frederica von Stade. Tatiana Troyanos sings Copland's setting of Robert Lowry's "At the river" with impressive, quiet dignity. Bernstein is the only composer who gets in three times – the Collegiate Chorale is on form for the first of the Chichester Psalms; Jerry Hadley sings "Maria"; and there's an ensemble from Candide. Finally, in case you didn't sign on for US citizenship, Marilyn Horne gives a truly commanding performance of Irving Berlin's classic God bless America. This is not just an anthology which works – it's a wow!

New review
Elisabeth Schwarzkopf Songbook Dame Elisabeth Schwarzkopf (sop); [a]Gerald Moore, [b]Geoffrey Parsons, [c]Nicolas Medtner, [d]Cyril Szalkiewicz (pfs). EMI mono/stereo Ⓜ CHS5 65860-2* (three discs: 230 minutes: ADD: 4/96). Texts and translations included. Recorded 1947-74. Ⓖ

Mozart Warnung, K433[a] (from Columbia LB73, 11/48). Der Zauberer, K472 (two versions; LB118[a], 2/52 and HMV ASD2844[b], 8/73). Das Veilchen, K476[b] (ASD2404, 12/68). **Schubert** Die schöne Müllerin, D795 – Ungeduld[a] (Columbia 33CX1044, 9/54). Claudine von Villa Bella – Liebe schwärmt auf allen Wegen[a] (Columbia SAX5268, 10/66). **Mendelssohn** Auf Flügeln des Gesanges, Op. 34 No. 2[a] (SAX2265, 3/59). **Schumann** Liederkreis, Op. 39[b] – In der Fremde; Intermezzo; Waldesgespräch; Die Stille; In der Fremde II; Im Walde (all from ASD3037, 1/75). Aufträge, Op. 77 No. 5[a] (LB122, 3/52). Widmung, Op. 25 No. 1[a] (SAX5268). **Liszt** Die drei Zigeuner, S320[b] (ASD2634, 3/71). **Brahms** Vergebliches Ständchen, Op. 84 No. 4[a] (33CX1044). Liebestreu, Op. 3 No. 1[b]. Vergebliches Ständchen, Op. 84 No. 4[b]. Der Jäger, Op. 95 No. 4[b]. Wie Melodien zieht es mir, Op. 105 No. 1[b]. Immer leiser wird mein Schlummer, Op. 105 No. 2[b]. Ständchen, Op. 106 No. 1[b] (ASD2844). **Jensen** Murmelndes Lüftchen, Op. 21 No. 4[a] (SAX2265). **Mahler** Lob des hohen Verstandes[b]. **R. Strauss** Wer lieben will, Op. 49 No. 7[b]. Ach, was Kummer, Op. 49 No. 8[b] (ASD2404). Drei Lieder der Ophelia, Op. 67[b] (previously unpublished. From a BBC broadcast performance on December 2nd, 1968). **Wolf** Italienisches Liederbuch – 25 Lieder[a] (SAX2366, 12/61). Goethe Lieder[a] – Blumengruss; Epiphanias; Gleich und Gleich; Frühling übers Jahr (SAX2333, mono 3/60); Hoch beglückt in deiner Liebe; Als ich auf dem Euphrat schiffte; Nimmer will ich dich verlieren!; Der Schäfer (SAX2589, 2/66). Mörike Lieder[b] – Verborgenheit; Lebe wohl (ASD2404); Auf eine Christblume I (ASD2844); Auftrag. Kleine gleicht von allen Schönen[b] (ASD3124, 3/76). Wiegenlied im Sommer[a]. Mausfallen-Sprüchlein[a] (33CX1044). Spanisches Liederbuch – In dem Schatten meiner Locken[a]. **Grieg** Farmyard Song, Op. 61 No. 3[a] (SAX2265). I love but thee, Op. 5 No. 3[b]. With a waterlily, Op. 25 No. 4[b]. Last Spring, Op. 33 No. 2[b] (ASD2634). The first meeting, Op. 21 No. 1[b]. The way of the world, Op. 48 No. 3[b]. The time of roses, Op. 48 No. 5[b]. With a primrose, Op. 26 No. 4[b] (ASD2844). **Dvořák** Songs my mother taught me, B104 No. 4[a]. **Tchaikovsky** None but the lonely heart, Op. 6 No. 6[a] (SAX2265). **Mussorgsky** Gathering mushrooms[b] (ASD2404). **Medtner**[c] The muse, Op. 29 No. 1 (Columbia LX1425, 10/51). The rose, Op. 29 No. 6 (LX1423, 10/51). The waltz, Op. 32 No. 5 (LX1425). Kaum welken hier die Rosen, Op. 36 No. 3. Elfenliedchen, Op. 6 No. 3. Im Vorübergehen, Op. 6 No. 4 (LX1423). Songs, Op. 15 – Selbstbetrug, Op. 15 No. 3 (LX1424, 10/51). Aus "Lila", Op. 15 No. 5 (LX1425). Meeresstille, Op. 15 No. 7. Glückliche Fahrt, Op. 15 No. 8 (LX1424). Einsamkeit, Op. 18 No. 3. Songs, Op. 46 – No. 1, Praeludium; No. 5, Winter Night (LX1426, 10/51); No. 6, The Fountain (LX1424). **Sibelius**[d] Songs, Op. 72 – No. 3, The kiss; No. 4, The echo nymph; No. 6, A hundred ways. The north, Op. 90 No. 1. Songs, Op. 36 – No. 1, Black roses; No. 4, Sigh, sedges, sigh. Songs, Op. 37 – No. 1, The first kiss; No. 4, Was it a dream? (prev. unpublished. Finnish broadcast performance, June 11th, 1955).

"For me, the supreme Lieder singer of our time": the writer, careful to present his judgement as personal as well as fully deliberate (he has Fischer-Dieskau in view and makes a close comparison to substantiate the point a little later on), was Eric Sams, and there can be no one whose opinion on Lieder and the performance of Lieder is more worth having. All three discs have their treasures. The first includes, rather unexpectedly, Mendelssohn's *Auf Flügeln des Gesanges*, gracefully combining an unspoilt legato line with an intelligent attention to meaning. Six songs from Schumann's Eichendorff *Liederkreis* are salvaged from the complete recording. Among the Brahms songs is *Immer leiser wird mein Schlummer*, one of the few performances of that song to go on the assumption that the poem means what it says. The three *Ophelia* Songs of Strauss are new: recorded live at the Ernest Newman Commemoration Concert in 1968, and affording a welcome alternative to the version with Glenn Gould on Sony (3/93). The second disc is entirely devoted to Wolf, and has a particularly lovely early (1954) recording of the *Wiegenlied im Sommer*. Then on the final disc, called "Rarities", we are given a delightful selection of Grieg, starting with the *Farmyard Song* in English, a complete run of the Medtner recordings made with the composer in 1950, and, most valuably, a Sibelius group, taken from a Finnish Radio concert of 1955 and here released for the first time. These capture the voice at its most radiant and the spirit at its most impassioned: deeply felt performances and a genuine enrichment of the archive. The transfers have the great modern virtue of clarity, and also the modern vice of achieving it at the expense of the warmth and the absence of hardness which were characteristic of the voice we knew 'in the flesh'. Adjusted to suit taste, they can still give great pleasure.

New review

A Shropshire Lad Songs and Poems. **Anthony Rolfe Johnson** (ten); **Graham Johnson** (pf).
Hyperion Ⓟ CDA66471/2 (two discs: 124 minutes: DDD: 8/95). Includes various poems from Housman's "A Shrophire Lad" read by Alan Bates. Texts included. Recorded 1994.
Barber With rue my heart is laden. **L. Berkeley** Because I liked you better. He would not stay for me. **Butterworth** Bredon Hill. When the lad for longing sighs. On the idle hill of summer. A Shropshire Lad – complete. **Horder** White in the moon. **Ireland** Hawthorn time. The heart's desire. The lent lily. Goal and wicket. The vain desire. The encounter. Epilogue. **Moeran** Far in a western brookland. O fair enough are sky and plain. **C.W. Orr** When I watch the living meet. Hughley steeple. Into my heart. O see how thick the goldcup flowers. The Isle of Portland. This time of year.

There should be a Hyperion 'Book of Essays'. Graham Johnson's introductions would probably make quite a handsome volume on their own, and there would certainly be room for Andrew Green's notes on this Housman anthology. If indeed (as he says) there has long been argument about the whys and wherefores of Housman's popularity among composers, with Ernest Newman claiming (where?) that *A Shropshire Lad* "cried out for music", then these discs should further the discussion, suggesting some very good reasons by simple juxtaposition of the speaking and the singing voice – or rather, of the sound of the text alone compared with the musical expression of feelings it evokes. The poems are presented in their printed order, all 63 of them (with two added from other volumes), 28 in musical settings, the rest recited. Alan Bates employs what may seem restricted means: he reads without any of the throb of poetry, the voice rarely extended in range or volume, the manner reflective yet dispassionate, almost dry. So may Housman himself have read, and one's first thought is that this probably accounts for it as a 'policy'. A little tentative experimentation (growing bolder) convinces that it is the right way, perhaps the only way; which is one reason why the poems, in Newman's words, cry out for music. The music lies within the lines as they pass, lovingly, through the mind, but the actual sound of the words, for all the prevalence of rhyme and rhythm, is curiously tight-lipped, prosaic, factual. Among the song-writers here, George Butterworth has an almost invariable rightness of note-catching. Others miss the sharpness, the more sardonic tone. The performances are sensitive to nuance, of both words and notes. Graham Johnson's touch is often uncannily suggestive, letting the melisma of the opening phrases of "Loveliest of trees" trickle deliciously through his fingers. Rolfe Johnson sings with all his customary gifts and skill, producing a rare (and right) effect of chilling uncertainty at the end of "Is my team ploughing?": as the ghost guesses, the lad clearly does *not* lie easy, for the dead man is within him, has taken his voice, his music.

Singers of Imperial Russia, Volumes 1-4. **35 singers with various accompaniments.** Pearl mono
Ⓜ GEMMCDS9997/9*, GEMMCDS9001/03*, GEMMCDS9004/06* and GEMMCDS9007/09* (four three-disc sets, oas: 207, 209, 222 and 221 minutes: AAD: 6/93). *Gramophone Award Winner 1993.* ⒼⒼⒼ
GEMMCDS9997/9: recorded 1900-11: *Soprano* – Medea Mei-Figner. *Tenors* – Ivan Ershov, Nikolai Figner and Leonid Sobinov. *Baritone* – Ioakim Tartakov. *Basses* – Adamo Didur and Vasili Sharonov. *GEMMCDS9001/03*: 1901-11: *Sopranos* – Natalia Ermolenko-Juzhina and Maria Michailova. *Mezzo-soprano* – Antonina Panina. *Tenors* – David Juzhin, Andrei Labinsky and Gavril Morskoi. *Baritones* – Oskar Kamionsky and Polikarp Orlov. *Basses* – Dmitri Bukhtoyarov, Vladimir Kastorsky, Vasili Sharonov and Lev Sibiriakov. *GEMMCDS9004/06*: 1901-24: *Sopranos* – Irena Bohuss, Anna El-Tour, Janina Korolewicz-Wayda, Maria Kuznetsova, Lydia Lipkowska and Nadezhda Zabela-Vrubel. *Contralto* – Evgenia Zbrueva. *Tenors* – Dmitri Smirnov and Eugene Witting. *Bass* – K. E. Kaidanov. *GEMMCDS9007/09*: 1901-14: *Sopranos* – Maria Michailova and Antonia Nezhdanova. *Mezzo-soprano* – Galina Nikitina. *Contralto* – Evgenia Zbrueva. *Tenors* – Alexandr Alexandrovich, Alexandr Bogdanovich, Alexandr Davidov, Andrei Labinsky and Eugene Witting. *Baritone* – Nikolai Shevelev. *Basses* – Vladimir Kastorsky and Lev Sibiriakov.
This is the equivalent, in terms of gramophone history, of one of those exhibitions for which queues form long and deep and daily outside the Tate Gallery or the Royal Academy: in fact, if a similar exhibition of paintings, furniture and porcelain from the Tsar's palaces were mounted in London it would surely be a sell-out. Quite simply, there has never been a published collection to match this, both in the quality of the items and in its extensiveness. Of the singers of Imperial Russia, the world came to know Chaliapin, who eclipsed the rest. He is not among the artists presented here, but we have, among the basses, two who at least for vocal splendour are his equal: Adamo Didur, the Pole who was New York's first Boris Godunov (preceding Chaliapin there), and Lev Sibiriakov, another giant of a man with a magnificently produced voice to match. The tenors include Smirnov and Sobinov, a kind of collector's Tweedledum and Tweedledee, though in fact very unalike indeed. New to most listeners will be Ivan Ershov, heard in Siegfried's Forging Song from St Petersburg, 1903, with piano and anvil accompaniment: an astonishing voice and most accomplished in technique. Evgenia Zbrueva the contralto, sopranos Nezhdanova, Ermolenko-Jushina, Mei-Figner and the superbly recorded Korolewicz-Wayda are also plentifully represented. Most amazing of all, perhaps, is the vividness of sound. These are some of the world's rarest recordings and, almost without exception, they are in pristine condition.

Songs by Finzi and his Friends ªIan Partridge (ten); ᵇStephen Roberts (bar); Clifford Benson (pf). Hyperion Ⓕ CDA66015 (51 minutes: ADD: 9/91). Texts included. From A66015 (9/81). Recorded 1981.
Finzi To a Poet, Op. 13aᵇ. Oh fair to see, Op. 13bª. **Milford**ª If it's ever spring again. The colour. So sweet love seemed. **Farrar** O mistress mine!ª. **Gurney**ᵇ Sleep. Down by the salley gardens. Hawk and Buckle. **Gill** In Memoriamᵇ.
This is a record that drew from its original reviewer, Trevor Harvey, high and unstinting praise when it appeared in 1981 as part of the commemoration of Finzi 25 years after his death. Finzi was never an avant-garde composer and during his lifetime received quiet and grateful acknowledgement from kindred spirits rather than anything more spectacular. In the last 20 years or so, appreciation has deepened and become more widespread. His songs, in particular, have a depth of feeling that is not always apparent at first hearing, and their idiom is that of a writer to whom overstatement or any other kind of cheapening would have been abhorrent. In this selection most of the chosen poems are

affectionate and gentle, but F.L. Lucas's *June on Castle Hill* contains "whispers of wars to come", and George Barker's "Ode on the Rejection of St Cecilia" is a strong and sombre utterance that evokes an uncommonly hard-hitting style in the composer. His friend, Robin Milford, sets Hardy and Bridges with comparable sensitivity, and Ernest Farrar (killed in 1918) is remembered by his charmingly nonchalant *O mistress mine!*. Stephen Roberts is an admirable singer of the songs by Ivor Gurney, and Ian Partridge gives a lovely account of Finzi's Op. 13b *Oh fair to see*. Clifford Benson is the excellent accompanist throughout and recording and presentation are first-rate.

Songs and Dances of Death Dmitri Hvorostovsky (bar); **Kirov Theatre Orchestra / Valery Gergiev.** Philips Ⓕ 438 872-2PH (62 minutes: DDD: 5/94). Texts and translations included. Recorded 1993.
   Rimsky-Korsakov Sadko – The paragon of cities; Beautiful city! Kashchey the Immortal – In this, night's darkest hour. Snow Maiden (second version) – Under the warm blue sea. The Tsar's Bride – Still the beauty haunts my mind. **Borodin** Prince Igor – No sleep, no rest. **Rubinstein** The Demon – Do not weep, my child; On the airy ocean; I am he whom you called. Nero – Vindex's Epithalamium: I sing to you, Hymen divine! **Rachmaninov** Aleko – Aleko's cavatina. **Mussorgsky** Songs and Dances of Death.

In the scenes from Rubinstein's *The Demon* Hvorostovsky, superbly supported by Valery Gergiev and his Kirov orchestra recorded in their own theatre, has done nothing better than his impersonation of the devil; in the scenes from the third he projects the gloating demon to the life. This is splendid stuff. So is Vindex's rollicking Epithalamium from the same composer's *Nero*, sung with wonderful breadth and confidence. Then he changes character again to bring before us the emotional torment of Rachmaninov's Aleko as he recalls the love Zemfira once had for him. The best of the Rimsky items as regards music and interpretation are Nizgir's aria from the *Snow Maiden* and Gryaznoy's musing on past triumphs in the field of love from *The Tsar's Bride*. Here Hvorostovsky varies his tone more successfully than in the other Rimsky items. Mussorgsky's *Songs and Dances of Death* really need an imposing bass rather than a lyric baritone to make their true mark, yet these are more than acceptable performances in a most enjoyable recital, immeasurably helped by the support and the excellent recording. This is a fascinating disc.

New review
Songs with Viola Mitsuko Shirai (mez); **Tabea Zimmermann** (va); **Hartmut Höll** (pf). Capriccio Ⓕ 10 462 (66 minutes: DDD: 9/95). Texts and translations included.   Ⓖ
   R. Strauss Stiller Gang, Op. 31 No. 4. **Brahms** Zwei Lieder, Op. 91. **A. Busch** Nun die Schatten dunkeln. Wonne der Wehmut. Aus den Himmelsaugen. **Loeffler** Quatre poèmes, Op. 5. **Dargomïzhsky** Elegy, "She is coming". **Marx** Durch Einsamkeiten. **Reutter** Fünf antike Oden, Op. 57. **Gounod** Evening song.

Voice and viola, we think, form a soothing combination: the sound of the words suggests as much, and memories of Brahms's Op. 91 (which is what we are likely to think of first and probably last) confirm it. The Brahms songs come second in this present programme, and on either side are compositions by Richard Strauss and Adolf Busch that are very much in keeping, the mood generally peaceful, the style essentially lyrical. Then come the *Quatre poèmes* of Charles Martin Loeffler (1861-1935). These, like the songs by Busch and, later, Hermann Reutter, are recorded now for the first time and they form a welcome addition to the small catalogue of Loeffler's works on record. In this programme, they, together with Reutter's "Sappho", provide a contrast, a more bracing and varied use of the combination: a relief from the soothing. Mitsuko Shirai, now mezzo-soprano, sings with almost consistently firm and beautiful tone. She lightens the voice skilfully, as in Brahms's "Gestillte Sehnsucht", and produces some beautifully sustained singing, as in the third of the Loeffler *Poèmes*, "Le son du cor". There is also an assured authority in this deeper voice with no less of the familiar charm. With fine playing by Tabea Zimmermann, especially in the Reutter cycle where the instrument is most imaginatively exploited, and with Hartmut Höll collaborating as sensitively as ever, the record clearly has a special place among song recitals.

New review
Songs from the Exotic Tapestry (Sandra Lissenden, sop; Andrew Sparling, cl; Katharine Durran, pf). British Music Label Ⓕ BML012 (73 minutes: DDD: 12/95). Texts included.
   N. Hayes The Basket. **Hallgrimsson** Syrpa. **Weir** (arr. Finnissy): Songs from the Exotic (on the rocks). **Finnissy** Beuk o' Newcassel Sangs. **G. Jackson** French Song. **S. Harrison** Nani ka itou. **Crane** Balanescu. **A. Fisher** Leviathan. **Skempton** Colomen.

Tapestry was formed about ten years ago, after its members had performed Schubert's *The Shepherd on the Rock* and wondered whether there was much else for this particular combination. That in its turn led to commissioning, and about 60 new works have been the result. What fun they've been having, if this selection is anything to go by. Michael Finnissy's *Newcassel Sangs* are the most immediately striking pieces here, but so they would be in pretty well any company. The nearest it is possible to get to describing them is to say that if Stravinsky had been a Geordie this is how his *Pribaoutki* would have sounded: there is rough humour to some of them, but pungency and anger as well: they are quite gripping. It says a good deal for Sandra Lissenden that she realizes that they need a quite different quality of voice from (say) the silvery pre-Raphaelite sound appropriate to Howard

Skempton's extended Mary Webb setting (a cunning example of *real* minimalism). Haflidi Hallgrimsson's and Judith Weir's short-cycles are both rooted (but not pot-bound) in folk music: both demonstrate that it can be vitally fruitful, he in a queer little nonsense-song for children, she throughout her four songs with the strong lines and spellbinding simplicity that are characteristic of her. Gabriel Jackson, too, proves that it is still possible to use very few notes and a memorable tune without seeming derivative. Sadie Harrison's and Aidan Fisher's pieces are tougher, hers not quite as epigrammatic and well-wrought as the Japanese poems she uses, he surely over-reacting to his text, eight minutes of gesturing for a four-line squib. Nick Hayes and Laurence Crane provide encore pieces: *The Basket* is catchy, euphonious, teasingly not quite as repetitive as it sounds; *Balanescu* (full title *I Saw Alexander Balanescu in Safeways*) is as minimal as you can get, and irresistibly droll. Expert performances throughout; the recordings are a touch dry and close.

New review

Spanish Baroque, Volume 1. **Al Ayre Español / Eduardo López Banzo.** Deutsche Harmonia
  Mundi Ⓔ 05472 77325-2 (70 minutes: DDD: 8/95). 🖎 Texts and translations included.   Ⓖ
  Anonymous Canción a dos tiples. Two Pasacalles. **Literes** Ah del rustico pastor. **C. Galán** Al
  espejo que retrata. Humano ardor. **J. de Torres** Más no puedo ser. Al clamor. **F. Valls** En un
  noble, sagrado firmamento. **F. de Iribarren** Quién nos dira de una flor. Viendo que Jil, hizo
  raya.
López Banzo could well be set to achieve for the Spanish baroque what William Christie and Les Arts Florissants have done for French music of the seventeenth and eighteenth centuries. There are many parallels between English and Spanish musical cultures in the baroque: French and Italian stylistic and structural elements are incorporated into a musical language that is nevertheless as clearly Spanish as the Purcell idiom is English. The melodiousness characteristic of the Spanish repertory and its distinctive rhythmic patterns are immediately apparent. The *villancicos* and *cantadas* by Torres, Literes, Iribarren and Valls are all sectional works that alternate recitative and arias in the manner of the Italian cantata, but they also introduce minuets, elegant slow movements, lively refrains and even Spanish dances of popular origin such as the *jácara*. Indeed, the disc ends with one of those characteristically foot-tapping pieces (performed in cathedrals and chapels on such joyous feasts as Christmas) by Iribarren who was chapelmaster at Malaga Cathedral. The performances are very fine. The instrumentalists seem to be completely at home with the style and point up the idiomatic syncopations with just the right degree of emphasis. Under the secure direction of López Banzo, they generally serve the music extremely well. The singers are Spanish which is probably essential, at least at this stage in our knowledge of the repertory. They, too, are consistently excellent. The soprano Marta Almajano's voice is agile and well-focused with a hint of that dark, enriching quality – like velvet-clad steel – that seems to characterize the Spanish voice (think of Victoria de los Angeles or even Plácido Domingo). She is, as the music demands, expressive or virtuoso, lyrical or brilliant, and in everything she has a superb sense of line.

A Spanish Songbook Jill Gomez (sop); John Constable (pf). Conifer Ⓕ CDCF243 (67 minutes:
  DDD: 9/94). Texts and translations included. Recorded 1994.
  Fuenllana Orphenica lyra – De los álamos vengo, madre; Duélete de mí, Señora. **Vásquez**
  Morenica, dame un beso. **Valderrébano** De dónde venís, amore? **Wolf** Spanisches Liederbuch –
  Klinge, klinge, mein Pandero; In dem Schatten meiner Locken. **Schumann** Der Hidalgo,
  Op. 30 No. 3. Tief im Herzen trag' ich Pein, Op. 138 No. 2. **Bizet** Guitare. **Ravel** Chanson
  espagnole. **Saint-Saëns** Guitares et mandolines. **Delibes** Les filles de Cadiz. **Granados**
  La maja dolorosa. **Walton** Noche espagnola. Through gilded trellises. **Gerhard** Cancionero
  de Pedrell – Farruquiño; La mal maridada; Muera yo. **Tarragó** Parado de Valldemosa.
  Rodrigo Adela. **Guridi** Mañanita de San Juan. **Obradors** El Vito. **Anonymous** Pase el
  aguo, Julieta.
Jill Gomez's imaginative and wide-ranging survey of songs in Spanish, or by German, French and English composers on Spanish themes, opens with what one might call a 'Victoria de los Angeles group' of Renaissance songs. Gomez has something of that plaintive, Moorish-influenced expression that de los Angeles used to bring to this repertory. Miguel de Fuenllana's *De los álamos vengo, madre* (arranged and popularized in our own time by Rodrigo) and the anonymous *Pase el aguo, Julieta*, are examples of courtly poetry, heavy with erotic symbolism, which is so typical of Spanish song. In the second 'Schwarzkopf group', two of Wolf's lighter essays in flirtation from the *Spanisches Liederbuch* frame Schumann's more obviously pastiche *Der Hidalgo* and then the deeply passionate *Tief im Herzen trag' ich Pein*. The four French songs might have been a speciality of Ninon Vallin – but enough of comparisons with singers of the past, for Jill Gomez has her own style, with a marvellous feeling for words and for the shape and mood of each piece. The most substantial, and best-known, are the three Granados *Tonadillas*. The two Walton songs are both lifted from *Façade*, one in an arrangement by the composer, the other by Christopher Palmer. There's a hint of an Edith Sitwell impersonation in one or two phrases. These, and the three songs by Roberto Gerhard, provide the English part of the recital, for Gerhard made these arrangements of songs collected by his teacher, Felipe Pedrell, when he was living in Cambridge in the 1940s. The disc ends with one of the most famous Spanish encores – Obradors's *El Vito*. Even if you know all these songs already, but especially if this repertory is unfamiliar, this sunny CD will bring nothing but delight.

New review

Elsie Suddaby Songs and Arias by M. Arne, T. Arne, Bach, Besly, Carey, Denza, Ford, German, Handel, Haydn, Jackson, MacCunn, Mendelssohn, Morley, Mozart, Purcell, Schubert, Somervell, Stanford and Warlock. **Elsie Suddaby** (sop) with various artists. Amphion mono
Ⓜ PHICD134* (80 minutes: ADD: 4/96). From HMV and Decca originals; Recorded 1924-52.
Elsie Suddaby (1893-1980) was a close contemporary of Isobel Baillie and Dora Labbette and in many ways she evinces the strongest personality of the three, and has a distinctive timbre very much her own. That can be heard in the first item, Michael Arne's *The lass with the delicate air*, a piece she virtually appropriated as her signature tune. She sings it with such variety of tone and, yes, such delicacy of accent, that one capitulates at once to so graceful an artist. In Dido's Lament, the singular quality of being able, simply and naturally, to move the listener is there: adding appoggiaturas to the recitative and discreetly employing portamento in the Lament itself she goes to the heart of the matter. There is also the joyfully affirmative side of her art, shown in a fresh account of "Rejoice greatly" from *Messiah* and "Endless pleasure", Semele wallowing in her conquest of Jupiter. Better still is a version of "Let the bright Seraphim" (*Samson*) that rings the rafters with its zealous delivery. Runs in all these Handel pieces are keenly accomplished though not quite with Baillie's assurance. These HMV recordings catch Suddaby in her prime, when she was in her thirties, yet on a Decca ten-inch of 1941 of Thomas Arne's *Where the bee sucks* and Morley's *It was a lover and his lass*, there is no diminution of her powers, and even the Warlock songs and Mozart's *Agnus Dei*, when Suddaby was in her late fifties, find the tone almost as fresh as ever and wholly free of wobble. The CD is a generous offering, the transfers are mostly well done and the booklet is obviously a labour of love.

Sweet Power of Song Felicity Lott (sop); **Ann Murray** (mez); **Graham Johnson** (pf) with [a]**Galina Solodchin** (vn) and [a]**Jonathan Williams** (va). EMI Ⓔ CDC7 49930-2 (62 minutes: DDD: 11/90). Texts and translations included. Recorded 1989.
Beethoven[a] 25 Irish Songs, WoO152 – Sweet power of song; English Bulls. 12 Irish Songs, WoO154 – The Elfin Fairies; Oh! would I were but that sweet linnet. **Berlioz** Pleure, pauvre Colette. Le trébuchet, Op. 13 No. 3. **Brahms** Vier Duette, Op. 61. **Chausson** Two duos, Op. 11. **Fauré** Pleurs d'or, Op. 72. Tarantelle, Op. 10 No. 2. **Gounod** D'un coeur qui t'aime. L'Arithmétique. **Saint-Saëns** Pastorale. El desdichado. **Schumann** Liederalbum für die Jugend, Op. 79 – No. 15, Das Glück; No. 19, Frühlings Ankunft; No. 23, Er ist's; No. 26, Schneeglöckchen.
This is a delightful presentation of an entertaining programme. The singers' careers have run concurrently with growing success on the international scene yet they remain faithful to Graham Johnson as founding members of the Songmakers' Almanac. Here they recall many evenings of happy duetting at that group's recitals. They sing together with an instinctive rapport that is most gratifying. Johnson has devised a programme for them that provides an ingenious variety of mood and style. Beethoven's Irish Songs may not be great music but they are given vivid advocacy here. So are the attractive and more profoun duets by Schumann and Brahms. The Berlioz pieces, nicely contrasted, are well done; so are the Gounod, Fauré and Chausson items, even if a shade more accenting of words would have been welcome here. The real winner among the French items – surely a collector's item of the future – is Gounod's *L'Arithmétique*, an amusing lesson in Victorian thrift delivered in both French and English. Johnson supplies appropriate accompaniments and interesting notes. The recording naturally balances voices and piano.

Maggie Teyte Songs by Berlioz, Chausson, Debussy, Duparc, Fauré, Hahn, Massenet and Ravel. **Dame Maggie Teyte** (sop); **Gerald Moore** (pf) with various artists. EMI Références mono •
Ⓜ CHS5 65198-2* (two discs: 157 minutes: ADD: 10/94). From HMV, Rimington Van Wyck, British Institute of Recorded Sound and Gramophone Shop of New York originals; recorded 1940-48.   ⒼⒼⒼ
"Je rapporte une rare émotion", the line from "Le martin-pêcheur", one of Ravel's *Histoires naturelles*, as Dame Maggie sings it, seems to signal the mood into which one is cast, listening to these famous recordings. The opening songs on the first CD, "Le spectre de la rose" and "Absence" from Berlioz's *Les nuits d'été* reveal at once all her positive virtues. The firmness of tone, the beauty of her high soft notes – like clear mountain spring water – which is not to say that there is anything watery about her interpretations; then the surprising sensuality of much of her phrasing and pronunciation – surprising because of the unmistakably British quality of her voice. She excelled above all in the *mélodie*, but her voice had none of the acid shrillness associated with French sopranos. Teyte's diction was excellent, but is not what one thinks of now as idiomatic French. "On ne chante pas comme on parle" she used to insist, and what one can hear is the Parisian fashion in the 1900s for affecting a slight English accent. That this came naturally to her must have added to her allure for audiences of the time. (Proust mentions her in his letters.) All the songs by Chausson are very fine. In *Le colibri* she demonstrates the richness of her low notes, and although the sound in *Poème de l'amour et de la mer* is somewhat restricted, this, too, is heady stuff. Chausson's *Chanson perpetuelle*, in which she is accompanied by Gerald Moore and the Blech String Quartet, has never been reissued before. This is one of Teyte's greatest records: the weight of sadness she brings to the poem by Charles Cros, with its tragic "Il est devenu mon amant", is reason enough to buy this new compilation. The Duparc songs

are superbly dramatic – Teyte wrote that "the deeper shades of pastel" were not enough for song recitals and that a singer needed to use as much power and expression as for opera. Her deep understanding of Ravel's *Shéhérazade* makes hers a fascinating version, even if at first those brought up on later, more expansive recordings may find it a little cool. All the items on the second CD are accompanied by Gerald Moore. In her autobiography she lamented the passing of "the lost art of the musicale". What she meant was the chance of intimate contact between artist and audience in a drawing-room – something she achieves immediately in the opening *Elégie* of Massenet. Then flow 13 songs by Fauré; *Soir* was a special favourite of Dame Maggie's – she had once sung it with Fauré as her accompanist – "Bravo, ma petite!" he exclaimed afterwards. There is not a single piece on this set that does not merit attention, and each song reveals something of Teyte's art. There are no texts or translations.

New review

Maggie Teyte Chansons Berlioz, Debussy, Duparc and Fauré. **Dame Maggie Teyte** (sop) with various artists. Pearl mono Ⓜ GEMMCD9134* (74 minutes: ADD: 11/95). From HMV and Rimington van Wyck originals; recorded 1936-41. Ⓖ

There was some sort of magic in the air at the EMI Abbey Road Studios in London on March 12th and 13th, 1936. Maggie Teyte, just short of her forty-eighth birthday, and Alfred Cortot, both of whom had been well acquainted with Claude Debussy, recorded 14 of his *mélodies*. This is no studio-bound recital but a performance, the passion and beauty of tone matched stroke for stroke by pianist and singer. These records, and the later ones Teyte made with Gerald Moore, are among the jewels of Debussy singing and playing. No one with an interest in French song should hesitate to acquire them, for they provide a lesson, not just in pronunciation of the French language (though like her contemporary and supposed rival, Mary Garden, Teyte sang with a pronounced English accent – something which entranced the French in the *belle époque*, when all things English were *à la mode*). The beauty of Teyte's tone, the freshness and girlish quality of her high notes – something which never deserted her, and she continued to sing for another 20 years – are constantly astonishing. So is the passion she puts into phrases such as "Qu'il était bleu, le ciel, et grand l'espoir!" in "Colloque sentimental" from the second book of *Fêtes galantes*, or the dark-hued "Il me dit: 'Les satyres sont morts,'" in "Le tombeau des Naïdes" from *Chansons de Bilitis*. Those who already have some of the other reissues of Teyte's Debussy recordings will find that this Pearl disc has a rather higher surface noise, perhaps the price one has to pay for getting the voice more forward. One wonders why Pearl have called the disc "Chansons", the correct term for these settings is *Mélodies* – or there is the good old English word 'song'.

The Three Tenors in Concert, 1994 [a]José Carreras, [b]Plácido Domingo, [c]Luciano Pavarotti (tens); [d]Los Angeles Music Center Opera Chorus; Los Angeles Philharmonic Orchestra / Zubin Mehta. Teldec Ⓕ 4509-96200-2 (74 minutes: DDD: 12/94). Texts and translations included. Recorded live in 1994.
Massenet Le Cid – O souverain, ô juge, ô pere[a]. Werther – Pourquoi me réveiller?[c]. **Moreno Torroba** Maravilla – Amor, vida de mi vida[b]. **Rodgers** Spring Is Here – With a song in my heart[a]. **Lara** Granada[b]. **De Curtis** Non ti scordar di me[c]. Tu, ca nun chiagne![a]. **Leoncavallo** Pagliacci – Vesti la giubba[b]. **Puccini** Turandot – Nessun dorma![c]. **Verdi** Rigoletto – La donna è mobile[abcd]. La traviata – Libiamo, ne'lieti calci[abcd]. **Various** (arr. and orch. Schifrin) A Tribute to Hollywood[abcd]. Around the World[abcd].

Domingo sings the first phrase of "Vesti la giubba" quite beautifully and sustains the broad climax well. With richness of tone, well-covered 'passage' notes, an exciting ring and, in the middle section, non-disruptive emphasis, he gives an exemplary demonstration of how to sing a popular song in his first solo, "Amor, vida de mi vida". In *Granada* he exercises the traditional charm of a good stylist at the point of leading back into the melody. Pavarotti still thrills with the clarity and resonance of his voice in the long line of high As in "Nessun dorma". The medleys include some pleasant quiet moments in "Santa Lucia lontana" and some unabashed big brassy ones in "Brazil". If one were to engage upon a balanced critical account it would have to start with the opening number, Carreras uneven and over-emphatic in the Prayer from *Le Cid*, and then continue with Pavarotti's Werther sung in *l'accent du Sud*. But it is not the sort of occasion, or the sort of record, for such commentary. Perhaps one might raise a quibble about the representation, in the *Around the World* medley, of Britain with "All I ask of you", and about the frequent returns in this geographically-guided selection, to Italy. For the rest, it's true there is a kind of pleasure in the lush, glitzy chorus swirling around in "With a song in my heart", and in The Three Tenors "Singing in the Rain" in unison like the football crowd of a dream.

Vocal Recital Régine Crespin (sop); [b]John Wustman (pf); [a]Suisse Romande Orchestra / Ernest Ansermet. Decca Ⓕ 417 813-2DH (68 minutes: ADD: 11/88). Texts and translations included. Items marked [a] from SXL6081 (3/64), [b]SXL6333 (6/68). Recorded 1963-7.
Berlioz Les nuits d'été. **Ravel** Shéhérazade[a]. **Debussy** Trois chansons de Bilitis[b]. **Poulenc** Fiançailles[b] – Chansons d'Orkenise; Hôtel. La courte paille[b] – Le carafon; La reine de coeur. Chansons villageoises[b] – Les gars qui vont à la fête. Deux poèmes de Louis Aragon[b].

Some recordings withstand the test of time and become acknowledged classics. This is one of them. Régine Crespin's voluptuous tone, her naturally accented French and her feeling for the inner meaning of the songs in the Berlioz and Ravel cycles are everywhere evident. Better than most single interpreters of the Berlioz, she manages to fulfil the demands of the very different songs, always alive to verbal nuances. In the Ravel, she is gorgeously sensuous, not to say sensual, with the right timbre for Ravel's enigmatic writing. The Debussy and Poulenc songs on this disc enhance its worth. Crespin offers an extremely evocative, perfumed account of the Debussy pieces and is ideally suited to her choice of Poulenc, of which her interpretation of "Hôtel" is a classic. Ansermet and his orchestra, though not quite note perfect, are – like the singer – right in timbre and colour for both these rewarding cycles. The sound is reasonable given the age of the recording. This is a most desirable acquisition.

New review

Voice and Harp Recital Charlotte de Rothschild (sop); David Watkins (hp). National Trust Ⓕ NTCD006 (73 minutes: DDD: 5/96). Texts and translations included. Recorded 1994.
Anonymous Have you seen but a white lily grow? Sumer is icumen in (arr. Watkins).
R. Johnson II As I walked forth. **Arne** Love's Labours Lost – When daisies pied. As You Like It – Blow, blow, thou winter wind. **Croft** Suite No. 3 in C minor – Sarabande and Ground.
Purcell Oedipus – Music for a while. **Parisotti** Se tu m'ami. **Gluck** Paride ed Elena – O del mio dolce ardor. **Durante** Danza, danza, fanciulla. **Schubert** An die Musik, D547. Heidenröslein, D257. Seligkeit, D433. **Meyer** Air de Sara. Air par M. Mereau. Du déserteur. **Watkins** Petite Suite. **Chausson** Mélodies, Op. 2 – Sérénade italienne; Le colibri. **Cannon** Chansons de femme – La bien aimée; La bien mariée. **Traditional** She moved through the fair. Scarborough Fair (arr. Watkins). Barbara Allen (arr. Watkins).

Charlecote Park, now National Trust property, was the ancestral home of the Lucy family, into which Mary Elizabeth married in 1823. Her harp, a wedding present from her husband, still resides in the parlour. Though we are not told in which room this recording was made, Charlecote Park is patently an apt venue for a recital such as this. There is an appropriate resonance, though it is not always kind to Rothschild's terminal consonants. The programme marks the 250th anniversary of the birth of the founding father of the Rothschilds and comprises music written by composers who were friends, teachers or ancestors of the family, a neat and unique package indeed. Rothschild has a fine and flexible voice, capable of subtle shading over a wide range of volume, a trifle hard-edged in the upper reaches when pushed and lacking a truly French nasal honk, but in general a splendid vehicle for this repertory. The various excellences of Watkins's harp playing, both as soloist and accompanist, will come as no surprise to those who have heard it before. What is on offer is some 73 minutes of intimate delights, with some old favourites in charming new dresses. Fear Morpheus only if you have eaten and drunk too well beforehand.

New review

Wings in the night Swedish Songs. Anne Sofie von Otter (mez); Bengt Forsberg (pf). DG Ⓕ 449 189-2GH (74 minutes: DDD: 5/96). Texts and translations included. Recorded 1995.
Gramophone Editor's choice. ⒼⒼ
Peterson-Berger Nothing is like the time of waiting. Swedish folk ballads, Op. 5 – No. 1, When I go myself in the dark forest; No. 3, Like stars in the heavens. Three Marit's Songs, Op. 12. Böljeby Waltz. Return. Aspåkers Polka. **Sigurd von Koch** Exotic Songs – No. 1, In the month of Tjaitra; No. 3, Of lotus scent and moonlight. The wild swans – Spring night's rain; Mankind's lot; The wild swans. **Stenhammar** Songs and Moods, Op. 26 – No. 1, The Wanderer; No. 4, Miss Blonde and Miss Brunette; No. 5, A ship sails; No. 9, Coastal song. Songs, Op. 37 – No. 1, Jutta comes to the Volkungs; No. 2, In the maple's shade. **Rangström** Poems by Bo Bergman – No. 1, Wings in the night; No. 3, Melody. The Dark Flower – No. 2, Prayer to the night; No. 4, Farewell. Pan. Old Swedish. **Alfvén** Songs, Op. 28 – No. 3, I kiss your hand; No. 6, The forest sleeps. **Sjögren** Lieder from Wolff's "Tannhäuser", Op. 12 – No. 4, Hab'ein Röslein dir gebrochen; No. 6, Ich möchte schweben. Du schaust mich an mit stummen Fragen.

If von Otter's and Forsberg's intention in compiling this recital was to provide an introduction to the riches of Swedish song so compelling that purchasers of it will hunger for more, they have succeeded. There are very few songs here that could not be programmed without apology or fear of comparison alongside the best German Lieder of the same period (the 40 years between 1884 and 1924). They contain considerable variety of mood and musical style, and the recital has been cleverly programmed to demonstrate in particular the range and the development of the two finest song composers here, Wilhelm Peterson-Berger and Wilhelm Stenhammar. Both were greatly gifted melodists, Peterson-Berger holding to an almost folk-like vein of simple lyricism, while Stenhammar reached further and touched darker moods, and the other composers here are by no means cast into the shade by these two masters. The performances are superb, quiet shadings of colour and subtle phrasings under immaculate control, a mere thread of voice often used to draw you into the heart of a song quite magically. Forsberg is an ideally imaginative and positive partner. You will probably find yourself playing several of these songs over and over again (for von Otter's exquisite little flourish of coloratura at the end of von Koch's *Of lotus scent*, for example, or for her delightful touch of humour and affection describing little chicks "who can hardly walk" stumbling into the first warm sun of summer in the first of Peterson-Berger's *Marit's Songs*).

Operatic highlights and recitals

Arias Angela Gheorghiu (sop); **Orchestra and** [a]**Chorus of Teatro Regio, Turin / John Mauceri.** Decca
Ⓕ 452 417-2DH (57 minutes: DDD: 6/96). Texts and translations included. Recorded 1995. Ⓖ
    Verdi Falstaff – Ninfe! Elfi! Silfi!; Sul fil d'un soffio etesio[a]. **Massenet** Chérubin – Aubade:
Vive amour qui rêve, embrasse et fuit[a]. Hérodiade – Celui dont la parole ... Il est doux, il est bon.
Catalani La Wally – Ebben? Ne andrò lontana. **Bellini** I Capuleti e i Montecchi – Eccomi in
lieta vesta ... Oh! quante volte. **Puccini** La bohème – Sì. Mi chiamano Mimì; Donde lieta uscì.
Boito Mefistofele – L'altra notte. **Gounod** Faust – O Dieu! que de bijoux! ... Ah! je ris.
Donizetti Don Pasquale – Quel guardo il cavaliere ... So anch'io la virtù magica. **Grigoriu**
Valurile Dunării – Muzica.

Here is a recital that begins in enchantment and ends in something a little less. If any two items are
individually responsible they are the arias from *Mefistofele* and *La Wally*. Perhaps Gheorghiu is
telling us to refine our ideas of these things: that the chesty Italian manner of Burzio and Muzio,
Callas and Scotto, should have 'gone out' with the actresses of the silent screen. Even so, what she
gives us in its place is surely incomplete. So it is that the most satisfying performances here are those
of a less overtly passionate nature. That does not include the Jewel song from *Faust*, where the rather
lazy tempo and lack of excitement in the style fail to catch the passionate impulses of laughter,
coquettishness, desire and even vanity in this naturally modest and simple girl. Massenet's Salomé and
Bellini's Giulietta are better suited; the Aubade from *Chérubin* is delightful; and we are back to the
beginning with Nannetta in Windsor Forest which is utter enchantment. The voice of course is a feast
in itself, the loveliest lyric soprano heard since Dame Kiri first came to us in the 1970s. The reticence,
which can be a limitation, has its positive side, and repeatedly one has to admire the way in which
fullness of volume and emotion is held in reserve for effective use at a climax.

The Art of the Prima Donna Dame Joan Sutherland (sop); **Chorus and Orchestra of the Royal
Opera House, Covent Garden / Francesco Molinari-Pradelli.** Decca Ⓜ 425 493-2DM2* (two discs:
109 minutes: ADD: 1/90). Texts and translations included. From SXL2556/7 (12/60). Recorded
1960. *Gramophone classical 100.* Ⓖ
    Arne Artaxerxes – The soldier tir'd. **Bellini** La Sonnambula – Care compagne ... Come per me
sereno ... Sopra il sen. Norma – Sediziose voci ... Casta diva ... Ah! bello a me ritorna. I Puritani
– Son vergin vezzosa; O rendetemi la speme ... Qui la voce ... Vien, diletto. **Delibes** Lakmé – Ah!
Où va la jeune Indoue. **Gounod** Faust – O Dieu! que de bijoux ... Ah! je ris. Roméo et Juliette –
Je veux vivre. **Handel** Samson – Let the bright Seraphim. **Meyerbeer** Les Huguenots – O beau
pays de la Touraine! **Mozart** Die Entführung aus dem Serail – Martern aller Arten. **Rossini**
Semiramide – Bel raggio lusinghier. **Thomas** Hamlet – A vos jeux, mes amis. **Verdi** Otello – Mia
madre aveva una povera ancella ... Piangea cantando. La traviata – È strano ... Ah fors' è lui ...
Sempre libera. Rigoletto – Gualtier Maldè ... Caro nome.

Those who have not heard Dame Joan until recent times can only speculate on the full beauty of her
voice in its prime. This album, from 1960, preserves the real Sutherland quality as well as any of her
records have done and it is a delight from start to finish. Sutherland and her husband, Richard Bonynge,
have long been interested in the history of opera and particularly of its singers, so *The Art of the Prima
Donna* was arranged to relate each of the solos to a famous soprano of the past. Arne's *Artaxerxes*
recalls Mrs Billington, and the final items are associated with more recent artists such as Tetrazzini and
Galli-Curci. It presents a brilliant conspectus, with Sutherland mastering the most fearsome of technical
demands and showing a wonderfully complete command of the required skills. She was then fresh from
the triumph at Covent Garden in *Lucia di Lammermoor* which brought her international fame in 1959.
Her voice was at its purest, and her style had not developed the characteristics which later partly limited
the pleasure of her singing. What the record may not quite convey is the sheer house-filling volume of
her voice. Even so, nobody who hears these recordings can be in any doubt about her mastery or about
the aptness of the title, bestowed on her by the Italians, of "la stupenda".

The Artistry of Fernando de la Mora Fernando de la Mora (ten); **Welsh National Opera
Orchestra / Sir Charles Mackerras.** Telarc Ⓕ CD80411 (64 minutes: DDD: 1/96).
    Gounod Roméo et Juliette – Ah! lève-toi, soleil. Faust – Salut! demeure chaste et pure. **Verdi** La
traviata – De' miei bollenti spiriti; O mio romorso! Rigoletto – Ella mi fu rapita!; Parmi veder le
lagrime; La donna è mobile. **Puccini** La bohème – Che gelida manina. Tosca – Recondita
armonia; E lucevan le stelle. **Cilea** L'arlesiana – È la solita storia. **Bizet** Carmen – La fleur que
tu m'avais jetée. Les pêcheurs de perles – Je crois entendre encore. **Donizetti** La fille du régiment
– Ah! mes amis. **Ponchielli** La Gioconda – Cielo e mar! **Massenet** Werther – Pourquoi me
réveiller? **Giordano** Fedora – Amor ti vieta.

The title draws attention to "the artistry" of this tenor, and very justifiably too; but what we want to
know about first is the voice. In his opening phrases the sound is tender and sweet, and we soon realize
that Fernando de la Mora is a name to be noted and remembered. This is in Roméo's cavatina: this

Mexican tenor sings with perhaps not such clean French definition but with rather more honey in the voice, perhaps more imaginatively too. But then in *La traviata* the production seems not quite so easy and secure, while a tendency to come up to a note from below (though no more than several eminent predecessors have done) compromises the style a little and a slightly nasalized quality intrudes in certain vowel-sounds. With "Che gelida manina", however, we are back with the charmer, the lyric tenor assured in his command of range and expression, the voice of the young lover and the reason why all the world loves a good young Italianate tenor. And so it goes on. Every item has it attractions, and many are very good indeed. In the now famous *Fille du régiment* solo he duly warms to his nine top Cs, and in the Flower song from *Carmen* he takes the high B flat softly but not falsetto. "Cielo e mar" is graced with a carefully preserved legato, though perhaps the tone is a bit limited in resources for this. "Salut! demeure" is sung gently and sensitively till it comes to the high C, a fine ringing note but isolated by the quietness of its context and by the prefatory breath taken before "la présence". Mackerras conducts, and the Welsh National Opera Orchestra play, with all due sympathy; and, yes, this is a tenor to note and remember.

Maria Callas Rarities. **Maria Callas** (sop); [a]**Paris Conservatoire Orchestra / Nicola Rescigno;** [b]**Maggio Musicale Fiorentino Orchestra / Tullio Serafin;** [c]**Rome RAI Orchestra / Alfredo Simonetto;** [d]**Philharmonia Orchestra / Antonio Tonini;** [e]**Paris Opera Orchestra / Georges Prêtre.** EMI Ⓟ CDC7 54437-2* (78 minutes: ADD: 2/93). Texts and translations included. Items marked [c] recorded at a concert in San Remo, Italy in 1954.
Beethoven Ah! perfido, Op. 65[a] (from Columbia SAX2540, 8/64). **Mozart** Don Giovanni – Non mi dir[b] (CMS7 63750-2, 11/91. Recorded in 1953). Die Entführung aus dem Serail – Martern aller Arten[c] (sung in Italian. New to UK). **Weber** Oberon – Ozean du Ungeheuer![d] (English. Previously unpublished. 1962). **Rossini** Armida – D'amore al dolce impero[c] (EX769741-1, 4/89). **Donizetti** Lucrezia Borgia – Tranquillo ei posa ... Com'è bello![d] (1961). **Verdi** Don Carlos – O don fatale[d] (1961). I vespri siciliani – Arrigo! ah, parli[d] (1960). Il trovatore – Vanne ... lasciami ... D'amor sull'ali rosee[a]. I lombardi – Te, Vergin santa[a] (all previously unpublished). Both recorded in 1964/5). Aida – Pur' ti riveggo ... Fuggiam gli ardor[e] (with Franco Corelli, ten. New to UK. 1964).

'Rarity' is one of those tricky words which, being really only quantitative, seems to imply something about quality as well. So the reader may well look doubtfully at the title: the "Callas Rarities" may indeed be rarities for the best of reasons, that of inferiority to versions and recordings that are less rare. In this instance, though, they are genuinely well worth having. For example, here is the Nile Duet from *Aida* with Franco Corelli, sole survivor of a projected album of duets to be recorded in 1964. Corelli provides the vocal thrills, sometimes even responding in kind to the dramatic intensity which characterizes Callas's performance from the start. Her voice is sometimes raw, and the soft B flat on "fuggiam" only just arrives and stays put. But always there is something distinctive: here it is the nostalgia, "Là tra foreste" being sung as a wistful, private vision of the homeland. Then there are the two incredibly brilliant solos from a concert at San Remo in 1954 ("Martern aller Arten" and "D'amore al dolce impero"); also previously unpublished versions, not alternative 'takes' but different performances, products of a different session. Usually one can see why they were not issued at the time, but here it is easier to see why they deserve to see the light of this later day.

New review

Caruso in Opera, Volume 2. Arias – L'africaine, Andrea Chenier, La bohème (Leoncavallo and Puccini), Carmen, Cavalleria Rusticana, Don Pasquale, Eugene Onegin, La favorita, Les huguenots, Macbeth, Martha, Nero, La reine de Saba, Rigoletto, Tosca and Il trovatore. **Enrico Caruso** (ten) with various artists. Nimbus Prima Voce mono Ⓜ NI7866* (79 minutes: ADD: 7/95). From Victor originals; recorded 1905-20.

The 1906 recording of "M'appari" from *Martha* comes first, and it introduces an aspect of Caruso's singing that rarely finds a place in the critical commentaries: his subtlety. Partly, it's rhythmic. The move-on and pull-back seems such an instinctive process that we hardly notice it (though no doubt a modern conductor would – and check it immediately). It makes all the difference to the emotional life of the piece, the feeling of involvement and spontaneous development. Then there is the phrasing, marvellously achieved at the melody's reprise. The play of louder and softer tones, too, has every delicacy of fine graduation; and just as masterly is the more technical (though still expressive) covering and (rare) opening of notes at the *passaggio*. An edition of the score which brought out all these features of Caruso's singing would be a densely annotated document. It would, even so, be a simplification, for accompanying all this is the dramatic and musical feeling, which defies analysis – and, of course, the voice. That voice! You may feel you know all these records and hardly need to play them, yet there is scarcely an occasion when the beauty of it does not thrill with a sensation both old and new (the first 'Ah!' is one of recognition, the second of fresh wonder). So it is with nearly all of the items here: all, in fact, save the *Eugene Onegin* aria, which remains external, and the late *L'africaine* recording with its saddening evidence of deterioration. The transfers are excellent.

Boris Christoff Opera Arias - Don Carlo, Don Giovanni, Ernani, La forza del destino, Iphigénie en Aulide, Mefistofele, Nabucco, Norma, Simon Boccanegra, La sonnambula and I vespri siciliani. **Boris Christoff** (bass) with various artists. EMI Références mono Ⓜ CDH5 65500-2* (80 minutes: ADD: 3/96). From HMV originals; recorded 1949-55.

The grieving king, the patriarchal priest, the smirking demon: these are all expected presences in Christoff's gallery of vivid characters, and one might well extend the list mentally by a dozen or so more before thinking of Leporello. Christoff sang very little Mozart but the Catalogue aria in *Don Giovanni* featured in his concert programmes. It is a marvellous performance, and alone provides a very good reason for buying this disc. Almost as unlooked for may be the Count's aria in *La sonnambula*, sung with affection and a nearly perfect legato. Warmth of tone perhaps is wanting, in both that and the "Infelice" (*Ernani*), but there is certainly no lack of emotional warmth in the fine solos from *I vespri siciliani* and *Simon Boccanegra*. Philip's great aria in *Don Carlo* ends with a too overt and prolonged tearfulness (avoided in later versions) but this recording is still among the supremely impressive mementos of its era. It comes from one of Christoff's first sessions in the studios, and is strikingly natural and lifelike, as are all the 78s heard here. In the 1955 recordings one is more aware of the microphone: for example, in his most authoritative vein, Christoff is splendidly represented by the Gluck aria (*Iphigénie en Aulide*) made in 1951, whereas the same magnificence is present in the excerpts from *Nabucco* (1955) but just slightly diminished by seeming to be made larger than life. When all is over, however, the first item demands a replay: that Catalogue song of Leporello's. John Hughes's admirable notes concede that the performance "may lack the necessary touch of humour" - but it surely does not! Gaiety, rhythm, even a chuckle, a swelling grandeur in the portrayal of the "maiestosa", a daintiness in "la piccina": it is all there, and with it a certain suavity of style, and, rarer still, the elegant phrases of "Nella bionda" sung with scrupulous legato. This disc goes into the 'Essential Christoff Collection' forthwith.

Covent Garden on Record, Volumes 1-4. **143 singers with various accompaniments.** Pearl mono Ⓜ GEMMCDS9923/6* (four three-disc sets, oas: 215, 227 and 222 minutes: AAD: 7/92). *Gramophone Award Winner 1992.*   ⒶⒶⒶ

An Aladdin's cave, where whatever the torch lights upon is treasure. At the entrance: Adelina Patti, well past her prime to be sure, but in that *Ah, non credea mirarti* what heartfelt pathos when she comes to the lines "Mi ravivar l'amore il pianto mio non puèo", what delicacy in the soft tones and the trill, and, after all, what a miracle that we should be able to hear as clearly as this, from the 63-year-old woman in retirement at her Welsh castle in 1906, the beauty remaining to the most world-renowned voice of her century. Further in among the treasures, the first Otello, the first Falstaff; near to them, a baritone, one Mario Ancona of 1904, almost forgotten today but truly superb in his Donizetti, as, by his side, is the bass Marcel Journet, sonorous and with a funny old chorus to support him in a passage from that epitome of nineteenth-century grand opera, *Les Huguenots*. Into the next chamber, and a voice arises celebrating the fickleness of womankind - the voice of the god of tenors, Enrico Caruso. His Irish friend McCormack, his business-partner Melba, his Neapolitan *amico* Scotti: all are there. Deeper in, and we have come through the First World War, to where British singers - Walter Widdop, Heddle Nash and Joan Cross among them mingle freely and quite rightly with tip-top company such as Lotte Lehmann, Elisabeth Rethberg and Friedrich Schorr. At the end of the journey we reach the ominous date 1939: for the chambers of this Aladdin's cave of records have also been the years of the Covent Garden Opera House, with singers heard there, in the present theatre, as early as 1871, up to the end of the international seasons and the outbreak of World War Two. The singers are heard in the roles they sang, and are sometimes recorded 'live' from the stage, as with Chaliapin in 1928 and Gigli in 1939. Many of the recordings are of extreme rarity, and thanks to the expertise of Keith Hardwick, who compiled the programme and effected the transfers, a sizeable proportion of them are heard to greater advantage than ever before on CD or LP. Not everything is perfect, either in the singers themselves (they don't always do what we want them to), or the selections (nothing of some famous Covent Garden roles such as Caruso's Canio and Turner's Turandot) or even the transfers (a certain harshness in some of the later recordings). But the four albums, three CDs to a volume and each volume available separately, comprise one of the best of anthologies. They also document a fascinating period in the history of a great opera house: an extraordinary concentration of enterprise, historical time, musical talent and in some instances genius, all within the compass of these 12 discs.

Zara Dolukhanova Opera Arias - Il barbiere di Siviglia, Don Carlo, Les huguenots, Kashchey the Immortal, Khovanshchina, The Maid of Orleans, Le nozze di Figaro, Samson et Dalila and Semiramide; Concert Arias by Prokofiev, Tchaikovsky and Verdi. **Zara Dolukhanova** (mez); **Moscow Philharmonic Orchestra / Grigory Stolarov.** Russian Disc mono Ⓜ RDCD15023* (66 minutes: AAD: 3/96). Recorded live in Moscow in 1954.

Zara Dolukhanova is all but forgotten in the West. She certainly doesn't deserve to be. Her voice was a faultlessly produced mezzo of great beauty, extending upwards well into the soprano range, downward far enough to make a formidably sultry Dalila, yet without any of that ugly barking which some mezzos use instead of low notes. Her range of character was even wider, from a really charming and stylish Cherubino ("Non so più cosa son" in Russian) to a full-voiced, devout and thoroughly Verdian account (in Italian) of the first of the *Four Sacred Pieces*. Her coloratura was accomplished, so her Rossini comes off well in both languages (in a Russian "Una voce poco fa" she is a smiling, rather than a vixenish Rosina). The Russian items give an excellent idea of her vocal range: generous and eloquent amplitude of voice in Joan's farewell from Tchaikovsky's *The Maid of Orleans* (a soprano role modified for a mezzo, but still needing soprano brightness), dark gravity and urgency in Marfa's soothsaying from *Khovanshchina* and, in a particularly Wagner-influenced Rimsky-Korsakov monologue (*Kashchey*) the sort of dramatic declamation that makes you wonder whether she ever dipped a toe into the Wagnerian repertory. The recordings were made at a public concert during, judging from the sound of the coughing, a damp Moscow January. The orchestral playing is at times a little unkempt, and the voice is placed well forward. Yet with such a voice, who's complaining? Only the extracts from Russian operas are provided with texts, and the insert-notes are effusive rubbish ("wearing a simple white dress which fitted her perfect body"), but when they speak of her "most beautiful voice, which is simultaneously so powerful and exquisitely graceful, dense and succulent as a peach", they do not exaggerate.

New review

Geraldine Farrar in French Opera Opera Arias and Duets – Carmen, Les contes d'Hoffmann, Manon, Mignon, Roméo et Juliette and Thaïs. **Geraldine Farrar** (sop) with various artists.
Nimbus Prima Voce mono Ⓜ NI7872* (79 minutes: ADD: 1/96). From Victor originals; recorded 1908-21. Recorded 1908-21.

This is a lovely addition to the Prima Voce series. Farrar's Carmen appears as a model of effectiveness within the restraints of good musical and dramatic behaviour. The "Séguedille" is sheer enchantment (irresistible promise in that breathed "je l'aimerai" and the dreamily provocative reprise of "Près des remparts"), while in the "Chanson bohème" we catch the energy of her personality as well as the carrying power of her by no means robust lyric soprano. These are all cherishable records, of the kind that on some pleasant desultory evening with the gramophone one will feel a prompting to take down from the shelves. Seasoned collectors should not necessarily assume that they already have everything on the disc: there is, for instance, the unpublished "Je veux vivre" (*Roméo et Juliette*) from 1911, a performance of surprising delicacy and charm. The Prelude to Act 4 is there, too, in a recording from 1921 said to be by the orchestra of La Scala conducted by Toscanini, one of those legendary sessions which put him off the gramophone for a decade. If he had heard the results as cleanly defined as they are here, he might have thought again.

New review

German Opera Arias Thomas Hampson (bar); [a]Pestalozzi Gymnasium Children's Choir; Munich Radio Orchestra / Fabio Luisi. EMI Ⓔ CDC5 55233-2 (79 minutes: DDD: 9/95). Texts and translations included. Recorded 1994.
Korngold Die tote Stadt – Mein Sehnen, mein Wähnen. **Lortzing** Zar und Zimmermann – Verraten! … Die Macht des Zepters. Der Wildschütz – Wie freundlich strahlt … Heiterkeit und Fröhlichkeit. **Marschner** Hans Heiling – An jenam Tag. Der Vampyr – Ha! Noch einen ganzen Tag. **Weber** Euryanthe – Wo berg' ich mich? … So weih' ich mich den Rachgewalten. **Spohr** Faust – Der Hölle selbst will ich...Liebe ist die zarte Blüthe. **Kreutzer** Das Nachtlager in Granada – Die Nacht ist schön. **Schreker** Der ferne Klang – In einem Lande ein bleicher König. **Humperdinck** Die Königskinder – Verdorben! Gestorben![a]. **Wagner** Tannhäuser – Wie Todesahnung … O du mein holder Abendstern. Die Walküre – Winterstürme wichen dem Wonnemond.

In addition to being a singer of outstanding gifts and versatility, Hampson is also scholarly in his approach. He himself, with Jens Mete Fischer, contributes an essay on "the baritone in German opera", making it clear that he is aware of the tradition in which he sings. It is not surprising, then, that voices from the past should come to mind and stay there quite contentedly during the course of this recital. Schlusnus (in *Hans Heiling*), Hüsch (in *Königskinder*), Janssen (*Tannhäuser*), and for just one phrase ("sie bringet Wünsche mancher Art mir dar" in *Der Wildschütz*) Fischer-Dieskau: a formidable array, and assuredly not assembled in order to bar the young American from entry to their ranks. His voice is uncommonly beautiful, he is scrupulous in his musicianship, and like the best Germans he knows the value of the Italian connection. If there is a limitation to his success in the chosen programme, it is simply the price that often has to be paid by a singer whose voice is an unmixed pleasure to the ear. For the villain of *Euryanthe* and the maniac of *Der Vampyr*, his voice-character is simply too good: goodness, not villainy, is its element. At times, too, there is need for more depth and body in the lower range (Spohr's Faust and Schreker's Count in *Der ferne Klang* are examples). Otherwise the singing is delightful, the *Zar und Zimmermann*, *Tannhäuser* and *Die tote Stadt* solos especially. In including Siegmund's "Winterstürme" from *Die Walküre*, Hampson was probably providing a talking-point as much as anything, and it is certainly interesting to hear how he will occasionally 'tenorize' while usually keeping to his normal baritone production, perhaps giving his admirers a moment's concern as he opens the voice for the F of "vereint" in the last phrase. The programme itself contains several rarities. The imaginative use of the solo violin in *Das Nachtlager in Granada* and the rich orchestration of *Der ferne Klang* are additional pleasures in a recital that is well accompanied, well recorded and informatively presented.

Great Singers at the Maryinsky Theatre Opera Arias with various accompaniments. Nimbus Prima Voce mono Ⓜ NI7865* (78 minutes: ADD: 3/95). Notes and some synopses included. From HMV originals; recorded 1908-13.

Sopranos – **Olimpia Boronat** (Les Huguenots), **Eugenia Bronskaya** (Hamlet, A life for the Tsar), **Elena Katulskaya** (Mireille, Thaïs), **Maria Kovalenko** (The Queen of Spades), **Lydia Lipkowska** (The Snow Maiden), **Antonina Nezhdanova** (Fra Diavolo, Lakmé, La traviata, Die Zauberflöte). *Mezzo-soprano* – **Evgenia Popello-Davidova** (Lakmé). *Contralto* – **Evgenia Zbrueva** (The Queen of Spades). *Tenors* – **David Juzhin** (La Gioconda), **Andrei Labinsky** (Halka), **Dmitri Smirnov** (Mefistofele, La traviata), **Leonid Sobinov** (The demon), **Eugene Vitting** (The Queen of Spades). *Baritone* – **Mikhail Karakash** (The Queen of Spades). *Basses* – **Vladimir Kastorsky** (Eugene Onegin), **Lev Sibiriakov** (Judith, Thaïs, Requiem – Verdi).

Here is a superb collection, "courtesy [we are told] of the Director of Staff of the St Petersburg State Museum of Theatre and Music". All of the originals are rare, and some must be practically unique. Among the soprano solos, particularly exciting is Boronat's account of the Queen's cabaletta in *Les Huguenots*, queenly indeed as far as the letter of the score is concerned but brilliant in technique and often exquisite in shading. Nezhdanova in both *Lakmé* excerpts (the Bell song and now even more famous 'flower' duet) sings with lovely purity and easy command. Lipkowska's *Snow Maiden* is an utter charmer, and also delightfully youthful in tone is Katulskaya's Mireille. Of the tenors, Labinsky's *Halka* solo has exemplary evenness of line, as has the baritone Karakash in Yeletsky's aria. Kastorsky's Gremin and Sibiriakov's admonition of the Israelites in *Judith* are among the finest of all; and how skilfully Sibiriakov subdues his mighty bass in the *Thaïs* duet with Katulskaya. The original copies used are all in pristine condition.

New review

Great Tenor Arias Ben Heppner (ten); [a]Bavarian Radio Chorus; Munich Radio Orchestra / Roberto Abbado. RCA Victor Red Seal Ⓕ 09026 62504-2 (61 minutes: DDD: 11/95). Texts and translations included. Recorded 1993-4.

Leoncavallo La bohème – Musette ! o gioia della mia dimora; Testa adorata. **Verdi** Luisa Miller – Oh! fede negar potessi; Quando le sere al placido. La forza del destino – La vita è inferno; Oh, tu che in seno. Aida – Se quel guerrier; Celeste Aida. Il trovatore – Ah! sì, ben mio; Di quella pira[a]. **Puccini** Manon Lescaut – Donna non vidi mai. Turandot – Nessun dorma![a]. La fanciulla del West – Ch'ella mi creda libero. **Bizet** Carmen – La fleur que tu m'avais jetée. **Meyerbeer** L'Africaine – Pays merveilleux; O Paradis. **Massenet** Hérodiade – Ne pouvant réprimer les élans de la foi; Adieu donc, vains objets. Le cid – Ah! tout est bien fini; O souverain, ô juge, ô père. **Giordano** Andrea Chenier – Colpito qui m'avete; Un dì all'azzurro spazio; Come un bel dì di maggio.

The name that immediately comes to mind in listening to this collection is that of Heppner's older contemporary, Domingo. Their timbre is similar, as is their vocal manner – consistently firm, plush tone brought to bear in a musically faultless approach to the piece in hand, with a fair understanding of the style required. A further likeness comes in Heppner's willingness to tackle Italian, French and German repertory with equal aplomb. Heppner immediately wins approval by beginning with Marcello's seldom-heard aria from Leoncavallo's *Bohème*, into which he pours forth generosity of tone and heart. Each of the Verdi items benefits from long-breathed phrasing, a sensitive attention to dynamic levels and excellent Italian. The Puccini arias are, if anything, even better. The *Manon Lescaut* and *Fanciulla* arias bear comparison with either Björling or Domingo in this music. Heppner is less confident and idiomatic in French, which may account for a fluently sung but matter-of-fact Flower Song and for a want of sheer flair in "O Paradis", where the big phrase doesn't open out as it should: here any comparison with Caruso is inadvisable. The Massenet pieces are better. John the Baptist's sorrowful aria from *Hérodiade* brings the most plangent performance of all, not least at "Je ne regrette rien", itself pre-echoing Piaf. The *Cid* Prayer begins, as it should, with an inward recitative and, as in all Heppner's performances, he manages to think himself into character and situation: this is no machismo tenor, but Rodrigue himself before us. As a whole this is a most rewarding recital, well accompanied and warmly recorded.

New review

Erich Kunz Opera Arias – Don Giovanni, Der lustige Krieg, Eine Nacht in Venedig, Le nozze di Figaro, Der Vogelhändler, Der Waffenschmied, Der Wildschütz, Zar und Zimmermann, Die Zauberflöte and Der Zigeunerbaron; Viennese songs by various composers. **Erich Kunz** (bar) with various artists. Testament mono Ⓕ SBT1059* (79 minutes: ADD: 9/95). From Columbia originals; recorded 1947-53.

Here is Kunz in his absolute prime, moving his agreeable voice around Figaro's, Leporello's and Papageno's music with the confidence derived from experience in the roles in Vienna, but without the slightest sense of routine. It should not be forgotten that he was one of the first German-speaking singers to learn his Da Ponte roles in Italian: his diction and accent in them, as we find here, are virtually perfect. Under Karajan, in Figaro's "Non più andrai" he is disciplined by a fast tempo, while Ackermann is more yielding in Leporello's "Madamina". Karajan also conducts the Giovanni/Zerlina duet (with the incomparable Seefried) It is a wonderful souvenir of two artists, their voices blending ideally, who sang so often together in that notable ensemble in Vienna. Kunz was also loved in his home city for his assumption of *buffo* parts in Lortzing's operas, and he brings to their arias, again with Ackermann in sympathetic support, a rich vein of comic characterization without ever resorting to caricature – Kunz was, above all, a sensitive musician. The second half of this issue is devoted to operetta items and Viennese songs. In the former it may be complained that he was often adopting, and transposing down, music written originally for a tenor: four songs from *Ein Nacht in Venedig*, in the Korngold rescension, rather suffer in that respect, yet Kunz's wholly idiomatic approach almost makes us forget the anomaly. In what are mostly Heurigen songs, he is absolutely in his element; only his older, tenor colleague, Julius Patzak was his peer in these. The accompanying Schrammel Ensemble are wholly authentic. Try, if you can, *Da draussen in der Wachau*, so beguiling in tone and style, and you will not be able to resist the rest.

New review

Claudia Muzio Opera Arias and Duets – Adriana Lecouvreur, Andrea Chénier, L'Arlesiana, La bohème, Cavalleria Rusticana, Cecilia, La forza del destino, Mefistofele, Norma, Otello, La sonnambula, Tosca, La traviata and Il trovatore; songs by Buzzi-Peccia, Debussy, Delibes, Donaudy, Parisotti, Refice and Reger. **Claudia Muzio** (sop) with various artists. Romophone mono Ⓕ 81015-2* (two discs: 155 minutes: ADD: 6/96). From Columbia and Italian Columbia originals; recorded 1934-5. Also contains part of Act 1 of Puccini's *Tosca*, recorded at a performance in the War Memorial Auditorium, San Francisco on October 15th, 1932. Ⓖ

This set completes Romophone's comprehensive survey of all Muzio's records, masterminded by Ward Marston. Since their first release, Muzio's Columbias of 1934-5 have always been her most accessible discs, but they have never, even on previous CD reissues, sounded so present and clear as they do here. This most eloquent of divas seems to be in the room with us and the music in hand is delivered with such sincere passion, such total conviction that tears are brought to the eyes. All those anonymous-sounding sopranos with their dull recitals today should sit down and listen to the individuality Muzio brings to every track here. Not for a moment can one be anything but enthralled by these readings. Since there is not enough material to fill two CDs, Romophone have added a substantial extract from Act 1 of a 1932 San Francisco *Tosca*, primitively recorded and so far known only to a few Muzio fanatics. However, as a whole this is an essential issue for anyone wanting to know about the art of one of the century's most lovable and vital interpreters.

The Incomparable Heddle Nash

Puccini La bohème – Act 4ª. **Lisa Perli** (sop) Mimì; **Heddle Nash** (ten) Rodolfo; **Stella Andreva** (sop) Musetta; **John Brownlee** (bar) Marcello; **Robert Alva** (bass) Schaunard; **Robert Easton** (bass) Colline; **London Philharmonic Orchestra / Sir Thomas Beecham**. Dutton Laboratories mono Ⓜ CDLX7012* (69 minutes: ADD: 2/95). Item marked ª from Columbia LX523/6 (10/36); remainder from HMV and Columbia originals; recorded 1929-35. Ⓖ
Opera Arias and Duets – Il barbiere di Siviglia, Così fan tutte, Don Giovanni, Die Fledermaus, La jolie fille de Perth and Rigoletto. **Heddle Nash** (ten) with various artists.

When he made this recording of Act 4 of *La bohème* in 1935 Nash was at the height of his powers and sings a spontaneous, quite Italianate Rodolfo. Perli makes a simple, heartfelt Mimì. The rest of the cast falls far short of the principals, but Beecham is at his most alert, and sensitive too. Nash's Mozart is most elegantly represented by the well-nigh faultless versions of Ottavio's arias, made at the time of his sensational Covent Garden début in 1929 in *Don Giovanni*. The phrasing is refined, the breath long, the big run in "Il mio tesoro" encompassed in a single span. The Duke of Mantua's three arias tell us just why this was one of Nash's favourite roles early in his career. He makes the most of the execrable translation by singing it with total conviction, and his lyric tenor rings out with just the right *élan*, matched by subtle colourings. The Serenade from *La jolie fille de Perth* is justly renowned because it displays to perfection the elegiac, minstrel-like quality of Nash's tone and his impassioned delivery – and yet he is said to have had a cold on the day it was made! The transfers (including the solo items) are superior to any previous issues, bringing the voices into one's room without let or hindrance.

New review

Serenade Opera Arias and Ensembles – La bohème, Carmen, Cavalleria Rusticana, Faust, Die Fledermaus, Friederike, La jolie fille de Perth, Les pêcheurs de perles, Rigoletto and Il trovatore; songs by Ascher, Delius, MacMurrough, Rossini and R. Strauss. **Heddle Nash** (ten) with various artists. Pearl mono Ⓜ GEMMCD9175* (72 minutes: AAD: 11/95). From HMV and Columbia originals; recorded 1928-44.

At last some of Nash's HMV titles are out of copyright and Pearl have swiftly taken advantage of the fact to give us his fluid, impassioned, graciously phrased account of the *Carmen* Flower song and Faust's *Cavatine*. Better still, indeed something of a collector's piece, is his version of Nadir's "Je crois entendre" from *Les pêcheurs de perles*, sung in a dreamy *mezza voce*. Also from these 1944 sessions (though the date is wrongly given here as 1939) comes Richard Strauss's *Ständchen*, a rarity in its original form, and sung so beguilingly as to charm any girl out of her eyrie, not forgetting Gerald Moore's light-fingered playing. No British tenor today sings so effortlessly off the words. From the Columbias of the early 1930s we have a nice contrast between Nash's buoyant account of Rossini's *La danza*, sung in the original, and his ardent, plaintive *Macushla* (MacMurrough). Most welcome, too, is the reappearance of his account of the two Shelley settings (*To the Queen of my Heart* and *Love's Philosophy*) always among the most desirable of his discs. "Wayside Rose" from Lehár's *Friederika* is a souvenir of his appearance in that operetta; but is it not transferred a semitone or so too high? As the Duke of Mantua, Nash launches the *Rigoletto* Quartet with spontaneous *élan* and sounds suitably tormented in the *Trovatore* "Miserere", Licette a notable partner in both. There are reservations about the transfers. With the example of the Dutton Laboratories' "Incomparable Nash" (reviewed above), these occasionally hazy Pearl transfers from 78s are questionable. In his otherwise informative note Charles Haynes again gives the tenor's birthday as 1896, when it has now been conclusively proved to have been 1894. In spite of these drawbacks, do not miss the many vocal delights enshrined here.

New review

Legendary Baritones Opera Arias and Songs with various accompaniments. Nimbus Prima Voce mono Ⓜ NI7867* (77 minutes: ADD: 10/95). From Columbia, Fonotipia, HMV, Victor, Polydor and German Odeon originals; recorded 1905-41.
  Lucien Fugère (Le jongleur de Notre Dame); **Victor Maurel** (Tosti: Au temps du grand roi); **Antonio Magini-Coletti** (Falstaff); **Mattia Battistini** (La traviata); **Mario Ancona** (Un ballo in maschera); **Maurice Renaud** (Le roi de Lahore); **Eugenio Giraldoni** (Otello); **Riccardo Stracciari** (Tosca); **Giuseppe de Luca** (Ernani); **Titta Ruffo** (Falstaff); **Pasquale Amato** (I due Foscari); **Joseph Schwarz** (Tannhäuser); **Heinrich Schlusnus** (Hans Heiling); **Renato Zanelli** (Zazà); **Carlo Galeffi** (Rigoletto); **John Charles Thomas** (Andrea Chenier); **Lawrence Tibbett** (Il barbiere di Siviglia); **Gerhard Hüsch** (Der Wildschütz); **Igor Gorin** (Attila).

Prizes for all here, except possibly John Charles Thomas. *Andrea Chenier* is not the subtlest of operas, and "Nemico della patria" does not call for the fine nuance of a Fischer-Dieskau, but it does want more than the mouthing of words and *tutta forza* for the notes. The voice is magnificent, but in this 'legendary' company we look also for taste. And in its various guises we find it: in the 80-year-old Fugère with his immaculate definition and unmawkish tenderness; in Maurel with a charm of old-world manners in his courtly song to Madame la Marquise; Magini-Coletti with his humorous but gentlemanly Falstaff; Battistini wearing his elegant paternal suit, and Ancona bestowing upon the outraged husband the dignity of more-in-sorrow-than-in-anger. After that comes Maurice Renaud, about whom one might raise a complaint concerning emotional expression achieved at the expense of the vocal line; yet there is stylistic refinement too, and a richly imaginative care for the Massenet aria, phrase by phrase. With Stracciari one might wonder about the voice production, so free one moment, throat-laden in another; then there is Amato with his rapid vibrancy, Galeffi with his weakness for the emotional quiver. Yet all are artists, and their work will repay study. The Germans are a distinguished trio too, and the Russian-born Igor Gorin is superb in his *Attila* aria. Ruffo, rich in vocal colours, de Luca gracious in the exercise of traditional virtues ... But there it is: a prize-giving here would have something for (almost) everybody, including those responsible for the transfers and booklet, for the choice of singers and their matching up with arias.

New review

John McCormack Opera and Operetta Arias – Il barbiere di Siviglia, Barry of Ballymore, La bohème, Carmen, L'elisir d'amore, Faust, La fille du régiment, La Gioconda, In a Persian garden, Lakmé, Lucia di Lammermoor, Naughty Marietta, Les pêcheurs de perles, Rigoletto and La traviata; songs by Balfe, Barker, Blumenthal, Cherry, Claribel, Crouch, MacMurrough, Marshall, Parelli, Rossini and Traditional. **John McCormack** (ten) with various artists. Romophone mono Ⓔ 82006-2* (two discs: 155 minutes: ADD: 4/96). From Victor and HMV originals; recorded 1910-11.

You think, at the start of this journey through the recordings of two years, that here is McCormack at his absolute best, in the first of the *Lucia di Lammermoor* solos; but no, for the second one ("Tu che a Dio spiegasti l'ali"), made two months later, is better still, a perfection of lyrical singing, the music lying ideally within his voice as it was at that time, and with the heart and imagination more evidently involved. A little later comes "Una furtiva lagrima", where the modulation into D flat major ("m'ama") brings surely some of the most beautiful, most unflawed tenor singing ever recorded. This album, from 1910 and 1911, presents him in finest voice. He was only 25 at the outset: in the first flush of his operatic success and already the partner of Melba (heard with him in the *Rigoletto* Quartet and *Faust* Trio) and Tetrazzini. His favourite baritone partner was Mario Sammarco, who turns up as a blustery Figaro to his elegant Almaviva, retiring to a more discreet distance behind the recording horn in the duet from *Les Pêcheurs de perles* (the deservedly rare version included here along with the more familiar ten inch). They also join in the *gondolieri*-like harmonies of Rossini's *Li marinari* (splendid high Bs from McCormack) and give each other a run for their money in a full-bodied, exciting account of the duet from *La Gioconda*. McCormack, it is true, had still to develop eloquence as a singer of songs, but his eventual mastery is clearly foretold in the old Irish song, *She is far from the land*, a haunting and heartfelt piece of tender nostalgia. The transfers are excellent.

Ezio Pinza Opera Arias – Aida, Attila, La bohème, Le caïd, Don Carlo, Don Giovanni, Faust,
La juive, Lucia di Lammermoor, Mignon, Norma, I puritani, Robert le diable, Il trovatore, I
vespri siciliani and Die Zauberflöte. **Ezio Pinza** (bass) with various artists. Nimbus Prima Voce
mono Ⓜ NI7875* (73 minutes: ADD: 6/96). From HMV and RCA Victor originals; recorded
1923-30.

There can surely be few dissenting voices where the quality of Pinza's singing is concerned. Play a
record of his to a hardened old collector or a green newcomer and they will undoubtedly join in
praising his golden, vibrant tone, seamless legato, the evenness of his vocal emission through a couple
of octaves. It has been said that he seldom sings below *forte*: that is wholly negated here by a
performance of the lullaby from Thomas's *Mignon*, sung almost entirely *mezza voce*, a lulling and
soft-grained song that would send any child into blissful slumber. Another French item, the famous
Tambour-major air from Thomas's lesser-known *Le caïd*, not only confirms Pinza's excellence in
French enunciation, but also shows quite another side of his personality: jocular, a smile in the tone,
exuberance in the delivery. The RCA Victors of Italian opera are well known, yet one marvels anew
at the easy command of Pinza's Oroveso, Procida, King Philip and Ramphis, the character of each
nicely etched in, even in extract. To complement these there is his grave Sarastro, his warmly sighing
Colline. All the phrases where other basses either exaggerate or lose focus in reaching a high or low
note are done quite effortlessly. His Giovanni suggests a formidable personality, and we end with him
in the distinguished company of Rethberg and Gigli for their glorious account of the *Attila* trio. All
the electrics are transferred carefully from RCA Victors in good condition. Where the six 1923-4
HMV acoustics are concerned you hear Nimbus's much-discussed additional resonance, room or
otherwise, come into play. It is an acceptable procedure if you understand that you are not hearing
exactly what the original sound is like. The most persuasive title here is "Cinta di fiori" from *Il
puritani*, where the *cantabile* rolls out with fabulous ease.

Opera Arias The bartered bride, Don Giovanni, Fidelio, Der Freischütz, Madama Butterfly, Der
Rosenkavalier, Tannhäuser and Tosca; songs by R. Strauss. **Hilde Konetzni** (sop) with various
artists. Preiser mono Ⓕ 90078* (74 minutes: AAD: 1/95). From Nixa, Telefunken, Columbia and
German Radio originals; recorded 1937-50.

Look no further than this disc to hear a near ideal tone and technique. A lovely singer suggesting the
very essence of natural, sincere, open-faced interpretation, Hilde Konetzni, leading soprano at the
Vienna State Opera from the late 1930s to the early 1950s, projects the varying emotions of Leonore,
Agathe, Elisabeth, Butterfly (albeit in German) and Mařenka (again in German) with an eager
sincerity that at once silences criticism and puts her in the class of her coevals in similar repertory –
the Marias Reining and Müller and Tiana Lemnitz (what a wealth of talent to draw on!). None of
these attempted Leonore, and Konetzni's "Abscheulicher!" is a totally convincing interpretation – and
marvellously sung. Here is the vulnerable, heroic wife to the life, pouring out her feelings in steady,
even, unfettered tones, negotiating the awkward intervals and the difficult tessitura as if they were no
problem at all. That performance comes from the series of Telefunken discs that Konetzni made in
1937, with the admirable support of Schmidt-Isserstedt as conductor. They include versions of
Agathe's "Wie nahte mir der Schlummer" and Elisabeth's arias that would be hard to better, so
radiant and unencumbered is the delivery. Konetzni must also have been a touching Butterfly: her
version of Cio-Cio-San's entrance and the Flower duet with Marie Luise Schilp as a warm Suzuki
touch the heart. The mind is dazzled by the exquisite refinement evinced at the end of "Vissi d'arte"
– or rather "Nur der Schönheit" as it is here. Ten years later Konetzni made a few treasured 78s for
Columbia with Karajan at the helm. Her account of Mařenka's "Endlich allein" from *The bartered
bride* shows no diminution of the singer's skills, only a deepening of the tone that also allowed her to
convey all the Marschallin's sadness in that character's Act 1 Monologue. Also included here are four
Richard Strauss songs made with the composer at the piano, in 1943. They are a trifle disappointing:
in terms of colour and inflexion they are penny-plain. Nevertheless, do get this disc if you want to
hear some truly heartfelt and wonderfully sung readings of these open excerpts.

Opera Arias Aida, Un ballo in maschera, La bohème, Carmen, Cavalleria Rusticana, Les contes
d'Hoffmann, Ernani, La forza del destino, Gianni Schicchi, La Gioconda, Guillaume Tell,
Louise, Madama Butterfly, Madame Sans-Gêne, Manon, Manon Lescaut, Mefistofele, Mignon,
Otello, Pagliacci, Il segreto di Susanna, Suor Angelica, Tosca, La traviata, Il trovatore, I vespri
siciliani and La Wally; songs by Braga, Burleigh, Buzzi-Peccia, Delibes, Donaudy, Giordano,
Mascheroni, Olivieri, Roxas and Sanderson. **Claudia Muzio** (sop) with various artists.
Romophone mono Ⓕ 81010-2* (two discs: 140 minutes: ADD: 1/95). From Pathé and Edison
originals; recorded 1917-25.   ⒼⒼⒼ

In the second set of Claudio Muzio, Romophone have put us further in their debt by issuing the 1917-
25 Pathés and adding four unpublished and fascinating Edison titles. Inevitably there is some
overlapping but it is surprising how many titles were not remade by the soprano. Here we have, on the
first disc, an impassioned and nicely shaded "Suicidio!" in a reading that is amazingly accomplished
when you realize Muzio was just 28 at the time. "O patria mia" and "Un bel di", neither repeated by

her, adumbrate the sheer beauty of the voice of the young *spinto*: strength is there, but also refinement and feeling, although the technical command, as often with this singer, isn't always faultless. Above all, we catch an echo over the years of what Muzio must have been like: deeply affecting, in these roles, confirming contemporary comment – and that is what records are about. The songs are, as ever with this singer, irresistible. Buzzi-Peccia's *Baciarmi* is poised sensuously on a skein of gossamer tone. In another song, Burleigh's *Jean*, we can delight in Muzio's excellent and clear English and also in the better sound. Then come the four 'new' Edisons, which include Donaudy's *O del mio amato ben*, later repeated in 1935 for Columbia: the performance here is just as plangent. Even more tenderly accented is a little-known and unattributed song, *Torna amore*, and the even more evocative traditional *Mon jardin*. Yes, a great singer indeed.

Opera Arias and Songs Adriana Lecouvreur, L'Africaine, L'amico Fritz, Andrea Chénier, Bianca e Fernando, La bohème, Carmen, Les contes d'Hoffmann, Eugene Onegin, La forza del destino, Hérodiade, I Lombardi, Loreley, Madame Sans-Gêne, Mefistofele, Pagliacci, Paride e Elena, Rinaldo, Salvator Rosa, La traviata, Il trovatore, I vespri siciliani, La Wally and Zazà; songs by Bachelet, Buzzi-Peccia, Chopin, Guagni-Benvenuti, Herbert, Mascheroni, Monahan, Pergolesi, Rossini and Sodero. **Claudia Muzio** (sop) with various artists. Romophone mono Ⓟ 81005-2* (two discs: 153 minutes: ADD: 1/94). From HMV and Edison originals; recorded 1911-25. ⒼⒼⒼ

The crackles and surface noise that usually afflict Edison reproduction have all but been eliminated, so that we can hear Muzio's voice in its absolute prime without, as it were, the effort of listening through a sea of interference. The sheer beauty of the soprano's voice and her wonderful intensity of expression can now be experienced with astonishing immediacy. All the Muzio gifts, including that of refined, exquisite phrasing combined with that peculiarly heart-rending intensity that was hers alone, are heard in that enchanting song by Bachelet, *Chère nuit* (first disc, track 8). If your dealer will let you hear that, even if you are sceptical about singers of the past, you are sure to make off home with this set, eager to hear the rest. A feast of captivating interpretations from one of the century's three or four greatest singing-actresses.

Opera Arias Le caïd, Le chalet, La damnation de Faust, Dinorah, Don Carlo, L'étoile du nord, Faust, Die Jahreszeiten, Martha, Mignon, Philémon et Baucis, Robert le diable, Roméo et Juliette, La Sonnambula, Stabat mater (Rossini) and Die Zauberflöte; songs by Adam, Bemberg, Faure, Ferrari, Flégier, Georges, Godard, Gounod, Massenet, Niedermeyer and Schumann. **Pol Plançon** (bass) with various artists. Romophone mono Ⓟ 82001-2 (two discs: 142 minutes: ADD: 12/94). From Victor originals; recorded 1903-08.

The new, inquiring collector will find copious writings on the merits of Plançon's unique voice and art. Perhaps Lord Harewood summed it all up when he commented on the bass's recording of Philip II's monologue: "He sings in French with a fullness and beauty of sound, a nobility of style, a smoothness of execution that have to be heard to be believed", to which one might add his plangency of tone – and these commendations apply to every single record he made, even if some are more amazing than others. So what is there new to say? That very few singers have seemed to *enjoy* performing on record as much as he, or evinced so much character; Gigli, Tauber, Supervia, and perhaps Bartoli, today. The smile and/or saturnine glee he brought to the music of Gounod's, Meyerbeer's and Berlioz's devils incarnate is superb: if you hear nothing else, listen to his insinuating "Voici des roses" from *La damnation de Faust* (the second disc, track 16). Then his *pièce de résistance* – "L'air du tambour-major" from Thomas's *Le caïd* – is unsurpassed for flexibility and lightness, and the treatment of grace notes, echoes of a lost art. But he is no less remarkable in 'serious' music such as "Pro peccatis" from Rossini's *Stabat mater*, where the tone rolls out in an effortless stream. Nor have his versions of the Porter's song from *Martha* and "O jours heureux" from *L'étoile du nord* been surpassed. Like most singers of his age, Plançon sang a deal of dross, but even these items are worth listening to for the pleasure of hearing a voice so immaculately produced throughout its range. Drawbacks? Well, to some modern ears his tone may be found lacking in resonance and vibrations. Plançon made many of his recordings twice, sometimes thrice. By and large the versions with orchestra of 1906-08 (on the second disc) are preferable to their predecessors with piano (the first disc): increasing familiarity with the recording horn seems to have allowed the bass to become ever more relaxed before it. As we have come to expect from this source, the transfers are virtually perfect – and prove quite conclusively that nothing has to be added to the sound to make old recordings thoroughly acceptable to today's collectors. Don't pass up this chance to hear one of the phenomenons of his – or any – day.

Opera Arias Gianni Schicchi, Die lustige Witwe and Rusalka; songs by Brahms, Dvořák, Kodály, Mahler, Mozart, Prokofiev and Rachmaninov. **Lucia Popp** (sop); **Geoffrey Parsons** (pf). Orfeo Ⓟ C363941B (69 minutes: ADD: 6/95). Recorded live in 1981. ⒼⒼ

The soprano is in most lovely voice, singing with warmth and delicacy, exercising a completely unostentatious mastery of perhaps a dozen facets of a singer's art. Her accompanist is what he always was, the superb professional; but, more than that, he works in complete sympathy with the singer and seems incapable of touching the simplest phrase without discovering its musical interest. At one point you can *see* him: it is in the last encore, the "Viljalied", where the piano introduction is pure Parsons.

The encores are probably what everybody present would remember years afterwards. They are finely graded – a Mozart song, happy and carefree after the subdued mood of Brahms's *In stiller Nacht* which ended the official programme: then there comes a little more concession to a romantic taste in Rachmaninov's *Lilacs*, and then, in order, Puccini, Dvořák and Lehár, all performed with taste and refinement, all yielding bigger returns with the drumming of feet and the shouting of bravos. Before this, the audience had enjoyed a recital with folk-song as its theme. The command of languages (Russian, Hungarian, Czech and German) is remarkable enough, and with it goes a musical expressiveness that can (at least to some extent) break the language barrier but texts would have been welcome. Recorded sound is excellent, and the disc a treasure.

Opera Arias and Duets Elisabeth Rethberg (sop) with various artists. Preiser Lebendige
Vergangenheit mono Ⓕ 89051* (71 minutes: AAD: 7/94). From Odeon and Brunswick originals; recorded 1920-25.   ⒼⒼ
L'Africaine, Andrea Chenier, The bartered bride, La bohème, Carmen, Madama Butterfly,
Le nozze di Figaro, Tosca, Die Zauberflöte and Der Zigeunerbaron; songs by Bizet, Mozart,
Pataky and R. Strauss.

Elisabeth Rethberg died in 1976, when little notice was taken of the passing of a singer once voted the world's most perfect. The year 1994 was the centenary of her birth, so this fine selection of her early recordings was well timed.The earliest catch her at the charming age of 26 (the voice settled, but still that of a young woman), and the last of them, made in 1925, find her just into her thirties, mature in timbre, feeling and artistry. It is doubtful whether a judicious listener would at any point cry "Ah, it's an Aida voice!", but Aida was the part for which she became most famous. In Countess Almaviva's first aria, her legato is the next thing to perfection; in Pamina's "Ach, ich fühl's" the head tones are beautifully in place, the portamentos finely judged, emotion always implicit in the singing. The duets with Richard Tauber include the music of Micaëla and Don José sung with unrivalled grace and intimacy, Rethberg shading off the end of her solo most elegantly, Tauber softening in his so as to welcome and not overwhelm the soprano's entry, and both singers phrasing like the consummate artists they were. The songs are equally delightful.

Opera Arias – Aida, Andrea Chenier, La bohème, Der Freischütz, Lohengrin, Madama Butterfly,
Le nozze di Figaro, Otello, Serse, Sosarme, Tannhäuser, Tosca and Die Zauberflöte; songs by
Bishop, Braga, Cadman, Densmore, Flies, Gounod, Grieg, Griffes, Hildach, Jensen, Korschat,
Lassen, Loewe, Massenet, Mendelssohn, Rubinstein, Schubert, Schumann, Taubert and
Tchaikovsky. **Elisabeth Rethberg** (sop) with various artists. Romophone mono Ⓕ 81012-2*
(two discs: 158 minutes: ADD: 2/95). From Brunswick originals; recorded 1924-29.   ⒼⒼⒼ

They're very collectable, these Romophone complete editions. Up they go on the shelves, and you know that there is another small but quite important area in the history of singing on records properly covered, ready for reference at any time, and reference that will be a pleasure because the standard of transfer is so reliable. In this instance it is the Rethberg Brunswicks: records which capture the voice in its lovely prime. Purely as a singer, Rethberg was surely the most gifted and accomplished lyric soprano of her age. The essential gift was a voice of exquisite quality, and her upbringing contributed to the purity of intonation and a feeling for musical style. Her production was even and fluent; on all these records there is scarcely a note or a phrase that is not delightful purely as singing. Some of the later records show it also as a voice capable of considerable expansion in volume. In Aida's "O patria mia" Rethberg is celestial, ample in volume, sensitive in feeling, phrasing beautifully, taking the C softly and in a broad single sweep. Equally lovely is her Mimì, and then in the *Andrea Chenier* aria there is such an unpressured beauty of utterance that it almost becomes a different composition. A previously unpublished delight is a blissful performance of Eugen Hildach's *Der Spielmann*, and among the less familiar songs is a charmer by Carl Taubert, *Es steht ein Baum in jenem Tal*.

New review
Opera Arias and Ensembles – L'africaine, Aida, Attila, Un ballo in maschera, Boccaccio,
Carmen, Cavalleria Rusticana, Don Giovanni, Faust, Die Fledermaus, Der fliegende Holländer,
Lohengrin, I lombardi, Madama Butterfly, Die Meistersinger von Nürnberg, Le nozze di Figaro,
Otello, Il rè pastore, Tannhäuser and Der Zigeunerbaron; songs by Brahms, Mendelssohn and
Wolf. **Elisabeth Rethberg** (sop) with various artists. Romophone mono Ⓕ 81014-2* (two discs:
155 minutes: ADD: 10/95). From HMV, Parlophone and Bell Telephone originals; recorded
1927-34.

To the older collector of vocal recordings it is to be feared that not many of these records will come as new. Attention can be directed, however, to the last three. These were made in 1932 in the Bell Telephone Laboratories as part of an experiment in improved recording methods. They were recorded at 33rpm, and they achieved startling results. The quality of the voice is captured to perfection, but most impressive is the freedom of emission, no longer confined within the studio but able to ring and expand, the contrasts of loud and soft tones being effective and often as exquisite as they would have been in the flesh. Most revealing is Elisabeth's Greeting from *Tannhäuser*, sung with piano accompaniment but with a dramatic conviction and enthusiasm far more vivid than that of the earlier orchestral version (reviewed above). Other new items are unpublished takes of the two Verdi trios with Gigli and Pinza, differing slightly in balance, but very little in style. The six electric Parlophones include the tender Micaëla's aria and the solo from *L'africaine* with its haunting unaccompanied introduction. Supreme among the Victors is the second *Un ballo in maschera* aria, the *Meistersinger* duet with Schorr running it close. It is also good to have the complete Nile scene from *Aida*, with Lauri-Volpi in his prime, de Luca somewhat past his. Transfers are of the usual high standard, and with the first volume mentioned above, this is clearly the primary source of a comprehensive Rethberg collection on disc.

Opera and Operetta Arias Maria Reining (sop) with various artists. Preiser Lebendige
  Vergangenheit mono Ⓕ 89065* (67 minutes: AAD: 9/94). From Electrola originals, including
  seven previously unpublished items and a 1943 radio broadcast; recorded 1942-3.
  Andrea Chénier, La bohème, Eva, Friederike, Madama Butterfly, Manon Lescaut, Le nozze di
  Figaro, Tannhäuser and Die toten Augen; songs by R. Strauss.
This is an important – and quite captivating – disc. It includes all Reining's Electrola discs, plus seven unpublished titles (presumably withheld at the time because of wartime restrictions). They are pure treasure. The three 'new' operatic titles, all cut in 1942, are "In quelle trine morbide" (*Manon Lescaut*), "Che tua madre" from *Madama Butterfly* (both sung in German) and "Psyche wandelt" (*Die toten Augen*). They show incontestably why Reining was considered the true successor to Lotte Lehmann in Vienna. The sheer beauty of her singing allied to its complete sincerity make all three moving experiences. Then there are four Strauss songs previously unpublished, also recorded in 1942, *Cäcilie* gloriously soaring as befits the ardent text, *Wiegenlied* and *Meinem Kinde* intimate and entrancing. Of the previously issued items, all display Reining's smiling tone, her judicious use of portamento. Any collector as yet unaware of Reining's virtues, so similar to those of Elisabeth Grümmer, her equally wonderful successor, should hurry to investigate this issue.

New review

Opera Arias and Duets [a]Angela Gheorghiu (sop); [b]Roberto Alagna (ten); Orchestra of the Royal
  Opera House, Covent Garden / Richard Armstrong. EMI Ⓕ CDC5 56117-2 (61 minutes: DDD:
  6/96). Texts and translations included. *Gramophone Editor's record of the month.*   ⒼⒼ
  Mascagni L'amico Fritz – Suzel, buon di ... Tutto tace[ab]. **Massenet** Manon – Je suis seul! ...
  Ah! fuyez, douce image[b]; Toi! Vous! ... N'est-ce plus ma main[ab]. **Donizetti** Anna Bolena – Al
  dolce guidami[a]. Don Pasquale – Tornami a dir[ab]. **Offenbach** La belle Hélène – Au mont Ida[b].
  Bernstein West Side Story – Only You ... Tonight, it all began tonight[ab]. **Gounod** Faust – Il se
  fait tard! ... O nuit d'amour[ab]. **G. Charpentier** Louise – Depuis le jour[a]. **Berlioz** Les troyens –
  Nuit d'ivresse![ab]. **Puccini** La bohème – O soave fanciulla[ab].
Ideally matched, the two young lyric artists of our day who have most taken the hearts and hopes of public and critics sing here in a programme that is both aptly and imaginatively selected. It ranges quite widely over the French and Italian repertoires, always combining instant satisfaction with a wish for more. The Cherry duet from *L'amico Fritz* comes first, and the voices have just the right freshness for it, the soprano warm-toned, the tenor elegant and cleanly defined; the style too is charming, natural and mutually responsive. Then with the excerpts from *Manon* they are not only well suited but show already a real dramatic impulse in their duet, again with its developments so well felt and understood. The Garden scene works unusual magic. The solos provide welcome opportunities: Gheorghiu, delightful in "Depuis le jour", is even more so in the aria from *Anna Bolena*, exquisitely phrased and shaded as though it were the slow movement of a sonata by Mozart. "Ah! fuyez, douce image" opens with the softness associated from long ago with Smirnov and Muratore; Alagna never forgets what he is singing about, is thrilling on his high B flats and finely controlled in the concluding *diminuendo*. His Mount Ida song from *La belle Hélène* has panache and humour, a deliciously promising *pianissimo* start to the last verse and a good robust C thrown in before he finishes. And then, inspiration on somebody's part, there is *West Side Story*. "Tonight" has never been better sung, and it also brings us to the other element in this recital – the playing of the Covent Garden orchestra under Richard Armstrong. In this, they make us realize afresh how distinctively flavoured (in harmony and orchestration) is Bernstein's marvellous score: the duet is intensely moving, yet the rhythm is kept strong and there is no sugar-coating or melting into slush. Repeatedly, in Gounod and Bernstein as in Mascagni and Puccini, one reacts with an 'I'd never noticed that before' or simply a smile or sigh of pleasure in the sound.

Opera Arias and Duets Giovanni Martinelli (ten); [a]Metropolitan Opera Chorus and Orchestra /
  Giulio Setti, [b]Josef Pasternack, [c]Rosario Bourdon. Preiser Lebendige Vergangenheit mono
  Ⓕ 89062* (68 minutes: AAD: 3/93). Recorded 1926-7.   ⒼⒼⒼ
  Verdi Rigoletto – La donna è mobile. Il trovatore – Quale d'armi fragor ... Di quella pira[a] (with
  Grace Anthony, sop). La forza del destino – Oh, tu che in seno; Invano Alvaro ... Le minacciei
  fieri accenti (with Giuseppe de Luca, bar). Aida – Se quel guerrier io fossi ... Celeste Aida[b];
  Nume, custode e vindici (with Ezio Pinza, bass). **Giordano** Andrea Chenier – Un dì all'azzurro
  spazio[b]; Come un bel dì di maggio[c]. Fedora[b] – Amor ti vieta; Mia madre, la mia vecchia madre.
  Mascagni Cavalleria Rusticana[c] – O Lola; Mamma, quel vino è generoso. **Leoncavallo**
  Pagliacci – Recitar! ... Vesti la giubba[c]; Per la morte! smettiamo ... No, Pagliaccio non son[a] (with
  Grace Anthony). Zaza – E un riso gentil[c]. **Puccini** La bohème – Che gelida manina[b]. Tosca –
  E lucevan le stelle[b].

Here is one of the most fascinating of singers. He can also be one of the most thrilling, his voice having at its best a beauty unlike any other, his art noble in breadth of phrase and concentration of tone. It also has to be said that his records hardly make easy or restful listening, but what at first may even repel soon becomes compulsive, the intensity of expression and individuality of timbre impressing themselves upon the memory with extraordinary vividness. Martinelli's career was centred on the Metropolitan, New York, where he sang first at the height of the Caruso era, inheriting Caruso's more dramatic roles in 1921. This selection makes an unrepresentative start with "La donna è mobile", but the excerpts from *Il trovatore* and *La forza del destino* have the very essence of the man, masterly in his shaping and shading of recitative, or in the long curves of his melodic line and the tension of his utterance. There are also superb performances of solos from *Andrea Chénier* and *Pagliacci*, the involvement of his "No, Pagliaccio non son" unequalled before or since. These are recordings from 1926 and 1927, the period in which his vocal and artistic qualities were probably best matched. The transfers are fine apart from the song from Leoncavallo's *Zazà* which plays below pitch.

Opera Arias and Duets Emma Eames (sop); Pol Plançon (bass) with various artists. Nimbus
   Prima Voce mono Ⓜ NI7860* (71 minutes: ADD: 1/95). From Victor originals; recorded
   1903-11.
   Emma Eames – Carmen, Don Giovanni, Faust, Lohengrin, Le nozze di Figaro, Roméo et Juliette
   and Die Zauberflöte; song by Schubert. **Pol Plançon** – Le caïd, La damnation de Faust, Dinorah,
   L'étoile du nord, Faust, Robert le diable, Roméo et Juliette, La Sonnambula, Stabat mater
   (Rossini) and Die Zauberflöte.

Here, in the first place, is a marvellous sense of period. The world of 'the real record collectors of old', and of their authorities P.G. Hurst and Herman Klein, the sense, too, of a calendar in which the digits had changed from 18 to 19, while in the great opera houses for just a few years longer the world stayed reassuringly the same: all of this is present. And we look at the photographs, with Eames's plaited tresses resting on the broad bosom without a hint of cleavage, and Plançon's suit, buttonhole and whiskers immaculately in place like the notes of his flawlessly even scale. Then the music itself, the programme opening (how appropriately) with Meyerbeer and ending with such essential nineteenth-century classics as *La Sonnambula* and Rossini's *Stabat mater*. Both of those are sung by Plançon, who has the slightly larger share. His was also the easier voice to record in those days, and the one which requires less adjustment of modern ears in listening. The incomparable mastery of style and technique, the beauty and resourcefulness of his voice, the life and variety of his characterizations, are all newly impressive. With the soprano, one sometimes wishes for a brighter tone; she is also no Susanna and in "Là ci darem" does some indefensible things with the time. Yet there are beauties here too, and, problematic as it may be for modern expectations to accept this, much can be gained from a study of her *Gretchen am Spinnrade*. The selection of recordings by both singers has been well made. The amount of hall-resonance in these Nimbus transfers is likely to be unacceptable only to people who have already made up their mind that they don't want any at all, and the horn-resonance points, troublesome in some of the earlier issues in the series, seem to have been virtually eliminated.

New review
Opera Arias and Songs Songs by Chausson, Clarke, Cui, Debussy, Duparc, Dupont, Dvořák,
   Fauré, Février, Fosse, Georges, Grieg, Grøndahl, Hahn, Henriques, Jordan, Koechlin, Křička,
   Milhaud, Mozart, Naginski, Poulenc, Ravel, Roussel, Schubert, Schumann, Sinding, Staub,
   Tchaikovsky, Thompson and Torelli; opera aria from Gluck's La Semiramide riconosciuta. **Povla
   Frijsh** (sop) with various artists. Pearl mono Ⓜ GEMMCDS9095* (two discs: 146 minutes: AAD:
   4/95). From HMV, Victor and Nordisk Polyphon originals and broadcast performances; recorded
   1926-42. Also includes part of an broadcast interview, recorded in 1953.

Frijsh's sound and manner may be described as an amalgam of Gerhardt, Lehmann (Lotte) and Teyte, the vocal style of the first, the total commitment of the second and the stylistic control in *mélodies* of the third. Or perhaps they could be characterized as the vocal equivalent of Garbo, with the same power to mesmerize. As an interpreter, she is the sort of free spirit rarely encountered in this day of uniformity (the recently retired Fassbaender is in the same category), one who takes liberties in the cause of conveying the full sense of a song, one who is a mistress of the lost art of portamento, particularly its downward variety, as a means of expression and of enhancing the line. She is no authenticist. If it suits her she will sing Scandinavian and German songs in the original; if it does not, she prefers translations, singing her Russian repertory in French. She is an explorer, tackling pieces well outside the regular repertory, at least as it is now conceived. Nothing here is more enthralling than Milhaud's *Chant de nourice*, the lullaby of a Jewish nurse telling her charge to be aware of its race, and that race's vicissitudes and pride. The inflexions at "O mon chéri" and "Dors ma fleur" rend the heart. A totally different but equally riveting singer seems to be in our presence in Grøndahl's *You meet me in the dance*, the very essence of seductive power. In *L'heure silencieuse* by one Victor Staub, the mystery of the twilight hour is perfectly conveyed. So is the miniature drama of Février's *L'intruse* and the wintry mystery of Koechlin's *L'hiver*. But she is no less remarkable in better-known pieces. The languorous description of Ravel's "Le paon" (from *Histoires naturelles*), the gentle melancholy of Hahn's *L'infidelité*, the haunting memory of Tchaikovsky's *At the ball*, these linger in the mind. Most of the performances were recorded by HMV (1932-3) or Victor (1939-42) when the artist was between 50 and 60. Obviously the tone isn't that of a young woman, and in Lieder that is a distinct disadvantage. Yet the triumph over a declining voice, and what she could achieve with it, is just as remarkable in the majority of the pieces here. The transfers are faultless.

Opera Arias and Songs Lucien Fugère (bar) with various artists. Symposium mono Ⓔ 1125* (78 minutes: AAD: 6/93). From French Columbia originals; recorded 1928-30.
 La basoche, Le jongleur de Notre-Dame, L'ombre, Die Zauberflöte, Don Giovanni, Le roi malgré lui, Dinorah, Le val d'Andorre, Louise, Les saisons, Le medecin malgré lui, La rencontre imprévue, Le maître de chapelle; songs by Chaminade, Couperin, Henrion, Levadé and Widor.
Dates to keep in mind: 1848, 1928, 1930, 1933 and 1935. On the first, Lucien Fugère was born, on the second he made the first of the records heard here, on the third he made the last; in 1933 he gave his last operatic performance, and two years later he died. A little mental arithmetic establishes that he was 80 when he recorded (for example) the solos from Massenet's *Le jongleur de Notre-Dame*; having listened to them, one has to do the sum again, this time counting up on one's fingers to make sure, for otherwise his age would be scarcely credible. Actually, the recordings made at 80 are not the best; 81 was better, 82 best of all. The year 1930 brought the 'Grand Air' from Paër's *Le maître de chapelle*, which is Fugère's masterpiece. This enacts in brief a miniature opera on the subject of Cleopatra, and vocally it uses every trick in the book: an exercise of brilliant resource, performed with wit, elegance, technical skill and the infinite variety of Cleopatra herself. And the voice does sound even younger, even more assured here than in the first sessions, the acoustic being less boxy and allowing more room for expansion. The transfers are clear and natural.

Opera Arias and Songs Amelita Galli-Curci (sop) with various artists. Conifer Happy Days mono Ⓜ CDHD201* (70 minutes: ADD: 3/94). From Victor originals; recorded 1917-29.
 Arias from Don Pasquale, The Golden Cockerel, Lucia di Lammermoor, Rigoletto, Semiramide, La sonnambula, La traviata and Il trovatore; songs by Bishop, A. Scarlatti and Yradier.
Opera Arias and Songs Amelita Galli-Curci (sop) with various artists. Romophone mono Ⓔ 81003-2* (two discs: 159 minutes: ADD: 3/94). From Victor originals; recorded 1916-20. Ⓖ Ⓖ Ⓖ
 Arias from Il barbiere di Siviglia, Dinorah, Don Pasquale, Lakmé, Lucia di Lammermoor, Manon Lescaut (Auber), Martha, Le nozze di Figaro, I puritani, Rigoletto, Roméo et Juliette, La sonnambula and La traviata; songs by Alvarez, Benedict, Bishop, Buzzi-Peccia, David, Delibes, Giordani, Grieg, Massenet, Proch, Samuels and Seppilli.
These two issues complement each other very happily, the Romophone going up to 1920, the Conifer concentrating on later recordings, with an overlap of only three items. In *Gramophone* in 1923 the Editor wrote: "One of the most solid grounds I have for facing the coming of old age with equanimity is the reasonable hope that I shall spend it listening to as many records of *la diva* Galli-Curci's voice as there are of Caruso's". The purity of her voice was certainly a delight; it was at that time firm and even throughout its wide compass; and her fluency in scalework, precision in staccato, and ability to swell and diminish on a long-held high note were exceptional. She was an artist who could phrase and nuance exquisitely and who, within the boundaries of a more or less pretty joy and sadness, could be quite poignantly expressive. In the years of her greatest fame and success, roughly the decade from 1916 to 1926, her operatic repertoire was the standard one for the 'coloratura' soprano, and it is well represented by her records. What they also have, making them treasurable beyond anything that such a summary might suggest, is a personal flavour, a caress, a way of making words sound like water purling gently on a summer's afternoon, a dreaminess that can awaken to fun and affection though she could also flatten rather sadly in pitch. For completeness and also for the fine quality of the transfers many will want the Romophone. The Conifer selection is certainly a good one, including rarities such as the Scarlatti cantata (*Solitudini amene, apriche collinetti*), "Bel raggio" and "Ah, non giunge". On the whole, the early records have been transferred on this CD more enjoyably than the electricals.

Opera Arias and Songs Beniamino Gigli (ten) with various artists. Memoir Classics mono Ⓔ CDMOIR417* (65 minutes: AAD: 6/93). From HMV originals. Recorded 1921-39.
 Arias from – L'Africaine, Andrea Chenier, La bohème, Cavalleria Rusticana, L'elisir d'amore, La forza del destino, Martha, Mefistofele, Les pêcheurs de perles and Rigoletto. Songs by Bixio, Cottrau, De Curtis, Denza, Di Chiara and Toselli
Of all the famous Italian tenors, Gigli was the one whose voice seemed most to embody the sweets of nature – the sunshine, the fruit filled "with ripeness to the core" and so forth. He sang as though for the love of it, though of course collecting a substantial fee too (and in fact rather than submit to the indignity of a reduction in salary he quit the Metropolitan in their financial crisis of 1932). The records included here come from the years either side of that date and show him in his magnificent prime, the leading lyric-dramatic tenor of the world. The programme begins with his "Che gelida manina" of 1931, one of the top best-sellers in the HMV catalogues for many a year. His appeal lies not only in the sweetness, the easy power and ring of his well-rounded voice, but also in a personality that is almost winsomely human: a chubby chuckle, a boyish pleading, lightens up the 'face' of his singing. There is fervour in his *Andrea Chenier*, good humour in his "La donna è mobile", and appropriate bad temper in his *Cavalleria Rusticana* duet with the formidable Dusolina Giannini. Then, in a selection of shamelessly tuneful Italian songs, he woos beguilingly, sometimes in the

honeyed half-voice, ultimately with the thrilling vibrancy of his *fortissimo*. Two of the items (from *Mefistofele* and *La forza del destino*) are reproduced a semitone too high, but in general the quality of transfers is fine and the selection excellent. A superb performance.

Opera Arias and Songs Maria Ivogün (sop); [a]Michael Raucheisen (pf); [b]orchestra; [c]Berlin State Opera Orchestra / Leo Blech. Nimbus Prima Voce Ⓜ NI7832* (78 minutes: ADD: 8/92).
Bishop Lo, here the gentle lark[b] (from Brunswick 10174, 11/25). **Handel** L'allegro, il penseroso ed il moderato, HWV55 – Sweet bird[b] (Polydor 85313, recorded 1925). **Donizetti** Don Pasquale – Ah! un foco insolito[b] (85302, recorded 1924). Lucia di Lammermoor – Ardon gl'incensi[b] (Odeon 76977, recorded 1917). **Rossini** Il barbiere di Siviglia – Una voce poco fa[b] (85309, recorded 1925). **Verdi** La traviata – E strano ... Ah, fors'è lui ... Sempre libera[b] (sung in German. 76982/3, recorded 1916). **Chopin** Nocturne in E flat major, Op. 9 No. 2[b] (arr. sop/orch. 76975). **Meyerbeer** Les Huguenots – Une dame noble et sage[b] (German. 76997). **Nicolai** Die Lustigen Weiber von Windsor – Nun eilt herbei[b] (76811. All recorded 1917). **Schubert** Ständchen (Horch! Horch! die Lerch), D899[b]. Winterreise, D911 – Die Post[b] (both from Brunswick 15075, 9/24). **J. Strauss II** Frühlingsstimmen, Op. 410[b] (85313, recorded 1924). G'schichten aus dem Wienerwald, Op. 325[b] (10174). An die schönen, blauen Donau, Op. 314[c]. Die Fledermaus – Klänge der Heimat[c] (HMV DB4412, 6/34). **Kreisler** Liebesfreud[b] (Brunswick 50050, 12/24). **Anonymous** O du liebs Angeli[a]. Z'Lauterbach han i'mein Strumpf verlor'n[a]. Gsätzli. Maria auf dem Berge[a] (all from HMV DA4402, 6/33).

Somewhere or other, after much searching of the memory, ransacking of the catalogues and phoning around among connoisseurs, it might be possible to discover a more delightful example of the coloratura's art than that of Maria Ivogün as displayed in her recording of Kreisler's *Liebesfreud*, made in 1924: if so, one such does not spring to mind now. With the most pure and delicate of tones, nothing shrill or piercing about them, she sings way above a normal mortal's reach, ease and accuracy in the purely technical feats going along with a lilt and feeling for the idiomatic give-and-take of waltz rhythm that are a joy musically. Turn to Handel, with the solo from *Il penseroso*, and the same art is put to lovely use in a different idiom. Her *Traviata* aria has warmth and spontaneity; her Frau Fluth in *Die lustigen Weiber von Windsor* is a woman of charm and energy; and the 1934 recording of the Czardas in *Die Fledermaus* shines as bright in spirit as in clarity of timbre. From the same period comes the set of four songs, Swiss and German, that show most touchingly her command of the art to be simple. This is an admirable introduction to a most lovely singer, and it represents the Prima Voce series at its best.

Opera Arias and Songs Adelina Patti (sop) with various artists. Nimbus Prima Voce mono Ⓜ NI7840/1* (two discs: 120 minutes: ADD: 7/93). Recorded 1902-28.
Mario Ancona, Mattia Battistini, Emma Calvé, Fernando De Lucia, Edouard de Reszke, Emma Eames, Lucien Fugère, Wilhelm Hesch, Lilli Lehmann, Félia Litvinne, Francesco Marconi, Victor Maurel, Dame Nellie Melba, Lillian Nordica, Adelina Patti, Pol Plançon, Maurice Renaud, Sir Charlles Santley, Marcella Sembrich, Francesco Tamagno and Francesco Viñas.

This is a 'historical' issue for straightforward enjoyment. Although the originals were made in the very earliest years of recording, they are reproduced here with a vividness that calls for very little in the way of 'creative listening', making allowances and so forth. It starts in party mood with the first Falstaff of all, Victor Maurel, singing to a bunch of cronies in the studio of 1907 the "Quand'ero paggio" which he sang at La Scala in the première of 1893. They cheer and call for an encore, which he gives them, then again (and best of all) this time in French. The record has been transferred many times to LP and CD, but never has it been so easy for the listener to 'see' it and feel part of it. The magnificent bass Pol Plançon follows with King Philip's solo from *Don Carlos*, beautifully even in production and deeply absorbed in the character and his emotions. The hauntingly pure, well-rounded soprano of Emma Eames in Tosti's *Dopo* (a real passion there despite its restraint), and then the miraculously spry and elegant 80-year-old Lucien Fugère lead to the first of the Patti records: the one her husband thought unladylike and asked to be withdrawn from the catalogue, *La calesera*, and the most joyous she ever made. Tamagno, Melba, Nordica, Renaud: they are all here, and on thrillingly good form. The copies of these rarities have been selected with great care, and, while other transfers have, technically, got more "off" the record, none has captured the beauty of the voices more convincingly.

Opera Recital Ezio Pinza (bass) with various artists. Pearl mono Ⓜ GEMMCD9306* (76 minutes: AAD: 2/89).　　　　　　　　　　　　　ⒼⒼ
Verdi Aida – Mortal diletto ai Numi (Metropolitan Opera Orchestra, New York / Giulio Setti); Nume custode vindici (Giovanni Martinelli, ten; Metropolitan Opera Chorus and Orchestra. Both from Victor 8111). Ernani – Che mai vegg'io ... Infelice! (orchestra / Rosario Bourdon. HMV DB1750). Don Carlos – Dormiro sol nel manto mio regal (orchestra / Bourdon. DB1087, 3/28). I vespri siciliani – O patria ... O tu Palermo (orchestra / Bourdon. DB1087). Messa da Requiem – Confutatis maledictis (orchestra / Bourdon. HMV AGSB103). Simon Boccanegra – A te l'estremo addio ... Il lacerato spirito (chorus and orchestra / Carlo Sabajno. DB699, 6/24). Il trovatore – Di due figli ... Abbietta zingara (chorus and orchestra / Sabajno. DB828). **Mozart** Don Giovanni – Finch'han dal vino; Deh vieni alla finestra (orchestra / Bourdon. HMV

DA1134, 10/31). Die Zauberflöte – O Isis und Osiris (sung in Italian. Orchestra / Bourdon. DB1088, 3/28). **Meyerbeer** Robert le Diable – Nonnes, qui reposez (sung in Italian. orchestra / Bourdon. DB1088). **Thomas** Le Caïd – Enfant chéri ... Le tambour-major (orchestra / Bourdon. DB1086, 3/28). **Gounod** Faust – Le veau d'or (Metropolitan Opera Chorus and Orchestra / Setti. DA1108, 9/38). **Bellini** Norma – Ah del tebro (Chorus and orchestra / Sabajno. DA566, 5/25). I Puritani – Cinta de fiori (Orchestra / Sabajno. HMV VB70, 6/52). **Donizetti** La favorita – Splendon più belle (orchestra. DA708). Lucia di Lammermoor – Dalle stanze (chorus and orchestra / Sabajno. VB70). **Boito** Mefistofele – Ave Signor (orchestra. DB829); Son lo spirito (orchestra / Sabajno. DA567). **Halévy** La Juive – Si la rigeur (sung in Italian. Orchestra / Sabajno. DB698, 11/24); Vous qui du Dieu vivant (sung in Italian. Orchestra. DB829).
The first half of the century brought forth three fine Italian basses: Nazzareno de Angelis, Tancredi Pasero and Ezio Pinza. Of these it was Pinza who gained the greatest international fame, partly through the beauty of his voice and partly through the strength and vividness of his personality. Eventually it was the musical *South Pacific* that made him a household name, but his success here owed much in turn to the fact that he came to the Broadway show from the Metropolitan Opera House where he was leading bass from his house début in 1926 until 1948. Before coming to America he had sung at La Scala under Toscanini, his repertoire then ranging from the role of Pimen in *Boris Godunov* (he was later to sing Boris himself) to King Mark in *Tristan und Isolde*. At the Metropolitan he sang mostly in the Italian and French operas, with an increasing interest in Mozart, whose Don Giovanni became his most famous role, which he sang also at Salzburg and Covent Garden. This is represented in the present selection (called "The Golden Years") by two short solos, which may well be found to be the least satisfying of the performances. Sarastro's "O Isis und Osiris", on the other hand, sung in Italian as "Possenti numi" is magnificent in the sonority of tone and dignity of style. There is also some superb Verdi, above all the aria from *Ernani*, sung with deep feeling and subtlety of shading, and the "Confutatis" from the Requiem, ideally smooth, resonant and authoritative. In these and the earlier pre-electrical recordings Pinza shows clearly why he is so widely regarded as having been the supreme *basso cantate* of the century.

New review

Pavarotti The Early Years, Volumes 1 and 2. **Luciano Pavarotti** (ten) with various artists. RCA Victor Gold Seal mono Ⓜ 09026 62541-2 and 09026 68014-2 (two discs, oas: 51 and 46 minutes: ADD: 10/95). Disc marked ᵃ recorded at various locations in Italy during 1967-9, ᵇ1964-9. Texts and translations included.
*09026 62541-2*ᵃ – **Puccini** La bohème – Che gelida manina; O soave fanciulla. **Donizetti** L'elisir d'amore – Quanto e bella; Una furtiva lagrima. La fille du régiment – Ah! mes amis; Pour mon âme. **Massenet** Manon – En ferment les yeux; Ah! fuyez, douce image. **Bellini** I puritani – Son gia lontani. **Rossini** Stabat mater – Cujus animam. *09026 68014-2*ᵇ – **Bellini** I Capuleti e i Montecchi – O di Cappelio generoso amici ... E' serbata a questa acciaro. I puritani – A te, o cara. **Verdi** I lombardi – Oh madre mia ... La mia letizia infondere. Luisa Miller – Oh! fede negar potessi ... Quando le sere al placido. Rigoletto – Questa o quella, Ella mi fu rapita! ... Parmi veder le lagrime; La donna è mobile. La traviata – Lunge da lei ... De' miei bollenti spiriti. **Donizetti** Lucia di Lammermoor – Tombe degl'avi miei ... Fra poco a me ricovero. **Puccini** Turandot – Nessun dorma!.
Probably the unique penalty of singing as well as Pavarotti has been doing in his late fifties is that records of 'the early years' come as less of a revelation than they do with most other tenors. The impact is also lessened by the relatively late age at which these years find him. We have one item from 1964, when he was 29, but most of the rest come from 1967-69 when he was in his thirties. On the whole, the famous Italian tenors of the century were well-established internationally and on record by then, and we would be unlikely to include recordings made at, say, the age of 34 among those of the early period. What we have from Pavarotti in these two discs is a voice already in its prime and an art already mature. The essential basis of the art is the legato style, the even binding of notes within the phrase. Listen to Pavarotti's legato in the waltz, "Qual destin", from *La fille du régiment*: of course it is the nine top Cs that take the attention, but those are incidentals, and the basis lies in the fine evenness with which the melody is sung. He also refrains from disrupting the surface of a melody with the intrusive H, about which so many of his countrymen (critics as well as singers) seem more or less indifferent: thus the end of the *Traviata* recitative does not go "tu-hu-tto-ho i-hil pa-ha-ssa-ha-ha (etc.)-to" but is a broad, smooth, respectable piece of singing. He can also be discovered singing softly, offering (for example) a gracefully quiet ending to the *Rigoletto* aria only to have its most testing note, the final G flat, drowned in cries of "Braviss!". For variety of touch try "La donna è mobile", for tenderness of expression "Che gelida manina", for bitterness the *Luisa Miller* excerpt. That aria also illustrates some of the artistic limitations, for the mood is too simply defined, just as the melodic line is too unimaginatively handled. The *Puritani* solos want light-and-shade and the more refined sensibility we gesture towards when we say 'poetry'. Never mind: it is a refined art compared with many, and the voice is a marvel. The two discs are not just another reassortment of the usual plentifully anthologized studio recordings, but instead come live from Rome, Catania, Modena, Turin and Milan. Recorded sound is always clear though rather variable in level and quality. The items are presented in no discernibly logical order, though at least the three *Rigoletto* solos are grouped together. Neither of the discs can be called generous in their timings, respectively, of 51 and 46 minutes.

New review

Pavarotti Plus Sixtieth Birthday Album. [a]Luciano Pavarotti (ten); [b]Nathalie Dessay, [c]Kallen
Esperian, [d]Nuccia Focile (sops); [e]Dolora Zajick, [f]Leah-Marian Jones (mezzos); [g]Giuseppe
Sabbatini (ten); [h]Dwayne Croft, [i]Leo Nucci, [j]Piero Cappuccilli (bars); [k]Francesco Ellero D'Artegna
(bass); [l]Philharmonia Chorus and Orchestra / James Levine; [m]Royal Philharmonic Orchestra /
Leone Magiera. Decca Ⓕ 448 701-2DH? (two discs: 131 minutes: DDD: 2/96). All items except
Inno delle Nazioni recorded live in 1995. All items in which Pavarotti sings are also available on
448 700-2DH (71 minutes: DDD). Recorded 1995.
Verdi Inno delle Nazioni[al]. Il trovatore – Madre, non dormi? ... Ai nostri monti[aem]. La traviata –
Libiamo, ne' lieti calici[a-k,m]; O mia Violetta ... Parigi, o cara[adm]. Aida – Fù la sorte dell'armi ...
Amore, amore[cem]. La forza del destino – Invano Alvaro[aim]. Macbeth – O figli, o figli miei! ... Ah,
la paterna mano[am]. Otello – Dio ti giocondi[acm]. Rigoletto – Giovanna, ho dei rimorsi ... E il sol
dell'anima[bfgm]. I Lombardi – L'acque sante del Giordano ... Qual voluttà[ackm]. **Puccini** Tosca –
Recondita armonia[am]. La bohème – Dunque, è proprio finita! ... Addio dolce svegliare[cdghm]; In
un coupé? ... O Mimì, tu più non torni[ahm]. Manon Lescaut – Tra voi, belle[am]. **Leoncavallo**
Pagliacci – Nedda! Silvio! a quest'ora[chm]. **Gounod** Faust – Alerte! alerte! ... Anges purs[dgkm].
Thomas Hamlet – Ophélie ... Doute de la lumière[bhm]. **Tchaikovsky** Eugene Onegin – Onegin,
I was younger then[dhm]. **Donizetti** L'elisir d'amore – Venti scudi[gim].
Although the event probably lives in the memory as the Pavarotti Sixtieth Birthday Party, it was
actually a gala to celebrate the 125th anniversary of the Red Cross, and its most memorable feature,
amongst all this exuberant sound, was probably a two-minute silence. The two CDs, well-filled as they
are, do not include everything in the programme, but, while the aria of Des Grieux in *Manon Lescaut*
is out, the shorter, opening solo, "Tra voi, belle", is in, and a most delightfully humorous,
idiosyncratic performance it receives, Pavarotti probably endearing himself more in that brief
pleasantry than in the desperations of *Macbeth* and *La forza del destino*, or in the bitter ironies (which
he does not quite catch) of Otello. With him are singers, mostly from the younger generation, each of
whom is given a generous share of the evening's opportunities. Most interest centres on Giuseppe
Sabbatini as the only other tenor and a possible 'successor'. His voice rings out well, with a full-
bodied timbre and an ample fund of high notes; stylishness, however, is not an element notable in his
performances, nor indeed in those of the others. Indeed, though the title is "Pavarotti Plus", the real
'plus' is still Pavarotti. In his sixtieth year he preserves, pre-eminently in this company, the two
qualities that contribute most to the pleasure which lies in the sound of a singing voice: purity of
timbre (no surface-scratch or breathiness) and evenness of emission. In essentials it is still a young
voice. As he confronts the heroic demands of Verdi's *Hymn to the Nations*, we can only marvel at the
stamina, and be grateful that in such a performance this most popular, and so most influential, of
living opera singers sets so wholesome an example.

New review

Alfred Piccaver Opera Arias – L'africaine, Aida, Andrea Chenier, La bohème, Cavalleria
Rusticana, La fanciulla del West, Faust, Fedora, Fidelio, La forza del destino, La Gioconda,
Lohengrin, Madama Butterfly, Manon, Martha, Die Meistersinger von Nürnberg, Pagliacci,
Requiem (Verdi), Tosca, Il trovatore, Turandot and Werther; songs by De Curtis, Geehl,
Leoncavallo, Nevin, Tirindelli, Tosti and Woodforde-Finden. **Alfred Piccaver** (ten) with various
artists. Preiser Lebendige Vergangenheit mono Ⓕ 89217* (two discs: 148 minutes: AAD: 4/96).
From Polydor originals; recorded 1928-30. Recorded 1928-30.
What a prize British opera missed, when Alfred Piccaver's parents moved to the USA. As a child,
Piccaver heard Caruso at the Metropolitan and it was his example that fired him to study singing,
initially in New York and then after his first season in Prague in 1907, moving on to Milan. His career,
however, was almost entirely devoted to Vienna, where from 1913 until 1937 he was the idol of the
Viennese public, singing opposite Lehmann and Jeritza. The soprano, Margit Angerer, who joins him
in six duets on these Polydor records (made between 1928 and 1930), while obviously a talented singer,
does not impress with much character. No such accusation could be levelled at Piccaver. His is one of
those outgoing, all-embracing personalities, with a voice of apparently inexhaustible warmth and
power. Piccaver phrases in a splendidly healthy way – listen to the opening of "E lucevan le stelle":
even an aria as well-known as this jumps out afresh when given such an relaxed outpouring of sound,
and unbroken legato. It's quite easy to imagine the thrill in the theatre. "The caressing velvet of his
voice was so unbelievably beautiful," wrote Lotte Lehmann. He certainly can act with the voice: the
farewell to the swan in the passage from Act 1 of *Lohengrin*, Florestan's aria (*Fidelio*), and the
absolutely glorious account of Vasco da Gama's "O Paradis" from Meyerbeer's *L'africaine* (in Italian)
all suggest a singer of such strength and presence that it is a wonder that Piccaver's name is not better
known. It is a tribute to his singing that one can listen to both these CDs in a single sitting without
tiring of his voice.

Russian Opera Choruses Bolshoi Theatre Chorus and Symphony Orchestra / Alexander Lazarev.
Erato Ⓕ 4509-91723-2 (65 minutes: DDD: 5/94). Recorded 1993.
Rimsky-Korsakov Snow Maiden – Carnival procession; Chorus of blind psalterists; Song of
the Grain. Mlada – Procession of the Nobles. The Tsar's Bride – Hop-Pickers' Chorus. Christmas

Eve – Koliadka. Invisible city of Kitezh – The disaster is approaching. **Glinka** A Life for the Tsar – Introduction, Polonaise and final chorus. **Mussorgsky** Boris Godunov – Kromy Forest scene. **Borodin** Prince Igor – Be firm, Countess; Villagers' Chorus; Polovtsian Dances.

Secretly, let's face it – or is this one of those heresies with which the guilty soul has to live companionless? – the moments in performances of Russian opera when the heart leaps up and gives a naïve little cry of "Oh, I *am* enjoying this!" tend to occur during the choruses. For one thing, they are often the most Russian part of it, having a basis of folk-song and bringing out of the voices something of the national character. More elemental and elementary, perhaps, is their colourfulness. All the choruses on this record are rich in colouring. Some (*Mlada* and the finale of *A Life for the Tsar*, for instance) are choruses of rejoicing; others (the psalterists in *Snow Maiden*, the *Christmas Eve* "Koliadka" carol) are religious; and it is good to have, for stiffening, the communal panic of the *Invisible city of Kitezh* and the Revolutionary scene in *Boris Godunov*. As for performance, chorus and orchestra are fine individually, and it is only this wretched habit in modern times of depriving choirs of any real immediacy of presence that limits enjoyment. The "Polovtsian Dances" bring the disc to a splendid conclusion.

New review

Stars of English Opera Opera Arias with various orchestras and conductors. Dutton Laboratories mono Ⓜ CDLX7018* (75 minutes: ADD: 4/96). From HMV and Columbia originals; recorded 1939-49. All items sung in English. Recorded 1938-49.
Sopranos – **Gwen Catley** (Rigoletto), **Joan Cross** (Così fan tutte), **Dame Joan Hammond** (Gianni Schicchi, Tosca); *Mezzos* – **Janet Howe** (Samson et Dalila), **Gladys Ripley** (Don Carlo), **Marjorie Thomas** (Alcina); *Tenors* – **Webster Booth** (Esmeralda), **James Johnston** (The bartered bride), **David Lloyd** (Don Giovanni, Die Zauberflöte), **Heddle Nash** (La favorita, Les pêcheurs de perles); *Baritones* – **John Hargreaves** (Rigoletto), **Redvers Llewellyn** (Falstaff), **Dennis Noble** (Il barbiere di Siviglia); *Bass* – **Oscar Natzke** (Die lustigen Weiber von Windsor).

The discs chosen come from that fruitful period in British singing in the years before, during and just after the war, when Columbia and HMV were busy recording a crop of native singers performing so eloquently in their native tongue. The group of tenors alone is a distinguished one, headed by Heddle Nash, whose dreamy, poised *mezza voce* is heard to perfection in Nadir's Romance from *Les pêcheurs de perles*, one of his most beguiling records. His ardent, refined singing of "Spirit so fair" from *La favorita*, made during the same 1944 Liverpool session, is equally desirable. So is James Johnston's account of Jenik's aria from *The bartered bride*. Most welcome of all are Don Ottavio's second aria and Tamino's Portrait solo as sung by David Lloyd, whose forthright, mellifluous tone and persuasive performances offer Mozart singing of the highest calibre. Joan Cross's account of Fiordiligi's Act 2 aria, is another fine piece of Mozart singing – and isn't that Dennis Brain playing the horn solos? Marjorie Thomas's refined art is recalled in her pure Handelian legato while Llewellyn offers character but a rather attenuated tone in Ford's aria, Hargreaves much feeling but stilted diction as Rigoletto. If these two baritones were limited in appeal, Noble was one of great distinction regarding tone, line and diction. His 1939 HMV "I'm the factotum" launches this disc in the most engaging way. Transfers, as usual from this source, are exemplary, surface noise wholly eliminated, voices clean and forward.

New review

Bryn Terfel Opera Arias. **Bryn Terfel** (bass-bar); **Orchestra of the Metropolitan Opera, New York /
James Levine**. DG Ⓕ 445 866-2GH (71 minutes: DDD: 6/96). Texts and translations included.
Gramophone Editor's choice.   ⒼⒼ
Mozart Le nozze di Figaro – Non più andrai. Don Giovanni – Madamina, il catalogo è questo; Deh! vieni alla finestra. Così fan tutte – Rivolgete a lui lo sguardo. Die Zauberflöte – Der Vogelfänger bin ich ja. **Wagner** Tannhäuser – Wie Todesahnung ... O du mein holder Abendstern. Der fliegende Holländer – Die Frist ist um. **Offenbach** Les contes d'Hoffmann – Allez! ... Pour te livrer combat ... Scintille, diamant. **Gounod** Faust – Vous qui faites l'endormie. **Borodin** Prince Igor – No sleep, no rest. **Donizetti** Don Pasquale – Bella siccome un angelo. **Rossini** La Cenerentola – Miei rampolli femminini. **Verdi** Macbeth – Perfidi! All'angelo caontra me v'unite! ... Pietà, rispetto, amore. Falstaff – Ehi! paggio! ... L'Onore! Ladri!.

In a careless moment we might describe Bryn Terfel as a very physical singer, and it would be true up to a point. His physical presence is much in evidence when he sings, or for that matter when he talks or just breathes. Having seen him 'in the flesh', one seems to see him while hearing the sound of his voice on records. But the crowning distinction of Terfel's art (granted the voice, the technique and, the general musicianship) is its intelligence. As with words, so with characters: each is a specific, sharp-minded creation, and none is a stereotype. This Leporello exhibits his master's catalogue with pride; it is the book of life and not to be taken lightly. This Don Magnifico recounts his dream in all good faith (he doesn't *know* that he's a complete idiot, and doesn't deliberately set himself up to sound like one). No less impressive, as an aspect of intelligence, is the linguistic command, and still more so the use he makes of it; the sheer mental concentration of his Dutchman carries intense conviction and an ever-specific understanding. This is, in short, a magnificent recital in which everything works together for good. The singer's concentration is matched by that of the conductor and in turn by his players. Balance and quality of recorded sound are fine.

Virtuoso Arias Sumi Jo (sop); [a]Monte-Carlo Philharmonic Orchestra / Paolo Olmi; [b]Paris Orchestral Ensemble / Armin Jordan. Erato Ⓕ 4509-97239-2 (74 minutes: DDD: 6/95). Texts included. Items marked [a] new to UK, [b]from 2292-45469-2 (5/90). Recorded 1994.
Rossini Il barbiere di Siviglia – Una voce poco fa ... Io son docile[a]. **Bellini** La sonnambula – Ah! non credea mirarti ... Ah! non giunge[a]. **Delibes** Lakmé – Ou va la jeune indouc ... La-bas dans la forêt plus sombre[a]. **Verdi** Rigoletto – Gualtier Maldè ... Caro nome[a]. **Meyerbeer** Dinorah – Ombre légère[a]. **Donizetti** Lucia di Lammermoor – Mad scene[a]. **R. Strauss** Ariadne auf Naxos – Noch glaub' ich dem einen ganz ... So war es mit Pagliazzo ... Als ein Gott kam jeder gegangen[a]. **Bernstein** Candide – Glitter and be gay[a]. **Mozart** Die Zauberflöte – Der Hölle Rache[b]. **Yoon** (arr. Constant) Barley Field[a].

Many listeners, well disposed towards most kinds of vocal recital, still tend to approach a new 'coloratura' programme with misgivings – all of which would seem to be obviated here. The emotional range of the music goes well beyond mere prettiness, whether of girlish glee or wilting pathos. The florid passages (commonly tagged 'display') are assumed by the singer to have an expressive purpose, which she then seeks out and fulfils. Her tone is bright but not piercing, her style clean but not cold; she understands perfectly well that, though these arias are famous for their high notes, far more of the singer's time is spent in the middle register, where a scrawny or breathy tone and flawed legato will not be excused on account of a few brilliances *in alt*. Intelligence is clearly at work from the start, in the enunciation of the words. "Una voce poco fa qui nel cuor mi risuono": the "qui" ("here") is the 'gesture-word', the one that makes it actual and individual. "La vincerò" is determined, but not doubly-underlined or given that arch, over-confident touch which may gain a point but, in doing so, forfeits likeableness. In *La sonnambula* sympathy is actually *strengthened* by the cleaning-up of all those downward portamentos that have threatened to become inseparable from the music since Callas and Sutherland introduced them. Similarly, the Mad scene from *Lucia di Lammermoor* is enacted as a genuinely dramatic piece but with a fresh realization, rather than from a mind loaded with memories of those illustrious predecessors. The only way in which Jo appears at a disadvantage is in the relative hardness of some high notes. Zerbinetta's aria, for instance, is a shade uncomfortable (clearly written with more of the German *Kopfstimme* in mind), while the Korean song, *Barley Field*, is entirely lovely in sound and does not rise above an A flat.

Vienna State Opera Live Recordings, Volume 6. **Vienna State Opera Chorus and Orchestra / Wilhelm Furtwängler, Leopold Reichwein, Hans Knappertsbusch, Leopold Ludwig and Clemens Krauss.** Koch Schwann mono Ⓜ 314562 (two discs: 143 minutes: ADD: 1/95). Recorded 1933-42.
Sopranos – **Helena Braun** (Parsifal; 1942), **Daniza Ilitsch** (Aida; 1942), **Anny Konetzni** (Siegfried; 1936. Die Walküre; 1937. Tristan und Isolde; 1941), **Viorica Ursuleac** (Die Meistersinger; 1933).
Mezzo-sopranos – **Margarete Klose** (Tristan und Isolde; 1941), **Elena Nicolai** (Aida; 1942).
Contralto – **Bella Paalen** (Die Meistersinger; 1933). *Tenors* – **Anton Arnold, Hermann Gallos** (both Die Meistersinger; 1933), **Josef Kalenberg** (Siegfried; 1936), **Max Lorenz** (Die Meistersinger; 1933. Tristan und Isolde; 1941. Parsifal, Götterdämmerung and Aida; all 1942), **William Wernigk, Herr Wolken, Erich Zimmermann** (all Die Meistersinger; 1933). *Baritones* – **Mathieu Ahlersmeyer** (Aida; 1942), **Hans Duhan, Alfred Jerger, Viktor Madin** (Die Meistersinger; 1933).
Bass-baritone – **Paul Schoeffler** (Parsifal and Götterdämmerung; 1942). *Basses* – **Herbert Alsen** (Aida; 1942), **Karl Ettl** (Die Meistersinger; 1933), **Ludwig Hofmann** (Die Walküre; 1937), **Josef von Manowarda** (Götterdämmerung; 1942), **Alfred Muzzarelli, Hermann Reich** (Die Meistersinger; 1933), **Sigmund Roth, Adolf Vogel** (Parsifal; 1942), **Hermann Wiedemann, Nikolaus Zec** (Die Meistersinger; 1933).

This set is devoted largely to the appreciable art of Anny Konetzni as Isolde and Brünnhilde, and Max Lorenz as Siegfried, Parsifal, Walther and Radames. Don't let anyone ever tell you that sopranos shouldn't tackle Wagner until they are 40. Providing they have the voice and their technique is secure (admittedly two big provisos), they should be in no trouble. Here is Konetzni, in her early thirties, offering a fully formed portrayal of Brünnhilde, sung in a steady, rounded, warm tone throughout a wide register that no Hochdramatische could rival today. Kalenberg (her Siegfried) is an ordinary tenor but Lorenz is her equally secure and sensitive Tristan. Elsewhere Lorenz proves maddening. Here is undoubtedly one of *the* Heldentenor voices of the century, but one that is sometimes crudely used. In the 1933 *Die Meistersinger* extracts he has not yet acquired bad habits, so his Walther comes forth in pristine state in both the Trial and Prize songs, which means they have seldom sounded better. By the time of the 1942 *Parsifal*, *Götterdämmerung* and *Aida* he had started to gulp and over-emote in a manner that exaggerates the passion of the moment to an extent that it becomes uncouth. Yet there is still no denying the sheer excitement of the sound, and its shining strength above the stave. He still (on occasion) sings fastidiously, as in the *Aida* finale, where he gives us a Radames full of remorse and sadness. But then he is partnering the revelation of this issue, the Aida of the Yugoslav soprano, Ilitsch who sings quite ravishingly here, in German, of course. The beauty and sensuousness of her singing is quite remarkable and most ingratiating. In the other operas, Helena Braun proves a strong, involving Kundry, one of the best on disc, and the brief example ("Nun zäume dein Ross" from *Die Walküre*) of Hofmann's Wotan leaves one wanting more; so, of course, do Konetzni's following "Hojotoho"s. In *Die Meistersinger*, Ursuleac's reputation is further restored by her readings of "O Sachs, mein Freund" and the start of the Quintet, so warm and outgoing, even if occasionally unfocused. The three famous conductors leading most of the performances confirm their justified reputations as Wagnerians, and Ludwig does well in *Aida*.

New review
Vienna State Opera Live Recordings, Volumes 22 and 24. **Vienna State Opera Chorus and Orchestra / Anton Paulik, Rudolf Moralt, Hans Knappertsbusch, Leopold Reichwein, Clemens Krauss.** Koch Schwann mono Ⓜ 314722* and 314742* (two two-disc sets, oas: 146 and 136 minutes: ADD: 5/96). Recorded at performances in the Vienna State Opera and at Salzburg in the years given.

314722 – Sopranos: **Irma Beilke** (Le nozze di Figaro; 1942), **Helena Braun** (Der fliegende Holländer; 1940. Le nozze di Figaro, Die Walküre and Götterdämmerung; all 1942), **Daga Söderqvist** (Götterdämmerung; 1942), **Gerda Sommerschuh** (Le nozze di Figaro; 1942), **Liane Timm** (Le nozze di Figaro; 1942). *Mezzo:* **Mela Bugarinovic** (Siegfried; 1941). *Contralto:* **Res Fischer** (Le nozze di Figaro; 1942). *Tenors:* **Joachim Sattler** (Siegfried; 1941), **William Wernigk** (Siegfried; 1941. Le nozze di Figaro; 1942), **Josef Witt** (Le nozze di Figaro; 1942). *Baritone:* **Erich Kunz** (Le nozze di Figaro; 1942). *Bass-baritones:* **Hans Hotter** (Der fliegende Holländer; 1940. Siegfried; 1941. Le nozze di Figaro, Parsifal and Die Walküre; 1942. Pagliacci; 1943), **Gustav Neidlinger** (Le nozze di Figaro; 1942). *Basses:* **Josef von Manowarda** (Der fliegende Holländer; 1940. Götterdämmerung; 1942), **Franz Normann** (Le nozze di Figaro; 1942). *314742 – Sopranos:* **Wanda Achsel** (Götterdämmerung; 1937), **Helena Braun** (Die Walküre; 1943), **Luise Helletsgruber** (Götterdämmerung; 1937), **Daniza Ilitsch** (Die Walküre; 1943), **Anny Konetzni** (Götterdämmerung; 1937), **Hilde Konetzni** (Die Walküre; 1943), **Olga Levko-Antosch** (Die Walküre; 1943), **Anne Michalsky** (Götterdämmerung; 1937), **Else Schulz** (Die Walküre; 1943), **Daga Söderqvist** (Die Walküre; 1943), **Adele Kern** (Siegfried; 1941), **Elisabeth Schumann** (Siegfried; 1937). *Mezzos:* **Mela Bugarinovic** (Siegfried; 1941), **Elena Nikolaidi** (Die Walküre; 1943), **Else Schürhoff** (Die Walküre; 1943), **Enid Szánthó** (Siegfried; 1936. Das Rheingold and Götterdämmerung; 1937), **Dora With** (Götterdämmerung; 1937. Die Walküre; 1943). *Contraltos:* **Rosette Anday** (Götterdämmerung; 1937), **Melanie Frutschnigg** (Die Walküre; 1943), **Bella Paalen** (Götterdämmerung; 1937). *Tenors:* **Josef Kalenberg** (Siegfried; 1936), **Max Lorenz** (Siegfried and Götterdämmerung; 1937. Die Walküre; 1943), **Set Svanholm** (Siegfried; 1941), **Erich Zimmermann** (Siegfried; 1936). *Baritones:* **Fred Destal** (Götterdämmerung; 1937), **Jaro Prohaska** (Götterdämmerung; 1937), **Emil Schipper** (Siegfried; 1936). *Bass-baritones:* **Hans Hotter** (Die Walküre; 1943), **Paul Schoeffler** (Siegfried; 1941). *Basses:* **Ludwig Hofmann** (Das Rheingold; 1937), **Nikolaus Zec** (Siegfried; 1937), **Alexander Kipnis** (Götterdämmerung; 1937).

This documents Hotter at the height of his powers as a young Heldenbariton in Vienna, giving us early glimpses of his Dutchman, Wotan/Wanderer and Amfortas. The voice at this stage of his career was lighter than it was to become. The top is not only produced more easily but has a brassy, focused quality less evident in later years. As an interpreter he seems more indulgent with his feelings: the readings have not yet become 'fixed' and in consequence they are deeply felt in a way that is different from the later versions. Most important perhaps are the extracts from Act 3 of *Die Walküre* and Acts 1 and 3 of *Siegfried*, since we have no substantial souvenirs of him, except of the Farewell, in these acts elsewhere at this stage of his career. Even in 1942, Hotter was supreme as the Wotan of *Die Walküre* Act 3, pouring out his anger and hurt to his erring daughter, then capitulating to her urgent demands for forgiveness. Hotter's tone seems to come forth as a stream of impassioned feeling, the phrasing eloquent in all respects, also firm in tone and long-breathed. The sheer authority of Hotter's singing would be hard to surpass, phrase after phrase filled with special meaning. Moralt and Knappertsbusch are respectively the yielding yet forward-moving conductors. His Amfortas must have been shattering, the character's long solos, even with passages missing, carrying the weight of the torture and agony in the injured and disturbed man's mind and heart: they have never been better done. The sound in all the above passages is very reasonable. That for the 1940 *Holländer*, however, is poor. Here he is partnered with Helena Braun's radiant Senta. Braun returns for Brünnhilde's Immolation. She sounds rather effortful at the end of a long evening and isn't helped by Reichwein's lacklustre conducting, but there's still much to admire in her thoughtful treatment of the text, always one of her strengths. Hotter reappears in Vol. 24 in another Act 3 of *Die Walküre* and another Farewell, distinguished not only by his presence, but also by Knappertsbusch in the pit. Indeed, he conducts all the extracts from *The Ring* in this, the final offering in this series, and it is perhaps the most persuasive reason for listening to them as he stamps his authority on everything. Schoeffler's Wanderer is lyrically sung but lacks Hotter's emotional charge. The 1936-7 extracts are lamed by indifferent sound. Fleetingly heard to good effect are Schumann as the Woodbird, Szánthó as Erda, Lorenz as Siegfried and, above all, Anni Konetzni, who again proves she was one of the great Brünnhildes, although heard all too briefly here.

The Harold Wayne Collection, Volume 8. **Suzanne Adams, Emma Calvé** (sops)); **Antonio Scotti, Maurice Renaud** (bars); **Anton van Rooy** (bass-bar); **Pol Plançon** (bass); **Sir Landon Ronald** (pf). Symposium mono Ⓕ 1100* (79 minutes: AAD: 3/93). From G&T originals. Recorded in 1902 with piano accompaniment.
Suzanne Adams excerpts from Faust and Roméo et Juliette; songs by Stern, Vidal and Bishop.
Emma Calvé Carmen and Cavalleria Rusticana. **Scotti** – Méssaline, Don Giovanni, Faust,

Carmen and Falstaff; songs by Rotoli and Tosti. **Maurice Renaud** – Tannhäuser; song by Holmès.
Anton Van Rooy – Die Walküre, Die Meistersinger von Nürnberg, Tannhäuser and Das
Rheingold. **Pol Plançon** – Philémon et Baucis, Roméo et Juliette, Le caïd and Les Huguenots;
songs by J-B. Faure and Godard.
Though this is the eighth volume of a remarkable series, it is probably the first that can be
recommended with assurance to a wider public than those listeners who have a specialized interest in
the singers recorded during the early years of the gramophone. Those on the present disc were all
made in London in 1902: they were the 'London Reds', beloved of collectors and now worth a small
fortune. The first likely surprise for a newcomer is how vividly the voices come through. The great
French bass Pol Plançon is heard in the opening tracks, and the immediacy and naturalness of
reproduction are often astonishing. So too is the singing, with sonority and refinement, superb
fluency of scales and triplets, a brilliantly articulated trill, the well-bound evenness of cello tone, and
a lively sense of fun. Not all are as satisfyingly caught as Plançon: the famous Carmen of the time,
Emma Calvé, proves more elusive, though her little asides and exclamations are entertaining. Harold
Wayne is the owner of one of the world's finest private collections, and his generosity has allowed
these rarities to become public property. It is an opportunity to gain a privileged glimpse of another
age and of singers who are far too special, both as voices and artists, to be merely forgotten.

The Harold Wayne Collection, Volume 15. **Félia Litvinne** (sop); **Léon Escalaïs** (ten); **Victor**
Maurel (bar) with various accompaniments. Symposium mono Ⓕ 1128* (80 minutes:
AAD: 12/94). From Fonotipia and French Odéon originals; recorded 1900s.
Litvinne – L'africaine, Aida, Carmen, Cavalleria Rusticana, Le Cid, La favorita, Lohengrin,
Samson et Dalila and Il trovatore. **Escalaïs** – Falstaff, Hérodiade, Mefistofele, Otello, Polyeucte
and Il trovatore. **Maurel** – Don Giovanni, Falstaff and Otello; songs by De Lara, d'Hardelot,
Paladilhe and Tosti.
The Harold Wayne Collection, Volume 21. **Ada Adini, Georgette Bréjean-Silver, Rose Caron**
(sops); **Marie De Reszke** (mez); **Victor Capoul, Léon David, Ernest van Dyck** (tens); **Pericles**
Aramis (bar); **Jean-François Delmas** (bass-bar); **Pedro Gailhard** (bass) with various
accompaniments. Symposium mono Ⓕ 1172* (79 minutes: ADD). From Fonotipia originals;
recorded 1904-05.
Adini – Hérodiade; song by Braga. **Bréjan-Silver** – La traviata. **Caron** – Sigurd; song by Gounod.
De Reszke – song by Gounod. **Capoul** – Jocelyn. **David** – Carmen and Mignon; song by
Bourgeois. **Van Dyck** – Die Walküre and Werther; songs by Nicolai and Schumann. **Aramis** –
songs by De Lara, Massenet and Tosti. **Delmas** – La damnation de Faust, Les Huguenots, Patrie
and Die Walküre; songs by Gounod and Schumann. **Gailhard** – L'Africaine and Faust; song by
Yradier.
Mezzo-soprano quality is much in evidence here, but rather remarkably it also serves as a foil for the
high notes, which are almost always as beautiful in their 'placing' as in the purity of tone. A fine
example is the aria "Sur mes genoux" from *L'Africaine*, which she recorded twice. The high A naturals
seem so easily taken and are admirably clear and firm. The two *Il trovatore* arias are also, if not quite
technically perfect, then at least the work of an artist who knows what perfection might be, and who
combines that vision with a fully human warmth of feeling. Best of all is "Pleurez, mes yeux" from
Le Cid, one of Massenet's loveliest arias and performed here with rare strength and sensitivity. With
Litvinne in this fifteenth volume are the heroic tenor Léon Escalaïs and the famous Maurel, 'creator'
of Iago and Falstaff, both of those characters having solos included here. Maurel is heard in the
complete run of Fonotipias (1904 and 1907), including an unedifying version of Don Giovanni's
Serenade and a song in English, *A year ago* by Guy d'Hardelot which, feeble as the music may be,
goes far to make amends. These are all rare enough, but for a concentration of super-rarities Vol. 21
must take the prize. Here, for instance, is Rose Caron, prima donna of the Paris Opéra in the 1880s
and 1890s, years rich in important premières in many of which the great bass Jean-François Delmas
would also take part, and perhaps the tenor van Dyck (the original Werther) too. Of these three,
Delmas is superb, Caron distinctive in the warm middle register, van Dyck (in euphemistic usage)
interesting. Pedro Gailhard sings Yradier's *La paloma*, which was written for him; Victor Capoul
(b.1839) sings the famous lullaby from *Jocelyn*, which he also sang at the première of the work in 1888.
Then there is the extraordinary survival of a single record, a unique copy, by Marie De Reszke
accompanied by her husband Jean. She sings Gounod's *Au rossignol*, and most beautifully, but the
record was never issued, for Jean, dissatisfied with his own vocal recordings, ordered the whole lot to
be destroyed, which the 'man from the company' hadn't quite the heart to do. When it came to copy
No. 11 of this song he desisted and put it secretly by. Eventually it came to Dr Wayne and hence,
thanks once more to his generosity and the enterprise of Symposium, to us.

New review
The Harold Wayne Collection, Volume 20. **Giuseppe Anselmi** (ten) with various artists.
Symposium mono Ⓕ 1170* (79 minutes: ADD: 7/95). From Fonotipia originals; recorded
1907-10.
Opera Arias – Cavalleria Rusticana, Don Pasquale, Il Duca d'Alba, Fedora, Iris, Luisa Miller,
Manon, Manru, Mignon, Pagliacci, Les pêcheurs de perles, Serse, La traviata and Werther; songs
by Alagna, Mendelssohn, Mugnone, Scarlatti, R. Strauss and Tosti.

It is surely one of the most lovely tenor voices ever heard: that is the first reaction and the most regularly recurrent. Then there are the special moments, individual notes or phrases, where one listens without breathing. For much of the time Anselmi moves with the utmost grace, his notes and the passage between them are managed so easily and evenly that he could be mistaken for a singer of faultless style and impeccable technique. But a mistake that would sadly be. So, for example, take the recitative and aria "Sogno soave" from *Don Pasquale*, which opens the programme and was the first record he made. The sheer immediacy of the voice in its recorded sound is gratifying, his emotional involvement draws one towards him, and his caress of the aria's first phrases is utterly winning. He has that lovely way, now lost, of 'holding' a moment in the melody and very lightly embellishing it; and all of this with a voice of such mellow warmth that the occasional aspirate and hint of 'frog' can be more or less ignored. There follows a most eloquent sadness in the aria from *Il Duca d'Alba*, and after that a treasurable, perhaps supreme, performance of "Quando le sere" from *Luisa Miller*. But the *Traviata* brings a multi-aspirated "tutto passato", and *Mignon* sees the temporary return of the 'frog'. There are also stylistic paradoxes, as he begins "Vesti la giubba" with an exquisite privacy of grief and yet gives vent to laughs and sobs without restraint. Surprising inclusions in the programme are songs by Mendelssohn and Strauss, whose *Morgen!* is beautifully sung (in Italian) and then, as John Freestone remarks in his notes, has its effect ruined by a totally misguided rewriting of the ending. Never mind. This is not a disc to miss.

Early music

Plainchant

New review

Gregorian Chant Mass for Christmas Day. **Ensemble Organum; Les Pages de la Chapelle: Maîtrise du centre de musique baroque de Versailles / Marcel Pérès** (org). Harmonia Mundi
Ⓕ HMC90 1480 (72 minutes: DDD: 1/96). Texts and translations included. Recorded 1993.

This disc is a welcome addition to the growing number of chant recordings illustrating various repertoires and styles of performance over the centuries. It is not the first time that seventeenth- and eighteenth-century organ chant *alternatim* has been recorded, but there cannot be many discs with a programme of pieces drawn from the old rite of Paris; a splendid rite destined, sadly, to disappear at the end of the nineteenth century. There are even fewer, if any, in which organ improvisation alternates with the chant, as is the case here, and since this form of performance would have been the norm during this period in the majority of cathedrals and churches – even in convent chapels – it is of the greatest interest to hear how it might have sounded to seventeenth- and eighteenth-century ears. It all seems to tie up extremely well: the utterly splendid Parisian chant, quite different from its Roman counterpart, provides the pieces of the Proper for Christmas Day. These are sung with appropriate ornamentation – only in two pieces, the *Alleluia* and the *Sequence*, does Pérès find the temptation to introduce his customary Eastern effects too strong to resist. As for the Ordinary, Campra's magnificently tuneful 'neo-Gallican' plainchant provides the organist with the material on which to base his improvisations, and the choir a chance to prove that a slow, dignified tempo will match up to the noble versets on the eighteenth-century Cliquot organ at Houdan far better than those hurried snatches of chant one so often hears. However, there is more: the introduction of the trebles (Les Pages de la Chapelle) was an inspired stroke, especially for a Mass of Christmas. They sing with strong, confident young voices, and have no fear of sustaining long phrases of slow notes, nor of adding some conventional ornamentation of the period.

Gregorian Chant The complete 1930 HMV Recordings. **Solesmes Abbey Choir / Dom Joseph Gajard.** Pearl mono Ⓜ GEMMCDS9152* (two discs: 96 minutes: ADD: 6/95). From HMV D1971/82 (4/31).
When in 1930 Solesmes, under Dom Gajard, produced their album of 12 records of Gregorian chant, it was a historic moment. They were making the first major contribution to the documentation of an art having its roots well back in the first millennium, an art underlying much of the subsequent development of Western music. The remarkable unity and flow of the chant was surely due to the fact that they were all singing this music day in, day out, and an occasional portamento, or lack of ensemble was a normal, understandable part of the package. This is a sound of youthful vigour, with all the hallmarks of the familiar Solesmes style already there, well in place: the soaring phrases with their softened peaks and quiet final syllables; the firm enunciation of first syllables; the lifted accents on short notes; the quaint interpretation of the salicus; but over it all, its own special, innate quality, which combines unmistakable spirituality with robust everyday living. That quality, and a certain quiet confidence, are present in this singing to a degree rarely attained by any other monastic choir. The remastering, naturally, has not succeeded in eliminating all the needle hiss. One hardly notices this, by the way, such is the selective power of the human ear! This collection is really Everyman's

basic anthology of Gregorian chant. It ranges from well-known hymns and pieces of the Ordinary, through gems from the Temporale and the Common of Saints, to some of the greatest masterpieces of the repertoire, including the Good Friday responsory *Tenebrae factae sunt* and the splendid first mode offertory *Jubilate Deo* for the second Sunday after Epiphany. It also contains some items one rarely hears nowadays, such as the powerfully moving *Media vita* – "In the midst of life we are in death".

Gregorian Chant Mass for the Feast of St Thomas of Canterbury. The Office of Matins for St Thomas of Canterbury. St Dunstan's Kyrie. **Lay Clerks of Canterbury Cathedral Choir / David Flood.** Metronome Ⓕ METCD1003 (74 minutes: DDD: 2/95). Texts and translations included. Recorded 1994.

A recording of music for the Feast of St Thomas à Becket by the Lay Clerks of Canterbury Cathedral is a delightful idea. The music for this feast in the Salisbury rite is rich and memorable, particularly that for the Offices. In this case the selection from Matins includes five magnificent responsories and two antiphons, as well as the hymn *Martyr Dei* and the Invitatory, *Assunt Thomas Martyris*. This last item is particularly valuable, since though the Invitatory has generally not found much favour in recordings and concerts (either as chant or set polyphonically), the cumulative effect of the form is extraordinary. This anthology also includes the Mass for the Feast of St Thomas (in which the Sequence, *Solemne canticum*, is especially impressive) and the *Kyrie, Rex Splendens*, attributed to St Dunstan. The singing is restrained and sober and somewhat lacking in colour. The problem seems to be that there is little response to the words on the part of the singers: the chant somehow does not sound 'organic', as though it were sung liturgically. This is a difficult problem to solve, but there is no doubt that the quality of the singing itself is very high. Certainly no one with an interest in Western chant should hesitate to buy this very worthwhile recording.

Holy Week and Easter at Benevento Cathedral Ensemble Organum / Marcel Pérès. Harmonia Mundi Ⓕ HMC90 1476 (73 minutes: DDD: 12/94). Texts and translations included. Recorded 1993.

Beneventan Chant Adoration of the Cross. Paschal Vigil. Easter Sunday Mass of the Day.

This is a recording of exceptional interest. Beneventan chant represents an area of early liturgical music about which, until recently, little has been generally known, and which has been almost entirely overshadowed by Gregorian chant. To a large extent, in past centuries, Benevento and its surrounds were geographically cut off from both Roman and Carolingian influence. Many Greek monastic communities had previously taken refuge and settled in Southern Italy. It was normal that the inhabitants of Benevento should have contacts with these communities and that they should establish cultural and political links with Greece itself. It is hardly surprising to find that the Latin rite of the Cathedral of Benevento contains substantial traces of Greek influence and numerous bilingual texts. The liturgy of Holy Week is a case in point, in particular the *Adoration of the Cross*: each antiphon is heard first in Greek and then in Latin, followed by Latin psalmody to slight variations of the more familiar Gregorian psalm tones. Some of this music, of purely Beneventan origin, is of quite extraordinary beauty. The responsory *Amicus meus* (sung by Josep Benet and Marcel Pérès) is one such piece, and for which alone one would wish to possess this recording. Ensemble Organum's normal recourse to a style of singing inspired by Greek Orthodoxy really comes into its own here: the choice seems entirely fitting for a repertoire such as this. The singers are to be congratulated on such a splendid result, the fruit of their study with Lycourcos Angelopoulos. The ornamentation is sounding more natural, the *ison* well controlled. Professor Thomas Kelly's concise and informative notes are an excellent introduction to the music.

Melchite Sacred Chant Hymns to the Blessed Virgin. **Sister Marie Keyrouz** (sop); **L'Ensemble de la Paix.** Harmonia Mundi Ⓕ HMC90 1497 (63 minutes: DDD: 9/94). Recorded 1993.

With very little hint of nasality or of singing from the throat, Sister Marie Keyrouz accomplishes the most florid ululations with the greatest of ease, the voice continuously and impressively set in relief by a reverberant acoustic and a drone bass provided by a small choir of male voices. The area touched on by this extremely rare repertory is a fascinating one, not much illuminated by the brief, at times almost impenetrable notes provided. The Melchite churches of the Near East in the fourth and fifth centuries AD were those that remained, in a period of frequent schism, faithful to Byzantium ('Melchite' derives from a Syriac word meaning 'Emperor'). The liturgy of these churches was very influential: many of the most famous hymns of the Orthodox church, for example, were composed in the sixth century by Romanos the Melodist in Syriac style; like Sister Marie, Romanos was born in what is now the Lebanon. So some of these melodies, if authentic, may be part of a repertory more ancient than any other surviving Christian chant. For the earlier part of their history, of course, they would have had to rely on oral transmission for their survival. How far they were changed in that process, how far they were affected by an Islamic tradition growing up around them and by translation of their texts from Greek and Syriac into Arabic, only a specialist could say; certainly the notes accompanying this collection do not. This would be only a quibble were not three of the longer chants attributed to Sister Marie herself, described either as "in improvised style" or as "written improvisation"; one of these is a setting of part of Romanos's most celebrated text, the Akathistos. The main difference between these and most of those whose origin is unattributed is their greater virtuosity: in them Sister Marie uses a wider vocal range, a rather more dramatic, declamatory utterance and still more florid melismata. It makes fascinating listening: a border territory between Christian and Islamic chant, at times revealing a modal simplicity beneath the flexible ornament, at others well-nigh hiding it in ecstatic, microtonal wailings.

St Petersburg Litany Priests and Choir of St Petersburg Cathedral. DG Ⓕ 445 653-2GH
(72 minutes: DDD: 2/95). Recorded live in 1994.

The subtitle "St Petersburg Litany" is neither here nor there: it really should be specified on the jewel-case somewhere that it is the Palm Sunday Vigil. This is the Russian tradition on a grand scale, starting with the great clanging bells out of which emerges the deacon's opening "Slava Svyatey ... " and the first huge choral "Amin" which sets the tone for what is to follow. The singing of the choir is generally first-rate, and if there are sometimes slips of intonation and smudged entries, who could blame the performers given that this disc is a distillation of a service which lasts for a little longer than three hours and that they choose such adventurous repertoire? In amongst some quite run-of-the-mill settings there appear richly scored works of Chesnokov and Rachmaninov (various settings from the Vigil Service or Vespers, notably *Nyne otpushchaeshi* on track 10) – a very difficult piece indeed to bring off in a liturgical celebration – and it is marvellous to hear how well they are integrated into their context, so used is one to hearing them in concert as part of a musical package rather than a liturgical rite: no need for "liturgical reconstruction" here. DG have sensibly provided the disc with tracks so that one can find one's way around easily and there is an excellent commentary on the structure and content of the service written by Fr Philip Steer. It is a shame that there are no texts provided, though it must be said that they would have taken up a great deal of room. A remarkable recording and at the same time a historical event: this disc must be heard.

Medieval-Renaissance — 12th-15th centuries

Music for the Lion-Hearted King Gothic Voices / Christopher Page. Hyperion Ⓕ CDA66336
(60 minutes: DDD: 10/89). Texts and translations included.
Anonymous Twelfth Century Mundus vergens. Novus miles sequitur. Sol sub nube latuit. Hac in anni ianua. Anglia, planctus itera. Etras auri reditur Vetus abit littera. In occasu sideris. Purgator criminum. Pange melos lacrimosum. Ver pacis apperit. Latex silice. **Gace Brulé** A la doucour de la bele seson. **Blondel de Nesle** L'amours dont sui espris. Ma joie me semont. **Gui IV, "Li chastelain de Couci"** Li nouviauz tanz.

Christopher Page has a remarkable gift for creating enthralling programmes of early music bound together by a brilliantly-chosen central theme, or appellation. This new collection is no less distinguished and every bit as fascinating, musically and historically. Whether or not Richard himself ever actually listened to any of these pieces is beside the point: they are all representative of the period of his lifetime and are gathered together here in his name for the 800th anniversary of his coronation (1189). Two types of twelfth-century vocal music are represented: the *conductus* – which can be written for one, two, three or even four voices and the *chanson*, or noble, courtly love song. The singers cannot be applauded too highly for performances marked by an extraordinary insight into how this music should be tackled, that is, with a fair degree of restraint as well as know-how, given the sort of audience it might have had in Richard's day: the royal court or the household of some high ranking ecclesiastical figure.

The Courts of Love Music from the time of Eleanor of Aquitaine. Sinfonye (Mara Kiek, voc; Andrew Lawrence-King, medieval hp; Jim Denley, perc) / Stevie Wishart. Hyperion Ⓕ CDA66367 (64 minutes: DDD: 8/90). ✒ Texts and translations included.
Gui d'Ussel Si be'm partetz, mala domna, de vos. **Raimbaut de Vaqeiras** Calenda maya (vocal and instrumental versions). **Anonymous Twelfth Century** L'on qui dit q'amors est dolce chose. **Bernart de Ventadorn** Ara'm conseillatz seignor. Conartz, ara sai au be. Quan vei la lauzeta mover. **Cadenet** S'anc fuy belha ni prezada (vocal and instrumental versions). **Giraut de Bornelh** S'ie'us queir conseil, bel' amig' Alamanda. **Gace Brulé** Quant je voi la noif remise. Quant voi le tens bel et cler. Quant flours et glais et verdues s'esloigne. Quant li tens reverdoie.

This recital consists of songs and instrumental pieces dating from the end of the twelfth century and derived from the "courts of love" of Aquitaine, Champagne, Flanders and elsewhere. These courts, created around aristocratic figures such as Marie of Champagne and Eleanor of Aquitaine, were essentially a charade of the medieval law courts, to which lovers could bring their complaints. Thus the texts of the songs are concerned with the dilemmas of infidelity, betrayal and unrequited love. All that survives of this music is melodies for singing: these have been sensitively arranged by Stevie Wishart for a small selection of medieval instruments, including the symphony, a sort of hurdy-gurdy, medieval fiddles, lutes and percussion. All the players of Sinfonye are both expert and relaxed, projecting the music with great character. Six of the pieces are sung by Mara Kiek with considerable feeling: her unusual voice production and tone help to give a sense of 'distance' to the performances, and throughout strike a suitably plaintive note. Hyperion's recording catches all the vocal and instrumental inflexions with great fidelity and a most natural sense of balance. All in all, a fascinating glimpse of music and manners from a remote if influential corner of medieval civilization.

New review

Eya Mater Gregorian Chant and Polyphony for the Blessed Virgin Mary, Elizabeth and Rachel. **Discantus / Brigitte Lesne.** Opus 111 Ⓕ OPS30-143 (72 minutes: DDD: 5/96). Texts and translations included. Recorded 1995. Ⓖ

Ave Eva Twelfth and Thirteenth Century Songs of Womanhood. **Brigitte Lesne** ([a]mez/[b]hp/[c]perc). Opus 111 Ⓕ OPS30-134 (61 minutes: DDD: 5/96). Texts and translations included.
Gautier de Coincy Entendez tuit ensemble[ac]. **Codax** Ondas de mar de vigo[b]. Mandad' ei comigo[ab]. Quantas sabedes amar amigo[ac]. **Alfonso el Sabio** Razon an os diabos de fugir (Cantiga de Santa Maria)[c]. Entre Av'e Eva[a]. **Robert de Reims** Qui bien vuet amors descrivre[ac]. **Beatriz de Dia** A chantar m'er de çò qu'eu no volria[ab]. **Adam de la Halle** Je muir, je muir d'amourettes[b]. **Anonymous** L'autrier m'en aloie[ab]. Li solaus luist et clers et bians (lai Y'Yseult)[ac]. Noches buenas[a]. Mes cuers est emprisonnés[b]. Nonne sui, nonne, laissiés, m'aler[ab]. Or piangiamo che piange Maria[a]. Onques n'amai tant con je fui amé[b]. Avant hier en un vert prea[c]. Nani, nani[a]. Se vos non pesar ende (Cantiga de amigo)[ac]. Ir me quieria yo[ac].

"Eya Mater" highlights two major features of eleventh- to twelfth-century liturgical development: the elaboration through troping of the long-established repertoire and its enrichment through experimentation with the recently discovered dimension of polyphony. Whoever devised the programme managed, deftly, to draw together its various strands by concentrating on a unifying theme well suited to an all-female ensemble: the theme of motherhood. Three mothers figure in the programme – Mary, the Virgin Mother of Christ; Elizabeth, the mother of John the Baptist; and Rachel, whose lamentation for her slaughtered offspring foreshadows the grieving of those mothers of the Holy Innocents slain, by order of Herod, during the infancy of the Christ Child. The skilful planning of the programme is fully matched by the ease and excellence of the performances. In the few pieces with neither tropes nor polyphony, the interpretation of the early neume notation is quietly convincing, with ornament dissolving into the basic melodic structure with a fluidity few other vocal groups seem able or willing to achieve.

Brigitte Lesne's solo recital, "Ave Eva", enters the world of the medieval woman from another angle, one more of flesh and blood. She extends her time-range to the thirteenth century and even beyond. Her starting-point is the somewhat rarefied theme of courtly love, but she comes down to earth with such delightfully homely subjects as a Jewish mother singing her baby to sleep (*Nani, nani*), or the portrait of the restless nun in her cell, longing for release (*Nonne sui, nonne, laissiés, m'aler*). Perhaps surprisingly, the singer's characteristic timbre, far from sounding monotonous or wearisome on the ear when sustaining such a full programme, has more of a mesmeric effect, and actually enhances the illusion that one is penetrating a new, enthralling and relatively unexplored world of human experience.

The Pilgrimage to Santiago New London Consort / Philip Pickett. L'Oiseau-Lyre Ⓕ 433 148-2OH2 (two discs: 126 minutes: DDD: 7/92). 🖉 Texts and translations included. *Selected by Sounds in Retrospect.*
Including Cantigas de Santa María (collected/composed by Alfonso el Sabio), the seven Cantigas de Amigo by Martin Codax and other medieval vocal and instrumental works from the Codices Las Huelgas and Calixtinus.
In recent years a far higher standard of performance together with more rigorous scholarship has come to be expected from those who choose to perform this kind of repertoire. Philip Pickett has been in the forefront of this impressive rise in confidence (as much about what is not known as is definitely known) as this two-disc set amply demonstrates. What may perhaps be surprising to some is the quality of the music itself. The *Cantigas* remain some of the most enticing melodies ever written, and the New London Consort do them full justice with an array of instrumentalists and singers who are, however, used with discretion. Similarly the moving *Cantigas de Amigo* of Martin Codax are beautifully sung with a restraint that pays expressive dividends, though they do not have quite the transcendent quality of Mara Kiek's recording with Sinfonye ("Bella Domna"; reviewed further on). The polyphonic music from the Las Huelgas and Calixtinus manuscripts completes, with a flourish, the survey tied together by the Santiago label. If there is early polyphony that sounds fresher than the four-part *Belial vocatur*, for example, it has yet to be recorded. In addition to polyphonic works of various genres, Pickett has also chosen to record the four *planctus* settings from the Las Huelgas Codex: moving in themselves, they are valuable pieces also for their historical associations, as is explained in the comprehensive notes to the set.

Vox Iberica I Sons of Thunder. **Sequentia / Benjamin Bagby, Barbara Thornton.** Deutsche Harmonia Mundi Ⓕ RD77199 (74 minutes: DDD: 12/92). Texts and translations included. Recorded 1989.
Codex Calixtinus Ad superni regis decus. Alleluia: Vocavit Ihesus Iacobum. Annua gaudia, Iacobe debita. Benedicamus Domino. Congaudeant catholici. Cum vidissent autem. Cunctipotens genitor deus. Dum pater familias. Dum esset. Exultet celi curia. Gratulantes celebremus festum. Huic Iacobo. Iacobe sancte tuum repettio. Iacobi virginei. In hac die laudes

cum gaudio. Jocundetur et letetur. Misit Herodes. Nostra phalans. O adiutor. Regi perhennis glorie. Rex immense, pater pie. Vox nostra resonet.

Vox Iberica II Codex Las Huelgas. **Sequentia / Benjamin Bagby, Barbara Thornton.** Deutsche Harmonia Mundi ℗ 05472-77238-2 (75 minutes: DDD: 12/92). Texts and translations included. Recorded 1989.

Codex Las Huelgas Audi, pontus. Ave Maria, gracia plena. Benedicamus Domino cum cantico. Benedicamus: Hic est enim precursor. Benedicamus virgini matri. Casta catholica. Catholicorum concio. Ex illustri. Fa fa mi fa/ut re mi ut. In hoc festo gratissimo. Maria, virgo virginum. Mater patris et filia. Mundi dolens de iactura. O gloriosa Dei genitrix. O, plangant nostri prelati. O plena gracia. Psallat chorus in novo carmina. Qui nos fecit ex nichilo. Resurgentis Domini. Salve regina glorie. Stabat iuxta Christi crucem. Verbum patris hodie. Virgo sidus aureum. Four Planctus – Plange Castella misera; Quis dabit meo aquam; Rex obiit et labitur Castelle gloria; O monialis concio Burgensis.

Vox Iberica III Cantigas de Santa Maria. **Sequentia / Benjamin Bagby, Barbara Thornton.** Deutsche Harmonia Mundi ℗ 05472-77173-2 (78 minutes: DDD: 12/92). Texts and translations included. Recorded 1989.

Alfonso el Sabio Por nos, Virgen Madre. Como o nome da Virgen. Sobelos fondos do mar. Nenbre-sse-e, Madre de. Dized', ai trobadores. Maldito seja quen non loara. Quantos me creveren loaran. Quen bõa dona querrá. Pero que seja a gente. Santa Maria, strela do dia. Pois que Deus quis da Virgen. Macar poucos cantares acabei e con son. En todo logar á poder. **Riquier** Humils, forfaitz, repres e penedens. **Anonymous Thirteenth Century** Kharajas – Que faray, mamma?; Meu sidi Ibrahim; Gar si yes devina; Gardi vos ay yermanellas.

These three generously-filled discs provide a fascinating insight into Spain between the twelfth and fourteenth centuries. The country's history and culture as encompassed in the texts and music of the three repertories recorded is brought to life by Sequentia with all the immediacy of an illuminated miniature in a mediaeval manuscript. The music comes from three famous Spanish mediaeval manuscripts – the Las Huelgas manuscript, the Codex Calixtinus, and the collection of Cantigas de Santa María compiled at the court of King Alfonso "El Sabio" of Castille. What strikes one immediately is the freshness and imagination of virtually every piece here recorded. Sequentia's performances are commensurate with these qualities – listen, for example, to the magical textures of the women's choir singing *Sobelos fondos do mar* from the Cantigas collection, or the robust, steely harmony projected by the men in the organa from the Calixtinus manuscript. Surely one of the most remarkable pieces of the Middle Ages is the enormous *Virgo sidus aureum*, a prosa *"de Sancta Maria"* lasting over 14 minutes, whose text is a radiant mystical contemplation of the Mother of God. Liturgico-poetic parallels for it may well be sought in the East rather than the West – the Greek *Akathist* hymn from several centuries earlier, for example – but if Hildegard of Bingen, the "feather on the breath of God" is brought to mind, that would also be no surprise. It must be said that the poetic quality of all three of these collections is so high that the music could hardly fail to be of the same level of inspiration. This astonishing piece is given a splendid, coherent rendition (no easy task with a monophonic work of this length) by two soloists, female choir and symphonia, and one only has to listen to it after one of the rather shorter three-part conductus, such as *Mundi dolens de iactura*, or one of the powerful *organa* for St James, the "Son of thunder", from the Calixtinus collection, to gain some idea of the impact and the extent of the variety to be found on these discs. The Cantigas collection convincingly conveys the accomplishments of the court of the king who "while he was pondering the heavens and looking at the stars…lost the earth and his kingdom", and places the Cantiga repertory in the context not only of the troubadours (in particular Guirault Riquier) but also the Mozarabic *kharjas* (or *jarchas*), whose music has been reconstructed, with some success, by Benjamin Bagby. This testament to the richness of musical life in medieval Spain should not be missed: it has lost none of its power over the centuries.

New review

Campus Stellae Twelfth-Century Pilgrims' Songs. **Discantus / Brigitte Lesne.** Opus 111 ℗ OPS30-102 (69 minutes: DDD: 7/95). Recorded 1994.

Tropes of "Benedicamus domino" – Ad superni regis decus; Dies ista celebris; Congaudeant catholici; Dies ista gaudium; Gregis pastor; Mira dies oritur. Conductus motets – Plebs domini; Flore vernans gratie. Prosae – Alleluia … Gratulemur et letemur; Res est admirabilis; Quam dilecta tabernacula; Clemens servulorum gemitus tuorum. Versi – Uterus hodie virginis floruit; Lilium floruit. Kyrie tropes – Rex immense; Cunctipotens genitor Deus. Judicii signum.

All-female ensembles have hitherto been rather thin on the ground, but following on from Anonymous 4 and the high-voice section of Sequentia, here is Discantus, a ten-member group of sopranos and contraltos, dedicated to breathing new life into the performance of sacred monody and early polyphony. This is an attractive and varied selection of pieces illustrating different aspects of twelfth-century French music, the main sources being two manuscripts from the school of St Martial de Limoges and the *Codex Calixtinus*, or *Liber Sancti Jacobi*, compiled in Burgundy, but relating to the famous pilgrimage to the shrine of St James of Compostela. The work which remains in the memory, after listening with delight to the whole of this absorbing programme, is undoubtedly a piece (from a rather later source) based on the Sibylline Oracles, *Judicii signum*, with its ominous, low-voiced announcement of the Last Judgement. Indeed, the alternation from piece to piece of high and low voices, of solo and choir, of monody and polyphony is adroitly and effectively managed throughout the recital, so that the musical interest of a well-balanced and well-planned programme is sustained. Brigitte Lesne and her singers have learnt how to make repercussion sound discreetly convincing. The cadential ornamentation, sometimes involving a kind of double polyphonic shake, might perhaps have gained from being allowed a little more panache. The vocal timbre is clear and fresh and the whole performance moves along with cheerful confidence.

Bella Domna The Medieval Woman: Lover, Poet, Patroness and Saint. **Sinfonye** (Mara Kiek, voc; Andrew Lawrence-King, medieval hp; Jim Denley, perc) / **Stevie Wishart** (medieval fiddle, symphony). Hyperion Ⓟ CDA66283 (60 minutes: DDD: 6/88). ✎ Texts and translations included.
    Martin Codax Cantigas de Amigo. **Anonymous Thirteenth Century** Domna, pos vos ay chausida. Estampies Royals – No. 3; No. 4; No. 6. Danse Royale. **de Fournival** Onques n'amai tant que jou fui amee. **La Comtesse de Die** A chantar m'er de so qu'ieu non volria.
    Anonymous Fourteenth Century Lasse, pour quoi refusai.   Ⓖ

This intriguing CD collection of medieval songs joined together by the themes of woman as lover, poet, patroness and saint was originally released in 1988 and represented the début of Stevie Wishart's group Sinfonye. The performances of this elusive music have all the freshness and excitement of first encounter. The musical centre stage is held predominantly by the extraordinary vocalist Mara Kiek, whose plaintive as well as idiosyncratic tone ideally matches the distance of the music between its composition and the present day: this is genuinely music from another time and place, with hardly any relationship to the twentieth century at all. Stevie Wishart's playing of the medieval fiddle, used predominantly as a drone instrument and the symphony, a kind of hurdy-gurdy, well matches in its freedom and espressivity Kiek's singing, as does the supportive percussion playing of Jim Denley on two types of medieval drum. The fourth and final member of the group is the harpist Andrew Lawrence-King, whose playing adds tremendous colour to these intriguing recreations of the medieval woman's expression of emotions such as betrayal and violation. The harshness as well as vigour of the medieval era is powerfully recreated in these performances. Hyperion's recording is appropriately neutral, catching at times some of the claustrophobia of the emotions expressed in the music. An extremely interesting recital of music unlikely to be encountered elsewhere.

L'Unicorne Medieval French Songs. [a]**Anne Azema** (sop); [b]**Jesse Lepkoff** (fl); [c]**Cheryl Ann Fulton** (hp); [d]**Shira Kammen** (vielle/rebec/hp). Erato Ⓟ 4509-94830-2 (57 minutes: DDD: 11/94). ✎ Texts and translations included. Recorded 1993.
    Philippe de Thaon Serena en mer hante[acd]. Monosceros[ad]. **Anonymous** En mai au douz tens nouvel[abc]. Ensement com la panthere[abc]. Au renouvel[bcd]. Bele Doette[ab]. **Marie de France** Issi avint qu'un cers[ad]. D'un gupil[ad]. La danse de gupil[d]. **Thibault de Champagne** Aussi come unicorne sui[ad]. **Gauthier de Coincy** Le Cycle de Sainte Leochade[abcd]. **Moniot de Paris** Je chevauchoie l'autrier[acd].

Anne Azema always seems to bring a breath of fresh air to whatever she does, whether reading or singing. Here she is singing of springtime and love, of beasts and miracles, of a woman's grief but also of her joy. The melodies, often unforgettable in their simplicity, are interpreted with tenderness and quiet understanding. Many are ravishingly beautiful, in particular those describing the panther and the unicorn and also several of the songs from the *Cycle de Sainte Leocadie* in Gauthier de Coincy's *Miracles of Our Lady*. One of the finest songs in the programme is the thirteenth-century *Bele Doette*, a saga of grief experienced by a noble lady on hearing the news of her beloved's untimely death during the jousting. Azema's control of the slow rhythm and deepening emotion is total, and she matches this with perfection, as the story unfolds, in her singing of the short sad refrain that ends each strophe. The occasional instrumental interludes, for example *D'un gupil* ("The fox's dance") or *Au renouvel* provide graceful linkage between songs and readings; the accompaniments are generally discreet and understated, though the flute comes into its own in one song – *En mai au douz tens nouvel* – with its charming imitations of birdsong.

Love's Illusion Motets from the Montpellier Codex. **Anonymous 4** (Ruth Cunningham, Marsha Genensky, Susan Hellauer, Johanna Rose, sngrs). Harmonia Mundi Ⓟ HMU90 7109 (64 minutes: DDD: 12/94). Texts and translations included. Recorded 1992-93.

One could easily imagine that a programme such as this, of 29 thirteenth-century motets, all composed around the same theme of *fin amours* and all sung unaccompanied by an all-female vocal ensemble, might end by becoming wearisome on the ear. Anonymous 4 have proved conclusively in this recording that this need not be so, that, in any case, there is already an infinite variety of mood and style among the songs and that it is possible further to vary them in performance, using no other means than the voices themselves. The directness of the group's approach is always refreshing: their tone is unaffected, their pitch secure. The songs are presented with simplicity in a clear acoustic. There is a total absence of any improvised doodling on reconstructed medieval instruments, which is rather a relief. One gets a sense of quiet satisfaction and enjoyment from the singers themselves, also the feeling that the singers are trying to teach us something about the music, the mechanics of the motet and how it works, almost as if they were demonstrating to a class of music students. They sometimes go out of their way to sing a single part and then to repeat it with another part added, and then finally to give us a polished rendering of the whole motet, complete with all its parts. Occasionally they add a drone – once with a doubling at the fifth above. The insert-notes are clear and informative.

New review

The Spirits of England and France, Volume 2. **Gothic Voices** (Emma Kirkby, sop; Margaret Philpot, mez; Rogers Covey-Crump, Leigh Nixon, tens; Henry Wickham, bar) / **Christopher Page** (medieval lte) with **Robert White** (bagpipes); **Nick Bicat** (perc); **Pavlo Beznosiuk** (fiddle). Hyperion Ⓕ CDA66773 (62 minutes: DDD: 8/95). Texts and translations included. Ⓖ
Songs of the Trouvères – **Richart de Semilli** Je chevauchai. **Gace Brulé** Desconfortez, plains de dolor. Quant define fueille et flor. De bien amer grant joie atent. Cil qui d'amours. **Gontier de Soignies** Dolerousement commence. **Guibert Kaukesel** Un chant novel. Fins cuers enamourés. **Gautier de Dargies** La doce pensee. **Adam de la Halle** Assenés chi, Grievilier. **Ernoul li Vielle** Por conforter mon corage. **Audefroi le Bastart** Au novel tens pascor. **Anonymous** Domna pos vos ay chausida. Quant voi la fleur nouvele. Amors m'art con fuoc am flamma. Trois Estampies.

This is a disc devoted to monophonic song and one of startling power and originality. Essentially it explores two repertories: the serious *grand chant*, particularly in the work of Gace Brulé, whose four songs here are presented with tremendous conviction and in wonderfully spacious readings; and the lighter dance songs, where Page often includes instruments, played with robust good humour. As regards the rhythmic approach, this is neatly varied to match the needs of particular songs: sometimes an equalist interpretation, sometimes syllabic, and sometimes in strict metre roughly derived from the principles of modal rhythm. That seems a thoroughly judicious and musical solution, and it gives the disc considerable variety of pace. Margaret Philpot shows her astonishing stylistic range in the five songs she sings, from Richart de Semilli's jovial *Je chevauchai* via Gace Brulé's wonderful *De bien amer* and concluding with *Au novel tens pascor*, the late *chanson de toile* by Audefroi le Bastart. Emma Kirkby makes a welcome return to Gothic Voices with two glorious performances: her success in later music has been so great over the last few years that it has been too easy to forget quite how expressive she can be in early monophony, especially with Page's rattling folk-style lute playing in *Domna pos vos ay chausida*. Beyond these it is particularly good that the disc includes a *descort* – that fascinating but undervalued genre – and a *jeu-parti*. Once again Gothic Voices have produced a record that sets new standards.

The Marriage of Heaven and Hell Thirteenth-Century French Motets and Songs. **Gothic Voices / Christopher Page.** Hyperion Ⓕ CDA66423 (46 minutes: DDD: 12/90). Texts and translations included.
Anonymous Je ne chant pas. Talens m'est pris. Trois sereurs/Trois sereurs/Trois sereurs. Plus bele que flors/Quant revient/L'autrier jouer. Par un martinet/Hé, sire!/Hé, bergier! De la virge Katerine/Quant froidure/Agmina milicie. Ave parens/Ad gratie. Super te Jerusalem/Sed fulsit virginitas. A vous douce debonnaire. Mout souvent/Mout ai esté en doulour. Quant voi l'aloete/Dieux! je ne m'en partiré ja. En non Dieu/Quant voi la rose. Je m'en vois/Tels a mout. Festa januaria. **Blondel de Nesle** En tous tans que vente bise. **Colin Muset** Trop volontiers chanteroie. **Bernart de Ventadorn** Can vei la lauzeta mover. **Gautier de Dargies** Autre que je ne seuill fas.

The reasons for the dazzling success of Gothic Voices both in the recording studio and in the concert-hall are once again evident in this collection. It is both an entertaining and well-planned recital and, if one chooses to take it that way, reading Christopher Page's insert-notes while listening, a detailed lecture-recital. The music, all French and dating from the thirteenth century, is that seemingly impenetrable repertoire of polytextual motets, unexpectedly compared and contrasted with monophonic trouvère songs. The comparison is illuminating, and the performances of both genres of music are up to Gothic Voices' usual high standards: intonation is perfect, textures are finely balanced, the performances are always conceived just as much melodically as harmonically, and the greatest respect is always paid to the words (even when there are three texts at the same time, as is often the case here!). The clever juxtaposition of the trouvère Bernart de Ventadorn's *Can vei la lauzeta mover* with the triple-texted motet *Quant voi l'aloete/Dieux! je ne m'en partiré ja/NEUMA* encapsulates the thinking behind this recording: a compelling musical experience and a provocative intellectual one.

The Spirits of England and France, Volume 1. **Gothic Voices) / Christopher Page;** [a]**Pavlo Beznosiuk** (medieval fiddle). Hyperion Ⓕ CDA66739 (63 minutes: DDD: 2/95). Texts and translations included. Recorded 1994.
The fourteenth and fifteenth centuries – **Anonymous** Quant la douce jouvencelle. En cest mois de May. Laus detur multipharia. Credo. La uitime estampie real[a]. **J. Cooke** Gloria. **M. da Perugia** Belle sans per. **Machaut** Ay mi! dame de valour. **Pykini** Plaisance, or tost. *The twelfth and thirteenth centuries –* **Anonymous** Deduc, Syon, uberrimas. Je ne puis/Par un matin/Le premier jor/Iustus. Beata nobis gaudia. Virgo plena gratie/Virgo plena gratie/Virgo. Crucifigat omnes. Flos in monte cernitur. In Rama sonat gemitus. Ave Maria. La septime estampie real[a]. La quarte estampie real[a]. **Pérotin** (attrib.) Presul nostri temporis.

From the beautifully swift and unsentimental reading of the opening song, *Quant la douce jouvencelle*, through to the magically perfumed close with what Page calls the "irredeemably English style" of *Ave

Maria, each piece has its own musical excellence. In the works of around 1400 it is usually Rogers Covey-Crump who leads the singing, with a skilled and nuanced grasp of the style that seems to grow with each recording: long may his career continue. For the earlier works the spoils are divided between Paul Agnew, Julian Podger, Andrew Tusa and Leigh Nixon, all tenors with spirit and individuality. Finally, as an innovation in Gothic Voices recordings, Pavlo Beznosiuk plays three *estampes* on the medieval fiddle, without percussion and without any embellishment or deviation from the notes of their single surviving manuscript. While not everybody will be happy about this literal attitude to the problem of early instrumental music, Beznosiuk's playing is so rhythmically alive and so irresistible as to justify the approach. Once again, then, a superb recording from Gothic Voices; one that raises questions, that stimulates, that charms.

Worcester Fragments English Sacred Music of the Late Middle Ages. **Orlando Consort**
(Robert Harre-Jones, alto; Charles Daniels, Angus Smith, tens; Donald Grieg, bar). Amon Ra
Ⓔ CD-SAR59 (58 minutes: DDD: 8/93). Texts and translations included. Recorded 1992.
In this recording the Orlando Consort provide the listener with the chance to gain an overall impression of how music developed in England during the thirteenth and early fourteenth centuries – a development distinguished by its intriguing variety, creativity and undoubted beauty, its peculiar sweetness being marked by the constant harmonic use of the interval of a third. The Orlando Consort manage to achieve a balance between the type of buzzing vocal timbre, believed to have been that of the Middle Ages with its roughness of approach, and their own good solid modern standards of professional musicianship. The Consort also attempt to reproduce what scholars now believe to have been the way in which ecclesiastical Latin was pronounced in medieval England.

The Study of Love French Songs and Motets of the Fourteenth Century. **Gothic Voices /
Christopher Page.** Hyperion Ⓔ CDA66619 (60 minutes: DDD: 6/93). Texts and translations
included. Recorded 1992.   Ⓖ
    Machaut Dame, je suis cilz/Fins cuer. Trop plus/Biauté paree/Je ne suis. Tres bonne et belle. Se
mesdisans. Dame, je vueil endurer. **Pycard** Gloria. **Solage** Le basile. **Anonymous** Pour vous
servir. Puis que l'aloe ne fine. Jour a jour la vie. Combien que j'aye (two versions). Marticius qui
fu. Renouveler me feïst. Fist on dame. Il me convient guerpir. Le ior. En la maison Dedalus. La
grant biaute. En esperent. Ay las! quant je pans.
The title of the disc speaks of the ways in which the discourses of love (and 'love') in the late Middle Ages are partly, perhaps largely, derived from books – the Bible, classical poetry and myths, the earlier medieval literary tradition – rather than some expression of unmediated personal feeling. But music was a powerful means for the late medieval artist to attempt to transcend the bookish intertextualities of the literary texts. Rarely have Gothic Voices, both as individuals and as a group, sounded more alive and present. The accord of vowel colour between the singers in some of the fully texted pieces is marvellous, a feature pointed up the more by juxtaposition with those works in which Page continues his experiments with lower-voice vocalization. Where some slight untidiness creeps in, the impression often (though not invariably) given is the positive one of risk being happily taken in the recording sessions, the very absence of which has so often been the downfall of lesser groups (and not just in medieval music). A wonderful addition to the catalogue, and the recorded sound is superlative.

Lancaster and Valois French and English Music, 1350-1420. **Gothic Voices** (Margaret Philpot,
contr. Rogers Covey-Crump, Andrew Tusa, Charles Daniels, Leigh Nixon, tens; Stephen
Charlesworth, Donald Grieg, bars; Andrew Lawrence-King, hp) **/ Christopher Page** (lte).
Hyperion Ⓔ CDA66588 (59 minutes: DDD: 9/92). Texts and translations included. Recorded
1991.
    Machaut Donnez, signeurs. Quand je ne voy ma dame. Riches d'amour et mendians. Pas de tor
en thies pais. **Solage** Tres gentil cuer. **Cesaris** Se vous scaviez, ma tres douce maistresse. Mon
seul voloir/Certes m'amour. **Cordier** Ce jur de l'an. **Pycard** Credo. **Sturgeon** Salve mater
domini/Salve templum domini. **Fonteyns** Regali ex progenie. **Anonymous** Puis qu'autrement
ne puis avoir. Soit tart, tempre, main ou soir. Le ior. Avrai je ja de ma dame confort? Sanctus. Je
vueil vivre au plaisir d'amours.
This is the tenth recording to come from Christopher Page's Gothic Voices and, the considerable success of their previous recordings notwithstanding, this is perhaps their best yet. In the space of 11 years, Page and his group have reinvented performance practice in medieval and fifteenth century music, as powerful and popularizing an influence as David Munrow and his Early Music Consort of London in the 1970s. "Lancaster and Valois" takes its name from the chosen repertoire: French secular songs of the late fourteenth and early fifteenth centuries juxtaposed with sacred English pieces from around 1400. Much thought has been given to the ordering of the pieces and the grouping of the voices, resulting in the greatest possible diversity. In *Tres gentil cuer* by Solage, Page sets an ideally lilting tempo, with the text finely enunciated by Margaret Philpot, the tenors (in this instance Charles Daniels and Leigh Nixon) adding definition but never threatening to engulf. This is followed by a *Credo* by the English composer Pycard, the longest and most stately piece on the disc, exploiting the richer timbres of tenors and baritones. With excellent sound and entertaining and scholarly notes by Christopher Page, this is an irresistible disc.

Balades a III chans Ferrara Ensemble / Crawford Young. Arcana Ⓕ A32 (59 minutes: DDD:
1/96). ✒ Texts and translations included. Recorded 1994.   Ⓖ
   Trebor Helas pitié envers moy dort si fort. Si Alexandre et Hector fussent en vie. **Cordier** Tout
par compas suy composés. **Matteo da Perugia** Rondeau-refrain. Pres du soloil deduissant
s'esbanoye. **Antonius de Civitate** Io vegio per stasone. **Grimace** Se Zephirus, Phebus et leur
lignie. **Anonymous** Adieu vous di, tres doulce compaynie. Lamech Judith et Rachel de plourer.
Le mont Aon de Thrace.
The *ballade*, that noblest form (in every sense) of fourteenth century secular music, was meant to honour
the dukes and counts who did so much to foster the fine arts while war, famine and plague raged round
them. Their musical protégés were by all accounts a slightly surreal bunch, dedicated seekers-out of
weirdness, addicted to the bottle – possibly even to hashish. Small wonder that so much of their music
seems hopelessly capricious on the page. Crawford Young's special achievement is to demonstrate what
many enthusiasts of *Ars subtilior* have felt all along. In performance, that wilful strangeness can
suddenly come across with astonishing naturalness: all it takes is the right singers, and here they are. Or
perhaps that last sentence should read: "here she is". It is no slight on the other members of the Ferrara
Ensemble to say that the mezzo-soprano, Lena Susanne Norin, steals the show. Her singing can only be
described as luscious. True, the quality of these performances is partly a matter of direction. Tempo is
of the first importance because it determines the specific gravity of the dissonances. Pitched too slow,
the phrases are weighed down by them; too fast, and the dissonances are trivialized. Beyond that,
however, the sensitivity to these details is down to Norin herself. This fierce-looking music, once tamed,
becomes almost unbelievably sensuous. The tone of the accompanying string instruments is perfectly
judged, the sound-recording outstanding – warm and glowing. The presentation of *ballades* is a tricky
business: to perform all three stanzas can take well over ten minutes. In the past, singers have tended to
confine themselves to just one or two stanzas. That has the advantage of fitting more music into a
recital, but aesthetically it makes about as much sense as trimming the tail of a peacock. Young gives all
three stanzas of the poem wherever possible, and in so doing he restores the *ballade*'s length, weight,
complexity, in a word, the *heroic* intent that is the form's very *raison d'être*. A glorious recital.

Il Solazzo The Newberry Consort / Mary Springfels. Harmonia Mundi Ⓕ HMU90 7038
(62 minutes: DDD: 7/93). ✒ Texts and translation included. Recorded 1990. *Gramophone
Editor's choice.*
   Anonymous Fourteenth Century Italian La Badessa. Bel fiore danza. Nova stella.
Cominciamento di gioia. Trotto. Principe di virtu. **Jacopo da Bologna** Non al suo amante.
Landini La bionda treccia. Dolcie signorie. Donna, s'i, t'o fallito. El gran disio. **Ciconia** O rosa
bella. Ligiadra donna. **Zacharo de Teramo** Rosetta. Un fior gentil. **Bartolino da Padova**
Alba columba.
If medieval Italian music pales somewhat in comparison to the glories of opera from the nineteenth
century onwards, there are still riches to be discovered in this collection of *trecento* vocal and
instrumental works. The Chicago-based ensemble, The Newberry Consort, use a mere five performers
to provide over an hour of entertainment. This was the era of writers such as Dante, Petrarch,
Boccaccio, but also of Simone Prodenzani – the author of a cycle of sonnets entitled *Il Solazzo*, many
of which were later set to music. Whilst some of the *Solazzo* texts are presented here in musical form
(the scurrilous *La Badessa* is one), Italian ballata from leading composers of the time are also
represented – Ciconia's *O rosa bella* and Landini's *La bionda treccia*, for example. The vocal numbers
are all taken by mezzo Judith Malafronte and countertenor Drew Minter who clear the hurdles of
tricky pronunciation and flamboyantly complex vocal lines to give a thoroughly communicative
performance of this wonderful music. Mary Springfels provides elegant and musical direction as well
as that essential ingredient to a disc such as this – the informative booklet. If the prospect of an hour
of early Italian song sounds daunting, fear not, for the instrumental dances on the disc (especially the
anonymous *Cominciamento di gioia*) are played with a vitality that will make you want to jump up
and join in! Explorers of the riches from Italian times long gone by need have no qualms when
sampling from this lively, superbly performed disc.

Popes and Antipopes Music for the courts of Avignon and Rome. Orlando Consort (Caroline
Trevor, mez; Robert Harre-Jones, alto; Charles Daniels, Angus Smith, tens; Donald Grieg, bar).
Metronome Ⓕ METCD1008 (71 minutes: DDD: 11/95). Texts and translations included.
Recorded 1994. *Gramophone Editor's choice.*   Ⓖ
   Anonymous Gloria, Clemens dens artifex tota clementia. Pictagore per dogmata/O terra sancta/
Rosa vernans. **Matheus de Sancto Johanne** Inclite flos orti Gebenensis. **Egidius** Courtois
et sages. **Philipoctus de Caserta** Par les bons Gedeons. **Ciconia** O Petre Christi discipule.
Gloria "Suscipe trinitas". **Bartolomeus da Bologna** Arts psalentes. **Velut** Benedicta
viscera/Ave mater gratie/Ora pro nobis Deum alleluya. **Tapissier** Eya dulcis adque vernans
rosa/Vale placens peroratrix. **Antonius de Civitate Austrie** Clarus ortu/Gloriosa mater.
Zacharias Gia per gran nobelta. **Brassart** Te dignitas presularis. **Dufay** Balsamus et munda
cera/Isti sunt agni novelli. Supremum est mortalibus bonum. Ecclesie militantis.

The music broadly known under the label *Ars subtilior* was conceived as connoisseurs' music, and so it remains to this day. Its sometimes fierce complexity does not make for easy listening (particularly the sacred music, which often avoids the more overt melodic sensuality of the songs). It is very much 'of its time', in that a fair proportion of what survives was composed to honour a patron or to commemorate a historical event. And it is little recorded, because there are very few multi-movement cycles around which to plan a recital. Hence the ingenious theme adopted here. During this period, a succession of rival candidates for St Peter's succession were elected and deposed by opposing factions. Quite a few of them were rogues, albeit very cultured ones. Their careers may be traced through the entire sequence of works, both secular and sacred (mostly the latter). The last pope to be represented is Eugenius IV (reigned 1431-48), patron of Dufay; but you don't need a degree in history to follow the story. Margaret Bent's informative insert-note lucidly clarifies the relationship between works, composers and patrons. The Orlando Consort are in a sense the unsung heroes of England's polyphonic ensembles. Quite simply, they keep getting better. One could comment on any number of 'discoveries' here, but there is one piece that must rank as core repertoire for this (indeed, for any) period, Dufay's gloriously exciting motet *Ecclesie militantis*. Previous recordings followed the Complete Edition in assigning the piece's three sections ratios of 3:2:3. but the Orlandos' choice of the ratios 3:4:3: is infinitely more satisfying. The use of *musica ficta*, too, underscores the work's status as a highly self-conscious summing-up of the musical style explored here. This project is musically the most successful of the Orlandos' frequent collaborations with leading musicologists, in this case, Margaret Bent. The balance of intellect and musicianship is just about perfect, and fits the repertory like a glove. To be savoured meditatively, like an Islay malt.

New review

The Spirits of England and France, Volume 3. **Gothic Voices / Christopher Page.**
Hyperion Ⓕ CDA66783 (67 minutes: DDD: 1/96). Texts and translations included. Recorded 1995.
Anonymous Abide, I hope it be the best. Exultavit cor in Domino. **Binchois** Qui veut mesdire si mesdie. Amoureux suy et me vient toute joye. Adieu mon amoureuse joye. Ay douloureux disant helas. Magnificat secundi toni. Se la belle n'a le voloir. **Bittering** En Katerina solennia/Virginalis concio/Sponsus amat sponsum. **Cardot** Pour une fois et pour toute. **Dunstable** Beata Dei genitrix. **Fontaine** J'ayme bien celui. **Johannes de Lymburga** Descendi in ortum meum. **Legrant** Se liesse. **Machaut** Il m'est avis qu'il n'est. **Power** Gloria. **Velut** Lassies ester vostres chans de liesse. Un petit oyselet chantant.

Gothic Voices continue their long-term exploration of early English and French polyphony with an offering devoted to the work of Binchois and his musical forebears of both 'nationalities'. Consistent with the ensemble's usual approach to this repertoire, voices and instruments are not mixed; instead, Christopher Page is joined by the lutenists Christopher Wilson and Shirley Rumsey in energetic renderings of several of the songs: light, and delightful, relief. The songs of Binchois are relatively late territory for Gothic Voices. It has been ten years or so – in "The Castle of Fair Welcome" (Hyperion, 11/86), to be exact – since they covered this repertoire in any depth (who can forget the chilly pathos of *Dueil angoisseux*?), and comparison with the new disc is instructive. Over the years there have been more, and deeper, men's voices; the hard-edged, polished chrome patina has perhaps mellowed and burnished with time. Perhaps, too, the almost obsessive concern with clarity and intonation has been allowed to ease a little, in favour of a heightened sensitivity to the affective projection of both text and music. Perhaps, but only just. The hard edge creeps back in when the programme strays from Binchois back on to earlier repertoire, such as Power's marvellous five-voice *Gloria* – here portrayed as an exercise in risk-taking for composer and singers alike. Its brashness, though glorious to listen to, leads to an inevitable query, for there seem to be not one but two programmes here. Binchois's songs, characterized by their restraint and understatement, seem uneasy in the company of so many of his exuberant contemporaries and immediate predecessors (and the not-so-immediate – what is Machaut doing here?). The singers do their utmost to reflect the difference in tone, but that only makes the discrepancy more telling. This is a pity, for the Binchois pieces are finely pitched, and deserved to have more space to themselves – more space also for the singers to acclimatize themselves to Binchois's languorous melancholy. Page knows a show-stopper when he hears one, and the haunted *Ay, douloureux*, clocking in at nearly nine minutes, stands out from other items in the collection like a hothouse plant. That is not meant to belittle the rest, but to suggest that, as a programme, this particular collection is perhaps not as well-rounded as so many of its predecessors: the sum of its parts. And yet there is so much that is deeply moving and magical that anything less than a warm recommendation would be positively Scrooge-like.

New review

Music from a Prague Manuscript, c1500 Codex Speciálník – excerpts. **Hilliard Ensemble**
(David James, alto; Rogers Covey-Crump, John Potter, tens; Gordon Jones, bass). ECM New Series Ⓕ 447 807-2 (77 minutes: DDD: 9/95). Texts and translations included. Recorded 1993.
The Hilliard Ensemble have been developing a knack for innovative programming. The idea behind their previous release, "Officium" (also on ECM) was unquestionably odd, whatever one thinks of the finished product. For this new offering, the Hilliard go back to what they do best, the singing of early polyphony. A few years ago they devoted an entire CD to music from a single source, the Old Hall

Manuscript. In terms of renown, the Codex Speciálník isn't a patch on Old Hall, but among musicologists it is notorious as one of the most unusual polyphonic sources in existence. Speciálník was copied in Prague c1500. Between its covers are some of the strangest bedfellows in medieval music: early-fifteenth-century local Czech composers rub shoulders with those of the Old Hall period (c1420) and others later still, including the generation active when the manuscript was copied. If this bizarre jumble reflects the musical tastes of the Prague congregation, then they were possessed of a rare degree of eclecticism. Nowadays, we jump from Perotin to Parry without a second thought, but even so, the differences in style are striking. There is something very touching about the Czech pieces in the collection, rough-hewn and jagged as they often are (they seem old-fashioned even by fourteenth-century standards); and some of the slightly later pieces (such as the jolly *In natali Domini*) have an unmistakably local, almost folksy flavour. A really fascinating collection, then, and one that should please all the constituents of the Hilliard's multifarious following. Although not always exempt from the criticism of uniformity that has sometimes been levelled at this ensemble, the best of these performances must count among their finest.

New review
Virtue and Vice German Secular Songs and Instrumental music from the time of Luther.
Convivium Musicum; Villanella Ensemble / Sven Berger. Naxos Ⓢ 8 553352 (70 minutes: DDD:
1/96). 🖝 Texts and translations included. Recorded 1994. *Gramophone Editor's choice.*
Isaac Carmen. In meinem Sinn (three versions). Greiner, zancker, schnöpffitzer. Mein Freud
allein. Ich stund an einem Morgen. La mi la sol. Las rauschen. **Obrecht** Tsat een meskin. **Senfl**
Will niemand singen. Ein Maidlein zue dem Brunnen ging. Dort oben auf dem Berge. Nun wöllt
ihr hören neue Mär. Ich soll und müess ein'n Büehlen haben. Oho, so geb' der Mann. Es wollt'
ein Maidlein Wasser hol'n. Es wollt' ein Frau zuem Weine gahn. Lamentatio. Ich stuend an einem
Morgen. Albrecht mirs schwer. Ich weiss nit was er ihr verheiss (two versions). **Hofhaimer** Erst
weis ich was die Liebe ist. Greyner, Zanner. Mein eynigs A (two versions). Zucht eer und lob.
Anonymous Zenner greyner. **Heinrich Finck** Greiner Zanner. Gloria laus. **Ammerbach** Die
Megdlein sind von Flandern. **A. Bruck** So trinken wir alle. Es ging ein Landsknecht. **Küffer**
Heth sold ein meisken garn om win. **G. Meyer** Bicinium germanicum. **Rhau** Ich stuend an
einem Morgen.
The programme here is very generous, yet it consists of works lasting no more than three minutes
apiece. That it manages in spite of this to be both coherent and immediately appealing speaks volumes
for its virtues. In Sven Berger's selection, the Franco-Flemish mainstream is chiefly represented by
Heinrich Isaac and his pupil Ludwig Senfl, though both are clearly writing in a Germanic vein. That
vein appears not to share the Italian concern with instrumental virtuosity: most of the non-vocal
pieces are obviously designed for dancing. Nor are there any of the lovelorn texts familiar from the
neighbouring Latin cultures. It is all country bumpkins and buxom wenches, yet the coarser
obscenities found in French *chansons* are scrupulously avoided. One song simply declaims a list of
herbs whose specific properties are left to the listener's sagacity. A variety of instrumental approaches
is on offer, including a solo clavichord, a mixed consort of flutes and fiddles, or quartets of high
instruments drawn from shawms, crumhorns, sackbuts, dulcians and curtal (a primitive bassoon).
Barring the odd fluff, these wind instruments are played with tremendous verve and careful
intonation. The players of Convivium Musicum occasionally lend their voices to the proceedings, but
the vocal palm goes to the singers of the Villanella Ensemble. Purists may wish to query the use of a
modern guitar on what is obviously a period instrument disc, but the combination of that instrument
with two women's voices and a recorder will come as a revelation. Does all this sound too good to
pass up? Then Naxos's super-bargain price should clinch the matter.

The Voice in the Garden Spanish Songs and Motets, 1480-1550. **Gothic Voices / Christopher
Page** with **Christopher Wilson** (vihuela) and **Andrew Lawrence-King** (hp). Hyperion
Ⓕ CDA66653 (52 minutes: DDD: 2/94). 🖝 Texts and translations included. Recorded 1993. Ⓖ
Gramophone Editor's choice.
Encina Mi libertad en sosiego. Los sospiros no sosiegan. **Peñalosa** Por las sierras de Madrid.
Ne reminiscaris, Domine. Precor te, Domine. Sancta Maria. **Mena** Yo creo que n'os dió Dios. La
bella malmaridada. **Enrique** Mi querer tanto vos quiere. **Anonymous** Pase el agoa, ma Julieta.
Harto de tanta porfía. Dindirín, dindirín. Ave, Virgo, gratia plena. Dentro en el vergel. Entra
Mayo y sale Abril. Instrumental works – **Narváez** Fantasía II tono; Fantasía III tono. Paseávase
el rey moro. **Fernández Palero** Paseávase el rey moro. **Milán** Fantasías 10, 12 and 18. **Segni**
Tiento. **Anonymous** A la villa voy.
As usual with Gothic Voices, there is a mixture of all-vocal and solo-instrument performances, never
the twain meeting and a mixture of what used to be called sacred and secular: motets by Peñalosa sit
cheek by jowl with love songs and instrumental fantasies, giving an unusual and intriguing picture of
the repertory. In general the record has all the qualities that make anything by Gothic Voices a
required purchase for collections that aim at serious coverage of early centuries; and the resourceful
selection of music makes it an important contribution to the understanding of Spanish culture. A
note of special praise for Christopher Wilson's performances of the vihuela solos which have a control
and eloquence that are truly impressive. Andrew Lawrence-King characteristically throws new light
on some of this repertory with his immaculate range of colours and textures on the harp.

New review

Al alva venid Spanish Secular Music of the Fifteenth and Sixteenth Centuries. **La Romanesca** (Marta Almajano, sop; Paolo Pandolfo, va da gamba; Juan Carlos de Mulder, vihuela/gtr; Pedro Estevan, perc) / **José Miguel Moreno** (vihuela). Glossa Ⓕ GCD920203 (60 minutes: DDD: 5/96). ☞ Texts and translations included. Recorded 1995. *Gramophone Editor's choice.*   Ⓖ
Anonymous Al alva venid. L'amor, dona, ch'io te porto. Rodrigo Martines. A los maitines era. Nina y vina. **Narváez** Paseavase el rey moro. Lós Seys libros del delphin – Diferencias de Guardame las vacas. **Encina** Más vale trocar. Si abrá en este baldrés! Qu'es de ti, desconsolado? Hoy comamos y bevamos. **D. Ortiz** Trattado de glosas – Recercarda segunda sobre el passamezzo moderno; Recercada tercera para viola de gamba sola; Recercada quarta sobre la folia; Recercada quinta sobre el passamezzo antiguo; Recercada settima sobre la Romanesca. **Pisador** Libro de música – En la fuente del rosel; La manana de Sant Juan. **Vásquez** Orphenica lyra – De los álamos vengo; Con qué la lavaré; Glosa sobre Tan que vivray; De Antequera sale el moro. **Mudarra** Tres libros de musica – Si me Ilaman a mi; Ysabel, perdiste la tu faxa; Guárdame las vacas.

Many of these pieces – songs and vihuela music from sixteenth-century Spain – have been recorded at least once, if not dozens of times before, but this CD takes pride of place in this repertory. La Romanesca perform with true *fantasía* but without any of the mannerisms – the excesses and the understatements – of many of their predecessors and rivals: they seem to hit it just right. They have mostly selected songs with a strong popular flavour – precisely those songs that have attracted most attention because they are simply so attractive – but their realizations are restrained in terms of instrumental accompaniment (plucked strings, viol and a smattering of percussion), but full of musical vitality – in other words, the emphasis is, justly, on the music and not the 'orchestrated' arrangement of it. The players, led by José Miguel Moreno, are brilliant, and the singer, Marta Almajano shines in this repertory. She brings out perfectly the lyricism inherent in the popular-inspired court song tradition – take, for example, Vásquez's lovely *De los álamos vengo*: these songs demand an elusive blend of sophistication and simplicity. The instrumentalists make the most of the virtuoso element already making itself felt in the works of the vihuelists and Ortiz's *recercadas*. It's good to have a 'straight' version of Encina's *Más vale trocar*, which is often treated in an upbeat manner at odds with the text. The same applies to Vásquez's *Con qué la lavaré* although this is, arguably, just a touch too slow. Overall, and above all, it is purely a pleasurable experience to listen to this disc. Take it with you wherever you go, and especially to that desert island.

The Rose and the Ostrich Feather Music from the Eton Choirbook, Volume 1. **The Sixteen / Harry Christophers.** Collins Classics Ⓕ 1314-2 (63 minutes: DDD: 4/92). Notes and texts included. *Gramophone Award Winner 1992.* Recorded 1990.
    Fayrfax Magnificat ("Regale"). **Hygons** Salve regina. **Turges** From stormy wyndis. Stabat iuxta Christi crucem. **Anonymous** This day day dawes. **Cornysh** Salve regina.   Ⓖ

The sacred music of early Tudor England (the end of the fifteenth century) has been unjustly neglected on CD and the welcome extended to this Collins release is further enhanced by the fact that Harry Christophers and his ensemble have since added three further volumes to this series dedicated to music from the Eton Choirbook (see below). The destruction of great swathes of manuscript in the sixteenth century has left us with only isolated jewels such as this to remind us in sound what the eye can behold in the Perpendicular style of the architecture of the cathedrals of Canterbury, Worcester, Winchester and the Minster at York. Both architecture and music present soaring vaulted vistas and an attention to florid and ornate tracery. The Rose and the Ostrich Feather? These were both potent symbolic emblems of members of the royal house of Tudor and the words are incorporated into the two secular songs with English texts. The white rose was also an image closely associated with the Virgin Mary and most of the scores in the Choirbook are dedicated to her. Sadly, the disc is without translations of the Latin works but there is a fascinating essay by John Milsom. This music finds The Sixteen at their best, especially attentive to the severe tuning demands placed on the singers, for whom there is no instrumental accompaniment. Particularly notable is the control that Christophers exerts over the sound of his performers in this very taxing music (four of the performances on the disc last for over ten minutes). The recorded sound expertly captures and balances the expressive singing. Whether used as an aural accompaniment to a great architectural style or enjoyed purely for its sharply-defined reflection of one of the greatest periods of English music (existing within the choral tradition which continues to this day), this disc is altogether outstanding and should not be missed.

The Pillars of Eternity Music from the Eton Choirbook, Volume 3. **The Sixteen / Harry Christophers.** Collins Classics Ⓕ 1342-2 (61 minutes: DDD: 7/93). Texts and translations included. Recorded 1992.
    Cornysh Ave Maria, mater Dei. **Davy** O Domine caeli terraeque. A myn hart remembir the well. A blessid Jhesu. **Lambe** Stella caeli. **Wilkinson** Credo in Deum/Jesus autem. Salve regina.

This disc opens with Richard Davy's *O Domine caeli*, a vast and complex work lasting just over a quarter of an hour in performance, but apparently composed within a single day at Magdalen College, Oxford. It goes on and on in the most exalted, but perhaps inconsequential manner until its final resounding "Amen". What should a choir do with it except sing it as well as possible in terms of ensemble and intonation, as The Sixteen certainly do, and let the glorious sounds wash over the dumbfounded listener? Still more perplexing is Robert Wilkinson's *Credo in Deum/Jesus autem*, a 13-voice canon in which the individual voice parts represent Jesus and the 12 disciples. The net effect has been aptly described as "harmonious chaos", which it surely is, although, in common with all multi-voiced works of this period, it is harmonically static in a way that should delight minimalist fans. Symbolism is also the key to the structure of Wilkinson's setting of the *Salve regina* – the nine voice parts each representing a designated rank in the nine-fold hierarchy of angels. This is vintage Eton Choirbook, the composer pitting the full and sonorous directness of the tutti acclamations against the flights of fantasy in the solo sections. Another must for any self-respecting collection of renaissance polyphony.

The Flower of all Virginity Music from the Eton Choirbook, Volume 4. **The Sixteen / Harry Christophers.** Collins Classics Ⓟ 1395-2 (63 minutes: DDD: 2/94). Texts and translations included. Recorded 1993.
> **Kellyk** Gaude flore virginali. **Nesbet** Magnificat. **Fayrfax** Most clere of colour. **Browne** O Maria Salvatoris mater. Salve regina. **Anonymous** Ah, my dear son. Afraid, alas.

We know a good deal about the context for which the Marian music in the Eton Choirbook was composed: each evening members of the College Choir were to gather before an image of the Virgin and sing an antiphon in her honour (the College was itself dedicated to Mary). During Lent they were to perform the *Salve regina*, and throughout the rest of the year 'an antiphon of the Blessed Virgin' is all that is stipulated in the College statutes. This is the repertory represented on this disc, together with a Magnificat and three songs with texts that can be loosely described as Marian. It is magnificent music: the sheer scale of the two Marian motets and the monumental approach of their composers Kellyk and Browne, is quite staggering. It is not difficult to imagine these works being sung on a major Marian feast with the chapel singers before the lectern in a supreme act of Marian piety. The Sixteen, of course, are now well sung in this repertory and they perform it wonderfully, with an instinctive feel for the contrasts of sonority that so often define its structure.

New review
The Voices of Angels Music from the Eton Choirbook, Volume 5. **The Sixteen / Harry Christophers.** Collins Classics Ⓟ 1462-2 (62 minutes: DDD: 3/96). Texts and translations included. Recorded 1995.
> **Davy** Salve regina. In honore summae matris. **Lambe** Salve regina. **Plummer** Tota pulchra es. Anna mater matris Christi. **William, Monk of Stratford** Magnificat.

These are vibrant performances, suitably varied in colour, nicely paced, and recorded with superb clarity. That is to say that The Sixteen continue to explore the astonishing riches of the Eton Choirbook with undiminished enthusiasm and imagination. The special spice in this particular issue is in the two works by John Plummer, that strangely individual composer who treated harmonic stillness more boldly than any other of his generation. His music makes a nice contrast and contains a few hints of the kinds of floridity you get elsewhere in the Eton repertory; moreover it has a direct expressive mood that comes across very effectively in these well-judged performances. Walter Lambe's *Salve regina* seems to be among the earlier works in the Eton Choirbook; it has a neatly wayward fantasy in its lovely textures. The truly fascinating works here are those of Richard Davy. You could think that his enormous *In honore summae matris* occasionally rambles, at over 15 minutes; and there are moments when even the patent virtuosity of The Sixteen seems challenged by the intricate floridity of the passages entirely for lower voices; but there seems to be no limit to the range of ideas and textures that Davy has at his disposal. His are unquestionably pieces that grow in stature on repeated listening. Nobody is likely to be disappointed by this new instalment.

French Chansons The Scholars of London. Naxos Ⓢ 8 550880 (60 minutes: DDD: 2/95). Texts and translations included. Recorded 1993.
> **Arcadelt** En ce mois délicieux; Margot, labourez les vignes; De temps que j'estois amoureux; Sa grand beauté. **Bertrand** De nuit, le bien. **Clemens Non Papa** Prière devant le repas; Action des Graces. **Costeley** Arrête un peu mon coeur. **Gombert** Aime qui vouldra; Quand je suis aupres. **Janequin** Le chant des oiseaux. Or vien ça, vien, m'amye. **Josquin Desprez** Faulte d'argent. Mille regretz. **Lassus** Beau le cristal. Bon jour mon coeur. Un jeune moine. La nuict froide et sombre. Si je suis brun. **Le Jeune** Ce n'est que fiel. **Passereau** Il est bel et bon. **Sandrin** Je ne le croy. **Sermisy** Tant que vivray en eage florissant. Venez, regrets. La, la Maistre Pierre. **Tabourot** Belle qui tiens ma vie. **Vassal** Vray Dieu.

Listening to this carefully crafted selection, one is struck by the flexibility of a style that accommodates so many distinctive temperaments – the verve of Janequin, the suavity of Sermisy, the gravity of Gombert. It is a democratic genre in the truest sense, appealing to the great (Josquin and Lassus) while permitting lesser figures to shine as well. The term 'democratic' also describes the *chanson*'s appeal, then as now: here are some of the most beguiling tunes of any period. To call these performances unobtrusive is to do them no injustice. The Scholars of London capture the wistful elegance of the courtlier pieces – for example, Le Jeune's *Ce n'est que fiel*. In some of the more scurrilous songs (such as Josquin's *Faulte d'argent*) there is a Gallic rambunctiousness but at times the tempos are a shade too brisk for comfort, and the choice of pitch-standard in Janequin's famous

Chant des oiseaux (sung here in its through-composed version) sets a strain on the singers' accustomed agility. But such details merely affect the odd piece. This is a disc that gives great pleasure: like ephemera trapped in amber, the music in this collection bears modest yet touching testimony to a period that produced much 'great' music. Its smaller creations are no less admirable.

New review

Forgotten Provence Martin Best Consort. Nimbus Ⓕ NI5445 (64 minutes: DDD: 3/96). 🖉 Recorded 1994.
    Anonymous Ne l'oseray-je/Voulez-vous que je vous dire?. Dessus la rive. Vecy le May. Ma charmante cadet. Alleluia justus ut palma. A l'entrada del temps clar. Li gelos. Air de cheval-Jupon. Ara Lauzatz. Laude jocunda. Pucelete/Je languis. Alle, psallite cum luya. Rossignolet du bois (two versions). Lo Sodard. Epiphanium Domino. **Beatriz de Dia** A chanter m'er de so qu'eu no volria. **Giraut de Bornelh** Reis glorios. **Petrus de Cruce** Aucun ont trouve/Lonc tans. **Rudel de Blaye** Lanquan li jorn son lonc en may.
Here is a generous offering of the warm south: four centuries of song from herb-scented Provence, songs of love, songs of spring, songs and dances of the troubadours, traditional songs, motets and sequences – a profusion of wonderful melodies, well-matched by the diversity of range and timbre of the performers. There are tenor and soprano soloists, groupings of altos, and tenors, by themselves or in alternation; and finally, some imaginative instrumentalists. There is a diversity of moods as well, ranging from the sprightly and boisterous to the languid. Martin Best displays his customary ease and wit, with those gliding ornaments that disappear discreetly into the fabric of the vocal line. Then there is Libby Crabtree with her clear, precise, yet glowing soprano voice. The highlights are surely *A chanter m'er*, by the twelfth-century troubadour Beatriz, Countess of Dia, sung by Crabtree; and its idealized counterpart *Lanquan li jorn*, composed by Jaufre Rudel de Blaye, a contemporary of Beatriz, and movingly performed by Best to a quiet accompaniment of psaltery and fidele. There are also some rollicking jollities, such as *Ara Lauzatz* and the traditional *Lo Sodard*. Three sequences complete these sketches of life in Provence between the twelfth and the sixteenth centuries, two with organum, the third, *Epiphanium Domino*, sung gently with the rhythmic interpretation suggested by Handschin in the old *Oxford History of Music*. Concise, illuminating insert-notes are offered, with translations but, sadly, no original texts.

Une fête chez Rabelais Clément Janequin Ensemble / Dominique Visse. Harmonia Mundi Ⓕ HMC90 1453 (59 minutes: DDD: 5/95). Texts and translations included. Recorded 1994.
    Certon La, la, la, je ne l'ose dire. **Clemens non Papa** Une fillette bien gorriere. Du laid tetin. Imcessament suis triste et doloreux. **G. Coste** Cette fillette. **Compère** Nous sommes de l'ordre de Saint Babouyn. **De Bussy** Las il n'a nul mal. **Fresneau** La Fricassée. Souspir d'amours. **Gombert** Mille regretz. A bien grant tort. Puisqu' ainsi est. Je prens congies. **Guiard** Or oiez les introites. **Hesdin** Ramonez moy ma cheminée. **Josquin Desprez** Scaramella va alla guerra. **La Rue** Autant en emporte le vent. **Ninot le Petit** N'as tu point. **Pipelare** Fors seulement. **Sermisy** Je ne menge point de porc. Las, je m'y plains, mauldicte soit fortune. Vien tost. **Vermont le Jeune** Ce n'est pas trop. **Willaert** Dessus le marché d'Arras. **Anonymous** La brosse. Pavane and gagliarde.
François Rabelais's deep love of music is evident throughout his work: song quotations, puns on musical terms, and a list of famous composers ranging from Ockeghem through to Sermisy, Janequin and beyond. Many of the songs from which Rabelais quotes extensively have already been recorded by the Janequin Ensemble, but there is plenty in this outstanding anthology to remind us of his inimitable blend of caustic wit and mock erudition. The Janequin Ensemble have made this repertoire their own. This is the tenth anthology of French *chansons* from Dominique Visse and his group, and with each new album their interpretations grow in freedom, confidence and emotional range. The instrumental component (organ, lute, viols) is now fully integrated into the ensemble, and its interventions on the disc are generally very convincing. One could single out many individual items, but it is one of the more lightweight pieces, the scatological *Je ne menge point de porc*, that shows how far the group has progressed: the lead-up to the punchline is marvellously paced, and the punchline itself is delivered with camp ferocity. The annotated insert-notes attempt to explain the many cross-references in both music and texts. Unfortunately, the translations give them in a severely condensed form, and (as usual with Harmonia Mundi) the bawdy bits are bowdlerized. Never mind: Rabelais himself was censored.

Late Renaissance   16th-17th centuries

Songs on Poems by Pierre de Ronsard Clément Janequin Ensemble / Dominique Visse (alto). Harmonia Mundi Ⓕ HMC90 1491 (59 minutes: DDD: 2/95). Texts included. Recorded 1993.
    Regnard Ni nuit ne jour. Dedans ce bois. Contre mon gré. Mon triste coeur. Heureux ennui. Las, toi qui es de moi. Bois Janin à moi. **Boni** Rossignol mon mignon. Las! sans espoir. Quand je dors. Ha, bel accueil. Comment au départir. **J. de Castro** Je suis tellement langoureux. Quand tu tournes tes yeux. De peu de bien. **Monte** Quand de ta lèvre. Si trop souvent. Le premier jour du mois de mai. **Rippe** Fantaisie II.

It has been far too easy in the past to see French chanson composers in the second half of the sixteenth century as lesser figures – too restrained in their mode of expression, faint epigones of their predecessors (particularly Claudin de Sermisy and Clément Janequin), less inventive and resourceful than the great Italian madrigalists who were their contemporaries. But in fact they just needed to be performed with the kind of skill and refinement we now hear from the Clément Janequin Ensemble. It is not just that everything is perfectly in place, that many years of experience have blended them into an ensemble of wonderful flexibility. It is also that they manage to find the mood of each piece with miraculous precision. Certainly the music is a little restrained – though 'refined' would be the better description. On the page, these pieces can look remarkably similar. But every time the Janequin Ensemble put their finger on the songs' individuality. Just once they let everything rip, in Regnard's *Bois Janin à moi*; but otherwise within a fairly restricted palette they ring all the changes with massive skill. Not that there is anything effete about their singing. They have an outward and vibrant sound, sometimes helped by the assertive lute playing of Eric Bellocq. That directness may be part of their success in bringing this little-heard music to vivid and irresistible fruition.

Tudor Church Music Worcester Cathedral Choir / **Donald Hunt** with **Raymond Johnston** (org). Abbey Alpha Ⓕ CDCA943 (51 minutes: DDD: 5/93). Texts included.
  Weelkes Hosanna to the Son of David. Gloria in exclsis Deo. When David heard. **Byrd** Teach me, O Lord. Cantate Domino. Ave verum corpus. Sing joyfully unto God our strength. **Tomkins** When David heard. Almighty God, the fountain of all wisdom. **Tallis** Salvator mundi, salva nos I. If ye love me. Hear the voice and prayer. **Gibbons** O Lord, in thy wrath rebuke me not. This is the record of John. Hosanna to the Son of David.

Its church music was one of the glories of Tudor England, and the standard as represented by relatively minor composers was as high as the output was generous. But here we have the masters, "the big five", all heard in some of their finest and most famous works, so that the recital presents a small but useful anthology, ideal for adding to collections which otherwise have nothing of this sort in them. The Choir of Worcester Cathedral have many recordings to their credit but probably none better than this. They are a fine example of the Cathedral tradition in England; and one does not have to have just finished reading Joanna Trollope's *The Choir* to feel strongly convinced of the need for its preservation. The first sound of Weelkes's *Hosanna to the Son of David* itself tells of a rich culture, especially when the luxury of a choice in settings arrives later with the version by Orlando Gibbons. There are also two settings of the lament *When David heard*, both of them superbly 'built' by the singers as well as the two composers, Weelkes and Tomkins. Some of the anthems have organ accompaniment and soloist; most are sung *a cappella*, in recorded sound that does not (as is frequently the case) place the choir in too distant a perspective.

New review
Exultate Deo Masterpieces of Sacred Polyphony. [a]**Alexander Semprini**, [a]**Francis Faux**, [a]**Raymond Winterflood** (trebs); [a]**Adrian Peacock** (bass); **Westminster Cathedral Choir / James O'Donnell** with [b]**Joseph Cullen** (org). Hyperion Ⓕ CDA66850 (72 minutes: DDD: 5/96). Texts and translations included. Recorded 1995.
  Palestrina Exultate Deo. Sicut cervus desi-derat. **Byrd** Ave verum corpus. Civitas sancti tui. Haec dies. **Parsons** Ave Maria. **Viadana** Exultate justi[b]. **Tallis** Salvator mundi, salva nos I. O nata lux de lumine. In manus tuas. **Philips** Ascendit Deus. Ave verum corpus Christi. **Allegri** Miserere mei[a]. **G. Gabrieli** Jubilate Deo I[b]. **Lotti** Crucifixus[b]. **Tye** Omnes gentes, plaudite. **Victoria** O quam gloriosum. **Monteverdi** Cantate Domino[b].

This anthology lives up to its billing: even those with only a nodding acquaintance with renaissance polyphony will probably have heard a fair proportion of these pieces. Most of them are mainstays, not just of the Catholic liturgical repertory, but of most major Anglican choral establishments. The selection of pieces here is wide-ranging and varied. More importantly, where pieces are especially famous, the standard of performance gives the competition a fair run for its money. There *is* the thrill in Allegri's *Miserere* of a boy treble (here, Alexander Semprini) hitting that high C – and no quibbles about the phrasing of the adjoining notes, either. The choir as a whole sound very well focused, and the unanimity of the trebles is admirable (though at times a slightly more veiled tone might have better suited the text). Where required, they sound very bright and forward (at the end of Tye's *Omnes gentes*, for example), despite a recording that could have appeared a touch withdrawn with a more timid choir.

New review
Utopia Triumphans Huelgas Ensemble / **Paul van Nevel**. Sony Classical Vivarte Ⓕ SK66261 (53 minutes: DDD: 4/96). Texts and translations included. Recorded 1994.
  Tallis Spem in alium. **Porta** Missa Ducalis – Sanctus; Agnus Dei. **Josquin Desprez** (attrib.) Qui habitat in adjutorio Altissimi. **Ockeghem** (attrib.) Deo gratias. **Manchicourt** Laudate Dominum. **G. Gabrieli** Symphoniae sacrae – Exaudi me Domine. **Striggio** Ecce beatam lucem.
Paul van Nevel describes this disc as a gallery of the renaissance's utopian visions, the musical counterparts of the seemingly miraculous discoveries and inventions that marked the period. Certainly these pieces stake out new realms of musical space, culminating in the two rival compositions for 40 voices by Striggio and Tallis. The most unexpected discovery here is the Mass by Costanzo Porta (d.1601) was one of the last composers outside the

Iberian peninsula to write in the purest Palestrinian idiom. The style is familiar enough, but the sheer opulence of the sound cannot fail to impress: one would like to have had more of it. By contrast, the 36-voice *Deo gratias* and the 24-voice *Qui habitat* (attributed to Ockeghem and Josquin respectively) are far less convincing. Both attributions have been called into question: the *Deo gratias* has no more than 18 voices sounding at any given time – could a composer of Ockeghem's reach have contented himself with such a sleight of hand? It seems unlikely. On a more positive note, the inclusion of Gabrieli's 16-voice motet brings a welcome hint of mannerism to this otherwise classical programme, and brings out the best in van Nevel's characteristic quirkiness. The Huelgas Ensemble are no strangers to such polyphonic behemoths. Their usual trademarks are in evidence here – a very Flemish depth and throatiness of timbre, captured in a warm acoustic – and if one disregards the odd fluffs, the balance between overall effect and attention to detail is finely judged. Even in the Tallis, where there is fierce competition, the Huelgas more than hold their own. One may prefer The Tallis Scholars for their more balanced casting, but this *Spem* presents the familiar work in the unfamiliar context of a distinctly un-English sound.

A Venetian Coronation, 1595 Gabrieli [a]Consort and Players / **Paul McCreesh.** Virgin Classics Veritas Ⓕ VC7 59006-2 (71 minutes: DDD: 5/90). 🎵 Texts and translations included. *Gramophone Award Winner 1990.*   ⒼⒼ
  G. Gabrieli Intonazioni – ottavo tono; terzo e quarto toni; quinto tono alla quarta bassa (James O'Donnell, org solo). Canzonas – XIII a 12; XVI a 15; IX a 10. Sonata VI a 8 pian e forte. Deus qui beatum Marcum a 10[a]. Omnes gentes a 16[a]. **A. Gabrieli** Intonazioni – primo tono (O'Donnell); settimo tono (Timothy Roberts, org). Mass Movements[a] – Kyrie a 5-12; Gloria a 16; Sanctus a 12; Benedictus a 12. O sacrum convivium a 5[a]. Benedictus Dominus Deus sabbaoth (arr. Roberts. O'Donnell, Roberts). **Bendinelli** Sonata CCC-XXXIII. Sarasinetta.
  M. Thomsen Toccata I.
The coronation of a new Doge of Venice was always a special occasion, and never more so than when Marino Grimani (1532-1605) was elected to that office. We do not know what music was played then, but the whole ceremony is notionally and credibly reconstructed in this recording by Paul McCreesh and his cohorts. The recording was made in Brinkburn Priory, a church whose acoustic (aided by some deft manipulation of the recording controls) is spacious enough to evoke that of the Basilica of St Mark, the site of the original event. Space *per se* is vital to the music of the Gabrielis, who excelled in using it by placing instrumental and vocal groups in different parts of the building – which thereby became an integral part of the music. A fine selection of music that *could* have been played then is enhanced by the opening tolling of a bell, a crescendo marking the leisurely approach of the ducal procession, and the impression of architectural space created by changing stereo focus. It would be difficult to speak too highly of the performances, supplemented by first-class annotation, in this memorable recording. A trip to Venice would cost a lot more than this disc but, though you could visit the real St Mark's, it would not buy you this superb musical experience.

New review
The Feast of San Rocco, Venice, 1608 [a]La Capella Ducale; Cologne Musica Fiata / **Roland Wilson** with **Christoph Lehmann** (org). Sony Classical Ⓕ S2K66254 (two discs: 126 minutes: DDD: 6/96). 🎵 Texts and translations included. Recorded 1994.   Ⓖ
  G. Gabrieli Toccata. Symphoniae sacrae, liber secundus – Benedictus es, Dominus[a]; Cantate Domino[a]; In ecclesiis[a]; Jubilate Deo[a]; Misericordia tua Domine. Canzoni et Sonate – Canzon V, a 7; Canzon X, a 8; Canzon XVII, a 12; Sonata XIX, a 15; Sonata per tre violini. Dulcis Jesu patris imago[a]. Sacrae symphoniae – Canzon primi toni, a 10; Canzon in echo duodecimi toni, a 12. Buccinate in neomenia tuba a 19. Timor et tremor[a]. Toccata primi toni. Magnificat[a]. **Grandi** Motets, Book 2 – Cantemus Domino[a]; Heu mihi[a]. O quam tu pulchra es[a]. Motets with sinfonie – Salvum me fac, Deus[a]. **Monteverdi** Salve, o Regina[a]. **Cima** Concerti ecclesiastici – Sonata per il violino, cornetto e violone; Sonata per il violino e violone. **Barbarino** Motets, Book 1, "Il Primo libro de motetti" – O sacrum convivium[a]. **Castaldi** Capricci a 2 stromenti – Capriccio detto svegliatoio[a].
Wilson's starting-point is the famous description of the festivities that took place on the patronal feast-day in the Scuola di San Rocco, the most luxurious of the six Venetian *scuole grandi*, written by the English eccentric and traveller Thomas Coryate. Frustratingly, although Coryate provides a well-observed and detailed account of the various instrumental and vocal groupings used, the names of neither performers nor composers are revealed. To this extent "The Feast of San Rocco" is something of a fiction; nevertheless, it is an intelligent one, a thoughtful and well-researched attempt to put flesh and blood on the bare bones of Coryate's anecdote. Three main repertories are drawn upon: Gabrieli's large-scale motets; canzonas and other purely instrumental works also mostly by him; and smaller-scale solo motets mostly by Alessandro Grandi. The latter are especially welcome. Evidence of Monteverdi's influence is everywhere in his music, but that doesn't detract from its freshness and charm. There are darker moments, too, as in the extraordinary four-voice dialogue *Heu mihi*, an essay in the affective, chromatic manner. More typical of Grandi's work is the exquisite *O quam tu pulchra es*, an atmospherically erotic text from the Song of Songs, delivered here with urgent rhetorical force by David Cordier and underpinned by the lightest of continuo accompaniments. And one of the most virtuosic of all Grandi's motets, *Salvum me fac, Deus*, with its range of more than two octaves, is

expertly negotiated by Harry van der Kamp in an engaged yet controlled performance. s regards the interpretation of the larger-scale festive pieces, Wilson has adopted the Praetorius approach to the thorny problem of instrumentation and voice distribution. Just occasionally the solo voices are overwhelmed by the instrumental forces, in the sense that vocal strain is evident and the words disappear; both *Buccinate in neomenia tuba* and *Dulcis Jesu patris imago* suffer from such moments. But at its best, as with *In ecclesiis*, this recording is as compelling as any comparative version on offer.

Sacred Music from Venice and Rome The Sixteen / **Harry Christophers** with [a]**Laurence Cummings** (org). Collins Classics Ⓕ 1360-2 (57 minutes: DDD: 10/93). Texts and translations included. Recorded 1992.
   Caldara Crucifixus. **A. Gabrieli** De profundis clamavi. **Frescobaldi** Fiori musicali, Op. 12 – Toccata cromatica per l'Elevatione; Toccata per l'Elevationea. **Cavalli** Salve regina. **Monteverdi** Domine, ne in furore. **G. Gabrieli** Hodie completi sunt. **Lassus** Tui sunt coeli. Missa Bell'Amfitrit altera.

Clearly the starting-point was the colour and richness of the Venetian tradition from the Gabrieli to Caldara, and it is certainly good to have available works such as Andrea's *De profundis* and Giovanni's *Hodie completi sunt*, comparatively little-known motets that are not otherwise currently available in the catalogue. But the Lassus Mass, which takes up more than a third of the record, fits rather awkwardly into this scheme despite its eight-voice texture and characteristic manipulation of sonority and texture. However, it is the performances themselves that matter, and here The Sixteen produce a sequence of finely-turned and thoughtful interpretations. Their approach is uniformly sturdy and muscular, with plenty of controlled power in the lower voices and an attractively clear brightness in the upper ones. Harry Christophers, guided by an unerring sense of mobility and contrast, encourages his singers in readings which never fail to extract every last nuance of the text. The dialogue exchanges in Cavalli's well-known *Salve regina* are beautifully executed, and the vivid sense of drama in that performance is carried through to particularly good effect in the Monteverdi which follows it. This is one of the best records of these repertories to appear for some time.

Venetian Vespers Gabrieli Consort and Players / **Paul McCreesh** with [a]**Timothy Roberts** (org). Archiv Produktion Ⓕ 437 552-2AH2 (two discs: 96 minutes: DDD: 4/93). 🖉 Texts and translations included. Recorded 1990. *Gramophone Award Winner 1993.*   Ⓖ
   Sacristy bell. **Gabrieli** (ed. Roberts) Intonazione[a]. Versicle and response: Deus in adiutorium; Domine ad adiuvandum. **Rigatti** Dixit Dominus. **Grandi** O intemerata. Antiphon; Beata es Maria. **Monteverdi** Laudate pueri. **Banchieri** Suonata prima[a]. Antiphon: Beatam me dicent. **Monteverdi** Laetatus sum. **Finetti** O Maria, quae rapis corda hominum. Antiphon: Haec est quae nescavit. **Rigatti** Nisi Dominus. **Banchieri** Dialogo secondo[a]. Antiphon: Ante thronum. **Cavalli** Lauda Jerusalem. **Grandi** O quam tu pulchra es. **Anonymous** Praeambulum[a]. Chapter: Ecce virgo. **Monteverdi** Deus qui mundum crimine iacentem. Versicle and response. Ave maria; Dominus tecum. Antiphon. Spiritus Sanctus. **Rigatti** Magnificat. **Marini** Sonata con tre violini in eco. Collect: Dominus vobiscum – Deus, qui de beatae Mariae. Dismissal: Dominus vobiscum – Benedicamus Domino. **Monteverdi** Laudate Dominum. **Fasolo** (ed. Roberts) Intonazione – excerpts[a]. **Rigatti** Salve regina.

Paul McCreesh's sense of adventure made quite an impact with his reconstruction of Doge Grimani's Coronation in 1595. This follow-up recording takes as its starting point a Vespers service "as it might have been celebrated in St Mark's, Venice 1643", and it is no less striking a speculation. McCreesh is wisely not attempting to re-create a historical event but to provide a rejuvenating context for some more wonderful Venetian church music. There can be little doubt that listening to psalm settings within a liturgical framework illuminates the theatricality and significance of the works in a unique way, barely possible in an ordinary format where one work simply follows another. Yet the quality of the music is what really counts and this is where McCreesh deserves the greatest praise. He has skilfully blended a range of diverse concerted works with equally innovative and expressive solo motets, each one offset by ornate organ interludes and home-spun plainchant. Monteverdi is well represented, as one would expect, but by introducing resident composers (who were regularly employed by the great basilica) a strong Venetian sensibility prevails in all these works despite the many contrasting styles of the new baroque age. The little-known Rigatti is arguably the sensation of this release with his highly dramatic and richly extravagant sonorities. The settings of *Dixit Dominus* and *Magnificat* are almost operatic at times though they maintain the spatial elements inspired by St Mark's. The Gabrieli Consort and Players are a group with an extraordinary homogeneity of sound and focused energy: Monteverdi's *Laetatus sum* is one of the many examples where they reach new heights in early seventeenth-century performance. The solo performances are deliciously executed too, particularly those involving the falsettists. The purity and control in Finetti's *O Maria, quae rapis* knows no bounds. This two-disc set is an achievement of the very highest order.

New review

Vanitas Vanitatum Rome 1650. Tragicomedia / **Stephen Stubbs.** Teldec Das Alte Werk Ⓕ 4509-98410-2 (74 minutes: DDD: 3/96). Recorded 1995.
   Carissimi Vanitas vanitatum II. **Marazzoli** Ogni nostro piacer, quanto. **Mazzocchi** Musiche sacre e morali – Da tutti gli horologi si cava moralità. **Rossi** Ergi la mente al sole. O si quis daret

concentum. **V. Mazzocchi** Sospirate bel lezze. **Landi** Arie – Superbe colli. **Anonymous**
Canzonette spirituali e morali – Ciaccona di Paradiso e dell'inferno; Passacalli della vita.
It is welcome to find Tragicomedia's disc beginning with something of a rarity, Carissimi's "Proposui in mente mea" (= *Vanitas vanitatum II*). Starting from this piece, Tragicomedia have constructed an ingenious sequence of works by Roman composers on the *vanitas* theme, including two little-known works by Luigi Rossi and an exquisite rarity by Marco Marazzoli. Marazzoli's music is constantly being reassessed as new works come to light, but from the pieces on this record it is clear that he was the equal of Carissimi himself. Structured around a hauntingly beautiful ritornello that is heard four times, *Ogni nostro piacer* is presented in bright tonal colours (occasionally, but only occasionally do the sopranos go over the top), and is delivered in a rather intense and highly rhetorical manner that is designed to underscore as effectively as possible the central theological message. Both here and elsewhere we are treated to some difficult passagework stunningly executed, and a particularly effective feature is the sensitive and delicate underpinning from a continuo grouping that opts for an intelligent variety of sound without indulging in over elaboration and intrusive ornamentation. The heroes of the hour are undoubtedly John Elwes and Harry van der Kamp, the former a delight in Domenico Mazzocchi's intensely compressed sonnet setting "Da tutti gli horologi si cava moralità", the latter on virtuoso form in Stefano Landi's brief but demanding "Superbe colli". This record is worth having for these two tracks alone, but there are many other good things to savour as well.

French Chamber Music [a]**Catherine Cantin** (fl); [b]**Maurice Bourgue** (ob); [c]**Michel Portal** (cl); [d]**Amaury Wallez** (bn); [e]**André Cazalet** (hn); **Pascal Rogé** (pf). Decca Ⓔ 425 861-2DH (67 minutes: DDD: 5/91). Recorded 1989.
Saint-Saëns Caprice sur des airs danois et russes, Op. 79[abc]. **d'Indy** Sarabande et menuet, Op. 72[abcde]. **Roussel** Divertissement, Op. 6[abcde]. **Tansman** Le Jardin du Paradis – Danse de la sorcière[abcde]. **Françaix** L'heure du berger[abce]. **Poulenc** Elégie[e]. **Milhaud** Sonata for Flute, Oboe, Clarinet and Piano, Op. 47[abc].

French composers are noted for their special fondness for writing for wind instruments, but their wide diversity of styles is illustrated by this attractive disc, which is notable for superbly clean and sensitive playing by musicians in complete accord with each other and in instinctive sympathy with the music. Of the three works here for wind quintet and piano, the Roussel *Divertissement* is a particular delight, in turn sprightly and seductive; the d'Indy movements (transcribed from an earlier suite for the curious combination of trumpet, two flutes and string quartet) are an expressively contrapuntal sarabande and an oddly chirpy minuet; and the pungent Tansman dance is from an unfinished ballet. Jean Françaix's habitual spirit of *gaminerie* reigns in his three portraits for wind quartet and piano, written with his usual consummate craftsmanship. The works for wind trio and piano could scarcely be more unlike: Saint-Saëns's suave confection on (reputedly bogus) Danish and Russian airs, with a brilliant piano part, and Milhaud's often abrasive sonata (despite a pastoral opening), which ends with a dirge for victims of a Spanish influenza epidemic. And there's Poulenc's elegy for Dennis Brain, its broad lament tinged with just a touch of the humour that Dennis himself would have enjoyed.

Music from Renaissance Portugal Cambridge Taverner Choir / Owen Rees. Herald Ⓔ HAVPCD155 (69 minutes: DDD: 1/94). Texts and translations included. Recorded 1992.
Gramophone Editor's choice.   Ⓖ
P. de Cristo Magnificat. Ave Maria. Sanctissimi quinque mar tires. De profundis. Lachrimans sitivit anima mea. Ave Regina caelorum. **D. Lôbo** Missa pro defunctis. **Anonymous** Si pie Domine. **A. Fernandez** Libera me Domine. Alma redemptoris mater. **Carreira** Stabat mater.

This is one of those rare examples of scholarship and musicianship combining to result in performances that are both impressive and immediately attractive to the listener in excellent music, totally neglected until now. There is a wonderful glow about this recording that reflects the skilful engineering on the part of Herald as well as the imagination of the sonority on Rees's part. The striking feature of his approach is the emphasis on the meaning of the words. This choir sing of the Day of Judgement or the rejoicing due to the Virgin as if they really mean it: Rees is not afraid to shape phrases, to use dynamics, to vary the intensity of the sound in the service of the words which, though even more familiar to the monks and chapel singers who originally performed these pieces at the monastery of Santa Cruz in Colmbra, would have had an immediacy and a reality for them that it is hard to recapture today. How graphic those texts, in fact, are, and how well this choir bring them to life.

Musica Mediterranea Kithara (Shirley Rumsey, [a]mez/lte/gtr/cittern; William Lyons, fl/rec; Jan Walters, hp; Christopher Wilson, lte/gtr; David Miller, theorbo/lte; Susanna Pell, bass viol). Chandos Chaconne Ⓔ CHAN0562 (62 minutes: DDD: 3/95). Texts and translations included. Recorded 1993.
Willaert A quand'haveva[a]. O bene mio[a]. **Nola** Cingari simo venit'a giocare. **D. Ortiz** La spagna. La gamba. O felici occhi miei. **Mudarra** Si me llaman a mi. **Barberiis** Madonna qual certezza. **Valderrábano** Discantar sobre un punto. **A. Valente** Tenore del passo e mezzo. **Molinaro** Ballo detto il Conte Orlando. **Picchi** Ballo e Saltarello ongaro. **Piccinini** Chiacconna. **Bottegari** Non se vedde giamai[a]. **Bassano** Vestiva i colli. **Rossi** Passacaglia. **Arañés** Un sarao de la Chacona[a]. **Anonymous** Riu, riu, chiu[a]. Recercar. Donna vagh'e leggiadra[a]. Folias.

This recording of music from renaissance Spain and Italy by the solo vocal and instrumental ensemble Kithara is a delight. The music, by Willaert, Ortiz, Mudarra, Valente, Picchi *et al.*, is charming and expressive by nature and the performances are above reproach, both at ensemble and solo level. Susanna Pell's excellent account of Ortiz's *La spagna* catches just the right slightly mournful feel with her rich-toned gamba-playing; William Lyons's divisions on the renaissance flute (which, quite exceptionally, he makes sound like a real musical instrument capable of varied timbres and expressive phrasing) in Bassano's *Vestiva i colli* are superbly executed; and the plucked string accompaniments and solo items, led by Christopher Wilson on a variety of instruments, are gossamer fine and rhythmically strong as and when required. Shirley Rumsey both sings and contributes to this colourful plucked string section. Her voice has a darker quality that is in many ways suitably Mediterranean. Dinko Fabris, in his accompanying notes, emphasizes "the true sensibility of the northern European travellers of that time" in Kithara's interpretations of this colourful music. He's right in that in many ways the group sound very 'English', given the excellent teamwork and high level of musicality that fights a little shy of anything too extrovert. A very enjoyable disc nevertheless.

New review

Dolcissima ed amorosa Paul O'Dette (lte). Harmonia Mundi Ⓕ HMU90 7043 (67 minutes: DDD: 10/95). Recorded 1990-92.

Francesco da Milano Fantasias – Castelfranco MS; Dolcissima et amorosa; Nos. 8, 26, 39, 56 and 83. Ricercar No. 13. **Borrono da Milano** Pavana chimata la Desparata. Tocha tocha la Canella. Pavana la Gombertina. Saltarello chiamato el Mazolo. Two saltarellos. Fantasia. **Ripa** Fantasias Nos. 8 and 22. L'Eccho. **Dall'Aquila** Ricercar. Il est bel est bon. Ricercar Lautre jour No. 101. Nous bergiers. La Traditora Nos. 2 and 3. Ricercars Nos. 16 and 33. La Battaglia.

The album's title summarizes a quotation from an encomium by Francesco Marcolini (1536) in praise of the lute playing of three of those whose music it contains, to which O'Dette adds Pietro Paolo Borrono (da Milano), some of whose works were published together with some by Francesco (da Milano) in 1546, not long after the latter's death. O'Dette draws on all the genres of lute music at that time: fantasias, character pieces, dances and intabulations of vocal music. Christopher Wilson's recent recording of music by Francesco (Naxos Ⓓ 8 550774) was inevitably focused on fantasias/ricercars and intabulations, which formed the bulk of his output, but though Marcolini's chosen composers wrote down few dances – they would have improvised them instead – Borrono wrote enough to make up for it, and by including several of them O'Dette has given an attractive variety to his programme. Three of the Francesco items (Ricercar No. 13 and Fantasias Nos. 56 and 83) are on both Wilson's and O'Dette's discs; it is O'Dette who takes the more energetic view of the last two of these, another contribution to overall variety. Guitarists may be surprised to know that their device of repeating a passage in a higher position on lower strings, to give a softer tone-colour, was used in Marco's intabulation of Gentian's chanson *L'Eccho* – is there nothing new under the sun? O'Dette is a brilliant technician and a consummate musician who considers the function of every note. These attributes, coupled with an astutely compiled and finely recorded programme, make this a disc that should have a wide appeal – academia plus entertainment holding the attention throughout.

Italian Harpsichord Works, 1550-1700 Rinaldo Alessandrini (hpd). Opus 111 Ⓕ OPS30-118 (77 minutes: DDD: 4/95). ✍ Recorded 1994.   ⒼⒼ

A. Valente Tenore del passo e mezzo. **Facoli** Pass'e mezzo moderno. **Giovanni de Macque** Due Gagliarde. Seconde Stravaganze. **A. Mayone** Partite sopra "Fidele". **Trabaci** Partite sopra "Rugiero". **Picchi** Balli – Ballo ongaro; Ballo alla polacha; Ballo ditto il Picchi. **Buono** Sonata quinta. **Frescobaldi** Toccata. **Lambardo** Gagliarda. Partite sopra "Fidele". **Merula** Capriccio cromatico. Toccata del secondo tono. **M. Rossi** Toccata settima. **Salvatore** Toccata prima. Canzon Francese terza. Due Correnti. **B. Storace** Toccata e Canzon. **B. Strozzi** Corrente terza. **Stradella** Toccata. **A. Scarlatti** Toccata per il cembalo.

Even harpsichordists and connoisseurs of seventeenth-century music are likely to find many of the items on this extremely interesting and unusual disc unfamiliar: Rinaldo Alessandrini has made a special study of sixteenth- and seventeenth-century Italian music, and here presents (with the co-operation of the West German Radio) two dozen pieces that illustrate changes of style there between 1576 (the year of Antonio Valente's pioneering harpsichord collection) and around 1700, and, to some extent, differences between the more austere northern school and the more extrovert southern one. It may perhaps not be generally realized that the keyboard virtuosity demanded by our own brilliant John Bull is matched by his Italian contemporaries: Alessandrini's rhythmically vital, stylish and engaged performances leave us in no doubt of that. He gives us a well-chosen range of forms. There are variations on the *passamezzo* ground, in the minor mode and in the major variant ("moderno") – both examples here of considerable elaboration: and there are other variations (*partite*) on the harmonic bass variously known as "Ruggiero" or "Fedele". Dance forms are represented by two examples of the *gagliarda* (both chordal in treatment), two of the *corrente* (that by Salvatore full of chromaticisms), and 'exotic' dances from Poland and Hungary. Of particular interest in several items is their composers' fascination with chromaticism (which produces some curious intonation in the unidentified tuning system of the 1678 Italian harpsichord used here): a *stravaganza* by de Macque (who was Flemish by birth but spent his life in Naples, where he taught Mayone and Trabaci) contains several bold surprises; a Merula *capriccio*, a contrapuntal Salvatore *canzona*, a

Buono 'sonata' and a Rossi *toccata* with a truly astonishing ending likewise feature chromaticism. The seven in this programme – mostly rhapsodic and improvisatory-sounding – include a splendid example by Frescobaldi and a sombrely declamatory one by Merula; but the eventual falling-off of this keyboard style is signalled by the toccata by Stradella, which is overly reliant on formulas.

Spanish and Portuguese Harpsichord Music Sophie Yates (hpd). Chandos Chaconne
     Ⓔ CHAN0560 (63 minutes: DDD: 11/94). ✒ Recorded 1993.
     A. de Cabezón Diferencias sobre "La dama le demanda". Diferencias sobre el Canto llano del Caballero. Diferencias sobre la Gallarda Milanesa. Pavana con su glosa. Tiento del primer tono. Farbordon del primer tono. Obra sobre Cantus firmus. **Ximénez** Obra del primer tono de lleno. **Coelho** Segunda Susana grosada a 4 sobre a de 5. Segunda Tento do primeiro tom. **Anonymous** Españoleta. **Carreira** Canção a Quatro glosada. **H. de Cabezón** "Dulce memoria" glosada. **Cabanilles** Pasacalles primero tono. Tiento de Batalla del octavo tono.

With an unusual and wholly admirable restraint Sophie Yates has chosen not any of the familiar showpieces of the harpsichord repertoire but the relatively little-known area of the early Iberian masters. That less of their music has survived than that of their contemporaries, the English virginalists, is attributed in the thoughtful insert-notes not only to composers jealously guarding their work for their own exclusive use, to economic reasons or to the great losses suffered in the Lisbon earthquake of 1755, but to the emphasis on improvised, rather than written-out, music. The techniques (often virtuosic) involved in this are illustrated in the many sets of *diferencias* (variations) which were a speciality of the time. Several examples are offered here, beginning with one on *La dama le demanda* (a version of the tune familiar as the "Pavane" in Warlock's *Capriol Suite*); others, also by the blind Cabezón, are on the *Gallarda Milanesa* and that favourite theme, the *Canto llano del Caballero*, in which the melody, instead of merely being treated with ever-increasing elaboration, successively passes to other voices in the texture. All these pieces are played with engaging vitality and commendably springy articulation by Sophie Yates on a copy of an Italian harpsichord of about 1600.

New review

Alfred Deller Songs and Airs – Anonymous, Bedyngham, Campion, Ciconia, Dowland,
     R. Joynson, Morley, Purcell, Rosseter and J. Wilson. **Alfred Deller** (alto) with various artists.
     EMI Références mono Ⓜ CDH5 65501-2* (77 minutes: ADD: 5/96). From HMV originals;
     recorded 1949-54.

All but two of the pieces here are by English composers of the late sixteenth and seventeenth centuries; the odd ones out are Johannes Ciconia's *O rosa bella* and John Bedyngham's setting of the same text, which belong to the fourteenth and fifteenth centuries, respectively. Curiously, some of these recordings reveal Deller on rather less than top form. Dowland's *Slow my tears*, for instance, is marred by a persistent huskiness while certain others display a marked expressive restraint. But, almost needless to say, there is also plenty of vintage Deller here, in which category Morley's Shakespeare settings, *It was a lover and a lass* and *O Mistress mine*, certainly belong. Comparably affecting are Robert Johnson's *Full fathom five* and the celebrated anonymous setting of Desdemona's *Sing, willow, willow, willow*. Most touching of all, though, is the anonymous *Caleno custure me!* from *Henry V*, which Deller sings with exquisite sensibility. That and the popular *Greensleeves* would be quite sufficient on their own to make you go at once in search of this disc. Sadly, the Purcell songs seem rather dated, not so much for Deller's singing of them as for the archaic sound of the harpsichord, the tuning, and the playing of them, sometimes technically insecure and often with quaintly realized continuo lines. Notwithstanding these reservations, the anthology is a precious one, with moments of real magic. The transfers to CD have been remastered skilfully with virtually no background noise at all.

New review

Sacred Choral Works ªVienna Hofburgkapella Schola; ᵇConcerto Palatino; Gradus ad Parnassum
     / Konrad Junghänel. Deutsche Harmonia Mundi Ⓔ 05472 77326-2 (74 minutes: DDD: 7/95). ✒
     Texts and translations included. Recorded 1994.
     Biber Missa allelujaᵃᵇ. **Schmelzer** Vesperae sollennesᵃᵇ. Sonata per Chiesa et Camera. Sacro-Profanus Concentus Musicus – Sonata XII. **Palestrina** Coelestis urbs Jerusalem. **Froberger** Fantasia II in A minor. **Anonymous** Gregorian Chant for the Dedication of a Church – Mass Propersᵃ. Gregorian Chant for Vespersᵃ.

What this record achieves above all else is to confirm the suspicion that Austrian choral music of the seventeenth century is not confined to a couple of Requiem settings by Biber and a few other works of little or no musical interest. The spatial and textural intricacy of Biber's 36-part setting of the Mass is a wonder in itself and the product of a composer who 'worked' the galleries of Salzburg Cathedral to his advantage. A degree of this multi-antiphonal style is Venetian in flavour but only superficially; the quicker harmonic rhythm and sophisticated groupings, as well as other colourful central European quirks, reveal a composer whose manipulation of singers and instrumentalists has more to offer than abstract sonic resplendence; Biber is admirably sensitive to the text he is setting. The performances are equally sensitive. Junghänel never allows his singers or players to overblow as can be the temptation with polychoral repertoire. Obtaining the right balance between wafting, majestic sonorities and clearly defined solo contributions takes direction of a high order and one is left in no doubt that Biber's detailed but solemn score is being taken with the utmost seriousness. There are a few moments where articulation is under-explored and the strings can sound a little too diffident. Schmelzer's *Vespers* are finely constructed, too, with an imaginative range of scorings which Junghänel and his musicians execute with tenderness and great nobility throughout. A fine and illuminating release.

Seventeenth-century English Organ works Robert Woolley (org). Chandos Chaconne
Ⓕ CHAN0553 (73 minutes: DDD: 9/94). Played on the Guilimiau organ, Brittany. Recorded
1993. Ⓖ
C. Gibbons Verses – D minor; A minor. **Locke** Voluntaries from "Melothesia" – Two in
A minor; for the Double Organ in D minor. **Anonymous** Voluntary for the Double Organ in
D minor. Voluntary for the Trumpet Stop. **Blow** Verses – G major; A minor; C major; for the
Double Organ in G major; G minor. Voluntary for the Cornet and Echo. **Purcell** Voluntaries –
C major, Z717; D minor for the Double Organ, Z718; G major, Z720. Verse in F major, Z716.
Clarke The Prince of Denmark's March, T435. Trumpet Tune, T438. **Croft** Voluntaries –
G major; G minor; D major.

England's greatest dynasty of organ builders in the early- and mid-seventeenth century, the Dallams, fled to Brittany to escape the organ-wrecking activities of Cromwell's cohorts in the 1640s, and so, ironically, more work survives in north-west France than in England. The magnificent 1989 reconstruction of the three-manual Thomas Dallam organ at Guilimiau, dating from around 1675-80, has given Robert Woolley the opportunity to produce an anthology in the vernacular, as it were, tracing the development of a re-emerging organ tradition over half a century, from the 1660 restoration of the monarchy to just before the advent of Handel in London. It is an opportunity magnificently seized. Restoration organ music is notoriously difficult to bring off, quirky in ornamentation, volatile in temper, erratic in idiom and invention. But at its best, and particularly in the works of Blow, who is not averse to unashamedly jackdaw-like raids on Frescobaldi's toccatas for lyrical interludes (tracks 9 and 10), it possesses an engagingly ramshackle virtuosity, an unpredictability of wit and an occasionally prodigal approach to chromaticism (try the end of the anonymous double organ voluntary, track 6). The disc cannily manages to squeeze in virtually all the best works of the period, including (forgiveably) Jeremiah Clarke's two famous Trumpet Tunes – properly harpsichord pieces. Woolley's playing integrates the curious English keyboard ornaments of the period within a thoroughly convincing rhetorical delivery, while never lapsing into eccentricity nor rushing his fences. And rightly, he doesn't hesitate to use the resonantly full resources of the Guilimiau organ (superbly recorded), even though these are a little more lavish than was typical of the English organs of the period. An important issue for the organ fraternity. For others, a Restoration byway vividly restor'd.

A High-Priz'd Noise Violin Music for Charles I. **Parley of Instruments Renaissance Violin Band /
Peter Holman.** Hyperion Ⓕ CDA66806 (67 minutes: DDD: 6/96). 🎵 Recorded 1995. Ⓖ
R. Johnson II The Prince's Alman and Coranto. Air in G minor. The Temporiser a 4. The
Witty Wanton. Fantasia in G minor. **A. Ferrabosco II** Pavan and Alman. **Webster** Four
Consort pieces. **Nau** Suite in F major. Ballet in F major. Pavan and Galliard in D minor. **Notari**
Variations on the "Ruggiero". **W. Lawes** Alman in D major "for the Violins of Two Trebles".
Airs for consort.

This recording is less concerned with musical monuments, such as Lawes's large consorts, than in rejuvenating a repertoire which might have accompanied the King's recreation, or been the actual means for it. Most of the works are written in dance forms, though we can be reasonably certain that the majority would not have been conceived for accompanying dance. The violin's specific association with active dance music – except of a more base and popular kind – goes only so far, as the seventeenth century progresses. Of the courtly violin bands it is the more expansive one in the Presence Chamber (performing for public rather than private space at court) which has the most instantly appealing repertory – the opening set of works by Robert Johnson and the wonderful *Pavan and Alman* by Alphonso Ferrabosco II; the latter composition, although timeless in its exquisite part-writing, is given new life with a period violin band. Both pieces gleam with an engaging transparency, a compelling sound for those who have yet to hear this ensemble. The *Pavan* is magically forthcoming in its gracious lines with just a hint of melancholy, a poignant fragility which gives way to the noble rapture of the *Alman*. The Parley's 14-strong group of four violins, six violas and four bass violins is marshalled with a degree of characterization that gleefully extricates this music from dusty library shelves. A high-priz'd noise indeed, with further insights into our rich instrumental heritage, performed here with fragrance and deep affection.

Three Parts upon a Ground John Holloway, Stanley Ritchie, Andrew Manze (vns); Nigel North
(theorbo); Mary Springfels (va da gamba); John Toll (hpd/org). Harmonia Mundi Ⓕ HMU90
7091 (65 minutes: DDD: 1/94). 🎵 Recorded 1993.
Purcell Fantasia upon a Ground, Z731. **G. Gabrieli** Canzone et Sonate – Sonata per tre violini.
Marini Sonata in Ecco con tre violini. Sonatae, Op. 22 – Sonata terza a tre. **Uccellini** Sinfonici,

Op. 9 – Sinfonia nona a tre violini. **Fontana** Sonate a 1, 2, 3 – Sonata seidici. **Buonamente** Sonata a tre violini. **Constantin** Pavan. **Schmelzer** Sonata a tre. **Hacquart** Harmonia parnassia – Sonata decima. **Rosier** Suite for Three Violins. **Pachelbel** Canon and Gigue in D major.

While everyone will know the Purcell and Pachelbel grounds that frame the programme, the rest will be revelatory. The early Italian sonatas for three violins are, like their vocal counterparts, rhetorical and virtuosic. There are solo passages, imitative passages, dialogues between one violin and the others (especially in the Gabrieli Sonata), thrusting scales and delicate asides (in the Uccellini *Sinfonia*), and harmonically directed passages of resonant homophony. The rapport between the violinists is particularly evident in Marini's *Sonata in Ecco*, where not only is the spatial effect of the echoes brought off extremely effectively, but the slowing, cascading echoes over an organ pedal enchant by their novelty. The performances are polished and interactive, with Holloway, Ritchie and Manze approaching the music with a mixture of enthusiasm, stylishness and control. In sum: extremely entertaining.

New review

Sweeter than Roses Catherine Bott (sop); Pamela Thorby (rec); Anthony Robson (ob); Pavlo Beznosiuk, Rachel Podger (vns); Paula Chateauneuf (theorbo/gtr); Richard Egarr (hpd); Mark Levy (bass viol). L'Oiseau-Lyre Ⓟ 443 699-2OH (58 minutes: DDD: 4/96). ✎ Texts included. **Purcell** The History of King Richard II – Retir'd from any mortal's sight. King Arthur – Fairest isle. Sir Anthony Love – Pursuing Beauty. Oedipus – Music for a while. Henry the Second, King of England – In vain 'gainst love I strove. Rule a Wife and Have a Wife – There's not a swain. The Fairy Queen – Thrice happy lovers; O let me weep ("The Plaint"). The Married Beau – See where repenting Celia lies. Timon of Athens – The cares of lovers. Tyrannic Love – Ah! how sweet it is to love. The Tempest – Dear pretty youth. Bonduca – O lead me to some peaceful gloom. Pausanias – Sweeter than roses. **Locke** My lodging it is on the cold ground. **Blow** Lovely Selina, innocent and free. **Draghi** Where art thou, God of Dreams? **Courteville** Creep, creep, softly, creep. **J. Eccles** The Villain – Find me a lonely cave. **Weldon** The Tempest – Dry those eyes; Halcyon days. Recorded 1994.

This recital is a well-balanced exposé of theatre songs, starting appropriately with a founding father of Restoration musical sensibility in Matthew Locke. Then via clusters of Purcell songs, the later generation of Weldon and Eccles are represented, poignantly, in songs from plays produced in the wake of Purcell's death. Not all the Purcell examples are blockbusters though "Fairest isle", with some contemporary embellishments, reinforces its show-stopping qualities; "Retir'd from any mortal's sight" and the much later "The cares of lovers" are genuine declamatory songs which tickle the senses through more arcane means than the measured melodic invention of the ground bass songs such as "Music for a while" or Blow's *Lovely Selina*. In every genre, Bott always seem to know the time and place to impose herself and when objective dignity is the most effective means of projecting the sentiment (such as "The Plaint" which is never cool but, still, distinctly unpersonal as it is in *The Fairy Queen*). Indeed, most impressive perhaps is the way Bott imparts a broadly self-contained context to each song, not an easy task given that the purpose of such songs in the Restoration theatre is anything but consistent; she warms to Draghi's noble incantation in a glowing and moving account of *Where art thou, God of Dreams?*. She also delivers a fine sense of colour (occasionally it sits a little too brightly) and perspective throughout, knowing when vocally to 'withdraw' the sound into something quietly hypnotic, as in Eccles's "Find me a lonely cave" and when plain speaking is in order, as in Purcell's "Pursuing Beauty". The instrumental contributions are worthy, if a touch undercharacterized. In short, this is a fine recital which deserves to be widely heard.

Films and Show music

Suggested listening ...

...Big War Themes. **Jarre** Lawrence of Arabia. Is Paris Burning?. **Tiomkin** The Guns of Navarone. **Goodwin** Battle of Britain. Where Eagles Dare. 633 Squadron. **Coates** The Dam Busters – march. Eighth Army march. **Anka** The Longest Day. **E. Bernstein** The Great Escape. **Rózsa** The Green Berets. **Myers** The Deer Hunter – Cavatina. **Cobert** The Winds of War. **Farnon** Colditz. **Parker** Sink the Bismark. **Rodgers** Victory at Sea – excerpts. **King** We'll Meet Again. **Addison** Reach for the Sky. **Geoff Love and His Orchestra.** Compacts for Pleasure CC211.

...Blood and Thunder: Parades, Processionals and Attacks from Hollywood's Most Epic Films. **Rózsa** Ben-Hur. **A. Newman** Captain from Castile. **North** Cleopatra. **Goldsmith** The Wind and the Lion. **Herrmann** North by Northwest. **E. Bernstein** The Ten Commandments. **Waxman** Taras Bulba. **Kaper** Mutiny on the Bounty. **Seattle Symphony Orchestra / Cliff Eidelman.** Varèse Sarabande VSD5561.

...Captain Blood: Classic Film Scores for Errol Flynn. **Steiner** The Adventures of Don Juan – Suite. They Died With Their Boots On – Suite. Dodge City – Suite. **Waxman** Objective, Burma! – Parachute drop. **Korngold** The Sea Hawk – Suite[a]. Captain Blood – Ship in the night. The Adventures of Robin Hood – Suite. **Friedhofer** The Sun Also Rises – Prologue; The lights of Paris. [a]**Ambrosian Singers; National Philharmonic Orchestra / Charles Gerhardt.** RCA Victor Gold Seal GD80912 (11/91).

...Casablanca: Classic Film Scores for Humphrey Bogart. **Steiner** Casablanca – Suite. Passage to Marseille – Rescue at sea. The Treasure of the Sierra Madre – Suite. The Big Sleep – Love Themes. The Caine Mutiny – March. Virginia City – Stagecoach; Love scene. Key Largo – Suite. **Waxman** To Have and Have Not – main title. The Two Mrs Carrolls – Suite. **Young** The Left Hand of God – Love Theme. **Hollander** Sabrina – main title. **Rózsa** Sahara – main title. **National Philharmonic Orchestra / Charles Gerhardt.** RCA Victor Gold Seal GD80422 (10/90).

...Classic British Film Music. **Vaughan Williams** Coastal Command – Suite. **Easdale** The Red Shoes – Ballet. **Schurmann** Attack and celebration. **Bliss** Conquest of the Air – Suite. **Philharmonia Orchestra / Kenneth Alwyn.** Silva Screen FILMCD713.

...Classic Film Scores for Bette Davis. **Steiner** Now, Voyager – It can't be wrong. Dark Victory – excerpts A Stolen Life – main title. In This Our Life – Suite. Jezebel – waltz. Beyond the Forest – Suite. The Letter – main title. All This and Heaven Too – Suite. **Korngold** The Private Lives of Elizabeth and Essex – Elizabeth. Juarez – Carlotta. **Waxman** Mr Skeffington – Forsaken. **Newman** All About Eve – main title. **National Philharmonic Orchestra / Charles Gerhardt.** RCA Victor Gold Seal GD80183 (3/90).

...A Gala Concert for Hal Prince. **Sondheim** A Funny Thing Happened on the Way to the Forum. Pacific Overtures. Sweeney Todd. Follies. A Little Night Music. Company. **L. Bernstein** West Side Story. Candide. **Bock** Fiddler on the Roof. She Loves Me. **Kander** Cabaret. Kiss of the Spider Woman. **Lloyd Webber** Evita. The Phantom of the Opera. **Kern** Show Boat. **1995 Munich Cast; Munich Radio Orchestra / Charles Prince.** First Night DOCRCD2 (8/96).

...The Great Fantasy Adventure Album. **Rózsa** El Cid. **Williams** Hook. Jurassic Park. **Kamen** Robin Hood, Prince of Thieves. **Doyle** Henry V. **Horner** Willow. The Rocketeer. **Silvestri** The Abyss. **Rosenthal** Clash of the Titans. **Herrmann** The Seventh Voyage of Sinbad. **Elfman** Beetlejuice. **Goldsmith** Total Recall. **Knopfler** The Princess Bride. **Holdridge** Wizards and Warriors. **Poledouris** Conan the Barbarian. The Hunt for Red October. **Fiedel** The Terminator. **Cincinnati Pops Orchestra / Erich Kunzel.** Telarc CD80342.

...The Great Waltz. **Tiomkin** The Great Waltz. **R.R. Bennett** Murder on the Orient Express. **Herrmann** The Snows of Kilimanjaro. **Loewe** Gigi. **Rózsa** Madame Bovary. **Waxman** Hotel Berlin. **Steiner** Jezebel. **Korngold** The Prince and the Pauper. **Ravel** La Valse. **R. Strauss** Der Rosenkavalier. **Prokofiev** Cinderella. **Sondheim** A Little Night Music. **L. Bernstein** Candide. **Hollywood Bowl Orchestra / John Mauceri.** Philips 438 685-2PH (6/94).

...A History of Hitchcock: Dial M for Murder. **Gounod** Funeral March of the Marionette. **Waxman** Rebecca – Suite; Suspicion – excerpts. **Rózsa** Spellbound – Concerto for Orchestra. **Addinsell** Under Capricorn – Suite. **Tiomkin** Dial M for Murder – Suite. **Herrmann** Vertigo; North by Northwest; Psycho; Marnie – excerpts. **Jarre** Topaz – March. **Goodwin** Frenzy – London Theme. **City of Prague Philharmonic Orchestra / Paul Bateman.** Silva Screen FILMCD137 (3/94).

...A History of Hitchcock: To Catch a Thief. **Murray** To Catch a Thief – Suite. **Beaver/Levy** The 39 Steps – Suite. **Williams/Levy** The Lady Vanishes – Prelude. **Friedhofer** Lifeboat Disaster. **Poulenc/Buttolph** Rope – main titles. **Lucas** Stage Fright – Rhapsody. **Tiomkin** Strangers on a Train – Suite. **Waxman** Rear Window – Lisa. **Herrmann** The Trouble with Harry – A Portrait of Hitch. Vertigo – Prelude/The Nightmare. North by Northwest – Conversation piece. **Addison** Torn Curtain – main title. **Williams** Family Plot – Finale. **City of Prague Philharmonic Orchestra / Paul Bateman.** Silva Screen FILMCD159.

...Hollywood '95. **Goldenthal** Batman Forever. **Horner** Apollo 13. Casper. Braveheart. **Silvestri** Judge Dredd. **Goldsmith** Judge Dredd – trailer music. First Knight. **Howard** Waterworld.

Rózsa That Hamilton Woman. **Royal Scottish National Orchestra / Joel McNeely.** Varèse Sarabande VSD5671 (9/96).

…Hollywood Dreams. **Schoenberg** Fanfare for the Hollywood Bowl. **Rodgers** Carousel – Waltz. **Steiner** Gone with the Wind – main title. **Stravinsky** The Firebird – Lullaby; Finale. **Newman** Twentieth Century-Fox fanfare. Street scene. **Waxman** A Place in the Sun – suite. **Bernstein** On the Waterfront – Love Theme. **Arlen/Stothart** The Wizard of Oz – Suite. **Prokofiev** Semyon Kotko – Southern night. **Gore** Defending Your Life – finale. **Barry** Dances with Wolves – Theme. **Korngold** The Adventures of Robin Hood – excerpts. **Williams** ET – Flying. **Hollywood Bowl Orchestra / John Mauceri.** Philips 432 109-2PH (9/91).

…Horror! **Schurmann** Horrors of the Black Museum. Konga. **Searle** The Haunting. The Abominable Snowman. **Orr** Corridors of Blood. Fiend Without a Face. **Parker** Night of the Demon. **Ferris** Witchfinder General. **Martelli** The Curse of the Mummy's Tomb. **Bernard** The Devil Rides Out. **Frankel** The Curse of the Werewolf. **Westminster Philharmonic Orchestra / Kenneth Alwyn.** Silva Screen FILMCD175 (9/96).

…The Prince and the Pauper. **Korngold** Between Two Worlds. The Constant Nymph. The Prince and the Pauper. Escape Me Never. **Williams** The Reivers. Jane Eyre. **Rózsa** The Lost Weekend. **Antheil** The Specter of the Rose. **Lewis** The Madwoman of Chaillot. **North** Cleopatra. Who's Afraid of Virginia Woolf? **Pennario** Julie. **Delerue** Anne of the 1000 Days. **Walton** Henry V. **National Philharmonic Orchestra / Charles Gerhardt.** Varèse Sarabande VSD5207 (6/90)….True Grit: Music from the Classic Films of John Wayne. **Hageman** Stagecoach – Suite; She Wore a Yellow Ribbon – Leaving the fort. **Young** The Quiet Man – Suite. **Tiomkin** The High and the Mighty; The Alamo – Overture. **Steiner** The Searchers – Suite. **Newman** How the West Was Won. **Anka** The Longest Day. **Goldsmith** In Harm's Way Suite. **Williams** The Cowboys – Overture. **City of Prague Philharmonic Orchestra / Paul Bateman.** Silva Screen FILMCD153 (11/94).

Information

Gramophone
Awards winners

Now in their nineteenth year, *The Gramophone Awards* have established themselves as the most important event in the classical record industry's year. Out of the 3,000 or so discs that are issued each year, here is an opportunity to focus on some of the truly outstanding releases in a variety of categories. The following list of Award winners from 1977 to 1995 bears witness not only to the extraordinary musical talent that has been preserved on record for posterity but also the soundness of the voting procedure in picking out the great recordings of a given year – many have gone on to become classics of the gramophone and first choices years after being released.

1977

Chamber
Shostakovich String Quartets Nos. 4 and 12 *Fitzwilliam Quartet*
Decca 433 078-2DM6 (contains Nos. 1-15, 6/92)
Choral
Elgar Coronation Ode Parry I was glad
Traditional (arr. Elgar) The National Anthem *Soloists; Kings College Choir, Cambridge; Cambridge University Musical Society; Band of the Royal Military School of Music, Kneller Hall; New Philharmonic Orchestra / Philip Ledger*
EMI CDZ7 62528-2
Concerto
Mozart Piano Concerto No. 22. Rondos, K382 and K386 *Alfred Brendel (pf); Academy of St Martin in the Fields / Sir Neville Marriner*
Philips 422 507-2 (4/86)
Contemporary
Berio Concerto for Two Pianos. Nones. Allelujah II *Bruno Canino, Antonio Ballista (pfs); London Symphony Orchestra; BBC Symphony Orchestra / Pierre Boulez, Luciano Berio*
RCA Victor Red Seal RL11674 (8/77) nla†
Early music
Dowland Lute works *Julian Bream*
RCA Victor Red Seal 09026 61586-2 (11/87)
Historic
The Record of Singing, Vol. 1 *Various artists and accompaniments*
HMV mono RLS724 (1/78) nla†
Instrumental
Beethoven Piano Sonatas Nos. 27-32. *Maurizio Pollini (pf)*
DG 419 199-2GH2 (12/86)
Opera and Record of the year
Janáček Kata Kabanová *Vienna State Opera Chorus; VPO / Sir Charles Mackerras*
Decca 421 852-2DH2 (10/89)
Orchestral
Elgar Symphony No. 1 *London Philharmonic Orchestra / Sir Adrian Boult*
EMI CDM7 64013-2
Solo vocal
Shostakovich Suite on Verses of Michelangelo, Op. 145. Six Songs to Lyrics by English poets. Six Songs to Poems by Marina Tsvetayeva *Soloists; Moscow Radio Symphony Orchestra / Maxim Shostakovich; Moscow Chamber Orchestra / Rudolf Barshai*
HMV Melodiya SLS5078 (5/77) nla†

1978

Chamber
Bartók Sonata for Two Pianos and Percussion Debussy En blanc et noir **Mozart** Andante and Variations, K501 *Martha Argerich, Stephen Kovacevich (pfs); Willy Goudswaard, Michael de Roo (perc)*
Philips 9500 434 (8/78) nla†
Choral
Handel Dixit Dominus. Zadok the Priest *Soloists; Monteverdi Choir and Orchestra / John Eliot Gardiner*
Erato 2292-45136-2
Concerto
Prokofiev Piano Concerto No. 1. Romeo and Juliet – excerpts **Ravel** Piano Concerto for the left-hand. Pavane pour une infante défunte *Andrei Gavrilov; London Symphony Orchestra / Simon Rattle*
EMI Studio Plus CDM7 64329-2 (9/78) nla†
Contemporary
Webern Complete works, Vol. 1 *Various artists and ensembles / Pierre Boulez*
Sony Classical SM3K45845 (6/91)
Early music
Handel Acis and Galatea *Soloists; English Baroque Soloists / John Eliot Gardiner*
Archiv Produktion 423 406-2AH2 (8/88)
Historic
Gluck Orfeo ed Euridice *Kathleen Ferrier (contr); Greet Koeman (sop); Nel Duval (sop); Netherlands Opera Chorus and Orchestra / Charles Bruck*
EMI mono CDH7 61003-2 (6/88)
Instrumental
Liszt Piano works *Alfred Brendel (pf)*
Philips 9500 286 (5/78) nla†
Opera and Record of the year
Puccini La Fanciulla del West *Soloists; Chorus and Orchestra of the Royal Opera House, Covent Garden / Zubin Mehta*
DG 419 640-2GH2 (11/87)
Orchestral
Mozart Symphonies Nos. 25 and 29 *English Chamber Orchestra / Benjamin Britten*
Decca 430 495-2DWO (10/91) nla†
Solo vocal
Chausson Poème de l'amour et de la mer **Duparc** Mélodies. *Dame Janet Baker; London Symphony Orchestra / André Previn*
HMV ASD3455 (4/78) nla†

1979

Chamber and Record of the year
Haydn Piano Trios *Beaux Arts Trio*
Philips 432 061-2PM9 (7/92)

Choral
Schoenberg Gurrelieder *Soloists; Tanglewood Festival Chorus; Boston Symphony Orchestra / Seiji Ozawa*
Philips 412 511-2PH2 (3/85)

Concerto
Bartók Piano Concertos Nos. 1 and 2 *Maurizio Pollini; Chicago Symphony Orchestra / Claudio Abbado*
DG 415 371-2GH (9/86)

Contemporary
Maxwell Davies Symphony No. 1 *Philharmonia Orchestra / Simon Rattle*
Decca HEAD21 (11/79) nla†

Early music
Mozart Symphonies, Vol. 3 *Academy of Ancient Music / Jaap Schröder, Christopher Hogwood*
L'Oiseau-Lyre 417 592-2OH3

Engineering
Debussy Images. Prélude à l'après-midi d'un faune. *London Symphony Orchestra / André Previn*
EMI CDZ7 62504-2

Historic
The Record of Singing, Vol. 2 *Various artists and accompaniments*
HMV mono RLS743 (1/80) nla†

Instrumental
Bach Organ works, Vol. 3 *Peter Hurford*
Argo 414 206-1ZX25 (11/85) nla†

Opera
Berg Lulu *Soloists; Paris Opéra Orchestra / Pierre Boulez*
DG 415 489-2GH3 (11/86)

Orchestral
Debussy Images. Prélude à l'après-midi d'un faune *London Symphony Orchestra / André Previn*
EMI CDZ7 62504-2

Solo vocal
Grechaninov Five children's songs, Op. 39
Mussorgsky The Nursery Prokofiev The Ugly Duckling *Elisabeth Söderström (sop); Vladimir Ashkenazy (pf)*
Decca SXL6900 (7/79) nla†

1980

Chamber
Brahms Piano Quintet *Maurizio Pollini; Quartetto Italiano*
DG 419 673-2GH (6/87)

Choral
Handel L'Allegro, il Penseroso ed il Moderato *Soloists; Monteverdi Choir; English Baroque Soloists / John Eliot Gardiner*
Erato 2292-45377-2 (7/85)

Concerto
Ravel Piano Concerto in G major. Piano Concerto for the left-hand *Jean-Philippe Collard; French National Orchestra / Lorin Maazel*
HMV ASD3845 (6/80) nla†

Contemporary
Birtwistle Punch and Judy *Soloists; London Sinfonietta / David Atherton*
Etcetera KTC2014 (12/89)

Early music
C.P.E. Bach Sinfonias *English Concert / Trevor Pinnock*
Archiv Produktion 415 300-2AH (5/86)

Engineering
Debussy Nocturnes. Jeux *Concertgebouw Orchestra / Bernard Haitink*
Philips 438 742-2PM2 (6/94)

Historic non-vocal
Bartók Mikrokosmos – excerpts. Contrasts *Béla Bartók (pf); Joseph Szigeti (vn); Benny Goodman (cl)*
Sony mono CD47676 (12/80)

Historic vocal
The Gramophone Company Recordings 1902-1909 *Fernando de Lucia (ten) with various accompaniments*
Rubini mono RS305 (3/80) nla†

Instrumental
Brahms Piano Sonatas Nos. 1 and 2. *Krystian Zimerman (pf)*
DG 2531 252 (6/80) nla†

Opera and Record of the year
Janáček From the House of the Dead. *Soloists; Vienna State Opera Chorus; Vienna Philharmonic Orchestra / Sir Charles Mackerras*
Decca 430 375-2DH2 (10/91)

Orchestral
Debussy Nocturnes. Jeux *Concertgebouw Orchestra / Bernard Haitink*
Philips 438 742-2PM2 (6/94)

Solo vocal
Butterworth A Shropshire Lad. Musical Settings of Housman *Graham Trew (bar); Roger Vignoles (pf)*
Meridian CDE84185 (11/90)

1981

Chamber
Bartók String Quartets Nos. 1-6, *Tokyo Quartet*
DG 445 241-2GC3 (10/94)

Choral
Delius The Fenby Legacy. *Soloists; Royal Philharmonic Orchestra / Eric Fenby*
Unicorn-Kanchana DKPCD9008/9 (12/87)

Concerto
Beethoven Violin Concerto *Itzhak Perlman (vn); Philharmonia Orchestra / Carlo Maria Giulini*
EMI CDC7 47002-2 (2/84)

Contemporary
Tippett King Priam *Soloists London Sinfonietta and Chorus / David Atherton*
Decca 414 241-2LH2 (1/90)

Early music
German Chamber music before Bach *Musica Antiqua Köln*
Archiv Produktion 2723 078 (10/81) nla†

Engineering
Massenet Werther *Soloists, Children's Choir; Orchestra of the Royal Opera House, Covent Garden / Sir Colin Davis*
Philips 416 654-2PH2 (2/87)

Historic non-vocal
Brahms Chamber works *Busch Quartet; Rudolf Serkin (pf); Reginald Kell (cl); Aubrey Brain (hn)*
World Records mono SHB61 (4/81) nla†

Historic vocal
The Hugo Wolf Society Lieder Vols. 1-7 *Various artists*
HMV mono RLS759 (3/81) nla†

Instrumental
Liszt Piano works *Brendel*
Philips 420 837-2PM nla†

Opera and Record of the year
Wagner Parsifal *Soloists; Chorus of the Deutsche Opera, Berlin; Berlin Philharmonic Orchestra / Herbert von Karajan*
DG 413 347-2H4 (10/84)

Orchestral
Mahler Symphony No. 9 *Berlin Philharmonic Orchestra / Herbert von Karajan*
DG 410 726-2GH2 (7/84)

Solo vocal
Liszt Lieder *Dietrich Fischer-Dieskau (bar); Daniel Barenboim (pf)*
DG 2740 254 (10/81) nla†

1982-83

Chamber
Borodin String Quartets Nos. 1 and 2. *Borodin Quartet*
EMI CDC7 47795-2 (5/88)

Choral
Bach Mass in B minor *Soloists; Bach Ensemble / Joshua Rifkin*
Elektra Nonesuch 7559-79036-2

Concerto and Record of the year
Tippett Triple Concerto *György Pauk; Nobuko Imai; Ralph Kirshbaum; London Symphony Orchestra / Sir Colin Davis*
Philips 420 781-2PH (3/89)

Contemporary
Boulez Pli selon pli *Phyllis Bryn-Julson (sop); BBC Symphony Orchestra / Pierre Boulez*
Erato 2292-45376-2 (3/89)

Early music – Baroque
Charpentier Actéon *Soloists; Les Arts Florissants / William Christie*
Harmonia Mundi HMA 190 1095

Early music – Medieval and Renaissance
Hildegard of Bingen Sequences and Hymns. *Gothic Voices / Christopher Page*
Hyperion CDA66039 (7/85)

Engineering
Shostakovich Symphony No. 5 *Concertgebouw Orchestra / Bernard Haitink*
Decca 425 066-2DH (9/83)

Historic non-vocal
Bartók At the piano, 1920-45, Vol. 1 *Béla Bartok(pf)*
Hungaraton mono HCD12326/31 nla†

Historic vocal
Schubert Historical recordings of Lieder (1898-1952) *Various artists*
HMV mono RLS766 (9/82) nla†

Instrumental
Liszt Piano Sonata in B minor. Légende. La lugubre gondola Nos. 1 and 2 *Alfred Brendel (pf)*
Philips 410 040-2PH (10/83) nla†

Opera
Janáček The Cunning Little Vixen *Soloists; Vienna State Opera Chorus; Bratislava Children's Choir; Vienna Philharmonic Orchestra / Sir Charles Mackerras*
Decca 417 129-2DH2 (11/86)

Orchestral
R. Strauss Metamorphosen for 23 solo strings. Tod und Verklärung *Berlin Philharmonic Orchestra / Herbert von Karajan*
DG 410 892-2GH (2/84)

Solo vocal
Brahms Lieder *Jessye Norman (sop); Dietrich Fischer-Dieskau (bar); Daniel Barenboim (pf)*
Philips 411 052-2PH (9/87)

1984

Chamber
Beethoven String Quartets Nos. 12-16 Grosse Fuge *Lindsay Quartet*
ASV CDDCS403 (1/89)

Choral
Mozart Requiem *Soloists; Leipzig Radio Chorus; Dresden Staatskapelle / Peter Schreier*
Philips 411 420-2PH (6/84)

Concerto
Mozart Piano Concertos Nos. 15 and 16 *English Chamber Orchestra / Murray Perahia (pf)*
CBS Masterworks CD37824

Contemporary
Carter String Quartet No. 3 Ferneyhough String Quartet No. 2 Harvey String Quartet No. 2 *Arditti Quartet*
RCA Victor Red Seal RS9006 (5/84) nla†

Early music – Baroque
Bach Chamber works *Musica Antiqua Köhn / Reinhard Goebel*
Archiv Produktion 2742 007 (1/84) nla†

Early music – Medieval and Renaissance
Dunstable Motets *Hilliard Ensemble / Paul Hillier*
HMV ASD146703-1 (5/84) nla†

Engineering and production
Bax Symphony No. 4. Tintagel *Ulster Orchestra / Bryden Thomson*
Chandos CHAN8312 (8/84)

Historic non-vocal
Beethoven Piano Sonatas Nos. 30-32 *Egon Petri (pf)*
dell'Arte mono DA9012 nla†

Historic vocal
Brahms. Schumann Historical Recordings of Lieder (1901-1952) *Various artists*
HMV mono RLS154700-3 (/84) nla†

Instrumental
Beethoven Piano Sonata No. 29, "Hammerklavier" *Emil Gilels (pf)*
DG 410 527-2GH (2/84)

Opera
Janáček Jenůfa *Soloists; Chorus; Vienna Philharmonic Orchestra / Sir Charles Mackerras*
Decca 414 483-2DH2 (12/85)

Orchestral and Record of the year
Mahler Symphony No. 9 *Berlin Philharmonic Orchestra / Herbert von Karajan*
DG 410 726-2GH2 (7/84)

Solo vocal
R. Strauss Four Last Songs. *Jessye Norman (sop); Leipzig Gewandhaus Orchestra / Kurt Masur*
Philips 411 052-2PH (2/84)

1985

Chamber
Beethoven String Quartets Nos. 12-16. Grosse Fuge *Alban Berg Quartet*
EMI CDS7 47135-8 (8/85)

Choral
Fauré Requiem (ed. Rutter). Cantique de Jean Racine (orch. Rutter) *Soloists; Cambridge Singers; City of London Sinfonia / John Rutter*
Collegium COLCD109 (1/89)

Concerto and Record of the year
Elgar Violin Concerto *Nigel Kennedy (vn); London Philharmonic Orchestra / Vernon Handley*
EMI CD-EMX2058 (12/84)

Contemporary
Kurtág Messages du feu Demoiselle R.V. Troussová Birtwistle ... agm ... *Adrienne Csengery (sop); Marta Fabian (cymbalum); John Alldis Choir; Ensemble InterContemporain / Pierre Boulez*
Erato STU71543 (9/84) nla†

Early music – Baroque
Charpentier Medée *Les Arts Florissants / William Christie*
Harmonia Mundi HMC90 1139/41 (3/85)

Early music – Medieval and Renaissance
Victoria Masses and Motets *Westminster Cathedral Choir / David Hill*
Hyperion CDA66114 (6/86)
Engineering
Ravel Ma mère l'oye. Pavane pour une infante défunte. Le tombeau de Couperin. Valses nobles et sentimentales *Montreal Symphony Orchestra / Charles Dutoit*
Decca 410 254-2DH (11/84)
Historic non-vocal
Nielsen Symphonies Nos. 1-6 *Danish Radio Symphony Orchestra / Erik Tuxen, Thomas Jensen, Launy Grøndahl*
Danacord mono DAC0121/3 (7/84)nla†
Historic vocal
Opera Arias and Songs *Claudia Muzio (sop); orchestra / Lorenzo Molajoli, Licinio Refice*
EMI Références mono CDH7 69790-2 (8/89) nla†
Instrumental
Liszt Annèes de Pélèrinage, Première année "Suisse" *Jorge Bolet (pf)*
Decca 410 160-2DH (12/84)
Opera
Mozart Don Giovanni *Soloists; Glyndebourne Festival Chorus; London Philharmonic Orchestra / Bernard Haitink*
EMI CDS7 47037-8 (12/84)
Orchestral
Prokofiev Symphony No. 6. Waltz Suite, Op. 110 – Nos. 1, 5 and 6 *Scottish National Orchestra / Neeme Järvi*
Chandos CHAN8359 (7/85)
Solo vocal
Sibelius Songs *Elisabeth Söderström (sop); Tom Krause (bar); Vladimir Ashkenazy, Irwin Gage (pfs)*
Argo 411 739-1ZH5 (2/85) nla†

1986

Chamber
Fauré Piano Quartets Nos. 1 and 2 *Domus*
Hyperion CDA66166
Choral
Janáček Glagolitic Mass *Soloists; Czech Philharmonic Chorus and Orchestra / Sir Charles Mackerras*
Supraphon C37-7448 (10/86)
Concerto
Beethoven Piano Concertos Nos. 3 and 4 *Murray Perahia (pf); Concertgebouw Orchestra / Bernard Haitink*
CBS Masterworks CD39814 (10/86)
Contemporary
Lutosławski Symphony No. 3. Les espaces du sommeil *John Shirley-Quirk (bar); Los Angeles Philharmonic Orchestra / Esa-Pekka Salonen*
CBS Masterwrks CD42271 (6/87)
Early music – Baroque
Bach The Art of Fugue *Davitt Moroney (hpd)*
Harmonia Mundi HMC90 1169/70 (5/86)
Early music – Medieval and Renaissance
Chansons de Toile *Esther Lamandier (sop)*
Alienor AL1011 (5/86) nla†
Engineering and production
Respighi Belkis, Queen of Sheba – orchestral suite. Metamorphosen modi XII *Philharmonia Orchestra / Geoffrey Simon*
Chandos CHAN8405 (5/86)
Historic non-vocal
Beethoven String Quartets Nos. 1, 9, 11-12 and 14-16. Violin Sonatas Nos. 3, 5 and 7 *Busch Quartet; Rudolf Serkin (pf)*
HMV mono EX290306-3 (11/85) nla†

Historic vocal
The Record of Singing, Vol. 3 *Various artists and accompaniments*
HMV mono EX290169-3 (10/85) nla†
Instrumental
Mozart Sonata for Two Pianos in D major Schubert Fantasia in F minor *Murray Perahia, Radu Lupu (pfs)*
Sony Classical SK39511 (10/86)
Opera and Record of the year
Rossini Il Viaggio a Reims *Soloists; Prague Philharmonic Chorus; Chamber Orchestra of Europe / Claudio Abbado*
DG 415 498-2GH2 (1/86)
Orchestral
Vaughan Williams Sinfonia antartica *Sheila Armstrong (sop); London Philharmonic Choir and Orchestra / Bernard Haitink*
EMI CDC7 47516-2 (1/87)
Remastered Compact Disc
Britten Peter Grimes *Soloists; Chorus and Orchestra of the Royal Opera House, Covent Garden / Benjamin Britten*
Decca 414 577-2DH3 (4/86)
Solo vocal
Schubert Winterreise *Peter Schreier (ten); Sviatoslav Richter (pf)*
Philips 416 289-2PH2 (3/86) nla†

1987

Chamber
Chausson Concert for Piano, Violin and String Quartet. String Quartet *Jean-Philippe Collard (pf); Augustin Dumay (vn); Muir Quartet*
EMI CDC74/548-2 nla†
Choral
Handel Athalia *Soloists; New College Choir, Oxford; Academy of Ancient Music / Christopher Hogwood*
L'Oiseau-Lyre 417 126-2OH2 (2/87)
Concerto
Hummel Piano Concertos – A minor; B minor *Stephen Hough (pf); English Chamber Orchestra / Bryden Thomson*
Chandos CHAN8507 (4/87)
Contemporary
Tippett The Mask of Time *Soloists; BBC Singers; BBC Symphony Orchestra / Andrew Davis*
EMI CMS7 64711-2 (10/87)
Early music and Record of the year
Josquin Desprez Masses – Pange lingua; La sol fa re mi *The Tallis Scholars / Peter Phillips*
Gimell CDGIM009 (3/87)
Engineering and production
Holst The Planets *Montreal Symphony Orchestra / Charles Dutoit*
Decca 417 553-2DH (4/87)
Historic non-vocal
Schubert String Quartets, D87, D112 and D810. Piano Trio, D929. Fantasia, D934 *Busch Quartet; Rudolf Serkin (pf)*
EMI mono EX290950-3 (10/86) nla†
Historic vocal
The Art of Tito Schipa *Tito Schipa (ten) with various artists and accompaniments*
EMI Treasury mono EX290948-2 (4/87) nla†
Instrumental
Haydn Complete Piano Sonatas *Alfred Brendel (pf)*
Philips 416 643-2PH4 (3/87)
Opera
Verdi La forza del destino *Soloists; Ambrosian Opera Chorus; Philharmonia Orchestra / Giuseppe Sinopoli*
DG 419 203-2GH3 (5/87)

Orchestral

Mahler Symphony No. 8 *Soloists; Tiffin Boys'
School Choir; London Philharmonic Choir and
Orchestra / Klaus Tennstedt*
EMI CDS7 47625-8 (5/87)

Period performance

Beethoven Symphonies Nos. 2 and 8 *London
Classical Players / Roger Norrington*
EMI CDC7 47698-2 (3/87)

Remastered Compact Disc

Beecham conducts Delius The Complete Stereo
Recordings *Royal Philharmonic Orchestra / Sir
Thomas Beecham*
EMI CDS7 47509-8 (6/87)

Solo vocal

Liszt. R. Strauss Lieder *Brigitte Fassbaender
(mez); Irwin Gage (pf)*
DG 419 238-2GH (4/87) nla†

1988

Chamber

Mendelssohn Violin Sonatas in F minor and
F major *Shlomo Mintz (vn); Paul Ostrovsky (pf)*
DG 419 244-2GH (8/87)

Choral

Verdi Messa da Requiem. Opera Choruses *Soloists;
Atlanta Symphony Orchestra and Chorus / Robert
Shaw*
Telarc CD80152 (3/88)

Concerto

Tchaikovsky Piano Concerto No. 2
(original version) *Peter Donohoe (pf); Bournemouth
Symphony Orchestra / Rudolf Barshai with Nigel
Kennedy (vn) and Steven Isserlis (vc)*
EMI CMS7 64887-2 (11/87)

Contemporary

Birtwistle Carmen Arcadiae Mechanicae
Perpetuum. Silbury Air. Secret Theatre *London
Sinfonietta / Elgar Howarth*
Etcetera KTC1052 (4/88)

Early music – Baroque

Leclair Scylla et Glaucus *Soloists; Monteverdi
Choir; English Baroque Soloists / John Eliot Gardiner*
Erato 2292-45277-2 (4/88)

Early music – Medieval and Renaissance

The Service of Venus and Mars *Andrew
Lawrence-King (medieval hp); Gothic Voices /
Christopher Page*
Hyperion CDA66238 (11/87)

Engineering and production

Mahler Symphony No. 2, "Resurrection" *Soloists;
City of Birmingham Symphony Orchestra and
Chorus / Simon Rattle*
EMI CDS7 47962-8 (12/87)

Historic non-vocal

Brahms Violin Concerto Sibelius Violin Concerto
*Ginette Neveu (vn); Philharmonia Orchestra / Issay
Dobrowen, Walter Susskind*
EMI Références mono CDH7 61011-2 (3/88)

Historic vocal

Feodor Chaliapin (1873-1938) *Feodor Chaliapin
(bass) with various artists and accompaniments*
EMI Treasury mono EX761065-1 (6/88) nla†

Instrumental

Poulenc Piano works *Pascal Rogé (pf)*
Decca 417 438-2DH (7/87)

Opera

Britten Paul Bunyan *Soloists; Plymouth Music
Series Chorus and Orchestra / Philip Brunelle*
Virgin Classics VCD7 59249-2 (8/88)

Orchestral and Record of the year

Mahler Symphony No. 2, "Resurrection" *Soloists;
City of Birmingham Symphony Orchestra and
Chorus / Simon Rattle*
EMI CDS7 47962-8 (12/87)

Period performance

Haydn Mass in D minor, "Nelson". Te Deum in
C major *Soloists; The English Concert and Choir /
Trevor Pinnock*
Archiv Produktion 423 097-2AH (2/88)

Remastered Compact Disc

R. Strauss Der Rosenkavalier *Soloists; Loughton
High School for Girls and Bancroft's School Choirs;
Philharmonia Chorus and Orchestra / Herbert von
Karajan*
EMI CDS7 49354-2 (1/88)

Solo vocal

Schubert Die schöne Müllerin *Olaf Bär (bar);
Geoffrey Parsons (pf)*
EMI CDC7 47947-2 (8/87)

1989

Chamber and Record of the year

Bartók String Quartets Nos. 1-6 *Emerson Quartet*
DG 423 657-2GH2 (12/88)

Choral

Handel Jephtha *Soloists; Monteverdi Choir; English
Baroque Soloists / John Eliot Gardiner*
Philips 422 351-2PH3 (6/89)

Concerto

Nielsen Violin Concerto Sibelius Violin Concerto
*Cho-Liang Lin (vn); Swedish Radio Symphony
Orchestra; Philharmonia Orchestra / Esa-Pekka
Salonen*
Sony SK44548 (1/89)

Contemporary

Simpson Symphony No. 9 *Bournemouth Symphony
Orchestra / Vernon Handley*
Hyperion CDA66299 (12/89)

Early music – Baroque

Corelli 12 Concerti grossi, Op. 6 *The English
Concert / Trevor Pinnock*
Archiv Produktion 423 626-2AH2 (1/89)

Early music – Medieval and Renaissance

A Song for Francesca *Andrew Lawrence-King
(medieval hp); Gothic Voices / Christopher Page*
Hyperion CDA66286 (12/88)

Engineering and production

Tubin Symphonies Nos. 3 and 8 *Swedish Radio
Symphony Orchestra / Neeme Järvi*
BIS CD342 (9/88)

Historic non-vocal

Mahler Symphony No. 9 *Vienna Philharmonic
Orchestra / Bruno Walter*
EMI Références mono CDH7 63029-2 (8/89)

Historic vocal

The Record of Singing, Vol. 4 *Various artists and
accompaniments*
EMI mono CHS7 69741-2 (4/89)

Instrumental

Mozart Complete Piano Sonatas *Mitsuko Uchida
(pf)*
Philips 422 115-2PH6 (2/89)

Music theatre

Kern/Hammerstein Show Boat *Soloists; Ambrosian
Chorus; London Sinfonietta / John McGlinn*
EMI CDS7 49108-2 (11/88)

Opera

Gershwin Porgy and Bess *Soloists; Glyndebourne
Chorus; London Philharmonic Orchestra / Simon
Rattle*
EMI CDS7 49568-2 (6/89)

Orchestral

Schubert Symphonies Nos. 1-6, 8 and 9. Overtures
Chamber Orchestra of Europe / Claudio Abbado
DG 423 651-2GH5 (2/89)

Remastered Compact Disc
Ravel L'enfant et les sortilèges *Soloists; Chorus and Children's Voices of French Radio; French Radio National Orchestra / Lorin Maazel*
DG 423 718-2GH (3/89)

Solo vocal
Schubert Lieder, Vol. 1 *Dame Janet Baker (mez); Graham Johnson (pf)*
Hyperion CDJ33001 (10/88)

1990

Baroque non-vocal
Bach Orchestral Suites, BWV1066-69 *Amsterdam Baroque Orchestra / Ton Koopman*
Deutsche Harmonia Mundi RD77864 (1/90)

Baroque vocal
Bach St Matthew Passion *Soloists; London Oratory Junior Choir; Monteverdi Choir; English Baroque Soloists / John Eliot Gardiner*
Archiv Produktion 427 648-2AH3 (10/89)

Chamber
Respighi Violin Sonata R. Strauss Violin Sonata *Kyung-Wha Chung (vn); Krystian Zimerman (pf)*
DG 427 617-2GH (2/90)

Choral
Schumann Das Paradies und die Peri *Soloists; Lausanne Pro Arte Choir; Suisse Romande Chamber Choir and Orchestra / Armin Jordan*
Erato 2292-45456-2 (4/90)

Concerto
Shostakovich Violin Concertos Nos. 1 and 2 *Lydia Mordkovitch (vn); Scottish National Orchestra / Neeme Järvi*
Chandos CHAN8820 (4/90)

Contemporary
G. Benjamin Antara Boulez Dérive. Memoriale J. Harvey Song Offerings *Penelope Walmsley-Clark (sop); Sebastien Bell (fl); London Sinfonietta / George Benjamin*
Nimbus NI5167 (10/89)

Early music
G. and A. Gabrieli A Venetian Coronation, 1595 *Gabrieli Consort and Players / Paul McCreesh*
Virgin Classics Veritas VC7 59006-2 (5/90)

Engineering
Britten Prince of the Pagodas *London Sinfonietta / Oliver Knussen*
Virgin Classics VCD7 59578-2 (7/90) nla†

Historic non-vocal
Delius Orchestral works *London Philharmonic Orchestra / Sir Thomas Beecham*
Sir Thomas Beecham Trust mono BEECHAM2 (6/89)

Historic vocal
Massenet Werther *Soloists; Cantoria Children's Choir, Chorus and Orchestra of the Opéra-Comique, Paris / Elie Cohen*
EMI Références mono CHS7 63195-2 (3/90) nla†

Instrumental
Debussy Piano works *Zoltán Kocsis (pf)*
Philips 422 404-2PH (2/90)

Music theatre
Porter Anything Goes *Soloists; Ambrosian Chorus; London Symphony Orchestra / John McGlinn*
EMI CDC7 49848-2 (12/89)

Opera and Record of the year
Prokofiev The Love for Three Oranges *Soloists; Chorus and Orchestra of Lyon Opéra / Kent Nagano*
Virgin Classics VCD7 59566-2 (12/89)

Orchestral
Vaughan Williams A Sea Symphony *Soloists; Cantilena; London Philharmonic Choir and Orchestra / Bernard Haitink*
EMI CDC7 49911-2 (1/90)

Solo vocal
Schubert Schwanengesang. Heine and Seidl Leider *Peter Schreier (ten); András Schiff (pf)*
Decca 425 612-2DH (6/90)

Special achievement
Bach Sacred Cantatas Vols. 1-45 *Soloists; Choruses; Vienna Concentus Musicus / Nikolaus Harnoncourt; Leonhardt Consort / Gustav Leonhardt*
Teldec – various catalogue numbers

1991

Baroque non-vocal
Biber Mystery Sonatas *John Holloway (vn); Davitt Moroney (org/hpd); Tragicomedia*
Virgin Classics Veritas VCD7 59551-2 (5/91)

Baroque vocal
Handel Susanna *Soloists; Chamber Chorus of the University of California, Berkeley; Philharmonia Baroque Orchestra / Nicholas McGegan*
Harmonia Mundi HMU90 7030/2 (10/90)

Chamber
Brahms Piano Quartets Nos. 1-3 *Isaac Stern (vn); Jaime Laredo (va); Yo-Yo Ma (vc); Emanuel Ax (pf)*
Sony Classical S2K45846 (3/91)

Choral and Record of the year
Beethoven Mass in D major, "Missa Solemnis" *Soloists; Monteverdi Choir; English Baroque Soloists / John Eliot Gardiner*
Archiv Produktion 429 779-2AH (3/91)

Concerto
Sibelius Violin Concerto *Leonid Kavakos (vn); Lahti Symphony Orchestra / Osmo Vänskä*
Bis CD500 (4/91)

Contemporary
Casken Golem *Soloists; Music Projects London / Richard Bernas*
Virgin Classics VCD7 59028-2 (8/91)

Early music
Palestrina Masses and Motets *The Tallis Scholars / Peter Phillips*
Gimell CDGIM020 (9/90)

Engineering
Wordsworth Symphonies Nos. 2 and 3 *London Philharmonic Orchestra / Nicholas Braithwaite*
Lyrita SRCD207 (11/90)

Historic non-vocal
Berg Violin Concerto. Lyric Suite *Louis Krasner (vn); Galimir Quartet; BBC Symphony Orchestra / Anton Webern*
Continuum mono SBT1004 (6/91)

Historic vocal
Fauré. Chausson French songs *Gérard Souzay (bar); Jacqueline Bonneau (pf)*
Decca mono 425 975-2DM (7/91)

Instrumental
Shostakovich 24 Preludes and Fugues. *Tatyana Nikolaieva (pf)*
Hyperion CDA66620 (3/91)

Music theatre
Sondheim Into the Woods *Original London Cast*
RCA Victor Red Seal RD60752 (9/91)

Opera
Mozart Idomeneo *Soloists; Monteverdi Choir; English Baroque Soloists / John Eliot Gardiner*
Archiv Produktion 431 674-2AH3 (6/91)

Orchestral
Nielsen Symphonies Nos. 2 and 3 *Nancy Walt Fromm (sop); Kevin McMillan (bar); San Francisco Symphony Orchestra / Herbert Blomstedt*
Decca 430 280-2DH (8/91)

Solo vocal
Schubert Die schöne Müllerin *Peter Schreier (ten);*
András Schiff (pf)
Decca 430 414-2DH (5/91)

Special achievement
Mozart Complete Edition *Various soloists,*
orchestras and conductors
Philips 422 501/45-2 (45 volumes: 180 discs)

1992

Baroque non-vocal
Rameau Harpsichord works *Christophe Rousset*
(hpd)
L'Oiseau-Lyre 425 886-2OH2 (12/91)

Baroque vocal
Handel Giulio Cesare *Soloists; Concerto Cologne /*
René Jacobs
Harmonia Mundi HMC90 1385/7 (4/92)

Chamber
Szymanowski String Quartets Nos. 1 and 2
Webern Slow Movement *Carmina Quartet*
Denon CO-79462 (3/92)

Choral
Britten War Requiem. Sinfonia da Requiem. Ballad
of Heroes *Soloists; St Paul's Cathedral Choir;*
London Symphony Chorus and Orchestra / Richard
Hickox
Chandos CHAN8983/4 (11/91)

Concerto
Medtner Piano Concertos Nos. 2 and 3 *Nikolai*
Demidenko (pf); BBC Scottish Symphony Orchestra
/ Jerzy Maksymiuk
Hyperion CDA66580 (4/92)

Contemporary
Tavener The Protecting Veil. Thrinos **Britten** Solo
Cello Suite No. 3 *Steven Isserlis (vc); London*
Symphony Orchestra / Gennadi Rozhdestvensky
Virgin Classics VC7 59052-2 (3/92)

Early music
The Rose and the Ostrich Feather Music from
the Eton Choirbook, Vol. 1 *The Sixteen / Harry*
Christophers
Collins Classics 1314-2 (4/92)

Engineering
Britten War Requiem. Sinfonia da Requiem. Ballad
of Heroes *Soloists; St Paul's Cathedral Choir;*
London Symphony Chorus and Orchestra / Richard
Hickox
Chandos CHAN8983/4 (11/91)

Historic non-vocal
The Elgar Edition, Vol. 1 *London Symphony*
Orchestra; Royal Albert Hall Orchestra / Sir Edward
Elgar
EMI mono CDS7 54560-2 (6/92)

Historic vocal
Covent Garden on Record, Vols. 1-4 *Various*
artists and accompaniments
Pearl mono GEMMCDS9923/6 (7/92)

Instrumental
Alkan 25 Préludes dans les tons majeurs et mineur,
Op. 31 **Shostakovich** 24 Preludes, Op. 34 *Olli*
Mustonen (pf)
Decca 433 055-2DH (10/91)

Music theatre
Bernstein Candide *Soloists; London Symphony*
Chorus and Orchestra / Leonard Bernstein
DG 429 734-2GH2 (8/91)

Opera
R. Strauss Die Frau ohne Schatten *Soloists; Vienna*
Boys' Choir; Vienna State Opera Chorus; Vienna
Philharmonic Orchestra / Sir Georg Solti
Decca 436 243-2DH3 (5/92)

Orchestral and Record of the year
Beethoven Symphonies Nos. 1-9 *Chamber*
Orchestra of Europe / Nikolaus Harnoncourt
Teldec 2292-46452-2 (11/91)

Solo vocal
Schubert Lieder *Brigitte Fassbaender (mez);*
Aribert Reimann (pf)
DG 429 766-2GH (6/92)

1993

Baroque non-vocal
Heinichen Dresden Concertos *Musica Antiqua*
Köln / Reinhard Goebel
Archiv Produktion 437 549-2AH2 (5/93)

Baroque vocal
Stradella San Giovanni Battista *Soloists; Les*
Musiciens du Louvre / Marc Minkowski
Erato 2292-45739-2 (10/92)

Chamber
Haydn String Quartets, Op. 20, "Sun" *Quatuor*
Mosaïques
Astrée Auvidis E8784 (5/93)

Choral
Mendelssohn Elijah *Soloists; Leipzig Radio*
Chorus; Israel Philharmonic Orchestra / Kurt Masur
Teldec 9031-73131-2 (5/93)

Concerto
Brahms Piano Concerto No. 1. Zwei Gesänge,
Op. 91 *Stephen Kovacevich (pf); Ann Murray*
(mez); Nobuko Imai (va); London Philharmonic
Orchestra / Wolfgang Sawallisch
EMI CDC7 54578-2 (10/92)

Contemporary
MacMillan Confession of Isobel Gowdie. Tryst
BBC Scottish Symphony Orchestra / Jerzy
Maksymiuk
Koch Schwann 31050-2 (10/92)

Early music
Venetian Vespers *Gabrieli Consort and Players /*
Paul McCreesh
Archiv Produktion 437 552-2AH2 (4/93)

Engineering and production
Debussy Le martyre de Saint Sébastien *Soloists;*
London Symphony Chorus and Orchestra / Michael
Tilson Thomas
Sony Classical SK48240 (3/93)

Historic non-vocal
Rachmaninov The Complete Recordings *Sergei*
Rachmaninov with various artists
RCA Victor Gold Seal mono 09026 61265-2 (3/93)

Historic vocal
Singers of Imperial Russia, Vols. 1-4 *Various*
artists
Pearl mono GEMMCDS9997/9, 9001/3, 9004/6,
9007/9 (6/93)

Instrumental
Eightieth Birthday Recital from Carnegie Hall
Shura Cherkassky (pf)
Decca 433 654-2DH (1/93)

Music theatre
Gershwin Lady, be Good *Soloists; chorus and*
orchestra / Eric Stern
Elektra Nonesuch 7559-79308-2 (7/93)

Opera
Poulenc Dialogues des Carmélites *Soloists; Chorus*
and Orchestra of the Opéra de Lyon / Kent Nagano
Virgin Classics VCD7 59227-2 (9/92)

Orchestral
Hindemith Kammermusik *Royal Concertgebouw*
Orchestra / Riccardo Chailly
Decca 433 816-2DH2 (11/92)

Solo vocal and Record of the year
Grieg Songs *Anne Sofie von Otter (mez);*
Bengt Forsberg (pf)
DG Grieg Anniversary Edition 437 521-2GH (6/93)

Special achievement
Richter. The Authorized Edition. *Sviatoslav Richter*
(pf)
Philips 438 613-2PH21 (8/94)

1994

Baroque non-vocal
Bach Goldberg Variations *Pierre Hantaï (hpd)*
Opus 111 OPS30-84 (4/94)

Baroque vocal
Monteverdi Il quarto libro de madrigali *Concerto*
Italiano / Rinaldo Alessandrini
Opus 111 OPS30-81 (12/93)

Chamber
Tchaikovsky String Quartets Nos. 1-3. Souvenir de
Florence *Borodin Quartet*
Teldec 4509-90422-2 (1/94)

Choral
Delius Sea Drift. Songs of Sunset. Songs of
Farewell *Soloists; Waynflete Singers; Southern*
Voices; Bournemouth Symphony Chorus and
Orchestra / Richard Hickox
Chandos CHAN9214 (11/93)

Concerto
Bartók Violin Concerto No. 2. Rhapsodies Nos. 1
and 2 *Kyung-Wha Chung (vn); City of Birmingham*
Symphony Orchestra / Simon Rattle
EMI CDC7 542112-2 (6/94)

Contemporary
Holloway Second Concerto for Orchestra *BBC*
Symphony Orchestra / Oliver Knussen
NMC NMCD105M (5/94)

Early music
Rore Missa Praeter rerum seriem. Motets.
The Tallis Scholars / Peter Phillips
Gimell CDGIM029 (6/94)

Engineering
Dutilleux Symphonies Nos. 1 and 2 *BBC*
Philharmonic Orchestra / Yan Pascal Tortelier
Chandos CHAN9194 (11/93)

Historic non-vocal
Schoenberg Verklärte Nacht Schubert String
Quintet *Hollywood String Quartet; Alvin Dinkin*
(va); Kurt Reher (vc)
Testament mono SBT1031 (4/94)

Historic vocal
Britten The Rape of Lucretia. Peter Grimes –
scenes. Folksong Arrangements *Soloists; Orchestra*
of the Royal Opera House, Covent Garden / Sir
Reginald Goodall, Benjamin Britten
EMI mono CMS7 64727-2 (2/94)

Instrumental and Record of the year
Debussy Préludes *Krystian Zimerman (pf)*
DG 435 773-2GH2 (3/94)

Music theatre
Bernstein On the town *Soloists; London Voices;*
London Symphony Orchestra / Michael Tilson
Thomas
DG 437 516 2GH (10/93)

Opera
Britten Gloriana *Soloists; Chorus and Orchestra of*
the Welsh National Opera / Sir Charles Mackerras
Argo 440 213-2ZHO2 (7/93)

Orchestral
Koechlin Le livre de la jungle *Soloists; Berlin Radio*
Chamber Choir; Berlin Radio Symphony Orchestra /
David Zinman
RCA Victor Red Seal 09026 61955-2 (6/94)

Solo vocal
Barber Songs *Cheryl Studer (sop); Thomas Hampson*
(bar); Emerson Quartet; John Browning (pf)
DG 435 867-2GH2 (4/94)

Baroque vocal
Rameau Grand Motets *Les Arts Florissants /*
Christie
Erato 4509-96967-2 (8/95)

1995

Baroque non-vocal
Biber Violin Sonatas *Romanesca*
Harmonia Mundi HMU90 7134/5 (2/95)

Chamber
Fauré Piano Quintets *Domus*
Hyperion CDA66766 (7/95)

Choral
Szymanowski Stabat mater. Symphony No. 3.
Litany to the Virgin Mary *Soloists; CBSO and*
Chor / Rattle
EMI CDC5 55121-2 (8/94)

Concerto and Record of the year
Prokofiev Violin Concerto No. 1
Shostakovich Violin Concerto No. 1 *Vengerov;*
LSO / Rostropovich
Teldec 4509-98143-2 (2/95)

Contemporary
Ligeti Concertos – Piano; Violin; Cello *Gawriloff;*
Queyras; Aimard; Ensemble InterContemporain /
Boulez.
DG 439 808-2GH (1/95)

Early music
Fayrfax Missa O quam Glorifica, etc.
The Cardinall's Musick / Carwood
ASV Gaudeamus CDGAU142 (6/95)

Early opera
Purcell King Arthur *Soloists; Les Arts Florissants /*
Christie
Erato 4509-98535-2 (6/95)

Engineering
Szymanowski Stabat mater. Symphony No. 3.
Litany to the Virgin Mary *Soloists; CBSO and*
Chor / Rattle
EMI CDC5 55121-2 (8/94)

Historic non-vocal
Beethoven Symphony No. 9 *Soloists, Lucerne*
Festival Chorus; Philharmonia / Furtwängler
Tahra FURT1003 (3/95)

Historic vocal
Ravel L'enfant et les sortilèges *Soloists; French*
Radio National Chorus and Orchestra / Bour
Testament SBT1044 (2/95)

Instrumental
Chopin Four Ballades. Mazurkas. Etudes.
Nocturne, Op. 15 *Perahia*
Sony Classical SK64399 (12/94)

Music theatre
I wish it so *Upshaw; Orchestra / Stern*
Elektra Nonesuch 7559-79345-2 (12/94)

Opera
Walton Troilus and Cressida *Soloists; Chorus and*
Orchestra of Opera North / Hickox
Chandos CHAN9370/1 (5/95)

Orchestral
Schoenberg Chamber Symphony No. 1.
Erwartung *Bryn-Julson; CBSO / Rattle*
EMI CDC5 55212-2 (4/95)

Solo vocal
Schubert Lieder *Terfel; Martineau*
DG 445 294-2GH (10/94)

Special Achievement
Entartete Musik. *Various*
Decca

nla† – These items are no longer available

Manufacturers and distributors

Entries are listed as follows: **Manufacturer** or **Label** – UK Distributor *(Series)*

Abbey Alpha Records (Oxford)
ABC Classics Select
Accent Complete Record Co.
Albany Select
Altarus Kingdom
Amon Ra (Saydisc) Harmonia Mundi
APR Harmonia Mundi
Arabesque Seaford Music
Arcana Koch International
Archiphon TradeLink Music Distribution
Archive Documents Complete Record Co.
  /Michael G Thomas
Archiv Produktion PolyGram Record
  Operations *(Archiv Produktion, Archiv
  Produktion Galleria)*
Arc of Light Sony Music Entertainment
Argo PolyGram Record Operations
Arion Discovery Records
Ars Musici Carlton/Complete Record Co.
ASV Koch International *(ASV, Gaudeamus,
  Quicksilva, White Line)*
Athene Priory
Auvidis Harmonia Mundi *(Astrée, Valois,
  Montaigne)*
Bayer Priory
BBC Radio Classics Carlton/Complete
  Record Co.
Beecham Trust Sir Thomas Beecham Trust
Belart Entertainment Today
Berlin Classics Complete Record Co.
Beulah Priory
Biddulph Select
BIS Select
Bongiovanni Kingdom
Bridge Koch International.
British Music Label Forties Distribution
British Music Society British Music Society
Cala Complete Record Co.
Calig Priory
Calliope Harmonia Mundi *(Calliope,
  Approche)*
Campion Records RRD Distribution
Canyon Classics Complete Record Co
Capriccio Target
Caprice Complete Record Co. *(Caprice,
  Collector's Classics)*
Catalyst BMG Conifer
CBC Records Kingdom *(CBC, Musica Viva)*
CBS Sony Music Entertainment *(Masterworks,
  Masterworks Portrait, Maestro)*
CdM Russian Season (Le Chant du Monde)
  Harmonia Mundi
Centaur Complete Record Co.
Chandos Chandos *(Chandos, Chaconne, New
  Direction, Premium, Collect)*
Channel Classics Select *(Channel Classics,
  Channel Crossings)*
Chanticleer RRD Distribution
Chatsworth (Future Classics)
  Complete Record Co.
Christophorus Discovery
  (Christophorus, Musica Practica)

Claremont Complete Record Co.
Clarinet Classics Select
Classical Collector (EPM) Discovery Records
Classics for Pleasure Music for Pleasure
Claves Complete Record Co.
Cloud Nine Silva Screen
Collegium Koch International
Collins Classics Complete Record Co.
Columbia Sony Music Entertainment
  (Columbia, Legacy)
Conifer Classics BMG Conifer *(Conifer
  Classics, Happy Days)*
Connoisseur Society Harmony Records
Consonance Koch International
Continuum Select
CPO Select
CRD Select
Crystal Impetus
Danacord Discovery Records
Da Capo (Marco Polo) Select
Decca PolyGram Record Operations *(Decca,
  New Line, London, The Classic Sound,
  Ovation, Double Decca, Entartete Musik,
  Enterprise, Headline Classics, Phase 4,
  Historic, Música Española, Serenata)*
Dell'Arte Symposium Records
Dolos BMG Conifer
Denon Complete Record Co. *(Denon, Aliare)*
Deutsche Harmonia Mundi BMG Conifer
  (Deutsche Harmonia Mundi, Editio Classica)
DG PolyGram Record Operations *(DG, DG
  Galleria, The Originals, DG Double, 20th
  Century Classics, Masters, Grand Opera,
  Karajan Symphony Edition, Karajan Gold,
  Grieg Edition, Classikon, Dokumente, Karajan
  Symphony Edition, Privilege)*
Doron Music Discovery Records
Doyen Recordings BMG Conifer
Dutton Laboratories Complete Record Co.
Dynamic Priory
Earthsounds Earthsounds
EBS TradeLink Music Distribution
ECM New Series New Note
Edelweiss (Planetarium) Discovery Records
Editions Abseits RRD Distribution
Elan Discovery Records
Elektra Nonesuch Warner Classics
EMI Eminence Music for Pleasure
EMI EMI *(Angel, EMI, Reflexe, Studio,
  Beecham Edition, Virtuosi, Profile, Mahler
  Edition, Anglo-American Chamber Music,
  Salzburg Festival Edition, Sawallisch Edition,
  Broadway Classics, Forte, Seraphim, British
  Composers, Composers in Person, Digital
  Classics, Elgar Edition, L'Esprit Français,
  Great Recordings of the Century, Matrix,
  Phoenixa, Références, Rouge et Noir, Studio
  Plus)*
L'Empreinte Digitale Harmonia Mundi
Epic Sony Music Entertainment
Erato Warner Classics *(Erato, MusiFrance,
  Libretto, Bonsai)*

Etcetera TradeLink Music Distribution
Eurodisc BMG Conifer
Everest Complete Record Co.
Eye of the Storm Complete Record Co.
Finlandia Warner Classics
First Night Records Pinnacle
Fonè UK Distribution
Forlane Target
Four Hands Music Priory
Fox BMG UK
Foyer RRD Distribution
Gallo RRD Distribution
Geffen BMG UK
Gimell PolyGram Record Operations
Globe Complete Record Co.
Glossa Harmonia Mundi
GRP Classical New Note
Guild Complete Record Co.
Hänssler Classic Select
Harmonia Mundi Harmonia Mundi
  *(Harmonia Mundi, Ibèrica, Les Nouveaux
  Interprètes, Musique d'abord)*
Harmonic Records Discovery Records
Hat Hut Harmonia Mundi
Helicon Helicon
Herald Koch International
Hungaroton Target
Hyperion Select *(Hyperion, Helios)*
IMG Records Carlton
IMP Carlton/Complete Record Co. *(IMP
  Masters, IMP Classics)*
Intrada Silva Screen
Isis Records Complete Record Co.
Jade BMG UK
Jecklin Vanderbeek and Imrie
Kiwi-Pacific Records Harmony Records
Kingdom Records Kingdom
Koch Discover International Koch
  International
Koch International Classics Koch
  International
Koch Schwann Koch International
Kontrapunkt Impetus
Largo Complete Record Co.
LaserLight (Capriccio) Target
Le Chant du Monde Harmonia Mundi
Legato Classics Parsifal Distribution
Léman Classics Kingdom
Linn Records PolyGram Record Operations
L'Oiseau-Lyre PolyGram Record Operations
London PolyGram Record Operations
Lyrita Nimbus
Marco Polo Select *(Marco Polo, British Light
  Music)*
John Marks Records May Audio Marketing
Maya Recordings Complete Record Co.
MCA BMG UK
Melodiya BMG Conifer
Memoir Classics Target
Mercury PolyGram Record Operations
  (Mercury, Living Presence)
Meridian Nimbus
Metier Priory
Metronome Complete Record Co.
Mezhdunarodnaya Kniga Priory
MGB Musiques Suisses Complete
  Record Co.
Milan BMG UK

Mirabilis Discovery Records
Mode Harmonia Mundi
Motette Priory
Multisonic Priory
Music and Arts Harmonia Mundi
Musica Oscura Complete Record Co.
Musica Sveciae Complete Record Co.
MusicMasters Nimbus
Myto Parsifal Distribution
National Trust (Droffig) Discovery Records
Naxos Select
New Albion Harmonia Mundi
New World Harmonia Mundi
Newport Classic RRD Distribution
  (Newport Classics, Premier)
Nightingale Classics Koch International
Nimbus Nimbus *(Nimbus, Prima Voce)*
NM Classics Impetus
NMC Complete Record Co.
Nonesuch Warner Classics
Northeastern Priory
Nuova Era Complete Record Co.
Ode Discovery Records
Olympia Priory *(Olympia, Explorer)*
Ondine Koch International
Onyx RRD Distribution
Opera Rara Opera Rara
Opus III Harmonia Mundi
Opus 3 May Audio Marketing/Pentacone
Orfeo Koch International *(Orfeo, Orfeo D'Or,
  Salzburg Festpieldokumente)*
Ottavo Priory
Panton RRD Distribution
Pavane Kingdom
Pearl (Pavilion) Harmonia Mundi
Philips PolyGram Record Operations *(Philips,
  Silver Line, Duo, Solo, The Early Years,
  Bernard Haitink Symphony Edition, Arrau
  Edition, Opera Collector, Insignia, Baroque
  Classics, Collector, Legendary Classics, Mozart
  Edition, Musica da Camara, Concert Classics)*
Pianissimo Kingdom
Pierre Verany Kingdom
Point Music PolyGram Record Operations
Polskie Nagrania Priory
Polydor PolyGram Record Operations
Praga Harmonia Mundi
Preiser Harmonia Mundi
Priory Priory
Proud Sound BMG Conifer
RCA BMG Conifer *(RCA Victor, Red Seal,
  Gold Seal, Navigator, Julian Bream Edition,
  Living Stereo, Papillon, Seon)*
Redcliffe Recordings Complete Record Co.
Reference Recordings May Audio Marketing
Regent Records Regent Records
REM Editions Priory
Romophone Complete Record Co.
Royal Opera House Records BMG Conifer
RPO Records Carlton/Complete Record Co.
Russian Disc Koch International
Saga Classics Complete Record Co.
Sain Sain
Salabert Actuels Harmonia Mundi
Silva Screen BMG Conifer *(Silva Screen,
  Silva Treasury, Silva Classics)*
Sine Qua Non Sine Qua Non Society
Somm Recordings Priory

Sonpact Seaford Music
Sony Classical Sony Music Entertainment
*(Sony Classical, Vivarte, Arc of Light,
Essential Classics, Broadway, British Pageant,
St Petersburg Classics, Boulez Edition, West
End, Portrait, Legendary Interpretations,
Casals Edition, Glenn Gould Edition, Bernstein
Royal Edition)*
Soundboard Records Soundboard Records
Stafford J. Martin Stafford
Stradivari Michèle International
Stradivarius Priory
Supraphon Koch International
Symposium Records Symposium Records
Tahra Records Priory
Tall Poppies Complete Record Co.
Telarc BMG Conifer
Teldec Warner Classics *(Teldec Classics,
British Line, Das Alte Werk, Digital
Experience)*
TER Classics Koch International
Testament Complete Record Co.

Tremula Symposium Records
Tring International Tring International/Priory
Troubadisc Complete Record Co.
Unicorn-Kanchana Harmonia Mundi
(Unicorn-Kanchana, Souvenir)
VAI Audio Parsifal Distribution
Vanguard Classics Complete Record Co.
*(Vanguard Classics, Bach Guild, Alfred Deller
Edition)*
Varèse Sarabande Pinnacle
Virgin Classics EMI *(Virgin Classics, Veritas,
Virgo, Ultraviolet)*
Voiceprint Voiceprint
Vox Carlton Home Entertainment.
(Turnabout, Vox box, Vox Legends)
Wergo Harmonia Mundi
3D Classics Discovery Records1

For additional information on Manufacturers
and distributors, refer to the Label Distribution
Directory published in *Gramophone*

Record company names and addresses

Unless otherwise indicated all the companies listed below are based in the UK; addresses for record
companies from outside the UK are given, where available (telephone numbers should be prefixed
with the appropriate international dialing code)

Accent Records Eikstraat 31, 1673 Beert,
BELGIUM. Telephone 32 2 356 1878
Albany Music Distributors
US PO Box 5011, Albany, NY12205 *USA.*
Telephone 1 518 453 2203
Albany Records UK *UK* PO Box 12,
Carnforth, Lancashire LA5 9PD.
Telephone 01524 735873
Alpha Records (Oxford) 1 Abbey Street,
Eynsham, Oxford OX8 1HF.
Telephone 01865 880240
Altarus Records *UK* Easton Dene, Bailbrook
Lane, Bath BA1 7AA. Telephone 01225 852323
US 31 Conant Road, Ridgefield, CT06877
USA. Telephone 1 203 438 8342
Appian Publications and Recordings (APR)
PO Box 1, Wark, Hexham, Northumberland
NE48 3EW. Telephone 01434 220627
Arabesque Recordings 10 West 37th Street,
5th Floor, New York, NY10018, *USA.*
Telephone 1 212 279 1414
Arcana 7 Rue de Valmy, 44000 Nantes,
FRANCE. Telephone 33 5188 2017
Archiv Produktion 22 St Peter's Square,
London W6 9NW. Telephone 0181-910 5000
Argo 22 St Peter's Square, London W6 9NW.
Telephone 0181-910 5000
Disques Arion 36, Avenue Hoche, 75008 Paris,
FRANCE. Telephone 33 1 4563 7670
ASV 1 Beaumont Avenue, London W14 9LP.
Telephone 0171-381 8747
Athene (D&J Recording) 7 Felden Street,
London SW6 5AE. Telephone 0171-736 9485
Auvidio *FRANCE* 47 Avenue Paul Vaillant
Couturier, 94250 Gentilly, *FRANCE.*

Telephone 33 1 4615 8800
UK 19-21 Nile Street, London N1 7LL.
Telephone 0171-253 0863
Bayer AG Ku-Mipine-Makrolon (Dept),
51368 Leverkusen, *GERMANY.*
Telephone 49 214 30 8507
Sir Thomas Beecham Trust The West Wing,
Denton House, Denton, Harleston, Norfolk
IP20 0AA. Telephone 01986 788780
Berlin Classics Edel, Wichmannstraße 4,
22607 Hamburg, *GERMANY.*
Telephone 49 40 890 85603
Beulah The Signal Box, 1 Breach Road,
Coalville, Leicestershire LE67 3SB.
Telephone 01530 810828
Biddulph Recordings 34 St George Street,
London W1R 0ND. Telephone 0171-408 2458
Grammofon AB BIS Bragevägen 2,
18264 Djursholm, *SWEDEN.*
Telephone 46 8 755 4100
BMG Conifer UK Bedford House,
69-79 Fulham High Street, London SW6 3JW.
Telephone 0171-973 0011
BMG UK Lyng Lane, West Bromwich,
West Midlands B70 7ST.
Telephone 0121-500 5678
Bongiovanni Via Rizzoli 28/e, 40125 Bologna,
ITALY Telephone 39 51 225 722
Bridge Records GPO Box 1864, New York,
NY10116, *USA.* Telephone 1 516 487 1662
British Music Society 7 Tudor Gardens,
Upminster, Essex RM14 3DE.
Telephone 01708 224795
Cala Records 17 Shakespeare Gardens,
London N2 9LJ. Telephone 0181-883 7306

Calig Musik und Video Nymphenburgerstraße 29, 80335 München, *GERMANY.* Telephone 49 89 5525650

Calliope 14 Rue de la Justice, Boîte Postale 166, 60204 Compiègne Cedex, *FRANCE.* Telephone 33 4423 2765

Campion Records 13 Bank Square, Wilmslow, Cheshire SK9 1AN. Telephone 01625 527844

Capriccio Zur Mühle 2, 50226 Frechen, *GERMANY.* Telephone 49 2234 60060

Caprice Records Box 1225, 111 82 Stockholm, *SWEDEN.* Telephone 46 8 791 4600

Carlton Home Entertainment The Waterfront, Elstree Road, Elstree, Hertfordshire WD6 3BS. Telephone 0181-207 6207

Catalyst Bedford House, 69-79 Fulham High Street, London SW6 3JW. Telephone 0171-973 0011

CBC Records PO Box 500, Station A, Toronto, Ontario M5W 1E6, *CANADA.* Telephone 1 416 205 3501

CBS Records *see* SONY MUSIC ENTERTAINMENT

Centaur Records 8867 Highland Road, Suite 206, Baton Rouge, LA70808, *USA.* Telephone 1 504 336 4877

Chandos Records Chandos House, Commerce Way, Colchester, Essex CO2 8HQ. Telephone 01206 225200

Channel Classics Records Jacob van Lennepkade 334 e, 1053 NJ Amsterdam, *THE NETHERLANDS.* Telephone 31 20 616 1775

Christophorus Heuauerweg 21, 69124 Heidelberg, *GERMANY.* Telephone 49 6221 785011

Clarinet Classics 77 St Albans Avenue, London E6 4HH. Telephone 0181-472 2057

Classics for Pleasure EMI House, Brook Green, London W6 7EF. Telephone 0171-605 5000

Claves Records Trüelweg 14, 3600 Thun, *SWITZERLAND.* Telephone 41 3323 1649

Cloud Nine Records Silva House, 261 Royal College Street, London NW1 9LU. Telephone 0171-284 0525

Collegium Records PO Box 172, Whittlesford, Cambridge CB2 4QZ. Telephone 01223 832474

Collins Classics Premier House, 10 Greycoat Place, London SW1P 1SB. Telephone 0171-222 1921

The Complete Record Co. 12 Pepys Court, 84 The Chase, London SW4 0NF. Telephone 0171-498 9666

Connoisseur Society 2211 Broadway, Suite 10E, New York, NY10024, *USA.* Telephone 1 212 873 6769

Continuum 20 Lochiel Road, Remuera, Auckland 5, *NEW ZEALAND.* Telephone 64 9 520 7499

CPO Lübeckerstraße 9, 49124 Georgsmarienhütte, *GERMANY.* Telephone 49 5401 8510

CRD PO Box 26, Stanmore, Middlesex HA7 4XB. Telephone 0181-958 7695

Crystal Records 28818 NE Hancock Road, Camas, WA98607, *USA.* Telephone 1 360 837 7022

Da Capo (Marco Polo) Christianshavns Torv 2, 1410 Copenhagen K, *DENMARK.* Telephone 45 32 960 602

Danacord Records Gernersgade 35, 1319 Copenhagen, *DENMARK.* Telephone 45 33 151 716

Decca Classics 22 St Peter's Square, London W6 9NW. Telephone 0181-910 5000

Dell'Arte Records PO Box 26, Hampton, Middlesex TW12 2NL. Telephone 0181-979 2479

Delos International Hollywood and Vine Plaza, 1645 North Vine Street, Suite 340, Hollywood, California CA90028, *USA.* Telephone 1 213 962 2626

Denon/Nippon Columbia 14-14, Akasaka 4-Chome, Minatu-Ku, Tokyo 107-11, *JAPAN.* Telephone 81 3 3584 8271

Deutsche Grammophon 22 St Peter's Square, London W6 9NW. Telephone 0181-910 5000

Discovery Records The Old Church Mission Room, King's Corner, Pewsey, Wiltshire SN9 5BS. Telephone 01672 563931

Doyen Recordings Doyen House, 17 Coupland Close, Moorside, Oldham, Lancashire OL4 2TQ. Telephone 0161-628 3799

Dutton Laboratories PO Box 576, Harrow, Middlesex HA3 6YW. Telephone 0181-421 1117

Dynamic Edizione Discografiche e Musicale, Via Mura Delle Chiappe 39, 16136 Genova, *ITALY.* Telephone 39 10 27 2284

Earthsounds PO Box 1, Richmond, North Yorkshire DL10 5GB. Telephone 01748 825959

EBS Records Postfach 1230, 72121 Pliezhausen, *GERMANY.* Telephone 49 7127 88633

ECM Postfach 600331, 81203 München, *GERMANY.* Telephone 49 89 851048

Elan PO Box 101, Riverdale, Maryland 20738, *USA.* Telephone 1 301 864 0499

EMI Records Customer Services Dept, EMI House, Brook Green, London W6 7EF. Telephone 0171-605 5000

EMI Sales & Distribution Centre, Hermes Close, Tachbrook Park, Leamington Spa, Warwickshire CV34 6RP. Telephone 01926 888888

Entertainment Today PO Box 1425, Chancellors House, 72 Chancellors Road, Hammersmith, London W6 9QB. Telephone 0181-910 5618

Erato: *FRANCE* 50 Rue des Tournelles, 75003 Paris, *FRANCE.* Telephone 33 1 4027 7000; *UK* The Warner Building, 28 Kensington Church Street, London W8 4EP. Telephone 0171-938 0167

First Night Records 2-3 Fitzroy Mews, London W1P 5DQ. Telephone 0171-383 7767

Fonè 50-54 Via Goldoni, 57125 Livorno, *ITALY.* Telephone 39 586 884069

Forlane 15 Rue de l'Ancienne Mairie, 92100 Boulogne Billancourt, *FRANCE.* Telephone 33 1 4825 0217

Forties Distribution Co 44 Challacombe, Furzten, Milton Keynes MK4 1DP. Telephone 01908 502836

Four Hands Music 15 Birchmead Close, St Albans, Herts AL3 6BS. Telephone 01727 858485

Future Classics 13 Cotswold Mews,
30 Battersea Square, London SW11 3RA.
Telephone 0171-223 7265

Gimell Records 4 Newtec Place,
Magdalen Road, Oxford OX4 1RE.
Telephone 01865 244557

Globe Tapuit 4, 1902 KP Castricum, *THE
NETHERLANDS.* Telephone 31 2518 55584

Glossa Españoleta SL, Infante 6, 28200
San Lorenzo de El Escorial, *SPAIN.*
Telephone 34 1 896 1480

Guild Music PO Box 5, Hadleigh, Ipswich,
Suffolk IP7 6QF. Telephone 01473 658026

Hänssler Classic Postfach 12 20, 73762
Neuhausen, *GERMANY.*
Telephone 49 7158 1770

Harmonia Mundi: *UK* 19-21 Nile Street,
London N1 7LL. Telephone 0171-253 0863;
FRANCE Mas de Vert, 13200 Arles.
Telephone 33 9049 9049;
USA 2037 Granville Avenue, Los Angeles,
CA90025-6103, *USA.* Telephone 1 310 478 1311

Harmonic Records Parc du Montigny,
Maxilly-sur-Léman, 74500 Evian-les-Bains,
FRANCE Telephone 33 5075 6900

Harmony Records Charborough Lodge,
Charborough Park, Wareham BH20 7EL.
Telephone 01929 459589

Hat Hut Box 461, 4106 Therwil,
SWITZERLAND. Telephone 41 61 721 6655

Helicon PO Box 9, Hastings, East Sussex
TN34 3UU. Telephone 01424 422061

Herald Audiovisual Publications The Studio,
29 Alfred Road, Farnham, Surrey GU9 8ND.
Telephone 01252 725349

Hungaroton Reitter Ferenc u 39-49, 1135
Budapest XIII, *HUNGARY.*
Telephone 36 1 270 2411

Hyperion Records PO Box 25, Eltham,
London SE9 1AX. Telephone 0181-294 1166

Impetus Distribution PO Box 1324,
London W5 2ZU. Telephone 0181-998 6411

Isis Records 52 Argyle Street, Oxford,
OX4 1SS. Telephone 01865 726553

Editions Jade 165 Boulevard de Valmy,
92706 Colombes Cedex, *FRANCE.*
Telephone 33 1 4786 3619

Jecklin and Co Rämistraße 42, 8024 Zürich,
SWITZERLAND. Telephone 41 1 261 7733

Kingdom Records 61 Collier Street, London
N1 9BE. Telephone 0171-713 7788

Koch International: *UK* 24 Concord Road,
London W3 0TH. Telephone 0181-992 7177;
USA 2 Tri-Harbor Court, Port Washington,
New York, 11050-4617, *USA.*
Telephone 1 516 484 1000

Koch Schwann PO Box 7640, AM Wehrahn
1000, 4000 Düsseldorf 1, *GERMANY.*

Kontrapunkt PO Box 35, Slottsalleen 16,
2930 Klampenborg, *DENMARK.*
Telephone 45 31 644 244

Largo Records Hohenstaufenring 43-45, 50674
Köln, *GERMANY* Telephone 49 221 2402234

Le Chant du Monde 31 Rue Vandrezanne,
75013 Paris, *FRANCE.* Telephone 33 1 5380 0222

Legato Classics Lyric Distribution, 18
Madison Avenue, Hicksville, NY11801, *USA.*
Telephone 1 516 932 5503

L'Empreinte Digitale Domaine de la Garde,
13510 Eguilles, *FRANCE.*
Telephone 33 4233 3324

Linn Records Floors Road, Waterfoot,
Eaglesham, Glasgow G76 0EP.
Telephone 0141-644 5111

L'Oiseau-Lyre 22 St Peter's Square,
London W6 9NW. Telephone 0181-910 5000

Lyrita 99 Green Lane, Burnham, Slough,
Bucks SL1 8EG. Telephone 01628 604208

Maya Recordings Bramleys House,
Shudy Camps, Cambridge CB1 6RA.
Fax only 01799 584856

May Audio Marketing Aireside Mills,
Cononley, Keighley, West Yorkshire
BD20 8LW. Telephone 01535 632700

Marco Polo 58 Pak Tai Street, 8th Floor,
Kai It Bldg, Tokwawan, Kowloon,
HONG KONG. Telephone 852 2760 7818

Memoir Classics PO Box 66, Pinner,
Middlesex HA5 2SA.
Fax only 0181-866 7804

Mercury 22 St Peter's Square,
London W6 9NW. Telephone 0181-910 5000

Meridian Records PO Box 317, Eltham,
London SE9 4SF. Telephone 0181-857 3213

Metier Sound and Vision PO Box 270,
Preston, Lancashire PR2 3LZ.
Telephone 01772 866178

Metronome Productions Magdalen Studio,
Chapel Lane, Farthinghoe, Braekeley,
Northamptonshire NN13 5PG.
Telephone 01295 710641

MGB Musiques Suisses Postfach 266,
8031 Zürich, *SWITZERLAND.*
Telephone 41 1 277 2071

Michèle International Michèle House,
The Acorn Centre, Roebuck Road, Hainault,
Essex IG6 3TU. Telephone 0181-500 1819

Editions Milan Music 165 Boulevard de
Valmy, 92706 Colombes Cedex, *FRANCE.*
Telephone 33 1 4786 3619

Mirabilis Records 5 King's Croft Gardens,
Leeds LS17 6PB. Telephone 0113-268 5123

Mode PO Box 375, Kew Gardens, New York,
NY11415, *USA.* Telephone 1 212 595 6089

Motette-Ursina Neusser Weg 63a, 40474
Düsseldorf, *GERMANY.*
Telephone 49 211 434864

Music and Arts Programs of America
PO Box 771, Berkeley, California CA94701,
USA. Telephone 1 510 525 4583

Musica Oscura 47 Leamington Road Villas,
London W11 1HT. Telephone 0171 229 5142

Musica Sveciae Knugl, Musikalaiska
Akademien, Blasieholmstorg 8,
11148 Stockholm, *SWEDEN.*
Telephone 46 8 611 0397

Music for Pleasure EMI House, Brook Green,
London W6 7EF. Telephone 0181-605 5000

MusicMasters 1710 Highway 35, Ocean,
NJ 07712-9885, *USA.* Telephone 1 908 531 3375

Naxos 58 Pak Tai Street, 8th Floor, Kai It
Bldg, Tokwawan, Kowloon, *HONG KONG.*
Telephone 852 2760 7818

Naxos and Marco Polo (UK) PO Box 576,
Sheffield, Yorkshire S10 1AY.
Telephone 0114-267 8958

New Albion Records 584 Castro Street, Suite 515, San Francisco, CA94114, *USA*. Telephone 1 415 621 5757

New Note Electron House, Cray Avenue, St Mary Cray, Orpington, Kent BR5 3RJ. Telephone 016898 77884

New World Records 701 Seventh Avenue, 7th Floor, New York, NY10036, *USA*. Telephone 1 212 302 0460

Newport Classic 106, Putnam Street, Providence, Rhode Island RI02909, *USA*. Telephone 1 401 421 8143

Nightingale Classics Nussdorferstraße 38, 1090 Wien, *AUSTRIA*. Telephone 43 1 310 4017

Nimbus Records Wyastone Leys, Monmouth, Gwent NP5 3SR. Telephone 01600 890682

NMC Francis House, Francis Street, London SW1P 1DE. Telephone 0171-828 3432

NM Classics Havenstraat 31, PO Box 1634, 12000 BP Hilversum, *THE NETHERLANDS*. Telephone 31 35 624 0957

Nonesuch: *US* 75 Rockefeller Plaza, New York NY10019, *USA*. Telephone 1 212 484 7200 ; *UK* The Warner Building, 28 Kensington Church Street, London W8 4EP. Telephone 0171-938 0167

Nuova Era Records Corso Marconi, 39, Torino 10125, *ITALY*. Telephone 39 11 669 8903

Ode Record Co 19 Earle Street, Parnell, Box 37-331, Auckland, *NEW ZEALAND*. Telephone 64 9 3095 132

Olympia Compact Discs 31 Warple Way, London W3 0RX. Telephone 0181-743 6767

Ondine Fredrikinkatu 77 A 2, 00100 Helsinki, *FINLAND*. Telephone 35 8 492 348

Opera Rara 25 Compton Terrace, Canonbury, London N1 2UN. Telephone 0171-359 1777

Opus 111 37 Rue Blomet, 75015 Paris, *FRANCE*. Telephone 33 1 4567 3344

Opus 3 Firma Ljundinspelning Harpungränd 54, 17547 Järfälla, *SWEDEN*. Telephone 46 8 580 18686

Orfeo International Music Augustenstraße 79, 8000 München 2, *GERMANY*. Telephone 49 89 522031

Ottavo Recordings Westeinde 10, 2512HD Den Haag, *THE NETHERLANDS*. Telephone 31 70 346 9494

Panton Radlická 99, 150 00 Praha 5, *CZECH REPUBLIC*. Telephone 42 202 5341 378

Parsifal Distribution Bridge Studios, Suite No. 7, 318-326 Wandsworth Bridge Road, London SW6 2TZ. Telephone 0171-610 6725

Pavane Records 17 Rue Ravenstein, 1000 Bruxelles, *BELGIUM*. Telephone 32 2 513 0965

Pavilion Records Sparrows Green, Wadhurst, East Sussex TN5 6SJ. Telephone 01892 783591

Pentacone 4 Cross Bank Road, Batley, West Yorkshire WF17 8PJ. Telephone 01924 445039

Philips Classics 22 St Peter's Square, London W6 9NW. Telephone 0181-910 5000

Pianissimo Ridgeway Road, Pyrford, Woking, Surrey GU22 8PR. Telephone 01932 345371

Pierre Verany 15 Rue Guyton-de-Morveau, 75013 Paris, *FRANCE*. Telephone 33 1 4581 1414

Pinnacle Electron House, Cray Avenue, St Mary Cray, Orpington, Kent BR5 3RJ. Telephone 016898 70622

Planetarium Recordings 78 Belsize Park, London NW3 4ET. Telephone 0171-794 6436

Polskie Nagrania 6, Goleszowska Street, 01249 Warsaw, *POLAND*. Telephone 48 2 373794

PolyGram Classics and Jazz 22 St Peter's Square, London W6 9NW. Telephone 0181-910 5000

PolyGram Record Operations PO Box 36, Clyde Works, Grove Road, Romford, Essex RM6 4QR. Telephone 0181-910 1799

Priory Records Unit 9b, Upper Wingbury Courtyard, Wingrave, Nr. Aylesbury, Bucks HP22 4LW. Telephone 01296 682255

Proud Sound 61 Iffley Road, Oxford OX4 1EB. Telephone 01865 723764

RCA Bedford House, 69-79 Fulham High Street, London SW6 3JW. Telephone 0171-973 0011

Redcliffe Recordings 68 Barrowgate Road, London W4 4QU. Telephone 0181-995 1223

Reference Recordings Box 7725X, San Francisco, California CA94107, *USA*. Telephone 1 415 355 1892

Regent Records PO Box 528, Wolverhampton WV3 9YW. Telephone 01902 24377

REM Editions 4 Rue Sainte Marie des Terreaux, 69001 Lyon, *FRANCE*. Telephone 33 7830 0571

Romophone PO Box 717, Oxford OX2 7YU. Telephone 01865 515353

Royal Opera House Records *see* BMG Conifer

RRD (Distribution) 13 Bank Square, Wilmslow, Cheshire SK9 1AN. Telephone 01625 549862

Russian Disc 577 Brown Brook Road, Southbury, CT06488, *USA*. Telephone 1 203 264 4073

Sain Llandwrog, Caernarfon, Gwynedd LL54 5TG. Telephone 01286 831111

Saydisc Chipping Manor, The Chipping, Wotton-under-Edge, Glos GL12 7AD. Telephone 01453 845036

Seaford Music 24 Pevensey Road, Eastbourne, East Sussex BN21 3HP. Telephone 01323 732553

Select Music and Video Distributors 34a Holmethorpe Avenue, Holmethorpe Estate, Redhill, Surrey. Telephone 01737 760020

Silva Screen 261 Royal College Street, London NW1 9LU. Telephone 0171-284 0525

Sine Qua Non Sine Qua Non Society, The Old Forge, 2 Bridge Street, Hadleigh, Suffolk IP7 6BT. Telephone 01473 828494

Somm Recordings 13 Riversdale Road, Thames Ditton, Surrey KT7 0QL. Telephone 0181-398 1586

Sony Music Entertainment 10 Great Marlborough Street, London W1V 2LP. Telephone 0171-911 8200

Sony Music Operations Rabans Lane, Aylesbury, Buckinghamshire HP19 3RT. Telephone 01296 395151

Soundboard Records PO Box 5, Derwentside, Stanley, Co. Durham DH9 7HR. Telephone 0191-512 1103

J Martin Stafford 298 Blossomfield Road, Solihull, West Midlands B91 1TH. Telephone 0121-711 1975

Stradivarius Via Andrea Costa 7, 20131 Milano, *ITALY.* Telephone 39 2 261 43119

Supraphon Palackého 1, 11299 Praha 1, *CZECH REPUBLIC.* Telephone 42 2 24 225831

Symposium Records 36 Paul's Lane, Overstrand, Cromer, North Norfolk NR27 0PF Telephone 01263579715

Tahra 1 Allée Georges Bizet, 95870 Bezons, *FRANCE* Telephone 33 1 3961 2690

Target Records 23 Gardner Industrial Estate, Kent House Lane, Beckenham, Kent BR3 1QZ. Telephone 0181-778 4040

Telarc International 23307 Commerce Park Road, Cleveland, Ohio OH44122, *USA.* Telephone 1 216 464 2313

Teldec Classics The Warner Building, 28 Kensington Church Street, London W8 4EP. Telephone 0171-938 0167

TER Classics 107 Kentish Town Road, London NW1 8PD. Telephone 0171-485 9593

Testament 14 Tootswood Road, Bromley, Kent BR2 0PD. Telephone 0181-464 5947

Michael G. Thomas 5a Norfolk Place, London W2 1QN. Telephone 0171-723 4935

Tremula 63 Sandringham Road, Maidenhead, Berkshire SL6 7PL. Telephone 01628 29142

TradeLink Associates 3 Regal Lane, Soham, Ely, Cambridgeshire CB7 5BA. Telephone 01353 722223

Tring International Triangle Business Park, Wendover Road, Aylesbury, Bucks HP22 5BL. Telephone 01296 615800

UK Distribution 23 Richings Way, Iver, Bucks SL0 9DA. Telephone 01753 652669

Unicorn-Kanchana Records PO Box 339, London W8 7TJ. Telephone 0171-727 3881

Vanderbeek and Imrie 15 Marvig, Lochs, Isle of Lewis PA86 9QP. Telephone 01851 880216

VAI Audio Video Artists International 158 Linwood Plaza, Suite 301, Fort Lee, NJ07024-3704, *USA.* Telephone 1 201 944 0099

Vanguard Classics Groningenhaven 18, PO Box 1308, 3430 BH Nieuwegein, *THE NETHERLANDS.* Telephone 31 3402 88400; *US* 27, West 72nd Street, New York, NY10023, *USA.* Telephone 1 212 769 0360

Varèse Sarabande 13006 Saticoy St, North Hollywood, CA91605, *USA.* Telephone 1 818 764 1172

Virgin Classics *see* EMI Records

Voiceprint PO Box 5, Derwentside, Co. Durham, DH9 7HR. Telephone 0191-512 1103

Warner Classics (UK) The Warner Building, 28 Kensington Church Street, London W8 4EP. Telephone 0171-938 0167

Wergo Postfach 3640, 55026 Mainz, *GERMANY.* Telephone 49 6131 246891

Index

Schütz

G

The Illustrated Lives of the Great Composers

A series of biographies of great composers which presents the subjects against the social background of their times. Each book draws on personal letters and recollections, engravings, paintings, and - where they exist - photographs, to build up a complete picture of the composer's life.

Bach
Tim Dowley

144pp, softcover
ISBN 0.7119.0262.3
OP 42480
$14.95

Bartók
Hamish Milne

122pp, softcover
ISBN 0.7119.0260.7
OP 42464
$14.95

Beethoven
Ates Orga

176pp, softcover
ISBN 0.7119.0251.8
OP 42373
$14.95

Berlioz
Robert Clarson-Leach

128pp, softcover
ISBN 0.7119.0829.X
OP 43744
$14.95

Brahms
Paul Holmes

168pp, softcover
ISBN 0.7119.0826
OP 43710
$14.95

Chopin
Ates Orga

144pp, softcover
ISBN 0.7119.0247.X
OP 42332
$14.95

Debussy
Paul Holmes

133pp, softcover
ISBN 0.7119.1752.3
OP 45244
$14.95

Dvořák
Neil Butterworth

136pp, softcover
ISBN 0.7119.0256.9
OP 42423
$14.95

Elgar
Simon Mundy

138pp, softcover
ISBN 0.7119.0263.1
OP 42498
$14.95

Gilbert & Sullivan
Andrew Codd

softcover
ISBN 0.7119.175
OP 45251
$14.95

Handel
Wendy Thompson

144pp, softcover
ISBN 0.7119.2997.1
OP 46796
$14.95

Haydn
Neil Butterworth

144pp, softcover
ISBN 0.7119.0249.6
OP 42357
$14.95

Liszt
Bryce Morrison

112pp, softcover
ISBN 0.7119.1682.9
OP 44999
$14.95

Mahler
Edward Seckerson

150pp, softcover
ISBN 0.7119.0259.3
OP 42456
$14.95

Mendelssoh
Mozelle Mosh

144pp, softcover
ISBN 0.7119.025
OP 42381
$14.95

Mozart
100th Anniversary Ed.
Peggy Woodford

44pp, softcover
ISBN 0.7119.0248.8
OP 42340 **$14.95**

Offenbach
Peter Gammond

166p, softcover
ISBN 0.7119.0257.7
OP 42431
$14.95

Paganini
John Sugden

168pp, softcover
ISBN 0.7119.0264.X
OP 42506
$14.95

Prokofiev
David Gutman

144pp, softcover
ISBN 0.7119.2083.4
OP 45681
$14.95

Rachmaninoff
Robert Walker

144pp, softcover
ISBN 0.7119.0253.4
OP 42399
$14.95

Ravel
David Burnett-James

44pp, softcover
ISBN 0.7119.0987.3
OP 44015
$14.95

Rossini
Nicholas Till

144pp, softcover
ISBN 0.7119.0988.1
OP 44023
$14.95

Schubert
Peggy Woodford

160pp, softcover
ISBN 0.7119.0255.0
OP 42415
$14.95

Schumann
Tim Dowley

144pp, softcover
ISBN 0.7119.0261.5
OP 42472
$14.95

Shostakovich
Eric Roseberry

192pp, softcover
ISBN 0.7119.0258.5
OP 42449
$14.95

Sibelius
David Burnett-James

28pp, softcover
ISBN 0.7119.1688.7
OP 45004
$14.95

Richard Strauss
David Nice

160pp, softcover
ISBN 0.7119.1686.1
OP 45038
$14.95

The Strauss Family
Peter Kemp

272pp, softcover
ISBN 0.7119.1726.4
OP 45194
$14.95

Verdi
Peter Southwell-Sander

160pp, softcover
ISBN 0.7119.0250.X
OP 42365
$14.95

Villa-Lobos
Lisa Peppercorn

144pp, softcover
ISBN 0.7119.1688.8
OP 45061
$14.95

Vivaldi
John Booth

8pp, softcover
ISBN 0.7119.1727.2
OP 45202
$14.95

Wagner
Howard Gray

144pp, softcover
ISBN 0.7119.1687.X
OP 44817
$14.95

Weber
Anthony Friese-Greene

144pp, softcover
ISBN 0.7119.2081.8
OP 45665
$14.95

Available at all good recordstores and bookstores. For more information contact your local dealer or Music Sales directly.

EUROPE

Music Sales Limited
8-9 Frith Street
London W1V 5TZ
England
Tel: 0171-434-0066

Distribution Center
Newmarket Road
Bury St. Edmunds
Suffolk IP33 3YB
Tel: 01284-702600

USA

Music Sales Corporation
257 Park Avenue South
New York, NY 10010
Tel: 212-254-2100

Distribution Center
5 Bellvale Road
Chester, NY 10918
Tel: 914-469-2271
or 800-431-7187